The National Guide

TO EDUCATIONAL CREDIT FOR TRAINING PROGRAMS

Edited by Jo Ann Robinson and Jacqueline E. Taylor

AMERICAN COUNCIL ON EDUCATION

The National Guide

TO EDUCATIONAL CREDIT FOR TRAINING PROGRAMS

1998 Edition

Edited by Jo Ann Robinson and Jacqueline E. Taylor

The National Guide is a publication of ACE/CREDIT, a national program within the American Council on Education's Center for Adult Learning and Educational Credentials.

AMERICAN COUNCIL ON EDUCATION

ISBN 1-57356-034-0
ISSN 0275-4142

Printed in the United States of America

printing number
1 2 3 4 5 6 7 8 9 10

Table of Contents

Foreword

This new *National Guide to Educational Credit for Training Programs* is one in a series of ACE guides designed to help institutions offer appropriate recognition for learning attained outside their sponsorship. As such, you will find it to be an important reference guide.

Since 1945, when the first edition of *A Guide to the Evaluation of Educational Experiences in the Armed Services* was published, the American Council on Education has assisted institutions in their efforts to serve adult learners. Since that time, learning what individuals know and are able to do has become ever more important in a global economy. Over the last 20 years, we have seen a significant growth in the breadth of educational offerings provided by "corporate universities" and other extrainstitutional learning providers—and as a result—an expansion of ACE/CREDIT and other evaluation activities of our Center for Adult Learning and Educational Credentials has occurred.

The ACE guide series now includes the *Guide to the Evaluation of Educational Experiences in the Armed Services, The National Guide to Educational Credit for Training Programs, Guide to Educational Credit by Examination*, and guides on external degree programs.

The American Council on Education urges colleges and universities to develop policies that enable students to move smoothly among various learning providers—be they higher education institutions, the military, or corporations—by awarding credit for learning acquired by students who have successfully completed courses listed in *The National Guide*. For many institutions, long-standing policies on the use of the military guide will pave the way for the formulation of a policy concerning this companion activity. The policies and procedures used by ACE/CREDIT were adapted from those governing the Military Evaluations Program, and the two programs are similar.

Institutions without policies on the award of credit for extrainstitutional learning are encouraged to develop them. The ACE Board of Directors, in the statement "Awarding Credit for Extrainstitutional Learning" that appears in this publication, brings this important matter to the attention of the academic community and encourages positive action in developing policies to meet the changing and growing educational needs of adult learners.

We are especially pleased to acknowledge the cooperation of the state agencies that enabled this program to provide better service to adult learners, educational institutions, and noncollegiate organizations in their states. The commitment of states to provide increased opportunities for adult learners and to foster more effective linkages between the collegiate and noncollegiate sectors of postsecondary education attests to a positive direction in American higher education.

We are especially pleased to acknowledge support from the Fund for the Improvement of Postsecondary Education, to the General Motors Foundation for its grants to cover developmental costs, to the W. K. Kellogg Foundation for its commitment to the program's support for five years, and to Dale Carnegie and Associates, Inc. and the Westinghouse Electric Foundation for their grants to support a special project.

As the importance of lifelong learning continues to grow, ACE will look to educational institutions, noncollegiate organizations, and state education agencies for continued support and advice. Again, we hope you find this important reference guide to be a valuable tool.

Stanley O. Ikenberry
President
American Council on Education

Introduction

The purpose of the American Council on Education's College Credit Recommendation Service (ACE/CREDIT) is to help people obtain academic credit for learning acquired outside the sponsorship of colleges and universities by providing educational institutions with reliable information to use in making decisions on credit awards. ACE/CREDIT evaluates and makes credit recommendations for formal educational programs and courses offered by organizations that provide courses to their employees, members, or customers. These organizations include business and industry, labor unions, professional and voluntary associations, schools, institutes, and government agencies.

The credit recommendations are intended to guide colleges and universities as they consider awarding credit to persons who have successfully completed college-level instruction. In this way, students will be assisted in receiving academic credit for learning gained through such instruction.

The program is based on the proposition that it is sound educational practice for colleges and universities to grant academic credit for high-quality educational programs conducted by noncollegiate organizations, provided that the courses are appropriate to an individual's educational program. Moreover, experience has shown that awarding credit for prior learning will, in many cases, motivate students to enroll in formal postsecondary programs of study.

The program was initiated in July 1974 upon the recommendation of the Carnegie Commission on Nontraditional Study that the American Council on Education's system of evaluating formal courses offered by the armed services be extended to civilian organizations. The criteria and procedures that ACE has used since 1945 in evaluating military courses were adapted for use by ACE/CREDIT.

The program is national in scope, with ACE coordinating activities of its twenty ACE/CREDIT state affiliate offices. State affiliate offices include: Rio Salado Community College, Arizona; Golden Gate University, California; Community College and Occupational Education System, Colorado; Charter Oak State College, Connecticut; Florida International University, Florida; Georgia State University, Georgia; Illinois Community College Board, Illinois; Ivy Technical State College, Indiana State University, Rose-Hulman Institute of Technology, St. Mary-of-the-Woods College, Indiana; St. Joseph's College, Maine; Central Michigan University, Michigan; Clarkson College, Nebraska; College of Lifelong Learning, New Hampshire; Thomas Edison State College, New Jersey; Sinclair Community College, Ohio; The University of Oklahoma, Oklahoma; College of Charleston, South Carolina; The University of Tennessee at Knoxville, Tennessee; Alliance for Higher Education, Texas; Community College of Vermont, Vermont; and Davis and Elkins College, West Virginia.

All course evaluations are conducted by ACE/CREDIT or its state affiliated offices according to the program policies and procedures approved by the Com-mission on Educational Credit and Credentials, the policy-making body for the Center for Adult Learning and Educational Credentials. These policies and procedures appear on page 1449. ACE's coordinating role ensures consistency in the evaluation process. A review committee, with members from each program office, reviews the results of course evaluations for the program. The review committee also recommends policy to the Commission on Educational Credit and Credentials.

The American Council on Education encourages other state agencies to participate in the program and invites them to cooperate with the Council in the conduct of the program in their respective states.

The National Guide also contains the results of evaluations for apprenticeship programs, which are included in this edition. The policies and procedures governing the evaluation of apprenticeship programs closely resemble those used in the evaluation of business- or corporation-sponsored instruction and were approved by the Commission on Educational Credit and Credentials in May 1978. (A description of the policies and procedures is available upon request.)

In addition, *The National Guide* contains credit recommendations for courses offered by home-study schools that are accredited by the Distance Education Training Council (formerly the National Home Study Council). Here, too, policies and procedures are similar to those used in the evaluation of business- or corporation-sponsored instruction and were adopted by the Commission on Educational Credit and Credentials in May 1977. Under these policies, eligibility for review extends only to those accredited home-study courses that include a proctored, comprehensive examination. (A description of the policies and procedures is available upon request.)

ACE/CREDIT State Affiliate Offices

ACE/College Credit Recommendation Service
Center for Adult Learning and Educational Credentials
American Council on Education
One Dupont Circle, Suite 250
Washington, DC 20036-1193
Telephone: (202) 939-9727, 9437, or 9431
Fax: (202) 775-8578

Arizona Affiliate Office of ACE/CREDIT
Rio Salado Community College
Corporate Training and Education
2323 West 14th Street, Third Floor
Tempe, AZ 85281-6950
Telephone: (602) 517-8510
Fax: (602) 517-8519

California Affiliate Office of ACE/CREDIT
Golden Gate University
536 Mission Street
San Francisco, CA 94105
Telephone: (415) 442-6540
Fax: (415) 442-7049

Colorado Affiliate Office of ACE/CREDIT
Community College and Occupational Education System
1391 North Speer Boulevard, Suite 600
Denver, CO 80204-2554
Telephone: (303) 620-4000
Fax: (303) 825-4295

Connecticut Affiliate Office of ACE/CREDIT
Charter Oak State College
66 Cedar Street
Newington, CT 06111
Telephone: (860) 666-4595 ext. 20
Fax: (860) 666-4852

Florida Affiliate Office of ACE/CREDIT
Florida International University
N.E. 151 Street and Biscayne Boulevard
North Miami, FL 33181
Telephone: (305) 919-5669
Fax: (305) 919-5484

Georgia Affiliate Office of ACE/CREDIT
Georgia State University
P.O. Box 4044
Atlanta, GA 30302-4044
Telephone: (404) 651-3450
Fax: (404) 651-0443

Illinois Affiliate Office of ACE/CREDIT
Illinois Community College Board
401 East Capitol Avenue
Springfield, IL 62701-1711
Telephone: (217) 785-5003
Fax: (217) 524-4981

Indiana Affiliate Offices of ACE/CREDIT
Ivy Technical State College
7991 U.S. Highway 41 South
Terre Haute, IN 47802
Telephone: (812) 299-1121
Fax: (812) 299-5723

Indiana State University
217 N. Sixth Street
Terre Haute, IN 47809

Rose-Hulman Institute of Technology
5500 Wabash Avenue
Terre Haute, IN 47803

St. Mary-of-the-Woods College
St. Mary of The Woods, IN 47876

Maine Affiliate Office of ACE/CREDIT
Saint Joseph's College
278 Whites Bridge Road
Standish, ME 04084-5263
Telephone: (800) 343-5498
Fax: (207) 892-7423

Michigan Affiliate Office of ACE/CREDIT
Central Michigan University
Sloan Hall 324
Mount Pleasant, MI 48859
Telephone: (517) 774-4714
Fax: (517) 774-6456

Nebraska Affiliate Office of ACE/CREDIT
Clarkson College
101 South 42nd Street
Omaha, NE 68131-2739
Telephone: (800) 647-5500
Fax: (402) 552-6058

New Hampshire Affiliate Office of ACE/CREDIT
College of Lifelong Learning
10 Ferry Street, Suite 438
Concord, NH 03301
Telephone: (603) 271-5450
Fax: (603) 271-5453

New Jersey Affiliate Office of ACE/CREDIT
Thomas Edison State College
101 West State Street
Trenton, NJ 08608-1176
Telephone: (609) 633-6271
Fax: (609) 984-3898

Ohio Affiliate Office of ACE/CREDIT
Sinclair Community College
444 West 3rd Street
Dayton, OH 45402
Telephone: (937) 512-2940
Fax: (937) 512-5192

Oklahoma Affiliate Office of ACE/CREDIT
The University of Oklahoma
1700 Asp Avenue, Box 13
Norman, OK 73072-6400
Telephone: (405) 325-1947
Fax: (405) 325-0860

South Carolina Affiliate Office of ACE/CREDIT
College of Charleston
66 George Street
Charleston, SC 29424
Telephone: (803) 953-5822
Fax: (803) 953-1454

Tennessee Affiliate Office of ACE/CREDIT
The University of Tennessee–Knoxville
440 Communications and University Extensions Building
Knoxville, TN 37996-0346
Telephone: (423) 974-3181
Fax: (423) 974-6629

Texas Affiliate Office of ACE/CREDIT
Alliance for Higher Education
17101 Preston Road
LB 107, Suite 250
Dallas, TX 75248-1373
Telephone: (972) 713-8170 ext.116
Fax: (972) 713-8209

Vermont Affiliate Office of ACE/CREDIT
Community College of Vermont
32 College Street
Montpelier, VT 05602
Telephone: (802) 868-4060
Fax: (802) 868-2801

West Virginia Affiliate Office of ACE/CREDIT
Davis & Elkins College
100 Campus Drive
Elkins,WV 26241
Telephone: (304) 637-1261
Fax: (304) 637-1982

Participating Organizations Course Exhibits Contents

Participating Organizations 1978–1997

The following organizations have appeared in the 1978 through 1997 editions of *The National Guide to Educational Credit for Training Programs*. Organizations are listed in alphabetic order with the years they appeared in *The National Guide*. If you would like to order back copies of courses for these organizations, send a check in the amount of $5.00 for each organization to ACE/CREDIT National Guide, One Dupont Circle, Suite 250, Washington, DC 20036-1193.

Years	Sponsor
1982-1993	Abu Dhabi National Oil Company Career Development Center
1982-1987	Advanced Systems, Inc.
1986-1987	Airco Computer Learning Center
1987-1987	Alamo Learning Systems
1978-1992	American Institute of Banking, Correspondence Program
1981-1990	American International Group
1980-1987	American Medical International
1980-1985	American Red Cross
1978-1991	American Sterilizer Company
1979-1985	Anaheim Savings and Loan Association
1987-1993	American Center for Technical Arts and Sciences
1990	Applied Learning, Inc.
1984-1991	Applied Power, Inc.
1988	ASI/DELTAK
1986-1991	ARA Services, Inc.
1984-1987	Atlantic Electric
1979-1984	Atlantic Richfield Company
1989-1997	AT&T Executive Education
1987-1996	AT&T Learning Systems
1993-1997	AT&T Network Education and Training, International
1993-1997	AT&T Network Operations and Engineering Training
1994-1997	AT&T Network Operations and Engineering Training/Information Movement and Management Curriculum
1995-1997	AT&T Network Operations and Engineering Training, Network Services Division
1980-1996	AT&T Technical Education Center
1989-1994	Bally's Park Place Casino Hotel
1978-1985	Baltimore Police Department
1978-1986	Bank of America
1989-1993	Baroid Corporation
1982-1986	Beckman Instruments, Inc.
1987-1988	Bell Atlantic Network Services, Inc.
1979-1988	Bell of Pennsylvania/Diamond State Telephone
1982-1997	Bell Communications Research, Inc.
1987-1995	Bell Communications Research Training and Education Center
1986-1987	Bell South Services
1982-1986	Bell System Comptrollers Training Center
1987	Blackhawk Automotive Division
1990	Blackhawk Automotive, Inc.
1987-1991	Blake Business School
1984-1988	Blue Cross Hospital Service, Inc.
1987	Blue Cross and Blue Shield of Missouri
1978-1985	Blue Cross of Northern California
1978-1987	Boy Scouts of America
1984-1994	Brick Computer Science Institute
1984-1987	Brookings Institution
1992-1997	Bureau of Information Technology Studies
1986	Burroughs Corporation
1978-1985	California Department of Forestry Fire Academy
1979-1986	California Department of General Services
1982-1987	California Department of Transportation
1978-1979	California Employment Development Department
1978-1985	California State Police
1979-1985	Capitol Radio Engineering Institute
1989-1994	Center for Leadership Development, U.S. Department of Commerce
1985-1997	Central Intelligence Agency
1981-1988	Chesapeake & Potomac Telephone Company
1992-1993	Chubb and Son, Inc.
1988-1993	Cittone Institute
1980-1985	Collins Foods International, Inc.
1981-1998	Columbia Broadcasting System
1978-1987	Communications Workers of America
1986 1987	Computer Training Center, Institute for Safety and Systems
1988	Computer and Advanced Technology Center, College of Systems Science
1982-1991	ConTel Data Services Corporation
1987	ConTel Corporation
1989	ConTel Service Corporation
1979-1989	Continental Telecom, Inc.
1979-1985	Crocker National Bank
1984-1985	Crossroads Rehabilitation Center
1989-1997	Data Processing Training, Inc.
1988-1993	David C.D. Rogers Associates
1978-1985	Defense Contract Audit Agency
1983-1990	Defense Mapping Agency, Inter American Geodetic Survey
1982-1989	Del Taco Corporation
1984-1991	Del Taco Incorporated
1988	Del Taco, Inc.
1984-1992	DELTAK, Inc.
1986-1997	Digital Equipment Corporation
1980-1985	Douglas Oil Company of California
1987-1996	Dow Jones and Company, Inc.

1979-1985	Dresser Industries, Inc.
1985-1996	Educational Information and Resource Center
1979-1993	Electrical Workers, Local 26
1989-1993	Electrical Workers, Local 102
1984-1993	Electrical Workers, Local 164
1979	Electrical Workers, Local 441
1981-1985	Electronics Association of California
1990-1993	Employee Benefits Education and Planning Service, Inc.
1984-1988	Energy Consultants, Inc.
1991-1997	Evelyn Wood Reading Dynamics
1984-1995	Fairlaine Training and Development Center
1979-1985	Far West Services, Inc.
1980-1986	Fireman's Fund Insurance Companies
1987-1993	First Fidelity Bank, N.A., N.J. Management Program
1979-1989	Florida Bankers Association, Florida School of Banking
1978-1985	Fluor Engineers and Constructors, Inc.
1979	Fluor Corporation
1986-1993	Fox and Lazo, Inc.
1978-1997	GE Aircraft Engines
1978-1997	GE Apprenticeship Program
1981-1985	GEICO
1979-1985	General Dynamics, Pomona Division
1987-1989	General Motors Corporation, Advanced Engineering Staff
1989	General Motors Corporation, Technical Staffs Group and Lansing
1978-1985	General Telephone Company of California
1981-1985	General Telephone Company of the Southwest
1984-1987	Georgia Computer Programming Project
1988-1989	Georgia Computer Programming Project for Severely Handicapped Persons
1990-1991	Georgia Computer Campus
1981-1986	Glendale Federal Savings and Loan Association
1978-1981	Graduate School of Banking at the University of Wisconsin
1982-1991	Prochnow, Herbert V. Graduate School of Banking
1986-1987	Greater Cincinnati Industrial Training Corporation
1986-1991	GTE Service Corporation
1992	GTE Telephone Operations
1990-1993	Hallmark Cards, Incorporated
1979-1981	Harbor General Hospital
1982-1985	Harbor, UCLA Medical Center
1981-1986	Heath Company
1986-1991	Henkels & McCoy, Inc.
1978-1985	Holiday Inns, Inc.
1984-1986	Humana, Inc.
1981-1985	Illinois Bell Telephone Company
1981-1985	Illinois Management Training Institute
1987-1991	Inacomp Computer Centers, Inc.
1986	Increased Sales, Inc.
1981-1982	Indian Health Service
1982-1993	Indian Health Service, Tribal Management Support Center
1987-1988	Institute for Business and Technology
1978	Institute for Certifying Secretaries
1986-1991	Institute for Citizen Involvement in Education
1984-1985	Insurance Company of North America
1981-1982	Inter American Geodetic Survey Cartographic School, Defense Mapping
1982-1988	International Business Machines, Inc. General Systems Division
1988-1989	International Monetary Fund
1992-1997	IRI SKYLIGHT TRAINING & PUBLISHING, INC.
1979-1989	Jerrico Corporation
1979-1985	Jet Propulsion Laboratory
1984-1989	Jewish Hospital of St. Louis
1978-1985	John Hancock Mutual Life Insurance Company
1978-1985	Juvenile Justice Center of Pennsylvania
1980-1985	Kaiser Permanente Medical Care Program
1982-1985	Kaiser Permanente Medical Care Program (Southern CA)
1984-1987	Kansas Gas and Electric Company
1984-1989	Katharine Gibbs School
1976-1994	Laubach Literacy Action
1978-1985	Lockheed Missiles and Space Company, Inc.
1980-1986	Los Angeles, City of, Department of Water and Power
1986-1988	Lyons Institute
1986	Mainline Paralegal Institute
1987-1993	Maynard Management Institute
1980-1985	Mattel Toy Company
1984-1985	MCI Telecommunications
1980-1985	Memorial Hospital Medical Center of Long Beach, CA
1981-1986	Mr. Steak, Inc.
1982-1987	Mountain Bell Training and Education Center
1982-1985	Mountainside Hospital
1984-1995	National Academy for Paralegal Studies, Inc.
1978-1982	National Affiliation for Literacy Advance
1982-1983	National Association of Mutual Savings Banks, National School of Bank
1984-1993	National Association of Realtors
1990-1995	National Baptist Publishing Board
1984-1987	National Council of Savings Institutions
1979	National Electrical Contractors Association, Orange County
1979	National Electrical Contractors Association, Washington, DC
1978-1985	National Institute on Drug Abuse
1980-1985	National Institute on Mental Health

1986-1990	National Photographic Interpretation Center
1985-1995	National Sheriff's Association
1978-1980	National Security Agency
1979-1991	National Union of Hospital and Health Care Employees, District 1199C
1982-1994	NCR Corporation
1986-1989	Negotiation Institute
1982-1994	New England School of Banking
1982-1983	New Jersey Bell
1984-1986	New Jersey Bell Corporate Training Center
1987-1988	New Jersey Bell, A Bell Atlantic Company
1982-1985	New Jersey Department of Civil Service Division of Employee Development
1984-1988	NL Industries, Inc.
1981-1995	Northern Telecom, Inc.
1984-1986	Northwestern Bell
1987	Northwestern Bell Telephone Company, Training and Education Department
1989-1995	NYNEX
1990-1997	NYNEX Corporation
1987-1993	O/E Learning, Inc.
1990-1995	Ohio Bell Telephone Company
1983-1994	Omaha Joint Electrical Apprenticeship and Training Committee
1979-1991	Opportunities Academy of Management Training, Inc.
1979-1985	Orange County Electrical Joint Apprenticeship and Training Trust
1982-1988	Pacific Health Resources
1986-1990	Palmer School
1986	Pennco Tech
1990-1992	Philadelphia Electric Company
1979-1985	Philadelphia Lithographic Institute
1978-1985	Picker Corporation
1984-1986	Pioneer Take Out, Inc.
1984-1989	Pitney-Bowes, Inc.
1978-1985	Pittsburgh Psychoanalytic Center, Inc.
1980-1997	Police Training Institute
1981-1985	Polygraph Personnel Research School
1984-1989	Ponderosa, Inc.
1978-1987	Portland Cement Association
1986-1989	Portsmouth Naval Shipyard Apprenticeship Training Program
1980-1990	Professional Insurance Agents
1987-1995	Professional Secretaries International
1989	Raymond James & Associates, Inc. and Employee Benefits Education
1984-1986	Research-Cottrell
1981-1985	Rockwell International
1978-1985	Sacramento, City of
1979-1985	Sacramento, County of
1979-1993	San Diego Employers Association, Inc.
1989-1991	Sandy Corporation, Marketing Educational Services
1984-1985	Saudi Charter Medical, Ltd.
1987	Schneider Engineers
1979-1989	School of Banking of the South
1984-1985	Schoolwatch
1980-1985	Security Pacific National Bank
1990-1992	Sheffield School for Nannies
1978-1986	Sheraton Corporation
1978-1985	Southern California Edison Company
1979-1985	Southern California Gas Company
1978-1992	State of California Employment Development Department
1989-1995	Sun Company, Inc.
1992-1997	Swiss Bank Corporation
1984-1989	Syntex Laboratories, Inc.
1984-1987	Texas Instruments, Inc.
1988-1995	Texas Utilities Electric Corporation
1988-1993	The Cittone Institute
1978-1985	Trans World Airlines, Inc.
1989-1995	Tritone Music
1992-1993	Twin City Purchasing Management Association
1988-1992	Unisys Corporation
1979-1985	United Airlines
1990-1997	U.S. Army Anniston Army Depot
1991-1997	U.S. Army Center for Civilian Human Resource Management
1989-1991	U.S. Army Intelligence and Threat Analysis Center
1992-1997	U.S. Army Management Engineering College
1993-1994	U.S. Department of Commerce
1991-1995	U.S. Department of Labor Academy
1990-1995	U.S. Environmental Protection Agency
1989-1995	U.S. Food and Drug Administration
1980-1997	U.S. Office of Personnel Management
1990-1995	United Training Institute, Inc.
1984-1986	Upgrade Unlimited
1980-1987	Vetco Offshore, Inc.
1991-1997	Washington Gas Light Company
1984-1995	Washington Level Review Center
1981-1997	Westinghouse Electric Corporation
1986-1989	Westinghouse Electric Corporation, Defense and Electronics Center
1979-1991	Westinghouse Electric Corporation, Education Center Department
1984-1988	Westinghouse Electric Corporation, Water Reactor Divisions
1986-1989	Whirlpool Corporation
1988-1993	Wolf Creek Nuclear Operating Corporation
1989-1992	Yankee Atomic Electric Company
1979-1985	Young Men's Christian Association of Metropolitan Los Angeles
1978-1993	Young Women's Christian Association of the U.S.A.
1975-1997	Xerox Corporation

ORDER FORM FOR OUT–OF–PRINT CREDIT RECOMMENDATIONS

To order back copies of courses that were reviewed by ACE/CREDIT between the years 1978 and 1997 and that are **not** listed in this *National Guide*, please complete the following order form; enclose a check made payable to ACE/CREDIT; and mail to ACE/CREDIT *National Guide*, Attn: Jackie Taylor, One Dupont Circle, Suite 250, Washington, DC 20036-1193.

Name of Organization: ______________________________

____

____

Year(s) Applicable: ______________________________

____

No. of copies at $5.00 each (includes shipping and handling) ______________

______________________________ Total $ ______________

****

Name of Organization: ______________________________

____

____

Year(s) Applicable: ______________________________

____

No. of copies at $5.00 each (includes shipping and handling) ______________

______________________________ Total $ ______________

****

Name of Organization: ______________________________

____

____

Year(s) Applicable: ______________________________

____

No. of copies at $5.00 each (includes shipping and handling) ______________

______________________________ Total $______________

****

Mail ___ Fax ___ to:

Name: ______________________________

Title: ______________________________

Organization: ______________________________

____

Dept.: ______________________________

Street: ______________________________

City/State/Zip: ______________________________

Phone: ______________________ Fax: ______________________

A check made payable to **ACE/CREDIT** in the amount of $__________ is enclosed.

How to Use This Guide

The National Guide is intended for use in the academic counseling of students. The credit recommendations and course descriptions provide information for education officials to consider when granting credit to students for learning acquired in ACE/CREDIT participating organizations.

In order to make the best use of *The National Guide*, careful consideration should be given to this section. It explains the types of courses found in *The National Guide*, how to locate a particular course exhibit, how to interpret course exhibits, how the credit recommendations might be used, and how to receive assistance from the program offices.

The courses listed in *The National Guide* represent only a small sample of the educational programs conducted by the participating organizations. In addition, many other organizations in the United States conduct a wide range of high-quality educational programs for their employees or members. These are not included in this edition of *The National Guide* because they have not been submitted for review. Readers are cautioned against making adverse judgments regarding the educational programs of any organization merely because they are not listed in *The National Guide*. Students who have completed such unlisted courses should be given every consideration in accordance with institutional policies and practices.

It is the policy of ACE/CREDIT to include in *The National Guide* only those courses for which credit recommendations have been made. The ACE/CREDIT office will inform college officials, upon request, if a particular course given by one of the participating organizations was reviewed but was not recommended for credit.

How to Locate a Course Exhibit

In the text of *The National Guide*, each course is listed alphabetically by title or numerically by course number under the name of the organization that offers it. Therefore, it is necessary to identify the ACE/CREDIT participating organization before a course can be located. When a group of courses in an integrated program is reviewed, the courses are listed alphabetically or numerically under the title of the program, along with a paragraph describing the program.

How to Read a Course Exhibit

After each organizational heading, an introduction provides general information about the organization, its training and educational activities, the source of official records of student performance in its courses, and the program office to contact for additional information about the courses. Following the introduction, each course exhibit identifies the course and provides specific information about the course content and credit recommendation. (See Sample Course Exhibit.)

Title. Names of courses parallel course titles used traditionally in colleges and universities. In most cases, the course titles are the official ones used by ACE/CREDIT participating organizations. However, the evaluation team occasionally assigns an alternate title to provide more explanation and clarity. When the evaluation team assigns a title, the title used by the participating organization appears in parentheses below the evaluation team's title. Similarly, a course title that a team assigns to a *group* of courses appears first and is followed by a list of the courses that have been evaluated together to arrive at the credit recommendation. The evaluation team sometimes divides a course into parts, in which case the titles assigned by the team are given first, followed by the organization's title in parentheses.

Course number. The official course number, when provided by the organization, appears in parentheses or brackets following the course title.

Location. The site(s) where the course is offered. Correspondence, distance learning, and independent study courses are identified as such.

Length. Duration of the course in contact hours and, when appropriate, in days or weeks. The length is followed by any additional relevant information describing the course. Course length is useful information but consideration of learning outcomes must be given. The term "residential" indicates that the students reside at the location where the course is given for the duration of the course. Correspondence, distance learning, and independent study courses are identified as such.

Dates. The beginning and ending dates of the course are expressed by month and year. The dates cover the period during which the course has been offered with substantially the same content and procedures used at the time of its review; the credit recommendation applies to an individual who successfully completed the course during that period. The first date indicates the time from which the recommendation first applies and the second date indicates the time at which the recommendation ceased to apply. When "Present" is given as the second date, the recommendation applies as of the publication date for this edition of *The National Guide*. Program policy is to backdate a credit recommendation no more than ten years prior to the review date.

Course versions. Generally, if a course has more than one version, the newer version of the course has replaced an earlier one. The reader should be guided by the dates section. When a course has been modified, a closing date will be indicated for the earlier version, with the newer one beginning shortly after the closing date of the first version. Most often, "Present" will be listed as the second date for the newer course, indicating that the course is still offered. When both versions have "Present" as the closing date, the two versions are offered concurrently.

The multiple-version format also is used to indicate that a course has undergone modification. The date of modification will be indicated under the dates section. Wherever a change has occurred—in the length, learning outcome, objective, instruction, or credit recommendation—the reader should be guided by the listing for each version in the dates section.

Objective. The purpose for which the course is offered.

Learning Outcome. The abilities or competencies acquired by the student upon successful completion of the course.

Instruction. A description of the major topics covered including teaching methods, materials, equipment used, and methods of evaluating learning outcomes. Together, the objective, learning outcome, instructional description, and methods of evaluation supplement the credit recommendation by providing essential information about the nature of the course.

Credit recommendation. The category of credit, the number of semester hours recommended, the subject area(s) in which credit might be applied, and the date the course was reviewed.

1. *Categories of Credit:*

   a. *Vocational Certificate.* Includes coursework normally found in year-long certificate programs that are designed to provide students with occupational skills; in many two-year institutions, this type of coursework also is found in curricula leading to associate degrees in technical programs. Course content is specialized, and the accompanying shop training emphasizes procedural rather than analytical skills.

   b. *Lower Division Baccalaureate/Associate Degree.* Includes coursework found in programs leading to the Associate in Arts, Associate in Science, and Associate in Applied Science degrees and introductory-level coursework normally found in baccalaureate programs. Emphasis is on learning basic principles that have broad, judgmental application.

   c. *Upper Division Baccalaureate.* Includes coursework usually completed during the last two years of a baccalaureate program. The courses generally involve specialization of a theoretical or analytical nature beyond the introductory level.

   d. *Graduate Degree.* Includes coursework leading to a graduate degree. The courses tend to be oriented toward independent study, original research, critical analysis, and the scholarly and professional application of the specialized knowledge within a discipline.

   NOTE: In some instances, credit is recommended in more than one category. A decision must be made by the college as to which category of credit best applies to a student's educational program.

2. *Semester Hours:* All credit recommendations are made in semester hours. Credit recommendations are not derived by simple arithmetic conversion of contact hours to semester hours; the review teams base their recommendations on both the range and level of complexity of the subject matter covered, learning outcomes, and the number of contact hours.

3. *Subject Area(s):* In alphabetical order, the recommended subject area(s) in which credit might be applied. The designation of these general areas does not exclude the application of credit recommendation to other areas not mentioned in the course exhibit.

4. *Date of Review:* The month and year in which the credit recommendation was established are listed in parentheses following the subject area(s).

Sample Course Exhibit

Course Title: Either the participating organization's title or ageneric title assigned by the review team followed by the organization's title in parentheses.

Location: All locations where course is taught (e.g., Chicago, IL and Miami, FL; or Various sites in the U.S.; or Various sites worldwide).

Length: Given in actual contact hours and the number of days or weeks over which the course extends.

Dates: Month and year when credit recommendations became effective, to the present time; or, if course is no longer offered, effective month and year when it ceased to be taught (e.g., January 1989–January 1994).

Objective: A brief statement of the purpose or general goal the course was designed to achieve.

Learning Outcome: A list of the intellectual, technical, or attitudinal abilities/behaviors/competencies the student will have acquired as a result of sucessful completion of this course.

Instruction: Includes two elements: a list of the major topics covered and a list of all instructional methods and techniques used in delivering the course. It is important to indicate how the course instructor evaluates student learning. Normally this is done by quizzes or final exams, but other evaluation tools (e.g., checklists, criteria to judge projects, etc.) are often used to assess the extent of student achievement.

Credit Recommendation: Credit may be recommended in one or more of four categories: vocational certificate; lower-division baccalaureate/associate degree; upper-division baccalaureate degree; or graduate degree. Credit is expressed in semester hours only, and the date of the course evaluation is given in parentheses, e.g., (1/89).

Newspaper Design and Graphics

Location: Miami, FL.

Length: 36 hours (5 days).

Dates: January 1989–Present.

Objective: To provide the technical skills needed by newspaper layout, picture, and design editors.

Learning Outcome: Upon successful completion of this course, the student will be able to apply basic principles of editing to newspaper layout; use of pictures; and overall design elements.

Instruction: Major topics covered in the course are news hole efficiency; instant-art capabilities; type selection; tools of the trade; graphic capabilities of computer editing systems; redesign and prototype development; news–art department coordination; and photo, art, and graphics editing. Methods of instruction include lecture, discussion, classroom exercises, audio/visual material, quizzes, and final examination.

Credit Recommendation: In the lower division baccalaureate/associate degree category, 2 semester hours in Journalism (1/89) (1/94).

Verifying Course Completion

Educational institutions should require the applicant to verify that he or she has successfully completed a program or course either by having an American Council on Education's Registry of Credit Recommendations transcipt sent to their institution or by having official records submited by the organization. The introduction for each organization listed in *The National Guide* indicates the appropriate source of official student records. If the student has registered successful course completion in the Registry, he or she can request that a transcript be sent to an institution by the Registry. For Registry of Credit Recommendatons information see page 1455.

Awarding Credit

Credit for courses evaluated by the American Council on Education should be considered on the same basis as credit accepted by transcript from another institution. Institutions generally will require the applicant to furnish full information about previous college-level studies and a proposed future program of study before granting credit for such courses.

Applying the Credit to a Student's Academic Program

Credit for a course may be applied to a student's program of study in various ways: applied to the major to replace a required course; applied as an optional course within the major; applied as a general elective; or applied to waive a prerequisite.

Credit for a course taken in a participating organization should be granted only if the student has not completed a comparable college course. Most often, these educational programs do not exactly duplicate college courses but do contain instruction applicable to a general area of collegiate study. In such cases, credit can be granted toward required or elective courses in the area, depending on the instructional program at the institution and the specific educational objectives of the individual.

Duplicating Credit

If a student has completed in one organization several courses which are apparently in the same subject area and at the same level, the college official should review the descriptions of these courses for possible duplication of coverage. If it appears that instruction is duplicated among the several courses, officials should apply the credit recommendations so as to avoid granting duplicate credit for the course. In *The National Guide*, duplication of course materials is noted only for courses of a single participating organization. Users of *The National Guide* must make their own determinations about duplication of course material in courses offered by different organizations.

Interpreting Grades from Participating Organizations

Grading systems vary widely among participating organizations. Most organizations award certificates of successful completion on a pass/fail basis, with no attempt to apply traditional grading practices. A recommendation of academic credit for a course taken in a participating organization therefore should be interpreted as being applicable when the student presents official evidence of having successfully completed or passed the course.

Awarding Credit for Courses Listed in *The National Guide* but not Covered by the Dates of the Recommendations

Sometimes a student will request credit for a course listed in *The National Guide* but completed by the student prior to the beginning date or after the closing date of the recommendation. The recommendations in *The National Guide* are backdated to the point that the course was first offered in substantially the same form. Sometimes the beginning date indicates the earliest records kept by the organization, even though the course was offered prior to that date. In these cases, institutions can use *The National Guide* as a point of departure when making their own assessments.

When a student requests credit for a course not covered by the recommendations, the institution should verify the student's completion with the official record. The student should provide additional information about the course, perhaps a course outline or a catalog from the participating organization so that the institution can compare that course with the one listed in *The National Guide*. Using *The National Guide*, the institution then can make its own assessment.

Interpreting Course Exhibits with Different Versions or Changes in Location, Length, Objectives, Outcomes, Instruction, or Credit Recommendations

The course exhibits of each organization are reviewed annually. The review is conducted using information provided on questionnaires completed by organizational educators and trainers. These persons are requested to make changes in course titles, lengths, objectives, outcomes, and methods of instruction. They also are asked to update the program descriptions preceding their course exhibits. If the program staff determines that any of these changes may affect the existing credit recommendations, re-evaluations of the courses are conducted. When changes occur to the other items listed above, the course exhibits are simply changed accordingly. Guide users who have questions about any of these kinds of changes are encouraged to call the Program Advisory Service at (202) 939-9437.

Questions and Answers for Counselors and Advisors of Adult Students

This section is intended for use by persons responsible for helping individuals make the best use of the credit recommendations. Further advice and assistance are available from the Program Advisory Service at (202) 939-9727.

How many credits is each course worth? The recommended number of credits for each course is listed at the end of each course exhibit in *The National Guide*. This recommendation is made by a team of subject-matter experts when it has been determined that the course is college level.

These are recommended credits. A college is not required to grant as much credit as is recommended by the reviewers, nor is a college limited to granting only that amount of credit. A college may feel that a person's performance in a course deserves additional credit.

How are the credit recommendations used? The credit recommendations are used primarily to obtain college credit or advanced college placement. It also may be possible to use the credit recommendations for entry into new areas of employment, for job advancement, to obtain salary benefits, and for personal assessment.

Is college credit earned automatically when someone successfully completes a course listed in *The National Guide*? No. Successful completion of such a course results in actual course credit only when the course is accepted toward a degree or certificate at a postsecondary institution. A student who already has taken one of the courses listed in *The National Guide*, or who plans to take one, should contact the admissions office at the college he or she plans to attend to determine the acceptability of the course for academic credit.

Are policies for granting credit the same at all colleges? No. Each college sets its own policies, and these vary from college to college. While one college might not grant credit for successful completion of a course conducted by an ACE/CREDIT participating organization, others might. It also should be noted that a college may not grant credit but may, instead, waive a prerequisite or a required course.

Each institution, and, in many cases, each academic unit and department within each institution, sets its own policies for granting credit. The admissions office at a college should be able to direct students to the official responsible for making the decision.

What should be done if it is found that the organization's official records or the credit recommendations are not being accepted by some colleges? The appropriate state affiliate office of ACE/CREDIT should be informed promptly. Often, mere lack of familiarity with the program accounts for a college's refusal to accept records or credit recommendations. A phone call or letter from ACE or the appropriate state affiliate office may solve the problem. Counselors and advisors should develop for their course participants a list of colleges whose policies are favorable toward the individuals' educational requirements. Course participants will then be spared the time and expense of trial and error.

How much credit may be earned for courses taken at ACE/CREDIT participating organizations? Institutions have different policies regarding the amount of credit that may be earned off campus. The individual should check with the college he or she plans to attend to determine both the amount of credit that will be granted for such courses and the subject areas in which the college will grant credit for these courses.

When will credit be awarded? In most cases, an individual should seek credit when formally applying for admission to a college. A college may grant credit only provisionally at that time and may withhold full credit until the individual successfully completes either some courses or a specific number of credits at that college.

Can credit be earned for a course completed in the past or taken from a former employer? Yes. The credit recommendation established for each course described in *The National Guide* can be used by anyone who successfully completed the course during the period listed in the dates section of the course exhibit. When "Present" is given as the second date, the course is still being offered by the organization as of the publication date for this edition of *The National Guide*. Each organization listed in *The National Guide* keeps records of its present and former employees who completed courses during the periods indicated and will supply those records upon request.

When will a college consider granting credit for a participating organization's instruction? A college will consider granting academic credit to a student for an ACE/CREDIT-participating organization's course only after receiving an official record from the organization or a transcript from the ACE Registry (see page 1455) verifying that the person successfully completed the course.

How are student records for courses listed in *The National Guide* reported to colleges? The ACE/CREDIT-participating organization provides the official transcript at the student's request. If the course completion is registered with the American Council on Education's Registry of Credit Recommendations, the Registry records office will issue an official record at the individual's request. Information about the ACE Registry is available from the Registry's office, (202) 939-9434.

The official record or transcript from the Registry will enable a college official to verify the individual's successful completion of the course and the date of completion. The source of official student records for each organization is noted in the introduction under each organizational heading.

How are courses listed in *The National Guide* selected for review? With the assistance of the ACE/CREDIT staff, each organization selects the courses it would like to have reviewed. Individual students may not submit courses for review. Only education programs conducted on a formal basis and with official approval of the participating organization are listed in *The National Guide*.

Can an individual earn credit for certification exams? Yes. Exams that have been evaluated by the American Council on Education's Credit by Examination Program are eligible for college credit recommendations and may be used toward an academic degree in the same way as ACE/CREDIT credit recommendations. See page xxxiii for a list of evaluated certification examinations.

Can an individual earn credit for courses offered by organizations that are not listed in *The National Guide*? Yes. Some institutions will evaluate students' knowledge individually, either by means of national standardized proficiency examination programs, such as the College-Level Examination Program (CLEP) and the College Proficiency Examination Program (CPEP), or by assessment of individual learning experiences through portfolios or institutional examinations. A student should consult with an advisor at the institution where he or she is enrolled or is contemplating enrollment to learn how credit might be awarded for prior learning.

Why do some companies that appeared in previous editions of *The National Guide* no longer appear? Organizations that no longer wish to participate in ACE/CREDIT or to adhere to the requirements and procedures of the program are dropped from *The National Guide*. However, information about the courses formerly evaluated for these organizations is available in previous editions of *The National Guide* and from the ACE/CREDIT Advisory Service for a $5.00 processing fee. See the list of former participating organizations on pages xix-xxi of this *National Guide*. **Send a check for $5.00 for each organization to ACE/CREDIT, One Dupont Circle, Suite 250, Washington, DC 20036-1193.**

How can an institution that accepts ACE/CREDIT credit recommendations be listed in the *National Guide* and ACE/CREDIT's book of Academic Institutions That Have Accepted ACE/CREDIT Credit Recommendations? Complete and return the card on the last page of this Guide.

Advisory/Advocacy Service

A continuing advisory/advocacy service is provided by each state affiliate office of ACE/CREDIT. Publication of *The National Guide* on a regular basis is part of that service. After each edition of *The National Guide* is published, ACE/CREDIT and its state affiliate offices continue to evaluate courses. The official results of a course review are sent as soon as possible to the participating organization for general distribution to its employees and members.

The advisory/advocacy service will:

- furnish information on courses awaiting publication;
- offer assistance in the interpretation of published results;
- furnish information on courses for organizations that have been evaluated but that no longer maintain an active status with the program;
- and intervene with a college or university on behalf of an organization or student.

Courses awaiting publication will be listed in *Update*, the newsletter of the Center for Adult Learning and Educational Credentials, which is distributed to educational institutions and participating organizations twice a year.

The appropriate state affiliate office of ACE/CREDIT to contact for assistance with a particular course is indicated in the introduction to each group of course exhibits. Complete addresses of these offices are listed in the ACE/CREDIT Affiliate State Offices Index (see pages xi-xii).

Evaluated Certification Examinations

The American Council on Education's Credit by Examination (CBE) Program evaluates individual examinations in terms of academic credit, thereby ensuring that college credit awarded on the basis of test results represents achievement comparable to that earned through traditional courses of study. The results of the evaluations are published in the *Guide to Educational Credit by Examination.*

The American Council on Education's Credit by Examination Program has evaluated the following certification examinations:

Associate Computer Professional (ACP) sponsored by the Institute for the Certification of Computer Professionals (ICCP)

Automotive Service Excellence (ASE) Examinations sponsored by the National Institute for Automotive Service Excellence

Cardiovascular Registry Examination - Invasive sponsored by Cardiovascular Credentialing International (CCI)

Cardiovascular Registry Examination - Non invasive sponsored by Cardiovascular Credentialing International (CCI)

Certificate of Merit Examination sponsored by the National Court Reporters Association (NCRA)

Certified Cardiographic Technician sponsored by Cardiovascular Credentialing International (CCI)

Certified Computing Professional (CCP) sponsored by the Institute for the Certification of Computer Professionals (ICCP)

Certified Data Processor (CDP) sponsored by the Institute for the Certification of Computer Professionals (ICCP)

Certified Novell Instructor Examination sponsored by Novell

Certified Payroll Professional sponsored by the American Payroll Association (APA)

Certified Professional Legal Secretary Examination sponsored by the National Association of Legal Secretaries

Certified Professional Secretaries Examination sponsored by Professional Secretaries International

Certified Systems Professional (CSP) sponsored by the Institute for the Certification of Computer Professionals (ICCP)

International Certification Reciprocity Consortium Examination sponsored by Alcohol and Other Drug Abuse Inc.

National Computing Centre (NCC) Examination sponsored by the National Computing Centre

Novell Certified NetWare Administrator sponsored by Novell

Novell Certified NetWare Engineer sponsored by Novell

Private Pilot Certificate sponsored by the Federal Aviation Administration

Registered Professional Reporter Examination sponsored by the National Court Reporters Association (NCRA)

Technologists Examination sponsored by the Magnetic Resonance Institute

The Credit by Examination Program also has evaluated the following Testing Programs: ACT-PEP: Regents College Examinations, Advanced Placement (AP) Program sponsored by The College Board, College Level Examination Program (CLEP) sponsored by The College Board, Central Intelligence Agency Foreign Language Examinations, Defense Language Program Tests (DLPTs) sponsored by the Defense Language Institute, Defense Subject Standardized Tests (DSSTs) sponsored by the Defense Activity for Nontraditional Educational Support (DANTES).

For more information about the examinations and the American Council on Education's Credit by Examination Program, including the credit recommendations as listed in the Guide to Educational Credit by Examination (4th edition), call (202) 939-9434 or write to ACE, Credit by Examination Program, One Dupont Circle, Suite 250, Washington, DC 20036-1193. Fax (202) 775-8578.

Course Exhibits

AchieveGlobal

AchieveGlobal is an 18-year old education, consulting, and training firm that specializes in helping companies measurably improve individual and organizational performance.

Toward this end, AchieveGlobal focuses on enabling executives to effectively implement their business strategies through customer focus, process management, and employee involvement.

AchieveGlobal's executive offerings focus on the management technologies of service/quality, strategic process management, re-engineering, and work teams. Application of these proven methodologies result in creating products and services better, faster, and cheaper to gain sustainable competitive advantage.

AchieveGlobal's skills training addresses meeting-facilitation, problem-solving, team-building and participation, communication, relationship, performance and development, and quality issues. This training is designed for those at all organizational levels-middle managers, supervisors, individual contributors, team leaders and participants, and non-supervisory employees. All AchieveGlobal training includes and reinforces "The Basic Principles"-a unique set of values that emphasize respect for the individual, maintenance of long term relationships, leading by example, and taking initiative.

Headquartered in San Jose, California, the company works with more than 3,000 public and private sector organizations worldwide, including half the Fortune 500. Their training is available in more than 10 languages in more than 50 countries through a network of direct and affiliate offices.

Source of official student records: Registry of Credit Recommendations, American Council on Education, One Dupont Circle, Washington, DC 20036-1193.

Additional information about the courses: College Credit Recommendation Service, American Council on Education, One Dupont Circle, Washington, DC 20036-1193.

Building Successful Teams

Location: Various sites worldwide.

Length: 24 hours (days vary).

Dates: June 1994-Present.

Objective: To provide understanding of the evolution of work teams and how work teams change the conventional leadership role of supervisors and managers.

Learning Outcome: Upon successful completion of this course, the student will be able to describe the new leadership role in a team-oriented environment and how to attain it; use the Basic Principles to build team trust; describe the dynamics of work team development; develop a work team initiation plan and a plan to maintain a team; set tasks and task boundaries; provide teams with adequate support and monitor progress; encourage methods of team cooperation; and identify and resolve conflicts between team members.

Instruction: Major topics covered in the course are the team leadership concept, leadership skills in the work team environment, trust building in work teams, and the four phases of team development (work team vision/goals/ground rules, work team support/coaching/monitoring, team members responsibilities, and identification and resolution of team conflict). Methods of instruction include lecture, discussion, behavior modeling, skills practice, videotapes, workbook exercises, out-of-class projects, and evaluation using observation forms, coaching logs, oral and written feedback, student written plans for applying behavior, and self-assessment of behavioral change.

Credit Recommendation: In the upper division baccalaureate degree category, 1 semester hour in Human Resource Development, Human Relations, Industrial Operations and Systems Engineering, Leadership, Management, or Sociology (6/94).

Certification Seminar for Facilitators

Location: Various sites worldwide.

Length: 42 hours (days vary).

Dates: June 1994-Present.

Objective: To provide knowledge and skills required of instructors to deliver the Zenger-Miller Training System.

Learning Outcome: Upon successful completion of this course, the student will be able to explain the steps in the basic learning process; use the Zenger Miller Basic Principles in teaching; identify appropriate learning materials for local audiences; demonstrate facilitation behaviors in delivering content; give and receive feedback; and demonstrate an understanding of the implementation of facilitative training within organizations.

Instruction: Major topics covered in the course are the learning process, using the Zenger Miller Basic Principles, learning materials, facilitation skills/behaviors/techniques, and constructive feedback. Methods of instruction include lecture, discussion, behavior modeling, skills practice, videotapes, workbook exercises, out-of-class projects, and evaluation using observation forms, coaching logs, oral and written feedback, student written plans for applying behavior, and self-assessment of behavioral change.

Credit Recommendation: In the upper division baccalaureate degree category, 2 semester hours in Education, Human Resource Development, Psychology, or Sociology (6/94).

Enhancing Performance for Managers and Others (0018)

Location: Various locations worldwide.

Length: 17 hours.

Dates: September 1994-Present.

Objective: To provide participants with approaches to manage priorities and to assist others in the organization maximize their performance.

Learning Outcome: Upon successful completion of this course, the student will be able to describe coaching, its importance and the behaviors that foster a coaching environment and demonstrate asking and listening techniques that support formal and informal coaching; demonstrate techniques for giving and receiving constructive feedback; explain the impact of recognition on individual and organizational success and identify behaviors that reinforce people's efforts to achieve organizational goals; understand the need to establish priorities and identify techniques to deal with the complexities of a modern organization.

Instruction: Major topics covered in the course are coaching; giving and receiving constructive feedback; giving recognition; managing priorities. Methods of instruction include video, group discussions, application exercises, skills practice, experiential activities, case studies, simulations, video case studies, self assessments, instructional games, and presentations.

Credit Recommendation: In the lower division baccalaureate/associate degree category, 1 semester hour in Supervision or Leadership (11/95).

Exercising Influence in a Changing Environment (0019)

Location: Various locations worldwide.

Length: 15 hours.

Dates: September 1994-Present.

Objective: To provide participants with the materials and methods for successfully impacting organizational processes and results by practicing interpersonal skills.

Learning Outcome: Upon successful completion of this course, the student will be able to explain ways of influencing people for win-win outcomes; describe the change process and develop personal strategies for navigating change; use key actions to listen proactively and deal with different communication styles; and describe basic characteristics of a collaborative workplace.

Instruction: Major topics covered in the course are proactive listening; understanding reasons for change and making change successful; influencing skills. Methods of instruction include video, group discussions, application exercises, skills practice, experiential activities, case studies, simulations, video case studies, self-assessments, instructional games, presentations and small group exercises.

Credit Recommendation: In the lower division baccalaureate/associate degree category, 1 semester hour in Management, Human Resource Development, or Industrial Relations (11/95).

Facilitating for Results

Location: Various sites worldwide.

Length: 16 hours (days vary).

Dates: June 1994-Present.

Objective: To provide leaders with skill needed to identify and address routine and complex organizational problems using problem-solving teams.

Learning Outcome: Upon successful completion of this course, the student will be able to plan and conduct focused, outcome-based group meetings; integrate facilitation techniques to encourage a wide range of views; explain differences between meeting process and content; maintain the appropriate meeting pace and focus on task; assign specific action items and action plans; evaluate meeting effectiveness and future application of leadership skills.

Instruction: Major topics covered in the course are effective meeting facilitation, valuing individual differences, gaining group consensus, and managing a changing organization. Methods of instruction include lecture, discussion, behavior modeling, skills practice, videotapes, workbook exercises, out-of-class projects, and evaluation using observation forms, coaching logs, oral and written feedback, student written plans for applying behavior, and self-assessment of behavioral change.

Credit Recommendation: In the upper division baccalaureate degree category, 1 semester hour in Business Administration, Human Resource Development, Industrial Operations and System Engineering, Management, Organizational Development, Psychology, or Sociology (6/94).

Facilitating Successful Teams

Location: Various sites worldwide.

Length: 28 hours (days vary).

Dates: June 1994-Present.

Objective: To provide knowledge and skills that enable team leaders to draw on the knowledge, ability, and creativity of teams to achieve productive results.

Learning Outcome: Upon successful completion of this course, the student will be able to encourage diverse views and discussion using facilitation techniques; assign action items and follow-up plans; describe guidelines for decision-making and evaluation; achieve team consensus; analyze and capitalize on team member similarities and differences; identify disruptive team differences that warrant intervention; determine effective ways to deal with obstacles to organizational improvement; and use forward thinking skills to influence organizational change.

Instruction: Major topics covered in the course are dealing constructively with individual differences, effective facilitation of meetings, action planning, creating an adaptable and flexible organization, and managing and responding to organizational change. Methods of instruction include lecture, discussion, behavior modeling, skills practice, videotapes, workbook exercises, out-of-class projects, and evaluation using observation forms, coaching logs, oral and written feedback, student written plans for applying behavior, and self-assessment of behavioral change.

Credit Recommendation: In the upper division baccalaureate degree category, 2 semester hours in Business Administration, Human Resource Development, Industrial Operations and Systems Engineering, Management, Organizational Development, Psychology, or Sociology (6/94).

Focusing on Quality and the Customer

Location: Various sites worldwide.

Length: 16 hours (days vary).

Dates: June 1994-Present.

Objective: To provide skills necessary to meet customer expectations through quality improvement interventions.

Learning Outcome: Upon successful completion of this course, the student will be able to explain the importance of meeting customer expectations; define quality; explain components of a quality plan; understand the role of workers, supervisors, and managers in quality initiatives; describe successful customer/company relations and the consequences of dissatisfied customers; and explain how to "defuse" angry customers.

Instruction: Major topics covered in the course are customer expectations, successful customer/company relations, key customer issues and concerns, internal /external customers, dissatisfied customers, basic principles of quality, quality skills of managers and employees, and quality improvement initiatives. Methods of instruction include lecture, discussion, behavior modeling, skills practice, videotapes, workbook exercises, out-of-class projects, and evaluation using observation forms, coaching logs, oral and written feedback, student written plans for applying behavior, and self-assessment of behavioral change.

Credit Recommendation: In the lower division baccalaureate/associate degree category, 1 semester hour in Human Resource Development, Industrial Operations and Systems Engineering, Management, or Sociology (6/94).

Individual Leadership Strategies for the New Millennium

Location: Various sites worldwide.

Length: 16 hours.

Dates: June 1996-Present.

Objective: To provide participants with the leadership skills necessary to be successful in a rapidly changing, challenging, and demanding work environment; how to effectively express their thoughts and ideas, learn the importance of collaboration, problem solving, and decision making, handle conflict and emotions; and expand their roles to take greater responsibility in the organization's success.

Learning Outcome: Upon successful completion of this course, the student will be able to explain why they need to fulfill expanded, flexible roles in organizations; discuss what that means for their own jobs; describe five strategies they can use to focus their efforts as they handle new responsibilities environments; assess their effectiveness as leaders; describe the three elements of speaking; explain the importance of considering listener's needs when planning to speak; understand the need to formulate a clear, concise statement of the objective; demonstrate a variety of delivery techniques; construct and deliver a formal or informal presentation, identify influences that are contributing to conflict in today's organizations; identify behavior patterns that undermine the ability to address conflict constructively; describe productive methods for dealing with undermining behaviors; distinguish between positions taken in a conflict and the underlying issues; explain why emotions are normal and can be helpful in work situations; identify situations where emotional behavior is inhibiting productive discussion; discuss why the ability to maintain composure at work, or to regain it quickly, is an important skill; identify ways to manage their own reactions to the emotional behavior of others; and to use appropriate techniques to diffuse emotional behavior when it hinders progress in a work discussion.

Instruction: Major topics covered in the course are behavior patterns, approaches to conflict, turning conflict into positive, productive results; pitfalls common to organizations for dealing with conflict; expanded flexible roles; greater responsibility for an organization's success; barriers that prevent organizations from adapting to business realities; and five critical leadership strategies to be more effective leaders; essential speaking elements, comfort zones, self-assessment, the listener's needs, techniques for planning, organizing, and sharing results-oriented messages, delivery techniques, handling emotions, remaining calm and objective, recovering quickly from a situation, assisting others to handle their own emotions, and taking charge in difficult situations. Methods of instruction include lecture, discussion, simulations, video tapes, behavior modeling, individual coaching and practice, workbook exercises, and evaluation using written planning for application on the job, insight and action planning forms, and self-assessment.

Credit Recommendation: In the lower division baccalaureate/associate degree category, 1 semester hour in Administration, Management, and Supervision (10/96).

Influential Management

Location: Various sites worldwide.

Length: 18 hours (days vary).

Dates: June 1994-Present.

Objective: To provide skills in effective use of time in addressing and resolving difficult work situations, and to enhance workplace relationships through prioritizing, soliciting feedback, and encouraging a supportive environment.

Learning Outcome: Upon successful completion of this course, the student will be able to focus meetings on desired outcomes; achieve agreement on resolution of performance problems; develop and maintain action plans for peer and manager support; and explain how recommendations benefit employees and the organization.

Instruction: Major topics covered in the course are planning for desired outcomes, conflict resolution, gaining support from others, and constructive and effective organizational change. Methods of instruction include lecture, discussion, behavior modeling, skills practice, videotapes, workbook exercises, out-of-class projects, and evaluation using observation forms, coaching logs, oral and written feedback, student written plan behavior, and self-assessment of behavioral change.

Credit Recommendation: In the lower division baccalaureate/associate degree category, 1 semester hour in Management, Sociology, Social Psychology, Industrial Operations and Systems Engineering, Human Relations, or Human Resource Development (6/94).

Interpersonal Skills for Leaders and Managers

Location: Various sites worldwide.

Length: 17 hours (days vary).

Dates: June 1994-Present.

Objective: To provide knowledge of critical interpersonal skills used in management.

Learning Outcome: Upon successful completion of this course, the student will be able to apply basic principles of management including giving employees constructive feedback, obtaining information by utilizing questioning and listening techniques, defusing emotional behavior, and recognizing achievement.

Instruction: Major topics covered in the course are basic principles of management, constructive feedback, questioning and listening techniques, communicating difficult decisions, defusing emotional behavior, and recognizing positive results. Methods of instruction include lecture, discussion, behavior modeling, skills practice, videotapes, workbook exercises, out-of-class projects, and evaluation using observation forms, coaching logs, oral and written feedback, student written plans for applying behavior, and student self-assessment of behavioral change.

Credit Recommendation: In the lower division baccalaureate/associate degree category, 1 semester hour in Human Relations, Human Resource Development, Management, Social Psychology, Sociology, or Industrial Relations (6/94).

Interpersonal Skills for the Workplace

Location: Various sites worldwide.

Length: 19 hours (days vary).

Dates: June 1994-Present.

Objective: To provide skills required on the job to ensure effective employee relationships and productivity.

Learning Outcome: Upon successful completion of this course, the student will be able to use basic principles in job interactions; listen effectively; give adequate feedback; display skill in learning new job assignments; know when to request help; communicate effectively with supervisors; understand methods of conflict resolution; play an appropriate role in group meetings; and accept unavoidable challenges in a positive manner.

Instruction: Major topics covered in the course are basic principles of job interaction; listening; feedback; accepting a new assignment; communication up, down, and across an organization; conflict resolution; meeting dynamics; and challenges in the workplace. Methods of instruction include lecture, discussion, behavior modeling, skills practice, videotapes, workbook exercises, out-of-class projects, and evaluation using observation forms, coaching logs, oral and written feedback, student written plans for applying behavior, and self-assessment of behavioral change.

Credit Recommendation: In the lower division baccalaureate/associate degree category, 1 semester hour in Human Relations, Human Resource Development, Leadership, Sociology, or Supervision (6/94).

Manager's New Role in Self-Directed Teams

Location: Various sites worldwide.

Length: 16 hours (days vary).

Dates: June 1994-Present.

Objective: To provide understanding of how the manager's role changes as the organization converts from a traditional organizational structure to a structure which includes self-directed work teams.

Learning Outcome: Upon successful completion of this course, the student will be able to describe what self-directed work teams are and the benefits associated with a work team structure; describe the phases of work team development and the role of managers in each phase; identify anticipated training needs of managers and team members as the work team assumes more autonomy; develop a plan leading to expanded responsibility for work teams; and identify future actions for managers once work teams reach maturity.

Instruction: Major topics covered in the course are self-directed work teams, developmental phases of work teams, training needs for managers and team members, planning for expanded responsibility, the manager's changing role, and the manager's future role. Methods of instruction include lecture, discussion, behavior modeling, skills practice, videotapes, workbook exercises, out-of-class projects, and evaluation using observation forms, coaching logs, oral and written feedback, student written plans for applying behavior, and self-assessment of behavioral change.

Credit Recommendation: In the upper division baccalaureate degree category, 1 semester hour in Business Administration, Human Resource Development, Industrial Operations and Systems Engineering, Management, or Sociology (6/94).

Managing Change and Managerial Problem-Solving

Location: Various sites worldwide.

Length: 22 hours (days vary).

Dates: June 1994-Present.

Objective: To provide skills needed to manage change and innovation, and to be an effective problem solver.

Learning Outcome: Upon successful completion of this course, the student will be able to help employees implement successful change, encourage innovation, utilize techniques for logical problem-solving, participate in group problem-solving, and lead problem-solving sessions.

Instruction: Major topics covered in the course are resistance to change, managing change, encouraging innovation, the logical problem-solving process, tools and techniques for problem-solving (including force-field analysis and control charts), and participating in and leading problem-solving sessions. Methods of instruction include lecture, discussion, behavior modeling, skills practice, videotapes, workbook exercises, out-of-class projects, and evaluation using observation forms, coaching logs, oral and written feedback, student written plans for applying behavior, and self-assessment of behavioral change.

Credit Recommendation: In the lower division baccalaureate/associate degree category, 1 semester hour in Management, Industrial Operations, Systems Engineering, Industrial Relations, and Industrial Psychology (6/94).

Performance Management

Location: Various sites worldwide.

Length: 19 hours (days vary).

Dates: June 1994-Present.

Objective: To provide skills to ensure adequate performance of employees through establishing clear expectations and utilizing motivational techniques.

Learning Outcome: Upon successful completion of this course, the student will be able to establish job expectations, give positive feedback to employees, identify the effect of employee recognition, identify skill gaps and methods of correction, determine when and how to coach, and determine when and how to take corrective action,

Instruction: Major topics covered in the course are establishing job expectations, feedback, motivation through recognition, employee coaching, and corrective action. Methods of instruction include lecture, discussion, behavior modeling, skills practice, videotapes, workbook exercises, out-of-class projects, and evaluation using observation forms, coaching logs, oral and written feedback, student written plans for applying behavior, and self-assessment of behavioral change.

Credit Recommendation: In the lower division baccalaureate/associate degree category, 1 semester hour in Management, Sociology, Social Psychology, Industrial Operations and Systems Engineering, Human Relations, or Human Resource Development (6/94).

Problem-Solving and Team Skills for the Workplace

Location: Various sites worldwide.

Length: 18 hours (days vary).

Dates: June 1994-Present.

Objective: To provide interpersonal skills that enhance the ability of work teams to achieve desired results, deal with change, and solve specific problems.

Learning Outcome: Upon successful completion of this course, the student will be able to prioritize team tasks and results; determine ways to achieve team goals; communicate need for team success; understand why change occurs and how it affects the organization; solve problems associated with change; contribute to team problem solving; and achieve team consensus on problem-solving action plans.

Instruction: Major topics covered in the course are team development, team member roles and responsibilities, interpersonal communication, and team problem-solving tools and techniques. Methods of instruction include lecture, discussion, behavior modeling, skills practice,videotapes, workbook exercises, out-of-class projects, and evaluation using observation forms, coaching logs, oral and written feedback, student written plans for applying behavior, and self-assessment of behavioral change.

Credit Recommendation: In the lower division baccalaureate/associate degree category, 1 semester hour in Human Relations, Human Resource Development, Leadership, Psychology, Sociology, or Supervision (6/94).

Process and Quality Improvement

Location: Various sites worldwide.

Length: 16 hours (days vary).

Dates: June 1994-Present.

Objective: To provide a four-step problem solving process and problem-solving tools to identify process improvement opportunities.

Learning Outcome: Upon successful completion of this course, the student will be able to list opportunities for process improvement; compare performance to key customer expectations; determine causes of problems and apply appropriate tools to solve problems; achieve a team problem-solving approach; and focus problem-solving teams on the task.

Instruction: Major topics covered in the course are process-improvement methods, problem-solving methods and tools, and team development and leadership. Methods of instruction include lecture, discussion, behavior modeling, skills practice, videotapes, workbook exercises, out-of-class projects, and evaluation using observation forms, coaching logs, oral and written feedback, student written plans for applying behavior, and self-assessment of behavioral change.

Credit Recommendation: In the upper division baccalaureate degree category, 1 semester hour in Business Administration, Human Resource Development, Industrial Operations and Systems Engineering, Management, or Supervision (6/94).

Self-Directed Work Team Skills

Location: Various sites worldwide.

Length: 16 hours (days vary).

Dates: June 1994-Present.

Objective: To provide knowledge of interaction skills necessary for successful membership on a self-directed work team.

Learning Outcome: Upon successful completion of this course, the student will be able to recognize effective work team performance, follow the basic principles of interaction, reinforce teamwork, practice listening skills, provide constructive feedback, and communicate ideas.

Instruction: Major topics covered in the course are effective team performance, internal and external customer relationships, basic principles of interaction, reinforcing teamwork, listening skills, constructive feedback, and communicating ideas. Methods of instruction include lecture, discussion, behavior modeling, skills practice, videotapes, workbook exercises, out-of-class projects, and evaluation using observation forms, coaching logs, oral and written feedback, student written plans for applying behavior, and self-assessment of behavioral change.

Credit Recommendation: In the lower division baccalaureate/associate degree category, 1 semester hour in Human Relations, Human Resource Development, Psychology, or Sociology (6/94).

Strategic Process Management

Location: Various sites worldwide.

Length: 40 hours (days vary).

Dates: June 1994-Present.

Objective: To provide understanding of the concepts of strategic process management and its application within an organization.

Learning Outcome: Upon successful completion of this course, the student will be able to understand concepts of strategic process management; analyze an organization to identify strategic cross-functional processes; develop a strategic team; diagram major parts of the strategic process; select improvement opportunities; and initiate spin-off teams to work on subprocesses selected for improvement.

Instruction: Major topics covered in the course are concepts of strategic process management, role of the executive team, selection of strategic processes needing improvement, selection of the strategic team, identification of improvement opportunities and assignment of them to strategic and spin-off teams, role of spin-off teams in improving subprocesses, and interaction of the executive team with the strategic team and the spin-off teams. Methods of instruction include lecture, discussion, behavior modeling, skills practice, videotapes, workbook exercises, out-of-class projects, and evaluation using observation forms, coaching logs, oral and written feedback, student written plans for applying behavior, and self-assessment of behavioral change.

Credit Recommendation: In the lower division baccalaureate/associate degree category, 3 semester hours in Business Administration, Industrial Operations and Systems Engineering, Management, or Organizational Development (6/94).

Team Member Skills

Location: Various locations worldwide.

Length: 23 hours (days vary).

Dates: June 1994-Present.

Objective: To provide understanding and skill needed by team members to meet team performance goals.

Learning Outcome: Upon successful completion of this course, the student will be able to explain why organizations are moving to the use of teams; appreciate the challenges and rewards of team membership; utilize team skills to meet demands for high quality; develop innovative products and services; and help develop a plan for a team project.

Instruction: Major topics covered in the course are why organizations are becoming more team oriented; challenges and benefits of working in teams; core skills for team success; tools and techniques for team effectiveness; meeting the critical demands for high quality, speed, cost effectiveness, and innovation; and team project planning and decision-making. Methods of instruction include lecture, discussion, behavior modeling, skills practice, videotapes, workbook exercises, out-of-class projects, and evaluation using observation forms, coaching logs, oral and written feedback, student written plans for applying behavior, and self-assessment of behavioral change.

Credit Recommendation: In the upper division baccalaureate degree category, 1 semester hour in Business Administration, Human Relations, Psychology, or Management (6/94).

Advance Learning Network

Advance Learning Network (ALN), formerly College Leadership Consultants, carries on a ten year tradition of serving the adult learner in creative and nontraditional fashions. For the past decade this organization has assisted corporations, colleges and universities in fifty different markets with cohort based modules using a curriculum entitled Organizational Management. In doing so, this program has been successfully placed in all six-regional accreditation areas as well its courses gaining the approval of ACE/ CREDIT. ALN is committed to designing curricula bases on andragogical methodologies with cohort and modular design. ALN also carries on the mission of utilizing its various curricula and resources for the purposes of assisting adult learners with degree completion. Our curricula are supported and continuously improved by a full-time staff of curriculum experts and contract consultants across the United States. Modular courses are offered throughout the nation in various locations including collegiate campuses and corporate training centers. These courses are facilitated by individuals carrying Master's degrees or higher in their area of expertise. Nation-wide, our adult learners are 37 years old on average. We offer business and industry this advanced training model which will assist adults in their desire to complete bachelor's degrees as well as significantly impact their organizations with action research designed to address significant workplace issues.

AUTHORIZED ADVANCE LEARNING NETWORK SITE

Advance Learning Network - Jamaica
University Program of Jamaica
5 1/2 Caledonia Road
PO Box 628
Mandeville, Jamaica
Contact: W. Val Chambers, Ph.D.
Phone No.: 876-961-5383
E-Mail: eurekapr@toj.com

Source of official student records: Registry of Credit Recommendations, American Council on Education, One Dupont Circle, Washington, DC 20036-1193.

Additional information about the courses: College Credit Recommendation Service, American Council on Education, One Dupont Circle, Washington, DC 20036-1193.

Organizational Management

Accounting Basics (Bus 345) (Formerly Accounting Basics [Bus 345])

Location: Various locations throughout the United States.

Length: 28 hours (7 weeks).

Dates: September 1986-Present.

Objective: To introduce students to accounting concepts and the key components used as information and communication guides, and as the basis for decision-making. Some financial concepts are presented.

Learning Outcome: Upon successful completion of this course, the student will be able to read and analyze financial statements, especially income statements; balance sheets; statements of cash flows; use the fundamental "bookkeeping" tools of accounting and understand how these tools are used to compile financial information; be familiar with internal cost concepts and how to make managerial decisions based on the use of this accounting information; develop various types of operating budgets and know their implications; and understand how not-for-profit organizations differ in terms of accounting structure and operating approach.

Instruction: Major topics covered in the course are accounting principles, financial statement analysis, managerial and cost accounting, budgeting, and capital budgeting. Methods of instruction include discussion, lecture, classroom exercises, short presentations, and final project.

Credit Recommendation: In the lower division baccalaureate/associate degree category, 3 semester hours in Accounting or Business Administration (8/96).

Adult Development and Life Assessment

Location: Various locations throughout the United States.

Length: 24 hours (6 weeks).

Dates: September 1996-Present.

Objective: To evaluate career development in light of adult development theory, various learning styles, and their application to the work environment.

Learning Outcome: Upon successful completion of this course, the student will be able to identify critical career experiences; examine developmental workplace skills; and document findings in a portfolio for review for career assessment credit.

Instruction: Major topics covered in the course are basic writing and library skills, career assessment, adult learning and development styles, and Kolb's model of experiential learning. Methods of instruction include discussion, classroom exercises, lecture, learner presentations, homework assignments, reports, and a summary paper.

Credit Recommendation: In the lower division baccalaureate/associate degree category, 3 semester hours in Adult Learning, Career Development, Psychology, or Organizational Behavior (8/96).

An Introduction to Research and Analysis Using Statistics

Location: Various locations throughout the United States.

Length: 20 hours (5 weeks).

Dates: September 1986-Present.

Objective: To introduce statistical research methodology and tools that will help students complete their research projects.

Learning Outcome: Upon successful completion of this course, the student will be able to use the appropriate descriptive statistics to describe a set of data, including measures of central tendency and measures of variability; select the appropriate statistical test for making inferences about a population based on a sample, including confidence intervals, the independent t-test, and chi-square tests; define, research, analyze, and evaluate a problem relevant to his or her own interests; and interpret and document the results of a statistical analysis as part of a research paper.

Instruction: Major topics covered in the course are descriptive and differential statistics, collecting samples, central tendency, normal dispersion, and estimation. Methods of instruction include discussion, classroom exercises, lecture, learner presentations, reports, and weekly problem sets.

Credit Recommendation: In the lower division baccalaureate/associate degree category, 3 semester hour in Business Administration or Statistics (8/96).

Biblical Perspectives

Location: Various locations throughout the United States.

Length: 20 hours (5 weeks).

Dates: September 1986-Present.

Objective: To create an open and inquiring study of the conceptual and historical framework of the Christian faith.

Learning Outcome: Upon successful completion of this course, the student will be able to gain a basic understanding of Christianity; examine various phases of biblical study; and examine the relevance of faith to daily life and individual purpose.

Instruction: Major topics covered in the course are a study of the literary, historical, and religious dimensions of the Old and New Testaments; and the themes of covenants, redemption, justice, righteousness, reconciliation, eschatology, and hope. Methods of instruction include discussion, classroom exercises, lecture, learner presentations, group activities, class participation, book review, and a summary paper.

Credit Recommendation: In the upper division baccalaureate degree category, 3 semester hours in Religious Studies, General Education, or Liberal Arts (8/96).

Business Law (Bus 420)

Location: New York, New Jersey, Seattle, WA.

Length: 28 hours (7 weeks).

Dates: February 1997-Present.

Objective: To provide the adult learner with an overview of the legal issues affecting businesses so that he or she will understand the fundamentals of Business Law sufficiently to make the majority of his or her business decisions relating to legal matters without assistance.

Learning Outcome: Upon successful completion of this course, the student will be able to understand the legal rights and social forces inherent in our American legal environment; understand the rules governing the principal-agent relationship; understand the nature of contractual arrangements, their elements, the rights and duties of contractual parties, and the remedies for their breach; understand the various forms of business organizations; understand the various security devices and their effects on debtors and creditors in and out of bankruptcy; and develop the skills and methods needed to analyze a given set of facts for the purpose of identifying the legal issues of problems involved and applying the appropriate rule of law in resolving the issue.

Instruction: Major topics covered in the course are Business Law studies in history, background, sources and influences of our modern day law as it pertains to the business activities of individuals, corporations and other legal entities with particular emphasis upon business litigation, legal liabilities, alternative dispute resolution techniques, and the laws governing contracts, creditors' rights, secured transactions, bankruptcy, agency, partnerships, and corporations. Methods of instruction include lecture, discussion, computer-assisted instruction, simulation or role play, reports, papers, journals, attendance, homework, and projects.

Credit Recommendation: In the upper division baccalaureate degree category, 4 semester hours in Business Law (4/97).

Group and Organizational Dynamics

Location: Various locations throughout the United States.

Length: 20 hours (5 weeks).

Dates: September 1986-Present.

Objective: To help students develop effective strategies for efficient and productive group management.

Learning Outcome: Upon successful completion of this course, the student will be able to demonstrate knowledge of types of group processes and the relationship of groups to organizations; examine the Strength Development Inventory and a variety of motivational patterns that influence small group dynamics; analyze group and individual decision-making techniques; demonstrate an awareness of organizational complexity; and identify the nature, management, and significance of group and organizational conflict.

Instruction: Major topics covered in the course are portfolio review, time management, strength bombardment, individual and group decisionmaking, small group interaction, group size and structure, brainstorming, and conflict resolution. Methods of instruction include discussion, classroom exercises, lecture, case studies, learner presentations, summary papers, reports, and homework assignments.

Credit Recommendation: In the upper division baccalaureate degree category, 3 semester hours in Group Dynamics, Organizational Behavior, or Management (8/96).

Human Resource Management (Orgd 445)

Location: Various locations throughout the United States.

Length: 20 hours (5 weeks).

Dates: September 1986-Present.

Objective: To provide a practical approach to the functions and practices of human resource management in the achievement of organizational objectives.

Learning Outcome: Upon successful completion of this course, the student will be able to understand the role of the personnel function; know the difference between Equal Employment Opportunity (EEO) and Affirmative Action Planning; be familiar with the components of a personnel planning and forecasting process; identify the advantages/disadvantages of various internal/external recruiting sources; be aware of the elements of effective performance appraisal; and become familiar with unions, and elements of labor relations, including grievance procedures, arbitration and mediation.

Instruction: Major topics covered in the course are Government regulation of Human Resource Management including EEO and Affirmative Action; recruitment, selection, orientation, and compensation of employees; performance appraisal practices; and unions, grievances, arbitration, and mediation. Methods of instruction include discussion, classroom exercises, lecture, case studies, role playing, summary papers, reports, and homework assignments.

Credit Recommendation: In the upper division baccalaureate degree category, 3 semester hours in Human Resource Management or Business Administration (8/96).

Issues In Management (Bus 330)

Location: Various locations throughout the United States.

Length: 20 hours (5 weeks).

Dates: September 1986-Present.

Objective: To introduce the student to concepts of management as they pertain to the dynamics of leadership, motivation, strategic planning, and controlling.

Learning Outcome: Upon successful completion of this course, the student will be able to understand and apply various management concepts including motivation, leadership styles and effectiveness, strategic planning, organizing principles, negotiation, and the principles of TQM.

Instruction: Major topics covered in the course are management theories, strategic planning, employee motivation, organization structure and design, leadership, conflict resolution, and the distinction between MBO and TQM. Methods of instruction include discussion, classroom exercises, case studies, lecture, learner presentations, reports, self-assessment surveys, observations, and a summary paper.

Credit Recommendation: In the upper division baccalaureate degree category, 3 semester hours in Management or Business Administration (8/96).

Managerial Accounting (Bus 340)

Location: New York, New Jersey, and Seattle, WA.

Length: 20 hours (5 weeks).

Dates: February 1997-Present.

Objective: To understand the use of financial accounting, budgeting, and financial analysis.

Learning Outcome: Upon successful completion of this course, the student will be able to understand financial and cost accounting and complete problems as applied to assets, bonds, financial statement analysis, and cost accounting.

Instruction: Major topics covered in the course are financial statement analysis, accounting for assets, liabilities and equity, present value analysis, standard costs, and a final research project on how a company applies generally accepted accounting principles, including financial analysis and cost accounting. Methods of instruction include discussion, classroom exercises, case studies, reports, and papers.

Credit Recommendation: In the upper division baccalaureate degree category, 3 semester hours in Accounting or Business Administration (4/97).

Managerial Economics (Bus 335)

Location: Various locations throughout the United States.

Length: 20 hours (5 weeks).

Dates: September 1986-Present.

Objective: To provide students with a foundation of economic principles and theory that can be used in making managerial decisions that relate to resource allocation.

Learning Outcome: Upon successful completion of this course, the student will be able to apply economic principles to business situations; predict outcomes of managerial economic decisions; use the logic of economics when making personal decisions and when solving business problems; and use terms correctly when describing economic principles.

Instruction: Major topics covered in the course are supply and demand, elasticities, present value analysis, production and costs, perfect competition, monopolistic competition, monopoly, oligopoly, and game theory. Methods of instruction include lecture, discussion, classroom exercises, learner presentations, homework assignments, and final project.

Credit Recommendation: In the lower division baccalaureate/associate degree category, 3 semester hours in Microeconomics or Managerial Economics (8/96).

Managerial Finance (Bus 350)

Location: New York, New Jersey, and Seattle, WA.

Length: 20 hours (5 weeks).

Dates: February 1997-Present.

Objective: To introduce the students to issues in managerial finance.

Learning Outcome: Upon successful completion of this course, the student will be able to develop a firm understanding of the field of corporate finance: short term finance, capital budgeting, and long term finance; use traditional financial statements and related accounting data for broad based financial planning; and apply capital budgeting techniques to the analysis of investment opportunities.

Instruction: Major topics covered in the course are the organization-wide use of financial planning within the firm and corporate finance topics covered are the importance of short-term finance in current operations, use of capital budgeting tools for investment analysis, and the foundation of long-term finance for defining the organization's cost of capital and optimal capital structure. Methods of instruction include lecture, discussion, simulation or role play, homework, class participation, and projects.

Credit Recommendation: In the upper division baccalaureate degree category, 3 semester hours in Managerial Finance (4/97).

Marketing

Location: Various locations throughout the United States.

Length: 20 hours (5 weeks).

Dates: September 1986-Present.

Objective: To understand the role and skills of marketing and apply these concepts to organizational planning and strategies.

Learning Outcome: Upon successful completion of this course, the student will be able to discuss the evolution of marketing; develop a personal selling plan; apply the functions of marketing to business situations; develop marketing programs; and understand the international implications for marketing.

Instruction: Major topics covered in the course are the evolution and nature of marketing; role of marketing; marketing functions; and marketing concepts, theory, and terminology. Methods of instruction include discussion, classroom exercises, lecture, case studies, audio/visual material, learner presentations, homework, and a summary paper.

Credit Recommendation: In the upper division baccalaureate degree category, 3 semester hours in Marketing or Business Administration (8/96).

Organizational Communication

Location: Various locations throughout the United States.

Length: 20 hours (5 weeks).

Dates: September 1986-Present.

Objective: To investigate communication and relationships in creating a productive work environment.

Learning Outcome: Upon successful completion of this course, the student will be able to understand the importance of communication and methods of communicating effectively in organizations; identify and analyze facilitating and hindering forces in effective communications; practice developing and delivering effective interpersonal communications; understand theory and practice of team-building, conflict resolution, and problem solving; understand how communication and organizational cultures relate to one another; and understand the role of verbal and nonverbal messages and how to use them effectively.

Instruction: Major topics covered in the course are the communication process and media, team building, and conflict resolution. Methods of instruction include discussion, classroom exercises, lecture, audio/visual material, role play, classroom participation, homework assignments, and a summary paper.

Credit Recommendation: In the upper division baccalaureate degree category, 3 semester hours in Organizational Communication or Business Administration (8/96).

Personal Values and Organizational Ethics

Location: Various locations throughout the United States.

Length: 20 hours (5 weeks).

Dates: September 1986-Present.

Objective: To help students better understand their own values and how such values relate to the "business world" in which they function.

Learning Outcome: Upon successful completion of this course, the student will be able to differentiate among the three basic types of ethical systems; understand how human values interface with organizational ethics; and identify implications and resolutions to ethical problems in the workplace.

Instruction: Major topics covered in the course are ethical principles in business; ethics in consumer production and marketing; and human value perspectives of four basic world views that dominate western cultures, including Christianity, Marxism, Skinner's Conditional Behaviorism, and Existentialism. Methods of instruction include discussion, classroom exercises, lecture, case studies, learner presentations, reports, homework assignments, and summary reports.

Credit Recommendation: In the upper division baccalaureate degree category, 3 semester hours in Business Ethics or Philosophy (8/96).

Research Project Seminar

Location: Various locations throughout the United States.

Length: 200-250 hours (77 weeks).

Dates: October 1986-Present.

Objective: To provide the student with the necessary skills to research, write, and present a final written project.

Learning Outcome: Upon successful completion of this course, the student will be able to demonstrate research writing skills; and make an oral presentation covering the process of a project.

Instruction: Major topics covered in the course are research writing and oral presentations. Method of instruction is directed independent study, which is reviewed chapter by chapter by an advisor who provides continual feedback; evaluation; and a final grade.

Credit Recommendation: In the upper division baccalaureate degree category, 5 semester hours in Research Methods or Business Administration (8/96).

Social Problems and Their Impact On the Workplace (Soc 402)

Location: Various locations throughout the United States.

Length: 20 hours (5 weeks).

Dates: September 1986-Present.

Objective: To gain insight and broaden the student perception of social problems affecting the workplace and to increase awareness of how the workplace can respond positively to them.

Learning Outcome: Upon successful completion of this course, the student will be able to identify and analyze the causes, conditions, and consequences; and propose strategies to alleviate social problems in five specific areas of poverty, racism, sexism, drug/alcohol abuse, and illiteracy.

Instruction: Major topics covered in the course are a sociological and systematic approach to problem analysis and solution via a seven-stage task force, experiential process, identification of six critical social problems that challenge the Workforce 2000 model, and introduces six perspectives of social problems. Methods of instruction include discussion, classroom exercises, lecture, learner presentations, reports, observations papers, homework assignments, and summary reports.

Credit Recommendation: In the upper division baccalaureate degree category, 3 semester hours in Sociology or Business Administration (8/96).

Strategic Planning (Bus 450)

Location: Various locations throughout the United States.

Length: 20 hours (5 weeks).

Dates: October 1986-Present.

Objective: To introduce the student to strategic planning methodology and its implications.

Learning Outcome: Upon successful completion of this course, the student will be able to understand the strategic planning process, the role of mission statements, and strength, weakness, opportunities, and threats (SWOT) analysis; and the role of "corporate-level" strategies and their implementation in an organization.

Instruction: Major topics covered in the course are mission statement development, internal and external environmental analysis, SWOT analysis, and strategy formulation. Methods of instruction include discussion, case studies, lecture, homework assignments, class participation, case study, and a take-home final.

Credit Recommendation: In the upper division baccalaureate degree category, 3 semester hours in Management or Business Administration (8/96).

Systems Approach to Organizational Change

Location: Various locations throughout the United States.

Length: 20 hours (5 weeks).

Dates: September 1986-Present.

Objective: To examine the formal and informal functions of organizations and analyze an agency or organization based on a systems model.

Learning Outcome: Upon successful completion of this course, the student will be able to understand organizational concepts; apply concepts of systems theory problem-solving and decision-making to a research project; understand implementation and management of change in organizations; use a systems model to examine his or her organization; and recognize major theorists and researchers.

Instruction: Major topics covered in the course are organizational concepts, implementation and management of change, systems theory problem solving, and systems analysis of organizations. Methods of instruction include discussion, classroom exercises, case studies, lecture, learner presentations, homework, and a summary paper.

Credit Recommendation: In the upper division baccalaureate degree category, 3 semester hours in Organizational Behavior or Management (8/96).

Advantec Institute

Advantec Institute, a division of Computer Learning Centers, Inc., was established in 1993 to provide the best possible advanced information technology training to business and industry. Currently, Advantec provides hands-on training to over 500 computer professionals annually in several curricula including computer programming, networking, and internet development. Courses are developed based on input from students, instructors, and an advisory board consisting of area business persons in tune with the needs of contemporary business. Detailed lectures as well as hands-on lab exercises performed in state-of-the-art computer labs provide students with the practical experience necessary to advance within their fields. Furthermore, these courses are delivered by instructors whose qualifications require that both educational and professional experiences have led them to experts in their fields. Each of these components works together to provide students with the technical skills necessary to succeed in today's competitive information systems industry. Advantec Institute offers classes at three locations in the Washington, DC area: Alexandria, Virginia; Vienna, Virginia; and Laurel, Maryland. There are plans to expand to other geographical areas in which Computer Learning Centers are located.

Source of official student records: Registry of Credit Recommendations, American Council on Education, One Dupont Circle, Washington, DC 20036-1193.

Additional information about the courses: College Credit Recommendation Service, American Council on Education, One Dupont Circle, Washington, DC 20036-1193.

Advanced C Programming (AI 432)

Location: Various.

Length: 35 hours (5 days).

Dates: January 1997-Present.

Objective: To provide students with more sophisticated techniques utilizing the C programming language.

Learning Outcome: Upon successful completion of this course, the student will be able to use a variety of data types appropriate to specific programming problems; utilize the modular features of the language; master the use pointers; utilize optimization techniques; use bit manipulation techniques; and write system calls directly into the UNIX operating system.

Instruction: Major topics covered in the course are sorting and searching techniques, optimization techniques, resolving portability issues, advanced low level operations, and the UNIX and C interface including I/O and process management calls. Methods of instruction include lecture, discussion, classroom exercises, and final examination.

Credit Recommendation: In the lower division baccalaureate/associate degree category, 1 semester hour in Computer Science, Computer Information Systems, C Programming, or Application Development (1/97).

Internetworking with TCP/IP (AI 441)

Location: Various.

Length: 35 hours (5 days).

Dates: January 1997-Present.

Objective: To provide students with an explanation and understanding of the various protocols comprising the TCP/IP suite and relate these protocols to the UNIX operating system.

Learning Outcome: Upon successful completion of this course, the student will be able to identify the seven layers of the OSI networking model and relate this to TCP/IP; configure host IP, netmask, and broadcast addresses; use operating system commands to monitor network problems; and identify the networking protocols that support the TCP/IP networking model.

Instruction: Major topics covered in the course are open vs. proprietary systems; protocol models, stacks, and suites; connecting networks with bridges, routers, and gateways; network physical layer; IP layer; transport layer protocol; domain name services; network file system; SMTP and SNMP protocols; and networking tools, remote login, and administration of a TCP/IP network. Methods of instruction include lecture, discussion, hands-on lab exercises, audio/visual material, laboratory exercises, and final examination.

Credit Recommendation: In the lower division baccalaureate/associate degree or upper division baccalaureate degree category, 2 semester hours in Networking, Data Communications, Computer Science, or Computer Information Systems (1/97).

Introduction to C

Location: Various.

Length: 140 hours (20 days).

Dates: January 1997-Present.

Objective: To provide students with fundamental programming techniques in using the C programming languages.

Learning Outcome: Upon successful completion of this course, the student will be able to identify and utilize appropriate data structures, language structure, and syntax of C; and use various control flow constructs (arrays, pointers, and calls to the UNIX operating system) to efficiently solve programming problems.

Instruction: Major topics covered in the course are data structures, language syntax, operators, control flow, the preprocessor, functions, strings, arrays, pointers, and stream and binary file I/O. Methods of instruction include lecture, discussion, classroom exercises, and final examination.

Credit Recommendation: In the lower division baccalaureate/associate degree category, 2 semester hours in Computer Science, Computer Information Systems, C Programming, or Application Development (1/97).

Introduction to C++ Programming (AI 442)

Location: Various.

Length: 35 hours (5 days).

Dates: January 1997-Present.

Objective: To provide students with an introduction to the C++ programming language.

Learning Outcome: Upon successful completion of this course, the student will be able to understand how object oriented software engineering enhances the software development process; identify the major elements in an object oriented programming language; implement data abstraction and encapsulation in the creation of abstract data types; implement operator overloading; derive classes using inheritance in C++; select the proper class protection mechanism; demonstrate the use of virtual functions to implement polymorphism; write programs utilizing the I/O classes in C++; and explain advanced concepts such as templates, exceptions, and multiple inheritances and modify programs which use them.

Instruction: Major topics covered in the course are creating new C data types; search and sort files; manipulating bit structures, using optimization techniques; and resolving portability issues within object oriented programming, classes, operator overloading, inheritance, polymorphism, virtual functions, and templates. Methods of instruction include lecture, discussion, classroom exercises, and final examination.

Credit Recommendation: In the lower division baccalaureate/associate degree category, 1 semester hour in Computer Science, Computer Information Systems,

C++ Programming, or Application Development (1/97).

*Introduction to Oracle Database and SQL (Client/Server and Oracle 7 Architecture for Application Developers [AI 311] and Introduction to SQL, SQL*PLUS [AI 321])*

Location: Various.

Length: 35 hours (5 days).

Dates: January 1997-Present.

Objective: To provide students with an introduction to Oracle Database concepts and SQL programming.

Learning Outcome: Upon successful completion of this course, the student will be able to describe introductory terminology and database concepts; and perform basic Oracle SQL functions.

Instruction: Major topics covered in the course are RDBMS database terminology, database design, Oracle data types, SQL syntax, ad-hoc Oracle SQL statements, construction of queries, data manipulation language, data definition language statements, and SQL*Plus formatting features. Methods of instruction include lecture, discussion, classroom exercises, and a final examination.

Credit Recommendation: In the upper division baccalaureate degree category, 1 semester hour in Database Management, Computer Information Systems, and 1 semester hour in laboratory in Computer Science, Computer Information Systems, or SQL Programming (1/97).

Introduction to PERL Programming (AI 313)

Location: Various.

Length: 35 hours (5 days).

Dates: January 1997-Present.

Objective: To provide students with an introductory study of PERL programming language.

Learning Outcome: Upon successful completion of this course, the student will be able to manipulate files and directories; use the powerful regular expression capabilities of PERL; generate "awk-like" reports; solve problems by using PERL's associative array capability; take advantage of PERL's powerful interface to UNIX; and perform some system administration functions.

Instruction: Major topics covered in the course are I/O, PERL operators, arrays and array functions, control flow, subroutines, packages, libraries, accessing system resources, and generating basic reports. Methods of instruction include lecture, discussion, hands-on lab exercises, student assessments, and final examination.

Credit Recommendation: In the lower division baccalaureate/associate degree category, 1 semester hour in Computer Science, Computer Information Systems, PERL Programming, or Application Development (1/97).

Introduction to PL/SQL (AI 331)

Location: Various.

Length: 35 hours (5 days).

Dates: January 1997-Present.

Objective: To provide students with an introduction to the main features of the Pl/SQL language to aid students in developing effective programming habits and coding styles.

Learning Outcome: Upon successful completion of this course, the student will be able to define Pl/S!L and how it differs from SQL; describe PL/SQL's block structure and its three components; create variables and constants in PL/SQL, and assign values to them; control program flow using loops and if-then logic; handle errors using the EXCEPTION block in PL/SQL; create cursors to handle multiple-row queries; write stored, named procedures, functions, and database triggers; pass parameters to a procedure; describe, invoke, and use the Oracle Procedure Builder; use the Oracle DEBUG package and DEBUG triggers to debug PL/SQL code; and define and take advantage of Module Overloading.

Instruction: Major topics covered in the course are variables and constraints, control program flow, error handling, cursors, procedures, functions, triggers and parameters, the Oracle Procedure Builder, Module Overloading, and the DEBUG package. Methods of instruction include lecture, discussion, classroom exercises, and final assessment.

Credit Recommendation: In the lower division baccalaureate/associate degree or upper division baccalaureate degree category, 1 semester hour in Computer Science, Computer Information Systems, SQL Programming, or Application Development (1/97).

Netware 4.1 Advanced System Administration (AI 121)

Location: Various.

Length: 28 hours (4 days).

Dates: January 1997-Present.

Objective: To provide students with the skills necessary to support advanced Novell 4.1 networks including configuration, maintenance, and management.

Learning Outcome: Upon successful completion of this course, the student will be able to implement advanced Netware Directory Services (NDS) structures including partitioning, replication, time synchronization, and security.

Instruction: Major topics covered in the course are managing bindery emulation, defining partition and replication concepts, merging different tree structures, custom partitioning, implementing custom time synchronization, defining server performance indicators, suggesting solutions to server performance problems, and designing and implementing network auditing. Methods of instruction include lecture, discussion, hands-on lab exercises, audio/visual material, laboratory exercises, and a final examination.

Credit Recommendation: In the lower division baccalaureate/associate degree category, 2 semester hours in Networking, Data Communications, Local Area Networks, or Computer Information Systems (1/97).

Netware 4.1 Design and Implementation (AI 132)

Location: Various.

Length: 21 hours (3 days).

Dates: January 1997-Present.

Objective: To provide students with the strategies and guidelines to design, analyze, and implement Netware 4 networks.

Learning Outcome: Upon successful completion of this course, the student will be able to design a directory tree structure based on a case scenario; propose a partitioning and replication strategy; create a time synchronization scheme; and decide on an accessibility model for administering a Netware 4 network.

Instruction: Major topics covered in the course are identifying and sequencing all processes in a design and migration project, planning and drawing the layers of a directory tree, determining partition boundaries, developing an accessibility plan, and developing a plan to transport users across the network from multiple geographic locations. Methods of instruction include lecture, discussion, hands-on lab exercises, audio/visual material, laboratory exercises, and a final examination.

Credit Recommendation: In the lower division baccalaureate/associate degree or upper division baccalaureate degree category, 2 semester hours in Networking, Data

Communications, Local Area Networks, or Computer Information Systems (1/97).

Netware 4.1 System Administration (AI 112)

Location: Various.
Length: 28 hours (4 days).
Dates: January 1997-Present.
Objective: To provide students with an understanding of the basic functioning of the Netware 4 operating system.
Learning Outcome: Upon successful completion of this course, the student will be able to implement a Netware Directory Services structure; understand object file, directory management, and file system security; perform printing setup and user environment configuration; understand the use of system utilities; and introduce data protection and backup services.
Instruction: Major topics covered in the course are system administration overview utilities (GUI, menu, command-line), file system and directory management, drive mapping, printer and print server installation, remote server access, file security, login scripts, and Netware Directory Services (NDS). Methods of instruction include lecture, discussion, hands-on lab exercises, audio/visual material, laboratory exercises, and a final examination.
Credit Recommendation: In the lower division baccalaureate/associate degree category, 2 semester hours in Networking, Data Communications, Local Area Networks, or Computer Information Systems (1/97).

Network Service and Support (AI 134) (Service and Support)

Location: Various.
Length: 28 hours (4 days).
Dates: January 1997-Present.
Objective: To provide students with hands-on experience with network related hardware and software installation and troubleshooting.
Learning Outcome: Upon successful completion of this course, the student will be able to use research skills and diagnostic tools to resolve network problems; install and troubleshoot different network cards and cabling; setup various storage devices; detect bottlenecks; and evaluate network performance.
Instruction: Major topics covered in the course are service and support tasks; developing a troubleshooting model; installation and configuration of various NICs; configuration, installation, and troubleshooting IDE and SCSI disks; troubleshooting IPX and ODI-based work stations; diagnosing and troubleshooting network patches and NLMs; utilizing a protocol analyzer to diagnose problems; and an introduction to network management and Managewise. Methods of instruction include lecture, discussion, hands-on lab exercises, audio/visual material, laboratory exercises, and a final examination.
Credit Recommendation: In the lower division baccalaureate/associate degree category, 2 semester hours in Networking, Data Communications, Local Area Networking, or Computer Information Systems (1/97).

Networking Essentials (AI 211)

Location: Various.
Length: 35 hours (5 days).
Dates: January 1997-Present.
Objective: To provide students with basic networking terminology, definitions, and concepts and the skills necessary to install and maintain various network operating systems.
Learning Outcome: Upon successful completion of this course, the student will be able to utilize the components of a local area network including hardware and network media, various transport protocols, the OSI model, network security, and resource management.
Instruction: Major topics covered in the course are networks, sending data through the OSI layers, physical characteristics of a LAN, cabling media, ethernet/token ring/arcnet, NICs, and various device interfaces. Methods of instruction include lecture, discussion, hands-on lab exercises, audio/visual material, laboratory exercises, and a final examination.
Credit Recommendation: In the lower division baccalaureate/associate degree category, 2 semester hours in Networking, Data Communications, Local Area Networks, or Computer Information Systems (1/97).

Oracle Developer/2000 Forms 4.5 (AI 341)

Location: Various.
Length: 35 hours (5 days).
Dates: January 1997-Present.
Objective: To provide students with the knowledge and skills necessary to use Oracle forms to develop database applications for queries, data entry, updates, and deletions.
Learning Outcome: Upon successful completion of this course, the student will be able to identify types of forms; create a form using object properties; add graphics and buttons; and utilize the Layout Editor.
Instruction: Major topics covered in the course are definitions of Oracle Forms 4.5, Forms 4.5 components, and Forms 4.5 modules; default forms in Oracle Forms 4.5, using the Object Navigator to select and move to objects on a form; single record and multiple record forms; master-detail forms, using the Layout Editor; changing object properties, creating radio buttons, check boxes, and lists; attaching an LOV (List of Values) to an item; creating, managing, and controlling property classes; adding graphics, images, and color to a block; adding buttons, display items, timers, and alerts to forms; and writing forms triggers and procedures, creating multiple canvases in a form, and create custom menus. Methods of instruction include lecture, discussion, hands-on lab exercises to reinforce concepts presented during lecture, and a final project.
Credit Recommendation: In the upper division baccalaureate degree category, 1 semester hour in Computer Science, Computer Information Systems, Database Programming, or Application Development (1/97).

Oracle Developer/2000 Reports 2.5 (AI 351)

Location: Various.
Length: 28 hours (4 days).
Dates: January 1997-Present.
Objective: To provide students with the knowledge and skills necessary to build reports in a wide variety of styles using Oracle.
Learning Outcome: Upon successful completion of this course, the student will be able to define and produce several types of reports using Oracle Developer 2000.
Instruction: Major topics covered in the course are creating a variety of reports and using Oracle Reports 2.5, Reports 2.5 objects, and Reports 2.5 modules; use the Reports 2.5 Layout Editor, Data Model, and the Object Navigator; Tabular Report; Break Report; Master-Detail Report; Form Letter Report; Mailing Label Report; Matrix Report; Formula Report; reports containing user defined parameters, graphics, headers, footers, and page numbers; reports using group filters; and reports using report and format triggers. Methods of instruction include lecture, discussion, hands-on lab exercises to reinforce concepts presented during lecture, and a final project.
Credit Recommendation: In the upper division baccalaureate degree category, 1 semester hour in laboratory in Computer

Science, Computer Information Systems, Oracle Database Design and Development, or Application Development (1/97).

Support Windows 95 (AI 212)

Location: Various.
Length: 35 hours (5 days).
Dates: January 1997-Present.
Objective: To provide students with the skills necessary to install, configure, and support the Windows 95 operating system.
Learning Outcome: Upon successful completion of this course, the student will be able to support LAN work station users running the Windows 95 operating system including scheduling, memory management, file I/O, tuning, use of utilities, conversion to W/95, and providing users with multimedia support.
Instruction: Major topics covered in the course are installation, configuration, establishing user interfaces, multi-tasking, utilities and memory management, naming conventions, Novell interoperability, local and network printing, backup, defragmenting and compression, dialup networking, and troubleshooting tools and resources. Methods of instruction include lecture, discussion, hands-on lab exercises, audio/visual material, laboratory exercises, and a final examination.
Credit Recommendation: In the lower division baccalaureate/associate degree category, 2 semester hours in Networking, Data Communications, Local Area Networks, or Computer Information Systems (1/97).

Supporting Windows NT (AI 221)

Location: Various.
Length: 35 hours (5 days).
Dates: January 1997-Present.
Objective: To provide students with the skills necessary to install, configure, and support the Windows NT operating system.
Learning Outcome: Upon successful completion of this course, the student will be able to support LAN work station users running the Windows NT operating system, including system architecture, file systems and resources, use of NT setup, supporting tasks via the registry, managing user accounts, and maintaining system integrity.
Instruction: Major topics covered in the course are installation and configuration, choosing a file system, system security, accessing network resources, printing, interoperating with IPX and TCP/IP, remote access services, monitoring and optimizing performance, and applications support. Methods of instruction include lecture, discussion, hands-on lab exercises, audio/visual material, laboratory exercises, and a final examination.
Credit Recommendation: In the lower division baccalaureate/associate degree category, 2 semester hours in Networking, Data Communications, Local Area Networks, or Computer Information Systems (1/97).

Supporting Windows NT Server 3.51 (AI 231)

Location: Various.
Length: 35 hours (5 days).
Dates: January 1997-Present.
Objective: To provide students with the skills necessary to successfully install, configure, and support the Windows NT 3.51 Server network operating system on Intel and RISC platforms.
Learning Outcome: Upon successful completion of this course, the student will be able to support LANs running the Windows NT 3.51 Server operating system including domain and resource configuration and management, directory sharing, establishing trust relationships, and relating NT to other network operating systems.
Instruction: Major topics covered in the course are installation and configuration using local and global user accounts, installing and configurating MS-DOS clients, using dynamic host configuration, integrate Novell and NT migrate files, and directing and resolving network bottlenecks by using the performance monitor. Methods of instruction include lecture, discussion, hands-on lab exercises, audio/visual material, laboratory exercises, and a final examination.
Credit Recommendation: In the lower division baccalaureate/associate degree or upper division baccalaureate degree category, 2 semester hours in Networking, Data Communications, Local Area Networks, or Computer Information Systems (1/97).

TCP/IP for Netware (AI 135)

Location: Various.
Length: 28 hours (4 days).
Dates: January 1997-Present.
Objective: To provide students with an understanding of networking terminology, a working familiarity with the OSI model, and the skills necessary to configure and manage TCP/IP on Netware 4 and 3 servers.
Learning Outcome: Upon successful completion of this course, the student will be able to identify and list the functions of the OSI model within the TCP/IP protocol stack; install, configure, and manage an IP network by assigning IP addresses; develop subnetwork masks; configure Netware servers as IP routers; and manage TCP/IP activities using Netware utilities.
Instruction: Major topics covered in the course are network terminology and elements; origin, purpose, and functions of the seven layer OSI model; relate the model to the TCP/IP stack; analyze and classify IP addresses; assign IP addresses and subnet masks to IP internetworks; configure TCP/IP on Netware servers; configure and customize SNMP on Netware servers; analyze different routing protocols; configure a Netware server as an IP router; setup tunneling; and troubleshoot IP problems. Methods of instruction include lecture, discussion, hands-on lab exercises, audio/visual material, laboratory exercises, and a final examination.
Credit Recommendation: In the lower division baccalaureate/associate degree or upper division baccalaureate degree category, 2 semester hours in Networking, Data Communications, Local Area Networking, Computer Science, or Computer Information Systems (1/97).

UNIX Administration (AI 431)

Location: Various.
Length: 35 hours (5 days).
Dates: January 1997-Present.
Objective: To provide students with the necessary tools to manage a UNIX system.
Learning Outcome: Upon successful completion of this course, the student will be able to install, startup, and shutdown the UNIX system.
Instruction: Major topics covered in the course are installation, troubleshooting, and maintenance of a UNIX system; use of the front end system administration tool (SYSADMSH, SMIT, SAM, SYSADM, ADMINTOOL, etc.) to add and delete users; add devices; partition the disk and perform other administrative functions; use the administrator files and commands in the /etc. directory; check file system integrity; provide user guidance; backup and restore all or parts of the system; monitor system performance; and establish and maintain network connectivity. Methods of instruction include lecture, discussion, classroom exercises, and a final project or examination.
Credit Recommendation: In the lower division baccalaureate/associate degree or upper division baccalaureate degree category, 1 semester hour in Computer Science, Computer Information Systems,

UNIX System Administration, or Application Development (1/97).

UNIX Fundamentals (AI 411)

Location: Various.

Length: 35 hours (5 days).

Dates: January 1997-Present.

Objective: To provide students with a basic study of the UNIX operating system including its evolution, structure, programming environment, and user interface.

Learning Outcome: Upon successful completion of this course, the student will be able to explain the UNIX shell, evolution, structure, programming environment, and user interface.

Instruction: Major topics covered in the course are login and logout of a UNIX system; recall commands for automatic execution; launch and control jobs; provide front ends to well known commands; create and use shell environment variables; customize the environment using many shell productivity aids such as aliases, variables, etc. and the startup files kshrc and cshrc; write shell functions; use the pattern matching operators of the Korn Shell; and write shell scripts incorporating features such as variables, aliases, and functions. Methods of instruction include lecture, discussion, classroom exercises, and final assessment.

Credit Recommendation: In the lower division baccalaureate/associate degree category, 1 semester hour in Computer Science, Computer Information Systems, UNIX Programming, or Application Development (1/97).

UNIX Shell Programming (AI 421)

Location: Various.

Length: 35 hours (5 days).

Dates: January 1997-Present.

Objective: To provide students with an examination of the UNIX Korn Shell.

Learning Outcome: Upon successful completion of this course, the student will be able to use the shell as a command line interface, a programming language, and a tool for customizing the UNIX environment.

Instruction: Major topics covered in the course are shell process creation, use of a variety of shell metacharacters, commands for automatic execution, controlling jobs, front ends to well known commands, use of shell environment variables, customization of the environment using aliases and the startup files, write shell functions, use the pattern matching operators of the Korn Shell, and write shell scripts incorporating features such as variables, aliases, and functions. Methods of instruction include lecture, discussion, classroom exercises, and final examination.

Credit Recommendation: In the lower division baccalaureate/associate degree category, 1 semester hour in Computer Science, Computer Information Systems, UNIX Programming, or Application Development (1/97).

Allied Business Schools, Inc.

Incorporated in 1992 Allied Business Schools, Inc. is a distance education training institute providing courses for people interested in meeting the California Department of Real Estate's educational requirements for obtaining a California real estate sales or broker license. On December 18, 1992 Allied Business Schools was approved by the Office of Real Estate Appraisers (OREA) to provide courses for people interested in meeting the educational requirements for becoming licensed residential real estate appraisers.

Allied Business Schools offers three levels of licensing curriculum and one for appraisal continuing education. Upon completion of the 75 clock hour Appraisal License Course (90 hours commencing January 1, 1998) approved by OREA students may sit for the Residential License Examination. Successful completion of the 45 clock hour Advanced Appraisal Course approved by OREA, in combination with the Appraiser License Course for a total of 120 hours satisfies the educational requirement for the Certified Residential License Examination. Successful completion of the 45 clock hour Income Property Valuation Course approved by OREA, in combination with both the Appraisal License Course and Advanced Appraisal Course for a total of 190 hours, satisfies the educational requirement for the Certified General License Examination. Upon completion of the required continuing education courses approved by the OREA, students receive a certificate of completion for their continuing education courses which satisfies the requirements for license renewal.

The mission of Allied Business Schools, Inc. is best described in this statement from our employee handbook: "We pledge to provide each of our students the best home study education at the lowest cost with enjoyable one-on-one personal service-the same treatment that we would want." Allied School's competent, full-time staff is committed to providing expert assistance to our students to prepare them for successful completion of their courses.

Our quality program and unique services allow students to set their own pace toward successfully completing their courses in order to achieve their career goals. The curriculum is designed to teach the items needed to meet the state educational requirements, pass the state license examination, and prepare a student for his or her appraisal career.

Source of official student records: Registry of Credit Recommendations, American Council on Education, One Dupont Circle, Washington, DC 20036-1193.

Additional information about the courses: College Credit Recommendation Service, American Council on Education, One Dupont Circle, Washington, DC 20036-1193.

Administrative Assistant

Location: Independent study by correspondence.

Length: 100 hours (4 modules).

Dates: December 1997-Present.

Objective: To develop knowledge of basic and advanced office procedures.

Learning Outcome: Upon successful completion of this course, the student will be able to understand and perform common secretarial functions.

Instruction: Major topics covered in the course are telephone usage, mail services and shipping, travel arrangements, office machines, telecommunications equipment, computer systems, database system, e-mail and other computer communications, spreadsheets, data security, and keyboarding skills. Methods of instruction include independent study, exercises, quizzes, self scored quizzes, submission of keyboarding and word processing projects, and a proctored final examination.

Credit Recommendation: In the lower division baccalaureate/associate degree category, 3 semester hours in Secretarial Science or Office Systems Technology (11/97).

Elements of California Real Estate Principles (Formerly California Real Estate Principles-OREA, Federal and State Laws and Regulations-OREA, and Uniform Standards of Professional Appraisal Practice-OREA)

Location: Independent study by correspondence.

Length: 64 hours.

Dates: January 1995-Present.

Objective: To provide students with an overview of the field of real estate in California, including the Uniform Standards of Professional Appraisal Practice and appraisal regulations.

Learning Outcome: Upon successful completion of this course, the student will understand the principles of real estate in California and the Uniform Standards of Professional Appraisal Practice and federal and state regulations applying to appraisal.

Instruction: Major topics covered in the course are regulation of real estate practice; legal, financial, economic, and political aspects of real estate; real estate practice; real estate math; Uniform Standards of Professional Appraisal Practice; and federal and state appraisal regulations. Methods of instruction include correspondence study involving directed text readings, special projects, and a proctored final examination.

Credit Recommendation: In the lower division baccalaureate/associate degree category, 3 semester hours in Real Estate or Business Administration (5/97). **NOTE:** The student must successfully complete all three courses in order to receive credit.

Fundamentals of Bookkeeping

Location: Independent study by correspondence.

Length: 110 hours (3 modules).

Dates: December 1997-Present.

Objective: To provide the student with an understanding of the bookkeeping process.

Learning Outcome: Upon successful completion of this course, the student will be able to demonstrate understanding of the bookkeeping cycle; and be familiar with special journals and ledgers, merchandising entries, and specific bookkeeping topics including negotiable instruments, depreciation, and payroll.

Instruction: Major topics covered in the course are the double-entry system; journalizing and posting transactions; financial statements; adjusting and closing procedures; sales, purchase, and cash journals; bookkeeping in a merchandising environment; costing and pricing of merchandise; negotiable instruments; cash controls; payroll; depreciation; and partnership and corporation entries. Methods of instruction include independent study, self-scored chapter quizzes, module examinations, practice project, and a proctored final examination.

Credit Recommendation: In the lower division baccalaureate/associate degree category, 3 semester hours in Bookkeeping (11/97).

Income Property Valuation

Location: Independent study by correspondence.

Length: 45 hours.

Dates: January 1997-Present.

Objective: To provide the student with an understanding of the theory, economics, and principles of valuation and how they relate to income producing properties.

Learning Outcome: Upon successful completion of this course, the student will be able to appraise all income producing properties.

Instruction: Major topics covered in the course are techniques used to analyze income property; how to differentiate between direct and yield capitalization; the time value of money including future value, present value, and amortization; future income and cash flows; income investment measures; expected cash flows; mortgage and equity interests; the effects of leases on the value of a leased fee; highest and best use analysis of vacant and improved sites; and valuation of proposed projects and distressed properties. Methods of instruction include directed text readings, case studies, and a proctored final examination.

Credit Recommendation: In the upper division baccalaureate degree category, 2 semester hours in Real Estate or Business Administration (5/97).

Intermediate Real Estate Appraisal (Formerly Advanced Appraisal)

Location: Independent study by correspondence.

Length: 45 hours.

Dates: January 1997-Present.

Objective: To provide the student with an introduction to appraising income property with emphasis on the nature of real estate as a unique asset with value based on its forecast income.

Learning Outcome: Upon successful completion of this course, the student will be able to appraise income property.

Instruction: Major topics covered in the course are techniques used to analyze income property; how to differentiate between direct and yield capitalization; the time value of money including future value, present value, and amortization; future income and cash flows; income investment measures; expected cash flows; mortgage and equity interests; the effect of leases on the value of a leased fee; and highest and best use analysis of vacant and improved sites. Methods of instruction include correspondence study involving directed text readings, special projects, and a proctored final examination.

Credit Recommendation: In the upper division baccalaureate degree category, 2 semester hours in Real Estate or Business Administration (5/97).

Professional Office Procedures

Location: Independent study by correspondence.

Length: 80 hours (12 chapters).

Dates: December 1997-Present.

Objective: To acquaint the student with basic office procedures.

Learning Outcome: Upon successful completion of this course, the student will be familiar with basic keyboarding, fundamental office terminology, and methodology.

Instruction: Major topics covered in the course are mail processing, filing, basic telephone communications, office technology, travel, business meetings, office security and safety, business terminology, and seeking employment. Methods of instruction include independent study, exercises, quizzes, self-graded quizzes, the submission of keyboarding projects, and a proctored final examination.

Credit Recommendation: In the lower division baccalaureate/associate degree category, 3 semester hours in Secretarial Science or Office Systems Technology (11/97).

Real Estate Appraisal (Formerly Appraiser License Course)

Location: Independent study by correspondence.

Length: 75 hours.

Dates: December 1992-Present.

Objective: To provide the student with an understanding of the principles and practices of real estate appraisal.

Learning Outcome: Upon successful completion of this course, the student will be able to demonstrate familiarity with generally accepted appraisal theory and practice.

Instruction: Major topics covered in the course are the real property appraisal process; the real estate marketplace; data collection; residential construction; the sales comparison, site valuation, and cost approach to property valuation; income capitalization approaches including direct capitalization and the discounted cash flow method; appraising partial interests; the URAR appraisal report; appraisal math and statistics; and the Uniform Standards of Professional Appraisal Practice (USPAP). Methods of instruction include correspondence study involving directed text readings, special projects, quizzes, and a proctored final examination.

Credit Recommendation: In the lower division baccalaureate/associate or the upper division baccalaureate degree category, 3 semester hours in Real Estate or Business Administration (5/97).

America's Community Bankers

America's Community Bankers (ACB), headquartered in Washington, DC, is a trade association representing more than 2,000 insured depository institutions dedicated to serving the financial services needs to their communities. ACB was created in 1992 through a merger of the National Council of Community Bankers with the United States League of Savings Institutions.

ACB's Department of Education is based at the Conference Center at Fairfield on the campus of Fairfield University in Fairfield, Connecticut. The National School of Banking operates under the auspices of this department. The School emphasizes the six curriculum areas of Principles of Management; Finance; Organizational and Strategic Planning; Marketing; Money and Banking; and Financial Products and Services. In addition to the National School, ACB's Education Department designs and conducts more than 70 other technical and development workshops and seminars annually.

Source of official student records: Registry of Credit Recommendations, American Council on Education, One Dupont Circle, Washington, DC 20036-1193 or America's Community Bankers, National School of Banking, Center for Financial Studies, 200 Barlow Road, Fairfield, CT 06430.

Additional information about the courses: College Credit Recommendation Service, American Council on Education, One Dupont Circle, Washington, DC 20036-1193.

Finance: Financial Management of Thrift Institutions
Financial Reporting
Mergers and Acquisitions
Future Financial Outlook

Location: Fairfield, CT.

Length: 38 hours (in residence); 250 hours (independent study).

Dates: January 1987-Present.

Objective: To provide the student with an introduction to financial management theory and practice as it relates to financial institutions.

Learning Outcome: Upon successful completion of this course, the student will be able to describe the financial environment in which modern thrift institutions operate; describe various investment vehicles available; describe basic principles of thrift asset and liability management; and discuss current and developing issues for the thrift industry.

Instruction: Major topics covered in the course are credit markets and savings plans, basic yield and pricing concepts, investment risk consideration, liquidity and marketability of investments, money market investments, mortgage loans, equity investments, hedge management, asset and liability management, mergers and acquisitions, and debt securities. Methods of instruction include lecture, discussion, case studies, individual and group exercises, and research papers that are the basis for assessment of student learning.

Credit Recommendation: In the upper division baccalaureate degree category or in the graduate degree category, 4 semester hours in Finance, Banking, or Investments (11/93).

Financial Products and Services: Business Analysis and Commercial Lending
Consumer Compliance
Pricing Financial Products
Consumer Lending
Electronic Banking and Payment Services
Mortgage Lending

Location: Fairfield, CT.

Length: 21.5 hours (in residence); 200 hours (independent study).

Dates: January 1991-Present.

Objective: To provide the student with an understanding of various financial products offered by financial institutions and the environment in which these institutions operate.

Learning Outcome: Upon successful completion of this course, the student will be able to analyze a financial statement, evaluate a potential borrower, develop policy to cope with regulatory compliance programs, construct a compliance audit, determine a price for a financial service that incorporates the cost of providing that service, assess quality, manage delinquent loans, identify lending risk, identify EFT alternative, and review bank loan products.

Instruction: Major topics covered in the course are the commercial lending process; types of loans, financial statements; compliance programs in the regulatory environment; consumer lending, risk analysis; and EFT technology. Methods of instruction include lecture, discussion, classroom exercises, and research papers which are the basis for assessment of student learning.

Credit Recommendation: In the upper division baccalaureate degree category or in the graduate degree category, 3 semester hours in Banking, Finance, or Business Administration (11/93).

Marketing: Bank Marketing and Demographics

Location: Fairfield, CT.

Length: 17.5 hours (in residence); 200 hours (independent study).

Dates: January 1988-Present.

Objective: To provide the student with knowledge of the theory and principles of marketing and a framework for applying this theory to the practice of marketing financial services.

Learning Outcome: Upon successful completion of this course, the student will be able to analyze competitive market dynamics, identify areas of competitive advantage, use market segmentation strategies, and develop a strategic marketing plan.

Instruction: Major topics covered in the course are market research, customer segmentation, market strategy, and marketing for financial services. Methods of instruction include lecture, discussion, case studies, group and individual exercises, and independent study projects that are the basis for assessment of student learning.

Credit Recommendation: In the upper division baccalaureate degree category or the graduate degree category, 3 semester hours in Marketing or Marketing Financial Services (11/93).

Money and Banking: Money and Capital Markets and Applied Money and Banking

Location: Fairfield, CT.

Length: 27 hours (in residence); 275 hours (independent study).

Dates: January 1990-Present.

Objective: To provide the student with an overview of U.S. financial institutions, monetary and fiscal policy, and the basics of financial forecasting.

Learning Outcome: Upon successful completion of this course, the student will be able to explain the process of intermediation, define the function and workings of the Federal Reserve System, explain the cause and effect of a change in exchange rates, construct an economic forecast, and use an economic model to determine the likely result of monetary and fiscal policy changes.

Instruction: Major topics covered in the course are economic theory, financial intermediation, Federal Reserve System, economic forecasting, and international exchange. Methods of instruction include lecture, discussion, classroom exercises, and research papers which are the basis for assessment of student learning.

Credit Recommendation: In the upper division baccalaureate degree category or in the graduate degree category, 4 semester hours in Banking, Finance, Business Administration, or Economics (11/93).

Organizational and Strategic Planning:
Strategic Planning
Bank Management
Banking Overview
Simulating Bank Operations: The Strategic Banker

Location: Fairfield, CT.

Length: 45 hours (in residence); 200 hours (independent study).

Dates: January 1991-Present.

Objective: To provide the student with knowledge of the theory of strategy, the process of strategic planning, and the development of skill in applying specific strategic models and techniques to financial services.

Learning Outcome: Upon successful completion of this course, the student will be able to analyze economic, social, political, technological, and regulatory trends for strategic opportunities and threats; assess organizational strengths and weaknesses; improvements; and develop a strategic plan including scheduling and implementation processes.

Instruction: Major topics covered in the course are environmental analysis, competitive advantage, strategic planning, and the changing environment of financial services. Methods of instruction include lecture, discussion, simulation, individual and group exercises, and independent study projects that are the basis for assessment of student learning.

Credit Recommendation: In the upper division baccalaureate or in the graduate degree category, 4 semester hours in Strategic Planning, Strategic Management, or Strategy (11/93).

Principles of Management:
Career Management Process
Presentation Skills
Team Management
Manager as Counselor
Management and Motivation
Human Resource Management
Lessons from the Classic Sexual Harassment Issues

Location: Fairfield, CT.

Length: 32 hours (in residence); 175 hours (independent study).

Dates: January 1983-Present.

Objective: To provide the student with an understanding of organizational dynamics of financial institutions and how these dynamics affect managers; and to develop skill in managerial communication that enhances productivity and effectiveness.

Learning Outcome: Upon successful completion of this course, the student will be able to analyze their own management style; develop specific team-building techniques; practice effective listening skills; construct and deliver corporate presentations; develop and implement appropriate career development strategies for employees and self; analyze own leadership style; promote gender equality in the workplace; and apply techniques of effective performance appraisal.

Instruction: Major topics covered in the course are the career management process, presentation skills, team management, the manager as motivator, performance appraisal skills, sexual harassment issues, human resource management, and the manager as counselor. Methods of instruction include lecture, discussion, case studies, diagnostic tools, individual and group exercises, and research papers that are the basis for assessment of student learning.

Credit Recommendation: In the upper division baccalaureate degree category or in the graduate degree category, 3 semester hours in Management, Organizational Behavior, Human Relations, Personnel, or Human Resources Management (11/93).

American Academy of Nutrition, College of Nutrition

The American Academy of Nutrition was founded in 1985 to provide comprehensive nutrition education through guided distance learning while maintaining the highest academic standards. Faculty members and instructors are highly qualified specialists in the field of nutrition who use an in-depth nutrition curriculum and the finest textbooks and videos available.

The materials used by the Academy incorporate the latest advances in the field of nutrition and present a wide range of ideas and practical information. In addition to utilizing basic nutrition textbooks used in hundreds of universities throughout America, the courses provide alternate views by highly respected experts.

Included in the student body are health professionals as well as people who simply want to improve their health. The Academy is approved to provide continuing education for nurses, dentists, pharmacists, home economists, and others. Also, the Academy is accredited by the Accrediting Commission of the Distance Education and Training Council (DETC).

The goal of the Academy is to provide the students with the most comprehensive nutrition education available anywhere, whether for career enhancement or personal health improvement.

Source of official student records: Registry of Credit Recommendations, American Council on Education, One Dupont Circle, Washington, DC 20036-1193 or Registrar's Office, American Academy of Nutrition, College of Nutrition, 1212 Kenesaw, Knoxville, TN, 37919, (800)637-8325.

Additional information about the courses: College Credit Recommendation Service, American Council on Education, One Dupont Circle, Washington, DC 20036-1193.

Anatomy and Physiology

Location: Independent study by correspondence.

Length: 135 hours (self-paced).

Dates: June 1989-Present.

Objective: To develop the knowledge of person's pursuing careers in allied health fields in the design and function of the human body.

Learning Outcome: Upon successful completion of this course, the student will be able to understand how the body is organized; describe the functions of the principal body systems; and explain the role of oxygen and nutrients in the health of the human body.

Instruction: Major topics covered in the course are organization of the body's support and movement; regulation of body activities; internal transport and defense; oxygen, nutrients, and energy; regulation of fluids and electrolytes; perpetuating the species; hypoglycemia; and critique of current nutrition trends. Methods of instruction include case studies, textbooks, videotapes, course assignments, and final examination.

Credit Recommendation: In the lower division baccalaureate/associate degree category, 3 semester hours in Anatomy and Physiology (9/94).

Community Nutrition

Location: Independent study by correspondence.

Length: 135 hours (self-paced).

Dates: September 1994-Present.

Objective: To provide an educational foundation for those who will guide individuals and communities to proper nutrition and good health.

Learning Outcome: Upon successful completion of this course, the student will be able to understand the role of nutrition in public health and be able to apply this knowledge to program planning, management, assessment, and influencing consumer behavior in a community (public or private) setting.

Instruction: Major topics covered in the course are the role of nutrition in public health, epidemiology, public health care, national nutrition agenda, program planning and management, community nutrition assessment, consumer behavior, marketing nutrition for health promotion, domestic hunger and food assistance programs, nutrition services for all age groups, global nutrition awareness, and community learning activities. Methods of instruction include learner presentations/reports, textbooks, videotapes, course assignments, and a final examination.

Credit Recommendation: In the lower division baccalaureate/associate degree category, 3 semester hours in Community Nutrition (9/94). **NOTE**: For individuals completing the Internship-Practical Experience, the credit recommendation is in the lower division baccalaureate/associate degree category, 4 semester hours in Community Nutrition (9/94).

Environmental Challenges and Solutions

Location: Independent study by correspondence.

Length: 135 hours (self-paced).

Dates: September 1994-Present.

Objective: To provide knowledge of the scope and severity of environmental illnesses.

Learning Outcome: Upon successful completion of this course, the student will be able to recognize causes and effects of chemically induced illness; know how to find alternative solutions to chemicals; and understand the role proper nutrition plays in avoiding and/or mitigating the damage these chemicals cause.

Instruction: Major topics covered in the course are clinical ecology and environmental illnesses, food safety, food additives, pesticides, alternatives to toxins, and poisons. Methods of instruction include case studies, audio/visual material, learner presentations/reports, textbooks, videotapes, course assignments, and a final examination.

Credit Recommendation: In the lower division baccalaureate/associate degree category, 3 semester hours in Food and Nutrition (9/94).

Human Biology

Location: Independent study by correspondence.

Length: 135 hours (self-paced).

Dates: September 1994-Present.

Objective: To teach the structure and function of the human body and the balance that maintains the integrity of the body's systems and good health while encouraging the development of critical thinking skills.

Learning Outcome: Upon successful completion of this course, the student will understand all types of cellular tissue; recognize how the various systems within the body control certain functions; and have a good overview of the ecology system and ways in which humans can alter their tolerance for environmental factors.

Instruction: Major topics covered in the course are cells, chromosomes, and heredity; the human organism; structure and function of the human body; reproduction and development; ecology and behavior; osteoporosis case study; and critique of current nutrition trends. Methods of instruction include case studies, learner presentations/

reports, textbooks, videotapes, course assignments, and a final examination.

Credit Recommendation: In the lower division baccalaureate/associate degree category, 3 semester hours in Human Biology (9/94).

Nutrition Counseling Skills

Location: Independent study by correspondence.

Length: 135 hours (self-paced).

Dates: June 1989-Present.

Objective: To provide education in the psychology of nutrition counseling as well as assessment, treatment, and evaluation tools.

Learning Outcome: Upon successful completion of this course, the student will be able to identify inappropriate eating behaviors; demonstrate effective use of interviewing skills; and utilize proper nutrition counseling techniques.

Instruction: Major topics covered in the course are the psychological aspects of interviewing and counseling clients, proper use of assessment and monitoring techniques, application of interviewing and counseling skills, and case studies. Methods of instruction include case studies, learner presentations/reports, textbooks, videotapes, course assignments, and a final examination.

Credit Recommendation: In the lower division baccalaureate/associate degree category, 3 semester hours in Human Nutrition (9/94). **NOTE**: For individuals completing the Internship-Practical Experience, the credit recommendation is in the lower division baccalaureate/associate degree category, 4 semester hours in Community Nutrition (9/94).

Pregnancy, Pediatric, and Adolescent Nutrition

Location: Independent study by correspondence.

Length: 135 hours (self-paced).

Dates: June 1989-Present.

Objective: To train dieticians, nutritionists, and educators in life cycle nutrition particularly reproduction and conception, and to help those who wish to provide better nutrition to their families.

Learning Outcome: Upon successful completion of this course, the student will understand the conception and pregnancy process; and know how to meet nutritional needs during this period as well as during infancy, early childhood, and adolescence.

Instruction: Major topics covered in the course are pre-conception and pregnancy nutrition, pregnancy and lactation, nutrition during infancy through adolescence, nutrition supplementation, learning and behavior, attention deficit disorder by case study, and current nutrition trends. Methods of instruction include case studies, learner presentations/reports, textbooks, videotapes, course assignments, and a final examination.

Credit Recommendation: In the lower division baccalaureate/associate degree category, 3 semester hours in Human Nutrition (9/94). **NOTE:** For individuals completing the Internship-Practical Experience, the credit recommendation is in the lower division baccalaureate/associate degree category, 4 semester hours in Community Nutrition (9/94).

Sports Nutrition

Location: Independent study by correspondence.

Length: 135 hours (self-paced).

Dates: April 1992-Present.

Objective: To present current, accurate information on nutrition and physical fitness which motivates the student to take action toward good health an fitness; and to prepare educational and health professionals for counseling in sports medicine.

Learning Outcome: Upon successful completion of this course, the student will understand the motivation and benefits and be able to plan an appropriate exercise and nutrition program for professional and non-professional athletic endeavors.

Instruction: Major topics covered in the course are motivation and the benefits of fitness, flexibility, strength and endurance, nutrition for physically active people, preventing exercise and environmental injuries, supplementation for athletes, how to design an exercise program, nutrition and body building, and critique of current nutrition trends. Methods of instruction include case studies, learner presentations/reports, textbooks, videotapes, course assignments, and a final examination.

Credit Recommendation: In the lower division baccalaureate/associate degree category, 3 semester hours in Sports Nutrition (9/94). **NOTE**: For individuals completing the Internship-Practical Experience, the credit recommendation is in the lower division baccalaureate/associate degree category, 4 semester hours in Community Nutrition (9/94).

Understanding Nutrition I

Location: Independent study by correspondence.

Length: 135 hours (self-paced).

Dates: June 1989-Present.

Objective: To provide a basic understanding of human nutrition.

Learning Outcome: Upon successful completion of this course, the student will understand and be conversant with the basic components of nutrition such as vitamins, minerals, carbohydrates, fats, proteins, etc.

Instruction: Major topics covered in the course are nutrient elements; carbohydrates, fats, and proteins; vitamins, minerals, and body fluids; digestion, metabolism, and weight management; nutritional approach to obesity; and current nutrition trends. Methods of instruction include case studies, learner presentations/reports, textbooks, videotapes, course assignments, and a final examination.

Credit Recommendation: In the lower division baccalaureate/associate degree category, 3 semester hours in Human Nutrition (9/94).

Understanding Nutrition II

Location: Independent study by correspondence.

Length: 135 hours (self-paced).

Dates: July 1994-Present.

Objective: To recognize the relationship between physical activity and nutrition, and to understand nutrient needs throughout the life span.

Learning Outcome: Upon successful completion of this course, the student will be familiar with nutritional needs for specific age groups; chronic disease risk factors; consumer concerns about foods; and environmental consciousness.

Instruction: Major topics covered in the course are nutrients and physical activity, life cycle nutrition, risk factors for chronic diseases, consumer concerns about foods, and environmental consciousness. Methods of instruction include case studies, learner presentations/reports, textbooks, videotapes, course assignments, and a final examination.

Credit Recommendation: In the lower division baccalaureate/associate degree category, 3 semester hours in Human Nutrition (9/94).

Vegetarian Nutrition

Location: Independent study by correspondence.

Length: 135 hours (self-paced).

Dates: April 1992-Present.

Objective: To provide education about vegetarian diets and the health benefits and risks for those adopting a vegetarian diet.

Learning Outcome: Upon successful completion of this course, the student will understand the risks of a non-vegetarian diet and be able to plan a healthy vegetarian lifestyle.

Instruction: Major topics covered in the course are planning a vegetarian diet, risks of a non-vegetarian diet, nutrient supplementation for vegetarians, and the scientific basis of vegetarianism. Methods of instruction include case studies, audio/ visual material, learner presentations/ reports, textbooks, videotapes, course assignments, and a final examination.

Credit Recommendation: In the lower division baccalaureate/associate degree category, 3 semester hours in Human Nutrition (9/94).

American Association of Direct Human Service Personnel

The American Association of Direct Human Service Personnel (AADHSP) is a national, professional association founded in 1991. AADHSP's goal is to advance the professional prominence of nonprofit direct human service personnel. One way this is accomplished is through widely accepted certification programs that focus on the enhancement of job skills and techniques. These certifications assist in increasing the overall awareness and value of the "role" of direct human service personnel.

The curriculums are open to anyone employed in a nonprofit organization and working with the organization's mission target clientele. Each course includes three main segments - two months at home study of text books, a three-and-one-half-day classroom experience followed by a forced choice exam covering the home study and the classroom course, and a take home assignment which includes submitting a formal report. To become certified, participants must successfully complete the examination and have their after class take home assignment approved. Certification can be maintained for three years provided they accumulate twelve continuing education units by the end of the renewal period.

The classes are given in central locations throughout the United States, are taught by instructors with college degrees who have a minimum of five years work experience in human service agencies.

Source of official student records: Registry of Credit Recommendations, American Council on Education, One Dupont Circle, Washington, DC 20036-1193.

Additional information about the courses: College Credit Recommendation Service, American Council on Education, One Dupont Circle, Washington, DC 20036-1193.

Human Service Provider (Formerly Certified Human Service Provider)

Location: Various locations throughout the United States.

Length: 26 hours (3.5 days classroom, 2 plus months home study, and 30 hours on-the-job supervised training).

Dates: April 1992-Present.

Objective: To give human service providers an overview of the requisite knowledge, skills, and values of the field.

Learning Outcome: Upon successful completion of this course, the student will be able to apply some contemporary models and theories in human service provision to his or her own work.

Instruction: Major topics covered in the course are psychology, sociology, marketing, elementary statistics, and techniques of case management. Methods of instruction include lecture, discussion, classroom exercises, use of video, and an internship experience.

Credit Recommendation: In the lower division baccalaureate/associate degree category, 3 semester hours as a general elective in Psychology, Sociology, Human Development and Family Studies, or Social Work (12/93).

Service Facilitator

Location: Various locations throughout the United States.

Length: 27 hours (3.5 days), 45 hours (8 weeks) assigned readings and 4 weeks of case studies.

Dates: January 1995-Present.

Objective: To provide the participant with the knowledge and skills needed by a Service Facilitator (Case Manager) to facilitate services to populations at risk.

Learning Outcome: Upon successful completion of this course, the student will be able to demonstrate knowledge and ability requirements of service facilitators; describe the typical roles and responsibilities of a service facilitator; understand motivation and how it functions; identify communication styles and understand how to achieve effective communication; understand the roles of values, diversity, and culture; demonstrate effective interviewing skills; perform needs assessment and develop care plans.

Instruction: Major topics covered in the course are service facilitator's roles and duties; assessment interview techniques; self confidence inventory; the roles of values, diversity, and culture; ethics; communication; care planning; community resources; quality assurance; an introduction to statistical methods of evaluation; and psychological stressors. Methods of instruction include lecture, discussion, classroom exercises/problem solving, audiovisual, videotaping, instructional game, and final examination.

Credit Recommendation: In the lower division baccalaureate/associate degree category or upper division baccalaureate degree category, 3 semester hours in Social Work, Case Management, Public Administration, Sociology, Psychology, Family Services or Human Services (11/95).

American Bankers Association

The mission of the American Bankers Association (ABA) is to serve its members by enhancing the role of banks and bank holding companies as the preeminent providers of financial services. With more than 1,000 bankers who volunteer their time on councils and committees, and a national staff of about 400, ABA accomplishes this mission through federal legislative and regulatory activities, legal action, communication and consumer education, research, and products and services that promote, educate, train, inform, and support members.

ABA's Professional Development Council, made up of senior-level bankers from around the country, guides the work of the Professional Development Group (PDG) within ABA. PDG's mission includes banker education and training, research, evaluation, and program development. The Professional Development Group is responsible for developing and overseeing a variety of educational programs, including more than 30 national, residential schools and conferences, ranging in duration from a few days to two weeks. PDG also sponsors BankSim and BankExec, computer-based management training tools, and the Stonier Graduate School of Banking.

The American Institute of Banking (AIB), one of the largest industry-sponsored adult education programs in the world, is also part of PDG. Approximately 160,000 students—primarily entry-level to middle management—take AIB courses and seminars annually. These programs are delivered locally through a national network of 70 chapters. Chapters are chartered franchises of ABA; their management is further guided by their local boards of directors.

Most chapters have classroom facilities within their offices for course and seminar offerings. They also have working relationships with banks, colleges and universities, high schools, and community centers for the use or rental of classroom space. These places are chosen in locations where there is maximum accessibility for bankers.

The American Institute of Banking recommends that its chapters use the ABA criteria when selecting their instructors. In general, AIB chapters are advised to recruit instructors from their local banks, businesses, and colleges. The criteria noted above include content knowledge, demonstrated academic and professional achievement, knowledge of and ability to accomplish instructional objectives, positive attitude toward teaching and students, and willingness to participate in faculty development activities. ABA offers its AIB chapters a free instructor-training workshop. Each year, over 1,000 AIB instructors participate in these day-long workshops, led by ABA-approved training consultants.

ABA's Professional Development Group is responsible for managing the course development and revision process of AIB courses to ensure that a systematic sequence of high-quality, cost-effective educational opportunities is available to bankers. Banking experts are identified as authors and reviewers of textbooks and other materials. These authors work with committees of bankers representing different-sized institutions and diverse geographic locations to ensure that all viewpoints and needs are represented in the resulting materials. All texts and other materials go through a comprehensive review process to ensure accuracy, currency, and comprehensiveness.

In most cases, professional instructional designers are called upon to develop instructor's manuals and correspondence courses. These materials guide instructors in the most effective use of the textbook or seminar in the classroom. In addition to schedules and teaching strategies, instructor's manuals include visual masters, quiz questions, and midterm and final examinations. The instructional designers, some of whom are experienced tests and measurements professionals, are given specific guidance on the development of examinations. Each question is keyed to a specific course objective, and the number of questions on a topic must be proportional to instructional time given to it. Content validity is assured through this process. In addition, feedback is solicited from instructors whose students take these exams, to help detect problem questions and guide revisions.

Source of official student records: Registry of Credit Recommendations, American Council on Education, One Dupont Circle, Washington, DC 20036-1193 or AIB: Registrar, American Institute of Banking, American Bankers Association, 1120 Connecticut Avenue, N.W., Washington, DC 20036. **State-sponsored schools:** Send to the Registrar for the applicable school.

Additional information about the courses: College Credit Recommendation Service, American Council on Education, One Dupont Circle, Washington, DC 20036-1193.

NOTE 1: Credit is also recommended for any courses offered through correspondence study, provided that efforts of students using this method are measured by a proctored examination at the conclusion of each course.

NOTE 2: The following American Institute of Banking (AIB) chapters are following guidelines and standards established by the American Bankers Association and are eligible to use the credit recommendations granted to the American Bankers Association by the College Credit Recommendation Service of the American Council on Education:

Arkansas AIB
PO Box 608
Little Rock, AR 72203
Contact: Debbie Sefcik
Phone: 501-372-0940
Fax: 501-372-1142

Birmingham AIB
1824 29th Avenue South
Suite 240
Birmingham, AL 35209
Contact: Kim Boyd
Phone: 205-879-4242
Fax: 205-879-4246

Capital Region AIB
1 Pine West Plaza
Washington Avenue Extension
Albany, NY 12205
Contact: Helen Rinaldi
Phone: 518-464-4091
Fax: 518-464-4093

Columbus AIB
30 Eden Alley
Suite 201
Columbus, OH 43215
Contact: Pat Baker
Phone: 614-228-6196
Fax: 614-228-7434

Delaware AIB
PO Box 494
Dover, DE 19903-0494
Contact: David G. Bakerian
Phone: 302-674-0202
Fax: 302-674-0496

Des Moines AIB
Iowa Bankers Association
418 6th Avenue
Suite 430
Des Moines, IA 50309
Contact: Ann Winkel
Phone: 515-286-4320
Fax: 515-280-4140

Memphis AIB
5118 Park Avenue
Suite 111
Memphis, TN 38117
Contact: Vicki Simmons
Phone: 901-682-4494
Fax: 901-682-9752

Northern New England AIB
PO Box 503
Portland, ME 04112
Contact: Tanya Kolonoski
Phone: 207-772-7842
Fax: 207-776-7324

Oregon AIB
777 13th Street SE
Suite 130
Salem, OR 97301
Contact: Jo Ann Wright
Phone: 503-581-3522
Fax: 503-581-8714

Puerto Rico AIB
209 Munoz Rivera Avenue
Suite 1014
San Juan, PR 00918-1002
Contact: Jose Justel
Phone: 787-767-1130
Fax: 787-754-6022

Regional New York AIB
Main-Seneca Building
237 Main Street
Suite 300
Buffalo, NY 14203
Contact: Thomas H. Owen
Phone: 716-847-6430
Fax: 716-847-6432

Rocky Mountain AIB
1050 17th Street
Suite 450
Denver, CO 80265
Contact: Kathy Smith
Phone: 303-825-1590
Fax: 303-629-1591

Southern New England AIB
PO Box 1213
Norwich, CT 06360-1213
Contact: Michael Meakem
Phone: 860-886-6153
Fax: 860-823-1410

Utah AIB
185 South State Street
Suite 201
Salt Lake City, UT 84111
Contact: Wendy Holloway
Phone: 801-328-8124
Fax: 801-364-4495

Virginia AIB
870 North Military Highway
Suite 217
Norfolk, VA 23502
Contact: Deborah Gallaway
Phone: 757-466-1830
Fax: 757-455-8694

Wisconsin East AIB
177 E. Silver Spring Drive
Whitefish Bay, WI 53217-4703
Contact: Patti Katzban
Phone: 414-332-6468
Fax: 414-332-6478

Wisconsin West AIB
1325 Greenway Cross
Suite 115
Madison, WI 53713
Contact: Dean Kesler
Phone: 608-273-8384
Fax: 608-273-8381

Accounting (1000)
(Formerly Accounting Principles I [1000])
(Formerly Accounting I)
(Formerly Accounting Principles and Applications I)

Location: AIB chapters nationwide operating under established ABA guidelines and standards.

Length: *Version 1:* 45 hours (15 weeks; three 1-hour sessions per week); *Version 2:* 30 hours (10 weeks; three 1-hour sessions per week) or by correspondence study with proctored final examination.

Dates: November 1985-Present.

Objective: To provide the student with the basic principles and practices of general accounting procedures.

Learning Outcome: Upon successful completion of this course, the student will be able to describe the content and purposes of a balance sheet and income statement; compare the basic characteristics of the accrual basis of accounting; explain the full accounting cycle and prepare all required journals, entries, and adjustments; outline the necessity for and features of internal control; identify the basic assumptions, principles, and modifying conventions of accounting; describe how inflation affects information presented in conventional financial statements; and define partnerships and explain their characteristics.

Instruction: Major topics covered in the course are current practices of accounting procedures and include coverage of the latest accounting principles as set forth by the Financial Accounting Standards Board. Coverage includes processing accounting information, the accounting cycle, accounting systems and special journals, and assets and liabilities. Methods of instruction include lecture, discussion, classroom exercises, and laboratory. The course is also offered by correspondence with a proctored final examination.

Credit Recommendation: *Version 1:* In the lower division baccalaureate/associate degree category, 3 semester hours in Accounting (11/85). *Version 2:* In the lower division baccalaureate/associate degree category, 2 semester hours in Accounting (2/91) (11/95).

Accounting II (1010)
(Formerly Accounting Principles II [1010])
(Formerly Accounting: Principles and Applications II)

Location: AIB chapters nationwide operating under established ABA guidelines and standards.

Length: *Version 1:* 45 hours (15 weeks; one 3-hour session per week); *Version 2:* 30 hours (10 weeks; one 3-hour session per week) or by correspondence study with proctored final examination.

Dates: November 1985-July 1995.

Objective: To expand upon the basic principles and practices of general accounting procedures. Introduces broader applications of accounting relative to responsibilities, operations, and control.

Learning Outcome: Upon successful completion of this course, the student will be able to contrast the advantages and disadvantages of the corporate form of business; summarize the various features of bonds and how they differ from shares of stocks, and the journal entries required to account for them on financial statements; list the major sources and uses of funds; explain how comparative financial statements may be used to analyze and appraise the financial position of a firm and the results of its operations; discuss the concept of a standard cost analysis system, specifically addressing how standards are set and the advantages achieved through their use; and define capital budgeting and explain the effects of making poor capital budgeting decisions.

Instruction: Major topics covered in the course are policy analysis and management with emphasis on detailed accounting functions and procedures. Presentation includes corporate accounting, bond and stock investments, analysis and interpretation of financial statements, budgeting, and taxes. Methods of instruction include lecture, discussion, and exercises. The course is also offered by correspondence.

Credit Recommendation: *Version 1:* In the lower division baccalaureate/associate degree category, 3 semester hours in Accounting (11/85). *Version 2:* In the lower division baccalaureate/associate degree category, 2 semester hours in Accounting (2/91). *Prerequisite:* Accounting I.

Analyzing Financial Statements (6920)

Location: AIB chapters nationwide operating under established ABA guidelines and standards.

Length: *Version 1:* 45 hours (15 weeks; one 3-hour session per week); *Version 2:* 30 hours (10 weeks; one 3-hour session per week) or by correspondence study with proctored final examination.

Dates: November 1985-Present.

Objective: To provide the student with the basic theory and skills necessary to apply financial analysis to the financial statements, including the statement of cash flows, to evaluate the current and future financial condition of business firms.

Learning Outcome: Upon successful completion of this course, student will be able to apply financial ratio analysis to the income statement and the balance sheet; evaluate the business firms financial condition; analyze cash flows to determine the firm's capacity to generate internal cash flows and its need for external financing; prepare pro forma financial statements; prepare cash budgets and use them for financial planning; analyze business operating cycles and classify financial statement concepts; and analyze personal financial statements.

Instruction: Major topics covered in the course are financial ratio analysis, statement of cash flows, pro forma financial statements, cash budgets, sensitivity analysis, break even analysis, business cycles, classification of financial statement concepts, the relationship of loan structure and competition to credit analysis, and analysis of personal financial statements. Methods of instruction include lecture, discussion, proctored exercises, and an examination. This course is also offered by correspondence with a proctored final examination.

Credit Recommendation: *Version 1:* In the upper division baccalaureate degree category, 3 semester hours in Finance or Accounting (11/85). *Version 2:* In the upper division baccalaureate degree category, 2 semester hours in Finance or Accounting (2/91) (11/95). **NOTE:** Students who receive credit for this course should not receive credit for the course Statement Analysis.

Bank Accounting (6000) (Formerly Bank Accounting [7520])

Location: AIB chapters nationwide operating under established ABA guidelines and standards.

Length: *Version 1:* 45 hours (15 weeks; one 3-hour session per week); *Version 2:* 30 hours (10 weeks; three 1-hour sessions per week) or by correspondence study with proctored final examination.

Dates: November 1985-July 1996.

Objective: To provide the principles of accounting as they apply to a financial institution.

Learning Outcome: Upon successful completion of this course, the student will be able to describe the nature of the accounting process within the banking industry with its similarities to and differences from other industries; demonstrate the flow of funds concept within a bank; define basic accounting terms and procedures; identify the components of financial statements; describe the accrual accounting process; identify nonearning assets and their relationship to the bank's financial performance; and interpret the financial statements of a bank.

Instruction: Major topics covered in the course are basic bank accounting statements of financial position; investments, loans, and depository accounting; bank performance analysis; and governmental reporting. Methods of instruction include lecture, discussion, and problem solving.

Credit Recommendation: *Version 1:* In the lower division baccalaureate/associate degree category, 3 semester hours in Bank Accounting (11/85). *Version 2:* In the lower division baccalaureate/associate degree category, 2 semester hours in Bank Accounting (2/91).

Bank Cards (6610) (Formerly Banking and the Plastic Card [6610])

Location: AIB chapters nationwide operating under established ABA guidelines and standards.

Length: *Versions 1 and 3:* 45 hours (15 weeks; one 3-hour session per week); *Versions 2 and 4:* 30 hours (10 weeks; one 3-hour session per week) or by correspondence study with proctored final examination; *Version 5:* 45 hours (15 weeks; one 3-hour session per week) or 30 hours (10 weeks; one 3-hour session per week).

Dates: *Version 1:* November 1985-January 1991; *Version 2:* November 1985-January 1991; *Version 3:* February 1991-Present; *Version 4:* February 1991-Present; *Version 5:* September 1996-Present.

Objective: To provide the student with an understanding of bank cards, their basic operation, and their role in a financial environment.

Learning Outcome: Upon successful completion of this course, the student will be able to understand the impact of bank cards on the banking industry; understand the effects of bank cards on the economy; have an awareness of the regulatory environment; understand the various credit vehicles and the differences between them; and recognize benefits of the bank cards to merchants, banks, and consumers; bank credit card fraud; and the role of ATM and other non-credit cards.

Instruction: Major topics covered in the course are the history and structure of the card system, operational aspects, legal and regulatory issues, and trends. Methods of instruction include lecture and discussion or correspondence.

Credit Recommendation: *Version 1:* In the vocational certificate or lower division baccalaureate/associate degree category, 2 semester hours in Banking or Consumer Credit (11/85). *Version 2:* In the vocational certificate or lower division baccalaureate/associate degree category, 1 semester hour in Banking or Consumer Credit (11/85). *Version 3:* In the lower division baccalaureate/associate degree category, 3 semester hours in Banking or Consumer Credit (2/91). *Version 4:* In the lower division baccalaureate/associate degree category, 2 semester hours in Banking or Consumer Credit (2/91). *Version 5:* In the vocational certificate or lower division baccalaureate/ associate degree category, 2 semester hours in Banking or Consumer Credit (10/96).

Bank Control and Audit (6150)

Location: AIB chapters nationwide operating under established ABA guidelines and standards.

Length: 30 hours (10 weeks; one 3-hour session per week).

Dates: November 1985-December 1991.

Objective: To present the basic concepts of auditing to the nonauditor. Develop a deeper understanding of the role, duties, and responsibilities of the bank auditor.

Instruction: Major topics covered in the course are the nature of bank control and audit, risk exposure, auditing information systems, and regulatory compliance. Methods of instruction include lecture, discussion, and classroom exercise.

Credit Recommendation: In the lower division baccalaureate/associate degree category, 2 semester hours in Bank Auditing (11/85).

Bank Investments (7200)

Location: AIB chapters nationwide operating under established ABA guidelines and standards.

Length: 30 hours (10 weeks; one 3-hour session per week).

Dates: November 1985-December 1991.

Objective: To provide students of banking with an introductory overview of the investment function in commercial banking.

Instruction: Major topics covered in the course are various concepts and institutions that are critical to good investment decision-making at commercial banks, investment math, treasury and agency securities, municipal securities, money-market investments, and bond management techniques. Methods of instruction include lectures, discussions, and classroom exercises.

Credit Recommendation: In the lower division baccalaureate/associate degree category, 2 semester hours in Banking or Finance (11/85).

Bank Investments and Funds Management (7201)

Location: AIB chapters nationwide operating under established ABA guidelines and standards.

Length: *Version 1:* 45 hours (15 weeks; one 3-hour session per week); *Version 2:* 30 hours (10 weeks; one 3-hour session per week) or by correspondence study with proctored final examination.

Dates: *Version 1:* January 1987-September 1996; *Version 2:* October 1996-December 1996.

Objective: To provide an introduction to the fundamental concepts and strategies of investment account management within the broader context of the overall management of bank funds.

Learning Outcome: Upon successful completion of this course, the student will be able to implement bank investment and funds management strategies to earn an acceptable return without undue risk; describe strategies generally used in the management of bank funds; list characteristics and identify uses of specific investment funds and instruments; and describe procedures of profit and risk analysis that apply to bank funds and investments.

Instruction: Major topics covered in the course are investment mathematics; liquidity, risk and profitability; bank funding instruments; bank investment instruments; financial markets; investment portfolio management; and asset/liability management. Methods of instruction include lecture, discussion, classroom exercises, and final examination.

Credit Recommendation: *Version 1:* In the lower division baccalaureate/associate degree category, 3 semester hours in Banking or Finance (2/91) (10/96). *Version 2:* In the lower division baccalaureate/associate degree category, 3 semester hours in Banking or Finance (2/91) (10/96).

Bank Management (7535) (Formerly Commercial Bank Management)

Location: AIB chapters nationwide operating under established ABA guidelines and standards.

Length: *Version 1:* 45 hours (15 weeks; one 3-hour session per week); *Version 2:* 30 hours (10 weeks; one 3-hour session per week) or by correspondence study with proctored final examination; *Version 3:* Accelerated 15 hours (5 weeks; 3 hours per week).

Dates: November 1985-December 1996.

Objective: To describe and analyze the profitability of various banking functions from the perspective of the simultaneous management of asset, liability, and capital decisions.

Learning Outcome: Upon successful completion of this course, the student will be able to explain how bank objectives and policies are formed; outline the sources and uses of funds; explain principles of funds management; describe the administration of deposits, loans, and other investments; and analyze bank performance.

Instruction: Major topics covered in the course are the analysis of techniques for managing asset and funding decisions, with special emphasis on the interaction between balance sheet items; lending and investment decisions; deposit functions; liability management; capital decisions; gap management; and planning and profitability analysis. Methods of instruction include lecture, discussions, case materials, and examination. This course is also offered by correspondence with a proctored final examination.

Credit Recommendation: *Version 1:* In the upper division baccalaureate degree category, 3 semester hours in Banking or Finance (11/85). *Version 2:* In the upper division baccalaureate degree category, 2 semester hours in Banking or Finance (11/85). *Version 3:* In the upper division baccalaureate degree category, 1 semester hour in Banking or Finance (2/91).

Branch Banking Series (6231)
1. Credit (6239)
2. Human Resources Management (6237)
3. Marketing (6235)
4. Managing Sales in the Branch (7597)

Location: AIB chapters nationwide operating under established ABA guidelines and standards.

Length: *Version 1:* 45 hours (15 weeks; one 3-hour session per week), includes all four areas; *Version 2:* 30 hours (10 weeks; one 3-hour session per week), includes three of the four parts.

Dates: January 1990-July 1995.

Objective: To assist new branch managers to prepare for their responsibilities with respect to credit, marketing, human resources management, and managing sales in the branch.

Learning Outcome: Upon successful completion of this series, the student will be able to—*Part 1:* List and describe the steps in the credit process; describe the functions and importance of the credit department; and identify types of commercial credit. *Part 2:* Make sound hiring decisions based on skillful interviewing techniques and knowledge of personnel law; conduct objective, productive performance evaluations; document situations that call for disciplinary action and deal with difficult employees and problems of turnover; and identify training needs and council employees on career development. *Part 3:* Identify current position vis-a-vis competitors by evaluating customer base, product lines, and market needs; develop a plan of action and implement it through product, sales, and systems training; develop marketing strategies; identify costs in developing products or services, such as interest rate/credit risk, fees, spreads, and non-interest expenses, and compliance and reporting requirements against product profitability; identify delivery systems and appropriate positioning; and estimate product life cycles. *Part 4:* Design and implement a plan for increasing the selling effectiveness of the staff; involve staff in developing techniques of meeting a variety of customer needs and managing difficult selling situations; coach and counsel individual staff members concerning sales skills; and implement a sales performance measurement, reporting, and reward system to help motivate staff.

Instruction: Major topics covered in the course are commercial and consumer credit; financial statements; hiring, performance appraisal reviews, employee problems; marketing research, marketing plans; and sales functions. Methods of instruction include lecture, classroom discussion, role playing, and small group discussion.

Credit Recommendation: *Version 1:* In the lower division baccalaureate/associate degree category, 3 semester hours in Business (2/91). *Version 2:* In the lower division baccalaureate/associate degree category, 2 semester hours in Business (2/91).

Branch Sales: Creating a Plan for the 90's (7597)

Location: AIB chapters nationwide operating under established ABA guidelines and standards.

Length: 15 hours (5 weeks) or 15 hours (2 days).

Dates: September 1994-Present.

Objective: To provide a forum for exchanging ideas with other professionals and to create a workable sales plan for a branch.

Learning Outcome: Upon successful completion of this course, the student will be able to help create a sales culture in a branch and develop the staff's effectiveness as salespeople; implement effective communication skills with customers; devise tools and sales aids to enhance the staff's selling behaviors and skills; devise a system or rewards and recognition for superior sales performance; conduct a well-organized and productive sales meeting; and simulate a sales presentation of senior officers.

Instruction: Major topics covered in the course are creating a selling environment, tools for successful selling, enhancing selling behaviors and skills, sales meeting, and sales plan presentation. Methods of instruction include lecture, discussion, classroom exercises, and an examination.

Credit Recommendation: In the lower division baccalaureate/associate degree category, 1 semester hour in Sales, Marketing, or Business (11/95). **NOTE:** To receive 1 credit, both this course and Understanding and Selling Bank Products (7766) must be completed.

Commercial Lending (6350)

Location: AIB chapters nationwide operating under established ABA guidelines and standards.

Length: *Version 1:* 45 hours (15 weeks; one 3-hour session per week); *Version 2:* 30 hours (10 weeks; one 3-hour session per week) or by correspondence study with proctored final examination, approximately 4 months.

Dates: November 1985-Present.

Objective: To provide a conceptual framework for the study of commercial lending.

Learning Outcome: Upon successful completion of this course, the student will be able to explain why good human relations skills are critically important to the successful lending officer; identify the functions of the loan interview and credit investigation; describe how the borrower's financing needs and business type can affect the structuring of a loan; list important elements of loan documents and describe their functions; name some warning signs of problem loans; and identify ways that problem loans can be prevented.

Instruction: Major topics covered in the course are loan interviewing and credit investigation; basic financial analysis; loan structuring; loan negotiation and selling a total banking relationship; loan documentation and closing; and loan followup. Methods of instruction include lecture, discussion, and examination. This course is offered by correspondence with a proctored final examination.

Credit Recommendation: In the lower division baccalaureate/associate degree category, 2 semester hours in Credit Management (11/85) (2/91) (11/95) (10/96).

Commercial Loan Officer Development (6360) (Formerly Loan Officer Development)

Location: AIB chapters nationwide operating under established ABA guidelines and standards.

Length: *Version 1:* 45 hours (15 weeks; one 3-hour session per week); *Version 2:* 30 hours (10 weeks; one 3-hour session per week).

Dates: November 1985-December 1991.

Objective: To provide new or prospective commercial loan officers with some of the basic technical and interpersonal skills needed to make successful commercial loans.

Instruction: Major topics covered in the course are how to conduct an initial loan interview and evaluate the borrower's request; how to gather information necessary to make a sound credit decision and present recommendations to senior loan officers; how to negotiate the terms of the loan with a borrower; how to write credit files and business development call reports; how to recognize and address problem loans; and how to manage both people and tasks more effectively. Methods of instruction include lecture and discussion.

Credit Recommendation: *Versions 1 and 2:* In the vocational certificate category, 1 semester hour in Banking/Finance (11/85). **NOTE:** This course is applicable to an associate degree program.

Concepts of Data Processing (2090)

Location: AIB chapters nationwide operating under established ABA guidelines and standards.

Length: *Version 1:* 45 hours (15 weeks; one 3-hour session per week); *Version 2:* 30 hours (10 weeks; one 3-hour session per week).

Dates: November 1985-December 1991.

Objective: To introduce the student to the essential concepts of computerized data processing and to familiarize the student with basic information on data processing, terminology, and current technological trends and developments.

Learning Outcome: Upon successful completion of this course, the student will be able to describe the advantages and limitations of computerized data processing; explain the basic concepts in data processing functions; define major input methods and devices and describe their impact on computer users; explain the concepts and uses of data communications; explain what programming languages are and what they do; describe the major functions of data base management systems; and describe the impact of computers on individual and corporate privacy and the means by which privacy can be protected.

Instruction: Major topics covered in the course are data processing concepts, principles and uses, the impact of technology change, how to manage change, and the implications and applications for the future. Methods of instruction include lecture, discussion, and some workshop material.

Credit Recommendation: *Version 1:* In the lower division baccalaureate/associate degree category, 3 semester hours in Business Administration or Bank Operations. *Version 2:* In the lower division baccalaureate/associate degree category, 2 semester hours in Business Administration or Bank Operations (11/85) (2/91).

Construction Lending for Income-Producing Properties (7801) (Formerly Income Property Construction Lending [7801])

Location: AIB chapters nationwide operating under established ABA guidelines and standards.

Length: Correspondence study with proctored final examination, approximately 4 months.

Dates: November 1985-May 1994.

Objective: To help the student understand the most important elements of construction lending for income-producing properties.

Learning Outcome: Upon successful completion of this course, the student will be able to apply the fundamental concepts of construction lending; discuss the theory of income-property construction lending; describe the application process; apply standards to underwrite a borrower and a project; calculate equity requirements; and close and administer a loan.

Instruction: Major topics covered in the course are the practice of construction lending, theory of commercial construction lending, marketing of financial services, underwriting commercial loans, and administration of construction loans.

Credit Recommendation: In the lower division baccalaureate/associate degree category, 2 semester hours in Credit Management (11/85) (2/91).

Construction Lending for Residential Properties (7802) (Formerly Residential Mortgage Lending [7802])

Location: AIB chapters nationwide operating under established ABA guidelines and standards.

Length: Correspondence study with proctored final examination, approximately 4 months.

Dates: November 1985-May 1994.

Objective: To provide an understanding of the most important elements of construction lending for residential real estate with the focus on single-family homes.

Learning Outcome: Upon successful completion of this course, the student will be able to apply the fundamental concepts of residential construction lending; describe the theory of construction lending; identify basic residential construction techniques; discuss construction loan policy and application procedures; explain how to underwrite a borrower and a project; structure a loan; and close and administer a loan.

Instruction: Major topics covered in the course are construction lending for residential real estate, including construction loan processing and administration; underwriting; loan structure; and loan documentation. Method of instruction is by correspondence.

Credit Recommendation: In the lower division baccalaureate/associate degree category, 2 semester hours in Credit Management (11/85) (2/91).

Consumer Lending (7008)

Location: AIB chapters nationwide operating under established ABA guidelines and standards.

Length: *Versions 1 and 3:* 45 hours (15 weeks; one 3-hour session per week); *Versions 2 and 4:* 30 hours (10 weeks; one 3-hour session per week).

Dates: *Version 1:* November 1985-October 1987; *Version 2:* November 1987-Present; *Version 3:* November 1985-October 1987; *Version 4:* November 1987-Present.

Objective: To provide an up-to-date view of consumer lending, an up-to-date view of technology applications and risk management techniques, and the regulations that govern credit practices, loan processing, cross-selling, and collections.

Learning Outcome: Upon successful completion of this course, the student will be able to identify components of the consumer installment credit market; describe various loan products; delineate the lending process; apply credit math and loan pricing principles; recognize variables that affect loan structure; and identify opportunities for cross-selling bank products.

Instruction: Major topics covered in the course are an overview of consumer credit including loan policy; and evaluation and processing of applications and consumer credit regulation. Methods of instruction include lecture, discussion, practical examples and case study, and examination.

Credit Recommendation: *Version 1:* In the vocational certificate or lower division baccalaureate/associate degree category, 2 semester hours in Banking, Consumer Credit, or Credit Management (11/85). *Version 2:* In the vocational certificate or lower division baccalaureate/ associate degree category, 2 semester hours in Banking, Consumer Credit, or Credit Management (11/85). *Version 3:* In the lower division baccalaureate/associate degree category, 3 semester hours in Credit Management (2/91). *Version 4:* In the lower division baccalaureate/associate degree category, 2 semester hours in Credit Management (11/95).

Corporate Securities Services (6347)

Location: AIB chapters nationwide operating under established ABA guidelines and standards.

Length: *Version 1:* 45 hours (15 weeks; one 3-hour session per week); *Version 2:* 30 hours (10 weeks; one 3-hour session per week) or by correspondence study with proctored final examination.

Dates: *Version 1:* January 1986-Present; *Version 2:* January 1986-Present.

Objective: To provide a broad understanding of corporate securities processing and administration and to describe how a bank's corporate securities services department serves as an intermediary between corporations, states, municipalities, investors, and public authorities that issue securities.

Learning Outcome: Upon successful completion of this course, the student will be able to identify the types of corporate and municipal securities handled by banks as agents and trustees for the issuers; describe the workings of the securities marketplace and the roles of the various participants in the issuance and trading process; discuss the multitude of services performed by banks, the laws that define them, and the procedures followed to deliver them; explain the purposes and content of a bond indenture and the duties of bond trustees; and summarize the managerial processes as they relate to the administration on the corporate securities function.

Instruction: Major topics covered in the course are securities industry; insurance, transfer, and registrar functions; recordkeeping functions; trust indenture administration; and corporate agency and trust management. Methods of instruction include lecture, discussion, classroom exercises, quizzes, and an examination. This course is also offered by correspondence with a proctored final examination.

Credit Recommendation: *Version 1:* In the upper division baccalaureate degree category, 3 semester hours in Banking Finance or Investments (2/91). *Version 2:* In the upper division baccalaureate degree category, 2 semester hours in Banking Finance or Investments (11/95) (10/96).

Current Issues in Bank Management (1375) (The New World of Commercial Banking) (Formerly Inside Commercial Banking [1375])

Location: AIB chapters nationwide operating under established ABA guidelines and standards.

Length: 45 hours (15 weeks; one 3-hour session per week).

Dates: November 1985-July 1995.

Objective: To explore significant competitive, regulatory, technological, and market-related developments currently affecting commercial bank management.

Instruction: Major topics covered in the course are analysis and discussion of non-bank competition, EFT technology, asset/liability management, interstate banking activities, the Monetary Control Act, global banking, and current issues of effective managerial strategies. Methods of instruction include lecture and discussion.

Credit Recommendation: In the lower division baccalaureate/associate degree category, 3 semester hours in Banking or Finance (11/85).

Customer Service for Bank Personnel (6490)

Location: AIB chapters nationwide operating under established ABA guidelines and standards.

Length: 15 hours (5 weeks) or 15 hours (2 days).

Dates: September 1989-Present.

Objective: To provide bankers with basic principles of dealing with customers.

Learning Outcome: Upon successful completion of this course, the student will be able to apply methods of conveying respect toward customers; identify effective strategies for handling customers; relate product benefits to customer concerns and needs; and apply methods of handling objections.

Instruction: Major topics covered in the course are effective ways of establishing contact, exploring customer needs, defining and resolving problems and closing the encounter. Methods of instruction include lecture, discussion, visual, case studies, role plays, small group activities, and an examination.

Credit Recommendation: In the lower division baccalaureate/associate degree category, 1 semester hour in Marketing Sales (11/95).

Deposit Operations (6204)

Location: AIB chapters nationwide operating under established ABA guidelines and standards.

Length: *Versions 1 and 3:* 45 hours (15 weeks; one 3-hour session per week); *Versions 2 and 4:* 30 hours (10 weeks; one 3-hour session per week) or by correspondence study.

Dates: *Version 1:* November 1985-June 1991; *Version 2:* November 1985-June 1991; *Version 3:* February 1991-Present; *Version 4:* February 1991-Present.

Objective: To examine the depository operations of banks within the context of the U.S. payments system.

Learning Outcome: Upon successful completion of this course, the student will be able to define the regulatory and procedural framework within which banks operate; explain U.S. payments systems; interpret the changing definitions and roles of the nation's depositories and the changing legal and regulatory environment in which they operate; describe the check collection process, the rules and practices that govern bank activities in effecting paper payment, and the risks banks incur in processing checks; describe the electronic components of the nation's payment system, including mechanisms, operational costs, risks, and regulatory guidelines; illustrate how banks create deposits and the factors that affect the process; and list the range of cash management services that banks offer.

Instruction: Major topics covered in the course are U.S. payments mechanism, deposits and depositories, Regulatory structure, paper payments, electronic payments, deposit creation, and sources and uses of bank funds. Methods of instruction include lecture, discussion, and classroom exercise or if by correspondence study a final proctored examination.

Credit Recommendation: *Version 1:* In the vocational certificate or lower division baccalaureate/associate degree category, 2 semester hours in Bank Operations. *Version 2:* In the vocational certificate or lower division baccalaureate/associate degree category, 1 semester hour in Bank Operations (11/85). *Version 3:* In the lower division baccalaureate/associate degree category, 3 semester hours in Banking Operations. *Version 4:* In the lower division baccalaureate/associate degree category, 2 semester hours in Bank Accounting (2/91).

Economics for Bankers (2310)

Location: AIB chapters nationwide operating under established ABA guidelines and standards.

Length: *Version 1:* 45 hours (15 weeks; 3 hours per week); *Version 2:* 30 hours (10 weeks; 3 hours per week) or by correspondence study with a proctored final examination.

Dates: January 1990-Present.

Objective: To provide an introduction to the fundamental principles of economics.

Learning Outcome: Upon successful completion of this course, the student will be able to interpret the economic indicators published in the media; relate basic principles of economic theory to the business cycle and business organizations; describe the causes of inflation, its effects and ways it is measured; compare and contrast economic systems; and relate the fundamental concepts of supply and demand theory and Keynesian economics.

Instruction: Major topics covered in the course are fundamental economic principles, national income accounting, classical and Keynesian economics, and current macroeconomic issues. Methods of instruction include reading, lecture, discussion, laboratory exercises, and examination. The course is also offered by correspondence with a proctored final examination.

Credit Recommendation: *Version 1:* In the lower division baccalaureate/associate degree category, 3 semester hours in Economics. *Version 2:* In the lower division baccalaureate/associate degree category, 2 semester hours in Economics (2/91) (11/95).

Financial Planning (6535) (Formerly Financial Planning for Bankers)

Location: AIB chapters nationwide operating under established ABA guidelines and standards.

Length: *Versions 1 and 3:* 45 hours (15 weeks; one 3-hour session per week); *Versions 2 and 4:* 30 hours (one 3-hour session per week).

Dates: *Version 1:* November 1985-June 1990; *Version 2:* November 1985-June 1990; *Version 3:* July 1990-July 1995; *Version 4:* July 1990-July 1995.

Objective: To provide an overview of the comprehensive financial planning process as it relates to the goals and objectives of the bank customer. To look at a customer's total financial picture and recommend strategies to achieve the customer's objectives.

Learning Outcome: Upon successful completion of this course, the student will be able to define financial planning and describe its features and benefits; explain the four types of financial plans and discuss the six steps in the financial planning process; identify four customer buying styles and describe why financial goals should be specific and measurable; identify five prerequisites to investment planning; define the role of a financial planner in estate planning; describe how investments, taxation, and saving for retirement affect financial plans; explain the role and responsibilities of a financial planner in a bank; and identify the factors that increase profitability in financial planning services in a bank.

Instruction: Major topics covered in the course are the financial planning process, analyzing the present financial position, effective cash flow strategies, insurance planning, investment planning, tax planning, retirement planning, and estate planning. Methods of instruction include lecture, discussion, exercises, and role play.

Credit Recommendation: *Version 1:* In the lower division baccalaureate/associate degree category, 2 semester hours in Banking or Business. *Version 2:* In the lower division baccalaureate/associate degree category, 1 semester hour in Banking or Business (11/85). **NOTE:** For an accurate description of Versions 1 and 2, see the 1990 edition of the *National Guide. Version 3:* In the lower division baccalaureate/associate degree category, 3 semester hours in Financial Planning or Business. *Version 4:* In the lower division baccalaureate/associate degree category, 2 semester hours in Financial Planning or Business (2/91).

Fundamentals of Analyzing Financial Statements (6955)

Location: AIB chapters nationwide operating under established ABA guidelines and standards.

Length: *Version 1:* 15 hours (5 weeks; 3 hours per week); *Version 2:* 24 hours (8 weeks; 3 hours per week).

Dates: September 1995-Present.

Objective: To provide practice in analyzing several types of commercial loans.

Learning Outcome: Upon successful completion of this course, the student will be able to apply the basic tools and techniques of financial statement analysis; conduct trend, ratio, and comparative statement analyses; evaluate pro formas, projections, and cash budgets; and analyze a workout situation.

Instruction: Major topics covered in the course are financial analysis; funds flow and cash flow analyses; trend, ratio, and comparative statement analysis; cash flow and working capital; financial projections; principles of financial statement presentation; seasonal lending analysis; contractor lending; term lending analysis; and work-out analysis. Methods of instruction include lecture, discussions, case studies, visuals, role play, small group activities, and examination.

Credit Recommendation: *Version 1:* In the vocational certificate category or lower division baccalaureate/associate degree category, 1 semester hour in Bank Credit Analysis, Accounting, or Finance (11/95). *Version 2:* In the vocational certificate category or lower division baccalaureate/associate degree category, 1 semester hour in Bank Credit Analysis, Accounting, or Finance (11/95).

Income Property Underwriting (7823)

Location: AIB chapters nationwide operating under established ABA guidelines and standards.

Length: Approximately 4 months, correspondence study with proctored final examination.

Dates: November 1985-May 1994.

Objective: To present the basic theory for underwriting income property loans.

Learning Outcome: Upon successful completion of this course, the student will be able to apply the fundamental concepts of income property underwriting; identify the most important questions to which a market analysis should be addressed; describe the process of correlating cost, income, and market values to arrive at a final property estimate; and define the most important underwriting terms and conditions and explain how they can be used in underwriting a loan.

Instruction: Major topics covered in the course are the market for permanent loans on income-producing properties and the unique underwriting requirements for different types of properties. Method of instruction is by correspondence.

Credit Recommendation: In the lower division baccalaureate/associate degree category, 2 semester hours in Real Estate Finance (8/85) (2/91).

International Banking (7110) (Formerly International Banking [7710])

Location: AIB chapters nationwide operating under established ABA guidelines and standards.

Length: *Version 1:* 45 hours (15 weeks; one 3-hour session per week); *Version 2:* 30 hours (10 weeks; one 3-hour session per week); *Version 3:* 45 hours (15 weeks), 30 hours (10 weeks), 15 hours; or by correspondence study with proctored final examination.

Dates: November 1985-Present.

Objective: *Versions 1 and 2:* To provide students with a comprehensive overview of the roles-functions banks play in international commerce. *Version 3:* To provide commercial bankers with a comprehensive understanding of how to meet the global banking needs of their customers and the functions that all financial institutions play in international commerce.

Learning Outcome: *Versions 1 and 2:* Upon successful completion of this course, the student will be able to describe the basic dynamics and overall complexities of the international arena; identify the various international services banks provide; explain international lending concepts, credit principles, and risk factors; describe the various legal and regulatory constraints/requirements that dominate international finance; explain the history and basic concepts of the Eurodollar market; identify the various international lending agencies and their roles in international finance; and define basic international banking terms including Incoterms. *Version 3:* Upon successful completion of this course, the student will be able to describe the basic dynamics, structure and risks of global banking and the interconnected relationships of the many participants; delineate the international services banks can provide to customers; explain the legal, regulatory, and accounting constraints and requirements that affect global financial activities; reconcile global and domestic banking activities on a bank's financial statement; and use the basic language of global banking and finance.

Instruction: *Versions 1 and 2:* Major topics covered in the course are foreign exchange, collections, letters of credit, international financing agencies, documents used in international financial markets, and the Eurodollar market. *Version 3:* Major topics covered in the course are global structure including bank organization and the environment in which international banking takes place, international payments including foreign exchange and money transfers, the role of banks enabling trade between nations, and international finance and global risk management. Methods of instruction include lecture, discussion, and examination. This course is also offered by correspondence with a proctored examination.

Credit Recommendation: *Version 1:* In the upper division baccalaureate degree category, 3 semester hours in International Banking. *Version 2:* In the upper division baccalaureate degree category, 2 semester hours in Banking (11/85) (2/91) (11/95). *Version 3:* In the lower division baccalaureate/associate degree category or in the upper division baccalaureate degree category,

3 semester hours in International Banking (10/96).

Introduction to Accounting/Bookkeeping (1002) (Accounting Basics)

Location: AIB chapters nationwide operating under established ABA guidelines and standards.

Length: *Version 1:* 45 hours (15 weeks; one 3-hour session per week); *Version 2:* 30 hours (10 weeks; one 3-hour session per week).

Dates: September 1995-Present.

Objective: To provide familiarity with the accounting recording and reporting process.

Learning Outcome: Upon successful completion of this course, the student will be able to analyze and journalize basic financial transactions; prepare a financial work sheet; prepare financial statements; and prepare payroll records.

Instruction: Major topics covered in the course are the accounting equation; transaction; adjusting and closing journal entries; general ledger maintenance; payroll accounting and related reports; and financial statement preparation. Methods of instruction include lecture, discussion, case studies, and examination.

Credit Recommendation: *Version 1:* In the vocational certificate category, 3 semester hours in Accounting. *Version 2:* In the vocational certificate category, 2 semester hours in Accounting (11/95).

Introduction to Mortgage Lending (7820) Residential Mortgage Lending

Location: AIB chapters nationwide operating under established ABA guidelines and standards.

Length: 30 hours (10 weeks; one 3-hour session per week) or by correspondence study.

Dates: January 1989-Present.

Objective: To provide an overview of the field of mortgage lending.

Learning Outcome: Upon successful completion of this course, the student will be able to understand the rapidly changing field of residential mortgage lending; work step-by-step through the mortgage loan origination process; understand the documents used at each step; understand technical terms used in mortgage loan origination and processing; and understand government regulations and compliance issues from the point-of-view of bank employees involved in interviewing mortgage loan applicants to processing loan applications.

Instruction: Major topics covered in the course are a profile of the mortgage-lending industry; the basics of real estate law; legal issues in real estate lending; appraising residential property; mortgage loan origination; the role of government in housing and mortgage lending; the secondary market and mortgage loan servicing. Methods of instruction include lecture, discussion, correspondence, and examination or if by correspondence study a proctored final examination.

Credit Recommendation: In the lower division baccalaureate/associate degree category, 2 semester hours in Credit Management (2/91) (11/95).

Introduction to Supervision (4265)

Location: AIB chapters nationwide operating under established ABA guidelines and standards.

Length: 15 hours (5 weeks).

Dates: September 1989-Present.

Objective: To provide knowledge of techniques to enhance supervisory skills.

Learning Outcome: Upon successful completion of this course, the student will be able to identify ways to supervise effectively; explain how self-esteem affects employee productivity; apply employee motivators and construct a model; describe methods to assess performance problems; identify creative problem-solving strategies; and apply methods of decreasing stress for supervisors and their employees.

Instruction: Major topics covered in this course are employee motivation, communicating effectively and problem solving. Methods of instruction include lecture, discussions, audio-visual material, case studies, small group activities, role play, and examination.

Credit Recommendation: In the lower division baccalaureate/associate degree category, 1 semester hour in Management, Business, or Personnel (11/95). **NOTE:** To receive credit both this course and Personnel and the Law must be completed.

Law and Banking: Applications (3670) (Formerly Law and Banking: Applications [3710])

Location: AIB chapters nationwide operating under established ABA guidelines and standards.

Length: *Version 1:* 45 hours (15 weeks; 3 hours per week); *Version 2:* 30 hours (10 weeks; 3 hours per week); *Version 3:* 15 hours, or by correspondence study with a proctored final examination.

Dates: June 1990-Present.

Objective: To introduce laws pertaining to secured transactions, letters of credit, and the bank collection process.

Learning Outcome: Upon successful completion of this course, the student will be able to explain the concept of negotiability; analyze the concept of holder-in-due-course status; describe the nature of primary and secondary contractual liability on an instrument; discuss the legal issues related to bank collections and check losses; define and explain the nature of a letter of credit; and identify the issues related to secured transactions.

Instruction: Major topics covered in the course are negotiable instruments; holder in due course; liability; bank collections; check losses and fraud; letters of credit; and secured transactions. Methods of instruction include reading, lecture, discussion, and laboratory exercises. The course is also offered by correspondence.

Credit Recommendation: *Versions 1, 2, and 3:* In the lower division baccalaureate/associate degree category, 2 semester hours in Business Law or Banking Law (2/91) (10/96).

Law and Banking: Principles (3660)

Location: AIB chapters nationwide operating under established ABA guidelines and standards.

Length: *Version 1:* 45 hours (15 weeks; one 3-hour session per week); *Version 2:* 30 hours (10 weeks; 3 hours per week) or by correspondence study with a proctored final examination; *Version 3:* Accelerated 15 hours (5 weeks; 3 hours per week).

Dates: November 1985-Present.

Objective: This course is a banker's guide to law and legal issues, with special emphasis on the Uniform Commercial Code.

Learning Outcome: Upon successful completion of this course, the student will be able to identify (contingent upon specific modules completed) the sources and applications of banking law; distinguish between torts and crimes and how they relate to banking situations; explain contracts, including the need for legal capacity, legal objective, mutual assent, and consideration; describe real and personal properties and their application to banking; discuss how bankruptcy affects banks and differentiate between the liquidation and rehabilitation goals of the Bankruptcy Code; and identify the legal implications of consumer lending.

Instruction: Major topics covered in the course are torts and crimes, legal entities, contracts, real and personal property, bankruptcy, and federal regulations.

Methods of instruction include reading, lecture, discussion, and laboratory exercises. This course is also offered by correspondence and an accelerated format.

Credit Recommendation: *Version 1:* In the lower division baccalaureate/associate degree category, 1 semester hour in Business Law or Banking Law. *Version 2:* In the lower division baccalaureate/associate degree category, 1 semester hour in Business Law or Banking Law. *Version 3:* In the lower division baccalaureate/associate degree category, 1 semester hour in Business Law or Banking Law (2/91) (10/96).

Letters of Credit (7140)

Location: AIB chapters nationwide operating under established ABA guidelines and standards.

Length: *Version 1:* 45 hours (15 weeks; one 3-hour session per week); *Versions 2 and 3:* 30 hours (10 weeks; one 3-hour session per week).

Dates: *Version 1:* November 1985-January 1991; *Version 2:* February 1991-November 1995; *Version 3:* November 1995-Present.

Objective: To train bank personnel to understand and evaluate letters of credit and related documents used in international commerce.

Learning Outcome: Upon successful completion of this course, the student will be able to describe the functions of shipping documents such as ocean bills of lading, commercial invoices, and marine insurance policies; summarize the nature of letters of credit and their applications; and outline the steps involved from the customers application to the issuance of the letter of credit.

Instruction: Major topics covered in the course are detailed examination of shipping documents and the mechanics of letters of credit, including payment procedures, issuing, advising, and transfer of letters of credit. Methods of instruction include lecture, discussion, and examination.

Credit Recommendation: *Version 1:* In the upper division baccalaureate degree category, 2 semester hours in International Finance (11/85). *Version 2:* In the upper division baccalaureate degree category, 1 semester hour in International Finance (2/91). *Version 3:* In the lower division baccalaureate/associate degree category or the upper division baccalaureate degree category, 1 semester hour in International Finance (11/95).

Management (4140) (Formerly Management Fundamentals [4140])

Location: AIB chapters nationwide operating under established ABA guidelines and standards.

Length: *Versions 1 and 2:* 45 hours (15 weeks; one 3-hour session per week); *Version 3:* 30 hours (10 weeks; one 3-hour session per week).

Dates: *Version 1:* November 1985-October 1990; *Version 2:* November 1990-December 1996; *Version 3:* November 1990-December 1996.

Objective: To provide a comprehensive introduction to modern management theory, practices, and applications.

Learning Outcome: Upon successful completion of this course, the student will be able to identify and apply effective managerial techniques; discuss practical methods of management planning and strategy; identify current management issues related to social responsibility and ethics; describe sound management for international competition; explain the principles of organization, setting work objectives, delegation, and motivating employees to excel in their performance; apply skillful and effective leadership techniques; and identify proper guidelines for managing groups, organizational control, operations management, and managing change.

Instruction: *Version 1:* Major topics covered in the course are planning, staffing, leading, and controlling. Methods of instruction include lecture, discussion, and case studies. *Versions 2 and 3:* Major topics covered in the course are evolution of management theory and practices, the functions of management, social and cultural issues in management, information systems management, and international management. Methods of instruction include reading, lecture, discussion, laboratory exercises, and examination. The course is also offered by correspondence with a proctored final examination.

Credit Recommendation: *Version 1:* In the lower division baccalaureate/associate degree category, 3 semester hours in Business Administration or Management (11/85). *Version 2:* In the upper division baccalaureate degree category, 3 semester hours in Management (2/91) (10/96). *Version 3:* In the upper division baccalaureate degree category, 2 semester hours in Management (11/95) (10/96).

Marketing for Bankers (7740)

Location: AIB chapters nationwide operating under established ABA guidelines and procedures.

Length: *Version 1:* 45 hours (15 weeks); *Version 2:* 30 hours (10 weeks); *Version 3:* 45 hours (15 weeks), 30 hours(10 weeks), or 15 hours or by correspondence study.

Dates: *Version 1:* November 1985-September 1996; *Version 2:* November 1985-September 1996; *Version 3:* October 1996-Present.

Objective: *Version 1:* To provide an understanding of consumer motivation to purchase financial services and skill in developing a marketing plan. *Version 2:* To provide an understanding of consumer motivation to purchase financial services and skill in developing a marketing plan. *Version 3:* To provide an understanding of marketing and key marketing concepts including the significance of customer orientation, the conception, pricing, promotion, and distribution of products and developing marketing plans.

Learning Outcome: *Version 1:* Upon successful completion of this course, the student will be able to recognize consumer motivation and buying behavior; integrate public relations, advertising, sales promotion, selling, and service distribution functions in the bank's overall marketing plan; conduct situation analysis and formulate a master marketing strategy; and monitor and evaluate performance. *Version 2:* Upon successful completion of this course, the student will be able to recognize consumer motivation and buying behavior; integrate public relations, advertising, sales promotion, selling, and service distribution functions in the bank's overall marketing plan; conduct situation analysis and formulate a master marketing strategy; and monitor and evaluate performance. *Version 3:* Upon successful completion of this course, the student will be able to explain the marketing concept; list and describe the marketing mix; discuss four broad marketing strategies and key issues relating to banking products and services; recognize consumer motivation and buying behavior; conduct situation analyses; and develop a marketing plan with objectives, monitoring, and evaluation components.

Instruction: *Version 1:* Major topics covered in the course are marketing in the organization; consumer motivations and buying behavior; marketing information and research; the marketing management process—situation analysis, formulation of a master marketing strategy, performance monitoring and evaluation; marketing and the wholesale side of banking; and public relations and communications. Focuses on the market, the marketing process, and the management of the marketing process. *Version 2:* Major topics covered in the course are marketing in the organization; consumer motivations and buying behavior; marketing information and research; the marketing management process—situation analysis, formulation of a master marketing strategy, performance monitoring and evaluation; marketing and the wholesale side of banking; and public relations and communications. Focuses on the market, the marketing process, and the management of the marketing process. *Version 3:* Major topics covered in the course are the marketing concept, strategic marketing including situation analysis and objective-setting, customer and organizational buying behavior, market research and target markets, marketing mix, strategies, and organizational structure, external communication, wholesale banking, and the future of marketing. Methods of instruction include lecture, discussion, classroom exercises, audio-visual material, case studies, computer-assisted instruction, and examination or if by correspondence study a proctored final examination.

Credit Recommendation: *Version 1:* In the lower division baccalaureate/associate degree category, 3 semester hours in Bank Marketing. *Version 2:* In the lower division baccalaureate/associate degree category, 2 semester hours in Bank Marketing (11/85) (2/91) (11/95). *Version 3:* In the lower division baccalaureate/associate degree category, 3 semester hours in Bank Marketing (10/96).

Money and Banking (1350)

Location: AIB chapters nationwide operating under established ABA guidelines and standards.

Length: *Version 1:* 45 hours (15 weeks; one-3 hour session per week); *Version 2:* 30 hours (10 weeks; 3 hours per week) or by correspondence study with a proctored final examination; *Version 3:* 15 hours.

Dates: *Version 1:* November 1985-November 1989; *Version 2:* December 1989-September 1996; *Version 3:* October 1996-Present.

Objective: To provide knowledge of key concepts, theories, processes, and economic and policy interrelationships that link money and banking to the U.S. and world economy.

Learning Outcome: Upon successful completion of this course, the student will be able to describe how commercial banks "create" money; identify the tools of monetary and fiscal policy; summarize and better interpret major trends and issues in banking; relate bank operations to the U.S. payments mechanism; and compare and contrast various types of financial institutions.

Instruction: Major topics covered in the course are definition and characteristics of money, financial intermediaries and commercial banks, the Federal Reserve System, monetary and fiscal policy, and major trends and issues in banking. Methods of instruction include reading, lecture, discussion, laboratory exercises, and examination. The course is also offered by correspondence with a proctored final examination.

Credit Recommendation: *Versions 1, 2, and 3:* In the lower division baccalaureate/associate degree or upper division baccalaureate degree category, 3 semester hours in Money and Banking (11/85) (2/91) (11/95) (10/96).

Mortgage Loan Documentation (7826)

Location: AIB chapters nationwide operating under established ABA guidelines and standards.

Length: 30 hours (3 hours per week for 10 weeks) or by correspondence study.

Dates: September 1994-Present.

Objective: To learn to use the tools, forms, and procedures related to mortgage loan documentations, including regulatory requirements and constraints.

Learning Outcome: Upon successful completion of this course, the student will be familiar with all current forms required for loan application files; pick out the compliance implications of the information required to complete each form; relate mortgage loan documentation to the secondary market; and avoid mistakes commonly made in completing mortgage loan forms.

Instruction: Major topics covered in this course are initiation and maintenance of a loan case file; determination of mortgage eligibility; review of loan application; verification of employment, income and other sources of funds; compliance with statutory requirements; interpretation of a mortgage credit report; and private mortgage insurance. Methods of instruction include lecture, discussion, case studies, role play, small group activities, and examination or if by correspondence study a proctored final examination.

Credit Recommendation: In the vocational certificate category, 2 semester hours in Real Estate (11/95).

Performance Based Compliance: Commercial Lending (7311)

Location: AIB chapters nationwide operating under established ABA guidelines and standards.

Length: 8 hours (1 day).

Dates: September 1995-Present.

Objective: To provide performance based compliance training to bankers who handle compliance issues on a day-to-day basis.

Learning Outcome: Upon successful completion of this course, the student will be able to perform the regulatory compliance tasks associated with commercial lending.

Instruction: Major topics covered in this course are compliance aspects of handling loan inquiries; applications; loan evaluation and processing; retaining records; and furnishing information and debt collection. Methods of instruction include lecture, discussion, case studies, role playing, small group activities, and examination.

Credit Recommendation: In the vocational certificate category, 1 semester hour in Management (11/95). **NOTE:** All 5 courses must be completed to receive 3 credits.

Performance Based Compliance: Consumer Lending (7313)

Location: AIB chapters nationwide operating under established ABA guidelines and standards.

Length: 8 hours (1 day).

Dates: September 1995-Present.

Objective: To provide performance based compliance training to bankers who handle compliance issues on a day-to-day basis.

Learning Outcome: Upon successful completion of this course, the student will be able to perform the regulatory compliance tasks associated with consumer lending.

Instruction: Major topics covered in this course are the steps in loan processing including inquiry, application, processing, and closing. Methods of instruction include lecture, discussion, visual materials, case studies, role play, small group activities, and examination.

Credit Recommendation: In the vocational certificate category, 1 semester hour in Management (11/95). **NOTE:** All 5 courses must be completed to receive 3 credits.

Performance Based Compliance: Consumer Loan Account Servicing (7316)

Location: AIB chapters nationwide operating under established ABA guidelines and standards.

Length: 8 hours (1 day).

Dates: September 1995-Present.

Objective: To provide performance based compliance training to bankers who handle compliance issues on a day-to-day basis.

Learning Outcome: Upon successful completion of this course, the student will be able to perform the regulatory compliance tasks associated with consumer loan servicing.

Instruction: Major topics covered in this course are statement and notification; reports and monitoring information; records retention and credit reporting and escrow accounts. Methods of instruction include lecture, discussion, visual material, case studies, role playing, small group activities, and examination.

Credit Recommendation: In the vocational certificate category, 1 semester hour in Management (11/95). **NOTE:** All 5 courses must be completed to receive 3 credits.

Performance Based Compliance: Deposit Operations (7315)

Location: AIB chapters nationwide operating under established ABA guidelines and standards.

Length: 8 hours (1 day).

Dates: September 1995-Present.

Objective: To provide performance based compliance training to bankers who handle compliance issues on a day-to-day basis.

Learning Outcome: Upon successful completion of this course, the student will be able to conduct the regulatory compliance tasks associated with deposit operations.

Instruction: Major topics covered in this course are handling general inquiries; account opening; maintenance; and record keeping. Methods of instruction include lecture, discussion, visual material, case studies, role play, small group activities, and examination.

Credit Recommendation: In the vocational certificate category, 1 semester hour in Management (11/95). **NOTE:** All 5 courses must be completed to receive 3 credits.

Performance Based Compliance: Real Estate Lending (7314)

Location: AIB chapters nationwide operating under established ABA guidelines and standards.

Length: 8 hours (1 day).

Dates: September 1995-Present.

Objective: To provide performance based compliance training to bankers who handle compliance issues on a day-to-day basis.

Learning Outcome: Upon successful completion of this course, the student will be able to use the tools needed to perform the regulatory compliance tasks associated with residential real estate lending.

Instruction: Major topics covered in this course are Real Estate; Loan Inquiries; Interviews; loan applications; processing; loan resolution; and closing. Methods of instruction include lecture, discussion, audio/visual material, case studies, role playing, small group activities, and examination.

Credit Recommendation: In the vocational certificate category, 1 semester hour in Management (11/95). **NOTE:** All 5 courses must be completed to receive 3 credits.

Personnel and the Law (4245)

Location: AIB chapters nationwide operating under established ABA guidelines and standards.

Length: 15 hours (2 days) or (3 hours for 5 weeks).

Dates: September 1994-Present.

Objective: To provide an introduction to the laws essential to management of bank personnel.

Learning Outcome: Upon successful completion of this course, the student will be able to describe the historical and governmental perspective of employment law; discuss the Civil Rights Act and other Equal Employment Opportunity (EEO) law; compare EEO laws with regulations of the office of the Federal Contract Compliance Program; identify and comply with legal issues of employment; discuss other laws affecting personnel, including the Immigration Reform and Control Act, Employee Retirement Income Security Act (ERISA), and the Occupational Safety and Health Act (OSHA).

Instruction: Major topics covered in this course are EEO laws, compliance programs, and other legal issues affecting personnel. Methods of instruction include lecture, discussions, audio-visual material, case studies, small group exercises, role play, and examination.

Credit Recommendation: In the lower division baccalaureate/associate degree category, 1 semester hour in Management, Business or Personnel (11/95). **NOTE:** To receive credit both this course and Introduction to Supervision must be completed.

Principles of Banking (1370)

Location: AIB chapters nationwide operating under established ABA guidelines and standards.

Length: *Version 1:* 45 hours (15 weeks; one 3-hour session per week); *Version 2:* 30 hours (10 weeks; one 3-hour session per week); *Version 3:* 15 hours (5 weeks).

Dates: *Version 1:* November 1985-November 1989; *Version 2:* December 1989-September 1996; *Version 3:* October 1996-Present.

Objective: To provide a comprehensive introduction to the commercial banking system.

Learning Outcome: Upon successful completion of this course, the student will be able (contingent upon specific modules completed) to explain the importance of full-service commercial banking as it affects the economy, the community, business, and the individual; describe the three major functions of commercial banks and their interrelationship; list the various products and services banks offer governments, businesses, individuals, and correspondents; contrast between demand and time deposits; illustrate the various types of bank loans and investments; explain the concepts of liquidity, safety, and income; and identify various banking regulations and regulatory agencies.

Instruction: Major topics covered in the course are the history and evolution of American banking; an introduction to the Federal Reserve; the depository; loan and check processing functions; basic bank accounting; and specialized bank services such as international services, trust functions, and bank regulation. Methods of instruction include lecture, discussion, classroom exercises, and examination; or by correspondence study with a proctored final examination.

Credit Recommendation: *Version 1:* In the lower division baccalaureate/associate degree category, 3 semester hours in Bank Operations (11/85). *Version 2:* In the lower division baccalaureate/associate degree category, 2 semester hours in Bank Operations. *Version 3:* In the lower division baccalaureate/associate degree category, 2 semester hours in Bank Operations (2/91) (10/96).

Real Estate Appraisal (7860)

Location: AIB chapters nationwide operating under established ABA guidelines and standards.

Length: *Version 1:* 45 hours (15 weeks; one 3-hour session per week); *Version 2:* 30 hours (10 weeks; one 3-hour session per week).

Dates: September 1995-Present.

Objective: To provide a comprehensive look at real estate appraisal, including different approaches to valuation of property.

Learning Outcome: Upon successful completion of this course, the student will be able to define the technical terms used in real estate appraisal reports; outline essential steps in the appraisal process; interpret the FNMA/FHLMC Uniform Residential Appraisal Report; explain the valuation risk associated with environmental hazards; and explain the major differences between the three approaches to value.

Instruction: Major topics covered in this course are the appraisal of both residential and commercial property using three approaches: the cost approach, the income capitalization approach, and sales comparison approach. Methods of instruction include lecture, discussion, case studies, role play, small group activities, and examination or if by correspondence study a proctored final examination.

Credit Recommendation: In the upper division baccalaureate degree category, 3 semester hours in Real Estate (for the 15-week course) or 2 semester hours in Real Estate (for 10 week course) (11/95) (10/96).

Real Estate Appraisal (7877) (Formerly Real Estate Appraisal, Real Estate Appraisal I [7860], and Real Estate Appraisal II [7870])

Location: AIB chapters nationwide operating under established ABA guidelines and standards.

Length: *Version 1:* 45 hours (15 weeks; one 3-hour session per week); *Version 2:* 30 hours (10 weeks; one 3-hour session per week).

Dates: November 1985-July 1995.

Objective: To provide an introduction to the valuation of real estate.

Learning Outcome: Upon successful completion of this course, the student will be able to define the technical terms used in real estate appraisal reports; outline essential steps in the appraisal process; interpret the FNMA/FHLMC Uniform Residential Appraisal Report; explain the valuation risk associated with environmental hazards; and explain the major differences among the three approaches to value.

Instruction: Major topics covered in the course are methods related to the appraisal of both residential property and commercial real estate; the three approaches to appraisal (Cost Approach, Income Capitalization Approach, and Sales Comparison Approach); valuation risk and environmental hazards. Methods of instruction include lecture and discussion, or correspondence.

Credit Recommendation: In the upper division baccalaureate degree category, 3 semester hours in Real Estate Appraisal (11/85) (2/91). **NOTE:** Both courses, Real Estate Appraisal I and II, must be taken to receive credit.

Real Estate Finance (7880)

Location: AIB chapters nationwide operating under established ABA guidelines and standards.

Length: *Version 1:* 45 hours (15 weeks); *Version 2:* 30 hours (10 weeks) or by correspondence study.

Dates: November 1985-Present.

Objective: To provide an introduction to construction lending and other areas of commercial real estate finance with particular emphasis on managing credit risk.

Learning Outcome: Upon successful completion of this course, the student will be able to identify and explain basic legal issues related to commercial real estate financing; describe the standard techniques used in appraising the value of commercial real estate property; explain the principles of risk management related to financing commercial real estate purchases; explain the basic formulas used in the analysis of commercial real estate investments; and discuss contemporary trends in commercial real estate finance.

Instruction: Major topics covered in the course are construction lending, other areas of commercial real estate finance; managing credit risk; real estate law; appraisal and investment analysis; and introduction of principles of finance related to the following real estate categories: condominiums, multifamily rental property, retail property, office warehouse and lodging property. Methods of instruction include lecture, discussions, correspondence, and examination or if by correspondence study a proctored final examination.

Credit Recommendation: *Version 1:* In the lower division baccalaureate/associate degree category, 2 semester hours in Real Estate Finance. *Version 2:* In the lower division baccalaureate/associate degree category, 2 semester hours in Real Estate Finance (11/85) (2/91) (11/95) (10/96).

Real Estate Law (3718)
Mortgage Law I (3715)
Mortgage Law II (3716)

Location: AIB chapters nationwide operating under established ABA guidelines and standards.

Length: *Version 1:* 45 hours (15 weeks; one 3-hour session per week); *Version 2:* 30 hours (10 weeks; one 3-hour session per week) or by correspondence study with proctored final examination.

Dates: *Version 1:* November 1985-August 1995; *Version 2:* September 1995-Present.

Objective: To provide an introduction to the specific elements of real estate law that are important to mortgage lenders.

Learning Outcome: Upon successful completion of this course, the student will be able to correctly define legal terms associated with real estate transactions; explain the scope and limits of real property; explain the rights and duties of landowners; explain the six basic types of property ownership; list the required provisions of a real estate contract; and outline the major provisions of government regulations controlling the financing of real estate purchases.

Instruction: Major topics covered in the course are a basic introduction to four areas of real estate law:the definition and nature of the real property, the transfer of real estate, land use and regulation, and landlord and tenant law; law related to financing real estate purchases; residential mortgage law; and commercial real estate law. Methods of instruction include lecture, discussion, and examination.

Credit Recommendation: *Version 1:* In the upper division baccalaureate/associate degree category, 2 semester hours in Business Law or Real Estate Finance (2/91) (11/95). *Version 2:* In the lower division baccalaureate/associate degree category, 3 semester hours in Real Estate (2/91) (11/95) (10/96).

Residential Mortgage Underwriting (7925)

Location: AIB chapters nationwide operating under established ABA guidelines and standards.

Length: 8 lessons (4 months); correspondence study with proctored final examination.

Dates: January 1988-May 1994.

Objective: To understand the concepts in evaluating borrowers in relation to residential properties and to apply bank lending policies.

Learning Outcome: Upon successful completion of this course, the student will be able to identify the fundamental concepts of residential mortgage lending; process a residential mortgage application; review a loan application and analyze the borrower's income; and apply basic principles of residential appraisal.

Instruction: Major topics covered in the course are analysis of mortgage loan applications, and the steps mortgage lenders use in reviewing a completed appraisal report and in the approval or denial of a residential loan application.

Credit Recommendation: In the lower division baccalaureate/associate degree category, 2 semester hours in Residential Mortgage Lending (2/91).

Securities Processing (7240)

Location: AIB chapters nationwide operating under established ABA guidelines and standards.

Length: *Versions 1 and 3:* 45 hours (15 weeks; one 3-hour session per week); *Versions 2 and 4:* 30 hours (10 weeks; one 3-hour session per week); *Version 5:* 45 hours (15 weeks; one 3-hour session per week).

Dates: *Version 1:* November 1985-May 1989; *Version 2:* November 1985-May 1989; *Version 3:* June 1989-December 1995; *Version 4:* June 1989-December 1995; *Version 5:* January 1996-Present.

Objective: *Versions 1, 2, 3, and 4:* To provide a broad knowledge of the financial securities in a banking environment; to identify the laws and regulations that govern their trading in the marketplace; and to describe a bank's trust and agency responsibilities with respect to securities. *Version 5:* To introduce the student to the operational aspects of various securities, and administering consumer and corporate trust accounts.

Learning Outcome: Versions 1, 2, 3, and 4: Upon successful completion of this course, the student will be able to describe the types of securities; identify the laws and regulations that govern securities; and describe the procedures used to settle securities. *Version 5:* Upon successful completion of this course, the student will be able to describe traditional instruments and more specialized and new instruments that are offered and traded, the marketplaces in which they are traded, the participants involved, and how automated trading and information systems enhance the trading process; understand the development of the securities industry, including the evolution of electronic clearing and settlement methods; and understand the importance of the recent expansion of international investment and the structures that support it.

Instruction: *Versions 1, 2, 3, and 4:* Major topics covered in the course are operational aspects of various securities and administration of consumer and corporate trust accounts. *Version 5:* Major topics covered in the course are a review of types of securities, the securities marketplace, the elements of a securities transaction, industry structures, securities and bank operation, and security management issues. Methods of instruction include lecture, classroom exercises, correspondence, and examination; or by correspondence study with a proctored final examination.

Credit Recommendation: *Version 1:* In the vocational certificate or lower division baccalaureate/associate degree category, 2 semester hours in Bank Operations. *Version 2:* In the vocational certificate or lower division baccalaureate/associate degree category, 1 semester hour in Bank Operations. *Version 3:* In the lower division baccalaureate/associate degree category, 3 semester hours in Bank Operations. *Version 4:* In the lower division baccalaureate/associate degree category, 2 semester hours in Bank Operations (11/85) (2/91). *Version 5:* In the lower division baccalaureate/associate degree category, 3 semester hours in Bank Operations (10/96).

Statement Analysis (6970)

Location: AIB chapters nationwide operating under established ABA guidelines and standards.

Length: 45 hours (15 weeks; one 3-hour session per week) or independent study.

Dates: November 1985-Present.

Objective: To teach new or prospective bank lenders or credit analysts the skills of financial statement analysis.

Learning Outcome: Upon successful completion of this course, the student will be able to create statement spreadsheets; calculate and interpret ratios; interpret balance sheets, income statements, net worth reconciliations, funds flow and cash flow statements, and cash forecasts; produce credit decisions and recommendations; prepare funds flow and cash flow statements; and compare a firm's statements with industry averages.

Instruction: Major topics covered in the course are basic tools to conduct financial analysis: statement spreading, ratio analysis, trend analysis, funds flow and cash flow analysis, cash forecasting, and working capital analysis. Method of instruction may be classroom or independent study with an examination.

Credit Recommendation: In the lower division baccalaureate/associate degree category, 3 semester hours in Finance (11/85) (2/91) (11/95). **NOTE:** Credit should not be given for this course and for the course Analyzing Financial Statements.

Strategic Skill Builders for Banking (3361)

Location: AIB chapters nationwide operating under established ABA guidelines and standards.

Length: Up to 72 hours; 12 modules of approximately 6 hours each (trainers select approximately 6 hours each)(trainers select appropriate modules for individual students needs).

Dates: January 1990-July 1995.

Objective: To teach reading, writing, verbal communication, math, and learning skills needed to perform banking tasks.

Learning Outcome: Upon successful completion of this course, the student will be able (contingent upon specific modules completed) to balance the cash drawer; perform complex calculations; use computer screens; proofread written work; prepare correspondence; and take effective notes.

Instruction: Major topics covered in the course are reading job aids; balancing the cash drawer; cross-selling using brochures and tables; performing complex calculations; using computer screens; proofreading written work; preparing customer correspondence; constructing job aids; developing internal correspondence; note taking for training programs and meetings; building communication skills; and studying training materials. Methods of instruction include reading, lecture, discussion, classroom exercises, and examination.

Credit Recommendation: In the vocational certificate category or lower division baccalaureate/associate degree category, 1 semester hour in Office Administration per each four modules completed (2/91). **NOTE:** A total of 3 credit hours if all modules are completed.

Supervision (4310)

Location: AIB chapters nationwide operating under established ABA guidelines and standards.

Length: *Version 1:* 45 hours (15 weeks); *Version 2:* 30 hours (10 weeks) or by correspondence study.

Dates: January 1986-Present.

Objective: To help new or potential supervisors become better managers by emphasizing broad perspectives and by combining fresh insights with the interpersonal relations required of today's successful managers.

Learning Outcome: Upon successful completion of this course, the student will be able to identify the characteristics of effective management; set objectives, make decisions, and manage time; explain the benefits of training and development; develop effective communication and interpersonal skills; work effectively with groups and teams; interview, select, appraise and compensate employees; respond to grievances, conduct disciplinary actions and handle conflict; meet today's challenges of diversity, safety and health, ethics, quality; management and organizational change.

Instruction: Major topics covered in the course are the supervisory environment; supervisory functions; supervision and communication; supervision and interpersonal relations; and motivation. Methods of instruction include reading, lecture, discussion, laboratory exercises, and examination or if by correspondence study a proctored final examination.

Credit Recommendation: *Version 1:* In the lower division baccalaureate/associate degree category, 3 semester hours in Supervision. *Version 2:* In the lower division baccalaureate/associate degree category, 2 semester hours in Supervision (2/91) (11/95).

Supervisory Training (4335)

Location: AIB chapters nationwide operating under established ABA guidelines and standards.

Length: 27.5 hours (11 weeks).

Dates: November 1985-Present.

Objective: To develop first-line supervisory skills by integrating sound managerial concepts with practical experience.

Learning Outcome: Upon successful completion of this course, the student will be able to communicate effectively with employees; implement techniques on hiring; motivate and discipline employees, understand how to increase productivity among the people supervised; and create a team environment and achieve positive staff performance.

Instruction: Major topics covered in the course are the challenge of management; improving communication skills; getting the job done; working with people; and using supervisory skills. Methods of instruction include lecture, discussion, laboratory exercises, and examination.

Credit Recommendation: In the vocational certificate category, 1 semester hour in Management or Supervision (11/85) (2/91) (11/95).

Teller Training (6830)

Location: AIB chapters nationwide operating under established ABA guidelines and standards.

Length: *Version 1:* 45 hours (15 weeks; one 3-hour session per week); *Version 2:* 30 hours (10 weeks; one 3-hour session per week).

Dates: January 1988-July 1995.

Objective: To provide the skills that tellers need in the banking industry.

Learning Outcome: Upon successful completion of this course, the student will be able to describe the banking industry and its impact on society and the economy; perform various banking transactions, including balancing and settling, with accuracy and speed; demonstrate quality customer service; identify bank product features and benefits; sell bank products or properly refer customers to other bank representatives; identify and apply bank security and loss prevention techniques; and demonstrate successful communication skills with customers, co-workers, and supervisors.

Instruction: Major topics covered in the course are history of money and banking; role of banking in society; Federal Reserve System; services offered by a bank; and position of a teller. Methods of instruction include lecture, discussion, classroom exercise, and problem solving.

Credit Recommendation: *Version 1:* In the vocational certificate category, 3 semester hours in Bank Operations. *Version 2:* In the vocational certificate category, 2 semester hours in Bank Operations (2/91).

Today's Teller: Developing Basic Skills (6830)

Location: AIB Chapters nationwide operating under established ABA guidelines and standards.

Length: *Version 1:* 36 hours (12 sessions, 3 hours per session); *Version 2:* 36 hours (4 days, 8 hours per day).

Dates: September 1995-Present.

Objective: To introduce entry level tellers to the banking industry and to give them experience in performing basic teller functions.

Learning Outcome: Upon successful completion of this course, the student will be able to describe the basic functions of the banking industry; define the teller's responsibility in banking; explain and perform a variety of daily transactions procedures; summarize the features and benefits of four basic banking products; and demonstrate quality customer service.

Instruction: Major topics covered in this course are the role of the teller; primary and secondary teller functions; bank security; and providing quality customer service. Methods of instruction include case studies, audio visuals, lecture, discussion, group activities, and examination.

Credit Recommendation: In the vocational certificate category, 2 semester hours in Banking Operations (11/95).

Today's Tellers: Developing Advanced Skills (6832)

Location: AIB chapters nationwide operating under established ABA guidelines and standards.

Length: *Version 1:* 24 hours (6 hours per session for four days); *Version 2:* 24 hours (3 hours per day for eight sessions).

Dates: September 1995-Present.

Objective: To help newly promoted senior tellers adapt to the demands of their expanded responsibilities.

Learning Outcome: Upon successful completion of this course, the student will be able to perform advanced teller duties such as meeting their bank's cash and currency needs; process interteller transactions, large commercial transactions, and night deposits; maintain and settle the automated teller machine (ATM); help their banks comply with laws and regulations, including completing currency transaction reports required by the Bank Security Act; train teller staff in appropriate security procedures; teach staff to interpret and meet customer expectations by using effective communication techniques; supervise staff in compliance with equal employment laws and regulations; perform both daily and intermittent supervisory duties; and contribute to a teamwork environment.

Instruction: Major topics covered in the course are basic responsibilities of a senior teller; your banks' money supply; processing commercial transactions; other sources of commercial deposits; ATM responsibilities; the drive-through teller and balancing and settling. Methods of instruction include lecture, discussion, case studies, and examination.

Credit Recommendation: In the vocational certificate category, 1 semester hour in Banking Operations (11/95).

Trust Business (8250)

Location: AIB chapters nationwide operating under established ABA guidelines and standards.

Length: *Version 1:* 45 hours (15 weeks); *Version 2:* 30 hours (10 weeks) or by correspondence study.

Dates: November 1985-Present.

Objective: To provide an understanding of the trust business, the function of the trust department and how it fits in a bank, its services and their delivery, and the changing role of the trust department.

Learning Outcome: Upon successful completion of this course, the student will be able to provide a thorough introduction to the business of trust; to remove the mystery that sometimes surrounds the trust department; to enable the students to identify and describe the functions and services of the trust department; to place the trust business in a contemporary context; and to emphasize the need for cooperation between a bank's trust department and its other departments.

Instruction: Major topics covered in the course are the role of the trust department in a commercial bank; assets and ownership; and services and operational activities of the trust department. Methods of instruction include lecture, discussion, classroom exercises, and examination or if by correspondence study a proctored final examination.

Credit Recommendation: *Version 1:* In the lower division baccalaureate/associate degree category, 2 semester hours in Banking or Finance. *Version 2:* In the lower division baccalaureate/associate degree category, 2 semester hours in Banking or Finance (11/85) (2/91) (11/95) (10/96).

Trust Investments (8300) (Formerly Trust Investments [3540])

Location: AIB chapters nationwide operating under established ABA guidelines and standards.

Length: *Version 1:* 45 hours (15 weeks); *Version 2:* 30 hours (10 weeks).

Dates: November 1985-December 1990.

Objective: To understand investments, portfolio management, and the investment function as they are applied in a bank trust department.

Learning Outcome: Upon successful completion of this course, the student will be able to explain the basic dynamics and complexities of the investment process; define the nature of the trust function within a bank and the purpose of investment to the bank's trust department; list the trust services available; explain economic forecasting principles and illustrate their application; describe the techniques of valuing stocks and other securities; and explain the concept of portfolio management.

Instruction: Major topics covered in the course are the securities market; investment alternatives; trust department investment operations; investment techniques and practical applications; and investment policies and portfolio management. Methods of instruction include lecture, classroom exercises, demonstration, problem solving, and examination.

Credit Recommendation: *Version 1:* In the lower division baccalaureate/associate degree category, 3 semester hours in Bank Management or Finance. *Version 2:* In the lower division baccalaureate/associate degree category, 2 semester hours in Bank Management or Finance (11/85) (2/91) (11/95).

Trust Operations (8325)

Location: AIB chapters nationwide operating under established ABA guidelines and standards.

Length: *Version 1:* 45 hours (15 weeks); *Version 2:* 30 hours (10 weeks) or by correspondence study.

Dates: November 1986-Present.

Objective: To provide basic trust terminology and discuss the concepts and ideas that comprise the various trust functions and translate them into workable procedures.

Learning Outcome: Upon successful completion of this course, the student will be able to describe the types of securities handled by a trust department, the kinds of investments typically made with trust account assets, how securities are traded; identify the role and functions of the various participants in the securities industry; explain the responsibilities inherent in the fiduciary and agency relationships that a trust department has with its customers; apply the laws and regulations that define and circumscribe trust activities; illustrate the concepts of trust accounting and relate them to trust accounting functions performed by a trust department; and describe the internal controls, recordkeeping, and reporting requirements necessary in trust activities.

Instruction: Major topics covered in the course are securities funds; securities ownership and transactions; types of trust accounts and services; management and operation of trust services; trust accounting; asset/liability transaction; and internal accounting controls. Methods of instruction include lecture, classroom exercises, simulations, problem solving, and examination or if by correspondence study a proctored final examination.

Credit Recommendation: *Version 1:* In the lower division baccalaureate/associate degree category, 3 semester hours in Banking or Finance. *Version 2:* In the lower division baccalaureate/associate degree category, 2 semester hours in Banking or Finance (2/91) (11/95).

Understanding and Selling Bank Products (7766)

Location: AIB chapters nationwide operating under established ABA guidelines and standards.

Length: 30 hours (10 weeks).

Dates: September 1992-Present.

Objective: To provide knowledge of bank products, understanding of their features and benefits, and techniques for identifying customer needs.

Learning Outcome: Upon successful completion of this course, the student will be able to understand the importance of cross-selling as an element of good customer service; recognize typical prospects for various categories of bank products; describe bank's products and services in a customer-focused framework; and suggest products to prospects, overcome their resistance and conclude the sale.

Instruction: Major topics covered in this course are focusing on the customer; human relations skills; active listening; consumer banking needs; small business banking needs, cross-selling; closing the sales; and making referrals and recommending trust services. Methods of instruction include lecture, discussion, visual materials, case studies, role play, small group activities, and examination.

Credit Recommendation: In the lower division baccalaureate/associate degree category, 1 semester hour in Sales, Marketing, or Business (11/95). **NOTE:** To receive 1 credit, both this course and Bank Sales: Creating a Plan for the 90's (7595) must be completed.

Verbal Communication (5465)

Location: AIB chapters nationwide operating under established ABA guidelines and standards.

Length: 16 hours (8 weeks) or 24 hours (8 weeks).

Dates: September 1992-Present.

Objective: To provide effective verbal communication skills.

Learning Outcome: Upon successful completion of this course, the student will be able to overcome barriers to effective communication; identify and interpret verbal and non-verbal messages; listen effectively; and be persuasive.

Instruction: Major topics covered in the course are communication myths, verbal symbols, non-verbal symbols, creating effective messages. Methods of instruction include lecture, discussion, classroom exercises, case studies, assessment procedures, and examination.

Credit Recommendation: In the lower division baccalaureate/associate degree category, 1 semester hour in General Business (11/95). **NOTE:** To receive 1 credit, both this course and Written Communication (1870) must be completed.

Written Communications (1870)

Location: AIB chapters nationwide under established ABA guidelines and standards.

Length: 16 hours (8 weeks) or 24 hours (8 weeks) or by correspondence study.

Dates: September 1992-Present.

Objective: To provide understanding of principles essential for effective written communication.

Learning Outcome: Upon successful completion of this course, the student will be able to identify the elements and purposes of writing; tailor writing to the intended audience; define objectives of a writing task; and develop a strong business like "on-paper" personality.

Instruction: Major topics covered in this course are writing to communicate; defining objectives; "on-paper" personality; grammar problems; and organizing for the reader. Methods of instruction include lecture, discussion, classroom exercises, case studies, and examination or if by correspondence study a proctored final examination.

Credit Recommendation: In the lower division baccalaureate/associate degree category, 1 semester hour in General Business (11/95). **NOTE:** To receive 1 credit, both this course and Verbal Communication (5465) must be completed.

American Compensation Association

The American Compensation Association (ACA) is a not-for-profit association with more than 23,000 members, engaged in the design, implementation and management of employee compensation and benefits programs in their respective organizations. Founded in 1955, ACA is governed by a Board of Directors elected from the membership. In association with the Canadian Compensation Association (CCA) and the Global Remuneration Organization (GRO), ACA is the premier organization dedicated to excellence in total compensation. ACA serves the professions educational, informational and research needs by conducting educational and certification programs, promoting and sponsoring research activities, producing a wide variety of educational and informational publications, and providing networking opportunities.

ACA offered its first CCP (Certified Compensation Professional) seminar in the Fall of 1976. Since that time, nearly 8,000 individuals have earned ACA CCP certification. In 1993, ACA introduced the Certified Benefits Professional (CBP) designation. Since that time, nearly 355 individuals have earned ACA CBP. In 1997, ACA introduced the specialty certificate options. ACA Certification and Certificates are earned by passing the required batteries of examinations. Developed initially in cooperation with Michigan State University's Graduate School of Labor and Industrial Relations, ACA's certification body of knowledge model has been recently validated by a research team from Rutgers University's Institute of Management and Labor Relations.

Source of official student records: Registry of Credit Recommendations, American Council on Education, One Dupont Circle, Washington, DC 20036-1193 or ACA Headquarters, located at 14040 N. Northsight Boulevard, Scottsdale, AZ 85260..

Additional information about the courses: College Credit Recommendation Service, American Council on Education, One Dupont Circle, Washington, DC 20036-1193.

Alternative Reward Systems: Improving Performance and Competitiveness (C12)

Location: Various sites in the United States.

Length: 19.5 hours (2.5 days).

Dates: July 1995-Present.

Objective: To provide a knowledge of alternative rewards systems and strategies as a means to improve performance and achieve business objectives.

Learning Outcome: Upon successful completion of this course, the student will be able to describe the strengths and limitations of alternative rewards programs, explain how rewards programs relate to corporate culture and organizational strategy and their relation to productivity and business results; determine the most effective rewards program to reinforce corporate culture and to achieve strategic goals and business objectives.

Instruction: Major topics covered in the course are linking organizational, human resources, and rewards strategies; base pay strategies; short-term cash incentive strategies; individual level; group unit; organization wide level; implementation; and assessment of alternative reward strategies. Methods of instruction include lecture, discussions, case studies, quizzes, and final examination.

Credit Recommendation: In the upper division baccalaureate degree category, 1 semester hour in Human Resource Management or Business Administration (12/96).

Benefits Issues in Acquisitions, Mergers, and Divestitures (B6)

Location: Various sites in the United States.

Length: 19.5 hours (2.5 days).

Dates: September 1996-Present.

Objective: To provide knowledge of practical guidelines to assess opportunities and pitfalls in mergers, acquisitions, divestitures, and similar transactions important to the experienced benefits practitioner.

Learning Outcome: Upon successful completion of this course, the student will be able to describe various methodologies for effective "due diligence" for plan design; cost and structures; identify when an organization should seek outside help to facilitate the processes; identify and describe the guidelines for benefits communication throughout the transaction; and explain how to identify and effectively respond to employee issues and concerns.

Instruction: Major topics covered in the course are introduction human resources in the merger, acquisition, and divestiture process; before the transaction: team selection, strategy, data collection, and analysis; during the transaction; and after the transaction. Methods of instruction include lecture, discussions, classroom exercises, case studies, audio/visual material, quizzes, and final examination.

Credit Recommendation: In the lower division baccalaureate/associate degree category, 1 semester hour in Human Resource Management or Business Administration (12/96).

Designing Executive Compensation Programs (C6A)

Location: Various sites in the United States.

Length: 19.5 hours (2.5 days).

Dates: September 1996-Present.

Objective: To provide an overview and understanding of the issues surrounding the design of executive compensation programs.

Learning Outcome: Upon successful completion of this course, the student will be able to describe the ideas and issues in the design of executive compensation programs using advanced tax and accounting dimensions which affect executive compensation design, and cost and design executive compensation programs given the needs and business strategies of the organization.

Instruction: Major topics covered in the course are elements of executive compensation, advanced issues in tax and accounting, strategic design issues, short-term incentive design—the annual bonus plan, long-term incentives, SEC proxy disclosure regulations, and other topics of interest. Methods of instruction include lecture, discussion, classroom exercises, case studies, audio/visual material, quizzes, and final examination.

Credit Recommendation: In the upper division baccalaureate degree category, 1 semester hour in Human Resource Management, or Business Administration (12/96).

Elements of Executive Compensation (C6)

Location: Various sites in the United States.

Length: 19.5 hours (2.5 days).

Dates: September 1996-Present.

Objective: To provide knowledge of executive compensation in relation to the business and compensation strategies.

Learning Outcome: Upon successful completion of this course, the student will be able to define key terminology; describe different types of executive compensation programs; analyze executive compensation plans; and explain how they operate and apply appropriate tax and accounting treatments.

Instruction: Major topics covered in the course are elements of executive pay; strategic concepts; accounting aspects; tax aspects; and short-term incentives and long-term incentives. Methods of instruction include lecture, discussion, classroom exercises, case studies, quizzes, and final examination.

Credit Recommendation: In the lower division baccalaureate/associate degree category, 1 semester hour in Human Resource Management or Business Administration (12/96).

Elements of Expatriate Compensation (C9)

Location: Various sites in the United States.

Length: 19.5 hours (2.5 days).

Dates: July 1996-Present.

Objective: To provide knowledge of common and emerging expatriate compensation policies and practices, linking compensation to business and staffing strategies.

Learning Outcome: Upon successful completion of this course, the student will be able to describe common and emerging expatriate compensation policies and practices; describe how to develop compensation policies that support business and staffing strategies; make basic computations; and apply various program options using case studies and actual data.

Instruction: Major topics covered in the course are principles and terminology of expatriate compensation; tax equalization basics; housing equalization; goods and services equalization; premiums and incentives; the balance sheet; compensation of third-country nationals; expatriate compensation strategies; tax equalization; application and planning; supplemental expatriate policies; and relocation issues. Methods of instruction include lecture, discussion, classroom exercises, case studies, quizzes, and final examination.

Credit Recommendation: In the upper division baccalaureate degree category, 1 semester hour in Human Resource Management or Business Administration (12/96).

Elements of Sales Compensation (C5)

Location: Various sites in the United States.

Length: 19.5 hours (2.5 days).

Dates: December 1996-Present.

Objective: To provide knowledge of the fundamental principles affecting the development and application of sales compensation programs.

Learning Outcome: Upon successful completion of this course, the student will be able to describe the fundamental principles affecting the development and application of sales compensation programs including base salary, straight commission, and combination plans of base salary and variable incentive compensation, with emphasis on selecting and designing the appropriate incentive formula.

Instruction: Major topics covered in the course are sales channels, compensation principles applied to sales compensation, types of sales jobs, formula types, design features, calculation techniques, program qualifiers, application exercises, and program changes. Methods of instruction include lecture, discussion, classroom exercises, quizzes, and final examination.

Credit Recommendation: In the lower division baccalaureate/associate degree category, 1 semester hour in Human Resource Management or Business Administration (12/96).

Fundamentals of Employee Benefits Programs (B1)

Location: Various sites in the United States.

Length: 19.5 hours (2.5 days).

Dates: July 1996-Present.

Objective: To provide knowledge of the design, administration, and regulatory environment of private-sector employee benefits plans and programs.

Learning Outcome: Upon successful completion of this course, the student will be able to define key benefits terminology; describe current practices in benefits, determine the best balance between cash and noncash compensation perspectives within a given organization; and describe the scope of current growth and changes affecting employee benefits.

Instruction: Major topics covered in the course include scope and classification of benefits plans; government regulation of benefits plans; design features of group welfare benefits plans; design and regulation of pension plans; time off with pay and other benefits; flexible benefits; and communicating employee benefits. Methods of instruction include lecture, discussion, classroom exercises, case studies, audio/visual material, quizzes, and final examination.

Credit Recommendation: In the lower division baccalaureate/associate degree category, 1 semester hour in Human Resource Management or Business Administration (12/96).

Health Care and Insurance Plans: Design and Management (B3)

Location: Various sites in the United States.

Length: 19.5 hours (2.5 days).

Dates: August 1996-Present.

Objective: To provide knowledge of health and welfare benefits with a focus on basic underwriting and funding issues.

Learning Outcome: Upon successful completion of this course, the student will be able to identify legal requirements in health and insurance plans, describe legislative changes taking place, identify trends and emerging issues in health care, identify areas for saving opportunities in existing plans, compare various design and funding issues, and identify advantages and disadvantages of potential solutions.

Instruction: Major topics covered in the course are health and welfare plans basics, the principles of health and welfare benefits, death benefit plans, integrated disability management, health care plan basic features, cost management, medical plans— retiree coverage, flexible benefits, and emerging issues. Methods of instruction include lecture, discussion, classroom exercises, case studies, audio/visual material, quizzes, and final examination.

Credit Recommendation: In the lower division baccalaureate/associate degree category, 1 semester hour in Insurance, Human Resource Management or Business Administration (12/96).

Health Care and Insurance Plans: Financial Management (B3A)

Location: Various sites in the United States.

Length: 19.5 hours (2.5 days).

Dates: June 1995-Present.

Objective: To provide knowledge of financial issues facing corporation and not-for- profit organizations for experienced benefits professionals.

Learning Outcome: Upon successful completion of this seminar, participants will be able to describe funding alternatives and tax consequences to employers, employees and trusts, determine funding for postretirement welfare plans liabilities, explain how to manage risk through insurance, trusts and self-funding vehicles, identify issues facing organizations today and describe cost constraints in health care and insurance plans.

Instruction: Major topics covered in the course are funding concepts; insured approaches; self-funding; group insurance; tax treatment, employers and employees; tax treatment, trusts and welfare benefits plans; tax and funding features, disability and death benefits; and postretirement employee benefits. Methods of instruction include lecture, discussion, classroom exercise, case studies, quizzes, and examinations.

Credit Recommendation: In the lower division baccalaureate/associate degree category, 1 semester hour in Human Resource Management or Business Administration (12/96).

International Benefits (B9)

Location: Various sites in the United States.

Length: 19.5 hours (2.5 days).

Dates: June 1996-Present.

Objective: To provide knowledge of design, underwriting, funding and management issues that are inherent in providing benefits programs in an international environment.

Learning Outcome: Upon successful completion of this course, the student will be able to describe how the different social, political and economic conditions throughout the world impact the design of benefits programs, identify global trends in benefits practices as well as specific country practices, describe the roles and objectives of retirement and health and welfare benefits, describe techniques and considerations involved in designing and funding these plans on both a local and global basis, identify the benefits issues to consider when transferring employees internationally, and explain how to develop a benefits package for international transfers.

Instruction: Major topics covered in the course are introduction; mandatory retirement plans; design of company-provided retirement plans; funding, accounting, and taxation Issues in retirement planning; design of welfare plans; funding of welfare plans; international transfers; and other benefits and issues. Methods of instruction include lecture, discussion, classroom exercises, case studies, quizzes, and final examination.

Credit Recommendation: In the upper division baccalaureate degree category, 1 semester hour in Human Resource Management, or Business Administration (12/96).

International Total Remuneration (T9)

Location: Various sites in the United States.

Length: 19.5 hours (2.5 days).

Dates: June 1995-Present.

Objective: To provide an overview of the role of total remuneration within global organizations.

Learning Outcome: Upon successful completion of this course, the student will be able to describe how practitioners in various countries manage compensation and benefits; compare how different governments apply employment laws and regulations; describe the business contexts in which various international staffing and compensation strategies are effective; use appropriate tools to become an effective international business partner; describe the critical differences between international and local compensation and benefits; and understand the importance of recognizing cultural differences when developing global policies.

Instruction: Major topics covered in the course are total remuneration around the globe: similarities and differences; definitions and demographics; local national staffing; compensation practices, career progression, compensation and government intervention around the World; common expatriate compensation methodologies; government-mandated programs around the World; company-sponsored benefits; cross-border mergers and acquisitions: impact on compensation and benefits plans; group exercise; and total remuneration around the world: where we are, where we are going. Methods of instruction include lecture, discussions, classroom exercises, case studies, video, quizzes, and examinations.

Credit Recommendation: In the upper division baccalaureate degree category, 1 semester hour in Human Resource, Management, or Business Administration (12/96).

Job Analysis, Job Documentation, and Job Evaluation (C2)

Location: Various sites in the United States.

Length: 19.5 hours (2.5 days).

Dates: October 1996-Present.

Objective: To provide an overview of the fundamentals of job analysis and documentation with a focus on job descriptions.

Learning Outcome: Upon successful completion of this course, the student will be able to describe various methods of job evaluation including quantitative plan design; explain how job evaluation plans are selected or developed; analyze the way in which plans are applied in an organization; and select an effective plan-type for a specific organization.

Instruction: Major topics covered in the course are strategic overview; job analysis; job design; job documentation; market-based job evaluation; nonquantitative methods; quantitative methods; and selection and implementation issues. Methods of instruction include lecture, discussion, classroom exercises, quizzes, and final examination.

Credit Recommendation: In the lower division baccalaureate/associate degree category, 1 semester hour in Human Resource Management or Business Administration (12/96).

Managing Diversity Through Flexibility in Benefits (B5)

Location: Various sites in the United States.

Length: 19.5 hours (2.5 days).

Dates: December 1996-Present.

Objective: To provide an overview of flexible benefits programs and other benefits plans that help address the needs of a diverse work force.

Learning Outcome: Upon successful completion of this course, the student will be able to describe the elements of flexible benefits design, pricing; implementation and legal compliance; identify key issues for administration of flexible benefits plans; identify common pitfalls that arise during the introduction and management of a flexible benefits program; and describe various alternative work and family benefits arrangements.

Instruction: Major topics covered in the course are benefits perspective and strategy, design alternatives, pricing strategies, process for implementing choice, legal and regulatory environment, and work life strategies. Methods of instruction include lecture, discussion, case studies, audio/visual material, quizzes, and final examination.

Credit Recommendation: In the upper division baccalaureate degree category, 1 semester hour in Human Resource

Management or Business Administration (12/96).

Pay Structures, Pay Rate Determination, and Base Pay Program Administration (C4)

Location: Various sites in the United States.

Length: 19.5 hours (2.5 days).

Dates: October 1996-Present.

Objective: To provide an overview of the principles, design, implementation, and evaluation of employee base pay programs.

Learning Outcome: Upon successful completion of this course, the student will be able to define the principles of employee base pay programs and describe their design, implementation, and evaluation methodology; and focus on resolving differences between internal worth for a job and market data for the same job in order to design a pay program that is fair, competitive, and supportive of an organization's compensation strategy.

Instruction: Major topics covered in the course are compensation strategy; current market position; designing base pay structures, alternative pay methods, and merit pay programs; costing base pay programs; evaluating base pay programs; and other pay considerations. Methods of instruction include lecture, discussion, classroom exercises, quizzes, and final examination.

Credit Recommendation: In the upper division baccalaureate degree category, 1 semester hour in Human Resource Management or Business Administration (12/96).

Performance Management: Strategy, Design, and Implementation (C11)

Location: Various sites in the United States.

Length: 19.5 hours (2.5 days).

Dates: December 1996-Present.

Objective: To provide knowledge of the strategic context of linking pay plans to organizational, unit, and individual measures of performance.

Learning Outcome: Upon successful completion of this course, the student will be able to describe the key concepts associated with measuring and rewarding performance at the organizational, unit, and individuals levels; describe the relationship between performance management and organization strategy; and explain measurement issues, using models for defining performance at various organizational levels and linking rewards to performance.

Instruction: Major topics covered in the course are the context of organizational measurement; objectives of measuring performance in organizations; performance management at the organization wide Level; performance management at the group level; performance management at the individual level; performance management system design; implementation; three keys to success; and emerging issues for performance management. Methods of instruction include lecture, discussion, classroom exercises, case studies, audio/visual material, quizzes, and final examination.

Credit Recommendation: In the upper division baccalaureate degree category, 1 semester hour in Human Resource Management or Business Administration (12/96).

Principles of Accounting and Finance (T2)

Location: Various sites in the United States.

Length: 19.5 hours (2.5 days).

Dates: December 1996-Present.

Objective: To provide an overview of accounting and finance as it applies to total compensation management.

Learning Outcome: Upon successful completion of this course, the student will be able to read their organizations' financial statements, including the balance sheet, the income statement, the statement of cash flows and the statement of shareholder equity, and explain where compensation and benefits costs appear and their effect; understand the impact of compensation and benefits decisions on their organizations' financial results; make computations; and use financial statements to select appropriate financial measures for group and individual incentive plans.

Instruction: Major topics covered in the course are overview of accounting and finance; balance sheet; income statement; statement of cash flows and shareholders' equity; accounting alternatives; finance and planning; financial analysis; and human resources functioning with the finance department. Methods of instruction include lecture, discussions, classroom exercises, quizzes, and examination.

Credit Recommendation: In the lower division baccalaureate/associate degree category, 1 semester hour in Accounting, Finance, or Business Administration (12/96).

Quantitative Methods (T3)

Location: Various sites in the United States.

Length: 19.5 hours (2.5 days).

Dates: November 1996-Present.

Objective: To provide basic knowledge and application of quantitative concepts in relation to total compensation management.

Learning Outcome: Upon successful completion of this course, the student will be able to define general quantitative concepts; use basic statistical tools; and apply the mathematics of compensation and benefits design and administration and mathematical modeling and regression analysis, using data from numerous sources and using various techniques for problem solving.

Instruction: Major topics covered in the course are qualitative and quantitative data; percents and related issues; developing and evaluating the cost of a corporate-sponsored retirement program; time value of money; actuarial issues; organizing and analyzing data, statistics; displaying relationships between data; modeling and regression analysis; developing a salary budget recommendation; and guidelines for individual salary increases. Methods of instruction include lecture, discussions, classroom exercises, quizzes, and examination.

Credit Recommendation: In the lower division baccalaureate/associate degree category, 1 semester hour in Math or Business Administration (12/96).

Regulatory Environments for Compensation Programs (C1)

Location: Various sites in the United States.

Length: 19.5 hours (2.5 days).

Dates: November 1996-Present.

Objective: To provide an overview of the regulatory requirements of a compensation program, with emphasis on major federal statues that affect compensation design and practice.

Learning Outcome: Upon successful completion of this course, the student will be able to describe the regulatory requirements of a compensation program; define the concepts involved in key legislation relating to compensation; and explain the implications of legal and regulatory compliance requirements to an organization.

Instruction: Major topics covered in the course are regulatory environment and related laws; fair labor standards act; equal employment opportunity statutes and civil rights; rights legislation and the Civil Rights Act of 1991; and regulatory environment case studies. Methods of instruction include lecture, discussion, classroom exercises, case studies, audio/visual material, quizzes, and final examination.

Credit Recommendation: In the lower division baccalaureate/associate degree category, 1 semester hour in Human Resource Management, Business Law, or Business Administration (12/96).

Retirement Plans: Design and Management (B2)

Location: Various sites in the United States.

Length: 19.5 hours (2.5 days).

Dates: September 1996-Present.

Objective: To provide knowledge of qualified retirement plans for the benefits practitioner and those preparing to manage the plans.

Learning Outcome: Upon successful completion of this course, the student will be able to explain how to effectively design and administer qualified retirement plans; describe the regulatory requirements that affect retirement plans; describe the differences between defined benefit and defined contribution plans; and list the advantages and disadvantages of each type of plan.

Instruction: Major topics covered in the course are retirement planning objectives; income replacement; basic concepts of defined benefit vs. defined contribution plans; legislative and regulatory environment; tax issues; defined contribution plans; defined benefit plans; hybrid plans; and current strategies. Methods of instruction include lecture, discussions, case study, audio/visual material, quizzes, and final examination.

Credit Recommendation: In the lower division baccalaureate/associate degree category, 1 semester hour in Human Resource Management or Business Administration (12/96).

Retirement Plans: Financial Management (B2A)

Location: Various sites in the United States.

Length: 19.5 hours (2.5 days).

Dates: July 1996-Present.

Objective: To provide knowledge of the financial aspects of retirement plans for experienced benefits professionals.

Learning Outcome: Upon successful completion of this course, the student will be able to explain funding and expending of defined benefit and defined contribution plans; describe issues and responsibilities in investing plan assets and the tax ramifications for employers and employees; define nonqualified plan alternatives and describe their role in executive retirement packages; determine appropriate investment performance guidelines; and understand actuarial assumptions that affect retirement plans.

Instruction: Major topics covered in the course are funding for defined benefit pension plans; investment of defined benefit plans; valuation reports; investment of defined contribution plans; accounting for defined benefit pension plans; taxation of participants, including penalties; taxation of plan, including penalties; and nonqualified retirement plans. Methods of instruction include lecture, discussions, classroom exercises, case study, audio/video material, quizzes, and final examination.

Credit Recommendation: In the upper division baccalaureate degree category, 1 semester hour in Human Resource Management or Business Administration (12/96).

Strategic Benefits Planning (B4)

Location: Various sites in the United States.

Length: 19.5 hours (2.5 days).

Dates: April 1996-Present.

Objective: To provide knowledge of how to plan an employee benefits strategy to enable the experienced benefits practitioner to assume management responsibilities.

Learning Outcome: Upon successful completion of this course, the student will be able to identify the trade-offs that occur when designing a benefits plan; explain how to ensure that a plan supports the organization's business strategy; identify key issues to consider when developing and coordinating benefits strategy; discriminate between strategic and tactical elements of a plan; and explain how to incorporate each into the design of a benefits program.

Instruction: Major topics covered in the course are strategic employee benefits issues; strategic benefits planning; evaluation and review; and case studies. Methods of instruction include lecture, discussion, case studies, audio/visual material, quizzes, and final examination.

Credit Recommendation: In the upper division baccalaureate degree category, 1 semester hour in Human Resource Management or Business Administration (12/96).

Strategic Communication in Compensation and Benefits (T4) (formerly Communicating Compensation and Benefits [T4])

Location: Various sites in the United States.

Length: 19.5 hours (2.5 days).

Dates: December 1996-Present.

Objective: To provide the fundamentals of communicating compensation and benefits programs effectively.

Learning Outcome: Upon successful completion of this course, the student will be able to apply basic communication principles to their own organizations' compensation and benefits communication strategies; evaluate communication items for effectiveness and measure their success; and explain the communications perspective when releasing information on new compensation and benefits programs.

Instruction: Major topics covered in the course are qualitative and quantitative data; percents and related issues; developing and evaluating the cost of a corporate-sponsored retirement program considering time and value of money; actuarial issues; organizing and analyzing data, statistics; displaying relationships between data; modeling and regression analysis; developing a salary budget recommendation; and guidelines for individual salary increases. Methods of instruction include lecture, discussions, case study, learner presentations, video, quizzes, and examinations.

Credit Recommendation: In the upper division baccalaureate degree category, 1 semester hour in Human Resource Management or Business Administration (12/96).

Total Compensation Management (T1)

Location: Various sites in the United States.

Length: 19.5 hours (2.5 days).

Dates: February 1996-Present.

Objective: To provide a basic understanding of total compensation management with emphasis on the development of a total compensation strategy.

Learning Outcome: Upon successful completion of this course, the student will be able to describe the role of the contemporary compensation and benefits professional; explain the components, definitions, and strategy of total compensation; and use the necessary tools to design and implement compensation and benefits policy and practices.

Instruction: Major topics covered in the course are developing a total compensation strategy; factors affecting total compensation; overview; factors affecting direct compensation; factors affecting indirect compensation; administration of total compensation; and audit and redesign. Methods of Instruction lecture, discussions, classroom exercises, case studies, quizzes, and final examination.

Credit Recommendation: In the lower division baccalaureate/associate degree category, 1 semester hour in Human Resource Management or Business Administration (12/96).

American Educational Institute, Inc.

American Educational Institute, Inc. was founded in 1969 for the purpose of developing law courses for the education of property/casualty claim adjusters. Since that time AEI has provided claims law training through a series of undergraduate and graduate level courses offered to insurance industry personnel.

From the four courses originally offered, AEI now offers 40 individual courses in the subject areas of: Legal Principles, Liability Insurance, Property Insurance, Workers' Compensation and Claims Fraud.

In 1969 there were fewer than 500 students from less than 25 companies. Today AEI enrolls over 3500 students from more than 300 insurance companies, independent adjusters, self-insureds, agencies and brokers. In addition to credit recommendations from ACE, AEI's courses are recognized as a source for continuing education credits by many state insurance departments, Chartered Property Casualty Underwriter (CPCU), National Association of Insurance Women (NAIW) and as a component in the professional career path of many insurance companies.

The Institute is proud of its accomplishments and continues to be committed to providing the very best in claims law training courses to the insurance industry.

Source of official student records: Registry of Credit Recommendations, American Council on Education, One Dupont Circle, Washington, DC 20036-1193.

Additional information about the courses: Office of Corporate-Higher Education Programs, Thomas Edison State College, 101 West State Street, Trenton, New Jersey 08608-1176.

Alternative Dispute Resolution (222)

Location: Independent study.

Length: 15 hours.

Dates: January 1996-Present.

Objective: To provide the student with an understanding of Alternative Dispute Resolution (ADR) methods for resolving disputed claims.

Learning Outcome: Upon successful completion of this course, the student will be able to recognize the importance of using negotiation, mediation, arbitration and other ADR methods in resolving disputed claims.

Instruction: Major topics covered in the course are negotiation, mediation, arbitration, and other ADR methods and their insurance and legal implications. Methods of instruction include taking a proctored examination and submitting a graduate level project to be eligible for the credit recommendation.

Credit Recommendation: In the upper division baccalaureate degree category or in the graduate degree category, 1 semester hour in Business Law or Insurance elective (10/96).

Arson and Fraud (313)
(Formerly Arson and Fraud [314])

Location: Independent Study.

Length: 13 hours.

Dates: *Version 1:* July 1990-March 1992; *Version 2:* March 1992-Present.

Objective: To provide the student with an understanding of both arson and fraud policy defenses.

Learning Outcome: Upon successful completion of this course, the student will be able to understand and apply the elements of policy defenses to determine the necessary proof for arson and fraud defenses.

Instruction: Major topics covered in the course are elements of the policy defenses of arson and fraud and the proof needed to sustain them; and explores potential liability of insurers for defamation and related torts. Methods of instruction include a proctored examination that must be administered for students to be eligible for credit.

Credit Recommendation: In the upper division baccalaureate degree category, 1 semester hour in Advanced Commercial Law, Arson and Fraud, or Insurance elective (10/91) (10/96).

Avoiding Bad Faith and Civil Liability in Handling Suspicious Claims (514)

Location: Independent Study.

Length: 15 hours.

Dates: October 1992-Present.

Objective: To provide the student with an understanding of how to avoid the imposition of liability during the investigation of fraudulent claims.

Learning Outcome: Upon successful completion of this course, the student will be able to effectively investigate fraudulent claims in good faith.

Instruction: Major topics covered in the course are both first and third party bad faith claims; and other tort actions such as defamation, invasion of privacy and malicious prosecution.

Credit Recommendation: In the graduate degree category, 1 semester hour in Insurance Law: Liability in Handling Claims (4/93).

Commercial Property Coverage (316)

Location: Independent Study.

Length: 28 hours.

Dates: July 1990-Present.

Objective: To provide the student with an understanding of commercial property coverages.

Learning Outcome: Upon successful completion of this course, the student will be able to understand the many different commercial coverages available and to better evaluate claims arising under commercial property coverages.

Instruction: Major topics covered in the course are special policies providing definitive areas of protection, including boiler and machinery, builder's risk, sprinkler leakage, equipment floater, burglary, time element (business interruption) and combination special multiperil; and analyzes available insurance covering bailed property and extent of liabilities imposed on carriers and other types of bailees. Methods of instruction include a proctored examination that must be administered for student to be eligible for credit.

Credit Recommendation: In the upper division baccalaureate degree category, 1 semester hour in Advanced Commercial Law, Commercial Property, or Insurance elective (10/91) (10/96).

Comparative Negligence, Contribution and Settlements (211) (Formerly Comparative Negligence [211] and also Comparative Negligence [210])

Location: Independent Study.

Length: 18 hours.

Dates: *Version 1:* July 1990-March 1992; *Version 2:* March 1992-Present.

Objective: To provide the student with knowledge of the concept of comparative negligence as used in tort law.

Learning Outcome: Upon successful completion of this course, the student will be able to analyze the various forms of comparative negligence and to determine applicability of state law; understand the three theories of comparative negligence and their application to a dollar and cents evaluation of claims; and give consideration to the effect of contract, indemnity, strict or absolute liability, joint and several liability, contribution among joint tortfeasors, products liability, subrogation, and other areas.

Instruction: Major topics covered in the course are the various forms of comparative negligence; the effect on statutory and common law doctrines and defenses; the effect of tort reform on joint tortfeasor cases, including joint and several liability; and settlement, set-off, and conflict of law problems. Methods of instruction include a proctored examination which must be administered for students to be eligible for the credit recommendation.

Credit Recommendation: *Version 1:* In the upper division baccalaureate degree category, 1 semester hour in Advanced Commercial Law, Law of Torts, or Insurance elective (10/91). **NOTE:** Students will receive 3 semester hours in the upper division baccalaureate degree category, if they take this course in combination with Courses 217 and 218. This combination is equivalent to Law of Torts II. *Version 2:* In the graduate degree category, 1 semester hour in Law of Torts, or Insurance elective (5/92).

Endorsements, Forms, and Clauses (312)

Location: Independent Study.

Length: 23 hours.

Dates: July 1990-March 1992.

Objective: To provide the student with knowledge of forms and clauses commonly attached to the standard fire policy.

Learning Outcome: Upon successful completion of this course, the student will be able to explain the legal interpretation of any modern combination policy; understand how the endorsement broadens the coverage of the standard policy by covering additional perils; and know some of the current forms which use the basic fire policy in combination with other special provisions to broaden the basic policy in various ways, such as the Dwelling, Building and Contents Form.

Instruction: Major topics covered in the course are legal effect of extended coverage endorsement and other forms and clauses commonly attached to the Standard Fire Form covering dwellings and commercial property; and understanding these various policy provisions, the student will understand legal interpretations of any modern combination policy. Methods of instruction include a proctored examination.

Credit Recommendation: In the upper division baccalaureate degree category, 1 semester hour in Advanced Commercial Law, Personal Property and Liability Insurance, or Insurance elective (10/91). **NOTE**: Students will receive 6 semester hours in the upper division baccalaureate degree category, in Personal Property and Liability Insurance if they take this course in combination with Courses 211, 212, 310, 311, and 315.

Federal Workers' Compensation Law (414)

Location: Independent Study.

Length: 16 hours.

Dates: July 1990-Present.

Objective: To provide the student with an understanding of federal workers' compensation statutes.

Learning Outcome: Upon successful completion of this course, the student will be able to determine the applicability of federal laws pertaining to Workers' Compensation; understand how federal statutes interact with state laws and with other federal laws; determine property jurisdiction for any particular claim; and predict whether a claimant who has a federal remedy might also be entitled to an additional state recovery.

Instruction: Major topics covered in the course are federal workers' compensation such as Longshore and Harbor Workers' Compensation Act, Outer Continental Shelf Lands Act and Black Lung Benefits Act; and federal jurisdiction and relationship with state laws. Methods of instruction include a proctored examination and graduate level research project.

Credit Recommendation: In the upper division baccalaureate degree or graduate degree category, 1 semester hour in Workers' Compensation Law or Insurance elective (10/91) (10/96).

Fire and Extended Coverage Perils (311) (Formerly Standard Fire Insurance [311])

Location: Independent Study.

Length: *Version 1:* 15 hours; *Version 2:* 18 hours.

Dates: *Version 1:* July 1990-March 1992; *Version 2:* March 1992-Present.

Objective: *Version 1:* To provide the student with knowledge of the standard fire insurance policy. *Version 2:* To understand the fire and extended coverage perils and apply that understanding to any modern package policy including fire coverage.

Learning Outcome: *Version 1:* Upon successful completion of the course, the student will be able to explain the elements of the standard fire policy and apply these principles to a modern package policy. *Version 2:* Upon successful completion of the course, the student will be able to explain the elements of the standard fire policy and apply these principles to a modern package policy; understand and utilize courts' decisions and statutes affecting fire insurance claims; and effectively deal with attorneys in the negotiating and settlement of claims involving fire insurance.

Instruction: *Version 1:* Major topics covered in the course are interpreting judicial decisions establishing rights and obligations of parties under the NY Standard Form; and explaining the elements of this most basic of fire coverages and how it has been adapted to form the foundation of modern homeowners and commercial policies. Methods of instruction include a proctored examination which must be administered for students to be eligible for the credit recommendation. *Version 2:* Major topics covered in the course are defining the fire and extended coverage perils; interpreting judicial decisions involving perils; explains the elements of basic fire coverages and how the fire and extended coverage perils as originally contained in the NY Standard Form and the Extended Coverage Endorsement form the foundation for modern homeowners and commercial policies.

Credit Recommendation: In the upper division baccalaureate degree category, 1 semester hour in Advanced Commercial Law, Personal Property and Liability Insurance, or Insurance elective (10/91) (5/92) (10/96). **NOTE:** Students will receive 6 semester hours in the upper division baccalaureate degree category, in Personal Property and Liability Insurance if they take this course in combination with Courses 210, 216, 310, and 314.

Fundamentals in Coverage and Claims Law (010)

Location: Independent study.

Length: 14 hours.

Dates: January 1994-Present.

Objective: To provide the student with an introduction to the insurance contract and claims law.

Learning Outcome: Upon successful completion of this course, the student will be able to understand the property/casualty insurance policy as a legal contract; understand the fundamentals of claims law; and apply knowledge to make sound decisions in underwriting and claims.

Instruction: Major topics covered in the course are legal aspects of insurance, indemnification and damages, litigation and arbitration, and dispute resolution. Methods of instruction include a proctored examination for students to be eligible for credit recommendation.

Credit Recommendation: In the upper division baccalaureate degree category, 1

semester hour in Insurance Law, Business Law, or Insurance elective (10/96).

Handling Suspicious Claims: The Policy and Its Requirements (513)

Location: Independent Study.

Length: 17 hours.

Dates: October 1992-Present.

Objective: To provide the student with an understanding of insurance policy language and how it affects the investigation of a fraudulent claim.

Learning Outcome: Upon successful completion of this course, the student will be able to identify and interpret applicable policy language so as to guide the handling of fraudulent claims.

Instruction: Major topics covered in the course are the construction and application of insurance policy conditions and exclusions that govern the rights and duties of an insurance company in investigating and disposing of suspected fraudulent claims; and reviews the insurer's remedies with respect to the handling of suspicious claims.

Credit Recommendation: In the graduate degree category, 1 semester hour in Insurance Law: Handling Suspicious Claims (4/93).

Homeowners: Liability Coverages (315)

Location: Independent Study.

Length: 21 hours.

Dates: May 1992-Present.

Objective: To instruct and give guidance to participants in understanding and interpreting liability coverages involving homeowners and learn the rules courts employ to interpret these policy provisions.

Learning Outcome: Upon successful completion of this course, the student will be able to understand and utilize courts' decisions and statutes affecting insurance claims; effectively consult with attorneys in the negotiating and settlement of claims; and analyze the Homeowners Section II coverages including liability and medical payments to others.

Instruction: Major topics covered in the course are policy definitions, the scope of coverage and the limitations on coverage, including exclusionary language; and recent litigation on the intentional acts and business pursuits exclusions and analyzes the duty to defend. Methods of instruction include a proctored examination for students to be eligible for the credit recommendation.

Credit Recommendation: In the upper division baccalaureate degree category, 1 semester hour in Homeowners Liability Insurance or Insurance elective (5/92) (10/96).

Homeowners: Property Coverage (314) (Formerly Homeowners Insurance [315])

Location: Independent Study.

Length: 24 hours.

Dates: *Version 1:* July 1990-March 1992; *Version 2:* March 1992-Present.

Objective: To provide the student with the working knowledge of homeowners insurance policy.

Learning Outcome: Upon successful completion of this course, the student will be able to determine the validity of claims by understanding the policy language and court interpretation.

Instruction: Major topics covered in the course are reviewing judicial interpretation of property and liability coverages under the Homeowners program including variation between the '76 and '84 forms. Methods of instruction include a proctored examination that must be administered for students to be eligible for credit.

Credit Recommendation: In the upper division baccalaureate degree category, 1 semester hour in Advanced Commercial Law, Personal Property and Liability Insurance, or Insurance elective (10/91) (5/92) (10/96). **NOTE:** Students will receive 6 semester hours in the upper division baccalaureate degree category, in Personal Property and Liability Insurance if they take this course in combination with Courses 210, 216, 310, and 311.

Inland Marine (317)

Location: Independent Study.

Length: 16 hours.

Dates: May 1992-Present.

Objective: To give participants an understanding of inland marine forms and coverages and the ability to analyze their interpretation and application.

Learning Outcome: Upon successful completion of this course, the student will be able to understand Inland Marine coverages, common policy provisions and exclusions and how they have been interpreted in the courts; and effectively place coverage and/or handle claims involving inland marine risks.

Instruction: Major topics covered in the course are the origin and development of Inland Marine insurance and the analyses of various coverages including transportation, bailees' customers, personal and commercial floaters, dealers block and builders risk, focusing on issues in legal interpretation and application. Methods of instruction include a proctored examination for students to be eligible for the credit recommendation.

Credit Recommendation: In the upper division baccalaureate degree category, 1 semester hour in Inland Marine Insurance or Insurance elective (5/92) (10/96).

Introduction to Workers' Compensation Law-Origin and Development (410)

Location: Independent Study.

Length: 15 hours.

Dates: July 1990-Present.

Objective: To provide the student with an understanding of the concept of workers' compensation.

Learning Outcome: Upon successful completion of this course, the student will be able to have a thorough understanding of the application of workers' compensation; and identify those claims that are subject to the exclusive remedy of workers' compensation.

Instruction: Major topics covered in the course are the statutory, no-fault basis for workers' compensation laws; and introduces different types of statutes and analyzes important principles of exclusive remedy and extra-territorial application. Methods of instruction include a proctored examination and a graduate level research project.

Credit Recommendation: In the upper division baccalaureate degree or graduate degree category, 1 semester hour in Introduction to Workers' Compensation Law or Insurance elective (10/91) (10/96). **NOTE**: Students will receive 3 semester hours in the graduate degree category, in Workers' Compensation Law, if they take this course in combination with Courses 411 and 412. This combination is equivalent to Introduction to Workers' Compensation Law.

Law of Agency (113)

Location: Independent Study.

Length: 12 hours.

Dates: July 1990-Present.

Objective: To enable the student to understand the principal and agent relationship.

Learning Outcome: Upon successful completion of this course, the student will be able to identify an agency relationship and determine the liability of the principal for the agent's acts; understand special circumstances as independent contracts, joint enterprise, ratification and the family purpose doctrine; understand various relationships, rules, and defenses which are applied in claims between principal and agent; agent and third parties, and principal and third parties in connection with contract and tort actions.

Instruction: Major topics covered in the course are creation, scope, and limitations of the agency relationship; differences between direct and vicarious liability, and agents and independent contractors; express duties of the parties and those implied by law; and ratification by the principal and how an agency is terminated. Methods of instruction include a proctored examination for students to be eligible for the credit recommendation.

Credit Recommendation: In the upper division baccalaureate degree category, 1 semester hour in Business or Commercial Law (10/91) (10/96). **NOTE:** Students will receive 3 semester hours in the upper division baccalaureate degree category, if they take this course in combination with Courses 110 and 111. This combination is equivalent to Business Law I; or taken in combination with Courses 110, 111, and 114, 4 semester hours in the upper division baccalaureate degree category in Business Law; this combination is equivalent to Business Law I, plus 1 semester hour in Business Law II; or taken in combination with Courses 111 and 112, 3 semester hours in the upper division baccalaureate degree category, in Introduction to Law of Torts I. This combination is equivalent to Law of Torts I.

Law of Automobile Insurance: First Party Coverage and No Fault (215)

Location: Independent Study.

Length: 22 hours.

Dates: May 1992-Present.

Objective: To teach students the major provisions of automobile liability and physical damage policy coverage and other applicable procedures.

Learning Outcome: Upon successful completion of this course, the student will be able to understand how courts interpret the policy to effectuate the intent of the no-fault legislation.

Instruction: Major topics covered in the course are collision, comprehensive, medical payments, and no-fault coverages; and the pertinent insuring agreements, definitions, exclusions, and conditions for each of these coverages including applicable statues and case law. Methods of instruction include a proctored examination and a graduate level project to be eligible for the credit recommendation.

Credit Recommendation: In the upper division baccalaureate degree or graduate degree category, 1 semester hour in Auto Property Insurance or Insurance elective (5/92) (10/96).

Law of Automobiles (214) (Formerly Law of Automobiles [216])

Location: Independent Study.

Length: 22 hours.

Dates: *Version 1:* July 1990-March 1992; *Version 2:* March 1992-Present.

Objective: To provide the student with the knowledge of the law of automobiles and the rights of motorists.

Learning Outcome: Upon successful completion of this course, the student will be able to apply Common Law and Statutory Law to determine the automobile liability; and have understanding of how to approach investigation and negotiation of auto claims.

Instruction: Major topics covered in the course are common law and comparative negligence principles which determine the rights of motorists; explains the rules of the road; analyzes specific conditions on public highways and private roads, and the effect of defenses such as comparative negligence and assumption or risk; and discusses new developments in the seat belt defense, dram shop, and social host liability. Methods of instruction include a proctored examination which must be administered for students to be eligible for the credit recommendation. A graduate level research project must also be submitted to receive the credit recommendation.

Credit Recommendation: In the graduate degree category, 1 semester hour in Advanced Commercial Law, Automobile Insurance, or Insurance elective (10/91) (5/92) (10/96). **NOTE:** Students will receive 3 semester hours in the upper division baccalaureate degree category, in Automobile Insurance if they take this course in combination with Courses 211 and 214. This combination is equivalent to Advanced Commercial Law.

Law of Bailments, Innkeepers, and Carriers (114)

Location: Independent Study.

Length: 14 hours.

Dates: July 1990-Present.

Objective: To enable the student to understand the rules of law applicable to situations where the personal property of one person is in the care, custody, and control of others.

Learning Outcome: Upon successful completion of this course, the student will be able to understand the Law of Bailments, explain the relationship between bailor and bailee; understand and interpret the Law of Innkeepers; and understand and be able to interpret the Law of Carriers.

Instruction: Major topics covered in the course are rules of contract law applied to claims situations where property is in care, custody, or control of others; pledges, hire of use, custody and service bailments; and duties, liabilities, rights of innkeepers, common carriers, and other classes of bailees to each other and to third persons. Methods of instruction include a proctored examination which must be administered for students to be eligible for the credit recommendation.

Credit Recommendation: In the upper division baccalaureate degree category, 1 semester hour in Business or Commercial Law (10/91) (10/96). **NOTE:** Students will receive 4 semester hours in the upper division baccalaureate degree category if they take this course in combination with Courses 110, 111, and 113. This combination is equivalent to Business Law I, plus 1 semester hour in Business Law II.

Law of Contracts (110)

Location: Independent Study.

Length: 25 hours.

Dates: July 1990-Present.

Objective: To enable the students to understand basic laws governing the obligations and rights involved in contracts.

Learning Outcome: Upon successful completion of this course, the student will be able to understand and utilize courts' decisions and statutes affecting insurance claims; effectively deal with attorneys in the negotiating and settlement of claims; interpret various types of contracts and be aware of the basic law governing obligations of a contract; knowing how and when a contract comes into existence and by what means it may be terminated; and understand the nature, effect, and use of a contract of release and examine the circumstances and conditions under which they should be used.

Instruction: Major topics covered in the course are explanations of elements necessary to all contracts, including the insurance policy contract; when and how a contract arises and is terminated; the law of beneficiary, hold-harmless, exculpatory, releases, and other contracts; and effect of judicial and statutory modifications governing the rights, obligations, and remedies of the contracting parties. Methods of instruction include a proctored examination which must be administered for students to be eligible for the credit recommendation.

Credit Recommendation: In the upper division baccalaureate degree category, 1 semester hour in Business/Commercial Law (10/91) (10/96). **NOTE:** Students will receive 3 semester hours in the upper division baccalaureate degree category if they take this course in combination with Courses 111 and 113. This combination is equivalent to Business Law I.

Law of Damages (115)

Location: Independent Study.

Length: 14 hours.

Dates: July 1990-Present.

Objective: To provide the student with an understanding of the basic types of damages and how they can be proved.

Learning Outcome: Upon successful completion of this course, the student will be able to evaluate claims efficiently and determine the nature and extent of recoverable damages; understand basic types of damages and how they can be proven; know recent changes in the law concerning the award of punitive damages, the collateral source rule and claims for loss of spousal and parent-child consortium; and examine distinctions between survival and wrongful death statutes and the types and measure of damages available through both.

Instruction: Major topics covered in the course are classifying damages, including punitives and the validity of statutory caps; plaintiff's burden to prove with certainty; mitigation of damages; recent developments in the collateral source rule on a state- by-state basis; and methods of evaluating claims and determining values including a discussion of wrongful death and survival statutes. Methods of instruction include a proctored examination that must be administered for students to be eligible for the credit recommendation.

Credit Recommendation: In the upper division baccalaureate degree category, 1 semester hour in Law of Damages, Business, Commercial Law, or Insurance elective (10/91) (10/96).

Law of Environmental Claims (221)

Location: Independent Study.

Length: 27 hours.

Dates: March 1993-Present.

Objective: To provide the student with a good working knowledge of current environmental law, both statutory and case law, and its interplay with liability and property coverage issues.

Learning Outcome: Upon successful completion of this course, the student will be able to identify environmental issues as they arise and develop effective strategies to deal with them.

Instruction: Major topics covered are the definition of pollutant and contaminant, theories of environmental liability and recoverable damages, and insurance coverage issues applicable to both liability and first party property claims; and the major components of environmental statutes such as CERCLA also known as "Superfund."

Credit Recommendation: In the graduate degree category, 2 semester hours in Environmental Law (4/93).

Law of Evidence (212)
(Formerly Law of Evidence [214])

Location: Independent Study.

Length: 22 hours.

Dates: *Version 1:* July 1990-March 1992; *Version 2:* March 1992-Present.

Objective: To provide the student with the basic understanding of the rules of evidence.

Learning Outcome: Upon successful completion of this course, the student will be able to understand the admissibility of evidence at trial by applying the basic Common Law and the Federal Rules of Evidence; and be aware of the possibilities inherent in any evidence situation.

Instruction: Major topics covered in the course are reasons for thorough investigation by discussing admissibility of evidence at trial; develops ability to analyze strength and weakness of defenses; and emphasizes Federal Rules of Evidence. Methods of instruction include a proctored examination which must be administered for students to be eligible for the credit recommendation and a graduate level research project.

Credit Recommendation: In the graduate degree category, 1 semester hour in Advanced Commercial Law, Law of Evidence, or Insurance elective (10/91) (10/96).

Law of Insurance: Automobile Liability and Uninsured Motorist (216)
(Formerly Course number 212)

Location: Independent Study.

Length: 30 hours.

Dates: *Version 1:* July 1990-March 1992; *Version 2:* March 1992-Present.

Objective: To provide the student with a working knowledge of automobile policy and uninsured motorist endorsement.

Learning Outcome: Upon successful completion of this course, the student will be able to examine automobile liability coverage and understand court interpretation of policies; and understand the issues associated with both uninsured and underinsured motorist claims, including definitions of what qualifies as a uninsured or underinsured auto, the application of the various reduction clauses, and the resolution of disputes that arise when more than one policy is available to pay the claims.

Instruction: Major topics covered in the course are automobile liability coverage; judicial definitions of insured, ownership, and use including concepts of loading, unloading, and severability of interests; considers how care, custody, control, and other exclusions have been treated in the courts; and discusses uninsured and underinsured motorists coverage, including detailed analysis of reduction and escape clauses and how they've been interpreted in the courts. Methods of instruction include a proctored examination which must be administered for students to be eligible for the credit recommendation.

Credit Recommendation: In the graduate degree category, 1 semester hour in Advanced Commercial Law, Personal Property and Liability Insurance, or Insurance elective (10/91) (5/92) (10/96). **NOTE:** Students will receive 6 semester hours in the upper division baccalaureate degree category in Personal and Liability Insurance, if they take this course in combination with Courses 210, 310, 311, and 314, or if students take this course in combination with Courses 210 and 214, they will receive 3 semester hours in the upper division baccalaureate degree category, in Automobile Insurance or Insurance elective.

Law of Insurance: General Liability (217)
Law of Insurance: General Liability (213)

Location: Independent Study.

Length: 26 hours.

Dates: *Version 1:* July 1990-March 1992; *Version 2:* March 1992-Present.

Objective: To provide the student with the knowledge of the comprehensive personal and general liability insurance policies, and the commercial general liability policy.

Learning Outcome: Upon successful completion of this course, the student will be able to analyze the court interpretation of basic general policy language affecting investigation of claims; understand varied coverage areas such as punitive damages, wrongful termination of employment and sexual misconduct, as well as other important policy exclusions, such as the intentional acts exclusion and the work product exclusions; and understand policy conditions and the duties of both insured and insurer once a loss has occurred, including the insurer's duty to investigate, defend and settle and ways to avoid allegations of bad faith.

Instruction: Major topics covered in the course are analyzing the Commercial General Liability Policy; clarifies coverage aspects of comprehensive personal and general liability policies; emphasizes duty to investigate, settle or defend; analyzes exclusions, products and completed operations, contractual liability and sistership, extra-contract, bad faith, pollution exclusion; and considers policy defenses, limits of liability, and effects of statutory regulation on underwriting intent. Methods of instruction include a proctored examination which must be administered for students to be eligible for the credit recommendation and a graduate level research project.

Credit Recommendation: In the graduate degree category, 1 semester hour in Advanced Commercial Law, Law of Insurance, General Liability, or Insurance elective (10/91) (10/96).

Law of Subrogation (116) (Formerly Subrogation, Indemnity and Contribution [116])

Location: Independent Study.
Length: 14 hours.
Dates: July 1990-Present.
Objective: To enable the student to understand the concepts of subrogation, indemnification, and contribution.

Learning Outcome: Upon successful completion of this course, the student will be able to apply the basic principles of the Law of Subrogation pertaining to loss; and to pay claims fairly and minimize the company's losses.

Instruction: Major topics covered in the course are knowledge of legal principles for recovery of claim-loss payments; explains elements of subrogation; waiver of subrogation rights; explains opportunities to share loss by way of indemnification and contribution; and specifies rules of arbitration forums. Methods of instruction include a proctored examination for students to be eligible for the credit recommendation.

Credit Recommendation: In the upper division baccalaureate degree category, 1 semester hour in Business, Commercial Law, Law of Subrogation, or Insurance elective (10/91) (10/96).

Legal Principles

Location: Independent Study.
Length: 116 hours (self-paced).
Dates: January 1981-July 1990.
Objective: To provide a general understanding of basic legal principles.

Instruction: Major topics covered in the course are the development of common law; legal principles involved in contracts, torts, agency, bailments, and damages; and the significance of subrogation, indemnity, and contribution. Case studies are used throughout to illustrate issues studied.

Credit Recommendation: In the upper division baccalaureate degree category, 3 semester hours in Legal Environment of Business or Business/Commercial Law (10/84) (3/89). **NOTE:** To be eligible for credit, student must also successfully complete the final examination under a proctor approved by the Examination Committee of the American Educational Institute.

Liability

Location: Independent Study.
Length: 194 hours (self-paced).
Dates: January 1981-July 1990.
Objective: To provide the student with an understanding of how selected legal aspects are related to liability insurance.

Instruction: Major topics covered in the course are comparative negligence, law of automobile insurance, professional liability, product liability, law of insurance, law of evidence, and pleading and practice. Case studies are used throughout to illustrate issues studied.

Credit Recommendation: In the upper division baccalaureate degree category, 3 semester hours in Advanced Commercial Law or Liability Insurance (10/84) (3/89). **NOTE:** To be eligible for credit, student must also successfully complete the final examination under a proctor approved by the Examination Committee of the American Educational Institute.

Liability Insurance Principles (210) (Formerly Introduction to Law of Insurance: First Party Coverage [211])

Location: Independent Study.
Length: *Version 1:* 22 hours; *Version 2:* 17 hours.
Dates: *Version 1:* July 1990-March 1992; *Version 2:* March 1992-Present.

Objective: *Version 1:* To provide the student with the knowledge of the basic concepts of insurance law needed to understand both first and third party coverage. *Version 2:* To give students knowledge of insurance coverage including public liability, automobile, employer's liability workers' compensation, fidelity, and surety.

Learning Outcome: *Version 1:* Upon successful completion of the course, the student will be able to analyze fundamental principles of insurance and the insurance contract to determine the coverage; understand basic concepts of insurance law for both first and third party coverages as they have been interpreted in the courts; and focus on factors common to first party coverages and study physical damage, medical payments, and no-fault coverages. *Version 2:* Upon successful completion of this course, the student will have knowledge of basic concepts of insurance law needed to understand third party coverages as they're interpreted in the courts; have a good working knowledge of liability insurance and common policy provisions; and understand the rights and duties of both the insured and insurer under a liability insurance policy.

Instruction: *Version 1:* Major topics covered in the course are the reviews of fundamental principles of insurance and the insurance contract, emphasizing the rationale of various courts deciding issues of coverage; and analyzes first party coverages including auto physical damage, medical payments and no-fault. Methods of instruction include a proctored examination which must be administered for students to be eligible for the credit recommendation. *Version 2:* Major topics covered in the course are fundamental principles of liability insurance and the insurance contract, emphasizing the rationale of various court's deciding issues of coverage, such as the insured's duty of cooperation and the insurer's duties to defend and settle; and also considers requirements of unfair claims practices statues and imposition of liability for bad faith. Methods of instruction include a proctored examination which must be administered for students to be eligible for the credit recommendation.

Credit Recommendation: *Version 1:* In the upper division baccalaureate degree category, 1 semester hour in Advanced Commercial Law, Personal Property and Liability Insurance, or Insurance elective (10/91). **NOTE:** Students will receive 6 semester hours in the upper division baccalaureate degree category in Personal Property and Liability Insurance, if they take this course in combination with Courses 212, 310, 311, 312, and 315; or if students take this course in combination with Courses 212 and 216, they will receive 3 semester hours in the upper division baccalaureate degree category, in Automobile Insurance. *Version 2:* In the graduate degree category, 1 semester hour in Liability Insurance or Insurance elective (5/92).

Loss, Adjustment, and Subrogation (312) *(Formerly Loss, Adjustment and Subrogation [313])*

Location: Independent Study.

Length: 22 hours.

Dates: *Version 1:* July 1990-March 1992; *Version 2:* March 1992-Present.

Objective: To provide the student with knowledge of the rights and responsibilities of both insured and insurer once a loss occurs.

Learning Outcome: Upon successful completion of this course, the student will be able to explain the rights and duties of insurer and insured in handling loss adjustments; understand legal interpretations of policy requirements for notice; and understand the importance of a non-waiver agreement and when it must be obtained.

Instruction: Major topics covered in the course are rights and duties of insured in handling loss adjustments; effect of waiver and estoppel, non-waiver, and reservation of rights; bad faith and punitive damages; and explains availability of subrogation and how to pursue it. Methods of instruction include a proctored examination that must be administered for students to receive credit.

Credit Recommendation: In the upper division baccalaureate degree category, 1 semester hour in Advanced Commercial Law, Loss Adjustments and Subrogation, or Insurance elective (10/91) (10/96).

Medical Malpractice (218)

Location: Independent Study.

Length: 21 hours.

Dates: May 1992-Present.

Objective: To recognize and understand theories of liability in order to investigate, negotiate, and settle medical malpractice claims.

Learning Outcome: Upon successful completion of this course, students will be able to recognize theories of liability which may be asserted against various health care providers; understand elements of those theories to develop an effective strategy for investigation, negotiation and settlement of medical malpractice claims; understand and utilize courts' decisions and statutes affecting insurance claims; and effectively consult with attorneys in the negotiation and settlement of claims.

Instruction: Major topics covered in the course are considering various health care professionals such as physicians, nurses, hospitals, nursing homes, and pharmacists; their rights and liabilities are analyzed, not only with respect to patients and customers, but also as to third parties who might be affected by their actions; the standard care is examined as to each health care provider as well as methods of proving deviation from that standard; and defenses such as statute of limitations, contributory negligence and assumption of risk, that may be raised on behalf of the medical professional. Methods of instruction include a proctored examination and a graduate level project to be eligible for the credit recommendation.

Credit Recommendation: In the upper division baccalaureate degree or graduate degree category, 1 semester hour in Insurance, Professional Liability Insurance, or Insurance elective (5/92) (10/96).

Pleadings Practice (213) *[Formerly Pleadings Practice (215)]*

Location: Independent Study.

Length: 30 hours.

Dates: *Version 1:* July 1990-March 1992; *Version 2:* March 1992-Present.

Objective: To provide the student with an understanding of pleadings, discovery, procedural rules and events at trial.

Learning Outcome: Upon successful completion of this course, the student will be able to identify the procedures and their functions involved in the litigation process, as well as various time periods within which action must be taken; and understand the jurisdictional basis for bringing actions in the state and federal courts.

Instruction: Major topics covered in the course are encouraging control of legal expenses and closer supervision of suit files through an understanding of pleadings, discovery, procedural rules and events at trial. Methods of instruction include a proctored examination which must be administered for students to be eligible for the credit recommendation and a graduate level research project.

Credit Recommendation: In the upper division baccalaureate degree or in the graduate degree category , 1 semester hour in Advanced Commercial Law, Civil Litigation, or Insurance elective (10/91) (10/96).

Practice and Procedures in Workers' Compensation (416)

Location: Independent Study.

Length: 23 hours.

Dates: July 1990-Present.

Objective: To provide the student with the understanding of how workers' compensation claims are handled from investigation through appeals.

Learning Outcome: Upon successful completion of this course, the student will be able to explain the elements of claim investigation, settlement, negotiation, and hearing procedures.

Instruction: Major topics covered in the course are hearing and filing procedures; discusses the petition and answer, including notice and statute of limitations defenses; discusses elements of claim investigation, settlement negotiations and reserving; and considers actions by and against third parties. Methods of instruction include a proctored examination and a graduate level research project.

Credit Recommendation: In the upper division baccalaureate degree or graduate degree category, 1 semester hour in Workers' Compensation Law or Insurance elective (10/91) (10/96). **NOTE:** Students will receive 3 semester hours in the graduate degree category, in Workers' Compensation Law if they take this course in combination with Courses 413 and 415.

Products Liability (220) *(Formerly Law of Products [220] and course number [218])*

Location: Independent Study.

Length: 23 hours.

Dates: *Version 1:* July 1990-March 1992; *Version 2:* March 1992-Present.

Objective: To provide the student with knowledge of the law of products as it relates to those who put defective or harmful products in the stream of commerce.

Learning Outcome: Upon successful completion of this course, the student will be able to examine common law and statutory law relating to damages arising from harmful or defective products; and know the differences in the common and statutory law approaches to the liability question.

Instruction: Major topics covered in the course are tracing development of product liability; analyzes negligence, breach of warranty and strict liability theories, including the Uniform Commercial Code and Restatement, Second, Torts, and Sec. 402-A; discusses modern theories affecting asbestos claims and market share liability; and examines defenses available; and considers opportunity for contribution and indemnity. Methods of instruction include a proctored examination which must be administered for students to be eligible for the credit recommendation and a graduate level research project.

Credit Recommendation: In the graduate degree category, 1 semester hour in Advanced Commercial Law, Law of Torts, or Insurance elective (10/91) (5/92) (10/96). **NOTE:** Students will receive 3 semester hours in the upper division baccalaureate degree category, in Law of Torts II if they take this course in combination with Courses 211 and 219.

Professional Liability (219) (Formerly Professional Liability [217])

Location: Independent Study.

Length: 31 hours.

Dates: *Version 1:* July 1990-March 1992; *Version 2:* March 1992-Present.

Objective: To provide the student with knowledge of the duties and liabilities of professionals to their patients or clients, and to third parties.

Learning Outcome: Upon successful completion of this course, the student will be able to explain duties, liabilities and defenses of those rendering professional services; and focus attention on those factors constituting negligence, giving rise to appropriate defenses, and better directing investigation to avoid unwarranted expense and unnecessary claim payments.

Instruction: *Version 1:* Major topics covered in the course are examining and explaining duties, liabilities and defenses of those rendering professional services including physicians, nurses, hospitals, nursing homes, pharmacists, attorneys, insurance agents and brokers, directors and officers, and architects and engineers; explains recent state imposed caps on recovery of pain and suffering damages in medical malpractice claims; analyzes and designates on a state-by-state basis applicable contracts, statutes and cases which may have an effect on claim evaluation. Methods of instruction include a proctored examination which must be administered for students to be eligible for the credit recommendation and submit a graduate level research project. *Version 2:* Major topics covered in the course are examining and explaining duties, liabilities and defenses of those rendering professional services including public accountants, attorneys, insurance agents and brokers, directors and officers, and architects and engineers; analyzes and designates applicable contracts, statutes and cases which may have an effect on claim evaluation. NOTE: Students are required to take a proctored examination and submit a graduate level research project.

Credit Recommendation: *Version 1:* In the graduate degree category, 1 semester hour in Advanced Commercial Law, Law of Torts, or Insurance elective (10/91). **NOTE:** Students will receive 3 semester hours in the upper division baccalaureate degree category, in Law of Torts II if they take this course in combination with Courses 210 and 218. *Version 2:* In the graduate degree category, 1 semester hour in Liability Insurance or Insurance elective (5/92).

Property

Location: Independent Study.

Length: 163 hours (self-paced).

Dates: January 1983-July 1990.

Objective: To provide the student with an understanding of how selected legal aspects are related to property insurance.

Instruction: Major topics covered in the course are the significant issues related to property insurance; property insurance; standard fire insurance; contract; loss adjustments under fire policy; arson; false swearing; extended coverage endorsement; and property insurance forms; homeowners, farmowners-ranchowners, and mobile homeowners insurance; boat-yacht insurance; commercial property; carriers, warehousemen, and other bailors; and agreements of guiding principles and subrogation. Case studies are used throughout to illustrate issues studied.

Credit Recommendation: In the upper division baccalaureate degree category, 3 semester hours in Advanced Commercial Law or Property Insurance (10/84) (3/89). **NOTE:** To be eligible for credit, student must also successfully complete the final examination under a proctor approved by the Examination Committee of the American Educational Institute.

Property Insurance Principles (310) (Formerly Property Insurance [310])

Location: Independent Study.

Length: *Version 1:* 14 hours; *Version 2:* 18 hours.

Dates: *Version 1:* July 1990-March 1992; *Version 2:* March 1992-Present.

Objective: To provide the student knowledge of the basics of property insurance.

Learning Outcome: Upon successful completion of this course, the student will be able to explain the legal rights and responsibilities of insurance agents, brokers, and adjusters in procuring and servicing property insurance; understand the meaning of insurable interest and how to recognize its importance in any investigation conducted; and have a thorough understanding of property insurance basics as a foundation for the study of specific coverages.

Instruction: Major topics covered in the course are insuring agreements, exclusions, and conditions of the insurance contract; "Insurable Interest;" responsibilities of insured, agent, broker, and company; and authority of the adjuster. Methods of instruction include a proctored examination for students to be eligible for the credit recommendation.

Credit Recommendation: In the upper division baccalaureate degree category, 1 semester hour in Advanced Commercial Law, Personal Property and Liability Insurance, or Insurance elective (10/91) (5/92) (10/96). **NOTE:** Students will receive 6 semester hours in the upper division baccalaureate degree category, in Personal Property and Liability Insurance if they take this course in combination with Courses 211, 214, 311, and 313.

Proving Fraud (512)

Location: Independent Study.

Length: 18 hours.

Dates: October 1992-Present.

Objective: To apprise the student of the various avenues available towards legal proof of fraud.

Learning Outcome: Upon successful completion of this course, the student will be able to understand the issues involved in how to prove fraud legally; and identify the relevant forms of evidence in investigating fraud claims.

Instruction: Major topics covered in the course are burden of proof, evidence of prior and subsequent incidents, constitutional issues involving the Fourth, Fifth and Sixth Amendments and the effect of original proceedings in a civil action.

Credit Recommendation: In the graduate degree category, 1 semester hour in Insurance Law: Proving Fraud (4/93).

Recognizing Fraud (510)

Location: Independent Study.

Length: 14 hours.

Dates: October 1992-Present.

Objective: To assist the student in recognizing the elements of fraud, misrepresentation, concealment, false swearing and arson and how they relate to claims.

Learning Outcome: Upon successful completion of this course, the student will be able to identify and understand fraudulent claims and begin to take the steps necessary to deal with them.

Instruction: Major topics covered in the course are the elements of fraud, misrepresentation, concealment, false swearing and arson; different types of fraud, such as padding, bogus claims and other common schemes; and resources such as fraud indicators and databases, available to assist in the identification of fraudulent claims.

Credit Recommendation: In the graduate degree category, 1 semester hour in Insurance Law: Recognizing Fraud (4/93).

Special Investigation (511)

Location: Independent Study.

Length: 18 hours.

Dates: October 1992-Present.

Objective: To examine the role of the Special Investigative Unit (SIU) in dealing with fraudulent claims.

Learning Outcome: Upon successful completion of this course, the student will be able to understand the nature and scope of the Special Investigative Unit in dealing with fraudulent claims.

Instruction: Major topics covered in the course are legal limits of the SIU investigation as it relates to undercover operations, informants, entrapment, etc.; the role of the SIU in obtaining commitment to the fraud, corroboration of the fraud and finally, confronting the insured or perpetrator to obtain the desired confession of fraud or at least, withdrawal of the claim.

Credit Recommendation: In the graduate degree category, 1 semester hour in Insurance Law: Investigating Fraudulent Claims (4/93).

The Course and Scope of Employment in Workers' Compensation (412)

Location: Independent Study.

Length: 16 hours.

Dates: July 1990-Present.

Objective: To provide the student with an understanding of when an injury or accident arises out of and in the course of employment.

Learning Outcome: Upon successful completion of this course, the student will be able to determine the compensability of a claim under Workers' Compensation Law.

Instruction: Major topics covered in this course are compensability in terms of accidents arising out of and in the course of employment; explains special rules relating to going to and coming from work and dual purpose trips; and analyzes compensability of heart attacks, stress claims and other special injuries. Methods of instruction include a proctored examination and a graduate level research project.

Credit Recommendation: In the upper division baccalaureate degree or graduate degree category, 1 semester hour in Workers' Compensation Law or Insurance elective (10/91) (10/96). **NOTE:** Students will receive 3 semester hours in the graduate degree category, in Workers' Compensation Law, if they take this course in combination with Courses 410 and 411.

The Employment Relationship in Workers' Compensation (411)

Location: Independent Study.

Length: 13 hours.

Dates: July 1990-Present.

Objective: To provide the student with an understanding of the employment relationship as the basic element of workers' compensation.

Learning Outcome: Upon successful completion of this course, the student will be able to determine which persons qualify for worker compensation benefits; and know how certain types of employees such as domestics and farm workers are treated under various state statutes.

Instruction: Major topics covered in the course are the employment relationship for workers' compensation purposes; distinguishes independent contractors and casual employees; and discusses statutory employment and loaned employees. Methods of instruction include a proctored examination and a graduate level research project.

Credit Recommendation: In the upper division baccalaureate degree or graduate degree category, 1 semester hour in Workers' Compensation Law or Insurance elective (10/91) (10/96). **NOTE:** Students will receive 3 semester hours in the graduate degree category, in Workers' Compensation Law, if they take this course in combination with Courses 410 and 412.

Tort Concepts (111)

Location: Independent Study.

Length: 19 hours.

Dates: July 1990-Present.

Objective: To provide the student with a working knowledge of the fundamental tort concepts necessary to understand and apply specific liability theories and defenses.

Learning Outcome: Upon successful completion of this course, the student will be able to describe the essential elements of tort law; and explains concepts of duty, foreseeability, proximate cause, joint tortfeasors, negligence, intent, and liability without fault in terms of common law and statutory modifications.

Instruction: Major topics covered in the course are the essential elements of tort law; and concepts of duty, foreseeability, proximate cause, joint tortfeasors, negligence, intent, and liability without fault in terms of common law and statutory modifications. Methods of instruction include a proctored examination for students to be eligible for the credit recommendation.

Credit Recommendation: In the upper division baccalaureate degree category, 1 semester hour in Business Law (10/91) (10/96). **NOTE:** Students will receive 3 semester hours in the upper division baccalaureate degree category in Business Law if they take this course in combination with Courses 110 and 113. This combination of courses is equivalent to Business Law I; or when this course is taken in combination with Courses 110, 113, and 114, students will receive 4 semester hours in the upper division baccalaureate degree category in Business Law. This combination of courses is equivalent to Business Law I, plus 1 semester hour in Business Law II; or when this course is taken in combination with Courses 112 and 113, students will receive 3 semester hours in the upper division baccalaureate degree category, in Introduction to Law of Torts I. This combination of courses is equivalent to Introduction to Law of Torts I.

Tort Theories and Defenses (112)

Location: Independent Study.

Length: 26 hours.

Dates: July 1990-Present.

Objective: To apply tort theories and defenses to specific torts.

Learning Outcome: Upon successful completion of this course, the student will be able to identify the appropriate defense for tort liability; understand theories and defenses associated with premises liability claims, emotional distress claims, prenatal torts and claims against government entities; and the law which governs a large percentage of the claims that he or she will be asked to handle.

Instruction: Major topics covered in the course are teaching through application to practical claims problems how tort concepts have evolved and been applied to create theories of liability; state-by-state analysis of premises liability and emotional distress; treats property owner's liability for criminal acts of third parties, prenatal injuries, rescue doctrine, and employment relationships; and defenses available to specific tort theories with state-by-state treatment of comparative negligence, interspousal immunity and intrafamily immunity. Methods of instruction include a proctored examination which must be administered for students to be eligible for the credit recommendation.

Credit Recommendation: In the upper division baccalaureate degree category, 1 semester hour in Business or Commercial Law (10/91) (10/96). **NOTE:** Students will receive 3 semester hours in the upper division baccalaureate degree category, if they take this course in combination with Courses 111 and 113. This combination is equivalent to Introduction to Law of Torts I.

Worker's Compensation

Location: Independent Study.

Length: 123 hours (self-paced).

Dates: January 1977-July 1990.

Objective: To provide the student with understanding of how selected legal aspects are related to workers' compensation.

Instruction: The Major topics covered in the course are the origin and development of workers' compensation; federal jurisdiction; workers' compensation and employers' liability policy; social, economic, and legislative effects; notice, statute of limitations, and other procedural matters; definitions of the essential components involved in workers' compensation (employer, employee, and injury) ; benefits; investigation; settlement; hearings; subrogation; contribution; and indemnity and reserves. Case studies are used throughout to illustrate all issues studied.

Credit Recommendation: In the upper division baccalaureate degree category or in the graduate degree category, 3 semester hours in Worker's Compensation or Social Insurance (10/84) (3/89). **NOTE:** To be eligible for credit, student must also successfully complete the final examination under a proctor approved by the Examination Committee of the American Educational Institute.

Workers' Compensation and Employers' Liability Policy (415)

Location: Independent Study.

Length: 13 hours.

Dates: July 1990-Present.

Objective: To provide the student with an understanding of the language of the terms and conditions of the Workers' Compensation and Employers' Liability Policy.

Learning Outcome: Upon successful completion of this course, the student will be able to explain the language of the Workers' Compensation and Employers' Liability Policy and its interpretation in court.

Instruction: Major topics covered in the course are the 1984 policy and how it has been interpreted in the courts; and distinguishes between Part One covering statutory compensation claims and Part Two covering common law actions. Methods of instruction include a proctored examination, and a graduate level research project.

Credit Recommendation: In the upper division baccalaureate degree or graduate degree category, 1 semester hour in Workers' Compensation Law or Insurance elective (10/91) (10/96). **NOTE:** Students will receive 3 semester hours in the graduate degree category, in Workers' Compensation Law if they take this course in combination with Courses 413 and 416.

Workers' Compensation Benefits (413)

Location: Independent Study.

Length: 22 hours.

Dates: July 1990-Present.

Objective: To provide the student with an understanding as to how workers' compensation benefits are computed.

Learning Outcome: Upon successful completion of this course, the student will be able to understand how benefits are computed, with reference to a particular workers' compensation statute, and determine the amount of workers' compensation benefits.

Instruction: Major topics covered in the course are medical, disability, and death benefits; computations of temporary and permanent disability benefits, partial, and total; and considers second injury funds, physical, and vocational rehabilitation. Methods of instruction include a proctored examination and submission of a graduate level research project.

Credit Recommendation: In the upper division baccalaureate degree or graduate degree category, 1 semester hour in Workers' Compensation Benefits or Insurance elective (10/91) (10/96). **NOTE:** Students will receive 3 semester hours in the graduate degree category, in Workers' Compensation Benefits if they take this course in combination with Courses 415 and 416.

Yacht Insurance (318) (Formerly Course 317)

Location: Independent Study.

Length: 17 hours.

Dates: *Version 1:* July 1990-March 1992; *Version 2:* March 1992-Present.

Objective: To provide the student with an understanding of laws pertaining to boat ownership and operation and the insurance policies designed to cover boats and their usage.

Learning Outcome: Upon successful completion of this course the student will be able to understand the laws surrounding boat ownership and operation and the coverages available to protect against first and third party losses through the Yacht and Boatowners policies; and explain the legal interpretation of hull and liability insuring agreements, policy conditions and exclusions.

Instruction: Major topics covered in the course are legal interpretation of hull and liability insuring agreements, policy conditions, and exclusion; compares application of common law with admiralty law concerning pleasure boat claims; and compares Yacht and Boatowners' policies. Methods of instruction include a proctored examination that must be administered for students to be eligible for credit.

Credit Recommendation: In the upper division baccalaureate degree category, 1 semester hour in Advanced Commercial Law, Yacht Insurance, or Insurance elective (10/91) (10/96).

American Health Information Management Association

The American Health Information Management Association (AHIMA) is a nonprofit membership association. Control of the association is by the membership of the association through action of the House of Delegates and of the Board of Directors of the association. The staff of the Independent Study Division, which is responsible for the administration of the Independent Study Programs, includes credentialed health information management professionals, administrative personnel, and clerical personnel. Independent Study Division personnel are full time. Instructors for all the Programs, after having been approved through Criteria for Instructors and Instructors Qualification Record for the State of Illinois, are required to complete an orientation program prepared by the American Health Information Management Association (AHIMA).

The Essentials of an Accredited Educational Program for the Medical Record Technician, established by the AHIMA Council on Accreditation in collaboration with the American Medical Association, were used to develop the Independent Study Program in Medical Record Technology. The Program has been reviewed and approved by the AHIMA Council on Accreditation (formerly Council on Education) and has been accredited by the Distance Education and Training Council (DETC). The Independent Study Program in Coding was developed to fulfill a need for alternative educational opportunities for the training of medical coders. The Independent Study Program in Coding has been reviewed and approved by the AHIMA Council on Accreditation and accredited by DETC. Each of the individual modules in the two Programs can also be enrolled in individually, along with Module 101: Introduction to Computers, in the Independent Study Modules Program. This program is primarily used by students for continuing education credits or college transfer courses.

External review and assistance in course development are available from the AHIMA Council on Accreditation, the professional staff of the AHIMA, instructors, and credentialed professionals who are subject experts.

Source of official student records: Registry of Credit Recommendations, American Council on Education, One Dupont Circle, Washington, DC 20036-1193 or Registrar, Independent Study Division, AHIMA, 919 N. Michigan, Suite 1400, Chicago, IL 60601-1683.

Additional information about the courses: College Credit Recommendation Service, American Council on Education, One Dupont Circle, Washington, DC 20036-1193.

Independent Study Module 101: Introduction to Computers

Location: Correspondence Program.

Length: 3 lessons.

Dates: December 1993-Present.

Objective: To provide the student with basic computer technology knowledge (purpose, function, utilization) in the processing and administration of healthcare information.

Learning Outcome: Upon successful completion of this course, the student will be able to understand the development of the electronic computer; identify the basic historical components of the computer system (hardware/software) and interrelationships of data and information; and understand the impact of computer technology in the healthcare field.

Instruction: Major topics covered in the course are principles and concepts underpinning computer technology, computer hardware and software, and the importance of computer systems and their impact on the healthcare industry. Methods of instruction include self-instructional lessons, exercises, and monitored examination.

Credit Recommendation: In the lower division baccalaureate/associate degree category, 1 semester hour in Introduction to Computers (12/93).

Independent Study Module 102: Human Anatomy and Physiology

Location: Correspondence Program.

Length: A 2 part course covering 13 major topics in a 73 (45 minutes each) taped lecture series.

Dates: October 1994-Present.

Objective: To provide the student with a basic understanding of the structure and function of the human body.

Learning Outcome: Upon successful completion of this course, the student will be able to identify the structures of the following organ systems; skeletal, muscular, nervous cardiovascular, immune, respiratory, digestive, urinary and endocrine; discuss the interrelationship of these systems and describe the physical mechanics for each system's overall purpose.

Instruction: Major topics covered in the course are cells and tissues, the skeletal system, the muscular system, the nervous system, the senses, the cardiovascular system, the immune system, gas exchange, the digestive system, the urinary system, acid-base balance the reproductive systems and the endocrine system. Methods of instruction include listening to 73 taped lectures prepared by an anatomy instructor, reading assignments, lecture, audio, self-tests and 10 monitored examinations.

Credit Recommendation: In the vocational certificate or lower division baccalaureate/associate degree category, 4 semester hours in Anatomy or Physiology (8/95).

Independent Study Program in Coding
Module 2: Health Record Content and Format
Module 3: Medical Terminology
Module 10: Basic Pathology of Disease Process
Module 11: International Classification of Disease 9th Edition Clinical Modification (ICD-9-CM)
Module 14: Nomenclatures, Classification Systems, and Coding for Reimbursement
Module 18: International Classification of Disease 9th Edition Clinical Modification: Beyond the Basics (ICD-9-CM)
Module 19: Common Procedural Terminology: Beyond the Basics (CPT)

Location: Correspondence Program.

Length: 63 lessons included in the following 7 modules (maximum time for completion is 24 months).

Dates: January 1993-Present.

Objective: To improve the quality of patient care through increased knowledge health information management practices and procedures, especially in the area of classification systems and coding for reimbursement.

Instruction: Major topics covered in the program are health record content and format; medical terminology; basic pathology of disease process; ICD-9-CM; nomenclatures, classification systems, and coding for reimbursement; ICD-9-CM beyond the basics; and common procedural terminology beyond the basics. Methods of instruction include self-instructional lessons, coding exercises, readings, self-test, and monitored examination.

Credit Recommendation: See credit recommendation for each individual module (12/93).

Independent Study Program in Medical Record Technology
Module 1: Orientation to the Healthcare Field
Module 2: Health Record Content and Format
Module 3: Medical Terminology
Module 4: Medical Transcription
Module 5: Numbering and Filing Systems: Indexes, Registers
Module 6: Legal Aspects of Health Information
Module 8: Health Statistics
Module 9: Medical Staff
Module 10: Basic Pathology of Disease Process
Module 11: International Classification of Disease 9th Edition Clinical Modification (ICD-9-DM)
Module 12: The Healthcare Environment
Module 13: Quality Management
Module 14: Nomenclatures, Classification Systems, and Coding for Reimbursement
Module 15: Supervisory Principles and Practice
Module 16: Management Principles and Practice
Module 17: Directed Clinical Practice
Module 20: Health Information Management Technology

Location: Correspondence Program.

Length: 95 lessons over 17 modules (maximum time for completion is 36 months).

Dates: March 1979-Present.

Objective: To improve the quality of patient care through an increased knowledge of health information management principles and practices.

Instruction: Major topics covered in the program are orientation to the healthcare field; health record content and format; medical terminology; medical transcription; numbering and filing Systems (indices, registers); legal aspects of health information; health statistics; medical staff; basic pathology of disease process; ICD-9-CM; healthcare environment; quality management; nomenclatures, classification systems, and coding for reimbursement; supervisory principles and practice; management principles and practice; directed clinical practice; and health information management technology. Methods of instruction include self-instructional lessons, exercises, readings, self-tests, and monitored examination.

Credit Recommendation: In the lower division baccalaureate/associate degree category or in the upper division baccalaureate degree category, 30-33 semester hours in Medical Record Technology (2/80) (7/86) (12/93).

Module 11: International Classification of Disease 9th Edition Clinical Modification (Formerly Nomenclature and Classification Systems)

Location: Correspondence Program.

Length: *Versions 1 and 2*: 3 lessons (Lessons 2, 3, 4). (Module 11 of a 17-module program in medical record technology). *Version 3*: 4 lessons.

Dates: *Version 1:* March 1979-May 1985; *Version 2:* June 1985-November 1993; *Version 3:* December 1993-Present.

Objective: *Version 1:* Knowledge of health record data classification systems. *Version 2:* Knowledge of nomenclature and health record classification systems and understanding of their value in health care settings. *Version 3:* To give students knowledge of the ICD-9-CM classification system including its basic characteristics, conventions, and principles.

Learning Outcome: Upon successful completion of this course, the student will be able to understand the purpose of classification and coding systems; identify the ICD-9-CM coding system; assign ICD-9-CM codes for diseases, conditions, operations, and nonsurgical procedures; and abstract, code, and sequence diagnostic information from health records using ICD-9-CM.

Instruction: Major topics covered in the course are ICD-9-CM coding principles and practice. Methods of instruction include self-instructional lessons, exercises, and monitored examination.

Credit Recommendation: *Version 1:* In the lower division baccalaureate/associate degree category or in the upper division baccalaureate degree category, 2 semester hours in Medical Record Science (2/80) (6/90). *Version 2:* In the lower division baccalaureate/associate degree category, 4 semester hours in Medical Record Classification Systems or Medical Record Science (6/85) (7/86)(6/90). *Version 3:* In the lower division baccalaureate/associate degree category or in the upper division baccalaureate degree category, 2 semester hours in Health Information Management (12/93).

Module 12: The Healthcare Environment (Formerly Federal Health Programs)

Location: Correspondence Program.

Length: 6 lessons (Module 12 of a 17-module program in medical record technology)

Dates: *Version 1:* March 1979-June 1986; *Version 2:* July 1986-November 1993; *Version 3:* December 1993-Present.

Objective: To provide an overview of the Department of Health and Human Services (DHHS), the objectives of Medicare and Medicaid programs, and the payment systems; billing processes, and data sets.

Learning Outcome: Upon successful completion of this course, the student will be able to identify and describe the function of the major operating agencies of the Department of Health and Human Services (DHHS); identify and describe the functions of medicare; discuss the impact of the prospective payment systems on the health information management department; describe the review activities conducted by peer review organizations; apply the definitions of the uniform hospital discharge data set (UHDDS); understand the content and use of the uniform bill; and describe some of the major challenges facing the healthcare delivery system and the practice of health information management.

Instruction: Major topics covered in the course are the federal government and healthcare; the prospective payment system; peer review organizations; uniform reporting; today's healthcare challenges; and the challenges and changes within the health information management profession. Methods of instruction include self-instruction with exercises, self-tests, and monitored examination.

Credit Recommendation: *Versions 1 and 2*: In the lower division baccalaureate/associate degree category or in the upper division baccalaureate degree category, 2 semester hours in Hospital Ad-ministration, Nursing Home Administra-tion, Public Health Administration, or in Programs for Physicians' Assistants (2/80) (7/86) (6/90). *Version 3*: In the lower division baccalaureate/associate degree category or in the upper division baccalaureate degree category, 2 semester hours in Health Information

Management, Healthcare Administration, or Public Health Administration (12/93).

Module 13: Quality Assurance (Formerly Medical Care Evaluation)

Location: Correspondence Program.

Length: 4 lessons (Module 13 of a 17-module program in medical record technology)

Dates: March 1979-Present.

Objective: Knowledge of the purpose and implementation of quality manager programs in the health care field.

Learning Outcome: Upon successful completion of this course, the student will be able to appreciate the evolution of quality management in health care from its multiple perspectives; perform quality assessment functions for a health care facility; perform utilization management functions for a health care facility; and understand the concept of risk management and contribute medical record technology expertise as appropriate.

Instruction: Major topics covered in the course are quality management perspective; quality assessment; utilization management; and risk management. Methods of instruction include self-instruction with exercises and monitored examination.

Credit Recommendation: In the lower division baccalaureate/associate degree category or in the upper division baccalaureate degree category, 2 semester hours in Health Care Quality Management Programs and Techniques, Introductory Medical Care Evaluation, or Peer Review in the Health Care Field (2/80) (7/86) (1/88) (6/90) (8/95). **NOTE**: This course had been reevaluated and continues to meet requirements for credit recommendations.

Module 14: Nomenclatures, Classification Systems, and Coding for Reimbursement (Formerly Trends in Health Care Delivery)

Location: Correspondence Program.

Length: 4 lessons.

Dates: *Version 1:* March 1979-November 1993; *Version 2:* December 1993-Present.

Objective: To enable the student to describe various nomenclatures and classification systems; apply ICD-9-CM and CPT rules and coding conventions to ambulatory care encounters; and understand the relationship between accurate coding and reimbursement.

Learning Outcome: Upon successful completion of this course, the student will be able to apply ICD-9-CM and CPT conventions and ambulatory care encounters; describe diagnosis related groups (DRG) and the attributes which affect DRG assignments; list the benefits and limitations of automated coding software; and describe the Healthcare Finance Adminis-tration's (HCFA) Common Procedure and Coding Systems (HCPCS).

Instruction: Major topics covered in the course are selected nomenclature and classification, HCPCS, ambulatory care coding, and using healthcare data for reimbursement. Methods of instruction include self-instruction with required exercises and readings, self-tests, and monitored examinations.

Credit Recommendation: *Version 1:* In the lower division baccalaureate/associate degree category or in the upper division baccalaureate degree category, 1-2 semester hours in Health Care Delivery Systems or Introduction to Hospital Administration (4/80) (7/86) (6/90). *Version 2:* In the lower division baccalaureate/associate degree category or in the upper division baccalaureate/associate degree category, 2 semester hours in Healthcare Classification Systems or Health Information Management (12/93).

Module 15: Supervisory Principles and Practice

Location: Correspondence Program.

Length: 3 lessons (Module 15 of a 17-module program in medical record technology)

Dates: March 1979-Present.

Objective: Knowledge and application of principles and techniques of effective supervision.

Learning Outcome: Upon successful completion of this module, the student will be able to explain the supervisory role and how the role addresses the needs of upper management and employees; discuss authority, responsibility, and leadership; discuss policies and procedures and the personnel aspects of supervision; discuss the interactive style, the hierarchy of human needs and the potential limitations imposed upon the supervisor; describe the resources the supervisor will manage; review four methods of interviewing; explain the six-step problem-solving approach; discuss supervisory problems and corresponding action; discuss orientation and ongoing training and evaluation.

Instruction: Major topics covered in the course are fundamental leadership principles and techniques for good management; also provides information on policies and procedures; the teamwork approach, 4 methods of influencing, scheduling, problem solving techniques, disciplinary actions, productivity measurement, performance valuation, and employee training techniques.

Credit Recommendation: In the lower division baccalaureate/associate degree category, 1 semester hour in Interpersonal Human Relations, Principles of Supervision and Management, or Supervisory Practices in a Health Care Setting (4/80) (7/86) (6/90) (8/95).

Module 16: Planning for Health Information Services

Location: Correspondence Program.

Length: 3 lessons (Module 16 of a 17-module program in medical record technology)

Dates: March 1979-Present.

Objective: Application of management principles and techniques to health information management services.

Instruction: Major topics covered in the course are planning techniques in designing the physical layout and workflow patterns of a department, including the department's organization, major functions, staffing requirements, recruitment sources, and kinds of intradepartmental communications. Some attention is also given to health care practitioner's role of providing consultation services to other health care facilities. Methods of instruction include self-instructional lessons with exercise and monitored examination.

Credit Recommendation: In the lower division baccalaureate/associate degree category or in the upper division baccalaureate degree category, 1 semester hour in Health Information Services, Medical Record Services, or Medical Record Personnel Supervision (4/80) (7/86) (6/90) (8/95).

Module 17: Directed Clinical Practice

Location: Correspondence Program.

Length: 11 activities divided into three parts. (Module 17 of a 17-module program in medical record technology).

Dates: March 1979-Present.

Objective: To provide an opportunity to obtain clinical practice in one or more health care facilities under the supervision of a registered record administrator or an accredited record technician.

Learning Outcome: Upon successful completion of this course, the student will be able to apply the principles of the clinical setting; understand procedures as they are performed in the clinical setting; understand employee relationships from the perspective of a supervisor; interact professionally with other practitioners in the health care field; and understand differences in services in various health care settings.

Instruction: Major topics covered in the course are health information science and health information management.

Credit Recommendation: In the lower division baccalaureate/associate degree category or in the upper division baccalaureate degree category, 4-6 semester hours in Clinical Practice in Medical Record Technology (4/80) (7/86) (6/90) (8/95).

Module 18: International Classification of Disease 9th Edition Clinical Modification: Beyond the Basics

Location: Correspondence Program.

Length: 4 lessons.

Dates: December 1993-Present.

Objective: To enable the student to explore complex coding areas including disease processes and procedures related to these areas. (Previous knowledge of ICD-9-CM coding conventions required.)

Learning Outcome: Upon successful completion of this course, the student will be able to interpret data from health documentations to identify all diagnoses and procedures that affect the in-patient stay; apply uniform hospital discharge data; set definitions to the coding process; apply knowledge of the prospective payment system to confirm DRG (diagnostic related group) assignments; optimize reimbursement processes through accurate coding and record review; and apply quality assessment techniques to coding processes.

Instruction: Major topics covered in the course are circulatory coding rules, respiratory coding rules, digestive complications and other complex coding areas, and optimizing reimbursement. Methods of instruction include self-instruction with readings, self-test, coding exercises, and monitored examinations.

Credit Recommendation: In the lower division baccalaureate/associate degree category or in the upper division baccalaureate degree category, 2 semester hours in Health Information Classification Systems or Health Information Management (ICD-9-CM) (12/93).

Module 19: Common Procedural Terminology: Beyond the Basics

Location: Correspondence Program.

Length: 4 lessons.

Dates: December 1993-Present.

Objective: To give the student an understanding of the application of CPT coding rules, physician services, and health documentation; and identify procedures performed during ambulatory care encounters.

Learning Outcome: Upon successful completion of this course, the student will be able to interpret health documentation; identify all services and procedures performed during ambulatory care encounters; apply the knowledge of CPT format, guidelines and notes to locate the correct codes for physician services; apply knowledge of the ICD-9-CM classification system to code the patients' diagnoses; and apply the knowledge of pay or reimbursement to ensure optimal reimbursement for the provider.

Instruction: Major topics covered in the course are health documentation services and procedures; CPT format, guidelines, and notes to locate the codes for physician services; ICD-9-CM classification system codes for patients' diagnoses; and pay or reimbursement requirements. Methods of instruction include self-instruction with readings, self-tests, coding exercises, and monitored examinations.

Credit Recommendation: In the lower division baccalaureate/associate degree category or in the upper division baccalaureate degree category, 2 semester hours in Health Information Classification Systems or Health Information Management (12/93).

Module 10: Basic Pathology of Disease Process

Location: Correspondence Program.

Length: 24 lessons (Module 10 of a 17-module program in medical record technology)

Dates: March 1979-Present.

Objective: Knowledge of basic pathology of disease processes.

Learning Outcome: Upon successful completion of this course, the student will be able to discuss the pathophysiology of major disease processes affecting the human body and classify diseases according to etiology.

Instruction: Major topics covered in this course are general principles of disease, diseases that affect specific organs of the body, and vocabulary. Methods of instruction include self-instruction with exercises and monitored examination.

Credit Recommendation: In the lower division baccalaureate/associate degree category or in the upper division baccalaureate degree category, 3 semester hours in introductory courses in Medical Science or Pathophysiology (2/80) (7/86) (6/90) (8/95).

Module 01: Orientation to the Healthcare Field

Location: Correspondence Program.

Length: Lessons 1-3 (Module 1 of a 17-module program in medical record technology). .

Dates: *Version 1:* March 1979-May 1985; *Version 2:* June 1985-June 1997.

Objective: *Version 1:* Knowledge of the health care field, including the history of medicine and health records, and of health care in the United States. *Version 2:* Knowledge of the health care delivery system and the role of medical record technicians.

Learning Outcome: Upon successful completion of this course, the student will be able to define the major components of the health care delivery systems; describe the content and purposes of the health record; explain the roles and responsibilities of health record practitioners in providing health information services; state the educational requirements for initial certification and continuing education of health record technicians and health record administrators; and describe the history, purpose, and organization of the American Health Information Management Association.

Instruction: *Version 1:* Overview of the history of medicine and health records from ancient times to the present; health care in the United States, including the growth, development, and role of health-related associations, organizations, and local, state, and federal agencies. Methods of instruction include self-instruction with exercises and monitored examination. *Version 2:* Overview of the health care delivery system, including health care facilities and services, practitioners, organizations and consumers, content and purposes of the medical record, and a description of American Health Information Management Association history and organization. Methods of instruction include self-instruction with exercises and monitored examination.

Credit Recommendation: *Version 1:* In the lower division baccalaureate/associate degree category or in the upper division baccalaureate degree category, 1 semester hour in Community Health, Historical Aspects of Medicine and Health Care, or Introduction to Allied Health Careers (2/80) (6/90). *Version 2:* In the lower division baccalaureate/associate degree category, 1 semester hour in Introduction to Health Care Delivery Systems or Introduction to Medical Record Tech-nology (6/85) (7/86) (6/90).

Module 02: Medical Record Content and Format

Location: Correspondence Program.

Length: 7 lessons (Module 2 of a 17-module program in medical record technology)

Dates: March 1979-Present.

Objective: Understanding of content and format of health records in various health care facilities.

Learning Outcome: Upon successful completion of this course, the student will be able to define the medical record and describe the purposes and uses of medical records; describe voluntary and mandatory requirements of selected agencies for medical records; distinguish between the various patterns of arrangement for medical record content; distinguish between quantitative and qualitative analysis; perform analyses on medical records for various types of health care facilities; describe systems for handling incomplete medical records; design forms for medical records in various types of health care facilities; describe the typical forms and content requirements for medical records in various types of health care facilities; and discuss how continuum of patient care is influenced by timely transfer of information among the various types of health care facilities.

Instruction: Major topics covered in the course are purpose of health records and regulations governing content of health records in various health care settings. Methods of instruction include self-instruction lessons with exercises and monitored examinations.

Credit Recommendation: In the lower division baccalaureate/associate degree category or in the upper division baccalaureate degree category, 3 semester hours in Hospital Administration, Medical Office Assisting, or Health Information Management (2/80) (7/86) (6/90) (8/95).

Module 03: Medical Terminology

Location: Correspondence Program.

Length: 16 lessons (Module 3 of a 17-module program in medical record technology)

Dates: March 1979-Present.

Objective: Knowledge of specialized vocabulary for reading and understanding the language of medicine and for communicating with other health care professionals.

Learning Outcome: Upon successful completion of this course, the student will be able to define medical terms related to various body systems, oncology, anesthesiology, and pharmacology.

Instruction: The module is based on a basic workbook text in medical terminology and is supplemented by 16 lessons. Methods of instruction include self-instruction with vocabulary exercises, assignments, and monitored examination.

Credit Recommendation: In the lower division baccalaureate/associate degree category or in the upper division baccalaureate degree category, 4 semester hours in Medical Terminology or other appropriate health-related programs (2/80) (7/86) (6/90) (8/95).

Module 04: Medical Transcription

Location: Correspondence Program.

Length: *Version 1:* 3 lessons (Module 4 of a 17-module program in medical record technology); *Versions 2 and 3:* 3 lessons (Module 4 of a 17-module program).

Dates: *Version 1:* March 1970-May 1985; *Version 2:* June 1985-August 1995; *Version 3:* August 1995-Present.

Objective: To prepare the student to supervise a medical transcription department. It provides an opportunity to transcribe authentic physician dictated reports so that students will gain an appreciation for the art & science of this skill. (It is not a medical transcription training program).

Learning Outcome: Upon successful completion of this course, the student will be able to define transcription and its relationship to health record and health care services; identify and describe dictation and transcription equipment, typewriters, and word processing equipment; describe legal, ethical, and confidential aspects of medical transcription; transcribe medical reports into accurate and acceptable format; and apply a work measurement and quality control system for a transcription unit.

Instruction: *Version 1:* Processing and medical reports on patient history, physicals, radiology, operations, pathology, discharge summaries, and autopsies. *Version 2:* Dictation and word processing equipment, punctuation and editing, and ethical/legal aspects of medical transcriptions. Methods of instruction include self-instruction with exercises and monitored examination. *Version 3:* Major topics include the medical transcription and the healthcare team, transcription guidelines including style, punctuation, grammar, editing rules; transcription practice and managing a medical transcription service. Methods of instruction include self-instruction with exercises, transcription practice and monitored examination.

Credit Recommendation: *Version 1:* In the lower division baccalaureate/associate degree category or in the upper division baccalaureate degree category, 2 semester hours in Medical Office Transcription, Medical Report Transcription, or Medical Secretarial Transcription (2/80) (6/90). *Version 2:* in the lower division baccalaureate/associate degree category, 3 semester hours in Medical Record Transcription or in the upper division baccalaureate degree category, 2 semester hours in Medical Record Transcription (6/85) (7/86) (6/90). *Version 3:* In the lower division baccalaureate/associate degree category 2 semester hours in Medical Record Transcription or in the upper division baccalaureate degree category 2 semester hours in Medical Record Transcription (8/95).

Module 05: Numbering and Filing Systems; Indexes, Registers

Location: Correspondence Program.

Length: 3 lessons (Module 5 of a 17-module program in medical record technology)

Dates: *Version 1:* March 1979-July 1995; *Version 2:* August 1995-Present.

Objective: Knowledge of numbering, filing, and indexing techniques commonly used in health care institutions.

Learning Outcome: Upon successful completion of this course, the student will be able to list and describe the various systems used for numbering and filing medical records; for a given situation, number and file medical records according to a designated system; describe the process of microfilming and its advantages and disadvantages; list and describe the various indexes maintained in health care facilities; for a given situation, index medical records according to a designated system; list and describe the various registers maintained in health care facilities; and perform tumor registry functions.

Instruction: Major topics covered in the course are acceptable practices in maintaining health records, including types of supplies and equipment used and the common indexes and registers used and the methods used to compile them. In addition, students complete the following practical assignments: organizing a terminal digit file; preparing papers justifying a new and/or existing numbering and filing system for a hospital health information service; practicing alphabetical and phonetical filing, completing an accession register, and thorough Tumor Registry and

Cancer Program coverage. Methods of instruction include self-instructional lessons with exercises and monitored examination.

Credit Recommendation: In the lower division baccalaureate/associate degree category or in the upper division baccalaureate degree category, 1 semester hour in Numbering and Filing Systems, Indexes, or Registers Related to Health Information (2/80) (7/86) (6/90) (8/95).

Module 06: Legal Aspects of Health Information

Location: Correspondence Program.

Length: 4 lessons (Module 6 of a 17-module program in medical record technology)

Dates: March 1979-Present.

Objective: To provide the student with a knowledge of the legal aspects of health information management.

Learning Outcome: Upon successful completion of this course, the student will be able to describe the basic components of the legal system in the United States; define terms related to legal aspects of health information; understand and be guided by the legal concept of privacy; define the requirements for who may sign consents for treatment; follow the regulations, policies, and procedures governing the release of health record information; and define statute of limitations and how it relates to record retention.

Instruction: Major topics covered in the course are an overview of the United States legal system; concepts of confidentiality, patient's rights, consents, and authorization for treatments; the health record as a legal document, release of health information; methods of retention and destruction of health records. Methods of instruction include self-instructional lessons with exercises and monitored examination.

Credit Recommendation: In the lower division baccalaureate/associate degree category or in the upper division baccalaureate degree category, 1 semester hour in Legal Aspects of Health Information Management, Public Health, or Legal Concepts for Allied Health Occupations. (2/80) (7/86) (6/90) (8/95).

Module 08: Health Statistics

Location: Correspondence Program.

Length: 5 lessons (Module 8 of a 17-module program in medical record technology)

Dates: March 1979-Present.

Objective: Knowledge and application of health statistics, and collections and graphic presentation of statistical data used in health care.

Learning Outcome: Upon successful completion of this course, the student will be able to define health statistics and identify their sources and uses; calculate basic mathematical measures of rounding, metric conversions, percentage, and central tendency; define and compute common health rates and percentages; define and compute inpatient census and related statistics; explain inpatient discharge analysis and compute average length of stay; distinguish between raw and displayed data and prepare various types of data displays.

Instruction: Major topics covered in the course are collection and display of descriptive statistical data such as average length of stay and occupancy, death, autopsy, and infection rates. Students are required to complete the following practi cal assignments: statistical calculations, census projects, discharge analysis projects, data abstracting, and graphic display. Methods of instruction include self-instruction with exercises and monitored examination.

Credit Recommendation: In the lower division baccalaureate/associate degree category or in the upper division baccalaureate degree category, 1 semester hour in Descriptive Statistical Techniques Applied to the Health Field, Health Information Statistics, or Hospital Statistics (2/80) (7/86) (6/90) (8/95).

Module 09: Medical Staff

Location: Correspondence Program.

Length: 3 lessons (Module 9 of a 17-module program in medical record technology)

Dates: March 1979-Present.

Objective: Understanding of the role of medical staff members in various health care settings and outpatient services.

Learning Outcome: Upon successful completion of this course, the student will be able to define the categories of medical staff membership and committee structure and describe the medical staff's review functions as required by the Joint Commission.

Instruction: Major topics covered in the course are organization and activities of the medical staff in the hospital; role of physicians in skilled and intermediate nursing facilities; and role of physicians in ambulatory care settings. Methods of instruction include self-instructional lessons with exercises and monitored examination.

Credit Recommendation: In the lower division baccalaureate/associate degree category or in the upper division baccalaureate degree category, 1 semester hour in Hospital Administration or Medical and Health-Related Career Programs (2/80) (7/86) (6/90) (8/95).

American Institute for Chartered Property Casualty Underwriter, Insurance Institute of America

The American Institute for Chartered Property Casualty Underwriters and the Insurance Institute of America are companion educational organizations directly supported by the property-liability insurance industry to help meet its personnel development and professional education needs.

The American Institute for Chartered Property Casualty Underwriters is responsible for administering the Chartered Property Casualty Underwriter (CPCU) Program. The Insurance Institute offers programs in general insurance, insurance claims, management studies, risk management, underwriting, loss control, insurance production, premium auditing, research and planning, insurance accounting and finance, marine insurance, automation management, reinsurance, and fidelity surety bonding. Boards of Trustees made up of representatives of all segments of the property-liability insurance community—mutual and stock companies, agency and brokerage firms, and educators—govern the Institutes.

Courses, offered throughout the United States and abroad, are of three types: (1) formal classes, which may be publicly offered on college campuses or privately conducted at insurance companies; (2) informal study groups, which may have a designated leader or shared leadership; and (3) independent study, which primarily benefits those individuals who, because of distance and time factors, choose to study at their own pace. The third type of instruction requires a high degree of self-discipline. Whether they use the formal class, the study group, or the independent study method, the Institutes supply all students with current topical outlines that list the assigned textbooks and their publishers, the weekly readings, illustrative questions applicable to each topic, and suggested study methods.

The Institutes national examinations, made up of a series of essay questions, test a candidate's ability to master a body of knowledge and to communicate it clearly to others. Most program examinations are three hours in length.

NOTE: The American Institute for Chartered Property Casualty Underwriters/Insurance Institute of America sponsors a variety of study programs with a wide range of possible combinations of individual courses from several programs. The credit recommendations which are listed below are based on independent evaluations of the programs.

Source of official student records: Registry of Credit Recommendations, American Council on Education, One Dupont Circle, Washington, DC 20036-1193 or Vice President, American Institute for Chartered Property Casualty Underwriters, Insurance Institute of America, 720 Providence Road, P.O. Box 3016, Malvern, PA 19355-0716.

Additional information about the courses: College Credit Recommendation Service, American Council on Education, One Dupont Circle, Washington, DC 20036-1193.

ACCREDITED ADVISER IN INSURANCE PROGRAM

Courses are listed in alphanumerical order, e.g., AAI 81, AAI 82, etc.

AAI 81: Foundations of Insurance Production (Formerly PRO 81 and AAI 81: Principles of Insurance Production)

Location: Various locations through formal classes, informal study groups, or independent study.

Length: 12 lessons plus additional preparation.

Dates: *Version 1:* December 1981-July 1995; *Version 2:* August 1995-Present.

Objective: To give students technical knowledge of insurance products required to meet needs of individuals for personal insurance and to provide students with an introduction to commercial insurance.

Learning Outcome: Upon successful completion of this course, the student will be able to provide professional level service to individual clients and maintain productive working relationships with insurance companies.

Instruction: Major topics covered in the course are insurance sales, exposure identification, legal liability, personal lines insurance, commercial insurance sales, package policies, property insurance, commercial general liability insurance, principles of insurance, insurance law, the sales process, personal insurance coverage, the risk management process with emphasis on exposure identification, and an introduction to commercial insurance. Methods of instruction include formal classes, small group study, independent study, and additional preparation based on the prescribed texts and study guide. Credit is contingent on passing a nationally administered three-hour essay examination.

Credit Recommendation: *Version 1:* In the upper division baccalaureate degree category, 2 semester hours in Insurance or General Business (4/87). *Version 2:* In the upper division baccalaureate degree category, 3 semester hours in Insurance or General Business (8/95).

AAI 82: Multiple-Lines Insurance Production (Formerly PRO 82)

Location: Various locations through formal classes, informal study groups, or independent study.

Length: 12 lessons plus additional preparation.

Dates: *Version 1:* May 1982-July 1995; *Version 2:* August 1995-Present.

Objective: To give students technical knowledge of commercial insurance products to meet clients' needs for commercial insurance.

Learning Outcome: Upon successful completion of this course, the student will be able to provide professional level service to commercial clients and maintain productive working relationships with insurance company staff.

Instruction: Major topics covered in the course are major commercial line insurance coverages; selling techniques successfully used by agents and brokers; the application of coverage knowledge in the sales process; account development and use of the case approach to tie together coverages and selling; the major commercial insurance products; package policies; account development; and insurance sales and coverage. Included is a case approach with four common cases applying to all commercial coverages. Methods of instruction include formal classes, small group study, independent study, and additional preparation based on the prescribed texts and study guide. Credit is contingent on passing a nationally administered three-hour essay examination.

Credit Recommendation: *Version 1:* In the upper division baccalaureate degree category, 2 semester hours in Insurance or General Business (4/87). *Version 2:* In the upper division baccalaureate degree category, 3 semester hours in Insurance or General Business (8/95).

AAI 83: Agency Operations and Sales Management (Formerly PRO 83)

Location: Various locations through formal classes, informal study groups, or independent study.

Length: 12 lessons plus additional preparation.

Dates: *Version 1:* December 1982-July 1995; *Version 2:* August 1995-Present.

Objective: To provide students with knowledge of agency operations and sales management in the insurance business.

Learning Outcome: Upon successful completion of this course, the student will be able to conduct effective operation of insurance agencies and apply sales management techniques.

Instruction: Major topics covered in the course are agency operations planning, organizing, staffing, directing, and controlling; sales management, ethics, and professionalism; agency management; financial management and other current topics; sales management; individual sales plans for producers; risk placement management; competition management; suspecting; prospecting; managerial operations affecting the sale of insurance; personal production planning; automation; and specific producer topics such as competition, time management, creating a sales proposal, how to sell to the underwriter; and approaching the prospect. Methods of instruction include formal classes, small group study, independent study, and additional preparation based on the prescribed texts and study guide. Credit is contingent on passing a nationally administered three-hour essay examination.

Credit Recommendation: *Version 1:* In the upper division baccalaureate degree category, 2 semester hours in Marketing or General Business (4/87). *Version 2:* In the upper division baccalaureate degree category, 3 semester hours in Marketing or General Business (8/95).

ASSOCIATE IN AUTOMATION MANAGEMENT PROGRAM

Courses are listed in alphanumeric order, e.g., AAM 131, AAM 132, etc.

AAM 131: Essentials of Automation

Location: Various locations through formal classes, informal study groups, or independent study.

Length: 12 lessons plus additional preparation.

Dates: December 1987-Present.

Objective: To enable students to understand computers, information systems, and selected software.

Learning Outcome: Upon successful completion of this course, the student will be able to define and use automation terms; describe automation equipment, systems, and software; and describe issues of system security and social concerns related to automation.

Instruction: Major topics covered in the course are central processing units; input and output devices; storage; large computer systems; microcomputers; communications; management information systems; programming languages; word processors; data managers; spreadsheets; graphics; and social concerns and issues. Methods of instruction include formal classes, small group study, independent study, and additional preparation based on the prescribed texts and study guide. Credit is contingent on passing a nationally administered three-hour essay examination.

Credit Recommendation: In the lower division baccalaureate/associate degree category, 2 semester hours in Business or Information Systems Management (7/90) (8/95).

AAM 132: Automation in Insurance

Location: Various locations through formal classes, informal study groups, or independent study.

Length: 12 lessons plus additional preparation.

Dates: December 1987-Present.

Objective: To enable students to understand the use of automation in the property and liability insurance industry and to provide knowledge of major automated systems in insurance companies and agencies.

Learning Outcome: Upon successful completion of this course, the student will be able to describe major automated systems used in insurance companies and agencies; explain technologies and problems involved in company/agency interface; and explain information flow between property and liability insurance organizations and related organizations.

Instruction: Major topics covered in the course are automation of insurance information; objectives of company automation; underwriting and claims; marketing; life and health insurance company automation; agency information management; interface procedures and problems; rate-making; and statistical services. Methods of instruction include formal classes, small group study, independent study, and additional preparation based on the prescribed texts and study guide. Credit is contingent on passing a nationally administered three-hour essay examination.

Credit Recommendation: In the upper division baccalaureate degree category, 2 semester hours in Business or Information Systems Management (7/90) (8/95).

AAM 133: Managing Automated Activities

Location: Various locations through formal classes, informal study groups, or independent study.

Length: 12 lessons plus additional preparation.

Dates: December 1987-Present.

Objective: To enable students to understand the methods and problems of introducing automation and the modification of automated insurance tasks.

Learning Outcome: Upon successful completion of this course, the student will be able to describe methods and problems of automation needs analysis, project management, systems analysis and design, data conversion, and management of automated systems and to analyze issues and problems in the use of automation in the property and liability insurance industry.

Instruction: Major topics covered in the course are the management process; office automation; planning automation projects; project management techniques; system design; purchasing, installation and conversion of hardware and software; and managing system growth, trends, and issues. Methods of instruction include formal classes, small group study, independent study, and additional preparation based on the prescribed texts and study guide. Credit is contingent on passing a nationally administered three-hour essay examination.

Credit Recommendation: In the upper division baccalaureate degree category, 2 semester hours in Business or Information Systems Management (7/90) (8/95).

ASSOCIATE IN CLAIMS PROGRAM

Courses are listed in alphanumeric order, e.g., AIC 31, AIC 32, etc.

AIC 31: Principles of Insurance and Property Loss Adjusting (Formerly ADJ 31)

Location: Various locations through formal classes, informal study groups, or independent study.

Length: 13 lessons plus additional preparation.

Dates: May 1967-May 1987.

Objective: To provide students with knowledge of selected basic principles of insurance and an understanding of property loss adjustment fundamentals.

Learning Outcome: Upon successful completion of this course, the student will be able to apply insurance principles to solve property loss adjustment problems.

Instruction: Major topics covered in the course are selected principles of insurance, key definitions, insurance contract analysis (including study of the various limitations on amounts of recovery under insurance contracts), fundamental procedures of property loss adjusting, investigation and reports to insurers, and estimation of building losses. Methods of instruction include formal classes, small group study, independent study, and additional preparation based on the prescribed texts and study guide. Credit is contingent on passing a nationally administered three-hour essay examination.

Credit Recommendation: In the upper division baccalaureate degree category, 3 semester hours in Business, Business Law, or Insurance (5/77) (3/82) (4/87). **NOTE:** This course was last offered during May 1987 and as of that date continued to meet the requirements for the credit recommendation.

AIC 32: Principles of Insurance and Liability Claims Adjusting (Formerly ADJ 32)

Location: Various locations through formal classes, informal study groups, or independent study.

Length: 13 lessons plus additional preparation.

Dates: May 1967-May 1987.

Objective: To provide students with knowledge of basic liability claims adjusting procedures and the human behavioral response associated with adjusting and knowledge of functional areas affecting company operations.

Learning Outcome: Upon successful completion of this course, the student will be able to initiate and complete the claims investigation process and have an understanding of its impact on company operations.

Instruction: Major topics covered in the course are the functions of the claims department, coverages, liability, claims investigation, negotiation, settlement, rehabilitation, organization of insurers, rate-making, financial structure, and insurance regulation. Methods of instruction include formal classes, small group study, independent study, and additional preparation based on the prescribed texts and study guide. Credit is contingent on passing a nationally administered three-hour essay examination.

Credit Recommendation: In the upper division baccalaureate degree category, 3 semester hours in Business, Business Law, or Insurance (5/77) (3/82) (4/87). **NOTE:** This course was last offered during May 1987 and as of that date continued to meet the requirements for the credit recommendation.

AIC 33: The Claims Environment (Formerly The Claims Person and the Public [AIC 33])

Location: Various locations through formal classes, informal study groups, or independent study.

Length: 13 lessons plus additional preparation.

Dates: *Version 1:* December 1987-November 1993; *Version 2:* December 1993-Present.

Objective: To provide students with an understanding of issues common in all property/liability insurance claims.

Learning Outcome: Upon successful completion of this course, the student will be able to understand how the claim representative's role is simultaneously determined by policyholders and other customers, the insurance policy, the insurance company and its management, and the law and appreciate the importance of good communication, negotiation skills, and the proper attitude in successful claim work.

Instruction: Major topics covered in the course are insurance and the claim representative's role; the claim representative's duties; human relations in claims; listening; communication; types of claim communications; the negotiation process; negotiation styles; bad faith excess verdicts; bad faith unfair practices; claim management; law and the legal system; and claim professionalism. Methods of instruction include formal classes, small group study, independent study, and additional preparation based on the prescribed texts and study guide. Credit is contingent on passing a nationally administered three-hour essay examination.

Credit Recommendation: *Version 1:* In the upper division baccalaureate degree category, 2 semester hours in Insurance or Business (7/90). *Version 2:* In the upper division baccalaureate degree category, 2 semester hours in Business, Insurance, or Business Law (8/95).

AIC 34: Workers' Compensation and Medical Aspects of Claims (Formerly Principles of Property and Liability Claims Adjusting [AIC 34])

Location: Various locations through formal classes, informal study groups, or independent study.

Length: 13 lessons plus additional preparation.

Dates: *Version 1:* December 1987-November 1991; *Version 2:* December 1991-Present.

Objective: *Version 1:* To enable students to understand the principles and practices of property and liability claims adjusting. *Version 2:* To provide students with a thorough knowledge of workers' compensation claims adjusting principles with a broad grounding in legal principles and medical terminology specific to this line of insurance.

Learning Outcome: *Version 1:* Upon successful completion of this course, the student will be able to understand insurance contract coverages relevant to property and liability and apply appropriate claims adjustment procedures in property and liability claims. *Version 2:* Upon successful completion of this course, the student will be able to appreciate the importance of the workers' compensation system to workers and to employers as well as the central role of claim settlements in that system, analyze compensability and benefits in given situations, evaluate the medical aspect of given injury claims, and appreciate the importance of medical knowledge and education.

Instruction: *Version 1:* Major topics covered in the course are collecting and recording information; investigations; legal liability; determination of coverage; and determination of loss value. *Version 2:* Major topics covered in the course are the role of the workers' compensation system; compensability regarding the types of employment and injuries covered; compensability arising out of and in the course of employment benefits; workers' compensation claim procedures; cost crisis in workers' compensation; anatomy and medical terminology; trauma; psychological injuries and conditions; disability; rehabilitation; evaluation of medical treatment; and medical cost control. Methods of instruction include formal classes, small group study, independent study, and additional preparation based on the prescribed texts and study guide. Credit is contingent on passing a nationally administered three-hour essay examination.

Credit Recommendation: *Version 1:* In the upper division baccalaureate degree category, 2 semester hours in Insurance or Business (7/90). *Version 2:* In the upper division baccalaureate degree category, 3 semester hours, or in the graduate degree category, 2 semester hours in Business, Insurance, or Business Law (8/95).

AIC 35: Property Loss Adjusting (Formerly Property Insurance Adjusting [ADJ 35])

Location: Various locations through formal classes, informal study groups, or independent study.

Length: 13 lessons plus additional preparation.

Dates: *Version 1:* May 1967-July 1995; *Version 2:* August 1995-Present.

Objective: To provide students with an understanding of concepts relevant to the adjustment of property losses.

Learning Outcome: Upon successful completion of this course, the student will be able to apply effective loss adjustment techniques to complex property insurance losses.

Instruction: Major topics covered in the course are apportionment of losses; insurable interest; estimating and adjusting losses (building, personal property, and merchandise); salvage; and business interruption. Methods of instruction include formal classes, small group study, independent study and additional preparation based on the prescribed texts and study guides. Credit is contingent on passing a nationally administered three-hour essay examination.

Credit Recommendation: *Version 1:* In the upper division baccalaureate degree category, 3 semester hours in Business, Business Law, or Insurance (5/77) (3/82) (4/87). *Version 2:* In the upper division baccalaureate degree category or graduate degree category, 3 semester hours in Business, Business Law, or Insurance (8/95).

AIC 36: Liability Claims Adjusting (Formerly Liability Insurance Adjusting [ADJ 36])

Location: Various locations through formal classes, informal study groups, or independent study.

Length: 13 lessons plus additional preparation.

Dates: *Version 1:* May 1967-July 1995; *Version 2:* August 1995-Present.

Objective: To provide students with an understanding of legal concepts relevant to adjustment of increasingly complex liability claims.

Learning Outcome: Upon successful completion of this course, the student will be able to initiate more complex claims investigation procedures leading to settlement.

Instruction: Major topics covered in the course are liability coverages; casualty claims practices; contract law; torts; claims evaluation; negotiations; settlement; automobile liability; and product liability. Methods of instruction include formal classes, small group study, independent study, and additional preparation based on the prescribed texts and study guide. Credit is contingent on passing a nationally administered three-hour essay examination.

Credit Recommendation: *Version 1:* In the graduate degree category, 3 semester hours in Business, Business Law, or Insurance (5/77) (3/82) (4/87). *Version 2:* In the upper division baccalaureate or graduate degree category, 3 semester hours in Business, Business Law, or Insurance (8/95).

ASSOCIATE IN FIDELITY AND SURETY BONDING PROGRAM

Courses are listed in alphanumeric order, e.g., AFSB 151, AFSB 152, etc.

AFSB 151: Principles of Suretyship

Location: Various locations through formal classes, informal study groups, or independent study.

Length: 13 lessons plus additional preparation.

Dates: January 1992-Present.

Objective: To provide students with a basic knowledge of the fidelity-surety bond industry and its practices.

Learning Outcome: Upon successful completion of this course, the student will have a basic understanding of suretyship production, underwriting, financial and credit analysis, and fidelity-surety industry practices.

Instruction: Major topics covered in the course are the types of bonds, production principles and practices, underwriting principles and practices, financial and credit analysis, bond rate-making, reinsurance, fidelity and surety claims handling, and ethical principles. Methods of instruction include formal classes, small group study, independent study, and additional preparation based on the prescribed texts and study guide. Credit is contingent on passing a nationally administered three-hour essay examination.

Credit Recommendation: In the upper division baccalaureate degree category, 3 semester hours in Business or Insurance (8/95).

AFSB 152: Contract Surety

Location: Various locations through formal classes, informal study groups, or independent study.

Length: 13 lessons plus additional preparation.

Dates: September 1992-Present.

Objective: To provide students with an in-depth knowledge of contract surety bonding.

Learning Outcome: Upon successful completion of this course, the student will be able to describe the legal framework for contract bonding, apply key production and underwriting contract-bond concepts and principles, analyze and evaluate construction contractor financial and credit information, and identify and apply contract-bond claim procedures.

Instruction: Major topics covered in the course are the types of contract-bond law, contract-bond documentation, the bid process, contract-bond underwriting, financial and credit analysis, trend analysis, financial forecasting, and contract-bond claims. Methods of instruction include formal classes, small group study, independent study, and additional preparation based on the prescribed texts and study guide. Credit is contingent on passing a nationally administered three-hour essay examination.

Credit Recommendation: In the upper division baccalaureate degree category, 4 semester hours, or in the graduate degree category, 3 semester hours in Insurance or Risk Management (8/95).

AFSB 153: Fidelity and Noncontract Surety

Location: Various locations through formal classes, informal study groups, or independent study.

Length: 13 lessons plus additional preparation.

Dates: January 1993-Present.

Objective: To provide students with an in-depth knowledge of fidelity bonding, financial institution bonding, and noncontract surety bonding.

Learning Outcome: Upon successful completion of this course, the student will be able to describe the various types of noncontract surety bonds, apply commonly accepted production and underwriting principles to specific cases, describe appropriate fidelity and crime coverages for specific exposures, and describe the exposures, coverages, forms, and standard practices associated with financial institution crime coverages.

Instruction: Major topics covered in the course are court bonds; fiduciary bonds; miscellaneous surety bonds; public official bonds; federal noncontract surety bonds; Surety Association of America fidelity, forgery, and financial institution coverage forms; ISO crime coverage forms; and fidelity claims. Methods of instruction include formal classes, small group study, independent study, and additional preparation based on the prescribed texts and study guide. Credit is contingent on passing a nationally administered three-hour essay examination.

Credit Recommendation: In the upper division baccalaureate degree category, 4 semester hours, or in the graduate degree category, 3 semester hours in Insurance or Finance (8/95).

ASSOCIATE IN INSURANCE ACCOUNTING AND FINANCE PROGRAM

Courses are listed in alphanumeric order, e.g., AIAF 111, AIAF 112, etc.

AIAF 111: Statutory Accounting for Property and Liability Insurers

Location: Various locations through formal classes, informal study groups, or independent study.

Length: 13 lessons plus additional preparation.

Dates: *Version 1:* January 1985-July 1995; *Version 2:* August 1995-Present.

Objective: To provide students with an understanding of statutory accounting requirements for property-liability insurers.

Learning Outcome: Upon successful completion of this course, the student will be able to use knowledge of statutory accounting for property-liability insurance to assemble applicable data needed for required financial statements and reports.

Instruction: Major topics covered in the course are the principles of statutory accounting (through detailed study of the NAIC Annual Statement for Property and Casualty Insurance Companies); contrasting them with generally accepted accounting principles; preparation of the Annual Statement and other required reports; aspects of statutory accounting requirements; an introduction to insurance accounting and finance; annual statement reporting; assets; liabilities and policyholders' surplus; estimated liabilities for losses and loss adjustment expenses; earned and unearned premiums; other liabilities; capital; surplus; insurance company revenues and expenses; written premiums; losses and loss adjustment expenses; investment income; other income; reinsurance accounting; and GAAP and other financial reporting requirements.

Methods of instruction include formal classes, small group study, independent study, and additional preparation based on the prescribed texts and study guide. Credit is contingent on passing a nationally administered three-hour essay examination.

Credit Recommendation: *Version 1:* In the upper division baccalaureate degree category, 2 semester hours in Accounting or Insurance (4/87). **NOTE:** Students who complete AIAF 111, 112, and 113 should receive 3 semester hours in the graduate degree category (4/87). *Version 2:* In the upper division baccalaureate degree category, 3 semester hours in Accounting or Insurance (8/95).

AIAF 112: Insurance Information Systems

Location: Various locations through formal classes, informal study groups, or independent study.

Length: 13 lessons plus additional preparation.

Dates: *Version 1:* January 1986-July 1995; *Version 2:* August 1995-Present.

Objective: To provide students with an understanding of fundamental needs, tools, and controls required for development and management of insurance information systems.

Learning Outcome: Upon successful completion of this course, the student will be able to design and effectively manage insurance information systems and coordinate needs of systems users.

Instruction: Major topics covered in the course are analyzing the recording, processing, and reporting of accounting information for insurance companies; statistical, managerial, and financial reporting requirements; the application of computers in insurance; aspects of information management systems; computers and insurance; an overview of insurance information systems; data flows and data storage; cycles (premium, loss, reserve, reinsurance, treasury investment, payroll, and nonpayroll expenditures); budgeting and planning; management reporting; statistical reporting; data integrity; system controls, and auditing. Methods of instruction include formal classes, small group study, independent study, and additional preparation based on the prescribed texts and study guide. Credit is contingent on passing a nationally administered three-hour essay examination.

Credit Recommendation: *Version 1:* In the upper division baccalaureate degree category, 2 semester hours in Insurance or Information Systems Management (4/87). **NOTE:** Students who complete AIAF 111, 112, and 113 should receive 3 semester hours in the graduate degree category. *Version 2:* In the upper division baccalaureate degree category, 3 semester hours in Insurance or Information Systems Management (8/95).

AIAF 113: Insurance Company Finance

Location: Various locations through formal classes, informal study groups, or independent study.

Length: 13 lessons plus additional preparation.

Dates: *Version 1:* September 1986-July 1995; *Version 2:* August 1995-Present.

Objective: To provide students with an understanding of basic financial management principles as applied to property-liability insurers as well as an understanding of the financial environment in which these companies operate.

Learning Outcome: Upon successful completion of this course, the student will be able to understand the application of basic financial management principles in insurance company operations.

Instruction: Major topics covered in the course are principles of finance from an insurance company's perspective; financial institutions and the larger financial environment; cash management, capital structure, taxation, financial planning, investment management, financial markets and instruments; finance in insurance, including financial systems; financial management; cash management; capital structure; insurance company income, taxation, and financial planning; the economic environment; financial markets; money markets; capital markets; investment policy; and financial analysis of insurance companies. Methods of instruction include formal classes, small group study, independent study, and additional preparation based on the prescribed texts and study guide. Credit is contingent on passing a nationally administered three-hour essay examination.

Credit Recommendation: *Version 1:* In the upper division baccalaureate degree category, 2 semester hours in Economics,

Finance, or Insurance. **NOTE:** Students who complete AIAF 111, 112, and 113 should receive 3 semester hours in the graduate degree category (4/87). *Version 2:* In the upper division baccalaureate degree category, 3 semester hours in Economics, Finance, or Insurance (8/95).

ASSOCIATE IN INSURANCE SERVICES PROGRAM

AIS 25: Delivering Insurance Services

Location: Various locations through formal classes, informal study groups, or independent study.

Length: 13 lessons plus additional preparation.

Dates: July 1994-Present.

Objective: To give employees in the insurance business an understanding of the language, tools, and concepts of total quality management.

Learning Outcome: Upon successful completion of this course, the student will be familiar with total quality management and will have had some opportunity to apply the techniques of total quality management to various aspects of the property and liability insurance business.

Instruction: Major topics covered in the course are the three primary aspects of total quality management - customer focus, process improvement, and total involvement. These areas are drawn together through the material which includes the theory of total quality management with practical applications that relate to the activities of the insurance business. Topics include insurance as a service; the history of quality; applying quality concepts; identifying the customer; understanding customer expectations; mechanisms for understanding customers; managing key processes; six steps to process improvement; measuring performance; sample applications; leadership; empowerment of the work force; and sample strategies. Methods of instruction include formal classes, small group study, independent study, and additional preparation based on the prescribed texts and study guide. Credit is contingent on passing a three-hour written examination.

Credit Recommendation: In the upper division baccalaureate degree category, 3 semester hours in Business Management or Quality Control (8/95).

ASSOCIATE IN LOSS CONTROL MANAGEMENT PROGRAM

Courses are listed in alphanumeric order, e.g. ALCM 71, ALCM 72, etc.

ALCM 71: Hazard Identification and Analysis (Formerly LCM 71)

Location: Various locations through formal classes, informal study groups, or independent study.

Length: 13 lessons plus additional preparation.

Dates: January 1979-December 1985.

Objective: To provide students with an understanding of the loss control management process. Students will know how to identify and analyze hazards and develop alternative loss control measures.

Learning Outcome: Upon successful completion of this course, the student will be able to use knowledge of hazard identification and analysis to implement loss control programs.

Instruction: The major topic covered in the course is an in-depth analysis of principles relating to the identification and control of workplace hazards with emphasis on property, accident, and health hazards.

Credit Recommendation: In the upper division baccalaureate degree category, 3 semester hours in Insurance, Risk Management, or Industrial Safety, or in the graduate degree category, 3 semester hours in Insurance, Risk Management, or Industrial Safety for completion of the two course sequence: ALCM 71 and ALCM 72 (3/82) (4/87). **NOTE:** This course was last offered during December 1985 and as of that date continued to meet the requirements for the credit recommendation.

ALCM 72: Loss Control Applications and Management (Formerly LCM 72)

Location: Various locations through formal classes, informal study groups, or independent study.

Length: 12 lessons plus additional preparation.

Dates: January 1980-May 1986.

Objective: To provide students with an understanding of loss control management processes, including selection of effective and economical controls to minimize hazards or losses resulting from hazards; implementing these controls and monitoring the results.

Learning Outcome: Upon successful completion of this course, the student will be able to apply loss control and management decision techniques to the control of losses.

Instruction: Major topics covered in the course are an application of principles taught in ALCM 71 to design integrated loss control programs for specific hazards associated with products; workers' compensation; crime; transport and cargo; general liability; and property losses. Special attention is given to problem solving and decision making techniques. Case studies are used. Methods of instruction include formal classes, small group study, independent study, and additional preparation based on the prescribed texts and study guide. Credit is contingent on passing a nationally administered three-hour essay examination.

Credit Recommendation: In the upper division baccalaureate degree category, 3 semester hours in Insurance, Risk Management, or Industrial Safety; or in the graduate degree category, 3 semester hours in Insurance, Risk Management, or Industrial Safety for completion of the two course sequence: ALCM 71 and ALCM 72 (8/82) (4/87). **NOTE:** This course was last offered during May 1986 and as of that date continued to meet the requirements for the credit recommendation.

ALCM 74: Accident Prevention

Location: Various locations through formal classes, informal study groups, or independent study.

Length: 13 lessons plus additional preparation.

Dates: December 1986-Present.

Objective: To enable students to understand the measures used for controlling accidents that cause employee injury or property damage.

Learning Outcome: Upon successful completion of this course, the student will be able to recognize and evaluate hazards that cause industrial accidents and recommend measures for reducing injuries and property damage caused by industrial accidents.

Instruction: Major topics covered in the course are causes and costs of industrial accidents; safeguards against hazards in industrial settings; and principles and practices for formulating recommendations to control hazards. Methods of instruction include formal classes, small group study, independent study, and additional preparation based on the prescribed texts and study guide. Credit is contingent on passing a nationally administered three-hour essay examination.

Credit Recommendation: In the upper division baccalaureate or graduate degree category, 3 semester hours in Insurance or Business (7/90) (8/95).

ALCM 75: Property Protection

Location: Various locations through formal classes, informal study groups, or independent study.

Length: 13 lessons plus additional preparation.

Dates: *Version 1:* May 1987-July 1995; *Version 2:* August 1995-Present.

Objective: To enable students to understand the recommendation of measures for controlling losses to property and injury to persons from fire, national perils, crime, and transportation accidents.

Learning Outcome: Upon successful completion of this course, the student will be able to recognize causes of damage to property and injury to persons, evaluate these causes of damage and injury, and recommend effective measures for reducing the severity of damage and injury.

Instruction: Major topics covered in the course are fire safety, including hazards of materials and particular occupancies; building design and indoor storage; principles of fire safety; fire detection/signaling/suppression; loss control for pressure vessels, boilers and machinery; property conservation; security management; transportation loss control; and catastrophic loss control. Methods of instruction include formal classes, small group study, independent study, and additional preparation based on the prescribed texts and study guide. Credit is contingent on passing a nationally administered three-hour essay examination.

Credit Recommendation: *Version 1:* In the upper division baccalaureate or graduate degree category, 2 semester hours in Insurance or Business (7/90). *Version 2:* In the upper division baccalaureate or graduate degree category, 3 semester hours in Insurance or Business (8/95).

ALCM 76: Occupational Health and Hygiene (Formerly Industrial and Environmental Hygiene [ALCM 76])

Location: Various locations through formal classes, informal study groups, or independent study.

Length: 13 lessons plus additional preparation.

Dates: December 1987-Present.

Objective: To enable students to understand industrial and environmental hygiene factors and their relationship to industrial accidents and environmental pollution.

Learning Outcome: Upon successful completion of this course, the student will be able to recognize industrial and environmental hazards; evaluate the causes of industrial damage, injury and environmental pollution; and to recommend effective measures for reducing the severity of damage and workplace injuries and environmental pollution.

Instruction: Major topics covered in the course are fundamental concepts of industrial hygiene and environmental protection; workplace hazards arising from biological, physical, ergonomic, and chemical stresses; hazards to the environment from various pollutants; and measures for controlling industrial and environmental hygiene hazards. Methods of instruction include formal classes, small group study, independent study, and additional preparation based on the prescribed texts and study guide. Credit is contingent on passing a nationally administered three-hour essay examination.

Credit Recommendation: In the upper division baccalaureate or graduate degree category, 3 semester hours in Insurance or Business (7/90) (8/95).

ASSOCIATE IN MANAGEMENT PROGRAM

Courses are listed in alphanumeric order, e.g. AIM 41, AIM 42, etc.

AIM 41: The Process of Management (Formerly MGT 41)

Location: Various locations through formal classes, informal study groups, or independent study.

Length: 12 lessons plus additional preparation.

Dates: December 1968-August 1992.

Objective: To provide students with knowledge of management concepts and managerial problem solving.

Learning Outcome: Upon successful completion of this course, the student will be able to apply concepts of management in solving insurance management problems.

Instruction: Major topics covered in the course are functions in the management process; organization, motivation, planning and control; and managerial analytical tools.

Credit Recommendation: In the upper division baccalaureate degree category, 3 semester hours in Business Administration or Management (5/77) (3/82) (4/87) (8/95). **NOTE:** This course was last offered during August 1992 and as of that date continued to meet the requirements for the credit recommendation.

AIM 42: Management and Human Resources (Formerly MGT 42)

Location: Various locations through formal classes, informal study groups, or independent study.

Length: 12 lessons plus additional preparation.

Dates: May 1969-August 1992.

Objective: To provide students with knowledge and understanding of human behavior in organizations.

Learning Outcome: Upon successful completion of this course, the student will be able to apply principles of human behavior to individuals and groups within an organization.

Instruction: Major topics covered in the course are organizational behavior; work groups; individual behavior; two-person work relationships; leadership; group behavior; and organizational change.

Credit Recommendation: In the upper division baccalaureate degree category, 3 semester hours in Business Administration or Management (5/77) (3/82) (4/87) (8/95). **NOTE:** This course was last offered during August 1992 and as of that date continued to meet the requirements for the credit recommendation.

AIM 43: Managerial Decision Making (Formerly MGT 43)

Location: Various locations through formal classes, informal study groups, or independent study.

Length: 12 lessons plus additional preparation.

Dates: December 1969-August 1992.

Objective: To provide students with an understanding of modern decision-making tools and techniques.

Learning Outcome: Upon successful completion of this course, the student will be able to use appropriate decision-making tools and techniques in making management decisions.

Instruction: Major topics covered in the course are a systematic framework for evaluation of decisions, sources of inaccuracy and error in decision-making, the individual human decision-making process, the organizational decision-making process, and the role of computers in that process.

Credit Recommendation: In the upper division baccalaureate degree category, 3 semester hours in Business Administration or Management (5/77) (3/82) (4/87) (8/95). **NOTE:** This course was last offered during August 1992 and as of that date continued to meet the requirements for the credit recommendation.

AIM 44: Human Resource Management (Formerly Management in a Changing World [AIM 44])

Location: Various locations through formal classes, informal study groups, or independent study.

Length: 12 lessons plus additional preparation.

Dates: *Version 1:* May 1970-August 1992; *Version 2:* September 1992-August 1995.

Objective: *Version 1:* To provide students with knowledge of management decision-making in a complex and changing world. *Version 2:* To provide students with a broad knowledge base of the functions of human resource management and its importance to the insurance organization.

Learning Outcome: *Version 1:* Upon successful completion of this course, the student will have the ability to apply management theory to business organizations in a changing world with special reference to organizational planning and control. *Version 2:* Upon successful completion of this course, students will have a thorough knowledge of techniques to manage human resources in insurance organizations.

Instruction: *Version 1:* Major topics covered in the course are organizational development, organizational systems, strategic planning, the systems approach to organizational development, performance appraisals, and stress management. *Version 2:* Major topics covered in the course are strategic human resources management, acquisition of human resources, building individual and organizational performance, performance appraisals and compensation, health and safety, and multinational human resource management. Methods of instruction include formal classes, small group study, independent study, and additional preparation based on the prescribed texts and study guide. Credit is contingent on passing a nationally administered three-hour essay examination.

Credit Recommendation: *Version 1:* In the upper division baccalaureate degree category, 3 semester hours in Business Administration or Management (5/77) (3/82) (4/87). *Version 2:* In the upper division baccalaureate degree category, 3 semester hours in Business Administration or Human Resource Management (8/95).

AIM 45: Organizational Behavior in Insurance

Location: Various locations through formal classes, informal study groups, or independent study.

Length: 12 lessons plus additional preparation.

Dates: September 1992-Present.

Objective: To provide students with the knowledge needed to understand individual, group, or organizational behavior in insurance organizations.

Learning Outcome: Upon successful completion of this course, the student will be able to identify behavior determinants and dynamics of human behavior in organizations, and be able to develop strategies to influence human behavior in insurance organizations.

Instruction: Major topics covered in the course are organizational behavior and culture, individual behavior, work group dynamics, group decision making, project management, and organizational change and development. Methods of instruction include formal classes, small group study, independent study, and additional preparation based on the prescribed texts and study guide. Credit is contingent on passing a nationally administered three-hour essay examination.

Credit Recommendation: In the upper division baccalaureate degree category, 3 semester hours in Business Administration or Management (8/95).

ASSOCIATE IN MARINE INSURANCE MANAGEMENT PROGRAM

Courses are listed in alphanumeric order, e.g., AMIM 121, AMIM 122.

AMIM 121: Ocean Marine Insurance

Location: Various locations through formal classes, informal study groups, or independent study.

Length: 12 lessons plus additional preparation.

Dates: *Version 1:* December 1988-July 1995; *Version 2:* August 1995-Present.

Objective: To enable students to understand the principles and practices of ocean marine insurance.

Learning Outcome: Upon successful completion of this course, the student will be able to identify and explain ocean marine loss exposures; analyze various ocean marine contracts; recommend appropriate insurance policies to cover ocean marine loss exposures; explain whether described losses are covered by particular ocean marine insurance policies; and describe underwriting criteria that apply to ocean marine insurance coverage.

Instruction: Major topics covered in the course are shipping fundamentals, ocean cargo insurance and underwriting, hull insurance and underwriting, protection and indemnity insurance, miscellaneous marine coverages, and yacht insurance. Methods of instruction include formal classes, small group study, independent study, and additional preparation based on the prescribed texts and study guide. Credit is contingent on passing a nationally administered three-hour essay examination.

Credit Recommendation: *Version 1:* In the upper division baccalaureate degree category, 2 semester hours in Insurance or Business, or in the graduate degree category, 3 semester hours for completing both AMIM 121 and AMIM 122 (7/90). *Version 2:* In the upper division baccalaureate degree category, 2 semester hours in Insurance, Risk Management, or Transportation Engineering (8/95).

AMIM 122: Inland Marine Insurance

Location: Various locations through formal classes, informal study groups, or independent study.

Length: 12 lessons plus additional preparation.

Dates: *Version 1:* May 1988-July 1995; *Version 2:* August 1995-Present.

Objective: To enable students to understand the principles and practices of inland marine insurance.

Learning Outcome: Upon successful completion of this course, the student will be able to identify and explain inland marine loss exposures; analyze various inland marine insurance contracts; explain whether described losses are covered by particular inland marine insurance policies; and recommend appropriate inland marine insurance policies and endorsements for covering inland marine loss exposures.

Instruction: Major topics covered in the course are transit and motor truck cargo, contractor's equipment, bailees and bailors, builder's risk and installation floaters, difference in conditions, instrumentalities of transportation and communication, dealers, miscellaneous commercial floaters, personal articles, and outboard motor coverages. Methods of instruction include formal classes, small group study, independent study, and additional preparation based on the prescribed texts and study guide. Credit is contingent on passing a nationally administered three-hour essay examination.

Credit Recommendation: *Version 1:* In the upper division baccalaureate degree category, 2 semester hours in Insurance or Business, or in the graduate degree category, 3 semester hours for completing both AMIM 121 and AMIM 122 (7/90). *Version 2:* In the upper division baccalaureate degree category, 2 semester hours in Insurance or Risk Management (8/95).

ASSOCIATE IN PERSONAL INSURANCE PROGRAM

Courses are listed in alphanumeric order, e.g., API 28, API 29, etc.

API 28: Personal Insurance: Underwriting and Marketing Practices

Location: Various locations through formal classes, informal study groups, or independent study.

Length: 12 lessons plus additional preparation.

Dates: May 1997-Present.

Objective: To provide students with a thorough understanding of personal insurance coverages, exposures, underwriting, and marketing practices.

Learning Outcome: Upon successful completion of this course, the student will be able to understand the operation of property insurance services, including products and results management and apply this understanding to customer, insurer, and regulator interactions in the personal insurance fields of property and liability coverages.

Instruction: Major topics covered in the course are insurance customer's needs and perceptions, marketing, risk assessment, personal insurance regulation, personal and premises liability coverage, auto insurance, residential property coverage, watercraft and other motor vehicles' coverage, and personal inland marine coverage. Methods of instruction include formal classes, small study groups, independent study, additional preparation based on the prescribed texts and study guide, and final examination. Credit is contingent upon passing a three-hour national essay examination.

Credit Recommendation: In the upper division baccalaureate degree category, 3 semester hours in Property Insurance or Business Administration (12/96).

API 29: Personal Insurance: Services, Management, and Issues

Location: Various locations through formal classes, informal study groups, or independent study.

Length: 11 lessons plus additional preparation.

Dates: December 1997-Present.

Objective: To provide students with a thorough understanding of personal insurance services, customer interaction, product and results management, and current societal issues involving personal insurance.

Learning Outcome: Upon successful completion of this course, the student will be able to manage portfolios of personal insurance, which include coverages for autos, residential property, and personal liability, and to satisfy customers by developing insurance products, and understand and manage insurance for profit.

Instruction: Major topics covered in the course are customer's perspective and customer relations, insurance regulation, underwriting and claims, required insurance such as auto liability, insurance sales process, developing insurance products, managing insurance for profit, rate determination including Law of large numbers. Methods of instruction include formal classes, small study groups, independent study, additional preparation based on the prescribed texts and study guide, and a final examination. Credit is contingent upon passing a three-hour national essay examination.

Credit Recommendation: In the upper division baccalaureate degree category, 3 semester hours in Property Insurance Management or Business Administration (12/96).

ASSOCIATE IN PREMIUM AUDITING PROGRAM

Courses are listed in alphanumeric order, e.g., APA 91, APA 92, etc.

APA 91: Principles of Premium Auditing

Location: Various locations through formal classes, informal study groups, or independent study.

Length: 13 lessons plus additional preparation.

Dates: *Version 1:* September 1981-July 1995; *Version 2:* August 1995-Present.

Objective: To provide students with an understanding of the premium audit function in insurance and of the process that serves as a framework for premium audits.

Learning Outcome: Upon successful completion of this course, students will have an enhanced competence in premium auditing.

Instruction: Major topics covered in the course are defining the premium auditing function; establishing its relationship to other insurance company operations and systematic development of the principles and procedures of insurance premium auditing; the nature of premium auditing; insurance company operations; underwriting; insurance law; planning premium audits; reviewing of the insured's operations; the insured's employees; evaluation of accounting systems; design of audit programs; auditing EDP accounting systems; verification and analysis; the auditor's report and communication in the premium audit. Methods of instruction include formal classes, small group study, independent study, and additional preparation based on the prescribed texts and study guide. Credit is contingent on passing a nationally administered three-hour essay examination.

Credit Recommendation: *Version 1:* In the upper division baccalaureate degree category, 2 semester hours in Accounting or Insurance (4/87). *Version 2:* In the upper division baccalaureate degree category, 3 semester hours in Accounting or Insurance (8/95).

APA 92: Premium Auditing Applications

Location: Various locations through formal classes, informal study groups or independent study.

Length: 13 lessons plus additional preparation.

Dates: *Version 1:* January 1982-July 1995; *Version 2:* August 1995-Present.

Objective: To provide students with an understanding of how premium auditing principles are used to determine premiums for specific lines of insurance.

Learning Outcome: Upon successful completion of this course, the student will be able to determine premiums accurately for various lines of insurance using accepted premium auditing principles.

Instruction: Major topics covered in the course are premium auditing determination in a wide variety of property and liability insurance contracts and application of the principles learned in APA 91 to a number of significant and complex premium auditing problems; insurance rates and premiums; workers' compensation insurance; workers' compensation premium determination; classification of workers' compensation insurance of maritime workers; general liability (coverages, premium bases, classification and audit procedures); commercial auto premium determination; truckers premium determination; garage policy premium determination; premium determination of commercial property insurance; other applications; and premium auditing careers. Methods of instruction include formal classes, small group study, independent study, and additional preparation based on the prescribed texts and study guide. Credit is contingent on passing a nationally administered three-hour essay examination.

Credit Recommendation: *Version 1:* In the upper division baccalaureate degree category, 2 semester hours in Accounting or Insurance (4/87). *Version 2:* In the upper division baccalaureate degree category, 3 semester hours in Accounting or Insurance (8/95).

ASSOCIATE IN REINSURANCE PROGRAM

Courses are listed in alphanumeric order, e.g., ARe 141, ARe 142, etc.

ARe 141: Principles of Reinsurance

Location: Various locations through formal classes, informal study groups, or independent study.

Length: 13 lessons plus additional preparation.

Dates: *Version 1:* January 1991-July 1995; *Version 2:* August 1995-Present.

Objective: To enable students to understand the principles of reinsurance and the structure and operation of the reinsurance business.

Learning Outcome: Upon successful completion of this course, the student will be able to understand the relationship between insurance and reinsurance, have a knowledge of accounting and financial analysis, and understand the financial function of reinsurance.

Instruction: Major topics covered in the course are implications for reinsurers of insurance exposures, coverages, and primary company operations; loss reserving, statutory accounting, and financial analysis. Methods of instruction include formal classes, small group study, independent study, and additional preparation based on the prescribed texts and study guide. Credit is contingent on passing a nationally administered three-hour essay examination.

Credit Recommendation: *Version 1:* In the upper division baccalaureate degree category, 2 semester hours in Insurance or Business or in the graduate degree category, 3 semester hours for completion of both ARe 141 and ARe 142 (7/90). *Version 2:* In the upper division baccalaureate degree category, 3 semester hours or in the graduate degree category, 2 semester hours in Insurance or Risk Management (8/95).

ARe 142: Reinsurance Practices

Location: Various locations through formal classes, informal study groups, or independent study.

Length: 13 lessons plus additional preparation.

Dates: *Version 1:* June 1991-July 1995; *Version 2:* August 1995-Present.

Objective: To provide students with a comprehensive understanding of reinsurance contract provisions, pricing, and reinsurance program design.

Learning Outcome: Upon successful completion of this course, the student will be able to understand reinsurance pricing, analyze clauses in reinsurance contracts, and assemble a reinsurance agreement.

Instruction: Major topics covered in the course are reinsurance contract provisions, precontract negotiations and documentation, common and negotiated reinsurance contract clauses, proportional and excess of loss contract pricing, and reinsurance program design. Methods of instruction include formal classes, small group study, independent study, and additional preparation based on the prescribed texts and study guide. Credit is contingent on passing a nationally administered three-hour essay examination.

Credit Recommendation: *Version 1:* In the upper division baccalaureate degree category, 2 semester hours in Insurance or Business or in the graduate degree category, 3 semester hours for completion of both ARe 141 and ARe 142 (7/90). *Version 2:* In the upper division baccalaureate degree category, 3 semester hours or in the graduate degree category, 2 semester hours in Insurance or Risk Management (8/95).

ASSOCIATE IN RESEARCH AND PLANNING PROGRAM

Courses are listed in alphanumeric order, e.g., ARP 101, ARP 102, etc.

ARP 101: Business Research Methods

Location: Various locations through formal classes, informal study groups, or independent study.

Length: 13 lessons plus additional preparation.

Dates: *Version 1:* September 1983-July 1995; *Version 2:* August 1995-Present.

Objective: To provide students with an understanding of methods of effective business research as they relate to property and liability insurance.

Learning Outcome: Upon successful completion of this course, the student will be able to apply research skills to property and liability issues and to translate management concerns into research questions.

Instruction: Major topics covered in the course are the elements of logical analysis and the use of research methods such as measurement, sampling, secondary research, surveys, qualitative techniques, and statistical analysis; an overview of the research process and the evaluation and reporting of results; the nature of business research; scientific thinking; logical arguments; the research process; research design; measurement; sampling; secondary data sources and survey instrument design; scaling and data collection; experimentation; simulation and qualitative research techniques; elements of analysis; statistical analysis, and research reports. Methods of instruction include formal classes, small group study, independent study, and additional preparation based on the prescribed texts and study guide. Credit is contingent on passing a nationally administered three-hour essay examination.

Credit Recommendation: *Version 1:* In the upper division baccalaureate degree category, 2 semester hours in Business Administration, Management, or Insurance (4/87). **NOTE:** Students who complete ARP 101 and 102 should receive 3 semester hours in the graduate degree category. *Version 2:* In the upper division baccalaureate degree category, 2 semester hours in Business or Insurance (8/95).

ARP 102: Strategic Management for Insurers (Formerly Strategic Planning for Insurers [ARP 102])

Location: Various locations through formal classes, informal study groups, or independent study.

Length: 13 lessons plus additional preparation.

Dates: *Version 1:* January 1984-July 1995; *Version 2:* August 1995-Present.

Objective: To provide students with an understanding of the methods of strategic planning as they relate to property and liability insurance.

Learning Outcome: Upon successful completion of this course, the student will be able to apply strategic planning tools and processes to management of property and liability insurance companies.

Instruction: Major topics covered in the course include the processes and factors involved in choosing policy directions for insurance firms including strategic planning, scanning the business, regulatory and social environments, competitive analysis, forecasting, resource assessment, market strategy, product strategy, systems development, human resource planning, aspects of planning, including corporate and social change, introduction to strategic planning, strategic decision situations, strategic plans, forecasting and corporate models, economic forecasting, assessing strengths and weaknesses, competitive positioning and market strategy, product planning and development, systems development, and human resource planning. Methods of instruction include formal classes, small group study, independent study, and additional preparation based on the prescribed texts and study guide. Credit is contingent on passing a nationally administered three-hour essay examination.

Credit Recommendation: *Version 1:* In the upper division baccalaureate degree category, 2 semester hours in Business Administration, Insurance, or Management (4/87). **NOTE:** Students who complete ARP 101 and 102 should receive 3 semester hours in the graduate degree category. *Version 2:* In the upper division baccalaureate category, 3 semester hours, or in the graduate degree category, 2 semester hours in Business or Insurance (8/95).

ASSOCIATE IN RISK MANAGEMENT PROGRAM

Courses are listed in alphanumeric order, e.g., ARM 54, ARM 55, etc.

ARM 54: Essentials of Risk Management (Formerly Structure of the Risk Management Process [RM 54])

Location: Various locations through formal classes, informal study groups, or independent study.

Length: 13 lessons plus additional preparation.

Dates: *Version 1:* May 1967-July 1995; *Version 2:* August 1995-Present.

Objective: To provide students with an understanding of exposure identification and evaluation in risk management decision-making and of the financial management foundation for choosing risk management alternatives; knowledge of business organization objectives; and general management principles.

Learning Outcome: Upon successful completion of this course, the student will be able to identify and analyze various loss and liability exposures and use forecasting techniques and cash flow analysis in making risk management decisions.

Instruction: Major topics covered in the course are procedures for identifying and analyzing property, income, liability, and personal loss exposures; characteristics of risk control and risk financing techniques; guidelines for selecting appropriate risk management techniques; and the contribution of proper risk management to an organization's profits and productivity. Methods of instruction include formal classes, small group study, independent study, and additional preparation based on the prescribed texts and study guide. Credit is contingent on passing a nationally administered three-hour essay examination.

Credit Recommendation: *Version 1:* In the graduate degree category, 3 semester hours in Business Administration, Insurance, or Risk Management (5/77) (3/82) (4/87). *Version 2:* In the upper division baccalaureate or in the graduate degree category, 3 semester hours in Business Administration, Insurance, Management, or Risk Management (8/95).

ARM 55: Essentials of Risk Control (Formerly Risk Control [RM 55])

Location: Various locations through formal classes, informal study groups, or independent study.

Length: 12 lessons plus additional preparation.

Dates: *Version 1:* May 1967-July 1995; *Version 2:* August 1995-Present.

Objective: To provide students with knowledge of risk control techniques that reduce the frequency and severity of accidental losses.

Learning Outcome: Upon successful completion of this course, the student will be able to use appropriate risk control techniques in dealing with risk management problems.

Instruction: Major topics covered in the course are guidelines for selecting risk management techniques, appropriate employment and administration of risk control techniques, and coordination of the total risk management effort. Methods of instruction include formal classes, small group study, independent study, and additional preparation based on the prescribed texts and study guide. Credit is contingent on passing a nationally administered three-hour essay examination.

Credit Recommendation: *Version 1:* In the graduate degree category, 3 semester hours in Business Administration, Insurance, or Risk Management (5/77) (3/82) (4/87). *Version 2:* In the upper division baccalaureate or graduate degree category, 3 semester hours in Business Administration, Insurance, Management, or Risk Management (8/95).

ARM 56: Essentials of Risk Financing (Formerly Risk Financing [RM 56])

Location: Various locations through formal classes, informal study groups, or independent study.

Length: 12 lessons plus additional preparation.

Dates: *Version 1:* December 1973-July 1995; *Version 2:* August 1995-Present.

Objective: To provide students with knowledge of risk financing techniques leading to minimization of financial consequences of losses and claims.

Learning Outcome: Upon successful completion of this course, the student will be able to formulate procedures leading to minimization of financial consequences of losses and claims.

Instruction: Major topics covered in the course are risk financing techniques; financing property, liability, and personal losses; accounting and tax aspects of accidental losses; risk retention; pricing; selection of insurers; and allocating costs. Methods of instruction include formal classes, small group study, independent study, and additional preparation based on the prescribed texts and study guide. Credit is contingent on passing a nationally administered three-hour essay examination.

Credit Recommendation: *Version 1:* In the graduate degree category, 3 semester hours in Business Administration, Insurance, Management, or Risk Management (5/77) (3/82) (4/87). *Version 2:* In the upper division baccalaureate or in the graduate degree category, 3 semester hours in

Business Administration, Insurance, Management, or Risk Management (8/95).

ASSOCIATE IN SURPLUS LINES PROGRAM

Courses are in alphanumeric order, e.g., ASLI 161, ASLI 162, etc.

ASLI 161: Surplus Lines Insurance Principles and Issues

Location: Various locations.

Length: 10 lessons plus additional preparation.

Dates: December 1996-Present.

Objective: To enable students to understand the principles of property and liability insurance provided by insurance companies not licensed in the state of the customer (surplus lines insurance).

Learning Outcome: Upon successful completion of this course, the student will be able to explain and apply the principles of non-admitted (surplus lines) insurance coverage, including its regulation, reinsurance, financial analysis of insurers, and its marketing.

Instruction: Major topics covered in the course are the evolution of the industry, insurance regulation, distribution systems, reinsurance, financial analysis of insurers, insurance cycles, and surplus lines marketing. Methods of instruction include formal classes, small study groups, independent study, and a final examination. Credit is contingent upon passing a three-hour national essay examination.

Credit Recommendation: In the upper division baccalaureate degree category, 2 semester hours in Property Insurance or Business Administration (12/96).

ASLI 162: Surplus Lines Insurance Practices

Location: Various locations.

Length: 10 lessons.

Dates: May 1997-Present.

Objective: To enable students to understand the marketing and underwriting of property-liability insurance from non-admitted insurers (surplus lines insurers).

Learning Outcome: Upon successful completion of this course, the student will be able to describe and perform the development, marketing, and underwriting of surplus lines products, such as catastrophic reinsurance.

Instruction: Major topics covered in the course are customer's insurance regulation, marketing issues, risk financing alternatives, retailers and the surplus lines market, solvency records, financial analysis of insurers, the property and casualty insurance cycle, and surplus lines intermediaries. Methods of instruction include formal classes, small study groups, independent study, and a final examination. Credit is contingent upon passing a three-hour national essay examination.

Credit Recommendation: In the upper division baccalaureate degree category, 2 semester hours in Property Insurance, Marketing, or Business Administration (12/96).

ASSOCIATE IN UNDERWRITING PROGRAM

Courses are listed in alphanumeric order, e.g., AU 61, AU 62, etc.

AU 61: Principles of Property and Liability Underwriting (Formerly UND 61)

Location: Various locations through formal classes, informal study groups, or independent study.

Length: 13 lessons plus additional preparation

Dates: *Version 1:* January 1977-March 1987; *Version 2:* April 1987-July 1995; *Version 3:* August 1995-Present.

Objective: To enable students to understand principles, tools, and techniques of property and liability underwriting.

Learning Outcome: Upon successful completion of this course, the student will be able to make appropriate property and liability underwriting decisions.

Instruction: Major topics covered in the course are the underwriting function and decision-making process with special attention to coverage analysis, loss control, reinsurance for underwriters, numerical tools, pricing, information/financial analysis, decision making and monitoring, and communications. Case studies are used. Methods of instruction include formal classes, small group study, independent study, and additional preparation based on the prescribed texts and study guide. Credit is contingent on passing a nationally administered three-hour essay examination.

Credit Recommendation: *Version 1:* In the upper division baccalaureate degree category, 3 semester hours in Business Administration or Insurance (5/77) (3/82). *Version 2:* In the upper division baccalaureate degree category, 3 semester hours in Business Administration or Insurance. AU 61, AU 62, AU 63, and AU 64 together carry an upper division baccalaureate degree recommendation of 6 semester hours or a graduate degree recommendation of 3 semester hours (4/87). *Version 3:* In the upper division baccalaureate degree category, 3 semester hours in Business Administration or Insurance (8/95).

AU 62: Personal Lines Underwriting (Formerly UND 62)

Location: Various locations through formal classes, informal study groups, or independent study.

Length: 13 lessons plus additional preparation.

Dates: *Version 1:* September 1977-March 1987; *Version 2:* April 1987-December 1994.

Objective: To enable students to identify, describe, and evaluate factors to consider in underwriting personal lines insurance.

Learning Outcome: Upon successful completion of this course, the student will be able to make appropriate personal lines underwriting decisions.

Instruction: Major topics covered in the course are the nature of personal lines insurance; understanding automobile, residential, farm, ranch, personal inland marine, pleasure boat, and personal liability insurance; electronic data processing; and account underwriting. Case studies are used. Methods of instruction include formal classes, small group study, independent study, and additional preparation based on the prescribed texts and study guide. Credit is contingent on passing a nationally administered three-hour essay examination.

Credit Recommendation: *Version 1:* In the upper division baccalaureate degree category, 2 semester hours in Business Administration or Insurance (5/77). *Version 2:* In the upper division baccalaureate degree category, 2 semester hours in Business Administration or Insurance. Students should receive a maximum of 3 semester hours at the upper division baccalaureate level for any combination of AU 62, AU 63, and AU 64 (9/87). AU 61, AU 62, AU 63, and AU 64 together carry an upper division baccalaureate recommendation of 6 semester hours or a graduate recommendation of 3 semester hours (4/87) (8/95).

AU 63: Commercial Liability Underwriting (Formerly UND 63)

Location: Various locations through formal classes, informal study groups, or independent study.

Length: 13 lessons plus additional preparation.

Dates: *Version 1:* September 1978-February 1982; *Version 2:* March 1982-July 1995; *Version 3:* August 1995-December 1995.

Objective: To enable students to identify, describe, and evaluate factors to consider in underwriting commercial liability insurance.

Learning Outcome: Upon successful completion of this course, the student will be able to make appropriate commercial liability underwriting decisions.

Instruction: Major topics covered in the course are legal foundations of liability; underwriting the commercial enterprise (commercial auto liability, general liability, product liability, workers' compensation); medical, professional, and special liability insurance; surety bonds; and account underwriting. Case studies are used. Methods of instruction include formal classes, small group study, independent study, and additional preparation based on the prescribed texts and study guide. Credit is contingent on passing a nationally administered three-hour examination.

Credit Recommendation: *Version 1:* In the upper division baccalaureate degree category, 3 semester hours in Insurance (7/79). *Version 2:* In the upper division baccalaureate degree category, 3 semester hours in Business Administration or Insurance. Students should receive a maximum of 3 semester hours at the upper division baccalaureate degree level for any combination of AU 62, AU 63, and AU 64. AU 61, AU 62, AU 63, and AU 64 together carry an upper division baccalaureate recommendation of 6 semester hours or a graduate recommendation of 3 semester hours (4/87). *Version 3:* In the upper division baccalaureate degree category, 3 semester hours in Insurance or Business Administration (8/95).

AU 64: Commercial Property and Multiple-Lines Underwriting (Formerly UND 64)

Location: Various locations through formal classes, informal study groups, or independent study.

Length: 13 lessons plus additional preparation.

Dates: *Version 1:* January 1979-March 1987; *Version 2:* April 1987-July 1995; *Version 3:* August 1995-December 1995.

Objective: To enable students to understand the basic information and the decision-making process involved in making underwriting decisions for commercial property and commercial multiple-lines insurance.

Learning Outcome: Upon successful completion of this course, students will effectively be able to use knowledge of commercial property and commercial multiple-lines underwriting to make appropriate underwriting decisions.

Instruction: Major topics covered in the course are applications of the underwriting process to commercial property and multiple-lines risks, with emphasis on analyzing frequency and severity of fire and other perils, construction, occupancy hazards and controls, indirect loss exposures, marine risks, crime insurance, and package policies. Methods of instruction include formal classes, small group study, independent study, and additional preparation based on the prescribed texts and study guide. Credit is contingent on passing a nationally administered three-hour essay examination.

Credit Recommendation: *Version 1:* In the upper division baccalaureate degree category, 2 semester hours in Business Administration (7/79) (3/82). *Version 2:* In the upper division baccalaureate degree category, 2 semester hours in Business Administration or Insurance. Students should receive a maximum of 3 semester hours at the upper division baccalaureate level for any combination of AU 62, AU 63, and AU 64. AU 61, AU 62, AU 63, and AU 64 together carry an upper division baccalaureate recommendation of 6 semester hours or a graduate recommendation of 3 semester hours. *Version 3:* In the upper division baccalaureate degree category, 3 semester hours in Business Administration (8/95).

AU 65: Commercial Underwriting: Principles and Property

Location: Various locations through formal classes, informal study groups, or independent study.

Length: 13 lessons plus additional preparation.

Dates: May 1996-Present.

Objective: To enable students to understand advanced underwriting principles and to help them evaluate factors to apply in underwriting commercial property insurance.

Learning Outcome: Upon successful completion of this course, the student will be able to understand advanced underwriting principles and make appropriate commercial underwriting decisions.

Instruction: Major topics covered in the course are the fundamentals of underwriting, the commercial organization, analysis of underwriting information, pricing, and coverage analysis. Content covered in the commercial portion includes construction, occupancy, protection and exposure, underwriting direct and indirect exposures, crime, and miscellaneous property. Methods of instruction include formal classes, small group study, independent study, and additional preparation based on the prescribed texts and study guide. Credit is contingent on passing a nationally administered three-hour essay examination.

Credit Recommendation: In the upper division baccalaureate degree category, 4 semester hours, or in the graduate degree category, 3 semester hours in Finance, Risk Management, or Property-Liability Insurance (8/95).

AU 66: Commercial Underwriting: Liability and Advanced Techniques

Location: Various locations through formal classes, informal study groups, or independent study.

Length: 13 lessons plus additional preparation.

Dates: May 1996-Present.

Objective: To enable students to understand advanced underwriting techniques and to help them evaluate factors to apply in underwriting commercial liability insurance.

Learning Outcome: Upon successful completion of this course, the student will be able to make appropriate commercial liability underwriting decisions and have an understanding of advanced underwriting topics.

Instruction: Major topics covered in the course are the legal foundations of liability; commercial auto, general liability, and workers' compensation. The advanced underwriting portion includes communication, reinsurance, quantitative tools, a case study, and current underwriting issues. Methods of instruction include formal classes, small group study, independent study, and additional preparation based on the prescribed texts and study guide. Credit is contingent on passing a nationally administered three-hour essay examination.

Credit Recommendation: In the upper division baccalaureate degree category, 4 semester hours, or in the graduate degree category, 3 semester hours in Finance,

Risk Management, or Property-Liability Insurance (8/95).

BUSINESS WRITING PROGRAM

Writing at Work: A Course for Insurance Personnel

Location: Various locations through formal classes, informal study groups, or independent study.

Length: 10 lessons plus additional preparation.

Dates: September 1993-Present.

Objective: To teach students the skills necessary for professional writing and to ensure that each student's writing skills improve.

Learning Outcome: Upon successful completion of this course, the student will be able to write clear and concise insurance-related memos, letters, and reports.

Instruction: Major topics covered in the course are the improvement of writing skills; critical reading and writing, including exercises in both and a discussion of how students can learn to read their own writing critically; a detailed discussion of the writing process with effective strategies for prewriting, drafting, and rewriting; practical discussions of common grammatical problems including the rules for writing complete sentences, using the parts of speech correctly, and a brief discussion of how language changes and the role the insurance industry played in one of those changes; the five decisions every business writer must make - pertaining to subject, purpose, audience, organization, and tone - before beginning to write; business writing style with such topics as readability, brevity, clarity, and obsolete and archaic language; lists of commonly misused, confused, and misspelled words; and how to apply the principles they have learned to memos, letters, and reports that must be written in their jobs. Each assignment contains examples from actual property-casualty insurance documents that illustrate pertinent principles. Methods of instruction include formal classes, small group study, independent study, and additional preparation based on the prescribed texts and study guide. Credit is contingent on passing the ten assignments.

Credit Recommendation: In the lower division baccalaureate/associate degree category, 2 semester hours in Business Writing (8/95).

CHARTERED PROPERTY CASUALTY UNDERWRITER PROGRAM

Students who satisfactorily complete all ten national examinations and meet the ethical and experience requirements are awarded the Chartered Property Casualty Underwriter professional designation. Prior to 1978, this program was composed of five parts (indicated by roman numerals) which are herein listed after the currently offered ten parts.

CPCU 01: Ethics, Insurance Perspectives, and Insurance Contract Analysis (Formerly CPCU 1-Principles of Risk Management and Insurance)

Location: Various locations through formal classes, informal study groups, or independent study.

Length: 15 lessons plus additional preparation.

Dates: *Version 1:* September 1978-August 1992; *Version 2:* September 1992-Present.

Objective: *Version 1:* To introduce students to the basic concepts of risk management and insurance. *Version 2:* To provide students with a sound understanding of ethics and professionalism in property-liability insurance; to examine insurance from evolutionary, risk management and regulatory perspectives; and to develop the ability to analyze and interpret property and liability insurance contracts in depth, taking into account not only the contract language but also legal principles and environmental factors outside the written contract.

Learning Outcome: *Version 1:* Upon successful completion of this course, the student will be able to understand the theories of risk management, the basic application of insurance coverages, and how insurance policies are interpreted. *Version 2:* Upon successful completion of this course, students will have demonstrated their ability to apply the Code of Professional Ethics in evaluating practical ethical situations; evaluate and apply both written contract language and unwritten principles in determining coverage, values, and amounts of recovery in practical case situations; and explain regulatory, risk management and evolutionary principles underlying the application of insurance in modern society.

Instruction: *Version 1:* Major topics covered in the course are risk management concepts; measurement and treatment of loss exposures; insurance and society; and related legal concepts such as indemnity and insurable interests; tort law; and fundamentals of insurance contracts. *Version 2:* Major topics covered in the course are professionalism and ethics both alone and within various contexts throughout the course, as well as an in-depth study of the Code of Professional Ethics; a survey of the historical evolution of insurance (with emphasis on U.S. insurance regulation): insurance as a risk management tool; and the regulation of insurance. Two-thirds of the course covers insurance contract analysis, beginning with the legal nature of insurance contracts and the structure of an insurance policy and how to read it, and continuing with a detailed analysis of insurable interests and insured parties; common insurance policy provisions; insured events; policy limits and loss valuation provisions; deductibles, coinsurance and related concepts; other insurance and other sources of recovery; and external factors affecting insurance policy analysis. The analysis of both personal lines and commercial lines, and both property and liability policies are discussed in depth, with comparisons to life and health insurance where appropriate. Methods of instruction include formal classes, small group study, independent study, and additional preparation based on the prescribed texts and study guide. Credit is contingent on passing a nationally administered three-hour essay examination.

Credit Recommendation: *Version 1:* In the upper division baccalaureate degree category, 3 semester hours in Insurance or Risk Management (7/79). **NOTE:** If students have completed both this course and CPCU 2-Personal Risk Management and Insurance, they should be granted 3 semester hours of graduate credit in Insurance or Risk Management. *Version 2:* In the upper division baccalaureate degree category, 3 semester hours or in the graduate degree category, 1 semester hour in Insurance Contract Analysis, Property-Liability Insurance, or Risk Management (8/95).

CPCU 02: Personal Insurance and Risk Management (Formerly CPCU 2-Personal Risk Management and Insurance)

Location: Various locations through formal classes, informal study groups, or independent study.

Length: 15 lessons plus additional preparation.

Dates: *Version 1:* January 1979-July 1995; *Version 2:* August 1995-Present.

Objective: To provide students with the ability to apply risk management techniques and insurance concepts to personal loss exposures.

Learning Outcome: Upon successful completion of this course, the student will be able to review the personal loss exposures of individuals and families and be able to make recommendations through risk management techniques and insurance coverages for dealing with personal loss exposures.

Instruction: Major topics covered in the course are the nature of various personal loss exposures and the risk management process as they apply to individuals and families; personal property and liability coverages including homeowners insurance and automobile coverages; personal financial planning; life and health insurance coverages; investment planning, retirement planning, estate planning, and business continuation planning. Methods of instruction include formal classes, small group study, independent study, and additional preparation based on the prescribed texts and study guide. Credit is contingent on passing a nationally administered three-hour essay examination.

Credit Recommendation: *Version 1:* In the upper division baccalaureate degree category, 3 semester hours in Insurance or Risk Management (7/79). **NOTE:** If students have completed both this course and CPCU 1-Principles of Risk Management and Insurance, they should be granted 3 semester hours of graduate credit in Insurance or Risk Management. *Version 2:* In the upper division baccalaureate degree category or graduate degree category, 3 semester hours in Insurance or Risk Management (8/95).

CPCU 03: Commercial Property Insurance and Risk Management (Formerly CPCU 3-Commercial Property Risk Management and Insurance)

Location: Various locations through formal classes, informal study groups, or independent study.

Length: 15 lessons plus additional preparation.

Dates: *Version 1:* September 1978-July 1995; *Version 2:* August 1995-Present.

Objective: To provide students with a detailed understanding of commercial property loss exposures and insurance coverages, along with some noninsurance alternatives.

Learning Outcome: Upon successful completion of this course, the student will be able to review commercial property loss exposures and make recommendations through risk management techniques and insurance coverages for dealing with commercial property loss exposures.

Instruction: Major topics covered in the course are the major property insurance policies and coverage forms available to businesses, institutions, and other organizations for dealing with property loss exposures, inland marine, ocean cargo, boiler and machinery, and some miscellaneous exposures. Methods of instruction include formal classes, small group study, independent study, and additional preparation based on the prescribed texts and study guide. Credit is contingent on passing a nationally administered three-hour essay examination.

Credit Recommendation: *Version 1:* In the upper division baccalaureate degree category, 3 semester hours in Insurance or Risk Management (7/79). **NOTE:** A total of 3 semester hours of graduate credit should be granted when both this course and CPCU 4-Commercial Liability Risk Management and Insurance have been completed, but only if CPCU 1-Principles of Risk Management and Insurance and CPCU 2-Personal Risk Management and Insurance have also been completed. *Version 2:* In the upper division baccalaureate degree category or the graduate degree category, 3 semester hours in Insurance or Risk Management (8/95).

CPCU 04: Commercial Liability Insurance and Risk Management (Formerly CPCU 4-Commercial Liability Risk Management and Insurance)

Location: Various locations through formal classes, informal study groups, or independent study.

Length: 15 lessons plus additional preparation.

Dates: *Version 1:* January 1979-July 1995; *Version 2:* August 1995-Present.

Objective: To provide students with a detailed understanding of commercial liability loss exposures, along with the insurance and noninsurance techniques to deal with commercial liability loss exposures.

Learning Outcome: Upon successful completion of this course, the student will be able to review commercial liability loss exposures and make recommendations through risk management techniques and insurance coverages for dealing with commercial liability loss exposures.

Instruction: Major topics covered in the course are the concept of legal liability; liability loss control; general liability insurance; marine hull and liability insurance; aviation insurance; worker's compensation insurance; professional liability insurance; surety; excess insurance; and alternative risk financing methods. Methods of instruction include formal classes, small group study, independent study, and additional preparation based on the prescribed texts and study guide. Credit is contingent on passing a nationally administered three-hour essay examination.

Credit Recommendation: *Version 1:* In the upper division baccalaureate degree category, 3 semester hours in Insurance or Risk Management (7/79). **NOTE:** A total of 3 semester hours of graduate credit should be granted when both this course and CPCU 3-Commercial Property Risk Management and Insurance have been completed, but only if CPCU 1-Principles of Risk Management and Insurance and CPCU 2-Personal Risk Management and Insurance have also been completed. *Version 2:* In the upper division baccalaureate degree category or in the graduate degree category, 3 semester hours in Insurance or Risk Management (8/95).

CPCU 05: Insurance Operations (Formerly CPCU 5-Insurance Company Operations)

Location: Various locations through formal classes, informal study groups, or independent study.

Length: 15 lessons plus additional preparation.

Dates: *Version 1:* September 1978-July 1995; *Version 2:* August 1995-Present.

Objective: To familiarize students with all of the major functional operations of insurance companies and the interrelationships among them.

Learning Outcome: Upon successful completion of this course, the student will be able to understand the functions of different departments within insurance companies and how they interact with each other.

Instruction: Major topics covered in the course are insurance marketing; underwriting; reinsurance; rate-making; claims adjusting; loss control activities; and other functions and activities. With respect to each, current status and development are explored; and the impact of regulation and other social/environmental factors are considered. Methods of instruction include formal classes, small group study, independent study, and additional preparation based on the prescribed texts and study guide. Credit is contingent on passing a nationally administered three-hour essay examination.

Credit Recommendation: *Version 1:* In the upper division baccalaureate degree category, 3 semester hours in Insurance or Risk Management (7/79). **NOTE:** Students who have also completed CPCU 10-Insurance Issues and Professional Ethics should be granted 3 semester hours of graduate credit in Insurance or Risk Management. *Version 2:* In the upper division baccalaureate degree category or in the graduate degree category, 3 semester hours in Insurance or Risk Management (8/95).

CPCU 06: The Legal Environment of Insurance

Location: Various locations through formal classes, informal study groups, or independent study.

Length: 15 lessons plus additional preparation.

Dates: January 1979-Present.

Objective: To provide students with a basic understanding of business and insurance law.

Learning Outcome: Upon successful completion of this course, students will have an enhanced understanding of business and insurance law, and should be able to (1) understand the origins, general classifications, and applications of common law, statutory law, and regulatory law; (2) apply the legal concepts and rules to various situations in business and personal life; and (3) apply legal concepts and rules to various situations in the insurance business.

Instruction: Major topics covered in the course are general business law; particularly the areas of contract, tort, and agency law; the application of business law to insurance situations; and the rapidly growing areas of employment and consumer law. Methods of instruction include formal classes, small group study, independent study, and additional preparation based on the prescribed texts and study guide. Credit is contingent on passing a nationally administered three-hour essay examination.

Credit Recommendation: In the upper division baccalaureate degree category, 3 semester hours in Business Law, Insurance, or Risk Management (7/79) (8/95).

CPCU 07: Management

Location: Various locations through formal classes, informal study groups, or independent study.

Length: 15 lessons plus additional preparation.

Dates: September 1978-Present.

Objective: To provide students with a basic understanding of management principles and management information systems as they relate to the insurance industry.

Learning Outcome: Upon successful completion of this course, students will have an understanding of the principles of management, organizational behavior, and an introduction to management information systems.

Instruction: Major topics covered in the course are the historical development of management; basic management functions; behavioral processes; environmental influences; and management information systems and the decision-making process. Methods of instruction include formal classes, small group study, independent study, and additional preparation based on the prescribed texts and study guide. Credit is contingent on passing a nationally administered three-hour essay examination.

Credit Recommendation: In the upper division baccalaureate degree category, 3 semester hours in Business or Management (7/79) (8/95).

CPCU 08: Accounting and Finance

Location: Various locations through formal classes, informal study groups, or independent study.

Length: 15 lessons plus additional preparation.

Dates: *Version 1:* January 1979-July 1995; *Version 2:* August 1995-Present.

Objective: To enable students to understand the basic principles of accounting and finance, and the accounting and financial practices of insurance companies.

Learning Outcome: Upon successful completion of this course, students will have a basic understanding of accounting and financial principles, as well as a basic understanding of statutory requirements for insurance company accounting.

Instruction: Major topics covered in the course are accounting fundamentals, valuation of balance sheet accounts, income statements, analysis of financial statements, financial management, and a detailed analysis of insurance company accounting and financial management and the relationship between financial analysis and insurance company solvency. Methods of instruction include formal classes, small group study, independent study, and additional preparation based on the prescribed texts and study guide. Credit is contingent on passing a nationally administered three-hour essay examination.

Credit Recommendation: *Version 1:* In the graduate degree category, 3 semester hours in Accounting, Finance, or Insurance (7/79). *Version 2:* In the upper division baccalaureate category or in the graduate degree category, 3 semester hours in Accounting, Finance, or Insurance (8/95).

CPCU 09: Economics

Location: Various locations through formal classes, informal study groups, or independent study.

Length: 15 lessons plus additional preparation.

Dates: *Version 1:* September 1978-July 1995; *Version 2:* August 1995-Present.

Objective: To enable students to understand general economic principles at both the micro and macro levels.

Learning Outcome: Upon successful completion of this course, the student will have an understanding of the principles of economics at both the micro and macro levels, and how economic trends affect the insurance industry as a whole.

Instruction: Major topics covered in the course are the fundamental concepts of micro and macro economics; product pricing; national income accounting; monetary and fiscal policy; inflation; unemployment; and the international economy. Methods of instruction include formal classes, small group study, independent study, and additional preparation based on the prescribed texts and study guide. Credit is contingent on passing a nationally administered three-hour essay examination.

Credit Recommendation: *Version 1:* In the upper division baccalaureate degree category, 3 semester hours in Economics (7/79). *Version 2:* In the upper division baccalaureate degree category, 4 semester hours in Economics (8/95).

CPCU 10: Insurance Issues and Professional Ethics

Location: Various locations through formal classes, informal study groups, or independent study.

Length: 15 lessons plus additional preparation.

Dates: *Version 1:* January 1979-July 1995; *Version 2:* August 1995-Present.

Objective: To provide students with an identification and analysis of major current insurance issues and an examination of professional ethics in the context of the American Institute's Code of Professional Ethics.

Learning Outcome: Upon successful completion of this course, students will have an understanding of current issues facing the insurance industry, standards of professional behavior, and the rules, guidelines and disciplinary procedures contained in the American Institute's Code of Professional Ethics.

Instruction: Major topics covered in the course are current issues relating to property and liability insurance; price discrimination and regulation; changes in tort law; captive and government insurers; international insurance; and an examination of professionalism and ethics, including rules, guidelines, and disciplinary procedures. Methods of instruction include formal classes, small group study, independent study, and additional preparation based on the prescribed texts and study guide. Credit is contingent on passing a nationally administered three-hour essay examination.

Credit Recommendation: *Version 1:* In the upper division baccalaureate degree category, 3 semester hours in Insurance or Risk Management (7/79). **NOTE:** Students who have also completed CPCU 5-Insurance Company Operations should be granted 3 semester hours of graduate credit in Insurance or Risk Management. *Version 2:* In the upper division baccalaureate degree category, 3 semester hours in Insurance or Risk Management (8/95).

CPCU I: Insurance Principles and Practices

Location: Various locations through formal classes, informal study groups, or independent study.

Length: 30 lessons plus additional preparation.

Dates: May 1967-June 1978.

Objective: To provide an in-depth understanding of insurance principles and practices as they relate to contract analysis and application.

Instruction: Major topics covered in the course are the nature of risk, risk-handling techniques, provisions of the standard fire insurance contract, and many loss exposures such as business interruption, ocean and inland marine, general liability, workers' compensation, automobile accidents, fidelity, surety, crime, and boiler and machinery. Included is an in-depth study of the insurance contracts applicable to the aforementioned risks, and a survey of individual and group life insurance, annuities, and social insurance.

Credit Recommendation: In the graduate degree category, 3 semester hours in Insurance or in the upper division baccalaureate degree category, 6 semester hours in Insurance (5/77). **NOTE:** This course was last offered in June 1978 and as of that date continued to meet the requirements for the credit recommendations.

CPCU II: Analysis of Insurance Functions

Location: Various locations through formal classes, informal study groups, or independent study.

Length: 30 lessons plus additional preparation.

Dates: May 1967-June 1978.

Objective: To develop a thorough understanding of the functional characteristics of insurance company operations, insurance products and services (including loss prevention), and the environment within which the insurance industry operates.

Instruction: Major topics covered in the course are an analysis of the formation and organization of insurers, insurance marketing, risk selection, reinsurance, rate making and reserves, loss prevention, the preparation and scope of insurers' financial statements, claim management, and human motivation and professional ethics. Students have the option of pursuing an in-depth study of one of three specialty areas of insurance—adjusting, risk management, or underwriting.

Credit Recommendation: In the graduate degree category, 3 semester hours in Insurance or in the upper division baccalaureate degree category, 6 semester hours in Insurance (5/77). **NOTE:** This course was last offered in June 1978 and as of that date continued to meet the requirements for the credit recommendation.

CPCU III: Economics, Government, and Business

Location: Various locations through formal classes, informal study groups, or independent study.

Length: 30 lessons plus additional preparation.

Dates: May 1967-June 1978.

Objective: To develop a basic understanding of micro and macro economics and the application of economics to public policy.

Instruction: Major topics covered in the course are national income accounting; price determination; income distribution; monetary and fiscal policy; the theory and practice of international trade; public finance; the economics of the firm under competition, oligopoly, and monopoly; government regulation of business, particularly of insurance, and in an era of growing social responsibility; and antitrust regulation and the control of competition receive special attention, as does the protection of consumers.

Credit Recommendation: In the upper division baccalaureate degree category, 6 semester hours in Business Administration or Economics (5/77). **NOTE:** This course was last offered in June 1978 and as of that date continued to meet the requirements for the credit recommendation.

CPCU IV: Insurance and Business Law

Location: Various locations through formal classes, informal study groups, or independent study.

Length: 30 lessons plus additional preparation.

Dates: May 1967-June 1978.

Objective: To develop a basic understanding of business and insurance law.

Instruction: Major topics covered in the course are the treatment of contract law followed by several topics on the distinctive features of insurance policies as contracts; the principles of agency and tort law are illustrated extensively with examples and special situations from an insurance setting; and the law of bailments, commercial paper, corporations, partnerships, real property, and sales.

Credit Recommendation: In the upper division baccalaureate degree category, 6 semester hours in Business Law or Insurance or in the graduate degree category, 3 semester hours in Business Law or Insurance (5/77). **NOTE:** This course was last offered in June 1978 and as of that date continued to meet the requirements for the credit recommendations.

CPCU V: Management, Accounting, and Finance

Location: Various locations through formal classes, informal study groups, or independent study.

Length: 30 lessons plus additional preparation.

Dates: May 1967-June 1978.

Objective: To develop an understanding of the principles and applications of accounting, corporate finance, and management.

Instruction: Major topics covered in the course are five basic management functions: planning, organizing, directing, leading, and controlling; accounting terms and concepts and their application in managerial decisions and in the interpretation of financial statements; the objectives of financial management; and the available methods of obtaining and using financial resources to maximize the profits of a firm.

Credit Recommendation: In the upper division baccalaureate degree category, 3 semester hours in Management and 4 semester hours in Accounting/Finance, or in the graduate degree category, 3 semester hours in Financial Management (5/77). **NOTE:** This course was last offered in June 1978 and as of that date continued to meet the requirements for credit recommendation.

INSURANCE REGULATION PROGRAM

IR 201: Insurance Regulation

Location: Various locations through formal classes, informal study groups, or independent study.

Length: 14 lessons plus additional preparation.

Dates: September 1995-Present.

Objective: To provide students with an understanding of insurance regulation as it applies to the property-liability insurance industry.

Learning Outcome: Upon successful completion of this course, the student will better understand and comply with the regulatory requirements placed on the property-liability insurance industry and will be able to help improve communications between insurance regulators and the regulated property-liability insurance industry.

Instruction: Major topics covered in the course are an overview of insurance regulation including the roles of state insurance departments, the National Association of Insurance Commissioners, state legislatures, the legal system, Congress and federal agencies, consumers, the insurance industry and the media; the theory of regulation; the history of insurance regulation in the United States; how state insurance departments regulate the operations and activities of insurance companies, agents, and brokers; various perspectives of insurance regulation; and current issues in insurance regulation. Methods of instruction include formal classes, small group study, independent study, and additional preparation based on the prescribed texts and study guide. Credit is contingent on passing a nationally administered three-hour essay examination.

Credit Recommendation: In the upper division baccalaureate degree category, 3 semester hours, or in the graduate degree category, 2 semester hours in Regulation of Business or Regulation of Insurance (8/95).

INTRODUCTION TO CLAIMS PROGRAM

Introduction to Claims

Location: Various locations through formal classes, informal study groups, or independent study.

Length: 7 lessons plus additional preparation.

Dates: April 1988-Present.

Objective: To provide students with an understanding of the claims function and practices in property-liability insurance.

Learning Outcome: Upon successful completion of this course, the student will be able to determine coverage, liability, and damages for typical homeowners, auto, and auto damage claims.

Instruction: Major topics covered in the course are the claim function; insurance contracts; adjusting property losses; adjusting auto physical damage claims; liability claim handling; and how liability insurance works. Methods of instruction include formal classes, small group study, independent study, and additional preparation based on the prescribed texts and study guide. Credit is contingent on passing a two-hour short answer examination.

Credit Recommendation: In the upper division baccalaureate degree category, 1 semester hour in Property-Liability Insurance or Claims (8/95).

INTRODUCTION TO PROPERTY AND LIABILITY INSURANCE (INTRO) PROGRAM

Introduction to Property and Liability Insurance (INTRO)

Location: Various locations through formal classes, informal study groups, or independent study.

Length: 11 lessons plus additional preparation.

Dates: June 1984-Present.

Objective: To provide students with an understanding of the dynamic operation of the property-liability insurance industry and the relationships among the various functions. Principles and terminology are introduced and related to various contexts.

Learning Outcome: Upon successful completion of this course, the student will be able to understand the nature, importance, and interrelationships among various insurance functions; develop a sound understanding of basic insurance principles; and develop an overall understanding of insurance that provides a sound foundation for further analysis in intermediate level courses.

Instruction: Major topics covered in the course are the nature of insurance; how insurance is sold, underwritten, and serviced; how claims are handled; what is found in an insurance policy; personal and commercial insurance and the needs they address; how premiums are determined; and insurance in a changing world. Methods of instruction include formal classes, small group study, independent study, and additional preparation based on the prescribed texts and study guide. Credit is contingent on passing a two-hour short answer examination.

Credit Recommendation: In the vocational certificate category, 1 semester hour in Introduction to Property and Liability Insurance (8/95).

INTRODUCTION TO UNDERWRITING PROGRAM

Introduction to Underwriting

Location: Various locations through formal classes, informal study groups, or independent study.

Length: 8 lessons plus additional preparation.

Dates: December 1994-Present.

Objective: To provide students with an understanding of how underwriting in property-liability insurance works and the terminology used in such underwriting.

Learning Outcome: Upon successful completion of this course, the student will be able to describe the process used and the factors evaluated by property-liability underwriters in making underwriting decisions.

Instruction: Major topics covered in the course are general underwriting principles and application of those principles to several lines of property and liability insurance; what is underwriting; underwriting as decision making, personal auto underwriting, homeowners underwriting, commercial lines underwriting, general liability underwriting, commercial property underwriting, and underwriting results. Methods of instruction include formal classes, small group study, independent study, and additional preparation based on the prescribed texts and study guide. Credit is contingent on passing a two-hour short answer examination.

Credit Recommendation: In the lower division baccalaureate/associate degree category, 1 semester hour in Insurance, Insurance Underwriting, or Property-Liability Insurance (8/95).

PROGRAM IN GENERAL INSURANCE

Courses are listed in alphanumeric order, e.g., INS 21, INS 22, etc.

INS 21: Property and Liability Insurance Principles (Formerly INS 21 - General Principles of Insurance)

Location: Various locations through formal classes, informal study groups, or independent study.

Length: 12 lessons plus additional preparation.

Dates: *Version 1:* May 1976-February 1982; *Version 2:* March 1982-November 1987; *Version 3:* December 1987-July 1995; *Version 4:* August 1995-Present.

Objective: To enable students to understand the basic principles of risk management, property and liability insurance, insurance contract analysis, and the nature and operation of the property and liability insurance business.

Learning Outcome: Upon successful completion of this course, the student will be able to understand the relationship between uncertainty and insurance, recognize property and liability exposures, understand the nature and provisions of property and liability insurance contracts, distinguish among insurance providers, and describe major functions of insurers and how they are regulated.

Instruction: Major topics covered in the course are uncertainty and insurance; loss exposures of individuals, families, and businesses; structure and provisions of property and liability insurance contracts; insurance providers; financial performance and regulation; and marketing, underwriting, claims, risk management, and other functions of insurers. Methods of instruction include formal classes, small group study, independent study, and additional preparation based on the prescribed texts and study guide. Credit is contingent on passing a nationally administered three-hour essay examination.

Credit Recommendation: *Version 1:* In the upper division baccalaureate degree category, 1 semester hour in Insurance or Business (7/90). *Version 2:* In the upper division baccalaureate degree category, 2 semester hours in Insurance or Business (7/90). *Version 3:* In the upper division baccalaureate degree category, 2 semester hours in Insurance or Business (7/90). *Version 4:* In the upper division baccalaureate degree category, 3 semester hours in Insurance or Business (8/95).

INS 22: Personal Insurance (Formerly INS 22 - Property Insurance)

Location: Various locations through formal classes, informal study groups, or independent study.

Length: 12 lessons plus additional preparation.

Dates: *Version 1:* May 1967-February 1982; *Version 2:* March 1982-November 1987; *Version 3:* December 1987-July 1995; *Version 4:* August 1995-Present.

Objective: To enable students to understand the insurance needs of individuals and families through analysis of their loss exposures and the available types of personal insurance.

Learning Outcome: Upon successful completion of this course, the student will be able to recognize loss exposures faced by individuals and families and understand insurance coverages available to meet loss exposures of individuals and families.

Instruction: Major topics covered in the course are loss exposures; coverages including homeowners and other residential insurance; auto insurance; other personal property and liability insurance; and government programs such as social security, workers' compensation, and unemployment compensation. Methods of instruction include formal classes, small group study, independent study, and additional preparation based on the prescribed texts and study guide. Credit is contingent on passing a nationally administered three-hour essay examination.

Credit Recommendation: *Version 1:* In the upper division baccalaureate degree category, 1 semester hour in Insurance or Business (7/90). *Version 2:* In the upper division baccalaureate degree category, 2 semester hours in Insurance or Business (7/90). *Version 3:* In the upper division baccalaureate degree category, 2 semester hours in Insurance or Business (7/90). *Version 4:* In the upper division baccalaureate degree category, 3 semester hours in Insurance or Business (8/95).

INS 23: Commercial Insurance (Formerly INS 23 - Casualty Insurance)

Location: Various locations through formal classes, informal study groups, or independent study.

Length: 12 lessons plus additional preparation.

Dates: *Version 1:* May 1967-November 1987; *Version 2:* December 1987-Present.

Objective: To provide students with an understanding of property and liability loss exposures of businesses and analysis of major types of insurance needed by businesses.

Learning Outcome: Upon successful completion of this course, the student will be able to recognize property and liability loss exposures of businesses, and to understand types of insurance that protect businesses from loss exposures.

Instruction: Major topics covered in the course are property and liability loss exposures of businesses and coverages available to insure business loss exposures. Methods of instruction include formal classes, small group study, independent study, and additional preparation based on the prescribed texts and study guide. Credit is contingent on passing a nationally administered three-hour essay examination.

Credit Recommendation: *Version 1:* In the upper division baccalaureate degree category, 3 semester hours in Insurance or Business (7/90) (8/95). *Version 2:* In the upper division baccalaureate degree category, 3 semester hours in Insurance or Business (7/90) (8/95).

PROGRAM IN SUPERVISORY MANAGEMENT

Courses are listed in alphanumeric order, e.g., SM 18, SM 19, etc.

SM 18: Essentials of Supervision

Location: Various locations through formal classes, informal study groups,or independent study.

Length: 9 lessons plus additional preparation.

Dates: January 1985-Present.

Objective: To provide students with the opportunity to develop the practical knowledge and skills necessary to be effective supervisors.

Learning Outcome: Upon successful completion of this course, the student will

be able to understand the basic functions of a supervisor and the process of making the transition to a supervisory role, and apply basic supervisory and management skills.

Instruction: Major topics covered in the course are the role of the supervisor, motivation, leadership, understanding others, communications, coaching, and fair employment laws. Methods of instruction include formal classes, small group study, independent study, and additional preparation based on the prescribed texts and study guide. Credit is contingent on passing a two-hour short answer examination.

Credit Recommendation: In the upper division baccalaureate degree category, 1 semester hour in Management (8/95). **NOTE:** If taken in connection with SM 19: Supervisory Skills, the credit recommendation is in the upper division baccalaureate degree category, 3 semester hours in Management.

SM 19: Supervisory Skills

Location: Various locations through formal classes, informal study groups,or independent study.

Length: 9 lessons plus additional preparation.

Dates: January 1985-Present.

Objective: To provide students with the opportunity to develop the practical knowledge and skills necessary to be an effective supervisor.

Learning Outcome: Upon successful completion of this course, the student will be able to understand and apply basic supervisory skills such as work management and performance appraisals.

Instruction: Major topics covered in the course are the basic functions of management, work management, training, appraising performance, time management, handling performance problems, and developing teamwork. Case studies are used. Methods of instruction include formal classes, small group study, independent study, and additional preparation based on the prescribed texts and study guide. Credit is contingent on passing a two-hour short answer examination.

Credit Recommendation: In the upper division baccalaureate degree category, 1 semester hour in Management (8/95). **NOTE:** If taken in connection with SM 18: Essentials of Supervision, the credit recommendation is in the upper division baccalaureate degree category, 3 semester hours in Management.

American Institute for Paralegal Studies, Inc.

The American Institute for Paralegal Studies, Inc., has been offering a comprehensive educational program in the preparation of legal assistants and paralegals since August 1978. The program embarked on providing a part-time, continuing education opportunity to individuals who desired to enter this novel market.

The Institute's main administrative headquarters is located in Southfield, Michigan. Regional offices are located in Chicago, Illinois, and Atlanta, Georgia. The Office of Academic Affairs houses a substantial library of proprietary, scholarly, and academic materials dedicated to the study of legal assistants and paralegals. Textbook preparation and production, as well as course development and revision, are responsibilities of this office. The Institute's curricula underwent a major review in March 1994; however, the curricula are continually reviewed for conceptual efficiency, ensuring that new areas of law and its interpretation are appropriately incorporated. The Curriculum Committee recommends any major changes to a course, which are then submitted to the Office of Academic Affairs to incorporate.

All classroom facilities are located in educational facilities, usually colleges and universities. This type of agreement between the Institute and educational institutions provides accessibility to libraries and resources necessary for students to succeed. The Institute annually searches for faculty by advertising in trade journals, periodicals, local newspapers, and by references of other teaching staff. Instructors are reviewed by the students, who complete evaluation forms during and at the end of a course.

A certificate is awarded to any student who successfully completes a course. Additionally, the Institute has provisions for re-examination, probation, and other academic policies and procedures that ensure a just and equitable opportunity to rectify poor performance as well as ensure that the Institute adheres to high academic standards. Student grades are recorded by the instructor, who then submits them to either the regional or main office. Once received by the office, grades are recorded in the Institute's data base for permanent recordation on a transcript.

Source of official student records: Registry of Credit Recommendations, American Council on Education, One Dupont Circle, Washington, DC 20036-1193 or Southfield National Office, Dean of Students, Honeywell Center, 17515 West Nine Mile Road, Suite 225, Southfield, MI 48075

Additional information about the courses: College Credit Recommendation Service, American Council on Education, One Dupont Circle, Washington, DC 20036-1193.

Administrative Law (A-106)

Location: Various locations throughout the country.

Length: 15 hours (3 hours per week for 5 weeks).

Dates: September 1994-Present.

Objective: To provide entry level paralegals with a full sense of the administrative process, administrative agencies, and corresponding judicial oversight.

Learning Outcome: Upon successful completion of this course, the student will be able to evaluate rules, legal customs, and procedural norms applicable to the typical administrative hearing; and will be aware of the "administrative process" whereby various players perform their duties.

Instruction: Major topics covered in the course are the general parameters of administrative law, laws or rules promulgated by agencies of government and administrative agencies, and procedural and substantive adjudication of administrative law questions. Methods of instruction include lecture, projects, presentations, practical exercises, and tests.

Credit Recommendation: In the upper division baccalaureate degree category, 1 semester hour in Administrative Law (9/94).

American Jurisprudence (B-201)

Location: Various locations throughout the country.

Length: 15 hours (3 hours per week for 5 weeks).

Dates: September 1989-Present.

Objective: To become familiar with the structure and functioning of the American legal system and the role of the paralegal.

Learning Outcome: Upon successful completion of this course, the student will be able to identify judicial officers and personnel, courts of various jurisdictions, the place of the paralegal in the legal system, and the ethical constraints governing paralegal conduct.

Instruction: Major topics covered in the course are the functions and processes of the judicial, administrative, and legislative branches of the government; the role of the legal assistant; the canons of ethics of the American Bar Association; and the ethical guidelines of paralegal groups and associations.

Credit Recommendation: In the upper division baccalaureate degree category, 1 semester hour in American Jurisprudence (1/89) (9/94).

Bankruptcy Law (B-206)

Location: Various locations throughout the country.

Length: 15 hours (3 hours per week for 5 weeks).

Dates: September 1994-Present.

Objective: To learn about the legal remedy called bankruptcy and its various procedures, legal requirements, and strategies in Chapter 7, 11, and 13 cases.

Learning Outcome: Upon successful completion of this course, the student will be acquainted with the bankruptcy process and the laws that guide its practice; understand how paralegals play an important role in the administration of bankruptcy cases; and organize all bankruptcy materials in preparation for a final examination.

Instruction: Major topics covered in the course are basic bankruptcy rules and their application in a bankruptcy situation, introduction to the overall bankruptcy laws and procedures, and the role of the paralegal in bankruptcy cases. Methods of instruction include lecture, projects, presentations, practical exercises, and final exam.

Credit Recommendation: In the lower division baccalaureate/associate degree category, 1 semester hour in Bankruptcy Law (9/94).

Business Law (B-202)

Location: Various locations throughout the country.

Length: 30 hours (3 hours per week for 10 weeks).

Dates: September 1989-Present.

Objective: To present the various business entities including the partnership association and the corporation; and to acquaint students with the law of contracts including an examination of an offer and an acceptance, the capacity to contract, and the policies on the enforcement of contracts.

Learning Outcome: Upon successful completion of this course, the student will be able to prepare and initiate contracts; adhere to Uniform Commercial Code requirements; and develop and monitor sole proprietorships, partnerships, and corporations.

Instruction: Major topics covered in the course are the rights and obligations of a corporation or other business institution;

corporate filing requirements, management, and administration; directions, dissolutions, mergers, and liquidations; general principles of agency law including the master/servant theory; and the major provisions of the Uniform Commercial Code.

Credit Recommendation: In the upper division baccalaureate degree category, 2 semester hours in Business Law (1/89) (9/94).

Criminal Law (A-104)

Location: Various locations throughout the country.

Length: 15 hours (3 hours per week for 5 weeks).

Dates: September 1989-Present.

Objective: To provide an overview of criminal law and the procedures and constitutional rights as they apply to criminal cases.

Learning Outcome: Upon successful completion of this course, the student will have a basic understanding and interpretative capacity when analyzing misdemeanors and felonies; be able to assist in the preparation of both defense and prosecution pleadings; and assist in trial advocacy and appellate tactics.

Instruction: Major topics covered in the course are the definition and elements of crimes including crimes against the person, crimes against property, procedural and constitutional safeguards, and procedures necessary from arrest through trial and sentencing and punishment.

Credit Recommendation: In the upper division baccalaureate degree category, 1 semester hour in Criminal Law (1/89) (9/94).

Employment Law (B-207)

Location: Various locations throughout the country.

Length: 30 hours (3 hours per week for 10 weeks).

Dates: September 1994-Present.

Objective: To give an overview of law and legislation relative to employment practices both in the private and public sectors.

Learning Outcome: Upon successful completion of this course, the student will be able to understand significant legislation governing the American workplace; demonstrate a working knowledge of laws dealing with wages, benefits, and labor relations; and demonstrate investigation, representation, and advocacy of employment claims.

Instruction: Major topics covered in the course are significant legislation governing the American workplace; setting out rights and obligations of both employers and employees; federal laws dealing with wages and benefits, labor relations, entitlement programs, and privacy and health concerns; and the role of the paralegal in the investigation, representation, and advocacy of employment claims.

Credit Recommendation: In the upper division baccalaureate degree category, 2 semester hours in Employment Law (9/94).

Estates, Trusts, and Probate (B-203)

Location: Various locations throughout the country.

Length: 30 hours (3 hours per week for 10 weeks).

Dates: September 1978-Present.

Objective: To provide a basic understanding of estate planning and administration of decedents' estates.

Learning Outcome: Upon successful completion of this course, the student will be able to assist the supervising attorney in preparation of trusts and will documents, and aid the client during the entire estate administration.

Instruction: Major topics covered in the course are intestacy, wills, probate, federal and state taxes, accounting, and distribution of assets.

Credit Recommendation: In the upper division baccalaureate degree category, 2 semester hours in Estates and Trusts (12/83) (1/89) (9/94).

Family Law (A-103)

Location: Various locations throughout the country.

Length: 15 hours (3 hours per week for 5 weeks).

Dates: September 1989-Present.

Objective: To provide an overview of family law and procedures for interviewing clients with family law problems.

Learning Outcome: Upon successful completion of this course, the student will be able to draft domestic relations pleadings from divorce action to support claims; and assimilate information on matters involving equitable distribution, custody determination, pre- and post-nuptial agreements, and adoption.

Instruction: Major topics covered in the course are the wide array of issues that are part of family law including marriage, annulments, divorce, property rights and distribution, child visitation, alimony, separation agreements, adoptions, parent and child law; and skills to interview clients with family law problems and prepare complaints and agreements.

Credit Recommendation: In the upper division baccalaureate degree category, 1 semester hour in Family Law (1/89) (9/94).

Internship (C-110)

Location: Various locations throughout the country.

Length: 90 hours (over several weeks to several months).

Dates: September 1993-Present.

Objective: To provide paralegal students with actual experiences that apply theoretical and practical knowledge in the performance of paralegal duties.

Learning Outcome: Upon successful completion of this course, the student will be able to have actual experience working within the legal system; gain confidence in their ability as a legal assistant; and develop legal skills that are most effectively mastered in an actual legal setting.

Instruction: Major topics covered in the course are an integration of the theoretical concepts learned in the classroom with real world employment situations under direct supervision. Methods of instruction include hands-on experience under supervision approved by the Institute, a formal and written review by the end of twenty-four hours to determine whether the apprenticeship is academically appropriate for the student, and that the learning objectives of the program will be accomplished by the end of the internship.

Credit Recommendation: In the upper division baccalaureate degree category, 2 semester hours in Paralegal Internship (9/94).

Legal Research and Writing (B-204)

Location: Various locations throughout the country.

Length: 30 hours (3 hours per week for 10 weeks).

Dates: December 1979-Present.

Objective: To familiarize the student with the essential skills needed to perform legal research and writing including factual analysis, issue resolution, and Shepardizing.

Learning Outcome: Upon successful completion of this course, the student will be able to work with numerous legal research tools including case location and analysis, legislative histories and topical interpretation, shepardizing, legal memoranda, and legal citation method.

Instruction: Major topics covered in the course are such various sources for research materials as digests, reports, statutory materials, and encyclopedias; the proper approach to legal writing, preparing memoranda, and using citations; and evaluating precedents and formulating logical legal conclusions. Methods of instruction include extensive library research to solve numerous problems raised in the course and extensive writing projects completed outside normal class time.

Credit Recommendation: In the upper division baccalaureate degree category, 3 semester hours in Legal Research or Legal Writing (3/83) (1/89) (9/94).

Legal Writing (C-301)

Location: Various locations throughout the country.

Length: 30 hours (3 hours per week for 10 weeks).

Dates: September 1994-Present.

Objective: To acquaint prospective paralegals with the standards and nuances applicable to legal writing.

Learning Outcome: Upon successful completion of this course, the student will be familiar with the process of legal writing and recognize its basic characteristics; recognize time, format, citation, and content constraints common to legal writing; and approach legal writing as a step-by-step process in order to build legal documents in a systematic way while maintaining the flexibility to accommodate different situations.

Instruction: Major topics covered in the course are an understanding of the process of legal writing; practical writing experience using specific techniques of legal writing; and planning, organizing, and drafting clear and effective legal documents. Methods of instruction include lecture, projects, practical exercises, and tests.

Credit Recommendation: In the upper division baccalaureate degree category, 2 semester hours in Legal Writing (9/94).

Litigation, Pleadings, and Arbitration (A-102)

Location: Various locations throughout the country.

Length: 45 hours (3 hours per week for 15 weeks).

Dates: September 1989-Present.

Objective: To introduce the major aspects of litigation, pleadings, and arbitration as they apply to the work of a paralegal.

Learning Outcome: Upon successful completion of this course, the student will be familiar with the requirements of a client's case including jurisdictional questions, means and methods of service, preliminary motions and objections discovery, pre-trial and trial activities, and strategy on appeal.

Instruction: Major topics covered in the course are client counseling, investigative techniques and processes, the paralegal and civil practice (i.e., commencement of a lawsuit, pleadings, settlement, pretrial activities), trial procedures, and arbitration and dispute resolution. Methods of instruction include lecture and discussion.

Credit Recommendation: In the upper division baccalaureate degree category, 3 semester hours in Litigations, Pleadings, and Arbitration (1/89) (9/94).

Real Estate Transfer and Ownership (A-105) (Formerly Real Estate Transfer and Ownership [A-106])

Location: Various locations throughout the country.

Length: 30 hours (3 hours per week for 10 weeks).

Dates: September 1978-Present.

Objective: To develop an understanding of ownership of real property, transfer of such ownership, and the use of legal forms incident thereto.

Learning Outcome: Upon successful completion of this course, the student will be able to gather information relative to real estate contracts; identify and relate to the various parties in real estate transactions; process a real estate transaction from agreement to closing; and be familiar with the typical types of litigation seen in real estate transactions.

Instruction: Major topics covered in this course are an overview of real property; deeds; liens and other incumbrances on real property; contracts for sale or purchase of real estate; financial instruments; search, examination, and title insurance; title closing; landlord and tenant relationships; surveys; mortgages and financing; an out-of-class assignment to prepare all the proper documents used in a "closing" by the buyer and seller; and drafting case pleadings and other additional writing assignments.

Credit Recommendation: In the upper division baccalaureate degree category, 3 semester hours in Principles and Practice of Real Estate, Real Estate Laws, or Survey of Real Estate (12/83) (1/89) (9/94).

Torts and Personal Injury (A-101)

Location: Various locations throughout the country.

Length: 30 hours (3 hours per week for 10 weeks).

Dates: September 1989-Present.

Objective: To provide a thorough overview of traditional and contemporary tort law.

Learning Outcome: Upon successful completion of this course, the student will be able to identify the various civil actions applicable in specific client circumstances; gather information relative to damages both medical and economic; and prepare complaints, answers, and motions seen in personal injury practices.

Instruction: Major topics covered in this course are a study of traditional tort law including intentional torts such as assault and battery, negligence, no-fault laws, product liability, nuisance, misrepresentation, defamation, invasion of privacy, trespassing, and workmens' compensation.

Credit Recommendation: In the upper division baccalaureate degree category, 2 semester hours in Tort Law (1/89) (9/94).

American Institute of Banking of New Jersey

The American Institute of Banking (AIB) is the educational division of the American Bankers Association, the national organization of the banking industry. Its total membership includes some 10,000 financial service institutions, comprising approximately 97 percent of the nation's commercial banks. AIB is part of the Education, Policy and Development Group, one of the six working divisions of the Association.

AIB has franchised more than 300 chapters throughout the United States. An organized chapter assures that the Institute's mission is carried out from year to year.

All activities are initiated by the local chapter, including the curriculum and faculty selection, education and training programs, and classroom facilities. While individual chapters work in cooperation with the national AIB office, each chapter is administratively autonomous. As a result, credit recommendations established for courses offered by a specific chapter apply only to that chapter.

AIBNJ sponsors a program in contemporary banking subjects for employees of financial service institutions throughout New Jersey.

Source of official student records: Registry of Credit Recommendations, American Council on Education, One Dupont Circle, Washington, DC 20036-1193.

Additional information about the courses: Office of Corporate-Higher Education Programs, Thomas Edison State College, 101 West State Street, Trenton, NJ 08608-1176.

Accounting I (ACC101)

Location: Locations throughout New Jersey.

Length: 45 hours (15 weeks).

Dates: January 1977-Present.

Objective: To enable the student to understand the basic concepts, theories, and practices of business accounting.

Learning Outcome: Upon successful completion of this course the student will be able to describe the content and purpose of a balance sheet and income statement; compare the basic characteristics of the accrual basis and cash basis of accounting; explain the full accounting cycle and prepare all required journal entries and adjustments; identify the basic assumptions, principles, and modifying conventions of accounting; and describe how inflation affects information presented on conventional financial statements.

Instruction: Major topics covered in the course are analysis of business transactions, the accounting cycle, special journal and ledgers, end-of-cycle procedures, payrolls and control systems, payables and receivables, valuation of other assets, taxes, and the accrual basis. Methods of instruction include lectures, discussion, classroom exercises, and problem solving.

Credit Recommendation: In the lower division baccalaureate/associate degree category, 3 semester hours in Accounting I (1/82) (4/87) (11/94).

Accounting II (ACC102)

Location: Locations throughout New Jersey.

Length: 45 hours (15 weeks).

Dates: January 1977-Present.

Objective: To build on the basic principles in the Accounting I offering.

Learning Outcome: Upon successful completion of this course, the student will be able to contrast the advantages of the corporate form of business; summarize the various features of bonds and how they differ from shares of stocks, and identify the journal entries required for them on financial statements; describe the uses and limitations of consolidated financial states; list the major sources of funds; explain how comparative financial statements may be used to analyze and appraise the financial position of a firm and results of the firm's operations.

Instruction: Major topics covered in the course are advanced concepts and techniques of departmentalized accounting, the partnership accounting cycle, branch and home office accounting, corporation accounting, responsibility and cost accounting, budgeting, reporting, statement analysis, and an overview of data processing. Methods of instruction include lectures, discussion, classroom exercises, and problem solving.

Credit Recommendation: In the lower division baccalaureate/associate degree category, 3 semester hours in Accounting II (1/82) (4/87) (11/94).

Analyzing Financial Statements (CRL101)

Location: Locations throughout New Jersey.

Length: *Version 1:* 45 hours (15 weeks); *Version 2:* 30 hours (10 weeks); *Version 3:* 45 hours (15 weeks).

Dates: *Version 1:* January 1977-December 1986; *Version 2:* January 1987-August 1991; *Version 3:* September 1991-Present.

Objective: To enable the student to understand financial statement analysis through evaluation of past and current financial conditions, diagnosis of and suggested remedies for any existing financial problems, and forecasting of future trends.

Learning Outcome: Upon successful completion of this course, the student will be able to explain why financial analysis is important in commercial lending; relate how a company's type of business, legal structure, size, and management strategies affect the way a lender conducts financial analysis; analyze financial statements, balance sheets, and pro forma statements; calculate key financial ratios and use them to compare a company's performance with that of the company's industry; and determine when a fund flow statement is required.

Instruction: Major topics covered in the course are cash inflows and outflows, an analysis on selected financial statements, tools of financial statement analysis, and techniques of financial statement analysis. Methods of instruction include lectures, discussion, classroom exercises, and problem solving.

Credit Recommendation: *Version 1:* In the upper division baccalaureate degree category, 3 semester hours in Analyzing Financial Statements (1/82). *Version 2:* In the upper division baccalaureate degree category, 2 semester hours in Analyzing Financial Statements (4/87). *Version 3:* In the upper division baccalaureate degree category, 3 semester hours in Analyzing Financial Statements (11/94).

Bank Control and Audit (SUP 101)

Location: Locations throughout New Jersey.

Length: 45 hours (15 weeks).

Dates: September 1986-December 1994.

Objective: To develop understanding among banker-students of industry standards and the need and nature of bank control and audit functions with particular emphasis on how the objectives, purpose, and value of control relate to overall bank performance.

Learning Outcome: Upon successful completion of the course, the student will be able to develop appreciation of how all departments of a bank work together for the same basic goals—a successful, sound, and profitable bank.

Instruction: Major topics covered in the course are the requirement for bank control, overall and in various banking functions, including an overview of the audit process; financial risk exposure and control objectives for each area of the balance sheet will be analyzed as well as operational/systems controls to ensure adherence to bank policies and guidelines; risks associated with ATMs and proof and transit items in the check collection process; risks associated with newer product applications; profitability auditing and issues of bank security and protection; records retention and storage; laws and regulations; and contingency planning .

Credit Recommendation: In the lower division baccalaureate/associate degree category, 2 semester hours in Bank Control and Audit Functions (8/89).

Bank Management (SUP103)

Location: Locations throughout New Jersey.

Length: 45 hours (15 weeks).

Dates: January 1977-December 1993.

Objective: To enable the student to apply management principles to banking operations.

Learning Outcome: Upon successful completion of this course, the student will be able to explain how bank objectives and policies are formed,outline the sources and uses of funds management, describe the administration of deposits, loans, and other investments, and analyze bank performance.

Instruction: Major topics covered in the course are the nature and objectives of banking, setting of objectives, organizational planning, staffing, management controls, and relationship between management principles and selected banking functions. Methods of instruction include lectures, discussion, classroom exercises, and problem solving .

Credit Recommendation: In the upper division baccalaureate degree category, 3 semester hours in Bank Management Seminar (1/82) (4/87).

Bank Management Seminar

Location: Locations throughout New Jersey.

Length: 45 hours (15 weeks).

Dates: January 1978-December 1985.

Objective: To enable the student to apply management principles to banking operations.

Instruction: Major topics covered in this course are the nature and objectives of banking, setting of objectives, organizational planning, staffing, management controls, and relationship between management principles and selected banking functions. Methods of instruction include lectures, discussion, classroom exercises, and problem solving. *This course duplicates Bank Management.

Credit Recommendation: In the upper division baccalaureate degree category, 3 semester hours in Bank Management Seminar (1/82).

Bank Payment Systems (BKF106)

Location: Locations throughout New Jersey.

Length: 45 hours (over 15 weeks).

Dates: September 1985-Present.

Objective: To provide students with knowledge and understanding of how and why banks operate the way they do, particularly concerning the check collection process and electronic payments transfer systems.

Learning Outcome: Upon successful completion of this course, the student will be able to understand the deposit mix of U.S. bank depositories and of the regulatory and procedural framework of the U.S. bank payments mechanisms, both paper and electronic-based, that largely govern bank operations.

Instruction: Major topics covered in the course are examination of the deposit and payment operations of U.S. depository institutions and national/international payment systems, governmental and institutional rules and procedures as they pertain to payment systems, deposits and depositories, regulatory structure and constraints, check clearing operations, electronic fund transfer systems, and future trends and development.

Credit Recommendation: In the lower division baccalaureate/associate degree or in the upper division baccalaureate degree category category, 3 semester hours in Bank Payment Systems (8/89) (11/94).

Business Communications (COM102)

Location: Locations throughout New Jersey.

Length: *Version 1:* 30 hours (10 weeks); *Version 2:* 45 hours (over 15 weeks).

Dates: *Version 1:* September 1983-August 1994; *Version 2:* September 1994-Present.

Objective: To develop in banker-students communication skills and understanding required for effective business relationships.

Learning Outcome: Upon successful completion of this course, the student will be able to exhibit improved business writing skills, listening skills, critical reading skills, and improved business speaking skills.

Instruction: Major topics covered in the course are the craft of writing; development of language skills; and the improvement of reading, listening, and speaking skills. Methods of instruction involve various writing projects with emphasis on good business techniques and listening and reading exercises .

Credit Recommendation: *Version 1:* In the lower division baccalaureate/associate degree category, 1 semester hour in Business Communications (8/89) *Version 2:* In the lower division baccalaureate/ associate degree category, 3 semester hours in Business Communications (11/94).

Business Today (COM115)

Location: Locations throughout New Jersey.

Length: 45 hours (over 15 weeks).

Dates: January 1994-Present.

Objective: To provide the banking student a comprehensive overview of the banking customer: the private sector business enterprise-corporate and sole proprietorships, large and small, including new ventures and franchises.

Learning Outcome: Upon successful completion of the course, the student will be able to understand the foundations and forms of American business and its ethical and social responsibilities; recognize how an American business is organized and managed to produce and market its products and services; and become acquainted with the government, risk and insurance environment of business.

Instruction: Major topics covered in the course are various forms of contemporary American private sector business enterprise; corporate and single proprietorship-large and small, including new ventures and franchises; ethical and social responsibilities of business management; fundamentals of management required to organize a business and produce and deliver goods and services into the American and international market place; and government relations and the U.S. legal and insurance environment.

Credit Recommendation: In the lower division baccalaureate/associate degree category, 3 semester hours in Introduction to Business (11/94).

Commercial Lending (CRL106)

Location: Locations throughout New Jersey.

Length: 45 hours (15 weeks).

Dates: September 1982-Present.

Objective: To provide retail banking students with knowledge of consumer loan markets, regulations, products, processes, and credit administration fundamentals of this vital segment of U.S. banking.

Learning Outcome: Upon successful completion of this course, the student will be able to identify the functions of the loan interview and credit investigation; describe how the borrower's financing needs and business type can affect the structuring of a loan; list important elements of loan documents and describe their functions; name some warning signs of problem loans; and identify ways the loan officer can prevent problem loans.

Instruction: Major topics covered in the course are a conceptual framework for the study of commercial lending, the organization of commercial lending and its contribution to bank profitability, and the commercial lending process from the initial loan request through collection.

Credit Recommendation: In the upper division baccalaureate degree category, 3 semester hours in Commercial Lending (8/89) (11/94).

Consumer Lending (CR103)

Location: Locations throughout New Jersey.

Length: 45 hours (15 weeks).

Dates: September 1982-Present.

Objective: To provide retail banking students with knowledge of consumer loan markets, regulations, products, and process, and credit administration fundamentals of this vital segment of U.S. banking.

Learning Outcome: Upon successful completion of this course, the student will be able to identify the components of the installment credit market; describe various loan products; delineate the lending process; apply credit math and loan pricing principles; recognize variables that affect loan structure; and identify opportunities for cross-selling bank products.

Instruction: Major topics covered in the course are the universe of consumer credit products and services now offered by a commercial bank; closed end loans and particularly open end loans; loan policy making; and management of the consumer credit area.

Credit Recommendation: In the upper division baccalaureate degree category, 3 semester hours in Consumer Lending or Finance elective (8/89) (11/94).

Economics (LEF102)

Location: Locations throughout New Jersey.

Length: 45 hours (15 weeks).

Dates: *Version 1:* January 1977-December 1986; *Version 2:* January 1987-Present.

Objective: To enable the student to understand the basic principles of economics.

Learning Outcome: Upon successful completion of this course, the student will be able to interpret the economic indicators published in the media; relate basic principles of economic theory to the business cycle and business organization; describe the cause of inflation, its effect, and ways it is measured; compare and contrast economic systems; and relate the fundamental concept of the supply and demand theory and Keynesian economics.

Instruction: *Version 1:* Covers basic economics concepts and macro and micro principles. Topics include supply and demand, income determination, business cycles and forecasting, prices and money, the banking system deposit creation, and monetary policy. Methods of instruction include lectures, discussion, classroom exercises and problem solving. *Version 2:* This course sets forth the current principles explaining how our economic system operates. It takes up the determination of relative value in markets with different types of competition and applies the underlying principles of incomes and commodities. The course also offers a basic introduction to the arenas of international economics and finance.

Credit Recommendation: *Version 1:* In the lower division baccalaureate/associate degree category, 2 semester hours in Economics (1/82) (4/87). *Version 2:* In the lower division baccalaureate/associate degree category, 3 semester hours in Economics (1/82)(4/87)(11/94).

Human Relations in Banking (SUP106)

Location: Locations throughout New Jersey.

Length: 45 hours (15 weeks).

Dates: *Version 1:* September 1985-October 1994; *Version 2:* November 1994-Present.

Objective: To develop in banker-students an understanding of their role in a work setting with a private sector business enterprise whether supervisor or supervised.

Learning Outcome: Upon successful completion of this course the student will be able to understand how human relations is a key to success; improve personal and organizational communications; identify your motivations; develop personal strategies for improving human relations; and learn to achieve emotional control.

Instruction: Major topics covered in the course are the role of human relations in the work setting; concepts of motivation, leadership, communications, personality theories, and dynamics of group behavior; the role and function of the individual within an organizational (especially bank) structure.

Credit Recommendation: *Version 1:* In the upper division baccalaureate degree category, 3 semester hours in Human Relations (8/89). *Version 2:* In the lower division baccalaureate/associate degree category or in the upper division baccalaureate degree category, 3 semester hours in Human Relations (11/94).

International Banking (BKF110)

Location: Locations throughout New Jersey.

Length: 45 hours (15 weeks).

Dates: September 1982-Present.

Objective: To provide students with an introduction to international banking processes and practices supporting international trade and finance.

Learning Outcome: Upon successful completion of this course, the student will be able to identify the various international services banks provide; describe the various legal and regulatory constraints/ requirements that dominate international finance; identify the various international lending agencies and their role in international finance; and define basic international banking terms including Incoterms.

Instruction: Major topics covered in the course are an overview of international trade and investments that are common to American business, government, and banking, the practices and processes developed by U.S. banks under the impetus of business and government; country risk assessment; correspondent relationships; money transfer; and foreign exchange.

Credit Recommendation: In the upper division baccalaureate degree category, 3

semester hours in International Banking (8/89) (11/94).

Law and Banking: Applications (LEF104) (Formerly Business and Banking Law II (LEF104), Bank Marketing and Marketing for Business)

Location: Locations throughout New Jersey.

Length: 45 hours (15 weeks).

Dates: September 1987-Present.

Objective: To provide banker-students with knowledge and understanding of negotiable instruments and the Uniform Commercial Code, Articles 3-5 and 9.

Learning Outcome: Upon successful completion of this course, the student will be able to explain the concept of negotiability; analyze the concept of holder-in-due course status; discuss the legal issues related to bank collections and check losses; define and explain the nature of a letter of credit; and identify the issues related to a secured transaction.

Instruction: Major topics covered in the course are the concept of negotiability, parties to each particular type of negotiable instrument; the elements comprising negotiable instruments; holder-in-due course, liability, and bank collections plus check losses and frauds are analyzed from a banker's perspective; commercial and standby letters of credit; and an examination of secured transactions.

Credit Recommendation: In the lower division baccalaureate/associate degree category or in the upper division baccalaureate degree category , 3 semester hours in Business Law II (8/89) (11/94).

Law and Banking: Principles (LEF101) (Formerly Business and Banking Law I (LEF101) and Law and Banking)

Location: Locations throughout New Jersey.

Length: 45 hours (15 weeks).

Dates: January 1977-Present.

Objective: To enable the student to understand general legal principles and selected legal issues of importance to bankers.

Learning Outcome: Upon successful completion of this course, the student will be able to identify sources and applications of banking law; distinguish between torts and crimes, and how they relate to banking situations, explain contracts, including the need for legal capacity, legal objective, mutual assent, and consideration; describe real and personal properties and their application to banking; discuss how bankruptcy affects and differentiates between the liquidation and rehabilitation goals of Bankruptcy Code; and identify the legal implications of consumer lending.

Instruction: Major topics covered in the course are the court system, civil procedure, contracts, personal property, real property, torts, crime trusts, agency and partnership, corporations, sales, commercial paper, secured transactions, and consumer regulations. Methods of instruction include lectures, discussion, classroom exercises, and problem solving.

Credit Recommendation: In the lower division baccalaureate/associate degree or in the upper division baccalaureate degree category, 3 semester hours in Business Law I (1/82) (4/87) (11/94).

Loan and Discount

Location: Locations throughout New Jersey.

Length: 45 hours (15 weeks).

Dates: January 1977-December 1990.

Objective: To enable the student to understand the loan and discount function in a commercial bank.

Instruction: Major topics covered in the course are notes, guarantees, collateral agreements, and secured transactions. Methods of instruction include lectures, discussion, classroom exercises, and problem solving .

Credit Recommendation: In the upper division baccalaureate degree category, 3 semester hours in Loan and Discount (1/82) (4/87).

Lotus 1-2-3 for Bankers

Location: Locations throughout New Jersey.

Length: 45 hours (14 weeks).

Dates: January 1987-December 1993.

Objective: To provide banker-students with a comprehensive introduction to microcomputer fundamentals with an emphasis on attaining practical hands-on proficiency in the use of Lotus 1-2-3.

Learning Outcome: Upon successful completion of this course, the student will be able to understand all the basic features of Lotus 1-2-3.

Instruction: Major topics covered in the course are an overview of microcomputer concepts, and the use of Lotus 1-2-3 for the preparation of business reports requiring spreadsheet and data base application; and Lotus1-2-3's key features, such as the use of command menu, file management, use of function keys and formula development, format display, spreadsheet creation, template design, understanding "what-if" analysis, graph building and viewing, Lotus macro language, add-on products, data base, and graphics product for financial forecasting, modeling, and analysis. Methods of instruction include lecture, problem-solving sessions emphasizing why and when to use this popular spreadsheet, and hands-on exercises.

Credit Recommendation: In the lower division baccalaureate/associate degree category, 3 semester hours in Lotus 1-2-3 for Bankers (8/89).

Marketing for Bankers (BKF108) (Formerly Financial Marketing, Bank Marketing, and Marketing for Business)

Location: Locations throughout New Jersey.

Length: 45 hours (15 weeks).

Dates: January 1977-Present.

Objective: To enable the student to understand the basic principles of marketing as applied to banking.

Learning Outcome: Upon successful completion of this course, the student will be able to recognize consumer motivational and buying behavior; integrate public relations, advertising, sales promotion, selling and service distribution functions in the bank's overall marketing plan; conduct situation analysis and formulate a master marketing strategy; and monitor and evaluate performance.

Instruction: Major topics covered in the course are the concepts and philosophies of marketing, including market research; consumer behavior; motivation; strategies related to product, price, promotion, and place; public relations; advertising and selling; and planning. Methods of instruction include lectures, discussion, classroom exercises, and problem solving.

Credit Recommendation: In the upper division baccalaureate degree category, 3 semester hours in Bank Marketing or Business elective (1/82) (4/87) (11/94).

Microcomputer Applications in Banking

Location: Locations throughout New Jersey.

Length: 45 hours (14 weeks).

Dates: September 1986-December 1993.

Objective: To provide banker students with a comprehensive introduction to microcomputer concepts and technology with emphasis on microcomputer and software applications used in banking.

Learning Outcome: Upon successful completion of the course students will be able to gain immediate confidence and success in using a PC; understand microcomputer components, operating system's role, and practical business uses; and realize familiarity with software applications most commonly used in banking.

Instruction: Major topics covered in the course are an introduction to microcomputer concepts, computer operations, operating system commands, and primary application areas for which a PC can be used in banking (spreadsheets, word processing, database management, data communications). Hands-on use of a PC with customized banking models reinforces newly acquired skills and provides carryover effect for learned skills.

Credit Recommendation: In the lower division baccalaureate/associate degree category, 3 semester hours in Introduction to Microcomputer Concepts and Technology (8/89).

Microcomputers in Banking

Location: Locations throughout New Jersey.

Length: 45 hours (7 sessions/6 hours each).

Dates: January 1994-Present.

Objective: To provide an overview of today's most commonly used microcomputers in banking. Terminology, technical concepts and hands-on exercises are incorporated into a 7-session series offering a complete learning experience.

Learning Outcome: Upon successful completion of this course the student will be able to exhibit the skills necessary to access and effectively utilize microcomputer programs in word processing, database management, and spread sheeting; understand basic PC and file maintenance; and transfer most manual banking office procedures

Instruction: Major topics covered in the course include introduction to PCs and DOS, Excel, introduction to Lotus1-2-3 or Excel, intermediate Lotus or Excel, Wordperfect or Word, intermediate DOS, introduction to Paradox or DBase, and introduction to Windows.

Credit Recommendation: In the lower division baccalaureate/associate degree or in the upper division baccalaureate degree category, 3 semester hours in Microcomputer Applications (11/94).

Money and Banking (LEF103)

Location: Locations throughout New Jersey.

Length: 45 hours (15 weeks).

Dates: *Version 1:* January 1977-December 1986; *Version 2:* January 1987-Present.

Objective: To enable the banking student to learn the practical aspects of money and banking and basic monetary theory.

Learning Outcome: Upon successful completion of this course, the student will be able to describe how commercial banks "create" money; identify the tools of monetary and fiscal policy; summarize and better interpret major trends and issues in banking; relate banking operations to the U.S. payments mechanism; and compare and contrast the various types of financial institutions.

Instruction: *Version 1:* Major topics covered in the course are economic stabilization, types of spending, the role of gold, limitations of central bank control, government fiscal policy, the balance of payments, and foreign exchange. Methods of instruction include lectures, discussion, classroom exercises, and problem solving. *Version 2:* This course applies basic economic principles to the field of banking. Major topics covered are the economy and how it works; the Federal Reserve System; the business of banking; monetary policy and its impact on financial markets and banks; alternate theories of money's role in the economy; fiscal policy; and trends in banking.

Credit Recommendation: *Version 1:* In the upper division baccalaureate degree category, 2 semester hours in Money and Banking (1/82). *Version 2:* In the upper division baccalaureate degree category, or in the lower division baccalaureate/associate degree category, 3 semester hours in Money and Banking (4/87)(11/94).

Principles of Banking (BKF113)

Location: Locations throughout New Jersey.

Length: 45 hours (15 weeks).

Dates: *Version 1:* January 1977-December 1986; *Version 2:* January 1987-Present.

Objective: To provide the student with a basic understanding of commercial banking.

Learning Outcome: Upon successful completion of this course, the student will be able to explain the importance of full-service commercial banking as it affects the economy; the community, business, and the individual; describe the three major functions of commercial banks and their interrelationships; list the various products and services banks offer governments, business, individuals, and correspondents, contrast between demand and time deposits; illustrate the various types of loans and investments; and explain the concepts of liquidity, safety and income.

Instruction: *Version 1:* Major topics covered in the course are internal operations of commercial banks, including documents and language of banking, deposit functions, relationships with depositors, specialized banking services, regulations, and examination. Methods of instruction include lectures, discussion, classroom exercises, and problem solving. *Version 2:* This course offers a comprehensive introduction to the diversified services offered by the banking industry today. Major topics covered are banking, history, and economic and community environment; documents and language of banking; bank services; deposit and check processing; bank loans and investments; trust departments; specialized services; and bank regulations.

Credit Recommendation: *Version 1:* In the lower division baccalaureate/associate degree category, 2 semester hours in Introduction to Banking (1/82). *Version 2:* In the lower division baccalaureate/associate degree category, 3 semester hours in Introduction to Banking (4/87) (11/94).

Real Estate and Mortgage Principles (BKF114)
(Formerly Real Estate Finance)

Location: Locations throughout New Jersey.

Length: 45 hours (15 weeks).

Dates: January 1977 Present.

Objective: To enable the student to understand real estate from the viewpoint of the mortgage loan officer.

Learning Outcome: Upon successful completion of this course the student will be able to identify the concepts and terminology specific to real estate law, explain special risk associated with different kinds of income properties, describe the role of government in housing, and analyze real-estate investment.

Instruction: Major topics covered in the course are the mortgage market acquisition of mortgage portfolio, mortgage plans and procedures, mortgage loan processing and servicing, and portfolio management. Methods of instruction include lectures, discussion, classroom exercises, and problem solving..

Credit Recommendation: In the lower division baccalaureate/associate degree or in the upper division baccalaureate degree category, 3 semester hours in Real Estate Finance (1/82) (4/87) (11/94).

Securities Processing (BKF116)

Location: Locations throughout New Jersey.

Length: 45 hours (over 15 weeks).

Dates: September 1986-Present.

Objective: To provide banker-students with a general knowledge and understanding of the whole range of securities-related activities.

Learning Outcome: Upon successful completion of this course the student will be able to describe the type of securities that are traded, the marketplaces in which they are traded and what players are involved in the process; identify the laws and regulations that govern securities trading; list the various elements of securities transactions that have a bearing on the obligations, options and rights of securities issuers and stockholders; describe the procedures used to settle securities issuers, and stockholders; and justify a bank's trust and agency responsibilities with respect to securities.

Instruction: Major topics covered in the course are emphasizing the operational aspects of processing various securities, administering consumer and corporate trust accounts and the bank's own investment portfolio, buying and selling securities as agents for the accounts of bank customers, purchasing selected investment securities, and dealing in or underwriting allowable federal obligations of states and municipalities.

Credit Recommendation: In the upper division baccalaureate degree category, 3 semester hours in Securities (8/89) (11/94).

Supervision Concepts and Practices (SUP105) (Formerly Fundamentals of Supervision, Supervision, and Personnel Administration)

Location: Locations throughout New Jersey.

Length: 45 hours (15 weeks).

Dates: *Version 1:* January 1977-December 1986; *Version 2:* January 1987-Present.

Objective: To provide an understanding of management philosophies and techniques for first-line supervisors. This course is designed to aid first-line supervisors in making a smooth transition from expert in a particular task to the role of a supervisor who must produce results through the efforts of other people.

Learning Outcome: Upon successful completion of this course the student will be able to identify the characteristics of effective management; practice effective communication while developing interpersonal skills; work effectively with groups; conduct interviews, select employees, and handle conflict; appraise employees; and respond to grievances and conduct disciplinary actions.

Instruction: *Version 1:* Major topics covered in the course are developing management-mindedness, self-development, communication, management of change; superior-subordinate relationships, understanding, motivation, training, and grievances handling; planning, delegating, decision making, and performance review. Methods of instruction include lectures, discussion, classroom exercises, and problem solving. *Version 2:* Major topics covered in the course are the managerial process: planning, organizing, staffing, directing, and controlling. Practical case studies are used to apply these concepts to realistic situations. The course also treats basic management considerations and the area of labor relations.

Credit Recommendation: *Version 1:* In the lower division baccalaureate/associate degree category, 2 semester hours in Supervisor Management or Business elective (1/82). *Version 2:* In the lower division baccalaureate/associate degree category, 3 semester hours in Supervisor Man-agement or Business Elective (4/87) (11/94).

Trust Business (BKF118) (Formerly Trust Functions and Services)

Location: Locations throughout New Jersey.

Length: 45 hours (15 weeks).

Dates: January 1977-Present.

Objective: To enable the student to understand the function and services offered by institutions engaged in the trust business.

Learning Outcome: Upon successful completion of this course, the student will be able to explain the role of the trust department in a bank, describe the services corporate and consumer customers receive, and identify assets and ownership related to trust services.

Instruction: Major topics covered in the course are trusts, wills, estate administration, personal agencies, corporate agencies, property rights, trust funds, and employee benefit accounts. Methods of instruction include lectures, discussion, classroom exercises, and problem solving.

Credit Recommendation: In the upper division baccalaureate degree category, 3 semester hours in Trust Functions and Services or Business elective (1/82) (4/87) (11/94).

Trust Operations (BKF119)

Location: Locations throughout New Jersey.

Length: 45 hours (15 weeks).

Dates: January 1977-Present.

Objective: To enable the student to understand the fundamental functions of trust operations.

Learning Outcome: Upon successful completion of this course, the student will be able to describe the types of securities handled by a trust department, the kinds of investments typically made with trust account assets; why securities are used and how they are traded; identify the roles and function of the various participants in the securities industry; explain the responsibilities inherent in the fiduciary and agency relationships a trust department has with its customers; identify the law and regulations that define and circumscribe trust activities; describe the internal controls, and record keeping, and reporting requirements necessary in trust activities.

Instruction: Major topics covered in the course are orientation and history of trust operations, central depositories and security movement and control, retirement trusts and common fund accounting, corporate trust, fiduciary tax, fiduciary accounting, statutes and regulatory requirements, trust auditors, and trust profitability. Methods of instruction include lectures, discussion, classroom exercises, and problem solving.

Credit Recommendation: In the upper division baccalaureate degree category, 3 semester hours in Trust Operations or Business electives (1/82) (4/87) (11/94).

American Institute of Banking, Mid-Atlantic Chapter

The Mid-Atlantic Chapter of the American Institute of Banking (AIB) is a not-for-profit educational affiliate of the American Bankers Association. It is one of 300 chapters serving the continuing education needs of bankers in the United States, Puerto Rico, and Guam.

Founded in 1901, the chapter's mission is to deliver bank-specific and general business training and education for the benefit of the employees, officers, and directors of its nearly 200 member organizations in Maryland, the District of Columbia, and northern Virginia.

The chapter adopts may of the courses developed by the national AIB office and helps maintain nationally prescribed banker education standards. However, it is an autonomous organization and exercises administrative control over its instructor selection, and facilities arrangement. Therefore, credit recommendations established for the Mid-Atlantic Chapter do no necessarily apply to other AIB chapters.

Bank officers, attorneys, certified public accountants, and other professionals are selected to teach the courses. Students may earn a variety of banking industry certificates and diplomas by successfully completing selected courses. The chapter also offers a wide range of not-for-credit training programs on contemporary banking topics, conducts contract training for banks and other organizations, and sponsors an in-residence commercial lending school.

Source of official student records: Registry of Credit Recommendations, American Council on Education, One Dupont Circle, Washington, DC 20036-1193 or Registrar, Mid-Atlantic Chapter, American Institute of Banking, 8120 Woodmont Ave., #410, Bethesda, MD 20814.

Additional information about the courses: College Credit Recommendation Service, American Council on Education, One Dupont Circle, Washington, DC 20036-1193.

Accounting I (201)

Location: Various locations in Washington, DC, Maryland, and northern Virginia.

Length: 45 hours (15 weeks).

Dates: August 1978-Present.

Objective: To present to the student the basic concepts, theory, and practices of accounting.

Learning Outcome: Upon successful completion of this course, the student will be able to understand basic accounting terms, concepts and principles, and the accounting cycle; prepare basic financial statements; and analyze, journalize, and post business transactions.

Instruction: Major topics covered in the course are accounting terminology; the recording and classifying of financial transactions, including analyzing and posting; the preparation of the trial balance, worksheet, and financial statements; and the handling of adjustments, bad debts, inventory, and depreciation. Methods of instruction include lecture, discussion, class participation, group project, and examinations.

Credit Recommendation: In the lower division baccalaureate/associate degree category, 3 semester hours in Accounting or Business Administration (3/84) (3/89) (11/95).

Accounting II (202)

Location: Various locations in Washington, DC, Maryland, and northern Virginia.

Length: 45 hours (15 weeks).

Dates: September 1978-Present.

Objective: To provide the student with a further understanding of accounting principles and practices, including corporation accounting, and basic statement analysis.

Learning Outcome: Upon successful completion of this course, the student will be able to apply managerial cost accounting concepts and procedures, including accounting for manufacturing companies and planning, control, and decision making, and perform basic financial statement analysis, including the statement of cash flows, the balance sheet, and the income statement.

Instruction: Major topics covered in the course are partnership accounting, corporation accounting, responsibility accounting, cost accounting, and basic statement analysis. Methods of instruction include lecture, discussion, class participation, group project, and examinations.

Credit Recommendation: In the lower division baccalaureate/associate degree category, 3 semester hours in Accounting (5/84) (3/89) (11/95). *Prerequisite:* Accounting I.

Analyzing Financial Statements (205)

Location: Various locations in Washington, DC, Maryland, and northern Virginia.

Length: 45 hours (15 weeks).

Dates: September 1975-Present.

Objective: To provide the student with the basic theory and skills necessary to apply financial analysis to the financial statements, including the statement of cash flows, to evaluate the current and future financial condition of business firms.

Learning Outcome: Upon successful completion of this course, the student will be able to apply financial ratio analysis to the income statement balance sheet to evaluate the business firm's financial condition; analyze the statement of cash flows to determine the firm's capacity to generate internal cash flows and its need for external financing; and prepare pro forma financial statements and cash budgets and use them for financial planning.

Instruction: Major topics covered in the course are financial ratio analysis, statement of cash flows, pro forma financial statements, cash budgets, financial assumptions, sensitivity analysis, and break even analysis. Methods of instruction include lecture, discussion, and proctored exercises.

Credit Recommendation: In the upper division baccalaureate degree category, 3 semester hours in Accounting or Finance (5/84) (3/89) (11/95).

Bank Investments (802)

Location: Various locations in Washington, DC, Maryland, and northern Virginia.

Length: 24 hours (3 hours per week for 8 weeks).

Dates: August 1984-Present.

Objective: To teach bankers the fundamentals of investments most often encountered in their work, i.e., treasury securities, government securities, money market investments, and securities markets.

Learning Outcome: Upon successful completion of this course, the student will be able to understand skills needed to coordinate inflows and outflows of bank funds; manage the bank's investment account; and understand key concepts of bank investments and fund management.

Instruction: Major topics covered in the course are an introduction to investment and investment analysis, financial markets, money market investments, federal agency securities, municipal securities, and U.S. Treasury securities. Methods of instruction include lecture, discussion, classroom exercises, quizzes, and examinations.

Credit Recommendation: In the upper division baccalaureate degree category, 2 semester hours in Banking, Business Administration, or Finance (3/89) (11/95).

Bank Management (102)

Location: Various locations in Washington, DC, Maryland, and northern Virginia.

Length: *Version 1:* 35 hours (10 weeks); *Version 2:* 45 hours (15 weeks).

Dates: *Version 1:* October 1981-May 1992; *Version 2:* September 1993-Present.

Objective: To provide the student with an understanding of the fundamentals of bank functions, including the organizational structure and financial management philosophy of banks.

Learning Outcome: Upon successful completion of this course, the student will be able to understand the organizational and financial management philosophy of banks; know the bank functions, including the deposit, lending, and investment functions; analyze bank performance and know bank planning techniques; and be familiar with branch banking, bank holding companies, and international banking.

Instruction: Major topics covered in the course are bank financial statements; management and internal organization of commercial banks; asset, liability, and capital management; profitability; credit analysis and loan policies; short-term and long-term loans; commercial and consumer lending; and bank investments. Methods of instruction include lecture, discussion, and an examination.

Credit Recommendation: In the upper division baccalaureate degree category, 3 semester hours in Banking or Finance (5/84) (3/89) (11/95).

Bank Management: Commercial Banking (102)

Location: Various locations in the Washington, DC metropolitan area.

Length: 45 hours (15 weeks).

Dates: September 1976-May 1979.

Objective: To provide an understanding of commercial banking and its role in the economy.

Instruction: Major topics covered in the course are commercial bank functions, bank capital and earnings, lending policies and procedures, bank investments, and bank audits.

Credit Recommendation: In the lower division baccalaureate/associate degree category, 3 semester hours in Banking (3/79).

Bank Marketing: Theory and Applications (510)

Location: Various locations in Washington, DC, Maryland, and northern Virginia.

Length: 45 hours (15 weeks).

Dates: January 1987-Present.

Objective: To provide the student with a basic introduction to marketing and to explore applications of these concepts within a bank setting.

Learning Outcome: Upon successful completion of this course, the student will be able to interrelate and coordinate the multifunctions involved in the marketing process; integrate customer behavior factors into plans and strategies; have a better understanding of service offering development processes, pricing decisions, promotional strategies, and delivery alternatives; and be able to specify and use marketing information in marketing decisions.

Instruction: Major topics covered in the course are basic marketing, strategic marketing, understanding the market, marketing mix strategies, and pricing. Methods of instruction include lecture, discussion, case studies, learner presentations/reports, and examinations.

Credit Recommendation: In the lower division baccalaureate/associate degree category, 3 semester hours in Business Administration, Finance, or Principles of Marketing (3/89) (11/95).

Business Law (701)
Banking Law

Location: Various locations in Washington, DC, Maryland, and northern Virginia.

Length: *Version 1:* 20 hours (10 weeks); *Version 2:* 30 hours (10 weeks).

Dates: *Version 1:* October 1981-February 1989; *Version 2:* March 1989-Present.

Objective: To acquaint students with general principles of commercial law emphasizing transactions.

Learning Outcome: Upon successful completion of this course, the student will be able to understand the various aspects of the Uniform Commercial Code; reason through simple legal problems; and understand contract law.

Instruction: Major topics covered in the course are principles of commercial law, reasoning through simple legal problems, the legal environment of business, contracts, government regulation, torts, and liability. Methods of instruction include lecture, discussion, cases, and graded examinations.

Credit Recommendation: *Version 1:* In the upper division baccalaureate degree category, 3 semester hours in Business Law (5/84). *Version 2:* In the upper division baccalaureate degree category, 2 semester hours in Accounting, Business Administration, Business Law, or Finance (3/89) (11/95).

Business Law: Selected Topics 1. Banking Law/Lending (702) 2. Banking Law/Operations (703)

Location: Various locations in Washington, DC, Maryland, and northern Virginia.

Length: *Version 1:* 15 hours (5 weeks); *Version 2:* 15 hours (5 weeks).

Dates: *Version 1:* May 1984-February 1989; *Version 2:* March 1989-December 1995.

Objective: *Banking Law/Operations:* To expand the students' legal knowledge in selected topics in Business Law with special emphasis on bank operations. *Banking Law/Lending:* To acquaint the student with selected topics in Business Law with special emphasis on bank lending, secured credit, and truth in lending.

Learning Outcome: Upon successful completion of this course, the student will be able to understand the application of business law to bank operations, and relate business law to selected topics, including bank lending, secured credit, and truth in lending.

Instruction: Major topics covered in the course are legal issues that affect the bank employee in a number of areas, including check clearance, bank liability, electronic funds transfers, and meeting customer requests for credit. Methods of instruction include lecture and discussion.

Credit Recommendation: *Version 1:* In the upper division baccalaureate degree category, 3 semester hours in Business Law (5/84). *Version 2:* In the upper division baccalaureate degree category, 2 semester hours in Accounting, Business Administration, Business Law, or Finance (3/89) (11/95). **NOTE:** Students can receive 1 semester hour for completing either Lending or Operations and 2 semester hours for completing both.

Cash Management I and II (820 & 821)

Location: Various locations in Washington, DC, Maryland, and northern Virginia.

Length: 45 hours (15 weeks).

Dates: August 1983-December 1990.

Objective: This two-part course provides bankers with concise understanding of current and emerging domestic commercial cash management services and systems.

Learning Outcome: Upon successful completion of this course, the student will be able to understand the marketing of cash management services; understand electronic trends related to cash management; and assess cash management needs and problems.

Instruction: Major topics covered in the course are cash collection, short-term investment, cash disbursement, information and control, cash management regulation, the corporate services mix, and cash management risk. Methods of instruction include lecture, discussion, exercises, video, and field visits.

Credit Recommendation: In the upper division baccalaureate degree category, 3 semester hours in Banking, Business Administration, or Finance (3/89) (11/95).

Commercial Loan Case Simulation (853)

Location: Various locations in the Washington, DC, metropolitan area.

Length: 10 weeks (3-hour meetings weekly).

Dates: March 1983-April 1986.

Objective: To enable students to analyze and understand actual commercial credit applications and loan pricing in a competitive environment.

Instruction: Major topics covered in the course are competitive pricing, business financial statement and management analysis, bank financial performance, goal setting and attainment, credit investigation, and cost/benefit analysis. Methods of instruction include Commercial Loan Case Simulation, a computer "game" played by teams of three or four lenders competing against each other as they track the decisions made about a group of actual loans over a "four-year" period, computer feedback, lectures, individual instructor attention for teams, and small group interaction. Teams of three or four people from the same bank are encouraged to compete against other teams for what is an invaluable learning experience.

Credit Recommendation: In the upper division baccalaureate degree category, 2 semester hours in Finance (5/84).

Consumer Lending (860)

Location: Various locations in Washington, DC, Maryland, and northern Virginia.

Length: 45 hours (15 weeks).

Dates: August 1987-Present.

Objective: To provide the student with a basic understanding of credit services available to consumers.

Learning Outcome: Upon successful completion of this course, the student will be familiar with state and federal regulations and laws governing consumer credit; know the various types of consumer loans and the consumer lending process; and understand the planning, organizing, directing, and controlling of the consumer credit function.

Instruction: Major topics covered in the course are consumer credit legislation and regulation; open-end and closed-end consumer credit; credit process, including investigation, decision making, documentation, and collection; and credit policies and credit management. Methods of instruction include lecture, discussion, practical exercises, and examinations.

Credit Recommendation: In the lower division baccalaureate/associate degree category, 3 semester hours in Business Administration, Consumer Credit Management, Finance, or Marketing (3/89) (11/95).

Economics (301)

Location: Various locations in Washington, DC, Maryland, and northern Virginia.

Length: 45 hours (15 weeks).

Dates: September 1976-Present.

Objective: To provide the student with knowledge of basic economic principles.

Learning Outcome: Upon successful completion of this course, the student will be able to understand the relationship between micro and macro economic principles and applications; apply the basic concepts of supply, demand, and pricing to banking activities; and understand the sources of business cycle fluctuations and productivity growth.

Instruction: Major topics covered in the course are basic economic concepts; measurement of national output and income; national income analysis; monetary and fiscal policy; and basic demand, supply, and price concepts. Methods of instruction include lectures, discussion, and examinations.

Credit Recommendation: In the lower division baccalaureate/associate degree category, 3 semester hours in Economics (5/84) (3/89) (11/95).

Fundamentals of Bank Data Processing

Location: Various locations in the Washington, DC, metropolitan area.

Length: 45 hours (15 weeks).

Dates: September 1978-December 1991.

Objective: To provide the student with a basic understanding of the fundamentals of data processing and the computer.

Instruction: Major topics covered in the course are data processing, business applications, punched card systems computer concepts, basic flowcharting, and the programming cycle.

Credit Recommendation: In the lower division baccalaureate/associate degree category, 3 semester hours in Business Administration (3/79) (11/95).

International Banking (912)

Location: Various locations in Washington, Maryland, and northern Virginia.

Length: 45 hours (15 weeks).

Dates: August 1987-Present.

Objective: To provide the student a broad introductory exposure to the area of international banking and financial transactions. The course covers international operations, credit, and trading exchange policies as they concern the international banking community.

Learning Outcome: Upon successful completion of this course, the student will be able to evaluate various country risk assessments as they pertain to economic and political factors; understand the international finance transaction; understand the role of correspondent banking as it pertains to international markets; appreciate the trends in international monetary exchange; and translate and evaluate letters of credit from both issuing and utilization standpoints.

Instruction: Major topics covered in the course are organization and structure of the international monetary markets, how transactions concern transfer of funds, foreign trade collection, letters of credit, basic principles of foreign trade and exchange, and development of policies for exchange by government agencies to facilitate international financial transactions. Methods of instruction include lecture, discussion, case preparation, and a presentation.

Credit Recommendation: In the upper division baccalaureate degree category, 3 semester hours in Business Administration, Finance, or International Business (3/89) (11/95).

Introduction to Financial Planning (826)

Location: Various locations in Washington, DC, Maryland, and northern Virginia.

Length: 45 hours (15 weeks).

Dates: *Version 1:* October 1983-August 1988; *Version 2:* September 1990-Present.

Objective: To develop the student's awareness of the role of the professional financial planner and how financial planning services are offered in commercial banks.

Learning Outcome: *Version 1:* Upon completion, students will have an overview of the planning process and what is required to be competitive in the environment of high inflation and taxes. *Version 2:* Upon successful completion of this course, the student will have an overview of the financial planning process, financial planning approaches, and sources of financial planning information.

Instruction: *Version 1:* Major topics covered in the course are a broad range of insights into the financial planning industry in which the bankers are becoming more involved as the result of deregulation and the text is used to provide a source of information in which case situations are applied. Methods of instruction include actual case situations of the instructor are used to reinforce the learning process and student actual case situations are encouraged. *Version 2:* Major topics covered in the course are an overview of financial planning including insurance, investment, retirement, tax, estate, and special situation planning. Methods of instruction include lecture, discussion, cases, and examinations.

Credit Recommendation: In the lower division baccalaureate/associate degree category, 3 semester hours in Personal Finance (5/84) (11/95).

Law and Banking I

Location: Various locations in the Washington, DC, metropolitan area.

Length: 45 hours (15 weeks).

Dates: September 1975-March 1981.

Objective: To provide the student with a basic knowledge of business law.

Instruction: Major topics covered in the course are introduction to business law; the Uniform Commercial Code, including legal rights, contracts, personal property, and bailments; risk and property rights in sales; partnerships; and corporations.

Credit Recommendation: In the upper division baccalaureate degree category, 3 semester hours in Business Administration (3/79).

Law and Banking: Principles (698)
Law and Banking I

Location: Various locations in Washington, D. C., Maryland, and northern Virginia.

Length: 45 hours (15 weeks).

Dates: January 1985-Present.

Objective: To provide the student with a guide to law and legal issues, with special emphasis on the Uniform Commercial Code.

Learning Outcome: Upon successful completion of this course, the student will be able to identify the sources and applications of banking law, distinguish between torts and crimes and how they relate to banking; explain contracts and their requirements; identify real and personal properties and their application to banking; how bankruptcy affects banks and differentiate between the liquidation and rehabilitation goals of the Bankruptcy Code; and identify the legal implications of consumer lending.

Instruction: Major topics covered in the course are an introduction to business law; the Uniform Commercial Code, including legal rights, contracts, personal property, and bailments; risk and property rights in sales; partnerships; and corporations. Methods of instruction include lecture, discussion, cases, and examinations.

Credit Recommendation: In the lower division baccalaureate/associate or upper division baccalaureate degree category, 3 semester hours in Business Administration, Banking, or Business Law (11/95).

Law: Bank Lending (702)
Business Law: Selected Topics-Banking Law/Lending

Location: Various locations in Washington, DC, Maryland, and northern Virginia.

Length: 15 hours (5 weeks).

Dates: January 1996-Present.

Objective: To provide an in-depth study of those principles of business law that apply to bank loans.

Learning Outcome: Upon successful completion of this course, the student will be able to understand the application of business law to lending.

Instruction: Major topics covered in the course are finance charges, collateral, interest rates, joint ownership, and disclosure. Methods of instruction include lecture, discussion, current issues, and a final examination.

Credit Recommendation: In the upper division baccalaureate degree category, 1 semester hour in Business Law or Finance (11/95). *Prerequisite*: Business Law: Banking Law (701).

Law: Bank Operations (703)
Business Law: Selected Topics—Banking Law/Operations

Location: Various locations in Washington, DC, Maryland, and northern Virginia.

Length: 15 hours (5 weeks).

Dates: January 1996-Present.

Objective: To provide in-depth study of those principles of business law that apply to bank operations.

Learning Outcome: Upon successful completion of this course, the student will be able to understand the application of business law to bank operations that relate to demand, and other deposits.

Instruction: Major topics covered in the course are law that affects registration, check collection, Truth in Savings, checks as related to bank customers, and electronic fund transfers. Methods of instruction include lecture, discussion, current issue handouts, and examinations.

Credit Recommendation: In the upper division baccalaureate degree category, 1 semester hour in Business Law or Finance (11/95). *Prerequisite*: Banking Law (701).

Management of Commercial Bank Funds (806)

Location: Various locations in the Washington, DC, metropolitan area.

Length: 45 hours (15 weeks).

Dates: September 1975-March 1981.

Objective: To provide the student with an understanding of the principles of funds management in commercial banks.

Instruction: Major topics covered in the course are the importance of funds management in coordinating policies on loans, deposits, investments, and capital.

Credit Recommendation: In the upper division baccalaureate degree category, 3 semester hours in Banking, Business

Administration, or Finance (3/79). *Prerequisite:* Accounting I or Economics.

Money and Banking (302)

Location: Various locations in Washington, DC, Maryland, and northern Virginia.

Length: 45 hours (15 weeks).

Dates: January 1976-Present.

Objective: To provide an understanding of the functions of money in the United States and how the Federal Reserve and commercial banking system influence the money supply, banking, credit, and the economy.

Learning Outcome: Upon successful completion of this course, the student will be able to understand the role of money in the economy; the role of banks in creating money and their part in the nation's payment system; and the Federal Reserve's structure, operating tools, and objective.

Instruction: Major topics covered in the course are the development of the U.S. monetary and banking system; Federal Reserve monetary policy and its effect on commercial banking; the quantity theory of money (monetarist approach) and the Keynesian approach; the effectiveness of monetary policy; determination of interest rates; and availability of credit. Methods of instruction include lecture, discussion, and examinations.

Credit Recommendation: In the upper division baccalaureate degree category, 3 semester hours in Economics (5/84) (3/89) (11/95). *Prerequisite*: Economics.

Principles of Banking (101) (Formerly Principles of Bank Operations)

Location: Various locations in Washington, DC, Maryland, and northern Virginia.

Length: 45 hours (15 weeks).

Dates: *Version 1:* March 1979-December 1995; *Version 2:* January 1996-Present.

Objective: *Version 1:* To provide the student with an understanding of the fundamentals of bank functions. *Version 2:* To provide the student with an overview of banking functions.

Learning Outcome: *Version 1:* Upon successful completion of this course, the student will be able to understand and apply the basic principles of banking operations to various types of situations surrounding banking activities; provide a full range of services to customers of a standard or basic banking institution; be able to apply the various banking functions such as check processing, bookkeeping, deposits, and others as they pertain to the public; and appreciate the relationship between banks, the community, and various governmental agencies. *Version 2:* Upon successful completion of this course, the student will be able to understand the basic principles of banking operations and the range of services to customers of a standard or basic banking institution; be able to explain banking functions such as check processing, bookkeeping, deposits, and others as they pertain to the public; and appreciate the relationship between banks, the community, and various governmental agencies.

Instruction: Major topics covered in the course are negotiable instruments; deposits and payments; loans and investments; basic accounting; marketing and advertising; and legal relations with depositors. Methods of instruction include lecture, discussion, and an examination.

Credit Recommendation: *Version 1:* In the lower division baccalaureate/associate degree category, 3 semester hours in Banking, Business Administration, or Finance (5/84) (3/89). *Version 2:* In the lower division baccalaureate/associate degree category, 2 semester hours in Banking, Business Administration, or Finance (11/95).

Real Estate Finance (859)

Location: Various locations in Washington, DC, Maryland, and northern Virginia.

Length: 45 hours (15 weeks).

Dates: February 1989-Present.

Objective: To provide the student with a broad understanding of real property finance and its role in meeting the needs of both the borrower and the financial institution.

Learning Outcome: Upon successful completion of this course, the student will be able to understand and appreciate the real estate finance industry; be familiar with underwriting, closing, and administration of both residential and income property loans; and apply the fundamental principles of an analysis to real property investment.

Instruction: Major topics covered in the course are real estate law, the lending process, appraisal of the borrowers as well as the properties, various types of properties and peculiarities associated with each, and the administrative process and tasks involved in managing most mortgage departments including construction loans. Methods of instruction include lecture, discussion, cases, and workshops.

Credit Recommendation: In the lower division baccalaureate/associate degree or upper division baccalaureate degree category, 3 semester hours in Business Administration, Finance, or Real Estate (3/89) (11/95).

Trust Banking (810)

Location: Various locations in Washington, DC, Maryland, and northern Virginia.

Length: 24 hours (8 weeks).

Dates: February 1984-Present.

Objective: To provide the student with a basic knowledge of trust management and operations.

Learning Outcome: Upon successful completion of this course, the student will be able to know the various types of assets managed by trust departments and the basis of wills and trusts; understand trust investment management; be familiar with corporate trusts, charitable trusts, consumer trusts, and trust operations.

Instruction: Major topics covered in the course are types of assets managed by trust departments; investment management; trusts and wills; fiduciary service to consumers, including estate settlements, and corporate and employee benefit trusts; and trust operations. Methods of instruction include lecture, discussion, and written examinations.

Credit Recommendation: In the lower division baccalaureate/associate degree category, 2 semester hours in Business Administration, Finance, or Trust Banking (3/89) (11/95).

American Institute of Medical Law

The American Institute of Medical Law (AIML), founded in 1985, is a Florida corporation providing education services to health care professionals. AIML's mission is to provide quality education programs in risk management, to promote quality health care compatible with sound risk management skills, and to integrate clinical knowledge with concepts of managed care, integrate delivery systems, and state and federal protocols.

The Health Care Risk Management Course is approved by the Florida Department of Insurance for the state certification of Health Care Risk Managers. This is a fifteen month course with a final examination. The curriculum includes medical malpractice, insurance management, and regulatory issues, including environmental, labor, and workers' compensation law. The course covers virtually the whole spectrum of risk management and health care law.

The Risk Management School currently operates in four Florida cities, and has recently added branch locations in California and Michigan. AIML's alumni include distinguished physicians, nurses, health care attorney's and administrators, located in Florida and throughout the United States.

The faculty includes a distinguished panel of physicians, attorneys, nurses, insurance professionals, and health care administrators.

Source of official student records: Registry of Credit Recommendations, American Council on Education, One Dupont Circle, Washington, DC 20036-1193 or American Institute of Medical Law, 2801 Ponce De Leon Boulevard, Suite 1060, Coral Gables, FL 33134, (800) 431-3878.

Additional information about the courses: College Credit Recommendation Service, American Council on Education, One Dupont Circle, Washington, DC 10036-1193.

Health Care Risk Management

Location: Various sites in the United States.

Length: 120 hours (1 day a month for 15 months).

Dates: November 1985-Present.

Objective: To provide understanding of principles and administrative practices of risk management and their application to the health care industry.

Learning Outcome: Upon successful completion of this course, the student will be able to identify various health care risk management applications relevant to the health care industry; demonstrate understanding or risk control techniques and risk management responsibilities; and describe characteristics of effective quality improvement programs.

Instruction: Major topics covered in the course are overview of risk management, the health care environment as a workplace, health care standards which impact on risk management, legal liability in the health care setting, risk identification and analysis, risk management techniques, controlling losses in the clinical environment, medical malpractice and workers compensation, planning a risk management program, implementation and evaluation of risk management programs, and quality improvement management methods and applications, including statistical quality control. Methods of instruction include lecture, discussion, classroom exercises, audio visual materials, and final examination.

Credit Recommendation: In the upper division baccalaureate degree category or the graduate degree category, 6 semester hours in Health Care Administration (9/95).

American Research Group/Global Knowledge Network

American Research Group (ARG), founded in 1991 and purchased by Global Knowledge Network in 1997, conducts "real-world," hands-on network training targeted to information technology professionals. ARG's mission is to meet the needs and exceed the quality expectations of every customer.

Many of our courses are developed internally and are constantly improved for quality and to ensure inclusion of the latest innovations and technical breakthroughs. To this end, instructors and course directors update materials regularly and utilize ARG's extensive network of resources to research and test new methods and real-life experiences. ARG's instructors work in real corporate IT organizations in addition to their responsibilities as ARG instructors which promotes the type of experience that students need in today's competitive training environment.

ARG is proud to combine a tremendous learning experience with the logistical talent it takes to offer the courses needed by IT professionals when they need it and where they need it. ARG's courses can be taught effectively at corporate locations, in conference facilities, or in our facility. The student receives the same high quality education in a way that best fits their schedule and learning style.

Source of official student records: Registry of Credit Recommendations, American Council on Education, One Dupont Circle, Washington, DC 20036-1193.

Additional information about the courses: College Credit Recommendation Service, American Council on Education, One Dupont Circle, Washington, DC 20036-1193.

Advanced Cisco Router Configuration

Location: Various locations throughout the United States.

Length: 35 hours (5 days).

Dates: April 1996-Present.

Objective: To describe the issues inherent in complex multiprotocol internetworks and introduce and configure Cisco routers for operation in the laboratory environment.

Learning Outcome: Upon successful completion of this course, the student will be able to demonstrate how to configure routers for IGRP, EIGRP, and OSPF; establish extended and complex access lists; utilize TCP/IP encapsulation; and implement IGRP to OSPF and OSPF to EIGRP migration strategies.

Instruction: Major topics covered in the course are complex internetworking, managing traffic and security, scalable routing protocols, OSPF configuration, enhanced IGRP configurations (EIGRP), border gateway protocol, scalability features of WANs, nonrouted network integration, and advanced bridging. Methods of instruction include lecture, discussion, audio/visual material, computer-assisted instruction, and16 hands-on laboratories.

Credit Recommendation: In the upper division baccalaureate degree category, 2 semester hours (1 semester hour in Computer Science, Telecommunications, or Computer Information Systems and 1 semester hour in Computer Science, Telecommunications, or Computer Information Systems Laboratory) (10/96).

ATM Essentials

Location: Various sites in the United States.

Length: 14 hours (2 days).

Dates: January 1997-Present.

Objective: To provide a general understanding of the ATM protocol including deployment strategies.

Learning Outcome: Upon successful completion of this course, the student will be able to understand ATM theory and diagram a multi-stage deployment strategy.

Instruction: Major topics covered in the course are networking overview, ATM Deployment Strategies, ATM standards, cell structure, switched and permanent virtual circuits, quality of service, and LAN emulation. Methods of instruction include lecture, discussion, classroom quizzes and exercises, demonstration labs, and final examination.

Credit Recommendation: In the upper division baccalaureate degree category, 1 semester hour in Computer Information Systems, Computer Science, or Telecommunications (4/97).

ATM Internetworking: Hands-on

Location: Various sites in the United States and Canada.

Length: 21 hours (3 days).

Dates: January 1994-Present.

Objective: To provide knowledge in installation, implementation, and troubleshooting of multi-vendor ATM networks.

Learning Outcome: Upon successful completion of this course, the student will be able to set up and configure an ATM switch; configure and test native ATM connections; implement and test LAN emulation techniques; and use an ATM protocol analyzer.

Instruction: Major topics covered in the course are ATM cell structure and protocol; UNI signaling; SSCOP connection-oriented protocol; ILMI ATM management; traffic management; network implementation strategies; LANE, MPOA, voice, and WAN applications. Methods of instruction include lecture, discussion, classroom exercises, hands-on laboratories, audio/visual materials, and final examination.

Credit Recommendation: In the upper division baccalaureate degree category, 1 semester hour in Computer Science, Computer Information Systems, or Telecommunications (10/96).

Bay Networks Hub Connectivity: Hands-on

Location: Various locations throughout the United States.

Length: 28 hours (4 days).

Dates: October 1996-Present.

Objective: To teach students how to install, maintain, and troubleshoot Bay Networks hub connectivity hardware. Students will perform basic hub component and software configuration using Bay Networks' 3000, 5000, Distributed 5000, and Baystack connectivity products.

Learning Outcome: Upon successful completion of this course, the student will be able to describe the features, functions, and components of Bay concentrators and modules; install and configure Bay concentrators and modules; and install, configure, and troubleshoot Bay networks Ethernet and token ring modules.

Instruction: Major topics covered in the course are protocol analyzer features and operations; Ethernet and token ring troubleshooting issues; WAN troubleshooting issues; network designs - how they affect performance, protocol characteristics, and architectures; troubleshooting strategies and techniques; and network management configurations. Methods of instruction include lecture, discussion, instructor demonstrations, hands-on laboratories, chapter and laboratory quizzes, and final examination.

Credit Recommendation: In the lower division baccalaureate/associate degree category, 2 semester hours (1 semester hour in Computer Science, Telecommunications, or Computer Information Systems and 1 semester hour in Computer Science,

Telecommunications, or Computer Information Systems Laboratory) (10/96).

Bay Networks Router Configuration and Management: Hands-on

Location: Various locations throughout the United States.

Length: 28 hours (4 days).

Dates: January 1996-Present.

Objective: To teach students how to use Bay Networks' Technician Interface, Script Files, and Site Manager to install and configure Bay Networks routers in Multi-protocol environments.

Learning Outcome: Upon successful completion of this course, the student will be able to load and configure IP, IPX, and AppleTalk software; load and configure bridge software; interpret routing tables, router statistics, and event logs; manage router boot images and configuration files; use script files and TI; display and trap events; and apply filters.

Instruction: Major topics covered in the course are routing and IP addressing, IP services and configuration, IPX and Appletalk network configuration, transparent bridge and spanning tree, source route bridging, SNMP management, MIB's, boot images, configuration files, and events and traps. Methods of instruction include lecture, discussion, instructor demonstrations, hands-on laboratories, chapter and laboratory quizzes, and final examination.

Credit Recommendation: In the upper division baccalaureate degree category, 2 semester hours (1 semester hour in Computer Science, Telecommunications, or Computer Information Systems and 1 semester hour in Computer Science, Telecommunications, or Computer Information Systems Laboratory) (10/96).

Bay Networks Router Installation and Basic Configuration: Hands-on

Location: Various locations throughout the United States.

Length: 21 hours (3 days).

Dates: January 1996-Present.

Objective: To teach students how to install, maintain, and troubleshoot Bay Networks router hardware. Students will perform basic router software configuration using Bay Networks' Technician Interface and Site Manager.

Learning Outcome: Upon successful completion of this course, the student will be able to install, maintain, and troubleshoot Bay Networks router hardware and configure basic router software.

Instruction: Major topics covered in the course are Bay Networks facts and features, router hardware architecture, router modules and indicators, router software overview, ez-install, Netboot and directed Netboot, initial router configuration, and general troubleshooting. Methods of instruction include lecture, discussion, instructor demonstrations, hands-on exercises and laboratories, chapter exercises, and quizzes.

Credit Recommendation: In the lower division baccalaureate/associate degree category, 1 semester hour in Computer Science, Telecommunications, or Computer Information Systems or in Computer Science, Telecommunications, or Computer Information Systems Laboratory (10/96).

Cabling Voice and Data Networks

Location: Various sites in the United States.

Length: 21 hours (3 days).

Dates: January 1996-Present.

Objective: To provide basic knowledge of how to design, install, and troubleshoot data network cabling systems.

Learning Outcome: Upon successful completion of this course, the student will be able to understand cabling for the latest technologies; troubleshoot and terminate cabling systems; and demonstrate knowledge of the standards, codes, emerging trends, capabilities, and costs of cabling systems.

Instruction: Major topics covered in the course are evolution of data connectivity, standards organizations, an overview of LAN architectures, the technology of copper wiring systems, components and termination, category 5 specifications, certification testing and troubleshooting copper, fiber optics, fiber optic cable plant design, procedures for installing fiber, fiber termination and testing techniques, LAN cabling design procedures, and future trends. Methods of instruction include lecture, discussion, and computer laboratory exercises.

Credit Recommendation: In the lower division baccalaureate/associate degree category, 1 semester hour in Computer Science, Networking, Telecommunications, or Management Information Systems (10/96).

Cisco Internetwork Troubleshooting

Location: Various locations throughout the United States.

Length: 28 hours (4 days).

Dates: April 1996-Present.

Objective: To provide indepth training and hands-on practice in identifying and correcting communication problems for large networks using TCT/IP, IPX/SPX, and AppleTalk.

Learning Outcome: Upon successful completion of this course, the student will be able to use specific Cisco troubleshooting commands; isolate LAN/WAN problems; troubleshoot Ethernet and Token Ring networks; use Network General and Wandel and Golterman protocol analyzers; troubleshoot IP, IPX, AppleTalk, HDLC, and X.25 traffic problems; and perform a Novell Netware core dump.

Instruction: Major topics covered in the course are CISCO router software, CISCO troubleshooting commands, troubleshooting methodologies and tools, CISCO internetworking operating systems, and modeling and simulation tools. Methods of instruction include lecture, discussion, classroom exercises, and 17 hands-on laboratories.

Credit Recommendation: In the upper division baccalaureate degree category, 2 semester hours (1 semester hour in Computer Science, Telecommunications, or Computer Information Systems and 1 semester hour in Computer Science, Telecommunications, or Computer Information Systems Laboratory) (10/96).

Cisco Internetworking Design

Location: Various locations throughout the United States.

Length: 35 hours (5 days).

Dates: April 1996-Present.

Objective: To introduce fundamentals internetwork design, design of campus LAN, IP networks, WAN, and SNA with CISCO products.

Learning Outcome: Upon successful completion of this course, the student will be able to demonstrate an understanding of the steps for designing internetwork solutions; analyze client's business and technical requirements and select appropriate internetwork topologies and technologies; and construct an internetwork design that meets a client's objectives.

Instruction: Major topics covered in the course are internetwork design fundamentals, campus LAN design, IP network design, Desktop protocols, and WAN design; incorporating SNA; security issues; and internetwork design case studies. Methods of instruction include lecture, case studies, audio/visual material, computer-assisted instruction, and final examination.

Credit Recommendation: In the upper division baccalaureate degree category, 2

semester hours in Computer Science, Telecommunications, or Computer Information Systems (10/96).

Cisco Security and Performance Tuning

Location: Various sites in the United States.

Length: 21 hours (3 days).

Dates: February 1997-Present.

Objective: To provide advanced experience in configuring Cisco routers.

Learning Outcome: Upon successful completion of this course, the student will understand Access list design for IP and IPX networks; implement bridging filters on Cisco routers, benefits of Cisco router buffer and queue allocation, DDR security considerations, and TACACS+ features; and maximize router CPU utilization.

Instruction: Major topics covered in the course are IP Route Filtering, Ip Route Redistribution Filters, blocking specific Client/Server connections, IPX Route Filtering, restoring access to server, NetBios IP and IPX Filtering, Buffer Allocation, and Priority Queue linked to Access List. Methods of instruction include lecture, discussion, classroom lab exercises, audio-visual material, and final examination.

Credit Recommendation: In the upper division baccalaureate degree category, 1 semester hour in Computer Information Systems or Telecommunications (4/97).

Essentials of Wide Area Networking

Location: Various sites in the United States.

Length: 21 hours (3 days).

Dates: September 1995-Present.

Objective: To provide an introduction to Wide Area Networks concepts.

Learning Outcome: Upon successful completion of this course, the student will be able to understand WAN protocols and architectures; recognize connection and connectionless orientation; understand WAN transmission services; understand typical applications of both data and voice communications; and focus on network performance while using a WAN.

Instruction: Major topics covered in the course are an overview of WAN networking, LAN interconnectivity issues, the wide-area network environment, physical transmission options, transmission equipment, data traffic, integration of voice and data, T1/T3, ISDN, frame relay, ATM, X.25, network protocol architectures, TCP/IP, and future technologies and services. Methods of instruction include lecture, discussion, and classroom demonstration laboratory exercises.

Credit Recommendation: In the upper division baccalaureate degree category, 1 semester hour in Computer Science, Telecommunications, or Computer Information Systems (10/96).

Fiber Optic Network Design

Location: Various sites in the United States.

Length: 14 hours (2 days).

Dates: August 1994-Present.

Objective: To provide knowledge of the concepts of general fiber optic network design.

Learning Outcome: Upon successful completion of this course, the student will be able to implement fiber designs for several types of networks; differentiate the different types of fiber optic cable; accurately estimate network costs when using fiber; know the correct steps to take when designing a fiber optic network; describe the standards and requirements that must be followed when designing a fiber optic network; and describe performance tradeoffs of connector types.

Instruction: Major topics covered in the course are current and future applications of fiber optics, where and when to use fiber optics, essential hardware options, structured fiber optic cable plants, FDDI, fiber optic cost analysis, installation and design considerations, and steps for structured network design. Methods of instruction include lecture, discussion, and case studies.

Credit Recommendation: In the lower division baccalaureate/associate degree category, 1 semester hour in Computer Science, Telecommunications, or Management Information Systems (10/96).

Fiber Optic Network Installation (Formerly Fiber Optic Cable Installation)

Location: Various sites in the United States.

Length: 21 hours (3 days).

Dates: August 1994-Present.

Objective: To provide the basic concepts of fiber optic installation.

Learning Outcome: Upon successful completion of this course, the student will be able to inspect, install, and test several types of ST and SC connectors on fiber optic cable; install connectors using hot melt, epoxy, and mechanical techniques; troubleshoot fiber optic cable; know guidelines for successful cable installation; use light sources and power meters to verify installation results; and understand cost and time differences for different types of termination techniques.

Instruction: Major topics covered in the course are the rules for successful cable installation and end preparation, installation of multimode and singlemode connectors, optical power loss measurements, OTDR measurements, fiber splicing, and troubleshooting fiber optic cable systems. Methods of instruction include lecture, discussion, classroom laboratory exercises, and final examination.

Credit Recommendation: In the lower division baccalaureate/associate degree category, 1 semester hour in Telecommunications or Computer Science Laboratory (10/96).

IBM 8260 Intelligent Switching Hub

Location: Various sites in the United States.

Length: 14 hours (2 days).

Dates: November 1996-Present.

Objective: To provide students with a practical introduction to IBM's 8260 Intelligent Switching Hub.

Learning Outcome: Upon successful completion of this course, the student will be able to install, configure, and troubleshoot IBM's 8260 Intelligent Switching Hub.

Instruction: Major topics covered in the course are an introduction to IBM's 8260 Intelligent Switching Hub as network center hub and for ATM deployment, 8260 chassis components, 8250 adapter kit components, distributed management modules, and ethernet interconnect module. Methods of instruction include lecture, laboratory exercises, and final examination.

Credit Recommendation: In the lower division baccalaureate/associate degree category, 1 semester hour in Computer Information Systems or Telecommunications (laboratory) (4/97).

IBM 8271/8272 LAN Switches

Location: Various sites in the United States.

Length: 14 hours (2 days).

Dates: November 1996-Present.

Objective: To provide students with the practical information and hands-on experience that will enable them to install and configure IBM's 8271 and 8272 LAN switches.

Learning Outcome: Upon successful completion of this course, the student will be able to install IBM 8271 and 8272 products into a customer's network; configure the products; manage them locally, and troubleshoot the installation.

Instruction: Major topics covered in the course are advantages of using LAN switches; distinguishing features of the IBM 8271 and 8272 switches; and detailed instruction in the installation, maintenance, and troubleshooting of these switches. Methods of instruction include lecture, laboratory exercises, and final examination.

Credit Recommendation: In the lower division baccalaureate/associate degree category, 1 semester hour in Computer Science, Computer Information Systems, or Telecommunications (4/97).

IBM 8273/8274 Nways RouteSwitch

Location: Various sites in the United States.

Length: 21 hours (3 days).

Dates: November 1996-Present.

Objective: To provide students with a practical introduction to field implementations of IBM's 8273 and 8274 Nways RouteSwitch products.

Learning Outcome: Upon successful completion of this course, the student will be able to install, configure, and troubleshoot IBM 8273 and 8274 Nways RouteSwitch products.

Instruction: Major topics covered in the course are fundamentals of route switches; creating groups and VLANS; installation, maintenance, and troubleshooting of 8273 and 8274 Nways RouteSwitch products; and bridging and trunking. Methods of instruction include lecture, laboratory exercises, and final examination.

Credit Recommendation: In the lower division baccalaureate/associate degree category, 1 semester hour in Computer Information Systems or Telecommunications (laboratory) (4/97).

IBM ATM Products

Location: Various sites in the United States.

Length: 21 hours (3 days).

Dates: November 1996-Present.

Objective: To provide students with a practical introduction to field implementations of IBM's ATM products.

Learning Outcome: Upon successful completion of this course, the student will be able to install, configure, and troubleshoot IBM's ATM products.

Instruction: Major topics covered in the course are theory and explanation of ATM, an introduction to IBM's ATM products, an overview of the makeup of the products, and a detailed look at the components of the products. Methods of instruction include lecture, laboratory exercises, and final examination.

Credit Recommendation: In the lower division baccalaureate/associate degree category, 1 semester hour in Computer Science, Computer Information Systems, or Telecommunications (4/97).

IBM NWays Manager for Windows

Location: Various sites in the United States.

Length: 21 hours (3 days).

Dates: November 1996-Present.

Objective: To provide students with a practical introduction to field implementations of IBM's NWays Manager for Windows products.

Learning Outcome: Upon successful completion of this course, the student will be able to install, configure, locally manage, and troubleshoot IBM's NWays Manager for Windows products.

Instruction: Major topics covered in the course are LAN management theory, SNMP agents, pre-management configuration, configuration modules, management station requirements, testing, and report generation. Methods of instruction include lecture, laboratory exercises, and final examination.

Credit Recommendation: In the lower division baccalaureate/associate degree category, 1 semester hour in Computer Information Systems or Telecommunications (laboratory) (4/97).

Implementing TCP/IP with Windows NT

Location: Various sites in the United States.

Length: 21 hours (3 days).

Dates: August 1996-Present.

Objective: To provide students with the ability to implement, administer, and troubleshoot information systems that incorporate Microsoft TCP/IP.

Learning Outcome: Upon successful completion of this course, the student will be able to install hardware and software; establish and repair network and communication connections; tune and optimize systems; customize system environments; recommend system products, versions, or upgrades; and troubleshoot systems.

Instruction: Major topics covered in the course are an introduction to networking, TCP/IP architecture, IP addressing and subnetting, installation of TCP/IP on Windows NT, IP routing, Dynamic Host Configuration Protocol, Domain Name Service, Windows Internet Name Service, TCP/IP monitoring, Internet and NT, and Remote TCP/IP access. Methods of instruction include lecture, classroom exercises, laboratory exercises, and audio/visual materials.

Credit Recommendation: In the upper division baccalaureate degree category, 1 semester hour in Computer Science, Telecommunications, or Computer Information Systems (10/96).

Installation and Maintenance of Cisco Routers

Location: Various locations throughout the United States.

Length: 28 hours (4 days).

Dates: April 1996-Present.

Objective: To provide hands-on experience and lecture instruction for the basic recovery/upgrade procedures and hardware troubleshooting common to all Cisco routing products.

Learning Outcome: Upon successful completion of this course, the student will be able to understand site preparation, installation guidelines, and basic troubleshooting techniques; understand router maintenance procedures for opening chassis, removing and adding network processor modules, and flash memory and DRAM SIMMS; and know how to perform software upgrades for operating system ROM, interface microcode, and flash memory upgrades.

Instruction: Major topics covered in the course are router hardware essentials, installing and maintaining core routers, installing and maintaining modular access routers, and router configuration and software. Methods of instruction include lecture, discussion, classroom exercises, 16 hands-on laboratories, and quizzes.

Credit Recommendation: In the lower division baccalaureate/associate degree category, 2 semester hours (1 semester hour in Computer Science, Telecommunications, or Computer Information Systems and 1 semester hour in Computer Science, Telecommunications, or Computer Information Systems Laboratory) (10/96).

Integrating ISDN

Location: Various sites in the United States.

Length: 21 hours (3 days).

Dates: January 1996-Present.

Objective: To provide knowledge of the structure and use of ISDN.

Learning Outcome: Upon successful completion of this course, the student will be able to know key ISDN terms, protocols, and definitions; understand how to install and configure a video conferencing system; identify the costs involved with installing ISDN; learn criteria for selecting ISDN equipment for a network; understand techniques to use when troubleshooting an ISDN network; and know how to properly configure terminal equipment.

Instruction: Major topics covered in the course are ISDN architecture, components, U-Loop, Ordering, S/T Bus, basic protocols, Layer 2 Protocol, Layer 3 Protocol, cause codes, bridge set-up, router set-up, applications, and troubleshooting. Methods of instruction include lecture, discussion, and classroom laboratory exercises.

Credit Recommendation: In the lower division baccalaureate/associate degree category, 1 semester hour in Computer Science, Telecommunications, or Management Information Systems (10/96).

Internetworking With Bridges, Routers, and Switches: Hands-on

Location: Various locations throughout the United States.

Length: 21 hours (3 days).

Dates: January 1996-Present.

Objective: To teach students how to design, install, configure, and interconnect multi-vendor/multi-protocol networking environments.

Learning Outcome: Upon successful completion of this course, the student will be able to delineate between LANs and WANs; describe the basic components and operations of a WAN; define and describe various bridge types; perform protocol analysis; integrate switching technology into existing networks; select the appropriate routing protocol; design an IP network; capture, decode, and decipher TCP/IP protocols; design a Novell addressing scheme; obtain network management information from a SNMP manager; determine an appropriate backbone topology; and design an appropriate Appletalk addressing scheme.

Instruction: Major topics covered in the course are an introduction to internetworking; data link protocols; MAC layer bridging; network layer routing; switching technologies; TCP/IP, AppleTalk, and Novell IPX communication protocols; bridging and switching vs. routing and backbone internetworking strategies; and network management. Methods of instruction include lecture, discussion, instructor laboratory demonstrations, hands-on laboratories, and chapter and laboratory quizzes.

Credit Recommendation: In the lower division baccalaureate/associate degree category, 1 semester hour in Computer Science Laboratory, Networking Laboratory, or Telecommunications Laboratory (10/96).

Internetworking with TCP/IP

Location: Various sites in the United States and Canada.

Length: 21 hours (3 days).

Dates: January 1992-Present.

Objective: To allow a network technician or manager to track TCP/IP on the enterprise network.

Learning Outcome: Upon successful completion of this course, the student will be able to explain the structure and function of each level of the TCP/IP protocol suite, including network layer protocols such as Ethernet, internet protocols such as IP, ARP, and RARP, host-to-host protocols such as TCP, UDP, and ICMP, and application layer protocols, including RIP, FTP, Telnet, SMTP, and SNMP.

Instruction: Major topics covered in the course are stacked protocols, using IP addresses, subnets, and name services; layer analysis for each protocol; application layer protocols; and the TCP/IP client/server model. Methods of instruction include lecture, discussion, classroom exercises, computer laboratory exercises, audio/visual materials, and final examination.

Credit Recommendation: In the upper division baccalaureate degree category, 1 semester hour in Computer Science, Telecommunications, or Computer Information Systems (10/96).

Introduction to Cisco Router Configuration

Location: Various locations throughout the United States.

Length: 35 hours (5 days).

Dates: April 1996-Present.

Objective: To provide hands-on experience and lecture instruction for configuring routers in multiprotocol networks.

Learning Outcome: Upon successful completion of this course, the student will be able to demonstrate an understanding of the Cisco IOS, TCP/IP protocol stack, Cisco IP routing protocol (RIP and IGRP), and multiprotocol configurations (IP, AppleTalk, IPX, Banyan Vines, and Decnet).

Instruction: Major topics covered in the course are an introduction to internetworking; TCP/IP overview; IP address configuration, IP routing configuration, Novell/IPX configuration, Banyan Vines configuration, AppleTalk configuration, and DECnet configuration; Wide Area connectivity, and bridging. Methods of instruction include lecture, discussion, classroom exercises, 16 hands-on laboratories, audio/visual material, and final examination.

Credit Recommendation: In the lower division baccalaureate/associate degree category, 2 semester hours (1 semester hour Computer Science, Telecommunications, or Computer Information Systems and 1 semester hour in Computer Science, Telecommunications, or Computer Information Systems Laboratory) (10/96).

Introduction to LAN/WAN Protocols

Location: Various locations throughout the United States.

Length: 14 hours (2 days).

Dates: January 1996-Present.

Objective: To teach students the performance features and internetworking requirements of communications protocols.

Learning Outcome: Upon successful complete of this course, the student will be able to understand the OSI model in depth; explain the working details of the different OSI levels (physical, link, network, transport, and upper layers); understand bandwidth concepts and issues; and understand the issues and differences between the IBM networking model and the OSI model.

Instruction: Major topics covered in the course are networking protocol fundamentals, physical interfaces, link level transmission procedures, network layer protocols, transport layer, upper layer services, high performance LANs, and SNA networking. Methods of instruction include lecture, discussion, instructor laboratory demonstrations, hands-on laboratories, chapter and laboratory quizzes, and final examination.

Credit Recommendation: In the lower division baccalaureate/associate degree category, 1 semester hour in Computer Science, Networking, or Telecommunications (10/96).

Introduction to PERL Programming

Location: Various sites in the United States.

Length: 21 hours (3 days).

Dates: January 1996-Present.

Objective: To provide students with the ability to write PERL programs to process text and binary files; automate UNIX, Novell, or Windows System Administration; and interface World-Wide-Web browsers via CGI.

Learning Outcome: Upon successful completion of this course, the student will be able to invoke PERL under various operating systems; process text files with search/replace; use associative arrays as lookup tables; use multidimensional arrays to store complex data sets; print the keys to an associative array in sorted order; normalize data; create and use arrays; pass parameters to a function; and return values from functions.

Instruction: Major topics covered in the course are creating PERL programs, simple data types, conditional execution, lists and arrays, list functions, using loops, reading and writing text files, associative arrays, string and pattern matching, pattern substitution, PERL short-cuts, creating subroutines, sorting arrays, creating reports, reading and writing binary files, and writing CGI scripts. Methods of instruction include lecture, discussion, laboratory exercises, demonstrations, major module reviews, and final examination.

Credit Recommendation: In the upper division baccalaureate degree category, 2 semester hours in Computer Science or Computer Information Systems (10/96).

Network Management

Location: Various sites in the United States and Canada.

Length: 21 hours (3 days).

Dates: November 1992-Present.

Objective: To provide knowledge of the SNMP protocol suite, SNMP MIBs, agents, and network management systems.

Learning Outcome: Upon successful completion of this course, the student will be able to explain the structure and function of each level of the SNMP protocol; identify the structure and function of a network management system, Management Information Bases (MIBs), and Agents; and explain the use of private MIB extensions and Remote Monitoring (RMON).

Instruction: Major topics covered in the course are network management and support, the SNMP protocol, SNMP and RMON MIBs, management applications, agents, RFCs, implementing network management, and troubleshooting. Methods of instruction include lecture, discussion, classroom exercises, hands-on laboratories, audio/visual material, and final examination.

Credit Recommendation: In the upper division baccalaureate degree category, 1 semester hour in Computer Science, Telecommunications, or Computer Information Systems (10/96).

Network Security Administration

Location: Various sites in the United States and Canada.

Length: 21 hours (3 days).

Dates: July 1995-Present.

Objective: To provide knowledge of network security tools and threats, experience identifying and closing potential security problems, and exposure to encryption tools, one-time password authentication, firewalls, and screening routers.

Learning Outcome: Upon successful completion of this course, the student will be able to identify and close potential security problems in UNIX and Windows NT systems; utilize screening routers and set up routing tables; configure firewalls and proxy servers; and utilize encryption and authentication mechanisms to reinforce security.

Instruction: Major topics covered in the course are host-based network security, building firewalls, filters, and gateways; utilizing screening routers; and examining principles and practices of secure communications. Methods of instruction include lecture, discussion, classroom exercises, hands-on laboratories, audio/visual materials, and papers.

Credit Recommendation: In the upper division baccalaureate degree category, 1 semester hour in Computer Science, Telecommunications, or Computer Information Systems (10/96).

Network Troubleshooting

Location: Various sites in the U.S.

Length: 21 hours (3 days).

Dates: January 1996-Present.

Objective: To use network troubleshooting tools to identify, isolate and eliminate multi-protocol network problems.

Learning Outcome: Upon successful completion of this course, the student will be able to address Ethernet, Token Ring, and FDDI capacity problems; diagnose common WAN problems; analyze and graph network performance trends; and remedy performance and latency issues of bridges, routers, and switches.

Instruction: Major topics covered in the course are protocol analyzer features and operations; Ethernet and Token Ring troubleshooting issues; WAN troubleshooting issues; and network designs: how they affect performance, protocol characteristics and architectures, troubleshooting strategies and techniques, and network management configurations. Methods of instruction include lecture, discussion, instructor lab demonstrations, hands-on labs, and final examination.

Credit Recommendation: In the upper division baccalaureate degree category, 1 semester hour in Computer Information Systems, Computer Science, or Telecommunications (4/97).

Networking Fundamentals

Location: Various sites in the United States.

Length: 21 hours (3 days).

Dates: June 1996-Present.

Objective: To provide an in-depth introduction on the concepts, history, and deployment of networks.

Learning Outcome: Upon successful completion of this course, the student will be able to understand networking terminology; describe how data is moved in a network environment; understand physical, data-link layer, and network layer functions; recognize when and where to use a repeater, a bridge, and a router; and describe major protocols, communication architecture, and standards.

Instruction: Major topics covered in the course are data communication basics, data packet structure, data transmission methods, transmission techniques, LAN basics, structured LAN wiring, WAN basics, internetworking, LAN and WAN problem areas and remedies, and future trends. Methods of instruction include lecture, discussion, and computer laboratory demonstrations.

Credit Recommendation: In the lower division baccalaureate/associate degree category, 1 semester hour in Computer Science, Computer Information Systems, Management Information Systems, or Telecommunications (10/96).

Troubleshooting TCP/IP Networks

Location: Various sites in the United States.

Length: 14 hours (2 days).

Dates: April 1997-Present.

Objective: To provide network technicians and managers knowledge and experience in troubleshooting TCP/IP-based internetworks.

Learning Outcome: Upon successful completion of this course, the student will be able to use a variety of troubleshooting tools, including protocol analyzers, network management systems, and hand-held field testers; identify problems on a TCP/IP network; and use appropriate tools to isolate and correct the problems.

Instruction: Major topics covered in the course are an overview of OSI and TCP/IP; layered protocol models; operation of

SNMP and network management systems; and troubleshooting tools such as protocol analyzers, field analyzers, troubleshooting methodology, and layer-by-layer issues. Methods of instruction include lecture, laboratory exercises, and final examination.

Credit Recommendation: In the upper division baccalaureate category, 1 semester hour in Computer Information Systems or Telecommunications (laboratory) (4/97).

Understanding Computer Networks

Location: Various sites in the United States.

Length: 14 hours (2 days).

Dates: January 1997-Present.

Objective: To provide the basic concepts of computer networks and how they operate in today's corporate environments.

Learning Outcome: Upon successful completion of this course, the student will be able to understand how networks transmit voice, data, and images; why LANs are used; and the components of a network: route, hub, bridge switch, and NIC.

Instruction: Major topics covered in the course are the basic concepts of communication protocols and network operating systems, the distinguishing characteristics of centralized and distributed computing environments, and emerging network technologies. Methods of instruction include lecture, laboratory assignments and exercises, and final examination.

Credit Recommendation: In the lower division baccalaureate/associate degree category, 1 semester hour in Data Processing, Data Communication, or Computer Information Systems (4/97).

UNIX Level I

Location: Various sites in the United States.

Length: 14 hours (2 days).

Dates: January 1996-Present.

Objective: To provide students with the knowledge necessary to become productive users while they learn the functions and features of UNIX.

Learning Outcome: Upon successful completion of this course, the student will be able to use UNIX; start and stop sessions; manipulate files; work at the command line; create and manage processes; use VI; customize their environment; create archives; and use the built-in communication tools.

Instruction: Major topics covered in the course are an introduction to UNIX, basic operations, file system basics, file commands and utilities, file permissions, working at the command line, creating and managing processes, using VI, customizing the user environment, creating archives, and communicating with users. Methods of instruction include lecture, discussion, laboratory exercises, major module reviews, and final examination.

Credit Recommendation: In the lower division baccalaureate/associate degree category, 1 semester hour in Computer Science or Computer Information Systems (10/96).

UNIX Level II

Location: Various sites in the United States.

Length: 14 hours (2 days).

Dates: January 1996-Present.

Objective: To provide the students with the knowledge and skills necessary to become advanced UNIX users.

Learning Outcome: Upon successful completion of this course, the student will be able to start and manage X-Windows sessions; create Shell programs; manipulate archive files; schedule commands; monitor resources; find files; use regular expressions; use the many different editors available under UNIX; and use the remote access utilities available under UNIX.

Instruction: Major topics covered in the course are UNIX fundamentals, using X-Windows, creating Shell procedures, Shell command line processes, pattern matching with regular expressions, pattern processing in Shell procedures, Shell programming essentials, file management utilities, resource management utilities, remote processing facilities, and advanced UNIX utilities and applications. Methods of instruction include lecture, discussion, laboratory exercises, reviews, major module reviews, and final examination.

Credit Recommendation: In the lower division baccalaureate/associate degree category, 1 semester hour in Computer Science or Computer Information Systems (10/96).

Upgrading and Repairing PCs

Location: Various sites in the United States.

Length: 21 hours (3 days).

Dates: January 1997-Present.

Objective: To enable the student to master PC preventive maintenance and system optimization and to provide the level of knowledge needed to install, configure, upgrade, maintain and troubleshoot PC-compatible system hardware and software.

Learning Outcome: Upon successful completion of this course, the student will be able to understand current bus architectures; upgrade and troubleshoot motherboards; and perform cost effective repairs and upgrades.

Instruction: Major topics covered in the course are an overview of system features and components, a detailed look at system components and how to build a system from scratch, video and audio hardware, hard disk installation and troubleshooting, and preventive maintenance. Methods of instruction include lecture, discussion, instructor lab demonstrations, hands-on labs, laboratory exercises, and final examination.

Credit Recommendation: In the lower division baccalaureate/associate degree category, 1 semester hour in Data Processing, Data Communication, or Computer Science (4/97).

American Society of Safety Engineers

The ASSE's mission is to promote the advancement of the safety profession and foster the technical, scientific, managerial and ethical knowledge, skills and competency of safety professionals. From this mission flows the Society commitment to provide quality, accessible educational opportunities for members and others to achieve educational and training goals advancing career objectives to obtain personal preeminence in the safety, health, and environmental fields. To present such opportunities in the area of distance learning the Society's Education and Training Department referred such learning modules to the Technical Services Department (TSD) where the expertise for developing self-study/correspondence courses resides.

Using Needs Assessments and other membership surveys the TSD has developed correspondence courses meeting the overall educational/training goals of the Society and its affected members and others pursuing similar educational needs. The student/enrollee is one who wishes to prepare for certification examinations, obtain credit for maintenance of credentials, remain current in the field, and begin the development of a career process or path to progress educationally through and to career objectives.

Once course subject areas and accompanying texts have been selected, TSD staff choose nationally recognized experts (P.E., CSPs, etc.) in specifically related disciplines to serve as the collective faculty for the correspondence courses. Based upon their review of the text materials and selection of relevant learning principles in their specific discipline the curriculum of study is developed under the auspices of a principal author. The instructional staff is representative of the highest qualified professionals in the field of safety and health whose credentials are ascertained by TSD staff through various means of quality review both external and internal to the Society.

The courses are offered through the ASSE and its 140 nationwide chapters and eight (8) specialty divisions. While there is a significant distribution chain, the courses are centrally administered from headquarters to facilitate the matriculation process. However, summary proctored examinations are administered locally under general control of the central administrative function.

Student records can be obtained from ASSE by writing to: Administrator, ASSE Self-Study Programs, 1800 E. Oakton Street, Des Plaines, Illinois 60018.

Source of official student records: Registry of Credit Recommendations, American Council on Education, One Dupont Circle, Washington, DC 20036-1193.

Additional information about the courses: College Credit Recommendation Service, American Council on Education, One Dupont Circle, Washington, DC 22036-1193.

Certified Safety Professional: Management Aspects Self-Study Correspondence Course

Location: Correspondence.

Length: 605 hours (24 months) (Section I: Legal/Regulatory and Professional Affairs, 70 hours; Section II: Applied Sciences, 80 hours; Section III: Management, 150 hours; Section IV: Engineering, 305 hours).

Dates: January 1992-Present.

Objective: To prepare students to receive certification as a "Certified Safety Professional" qualified to manage a safety program, with special emphasis on legal/ regulatory, applied sciences, management and engineering.

Learning Outcome: Upon successful completion of this course, the student will be able to recognize, evaluate, and specify safe practices and procedures; with experience, administer a safety program; keep appropriate records and interact with regulatory agencies; and reasonably expect to pass the Board of Certified Professional Management Aspects Specialty Examination.

Instruction: Major topics covered in the course are Legal/Regulatory and Professional Affairs, 20 chapters and tests; Applied Sciences, 23 chapters and tests; Management, 43 chapters and tests; and Engineering, 87 chapters and tests. Methods of instruction include correspondence, consultation with ASSE staff, mail-in examinations (independently graded), and a proctored final examination.

Credit Recommendation: In the lower division baccalaureate/associate degree category, Section I: 2 semester hours; Section II: 3 semester hours; Section III: 5 semester hours; and Section IV: 10 semester hours in Health/Safety or Facilities Management (2/96).

Ergonomics Self-Study Correspondence Course

Location: Correspondence.

Length: 88 hours (3 months).

Dates: January 1993-Present.

Objective: To obtain or enhance knowledge in the field of ergonomics and to partially prepare an individual to complete the "Certified Safety Professional" examination.

Learning Outcome: Upon successful completion of this course, the student will be able to recognize the relationships between humans and their work environment; identify capabilities and limitations of humans and machines; evaluate and design workstations; and recommend countermeasures in preventing injury, fatigue, or other stressors.

Instruction: Major topics covered in the course are human factors and systems; information input; physical work and manual materials handling; work place design; environmental conditions; and human factors applications. Methods of instruction include correspondence, consultation with ASSE staff, 22 mail-in tests (independently graded), and a proctored final examination.

Credit Recommendation: In the lower division baccalaureate/associate degree category, 3 semester hours in Human Factors, Facilities Management, or Health/ Safety (2/96).

Industrial Hygiene: General Safety Aspects

Location: Home Study.

Length: 110 hours (5 months).

Dates: November 1996-Present.

Objective: To help the student prepare for the Occupational Health and Safety Technologist examination conducted by the Board of Certified Safety Professionals. Helps student obtain or enhance knowledge of the field of industrial hygiene, especially where such knowledge may be deficient. Serves as a means to accumulate Continuing Education Units to satisfy requirements for maintenance of technologist designation.

Learning Outcome: Upon successful completion of this course, the student will be able to lay the groundwork for understanding the anatomy, physiology, hazards, and pathology of lungs, eyes, ears, and skin; assist in the recognition of environmental factors or stresses, such as chemical substances, physical agents, and biological and ergonomic hazards in the workplace; provide basic information on the evaluation of hazards which include the use of various instruments to measure air quality and the presence of gas or vapors; and provide guidance in the control of hazards by special ventilation equipment and procedures, as well as, proper selection and use of respiratory protection.

Instruction: Major topics covered in the course are industrial hygiene programs and administration, including roles of professionals; use of control equipment and instruments; target organs; and related hazards and controls, as well as physical stressors such as radiation, noise, bio hazards, and air quality. Methods of instruction include correspondence, consultation with ASSE staff, 30 mail-in tests (independently graded), and a proctored final examination.

Credit Recommendation: In the lower division baccalaureate/associate degree category, 4 semester hours in Health Safety, Industrial Safety, or Facilities Management (11/97).

Occupational Safety and Health Self-Study Correspondence Course

Location: Home Study.

Length: *Version 1:* 176 hours (6 months); *Version 2:* 191 hours (7 months).

Dates: January 1994-Present.

Objective: To provide a thorough introduction to basic concepts and fundamentals of occupational health and safety, regulatory requirements, and safety program implementation.

Learning Outcome: Upon successful completion of this course, the student will be able to recognize a wide variety of unsafe conditions or practices; recommend or implement corrective measures; identify requirements of safety regulations as applied to a variety of work-sites and activities; and maintain records as required for regulations and for analysis of problem areas and trends.

Instruction: *Versions 1 and 2:* Major topics covered in the course are health and safety programs and administration, including regulations, safety training, record-keeping requirements, and analysis and engineering and technology, including safety and health aspects of construction, plant and process operations, industrial equipment, safety equipment, etc. *Version 1:* Methods of instruction include correspondence, consultation with ASSE staff, 44 mail-in tests (independently graded), and a proctored final examination. *Version 2:* Methods of instruction include correspondence, consultation with ASSE staff, 51 mail-in tests (independently graded), and a proctored final examination.

Credit Recommendation: In the lower division baccalaureate/associate degree category, 6 semester hours in Industrial Safety, Health/Safety, or Facilities Management (11/97).

Ameritech

Ameritech is one of the nation's leading information companies, helping 13 million U.S. customers communicate and manage information through cellular, telephone, data, and video networks. Sixty-five thousand employees, distributed over 15 business units, focus on the unique needs of customers ranging from consumers to businesses to other communications companies.

Ameritech's goal is to become a single source of communications solutions for customers. The company is therefore expanding beyond today's core business of local telephone service, cellular, and advertising into new growth businesses such as security monitoring, cable TV, and long-distance.

Ameritech is at present the second-largest U.S. security monitoring company, serving customers in the U.S. and Canada. A cable TV network is under construction, and the company has formed Americast — a joint venture with the Walt Disney Company, BellSouth, GTE, and SBC Communications — to create innovative and imaginative video programming and interactive services for consumers.

Ameritech serves over 300,000 customers with cellular long-distance service, and is moving forward to meet regulatory requirements that will enable them to offer long-distance to our telephone customers.

International operations bring better communications to countries such as China, Hungary, New Zealand, Belgium, and Norway. In addition, Ameritech has successfully completed two of the largest international privatizations — Telecom New Zealand and Matav, the Hungarian communications company. International investments are valued at almost $4 billion.

Source of official student records: Registry of Credit Recommendation, American Council on Education, One Dupont Circle, Washington, DC 20036-1193.

Additional information about the courses: College Credit Recommendation Service, American Council on Education, One Dupont Circle, Washington, DC 20036-1193.

Accelerated Learning (A10054)

Location: Region-wide various locations in Illinois, Indiana, Michigan, Ohio and Wisconsin.

Length: 24 hours (3 days).

Dates: August 1987-Present.

Objective: To teach participants how to design and deliver enhanced accelerated learning within organizations.

Learning Outcome: Upon successful completion of this course, the student will be able to make teaching and learning more enjoyable and rewarding for everyone; accelerate learning and reduce training time; appeal to different learning styles in teaching; teach with less stress and more success; help people optimize their natural abilities for learning; and unlock creative ability for designing and delivering winning training courses.

Instruction: Major topics covered in the course are expectations and goal sharing, understanding benefits of accelerated training, industrial vs. informational age learning from linear to geodesic, accelerated training presentation methods, learning styles and curriculum, keys to success in implementing accelerated training, case studies in accelerated learning, and feedback. Methods of instruction include lecture, demonstration, and case studies.

Credit Recommendation: In the upper division baccalaureate degree category, 1 semester hour in Methods in Teaching, Instructional Technology, or Education elective (11/91).

Building the Distributor Partnership (A10037)

Location: Within the five-state Ameritech Region.

Length: 20 contact hours (3 days).

Dates: May 1991-Present.

Objective: To help the distributor manager understand what it is like to be an owner of a small, profit-driven, entrepreneurial business and to understand the success factors a distributor manager must exhibit to be successful.

Learning Outcome: Upon successful completion of this course, the student will have a clearer definition of his or her role as distributor manager; have a system for evaluating and improving his or her position with each distributor; and process new knowledge, skills, and ideas for developing long-term partnerships with the distributors.

Instruction: Major topics covered in the course are role of distributor manager and research findings, the entrepreneurial mind (moving toward win-win), three partnership principles (how to achieve win-win), financial trouble (warning and action), Ameritech channel strategy (rule of third party), earning the right to partner "knowing the distributor's business", establishing trust, demonstrating commitment, and application—using the process with the distributor and partnership through planning. Methods of instruction include lecture, activities and exercises, videotapes, evaluation-in-basket exercise, and financial exercises.

Credit Recommendation: In the lower division baccalaureate/associate degree category, 1 semester hour in Small Business Management (11/91).

Computer Network Architectures (A220)

Location: Waukesha, WI.

Length: 40 hours (5 days).

Dates: May 1987-Present.

Objective: To understand architectural elements involved in modern computer networks.

Learning Outcome: Upon successful completion of this course, the student will be able to describe the importance of a computer network architecture with relation to customers, vendors, and a central carrier; describe the corporate networking market; extrapolate the evolution to open systems interconnection (OSI); identify and describe major components of the seven protocol layers of the OSI reference model; explain the technical issues involved in computer network design; differentiate between major commercial computer network architectures and contrast strengths and weaknesses; and list major OSI protocols.

Instruction: Major topics covered in the course are corporate networking marketing overview, network design, physical layer protocols, data link layer, network layer, transport layer, session layer, presentation layer, application layer, and computer network architecture trends. Methods of instruction include lecture, discussion, classroom and laboratory exercises, and a final examination.

Credit Recommendation: In the upper division baccalaureate degree category, 2 semester hours in Electrical Engineering, Computer Science, Telecommunications, Computer Engineering, or Management Information Systems (11/90).

Craft of Training (A10052)

Location: Region-wide, various locations in Illinois, Indiana, Michigan, Ohio, and Wisconsin.

Length: 40 hours (5 days).

Dates: April 1991-Present.

Objective: To develop practical effective skills for improving impact and credibility and increasing group involvement and learning in a training situation and to provide technical training skills.

Learning Outcome: Upon successful completion of this course, the student will be able to use body language to support and enhance delivery of materials; organize teaching materials; practice basic components of instruction including presentation, demonstration, activity, and practice; respond to questions and give feedback; use audio/visual aids; use listening skills for group facilitation; and deal with difficult participants.

Instruction: Major topics covered in the course are the body language of presenting, the presentation component-demonstration, listening and reflective skills, handling questions and responses, use of audio/visual aids, interactive presentations, leading presentations, debriefing, introduction to coaching, feedback and resistance, group problem solving, strengths and self-esteem, and core qualities needed for successful training of individuals. Methods of instruction include lecture, demonstrations, and exercises.

Credit Recommendation: In the upper division baccalaureate degree category, 2 semester hours in Methods in Teaching or Education elective (11/91).

Current Topics in the Communications Industry (Managing Ameritech in the 90s) (A10014)

Location: Various locations in Illinois, Indiana, Michigan, Ohio, Wisconsin, and other regional training facilities.

Length: 17 hours (2 days).

Dates: August 1990-Present.

Objective: To help managers understand competition in the marketplace and implications of moving from a regulated utility to a competitive environment.

Learning Outcome: Upon successful completion of this course, the student will be able to deal with competitive marketplace processes; understand the market/customer focus; understand the changing competitive marketplace; understand strategic response to marketplace elements (customer service, quality, empowerment, timeliness, low unit cost, mass customization, and alternative channels); implement a strategic plan; and identify action to make a company market/customer focused.

Instruction: Major topics covered in the course are team building, the competitive challenge, competitive response, the changing customer, customer perspectives, customer focus, and personal action plans. Methods of instruction include lecture, discussion, case studies, and videotapes.

Credit Recommendation: In the upper division baccalaureate degree category, 1 semester hour in Management or Strategic Planning (11/90).

Enhanced Team Dynamics (A10030)

Location: Within the 5-state Ameritech Region.

Length: 16 hours (2 days).

Dates: September 1990-Present.

Objective: To understand how to build and maintain work teams; how the talents of team members are tapped and linked to larger goals such as improved productivity; or how groups influence the performance of individual employees.

Learning Outcome: Upon successful completion of this course, the student will be able to develop capability to create an environment in which the team flourishes and appreciate and understand stages of group development, styles of team leadership, managing conflict, characteristics of high and low performing teams; and relations of team leader characteristics to various styles of leadership and group need.

Instruction: Major topics covered in the course are techniques for maintaining teams, techniques for building trust, factors that create or operate against harmony, and communication of team purposes in securing adherence or agreement. Methods of instruction include lecture, problem-solving exercises, and case studies.

Credit Recommendation: In the lower division baccalaureate/associate degree category, 1 semester hour in Management or Organizational Behavior (11/91).

Financial Orientation (A10005)

Location: Various locations in Illinois, Indiana, Michigan, Ohio, Wisconsin, and other regional training facilities.

Length: 16 hours (2 days).

Dates: January 1987-Present.

Objective: To understand the elementary process of accounting and to obtain introductory knowledge of structure and components of financial statements.

Learning Outcome: Upon successful completion of this course, the student will be able to understand the elementary process of accounting; read and understand income statements and balance sheets; calculate ratios from a balance sheet and income statement; understand company cash flow management; understand book depreciation as a non-cash expense; and understand elementary budgeting processes.

Instruction: Major topics covered in the course are accounting and financial statements, cash management, depreciation and taxes, and capital and construction budgeting and regulation. Methods of instruction include lecture, discussion, and classroom exercises.

Credit Recommendation: In the lower division baccalaureate/associate degree category, 1 semester hour in Financial Management or Accounting (11/90).

Impression Management (A10006)

Location: Various locations in Illinois, Indiana, Michigan, Ohio, Wisconsin, and other regional training facilities.

Length: 16 hours (2 days).

Dates: January 1987-Present.

Objective: To improve manager's professionalism in appearance and in making formal and informal presentations.

Learning Outcome: Upon successful completion of this course, the student will be able to dress appropriately for the occasion; identify personal style of interaction and make necessary modifications; deliver a presentation synthesizing verbal and visual systems; and understand the impact on others and be able to identify appropriate responses, respond flexibly, and use feedback to plan for further growth.

Instruction: Major topics covered in the course are professional appearance (visual presentation system), professional interactions (verbal interaction system), approaching professional situations confidently, and dimensional intensity. Methods of instruction include lecture, discussion, classroom exercises, and videotaped presentations with feedback.

Credit Recommendation: In the lower division baccalaureate/associate degree category, 1 semester hour in Business Administration (11/90).

Innovative Problem Solving (A10008)

Location: Various locations in Illinois, Indiana, Michigan, Ohio, Wisconsin, and other regional training facilities.

Length: 17.5 hours (2.5 days).

Dates: January 1989-Present.

Objective: To identify, analyze, and solve problems creatively.

Learning Outcome: Upon successful completion of this course, the student will be able to size up a situation and identify a problem; analyze and define the probable causes of a problem; develop information needed to solve a problem; generate alternative solutions and make an appropriate decision; and develop and implement a strategy for solving a problem.

Instruction: Major topics covered in the course are identifying a problem situation, analyzing problems and determining causes, evaluating information, and decision making. Methods of instruction include lecture, discussion, classroom exercises, case studies, role playing, and problem solving.

Credit Recommendation: In the upper division baccalaureate degree category, 1 semester hour in Management (11/90). **NOTE:** The course with this title offered by Ohio Bell was recommended for 2 semester hours credit, but subsequently it was reduced in duration from 4 days to 2.5 days. Thus, the credit recommendation has been lowered to 1 semester hour.

Integrated Information Transport (A320)

Location: Waukesha, WI.

Length: 40 hours (5 days).

Dates: May 1987-Present.

Objective: Understanding of voice/data integration techniques from functional, technical, economic, and problem-solving points of view.

Learning Outcome: Upon successful completion of this course, the student will be able to describe the methods used to integrate voice and data in today's networks, including its application to digital carriers, time slot interchangers, the digital hierarchy, PBX uses of voice/data integration, etc.; and describe various multiplexing forms.

Instruction: Major topics covered in the course are introduction to integrated information transport, T-1 carrier fundamentals, alternative digitization techniques, data networks, voice/data integration, image integration, transmission media techniques, intelligent networks, and customer-owned equipment. Methods of instruction include lecture, discussion, classroom exercises, computer-assisted visuals, case studies, and a final examination.

Credit Recommendation: In the upper division baccalaureate degree category, 2 semester hours in Telecommunication and Data Networking, Management Information Systems, or Electrical Engineering (11/90).

ISDN and Intelligent Networks (A340)

Location: Waukesha, WI.

Length: 40 hours (5 days).

Dates: May 1987-Present.

Objective: Understanding of structure, function, and application of an integrated service data network (ISDN).

Learning Outcome: Upon successful completion of this course, the student will be able to discuss the motivation for and the market projection of ISDN; use ISDN terminology appropriately; define channel characteristics; define the establishment of communication links, addressing assignments, and message exchange of the Q.931 protocol; discuss features and terminology of the common channel interoffice signaling system with SS7; and discuss the objectives and issues relating to an advanced information network.

Instruction: Major topics covered in the course are ISDN overview, ISDN technology, ISDN evolution, ISDN protocols, and SS7 and the intelligent network. Methods of instruction include lecture, discussion, laboratory exercises, computer-assisted visuals, and a final examination.

Credit Recommendation: In the upper division baccalaureate degree category, 2 semester hours in Electrical Engineering, Data Networking, Computer Engineering, Telecommunications, or Management Information Systems (11/90).

Leadership Strategies (A10004)

Location: Various locations in Illinois, Indiana, Michigan, Ohio, Wisconsin, and other regional training facilities.

Length: 28 hours (4 days).

Dates: October 1986-Present.

Objective: To understand contemporary management techniques for optimum leadership in the work environment.

Learning Outcome: Upon successful completion of this course, the student will be able to create a climate of performance with fulfillment; identify, communicate, and operationalize core values and purposes of work units; create goals responsive to needs of work-unit members; provide information to improve employees' performance, learning, and growth; identify worker's personal rewards framework and relate this to performance; and be proactive in providing and receiving support and creating a climate of trust and learning.

Instruction: Major topics covered in the course are contemporary leadership styles and their application to management, communication techniques, decision making, and supervisory theory. Methods of instruction include lecture, discussion, classroom exercises, videotapes, and a leadership survey profile.

Credit Recommendation: In the lower division baccalaureate/associate degree category, 2 semester hours in Organizational Behavior or Management (11/90).

Local and Metropolitan Networks (A310)

Location: Waukesha, WI.

Length: 40 hours (5 days).

Dates: May 1987-Present.

Objective: To understand local and metropolitan networks.

Learning Outcome: Upon successful completion of this course, the student will be able to identify major trends and directions pertaining to LANS; analyze telecommunication carriers in the PC LAN interconnection arena; explain the evolution of LAN technologies through the newer standards to FDDI, SMDS, and BISDN; explain the techniques and implementations associated with the upper layers of the OSI reference model; examine various types of LAN communications products; and evaluate LAN throughput and user interfaces.

Instruction: Major topics covered in the course are networking vs. multiuser systems, needs analysis, LANS, OSI, PS/2 and OS/2 servers, group productivity software, LAN products for micros, mainframe connections, and trends and directions. Methods of instruction include lecture, discussion, laboratory exercises, and a final examination.

Credit Recommendation: In the lower division baccalaureate/associate degree category, 2 semester hours in Telecommunications, Computer Information Systems, Computer Science, or Management Information Systems (11/90).

Major Competitive Architectures (A350)

Location: Waukesha, WI.

Length: 40 hours (5 days).

Dates: May 1987-Present.

Objective: Application of knowledge of the major computer network architectures, including IBM and DEC.

Learning Outcome: Upon successful completion of this course, the student will be able to compare and contrast network architecture of IBM and DEC; discuss issues concerning other vendors' architectures and technical computer internetworking schemes; describe some typical network management plans; understand the major protocols used in popular computer networks; and compare existing network architectures with the OSI reference model.

Instruction: Major topics covered in the course are SNA overview, services, and messages; synchronous data link control; path control; and other architectures. Methods of instruction include lecture, discussion, laboratory exercises, and a final examination.

Credit Recommendation: In the upper division baccalaureate degree category, 2 semester hours in Telecommunications, Computer Science, Computer Engineering, or Management Information Systems (11/90).

Managing Development and Diversity (A10055)

Location: Within 5-State Ameritech Region.

Length: 15 hours (2 days).

Dates: June 1991-Present.

Objective: To enable managers or team leaders to solve workplace problems that arise within the context of a diverse work force.

Learning Outcome: Upon successful completion of this course, the student will be able to appreciate the impact of diversity on individual and group performance; understand the nature of cultural diversity; and formulate means to interact and communicate with an array of individuals—women, Hispanics, Asians, Blacks, Native Americans, and older persons—in a sensitive and effective manner.

Instruction: Major topics covered in the course are premise of linkage of expectancy theory, attribution theory, complicity, stereotyping, and creation of a performance model; application of a development model that will affect students personal growth by eliciting productivity upon insight into one's beliefs (and values); the generation of feelings of self-worth and belonging as mechanisms to emeloriate or bridge interpersonal relationships; and demographics that will influence the need for this knowledge. Methods of instruction include lecture and case studies.

Credit Recommendation: In the lower division baccalaureate/associate degree category, 1 semester hour in Sociology or Management (11/91).

Managing Interpersonal Skills (Communication Skills Workshop) (A10003)

Location: Various locations in Illinois, Indiana, Michigan, Ohio, Wisconsin, and other regional training facilities.

Length: 20 hours (3 days).

Dates: December 1987-Present.

Objective: To promote and sustain better communications in the workplace.

Learning Outcome: Upon successful completion of this course, the student will be able to recognize successful performance of others; seek ideas and opinions of others to ensure adequate flow of information; foster desire for improved performance of others; make better use of human resources; and resolve conflicts in productive ways.

Instruction: Major topics covered in the course are delivering messages, giving and receiving feedback, listening, negotiating and managing differences, and responding. Methods of instruction include lecture, discussion, visual aids, classroom exercises, and role playing.

Credit Recommendation: In the lower division baccalaureate/associate degree category, 1 semester hour in Communications or Personnel Management (11/90).

Managing Multiple Priorities (A10029)

Location: Within the 5-State Ameritech Region.

Length: 16 hours (2 days).

Dates: September 1990-Present.

Objective: To enable the student to manage and organize assignments and tasks; to establish priorities among them as necessary; and to meet individual and organizational goals in an efficient and timely manner.

Learning Outcome: Upon successful completion of this course, the student will be able to manage priorities with skill and efficiency; identify priorities according to their seriousness, urgency, or trend of development and devise means for securing agreement or consensus among the interests; achieve closure on assignment of priorities; and engage in experiential learning to develop insight into problems associated with priority setting or handling multiple tasks simultaneously.

Instruction: Major topics covered in the course are how priorities came to be established; insights into elements that affect one's ability to negotiate priorities; imperativeness of the task or assignment to be accomplished; one's status or position in the organization; organizational and interpersonal interaction; insights into one's self and position in the negotiating process; maximizing one's effectiveness; barriers to agreement; structure, timing, misperceptions of interests; techniques of negotiation and securing agreement; and meshing one's self interest and that of the organization. Methods of instruction include lecture, classroom problem-solving exercises, role playing, and case studies.

Credit Recommendation: In the lower division baccalaureate/associate degree category, 1 semester hour in Management or Organizational Behavior (11/91).

Managing Personal Growth (A10022)

Location: Various locations in Illinois, Indiana, Michigan, Ohio, Wisconsin, and other regional training facilities.

Length: 14 hours (2 days).

Dates: December 1984-Present.

Objective: Sensitivity of managers and support staff to individual concerns and their relationship to organizational needs.

Learning Outcome: Upon successful completion of this course, the student will be able to identify skills needed for a specific job; assess skill deficiencies; and develop plans for enhancing skill deficiencies in relation to organizational needs.

Instruction: Major topics covered in the course are individual and group analysis of skills using Skills Inventory, personal talents and skills, development needs, job satisfaction, performance priorities, and individual development plan. Methods of instruction include lecture, discussion, classroom exercises, and post-course review and reinforcement with supervisors.

Credit Recommendation: In the lower division baccalaureate/associate degree category, 1 semester hour in Supervision, Management, or Human Resource Development (11/90).

Managing Quality Improvement (A10032)

Location: Within the 5-State Ameritech Region.

Length: 24 hours (3 days).

Dates: January 1991-Present.

Objective: To equip leaders with the knowledge and skills necessary to lead and support quality improvement teams and strengthen leadership's understanding of and commitment to the quality team.

Learning Outcome: Upon successful completion of this course, the student will be able to identify and support the principles, practices, and behaviors that characterize total quality management; identify and support the steps necessary in the quality improvement process; identify structures that facilitate or impede participation in quality improvement processes within an organization; understand the leaders' role in supporting the implementation of the quality improvement process;

and recognize the importance of achieving consensus in quality team activities.

Instruction: Major topics covered in the course are introductions to quality concepts and philosophy, such as quality principles; three phases of Ameritech quality; a seven-step quality improvement process; interface with quality advisors-team leaders; enhancing team members' development; acquiring team promotion skills; and selecting team leaders. Methods of instruction include lecture, case studies, and problem-solving exercises.

Credit Recommendation: In the upper division baccalaureate degree category, 1 semester hour in Managing Quality Control or Management (11/91).

Marketing Management at Ameritech (A10026)

Location: Woodfield Hilton, Arlington Heights, Illinois.

Length: 34 hours (4 days).

Dates: April 1991-Present.

Objective: To establish a market/customer focus for decision making and performance.

Learning Outcome: Upon successful completion of this course, the student will be able to understand the urgency for change in order to deal with a competitive marketplace process; understand the organizations' strategic responses to the market place i.e., customer service, quality environment, timeliness, low unit cost, mass customization, and alternative channels and commit to strategies; and apply strategies to jobs.

Instruction: Major topics covered in the course are the changing environment; Ameritech's strategic direction; wireless; customer buying behavior; segmentation, targeting, and positioning; product development; managing product offering; Ameritech Bell Group pricing strategy; pricing decisions; communication and promotion; accessing the market; Ameritech Bell Company channel management; and Ameritech marketing problems. Methods of instruction include pre-course packet of materials, student binder for study, lecture, videotapes, and case studies.

Credit Recommendation: In the lower division baccalaureate/associate degree category, 2 semester hours in Marketing elective (11/91).

Network Management Systems (A300)

Location: Waukesha, WI.

Length: 40 hours (5 days).

Dates: May 1987-Present.

Objective: Understanding of trends, issues, and products of network management systems.

Learning Outcome: Upon successful completion of this course, the student will be able to describe the rationale behind use of network management systems; understand internal workings of a network management system; compare similarities and differences of various network management systems; understand preliminary OSI standards for network management; and be receptive to future trends in network management systems, including addition of expert systems.

Instruction: Major topics covered in the course are network management overview, recognized needs for network management, designing network systems, case study of a network management system, analysis of network components, OSI network management, and future trends and directions. Methods of instruction include lecture, discussion, classroom exercises, case studies, and an oral examination of a team case study.

Credit Recommendation: In the upper division baccalaureate degree category, 2 semester hours in Business Administration, Management, Telecommunications Management, Network Management, or Management Information Systems (11/90).

Packet Switched Networks (A330)

Location: Waukesha, WI.

Length: 40 hours (5 days).

Dates: May 1987-Present.

Objective: Understanding of terminology and issues and their application in functioning packet switched networks.

Learning Outcome: Upon successful completion of this course, the student will be able to describe packet technology; and discuss the history of public packet networks—their practical implementation and management issues related to implementation.

Instruction: Major topics covered in the course are packet switching overview, evolution of packet switching and public networks, physical level protocols, link level protocols, packet level protocols, network services, asynchronous connections, BISYNC connections, SNA SDLC connections, and packet switched networks. Methods of instruction include lecture, discussion, laboratory exercises, videotapes, and a final examination.

Credit Recommendation: In the upper division baccalaureate degree category, 2 semester hours in Electrical Engineering, Data Networking, Telecommunications, or Management Information Systems (11/90).

Performance Planning for Goal Achievement (A1007)

Location: Various locations in Illinois, Indiana, Michigan, Ohio, Wisconsin, and other regional training facilities.

Length: 16 hours (2 days).

Dates: January 1987-Present.

Objective: For managers to define their jobs clearly, establish meaningful goals, and interact reflectively with their supervisors.

Learning Outcome: Upon successful completion of this course, the student will be able to develop clear job descriptions; define goals using specific criteria for selected responsibilities and functions; plan and participate in job definition and goal-setting discussions; and relate goals and job definition to overall corporate performance system.

Instruction: Major topics covered in the course are job definition and goal-setting process; job summary; responsibility statements; function statements; latitudes and constraints; writing, reviewing, and critiquing job definition; definition, value, and criteria for writing goals; planning and conducting the goal setting-discussion; and the performance system. Methods of instruction include lecture, discussion, classroom exercises, and post-course interview with supervisor.

Credit Recommendation: In the lower division baccalaureate/associate degree category, 1 semester hour in Human Resource Development or Personnel Management (11/90).

Quality Advisor (A10033)

Location: Within the 5-State Ameritech Region.

Length: 40 hours (5 days).

Dates: January 1991-Present.

Objective: To increase participants' knowledge of quality concepts and gain insight and experience in the skills necessary to assist quality improvement teams in their objectives.

Learning Outcome: Upon successful completion of this course, the student will be able to facilitate and evaluate the group dynamics of teams; promote a culture that emphasizes teamwork; understand administrative requirements associated with quality efforts; facilitate consensus building in teams; and understand the behaviors associated with the various quality advisor roles.

Instruction: Major topics covered in the course are quality concepts, facilitation and evaluation of the group dynamics of teams, promoting a culture of teamwork, consensus-building skills, administrative requirements of quality improvement efforts, role of quality improvement teams, and technical and organizational issues in quality process. Methods of instruction include lecture, problem-solving exercises, and case studies.

Credit Recommendation: In the upper division baccalaureate degree category, 2 semester hours in Leadership Management or Quality Control (11/91).

Quality Team Leader (A10034)

Location: Within the 5-State Ameritech Region.

Length: 40 hours (5 days).

Dates: January 1991-Present.

Objective: To equip participants with the knowledge and skills to lead quality improvement teams and to develop problem-solving and group leadership skills.

Learning Outcome: Upon successful completion of this course, the student will be able to understand the purpose of and apply mechanics of the quality improvement processes; identify percentage; analyze and solve work-related problems; and build and maintain quality teams.

Instruction: Major topics covered in the course are review of the purpose and mechanics of a quality continuous improvement process; review of the techniques of identifying, prioritizing, analyzing, and solving work-related problems; and group dynamics and group leadership concepts necessary to build and maintain quality teams. Methods of instruction include lecture, problem solving, and case studies.

Credit Recommendation: In the upper division baccalaureate degree category, 2 semester hours in Leadership or Management of Quality Control (11/91).

Quality Team Member (A10035)

Location: Within the 5-State Ameritech Region.

Length: 16 hours (2 days).

Dates: January 1991-Present.

Objective: To provide participants with an overview of quality principles and practices and the role of quality teams, and provide participants with experience in the process of working as a team.

Learning Outcome: Upon successful completion of this course, the student will be able to understand in general terms quality principles and practices; follow guidelines for effective meetings; follow analytical problem-solving steps; and understand the Ameritech quality improvement process.

Instruction: Major topics covered in the course are an overview of quality principles and practices with specific emphasis on the role of the team, introduction to the Ameritech quality improvement story, and the use of analytical problem-solving tools. Methods of instruction include lecture, role playing, and case studies.

Credit Recommendation: In the lower division baccalaureate/associate degree category, 1 semester hour in Management (11/91).

ServiceMAX Construction (A10041 and A10046))

Location: Illinois Bell Learning Center, Chicago, IL.

Length: 37.5 hours (1 week).

Dates: September 1991-Present.

Objective: To understand contemporary management techniques for optimum leadership in a telecommunications environment specific to construction.

Learning Outcome: Upon successful completion of this course, the student will be able to explain the major components of the telephone network and the organizations responsible for the operations of each network component; and develop managerial expertise applicable to the construction phase.

Instruction: Major topics covered in the course are major components in network activities, workforce, customers, standard operating environments, causes and effects of customer expectations, workforce management, forecasting management, forecasting load and force requirements, and project management techniques. Methods of instruction include lecture, discussion, case studies, videotapes, and course assignments.

Credit Recommendation: In the upper division baccalaureate degree category, 1 semester hour in Telecommunications or Technical Management (11/91).

ServiceMAX Installation and Maintenance (A10040 and A10045)

Location: Illinois Bell Learning Center, Chicago, IL.

Length: 36 hours.

Dates: September 1991-Present.

Objective: To understand contemporary management techniques for optimum leadership in a telecommunications environment specific to installation and maintenance.

Learning Outcome: Upon successful completion of this course, the student will be able to explain the functions of major installation and maintenance organizations; identify the major installation and maintenance support systems; identify and discuss ways to manage better the service provision process; explain the importance and key components of the workforce management process; explain appropriate techniques to develop an effective preventive maintenance program; use system output reports to plan corrective actions; and analyze performance measurements and determine corrective action plans.

Instruction: Major topics covered in the course are installation and maintenance operational fundamentals, maintenance, workforce management, preventive maintenance, and performance measurements. Methods of instruction include lecture, discussion, classroom exercises, and videotapes.

Credit Recommendation: In the upper division baccalaureate degree category, 1 semester hour in Telecommunications or Technical Management (11/91).

ServiceMAX Outside Plant Engineering (A10042 and A10047)

Location: Illinois Bell Learning Center, Chicago, IL.

Length: 39 hours (1 week).

Dates: October 1991-Present.

Objective: To understand contemporary management techniques for optimum leadership in a telecommunications environment specific to outside plant engineering.

Learning Outcome: Upon successful completion of this course, the student will be able to identify and discuss major components of a capital program; identify and discuss telecommunications engineering functions from an outside plant perspective; identify and discuss engineering roles in project management; and discuss and use project management techniques.

Instruction: Major topics covered in the course are engineering network overview; capital program planning and monitoring; project management techniques; resource planning, scheduling, and management; and planning and management of project teams. Methods of instruction include lecture, discussion, case studies, computer-assisted videotape, and course assignments.

Credit Recommendation: In the upper division baccalaureate degree category, 1 semester hour in Telecommunications or Technical Management (11/91).

ServiceMAX Special Services (A10044 and A10049)

Location: Illinois Bell Learning Center, Chicago, IL.

Length: 36.5 hours (1 week).
Dates: September 1991-Present.
Objective: To understand contemporary management techniques for optimum leadership in telecommunications environment specific to special services.
Learning Outcome: Upon successful completion of this course, the student will be able to explain the major components of the telephone network and the organizations responsible for the operations and maintenance of each network component; and develop the managerial expertise applicable to the special services phase.
Instruction: Major topics covered in the course are major types of special services, and identifying those that are most competitive; personnel utilization, workload, and planning; trouble report administration; network facilities; statistical elements in provisioning services; and project management skills. Methods of instruction include lecture, discussion, case studies, and videotape.
Credit Recommendation: In the upper division baccalaureate degree category, 1 semester hour in Telecommunications or Technical Management (11/91).

ServiceMAX Switching (A10043 and A10048)

Location: Illinois Bell Learning Center, Chicago, IL.
Length: 36.9 hours (1 week).
Dates: October 1991-Present.
Objective: To understand contemporary management techniques for optimum leadership in a telecommunications environment specific to switching.
Learning Outcome: Upon successful completion of this course, the student will be able to describe the major components of a switched network; manage a workforce charged with switched network; and relate switching capabilities to company resources, strategic planning, and technical advantages.
Instruction: Major topics covered in the course are network configuration overview, workforce management, customer service, management of technical functions, and implementation of new technologies. Methods of instruction include lecture, discussion, course assignments, case studies, and computer-assisted videotape.
Credit Recommendation: In the upper division baccalaureate degree category, 1 semester hour in Telecommunications or Technical Management (11/91).

The Information Technology Environment (A200)

Location: Waukesha, WI.
Length: 40 hours (5 days).
Dates: May 1987-Present.
Objective: To know data communications and integrated transport systems.
Learning Outcome: Upon successful completion of this course, the student will be able to identify major components of modern information systems and describe their functions; identify trends in information system technology and describe the significance of these trends in a business environment; recognize and state applications for selected technology within the information system environment in terms of specific product sales opportunities; and identify and assess the activity of major vendors in the information systems environment.
Instruction: Major topics covered in the course are information technology, computer system applications, networking and network management, OSI standards, systems network architecture (SNA), local area networks, ISDN, and packet switched networks. Methods of instruction include lecture, discussion, case studies, and a final examination.
Credit Recommendation: In the lower division baccalaureate/associate degree category, 2 semester hours in Telecommunications, Computer Science, Computer Engineering, or Management Information Systems (11/90).

Armenian National Education Committee

The Siamanto Academy of the Armenian National Education Committee has been headquartered in New York City since September 1983. The educational setting is currently situated at the Armenian National Education Commit-tee's location in the Prelacy Building of the Armenian Apostolic Church of America. The Prelacy houses a library and offers advantages of a variety of technical and cultural resources.

Source of official student records: Registry of Credit Recommendations, American Council on Education, One Dupont Circle, Washington, DC 20036-1193 or Administrator, Siamanto Academy, Armenian National Education Committee, 138 East 39th Street, New York, NY 10016.

Additional information about the courses: Office of Corporate-Higher Education Programs, Thomas Edison State College, 101 West State Street, Trenton, NJ 08608-1176.

Armenian Ancient and Medieval History

Location: St. Illuminator Cathedral, 221 East 27th Street, New York, NY.

Length: 70 hours (60 weeks).

Dates: January 1983-May 1996.

Objective: To introduce students to ancient and medieval Armenian history, covering the period from 1500 B.C. to 1375 A.D.

Instruction: Major topics covered in the course are the relationship between the Armenians and the following empires: Persia, Alexander the Great, Rome, Byzantine, Arab, and early Ottomans; tracing of Armenian religious expression including early duties and Zoroastrian traditions; and the analysis of impact of Christianity on the Armenian people including the role of the Armenians during the Crusades.

The material is presented through staff and guest lectures. Homework is assigned regularly, and frequent quizzes and examinations are given in class.

Credit Recommendation: In the lower division baccalaureate/associate degree category, 3 semester hours in Ancient/ Medieval Armenian History (1/83) (5/91). The requirements for credit recommendation. All three courses offered by the Siamanto Academy form an integrated program and the credit recommendations only apply upon successful completion of the entire program.

Introduction to Armenian Civilization and Culture

Location: St. Illuminator Cathedral, 221 East 27th Street, New York, NY.

Length: 180 hours (90 weeks).

Dates: January 1983-May 1996.

Objective: To introduce students to Armenian civilization and culture through the study of literature, drama, history of the Armenian Church, music, and folk dance.

Instruction: In this course an historical perspective is presented and, when applicable, students participate in the performance of theater, music, and folk dance. Through the analysis of selected readings, the student will correlate and integrate the historical and geographical trends in Armenian literature, music, theater, and folk dance. The course also covers topics in ethics, the Church fathers, Church history, and the Armenian religious tradition.

The material is presented through staff and guest lectures. Rehearsals and public performances are part of the program. Homework is assigned regularly, and frequent quizzes and examinations are given in class.

Credit Recommendation: In the lower division baccalaureate/associate degree category, 3 semester hours in Introduction to Armenian Civilization and Culture (1/83) (5/91). The requirements for credit recommendation. All three courses offered by the Siamanto Academy form an integrated program and the credit recommendations only apply upon successful completion of the entire program.

Modern (East and West) Armenian History

Location: St. Illuminator Cathedral, 221 East 27th Street, New York, NY.

Length: 35 hours (30 weeks).

Dates: January 1983-May 1996.

Objective: To introduce students to modern Armenian history, covering the period from 1375 A.D. to the present.

Instruction: The course includes the analysis of modern West and East Armenian history; identification of related events in Ottoman, late Byzantine, European, Arabian, Russian, Persian, Georgian, and Azeri histories; the analysis of the relationship between the Armenian community and the Ottoman government as reflected in the Millet system; the rise of Armenian nationalism; the course and consequences of the massacres of 1895 and 1915; identification of the events leading to the Armenian Republic of 1918-20; survey of the history of Soviet Armenia, 1920 to present; survey of the selected developments of Turkish history from 1920 to present; and survey of the development of the Armenian communities in the Diaspora, 1920 to present.

The material is presented through staff and guest lectures. Homework is assigned regularly, and frequent quizzes and examinations are given in class.

Credit Recommendation: In the lower division baccalaureate/associate degree category, 3 semester hours in Modern Armenian History (1/83) (5/91). The requirements for credit recommendation. All three courses offered by the Siamanto Academy form an integrated program and the credit recommendations only apply upon successful completion of the entire program.

Art Instruction Schools, Inc.

Art Instruction Schools is a wholly owned subsidiary of the Bureau of Engraving, Inc., a privately owned corporation. Located in Minneapolis, Minnesota, the school has offered art courses by correspondence since 1914.

Art Instruction Schools offers Fundamentals of Art and Specialized Art. The Fundamentals of Art course consists of 27 lessons and requires a typical student two years and over 1,000 hours to complete. The Specialized Art course consists of 27 lessons and requires a typical student two years and over 1,400 hours to complete. Fundamentals of Art is a prerequisite for Specialized Art. For each lesson students must submit artwork that demonstrates proficiency in the techniques and concepts presented in the lesson. The assigned artwork evaluates only a portion of the material presented in the lesson, so students may, through independent work and practice, learn more than they are required to demonstrate in the assignments. Institutions are urged to evaluate portfolios individually to determine the exact amount of credit to be awarded.

Students applying for college credit are required to take proctored, objective art examinations. In Fundamentals of Art, an examination may be taken after Lessons 8, 14, 18, 22, 26 (at which time a student may apply for credit for the portion completed) or upon completion of the entire Fundamentals of Art program. Similarly, in Specialized Art, students may take an examination after Lesson 6, 9, 12, 17, 20, or upon completion of Specialized Art. Students are also required, as part of the examination, to submit a portfolio which is evaluated by a faculty committee and is part of the final grade. Institutions should review the portfolio in determining the credit award.

These examinations were instituted in January 1978, but students who began the programs as early as August 1973 may take the art examination to have the credit recommendations apply to them. Successful completion of the examinations is indicated on the student's record.

Source of official student records: Director of Education, Art Instruction Schools, Inc., 500 South Fourth Street, Minneapolis, MN 55415.

Additional information about the courses: College Credit Recommendation Service, American Council on Education, One Dupont Circle, Washington, DC 20036-1193.

Fundamentals of Art
Part 1: Basic Drawing and Design I
Part 2: Ink and Color Rendering and Design II
(Formerly Basic Drawing and Design II)
Part 3: Animal Drawing and Perspective
(Formerly Figure Drawing and Studio Techniques)
Part 4: Art Mediums and Techniques
Part 5: Figure Drawing
Part 6: Studio Techniques

Location: Correspondence program.

Length: 27 lessons (typical student requires two years and over 1,000 hours to complete).

Dates: *Version 1:* January 1978-February 1983; *Version 2:* March 1988-June 1988; *Version 3:* July 1988-March 1994; *Version 4:* April 1994-Present.

Objective: *Versions 1, 2, 3, Part 1:* To introduce students to drawing, design principles, and color concepts. *Versions 1, 2, 3, Part 2:* To enable students to use a variety of art media and techniques creatively. *Versions 1, 2, 3, Part 3:* To provide students with an understanding of human anatomy that will enable them to draw the nude and draped figure. *Version 4, Part 1 (lessons 1-8):* To introduce the student to drawing accurately while showing realistic form and structure. *Version 4, Part 2 (lessons 9-14):* To provide students with an understanding of ink rendering, color concepts, and design principles. *Version 4, Part 3 (lessons 15-18):* To provide students with an understanding of animal form and construction, and the use of perspective in drawing. *Version 4, Part 4 (lessons 19-22):* To enable students to use a variety of art media and techniques creatively. *Version 4, Part 5 (lessons 23-26):* To provide students with an understanding of human anatomy in drawing the nude and draped figure. *Version 4, Part 6 (lesson 27):* To provide students with an understanding of techniques used to present art work professionally for reproduction.

Learning Outcome: Upon successful completion of this course, the student will be familiar with basic drawing, basic color, form, basic design, various media and techniques, studio techniques, cartooning, animal drawing, figure drawing, lettering, and composition.

Instruction: *Versions 1, 2, 3, Part 1:* Fundamental techniques of drawing to achieve accurate proportions, form, foreshortening, and textures; fundamentals of representational, abstract, and nonobjective designs; application of color principles through planning, mixing, and use. *Versions 1, 2, 3, Part 2:* Drawing and rendering animals; perspective, including one-point to multiple-point, and spacing, shadows, reflections, and plane projections; history and techniques of lettering; identification of lettering styles; lettering tools; pen and brush lettering and creative lettering; still life art, including positive and negative shapes, sight-size drawing, lighting, backgrounds, enlarging and reducing; pictorial composition. *Versions 1, 2, 3, Part 3:* Figure drawing, including proportions, skeleton, and muscles; action and expressions; foreshortening and distortion; head, hand, and foot studies; drawing the draped figure—with an introduction to fashion illustration; studio techniques, including art studios, care and use of tools and materials, tricks of the trade, the airbrush, mounting photographs and artwork, matting, preparation of keylines (mechanicals or paste-ups), and instructional aids such as the use of a grid. *Version 4, Part 1 (lessons 1-8):* Major topics covered in the course are fundamental techniques of drawing to achieve accurate proportions, basic shapes, three-dimensional shapes and structure; techniques of using various pencil strokes to show texture, tone, depth, and color; and fundamentals of form to draw realistically. *Version 4, Part 2 (lessons 9-14):* Major topics covered in the course are drawing and shading with pen and ink and brush and ink; introduction to cartooning; techniques for combining pen and brush work; fundamentals of the color wheel; psychology of color, value, and scale of colors; and mixing and applying color schemes, elements, and principles of design as applied to realistic, decorative or abstract artwork. *Version 4, Part 3 (lessons 15-18):* Major topics covered in the course are techniques of drawing and rendering basic animal forms, skeletons and muscle structure; study of construction of fish and birds; rules of linear perspective to capture illusion from one point to multiple points; and the use of aerial perspective as applied to vanishing trace, shadows, reflections, and projections. *Version 4, Part 4 (lessons 19-22):* Major topics covered in the course are sight-size method of drawing, lighting setups; enlarging or reducing single subject; history and techniques of lettering; identification of lettering styles; lettering tools; pen and brush lettering; creative lettering; and still life art including positive and negative shapes, sight-size drawing, and pictorial composition. *Version 4, Part 5 (lessons 23-26):* Major topics covered in the course are figure drawing including proportions, skeleton and muscles, action and expressions; foreshortening and distortion; head, hand, and foot studies; and drawing the draped figure with an introduction to fashion illustration. *Version 4, Part 6 (lesson 27):* Major topics covered in the course are studio techniques including art studios, use of tools and materials, tricks of the trade, airbrush, mounting photographs and artwork, matting, preparation of keylines (mechanicals and pasteups), and instructional aids such as the use of the grid.

Credit Recommendation: *Version 1:* In the lower division baccalaureate/associate degree category, 4-6 semester hours in Art Education or Studio Art for each part, for a total of 12-18 semester hours (1/78). *Version 2:* In the lower division baccalaureate/associate degree category, 4-8 semester hours in Art Education or Studio Art for each part, for a total of 12-24 semester hours (3/83). *Version 3:* In the lower division baccalaureate/associate degree category, 24 semester hours in Art Education or Studio Art (7/88). *Version 4: Part 1: (lessons 1-8):* In the lower division baccalaureate/associate degree category, 4 semester hours in Art Education or Studio Art. *Version 4: Part 2 (lessons 9-14):* In the lower division baccalaureate/associate degree category, 4 semester hours in Art Education or Studio Art. *Version 4: Part 3 (lessons 15-18):* In the lower division baccalaureate/associate degree category, 4 semester hours in Art Education or Studio Art. *Version 4: Part 4 (lessons 19-22):* In the lower division baccalaureate/associate degree category, 4 semester hours in Art Education or Studio Art. *Version 4: Part 5 (lessons 23-26):* In the lower division baccalaureate/associate degree category, 6 semester hours in Art Education or Studio Art. *Version 4: Part 6 (lesson 27):* In the lower division baccalaureate/associate degree category, 2 semester hours in Art Education or Studio Art. *Version 4: Parts 1-6,* carry a total credit recommendation in the lower division baccalaureate/associate degree category, 24 semester hours in Art Education or Studio Art (4/94).

Specialized Art
Part 1. Design, Composition, and Reproduction
Part 2. Painting Techniques
Part 3. Cartooning
Part 4. Art in Advertising
Part 5. Advanced Drawing and Painting
Part 6. Advanced Illustration

Location: Correspondence program.

Length: 27 lessons (typical student requires two years and over 1,400 hours to complete).

Dates: *Version 1:* January 1978-June 1988; *Version 2:* July 1988-March 1994; *Version 3:* April 1994-Present.

Objective: *Versions 1, 2, 3, Part 1 (lessons 1-6):* To provide an understanding of advanced problems in design, reproduction, and composition. *Versions 1, 2, 3, Part 2 (lessons 7-9):* To provide an understanding of various painting techniques and media. *Versions 1, 2, 3, Part 3 (lessons 10-12):* To provide an understanding of cartooning as a creative and expressive art including the history of cartooning styles and techniques. *Versions 1, 2, 3, Part 4 (lessons 13-17):* To provide an understanding of the functions and responsibilities of an art director and an advertising agency; to provide an awareness of the creative process for an advertisement by analyzing client's needs, researching, and choosing visuals, layout tools, and techniques; to develop an understanding of cartoons as part of the advertising message; and to experiment with the styles and techniques involved in preparing advertising cartoons. *Versions 1, 2, 3, Part 5 (lessons 18-20):* To enable students to select subjects, compose, use perspective, and apply color theory to drawing from nature and painting portraits. *Versions 1, 2, 3, Part 6 (lessons 21-27):* To familiarize students with the tools and techniques used by professional illustrators; and provide an understanding of the problems of creating artworks for book, fashion, editorial, and advertising illustrations.

Learning Outcome: Upon successful completion of this course, the student will be able to design, compose, and reproduce; paint; use effective art techniques in cartooning, advertising, drawing, and painting; and illustration.

Instruction: *Versions 1, 2, 3, Part 1 (lessons 1-6):* Major topics covered in the course are commercial printing processes (letterpress and offset lithography), reproduction of art screens, applying tone to line art, color reproduction, silk screening; advanced design problems, processes, techniques, and commercial applications; advanced study of composition, underlying picture patterns, rendering styles, analysis of shapes, values, and color in picture arranging. *Versions 1, 2, 3, Part 2 (lessons 7-9):* Major topics covered in the course are value and color problems in transparent and opaque media; their application to fine art and advertising art. *Versions 1, 2, 3, Part 3 (lessons 10-12):* Major topics covered in the course are study of cartooning using ink, acrylics, Zip-A-Tone shading sheets, colored papers, felt cloth, and other media on illustration boards, texture sheets, acetate, and other surfaces doing dry brush renderings, creating collages, and using other techniques. *Versions 1, 2, 3, Part 4 (lessons 13-17):* Major topics covered in the course are construction of an advertising campaign; service and institutional advertisements; psychology of advertising; functions and responsibilities of the art director; functions of the advertising agency; tools and techniques used in advertising art studios and agencies. *Versions 1, 2, 3, Part 5 (lessons 18-20):* Major topics covered in the course are composition as it relates to landscape space, aerial perspective, drawing and painting portraits, review of head anatomy and form; placement, background considerations, color mixing, and painting methods. *Versions 1, 2, 3, Part 6 (lessons 21-27):* Major topics covered in the course are developing illustrating skills and advanced rendering techniques for book, fashion, editorial, and advertising illustration.

Credit Recommendation: *Version 1: Part 1:* In the upper division baccalaureate degree category, 4-6 semester hours in Art Education or Studio Art (1/78). *Part 2:* In the upper division baccalaureate degree category, 2 semester hours in Art Education or Studio Art (1/78). *Part 3:* In the upper division baccalaureate degree category, 2 semester hours in Art Education or Studio Art (1/78). *Part 4:* In the upper division baccalaureate degree category, 4-6 semester hours in Art Education or Studio Art (1/78). *Part 5:* In the upper division baccalaureate degree category, 2 semester hours in Art Education or Studio Art (1/78). *Part 6:* In the upper division baccalaureate degree category, 6-10 semester hours in Art Education or Studio Art (1/78). Total credit of 20-28 semester hours (1/78) (3/83). *Version 2:* In the upper division baccalaureate degree category, 28 semester hours in Art Education or Studio Art (7/88). *Version 3: Part 1:* In the upper division baccalaureate degree category, 8 semester hours in Art Education or Studio Art (4/94). *Version 3: Part: 2:* In the upper division baccalaureate degree category, 3 semester hours in Art Education or Studio Art (4/94). *Version 3: Part 3:* In the upper division baccalaureate degree category, 3 semester hours in Art Education or Studio Art (4/94). *Version 4: Part 4:* In the upper division baccalaureate degree category, 3 semester hours in Art Education or Studio Art (4/94). *Version 3: Part 5:* In the upper division baccalaureate degree category, 3 semester hours in Art Education or Studio Art (4/94). *Version 3:*

Part 6: In the upper division baccalaureate degree category, 8 semester hours in Art Education or Studio Art (4/94). *Version 3: Parts 1-6,* carry a total credit recommendation in the upper division baccalaureate degree category of 28 semester hours in Art Education or Studio Art (4/94).

AT&T Network and Computing Services/Network Operations and Engineering Training

Network Operations and Engineering Training (NOET) is the primary provider of network training and performance solutions for AT&T. Courses provide in-depth global network telecommunications training to improve the job performance of all AT&T associates who touch the communications network. Actively moving forward to the next technological level, NOET has introduced interactive multimedia methods like CD-ROM and Web-based applications to complement traditional classroom training.

Training is targeted for members of the Network and Computing Services (NCS), its Business Operating Unit customers and suppliers, and for end-user customers and suppliers of AT&T.

The NOET training center in Kansas City (KCTEC) is equipped with a digital facilities laboratory. The equipment in the lab is interconnected in exactly the same manner as the actual NSD technology transport network. This facility is a fully networked end-to-end environment which provides students with both network and technology training. The emphasis in the lab is on hands-on exercises which allows the student to experience actual troubleshooting techniques.

KCTEC is the source of interactive video training delivered to the On-Site Work Force (OSWF) within NCS. Currently, NCS central offices are equipped with video receive capability over the existing satellite communications network. This video receive capability provides a medium for NCS-NOET to develop and deliver live broadcast video training sessions directly to NCS technicians and supervisors. The system is designed to deliver high quality training quickly and cost effectively.

Included in this medium is an interactive support tool called the "One Touch" Student Response System which provides the instructor and students two-way audio capability to enhance the one-way video broadcast. "One Touch" also provides the instructor with on-screen note cards and individual student identification. Each student responds via an individual key pad.

A "One Touch" host system at the broadcast studio collects data for post course utilization such as a student's name, location, and individual response to questions which can be used for pre- and post-testing.

The video production studio, integrated with the comprehensive digital facilities laboratory, gives the KCTEC the capability to originate video broadcasts directly from the lab in order to present live demonstrations of typical technician work.

Source of official student records: Registry of Credit Recommendations, American Council on Education, One Dupont Circle, NW, Washington, DC 20036-1193.

Additional information about the courses: Office of Corporate-Higher Education Programs, Thomas Edison State College, 101 W. State Street, Trenton, NJ 08608-1176.

3B20D Processor Hardware Interrupts (ON-0515)

Location: Denver, Colorado.

Length: 32 hours (4 days).

Dates: December 1992-Present.

Objective: To provide the student with the knowledge and skills required to deal with various 3B20D Processor interrupts.

Learning Outcome: Upon the successful completion of this course, the student will be able to identify a 3B20D Processor interrupt and use the job aid provided to troubleshoot the interrupt.

Instruction: Major topics covered in the course are recognition and resolution of 3B20D Processor interrupts and the use and understanding of 3B20D Processor job aids. Methods of instruction include testing and practical assignments.

Credit Recommendation: In the lower division baccalaureate/associate degree category, 2 semester hours in Computer Systems (3/95).

3B20D Processor Maintenance (ON-0074B)

Location: Denver, Colorado.

Length: 40 hours (5 days).

Dates: June 1988-Present.

Objective: To provide the student utilization of printed material, hands-on practices, with a working 3B20D, a video tape, and simulation for troubleshooting and analysis practice.

Learning Outcome: Upon successful completion of this course, the student will be able to identify a 3B20D Processor, understand cause and effect of a 3B20D Processor recovery action, state the function of the three major components of the 3B20D Processor, locate the fault circuit pack using TLP, use the MCRT to perform various maintenance operations, and safely remove, clean and reinstall circuit packs.

Instruction: Major topics covered in the course are recognition, function, and description of all 3B20D Processor equipment, as well as proper maintenance procedures; and the use and understanding of 3B20D Processor documentation. Methods of instruction include testing and practical assignments.

Credit Recommendation: In the upper division baccalaureate degree category, 2 semester hours in Computer Systems or Technical elective (3/95).

4ESS Advanced 1B Processor Diagnostics (ON-0495X)

Location: Denver, Colorado.

Length: 24 hours (3 days).

Dates: December 1994-Present.

Objective: To repair 1B Processor equipment.

Learning Outcome: Upon successful completion of this course, the student will be able to resolve faulty cable and single lead problems in the 1B Processor and understand and use the 1B Processor's electronic support programs.

Instruction: Major topics covered in the course are in-depth diagnostics for the 1B Processor; and cable and single lead troubles using electronic systems such as program listings, electronic schematic drawings, and the pack-to-cable programs.

Credit Recommendation: In the lower division baccalaureate/associate degree category or upper division baccalaureate degree category, 1 semester hour in Telecommunications Technology or Technical elective (3/95).

4ESS Advanced 1B Processor Maintenance (ON-0494)

Location: Conyers, GA; Denver, CO; Warrenville, IL.

Length: 80 hours (10 days).

Dates: October 1993-Present.

Objective: To train personnel to maintain and repair 1B Processor equipment.

Learning Outcome: Upon successful completion of this course, the student will be able to identify the function of each of the 1B Processor's circuit packs, identify the internal and external connections to the 1B Processor, interpret interrupt data, and identify faulty hardware from diagnostic printouts.

Instruction: Major topics covered in the course are in-depth maintenance of the 1B Processor; and fault resolution using program listings (PRs) and schematic diagrams (SDs).

Credit Recommendation: In the lower division baccalaureate/associate degree category or upper division baccalaureate degree category, 2 semester hours in Telecommunications Technology or Technical elective (3/95).

4ESS Maintenance Diagnostic Seminar (ON-0489)

Location: Upon request.

Length: 40 hours (5 days).

Dates: June 1994-September 1996.

Objective: To resolve a 4ESS diagnostic using the Maintenance Reference Handbook and Schematic Drawings.

Learning Outcome: Upon successful completion of this course, the student will be able to determine which tools to use most frequently, effectively use those tools, interpret and use the basic layout of DIAL statements used in Peripheral PRs, assemble an interactive diagnostic input message given a Peripheral diagnostic printout, and determine when to use: Diagnostic printouts, I/O Manuals, PKs, OPAD/OP-CODEs, Maintenance Reference Handbook, SDs, PRs, and extended use of TLP.

Instruction: Major topics covered in the course are refresher information for those who have been in the field working on 4ESS switching equipment, how to resolve diagnostic failures using beyond TLP (Trouble Locating Program) methods taught previously, and the use of interactive diagnostics.

Credit Recommendation: In the lower division baccalaureate/associate degree category or upper division baccalaureate degree category, 2 semester hours in Telecommunications Technology or Technical elective (3/95).

4ESS Maintenance Interrupt Seminar (ON-0488)

Location: Where requested.

Length: 40 hours (5 days).

Dates: June 1994-September 1996.

Objective: To resolve a 4ESS interrupt using the Maintenance Reference Handbook and Schematic Drawings.

Learning Outcome: Upon successful completion of this course, the student will be able to list the possible causes for any level of interrupt; determine and list the circuits which are matched and the time the match occurs during the normal execution of any Assembly Language Instruction; resolve hardware C-Level interrupts that cannot be resolved by diagnostic analysis; determine the most suspect pack by type and location based upon a TSI interrupt printout; and determine the most suspect pact by type and location based upon a TMS interrupt printout.

Instruction: Major topics covered in the course are refresher information for those who have been in the field working on 4ESS switching equipment, how to resolve interrupt failures (C,D,E and F levels) using TOPs (Task Oriented Practices), Maintenance Reference Handbook, and strong emphasis on schematic diagrams.

Credit Recommendation: In the lower division baccalaureate/associate degree category or upper division baccalaureate degree category, 1 semester hour in Telecommunications Technology or Technical elective (3/95).

4ESS Network Clock Seminar (ON-0492E)

Location: Denver, CO.

Length: 24 hours (3 days).

Dates: January 1993-Present.

Objective: To maintain 4ESS Network Clock.

Learning Outcome: Upon successful completion of this course, the student will be able to describe the function of the Network Clock (NCLK) frame and its components; resolve a diagnostic and interrupt failure in the NCLK; describe the function of the Network Clock Sync Unit (NCSU) frame and its components; resolve a diagnostic and interrupt failure in the NCSU; describe the function of the System Clock (SCLK) frame and its components; and resolve a diagnostic and interrupt failure in the SCLK.

Instruction: Major topics covered in the course are in-depth maintenance of the 4ESS network clock, fault resolution using PRs and SDs, network clock frame, network clock sync unit, system clock, Primary Reference Clock (PRC) Timing Monitoring System (TMS), Clock Distribution Unit (CDU), and Global Positioning Systems (GPS).

Credit Recommendation: In the lower division baccalaureate/associate degree category or upper division baccalaureate degree category, 1 semester hour in Telecommunications Technology or Technical elective (3/95).

4ESS Peripheral Maintenance (ON-0492)

Location: Denver, CO.

Length: 240 hours (6 weeks).

Dates: June 1985-Present.

Objective: To maintain 4ESS peripheral equipment.

Learning Outcome: Upon successful completion of this course, the student will be able to know the functional layout of the Peripheral Unit Bus (PUB) System and the physical layout of the PUB units and their function; describe the Peripheral Unit Bus Branching frame and its two major functions (branching and looping); from a diagnostic failure: list the failing bit number and indicate if it should be an "0" or a "1;" find first monitor point address; use the monitor point address PK (Test Access) to determine the SC (Schematic Drawing) where the first failure occurred; list the diagnostic phase being tested and find: the pident number, the equipment being tested, the failing sub-routine, the number of Do-Loops; determine the PR page and line number where the failure occurred; understand a DIAL statement layout and determine what it does; assemble an interactive diagnostic; describe the function of the Terminal Access Group (TGR) frame and Terminal Unit (TER) in the TGR; Analyze Operational Codes (OPCODES) and sequence charts developing gating leads in the frame; analyze Error Source (ESR), Status Registers and diagnostic failures to determine a failing circuit pack; describe the function of the Time Slot Interchange (TSI) and the Time Multiplex Switch (TMS) frames; analyze OPCODES, diagnostic and interrupts to determine a failing circuit pack; describe the function of the Network Clock (NCLK), Network Clock Sync Units (NCSU) and System Clock (SCLK) frames; describe the function of the SIgnal Processor 1 (SP1) frame; describe the function of the Digital Interface (DIF) frame; describe the function of the Di-Group Terminal (DT) frame.

Instruction: Major topics covered in the course are providing OSWF and the TCC (Technology Control Center) technician focus on in-depth maintenance of the 4ESS switching equipment peripheral beyond TLP (Trouble Locating Program) and fault resolution using PRs (Program Records) and SDs (Schematic Drawings). Each frame will be covered in detail and handout packages will be given.

Credit Recommendation: In the lower division baccalaureate/associate degree category or upper division baccalaureate degree category, 6 semester hours in Telecommunications Technology or Technical elective (3/95).

Advanced Excel for Windows (IMM-940)

Location: Atlanta, GA and other locations.

Length: 16 hours (2 days).

Dates: July 1994-December 1997.

Objective: To teach students how to apply advanced techniques to their spreadsheets for financial management, database management and the use of visual display of data as graphs and charts.

Learning Outcome: Upon successful completion of this course, the student will be able to apply range names, absolute references, and special past commands; apply advanced functions to perform more complex calculations; use and create outlines; link worksheets to transfer automatically, import and export data; and create workbooks to group worksheets.

Instruction: Major topics covered in the course are manipulating ranges, performing complex calculations, creating and using outlines, linking worksheets, and group worksheets.

Credit Recommendation: In the lower division baccalaureate/associate degree category, 1 semester hour in Advanced Excel for Windows (4/94).

Advanced Microsoft Word for Windows (IMM-944)

Location: Atlanta, GA and other locations.

Length: *Version 1:* 16 hours (2 days); *Version 2:* 24 hours (3 days).

Dates: *Version 1:* July 1994-December 1996; *Version 2:* January 1997-December 1997.

Objective: To enable students who are versed in word processing, to create columns, separate a document into sections, create merged documents, and apply a higher level of formatting techniques to already created documents.

Learning Outcome: Upon successful completion of this course, the student will be able to address and print envelopes; apply borders, shading, bullets and numbers to paragraphs; create and apply different styles; create and print merged documents; divide documents into sections; create columns; and create a table of contents and an index.

Instruction: Major topics covered in the course are the creating and using style sheets, addressing and printing envelopes, manipulating paragraphs and columns, merging documents, creating columns, and creating a table of contents and indexes.

Credit Recommendation: In the lower division baccalaureate/associate degree category, 1 semester hour in Advance Microsoft Word for Windows (4/94).

Advanced PMX/TERM (IMM-703)

Location: Atlanta, GA and other locations.

Length: 16 hours (2 days).

Dates: August 1990-December 1997.

Objective: To teach students to proficiently use electronic mail in day-to-day activities such as creating a form, creating broadcast codes, and learning further editing capabilities.

Learning Outcome: Upon successful completion of the course, the student will be able to review reading, printing, answering, and forwarding messages; prepare, revise and answer forms; create and revise Broadcast codes then send messages using a Broadcast Code; access the personal directory, create and update index data, apply the UNIX editor for creation or revision of messages; attach and detach files using UNIX to attach to other messages or to hold for later use; mark messages to delete or move to folders and use Search to locate files in folders.

Instruction: Major topics covered in the course are the features in lesson one, features in lesson two, how to perform all the functions, how to display the output on their screen, and how to print an output through the system. Methods of instruction include section review questions, discussion, and hands-on exercises.

Credit Recommendation: In the lower division baccalaureate/associate degree category, 1 semester hour in Advanced PMX/TERM (4/94).

Advanced Samna UNIX (IMM-913)

Location: Atlanta, GA and other locations.

Length: 24 hours (3 days).

Dates: June 1992-December 1997.

Objective: To enable the student to create columns, use the outline format; use different styles, establish tables and merge documents; use additional marks and enhancements such as pitch and type style within the documents.

Learning Outcome: Upon successful completion of this course, the student will be able to create, edit, sort and print using merge functions; apply and remove character attributes, such as pitch and type style; copy and move text within and between documents; use the mark functions and further define the default settings, including adding a subdirectory; and create columns and outlines.

Instruction: Major topics covered in the course are the features learned in the Introduction to SAMNA class are built upon and reviewed in lesson one; how to perform all the functions; how to display the output on their screen; how to print the output through the system; and how to relate the new information to the work environment by examples of how one might use the merge function, character attributes, columns, and outlining. Methods of instruction include section review questions, discussion, and hands-on exercises.

Credit Recommendation: In the lower division baccalaureate/associate degree category, 1 semester hour in Advanced Samna UNIX (4/94).

AT&T Switched Network Call Flow (ON-0200) (Formerly Overview of the AT&T Switched Network)

Location: Suitcased to AT&T locations when requested.

Length: *Version 1:* 32 hours (4 days); *Version 2:* 24 hours (3 days).

Dates: *Version 1:* June 1994-December 1996; *Version 2:* January 1997-Present.

Objective: To explain call-flow and routing of services and features provided by the AT&T Switched Network.

Learning Outcome: Upon successful completion of this course, the student will be able to describe the basic network hardware configurations, CNI Ring and its components, MF, CCIS6 and CCS7 signaling, Q.931 protocol, CCS7 protocol and point code structure, POTS call set-up, complex NCP services and their Network Routing.

Instruction: Major topics covered in the course are fundamental theories and principles; various types of calls and data transported through the AT&T switched Network; the functions and duties of other groups, whose interaction provide an end service; and simulate making a Plain Old Telephone Service (POTS) call using AT&T as the long distance carrier, the call originates on the east coast using a local carrier, travels through the necessary AT&T network components and terminates through another local carrier on the west coast.

Credit Recommendation: In the upper division baccalaureate degree category, 2 semester hours in Telecommunication Networks or Technical elective (3/95).

Basic Signalling Theory (TF-0005) (Formerly Basic Signalling Theory [ECO270])

Location: AT&T locations or home personal computers.

Length: Self-paced instruction (approximately 4 hours).

Dates: November 1988-Present.

Objective: To provide the student with a comprehensive introduction to the terms and fundamental principles of signalling within the telecommunications industry.

Learning Outcome: Upon successful completion of this course, the student will be able to define the three functions of signalling; define the purpose of four common types of signalling equipment; identify AC and DC portions of a circuit; relate tone on/off signalling conditions on the line to idle/busy conditions in an SF unit; relate E&M leads to transmit/receive directions; differentiate between manual ringdown, coded ringing and code selective ringing; and define the purpose of CCS, MF, SF, and out-of-band/built-in signalling.

Instruction: Major topics covered in the course are types of signals, characteristics of signalling equipment, and identification of various signalling arrangements. Methods of instruction include computer-based, self-paced instruction.

Credit Recommendation: In the lower division baccalaureate/associate degree category, 1 semester hour in Electronic Technology or Telecommunications (12/89). **NOTE:** In order to receive credit, students must successfully complete this course and Broadband Facility Fundamentals (ECO165) or Digital Introduction (OPOO12).

Basic UNIX for the TCC (ON-0466)

Location: Denver, CO and Conyers, GA.

Length: 24 hours (3 days).

Dates: February 1993-April 1996.

Objective: To provide the basic skills and knowledge necessary to use the UNIX operating system in the TNM environment.

Learning Outcome: Upon the successful completion of this course, the student will be able to create and manipulate files and directories; determine and change access permissions for files and directories; identify and communicate with other users; sort files and data bases on any field; connect processes and run processes in the background; perform searches using wildcards, commands and patterns; and use the VI editor to create simple shell scripts.

Instruction: Major topics covered in the course are the skills and knowledge to become basic users of the UNIX Operating System; UNIX commands, their format, and the use of the VI editor; and how to apply concepts using the TNM (Total Network Management) system at the SUN Workstation. Method of instruction includes hands-on exercises.

Credit Recommendation: In the lower division baccalaureate/associate degree category, 2 semester hours in Computer Literacy (3/95).

Broadband Facility Fundamentals (TF-0203) (Formerly Broadband Facility Fundamentals [ECO165])

Location: AT&T locations or home personal computers.

Length: Self-paced instruction (approximately 4 hours).

Dates: October 1988-Present.

Objective: To provide the student with background knowledge for intercity facilities.

Learning Outcome: Upon successful completion of this course, the student will be able to define frequency and identify its application to the Broadband Network; define the terms carrier and modulation; recognize the components that comprise the analog and digital hierarchy; and describe the term spans and how they relate to the facility system.

Instruction: Major topics covered in the course are frequency, carrier and modulation, analog hierarchy, digital hierarchy, and spans. Methods of instruction include computer-based, self-paced instruction.

Credit Recommendation: In the lower division baccalaureate/associate degree category, 1 semester hour in Electronic Technology or Telecommunications (12/89). **NOTE:** In order to receive credit, students must successfully complete this course and Basic Signalling Theory (ECO270) or Digital Introduction (OPOO12).

Common Channel Signaling (CCS) Network Overview (ON-0010)

Location: On-Site.

Length: 16 hours (2 days).

Dates: September 1991-Present.

Objective: To provide the student with basic knowledge of the Common Channel Signaling (2STP) Network, CCS6, CCS7 protocols and high level overview of services.

Learning Outcome: Upon successful completion of this course, the student will be able to identify and functionally describe the components which make up the Common Channel Signaling Network; trace signaling paths through the network; and define and describe the function and make-up of messages traversing the network.

Instruction: Major topics covered in the course are Common Channel Signaling concepts, components, signaling methods, overview of the 2STP network, and calling services. Methods of instruction include self-paced study and lesson tests to reinforce the course objectives.

Credit Recommendation: In the upper division baccalaureate degree category, 1 semester hour in Telecommunication Network or Technical elective (3/95).

Cost of Quality Workshop (QU-0160)

Location: Various AT&T locations.

Length: 8 hours, plus 8 hours outside independent study and project.

Dates: October 1989-September 1992.

Objective: To train managers to assess the efficiency of their operations with regard to Quality and identify improvement opportunities.

Learning Outcome: Upon successful completion of this course, the student will be able to conduct a cost of quality data collection effort; analyze quality cost data; define organizational cost of quality performance; and establish any prioritized cost of quality improvement opportunities.

Instruction: Major topics covered in the course are cost of quality concepts and a cost of quality process; purpose of a cost of quality process in providing a structured approach to the identification and prioritization of opportunities for quality improvement which result in optimizing operating costs. Methods of instruction include a comprehensive written case analysis project.

Credit Recommendation: In the upper division baccalaureate degree category, 1 semester hour in Quality Management (12/92).

DACS III Operations and DTMS Maintenance (OF-0150)

Location: Kansas City Technical Education Center.

Length: 56 hours.

Dates: January 1989-Present.

Objective: To teach students the concepts associated with the DACS III (Digital Access Cross-Connect System, technology series III) and DTMS (Digital Test Maintenance System), and to familiarize students with the DACS III and DTMS equipment and troubleshooting techniques.

Learning Outcome: Upon successful completion of this course, the student will be able to understand the concepts and functions of cross connecting digital transmission systems; perform frame provisioning, cross-connection, re-routing of facilities, back-up procedures, and protection switching; and perform hands-on diagnostics.

Instruction: Major topics covered in the course are providing students with the skills and knowledge necessary to identify and perform maintenance tasks in the DACS III technology at a terminal office; and hands-on experience in the laboratory to learn how to operate and maintain DACS III and DTMS equipment.

Credit Recommendation: In the lower division baccalaureate/associate or upper division baccalaureate degree category, 2 semester hours in Operations and Test Measurement of Digital Transmission Systems (6/93).

DACS IV/DTMS Operations and Maintenance (OF-0151)

Location: Kansas City Technical Education Center.

Length: 56 hours.

Dates: April 1991-Present.

Objective: To teach students the concepts associated with the DACS IV (Digital Access Cross-Connect System, technology series IV) and DTMS (Digital Test Maintenance System), and to familiarize students with the DACS IV and DTMS equipment and troubleshooting techniques.

Learning Outcome: Upon successful completion of this course, the student will be able to identify the DACS IV frame components; identify the functions of the DTMS frame components; identify the tasks performed by the various input commands; execute appropriate commands to administer a DACS IV system; interpret DACS IV output messages; analyze and correct trouble associated with the DTMS; specify and perform appropriate tests for out-of-service circuits; and identify Transport Service Center (TSC) functions that support DACS IV.

Instruction: Major topics covered in the course describe the Digital Access and Cross-Connect System (DACS IV) and the Digital Test Maintenance System (DTMS) in the detail necessary for technicians responsible for normal day-to-day activities and for trouble analyzation; DACS IV system overview; operations and maintenance procedures; trouble analyzation; DACS IV hardware and software functions; and DTMS hardware and software functions.

Credit Recommendation: In the lower division baccalaureate/associate or upper division baccalaureate degree category, 2 semester hours in Advanced Operations and Test and Measurement of Lightwave Digital Systems (6/93).

Digital Basic Introduction (TF-0201) (Formerly Digital Introduction [OP0012])

Location: AT&T locations or home personal computers.

Length: Self-paced instruction (approximately 4 hours).

Dates: October 1989-Present.

Objective: To provide the student with a comprehensive introduction to digital transmission of analog signals (T1 transmissions).

Learning Outcome: Upon successful completion of this course, the student will be able to explain T1 transmission basics; identify functions of a regenerative repeater; and describe the components of pulse code modulation.

Instruction: Major topics covered in the course are T1 transmission concepts and pulse code modulation components. Methods of instruction include computer-based, self-paced instruction.

Credit Recommendation: In the lower division baccalaureate/associate degree category, 1 semester hour in Electronic Technology or Telecommunications (12/89). **NOTE:** In order to receive credit, students must successfully complete this course and Basic Signalling Theory (ECO270) or Broadband Facility Fundamentals (ECO175).

Digital Microwave Radio Fundamentals (OF-0309)

Location: Kansas City Technical Education Center.

Length: 40 hours.

Dates: March 1990-Present.

Objective: To teach students the concepts of digital microwave radio and to familiarize the students with the radio bay equipment and troubleshooting techniques.

Learning Outcome: Upon successful completion of this course, the student will be able to identify characteristics of waveguide as a transmission line; select the primary functions of radio transmitter; select two methods of reducing transmitter intermodulation; select two methods of reducing effect of multipath fading; select primary function of a dehydrator; identify the need for fade margin testing; perform microwave radio test set calibration; perform received signal level measurement; perform fade margin; test perform back-to-back calibration of microwave link analyzer distortion tests and amplitude response tests; and perform DADE tests and equalization.

Instruction: Major topics covered in the course are the concepts and theories of waveguide, antennas, signal propagation, fade margins, delay causes and testing and test set functions; calibrating test sets and using the test sets to perform radio hop tests.

Credit Recommendation: In the lower division baccalaureate/associate degree category or in the upper division baccalaureate degree category, 2 semester hours in Principles of Digital Microwave Radio (6/93).

Digital Technology in the Network (NI-0168)

Location: AT&T locations worldwide.

Length: 24 hours.

Dates: August 1990-Present.

Objective: To summarize the digital components of the AT&T Switched Network (ASN) and illustrate the interaction of these components so that the students will understand the applications and benefits of digital technology.

Learning Outcome: Upon successful completion of this course, the student will be able to explain some relevant basic digital theory; define terms used in digital networks; list components and their functionality; describe digital hierarchy; identify equipment used in the Gateway Office; list the benefits of digital technology; and explain the need for synchronization.

Instruction: Major topics covered in the course are an overview of digital technology used in the AT&T Switched and Private Networks in both domestic and international environments.

Credit Recommendation: In the lower division baccalaureate/associate degree category or upper division baccalaureate degree category, 2 semester hours in Introduction to Digital Data Communications (3/93).

DMB Theory—DACS I (EC-0623)

Location: AT&T locations or home personal computers.

Length: Self-paced instruction (approximately 12 hours).

Dates: April 1989-Present.

Objective: To provide the student with an understanding of digital multipoint bridges (DMBs) as used in the DACS I environment.

Learning Outcome: Upon successful completion of this course, the student will be able to identify the function of DMB and recognize at least four benefits of

DMB utilization; recognize differences between working DACS frames and concentrator bridge frames as well as non-concentrator and concentrator locations as related to DMB usage; and using a completed CD, identify DMB fields residing on the CD either discussed or not discussed in previous modules.

Instruction: Major topics covered in the course are the definition of DMB, DMB capacity, typical DMB arrangements in concentrator and non-concentrator locations, modes of operation and DMB options and the integration of all components. Methods of instruction include computer-based, self-paced instruction.

Credit Recommendation: In the lower division baccalaureate/associate degree category, 1 semester hour in Electronic Technology or Telecommunications (12/89).

DR4 Digital Radio System Maintenance (OF-0305)

Location: Kansas City Technical Education Center.

Length: 40 hours.

Dates: December 1988-Present.

Objective: To teach students the digital microwave radio techniques to perform pre-service and maintenance tests and to use system documentation on the DR4.

Learning Outcome: Upon successful completion of this course, the student will be able to use documentation to isolate alarmed troubles; identify DR4 radio transmitter and receiver units, tests, and functions; identify 90C digital terminal and regenerator units, functions, and tests; use documentation to perform tests on DR4 radio transmitters, radio receivers, digital terminal and regenerators and protection switching; identify characteristics and functions of error measurements, error detection, and error correction; and identify Transport Service Center (TSC) functions that support DR4 Digital Radio.

Instruction: Major topics covered in the course provide the knowledge and hands-on practice that will enable the student to perform DR4 pre-service and maintenance tests and to use system documentation to isolate and repair alarm reported equipment troubles.

Credit Recommendation: In the lower division baccalaureate/associate degree category or in the upper division baccalaureate degree category, 2 semester hours in 4 GHz Digital Radio System Maintenance (6/93).

DR6/11-135 Digital Radio System Maintenance (OF-0303)

Location: Kansas City Technical Education Center.

Length: 40 hours.

Dates: September 1985-Present.

Objective: To teach students the digital microwave radio techniques to perform pre-service and maintenance tests and to use system documentation on the DR6/11-135.

Learning Outcome: Upon successful completion of this course, the student will be able to use documentation to isolate alarmed troubles; identify DR6/11-135 radio transmitter and receiver units, tests, and functions; identify digital terminal and regenerator units, functions, and tests; use documentation to perform tests on DR-135 radio transmitters, radio receivers, digital terminal, and regenerators and protection switching; identify characteristics and functions of error measurements, error detection, and error correction; and identify Transport Service Center (TSC) functions that support DR6/11-135 Digital Radio.

Instruction: Major topics covered in the course are knowledge and hands-on practice that will enable the student to perform DR6/11-135 pre-service and maintenance tests and to use system documentation to isolate and repair alarm reported equipment troubles.

Credit Recommendation: In the lower division baccalaureate/associate degree category or in the upper division baccalaureate degree category, 2 semester hours in Digital 6 GHz Radio System Maintenance (6/93).

Enhancing Individual and Team Success (QU-0180)

Location: AT&T client locations.

Length: 30 hours (4 days).

Dates: May 1995-Present.

Objective: To prepare participants to understand and practice open and honest conversation based on the concepts of self awareness, choice and openness, as well as team compatibility.

Learning Outcome: Upon successful completion of this course, the student will be able to recognize the stages in adult learning and change; understand one's own behavior and its relationship to other team members; create a working and learning environment that assures individual and team success; work and learn with others for the purpose of assuring individual and organizational success; and understand and manage the relationships among desired outcomes, individuals, teams and the organization.

Instruction: Major topics covered in the course are exploring and solving the causes for less than honest communication; Form and Storm stages of group development and beyond; "working agreement" types of behaviors and beyond; and prepares participants to understand and practice open and honest conversation and feedback based on the concepts of self-awareness, choice and openness, as well as team compatibility. Methods of instruction include a combination of lecture, class discussion, and small group discussion.

Credit Recommendation: In the lower division baccalaureate/associate degree category, 1 semester hour in Individual and Group Behavior (10/97).

FT Series G 1.7 Gb/s Lightwave Digital Transmission System (OF-0140)

Location: Kansas City Technical Education Center.

Length: 40 hours.

Dates: January 1989-Present.

Objective: To teach students the concepts associated with lightwave technology and to familiarize students with the FT Series G 1.7 Gb/s lightwave equipment and troubleshooting techniques.

Learning Outcome: Upon successful completion of this course, the student will be able to identify and understand the operation of the major components of the 1.7 Gigabit (Gb) Lightwave Digital System.

Instruction: Major topics covered in the course are skills and knowledge necessary to identify and perform maintenance tasks in the 1.7 Gb/s Lightwave System at terminal offices and line repeater stations; and maintenance of the Dual Quad Assembly (DQA) and Terminating Muldem Assembly (TMA) are included. Methods of instruction include hands-on training in a laboratory using functional equipment.

Credit Recommendation: In the lower division baccalaureate/associate degree category, 1 semester hour in Elements of Lightwave Digital System II (6/93).

FT Series G 417 Mb/s Lightwave Digital Transmission System (OF-0126)

Location: Kansas City Technical Education Center.

Length: 40 hours.

Dates: January 1989-Present.

Objective: To teach students the concepts associated with lightwave technology and to familiarize students with the FT Series G 417 Mb/s lightwave equipment and troubleshooting techniques.

Learning Outcome: Upon successful completion of this course, the student will be able to identify and understand the operation of the major components of the 417 Megabit (Mb) Lightwave Digital System; apply knowledge of state-of-the-art digital test equipment; and understand troubleshooting procedures.

Instruction: Major topics covered in the course provides students with the skills and knowledge necessary to identify and perform maintenance tasks in the 417 Mb/s Lightwave System at terminal offices and line repeater stations. Methods of instruction include hands-on training in a laboratory using functional equipment.

Credit Recommendation: In the lower division baccalaureate/associate degree category, 1 semester hour in Elements of Lightwave Digital System I (6/93).

FT-2000 Series OF0122A SONET Overview; OF0145A FT-2000 SONET Applications; OF0145B FT-2000 OC-48 Lightwave System Fundamentals; OF0147 FT-2000 Large Capacity Terminal; OF0148 FT-2000 Optical Line System; and OF0149 FT-2000 Laboratory

Location: All courses except for OF0149 are available at any of AT&T's 267 locations that are part of AT&T's Interactive Video Broadcast Network (IVBN). OF0149 is taught in the Next Generation Lightguide Laboratory of AT&T's Kansas City Technical Education Center in Kansas City, MO.

Length: 44 hours Breakdown: OF0112A: 4 hours; OF0145A: 3 hours; OF1145B: 3 hours; OF0147: 6 hours; OF0148: 4 hours; and OF0149: 24 hours (3 days).

Dates: June 1997-Present.

Objective: To provide the students with a working knowledge of Lucent Technology's FT-2000 family of equipment and the skills necessary to function competently in the operations, maintenance, and repair of the FT-2000 OC-48 Lightwave System.

Learning Outcome: Upon successful completion of this course, the student will be able to become familiarized with the new terminology, SONET/SDH data frames and overhead bytes, new network devices and network architectures that are defined by the SONET/SDH standards, and how Asynchronous Transfer Mode will transport data using these standards; given a block diagram, identify the equipment application and configuration, and identify information flow through functional areas of the system; recognize the Craft Interface Terminal, know its purpose and use it to retrieve alarms, alerts, and performance monitoring; using a block diagram, explain the basic function and operation of the circuit packs; and given alarm conditions, recognize and identify equipment failures and perform necessary repair tasks to restore system operation.

Instruction: Major topics covered in the course are technical explanations of Lucent Technologies FT-2000 family of equipment and the processes necessary to function as an On Site Work Force technician responsible for the operations, maintenance, and repair of the FT-2000 OC-48 Lightwave System. Methods of instruction include lecture and lab.

Credit Recommendation: In the lower division baccalaureate/associate degree category or in the upper division baccalaureate degree category, 2 semester hours in Network Technology or Network Architecture (10/97). **NOTE:** Students must complete FT-2000 series (OF0112A, OF0145B, OF0147, OF0148 and OF0149) to receive the credit recommendation.

International Signaling Overview (NI-0107)

Location: AT&T locations worldwide.

Length: 20 hours.

Dates: May 1992-Present.

Objective: To provide the student with a basic understanding of how signaling (R1, R2, CCITT5, 6, and 7) takes place between international telecommunications networks.

Learning Outcome: Upon successful completion of this course, the student will be able to describe International signaling functions; distinguish between the various types of International signaling architectures; differentiate call flows of various types of signaling functions; list components of each type of signaling architecture; define terms used in International signaling; list advantages of each type of signaling system; allow technicians a methodology for isolating CCITT5, 6, and 7 call irregularities; and provide the technician with a method of escalation.

Instruction: Major topics covered in the course are teaching how signaling takes place between International Telecommunications Networks; specific types of signaling covered are R1 and R2 (Analog and Digital), CCITT5, CCITT6, and CCITT7; and an understand of what signaling can be used in a network, the architecture of each signaling type along with call flow that takes place between International Switches, and the advantages of current technology in signaling over previous technology.

Credit Recommendation: In the lower division baccalaureate/associate degree category or in the upper division baccalaureate degree category, 1 semester hour in Introduction to Telecommunications (3/93).

Introduction to 4ESS Maintenance (ON-0490)

Location: Kansas City, MO.

Length: 80 hours (2 weeks).

Dates: June 1994-Present.

Objective: To provide the student with the knowledge and skills required to maintain 4ESS switching equipment at the Trouble Locating Procedure (TLP) level using current office documentation.

Learning Outcome: Upon the successful completion of this course, the student will be able to identify 4ESS switching equipment; use available 4ESS switching equipment documentation; state the function of the frames; locate the fault circuit pack using TLP; interpret and retire alarms; and safely remove, clean, and reinstall circuit packs.

Instruction: Major topics covered in the course are recognition, function, and description of all 4ESS switching equipment as well as proper maintenance procedures, use of 4ESS office documentation, and tours of a 4ESS switch. Methods of instruction include practical assignments, classroom discussions, and testing.

Credit Recommendation: In the lower division baccalaureate/associate degree category or in the upper division baccalaureate degree category, 2 semester hours in Telecommunications Technology or Technical elective (3/95).

Introduction to 4ESS Maintenance and Analysis (ON-0496)

Location: Kansas City, MO.

Length: 40 hours (5 days).

Dates: July 1993-Present.

Objective: To provide the student with the knowledge and skills required to maintain 4ESS switching equipment beyond the Trouble Locating Procedure (TLP) level using current office documentation.

Learning Outcome: Upon successful completion of this course, the student will be able to describe the maintenance process; use available 4ESS switching equipment documentation (TOPs, PR, PK and SDs); and locate in a phase PR the PIDENT prologue, Program Unit prologue, Failing test and Macro statement.

Instruction: Major topics covered in the course are the knowledge and skills required to follow the maintenance process beyond TLP (TOPs, to PR, to PK, to SD). This is achieved by the practice in using this process to analyze diagnostic failures.

Credit Recommendation: In the lower division baccalaureate/associate degree category or in the upper division baccalaureate degree category, 1 semester hour in Telecommunications Technology or Technical elective (3/95).

Introduction to Ami Pro (IMM-945)

Location: Atlanta, GA and other locations.

Length: 16 hours (2 days).

Dates: April 1993-December 1997.

Objective: To enable to student who is new to word processing, to create and modify documents, use enhancements, copy and move text, change margins, and print and save documents using the Windows vocabulary.

Learning Outcome: Upon successful completion of this course, the student will be able to type, print and save a simple document; use editing skills to include fonts, bold, underline, etc.; insert, delete, copy and move text; use spelling and grammar check functions; format a document; and create new documents and open existing documents.

Instruction: Major topics covered in the course are creating; saving; editing; formatting and outputing documents in Ami Pro for Windows; and how to use the spelling, grammar checker, and thesaurus tools.

Credit Recommendation: In the lower division baccalaureate/associate degree category, 1 semester hour in Introduction to Ami Pro for Windows (4/94).

Introduction to Excel for Windows (IMM-939)

Location: Atlanta, GA and other locations.

Length: 16 hours (2 days).

Dates: October 1993-December 1997.

Objective: To teach the student how to create spreadsheets for financial management, database management and the use of visual display of data as graphs and charts.

Learning Outcome: Upon successful completion of this course, the student will be able to create, open, save and delete Excel files; apply worksheet formatting: bold, italics, fonts, alignment, borders and shading; design and create spreadsheets, charts and graphs; create a database; number and sort records; apply copy, move, past, edit, and print commands for worksheets; and create formulas: sum, autosum, max, and average.

Instruction: Major topics covered in the course are managing Excel files; formatting worksheets; manipulating and outputting worksheet data; using formulas; creating charts and graphs; and creating and sorting a database.

Credit Recommendation: In the lower division baccalaureate/associate degree category, 1 semester hour in Introduction to Excel for Windows (4/94).

Introduction to Harvard Graphics for Windows (IMM-937)

Location: Atlanta, GA and other locations.

Length: 16 hours (2 days).

Dates: May 1993-December 1997.

Objective: To teach the student to design and create quality business graphics and charts using Harvard Graphics for Windows.

Learning Outcome: Upon successful completion of this course, the student will be able to create, open, and save presentation files; create and edit dataforms; create title, bullet, table, pie, vertical and horizontal bar, line and organization; edit chart features, add clip art; and apply formatting options: bold, italics, fonts, alignments, and text.

Instruction: Major topics covered in the course include creating, saving and outputing presentation files; creating and editing data forms; creating and editing bullet, table, pie, vertical and horizontal bar, line and organization charts; applying formatting options; and adding clip art.

Credit Recommendation: In the lower division baccalaureate/associate degree category, 1 semester hour in Introduction to Harvard Graphics for Windows (4/94).

Introduction to Local Area Networks (TF-0070) (Formerly Introduction to Local Area Networks [NT-0031])

Location: AT&T locations or home personal computers.

Length: Self-paced instruction (approximately 8 hours).

Dates: October 1989-Present.

Objective: To provide the student with a comprehensive introduction to Local Area Networks (LANs).

Learning Outcome: Upon successful completion of this course, the student will be able to describe the basic terms, features, functions, and building blocks of LANs; identify and describe how three LAN topologies work; describe characteristics for twisted pair, coaxial cable, and fiber optic cable; define CSMA, manchester encoding, collision, CSMA/CD, and token passing as it relates to LAN access methods; and describe the implementation of a token ring.

Instruction: Major topics covered in the course are introduction to Local Area Networks (LANs), LAN topologies, LAN media, LAN access methods, and LAN applications. Methods of instruction include computer-based, self-paced instruction.

Credit Recommendation: In the lower division baccalaureate/associate degree category, 1 semester hour in Computer Information Systems or Telecommunications (12/89).

Introduction to Lotus 1-2-3 for Windows (IMM-935)

Location: Atlanta, GA and other locations.

Length: 16 hours (2 days).

Dates: April 1994-December 1997.

Objective: To teach students to create spreadsheets for financial management, database managements and the use of visual display of data as graphs and charts.

Learning Outcome: Upon successful completion of this course, the student will be able to create, open and save Lotus files; apply worksheet formatting: bold, italics, fonts, alignment, borders and shading; design and create spreadsheets, charts and graphs; create a database, number and sort records; apply copy, move, paste, edit, and print commands for worksheets; and create formulas: sum, autosum, max and average.

Instruction: Major topics covered in the course are managing Lotus files; formatting worksheet; manipulating and outputing worksheet data and using forumulas; creating charts and graphs; and creating and sorting databases.

Credit Recommendation: In the lower division baccalaureate/associate degree category, 1 semester hour in Introduction to Lotus 1-2-3 for Windows (4/94).

Introduction to Microsoft Windows (IMM-930)

Location: Atlanta, GA and other locations.

Length: 16 hours (2 days).

Dates: January 1993-December 1997.

Objective: To enable the student to understand and be able to perform basic Window's functions using the mouse to select and move around in the Windows environment.

Learning Outcome: Upon successful completion of this course, the student will be able to start-up Windows and exit Windows correctly; use a mouse; use many of the icons, and File Manager; create and save files; and perform basic editing functions and copy, cut, and paste using the clipboard.

Instruction: Major topics covered in the course include starting and exiting Windows; running and closing Windows applications; using the File Manager; and positioning windows and icons and using desktop accessories.

Credit Recommendation: In the lower division baccalaureate/associate degree category, 1 semester hour in Introduction to Microsoft Windows (4/94).

Introduction to Microsoft Word for Windows (IMM-943)

Location: Atlanta, GA and other locations.

Length: 16 hours (2 days).

Dates: March 1993-December 1997.

Objective: To enable the student who is new to word processing, to create and modify documents, use enhancements, copy and move text, change margins and print and save documents using the Win-dows vocabulary in the Windows environment.

Learning Outcome: Upon successful completion of this course, the student will be able to type, print and save a simple document; use editing skills to include fonts, bold, underline, etc.; insert, delete, copy and move text; use spelling and grammar check functions; format a document; and create new documents and open existing documents.

Instruction: Major topics covered in the course are creating, saving, editing, formatting, outputting Microsoft Word documents, spelling, grammar checker, and thesaurus.

Credit Recommendation: In the lower division baccalaureate/associate degree category, 1 semester hour in Introduction to Microsoft Word for Windows (4/94).

Introduction to PC Networking (TF-0902)
(Formerly Introduction to PC Networking [I-902])

Location: AT&T locations or home personal computers.

Length: Self-paced instruction (approximately 8 hours).

Dates: March 1989-December 1997.

Objective: To provide the student with an introduction to the concepts and terminology required in the telecommunications industry.

Learning Outcome: Upon successful completion of this course, the student will be able to identify the concepts, terminology, and applications required to use the PC; recognize the terms used in file program transfer and list online services available to PC users; and recognize the problems of hardware and information compatibility.

Instruction: Major topics covered in the course are the concepts and terminology required in the telecommunications industry, various types of transmission, protocols, physical components in a network, different LAN configurations, transmission techniques, and the functions of the physical components in a network. Methods of instruction include computer-based, self-paced instruction.

Credit Recommendation: In the lower division baccalaureate/associate degree category, 1 semester hour in Computer Information Systems or Telecommunications (12/89).

Introduction to Personal Computers and Microsoft DOS (IMM-920)

Location: Atlanta, GA and other locations.

Length: 16 hours (2 days).

Dates: July 1994-December 1997.

Objective: To familiarize the student with the basic concepts and commands required to understand and use the current version of MS-DOS and the hardware of the computer.

Learning Outcome: Upon successful completion of the course, the student will be able to identify the components of a personal computer; use basic MS-DOS commands; understand the concepts of: software and hardware, paths, directories and subdirectories, LAN, and special files: autoexec.bat and config.sys; edit; and use the DOS shell.

Instruction: Major topics covered in the course are PC components, DOS commands, paths and directories, LAN, special files, DOS shell, and editing.

Credit Recommendation: In the lower division baccalaureate/associate degree category, 1 semester hour in Introduction to PCs and DOS (4/94).

Introduction to PMX/TERM (IMM-702)

Location: Atlanta, GA and other locations.

Length: 8 hours (1 day).

Dates: May 1990-December 1997.

Objective: To enable the student to read, create, edit, print, answer, forward, save, send and organize PMX/TERM messages (files) into folders in a UNIX 3B environment.

Learning Outcome: Upon successful completion of the course, the student will be able to read, print, answer and forward messages; prepare and revise messages; send and receive messages; create folder for message storage; and file and organize messages in folders.

Instruction: Major topics covered in the course are a progressive learning style where the features learned in lesson one are repeated in lesson two with new features added and the create and send message commands will be introduced to provide the overall electronic mail process. Methods of instruction include section review questions, discussion, a hands-on class where the student will perform all the functions and the output will be displayed on their screen, the students will receive incoming messages from the instructor which they read, edit, forward, or answer where appropriate.

Credit Recommendation: In the lower division baccalaureate/associate degree category, 2 semester hours in Introduction to PMX TERM and Introduction to UNIX (4/94). **NOTE:** There is no credit recommendation for this class if taken alone, but if taken in combination with "Introduction to UNIX (TF0720)" the credit recommendation is as stated above.

Introduction to PowerPoint (IMM-949)

Location: Atlanta, GA and other locations.

Length: 16 hours (2 days).

Dates: September 1993-December 1997.

Objective: To teach the student to understand and be able to design and create quality business graphics using the current version of PowerPoint for Windows.

Learning Outcome: Upon successful completion of this course, the student will be able to create, open and save presentations; apply format options: bold, italics, etc.; design and create charts and graphs; edit charts and graphs features; create title, bullet, bar, line and pie charts; and add clip art to presentations.

Instruction: Major topics covered in the course are creating, saving and outputting presentation files; applying format options, designing and editing various types of charts and graphs; and adding clip art to presentations.

Credit Recommendation: In the lower division baccalaureate/associate degree category, 1 semester hour in Introduction to PowerPoint (4/94).

Introduction to Samna UNIX (IMM-912)

Location: Atlanta, GA and other locations.

Length: 16 hours (2 days).

Dates: June 1992-December 1997.

Objective: To enable the student to create and save a Samna file in a UNIX 3B environment and use Samna as a word processor; write and print memos and letters with enhancements; and use copy and move, margins, tabs and character attributes features.

Learning Outcome: Upon successful completion of this course, the student will be able to create, edit and print multi-page documents; apply and remove character attributes such as bolding, capitalizing, justifying, underlining; copy and move text within and between documents; insert headers/footers into a document and place page number marks; perform file functions (i.e. copy, delete and rename files); and display and edit two files at the same time.

Instruction: Major topics covered in the course are using the Samna word processor for creating, editing, printing, formatting, copying, and moving documents in a UNIX environment.

Credit Recommendation: In the lower division baccalaureate/associate degree category, 1 semester hour in Introduction to Samna UNIX (4/94).

Introduction to Telecommunications (TF-0002) (Overview of the Telecommunication Industry [NT0002]) (Formerly Introduction to Telecommunications [NT-00021])

Location: AT&T locations or home personal computers.

Length: Self-paced instruction (approximately 8-12 hours).

Dates: March 1989-Present.

Objective: To provide the student with an introduction to the history, terminology, and components of the telecommunications industry.

Learning Outcome: Upon successful completion of this course, the student will be able to identify the events and contributions that form the history of early telephone communications; identify the terms and components for analog carrier systems, digital carrier systems, and switching; and identify the terms, functions, and equipment used in data communications.

Instruction: Major topics covered in the course are early telephone communications, switching concepts, birth of a national network, 20th-century technologies, pre-divestiture network, post-divestiture network, private systems and networks, special business circuits, and computers and data communications. Methods of instruction include computer-based, self-paced instruction.

Credit Recommendation: In the lower division baccalaureate/associate degree category, 2 semester hours in Telecommunications (5/89).

Introduction to UNIX (IMM-720)

Location: Atlanta, GA and other locations.

Length: 24 hours (3 days).

Dates: November 1989-December 1997.

Objective: To teach the student to perform basic UNIX commands. A file structure overview with emphasis on file pathing is delivered. A brief introduction to the Vi editor and Shell programming is introduced.

Learning Outcome: Upon successful completion of the course, the student will be able to use the command structure in the UNIX operating system; identify and perform basic UNIX commands; identify file management, pathing, and structures; use permissions and ownership of files and directories; invoke and exit the Vi editor; and create and execute ascii files.

Instruction: Major topics covered in the course are UNIX and UNIX commands; file management; permissions and ownership; and the Vi editor.

Credit Recommendation: In the lower division baccalaureate/associate degree category, 1 semester hour in Introduction to UNIX, if course is taken alone (4/94). **NOTE:** If this course is taken in combination with "Introduction to PMX/TERM (TF0702)", the credit recommendation is 2 semester hours in the lower division baccalaureate/associate degree category in Introduction to PMX/TERM or Introduction to UNIX. If this course is taken in combination with "Introduction to Vi Editor (TF0725)", the credit recommendation is 2 semester hours in the lower division baccalaureate/associate degree category in Introduction to Vi Editor or Introduction to UNIX.

Introduction to Vi Editor (IMM-725)

Location: Atlanta, GA and other locations.

Length: 8 hours (1 day).

Dates: November 1989-December 1997.

Objective: To teach the student how to use the unix text editor in creating and revising ascii files on the UNIX operating system.

Learning Outcome: Upon successful completion of this course, the student will be able to enter and exit Vi, create, edit and delete text; copy and move text, split and join lines; undo a change; search for and change text; copy contents of an ascii file into another ascii file; and run a UNIX shell command while in Vi and set Vi options.

Instruction: Major topics covered in the course are using the Vi editor to create, edit, and save text; and using the UNIX shell.

Credit Recommendation: In the lower division baccalaureate/associate degree category, 2 semester hours in Introduction to UNIX and Introduction to Vi Editor (4/94). **NOTE:** There is no credit recommendation for this course alone, but if it is taken in combination with "Introduction to UNIX (TF0720)", the credit recommendation is as stated above.

Introduction to WordPerfect 5.2 for Windows (IMM-941)

Location: Atlanta, GA and other locations.

Length: 16 hours (2 days).

Dates: September 1993-December 1997.

Objective: To enable the student who is new to word processing, to create and modify documents, use enhancements, copy and move text, change margins and print and save documents using the Windows environment.

Learning Outcome: Upon successful completion of this course, the student will be able to type, print and save a simple document; use editing skills to include fonts, bold, underline, etc.; insert, delete, copy and move text; use spelling and grammar check functions; format a document; and create new documents and open existing documents.

Instruction: Major topics covered in the course are creating; saving; editing; formatting; outputting WordPerfect for

Windows documents; and use of the spelling, grammar checker, and thesaurus.

Credit Recommendation: In the lower division baccalaureate/associate degree category, 1 semester hour in Introduction to WordPerfect for Windows (4/94).

Introduction to X.25 (TF-0101) (Formerly Introduction to X.25 [I-901])

Location: AT&T locations or home personal computers.

Length: Self-paced instruction (approximately 8 hours).

Dates: March 1989-December 1997.

Objective: To provide the student with the technical and economic considerations of X.25 communications—packet mode, data communications protocol.

Learning Outcome: Upon successful completion of this course, the student will be able to describe the functions and layers of the X.25 architecture; define frame and packet formats and functions; and identify the advantages and uses for a variety of virtual circuits and communications services.

Instruction: Major topics covered in the course are events that led to the evolution of electronic data communications, the terms and standards that relate to packet switching, the differences between time division and statistical time division multiplexing, the components of X.25, and the use of private network versus public data network. Methods of instruction include computer-based, self-paced instruction.

Credit Recommendation: In the lower division baccalaureate/associate degree category, 1 semester hour in Electronic Technology or Telecommunications (12/89).

Modularized Process Management Steps 1, 2a, and 2b (QU0220AM/QU0220BM) and QU0220CM

Location: AT&T locations nationwide.

Length: 16 hours (2 days).

Dates: February 1997-Present.

Objective: To teach Process Quality Management using the Process Quality Management & Improvement methodology for steps 1, 2A & 2B, which is sanctioned by "Network & Computing Services" (NCS business organization within AT&T).

Learning Outcome: Upon successful completion of this course, the student will be able to describe the steps of Process Quality Management & Improvement methodology (PQMI): PQMI step 1: establish Process Management responsibilities and apply this step to their team/process; roles of Process Management team members, scope and purpose of a process and how it relates to the QMS process structure; describe Step 2A of the PQMI methodology; demonstrate the correct usage of Operations Engineering Workbook (OEW) flow diagramming symbols and conventions as applicable to your process; identify and document customer and supplier requirements for their process; and explain correct usage of Customer Needs Analysis and Surveys.

Instruction: Major topics covered in the course are the Process Element of NCS's QMS (Quality Management System); how to implement steps 1, 2A, & 2B of PQMI within a process management framework, including how to use OEW (Operations Engineering Workbook) conventions to document the process. Methods of instruction include a comprehensive case study to integrate the concepts of Steps 1, 2A, & 2B and OEW, lecture and interactive components.

Credit Recommendation: In the lower division baccalaureate/associate degree category, 1 semester hour in Business Process/Statistical Process Control or Operations Management (10/97).

Modularized Process Management Steps 3 and 4 (QU0220DM)

Location: AT&T locations nationwide.

Length: 16 hours (2 days).

Dates: May 1997-Present.

Objective: To teach Process Quality Management using the Process Quality Management & Improvement methodology for Steps 3 & 4, which is sanctioned by "Network & Computing Services" (NCS business organization within AT&T).

Learning Outcome: Upon successful completion of this course, the student will be able to apply the activities of PQMI steps 3&4, and the NCS QMS Metrics Framework to their process; describe the linkage of metrics to goals; determine if existing measures ar appropriate according to customer requirements and comparison of ideal best and existing metrics and measurements; and compare process output performance to requirements, determine problem areas and document findings on templates 2.1, 2.2, 2.3, and 2.4.

Instruction: Major topics covered in the course are Process Element of NCS's QMS (Quality Management System); how to implement steps 3&4 of PQMI within a Process Management framework, including the AT&T problem solving methodology, Gap Analysis Worksheet, and Metrics Framework. Methods of instruction include a comprehensive case study to integrate the concepts of Steps 3&4, lecture and interactive components.

Credit Recommendation: In the lower division baccalaureate/associate degree category, 1 semester hour in Process or Statistical Process Control or Operations (10/97).

Modularized Process Management Steps 5, 6, and 7 (QU0220EM)

Location: AT&T locations nationwide.

Length: 24 hours (3 days).

Dates: August 1997-Present.

Objective: To teach Process Quality Management using the Process Quality Management and Improvement Methodology for Steps 5, 6, and 7, which is sanctioned by "Network & Computing Services" (NCS business organization within AT&T).

Learning Outcome: Upon successful completion of this course, the student will be able to apply the activities of PQMI steps 5, 6, and 7 and the NCS QMS Metrics Framework to their process; identify critical internal problems impacting customer satisfaction and costs; relate improvement areas to customer requirements and business needs; verify and remove root causes of internal problems in their process; and document findings on templates 3.1, 3.2, 3.3, 3.4, 3.5, 3.6, 4.1, 4.2, 4.3, and 4.4.

Instruction: Major topics covered in the course are the Process Elements of NCSs QMS (Quality Management System), how to implement steps 5, 6, and 7 of PQMI within the Process Management framework, including the AT&T Problem Solving Methodology and the Metrics Framework. Methods of instruction include a comprehensive case study to integrate the concepts of steps 5, 6, and 7, lecture and interactive components.

Credit Recommendation: In the lower division baccalaureate/associate degree category, 1 semester hour in Process or Statistical Process Control or Operations (10/97).

Network Management (NI-0110 and NI-0110A)

Location: AT&T locations worldwide.

Length: *Version 1:* 24 hours; *Version 2:* 24 hours plus 6-month internship.

Dates: *Version 1:* May 1991-December 1996; *Version 2:* March 1993-December 1996.

Objective: To provide the student with an overview of International Network

Management responsibilities and explain how this role supports the integrity and performance of the AT&T Switched Network.

Learning Outcome: Upon successful completion of this course, the student will be able to define the history and direction of the Network Management role; define the responsibilities of the Regional and Worldwide Network Management Centers; identify the ASN design with an emphasis on Network Management capabilities and controls; explain data computations and interpretations for the proper analysis of network traffic patterns and abnormalities; list some systems and tools available to control the network; and prepare the student to perform "normal" daily Network Management activities under the guidance of a qualified Network Manager.

Instruction: Major topics covered in the course are an overview of International Network Management responsibilities and an understanding of how this role supports the integrity and performance of the AT&T Switched Network (ASN); introduces the systems and tools used for determining network abnormalities; and principles and philosophies for the management of the ASN are defined and Network irregularities.

Credit Recommendation: *Version 1:* In the lower division baccalaureate/associate degree category or in the upper division baccalaureate degree category, 2 semester hours in Network Management. *Version 2:* In the lower division baccalaureate/associate or in the upper division baccalaureate degree category, 4 semester hours in Network Management (3/93).

Network Service Complex (NSCX)-Maintenance Generic (ON-0474)

Location: Denver, CO and Conyers, GA.

Length: 32 hours (3 days).

Dates: December 1991-Present.

Objective: To provide the student with the knowledge and skills required to maintain the Network Service Complex at the Trouble Locating Plan (TLP) level using current office documentation.

Learning Outcome: Upon successful completion of this course, the student will be able to identify NSCX equipment and its function; identify the criticality of an INIT level; select messages to change the NSCX operational state; locate the fault circuit pack using TLP; interpret an error message printout; and interpret an audit printout.

Instruction: The purpose of this course is to provide the student with a basic understanding of what the Network Service Complex is, its function and its place in the AT&T Switched Network. Also the course illustrates the use of various NSCX types of documentation and how to deal with various maintenance occurrences.

Credit Recommendation: In the upper division baccalaureate degree category, 2 semester hours in Telecommunication Systems or Technical elective (3/95). **NOTE:** Students must also complete ON0472 to earn the credit recommendation.

Network Service Complex-Automatic Speech Recognition (ON-0477)

Location: On-Site.

Length: 4 hours (1 day).

Dates: April 1993-Present.

Objective: To provide the student with the knowledge and skills required to maintain the NSCX automatic speech recognition equipment at the Trouble Locating Plan (TLP) level.

Learning Outcome: Upon successful completion of this course, the student will be able to identify operation of the NSCX automatic speech recognition equipment; understand the need for echo cancellers; understand the changes made to tone receivers; list the components of automatic speech recognition; and know the function of ASR interface unit.

Instruction: This course is designed as a self-paced study to provide the student with the basic knowledge required to understand NSCX automatic speech recognition concepts, components and call flow. This is achieved by systematically presenting the material in a logical sequence with lesson tests to reinforce the course objectives.

Credit Recommendation: In the upper division baccalaureate degree category, 3 semester hours in Telecommunication Systems or Technical elective (3/95). **NOTE:** Students must also complete ON0475, ON0476 (laboratory sequence), ON0472, and ON0474 to earn the credit recommendation.

Network Service Complex-Hard Disk Units (ON-0476)

Location: On-Site.

Length: 4 hours (1 day).

Dates: June 1992-Present.

Objective: To provide the student with the knowledge and skills required to maintain the new Network Service Complex hard disk units at the Trouble Locating Plan (TLP) level.

Learning Outcome: Upon successful completion of this course, the student will be able to identify the new circuit pack changes in the NSCX; identify new frame and equipment arrangements; understand the function and operation of the hard disk units; and understand the power controls and arrangements for the hard disk units.

Instruction: This course focuses on the recognition, function and description of the hard disks units added to the NSCX by Generic 8, as well as proper maintenance procedures. This is achieved by the use and understanding of NSCX documentation through testing and practical assignments.

Credit Recommendation: In the upper division baccalaureate degree category, 3 semester hours in Telecommunication Systems or Technical elective (3/95). **NOTE:** Students must also complete ON0475, ON0477 (laboratory sequence), ON0472, and ON0474 to earn the credit recommendation.

Network Service Complex-Overview (ON-0472)

Location: On-Site.

Length: 4 hours (1 day).

Dates: May 1991-Present.

Objective: To provide the student with an overview of what the Network Service Complex is and how it is part of the AT&T Switched Network.

Learning Outcome: Upon successful completion of this course, the student will be able to identify the types of NSCXs; match the organization with its responsibility in relation to the NSCX; identify the architecture of the NSCX system; and identify NSCX equipment and match it to its function in the NSCX.

Instruction: This course provides the student with a basic understanding of what the Network Service Complex is, its functions, its place in the AT&T Switched Network and the organizations related to its operation.

Credit Recommendation: In the upper division baccalaureate degree category, 2 semester hours in Telecommunication Systems or Technical elective (3/95). **NOTE:** Students must also complete ON0474 to earn the credit recommendation.

Network Service Complex-Teleconference (ON-0475)

Location: On-Site.

Length: 4 hours (1 day).

Dates: May 1995-Present.

Objective: To provide the student with the knowledge and skills required to maintain Network Service Complex-Teleconference locations at the Trouble Locating Plan (TLP) level.

Learning Outcome: Upon successful completion of this course, the student will be able to identify the three features offered by the NSCX Teleconference; diagram the call-flow for the various teleconferencing features; identify the equipment of the NSCX-Teleconference office; and understand the location of the NSCX-Teleconference in the AT&T Switched Network.

Instruction: Major topics covered in the course are the areas of operations, call-flow, administration, maintenance, and the equipment. The course is designed to present a comprehensive view of the Teleconference Network Service Complex.

Credit Recommendation: In the upper division baccalaureate degree category, 3 semester hours in Telecommunication Systems or Technical elective (3/95). **NOTE:** Students must also complete ON0476 and ON0477 (laboratory sequence), ON0472, and ON0474 to earn the credit recommendation.

Number 1 Packet Switch System Release 4(1PSS) Operations and Maintenance (ON-0541)

Location: Denver, CO and Conyers, GA.

Length: 24 hours (3 days).

Dates: January 1990-Present.

Objective: To provide the student with the knowledge and skills required to maintain a No. 1 Packet Switch switching equipment at the Trouble Locating Plan (TLP) level using current office documentation.

Learning Outcome: Upon successful completion of this course, the student will be able to understand the function of the #1PSS network; use available #1PSS switching equipment documentation; state the function of the frames; locate the fault circuit pack using TLP; understand the call-flow for a Packet Switch; and safely remove, clean, and reinstall circuit packs.

Instruction: Major topics covered in the course are the recognition, function, and description of all #1PSS switching equipment as well as proper maintenance procedures. This is achieved by the use and understanding of #1PSS office documentation through testing and practical assignments.

Credit Recommendation: In the lower division baccalaureate/associate degree category or in the upper division baccalaureate degree category, 2 semester hours in Telecommunication Technology or Technical elective (3/95).

Overview of Network Architecture (NI-0100)

Location: AT&T locations worldwide.

Length: 24 hours.

Dates: January 1990-December 1996.

Objective: To provide a comprehensive overview of the basic concepts of telecommunications and how it relates to the Network Architecture of the AT&T Switched Network (ASN), which supports both the domestic and international services.

Learning Outcome: Upon successful completion of this course, the student will be able to list network access arrangements (i.e., describe network elements, facilities, and switching systems; identify types of telecommunications signaling; describe telecommunications routing and switching; describe Nodal Services; and explain Integrated Service Digital Network (ISDN).

Instruction: Major topics covered in the course are teaching the overall make-up of the ASN to include facilities, signaling, routing configurations and switches; and included will be examples of International and Domestic Services and how they are routed through the Network.

Credit Recommendation: In the lower division baccalaureate/associate degree category or in the upper division baccalaureate degree category, 2 semester hours in Introduction to Telecommunications (3/93).

Overview of the AT&T Switched Network (ON-0200)

Location: Suitcased to AT&T locations.

Length: 32 hours (4 days).

Dates: June 1994-Present.

Objective: To explain call-flow and routing of services and features provided by the AT&T Switched Network.

Learning Outcome: Upon successful completion of this course, the student will be able to describe the basic network hardware configurations, CNI Ring and its components, MF, CCIS6 and CCS7, signaling, Q.931 protocol, CCS7 protocol and point code structure, POTS call set-up, and complex NCP services and their Network Routing.

Instruction: Major topics covered in the course are the fundamental theories and principles of the AT&T Switched Network, the various types of calls and stat transported through the AT&T Switched Network, and the functions and duties of other groups whose interaction provide an end service. Methods of instruction include lecture, discussion, and classroom exercises.

Credit Recommendation: In the upper division baccalaureate degree category, 2 semester hours in Telecommunication Networks or Technical elective (3/95).

Process Management Workshop (QU-0200)

Location: Various AT&T locations.

Length: 24 hours.

Dates: October 1992-Present.

Objective: To provide managers with the Statistic tools needed to manage the quality process.

Learning Outcome: Upon successful completion of this course, the student will be able to apply statistical tools to quality issues; describe the process focused management model and integrate it into decision making; and describe the customer-supplier model showing the importance of linking process/product performance requirements.

Instruction: Major topics covered in the course are an overview of the forces which drove NSD's transformation to a Process driven Management System; NSD's Organization Hierarchy and the Support Systems being implemented to Support Process Management; review of the Process Quality Management and Improvement (PQMI) Methodology and implementation within NSD; and an introduction to Statistical Process Control (SPC), a key tool for Process Managed Organizations. Additional Requirements: Take home exam of at least 4 problems applying the statistical tools to the quality process.

Credit Recommendation: In the lower division baccalaureate/associate degree category or in the upper division baccalaureate degree category, 2 semester hours in Statistical Techniques in Decision Making (12/92).

Process Management Workshop (QU-0200)

Location: Various AT&T locations.

Length: *Version 1:* 24 hours (3 days); *Version 2:* 185 hours (25 days).

Dates: *Version 1:* October 1992-November 1996; *Version 2:* December 1996-Present.

Objective: *Version 1:* To provide managers with the statistical tools needed to manage the quality process. *Version 2:* To teach Process Quality Management using the Process Quality Management and Improvement (PQMI) methodology, which is sanctioned by "Network & Computing Services".

Learning Outcome: *Version 1:* Upon successful completion of this course, the student will be able to apply statistical tools to quality issues; describe the process focused management model and integrate it into decision making; and describe the customer-supplier model showing the importance of linking process and product performance requirements. *Version 2:* Upon successful completion of this course, the student will be able to understand and implement the seven steps of Process Quality Management & Improvement (PQMI) methodology; define a "process" using the OEW conventions for process flow diagramming; and work through as AT&T case study, using PQMI, the OEW conventions for process flow diagramming, and the OEW templates.

Instruction: *Version 1:* Major topics covered in the course are an overview of the forces which drove NSD's transformation to a process driven management system; introduces NSD's organizational hierarchy and the support systems being implemented to support process management; review the Process Quality Management and Improvement (PQMI) Methodology and its implementation within NSD; and an introduction to Statistical Process Control (SPC), a key tool for process managed organizations. Methods of instruction include a take home examination of at least 4 problems applying the statistical tools to the quality process. *Version 2:* Major topics covered in the course are the Process Element of NCS's QMS (Quality Management System), how to implement PQMI with a process management framework, including how to use OEW (Operations Engineering Workbook) conventions to document the process. Methods of instruction include a comprehensive case study to integrate the concepts of PQMI and OEW, lecture, and interactive components.

Credit Recommendation: *Version 1:* In the lower division baccalaureate/associate degree category or the upper division baccalaureate degree category, 2 semester hours in Statistical Techniques in Decision Making (12/92). *Version 2:* In the upper division baccalaureate degree category, 1 semester hour in Statistical Techniques in Decision Making or Operations Manager (10/97).

Ring Concepts and Maintenance (ON0013)

Location: On-Site.

Length: 16 hours (2 days).

Dates: March 1992-Present.

Objective: To provide job aids and procedures to resolve faults on the basic CNI ring and its peripheral equipment used in all Common Channel Signaling Applications.

Learning Outcome: Upon successful completion of this course, the student will be able to state the function of the ring; identify software and hardware in the ring; and identify and resolve faults on the ring.

Instruction: Major topics covered in the course are how to apply the fundamental principles by resolving faults on the CNI ring at their work location.

Credit Recommendation: In the upper division baccalaureate degree category, 1 semester hour in Telecommunication Systems or Technology elective (3/95).

Team Dynamics and Problem Solving Workshop (TDAPS) (QU-0500)

Location: AT&T locations nationwide.

Length: 26 hours (35 days).

Dates: April 1997-Present.

Objective: To enable students to apply quality tools and techniques useful to a team environment using the AT&T Problem-Solving Method.

Learning Outcome: Upon successful completion of this course, the student will be able to define a team through dialogue and role play; apply the seven steps of the AT&T Problem-Solving Method and corresponding tools/techniques; demonstrate effective meeting facilitation skills; demonstrate observation skills; and participate in team meetings in an effective, efficient manner with emphasis on team dynamics.

Instruction: Major topics covered in the course are team building exercises and experiences using the AT&T Problem-Solving Method, fundamentals of team membership, leadership and team dynamics. Interactive exercises throughout this course will allow participants to experience the various roles on the team. The exercises emphasize the use of quality tools to solve problems according the the seven steps of the AT&T Problem-Solving Method. Methods of instruction include interactive exercises, discussion, lecture and simulation.

Credit Recommendation: In the upper division baccalaureate degree category, 2 semester hours in Problem Solving or Decision Making (10/97).

Team Leader Training (QU-0130)

Location: Various locations throughout the U.S.

Length: 40 hours.

Dates: January 1990-December 1997.

Objective: To prepare individuals to be effective team leaders and understand the nature of group dynamics.

Learning Outcome: Upon successful completion of this course, the student will be able to describe the Quality Improvement Cycle; describe the role of the Team Leader in the Quality Improvement Cycle; utilize the eight steps of the Quality Improvement Cycle and supporting tools/techniques; introduce Team Leaders to the concepts of group dynamics and their impact on the Team; and introduce the Quality Improvement Process administrative support structure.

Instruction: Major topics covered in the course are how to guide the Quality Improvement Teams in pursuit of customer satisfaction, development of the Team Leader's role through the use of the NSD eight step Quality Improvement Cycle and the supporting tools and techniques required to implement the cycle, concepts of group dynamics and their impact on the Quality Improvement Team, and administrative support structures for maintenance of the Quality Improvement Process. Methods of instruction include a graded oral and written project pertaining to some aspect of the job.

Credit Recommendation: In the upper division baccalaureate degree category, 3 semester hours in Group Dynamics and Leadership (12/92). **NOTE:** A passing score on the examination is required to earn the credit recommendation.

Telecommunications Theory (TF-0204) (Basic Transmission Theory [EC0233]) (Formerly Telecommunications Theory [EC-0233])

Location: AT&T locations or home personal computers.

Length: Self-paced instruction (approximately 8-12 hours).

Dates: March 1989-December 1996.

Objective: To provide the student with an introduction to the terminology and fundamental principles of transmission within the telecommunications industry.

Learning Outcome: Upon successful completion of this course, the student will be able to define basic terms used to discuss telecommunication systems and transmissions; identify the principle types of transmission media; and define multiplexing and distinguish between FDM (Frequency Division Multiplexing) and TDM (Time Division Multiplexing).

Instruction: Major topics covered in the course are the introduction to telecommunications, concepts of transmission, transmission media, multiplexing, and transmission impairment and distortion. Methods of instruction include computer-based, self-paced instruction.

Credit Recommendation: In the lower division baccalaureate/associate degree category, 1 semester hour in Telecommunications (5/89). **NOTE:** Credit is awarded only if both this course and Introduction to Telecommunications (NT0002) have been successfully completed.

Tools and Process Overview (QU-0140)

Location: Various AT&T locations throughout the country.

Length: 16 hours.

Dates: April 1987-January 1994.

Objective: To describe the application of the eight step Quality Improvement Cycle and its supporting tools and techniques as a problem solving methodology.

Learning Outcome: Upon successful completion of this course, the student will be able to describe the activities of the eight step (QIC), and apply the Quality Improvement Tools/Techniques.

Instruction: Major topics covered in the course are the eight step Quality Improvement Cycle, this QIC is an eight step problem identification and solving methodology; and the appropriate Quality Improvement Tools/Techniques. Methods of instruction include performance evaluation in the case study and take-home examination on applications of problem solving tools and techniques.

Credit Recommendation: In the upper division baccalaureate degree category, 1 semester hour in Quality Improvement Techniques (12/92).

Working Together as a Workplace of the Future Team (QU-0405)

Location: Various locations as requested.

Length: 24 hours (3 days).

Dates: April 1997-Present.

Objective: To teach Workplace of the Future Teams how to implement WPOF concepts and principles as they function as a team.

Learning Outcome: Upon successful completion of this course, the student will be able to apply the principles of WPOF in a team situation; better understand how WPOF principles apply in any problem solving or decision making process; utilize various tools and techniques which support problem solving; assess your team dynamics with respect to your approach to problem solving and decision making; assess your personal and your team's approach to conflict resolution; and begin work on an issue related to team functioning within the context of problem solving and decision making.

Instruction: Major topics covered in the course are building on WPOF concepts and principles taught in the prerequisite course, "WPOF Team Orientation Workshop-QU0400," how to work together as a WPOF team; approach to problem solving and decision making that is effective and consistent with WPOF principles; examines team dynamics with respect to their (teams) problem solving and decision making approach. Exercises and a case study enable participants to practice the skills and knowledge, and assess their team performance using behavioral checklists. Methods of instruction include discussion, lecture, and interactive exercises.

Credit Recommendation: In the upper division baccalaureate degree category, 2 semester hours in Organizational Dynamics or Group Process (10/97).

Workplace of the Future Team Member Orientation Workshop (Phase IIA) (QU-0401)

Location: AT&T locations nationwide.

Length: 24 hours (3 days).

Dates: September 1997-Present.

Objective: To teach the concepts and principles that are the foundation of the Workplace of the Future, and to bring new team members to the education level of the existing team members.

Learning Outcome: Upon successful completion of this course, the student will be able to develop an understanding of WPOF and its rationale; why the company and the unions have decided to work together in this way; develop an understanding of fundamental interests and values of those involved in WPOF - especially those of the unions and of the business; develop understanding of and practice the concept of interactivity; and to introduce aspects of group dynamics relating to new team membership.

Instruction: Major topics covered in the course are the concepts and principles of WPOF including the key elements of WPOF; a discussion of investors, employees and customers as stakeholders; group dynamics; and the win-win problem solving approach. This course is intended for new members joining an existing WPOF team. Methods of instruction include discussion, lecture, simulation, and interactive exercises.

Credit Recommendation: In the lower division baccalaureate/associate degree category, 2 semester hours in Labor Relations (10/97).

Workplace of the Future Team Orientation Workshop (Phase II) (QU0400)

Location: AT&T locations nationwide.

Length: 28 hours (35 days).

Dates: September 1997-Present.

Objective: To teach the concepts and principles that are the foundation of the Workplace of the Future.

Learning Outcome: Upon successful completion of this course, the student will be able to develop an understanding of Workplace of the Future and its rationale; why the company and the union have decided to work together in this way; develop an understanding of fundamental interests and values of those involved in WPOF-especially those of the union and of the business; build interaction among different parties so that they can effectively solve problems together; develop or reinforce skills in joint problem solving; and start/continue working together incorporating the WPOF principles.

Instruction: Major topics covered in the course are the concepts and principles of WPOF, including NPG's Ideal Future-it involves a high degree of interactivity, including small group breakout sessions; and process of dealing with actual team issues and problems, as well as designing their own Ideal Future. Methods of instruction include discussion, lecture, simulation, and interactive exercises.

Credit Recommendation: In the upper division baccalaureate degree category, 2 semester hours in Labor Relations (10/97).

Workplace of the Future-Train-The-Trainer (QU-0403)

Location: AT&T locations nationwide.

Length: 60 hours (2 weeks).

Dates: March 1995-Present.

Objective: To prepare trainers to deliver WPOF Team Orientation Workshop to WPOF teams outside of NCS.

Learning Outcome: Upon successful completion of this course, the student will be able to convey the course objectives; facilitate team breakout sessions; help teams realize the significance of making business decisions that honor the interests of all three stakeholders while transforming the organization; help teams develop ways to constantly measure their impact to EVA, PVA, & CVA; and convey the institutional needs of the business and the union so teams can build on the commonalities to ensure the success of the business and our business partners and customers.

Instruction: Major topics covered in the course are information concerning the evolution of WPOF that traces its history and principles expanded through the NCS Ideal Future and Operational Framework; content is linked to the Common Bond and Covey principles; history and structure of the CWA (our partner); a case study that shows the success and non-success of Eastern Airlines. Built into this content are a number of opportunities to practice interactivity (one of the underlying concepts) while exploring the learning points. Methods of instruction include discussion, lecture, lab, simulation, computer-aided instruction, but most learning is based on interactive exercises. Members are constantly combined in different combinations to ensure a good mixture of ideas and creativity.

Credit Recommendation: In the upper division baccalaureate degree category, 3 semester hours in Training and Development (10/97).

AT&T School of Business and Technology

AT&T School of Business and Technology, (formerly the AT&T School of Business, the AT&T Technical Education Center, and the AT&T Learning Services Division), provides a wide range of training, educational, and consulting services. Such services include determining training needs for organizations, developing and delivering courses anywhere in the world, customizing existing courses to fit individual client's needs, and providing technical consulting in specialty areas for a client's programs or projects.

Business and Leadership Programs provide fundamental and advanced learning. Courses include principles, theory, and practical application in a broad range of subject areas. Topics include diversity, finance, accounting and auditing, global business, instructor education and training, leadership skills, marketing and product management, multimedia, procurement, project management and human factors, voice communications technology, internet and data communications technologies, programming technologies and business systems engineering and UNIX/PC/Open systems.

Courses are available to management and occupational personnel within each of AT&T's business operating units and divisions as well as external companies. The instructional staff is composed of university faculty, business and industry leaders, and internal subject matter experts. Each faculty member is viewed as a leading authority by business and academia. Many have advanced degrees and are recognized for their contributions and expertise in their fields.

Source of official student records: Registry of Credit Recommendations, American Council on Education, One Dupont Circle, Washington, DC 20036-1193.

Additional information about the courses: Office of Corporate-Higher Education Programs, Thomas Edison State College, 101 West State Street, Trenton, New Jersey 08608-1176.

A Certificate in Innovation: Take Charge of Your Business Ideas! (ME2075)

Location: Somerset, NJ; Lisle, IL; Atlanta, GA; and Mesa, AZ.

Length: 48 hours (6 days).

Dates: April 1995-Present.

Objective: To spur innovation and promote an entrepreneurial spirit among managers.

Learning Outcome: Upon successful completion of this course, the student will be able to recognize the need for innovation; identify opportunities and pick winning projects; benchmark the right role models in other corporations; develop written proposal - make the sale; and present the project effectively for a win/win situation.

Instruction: Major topics covered in the course are how to implement real ideas from concept to final product resulting in a certificate from Columbia University and how to develop specific action plans to implement back on the job. Methods of instruction include one-on-one coaching with peers and instructors from Columbia University builds support and encourages risk-taking and an appropriate graduate level project.

Credit Recommendation: In the graduate degree category, 3 semester hours in Entrepreneurship (12/95).

A Cost Model for Communications Private Line Cost Models and Studies- PLIAC (AT&T 108, PUB 303 or SA1060)

Location: Somerset Seminars Center, Somerset, NJ.

Length: 40 hours (5 days).

Dates: January 1984-December 1986.

Objective: To provide the expertise to prepare and use effectively the Private Line Cost Models and Studies to develop incremental or resource investments and annual costs relevant to Private Line Services. The seminar further provides an understanding of the functions of other models interfacing with Private Line Cost Models and Studies.

Instruction: Major topics covered in the course are definitions for the makeup, structure, and content of the PLIAC Model; an understanding of capabilities and limitations of PLIAC as well as the purpose, content, and interrelationship of supporting files; and the procedures required to first establish PLIAC data bases, and subsequently to make actual PLIAC runs and analyze the results.

Credit Recommendation: In the graduate degree category, 1 semester hour in Finance or Accounting, which would be appropriate in the following degree programs: Operations Research, Finance, Business Administration, Economics, or Accounting (11/85).

Accelerated Microsoft Project for Windows (IE1693)

Location: Piscataway, NJ and various other locations nationwide.

Length: 24 hours (3 days).

Dates: July 1995-December 1996.

Objective: To teach participants to use Microsoft Project 4.0 to effectively create and manage single and multiple project schedules using accepted project management principles.

Learning Outcome: Upon successful completion of this course, the student will be able to create a new project, enter task and resource information for the project, organize the project in outline form, display various views of project information, analyze and adjust schedules, resources and costs as the project progresses, preview and print reports on the project, create Master project to subproject relationships, combine multiple projects, share a common resource pool between projects, analyze resource conflicts between multiproject assignments, customize Microsoft Project filters, reports, tables and tool bars.

Instruction: Customization of Microsoft Project is introduced by creating custom views, tables, filters, reports and tool bars. The principles of sharing customized objects among projects are also taught. Project management principles are also discussed along with their application in Microsoft Project.

Credit Recommendation: In the upper division baccalaureate degree category or in the lower division baccalaureate/associate degree category, 2 semester hours in Microsoft Projects for Windows I & II (6/95).

Accelerating Quality Through Leadership (CQ1006)

Location: AT&T locations nationwide.

Length: 16 hours (2 days).

Dates: October 1988-December 1994.

Objective: To prepare participants to develop skills needed for managing customer relationships, empowerment, and change.

Learning Outcome: Upon successful completion of this course, the student will be able to identify the behaviors needed for change and to support quality; identify gaps between ideal and current practices; and plan individual and council development.

Instruction: Major topics covered in the course are three modules: the first module traces the continuing process of implementing quality at AT&T, skills, behaviors and work situations that support or detract from your ability to accelerate quality in the organization will be assessed; the second module shows there are two parts to the negotiation process. Students will concentrate on the first part, establishing valid customer requirements, will conduct negotiation sessions in their roles as customers and suppliers, they will give and receive feedback on their negotiation skills, and decide what can be done to improve customer-supplier negotiations in the organizations they manage. The third module focuses on the second part of the negotiation process, making sure suppliers are empowered to do the right things and meet customer requirements.

Credit Recommendation: In the graduate degree category, 1 semester hour in Organizational Leadership (10/91).

Acquisitions and Joint Ventures: A Strategic Marketing Approach to New Business Growth (SA6040)

Location: Somerset, NJ.

Length: 24 hours plus lab.

Dates: December 1989-March 1994.

Objective: To assess the need for and role of external development in creating increased owner equity, through country, industry, company, and candidate evaluation, selection, approach and negotiation to the implementation/integration phases.

Learning Outcome: Upon successful completion of this course, the student will be able to develop a meaningful business definition in order to do a relevant country, industry, company and candidate evaluation; apply the principles and tactics involved in acquisitions and/or joint ventures; develop a set of acquisition/joint venture criteria (strategies, financial and tactical) to guide the search and screening process; demonstrate the ability to search out legitimate public and private candidates and screen appropriately versus the criteria; reasonably value a target company, setting lo/mid/hi values and explain variations; establish a negotiating strategy that covered all meaningful aspects and negotiate with owners; articulate what a post acquisition integration plan would look like; laying out steps, procedures and timing, assuming deal takes places; and implement any/all of the above.

Instruction: This course focuses on the process of new business development via the alternative strategic approach of acquisition and/or joint ventures. It presents a tested framework for rigorously assessing external business opportunities, domestic and international. It overviews the entire process from assessing the need for and role of external development in creating increased owner equity, through country, industry, company and candidate evaluation, selection, approach and negotiation, to the due diligence and implementation/integration phases. It also addresses candidate evaluate and premium recapture.

Credit Recommendation: In the graduate degree category, 3 semester hours in Acquisitions and Joint Ventures (8/91).

Active Communicating: Professional Presence and Creativity (MD6411)

Location: Somerset, NJ and other School of Business sites.

Length: 21 hours (3 days).

Dates: July 1990-Present.

Objective: To develop more conscious and competent communication within a business environment.

Learning Outcome: Upon successful completion of this course, the student will be able to understand the relationship between language and its expression through the voice and the body; improve interpersonal communication skills, including listening, sensitivity to others and team building skills; improve presentation skills, including use of voice, body and the ability to think quickly under pressure; develop a more self-confident overall communication style.

Instruction: This course involves the use of theater-based exercises to bring to awareness and improve the various components which determine effective communication, such as voice use; concentration; creativity and imagination; timing; listening; body awareness; sensitivity to others; pacing; memory; ability to improvise; emotional expressiveness and self-confidence in speaking. Course readings, lectures and discussions relate the exercises to the interpersonal communication dynamics of the workplace and how individuals can make a contribution towards their improvement.

Credit Recommendation: In the lower division baccalaureate/associate degree category, 1 semester hour in Oral Business Communication (6/94).

Activity Based Management: Fundamentals and Applications (FE0203)

Location: Somerset, NJ and Atlanta, GA.

Length: 16 hours (2 days).

Dates: March 1995-Present.

Objective: To learn to improve your organization's profitability, productivity and operational processes through a hands-on introduction to Activity-Based Costing/ Activity-Based Management.

Learning Outcome: Upon successful completion of this course, the student will be able to understand the concepts, applications and importance of ABC and ABM; understand how ABC/ABM can help your organization increase profitability and productivity, improve business processes and enrich decision making; learn the tools and techniques necessary to design and implement an ABC/ABM project within your organization; learn how ABC/ABM has been applied within AT&T; locate experienced internal and external resources to help you implement an ABM project.

Instruction: This course includes the need for ABC/ABM, ABC/ABM as the foundation for increasing profitability and productivity, improving business processes and highlighting opportunities, ABC and ABM concepts and techniques, managing and implementing a successful ABC/ABM project, and ABC/ABM in AT&T. A comprehensive paper is required as part of this course.

Credit Recommendation: In the graduate degree category or in the upper division baccalaureate degree category, 1 semester hour in Production/Operations Management (7/95).

Advanced Economic Principles of Network Services Pricing

Location: Somerset Seminars Center, Somerset, NJ.

Length: 24 hours (3 days).

Dates: January 1984-December 1986.

Objective: This two-day seminar increases the understanding of the application of microeconomic theory in the pricing/costing of intrastate intraLATA services.

Instruction: This seminar's primary emphasis is on the use of microeconomic principles in analyzing the issues relating to pricing and costing intraLATA services. It includes a brief review of economic analysis; a brief review of market mechanisms and the concept of economic efficiency; a discussion of pricing decisions by the firm and by regulatory bodies. The focus is on intraLATA services pricing issues, emphasizing the local area services.

Credit Recommendation: In the lower division baccalaureate/associate degree category or in the upper division baccalaureate degree category, 2 semester hours in Economics (11/85).

Advanced Field Management (SM0130)

Location: Somerset, NJ and other AT&T locations.

Length: 16 hours (2 days).

Dates: December 1993-Present.

Objective: To aid participants in developing effective sales strategies and reliable forecasts based on company/division goals and market understanding.

Learning Outcome: Upon successful completion of this course, the student will be able to develop effective sales strategies and reliable forecasts based on company/division goals and market understanding; build skills required to work effectively with internal function (e.g., marketing, distribution, manufacturing); increase ability to provide direction and motivation to a sales team; learn methods to develop the skills of a sales team; and learn how to develop a sales team to become the preferred supplier in the customer's eyes.

Instruction: Major topics covered in the course are designed for students with previous field management experience. It includes strategic planning, sales marketing, sales forecasting, international functions, winning with customers, and motivation skills. Methods of instruction include case studies, lectures, and discussions.

Credit Recommendation: In the upper division baccalaureate degree category, 1 semester hour in Sales Management or General Management (12/93).

Advanced Finance in Global Markets (FM1070) (Formerly Overview of Global Finance [GM1040] and Finance in the Global Marketplace [GM1040])

Location: Somerset, NJ.

Length: 21 hours (3 days).

Dates: November 1989-Present.

Objective: To explain to participants the global financial issues involved in doing business internationally.

Learning Outcome: Upon successful completion of this course, the student will be able to understand the workings of the foreign exchange markets and the impact of macro-economic policy on exchange rates; relate AT&T's international operating agreements to the foreign exchange risks and explain the pros and cons of the foreign exchange risk management tools available in the market; develop a strategy for currency of invoice selection in the case of accounts receivable, accounts payable, and short-term financing; describe the institutional structure of the international financial instruments offered; and identify the critical differences in the foreign versus domestic direct investment decision.

Instruction: This course introduces participants to the world of global financial issues. The objective of the course is to enhance participants' abilities to incorporate various facets of international finance into their pricing, sourcing, and sales decisions.

The program also addresses the issues of AT&T's international operating agreements and discusses the foreign exchange risk management and global financing issues associated with such agreements. An appropriate graduate level project is included as part of the course requirement for students to earn the credit recommendation.

Credit Recommendation: In the graduate degree category or in the upper division baccalaureate degree category, 2 semester hours in Global Finance (12/90) (7/95).

Advanced Management Program (ATT01)

Location: The Learning Center, Basking Ridge, NJ.

Length: *Version 1:* 140 hours; *Version 2:* 98 hours; *Version 3:* 2 weeks.

Dates: *Version 1:* January 1980-December 1990; *Version 2:* January 1991-June 1996; *Version 3:* July 1996-Present.

Objective: To provide an intense two-week developmental, leadership and general management experience designed to exponentially enhance the leadership capacity of division level high performing managers and to increase their ability to assume higher level responsibilities.

Learning Outcome: Upon successful completion of this course, the student will be able to understand leadership behaviors, skills and mindset to be an effective agent of change; understand AT&T's latest strategies through interaction with senior AT&T executives; exercise strategic thinking and strategy execution; develop a global, general management perspective and an understanding of the information industry; develop an innovative action plan to address critical business challenge; understand impact on bottom line and be clear on contributions toward success of AT&T.

Instruction: Major topics covered in the course are business capabilities needed to address global business challenges, leadership skills required to effect change and align teams behind change efforts, and personal effectiveness skills essential to continual renewal and growth. The program is holistic and integrates several learning modalities. These include Action Learning, Cognitive and Experiential Learning, Feedback, Leadership, Wellness/Fitness, Organizational and Personal Change Strategies. Participants identify and address their key business issues and personal leadership challenges throughout the program in small group sessions called "GAP" groups. They offer one another candid but caring feedback and help develop innovative action plans to address business and leadership challenges. Participants are also given a 360 degrees feedback instrument prior to their participation and then get the results of the feedback during the program. An experienced consultant is available to offer individual counsel to the participants to help them act on their feedback results. Methods of instruction include classroom discussion, lecture, simulation, independent study and other experiential/action learning. **NOTE:** An appropriate graduate level research project is included as part of the course requirement for each student who seeks the credit recommendation.

Credit Recommendation: *Version 1:* In the graduate degree category, 4 semester hours in Advanced Case Analysis I, and 4 semester hours in Advanced Case Analysis II, for a total of 8 semester hours (9/89). *Version 2:* In the graduate degree category, 3 semester hours in Advanced Case Analysis I, and 3 semester hours in Advanced Case Analysis II, for a total of 6 semester hours (Special Annual Review 1/91). *Version 3:* In the graduate degree category, 6 semester hours in Organizational Leadership (10/97).

Advanced Management Program

Location: Hamilton Park Conference Center, Florham Park, NJ.

Length: *Version 1:* 140 hours; *Version 2:* 98 hours.

Dates: *Version 1:* January 1980-December 1990; *Version 2:* January 1991-June 1996.

Objective: To prepare participants with senior management potential for executive-level responsibilities in a competitive business environment.

Learning Outcome: Upon successful completion of this course, the student will be able to develop and implement strategic initiatives; develop a financial perspective; enhance management effectiveness in a changing, competitive environment; understand and anticipate the changing marketplace; and develop a perspective on global markets.

Instruction: Major topics covered in the course are business strategy, allocating resources/obtaining technology, cash flow analysis, sources of capital, linkages of financial decisions and corporate strategy, responding to the marketplace, the leadership role, management norms and values, the multinational corporation, and the global marketplace. Methods of instruction include utilizing computer-based management simulation, "7S" analysis of AT&T entities, and seminars led by senior AT&T management and by distinguished graduate school faculty members. Students seeking the credit recommendation have each completed formal management coursework, in addition to extensive management experience prior to attending this course; and are involved in significant case analysis as part of their involvement with this course.

Credit Recommendation: *Version 1:* In the graduate degree category, 4 semester hours in Advanced Case Analysis I, and 4 semester hours in Advanced Case Analysis II, for a total of 8 semester hours (9/89). *Version 2:* In the graduate degree category, 3 semester hours in Advanced Case Analysis I and 3 semester hours in Advanced Case Analysis II, for a total of 6 semester hours (Annual Review).

Advanced Market Planning (SE1000) (Formerly Computer Assisted Market Planning [UMMC])

Location: Somerset Seminars Center, Somerset, NJ.

Length: 32 hours (4 days).

Dates: January 1984-December 1988.

Objective: To show participants how to implement market strategies through computer simulation.

Instruction: Course uses an interactive computer model that simulates the competitive situation faced by contemporary market planners. Teams of 3-5 persons strive to achieve market share and profit over a several year period. Participants make decisions about cost dynamics, segmentation and positioning, market evolution new product/service development, resource allocation, and the use of market research data. The computer simulation model feeds back the results of team decisions before other decisions can be made. The simulation plus integrated materials, lectures, and assistance by the seminar faculty leads participants to study a situation in depth, implement a plan, and test decision-making processes. This allows participants to: understand the relationships among the elements of a marketing plan and their impact on company performance, combine tactical with strategic plans and evaluate their effectiveness, develop insight into the dynamics of the marketing process, and learn new ideas for application of marketing resources.

Credit Recommendation: In the upper division baccalaureate degree category, 2 semester hours in Business Administration, Industrial Marketing, Marketing, or Marketing Management (9/83).

Advanced Microsoft Project for Windows (IE1692)

Location: Piscataway, NJ and various other locations nationwide.

Length: 14 hours (2 days).

Dates: July 1995-Present.

Objective: To teach those students who have mastered the essential functions, features, commands and keystrokes of Microsoft Project for Windows 4.0 to manage their projects.

Learning Outcome: Upon successful completion of this course, the student will be able to exchange information with other products; build a resource pool which can be shared by multiple projects; manage Master Project/Subproject relationships; resolve resource conflicts and over-allocation in a multiple project environment; control file access and update protection by managing file security; and understand macro syntax.

Instruction: This advanced level course is for those who have mastered the essential functions, features, commands and keystrokes of Microsoft Project for Windows to manage their projects. For those involved in Multiple Projects, Master projects/Subprojects and shared resource pools.

Credit Recommendation: In the upper division baccalaureate degree category, or in the lower division baccalaureate/associate degree category, 1 semester hour in Microsoft Project for Windows II (6/95).

Advanced Quantitative Methods in Marketing Application of Multivariate Techniques

Location: Mt. Laurel, NJ; Atlanta, GA; Denver, CO.

Length: 34 hours (4 days).

Dates: January 1980-December 1982.

Objective: To help students apply advanced statistical techniques to marketing problems.

Instruction: Covers the fundamentals of multivariate methods and applications to research strategies. Methods of instruction include lectures, workshops, practicums, case histories, and criterion testing.

Credit Recommendation: In the upper division baccalaureate degree category, 2 semester hours in Business Analysis, Marketing Research, Quantitative Methods, or Statistics (9/80). *Prerequisite*: Statistics course or Quantitative Analysis of Marketing Data within the last three years.

Advanced Service Management Seminar (BUASM)

Location: Somerset Seminars Center, Somerset, NJ.

Length: 40 hours (5 days).

Dates: January 1984-December 1984.

Objective: To provide techniques, practices, and systems to select, organize, implement, and evaluate projects successfully. Particular emphasis is placed on management of service operations with project accounting and finance, project organization/control, human resources management, and implementation issues.

Instruction: Course is divided into three segments: (1) Project Accounting and Financial Management emphasizes project selection and evaluation and develops criteria for definition of project goals and objectives; (2) Project Organization/ Control covers project control, cost control, PERT diagrams, control path management and other techniques for successful management and implementation; (3) Human Resources Management discusses the project team/organization, motivation, implementation factors, and management of change created by the project.

Credit Recommendation: In the graduate degree category, 2 semester hours in Financial Management, Management, or Business Administration (11/85).

Advanced Techniques of Instruction (IE8211)

Location: Piscataway, NJ, and other AT&T locations.

Length: 37.5 hours (5 days).

Dates: September 1983-December 1986.

Objective: To help participants identify student/instructor problems and derive solutions for them.

Instruction: Major topics covered in the course are how to identify and deal with an assortment of classroom problems; knowledge of desirable instructor characteristics and roles; the principles of small group dynamics and learning theory; how to identify areas of instructional techniques that require improvement; and advanced concepts of human interaction/ teaching methods/human learning. Methods of instruction include lecture, discussions, team exercises, videotaped microteaching sessions, role play, and guided practice.

Credit Recommendation: In the upper division baccalaureate degree category, 2 semester hours in Education or Instructional Technology (7/85).

Analytical Tools for Purchasers (PR5053)

Location: All AT&T training locations.

Length: 24 hours (3 days).

Dates: January 1995-Present.

Objective: To expand the student's knowledge of financial concepts and ratios and increase their ability to negotiate, based on cost analysis.

Learning Outcome: Upon successful completion of this course, the student will be able to successfully work with suppliers to keep their costs competitive, determine total cost and life-cycle costs, and prepare break-even analysis.

Instruction: Major topics covered in the course are financial concepts and ratios; how to interpret a financial statement; how to evaluate a supplier's financial condition; cost/price analysis/break-even analysis; how to determine total cost and life-cycle cost; and how to make buy and lease/buy decision. Methods of instruction include classroom discussion and lecture. An appropriate graduate level project is included as part of the course requirement.

Credit Recommendation: In the upper division baccalaureate degree category, 2 semester hours in Purchasing or in the graduate degree category, 1 semester hour in Purchasing (11/96).

Annoyance Calls and Bomb Threat Tactics (NW2501)

Location: AT&T locations worldwide.

Length: 16 hours (2 days).

Dates: July 1991-Present.

Objective: To enable students to comprehend the safest alternatives to a bomb threat situation.

Learning Outcome: Upon successful completion of this course, the student will be able to analyze and describe various callers' significant speech patterns; apply the four basic steps to follow after reception of an annoyance call; and understand negotiating techniques and the ability to plan and execute a strategy to handle these problems.

Instruction: Major topics covered in the course are first-hand knowledge about the right questions to ask; documentation; types of bombs; nature of bombs threats; proper awareness attitude; major mail bomb recognition points; response to demands; negotiating techniques; observation/perception; and parking lot/garage security. Methods of instruction include case studies, lectures, group discussion, practice exercises, simulations, and job aids.

Credit Recommendation: In the lower division baccalaureate/associate degree category, 1 semester hour in Security Techniques (12/94).

Applications in Global Product Management (ME2030) (Formerly Product Management for Global Markets [GM1065])

Location: Somerset, NJ and other AT&T locations.

Length: 36 hours.

Dates: December 1991-April 1997.

Objective: To explore key strategic marketing and management concepts in focused cases and lectures and experience the product management process in a challenging and dynamic simulation exercise.

Learning Outcome: Upon successful completion of this course, the student will be able to integrate strategic marketing and product management concepts into your own business activity; apply new management skills and insights; develop action-oriented market strategies; identify new global market challenges and opportunities; and put analytic skills, strategic thinking and a new understanding of the global marketplace to work.

Instruction: Major topics covered in the course are the product management process in a challenging and dynamic simulation exercise; applying critical lessons and insights to AT&T businesses and the current global environment. Methods of instruction include simulation, cases, lectures, and workshops and students are required to complete a research paper at the graduate level that focuses on some aspect of global marketing.

Credit Recommendation: In the graduate degree category, 3 semester hours in Strategic Global Marketing (4/92).

Applied Business Forecasting (SA4090)

Location: Somerset, New Jersey.

Length: 21 hours plus lab.

Dates: August 1990-August 1996.

Objective: To introduce the student to the methods of forecasting, and impart an ability to carry out simple forecasting studies.

Learning Outcome: Upon successful completion of this course, the student will be able to state the several approaches to forecasting,and give their areas of application and carry out simple forecasting studies and interpret forecasting results.

Instruction: Major topics covered in the course include using in-house mainframe software to learn principles and practices of business forecasting; time series forecasting (moving average and autoregressive models, seasonality, and other advanced models and issues) and econometric models (regression analysis), model building, forecasting using econometric models and additional issues in econometric models and additional issues in econometric forecasting; students will become familiar with issues of new product forecasting, and will cover conjoint analysis and logistic models; and students will made aware of the computing and data resources available to the AT&T analyst.

Credit Recommendation: In the upper division baccalaureate degree category, 3 semester hours in Applied Business Forecasting or in the graduate degree category, 2 semester hours in Applied Business Forecasting (8/91).

Applied Physical Security Plus (FE0702)

Location: AT&T locations nationwide.

Length: 21.5 hours (3 days).

Dates: November 1988-December 1993.

Objective: To provide a thorough knowledge of the strengths and weaknesses of the latest state-of-the-art security technology.

Learning Outcome: Upon successful completion of this course, the student will be able to understand preventative physical security technologies and the emerging role of physical security; and analyze performance and control deficiencies in mechanical devices, life safety systems, alarm systems and access systems.

Instruction: Major topics covered in the course are strengths and weaknesses of the latest state-of-the-art security technology; extensive hands-on lab where access, alarm, mechanical and life safety systems are discussed and displayed; physical security strategy, risk assessment and vendor interface are also covered by a guest speaker from Sandia National Labs; evaluate the usefulness of the equipment and techniques in the many kinds of asset protection situations. Methods of instruction include a five page single-spaced term paper, prior reading assignments, case studies, lectures, group discussions, practice exercises, equipment lab, and job aids.

Credit Recommendation: In the lower division baccalaureate/associate degree category, 1 semester hour in Physical Security Systems (8/91).

Applied Quality Principles in Computer Systems (IE1954) (Formerly Applied Quality Principles for System Developers)

Location: Piscataway, NJ and other locations nationwide.

Length: *Version 1:*18 hours (3 days); *Version 2:* 21 hours (3 days).

Dates: *Version 1:* September 1988-December 1993; *Version 2:* January 1994-Present.

Objective: To focus on the qualitative approaches used by project managers to ensure that projects meet quality and cost requirements.

Learning Outcome: Upon successful completion of this course, the student will be able to demonstrate a knowledge of basic quality concepts; use quality in the system development process; and use tools and techniques in the use of quality in the process management.

Instruction: This course focuses on the qualitative and quantitative approaches used by project managers to ensure that projects and ongoing operations meet quality requirements as well as cost and schedule demands. Practical tools and techniques are introduced to help manage and improve quality in the development and operation of computer systems.

Credit Recommendation: *Version 1:* In the upper division baccalaureate degree category, 1 semester hour in Management Information/Quality Systems (7/90); *Version 2:* In the graduate degree category, 1 semester hour in Applied Quality Principle (6/95).

Applying SQC Troubleshooter to Improve Quality (MF3449)

Location: Piscataway, NJ.

Length: 16 hours (2 days).

Dates: March 1990-December 1995.

Objective: To provide in-depth instruction on the application of SQC Troubleshooter (statistical quality control software) in the improvement of any process.

Learning Outcome: Upon successful completion of this course, the student will be able to use the SQC Troubleshooter approach to problem solving; apply SQC Troubleshooter to improve quality, use control charts to perform process capability studies and monitor process performance; use histograms, normal probability plots, and Pareto analysis to identify the type and severity of process problems; use scatterplots, boxplots, and Analysis of Means to determine the relationship between explanatory variables and the response; use the statistics associated with the various graphical tools to help in decision making; use sorting and filtering to restrict the analysis; produce and modify graphics with SQC Troubleshooter; and transfer data from other information systems to SQC Troubleshooter.

Instruction: Major topics covered in this course are how to work step-by-step through the process improvement process using SQC Troubleshooter's capabilities; SQC Troubleshooter offers an assortment of powerful graphical and statistical tools to monitor, control, and improve the most repetitive processes; some key topics include Control Charts, Data Management, Process Capability, Pareto Analysis, Process Control, Loading Data, Analysis of Means (ANOM), Scatterplots, Problem Indicators, Archiving Data, Statistics, Boxplots, Problem Diagnosis, Process Improvement, Histograms, and Pretty Graphs.

Credit Recommendation: In the upper division baccalaureate degree category, 1 semester hour in Applied Statistical Quality Control (10/91).

Assembler Language Coding (IE3135) Introduction to Assembler Language Coding

Location: Piscataway, NJ, and other AT&T locations; Bell Operating Company locations.

Length: 30 hours (5 days).

Dates: January 1984-December 1988.

Objective: To introduce students to the elements of IBM 370 assembler language coding.

Instruction: Major topics covered in the course introduce the basic commercial Instruction Set and the use of basic I/O macros. Topics covered include introduction to Assembler, basic instructions, looping and branching, decimal instructions, character handling, and QSAM data management. Methods of instruction include lecture and labs.

Credit Recommendation: In the lower division baccalaureate/associate degree category, 2 semester hours in Computer Science or Data Processing (7/85).

Assessing and Designing System Controls (IE2912)

Location: Piscataway, NJ, and other AT&T locations.

Length: *Version 1:* 18-24 hours (3 days); *Version 2:* 12-16 hours (2 days).

Dates: *Version 1:* April 1989-April 1993; *Version 2:* May 1993-June 1996.

Objective: To teach participants to be able to build controls into information systems.

Learning Outcome: Upon successful completion of this course, the student will be able to identify and review the project controls situation and its boundaries; design controls for the manual and automated aspects of a system focusing on business events and business risks using a simple but comprehensive set of control objectives that can be used on all systems; identify and select the best control technique for each control objective based on the degree of risk and volume of transactions; and assess and define the testing requirements and techniques for controls.

Instruction: Major topics covered in the course are instructor-led course teaches the student the skills and knowledge to build controls into information systems. The course uses a rigorous process to determine risks. These risks are then assessed and control for completeness, accuracy, authorization, continuity, and timeliness are built into the system to prevent and/or mitigate each risk. Methods of instruction include a pre-reading assignment and homework reading assignments from the Controls Handbook.

Credit Recommendation: In the lower division baccalaureate/associate degree category, or upper division baccalaureate degree category, 1 semester hour in Control Systems or Information Systems (7/90).

AT&T Business Case: Advanced Decision Making and Risk Analysis (FE0450) (Formerly Advanced Decision Making and Risk Analysis)

Location: Somerset, NJ.

Length: 40 hours (5 days).

Dates: July 1990-Present.

Objective: To teach managers the capability of preparing business cases for AT&T's most complex, high-risk ventures.

Learning Outcome: Upon successful completion of this course, the student will be able to use a variety of issue-raising approaches to examine industry structure, customer value, and competitive position; determine the appropriate membership of the decision board, project team, and subject matter experts; use a variety of strategy-generation techniques to create a wide range of alternative strategies; use the influence diagram to structure uncertainty and talk at, rather than around, the real issues; build complex cash flow models using the AIM system; assess ranges of uncertainty and probability distributions on continuous and discrete variables, recognizing dependence where appropriate; use decision tree and influence diagram software to compute the probability distributions on NPV, the value of perfect and imperfect control; communicate business case results and recommendations; and develop functional support plans, milestones and responsibility assignments, and a tracking system.

Instruction: This course provides in-depth decision and risk analysis training and builds on the techniques learned in the prerequisite courses. Advanced business case techniques are applied to unique, complex, high-risk ventures. An appropriate graduate level project is required as part of the course for students to earn the credit recommendation.

Credit Recommendation: In the graduate degree category or in the upper division baccalaureate degree category, 2 semester hours in Advanced Decision Making and Risk Analysis (12/90) (7/95).

AT&T Business Case: Business Strategy and Risk Analysis (FE0445) (Formerly Business Case: Business Strategy & Risk Analysis)

Location: Somerset, NJ.

Length: 16 hours (2 days).

Dates: March 1990-Present.

Objective: To build upon the basic skills developed in "Business Case: Decision-Making and Financial Analysis" and provide an overview of the AT&T Business Case Process.

Learning Outcome: Upon successful completion of this course, the student will be able to understand decision quality principles and use AT&T's Business Case Process to develop quality business cases; "frame" a business case properly to raise all pertinent issues, get the participation of appropriate decision-makers and staff, consider all the alternatives, and identify questions to be addressed; "analyze" various alternatives, including evaluation of information and control, to gain insight into sources of value and risk; and "connect" the results of the business case to the business plan that addresses functional support, budgeting, and implementation.

Instruction: This course presents the AT&T Business Case Process and the principles of decision quality embedded in the process stages to build quality business cases from discovery to implementation. Major topics covered in the course are techniques for issue-raising, taking into consideration the dynamics of industry structure, customer value, and competitive position; techniques for creating a wide range of alternative strategies; techniques for structuring and assessing uncertainty; techniques for comparing and communicating opportunity versus risk; and techniques for getting a shared commitment to the recommendation. Through a case study, combining R&D, manufacturing and marketing decisions, participants develop a business case using the techniques taught in the course.

Credit Recommendation: In the upper division baccalaureate degree category, 1 semester hour in Strategic Planning or Analysis (12/90) (7/95).

AT&T Business Case: Decision Making and Financial Analysis (FE0400) (Formerly Business Case: Decision Making and Financial Analysis [FE0400])

Location: Locations throughout the continental U.S.

Length: 24 hours (3 days).

Dates: *Version 1:* March 1990-February 1993; *Version 2:* March 1993-Present.

Objective: To teach students basic decision-making and financial analysis skills required in developing business cases, and prepare them to analyze routine projects.

Learning Outcome: Upon successful completion of this course, the student will be able to systematically identify decisions and critical issues in business cases; build a cash flow model using the AT&T Investment Modeling Software (AIM) System; correctly use discounted cash flow analysis, NPV, IRR, and MOI; assess ranges of uncertainty on important variables; and conduct sensitivity analysis and present results.

Instruction: Participants learn a systematic process to define the decision, identify important questions, model cash flows, assess uncertainty and risk, and conduct and interpret sensitivity analysis. These topics are integrated via two investment cases: the first, a simple tutorial example; and the second, a potential multimillion dollar investment in cost reduction. An application project is required as part of the course for students to earn the credit recommendation.

Credit Recommendation: *Version 1:* In the upper division baccalaureate degree category, 1 semester hour in Financial Analysis. *Version 2:* In the graduate degree category or in the upper division baccalaureate degree category, 2 semester hours in Decision Making and Financial Analysis (7/95).

AT&T CQA Examiner Workshop (CQ9018)

Location: AT&T locations in the US and worldwide.

Length: 18 hours (2 days); plus minimum of 40 hours pre-class asignment and 20-day, post-class exercises.

Dates: April 1990-Present.

Objective: To coach business managers to work within a team to asses TQM applications and communicate the strengths and areas for improvement that impact the business unit being assessed.

Learning Outcome: Upon successful completion of this course, the student will be able to understand the Baldridge model criteria as applied to business units, assess and evaluate a TQM award application which was prepared according to the Baldridge model, and communicate effectively to the business unit the strengths and areas for improvement found in the assessment.

Instruction: Major topics covered in the course are the Baldridge model application, site visits, and assessing and reporting findings to business leaders. the course presupposes that students are familiar with TQM and have completed a preclass component, students are then engaged in an extensive review of an actual Baldridge model application and carry it through all stages to final reporting of results to business leaders.

Credit Recommendation: In the graduate degree category, 4 semester hours in TQM Application/Baldridge Model (6/94).

Auditing Internal Controls (FE0604)

Location: AT&T locations throughout the world.

Length: 24 hours (3 days).

Dates: September 1993-Present.

Objective: To provide understanding of internal controls.

Learning Outcome: Upon successful completion of this course, the student will be able to identify and document the internal controls of a business operation and apply all techniques learned in class in the course case study audit.

Instruction: Major topics covered in the course are identifying and documenting internal controls of a business operation. Methods of instruction include lecture, exercises and application, completion of a pre-course assignment, and a case study audit.

Credit Recommendation: In the lower division baccalaureate/associate degree category, or in the upper division baccalaureate degree category, 2 semester hours in Auditing Control or Managing Internal Control (12/94).

Auditing Standards and Principles (FE0601)

Location: Somerset, NJ.

Length: 80 hours.

Dates: January 1986-August 1996.

Objective: To provide AT&T managers with the skills and background to effectively perform an audit or operational review.

Learning Outcome: Upon successful completion of this course, the student will be able to prepare for an audit by identifying resources needed; document the audit program using flowchart work operations, identify controls, recognize objectives and design audit tests; conduct pre-audit fieldwork by applying statistical sampling techniques, conduct field interviews, review work operation and documentation; analyze results of test actions by summarizing and analyzing audit test results, evaluate controls and determine significance of findings; communicate results to management, perform exit interviews, write audit report, conduct post audit reviews; and organize audit documentation in accordance with AT&T standards.

Instruction: This course is designed to instruct AT&T managers on how to conduct an audit or operational review. The practical understanding of the audit process will be gained through lecture, discussions, exercises, role plays and a comprehensive case study; Internal Control Theory and Methodology, risk analysis, auditing tools (coupling, flowcharting, etc.) and communication techniques.

Credit Recommendation: In the graduate degree category, 6 semester hours in Auditing (8/91).

Basic FORTRAN (IE3130) (Introduction to FORTRAN)

Location: Piscataway, NJ, and other AT&T locations.

Length: 30 hours (5 days).

Dates: August 1983-August 1988.

Objective: An introductory level course which will enable programmers to write FORTRAN IV programs which are readable and maintainable.

Instruction: Major topics covered in the course are standard FORTRAN statements, data representation and expressions, arithmetic and logical statements, input/output statements, and structured programming in FORTRAN. Methods of instruction include lecture and laboratory.

Credit Recommendation: In the lower division baccalaureate/associate degree category, 2 semester hours in Computer Science or Data Processing (7/85) (7/90).

Basic Negotiations: Negotiating to Yes (MS6420)

Location: Worldwide.

Length: 16 hours (2 days).

Dates: April 1990-Present.

Objective: To provide managers with a method of negotiating with integrity; a way to reach satisfying agreements while maintaining the relationship.

Learning Outcome: Upon successful completion of this course, the student will be able to have a conceptual framework for understanding negotiations - a language and a process to use before, during, and after a negotiation; apply a simple strategy for negotiating that enables them to pursue their interests without giving in or getting into confrontation; and follow a preparation procedure that covers a crucial step in negotiation.

Instruction: Major topics covered in the course are the techniques to successfully implement the negotiating process, using personal application and the win-win negotiation strategy and tactics. Methods of instruction include lecture, experiential exercises, discussion, video tapes, and an appropriate graduate level project.

Credit Recommendation: In the graduate degree category, 1 semester hour in Negotiations (5/96). **NOTE:** This course was originally evaluated combined with MD7790, "Negotiating Collaboratively," in October 1991. MD7790 is now closed, but this course is still open.

Basic Telecommunications Principles and Networks for Engineering Services (TC6179)

Location: All AT&T training locations.

Length: 32 hours (4.5 days).

Dates: January 1993-Present.

Objective: To have the student learn about the concepts and major telecommunications product groups that support the domestic and overseas markets.

Learning Outcome: Upon successful completion of this course, the student will be able to understand the basic architecture of telecommunications networks, know and understand the telecommunications products, and understand the design process used to build local and long distance carrier networks.

Instruction: Major topics covered in the course are the major elements of the telecommunications environment, switching concepts, ESS stored program control, transmission principles, and the basics of analog digital systems, telephony, numbering plans, LATA and interLATA, communication channels, modulation and multiplexing, synchronization, Common Channel Signaling System 7, Switching, management systems, SONET/SDH, cellular and PCS, data and integrated services, protocols, LANs, MANs, and WANs.

Credit Recommendation: In the upper division baccalaureate degree category, 2 semester hours Telecommunications Principles (11/96).

Basic Training Development Skills Workshop (IE8101)

Location: Piscataway, NJ, and other AT&T locations.

Length: 35 hours (5 days).

Dates: *Version 1:* August 1979-May 1983; *Version 2:* May 1983-December 1986.

Objective: To introduce the new course developer to a systematic approach to the training development process and to provide "tools" to use in achieving course development goals.

Instruction: Major topics covered in the course are training requirements analysis; preparation of course objectives; test construction; learning strategies; development of course materials; use of audiovisual media; and course evaluation. Methods of instruction include lecture, discussion, and classroom exercises.

Credit Recommendation: *Version 1:* In the lower division baccalaureate/associate degree category, 2 semester hours in Education (2/80). *Version 2:* In the upper division baccalaureate degree category, 2 semester hours in Human Resources Management, Training and Development, or Education (7/85).

Benchmarking Workshop (CQ1016) (Formerly Seminar in Benchmarking [CQ1016])

Location: AT&T locations nationwide.

Length: 16 hours (2 days).
Dates: February 1991-Present.
Objective: To understand the benchmarking process, its underlying concepts, and how it can lead to superior performance; and apply benchmarking techniques to specific work situations.
Learning Outcome: Upon successful completion of this course, the student will be able to effectively benchmark a function within an organization; determine which companies to benchmark against based upon the needs of your organization; and assess competition and refocus business strategies and goals.
Instruction: Major topics covered in the course are a detailed step-by-step blueprint to benchmarking, which supplies concepts, cases, and job applications in critical areas of the benchmarking process; and students learn how to incorporate benchmarking into their strategic quality planning and quality improvement processes. Methods of instruction include lecture, discussion, and an appropriate graduate level project.
Credit Recommendation: In the graduate degree category, 1 semester hour in Strategic Quality Management (8/91) (5/96).

Bisync Protocol Analysis (DC7130) (IE7130)

Location: Piscataway, NJ, and other AT&T locations.
Length: 24 hours (4 days).
Dates: January 1976-June 1996.
Objective: To introduce the student to traffic characteristics across the line in a multipoint, leased-line, or polling-mode environment; the establishment and control of the communications link via Bisync framing characters; and the various commands, orders, and codes transmitted as message-text for screen formatting in support of transaction processing.
Instruction: Major topics covered in the course are interpretation of a variety of message types flowing across the link; identification of the processes under way between host and the remote station; identification of the external causes and effects of these messages in terms of screen appearance, user actions, and error recovery; identification of error situations and their probable causes; and the creation of control and text messages required to produce particular screens. Methods of instruction are lecture and discussion.
Credit Recommendation: In the upper division baccalaureate degree category, 1 semester hour in Data Communications or Operations, Data Processing, or Computer Science (7/85) (7/90).

Business Case: Advanced Decision Making and Risk Analysis (FE0450)

Location: AT&T locations throughout the United States.
Length: 40 hours (5 days).
Dates: July 1990-Present.
Objective: To teach managers the capability of preparing business cases for AT&T's most complex, high-risk ventures.
Learning Outcome: Upon successful completion of this course, students will be able to use a variety of issue-raising approaches to examine industry structure, customer value, and competitive position; determine the appropriate membership of the decision board, project team, and subject matter experts; use a variety of strategy-generation techniques to create a wide range of alternative strategies; use the influence diagram to structure uncertainty and talk at, rather than around, the real issues; build complex cash flow models using the AIM system; assess ranges of uncertainty and probability distributions on continuous and discrete variables, recognizing dependence where appropriate; use decision tree and influence diagram software to compute the probability distributions on NPV, the value of perfect and imperfect control; communicate business case results and recommendations; and develop functional support plans, milestones and responsibility assignments, and a tracking system.
Instruction: This course provides in-depth decision and risk analysis training and builds on the techniques learned in the prerequisite courses. Advanced business case techniques are applied to unique, complex, high-risk ventures. An appropriate graduate level project is required as part of the course for students to earn the credit recommendation.
Credit Recommendation: In the upper division baccalaureate degree category, or in the graduate degree category, 2 semester hours in Advanced Decision Making and Risk Analysis (12/90) (7/95).

Business Ethics: Making Tough Choices (MD7734) (Formerly [#BM0106])

Location: Somerset, NJ, and other AT&T regional facilities.
Length: 16 hours (2 days).
Dates: June 1990-December 1994.
Objective: To provide students an understanding of business ethics as an aspect of many business decisions and to provide students with an opportunity to use a structured approach to solving ethical dilemmas.
Learning Outcome: Upon successful completion of this course, students will be able to understand the value of business ethics and ethical reasoning techniques; be aware of the ethical dimension of thinking, reasoning, and decision making; and use a structured approach to ethical decision making.
Instruction: Major topics covered in the course are ethical aspects of business decisions, the psychology of ethical development, and the relationship of ethical reasoning to behavior. Each student will be asked to bring a decision that they are facing in their jobs to be used/analyzed in the course.
Credit Recommendation: In the graduate degree category, 1 semester hour in Business Ethics (12/90).

Business of Doing Business on the Internet (OL1200)

Location: All AT&T training locations.
Length: 16 hours (2 days).
Dates: January 1996-Present.
Objective: To provide a comprehensive examination of the on-line business environment to anyone with an interest in using the Internet and World Wide Web for business activities, and to provide a relevant background for anyone involved in the creative process, such as designers and publishers.
Learning Outcome: Upon successful completion of this course, the student will be able to assess the current and future impact that the Internet will have on business, create an Internet Business Plan that includes a cost benefit analysis of a planned Internet presence, and describe the potential and actual ways the Internet can be used in business.
Instruction: Major topics covered in the course are the Internet, the World Wide Web; Internet presence of key competitors, successful and unsuccessful ventures, identification of real opportunities, the economies of creating an on-line presence, and a step-by-step process for defining and developing a business on the Internet. Methods of instruction include lecture, discussion, hands-on Internet learning, hands-on group and individual activities on the Internet, case studies, and analysis of case examples on-line.
Credit Recommendation: In the upper division baccalaureate degree category, 1

semester hour in Business Development (11/96).

Business Planning (BM0103)

Location: Somerset, NJ, and other AT&T regional facilities.

Length: 16 hours (2 days).

Dates: May 1989-October 1994.

Objective: To help the participant develop/upgrade skills in the creative and systematic use of business concepts, analytic methods, and strategies for the planning design and evaluation of strategies and tactics for the organization.

Learning Outcome: Upon successful completion of this course, students will be able to improve skills in the use of business concepts; apply analytic methods and techniques; apply methods and concepts in design, development, and evaluation of strategic/tactical plans; and use step-by-step methodologies and approaches for preparing a plan at any level.

Instruction: Major topics covered in the course are a review of the four general dimensions of a planning module; a review of a number of analytical techniques useful in making sense out of the vast array of internal and external data to be considered; the opportunity to begin applying the planning techniques to a case study situation; the basics of writing a plan, i.e., plan content, format, resulting objective, and strategy development; and preparation of an executive summary for the attendant's business area of responsibility using the analytical tools, plan content, and format provided.

Credit Recommendation: In the upper division baccalaureate degree category, 1 semester hour in Business Planning (12/90).

Business Requirements Interviewing Techniques (IE 2537)

Location: Piscataway, NJ and other AT&T locations.

Length: 48 hours (5 days).

Dates: October 1992-June 1996.

Objective: To learn and apply skills and specific questioning methods required to collect fundamental business requirements in a single Universal Interview.

Learning Outcome: Upon successful completion of this course, the student will be able to apply three requirements "perspectives: to interview for relevant business facts"; use business topics to structure the interview and focus the client; assemble the basic communications constructs for effective requirements interviewing; translate analysis terms into keywords the client will understand; probe for all the business facts needed to construct each analysis diagram; and adopt the "single interview" concept for requirements collection to find all the fundamental business needs.

Instruction: Major topics covered in the course are a hands-on workshop focusing on the interviewing skills required to find all the fundamental business needs. Attendees practice ten levels of questioning in each category of requirements. Specific analysis questioning methods focus on the evidence needed to construct linkage diagrams, interface diagrams, and process hierarchies. The course culminates in a full Universal Interview. The different roles for a team interviewing approach are explained and practiced. Attendees prepare for, structure and conduct the session, to collect the full spectrum of client business needs.

Credit Recommendation: In the lower division baccalaureate/associate degree category, or in the upper division baccalaureate degree category, 3 semester hours in Interviewing Techniques (9/94).

Business Statistics Application (SA4085) (Formerly Analysis of Marketing Data for Management Decision Making [SA4085] and Quantitative Analysis of Marketing Data)

Location: Somerset, NJ.

Length: *Version 1:* 34 hours (4 days); *Version 2:* 28 hours (4 days).

Dates: *Version 1:* January 1980-May 1990; *Version 2:* June 1990-August 1996.

Objective: *Version 1:* To help managers prepare more meaningful reports, assist them in decision making, and heighten their understanding of statistical analysis. *Version 2:* To provide an overview of statistical techniques most often used in analyzing data.

Learning Outcome: Upon successful completion of this course, the student will be able to select appropriate techniques; interpret data; relate data to analysis; understand assumptions behind results; and understand and be able to use a statistical software package.

Instruction: *Version 1:* Major topics covered in the course are the application of appropriate statistical techniques. Methods of instruction include lectures, individual and group projects, problem solving, and criterion testing. *Version 2:* Major topics covered in the course are reviewing basic statistics, then continues to more advanced topics including hypothesis testing-used to test the truth of an assertion against sample data, which can be used to test for a difference between two sample means; regression analysis-used to detect and specify forms and strengths of relationships among variables; and analysis of variance-used to test for differences among three or more sample means. Methods of instruction include lectures by AT&T statisticians and group exercises using statistical software on a PC.

Credit Recommendation: *Version 1:* In the upper division baccalaureate degree category, 2 semester hours in Business Analysis, Marketing, Marketing Research, Quantitative Methods, or Statistics (9/80) (11/85). *Version 2:* In the upper division baccalaureate degree category, 2 semester hours in Analysis of Marketing Data (8/91).

Business Writing/Support Staff (MS6521)

Location: Somerset, NJ and other AT&T locations.

Length: 16 hours (2 days).

Dates: January 1987-June 1994.

Objective: To apply the principles of contemporary business writing to the writing of letters, memos, and reports.

Learning Outcome: Upon successful completion of this course, the student will be able to write and edit documents following contemporary writing principles; use appropriate style and grammar; and write for someone else's signature.

Instruction: Major topics covered in the course are examples from actual AT&T correspondence and documents; editing, rewriting, and composing documents following a style guide and a standard reference text; individually and in groups, critique various samples of business writing and apply basic principles of editing for correct spelling, appropriate usage and effective style.

Credit Recommendation: In the lower division baccalaureate/associate degree category, 1 semester hour in Business Communications (4/92).

Call Center Implementation and Management (ME9100)

Location: Locations worldwide.

Length: 16 hours (2 days).

Dates: November 1993-Present.

Objective: To evaluate and experience the techniques and strategies required in marketing strategy, advertising, promotions, call management, information systems, human resources and operations for designing and ongoing management of a call center.

Learning Outcome: Upon successful completion of this course, the student will be able to implement the seven components of effective call center management; analyze and assess typical problems and challenges faced in a call center environment; integrate call programs into the overall marketing strategy of the center; and design effective hiring, training, and professional development programs.

Instruction: Major topics covered in the course are experiments with new ways to qualify sales leads, increase and improve the productivity of the call center representatives and motivate the team for success; a variety of measurement and control systems will be presented to enable participants to ensure the profitability of their centers; effective techniques for hiring, recruiting and training staff.

Credit Recommendation: In the upper division baccalaureate degree category, 1 semester hour in Office Management/ Customer Service (7/95).

Capital Cost Methodology (AT&T 312 or PUB 301)

Location: Somerset Seminars Center, Somerset, NJ.

Length: 40 hours (1 week).

Dates: January 1982-September 1984.

Objective: To provide in-depth knowledge of methodologies and algorithms used in the calculations of the depreciation, post-tax income, and taxes associated with cost studies.

Instruction: This seminar equips managers with the in-depth knowledge required to explain calculations and algorithms of the CAPCOST 2 Model (a cost study tool used to determine capital costs attributable to specific project investments recognizing plant survivor characteristics, accelerated tax depreciation procedures, and investment credit); to understand and make necessary decisions regarding the appropriateness of the variable inputs to the Model (life curves, life tables, service life, etc.); and to understand and explain the various elements of the output data.

Credit Recommendation: In the upper division baccalaureate degree category, 3 semester hours, or in the graduate degree category, 2 semester hours in Finance, which is appropriate for degree programs in Finance, Public Administration, Management, Economics, or Business Administration (8/83).

Cash Flow Analysis I (AT&T 401A)

Location: Somerset Seminars Center, Somerset, NJ.

Length: 32 hours (4 days).

Dates: January 1984-May 1987.

Objective: To provide the participants with the skills to perform a valid cash flow analysis without the details of the calculations.

Instruction: The course provides participants with an understanding of the components of the financial decision environment. Cash flows, including representation and reduction to net cash flows, are calculation and interpretation of summary measures (net present value) presented. This course provides an overview of the Economic Impact and Study System (EISS) and trains participants to enter data and interpret output results.

Credit Recommendation: In the upper division baccalaureate degree category, 2 semester hours in Finance or Accounting applicable to Business Administration, Accounting, Finance, Management, or General Business degree programs (11/85). **NOTE:** If this course is followed by and combined with Cash Flow Analysis II (AT&T 401B), then the combined credit recommendation would be 3 semester hours in the above cited level and categories.

Coaching and Communicating with a Diverse Workforce (AA5600)

Location: All AT&T training locations.

Length: 16 hours (2 days).

Dates: October 1996-Present.

Objective: To focus on increasing the quality, productivity and sense of team required to thrive in today's diverse business world.

Learning Outcome: Upon successful completion of this course, the student will be able to understand self-assess awareness and diagnose self and others' values, attitudes and behavior regarding differences, develop strategies and skills for effective interpersonal communication in a diverse environment, understand issues and organizational impact to a diverse workforce, and develop coaching skills for communicating work assignments, giving feedback and resolving conflict effectively with all employees.

Instruction: Major topics covered in the course are the real issues faced when problem-solving and coaching and managing work in a diverse workplace. Methods of instruction include classroom discussion, lecture, simulation, case studies, and exercises.

Credit Recommendation: In the upper division baccalaureate degree category, 1 semester hour in Organizational Behavior or Human Resource Management (11/96).

Coaching Skills for Working with Others (MS6403)

Location: All AT&T training locations.

Length: 16 hours (2 days).

Dates: January 1996-Present.

Objective: To provide the student with the tools of coaching necessary to coach others in order to encourage each other's quest for growth and development.

Learning Outcome: Upon successful completion of this course, the student will be able to effectively use the five key skills of giving/receiving feedback, observing, listening, questioning, and resolving conflict, identify which coaching approach (counseling, mentoring, tutoring or confronting/challenging) is the most effective in the situation, and develop a plan to use when coaching others.

Instruction: Major topics covered in the course are what is coaching in a learning environment, what skills support the coaching function, various coaching approaches, and the coaching process. Methods of instruction include classroom discussion and role playing.

Credit Recommendation: In the upper division baccalaureate degree category, 1 semester hour in Organizational Behavior (11/96).

COBOL Workshop (IE3105)

Location: Piscataway, NJ, and other AT&T locations.

Length: 75 hours (10 days).

Dates: November 1983-December 1989.

Objective: To present advanced COBOL Coding, Report Writer, COBOL Sorts, and VSAM Access.

Instruction: Major topics covered in the course are providing VSAM files in COBOL; processing variable length records in COBOL; data representation and manipulation in COBOL; use of special registers in COBOL maintenance and enhancement of nonstructured COBOL programs; use of COBOL Report Writer features; and testing and debugging of COBOL modules and external and internal sorts. Methods of instruction include lecture and laboratory.

Credit Recommendation: In the lower division baccalaureate/associate degree category, 4 semester hours in Data Processing or Management Information Systems (7/85).

Collaborating Across Organizational Boundaries (MS6477)

Location: All AT&T training locations.

Length: 16 hours (2 days).

Dates: January 1996-Present.

Objective: To challenge the traditional practices and mindsets of managers while offering a new way or organizational cooperation.

Learning Outcome: Upon successful completion of this course, the student will be able to leverage the diverse talents between organizations, identify when a collaborative effort is and isn't appropriate, overcome divided loyalty across organizations, leverage conflict as a productive force across organizations, and share responsibility for the collaborative process.

Instruction: Major topics covered in the course are the skills of the Collaborative Success Model, thinking strategically, inspiring a shared purpose, and building partnerships. The course challenges the traditional practices and mindsets of managers and offers a new way of organizational cooperation. It uses the power of diversity through the confrontation of ideas and options-not for the sake of self-interests or getting along, but for the sake of seizing the business opportunity and satisfying the customer. Fifty percent of the program focuses on participant issues.

Credit Recommendation: In the upper division baccalaureate degree category, 1 semester hour in Organizational Behavior (11/96).

Communication Workshop (MS6410)

Location: Throughout the continental United States and global locations.

Length: 21 hours (3 days).

Dates: January 1990-Present.

Objective: To provide the principles upon which communications are based for the student to gain knowledge and insight to communicate more effectively.

Learning Outcome: Upon successful completion of this course, the student will be able to achieve more powerful results in communication situations; use the style option that best adapts to others' styles; apply key patterns of assertiveness behavior; resolve conflict situations constructively; listen actively; and clarify both verbal and nonverbal messages.

Instruction: This course is designed to improve the students' effectiveness by increasing their understanding of how their communication styles impact others' styles. It will help them develop assertiveness techniques they can use to identify and achieve their objectives as well as help them assess their conflict management skills. The course also focuses on sharpening the students' ability to listen actively to verbal messages, to interpret non verbal messages, and to clarify the intended meaning of both.

Credit Recommendation: In the upper division baccalaureate degree category, or in the lower division baccalaureate/associate degree category, 1 semester hour in Communications (12/90) (12/95).

Competitive Intelligence: Analyzing and Collecting Competitive Information (ME2022)

Location: Somerset, NJ and other AT&T locations.

Length: 21 hours (3 days).

Dates: March 1994-Present.

Objective: To have a better understanding of how to collect relevant information and effectively use it on your competitors.

Learning Outcome: Upon successful completion of this course, the student will be able to gather, analyze and integrate competitive information; apply a systematic framework for developing a competitor analysis; and better utilize the competitive information available within AT&T.

Instruction: This course provides an overview of competitor and competitive analysis, with an emphasis on those aspects of product development and marketing that are competitor driven. Students will explore how competitive information affects marketing and the product decision. They will learn how competitive analysis is done, who does it, and the role of a R&D professional. Methods of instruction include lectures and guided class discussions based on competitive analysis activities.

Credit Recommendation: In the upper division baccalaureate degree category, 2 semester hours in Competitive Intelligence (6/94).

Competitive Marketing Strategies

Location: Somerset Seminars, Somerset, NJ.

Length: 195 hours (3 days).

Dates: February 1984-December 1986.

Objective: To acquaint managers with the issues and problems in development of marketing strategies.

Instruction: Major topics covered in the course are competitive strategy under deregulation as well as segmenting deregulated markets. It contrasts the goals and objectives of regulatory bodies with those of the ultimate consumer, both business and residential. This course includes lectures, discussions, classroom exercises, simulations, problem solving, and case studies.

Credit Recommendation: In the upper division baccalaureate degree category, or in the graduate degree category, 1 semester hour in Marketing (11/85).

Competitive Pricing Strategy and Tactics (BUCP and SA6010) (Formerly Competitive Pricing Strategy and Planning [BUCP or SA6010])

Location: Somerset Seminars Center, Somerset, NJ.

Length: 32 hours (4 days).

Dates: January 1984-September 1992.

Objective: To provide current approaches and techniques for integrating competitive pricing and marketing strategies and improve pricing decision process skills.

Instruction: Course is designed to prepare participants to develop competitive marketing strategies including definition of a service, selection of the most appropriate strategies to exploit market opportunities, and pricing and distribution strategies. Competitive pricing will be stressed. Competitor analysis for pricing decision making and evaluation of pricing performance will be included. A computer simulation that integrates these marketing and pricing concepts will be used.

Credit Recommendation: In the graduate degree category, 2 semester hours in Marketing, Marketing Management, or Business Administration (11/85) (8/91).

Computer Communications System Architecture (IE7165)

Location: Piscataway, NJ, and other AT&T locations.

Length: 30 hours (5 days).

Dates: January 1976-December 1986.

Objective: To introduce the student to the major steps involved in defining communications needs, collecting relevant data, and examining alternative considerations in the selection of appropriate hardware, software, facilities, protocols, and switching methods.

Instruction: Major topics covered in the course are major areas of computer communications service categories; definition of major components of a computer communications network; differences between bit and character-oriented protocols; identification of traffic-dependent criteria; and the identification of elements in the design of a computer communications network. Methods of instruction include lecture and discussion.

Credit Recommendation: In the upper division baccalaureate degree category, 2 semester hours in Data Processing or Data Communications or Computer Science (7/85).

Computer Communications System Operations (IE7115)

Location: Piscataway, NJ, and other AT&T locations.

Length: 24 hours (4 days).

Dates: January 1976-March 1986.

Objective: To develop basic skills required to operate in the computer communications environment, which demands knowledge of the network configuration and functions, terminal user functions, and the ability to perform trouble analysis and fault isolation.

Instruction: Major topics covered in the course are description of various hardware, software, and facilities that make up a computer communications network; the major functions of the control center and the responsibilities of its personnel; tools used in performing network monitoring, network control, network analysis, and network diagnostics; and identification of discrete steps in a procedure used to resolve network trouble encountered by a terminal user. Methods of instruction include lecture and discussion.

Credit Recommendation: In the upper division baccalaureate degree category, 1 semester hour in Data Communications or Operations, Data Processing, or Computer Science (7/85).

COMTEN and the XNA Network (IE7135)

Location: Piscataway, NJ, and other AT&T locations.

Length: 16 hours (2 days).

Dates: January 1990-July 1992.

Objective: To introduce data communications personnel to COMTEX and the XNA Network.

Learning Outcome: Upon successful completion of this course, the student should be able to describe the functions of the COMTEN FEP; describe the functions of the XNA network, DSP, NCP, and SRM; explain the use of the COMTEN commands; explain the operation of the COMTEN; and explain network generations and their design.

Instruction: Major topics covered in this instructor-led course provide the student with an explanation of what the COMTEN Front End Processor (FEP) does and its operation; explains the XNA Network; and a description of EP, COS, NCP, SRM, CSN, MAF, and DSP.

Credit Recommendation: In the lower division baccalaureate/associate degree category, 1 semester hour in Data Communications (7/90). **NOTE:** Students who have taken IE7125 (Terminals and Line Protocol) will receive no credit for this course because of content duplication.

Concepts in Industrial Marketing (ME 0891)

Location: Somerset, NJ, and other AT&T locations throughout the country.

Length: 40 hours (5 days).

Dates: January 1986-December 1991.

Objective: To acquaint marketing managers with selected key concepts in industrial marketing.

Learning Outcome: Upon successful completion of this course, the manager will be able to describe the concept of organizational buying and use this concept as a marketing strategy; define product marketing, including product life cycle, product cannibalism, and economic value to the customer, explain the nature of industrial pricing and perform a pricing analysis; describe how and why industrial markets are segmented and assess various market segmentation alternatives; and apply the appropriate tools and techniques to develop strategies for AT&T.

Instruction: This course applies marketing principles to industrial, real-world case situations. It emphasizes sales techniques, market segmentation, organization buyer behavior, and pricing.

Credit Recommendation: In the upper division baccalaureate degree category, 3 semester hours in Industrial Marketing Applications (11/86) (8/91).

Concepts of Capital Costs (CAP-COST)

Location: Somerset Seminars Center, NJ.

Length: 35 hours (1 week).

Dates: January 1981-December 1984.

Objective: To provide the detailed tax and accounting methods used in the CAP-COST 2 Model and the development of the components of a capital cost (depreciation, post-tax income, and income tax expense) as implemented in the CAP-COST 2 Model and to provide a thorough analysis of the calculations performed by the CAPCOST 2 Model.

Instruction: Major topics covered in the course are the concepts of capital costs, accelerated depreciation, book basis versus tax basis of investment, investment tax credit, and present worth levelized costs are addressed in general terms. The seminar also provides through casework hands-on experience in such areas as procedures for modeling the survivor characteristics of plant investment, ACRS depreciation with salvage and cost of removal, and use of the CAPCOST 2 Model. The seminar concludes with an extensive casework using the CAPCOST 2 Model. Methods of instruction include lecture, audiovisuals, discussion, casework, and use of time-share computer.

Credit Recommendation: In the upper division baccalaureate degree category, 2 semester hours in Business Administration, Public Administration, or Finance and Engineering Economics (12/81).

Concepts of Promotional Strategy (ME0899)

Location: Somerset, NJ, and other AT&T locations throughout the country.

Length: 16 hours (2 days).

Dates: December 1986-December 1992.

Objective: To introduce AT&T participants to various promotional concepts and how these concepts can be integrated into an effective promotional strategy.

Learning Outcome: Upon successful completion of this course, the student will be able to define the promotional components: advertising, sales promotion, public relations, and personal selling; illustrate the interaction between segmentation, differentiation and positioning; illustrate the campaign; provide an overview of the creative and tactical strategies used in promotion; and demonstrate techniques employed to assess promotional effectiveness.

Instruction: This course is designed for AT&T employees who interface with customers or design marketing strategies. Various promotional concepts are studied and students are given an opportunity to integrate appropriate concepts into effective promotional strategy. After the two days of class, the students must individually write a complete promotional plan and submit this for review and grading by the instructor.

Credit Recommendation: In the graduate degree category, 2 semester hours or in the upper division baccalaureate degree category, 3 semester hours in Marketing

Communications, or Sales Promotion and Advertising Concepts of Effective Promotion or Advertising Principles (11/86) (8/91). *Prerequisites*: Successful completion of at least one college or graduate level marketing course. Also, students must read "Guide to Marketing, Media and Production" by Ann Grossman prior to attending course.

Concepts of the Integrated Systems Provisioning Process (IE2000) (Formerly Concepts of Total System Development [IE2000])

Location: Piscataway, NJ, and other AT&T locations.

Length: *Version 1:* 18 hours (3 days); *Version 2:* 12 hours (2 days).

Dates: *Version 1:* January 1979-December 1989; *Version 2:* January 1990-June 1996.

Objective: To cover the phases and activities required for information systems development projects and to provide an overview of the total system development methodology.

Learning Outcome: Upon successful completion of this course, the student will be able to identify the steps and characteristics of the total system development (TSD) process; define a system and list system characteristics; indicate the phase in which the major activities take place in the TSD process; identify subactivities and characteristics that occur during each phase of the TSD process; list the make-up of the system development project team and identify the roles of the team members; identify and list the areas in which documentation is essential in a system development effort; identify and indicate the functions of project management; and identify and list the methods for estimating resources required for a system development effort.

Instruction: Major topics covered in the course are the steps and characteristics of the total system development (TSD) process, the make-up of the system development project team and the roles of the team members, the areas in which documentation is essential in a system development effort, the functions of project management, and the methods for estimating resources required for a system development effort.

Credit Recommendation: In the lower division baccalaureate/associate degree category, 1 semester hour in Computer Information Systems, Business Administration, or Information Science (7/85) (7/90).

Consumer Marketing (SA4100) (Formerly Applied Consumer Behavior)

Location: Somerset, NJ. and other AT&T locations worldwide.

Length: 21 hours (3 days).

Dates: January 1985-August 1996.

Objective: To provide an understanding of the basic concepts of consumer marketing and how they apply to the AT&T residence marketplace. To enumerate ways in which the consumer market can be segmented. To identify the synergies among environmental influences, market research and segmentation, demographics, psychological dimensions, and social and cultural factors in understanding the consumer marketplace. To distinguish among the various elements of the marketing mix and how they affect the analysis, development, and implementation of marketing strategies, plans, and programs in the residence market.

Instruction: Major topics covered in the course are an understanding of consumer marketing and the application of the concepts and practices to the AT&T residence market; an introduction to marketing in a competitive environment, focusing on the consumer; analyzing the residence marketplace; and developing and implementing marketing plans and programs. Methods of instruction include lectures, group participation, and case analysis.

Credit Recommendation: In the upper division baccalaureate degree category, 1 semester hour in Marketing (11/85) (8/91).

Consumer Marketing Strategies (ME 0894)

Location: Somerset, NJ, and other AT&T locations throughout the country.

Length: 24 hours (3 days).

Dates: July 1986-December 1989.

Objective: To introduce managers to selected aspects of consumer marketing.

Learning Outcome: Upon successful completion of this course, the manager will be able to recognize and be effective in working with the marketing environment; consumer buyer behavior; advertising and promotion decisions; and product management.

Instruction: Major topics covered in the course are the planning, development and execution of a marketing program directed at consumer markets.

Credit Recommendation: In the upper division baccalaureate degree category, 2 semester hours in Consumer Marketing Management (11/86).

Contemporary Accounting and Financial Concepts (FE0200)

Location: Somerset, NJ, and other AT&T regional facilities.

Length: 16 hours (2 days).

Dates: March 1987-December 1995.

Objective: To provide managers with an understanding of contemporary accounting and financial concepts as applied to the AT&T accounting framework and its related reports and functions.

Learning Outcome: Upon successful completion of this course, students will be able to explain the different uses and users of financial information; name and explain the Generally Accepted Accounting Principles (GAAP); describe the importance of each GAAP; describe the difference between cash and accrual accounting and decide which terms belong to each system; recount the six-step accounting system; name the elements of a balance sheet, income statement, and statement of changes in financial position; use T-accounts; calculate and apply financial ratios, particularly with reference to the AT&T Financial Report; and describe financial flexibility, using degrees of operating and financial leverage.

Instruction: This course enables managers to understand AT&T financial statements, Generally Accepted Accounting Principles, financial information flows, differences between cash and accrual accounting, and operating and financial leverage. AT&T financial reports and a sample company are used to illustrate contemporary accounting and financial concepts.

Credit Recommendation: In the upper division baccalaureate degree category, 1 semester hour in Accounting (12/90).

Cost Analysis and Cost Reduction (FE0104)

Location: Pleasanton, California and other AT&T locations.

Length: 16 hours (2 days).

Dates: April 1992-December 1992.

Objective: To teach students to effectively reduce expenses in their operations while simultaneously increasing customer satisfaction and employee involvement.

Learning Outcome: Upon successful completion of this course, the student will be able to identify the activities that do not add value to the customer and begin to eliminate or reduce these activities; and apply several cost reduction strategies to their operations that will enhance efficiency and effectiveness.

Instruction: Major topics covered in the course are a series of strategies and tips to successfully reduce expenses, e.g. mapping the workflow, value analysis, benchmarking, group problem solving, and the cost of poor quality; and framework by which students can systematically reduce expenses and apply those strategies that are best suited to the student's particular situation.

Credit Recommendation: In the upper division baccalaureate degree category, 2 semester hours in Financial Analysis and Control (4/92).

Cost Analysis for Marketing Studies (AT&T 202 and SA2010) (Formerly Fundamentals of Costing for Pricing Decisions [AT&T 202])

Location: Somerset Seminars Center, Somerset, NJ.

Length: 32 hours (4 days).

Dates: January 1984-November 1990.

Objective: To provide an awareness and knowledge of the fundamentals of cost and rate functions.

Instruction: This seminar is designed to describe and discuss conceptually the service management approach. It gives an overview of the role of the Federal Communications and State Commissions in pricing decisions. The seminar describes the questions that an incremental analysis, cash flow analysis, and a fully distributed cost study will answer. The seminar also describes the microeconomics concepts used in service costs work including price demand curve, marginal revenue, marginal costs, elasticity of demand, and cross elastic effects. Participants will identify and compute the components of investment costs and capital-related costs, and operating expenses. The course describes and defines the purpose of the cost model in regard to translators, unit investments, and annual cost factors.

Credit Recommendation: In the upper division baccalaureate degree category, 3 semester hours in Economics, Finance, Management, or Business Administration (11/85).

Cost of Quality (CQ1008) (Quality Control Techniques I)

Location: AT&T locations nationwide.

Length: 8 hours.

Dates: October 1990-December 1994.

Objective: To assist students in understanding data analysis as it relates to quality costs in ongoing processes.

Learning Outcome: Upon successful completion of this course, the student will be able to use Cost of Quality techniques within the context on ongoing process management; define Cost of Quality and describe the Cost of Quality identification process; and identify Cost of Quality workplan, conduct data collection, and analyze Cost of Quality data.

Instruction: Major topics covered in the course are a hands-on application of the AT&T Cost of Quality (COQ) Guidelines; learn COQ concepts, identify, analyze, and use data to learn how to reduce process costs; gain in-depth knowledge of the Cost of Quality Guidelines and long term cost reductions when implementing Quality initiatives.

Credit Recommendation: In the upper division baccalaureate degree category, 1 semester hour in Quality Control Techniques I (8/91). **NOTE:** The credit recommendation applies only to those students who successfully complete an Implementation project or plan to be assessed by the instructor.

Creating Business Value: Workshop on EVA, CVA and PVA (FE2020)

Location: Somerset, NJ and other AT&T locations.

Length: 16 hours (2 days).

Dates: September 1993-Present.

Objective: To teach managers techniques to create and/or improve value in three key business dimensions — customers, people and shareholders.

Learning Outcome: Upon successful completion of this course, the student will be able to choose actions, behaviors and decisions that best satisfy customers, employees and shareholders — short-term and long-term; promote innovation and develop win-win supplier relationship; and implement a business impact plan to initiate a process of continuous value creation in various aspects of your job.

Instruction: This workshop examines specific techniques one can use to create or improve value in three key business dimensions - customers, people and shareholders - and connect value concepts and measures such as Economic Value Added (EVA) with specific actions, behaviors, and decisions to improve or create value in the job.

Credit Recommendation: In the upper division baccalaureate degree category, 1 semester hour in Business Value Concepts (6/94).

Cross-Cultural Effectiveness (GM1075) (Formerly Intercultural Training Seminar)

Location: Somerset, NJ and other AT&T locations.

Length: 16 hours (2 days).

Dates: *Version 1:* January 1989-September 1992; *Version 2:* October 1992-Present.

Objective: To make the student aware of how cross-cultural factors impact his/her effectiveness and success when working with people from other cultures.

Learning Outcome: *Version 1:* Upon successful completion of this course, the student will be able to identify the role that cultural factors play in interpersonal interaction; identify how cultural differences impact on performance; identify the traits and skills necessary for success overseas; identify American values, assumptions and stereotypes and contrast these with those of other cultures; recognize potential intercultural adjustment problems and identify three steps for reducing the stress and anxiety associated with working in a new culture; *Version 2:* Upon successful completion of this course, the student will be able to identify the cultural factors which facilitate or inhibit interaction; and identify specific situations where misunderstandings are likely to occur and develop a strategy to prevent these misunderstandings.

Instruction: *Version 1:* This course combines a variety of learning strategies to facilitate instruction. It includes simulations, video tapes, self assessments, lecturettes, group discussions, and workshops using the very latest cross-cultural research and training techniques to enable the participants to develop strategies for success when working with people from other cultures. *Version 2:* This course is designed for those who require an intensive examination of the impact of cross-cultural factors on their effectiveness and success when working with people from other cultures. It includes globalization, cultural values, language insights, critical incidents, four dimensions of national cultures. Methods of instruction include case study, group role plays, lecture and discussion.

Credit Recommendation: *Version 1:* In the upper division baccalaureate category, 1 semester hour in Intercultural Education or Business Elective (8/91). **NOTE:** Students complete a major project on intercultural issues. *Version 2:* In the graduate degree category, 1 semester hour in International Business (12/93).

Customer Service Calling Skills (ME9020)

Location: Locations worldwide.

Length: 8 hours (1 day).

Dates: March 1994-Present.

Objective: To provide participants with the tools and techniques to enable them to gain a competitive advantage in the marketplace, elevating their companies to world class status as they differentiate themselves by delivering quality customer service.

Learning Outcome: Upon successful completion of this course, the student will be able to create a win-win partnership with customers; delight customers by anticipating their needs; soothe irate customers with specific proven techniques; and build rapport and create goodwill for future sales.

Instruction: Major topics covered in this course are how to communicate effectively with their customers, becoming service leaders who are capable of handling diverse and demanding customers and situations with poise and confidence. Agents will become CEO's of customer care after attending this course. They will gain practice with techniques to delight their customers and build relationships.

Credit Recommendation: In the upper division baccalaureate degree category, 1 semester hour in Sales (7/95). **Note:** Student must also complete ME9010 to earn the credit recommendation.

Data Analysis and Logical Data Structuring (IE2530)

Location: Piscataway, NJ, and other AT&T locations.

Length: 30 hours (5 days).

Dates: May 1984-December 1993.

Objective: To provide systems analysts with the basic skills and knowledge needed to perform a feasibility data analysis.

Learning Outcome: Upon successful completion of this course, participants will be able to explain the purpose of logical data analysis; determine the difference between a data base and traditional files; construct a complete and accurate relational view of sample data using "top-down" analysis techniques; verify that a data structure is normalized by using "bottom-up" normalization techniques; develop a complete and accurate usage view of sample data; and compare the relational and usage views to verify the accuracy and completeness of the logical data structure.

Instruction: Major topics covered in the course are a "top-down" approach (entity analysis) to construct and document the "relational" and "usage" views of sample data and how to use normalization procedures to clarify and verify a logical data structure.

Credit Recommendation: In the upper division baccalaureate degree category, 2 semester hours in Computer Science or Computer Information Systems (7/85) (7/90). **NOTE:** Students who already received credit for Logical Data Structuring should receive only 1 semester hour of credit for this course.

Data Analysis and Regression (AT&T 313)

Location: Somerset Seminars Center, Somerset, NJ.

Length: 80 hours (2 weeks).

Dates: January 1982-December 1983.

Objective: This seminar provides participants with the skills to apply a variety of data-analytic and regression techniques for modeling and forecasting situations to interpret the statistical and computational output of a variety of regression techniques with particular emphasis on robust and resistant methods; to use effectively computer-generated graphics in data display, model building, and management presentations; to recognize an appropriate modeling strategy to arrive at practical regression models at reasonable costs; to use effectively statistical computing software for data analysis and regression in an interactive mode; and to prepare, present, and document modeling results for both technical and higher management audiences.

Credit Recommendation: In the graduate degree category, 3 semester hours in Data Analysis and Regression (8/83).

Data Display Tools Workshop (MQ1002)

Location: Somerset, NJ and other AT&T locations.

Length: 16 hours (2 days).

Dates: November 1991-October 1992.

Objective: To understand and effectively use a set of nine advanced data display tools and methodologies.

Learning Outcome: Upon successful completion of this course the student will be able to understand the strengths and weaknesses of the nine advanced tools in data information display formats; and effectively choose the appropriate tool to manipulate data and information for display (report) purposes to obtain a decisive outcome.

Instruction: Major topics covered in the course are benefits and pitfalls of nine data and information display tools; Pareto diagrams, histograms, control charts, problem selection matrices, and solution selection matrices; strengths and weaknesses of data display tools; which tool to use to process data to an informative outcome; and team leadership. **NOTE:** A graduate level project is required to complete this course.

Credit Recommendation: In the graduate degree category, 1 semester hour in Data Analysis (4/92).

Data Gathering for System Development (IE2510)

Location: Piscataway, NJ, and other AT&T locations.

Length: 24 hours (4 days).

Dates: October 1983-September 1992.

Objective: To cover data gathering plans, interviewing techniques, questionnaire design, content analysis, observation, and paperwork flow.

Learning Outcome: Upon successful completion of this course, the student should be able to plan and organize a data collection project; discuss the advantages and disadvantages of the five major data collection techniques; and plan, conduct, and record an interview.

Instruction: Methods of instruction include lectures, discussions, students practice data gathering techniques in group exercises, and role plays.

Credit Recommendation: In the upper division baccalaureate degree category, 1 semester hour in Business Administration, Computer Science, or Computer Information Systems (7/85) (7/90).

Data Gathering Methods: Overview (HP3405)

Location: All AT&T training locations.

Length: 24 hours (3 days).

Dates: October 1996-Present.

Objective: To teach participants how to collect useful information which may be used for a variety of purposes.

Learning Outcome: Upon successful completion of this course, the student will be able to plan the data gathering effort, know how to sample the population, understand the different methods:observation, interviews, questionnaires, understand data analysis:quantitative and qualitative, and prepare graphic and tabular reporting.

Instruction: Major topics covered in the course are the methods of collecting useful information, voice of the customer data to determine quality attributes, customer requirements, benchmarking information, customer satisfaction and employee satisfaction data, a systematic process for data collection, and specific data collection methods including questionnaires, interviews (face-to-face, telephone, and focus group), and observation. Methods of instruction include discussion and review.

Credit Recommendation: In the upper division baccalaureate degree category, 2 semester hours in Research Methods (11/96).

Data Gathering, System Analysis, and Design

Location: AT&T Training Center, South Plainfield, NJ; and various operating company training centers.

Length: 26 hours (4 days).

Dates: October 1980-December 1983.

Objective: To enable the student to use four major gathering techniques to analyze and design a business system, use data flow diagrams to graphically depict a customer business system, construct decision trees and tables, correctly define data structures and elements, and explain the purpose and function of a data dictionary.

Instruction: Students are introduced to the top-down approach to systems analysis and design. The key point that students should understand is that systems analysis and design is not a straight-line process. Rather, it requires multiple iterations. Data collection plans and techniques are discussed in detail and students complete exercises requiring the use of interviews, content analysis, and questionnaires to acquire information to be used in system design. Several tools for analysis and design are discussed: flowcharting, DFDs, and HIPO. Data Flow Diagramming is covered in detail and students are asked to complete a high-level DFD for a customer system and a structured walkthrough. Additional symbols and conventions for lower-level DFDs are covered next, and students complete another exercise in charting and presenting a lower-level DFD. Data base concepts addressed are nest-data element, data structures, common files, etc. Process logic is also reviewed, and students are asked to complete exercises in constructing decision trees, decision tables, and writing logic in structured English.

Credit Recommendation: In the lower division baccalaureate/associate degree category, 1 semester hour in Systems Analysis (7/81).

Data Requirements Analysis & Modeling (IE2533)

Location: Piscataway, NJ and other AT&T locations.

Length: 32 hours (5 days).

Dates: June 1993-Present.

Objective: To learn and apply the principles and concepts needed to formulate an entity-relationship model for a business; gain a full set of practical skills in all aspects of entity modeling.

Learning Outcome: Upon successful completion of this course, the student will be able to appreciate the purpose and the work involved in each state of the business system life cycle; explain the difference between requirements analysis, the different types of analysis activities involved and the relationships between these activities; identify valid entity types and relationship diagram (ERD), and make appropriate adjustments to improve the data model; understand the principles of normalization and the subsequent impact on the formation of entity types and the assignment of data elements to the entity types; assign data elements to the correct entity type based on the principles of normalization; explain the purpose and need for logical access path diagrams; and create basic logical access path diagrams for given business functions.

Instruction: This course goes beyond the theory and teaches the practical application of entity modeling. Self-assessment skills are developed for entity modeling (data requirements) products.

A full set of practical skills in all aspects of entity modeling is gained. What an entity model illustrates about a business is explored.

The methodology taught in this course is a top-down, business resource-driven approach. Students discover how to find the business's most vital objects that are the basis of object-oriented design, and develop the key skills and foundations that leverage organizational investment in CASE tools.

Credit Recommendation: In the upper division baccalaureate degree category, or in the lower division baccalaureate/associate degree category, 2 semester hours in Organizational Analysis (9/94).

Data Security and Controls

Location: Data Systems Education Center, Piscataway, NJ, and other Bell locations.

Length: 31 hours (1 week).

Dates: April 1979-December 1984.

Objective: To familiarize the student with the need for data security and the basic methods used to provide good security.

Instruction: Major topics covered in the course are the need for systems security development, design of countermeasures to meet documented security requirements, and continued security maintenance of a data system. Methods of instruction include lecture and laboratory.

Credit Recommendation: In the upper division baccalaureate degree category, 2 semester hours in Computer Science or Data Processing (2/80).

DB2 Application Programmers (IE3604)

Location: All AT&T training locations.

Length: *Version 1:* 30 hours; *Version 2:* 32.5 hours (5 days).

Dates: July 1988-June 1996.

Objective: To prepare application programmers to produce DB2 applications.

Learning Outcome: Upon successful completion of this course, the student will be able to code SQL statements to modify a DB2 database and extract information from it, compile and execute programs that access DB2 databases, use DB2 built-in functions, discuss concepts of data security and data integrity as they relate to DB2 databases, and discuss concepts of performance and efficiency as they relate to DB2 requests.

Instruction: Major topics covered in the course are how to implement programs interacting with DB2 Relational Databases in an MVS/ESA environment; COBOL and PL/1 considerations for all DB2 environments (TSO/ISPF with Dialog Manager, CICS/VS and IMS/VS); and programming techniques including database loading, retrieval, and updating.

Credit Recommendation: *Version 1:* In the upper division baccalaureate degree category, 2 semester hours in DB2 Applications or Computer Science (7/90). *Version 2:* In the upper division baccalaureate degree category, 1 semester hour in DB2 Applications or Computer Science (11/96).

Decision and Risk Analysis (SE9000)

Location: Somerset Seminars Center, Somerset, NJ.

Length: 21 hours (3 days).

Dates: May 1985-October 1987.

Objective: To provide students with a set of concepts and techniques that furnish the logic for decision making in the face of uncertainty.

Instruction: Course examines the role of risk and uncertainty in the managerial decision-making process. Lecture, discussion, and demonstrations are used.

Credit Recommendation: In the upper division baccalaureate degree category, or in the graduate degree category, 1 semester hour in Decision and Risk Analysis (11/85).

Demand Analysis Techniques (PUB 302)

Location: Somerset Seminars Center, Somerset, NJ.

Length: 80 hours (10 days).

Dates: January 1979-December 1984.

Objective: To provide a foundation in practical applications of regression analyses and econometric modeling to estimate and forecast demand and revenues for telecommunications products and services.

Instruction: Course translates microeconomic theory into empirical demand models for telecommunication needs. It teaches participants to define and select appropriate dependent and independent variables when specifying a demand model. Course also offers an understanding of major data sources, collection and validity problems with those sources, and identifies potential solutions to these problems.

Credit Recommendation: In the graduate degree category, 5 semester hours in Business Administration, Economics, Industrial Engineering, Operations Research, Public Administration, Systems Analysis, or Econometrics (9/83).

Demand Analysis Techniques Seminar (DATS)

Location: Bell System Tariffs and Costs Seminars, Somerset, NJ.

Length: 85 hours (2 weeks).

Dates: January 1979-December 1984.

Objective: To provide the participant with a foundation in the practical applications of regression analysis and econometric modeling to estimate and forecast demand and revenues for telephone products and services. Particular emphasis is given to quantifying the individual factors that affect demand, e.g., elasticity estimation.

Instruction: This seminar will enable the participant to translate microeconomic theory into empirical demand models for telecommunication needs and to define and select appropriate dependent and independent variables when specifying a demand model. It will provide an understanding of major data sources, collection and validity problems with those sources, and potential solutions to those problems. In general, the seminar will allow the participant to understand and experience the various aspects of demand analysis, ranging from model specifications to model building, and documentation. Lectures, audiovisuals, individual and group tasks, and guest speakers are used.

Credit Recommendation: In the graduate degree category, 5 semester hours in Business Administration, Economics, Industrial Engineering, Operations Research, or Systems Analysis (2/81). *Prerequisite*: Background in regression analysis, calculus, and economics.

Developing and Implementing Successful Product Strategies (ME2018) (Formerly Product Management Strategy [ME2018])

Location: Somerset, NJ. and other AT&T locations.

Length: 24 hours plus lab.

Dates: September 1990-August 1996.

Objective: To improve the effectiveness of AT&T Managers by imparting to them an awareness and understanding of industry structure, competitive strategy, and product positioning.

Learning Outcome: Upon successful completion of this course, the student will be able to anticipate the competitors' moves and counter moves; apply competitive analysis techniques to their ongoing decision making process; and apply competitive frameworks to improve the competitive position.

Instruction: Major topics covered in the course are an understanding of the principles of competitive strategy; applying competitive strategy concepts to own business; industry analysis, competitive positioning, value chain analysis and marketing segmentation.

Credit Recommendation: In the graduate degree category, 1 semester hour in Competitive Strategies (8/91).

Direct Mail Marketing in Business Markets (ME 0897) (Formerly Business/Consumer Direct Marketing Applications)

Location: Somerset, NJ, and other AT&T locations throughout the country.

Length: 16 hours (2 days).

Dates: September 1986-December 1994.

Objective: To introduce managers to direct marketing applications.

Learning Outcome: Upon successful completion of this course, the manager will be familiar with business-to-business megatrends and direct marketing fundamentals; why direct mail is a unique marketing medium; the mathematics used by direct marketers; and business lists and market segmentation.

Instruction: Major topics covered in the course are direct marketing techniques aimed at the business consumer and international markets. Topics include direct marketing as a cost-effective delivery channel and state-of-the-art techniques and applications.

Credit Recommendation: In the upper division baccalaureate degree category, 1 semester hour in Business/Consumer Direct Marketing Applications (11/86) (8/91).

Direct Marketing for Consumer Markets (SA4110) (Formerly Direct Marketing)

Location: Somerset Seminars Center, Somerset, NJ.

Length: 17 hours (3 days).

Dates: June 1985-December 1994.

Objective: To provide managers with an overview of the fundamentals of direct marketing.

Instruction: This course is designed to provide managers with an overview of the field of direct marketing with special emphasis on telemarketing. This course includes lectures, discussion, classroom exercises, simulation, problem solving, and case studies.

Credit Recommendation: In the upper division baccalaureate degree category, 1 semester hour in Direct Marketing or Business elective (11/85) (8/91).

Doing Business in Developing Countries (GM1025)

Location: Somerset, NJ and other AT&T locations.

Length: 24 hours (3 days).

Dates: November 1992-December 1994.

Objective: To teach students to operate within the decision making framework that guides purchasing decisions when governments and "undefined forces" dictate business practices.

Learning Outcome: Upon successful completion of this course, the student will be able to analyze and positively impact corporate results; understand differences in financial policies; apply basic financial concepts, such as risk, reward, and the time value of money; and understand capital markets and implications of bond and stock financing.

Instruction: Major topics covered in the course are designed for students with job responsibilities for planning, selling, or managing throughout the developing world. It instructs students on developing strategies and sales plans. Methods of instruction include lectures, discussions, case studies, and exercises. Appropriate graduate level research project is submitted as part of the course requirements.

Credit Recommendation: In the graduate degree category, 2 semester hours in International Business (12/93).

Doing Business In (Specific Country) (GM1073) *(Formerly Doing Business in (Specific Country) [GM1075])*

Location: Somerset, NJ and other AT&T locations.

Length: 14 hours (2 days).

Dates: May 1991-April 1997.

Objective: To enable students to feel more comfortable with cultural differences and to work and interact more effectively with the people of a specific country.

Learning Outcome: Upon successful completion of this course, the student will be able to understand key concepts of cultural behavior and the role of culture in shaping perceptions, thoughts, and behavior; explore aspects of doing business with a specific country such as protocol, presentations, expectations at meetings, management styles, decision making, work attitudes and motivation, skill transfer, boss-subordinate relations, role of business women, business entertaining and executive gift-giving; learn verbal and nonverbal communication skills for more effective communications and negotiations; identify critical points on the job where misunderstandings could occur using a problem solving model, and discuss strategies and tactics for handling these situations more effectively; gain a better understanding of the people, country, and customs, as well as an understanding of the underlying political issues; and learn a few important language phrases.

Instruction: Major topics covered in the course are a need to understand, communicate, and interface successfully with their counterparts in a targeted country; training focuses on cultural differences and how these impact work effectiveness; and a research paper on the country studied in order to complete the course.

Credit Recommendation: In the lower division baccalaureate/associate degree category, 1 semester hour in Socio-cultural Aspects of Business (4/92).

Dynamic Tools Workshop (MQ1001)

Location: Somerset, NJ and other AT&T locations.

Length: 16 hours (2 days).

Dates: November 1991-October 1992.

Objective: To understand and effectively use a set of nine advanced group dynamic tools to lead groups to a desired outcome and understand group interactions.

Learning Outcome: Upon successful completion of this course, the student will be able to understand the strengths and weaknesses of nine advanced group dynamic tools; and effectively choose the appropriate tool and use it to lead a group to a desired outcome.

Instruction: Major topics covered in the course are a highly interactive workshop where participation is required; learn strengths, weaknesses and effective use of nine different group dynamic tools, such as Nominal Group Technique, Block diagram, Force Field Analysis, Customer Needs Analysis, and many more; gain confidence in facilitating these tools in teams; and a graduate level project is required to complete this course. This is a first in a triad of workshops leading to a Certificate of Mastery in Process Management and Improvement.

Credit Recommendation: In the graduate degree category, 1 semester hour in Techniques for Quality Improvement (4/92).

Economics for Pricing Network Services (PUB 102)

Location: Somerset Seminars Center, Somerset, NJ.

Length: 24 hours (3 days).

Dates: January 1984-December 1984.

Objective: To provide economic perspectives for understanding the foundation of pricing and costing decisions for intrastate intraLATA services.

Instruction: This course presents a basic introduction to microeconomics with examples drawn from and related to the telecommunications field. In this course market mechanisms, market analysis, and cost analysis are discussed. A session on pricing strategies used by the different regions on specific lines of business will also be presented. Course uses a high degree of lecture and instructor/student interaction to achieve its objectives.

Credit Recommendation: In the lower division baccalaureate/associate degree category, or in the upper division baccalaureate degree category, 1 semester hour in Applied Economics, Pricing Strategies, or Business Administration (11/85).

Emerging Leaders Program

Location: AT&T Corporate Education Center, Hopewell, NJ.

Length: 40 hours.

Dates: June 1989-December 1991.

Objective: To increase the ability of lower level managers to assume middle management responsibilities.

Learning Outcome: Upon successful completion of this course, the student will be able to assess the strategic context through the SBU (strategic business unit) process; understand and take risk from the position of a middle manager; innovate and be creative from inside the organization; improve leadership and interpersonal effectiveness; and create organizational ownership and high performance implementation.

Instruction: Major topics covered in the course are managing from the middle management level; strategy implementation within the SBU (strategic business unit) context; an examination of leadership styles, effectiveness, and change; and innovation and new product development. Methods of instruction include lecture, discussion, led by distinguished practitioners and academicians. Students seeking the credit recommendation for this course have completed management coursework, in addition to their management experience, prior to beginning this course. In addition these students submit a graduate level research paper on a specific topic, integrating the subject areas covered in this course, and including a bibliography with relevant material from academic journals.

Credit Recommendation: In the graduate degree category, 3 semester hours in Intrapreneurial Management or Management elective (9/89).

Ensuring Business Results: How to Read and Monitor the Vital Signs of Your Business (RB1014)

Location: Somerset, NJ and other AT&T locations.

Length: 24 hours (3 days), plus extensive guided, independent study.

Dates: April 1992-April 1997.

Objective: To teach students a systematic approach for identifying, quantifying and monitoring the vital signs that project their business' health.

Learning Outcome: Upon successful completion of this course, the student will be able to develop an integrated set of measures for Strategic Global Intent, Near-Term Intent, and day-to-day vital signs that indicate business direction; identify characteristics and criteria for developing vital signs and other key business measures; determine methods and techniques for collecting and reporting measures and results of near and long-term performance data; create visual displays, data collection responsibilities, and communication networks for reporting data-based business results; and analyze results and develop action and contingency plans for making key business decisions based on the data.

Instruction: Major topics covered in the course are a series of four integrated workshops designed to give students the tools they need to successfully run their jobs as a business; the workshops are a set of hands-on, market-focused clinics, not simply training classes, where students acquire and sharpen skills they can immediately apply to running their jobs; while students focus on their jobs, instructors consult and facilitate the process; and students read and learn the material through pre-course and evening assignments, discuss material in class, then apply the tools and skills to their own businesses in class with the aid of the instructor. Methods of instruction include hands-on involvement and a lengthy and detailed post-course assignment is required for credit and certification.

Credit Recommendation: In the graduate degree category, 3 semester hours in Management Analysis and Control (4/92).

Entrepreneurial Manager (ME0990) (Formerly Marketing Entre/Intrapreneurship [ME 0990])

Location: Somerset, NJ; and other AT&T locations throughout the country.

Length: 34 hours (3 days).

Dates: August 1986-January 1994.

Objective: To make executives think like entrepreneurs both within and outside a company environment.

Learning Outcome: Upon successful completion of this course, the manager will be able to better take appropriate business risks; to evaluate the role of the entrepreneur within the business environment, and to understand the role of the pro-active manager in the business environment.

Instruction: Major topics covered in the course are a series of topics designed to address and encourage innovation, creativity and entrepreneurship and intrapreneurship within a business enterprise.

Credit Recommendation: In the graduate degree category, 2 semester hours in New Venture Management (11/86) (8/91).

Establishing Your Business Focus (RB1012) (Formerly Making Your Move: Establishing Business Focus [RB-1012])

Location: Somerset, NJ and other AT&T locations.

Length: 32 hours.

Dates: September 1991-August 1996.

Objective: To teach students how to establish a global vision for their business, align their resources, and build an action plan to achieve their global vision.

Learning Outcome: Upon successful completion of this course, the student will be able to develop a global vision for their business and communicate the vision to stakeholders; align and motivate stakeholders and resources towards the vision, and maintain constant focus; build and implement an action plan, detailing strategies and tactics, priorities and contingencies; and establish performance measures and track the key indicators of business success.

Instruction: Major topics covered in the course are establishing business focus; course consists of six modules: A Framework for Leadership, Developing Global Intent, Aligning Key Stakeholders, Leading and Planning for Success, Staying On Track, and Visualizing and Signalling Success. Methods of instruction is in three parts: an advanced simulation case allows students to implement strategy and see immediate results, followed by a clinic-type discussion of the issues and techniques of the module; and the students apply the techniques to their own businesses.

Credit Recommendation: In the graduate degree category, 3 semester hours in Strategic Planning (8/91). **NOTE:** The credit recommendation applies only to those students who successfully complete a Job Application Project to be assessed by the instructor, and using the strategy techniques taught in the course.

Facilitation Workshop (MS6460)

Location: All AT&T regional and international training centers and business units.

Length: 24 hours (3 days).

Dates: June 1988-Present.

Objective: To train people to facilitate quality teams.

Learning Outcome: Upon successful completion of this course, the student will be able to effectively provide feedback to groups and/or individuals; recognize key indices of a team's growth and development and the actions needed to move the group forward at each stage of their development; select appropriate data gathering tools and instruments for assessing team/group development; and identify your strengths and weaknesses as a facilitator.

Instruction: This course covers those skills necessary to effectively facilitate groups through experiential, knowledge-based, practice, and self-awareness exercises. These experiences will involve: group and team growth and development, leadership, facilitation and intervention styles; data gathering; conflict resolution; and questioning and processing techniques.

Credit Recommendation: In the upper division baccalaureate degree category, 2 semester hours in Group Dynamics (6/94).

Finance and Accounting for Business Managers (FEO103)

Location: Pleasanton, California and other AT&T locations.

Length: 16 hours (2 days).

Dates: April 1991-December 1992.

Objective: To teach students financial terminology and how to use financial tools to measure their organization's effectiveness.

Learning Outcome: Upon successful completion of this course, the student will be able to analyze your department, division, or company financial statements; and make managerial and organizational decisions by tracking and monitoring your financial results.

Instruction: Major topics covered in the course are basic accounting principles, such as debit and credit entries and thoroughly examines the income statement balance sheet, and statement of cash flows; learn to interpret theses statements and track organizational and financial effectiveness through the use of financial ratio analysis; contingency budgets will be explored and students will construct contingency budgets for their own areas of responsibility; and AT&T financial documents will be used for examples and students will see how AT&T compares to its competitors.

Credit Recommendation: In the upper division baccalaureate degree category, 2

semester hours in Financial Accounting (4/92).

Finance Applications Using Excel (FM2030)

Location: Somerset, NJ and Liele, IL.
Length: 16 hours (2 days).
Dates: August 1995-Present.
Objective: To learn to develop and utilize spreadsheets for many different financial applications, and to use sophisticated spreadsheeting techniques.
Learning Outcome: Upon successful completion of this course, the student will be able to more productively create and utilize spreadsheet programs for financial analysis; create spreadsheets to analyze financial statements, perform financial forecasts and sensitivity analysis; evaluate projects using NPV, assess product profitability and others; utilize sophisticated spreadsheeting methods, including linking, graphing and macros; and learn to unlock the power of Excel, Version 5.
Instruction: This course includes applications for EVA analysis, financial statement analysis, ratio analysis, financial forecasting, NPV analysis, sensitivity/what if analysis, variance analysis, pricing and break-even analysis and budgeting; and techniques for graphing, linking spreadsheets, macros and exporting data to documents.
Credit Recommendation: In the upper division baccalaureate degree category, 1 semester hour in Financial Analysis Using Excel (12/95).

Finance for the Non-Finance Manager (FE0120)

Location: Somerset, NJ and other locations throughout the world.
Length: 24 hours (3 days).
Dates: July 1994-Present.
Objective: To teach both general and finance managers to use financial concepts and techniques to improve the management and profitability of their business.
Learning Outcome: Upon successful completion of this course, the student will be able to understand financial statements and utilize financial statement information to improve business performance; understand EVA concepts; apply contribution margin and break-even analysis to manage for profitability; perform activity-based costing techniques to increase profitability, productivity, and operational processes; and utilize capital budgeting and net present value analysis to accept projects that add value to the corporation.
Instruction: Through a combination of lecture and class exercises participants learn the fundamentals of financial management. The class progresses from GAAP principles to the three basic financial statement analysis. With this as a base, management accounting, contribution margins breakevens, time value of money and capital budgeting are covered. Students in the course complete a comprehensive case study.
Credit Recommendation: In the graduate degree category, or in the upper division baccalaureate degree category, 2 semester hours in Financial Management (12/94).

Financial Awareness Plus Seminar (SA9001)

Location: Somerset Seminars Center, Somerset, NJ.
Length: 18 hours (2.5 days).
Dates: November 1984-October 1987.
Objective: To improve the level of financial awareness and competency of AT&T managers.
Instruction: The course content stresses the Wall Street perspective, the use of financial analysis, the management of business and financial analysis, the management of business and financial risk, cost of capital, and net present value. Learning points are reinforced through a group exercise, discussion of financially excellent companies, and analysis of a sample case.
Credit Recommendation: In the graduate degree category, 1 semester hour in Business Finance, Principles of Finance, or Corporate Finance (11/85).

Financial Awareness Seminar (SE9000)
Introduction to Finance

Location: Somerset Seminars Center, Somerset, NJ.
Length: 14 hours (2 days).
Dates: November 1984-November 1990.
Objective: The course focuses on the financial objectives and structure of AT&T and achieving financial excellence.
Instruction: Major topics covered in the course are the use of financial analysis, the management of business and financial risk, cost of capital, and net present value.
Credit Recommendation: In the upper division baccalaureate degree category, or in the graduate degree category, 1 semester hour in Business Finance, Principles of Finance, Introduction to Finance, or Corporate Finance (11/85).

Financial Awareness: Understanding AT&T Finances (FE0300) (Financial Awareness [FE0300])

Location: Somerset, NJ, and other regional AT&T facilities.
Length: 16 hours (2 days).
Dates: *Version 1:* January 1988-June 1995; *Version 2:* July 1995-Present.
Objective: To acquaint and involve participants at all levels with the fundamentals of AT&T's current and future strategic and financial performance.
Learning Outcome: Upon successful completion of this course, students will be able to demonstrate how to assess business strategy through analysis of financial performance and the basis for stock valuation and its relationship to strategy; report on AT&T's financials that show where we have been, where we are today, and where we want to be in terms of profit and loss statements, the balance sheet, cash flow, and stock price; and as employees and shareholders, understand critical factors for success and how their collective efforts can help.
Instruction: Major topics covered in the course are how to analyze and assess business strategy performance through analysis of financial performance; and key competitors, their strategies and financial performance, and the basis for stock valuation. This seminar invites participants to take a leadership position and recommend/input to the critical success factors that can effect positive changes to the company's long-term results.
Credit Recommendation: *Version 1:* In the upper division baccalaureate degree category, 1 semester hour in Finance (12/90). *Version 2:* In the graduate degree category or in the upper division baccalaureate degree category, 1 semester hour in Finance (7/95). **NOTE:** A comprehensive project is required as part of the course for students to earn the credit recommendation.

Financial Leadership Program (Module 1): Accounting and Reporting

Location: Basking Ridge, NJ.
Length: 72 hours (over 12 weeks).
Dates: September 1994-Present.
Objective: To provide participants with the skills to successfully perform in an accounting or reporting function in the CFO organization.

Learning Outcome: Upon successful completion of this course, the student will be able to apply appropriate accounting skills to specific business processes; demonstrate knowledge of the effects of regulatory, economic, legal, and political events on accounting and reporting policies and processes; understand the role the CFO community plays in supporting business decisions; appropriately respond to external shareholders and agencies; recognize the need for appropriate controls and technology to insure the welfare of corporate assets and information; and understand contemporary financial issues and their impact upon the corporation.

Instruction: Major topics covered in the course are supporting business opportunities, performance evaluation, current finance issues, control issues, and accounting for specific business processes. Methods of instruction include lecture, dialogue, team assignments, in-class presentations, precourse reading, homework, quizzes, and examinations.

Credit Recommendation: In the graduate degree category, 4 semester hours in Accounting and Financial Reporting or Accounting elective (5/96).

Financial Leadership Program (Module 2): Managing Risk

Location: Basking Ridge, NJ.

Length: 67 hours (over 12 weeks).

Dates: April 1995-Present.

Objective: To provide participants with the skills to successfully perform in a risk or internal control function and to demonstrate knowledge of the importance of risk management for all managers.

Learning Outcome: Upon successful completion of this course, the student will be able to apply appropriate risk assessment activities to business functions, understand internal control objectives, apply knowledge of the audit process to a case study, and understand the role of financial security within the greater corporate community.

Instruction: Major topics covered in the course are control theory and audit process methodology and application related to the following significant business processes: information management, financial reporting, billing, payments, security, and network reliability. Methods of instruction include lecture, dialogue, team and individual assignments, precourse reading, flowcharting, case study analysis, quizzes, examinations, and an on-site visit to observe control activities is completed and documented.

Credit Recommendation: In the graduate degree category, 4 semester hours in Internal Auditing and Control or Accounting elective (5/96).

Financial Leadership Program (Module 3): Taxation, Treasury, and Financial Services

Location: Basking Ridge, NJ.

Length: 75 hours (over 12 weeks).

Dates: September 1995-Present.

Objective: To provide students with an understanding of taxation, cash and risk management, international finance, and credit and capital management.

Learning Outcome: Upon successful completion of this course, the student will be able to demonstrate understanding of taxation issues; demonstrate understanding of key treasury functions; demonstrate knowledge of discounted cash flow analysis and the time value of money; recognize the role of Wall Street analysts, investment banks, commercial banks, and agencies; understand risk management in the area of property and casualty risks; demonstrate knowledge of the use of short term borrowing and derivatives, cash management; demonstrate understanding of managing foreign exchange exposure; understand the nature of the credit and financing industries and their associated risk; and demonstrate understanding of the concept of securitization.

Instruction: Major topics covered in the course are tax accounting and minimization strategies; corporate finance, investment management and cash and credit management; economics of financial services; financial services risk management; and financial services accounting. Methods of instruction include lecture, dialogue, team projects, homework, precourse reading, and examinations.

Credit Recommendation: In the graduate degree category, 4 semester hours in Selected Topics in Financial Management: Taxation, Treasury, and Financial Services or Finance elective (5/96).

Financial Leadership Program (Module 4): Business Analysis and Decision Support

Location: Basking Ridge, NJ.

Length: 80 hours (2 weeks).

Dates: May 1996-Present.

Objective: To provide participants with the skills to perform financial analysis and support business decision-making.

Learning Outcome: Upon successful completion of this course, the student will be able to demonstrate the ability to perform financial statement analysis to support business decision-making; demonstrate understanding of cost and managerial accounting for management planning and control, performance measurement, and process improvement; demonstrate knowledge of foreign exchange risk and financing; and demonstrate understanding of financial implications of common business events and decisions (PC simulation).

Instruction: Major topics covered in the course are financial statement analysis, managerial accounting issues, how to manage a corporation for a one-year cycle, and practicing the financial implications of business events and decisions. Methods of instruction include a PC simulation and extensive work with problem solving and case studies.

Credit Recommendation: In the graduate degree category, 4 semester hours in Financial Analysis and Business Decision-Making, Accounting elective, or Finance elective (5/96).

Financial Management in Telecommunications (SE3000)

Location: Somerset Seminars Center, Somerset, NJ.

Length: 24 hours (3 days).

Dates: January 1985-October 1987.

Objective: To provide a financial analyst's view of telecommunications in a post-divestiture environment.

Instruction: The course provides participants an introduction to basic financial principles. The course surveys the basic techniques used by money managers to evaluate and improve profit performance by reviewing the financial indicators and ratios used in appraising performance. The course provides an understanding of the various forces that currently affect the telecommunications industry, i.e., competition, technology, regulation, social changes, judicial and legislative factors, and inflation.

Credit Recommendation: In the upper division baccalaureate degree category, 1 semester hour in Financial Statement Analysis (11/85).

Financial Management in Telecommunications (a) Financial Perspectives on Telecommunications (WSS1) (b) Financial Management for Services Managers (WSS4)

Location: Somerset Seminars Center, Somerset, NJ.

Length: (a) 8 hours (1 day); (b) 16 hours (2 days).

Dates: January 1984-December 1984.

Objective: (a) To provide participants with a financial analyst's view of telecommunications in a post-divestiture environment. (b) To help participants gain skills to interpret financial strength, expand profits, strengthen cash flow and cash position, locate and determine capital needs, analyze profit margins, and measure and improve operating performance.

Instruction: (a) Major topics covered in the course are an understanding of the various forces that affect current telecommunications, e.g., competition, technology, regulation, social changes, judicial and legislative actions, and inflation; new distinct businesses in telecommunications—customer premises, services, local exchange, enhanced services, and manufacturing. (b) Major topics covered in the course are an overview for understanding the return-on-investment concept and using it effectively to control and spot developing financial problems; an understanding of cash flows through a company and how to forecast that flow of cash; how to analyze changes in volume, price, and cost, elements in the cost of producing a service, what variables affect gross margin, break-even strategies, cost behavior patterns, and the "margin of safety."

Credit Recommendation: In the upper division baccalaureate degree category, 1 semester hour in Financial Management (11/85). **NOTE:** Parts (a) and (b) must both be completed for credit recommendation to apply. No credit recommended for either part alone.

Financial Planning Control and Decision Making (UMMD and SG1010) (Formerly Managerial Decision Making Through Financial Planning and Control [UMMD])

Location: Somerset Seminars Center, Somerset, NJ.

Length: 24 hours (3 days).

Dates: January 1984-December 1988.

Objective: To enable participants to apply financial information to service marketing decisions, perform financial analysis of alternative courses of action, and improve profit planning and control processes.

Instruction: Major topics covered in the course are the financial analysis of ratios and the time value of money; knowledge for management planning and control; relationship between measurement systems and business strategies; designing the measurement system for specific organizational units; the budgeting process and its behavioral implications; the relationship between budgeting and the long-range planning systems; how to identify costs relevant to various decisions, cost-volume-profit relationships, treatment of sunk costs and operating costs, and analyses of complex alternatives.

Credit Recommendation: In the upper division baccalaureate degree category, 1 semester hour in Financial Decision Making, Financial Analysis, Business Administration, or Management (11/85).

Financial Statement Analysis (a) Understanding Financial Statements (WSS2) (b) Effective Financial Analysis (WSS3)

Location: Somerset Seminars Center, Somerset, NJ.

Length: (a) 8 hours (1 day); (b) 16 hours (2 days).

Dates: January 1984-December 1984.

Objective: (a) To help participants gain a solid foundation in basic financial principles. (b) To gain a clear understanding of financial statements. Course provides participants with knowledge of how to predict future financial positions, how to measure the degree of risk in marginal accounts, how to use financial ratios, and how to compare financial standings and operating results of similar businesses.

Instruction: (a) Major topics covered in the course are simplifying financial records, constructing financial statements, providing evaluations to determine progress by examining balance sheet relationships, and measuring costs and margins. (b) Major topics covered in the course are financial statements, internal analyses of the effectiveness of operations and management decisions, capital analyses to determine how management handles money, comparative analyses revealing trends in finances and uncovering problems in marketing and management decisions, and marginal risk analyses in predicting future business prospects.

Credit Recommendation: In the upper division baccalaureate degree category, 1 semester hour in Financial Statement Analysis (11/85). **NOTE:** Parts (a) and (b) must both be completed for credit recommendation to apply. No credit recommended for either part alone.

Fire Safety for Building Management (BM2001) (Formerly Course FE0803 and MF2803)

Location: AT&T locations nationwide.

Length: 16 hours.

Dates: November 1989-August 1996.

Objective: To attain the ability to successfully implement AT&T's fire protection strategies, and to gain an overview of the principles of fire safety.

Learning Outcome: Upon successful completion of this course, the student will be able to better understand building/facility compartmentalization philosophies; know Egress and Access requirements; perform orientations with local fire departments; and develop emergency action plans.

Instruction: Major topics covered in the course are implementing AT&T's protection strategies, portable fire extinguishers, trends in fire codes and the latest detection and signalling systems; fire stopping methodologies and will have an opportunity to view the testing of fire suppression systems; maintenance of water suppression systems and learn first hand the importance of adequate alarm systems. Methods of instruction include case studies, lectures, group discussions, practice exercises, simulations, job aids, prior readings and a term paper.

Credit Recommendation: In the upper division baccalaureate degree category, 1 semester hour in Fire Safety for Building Management (8/91).

Focus Group Workshop (ME0958) (Formerly Industrial Interviewing and Focus Group Techniques [ME0958])

Location: Somerset, NJ, and other AT&T locations throughout the country.

Length: *Version 1:* 32 hours (4 days); *Version 2:* 24 hours (3 days).

Dates: *Version 1:* October 1986-June 1989; *Version 2:* June 1989-August 1996.

Objective: To prepare students to conduct focus group depth interviews and other group techniques pertaining to individual market research.

Learning Outcome: Upon successful completion of this course, the participant will be able to describe the elements of telephone and personal interviewing; identify the proper use of interviewing as a data collection device; conduct personal and telephone interviews to obtain desired market research data; identify the proper uses of focus groups for preliminary market research data collection; list the requirements for designing, conducting, and evaluating industrial focus groups; and use focus group results to guide subsequent market research design development.

Instruction: Major topics covered in the course are the critical elements of professional telephone, personal interviewing, and focus group interviewing techniques. Methods of instruction include extensive individual exercises, lecture, discussion to demonstrate how essential interviewing is for gathering market research data, and an intensive workshop.

Credit Recommendation: In the upper division baccalaureate degree category, 2 semester hours, or in the graduate degree category, 1 semester hour in Industrial Interviewing and Focus Group Techniques (11/86) (8/91).

Forecasting (SA4090) (Formerly Sales Forecasting)

Location: Somerset Seminars Center, Somerset, NJ.

Length: 34 hours (4 days).

Dates: January 1980-November 1990.

Objective: To present an intensive treatment of time series analysis, national and regional forecasts, and product and/or service forecasts.

Instruction: Emphasizes the Delphi technique, sales-force opinions method, executive judgment forecasts, customer surveys, as well as statistical and graphical presentation. Lectures, discussion, and group exercises are used.

Credit Recommendation: In the upper division baccalaureate degree category, 2 semester hours in Sales Forecasting (9/80) (11/85).

Function Analysis Workshop (IE2535)

Location: Piscataway, NJ and other AT&T locations.

Length: 32 hours (5 days).

Dates: June 1991-Present.

Objective: To learn and apply the principles, concepts and skills needed to bound partition and hone-in on specific logical, functional needs.

Learning Outcome: Upon successful completion of this course, the student will be able to explain the purpose and results of business requirements analysis; describe, contrast and list the basic specification components of each of the six building blocks of event and function analysis; explain the purpose, the work involved, and the products that are created in each of the major activities in event and function analysis; describe what an analysis scope represents; discover and validate interfaces for a given scope of analysis; explain the significance and characteristics of processes; identify and differentiate various types of business events for a given analysis scope, and allocate the events to processes and functions; subdivide a process for a given scope of analysis into appropriately shaped/sized business functions; apply the criteria to ensure that the business functions are leveled to elementary; explain the purpose, the relevant supporting analysis work products, and the principles which apply to analysis data flow diagrams; and build an analysis data flow diagram, given relevant event and function analysis products.

Instruction: This instructor-led workshop teaches the basic skills and knowledge needed to perform event and function analysis. Case study activities include bounding the business scope, recognizing and correlating business events, interfaces and processes, decomposing functions to the elementary level, and defining function precedence via data flow diagrams.

Function analysis techniques (as they would be applied to new system development, prior to a solution being determined or designed) are also covered.

Credit Recommendation: In the upper division baccalaureate degree category, 2 semester hours in Organizational Processes (9/94).

Function Point Workshop (IE1660)

Location: Somerset, NJ and other training locations.

Length: 16 hours (2 days).

Dates: February 1988-June 1996.

Objective: To enable participants to estimate the development time of a system or application.

Learning Outcome: Upon successful completion of this course, the student will be able to recognize the components necessary for a function point analysis, perform a function point analysis on a new and continuing development application, complete all the worksheets, forms and calculations necessary to achieve an accurate function point count for each application, and apply the 4.0 methodology based on instructor-led examples and more comprehensive case exercises.

Instruction: Major topics covered in the course are a methodology of measurement which is used to estimate the development time of a system, application, or project and to measure productivity and quality of such applications. Methods of instruction include classroom discussion, lecture, and lab.

Credit Recommendation: In the upper division baccalaureate degree category, 1 semester hour in Business Administration or Computer Information Systems (7/90) (11/96).

Fundamental Legal Concepts of Global Procurement (GP1020)

Location: All AT&T Training Locations in the U.S.

Length: 16 hours (2 days).

Dates: June 1994-Present.

Objective: To prepare the student to practice up-to-date skills as they relate to the ever-changing legal concept of Global Procurement.

Learning Outcome: Upon successful completion of this course, the student will be able to understand terminology and specifications of UCC; understand the basics and usage of contracts; define major clauses, e.g., warranty, insurance; understand intellectual property; and execute a model contract.

Instruction: This course covers the elements of contracts and their applicability to global business practice.

Credit Recommendation: In the upper division baccalaureate degree category, 1 semester hour in Fundamentals of Global Contracts Law (7/95).

Fundamental Marketing Concepts and Practices in Emerging Economies (GB1020)

Location: Somerset, NJ and other AT&T locations.

Length: 24 hours (3 days).

Dates: November 1993-Present.

Objective: To introduce marketing practices to managers in emerging market economies.

Learning Outcome: Upon successful completion of this course the student will be able to explain the principles of marketing and position of marketing in the overall structure of a business operating in a market economy; identify marketing structure, processes, and relationships (interconnections) to other business functions; achieve an understanding of the marketing mix and plan marketing activities associated with managing them.

Instruction: This course deals with the basic understanding of marketing concepts and their importance in managing a business. The focus, however, will be on the role of marketing in managing a company in an emerging market economy.

Credit Recommendation: In the upper division baccalaureate degree category, 2 semester hours in Marketing Fundamentals in Emerging Market Economies (6/94).

Fundamentals of Finance and Accounting (UPFF or SE2000)

Location: Somerset Seminars Center, Somerset, NJ.

Length: 24 hours (3 days).

Dates: January 1984-December 1987.

Objective: To provide the fundamentals of finance and accounting and furnish an overall understanding of the role of accounting and finance in the success of an enterprise.

Instruction: Major topics covered in the course are an analysis of financial statements, including the nature of assets, liabilities, and equity. Course includes an examination of financial data, factors that cause fluctuations in the performance of different divisions and service/product lines, and decision rules for top management to improve assessments and predictive ability as well as cash flow and project return on investment.

Credit Recommendation: In the upper division baccalaureate degree category, 1 semester hour in either Finance or Accounting (11/85).

Fundamentals of Marketing Research (ME0955)

Location: Somerset, NJ and other AT&T locations.

Length: *Version 1:* 40 hours (5 days); *Version 2:* 24 hours (3 days).

Dates: *Version 1:* January 1986-April 1993; *Version 2:* May 1993-Present.

Objective: *Version 1:* To acquaint students with methodologies of marketing research and measurement. *Version 2:* To give participants an overview of all aspects of marketing research.

Learning Outcome: *Version 1:* Upon successful completion of this course, the student will be able to list the considerations in selecting appropriate research strategies; recognize the various data collection techniques and identify the strengths and weaknesses of each; describe the basic data analysis procedures and their proper application; translate marketing research findings into management recommendations regarding applications to forecasting, market segmentation, and product innovation decision making; and effectively organize and communicate marketing research findings and recommendations. *Version 2:* Upon successful completion of this course, the student will be able to identify and solve common marketing research design problems; describe basic data analysis procedures and their proper application and translate marketing research findings into management recommendations.

Instruction: *Version 1:* This course provides an introduction to marketing research for individuals conducting research projects, managing the marketing research function, or making decisions based on study results. *Version 2:* This course provides an end-to-end overview of the marketing research process from research problem definition and design through sampling, survey methods, and data analysis. Students learn how to choose the right marketing research design to meet objectives and avoid common marketing research problems. Methods of instruction include lecture and objectives.

Credit Recommendation: *Version 1:* In the graduate degree category, 2 semester hours, or in the upper division baccalaureate degree category, 3 semester hours in Fundamentals of Marketing Research (11/86) (8/91). **NOTE:** This course has been reevaluated and continues to meet requirements for credit recommendations. *Version 2:* In the graduate degree category, 2 semester hours in Fundamentals of Marketing Research (12/93).

Fundamentals of Modern Marketing (SA4060)

Location: Somerset, NJ and other AT&T locations worldwide.

Length: *Version 1:* 36 hours (1 week); *Version 2:* 24 hours (3 days); *Version 3:* 16 hours (2 days).

Dates: *Version 1:* January 1983-December 1990; *Version 2:* January 1991-December 1995; *Version 3:* January 1996-Present.

Objective: To provide new marketing personnel and those from related areas with the principles and concepts which they will need to manage effectively in their new environment.

Learning Outcome: Upon successful completion of this course, the student will be able to identify and describe the challenges, activities, and institutions involved in the managing marketing process; analyze the dynamic relationship between marketing and its environment; identify and explain the major elements of the marketing program; and develop a strategic approach for capitalizing on marketing opportunities.

Instruction: Major topics covered in the course are a general overview of the marketing process as it relates to service marketing and a basic overview of those marketing principles needed to function effectively in AT&T's new marketing environment. Methods of instruction include case studies, guest lectures, and relevant current literature.

Credit Recommendation: *Versions 1 and 2:* In the upper division baccalaureate degree category, 1 semester hour in Introduction to Marketing (9/84) (8/91). *Version 3:* In the upper division baccalaureate degree category, 1 semester hour in Fundamentals of Marketing (5/96).

Fundamentals of Procurement (PR5051)

Location: All AT&T Training Locations in the U.S.

Length: 24 hours (3 days).

Dates: October 1995-Present.

Objective: To provide a broad-based overview of the responsibilities and tools of purchasing management.

Learning Outcome: Upon successful completion of this course, the student will be able to understand the procurement environment; manage procurement personnel; manage cost and price analysis inventory; select and manage suppliers; understand competitive bidding and negotiation; and understand financial and value analysis.

Instruction: By way of classroom instruction over a 3-day period, the course will cover concepts including opportunities and challenges of purchasing, managing purchasing responsibilities, legal concepts of purchasing, analytical tools for purchasers, sources of supply, bidding and negotiation, introduction to contracts, code of conduct, standard clauses, and supplier quality management. An appropriate graduate level project is required to earn the graduate credit recommendation.

Credit Recommendation: In the graduate degree category, 1 semester hour in Purchasing Management, or in the upper division baccalaureate degree category, 2 semester hours in Purchasing Management (12/95).

Fundamentals of the UNIX Operating System for Programmers (UC1080)

Location: Somerset, NJ and other AT&T locations.

Length: *Version 1:* 24 hours; *Version 2:* 32 hours (1 week).

Dates: January 1987-Present.

Objective: To introduce programmers to the fundamentals of the UNIX Operating System.

Learning Outcome: Upon successful completion of this course, the student will

be able to use the UNIX System User's Manual to locate commands by name or description and recognize syntax conventions, use the UNIX system's basic commands. Communicate with other users of the system, Create, list and manipulate files and directories, use the UNIX system full screen editor-"vi"; use file generation characters; and name features included in the UNIX system.

Instruction: Major topics covered in the course are an instructor-led course which includes basic UNIX operating system characteristics; accessing a UNIX system; the Shell command language architecture; the hierarchical file system; the UNIX system full screen editor-"vi"; Interuser communications; using the UNIX system documentation; a summary of the UNIX system features. Methods of instruction include classroom discussion, lecture, and lab.

Credit Recommendation: *Version 1:* In the lower division baccalaureate/associate degree category, 1 semester hour in UNIX Fundamentals or Computer Science or Data Processing (7/90). **NOTE:** If a student has taken UC1070, this course duplicates the information and no credit will be given. *Version 2:* In the lower division baccalaureate/associate degree category, 1 semester hour in Computer Information Systems (lecture) and 1 semester hour in Computer Information Systems (lab), for a total of 2 semester hours (11/96).

Fundamentals of the UNIX Operating System for Users (UC1070) Formerly [IE5001])

Location: Piscataway, NJ.

Length: 30 hours (5 days).

Dates: January 1987-June 1996.

Objective: To provide users with an introduction to the fundamentals of the UNIX operating system.

Learning Outcome: Upon successful completion of this course, the student will be able to gain access (logon) to the UNIX system; send and manage UNIX system mail; control the input and output of commands; use redirection and pipelining; use the UNIX System V User Reference Manual to obtain information about new commands and options; locate and use files on the UNIX file system; use the "vi" editor to create and change text files; create a profile file to customize one's login environment; print the contents of text files and directories; copy, move, remove, and rename files; organize files by creating, removing, and renaming directories; control who has permission to access files; sort, search, and manipulate information in files; run and manage commands in the background; write shell procedures to combine commands; and communicate with users on the local UNIX system and on remote UNIX systems.

Instruction: Major topics covered in the course provide the user with an understanding of the basic concepts of the UNIX operating system through a combination of class lectures and hands-on exercises. Topics include the file system hierarchy, commonly used UNIX system commands, the UNIX system editor "vi," shell programming, and communicating with and transferring files to other UNIX systems.

Credit Recommendation: In the lower division baccalaureate/associate degree category, 2 semester hours in UNIX Fundamentals, Computer Science, or Data Processing (7/90). **NOTE:** If the student has already completed IE5101 (Fundamentals of the UNIX Operating System for Programmers), then only 1 semester hour may be granted because of content overlap.

Fundamentals of UNIX Operating System for Users (UC1070)

Location: Somerset, NJ and other AT&T locations.

Length: *Version 1:* 30 hours; *Version 2:* 40 hours (1 week).

Dates: *Version 1:* January 1987-February 1993; *Version 2:* March 1993-Present.

Objective: To provide users with an introduction to fundamentals of UNIX Operating Systems.

Learning Outcome: Upon successful completion of this course, the student will be able to gain access (logon) to the UNIX System; send and manage UNIX System mail; control the input and output of commands, use redirection and pipelining; use the UNIX System V User reference manual to obtain information about new commands, locate and use files on the UNIX file system; use the vi editor to create and change text files, and create a profile file to customize one's login environment; and print the contents of text files and directories.

Instruction: Major topics covered in the course are an understanding of the basic concepts of the UNIX operating system, file system hierarchy, commonly used UNIX system commands, the UNIX system editor, vi, shell programming, and communicating with and transferring files to other UNIX systems. Methods of instruction include lectures and hands-on exercises.

Credit Recommendation: In the lower division baccalaureate/associate degree category, 2 semester hours in UNIX Fundamentals, or Computer Science, or Data Processing (7/90) (11/96). **NOTE:** If student has already completed UC1080, then student will receive only 1 semester hour because of content overlap.

Gap Analysis (ME0871) (Applying Gap Analysis [ME0871])

Location: Somerset, NJ.

Length: 16 hours.

Dates: July 1990-August 1992.

Objective: To provide AT&T managers with the skills to develop a marketing strategy that will uncover new sales and profit opportunities.

Learning Outcome: Upon successful completion of this course, the student will be able to assess present market position; evaluate their current service/product objectives and strategies; and estimate sales and profit potential for products and services.

Instruction: Major topics covered in the course are developing a marketing strategy and who must uncover new sales and profit opportunities. Methods of instruction include a combination of lecture and hands-on worksheets in which managers will complete a situation analysis and then apply the three primary uses of Gap Analysis to their products.

Credit Recommendation: In the upper division baccalaureate degree category, 2 semester hours in Marketing or Business elective (8/91).

Global Account Management 1) Coordinated Global Account Management (SM150) 2) Global Marketing Overview (ME1212)

Location: Somerset, NJ and other AT&T locations.

Length: *Course 1:* 24 hours (3 days); *Course 2:* 16 hours (2 days).

Dates: *Course 1:* December 1993-Present; *Course 2:* June 1994-Present

Objective: *Course 1:* To help account managers master the skills needed to be successful selling to global accounts. *Course 2:* To provide an overview to Global Marketing and the impact of global competition on marketing strategy and tactics.

Learning Outcome: *Course 1:* Upon successful completion of this course, the student will be able to improve his understanding of the major global forces as they impact markets and customers; develop strategies to build long-term customer/supplier relationships. Realize the steps needed to institutionalize a global account management mindset; and develop a global orientation in account management. *Course 2:* Upon successful completion of this course, the student will be able to develop awareness of the globalization of markets and the factors that drive globalization; identify market groupings across countries at a macro level. Evaluate business, government and consumer markets at a micro level and estimate demand; and develop global marketing strategies.

Instruction: *Course 1:* Major topics covered in the course are how to overcome organizational hurdles as part of a global account team, the major global forces impacting markets and customers, and realize the steps that must be taken to institutionalize a global account management mindset. *Course 2:* This course will provide an overview to global marketing and will examine a variety of areas, including the effects competing globally has on each element of the marketing mix. It will show the impact of competing in a global marketplace on marketing strategy and tactics.

Credit Recommendation: In the upper division baccalaureate degree category, 3 semester hours in Global Account Management (6/94). **NOTE:** Students must take both courses 1 and 2 to successfully complete the course.

Global Business Fundamentals (GM1000) (Formerly Elements of Global Business (GM1000)

Location: Somerset, NJ, and other AT&T regional facilities.

Length: 21 hours (3 days).

Dates: January 1989-February 1995.

Objective: To give participants a general understanding of global business, touching on finance, marketing, competition, and cultural difference issues.

Learning Outcome: Upon successful completion of this course, the student will be able to identify and understand the different stages in the evolution of global business strategy and the difference between a global business strategy and domestic, multinational, or international business strategies; appreciate the broad context of global business markets, scan the globe for relevant information (including using the IRC and AT&T), spot trends, and learn where income, population, market potential, and competition are located today and where they will be tomorrow; and appreciate the importance of culture on doing business internationally, understand global brands/products and how they are created, and learn how to formulate a market-entry strategy for penetrating a new global market.

Instruction: Major topics covered in the course are a broad look at the global business environment, identifying significant trends and events, examples of effective and ineffective global strategies, and requirements for success in the global marketplace. As the introductory course to the Global Management curriculum, the material will touch on many of the topics covered later in the curriculum (competition, finance, marketing, cross-cultural communications, and product management) and integrate them into a coherent whole.

Credit Recommendation: In the graduate degree category, 2 semester hours in International Business (12/90) (12/94).

Global Joint Ventures and Strategic Alliances (SA6040)

Location: Somerset, NJ and other AT&T locations.

Length: 16 hours (2 days).

Dates: April 1994-Present.

Objective: To develop student skills to promote successful strategic alliances in a global environment.

Learning Outcome: Upon successful completion of this course the student will be able to decrease the time and costs of developing an alliance by effectively identifying and evaluating potential partners;. improve the chances for success of a joint venture project by understanding the strengths and weaknesses of various structures; and ensure proper operation of a new alliance by employing techniques for coordinating resources and ensuring cooperative decision-making.

Instruction: Major topics covered in the course are how to formulate cooperative venture strategies, promote successful alliance management, structure deals, develop joint ventures and create action plans for alliances. The course will look not only at formation and structuring strategies, but also techniques for integrating cultures and identifying warning signs in global joint ventures.

Credit Recommendation: In the upper division baccalaureate degree category, 1 semester hour in Global Strategic Alliances (6/94).

Global Leader (GM1090)

Location: Somerset, NJ and other AT&T locations.

Length: 24 hours (3 days).

Dates: April 1993-Present.

Objective: To look at the globalization process and how it impacts the strategy, structure, culture and people of AT&T, while addressing leadership behavior for the global environment.

Learning Outcome: Upon successful completion of this course, the student will be able to apply leadership skills and mindsets as well as AT&T's values to specific job/team-related issues in order to get immediate results; and practice those leadership skills and begin applying them immediately, both in a domestic and global concept.

Instruction: Major topics covered in the course are designed for students who want to keep pace with global changes. It includes success factors, mindsets of the leader, managing conflict, win/win, cultural self-awareness, cultural differences, and targeting results. Methods of instruction include case discussions, case study, and lectures. An appropriate graduate level research project is submitted as part of the course requirements. In addition, students must also read five journal articles.

Credit Recommendation: In the graduate degree category, 2 semester hours in International Business (12/93).

Global Management: An Advanced Business Simulation (GM1050)

Location: Somerset, NJ and other AT&T locations.

Length: 40 hours (5 days).

Dates: *Version 1:* December 1989-October 1992; *Version 2:* November 1992-Present.

Objective: To provide students with the experience of running a global business from production-to-finance-to-sales, using computer-based advanced business simulation.

Learning Outcome: *Version 1:* Upon successful completion of this course, the student will be able to outline the changing role of managers as they move up the organization ladder and identify major elements in the development of a management team; explain the natural conflicts between functional areas of a business and present conflict resolution alternatives; show how market forces drive decisions in all functional areas; explain the role of sales forecasts in decision making, and show why forecasting international sales may be less reliable than forecasting national sales; and help students understand the totality of an organization as a vibrant organism with changing and evolving units which follow self interests. *Version 2:* Upon successful completion of this course, the student will be able to make decisions related to product pricing, quality improvement, marketing efforts, technological levels, asset deployment and quality of personnel.

Instruction: *Version 1:* Major topics covered in the course are management of a 16-country multinational enterprise; and students will participate in discussions analyzing the complexities of global business and gain hands-on experience in sales forecasting, strategy formulation, budgeting and other aspects of operating a global business. *Version 2:* Major topics covered in the course are designed for students with previous exposure to the global business environment. It includes international decision making, team dynamics, financial analysis, competitive tactics and product management strategies. Methods of instruction include team exercises, lecture, and discussion.

Credit Recommendation: *Version 1:* In the upper division baccalaureate degree category, 3 semester hours in Global Management (4/92). *Version 2:* In the upper division baccalaureate degree category, 3 semester hours in Global Management or Strategic Management (12/93).

Global Product and Service Management in the Information Age (ME2030)

Location: Locations throughout the U.S.

Length: 24 hours (3 days).

Dates: January 1994-Present.

Objective: To gain a better understanding of global product/service management strategies and identify global market opportunities and challenges in one's work environment.

Learning Outcome: Upon successful completion of this course, the student will be able to relate product management concepts from a global setting to the demands of your work; design action-oriented strategies for your business unit created from information about changing markets; apply marketing, management, and competitive frameworks to your products in the global marketplace; and evaluate product and market strategies and identify opportunities and challenges.

Instruction: Major topics covered in the course are how to plan and manage an international product portfolio; explain his/her role in international opportunity analyses, global product planning and resource, and profitability management; how to better deal with the traps and pitfalls of foreign market entry; and the movement of goods and services across national borders.

Credit Recommendation: In the upper division baccalaureate degree category, 1 semester hour in Global Product Management (7/95).

Global Sourcing (PR5103)

Location: All AT&T training locations.

Length: 24 hours (3 days).

Dates: January 1995-Present.

Objective: To provide the participants with global sourcing strategies designed to provide their organizations with a competitive advantage.

Learning Outcome: Upon successful completion of this course, the student will be able to identify and serve global needs through worldwide operations, seize sourcing opportunities around the globe, and effectively negotiate with overseas suppliers by understanding cultural and legal differences.

Instruction: Major topics covered in the course are how to identify and seize sourcing opportunities around the globe to improve the organization's competitiveness, global sourcing and competitive advantage, understanding cultural differences, legal aspects of global sourcing, capitalizing on countertrade, researching global sourcing opportunities, global procurement strategies, and negotiating with overseas suppliers and global partnering. An appropriate graduate level project is included as part of the course requirement.

Credit Recommendation: In the upper division baccalaureate degree category, 2 semester hours in Logistics or in the graduate degree category, 1 semester hour in Logistics (11/96).

Guidelines for Effective Character-Based Screen Design (IE1013) (Formerly Fundamentals of Screen Design: A Workshop [IE1302])

Location: All AT&T training locations.

Length: *Version 1:* 30 hours; *Version 2:* 21 hours (3 days).

Dates: March 1988-December 1996.

Objective: To teach the major principles of effective screen layout for a variety of screen types.

Learning Outcome: Upon successful completion of this course, the student will be able to apply the steps of the screen design process and identify where and how screen design fits into the system development process, develop a user profile as a prelude to choosing a dialog type and designing screens, apply human performance research-based guidelines to choose between and design the following types of dialogs:menus, form fill, inquiry, question/answer, command language, choose appropriate screen colors and organize, group and lay out screen elements to allow for optimized user performance, develop effective user guidance and error handling screens and messages, link displays to move easily from task to task, develop a user interface prototype, test user interface screens for user preference and performance.

Instruction: Major topics covered in the course are the major principles of effective screen layout for a variety of screen types (form fill, display-only, menus, etc.); alignment, symmetry, organization, and chunking of information; use of color; creation of screen templates; character-based or ASCII screen layout; and guidelines and techniques for effective screen design lead to easier to use applications, shorter training times, higher user productivity, and lower error rates. Methods of instruction include a highly interactive workshop which allows students to practice designing, testing, and linking screens using a PC-based software tool to produce working prototypes.

Credit Recommendation: In the lower division baccalaureate/associate degree category or in the upper division baccalaureate degree category, 1 semester hour in Human Factors or Computer Science (7/90) (11/96).

Human Factors in Computer Systems (IE1002)

Location: Somerset, NJ and other AT&T locations.

Length: 90-95 hours (15 days over 3 months).

Dates: July 1982-June 1996.

Objective: To provide the base education needed to perform Human Factors activities.

Learning Outcome: Upon successful completion of this course, the student will be able to make and support Human Factors decisions and recommendations, conduct research in the various subtopics within Human Factors, perform various analysis techniques required to produce HF products, analyze error rates and costs, design dialog, command language, codes and error messages, critique the effectiveness of various forms of user documentation for specific use, evaluate screens and forms and make recommendations for improvements, conduct experiments to evaluate problem situations, and apply ergonomic principles to work station design.

Instruction: Major topics covered in the course are basic human information processing principles via discussions, research, experiments and testing, and then apply the results to design activities. Methods of instruction include discussions, research, experiments, and testing. An appropriate graduate level project is included as part of the course requirement.

Credit Recommendation: In the graduate degree category, 3 semester hours in Industrial Engineering, Computer Science, or Computer Information Systems (7/85) (7/90) (11/96).

Human Factors Usability Design Strategies (IE1001)

Location: Somerset, NJ and other AT&T locations.

Length: 24.25 hours.

Dates: January 1988-June 1996.

Objective: To teach system developers the issues and problems affecting the usability of computer systems.

Learning Outcome: Upon successful completion of this course, the student will be able to identify how and when human factors methods and techniques can be applied throughout the development cycle to increase the accuracy, speed and acceptance of systems, demonstrate the cost benefits of greater usability in systems and conduct cost/benefit analyses, and design systems which conform to users' psychological, physical and physiological requirements and limits, based on human factors research.

Instruction: Major topics covered in the course are identification of human performance problems and issues related to user documentation, training, and help systems; hardware ergonomics issues and the effect of the physical environment on human performance in systems; demonstrates how to conduct simple human factors tests and studies for evaluating and measuring human performance of individual system functions; and identifies sources of information for further study and research. Methods of instruction include lecture and collaborative learning formats.

Credit Recommendation: In the upper division baccalaureate degree category, 1 semester hour in Systems (7/90) (11/96).

IM Report and Memo Writing for Technical Managers (IE1201)

Location: Piscataway, NJ, and other AT&T locations.

Length: 14 hours (2 days).

Dates: March 1988-June 1996.

Objective: To provide an introductory overview of information mapping (IM).

Learning Outcome: Upon successful completion of this course, the student will be able to given the information for a business memo, apply the six-task approach and imaginary dialogue strategy by planning and writing a short memo; given information for common kinds of memos, apply the method by writing clear and concise memos; and given a case study, apply the principles, components, and organization and analysis techniques to a longer report.

Instruction: Major topics covered in the course are how to solve complex, technical communication tasks using the IM method to organize and analyze material, test it for completeness and accuracy, and determine its content and format. They learn skills to solve problems of sequencing, structure, level of detail, consistency, and the management of large amounts of complex information. Methods of instruction include realistic problem scenarios are used in the seminar for hands-on format.

Credit Recommendation: In the lower division baccalaureate/associate degree category, 1 semester hour in Technical Report Writing (7/90).

Improving Quality and Productivity by Industrial Experimentation (MF3401)

Location: Piscataway, NJ and other AT&T locations.

Length: 36 hours (5 days).

Dates: June 1989-June 1996.

Objective: To teach students how to use designed experiments to identify and solve problems and to improve quality and productivity of manufacturing processes.

Learning Outcome: Upon successful completion of this course, the student will be able to state the problem or objective of the experiment, determine a criterion, and decide how to combine the experimental factors that might affect the criterion; design the experiment: determine order of experimentation and method of randomization, develop mathematical model, and establish null hypothesis; run the experiment and collect response data; analyze and interpret the results; contrast Taguchi robust design methods to classical approaches.

Instruction: Major topics covered in the course include how to use designed experiments to identify and solve problems and to improve quality and productivity of manufacturing processes; designs for single and multifactor experiments, including completely randomized designs and designs with restrictions on randomization; the classical and Taguchi approaches are compared; analysis of variance (ANOVA) and normal plots are used as the analysis methods, and a PC software package Statgraphics is used for data analysis.

Credit Recommendation: In the upper division baccalaureate degree category, 3 semester hours in Research Methodology or Experimental Design (10/91). **Note:** The credit recommendation applies only to those students who also successfully complete an independent project employing appropriate experimental design applications.

IMS Physical Data Base Design (Introduction & Techniques) (IE320 and IE3324) (Formerly IMS/VS Physical Data Base Design (Introduction and Techniques) [IE3320 and IE3324})

Location: Piscataway, NJ and other AT&T locations.

Length: *Version 1:* 60 hours (10 days); *Version 2:* 42 hours (7 days); IE3320: 2 days; IE3324: 5 days.

Dates: *Version 1:* January 1985-November 1991; *Version 2:* December 1991-July 1995.

Objective: To provide the transition from logical to physical data base design and also to provide the student with the skills and knowledge necessary to complete IMS physical data base design. The student will also learn the concepts, structure, and terminology of IMS and the basics of evaluating and tuning a particular physical data base design.

Instruction: Major topics covered in the course include structural and physical view of data; translating conceptual models into physical design; the use of modeling techniques and tools; and the development of test procedures for a data base to be implemented under a physical design. Methods of instruction include lecture and laboratory.

Credit Recommendation: In the upper division baccalaureate degree category, 3 semester hours in Computer Science or

Data Processing (7/85) (7/90). **NOTE:** Students are required to complete both of these courses in order to receive the full credit recommended.

IMS Physical Data Base Implementation IMS/VS Physical Data Base Implementation (IE3304)

Location: Piscataway, NJ and other AT&T locations.

Length: 30 hours (5 days).

Dates: January 1985-July 1995.

Objective: To provide the student with an understanding of the physical characteristics of IMS data bases, and the coding of the necessary control blocks to define data bases and programs to IMS.

Instruction: Major topics covered in the course are the characteristics of multiple data set groups; pointer options; segment edit/compression; and variable length segments; coding physical data base descriptions (DBDs) for the various data base organizations; coding of program specification blocks (PSBs) required for data base processing; coding of the control statements necessary to pre-build application control blocks; and implementation physical IMS data bases. Methods of instruction include lecture and laboratory.

Credit Recommendation: In the upper division baccalaureate degree category, 2 semester hours in Computer Science or Data Processing (7/85) (7/90).

IMS Programming-Batch (IE3204) (Formerly IMS/VS Batch Programming [IE3204])

Location: Piscataway, NJ and other AT&T locations.

Length: 30 hours (1 week).

Dates: January 1985-June 1996.

Objective: To teach the student how to process data stored in an integrated IMS/VS data base in the batch mode.

Instruction: Major topics covered in the course are IMS/VS data base concepts, Data Language/I calls and segment search arguments, manipulation of data in a batch environment; additional IMS/VS features such as multiple positioning, variable length segments, segment edit/compression, AND, and checkpoint/restart. Methods of instruction include lecture and laboratory.

Credit Recommendation: In the upper division baccalaureate degree category, 2 semester hours in Computer Science or Data Processing (7/85) (7/90).

IMS Programming-Teleprocessing (IE3208) (Formerly IMS/VS Programming - Teleprocessing [IE3208]) (Formerly IMS/ESA Programming - Teleprocessing [IE3208])

Location: Piscataway, NJ and other AT&T locations.

Length: 30 hours (1 week).

Dates: January 1985-June 1996.

Objective: To teach students the difference between the methodology of teleprocessing and batch processing and to introduce students to MFS and BTS concepts and usages.

Instruction: Major topics covered in the course include IMS teleprocessing concepts; coding of message processing, batch message processing, and conversational programs; introduction to the use of Message Format Services; and use of the Batch Terminal Simulator. Methods of instruction include lecture and laboratory.

Credit Recommendation: In the upper division baccalaureate degree category, 2 semester hours in Computer Science or Data Processing (7/85) (7/90).

IMS/ESA Programming-Batch (IE3204) IMS Programming (IE3204); IMS/VS Batch Programming (IE3204)

Location: All AT&T training locations.

Length: 30 hours (5 days).

Dates: January 1985-Present.

Objective: To teach the student how to write programs that process data stored in an IMS database.

Learning Outcome: Upon successful completion of this course, the student will be able to retrieve, insert, replace, and delete segments from an IMS database, provide linkage between DL/1 and COBOL or PL/1 language for a batch environment using: the segment search argument, the segment input/output areas, the program communication blocks, the call to DL/1, check and analyze DL/1 status codes from requests made in a batch mode, and write application programs that execute in a batch mode.

Instruction: Major topics covered in the course are IMS database concepts, Data Language/1 calls and segment search arguments, and manipulation of data in a batch environment. Methods of instruction include lecture and lab.

Credit Recommendation: In the upper division baccalaureate degree category, 2 semester hours in Computer Science or Data Processing (1 hour lecture and 1 hour lab) (7/85) (7/90) (11/96).

IMS/ESA Programming-Teleprocessing (IE3208) IMS Programming-Teleprocessing IE3208; IMS/ESA Programming-Teleprocessing IE3208; IMS/VS Programming-Teleprocessing IE3208

Location: All AT&T training locations.

Length: 30 hours (4.5 days).

Dates: January 1985-Present.

Objective: To teach the student to program within the IMS DC environment using Message Format Service (MFS) and Batch Terminal Simulation (BTS).

Learning Outcome: Upon successful completion of this course, the student will be able to understand IMS teleprocessing concepts, understand the flow of messages between the terminal and application program, understand some of the system parameters which are needed to support the DC environment, code application programs to execute in Message Processing regions, invoke Message Format Services using application code, and use BTS to test an on-line application in a batch environment.

Instruction: Major topics covered in the course are IMS teleprocessing concepts, coding of message processing, batch message processing and conversational programs, introduction to the use of Message Format Services, and use of Batch Terminal Simulator. Methods of instruction include lecture and laboratory.

Credit Recommendation: In the upper division baccalaureate degree category, 2 semester hours in Computer Science or Data Processing (1 hour lecture and 1 hour lab) (7/85) (7/90) (11/96).

IMS/VS Data Base Implementation

Location: Data Systems Education Center, Piscataway, NJ and other Bell locations.

Length: 60 hours (2 weeks).

Dates: June 1978-December 1984.

Objective: To enable students responsible for implementing IMS/VS data base(s) to choose and use the most appropriate method.

Instruction: Major topics covered in this course include physical data base descriptions from hierarchical structures; appropriate data base organizations and access methods and related factors.

Methods of instruction include lecture, discussion, and workshops.

Credit Recommendation: In the lower division baccalaureate/associate degree category, 2 semester hours in Computer Science or Data Processing (2/80).

IMS/VS Logical Data Base Implementation (IE3308)

Location: Piscataway, NJ and other AT&T locations.

Length: 18 hours (3 days).

Dates: January 1985-June 1996.

Objective: To teach the concepts and implementation techniques of IMS logical relationships. Logical relationships enable the use of network structures in IMS.

Instruction: Major topics covered in the course include description of the characteristics and uses of the three types of IMS logical relationships; coding the physical data base description (DBD) parameters necessary to implement logical relationships; drawing the data structures made possible by a given logical relationship; coding logical data base descriptions (logical DBDs); describing the implications of the logical update rules; and describing the procedures necessary to reorganize a data base involved in a logical relationship. Methods of instruction include lecture and laboratory.

Credit Recommendation: In the upper division baccalaureate degree category, 1 semester hour in Computer Science or Data Processing (7/85) (7/90).

IMS/VS Programming (Batch and Teleproces)

Location: Data Systems Education Center, Piscataway, NJ; and other Bell locations.

Length: 60 hours (2 weeks).

Dates: June 1976-December 1984.

Objective: To teach the student how to process data stored in an integrated IMS/VS data base in the batch mode.

Instruction: Major topics covered in the course are data base concepts; data language/I calls; manipulation of data in a batch environment; program debugging in an IMS/VS environment; advanced IMS/VS features such as variable length segments, segment edit/compression, independent versus dependent AND, and system service calls. Methods of instruction include lecture, discussion, and workshops.

Credit Recommendation: In the lower division baccalaureate/associate degree category, 2 semester hours in Computer Science or Data Processing (2/80).

Information Mapping, Structured Writing (IE1202)

Location: Somerset, NJ and other AT&T locations.

Length: *Version 1:* 24 hours; *Version 2:* 18 hours.

Dates: *Version 1:* June 1980-December 1995; *Version 2:* January 1996-June 1996.

Objective: To teach participants to use this systematic method (Information Mapping) which makes writing simple, clear, more efficient and more effective.

Learning Outcome: Upon successful completion of this course, the student will be able to describe Information Mapping Structured Writing; write and edit a training unit according to the course standards; write and edit basic and supplementary types of maps; identify good applications of the structured writing methods; and survey other aspects of this approach, i.e., memos and reports.

Instruction: Major topics covered in the course are a modular way of organizing and presenting written materials and a carefully-structured format combining simple graphics and words. Methods of instruction include classroom discussion, lecture, and collaborative learning.

Credit Recommendation: *Version 1:* In the lower division baccalaureate/associate degree category, 2 semester hours in Business or Managerial Communications (7/85)(7/90). *Version 2:* In the upper division baccalaureate degree category, 1 semester hour in Business or Managerial Communications (11/96).

Information System Seminar for the Executive (IE2104)

Location: Central New Jersey "off work" locations.

Length: 18 hours (3 days).

Dates: October 1980-December 1986.

Objective: To convey the systems development process to students who require a non-technical (user) perspective of information system applications.

Instruction: Major topics covered in the course are data processing concepts; the project development life cycle; managing and controlling the project; the project approval process; the role of systems people; systems analysis and design; human factors development; the role of the support organizations; hardware/software/programming languages; data administration; data security and controls; the purpose of EDP audits; data communications; system documentation; and current and future technologies.

Credit Recommendation: In the lower division baccalaureate/associate degree category, 1 semester hour in General Education (Computer Literacy) (7/85). **NOTE:** This course is not applicable to a computer science degree. Students who receive credit for this course should not receive credit for Data Processing Concepts for Users (IE2002).

Information System Technologies & Concepts (IE2002) (Formerly Data Processing Concepts for Users [IE2002])

Location: Piscataway, NJ, and other AT&T locations.

Length: 18 hours (3 days).

Dates: May 1984-June 1996.

Objective: To familiarize people lacking backgrounds in data processing with some of the most common concepts and terminology encountered in a mechanized environment.

Instruction: Major topics covered in the course are how and why computers are used; how computers work; peripheral equipment; data communications; data base principles; types of software; languages and programming; and current future trends.

Credit Recommendation: In the lower division baccalaureate/associate degree category, 1 semester hour in General Education (Computer Literacy) (7/85) (7/90). **NOTE:** This course is not to be used for credit in computer-related or other technical degree programs. Students who receive credit for this course should not receive credit for Information Systems Seminar for the Executive.

Information Systems Analysis Workshop (ISAW) (IE2540)

Location: All AT&T training locations.

Length: 90 hours (10 days).

Dates: *Version 1:* June 1984-December 1995; *Version 2:* January 1996-June 1996.

Objective: To have the students learn how to apply and integrate the latest techniques and methodologies of systems engineering as part of a process for performing systems analysis.

Learning Outcome: Upon successful completion of this course, the student will be able to recognize business objectives and fundamental business needs, create an entity-relationship diagram by identifying business factors and practices and rules, identify logical business events, define business processes, high level functions and elementary functions, and integrate developmental techniques and methods.

Instruction: Major topics covered in the course are a "development team" simulating a live environment, performing the data and function analysis to be included in the system requirements; practical analysis that exercises all the analysis modeling skills; using a telecommunications business case study, detailed business requirements are progressively developed throughout the course; and client interviews. Methods of instruction include extensive evening and weekend reading assignments, Information Systems Analysis Workshop, individual and group case studies, and application of advanced techniques that are needed in real projects. ISAW gives practical answers to questions that analysts develop from their job experiences. An appropriate graduate level project is included as part of the course requirement to earn the credit recommendation covered under Version 1.

Credit Recommendation: *Version 1:* In the upper division baccalaureate degree category, 5 semester hours in Business Administration or Computer Information Systems; or in the graduate degree category, 3 semester hours in Business Administration or Computer Information Systems (7/85) (7/90). *Version 2:* In the upper division baccalaureate degree category, 3 semester hours in Business Administration or Computer Information Systems (lecture) and 2 semester hours in Business Administration or Computer Information Systems (lab) for a total of 5 semester hours (11/96).

Initial Analyst Training (IE 2500)

Location: Piscataway, NJ and other AT&T locations.

Length: 320 hours (8 weeks).

Dates: January 1992-June 1996.

Objective: To develop data analysis and modeling skills, function analysis modeling skills and interviewing skills needed by business system analysts.

Learning Outcome: Upon successful completion of this course the student will be able to apply the tools of data analysis to produce the entity relationship model; apply the tools of function analysis to define the business functions; identify, through data gathering and effective interpersonal and communication skills, business requirements for users, subject matter experts; perform business event analysis; document the logical access requirements for business functions; and act as a contributing system analysis member of a project team.

Instruction: Major topics covered in the course teach modeling skills and analysis concepts fundamental to the system analyst role. The student adopts an in-depth view of the structure of business system requirements. Through demonstrations, exercises, and role-playing, the student learns analysis techniques that effectively discover and specify business system requirements. Analysis Scope: The student learns the significance of defining a business boundary of an analysis effort through the analysis of business objectives. Entity-Relationship Modeling: The student learns how to discover and model the structure of data requirements of an analysis scope. Data Element Analysis: The student learns how to discover the business facts that need to be retained by an analysis scope and methods of normalizing the association of business facts to business entities. Interface Discovery: The student learns how to discover and specify the business systems that interface with an analysis scope. Event Analysis: The student learns how to discover and model the business decisions and conditions of significance to an analysis scope. Function Decomposition: The student learns how to progressively partition business decisions and conditions of significance to an analysis scope. Logical Access Path Analysis: The student learns how to analyze and model the data access requirements of a function. Data Flow Analysis: The student learns how to discover and specify the necessary communication requirements of functions within the scope. Function Logic Specification: The student learns to how to form and document the detailed logic of functions within the analysis scope. Data Gathering: Through instructor role playing, the student interacts with business people to discover business needs. Computer Aided Software Engineering (CASE) Tools: Through lecture and software demonstrations, the student becomes acquainted with the capabilities and uses of CASE tools. Human Factors: The student is introduced to the role of Human Factors Design in the development and enhancement of business systems. Teaching Approach: Students learn analysis skills through actual application of techniques. Concepts are initially introduced through instructor lectures and demonstrations. Students then perform individual exercises to learn how to apply the techniques. Detailed exercise reviews and multiple opportunities to apply each technique further reinforce skills. Students are provided formal feedback on an ongoing basis. Formal feedback is provided at midterm and course completion. Assessment of student performance at course completion is based on the completion of a final case study performed during the last week of class.

Credit Recommendation: In the upper division baccalaureate degree category, 8 semester hours in Business Systems and Analysis (9/94).

Initial Designer Training 2 (IDT2) (IE3000)

Location: All AT&T training locations

Length: 52 days.

Dates: *Version 1:* June 1983-December 1995; *Version 2:* January 1996-June 1996.

Objective: To teach entry level programmers the programming design, testing and implementation methods needed to perform the job of an application or system programmer in an AT&T IBM mainframe environment.

Learning Outcome: Upon successful completion of this course, the student will be able to use transfer analysis tools describing "what" has to be accomplished into design tools describing "how" it will be accomplished, analyze and improve designs using analytical tools, prepare implementation plans, design a solution using structure charts and pseudo-code, partition the structure chart into modules and develop an implementation plan, develop module verification and integration test plans, code a structured COBOL II language solution to relatively complex multi-module multi-step process, develop, use and code TSO CLISTs and JCL, use an interactive debugger (XPEDITER) to test and debug modules, and given an existing module, debug problems with the module and implement a change specification.

Instruction: Major topics covered in the course are programming design and testing and implementation methods needed to perform the job of an application or system programmer in an AT&T IBM-mainframe environment. Methods of instruction include exercises (paper and computer), an intensive final case problem, and trainee evaluation. IDT2 graduates will require follow-up environment and language training prior to their first assignment.

Credit Recommendation: *Version 1:* In the lower division baccalaureate/associate degree category, 3 semester hours in Introduction to COBOL and 3 semester hours in Systems Analysis and Design for a total of 6 semester hours (7/85)(7/90). *Version 2:* In the lower division baccalaureate/associate degree category, or in the upper division baccalaureate degree category, 6 semester hours in Introduction to COBOL and 6 semester hours in Systems Analysis and Design for a total of 12 semester hours (11/96).

Initial Designer Training C (IDTC) (IE3001)

Location: Somerset, NJ and other locations throughout the country.

Length: 375 hours (10 weeks).

Dates: *Version 1:* February 1985-December 1995; *Version 2:* January 1996-June 1996.

Objective: To teach the design skills and C Language programming concepts needed by a programmer/analyst in a UNIX operating system environment.

Learning Outcome:

Instruction: Major topics covered in the course are the identification and utilization of various steps for systems development; C Language programming, including coding, testing, and debugging under UNIX; and the creation of all necessary documentation. Methods of instruction include lecture, laboratory, discussion, case study, and oral presentation.

Credit Recommendation: *Version 1:* In the lower division baccalaureate/associate degree category, 3 semester hours in C Language and 3 semester hours in Systems Analysis and Design for a total of 6 semester hours (7/85) (7/90). *Version 2:* In the the lower division baccalaureate/associate degree category, or in the upper division baccalaureate degree category, 6 semester hours in C Language and 6 semester hours in Systems Analysis and Design for a total of 12 semester hours (11/96).

Initiating Change: Unleashing Competitive Advantage (MD7630) Mastering Change: Unleashing Competitive Advantage MD7630

Location: All AT&T training locations.

Length: 16 hours (2 days).

Dates: January 1996-Present.

Objective: To provide the student with the tools to initiate change and reshape their current/future organizations to meet the increasingly competitive demands of the marketplace.

Learning Outcome: Upon successful completion of this course, the student will be able to describe and use a model for change, initiate and advocate change initiatives to create new opportunities, anticipate and seize opportunities to cause meaningful change, recognize and overcome resistance to change, and apply diverse thinking to change initiative.

Instruction: Major topics covered in the course are power of envision, the force of invention, and energy of involvement. Methods of instruction include lecture, discussion, and role-playing.

Credit Recommendation: In the upper division baccalaureate degree category, 1 semester hour in Organizational Behavior (11/96).

Instructional Design & Development Workshop (TD0930) (Formerly [QL0303])

Location: Morristown, NJ and other AT&T locations throughout the country.

Length: *Version 1:*40 hours (5 days); *Version 2:* 32 hours (4 days).

Dates: October 1984-Present.

Objective: *Version 1:* To provide the new course developer with the knowledge and skills needed to design courses successfully and effectively. *Version 2:* To enable employees to demonstrate effective skills to design and develop courses that reflect methods that support learning and retention.

Learning Outcome: *Version 1:* Upon successful completion of this course, the student will be able to describe techniques to determine performance problems; gather and analyze data about job tasks; determine what skills and knowledge should be taught; choose the instructional strategies, methods and media for the course; describe the balanced instruction technique; describe learning styles and how they relate to the instructional design and development process. *Version 2:* Upon successful completion of this course, the student will be able to identify the major phases of the systematic training development model, as well as the purpose and outputs of each phase; identify the major cost and time variables associated with course development; demonstrate methods for determining performance problems and opportunities; demonstrate methods for performing task analysis and skill/knowledge derivation; demonstrate how to derive and write performance related objectives and test items; define and develop learning strategies and methods appropriate for different learning outcomes; and demonstrate techniques for evaluating course material.

Instruction: *Version 1:* No prior teaching experience is required. Students receive precourse materials two weeks prior to the class and must have these assignments completed before class begins. The course covers the fundamental principles of instructional design, as presented in a four (4) step model. Practical application of the model and its underlying principles are emphasized as students design and develop a training package. Students will study task analysis, needs analysis and job analysis. *Version 2:* This course teaches the fundamental principles of instructional design. Practical application of the systematic development process and its underlying principles are emphasized and practiced.

Credit Recommendation: *Version 1:* In the graduate degree category, 3 semester hours in Instructional Design and Development, (for those students who already possess a baccalaureate degree or above) or in the upper division baccalaureate degree category, 3 semester hours for those students who do not already possess a baccalaureate degree (1/87). **NOTE:** Evaluators determined that if students did not already possess a BA degree or above, there was not sufficient indication that they would master the graduate level of the course. *Version 2:* In the upper division baccalaureate degree category, 3 semester hours in Instructional Design and Development (7/93).

Instructor Skills Practicum (TD0910)

Location: Morristown, NJ and other locations throughout the country.

Length: 24 hours (3 days).

Dates: February 1991-Present.

Objective: To enable subject competent employees to demonstrate effective teaching skills reflecting appropriate learning principles, instructional methods and techniques that facilitate learning.

Learning Outcome: Upon successful completion of this course, the student will be able to identify and practice using principles of learning and the application of adult learning theory; describe and demonstrate classroom motivational strategies to ensure interesting and challenging instructional delivery; practice introducing, managing and debriefing group and team exercises; demonstrate effective questioning techniques, experiential learning strategies and proper use of instructional media; and describe how to deal with disruptive student behaviors and classroom conflicts.

Instruction: The Instructor Skills Practicum (ISP) is an intensive three-day workshop designed to help students develop instructional delivery skills through practice. By engaging in a series of structured videotaped practice sessions, they are encouraged to take risks, incorporate new teaching strategies and skills into their teaching repertoires - and then receive precise and constructive feedback on performance from a skilled master trainer as well as "instructor" peers.

Credit Recommendation: In the upper division baccalaureate degree category, 2 semester hours in Instructor Skills Methods (7/93).

Instructor Training Workshop (TD0911)
(Formerly Basic Instructor Skills [QL0101-A])

Location: Morristown, NJ and other AT&T locations throughout the country.

Length: *Version 1:* 28 hours (4 days); *Version 2:* 40 hours (5 days).

Dates: *Version 1:* September 1985-June 1988; *Version 2:* July 1988-Present.

Objective: To enable subject competent employees to demonstrate effective teaching skills reflecting appropriate learning principles, instructional methods and techniques that facilitate learning.

Learning Outcome: *Version 1:* Upon successful completion of this course, the student will be able to describe the four learning styles and implications of those styles for instructing; explain the 3-step intervention process for handling problem situations in the classroom; explain the ARCS model of motivation and major strategies for stimulating desire to learn; demonstrate effective techniques for giving and receiving feedback; demonstrate the effective use of questioning skills and presentation skills as major tools for enhancing learning. *Version 2:* Upon successful completion of this course, the student will be able to identify and apply sound learner-centered principles of instruction that support learning; describe and demonstrate classroom motivational strategies to ensure interesting and challenging instructional delivery; identify instructional factors that promote (and hinder) student interaction and learning; identify and apply classroom delivery behaviors that support and enhance instructor credibility; describe instructor preparation strategies; demonstrate effective questioning techniques, experiential learning strategies and proper use of instructional media; and describe how to deal with disruptive student behaviors and classroom conflicts.

Instruction: *Version 1:* The course presents various concepts and skills for effective stand-up instruction and participate student-centered lecture. Course covers the 3-step intervention process and uses the ARCS model of motivation. Students prepare and deliver two 20-minute balanced instruction lectures. Also instructor observation, an instructor skills inventory and quizzes are used. *Version 2:* This course provides instruction in learning principles, instructional methods, and techniques that facilitate learning. It also provides practice in the planning and delivery of instructional sessions to demonstrate newly acquired skills.

Credit Recommendation: *Version 1:* In the upper division baccalaureate degree category, 2 semester hours in Basic Instructor Skills (1/87). *Version 2:* In the upper division baccalaureate degree category, 3 semester hours in Basic Instructor Skills (7/93).

Integrated Business and Financial Strategies (BM0114)

Location: Somerset, NJ and other AT&T locations.

Length: 32 hours.

Dates: December 1991-December 1993.

Objective: To empower students to perform their work in a more proactive, productive fashion, focusing on key strategic issues and questions relevant to OBS.

Learning Outcome: Upon successful completion of this course, the student will be able to identify the basic principles of business and the role of a business manager; demonstrate a working knowledge of business management with the skills required to define business strategies; identify the skills required to manage profitability and increase shareholder value; identify the issues associated with channel strategy, plans, and tactics; enhance knowledge of the business environment by focusing on the data-to-information process; defining the relationship between the data-to-information process and decision making; define and apply the techniques used to develop a situational analysis; and apply the techniques used to develop a situational analysis toward making a strategic business recommendation.

Instruction: Major topics covered in the course are instructing students on how to integrate the business, marketing, and financial aspects of a business operation; provide a framework for developing a situation analysis and translating this into an overall business vision, mission, objectives, and core strategic thrusts; also deals with developing a marketing plan; targeting key customers and establishing competitive advantage; and learn how to establish specific financial and marketing targets and how to monitor performance against these metrics.

Credit Recommendation: In the upper division baccalaureate degree category, 2 semester hours in Financial Analysis and Planning (4/92).

Integrated Marketing and Financial Strategies (SA4500)

Location: Locations throughout the U.S.

Length: *Version 1:* 21 hours (3 days); *Version 2:* 24 hours (3 days).

Dates: *Version 1:* October 1985-February 1993; *Version 2:* March 1993-Present.

Objective: *Version 1:* To acquaint students with the role of financial analysis in marketing. *Version 2:* To use financial and market measures to evaluate strategic and tactical marketing alternatives and make decisions, and to understand the bottom line impact of these decisions.

Learning Outcome: Upon successful completion of this course, the student will be able to use an integrated spreadsheet program to model the costs and benefits of specific programs; translate your marketing strategies into specific tactics and objectives; for example, awareness, CVA, repeat consumption, and market volume share; and accurately measure the impact of your marketing decisions using specific financial and marketing metrics, including variable contribution/margin, EVA, market share, and net present value.

Instruction: *Version 1:* This course presents strategic alternatives in the areas of promotion, price and distribution as related to the marketing of products and services. The role of financial analysis in the control marketing mix decisions is also emphasized. *Version 2:* This course will help students assess the bottom-line impact of your strategic and tactical marketing decisions. Participants will review the financial and market measure used to determine the impact decisions have, and learn to calculate the costs and benefits of alternative marketing strategies and tactics. An appropriate graduate level project is included as part of the course requirement for students to earn the credit recommendation.

Credit Recommendation: In the graduate degree category or in the upper division baccalaureate degree category, 1 semester hour in Integrated Marketing Strategies (11/85) (7/95).

International Business Ethics (GM1035)

Location: Somerset, NJ and other AT&T locations.

Length: 16 hours (2 days).

Dates: October 1992-Present.

Objective: To raise awareness of the issues of business ethics in different countries and provide students with the necessary skills to deal with situations in which they will be forced to make decisions.

Learning Outcome: Upon successful completion of this course, the student will be able to build stable, profitable business relationships in the global marketplace; develop a structure and strategy for resolving dilemmas; and strengthen employee loyalty and morale while enhancing business efficiency.

Instruction: Major topics covered in the course help raise students' awareness of the issues of business ethics in different countries and provides the necessary skills to deal with situations in which students will be forced to make decisions. The course includes ethical values, honesty, trust, respect and fairness, law and government regulation, strategies and implementation plans. Methods of instruction include discussion, lecture, case studies, video presentations and guest speakers. An appropriate graduate level research project is submitted as part of the course requirements.

Credit Recommendation: In the graduate degree category, 1 semester hour in International Business Ethics (12/93).

International Marketing (AT&T 411 SA4080)
SA4080, & 19F

Location: Somerset, NJ.

Length: 24 hours (3 days).

Dates: November 1983-December 1993.

Objective: To provide participants with an overview of foreign market opportunities.

Instruction: Major topics covered in the course are an appreciation of the similarities and differences of doing business in the service sector internationally versus domestically. Methods of instruction include case studies, guest lectures, and relevant materials from journals and trade magazines.

Credit Recommendation: In the upper division baccalaureate degree category, 2 semester hours in Introduction to World Resources (9/84) (8/91).

International Travel Security (FE0706)

Location: AT&T locations nationwide.

Length: 8 hours.

Dates: May 1991-March 1992.

Objective: To gain first hand knowledge about living and working in a risk environment, hostage survival, kidnap and extortion, political detention, and emergency evacuation.

Learning Outcome: Upon successful completion of this course, the student will be able to comprehend the safest and most risk-free travel alternatives; analyze current security descriptions for various countries; understand the basics of kidnapping and extortion; and describe various aspects of political detention and emergency evacuation.

Instruction: Major topics covered in the course are first hand knowledge about living and working in a risk environment, hostage survival, kidnap and extortion, political detention and emergency evacuation. Methods of instruction include case studies, lectures, group discussions, practice exercises, simulations and job aids; a series of guest speakers from the Corporate Security Organization, the Corporate Travel Group and American Express who can provide students with ample opportunity to "try out" the tactics and their countermeasures and evaluate their usefulness in the many kinds of travel situations; prior reading assignments and a term paper are also required.

Credit Recommendation: In the upper division baccalaureate degree category, 1 semester hour in International Terrorism (8/91).

Interpersonal Management Skills for Information Systems (IE1800)

Location: All AT&T training locations.

Length: 21 hours (3 days).

Dates: June 1979-June 1996.

Objective: To understand the basics of interpersonal skills as they relate to management.

Learning Outcome: Upon successful completion of this course, the student will be able to effectively use the skills of CLARIFYING and CONFIRMING, give balanced, critical feedback so the feedback will be used and accepted, appropriately use the discussion skills, select appropriate tactics in MANAGING DIFFERENCES, and give timely and high-impact CREDIT for performances.

Instruction: Major topics covered in the course are CLARIFYING and CONFIRMING-understanding what is said and/or implied and why; CONSTRUCTIVE CRITICISM-changing performance without stifling initiative by providing critical feedback so that the feedback will be used and accepted; DISCUSSION SKILLS-establishing a two-way communication link by appropriately using the skills of acknowledging others' ideas, brainstorming, and summarizing in discussions, interpersonal managing skills for information systems; MANAGING DIFFERENCES-selecting appropriate tactics in managing differences and avoiding win-lose conflicts; and CREDITING -giving timely and high-impact credits to reinforce standards of excellence by acknowledging good performance. Methods of instruction include programmed instruction, video, small group discussions, and role-playing.

Credit Recommendation: In the upper division baccalaureate degree category, 1 semester hour in Business Management, Psychology, or Communications (7/85) (7/90) (11/96).

Introduction to Accounting (FE0100)

Location: Locations throughout the U.S.

Length: 21 hours (3 days).

Dates: January 1988-Present.

Objective: To teach students the basic principles of accounting and the six-step accounting process.

Learning Outcome: Upon successful completion of this course, the student will be able to explain basic accounting concepts; define the accounting process; match AT&T main accounts to the appropriate categories on AT&T financial reports; describe the balance sheet equation; record written financial transactions in T-accounts, journal entries, and post and balance ledger accounts; prepare trial balance worksheet; perform closing process; and develop financial statements.

Instruction: The course includes an introduction to "T" accounts, discussion of recording financial transactions, posting and balancing worksheets, and culminates with the preparation of financial statements.

Credit Recommendation: In the upper division baccalaureate degree category, 1 semester hour in Accounting (12/90) (7/95).

Introduction to Basic Statistics (SE6000)
(Formerly Basic Statistics [SE6000])

Location: AT&T locations nationwide.

Length: 21 hours (3 days).

Dates: January 1983-Present.

Objective: To provide the student an understanding of basic statistics to improve the quality of communication between AT&T statisticians and their clients.

Learning Outcome: Upon successful completion of this course, the student will be able to apply statistics in daily work environments to improve productivity, use statistics to improve data gathering and evaluation techniques, and use statistical terminology with subject matter experts to bridge the communication gap.

Instruction: Major topics covered in the course are probability and statistics at the most basic level; knowledge of measures of central tendency (mean, median, mode); measures of variability (variance, standard deviation); random variables; continuous and discrete probability distributions; the binomial distribution; the normal distribution; the concepts of sampling distributions and confidence intervals; sampling theory; and the language of statistics and how to communicate effectively with statisticians. Methods of instruction include lecture, discussion, and exercises.

Credit Recommendation: In the upper division baccalaureate degree category, 2 semester hours in Statistics (8/91) (5/96).

Introduction to Budgeting Workshop (FE0108)

Location: Somerset, NJ; Atlanta, GA; Chicago, IL; and Orlando, FL.

Length: 16 hours (2 days).

Dates: May 1995-Present.

Objective: To learn the purpose and principles of budgeting and how to develop, implement, and manage a budget in AT&T.

Learning Outcome: Upon successful completion of this course, the student will be able to understand the budgeting process; develop, implement, and manage a budget for your business unit using a spreadsheet or budget software program; pinpoint budget variances, analyze budget vs. actual results and recommend solutions to problems; and use a budge as a managerial tool to achieve corporate/business unit objectives and improve profitability and cash flow.

Instruction: Major topics covered in the course are an introduction to the principles of budgeting; the structure of a budgeting report; master budget and operational/financial budgets, includes how to evaluate financial results, budget preparation, and capital assets; how to manage a budget; and variances: Budget vs. Actual. Methods of instruction include hands-on exercises using a manual spreadsheet and AT&T sample budget forms.

Credit Recommendation: In the upper division baccalaureate degree category, 1 semester hour in Financial Management: Budgeting (12/95).

Introduction to Expert Systems (IE1910)

Location: Piscataway, NJ and other AT&T locations.

Length: 22.5 hours (3 days).

Dates: May 1989-June 1992.

Objective: To introduce participants to the uses of expert systems.

Learning Outcome: Upon successful completion of this course, the student will be able to understand knowledge representation schemes (rules, frames, and semantic nets); choosing an appropriate representation scheme; languages and tools used in building expert systems; and using prototyping to solve ill-defined problems.

Instruction: Major topics covered in the course are various uses of expert systems, successful applications, programming languages and techniques used for building expert systems, and features of expert system shells. Methods of instruction include knowledge structuring exercises and hands-on lab are included to demonstrate how knowledge is encoded using a rule-based tool and how to interact with an expert system.

Credit Recommendation: In the lower division baccalaureate/associate degree category or the upper division baccalaureate degree category, 1 semester hour in Introduction to Expert Systems or Computer Science elective; however, if taken in combination with IE1911 (Knowledge Engineering), 3 semester hours in Artificial Intelligence in the upper division baccalaureate degree category (7/90).

Introduction to Finance

Location: Somerset, NJ and other AT&T regional facilities.

Length: 16 hours (2 days).

Dates: December 1988-Present.

Objective: To introduce basic financial concepts, including the components of financial statements by allowing the student to construct his/her personal financial position and cash flow statement.

Learning Outcome: Upon successful completion of this course, the student will be able to, using data from personal experience and the Balance Sheet Equation, identify an asset and its component parts and the two categories of liabilities; given interest tables and the "Rule of 72," describe the concept, Time Value of Money; provided with cash expenditures data and the categories of revenues and expenses, accurately develop a pro-forma cash flow statement; given examples of financial statements and their components, identify and describe the elements of a corporate financial statement; using personal financial concepts developed in the program, correctly relate the concepts developed in a financial environment; and using financial reports and ratios, interpret the reports using ratios to make financial decisions.

Instruction: This course is for the student with little or no background in finance. Students will learn the concept of compound interest and apply it to the theory of time value of money. They will also learn how to apply personal financial concepts to corporate finance to better understand the components of financial reports and analysis. Other topics include: Wall Street, income tax, and financing a business.

Credit Recommendation: In the upper division baccalaureate degree category, 1 semester hour in Finance (12/90) (7/95).

Introduction to Project Management (MS6310)

Location: Somerset, NJ and other AT&T locations.

Length: 24 hours (3 days).

Dates: *Version 1:* January 1988-December 1992; *Version 2:* January 1993-Present.

Objective: To provide concepts, tools, and techniques to plan, schedule, organize and implement projects to enable students to better manage projects instead of projects managing them.

Learning Outcome: *Version 1:* Upon successful completion of this course, the student will be able to define project management and its phases in terms of an information systems model; describe the characteristics of effective project managers and team members; plan, organize, monitor, and control a project using a work breakdown structure and an analysis of critical and high-risk factors; use several scheduling techniques, develop an activity network diagram, and calculate the critical path and slack for activities; describe the uses of project management PC software and the types of outputs that can be generated for all phases of a project; describe how team building, managing differences, and personal style can affect team and interpersonal effectiveness and the strategies that can be used to improve them. *Version 2:* Upon successful completion of this course, the student will be able to develop a step-by-step process to plan, organize, monitor and control a project; determine the life cycle of a project and what must be done at each stage; identify the characteristics, roles and responsibilities of the project manager; and to introduce and provide practical application of the principles and concepts of the Project Management Institute Body of Knowledge (PMBOK).

Instruction: *Version 1:* This course considers a number of behavioral and organizational issues associated with projects. These topics can help both project team members and team leaders get the right expected level of quality. *Version 2:* This course is designed for students managing projects or members of a project team. It includes project management, project planning, scheduling and budget, monitoring and controlling, using PC software for project management, and project teams. Methods of instruction include lecture and discussion.

Credit Recommendation: *Version 1:* In the upper division baccalaureate degree category, 1 semester hour in Introduction to Project Management; *Version 2:* In the upper division baccalaureate degree category, 2 semester hours in Project Management (12/93).

Introduction to Regulated Utilities (PUB 201)

Location: Somerset Seminars Center, Somerset, NJ.

Length: 40 hours (5 days).

Dates: January 1984-December 1984.

Objective: To provide an overview of the components of utility pricing and rate case processing.

Instruction: Course provides an introduction to the elements of a regulated utility. It describes the factors considered in determining the need for rate changes, examines the price structure for key intraLATA service, and explains financial and capital components. It also provides an overview of major accounting and reporting systems used by a utility in operation. Course uses lectures, group discussions, and workshops.

Credit Recommendation: In the upper division baccalaureate degree category, 2 semester hours in Business Administration, Marketing, or Public Administration (9/83).

Introduction to SPC (MF3405)

Location: Any AT&T location as requested.

Length: 36 hours (5 days).

Dates: *Version 1:* June 1988-December 1992; *Version 2:* January 1993-December 1996.

Objective: To teach statistical process control techniques for use in manufacturing environments.

Learning Outcome: Upon successful completion of this course, the student will be able to use scatter plots, frequency distributions, cause and effect diagrams, Pareto and box-and-whisker charts and defect concentration analysis, calculate the centerline and control limits for variables and attributes control charts, plot the charts, identify out-of-control conditions, know when to apply attributes or variables control charts, calculate the coefficient of correlation, the coefficient of determination, and the regression equation for a set of data, use analysis f means and test of hypotheses to compare groups of data, and discuss the applications of statistically designed experiments.

Instruction: Major topics covered in the course are an overview of statistical process control methods for manufacturing professionals, the application of statistical tools to control a process and how to assess changes in process, a PC software package SQC Troubleshooter is used to analyze data. This course is presented on a level suitable to engineers. Methods of instruction include classroom discussion, lecture, and simulation. Students must successfully complete the specified examination, or an independent project utilizing appropriate statistical process control techniques.

Credit Recommendation: *Version 1:* In the upper division baccalaureate degree category, 3 semester hours in Statistical Methods for Quality Control or Statistical Quality Control (10/91). *Version 2:* In the upper division baccalaureate degree category, 2 semester hours in Statistical Methods for Quality Control or Statistical Quality Control (11/96).

Introduction to Technical Mathematics and Electricity and Electronics

Location: Offered at various corporate locations throughout the United States.

Length: 48 hours, two 3 hour sessions weekly for eight weeks.

Dates: October 1995-Present.

Objective: To take a student with a limited mathematical background and no previous knowledge of electricity into the field of electricity and electronics with an emphasis on its use in telephony.

Learning Outcome: Upon successful completion of this course, the student will have the mathematical ability to do problem solving in electronics. The knowledge gained in electricity and electronics will go from the basic level of electron theory through electric and electronic circuits of both direct current and alternating current.

Instruction: Major topics covered in the course are scientific notation, equation solving, graphing, electron theory, electric circuits, Ohm's Law, series and parallel circuits, magnetic fields, inductance, capacitance, timing circuits, reactance, impedance and introduction to telephony. Methods of instruction include lecture, circuit and instrument demonstrations, classroom problem sessions, homework assignments and tests. Evaluation methods include tests, home work assignments, in-class worksheets and final exam.

Credit Recommendation: In the lower division baccalaureate/associate degree category, 2 semester hours in Introduction to Electricity and Magnetism (1/98).

Introduction to Total Quality Management Series (MF3414)
a) Organizational Self-Assessment Using Baldridge Criteria (CQ1018)
b) Sharing the Quality Vision (CQ1002)
c) SPC Overview for Managers (MF3414)

Location: Various AT&T locations nationwide.

Length: A) 8 hours; B) 8 hours; C) 8 hours.

Dates: A) September 1990-December 1993; B) December 1989-December 1993; C) December 1989-December 1993.

Objective: A) To enable a work team to assess their organization's total quality system based on the Malcolm Baldridge National Quality Award; B) to teach the basic theories and principles of total Quality Management; C) to familiarize managers with SPC and how it relates to improving the quality of their processes.

Learning Outcome: Upon successful completion of course A, the student will be able to understand the Malcolm Baldridge National Quality Award Criteria; understand the relationship of the Malcolm Baldridge Quality Award and the AT&T Chairman's Award; gain working knowledge of the self-award assessment process; adopt the Baldridge criteria as a framework for running a successful business. Upon successful completion of course B, explain Total Quality in current management practices; understand and apply the customer-supplier model to various business relationships; and understand the roles and responsibilities of Quality teams and team members. Upon successful completion of course C, the student will be able to define process capability, process control, and process improvement; calculate and interpret several descriptive statistics; and interpret control charts, Pareto diagrams, histograms, scatterplots, and analysis of means.

Instruction: A) Major topics covered in the course are a natural work team to assess their total quality system based on recognized national quality standards and to plan improvements based on their findings. B) Major topics covered in the course are how to establish a common language of quality by examining AT&T's Quality Policy and the five principles of quality; the opportunity to consider what is currently happening in the organization in regard to the principles and policy; focus on the types of activities that will be necessary to turn AT&T's business around to a total quality approach; looks at the quality support, policy, implementation, results, and business results that will be necessary to transform the business; and students will use the quality grid to identify potential improvement opportunities in their work and organizations. C) Major topics covered in the course are SPC to the manager's role in applying quality-improvement techniques to their processes; managers will learn which tools to apply, when to apply them, and what results to expect, emphasis is on the interpretation of various graphical presentations; the course addresses what it means to have a "6 process" and what to do to get there; and many examples of the use of SPC to improve quality and decision making.

Credit Recommendation: In the upper division baccalaureate degree category, 1 semester hour in Management when this course is taken in combination with CQ1002 and MF3414 as a series (10/91). **NOTE:** The student must also complete an Application Project and have it reviewed by one of three course instructors to be eligible for the credit recommendation.

Introductory Project Management 1. Project Management Essentials (IE1602) (Formerly 1. Introduction to Project Management) 2. Project Management Workshop (IE1604)

Location: Piscataway, NJ and other AT&T locations.

Length: *Course 1:* 18 hours (3 days); *Course 2:* 34 hours (5 days).

Dates: *Courses 1 and 2:* November 1979-December 1993.

Objective: To provide the student with detailed conceptual knowledge of the project management process.

Instruction: Major topics covered in the course are the characteristics of a complex systems project and the important aspects of the structure, environment, and vocabulary of project management. Methods of instruction include lecture, discussion, and workshops.

Credit Recommendation: In the upper division baccalaureate degree category, 3 semester hours in Business Administration or Management (5/80) (7/85) (7/90). **NOTE:** Students must complete both courses to receive credit for Introductory Project Management.

Job Aids Workshop (IE1204)

Location: Piscataway, NJ and other AT&T locations.

Length: 18 hours (3 days).

Dates: January 1983-June 1996.

Objective: To provide an introduction to job aids for trainers.

Learning Outcome: Upon successful completion of this course, the student will be able to decide how a deficiency in skill or knowledge will be treated—job aid only, instruction-to-recall only, or a combination of instruction and job aid(s); describe performance criteria to a level of detail required to construct job aids; and analyze the characteristics of the performance to select the most appropriate format or combination of formats for job aids.

Instruction: Major topics covered in the course are combination facilitator-led/programmed instruction offering. Opportunities for questions and student interaction are strongly emphasized. Job aids of every type are available as models. The course gives practice in the selection and construction of various types of job aids, including one which the student must bring to class for development.

Credit Recommendation: In the upper division baccalaureate degree category, 1 semester hour in Business Administration (7/90).

Knowledge Engineering (IE1911)

Location: Piscataway, NJ and other AT&T locations.

Length: 37.5 hours (5 days).

Dates: July 1989-June 1992.

Objective: To introduce participants to the process and techniques used in building expert systems.

Learning Outcome: Upon successful completion of this course, the student will be able to understand: (1) potential expert system applications; (2) the management of an expert system development project; (3) knowledge acquisition; (4) knowledge structuring; (5) prototyping; and (6) deployment issues.

Instruction: Major topics covered in the course are centered around a successful methodology that offers a practical approach to beginning knowledge engineering training through classroom lecture, case studies, supplementary reading, and group discussions. Methods of instruction include intensive exercises as well supplemental knowledge acquisition.

Credit Recommendation: In the lower division baccalaureate/associate degree or the upper division baccalaureate degree category, 2 semester hours in Knowledge Engineering or Computer Science elective; however, if taken in combination with IE1910 (Introduction to Expert Systems), 3 semester hours in Artificial Intelligence in the upper division baccalaureate degree category (7/90).

Leadership Development Program (ATT03)

Location: The Learning Center, Basking Ridge, NJ.

Length: *Version 1:* 140 hours; *Version 2:* 98 hours; *Version 3:* 2 weeks.

Dates: *Version 1:* January 1985-December 1990; *Version 2:* January 1991-June 1996; *Version 3:* July 1996-Present.

Objective: To provide an intense two-week developmental, leadership and general management experience designed to exponentially enhance the leadership capacity of second level and district level high performing managers and to increase their ability to assume higher level responsibilities.

Learning Outcome: Upon successful completion of this course, the student will be able to understand leadership behaviors, skills and mindset to be an effective agent of change; understand AT&T's latest strategies through interaction with senior AT&T executives; exercise strategic thinking and strategy execution ; develop a global, general management perspective and an understanding of the information industry; develop an innovative action plan to address critical business challenge; and understand impact on the bottom line and be clear on contributions toward the success of AT&T.

Instruction: Major topics covered in the course are business capabilities needed to address global business challenges; leadership skills required to effect change and align teams behind change efforts; and personal effectiveness skills essential to continual renewal and growth. The program is holistic and integrates several learning modalities. These include Action

Learning, Cognitive and Experiential Learning, Feedback, Leadership, Wellness/Fitness, Organizational and Personal Change Strategies. Participants identify and address their key business issues and personal leadership challenges throughout the program in small group sessions called "GAP" groups. They offer one another candid but caring feedback and help develop innovative action plans to address business and leadership challenges. Participants are also given a 360 degrees feedback instrument prior to their participation and then get the results of the feedback during the program. An experienced consultant is available to offer individual counsel to the participants to help them act on their feedback results. Methods of instruction include classroom discussion, lecture, simulation, independent study and other experiential/action learning. **NOTE:** An appropriate graduate level research project is included as part of the course requirement for students who seek the credit recommendation.

Credit Recommendation: *Version 1:* In the graduate degree category, 4 semester hours in Business Strategy and Policy, and 4 semester hours in Market Planning and Strategy, for a total of 8 semester hours (9/89). *Version 2:* In the graduate degree category, 3 semester hours in Business Strategy and Policy, and 3 semester hours in Market Planning and Strategy, for a total of 6 semester hours (Special Annual Review 1/91). *Version 3:* In the graduate degree category, 3 semester hours in Business Strategy and Policy, and 3 semester hours in Market Planning and Strategy, for a total of 6 semester hours (10/97).

Leadership Development Program

Location: Hamilton Park Conference Center, Florham Park, NJ.

Length: *Version 1:* 140 hours; *Version 2:* 98 hours.

Dates: *Version 1:* January 1985-December 1990; *Version 2:* January 1991-Present.

Objective: To develop in emerging executives the strategic and managerial competencies required to succeed in a high technology, competitive business environment.

Learning Outcome: Upon successful completion of this course, the student will be able to understand the executive role and responsibilities; identify and diagnose the impact of relevant external forces (global, domestic, business, social, and legislative); translate external corporation; effectively communicate and implement strategic directions and plans; be more effective in interpersonal and leadership working with individuals of all levels, inside and outside the organization; and employ increased managerial competence in all phases of the corporation.

Instruction: Major topics covered in the course are global and domestic environmental forces; customers, markets, and competition; organization culture and effectiveness; strategic planning, thinking, and management; business functions and interrelationships; and executive approaches to managing people and organizations. Methods of instruction include lecture, discussion, led by distinguished consultants and graduate school academicians; and case-study analyses. All students qualifying for credit recommendations have also completed previous formal coursework in management principles, in addition to their experience as mid-level managers. These students also complete a comprehensive and exhaustive case analysis (corresponding to at least a 40-page case study) drawn from either a specific AT&T corporate situation or from an appropriate academic source (e.g., University of Michigan case study) including overall business strategy, market planning, product positioning, etc. The case analysis is evaluated by appropriate faculty associated with this program.

Credit Recommendation: *Version 1:* In the graduate degree category, 4 semester hours in Business Strategy and Policy, and 4 semester hours in Market Planning and Strategy for a total of 8 semester hours (9/89). *Version 2:* In the graduate degree category, 3 semester hours in Business Strategy and Policy, and 3 semester hours in Market Planning and Strategy, for a total of 6 semester hours (Annual Review).

Leadership for the Future: A Principle-Centered Leadership-Based Model (MD7603) (Formerly Leadership for the Future [MD7603])

Location: Worldwide with AT&T /Lucent Technologies.

Length: 32 hours (4 days).

Dates: *Version 1:* March 1989-April 1996; *Version 2:* May 1996-Present.

Objective: To stimulate personal and organizational development, increase the levels of trust in the workplace, and create an awareness around leadership development.

Learning Outcome: Upon successful completion of this course, the student will be able to identify the principles through which lasting and effective leadership is developed, and assess how their current behaviors relate to these principles; state how applying these principles fosters the development of the AT&T Dimensions of Leadership; develop unity in their organization or work team around a commonly shared mission and values; establish a foundation around mission and values as a way of productively preparing the work team/organization for change; cultivate trust, strength, and desire in work group members to be proactive and take risks; manage interpersonal conflicts in a courageous yet collaborative manner; maximize group members' individual contribution while nurturing their personal satisfaction and development; and develop plans for assessing their progress, as well as a work group's progress, toward fulfilling the mission of the organization.

Instruction: *Version 1:* Major topics covered in the course are a leadership perspective that will enhance their manager's management skills; the critical role of AT&T's first- and second-level managers and how they can positively affect their organization, mission, and strategy by exercising judgment, initiative, and leadership behaviors; and "principle-centered leadership," experience has shown that this approach to leadership translates into greater organizational unity, interpersonal flexibility, and personal productivity. Methods of instruction include lecture, discussion, exercises. *Version 2:* Major topics covered in the course are a leadership perspective that will enhance their manager's management skills; the critical role of AT&T's first- and second-level managers and how they can positively affect their organization, mission, and strategy by exercising judgment, initiative, and leadership behaviors; and "principle-centered leadership," experience has shown that this approach to leadership translates into greater organizational unity, interpersonal flexibility, and personal productivity. Methods of instruction include lecture, discussion, exercises, and an application project.

Credit Recommendation: *Version 1:* In the lower division baccalaureate/associate degree category, 2 semester hours in Leadership Principles, Management, or Human Resources Development (12/90). *Version 2:* In the lower division baccalaureate/associate degree category or upper division baccalaureate degree category, 2 semester hours in Leadership Principles, Management, or Human Resources (5/96).

Leadership for the Future: A Principle-Centered Leadership-Based Model (Occupational) (MD7604) (Formerly Leadership for the Future-Occupational [MD7613]) (Formerly Leadership for the Future-Occupational [MD7604])

Location: Worldwide with AT&T.

Length: 24 hours (3 days).

Dates: *Version 1:* June 1990-April 1996; *Version 2:* May 1996-December 1996.

Objective: To stimulate personal and organizational effectiveness that provides the basis for leadership development.

Learning Outcome: *Version 1:* Upon successful completion of this course, the student will be able to write and use a personal mission statement as a guide to daily activities; apply the development process based on Steven R. Covey's *7 Habits of Highly Effective People*; use the tools and processes that will effectively help you respond to the feedback you receive from your boss, colleagues, and key contacts; and write and establish win/win agreements with your boss, colleagues, and customers. *Version 2:* Upon successful completion of this course, the student will be able to write and use a personal mission statement as a guide to daily activities; create goals and plans (based on The 7 Habits of Highly Effective People) to increase personal performance; have the ability to respond to feedback from their boss, colleagues, and customers; make win-win agreements with your boss, colleagues, and customers; and establish coaching partnerships and build productivity.

Instruction: *Version 1:* Major topics covered in the course are the first two phases of leadership development: personal self-mastery and interpersonal effectiveness; self-empowering principles; how to avoid management fads and short-term quick fix solutions; examining and experiencing the phases of leadership development that lead to personal and interpersonal effectiveness; how to develop and complete specific implementation plans; and how to set goals to achieve dramatic increases in personal performance. Methods of instruction include lecture, discussion, and extensive feedback from boss and colleagues based upon Steven R. Covey's *7 Habits of Highly Effective People*. *Version 2:* Major topics covered in the course are high-powered concepts and principles everyone needs to prepare for the future and the concepts of "Principle-Centered Leadership" experience, this approach to leadership translates into greater organizational unity, interpersonal flexibility, and personal productivity. Methods of instruction include lecture, discussion, and an application project.

Credit Recommendation: *Version 1:* In the lower division baccalaureate/associate degree category, 2 semester hours in Principles of Management (10/91). *Version 2:* In the lower division baccalaureate/associate degree category or upper division baccalaureate degree category, 2 semester hours in Fundamentals of Leadership (5/96).

Leading for Results (MD7704)

Location: All AT&T training locations.

Length: 16 hours (2 days).

Dates: January 1996-Present.

Objective: To build on the personal leadership principles learned in "Principle-Centered Leadership/Leadership for the Future"/MD7603 and offer the participants the opportunity to work through a real organizational management which they bring to the workshop.

Learning Outcome: Upon successful completion of this course, the student will be able to set and/or transform already set strategy into results, recognize and deal with paradoxes, list and describe the Transformational Leadership Framework, Global Mindsets and the SABLE, and work with colleagues to create results regardless of reporting relationships.

Instruction: Major topics covered in the course are the application of learning and leadership skills to actual job challenges and to formulate plans of action to be taken back to the workplace. Methods of instruction include lecture, discussion, and role-playing.

Credit Recommendation: In the upper division baccalaureate degree category, 1 semester hour in Organizational Behavior (11/96).

Leading Performance Improvement Teams (MQ6012) (Formerly Quality Improvement Team Leader Workshop [MQ6012])

Location: Somerset, NJ and other AT&T locations.

Length: 24 hours (3 days).

Dates: February 1992-Present.

Objective: To give quality improvement team leaders a practical workshop dealing with the issues they will face as a team facilitator.

Learning Outcome: Upon successful completion of this course, the student will be able to lead a quality improvement team using QIC, QIS or PQMI methodology and acquire the facilitation skills needed to manage effectively in a team oriented improvement process.

Instruction: This course is recommended for team leaders having prior exposure to PQMI, QIC, or QIS methodology. It is a practical workshop using exercises and role plays to establish facilitation skills essential to success as a team leader. **NOTE:** An application project at the graduate level is required to complete the course.

Credit Recommendation: In the graduate degree category, 2 semester hours in Group Dynamics (4/92).

Leading Policy Deployment (CQ8058)

Location: Somerset, NJ and other AT&T locations.

Length: 7.5 hours.

Dates: December 1991-December 1993.

Objective: To enable a management team to begin the policy deployment process.

Learning Outcome: Upon successful completion of this course, the student will be able to determine how policy deployment will be used to improve business capabilities in their organization; and begin to implement their organizational specific policy deployment process.

Instruction: Major topics covered in the course are helping leaders of an organization to establish breakthrough objectives as well as a conducive environment that will enable a successful implementation of Policy Deployment within their organization; and students must submit a graduate level research project to earn the graduate credit recommendation.

Credit Recommendation: In the graduate degree category, 1 semester hour in Business Policy (4/92).

Lease Versus Buy Decision (FE0460)

Location: AT&T locations throughout the United States.

Length: 8 hours (1 day).

Dates: December 1989-October 1993.

Objective: To teach managers the fundamentals of ownership versus lease analysis.

Learning Outcome: Upon successful completion of this course, the student will be able to understand the rationale and terminology for leasing; perform a lease analysis; and understand the financial implications of leasing.

Instruction: Major topics covered in the course are the fundamentals of lease-versus-buy analysis; topics include leasing, reasons for and against leasing, economic analysis of the lease-versus-buy decision, and criteria for selecting an alternative.

Credit Recommendation: In the graduate degree category, 1 semester hour in Finance or Accounting (12/90).

Local Network Services Seminar (LNSS) (Formerly Exchange Services Seminar [EXS])

Location: Bell System Tariffs and Costs Seminars, Somerset, NJ.

Length: 35.5 hours (1 week).

Dates: *Version 1:* May 1980-November 1981; *Version 2:* December 1981-December 1984.

Objective: *Version 1:* To provide information and knowledge fundamentals to the understanding of key exchange issues and techniques. *Version 2:* To provide a forum for identification and discussion of the pertinent issues affecting the implementation of local measured service and the provision of attendant local area services.

Instruction: *Version 1:* Major topics covered in the course are exchange service definitions, concepts, and pricing and costing methodologies; cost models; and economic and market impacts. In addition, the seminar discusses interrelationships between exchange and network services, extended area service optional calling plans, coin operation and service, radio services, and measured service. The seminar provides a group exercise that involves rate structures and levels, the critical need for long-range plans, and awareness of various market impacts. Methods of instruction include lectures, audiovisuals, guest speakers, group task performances, and field observations. *Version 2:* Major topics covered in the course are various instructional strategies so that the participants have a high-level perception of the application of strategy and development of pricing principles and provides discussion of pertinent issues, primarily from a public acceptance view; current viewpoints on the key local area service issues; the economic rationale for local area service ratemaking decisions, and the need for specific long-range planning.

Credit Recommendation: In the upper division baccalaureate degree category, 1 semester hour in Business Administration, Engineering, or Public Administration (2/81).

Logical Data Base Design

Location: Data Systems Education Center, Piscataway, NJ and other Bell locations.

Length: 32 hours (1 week).

Dates: May 1978-August 1984.

Objective: To provide the student with skills and knowledge necessary to complete logical data base design.

Instruction: Major topics covered in the course are logical design of a data base, relational and usage requirements of the data base, and the need for controls and security requirements. Methods of instruction are lecture and laboratory.

Credit Recommendation: In the upper division baccalaureate degree category, 1 semester hour in Computer Science or Data Processing (2/80).

Logical Data Structuring (IE2532)

Location: Piscataway, NJ and other AT&T locations.

Length: 18 hours (3 days).

Dates: September 1984-December 1986.

Objective: To provide programmers with the skills needed to complete logical data base "relational" and "usage" views.

Learning Outcome: Upon successful completion of this course, the student should be able to explain how a data base differs from traditional file processing; describe how the four phases of data base design are related to each other; construct a relational view of sample; verify that a data structure is normalized; develop a usage view of sample data; and compare relational and usage views to verify the completeness and accuracy of the logical data structure.

Instruction: Major topics covered in the course are how to perform 3-step normalization, how to verify that a data structure is in 3rd Normal Form, and how to document data access and usage requirements.

Credit Recommendation: In the upper division baccalaureate degree category, 1 semester hour in Computer Information Systems or Computer Science (7/85). **NOTE:** Students who already received credit for IE2530 (Data Analysis and Logical Data Structuring) should receive no credit for this course.

Malcolm Baldridge National Quality Award-A Guide to Quality Improvement (MF3412)

Location: Piscataway, NJ.

Length: 16 hours (2 days).

Dates: June 1990-June 1996.

Objective: To develop the student's understanding of the MBNQA criteria and to have students apply the criteria to improve their organization's quality.

Learning Outcome: Upon successful completion of this course, the student will be able to explain the MBNQA and the Award criteria; describe the incentives, tools, and data required for a self-assessment; and describe how to use the Award criteria to track the results of your quality-improvement efforts.

Instruction: Major topics covered in the course teach how the Award criteria can be used by any organization in AT&T for self-assessment and how to use the results of the assessment to improve the quality of an organization's processes, products, and services; how to systematically divide their processes into carefully defined areas and how to evaluate them by considering the Award criteria and the critical aspects of each; and also learn what kind of information is needed for a self-assessment.

Credit Recommendation: In the upper division baccalaureate degree category, 1 semester hour in Organizational Assessment (10/91). **NOTE:** The credit recommendation applies only to those students who also successfully complete an independent exam on the subject of "Organizational Assessment."

Management Workshop on AT&T's Business Case Process (FE9000) (Business Case and Risk Analysis: An Executive Workshop (FE9000)

Location: AT&T locations throughout the country.

Length: 24 hours (3 days).

Dates: June 1990-Present.

Objective: To teach students the business case process from the perspective of the decision maker.

Learning Outcome: Upon successful completion of this course, the student will be able to understand principles of decision quality; perform the critical review function as a "decision board" member for business cases; and understand the framing, analysis, and connection stages of the business case process to be an effective participant on the project team.

Instruction: Major topics covered in the course are three separate business case studies, reviewing the quality of the work done by the project team at critical review points: the issues and alternative strategies, the framework for analysis, the sensitivity results, the opportunity versus risk evaluations, and the implementation plan. An appropriate graduate level project is included as part of the course requirement for students to earn the credit recommendation.

Credit Recommendation: *Version 1:* In the graduate degree category, 1 semester hour in Decision Making (12/90). *Version 2:* In the graduate degree category or in the upper division baccalaureate degree category, 1 semester hour in Business Strategies and Decision Making (7/95).

Managing a Global Business: Money and Results (GM1010)

Location: Somerset, NJ and other AT&T locations.

Length: 30 hours.

Dates: October 1988-April 1997.

Objective: To teach students to run their own global business as part of a team, using a unique board game simulation.

Learning Outcome: Upon successful completion of this course, the student will be able to understand and visualize the business cycle of the firm, from marketing and finance through production and labor management; use strategic and competitor analysis in conjunction with budgets and cash flow forecasts to set prices in a competitive market; create and use financial statements, and understand and control situations through Competitor Analysis, Income Statement Analysis, Breakeven Analysis and Ratio Analysis; better identify and respond to cross-cultural problems in both interpersonal skills and business structures; understand the structure of financial statements in the global marketplace, including discrepancies in accounting principles and practices in different countries; and compare investment opportunities in different countries in terms of payback, choice of investment structure, and long-term strategic advantage.

Instruction: Major topics covered in the course include a simulation methodology which calls for the student to participate in a unique board game and allows the student to "run" their own global business as part of a team; students experience the difficulties and challenges of managing cash flow, budgeting for expenses and estimating sales; and they compete in the "open market" by pricing competitively to sell products.

Credit Recommendation: In the upper division baccalaureate degree category, 1 semester hour in Financial Analysis for Global Markets (4/92).

Managing a Strategic Business Unit (SA5100)

Location: Somerset, NJ.

Length: 24 hours plus lab.

Dates: September 1988-October 1992.

Objective: To provide students an understanding of the strategic, financial, cross-functional and organizational tradeoffs necessary to run a successful business in a dynamic and competitive global marketplace.

Learning Outcome: Upon successful completion of this course, the student will be able to perform industry analysis to identify factors influencing profitability; develop a strategy which entails understanding customer needs worldwide, segmenting the marketplace, analyzing competitors and the industry, and evaluating key trade-offs for meeting customer requirements; understand cross-functional relationships and resource allocations involved in operating a business; evaluate the impact of competition and other external forces on customer relationships and overall company performance; interpret financial statements, cash flows and profitability ratios; use proformas for planning and analyzing strategies; work together as a team; and develop processes for decision making ad communications.

Instruction: Major topics covered in the course are an introduction to industry analysis and strategy formulation; analyze the simulation industry; formulate strategies and make the tactical business decisions necessary to run their businesses; business concepts are reinforced, and challenging and thought-provoking questions are asked to ensure that students receive a maximized learning experience. Methods of instruction include in-depth research for a substantial written document on some strategic or cross-functional aspect of business operations, using footnotes with annotated bibliography; formal presentation of the proposed topic after discussion in class. The maximum time period for the completion of this project is 8 weeks from the end of the course.

Credit Recommendation: In the upper division baccalaureate degree category, 3 semester hours in Managing a Strategic Business Unit, or in the graduate degree category, 3 semester hours in Managing a Strategic Business Unit, provided specific requirements are completed (8/91).

Managing and Improving Processes with Quality (CQ1004)

Location: AT&T locations nationwide.

Length: 16 hours.

Dates: June 1989-August 1996.

Objective: To teach quality methods to improve the effectiveness and efficiency of functional processes.

Learning Outcome: Upon successful completion of this course, the student will be able to define the 7-steps in PQMI; learn basic data collection and basic tools in applying the PQMI methodology; understand and describe the responsibilities of those implementing PQMI; and determine the next steps for implementing PQMI in your own work.

Instruction: Major topics covered in the course is Process Quality Management and Improvement (PQMI) a 7-step methodology used to successfully manage product and service processes. Methods of instruction include case study as well as their own work process.

Credit Recommendation: In the upper division baccalaureate degree category, 1 semester hour in Introduction to Quality Control (8/91). **NOTE:** The credit recommendation applies only to those students who successfully complete an Implementation Project or Plan to be assessed by the Instructor.

Managing Conflict (MS6430)

Location: AT&T locations throughout the United States.

Length: 24 hours (3 days).

Dates: January 1986-June 1992.

Objective: To provide experiences and theory to evaluate and respond constructively to conflicts between and within groups and between individuals.

Learning Outcome: Upon successful completion of this course, students will be able to explain how conflict is inevitable in a variety of interpersonal and organizational settings; define and distinguish, by using models and exercises, conflict behavior for interpersonal, intragroup, and intergroup settings; identify one's own individual conflict style in interpersonal and group settings; and identify and apply appropriate intervention and resolution skills in the three conflict settings by considering the nature of the conflict and the appropriateness of collaborative/competitive behavior; structural/situational preconditions in the organization; prior conflict history; strengths and weaknesses of one's own personal style; and barriers and aids to resolution.

Instruction: Major topics covered in the course are how conflict is inevitable in a variety of interpersonal and organizational settings; defines and distinguishes by using theoretical models of conflict behavior in interpersonal, intragroup, and intergroup settings; identifies one's own individual conflict style in interpersonal and group settings with emphasis on conflict-provoking situations, extreme or excessive personal reactions to other personal styles or circumstances, personal strengths and weaknesses, and self-management during conflict; and identifies and applies appropriate intervention and resolution skills in the three conflict settings by consideration of the nature of the conflict and the appropriateness of collaborative/competitive behavior, the structural/situational preconditions in the organization, prior conflict history, the strengths and weaknesses of one's own personal style, and barriers and aids to resolution.

Credit Recommendation: In the upper division baccalaureate degree category, 1 semester hour in Managing Conflict (12/90).

Managing Development and Diversity (MD2020)

Location: Somerset, NJ and other AT&T locations.

Length: 16 hours (2 days).

Dates: November 1990-December 1994.

Objective: To provide managers with concrete strategies to maximize performance and productivity using a results oriented approach.

Learning Outcome: Upon successful completion of this course, the student will be able to analyze the obstacles to development for women and minorities; employ a problem solving approach to remove such barriers or minimize their impact; build employee's confidence and increase their willingness to take on challenging projects; encourage the independence and initiative of all employees; and write detailed action plans that apply the seminar concepts to the management of particular employees.

Instruction: Major topics covered in the course are the ability to confront questions about the performance capabilities of minorities and women, addresses the tensions sometimes present in a multicultural workplace and offers an operational perspective on managing a diverse workforce; using a results-oriented approach, the program focuses on methods for improving productivity the manager can control directly; and the student is required to complete an application project by the end of the course.

Credit Recommendation: In the lower division baccalaureate/associate degree category, 1 semester hour in Managing Diversity (4/92).

Managing Emerging Technologies (IE1623)

Location: Piscataway, NJ and various other locations nationwide.

Length: 12 hours (2 days).

Dates: January 1994-Present.

Objective: To identify recent advances in the information technology industry, the organizational dynamics of their adoption and their impact on Project Management.

Learning Outcome: Upon successful completion of this course, the student will be able to understand and manage the organizational issues of emerging technology adoption; recognize and evaluate emerging technologies; understand and manage the effect of technical issues on system development: building the system right; understand the management of a project when emerging technologies are involved; and plan for implementing new technologies and management philosophies.

Instruction: This course identifies recent advances in the information technology industry and their impact on organizations and project management. Future technologies and their impact on current usage are defined, including their effect on the project life cycle.

Credit Recommendation: In the graduate degree category, 1 semester hour in Managing Change (6/95). **NOTE:** In order for student to receive this credit recommendation, student must also complete IE1620.

Managing in the Virtual Workplace (VO2006)

Location: Open/General Enrollments: Somerset, NJ; Atlanta, GA; Chicago, IL; and Pleasanton, CA. Suitcased/On-site Delivery: Internationally.

Length: 7 hours (1 day).

Dates: September 1995-Present.

Objective: To provide managers with an understanding of the issues associated with managing remote workers and how to supervise for success and maintain teamwork and synergy with associates working in a remote environment.

Learning Outcome: Upon successful completion of this course, the student will be able to identify the major concerns of Virtual Workplace managers and the adjustments they might need to make to effectively supervise remotely; apply the principles and tools of performance management to enhance productivity and create the necessary results-oriented mindsets; identify techniques for establishing and maintaining trust with virtual workers as well as fostering location independent teamwork; and plan for the resources, policies and procedures, and monitoring program that you will need to support virtual workers.

Instruction: Major topics covered in the course are How do you manage people when they are physically out-of-sight?; How do you measure productivity if you can't see the work as it is being completed?; How do you maintain an atmosphere of trust and productivity, not just with people outside the traditional office, but also with those remaining?; and managing by results and output rather than hours worked, activity level, or personal style. Methods of instruction include interactive and diagnostic exercises with practical guidelines you can use to make this important paradigm shift.

Credit Recommendation: In the lower division baccalaureate/associate degree category, 1 semester hour in Telecommunication Management (12/95). **NOTE:** to earn this credit recommendation, the student must complete this course and one of the following courses: The Telecommuting and Virtual Workplace Seminar (VO2000) or Working in the Virtual Workplace (VO2005).

Managing People's Performance (MD7601)

Location: AT&T Locations worldwide.

Length: 32 hours (4 days).

Dates: *Version 1:* January 1988-June 1994; *Version 2:* July 1994-Present.

Objective: To provide managers with the ability to assess and enhance their management skills and to emphasize achieving results through people.

Learning Outcome: Upon successful completion of this course, the student will be able to understand the roles/responsibilities of the 1st and 2nd level managers; receive feedback from subordinates on management skills and develop personal development plans; implement the Management Practices that positively impact the work group climate; become familiar with the work group climate; become familiar with the work group development process; conduct effective goal setting and performance appraisal sessions; analyze performance problems and establish developmental plans for improved work performance; and utilize the supportive roles of Corporate resource organizations.

Instruction: This intensive, comprehensive workshop provides managers with the ability to assess and enhance their management skills and emphasizes achieving results through people. It will help supervisors identify and examine practices, communication style and leadership behavior and practice handling typical work situations. Based on feedback, participants in this course will develop specific plans to assist them in achieving personal and organizational effectiveness.

Credit Recommendation: *Version 1:* In the lower division baccalaureate/associate degree category, 1 semester hour in Managing People and Performance (12/90). *Version 2:* In the lower division baccalaureate/associate degree category, 2 semester hours in Management (7/95).

Managing Policy Deployment (CQ8056)

Location: Somerset, NJ and other locations throughout the country.

Length: 16 hours (2 days).

Dates: May 1991-June 1996.

Objective: To prepare Quality Professionals to facilitate the implementation and assist with the ongoing management of Policy Deployment within their organization.

Learning Outcome: Upon successful completion of this course, the student will be able to introduce Policy Deployment within their organization; facilitate the integration of Policy Deployment with other Quality Initiatives; support the preparation of a plan for implementation and ongoing management of Policy Deployment; and guide the alignment of resources and activities required to support Policy Deployment.

Instruction: Major topics covered in the course are the Policy Deployment Process, how it works, its benefits, the tools that support the process and the Quality Manager's role; developing an organizational vision and breakthrough objectives; review of the link between Policy Deployment, Business Planning, and other Quality programs; and how Policy Deployment can be employed to increase business success.

Credit Recommendation: In the upper division baccalaureate degree category, 1 semester hour in Business Policy (10/91) (11/96).

Managing Product Profitability (FE0895)

Location: Locations throughout the U.S.

Length: 16 hours (2 days).

Dates: June 1986-Present.

Objective: To improve participants' financial and planning skills and help ensure profitable management of products and services.

Learning Outcome: Upon successful completion of this course, the student will be able to define, calculate and manage profitability at all levels (i.e., Corporate, Business Unity, Program/Function); read and comprehend basic financial statements; analyze an AT&T report card to determine key ratios and information required to measure profit margins; and demonstrate improved planning and financial skills and use these skills to manage products, services or functions for greater profitability.

Instruction: With the continuing pressure to reduce costs and stimulate revenue, this course improves participants' financial and planning skills and helps to ensure profitable management of products and services. Topics covered include profitability calculation and management methods, managerial accounting techniques and analysis of marketing decisions. Participants will learn to analyze decisions to determine cost vs. revenue and overall impact on financial results. An Application project is required as part of the course requirement for students to earn the credit recommendation.

Credit Recommendation: In the upper division baccalaureate degree category, 1 semester hour in Product Management (12/90) (7/95).

Managing the Data Systems Manager (IE1804)

Location: Piscataway, NJ and other AT&T locations.

Length: 20 hours (3 days).

Dates: July 1980-December 1989.

Objective: To examine advanced techniques to maintain manager motivation and to build high-performing teams.

Learning Outcome: Upon successful completion of the course, the participant will be able to understand new techniques for managing subordinate managers; coach and develop subordinates; understand advanced techniques to maintain manager motivation; prevent crisis management situations through the use of anticipatory management techniques; and improve the performance evaluation and ranking process.

Credit Recommendation: In the upper division baccalaureate degree category, 1 semester hour in Business Management (7/85).

Managing the D.P. Professional (IE1802)

Location: Piscataway, NJ and other AT&T locations.

Length: 18 hours (3 days).

Dates: August 1981-July 1995.

Objective: To improve the understanding of the traits, behaviors, and attitudes that are unique to D.P. professionals and to develop strategies to manage them successfully.

Learning Outcome: Upon completion of the course, the student will be able to understand today's DP environment—the changing DP industry and its short- and long-term effect of managers; identify and discuss the problems of managing in the new restructured organization; explore more effective leadership styles for managing DP workers; and understand the team concept and how to build a stronger team.

Credit Recommendation: In the upper division baccalaureate degree category, 1 semester hour in Business Management (7/85) (7/90).

Managing Your Building Service Contract (NW2002) (Formerly Course FE0804 and Managing Your Building Service Contract [MF2804])

Location: AT&T locations nationwide.

Length: 16 hours.

Dates: May 1991-December 1995.

Objective: To give students a first-hand knowledge of contracting techniques with emphasis on the ability to successfully implement them.

Learning Outcome: Upon successful completion of this course, the student will be able to understand up front considerations and planning necessary when establishing a contract; identify all pertinent legal issues associated with a building services contract; state the elements of a contract; develop quality specifications; understand cost elements of a contract; define contract administration responsibilities; and distinguish between building management and purchasing responsibilities.

Instruction: Major topics covered in the course are first-hand knowledge of contracting techniques with emphasis on the ability to successfully implement them; examine legal issues; types of contracts; cost factors; contract administration techniques; and new ways to resolve problems; establishing contracts; planning contracts; the pre-award conference; writing specifications; development of an inspection checklist; planning for contract changes and dealing with supplier employees. Methods of instruction include lectures, learning dialogues, exercises, role plays, students will "try out" the negotiation strategies and tactics and evaluate their usefulness in negotiation situations, and prior readings and a term paper are required.

Credit Recommendation: In the upper division baccalaureate degree category, 1 semester hour in Principles of Contract Administration (8/91) (5/96).

Manufacturing Leadership Program (MF3000)

Location: Princeton, NJ.

Length: 168 hours (4 weeks).

Dates: April 1987-December 1995.

Objective: To educate influential manufacturing managers in current topics of technologic and managerial techniques needed to insure AT&T as a world class competitor.

Learning Outcome: Upon successful completion of this course, the student will be able to implement many changes using leading edge processes; impart leadership skills to change and establish a culture that promotes organizational effectiveness and commitment; understand latest technologic systems and future trends; benchmark your operation; and meet with classmates in future reviews to share experiences.

Instruction: Major topics covered in the course provide middle managers with an opportunity to increase their abilities to manage technological change and implement the manufacturing strategy. The program consists of three weeks of classroom work utilizing state-of-the-art learning methods; manufacturing systems simulation, business simulations, case studies, and hands-on laboratories; discussions are led by external and internal corporate executives, leading business consultants and prominent university faculty; and each session of the Manufacturing Leadership Program offers a sound practical approach that translates today's critical leadership and management trends into learnable concepts and skills.

Credit Recommendation: In the graduate degree category, 5 semester hours in Manufacturing Management (10/91).

Manufacturing Process Optimization (MF3400)

Location: Piscataway, NJ and other AT&T locations.

Length: 24 hours (3 days).

Dates: August 1990-June 1996.

Objective: To teach optimization of in-process variables to improve yield.

Learning Outcome: Upon successful completion of this course, the student will be able to recognize and apply informative inspection methods and foolproofing to remove special causes of variation; understand the concepts of the cause-and-effect relationship and the role of variation in the analysis of data; select design elements and conduct an experiment; collect and analyze data to determine process inputs that influence variability; and stabilize processes and reduce variation by exploiting functional relationships.

Instruction: Major topics covered in the course are special tools for process yield improvement, learn how to improve yield by using new techniques to optimize the in-process variables that affect yield; other topics include variation reduction, optimization, cost impacts, process yield, design of experiments, cost reduction; informative inspection, input-output relationships; and cause and effect relationships.

Credit Recommendation: In the upper division baccalaureate degree category, 2 semester hours in Manufacturing Management (10/91).

Market Knowledge/Economics (PR5052)

Location: All AT&T training locations.

Length: 24 hours (3 days).

Dates: January 1995-Present.

Objective: To enhance managers' knowledge of market changes and the economy.

Learning Outcome: Upon successful completion of this course, the student will be able to employ a broad understanding of business cycles, supply and demand, market structure and pricing to the way you develop purchasing decisions and analyze and predict market conditions.

Instruction: Major topics covered in the course are pertinent economic concepts and tools, business cycles, inflation and monetary policy, supply and demand, price elasticity, market structure and pricing, and analyzing and predicting market conditions and using economic indicators. Methods of instruction include classroom discussion, lecture, and role-playing. An appropriate graduate level project is included as part of the course requirement.

Credit Recommendation: In the upper division baccalaureate degree category, 2 semester hours in Procurement or Economics or in the graduate degree category, 1 semester hour in Procurement or Economics (11/96).

Market Positioning Research (ME 0957)
(Formerly Applications in Industrial Marketing Research [ME 0957])

Location: Somerset, NJ, and other AT&T locations.

Length: *Version 1:* 40 hours (5 days); *Version 2:* 16 hours (2 days).

Dates: *Version 1:* March 1986-May 1994; *Version 2:* June 1994-January 1994.

Objective: *Version 1:* To acquaint students with skills to conduct industrial marketing research using conjoint analysis and cluster analysis and multidimensional scaling. *Version 2:* To teach students the different methodologies for conducting and analyzing market positioning research.

Learning Outcome: *Version 1:* Upon successful completion of this course, the student will be able to identify the uses of questionnaires in acquiring market research data; design questionnaires for use in direct mail, telephone, and personal interviews; list questionnaire difficulties and possible solutions; use MDPREF, MONANOVA, and HCLUSTER software for concept testing and product positioning; and interpret and apply the computer-generated results to concept and product decisions. *Version 2:* Upon successful completion of this course, the student will be able to conduct marketing positioning research studies; and test product and service concepts by applying multidimensional scaling and conjoint analysis.

Instruction: *Version 1:* Major topics covered in the course are the critical topics of designing questionnaires and developing and analyzing concept testing methodologies. The course covers the mechanics of questionnaire development for industrial market research. Design issues and execution issues are discussed and resolved with practical recommendations. Concept testing techniques will be discussed and Bell Laboratories-developed software for concept testing and product positioning will be used. The workshop will demonstrate how conjoint analysis, cluster analysis, and multidimensional scaling may be applied to concept testing and product positioning situations. Prerequisite: ME 0955. *Version 2:* Major topics covered in the course are designed for students who want to learn how to apply conjoint analysis or multidimensional scaling to product concepts. It includes alternative market positioning methods, determining the research methodology, isolating relevant dimensions for research, questionnaire issues, data gathering issues, data analysis alternatives, multidimensional scaling, and conjoint analysis. Methods of instruction include lectures and discussions. An appropriate graduate level research project is submitted as part of the course requirements.

Credit Recommendation: *Version 1:* In the graduate degree category, 3 semester hours in Applications in Industrial Marketing Research or Advanced Market Research (11/86) (8/91). *Version 2:* In the graduate degree or upper division baccalaureate degree categories, 1 semester hour in Marketing Research or Marketing elective (12/93).

Marketing and Business Plans: Design and Implementations (SA4600)

Location: Somerset, NJ and other AT&T locations.

Length: *Version 1:* 16 hours, plus laboratory; *Version 2:* 24 hours (3 days).

Dates: *Version 1:* June 1989-December 1994; *Version 2:* January 1995-Present.

Objective: To teach students how to design and build a marketing plan.

Learning Outcome: Upon successful completion of this course, the student will be able to develop a business definition and demonstrate bridging to other strategic decisions such as organizational/functional strategies and understand the analytical techniques required to determine appropriate goals and strategic alternatives, e.g., market opportunities, cost dynamics, scale and experience effects, and portfolio analysis.

Instruction: Major topics covered in the course are how to improve skills in the planning, design, and evaluation of strategic and tactical plans of the organization and how to develop and fine-tune market/business plans that translate corporate goals into effective marketplace behaviors. Methods of instruction include case studies, lectures, group discussions, practice exercises, and a substantial graduate level paper.

Credit Recommendation: In the graduate degree category, 2 semester hours in Marketing (8/91) (5/96).

Marketing Communications (ME0885)

Location: Various AT&T locations throughout the U.S.

Length: 16 hours (2 days).

Dates: March 1995-Present.

Objective: To learn how to plan and manage advertising, public relations, and general communications plans to meet tight budgets and achieve profitability.

Learning Outcome: Upon successful completion of this course, the student will be able to understand the relationship of marketing communications to business goals and objectives; understand the key steps in the marketing communications process; understand the management of the marketing communications process from strategic development through execution; and gain experience in the application of the marketing communications process to situations related to the student's real business needs.

Instruction: This course examines the various communications tools and tactics used to reach business and consumer markets, then develop an integrated marketing communications plan to support your umbrella market strategy. Through various exercises you will consider numerous marketing approaches, such as public relations, trade shows, logos and design, and direct marketing.

Credit Recommendation: In the upper division baccalaureate degree category, 1 semester hour in Marketing Promotions (7/95).

Marketing Decision Making (ME 0954)

Location: Somerset, NJ; and other AT&T locations throughout the country.

Length: 32 hours (4 days).

Dates: August 1986-December 1990.

Objective: To enable managers to make more effective decisions through an understanding of the techniques of marketing decision-making.

Learning Outcome: Upon successful completion of this course, the student will have an understanding of: the decision making process; market analysis; market and sales potential; strategic planning; and developing an integrated marketing plan.

Instruction: The three main areas covered in the course are marketing research, statistical analysis of marketing data, and sales forecasting. The emphasis is on interpretations, not computations. No specific statistical nor quantitative background is required. Students must submit a paper (for grading) after completion of class time.

Credit Recommendation: In the graduate degree category, 2 semester hours in Marketing Decision Making (11/86).

Marketing Principles in a High-Tech Environment (ME0880)

Location: Somerset, NJ.

Length: 16 hours.

Dates: June 1988-December 1993.

Objective: To provide an overview of marketing concepts and practices as they relate to AT&T.

Learning Outcome: Upon successful completion of this course, the student will be able to understand the strategic marketing planning process; and explain AT&T's changing marketing environment with emphasis on market, technological and competitive changes.

Instruction: Major topics covered in the course are knowledge of marketing and its role in a rapidly changing technological environment; an overview of marketing concepts and practices and their application to AT&T and the telecommunications industry. Methods of instruction include class discussion, case studies, and other participatory learning materials will be used to illustrate key marketing strategies and their application to AT&T's markets and technologies.

Credit Recommendation: In the upper division baccalaureate degree category, 2 semester hours in Marketing Principles in a High Tech Environment (8/91).

Marketing Research (SA4075)

Location: Somerset Seminars Center, Somerset, NJ.

Length: 34 hours (4 days).

Dates: January 1980-December 1990.

Objective: To provide students with the basic tools, concepts, and approaches used in data collection in marketing.

Instruction: Major topics covered in the course are different approaches to data collection, with emphasis on secondary sources, as well as the use of quantitative and qualitative procedures.

Credit Recommendation: In the upper division baccalaureate degree category, 2 semester hours in Marketing or Marketing Research (9/80)(11/85).

Marketing Strategy (SA4065)

Location: Somerset Seminars Center, Somerset, NJ.

Length: 34 hours (4 days).

Dates: January 1980-December 1990.

Objective: To survey marketing operations, market planning, and market research.

Instruction: Major topics covered in the course are subjects related to planning, evaluation, and control in the marketing of services.

Credit Recommendation: In the upper division baccalaureate degree category, 2 semester hours in Marketing (9/80) (11/85).

Maximizing the Value of Your Resources: How to Leverage the Hidden Opportunities (RB1013)

Location: Somerset, NJ and other AT&T locations.

Length: 24 hours, plus extensive guided-independent study.

Dates: February 1992-April 1997.

Objective: To help students identify their business' core competencies (long and short term), establish a Resource Network and Resource Portfolio, and learn how to creatively leverage all their business assets.

Learning Outcome: Upon successful completion of this course, the student will be able to determine both the long-term and the near-term core competencies your business will require to achieve your Strategic Global Intent (SGI); identify the Near-Term Intent (one year out) that must be fulfilled in order to achieve your requisite near-term results and advance towards your SGI; identify your business's Resource Portfolio-the fullest set of available resources that can be deployed in fulfilling Near-Term Intent; demonstrate methods for leveraging resources to identify and seize new opportunities which are traditionally overlooked; illustrate methods for optimizing the use of resources, particularly for effectively exploiting use of slack resources; determine the criteria for evaluating resources as well as options for building a diverse Resource Portfolio and Resource Network for business; identify types of resource alliances and the necessity for "Win-Win" relationships; and develop a resourcing plan based on Near Term Intent, available resource pool, and external alliances that will ensure success.

Instruction: Major topics covered in the course are one series in a series of four integrated workshops designed to give students the tools they need to successfully run their jobs as a business; the workshops are a set of hands-on, market-focused clinics, not simply training classes, where students acquire and sharpen skills they can immediately apply to running their jobs; and while students focus on their jobs, instructors consult and facilitate the process. Methods of instruction include students reading and learning the material through pre-course and evening assignments, discussing materials in class, then applying the tools and skills to their own businesses in class with the aid of the instructor; and lengthy and detailed post-course assignment is required for credit and certification.

Credit Recommendation: In the graduate degree category, 3 semester hours in Resource Planning and Management (4/92). **NOTE:** The credit recommendation applies only to those students who successfully complete the Job Application Project contained within the Application Book. This will be assessed by the instructor and the student will use the strategy techniques taught in the course.

Measured Service Issues Seminar

Location: Bell System Tariffs and Cost Seminars, Somerset, NJ.

Length: 445 hours (1 week).

Dates: October 1979-October 1981.

Objective: To concentrate on all the internal and external issues associated with addressing measured service implementation proposals in both testimony preparation and presentation.

Instruction: This seminar assumes in-depth knowledge of the measured service issue and familiarity with the preparation as discussed in the General Rate and Cost Issue Seminar. MSIS-1 provides participants with the opportunity to discuss the issues with subject matter experts, to monitor lectures by non-Bell consultants, and to receive a high ratio of videotaped role play. This seminar relies on intergroup discussions and task performances to achieve the level of preparedness needed to address effectively the issue before the regulatory bodies. Panel discussions, lectures, individual and group task performances, videotaped role play, evaluation by subject matter experts, and lectures by consultants are used.

Credit Recommendation: In the graduate degree category, 2 semester hours in Business Administration, Law, or Public Administration (2/81).

Methods Workshop-Process Quality Management Improvement/Quality Improvement C (PQMI/QIC) (MQ1003)

Location: Somerset, NJ and other AT&T locations.

Length: 16 hours (2 days).

Dates: November 1991-November 1992.

Objective: To equip the student to apply PQMI and QIC methodologies through an understanding of the relationship and dynamics between the methodologies and the Malcolm Baldridge Award Criteria.

Learning Outcome: Upon successful completion of this course, the student will be able to apply PQMI and QIC with a deeper understanding of relational dynamics; and understand the relation of outcome number 1 to the use of the Malcolm Baldridge Award Criteria as a management guide.

Instruction: Major topics covered in the course are final workshop in triad of workshops leading to a Certificate of Mastery in Process Management and Improvement; ties together PQMI and QIC, the relationship of the two methodologies, team structure to support PQMI and QIC, and their relationship to Malcolm Baldridge National Quality Award Criteria; and an application project showing evidence that tools are used and applied is required for the student to complete the course.

Credit Recommendation: In the graduate degree category, 1 semester hour in Data Management (4/92).

Micro Focus COBOL/2 Workbench and Associated Products IE 3116 and one of the following elective modules: IE 3117, IE 3118 or IE 3119

Location: Piscataway, NJ and other AT&T locations.

Length: Minimum: 19 hours (3 days); Maximum: 22 hours (5.5 days).

Dates: January 1991-June 1996.

Objective: To enable the students to develop mainframe compatible COBOL applications in the Micro Focus COBOL/2 Workbench PC environment.

Learning Outcome: Upon successful completion of this course, the student will be able to use the relevant Micro Focus file utilities to transfer mainframe data to the PC in proper format for testing; use the development utilities to edit, compile, execute and debug COBOL programs on the PC; and use the associated IMS, CICS, and DB2 emulators to test DB/DC applications.

Instruction: Major topics covered in the course are designed for COBOL programmers; students learn to use the Microsoft Focus COBOL environment; and file transfers and file conversions between the PC and the mainframe. After completing IE 3116, students choose an option in IMS (IE 3117) CICS (IE 3118) or XDB (IE 3119).

Credit Recommendation: In the lower division baccalaureate/associate degree or upper division baccalaureate degree category, 1 semester hour in Micro Focus

COBOL (9/94). **NOTE:** To be eligible for the credit recommendation, the student must successfully complete Module IE 3116, and any one of the other three elective modules (IE 3117, 3118, or 3119).

Microeconomics Seminar (MES)

Location: Bell Systems Tariffs and Cost Seminars, Somerset, NJ.

Length: 23 hours (3 days).

Dates: October 1977-December 1984.

Objective: To increase the awareness and understanding Bell System managers have of the microeconomic theory and the application of that theory in the pricing/costing of telecommunication services.

Instruction: This seminar's primary emphasis is on the use of microeconomics theory in pricing and in regulatory proceedings. The seminar includes introduction to economic analysis; discussion of market mechanisms, e.g., principle components of the market, interplay of supply and demand; analysis of supply and demand, e.g., economic concept, of consumer decision making, price elasticity and cross elasticity, repression, definition of various costs; discussion of pricing decisions by the firm, pricing decisions by regulatory bodies; discussion of satisfying business objectives and regulatory objectives in a single telephone's pricing policy. The seminar concludes with a discussion of the trends and current issues in the intrastate regulatory arena as seen by a non-Bell consultant. Methods of instruction include lecture, discussion, and question/answer sessions.

Credit Recommendation: In the lower division baccalaureate/associate degree category or in the upper division baccalaureate degree category, 2 semester hours in Economics (2/81).

Microsoft Windows Programming (IE3180)

Location: All AT&T training locations.

Length: 32 hours (5 days).

Dates: January 1995-June 1996.

Objective: To teach the skills and knowledge necessary to create an application that runs in the Windows environment.

Learning Outcome: Upon successful completion of this course, the student will be able to know how to implement the text and visual editors of the Microsoft C++ workbench; understand Windows Architecture; know message processing in the Windows event-driven environment; and implement resources such as icons, cursors, menus, accelerators, and dialog boxes.

Instruction: Major topics covered in the course are how to create a basic application that displays a window, menus, dialog boxes, text, how to apply the basic elements of the Windows application programming interface (API), how to use the Windows messaging system and basic memory management techniques, how to implement basic user interface objects, and create basic windows-based applications.

Credit Recommendation: In the upper division baccalaureate degree category, 2 semester hours in Computer Information Systems (1 hour lecture and 1 hour lab) (11/96).

Mini-MBA in Competitive Advantage (ME2050) (Formerly Understanding Your Customers, Markets & Competitors [RB1011], Establishing Your Business Focus [RB1012], Maximizing Value of Resources: How to Leverage [RB1013], Ensuring Business Results: How to Read & Monitor Vital Signs of Your Business [RB1014])

Location: All AT&T locations nationwide.

Length: 64 hours (8 days-2/4-day sessions/one month apart).

Dates: April 1995-Present.

Objective: To address the concepts of identifying, enhancing, and implementing your competitive advantage through direct application to your business.

Learning Outcome: Upon successful completion of this course, the student will be able to develop a situation analysis to understand your customers, markets, and competitors in developing your point of competitive advantage; identify a strategic direction to establish long-term direction and focus while identifying and gaining alignment among key stakeholders; determine a resourcing plan to maximize the value of your resources while focusing on continuous improvement and innovation; and create a vital sign system to ensure business success in marketplace execution.

Instruction: The Mini-MBA in Competitive Advantage integrates advanced business concepts by leveraging your business' core competencies. You use your energy to align your customers, your resources, and your stakeholders. This program focuses not only on the key concepts and brings them to life through real examples, multi-media presentations, and in-class case studies, but more importantly, provides actual application directly to your business with expert consulting to guide your work. Sponsorship for certificate is pending from Lehigh University. An appropriate graduate level research project is required to earn the graduate level credit recommendation.

Credit Recommendation: In the graduate degree category, 3 semester hours in Strategic Management; or in the upper division baccalaureate degree category, 4 semester hours in Strategic Management (12/95).

Mini-MBA in Finance (FM3000)

Location: Somerset, NJ and other locations throughout the world.

Length: 64 hours, (8 days over a 6 week period).

Dates: June 1994-Present.

Objective: To provide participants with a good working understanding of the key concepts in financial management and how to apply them to improve business performance and increase shareholder value.

Learning Outcome: Upon successful completion of this course, the student will be able to analyze financial statements to improve business results; utilize management accounting principles to improve business operations; manage cash flow and working capital; manage foreign exchange risk; and select among various budgeting techniques to project decisions.

Instruction: There is an extensive pre-course assignment covering accounting fundamentals and time value of money. This is designed to replace prerequisites and introduce the participants to basic accounting prior to the class. This is an 8 day class which is taught in two four-day sections. The class is composed of 17 modules. The instructional focus is on lecture with exercises used to give students a chance to practice what they have learned. The coursework becomes more complex over the eight days. Beginning with a look at the financial statements, the course prepares the participants to make financial decisions considering all aspects from time value of money to global finance.

Credit Recommendation: In the graduate degree category, 4 semester hours in Finance or in the upper division baccalaureate degree category, 6 semester hours in Finance (12/94).

Mini-MBA in General Management (ME2025)

Location: Somerset, NJ and other AT&T locations.

Length: 64 hours (8 days).

Dates: January 1993-Present.

Objective: To expose students to the main ideas, techniques, and paradigms taught in traditional two-year MBA programs.

Learning Outcome: Upon successful completion of this course, the student will be able to make more efficient day-to-day business decisions; identify strategies and tactics to use to be a more effective manager; apply various frameworks to decisions and issues he/she faces; and analyze how his/her decisions affect other people and other organizations.

Instruction: Major topics covered in the course provide all the elements in a typical MBA program. Topics include marketing, strategy, research, finance, forecasting, organizational behavior, ethics and the global marketplace. Methods of instruction include discussion, lecture, case studies, and guest speakers. An appropriate graduate level research project is submitted as part of the course requirements.

Credit Recommendation: In the graduate degree category, 2 semester hours in General Management and 2 semester hours in Marketing for a total of 4 semester hours; or in the upper division baccalaureate degree category, 2 semester hours in Marketing, 1 semester hour in Business Strategy, 1 semester hour in Global Economics, 1 semester hour in Finance, 1 semester hour in Forecasting and Statistics, 1 semester hour in Organizational Behavior and 1 semester hour in Decision-making, for a total of 8 semester hours (12/93).

Mini-MBA in Global Business (GM3000)

Location: Somerset, NJ and other AT&T locations.

Length: 64 hours (8 days).

Dates: November 1994-Present.

Objective: To expose students to various functional aspects of global business from the strategic point of view.

Learning Outcome: Upon successful completion of this course, the student will be able to appreciate and understand the similarities and differences in global markets; develop skills and knowledge to effectively compete in global markets; develop a global strategy for products and services; and identify and measure various financial aspects of global business, including exchange rate risk.

Instruction: This course deals with the various environmental aspects of global business. The topics included are economic and socio-cultural, international organizational behavior, global finance and accounting, and multinational marketing strategies.

Credit Recommendation: In the graduate degree category, or in the upper division baccalaureate degree category, 4 semester hours in Advanced Global Management (6/94).

Mini-MBA in Global Technology (ME2035)

Location: AT&T locations though U.S. & the International Marketplace.

Length: 64 hours (8 days).

Dates: March 1995-Present.

Objective: To gain new insights into the dynamics of the evolving global market technology, the course will analyze the ways in which globalization and regionalization have affected strategic attitudes and practices towards the development and diffusion of technology.

Learning Outcome: Upon successful completion of this course, the student will be able to learn a strategic perspective on the Global Management of Technology; understand how technology (hardware & software) can be harnessed to meet both long term and short term corporate marketing and profit objectives; forecast the alternative perspectives on cross-border movement through technological transfer and joint ventures; and understand the new challenges to global management of technology including time-based competition and managing cross-cultural teams.

Instruction: This course is designed to provide AT&T with a strategic perspective on the Global Management of Technology, highlighting those ways in which technology - hardware and software- can be harnessed to meet both short and long-term corporate marketing and profit objectives. Along with providing new insight into the dynamics of the evolving global market technology, the course will analyze the ways in which globalization and regionalization have affected strategic attitudes and practices towards the development and diffusion of technology. A comprehensive application project is part of the course requirement for students to earn the credit recommendation.

Credit Recommendation: In the graduate degree category or in the upper division baccalaureate degree category, 4 semester hours in Strategic Global Marketing (7/95).

Mini-MBA in Management of Information (IM2025)

Location: AT&T locations worldwide.

Length: 64 hours (8 days over a 6-8 week period).

Dates: May 1994-Present.

Objective: To provide managers with a working knowledge and skills for managing information in the life cycle process.

Learning Outcome: Upon successful completion of this course, the student will be able to develop a management process for creating and/or collecting quality data and information in the corporate environment; enhance techniques for analyzing information systems; identify the expanding world of management information and its impact on business; develop strategic, tactical and operational views of data information and knowledge; and apply content of knowledge, information, and data management processes to the business environment.

Instruction: Course provides an overview of the data and information life cycle.

Credit Recommendation: In the graduate degree category, 4 semester hours in Management of Information or in the upper division baccalaureate degree category, 6 semester hours in Management of Information (12/94).

Modems and Facilities (DC7120) (IE7120)

Location: Piscataway, NJ and other AT&T locations.

Length: 24 hours (4 days).

Dates: June 1982-June 1996.

Objective: To provide the student with an overview of facilities operation techniques and modulation techniques used by AT&T and approved vendor-supplied modems and DSUs.

Instruction: Major topics covered in the course are a description of how data is transmitted over telephone facilities; the functions and characteristics of modems and multiplexors; and troubleshooting data transmission problems on facilities, modems, and multiplexors. Methods of instruction include lecture and workshops.

Credit Recommendation: In the upper division baccalaureate degree category, 1 semester hour in Data Communications or

Operations, Data Processing, or Computer Science (7/85) (7/90).

MVS Workshop (IE4100)

Location: Piscataway, NJ and other AT&T locations.

Length: 90 hours (15 days).

Dates: August 1983-December 1993.

Objective: To teach MVS batch processing concepts, job control language cataloged procedures and utilities and their use.

Instruction: Major topics covered in the course are MVS concepts, coding of JCL statements, creating and maintaining cataloged procedures, introduction to storage facilities, and selecting and coding JCL required to execute utilities. Methods include lecture and laboratory.

Credit Recommendation: In the lower division baccalaureate/associate degree category, 3 semester hours in Computer Science or Data Processing (7/85) (7/90).

Negotiating Across Borders (GM1070) (Formerly Cross Cultural Business Negotiations and Communications [GM1070])

Location: Somerset, NJ and other AT&T locations.

Length: 14 hours (2 days).

Dates: January 1989-July 1997.

Objective: To develop cultural sensitivity and techniques for negotiating and communicating with other cultures effectively.

Learning Outcome: Upon successful completion of this course, the student will be able to appreciate the overall context of an international business negotiation; recognize, with the self-awareness gained from role-plays and videotape feedback, how you and your American colleagues generally conduct business negotiations; anticipate common negotiating styles and practices in diverse regions and countries such as China, France, Japan, Mexico, Nigeria, and Saudi Arabia; and apply within this context, the skills and insights essential for you and other individuals to negotiate effectively.

Instruction: This course concentrates on the negotiating skills individuals need in international and cross-cultural business settings. Topics include the complex context of international business negotiations, determinants of negotiation outcomes, cultural aspects of negotiation, and three skill areas (preparing, communicating and problem-solving). **NOTE:** A graduate level project is required to complete this course.

Credit Recommendation: In the graduate degree category, 1 semester hour in International Business Negotiations (4/92).

Negotiating Collaboratively (MD7790) Negotiating to Yes (MS6420)

Location: AT&T locations nationwide.

Length: 16 hours (2 days).

Dates: April 1990-May 1996.

Objective: To provide managers with a method of negotiating with integrity; a way to reach satisfying agreements while maintaining the relationship.

Learning Outcome: Upon successful completion of this course, the students will be able to have a conceptual framework for understanding negotiations-a language and a process to use before, during, and after a negotiation; apply a simple strategy for negotiating that enables them to pursue their interests without giving in or getting into confrontation; and follow a preparation procedure that covers a crucial step in negotiation.

Instruction: Major topics covered in the course include knowledgeable in a proved negotiating process; learn techniques to successfully implement the process, using personal application; and throughout the course will examine win-win negotiation strategy and tactics.

Credit Recommendation: In the graduate degree category, 1 semester hour in Negotiations (10/91).

Network Building Operations 101 (NW2522)

Location: AT&T locations worldwide.

Length: 41 hours (4 days).

Dates: June 1993-Present.

Objective: To provide a comprehensive overview of building operations and management methodologies.

Learning Outcome: Upon successful completion of this course, the student will be able to understand and implement the basic principles and methods for contract administration, house services, building emergency action plans, and environmental and safety administration; comprehend the fundamentals of heating, ventilation and air-conditioning, plumbing, elevators, and the electrical plant; and understand basic technical concepts and be able to recommend procedures for maintaining complex, strategic telephone apparatus.

Instruction: Major topics covered in the course are a comprehensive overview suitable for managers new to the area of building operations or experienced managers who require updating and refreshing knowledge of building management issues. Methods of instruction include case studies, real world exercises, and hands on practice with the equipment.

Credit Recommendation: In the lower division baccalaureate/associate degree category, 3 semester hours in Building Management (12/94).

Network Cost System and Workshop (AT&T 103 A&B)

Location: Somerset Seminars Center, Somerset, NJ.

Length: *103A*. 16 hours (2 days); *103B*. 24 hours (2 days).

Dates: January 1984-December 1988.

Objective: *103A*. To provide a perspective on the interstate network cost system (NCS) and its application to the costs process for the interstate public switched network (PSN) *103B*. This seminar is sequential to AT&T 103A; it provides the details and specifics of the interstate network service cost system.

Instruction: *103A*. The main emphasis of the course is on NCS as a financial analysis tool, building on principles presented in the Fundamentals of Costing for Pricing Decisions. The course starts with a review and background material on cost concepts and public switched network calls and its network components used throughout this course and aggregates the various NCS investment/cost analyses. The NCS functions module introduces a six-step flowchart of the cost development process. The final two modules are designed to "round out" the NCS course by positioning the NCS in the financial analysis process and presenting an overview of the mechanics of executing NCS.

103B. Section I of the workshop begins by linking with the NCSI courses, providing a "systems approach" diagram and details the various inputs and outputs of NCS. The modules that follow address each of the input/output items individually and will detail the data selection/specification required to set up NCS. The final module in Section I examines the NCS output and how results are extracted and analyzed based on the study objective. Section II offers the participant the opportunity to apply NCS to three case problems that cover a range of basic NCS studies conducted by the PSN service groups: a marginal analysis, an incremental cost analysis with data extraction for NPCS and cash flow, and a new service analysis for initial rate-setting. The participants will be required to identify the study objective, complete the NCS run request form, and extract/analyze the NCS output.

Credit Recommendation: In the upper division baccalaureate degree category, 2 semester hours in Systems Analysis, Quantitative Methods, or Economics (11/85).

Network Services Issues Seminar (NSIS) (Formerly General Rate and Cost Issue Seminar [GIS])

Location: Bell System Tariffs and Costs Seminars, Somerset, NJ.

Length: 43.5 hours (1 week).

Dates: February 1977-December 1984.

Objective: To provide participants with a clear understanding of the techniques for effective presentation of testimony before regulatory bodies, of the need for consistent approaches in addressing fundamental issues, and of the process for achieving the proper regulatory team (rate, cost, marketing, legal, etc.) interactions.

Instruction: This seminar is considered the foundation of discipline and involves writing testimonies, implementing the methodology for effective presentation of each testimony, presenting the testimony in a simulated role-play performance by subject matter experts. Lectures, guest speakers, videotaped presentations, and individual group tasks are used. The seminar also includes videotaping of role plays and evaluation of participants' performances.

Credit Recommendation: In the graduate degree category, 2 semester hours in Business Administration, Law, or Public Administration (2/81).

New Product Introduction (ME2010) (Formerly Effective Strategies for Launching New Products/Services [ME2010] and Fundamentals of New Product Development [ME2003]).

Location: Somerset, NJ and other AT&T locations.

Length: 16 hours.

Dates: June 1989-December 1997.

Objective: To provide AT&T managers with the skills to source, screen and evaluate new product/service ideas.

Learning Outcome: Upon successful completion of this course, the student will be able to understand the issues faced in the concept, design and development phases of the product life cycle; apply the Product Management Process during the early phases of the product life cycle; and evaluate and screen new product ideas.

Instruction: This course provides product managers with the tools to maximize their effectiveness in the search for additional sources of revenue for their products and services. Through a combination of lectures and case studies they explore methods to improve their success rate and reduce their cost.

Participants will examine the steps involved in developing an overall new business strategy and they learn how to write a Product Innovation Charter (PIC).

Credit Recommendation: In the upper division baccalaureate category, 2 semester hours in Advanced Marketing or Business elective (8/91).

ODBC and OLE for Visual Basic (IE3198)

Location: All AT&T training locations.

Length: 28 hours (4 days).

Dates: January 1995-Present.

Objective: To teach Visual Basic programmers the advanced features of ODBC and OLE.

Learning Outcome: Upon successful completion of this course, the student will be able to know the Visual Basic Data Access Objects, know how to access databases, both ODBC and non-ODBC, know how to create tables and indexes, be able to do program and data maintenance, and be able to use OLE automation and other OLE controls.

Instruction: Major topics covered in the course are how to access both ODBC and non ODBC databases, advanced features of OLE, how to access data dictionary information as well as user data, Visual Basic Data Access Objects, database management, ODBC concepts, OLE Control, and OLE automation. Methods of instruction include group projects, lecture, and lab.

Credit Recommendation: In the upper division baccalaureate degree category, 2 semester hours in Computer Information Systems (1 hour lecture and 1 hour lab) (11/96).

Operations/Process Knowledge for Purchasers (PR5054)

Location: All AT&T training locations.

Length: 24 hours (3 days).

Dates: January 1995-Present.

Objective: To provide the student with insight into the ways in which suppliers organize and manage their processes and desire to help suppliers improve the efficiency of their operations.

Learning Outcome: Upon successful completion of this course, the student will be able to understand the linkages involved in providing goods and services, understand supplier operations and processes, and understand basic operations models.

Instruction: Major topics covered in the course are supplier operations and processes, the ways in which suppliers of goods and services organize and manage the processes by which they create and deliver the outputs that purchasers acquire, and how the suppliers can improve the efficiency of their operations and the effectiveness of their linkages with customer operations. An appropriate graduate level project is included as part of the course requirement.

Credit Recommendation: In the upper division baccalaureate degree category, 2 semester hours in Operations Management or in the graduate degree category, 1 semester hour in Operations Management (11/96).

Overview of Global Finance (GM1040) (formerly Finance in the Global Marketplace [GM1040])

Location: Somerset, NJ.

Length: 21 hours (3 days).

Dates: November 1989-Present.

Objective: To explain to participants the global financial issues involved in doing business internationally.

Learning Outcome: Upon successful completion of this course, students will be able to understand the workings of the foreign exchange markets and the impact of macro-economic policy on exchange rates; relate AT&T's international operating agreements to the foreign exchange risks faced by the company; identify and measure the various types of foreign exchange risks and explain the pros and cons of the foreign exchange risk management tools available in the market; develop a strategy for currency of invoice selection in the case of accounts receivable, accounts payable, and short-term financing; describe the institutional structure of the international financial system and the benefits of the various financial instruments offered; and identify the critical differences in the foreign versus domestic direct investment decision.

Instruction: This course introduces participants to the world of global financial issues. The objective of the course is to enhance participants' abilities to incorporate various facets of international finance into their pricing, sourcing, and sales decisions. The program also addresses the issues of AT&T's international operating agreements and discusses the foreign exchange risk management and global financing issues associated with such agreements. An appropriate graduate level project is included as part of the course requirement for students to earn the credit recommendation.

Credit Recommendation: *Version 1:* In the graduate degree category, 2 semester hours in International Finance (12/90). *Version 2:* In the graduate degree category or in the upper division baccalaureate degree category, 2 semester hours in Global Finance (7/95).

Personnel Subsystem Testing and Evaluation (IE1400)

Location: Piscataway, NJ and other AT&T locations.

Length: *Version 1:* 18 hours (3 days); *Version 2:* 24 hours (4 days).

Dates: *Version 1:* June 1978-February 1988; *Version 2:* February 1988-May 1990.

Objective: *Version 1:* To present techniques of testing the design of a computer-based system for compatibility with human performance, and for evaluating whether user-related products or documents meet acceptable levels of performance. *Version 2:* To enable participants to test the design of computer-based systems for usability, i.e. the personnel subsystem components.

Learning Outcome: Upon successful completion of this course, the student will be able to state benefits and provide examples of how PSS testing and evaluation can improve system design and performance; design and construct a PSS testing and evaluation plan; identify strengths and weaknesses of different testing and evaluation methods for commonly produced PSS products; conduct tests and analyze results using representative test subjects; and evaluate all PSS products for accuracy and quality, including procedures, manuals, screens, and training materials.

Instruction: *Version 1:* Major topics covered in the course are how to design and construct a test plan; how to design and construct test items and instructions; how to conduct a test and analyze results using representative test subjects; and how to evaluate all user-related products for accuracy and quality including procedures, manuals, screens, and training materials. *Version 2:* Major topics covered in the course are techniques for evaluating whether user-related products or documents produce acceptable levels of performance. Any human factors product that requires testing can be applied to the methodology presented in the course.

Credit Recommendation: In the lower division baccalaureate/associate degree category, 1 semester hour in Computer Information Systems or Management (7/85) (7/90). **NOTE:** Students who have received credit for IE2710 (Structured Test Plans) should not receive credit for this course.

Physical Data Base Design (Introduction and Tec)

Location: Data Systems Education Center, Piscataway, NJ, and other Bell locations.

Length: 60 hours (2 weeks).

Dates: May 1978-December 1984.

Objective: To enable the student to make the transition from logical to physical data base design.

Instruction: Major topics covered in the course are the construction of an Information Management System (IMS) that provides a structural view of the data, understanding of the flexibility of the logical data base design, identification of potential back-up and recovery problems. Methods of instruction include lecture and laboratory.

Credit Recommendation: In the upper division baccalaureate degree category, 2 semester hours in Computer Science or Data Processing (2/80).

PL/1 Workshop (IE3125)

Location: Piscataway, NJ other AT&T locations.

Length: *Version 1:* 30 hours (5 days); *Version 2:* 60 hours (10 days).

Dates: June 1981-June 1996.

Objective: To teach students the structure, syntax, and instruction set of the PL/1 language.

Instruction: Major topics covered in the course include requiring students to code, execute, and debug sample programs in PL/1 using checkout and optimizing compilers. Topics covered include PROCEDURE blocks, sequence of control, stream I/O, built in functions—SUBSTR, INDEX, LENGTH, and VERIFY, storage allocation, record I/O PL/1 subroutines.

Credit Recommendation: In the lower division baccalaureate/associate degree category, 2 semester hours in Computer Science or Data Processing (7/85) (7/90).

Policy Deployment Tools (CQ8057) (Seminar in Planning)

Location: AT&T locations nationwide.

Length: 16 hours.

Dates: May 1991-August 1996.

Objective: To provide participants with working knowledge and hands-on experience with the Management and Planning Tools.

Learning Outcome: Upon successful completion of this course, the student will be able to apply the Management and Planning Tools to Policy Deployment; and identify opportunities to apply the Tools to other business situations.

Instruction: Major topics covered in the course are understanding of the Management and Planning Tools and an opportunity to practice using the Tools; the tools directly support Policy Deployment as well as other business situations.

Credit Recommendation: In the graduate degree category, 1 semester hour in Business Policy (8/91). **NOTE:** The credit recommendation applies only to those students who successfully complete an Application Project to be assessed by the instructor.

PowerBuilder Workshop (IE3194)

Location: All AT&T training locations.

Length: 35 hours (5 days).

Dates: January 1995-Present.

Objective: To provide the skills and knowledge to develop applications using PowerBuilder in a windows-based client server environment.

Learning Outcome: Upon successful completion of this course, the student will be able to understand the components of a PowerBuilder constructed application, use the PowerBuilder toolset (Painters), understand and use the PowerScript language, use the on-line help facilities of PowerBuilder, understand how to distribute PowerBuilder built applications, administer the database through PowerBuilder, understand and use basic Data Windows for both database management and reporting, and understand the object oriented features of PowerBuilder.

Instruction: Major topics covered in the course are skills needed to develop client/server windows-based production applications using the PowerBuilder development environment, the procedures required to build an application, and how to use Painters to implement the procedures. Methods of instruction include laboratory exercises and lecture.

Credit Recommendation: In the upper division baccalaureate degree category, 2 semester hours in Computer Information

Systems (1 hour lecture and 1 hour lab) (11/96).

Preparing Technical Presentations (IE8320)

Location: Piscataway, NJ and other AT&T locations.

Length: 28 hours (4 days).

Dates: November 1981-December 1986.

Objective: To prepare managers to be able to plan, prepare, and deliver a presentation.

Learning Outcome: Upon successful completion of this course, the student will be able to use an efficient and creative approach to prepare a presentation; organize a presentation based on its purpose—persuade, inform, and/or influence attitudes; plan and use visual aids; plan and control audience participation; and plan and deliver a presentation that communicates at the sensory, emotional, and rational levels.

Instruction: Major topics covered in the course are both informative and persuasive presentations. Methods of instruction include two presentations, one planned and one impromptu, given by each student, the planned presentation is videotaped, and a class critique of the presentation.

Credit Recommendation: In the lower division baccalaureate/associate degree category, 2 semester hours in Public Speaking or Managerial Communications (7/85).

Presentation Techniques (MS6515)

Location: Throughout the continental United States and global locations.

Length: 21 hours (3 days).

Dates: January 1990-Present.

Objective: To incorporate effective platform skills, both vocal and physical delivery, into a presentation.

Learning Outcome: Upon successful completion of this course, the student will be able to incorporate effective platform skills into a presentation (Platform skills in this sense would encompass both vocal and physical delivery); analyze an audience and understand how it will relate to the presentation; utilize patterns of organization and methods of preparation, including the Monroe Motivated Sequence; effectively handle question and answer sessions; and integrate visual aids into a presentation.

Instruction: This course helps participants master the skills needed to plan, structure and deliver oral presentations. The course provides the participants with the opportunity to deliver numerous presentations; most are videotaped for playback critique. The focus of the course is on delivering convincing presentations with confidence, credibility, and personal impact.

Credit Recommendation: In the lower division baccalaureate/associate degree category, 1 semester hour in Presentation Techniques or Business Communications (12/90) (12/95).

Pricing Your Products or Services (ME2009)

Location: Somerset, NJ and other AT&T locations.

Length: 16 hours (2 days).

Dates: May 1993-Present.

Objective: To teach participants how to develop effective pricing strategies and tactics.

Learning Outcome: Upon successful completion of this course, the student will be able to make intelligent pricing decisions; develop pricing strategies and tactics; analyze what impact costs, demand, customers, and competitors have on price; determine how marketing research can be used to help establish price; avoid pricing traps; and establish pricing objectives.

Instruction: This course provides students with techniques to develop effective pricing strategies and tactics for both new and existing products and services. Topics include pricing research, upward and downward price limits, the role of cost in pricing decisions, pricing analysis, pricing objectives, pricing strategies and tactics. Methods of instruction include discussion and lecture. An appropriate graduate level research project is submitted as part of the course requirements.

Credit Recommendation: In the graduate degree category, 1 semester hour in Marketing elective; or in the upper division baccalaureate degree category, 2 semester hours in Marketing elective (12/93).

Principle-Centered Leadership (MD7701)

Location: AT&T locations throughout the United States.

Length: 32 hours (4 days).

Dates: March 1989-December 1995.

Objective: To stimulate personal and organizational development, increase the levels of trust in the workplace, and create an awareness around leadership development.

Learning Outcome: Upon successful completion of this course, students will be able to increase personal and organization effectiveness through learning and living principle-centered leadership; build an environment that empowers people and energizes them to develop and pursue a shared vision; create and sustain successful partnerships with team members, customers, suppliers, peers, and bosses; align personal and career roles and goals; and teach the course concepts to peers, bosses, and subordinates and thereby reinforce their own learning experience.

Instruction: This course will equip AT&T middle managers with the vital foundations of leadership needed to achieve the critical business results of the 1990s. The principles of leadership, along with feedback and action planning, support the AT&T Dimension of Leadership.

Credit Recommendation: In the upper division baccalaureate degree category, 2 semester hours in Leadership Principles, Management, or Human Resources Development (12/90).

Principles of Marketing Management (SE1030) (Marketing Management Program) (UMMP)

Location: Somerset Seminars Center, Somerset, NJ.

Length: 24 hours (3 days).

Dates: January 1984-December 1987.

Objective: To provide an understanding of service marketing issues and principles and the roles and tasks of marketers in the strategic planning process. Course also provides a framework for strategic thinking and understanding the role that marketing research plays in decision making.

Instruction: Within this program, one module focuses on the fundamentals of marketing, which cover such topics as marketing planning, buyer behavior, market strategies, product, pricing, distribution, and promotional policies and strategies, and monitoring the marketing plan. Another module provides participants with the understanding of the market research system, the management interface, validity, and approaches to conclusive research. Another module provides product management discussion, market segmentation, trade-off analysis, marketing research, and forecasting. The final module provides participants with knowledge of strategic marketing management, the planning concepts and tools.

Credit Recommendation: In the upper division baccalaureate degree category, 1 semester hour in Business Administration,

Marketing, or Marketing Management (9/83).

Problem Solving and Decision Making (MS6315)

Location: Somerset, NJ and other AT&T locations.

Length: 24 hours (3 days).

Dates: February 1991-April 1997.

Objective: To understand and utilize five problem solving processes; Cause Analysis, Creative Problem Solving, Decision Making, Anticipating Problems and Situation Analysis.

Learning Outcome: Upon successful completion of this course, the student will be able to determine most appropriate problem solving process and methodology, and recognize when each is the most appropriate; utilize the five problem solving processes; understand and practice the most important teamwork skills during problem solving and decision making meetings; have the opportunity for full or partial resolution of at least one important job concern; and develop a plan to apply what they have learned on the job.

Instruction: Major topics covered in the course are a unique blend of all three of the major problem solving approaches: Rational, Creative and Applied Group Dynamics; and the resulting synergism leads to more effective solutions and greater commitment to action for both object and people concerns.

Credit Recommendation: In the upper division baccalaureate degree category, 2 semester hours in Problem Solving and Decision Making (4/92).

Problem Solving Method (MQ7017)

Location: All AT&T training locations.

Length: 16 hours (2 days).

Dates: March 1996-Present.

Objective: To have the student learn and practice the basics of problem solving under the guidance of an experienced facilitator.

Learning Outcome: Upon successful completion of this course, the student will be able to identify and prioritize ways to improve the speed, cost and quality of your work processes, win support of key stakeholders and co-workers, find and remedy the root causes of problems, practice the steps of the AT&T Problem-Solving Method and apply them back on the job, and use a variety of tools and checklists for collecting, analyzing and communicating information.

Instruction: Major topics covered in the course are how to analyze performance and customer satisfaction data. Methods of instruction include lecture, discussion, and team or individual practice (role playing), and problem-solving. This course is a core requirement for the Process Quality Management Professional Certificate.

Credit Recommendation: In the upper division baccalaureate degree category, 1 semester hour in Organizational Behavior (11/96).

Process Quality Management and Improvement (CQ1004)

Location: Somerset, NJ and other locations around the world based on customer needs.

Length: 16 hours (2 days) plus extensive independent study/project.

Dates: July 1994-Present.

Objective: To prepare students to use a proven approach to managing and improving process performance to become the supplier of choice by consistently delivering superior value as measured against customer requirements.

Learning Outcome: Upon successful completion of this course, the student will be able to understand and apply the basics of process management and improvement; explain the role and importance of customer requirements in PQMI; construct a block diagram of a business process and interpret basic data display tools such as histograms, control charts and trend lines.

Instruction: PQMI is widely recognized as a world-class approach to process management. Using the core methodology for process management the student learns to apply PQMI's 7 basic steps and basic tools to a process you manage and wish to improve. Topics include diagramming and mapping process, identifying customer requirements and translating them into effective measures, gathering and using data, objectives for improvement, and roles of process management and quality improvement teams. Student receives the AT&T Quality library book PQMI Guidelines as part of this workshop. This course was revised to include lessons learned since 1992.

Credit Recommendation: In the upper division baccalaureate degree category, 2 semester hours in Process Quality Management & Improvement (12/94).

Procurement Leadership (PR5101)

Location: All AT&T training locations.

Length: 24 hours (3 days).

Dates: January 1995-Present.

Objective: To strengthen the student's understanding of customer-focused techniques, procurement empowerment and procurement leadership; and it also enables a better understanding of how to build successful procurement teams.

Learning Outcome: Upon successful completion of this course, the student will be able to understand procurement image problems, understand the nature of leadership, and exercise procurement leadership.

Instruction: Major topics covered in the course are how to become more customer-focused and market the procurement function both internally and externally, procurement empowerment, how to build and manage high-performance teams, and how to exercise procurement leadership. Methods of instruction include classroom instruction, discussion, and role playing. An appropriate graduate level project is included as part of the course requirement.

Credit Recommendation: In the upper division baccalaureate degree category, 2 semester hours in Organizational Behavior or in the graduate degree category, 1 semester hour in Organizational Behavior (11/96).

Product Exit Planning (ME2004)

Location: Somerset, NJ.

Length: 8 hours.

Dates: September 1990-December 991.

Objective: To provide AT&T managers with the skills to maximize profits and minimize expenses when exiting a product from the market.

Learning Outcome: Upon successful completion of this course, the student will be able to evaluate alternative strategies for declining businesses; apply the AT&T Exit Planning Methods and Procedures Guidelines to products or services; and write an exit plan that covers all the issues and decisions to be made during the withdrawal of a product or service from the marketplace.

Instruction: Major topics covered in the course are how to plan and implement a successful withdrawal from the market; procedures to be followed according to AT&T Guidelines; students guided to maximize profit while insuring customer satisfaction; and the adequate control of inventory will be addressed as well as the integration with appropriate manufacturing facilities.

Credit Recommendation: In the upper division baccalaureate degree category, 1

semester hour in Marketing elective or Business elective (8/91).

Product Logistics Management (ME 2007) (Formerly Strategic Physical Distribution Management [ME 0960])

Location: Somerset, NJ, and other AT&T locations throughout the country.

Length: *Version 1:* 24 hours (3 days) on site; *Version 2:* 32 hours (4 days).

Dates: July 1986-August 1996.

Objective: To provide an understanding of the physical distribution management concept and to encourage interfunctional teamwork necessary for cost-effective provision of products to customers.

Learning Outcome: Upon successful completion of this course, managers will have an understanding of integrated physical distribution management concept; physical distribution management in international marketing; order processing to improve profitability; managing customer service to build market share; computer use in physical distribution; and the functions of inventory.

Instruction: This course examines the linkages and information flows necessary between marketing, manufacturing, finance, and data systems to ensure the optimal, cost-effective provision of products to meet customer needs. The course addresses the integration of distribution-related activities including inventory management, customer service, order processing, and production planning. Before coming to the class, participants must complete more than 18 hours of work (readings and case problems) to be presented to the instructor on arrival. During the class, case study analyses are used and a paper is submitted to the instructor following completion of the class time.

Credit Recommendation: In the graduate degree category, 2 semester hours in Physical Distribution Management (11/86) (8/91).

Product Management Concepts (ME2001) (Formerly [ME0896])

Location: AT&T locations nationwide.

Length: 40 hours (5 days).

Dates: July 1986-Present.

Objective: To provide managers with the purposes and techniques of product management.

Learning Outcome: Upon successful completion of this course, the student will be able to understand the key marketing, management, and strategic issues product managers face; identify strategies and tactics to use in meeting market and financial goals; apply various pricing, life cycle, and product portfolio models to the products; and lead or participate in a more effective product team.

Instruction: Major topics covered in the course are the key concepts pertaining to the planning, developing, and marketing of existing and new products and various techniques such as: competitive analysis, environmental analysis, market research and segmentation, and forecasting. Methods of instruction include lecture, discussion, and an appropriate graduate level project.

Credit Recommendation: In the graduate degree category, 3 semester hours in Product Planning and Management, Applied Marketing Management, Advanced Marketing, or Strategic Marketing (11/86) (8/91) (5/96).

Product Management for Global Markets (GM1065) (Formerly Product Management in Global Markets [GM1060])

Location: Somerset, NJ.

Length: 21 hours (3 days).

Dates: May 1990-December 1994.

Objective: To explain to participants the complexities involved in product management in global markets, including AT&T examples and factors for success.

Learning Outcome: Upon successful completion of this course, students will be able to distinguish between the skills and strategies required for domestic versus international product management; integrate individual product/service strategies with AT&T's global strategy as a whole and, operate within the AT&T environment and utilize country managers and other sources of expertise; evaluate the pros and cons of partnerships, joint ventures, and other strategic sharing arrangements; analyze make/buy decision; use agents and other third parties to implement and expedite strategy in foreign markets; and perform pertinent market research (including customer feedback), bid creatively on contracts, assure compliance with regulations and standards and structure financing, and arrange strategic sourcing and distribution within foreign markets.

Instruction: This course examines the issues involved in taking the product management function into the global arena. The course highlights the skills necessary for success in the global marketplace by addressing challenges such as market planning, competitive analysis, channel management, bidding and pricing strategy, and promotion. Lecture, discussion, case studies, and guest presentations by experienced AT&T product managers are used to illustrate and analyze the complexities of product management in global markets.

Credit Recommendation: In the graduate degree category, 2 semester hours in International Product Management (12/90).

Programmer Basic Training (PBT)

Location: Data Systems Education Center, Piscataway, NJ.

Length: 476.25 hours (12.7 weeks).

Dates: January 1975-December 1983.

Objective: To acquaint students with the physical structure and major concepts of a computer, enable students to design and implement a structured COBOL program, test and debug, modify the source statements, understand job control language, and execute various IBM programs.

Instruction: Major topics covered in the course are data processing concepts; data representation; structured programming, design, implementation, and case problems; COBOL; JCL; utilities; cataloged procedures. The COBOL unit of the course emphasizes understanding diagnostic messages, making appropriate corrections to COBOL code, debugging. Students are required to take written tests and execute case studies which adhere to the principles of structured programming, the major emphasis of the course. Methods of instruction lecture, discussion, workshop, and independent study.

Credit Recommendation: In the lower division baccalaureate/associate degree category or in the upper division baccalaureate degree category, 6 semester hours in Business, Computer Science, Engineering, Engineering Technology, or Information Science (12/79).

Programmer Productivity Techniques

Location: Data Systems Education Center, Piscataway, NJ.

Length: 30 hours (1 week).

Dates: June 1974-December 1983.

Objective: To enable programmers and managers who develop data processing applications to create error-free programs which are readable, maintainable, and changeable while producing the needed documentation as the program is designed and written.

Instruction: Major topics covered in the course are structured programming;

using and creating a HIPO package; translating pseudo-English into a high-level programming language, such as PL/1 or FORTRAN; writing readable COBOL; and conducting and participating in walk-through. Methods of instruction lecture, discussion, and workshops.

Credit Recommendation: In the lower division baccalaureate/associate degree category, 1 semester hour in Computer Programming (2/80).

Programming in C Language (IE5142)

Location: Piscataway, NJ.

Length: 30 hours (5 days).

Dates: March 1989-June 1996.

Objective: To enable programmers to use the basic structure and syntax of "C" Language.

Learning Outcome: Upon successful completion of this course, the student will be able to describe how an application program interfaces with the UNIX system; discuss the basic structure and syntax of the "C" programming language; design programs using arrays, pointers, and structured programming concepts; handle file control via storage management and I/O processing; design and code "C" programs in a UNIX system environment; and compile and execute "C" programs.

Instruction: Major topics covered in this instructor-led course provide programmers the ability to design, code, test, and execute programs using "C" language. Topics include the structure of the language, declaration of variables, arithmetic processing, logical constructs, array processing, pointer processing, storage management, I/O processing, and many other "C" language functions.

Credit Recommendation: In the upper division baccalaureate degree category, 2 semester hours in "C" Language or Computer Science (7/90).

Programming Methods and Design (UNIX/C) (IE3055)

Location: Somerset, NJ and other training locations.

Length: 35 days.

Dates: *Version 1:* June 1988-June 1996; *Version 2:* July 1996-Present.

Objective: To train newly hired programmers to program in a UNIX system environment.

Learning Outcome: Upon successful completion of this course, the student will be given a narrative of high-level specification and able to recognize and use analysis and design tools; use transform analysis tools describing "what" has to be accomplished into design tools describing "how" it will be accomplished; design a solution using structure charts and pseudo-code; code a structured "C" language solution to a relatively complex multi-module process; and (5) develop, code, and use UNIX shells.

Instruction: Major topics covered in the course teach programmers the design, testing, and implementation methods needed to perform the job of an application or system programmer in a UNIX system environment. Often these students already possess a degree in computer science. The student is expected to be proficient in "C" language. Methods of instruction include practice exercises (paper and computer) and the completion of an intensive final case problem is required.

Credit Recommendation: *Version 1:* In the upper division baccalaureate degree category, 4 semester hours in UNIX/"C" or Computer Science (7/90). *Version 2:* In the upper division baccalaureate degree category or in the lower division baccalaureate/associate degree category, 3 semester hours in C Programming Language and 2 semester hours in UNIX Operating System for a total of 5 semester hours (10/97).

Programming Methods and Design-MVS (IE3050) (Formerly Programming Methods and Design (MDS/COBOL))

Location: Somerset, NJ and other training locations.

Length: 40 days.

Dates: *Version 1:* June 1988-June 1996; *Version 2:* July 1996-Present.

Objective: To train newly hired programmers to program COBOL in AT&T IBM mainframe environment.

Learning Outcome: Upon successful completion of this course, the student will be given a narrative high-level specification, the student should be able to recognize and use analysis and design tools used to create physical and logical system views; use transform analysis tools describing "what" has to be accomplished into design tools describing "how" it will be accomplished; design a solution using structure charts and pseudo-code; code a structured COBOL or PL/1 language solution to relatively complex multi-module multi-step process; and develop, use, and code TSO CLISTs.

Instruction: Major topics covered in the course are teaching programmers the programming design, testing, and implementation methods needed to perform the job of an application or system programmer in an AT&T IBM-mainframe environment. Often these students already possess a degree in computer science. Students in this course are expected to be proficient in COBOL. Methods of instruction include practice exercises (paper and computer) and the completion of an intensive final case problem is required.

Credit Recommendation: *Version 1:* In the upper division baccalaureate degree category, 4 semester hours in Programming Methods or Computer Science (7/90). **NOTE:** This course duplicates IE3055 (Programming Methods and Design [UNIX System]) and credit will be awarded for only one of these courses taken by the student. *Version 2:* In the upper division baccalaureate degree category or in the lower division baccalaureate/associate degree category, 4 semester hours in COBOL Programming Applications and 1 semester hour in IBM Job Control Language for a total of 5 semester hours (10/97).

Project Contract-Procurement Management (IE1622)

Location: Piscataway, NJ and various locations nationwide.

Length: 26 hours (4 days).

Dates: January 1994-Present.

Objective: To enable project managers to positively impact quality, cost and schedule of any project through the tools of contract development and procurement management process.

Learning Outcome: Upon successful completion of this course, the student will be able to understand the role the Project Manager has in the Contract and Procurement processes; appreciate the interrelationship of the skills of Contracts knowledge, Procurement, Marketing and Negotiations, and how this interrelationship is an important element in project success; understand the role Needs Identification plays in the proposal process; understand the Basic Elements of Contracts and the factors to consider in the proposal process; understand the components to review when determining a Make or Buy decision; develop a Bid Package; and appreciate the importance of preparation in the Negotiations process.

Instruction: This course examines the process by which goods and services are acquired in project management environments and the legal issues project managers face. This course also explores the evolution of the contractual relationship from initial formation through completion of the services and delivery of goods.

Credit Recommendation: In the graduate degree category, 2 semester hours in Procurement Management (6/95).

Project Cost Management: Estimating, Budgeting and Controlling (IE1621)

Location: Piscataway, NJ and various locations nationwide.

Length: 26 hours (4 days).

Dates: January 1994-Present.

Objective: To provide a broad overview of the differing perspectives of cost within a project, various financial techniques and the factors influencing cost data.

Learning Outcome: Upon successful completion of this course, the student will be able to identify types of costs in your industry and others, and classify them by direct, indirect and overhead categories; recognize sources of cost problems and develop ways to minimize them; understand financial and cost accounting terminology and know how it is used in your projects; review cash flow estimations and financial projections for reasonableness; and understand various methods of estimating, budgeting, and monitoring and the appropriate situations for their use.

Instruction: This course presents a broad overview of the differing perspectives of cost within a project and an organization, various financial techniques, and the factors influencing cost data and control methods.

Credit Recommendation: In the graduate degree category, 2 semester hours in Capital Budgeting (6/95).

Project Management and Leadership 1. Introduction to Project Management 2. Project Leadership Workshop

Location: Data Systems Education Center, Piscataway, NJ.

Length: 1. 20 hours (3 days); 2. 26 hours (4 days). Total 46 hours.

Dates: November 1979-December 1984.

Objective: To provide the student with skills and knowledge required to use methods, tools, and techniques that assure effective performance of project leader responsibilities.

Instruction: Major topics covered in these courses are the responsibilities and characteristics of a data systems project leader; appropriate organizing and controlling techniques needed to administer a selected project phase subsystem of a test case. Methods of instruction include lecture and workshops.

Credit Recommendation: In the upper division baccalaureate degree category, 3 semester hours in Business Administration or Management (5/80). **NOTE:** Students who receive credit for this course should not receive credit for Introductory Project Management.

Project Management Essentials (IE1602) (Formerly Introduction to Project Management)

Location: Piscataway, NJ and various locations nationwide.

Length: *Version 1:* 18 hours (3 days); *Version 2:* 215 hours (3 days).

Dates: *Version 1:* November 1979-December 1993; *Version 2:* January 1994-Present.

Objective: To introduce the participant to the principles, methods and tools of project management.

Learning Outcome: Upon successful completion of this course, the student will be able to define a project, list the important characteristics of any project, define the primary functions of project management, describe the relationship between project management process and any product development process, and list the project management roles and their major responsibilities.

Instruction: This course introduces the participant to the principles, methods, and tools of project management. Project management techniques and methods are discussed from the standpoint of the manager who must plan, schedule, organize and control non-routine activities to achieve schedule, budget and performance objectives. An appropriate graduate level research project is included as part of the course requirement for each student who seeks the credit recommendation.

Credit Recommendation: *Version 1:* In the upper division baccalaureate degree category, 3 semester hours in Business Administration or Management (5/80) (7/85) (7/90). **NOTE:** Students must complete both modules to receive credit for the Introductory Project Management. *Version 2:* In the graduate degree category, 1 semester hour in Principles of Project Management I (6/95).

Project Management Using Microsoft Project for Windows (IE1691)

Location: Piscataway, NJ and various locations nationwide.

Length: 14 hours.

Dates: July 1995-Present.

Objective: To provide students hands-on exercises with the latest version of Microsoft Project for Windows (version 4.0).

Learning Outcome: Upon successful completion of this course, the student will be able to enter and access data, view screens, set preferences and use dialog boxes; breakdown the structure and outline features to group project tasks; prepare resource management capabilities for more realistic resource constrained scheduling of projects; use the table, filter, tool bar, and sorting capabilities including customization; and use track and control features to ensure project completion within budget.

Instruction: This course provides hands-on exercises with the latest version of Microsoft Project for Windows (version 4.0). The major functions and features of the software and how to use them to plan, organize, control and report progress are exercises. Emphasis is placed on using the software to effectively create and manage project schedules using accepted project management principles.

Credit Recommendation: In the upper division baccalaureate degree category or in the lower division baccalaureate/associate degree category, 1 semester hour in Microsoft Project for Windows I (6/95).

Project Management Workshop (IE1604)

Location: Piscataway, NJ and various locations nationwide.

Length: *Version 1:* 34 hours (5 days); *Version 2:* 38 hours (5 days).

Dates: *Version 1:* November 1979-December 1993; *Version 2:* January 1994-Present.

Objective: To provide exposure to the project management functions of planning, organizing and controlling using computer based simulation.

Learning Outcome: Upon successful completion of this course, the student will be able to produce Network and Gantt charts; identify Gantt charts, Critical Path Methods and work breakdown structures; recognize the terms: Slack, CPM, Concurrent Activity, Bar Chart, and Network.

Instruction: The intent of this interactive workshop is to practice the project management functions of planning, organizing and controlling. Students will utilize a computer-based simulator to exercise the skills required to project manage a non-trivial development project. Scheduling and cost-control techniques are emphasized. An appropriate level research project is included as part of the course requirement for each student who seeks the credit recommendation.

Credit Recommendation: *Version 1:* In the upper division baccalaureate degree category, 3 semester hours in Business Administration or Management (5/80) (7/85) (7/90). **NOTE:** Students must complete both modules to receive credit for the Introductory Project Management. *Version 2:* In the graduate degree category, 2 semester hours in Principles of Project Management II (6/95).

Project Quality Management (IE1624)

Location: Piscataway, NJ and various locations nationwide.

Length: 35 hours (5 days).

Dates: January 1994-Present.

Objective: To provide students with a focus on both the qualitative and quantitative approaches used by project managers to ensure that project and ongoing operations meet quality requirements as well as cost and schedule demands.

Learning Outcome: Upon successful completion of this course, the student will be able to demonstrate a knowledge of basic quality concepts; use quality in the system development process; and apply quality tools and techniques in the process management.

Instruction: This course focuses on both the qualitative and quantitative approaches used by project managers to ensure that project and ongoing operations meet quality requirements as well as cost and schedule demands. Emphasis is placed upon the use of continuous process improvement techniques as a means of improving productivity and performance within an organization. An appropriate graduate level research project is included as part of the course requirement for each student who seeks the credit recommendation.

Credit Recommendation: In the graduate degree category, 2 semester hours in Quality Management (6/95).

Project Risk Management (IE1625)

Location: Piscataway, NJ and various locations nationwide.

Length: 35 hours (5 days).

Dates: January 1994-Present.

Objective: To enable a student to understand risk management, identify project risks and develop strategies which significantly reduce them or take steps to avoid them.

Learning Outcome: Upon successful completion of this course, the student will be able to define risk in a project environment; understand the project manager's role in managing risk; define the role of risk in project selection; recognize external and internal forces that cause risk on the project; develop a method of identifying risks and dependencies; apply statistical methods in quantifying risk; develop techniques for developing contingency plans; control risk throughout the project life cycle; and prepare for the Project Risk Management portion of the PMP exam.

Instruction: This course integrates risk and estimating technologies that have been established to ensure optimum project decision making. All projects involve a degree of uncertainty due to factors both internal and external to the company. By their nature, projects are more risky than ongoing operations. This course is the study of ways a project manager can identify, analyze, quantify, mitigate and plan contingencies and manage risks in projects.

Credit Recommendation: In the graduate degree category, 2 semester hours in Principles of Risk Management (6/95).

Project Team Leadership: Human Resources and Communications (IE1620)

Location: Piscataway, NJ and various locations nationwide.

Length: 325 hours (5 days).

Dates: January 1994-Present.

Objective: To prepare the student for leading teams to successfully complete a technical project.

Learning Outcome: Upon successful completion of this course, the student will be able to identify student's and others' interpersonal styles to use in motivating and goal setting; understand the characteristics of people and processes on a Systems Project Team; demonstrate interpersonal skills to involve team members in win-win solutions to conflict; identify student's own strengths as they relate to team building and project management; define and demonstrate group leadership and communication skills; list project management roles and major responsibilities; use negotiation and delegation to aid in reaching group goals; demonstrate understanding of group dynamics and group process; and demonstrate knowledge of appropriate strategies for balancing participation, correcting confusion and bringing team goals to closure.

Instruction: This course examines the leadership skills required of project managers to organize and motivate people in a manner that achieves results in complex organizational environments. Participants will be actively involved in class discussions, case studies and simulations.

Credit Recommendation: In the graduate degree category, 2 semester hours in Organizational Behavior (6/95).

Public Switched Network Seminar (PSNS)

Location: Bell System Tariffs and Costs Seminars, Somerset, NJ.

Length: 355 hours (1 week).

Dates: February 1980-December 1984.

Objective: To provide an in-depth review of the issues associated with the pricing of public switched network services. The material will be of critical importance for understanding the appropriate future pricing policies for PSN services.

Instruction: This seminar addresses basic components of the public switched network, presents economic theory, and discusses service offering guidelines. It also provides an understanding of various rate design tools, e.g., Message Analysis of Revenue and Customers (MARC); Centralized Message Data Systems (CMDS); WATS Information Systems (WIS); Demand Analysis and cost inputs, such as MIMIC, ODOD, EDA, SCORE; and other appropriate cost supports. Lecture, audiovisuals, group interaction, discussion, and field observations are used.

Credit Recommendation: In the upper division baccalaureate degree category, 2 semester hours in Business Administration, Communications, Economics, Engineering Economics, Finance, Industrial Engineering, or Public Administration (2/81).

Quality Improvement Story (QIS) Process Overview (MQ7015) (Formerly Quality Improvement Story (QIS) for Team Members [MQ7015])

Location: Somerset, NJ and other AT&T locations.

Length: 8 hours.

Dates: January 1992-December 1994.

Objective: To introduce team members to the tools and steps of the 7-step QIS methodology.

Learning Outcome: Upon successful completion of this course, the student will be able to understand and follow the 7-step QIS process to solve work related problems; and understand how QIS relates to other quality methodologies used by AT&T.

Instruction: Major topics covered in the course are introducing the 7 steps of QIS methodology to solve work related quality improvement problems.

Credit Recommendation: In the upper division baccalaureate degree category, 1 semester hour in Process Quality I (4/92).

Quality Improvement Story (QIS) Tools and Process (MQ7016)

Location: Somerset, NJ and other AT&T locations.

Length: 16 hours (2 days).

Dates: January 1992-April 1997.

Objective: To introduce the environment, framework, foundation, and tools of the 7-step QIS using actual team stories and examples.

Learning Outcome: Upon successful completion of this course, the student will be able to understand and follow the 7-step QIS methodology using appropriate tools and techniques to solve job related problems; and evaluate presentation formats to effectively communicate team progress and goals.

Instruction: Major topics covered in the course are an in-depth discussion of QIS methods with illustrations of real team stories. Methods of instruction include submitting a graduate level research project to earn the graduate credit recommendation.

Credit Recommendation: In the upper division baccalaureate degree category, 2 semester hours or in the graduate degree category, 1 semester hour in Process Quality II (4/92).

Quality Leadership Workshop (CQ1011)

Location: Somerset, NJ.

Length: 20 hours (3 days).

Dates: December 1989-December 1993.

Objective: To describe the basic principles of quality (PQMI, QIC, and Policy Responsibilities) and how they affect day-to-day work.

Learning Outcome: Upon successful completion of this course, the student will be able to use PQMI tools within the framework of QIC to define work processes and identify possible process improvement opportunities; understand multiple roles managers have in implementing PQMI and identify needed changes to support the implementation of quality; understand the cultural factors of change and the implementation of the nine quality policy responsibilities in your organization; and identify initial steps of your quality action plan and describe your vision of quality.

Instruction: Major topics covered in the course are principles, concepts, and methodology that enable quality implementation; the workshop is designed to make an organizational shift from talking about quality to doing it.

Credit Recommendation: In the graduate degree category, 2 semester hours in Organizational Leadership II (10/91). **NOTE:** The credit recommendation applies only to those students who also successfully complete an independent project integrating the theory and practice of this course and demonstrate an integration of the instruction presented each day.

Rate Seminar (RS)

Location: Bell System Tariffs and Cost Seminars, Somerset, NJ.

Length: 80 hours (2 weeks).

Dates: January 1980-December 1984.

Objective: To provide participants with an overview of the requirements for preparation, design, and implementation of basic, nonbasic, network, and special network service rate structures; to expand the knowledge level of those assigned to rate structure work; and to provide understanding for those who must relate with rate personnel.

Instruction: This seminar uses subject matter experts (SME) from the various rate and cost disciplines to address the historical and developing principles and concepts used in rate structure design. The seminar presents marketing approaches, changes and challenges to the industry, cost/price theory and application, competition, current proposals in the exchange network, special network services, terminal products, and rate costs preparation. A simulated rate case concludes the seminar with an illustrative experience of rate structure implementation. SME lectures, audiovisuals, individual and group task performance, group discussion, and guest speakers form the seminar process.

Credit Recommendation: In the upper division baccalaureate degree category, 3 semester hours in Business Administration, Management, Marketing, or Public Administration (2/81).

Regulated Pricing and Marketing (AT&T 201)

Location: Somerset Seminars Center, Somerset, NJ.

Length: 40 hours (5 days).

Dates: January 1983-May 1985.

Objective: To provide an overview of marketing, pricing, and costing in a regulated environment.

Instruction: The instruction includes marketing and services planning overviews; plus hands-on exercises in marketing of MTS, WATS/800 and special network services. A module addressing basic through advanced service management concepts and techniques is included.

Credit Recommendation: In the upper division baccalaureate degree category, 2 semester hours in Marketing applicable to degree programs in Marketing, Business Administration, or Management (9/83).

Resolving Conflict and Differences (MD7785)

Location: AT&T locations nationwide.

Length: 16 hours (2 days).

Dates: June 1989-December 1993.

Objective: To provide a framework for identifying, surfacing, clarifying, and resolving systematic and interpersonal types of conflict.

Learning Outcome: Upon successful completion of this course, the student will be able to apply a framework for identifying, surfacing, clarifying, and resolving systematic conflict; increase your set of behaviors to use in conflict to avoid getting stuck, losing altogether, or annihilating your "adversary."

Instruction: Major topics covered in the course include presentation, experiential exercises, small group discussion, and practice sessions, interpersonal and organizational conflict resolution; basic principle of respect and working toward "win/win" solutions complements the learning in "Principle Centered Leadership" and "Negotiating Collaboratively."

Credit Recommendation: In the graduate degree category, 1 semester hour in Conflict Management (10/91).

Restructure of Private Line Issues (RPLS-1)

Location: Bell System Tariffs and Cost Seminars, Somerset, NJ.

Length: 44.75 hours (1 week).

Dates: October 1979-September 1981.

Objective: To concentrate on all the internal and external issues associated with the re-price re-structure of private line services as they apply to testimony preparation and presentation.

Instruction: This seminar assumes in-depth knowledge of the private line or special switched network services and familiarity with the preparation and presentation techniques as discussed in the General

Rate and Cost Issue Seminar. RPLS-1 provides an overview of pricing/costing principles presented by subject-matter experts; lectures by non-Bell consultants; and a high ratio of videotaped role play. This seminar relies on intergroup discussions and task performances to achieve the level of preparedness needed to address effectively the issues before the regulatory bodies. Panel discussion, lectures, individual and group task performances, videotaped role play, consultants, and evaluations by subject matter experts are used.

Credit Recommendation: In the graduate degree category, 1 semester hour in Business Administration, Law, or Public Administration (2/81).

Sales Calling Skills (ME9010)

Location: Locations worldwide.

Length: 8 hours (1 day).

Dates: March 1994-Present.

Objective: To position participants to be able to increase sales, qualify leads and utilize effective sales call process, establishing long-term customer relationships.

Learning Outcome: Upon successful completion of this course, the student will be able to maximize bottom line results by effective listening to customers; respond to customer objections and learn to deal effectively and efficiently with resistance; and effectively manage customer contacts from start to finish and close the sale.

Instruction: This course will help enable participants to recognize that the goal is not simply winning sales but rather winning customers, as long term partners. Sales agents will learn how to qualify leads, reach decision makers, uncover and use benefits oriented presentations to gain sales.

Credit Recommendation: In the upper division baccalaureate degree category, 1 semester hour in Sales (7/95). **NOTE:** Student must also complete ME9020 to earn the credit recommendation.

Sales Presentation Techniques (SE7000)
(Formerly Get to the Point Sales Presentation Techniques [SE7000] and also Marketing Communications Workshop [AT&T 502 and SE7000] and Media Interaction for Managers [AT&T 502 and SE7000])

Location: Somerset, NJ and other AT&T locations.

Length: *Version 1:* 164 hours (2 days); *Version 2:* 24 hours (3 days).

Dates: *Version 1:* January 1984-October 1985; *Version 2:* November 1985-Present.

Objective: *Version 1:* To provide managers with the communication skills required in an evolving management and marketing culture. *Version 2:* To provide managers with the communication skills required in an evolving management, marketing, and sales culture.

Learning Outcome: Upon successful completion of this course, the student will be able to understand the demands and dynamics of sales-oriented presentations, for both internal and external customer groups; successfully prepare audience profile to assist in targeting key messages; plan, prepare, and deliver an effective, focused, oral presentation using enhanced communications skills techniques; plan, design, and use proper visual aids that enhance a presentation; develop strategies for handling Q&A sessions; and identify personal strengths and areas for improvement regarding group and one-on-one presentations.

Instruction: *Version 1:* Major topics covered in the course are audience analysis, lecture techniques, effective use of visuals, handling a question/answer sequence, handling adversary questions, panel discussion techniques, effective meeting techniques, television techniques, interview techniques, body language, and proper dress. Methods of instruction include a high degree of videotaping and individual feedback and critique. *Version 2:* Major topics covered in the course are audience/client/customer analysis, presentation organization techniques, Q&A sessions, selling technique trends, and presentation components: visual aids, listening techniques, and memory enhancers. Methods of instruction include videotaped presentations made by students and critiqued by instructors in one-on-one sessions, lecture, discussion, and a highly interactive workshop.

Credit Recommendation: *Version 1:* In the graduate degree category, 1 semester hour is appropriate for use in degree programs in Business Communication, Public Administration, Management, or Organizational Behavior (11/85) (8/91). *Version 2:* In the graduate degree category, 1 semester hour in Sales Presentation Marketing Communications (12/93). **NOTE:** An appropriate graduate level research project is submitted as part of the course requirements.

Sales Skills Application Workshop (ME1050)

Location: Somerset, NJ and other AT&T locations.

Length: 24 hours (3 days).

Dates: June 1993-Present.

Objective: To improve confidence in face-to-face selling situations; increase ability to productively control the tone, flow and outcome of sales calls; and enhance ability to build business partnerships.

Learning Outcome: Upon successful completion of this course, the student will be able to implement a structured approach for conducting sales calls; tailor his/her approach to specific selling situations; and develop sales relationships based on understanding client needs.

Instruction: Major topics covered in the course are designed to build face-to-face selling skills for students involved in selling and those who want to learn skills for effective management of sales situations. It includes sales call planning, presenting solutions, handling objections, and closing the sale. Methods of instruction include videotaped role play, lecture, and discussion.

Credit Recommendation: In the lower division baccalaureate/associate degree category, 1 semester hour in Sales Management (12/93).

Service Marketing (AT&T 504 and SA4040)
(Formerly Concepts of Service and Segment Management)

Location: Somerset Seminars Center, Somerset, NJ.

Length: 24 hours (3 days).

Dates: January 1984-December 1989.

Objective: To provide AT&T Marketing personnel with an overview of service and segment management and their interrelationship.

Instruction: This seminar addresses marketing within the AT&T structure, the service development management processes. Participants will be aware of the roles and responsibilities of service and segment management. Sessions on life cycle management, decision and risk analysis, the regulatory process, marketing research, market segmentation, forecasting, and tracking are presented in this seminar.

Credit Recommendation: In the upper division baccalaureate degree category, 2

semester hours in Marketing (Marketing Segmentation) for use in degree programs in Marketing or Business Administration (11/85).

Service Plan Financial Analysis (AT&T 404)
Analysis for Service Decisions

Location: Somerset Seminars Center, Somerset, NJ.

Length: 32 hours (4 days).

Dates: January 1984-November 1984.

Objective: To provide participants with the training to perform and interpret the types of analysis used in the work of the service groups, and to adapt to changing or unusual analysis requirements.

Instruction: Major topics covered in the course are an understanding of the analysis tools used in service group work, interrelationships, and the use of these tools to perform any of the economic, regulatory, accounting, and tracking analyses normally encountered, and analysis systems such as inputs and interpretation of outputs.

Credit Recommendation: In the upper division baccalaureate degree category, 2 semester hours in Financial Management which could apply to degree programs in Business Administration, Management, or Marketing (11/85).

Software Prototyping (IE 1004)

Location: Piscataway, NJ and other AT&T locations.

Length: 18 hours (3 days).

Dates: April 1994-June 1996.

Objective: To enable a student to understand, develop and evaluate software prototypes.

Learning Outcome: Upon successful completion of this course, the student will be able to know when to begin prototyping, and when to stop; know how to select appropriate prototyping software; and know how to use two popular prototyping packages.

Instruction: Major topics covered in the course are software prototyping, i.e., the development of computer system models, these models can simulate both system functionality and the user interface; how prototyping can be used in the design and development of software products; then, using "hands-on" exercises, participants create, modify, evaluate, and test many different types of prototypes. Methods of instruction include several case problems and participants use PC-based prototyping tools to complete the prototyping exercises.

Credit Recommendation: In the upper division baccalaureate degree or the graduate degree category, 1 semester hour in Software Prototyping (9/94).

Special Network Services Seminar (SNSS)

Location: Bell System Tariffs and Cost Seminars, Somerset, NJ.

Length: 38 hours (1 week).

Dates: March 1980-December 1984.

Objective: To provide personnel in the operating companies' private-line and data-channel organizations with a basic level of job effectiveness.

Instruction: This seminar provides participants with an understanding of the basic plant network components used by each of the private-line and data services; provides a description of each service offering, including the market needs and recommended rate structures; and analyzes the nature and application of the private-line and general exchange tariffs related to these offerings. Lectures, audiovisuals, casework, discussions, and field observation are used.

Credit Recommendation: In the upper division baccalaureate degree category, 2 semester hours in Business Administration, Electrical Engineering, Engineering Communications, Industrial Engineering, or Public Administration (2/81).

Stakeholder Analysis (AT&T 503)
Evaluation of AT&T Interexchange Culture: A Management Technique

Location: Somerset Seminars Center, Somerset, NJ.

Length: 40 hours (1 week).

Dates: January 1984-December 1987.

Objective: To provide participants with an understanding of the evolution occurring in the AT&T culture, to provide the participant with the techniques to cope with the corporate changes, and to provide those techniques needed to address the new stakeholders in the unregulated marketplace.

Instruction: This seminar addresses the changing environment of business, the stakeholder management philosophy and process, and human skills and negotiations. This seminar provides participants with a realistic experience of stakeholder applications by making various external and internal resource people available for each role play required in the specific stakeholder process. This seminar is designed to be easily adaptable to a variety of current issues and concerns. It will constantly be modified to meet identified needs.

Credit Recommendation: In the upper division baccalaureate degree category, 2 or 3 semester hours, or in the graduate degree category, 2 semester hours in Business Administration, Organizational Behavior, Management, or Public Administration (11/85).

Statistical Process Control (SPC) for Process Management (CQ1009)

Location: All AT&T training locations.

Length: *Version 1:* 36 hours (5 days); *Version 2:* 32 hours (4.5 days).

Dates: *Version 1:* May 1990-May 1996; *Version 2:* June 1996-Present.

Objective: To teach statistical process control (SPC) to those working in a service or administrative function.

Learning Outcome: Upon successful completion of this course, the student will know data collection and analysis to improve customer satisfaction, understand Histograms and Pareto analyses to determine the types of process problems, construct and analyze various control charts to monitor process performance over time, use scatterplots and analysis of means (ANOM) to detect causes of problems, and use consulting tips to help lead co-workers to continuous quality improvement.

Instruction: Major topics covered in the course are statistical process control to those working in a service or administrative function, how and when to collect useful data, graphical and statistical tools for analyzing the data, and SQC Troubleshooter. Method of instruction includes an independent project applying several of the identified statistics procedures.

Credit Recommendation: In the upper division baccalaureate degree category, 1 semester hour In Statistical Quality Control (lecture) and 1 semester hour in Statistical Quality Control (lab) for a total of 2 semester hours (10/91) (11/96).

Statistical Sampling Seminar (FE0606)

Location: Somerset, NJ.

Length: 24 hours.

Dates: December 1989-August 1996.

Objective: To provide the student with an understanding of statistical sampling and how to use it effectively on the job.

Learning Outcome: Upon completion of this course, the student will be able to determine the applicability of using sampling as a measurement technique; determine the proper use of both scientific and non-scientific sampling; understand the mathematical theory behind statistical sampling; discuss sampling methods, techniques, and sample design with management and external auditors; apply the requirements of SAS39 and SAS47 on several case studies, using appropriate tools during the selection of test samples; and draw a statistically valid sample, determine and evaluate results, properly communicate results to management, and document the test in workpapers.

Instruction: Major topics covered in the course are understanding of statistical sampling and its use; conduct tests using several sampling techniques and will report on the results; and focus on the practical aspect of sampling when dealing with large numbers of transactions.

Credit Recommendation: In the graduate degree category, 2 semester hours in Statistical Sampling (8/91).

Statistics I: Introduction to Statistics and Probability (QU1135)

Location: All AT&T training locations.

Length: 24 hours (3 days).

Dates: January 1995-Present.

Objective: To provide the student with the fundamental concepts of statistics and probability.

Learning Outcome: Upon successful completion of this course, the student will be able to understand the different types of data, know the measure of central tendency and dispersion, know the graphical tools used for summarizing data, understand regression and correlation, understand the concepts of probability, and master the calculation of probability using different models.

Instruction: Major topics covered in the course are fundamental concepts of statistics; measures of location and dispersion, graphical tools for summarizing data, correlation and regression analyses, the fundamental concept of probability theory including calculations of probabilities, concepts of random variables, and discrete and continuous theoretical distribution. Methods of instruction include lecture.

Credit Recommendation: In the upper division baccalaureate degree category, 2 semester hours in Business Statistics (11/96).

Strategic Marketing and Process Service Planning Seminar [PUB 401]

Location: Somerset Seminars Center, Somerset, NJ.

Length: 24 hours (3 days).

Dates: January 1983-December 1984.

Objective: To provide an understanding of strategic marketing concepts and processes as they relate to service management and products.

Instruction: Major topics covered in the course are marketing fundamentals and the basics of strategic marketing. It addresses the process of strategic marketing decision making, especially decisions involving telecommunications services and product lines.

Credit Recommendation: In the graduate degree category, 1 semester hour in Marketing, Strategic Marketing, or Business Administration (9/83).

Strategic Marketing for Maximum Profitability (ME0872)

Location: Somerset, NJ and other AT&T locations worldwide.

Length: 24 hours, plus laboratory.

Dates: *Version 1:* September 1990-June 1996; *Version 2:* July 1996-Present.

Objective: To teach students how to utilize the latest theories and practices in Strategic Marketing.

Learning Outcome: Upon successful completion of this course, the student will be able to develop and implement directly job applicable SBU oriented strategic and tactical marketing strategies; strategically protect and win market share; formulate an umbrella marketing strategy; optimally manage the marketing mix through all stages of the product/service life cycle to maximize profits; implement strategies to increase revenue/profits from your current market base; construct and write a short range and long range marketing plan for a business case; participate in developing and implementing an SBU market information system, designing focus groups, writing questionnaires, collecting data, interpreting research findings, and presenting results to management for AT&T actionable marketing decision-making; analyze your SBU's micro and macro environment; identify whether your product/service should be marketed as a market leader, challenger, or nicher and how to implement the strategy; and apply seminar material to the international market.

Instruction: Major topics covered in the course are the concept of strategic marketing, formulating an umbrella marketing strategy, developing and implementing an SBU market information system, analyzing an SBU's micro and macro environment, strategically targeting market segments, market analysis and demand, constructing a short-range tactical marketing plan for a business case, constructing a long-range marketing plan for a business case, strategic marketing for market leader SBUs and challenger SBUs, market strategies to protect and win back market share, developing and implementing tactical marketing decisions, developing and implementing long range marketing decisions, strategic marketing formula for success, strategies for new product/service development, strategic marketing for new products/services, strategic marketing for mature products/services, product/service strategic marketing, customer focused strategic pricing, strategic marketing communications and promotion, strategic channel marketing, identifying and strategically marketing to business and consumer innovators, international strategic marketing, applying seminar material to the international market, and strategic marketing customer focus and quality application. Methods of instruction include lecture, discussion, and a graduate level project related to Strategic Marketing.

Credit Recommendation: *Version 1:* In the graduate degree category, 3 semester hours in Strategic Marketing (8/91). *Version 2:* In the graduate degree category, 2 semester hours in Marketing (5/96).

Strategic Pricing for Profitability (ME 2006) (Formerly ME 0898)

Location: Somerset, NJ, and other AT&T locations throughout the country.

Length: 16 hours (2 days).

Dates: July 1986-December 1989.

Objective: To acquaint managers with cost and demand oriented approaches to pricing.

Learning Outcome: Upon successful completion of this course, managers will be able to recognize various pricing techniques; recognize the difference between cost-based and market-based pricing; and recognize a role of market segmentation for better pricing decisions.

Instruction: This course illustrates selected pricing procedures. The perceived value concept as an element of pricing strategy is explained through various exercises in which managers can apply the principles to specific products and situations. Case study analysis is used throughout the course and a separate term paper must be submitted to the instructor after the class time as part of the course requirements. Prerequisite: Submission of a pricing plan.

Credit Recommendation: In the graduate degree category, 1 semester hour in Fundamentals of Pricing (11/86).

Strategies for Competing Globally (GM1020)

Location: AT&T locations worldwide.

Length: *Version 1:* 21 hours (3 days); *Version 2:* 16 hours (2 days).

Dates: *Version 1:* April 1990-January 1995; *Version 2:* February 1995-Present.

Objective: *Version 1:* To help participants identify the elements involved in formulating successful global strategies and describe AT&T's current approach/position. *Version 2:* To provide participants a conceptual framework for strategic competitive analysis and planning.

Learning Outcome: *Version 1:* Upon successful completion of this course, the student will be able to understand the major trends, variables, and factors (external and internal) that have an impact on global competitive advantage - in general and with reference to AT&T's business; analyze foreign buying behavior, with emphasis on market research and information acquisition; understand how to use concepts, methodologies, and market information to formulate strategies and courses of action that will improve AT&T's competitive position; discuss product/service planning, including sourcing, offshore manufacturing, countertrade agreements, market segmentation, pricing policies, and international sales management; understand AT&T's current global presence, competitive position, and stated competitive strategy. *Version 2:* Upon successful completion of this course, the student will be able to evaluate major trends, including internal and external variables that impact global competition with reference to AT&T's businesses; use concepts, methodologies and market information to formulate strategies and courses of action that will improve competitive position; and understand and discuss AT&T's global business strategy.

Instruction: *Version 1:* This course is designed for AT&T managers with international managerial responsibilities. The course discusses in depth the competitive forces AT&T is facing in global markets and provides a comprehensive and integrated framework for: a) analyzing and interpreting relevant competitive information, and b) designing effective global strategies. Methods of instruction include lectures, exercises, and discussions centering on vital aspects of competitive strategic planning in a global context. *Version 2:* This program will provide a conceptual framework for strategic competitive analysis and planning. Students will closely examine both competitive analysis and strategic positioning for success in the telecommunications market. Students will gain an overall perspective of global structure and strategy, and understand global presence, competitive position and competitive strategy. An appropriate graduate level project is included as part of the course requirement for students to earn the credit recommendation.

Credit Recommendation: *Version 1:* In the graduate degree category, 2 semester hours in International Business Strategies (12/90). *Version 2:* In the graduate degree category, 1 semester hour in Global Business Strategies (7/95).

Strategy Analysis for Finance and Marketing (UPSA and SE2010)

Location: Somerset Seminars Center, Somerset, NJ.

Length: 24 hours (3 days).

Dates: January 1984-October 1987.

Objective: To focus on the convergence of two functions (finance and marketing) and to address marketing/finance issues at both the level of the managers of individual product-market business/service units and at the level of the overall corporate financial managers.

Instruction: The program uses a decision-making orientation and discusses the elements of a comprehensive marketing strategy with respect to their cost profiles and in developing sustainable competitive roles. Also, measurement of financial performance is developed and applied to a particular firm in order to determine its success in investing its financial objectives. This course discusses the impact of competitive marketing decisions on the business's income statement and balance sheet and considers a systematic approach to analyzing profitability and risk. Procedures for unbundling top-down budget objectives into product-marketing strategy are discussed and the importance of the consistency of a firm's financial planning is stressed.

Credit Recommendation: In the upper division baccalaureate degree category, 1 semester hour as an upper level Business elective (11/85).

Structured Program Design (CS7200) (Formerly Analysis and Design Strategies [ADS] [IE3010])

Location: Piscataway, NJ, other AT&T locations, and Bell Operating Company locations.

Length: *Version 1:* 30 hours (5 days); *Version 2:* 24 hours (4 days).

Dates: *Version 1:* June 1981-December 1991; *Version 2:* January 1992-June 1996.

Objective: To provide students with the overall concepts of structured system development.

Learning Outcome: Upon successful completion of this course, the student will be able to distinguish between logical and physical views of a system; identify the analysis and design tools used to create physical and logical views of a system; identify the products produced by analysis and design; convert the products of analysis into the products of design; identify design tools and how to use them; and convert a properly produced system analysis (standard system specification) into an efficient structured design document.

Credit Recommendation: In the upper division baccalaureate degree category, 2 semester hours in Computer Information Systems or Computer Science (7/85) (7/90).

Structured Test Plans (IE2710)

Location: Piscataway, NJ and other AT&T locations.

Length: 24 hours (4 days).

Dates: January 1978-June 1996.

Objective: To specify how and when testing activities interact with the Total System Development process; to prepare a test plan and identify various testing methods and test aids.

Instruction: Major topics covered in the course are testing principles and test planning and includes a presentation of a testing methodology applied to each phase of the "total system development" process. Methods of instruction include lecture, discussion, and workshops.

Credit Recommendation: In the lower division baccalaureate/associate degree category, 1 semester hour in Computer Science or Computer Information Systems (2/80) (7/85) (7/90).

Supplier Quality Management (CQ9001)

Location: U.S. and locations globally.

Length: 16 hours (2 days).

Dates: February 1994-Present.

Objective: To provide guidelines to assist organizations in helping their suppliers deliver customer-focused value.

Learning Outcome: Upon successful completion of this course, the student will be able to develop a supply strategy for managing suppliers in support of business goals; determine the appropriate type of relationship to develop with suppliers; and monitor and improve supplier performance to achieve business goals.

Instruction: This course links supplier relationships to a customer-focused business plan designed to produce superior value through continuous improvement of performance in the supply channels. It focuses on developing a supply strategy, selecting and qualifying suppliers, and monitoring and improving their performance based on the desired relationship identified for specific suppliers.

Credit Recommendation: In the graduate degree category, 1 semester hour in Supplier Quality Management (6/94).

Supply Chain Management (PR5102)

Location: All AT&T training locations in the U.S.

Length: 24 hours (3 days).

Dates: October 1995-Present.

Objective: To provide an overview of what constitutes effective and efficient management of the organization's supply chain.

Learning Outcome: Upon successful completion of this course, the student will be able to design effective supply chains, manage supplier relationships, improve supply chain efficiency, continue quality improvement, understand supplier certification, and understand cost containment strategies.

Instruction: Major topics covered in the course are designing effective supply chains; managing supplier relationships; improving supply chain efficiency; continuing quality improvement; supplier certification; cost containment strategies; and the power of strategic partnership. Methods of instruction include classroom instruction and an appropriate graduate level research project for those students seeking the graduate credit recommendation.

Credit Recommendation: In the upper division baccalaureate degree category, 2 semester hours, or in the graduate degree category, 1 semester hour in Purchasing (12/95).

Support Services Strategy for the 90's (FE0807)

Location: AT&T locations nationwide.

Length: 8 hours.

Dates: February 1990-November 1992.

Objective: To teach students the new Support Services organization structure, explore our roles and responsibilities in the new organization; reinforce the CSO shared values, and accept the challenge of commitment to the new course being charted.

Learning Outcome: Upon successful completion of this course, the student will be able to understand the principles of Product Management; understand and participate in the AT&T Team Leader and Product Management Concept; and understand and describe the role of the Team Leader and associated financial performance accountability.

Instruction: Major topics covered in the course include implementing AT&T's Team Leader and Product Management concept in a partnership relationship between Product Management, Team Leaders and Clients; learn aspects of quality requirements for tracking organizational architecture and associated financial data; and they will construct a scenario which demonstrates interdependencies between Team Leaders, Product Management Teams and Clients. Methods of instruction include a series of lectures, practice exercises, simulations, and job aids; prior reading assignments and a term paper which are required for completion of the course.

Credit Recommendation: In the upper division baccalaureate degree category, 1 semester hour in Strategies for Organizational Behavior (8/91).

Support Services Strategy for the 90's-Occupational (FE0808)

Location: AT&T locations nationwide.

Length: 6 hours.

Dates: February 1990-November 1992.

Objective: To teach students AT&T's new Support Services organization structure; explore the roles and responsibilities in the new organization; reinforce the CSO shared values; and accept the challenges of commitment to the new course being chartered by AT&T.

Learning Outcome: Upon successful completion of this course, the student will be able to understand and participate in the Team Leader and Product Management Concept; obtain an overview of the principle of Product Management; identify and describe elements of organizational strategies for Building Management and Administrative Services Personnel; and develop a matrix of accountability.

Instruction: Major topics covered in the course are implementing AT&T's Team Leader and Product Management concept in a partnership relationship between Product Management, Team Leaders and Clients; aspects of quality requirements for tracking organizational architecture and associated financial data; and they will construct a scenario which demonstrates interdependencies between Team Leaders, Product Management Teams and Clients. Methods of instruction include a series of lectures, practice exercises, simulations, and job aids. Prior readings and a term paper are also required for the completion of the course.

Credit Recommendation: In the upper division baccalaureate degree category, 1 semester hour in Strategies for Organizational Behavior (8/91).

System Design

Location: Data Systems Education Center, Piscataway, NJ.

Length: 60 hours (2 weeks).

Dates: December 1978-December 1984.

Objective: To provide students with the background necessary to enable them to identify and analyze an entity problem and create a logical model of the problem using system analysis methodology.

Instruction: Major topics covered in the course are systems data structure, data flow, function structure, function flow, control, performance criteria, logical subsystems, system implementation, and testing. Methods of instruction include lecture, discussion, and workshops.

Credit Recommendation: In the upper division baccalaureate degree category, 3 semester hours in Information Systems Design (5/80).

Tactics for Competing Globally (GM1030)

Location: Somerset, NJ.

Length: 21 hours (3 days).

Dates: August 1990-October 1992.

Objective: To identify and explain specific tactics for success in the global marketplace, showcasing specific AT&T examples.

Learning Outcome: Upon successful completion of this course, the student will be able to analyze the competitive strengths and weaknesses of major competitors in specific markets; identify the current opportunities and threats in specific markets and anticipate future opportunities and threats based on trends in the industry; understand AT&T's approach to global market penetration and create competitive synergies with other AT&T entities, e.g., matrixing with AT&T International, interfacing with country managers, etc., and effectively deploy local resources in foreign markets, gathering competitive information, overcoming regulatory obstacles, expediting transactions, etc.

Instruction: This course discusses specific, micro-level tactics that will help managers compete more effectively in the following markets: Europe, Far East, Americas, India, Middle East, and Africa. The course addresses certain lines of business only—network systems, ICS, PBX markets, and DSG products—and analyzes AT&T's competitive position in relation to the top three competitors in each market. Through examples and case studies of recent AT&T experiences, as well as lecture, discussion, and guest speakers, participants learn to formulate their own product-specific competitive strategies.

Credit Recommendation: In the graduate degree category, 2 semester hours in International Business Tactics (12/90).

Targeting Your Markets for Today's Changing Environment: Tools for the External and Internal Markets (SA4070) (Formerly Targeting Your Customer: Segmenting Markets for Profitability [SA4070]) (Formerly Market Segmentation/Buyer Behavior)

Location: Somerset, NJ and various other AT&T locations.

Length: *Version 1:* 34 hours (4 days); *Version 2:* 24 hours (3 days); *Version 3:* 16 hours (2 days).

Dates: *Version 1:* January 1980-December 1990; *Version 2:* January 1991-December 1993; *Version 3:* January 1994-Present.

Objective: *Version 1:* To develop the theory of buyer behavior and its impact on market segmentation strategy. *Versions 2 and 3:* To teach participants the core elements of the market segmentation process and the criteria used to assess potential alternative market segments.

Learning Outcome: Upon successful completion of this course, the student will be able to review the concepts of market segmentation and explore the importance of micro marketing or niche marketing in today's marketplace and analyze the relationship between customer behavior and segmenting in the market.

Instruction: *Version 1:* Major topics covered in the course stress individual market segmentation in terms of different types of organizations, their sizes, distribution, number, geographical location, and types of purchasing organizations. The customer is studied from a behavioral point of view. *Versions 2 and 3:* Major topics covered in the course provides participants with market segmentation concepts, explores the interrelationship between customer behavior and segmentation, and discusses in-depth how to implement a market segmentation strategy to achieve profitability.

Credit Recommendation: *Versions 1 and 2:* In the upper division baccalaureate degree category, 2 semester hours in Marketing (9/80) (11/85) (8/91). *Version 3:* In the upper division baccalaureate degree category, 1 semester hour in Marketing (5/96).

Task Analysis (IE1104)

Location: Piscataway, NJ and other AT&T locations.

Length: 15 hours (3 days).

Dates: January 1985-June 1996.

Objective: To present the fundamental characteristics and applications of task analysis in order to evaluate and improve current systems, modify existing systems, or as a part of total system development in the creation of new systems.

Learning Outcome: Upon successful completion of this course, the student should be able to identify the sequence of procedures required to perform task analysis; identify the uses of task analysis in the design of user products and development of systems, modified and new; perform and document task analysis process from planning through the detail analysis phase; and make recommendations for design based upon the task analysis results.

Credit Recommendation: In the upper division baccalaureate degree category, 1 semester hour in Computer Information Systems or Management (7/85) (7/90).

Team Leader Training (CQ1012) (Formerly Total Quality Management (TQM) Team Leader Training [CQ1012])

Location: Somerset, NJ and other AT&T locations.

Length: 40 hours (plus extensive guided-independent study).

Dates: May 1989-December 1994.

Objective: To prepare students to function effectively as the leader of a Quality Improvement Cycle (QIC) Team.

Learning Outcome: Upon successful completion of this course, the student will be able to understand, explain, and apply the Quality Improvement Cycle Tools and Techniques to lead teams in solving job related problems; understand and apply leadership principles to manage group dynamics; and fulfill the administrative and support roles required of a team leader.

Instruction: Major topics covered in the course are coaching students in facilitation skills, group dynamics, and on their duties as a team leader; and Quality Assurance and Statistical Analysis. Methods of Instruction include role play, case study, and the student must complete an application project that exhibits the ability to apply the tools and group leadership techniques learned in the course.

Credit Recommendation: In the graduate degree category, 3 semester hours in Team Leadership for Quality Assurance (4/92).

Technical Consulting Skills Workshop (IE1500)

Location: All AT&T training locations.

Length: *Version 1:* 24 hours; *Version 2:* 28 hours.

Dates: *Version 1:* December 1979-December 1987; *Version 2:* January 1988-June 1996.

Objective: To enable the manager to understand and practice the interpersonal skills necessary for a successful client/consultant relationship.

Learning Outcome: Upon successful completion of this course, the student will be able to describe the kind of problems which may arise from ineffective consulting, determine the suitability of a potential client for consulting work, utilize active listening techniques to draw out client needs and expectations, identify different client styles and adopt appropriate consulting roles, perform the appropriate tasks at each phase of a consulting project, and identify and deal effectively with dilemmas using appropriate strategies.

Instruction: Major topics covered in the course are the interpersonal skills needed to conduct a successful consulting project; the project-orientation and interpersonal aspects of consulting; the phases of a consulting project; the roles a consultant might take in working with a client; and problems that can arise at each phase, suggests ways of dealing with them, and gives students practice applying the techniques. Methods of instruction include discussion, exercises, role plays, and video taping. There is a pre-course reading assignment.

Credit Recommendation: In the upper division baccalaureate degree category, 2 semester hours in Management (7/85) (7/90) (11/96).

Techniques of Instruction (IE8210)

Location: Piscataway, NJ and other AT&T locations.

Length: 35 hours (5 days).

Dates: March 1978-December 1986.

Objective: To enable the student to instruct a class efficiently and effectively using balanced instructional techniques and objective performance criteria.

Instruction: Major topics covered in the course include pre-class preparation, ice-breaking, motivation, classroom management, instructional techniques, and end-of-course evaluation. Methods of instruction include lecture, discussion, classroom exercises, and microteaching.

Credit Recommendation: In the lower division baccalaureate/associate degree category, 2 semester hours in Education, Human Resources Management, or Training and Development (2/80) (7/85).

Telephone Bypass Opportunities and Local Access (PUB 402)

Location: Somerset Seminars Center, Somerset, NJ.

Length: 16 hours (2 days).

Dates: January 1984-December 1984.

Objective: To demonstrate the significance of the telephone bypass industry, the innovative application opportunities, and the emerging market structure.

Instruction: This seminar provides a systematic review of today's telephone network services marketplace and offers participants an overview of telecommunications, highlighting expected local access marketing strategies for AT&T, other common carriers, and large corporate users. These keys for success in the new marketplace are covered: (1) bypass technology economics, (2) local access and charges, and (3) joint venture contracts.

Credit Recommendation: In the graduate degree category, 1 semester hour in Marketing or Business Administration (11/85).

Teleprocessing (T.P.) in the Host (IE7145) (Formerly Main Frame Data Communications Software Interfaces)

Location: Piscataway, NJ and other AT&T locations.

Length: 24 hours (4 days).

Dates: February 1984-November 1989.

Objective: To introduce the student to teleprocessing channel programs, control blocks, and the relationships between teleprocessing access method software and hardware components.

Instruction: Major topics covered in the course emphasize teleprocessing trouble identification and resolution tools. Lecture, discussion, and laboratory are used. The Major topics covered in the course are the identification of teleprocessing software-related trouble indications that may originate from various sources the network performance monitor; T.P. access method console; operating system console; user contact; also included are identification of the proper procedures used to isolate/locate the troubles; identification of the conditions that most likely caused the troubles to occur; and description of the steps necessary to resolve or refer the troubles.

Credit Recommendation: In the upper division baccalaureate degree category, 1 semester hour in Data Communications/ Operations, Data Processing, or Computer Science (7/85).

Terminal Products Issues Seminar (TPIS)

Location: Bell System Tariffs and Costs Seminars, Somerset, NJ.

Length: 30 hours (4 days).

Dates: November 1980-December 1981.

Objective: To concentrate on all the internal and external issues associated with the implementation of terminal product/ service rate proposals before the regulatory bodies.

Instruction: This seminar assumes in-depth knowledge of the concepts, principles, and market considerations associated with the rate design and levels of terminal products and services and familiarity with the preparation and presentation techniques as discussed in the General Rate and Cost Issue Seminar. TPIS also provides experience in using tariff-filing support materials in a simulated regulatory implementation process.

Credit Recommendation: In the graduate degree category, 2 semester hours in Business Administration, Law, or Public Administration (2/81). **NOTE:** If the student has taken General Rate and Cost Issue Seminar (GIS), then TPIS is recommended for 1 semester hour in the graduate degree category because of duplication.

Terminals and Line Protocol (DC7125) (IE7125)

Location: Piscataway, NJ and other AT&T locations.

Length: 30 hours (5 days).

Dates: September 1983-June 1996.

Objective: To teach the fundamentals of how terminals operate in a telecommunications environment. Specifically, students will acquire skills on interpreting various forms of asynchronous and synchronous protocols.

Instruction: Major topics covered in the course are asynchronous and synchronous transmissions; the ASCII code set and its control characters; the use of the ANSI X3.64 code; options available on asynchronous terminals, decoding various implementations of BSC protocol; and trouble isolation for asynchronous and synchronous terminals. Methods of instruction include lecture, laboratory, and discussion.

Credit Recommendation: In the upper division baccalaureate degree category, 2 semester hours in Data Communications or Operations, Data Processing, or Computer Science (7/85) (7/90).

Test Design for Course Developers (IE8104)

Location: Piscataway, NJ and other AT&T locations.

Length: 12 hours (2 days).

Dates: August 1983-December 1986.

Objective: To provide basic information about test design and evaluation for course developers.

Learning Outcome: Upon successful completion of the course, the student will be able to determine which type of test is appropriate for specific applications; design test items that match objectives; create a test document following the recommended format; and evaluate the test data.

Instruction: Major topics covered in the instructor-led course are more information about designing tests; general information about testing, test items and format, and test data evaluation.

Credit Recommendation: In the lower division baccalaureate/associate degree category, 1 semester hour in Education (7/85).

The Scheuing Method (PR5001)

Location: AT&T training locations in the U.S.

Length: 40 hours (5 days).

Dates: June 1995-Present.

Objective: To prepare the student to pass the Certified Purchasing Manager (CPM) examination.

Learning Outcome: Upon successful completion of this course, this student will be able to pass the CPM examination from having studied major topics such as: reading and interpreting questions, administrative aspects of the purchasing department, personnel issues, updates on exam content, and suggestions for preparation.

Instruction: This course helps participants enhance their chances of passing the examination to receive NAPM certification in Purchasing Management by participating in a lecture presentation with videos on the Purchasing function; gaining a better understanding of preparation techniques for completing exam requirements; reviewing the organizational functions of Purchasing; understanding the continuing education function of Purchasing. An appropriate graduate level project is included as part of the course requirement for students to earn the credit recommendation.

Credit Recommendation: In the graduate degree category or in the upper division baccalaureate degree category, 3 semester hours in Purchasing Management (7/95).

The Telecommuting and Virtual Workplace Seminar (VO2000)

Location: Open/General Enrollments: Somerset, NJ; Atlanta, GA; Chicago, IL; Pleasanton, CA. Suitcased/On-Site Delivery: Internationally.

Length: 7 hours (1 day).

Dates: June 1995-Present.

Objective: To establish a foundation by which participants can understand the trends, issues, opportunities and challenges associated with implementing non-traditional work environments such as telecommuting, satellite officing and hoteling.

Learning Outcome: Upon successful completion of this course, the student will be able to define the key concepts associated with alternative work arrangements; recognize the driving forces and the many benefits of non-traditional work environments; and understand the human factor issues associated with non-traditional work environments.

Instruction: For people who are interested in or curious about the emerging new ways of "working." This interactive workshop provides an overview of the issues and trends driving businesses to explore a variety of non-traditional work arrangements such as telecommuting, satellite officing, hoteling and the virtual office and how these trends affect business and operational results. Participants also gain valuable insight into a step-by-step process that enables one to assess whether or not a non-traditional work environment is appropriate for the individual and/or organization.

Credit Recommendation: In the lower division baccalaureate/associate degree category, 1 semester hour in Telecommunication Management (12/95). **NOTE:** To earn this credit recommendation, student must complete this course and one of the following courses: VO2005 or VO2006.

Theory and Practice of Promotion Management (Formerly Advanced Consumer Promotion Management I and II)

Location: Somerset Seminars Center, Somerset, NJ.

Length: 35 hours (5 days).

Dates: July 1985-August 1985.

Objective: To familiarize the student with the design and implementation of advertising and promotional strategies as part of the overall marketing planning process.

Instruction: Major topics covered in the course are market segmentation and positioning, scheduling, market selection, message design, media selection, budgeting, and measurement. Particular attention is paid to implementing an advertising/promotion strategy for new products and formulating an annual advertising/promotion calendar for existing products. This course includes lectures, discussions, classroom exercises, simulations, problem solving, and case studies.

Credit Recommendation: In the upper division baccalaureate degree category, 2 semester hours, or in the graduate degree category, 1 semester hour in Promotion and Advertising (11/85). **NOTE:** Both sections need to be completed to receive credit.

Transportation Strategies for the Year 2000 (PR5055)

Location: All AT&T training locations.

Length: 24 hours (3 days).

Dates: January 1995-Present.

Objective: To provide managers who are in transportation and procurement the ability to develop non-price strategies for gaining competitive advantage. Also for shippers who want to enhance their firm's profitability and corporate performance through value-added transportation service.

Learning Outcome: Upon successful completion of this course, the student will be able to successfully determine customer requirements and shipper and carrier perspective, develop customer-oriented strategies for world-class performance, and understand benchmarking and performance measures.

Instruction: Major topics covered in the course are how carriers and shippers can build strategic alliances and partnerships to maximize carrier efficiency, shipper satisfaction and profits, determining customer requirements, shipper and carrier perspectives, implementing EDI in transportation, using GAP analysis, developing customer oriented strategies for "world class" performance, developing partnerships between shippers and carriers, implementing transportation service quality programs, benchmarking and performance measures, and meeting the challenge of NAFTA. An appropriate graduate level project is included as part of the course requirement.

Credit Recommendation: In the upper division baccalaureate degree category, 2 semester hours in Logistics or in the graduate degree category, 1 semester hour in Logistics (11/96).

Understanding Your Customers, Markets and Competitors (RB1011) (Formerly Dealing Your Customers a Winning Hand [RB1011])

Location: Somerset, NJ and other AT&T locations.

Length: *Version 1:* 32 hours; *Version 2:* 24 hours (3 days).

Dates: *Version 1:* November 1990-December 1993; *Version 2:* January 1994-Present.

Objective: *Version 1:* To teach students to analyze their markets, competitors, and products so that they can run their businesses competitively and successfully. *Version 2:* To build insights and skills to analyze your industry and your business and to be able to incorporate "real world" considerations that are prime requisites for long-term success.

Learning Outcome: *Version 1:* Upon successful completion of this course, the student will be able to define the parameters of the business they want to be in, set targets for the business, and determine the means by which to achieve the targets; analyze and fully understand the trends and dynamics of the industry and markets they want to compete in; perform in-depth market analyses, segment the market accurately, and identify the customer segments they want to serve; identify competitors, perform in-depth competitive analyses (using benchmarking, SWOT analysis and other tools) and develop effective competitive strategies; and position and differentiate their product or service for maximum competitive advantage, using value chain analysis and other tools. *Version 2:* Upon successful completion of this course, the students will be able to examine your value chain against your customer's expectations; analyze the dynamics of your industry; benchmark against your potential and present competitors; and identify your competitor's strengths and weaknesses.

Instruction: *Version 1:* Major topics covered in the course are a series of concepts, tools and skills for running a business successfully-e.g., business definition, industry and market analysis, market segmentation, competitive positioning, and others; the course integrates these elements into a coherent business analysis framework in which attention to Quality and a Global Perspective are fundamental; the instructional focus is on immediate application to students' businesses; students read and learn the material through pre-course and evening assignments, discuss material in class, then apply the tools and skills to their own businesses in class with the aid of the instructor. Methods of instruction include hands-on involvement, and a lengthy and detailed post-course assignment is required. *Version 2:* Major topics covered in the course are designed for students who need to run their job as a business. It includes SWOT analysis, global market life cycle, industry structure, market segmentation principles, target market segments, competitive position, value chain, and benchmarking. Methods of instruction is an application workshop; lectures are minimized to devote time to applying skills and developing a winning competitive game plan. An appropriate graduate level research project is submitted as part of the course requirements.

Credit Recommendation: *Version 1:* In the graduate degree category, 3 semester hours in Business Policy (8/91). *Version 2:* In the graduate degree category, 2 semester hours in Business Policy (12/93).

UNIX System Resource Efficiencies (IE5004)

Location: Somerset, NJ and other AT&T locations.

Length: *Version 1:* 30 hours (5 days); *Version 2:* 40 hours (1 week).

Dates: *Version 1:* December 1987-January 1995; *Version 2:* February 1995-June 1996.

Objective: To enable programmers and administrators to identify and make use of many system resources.

Learning Outcome: Upon successful completion of this course, the student will be able to describe the division of UNIX system memory among the kernel and the user processes, describe a UNIX system process and its attributes, use various commands for effective management of files and processes, and compare efficient versus inefficient usage of system resources in UNIX system programming or administration.

Instruction: Major topics covered in the course are background information about the internal operations of the UNIX system to enable them to identify and make efficient use of the many important system resources, and commands that increase human efficiency in the management of UNIX system files and processes.

Credit Recommendation: *Version 1:* In the lower division baccalaureate/associate degree category, 1 semester hour in Topics in Computer Science (7/90). *Version 2:* In the upper division baccalaureate degree category, 2 semester hours in Computer Science or Computer Information Systems (1 hour lecture and 1 hour lab) (11/96).

UNIX System Tools for End Users (IE5012)

Location: Piscataway, NJ.

Length: 18 hours (3 days).

Dates: May 1986-November 1991.

Objective: To enable participants to do information processing on a UNIX system.

Learning Outcome: Upon successful completion of this course, the student should be able to: (1) identify the functions of various commands; (2) use these commands to increase information processing effectiveness and efficiency; and (3) define and construct UNIX system tools.

Instruction: Major topics covered in this instructor-led course cover the use of various commands for organizing, updating, selecting, and comparing files; and also covers the use of various shell features to combine these commands to produce new tools.

Credit Recommendation: In the lower division baccalaureate/associate degree category, 1 semester hour in UNIX System Tools or Computer Science elective (7/90). **NOTE:** This course duplicates course IE5112 (UNIX System Tools for Programmers) and credit will be awarded for only one of these courses taken by the student.

UNIX System Tools for Programmers (IE5112)

Location: Piscataway, NJ.

Length: *Version 1:* 18 hours (3 days); *Version 2:* 12 hours (2 days).

Dates: *Version 1:* May 1986-December 1992; *Version 2:* January 1993-June 1996.

Objective: To enable programmers to do information processing on a UNIX system.

Learning Outcome: Upon successful completion of this course, the student should be able to identify the functions of various commands; use these commands to increase information processing effectiveness and efficiency; and define and construct UNIX system tools.

Instruction: Major topics covered in this instructor-led course cover the use of various commands for organizing, updating, selecting, and comparing files; examples and extensive terminal exercises; and also covers the use of various shell features to combine these commands to produce new tools.

Credit Recommendation: In the lower division baccalaureate/associate degree category, 1 semester hour in UNIX System Tools or Computer Science elective (7/90). **NOTE:** This course duplicates IE5012 (UNIX System Tools for End Users) and credit will be awarded for only one of these courses taken by the student.

User Documentation/Performance Aids Workshop (IE1200)

Location: Piscataway, NJ and other AT&T locations.

Length: 18 hours (3 days).

Dates: June 1980-June 1988.

Objective: To assist students develop their skill in the design and construction of performance aids and work procedures for use on the job.

Learning Outcome: Upon successful completion of this course, the student should be able to identify the common pitfalls and problems of existing documentation products; reference and apply state-of-the-art documentation principles to the design and presentation of user documents; design documentation products that are clear, legible, easy to scan, and easy to reference; redesign existing products to enhance accessibility, clarity, and organization; and identify strengths, weaknesses, and optimum applications for six documentation formats.

Instruction: Major topics covered in this instructor-led workshop addresses products from the Detail and Implementation phases of Total Systems Development, but many of the principles discussed are applicable to other documentation products such as administrative guides, run books, and user guides.

Credit Recommendation: In the lower level baccalaureate/associate degree category or in the upper division baccalaureate degree, 1 semester hour in Human

Resources Management, Training and Development, or Education (7/85).

User Interface Specialist Training (IE1002) (Formerly Human Factors in Computer Systems [IE1002])

Location: Somerset, NJ and other AT&T locations.

Length: 90-95 hours (15 days over 3 months).

Dates: July 1982-Present.

Objective: To provide the base education needed to perform Human Factors activities.

Learning Outcome: Upon successful completion of this course, the student will be able to make and support Human Factors decisions and recommendations; conduct research in the various subtopics within Human Factors; perform various analysis techniques required to produce HF products; analyze error rates and costs; design dialog, command language, codes and error messages; critique the effectiveness of various forms of user documentation for specific use; evaluate screens and forms and make recommendations for improvements; conduct experiments to evaluate problem situations; and apply ergonomic principles to work station design.

Instruction: Students are exposed to basic human information processing principles via discussions, research, experiments and testing, and then they apply the results to design activities. An appropriate graduate level project is included as part of the course requirement.

Credit Recommendation: In the graduate degree category, 3 semester hours in Industrial Engineering, Computer Science or Computer Information Systems (7/85) (7/90) (11/96).

Using the Business Case Process in Sales (FE0455)

Location: Somerset, NJ and other AT&T locations.

Length: 16 hours (2 days).

Dates: April 1994-Present.

Objective: To teach marketing and sales personnel how to use the business case process in preparing sales presentations from their customer's perspective.

Learning Outcome: Upon successful completion of this course the student will be able to understand the business investment decision making process; utilize this investment process to understand and address customer needs at each step of the investment process; identify and create value for the customer; frame the customer sales opportunity; perform a value analysis; and use a business case format to present the value analysis to the customer.

Instruction: Major topics covered in the course are how to frame the customer sales opportunity and perform a value analysis, including economic value added (EVA). Designed for marketing and sales personnel, this course will cover how to use the business case format in sales presentation and how to develop business cases from the customer's perspective.

Credit Recommendation: In the upper division baccalaureate degree category, 1 semester hour in Sales Analysis-Case Method (6/94).

Visual Basic Programming (IE3190)

Location: Piscataway, NJ; Cincinnati, OH; Herndon, VA; Alpharetta, GA; Altamonte Springs, FL; Kansas City, MO.

Length: 30 hours (5 days).

Dates: June 1993-Present.

Objective: To enable the student to effectively design and implement a graphical user interface using Visual Basic.

Learning Outcome: Upon successful completion of this course, the student will be able to explain the function of individual components of the Visual Basic environment; use Visual Basic Controls to interactively exchange information with users; code Visual Basic statements, methods and function calls within Event and General Procedures; create and access application data files; use the data control to access Databases; and use Dynamic Data Exchange facilities for cross applications communication.

Instruction: This course provides the students with the skills and knowledge to develop Microsoft Windows based applications. Lectures, on-line demonstrations and extensive hands-on exercises are used in the class. Students develop an application using multiple Visual Basic controls.

Credit Recommendation: In the lower division baccalaureate/associate degree category, 2 semester hours in Visual Basic Programming (9/94).

Visual C++ Programming (IE3193)

Location: All AT&T training locations.

Length: 35 hours (5 days).

Dates: January 1995-Present.

Objective: To teach the skills and knowledge necessary to create an application that runs in the Microsoft Windows environment using the Microsoft Visual C++ Workbench and the Microsoft Foundation Class Library (MFC).

Learning Outcome: Upon successful completion of this course, the student will be able to implement a Windows event-driven application using MFC, use App Wizard to create a new application based on the document/view applications framework, use resource editors to create resources such as icons, cursors, menus, accelerators and dialog boxes, use Class Wizard to create implementation code, implement disk I/O for data and objects, use debugging features to trace execution, trap errors, detect memory leaks and print objects, implement basic text and graphics in a window, use collection of objects, implement both SDI and MDI applications, and build simple database applications.

Instruction: Major topics covered in the course are how to use MFC class library and visual C++ to construct Windows programs, coding Windows programs, debugging programs with the interactive debuggers and trace options, and implementing the MFC architecture.

Credit Recommendation: In the upper division baccalaureate degree category, 1 semester hour in Visual C++ Programming (lecture) and 1 semester hour in Visual C++ Programming (lab) for a total of 2 semester hours (11/96).

Voice of the Customer (CQ1020)

Location: Somerset, NJ and other AT&T locations.

Length: 15 hours (2 days).

Dates: April 1993-Present.

Objective: To prepare participants to utilize the Voice of the Customer approach in decision making, the development of measurements and managing business improvements.

Learning Outcome: Upon successful completion of this course, the student will be able to develop measures of customer satisfaction, service standards and process requirements that are linked to customer needs; identify and manage critical Moments of Truth when customers form their opinions about your products and services; identify and measure gaps between current performance and key measures and target performance needed to satisfy customers.

Instruction: This course is designed for students making business decisions and want the Voice of the Customer represented in those decisions. It includes VOC framework, customer information processes, managing moments of truth, family of measures, customer driven improvement strategies. Methods of instruction include lecture and discussions. An appropriate graduate level research project is submitted as part of the course requirements.

Credit Recommendation: In the upper division baccalaureate degree category, 2 semester hours in Marketing or General Business (12/93).

Windows NT Administration-Accelerated Training (IE4003)

Location: All AT&T training locations.

Length: 40 hours (5 days).

Dates: June 1996-Present.

Objective: To teach the skills necessary for installation and maintenance of Windows NT, systems administration using Windows NT Server, and how to work with Domain Models in network design and effective system troubleshooting.

Learning Outcome: Upon successful completion of this course, the student will be able to understand Windows NT Micro-Kernel Architecture, install Windows NT Workstation, manage Security and File Access, and install and configure a NT Server.

Instruction: Major topics covered in the course are bootstapping and configuration, running applications and printing, domains and networking, user and group management, domain models and management, interoperability, remote access services (RAS), fault tolerance and disaster recovery, performance monitoring, and tuning and troubleshooting.

Credit Recommendation: In the upper division baccalaureate degree category, 2 semester hours in Windows NT Administration (11/96).

Witness Preparation (AT&T 204, PUB 202, a)
114 (Formerly General Witness Preparation [AT&T 204 or PUB 202])

Location: Somerset Seminars Center, Somerset, NJ.

Length: 40 hours (5 days).

Dates: January 1982-September 1987.

Objective: To provide an understanding of the issues and concerns associated with interstate and intrastate interLATA filings with skill training for presenting testimony by experiencing the rate case process.

Instruction: This seminar provides skill training in writing testimony that addresses interstate and intrastate interLATA issues; implements the methodology for effective witnessing to each type of testimony; provides the opportunity to present the testimony in a simulated role- playing experience of the state and federal regulatory process; describes cross-examination tactics and techniques for dealing with them; identifies the stress associated with formal regulatory presentations; and reviews techniques for managing stress levels.

Credit Recommendation: In the graduate degree category, 2 semester hours in Business Communications, Finance, Organizational Behavior, Business Law, or Management (9/83).

Witness Support (AT&T 205, PUB 203, o)

Location: Somerset Seminars Center, Somerset, NJ.

Length: 40 hours (5 days).

Dates: January 1983-August 1988.

Objective: To provide expertise in the process of supporting witnesses; provide skill training for writing testimony; provide participants with the techniques for effective decision making; and provide background in persuasive presentation of ideas and concepts.

Instruction: The testimony-writing module incorporates successful writing techniques. The seminar concentrates on the management structure and process to ensure that all relevant issues are addressed in a timely manner. It also provides a case management model and the experience of debating deregulation issues. The course concludes with a simulation of a public hearing by a regulatory body.

Credit Recommendation: In the graduate degree category, 3 semester hours in Business Communications, Business Law, Management, Organizational Behavior (8/83). **NOTE:** Only the full 40-hour version of this course carries credit recommendations.

Working in the Virtual Workplace (VO2005)

Location: Open/General Enrollments: Somerset, NJ; Atlanta, GA; Chicago, IL; Pleasanton, CA. Suitcased/On-Site Delivery: Internationally.

Length: 7 hours (1 day).

Dates: August 1995-Present.

Objective: To provide participants with an understanding of how to achieve success and maintain communication with customers, managers and peers while working in a remote environment.

Learning Outcome: Upon successful completion of this course, the student will be able to describe the key success factors for working in the Virtual Workplace/Telecommuting; identify techniques for maintaining effective communications with customers, team members and management; and apply key principles of performance management to enhance productivity and effectiveness in attaining business objectives when working remotely.

Instruction: People who are currently or are planning to telecommute, satellite office or work "virtually" face many challenges. These challenges include but are not limited to how to manage time efficiently and effectively; how to maintain effective communication with customers, suppliers, managers and peers; how to ensure that "out of sight" does not turn into "out of mind," and how to ensure consistent levels of performance. This interactive workshop was designed to provide remote workers with practical tools, techniques, and job aids and hands-on practice to maximize their ability to effectively overcome these challenges.

Credit Recommendation: In the lower division baccalaureate/associate degree category, 1 semester hour in Telecommunication Management (12/95). **NOTE:** To earn this credit recommendation, student must complete this course and one of the following courses: VO2000 or VO2006.

Workshop for Improving Productivity in the Information Systems Environment (IE1805)

Location: Piscataway, NJ; Altamonte Springs, FL.

Length: 23 hours (3 days).

Dates: February 1990-June 1991.

Objective: To assist managers to be more effective with Information Systems (IS) personnel and project teams.

Learning Outcome: Upon successful completion of this course, the student will be able to demonstrate the five major techniques for leading an IS team that integrates past cultures; define the characteristics of a High Performing Team and describe techniques for building such a team; demonstrate how to plan for, manage, and control quality in one's own project environment; and describe the performance management cycle for IS personnel and demonstrate how to write performance goals and set performance level criteria for Programmer/Application Developers and System Analysts.

Instruction: Major topics covered in this instructor-led workshop focuses on the problems of managing a development team in today's integrated environment; and the emphasis of the workshop is on the application of management principles and techniques tailored to managing IS professionals.

Credit Recommendation: In the upper division baccalaureate degree category, 1 semester hour in Management or Business Administration (7/90).

World Class Procurement (PR5104)

Location: All AT&T training locations.
Length: 24 hours (3 days).
Dates: January 1995-Present.
Objective: To provide the participants with an understanding of current and projected trends affecting firms and the advanced strategies and practices that create a competitive advantage.
Learning Outcome: Upon successful completion of this course, the student will be able to understand advanced strategies and practices that provide an advantage in today's marketplace and identify the trends and forces on today's business and apply quality improvement initiatives.
Instruction: Major topics covered in the course are the current and projected trends and forces affecting firms in competitive industries; through the procurement and sourcing process, leading-edge firms will respond to these trends or forces by pursuing advanced strategies and concepts that create competitive advantages in cost, quality, time delivery, and technology; specific cost-reduction initiatives; cross-functional integration to support sourcing decisions; longer-term contracting relationships, partnerships, and alliances; quality improvement initiatives with suppliers, including supplier certification; cost-based pricing; total cost of ownership; corporate-wide consolidation of purchases; and use of full-service suppliers. Methods of instruction include discussion, lecture, and an appropriate graduate level project.
Credit Recommendation: In the upper division baccalaureate degree category, 2 semester hours in Purchasing Management or Procurement, or in the graduate degree category, 1 semester hour in Purchasing Management or Procurement (11/96).

Write to the Top (MD7795)

Location: Somerset, NJ and other AT&T locations.
Length: 12 hours (1.5 days).
Dates: August 1991-December 1994.
Objective: To provide managers with techniques for improving job quality by creating customer-focused documents.
Learning Outcome: Upon successful completion of this course, the student will be able to apply new skills and strategies to on-the-job writing; increase writing speed and impact; and write in a highly readable style.
Instruction: Major topics covered in the course are writing tools for success and helping students write faster and organize written documents better; and teaches reader-centered writing.
Credit Recommendation: In the upper division baccalaureate degree category, 1 semester hour in Business Communications (4/92).

Writer's Workbench (IE5026)

Location: Piscataway, NJ.
Length: 18 hours (3 days).
Dates: February 1985-September 1992.
Objective: To prepare the individual to use the UNIX system to evaluate and improve their written on-line documentation.
Learning Outcome: Upon successful completion of this course, the student will be able to: (1) describe the function and purpose of Writer's Workbench (WWB); (2) recognize WWB commands; (3) use WWB commands to analyze and modify text files; (3) interpret reports and suggested modifications generated by the WWB package; (4) interpret reports and suggested modifications generated by the WWB package; and (5) modify user-specified files to incorporate the students' own or departmental standards.
Instruction: Major topics covered in the course are the concepts and use of the WWB software package; the purpose of WWB; use of the WWB commands; use of interface program commands; interpretation of suggested modifications to your written material; and modification of user-specified terms and phrases.
Credit Recommendation: In the lower division baccalaureate/associate degree category, 1 semester hour in Word Processing (7/90).

Writing Better Documentation for Users (IE1222)

Location: Piscataway, NJ and other AT&T locations.
Length: 28 hours (4 days).
Dates: March 1988-June 1996.
Objective: To enable participants to write accurate and clearly understood computer documentation.
Learning Outcome: Upon successful completion of this course, the student will be able to write accurate and clearly understood computer documentation; take a systematic approach to writing manuals, procedures, and on-line documentation in an information systems environment; present documentation on paper as well as on screens; and use recent innovations in the packaging of documentation, in graphics, and in project management.
Instruction: Major topics covered in this instructor-led workshop are an overview of documentation; the step-by-step process of developing a good piece of documentation; the development of graphics and desktop publishing techniques for designing; reference aids and packaging; the significance of on-line documentation; and individual documentation and critique conferences.
Credit Recommendation: In the lower division baccalaureate/associate degree category, or in the upper division baccalaureate degree category, 2 semester hours in Technical Writing (7/90).

Writing Winning Sales Proposals (ME1277)

Location: Somerset, NJ and other AT&T locations.
Length: 16 hours (2 days).
Dates: March 1993-Present.
Objective: To improve the quality of the sales process by focusing on producing a winning proposal of better quality, in less time, and at less cost.
Learning Outcome: Upon successful completion of this course the student will be able to improve success rate by eliminating proposal efforts he/she has little chance of winning; and improve his/her win percentage in those proposal efforts consistent with corporate and office objectives through effective proposal planning and writing.
Instruction: Major topics covered in the course are for students working on proposals. It includes client evaluation, selecting winning proposals, analyzing opportunities, planning the proposals and writing the proposal. Methods of instruction include lecture and discussion.
Credit Recommendation: In the lower division baccalaureate/associate degree category, 1 semester hour in Business Writing (12/93).

Written Communications (MS6522)

Location: Somerset, NJ and other AT&T locations.
Length: 40 hours (5 days).
Dates: January 1983-April 1997.
Objective: To apply the principles of contemporary business writing to the writing of letters, memos, and reports.
Learning Outcome: Upon successful completion of this course, the student will be able to set and meet objectives for each writing task; apply principles of contem-

porary writing; and choose and use the most effective format and style.

Instruction: Major topics covered in the course are a full review of functional grammar and business style; provide a basic foundation for business writing, including letters, memos, and reports; study actual AT&T documents and rewrite them according to the principles of style and usage explained and demonstrated in class; apply principles of basic grammar and punctuation to numerous examples of actual business writing. Methods of instruction include writing samples which will be critiqued in detail by the instructor.

Credit Recommendation: In the upper division baccalaureate degree category, 3 semester hours in Written Communications (4/92).

X.25 Network Architecture (DC7170) (IE7170)

Location: Piscataway, NJ and other AT&T locations.

Length: 24 hours (1 week).

Dates: March 1983-June 1996.

Objective: To provide a detailed description of X.25 Network Architecture including frame and packet formats with applicable scenarios.

Instruction: Major topics covered in the course are concepts and basic function of packet switching public data networks; BS.25 protocol characteristics; data transfer and flow control scenarios involving BX.25 packets; major difference between X.25 and BX.25; and a description of packet switching as used by various public networks. Methods of instruction include lecture and laboratory.

Credit Recommendation: In the upper division baccalaureate degree category, 1 semester hour in Data Processing, Data Communications, or Computer Science (7/85) (7/90).

Automatic Sprinkler Apprenticeship Program

All educational/training programs are administered through the educational funds of Local 669 Joint Apprenticeship Training Committee (JATC). The United States Department of Labor approved the apprentice training program and related training in April 1953. The apprentice training program is also recognized by the Federal Bureau of Apprenticeship Training.

This program of courses is offered by correspondence delivery system. Courses are reviewed on a continuous basis. Course development and revisions are based on changes in the codes governing construction, hardware, and procedures and methods relating to the industry. The Department of Distance Education of The Pennsylvania State University provides instruction and course development, as well as using experts in the trade to provide external review. Tutors/proctors are responsible for assisting apprentices with course-related problems and proctoring examinations. If an apprentice is not in the vicinity of a tutor/proctor, the JATC with the agreement of Penn State has designated the apprentice's supervisor as an acceptable proctor.

To complete a course successfully, the apprentice is required to submit all lessons and examinations associated with a specific course. Students are not permitted to advance to the next course in the program until they have satisfactorily completed (average grade of 60 percent or better) the previous course. Certificates are only issued upon successful completion of the 19-course program.

Source of official student records: Registry of Credit Recommendations, American Council on Education, One Dupont Circle, Washington, DC 20036-1193 or Transcript Department, 112 Shields Building, Pennsylvania State University, University Park, PA 16802.

Additional information about the courses: College Credit Recommendation Service, American Council on Education, One Dupont Circle, Washington, DC, 20036-1193.

Architectural Working Drawings for Sprinkler Fitters(ME 5010A, ME 5010B, ME 5010C) (Formerly ME 5010 and ME 990-501)

Location: Correspondence program.

Length: 12 independent study lessons.

Dates: July 1976-Present.

Objective: To provide an understanding of different architectural construction materials and their effect on sprinkler piping installations.

Learning Outcome: Upon successful completion of this course, the student will be able to analyze the relationship of the sprinkler systems in the particular architectural mode used by a designer.

Instruction: Major topics covered in the course are the use of symbols, abbreviations and print types; defining conventions, schedules, and use of scales; drawing interpretation; plan projections, plan scale, and foundation construction types; inspection of floor plans; use of elevations; sectioning, detailing, lumber sizing, and steel framing; mechanical equipment drawings; and plumbing system and sprinkler system types. Methods of instruction include independent study with course guide, optional tutoring, supplemental materials, and proctored final examination.

Credit Recommendation: In the vocational certificate category, 20 semester hours in Fire Sprinkler System Technology if taken with ME courses 5001 through 5019, or in the lower division baccalaureate/associate degree category, 12 semester hours in Fire Sprinkler System Technology if taken with ME courses 5004, 5006, 5007, 5009, 5012, 5013, 5015, 5017, 5018, and 5019 (3/89) (11/94).

Basic Drawing for the Sprinkler System (ME 5004) (Formerly ME 990-530)

Location: Correspondence program.

Length: 12 independent study lessons.

Dates: February 1987-Present.

Objective: To introduce the student to the basic elements of graphical representation using both 2D and 3D layouts and how they relate to a fire sprinkler system.

Learning Outcome: Upon successful completion of this course, the student will be able to understand 2D and 3D layouts for graphical representation of geometric figures; and apply the appropriate rules of geometry to piping projects using 3D graphics and sketching tools.

Instruction: Major topics covered in the course are blueprint reading, multiview drawings, applications of drawings, size and location dimensioning, rules for dimensioning, scales, thread representation and dimensioning, sections, principles of sketching, the working sketch, isometric drawings, and isometric drawings for piping layouts. Methods of instruction include independent study with course guide, optional tutoring, and proctored examination.

Credit Recommendation: In the vocational certificate category, 20 semester hours in Fire Sprinkler System Technology if taken with ME courses 5001 through 5019, or in the lower division baccalaureate/associate degree category, 12 semester hours in Fire Sprinkler System Technology if taken with ME courses 5004, 5006, 5007, 5009, 5010, 5012, 5013, 5015, 5017, 5018, and 5019 (3/89) (11/94).

Blueprint Reading for the Sprinkler Fitter (ME 5011) (Formerly ME 5009)

Location: Correspondence program.

Length: 12 independent study lessons.

Dates: July 1985-Present.

Objective: To provide the ability to read, understand, and analyze piping graphical representation using piping industry notation.

Learning Outcome: Upon successful completion of this course, the student will be able to understand piping 2D and 3D drawing; and understand and interpret piping industry notation for geometry, materials and pipe fastening practice/code.

Instruction: Major topics covered in the course are isometric drawing in pipe fitting, piping and equipment symbols and nomenclature, progress and instrumentation drawings, orthographic drawings, detailed isometric drawing, spool (shop) drawings, hanger details, and blueprint reading. Methods of instruction include independent study with course guide, optional tutoring, supplemental materials, and proctored final examination.

Credit Recommendation: In the vocational certificate category, 20 semester hours in Fire Sprinkler System Technology if taken with ME courses 5001 through 5019, or in the lower division baccalaureate/associate degree category, 12 semester hours in Fire Sprinkler System Technology if taken with ME courses 5004, 5006, 5007, 5009, 5010, 5012, 5013, 5015, 5017, 5018, and 5019 (3/89) (11/94).

Economics of the Sprinkler Industry (ME 5017) (Formerly ME 990-544)

Location: Correspondence program.

Length: 9 independent study lessons.

Dates: August 1986-Present.

Objective: To provide the student with an understanding of the economics of the sprinkler industry within the American economic system.

Learning Outcome: Upon successful completion of this course, the student will be able to recognize the place of money in a capitalist society; and explain the economic terms used by labor and management that define their differing views.

Instruction: Major topics covered in the course are the free enterprise system, needs of people, capital and money, analysis of financial statements, costs, profits, competition, and productivity. Methods of instruction include independent study with course guide, optional tutoring, and proctored final examination.

Credit Recommendation: In the vocational certificate category, 20 semester hours in Fire Sprinkler System Technology if taken with ME courses 5001 through 5019, or in the lower division baccalaureate/associate degree category, 12 semester hours in Fire Sprinkler System Technology if taken with ME courses 5004, 5006, 5007, 5009, 5010, 5012, 5013, 5015, 5017, 5018, and 5019 (3/89) (11/94).

Human Relations (ME 5018) (Formerly ME 990-545)

Location: Correspondence program.

Length: 12 independent study lessons.

Dates: February 1987-Present.

Objective: To provide an understanding of the basics of human relations in a "team effort" environment.

Learning Outcome: Upon successful completion of this course, the student will be able to describe the scope and focus of a supervisor's/foreman's efforts to coordinate staff productivity; and accept need for and make plans for a job; practice good communication with superiors and co-workers/customers in a team function.

Instruction: Major topics covered in the course are the duties and responsibilities of foremen, understanding human nature, planning, the foreman's responsibility for training, giving orders, directions, and suggestions, record keeping and written reports, the foreman and operational costs, other phases of communication, safety, improving work methods and procedures, and getting the job done right in a team environment with management-leadership hierarchy. Methods of instruction include independent study with course guide, optional tutoring, and proctored final examination.

Credit Recommendation: In the vocational certificate category, 20 semester hours in Fire Sprinkler System Technology if taken with ME courses 5001 through 5019, or in the lower division baccalaureate/associate degree category, 12 semester hours in Fire Sprinkler System Technology if taken with ME courses 5004, 5006, 5007, 5009, 5010, 5012, 5013, 5015, 5017, 5018, and 5019 (3/89)(11/94).

Hydraulics for the Sprinkler Apprentice (ME 5015) (Formerly ME 990-542)

Location: Correspondence program.

Length: 6 independent study lessons.

Dates: August 1982-Present.

Objective: To provide knowledge of fluids under pressure used in the operation of fire protection systems and their installation requirements.

Learning Outcome: Upon successful completion of this course, the student will be able to perform calculations relative to specific weight, dry valve differentials, static pressure from gravity tanks, head pressure, velocity, and equivalent length.

Instruction: Major topics covered in the course are specific weight, specific gravity, pressure generation, pressure measurement, sprinkler system design, and pressure losses. Methods of instruction include independent study with course guide, optional tutoring, and proctored final examination.

Credit Recommendation: In the vocational certificate category, 20 semester hours in Fire Sprinkler System Technology if taken with ME courses 5001 through 5019, or in the lower division baccalaureate/associate degree category, 12 semester hours in Fire Sprinkler System Technology if taken with ME courses 5004, 5006, 5007, 5009, 5010, 5012, 5013, 5015, 5017, 5018, and 5019 (3/89) (11/94).

Installation of Sprinkler Systems (ME 5008A, ME 5008B, ME 5008C) (Formerly ME 5008 and ME 990-535)

Location: Correspondence program.

Length: 15 independent study lessons.

Dates: June 1987-Present.

Objective: To provide knowledge of the rules and regulations governing the design, installation, and testing of fire sprinkler systems.

Learning Outcome: Upon successful completion of this course, the student will be able to apply NFPA 13, NFPA 13D, and NFPA 13R to the design, installation, and testing of sprinkler systems.

Instruction: Major topics covered in the course are the National Fire Protection Association Standards; water supply and system components, spacing, location and position of sprinklers, and hydraulically designed sprinkler systems. Methods of instruction include independent study with course guide, optional tutoring, supplemental materials, and open-book proctored final examination.

Credit Recommendation: In the vocational certificate category, 20 semester hours in Fire Sprinkler System Technology if taken with ME courses 5001 through 5019 (3/89) (11/94).

Introduction to Automatic Sprinkler Protection (ME 5005A, ME 5005B, ME 5005C) (Formerly Introduction to Automatic Sprinklers ME 5005 and ME 990-531)

Location: Correspondence program.

Length: 12 independent study lessons.

Dates: August 1986-Present.

Objective: To provide knowledge of automatic fire sprinkler systems and their installation and inspection.

Learning Outcome: Upon successful completion of this course, the student will be able to demonstrate an understanding relative to the economic and protection value that sprinkler systems provide in buildings of varying construction; and apply installation rules to Automatic Sprinkler Systems.

Instruction: Major topics covered in the course are fire and its extinguishment, history, value and performance of automatic sprinkler protection, organizations related to the automatic sprinkler industry, factors affecting sprinkler performance, hazard rating and special occupancy conditions, wet-pipe and dry-pipe systems, other types of sprinkler systems, acceptance tests, and flushing sprinkler piping. Methods of instruction include independent study with course guide, optional tutoring, and proctored examination.

Credit Recommendation: In the vocational certificate category, 20 semester hours in Fire Sprinkler System Technology if taken with ME courses 5001 through 5019 (3/89) (11/94).

Job Safety and Health (ME 5001A, ME 5001B, ME 5001C) (Formerly Safety, Rigging, and Scaffolding ME 5001 and ME 990-533)

Location: Correspondence program.

Length: 9 independent study lessons.

Dates: July 1985-Present.

Objective: To provide an awareness of safety requirements common to building construction sites.

Learning Outcome: Upon successful completion of this course, the student will be able to understand good practices for worker job safety and health in the piping industry using manual and powered equipment; and understand and apply appropriate regulatory documents appropriate to the work environment within which piping tools are to be used.

Instruction: Major topics covered in the course are safe and proper use of personal protective equipment and tools, handling and storage of materials, fire protection, trenches, welding, first aid, ladders, scaffolding, lift equipment, rigging, signals, safety aspects of working with radiation, contaminates, asbestos, noise, hazardous energy, and applicable laws and regulations. Methods of instruction include independent study with course guide, optional tutoring, and proctored final examination.

Credit Recommendation: In the vocational certificate category, 20 semester hours in Fire Sprinkler System Technology if taken with ME courses 5001 through 5019 (3/89) (11/94).

Reading Automatic Sprinkler Piping Drawings (ME 5006) (Formerly ME 990-532)

Location: Correspondence program.

Length: 12 independent study lessons.

Dates: October 1984-Present.

Objective: To provide knowledge of automatic fire sprinkler system drawings.

Learning Outcome: Upon successful completion of this course, the student will be able to interpret sprinkler piping drawings; and analyze sprinkler piping drawings for coordination with contractor working drawings.

Instruction: Major topics covered in the course are an introduction to piping drawings, sprinkler piping, sectional views, underground piping, hydraulically calculated systems, use of materials, deluge system, computer-aided blueprints, and halon system. Methods of instruction include independent study with course guide, optional tutoring, supplemental materials, and proctored final examination.

Credit Recommendation: In the vocational certificate category, 20 semester hours in Fire Sprinkler System Technology if taken with ME courses 5001 through 5019, or in the lower division baccalaureate/associate degree category, 12 semester hours in Fire Sprinkler System Technology if taken with ME courses 5004, 5006, 5007, 5009, 5010, 5012, 5013, 5015, 5017, 5018, and 5019 (3/89) (11/94).

Special Application Sprinkler Systems (ME 5014A, ME 5014B, ME 5014C) (Formerly ME 5014 and ME 990-541)

Location: Correspondence program.

Length: 12 independent study lessons.

Dates: July 1984-Present.

Objective: To provide the student with an understanding of sophisticated fire detection technology used in conjunction with fire protection systems.

Learning Outcome: Upon successful completion of this course, the student will be able to repair and maintain specialized releasing systems and detection systems, both older and technologically advanced.

Instruction: Major topics covered in the course are rate-of-rise releasing systems, reaction systems, and specialized valves. Methods of instruction include independent study with course guide, optional tutoring, and proctored open-book final examination.

Credit Recommendation: In the vocational certificate category, 20 semester hours in Fire Sprinkler System Technology if taken with ME courses 5001 through 5019 (3/89) (11/94).

Sprinkler System Water Supply (ME 5012A, ME 5012B, ME 5012C) (Formerly ME 5012 and ME 990-539)

Location: Correspondence program.

Length: 12 independent study lessons.

Dates: August 1985-Present.

Objective: To provide the student with an understanding of the various types of fire sprinkler water supply sources.

Learning Outcome: Upon successful completion of this course, the student will be able to understand the design, installation, and operation of water supply sources for fire protection systems.

Instruction: Major topics covered in course are the occupancy classification, water supply requirements, supply connections, public water supply systems, fire department connections, backflow prevention, gravity tanks, water level indicators, tank heaters, pressure tanks, embankment tanks, centrifugal fire pumps, horizontal pumps, vertical shaft turbine-type pumps, controllers, and installation of private fire service mains. Methods of instruction include independent study with course guide, optional tutoring, and proctored final examination.

Credit Recommendation: In the vocational certificate category, 20 semester hours in Fire Sprinkler System Technology if taken with ME courses 5001 through 5019, or in the lower division baccalaureate/associate degree category, 12 semester hours in Fire Sprinkler System Technology if taken with ME courses 5004, 5006, 5007, 5009, 5010, 5012, 5013, 5015, 5017, 5018, and 5019 (3/89) (11/94).

Sprinkler Systems Alarms (5016) (Formerly ME 990-543)

Location: Correspondence program.

Length: 6 independent study lessons.

Dates: November 1979-Present.

Objective: To provide the student with an understanding of alarm and supervisory devices.

Learning Outcome: Upon successful completion of this course, the student will be able to apply installation requirements for supervisory devices and the application of NFPA standards for fire alarm system design and installation.

Instruction: Major topics covered in the course are the principles of sprinkler system alarms, wet system water flow alarm methods, water-motor gongs and circuit closers, central station system requirements, and supervisory protection. Methods of instruction include independent study with course guide, optional tutoring, and proctored final examination.

Credit Recommendation: In the vocational certificate category, 20 semester hours in Fire Sprinkler System Technology if taken with ME courses 5001 through 5019 (3/89) (11/94).

Sprinkler Systems Calculations (ME 5007) (Formerly ME 990-534)

Location: Correspondence program.

Length: 18 independent study lessons.

Dates: August 1979-Present.

Objective: To provide knowledge of basic mathematics relevant to installation of fire sprinkler systems.

Learning Outcome: Upon successful completion of this course, the student will be able to perform calculations to determine proper piping layout for fire protection systems.

Instruction: Major topics covered in the course are basic arithmetic operations and functions, simple geometry, piping measurement and offsets, pipe bends and piping, piping layouts, piping offsets, and the metric system. Methods of instruction include independent study with course guide, optional tutoring, and proctored open-book final examination.

Credit Recommendation: In the vocational certificate category, 20 semester hours in Fire Sprinkler System Technology if taken with courses ME 5001 through 5019, or in the lower division baccalaureate/associate degree category, 12 semester hours in Fire Sprinkler System Technology if taken with ME courses 5004, 5006, 5007, 5009, 5010, 5012, 5013, 5015, 5017, 5018, and 5019 (3/89) (11/94).

Technical Reports (ME 5019) (Formerly ME 990-546)

Location: Correspondence program.
Length: 6 independent study lessons.
Dates: July 1974-Present.
Objective: To provide the skills necessary to write relevant technical reports.

Learning Outcome: Upon successful completion of this course, the student will be able to understand the need for clear and complete written communication on a timely basis; and understand the function of and rationale for specialized "forms" to organize data.

Instruction: Major topics covered in the course are accident reports, weekly reports (hourly time ticket, weekly progress report), special reports (daily contract change order, day work order), final reports (final "progress" report, contractor's material and test certificate), and adjunct reports (bill of lading, report of inspection). Methods of instruction include independent study with course guide, optional tutoring, and proctored final examination.

Credit Recommendation: In the vocational certificate category, 20 semester hours in Fire Sprinkler System Technology if taken with ME courses 5001 through 5019, or in the lower division baccalaureate/associate degree category, 12 semester hours in Fire Sprinkler System Technology if taken with ME courses 5004, 5006, 5007, 5009, 5010, 5012, 5013, 5015, 5017, 5018, and 5019 (3/89) (11/94).

The Automatic Sprinkler (ME 5009A, ME 5009B, ME 5009C) (Formerly Automatic Fire Sprinkler [ME 5011] and The Sprinkler Head [ME 990-538])

Location: Correspondence program.
Length: 15 independent study lessons.
Dates: March 1985-Present.
Objective: To provide a basic understanding of operating principles of automatic fire sprinklers, new sprinkler technology and the effect on use, regulations applicable to all types of sprinklers and governing each specific type of sprinkler, the importance of recognizing and installing the proper sprinkler for the application, and how sprinklers are modified to address specific needs.

Learning Outcome: Upon successful completion of this course, the student will be able to understand the operation, installation, and maintenance of the major types of fire sprinklers used on modern fire protection systems.

Instruction: Major topics covered in the course are history, operating principles, sensitivity, the NFPA regulations covering standard upright and pendent sprinklers, standard sidewall sprinklers, extended coverage upright and pendent sprinklers, extended coverage sidewall sprinklers, large drop sprinklers, ESFR sprinklers and residential sprinklers. The course also covers specialty sprinklers including corrosion resistant, flush, dry, cycling, intermediate level, attic and exposure protection. Methods of instruction include independent study with course guide, optional tutoring, supplemental materials, and proctored open book final examination.

Credit Recommendation: In the vocational certificate category, 20 semester hours in Fire Sprinkler System Technology if taken with ME courses 5001 through 5019 (3/89) (11/94).

Types of Fire Protection Systems (ME 5013A, 5013B, ME 5013C) (Formerly Types of Fire Protection Systems ME 5013 and ME 990-540)

Location: Correspondence program.
Length: 15 independent study lessons.
Dates: December 1984-Present.
Objective: To provide an understanding of the various types of fire protection systems and their application.

Learning Outcome: Upon successful completion of this course, the student will be able to understand the differences among fire protection systems; properly diagnose problems associated with each type of system; and system maintenance.

Instruction: Major topics covered in the course are wet-pipe, anti-freeze, dry-pipe, pre-action, and deluge systems; combined dry-pipe and pre-action systems; automatic sprinkler systems with nonfire protection connections; combined sprinkler-standpipe, foam-water, carbon dioxide, and halon systems. Methods of instruction include independent study with course guide, optional tutoring, and proctored final examination.

Credit Recommendation: In the vocational certificate category, 20 semester hours in Fire Sprinkler System Technology if taken with ME courses 5001 through 5019, or in the lower division baccalaureate/associate degree category, 12 semester hours in Fire Sprinkler System Technology if taken with ME courses 5004, 5006, 5007, 5009, 5010, 5012, 5013, 5015, 5017, 5018, and 5019 (3/89) (11/94).

Use and Care of Tools (ME 5003A, ME 5003B, ME 5003C) (Formerly ME 5003 and ME 990-529)

Location: Correspondence program.
Length: 12 independent study lessons.
Dates: February 1987-Present.
Objective: To provide knowledge of the purpose of tools and materials in the piping industry and their safe and efficient use.

Learning Outcome: Upon successful completion of this course, the student will be able to understand the safe use and care of tools as the means to effective workmanship; understand/apply safe practice in both manual and powered tool usage across a spectrum of piping materials; and apply standard pipe fastening practices including threaded joints and clamped joints, pipe cutting for various joint systems, and use of the appropriate tools required.

Instruction: Major topics covered in the course are rules for good practice and safety, OSHA standards, and the use and care of tools used in the pipe trades. Methods of instruction include independent study with course guide, optional tutoring, supplemental materials, and proctored final examination.

Credit Recommendation: In the vocational certificate category, 20 semester hours in Fire Sprinkler System Technology if taken with ME courses 5001 through

Baltimore Gas & Electric Company

The Nuclear Security Officer Basic Training Program is administered by the Security Training and Education Unit of the Baltimore Gas & Electric Company. The program is presented at the Calvert Cliffs Nuclear Power Plant at Lusby, Maryland.

The program is offered one or two times throughout the year and consists of ten consecutive weeks of classroom instruction, firearms training, and response force tactical training. Its purpose is to train and qualify individuals as Nuclear Security Officers as mandated by federal regulation.

Source of official student records: Registry of Credit Recommendations, American Council on Education, One Dupont Circle, Washington, DC 20036-1193 or Supervisor, Security Training and Education Unit, Baltimore Gas & Electric Company, Calvert Cliffs Nuclear Power Plant, Lusby, MD 20657.

Additional information about the courses: College Credit Recommendation Service, American Council on Education, One Dupont Circle, Washington, DC 20036-1193.

Nuclear Security Officer Basic Training Program (152)

Location: Calvert Cliffs Nuclear Plant, Lusby, MD.

Length: *Version 1:* 400 hours (10 weeks).

Dates: *Version 1:* February 1980-January 1993.

Objective: To assure that the training requirements of the Security Training and Qualification Plan are met and to assure that the students are capable of fulfilling the mandates of company security plans and other licensing documents approved by the Nuclear Regulatory Commission.

Learning Outcome: Upon successful completion of this course, the student will be able to understand the various techniques/programs that have been successful in the security area, especially as applicable to the nuclear industry; understand the differences and similarities between the criminal justice system and the private security sector; identify specific criminal activity affecting the need for upgrading security programs; develop an understanding of the many management problems involved in controlling the factors relating to security; effectively administer cardiopulmonary resuscitation (CPR) and emergency first aid whenever required; understand principles and techniques of boating safety; and understand and practice techniques of self-defense and physical fitness and conditioning.

Instruction: The program includes an overview of private security in the nuclear industry (introduction to laws and legal issues that apply to private security forces), rationale for physical protection in terms of adversary threats, regulatory requirements, and security-related tasks. As part of this course, students learn the historical, philosophical, and legal bases for security. The role of security and security personnel in modern society and in the nuclear industry are covered. The concepts of professionalism, administrative, personnel, and physical aspects of security are covered. The program also covers the basics of emergency first aid and CPR procedures; students must meet all Red Cross certification requirements in each of these areas and must renew their certification every twelve months. The program also has stringent physical education requirements, including instruction in self-defense, physical fitness, conditioning, and boating safety and operating techniques.

Credit Recommendation: *Version 1:* In the lower division baccalaureate/associate degree category, 3 semester hours in Introduction to Security, 2 semester hours in First Aid and CPR, 1 semester hour in Introduction to Criminal Justice or Introduction to Law Enforcement, and 2 semester hours in Physical Education, for a total of 8 semester hours (11/89) (2/95).

Nuclear Security Officer Basic Training Program (152)

Location: Calvert Cliffs Nuclear Plant, Lusby, MD.

Length: *Version 2:* 416 hours (10 weeks).

Dates: *Version 2:* February 1993-Present.

Objective: To provide security personnel with an overview of knowledge and skills relevant to nuclear industry security, including legal, operational, technical, and safety aspects in compliance with industry and national standards.

Learning Outcome: Upon successful completion of this course, the student will be able to discuss laws and legal issues relevant to nuclear security; perform basic tasks of security operations, protection, and response to threatening circumstances; display skills of safety, first aid, CPR, self-defense, and provide evidence of physical fitness; explain basic techniques of radiation protection; perform basic site security procedures; operate, inspect, and maintain security systems; explain functions of security clerical personnel, and perform duties of watchpersons and escort personnel; demonstrate weapons safety and proficiency; and perform basic microcomputer operations.

Instruction: Major topics covered in this course include points of law and legal issues; nuclear facility security operations and safety standards; first aid, safety, security communications, self-defense, and physical fitness; security plan, access control, and protecting and controlling proprietary information; nuclear facility security systems; access authorization and records; radiation protection; armorer duties; watchperson and escort duties; weapons safety and training, and basic computer operations. Methods of instruction include lecture, discussion, classroom exercises, audio-visual material, computer-assisted instruction, computer laboratory, practical exercises, on-the-job training, graded and written practical tests, and a comprehensive final examination.

Credit Recommendation: *Version 2:* In the lower division baccalaureate/associate degree category, 3 semester hours in Introduction to Security or Introduction to Safety and Security, 3 semester hours in Occupational Safety, First Aid and CPR, 3 semester hours in Introduction to Law Enforcement, 2 semester hours in Physical Education, and 1 semester hour in Computer Applications (2/95).

Bell Atlantic Corporation

Since its incorporation in late 1983, Bell Atlantic Corporation has evolved from the parent of a group of regulated telephone utilities serving the mid-Atlantic region of the United States into a major source of information-management and communications services and systems, with subsidiary companies operating in regional, national, and international markets.

With revenues exceeding $12 billion and assets of $28 billion, Bell Atlantic, through its core business, is providing state-of-the-art voice and data communications and exchange access services to one of the fastest growing, most densely populated and communications-intensive regions of the United States.

Bell Atlantic's operating telephone companies serve the states of New Jersey, Delaware, Pennsylvania, Maryland, Virginia, West Virginia, and the District of Columbia, which have over 12 million residential, business, and government customers in a geographic area that is home to the U. S. federal government and 77 of the nation's Fortune 500 companies. Its telecommunications network is one of the most technologically advanced in the world and the most cost efficient in the United States.

Bell Atlantic also is the parent of one of the nation's largest cellular carriers and provides customers throughout the United States and overseas with a range of quality communications services, information products, and related business services.

Source of official student records: Registry of Credit Recommendation, American Council on Education, One Dupont Circle, Washington, DC 20036-1193 or CREDIT Coordinator, Bell Atlantic Corporation, Network Services, Inc., 13100 Columbia Pike, D16, Silver Spring, MD 20904.

Additional information about the courses: College Credit Recommendation Service, American Council on Education, One Dupont Circle, Washington, DC 20036-1193.

Account Executive Selling Skills

Location: Silver Spring, MD.

Length: 75 hours (2 weeks).

Dates: January 1978-December 1984.

Objective: To instruct personnel in the basic sales skills including preparatory financial analysis and systems theory.

Instruction: Major topics covered in the course are financial calculations, sales planning and preparation, conducting a systems study, presentation of results, and cost justification. Methods of instruction include lecture, case studies, and role playing.

Credit Recommendation: In the upper division baccalaureate degree category, 3 semester hours in Marketing (12/79).

Advanced Lotus 1-2-3

Location: South Plainfield, NJ.

Length: 21 hours (3 days).

Dates: June 1985-January 1993.

Objective: To present advanced concepts of Lotus 1-2-3 to students who have already mastered fundamentals of Lotus 1-2-3.

Instruction: Major topics covered in the course are advanced macros, database and statistical analysis, and financial modeling. Methods of instruction include leader-led tutorials and laboratory exercises.

Credit Recommendation: In the lower division baccalaureate/associate degree category, 1 semester hour in Business Administration (3/86) (1/95).

Advanced Peripheral Processor Maintenance (1 A ESS Advanced Peripheral Processor Maintenance; No. N691OSC)

Location: South Plainfield, NJ.

Length: Self-paced (approximately 260 hours).

Dates: August 1985-December 1993.

Objective: To provide the training necessary to perform in-depth troubleshooting on the 1 A ESS system.

Instruction: Major topics covered in the course are an in-depth troubleshooting by performing the analyzer's function; 1 A ESS Central Control; 1 A Memory Storage Unit Hardware, and Maintenance; 1 A Processor Interface Units, Hardware and Maintenance; and 1 A ESS Documentation. **NOTE:** The 1 A ESS is a more advanced and more complex version of the 1 ESS switching machine.

Credit Recommendation: In the upper division baccalaureate degree category, 3 semester hours in Electronics Technology (6/86). **NOTE:** Not applicable as core course in Electrical Engineering or Engineering Technology.

Advanced Peripheral Processor Maintenance (1 ESS Advanced Peripheral Processor Maintenance; No. N691ASC)

Location: South Plainfield, NJ.

Length: Self-paced (approximately 130 hours).

Dates: August 1985-December 1993.

Objective: To provide the training necessary to perform in-depth troubleshooting on the 1 ESS system.

Instruction: Major topics covered in the course are an in-depth troubleshooting by performing the analyst's function; 1 ESS Control Center and Program Fund-amentals; 1 ESS Program Store, Call Store, and Signal Processor; 1 ESS AMA and TTY Diagnosis; 1 ESS Software and Software Fault Identification; and 1 ESS Processor Troubleshooting Work Assign-ments. **NOTE:** This course is similar to 1 A ESS Advanced Peripheral Processor Maintenance except that all work is done on the 1 ESS machine.

Credit Recommendation: In the upper division baccalaureate degree category, 2 semester hours in Electronics Technology (6/86). **NOTE:** Not applicable as core courses in Electrical Engineering or Engineering Technology.

Advanced Systems Selling for Accounting Executives

Location: Silver Spring, MD.

Length: 132 hours (3 weeks).

Dates: October 1977-December 1984.

Objective: To instruct personnel in advanced sales skills including financial analysis, systems analysis, and the various phases of the sales process.

Instruction: Major topics covered in the course are systems theory, ratio analysis, benefit and investment analysis, economic modeling, behavior modification techniques, and the administration and execution of a sales plan through the phases of the systems selling process. Methods of instruction include lecture, discussions, case studies, and role playing.

Credit Recommendation: In the upper division baccalaureate degree category, 6 semester hours in Marketing (12/79). **NOTE:** Students must have successfully completed the course on Account Executive Selling Skills before receiving credit for this course.

ALPHA IV: Unit 1

Location: *Version 1 (Module 1/Chapters 1 and 2 of Module 2):* White Plains, NY; *Version 1 (Module 2/Chapters 3-10):* White Plains, NY; *Version 2:* Marlboro, MA.

Length: *Version 1 (Module 1/Chapters 1 and 2 of Module 2):* 42 hours (6 days); *Version 1 (Module 2/Chapters 3-10):* 28 hours (4 days); *Version 2:* 80 hours.

Dates: *Version 1(Module 1/Chapters 1 and 2 of Module 2):* October 1988-December 1996; *Version 1 (Module 2/ Chapters 3-10):* October 1988-December 1996; *Version 2:* January 1997-Present.

Objective: *Version 1 (Module 1/ Chapters 1 and 2 of Module 2):* To provide students with an understanding of computer systems and elements of communications. *Version 1 (Module 2/Chapters 3-10):* To provide students with an overview of data communications and networking. *Version 2:*To provide an in-depth knowledge of the origins of today's technology of computers and data communications through the study of hardware, operating systems, desktop software, and communication protocols.

Learning Outcome: *Version 1 (Module 1/Chapters 1 and 2 of Module 2):* Upon successful completion of this course, the student will be able to understand the basic concepts of information systems, including computer systems, software, and data communications. *Version 1 (Module 2/Chapters 3-10):* Upon successful completion of this course, the student will be able to define and discuss the fundamentals of data communications and network architecture. *Version 2:* Upon successful completion of this course, the student will be able to demonstrate knowledge of computer and communications systems; compare and contrast choices of hardware, applications and operating systems as well as identifying and explaining the layers of the OSI protocol stack.

Instruction: *Version 1 (Module 1/ Chapters 1 and 2 of Module 2):* Major topics covered in the course are computer systems, information systems, and communication systems. Methods of instruction include lecture, laboratory, discussion, and case studies. *Version 1 (Module 2/Chapters 3-10):* Major topics covered in the course are protocols, circuits, message and packet networks, and Local Area Net-works (LANs). Methods of instruction include lecture, laboratory, discussion, and case studies. *Version 2:* Major topics covered in the course are computer architecture, operating systems and desktop applications, comparison of past and current technologies, introductions to the internet, and the OSI reference model. Methods of instruction include lecture, discussion, classroom exercises, case studies, audio/ visual material, learner presentations/ reports, computer lab with interactive computer exercises. Methods of evaluating learning outcomes include: quizzes, observations, and presentation of case studies.

Credit Recommendation: *Version 1 (Module 1/Chapters 1 and 2 of Module 2):* In the lower division baccalaureate/associate degree category, 3 semester hours in Introduction to Computer Systems and Communications (applicable to Information Systems), Information Technology, or Management Information Systems (12/90). *Version 1 (Module 2/Chapters 3-10):* In the upper division baccalaureate degree category, 2 semester hours in Introduction to Data Communications and Networking (applicable to Computer Science or Information Systems) (12/90). *Version 2:* In the upper division baccalaureate degree category, 5 semester hours in Computer Science; Computer Information Systems; Data Communications; or Telecommunications (11/97).

ALPHA IV: Unit 2

Location: *Version 1:* White Plains, NY; *Version 2:* Marlboro, MA.

Length: *Version 1:* 98 hours (14 days); *Version 2:* 80 hours.

Dates: *Version 1:* October 1988-December 1996; *Version 2:* January 1997-Present.

Objective: *Version 1:* To enable students to understand programming languages, operating systems, computer architecture, and protocol design. *Version 2:* To provide students with an understanding of various layered protocols using transporting, switching, and error correction data.

Learning Outcome: *Version 1:* Upon successful completion of this course, the student will be able to understand software, computer operating systems, computer architecture, and protocol design. *Version 2:* Upon successful completion of this course, the student will be able to explain the functions of the various parts of a network and discuss the roles SNA, DNA, TC/IP, and the ISO model play in data switching and communications.

Instruction: *Version 1:* This overview course consists of six modules. Module 1 covers BASIC programming and overview of programming languages. Modules 2 and 3 cover elements of computer architecture and operating systems. Modules 4, 5, and 6 cover operating systems and protocol design. Methods of instruction include lecture, laboratory, and discussion. *Version 2:* Major topics covered in the course are the physical layer, the integrated information transport layer, CATV and Video, the data link layer, network and upper layers. Methods of instruction include lecture, discussion, classroom exercise, case studies, computer-assisted instruction, and learner presentations/ reports. Methods of evaluating learning outcomes include quizzes, reports, observations, and oral examinations.

Credit Recommendation: *Version 1:* In the lower division baccalaureate/associate degree category, 5 semester hours in Survey of Programming languages or Computer Systems and Communication (applicable to Computer Information Systems or Information Systems) (12/90). *Prerequisite:* ALPHA IV-Unit 1. *Version 2:* In the upper division baccalaureate degree category, 5 semester hours in Computer Science, Computer Information Systems, Data Communications or Telecommunications (11/97).

ALPHA IV: Unit 3

Location: *Version 1:* White Plains, NY; *Version 2:* Marlboro, MA.

Length: *Version 1:* 98 hours (14 days); *Version 2:* 80 hours.

Dates: *Version 1:* October 1988-December 1996; *Version 2:* January 1997-Present.

Objective: *Version 1:* To provide the student with an in-depth knowledge of computer networks. *Version 2:* To give the student an in-depth understanding of X.25 standard, TCP/IP Stack and Internet Operations, Systems Network Architecture (SNA), Integrated Services Digital Networks (ISDN), and SS7 architecture.

Learning Outcome: *Version 1:* Upon successful completion of this course, the student will be able to analyze and evaluate computer networks and their protocols. *Version 2:* Upon successful completion of this course, the student will be able to analyze, evaluate, and describe the function of X.25 packet switching standard; TCP/IP protocol architecture, current issues with internet, network interface layer, network security: System Network Architecture, telephone signaling and telecommunication environment; and SS7 network components and their functions; basic terms and concepts of ISDN protocols.

Instruction: *Version 1:* Major topics covered in the course are protocols, open system architecture, and TCP/IP, SNA and DNA at the network transport and session levels. Methods of instruction include lecture, discussion, laboratory, and case studies. *Version 2:* Major topics covered in the course are data communications of a network, packet switching, X.25 standard, physical and data link layers, packet layer protocol INFOPATH; Internet and TCP/IP layers, application services; network security, world wide web; SNA concepts, subarea and peer-to-peer networks, data link options, signaling; SS7 objectives, standards, components, applications, protocol and operation; introduction to ISDN, deployment, basic service, signaling and relationship between ISDN and SS7. Methods of instruction include lecture, classroom exercises, case studies, audio/visual material, computer-assisted instruction (interactive), learner presentations/reports, and study groups. Methods of evaluating learning outcomes include quizzes, reports, and oral examination.

Credit Recommendation: *Version 1:* In the upper division baccalaureate degree category, 5 semester hours in Computer Networking I (applicable to Computer Information Systems or Information Systems) (12/90). *Version 2:* In the upper division baccalaureate degree category, 5 semester hours in Computer Networking I (11/97). *Prerequisite:* ALPHA IV, Unit 2.

ALPHA IV: Unit 4

Location: *Version 1:* White Plains, NY; *Version 2:* Marlboro, MA.

Length: *Version 1:* 98 hours (14 days); *Version 2:* 80 hours.

Dates: *Version 1:* October 1988-December 1996; *Version 2:* January 1997-Present.

Objective: *Version 1:* To give students an in-depth understanding of Local Area Networks (LANs), their extension to Metropolitan Area Networks (MANs), Wide Are Networks (WANs), Integrated Services Digital Networks (ISDNs), X.25, Frame Relay, ATM, SONET, and SS7. *Version 2:* To give students an in-depth understanding of Local Area Networks (LAN), their extension to Metropolitan Area Networks (MAN), Wide Area Networks (WAN), Broadband Integrated Services Digital Networks (B-ISDN), Frame Relay, and Asynchronous Transfer Mode (ATM) service characteristics.

Learning Outcome: *Version 1:* Upon successful completion of this course, the student will be able to analyze and evaluate LANs, MANs, WANs, X.25, Frame Relay, ATM, SONET, ISDNs, and signaling systems. *Version 2:* Upon successful completion of this course, the student will be able to analyze and evaluates LANs, MANs, WANs, Frame Relays, B-ISDN, ATM Components, Media Access Control (MAC) Schemes, topologies, standards, network operating systems, and interconnection technologies. Explain fast packet technologies of frame relay.

Instruction: *Version 1:* Major topics covered in the course are topologies, media, and protocols of LANs, MANs, WANs, X.25, Frame Relay, ATM, SONET, and SS7. Methods of instruction include lecture, discussion, case studies, and laboratory exercises. *Version 2:* Major topics covered in the course are LAN technology, standards and products (IEEE 802), bridges, routers, building internetworks, fast packet services, Broadband ISDN; ATM principles, services, networking, applications, products, and services. Methods of instruction include lecture, discussion, classroom ex-ercises, case studies, learner presentations/reports, and lab exercises. Methods of evaluating learning outcomes include quizzes, final examination, observations, and oral examination.

Credit Recommendation: *Version 1:* In the upper division baccalaureate degree category, 5 semester hours in Computer Networking II (applicable to Computer Information Systems or Information Systems) (12/90). *Version 2:* In the upper division baccalaureate degree category, 5 semester hours in Computer Networking II or Networking Applications (11/97). *Prerequisite:* ALPHA IV, Unit 3.

ALPHA IV: Unit 5

Location: *Version 1:* White Plains, NY; *Version 2:* Marlboro, MA.

Length: *Version 1:* 70 hours (10 days); *Version 2:* 80 hours.

Dates: *Version 1:* October 1988-December 1996; *Version 2:* January 1997-Present.

Objective: *Version 1:* To give students an understanding of network management and to integrate the work of the previous four units into capstone cases. *Version 2:* To provide students with an understanding of imaging techniques, network management, and wireless technologies.

Learning Outcome: *Version 1:* Upon successful completion of this course, the student will be able to integrate the knowledge obtained in the first four units into real-world network solutions and management. *Version 2:* Upon successful completion of this course, the student will be able to explain image and video compression technologies and standards; network management standards and functions, and cellular, PCS, and satellite technologies.

Instruction: *Version 1:* The course is divided into two parts. Part 1 discusses the management of computer networks. Part 2 uses capstone cases to integrate the materials covered in the earlier units of the program. Methods of instruction include lecture, discussion, and case studies. *Version 2:* Major topics covered in the course are analog and digital signals; concepts of signal spectrum; analog-to-digital conversion; compression techniques; spatial and temporal redundancy; fundamentals of cellular radio, and wireless telephony. Methods of instruction include lecture, discussion, classroom exercises, case studies, computer-assisted instruction, learner presentations/reports, and study group. Methods of evaluating learning outcomes include quizzes and one-on-one oral exam.

Credit Recommendation: *Version 1:* In the upper division baccalaureate degree category, 3 semester hours in Computer Sciences or Information Systems (12/90). *Version 2:* In the upper division baccalaureate degree category, 3 semester hours in Computer Science; Computer Information Systems, or Telecommunications (11/97). *Prerequisite:* ALPHA IV, Unit 4.

Assembly Language Programming (IS05-1100)

Location: Silver Spring, MD and Philadelphia, PA.

Length: 105 hours (15 days).

Dates: January 1983-December 1997.

Objective: To bring the student with programming experience to an understanding of and ability to write in assembly language.

Learning Outcome: Upon successful completion of this course, the student will be able to understand the basic concepts of assembly language programming and be able to apply them to the IBM 370.

Instruction: Major topics covered in the course are basic instructions, loop instructions, decimal instructions, character handling, output editing, and program segmentation techniques. Methods of instruction include lecture, case problems, and classroom exercises.

Credit Recommendation: In the lower division baccalaureate/associate degree category, 4 semester hours in Assembly Language, Computer Science, or Information Science (12/92).

Basic Data Protocol (354)

Location: South Plainfield, NJ.

Length: 32.5 hours (self-paced).

Dates: September 1980-December 1993.

Objective: Upon successful completion of this course, the student will have the basic protocol knowledge to establish, maintain, and repair data circuits that use protocols in interactive data communication equipment.

Instruction: Major topics covered in the course are protocol test equipment and its uses; data speed terminal equipment; protocol trouble isolation; numbering systems/hex, octal, binary, and BCD; formatting and coding of standard data characters; and protocol error and detection systems.

Credit Recommendation: In the lower division baccalaureate/associate degree category, 2 semester hours in Basic Data Protocol (6/82).

Basic Electricity and Electronics Course (492)

Location: South Plainfield, NJ.
Length: 78 hours (self-paced).
Dates: December 1973-September 1994.
Objective: Upon successful completion of this course, the student will be able to operate test equipment on alternating and direct circuit power supplies, and test various electrical and electronic components using the electronic AC-DC voltmeter, function generators, and oscilloscopes.
Instruction: Major topics covered in the course are use of meters, reading circuit diagrams, capacitors, series and parallel circuits, electromagnetism, alternating current, calculating resistance, inductance, RL circuits, effects of capacitance, RC circuits, RLC circuits, transformers, diodes and tubes, transistors, power supplies, and amplifiers, and oscillators.
Credit Recommendation: In the lower division baccalaureate/associate degree category, 3 semester hours in Basic Electricity and Electronics (6/82) (1/95).

Basic Mathematics (Developmental Studies)

Location: Various locations throughout Bell Atlantic Region.
Length: 32 weeks; individual sessions ranging from 1 to 3 hours per week.
Dates: September 1975-December 1996.
Objective: To review and master the basic operations with whole numbers, integers, and rational numbers as well as solve algebraic equations and problems in basic geometry.
Learning Outcome: Upon successful completion of this course, the student will be able to perform with proficiency all basic operations relating to the manipulation of whole numbers, integers, and rational numbers, and will successfully compute such geometric concepts as perimeter, area, and volume.
Instruction: Major topics covered in the course are demonstrating professionalism in solving algebraic equations, using whole numbers, fractions, decimals, percents, algebra, and measurements. Methods of instruction are individualized and self-paced, with tutorial assistance and evaluation provided by the instructor.
Credit Recommendation: In the lower division baccalaureate/associate degree category, 3 semester hours in Basic Mathematics (5/80) (12/84) (12/91).

Black Managers Workshop (ME0801)

Location: Resident locations throughout Bell Atlantic Region.
Length: 45 hours (1 week).
Dates: December 1981-Present.
Objective: To serve as a development tool for enabling black managers to become viable assets to the company and better manage themselves; to enhance the level of communication between black management coworkers; and to increase awareness of barriers that have impact on effectiveness, morale, and productivity.
Learning Outcome: Upon successful completion of this course, the student will be able to have more self-awareness about black managers' self-esteem and career goal; understand organization culture and individual values; become knowledgeable about leadership style, organization power, stress management, and interpersonal communication; and have knowledge about company's image.
Instruction: Major topics covered in the course are black manager and self-esteem, methods of career and self-development, methods of goal attainment, individual values, organization norms and leadership styles; race-related stress; and organizational development goals and methods for black managers. Methods of instruction include lecture, exercises, project, action plan, self-report, and classroom exercises.
Credit Recommendation: In the upper division baccalaureate degree category, 2 semester hours in Introduction to Management, Organization Behavior, or Business Administration (12/91).

Computer Network Architecture (Top Gun: Unit Three)

Location: Eagle Lodge, Lafayette Hill, PA.
Length: 112 hours (14 days).
Dates: January 1987-December 1993.
Objective: To give the student an in-depth understanding of computer networking at the data-link, network, transport, and session layers.
Learning Outcome: Upon successful completion of this course, the student will be able to analyze and evaluate complex computer networks and their protocols.
Instruction: Major topics covered in the course are the major protocols at the data-link, network, transport, and session layers of the ISO OSI (International Standards Organization Open Systems Interconnection) model. Methods of instruction include lecture, discussion, and laboratory exercises.
Credit Recommendation: In the upper division baccalaureate degree category, 4 semester hours in Computer Networking (4/89) (1/95). *Prerequisite:* Programming Languages, Architecture and Operating Systems, and Communications (Top Gun—Unit Two). College-level mathematics is desirable but not required for this course.

Computer-Based PBX Systems (Dimension 400 Tier 1)

Location: South Plainfield, NJ.
Length: 169 hours (8.5 weeks).
Dates: September 1978-January 1984.
Objective: To train advanced personnel to install and maintain computer-based PBX systems.
Instruction: Major topics covered in the course are operation, installation, and maintenance of computer-based PBX systems; central processor operation and maintenance; software descriptions; installation testing; and software diagnostic systems. Methods of instruction include instructor-led course that uses audiovisual materials and laboratory exercises.
Credit Recommendation: In the lower division baccalaureate/associate degree category, 2 semester hours in Computer, Industrial, or Electrical Technology technical electives (6/82).

Custom Telephone Service System
1. Dimension 400 Tier 1 Installation and Repair (208)
2. Dimension 400 Repair-Tier 2 (209)
3. Horizon Computer Communications Systems (237)

Location: South Plainfield, NJ.
Length: 117 hours (3.6 weeks).
Dates: September 1978-January 1984.
Objective: To operate, install, test, and maintain computer-based PBX systems.
Instruction: Major topics covered in the course are installation, operation, and maintenance of custom telephone systems related to dimension 400 PBX. Methods of instruction include instructor-led course, lectures, and laboratories.
Credit Recommendation: In the vocational certificate category, 3 semester

hours in Communications Systems Practices (3/87).

Data Communications (Formerly Data Processing/Data Communications)

Location: Philadelphia, PA.
Length: 48.5 hours (2 weeks).
Dates: May 1980-December 1988.
Objective: To familiarize the student with data processing concepts.
Instruction: Major topics covered in the course are survey of data processing, including description of hardware, software, flowcharting, programming, systems, and related applications. Methods of instruction include lecture, discussion, and laboratory exercises.
Credit Recommendation: In the lower division baccalaureate/associate degree category, 1 semester hour in Data Processing (4/81) (2/85).

DB2 Overview and DB2 Application Programming (IS15-1200 and IS15-1)

Location: Silver Spring, MD; Madison and Freehold, NJ; Philadelphia, PA.
Length: 35 hours (5 days).
Dates: January 1992-December 1993.
Objective: To introduce the student to relational database using DBs, and to provide the student with a working knowledge of Structural Query Language (SQL) and the "how to's" of incorporating SQL into application programs.
Learning Outcome: Upon successful completion of this course, the student will be able to write SQL/DML statements to retrieve, update, add and delete data; describe components of a DB2 application pro-gram; write a DB2 application program using either COBOL or PL/1; prepare, execute, and test DB2 application programs; identify basic components and characteristics of the DB2 environment; and identify issues related to DB2 performance.
Instruction: Major topics covered in the course are operating environment, interactive tools, DB2 objects, object relationships, referential integrity, DB2 catalog, creating and maintaining DB2 objects, accessing DB2 data, application program preparation, SQL/select statement usage; and DB2 security, locking and recovery. Methods of instruction include lecture, discussion, and lab exercises.
Credit Recommendation: In the lower division or upper division baccalaureate degree category, 3 semester hours in Relational Databases, Database Management Systems or Computer Information Systems (12/92). **NOTE**: Student must successfully complete both courses (Overview and Application) to receive credit recommendation.

Drafting (NE1901C)
1. Basic Drafting (NE1801C)
2. Conduit Drafting

Location: South Plainfield, NJ; Newark, NJ.
Length: 1. 70 hours (10 days); 2. 49 hours (7 days).
Dates: April 1979-December 1992.
Objective: (1) To present the basic drafting skills required for performing the duties of an Outside Plant Drafter. (2) To present the basic skills required for the preparation of scaled conduit work prints.
Learning Outcome: Upon successful completion of this course, the student will be able to understand basic drafting techniques, the technology and principles necessary to prepare outside plant records, and prepare scaled work prints.
Instruction: (1) Major topics covered in the course are length and gauges (route records, symbols, cable capacitors, cross connecting fixtures); and work orders (forms, title block, account codes, MCF, terminals involved). (2) Major topics covered in the course are field notes, profile, angles, scaled work prints, drafting techniques, and interpretation of other utility prints. Methods of instruction include lecture, discussion, classroom exercises, audio/visual materials, labs, and evaluation of exercises.
Credit Recommendation: In the lower division baccalaureate/associate degree category, 1 semester hour in Conduit Layout (1/85) (1/95). **NOTE:** Credit recommendation is based on successful completion of Courses 1 and 2.

Effective Writing

Location: Various locations throughout C&P Telephone Company business area.
Length: 30 hours (15 weeks).
Dates: September 1977-December 1992.
Objective: To improve students' ability to write clear and concise paragraphs, letters, memoranda, and other communications.
Instruction: Major topics covered in the course are the qualities of effective writing; offers opportunity to receive critiques and to revise. Methods of instruction include lectures and discussions followed by writing laboratory sessions.
Credit Recommendation: In the lower division baccalaureate/associate degree category, 1 semester hour in Composition, Written Communication, or Writing Skills (5/80) (12/84).

Electronic Switching Systems Method of Operation 5

Location: South Plainfield, NJ.
Length: 35 hours (1 week).
Dates: December 1984-September 1994.
Objective: To present a comprehensive data communications course using the #5 ESS (electronic switching) system as a vehicle to explain data communications.
Instruction: Major topics covered in the course are a comprehensive overview of the #5 ESS system architecture, hardware options, and generic capabilities; knowledge of terminology and method of operation; multimodule configuration including host and remote operation, 3B-20 processor, call processing, software architecture, traffic measurement capability, and the maintenance philosophy. Methods of instruction include lecture, demonstrations, and exercises.
Credit Recommendation: In the upper division baccalaureate degree category, 3 semester hours in Data Communications, Computer Science, or MIS (3/86) (1/95).

Electronic Switching Systems: 431 (Number 1 ESS)

Location: South Plainfield, NJ.
Length: 897 hours (138 days).
Dates: December 1973-December 1993.
Objective: To characterize data failures, interpret program instructions, apply software diagnostic strategies in troubleshooting, interpret and use program documentation, and use diagnostics in hardware maintenance.
Instruction: Major topics covered in the course are computer concepts, hardware fundamentals, common peripherals, processor and program fundamentals, and memory organization. The self-paced course orients students to software use and analysis.
Credit Recommendation: In the lower division baccalaureate/associate degree category, 3 semester hours in Industrial, Electrical, or Computer Technology technical electives (10/82).

Electronic Switching Systems: 458 (Number 1A ESS)

Location: South Plainfield, NJ.
Length: 670 hours (103 days).

Dates: April 1977-September 1994.

Objective: Individuals will be able to characterize data failures, interpret program instructions, apply software diagnostic strategies in troubleshooting, interpret and use program documentation, and use diagnostics in hardware maintenance.

Instruction: Major topics covered in the course are computer concepts, hardware fundamentals, common peripherals, processor and program fundamentals, and memory organization. This self-paced course orients students to software use and analysis.

Credit Recommendation: In the lower division baccalaureate/associate degree category, 3 semester hours in Industrial, Electrical, or Computer Technology technical electives (10/82) (1/95).

English Grammar and Usage

Location: Various locations throughout the Bell Atlantic Region.

Length: 32 weeks; individual sessions ranging from 1-3 hours per week.

Dates: September 1978-December 1996.

Objective: To teach fundamental grammar and punctuation usage, which are necessary for correct writing structure.

Learning Outcome: Upon successful completion of this course, the student will be able to construct sensible sentences; use parts of speech correctly; form simple, compound, and complex sentences; punctuate sentences correctly; and use subject/verb constructions correctly.

Instruction: Major topics covered in the course are subject and verb usage; sentence patterns; capitalization usage; and punctuation rules and usage.

Credit Recommendation: In the lower division baccalaureate/associate degree category, 1 semester hour in Basic English, Composition, Grammar, or Written Communications (5/80) (12/84) (12/91).

Fiber Optics Design/Loop Electronics Design (EN4121)

Location: Silver Spring, MD, South Plainfield, NJ, and on-site locations.

Length: 66 hours (2 weeks).

Dates: July 1991-Present.

Objective: To provide details required to prepare an engineering job order for digital loop carriers on fiber.

Learning Outcome: Upon successful completion of this course, the student will be able to understand analog to digital conversion; understand the types of digital facilities; plan and design digital loop carrier configuration; and plan, design, and administer fiber cables, multiplexers, and other component equipment.

Instruction: Major topics covered in the course are analog and digital system, multiplexing, digital system's operation and components, diagnostics, system capabilities and digital architecture including switching components. Methods of instruction include lecture, discussion, workshops, exercises, and casework.

Credit Recommendation: In the lower division baccalaureate/associate degree category, 3 semester hours in Electrical Technology, Electronic Technology, or Telecommunications (12/92) (1/95).

Fundamentals of Data Transmission (Introduction to Data)

Location: South Plainfield, NJ.

Length: 66 hours (self-paced).

Dates: February 1975-September 1994.

Objective: To identify forms of data communications; define binary, octal, and hex numbering systems; describe basic computer components; describe modem connections (e.g., RS-232); write simple programs; and perform various tests related to transmission loss.

Instruction: Methods of instruction include textbook instruction, media aids, and laboratory experiences.

Credit Recommendation: In the lower division baccalaureate/associate degree category, 2 semester hours in Computer, Electrical, or Industrial Technology; Medical Instrumentation Technology; or Humanities electives (10/82) (1/95).

Fundamentals of Data Transmission: Testing and Service (921A Data Test Set I)

Location: South Plainfield, NJ.

Length: 91 hours (self-paced).

Dates: September 1980-September 1994.

Objective: To install, test, and service 200 series Data Sets and Dataphone II sets.

Instruction: Self-paced course includes operating specialized test sets used to test synchronous and asynchronous modems; installation, use, testing, and maintenance of various speed modem units.

Credit Recommendation: In the lower division baccalaureate/associate degree category, 1 semester hour in Computer, Electrical, or Industrial Technology; Medical Instrumentation Technology; Business; or Humanities electives (10/82) (1/95). *Prerequisite:* Basic Data Transmission Fundamentals.

Fundamentals of Digital Circuits (Advanced Electronics Course [493])

Location: South Plainfield, NJ.

Length: 78 hours (self-paced).

Dates: December 1973-December 1993.

Objective: To demonstrate to students computer terminology; solve problems using numbering systems of bases 2, 8, 10; demonstrate use of Boolean functions; describe operation of core memories, twister memories, ferrods and fereeds, stored program methods, transistors, pulse nomenclature, clippers, clampers, and wave shaping; and use oscilloscope for digital test measurements.

Instruction: Major topics covered in the course are oscilloscope, diodes, transistors, pulse waveshaping, clippers and clampers, numbering systems, basic logic fundamentals, and memory systems. Methods of instruction for this self-paced course are tutoring and laboratory work.

Credit Recommendation: In the lower division baccalaureate/associate degree category, 3 semester hours in Fundamentals of Digital Circuits (6/82).

Fundamentals of Outside Plant Engineering (EN4011, EN4012, EN4013)

Location: South Plainfield, NJ and Silver Spring, MD.

Length: 250 hours (35 days).

Dates: February 1976-Present.

Objective: To provide training in basic skills required by outside plant facility engineers and to enable them to effect the design of the outside components of a communications system.

Learning Outcome: Upon successful completion of this course, the student will be able to identify network configurations, define routing patterns, identify trunking types by their applications, define distribution requirements, and prepare planning documents.

Instruction: Major topics covered in the course are reading, drawing and interpreting communication line construction work plans; basic electrical communication topics including sections on electrical protection procedures, estimate preparation, engineering economics, distribution cable design, problem solving, and subscriber loop design. Methods of instruction include lecture, discussion, problem solving, and case studies.

Credit Recommendation: In the lower division baccalaureate/associate degree

category, 4 semester hours in Planning and Operations or Industrial Engineering Technology (1/85) (12/92).

Human Relations in Business

Location: Various locations throughout C&P Telephone Company business area.

Length: 30 hours (15 weeks).

Dates: February 1981-December 1994.

Objective: To develop understanding and practice of human relations skills as they relate to the business setting, emphasizing the development of awareness and personal skills in the areas of interpersonal communication, problem solving, and conflict in organizations.

Instruction: Major topics covered in the course are interpersonal communication and dynamic listening. Methods of instruction include role playing, problem solving, and case studies through lecture and discussions.

Credit Recommendation: In the upper division baccalaureate degree category, 2 semester hours in Business Administration, Human Relations, Leadership, or Management (2/81) (12/84) (1/95).

Information Networks (Top Gun: Unit Four)

Location: Eagle Lodge, Lafayette Hill, PA.

Length: 112 hours (14 days).

Dates: January 1987-December 1993.

Objective: To give the student an in-depth understanding of Local Area Networks (LANs) and Integrated Services Digital Networks (ISDNs).

Learning Outcome: Upon successful completion of this course, the student will be able to analyze and evaluate Local Area Networks (LANs) and Integrated Services Digital Networks (ISNDs).

Instruction: Major topics covered in the course are topologies, media, and protocols of LANs and the operation and function services of ISDN and voice/data communication. Methods of instruction include lecture, discussion, and case studies.

Credit Recommendation: In the upper division baccalaureate degree category, 4 semester hours in Computer Networking (4/89) (1/95). *Prerequisite:* Computer Network Architecture (Top Gun—Unit Three). College-level mathematics is desirable but not required for this course.

Information Transmission and Networking (The Network)

Location: New Jersey, Pennsylvania, Delaware, Maryland, Virginia, West Virginia, and Washington, DC.

Length: 72 hours (9.5 days).

Dates: August 1984-December 1993.

Objective: To provide the student with information in the areas of transmission and networking fundamentals, telephone system functions, data communications concepts, data transmission digital and analog (microwave satellite and fiber optic), and existing and proposed network protocols.

Instruction: Major topics covered in the course are preparing students for a future in data communications with emphasis on services provided by regulated carriers. Methods of instruction include applications, exercises, and mock presentations.

Credit Recommendation: In the upper division baccalaureate degree category, 2 semester hours in Computer Science (12/85).

Installation and Service of Key Telephone Customer Equipment (COM KEY 2152 Install)

Location: South Plainfield, NJ.

Length: 27 days (6 weeks).

Dates: March 1979-December 1993.

Objective: To teach students to install and service key telephone customer credit.

Instruction: Major topics covered in the course are basic and optional equipment components, planning locations of equipment and cables, installing equipment, and installing and troubleshooting key telephone systems. Methods of instruction include texts, audiovisual aids, and extensive laboratory experience.

Credit Recommendation: In the vocational certificate category, 3 semester hours in Key Telephone Customer Equipment Installation Repair (10/82).

Introduction to dBASE III

Location: South Plainfield, NJ.

Length: 14 hours (2 days).

Dates: June 1985-January 1993.

Objective: To present students with the fundamentals of dBASE III.

Instruction: Major topics covered in the course are leader-led tutorials; and creation of basic files and data entry techniques as well as file manipulation, editing, and output.

Credit Recommendation: In the lower division baccalaureate/associate degree category, 1 semester hour in Business Administration (3/86) (1/95).

Introduction to Information Technology: Basic Concepts and Market Structure (Top Gun: Unit One)

Location: Eagle Lodge, Lafayette Hill, PA.

Length: 112 hours (14 days).

Dates: January 1987-December 1993.

Objective: To provide the student with an understanding of information technology and its marketplace.

Learning Outcome: Upon successful completion of this course, the student will be able to define the technological components of the information systems marketplace including computer and distributed systems, fundamentals of network architecture, and strategic competition in the marketplace.

Instruction: Major topics covered in the course are communications marketplace, information systems, computer systems, communications systems, and communications architecture. Methods of instruction include lecture, discussion, and case studies.

Credit Recommendation: In the lower division baccalaureate/associate degree category, 6 semester hours in Information Technology (4/89) (1/95).

Introduction to Lotus 1-2-3

Location: South Plainfield, NJ.

Length: 14 hours (2 days).

Dates: February 1985-January 1993.

Objective: To present students with the fundamental concepts of Lotus 1-2-3.

Instruction: Major topics covered in the course are creation, printing, and graphing of spreadsheets. Methods of instruction include leader-led tutorials and laboratory exercises.

Credit Recommendation: In the lower division baccalaureate/associate degree category, 1 semester hour in Business Administration (3/86) (1/95).

Loop Electronics Design Advanced (EN4201)

Location: South Plainfield, PA, Silver Spring, MD, and on-site locations.
Length: 20 hours (3 days).
Dates: January 1992-August 1992.
Objective: To provide the basic concepts on the planning and design of a digital loop carrier system.
Learning Outcome: Upon successful completion of this course, the student will be able to list the components of a digital loop carrier system; describe compatibility requirements between a digital loop carrier system and a local digital switch; design a Remote Electronics Site (RES); explain the function of a Synchronous Optical Network and how it impacts the local loop; explain the advantage of using fiber optics in the distribution loop; and list the components and purpose of an operations system.
Instruction: Major topics covered in the course are basic concepts of a loop carrier system including compatibility, network survival, synchronized optical networks (SONET), fiber optics in the distribution loop (FITL), and operations systems. Methods of instruction include lecture, discussion, and case studies.
Credit Recommendation: In the upper division baccalaureate degree category, 1 semester hour in Telecommunications (12/92).

Loop Electronics Inventory Module (EN5140)

Location: South Plainfield, PA, and Silver Spring, MD.
Length: 34 hours (5 days).
Dates: January 1988-Present.
Objective: To train the student in the design and maintenance of loop electronics inventory using the Loop Electronics Inventory Module (LEIM).
Learning Outcome: Upon successful completion of this course, the student will be able to develop a LEIM wire center database; retrieve and printout reports; and access and utilize data management programs.
Instruction: Major topics covered in the course are the design and operation of the LEIM architecture including hardware, UNIX operating system, relational database and LEIM. Methods of instruction include lecture, discussion, and casework.
Credit Recommendation: In the upper division baccalaureate degree category, 2 semester hours in Information Systems or Operations Management (12/92).

Loop Engineering Assignment Data (EN5130)

Location: South Plainfield, PA, and Silver Spring, MD.
Length: 33 hours (5 days).
Dates: January 1987-Present.
Objective: To understand the Utilization of Loop Engineering Assignment Data (LEAD) to analyze various reports in order to determine the status of local access loop plant facilities.
Learning Outcome: Upon successful completion of this course, the student will be able to define the purpose and structure of the LEIS; use basic UNIX commands relating to LEIS; generate LEAD reports; and use the cable transfer program to test potential cable pair transfers.
Instruction: Major topics covered in the course are introduction to LEIS; UNIX basics; LEAD interaction; LEAD reports; and creation and utilization of LEAD tables. Methods of instruction include lecture, discussion, and case studies.
Credit Recommendation: In the upper division baccalaureate degree category, 1 semester hour in Information Systems (12/92).

Microcomputer-Based PBX Systems: Installation and Maintenance
1. Dimension 400-Installation and Maintenance (208)
2. Dimension 2000-Installation (136)
3. Horizon-Installation (237)

Location: South Plainfield, NJ.
Length: 2 .8 weeks (91 hours).
Dates: September 1975-January 1984.
Objective: To train advanced personnel to install and maintain microcomputer-based PBX systems.
Instruction: Major topics covered in the course are operation, installation, and maintenance of microcomputer based systems include central processor operation and maintenance, software descriptions, installation testing, and software diagnostic systems. Methods of instruction include instructor-led course using audio-visual materials and laboratory exercises.
Credit Recommendation: In the vocational certificate category, 2 semester hours in Computer, Industrial, or Electrical Technology technical electives (6/82).

Network Management and Applications (Top Gun: Unit Five)

Location: Eagle Lodge, Lafayette Hill, PA.
Length: 112 hours (14 days).
Dates: January 1987-December 1993.
Objective: To give the student an understanding of the services provided by the local metropolitan and wide area networks.
Learning Outcome: Upon successful completion of this course, the student will be able to analyze, evaluate, and propose solutions for actual real-world networking problems.
Instruction: Major topics covered in the course are a thorough understanding of the services, management, and protocols provided by computer networks and serves as a capstone, integrating material presented in Units two, three, and four through the use of a series of case studies. Methods of instruction include lecture, discussion, and case studies.
Credit Recommendation: In the upper division baccalaureate degree category, 3 semester hours in Computer Science or Information Systems (4/89) (1/95). *Prerequisite:* Information Networks (Top Gun—Unit Four)

New Jersey Bell 1 A ESS Overview and Maintenance
1. System Overview and Software Documentation; No. N 687 OSC
2. 1/1A SCC ESS Translations; No. 688 OSC
3. 1 A ESS Peripheral Processor Maintenance; No. N 689 ASC

Location: South Plainfield, NJ.
Length: 1. Self-paced (approximately 19 hours); 2. self-paced (approximately 52 hours); 3. self-paced (approximately 260 hours).
Dates: August 1985-December 1993.
Objective: 1: To introduce students to the processor and peripheral equipment associated with 1 A ESS. 2: To provide the training necessary to input and verify different types of changes related to SCC translation function. 3: To train technicians to perform normal maintenance tasks associated with processor and peripheral equipment in 1 A ESS.
Instruction: 1: Major topics covered in the course are switching technicians

assigned to work with the SCC translations function of SCC field function are introduced to the processor and peripheral equipment associated with 1 A ESS; students also become familiar with the hardware and software documentation that support the 1 A ESS. 2: Major topics covered in the course are translation introduction, translation forms, translations and recent change verification, recent change procedures, and translation updates. Simulated work assignments are employed to provide on-the-job conditions. 3: Major topics covered in the course are normal maintenance tasks associated with an SCC field assignment and includes peripheral and processor maintenance in 1 A ESS. Other topics include 1/1A digital trunk carrier; 1 A ESS processor; 3 B processor; and attached processor interface.

Credit Recommendation: In the lower division baccalaureate/associate degree category, 4 semester hours in Microprocessor-Based Systems: Maintenance and Troubleshooting (6/86).

New Jersey Bell 1 ESS System Overview and Maintenance
1. System Overview and Software Documentation (No. N 687 ASC)
2. 1/1A SCC ESS Translations; (No. 688 OSC)
3. 1 ESS Peripheral Processor Maintenance (No. N 689 ASC)

Location: South Plainfield, NJ.

Length: 1. Self-paced (approximately 19 hours); 2. self-paced (approximately 52 hours); 3. self-paced (approximately 182 hours).

Dates: August 1985-December 1993.

Objective: 1: To introduce students to the processor and peripheral equipment associated with 1 ESS. 2: To provide the training necessary to input and verify different types of changes related to SCC translation function. 3: To train technicians to perform normal maintenance tasks associated with processor and peripheral equipment in 1 E ESS.

Instruction: 1: Major topics covered in the course are switching technicians assigned to work with the SCC translations function or SCC field function are introduced to the processor and peripheral equipment associated with 1 ESS. 2: Major topics covered in the course are translation introduction, translation forms, translations and recent change verification, recent change procedures, and translation updates. Simulated work assignments are employed to provide on-the-job conditions. 3: Major topics covered in the course are normal maintenance tasks associated with an SCC field assignment and includes peripheral and processor maintenance in 1 E ESS. Other topics include 1/1A remreed frames; 1/1A digital carrier trunk; 1 ESS processor; and 1 ESS 8K, 32K call store hardware and maintenance.

Credit Recommendation: In the lower division baccalaureate/associate degree category, 3 semester hours in Microprocessor-Based Systems: Maintenance and Troubleshooting (6/86). **NOTE:** Modules 1, 2, and 3 need to be completed for credit recommendation.

New Jersey Bell 534 (A-E)
1. 534A No. 1 ESS Central Control Language, Hardware, and Maintenance
2. 534B Program Store Hardware and Maintenance
3. 534C Call Store Maintenance
4. 534D No. 1 ESS Central Processor Hardware and Maintenance
5. 534E Master Control Centers and Associated Frames Diagnostics

Location: South Plainfield, NJ.

Length: 206 hours (self-paced).

Dates: December 1973-December 1993.

Objective: To provide the student with the skills, knowledge, and techniques required to maintain the central processor free of hardware faults.

Instruction: Major topics covered in the course are central control, program store, call store, signal processor, and master control center. Five modules contain a total of 15 individual units. Tests after each unit. Must obtain 100.

Credit Recommendation: In the vocational certificate category, 6 semester hours in Digital Hardware Maintenance (6/82).

New Jersey Bell 534K Sequence
1. 534KA 1A Central Control Organization, Language and Maintenance
2. 534KB 1A Memory Storage Units Hardware and Maintenance
3. 534KC 1A Processor Interface Units Hardware and Maintenance

Location: South Plainfield, NJ.

Length: 96 hours (self-paced).

Dates: April 1977-December 1993.

Objective: To provide the student with the skills, knowledge, and techniques required to maintain the central processor free of hardware faults.

Instruction: Major topics covered in the course are central control, program store, call store, signal processor, and master control center. Three modules contain a total of nine individual units. Tests after each unit. Must obtain 100.

Credit Recommendation: In the vocational certificate category, 6 semester hours in Digital Hardware Maintenance (6/82).

New Jersey Bell 539 (A-F)
1. 539A No. 1 ESS Stored Program Organization
2. 539B No. 1 ESS Parameters
3. 539C No. 1 ESS Translations
4. 539D No. 1 ESS Call Processing
5. 539E No. 1 ESS Maintenance and Alarm Printouts
6. 539F No. 1 ESS Maintenance Procedures

Location: South Plainfield, NJ.

Length: 212 hours (self-paced).

Dates: December 1973-December 1993.

Objective: To develop the skills that will enable an individual to perform tasks in the area of software maintenance for No. 1 Electronic Switching Systems (ESS).

Instruction: Major topics covered in the course are the use of generic program documentation, locating and clearing parameter and translation problems, applied knowledge of No. 1 ESS call processing, resolving audit error printouts, and off-line testing. Methods of instruction include self-paced instruction with graded exams.

Credit Recommendation: In the vocational certificate category, 6 semester hours in Switching System Software Diagnostics (6/82).

New Jersey Bell 539K Sequence
1. 539KA 1A ESS Documentation
2. 539KB ESS Translations and Recent Change
3. 539KC 1A Parameters and Call Processing Audits
4. 539KD 1A Memory Administration, Features, and Programs
5. 539KE Program Interrupts, Deferred Fault Recovery, and Error Analysis
6. 539KF 1A System Recovery

Location: South Plainfield, NJ.

Length: 209 hours (self-paced).

Dates: April 1977-December 1993.

Objective: To develop the skills that will enable an individual to perform tasks in the area of software maintenance for No. 1A Electronic Switching System (ESS).

Instruction: Major topics covered in the course are generic program documentation, locating and clearing parameter and translation problems, applied knowledge of No. 1A ESS call processing, resolving audit error printouts, and off-line testing. Methods of instruction include self-paced instruction with graded examinations.

Credit Recommendation: In the vocational certificate category, 6 semester hours in Switching System Software Diagnostics (6/82).

New Jersey Bell 507AA/AA Sequence
1. 507AA Introduction to Electronic Switching Systems/Second Generation
2. 508A Common Peripheral Units/Second Generation
3. 508AA 1A Technology Common Peripheral Units

Location: South Plainfield, NJ.

Length: 221 hours (self-paced).

Dates: December 1973-December 1993.

Objective: To provide the student with entry-level skills and knowledge for first- and second-generation electronic switching technology.

Instruction: Major topics covered in the course are electronic switching systems overview, numbering systems, diodes and transistors, logic circuits, hardware, oscilloscope usage, basic ESS communication buses, principal components, and skills required for locating trouble. Meth-od of instruction is self-paced, practical exercises under supervision of an administrator.

Credit Recommendation: In the lower division baccalaureate/associate degree category, 3 semester hours in Introduction to Electronic Switching Systems (6/82).

New Jersey Bell 507B
1. Introduction to No. 1 Electronic Switching Systems (ESS)
2. No. 1 ESS Peripheral Units—On-the-Job Training

Location: South Plainfield, NJ.

Length: 18 hours (self-paced).

Dates: December 1973-December 1993.

Objective: To provide the student with the skills needed to progress to more advanced No. 1-level ESS and to provide the student with practice and skills associated with No. 1 ESS peripheral equipment maintenance.

Instruction: Major topics covered in the course are operations, use, fault diagnostics, and repair of No. 1-level ESS and their related peripheral units including component identification from schematics, block diagram analysis, program diagnostics and listing, testing procedures for service lines and equipment, logic circuit testing, and central processor hardware operations. Methods of instruction include self-paced instruction and practical on-the-job exercises.

Credit Recommendation: In the vocational certificate category, 1 semester hour in Switching System Maintenance (6/82).

New Jersey Bell 507K: Introduction to the IA Processor

Location: South Plainfield, NJ.

Length: 18 hours (self-paced).

Dates: April 1977-December 1993.

Objective: To provide the student with the skills needed to progress to more advanced No. 1A-level ESS (electronic switching system) and with practice and skills associated with No. 1A ESS peripheral equipment maintenance.

Instruction: Major topics covered in the course are operations, use, fault diagnosis, and repair of No. 1A-level ESS and their related peripheral units including component identification from schematics, block diagram analysis, program diagnostics and listing, testing procedures for service lines and equipment, logic circuit testing, and central processor hardware operations.

Credit Recommendation: In the vocational certificate category, 1 semester hour in Switching System Maintenance (6/82).

New Jersey Bell 508K Sequence
1. 508KA No. 1/1A Remreed Peripheral Maintenance
2. 508KB No. 1/1A ESS CMT/MUT Peripheral Unit Maintenance
3. 508KD No. 1/1A ESS PUC/DCT—Operation and Maintenance
4. 508KF No. 1 ESS Ferreed Operation and Maintenance

Location: South Plainfield, NJ.

Length: 125.5 hours (self-paced).

Dates: December 1973-December 1993.

Objective: To provide the student with the general knowledge and maintenance procedures required to work on first- and second-generation electronic switching system (ESS) peripherals.

Instruction: Major topics covered in the course are operation, design, maintenance, and fault diagnosis of first- and second-generation ESS Remreed switching network and its related equipment including switching path network, trunk switching frames, junction switching, network maintenance, pulse distributing diagnostics, trunk circuit analysis, and digital switching diagnostics. Methods of instruction include self-paced instruction and practical exercises.

Credit Recommendation: In the vocational certificate category, 5 semester hours in Switching System Maintenance (6/82).

New Jersey Bell 509B (No. 1 ESS Central Processor and Program Fundamentals)

Location: South Plainfield, NJ.

Length: 108 hours (self-paced).

Dates: December 1973-December 1993.

Objective: To provide the student with the skills necessary to characterize data failures in No. 1 Electronic Switching Systems (ESS) Program Store or Call Store memory systems and to identify the specific location of hardware failure.

Instruction: Major topics covered in the course are operation, maintenance, and repair of an advanced-level ESS control unit including logic circuit analysis, block diagram and timing analysis, address operations, computer system operations, memory addressing (32K and 8K), program instruction codes, core memory operations, program diagnostics, troubleshooting procedures, and repair methods. Methods of instruction include self-paced instruction and practical exercises.

Credit Recommendation: In the lower division baccalaureate/associate degree category, 3 semester hours in Computer Systems or Logic Circuit Fundamentals (6/82).

Office Control (1/1A ESS SCC Office Control; No. N690OSC)

Location: South Plainfield, NJ.

Length: Self-paced (approximately 65 hours).

Dates: August 1985-December 1993.

Objective: To familiarize students with Switching Control Center (SCC) Office Control basic workstation procedures.

Instruction: Major topics covered in the course are SCC Office Control basic workstation procedures including browsing, making patterns, and file manipulation; and key topics include SCC Opera-tions, Office Control Operations, alarms, audits, and emergency action. Methods of instruction include simulated work assignments which reinforce self-paced course material.

Credit Recommendation: In the lower division baccalaureate/associate degree

category, 1 semester hour as a Technical Elective (6/86).

Oral Communication

Location: Various locations throughout C&P Telephone Company business area.
Length: 24 hours (12 weeks).
Dates: September 1978-December 1994.
Objective: To foster verbal skills in dialogue and public speaking.
Instruction: Major topics covered in the course are basic communication theory and models; listening, perception, and self-awareness; verbal and nonverbal language systems; interpersonal communication; group discussion theory; and public communication. Methods of instruction include lectures, role playing, group discussions; and presentation and evaluation of prepared talks.
Credit Recommendation: In the lower division baccalaureate/associate degree category, 2 semester hours in Communications or Speech (5/80) (12/84) (1/95).

Oscilloscopes

Location: South Plainfield, NJ.
Length: 13 hours (self-paced).
Dates: January 1975-September 1994.
Objective: To develop proficiency in using oscilloscopes.
Instruction: Major topics covered in the course are setting up and calibrating the oscilloscope, measuring wave form amplitude polarity and time duration, and using dual trace and delayed sweep features.
Credit Recommendation: In the vocational certificate category, 1 semester hour in Oscilloscopes (10/82) (1/95).

Outside Plant Trunk Facilities Design (NE100ICO)

Location: South Plainfield, NJ; Newark, NJ.
Length: 35 hours (5 days).
Dates: December 1976-December 1993.
Objective: To provide basic knowledge of the fundamentals required to design outside plant analog/digital trunk cable facilities.
Instruction: Major topics covered in the course, intended for all engineers involved with the function of providing OSP trunk facilities, are the ability to list all forces included in the company function of providing trunk facilities; describe the job responsibilities of each force; design a loaded and a nonloaded trunk cable facility for wire circuit; design a trunk cable for T-1 carrier; and demonstrate ability to define the job responsibilities of all forces included in the function of providing trunk facilities.
Credit Recommendation: In the lower division baccalaureate/associate degree category, 2 semester hours as a Communications elective (1/85).

PC Courses
Introduction to IBM PC-XT and DOS
2. Computer Literacy/Do I Need a PC?

Location: South Plainfield, NJ.
Length: 1. 7 hours (1 day); 2. 7 hours (1 day).
Dates: June 1985-January 1993.
Objective: To determine if an employee needs a PC to help perform job in accordance with New Jersey Bell regulations and procedures and to provide an introduction to IBM PC and disk operating systems.
Instruction: Major topics covered in the course are to determine the types of tasks best performed by PC and to provide an introduction to available software to perform these tasks; a general overview of typical hardware/software is presented with a review of NJ Bell policies regarding computer acquisition and usage; and provides an introduction to operating procedures of the keyboard and peripherals with detailed PC-DOS commands. Methods of instruction include instructor-led tutorials, slide presentations, and hands-on IBM PC lab.
Credit Recommendation: In the lower division baccalaureate/associate degree category, 1 semester hour in Business Administration (3/86) (1/95). **NOTE:** Students can be admitted directly into the Introduction to IBM PC-XT and DOS course; if they successfully complete this course; they are eligible for the credit recommendation.

Peripheral Installation and Maintenance
1. Data Speed 40 Dataphone Service, Course 313
2. Synchronous Data Speed 40 (DS40/4) (4540), Course 341
3. COMM-STOR II CSU, Course 355

Location: South Plainfield, NJ.
Length: 130 hours (self-paced).
Dates: February 1974-December 1993.
Objective: Students will be able to install, test, and troubleshoot peripheral device controllers, printers, and floppy disks.
Instruction: Major topics covered in the course are ASCII/EBCDIC/HEX code synchronous message formats, floppy disks formats and control characteristics, and troubleshooting using diagnostic diskettes. Methods of instruction include a self-paced course with texts, audiovisual aids, and laboratory experiences.
Credit Recommendation: In the lower division baccalaureate/associate degree category, 2 semester hours in Computer, Electrical or Industrial Technology, Medical Instrumentation Technology, Business, or Humanities electives (6/82).

Peripheral Installation and Maintenance (Data Speed 40 Dataph)

Location: South Plainfield, NJ.
Length: 98 hours (self-paced).
Dates: October 1976-December 1993.
Objective: To be able to install, test, and troubleshoot peripheral device controllers, printers, and floppy disks.
Instruction: Major topics covered in the course are ASCII/EBCDIC/HEX code synchronous message formats, floppy disk formats and control characteristics, troubleshooting using diagnostic diskettes. Methods of instruction include a self-paced course with texts, audiovisual aids, and laboratory experiences.
Credit Recommendation: In the lower division baccalaureate/associate degree category, 2 semester hours in Computer, Electrical or Industrial Technology, Medical Instrumentation Technology, Business, or Humanities electives (10/82).

Personal Selling I (Account Executive Phase I)

Location: Philadelphia, PA; Silver Spring, MD.
Length: 85 hours (6 weeks).
Dates: January 1984-December 1993.
Objective: To teach students basic selling skills.
Instruction: Major topics covered in the course are developing skills for one-to-one promotion based on customer analyses and benefits selling. Methods of instruction include lecture, discussion, role playing, and case analyses.
Credit Recommendation: In the lower division baccalaureate/associate degree

category, 3 semester hours in Personal Selling (12/85).

Personal Selling II (Account Executive Phase II)

Location: Philadelphia, PA; Silver Spring, MD.

Length: 91.5 hours (6 weeks).

Dates: January 1985-December 1993.

Objective: To teach students advanced selling skills.

Instruction: Major topics covered in the course are developing a strategic selling approach and includes competitor analyses, sales plans, presentations, and closing skills. Methods of instruction include lecture, discussion, role playing, and case analysis.

Credit Recommendation: In the upper division baccalaureate degree category, 3 semester hours in Personal Selling (12/85).

Programming Languages, Architecture and Operating Systems, and Communications (Top Gun: Unit Two)

Location: Eagle Lodge, Lafayette Hill, PA.

Length: 112 hours (14 days).

Dates: January 1987-December 1993.

Objective: To allow the student to examine key elements of information technology.

Learning Outcome: Upon successful completion of this course, the student will be able to understand software management and construction, computer operating systems, and communications.

Instruction: Major topics covered in the course are BASIC programming, dBASE III, and a comparison of programming languages; elements of computer architecture and operating systems; and communications channels including components and signal processing and underlying principles of data communications. Methods of instruction include lecture, discussion, and laboratory exercises.

Credit Recommendation: In the lower division baccalaureate/associate degree category, 6 semester hours in Communications, Computer Systems, or Survey of Programming Languages (4/89) (1/95). *Prerequisite:* Introduction to Information Technology—Basic Concepts and Market Structure (Top Gun—Unit One).

Radio License: Second Class (326)

Location: South Plainfield, NJ.

Length: 200 hours (self-paced).

Dates: March 1974-January 1994.

Objective: To pass the Federal Communications Commission (FCC) Second Class Radio-Telephone License test.

Instruction: Major topics covered in the course are DC elements; DC theory; AC theory; inductance—transformers; capacitors; AC circuits; resonance—filters; tubes; basic solid state devices; batteries; motors—generators; AC power supplies; meters, oscilloscopes—decibels, oscillators; AF amplifiers, RF amplifiers; transmitters; AM transmitters; AM receivers; FM receivers, antennas; measuring frequency; microwave; rules/regulations; basic radio law; and basic operation practice.

Credit Recommendation: In the lower division baccalaureate/associate degree category, 2 semester hours in Electronic Communications (6/82) (1/95).

Repair Transmission (224)

Location: South Plainfield, NJ.

Length: 32.5 hours (self-paced).

Dates: December 1973-December 1992.

Objective: To select and apply appropriate test equipment to troubleshoot electrical systems and analyze test results to sectionalize circuit trouble conditions.

Instruction: Major topics covered in the course are applications of troubleshooting techniques to foreign exchange circuits; tie lines; PBX off-premise circuits; and radio circuits.

Credit Recommendation: In the lower division baccalaureate/associate degree category, 1 semester hour in Electronic Maintenance (6/82) (1/95).

Selling Skills (Market Administrator—Voice, Intercity, PBX)

Location: Philadelphia, PA.

Length: *Version 1:* 297 hours (9 weeks); *Version 2:* 468 hours (16 weeks).

Dates: *Version 1:* January 1968-April 1981; *Version 2:* September 1979-December 1982.

Objective: To introduce the student to basic marketing and sales techniques and to develop the student's selling skills.

Instruction: Major topics covered in the course are principles of business management and economics, pricing tariffs, credit, marketing organization, servicing, selling skills, and preparing proposals. Methods of instruction include videotape modules, field training, role playing, and program text.

Credit Recommendation: *Version 1:* In the lower division baccalaureate/associate degree category, 4 semester hours in Marketing (Selling Skills) (4/81). *Version 2:* In the lower division baccalaureate/associate degree category, 4 semester hours in Marketing (Selling Skills) (4/81).

Skillful Reading

Location: Various locations throughout the Bell Atlantic Region.

Length: 32 weeks; individualized instruction ranging from 1-3 hours per week.

Dates: *Version 1:* September 1975-November 1991; *Version 2:* December 1991-December 1994.

Objective: To improve students' reading comprehension.

Learning Outcome: Upon successful completion of this course, the student will be able to improve skills, knowledge, and understanding of contemporary literature; comprehend more fully and accurately materials; and read short stories and technical books.

Instruction: Major topics covered in the course are to understand the main idea, draw a conclusion, make a judgment, make an influence, recognize tone, understand characters, appreciate literary forms, and understand vocabulary.

Credit Recommendation: *Version 1:* In the vocational certificate category, 3 semester hours in Reading Comprehension or Basic Skills Development (5/80) (12/84). *Version 2:* In the lower division baccalaureate/associate degree category, 3 semester hours in Freshman English, Freshman Literature, or Reading Skills (12/91) (1/95).

Subscriber Carrier: Lightwave Design (NE31OIC)

Location: South Plainfield, NJ; Newark, NJ.

Length: 42 hours (6 days).

Dates: January 1981-December 1993.

Objective: To become familiar with lightwave principles and proper procedures for lightwave cable installation; and to provide information required to design a SLC-96 system.

Instruction: Major topics covered in the course provide familiarization with lightwave theory, lightguide cable manufacturing processes, lightguide cable characteristics and SLC-96 lightwave features; lightguide digital line design rules, lightguide bable grade selection, accounting codes, and documentation; and an understanding of an application of the SLC-96 system.

Credit Recommendation: In the lower division baccalaureate/associate degree category, 2 semester hours in Lightwave Cable Application or Electric Technology (1/85). **NOTE:** Credit recommendation applies when both modules are successfully completed.

T-Span Design

Location: Silver Spring, MD, South Plainfield, NJ, and on-site locations.

Length: 33 hours (1 week).

Dates: July 1991-December 1992.

Objective: To develop an understanding of T-1 Digital Line Design, and to determine power requirements, diagnostics design, and fault isolation requirements for T-1 facilities.

Learning Outcome: Upon successful completion of this course, the student will be able to understand loop technology evolution; understand the design and operation of T-1 facilities; and identify the components of a T-1 digital facility.

Instruction: Major topics covered in the course are history of digital technology, T-1 technology, operations of a T-1 facility and components; and design and maintenance of T-1 facilities. Methods of instruction include lecture, discussion, exercises, and case studies.

Credit Recommendation: In the lower division baccalaureate/associate degree category, 2 semester hours in Telecommunications or Information Systems (12/92) (1/95).

Teletype Fundamentals (328)

Location: South Plainfield, NJ.

Length: 45.5 hours (self-paced).

Dates: December 1973-December 1992.

Objective: To introduce teletypewriter apparatus and related gear.

Instruction: Major topics covered in the course are teletype signal make-up and selecting codes, transmitting devices, printer mechanisms, tape punches, electrical service units and call controls, motors, data sets, tools and equipment, and troubleshooting.

Credit Recommendation: In the vocational certificate category, 2 semester hours in Hardware Maintenance (6/82) (1/95).

Traffic Theory/Basic Network Design (Formerly Traffic Theory and Communications Engineering)

Location: Philadelphia, PA.

Length: 30 hours (5 days).

Dates: August 1980-December 1988.

Objective: To teach the student the statistical skills and traffic theories necessary for traffic management.

Instruction: Major topics covered in the course are principles of data collection concepts sampling, probability, and traffic theory. Methods of instruction include lecture, discussion, and laboratory exercises.

Credit Recommendation: In the upper division baccalaureate degree category, 1 semester hour in Statistics (4/81) (12/85).

Trunk Tester (1/1A SCC Trunk Tester; No. N686OSC)

Location: South Plainfield, NJ.

Length: Self-paced (approximately 65 hours).

Dates: August 1985-December 1993.

Objective: To familiarize students with the SCC trunk work station.

Instruction: Major topics covered in the course are SCC trunk work station and the SCC procedures as they apply to trunk installation/maintenance; and to perform basic trunk testing, trunk installation, and field maintenance.

Credit Recommendation: In the lower division baccalaureate/associate degree category, 1 semester hour in Telephone Switching or as a Technical Elective (6/86).

Underground Conduit Design and Administration (EN4031)

Location: South Plainfield, NJ; Newark, NJ.

Length: 35 hours (5 days).

Dates: September 1983-Present.

Objective: To present major aspects of engineering outside plant (OP) underground conduit systems.

Learning Outcome: Upon successful completion of this course, the student will be able to select appropriate piping material; economically size conduits; design manholes; design right of way routes for installation and maintenance safety; evaluate alternate routes; review final work prints for accuracy and standards compliance; and determine site restoration requirements.

Instruction: Major topics covered in the course are designed for first and second level managers involved in any portion of the O.P. engineer's job that in-cludes design, cost estimating, contract preparation, and control of expenditures for underground conduit jobs; emphasis will be placed on designing systems within the context of the approved standards; provide instruction in the following objectives: material selection; structure sizing; manhole sizing and construction; pulling-in-tension; design-for-safety; route selection; research, R/W, liaison, environment; field survey, work prints; restoration requirements, and special construction. Methods of instruction include lecture, discussion, classroom exercises, and lab exercises.

Credit Recommendation: In the lower division baccalaureate/associate degree category, 2 semester hours in Underground Conduit Design and Administration (1/85) (1/95).

Vocabulary Development (Wordpower Workshop)

Location: Various locations throughout the Bell Atlantic Region.

Length: *Version 1*: 32 weeks; individual sessions ranging from 1 to 3 hours per week; *Version 2*: 20-60 contact hours.

Dates: *Version 1:* September 1975-August 1988; *Version 2:* September 1988-Present.

Objective: To help students' improve their ability to increase their vocabulary at the seventh grade level through undergraduate freshman reading levels.

Learning Outcome: Upon successful completion of this course, the students will be able to add 600 to 2,700 words to their vocabulary; match at least 80% of the words presented exercising their synonyms and antonyms; and concentrate on vocabulary development.

Instruction: Major topics covered in the course are enhancement of the vocabulary resources; promotion of more effective communication in today's world; and improvement of vocabulary skills assessed on standardized or college admissions tests. Methods of instruction include self-study tests, tutorial assistance, lecture, programmed texts, and post-tests.

Credit Recommendation: In the lower division baccalaureate/associate degree category, 1 semester hour in Written Communications, Composition, or Basic English (5/80) (12/84) (12/91).

ENGINEERING TRAINING PROGRAM

The Engineering Training program conducts technical courses for managers in Pennsylvania, Delaware, New Jersey, Maryland, Virginia, West Virginia, and the District of Columbia.

Basic Accounting (Accounting for Equipment Engineers)

Location: Philadelphia Engineering Training Center.

Length: 33 hours (1 week).
Dates: January 1983-December 1992.
Objective: To explain basic telephone account concepts including assets, liabilities, retained earnings, operating revenues, and operating expense accounts.
Instruction: Major topics covered in the course are explaining various accounting terminology and concepts relating to equipment engineering.
Credit Recommendation: In the lower division baccalaureate/associate degree category, 2 semester hours in Principles of Accounting (12/85) (1/95).

Basic Engineering Economy

Location: Philadelphia Engineering Training Center.
Length: 33 hours (1 week).
Dates: February 1985-December 1992.
Objective: To identify the various types of cost studies and where they are used as well as identify common intangible factors and the effect they have on final decisions.
Instruction: Major topics covered in the course are use of time value factors, treatment of inflation, books, and tax depreciation.
Credit Recommendation: In the lower division baccalaureate/associate degree category, 2 semester hours in Engineering or Engineering Technology (12/85) (01/95). **NOTE:** Credit should be granted as an elective.

Capital Utilization Criteria (CUCRIT)

Location: Philadelphia Engineering Training Center.
Length: 33 hours (1 week).
Dates: January 1981-December 1993.
Objective: To explain and calculate various capital utilization criteria (CUCRIT). To input and run CUCRIT programs. To make reasonable decisions based upon CUCRIT.
Instruction: Major topics covered in the course are a "hands-on" course in advanced topics in Engineering Economy within problem solving and computer applications are stressed. Methods of instruction include a case study and extensive use of the computer which is incorporated into the instruction.
Credit Recommendation: In the lower division baccalaureate/associate degree or in the upper division baccalaureate degree category, 2 semester hours in Engineering or Engineering Technology (12/85). **NOTE:** Credit should be granted as an elective.

Concepts of Engineering for Nontechnical Majors (General Engineering)

Location: Philadelphia, PA.
Length: 66 hours (2 weeks).
Dates: January 1970-December 1993.
Objective: To expose the nontechnical student to the functions of engineering, including responsibilities, problems, and terminology.
Instruction: Major topics covered in the course are surveys basic switching, traffic engineering, transmission concepts, business information systems, construction programs, development engineering, effective writing, engineering economics, probability, rate engineering, sound, speech and hearing, special networks, special services, switching networks, and time-shared computers. Methods of instruction include lecture, discussion, and laboratory.
Credit Recommendation: In the lower division baccalaureate/associate degree category or in the upper division baccalaureate degree category, 3 semester hours in a Nontechnical Curriculum (8/78).

Digital Technology

Location: Philadelphia Engineering Training Center.
Length: 33 hours (1 week).
Dates: January 1982-December 1993.
Objective: To identify the systems and methods available for management of the digital network, and to identify interdisciplinary issues that must be resolved when introducing digital technology.
Instruction: Major topics covered in the course are instruction on basic digital theory and terminology; digital switching machines; and digital interoffice facilities equipment.
Credit Recommendation: In the lower division baccalaureate/associate degree category, 2 semester hours in Electrical Technology or Electronic Technology (12/85).

Economic Study Module (EN5110)

Location: South Plainfield, PA, Silver Spring, MD and on-site locations.
Length: 20 hours (3 days).
Dates: January 1986-Present.
Objective: To become knowledgeable about the basic ESM menus, create and modify a study including general economic parameters and cost data; and to generate and analyze ESM and CUCRIT reports.
Learning Outcome: Upon successful completion of this course, the student will be able to prepare input for the ESM problem file, and user cost and data file; and to analyze the output report and select the best alternative.
Instruction: Major topics covered in the course are basic ESM menus and masks; creation and modification of an ESM study; modification general economic parameters and cost data; generation and analysis of ESM and CUCRIT reports. Methods of instruction include lecture, and instructor-led student interaction with ESM software.
Credit Recommendation: In the upper division baccalaureate degree category, 1 semester hour in Engineering Economics, Planning and Operations, Industrial Engineering, or 1 semester hour in a self-study Database course (12/92).

Engineering Economy

Location: Philadelphia, PA.
Length: 66 hours (2 weeks).
Dates: January 1970-December 1988.
Objective: To provide the information necessary to perform a complete engineering economy study.
Instruction: Major topics covered in the course are accounting, mathematics and money, depreciation, division of revenue, inflation, accelerated depreciation, investment tax credit, and study techniques. Methods of instruction include lecture, workshop, and laboratory.
Credit Recommendation: In the lower division baccalaureate/associate degree category or in the upper division baccalaureate degree category, 3 semester hours in Engineering or Engineering Technology (8/78). **NOTE:** Credit should be granted as an elective.

Feeder Administration

Location: Philadelphia, PA.
Length: 60 hours (2 weeks).
Dates: May 1979-December 1993.
Objective: To provide knowledge and skills in the application of existing economic, electronic, and feeder wire routing programs for the purpose of developing plans for optimum expanded phone usage.
Instruction: Major topics covered in the course are appropriate economic, electronic, and feeder wire programs; commitment strategies; and monitoring and decision studies. Methods of instruction include case studies, lectures, discussion, and laboratories.

Credit Recommendation: In the lower division baccalaureate/associate degree category, 2 semester hours in Electrical Technology or Electronic Technology (4/81).

General Transmission Concepts

Location: Philadelphia Engineering Training Center

Length: 76 hours (2 weeks).

Dates: June 1983-December 1993.

Objective: To examine the general design requirements for a telephone system using analog and digital carrier and radio or light wave systems.

Instruction: Major topics covered in the course are basic telephone equipment operations, design parameters, metallic facilities, introduction to carrier systems, and transmission of data.

Credit Recommendation: In the lower division baccalaureate/associate degree category, 4 semester hours in Electrical Technology (12/85).

Interoffice Facilities Current Planning (EN2100)

Location: Philadelphia Engineering Training Center.

Length: 40 hours (1 week).

Dates: February 1983-December 1993.

Objective: To develop a current facility and equipment plan.

Instruction: Major topics covered in the course are developing and maintaining a planning model, identifying options for relief, and appropriate support documentation. Methods of instruction include lecture, discussion, and workshop.

Credit Recommendation: In the lower division baccalaureate/associate degree category, 2 semester hours in Electrical Technology, Electronic Technology, or Telecommunications (12/85) (12/92).

Light Wave Design (Fiber Optics Design)

Location: Philadelphia Engineering Training Center.

Length: 34 hours (1 week).

Dates: November 1984-June 1991.

Objective: To provide details required to prepare an engineering job order for digital loop carrier on fiber.

Instruction: Major topics covered in the course are how to prepare fiber cable work prints specifying remote terminal/fiber hub configurations, hardwired equipment, plug-in equipment, and cable details.

Credit Recommendation: In the lower division baccalaureate/associate degree category, 2 semester hours in Electrical Technology or Electronic Technology (12/85).

Loop Electronics Design

Location: Philadelphia Engineering Training Center.

Length: 36 hours (1 week).

Dates: January 1982-June 1991.

Objective: To be able to provide details required to prepare an engineering job order for digital loop carrier systems.

Instruction: Major topics covered in the course are determining power requirements for remote terminals, specifying types and locations for terminal plug-ins, and determining splice locations.

Credit Recommendation: In the lower division baccalaureate/associate degree category, 2 semester hours in Electrical Technology or Electronic Technology (12/85).

Loop Electronics Planning

Location: Philadelphia, PA.

Length: 37.5 hours (5 days).

Dates: March 1981-December 1993.

Objective: To provide the student with the tools to make decisions and develop plans for phone company feeder line relief.

Instruction: Major topics covered in the course are economic analysis for alternate feeder designs, techniques for developing decisions, and plans for optimum feeder system. Methods of instruction include lecture, discussion, and case studies.

Credit Recommendation: In the lower division baccalaureate/associate degree category, 1 semester hour in Electrical Technology or Electronic Technology (4/81).

LROPP (Long-Range Outside P)

Location: Philadelphia, PA.

Length: 64 hours (2 weeks).

Dates: September 1979-December 1993.

Objective: To provide the student with the economic and technical skills and knowledge necessary to develop long-range plans for phone company wire centers.

Instruction: Major topics covered in the course are tools involved in facilities, forecasting, and planning necessary for phone company wire center development. Methods of instruction include lecture, discussion, and classroom exercises.

Credit Recommendation: In the lower division baccalaureate/associate degree category, 2 semester hours in Electrical Technology or Electronic Technology as a technical elective (4/81).

Mobile Radio Systems Engineering (MRSE)

Location: Philadelphia, PA.

Length: 124 hours (3 weeks).

Dates: April 1980-December 1993.

Objective: To develop the necessary skills for the design of two-way mobile radio systems and one-way radio paging systems.

Instruction: Major topics covered in the course are frequency, site, receiver, antenna, and transmitter power selection procedures; the fundamentals of co-channel and intermodulation interference; and study of signaling systems, remote transmitter control, coupling loss between antennas, and site noise tests. Methods of instruction include lectures, discussion, and laboratories.

Credit Recommendation: In the lower division baccalaureate/associate degree category, 3 semester hours as a technical elective, or in the upper division baccalaureate degree category, 3 semester hours as a free elective (4/81).

Time Share Cable Sizing Program ALLOC II, Economic Feeder Admin and Relief, Economic Alternative Selection OSP[NE060IIC, NE130IIC, NE080IIC, NE040IIC]

Location: South Plainfield, NJ; Newark, NJ.

Length: 56 hours (8 days).

Dates: January 1981-December 1993.

Objective: To enable the student to use TICS program, to create FAS tables and use ALLOC and computer program, to prepare for and conduct an EFAR analysis, and to use the EASOP program to test the economic impact of alternative plans.

Instruction: Major topics covered in the course are use of TICS program to develop economic cable sizing for feeder cable relief; next module includes information needed to write the necessary file and run a program using the ALLOC computer program to produce initial run and to analyze the initial output; following module covers EFAR analysis to determine optimum fill and relief and proper utilization of feeder route in accord with NJB practices; final module covers gathering necessary information, developing comparable alternatives to be tested, and running the EASOP program and evaluating output of the program.

Credit Recommendation: In the lower division baccalaureate/associate degree category, 2 semester hours in Engineering Economics (1/85).

nstructor Training Workshop (MS0401)

Location: Philadelphia, PA.
Length: 25 hours (4 days).
Dates: September 1970-Present.
Objective: To prepare teachers to use a variety of instructional techniques to enhance the teaching/learning process.
Learning Outcome: Upon successful completion of this course, the student will be able to define learning theory; describe instructional methodology; write learning objectives; and use visual aids in a classroom environment.
Instruction: Major topics covered in the course are learning theory, instructional methodology, writing learning objectives, and the use of visual aids. Methods of instruction include group discussions and simulations.
Credit Recommendation: In the upper division baccalaureate degree category, 1 semester hour in Education (8/78) (12/92).

INFORMATION SYSTEMS EDUCATION CENTER

Information Systems Education Center trains employees involved in data systems work and provides education in many disciplines concerned with the development of primarily mainframe computer-based data systems. Courses offered range from basic programmer training to operating systems and system analyst training.

Advanced UNIX-Using the Shell (IS05-2550)

Location: Silver Spring, MD; Freehold, NJ; Philadelphia, PA.
Length: 80 hours (2 weeks).
Dates: April 1991-December 1996.
Objective: To provide students with the concepts and skills required to develop a customized UNIX environment, and to develop and debug shell programs (scripts).
Learning Outcome: Upon successful completion of this course, the student will be able to create, customize, and debug shell scripts (programs) using shell command options and variables.
Instruction: Major topics covered in the course are shell built-in commands, shell processes, logical constructs, signal handling, pipelines, positional parameters, special substitution, and sed and debugging aids. Methods of instruction include lecture, lab exercises, and an overall programming project.
Credit Recommendation: In the lower division baccalaureate/associate degree category, 1 semester hour in UNIX System Tools or Computer Science elective (12/92).

An Introduction to Time Share and BASIC Language Programming
1. Time Share BASIC
2. Introduction to Honeywell Time Share

Location: C&P Telephone Company's Information Systems Education Center, Silver Spring, MD; and on-site work locations.
Length: 1. 18 hours (3 days); 2. 23.5 hours (4 days).
Dates: February 1983-December 1992.
Objective: To introduce students to time sharing commands, operations, editors, and file structures. In the "BASIC" programming portion, students design, code, and execute programs.
Instruction: Major topics covered in the course are BASIC programming language; functions of current/collector file, system commands, and subsequent operation; use of the text editor to create and modify files; and understanding the file management supervisor. Methods of instruction include video presentation, lecture, labs, and discussion combined with hands-on terminal usage.
Credit Recommendation: In the lower division baccalaureate/associate degree category, 1 semester hour in Data Processing (12/85) (1/95). **NOTE:** Students must take both courses to receive credit.

C Language Programming
Module A: Basic C Programming (IS10-1360)
Module B: Advanced "C" Programming (IS10-1370)

Location: Silver Spring, MD; Freehold, NJ; Philadelphia, PA.
Length: *Module A*: 32.5 hours (5 days); *Module B*: 32.5 hours (5 days).
Dates: November 1992-December 1996.
Objective: To present the basic structure, syntax, and all essential constructs of the "C" programming language along with advanced programming facilities available in "C".
Learning Outcome: Upon successful completion of this course, the student will be able to write, execute, and debug "C" language programs; understand program flow constructs, storage classes, pointers to data types, and standard I/0 libraries; and understand memory management issues and linked lists.
Instruction: Major topics covered in the course are basic structures, syntax and all essential constructs of the "C" language, and advanced facilities available in "C" language with attention to portability issues. Methods of instruction include lecture, discussion, and lab exercises.
Credit Recommendation: In the lower division baccalaureate/associate degree category, 4 semester hours in "C" Language, Computer Science, or Computer Information Systems (12/92). **NOTE**: Student must successfully complete Modules A and B to receive the credit recommendation.

C Programming

Location: C&P Telephone Company's Information Systems Education Center, Silver Spring, MD.
Length: 24 hours (4 days).
Dates: February 1983-December 1996.
Objective: To enable a student to develop, maintain, or modify C language programs.
Instruction: Major topics covered in the course are C language including basics, time share, basic structures and syntax, program design, arrays, pointers, structured programming concepts, file control, and I/O processing.
Credit Recommendation: In the lower division baccalaureate/associate degree category, 1 semester hour in Data Processing (12/85).

Information Management System (IMS)

Location: Silver Spring, MD; Philadelphia, PA; Freehold, NJ.
Length: 62 hours (2 weeks).
Dates: July 1978-December 1996.
Objective: To introduce students with programming experience to data base concepts and IMS data base management system; to develop skills in access methods of data bases; to process data stored in an IMS data base, and to retrieve data from online systems.
Learning Outcome: Upon successful completion of this course, the student will be able to understand the basic concepts and terms used to define IMS/VS DBMS structure; compare and contrast various IMS access methods; discuss a transaction manager data communications environment; describe the various database utilities and their use; use the JCL required to

employ IMS programming; and program IMS in batch and teleprocessing modes.

Instruction: Major topics covered in the course are Information Management System overview; batch processing and teleprocessing; overview unit emphasizes the building of data base and various access methods used; batch unit stresses the use of Data Language One pointers, and command codes; and teleprocessing unit emphasizes message formats, program structure, calls, and conversational processing. Methods of instruction include computer programming exercises that are evaluated.

Credit Recommendation: In the upper division baccalaureate degree category, 3 semester hours in Data Base Management (12/79) (12/84) (1/95).

Initial Programming Skills for MVS (ISO1-5000)

Location: Silver Spring, MD; Freehold, NJ; Philadelphia, PA.

Length: 562 hours (15 weeks).

Dates: February 1992-Present.

Objective: To prepare students for entry-level programming positions.

Learning Outcome: Upon successful completion of this course, the student will be able to analyze a problem, develop an appropriate algorithm, use proper syntax to code the algorithms; and the programming language used is COBOL in an MVS environment.

Instruction: Major topics covered in the course are data processing, concepts, data representation, programming structures and design, introduction to MVS and TSO/ISPF, introduction to JCL and advanced JCL, COBOL programming, software testing and system maintenance. Methods of instruction include lecture, programming exercises, laboratory, and video.

Credit Recommendation: In the lower division baccalaureate/associate degree category, 4 semester hours in COBOL and 4 semester hours in Introduction of Information Processing for a total of 8 semester hours; also applicable to Com-puter Science or CIS (12/92).

Introduction to SQL and Sybase (Introduction to SQL-I555-0320; and Fast Track to Sybase I555-0350)

Location: Silver Spring, MD; Philadelphia, PA; Freehold, NJ.

Length: 35 hours (5 days).

Dates: January 1992-Present.

Objective: To introduce the basic concepts and commands of SQL and its application to the client/server architecture in Sybase.

Learning Outcome: Upon successful completion of this course, the student will be able to perform basic retrieval and modification of databases using Sybase SQL; perform Sybase SQL joins and subqueries; develop and run queries; create databases and objects; manipulate data and programs using Transact-SQL; write and employ stored procedures; and backup and restore databases.

Instruction: Major topics covered in the course are basic concepts and terms; basic data retrieval techniques; organizing data and summarizing results; joins, subqueries and unions; data definition and manipulation; client/server architecture and the SQL server; creating databases and objects; retrieving, modifying data, and programming in Transact-SQL; data control statements; stored procedures; transaction management; backup and restore; and open clients and open servers. Methods of instruction include lecture, discussion, classroom exercises, classroom participation, and successful completion of database exercises.

Credit Recommendation: In the lower division baccalaureate/associate degree category, 2 semester hours in Database Management, Data Processing, or Information Systems (1/95). **NOTE:** To achieve 2 semester hours credit, both courses must be completed).

Introduction to UNIX Fundamentals (IS05-2500)

Location: Silver Spring, MD; Freehold, NJ; Philadelphia, PA.

Length: 40 hours (5 days).

Dates: March 1991-Present.

Objective: To introduce the student to the UNIX operating system and environment.

Learning Outcome: Upon successful completion of this course, the student will be able to have a beginning knowledge of the UNIX Operating System.

Instruction: Major topics covered in the course are login procedures, basic file and directory manipulation commands, UNIX file system hierarchy, vi editor, file and directory permissions, file transfer, and shell programming topics. Methods of instruction include lecture, discussion, and hands-on exercises.

Credit Recommendation: In the vocational certificate category, 2 semester hours in Introduction to UNIX (12/92).

Programmer Basic Training

Location: Silver Spring, MD.

Length: 472.5 hours (13 weeks).

Dates: June 1978-December 1992.

Objective: To introduce students with no programming experience to the physical structure, major concepts, and application of computers; to develop skills in designing and implementing structured COBOL programs and required documentations, and to prepare students to create and modify JCL to execute programs and procedures.

Instruction: Major topics covered in the course are data processing concepts; data representation, structured programming, design, implementation, and case problems; COBOL; JCL; utilities; the COBOL unit of the course emphasizes understanding diagnostic messages; and making appropriate corrections to COBOL case, and debugging. Methods of instruction include written tests, case studies, lecture, discussion, workshop, and independent study.

Credit Recommendation: In the lower division baccalaureate/associate degree category or in the upper division baccalaureate degree category, 6 semester hours in Business, Computer Science, Engineering, Information Science, or Technology (12/79) (12/84) (1/95). **NOTE:** Students may also be awarded credit recommendations in the following manner: in the lower division baccalaureate/associate degree category, 3 semester hours in Introduction to Data Processing; in the upper division baccalaureate degree category, 3 semester hours in Programming; in the lower division baccalaureate/associate degree category, 3 semester hours in Introduction to Computer Systems.

Programmer Basic Training COBOL

Location: Philadelphia, PA.

Length: 473 hours (13 weeks).

Dates: February 1977-December 1992.

Objective: To introduce students with no programming experience to the physical structure and major concepts of a computer; to develop skills in designing and implementing structured COBOL programs and required documentation; and to prepare students to create and modify JCL to execute programs and procedures.

Instruction: Major topics covered in the course are data processing concepts; data representation; structured programming, design, implementation, and case problems; COBOL; JCL; utilities; cataloged procedures; the COBOL unit of the course emphasizes understanding diagnostic messages, making appropriate corrections to COBOL code, debugging, modularity, the SORT verb, and modular debugging. Methods of instruction include written tests, case studies, lecture, discussion, workshop, and independent study.

Credit Recommendation: In the lower division baccalaureate/associate degree category or in the upper division baccalaureate degree category, 6 semester hours in Computer Sciences, Engineering, Information Sciences, or Technology (8/78) (1/95).

Programmer Workshop I

Location: Silver Spring, MD.

Length: 32.5 hours (1 week).

Dates: February 1979-December 1992.

Objective: To introduce systems application.

Instruction: Major topics covered in the course are linkage editor functions, IBM time sharing option, and C&P conventions for JCL. Methods of instruction include lecture and laboratory activities.

Credit Recommendation: In the upper division baccalaureate degree category, 1 semester hour in Information Systems or Systems Application (5/80) (12/84) (1/95).

Software Testing Methodology and Techniques
Module A: Software Testing and Overview (IS80-1000)
Module B: Elements of Testing/Unit Testing (IS80-2000)
Module C: Advanced Testing Topics (IS80-3000)

Location: Silver Spring, MD; Madison and Freehold, NJ; Philadelphia, PA.

Length: *Module A:* 6.5 hours (1 day), *Module B:* 13 hours (2 days), *Module C:* 13 hours (2 days).

Dates: May 1992-Present.

Objective: To present levels, types, techniques, roles, and responsibilities required in software testing.

Learning Outcome: Upon successful completion of this course, the student will be able to define levels of testing, select appropriate test metrics, identify test deliverables, and generate test cases.

Instruction: Major topics covered in the course are general view of testing in terms of SDLC, all levels of testing deliverables, test planning, walk throughs and inspections, and system testing objectives. Methods of instruction include lecture, discussion, role playing, and laboratories.

Credit Recommendation: In the upper division baccalaureate degree category, 2 semester hours in Computer Information Systems or Systems Analysis (12/92).

NOTE: Students must successfully complete Modules A, B, and C to receive credit recommendation.

Structured Systems Analysis

Location: Silver Spring, MD; Madison and Freehold, NJ; Philadelphia, PA.

Length: 35 hours (5 days).

Dates: May 1992-Present.

Objective: To introduce the student to concepts and use of structured analysis and design techniques, and the development of software systems.

Learning Outcome: Upon successful completion of this course, the student will be able to apply structured analysis and design techniques to all phases of SDLC (System Development Life Cycle).

Instruction: Major topics covered in the course are methodology related to product life cycle, process-oriented and data-oriented analysis and design techniques, use of both logical and physical process models, perform event modeling, utilize appropriate data definition techniques, interpret a data model, and discuss model/design evaluation criteria. Methods of instruction include lecture, discussion, and lab exercises.

Credit Recommendation: In the upper division baccalaureate degree category, 3 semester hours in Structured System Analysis and Design, Computer Science, or Computer Information Systems (CIS) (12/92).

LEADERSHIP DEVELOPMENT

The Leadership Development program offers clients several activities to improve their organizations' effectiveness. These include performance improvements, organization development, team building, communications, planning, management education courses to enhance managerial skills.

Basic Telephone Accounting

Location: Silver Spring, MD.

Length: 35 hours (1 week).

Dates: December 1975-December 1993.

Objective: To understand the nature and purpose of accounting.

Instruction: Major topics covered in the course are use of the account to record and accumulate increases and decreases in the items that appear on the financial reports; the processes employed in recording financial data; the eight-step accounting process; and application of principles and processes of telephone accounting in preparing financial reports for a small telephone company. Methods of instruction include lecture with visual aids, slide/tape presentations, workbook problems and lesson tests, instructor-led discussions, and case problems involving operations of a small telephone company.

Credit Recommendation: In the lower division baccalaureate/associate degree category, 2 semester hours in Principles of Accounting (12/79) (12/84).

Cost and Accounting Systems (DOPAC Disk Oriented Property and Cost [2664])

Location: Silver Spring, MD.

Length: 44.5 hours (5 days).

Dates: December 1982-December 1988.

Objective: To enable the student to define the overall processing performed on data provided and evaluate when incorrect processing has occurred; identify how transactions are batched, balanced, controlled, generated, corrected, posted, and reported within the system process; ensure reasonably complete and accurate financial reporting; and evaluate and respond appropriately to feedback received from system users.

Instruction: Major topics covered in the course are a basic overview of the inputs, processes, outputs, and interfaces of a cost accounting system. Methods of instruction include lecture, visual aids, group discussions, student materials/reference binders, case problems, and group exercises.

Credit Recommendation: In the upper division baccalaureate degree category, 2 semester hours in Accounting (8/85).

Data Management for Switching Networks (Data Management No. 5 Crossbar [DM-5])

Location: Silver Spring, MD.

Length: 90 hours (2 weeks).

Dates: November 1978-December 1993.

Objective: To enable the student to validate and analyze data and suggest proper solutions for all problems.

Instruction: Major topics covered in the course are validation and analysis of the traffic data for switching purposes; the interpretation and application of data directed at each system component including equipment operation, register scoring sequence, validation of data, and analysis of data; problem analysis and solutions including dial tone speed, incoming failure to match, overflows; and equipment irregularity. Methods of instruction include lecture, workshops, flow charts, simulations, classroom and problem-solving exercises.

Credit Recommendation: In the lower division baccalaureate/associate degree category, 3 semester hours in Electrical Engineering (12/79) (12/84).

Designing and Conducting Role Play

Location: Various locations throughout C&P Telephone Company business area.

Length: 22.5 hours (3 days).

Dates: August 1978-December 1993.

Objective: To enable participants to understand different role-play concepts and techniques; to improve skills in writing, conducting, and critiquing role plays; and to apply role-play knowledge and skill to their own specific uses.

Instruction: Major topics covered in the course are developing, designing, and conducting a variety of role plays. Methods of instruction include role playing.

Credit Recommendation: In the vocational certificate category, 1 semester hour in Communication Skills (12/79) (12/84) (1/95).

Developing Additional Managerial Skills

Location: Silver Spring, MD.

Length: 51 hours (1 week).

Dates: June 1971-June 1980.

Objective: To develop and reinforce an understanding of managerial styles and interpersonal skills to promote the growth of management.

Instruction: Major topics covered in the course are application of theories about managerial functions, interpersonal relationships, and human development in organizations. Methods of instruction include discussion, lecture, and classroom exercises.

Credit Recommendation: In the upper division baccalaureate degree category, 3 semester hours in Business Administration, Educational Administration, or Social Sciences (12/79). **NOTE:** Students receiving credit for this course should not receive credit for Developing Managers.

Developing Managers

Location: Silver Spring, MD.

Length: 51 hours (1 week).

Dates: June 1971-December 1993.

Objective: To develop an understanding of managerial styles and interpersonal skills to promote the growth of newly hired or newly promoted management personnel.

Instruction: Major topics covered in the course are introductory application of theories about managerial functions, interpersonal relationships, and human development in organizations. Methods of instruction include discussion, lecture, and classroom exercises.

Credit Recommendation: In the upper division baccalaureate degree category, 3 semester hours in Business Administration, Educational Administration, or Social Sciences (12/79) (12/84). **NOTE:** Students receiving credit for this course should not receive credit for Developing Additional Managerial Skills.

Developing Managers (G199AIC and G199BIC)

Location: South Plainfield, NJ, and other locations throughout the state.

Length: 35 hours (5 days).

Dates: January 1974-December 1993.

Objective: To provide managers new to the company or employees newly promoted to management with a knowledge and understanding of their new role.

Learning Outcome: Upon successful completion of this course, the participant will be able to use the management appraisal process; develop clear, measurable job objectives; focus on the attributes of competent management; and define managerial roles as they relate to corporate objectives.

Instruction: Major topics covered in the course are designed to provide a smooth transition into management and help new management employees better understand their roles as managers of the business. Methods of instruction include guest speakers from various departments, discussion, role-play, and trainer observation. Participants are evaluated by this discussion and role play to assure that they meet course objectives.

Credit Recommendation: In the lower division baccalaureate/associate degree category, 1 semester hour in Management Development (6/81) (8/86).

Dynamics of Management
a. Developing Managers (G199AIC and G199BIC)
b. Managing the Work (G759OIC)
c. Problem Solving (G763OIC)
d. Situational Leadership (G763OIC)
e. Time Management (G190OIC)

Location: South Plainfield, NJ, and other locations throughout the state.

Length: a. 35 hours (5 days); b. 21 hours (3 days); c. 7 hours (1 day); d. 14 hours (2 days); e. 7 hours (1 day).

Dates: April 1976-December 1993.

Objective: To enable participants to understand their role as manager, to manage work flow, to have a systematic approach for solving problems, to become effective with the situational leadership approach, and to learn practical techniques to manage time and gain control of work.

Learning Outcome: Upon successful completion of this series of modules, the student will be able to: (a) *Developing Managers*—develop clear, measurable job objectives; focus on the attributes of competent management; and use skillful communication to enhance managerial style; (b) *Managing the Work*—plan and organize work more effectively and prepare written plans, checkpoint logs, and work schedules; (c) *Problem Solving*—accurately define a problem and determine if it is worth solving, and select the most efficient solution to the problem; (d) *Situational Leadership*—diagnose the readiness of followers to do a specific task or function, and vary leadership styles depending on the situation and the development level of the follower; and (e) *Time Management*—set long, and short term goals, and handle paperwork, deal with procrastination, and manage interruptions.

Instruction: Major topics covered in the course are a sequence of modules that provide an introduction to the role of the manager at New Jersey Bell; in addition to the overview of a corporate manager, the modules focus on specific areas, managing work, problem solving, situational leadership, and time management; the modules clarify the issues involved in each of these types and present a variety of methods of response; and the modules are presented only to those in managerial positions and use extensive class exercises. Methods of instruction include individual activities, projects, or presentations are employed by the instructor to determine that participants are meeting course objectives.

Credit Recommendation: In the lower division baccalaureate/associate degree category, 5 semester hours in Dynamics of Management (8/86) (1/95).

Effective Communicating
a. Effective Communications Workshop (G761OIC)
b. Effective Reading (G212OIC)
c. Effective Writing (G197OIC)

Location: South Plainfield, NJ, and other locations throughout the state.

Length: a. 14 hours (2 days); b. 14 hours (2 days); c. 14 hours (2 days).

Dates: January 1976-December 1992.

Objective: To enable participants to communicate in a more effective and businesslike manner whether reading, writing, or speaking in public.

Learning Outcome: Upon successful completion of these courses, the participant will be able to organize a presentation quickly and effectively; give talks confidently and convincingly; determine a purpose and objective for reading; adjust reading rate and technique based on the purpose; organize writing logically; use simple, clear, precise language; and analyze the readability of letters.

Instruction: Major topics covered in these courses are presenting a speech that is videotaped and subsequently critiqued; also pre-testing and post-testing to measure reading speed and comprehension; and finally, students are required to demonstrate the principles of business writing by applying proper techniques to make sure their writing is clear, concise, and understandable.

Credit Recommendation: In the lower division baccalaureate/associate degree category, 3 semester hours in Effective Communications (8/86).

Effective Oral Presentations (ME0605)
Oral Communication Skills

Location: *Version 1:* Various locations throughout the Bell Atlantic Region. *Version 2:* Various locations throughout the Bell Atlantic Region.

Length: *Version 1*: 28.5 hours (3 days); *Version 2*: 15 hours (2 days).

Dates: *Version 1:* April 1978-November 1991; *Version 2:* December 1991-Present.

Objective: *Version 1:* To enable participants to prepare and present several oral presentations. *Version 2:* To enable participants to speak in a manner that demonstrates management of language and knowledge of audience composition.

Learning Outcome: Upon successful completion of this course, the student will learn to make effective oral presentations in front of large or small audiences; understand the importance of a high self-esteem relative to oral presentation; organize thoughts into spoken words; hold the interest of an audience; participate in dialogue with audience after presentation; and use visual aids to enhance presentation.

Instruction: *Version 1:* Major topics covered in the course are the criteria for a good oral presentation and identifies future developmental needs in oral skills for individual students. Methods of instruction include discussion, classroom presentations, and films. *Version 2:* Major topics covered in the course are brain power, knowing self, overcoming fears, organizing subjects, knowing audience; and leaving positive impressions. Methods of instruction include lectures, videos, and extemporaneous discussions.

Credit Recommendation: In the vocational certificate category, 1 semester hour in Speech (12/79) (12/84) (12/91).

First Level Curriculum: Managing Performance

Location: C&P Learning Center, Silver Spring, MD.

Length: 30 hours (4 days).

Dates: July 1982-December 1993.

Objective: To enable the student to apply and implement such developmental processes as performance feedback, coaching, career counseling, establishing a motivating atmosphere, and handling formal and informal communication.

Instruction: Major topics covered in the course provide new first-level managers with an organized process for conducting work-related discussions with their employees including ways to plan and follow up on these discussions; stresses the use of appropriate communication skills; the provision of a motivating climate; and the removal of roadblocks to effective performance. Methods of instruction include lecture and discussion.

Credit Recommendation: In the lower division baccalaureate/associate degree category, 1 semester hour in Human Relations or Introductory Management (12/84).

Fundamentals of Revenue Accounting

Location: C&P Learning Center, Silver Spring, MD.

Length: 32 hours (5 days).

Dates: December 1984-December 1993.

Objective: To provide students with the fundamental principles and concepts of revenue accounting.

Instruction: Major topics covered in the course are general revenue accounting concepts including accrual accounting, estimates of uncollectability, billing, journalization, source documents, transaction management, and preparation of the associated financial reports. Methods of instruction include lecture, discussion, and classroom exercises.

Credit Recommendation: In the lower division baccalaureate/associate degree category, 2 semester hours in Principles of Accounting, or in the upper division baccalaureate degree category, 1 semester hour in Intermediate Accounting, or as an elective in the upper division baccalaureate degree category, 2 semester hours in Accounting (12/84).

Initial Management Training (113)

Location: Harrisburg, Philadelphia, and Pittsburgh, PA.

Length: 32 hours (1 week).

Dates: January 1969-January 1984.

Objective: To identify the functions of management, their applications, and the relationship of managerial behavior to the work situation.

Instruction: Major topics covered in the course are the initial management principles, behavior, work situation, basic communications, and role playing. Methods of instruction include group discussion, lectures, and simulations.

Credit Recommendation: In the lower division baccalaureate/associate degree category, 1 semester hour in Management (8/78).

Initial Supervisory Training (114)

Location: Harrisburg, Philadelphia, and Pittsburgh, PA.

Length: 32 hours (1 week).

Dates: January 1969-January 1984.

Objective: To identify attitudes and behavior appropriate to a supervisor's position and to enhance the supervisor's relationship with others.

Instruction: Major topics covered in the course are decision-making processes, motivation, behavior and attitudes, management by objectives, and interrelations. Methods of instruction include group discussion, lectures, and simulations.

Credit Recommendation: In the lower division baccalaureate/associate degree category, 1 semester hour in Management (8/78).

Instructor Training Workshop

Location: South Plainfield, NJ.

Length: 31 hours (5 days).

Dates: June 1976-December 1993.

Objective: To familiarize students with principles, methods, and techniques of instruction to increase their effectiveness as trainers and instructors; to enable students to analyze their own performances through the use of television recording and replay; and to aid students in applying principles of learning.

Instruction: Major topics covered in the course are an examination of the relationship between learners, trainers, and topic; exploration of the effectiveness of the trainer and methods of training; analysis of effective organization of information; and examination of methods to motivate learners. Methods of instruction include lectures, case studies, observable behavior, and mastery of tests.

Credit Recommendation: In the lower division baccalaureate/associate degree category, 1 semester hour in Workshop Leadership Methods (6/81) (12/93).

Introduction to Management (First Level Curriculum—Managing Performance)

Location: Various locations throughout the C&P Telephone Company network.

Length: 30 hours (4 days).

Dates: July 1982-December 1993.

Objective: To provide students with an introduction to management techniques with an emphasis on managing performance.

Instruction: Major topics covered in the course are specific management techniques including employee motivation, performance standards, performance appraisal, and career counseling. Methods of instruction include lecture, discussion, and role playing.

Credit Recommendation: In the lower division baccalaureate/associate degree category, 2 semester hours in Basic Management (12/85).

Introduction to Property and Cost Accounting

Location: C&P Learning Center, Silver Spring, MD.

Length: *Version 1:* 35 hours (1 week); *Version 2:* 37.5 hours (5 days).

Dates: *Version 1:* December 1972-February 1984; *Version 2:* March 1984-December 1993.

Objective: To provide the student with a basic knowledge and understanding of the theory behind each major function of the Property and Cost Office, and a working knowledge of telephone plant accounts and how they affect the financial and productivity reports.

Instruction: *Version 1:* Major topics covered in the course are the accounting process used in classifying, recording, summarizing, and reporting financial transactions involving the addition, retirement, and maintenance of telephone plant accounts. Methods of instruction include instructor-led lectures, visual aids, student case problems, discussions, and tests. *Version 2:* Major topics covered in the course are reviewing basic telephone accounting; defines the nature and purpose of property and cost accounting; defines the concept of net plant; provides for the integration of information flow, the allocation of personnel costs, the use of overhead accounts, and preparation of managerial reports. Methods of instruction include lecture, discussion, and classroom exercises.

Credit Recommendation: In the lower division baccalaureate/associate degree category, 2 semester hours in Cost Accounting, Managerial Accounting, or Principles of Accounting (12/84).

Investment in Excellence (ME0809) New Age Thinking (G764OIC)

Location: Various locations throughout the Bell Atlantic Region.

Length: 15 hours (2 days).

Dates: April 1983-December 1993.

Objective: To assist students in identifying and achieving personal goals, financial goals, spiritual goals, corporate goals, and group goals.

Learning Outcome: Upon successful completion of this course, the student will be able to develop personal growth and excellence; align self-image with professional goals; identify ways to reduce stress and relax; make affirmations for increased performance; motivate self and others; make meaningful changes; and plan for success.

Instruction: Major topics covered in the course are possibility thinking; process of thought, self-image, habits and attitudes, formation of self-image; self-esteem and performance, maintaining self and others; and philosophy of goal-setting and guide to goal-setting. Methods of instruction include lecture, discussion, and classroom exercises.

Credit Recommendation: In the upper division baccalaureate degree category, 1 semester hour in Actualized Manager, Management Psychology, New Age Thinking, or Corporate Culture (8/86) (12/91).

Job Study Workshop

Location: Silver Spring, MD.

Length: 32 hours (1 week).

Dates: May 1978-December 1993.

Objective: To enable the student to perform a content analysis of documents used in job performance.

Instruction: Major topics covered in the course are conducting a job study interview; recording, referencing, and summarizing data; flow chart work activities; and analysis for completeness; and students must demonstrate mastery of subject by providing group outputs that conform to programmed results. Methods of instruction include lecture, discussions, classroom exercises, interviews, videotapes, and flow charts.

Credit Recommendation: In the upper division baccalaureate degree category, 1 semester hour in Personnel (12/79) (12/84).

Leadership Challenge Development Program (Leaders of Managers and Leaders of Organizations)

Location: Aresty Institute of Executive Education, The Wharton School, University of Pennsylvania, Philadelphia, PA.

Length: 51 hours (5.5 days) plus 24 hours (3 days) of post review and assessment.

Dates: December 1992-Present.

Objective: To develop a practical understanding of the leadership requirements for integrating strategic initiatives with functional priorities. To enhance participants' ability to focus their organizations strategically and to facilitate team involvement that maximizes employee contribution and commitment.

Learning Outcome: Upon successful completion of this course, the student will be able to identify major challenges and skills required to play a leadership role in world class companies; to understand the complexities of managing massive change in large scale work systems; to facilitate high performance change management teams; to develop an integrated management approach that includes customer focus, quality orientation, competitive marketing, and financial performance; to integrate strategic initiatives with functional priorities; and to operate as general corporate mangers.

Instruction: Major topics covered in the course are critical incident analyses, leadership challenges, learning organization, strategic thinking, strategic marketing, shareholder value, organization structure and politics, and managing radical change. Methods of instruction include lecture, discussion, classroom exercises, case studies, audio/visual material, learner presentations/reports, formal evaluation of participant presentations, project evaluation, daily self-evaluation of learning outcomes, two periodic follow-up sessions, and pre and post evaluation.

Credit Recommendation: In the graduate degree category, 3 semester hours in Management or Business Administration (1/95).

Left/Right Brain Applications: Power Thinking (ME0812)

Location: Various locations throughout Bell Atlantic Region.

Length: 20 hours (3 days).

Dates: October 1986-December 1991.

Objective: To provide the student with hands-on practice of a variety of "whole brain" learning techniques.

Learning Outcome: Upon successful completion of this course, the student will be able to expand as individuals while developing new ways of thinking; understand how the mind works; identify commonalities shared in the thought process; identify challenges of motivation; and stress concentrations and study habits.

Instruction: Major topics covered in the course are introduction to mind mapping, range reading techniques to improve both speed and comprehension of reading material, and techniques to stimulate and improve memory. Methods of instruction include lectures, exercises, and computer-assisted videotapes.

Credit Recommendation: In the vocational certificate category, 1 semester hour in Introduction to Adult Psychology, Personality, or Human Relations (12/91).

Management Appraisal Plan Training

Location: Various locations throughout C&P Telephone Company business area.

Length: 18 hours (2 days).

Dates: June 1977-December 1988.

Objective: To develop the ability to make overall determinations of management potential on the basis of documented behavior and ratings of potential.

Instruction: Major topics covered in the course are a program for new managers who will be doing performance appraisals of subordinates; provides a background in appraisals; definition of performance; and factors and practical experience in classifying behavior, rating behavior, and giving evaluation feedback. Methods of instruction include lecture, discussion, and classroom exercises.

Credit Recommendation: In the vocational certificate category, 1 semester hour in Personnel (12/79).

Management/Union Relations Workshop

Location: Various locations throughout the Bell Atlantic Region.

Length: 15 hours (2 days).

Dates: February 1982-Present.

Objective: The participants will gain understanding and develop basic skills in establishing and maintaining good management/union relations.

Learning Outcome: Upon successful completion of this course, the student will understand the role of labor relations; basic steps in progressive corrective discipline; recommended procedure for handling insubordination; steps in handling a grievance meeting; and communication techniques.

Instruction: Major topics covered in the course are an understanding of and methods for dealing with selected management/union matters. Skills are developed in corrective progressive discipline, handling grievances, refusals to follow instructions, introducing company-initiated change, and documenting employee discussions. Methods of instruction include practice sessions, written exercises, and group discussions.

Credit Recommendation: In the vocational certificate category, 1 semester hour in Industrial Relations or Personnel Management (12/84) (12/91).

Managing the Flow of Work
2. Developing Subordinates
3. Managing the Job

Location: South Plainfield, NJ.

Length: 38.5 hours (6 days).

Dates: June 1981-December 1993.

Objective: To enable the participant to use a systematic process for planning and monitoring the work flow, develop satisfactory subordinates, and manage his or her job effectively.

Instruction: Major topics covered in the course are managing, supervising, planning, organizing, delegating, problem solving, interviewing, and negotiating, time management, and interpersonal skills. Methods of instruction include lectures, case studies, observable behavior, and mastery of tests.

Credit Recommendation: In the lower division baccalaureate/associate degree category, 2 semester hours in Job Definition and Management (6/81).

Managing the Problem-Solving Process
2. Managing to Write
3. Defining the Job

Location: South Plainfield, NJ.

Length: 36 hours (6 days).

Dates: February 1981-December 1993.

Objective: To enable the participant to demonstrate a process for solving problems; write memos, letters, and reports, and produce documents that provide maximum impact on the reader; and define thoroughly the job and improve the work group's effectiveness.

Instruction: Major topics covered in the course are describing the problem situation and problem characteristics, determining the problem causes, and selecting and evaluating solutions; writing memos, letters, reports, and producing documents that provide maximum impact on the readers; defining thoroughly the job and to improve the work group's effectiveness; and producing a job definition, reviewing and verifying the job definition, and defining and reviewing the work groups. Methods of instruction include lectures, case studies, observable behavior, and mastery of tests.

Credit Recommendation: In the lower division baccalaureate/associate degree category, 2 semester hours in Problem Solving (6/81).

Methods Developers' Workshop

Location: C&P Learning Center, Silver Spring, MD.

Length: 60 hours (2 weeks).

Dates: February 1982-December 1993.

Objective: To enable the student to demonstrate a basic understanding of methods development by analyzing case study documents and developing appropriate methods material.

Instruction: Major topics covered in the course focuses on analyzing and writing methods, including job aids throughout the course. Methods of instruction include group and individual exercises are used to enable participants to practice developing methods in a systematic way, participants receive a workbook containing several job aids for use back on the job.

Credit Recommendation: In the upper division baccalaureate degree category, 2 semester hours in Technical Writing or Operations (12/84).

Methods Development Standards
1. Methods Development Standards (Module I)
2. Methods Development Standards (Module II)

Location: South Plainfield, NJ.

Length: *Module I*: 30 hours (5 days); *Module II*: 60 hours (10 days).

Dates: June 1980-December 1993.

Objective: To enable the participant to develop uniform, high quality methods documents for systems use.

Instruction: Major topics covered in the course are the standards by which methods should be developed. The standards comprise nine phases. Each phase embodies a list of activities to perform and disciplines to apply, enabling a project to develop ever increasing levels of detail in a systematic approach toward performance-oriented practices. Methods of instruction include lectures, case studies, observable behavior, and mastery of tests.

Credit Recommendation: *Module I:* In the lower division baccalaureate/associate degree category, 2 semester hours in Methods Development. *Module II:* In the lower division baccalaureate/associate degree category, 2 semester hours in Methods Development (6/81).

Negotiation and Conflict Resolution (Negotiation Skills Workshop)

Location: Various locations throughout the Bell Atlantic Region.

Length: 22.5 hours (3 days).

Dates: June 1981-December 1993.

Objective: To gain understanding and develop skills that are essential to successful negotiating and conflict resolution.

Learning Outcome: Upon successful completion of this course, the student will be able to define power and power currencies; assess their strengths and weaknesses in handling conflict; acquire the skills of negotiation; and understand the theories of negotiations and conflict resolution.

Instruction: Major topics covered in the course are information pertinent to the components of negotiation, which include power and conflict; identification of the participants' negotiating skills, strengths, and growth areas; and preparation and practice of these skills through videotaped role-plays and feedback.

Credit Recommendation: In the lower division baccalaureate/associate degree category, 1 semester hour in Human Relations or Personnel Relations (12/84) (12/91).

Orientation for New Managers/Supervisors
1. Orientation for New Managers
2. Orientation for New Supervisors

Location: Philadelphia, Harrisburg, and Pittsburgh, PA.

Length: 1. 21 hours (3 days); 2. 32 hours (1 week).

Dates: May 1980-June 1983.

Objective: To acquaint prospective managers and supervisors with basic management skills.

Instruction: Major topics covered in the course are basic management objectives, communications skills, personnel problems, leadership styles, and motivation. Methods of instruction include classroom exercises.

Credit Recommendation: In the lower division baccalaureate/associate degree category, 2 semester hours in Management (4/81). **NOTE:** To be eligible for credit, student must successfully complete both courses.

Payroll Accounting (2666)

Location: Silver Spring, MD.

Length: 21 hours (3 days).

Dates: January 1983-December 1993.

Objective: To enable the student to understand the nature and purpose of payroll accounting; journalize the various employee cash and noncash payments and understand the related tax treatment; and calculate and journalize the dollar amounts for gross wages, federal income taxes, FICA taxes, allotment withholdings, special payroll transactions, and net pay.

Instruction: Major topics covered in the course are the payroll accounting system; familiarizes the student with the inputs, outputs, and the related processing functions of payroll accounting. Methods of instruction include an instructor-led course using lecture and visual aids, student workbook problems and tests, and instructor-led discussions.

Credit Recommendation: In the lower division baccalaureate/associate degree category, 1 semester hour in Accounting (8/85).

Performance Analysis Workshop (204)

Location: South Plainfield, NJ.

Length: 19 hours (3 days).

Dates: February 1980-December 1993.

Objective: To enable the participant to apply performance analysis strategies to organizational performance problems; recommend and implement nontraining solutions—such as feedback systems, incentive systems, and job engineering—for appropriate nontraining problems; conduct a worth analysis of training solutions; and increase the effectiveness of the training organization by adopting performance analysis strategies, worth analysis techniques, and the systems approach to training.

Instruction: Major topics covered in the course are identification or isolation of organizational performance problems; determination of the value of correcting the problems; determination of the cause of the problems by separating problems into those caused by lack of knowledge and those caused by work environment factors such as lack of feedback, punishment, and poor job design; and selection of strategies for solving problems. Methods of instruction include lectures, case studies, observable behavior, and mastery of tests.

Credit Recommendation: In the lower division baccalaureate/associate degree category, 1 semester hour in Performance Analysis (6/81).

Performance Appraisal
a. Communicating for Improved Performance (G770OIC)
b. Evaluation of Potential (G765OIC)
c. Managing Performance (G760OIC)

Location: South Plainfield, NJ, and other locations throughout the state.

Length: a. 21 hours (3 days); b. 7 hours (1 day); c. 28 hours (4 days).

Dates: December 1985-August 1991.

Objective: To enable managers to deal effectively with people-related performance problems, to determine a subordinate's potential for promotion, and, in general, to manage subordinates in a successful manner.

Learning Outcome: Upon successful completion of Course a, the participant will be able to use a systematic procedure to analyze and respond to performance problems, and conduct problem-solving conversations that help solve the problem and maintain or improve relationships; Course b: observe and classify behaviors relevant to promotion, and document, rate, and evaluate behavior related to promotion potential; Course c: use performance standards as a basis for discussion; reinforce good performance, improve performance, coach, career counsel, and give performance reviews; and create an action plan to remove roadblocks and encourage employees so that they can and desire to do the work.

Instruction: Major topics covered in the course are designed to enable managers to manage their staff more effectively; evaluate individuals for promotion; and resolve job performance problems. Methods of instruction include evaluating participants by their specific individual class assignments to demonstrate that they have mastered the course objectives, videotaped lectures, case studies, and role playing, as well as a review of pre-class assigned readings.

Credit Recommendation: In the upper division baccalaureate degree category, 3

semester hours in Performance Appraisal or Performance Management (8/86).

Procurement Management Fundamentals

Location: C&P Learning Center, Silver Spring, MD; New Jersey Bell Training Center, South Plainfield, NJ; Bell of Pennsylvania (various locations).

Length: Approximately 30 hours (3 days).

Dates: July 1983-December 1993.

Objective: To provide an introductory orientation to the process of procurement of materials and contracting.

Instruction: Major topics covered in the course are an introduction to the procurement field for persons performing procurement functions; provides an overview of all procurement functions, from needs identification to disposition; and defines policies and principles that govern the various functions. Methods of instruction include lecture, discussion, and case studies.

Credit Recommendation: In the upper division baccalaureate degree category, 2 semester hours in Procurement and Contracting or Logistics and Materials Management (12/84).

Rate Regulations (Accounting Witness Support Training [2693])

Location: Silver Spring, MD.

Length: 37.5 hours (5 days).

Dates: December 1979-December 1993.

Objective: To teach the student the components of the rate base and income statement required to produce an accounting exhibit and the general methodologies and sources of information necessary to develop an accounting exhibit including income statement analysis, computation of the cost of capital, and all other accounting issues.

Instruction: Major topics covered in the course are major areas and issues in the preparation and presentation of testimony for Rate Case filings with state commissions. Methods of instruction include an instructor-led course using lecture, visual aids, and discussions.

Credit Recommendation: In the upper division baccalaureate degree category, 2 semester hours in Finance (8/85).

Stress Management (G769OIC)

Location: South Plainfield, NJ, and other locations throughout the state.

Length: 14 hours (2 days).

Dates: October 1984-December 1993.

Objective: To enable participants to identify their own best range of stress for effective functioning.

Learning Outcome: Upon successful completion of this course, the participant will be able to recognize what stress is and what triggers it; examine coping styles and behavior patterns that are developed to deal with stress; manage internal reactions to stress; and apply problem-solving skills to stress management.

Instruction: Major topics covered in the course are stress management to increased productivity, better physical health, more satisfying relationships, a greater sense of well-being, and it also relates physical fitness, health, and nutrition to stress management.

Credit Recommendation: In the lower division baccalaureate/associate degree category, 1 semester hour in Stress Management (8/86).

Supervisory Relationships Training

Location: Various locations throughout C&P Telephone Company business area.

Length: 18 hours (one session a week for 5 weeks).

Dates: December 1972-December 1993.

Objective: To give first-level managers supervisory skills in solving problems, maintaining open communication, and maintaining an employee's self-esteem.

Instruction: Major topics covered in the course are guidelines for handling problem situations on the job, supervisory theory, communication techniques, questioning techniques, and interpretive skills. Methods of instruction include classroom exercises, lecture, and discussion.

Credit Recommendation: In the lower division baccalaureate/associate degree category, 1 semester hour in Personnel (12/79) (12/84).

Supervisory Relationships: Trainer Workshop

Location: Various locations throughout C&P Telephone Company business area.

Length: 40 hours (5 days).

Dates: December 1972-December 1993.

Objective: To train second-level managers with the skills necessary to conduct supervisory relationships training courses for first-level managers.

Instruction: Major topics covered in the course are guidelines for handling problem situations on the job, supervisory theory, communication techniques, feedback techniques, questioning techniques, techniques for conducting a workshop and handling resistance in the classroom, leadership skills; interpretive skills, and skills for working with an adult learner. Methods of instruction include lecture, discussion, and classroom exercises.

Credit Recommendation: In the upper division baccalaureate degree category, 3 semester hours in Personnel (12/79) (12/84).

Supervisory Skills
1. Supervisory Relationships Training
2. Time Management (#190)
3. Handling Grievances
4. Social Awareness (#196)

Location: South Plainfield, NJ.

Length: 33.75 hours (5.5 days).

Dates: November 1979-December 1993.

Objective: To enable the student to teach methods that solve problems supervisors face everyday and sustain open communications between supervisors and subordinates while maintaining the self-esteem of the employees; set long- and short-term goals; set priorities; maintain a daily to-do list; identify time wasters, and take corrective action to eliminate time wasters; locate union contract information when necessary; answer questions about provisions of the contract agreement; recognize a grievance situation, and take necessary actions to see a grievance to its conclusion; and have each participant assess his or her knowledge and beliefs against a set of questions requiring some individual interpretation, and have this individual's knowledge and belief tested in a group situation where different interpretations may exist.

Instruction: Major topics covered in the course are encouraging the average employee and increasing the work quantity of subordinates, improving work quality, handling charges of equal employment opportunity discrimination, reducing employee resistance to a new supervisor, handling problems and discrimination complaints in the absence of written policy, and the steps to take if the initial approach fails; delegating work to subordinates and applying the course principles to other situations; the evaluation of resources, examination of principles, time wasters, how to prioritize short- and long-term goals, and the maintenance of a time diary; how to recognize and handle grievances and union agreement and arbitration cases; and problems of managing different individuals and probable causes of these problems. Methods of instruction include lectures, case studies, observable behavior, and mastery of tests.

Credit Recommendation: In the lower division baccalaureate/associate degree category, 1 semester hour in Management of Human Resources (6/81).

The Total Manager a. New Age Thinking (G764OIC) b. Whole Brain Applications (G772OIC)

Location: South Plainfield, NJ, and other locations throughout the state.

Length: a. 24 hours (3 days); b. 21 hours (3 days).

Dates: April 1983-November 1991.

Objective: To enable managers to perform more effectively through identifying a self-image that supports professional goals and using creative and analytical skills to accomplish professional goals.

Learning Outcome: Upon successful completion of these modules, the student will be able to align self-image with professional goals; correct "mistakes" made by others over whom one has leadership responsibility; become more effective in activities that require studying and memory; balance academic and creative mental functions to increase learning ability; and remember facts, consolidate information and recall information more effectively.

Instruction: Major topics covered in these courses are designed to make managers much more effective in achieving their professional and organizational goals by a fuller understanding and application of affirmations and visualizations and maximizing use of academic and creative mental functions; and students are evaluated in meeting course objectives by their individual contributions and specific individual activities. Methods of instruction include audiovisual information presentations, extensive instructor-led discussion, and class activities.

Credit Recommendation: In the upper division baccalaureate degree category, 3 semester hours in The Actualized Manager or Management Psychology (8/86). **NOTE:** Student must complete both courses for 3 semester hour credit recommendations. Each course alone carries 1 semester hour credit recommendation (see separate listing under individual titles).

Trainer Skills Workshop (G762OIC)

Location: South Plainfield, NJ, and other locations throughout the state.

Length: 70 hours (10 days).

Dates: April 1982-December 1992.

Objective: To provide trainers with the knowledge and skills necessary to instruct in an adult learning environment.

Learning Outcome: Upon successful completion of this course, the participant will be able to: identify various learning styles and adapt teaching methods; instruct effectively in the following formats: lecture, group discussion, demonstration, programmed instruction, role playing, and case study; apply the following skills successfully: oral presentation, use of AV, questioning, listening, nonverbal communication, counseling/coaching, and managing group dynamics; apply professional and ethical considerations in training; and plan ongoing professional development.

Instruction: Major topics covered in the course are a workshop that provides trainers with the knowledge and skills necessary to create an effective learning environment; describes the key role of the trainer in a climate of rapid change; and assumes that they possess subject matter expertise and course-specific instructional materials, such as a leader's guide and student materials, as required.

Credit Recommendation: In the upper division baccalaureate degree category, 3 semester hours in Training and Development or Manager as Trainer (applicable to a Business or Education curriculum) (8/86).

Trainer Workshop

Location: Various locations throughout C&P Telephone Company business area.

Length: 40 hours (5 days).

Dates: August 1978-December 1993.

Objective: To provide basic learning concepts, training methodologies/techniques, and skill practice for trainers of adult learners.

Instruction: Major topics covered in the course are training methods and learning behavior; emphasis is placed on the needs of the individual trainer as he/she learns to improve performance of management and nonmanagement employees in industry. Methods of instruction include lecture, discussion, group exercises, and individual practice in a simulated training environment.

Credit Recommendation: In the lower division baccalaureate/associate degree category, 1 semester hour in Educational Methodology or Training Techniques (5/80) (12/84).

Transactional Analysis (Management Relationships Training [105])

Location: Harrisburg, Philadelphia, Pittsburgh, PA.

Length: 26 hours (4 days).

Dates: January 1975-December 1993.

Objective: To recognize major sources of behavior for particular situations and to demonstrate skills in conducting productive communications and promoting mutual understanding.

Instruction: Major topics covered in the course are surveying ego states, diagramming, ulterior transactions, stroking patterns, psychological positions, games, and time structuring. Methods of instruction are group discussion, lectures, and simulations.

Credit Recommendation: In the lower division baccalaureate/associate degree category, 1 semester hour in Management (8/78).

Whole Brain Applications (G772OIC)

Location: South Plainfield, NJ, and other locations throughout the state.

Length: 21 hours (3 days).

Dates: October 1986-December 1993.

Objective: To provide participants with understanding and techniques to increase the mental abilities by using both areas of the brain.

Learning Outcome: Upon successful completion of this course, the participant will be able to be more effective in activities that require studying and memory; remember facts, consolidate information, and recall information more effectively; and maximize the use of both areas of the brain.

Instruction: Major topics covered in the course are to acquaint managers with the techniques needed to increase mental abilities, learning potential, and organizational skills through proper use of both areas of the brain, is offered to management staff in small group settings. Methods of instruction include evaluation through the extensive class participation activities and the specific application of techniques as supervised by the instructor.

Credit Recommendation: In the upper division baccalaureate degree category, 1 semester hour in Whole Brain Applications or Management Psychology (8/86).

Written Communication Skills

Location: Various locations throughout C&P Telephone Company business area.

Length: 24 hours (four 6-hour sessions spread over a 4-week period).

Dates: May 1977-December 1993.

Objective: To enable managers to write more effectively.

Instruction: Major topics covered in the course are focusing on skills necessary for organized, clear, accurate, and effective business writing. Methods of instruction include videotapes, exercises, and discussion.

Credit Recommendation: In the vocational certificate category, 1 semester hour in English (12/79) (12/84).

Written Communication Skills: Put It in Writing (ME0606)

Location: Various locations throughout the Bell Atlantic Region.

Length: 20 hours (3 days).

Dates: December 1981-December 1992.

Objective: To enhance students' ability to write expediently, clearly, and orderly in the vernacular of the intended reader(s).

Learning Outcome: Upon successful completion of this course, the student will learn the purpose and influence of good communication skills and will be able to convert ideas into words; apply six principles of writing; express ideas clearly and accurately; write in an organized expository manner; and meet writing deadlines.

Instruction: Major topics covered in the course are a brief history of the English language, grammar fundamentals, writing fundamentals, and organization of ideas. Methods of instruction include videotapes, books and manuals, lectures, and exercises.

Credit Recommendation: In the lower division baccalaureate/associate degree category, 1 semester hour in English (12/91).

Bergen County Police and Fire Academy

The Bergen County Police and Fire Academy is a 26-acre facility located in Mahwah, New Jersey. It was established in 1965 and is operated and maintained by the Division of Public Safety Education under the aegis of the Bergen County executive form of government.

Police Academy. A paid staff of fifty-two (52) and a volunteer instructor staff of over 500 share their expertise through a full range of comprehensive police basic, in-service, specialized, and refresher training courses provided to over 12,000 officers in northern New Jersey each year.

Fire Academy. The Fire Training and Education Section is staffed by four (4) full-time instructors and thirty-two (32) part-time instructors, who teach fire suppression and fire prevention through a variety of courses. In addition, Fire Brigade Training is offered for industries interested in enhancing their own fire protection.

The Fire Training and Education Section provides educational programs for approximately 5,000 firefighters from Bergen, Passaic, Essex, and Hudson counties, annually.

Bergen County Sheriff's Department. The Sheriff's Department consists of over 450 sworn and civilian personnel. The department is responsible for the care and custody of approximately 850-1,000 inmates at the Bergen County Jail, located in Hackensack, NJ. Additional duties of the department consist of, but are not limited to: security within the Bergen County Justice Center, transportation of inmates from the correctional facility to various courts throughout the state as well as acute care facilities, Community Policing, Detective Bureau, Missing Persons Unit, Domestic Violence Unit, Warrant Squad, Internal Affairs Unit, and Operations Unit. As a result of cooperative working relationships with the FBI, DEA, and Narcotics Task Force, several members of the department are on temporary assignment to the aforementioned agencies. The department's Bureau of Criminal Identification gathers evidence at crime scenes throughout Bergen County (encompassing 70 municipalities). BCI utilizes state of the art laser, photographic, and computer equipment, including the AFIS System, which provides an automated process for researching fingerprints to identify suspects through latent fingerprints.

Source of official student records: Registry of Credit Recommendations, American Council on Education, One Dupont Circle, Washington, DC 20036-1193, (202) 939-9434.

Additional information about the courses: Office of Corporate-Higher Education Programs, Thomas Edison State College, College Credit Recommendation Service, 101 West State Street, Trenton, NJ 08608-1176, (609) 633-6271.

FIRE ACADEMY

Building Construction

Location: Mahwah, NJ.

Length: 21 hours .

Dates: January 1986-Present.

Objective: To provide the student with the ability to recognize construction types, design, alteration consequences, materials used, and their influence on the building's reaction to fire.

Learning Outcome: Upon successful completion of this course, the student will be able to identify dangerous building conditions created by fire; list five indicators of structural instability; identify the characteristics of basic building materials and their behavior under fire conditions; and describe how to control the spread of fire within the building.

Instruction: Major topics covered in the course are an understanding of how the construction type, alterations, design, and materials will influence a building's reaction to fire. The goals are to reduce fire fighter injuries in building fires, with emphasis on fire protection and life safety. There is also a review of pertinent standards and codes.

Credit Recommendation: In the lower division baccalaureate/associate degree category, 2 semester hours in Building Construction (12/89) (11/95).

Emergency Medical Care - First Responder

Location: Mahwah, New Jersey.

Length: 46 hours.

Dates: October 1985-Present.

Objective: To provide the training to assist with emergency medical care.

Learning Outcome: Upon successful completion of this course, the student will be able to assist with emergency medical care as a first responder or with crash injury management.

Instruction: Major topics covered in the course are emergency medical care and crash injury management. Methods of instruction include lecture, video, exercises, and other methodologies designed to help students learn thoroughly and master all the objectives of the course.

Credit Recommendation: In the lower division baccalaureate/associate degree category, 3 semester hours in Emergency Medical Technician (12/95).

Emergency Medical Technician - Ambulance

Location: Mahwah, New Jersey.

Length: 150 hours.

Dates: August 1988-Present.

Objective: To provide the training and to qualify to sit for the state EMT-A examination.

Learning Outcome: Upon successful completion of this course, the student will be able to assist with emergency medical care as a first responder or with crash injury management, prepare to be eligible to sit for the state EMT examination, develop and display the desirable skills of an Emergency Medical Technician (EMT), and provide EMT level care as defined by law and regulations.

Instruction: Major topics covered in the course are the knowledge and practical skills needed to respond to various situations including: burns, respiratory and cardiac problems, broken bones, etc.; the opportunity to qualify for Emergency Medical Technician (EMT) licensing, and CPR. Methods of instruction include lecture, video, exercises, and other methodologies designed to help students learn thoroughly and master all objectives of the course. Students receive certificates in CPR.

Credit Recommendation: In the lower division baccalaureate/associate degree category, 4 semester hours in Emergency Medical Technician - Ambulance (12/95).

Fire and Arson Detection

Location: Mahwah, NJ.

Length: 15 hours.

Dates: January 1986-Present.

Objective: To give the student information on topics dealing with the responsibilities for determination of fire cause and fire scene procedures.

Learning Outcome: Upon successful completion of the course, the student will be able to identify the probable motives and the relationship between motives and probable suspects; determine the point of origin; determine accidental and incendiary fire causes in both structural and vehicle fires; explain the special considerations in fatal fires; and determine considerations necessary in the collection of evidence and identifying the legal problems associated with arson prosecutions.

Instruction: Major topics covered in the course are six areas of study from motivation of the fire setter to the legal aspects of fire scene searches, and suggested demeanor for courtroom testimony.

Credit Recommendation: In the lower division baccalaureate/associate degree category, 1 semester hour in Fire Investigation (12/89) (11/95).

Fire Fighter
Fire Fighter I
Fire Fighter II
Fire Fighter III

Location: Mahwah, NJ.

Length: *Version 1:* I: 60 hours; II: 63 hours; III: 36 hours; *Version 2:* I: 120 hours; II: 69 hours; III: 36 hours.

Dates: *Version 1:* I: March 1981-December 1991; *Version 1:* II: March 1982-December 1991; *Version 1:* III: August 1983-December 1991; *Version 2:* I, II, III: January 1992-Present.

Objective: *Fire Fighter I:* To provide the student with sufficient skill and knowledge to allow him/her to function as an effective fire ground participant under direct supervision of department officers. *Fire Fighter II:* To provide the student with sufficient knowledge and skill to allow him/her to function as an effective fire ground participant to the extent that direct supervision is not required and be capable of some decision making. *Fire Fighter III:* To provide the fire fighter with sufficient skill and knowledge to function as a fire ground participant under little or no supervision.

Learning Outcome: *Fire Fighter I:* Upon successful completion of this course, the student will be able to describe the needed requirements of a fire fighter under the National Fire Protection Association Standard 1001, Fire Fighter Professional Qualifications; identify the organization of the fire department; identify and demonstrate the proper use of protective equipment and all types of fire service tools and appliances; and have basic knowledge of the elements of fire and burning process. *Fire Fighter II:* Upon successful completion of this course, the student will be able to describe the needed requirements of a fire fighter under the National Fire Protection Association Standard 1001, Fire Fighter Professional Qualifications; identify and explain the function of fixed fire suppression systems; demonstrate and select the appropriate size, strength, and length of rope for a given task; demonstrate the concepts of mechanical ventilation; and identify observable result that is obtained when proper application of a fire stream is accomplished. *Fire Fighter III:* Upon successful completion of this course, the student will be able to describe the four main fire service objectives; name the five major fire ground activities; and describe the concepts used to make tactical decisions at a fire emergency.

Instruction: *Fire Fighter I:* Major topics covered in the course are all information concerned with making the student a safe working member of the fire fighting force. Methods of instruction include lecture, practical exercises, written final examinations, a practical evaluation, and written and practical hands-on evaluations. *Fire Fighter II:* Major topics covered are National Fire Protection Association Standard 1001, Fire Fighter Professional Qualifications and fixed fire suppression systems. Methods of instruction include lecture, practical exercises, written final examinations, and a practical evaluation. All students also receive cardiopulmonary resuscitation certification upon completion. *Fire Fighter III:* Major topics covered in the course are the knowledge to carry out fire ground evaluations under minimum supervision and how to take charge of a group and direct them toward completing an assignment, in accordance with nationally accepted safe practices. Methods of instruction include lecture, practical exercises, written final examinations, and a practical evaluation.

Credit Recommendation: In the lower division baccalaureate/associate degree category, 4 semester hours in Fire Department Orientation and Indoctrination (12/89) (11/95). **NOTE:** These three courses are offered together to attain the 4 semester hour credit recommendation.

Fire Fighter Safety and Survival

Location: Mahwah, NJ.

Length: 18-21 hours.

Dates: January 1986-Present.

Objective: To give the student a depiction and explanation of the most common causes of injuries and deaths to fire service personnel.

Learning Outcome: Upon successful completion of this course, the student will be able to identify the most common causes of personal injury to the fire fighter; given specific hazards, develop an accident prevention program applicable to his/her duty assignment; and given actual or simulated accident and injury reports, evaluate the reports and describe appropriate prevention measures.

Instruction: Major topics covered in the course are the responsibilities of the student for fire fighter safety and survival and an overview of the need for attitude changes regarding safety.

Credit Recommendation: In the lower division baccalaureate/associate degree category, 1 semester hour in the Principles of Fire Fighter Safety (12/89) (11/95).

Fire Inspector I

Location: Mahwah, NJ.

Length: 48 hours.

Dates: August 1985-Present.

Objective: To teach the student the proper procedures to make a basic fire prevention inspection, interpret code requirements, and use the proper inspection forms.

Learning Outcome: Upon successful completion of this course, the student will be able to present a clear argument for the enforcement of fire prevention codes; explain where the authority for fire code enforcement comes from; list the requirements of all fire rated building assemblies; identify the hazards of storing hazardous materials in buildings; and identify heating and cooking hazards and use of portable and fixed fire suppression systems.

Instruction: Major topics covered in the course are basic fire prevention inspections and interpretation of code requirements, and is approved to meet the educational requirements to obtain a license as a fire inspector or fire official from the State of New Jersey Bureau of Fire Safety.

Credit Recommendation: In the lower division baccalaureate/associate degree category, 3 semester hours in Fire Prevention and Inspection or Fire Prevention and Inspection Practices (12/89) (11/95).

Fire Official

Location: Mahwah, NJ.

Length: 36 hours.

Dates: January 1992-Present.

Objective: To provide the student with a planned pattern of instruction and experiences for Fire Officials in Administration, legal methods of code enforcement, and how to interpret and implement the administrative requirements of the Uniform Fire Code.

Learning Outcome: Upon successful completion of this course, the student will be able to define and describe the administrative functions of Sub-Chapters 1 and 2 of the New Jersey Uniform Fire Code, describe the role of the Fire Official within the framework of local government, summarize and present and/or substantiate a case before a legal body, and describe the management principles and techniques related to the supervision of a fire inspection.

Instruction: Major topics covered in the course are administration of the Fire Code Enforcement Agency, the role of the fire official as it relates to administration, management, report, and record-keeping, and legal issues of code enforcement are reviewed through the case study methods.

Credit Recommendation: In the lower division baccalaureate/associate degree category, 2 semester hours in Fire Science/ Fire Administration (11/95).

Hazardous Materials Incident Analysis

Location: Mahwah, NJ.

Length: 15 hours.

Dates: November 1987-Present.

Objective: To give the student the ability to assess the hazardous materials emergency threat to people, property, and systems through an analytical study of general hazardous materials emergency behaviors.

Learning Outcome: Upon successful completion of this course, the student will be able to define hazardous materials and the Department of Transportation categories and classifications; describe five areas in which hazardous materials are present in the community and five modes of hazardous materials transportation; explain the purpose of an emergency response effort; and explain the process of identifying hazardous materials.

Instruction: Major topics covered in the course are how to identify hazardous materials incident potential and analyze what possible steps can be taken to mitigate the situation in a safe manner; chemical characteristics and reactions related to storage, transportation, and handling of hazardous materials such as flammable liquids, combustible solids, oxidizing and corrosive materials, and radioactive compounds; and emergency situations and fire fighting control.

Credit Recommendation: In the lower division baccalaureate/associate degree category, 1 semester hour in Introduction to Hazardous Materials (12/89) (11/95).

Initial Company Tactical Operations

Location: Mahwah, NJ.

Length: 15 hours.

Dates: January 1986-Present.

Objective: To provide students with an understanding of incident management and familiarization with tactics and strategies associated with fire control methods.

Learning Outcome: Upon successful completion of this course, the student will be able to describe his/her responsibility in decision-making based on fire behavior characteristics; perform an incident analysis on the fire ground; define the primary duties of engine and truck companies at a fire emergency; and describe the major problem he/she may encounter at residential and small commercial fires.

Instruction: Major topics covered in the course are basic fire officer consideration of initial operations and fire fighting methods for typical occupancies. Methods of instruction include role playing, simulated exercises, and case studies.

Credit Recommendation: In the lower division baccalaureate/associate degree category, 1 semester hour in Fire Fighting Strategy and Tactics for Company Officers (12/89) (11/95).

Instructional Techniques for Company Officers

Location: Mahwah, NJ.

Length: 16 hours.

Dates: January 1986-Present.

Objective: To give the student the ability to identify and use the four-step approach to instruction as identified in the National Fire Protection Fire Service Instructor Qualifications, Standard 1041.

Learning Outcome: Upon successful completion of this course, the student will be able to identify and use the four steps of the teaching techniques; demonstrate the ability to properly position, make ready, and operate audiovisual teaching aids; and prepare and deliver a five-minute presentation using the four-step teaching method.

Instruction: Major topics covered in the course are educational concepts necessary to train prospective trainers and refining of the techniques they will apply as trainers.

Credit Recommendation: In the lower division baccalaureate/associate degree category, 1 semester hour in Instructional Techniques for Company Officers (12/89) (11/95).

Pump Operator

Location: Mahwah, NJ.

Length: 36 hours.

Dates: January 1981-Present.

Objective: To give the student the necessary knowledge and skill to operate a fire department pumper at a fire emergency.

Learning Outcome: Upon successful completion of this course, the student will be able to describe the qualification needed under the 1002 standard of the National Fire Protection Association for fire apparatus drivers; explain how a fire department pump operates and describe some of the problems that occur when operating fire department pumps; have sufficient knowledge to utilize hydraulic formulas to establish friction loss charts for his/her own pump; and establish simple, reliable methods to determine proper pump pressures within the design parameters of the pump and meet the demands of various fire ground hose evolutions.

Instruction: Major topics covered in the course are information on fire department hydraulics necessary to operate a fire department pump for the various fire ground situations, fire service hydraulics, principles of pressure, fire department sprinkler and standpipe systems, and the New Jersey driving laws applicable to the apparatus driver. Methods of instruction include lecture, live pumping situations, and class projects.

Credit Recommendation: In the lower division baccalaureate/associate degree category, 2 semester hours in Fire Service Hydraulics (Principles of Hydraulics) (12/89) (11/95).

POLICE ACADEMY

Basic Police Training Course

Location: Mahwah, NJ.

Length: *Version 1:* 710 hours (17 weeks); *Version 2:* 890 hours (19.5 weeks); *Version 3:* 890 hours (19.5 weeks).

Dates: *Version 1:* October 1985-July 1988; *Version 2:* August 1988-December 1992; *Version 3:* January 1993-Present.

Objective: To provide the training (as mandated by New Jersey Police Training Act) to enable the trainee to meet the physical, psychological, legal, and social responsibilities of a police officer within the state of New Jersey.

Learning Outcome: *Version 1:* Upon the successful completion of this course, the student will be able to describe the history and development of enforcement, and the morals and ethics involved in law enforcement; understand the functional components of the criminal justice system and the New Jersey Correctional System; identify factors affecting vehicle operations (maintenance, accidents, etc.); describe and demonstrate the officer's role at an accident and in traffic law enforcement; be familiar with the basics of criminal law, covering topics such as: theft, forgery, disorderly conduct, use of force, controlled dangerous substances, alcohol use, laws concerning juveniles, etc.; understand and apply the constitutional provisions relating to arrest, search, seizure, and evidence; pursue a criminal investigation, including: preliminary investigation, serious crimes against persons or property, courtroom testimony, etc.; assist with emergency medical care as a first responder (a EMT-A) or with crash injury management; understand the physical and stress problems that typically affect police officers; and understand the "how, why, and what" of physical education and participate in a newly created cultural diversity course. *Version 2:* Upon the successful completion of this course, the student will be able to describe the history and development of enforcement, and the morals and ethics involved in law enforcement; understand the functional components of the criminal justice system and the New Jersey Correctional System; identify factors affecting vehicle operations (maintenance, accidents, etc.); describe and demonstrate the officer's role at an accident and in traffic law enforcement; be familiar with the basics of criminal law, covering topics such as: theft, forgery, disorderly conduct, use of force, controlled dangerous substances, alcohol use, laws concerning juveniles, etc.; understand and apply the constitutional provisions relating to arrest, search, seizure, and evidence; pursue a criminal investigation, including: preliminary investigation, serious crimes against persons or property, courtroom testimony, etc.; assist with emergency medical care as a first responder (a EMT-A) or with crash injury management; understand the physical and stress problems that typically affect police officers; understand the "how, why, and what" of physical education and participate in a newly created cultural diversity course; prepare for state EMT examination; develop and display the desirable skills of an Emergency Medical Technician (EMT); and provide EMT level care as defined by law and regulations. *Version 3:* Upon the successful completion of this course, the student will be able to describe the history and development of enforcement, and the morals and ethics involved in law enforcement; understand the functional components of the criminal justice system and the New Jersey Correctional System; identify factors affecting vehicle operations (maintenance, accidents, etc.); describe and demonstrate the officer's role at an accident and in traffic law enforcement; be familiar with the basics of criminal law, covering topics such as theft, forgery, disorderly conduct, use of force, controlled dangerous substances, alcohol use, laws concerning juveniles; understand and apply the constitutional provisions relating to arrest, search, seizure, and evidence; pursue a criminal investigation, including preliminary investigation, serious crimes against persons or property, courtroom testimony; assist with emergency medical care as a first responder (a EMT-A) or with crash injury management; understand the physical and stress problems that typically affect police officers; understand the "how, why, and what" of physical education and participate in a newly created cultural diversity course; prepare for state EMT examination; develop and display the desirable skills of an Emergency Medical Technician (EMT); provide EMT level care as defined by law and regulations; and recognize preconceived notions as it relates to stereotypes and the significance of individual groupings.

Instruction: *Version 1:* Major topics covered in course are the 13 critical learning areas and the 714 specific objectives mandated by the state of New Jersey for the instruction of police officers; the history, development, and function of police in a free society; the relationships among the various components of the criminal justice system; the philosophy, development, and application of the law of criminal procedure and its constitutional provisions; issues of police authority relative to laws of arrest, search and seizure; review of relevant court decisions; analysis of the essential elements of investigation as a science of inquiry with an emphasis on the legal significance of evidence; methods of searching for, collecting, preserving, and evaluating physical evidence; organizational investigative functions; emergency medical care, students gain the knowledge and practical skills needed to respond to various situations including burns, respiratory and cardiac problems, and broken bones; how to develop and participate in an individualized exercise activity program; and a theoretical study of the nature of exercise and its effect on the human body, this includes topics of health and fitness, cardiovascular functioning, strength, flexibility, stress, and motor fitness. In addition to their normal academic qualifications, all instructors are qualified in their specific area of instruction, complete a methods of instruction course, and are certified to teach by the state. Methods of instruction include lecture, video, exercises, and other methodologies designed to help students learn thoroughly and master all the objectives of the course. Students receive certificates in CPR and First Aid. *Version 2:* Major topics covered in course are the 13 critical learning areas and the 714 specific objectives mandated by the state of New Jersey for the instruction of police officers; the history, development, and function of the police in a free society; the relationships among the various components of the criminal justice system; the philosophy, development, and application of the law of criminal procedure and its constitutional provisions; issues of police authority relative to laws of arrest, search and seizure, and a review of relevant court decisions; analysis of the essential elements of investigation as a science of inquiry with an emphasis on the legal significance of evidence; methods of searching for, collecting, preserving, and evaluating physical evidence; organizational investigative functions; in emergency medical care, students gain the knowledge and practical skills needed to respond to various situations including: burns, respiratory and cardiac problems, broken bones, etc.; how to develop and participate in an individualized exercise activity program; a theoretical study of the nature of exercise and its effect on the human body and include topics of: health and fitness, cardiovascular functioning, strength, flexibility, stress, and motor fitness; and provides the student the opportunity to qualify for Emergency Medical Technician (EMT) licensing. All instructors are qualified in their specific area of instruction, complete a methods of instruction course, and are certified to teach by the state, in addition to their normal academic qualifications. Methods of instruction include lecture, video, exercises, and other methodologies designed to help students learn thoroughly and master all the objectives of the course. Students receive certificates in CPR and First Aid. *Version 3:* Major topics covered in course are the 13 critical learning areas and the 714 specific objectives mandated by the state of New Jersey for the instruction of police officers; the history, development, and function of the police in a free society; the relationships among the various components of the criminal justice system; the philosophy, development, and application of the law of criminal procedure and its constitutional provisions; issues of police authority relative to laws of arrest, search and seizure, and a review of relevant court decisions; analysis of the essential elements of investigation as a science of inquiry with an emphasis on the legal significance of evidence; methods of searching for, collecting, preserving, and evaluating physical evidence; organizational investigative functions; in emergency medical care, students gain the knowledge and practical skills needed to respond to various situations including: burns, respiratory and cardiac problems, broken bones, etc.; In physical fitness, students develop and participate in an individualized exercise activity program. They cover a theoretical study of the nature of exercise and its effect on the human body and include topics of: health and fitness, cardiovascular functioning, strength, flexibility, stress, and motor fitness; provides the student the opportunity to qualify for Emergency Medical Technician (EMT) licensing; and students will be made aware of minority cultural groups with emphasis placed on prejudice as learned behavior. All instructors are qualified in their specific area of instruction, complete a methods of instruction course, and are certified to teach by the state, in addition to their normal academic qualifications. Methods of instruction include lecture, video, exercises, and other methodologies designed to help students learn thoroughly and master all the objectives of the course. Students receive certificates in CPR and First Aid.

Credit Recommendation: *Version 1:* In the lower division baccalaureate/associate degree category, 3 semester hours in Introduction to Criminal Justice, 3 semester hours in Criminal Law, 3 semesters hours in Law Enforcement electives, 3 semester hours in Emergency Medical Care, 1 semester hour in Body Conditioning, and 2 semester hours in Foundations of Physical Education, for a total of 15 semester hours (11/87) (4/88). *Version 2:* In the lower division baccalaureate/associate degree category, 3 semester hours in Introduction to Criminal Justice, 3 semester hours in Criminal Law, 3 semester hours in Law Enforcement elective, 3 semester hours in Emergency Medical Care, 4 semester hours in Emergency Medical Technician (Ambulance), 1 semester hour in Body Conditioning, and 2 semester hours in Foundations of Physical Education, for a total of 19 hours (5/93). *Version 3:* In the lower division baccalaureate/associate degree category, 3 semester hours in Introduction to Criminal Justice, 3 semester hours in Criminal Law, 3 semesters hours in Law Enforcement elective, 3 semester hours in Emergency Medical Care, 4 semester hours in Emergency Medical Technician (Ambulance), 1 semester hour in Body Conditioning, and 2 semester hours in Foundations of Physical Education, and 1 semester hour in Cultural Diversity, for a total of 20 semester hours (5/93).

SHERIFF'S DEPARTMENT

Basic Course for County Corrections Officer (140)

Location: Mahwah, New Jersey.

Length: *Version 1:* 12 weeks.

Dates: *Version 1:* September 1989-February 1992.

Objective: *Version 1:* To enable Basic Corrections recruits to meet the physical, psychological, social and legal responsibilities of a County Correction Officer in the State of New Jersey as mandated by the Police Training Commission.

Learning Outcome: *Version 1:* Upon successful completion of this course, the student will be able to describe the history and development of Corrections in America and the morals, ethics, and professional conduct involved in Law Enforcement; understand the functional components of the Criminal Justice System; understand and apply the constitutional provisions relating to arrest, search, and seizure; understand the physical and psychological stress problems that typically affect Corrections Officers; assist with emergency medical care; understand the process of a criminal investigation including marking, preserving, and packaging evidence, and courtroom testimony; and be familiar with basics of Title 2C Criminal Law covering areas such as: theft, forgery, disorderly conduct, use of force, laws pertaining to juveniles, etc.

Instruction: *Version 1:* Major topics covered in the course are 13 critical functional areas and specific performance objectives mandated by the State of New Jersey Police Training Commission for the instruction of County Corrections Officers; the knowledge and practical skills needed to respond to various emergencies; physical fitness conditioning through participation in various exercise activity programs; the theoretical study of the nature of exercise and its effects on the human body; and reduction of stress related disorders. Methods of instruction include lecture, discussion, case study, and practical hands-on exercises.

Credit Recommendation: *Version 1:* In the lower division baccalaureate/associate degree category, 3 semester hours in Introduction to Criminal Justice, 3 semester hours in Criminal Law, 3 semester hours in Contemporary Corrections, 3 semester hours in Emergency Medical Care, 1 semester hour in Body Conditioning, 2 semester hours in Foundations of Physical Education, and 1 semester hour in Cultural Diversity, a total of 16 semester hours (11/94).

Basic Course for County Corrections Officer (140)

Location: Mahwah, New Jersey.

Length: *Version 2:* 17 weeks.

Dates: *Version 2:* March 1992-January 1994.

Objective: *Version 2:* To enable Basic Corrections recruits to meet the physical, psychological, social, and legal responsibilities of a County Correction Officer in the State of New Jersey as mandated by the Police Training Commission.

Learning Outcome: *Version 2:* Upon successful completion of this course, the student will be able to describe the history and development of Corrections in America and the morals, ethics, and professional conduct involved in Law Enforcement; understand the functional components of the Criminal Justice system; understand and apply the constitutional provisions relating to arrest, search, and seizure; understand the physical and psychological stress problems that typically affect Corrections Officers; assist with emergency medical care; understand the process of a criminal investigation including marking, preserving, and packaging evidence, and courtroom testimony; and be familiar with basics of Title 2C Criminal Law covering areas such as: theft, forgery, disorderly conduct, use of force, laws pertaining to juveniles, etc.

Instruction: *Version 2:* Major topics covered in the course are the critical functional areas and specific performance objectives mandated by the State of New Jersey Police Training Commission for the instruction of County Corrections Officers; the knowledge and practical skills needed to respond to various emergencies including burns, respiratory and cardiac problems, fractured bones, etc.; CPR; physical fitness conditioning through participation in various exercise activity programs; the theoretical study of the nature, exercise and its effects on the human body; reduction of stress related disorders; health and fitness; nutrition; cardiovascular functioning; strength; flexibility; and stress and motor fitness. Methods of instruction include lecture, discussion, case study, and practical hands-on exercises.

Credit Recommendation: *Version 2:* In the lower division baccalaureate/associate degree category, 3 semester hours in Introduction to Criminal Justice, 3 semester hours in Criminal Law, 3 semester hours in Contemporary Corrections; 4

semester hours in EMT; 1 semester hour in Body Conditioning; 2 semester hours in Foundations of Physical Education; and 1 semester hour in Cultural Diversity, a total of 17 semester hours (11/94).

Basic Course for County Corrections Officer (140)

Location: Mahwah, New Jersey.

Length: *Version 3:* 19 weeks.

Dates: *Version 3:* February 1994-Present.

Objective: *Version 3:* To enable Basic Corrections recruits to meet the physical, psychological, social, and legal responsibilities of a County Correction Officer in the State of New Jersey as mandated by the Police Training Commission.

Learning Outcome: *Version 3:* Upon successful completion of this course, the student will be able to describe the history and development of Corrections in America and the morals, ethics, and professional conduct involved in Law Enforcement; understand the functional components of the Criminal Justice system; understand and apply the constitutional provisions relating to arrest, search, and seizure; understand the physical and psychological stress problems that typically affect Corrections Officers; assist with emergency medical care; understand the process of a criminal investigation including marking, preserving, and packaging evidence, and courtroom testimony; and be familiar with basics of Title 2C Criminal Law covering areas such as: theft, forgery, disorderly conduct, use of force, laws pertaining to juveniles, etc.

Instruction: *Version 3:* Major topics covered in the course are the critical functional areas and specific performance objectives mandated by the State of New Jersey Police Training Commission for the instruction of County Corrections Officers; the knowledge and practical skills needed to respond to various emergencies including burns, respiratory and cardiac problems; fractured bones, etc.; CPR; EMT; physical fitness conditioning through participation in various exercise activity programs; the theoretical study of the nature of exercise and its effects on the human body; reduction of stress related disorders; health and fitness; nutrition; cardiovascular functioning; strength; flexibility; stress, and motor fitness. Methods of instruction include lecture, discussion, case study, and practical hands-on exercises.

Credit Recommendation: *Version 3:* In the lower division baccalaureate/associate degree category, 3 semester hours in Introduction to Criminal Justice, 3 semester hours in Criminal Law, 3 semester hours in Contemporary Corrections, 3 semester hours in Crisis Intervention, 4 semester hours in EMT, 1 semester hour in Body Conditioning, 2 semester hours in Foundations of Physical Education, and 1 semester hour in Cultural Diversity, a total of 20 semester hours (11/94).

Field Training Officer Internship

Location: Bergen County Jail, Hackensack, NJ.

Length: 120 hours (15 days).

Dates: April 1995-Present.

Objective: To provide basic knowledge and skill applications through the evaluation process.

Learning Outcome: Upon successful completion of this course, the student will be able to become familiar with the Field Training Officer Manual; understand the daily observation report (ODR); work in unsupervised assignments within the facility; and provide basic guidelines for all corrections operations necessary for the safety, security, and welfare of both staff and inmates.

Instruction: Major topics covered in the course are the Field Training Officer Manual; how to write and understand a daily observation report (ODR); and the basic guidelines for all corrections operations necessary for the safety, security, and welfare of both staff and inmates. Methods of instruction include one-to-one individualized training, screening, and evaluation which will take place on a daily basis, keeping a journal, and tests.

Credit Recommendation: In the lower division baccalaureate/associate degree category, 3 semester hours in Criminal Justice Internship (4/95).

Field Training Program for Sheriffs Officers

Location: Bergen County Justice Center, Hackensack, NJ.

Length: 120 hours (15 days).

Dates: January 1996-Present.

Objective: To provide basic knowledge and skill applications through modeling, coaching, and the evaluation process.

Learning Outcome: Upon successful completion of this course, the student will be able to be familiar with the Field Training Officer Manual; understand the daily observation report (ODR); work in unsupervised assignments within the complex; and provide basic guidelines for all operations necessary for the safety, security, and welfare of staff, inmates, and the community at large.

Instruction: Major topics covered in the course are how to perform the Sheriff Officer's role at an acceptable level and how to make yourself worthy to the facility and department. Methods of instruction include maintaining a journal of daily experiences; one-to-one individualized training, screening, and evaluation on a daily basis; and a test to ensure the trainee's ability to perform the Sheriff Officer's role at an acceptable level. This program provides direct supervision, training, and assistance to the new probationary Sheriff's officer.

Credit Recommendation: In the lower division baccalaureate/associate degree category, 3 semester hours in Field Experience or Internship in Criminal Justice (6/96).

Berlitz International, Inc.

Berlitz International, Inc. is the world's oldest and largest organization exclusively devoted to language instruction and related services such as translation and interpretation. It teaches language in response to a full spectrum of needs and to the broadest possible range of students. Courses can be arranged at any of Berlitz's nearly 300 centers worldwide or, by special arrangement, in other locations. Berlitz has served the international community for over a century. It pioneered the "direct method" of language instruction and its distinctive form of that method has become its hallmark. The essential principle of the Berlitz Method is that one learns to speak a language by speaking it. From the moment the student begins the course, the target language will be used exclusively in class. Everything from vocabulary to grammatical structures is presented in such a way that it is either immediately intelligible or can be made immediately intelligible using only material that has already been taught. This building block approach ensures that the students think directly in their new language at all times. In a Berlitz lesson, there is a continuous exchange between the teacher and students and in this exchange the students speak at least half the time, often leading the conversation. This ensures that the students have sufficient practice to develop an active command of the material they are learning.

Berlitz has at each of its centers a staff of instructors who have native fluency in the languages they teach. There is, in addition, a Pedagogical Director who oversees the quality of instruction and directs special projects.

In the United States, as in Europe, Asia, and Latin America, there is a network of regional and national managers who ensure that the quality of Berlitz language services remains uniformly high and they, in turn, report to the International Headquarters in Princeton, New Jersey. Berlitz's publishing division produces a wide range of instructional materials for use in conjunction with Berlitz courses as well as books, tapes, and videos for the retail trade.

Berlitz Language Centers-North American Locations: Akron, OH; Atlanta, GA; Austin, TX; Baltimore, MD; Bellevue, WA; Beverly Hills, CA; Bingham Farms, MI (Detroit); Boston, MA; Campbell, CA; Charlotte, NC; Chicago, IL (2 sites); Cincinnati, OH; Cleveland, OH; Coral Gables, FL; Dallas, TX; Indianapolis, IN; Irvine, CA; Irving, TX (Las Colinas); Los Angeles, CA; Miami, FL; Milwaukee, WI; Mineola, NY; Minneapolis, MN; Nashville, TN; New York, NY (2 sites); Northbrook, IL; Oak Brook, IL; Orange, CA; Palo Alto, CA; Pasadena, CA; Philadelphia, PA; Phoenix, AZ; Pittsburgh, PA; Princeton, NJ; Raleigh, NC; Ridgewood, NJ; Rochester, NY; Rockville, MD; St. Louis, MO; San Antonio, TX; San Diego, CA; San Francisco, CA; Santa Monica, CA; Schaumburg, IL; Stamford, CT; Summit, NJ; Tampa, FL; Torrance, CA; Vienna, VA; Walnut Creek, CA; Washington, DC; Wayne, PA; Wellesley Hills, MA; West Hartford, CT; White Plains, NY; and Woodland Hills, CA. *Canada*: Calgary, Alberta; Mississauga, Ontario; Montreal, Quebec (2 sites); Ottawa, Ontario; Quebec City, Quebec; Toronto, Ontario; and Vancouver, BC.

Source of official student records: Registry of Credit Recommendations, American Council on Education, One Dupont Circle, Washington, DC 20036-1193.

Additional information about the courses: College Credit Recommendation Service, American Council on Education, One Dupont Circle, Washington, DC 20036-1193.

Arabic I

Location: Berlitz Language Centers around the world.

Length: 112-150 hours.

Dates: *Version 1:* June 1986-December 1995; *Version 2:* January 1996-Present.

Objective: To enable the student to communicate in basic, everyday conversational situations in the Levantine Arabic dialect.

Learning Outcome: Upon successful completion of this course, the student will be able to understand and speak colloquial Levantine Arabic of a general social nature at a level 1 proficiency on the government scale (ACTFL intermediate low).

Instruction: Major topics covered in the course are greetings; courtesy expressions; geography; counting; telling time; food; clothing; shopping; banking; travel; weather; health; professions; and personal, family, and home life. All basic dialogues and drills are in transliteration. Methods of instruction include the direct situational method, which uses visual demonstration and dramatization to introduce new lexical expressions and grammatical constructions, with special emphasis on extensive drilling practice and role playing.

Credit Recommendation: *Version 1*: In the lower division baccalaureate/associate degree category, 4 semester hours in Colloquial Levantine Arabic (4/91). *Version 2*: In the lower division baccalaureate/associate degree category, 6 semester hours in Colloquial Levantine Arabic (10/96).

Chinese Mandarin

Location: Berlitz Language Centers around the world.

Length: 180 hours.

Dates: January 1985-Present.

Objective: To enable the student to master a basic conversational ability in standard Mandarin Chinese (Putonghua or Guoyu).

Learning Outcome: Upon successful completion of this course, the student will be able to have a functional knowledge of spoken Mandarin Chinese that is at least at, and probably beyond, the level of a six-credit, beginning Chinese course. This Berlitz course could be used to satisfy the basic language requirement of, for example, a business major. However, since the student will have little or no ability to read or write Chinese, a Chinese language major would probably need remedial work to qualify for admittance into an intermediate course.

Instruction: Major topics covered in the course are approximately 1,200 words of basic conversational and travel vocabulary; basic patterns including questions (including -ma, -we and choice-type) and responses; imperatives; demonstratives; interrogatives; numbers and measures; noun modification; location and direction; copula and stative verb constructions; coverbs and auxiliary verbs; potentials and resultatives; comparison; and experiential.

Credit Recommendation: In the lower division baccalaureate/associate degree category, 6 semester hours in spoken standard Mandarin Chinese (4/91) (10/96).

French I

Location: Berlitz Language Centers around the world.

Length: 90-112 hours.

Dates: July 1990-Present.

Objective: To be able to understand and converse in everyday conversation.

Learning Outcome: Upon successful completion of this course, the student will be able to converse in most common situations using the present, past, and future tenses; and can follow the general sense of a conversation between native speakers.

Instruction: Major topics covered in the course are approximately 1,200 frequently used words including vocabulary relating to personal, family, and social life;

travel, hotel, and restaurant situations; and telephone usage. The principal grammatical structures and the present, past, and future verb tenses are taught. Methods of instruction include direct method (oral); drill exercises; tutorial; and role plays.

Credit Recommendation: In the lower division baccalaureate/associate degree category, 6 semester hours in French (4/91) (10/96).

German I

Location: Berlitz Language Centers around the world.

Length: 90-112 hours.

Dates: January 1990-Present.

Objective: To provide a basic conversational skill in German.

Learning Outcome: Upon successful completion of this course, the student will be able to conduct simple conversation using basic vocabulary to handle everyday situations.

Instruction: Major topics covered in the course are grammar, basic tenses and vocabulary, gender, cases, directions, comparisons; pronouns, time expressions, prepositions, and word order; and travel and everyday situations. Methods of instruction include all oral instruction in German with some written exercises.

Credit Recommendation: In the lower division baccalaureate/associate degree category, 6 semester hours in Introductory German (101, 102) with emphasis on conversation (4/91) (10/96).

Italian I

Location: Berlitz Language Centers around the world.

Length: 90-112 hours.

Dates: April 1981-Present.

Objective: Basic conversational ability in the language.

Learning Outcome: Upon successful completion of this course, the student will be able to conduct simple conversations in the language (social or business in nature) and handle everyday situations.

Instruction: Major topics covered in the course are basic vocabulary relating to everyday situations; gender; articles (definite and indefinite); pronouns (direct and indirect); use of partitive; prepositions; auxiliary verbs (esseae, aveae); adjectives; practical situations; numbers; subjunctive (present); and simple and compound tenses:present, imperfect, imperative, and preterit. Methods of instruction include all instruction in Italian using basic conversational exercises with some written exercises.

Credit Recommendation: In the lower division baccalaureate/associate degree category, 6 semester hours in Introduction to Italian with emphasis on conversation (4/91) (10/96).

Japanese I

Location: Berlitz Language Centers around the world.

Length: 150-180 hours.

Dates: January 1986-Present.

Objective: A basic conversational ability in Japanese.

Learning Outcome: Upon successful completion of this course, the student will be able to have a functional knowledge of spoken Japanese that is at least at, and almost surely beyond, the level of a six-credit, beginning Japanese course. The speech level taught is distal (desu/masu) with some introduction of more polite speech. (The "distal" level is usually considered the "safest" for non-Japanese to use.) This Berlitz course could be used to satisfy a basic language requirement of, for example, a business major. However, since the student will have no ability to read or write Japanese, a Japanese language (or culture, history, etc.) major would probably need remedial work to qualify for admittance into an intermediate course.

Instruction: Major topics covered in the course are approximately 1,200 words of basic conversational and travel vocabulary, basic structural patterns, including desu/masu verb forms; use of verbal aspect and auxiliaries to locate action in time; existence and location; comparison; in-group/out-group nouns (e.g., "my wife," "your wife"); change of state ("become"); noun modification with and without no; numbers and classifiers; clause formation; indirect discourse (... to iimashita); verbs of giving and receiving (e.g., -te ageru); conditional (-ba...); and passive.

Credit Recommendation: In the lower division baccalaureate/associate degree category, 6 semester hours in spoken Japanese (4/91) (10/96).

Portuguese I

Location: Berlitz Language Centers around the world.

Length: 90-112 hours.

Dates: January 1986-Present.

Objective: A basic conversational ability in Portuguese.

Learning Outcome: Upon successful completion of this course, the student will be able to understand and use simple and complex sentences with verbs in the present, past, and future indicative and the present subjunctive. Practical ability in communication covers social and everyday functions such as making travel arrangements, completing exchanges in a bank, ordering food in a restaurant, handling common idiomatic phrases, and reading familiar subjects in newspapers or short messages.

Instruction: Major topics covered in the course range from basic greetings to extended use of practical Portuguese needed by visitors in Brazil and Portugal; verbs in the present, past (perfect and imperfect), and future of the indicative; regular and most used irregular verbs; use of present of the subjunctive and of auxiliary verbs in connection with main actions; and practical uses of the language such as exchanges at a hotel, restaurant, store or office.

Credit Recommendation: In the lower division baccalaureate/associate degree category, 6 semester hours in Portuguese I (4/91) (10/96).

Russian I

Location: Berlitz Language Centers around the world.

Length: 90-112 hours.

Dates: January 1990-Present.

Objective: To provide a basic conversational skill in Russian.

Learning Outcome: Upon successful completion of this course, the student will be able to conduct simple conversation using basic vocabulary and will be able to handle everyday situations.

Instruction: Major topics covered in the course are grammar, basic tenses, and vocabulary; prepositions; gender; some basic grammatical constructions and some cases; and everyday situations encountered by travelers, e.g., food, taxis, and hotels. All instruction is done in Russian, with some outside written exercises.

Credit Recommendation: In the lower division baccalaureate/associate degree category, 6 semester hours in Introductory Russian with emphasis on conversation (4/91) (10/96).

Spanish I

Location: Berlitz Language Centers around the world.

Length: 90-112 hours.

Dates: January 1986-Present.

Objective: A basic conversational ability in Spanish.

Learning Outcome: Upon successful completion of this course, the student will be able to understand and use simple and complex sentences in the present, past, and future of the indicative and the present subjunctive. Practical ability in communication covers social and everyday functions such as making travel arrangements; completing exchanges in a bank; ordering food in a restaurant; handling common idiomatic phrases; and reading subjects in newspapers or short messages.

Instruction: Major topics covered in the course proceed up to extended use of practical Spanish needed by visitors in Spanish America and Spain; verbs in the three tenses of the indicative; the present of the subjunctive; and vocabulary related to everyday situations encountered in any country of Spanish America or in Spain.

Credit Recommendation: In the lower division baccalaureate/associate degree category, 6 semester hours in Spanish I (4/91) (10/96).

Beth Jacob Academy of Higher Learning

The Jewish community has been established in Toronto since Canada's Confederation in 1867. Yet, it was the post second World War era which saw the founding of a new thriving community based on the influx of orthodox Ashkenazic Jewry.

During the 1950's, Jewish elementary schools became firmly established within the community. In 1960, Beth Jacob High School was started as the first Jewish High School for girls in Ontario. Graduates of the school receive a comprehensive education in Jewish and secular studies, true to the Beth Jacob tradition. In 1969, a post-graduate institute, Beth Jacob's Teachers' Seminary, was brought into existence to meet the expanding educational needs within the orthodox Jewish community. In 1996, Beth Jacob Academy was founded as an affiliate to the existing Beth Jacob Institutions. The Academy provides a post-high school, college-level, career-oriented education. The student body consists of primarily of young Jewish women with substantial prior Judaic and secular education.

The Academy's mission is to meet the needs of seminary graduates seeking a suitable, rigorous continuing education. It was with this in mind, that the Academy designed a curriculum and recruited a qualified faculty which offers the committed Jewish woman a quality baccalaureate degree within a supportive, spiritual environment.

The Academy currently offers degree courses in the areas of psychology, computer science, Jewish philosophy and religious studies. These courses lead to degrees in one of three tracks developed to articulate with degree programs offered through Thomas A. Edison State College of New Jersey. These are (1) Bachelor of Arts in Humanities; (2) Bachelor of Arts in Psychology; and (3) Bachelor of Arts in Liberal Studies.

Source of official student records: Registrar, Beth Jacob Academy of Higher Learning, 410 Lawrence Avenue West, Toronto, Ontario, M5M 1C2, Canada.

Source of official student records: Registry of Credit Recommendations, American Council on Education, One Dupont Circle, Washington, DC 20036-1193.

Additional information about the courses: College Credit Recommendation Service, American Council on Education, One Dupont Circle, Washington, DC 20036-1193.

Abnormal Psychology (PSY 430)

Location: Beth Jacob Academy of Higher Learning, Toronto, Ontario, Canada.

Length: 39 hours (13 weeks).

Dates: March 1997-Present.

Objective: To introduce the student to the concept of normal vs. abnormal behavior and to understand its causes, manifestations, and treatment.

Learning Outcome: Upon successful completion of this course, the student will be able to understand historical perspectives toward abnormal behavior; be familiar with all the major DSM-IV classifications of abnormal behavior — their causes, manifestations, and treatment (neuroses, psychosomatic disorders, personality disorders, addictive disorders, psychoses, organic disorders, eating disorders, suicide, and developmental disorders of childhood); understand the psychoanalytic, environmental, behavioral, and humanistic theories about mental illness; and be familiar with the major forms of treatment available today.

Instruction: Major topics covered in the course are historical perspective, major psychiatric (DSM-IV) categories, causes and treatment, and three major therapeutic orientations: Psychoanalytical, Behavioral, and Humanistic. Methods of instruction include lecture and case study analysis.

Credit Recommendation: In the upper division baccalaureate degree category, 3 semester hours in Abnormal Psychology (2/97). *Prerequisites:* Introduction to Psychology and Theories of Personality.

Analysis of Hebrew Scriptures: Deuteronomy (REL 260)

Location: Beth Jacob Academy of Higher Learning, Toronto, Ontario, Canada.

Length: 39 hours (13 weeks).

Dates: September 1996-Present.

Objective: To examine the Book of Deuteronomy in the original Hebrew with the 11th century commentary of Rashi.

Learning Outcome: Upon successful completion of this course, the student will be able to articulate an in-depth understanding of the major religious and historical elements of the Book of Deuteronomy.

Instruction: Major topics covered in the course are Jewish creed declarations and their philosophical implications, the Decalogue, charity, Biblical poetry, and Moses' farewell oration. Methods of instruction include lecture, discussion, and textual analysis.

Credit Recommendation: In the lower division baccalaureate/associate or in the upper division baccalaureate degree category, 3 semester hours in Analysis of Hebrew Scriptures: Deuteronomy, Religious Studies, or Hebraic/Judaic Studies (2/97).

Analysis of Hebrew Scriptures: Genesis (REL 220)

Location: The Zaidner Institute, Neve Yerushalayim, Jerusalem.

Length: 39 hours (13 weeks).

Dates: September 1997-Present.

Objective: To examine the Book of Genesis in the original Hebrew with the 11th century commentary of Rashi.

Learning Outcome: Upon successful completion of this course, the student will be able to articulate an in-depth understanding of the major religious and historical elements of the book of Genesis.

Instruction: Major topics covered in the course are account of creation, the Sabbath day, the nature of man, deluge and dispersion, the covenant with Abraham, and the patriarchs. Methods of instruction include lecture, discussion, and textual analysis.

Credit Recommendation: In the lower division baccalaureate/associate degree category or in the upper division baccalaureate degree category, 3 semester hours in Analysis of Hebrew Scriptures: Genesis, Religious Studies, or Hebraic/Judaic Studies (2/97).

Analysis of Hebrew Scriptures: Leviticus (REL 240)

Location: Beth Jacob Academy of Higher Learning, Toronto, Ontario, Canada.

Length: 39 hours (13 weeks).

Dates: September 1996-Present.

Objective: To examine the Book of Leviticus in the original Hebrew with the 11th century commentary of Rashi.

Learning Outcome: Upon successful completion of this course, the student will be able to articulate an in-depth understanding of the major religious elements of the Book of Leviticus.

Instruction: Major topics covered in the course are sacrificial rite, rationale for sacrifices, identification of ritually pure and impure animals, ritual defilement, laws of sexual relationship, business and social behavior, and priestly code. Methods of instruction include lecture, discussion, and textual analysis.

Credit Recommendation: In the lower division baccalaureate/associate or in the upper division baccalaureate degree category, 3 semester hours in Analysis of

Hebrew Scriptures: Leviticus, Religious Studies, or Hebraic/Judaic Studies (2/97).

Curriculum in Education I (EDU 103)

Location: Beth Jacob Academy of Higher Learning, Toronto, Ontario.

Length: 39 hours (13 weeks).

Dates: September 1996-Present.

Objective: To present student with a good overview of the role and significance of language arts in the classroom and the learning environment.

Learning Outcome: Upon successful completion of this course, the student will be aware of the strengths and weaknesses of the major approaches within contemporary education theory. The student will have a fundamental understanding of how the competing educational theories are implemented within a classroom.

Instruction: Major topics covered in the course are an introduction to the reading process; pre-reading skills and goals; two approaches to teaching reading: sight approach and the phonetic approach; directed reading lessons; reading diagnosis; reading miscues; close procedure, focus on language and comprehension; micro teaching; sampling of children's literature; poetry; spelling; the writing process; evaluating writing; learner penmanship; teacher's penmanship; and integrating grammar in the language arts curriculum. Methods of instruction include lecture, audio/visual material, classroom exercises, learner presentations/reports, examinations, presentations, demonstrations, supervisor observation, and projects.

Credit Recommendation: In the lower division baccalaureate/associate or upper division baccalaureate degree category, 3 semester hours in Language Arts Education or Education Elective (8/97).

Curriculum in Education II (EDU 104)

Location: Beth Jacob Academy of Higher Learning, Toronto, Ontario.

Length: 39 hours (13 weeks).

Dates: February 1997-Present.

Objective: To teach students the art of teaching Jewish Studies, with particular emphasis on instruction in the Bible at the elementary grade level.

Learning Outcome: Upon successful completion of this course, the student will be able to appreciate the essential skills required for Biblical instruction; and answer such key questions as: How does one plan for a unit of instruction concerning the Sabbath or Passover?, How does the teaching of the Prophets differ from the teaching of Pentateuch?, and How do the goals for instruction in these different parts of biblical literature differ?

Instruction: Major topics covered in the course are an overview of skills and decision making of teachers of religious studies; the structure of the lesson in primary grades; Pentateuch Skills-Using Language To Build Independent Study; Pentateuch Skills-Rashi; Pentateuch Skills-Rashi vs. Other Commentaries; guidelines; using the blackboard and other aids to keep children focused; alternate approaches to teaching the Pentateuch; practice teaching; unit planning- the festivals, prophets in the junior grades-the process, prophets in the junior grades-skills; the social sciences: an overview of the curriculum note taking, presentation of material; arts and crafts; and course summation. Methods of instruction include lecture, audio/visual material, classroom exercises, learner presentations/reports, examinations, presentations, demonstrations, projects, and supervisor observation.

Credit Recommendation: In the lower division baccalaureate/associate or upper division baccalaureate degree category, 3 semester hours in Elementary Education, Educational Curriculum, or Education Elective (8/97).

Daniel (REL 450)

Location: Beth Jacob Academy of Higher Learning, Toronto, Ontario, Canada.

Length: 39 hours (13 weeks).

Dates: December 1996-Present.

Objective: To examine the Book of Daniel in the original Hebrew and Aramaic, with English translations and with the 11th century commentary of Rashi and other classical commentaries.

Learning Outcome: Upon successful completion of this course, the student will be able to articulate an in-depth understanding of the major religious, moral, and apocalyptic themes of the Book of Daniel.

Instruction: Major topics covered in the course are literary structure, language, and history of the book of Daniel; structures of history; apocalyptic revelations and their interpretations; redemption; theodicy; and eschatology. Methods of instruction include lecture, discussion, and textual analysis.

Credit Recommendation: In the upper division baccalaureate degree category, 3 semester hours in The Book of Daniel, Religious Studies elective, or Hebraic/ Judaic Studies (2/97).

Data Structures (CMP 275)

Location: The Zaidner Institute, Neve Yerushalayim, Jerusalem.

Length: 39 hours (13 weeks).

Dates: December 1997-Present.

Objective: To give the student an understanding of the various abstract data structures and the means to implement them.

Learning Outcome: Upon successful completion of this course, the student will be able to understand what different data structures are, how they aid us in problem-solving, and how to actually create and use them in a program (included are queues, stacks, linked lists, circular lists, doubly-linked lists, binary trees, genealogical trees, and graphs).

Instruction: Major topics covered in the course are dynamic storage allocation, linked lists, recursion, stacks, queues, other list structures, binary trees, graphs, and sorting and searching methods. Methods of instruction include lectures, labs, examinations, and programs.

Credit Recommendation: In the lower division baccalaureate/associate degree category or in the upper division baccalaureate degree category, 3 semester hours in Data Structures or Computer Science elective (2/97).

Developmental Psychology I (PSY 210)

Location: Beth Jacob Academy of Higher Learning, Toronto, Ontario, Canada.

Length: 39 hours (13 weeks).

Dates: December 1996-Present.

Objective: To provide the student with an in-depth understanding of the growth and development of human beings from conception through middle childhood, focusing on physical, intellectual, emotional, and social components.

Learning Outcome: Upon successful completion of this course, the student will be able to understand the physiology of conception, prenatal development, and birth; have a working knowledge of Piaget's theory of cognitive development; apply Piaget's principles to develop a practical understanding of how children think and learn; be familiar with Erikson's theory of psychosocial development and be able to apply it to understanding human behavior; learn to recognize the various social and emotional states a child passes through from birth to adolescence; learn about the physical capabilities of neonates and the changes they undergo in the first year; learn about the concept of intelligence — what it is, how it is measured, and nature vs. nurture controversy; understand the role and importance of attachment in normal development; and comprehend the major types of abnormal development — autism, schizophrenia, mental retardation, depression, etc.

Instruction: Major topics covered in the course are theory and research on physical, mental, emotional, and social development from birth through mid-childhood; Erikson's stages of psychosocial development; language development; intellectual development; and Piaget's theory. Methods of instruction include lectures and individual projects.

Credit Recommendation: In the lower division baccalaureate/associate degree category, 3 semester hours in Child Developmental Psychology (2/97). *Prerequisite:* Introduction to Psychology.

Developmental Psychology II (PSY 211)

Location: Beth Jacob Academy of Higher Learning, Toronto, Ontario, Canada.

Length: 39 hours (13 weeks).

Dates: March 1997-Present.

Objective: To give students an in-depth understanding of the physical, emotional, social, and intellectual changes one undergoes in adolescence, adulthood, and life span development.

Learning Outcome: Upon successful completion of this course, the student will be able to understand such factors in adolescence as a stormy period, physical and cognitive changes over the life span, Erikson's psychosocial stages 5-8, mid-life crises, death and dying, and Kubler-Ross stages.

Instruction: Major topics covered in the course are physical, cognitive, emotional, and social aspects of various stages of adult development; transition from child to adult; marriage; career; raising a family; growing old; and facing death. Methods of instruction include lectures, field observations, and projects.

Credit Recommendation: In the lower division baccalaureate/associate degree category, 3 semester hours in Adolescent and Adult Developmental Psychology (2/97). *Co-requisites:* Introduction to Psychology and Developmental Psychology I.

Ethics of the Fathers (PHI 250)

Location: The Zaidner Institute, Neve Yerushalayim, Jerusalem.

Length: 39 hours (13 weeks)..

Dates: September 1997-Present.

Objective: To examine the ethical, moral and theological teachings of the Mishnaic tract, Avot, utilizing various schools of interpretation.

Learning Outcome: Upon successful completion of this course, the student will be able to analyze the ethical, moral, and theological teachings represented in the Avot tract and the various interpretations reflected in the accompanying Avot commentaries.

Instruction: Major topics covered in the course are charity, altruism and selfishness, humility, asceticism, spirituality, judicial ethics, theodicy, and eschatology. Methods of instruction include lecture and discussion.

Credit Recommendation: In the lower division baccalaureate/associate degree category, 3 semester hours in Ethics of the Fathers, Religious Studies, or Philosophy (2/97).

Feminism and Jewish Perspectives of Women (REL 410)

Location: The Zaidner Institute, Neve Yerushalayim, Jerusalem.

Length: 39 hours (13 weeks)..

Dates: September 1997-Present.

Objective: To examine major issues of feminism with an emphasis on the role of women in Jewish law and thought.

Learning Outcome: Upon successful completion of this course, the student will be able to understand the underlying concerns motivating the broader feminist movement; understand the specific concerns felt by Jewish feminists seeking to reconcile their sense of independence with an authentic Jewish connection; and understand the feminist concerns as articulated in primary and secondary traditional sources.

Instruction: Major topics covered in the course are contemporary feminism, social position of women in the bible, historical perspectives, love, marriage, purity, motherhood and career, sexuality, divorce and widowhood, and women and ritual law. Methods of instruction include lecture and discussion.

Credit Recommendation: In the lower division baccalaureate/associate degree category or in the upper division baccalaureate degree category, 3 semester hours in Feminism and Jewish Perspectives of Women, Women's Studies, Religious Studies, or Judaic Studies (2/97).

Fundamentals of Speech (COM 101)

Location: The Zaidner Institute, Neve Yerushalayim, Jerusalem.

Length: 39 hours (13 weeks).

Dates: September 1997-Present.

Objective: To enhance students' communication skills in the area of public speaking, emphasis is placed on practical situations that they are likely to face in employment or social interaction. Also, the course strives to develop skills in public speaking in an environment of controlled criticism.

Learning Outcome: Upon successful completion of this course, the students will be able to more effectively define and articulate the objective they seek to achieve by speaking; better evaluate the nature of the audience and its effect on basic types of speeches; compose a speech appropriate to achieve a given objective for a given audience; deliver a speech with greater confidence; appreciate the speeches of others and more precisely analyze the elements of their speeches; chair an informal business meeting; participate more constructively in informal business meetings; and recognize other forms and applications of oral communication (radio, television, etc.).

Instruction: Major topics covered in the course are principles of and obstacles to public communication, basic types of speeches, use of audiovisual aids, communication in meetings, interviewing techniques, print and audiovisual media, and role of criticism. Methods of instruction include lecture, discussion, student presentations and criticism, role-playing, and analysis of recorded speeches.

Credit Recommendation: In the lower division baccalaureate/associate degree category, 3 semester hours in Communication, Rhetoric, or Speech (2/97).

Introduction to Computers (CMP 101)

Location: Beth Jacob Academy of Higher Learning, Toronto, Ontario, Canada.

Length: 39 hours (13 weeks).

Dates: September 1996-Present.

Objective: To introduce the elementary programming concepts to the student and develop proficiency in programming in BASIC.

Learning Outcome: Upon successful completion of this course, the student will be able to analyze a problem, write an algorithm for it, and code its solution in BASIC; debug and thoroughly test the program; and decide which sort or search methods are most efficient for a particular case and implement the method.

Instruction: Major topics covered in the course are processing numeric and character information, debugging and testing (verification) of programs, program structure, arithmetic operations, looping, input/output operations, arrays, subroutines, character string manipulation, and sorting and searching. Methods of instruction include lectures, lab, examinations, and programs.

Credit Recommendation: In the lower division baccalaureate/associate degree category, 3 semester hours in Computer Science or as a Computer Science elective (2/97).

Introduction to Counseling (PSY 250)

Location: Beth Jacob Academy of Higher Learning, Toronto, Ontario, Canada.

Length: 39 hours (13 weeks).

Dates: December 1996-Present.

Objective: To provide an introduction to the dynamics of the counseling relationship.

Learning Outcome: Upon successful completion of this course, the student will be able to define and structure the counseling situation; identify the elements of effective helping; conduct initial, fact-finding interviews for a mental-status examination; use the Carkhuff model of helping and problem-solving; understand the effective use of self in the counseling process; understand Roger's theory of counseling; use specific skills that facilitate good communication; and deal with hostile and resistant clients.

Instruction: Major topics covered in the course are the nature of helping relationships, goals in counseling, counseling skills and techniques, ethics in counseling, and the necessary components of effective helping in a theoretical as well as a practical framework. Methods of instruction include lecture, role play, and video.

Credit Recommendation: In the upper division baccalaureate degree category, 3 semester hours in Introduction to Counseling (2/97). *Prerequisite:* Introduction to Psychology. Theories of Personality is suggested.

Introduction to Methodology (EDU 101)

Location: Beth Jacob Academy of Higher Learning, Toronto, Ontario.

Length: 39 hours (13 weeks).

Dates: September 1996-Present.

Objective: To introduce students to basic teaching methodology.

Learning Outcome: Upon successful completion of this course, the student will be able to appreciate the various fundamentals of effective teacher communication; and have the basic tools to introduce these skills into the classroom.

Instruction: Major topics covered in the course are the child in the classroom, teaching a child as an individual, desirable teacher traits, Mager's Behavioral Objectives, Bloom's Taxonomy-The Cognitive Domain, Bloom's Taxonomy-The Affective Domain, goals and objectives in general education, goals and objectives in jewish education, designing a lesson plan, integrating principles of good teaching in the lesson plan, micro-teaching, questioning techniques, kinds of lessons, teaching a new concept, drills, review lessons, communication skills, multi-media, the television in the classroom, the computer in the classroom, and a teacher's realization. Methods of instruction include lecture, audio/visual material, discussion, classroom exercises, learner presentations /reports, examinations, presentations, demonstrations, and projects.

Credit Recommendation: In the lower division baccalaureate/associate degree category, 3 semester hours in Educational Methodology, Introduction to Education, or Concepts of Learning (8/97).

Introduction to Psychology (PSY 101)

Location: Beth Jacob Academy of Higher Learning, Toronto, Ontario, Canada.

Length: 39 hours (13 weeks).

Dates: September 1996-Present.

Objective: To provide an overview of the various theories, methods, and fields of basic and applied psychology.

Learning Outcome: Upon successful completion of this course, the student will be able to demonstrate familiarity with biological and physiological influences on psychology (sensation and perception) and with major personality theories, mental health/illness, and social influences upon people.

Instruction: Major topics covered in the course are biological bases of behavior, human intellect, personality, mental health, psychodevelopment, and social psychology. Method of instruction includes lecture.

Credit Recommendation: In the lower division baccalaureate/associate degree category, 3 semester hours in Introduction to Psychology or Principles of Psychology (2/97).

Introduction to Statistics (MAT 201)

Location: Beth Jacob Academy of Higher Learning, Toronto, Ontario, Canada.

Length: 39 hours (13 weeks).

Dates: December 1996-Present.

Objective: To give the student an appreciation of statistical methods and techniques and the ability to use these methods in varied business data contexts.

Learning Outcome: Upon successful completion of this course, the student will be able to describe a given data set in statistical terms; calculate all standard statistical parameters; use simple probability notions; handle normal distribution problems; appreciate the techniques of comparative statistics; identify problems requiring advanced statistics; and convey statistical information to decision-makers.

Instruction: Major topics covered in the course are measurement scales, sources of data, descriptive statistics, data display, univariate measure of location and variability, basic probability, normal curve and applications, correlation and regression, inferential statistics, probability theory, binomial distribution, and parametric and nonparametric tests of significant difference. Methods of instruction include lectures, analytic lab, examinations, and presentations.

Credit Recommendation: In the lower division baccalaureate/associate or in the upper division baccalaureate degree category, 3 semester hours in Statistics (2/97).

Jewish Philosophy: Interpersonal Relationships (PHI 380)

Location: The Zaidner Institute, Neve Yerushalayim, Jerusalem.

Length: 39 hours (13 weeks).

Dates: September 1996-Present.

Objective: To examine and analyze the Biblical and Rabbinic perspectives on the ethico-legal dynamic of interpersonal relations.

Learning Outcome: Upon successful completion of this course, the student will be able to demonstrate an understanding of the substance of the ethico-legal teachings addressing the interpersonal dynamic and the Hebrew linguistic and literary elements characteristic of the relevant Biblical and rabbinic text materials.

Instruction: Major topics covered in the course are examining issues of hatred, reproof, revenge, cynical and deceptive abuse, friendship, greed, and charity. Methods of instruction include lecture, discussion, and textual analysis.

Credit Recommendation: In the lower division baccalaureate/associate degree or the upper division baccalaureate degree category, 3 semester hours in Jewish Philosophy: Interpersonal Relationships; Hebraic; or Judaic Studies elective (2/97).

Literature and History of the Mussar Movement (REL 340)

Location: Beth Jacob Academy of Higher Learning, Toronto, Ontario, Canada.

Length: 39 hours (13 weeks).

Dates: September 1996-Present.

Objective: To examine the historical context, central personalities, and ideological and methodological principles of the Mussar movement.

Learning Outcome: Upon successful completion of this course, the student will be able to demonstrate a knowledge of the historical and cultural setting in which the Mussar movement arose and of the central Mussar figures and their ideological and pedagogical profiles.

Instruction: Major topics covered in the course are the nineteenth century Jewish cultural climate, biographies of major Mussar figures, analysis of the ethical system, and ideology and methodology of major Mussar figures. Methods of instruction include lecture and discussion.

Credit Recommendation: In the upper division baccalaureate degree category, 3 semester hours in Literature and History of the Mussar Movement, Religious Studies elective, or Hebraic/Judaic Studies (2/97).

Macroeconomics (BUS 260)

Location: The Zaidner Institute, Neve Yerushalayim, Jerusalem.

Length: 39 hours (13 weeks).

Dates: September 1997-Present.

Objective: To give the student an understanding of the nature of macroeconomics theory as applied to economic output, price levels, and unemployment.

Learning Outcome: Upon successful completion of this course, the student will be able to appreciate the circular flows in economic environments; understand the history and nature of macroeconomics; understand the means of determining economic outputs; appreciate the role of government and fiscal policy; understand the banking system and monetary policy; relate to the issues of unemployment; relate the the issues of inflation; and appreciate the interrelation between economic and political considerations.

Instruction: Major topics covered in the course are macroelements of supply and demand; measuring national output; consumption and investment; government fiscal and monetary policy (FRB); income distribution and wealth; and inflation and unemployment. Methods of instruction include lecture, discussion, case studies, and presentations.

Credit Recommendation: In the lower division baccalaureate/associate degree category, 3 semester hours in Principles of Macroeconomics (2/97).

Megillat Esther (REL 267)

Location: The Zaidner Institute, Neve Yerushalayim, Jerusalem.

Length: 39 hours (13 weeks).

Dates: March 1998-Present.

Objective: To examine the Book of Esther in the original Hebrew text together with the commentary of Rashi; to explicate major themes as well as provide answers to questions of detail, sequence, and syntactical analysis; to review the Talmudic and Midrashic statements regarding the matter as a source for additional detail and amplification of the text; to refer to the commentary of Ibn Ezra for concomitant interpretation when necessary; and to study The Book of Esther narrative in light of its historical referents.

Learning Outcome: Upon successful completion of this course, the student will be able to correctly identify the authorship and sequence of events recorded in the Book of Esther; analyze the central philosophical and theological themes in the Book of Esther; and articulate the laws of Purim.

Instruction: Major topics covered in the course are a close reading of the Book of Esther focusing on its homiletic interpretation and the theological implications. Methods of instruction include lecture and discussion.

Credit Recommendation: In the lower division baccalaureate/associate degree category or in the upper division baccalaureate degree category, 3 semester hours in The Book of Esther, Religious Studies, or Hebraic/Judaic Studies (2/97).

Megillot II: Song of Songs, Ecclesiastes, Lamentations (REL 365)

Location: The Zaidner Institute, Neve Yerushalayim, Jerusalem.

Length: 39 hours (13 weeks).

Dates: September 1997-Present.

Objective: To examine the Books of Song of Songs, Ecclesiastes, and Lamentations in the original Hebrew with the 11th century commentary of Rashi and other classical commentaries.

Learning Outcome: Upon successful completion of this course, the student will be able to articulate an understanding of the major religious, literary, and moral symbolic elements of the Books of Song of Songs, Ecclesiastics, and Lamentations.

Instruction: Major topics covered in the course are Song of Songs—issues of authorship, literary issues (allegorical interpretation, structure, and style); Ecclesiastes—authorship, canonic issues, wisdom, wisdom literature, pessimism, and optimism; Lamentations—historical context; the role of Jerusalem; and Theodicy. Methods of instruction include lecture, discussion, and textual analysis.

Credit Recommendation: In the lower division baccalaureate/associate degree category or in the upper division baccalaureate degree category, 3 semester hours in Song of Songs, Ecclesiastes, Lamentations, Religious Studies elective, or Hebraic/Judaic Studies (2/97).

Microeconomics (BUS 250)

Location: The Zaidner Institute, Neve Yerushalayim, Jerusalem.

Length: 39 hours (13 weeks).

Dates: February 1998-Present.

Objective: To give the successful student an understanding of the nature and practice of the function of the market, price, production, and the economic behavior of the firm.

Learning Outcome: Upon successful completion of this course, the student will be able to understand utility and demand theory; analyze cost; recognize imperfect competition in the market place; understand the firm and the labor market; understand the role of government in the markets; and appreciate the elements of international trade.

Instruction: Major topics covered in the course are output and price and supply and demand; theories of utility and demand; production cost analysis and marginal products, marginal costs; pricing input factors; land, resources, wages, salaries, and the labor market; competition—perfect and imperfect, oligopoly, monopoly, regulation, and antitrust policy; and government policy and public choice, economic growth, and international trade. Methods of instruction include lecture and discussion.

Credit Recommendation: In the lower division baccalaureate/associate degree

category, 3 semester hours in Microeconomics (2/97).

Midrashic and Aggadic Literature (REL 440)

Location: Beth Jacob Academy of Higher Learning, Toronto, Ontario, Canada.

Length: 39 hours (13 weeks).

Dates: September 1996-Present.

Objective: To enable the student to examine the distinctive characteristics of midrashic literature.

Learning Outcome: Upon successful completion of this course, the student will be able to demonstrate an understanding of linguistic and literary elements of midrashic literature and identify various midrashic types and historical approaches to the interpretation of aggadah and midrash.

Instruction: Major topics covered in the course are attitudes toward midrashic and aggadic literature, literary forms in aggadic literature, rabbinic theology as reflected in the midrash, esotericism and exotericism in aggadic literature, and a survey of major works of aggadic literature. Methods of instruction include lecture and discussion.

Credit Recommendation: In the lower division baccalaureate/associate or in the upper division baccalaureate degree category, 3 semester hours in Midrashic and Aggadic Literature, Religious Studies elective, or Hebraic/Judaic Studies elective (2/97).

Philosophical and Theological Foundations of Jewish Prayer (PHI 180)

Location: Beth Jacob Academy of Higher Learning, Toronto, Ontario, Canada.

Length: 39 hours (13 weeks).

Dates: September 1996-Present.

Objective: To examine the philosophical and theological underpinnings of Jewish prayer.

Learning Outcome: Upon successful completion of this course, the student will be able to analyze the philosophical and theological centrality of prayer in Judaism; identify central themes in specific parts of the prayers; and define central terms and activities connected with prayer and their conceptual implications.

Instruction: Major topics covered in the course are examinations of the texts of prayers; the setting of prayer; preparation for prayer; intention and devotion during prayer; and the silent prayer (Shemonah Esreh) — its components, themes, laws, and explanation of those items. Methods of instruction include frontal lecture, discussion, and textual preparation.

Credit Recommendation: In the lower division baccalaureate/associate or in the upper division baccalaureate degree category, 3 semester hours in Philosophical and Theological Foundations of Jewish Prayer, Religious Studies, or Theology (2/97).

Principles of Management (BUS 370)

Location: The Zaidner Institute, Neve Yerushalayim, Jerusalem.

Length: 39 hours (13 weeks).

Dates: February 1998-Present.

Objective: To give the student an understanding of the importance of the firm to modern society, role and tasks of management, the impact of rapid change on managers and businesses.

Learning Outcome: Upon successful completion of this course, the student will be able to understand the profound changes in current worldwide markets and competition and the requirements for firms and their leaders in the new era; understand the role and process of planning in a contemporary business; be familiar with issues of ethics, culture, organization, and design in large businesses and corporations; have a basic understanding of the principles of organization behavior, motivation, communication, and decision making in contemporary business organizations; be stimulated to think about their own personal and professional goals; and consider what type of professional settings they might find the most satisfactory.

Instruction: Major topics covered in the course are the importance of the firm to modern society, role and tasks of management, ethical issues and societal responsibility of the firm, decision making, international business, importance and process of planning, individual and group behavior, theories of motivation, control, managing for quality, leadership, and the impact of rapid change on managers and businesses. Methods of instruction include lecture with extensive outside reading from business periodicals and journal linking theory and techniques discussed in class to the real world of business.

Credit Recommendation: In the lower division baccalaureate/associate degree category, 3 semester hours in Principles of Management (2/97).

Principles of Methodology (EDU 102)

Location: Beth Jacob Academy of Higher Learning, Toronto, Ontario.

Length: 39 hours (13 weeks).

Dates: February 1997-Present.

Objective: To present to future teachers the fundamentals of classroom dynamics and effective classroom management and the role of evaluation in the classroom.

Learning Outcome: Upon successful completion of this course, the student will be able to appreciate the essential skills required for effective classroom management and constructive evaluation procedures.

Instruction: Major topics covered in the course are defining good classroom management, looking at misbehavior, preventive class discipline, the importance of routines, discipline with dignity, principles, professional development, classroom management, levels of response, micro teaching, practice teaching, introduction to evaluation, formative evaluation, summative evaluation, designing effective tests, report cards, and communicating effectively with parents: PTA and role playing, creating the right classroom environment, and starting your new year. Methods of instruction include lecture, audio/visual material, classroom exercises, learner presentations/reports, examinations, presentations, demonstrations, and projects.

Credit Recommendation: In the lower division baccalaureate/associate degree category, 3 semester hours in Educational Methodology, Classroom Management, or Educational Elective (8/97).

Psychological Foundations of Education (PSY 260)

Location: Beth Jacob Academy of Higher Learning, Toronto, Ontario, Canada.

Length: 39 hours (13 weeks).

Dates: March 1997-Present.

Objective: To provide the necessary information concerning the philosophies and psychological processes associated with the educational experience.

Learning Outcome: Upon successful completion of this course, the student will be able to formulate a personal definition of a teacher, student, and classroom; devise and utilize behavioral objectives in support of a teaching task and construct taxonomies of objectives; comprehend contemporary learning theories, cognitive theories, and information processing models; understand theories of motivation and apply them to classroom management; assess and effectively relate to pupil variability in terms of stage theories of normal development and typical age-level characteristics; and demonstrate familiarity with different means of evaluating classroom learning.

Instruction: Major topics covered in the course are theoretical perspectives and research pertinent to classroom teaching; how children develop, interact, and learn within educational settings; and psychological evaluation of school achievement. Methods of instruction include lecture and discussion.

Credit Recommendation: In the upper division baccalaureate degree category, 3 semester hours in Psychological Foundations of Education (2/97). *Prerequisites:* Introduction to Psychology and Developmental Psychology I.

Psychological Testing and Measurement (PSY 410)

Location: Beth Jacob Academy of Higher Learning, Toronto, Ontario, Canada.

Length: 39 hours (13 weeks).

Dates: September 1996-Present.

Objective: To provide the theoretical and practical information necessary to competently understand and evaluate the major psychological tests used today.

Learning Outcome: Upon successful completion of this course, the student will be able to interpret psychiatric test results; understand statistical analysis of tests; know major components of I.Q. tests; understand the nature of personality tests and the difference between projective and standardized tests; and be aware of ethical issues in testing.

Instruction: Major topics covered in the course are the characteristics of psychological tests, intelligence tests, aptitude and interest tests, and personality tests. Methods of instruction include lecture and class demonstration.

Credit Recommendation: In the upper division baccalaureate degree category, 3 semester hours in Psychological Tests and Measurements (2/97). *Prerequisite:* Introduction to Psychology, and Developmental Psychology I and/or Theories of Personality are suggested.

Scriptural Teaching Skills Based on the Book of Deuteronomy (EDU 222)

Location: Beth Jacob Academy of Higher Learning, Toronto, Ontario.

Length: 52 hours (4 hours for 13 weeks).

Dates: September 1993-Present.

Objective: To teach the students how to develop their skills as instructors in scripture.

Learning Outcome: Upon successful completion of this course, the student will be able to prepare, plan, and execute vibrant and meaningful scriptural lessons at a secondary level.

Instruction: Major topics covered in the course are commentary (Miforshim) skills; an ability to read all commentaries (miforshim); a familiarity with particular commentary (miforshim) styles as well as the relationships between various commentaries (miforshim); teaching skills at different levels; choosing commentaries (miforshim) as a means of teaching skills; integrating commentaries (miforshim) into the Scriptural verse; finding the textual difficulty and the resolution in the verse; interpretation of the verse according to the commentator (miforesh); identifying the message in the commentator and setting goals; choosing commentaries for their message; personalizing the message and rewording the concepts into present day terminology and ideas; the values of student preparation; tailoring the preparation for the appropriate skills/interest level; following and building on preparation; integrating all the earlier components into a seamless lesson; identifying units; the lesson plan; and various methods of testing and their respective strengths, weaknesses and academic validity. Methods of instruction include lecture, discussion, examinations, presentations, demonstrations, and projects.

Credit Recommendation: In the lower division baccalaureate/associate or upper division baccalaureate degree category, 3 semester hours in Secondary Methodology or Education Elective (8/97).

Social Psychology (PSY 340)

Location: Beth Jacob Academy of Higher Learning, Toronto, Ontario, Canada.

Length: 39 hours (13 weeks).

Dates: December 1996-Present.

Objective: To evaluate the theoretic and scientific methods of how people perceive, influence, and relate to one another.

Learning Outcome: Upon successful completion of this course, the student will be able to know the experimental method in social psychology, causes and effects of prejudice, learned social behavior, competition and cooperation in social situations, and altruism in human behavior.

Instruction: Major topics covered in the course are theory and research on how an individual affects and is affected by his or her social environment; membership in groups, both formal and informal; conformity, prejudice, competition, and cooperation; and a basic understanding of the major principles and theories regarding how an individual is affected by the groups of which he or she is a part. Methods of instruction include lecture, discussion, and written examinations.

Credit Recommendation: In the upper division baccalaureate degree category, 3 semester hours in Social Psychology (2/97). *Prerequisite:* Introduction to Sociology or Introduction to Psychology.

Studies in Jewish Law: Interpersonal Relationships (REL 315)

Location: The Zaidner Institute, Neve Yerushalayim, Jerusalem.

Length: 39 hours (13 weeks).

Dates: February 1998-Present.

Objective: To examine the Biblical and halakhic texts dealing with various interpersonal relationships.

Learning Outcome: Upon successful completion of this course, the student will be able to demonstrate an understanding of diverse Rabbinic approaches to complex psychological, social, moral, and theological issues of interpersonal relationships.

Instruction: Major topics covered in the course are respect in family relationships, adoption, love for fellow humans, care for the ill, and labor relations. Methods of instruction include textual analysis, lecture, and discussion.

Credit Recommendation: In the lower division baccalaureate/associate degree category or in the upper division baccalaureate degree category, 3 semester hours in Studies in Jewish Law: Interpersonal Relationships, Religious Studies elective, Hebraic/Judaic Studies, or Liberal Arts (2/97).

Studies in Jewish Law: Laws and Customs of the Shabbat I (REL 120)

Location: Beth Jacob Academy of Higher Learning, Toronto, Ontario, Canada.

Length: 39 hours (13 weeks).

Dates: September 1996-Present.

Objective: To equip the student with the knowledge of the laws of the Sabbath and their biblical and rabbinic sources.

Learning Outcome: Upon successful completion of this course, the student will be able to articulate the philosophical-theological basis for the Sabbath and its centrality to the faith of the traditional Jew; the cultural significance of Sabbath symbols; and the motifs of Sabbath prayer.

Instruction: Major topics covered in the course are biblical and rabbinic sources for Sabbath observance, including concepts of labor and rest. Methods of instruction include lecture, discussion, and textual analysis.

Credit Recommendation: In the lower division baccalaureate/associate degree category, 3 semester hours in Studies and Jewish Law: Laws and Customs of the Sabbath I or Hebraic/Judaic Studies elective (2/97).

Studies in Jewish Philosophy and Ethics (PHI 455)

Location: Beth Jacob Academy of Higher Learning, Toronto, Ontario, Canada.

Length: 39 hours (13 weeks).

Dates: September 1996-Present.

Objective: To examine selected ethical/philosophical themes from the text of Pirkei Avot, a moralistic Mishnaic text, with the accompanying sixteenth century Derekh Hayyim gloss of Judah Loew ben Bezalel (Maharal of Prague).

Learning Outcome: Upon successful completion of this course, the student will be able to analyze the ethical/philosophic thematics addressed in the mishnaic and accompanying Derekh Hayyim texts, as well as talmudic source references cited and exposited in the Derekh Hayyim gloss.

Instruction: Major topics covered in the course are the ideas of R. Judah Loew of Prague vis a vis judicial integrity, the learning process, political leadership, definition of virtue, and a wide selection of ethical and philosophical ideas. Methods of instruction include lecture, discussion, and textual analysis.

Credit Recommendation: In the lower division baccalaureate/associate or in the upper division baccalaureate degree category, 3 semester hours in Jewish Philosophy and Ethics or Philosophy elective (2/97).

Studies in the Writings of Luzatto (PHI 370)

Location: The Zaidner Institute, Neve Yerushalayim, Jerusalem.

Length: 39 hours (13 weeks).

Dates: September 1997-Present.

Objective: To systematically analyze Rabbi Luzatto's ethical system and exposition of the biblical and rabbinic sources.

Learning Outcome: Upon successful completion of this course, the student will be able to appreciate the major themes in the author's ethical teaching and the author's particular methodology in interpretation of supportive biblical and rabbinic references cited within the work.

Instruction: Major topics covered in the course are the moral values of vigilance, diligence, cleanliness, self-denial, purification, piety, humility, fear of sin, and holiness. Methods of instruction include lecture and discussion.

Credit Recommendation: In the lower division baccalaureate/associate degree category or in the upper division baccalaureate degree category, 3 semester hours in Ethics/Philosophy, Religious Studies, or Hebraic/Judaic Studies (2/97).

Studies in the Writings of the Maharal of Prague (PHI 360)

Location: The Zaidner Institute, Neve Yerushalayim, Jerusalem.

Length: 39 hours (13 weeks).

Dates: February 1998-Present.

Objective: To examine the ethical/theological system of the Maharal of Prague.

Learning Outcome: Upon successful completion of this course, the student will be able to demonstrate an understanding of the fundamental substances of the author's writings; the terminology characteristic of the author's literary style, with its philosophic/mystical connotations; and the author's distinctive methodology in interpretation of biblical and rabbinic sources.

Instruction: Major topics covered in the course are a reflection of the specific text which will be studied comprehensively. Text selections will vary. Methods of instruction include lecture and discussion.

Credit Recommendation: In the upper division baccalaureate degree category, 3 semester hours in Studies in the Writings of the Maharal of Prague, Hebraic/Judaic Studies, Theology, or Religious Studies (2/97).

Survey of Biblical Themes (REL 385)

Location: The Zaidner Institute, Neve Yerushalayim, Jerusalem.

Length: 39 hours (13 weeks).

Dates: September 1997-Present.

Objective: To examine selected Biblical topics with their classical commentaries.

Learning Outcome: Upon successful completion of this course, the student will be able to demonstrate an understanding of the breadth of ethical, moral, and theological motifs implicit in the given narratives; and the diversity of interpretive positions reflected in the accompanying Talmudic, midrashic, and exegetical sources.

Instruction: Major topics covered in the course are selected ethical, moral, and theological themes from the Books of Genesis and Exodus. Methods of instruction include lecture and discussion.

Credit Recommendation: In the lower division baccalaureate/associate degree category or in the upper division baccalaureate degree category, 3 semester hours in Survey of Biblical Themes, Hebraic/Judaic Studies, or Religious Studies (2/97).

Survey of Exceptional Children (PSY 310)

Location: Beth Jacob Academy of Higher Learning, Toronto, Ontario, Canada.

Length: 39 hours (13 weeks).

Dates: September 1996-Present.

Objective: To provide the student with a brief overview of all the major exceptionalities dealt with in the school environment.

Learning Outcome: Upon successful completion of this course, for each of the exceptionalities presented, the student will be able to identify its symptoms in pupils in the classroom; understand basic diagnostic procedures; understand relevant terms (i.e., decibels, adventitious deafness, etc.); read and interpret IEPs; understand the necessary physiology; understand the causative factors; and know basic treatment techniques and specific classroom management techniques.

Instruction: Major topics covered in the course are an introduction to the study of exceptional children, hearing impaired, visually impaired, mental retardation, emotionally disturbed (behavior disordered), physically handicapped, speech and language disorders, gifted, and normalization; incidence; causation; diagnosis; treatment; behavior management; and suggestions for the classroom teacher. Methods of instruction include lecture, observation, and discussion.

Credit Recommendation: In the upper division baccalaureate degree category, 3 semester hours in Survey of Exceptional Children (2/97).

The Early Prophets: Kings I and II (REL 275)

Location: The Zaidner Institute, Neve Yerushalayim, Jerusalem.

Length: 39 hours (13 weeks).

Dates: February 1998-Present.

Objective: To examine the Book of Kings in the original Hebrew with the 11th century commentary of Rashi and other classical commentaries.

Learning Outcome: Upon successful completion of this course, the student will be able to articulate an in-depth understanding of the major religious and historical elements of the Book of Kings.

Instruction: Major topics covered in the course are biographies of the Kings of Judah and Israel, the split in the kingdoms, the personalities of Elijah and Elisha, the exile of ten tribes, and the destruction of the first Temple. Methods of instruction include lecture, discussion, and textual analysis.

Credit Recommendation: In the lower division baccalaureate/associate degree category or in the upper division baccalaureate degree category, 3 semester hours in The Book of Kings I and II, Religious Studies elective, or elective in Hebraic/Judaic Studies (2/97).

The Early Prophets: Samuel I and II (REL 270)

Location: Beth Jacob Academy of Higher Learning, Toronto, Ontario, Canada.

Length: 39 hours (13 weeks).

Dates: September 1996-Present.

Objective: To examine the Book of Samuel in the original Hebrew with the 11th century commentary of Rashi and rabbinic sources.

Learning Outcome: Upon successful completion of this course, the student will be able to articulate an in-depth understanding of the major personalities and events of the period.

Instruction: Major topics covered in the course are the narrative of Samuel I and II; the personalities of Samuel, Saul, David, and other biblical figures; and moral and religious teachings implicit in the biblical text. Methods of instruction include lecture, discussion, and textual analysis.

Credit Recommendation: In the lower division baccalaureate/associate degree category or in the upper division baccalaureate degree category, 3 semester hours in The Book of Samuel I and II, Religious Studies elective, or Hebraic/Judaic Studies (2/97).

Theories of Personality (PSY 420)

Location: Beth Jacob Academy of Higher Learning, Toronto, Ontario, Canada.

Length: 39 hours (13 weeks).

Dates: September 1996-Present.

Objective: To give the student an understanding of and appreciation for the historical process in the development of modern psychology, comparing the major theories of personality, with an emphasis on practical application.

Learning Outcome: Upon successful completion of this course, the student will be able to understand the theoretical underpinnings of each major personality theory based on the impact of historical and social influences upon its originator; be conversant with all the major theories that have contributed to and shaped modern psychological thought; and be able to evaluate the contributions of each theory and to assess the current status of each theory.

Instruction: Major topics covered in the course are major personality theories, development of normal and abnormal behavior, and historical influences on the development of various personality theories. The course provides a comprehensive view of the development of personality theory over the last 100 years. Methods of instruction include lectures, video presentations, reading of selected literature, and workshop discussions.

Credit Recommendation: In the upper division baccalaureate degree category, 3 semester hours in Theories of Personality (2/97). *Prerequisite:* Introduction to Psychology.

Topics in Chassidic Thought (PHI 420)

Location: The Zaidner Institute, Neve Yerushalayim, Jerusalem.

Length: 39 hours (13 weeks).

Dates: February 1998-Present.

Objective: To analyze the fundamental concepts of Hasidic thought, through the examination of primary and secondary source materials.

Learning Outcome: Upon successful completion of this course, the student will be able to demonstrate an understanding of the fundamental concepts of the Hasidic world view; and the ideological conflict separating Hasidim and Mitnagdim.

Instruction: Major topics covered in the course are worship, prayer, Torah study, ritual performance, the righteous master, and conceptions of God. Methods of instruction include lecture and discussions.

Credit Recommendation: In the lower division baccalaureate/associate degree category or in the upper division baccalaureate degree category, 3 semester hours in Topics in Chassidic Thought, Religious Studies, Theology, or Hebrew/Judaic Studies (2/97).

Bisk-Totaltape Publishing Company

Bisk-Totaltape Publishing Company is a Florida-based national communications company which provides training for the Uniform CPA Exam, Continuing Professional Education (CPE) to CPAs and other tax and accounting professionals, and in partnership with Regis University, and MBA Program (distance learning). The company publishes textbooks, software, CD-ROM, audio and video educational materials, and provides on-line services through the Internet. Bisk-Totaltape was founded in Gainesville, Florida in 1971, and moved to its present location in Tampa in 1987.

Totaltape CPA Review Division courses are designed to help accountants pass the CPA exam, considered to be the toughest professional certification exam in the country. Totaltape CPA Review is a complete study system, providing a personal choice of textbooks, software, CD-ROM, video and audio cassettes, and on-line classes, including email, chat rooms, and threaded bulletin board discussions. The primary audience is accounting students and CPA Exam candidates.

Bisk-Totaltape courses combine the most advanced multimedia and Internet technology with the finest attributes of classroom and self-study, thereby providing options in CPA exam preparation unsurpassed by any other CPA Review provider. Structured assignments and personal guidance help students stay on target for CPA exam success, while studying in the comfort of their own home or office.

CPA exam candidates spend more than 400 hours preparing for all four sections of the CPA exam - Financial Accounting and Reporting: Business Enterprises; Accounting and Reporting: Taxation, Managerial, and Governmental and Not-for-Profit Organizations; Auditing; and Business Law and Professional Responsibilities. Professors and instructors are always available on a toll-free "help line" or via email to provide information, assist with difficult subject material, and answer questions. If you wish to receive information about your student record or would like more information, please write the Registrar's Office, Bisk-Totaltape Publish-ing Company, 9417 Princess Palm Ave-nue, Tampa, FL 33619 or call toll-free, 1-800-874-7877.

Source of official student records: Registry of Credit Recommendations, American Council on Education, One Dupont Circle, Washington, DC 20036-1193.

Additional information about the courses: College Credit Recommendation Service, American Council on Education, One Dupont Circle, Washington, DC 20036-1193.

CPA Exam Review: Accounting and Reporting - Taxation, Managerial, and Governmental and Not-for-Profit Organizations (Self-Study)

Location: Independent study.

Length: Approximately 102 hours (independent study).

Dates: February 1998-Present.

Objective: To help students understand the concepts of accounting and reporting. This includes federal taxation, accounting for governmental and nonprofit organizations and managerial accounting.

Outcome: Upon successful completion of this course, the student will be able to demonstrate knowledge of federal taxation of individuals, corporations, partnerships, estates, and trusts; demonstrate proficiency in accounting for Governmental and Not-for-Profit organizations; and show mastery of managerial accounting and cost accounting.

Instruction: Major topics covered in the course are calculation of adjusted gross income, taxable income, partnership share of income, tax accounting methods, tax liability, tax credits, corporate taxation, tax-exempt organizations, capital gains, estate and trust taxations, preparers re-sponsibilities, accounting and financial reporting for governmental organizations, accounting and financial reporting for non-profit organizations, and costing and analysis methods including product, standard, and cost volume profit and budgeting. Methods of instruction include self-study with individual choice of formats, including books, software in a floppy disk or CD-ROM format, video tapes, and audio tapes. The student must complete all 13 lessons, including a quiz for each topic, must answer all 1,164 questions correctly, and pass a proctored final exam.

Credit Recommendation: In the upper division baccalaureate degree category, 1 semester hour in Taxation, 1 semester hour in Managerial Accounting, 1 semester hour in Governmental and Not-for-Profit Organizations or 3 semester hours in Accounting (2/98).

CPA Exam Review: Accounting and Reporting - Taxation, Managerial, and Governmental and Not-for-Profit Organizations (Online)

Location: Online and independent study.

Length: Approximately 102 hours (independent study).

Dates: February 1998-Present.

Objective: To help students understand the concepts of accounting and reporting. This includes federal taxation, accounting for governmental and nonprofit organizations and managerial accounting.

Outcome: Upon successful completion of this course, the student will be able to demonstrate knowledge of federal taxation of individuals, corporations, partnerships, and estates and trusts; demonstrate proficiency in accounting for Governmental and Not-for-Profit organizations; and show mastery of managerial accounting and cost accounting.

Instruction: Major topics covered in the course are calculation of adjusted gross income, taxable income, partnership share of income, tax accounting methods, tax liability, tax credits, corporate taxation, tax-exempt organizations, capital gains, estate and trust taxations, preparers responsibilities, accounting and financial reporting for governmental organizations, accounting and financial reporting for non-profit organizations, and costing and analysis methods including product, standard, and cost volume profit and budgeting. Methods of instruction include distance learning including online assignments, weekly chat rooms, and assigned discussion on the bulletin board. The course includes books, software in a floppy disk or CD-ROM format, and video tapes. The software includes self-grading, "cheat-proof" examinations that are created new every time students take them; instant, on-screen essay grading using AICPA-style key words and phrases. Students can participate in the weekly chat room, and are required to participate in the discussion questions posted on the bulletin board. Students can e-mail questions to professors, or can call toll-free for assistance on the Bisk-Totaltape "Help Line."

Credit Recommendation: In the upper division baccalaureate degree category, 1 semester hour in Taxation, 1 semester hour in Managerial Accounting, 1 semester hour in Governmental and Not-for-Profit Organizations or 3 semester hours in Accounting (2/98).

CPA Exam Review: Auditing (Self-Study)

Location: Independent study.

Length: Approximately 92 hours (independent study).

Dates: February 1998-Present.

Objective: To help students understand the concepts of auditing.

Outcome: Upon successful completion of this course, the student will be able to demonstrate mastery of reviewing the engagement to provide reasonable assurance that objectives are achieved, and evaluating information obtained to reach and to document engagement conclusions, including performing analytical procedures, evaluating the sufficiency and competence of audit evidence and document engagement conclusions, and reviewing the work performed to provide reasonable assurance that objectives are achieved; and show proficiency in preparing communications to satisfy engagement objectives, including preparing reports, preparing letters and other required communications, and other matters.

Instruction: Major topics covered in the course are audit standards, quality control standards, governmental auditing, planning the audit, internal control, audit procedures, sampling, EDP systems, reports on audited financial statements, other reports, and other professional services. Methods of instruction include self-study with individual choice of formats, including books, software in a floppy disk or CD-ROM format, video tapes, and audio tapes. The participant must complete all 9 lessons, including a quiz for each topic, must answer all 836 questions correctly, and pass a proctored final exam.

Credit Recommendation: In the upper division baccalaureate degree category, 3 semester hours in Auditing (2/98).

CPA Exam Review: Auditing (Online)

Location: Online and independent study.

Length: Approximately 92 hours (independent study).

Dates: February 1998-Present.

Objective: To help students understand the concepts of auditing.

Outcome: Upon successful completion of this course, the student will be able to demonstrate mastery of reviewing the engagement to provide reasonable assurance that objectives are achieved; evaluating information obtained to reach and to document engagement conclusions, including performing analytical procedures, evaluating the sufficiency and competence of audit evidence and document engagement conclusions, and reviewing the work performed to provide reasonable assurance that objectives are achieved; and show proficiency in preparing communications to satisfy engagement objectives, including preparing reports, preparing letters and other required communications, and other matters.

Instruction: Major topics covered in the course are audit standards, quality control standards, governmental auditing, planning the audit, internal control, audit procedures, sampling, EDP systems, reports on audited financial statements, other reports, and other professional services. Methods of instruction include distance learning including online assignments, weekly chat rooms, and assigned discussion on the bulletin board. The course includes books; software in a floppy disk or CD-ROM format, and video tapes. The software includes self-grading, "cheat-proof" examinations that are created new every time students takes them; instant, on-screen essay grading using AICPA-style key words and phrases. Students can participate in the weekly chat room, and are required to participate in the discussion questions posted on the bulletin board. Students can e-mail questions to professors, or can call toll-free for assistance on the Bisk-Totaltape "Help Line".

Credit Recommendation: In the upper division baccalaureate degree category, 3 semester hours in Auditing (2/98).

CPA Exam Review: Business Law and Professional Responsibilities (Online)

Location: Online and independent study.

Length: Approximately 82 hours (independent study).

Dates: February 1998-Present.

Objective: To help students understand the concepts of business law and professional responsibilities.

Outcome: Upon successful completion of this course, the student will have knowledge of professional and legal responsibilities, business organizations, contracts, debtor-creditor relationships, government regulation of business, uniform commercial code, and property.

Instruction: Major topics covered in the course are contracts, sales, commercial paper, bailments, documents of title and investments securities, secured transactions, bankruptcy, suretyship, business organizations, government regulation of business, property, insurance, and ethics and professional liability. Methods of instruction include distance learning including online assignments, weekly chat rooms, and assigned discussion on the bulletin board. The course includes books, software in a floppy disk or CD-ROM format, and video tapes. The software includes self-grading, "cheat-proof" examinations that are created new every time students take them; instant, on-screen essay grading using AICPA-style key words and phrases. The student must complete a quiz for each chapter; completion of all 17 lessons, including a quiz for each topic, must answer all 808 questions correctly; and pass a proctored final exam. Students can participate in the weekly chat room, and are required to participate in the discussion questions posted on the bulletin board. Students can e-mail questions to professors, or can call toll-free for assistance on the Bisk-Totaltape "Help Line."

Credit Recommendation: In the upper division baccalaureate degree category, 3 semester hours in Business Law (2/98).

CPA Exam Review: Business Law and Professional Responsibilities (Self-Study)

Location: Independent study.

Length: Approximately 82 hours (independent study).

Dates: February 1998-Present.

Objective: To help students understand the concepts of business law and professional responsibilities.

Outcome: Upon successful completion of this course, the student will have knowledge of professional and legal responsibilities, business organizations, contracts, debtor-creditor relationships, government regulation of business, uniform commercial code, and property.

Instruction: Major topics covered in the course are contracts, sales, commercial paper, bailments, documents of title and investments securities, secured transactions, bankruptcy, suretyship, business organizations, government regulation of business, property, insurance, and ethics and professional liability. Methods of instruction include self-study with individual choice of formats, including books, software in a floppy disk or CD-ROM format, video tapes, and audio tapes. The student must complete a quiz for each chapter; completion of all 17 lessons, including a quiz for each topic, must answer all 808 questions correctly; and pass a proctored final exam.

Credit Recommendation: In the upper division baccalaureate degree category, 3 semester hours in Business Law (2/98).

CPA Exam Review: Financial Accounting and Reporting - Business Enterprises (Online)

Location: Online and independent study.

Length: Approximately 144 hours (independent study).

Dates: February 1998-Present.

Objective: To help students understand the concepts of financial accounting and reporting.

Outcome: Upon successful completion of this course, the student will be able to demonstrate knowledge of the concepts and standards for financial statements, including financial accounting concepts, financial accounting standards for presentation and disclosures in general purpose financial statements, other presentations of financial data, and financial statement analysis. The student will also demonstrate proficiency in recognition, measurement, valuation, and presentation of typical items and specific types of transactions and events in financial statements in conformity with Generally Accepted Accounting Principles.

Instruction: Major topics covered in the course are consolidated and combined financial statements, balance sheet, statements of income, comprehensive income, changes in equity accounts, and cash flows, and related notes, disclosures, and analysis. Also covered are the various combinations, cash flow components, contingent liabilities, discontinued operations, earnings per share, employee benefits, financial instruments, foreign currency transactions and translation, income tax accounting, interim financial reporting, leases, nonmonetary transactions, reorganizations and changes in entity, related party transactions, research and development costs, and segment reporting. Methods of instruction include distance learning including online assignments, weekly chat rooms, and assigned discussion on the bulletin board. The course includes books; software in a floppy disk or CD-ROM format, and video tapes. The software includes self-grading, "cheat-proof" examinations that are created new every time students takes them; instant, on-screen essay grading using AICPA-style key words and phrases. The student must complete a quiz for each chapter; completion of all 20 lessons, including a quiz for each topic, must answer all 1,053 questions correctly; and pass a proctored final exam. Students can participate in the weekly chat room, and are required to participate in the discussion questions posted on the bulletin board. Students can e-mail questions, or can call toll-free for assistance on the Bisk-Totaltape "Help Line."

Credit Recommendation: In the upper division baccalaureate degree category, 3 semester hours in Financial Accounting (2/98).

CPA Exam Review: Financial Accounting and Reporting - Business Enterprises (Self-Study)

Location: Independent study.

Length: Approximately 144 hours (independent study).

Dates: February 1998-Present.

Objective: To help students understand the concepts of financial accounting and reporting.

Outcome: Upon successful completion of this course, the student will be able to demonstrate knowledge of the concepts and standards for financial statements, including financial accounting concepts, financial accounting standards for presentation and disclosures in general purpose financial statements, other presentations of financial data, and financial statement analysis. The student will also demonstrate proficiency in recognition, measurement, valuation, and presentation of typical items and specific types of transactions and events in financial statements in conformity with Generally Accepted Accounting Principles.

Instruction: Major topics covered in the course are consolidated and combined financial statements, balance sheet, statements of income, comprehensive income, changes in equity accounts, and cash flows, and related notes, disclosures, and analysis. Also covered are the various combinations, cash flow components, contingent liabilities, discontinued operations, earnings per share, employee benefits, financial instruments, foreign currency transactions and translation, income tax accounting, interim financial reporting, leases, nonmonetary transactions, reorganizations and changes in entity, related party transactions, research and development costs, and segment reporting. Methods of instruction include self-study with individual choice of formats, including books, software in a floppy disk or CD-ROM format, video tapes, and audio tapes. The student must complete all 20 lessons, including a quiz for each topic, must answer all 1,053 questions correctly, and pass a proctored final exam.

Credit Recommendation: In the upper division baccalaureate degree category, 3 semester hours in Financial Accounting (2/98).

BOMI Institute

BOMI Institute is a nonprofit, educational institution serving the commercial property management industry. The purpose of the BOMI Institute is to provide practical educational programs for professionals in property management, facilities management, and building engineering.

The education applies to all aspects of the building to include the facilities, technical systems and management. It is aimed at the mid-career professional and is accomplished through four programs; the Real Property Administrator (RPA), the Facilities Management Administrator (FMA), the Systems Maintenance Technician (SMT), and the Systems Maintenance Administrator (SMA).

Classrooms are available in over 60 cities throughout the US and Canada, sponsored by local Building Owners and Managers Associations, corporations, unions, and others. In addition, courses are offered by various colleges, universities, and technical schools. Students may also choose an accelerated review or self-study format.

Source of official student records: Registry of Credit Recommendations, American Council on Education, One Dupont Circle, Washington, DC 20036-1193 or BOMI Institute, 1521 Ritchie Highway, Arnold, MD 21012.

Additional information about the courses: College Credit Recommendation Service, American Council on Education, One Dupont Circle, Washington, DC 20036-1193.

Air Handling, Water Treatment, and Plumbing Systems (12031)

Location: Various sites in the United States and Canada.

Length: 24 hours (12 weeks); Accelerated course, 24 hours (3 days); Self-study, 12 lessons (est. 48 hours).

Dates: January 1985-Present.

Objective: To provide knowledge of climate control for human comfort, components of HVAC systems, and basics of water treatment and plumbing systems.

Learning Outcome: Upon successful completion of this course, the student will be able to perform common water tests, maintain air conditioning systems, maintain water services, and inspect portable fire extinguishers.

Instruction: Major topics covered in the course are HVAC systems; air cleaning devices, indoor air quality; water conditioning and treatment; plumbing; fire protection and alarm systems. Methods of instruction include lecture, discussion, class exercises, audio/visual materials, pre-test, quizzes, and a final examination; or self-study and a proctored final examination.

Credit Recommendation: In the lower division baccalaureate/associate degree category, 2 semester hours in Building Systems, Facilities Management, or Stationary Engineering (11/94).

Asset Management (11101)

Location: Various sites in the United States and Canada.

Length: Semester course, 30 hours + 2 hour examination (15 weeks); Accelerated course, 30 hours + 2 hour examination (4 days); Self-study, 15 lessons (est. 60 hours) + proctored examination.

Dates: March 1995-Present.

Objective: To provide the students with knowledge about the asset manager's role and function and its place in real estate and business.

Learning Outcome: Upon successful completion of this course, the student will be able to describe the role and responsibilities of asset management; develop an asset management plan, including appropriate human, physical and financial resources; understand the measurement of financial objectives, audits and reasoning thereof; understand property acquisition; disposition, and evaluation of troubled property alternatives.

Instruction: Major topics covered in the course are maximizing a property's or portfolio of properties' acquisition to disposition, utilizing strategic planning including investment and operations analysis. Methods of instruction include lecture, discussion, classroom exercises, audio/visual material, case studies, and an examination; or self-study with a proctored final examination.

Credit Recommendation: In the vocational certificate category, or lower division baccalaureate/associate degree category, 2 semester hours in Real Estate, Property Management, Corporate Real Estate Asset Management, or Business Administration (11/95).

Boilers, Heating Systems, and Applied Mathematics (12011)

Location: Various sites in the United States and Canada.

Length: Semester course, 24 hours (12 weeks); Accelerated course, 24 hours (3 days); Self-study, 12 lessons (est. 48 hours).

Dates: April 1991-Present.

Objective: To provide skill in operating boilers and heating systems using relevant mathematical calculations.

Learning Outcome: Upon successful completion of this course, the student will be able to operate and maintain heating systems including steam and hot water, warm air and radiant heat, and the auxiliary pumps and fans used in these systems.

Instruction: Major topics covered in the course are heating systems operations, mechanical components of heating systems, thermodynamics as applied to heating systems, and basic mathematics needed to operate heating systems. Methods of instruction include lecture, discussion, classroom exercises, pre-test, quizzes, and a final examination; or self-study and a proctored final examination.

Credit Recommendation: In the lower division baccalaureate/associate degree category, 2 semester hours in Building Systems or Stationary Engineering (6/94).

Building Control Systems (12051)

Location: Various sites in the United States and Canada.

Length: Semester course, 24 hours (12 weeks); Accelerated course, 24 hours (3 days); Self-study, 12 lessons (est. 48 hours).

Dates: October 1992-Present.

Objective: To provide knowledge of heating, ventilating, and air conditioning (HVAC) control systems.

Learning Outcome: Upon successful completion of this course, the student will be able to explain components, principles, adjustment, and maintenance of system controller, auxiliary devices, electronic, pneumatic, and computer control systems; describe the operation of heating, cooling, humidification, and dehumidification control applications; and explain variable air volume design and building pressurization control devices.

Instruction: Major topics covered in the course are control system basics; auxiliary and electronic controls and their application to heating, cooling, humidifying, dehumidifying and volume control; and computerized automatic control systems. Methods of instruction include lecture, discussion, classroom exercises, pretest, quizzes, and a final examination; or self-study and a proctored final examination.

Credit Recommendation: In the lower division baccalaureate/associate degree category, 2 semester hours in Stationary

Engineering or Facilities Management (6/94).

Building Design and Maintenance (12061) (Formerly Building Design and Maintenance [01206])

Location: Various sites in the United States and Canada.

Length: *Versions 1 & 2:* Semester course, 24 hours + 2 hour examination (12 weeks); Accelerated course, 24 hours + 2 hour examination (3 days); Self-study, 12 lessons (est. 48 hours) + proctored examination.

Dates: November 1995-Present.

Objective: *Version 1:* To equip the student to properly select and utilize building materials and minimize building maintenance in the safe operation of building systems. *Version 2:* To equip students with basic information on building design, materials, structural systems and finishes, maintenance procedures and equipment, grounds maintenance, reading and using construction documents, and preventive maintenance necessary for the operation and maintenance of building systems.

Learning Outcome: *Version 1:* Upon successful completion of this course, the student will be able to select and properly use construction materials which meet requirements, and standard codes with consideration for maintenance costs. *Version 2:* Upon successful completion of this course, the student will be able to describe characteristics, uses, properties of common building materials, and codes and standards; compare building system components; identify appropriate inspection and maintenance techniques; establish procedures and standards for monitoring building operations, preventive maintenance, and cleaning for a facility; and read and interpret construction documents.

Instruction: *Version 1:* Major topics covered in the course are proper utilization of various building materials and equipment and the care and maintenance of the building, the equipment, and the site for safe access and transportation of people. Methods of instruction include lecture, discussion, audio/visual material, and an examination; or self-study and a proctored final examination. *Version 2:* Major topics covered in the course are common building materials and systems found in foundations; curtain walls; windows; roofing systems; interior finishes; vertical transportation; grounds and their maintenance and inspection; and the reading, scaling, interpretation, care, and use of construction documents. Methods of instruction include lecture, discussion, classroom exercises, audio/visual material, pretests (self study pretests-self evaluation), and a final proctored examination.

Credit Recommendation: *Version 1:* In the vocational certificate category or lower division baccalaureate/associate degree category, 2 semester hours in Construction Technology or Architecture (11/95). *Version 2:* In the upper division baccalaureate degree category, 2 semester hours in Building Systems, Facilities Management, Construction Management, or Architecture (9/96).

Electrical Systems and Illumination (12041)

Location: Various sites in the United States and Canada.

Length: 26 hours (12 weeks); Accelerated course, 26 hours (4 days); Self-study, 12 lessons (est. 48 hours).

Dates: October 1985-Present.

Objective: *Version 1:* To provide a working knowledge of electrical and illumination systems. *Version 2:* To provide a clear understanding of electricity basics, the skills needed to measure electrical consumption, and the ability to recognize, set up, and maintain reliable and effective maintenance and safety systems.

Learning Outcome: *Version 1:* Upon successful completion of this course, the student will be able to maintain the electrical systems of a building; manage electrical energy usage; assess when to contract for work; and explain safety rules for working on electrical equipment. *Version 2:* Upon successful completion of this course, the student will know how to safely operate and maintain a building's electrical equipment; and understand the components of electrical systems and how to measure the electricity the building consumes.

Instruction: *Version 1:* Major topics covered in the course are basic electrical principles; lighting, maintenance, safety, conductors, insulators, switches, motors, and the measurement of electrical consumption. Methods of instruction include lecture, discussion, classroom exercises, audio/visual materials, pre-test, quizzes, and a final examination; or self-study and a proctored final examination. *Version 2:* Major topics covered in this course are sources of electricity; electrical safety and circuits; electric meters; cables, terminations, and conduits; light sources, fixtures, and maintenance; and electric motor basics and maintenance. Methods of instruction include lecture, discussion, classroom exercises, audio/visual materials, pre-test, quizzes, and a final examination; or self-study and a proctored final examination.

Credit Recommendation: *Version 1:* In the vocational certificate category or in the lower division baccalaureate/associate degree category, 2 semester hours in Building Systems, Facilities Management, or Stationary Engineering (11/94). *Version 2:* In the lower division baccalaureate/associate degree category, 2 semester hours in Electrical Systems, Industrial Electricity, or Facilities Operations (9/97).

Energy Management (12071)

Location: Various sites in the United States and Canada.

Length: Semester course, 24 hours + 2 hour examination (12 weeks); Accelerated course, 24 hours + 2 hour examination (3 days); Self-study, 12 lessons (est. 48 hours) + proctored examination.

Dates: April 1994-Present.

Objective: To provide the student with a knowledge of energy management strategies for facility HVAC, electronic and lighting systems.

Learning Outcome: Upon successful completion of this course, the student will be able to perform cost/benefit analysis of HVAC, electric and lighting systems and create an energy management program for their facility.

Instruction: Major topics covered in the course are factors determining energy consumption in HVAC, electronic and lighting systems; preventive maintenance measures in energy management and energy management control system applications. Methods of instruction include lecture, discussion, classroom exercises, audio/visual material, an examination, pretests, a final examination; or self-study with a proctored final examination.

Credit Recommendation: In the upper division baccalaureate degree category, 2 semester hours in Building Systems, Stationary Engineering, Facilities Management, or Construction Management (11/95).

Environmental Health and Safety Issues (19091) (Formerly Environmental Health and Safety Issues [01909])

Location: Various sites in the United States and Canada.

Length: *Versions 1 & 2:* 32 hours (15 weeks); Accelerated course, 32 hours (4 days): Self-study, 15 lessons (est. 60 hours).

Dates: *Version 1:* January 1994-August 1996; *Version 2:* September 1996-Present.

Objective: *Version 1:* To provide knowledge needed to manage environmental health and safety concerns in the workplace. *Version 2:* To provide an overview of environmental health and safety considerations in facilities operations and the maintenance of a proactive management program.

Learning Outcome: *Versions 1 & 2:* Upon successful completion of this course, the student will be able to develop and manage proactive environmental/occupational health and safety programs, comply with regulatory standards and guidelines governing facility health and safety issues, and assess when to obtain technical assistance.

Instruction: *Version 1:* Major topics covered in the course are asbestos; indoor air quality; pollution control, hazardous waste, storm water, and waste water; OSHA and EPA regulations; recordkeeping; site assessments and audits; emergency response; and legal issues. Methods of instruction include lecture, discussion, classroom exercises, audio/visual materials, pre-test, quizzes, and a final examination; or self-study and a proctored final examination. *Version 2:* Major topics covered in the course are regulatory overview, OSHA and EPA regulations, hazard communication, emergency response, asbestos and lead management, office and industrial ergonomics, indoor air quality, air emissions and pollution control, storage tanks, hazardous waste, site assessment and audits, record keeping, and legal issues. Methods of instruction include lecture, discussion, classroom exercises, audio/visual material, pretests (self study quizzes and pretests-self evaluation) and a proctored final examination for self-study.

Credit Recommendation: *Version 1:* In the lower division baccalaureate/associate degree category or in the upper division baccalaureate degree category, 2 semester hours in Facilities Management, Environmental, Occupational Safety, or Business Administration (11/94). *Version 2:* In the upper division baccalaureate degree category, 3 semester hours in Facilities Management, Environmental or Occupational Safety, or Business Administration (9/96).

Facilities Management and the Work Environment (13031)

Location: Various sites in the United States and Canada.

Length: 32 hours (15 weeks); Accelerated course, 32 hours (4 days); Self-study, 15 lessons (est. 60 hours).

Dates: September 1991-June 1997.

Objective: To provide an introduction to facilities management as it relates to the corporate and other business environments.

Learning Outcome: Upon successful completion of this course, the student will be able to create a facilities management plan and implement strategic facilities management techniques.

Instruction: Major topics covered in the course are strategic planning and management; corporate finance and capital investment; management information systems; resource maximization; physical asset management; and the facilities management plan. Methods of instruction include lecture, discussion, classroom exercises, audio/visual materials, pre-test quizzes, and a final examination; or self-study and a proctored final examination.

Credit Recommendation: In the upper division baccalaureate degree category, 2 semester hours in Facilities Management or Business Administration (11/94).

Facilities Planning and Project Management (13051)

Location: Various sites in the United States and Canada.

Length: Semester course, 32 hours (15 weeks); Accelerated course, 32 hours (4 days); Self-study, 15 lessons (est. 60 hours).

Dates: April 1989-Present.

Objective: To provide knowledge of planning facilities from inception to occupancy.

Learning Outcome: Upon successful completion of this course, the student will be able to assemble and manage facilities teams; plan and implement facilities projects and control key elements of the process; coordinate logistics; close out projects; and complete facility annual reports.

Instruction: Major topics covered in the course are value of planning, organizing to plan; planning models; identifying and rating user needs; owned vs. leased vs. developed facilities; managing planning; classifying facility projects; roles of players; specifications for facilities performance; design development and review; implementing projects; planning occupancy; project close-out; and post-occupancy evaluation using facility annual reports. Methods of instruction include lecture, discussion, classroom exercises, pre-test, quizzes, and a final examination; or self-study and a proctored final examination.

Credit Recommendation: In the lower division baccalaureate/associate degree category, 2 semester hours in Facilities Management, Planning, or Construction Management (6/94).

Fundamentals of Facilities Management (13031.2)

Location: Various sites in the U.S. and Canada.

Length: 30 hours plus a 2 hours examination (2 hours/week for 16 weeks or accelerated review-8 hours/day for 4 days or 10 hours/day for 3 days including a 2 hour examination).

Dates: May 1997-Present.

Objective: To provide a broad scope of technical knowledge as the base from which to build a career in facilities management.

Learning Outcome: Upon successful completion of this course, the student will know how to structure and manage operations and maintenance programs; effectively staff to control workload; utilize strategies for internal marketing; and apply project management and leadership skills.

Instruction: Major topics covered in the course are facilities management within the organizational structure; principles of information management; investment, cost controls, and budgeting strategies; operating levels of facilities activities; outsourcing principles; and benefits of leasing vs. ownership. Methods of instruction include lecture, discussion, classroom exercises, audio/visual material, quizzes, and final examination.

Credit Recommendation: In the lower division baccalaureate/associate degree or upper division baccalaureate degree category, 2 semester hours in Facilities Management (9/97) (11/97).

Fundamentals of Real Property Administration (11071)

Location: Various sites in the United States and Canada.

Length: Semester course, 32 hours (15 weeks); Accelerated course, 32 hours (4 days; Self-study, 15 lessons (est. 60 hours).

Dates: January 1994-Present.

Objective: To provide an introduction and overview of the property management profession.

Learning Outcome: Upon successful completion of this course, the student will be able to understand and apply knowledge of the duties and responsibilities of a property manager.

Instruction: Major topics covered in the course are ethics, history, tasks, and responsibilities of property managers; asset management; economics; owner/tenant relations; retention, improvements, marketing, and leases; safety and security; contracting services; reporting and control systems; and environmental issues. Methods of instruction include lecture, discussion, classroom exercises, pre-test, quizzes, and a final examination; or self-study and a proctored final examination.

Credit Recommendation: In the upper division baccalaureate degree category, 2 semester hours in Real Estate (6/94).

Law for Property Managers (11052)

Location: Various sites in the United States and Canada.

Length: Semester course, 30 hours + 2 hour examination (15 weeks); Accelerated course, 30 hours + 2 hour examination (4 days); Self-study, 15 lessons (ext. 60 hours) + proctored examination.

Dates: July 1988-December 1997.

Objective: To provide students with information about contracts, owner liabilities, law of agency, real and personal property transfer agreements and other legal aspects of property management.

Learning Outcome: Upon successful completion of this course, the student will be able to describe the legal system; classify actions and situations according to legal designations; evaluate contracts for completeness, legality, and potential violation; analyze agency relationships for appropriateness to a contract agreement; evaluate simple real property agreements.

Instruction: Major topics covered in the course are premises liability: negligence, strict liability, intentional torts and crimes; contract law; agency; real personal property transfer; real property title, mortgages and liens; and leases, environmental law and fair housing laws. Methods of instruction include lecture, discussion, examinations, and audio/visual material; or self-study and a proctored final examination.

Credit Recommendation: In the lower division baccalaureate/associate degree category or upper division baccalaureate degree category, 2 semester hours in Real Estate, Real Property Law, or Law for Property Managers (11/95).

Leasing and Marketing for Property Managers (11081)

Location: Various sites in the United States and Canada.

Length: Semester course, 32 hours (15 weeks); Accelerated course, 32 hours (4 days); Self-study, 15 lessons (est. 60 hours).

Dates: August 1999-Present.

Objective: To provide analytical skills needed to successfully lease and market building space under favorable as well as adverse economic conditions.

Learning Outcome: Upon successful completion of this course, the student will be able to conduct targeted market surveys, and to apply market survey and plan information needed to make day-to-day marketing and leasing decisions under all market conditions.

Instruction: Major topics covered in the course are market analysis, survey, conditions, and planning; ownership and investment; renewal and tenant satisfaction; the leasing plan; public relations and advertising; tenant prospecting and space allowance; finish; and the leasing organization and document. Methods of instruction include lecture, discussion, classroom exercises, pre-test, quizzes, and a final examination; or self-study and a proctored final examination.

Credit Recommendation: In the upper division baccalaureate degree category, 2 semester hours in Real Estate or Marketing (6/94).

Managing Real Estate and General Service Activities (13071)

Location: Various sites in the United States and Canada.

Length: 32 hours (15 weeks); Accelerated course, 32 hours (4 days); Self-study, 15 lessons (est. 60 hours).

Dates: January 1990-June 1996.

Objective: To provide knowledge of the facility manager's role in real estate management from site selection to ancillary services.

Learning Outcome: Upon successful completion of this course, the student will be able to assemble information about possible sites into a matrix, complete a site evaluation, and negotiate a lease.

Instruction: Major topics covered in the course are acquisition and disposition; site selection; negotiating with agents and brokers; contract development and negotiation; risk management; and the facilities management process. Methods of instruction include lecture, discussion, classroom exercises, audio/visual materials, pre-tests, quizzes, and a final examination.

Credit Recommendation: In the upper division baccalaureate degree category, 2 semester hours in Real Property Management or Facilities Management Process (11/94).

Property Manager's Guide to Commercial Real Estate Law (11052.2)

Location: Various sites in the US and Canada.

Length: 30 hours plus a 2 hour examination (2 hours/week for 16 weeks) or accelerated review - 8 hours/day for 4 days or 10 hours/day for 3 days including a 2 hour examination.

Dates: January 1998-Present.

Objective: To provide a foundation in the basic principles of the law, to help property managers deal with everyday legal issues surrounding their business.

Learning Outcome: Upon successful completion of this course, the student will know contract law; have insight into real estate financing; have an awareness of environmental law and land use; and be skilled in recognizing potential legal liability situations.

Instruction: Major topics covered in the course are real property financing; contracts; property possession and premises liability; environmental law; and employment relationships and agency. Methods of instruction include lecture, discussion, classroom exercises, audio/visual material, and also self-study. Methods of evaluating learning outcomes include quizzes and final examination.

Credit Recommendation: In the upper division baccalaureate degree category, 2 semester hours in Real Estate Property Law, or Law for Property Managers or in the lower division baccalaureate/associate degree category, 2 semester hours in Real Estate Property Law, or Law for Property Managers (1/98).

Real Estate Investment and Finance (19062)

Location: Various sites in the United States and Canada.

Length: Semester course, 32 hours (15 weeks); Accelerated course, 32 hours (4 days); Self-study, 15 lessons (est. 60 hours).

Dates: *Version 1:* July 1991-September 1995; *Version 2:* September 1995-Present.

Objective: *Version 1:* To provide knowledge of market value appraisal, land and real estate taxation, depreciation, obsolescence, and the use of space. *Version 2:* To provide the student with basic financial concepts as they relate to real estate including valuation, analysis, taxation, depreciation, and use of space (life-cycle) costing.

Learning Outcome: *Version 1:* Upon successful completion of this course, the student will be able to understand basic real estate financial concepts; evaluate a real estate investment; develop a property budget and estimate net operating income; and understand the tax implications involved in ownership and disposal of property. *Version 2:* Upon successful completion of this course, the student will be able to evaluate a real estate investment and develop a budget that estimates net operating income; also will be able to do discounted cash flow analysis, income capitalization approach; property taxation costs and strategy to offset costs; and calculate net present value and internal rate of return.

Instruction: *Version 1:* Major topics covered in the course are real estate finance, real estate as an investment, investment objectives, tax factors, real estate appraisal factors, use of financial calculator, and spreadsheets. Methods of instruction include lecture, discussion, classroom exercises, case studies, pre-test, quizzes, and a final examination; or self-study and a proctored final examination. *Version 2:* Major topics covered in the course are commercial property management and facilities management, asset valuation and enhancement, and costs and taxes, with extensive use of hand-held calculators with exercises. Methods of instruction include lecture, discussion, classroom exercises, audio/visual material, case studies, an examination, and extensive practical exercises using calculators; or self-study and a proctored final examination.

Credit Recommendation: *Version 1:* In the upper division baccalaureate degree category, 2 semester hours in Real Estate (6/94). *Version 2:* In the upper division baccalaureate degree category, 3 semester hours in Real Estate, Property Management, and Finance and/or Business Administration (11/95).

Real Property Accounting (11031)

Location: Various sites in the United States and Canada.

Length: Semester course, 32 hours (15 weeks); Accelerated course, 32 hours (4 days); Self-study, 15 lessons (est. 60 hours).

Dates: July 1990-June 1996.

Objective: To provide knowledge of accounting as applied to real property management.

Learning Outcome: Upon successful completion of this course, the student will be able to describe the accounting cycle; prepare budgets and cash flow statements; use the checklist of documents in assuming management of a building; and understand the purpose and use of appropriate statements, procedures, and technology relevant to property management accounting.

Instruction: Major topics covered in the course are the accounting cycle; preparation of internal reports, external financial statements, cash and cost controls, financial and other documents necessary for building management; billing and collecting rents; expenditure cycle; cash flow statements; analysis of financial statements; lease abstraction; budgeting; and use of computers. Methods of instruction include lecture, discussion, visual aids, a case study, pre-tests, quizzes, and a final examination; or self-study and a proctored final examination.

Credit Recommendation: In the lower division baccalaureate/associate degree category, 2 semester hours in Managerial Accounting (6/94).

Refrigeration Systems and Accessories (12021)

Location: Various sites in the United States and Canada.

Length: Semester course, 24 hours + 2 hour examination (12 weeks); Accelerated course, 24 hours + 2 hour examination (3 days); Self-study, 12 lessons (est. 48 hours) + proctored examination.

Dates: April 1991-Present.

Objective: To provide the student with knowledge of refrigeration systems and processes and the related maintenance and operation requirements.

Learning Outcome: Upon successful completion of this course, the student will be able to describe the principles of refrigeration and identify the performance characteristics of refrigeration components; and establish maintenance processes and troubleshoot sequences.

Instruction: Major topics covered in the course are refrigeration cycles and principles, mechanical components of refrigeration systems, systematic troubleshooting, and general maintenance procedures. Methods of instruction include lecture, discussion, classroom exercises, audio/visual material, pre-tests, and a final examination; or self study and a proctored final examination.

Credit Recommendation: In the lower division baccalaureate/associate degree category, 2 semester hours in Stationary Engineering, Building Technology, or Facilities Management (11/95).

Risk Management and Insurance (11042)

Location: Various sites in the United States and Canada.

Length: Semester course, 30 hours + 2 hour examination (15 weeks); Accelerated course, 30 hours + 2 hour examination (4 days); Self-study, 15 lessons (est. 60 hours) + proctored examination.

Dates: July 1989-Present.

Objective: To provide the student with information for identifying, measuring, and dealing with loss exposure in running a business and in the property management field.

Learning Outcome: Upon successful completion of this course, the student will be able to apply the steps of risk management; identify the different types of insurance companies; understand the concepts of insurable interest and liability claims; evaluate insurance needs and policies; understand the claims adjustment process; and explain the role of environmental hazards and the associated concern.

Instruction: Major topics covered in the course are introduction to risk management and insurance, insurance company operations, principles of insurance and insurable risk; property and income loss insurance; liability insurance; employee benefit plans; real estate loss exposure; and environmental concerns. Methods of instruction include lecture, discussion, classroom exercises, audio/visual material, case studies, and an examination; or self-study with a proctored final examination.

Credit Recommendation: In the lower division baccalaureate/associate degree category or upper division baccalaureate degree category, 2 semester hours in Insurance (11/95).

Supervision (12081)

Location: Various sites in the United States and Canada.

Length: Semester course, 24 hours (12 weeks); Accelerated course, 24 hours (4 days); Self-study, 2 lessons (est. 48 hours).

Dates: March 1988-June 1997.

Objective: To provide supervisory skills needed to motivate staff and communicate with other levels of management.

Learning Outcome: Upon successful completion of this course, the student will be able to use techniques for setting objectives and decision-making including management by objectives; plan and control a supervisory process; display understanding of the relationship of authority and responsibility; create conditions to motivate employees; utilize communication, listening, and counseling techniques; manage conflict and handle complaints; relate to minority employees; understand ethical issues; and use time management techniques.

Instruction: Major topics covered in the course are decision-making and leadership; planning and controlling; delegation and motivation; communication and listening skills; counseling and evaluation; conflict management and discipline; supervision of minority employees; budgets, ethics, safety, and time management. Methods of instruction include lecture, discussion, classroom exercises, pre-tests, quizzes, and a final examination; or self-study and a proctored final examination,

Credit Recommendation: In the lower division baccalaureate/associate degree category, 2 semester hours in Supervision or Management (6/94).

Technologies for Facilities Management (13041)

Location: Various sites in the United States and Canada.

Length: .

Dates: *Version 1:* January 1989-May 1995; *Version 2:* June 1995-Present.

Objective: *Version 1:* To provide understanding of available technologies to plan, maintain, and upgrade office and business facilities. *Version 2:* To provide the student with an understanding of the technology commonly used in the facilities environment, justifying the usage of technology and its impact on both workers and the work place.

Learning Outcome: *Version 1:* Upon successful completion of this course, the student will be able to develop policies and procedures for planning and construction of facilities; specify environmental conditions, equipment and furniture compatible with ergonomic requirements for office workers; apply various software management systems; use computer-aided design (CAD, CAFM) systems; plan teleconferencing, audio-visual, and computer facilities; assemble and analyze reports; and evaluate telecommunications systems, data-transmission systems, and existing electric services. *Version 2:* Upon successful completion of this course, the student will be able to acquire knowledge of the role of technology, the application of appropriate technologies, determine the adequacy of technological services and systems, specify software, evaluate telecommunications systems; and data transmissions and existing electrical services.

Instruction: *Version 1:* Major topics covered in the course are office personnel issues; equipment selection and cost; utilization of software; data storage, retrieval, and distribution; and communication systems and cost. Methods of instruction include lecture, discussion, classroom exercises, pre-tests, quizzes, and a final examination; or self-study and a proctored final examination. *Version 2:* Major topics covered in the course are the evolution of technology in the workplace, the usage and effect of computer aided facilities management (CAFM) local area networks, CAD systems, telecommunication systems, power distributions, electrical lighting, HVAC systems, internal special room and space requirements; laboratories and interior environment, high security and surveillance systems, and data retrieval and distribution systems. Methods of instruction include lecture, discussion, classroom exercises, audio/visual material, case studies, an examination, and extensive practical exercises using calculators; or self-study and a proctored final examination.

Credit Recommendation: *Version 1:* In the lower division baccalaureate/associate degree category, 2 semester hours in Computer Science, Information Systems Management, or Facilities Management (6/94). *Version 2:* In the upper division baccalaureate category, 2 semester hours in Computer Science, Information Systems Management, and/or Facilities Management (11/95).

The Design, Operation, and Maintenance of Building Systems, Part I (19011)

Location: Various sites in the United States and Canada.

Length: Semester course, 32 hours (15 weeks); Accelerated course, 32 hours (4 days); Self-study, (est. 60 hours).

Dates: December 1992-Present.

Objective: To provide knowledge of building design and construction including codes, renovation, life cycle costing, maintenance, and building systems.

Learning Outcome: Upon successful completion of this course, the student will be able to manage the ongoing operation and maintenance of building systems; perform life cycle costing on a building project; assist a design team on construction or renovation projects; contract for building services; and monitor performance of contractors.

Instruction: Major topics covered in the course are design and construction; construction materials; structural systems; finish materials, heating, ventilating, and air conditioning; building system controls; life cycle costing; and role of managers in the design and construction process. Methods of instruction include lecture, discussion, classroom exercises, pre-tests, quizzes, and a final examination; or self-study and a proctored final examination.

Credit Recommendation: In the lower division baccalaureate/associate degree category, 2 semester hours in Facilities Management, Stationary Engineering, Construction Management, or Architectural Technology (6/94).

The Design, Operation, and Maintenance of Building Systems, Part II (19021)

Location: Various sites in the United States and Canada.

Length: Semester course, 30 hours + 2 hour examination (15 weeks); Accelerated course, 30 hours + 2 hour examination (4 days); Self-study, 15 lessons (est. 60 hours) + proctored examination.

Dates: December 1994-Present.

Objective: To prepare students to analyze and manage building systems including electrical, vertical transportation, and energy. Also includes managing pest control, landscaping and fire protection.

Learning Outcome: Upon successful completion of this course, the student will make safe management decisions about the various building systems and site with consideration for comfort and efficiency.

Instruction: Major topics covered in the course are electricity (AC and DC) and its applications in building systems; energy management; preventative maintenance; pest and waste control; vertical transportation; cleaning; and landscaping and fire protection. Methods of instruction include lecture, discussion, classroom exercises, audio/visual material, and an examination; or self-study with a proctored final examination.

Credit Recommendation: In the vocational certificate category or lower division baccalaureate/associate degree category, 2 semester hours in Stationary Engineering or Building Engineering (11/95). **NOTE:** Credit should not be given for both this course and specific courses with the same content, i.e., Part I and II of this course duplicates Refrigeration Systems and Accessories and Building Design and Maintenance.

Caesars Atlantic City

Caesars Atlantic City Hotel/Casino is located at the center of the Monopoly-famed Boardwalk in Atlantic City, New Jersey. Since its inception in June 1979 as the second casino to open in New Jersey, Caesars Atlantic City has watched Atlantic City grow to become America's most visited city in America. Once named "Casino of the Decade," Caesars prides itself on award-winning service and premium entertainment and gaming features. Caesars Atlantic City continues to present the latest forms of gaming, which is rapidly becoming America's favorite pastime, second only to motion pictures.

The Training and Development department of Caesars Atlantic City provides education and training services to its over 3600 employees as well as the employees of Caesars Pocono Properties in the Pennsylvania Pocono Mountains. The training offered, encompasses a broad range of subjects such as Basic Skills/ E.S.L, Management, and Computer Software.

Source of official student records: Registry of Credit Recommendations, American Council on Education, One Dupont Circle, Washington, DC 20036-1193.

Additional information about the courses: Office of Corporate-Higher Education Programs, Thomas Edison State College, 101 West State Street, Trenton, NJ 08608-1176.

Front Office Procedures

Location: Atlantic City, New Jersey.

Length: 48 hours (over 16 weeks).

Dates: September 1997-Present.

Objective: To provide the student with an understanding of front office applications within the context of property operations.

Learning Outcome: Upon successful completion of this course, the student will be able to: Explain and understand the functions and operations of a front office system; Demonstrate proficiency in the use of front office technology; Understand the concepts of yield management.

Instruction: Major topics covered in the course are: the Lodging Industry; Hotel Organization, Front Office Operations, Front Office Operations/Computer Applications, the Guest Cycle, Planning and Evaluating Operations, Yield Management, and Managing Human Resources. Methods of instruction include classroom discussion, lecture, lab and simulation.

Credit Recommendation: In the lower division baccalaureate/associate degree category, or in the upper division baccalaureate degree category, 3 semester hours in Front Office Operations (8/97).

Hospitality Industry Computer Systems

Location: Atlantic City, New Jersey.

Length: 48 hours (over 16 weeks).

Dates: February 1997-Present.

Objective: To provide students a basic understanding of computer systems used in the hospitality industry.

Learning Outcome: Upon successful completion of this course, the student will be able to identify and explain the components of computer-based property management systems; explain the common property management information system interfaces; explain the use of a Property Management Information System to provide efficient and effective customer service.

Instruction: Major topics covered in the course are Introduction to Computer Systems, Computer-Based Hotel Property Management Systems, Other Hospitality Applications, and Management Responsibilities. Methods of instruction include classroom discussion, lecture and lab.

Credit Recommendation: In the lower division baccalaureate/associate degree category, 3 semester hours in Survey of Integrated Property Management Information Systems (8/97).

Hospitality Law

Location: Atlantic City, New Jersey.

Length: 48 hours (over 16 weeks).

Dates: September 1997-Present.

Objective: To provide the student with a basic understanding of the law as it relates to the operation of a lodging property and relations with employees.

Learning Outcome: Upon successful completion of this course, the student will be able to describe the laws regarding the rights and liabilities of hotelkeepers; describe the hotel's obligation to protect its guests; explain the laws relating to employers and employment.

Instruction: Major topics covered in the course are Basic Legal Principles Governing Hospitality Operations, Hotel's Duty to Receive Guests and its Right to Refuse guests, Hotel's Duties to the Guest and Others, Restaurant, Food Service and Bars, Hotel and its employees, Laws Relating to General Hotel Operation. Methods of instruction include classroom discussion, lecture and lab.

Credit Recommendation: In the lower division baccalaureate/associate degree category, or in the upper division baccalaureate degree category, 3 semester hours in Hospitality Law (8/97).

Introduction to the Hospitality Industry

Location: Atlantic City, New Jersey.

Length: 48 hours (over 16 weeks).

Dates: October 1996-Present.

Objective: To provide the student with a basic understanding of the history, structure, operation, internal and external function of the hospitality industry.

Learning Outcome: Upon successful completion of this course, the student will be able to explain the history and development of the hospitality industry; describe the common divisions of hospitality organizations; identify the goals and emphasis of managing operational areas; describe the interaction of all functional areas.

Instruction: Major topics covered in the course are Travel and Tourism Industry; Career Opportunities; the Early History of Lodging; the Globalization of the Lodging Industry; Organization and Structure of the Lodging Industry; the Rooms Division; Growth and Development of Food Service; Organization and Structure of the Food Service Industry; Management and Operation of Food Services; Engineering and Maintenance Division; Marketing and Sales Division; Accounting Division; Human Resources; Security Division. Methods of instruction include classroom discussion, lecture and assignments.

Credit Recommendation: In the lower division baccalaureate/associate degree category, 3 semester hours in Introduction to the Hospitality Industry (8/97).

Management Development Program Series

Location: Caesars Atlantic City/ Caesar's Pocono Resorts.

Length: 21 hours (6 sessions).

Dates: April 1992-Present.

Objective: To enhance the skills of managers in the areas of interviewing, motivation, managing stress, teamwork/ team building, recognizing various workplace behavior patterns and managing for customer service.

Learning Outcome: Upon the successful completion of this course, the student will be able to recognize and value various workplace behavior patterns and use them to create and maintain an atmosphere conducive to peak performance; develop their own stress coping strategies that are practical and effective; effectively prepare for and facilitate an employment interview that results in sound and legal hiring decisions; and use various techniques to maintain a team environment.

Instruction: Major topics covered in the course are "MDP", a career development program designed for managers and experienced supervisors who have successfully completed Caesars "Supervisory Skills Training Program" (Employees may enroll in individual workshops or take the entire series. In order to earn the MANAGEMENT DEVELOPMENT certificate, employees must complete all six workshops. Each workshop addresses key challenges facing today's managers.); a broad understanding and appreciation of their role in the organization; vital skills in the areas of effective interviewing, motivation, team building and managing, effective customer service; stress management; and understanding various workplace behaviors. Methods of instruction include lecture, role play simulations, discussion, and independent study.

Credit Recommendation: In the lower division baccalaureate/associate degree category, 1 semester hour in Principles of Management (2/95).

Supervisory Skills Training Program

Location: Caesars Atlantic City/ Caesar's Pocono Resorts.

Length: 20 hours (2 hours per week over 10 weeks).

Dates: March 1990-Present.

Objective: To provide supervisors with the fundamental skills to be an effective leader.

Learning Outcome: Upon successful completion of this course, the student will be able to identify various management styles and their effect on manager/employee relationships; recognize the role and responsibility of the manager in the performance appraisal process; identify the benefits of effective delegation; create and manage an environment that encourages expression of different ideas and opinions; recognize the benefits of a well-planned 1-on-1 training process; and effectively use 1 and 2-way communication.

Instruction: Major topics covered in the course are developing and enhancing the potential of new and experienced supervisor's management, administration, and human relations skills; assisting the front line supervisor in making the difficult transition from employee to supervisor; and reinforces good, fundamental management skills for the more experienced supervisor. Methods of instruction include lecture, discussion, role playing, and independent study.

Credit Recommendation: In the lower division baccalaureate/associate degree category, 1 semester hour in Principles of Supervision (2/95).

Upward Mobility Program

Location: Caesars Atlantic City.

Length: 64 hours (2 hour sessions over 32 weeks).

Dates: October 1990-Present.

Objective: To provide participants with a fundamental managerial and business practice overview.

Learning Outcome: Upon successful completion of this course, the student will be able to create a strong professional presence through appropriate business dress, etiquette, and image; develop strategies that can help plan, direct, and control their careers; write more effective business correspondence by writing more efficiently and persuasively; use speech organization, voice control, and body language to deliver effective platform communications; better understand the internal policies and procedures and external laws that govern our industry and how they are enforced; and utilize fundamental leadership skills.

Instruction: Major topics covered in the course are the professional development of employees, fundamental supervisory skills, and current issues and challenges facing Caesars and the hotel/casino industry. Methods of instruction include lectures, case studies, role plays, exercises, tours, and workshops.

Credit Recommendation: In the lower division baccalaureate/associate degree category, 3 semester hours in Business Communications (2/95).

Calhoon MEBA Engineering School

Established in 1966 as a training facility for both merchant marine engineering cadets and licensed MEBA marine officers serving aboard United States Merchant vessels, the school now provides only continuing education and license upgrading opportunities for MEBA marine officers. The director and the staff of the school operate within the specific guidelines and requirements established by a board of trustees composed of an equal number of shipping company representatives and elected officers from the Marine Engineers Beneficial Association (MEBA).

Dedicated to providing training that enhances the qualifications of MEBA marine officers to operate U.S. merchant vessels safely, efficiently, and in compliance with all applicable maritime laws, the school offers courses utilizing state of the art equipment in conjunction with proven instructional techniques. All course documentation, development, and revision reflecting changes in industry or regulatory body requirements is conducted under the guidelines established by the International Maritime Organization (IMO), implemented under the direction of the U.S. Coast Guard, and are consistent with generally accepted curriculum design models.

Instructors must meet rigorous standards that include certification and demonstrated proficiency in their field of expertise. Additionally, seminars, conferences, and courses of study offered by accredited institutions are an integral part of required staff development.

Source of official student records: Registry of Credit Recommendations, American Council on Education, One Dupont Circle, Washington, DC 20036-1193 or Registrar, Calhoon MEBA Engineering School, 27050 St. Michaels Road, Easton, MD 21601-7550.

Additional information about the courses: College Credit Recommendation Service, American Council on Education, One Dupont Circle, Washington, DC 20036-1193.

Advanced Firefighting

Location: Calhoon MEBA Engineering, Easton, MD.

Length: 30 hours (1 week).

Dates: August 1996-Present.

Objective: To prepare the student to handle a fire emergency aboard a vessel by effectively applying the Incident Command System and Fire Command Practices.

Learning Outcome: Upon successful completion of this course, the student will be able to define the properties of flammable materials and list the common types of sources of ignition found aboard ship; develop pre-plans for fire related emergencies; organize a command structure for shipboard firefighting; and list, define, and discuss the phases of fire development aboard ship and how to handle them.

Instruction: Major topics covered in the course are, but are not limited to, properties of extinguishing agents, pre-fire plans, shipboard firefighting procedures, and protective equipment. Methods of instruction include lecture, discussion, classroom exercises, case studies, computer-assisted/video tape, tests, quizzes, and competency based exercises.

Credit Recommendation: In the lower division baccalaureate/associate degree category, 2 semester hours (1 hour lecture and 1 hour laboratory) in Fire Science (12/96).

Analog Electronics

Location: Easton, Md.

Length: 120 hours (4 weeks).

Dates: May 1996-Present.

Objective: To provide the student with knowledge of discrete and integrated semiconductor devices with emphasis on their utilization in industrial instrumentation and control applications.

Learning Outcome: Upon successful completion of this course, the student will be able to know the linear characteristics of discrete and integrated semiconductor devices and understand the operation of common circuit arrangements for each device; demonstrate skills in PC board soldering, reading schematic diagrams, and using standard electronic test equipment; and identify and test all common electronic components.

Instruction: Major topics covered in the course are, but not limited to, an overview of DC resistive and capacitive circuits used in electronics, analog waveform analysis, the use of electronic test equipment including oscilloscopes, device packaging and testing, soldering skills, semiconductor theory, diodes, rectification, power supplies, zener regulators, LEDs, bipolar and field-effect transistor amplifiers, thyristor power control, operational amplifiers, analog sensors, and signal conditioning. Methods of instruction include lectures; demonstrations; audio/visual presentations; competency-based laboratory exercises which provide practical skills in device packaging and testing, breadboard wiring techniques, circuit measurement and analysis, and the use of electronic test equipment; quizzes; homework assignments; and final examination.

Credit Recommendation: In the vocational certificate category, 1 semester hour in Basic Circuits Fundamentals; in the lower division baccalaureate/associate degree category, 2 semester hours in Electronic Devices, and in the lower division baccalaureate/associate degree category, 1 semester hour in Basic Electronics Laboratory (5/97).

Electrical Troubleshooting

Location: Calhoon MEBA Engineering, Easton, MD.

Length: 60 hours (2 weeks).

Dates: September 1995-Present.

Objective: To provide classroom instruction and hands-on training of a wide range of electrical troubleshooting topics directed to the needs of a marine engineer. Emphasis is on electromechanical and programmable logic controller control of three phase induction motors.

Learning Outcome: Upon successful completion of this course, the student will be able to discuss the theory and operation of AC motor controllers as well as become proficient in their troubleshooting and repairing.

Instruction: Major topics covered in the course are a review of R, L & C components and associated circuits, test equipment, understanding shock hazards, circuit protection systems, three phase motors and their characteristics, full voltage and reduced voltage motor starter systems, programmable logic controllers, and the theory and application of electrical troubleshooting and repair techniques. Methods of instruction include lecture, laboratory time, classroom exercises, case studies, computer-assisted/video tape, tests, quizzes, and competency based exercises.

Credit Recommendation: In the lower division baccalaureate/associate degree category, 2 semester hours (1 hour lecture and 1 hour laboratory) in Troubleshooting Motor Controllers (12/96).

Electricity

Location: Calhoon MEBA Engineering, Easton, MD.

Length: 120 hours (4 weeks).

Dates: November 1995-Present.

Objective: To provide a theoretical background, reinforced by practical experience, in basic electricity with an emphasis on motor control systems.

Learning Outcome: Upon successful completion of this course, the student will be able to demonstrate a basic understanding of passive AC and DC electric circuits; perform electrical troubleshooting and repair of electromechanical motor control systems; discuss the theory and operation of programmable logic controllers; and develop a basic programming ability with one specific typical Programmable Logic Controller.

Instruction: Major topics covered in the course are fundamentals of electricity, understanding shock hazards, DC circuits, electrical measurement techniques, magnetism, AC fundamentals and circuits, power and circuit protection devices, three-phase fundamentals and transformers, three-phase motors and their various characteristics, full voltage and reduced voltage motor starter systems, programmable logic controllers, and electrical troubleshooting techniques. Methods of instruction include lecture, discussion, classroom exercises, case studies, computer-assisted/video tape, laboratory, tests, quizzes, and competency based exercises.

Credit Recommendation: In the vocational certificate category, 2 semester hours in Basic Electricity or in the lower division baccalaureate/associate degree category, 2 semester hours (1 hour lecture and 1 hour laboratory) in Motors and Motor Controllers (12/96).

Hazardous Materials Technician

Location: Calhoon MEBA Engineering, Easton, MD.

Length: 30 hours (1 week).

Dates: August 1996-Present.

Objective: To prepare the student to function as a member of a Hazardous Materials Response Team or be able to set up a hazardous materials program aboard ship. This course is designed to meet or exceed the requirements of OSHA 29 CFR 1910.120 and NFPA Standards 471 and 472 for Hazardous Materials Technician-level response personnel.

Learning Outcome: Upon successful completion of this course, the student will be able to apply the hazardous materials laws as they relate to the shipboard environment; develop and implement an emergency response plan; and identify, classify, and verify a hazardous material and select appropriate decontamination procedures associated with it.

Instruction: Major topics covered in the course are, but are not limited to, hazardous materials legislation, recognition of hazardous materials, risk assessment, medical evaluations and toxicology, decontamination, tactical operations, and local emergency response team development. Methods of instruction include lecture, discussion, classroom exercises, case studies, computer-assisted/video tape, tests, quizzes, and competency based exercises.

Credit Recommendation: In the lower division baccalaureate/associate degree category, 2 semester hours (1 hour lecture and 1 hour laboratory) in Emergency Management or Fire Science (12/96).

LNG Tankship/Liquefied Gas (PIC)

Location: Calhoon MEBA Engineering, Easton, MD.

Length: 60 hours (2 weeks).

Dates: March 1986-Present.

Objective: Students successfully completing this course should be qualified to take immediate responsibility for the loading, discharging, care in transit, and handling of cargo on a liquefied gas tanker.

Learning Outcome: Upon successful completion of this course, the student will be able to describe the production of liquefied gas; interpret the Rules and Regulations for Gas Carriers; cite the specific design features associated with Gas Carriers; explain how to utilize the various piping systems found aboard Gas Carriers to manipulate the cargo; and implement the safety procedures associated with the transport of liquefied gas.

Instruction: Major topics covered in the course are Code of Federal Regulations (CFR), Ship Design, Stability of the Vessel, Chemistry and Physics of liquefied gases, Cargo Systems and their uses, and Vessel Operation. Methods of instruction include lecture, discussion, classroom exercises, case studies, written formal examinations, and quizzes.

Credit Recommendation: In the upper division baccalaureate degree category, 2 semester hours in Petroleum Engineering or Liquid Cargo Operations (12/96).

Ship's Medicine

Location: Calhoon MEBA Engineering, Easton, MD.

Length: 63 hours (2 weeks).

Dates: January 1994-Present.

Objective: To provide students with a sufficient understanding of various emergency care principles so that they are able to assist an ill or injured shipmate in an emergency situation while on board ship, at sea.

Learning Outcome: Upon successful completion of this course, the student will be able to perform basic emergency medical care and the advanced skills of IV therapy and medication administration, suturing, urinary catheterization, and some emergency dentistry skills.

Instruction: Major topics covered in the course are anatomy and physiology of the body; patient assessment; bleeding control, wound care, suturing, and shock management; fracture management; MAST application; emergency dentistry; IV therapy and medication administration; urinary catheterization; oxygen therapy and adjunctive airway management; reports and recordkeeping; alcohol and drug abuse awareness; post mortem care; and sustained nursing care. Methods of instruction include lecture, discussion, classroom exercises, case studies, computer-assisted/video tape, tests, quizzes, and competency based exercises.

Credit Recommendation: In the lower division baccalaureate/associate degree or upper division baccalaureate degree category, 3 semester hours in Emergency Medical Technology or Health Science (12/96).

Steam Engineering

Location: Calhoon MEBA Engineering, Easton, MD.

Length: 174 hours (6 weeks) (156 lecture hours and 18 laboratory hours).

Dates: March 1997-Present.

Objective: To prepare the student to assume the duties and responsibilities appropriate for the level of their license on board steam powered vessels. Emphasis is placed on the theory, construction, operation, and casualty control of steam power plants, especially marine propulsion systems.

Learning Outcome: Upon successful completion of this course, the student will be able to explain the construction, operation, maintenance, and casualty control procedures associated with steam power plants, especially marine propulsion systems. In addition, successful completion of the course also allows a licensed diesel engineer to take the USCG Steam Endorsement examination and cross over a current Motor license to a Steam license at its current grade, or receive 90 days steam service towards any license upgrade of a current Steam license.

Instruction: Major topics covered in the course are general steam principles, steam generation, turbine construction and operation, boiler feedwater systems and basic chemistry, and combustion control systems. Methods of instruction include lecture, discussion, laboratory demonstration, practical exercises, field trips, tests, quizzes, and competency based exercises.

Credit Recommendation: In the lower division baccalaureate/associate degree category, 7 semester hours (6 hours lecture and 1 hour laboratory) in Power Plant Technology, Steam Generation Systems, or Marine Engineering (12/96).

Tankship Safety/Dangerous Liquids (PIC)

Location: Calhoon MEBA Engineering, Easton, MD.

Length: 60 hours (2 weeks).

Dates: September 1992-Present.

Objective: Those successfully completing this course will meet certification requirements to serve as any deck or engine officer immediately responsible for the handling or care of dangerous liquid cargo or cargo handling systems aboard an oil or chemical tanker.

Learning Outcome: Upon successful completion of this course, the student will be able to describe the characteristics of dangerous liquids; explain the necessary safety precautions to be followed when handling dangerous liquids; list the rules concerning protection of the environment from the uncontrolled release of cargo; identify the general arrangement of cargo tanks and associated equipment including free flow type; calculate loading rates and completion times; and state the operational procedures for primary inerting using various methods.

Instruction: Major topics covered in the course are cargo systems; cargo handling; instrumentation systems; auxiliary systems; loading and discharge operations; stability requirements; safety precautions; and pollution prevention. Methods of instruction include lecture, discussion, video tapes, practical demonstrations, laboratory, tests, quizzes, and competency based exercises.

Credit Recommendation: In the lower division baccalaureate/associate degree category, 2 semester hours in Environmental Science, Nautical Science, Cargo Handling, or Liquid Cargo Operations (12/96).

California College for Health Sciences

California College for Health Sciences (CCHS) is a private postsecondary institution licensed by the State of California to operate as a degree-granting school of higher education. The school was founded in 1975 as a resident campus for respiratory care education. In 1978, the school launched a distance education component in the field of respiratory care. Since that time, the distance education curriculum has been expanded to include Associate of Science degrees in: Respiratory Tech-nology, Respiratory Therapy, Medical Transcription, Electroencepholographic Technology, and Early Childhood Education; Bachelor of Science degrees with emphasis in: Management, Poly-somnography, and Respiratory Care; a Master of Science degree in Community Health Administration and Wellness Promotion, and courses in basic science and general education.

As an educational institution, CCHS is accredited by the Accrediting Commission of the Distance Education and Training Council and by the Accrediting Commission of Career Schools and Colleges of Technology. In addition, the entry-level and advanced practitioner programs in respiratory care education are accredited by the Commission on Accreditation of Allied Health Education Programs (CAAHEP).

The mission of the College is "to assist prospective and working health and human services professionals in the achievement of their individual career objectives with comprehensive, highly accessible and practical education that meets national professional academic standards." The independent study format of distance education enables students to design a study schedule that meets their individual needs, taking into consideration career and family obligations.

CCHS is a leader in distance education for health care practitioners. Located in a suburb of San Diego, California, CCHS employs more than 50 full-time faculty and staff to assist students by providing a timely response to inquiries and requests for assistance. Courses are developed by subject matter experts working in conjunction with professional instructional designers. Course formats include both textbooks accompanied by study guides and stand-alone resources that integrate course content and study materials into a single student manual. Academic assistance is provided by qualified faculty and staff via correspondence and electronic communication modalities.

Instructional staff members with subject matter expertise are available at CCHS to answer questions and to provide tutorial assistance. Additional assistance is provided by adjunct faculty and other resource personnel in hospitals and other employment settings. Support staff are also in frequent contact with students to resolve nonacademic concerns that tend to influence student success and satisfaction with the program. A computerized management system is used for evaluating learning outcomes and for tracking student progress.

Source of official student records: Registry of Credit Recommendations, American Council on Education, One Dupont Circle, Washington, DC 20036-1193 or Office of the Registrar, California College for Health Sciences, 222 W. 24th Street, National City, CA 91950.

Additional information about the courses: College Credit Recommendation Service, American Council on Education, One Dupont Circle, Washington, DC 20036-1193.

Accounting I (ACC 220)

Location: Independent study by correspondence.

Length: Self-study.

Dates: June 1997-Present.

Objective: To introduce the basic principles of accounting.

Learning Outcome: Upon successful completion of this course, the student will be able to demonstrate an understanding of the basic principles of accounting.

Instruction: Major topics covered in the course are the accounting cycle; accounting systems, internal controls, and special journals; accounting for merchandising businesses; and accounting for cash, receivable, temporary investments, inventories, assets, and payable. Methods of instruction include directed, text-based independent study (distance education course), tests, projects, and final examination.

Credit Recommendation: In the lower division baccalaureate/associate degree category, 3 semester hours in Accounting or Business Administration (6/97).

Algebra Essentials (MAT 101)

Location: Independent study by correspondence.

Length: 115 hours (9 units covering 12 chapters).

Dates: October 1984-Present.

Objective: To provide the student with knowledge of the use of number systems and algebraic expressions, scientific notation, and the evaluation and solving of algebraic equations and word problems.

Learning Outcome: Upon successful completion of this course, the student will be able to perform real number operations; translate word problems into equations; write numbers in scientific notation form; solve problems involving polynomial expressions; graph straight line and curvilinear equations; solve systems of equations; and solve quadratic equations.

Instruction: Major topics covered in the course are real number operations, inequalities, translating word problems into equations, exponents and scientific notation, polynomials, factoring, finding least common denominators, graphing, systems of equations, radicals, and quadratic equations. Methods of instruction include independent study with open book unit examinations and a proctored final examination.

Credit Recommendation: In the lower division baccalaureate/associate degree category, 3 semester hours in Mathematics, College Algebra, or Basic Algebra (10/93).

Cardiology Transcription (MDT 124)

Location: Independent study by correspondence.

Length: Self-study.

Dates: June 1997-Present.

Objective: To help the experienced medical transcriptionist develop expertise in cardiology transcription.

Learning Outcome: Upon successful completion of this course, the student will be able to transcribe cardiology dictation with a high degree of accuracy; proofread transcribed reports; select proper formats; demonstrate proper editing techniques with identification and correction of errors of style, format, punctuation, and grammar; utilize appropriate reference material; describe and spell common cardiology symptoms, diseases, laboratory tests, x-ray procedures, and surgical instruments; describe the main categories of cardiac drugs; differentiate between generic and trade name drugs; give common drug dosage forms and routes of administration; and name common intravenous solutions.

Instruction: Major topics covered in the course are cardiology terminology; symptoms and disease processes impacting cardiology reports; cardiology laboratory and x-ray practices and procedures; cardiology surgical indications and procedures; medical grammar, proofreading, and editing; and standard transcription practices. Methods of instruction directed, text-based independent study (distance education course), audio/visual material, readings, significant practice at transcribing cardiology dictation, quizzes, tests, transcription of cardiology dictation, and final examination.

Credit Recommendation: In the lower division baccalaureate/associate degree category, 3 semester hours in Cardiology Transcription (6/97).

Child Abuse and Neglect (ECE 112)

Location: Independent study by correspondence.

Length: 3 self-paced units (8 lessons).

Dates: February 1994-Present.

Objective: To provide the student understanding of child abuse and neglect, proper identification and reporting procedures, and methods for treating and preventing child abuse and neglect.

Learning Outcome: Upon successful completion of this course, the student will be able to define what is meant by child abuse and neglect; identify child abuse and neglect; understanding reporting procedures; understand treatment and prevention strategies; and understand the child care professional's role in the child abuse reporting process.

Instruction: Major topics covered in the course are child abuse recognition, identification, reporting procedures, and the teacher's role. Methods of instruction include independent study, course manual, projects, video, self-administered unit quizzes, and a proctored final examination.

Credit Recommendation: In the lower division baccalaureate/associate degree category, 3 semester hours as an elective in Early Childhood Education (4/94).

Curriculum for Early Childhood Education (ECE 115)

Location: Independent study by correspondence.

Length: 19 self-paced lessons.

Dates: May 1992-Present.

Objective: To provide the student with the knowledge and skill in designing an age-appropriate curriculum for your children.

Learning Outcome: Upon successful completion of this course, the student will be able to implement a curriculum for young children by focusing on competencies in emotional, social, physical, cognitive, and creative development; and to develop skills in interacting with families.

Instruction: Major topics covered in the course are preparing a stimulating learning environment, planning activities and experiences to facilitate development of "the five selves," and working with families. Methods of instruction include independent study, course manual, projects, self-administered unit quizzes, and a proctored final examination.

Credit Recommendation: In the lower division baccalaureate/associate degree category, 3 semester hours in Early Childhood Education (4/94).

Dealing with Death and Dying (SOC 110)

Location: Independent study by correspondence.

Length: 90 hours (11 lessons).

Dates: October 1984-Present.

Objective: To provide the student with an understanding of the social, cultural, and ethical aspects of dying with emphasis on the role of the caregiver.

Learning Outcome: Upon successful completion of this course, the student will be able to identify and describe important aspects of death and dying, including commonly held perceptions; ethical issues; stages of grief; and bereavement.

Instruction: Major topics covered in the course are attitudes toward death, modes of immorality, the hospice movement, the dying process and death perceptions, the role of the hospital and helping professions, the dying child, ethical issues, suicides, functions of funerals, stages of grief, cross-cultural perspectives, and major concerns for the future of death education and counseling. Methods of instruction include independent study with open-book unit examinations and a proctored final examination.

Credit Recommendation: In the lower division baccalaureate/associate degree category, 3 semester hours in Sociology or Health Education (10/93).

Developing Math and Science Skills in Young Children (ECE 117)

Location: Independent study by correspondence.

Length: Self-study.

Dates: June 1997-Present.

Objective: To teach the knowledge and skills needed to effectively teach math and science to young children in an organized sequential approach, and to create and develop appropriate math and science curriculum for preschool children.

Learning Outcome: Upon successful completion of this course, the student will be able to correctly identify children's developing concepts; correctly describe commonalties between math and science; label Piaget's and Vygotsky's developmental stages; explain how young children acquire knowledge; define one-to-one correspondence; assess and evaluate a child's ability to use math sets and symbols; develop instructional activities and materials for whole number operations; develop lessons that guide students in primary science investigations; integrate science and math with other subjects; and select appropriate materials for teaching math and science.

Instruction: Major topics covered in the course are concept development in math and science; and fundamental concepts and skills in identifying symbols and higher level activity. Methods of instruction include directed, text-based independent study (distance education course), papers, tests, and final examination.

Credit Recommendation: In the lower division baccalaureate/associate degree category, 3 semester hours in Developing Math and Science Concepts in Young Children (6/97).

Effective Communication Through Technical Writing (ENG 110)

Location: Independent study by correspondence.

Length: 120 hours (7 lessons).

Dates: October 1984-Present.

Objective: To provide the student with skill in writing, especially for business and scientific purposes, and with practice in writing business letters, memos, and scientific papers.

Learning Outcome: Upon successful completion of this course, the student will be able to develop a technical writing style that incorporates correct grammar and the four step method for technical prose; write a business letter using the correct layout, parts, and format; write an interoffice memo using the basic principles regarding conciseness and function; recognize the different types of proposals, select an appropriate proposal style, and write a proposal; identify the services that index medical literature; identify the eight parts of a scientific paper; describe the basic elements in book or article reviews, case reports, editorials, and letters to the editor; and describe the procedure of preparing and submitting a manuscript to a scientific journal.

Instruction: Major topics covered in the course are writing style and technical prose; writing the business letter, interoffice memo, proposal, scientific paper, and other forms of medical and scientific prose; and writing for publication. Methods of instruction include independent study, writing assignments, open-book unit exams, and a proctored final exam.

Credit Recommendation: In the lower division baccalaureate/associate degree category, 3 semester hours in English or Communications (10/93).

Electroencephalographic Technology Program
General Anatomy/Physiology and Human Disease
Medical Terminology
Neuroanatomy and Neurophysiology
Patient Care and Infection Control
Fundamental Electroencephalography
Normal Adult EEG and Normal Variants
Normal Neonatal and Pediatric EEG
Applied Pharmacology
Neurological Disorders and Neuropathology
Advanced EEG
Abnormal EEG and Clinical Correlations-Adults
Abnormal EEG and Clinical Correlations-Newborn and Ped.
Introduction to Computers
Overview of EEG Specialties and Trends

Location: Independent study by correspondence.

Length: 1,400 hours over 18 months.

Dates: October 1994-Present.

Objective: To prepare students with didactic knowledge and clinical skills, to perform routine and specialized EEGs, have a basic knowledge of Neuroanatomy & Neurophysiology, describe the structure & function of the neurological systems with clinical correlations, describe the applications of neurodiagnostic testing equipment, apply infection control and patient safety procedures.

Learning Outcome: Upon successful completion of this course, the student will be able to perform routine and specialized EEG's; have a basic knowledge of Neuroanatomy & Neurophysiology; describe the structure & functions of neurological systems with clinical correlations; describe the applications of neurodiagnostic testing equipment; and apply infection control and patient safety procedures.

Instruction: Major topics covered in the course are Neuroanatomy and Neuro-physiology, patient care and infection control, fundamental Electroencepahlography, applied pharmacology, Neurological disorders and Neuropathology, Advanced Electroencephalography, Normal and Abnormal EEG, and clinical correlations.

Credit Recommendation:

General Anatomy/Physiology and Human Disease

In the lower division baccalaureate associate or upper division baccalaureate degree category, 3 semester hours in General Anatomy/Physiology and Human Diseases (10/95).

Medical Terminology

In the lower division baccalaureate/associate or upper division baccalaureate degree category, 1 semester hour in Medical Terminology(10/95).

Neuroanatomy and Neurophysiology

In the lower division baccalaureate/associate or upper division baccalaureate degree category, 3 semester hours in Neuroanatomy and Neurophysiology (10/95).

Patient Care and Infection Control

In the lower division baccalaureate/associate or upper division baccalaureate degree category, 3 semester hours in Patient Care and Infection Control (10/95).

Fundamental Electroencephalography

In the lower division baccalaureate/associate or upper division baccalaureate degree category, 4 semester hours in Fundamental Electroencephalography (10/95).

Normal Adult EEG and Normal Variants

In the lower division baccalaureate/associate or upper division baccalaureate degree category, 2 semester hours in Normal Adult EEG and Normal Variants (10/95).

Normal Neonatal and Pediatric EEG

In the lower division baccalaureate/associate or upper division baccalaureate degree category, 2 semester hours in Normal Neonatal and Pediatric EEG (10/95).

Applied Pharmacology

In the lower division baccalaureate/associate or upper division baccalaureate degree category, 2 semester hours in Applied Pharmacology (10/95).

Neurological Disorders and Neuropathology

In the lower division baccalaureate/associate or upper division baccalaureate degree category, 1 semester hour in Neurological Disorders and Neuropahtology (10/95).

Advanced EEG

In the lower division baccalaureate/associate or upper division baccalaureate degree category, 3 semester hours in Advanced EEG (10/95).

Abnormal EEG and Clinical Correlations - Adults

In the lower division baccalaureate/associate or upper division baccalaureate degree category, 2 semester hours in Abnormal EEG and Clinical Corrections - Adults (10/95).

Abnormal EEG and Clinical Correlations - Newborn and Ped.

In the lower division baccalaureate/associate or upper division baccalaureate degree category, 2 semester hours in Abnormal EEG and Clinical Corrections - Newborns and Peds (10/95).

Introduction to Computers

In the lower division baccalaureate/associate or upper division baccalaureate degree category, 1 semester hour in Introduction to Basic Elements to Computers (10/95).

Overview of EEG Specialties and Trends

In the lower division baccalaureate/associate or upper division baccalaureate degree category, 2 semester hours in Overview of EEG Specialties and Trends (10/95).

In the lower division baccalaureate/associate or upper division baccalaureate degree category, 15 semester hours in Clinical Practicum (for a total of 46 hours) (10/95).

English Essentials (ENG 101)

Location: Independent study by correspondence.

Length: 3 self-paced lessons (completion takes up to 6 months).

Dates: September 1995-Present.

Objective: To refine the essential English language skills needed to communicate ideas successfully.

Learning Outcome: Upon successful completion of this course, the student will be able to identify and utilize the basic techniques of the English language, including grammar, punctuation, spelling, and composition.

Instruction: Major topics covered in the course are the parts of speech, sentence structure, capitalization, punctuation, spelling, paragraph structure, types of evidence, and composition structure. Methods of instruction include self-paced independent study, textbook/study guide, tests, papers, and a final examination.

Credit Recommendation: In the vocational certificate or lower division baccalaureate/associate degree category, 3 semester hours in English (11/95) (6/96).

Fundamentals of Child Care Education Overview (ECE 111)

Location: Independent study by correspondence.

Length: 9 self-paced lessons.

Dates: December 1991-Present.

Objective: To provide the student with the knowledge to develop an age appropriate child care facility.

Learning Outcome: Upon successful completion of this course, the student will be able to effectively work with young children; provide an environment that is conducive for learning; involve parents in the education and developmental processes of their child; provide a healthy and safe atmosphere for young children; and familiarize himself/herself with meeting the nutritional needs of young children.

Instruction: Major topics covered in the course are attributes for a child care professional, conducive learning environment for young children, various discipline styles, health and safety for a children, nutritional ideas, and parent involvement. Methods of instruction include correspondence study, quick quizzes, projects, self-evaluation, hands-on activities, and examinations.

Credit Recommendation: In the vocational certificate or lower division baccalaureate/associate degree category, 3 semester hours in Early Childhood Education (11/95).

Fundamentals of Child Development (ECE 100)

Location: Independent study by correspondence.

Length: 7 self-paced lessons (15 learning exercises).

Dates: March 1993-Present.

Objective: To provide the student with an understanding of physical, cognitive, social, and emotional development of young children, and of factors that hinder their normal development.

Learning Outcome: Upon successful completion of this course, the student will be able to identify and describe several learning theories; analyze physical, social, cognitive, and emotional development; and recognize environmental and hereditary factors which influence normal growth and development of young children.

Instruction: Major topics covered in the course are history and theory; physical and motor development; cognitive, social, and emotional development; factors that hinder normal development in children; and characteristics of preschoolers. Methods of instruction include independent study utilizing course manual, projects, audio visual aids, self-administered unit examinations, and a proctored final examination.

Credit Recommendation: In the lower division baccalaureate/associate degree category, 3 semester hours in Early Childhood Education (4/94).

Fundamentals of Supervision: The New Supervisor (BUS 101)

Location: Independent study by correspondence.

Length: 90 hours (3 lessons covering 13 chapters).

Dates: September 1987-Present.

Objective: To provide the student with the knowledge required to supervise others effectively and to provide leadership that contributes to a productive work unit.

Learning Outcome: Upon successful completion of this course, the student will be able to describe the responsibilities of a manager; identify sources of conflict; discuss the differences between verbal and nonverbal communication; and manage a diverse workforce with understanding and effectiveness.

Instruction: Major topics covered in the course are promotion, getting to know your workers and bosses, communication, managing time and stress, interviewing techniques, orienting and training workers, managing a diverse workforce, team building and group skills, and power politics. Methods of instruction include independent study with open-book unit examinations and a proctored final examination.

Credit Recommendation: In the vocational certificate or lower division baccalaureate/associate degree category, 3 semester hours in Business Administration, Office Management, or Communications (10/93).

Human Anatomy and Physiology (BIO 110)

Location: Independent study by correspondence.

Length: 125 hours (9 lessons).

Dates: October 1984-Present.

Objective: To provide the student with basic knowledge of the structure and functions of the human body.

Learning Outcome: Upon successful completion of this course, the student will be able to describe the structure and function of all the major organ systems of the human body.

Instruction: Major topics covered in the course are anatomical structure; functions of cells, tissues, and skin; skeletal structure; muscular system; nervous system; endocrine system; digestive system; renal system; circulatory system; and respiratory anatomy and physiology. Methods of instruction include independent study with open-book lesson examinations and a proctored final examination.

Credit Recommendation: In the lower division baccalaureate/associate degree category, 3 semester hours in Human Anatomy and Physiology or Human Biology (10/93). **NOTE**: If both BIO 110 and BIO 120 are successfully completed, students could seek credit for 6 semester hours in Health Sciences (10/93).

Infant and Toddler Care (ECE 120)

Location: Independent study by correspondence.

Length: 13 self-paced modules.

Dates: March 1992-Present.

Objective: To provide the student with an understanding of the special attention and supervision required by infants and toddlers.

Learning Outcome: Upon successful completion of this course, the student will be able to understand the development of infants and toddlers and provide them with an enriching environment that will encourage the infants and toddlers to reach their optimal potential.

Instruction: Major topics covered in the course are health and safety; the learning environment; and physical, cognitive, and language development. Methods of instruction include independent study, course manual, textbooks, projects, self-administered unit quizzes, and a proctored final examination.

Credit Recommendation: In the lower division baccalaureate/associate degree category, 3 semester hours in Early Childhood Education (4/94).

Integrated Respiratory Care Sciences (RT 200)

Location: Independent study by correspondence.

Length: 120 hours (5 lessons).

Dates: September 1992-Present.

Objective: To provide the student with basic principles of chemistry, physics, mathematics, biochemistry, and microbiology that relate to respiratory care.

Learning Outcome: Upon successful completion of this course, the student will

be able to perform calculations and chemical conversions associated with respiration; relate principles of physics to the properties of gases and liquids; describe characteristics of basic cell physiology, principles of physiology, and procedures for sterilization; and discuss the relationship of certain microorganisms to specific respiratory diseases.

Instruction: Major topics covered in the course are ratios, proportions, exponents, scientific notation, gas laws, molarity, normality, acid-base balance, kinetic forces, fluid dynamics, hemoglobin structure and function, chemical bonding, microbial respiratory diseases, and equipment sterilization. Methods of instruction include independent study with open-book lesson examinations and a proctored final examination.

Credit Recommendation: In the lower division baccalaureate/associate degree category, 3 semester hours as a Respiratory Science elective, or Basic Science for Respiratory Therapists (10/93). **NOTE**: The course is also offered as a part of the Advanced Practitioner Respiratory Therapy program that is described in the following section. Students who enroll in Respiratory Therapy: An Advanced Practitioner Program in Respiratory Care, cannot receive duplicate credit for this course.

Introduction to Biology (BIO 101)

Location: Independent study by correspondence.

Length: 100 hours (4 units covering nine lessons).

Dates: October 1984-Present.

Objective: To provide the student with an introduction to the structure and function of the human body and the relationship of humans to the environment.

Learning Outcome: Upon successful completion of this course, the student will be able to identify the basic structure and function of the cell; identify the macro-functions of each human body system; explain the basic principles of human genetics; and list major factors influencing the environment.

Instruction: Major topics covered in the course are the cell, nutrition and digestion, circulatory system, respiratory system, immunity, nervous system, sensory system, muscles and skeleton, reproduction, human heredity, and environmental issues. Methods of instruction include independent study with open-book unit examinations and a proctored final examination.

Credit Recommendation: In the lower division baccalaureate/associate degree category, 3 semester hours in Human Biology (10/93).

Introduction to Business (BUS105)

Location: Independent study by correspondence.

Length: Self-study.

Dates: June 1997-Present.

Objective: To provide the students with knowledge of the essential elements and key participants of a business enterprise and a foundation on which to build their business skills.

Learning Outcome: Upon successful completion of this course, the student will be able to describe key business functions; develop a plan for a new business; explain key components of organization management and of the structure of business enterprises; discuss accounting, financial, and investment management of a business; and explain how businesses use technology to manage the information they need to succeed.

Instruction: Major topics covered in the course are organization of a business; planning a business; selecting a form of business ownership; business ethics and social responsibility; environmental factors affecting businesses; management of a business; improving production, quality, and efficiency; motivating employees; marketing and promotion, pricing, and distribution strategies; financial management; business investment; and management information systems. Methods of instruction include directed, text-based independent study (distance education course), quizzes (self-appraisals), tests, and final examination.

Credit Recommendation: In the lower division baccalaureate/associate degree category, 3 semester hours in Business (6/97).

Introduction to Chemistry (101)

Location: Independent study by correspondence.

Length: 10 self-paced lessons.

Dates: September 1992-Present.

Objective: To enable students to read, write, and talk about chemistry; to understand chemical formulas and equations; to set up and solve routine chemical problems; and to think chemistry on atomic or molecular levels, visualizing what happens in a chemical change.

Learning Outcome: Upon successful completion of this course, the student will be able to define and give examples of mass, matter, and chemical property and physical property; distinguish between physical change and chemical change and give examples of each; define and give examples of an element atom compound and mixture; distinguish between the units of measurement used in the english, metric, and si systems; define density, mass, and volume; use scientific notation; define mole and recognize its uses in calculating chemical formulas; give percent composition; calculate the empirical formula of a compound; identify structural or chemical properties that can be changed when an ion is formed; distinguish between the solute and solvent components of a solution; identify the characteristics of water-soluble compounds; define and give examples of conjugate acid-base pairs; define organic chemistry and biochemistry; and understand the significance of amino acids to protein structure.

Instruction: Major topics covered in the course are atomic and molecular structure, chemical formulas and calculations, acid-base chemistry, and biochemistry. Methods of instruction include independent study, textbook, course manual, self-administered unit quizzes, and a proctored final examination.

Credit Recommendation: In the lower division baccalaureate/associate degree, 3 semester hours in Chemistry (11/95).

Introduction to Medical Microbiology (BIO 120)

Location: Independent study by correspondence.

Length: 130 hours (11 lessons).

Dates: March 1986-Present.

Objective: To provide the student with basic principles of microbiology and the relationship of microorganisms to human disease.

Learning Outcome: Upon successful completion of this course, the student will be able to describe the characteristics and habits of microbial groups and discuss their effect on the human body.

Instruction: Major topics covered in the course are microbial growth, structure, metabolism, and classification; principles of disease and epidemiology; practical applications of immunology; microbial diseases; antimicrobial drugs; and applied microbiology. Methods of instruction include independent study with open-book lesson examinations and a proctored final examination.

Credit Recommendation: In the lower division baccalaureate/associate degree category, 3 semester hours in Medical Microbiology or Microbiology for Allied Health (10/93). **NOTE**: If BIO 110 and

BIO 120 are successfully completed, students could seek credit for 6 semester hours in Health Sciences (10/93).

Introduction to Perinatal Development and General Care (RCP 304)

Location: Independent study by correspondence.

Length: 120 over 6 months.

Dates: January 1994-Present.

Objective: To provide students with knowledge at introductory level of perinatal history, gestational development of cardiorespiratory system; lab procedures, neonatal care and assist students to prepare for NBRC pediatric/neonatal specialist credentialing exam.

Learning Outcome: Upon successful completion of this course, the student will be able to define neonatology and perinatology, and discuss historical advancements, and iatrogenic conditions resulting from the application of technological advance used to treat pulmonary disease; explain and discuss the various stages of fetal development; delineate the significant landmark times associated with gestation age; define viability; describe the circulatory changes that occur prior to and after birth; explain how to perform an initial assessment on a newborn; know how to assess gestational age; when physical and neurologic assessment should be performed, and how to perform these assessments; and laboratory assessment and radiologic examinations on neonatal and pediatric patients.

Instruction: Major topics covered in the course are Introduction to Perinatal Care; Fetal Development; Pregnancy, Labor and Delivery; Physical Examination; Gestational Age Assessment; Laboratory Assessment; and Radiologic Evaluation. Methods of instruction include independent study, and a proctored open book final examination.

Credit Recommendation: In the lower division baccalaureate/associate degree or upper division baccalaureate degree category, 3 semester hours in Introduction to Perinatal Development and General Care (10/95).

Introduction to Psychology (PSY 101)

Location: Independent study by correspondence.

Length: 115 hours (4 modules covering 18 chapters).

Dates: September 1990-Present.

Objective: To enable the student to examine biological and environmental factors that influence human development and behavior through an overview of the applications of psychology.

Learning Outcome: Upon successful completion of this course, the student will be able to recognize the goals and methods of psychology; functions of the human system; effects of heredity and environment; problems of childhood, adolescence, and adulthood; effects of hypnosis and drugs on processes of learning and memory; how intelligence is defined and measured; physical health and stress; personality types and abnormal behavior; origins of prejudice; and origins of the sex drive.

Instruction: Major topics covered in the course are goals and methods of psychology; nervous system and brain, cognitive, and moral development; challenges of childhood, adolescence, adulthood, and dying; sensory system and role of perception; hypnosis, sleep, and drugs; learning and memory; intelligence, motivation, and stress; abnormal behavior and therapy; sexual behavior and romantic love; and origins of prejudice. Methods of instruction include independent study with open-book module examinations and a proctored final examination.

Credit Recommendation: In the lower division baccalaureate/associate degree category, 3 semester hours in Introduction to Psychology (10/93).

Language Development in Young Children (ECE116)

Location: Independent study by correspondence.

Length: Self-study.

Dates: June 1997-Present.

Objective: To help persons working in the child care field provide an opportunity-rich program full of interesting, appropriate, and developmental language arts activities.

Learning Outcome: Upon successful completion of this course, the student will be able to understand the four interrelated areas of language arts and young children's growth and development potential; understand the concept of emerging literacy; recognize children's literacy behaviors; identify adult behaviors that aid speech development; explain how playing with others helps vocabulary development and language acquisition in settings where children interact in real and make-believe situations; develop specific activities using puppetry, props, playacting, and pantomime that will aid children's acquisition of dramatization abilities; state the three developmental stages a child must master before he gains the ability to print; name the one activity which is the strongest predictor of first grade reading success; describe specific teacher techniques that promote children's expression of ideas; and identify ways in which parents can strengthen a child's language growth.

Instruction: Major topics covered in the course are language development and emerging literacy in the young child; development of language arts programs; introducing literature in the classroom; speech growth related to conversation, expression, and dramatization; writing awareness and use; and settings promoting literacy. Methods of instruction include directed, text-based independent study (distance education course), tests, and final examination.

Credit Recommendation: In the lower division baccalaureate/associate degree category, 3 semester hours in Language Development in Young Children (6/97).

Medical Transcription I Program
Medical Terminology (MDT 105)
Anatomy and Physiology (MDT 110)
Basic Medical Science (MDT 115)
Medical Transcription Practice (MDT 120)
Medical Grammar (MDT 121)

Location: Independent study by correspondence.

Length: 850 hours (5 courses).

Dates: January 1993-Present.

Objective: To provide the student with the knowledge of basic grammar, medical terminology, anatomy and physiology, pharmacology, laboratory testing, medical records, and of the role of the medical transcriptionist as a member of the health-care team; and with the skill in transcribing dictated medical reports needed for entry-level practice of medical transcription.

Learning Outcome: Medical Terminology (MDT 105)

Length: 90 hours (15 lessons).

Learning Outcome: Upon successful completion of this course, the student will be able to spell and define common prefixes, suffixes, word roots, and combining forms for the skeletal, muscular, integumentary, nervous, cardiovascular, lymphatic, respiratory endocrine, digestive, renal, and reproductive systems and the body as a whole; build medical words using prefixes, suffixes, and root words; spell and define common medical terms; identify and translate common medical abbreviations and acronyms; and list examples of words whose spellings vary in different forms.

Anatomy and Physiology (MDT 110)

Length: 90 hours (15 lessons).

Learning Outcome: Upon successful completion of this course, the student will be able to describe the structure of cells and movements of materials through all membranes; describe the anatomical position and function of structures or organs within body systems; and describe the structure and function of the skeletal, muscular, integumentary, nervous, cardiovascular, lymphatic, respiratory endocrine, digestive, renal, and reproductive systems.

Basic Medical Science (MDT 115)

Length: 180 hours (15 lessons).

Learning Outcome: Upon successful completion of this course, the student will be able to describe the pharmacological action of common drugs within all major drug categories by body system; identify drug category of common drugs when given common generic or trade names; describe routes of administration and steps in drug cycle; differentiate between local, systemic, therapeutic, toxic, and side effects of drugs; demonstrate proper use of drug references and laboratory materials; identify and define common laboratory tests and procedures and give the medical meaning of their results; and describe the purpose and general contents under each main heading of a history and physical examination report.

Medical Transcription Practice (MDT 120)

Length: 400 hours (15 lessons).

Learning Outcome: Upon successful completion of this course, the student will be able to describe and use WordPerfect commands as utilized in medical transcription; accurately transcribe physician dictation for ambulatory and hospital reports involving such topics as health record history, physical examination reports, pharmacology and laboratory tests, dermatology, gastroenterology, urology, orthopedics, cardiology, pulmonary medicine, endocrinology, obstetrics, gynecology, otorhinolaryngology, ophthalmology, and neurology; and accurately and efficiently proofread transcription of dictation.

Medical Grammar (MDT 121)

Length: 90 hours (15 lessons).

Learning Outcome: Upon successful completion of this course, the student will be able to demonstrate correct sentence structure, correctly observing rules of punctuation, and capitalization; define parts of speech; identify homonyms, synonyms, and eponyms; distinguish between various sentence types; demonstrate correct subject-verb and pronoun-antecedent agreement; demonstrate correct form for typing numbers and measurements; and proofread and correct manuscripts.

Instruction: The Medical Transcription I Program consists of five related and integrated courses, each comprised of 15 lessons and collectively requiring approximately 850 hours of study for completion. The program provides the basic knowledge and skills required to enter the practice of medical transcription. The curriculum integrates content from the five courses (Anatomy and Physiology, Basic Medical Science, Medical Terminology, Medical Grammar, and Medical Transcription Practice) and presents it in units organized by body systems. These courses are not available separately because of the integrated and interrelated curriculum design.

The average student in the Medical Transcription I Program is expected to complete the coursework in approximately 12 months. Because the program is offered only in independent study format, however, the time spent by students in completing the five integrated courses may vary by as many as six months. Instructional assistance is provided by CCHS faculty through correspondence and electronic communication. Completion of the program prepares the student to assume an entry-level transcriptionist position with the ability to transcribe reports that have been recorded by medical practitioners.

The method of instruction is independent study with open-book lesson exams and a proctored final exam for all 5 courses. An indication of course length and a description of the learning outcomes for each course follows. Although the information is presented by individual course, credit is not awarded to students until they have completed the entire curriculum.

Credit Recommendation: Upon completion of all 5 courses in the Medical Transcription I Program (MDT 105, MDT 110, MDT 115, MDT 120, and MDT 121) in the lower division baccalaureate/associate degree category, 15 semester hours in Medical Transcription (10/93).

Nutrition, Health, and Safety (ECE 130)

Location: Independent study by correspondence.

Length: 9 self-paced lessons .

Dates: November 1995-Present.

Objective: To introduce the student to the fundamentals of health, safety, and nutrition in a childcare setting.

Learning Outcome: Upon successful completion of this course, the student will be able to implement health, safety, and nutritional aspects into their childcare program; promote a healthy environment for children and staff; manage and control the spread of infectious diseases in the childcare setting; and identify different types of child abuse.

Instruction: Major topics covered in the course are promoting and planning a healthy environment, understanding the importance of nutrition, creating a safe environment, and child abuse and neglect. Methods of instruction include independent study (distance education course), activity assignments, written examinations, and a final examination.

Credit Recommendation: In the lower division baccalaureate/associate degree category, 3 semester hours Nutrition, Health, or Safety (11/95).

Organizational Behavior and Leadership (BUS 110) (Effective Management)

Location: Independent study by correspondence.

Length: 90 hours (4 lessons covering 17 chapters).

Dates: September 1987-Present.

Objective: To provide the student with knowledge of organizational and human relations skills needed for successful management and supervision within an organization.

Learning Outcome: Upon successful completion of this course, the student will be able to communicate effectively; analyze management techniques; make effective decisions; discuss ethical responsibilities; manage stress; improve motivation; and apply effective organizational behavior skills to improve the organizational climate.

Instruction: Major topics covered in the course are organization and human behavior, decision making, communication, small group behavior, organizational climate and structure, needs and motivation, morale, leadership techniques, managing change, and organizational diversity. Methods of instruction include independent study with open-book unit examinations and a proctored final examination.

Credit Recommendation: In the lower division baccalaureate/associate degree category, 3 semester hours in Business Administration, Health Care Administration, Personnel Administration, or Public Administration (10/93).

Orthopedic Transcription (MDT 128)

Location: Independent study by correspondence.

Length: Self-study.

Dates: June 1997-Present.

Objective: To help the experienced medical transcriptionist develop an expertise in orthopedic transcription.

Learning Outcome: Upon successful completion of this course, the student will be able to transcribe orthopedic dictation with a high degree of accuracy; proofread transcribed reports; select proper formats; demonstrate proper editing techniques with identification and correction of errors of style, format, punctuation, and grammar; utilize appropriate reference material; describe and spell common orthopedic diseases and symptoms, including terms related to fractures; define common orthopedic abbreviations; pronounce common orthopedic symptoms, diseases, laboratory tests, x-ray procedures, and surgical procedures; describe standard operating room procedures; describe common orthopedic surgical procedures and surgical instruments; describe the main categories of orthopedic drugs; differentiate between generic and trade name drugs; give common drug dosage forms and routes of administration; name common intravenous solutions; and describe the process of bone formation and growth.

Instruction: Major topics covered in the course are orthopedic terminology; symptoms and disease processes impacting orthopedic reports; orthopedic laboratory and x-ray practices and procedures; orthopedic surgical indications and procedures; medical grammar, proofreading, and editing; and standard transcription practices. Methods of instruction include directed, text-based independent study (distance education course), readings, audio/visual material, significant practice at transcribing orthopedic dictation, quizzes, tests, and final examination.

Credit Recommendation: In the lower division baccalaureate/associate degree category, 3 semester hours in Orthopedic Transcription (6/97).

Pathology Transcription (MDT 122)

Location: Independent study by correspondence.

Length: Self-study.

Dates: June 1997-Present.

Objective: To help the experienced medical transcriptionist develop expertise in pathology transcription.

Learning Outcome: Upon successful completion of this course, the student will be able to transcribe pathology dictation with a high degree of accuracy; proofread transcribed reports; select proper formats; demonstrate proper editing techniques with identification and correction of errors of style, format, punctuation, and grammar; utilize appropriate reference material; describe the main branches of pathology; spell and pronounce pathology terms; define common abbreviations used in pathology; describe the steps followed in performing an autopsy; explain the difference between microscopic and gross anatomic description; name and describe standard pathology tests and procedures; describe tumor classification and staging protocols.

Instruction: Major topics covered in the course are pathology terminology; body systems and disease processes impacting pathology reports; pathology laboratory practices and procedures; medical grammar, proofreading, and editing; and standard transcription practices. Methods of instruction directed, text-based independent study (distance education course) utilizing audio/visual material, readings, significant practice at transcribing pathology dictation, quizzes, tests, transcription of pathology dictation, and final examination.

Credit Recommendation: In the lower division baccalaureate/associate degree category, 3 semester hours in Pathology Transcription (6/97).

Perinatal Diseases and Congenital Disorders (RCP 308)

Location: Independent study by correspondence.

Length: 110 hours.

Dates: January 1994-Present.

Objective: To provide students with advanced knowledge of pathopysiology, diagnosis of respiratory problems of premature newborns, cardiac anomalies at or soon after birth, congenital malformations and therapeutic approaches to care of the neonate.

Learning Outcome: Upon successful completion of this course, the student will be able to describe the wide range of neonatal respiratory diseases and treatments; and explain the various congenital cardiac anomalies and congenital malformations.

Instruction: Major topics covered in the course are Neonatal Respiratory Diseases, Congenital Cardiac Anomalies, and Congenital Malformations. Methods of instruction include independent study with open book unit examinations and a proctored final examination.

Credit Recommendation: In the lower division baccalaureate/associate degree or upper division baccalaureate degree, 3 semester hours in Perinatal Diseases and Congenital Disorders (10/95).

Perinatal/Pediatric Respiratory Therapeutics (RCP 306)

Location: Independent study by correspondence.

Length: 120 hours over 6 months.

Dates: January 1994-Present.

Objective: To provide students with advanced knowledge of airway management; oxygen therapy; continuous blood gas monitoring; continuous positive airway pressure; mechanical ventilation; bronchial hygiene; pharmacology; membrane oxygenation (ECMO); perinatal transport; and the latest treatments and techniques for providing respiratory care for perinatal/pediatric patients.

Learning Outcome: Upon successful completion of this course, the student will be able to describe the various techniques and indications for proactive management of neonatal airways; explain the indications and techniques for applying oxygen therapy for neonates; list techniques for employing trancutaneous monitoring and pulse oximetry; describe the criteria for the techniques and guidelines for implementing continuous positive airway pressure (CPAP), explain the various techniques, indications and complications of mechanical ventilation, techniques for maintaining neonatal bronchial hygiene, list the reasons and options available for pharmacological intervention with neonatal patients; explain the indications for and the techniques associated with extracorporeal membrane oxygenation (ECMO); and discuss the various considerations and technical aspects involved with perinatal transport.

Instruction: Major topics covered in the course are Airway Management, Oxygen Therapy, Continuous Blood Gas Monitoring, Continuous Positive Airway Pressure; Mechanical Ventilation; Bronchial hygiene; Pharmacology, Respiratory Care; Exracorporeal membrane Oxygenation (ECMO); and transport of neonate and pediatric patients. Methods of instruction include independent study and open book examinations and a proctored final examination.

Credit Recommendation: In the lower division baccalaureate/associate degree or upper division baccalaureate degree, 3 semester hours in Perinatal/Pediatric Respiratory Therapeutics (10/95).

Physics Concepts (101)

Location: Independent study by correspondence.

Length: Self-paced lessons.

Dates: September 1991-Present.

Objective: To give non-science students, with limited mathematical backgrounds, an overview of classical physics.

Learning Outcome: Upon successful completion of this course, the student will be able to identify the steps in the scientific method; recognize the qualities of a good theory and a natural law; explain the contributions of various philosophers and astronomers to the understanding of celestial motion; define speed, velocity ,and acceleration and recognize their relationships; define torque, rotational inertia, and center of gravity and how they relate to Newton's laws of motion; understand Hooke's law, and explain how it relates to elasticity; understand and give examples of kinetic and potential energy; identify the common properties of gases; explain the composition of the atmosphere and its behavior; interpret the functions of different types of pumps in moving fluids; explain the kinetic theory of gases, solids, and liquids; explain the relationship of heat, energy, and temperature; distinguish between conduction, convection, and radiation and identify examples of each; identify the origin and characteristics of electric charge and interpret coulomb's law; give examples of conductors, nonconductors, and semiconductors; and identify the basic concepts of nuclear physics.

Instruction: Major topics covered in the course are laws of motion; work, energy, and kinetic theory of gases; heat and electricity. Methods of instruction include independent study, textbook course manual, self-administered unit quizzes, and a proctored final examination.

Credit Recommendation: In the lower division baccalaureate associate degree category, 3 semester hours in Physics (11/95).

Principles of Finance (FIN 341)

Location: Independent study by correspondence.

Length: Self-study.

Dates: June 1997-Present.

Objective: To introduce a variety of responsibilities of the corporate financial manager to maximize shareholder wealth while increasing the value of the firm.

Learning Outcome: Upon successful completion of this course, the student will be able to describe the role and responsibilities of the corporate financial management professional; analyze a firm's financial statements to identify its financial performance, on its own and in comparison to the industry; understand the net present value and the time value of money, and use these concepts to determine the value of various securities, especially bonds, preferred stock, and common stock; describe the concept of risk, its causes, and its effects on shareholder wealth; understand and calculate the cost of capital; analyze a firm's capital structure; understand the capital budgeting process; and analyze different capital budgeting options and how each will affect shareholder wealth.

Instruction: Major topics covered in the course are asset valuation, capital valuation, cost and structures, and long and short-term assets of financial management. Methods of include directed, text-based independent study (distance education course), tests, quizzes, and final examination.

Credit Recommendation: In the upper division baccalaureate degree category, 3 semester hours in Business Administration or Financial Management (6/97).

Principles of Microeconomics (ECO 211)

Location: Independent Study by correspondence.

Length: Self-study.

Dates: June 1997-Present.

Objective: To understand the basic principles of microeconomics.

Learning Outcome: Upon successful completion of this course, the student will be able to explain the relationship between the scarcity of resources and want for products; explain the relationships between the price and supply of products; and explain the rationale for government intervention and regulation of business practices that influence the supply and demand for goods and services.

Instruction: Major topics covered in the course are production possibilities and opportunity consumer choices, price ceilings and floors, and business ownership and microeconomics of factory markets. Methods of instruction include directed, text-based independent study (distance education course), tests, projects, and final examination.

Credit Recommendation: In the lower division baccalaureate/associate degree category, 3 semester hours in Business Administration (6/97).

Radiology Transcription (MDT 130)

Location: Independent study by correspondence.

Length: Self-study.

Dates: June 1997-Present.

Objective: To help the experienced medical transcriptionist develop an expertise in radiology transcription.

Learning Outcome: Upon successful completion of this course, the student will be able to transcribe radiology dictation a high degree of accuracy; proofread transcribed reports; select proper formats; demonstrate proper editing techniques with identification and correction of errors of style, format, punctuation, and grammar; utilize appropriate reference material; describe and spell common radiology terms and procedures; define common radiology abbreviations; pronounce common radiology procedures and equipment; describe and pronounce common indications for radiology procedures; describe common radiology contrast media and routes of administration; describe standard radiology views and positions; and explain the procedures common to the divisions of radiology, nuclear medicine, and radiation therapy.

Instruction: Major topics covered in the course are radiology terminology; radiology practices and procedures; radiology medical and surgical indications and procedures; medical grammar, proofreading, and editing; and standard transcription practices. Methods of instruction include directed, text-based independent study (distance education course), audio/visual material, readings, significant practice at transcribing radiology dictation, quizzes, tests, and final examination.

Credit Recommendation: In the lower division baccalaureate/associate degree category, 3 semester hours in Radiology Transcription (6/97).

Respiratory Care Assistant (RCA 101)

Location: Independent study by correspondence.

Length: 400 hours (5 lessons covering 22 units).

Dates: April 1992-Present.

Objective: To provide the student with the knowledge and skills required to perform nontherapeutic respiratory care procedures without direct supervision and to provide the nonclinical preparation needed to qualify for entering the advanced standing Respiratory Therapy Technology program offered by CCHS.

Learning Outcome: Upon successful completion of this course, the student will be able to describe expected professional behaviors of a respiratory care practitioner; describe the functions of a respiratory care unit; discuss cardiopulmonary anatomy and physiology; describe the structure and function of the cardiovascular and respiratory systems; discuss acute and chronic pulmonary diseases; describe the use of respiratory care equipment in a noncritical care environment; discuss the clinical basis for respiratory therapy; and apply infection control and patient safety procedures.

Instruction: Major topics covered in the course are professional ethics, cardiopulmonary anatomy and physiology, pulmonary diseases, respiratory treatment concepts and equipment, infection control, and patient safety and observation. Methods of instruction include independent study with open-book lesson examinations, a proctored final examination, and performance assessment by an on-site evaluator.

Credit Recommendation: In the vocational certificate category, 6 semester hours in Respiratory Therapy Technology (10/93).

Respiratory Therapy Program: An Advanced Practitioner Program in Respiratory Care
Integrated Respiratory Care Sciences (RT 200)
Ethical Considerations in Health Care Delivery (RT 201)
Advanced Cardiopulmonary Assessment & Diagnostic Techniques (RT 202)
Clinical Practice Guidelines (RT 203)
Advanced Ventilatory Care Concepts (RT 204)
ICU Crisis Management (RT 205)
Neonatal Critical Care (RT 206)
Home Care and Pulmonary Rehabilitation (RT 207)
Clinical Practicum (RT 240)

Location: Independent study by correspondence.

Length: 700 hours accompanied by 800 hours of clinical experience (8 courses).

Dates: October 1984-Present.

Objective: To provide the student with the knowledge and skills necessary to become a Registered Respiratory Therapist (RRT) by successfully completing the Written Registry Examination and the Clinical Simulation Examination, the two advanced practitioner credentialing exams administered by the National Board for Respiratory Care (NBRC).

Integrated Respiratory Care Sciences (RT 200)

Length: 120 hours (5 lessons).

Learning Outcome: Upon successful completion of this course, the student will be able to perform calculations and chemical conversions associated with respiration; relate principles of physics to the properties of gases and liquids; describe characteristics of basic cell physiology, principles of physiology, and procedures for sterilization; and discuss the relationship of certain microorganisms to specific respiratory diseases.

Credit Recommendation: This course may be taken for 3 semester hours of lower division baccalaureate/associate degree credit by students who are not enrolled in the Advanced Practitioner Respiratory Therapy program. For additional information about this course, see the discussion of Integrated Respiratory Care Sciences (RT 200). (10/93)

Ethical Considerations in Health Care Delivery (RT 201)

Length: 100 hours (11 lessons).

Learning Outcomes: Upon successful completion of this course, the student will be able to recognize principles of problem solving and conflict management; distinguish between law and ethics; define terms and concepts frequently encountered in the ethics of patient care; recognize the values underlying all ethical issues; understand the role of ethics committees in the context of the hospital organization and the JCAHO's guidelines; recognize and be able to discuss moral/ethical issues such as the allocation of limited resources, DNR, selection of transplant recipients, honesty with dying patients, euthanasia, and practitioner incompetence.

Advanced Cardiopulmonary Assessment and Diagnostic Techniques (RT 202)

Length: 60 hours (1 lesson).

Learning Outcome: Upon successful completion of this course, the student will be able to describe a common method for observing all body systems during a physical assessment of adults and infants; describe physical assessment of the chest; summarize the usefulness of chest roentgenography in patient assessment; describe the method for gross examination of properly obtained sputum specimen; describe applications of invasive cardiac monitoring; discuss fundamentals of cardiac anatomy and physiology and of EKGs; and explain the systematic approach to the interpretation of arrhythmias.

Clinical Practice Guidelines (RT 203)

Length: 140 hours (9 lessons).

Learning Outcome: Upon successful completion of this course, the student will be able to differentiate between and explain the relationship between clinical practice guidelines and therapist-driven protocols; understand and be able to teach others how to implement clinical practice guidelines; list the strengths and weaknesses of various patient assessment techniques; design patient treatment protocols based on established clinic practice guidelines; demonstrate how the use of practice guidelines and protocols can help the hospital to move towards patient-focused care and reduce the misallocation of services.

Advanced Ventilatory Care Concepts (RT 204)

Length: 60 hours (1 lesson).

Learning Outcome: Upon successful completion of this course, the student will be able to relate knowledge of cardiopulmonary physiology to mechanical ventilation; explain the principles of mechanical ventilators; perform patient assessment and monitoring; recognize complications associated with mechanical ventilation; describe the principles and procedures for implementing mechanical ventilation, PEEP, IMV, high frequency ventilation, and for weaning patients from ventilation; set up a ventilator and prepare a patient for mechanical ventilation; and manage a patient receiving mechanical ventilation.

ICU Crisis Management (RT 205)

Length: 70 hours (4 lessons).

Learning Outcome: Upon successful completion of this course, the student will be able to describe emergency and intensive care procedures including positive physiological effects, hazards, and side effects; interpret gas and laboratory results in terms of acid-base and fluid-electrolyte balance; describe and demonstrate patient evaluation, bedside monitoring, airway maintenance, initiation of and weaning from mechanical ventilation; describe extracorporeal membrane oxygenation and closed-chest drainage; and discuss various diseases requiring ventilation assistance.

Neonatal Critical Care (RT 206)

Length: 70 hours (1 lesson).

Learning Outcome: Upon successful completion of this course, the student will be able to discuss and assess fetal respiratory anatomy and physiology; perform fetal and newborn monitoring and assessment; recognize and identify at risk neonates; identify elements of newborn resuscitation; list four signs of Respiratory

Distress Syndrome (RDS) and discuss appropriate and pulmonary complications of RDS; discuss patent ductus arteriosus (PDA) and arterial bloods; list factors that affect body systems other than the lungs; and discuss neonatal intervention techniques including oxygen therapy, mechanical ventilation, and extracorporeal membrane oxygenation.

Home Care and Pulmonary Rehabilitation (RT 207)

Length: 100 hours (1 lesson).

Learning Outcome: Upon successful completion of this course, the student will be able to explain the pathophysiology of chronic and acute lung disease; describe the operation and maintenance of home oxygen systems; describe conditions which meet Medicare coverage for home oxygen therapy; describe techniques for training patients in the use of home respiratory therapy; describe psychosocial aspects and purposes of pulmonary rehabilitation; and describe the implementation of patient assessment and pulmonary rehabilitation programs.

Clinical Practicum (RT 240)

Learning Outcome: Upon successful completion of this course, the student will be able to demonstrate practical experience in working with patients in clinical settings.

Instruction: The Respiratory Therapist program is an advanced standing program for students who have completed a respiratory therapy technician program or the equivalent. A majority of the applicants to the program are Certified Respiratory Therapy Technicians (CRTT) with several years of respiratory care experience. Admission to the program requires evidence of current employment or affiliation with a respiratory care department in which proficiency in performing clinical procedures required of the advanced respiratory care practitioner can be developed.

Instructional assistance is provided by CCHS faculty through correspondence and electronic communication and by special adjunct faculty. An adjunct faculty member is an employee of the healthcare institution in which the student works, who volunteers to assist the fellow employee with his or her studies. The adjunct faculty member is an experienced respiratory care professional who serves the student as a mentor and role model and who provides the supervision and assistance necessary for the student to become clinically competent.

The program consists of an 9-course, modular curriculum that is completed by the respiratory care practitioner who is seeking eligibility for the NBRC Written Registry and Clinical Simulation Examinations. With the exception of RT 200 Integrated Respiratory Care Sciences, the courses are available only as part of the integrated curriculum in Respiratory Therapy. Although the following program description is presented by individual course, credit is not awarded to students until they have completed the entire curriculum.

The method of instruction is independent study with open-book lesson exams, and a proctored final exam for all 9 courses. An indication of course length and a description of the learning outcomes for each course follows.

Credit Recommendation: In the lower division baccalaureate/associate degree category, 30 semester hours (22 hours for didactic course work and 8 hours for clinical experiences) in Respiratory Therapy (therapist level) is recommended upon completion of all 8 courses in the Advanced Respiratory Therapy program (RT 200-RT 207 described above)(10/93) (1/95) (7/95).

Respiratory Therapy Technology Program: An Entry Level Program in Respiratory Care

General Anatomy and Physiology (RTT 100)
Cardiopulmonary Anatomy and Pathophysiology (RTT 102)
Pulmonary Related Math and Physics (RTT 104)
Microbiology and Infection Control (RTT 106)
Cardiopulmonary Resuscitation (RTT 108)
Pharmacology (RTT 110)
Contemporary Topics in Respiratory Care (RTT 112)
Airway Management and Advanced Cardiac Life Support (RTT 114)
Cardiopulmonary Diagnostics (RTT 116)
Basic Patient Assessment (RTT 118)
Medical Gas Therapy (RTT 120)
Aerosol and Humidity Therapy (RTT 122)
Lung Expansion Therapy (RTT 124)
Chest Physical Therapy and Rehabilitation (RTT 126)
Mechanical Ventilation (RTT 128)
Neonatal and Pediatric Respiratory Care (RTT 130)

Location: Independent study by correspondence.

Length: 900 hours accompanied by 800 hours of clinical experience (16 courses).

Dates: October 1984-Present.

Objective: To provide the student with the knowledge and skills necessary to become a Certified Respiratory Therapy Technician (CRTT) by successfully completing the Entry Level Examination, a credentialing exam administered by the National Board for Respiratory Care (NBRC).

General Anatomy and Physiology (RTT 100)

Length: 110 hours (7 lessons).

Learning Outcome: Upon successful completion of this course, the student will be able to describe the structure and function of cells, tissues, organs, and of the skeletal, muscular, nervous, digestive, renal, endocrine, and reproductive systems.

Cardiopulmonary Anatomy and Pathophysiology (RTT 102)

Length: 110 hours (3 lessons).

Learning Outcome: Upon successful completion of this course, the student will be able to describe the circulatory system and blood composition; describe normal dynamics of chest movement, muscles of ventilation, and ventilation perfusion ratios; define respiratory disease; define chronic obstructive, restrictive, and infectious pulmonary disease; and describe pulmonary pathology due to trauma.

Pulmonary Related Math and Physics (RTT 104)

Length: 70 hours (1 lesson).

Learning Outcome: Upon successful completion of this course, the student will be able to describe the physical composition and behavior of matter; describe the behavior of gases and their relationship to various gas laws; define and apply respiratory therapy formulae, variables, constants, theories and gas laws; and describe the effects of water vapor and airway resistance on the function of the respiratory system.

Microbiology and Infection Control (RTT 106)

Length: 70 hours (1 lesson).

Learning Outcome: Upon successful completion of this course, the student will be able to describe the field of microbiology; recognize and describe disease causing organisms; identify aspects of bacterial growth patterns and describe how they are affected by water, temperature, pH light, and oxygen; define terms related to infection control, sterilization, and decontamination; identify methods of transmission of infectious organisms and the nature of nosocomial infections; and list elements of effective surveillance programs to prevent nosocomial infections.

Cardiopulmonary Resuscitation (RTT 108)

Length: 35 hours (1 lesson).

Learning Outcome: Upon successful completion of this course, the student will be able to compare CPR measures for infants, children, and adults; define cardiac arrest and clinical and biological death; list procedures of effective CPR; explain basics of life support measures; describe hazards and common errors of CPR; compare partial and complete airway obstruction; and describe airway clearance procedures.

Pharmacology (RTT 110)

Length: 35 hours (1 lesson).

Learning Outcome: Upon successful completion of this course, the student will be able to recognize and interpret components of a prescription; describe the correct procedures and rules for administering drugs; describe drug indications, contraindications, and doses; identify routes and methods of drug administration; describe stimulation of bronchodilation and functions of alpha, beta-1, and beta-2 receptors; describe groups of drugs used in respiratory therapy and their intended effects and possible side effects; and discuss the name and function of related drugs commonly used in hospitals.

Contemporary Topics in Respiratory Care (RTT 112)

Length: 34 hours (1 lesson).

Learning Outcome: Upon successful completion of this course, the student will be able to list important psychosocial characteristics of patient care; identify body-image components and factors that distort body image; discuss sick role behavior and interventions of healthcare workers; describe the difference between acute and chronic illness and the interventions of healthcare workers; describe the grieving process and identify the steps in Kubler/Ross' grieving process; and describe basic computer hardware and software utilized in pulmonary medicine.

Airway Management and Advanced Cardiac Life Support (RTT 114)

Length: 35 hours (2 lessons).

Learning Outcome: Upon successful completion of this course, the student will be able to identify steps in emergency airway care and endotracheal intubation; identify equipment used in establishment and maintenance of airways; discuss airway suctioning and associated hazards; discuss the indications, hazards, and complications of airway management; and describe the indications and procedures for performing a cricothyrotomy.

Cardiopulmonary Diagnostics (RTT 116)

Length: 70 hours (2 lessons).

Learning Outcome: Upon successful completion of this course, the student will be able to discuss the mechanism of oxygen and carbon dioxide transport; discuss the mechanism of acid-base balance; identify the body buffer systems; list abnormalities of acid-base balance; discuss techniques of blood gas sampling; identify the purpose and methods of pulmonary function testing; describe chronic obstructive and restrictive lung disease; and describe the devices that are commonly used in pulmonary function testing.

Basic Patient Assessment (RTT 118)

Length: 35 hours (1 lesson).

Learning Outcome: Upon successful completion of this course, the student will be able to describe the procedures for obtaining an accurate and useful history of a hospitalized patient; describe patient observation methods; demonstrate physical assessment of the chest; explain the usefulness of chest roetgenography in patient assessment; describe the method for obtaining sputum specimens; discuss normal and abnormal EKGs; and list the differences between adult, pediatric, and infant assessment.

Medical Gas Therapy (RTT 120)

Length: 35 hours (1 lesson).

Learning Outcome: Upon successful completion of this course, the student will be able to list the properties of medical gases, cylinder marking, and medical gas safety systems; identify the organizations that regulate medical gases and their functions; describe the use and function of each device used in medical gas therapy; list indications for oxygen therapy and types of hypoxia; and discuss the hazards and precautions to be taken in oxygen.

Aerosol and Humidity Therapy (RTT 122)

Length: 70 hours (1 lesson).

Learning Outcome: Upon successful completion of this course, the student will be able to describe normal mucociliary clearance; list the purposes of aerosol and humidity therapy and the hazards of dry gas administration; discuss the types of humidifiers and nebulizers and their clinical applications; discuss the effects of various factors upon the administration of humidity; and list the hazards of aerosol therapy.

Lung Expansion Therapy (RTT 124)

Length: 35 hours (1 lesson).

Learning Outcome: Upon successful completion of this course, the student will be able to discuss the indications, goals, contraindications, and complications of IPPB therapy; discuss hazards of IPPB therapy; list the goals of incentive spirometry; and describe the current procedures for performing incentive spirometry and IPPB therapy.

Chest Physical Therapy and Rehabilitation (RTT 126)

Length: 70 hours (1 lesson).

Learning Outcome: Upon successful completion of this course, the student will be able to list the basis and goals for chest physical therapy (CPT) rehabilitation, home care, and concomitant techniques; list the indications, goals, positions, hazards and contraindications of CPT; discuss the definition of pulmonary rehabilitation; discuss the rationale for the techniques used in home care and the need of patients for home respiratory therapy; and list the procedures for the decontamination and sterilization of home respiratory care equipment.

Mechanical Ventilation (RTT 128)

Length: 110 hours (2 lessons).

Learning Outcome: Upon successful completion of this course, the student will be able to discuss the application of any type of ventilator, describe the indications for mechanically assisting a patient's breathing; describe different types of ventilators, their indications and precautions; discuss weaning criteria and techniques; discuss blood gas results and correlate them to ventilator management; list complications of mechanical ventilation and how to prevent them; and explain the precautions to be taken when delivering mechanical ventilation.

Neonatal and Pediatric Respiratory Care (RTT 130)

Length: 35 hours (1 lesson).

Learning Outcome: Upon successful completion of this course, the student will be able to describe embryonic lung development and fetal circulation; discuss high risk pregnancy and high risk infants; describe the newborn infant scoring system and the signs of cardiac and pulmonary diseases; describe child and infant ventilation techniques; describe infant ventilators; describe PEEP and CPAP; and describe the treatment of respiratory pediatric diseases and the emotional support of sick children.

Instruction: The Respiratory Therapy Technology program is an advanced standing program with an entrance requirement of at least six months of hands-on experience in the field of respiratory care. At a minimum, the experience must include the following areas of routine "floor" care: equipment sterilization and maintenance, oxygen therapy, IPPB therapy, and incentive spirometry. A majority of the applicants to the program are experienced practitioners with prior on-the-job training in a respiratory care department. In addition, admission to the program requires evidence of current employment or affiliation with a respiratory care department in which proficiency in performing all clinical procedures required of the entry-level practitioner can be developed.

Instructional assistance is provided by CCHS faculty through correspondence and electronic communication and by special adjunct faculty. An adjunct faculty member is an employee of the healthcare institution in which the student works, who volunteers to assist the fellow employee with his or her studies. The adjunct faculty member is an experienced respiratory care professional who serves the student as a mentor and role model and who provides the supervision and assistance necessary for the student to become clinically competent.

The program consists of a 16-course, modular curriculum that is completed by the respiratory care practitioner who is seeking eligibility for the NBRC Entry Level Examination. The courses are available only as a part of the integrated curriculum in respiratory therapy technology.

The method of instruction is independent study with open-book lesson examinations, and a proctored final examination for all 16 courses. An indication of course length and a description of the learning outcomes for each course follows.

Credit Recommendation: In the lower division baccalaureate/associate degree category, 35 semester hours (27 hours for didactic course work and 8 hours for clinical experiences) in Respiratory Therapy or Health Science upon completion of all 16 courses in Respiratory Therapy Technology: An Entry Level Program in Respiratory Care (10/93) (1/95).

The Child, Family, and Community (ECE 110)

Location: Independent study by correspondence.

Length: 9 self-paced units (9 lessons).

Dates: December 1992-Present.

Objective: To provide the student with knowledge and understanding of the importance of parent, community, and center involvement in the development and delivery of education and other services to young children.

Learning Outcome: Upon successful completion of this course, the student will be able to exhibit an understanding of working with parents; identify factors families consider important when selecting child care programs; develop effective methods of verbal and written communication; conduct parent conferences; develop parent newsletters; develop strategies for indirect and direct parental involvement in child care programs; identify community resources; and develop a parent resource center.

Instruction: Major topics covered in the course are working with parents, understanding individual differences, what parents want to know, good communication skills, personal and written contact with parents, parent involvement, parent education programs, and community resources and services. Methods of instruction include independent study, course manual, projects, audio tapes, self-administered unit quizzes, and a proctored final examination.

Credit Recommendation: In the lower division baccalaureate/associate degree category, 3 semester hours in Early Childhood Education (4/94).

Theory and Practice in the Human Services (SOC 120)

Location: Independent study by correspondence.

Length: Self-study.

Dates: June 1997-Present.

Objective: To broaden the student's understanding of the human services professions and to provide an introduction to the skills necessary to function effectively as a human services professional.

Learning Outcome: Upon successful completion of this course, the student will be able to recognize the needs of human services consumers and apply the skills and procedures for effective human services case management.

Instruction: Major topics covered in the course are an orientation to human services, the delivery of human services, and effective human services case management. Methods of instruction include directed, text-based independent study (distance education course); exercises; quizzes; and final examination.

Credit Recommendation: In the lower division baccalaureate/associate degree category, 3 semester hours in Sociology or Health Care Management (6/97).

Therapist Driven Protocols (RCP 302)

Location: Independent study by correspondence.

Length: 110 hours over 6 months.

Dates: September 1993-Present.

Objective: To provide students with the knowledge and skill in the development and implementation of therapist driven protocols.

Learning Outcome: Upon successful completion of this course, the student will be able to explain the rationale for giving more patient care responsibility to allied healthcare professionals; describe the evolution of TDP's; define and explain the elements of TDP's; AARC's Clinical Practice Guidelines; techniques for introducing the implementation of TDP's in a respiratory care department; the key steps in developing a TDP; become proficient in respiratory care assessment techniques; and discuss and explain specific therapist driven protocol.

Instruction: Major topics covered in the course are development of a Therapist Driven Protocol; developing Therapist Driven Protocols and formatting a TDP; learning the TDP; Respiratory Care Assessment techniques and specific TDP's. Methods of instruction include independent study with open book examination, five critical thinking exercises, two writing projects, and a proctored final examination.

Credit Recommendation: In the lower division baccalaureate/associate degree or upper division baccalaureate degree, 3 semester hours in Therapist Driven Protocols (10/95).

Working with Children with Special Needs (ECE 103)

Location: Independent study by correspondence.

Length: 3 self-paced units (30 topics).

Dates: November 1993-Present.

Objective: To provide the student with an overview of disabling conditions that could affect young children, the early intervention process, and the integration of children with disabilities into early childhood education center programs.

Learning Outcome: Upon successful completion of this course, the student will be able to identify disabling conditions; identify early intervention procedures; understand learning conditions such as mainstreaming; and become familiar with educational strategies relevant to specific disability conditions.

Instruction: Major topics covered in the course are disabilities that may affect young children, benefits of early identification, mainstreaming, and educational strategies to be used with specific disabilities. Methods of instruction include independent study, course manual, projects, observations, visual aids, self-administered unit quizzes, and a proctored final examination.

Credit Recommendation: In the lower division baccalaureate/associate degree category, 3 semester hours in Early Childhood Education (4/94).

Cambridge College Programme

Established in 1986, the Cambridge College Programme is the oldest American summer programme in Cambridge, England. It is the only American teen summer programme in Cambridge or Oxford that exclusively employs faculty who are British educators. The educational experience is enhanced by the Programme's small student-faculty ratio; class sizes are limited to 18, and historically the Programme's student body has been approximately 100 and comprised of students from all over the United States.

The teaching faculty are members and graduates of Cambridge University and other distinguished United Kingdom universities. Students enrolled in the Programme are therefore immersed both academically and residentially in British culture, education, and history. Morning and afternoon courses present a diverse and rich variety of learning opportunities, and an afternoon lecture and excursion series explores the historical ties between Great Britain and the United States with a focus on the evolution of constitutional democracy. Classroom and experiential excursion are balance for optimum exposure to those ends.

Source of official student records: Registry of Credit Recommendations, American Council on Education, One Dupont Circle, Washington, DC 20036-1193 or the Cambridge College Programme, 218 W. St. Paul, Chicago, IL 60614.

Additional information about the courses: College Credit Recommendation Service, American Council on Education, One Dupont Circle, Washington, DC 20036-1193.

Principles of Scientific Discovery (Formerly Cambridge Scientific Discoveries: Math, Physics, Chemistry, Biology, Astronomy, and Medicine)

Location: Queens' College, University of Cambridge, Cambridge, England.

Length: 18 hours (3 weeks).

Dates: June 1992-Present.

Objective: To gain an overall view of Cambridge science and scientists. This comprehensive series of lectures and excursions exposes students to leading science figures in their own disciplines (biology, chemistry, engineering, astronomy, mathematics, and physics).

Learning Outcome: Upon successful completion of this course, students will be exposed to scientific research projects in Cambridge.

Instruction: Major topics covered in the course are the structure of scientific research within the University of Cambridge; the history of science and scientific discoveries at the University of Cambridge; current research in applied mathematics and theoretical physics, astronomy, earth sciences, forensic science, genetics, geology, physics and applied physics, polar exploration, radio astronomy, and zoology. Methods of instruction include lecture, projects, presentations, team work, video, interactive computer, excursions and lectures on site at a number of museums, laboratories, observatories, in-class discussions, classroom exercises (supervised experiments and museum "treasure hunt"), out-of-class written assignments, tests, quizzes, projects, final examinations, class participation and on-site contributory effort, and written evaluation of out-of-class assignments.

Credit Recommendation: In the lower division baccalaureate/associate degree category, 1 semester hour in General Science (11/97).

The Literary History of Jane Austen

Location: Queens' College, University of Cambridge, Cambridge, England.

Length: (total duration or division of time in course, in hours and weeks [i.e., 30 hours for 15 weeks; 2 one-hour meetings per week]). 15 hours, 3 weeks.

Dates: June 1997-Present.

Objective: Upon successful completion of this course, the student will be able to understand the evolving writing style of Jane Austen, as she chronicled life during England's Regency period; develop an understanding of English society's marital structure (gender roles and expectations, function of marriage, and threats to marriage), the family (the small social unit, the function of the family, and types of family), the wider social structure (social class, property, inheritance, England's structure), and education (how women in particular are educated, and male educators as heroes).

Learning Outcome: Upon successful completion of this course, students will be able to understand the evolving writing style of Jane Austen's contributions to the literary canon as well as her own evolution as a writer as she chronicled her period's English society.

Instruction: Major topics covered in the course are Austen's writing content; Marriage: gender roles and expectations; function of marriage; threats to marriage; the family: the small social unit: the function of the family; types of family; the wider social structure: social class; property; inheritance; England's structure; Education: how women in particular are educated; male educators as heroes; Austen's writing form: Humor: irony; satire; parody; how they are "female" narrative traits; Characterization: openings of novels; major/minor characters; deceiving characters; Closure: the "happy ending"; the sense of finality/fitness; sequels and rewritings. Methods of instruction in-clude lecture, projects, presentations, team work, video, interactive computer, etc. Lectures, in-class discussions, out-of-class written assignments. Evaluation methods used are: tests, quizzes, projects, final exams, etc. Class participation and written evaluation of out-of-class assignments.

Credit Recommendation: In lower division baccalaureate/associate degree category, 1 semester hour in Humanities (11/97).

Carolina Power & Light Company

Carolina Power & Light Company's (CP&L) is organized with three nuclear plant training sections (PTS) which are responsible for providing technical education and training to reactor operators and senior reactor operators, as well as craft and technical classifications at each site. This is accomplished through a combination of classroom, simulator, lab, and on-the-job training conducted at each nuclear plant. The reactor operator training programs at Harris Nuclear Plant also includes courses on the PULSTAR research reactor and scaled PWR facility at North Carolina State University.

Each PTS is part of the Plant Department of the Nuclear Generation Group and consists of two functional units at the Brunswick and Harris Nuclear Plants-Operations Training and Technical Training. The Robinson Nuclear Plant has three functional units: Operations Train-ing, Technical Training, and Support Training. Corporate management training, including the supervisory development training, is the responsibility of the Human Resources Administration Section of the Human Resources Department.

Carolina Power & Light Company's training programs are developed through job and task analyses. Training programs derived from job and task analyses utilize criterion-referenced technology in lesson plans and other training materials. The training programs are conducted by individuals who are highly qualified in both technical and instructional skills. Supervisory development programs are developed through an assessment of supervisory needs, INPO guidelines, and management direction.

Each training program is designed to facilitate the evaluation and appraisal of each student's comprehension and degree of mastery of the subject by written, performance, and oral examinations. Training programs embody both the academic and practical aspects of the subject. Training programs are modified as necessary to reflect new regulatory requirements, operating experiences of CP&L and the nuclear industry, INPO evaluations, CP&L audits, and plant modifications.

Source of official student records: (A) H.B. Robinson Training Manager, Carolina Power & Light Company, H.B. Robinson Steam Electric Plant, 3581 West Entrance Road, Hartsville, SC 29550; (B) Harris Training Manager, Carolina Power & Light Company, Harris Energy & Environmental Center, Route 1, Box 327, New Hill, NC 27562; (C) Brunswick Training Manager, Carolina Power & Light Company, Brunswick Steam Electric Plant, P.O. Box 10429, Southport, NC 28461; (D) Director, Nuclear Reactor Program, Department of Nuclear En-gineering, Box 7909, North Carolina State University, Raleigh, NC 27695-7909; and (E) Director, Management Training, Carolina Power and Light Company, 2700 Wycliff Road, Suite 101, Raleigh, NC 27607.

Additional information about the courses: College Credit Recommendation Service, American Council on Education, One Dupont Circle, Washington, DC 20036-1193.

Brunswick Steam Electric Plant

Primary, Secondary & Electrical Systems and Procedures (ROA01B-PRISEC Systems)

Location: Brunswick Nuclear Power Plant, Southport, NC.

Length: 760 hours (19 weeks - classroom); 600 hours (15 weeks - On-the-Job-Training [OJT]).

Dates: December 1994-Present.

Objective: To provide the student with instruction on nuclear steam supply systems and the governing operating procedures as they apply to nuclear power plant operation. In addition, the course provides the student with actual hands on experience in the plant main control room.

Learning Outcome: Upon successful completion of this course, the student will be able to identify and describe the operational characteristics of the reactor primary and secondary systems and plant electrical systems; and apply this knowledge while operating the systems from the control room.

Instruction: Major topics covered in the course are reactor primary and secondary heat transfer, instrumentation control and safety systems, electrical control and safety systems, radwaste systems, and administrative and control documentation. Methods of instruction include lecture, discussion, OJT, and periodic and final examinations, plus an oral exam in the plant control room.

Credit Recommendation: In the upper division baccalaureate degree category, 15 semester hours in Nuclear Engineering Technology (2/95).

Reactor Operator Systems: Nuclear Steam Supply Systems and Design Considerations (ROAO1B-Prim. Syst.)

Location: Brunswick Steam Electric Plant, Southport, NC.

Length: 420 hours (13 weeks); 100 hours classroom instruction and 320 hours on-the-job training (OJT).

Dates: January 1984-November 1994.

Objective: To provide the student with instruction on nuclear steam supply systems and design considerations (primary systems) as they apply to a nuclear power plant reactor operator.

Learning Outcome: Upon successful completion of this course, the student will be able to describe the design and operation of the following general systems: reactor coolant systems; fuel handling system; instrumentation and control systems; containment and support systems; reactor protection systems; and engineering safety systems.

Instruction: Major topics covered in the course are classroom and OJT related to nuclear steam supply system and design considerations including the design and operation of a boiling water reactor, its support system, emergency safeguards, and the licensing and technical specifications under which the operating license is issued.

Credit Recommendation: In the lower division baccalaureate/associate degree category, 4 semester hours in Nuclear Engineering Technology (12/87) (7/92).

Reactor Operator Systems: Power Plant Engineering Systems (ROA01B-Sec. and Elec)

Location: Brunswick Steam Electric Plant, Southport, NC.

Length: 300 hours (10 weeks); 100 hours classroom instruction and 200 hours on-the-job training (OJT).

Dates: January 1984-November 1994.

Objective: To provide the student with instruction on power plant engineering systems (secondary and electrical) as they apply to a nuclear power plant reactor operator.

Learning Outcome: Upon successful completion of this course, the student will be able to describe the design and operation of the following general systems: main and auxiliary steam systems; condensate and feedwater systems; main turbine and associated support systems; and electrical systems associated with the secondary plant.

Instruction: Major topics covered in the course are classroom and OJT related to power plant engineering systems including steam distribution systems, electrical distribution and operation, condensate and feedwater, main turbine and generator, and auxiliary systems including emergency power.

Credit Recommendation: In the lower division baccalaureate/associate degree category, 3 semester hours in Nuclear Engineering Technology (12/87) (7/92).

Reactor Operator Theory: Chemistry (ROA01B-CH)

Location: Brunswick Steam Electric Plant, Southport, NC.

Length: 16 hours (2 days).

Dates: January 1984-June 1991.

Objective: To provide instruction on chemistry as it applies to a nuclear power plant reactor operator.

Learning Outcome: Upon successful completion of this course, the student will have an understanding of the importance associated with maintaining chemistry controls.

Instruction: Major topics covered in the course are subjects related to chemistry, including structure of matter; atomic structure; chemical activity (valence bonding and covalent bonding); solutions; ionization; acid, bases, and salts; conductivity; boiling water reactor (BWR) chemistry (corrosion and water quality control); BWR radiochemistry; and removal of activation products.

Credit Recommendation: In the lower division baccalaureate/associate degree category, 1 semester hour in Chemistry (12/87) (7/92).

Reactor Operator Theory: Heat Transfer, Fluid Flow, and Thermodynamics (ROA01B-HT, FF, TH) (A and B)

Location: Brunswick Steam Electric Plant, Southport, NC.

Length: *Version A:* 40 hours (1 week); *Version B:* 80 hours (2 weeks).

Dates: *Version A:* January 1984-October 1987; *Version B:* October 1987-June 1991.

Objective: To provide the student with sufficient instruction on heat transfer, fluid flow, and thermodynamics as they apply to nuclear power plant operation.

Learning Outcome: Upon successful completion of this course, the student will be able to understand the essential heat transfer, fluid mechanics, and thermodynamic principles relative to nuclear power plant operation; perform calculations to estimate temperatures, pressures, and thermodynamic properties associated with essential plant systems.

Instruction: Major topics covered in the course are subjects related to heat transfer, fluid flow, and thermodynamics including laws and methods of heat transfer; boiling heat transfer (critical heat flux, two-phase flow, and flow patterns in heated vertical tube); thermal stresses; fluid statics; fluid flow; pumps, valves, and turbine theory; and nozzles.

Credit Recommendation: In the upper division baccalaureate degree category, 3 semester hours in Nuclear Engineering Technology (12/87) (7/92). **NOTE:** Credit cannot be given for the Version A course and the Control Operator Candidate course.

Reactor Operator Theory: Reactor Core Analysis and Mitigating Core Damage (ROA01B-RCA and MCD) (A and B) (Reactor Core Analysis and Mitigating Core Damage (R0A01B-RCA & MCD)

Location: Brunswick Steam Electric Plant, Southport, NC.

Length: *Version A:* 24 hours (1 week); *Version B:* 38 hours (1 week).

Dates: *Version A:* January 1984-October 1994; *Version B:* October 1994-Present.

Objective: To provide the student with instruction on reactor core analysis and mitigating core damage as they apply to a nuclear power plant reactor operator.

Learning Outcome: Upon successful completion of this course, the student will be able to state expected responses to various events; explain instrument responses to various events; define various terms; state radiological consequences both on-site and off-site; and become familiar with process computer.

Instruction: Major topics covered in the course are reactor core analysis and mitigating core damage including transient analysis, accident analysis, mitigating core damage, thermal limits, core power response, and process computer. Methods of instruction include lecture and periodic examinations.

Credit Recommendation: In the lower division baccalaureate/associate degree category, 1 semester hour in Nuclear Engineering Technology or Nuclear Science (7/92) (2/95). **NOTE:** Credit should not be awarded for both this course and Reactor Core Analysis and Mitigating Core Damage (ROAO2B-RCA & MCD).

Reactor Operator Theory: Reactor Theory (ROA01B-RT) (A and B)

Location: Brunswick Steam Electric Plant, Southport, NC.

Length: *Version A:* 80 hours (2 weeks); *Version B:* 120 hours (3 weeks).

Dates: *Version A:* June 1983-October 1987; *Version B:* October 1987-June 1991.

Objective: To provide instruction on reactor theory as it applies to a nuclear power plant reactor operator.

Learning Outcome: Upon successful completion of this course, the student will be able to define some physics terms; describe the structure of the atom; make radioactive decay calculations; make static and dynamic reactor calculations using the six-factor equation and the reactor equation; describe and calculate various coefficients; and describe and calculate reactivity effects.

Instruction: Major topics covered in the course are subjects related to reactor theory, including properties of matter and energy, nuclear physics and reactions, reactor physics, reactivity effects and variations, reactor kinetics, subcritical theory, various coefficients, poisoning, power distribution, and reactivity control during operation.

Credit Recommendation: *Version A:* In the lower division baccalaureate/associate degree category, 2 semester hours in Nuclear Engineering Technology (12/87). *Version B:* In the lower division baccalaureate/associate degree category, 3 semester hours in Nuclear Engineering Technology (12/87) (7/92).

Reactor Operator: Simulator (ROA01B-RO-Simul)

Location: Brunswick Steam Electric Plant, Southport, NC.

Length: 368 hours (20 weeks); 28 hours classroom instruction and 340 hours simulator.

Dates: January 1984-October 1994.

Objective: To provide the student with instruction and practical operating experience to conduct normal, abnormal, and emergency power plant operation as they apply to a boiling water reactor (BWR) nuclear power plant reactor operator.

Learning Outcome: Upon successful completion of this course, the student will be able to perform plant startups and shutdowns under normal and abnormal operating conditions; diagnose and mitigate malfunctions; and initiate appropriate emergency operating procedures in nuclear power plants.

Instruction: Major topics covered in the course are subjects related to BWR power plant operations including plant startups, shutdowns, normal operation, abnormal operation, and emergency conditions.

Credit Recommendation: In the upper division baccalaureate degree category, 3 semester hours in Nuclear Engineering Technology (12/87) (7/92).

Reactor Operator: Simulator Training (ROA01B-RO)

Location: Brunswick Nuclear Power Plant, Southport, NC.

Length: 240 hours (16 weeks).

Dates: October 1994-Present.

Objective: To provide the student with instruction and practical operating experience as it applies to a boiling water reactor (BWR).

Learning Outcome: Upon successful completion of this course, the student will be able to perform plant startup and shutdowns under normal and abnormal operating conditions; diagnose and mitigate malfunctions; and initiate appropriate emergency operating procedures for the Brunswick Nuclear Plant.

Instruction: Major topics covered in the course are BWR power plant operations including startups, shutdowns, normal operation, abnormal operation, and emergency conditions. Methods of instruction include lecture, simulator operation, simulator examinations, and a final examination.

Credit Recommendation: In the upper division baccalaureate degree category, 2 semester hours in Nuclear Engineering Technology (2/95).

ROGF: Heat Transfer, Fluid Flow, and Thermodynamics

Location: Brunswick Nuclear Power Plant, Southport, NC.

Length: 68 hours (1.7 weeks).

Dates: August 1993-Present.

Objective: To provide the student with basic instruction on heat transfer, fluid flow and thermodynamics as applied to nuclear power plant operation.

Learning Outcome: Upon successful completion of this course, the student will be able to understand the basic heat transfer, fluid mechanics; and thermodynamic principles relative to nuclear plant operations; perform calculations to estimate and identify thermodynamic states of steam and perfect gases; and calculate simple energy balances and heat transfer.

Instruction: Major topics covered in the course are heat transfer, fluid flow and thermodynamics; thermodynamic units and properties; basic energy equations; thermodynamic processes and cycles; basic fluids and heat transfer; boiling heat transfer (critical heat flux, two-phase flow and flow patterns in a heated vertical tube); core thermal limits; thermal stresses; fluid statics; fluid flow; pumps; valves; nozzles; and turbines. Methods of instruction include lecture, discussion, classroom exercises, and periodic and final examinations.

Credit Recommendation: In the upper division baccalaureate degree category, 2 semester hours in Nuclear Engineering Technology (2/95).

ROGF: Reactor Theory

Location: Brunswick Nuclear Power Plant, Southport, NC.

Length: 59 hours (1.5 weeks).

Dates: August 1993-Present.

Objective: To provide instruction on reactor theory as it applies to a nuclear plant reactor operator.

Learning Outcome: Upon successful completion of this course, the student will be able to define reactor physics terms, describe the structure of the atom, make radioactive decay calculations, make static and dynamic reactor calculations using the reactor equation and the 6 factor formula, and describe and calculate reactor coefficients and reactivity effects.

Instruction: Major topics covered in the course are reactor theory, including properties of matter and energy, nuclear physics and reactions, reactor physics, reactivity effects and variations, reactor kinetics, subcritical theory, reactor coefficients, poisoning, and power distribution and reactivity control during operation. Methods of instruction include lecture and periodic examinations.

Credit Recommendation: In the lower division baccalaureate/associate degree category, 2 semester hours in Nuclear Engineering Technology or Nuclear Science (2/95).

Senior Reactor Operator: Operational Administration (ROA02B-OPADMIN)

Location: Brunswick Steam Electric Plant, Southport, NC.

Length: *Version A:* 88 hours (4 weeks); *Version B:* 48 hours (1 week).

Dates: *Version A:* January 1984-August 1993; *Version B:* August 1993-Present.

Objective: To provide instruction on operational administration as it applies to a nuclear power plant senior reactor operator.

Learning Outcome: Upon successful completion of this course, the student will be able to describe and explain the implications, definitions, limitations, compliance, and bases for technical specifications and the various parts of the code of federal regulations; describe the interrelationships between on-site and off-site emergency organizations; and perform administrative aspects for various maintenance tasks.

Instruction: Major topics covered in the course are plant operating license, administrative procedures and instructions, operating procedures and instructions, appropriate sections of the code of federal regulations, regulatory compliance instructions, maintenance procedures, technical specifications and their bases, the emergency plan, and environmental and radiation control procedures. Methods of instruction include periodic and final examinations.

Credit Recommendation: *Version A:* In the upper division baccalaureate degree category, 3 semester hours in Nuclear Plant Management (12/87) (7/92). *Version B:* In the upper division baccalaureate degree category, 2 semester hours in Nuclear Plant Management (2/95).

Senior Reactor Operator: Plant Systems Review and Upgrade (ROA02B-Review)

Location: Brunswick Nuclear Plant, Southport, NC.

Length: 240 hours (6 weeks).

Dates: October 1994-Present.

Objective: To provide the student with a review of reactor operations and systems courses as they apply to a nuclear plant senior reactor operator. This course provides the student with an indepth and integrated understanding of essential plant systems and their interrelationships.

Learning Outcome: Upon successful completion of this course, the student will be able to demonstrate a thorough and integrated understanding of plant systems relative to operating procedures, technical specifications and design limitations, and understand the operational procedures and limits for standard operations and for abnormal operational procedures.

Instruction: Major topics covered in the course are primary and secondary containment control, plant startup and shutdown, fuel handling, fire protection, and emergency and abnormal operating procedures. Methods of instruction include lecture, discussion, simulator, on-the-job training, and periodic and final examinations.

Credit Recommendation: In the upper division baccalaureate degree category, 5 semester hours in Nuclear Engineering Technology (2/95).

Senior Reactor Operator: Plant Systems Review and Upgrade (ROA02B-Review)

Location: Brunswick Steam Electric Plant, Southport, NC.

Length: 240 hours (6 weeks).

Dates: January 1984-October 1994.

Objective: To provide the student with a review of reactor operator theory and systems courses as they apply to a nuclear power plant senior reactor operator. It should provide the student with an in-depth and integrated understanding of essential plant systems and their interrelationships.

Learning Outcome: Upon successful completion of this course, the student will be able to demonstrate a thorough and integrated understanding of plant systems relative to operating procedures, technical specifications, and design limitations. This level of understanding should also be evident with respect to operational procedures and limits imposed by reactor physics, heat transfer, fluid flow, thermodynamics, and general laws of physics and chemistry.

Instruction: Major topics covered in the course are subjects related to a review of reactor operator theory and systems course including reactor theory; heat transfer, fluid flow, and thermodynamics; chemistry; radiological control; instrumentation; and plant systems.

Credit Recommendation: In the upper division baccalaureate degree category, 5 semester hours in Nuclear Engineering Technology (12/87) (7/92).

Senior Reactor Operator: Reactor Core Analysis and Mitigating Core Damage (ROA02B-RCA & MCD)

Location: Brunswick Steam Electric Plant, Southport, NC.

Length: *Version A:* 20 hours (.5 week); *Version B:* 38 hours (1 week).

Dates: *Version A:* January 1984-October 1994; *Version B:* October 1994-Present.

Objective: To provide the student with instruction on reactor core analysis and mitigating core damage as they apply to a nuclear power plant senior reactor operator.

Learning Outcome: Upon successful completion of this course, the student will be able to state expected responses to various events; explain instrument responses to various events; define various terms; state radiological consequences both on-site and off-site; and become familiar with process computers.

Instruction: Major topics covered in the course are reactor core analysis and mitigating core damage including transient analysis, accident analysis, mitigating core damage, thermal limits, core power response, and process computers. Methods of instruction include lecture and periodic examinations.

Credit Recommendation: In the lower division baccalaureate/associate degree category, 1 semester hour in Nuclear Engineering Technology or Nuclear Science (7/92) (2/95). **NOTE:** Credit should not be awarded for both Reactor Operator: Reactor Core Analysis and Mitigating Core Damage (ROAO1B-RCA & MCD) and this course.

Senior Reactor Operator: Simulator (ROA02B-SRO Simul)

Location: Brunswick Steam Electric Plant, Southport, NC.

Length: 200 hours (10 weeks); 60 hours classroom instruction and 140 hours simulator.

Dates: January 1984-October 1994.

Objective: To provide the student with instruction and practical operating experience to supervise normal, abnormal, and emergency power plant operation as it applies to a boiling water reactor (BWR) nuclear power plant reactor operator.

Learning Outcome: Upon successful completion of this course, the student will be able to supervise normal and abnormal plant startups and shutdowns; perform transient and accident analyses; direct emergency operations; and evaluate plant operations relative to technical specifications.

Instruction: Major topics covered in the course are subjects related to the supervision of power plant operation including diagnosing problems and applying technical specifications to plant start-ups, shutdowns, normal operations, abnormal operation, and emergency conditions.

Credit Recommendation: In the upper division baccalaureate degree category, 2 semester hours in Nuclear Engineering Technology (12/87) (7/92).

Senior Reactor Operator: Simulator Training (ROA02B)

Location: Brunswick Nuclear Power Plant, Southport, NC.

Length: 240 hours (16 weeks).

Dates: October 1994-Present.

Objective: To provide the student with instruction and practical operating experience to supervise normal, abnormal and emergency power plant operation as it applies to a boiling water reactor (BWR) nuclear power plant reactor operator.

Learning Outcome: Upon successful completion of this course, the student will be able to supervise reactor plant startups and shutdowns, perform transient and accident analysis, direct emergency operations, and evaluate plant operations relative to the technical specifications.

Instruction: Major topics covered in the course are supervision of power plant operation including diagnosing problems, and applying the plant technical specifications as they relate to normal and off normal plant conditions including emergency conditions. Methods of instruction include simulator operation and periodic and final simulator examinations.

Credit Recommendation: In the upper division baccalaureate degree category, 3 semester hours in Nuclear Engineering Technology (2/95).

Carolina Power & Light Company Courses

COC: Chemistry and Material Science (COB01N-CH, MS)

Location: Shearon Harris Energy & Environmental Center, New Hill, NC.

Length: 33 hours (10 weeks).

Dates: January 1983-December 1986.

Objective: To provide the student with instruction on chemistry and material science as they apply to a nuclear power plant reactor operator.

Learning Outcome: Upon successful completion of this course, the student will be able to define and explain basic chemical terms and reactions, understand corrosion, radiation chemistry and hazardous chemicals, and understand properties associated with nuclear power plant materials.

Instruction: Major topics covered in the course are subjects related to chemistry and material science including: chemistry fundamentals, corrosion, radiation chemistry, feed and condensate chemistry, hazardous chemicals, water treatment, and the fundamentals of material science from stress and strain through the use of testing to determine the properties of metals.

Credit Recommendation: In the lower division baccalaureate/associate degree category, 1 semester hour in Chemistry (12/87) (7/92).

COC: Electrical Science, Instrumentation, and Control (COB01N-EL, IC)

Location: Shearon Harris Energy & Environmental Center, New Hill, NC.

Length: 35 hours (10 weeks).

Dates: January 1983-December 1986.

Objective: To provide instruction on the science of electricity generation and instrumentation and control as they apply to a nuclear power plant reactor operator.

Learning Outcome: Upon successful completion of this course, the student will be able to describe, define, and calculate the basic properties of electrical circuits and devices.

Instruction: Major topics covered in the course are subjects related to electrical science and instrumentation and control including AC circuits through three-phase generators, AC and DC motors, power system control and protection, and semiconductor theory.

Credit Recommendation: In the upper division baccalaureate degree category, 2 semester hours in Electrical Engineering Technology (12/87) (7/92).

COC: Health Physics (COB01N-HP)

Location: Shearon Harris Energy & Environmental Center, New Hill, NC.

Length: 25 hours (10 weeks).

Dates: January 1983-December 1986.

Objective: To provide instruction on health physics as it applies to a nuclear power plant reactor operator.

Learning Outcome: Upon successful completion of this course, the student will have an understanding of radioactive decay, biological effect, radiation dose, radiation monitoring, dose levels, and emergency plans.

Instruction: Major topics covered in the course are subjects related to health physics including how to control exposure to radioactive isotopes, measurement of radiation fields, identification and exposure limits for radioactive isotopes, the use of protective clothing and respirators, and the calculation of possible effects of a release of radioactive isotopes.

Credit Recommendation: In the lower division baccalaureate/associate degree category, 1 semester hour in Nuclear Science (Health Physics) (12/87) (7/92).

COC: Heat Transfer, Fluid Flow, and Thermodynamics (COB01N-TH, HT and FF)

Location: Shearon Harris Energy & Environmental Center, New Hill, NC.

Length: 68 hours (10 weeks).

Dates: January 1983-December 1986.

Objective: To provide instruction on thermodynamics, heat transfer, and fluid flow as they apply to a nuclear power plant reactor operator.

Learning Outcome: Upon successful completion of this course, the student will be able to understand heat transfer, fluid mechanics, thermodynamic principles, and perform calculations to estimate temperatures, pressures, and thermodynamic properties associated with essential plant systems.

Instruction: Major topics covered in the course are subjects related to thermodynamics, heat transfer, and fluid flow including the first and second laws of thermodynamics through energy, enthalpy, entropy, and the general energy equation; the properties of water in all phases, steam tables, Mollier diagram; conductive, convective, and radioactive heat transfer; and pump head and head loss calculations.

Credit Recommendation: In the upper division baccalaureate degree category, 3 semester hours in Nuclear Engineering Technology (12/87) (7/92).

COC: Mathematics and Physics (COB01N-MA, PHY)

Location: Shearon Harris Energy & Environmental Center, New Hill, NC.

Length: 33 hours (10 weeks).

Dates: January 1983-December 1986.

Objective: To provide the student with instruction on mathematics and physics as they apply to a nuclear power plant reactor operator.

Learning Outcome: Upon successful completion of this course, the student will be able to define, explain, and solve various arithmetic operations, algebraic terms, systems of linear equations, trigonometric functions, and physics problems for nuclear power plants.

Instruction: Major topics covered in the course are subjects related to mathematics and physics including: arithmetic operations, algebra, logarithms, geometry, trigonometry, unit conversion, differential and integral calculus, and basic physics from Newton's laws through the concepts of work and energy.

Credit Recommendation: In the lower division baccalaureate/associate degree category, 1 semester hour in Science (12/87) (7/92).

COC: Reactor Theory (COB01N-RT)

Location: Shearon Harris Energy & Environmental Center, New Hill, NC.

Length: 69 hours (10 weeks).

Dates: January 1983-December 1986.

Objective: To provide instruction on reactor theory as it applies to a nuclear power plant reactor operator.

Learning Outcome: Upon successful completion of this course, the student will have knowledge of concepts related to atomic and nuclear physics as well as basic nuclear reactor theory.

Instruction: Major topics covered in the course are subjects related to reactor theory including the details of atomic structure and radioactive decay of elements, the behavior and control of the neutron flux in a power reactor, and those factors necessary to achieve and maintain a critical reactor.

Credit Recommendation: In the lower division baccalaureate/associate degree category, 2 semester hours in Nuclear Engineering Technology (12/87) (7/92).

Nuclear Engineering Fundamentals Laboratory (ROT-301)

Location: Burlington Laboratory, NCSU Campus, Raleigh, NC.

Length: 31.5 hours (1 week); 11.5 hours lecture and 20 hours laboratory.

Dates: February 1985-December 1989.

Objective: To provide knowledge and experience relating to radiation control and thermal hydraulic processes applicable to nuclear reactors.

Learning Outcome: Upon successful completion of this course, the student will have been introduced to radiation monitoring concepts, fluid systems, and heat transfer.

Instruction: Major topics covered in the course are radiation measurement, radiation shielding, heat transfer and fluid flow in reactors, and power plant thermodynamics.

Credit Recommendation: In the lower division baccalaureate/associate degree category, 1 semester hour in Nuclear Engineering Technology (12/87) (7/92).

Radiation Control and Measurement Laboratory (ROT-201)

Location: Burlington Laboratory, NCSU Campus, Raleigh, NC.

Length: 28 hours (1 week); 10.5 hours lecture and 17.5 hours laboratory.

Dates: January 1978-January 1981.

Objective: To introduce techniques relating to health physics measurements at nuclear power plants.

Learning Outcome: Upon successful completion of this course, the student will have knowledge of survey instrument operation, monitoring techniques, water chemistry procedures, and the use of anti-contamination clothing.

Instruction: Major topics covered in the course are the basic principles used in radiation detection and process instrumentation in commercial nuclear power plants, various techniques of radiation monitoring, personnel monitoring, reactor nuclear instrumentation, contamination control, process measurement, and water chemistry analysis as applicable to commercial power reactor plants.

Credit Recommendation: In the lower division baccalaureate/associate degree category, 1 semester hour in Nuclear Science (Health Physics) (12/87) (7/92). **NOTE:** Credit should not be awarded for both Nuclear Engineering Fundamentals Laboratory (ROT-301) and this course.

Supervisory Development Program MD 126

Location: Carolina Power and Light Company Management Training Center.

Length: 140 hours (4 weeks).

Dates: January 1992-December 1995.

Objective: To present (in discrete modules) basic concepts and methods of effective management at the supervisory level.

Learning Outcome: Upon successful completion of this course, the student will be able to understand the conceptual role of supervisors, team dynamics and problem-solving, more effective communication skills, how to better manage stress, and basic performance management and measurement.

Instruction: Major topics covered in the course are personal organization, problem-solving, EEO/Affirmative Action, written business communication, communication (interpersonal), meeting & presentation skills, leadership, stress management, and team building. Methods of instruction include lecture, audio/visual material, discussion, classroom exercises, learner presentations/reports, case studies, group activity, examinations, class performance, team exercises, and assignments.

Credit Recommendation: In the upper division baccalaureate degree category, 3 semester hours in General Management or Leadership (2/95).

Supervisory Development Program: Assessment & Development Center (CPD002)

Location: Carolina Power & Light Management Training Center.

Length: 20 hours (2.5 days).

Dates: January 1996-Present.

Objective: To assess the supervisory/managerial potential of senior lead personnel using an exercise/simulation based manager assessment center process. Assessors provide individual evaluation and participants receive feedback in a focused developmental system to enhance their self-knowledge of skills to improve.

Learning Outcome: Upon successful completion of this course, the student will be able to identify management dimensions analyzed and tested; measure self-performance against an objective standard validated by the Assessment Center instrument; and demonstrate knowledge and experience with exercises conducted in the development assessment process.

Instruction: Major topics covered in the course are Assessment/Development Center Process, role-play interview simulation, in-basket simulation, scheduling simulation (craft only), Assessor feedback, negotiation exercise (professional support only), and group discussion for leader identification exercise (craft only). Methods of instruction include lecture, classroom exercises, case studies, learner presentations/reports, self-study, observations, examinations, and assessor evaluations.

Credit Recommendation: In the upper division baccalaureate degree category, 1 semester hour in General Management, Organizational/Individual Development, or Leadership (7/97).

Supervisory Development Program: Pre-Supervisory Training (MD132)

Location: Carolina Power & Light Management Training Center.

Length: 21 hours (3 days and 8-24 hours of self-study).

Dates: January 1996-Present.

Objective: To introduce concepts and functions of management to Pre-Supervisory candidates and to provide opportunity for self-assessment, practical application of supervisory principles, and individual self-study for improvement.

Learning Outcome: Upon successful completion of this course, the student will be able to understand the conceptual and operational role of a supervisor; gain information via role simulations of supervisory potential; complete a supervisory training exercise; and complete self-study exercises based on self-assessment modules completed.

Instruction: Major topics covered in the course are supervisory-subordinate/peer skills scenarios on supervisory functions and situations; in-basket simulation assessing eight dimensions of the supervisor; and leadership series focusing on the role of the manager, styles of leadership, communication skills, and delegation/direction skills. Methods of instruction include discussion, classroom exercises, case studies, audio/visual material, self-study, observations, examinations, and self-assessment exercises/simulations.

Credit Recommendation: In the upper division baccalaureate degree category, 1 semester hour in General Management, Organizational/Individual Development, or Leadership (7/97).

Supervisory Development Program: Supervisory Development (MD154)

Location: Carolina Power & Light Management Training Center.

Length: 84 hours (12 days).

Dates: January 1996-Present.

Objective: To present concepts, methods, and case studies of effective and efficient management at the supervisory level.

Learning Outcome: Upon successful completion of this course, the student will be able to demonstrate understanding and knowledge of management principles and methods; exhibit teamwork skills in preparation of case studies; and demonstrate understanding and use of supervisor's skills in problem-solving, change management, performance management, and other functions.

Instruction: Major topics covered in the course are leadership and team building, managing organizational change, EEO/AA, problem-solving/decision making, presentation skills, labor relations, business controls, employee empowerment and assistance, interpersonal supervisory skills, and case study (team) presentations. Methods of instruction include lecture, discussion, classroom exercises, case studies, audio/visual material, learner presentations/reports, self-study, observations, examinations, quizzes, reports, team case study presentations, a 24-36 hour case study assignment, and final examination.

Credit Recommendation: In the upper division baccalaureate degree category, 3 semester hour in General Management,

Organizational/Individual Development, or Leadership (7/97).

H.B. Robinson Steam Electric Plant

Reactor Operator Systems: Nuclear Steam Supply Systems and Design Considerations (ROA01R)

Location: H.B. Robinson Steam Electric Plant, Hartsville, SC.

Length: 495 hours (12.4 weeks); 135 hours classroom instruction and 360 hours on-the-job training (OJT).

Dates: January 1983-Present.

Objective: To provide the student with instruction on nuclear steam supply systems and design considerations (primary systems) as they apply to a nuclear power plant reactor operator.

Learning Outcome: Upon successful completion of this course, the student will be able to describe the design and operation of the following general systems: reactor coolant systems, fuel handling system, instrumentation and control systems, chemical and volume control system, containment and support system, reactor protection systems, and radioactive waste handling and processing systems.

Instruction: Major topics covered in the course are classroom and on-the-job training related to nuclear steam supply systems and design considerations including: reactor coolant systems, nuclear fuel, incore instrumentation, nuclear instrument systems, chemical volume control system, fuel handling, residual heat removal, primary sampling, component coolant water, spent fuel pit, containment and support, HVAC, engineered safety features, rod control, rod position indication, snubbers, reactor protection, radiation monitoring, solid waste, liquid rad waste, and gaseous rad waste. Methods of instruction include lecture, discussion, self-study, and examinations.

Credit Recommendation: In the lower division baccalaureate/associate degree category, 5 semester hours in Nuclear Engineering Technology (12/87) (7/92) (2/95).

Reactor Operator Systems: Plant Systems Review and Upgrade (Prelicense Review) (ROA01R-PLR)

Location: H.B. Robinson Steam Electric Plant, Hartsville, SC.

Length: *Version 1:* 100 hours (2.5 weeks); *Version 2:* 80 hours (2 weeks).

Dates: *Version 1:* January 1983-May 1994; *Version 2:* June 1994-Present.

Objective: To provide the student with instruction on plant systems review and upgrade (prelicense review) as they apply to a nuclear power plant reactor operator. The student should obtain an integrated knowledge of essential plant systems and their interrelationships.

Learning Outcome: Upon successful completion of this course, the student will be able to demonstrate an improved and integrated knowledge of plant systems relative to plant operating procedures, technical specifications, and design limitations.

Instruction: Major topics covered in the course are the plant system review and update. Methods of instruction include lecture, class discussion, self-study, and examinations.

Credit Recommendation: In the upper division baccalaureate degree category, 2 semester hours in Nuclear Engineering Technology (12/87) (7/92) (2/95). **NOTE:** A student should not simultaneously receive credit for this course and (ROA02R - PLR).

Reactor Operator Systems: Power Plant Engineering Systems (ROA01R-Sec. and Elec)

Location: H.B. Robinson Steam Electric Plant, Hartsville, SC.

Length: 265 hours (6.6 weeks); 105 hours classroom instruction and 160 hours on-the-job training (OJT).

Dates: January 1983-Present.

Objective: To provide the student with instruction on nuclear power plant secondary and electrical engineering systems.

Learning Outcome: Upon successful completion of this course, the student will be able to describe the design and operation of the following systems associated with the secondary plant: main and auxiliary steam, condensate, feedwater, main turbine, steam generator, fire protection, and electrical.

Instruction: Major topics covered in the course are power plant engineering systems including: secondary sampling, service water, main and auxiliary steam, steam generator, water level control, main turbine and reheaters, turbine auxiliary system, oil analysis, turbine control, condensate, feedwater, extraction steam, feedwater heater, vents and drains, fire protection, main generator, generator auxiliaries, AC and DC electrical, diesel generators, plant computer (ERFIS), circulating water, plant air handling, gland sealing, cooling water, HVAC, and emergency response. Methods of instruction include lecture, on-the-job training, and weekly examinations.

Credit Recommendation: In the upper division baccalaureate degree category, 3 semester hours in Nuclear Engineering Technology (12/87) (7/92) (2/95).

Reactor Operator Theory: Chemistry (ROA01R-CHEM)

Location: H.B. Robinson Steam Electric Plant, Hartsville, SC.

Length: 20 hours (0.5 week); 15 hours lecture/discussion and 5 hours self-study.

Dates: January 1983-June 1991.

Objective: To provide the student with instruction in chemistry as it applies to a nuclear plant reactor operator.

Learning Outcome: Upon successful completion of this course, the student will have an understanding of fundamental chemistry concepts and the important role chemistry plays in the performance and safety of a nuclear power plant.

Instruction: Major topics covered in the course are subjects related to chemistry including: chemistry fundamentals review, corrosion and corrosion control, radiation chemistry, secondary water chemistry, hazardous chemicals, sampling techniques, and water treatment.

Credit Recommendation: In the lower division baccalaureate/associate degree category, 1 semester hour in Chemistry (12/87) (7/92).

Reactor Operator Theory: Heat Transfer, Fluid Flow, and Thermodynamics (ROA01R-HT, FF, TH)

Location: H.B. Robinson Steam Electric Plant, Hartsville, SC.

Length: 80 hours (2 weeks); 60 hours lecture/discussion and 20 hours self-study.

Dates: January 1983-June 1991.

Objective: To provide the student with sufficient instruction in heat transfer, fluid flow, and thermodynamics as they apply to nuclear power plant operation.

Learning Outcome: Upon successful completion of this course, the student will be able to understand the essential heat transfer, fluid mechanics, thermodynamic principles relative to nuclear power plant operation, and perform calculations to estimate temperatures, pressures, and thermodynamic properties associated with essential plant systems.

Instruction: Major topics covered in the course are subjects related to heat transfer, fluid flow, and thermodynamics including: properties of working fluids, phases of matter, laws of thermodynamics, steam tables, limits, Bernoulli's equation, pump laws, heat balance, and Rankine cycle.

Credit Recommendation: In the upper division baccalaureate degree category, 3 semester hours in Nuclear Engineering Technology (12/87) (7/92).

Reactor Operator Theory: Material Science (ROA01R-Mt Sc)

Location: H.B. Robinson Steam Electric Plant, Hartsville, SC.

Length: 20 hours (0.5 week); 15 hours lecture/discussion and 5 hours self-study.

Dates: January 1983-June 1991.

Objective: To provide instruction in material science as it applies to a nuclear power plant reactor operator.

Learning Outcome: Upon successful completion of this course, the student will be able to describe, state, list, define, and explain the concepts and phenomena covered in the course description.

Instruction: Major topics covered in the course are subjects related to material science including atomic interactions and order in microstructures, classification of crystalline materials, imperfection in materials, stress and strain, mechanical properties of materials, mechanisms of deformation and fracture, toughness testing, effects of radiation on materials, alloys, nuclear fuel and cladding, brittle fracture in reactor vessels, and heat-up and cool-down considerations.

Credit Recommendation: In the lower division baccalaureate/associate degree category, 1 semester hour in Material Science (12/87) (7/92).

Reactor Operator Theory: Mathematics (ROA01R-Math)

Location: H.B. Robinson Steam Electric Plant, Hartsville, SC.

Length: 28 hours (3.5 days); 21 hours lecture/discussion and 7 hours self-study.

Dates: January 1983-June 1991.

Objective: To provide the student with sufficient instruction to perform essential calculations for operating a nuclear power plant.

Learning Outcome: Upon successful completion of this course, the student will be able to perform calculations required to operate a nuclear power plant.

Instruction: Major topics covered in the course are fundamentals of algebra, graphs and functions, exponential and logarithmic functions, and trigonometry.

Credit Recommendation: In the lower division baccalaureate/associate degree category, 1 semester hour in Mathematics (12/87) (7/92).

Reactor Operator Theory: Mitigating Core Damage (ROA01R-MCD)

Location: H.B. Robinson Steam Electric Plant, Hartsville, SC.

Length: *Version A:* 60 hours (1.5 weeks), 45 hours lecture/discussion and 15 hours self-study; *Version B:* 40 hours.

Dates: *Version A:* January 1983-April 1989; *Version B:* May 1989-Present.

Objective: To provide instruction on mitigating core damage as it applies to a nuclear power plant reactor operator.

Learning Outcome: Upon successful completion of this course, the student will be able to list, describe, and explain the parameters, symptoms, alarms, causes, and indications that could result in core damage and to state, explain, and list the actions, procedures, and conditions that would mitigate core damage.

Instruction: Major topics covered in the course are mitigating core damage, including: fuel rod temperature profiles, core thermal limits, natural circulation, fission product containments, post-accident radiation monitoring, Three Mile Island-2 event, reactivity and power distribution anomalies, heat removal by secondary system, expected transients, and integrated system responses. Methods of instruction include lecture, discussion, self-study, and examinations.

Credit Recommendation: *Version A:* In the lower division baccalaureate/associate degree category, 2 semester hours in Nuclear Engineering Technology (12/87) (7/92). *Version B:* In the upper division baccalaureate degree category, 1 semester hour in Nuclear Engineering Technology (2/95).

Reactor Operator Theory: Radiological Control (Health Physics) (ROA01R-HP)

Location: H.B. Robinson Steam Electric Plant, Hartsville, SC.

Length: 28 hours (3.5 days); 21 hours lecture/discussion and 7 hours self-study.

Dates: January 1983-June 1991.

Objective: To provide the student with instruction in radiological control as it applies to a nuclear power plant reactor operator.

Learning Outcome: Upon successful completion of this course, the student will have an understanding of radioactivity, contamination, health effects, and emergency responses.

Instruction: Major topics covered in the course are subjects related to radiological control (health physics) including terminology and decay equations, properties and interactions of radiation, units of exposure and dose, biological effects of radiation, dose rate and shielding, detector principles, emergency response plan, and initial dose projections.

Credit Recommendation: In the lower division baccalaureate/associate degree category, 1 semester hour in Nuclear Engineering Technology (12/87) (7/92).

Reactor Operator Theory: Reactor Theory (ROA01R-RT)

Location: H.B. Robinson Steam Electric Plant, Hartsville, SC.

Length: 80 hours (2 weeks); 60 hours lecture/discussion and 20 hours self-study.

Dates: January 1983-June 1991.

Objective: To provide instruction in reactor theory as it applies to a nuclear power plant reactor operator.

Learning Outcome: Upon successful completion of this course, the student will be able to define some physics terms; describe the structure of the atom; make radioactive decay calculations; make static and dynamic reactor calculations using the six-factor equation and the reactor equation; describe and calculate various coefficients; and describe and calculate reactivity effects.

Instruction: Major topics covered in the course are subjects related to reactor theory, including: properties of matter and energy, nuclear physics and reactions, reactor physics, reactivity effects and variations, reactor kinetics, subcritical theory, various coefficients, poisoning, power distribution, and reactivity control during operation.

Credit Recommendation: In the lower division baccalaureate/associate degree category, 2 semester hours in Nuclear Engineering Technology (12/87) (7/92).

Reactor Operator: Emergency Operating Procedures (Including Dedicated Shutdown Procedures) (ROA01R-EOP, ARP)

Location: H.B. Robinson Steam Electric Plant, Hartsville, SC.

Length: *Version 1:* 56 hours (1.4 weeks); 42 hours lecture/discussion and 14 hours self-study; *Version 2:* 57 hours (2 weeks), 42 hours lecture/discussion, and 15 hours self-study.

Dates: January 1983-Present.

Objective: To provide instruction on emergency operating procedures and dedicated shutdown procedures as they apply to a nuclear power plant reactor operator.

Learning Outcome: Upon successful completion of this course, the student will be able to state, list, discuss, and describe conditions that require the initiation of the various procedures, and will be familiar with and understand the steps, actions, and equipment necessary to effect the various procedures.

Instruction: Major topics covered in the course are subjects related to emergency operating procedures, dedicated shutdown procedures including plant emergency operating procedures, and fire protection. Methods of instruction include lecture, self-study, and examinations.

Credit Recommendation: In the lower division baccalaureate/associate degree category, 2 semester hours in Nuclear Engineering Technology (12/87) (7/92) (2/95). **NOTE:** Credit should not be awarded for both Senior Reactor Operator: Emergency Operating Procedures (Including Dedicated Shutdown Procedures) (ROA02R, EOP, ARP) and this course.

Reactor Operator: Generic Fundamentals (ROGF- HT & FF)

Location: H.B. Robinson Steam Electric Plant, Hartsville, SC and other company locations.

Length: 66 hours (48 hours lecture, 18 hours of self-study).

Dates: August 1993-Present.

Objective: To provide the student with sufficient knowledge in heat transfer, fluid flow, and thermodynamics as it applies to nuclear power plant operators.

Learning Outcome: Upon successful completion of this course, the student will be able to understand the essential heat transfer, fluid mechanics, thermodynamic principles relative to nuclear power plant operation; and perform calculations to estimate temperatures, pressures, and thermodynamic properties associated with essential plant systems.

Instruction: Major topics covered in the course are thermodynamics, heat transfer, and fluid flow including the first and second laws of thermodynamics through energy enthalpy, entropy, and the general energy equations; the properties of water in all phases; steam tables; Mollin diagrams; conductive; convective; radiation heat transfer; and pump heat laws. Methods of instruction include lecture, discussion, self-study, and examinations.

Credit Recommendation: In the lower division baccalaureate/associate degree category, 2 semester hours in Nuclear Science in the upper division baccalaureate degree category, 2 semester hours in Nuclear Engineering Technology (2/95).

Reactor Operator: Generic Fundamentals (ROGF-RT)

Location: H.B. Robinson Steam Electric Plant, Hartsville, SC and other company locations.

Length: 66 hours (48 hours lecture, 18 hours of self-study).

Dates: August 1993-Present.

Objective: To provide the student with sufficient knowledge in reactor theory and kinectics as it applies to nuclear plant operation.

Learning Outcome: Upon successful completion of this course, the student will be able to define some physics terms, describe the structure of an atom, make radioactive delay calculations using the six-factor equation and the reactor equation, describe and calculate various coefficients, and describe and calculate reactivity effects.

Instruction: Major topics covered in the course are reactor theory, including: properties of matter and energy, nuclear physics and reactions, reactor physics, reactivity effects and variations, reactor kinetics, subcritical theory, various coefficients, poisoning, power distribution, and reactivity control during operation. Methods of instruction include lecture, discussion, self-study, and examinations.

Credit Recommendation: In the lower division baccalaureate/associate degree category, 2 semester hours in Nuclear Science or in the upper division baccalaureate degree category, 2 semester hours in Nuclear Engineering Technology (2/95).

Reactor Operator: Simulator (ROA01R-RO Simul)

Location: H.B. Robinson Steam Electric Plant, Hartsville, SC.

Length: *Version A:* 240 hours (6 weeks); *Version B:* 272 hours (6.8 weeks).

Dates: *Version A:* January 1983-January 1988; *Version B:* February 1988-Present.

Objective: To provide the student with instruction and practical operating experience to conduct normal, abnormal, and emergency plant operation as they apply to a pressurized water reactor (PWR) nuclear plant reactor operator.

Learning Outcome: Upon successful completion of this course, the student will be able to perform plant startups and shutdowns under normal and abnormal operating conditions; diagnose and mitigate malfunctions; and initiate appropriate emergency operating procedures in nuclear power plants.

Instruction: Major topics covered in the course are PWR power plant operations including startups, shutdowns, normal operations, abnormal operations, emergency conditions, and basic exercises performed by the students on a nuclear power plant simulator. Methods of instruction include simulator usage, job performance evaluations, written examinations, and simulator examinations.

Credit Recommendation: *Version A:* In the upper division baccalaureate degree category, 2 semester hours in Nuclear Engineering Technology (12/87) (7/92). *Version B:* In the upper division baccalaureate degree category, 3 semester hours in Nuclear Engineering Technology Laboratory (2/95). **NOTE:** A student should not simultaneously receive credit for this course and (ROA01R - PLR).

Senior Reactor Operator Theory: Electrical Science (ROA02R-ELEC)

Location: H.B. Robinson Steam Electric Plant, Hartsville, SC.

Length: 60 hours (1.5 weeks); 45 hours lecture/discussion and 15 hours self-study.

Dates: January 1983-October 1993.

Objective: To provide the student with instruction on electrical science as it applies to a nuclear power plant senior reactor operator.

Learning Outcome: Upon successful completion of this course, the student will be able to describe, define, and calculate the basic properties of electrical circuits, components, and devices.

Instruction: Major topics covered in the course are electrical science including fundamental concepts, AC circuit fundamentals, three-phase generation, transformer theory, power system control and protection, station AC, emergency diesel generators, electrical components and systems, DC electrical system, transistors, and thermocouples. Methods of instruction include self-study and examinations.

Credit Recommendation: In the upper division baccalaureate degree category, 2 semester hours in Electrical Engineering Technology (12/87) (7/92) (2/95).

Senior Reactor Operator: Administration, Procedures and Bases (ROA02R-PROC, AOP)

Location: H.B. Robinson Steam Electric Plant, Hartsville, SC.

Length: 628 hours (15.5 weeks); 100 hours lecture/discussion and 528 hours on-the-job training.

Dates: January 1983-Present.

Objective: To provide instruction on administration, procedures, and bases as they apply to a nuclear power plant senior reactor operator.

Learning Outcome: Upon successful completion of this course, the student will be able to describe and explain the implications, definitions, limitations, compliance, and bases for technical specifications and the various parts of the code of federal regulations; describe the interrelationships between on-site and off-site emergency organizations; perform administrative aspects for various plant maintenance tasks; and list responsibilities of personnel from general plant manager to radiation control technician under certain circumstances.

Instruction: Major topics covered in the course are administration, procedures, and bases including: health physics administrative guidelines, procedures, off-site release of gaseous and liquid radioactive effluents, health administrative radiation work permits, emergency response plans, technical specifications, and fuel follow procedures. Methods of instruction include lecture, discussion, on-the-job training, and examinations.

Credit Recommendation: In the upper division baccalaureate degree category, 3 semester hours in Nuclear Plant Management (12/87) (7/92) (2/95).

Senior Reactor Operator: Advanced Transient and Accident Analysis (ROA02R-ATAA)

Location: H.B. Robinson Steam Electric Plant, Hartsville, SC.

Length: 70 hours (1.8 weeks).

Dates: January 1983-Present.

Objective: To provide the student with instruction on advanced transient and accident analysis as it applies to a nuclear power plant senior reactor operator.

Learning Outcome: Upon successful completion of this course, the student will be able to list, state, explain, and describe indications or situations that could be potentially damaging to the reactor system, and describe action that should be taken by the operator to prevent such damage.

Instruction: Major topics covered in the course are advanced transient and accident analysis including: fuel rod temperature profiles, reactor heat generation, core thermal limits, natural circulation, fission product containment, post-accident radiation monitoring, incore thermocouple system, large and small break loss of coolant accident, steam generator tube rupture, and brittle fracture and the reactor vessel. Methods of instruction include lecture, discussion, self-study, and examinations.

Credit Recommendation: In the upper division baccalaureate degree category, 2 semester hours in Nuclear Engineering Technology (12/87) (7/92) (2/95).

Senior Reactor Operator: Emergency Operating Procedures (Including Dedicated Shutdown Procedures) (ROA02R-EOP, ARP)

Location: H.B. Robinson Steam Electric Plant, Hartsville, SC.

Length: *Version 1:* 56 hours (1.4 weeks); 42 hours lecture/discussion, 14 hours self study; *Version 2:* 57 hours (2 weeks) 42 hours lecture/discussion and 15 hours self-study.

Dates: January 1983-Present.

Objective: To provide instruction on emergency operating procedures and dedicated shutdown procedures as they apply to a nuclear power plant senior reactor operator.

Learning Outcome: Upon successful completion of this course, the student will be able to state, list, discuss, and describe conditions that require the initiation of the various procedures and will be familiar with and understand the steps, actions, and equipment necessary to effect the various procedures.

Instruction: Major topics covered in the course are subjects related to emergency operating procedures, dedicated shutdown procedures, including plant emergency operating procedures, and fire protection. Methods of instruction include lecture, discussion, computer-assisted instruction, self-study, simulator training, and examinations.

Credit Recommendation: In the lower division baccalaureate/associate degree category, 1 semester hour in Nuclear Engineering Technology (12/87) (7/92) (2/95). **NOTE:** Credit should not be awarded for both Reactor Operator: Emergency Procedures (Including Dedicated Shutdown Procedures) (ROA01R-EOP, ARP) and this course.

Senior Reactor Operator: Plant Systems Review and Upgrade (Prelicense Review) (ROA02R-PLR)

Location: H.B. Robinson Steam Electric Plant, Hartsville, SC.

Length: 100 hours (2.5 weeks); 75 hours lecture/discussion and 25 hours self-study.

Dates: January 1983-Present.

Objective: To provide the student with a review of reactor operator theory and systems courses as they apply to a nuclear power plant senior reactor operator. It should provide the student with an in-depth and integrated understanding of essential plant systems and their interrelationships.

Learning Outcome: Upon successful completion of this course, the student will be able to demonstrate a thorough and integrated understanding of plant systems relative to operating procedures, technical specifications, and design limitations. This level of understanding should also be evident with respect to operational procedures and limits imposed by reactor physics, heat transfer, fluid flow, thermodynamics, and general laws of chemistry.

Instruction: Major topics covered in the course are plant systems review and upgrade (prelicense review) including: reactor theory, heat transfer, fluid flow, and thermodynamics, chemistry, health physics, systems, routine and emergency reporting requirements, and Westinghouse major design base accidents. Methods of instruction include lecture, discussion, classroom exercises, self-study, simulator performance, and examinations.

Credit Recommendation: In the upper division baccalaureate degree category, 3 semester hours in Nuclear Engineering Technology (12/87) (7/92) (2/95). **NOTE:** A student should not simultaneously receive credit for this course and (ROA01R - PLR).

Senior Reactor Operator: Simulator (ROA02R-SRO Simul)

Location: Shearon Harris Energy and Environmental Center, New Hill, NC and H.B. Robinson Steam Electric Plant, Hartsville, SC.

Length: *Version A:* 120 hours (3 weeks); *Version B:* 280 hours.

Dates: *Version A:* January 1983-January 1988; *Version B:* February 1988-Present.

Objective: To provide the student with instruction and practical operating experience to supervise normal, abnormal, and emergency power plant operation as they apply to a pressurized water reactor (PWR) nuclear power plant senior reactor operator.

Learning Outcome: Upon successful completion of this course, the student will be able to supervise normal and abnormal plant startups and shutdowns; perform transient and accident analyses; direct emergency operations; and evaluate plant operations relative to technical specifications.

Instruction: Major topics covered in the course are supervising and directing operators during plant startups, shutdowns, normal operations, abnormal operations, emergency conditions, and advanced exercises performed by the students on a nuclear power plant simulator. Methods of instruction include simulator usage, job performance evaluations, written examinations, and simulator examinations.

Credit Recommendation: *Version A:* In the upper division baccalaureate degree category, 1 semester hour in Nuclear Engineering Technology (12/87) (7/92). *Version B:* In the upper division baccalaureate degree category, 1 semester hour in Nuclear Engineering Technology; or 3 semester hours in Nuclear Engineering Technology Laboratory (2/95).

Shearon Harris Nuclear Power Plant

Nuclear Reactor Operations Laboratory (ROT401)

Location: Burlington Laboratory, NCSU Campus, Raleigh, NC and other company locations.

Length: *Version A:* 38 hours (1 week); *Version B:* 80 hours (2 weeks).

Dates: *Version A:* January 1978-December 1989; *Version B:* January 1990-Present.

Objective: To provide the student with knowledge and experience relating to operation of light water reactors using laboratory experiments performed on the PULSTAR reactor at North Carolina State University.

Learning Outcome: Upon successful completion of this course, the student will be able to perform normal start-ups of the PULSTAR reactor with minimum assistance from instructor; relate functions and operations of instrumentation to reactor conditions; explain significance of reactor symptoms that require immediate and follow-up actions in emergency procedures; calculate reactivity balances for various conditions; and explain how neutron flux, reactivity, and other factors are related to heat and power generation.

Instruction: Major topics covered in the course are reactor start-up and operation procedures, subcritical behavior, reactor statics and kinetics, transient analysis, and reactor safety considerations. Methods of instruction include lecture, laboratory, task performance, and both written and oral examinations.

Credit Recommendation: In the upper division baccalaureate degree category, 3 semester hours in Nuclear Science (7/92) (2/95).

Radiation Control Technician Level I Generic Training RC200N

Location: Shearon Harris Nuclear Power Plant, New Hill, NC and other company locations.

Length: 187 hours (5 weeks).

Dates: January 1986-Present.

Objective: To introduce the student to the basic concepts and practices of health physics that apply in nuclear power plants. In addition, the course includes a review of math, an introduction to plant chemistry, and an introduction to personal computers.

Learning Outcome: Upon successful completion of this course, the student will be able to describe and discuss radiation and its interaction with matter; radiation detectors; radiation surveys; radioactive material handling and control procedures; regulations; ALARA concepts; and radioactive contamination and decontamination. The student will also be able to perform algebraic operations, solve equations, use logarithms, and convert units.

Instruction: Major topics covered in the course are basic math, plant chemistry, radioactive material handling and control, procedures, regulations, basic detector theory, respiratory protection, radiation surveys, nuclear physics, radioactive contamination and decontamination, ALARA concepts, emergency preparedness, industrial hygiene, TLD dosimetry, air sampling, hot particles, and personal computer concepts. Methods of instruction include lecture and classroom exercises.

Credit Recommendation: In the lower division baccalaureate/associate degree category, 1 semester hour in Basic Math, 1 semester hour in Chemistry, and 4 semester hours in Nuclear Engineering Technology, for a total of 6 semester hours (2/95).

Radiation Control Technician Level II Generic Training RC300N

Location: Shearon Harris Nuclear Power Plant and other company locations.

Length: 120 hours (3 weeks).

Dates: January 1986-Present.

Objective: To introduce the student to the concepts, theory, and practices of health physics. This course prepares students for further plant specific training.

Learning Outcome: Upon successful completion of this course, the student will be able to discuss radioactive decay, interactions of radiation with matter, dose, biological effects, radiation instruments, monitoring and counting; calculate doses, calibrate radiation measuring instruments, and determine requirements for shipping radioactive waste.

Instruction: Major topics covered in the course are nuclear physics, radioactive decay, radiation monitoring, instrument calibration and use, biological effects of radiation, internal dose assessment, single and multichannel analyzers, shielding, and shipping radioactive materials. Methods of instruction include lecture and laboratory.

Credit Recommendation: In the upper division baccalaureate degree category, 4 semester hours in Nuclear Engineering Technology (2/95).

Reactor Operator Systems: Nuclear Steam Supply Systems and Design Considerations (RO6C02H-Prim. Syst.)

Location: Shearon Harris Nuclear Power Plant, New Hill, NC.

Length: 240 hours (15 weeks); 80 hours classroom instruction and 160 hours on-the-job training (OJT).

Dates: March 1983-Present.

Objective: To provide the student with instruction on nuclear steam supply systems and design considerations (primary systems) as they apply to a nuclear power plant reactor operator.

Learning Outcome: Upon successful completion of this course, the student will be able to describe the design and operation of the following general systems: reactor coolant systems; safety systems; containment systems; safety-related auxiliary systems; and instrumentation and control systems.

Instruction: Major topics covered in the course are classroom and on-the-job training related to nuclear steam supply systems and design considerations including reactor coolant systems, safety systems, containment systems, safety-related auxiliary systems, and instrumentation and control systems. Methods of instruction include lecture, audio/visual material, discussion, on-the-job training, written examinations, performance testing, and qualifications cards.

Credit Recommendation: In the upper division baccalaureate degree category, 3

semester hours in Nuclear Engineering Technology (12/87) (7/92) (2/95).

Reactor Operator Systems: Plant Systems Review and Upgrade (Prelicense Review) (RO6C02H-PLR)

Location: Shearon Harris Nuclear Power Plant, New Hill, NC.

Length: 150 hours (5 weeks).

Dates: October 1982-Present.

Objective: To provide the student with instruction on plant systems review and upgrade (prelicense review) as they apply to a nuclear plant reactor operator. The student should obtain an integrated knowledge of essential plant systems and their interrelationships.

Learning Outcome: Upon successful completion of this course, the student will be able to demonstrate an improved and integrated knowledge of plant systems relative to plant operating procedures, technical specifications, and design limitations.

Instruction: Major topics covered in the course are plant systems review and upgrade. Methods of instruction include lecture, audio/visual material, discussion, written examinations, and performance testing.

Credit Recommendation: In the upper division baccalaureate degree category, 2 semester hours in Nuclear Engineering Technology (12/87) (7/92) (2/95).

Reactor Operator Systems: Power Plant Engineering Systems (RO6C02H-Sec. and Ele)

Location: Shearon Harris Nuclear Power Plant, New Hill, NC.

Length: 573 hours (20 weeks); 213 hours classroom instruction and 360 hours on-the-job training (OJT).

Dates: March 1983-Present.

Objective: To provide the student with instruction on power plant engineering systems (secondary and electrical) as they apply to a nuclear power plant reactor operator.

Learning Outcome: Upon successful completion of this course, the student will be able to describe the design and operation of the following general systems: main and auxiliary steam systems, condensate and feedwater systems, main turbine and associated support systems; steam generator and associated support systems; and electrical systems associated with the secondary plant.

Instruction: Major topics covered in the course are classroom and OJT related to power plant engineering systems including secondary pressurized water reactor systems and electrical systems. Methods of instruction include lecture, audio/visual material, discussion, OJT, written examinations, performance testing, and qualification cards.

Credit Recommendation: In the upper division baccalaureate degree category, 6 semester hours in Nuclear Engineering Technology (12/87) (7/92) (2/95).

Reactor Operator Theory: Electrical Sciences (RO6C02H-ELEC)

Location: Shearon Harris Nuclear Power Plant, New Hill, NC.

Length: 30 hours (1.25 weeks); 22 hours lecture/discussion and 8 hours self-study.

Dates: October 1982-June 1991.

Objective: To provide the student with instruction on electrical sciences as they apply to a nuclear power plant reactor operator.

Learning Outcome: Upon successful completion of this course, the student will have a basic knowledge of voltage, current, and resistance in DC and AC electrical circuits, circuit laws and nomenclature, as well as the operation of electrical instruments.

Instruction: Major topics covered in the course are subjects related to electrical sciences including AC circuit fundamentals, DC theory and circuits, DC measurement, AC generation, motors, load sharing, and voltage regulation.

Credit Recommendation: In the lower division baccalaureate/associate degree category, 1 semester hour in Electrical Engineering Technology (12/87) (7/92).

Reactor Operator Theory: Heat Transfer, Fluid Flow, and Thermodynamics (RO6C02H-HT, FF, TH)

Location: Shearon Harris Nuclear Power Plant, New Hill, NC.

Length: 80 hours (2 weeks); 60 hours lecture/discussion and 20 hours self-study.

Dates: October 1982-June 1991.

Objective: To provide the student with sufficient instruction on heat transfer, fluid flow, and thermodynamics as they apply to nuclear power plant operation.

Learning Outcome: Upon successful completion of this course, the student will be able to understand the essential heat transfer, fluid mechanics, thermodynamic principles relative to nuclear power plant operation, and perform calculations to estimate temperatures, pressures, and thermodynamic properties associated with essential plant systems.

Instruction: Major topics covered in the course are subjects related to heat transfer, fluid flow, and thermodynamics including reactor heat transfer, heat exchangers, and design and operational limits: reactor core thermal parameters, fluid statics, fluid flow dynamics, fluid mechanics in pumps and piping, fluid mechanics in the turbine, natural circulation, instrumentation, the properties of water, reactor and pressurizer thermo, steam generator thermodynamics, turbine thermodynamics and the Rankine cycle, and condenser/tertiary system thermodynamics.

Credit Recommendation: In the upper division baccalaureate degree category, 3 semester hours in Nuclear Engineering Technology (12/87) (7/92).

Reactor Operator Theory: Material Sciences (RO6C02H-MtSc, PTS)

Location: Shearon Harris Nuclear Power Plant, New Hill, NC.

Length: 30 hours (4 days); 22 hours lecture/discussion and 8 hours self-study.

Dates: October 1982-June 1991.

Objective: To provide instruction on material sciences and pressurized thermal shock as they apply to a nuclear power plant reactor operator.

Learning Outcome: Upon successful completion of this course, the student will be able to describe, state, list, define, and explain the concepts and phenomena covered in the course description.

Instruction: Major topics covered in the course are subjects related to material science including mechanical metallurgy, material properties, nuclear core design, plant materials, reactor vessel stress and embrittlement, and pressurized thermal shock.

Credit Recommendation: In the lower division baccalaureate/associate degree category, 1 semester hour in Material Science (12/87) (7/92).

Reactor Operator Theory: Mathematics (RO6C02H-Math)

Location: Shearon Harris Nuclear Power Plant, New Hill, NC.

Length: 36 hours (1 week); 26 hours lecture/discussion and 10 hours self-study.

Dates: October 1982-June 1991.

Objective: To provide the student with sufficient instruction to perform essential calculations for operating a nuclear power plant.

Learning Outcome: Upon successful completion of this course, the student will be able to perform all essential calculations required to operate a nuclear power plant.

Instruction: Major topics covered in the course are fundamentals of algebra, graphs and functions, exponential and logarithmic functions, trigonometry, and introductory calculus.

Credit Recommendation: In the lower division baccalaureate/associate degree category, 1 semester hour in Mathematics (12/87) (7/92).

Reactor Operator Theory: Operation and Administration (RO6C02H-OPADMIN)

Location: Shearon Harris Nuclear Power Plant, New Hill, NC.

Length: 185 hours (5 weeks).

Dates: October 1987-Present.

Objective: To provide instruction on plant operation procedures and administration as they apply to a nuclear power plant reactor operator.

Learning Outcome: Upon successful completion of this course, the student will be able to state, list, and define terms, safety limits, and certain requirements for technical specifications as they relate to nuclear power plant reactor operations.

Instruction: Major topics covered in the course are plant operation procedures and administration including: technical specifications, general procedures, emergency procedures, plant procedures, and abnormal operating procedures. Methods of instruction include lecture, audio/visual material, discussion, written examinations, and performance testing.

Credit Recommendation: In the lower division baccalaureate/associate degree category, 3 semester hours in Nuclear Engineering Technology (12/87) (7/92) (2/95).

Reactor Operator Theory: Radiation Protection and Chemistry (RO6C02H-RP, CH)

Location: Shearon Harris Nuclear Power Plant, New Hill, NC.

Length: 40 hours (1 week).

Dates: October 1982-June 1991.

Objective: To provide the student with instruction on radiation protection and chemistry as it applies to a nuclear power plant reactor operator.

Learning Outcome: Upon successful completion of this course, the student will have an understanding of radioisotopes, the interaction and health effects of ionizing radiation, as well as nuclear power plant chemistry.

Instruction: Major topics covered in the course are subjects related to radiation protection and chemistry including: radioactivity concepts, radiation interaction with matter, health effects, radiation detection, chemistry fundamentals, corrosion, primary and secondary water chemistry, and hazardous chemicals.

Credit Recommendation: In the lower division baccalaureate/associate degree category, 2 semester hours in Nuclear Engineering Technology (12/87) (7/92).

Reactor Operator Theory: Reactor Theory (RO6C02H-RT)

Location: Shearon Harris Nuclear Power Plant, New Hill, NC.

Length: 80 hours (2 weeks); 70 hours lecture/discussion and 10 hours self-study.

Dates: October 1982-June 1991.

Objective: To provide instruction on reactor theory as it applies to a nuclear power plant reactor operator.

Learning Outcome: Upon successful completion of this course, the student will be able to define some physics terms; describe the structure of the atom; make radioactive decay calculations; make static and dynamic reactor calculations using the six-factor equation and the reactor equation; describe and calculate various coefficients; and describe and calculate reactivity effects.

Instruction: Major topics covered in the course are subjects related to reactor theory, including: properties of matter and energy, nuclear physics and reactions, reactor physics, reactivity effects and variations, reactor kinetics, subcritical theory, various coefficients, poisoning, power distribution, and reactivity control during operation.

Credit Recommendation: In the lower division baccalaureate/associate degree category, 2 semester hours in Nuclear Engineering Technology (12/87) (7/92).

Reactor Operator: Simulator (SHNPP) (RO6CO2H-RO Simul)

Location: Shearon Harris Nuclear Power Plant, New Hill, NC.

Length: 248 hours (6 weeks).

Dates: January 1983-Present.

Objective: To provide the student with instruction and practical operating experience on normal, abnormal, and emergency power plant operation as they apply to a pressurized water reactor (PWR) nuclear power plant reactor operator.

Learning Outcome: Upon successful completion of this course, the student will be able to perform plant startups and shutdowns under normal and abnormal operating conditions; diagnose and mitigate malfunctions; and institute appropriate emergency operating procedures in nuclear power plants.

Instruction: Major topics covered in the course are PWR power plant operation including: plant startups, shutdowns, normal operation, abnormal operation, and emergency conditions. Methods of instruction include lecture, simulator training, written examinations, and performance testing.

Credit Recommendation: In the upper division baccalaureate degree category, 3 semester hours in Nuclear Engineering Technology (12/87) (7/92) (2/95).

ROGF: Heat Transfer, Fluid Flow, and Thermodynamics

Location: Shearon Harris Nuclear Power Plant, New Hill, NC and other company locations.

Length: 68 hours (17 weeks).

Dates: August 1991-August 1993.

Objective: To provide the student with basic instruction on heat transfer, fluid flow, and thermodynamics as applied to nuclear power plant operation.

Learning Outcome: Upon successful completion of this course, the student will be able to understand the basic heat transfer, fluid mechanics, and thermodynamics principles relative to nuclear plant operation; and perform simple/noncalculus-based calculations to estimate temperatures, pressures, and thermodynamic properties, energy balances, and heat transfer associated with essential plant systems.

Instruction: Major topics covered in the course are heat transfer, fluid flow, and thermodynamics, basics of flat plate heat transfer, perfect gases, steam tables, simple first law analysis of control volume and control mass systems, fluid statics, pumps, valves, and nozzles. Methods of instruction include lecture, discussion, classroom exercises, and periodic and final examinations.

Credit Recommendation: In the lower division baccalaureate/associate degree category, 2 semester hours in Engineering Technology (2/95).

ROGF: Reactor Theory

Location: Shearon Harris Nuclear Power Plant, New Hill, NC and other company locations.

Length: 59 hours (1.5 weeks).

Dates: August 1991-August 1993.

Objective: To provide instruction on reactor theory as it applies to a nuclear power plant reactor operator.

Learning Outcome: Upon successful completion of this course, the student will be able to define reactor physics terms, describe the structure of the atom, make radioactive decay calculations, and make static and dynamic reactor calculations using the reactor equation and the 6 factor formula. Also the student will describe and calculate reactor coefficients and reactivity effects.

Instruction: Major topics covered in the course are reactor theory, including: properties of matter and energy, nuclear physics and reactions, reactor physics, reactivity effects and variations, reactor kinetics, subcritical theory, reactor coefficients, poisoning, power distribution, and reactivity control during operation. Methods of instruction include lecture and periodic examinations.

Credit Recommendation: In the lower division baccalaureate/associate degree category, 2 semester hours in Nuclear Engineering Technology or Nuclear Science (2/95).

Senior Reactor Operator Theory: Electrical Science S06C00H-ELEC; Version A

Location: Shearon Harris Nuclear Power Plant, New Hill, NC.

Length: 40 hours (1 week), 26 hours lecture/discussion and 14 hours self-study .

Dates: October 1982-September 1993.

Objective: To provide the student with instruction on electrical science as it applies to a nuclear power plant senior reactor operator.

Learning Outcome: Upon successful completion of this course, the student will be able to describe, define, and calculate the basic properties of electrical circuits, components, and devices.

Instruction: Major topics covered in the course are electrical sciences including: AC circuit fundamentals; three-phase power generation; generator paralleling and sharing of real and reactive load; generator voltage regulation; generator operational limitations; brushless excitation system; transformer theory; protective relaying; diesel generator operation; lead acid batteries; and electrical specifications. Methods of instruction include lecture, audio/visual material, discussion, written examinations, and performance testing.

Credit Recommendation: In the upper division baccalaureate degree category, 2 semester hours in Electrical Engineering Technology (12/87) (7/92).

Senior Reactor Operator Theory: Electrical Science S06C00H-ELEC; Version B

Location: Shearon Harris Nuclear Power Plant.

Length: 40 hours (1 week); 32 hours lecture/discussion and 8 hours self-study.

Dates: October 1993-Present.

Objective: To provide the student with instruction on electrical science as it applies to a nuclear power plant senior reactor operator.

Learning Outcome: Upon successful completion of this course, the student will be able to describe, define, and monitor the plant electrical system.

Instruction: Major topics covered in the course are electrical sciences including: AC circuit fundamentals, three-phase power generation, generator voltage regulation, generator paralleling and sharing of real and reactive load, generator operational limitations, brushless excitation system, transformer theory, protective relaying, lead acid batteries, diesel generator operation, and electrical specifications. Methods of instruction include lecture, audio/visual material, discussion, written examinations, and performance testing.

Credit Recommendation: In the upper division baccalaureate degree category, 2 semester hours in Electrical Engineering Technology (2/95).

Senior Reactor Operator Theory: Mitigating Core Damage S06C00H-MCD, Version A

Location: Shearon Harris Nuclear Power Plant, New Hill, NC.

Length: 25 hours (4 days); 23 hours lecture/discussion and 2 hours self-study.

Dates: October 1984-August 1993.

Objective: To provide instruction on nuclear mitigating core damage as it applies to a nuclear power plant senior reactor operator.

Learning Outcome: Upon successful completion of this course, the student will be able to state expected plant response to various core damaging events; recognize core damage characteristics; describe the parameters, symptoms, and indications that could result in core damage; explain operator actions and conditions that would mitigate core damage; understand the basis supporting the mitigation strategies; and state radiological consequences both on-site and off-site for various events.

Instruction: Major topics covered in the course are mitigating core damage including: post-accident cooling, small break loss of coolant accident (LOCA) with no high head safety injection, loss of feedwater-induced LOCA, vital process instrumentation, accident response of incore and excore instrumentation, post-accident primary radiochemistry, radiological aspects of core damage, and loss of all AC power. Methods of instruction include lecture, on-the-job training (OJT), task performance evaluations during the OJT phase, and periodic examinations.

Credit Recommendation: In the lower division baccalaureate/associate degree category, 1 semester hour in Nuclear Engineering Technology (12/87) (7/92).

Senior Reactor Operator Theory: Mitigating Core Damage S06C00H-MCD Version B

Location: Shearon Harris Nuclear Power Plant.

Length: 190 hours (5 weeks).

Dates: September 1993-Present.

Objective: To provide instruction on nuclear accident response and mitigating core damage as it applies to nuclear power plant Senior Reactor Operators.

Learning Outcome: Upon successful completion of this course, the student will be able to state the expected plant response to various core damaging events, recognize core damage characteristics, state radiological consequences both on-site and off-site for various events, describe the parameters, symptoms, and indications that could result in core damage, explain the operator actions and conditions that would mitigate core damage, and understand the basis supporting the mitigation strategies.

Instruction: Major topics covered in the course are industry events, including: Three Mile Island, Chernobyl, and various stream generator tube ruptures, mitigating core damage, and abnormal and emergency operating procedures. Classroom instruction is reinforced through the use of On-The-Job Training stressing the role of the Senior Reactor Operator in directing crew response to an accident situation. This includes accident diagnosis, procedure implementation, and maintaining critical safety functions to prevent core damage. Methods of instruction include lecture, on-the-job training (OJT), task performance evaluations during the OJT phase, and periodic examinations.

Credit Recommendation: In the lower division baccalaureate/associate degree

category, 3 semester hours in Nuclear Engineering Technology (2/95).

Senior Reactor Operator Theory: Transient and Accident Analysis (S06C00H-T&AA)

Location: Shearon Harris Nuclear Power Plant, New Hill, NC.

Length: 47 hours (1.5 weeks).

Dates: October 1982-Present.

Objective: To provide instruction on transient and accident analysis as it applies to a nuclear power plant senior reactor operator.

Learning Outcome: Upon successful completion of this course, the student will be able to analyze indications from instruments relative to possible abnormal events and be capable of specifying appropriate corrective actions.

Instruction: Major topics covered in the course are transient and accident analysis including: instrument failure analysis, introduction to accident analysis, primary induced reactivity addition accidents, increased secondary heat removal, decreased secondary heat removal, loss of coolant accident, steam generator tube rupture, loss of flow accident, anticipated transients without trip, heat source and hot channel factors, hydrogen generation and control, fission product containment, normal and abnormal transient analysis, operational experience reports, and brittle fracture and the reactor vessel. Methods of instruction include lecture, audio/visual material, discussion, written examinations, and performance testing.

Credit Recommendation: In the upper division baccalaureate degree category, 2 semester hours in Nuclear Engineering Technology (12/87) (7/92) (2/95).

Senior Reactor Operator: Operation and Administration S06C00H-OPADMIN, Version A

Location: Shearon Harris Nuclear Power Plant, New Hill, NC.

Length: 70 hours (2 weeks).

Dates: October 1982-June 1991.

Objective: To provide instruction on plant operation procedures and administration as they apply to a nuclear power plant senior reactor operator.

Learning Outcome: Upon successful completion of this course, the student will be able to describe and explain the implications, definitions, limitations, compliance, and bases for technical specifications; describe interrelationships between on-site and off-site emergency organizations; perform administrative aspects for various plant tasks; and list responsibilities of personnel from general plant manager to radiation control technicians under certain circumstances.

Instruction: Major topics covered in the course are plant operation procedures and administration including technical specifications, emergency plan plant procedures, and advanced operating practices. Methods of instruction include lecture, audio/visual material, and discussion.

Credit Recommendation: In the upper division baccalaureate degree category, 2 semester hours in Nuclear Plant Management (12/87) (7/92).

Senior Reactor Operator: Operation and Administration S06C00H-OPADMIN; Version B

Location: Shearon Harris Nuclear Power Plant, New Hill, NC.

Length: 460 hours (11.5 weeks); 40 hours lecture/discussion and 420 hours on-the-job training (OJT).

Dates: July 1991-Present.

Objective: To provide instruction on plant operation procedures and administration as they apply to a nuclear power plant senior reactor operator.

Learning Outcome: Upon successful completion of this course, the student will be able to describe and explain the implications, definitions, limitations, compliance, and bases for technical specifications; describe interrelationships between on-site and off-site emergency organizations; perform administrative aspects for various plant tasks; and list responsibilities of personnel for general plant manager to radiation control technicians under certain circumstances.

Instruction: Major topics covered in the course are plant operation procedures and administration including technical specifications, emergency plan plant procedures, and advanced operating practices. Methods of instruction include lecture, audio/visual material, discussion, written examinations, performance testing, and qualification cards.

Credit Recommendation: In the upper division baccalaureate degree category, 4 semester hours in Nuclear Plant Management (2/95).

Senior Reactor Operator: Plant Systems Review and Upgrade (Prelicense Review) (S06C00H-PLR)

Location: Shearon Harris Nuclear Power Plant, New Hill, NC.

Length: 130 hours (4 weeks); 92 hours lecture/discussion and 38 hours self-study.

Dates: October 1982-Present.

Objective: To provide the student with a review of reactor operator theory and systems courses as they apply to a nuclear power plant senior reactor operator. It should provide the student with an in-depth and integrated understanding of essential plant systems and their interrelationships.

Learning Outcome: Upon successful completion of this course, the student will be able to demonstrate a thorough and integrated understanding of plant systems relative to operating procedures, technical specification, and design limitations. This level of understanding should also be evident with respect to operational procedures and limits imposed by reactor physics, heat transfer, fluid flow, thermodynamics, and general laws of physics and chemistry.

Instruction: Major topics covered in the course are plant systems review and upgrade (prelicense review) including: reactor theory, heat transfer, fluid flow, and thermodynamics; chemistry; radiation protection; and general procedures, emergency operating procedures, and plant procedures. Methods of instruction include lecture, audio/visual material, discussion, written examinations, and performance testing.

Credit Recommendation: In the upper division baccalaureate degree category, 3 semester hours in Nuclear Engineering Technology (12/87) (7/92) (2/95).

Senior Reactor Operator: Simulator (SHNPP) (S06C00H-SRO Simul)

Location: Shearon Harris Energy & Environmental Center, New Hill, NC.

Length: 157 hours (4 weeks).

Dates: January 1983-Present.

Objective: To provide the student with instruction and practical operating experience to supervise normal, abnormal, and emergency power plant operation as they apply to a pressurized water reactor nuclear power plant senior reactor operator.

Learning Outcome: Upon successful completion of this course, the student will be able to supervise normal and abnormal plant startups and shutdowns; perform transient and accident analyses; direct emergency operations; and evaluate operations relative to technical specifications.

Instruction: Major topics covered in the course are supervision of power plant operation including: transient and accident analysis, diagnosing problems and applying technical specifications to plant startups, shutdowns, normal operation, abnormal operation, and emergency conditions. Methods of instruction include lecture, audio/visual material, discussion, simulator, written examinations, and performance and simulator testing.

Credit Recommendation: In the upper division baccalaureate degree category, 2 semester hours in Nuclear Engineering Technology (12/87) (7/92) (2/95).

Carpenters Health and Safety Fund of North America

The Carpenter's Health & Safety Fund of North America is a non-profit, labor management trust fund, established in 1990 to provide health and safety training and other services to participating contractors and to members of the United Brotherhood of Carpenters. Courses are provided in Hazardous Waste, Lead, Asbestos, Confined Space, Ergonomics, Radiology, BloodBorne Diseases, First Aid/CPR, and Hazard Communication. Students are journey level carpenters or other tradespeople who have completed a four year apprenticeship program through the United Brotherhood of Carpenters or through other construction unions. The training assists in the Carpenters Funds' long term goal of protecting the health and safety of their members, and family members.

The courses are available at the United Brotherhood of Carpenters' 225 Joint Apprenticeship Training Centers, throughout the country. The training is provided by a team of trainers or experienced tradespeople, who have taken the courses, had 40 hour Train-the-Trainer training, and are lead by Master Trainers. Annual technical enhancement and training techniques courses are provided for trainers. The courses rely heavily on interactive, small group activities, in which participants interrelate pieces of information and concepts, discuss them in small groups, and draw their own conclusions. Students are actively involved in learning with as many hands-on activities as possible.

The courses are developed when requested, or when a need is perceived, with the cost of development assisted by federal grants. Carpenter's has a large training and Education Program with extensive expertise. Quality control is setup both externally and internally and instructors are trained, monitored and provided with updated and in-service training on an annual basis.

Source of official student records: Registry of Credit Recommendations, American Council on Education, One Dupont Circle, Washington, DC 20036-1193.

Additional information about the courses: College Credit Recommendation Service, American Council on Education, One Dupont Circle, Washington, DC 20036-1193.

Asbestos Supervisor/Contractor Course (UBC OHS L02)

Location: Varies, Continental United States.

Length: 40 hours.

Dates: November 1990-Present.

Objective: To provide workers with information on asbestos hazards, engineering controls, proper personal protective clothing and equipment, and abatement technologies with appropriate supervisory skills to safely manage abatement activities. To provide EPA approved training and meet OSHA requirements.

Learning Outcome: Upon successful completion of this course, students will be able to recognize the hazards of asbestos; exposure; understand the applicable regulations governing asbestos abatement; safely perform asbestos abatement tasks; understand workers' rights pertaining to asbestos work; perform and supervise asbestos abatement tasks and maintain appropriate documentation and records at an asbestos abatement site.

Instruction: Major topics covered in the course are history, uses of asbestos and health effects of asbestos; exposure; proper air and bulk sampling techniques; proper respiratory protection and elements of a respiratory protection program; federal and state asbestos laws; medical surveillance program requirements; project management and supervisory techniques to manage appropriate legal, insurance and contractual specifications; and recordkeeping requirements. Methods of instruction include lecture, discussion, classroom exercises, audio/visual material, pre and post tests, successful completion of a written examination (70% or higher), and satisfactory demonstration of knowledge and understanding through simulated hands-on exercises.

Credit Recommendation: In the lower division baccalaureate/associate degree category, 2 semester hours in Industrial Hygiene, Industrial/Occupational Education, Occupational Health and Safety, Hazardous Waste Management, or Environmental Science (4/95). **NOTE:** This course is also taught under the title Asbestos Hazard Emergency Response Act (AHERA) Contractor/Supervisor Course in Illinois.

Asbestos Worker Course (UBC OHS L01)

Location: Varies, Continental United States.

Length: 32 hours.

Dates: November 1990-Present.

Objective: To provide workers with information on asbestos hazards, engineering controls, proper personal protective clothing and equipment, and abatement technologies. To provide EPA approved training and meet OSHA requirements.

Learning Outcome: Upon successful completion of this course, students will be able to recognize the hazards of asbestos; understand the applicable regulations governing asbestos abatement; safely perform asbestos abatement tasks; and understand workers' rights pertaining to asbestos work.

Instruction: Major topics covered in the course are history, uses of asbestos and health effects of asbestos; exposure; proper air and bulk sampling techniques; proper respiratory protection and elements of a respiratory protection program; and federal and state asbestos laws. Methods of instruction include lecture, discussion, classroom exercises, audio/visual material, pre and post tests, successful completion of a written examination (70% or higher), and simulated hands-on exercises.

Credit Recommendation: In the lower division baccalaureate/associate degree category, 2 semester hours in Industrial Hygiene, Industrial/Occupational Education, Occupational Health and Safety, or Hazardous Waste Management (4/95). **NOTE:** This course is also taught under the title *Asbestos Hazard Emergency Response Act (AHERA) Worker Course* in Colorado, Delaware, Virginia, Montana, and Louisiana. In New York this course is taught under the title *Asbestos Handler.*

Hazardous Waste Worker Course (UBC OHS H01)

Location: Varies, Continental United States.

Length: 40 hours.

Dates: November 1990-Present.

Objective: To provide workers with health and safety training to perform activities safely at hazardous waste sites in accordance with the requirements of 29 CFR 1910.120.

Learning Outcome: Upon successful completion of this course, the student will be able to prepare a site safety and health plan; recognize hazards and safe work practices; use respiratory and personal protective clothing and equipment safely; perform patching and plugging activities; and demonstrate proper spill containment and decontamination methods.

Instruction: Major topics covered in the course are recognition, evaluation, and control of hazards; basics of toxicology; respiratory protection; personal protected clothing and equipment; safe operating practices; and elements of a site safety and health plan. Methods of instruction include lecture, discussion, classroom exercises, case studies, audio/visual material, participation in hands-on workshops (demonstrate performance), small group and interactive activities, and successful completion of a written examination (70% or higher).

Credit Recommendation: In the lower division baccalaureate/associate degree category, 2 semester hours in Environmental Science, Industrial/ Occupational Education, Occupational Health and Safety, or Hazardous Waste Management (4/95).

Lead Abatement Supervisor Course (UBC OHS L02)

Location: Varies, Continental United States.

Length: 40 hours.

Dates: November 1991-Present.

Objective: To teach students the hazards and regulations for lead removal operations, appropriate supervisory skills and information, and the procedures and technologies to perform and supervise safe lead abatement. To meet OSHA and HUD requirements and lead abatement training.

Learning Outcome: Upon successful completion of this course, students will be able to identify regulatory agencies involved in lead; abatement; recognize and explain health effects of lead; exposure; specify permissible exposure limits; exhibit proper selection and uses of respirators; describe medical monitoring; perform proper decon; perform procedures for measuring lead levels in paint and air; and read and understand MSDS.

Instruction: Major topics covered in the course are history, uses of lead and health effects of lead; exposure; proper air and bulk sampling techniques; proper respiratory protection and elements of a respiratory protection program; federal and state lead laws; liability; conflict of interest; insurance issues; and proper recordkeeping. Methods of instruction include lecture, discussion, classroom exercises, audio/visual material, pre and post tests, successful completion of a written examination (70% or higher), and satisfactory demonstration of knowledge and understanding through simulated hands-on exercises.

Credit Recommendation: In the lower division baccalaureate/associate degree category, 2 semester hours in Industrial Hygiene, Industrial/Occupational Education, Occupational Health and Safety, or Hazardous Waste Management (4/95). **NOTE:** This course is also taught under the title *Lead-Related Construction Supervision and Project Monitoring Course* in California. The course is also approved by Massachusetts, Minnesota, and Wisconsin.

Lead Worker Course (UBC OHS L001 - 11/92)

Location: Varies, Continental United States.

Length: 32 hours (Actual contact hours 29.3 hours).

Dates: November 1991-Present.

Objective: To teach students the hazards and regulations for lead removal operations and the procedures and technologies to perform safe lead abatement work. To meet OSHA and HUD requirements to lead abatement training.

Learning Outcome: Upon successful completion of this course, students will be able to identify regulatory agencies involved in lead; abatement; recognize and explain health effects of lead; exposure; specify permissible exposure limits; exhibit proper selection and use of respirators; describe medical monitoring; perform proper decon; perform procedures for measuring lead levels in paint and air; and read and understand MSDS.

Instruction: Major topics covered in the course are health hazards of lead; uses of lead; respirator use; air testing; abatement practices; decontamination; disposal of lead; and medical surveillance. Methods of instruction include lecture, discussion, classroom exercises, audio/visual material, much emphasis of hands-on activities, and a final examination with passing grade of 70% or higher (examination is read to students with literacy problems).

Credit Recommendation: In the lower division baccalaureate/associate degree category, 2 semester hours in Environmental Science, Industrial/Occupational Education, Occupational Health and Safety, or Hazardous Waste Management (4/95). **NOTE:** This course is also taught under the title *Lead-Related Construction Worker Course* in California, *32-hour Lead Abatement Worker Course* in Wisconsin, and *32-hour Deleader Worker Abatement Course* in Massachusetts.

Case Corporation

Case Corporation, with net sales of nearly $5 billion in 1995, is headquartered in Racine, Wisconsin, and is a leading worldwide designer, manufacturer and distributor of construction and agricultural equipment. The company's products are sold through a network of approximately 4,100 independent dealers and distributors in more than 150 countries.

The training department supports the Case Corporation Mission Statement "Case will lead the industry by providing our agricultural and construction equipment customers around the world with superior products and services that maximize their productivity and success." The stated purpose of the training department is "...to measurably improve the performance capability of dealership and field personnel."

Courses offered include classes on technical support, sales skills, product knowledge, and business management through a variety of delivery methods including Face to Face at a central location, Face to Face at a remote location, and Self Directed Learning in print, video and CD-Rom formats. Participants in these classes include internal clients from through out the North American Case operation and external clients such as dealer personnel from Sales, Service, Parts, and Management backgrounds. 8,000 students pass through one or more of the over 80 classes available per year.

Source of official student records: Registry of Credit Recommendations, American Council on Education, One Dupont Circle, Washington, DC 20036-1193.

Additional information about the courses: College Credit Recommendation Service, American Council on Education, One Dupont Circle, Washington, DC 20036-1193.

Business Organization and Policy (Dealer Organizational Structures, Dealership Computer Systems, Competitor's Business Strategies, Policies and Procedures, Best Practices and Dealer Processes)

Location: Self directed learning in print.

Length: Self paced (25-35 hours estimated).

Dates: February 1996-Present.

Objective: The learner will be able to identify the business impact of policies, procedures, organization and practices of the firm and its competitors. Learners will be capable of applying this knowledge to business environments.

Learning Outcome: Upon successful completion of this course, the learner will be able to identify business policies and strategies and apply the appropriate policy in the business, organization and practice in computerized business environment.

Instruction: Major topics covered in the course are policy and practice application to operational needs and guidelines in computerized business system, to include a firm's best practices, competitors strategies, appropriate organizations, and general business action planning. Methods of instruction include self paced learning, final exams, case studies, and performance observation.

Credit Recommendation: In the graduate division degree category, 2 semester hours in Executive MBA (1/97).

Credit Policies, Products, and Sales Support (Case Sales Support Offerings, Credit Products and Services, Wholesale Credit Policies and Procedures)

Location: Self directed learning in print.

Length: Self paced (12-14 hours estimated).

Dates: January 1997-Present.

Objective: To understand sales support options such as lease versus purchase, wholesale credit policies and procedures, and a variety of credit options to enhance sales.

Learning Outcome: Upon successful completion of the course, the student will be able to customize credit options to individual customers needs; identify a variety of credit, lease, rent and floor plan alternatives to enhance sales; develop competitive analysis; and design strategies to maintain and enhance market share through increased sales.

Instruction: Major topics covered in the course are leasing and financial packages; wholesale credit and financing agreements; and financial products and services. Methods of instruction include self paced learning, final exams, case studies, and performance observation.

Credit Recommendation: In the graduate division degree category, 1 semester hour in Executive MBA (1/97).

Developmental Management Skills (The Adult Learner, Continuous Improvement, Meeting Administration Skills, Effective Writing Skills, Innovation Skills, Problem Solving)

Location: Self directed learning in print.

Length: Self paced (36-46 hours estimated).

Dates: January 1996-Present.

Objective: The adult learner will develop problem solving, innovation, writing, group dynamics and continuous improvement skills.

Learning Outcome: Upon successful completion of the course, the student will be able to implement a continuous improvement process; conduct effective meetings; communicate in writing effectively; apply innovative and appropriate routine solutions to problems; and understand self and others' diversified learning styles.

Instruction: Major topics covered in the course are learning styles; business problem solving methods; effective writing and meeting administration skills; and innovative and continuous improvement process skills. Methods of instruction include self paced learning, final exams, case studies, and performance observation.

Credit Recommendation: In the graduate division degree category, 3 semester hours in Executive MBA (1/97).

Fundamentals of Accounting and Finance (Basic Accounting, Banking Relationships, Key Economic Trends, Financial Management)

Location: Computer Based Training.

Length: Self paced (20-28 hours estimated).

Dates: December 1996-Present.

Objective: To understand accounting, economics, financial principles and their use in the business environment.

Learning Outcome: Upon successful completion of the course, the student will be able to develop financial statements; identify and understand key economic indicators; calculate and understand ratio analysis; identify alternative sources of funds; and calculate and understand the implications of time value analysis.

Instruction: Major topics covered in the course are financial statements, cash flow, ratio analysis, source of funds, time value models, leverage and economic indicators. Methods of instruction include computer assisted self-paced instruction, final exams, case studies, and performance observation.

Credit Recommendation: In the graduate division degree category, 3 semester hours in Executive MBA (1/97).

Introduction to Marketing (Value Added Selling, Basics of Planning Marketing and Communication, Marketing Communications Planning, Opportunity and Risk Assessment, Pricing Strategy Development, Market Analysis and Product Application)

Location: Self directed learning in print and video.

Length: Self paced (35-45 hours estimated).

Dates: May 1996-Present.

Objective: To analyze marketing strategies including market opportunities, value added selling, competitors sales programs, target markets, product development, and tactics into a marketing communication and pricing plan.

Learning Outcome: Upon successful completion of the course, the student will be able to define and implement the strategic marketing plan; and communicate it to the target market audience in line with the companies mission and resources and pricing strategy.

Instruction: Major topics covered in the course are business mission, strategy, tactics, planning, process and design, communication and measurement in a legal competitive pricing strategic environment. Methods of instruction include audio/visual material, self paced learning, final exams, case studies, and performance observation.

Credit Recommendation: In the graduate division degree category, 3 semester hours in Executive MBA (1/97).

Marketing Research (Collect and Analyze Competitive Information, Local Area Market and Community Profile, Developing a Customer Database, Customer Satisfaction Practices, Designing and Interpreting Questionnaires, Focus Group Data Interpretation)

Location: Self directed learning in print.

Length: Self paced (30-42 hours estimated).

Dates: March 1996-Present.

Objective: To develop, interpret, and use information in the marketing decision making process.

Learning Outcome: Upon successful completion of the course, the student will be able to identify Information needs, engage in data collection, interpret and utilize information to support the marketing planning and decision making process.

Instruction: Major topics covered in the course are identification of information sources, data collection and analysis, questionnaire design, developing databases, focus group planning and implementation. Methods of instruction include self paced learning, final exams, case studies, and performance observation.

Credit Recommendation: In the graduate division degree category, 3 semester hours in Executive MBA (1/97).

Catholic Distance University

The Catholic Distance University (CDU) was established in 1983 to teach college-level Catholic theology and religious education courses through distance learning. The University, accredited by the Accrediting Commission of the Distance Education and Training Council (DETC), is governed by a board of Catholic bishops, clergy, and laity with extensive experience in Catholic education.

In 1983 the Vatican Congregation for the Clergy officially recognized CDU as a Catechetical Institute with the authority to grant the Catechetical Diploma (an ecclesiastical teaching certificate) through distance learning. This is the first time in the United States that such recognition was given to a Catechetical Institute using distance learning. In 1997, two Masters Degree Programs will be available.

CDU uses a computerized data base to maintain student records which is updated daily and generates a grade report/transcript. Information such as enrollment and completion dates, personal and geographic information, education levels, credits earned, payment history, mailing history, and grades are kept in the student database.

Given the unique nature of distance learning, the teaching staff includes the course author who writes the course manual; the staff instructor who is a trained religious educator who evaluates the written assignments and examinations, maintains personal contact through motivational letters and telephone calls, and is responsible for calculating the final grade; and the staff theologian who handles specific theological inquiries from students and is available for consultation by letter, telephone, or e-mail. In some cases, such as the Masters, the course author also serves as course instructor for his or her course.

The Provost supervises course development. Most course authors are recruited from seminary faculties. The Provost chairs the Academic Committee which serves in an advisory capacity. Editors, skilled in distance course design, work with course authors and the Provost as a team. Courses are scheduled for revision every five years. The Academic Committee serves as an external review, as well as the Accrediting Commission of the DETC.

A certificate of completion is awarded to students who master learning objectives as measured by the quality of written assignments and examinations. A proctored final examination is required. The Provost monitors staff instructors and the evaluation of student work. Students who do not demonstrate an acceptable level of learning are identified as early as possible and advised to seek programs at a more appropriate level, either through CDU or through another institution. However, this is rare since the majority of CDU students have at least a baccalaureate degree upon enrollment.

The performance of the teaching staff is monitored directly by the Provost, who responds to the Executive Vice President, who reviews all incoming mail daily. Student course evaluations, correspondence, re-enrollment rates which average over 50%, and a complaint file are all reviewed weekly by the Executive Vice President.

Course authors must have a Ph.D. or equivalent credential and should have at least three years teaching experience at the college level. Authors with their own textbook are given preference.

Courses adhere to standards of the Accrediting Commission of the DETC. A course can be completed in six months or less (a full year is allowed). Distance courses contain from nine to twenty lessons in a three-ring binder course manual. The manual includes a glossary, bibliography, and anthology of supplementary reading material. CDU provides all textbooks, official Church documents, and papal encyclicals. Students in the Masters Programs must supply their own textbooks. CDU uses the new Catechism of the Catholic Church as a recommended or required text in every course. CDU courses are print-based but may include an audio-taped introduction by the course author.

Source of official student records: Registry of Credit Recommendations, American Council on Education, One Dupont Circle, Washington, DC 20036-1193 or Department of Student Services, The Catholic Distance University, 120 East Colonial Hwy, Hamilton, VA 20158-9012.

Additional information about the courses: College Credit Recommendation Service, American Council on Education, One Dupont Circle, Washington, DC 20036-1193.

A Survey of Catholic Spirituality (101-0701) (Formerly Ways of Praying: A Historical Introduction to Catholic Spiritual Traditions [101-0701] and Christian Spirituality in the Catholic Tradition)

Location: Distance education by correspondence.

Length: 10 lessons (approximately 6 months required for course completion).

Dates: May 1987-Present.

Objective: To examine the historical development and theological elements of Catholic spiritual traditions from the early Church Fathers to the nineteenth century.

Learning Outcome: Upon successful completion of this course, the student will be able to explain the origin of Christian asceticism; identify and explain the various schools of spirituality that emerged in the West; and explain the significant roles of Augustine and Benedict in the spirituality of the West.

Instruction: Major topics covered in the course are an introduction to the origin and development of Christian asceticism; identifying the early and subsequent spiritual schools and their leaders; emergence of western monasticism with emphasis on Augustine and Benedict; development of spirituality through the subsequent centuries up until modern times. Methods of instruction include independent study, quizzes, graded term paper, and a final examination.

Credit Recommendation: In the upper division baccalaureate degree category, 3 semester hours in Religious Studies or Theology (1/87) (1/95).

Catholic Apologetics (101-1101)

Location: Distance study.

Length: 6 months (9 months allowed).

Dates: November 1996-Present.

Objective: To examine the foundations for belief, the authoritative sources for belief, and the modern problems associated with belief.

Learning Outcome: Upon successful completion of this course, the student will be able to demonstrate knowledge of principles of belief, characteristics of religious belief, the foundations for apologetics, revealed knowledge and natural knowledge, relation of faith to reason, distortions in faith's relation to reason, kerygma, early apologists, later apologists and their principal works, relationship between pastoral theology and apologetics, obstacles to apologetics, the Magisterium, magisterial documents on apologetics, characteristics of faith in the *Catechism of the Catholic Church*, four aspects of faith, problems connected to theology's understanding of fa ith, catechesis and apologetics, early catechesis in the Church, relationship between catechetics and apologetics, St. Augustine, St. Thomas Aquinas, Cardinal Newman as apologists, themes of apologetics related to spirituality, apologetics and spiritual formation, apologetics and missionary work, and constructing an apologetic.

Instruction: Major topics covered in the course are Principles of Belief, Four Cornerstones of Apologetics, History of Apologetics in the Catholic Church, Apologetic Imperative, Magisterium Teaches-Apologetics Explains, Theological Dimensions of Apologetic, Relationship Between Catechesis and Apologetics, Masters of Apologetics, Apologetics and Spiritual Formation, Role of Apologetics in the Missionary Work of the Church, and On Constructing an Apologetic. Methods of instruction include distance learning, including print-based correspondence materials and a variety of communication technologies; essays; tests, quizzes; a term paper; and a proctored final examination.

Credit Recommendation: In the upper division baccalaureate degree category, 3 semester hours in Theology or Religious Studies (10/96).

Catholic Fundamental Moral Theology, Part A (201-0304)

Location: Distance study.

Length: 6-8 months (9 months allowed).

Dates: January 1997-Present.

Objective: To explore both the foundations of Catholic morality in the creating, redeeming, and sanctifying activity of the Father, Son, and Holy Spirit and our graced response to God as members of the Body and Bride of Christ, the Church, the graduate student, on a deeper level, will study the reasons for the Second Vatican Council's call for the renewal of moral theology and strive for understanding more deeply and profoundly the connectedness o f moral theology with spirituality, Scripture, philosophy, and the behavioral sciences.

Learning Outcome: Upon the successful completion of this course, the student will be able to demonstrate knowledge of ethics and moral theology; why life and activity of the Triune God is important for moral theology; what Genesis I teaches us about God, creation, and our being created in the image and likeness of God; God's risk in creating us in His image and likeness and the temptation we must constantly face; the original sin of Adam and Eve, and the effect of the original sin on the descendants of Adam and Eve; why evil exists; difference between moral and physical evil; how human free will can be a cause of action; how God manifests His omnipotence in relation to the evil that man does; God's transcendence and immanence; the new pattern and meaning of ethics; the significance of the negative and positive precepts of the Decalogue; significance of the family in the context of the Ten Commandments; The Beatitudes; stages of discipleship in Mark's gospel; the radical mystery of sin; power of sin according to St. Paul in Letter to the Romans; internal life of God; two principles that guide our reflection on the Blessed Trinity; difference and relationship between Father, Son, and Holy Spirit and Creator, Redeemer, and Sanctifier; Resurrection of Christ and the outpouring of the Holy Spirit; the Church as the Bride and Body of Christ; how and why Mary is most perfectly both the Bride of Christ and the Mother of the Church; relationships among the Church Triumphant; Church Suffering and the Pilgrim Church; sacraments and moral theology; seven sacraments as actions of Christ; and actions of the Church and the Sacraments of Initiation.

Instruction: Major topics covered in the course are *Part One:* the Triune; God's constant risk and our constant temptation; man and woman and the original sin; free will, time, and the Mystery of Evil: God Participates in the Human Story; *Part Two:* the Triune God redeems; discipleship and the Way of the Cross: God's Human Story; the Beatitudes: Discipleship is a Call to Perfection; *Part Three:* the Triune God sanctifies; Father, Son, and Holy Spirit: Origin and Destiny of any Sense in Our Lives; Trinification of the Human Story: The Resurrection of Christ and the Outpouring of the Holy Spirit; The Church: The Bride and Body of Christ; and Life in Christ: The Seven Sacraments. Methods of instruction include distance learning, including print-based correspondence materials and a variety of communication technologies; essays; tests; quizzes; a term paper; and a proctored final examination.

Credit Recommendation: In the graduate degree category, 3 semester hours in Theology or Religious Studies (10/96).

Catholic Fundamental Moral Theology, Part A (101-0304)

Location: Distance Education by correspondence.

Length: 12 lessons (6 months).

Dates: January 1995-Present.

Objective: To present an introduction to the foundations of Catholic morality in the creating, redeeming, and sanctifying activity of the Father, Son, and Holy Spirit.

Learning Outcome: Upon successful completion of this course, the student will be able to understand the foundations of Catholic morality in the creating, redeeming, and sanctifying activity of the Father, Son, and Holy Spirit; explore how Catholic morality is our graced response to God as members of the Body and Bride of Christ (the Church); and emphasize the intimate link between spirituality and morality.

Instruction: Major topics covered in the course are God's created order and the image and likeness of God; God's constant risk and our constant temptation; man and woman and the original sin; free will, time, and the mystery of evil; God of the covenant; discipleship and the way of the cross; the Beatitudes; the radical mystery of sin; the Father, Son, and Holy Spirit; the Resurrection of Christ and the Outpouring of the Holy Spirit; the Church (the Bride and Body of Christ); and the seven sacraments. Methods of instruction include print-based home study course manual and textbooks, tests, and final examination.

Credit Recommendation: In the upper division baccalaureate degree category, 3 semester hours in Religious Studies or Theology (1/95).

Catholic Fundamental Moral Theology, Part B (101-0305)

Location: Distance study.

Length: 6 months (9 months allowed).

Dates: January 1997-Present.

Objective: Building on the study of the foundations of Catholic morality in Part A, to explore the three components of Catholic Morality: motives (the cardinal and theological virtues), actions (the various dimensions of the human act that call for moral responsibility), and norms (the eternal, natural, civil, and divine laws).

Learning Outcome: Upon successful completion of this course, the student will be able to demonstrate knowledge of the ultimate good; motives; the relationship between the ultimate good, happiness, the soul, and virtue; the relationship between affective and spirited emotions; importance of virtue; cardinal virtues; capital sins; theological virtues; trinification; the relationship between Jesus and Mary as the new Adam and the second Eve; the structure of human actions; the species of an act; components of a moral act and how its morality is determined; norms of morality; The Ten Commandments; formation of conscience; a theology of conscience; and the mission of the moral life and its relationship to the New Envangelization.

Instruction: Major topics covered in the course are motives, morals and emotions, morals and habits, the theological virtues, the structure of human actions, the ends, means, and consequences of human action, norms of morality, the Ten Commandments, moral theology and the formation of conscience, and Catholic morality for the Third Millennium—the New Evangelization. Methods of instruction include distance learning, including print-based correspondence materials and a variety of communication technologies; essays; tests; quizzes; a term paper; and a proctored final examination.

Credit Recommendation: In the upper division baccalaureate degree category, 3 semester hours in Theology or Religious Studies (10/96).

Divine Revelation: An Introduction to Dei Verbum (101-0402)

Location: Distance education by correspondence.

Length: 5 lessons (2 months).

Dates: January 1995-Present.

Objective: To analyze the Constitution on Divine Revelation (Dei Verbum) of Vatican II.

Learning Outcome: Upon successful completion of this course, the student will be able to describe something of the history which lies behind the document as we have it in final form, enabling the student to discern special emphasis of the Council which might otherwise elude us; outline the overall structure of the document and the interrelationship of its various parts; define the meaning of revelation, Sacred Tradition, and Sacred Scripture with regard to their place in the Church and their relationship to the Magisterium; and explain the implications for the Church's life and worship of renewed emphasis on Scripture, including insight into the use of Scripture for prayer, both within and outside the liturgy.

Instruction: Major topics covered in the course are the nature of revelation, transmission of divine revelation, inspiration and interpretation of Scripture, and Sacred Scripture in the life of the Church. Method of instruction is independent study, including quizzes, a graded term paper, and a final examination.

Credit Recommendation: In the lower division baccalaureate/associate or upper division baccalaureate degree category, 1 semester hour in Religious Studies or Theology (1/95).

Early Church History: The Church From Its Beginnings Through the Middle Ages (201-0501)

Location: Distance study.

Length: 6-8 months (9 months allowed).

Dates: January 1997-Present.

Objective: To give the student an in-depth examination of the history of the Christian Church from the time of Christ to Charlemagne, using primary and secondary readings as the basis of discussion.

Learning Outcome: Upon successful completion of this course, the student will be able to demonstrate knowledge of the Apostolic Church; classical culture; roman emperors who influenced development of the Church; events leading up to Constantine's legalization of Christianity; the Greek Fathers; basic teaching of the Cappadocian Fathers; the Latin Fathers; key points of the City of God; Jerome's impact on Scripture; Cardinal Newman's appraisal of the Fathers of the Church; Church belief in Creed and Council; major heresies; crisis of the New Israel; development of Christian monasticism; Celtic and Roman monasticism; contributions of Boethius and Cassiodorus; Pope Gregory the Great; the mission of Augustine of Canterbury to England; Byzantine culture; barbarian assaults; emperor Justinian; concept of caesaropapism; Dark Ages; efforts of evangelization by St. Patrick in Ireland; origins of the Moslem faith; impact of the Moslem faith on Christian world; Carolingian renaissance; Venerable Bede; Charlemagne; reforms achieved by Charlemagne; SS Cyril , Methodius and St. Ansgar in evangelization; and the impact of the Vikings, Saxons, and Normans on Western Europe.

Instruction: Major topics covered in the course are the Apostolic Church, the Church of the Martyrs and Apologists, Greek Fathers, Latin Fathers, formation of Church belief in Creed and Council, Monastic Achievement, Rome and Byzantium, stability of the Church in the face of babarian chaos, Christianity and Islam, Carolingian Renaissance, and the Church confronts the new millennium. Methods of instruction include distance learning, print-based correspondence materials and a variety of communication technologies, essays, tests, quizzes, a term paper, and a proctored final examination.

Credit Recommendation: In the graduate degree category, 3 semester hours in Theology or Religious Studies (10/96).

Early Church History: The Church From Its Beginnings Through the Middle Ages (101-0501)

Location: ICIU centers or various resident training sites worldwide and home study.

Length: 12 lessons (6 months).

Dates: *Version 1:* March 1992-September 1995; *Version 2:* October 1995-Present.

Objective: To focus on the unique role and responsibilities of the minister, including the call to ministry, preparation for service, personal life and ethics, family life and general leadership responsibilities in the church.

Learning Outcome: Upon successful completion of this course, the student will be able to describe the biblical principles which guide the minister's work, understand the preparation needed for functioning as an effective minister, describe the major duties and responsibilities required of the minister.

Instruction: Major topics covered in the course are biblical principles of ministry; the minister's spiritual life, calling, ethics, and family life; principles of leadership for the minister; and the major roles and responsibilities of the minister. Methods of instruction include study guide, textbook, study questions, independent study, self tests, unit progress evaluations, written project, and final examination.

Credit Recommendation: *Version 1:* In the lower division baccalaureate/associate degree category, 3 semester hours Practical Ministries, Bible, or Religion (12/94). *Version 2:* In the upper division baccalaureate degree category, 3 semester hours in Religion, or Practical Ministries (9/95).

General Catechetics: Methods and Materials (101-0901)

Location: Distance education by correspondence.

Length: *Version 1:* 11 lessons (approximately 112 hours); *Version 2:* 12 lessons.

Dates: *Version 1:* December 1991-March 1992; *Version 2:* April 1992-February 1996.

Objective: To enable prospective religion teachers to apply appropriately the principles of learning theory and the directives and teachings of the Catholic Church.

Learning Outcome: Upon successful completion of this course, the student will be able to discuss the nature of Catechetics as religious instruction and have a practical knowledge of the constitutive elements of sound Catechesis.

Instruction: Major topics covered in the course are Catechetics, its definitions and forms; Catechetics vis-a-vis stages of human development and moral development; and Catechetics in relation to sacramental preparation, to liturgy, to prayer, to the classroom, and to the Church's social teaching. Methods of instruction include independent study, quizzes, a graded term paper, and a final examination.

Credit Recommendation: In the upper division baccalaureate degree category, 3 semester hours in Religious Education or Religious Studies (2/91).

God, Man, and the Universe (201-0101)

Location: Distance study.

Length: 6 months (9 months allowed).

Dates: January 1997-Present.

Objective: To present to the student the fundamental principles for studying the Faith based on the three essential tools: Sacred Scripture, Sacred Tradition, and the Magisterium. Readings enable the student to understand God's knowledge of man and man's knowledge of God.

Learning Outcome: Upon successful completion of this course, the student will be able to demonstrate knowledge of the following: revelation, faith, reason, the difference between natural revelation and supernatural revelation, when revelation ended, two sources of Divine Revelation, five books of the Pentateuch, two or more councils of the Church that dealt with Catholic canon of the Bible, Deposit of Faith, difference between Sacred Scripture and Sacred Tradition, development of doctrine, rationalism, literary criticism, Pontifical Biblical Commission, internal attributes of God, atheism, pantheism, disbelief, agnosticism, nominalism, positivism, empiricism, relativism, humanism, indifference, the Trinity, external attributes of God as Creator, Divine Providence, Angels, fallen angels, possession and obsession, the Church's teaching on Evolution, relationship between faith and reason, the Fall of man, and original sin and the dignity of the human person.

Instruction: Major topics covered in the course are revelation, Sacred Scripture, Sacred Tradition, development of Doctrine, the Trinity, God, the Creator, Divine Providence, angels, the Devil, the Origin of Man, the Fall of man, and the human person. Methods of instruction include distance learning, including print-based correspondence materials and a variety of communication technologies, essays, tests, quizzes, a term paper, and a proctored final examination.

Credit Recommendation: In the graduate degree category, 3 semester hours in Theology or Religious Studies (10/96).

God, Man, and the Universe (101-0101)

Location: Distance education by correspondence.

Length: 13 lessons (approximately 6 months required for course completion).

Dates: May 1986-Present.

Objective: To introduce the student to doctrinal theology that examines the fundamental teachings of the Catholic Church as contained in the first article of the Apostles Creed—God the Creator, original sin, and the fall of man.

Learning Outcome: Upon successful completion of this course, the student will be able to identify and explain the ways in which God revealed and continues to reveal himself; understand the development of doctrine that leads to a deeper understanding of God's revelation; and identify the principal truths that pertain to God in Himself, the creation of angels, and of man and his fall.

Instruction: Major topics covered in the course are an introductory study of Revelation, the relationship between Sacred Scripture and Sacred Tradition; and first articles of the Creed: God the Creator, the Trinity, Providence, the Angels, Satan, Original Sin—the fall of man and evolution. Method of instruction is independent study, including quizzes, a graded term paper, and final examination.

Credit Recommendation: In the lower division baccalaureate/associate degree category, 3 semester hours in Religious Studies or Theology (1/87) (1/95).

Introduction to Sacred Scripture (201-0401)

Location: Distance study.

Length: 6-8 months (9 months allowed).

Dates: January 1997-Present.

Objective: To give the student a comprehensive preparation in essential scriptural concepts for biblical study and for use in catechesis: inspiration, inerrancy, and canonicity.

Learning Outcome: Upon successful completion of this course, the student will be able to demonstrate knowledge of the following: the concept of inspiration; theories of inspiration rejected by the Church; principles of the Church's pronouncements on inspiration; concept of inerrancy; canonicity; gradual development of the Canon; Protestant differences in the content of the Canon; process of writing; redaction and transmission by which Bible comes to us; extant texts of the Bible; Dei Verbum; summary of the major Church pronouncements concerning the Bible; scope, purpose, and nature of hermeneutics; history of interpretation of the Bible; interpretational approaches; theories of interpretation rejected and those consistent with Church teaching; language study; contribution of archaeology and geography to Scripture study; textual criticism; criteria for establishing a reading of the text; source criticism; form criticism; redaction criticism; structural exegesis; historical-critical exegesis; literal meaning; meaning of fuller sense; typical sense; and accommodated sense.

Instruction: Major topics covered in the course are inspiration, inerrancy, canonicity, texts and versions, Church documents, Hermeneutics, history of interpretation, textual criticism, Scripture and science, source criticism, form criticism, redaction criticism, interpretation, and meaning of the text. Methods of instruction include distance learning, including print-based correspondence materials and a variety of communication technologies; essays; tests; quizzes; a term paper; and a proctored final examination.

Credit Recommendation: In the graduate degree category, 3 semester hours in Theology or Religious Studies (10/96).

Introduction to Sacred Scripture (101-0401)

Location: Distance education by correspondence.

Length: 14 lessons (approximately 6 to 9 months required for course completion).

Dates: *Version 1:* March 1987-August 1989; *Version 2:* September 1989-Present.

Objective: This is a substantial course intended to acquaint the student with scriptural concepts and terminology and to provide the requisite tools for understanding the Bible as a divine and human document.

Learning Outcome: Upon successful completion of this course, the student will be able to better appreciate the meaning of the Scriptures and integrate this knowledge into personal and religious practice; intelligently participate in Biblical discussion and study; and have a Scriptural foundation for Ecumenical dialogue.

Instruction: Major topics covered in the course are fundamental notions of inspiration, inerrancy, and canonicity and treats the science of biblical interpretation (hermeneutics) with its tools of textual, source, form, and redaction criticism.

Method of instruction is independent study, with quizzes, a graded term paper, and a final examination.

Credit Recommendation: *Version 1:* In the lower division baccalaureate/associate degree category, 3 semester hours in Religious Studies or Theology (4/87). *Version 2:* In the lower division baccalaureate/associate degree, or in the upper division baccalaureate degree category, 3 semester hours in Humanities, Religious Studies, or Theology (9/89) (1/95).

Jesus Christ, Mary, and the Grace of God (101-0102)

Location: Distance education by correspondence.

Length: 16 lessons (approximately 6 months required for course completion).

Dates: May 1986-Present.

Objective: To introduce the student to doctrinal theology that examines the fundamental teachings of the Catholic Church as contained in the second article of the Apostles Creed—Jesus Christ, Mary, and divine grace.

Learning Outcome: Upon successful completion of this course, the student will be able to explain the theology of Christ as reflected in the Synoptic Gospels and the writings of Paul and John; describe the theology of Mary and its primary relationship to the theology of Christ; and discuss the theology of grace, both sanctifying and actual and their relationship to the Christian virtues and the gifts of the Holy Spirit.

Instruction: Major topics covered in this course are the second article of the Creed: Jesus Christ in Sacred Scripture, the Church's teaching on the Person and work of Jesus Christ, the Hypostatic Union, heresies, the role of Mary, the doctrine of grace, and the virtues and gifts of the Holy Spirit. Method of instruction is independent study, including quizzes, a graded term paper, and final examination.

Credit Recommendation: In the lower division baccalaureate/associate degree category, 3 semester hours in Religious Studies or Theology (1/87) (1/95).

Lumen Gentium: An Introduction to Ecclesiology (101-1001)

Location: Distance education by correspondence.

Length: 4 lessons (2 months).

Dates: January 1995-Present.

Objective: To present the Church's understanding of itself revealed in the Vatican II Constitution, Lumen Gentium.

Learning Outcome: Upon successful completion of this course, the student will be able to discuss the historical perspective of Vatican II in relation to the Council of Trent and Vatican I; describe the structure of the document, Lumen Gentium (LG); explain the Church as mystery; define People of God, hierarchy, and laity as they are used in LG; specify the relationships that exist about the three terms; clarify the meaning of the "priesthood of the baptized" and that of the "ministerial priesthood"; clarify and explain the Church's holiness, and explain the meaning of the Church's eschatological nature; describe the proper role of Mary within the life of the Church, and evaluate the contribution of Vatican II toward understanding the mystery of the Church.

Instruction: Major topics covered in the course are the Church's understanding of itself revealed in the Vatican II Constitution Lumen Gentium, the mystery of the Church, the people of God (the hierarchy and the laity), and the call to holiness (religious life and the pilgrim church, and the role of the blessed mother). Methods of instruction include print-based home study course manual and textbook, tests, and a final examination.

Credit Recommendation: In the upper division baccalaureate or lower division baccalaureate/associate degree category, 1 semester hour in Religious Studies in Theology (1/95).

Madonna: Mary in the Catholic Tradition (201-0104)

Location: Distance study.

Length: 6-8 months (9 months allowed).

Dates: January 1997-Present.

Objective: To have the student examine and reflect upon the biblical modonnas, the development of the marian dogmas in the Tradition and their special significance today with particular consideration of the unique relationship between Mary and the Holy Spirit, the place of marian doctrine and devotion in the ecumenical and interfaith dialogues, and in the Catechism of the Catholic Church.

Learning Outcome: Upon successful completion of this course, the student will be able to demonstrate knowledge of the following: types of mariology (Chistocentric and ecclesiotypical); Vatican II's approach to Mariology; interrelationship of Scripture, Tradition, and the Magisterium in Mariology; the Old Testament development of the theme "daughter of Sion;" the relationship of Mary to Abraham and David; Mary in the New Testament; Mary as the Woman at Cana; Mary as the Woman at the Cross; the New Eve; Irenaeus' concept of recircumlatio and recapitulation and further development of the New Eve imagery; Mary's virginal conception of Jesus; the theology of Mary's virginity prior to childbirth, during childbirth, and after childbirth; the meaning of theotokos; the spiritual, ecumenical, and theological significance of belief in Mary as the Virgin Theotokos today; the truths contained in the dogma of Mary's Immaculate Conception; the contributions of Eadmer of Canterbury to the medieval development of the dogma; the contribution of Duns Scotus; the dogma of the Assumption; the historical development of the dogma in the Eastern and Western Church; the treatment of Mary by St. Thomas Aquinas; the Communion of Saints; the history of devotion to St. Joseph; Mary's unique intercessory power for those on earth; Mary in the liturgical year; Church guidelines for private Marian devotions; the Rosary as a contemplative form of private prayer; Marian apparitions; and difficulties and hopeful signs for Marian unity.

Instruction: Major topics covered in the course are One Mary, Many Madonnas, Daughter of Sion, The Perfect Disciple, Mother of God's Son, The Woman of Faith, Mother of God's People, The New Eve, Ever-Virgin, Theotokos, The Immaculate Conception, the Assumption, Mary in the Theology of the Church's Common Doctor, Mary and Joseph in the Communion of Saints, Mary in the Liturgical Year, Mary in Private Devotions and Apparitions, and a Madonna for All Christians. Methods of instruction include distance learning, including print-based correspondence materials and a variety of communication technologies; essays; tests; quizzes; a term paper; and a final examination.

Credit Recommendation: In the graduate level category, 3 semester hours in Theology or Religious Studies (10/96).

Madonna: Mary in the Catholic Tradition (101-0104)

Location: Distance education by correspondence.

Length: 14 lessons (approximately 6 months required; 9 months allowed for completion).

Dates: January 1992-May 1997.

Objective: To present an authentic portrait of Mary, the Madonna, drawn from Scripture and Church Tradition.

Learning Outcome: Upon successful completion of this course, the student will

be able to appreciate the theological field of study called "Mariology" in which the author considers Mary in her reality as Daughter of Sion, perfect disciple, woman of faith, new Eve, ever-Virgin, Theotokos, etc. and her place in the theology of Thomas Aquinas, in the liturgical year, in private devotion and in ecumenism.

Instruction: Major topics covered in the course are Mariology, Mary's place in the theology of Thomas Aquinas, in the liturgical year, in private devotion and in ecumenism. Methods of instruction include reading, written and audio lectures, written assignments, and term paper.

Credit Recommendation: In the upper division baccalaureate degree category, 3 semester hours in Religious Studies or Theology (5/92).

Medicine and Christian Morals (101-0303)

Location: Distance education by correspondence.

Length: 17 lessons (approximately 6 to 9 months required for course completion).

Dates: June 1989-Present.

Objective: To introduce the student to basic concepts in the field of morality in order to apply them to medical issues such as euthanasia, organ transplants, contraception, sterilization, abortion, genetic engineering, and ethical practices pertaining to the field of medicine.

Learning Outcome: Upon successful completion of this course, the student will be able to explain the basic principles and application of ethical and moral judgment making; understand the moral problem of multiple effects of human actions and how properly to make moral decisions in choosing the good while permitting evil; and understand and respond to the moral problems of diverse modern medical procedures and life practices.

Instruction: Major topics covered in the course are the nature of morality, freedom, the human act, moral conscience, and the practical application in the medical sphere and the key principles of double effect, formal/material cooperation, and confidentiality. Method of instruction is independent study, including quizzes, a graded term paper, and final examination.

Credit Recommendation: In the upper division baccalaureate degree category, 3 semester hours in Ethics, Moral Theology, Philosophy, or Religious Studies (9/89) (1/95).

Nature of Christian Spirituality (101-0702)

Location: Distance education by correspondence.

Length: *Version 1:* 13 lessons; *Version 2:* 15 lessons.

Dates: *Version 1:* March 1987-February 1989; *Version 2:* March 1989-Present.

Objective: To define the nature and source of Christian Spirituality and demonstrate how it differs from all other religions, i.e., its peculiarities and uniqueness.

Learning Outcome: Upon successful completion of this course, the student will be able to understand basic concepts of Biblical theology and the relationship of spirituality to theology; explain the uniqueness of Christian spirituality; describe characteristics of God's love and the relation between the old and new covenants; and understand the significance for Christian spirituality of the role of Jesus Christ, the work of the Holy Spirit, especially through the Sacraments.

Instruction: Major topics covered in the course are the instruments employed by the Holy Spirit in leading Christians to union with God's grace, revelation, relation of old and new covenants, significance of the cross, and the role of the Son and Spirit in the spiritual life of the human person. Methods of instruction include independent study, graded essays, quizzes, and a final examination.

Credit Recommendation: In the upper division baccalaureate degree category, 3 semester hours in Religious Studies or Theology (4/87) (1/95).

Orientale Lumen: On the Eastern Churches (101-0602)

Location: Distance study.

Length: 2 months (9 months allowed).

Dates: January 1996-Present.

Objective: To examine Pope John Paul II's recent document on reconciliation between the Eastern and Western Churches.

Learning Outcome: Upon successful completion of this course, the student will be able to demonstrate knowledge of purpose, structure of document, significance of title, meaning of the term Eastern Churches; main centers of early Eastern Christianity; differences between Roman Catholics and Eastern Christians; spiritual heritage of Eastern Christians; role of Eastern churches in the spread of monastic life; characteristics of Eastern monasticism and its spirituality; estrangement from the Church of Rome; how Christians of the West can foster friendship with Christians of the East; and the importance of union between the Eastern and Western churches for the successful evangelization of the world.

Instruction: Major topics covered in the course are the elements of Eastern Christianity, monasticism, the schism between East and West, and issues today for the re-unification of East and West. Methods of instruction include distance learning; including print-based correspondence materials and a variety of communication technologies, essays, tests, quizzes, a term paper, and a proctored final examination.

Credit Recommendation: In the lower division baccalaureate/associate or upper division baccalaureate degree category, 1 semester hour in Theology or Religious Studies (10/96).

Philosophy for Theology (101-1201)

Location: Distance study.

Length: 6 months (9 months allowed).

Dates: February 1997-Present.

Objective: To present the student with an introduction to the field of philosophy as it serves the study of theology by exploring the nature and scope of philosophy, compatibility of faith and reason as a justification for the study of philosophy, distinction between God's wisdom and man's wisdom in Scripture, the method of Plato, use of logic as a tool for understanding faith, and St. Thomas and modern philosophy.

Learning Outcome: Upon successful completion of this course, the student will be able to demonstrate knowledge of philosophy as a rational enterprise; the attitude of some Church Fathers toward philosophy; familiarity with Plato's manner of philosophizing; dialectic as a method; Plato's doctrine of forms; the content of logic; logic as a tool for understanding faith; Plato's theory of forms; notion of metaphysical dualism; Plato's view of immortality of the soul; Plato's cosmology; Stoic view of the universe; significance of natural law in the Stoic system; Plotinus' mystical project of bringing the human mind into contact with the One; negative theology originating from Pseudo-Dionysius; univocity from equivocity from analogy; Aristotle's realism; how St. Thomas reconciles Aristotle with Christian belief in God's creation of the world; God's knowledge and providence of the world and the soul's immortality; Anselm's argument for God's existence; Thomas' five ways of rationally proving God's existence; St. Thomas' theory of knowledge; a summary of modern philosophy as characterized by Descartes; Locke and Kant; recent Catholic theology, especially Rahner; and the historical critical method.

Instruction: Major topics covered in the course are What is Philosophy?; Dialetic and Logic; Forms and the Real World; Cosmology of Neo-Platonism; Aristotle's Realism; Anselm and Aquinas on God's Existence; St. Thomas' Theory of Knowledge; Modern Philosophy: Decartes, Locke, and Kant; Recent Catholic Theology: Rahner and St. Thomas; and The Historical Critical Method. Methods of instruction include distance learning; including print-based correspondence and a variety of communication technologies, essays, tests, quizzes, a term paper; and proctored final examination.

Credit Recommendation: In the lower division baccalaureate/associate or upper division baccalaureate degree category, 3 semester hours in Theology or Religious Studies (10/96).

Survey of Catholic Spirituality (201-0701)

Location: Distance study.

Length: 6-8 months (9 months allowed).

Dates: January 1997-Present.

Objective: To introduce the student to the evolution and development of Catholic spirituality from the earliest days of the Church to the present time.

Learning Outcome: Upon successful completion of this course, the student will be able to demonstrate knowledge of the following: basic principles of Gospel spirituality; dogmatic and moral theology; Old Testament as a preparation for the mission of Jesus Christ; spirituality of the Early Church; monasticism in the East; differences between the cenobitic and eremitical life of monks; difference between the monastic life of St. Pachomius and St. Basil; monasticism in the West; basic principles of St. Augustine's teaching; rule of St. Benedict; the importance of St. Gregory the Great; influence of Cassian on Western monasticism; Christian life in the 9th and 10th centuries; origins of the Camaldolese and Carthusians; role of St. Bernard; life of nuns and lay brothers; Christian life of the 12th century; rise of scholasticism; nature and mission of the mendicant friars; difference in emphasis between St. Thomas Aquinas and St. Bonaventure; spiritual teaching of the Rhineland mystics; outstanding English spiritual writers of the 14th century; John Gerson's contribution to spirituality; post-tridentine spirituality; teaching of St. Teresa of Avila; St. John of the Cross and St. Ignatius Loyola; modern spirituality; French spirituality; rise and fall of Jansenism; teachings of the Quietists; life and work of St. Alphonsus Liguori; Oxford Movement in England; 20th century spirituality; contributions of St. Therese of Lisieux; Elizabeth of the Trinity; Catholic Action; Secular Institutes; and theology of Christian perfection.

Instruction: Major topics covered in the course are Sacred Scripture and the Spiritual Life, spirituality of the Early Church, monasticism in the East, monasticism in the West, Benedictine Monasticism, medieval spirituality, dionysian spirituality and devotion moderna, Post-Tridentine Spirituality, modern spirituality, and Twentieth Century Spirituality. Methods of instruction include distance learning, including print-based correspondence materials and a variety of communication technologies; essays; tests; quizzes; a term paper; and a proctored final examination.

Credit Recommendation: In the graduate degree category, 3 semester hours in Theology or Religious Studies (10/96).

The Catechism of the Catholic Church: Evangelization for the Third Millennium (101-0800)

Location: Distance education by correspondence.

Length: 16 lessons.

Dates: February 1995-Present.

Objective: To present an organic synthesis of the essential and fundamental content of Catholic doctrine, as regards both faith and morals, in the light of the Second Vatican Council and the whole of the Church's Tradition.

Learning Outcome: Upon successful completion of this course, the student will be able to understand and explain the nature of catechesis, the history and functions of catechisms in general, and the development and content of the Catechism of the Catholic Church in particular.

Instruction: Major topics covered in the course are history and development of catechisis and catechisms; relation of catechetics to prayer and spirituality; the sacramental life and its catechetical significance; the Creed; and catechetical significance of moral teachings of the Catholic Church. Methods of instruction include quizzes, graded term paper, independent study, and a final examination.

Credit Recommendation: In the upper division baccalaureate degree category, 4 semester hours in Religious Studies or Theology (12/95).

The Church and Human Destiny (101-0103)

Location: Distance education by correspondence.

Length: 17 lessons (approximately 6 months required for course completion).

Dates: May 1986-Present.

Objective: To introduce the student to doctrinal theology that examines the fundamental teachings of the Catholic Church as contained in the third article of the Apostles Creed-the Church and Eschatology.

Learning Outcome: Upon successful completion of this course, the student will be able to explain the foundational role of Jesus Christ as the Head of the Body, the Church; develop an understanding of the nature of the Church in light of Vatican II; and summarize introductory concepts of Christian eschatology.

Instruction: Major topics covered in the course are the final articles of the Creed: the foundation of the Church, its four marks, ecumenism, church-state relations, religious freedom, and eschatology: the four last things (heaven, hell, death, and judgment). Method of instruction is independent study, including quizzes, a graded term paper, and final examination.

Credit Recommendation: In the lower division baccalaureate/associate degree category, 3 semester hours in Religious Studies or Theology (1/87) (1/95).

The Historical Development of Marriage in the Church (201-0203)

Location: Distance study.

Length: 6-8 months (9 months allowed).

Dates: January 1997-Present.

Objective: To give the student a comprehensive presentation of marriage: the history and development of marriage theology through Vatican documents and Pope John Paul II.

Learning Outcome: Upon successful completion of this course, the student will be able to demonstrate knowledge of the following: the sacramental nature of marriage; effects of secularization upon marriage in the 20th century; prominent theologians within the historical development of a theology of marriage; marriage and family in the Early Church; the Roman model of marriage; major historical periods of challenge to Christian marriage; societal and cultural forces affecting Christian marriage in the 20th century; marriage theology; historical development of Catholic marriage theology; marriage theology in Biblical times; marriage in the Synoptic Gospels; the influence of the Dead Sea Scrolls; Christ's teachings about divorce and remarriage; marriage theology in the Patristic Period; early Christian writings on marriage; Augustine's notion of the essence of marriage; the "three goods of marriage," later influence of Augustine on marriage theology; marriage during the Middle Ages; St. Thomas' understanding of marriage as a natural institution; St. Thomas' contribution to marriage theology; major decisions of the Council of Trent affecting marriage, roots, and effects of the 20th century theological revival, notably Personalism; marriage theology and Vatican II; *Humanae Vitae*; Pope John Paul II's contribution to marriage theology; marriage as a sacrament; marriage in the new Code of *Canon Law*; annulments; marriage preparation; diocesan marriage tribunals; three major changes in handling marriage cases since Vatican II; the wedding ceremony; and marriage and the Christian family.

Instruction: Major topics covered in the course are marriage in society and the Church; marriage and family in the Early Church; the challenges of Christian marriage in later centuries; what marriage theology is about; marriage theology and biblical times; marriage theology in the Patristic Period; marriage theology in the medieval period; marriage theology in the post-medieval period through the early 20th century; Vatican II and marriage theology; Pope John Paul II's development of marriage theology; marriage as a sacrament; marriage in the New *Code of Canon Law*, Parts I-II; the wedding ceremony; and marriage and the Christian family. Methods of instruction include distance learning, including print-based correspondence materials and a variety of communication technologies; essays; tests; quizzes; a term paper; and a proctored final examination.

Credit Recommendation: In the graduate degree category, 3 semester hours in Theology or Religious Studies (10/96).

The Historical Development of Marriage in the Church (101-0203) (Formerly Theology of Christian Marriage)

Location: Distance education by correspondence.

Length: 16 lessons (approximately 161 hours).

Dates: April 1991-February 1996.

Objective: To study marriage as a social reality situated in human history, as a religious reality seen through the eyes of the Catholic Church, and as a canonical (legal) reality.

Learning Outcome: Upon successful completion of this course, the student will be able to explain marriage as a social and religious reality; discern its historical and legal evolution; understand its essential development from biblical times through the patristic, medieval, and post-medieval periods into the twentieth century; and appreciate it as a sacrament and as a vocation.

Instruction: Major topics covered in the course are marriage as a natural institution in society, in the early Church, in later centuries, theology of marriage and its progressive understanding in the biblical, patristic, medieval, and modern eras; marriage as sacrament; canon law of marriage; the wedding ceremony, marriage and the family. Method of instruction is independent study with quizzes, graded term paper, and final examination.

Credit Recommendation: In the upper division baccalaureate or graduate degree category, 3 semester hours in Religious Studies or Theology (2/91).

The Sacraments of Initiation (101-0204)

Location: Distance education by correspondence.

Length: 4 lessons (2 months).

Dates: February 1995-Present.

Objective: To introduce the student to the theology of the Sacraments of Baptism, Eucharist, and Confirmation.

Learning Outcome: Upon successful completion of this course, the student will be able to explain the meaning of the term sacrament as used by the Church; and to explain key elements of Church teaching on Baptism, Eucharist, and Confirmation, with respect to Scripture, Tradition, and Canon Law.

Instruction: Major topics covered in the course are sacramental theology, Scriptural sources, Church traditions, and Canon Law regarding these sacraments. Method of instruction is independent study, including quizzes, graded term paper, and final examination.

Credit Recommendation: In the lower division baccalaureate/associate degree category, 1 semester hour in Religious Studies or Theology (1/95).

The Ten Commandments Today, Part A (101-0301)

Location: Distance education by correspondence.

Length: 10 lessons (approximately 6 months required for course completion).

Dates: May 1986-Present.

Objective: To introduce the student to moral theology, its terms and concepts and to provide detailed application of concepts to first five commandments of the Decalogue seen from the point of view of Scripture and Church teaching.

Learning Outcome: Upon successful completion of this course, the student will be able to explain the introduction to basic principles and language of moral theology; the guidelines for the proper formation of Christian conscience; and explain and apply the first five Commandments.

Instruction: Major topics covered in the course are introduction to moral theology: moral responsibility, conscience, objective moral principles, and the first five commandments according to Scripture and Church teaching. Method of instruction is independent study, with quizzes, graded term paper, and final examination.

Credit Recommendation: In the lower division baccalaureate/associate degree category, 3 semester hours in Religious Studies or Theology (1/87) (1/95).

The Ten Commandments Today, Part B (101-0302)

Location: Distance education by correspondence.

Length: 13 lessons (approximately 6 months required for course completion).

Dates: May 1986-Present.

Objective: To continue the study of basic moral theological principles, the last five commandments of the Decalogue in Scripture and Church teaching.

Learning Outcome: Upon successful completion of this course, the student will be able to explain and apply the last five Commandments of the Decalogue; and develop the understanding of basic Christian virtues with emphasis on the theological virtues of faith, hope, and charity.

Instruction: Major topics covered in the course are a continuation of 101-0301: the basic principles of moral theology, and the last five Commandments. Method of instruction is independent study, including quizzes, graded term paper, and final examination.

Credit Recommendation: In the lower division baccalaureate/associate degree category, 3 semester hours in Religious Studies or Theology (1/87) (01/95).

The Vocation and Mission of the Laity (201-0601)

Location: Distance study.

Length: 6-8 months (9 months allowed).

Dates: January 1997-Present.

Objective: To have an introductory discussion of the nature and mission of the Church, the course explains how the term "the faithful" embraces all the members of the Church: clergy, religious, and laity.

Learning Outcome: Upon successful completion of this course, the student will be able to demonstrate knowledge of the following: the nature of the Church, conditions for membership, the People of God, the mission of the Church, evangelization, classes of members in the Church, the Faithful of Christ, rights of the faithful, duties of the faithful, laity, duties of the laity, fostering lay participation in the Church, the lay apostolate, and spirituality of the laity.

Instruction: Major topics covered in the course are the nature of the Church, the mission of the Church, the Faithful of Christ, the rights and duties of the Faithful, a definition of the laity, duties of the laity, rights of the laity, the lay apostolate, and the spirituality of the laity. Methods of instruction include distance learning, including print-based correspondence materials and a variety of communication technologies; essays; tests; quizzes; a term paper; and a proctored final examination.

Credit Recommendation: In the graduate degree category, 3 semester hours in Theology or Religious Studies (10/96).

The Wisdom of St. Elizabeth Ann Seton (101-0703)

Location: Distance study.

Length: 4 months (9 months allowed).

Dates: January 1996-Present.

Objective: To explore the sanctifying mission of the Spirit in the life of Saint Elizabeth Ann Seton, and show how certain formative events in her human history marked her vocation and spiritual teaching in a fruitful and definitive way.

Learning Outcome: Upon successful completion of this course, the student will be able to demonstrate knowledge of identification of certain formative personalities and experiences in St. Elizabeth Ann Seton's childhood and youth; identification of distinctive features of her adult spirituality; the role of suffering and the cross in her life; importance of the Eucharist; spiritual contributions of her vocations of marriage and motherhood to her sanctity and their contribution to her role as religious foundress; her conversion to Catholicism; her challenges in founding a religious community and her dual role of mother superior and mother of her children; the role of the Blessed Mother; and Mother Seton's spiritual instructions to her sisters and her devotion to the will of God.

Instruction: Major topics covered in the course are St. Elizabeth Ann Seton's childhood and Protestant heritage; the cross in her life; importance of the Eucharist in her conversion; her mission and call to religious life; founding of the religious community; and her spiritual heritage to her religious sisters. Methods of instruction include distance learning; including print-based correspondence materials and a variety of communication technologies, essays, tests, quizzes, a term paper, and proctored final examination.

Credit Recommendation: In the lower division baccalaureate/associate or upper division baccalaureate degree category, 2 semester hours in Theology or Religious Studies (10/96).

Theology of the Sacraments, Part I (201-0201)

Location: Distance study.

Length: 6 months (9 months allowed).

Dates: January 1997-Present.

Objective: To introduce the student to the study of the Sacraments including their nature, number, and situation within the sacred Liturgy. Special emphasis is given to the Sacraments of the Eucharist and Penance.

Learning Outcome: Upon successful completion of this course, the student will be able to demonstrate knowledge of the nature of liturgy, adaptation and development; meaning of sacraments in the Church; the Eucharist as Real Presence; Sacrifice of the Mass; Holy Communion; worship of the Blessed Sacrament; Spiritual treasures of the Eucharist; Sacrament of Penance: its historical development, a theological analysis; and contemporary issues.

Instruction: Major topics covered in the course are Liturgy: adaptation and development; Sacraments in the Church; The Eucharist: Real Presence; The Eucharist: The Sacrifice of the Mass; The Eucharist: Holy Communion; The Eucharist: Worship of the Most Blessed Sacrament; Spiritual Treasures of the Eucharist; The Sacrament of Penance: Historical Development; The Sacrament of Penance: a Theological Analysis; and The Sacrament of Penance: Some Contemporary Issues. Methods of instruction include distance learning; including print-based correspondence materials and a variety of communication technologies, essays, tests, quizzes, a term paper, and proctored final examination.

Credit Recommendation: In the graduate degree category, 3 semester hours in Theology or Religious Studies (10/96).

Theology of the Sacraments, Part I (101-0201)

Location: Distance education by correspondence.

Length: *Version 1:* 9 lessons (approximately 6 months required for course completion); *Version 2:* 11 lessons (approximately 6 months required for course completion).

Dates: *Version 1:* April 1986-September 1992; *Version 2:* October 1992-Present.

Objective: To introduce the student to sacramental theology, to liturgy, and to the theological/historical development of Eucharist and Penance.

Learning Outcome: Upon successful completion of this course, the student will be able to explain the nature of the Liturgy and the teaching of the Church concerning the Sacraments of Eucharist (Presence, the Mass, Communion); and Penance.

Instruction: Major topics covered in the course are the nature of the liturgy, the Sacraments of the Church; their adaptation and development; the Eucharist: Real Presence, the Mass and Communion; and Penance: historical development, theological analysis, and contemporary issues. Methods of instruction include independent study, quizzes, graded term paper, and a final examination.

Credit Recommendation: In the lower division baccalaureate/associate or upper division baccalaureate degree category, 3 semester hours in Religious Studies or Theology (1/87) (1/95).

Theology of the Sacraments, Part II (101-0202)

Location: Distance education by correspondence.

Length: 12 lessons (approximately 6 months required for course completion).

Dates: April 1987-Present.

Objective: To provide a continuation of the study of sacramental theology dealing with the historical and theological development of the Sacraments of Baptism, Confirmation, Marriage, Holy Orders, and

Anointing of the Sick. A brief study is made of related subjects such as sacramentals, Liturgy of the Hours, and indulgences.

Learning Outcome: Upon successful completion of this course, the student will be able to articulate the meaning of the Sacraments of Baptism, Confirmation, Holy Orders, Marriage, and Anointing of the Sick; explain the complementary nature of related prayer and liturgical practices such as Liturgy of the Hours, Sacraments, and indulgences; and course lays a foundation for developed practices since Vatican II and their value for the practices of the Faithful in the life of the Church.

Instruction: Major topics covered in the course are the continuation of the study of the Sacraments not treated in Part One: Baptism, Confirmation, Holy Orders, Marriage, and the Anointing of the Sick. Explains "Sacramental character," the ministers of the Sacraments, the requirements for valid reception, the appropriate grace of each Sacrament and discusses sacramentals. Method of instruction is independent study, including quizzes, graded term paper, and final examination.

Credit Recommendation: In the lower division baccalaureate/associate degree category, 3 semester hours in Religious Studies or Theology (1/87) (1/95).

Vocation and Mission of the Laity (101-0601)

Location: Distance education by correspondence.

Length: 10 lessons (approximately 6 months required; 9 months allowed for completion).

Dates: March 1992-March 1997.

Objective: To inform the lay Catholic of his or her vocation and mission in the Church and his or her rights and duties.

Learning Outcome: Upon successful completion of this course, the student will be able to understand within the reality of the Church and the canonical status of the lay person, his or her rights and duties and the nature of the lay apostolate and lay spirituality.

Instruction: Major topics covered in the course are the nature and mission of the Church; definition of terms; the rights and duties of the Faithful in general and the lay person in particular; the lay apostolate; the spirituality of the laity. Methods of instruction include reading, written lecture, written assignments, term papers, and final examination.

Credit Recommendation: In the upper division baccalaureate degree category, 3 semester hours in Religious Studies or Theology (3/92).

Center for Lactation Education

Breastfeeding Support Consultants, Inc. established in 1981, is a nonprofit, self-sustaining educational institution. The mission of BSC is to improve the health of women and infants through education and promotion of breastfeeding to health professionals. BSC provides instruction for professional members of the health care team as well as peer counselors. Courses prepare the lactation consultant, nurse practitioner, physician, midwife, physician assistant, and peer counselor in the core knowledge and skills necessary for helping mothers to breastfeed and, in the lactation consultant courses, the advanced skills needed for problem solving. BSC is recognized as a long term provider of continuing education through Pennsylvania Nurses Association (PNA) and the International Board of Lactation Consultant Examiners (IBLCE). BSC is accredited by the Accrediting Commission of the Distance Education and Training Council (DETC).

BSC courses offer self-paced instruction based on adult learning theory. Guided with one-on-one personal instruction and mentoring, students learn to consider individual needs of every mother and infant with an approach of prevention counseling and empowerment. Course content is guided by the Standards of Practice for Lactation Consultants developed by the International Lactation Consultant Association. Programs are available exclusively through home study or through combination of home study and residence training in several U.S. cities.

Instructors are practicing certified lactation consultants with advanced professional degrees from throughout North America. They have completed the BSC Lactation Consultant course and are certified through the IBLCE. Because BSC faculty are involved in all aspects of the field, BSC becomes aware of new practices and recommendations and is able to incorporate them into programs in a timely fashion to remain on the cutting edge of lactation management training.

Source of official student records: Registry of Credit Recommendations, American Council on Education, One Dupont Circle, Washington, DC 20036-1193 or Executive Director, Breastfeeding Support Consultants, 228 Park Lane, Chalfont, PA 18914.

Additional information about the courses: College Credit Recommendation Service, American Council on Education, One Dupont Circle, Washington, DC 20036-1193.

Lactation Consultant Track 1

Location: Home Study.

Length: 24-30 months.

Dates: January 1984-Present.

Objective: To provide the student with the skills and knowledge needed to serve as an entry level Lactation Consultant rendering appropriate advice and services to breastfeeding mothers, their families, and other health care professionals.

Learning Outcome: Upon successful completion of this course, the student will be prepared to function as an entry level Lactation Consultant able to participate as a member of the health care team; promote breastfeeding in the lay socio-political arena as well as among other health care professionals; assist and advise breastfeeding mothers; evaluate breastfeeding mothers and babies, recognizing and assessing problems, and recommending and/or implementing appropriate interventions; employ appropriate counseling skills and techniques; submit consultative reports to physicians and other health care providers; and apply appropriate current research findings to these professional decisions.

Instruction: Major topics covered in the course are the content needed by the Lactation Consultant including, counseling skills; social, political, and financial factors influencing breastfeeding; anatomy and physiology of the breast; anatomy and physiology of the infant's sucking mechanism; maternal and infant nutrition and common problems; societal, emotional, and family adjustments; racial, ethnic, and cultural influences on breastfeeding; physical assessment of the mother-baby breastfeeding dyad; appropriate interventions for specific problems; breastfeeding devices and alternatives; mothers and babies with long term special needs; and clinical practice in Lactation Consulting.

Credit Recommendation: In the upper division baccalaureate or graduate degree category, 15 semester hours in Lactation Consultancy (6/95). **NOTE**: Students receiving credit for Track 1 may not receive credit for Tracks 2, 3, or 4.

Lactation Consultant Track 2

Location: Home Study.

Length: 6-12 months.

Dates: January 1995-Present.

Objective: To provide the student with the skills and knowledge needed to serve as an entry level Lactation Consultant rendering appropriate advice and services to breastfeeding mothers, their families, and other health care professionals in hospitals and in private practice.

Learning Outcome: Upon successful completion of this course, the student will be able to function as an entry level Lactation Consultant able to: participate as a member of the health care team; promote breastfeeding in the lay socio-political arena as well as among other health care professionals; assist and advise nursing mothers with breastfeeding; evaluate breastfeeding mothers and babies, recognizing and assessing problems, and recommending and/or implementing appropriate interventions; employ appropriate counseling skills and techniques; submit consultative reports to physicians and other health care providers; and apply appropriate current research findings to these professional decisions.

Instruction: Major topics covered in the course are the content needed by the Lactation Consultant including, counseling skills; social, political, and financial factors influencing breastfeeding; anatomy and physiology of the breast; anatomy and physiology of the infant's sucking mechanism; maternal and infant nutrition and common problems; societal, emotional, and family adjustments; racial, ethnic, and cultural influences on breastfeeding; physical assessment of the breastfeeding dyad; appropriate interventions for specific problems; breastfeeding devices and alternatives; mothers and babies with long term special needs; and clinical practice in Lactation Consulting.

Credit Recommendation: In the upper division baccalaureate or graduate degree category, 15 semester hours in Lactation Consultancy (6/95). **NOTE**: Students receiving credit for Track 2 may not receive credit for Tracks 1, 3, 4, or 5.

Lactation Peer Counselor Track 3 (Breastfeeding Peer C)

Location: Home Study.

Length: 16-24 months.

Dates: January 1984-Present.

Objective: To provide the student with the skills and knowledge necessary to function as an entry level Lactation Peer Counselor assisting nursing mothers and their families with normal breastfeeding issues and practices.

Learning Outcome: Upon successful completion of this course, the student will be able to function as an entry level Lactation Peer Counselor able to promote breastfeeding in the socio-political arena; employ appropriate counseling skills and techniques; assist and advise nursing mothers with normal breastfeeding; evaluate breastfeeding mothers and babies and recognize problems; and refer problems to the Lactation Consultant or other member of the health care team.

Instruction: Major topics covered in the course are a study of all of the topics needed by the Lactation Peer Counselor including counseling skills; social, political, and financial factors influencing breastfeeding; normal anatomy, physiology, and minor problems of the breast; normal anatomy, physiology, and minor problems of the infant's sucking mechanism; maternal and infant nutrition and common problems; societal, emotional, and family adjustments; racial, ethnic, and cultural influences on breastfeeding; physical assessment of the breastfeeding dyad with reference to normalcy; appropriate interventions for specific problems and referral of other problems; breastfeeding devices and alternatives; and clinical practice in Lactation Peer Counseling.

Credit Recommendation: In the lower division baccalaureate/associate or upper division baccalaureate degree category, 4 semester hours in Lactation Peer Counseling (6/95). **NOTE**: Students receiving credit for Track 3 may not receive credit for Tracks 1, 2, or 4.

Lactation Peer Counselor Track 4 (Breastfeeding Peer C)

Location: Home Study.

Length: 6-12 months.

Dates: March 1995-Present.

Objective: To provide the student with the skills and knowledge necessary to function as an entry level Lactation Peer Counselor assisting nursing mothers and their families with normal breastfeeding issues and practices.

Learning Outcome: Upon successful completion of this course, the student will be able to function as an entry level Lactation Peer Counselor able to promote breastfeeding in the socio-political arena; employ appropriate counseling skills and techniques; assist and advise nursing mothers with normal breastfeeding; evaluate breastfeeding mothers and babies and recognize problems; and refer problems to the Lactation Consultant or other member of the health care team.

Instruction: Major topics covered in the course are a study of the topics needed by the Lactation Peer Counselor including counseling skills; social, political, and financial factors influencing breastfeeding; normal anatomy, physiology, and minor problems of the breast; normal anatomy, physiology, and minor problems of the infant's sucking mechanism; maternal and infant nutrition and common problems; societal, emotional, and family adjustments; racial, ethnic, and cultural influences on breastfeeding; physical assessment of the mother-baby breastfeeding dyad with reference to normalcy; appropriate interventions for specific problems and referral of other problems; and breastfeeding devices and alternatives; and clinical practice in Lactation Peer Counseling.

Credit Recommendation: In the lower division baccalaureate/associate or upper division baccalaureate degree category, 4 semester hours in Lactation Peer Counseling (6/95). **NOTE**: Students receiving credit for Track 4 may not receive credit for Tracks 1, 2, or 3.

Lactation Management Track 5

Location: Chicago, IL and Philadelphia, PA.

Length: 89 hours (6 days) residential.

Dates: January 1995-Present.

Objective: To provide the student with some of the skills and knowledge needed to serve as an entry level Lactation Consultant in hospitals and in private practice.

Learning Outcome: Upon successful completion of this course, the student will be able to participate as a member of the health care team; promote breastfeeding in the socio-political arena as well as among other health care professionals; assist and advise nursing mothers; evaluate breastfeeding mothers and babies, recognizing and assessing problems, and recommending or implementing appropriate interventions; employ appropriate counseling skills and techniques; submit consultative reports to physicians and other health care providers; and apply current research findings to these professional decisions.

Instruction: Major topics covered in the course are counseling skills; social, political, and financial factors influencing breastfeeding; normal anatomy, physiology, and minor problems of the breast; normal anatomy, physiology, and minor problems of the infant's sucking mechanism; maternal and infant nutrition and common problems; societal, emotional, and family adjustments; racial, ethnic, and cultural influences on breastfeeding; physical assessment of the mother-baby breastfeeding dyad; appropriate interventions for specific problems; breastfeeding devices and alternatives; and mothers and babies with long term special needs.

Credit Recommendation: In the upper division baccalaureate or graduate degree category, 3 semester hours in Lactation Consultancy (6/95).

Central States Health and Life Company

Founded in 1932, Central States Health & Life Co. of Omaha (CSO) markets a diversified portfolio of life, health, and disability insurance products. Located in Omaha, Nebraska, CSO has developed a well-educated and productive group of professionals through a work environment that supports personal and career goals.

CSO's Training and Development Department mission is to enhance employee's performance skills and team effectiveness by offering leading-edge educational services. A high-quality training staff assists and encourages employees to aspire to personal excellence, thus promoting company loyalty and pride.

CSO offers a full range of courses taught by baccalaureate or advanced-degreed trainers who offer the most current experience and educational techniques. CSO's courses are also offered on contract to employees of agent/partner firms in the financial services industry.

Source of official student records: Registry of Credit Recommendation, American Council on Education, One Dupont Circle, Washington, DC 20036-1193.

Additional information about the courses: College Credit Recommendation Service, American Council on Education, One Dupont Circle, Washington, DC 20036-1193.

General Management Sequence:
Basic Communications (CSC-051)
Business Ethics (CDT-003)
Quality Improvement (MSC-114)
Supervision (MSC-102)

Location: Omaha, NE.

Length: Courses range from 2 hours (Quality Improvement) to 7 hours (Supervision), and some to 15 class hours plus readings and outside discussion.

Dates: January 1986-Present.

Objective: To provide the student with the essential skills of speaking and listening; different managerial styles and protocols for handling ethical dilemmas; quality assurance and teamwork for the improvement of quality work in the organization; and the role of motivation, leadership and decision making in supervising a diverse workforce.

Learning Outcome: Upon successful completion of this course, the student will be able to demonstrate a knowledge of practical speaking and listening skills, recognize and critically evaluate ethical dilemmas, identify the processes that contribute to increased profit through quality improvement, and refine their basic supervisory skills.

Instruction: Major topics covered in the course are Berlo's communication model, Johari Window, speaking skills, listening skills, ethical styles, company ethics policy, various interpretations of ethics, ethics cases/problems, various dimensions of work quality, quality assurance, quality measurement exercises, role of supervision in motivation and effective communications, supervisor style, and supervision exercises, and problems. Methods of instruction include lecture, discussion, problems, exercises, and examinations.

Credit Recommendation: In the lower division baccalaureate/associate degree category, 1 semester hour in Management Principles or Fundamentals or Business or Management elective (9/93).

Human Relations Management Course Segments:
Sexual Harassment (MSC-107)
Performance Appraisal (MSC-111
Guidelines for Counseling (MST-150)
EEO/Interviewing (MSC-109)
Salary-Payroll (MSC-115)

Location: Omaha, NE.

Length: 15 hours (5 days).

Dates: January 1986-Present.

Objective: To provide the student with the skills to examine the procedures of employee performance appraisal; the laws, attitudes and procedures that relate to sexual harassment; the fundamentals of counseling problem employees; and the EEO laws that pertain to interviewing and hiring employees, salary administration, and payroll procedures.

Learning Outcome: Upon successful completion of the five course series, the student will be able to better utilize and manage the human resources of an organization including understanding the legal environment, salary administration, performance appraisal, sexual harassment, interviewing, and employee counseling techniques.

Instruction: Major topics covered in the series are legal history and current policy on sexual harassment in the workplace; identification and sensitivity to sexually harassing behavior and patterns; evaluation of videos (role enactment); investigation of sexual harassment allegations; employee and employer liability aspects; continuous cycle of performance appraisal; theory and practical exercises in performance appraisal; definition and specific mandate on counseling; disciplinary process as a vehicle for positive outcomes; corrective feedback; legal (EEO) considerations in interviewing and hiring; the professional interview; salary administration in terms of positions, grades and scales; justifying variance from salary standards, job criteria for additional compensation; and advancement. Methods of instruction include lecture, discussion, problems/exercises, videos, and examinations.

Credit Recommendation: In the lower division baccalaureate/associate category, 1 semester hour in Human Relations, Organization and Behavioral Management Fundamentals, or Business or Management elective (9/93).

Certified Employee Benefit Specialist Program

The International Foundation of Employee Benefit Plans and the Wharton School of the University of Pennsylvania jointly sponsor the Certified Employee Benefit Specialist (CEBS) Program. The International Foundation is responsible for the overall administration of the program, while the Wharton School is responsible for the academic content and educational standards.

The International Foundation is the largest educational organization in the employee benefits field and is dedicated to enhancing the skills and knowledge of those who have responsibility for employee benefit plans. The Foundation annually sponsors educational meetings; administers the CEBS Program; publishes news and information periodicals, research reports, and books; and makes available the services of its Library/Information Center.

The Wharton School's joint sponsorship of the CEBS Program with the International Foundation is an extension of its long interest in adult education.

This ten-course, professional designation program has a threefold purpose:

(1) to enhance individual capabilities for fulfilling responsibilities in the employee benefit sector at a high performance level;

(2) to bestow a measure of professional recognition on those persons who achieve significant competence in the field, as evidenced by passing a series of national examinations; and

(3) to assist the public in evaluating the academic qualifications and competence of persons having responsibilities for employee benefit plans.

To provide participants maximum flexibility for taking courses and preparing for examinations, three different study methods are available: (1) formal classes, which are offered at more than95 colleges and universities throughout the United States, (2) study groups, and (3) independent study.

Study materials for the courses can be ordered directly from the International Foundation or can be obtained from some university bookstores offering the CEBS Program. CEBS examinations are administered through computer-based testing at over 240 locations throughout the country.

Successful completion of a CEBS course is based on passing the national examination. In order to qualify for the CEBS designation, candidates must pass all ten examinations, meet Precertification Standards, and abide by the Principles of Conduct.

Source of official student records: Registry of Credit Recommendations, American Council on Education, One Dupont Circle, Washington, DC 20036-1193 or CEBS Department, International Foundation for Employee Benefit Plans, P.O. Box 1270, 18700 West Bluemound Road, Brookfield, WI 53008-1270.

Additional information about the courses: College Credit Recommendation Service, American Council on Education, One Dupont Circle, Washington, DC 20036-1193.

CEBS Course I: Employee Benefit Concepts and Medical Care Benefits (Formerly Course 1: Life, Health and Other Group Benefit Programs)

Location: Various locations throughout the U.S.

Length: 75 hours (self-study) and 94 hours (formal class sessions).

Dates: *Version 1:* June 1977-December 1992; *Version 2:* January 1993-Present.

Objective: *Version 1:* To provide the student with knowledge of the various methods used to protect against the financial consequences resulting from illness, disability, unemployment, and premature death using both public and private sector institutional arrangements. *Version 2:* To survey the employee benefit field, provide concepts and working definitions, basic legal and institutional knowledge and factual information.

Learning Outcome: Upon successful completion of this course, the student will possess working knowledge and understanding of employee benefit plans and the medical care environment in the U.S.

Instruction: *Version 1:* Covers the functional approaches to employee benefit planning, social insurance, the group insurance mechanism, life insurance benefits, medical expense benefits, disability income, dental and vision care, prepaid legal services, property and liability insurance benefits, and other benefit plans. Self-study, group study, or formal class sessions are used. *Version 2:* Major topics covered in the course are risk management and insurance; Medicare and Worker's Compensation; hospital and medical expense plans; comprehensive care and cost-containment; HMO/PPO; dental plans; chemical dependency coverage; retiree medical benefits and long term care. Methods of instruction include self-study, study groups or formal class sessions, and national examinations.

Credit Recommendation: *Version 1:* In the upper division baccalaureate degree category, 4 semester hours, or in the graduate degree category, 3 semester hours in Life and Health Insurance, Group Life and Health Insurance, or Employee Benefit Programs (3/81) (4/86). *Version 2:* In the upper division baccalaureate degree category, 3 semester hours in Insurance, Business, Public Administration, Health Care, or Industrial Relations (1/93).

CEBS Course II: Life, Disability Income and Other Welfare Benefit Plans: Design and Administration (Formerly Course II: Retirement Plans: Basic Features and Defined Benefit Approaches and also formerly Pension Plans)

Location: Various locations throughout the U.S.

Length: 75 hours (self-study) and 94 hours (formal class sessions).

Dates: *Version 1:* June 1977-December 1992; *Version 2:* January 1993-Present.

Objective: *Version 1:* To teach the student contemporary fundamentals of pension plans as well as the federal tax considerations and the reporting, disclosure, and other regulations in the management of pension plans. *Version 2:* To provide students with a background in a wide variety of employee benefit plans including life insurance, disability income protection, unemployment compensation, family leave, flexible benefit plans, financial counseling and also in the regulation and administration of employee benefit plans.

Learning Outcome: Upon successful completion of this course, the student will be able to apply the knowledge of employee benefit plans and their administration to problems in the design and management of employee benefit programs.

Instruction: *Version 1:* The Major topics covered in the course are the history and development of pension plans, plan design, funding aspects, disclosure requirements, taxation, and plan termination insurance. Self-study, group study, or formal class sessions are used. *Version 2:* Major topics covered in the course are individual and group, term and permanent life insurance, disability income benefits and plans, dependent care and family leave benefits, unemployment compensation, a variety of miscellaneous benefit programs such as legal services, property-liability benefits and financial planning; plan administration and tax aspects of employee benefit plans. Methods of instruction include self-study, study groups or formal class sessions, and national examinations.

Credit Recommendation: *Version 1:* In the upper division baccalaureate degree category, 4 semester hours, or in the graduate degree category, 3 semester hours in Advanced Life Insurance and Pension Plans, or Pension Plans. (3/81) (4/86). *Version 2:* In the upper division baccalaureate degree category, 3 semester hours in Compensation Administration, Employee Benefit, Business Administration, or Industrial Relations (1/93).

CEBS Course III: Retirement Plans: Basic Features and Defined Contribution Approaches (Formerly Retirement Plans: Defined Contribution Approaches and Plan Administration and also formerly Social Security, Savings Plans and Other Retirement Arrangements)

Location: Various locations throughout the U.S.

Length: 75 hours (self-study) and 94 hours (formal class sessions).

Dates: *Version 1:* June 1977-December 1988; *Version 2:* January 1989-Present.

Objective: *Version 1:* To provide the student with knowledge and understanding of the individual account or defined contribution approach toward providing post-retirement income. *Version 2:* To provide the student with knowledge and understanding of basic features of qualified retirement plans and defined contribution approaches.

Learning Outcome: *Version 1:* Upon successful completion of this course, the student will be able to demonstrate mastery in the administration and utilization of defined contribution plans. *Version 2:* Upon successful completion of this course, the student will be able to explain the tax law retirement plan qualification requirements, define money purchase pension plans, define and explain Section 401(k) and 403(b) plans, and list and explain plans for self-employed and IRA plans.

Instruction: *Version 1:* Major topics covered in the course are defined contribution *vs.* defined benefit plans; profit-sharing plans; thrift and savings plans; cash or deferred plans (CODAs); employee stock ownership plans; individual retirement arrangements and simplified employee pensions; tax-deferred annuities; plan installation; fiduciary responsibilities and disclosure; taxation of distributions; executive retirement arrangements; accounting and reporting by employee benefit plans; and Section 457 plans and retirement plans for government employees. Methods of instruction include self-study, group study, or formal class sessions. *Version 2:* Major topics covered in the course are development of private pension plans, benefit plan objectives, tax law qualifications, nontax legal requirements, money purchase pension plans, and section 401(k) plans. Methods of instruction include self-study, study groups or formal class sessions, and national examinations.

Credit Recommendation: *Version 1:* In the upper division baccalaureate degree category, 4 semester hours or in the graduate degree category, 3 semester hours in Retirement Social Insurance, Social Security, Savings Plans and Other Retirement Arrangements (3/81) (4/86). *Version 2:* In the upper division baccalaureate degree category, 3 semester hours or in the graduate degree category, 2 semester hours in Retirement Planning, Business Administration, or Human Resource Management (1/93).

CEBS Course IV: Retirement Plans: Defined Benefit Approaches and Plan Administration (Formerly Management Principles)

Location: Various locations throughout the U.S.

Length: 75 hours (self-study) and 94 hours (formal class sessions).

Dates: *Version 1:* June 1978-December 1992; *Version 2:* January 1993-Present.

Objective: *Version 1:* To provide the student with knowledge of the universal concept of management as a process with special emphasis on the environment, structure, and methodology of employee benefits management. The principles, theories, and concepts covered will be used by an individual to staff and administer employee benefit plan operations effectively. *Version 2:* To provide the student with an understanding of the contemporary fundamentals of pension plans with emphasis on defined benefit approaches and retirement plan administration.

Learning Outcome: Upon successful completion of this course, the student will be able to explain retirement benefits covered by Social Security, list the advantages of a defined benefit plan, determine compensation under a defined benefit plan, and explain target benefit plans.

Instruction: *Version 1:* The course includes management organization, human factors in organizing, decision-making, planning, controlling, and activation. The principles, concepts, and terminology are applicable to any type of management setting, such as employee benefit systems, manufacturing enterprises, hospitals, sales organizations, and educational institutions. Self-study, group study, or formal class sessions are used. *Version 2:* Major topics covered in the course are Social Security and Medicare, defined benefit plan features, cash balance and target benefit plans, cost and funding considerations and actuarial cost methods for defined benefit pension plans. Methods of instruction include self-study, study groups or formal class sessions, and national examinations.

Credit Recommendation: *Version 1:* In the upper division baccalaureate degree category, 3 semester hours in Management or Organizational Behavior (3/81) (4/86). *Version 2:* In the upper division baccalaureate degree category, 3 semester hours or in the graduate degree category, 2 semester hours in Retirement Plans, Business Administration, or Human Resource Management (1/93).

CEBS Course IX: Employee Benefit Plans and the Economy

Location: Various locations throughout the U.S.

Length: 75 hours (self-study) and 94 hours (formal class sessions).

Dates: January 1980-Present.

Objective: To provide the student with a general knowledge of macroeconomic principles and how they affect employee benefit plans.

Learning Outcome: Upon successful completion of this course, the student will be able to describe basic economic principles underlying inflation and employment levels, explain the business cycle, and describe the economic impact of pension plans.

Instruction: Major topics covered in the course are economic principles underlying inflation; national income; business cycles; employment levels; money and banking; monetary and fiscal policy; international economics; the economic impact of pension plans; and the ways in which unemployment and inflation affect Social Security, pension plans, and health and welfare plans. Methods of instruction include self-study, group study, formal class sessions, and national examinations .

Credit Recommendation: In the upper division baccalaureate degree category, 3 semester hours in Economic Principles, General Economics, or Macroeconomics (3/81) (4/86) (1/93).

CEBS Course V: Contemporary Legal Environment of Employee Benefit Plans

Location: Various locations throughout the U.S.

Length: 75 hours (self-study) and 94 hours (formal class sessions).

Dates: *Version 1:* June 1977-December 1992; *Version 2:* January 1993-Present.

Objective: To provide a working knowledge of the U.S. legal system and basic understanding of concepts and principles of the legal environment in which employee benefit plans exist and function.

Learning Outcome: Upon successful completion of this course, the student will be able to define torts and crimes, explain insurance regulations, list the requirements for an enforceable contract, explain forms of property ownership and define legal structures of forms of business organizations.

Instruction: Major topics covered in the course are legal procedure, agency contracts, personal and real property, mortgages, wills, estates, commercial paper, partnerships, corporations, and trusts. Methods of instruction include self-study, group study, formal class sessions, and national examinations.

Credit Recommendation: *Version 1:* In the upper division baccalaureate degree category, 3 semester hours in Business/ Commercial Law or Legal Environment of Business (3/81) (4/86). *Version 2:* In the upper division baccalaureate degree category, 3 semester hours in Business or Commercial Law, Legal Environment in Business Administration, Public Administration, or Health Administration (1/93).

CEBS Course VI: Accounting and Finance (Formerly Accounting and Information Systems)

Location: Various locations throughout the U.S.

Length: 75 hours (self-study) and 94 hours (formal class sessions).

Dates: *Version 1:* June 1977-December 1989; *Version 2:* January 1990-Present.

Objective: To provide the student with a basic knowledge of accounting and financial concepts essential to the administration of employee benefit plans.

Learning Outcome: Upon successful completion of this course, the student will be able to understand accounting concepts and statements and the fundamental concepts of business finance.

Instruction: Major topics covered in the course are accounting statements, time value, valuations, basics of capital budgeting, working capital management, characteristics of debt and equity investments; and cost of capital and dividend policy. Methods of instruction include self-study, study groups or formal class sessions, and national examinations.

Credit Recommendation: *Version 1:* In the upper division baccalaureate degree category, 3 semester hours in Accounting or Management Information Systems. *Version 2:* In the upper division baccalaureate degree category, 3 semester hours in Finance or Business Administration (3/81) (4/86) (1/93).

CEBS Course VII: Asset Management

Location: Various locations throughout the U.S.

Length: 75 hours (self-study) and 94 hours (formal class sessions).

Dates: July 1979-Present.

Objective: To provide the student with an understanding of the investment process, to include both theory and practical application.

Learning Outcome: Upon successful completion of this course, the student will be able to understand and apply several principles of investment analysis and management.

Instruction: Major topics covered in the course are securities markets, investment objectives, investment timing, portfolio theory, capital asset pricing theory, portfolio management, technical analysis, and evaluation of financial performance. Methods of instruction include self-study, study groups, formal class sessions, and national examinations.

Credit Recommendation: In the upper division baccalaureate degree category, 3 semester hours in Principles of Investments or Investments (3/81) (4/86) (1/93).

CEBS Course VIII: Human Resources and Compensation Management (Formerly Personnel and Labor Relations [Industrial Relations])

Location: Various locations throughout the U.S.

Length: 75 hours (self-study) and 94 hours (formal class sessions).

Dates: *Version 1:* June 1977-May 1989; *Version 2:* June 1989-Present.

Objective: To provide the student with a basic understanding of human resources and compensation administration by providing an overview of current issues and innovative practices.

Learning Outcome: Upon successful completion of this course, the student will be able to demonstrate mastery in the basics of human resource management and compensation administration.

Instruction: Major topics covered in the course are human resources management; motivation; equal employment opportunity; job analysis; human resources planning; recruitment and selection; human resources development; economic analysis and compensation determination; institutional constraints on compensation administration; job evaluation; compensation structure design and job pricing; performance assessment; incentive compensation systems; employee benefits and noneconomic rewards; compensation discrimination; compensation control; labor relations; labor contract administration; discipline; safety; and human resources audits. Methods of instruction include self-study, study groups, formal class sessions, and national examinations.

Credit Recommendation: *Version 1:* In the upper division baccalaureate degree category, 3 semester hours or in the graduate degree category, 2 semester hours in Human Resources Management, Labor Relations/Industrial Relations or Personnel Administration (3/81) (4/86). *Version 2:* In the upper division baccalaureate degree category, 3 semester hours or in the graduate degree category, 2 semester hours in Human Resources Management or Personnel Administration (10/90) (1/93).

CEBS Course X: Contemporary Benefit Issues and Administration

Location: Various locations throughout the U.S.

Length: 75 hours (self-study) and 94 hours (formal class sessions).

Dates: *Version 1:* June 1980-December 1992; *Version 2:* January 1993-Present.

Objective: To provide the student with perspective knowledge of contemporary issues affecting employee benefit plan provisions and administration.

Learning Outcome: Upon successful completion of this course, the student will be able to apply the knowledge of contemporary issues affecting employee benefit programs in the design and management of employee benefit programs.

Instruction: Major topics covered in the course are contemporary issues affecting the provisions and administration of employee benefit plans. Methods of instruction include self-study, study groups, formal class sessions, and national examinations.

Credit Recommendation: *Version 1:* In the upper division baccalaureate degree category, 4 semester hours or in the graduate degree category, 3 semester hours in Advanced Personnel Administration, Contemporary Benefit Issues and Administration or Employee Benefits (3/81) (4/86). *Version 2:* In the upper division baccalaureate degree category, 3 semester hours or in the graduate degree category, 2 semester hours in Contemporary Benefit Issues and Administration or Employee Benefits (1/93).

Certified Medical Representatives Institute, Inc.

The Certified Medical Representatives Program was established to provide and administer a complete educational and professional development program designed primarily for the needs of medical representatives employed in the United States.

The curriculum has been designed in a broad manner to enforce and complement the sales training programs offered by pharmaceutical companies. Courses and examinations have been developed under the supervision of educators in various universities throughout the United States.

Upon successful completion of required foundation courses and other elective courses closely related to his or her professional responsibilities, the medical representative is awarded the CMR designation by the Institute. The CMR award certifies the professional competency of the representative in pertinent areas of knowledge and signifies a certified career representative.

Source of official student records: Registry of Credit Recommendations, American Council on Education, One Dupont Circle, Washington, DC 20036-1193 or Certified Medical Representatives Institute, Inc., 4950 Brambleton Avenue, S.W., Roanoke, VA 24018.

Additional information about the courses: College Credit Recommendation Service, American Council on Education, One Dupont Circle, Washington, DC 20036-1193.

Advanced Concepts in Managed Healthcare (71)

Location: Independent self-study by correspondence.

Length: 39 hours (10 weeks) (approximately 36 hours of study time).

Dates: September 1995-Present.

Objective: To provide a broad understanding of the trend towards integrated healthcare delivery systems and its implications for the pharmaceutical industry and healthcare representatives.

Learning Outcome: Upon successful completion of this course, the student will be able to discuss the evolution of integrated healthcare systems in response to the success of managed care; discuss the nature of integrated healthcare systems and their major approaches to cost containment; identify the five most common organizational models of provider integration; discuss the role of healthcare providers (including pharmacy benefit management companies or PBMs) in integrated systems; and discuss the changing role of the pharmaceutical industry in the evolving healthcare delivery landscape.

Instruction: Major topics covered in the course are managed care today, rising costs of healthcare, rising competition in the managed care marketplace, the move to integrate, approaches to cost containment, total disease management, integrated information systems, healthcare providers in integrated systems, and trends and forces in healthcare delivery. Methods of instruction include self-study with text, audiotape, pre- and post tests, progress checks, course summary, and proctored final examination.

Credit Recommendation: In the upper division baccalaureate category, 3 semester hours or in the graduate category, 1 semester hour in Healthcare Administration (11/97). **NOTE:** Graduate credit is only applicable at the introductory level.

Asthma: Approaches In Disease Management (9A)

Location: Independent self-study by correspondence.

Length: 39 hours (10 weeks) (approximately 36 hours of study time).

Dates: May 1996-Present.

Objective: To provide an overview of the pathophysiology, epidemiology, and treatment of asthma including general guidelines and elements of asthma management programs within healthcare systems.

Learning Outcome: Upon successful completion of this course, the student will be able to discuss the causes, epidemiology, diagnosis, and treatment of asthma; describe the guidelines used to treat chronic mild, moderate, and severe cases of asthma; describe the rationale and application of asthma disease management programs in healthcare organizations; and discuss the important role that the pharmaceutical industry and the healthcare representative can play in the development of asthma management programs.

Instruction: Major topics covered in the course are an overview of asthma, approaches to asthma management, asthma management applications in healthcare, and the role of the pharmaceutical industry in asthma management. Methods of instruction include self-study with text, audiotape, pre- and post tests, progress checks, course summary, and proctored final examination.

Credit Recommendation: In the upper division baccalaureate category, 3 semester hours in Health Sciences/Nursing (11/97).

Behavioral Pathology and Treatment (7-A)

Location: Throughout the United States.

Length: Self-study.

Dates: January 1989-Present.

Objective: To provide an overview of the major categories of behavioral disorders and to describe the methods of psychotherapy and pharmacotherapy used in their treatments.

Learning Outcome: Upon successful completion of this course, the student will be able to process basic knowledge in psychotherapy and become familiar with the pharmacology and terminology related to behavioral disorders.

Instruction: Major topics covered in the course are psychotherapy, psychoanalytic theory and modern psychotherapy, nerve cell structures and neurotransmitter actions and activity, related pharmacology and terminology; and an overview of behavioral disorders including anxiety disorders, affective (mood) disorders, psychotic disorders, organic mental disorders and impulse control disorders, pharmacology, and neurotransmitter activity. Methods of instruction include self-study with text, audiotape, and pre- and post-tests, progress checks, and proctored final examination.

Credit Recommendation: In the upper division baccalaureate degree category, 3 semester hours in Abnormal Psychology (1/89) (7/94).

Business Alliances and Partnerships In Healthcare (10B)

Location: Independent self-study by correspondence.

Length: 39 hours (10 weeks) (approximately 36 hours of study time).

Dates: September 1996-Present.

Objective: To provide an overview of the strategic alliances and partnering arrangements occurring in the healthcare industry and to provide healthcare representatives with the skills necessary to support the alliances their pharmaceutical companies form with healthcare systems.

Learning Outcome: Upon successful completion of this course, the student will be able to describe the current trend toward pharmaceutical companies developing long-term alliances with healthcare organizations; discuss the importance of correctly identifying customer needs and the importance of meeting and exceeding customer expectations; describe the negotiation and communication skills healthcare representatives may use in supporting long-term alliances; and discuss how these alliances are changing the role of healthcare representatives.

Instruction: Major topics covered in the course are key concepts in forming strategic alliances, identifying customer needs, achieving customer satisfaction, supporting long-term alliances, effective communication, and effective partnering. Methods of instruction include self-study with text, audiotape, pre- and post tests, progress checks, course summary, and proctored final examination.

Credit Recommendation: In the lower division baccalaureate/associate degree category, 3 semester hours in Pharmaceutical Marketing (11/97).

Business and Management Strategies In Healthcare (10A)

Location: Independent self-study by correspondence.

Length: 39 hours (10 weeks) (approximately 36 hours of study time).

Dates: May 1996-Present.

Objective: To provide an overview of the business and management strategies that are being applied to transform the healthcare and pharmaceutical industries.

Learning Outcome: Upon successful completion of this course, the student will be able to discuss the management restructuring and change of focus towards business that is now occurring in the healthcare industry; describe the business and management strategies being applied in the healthcare industry today; and discuss the reorganization of the pharmaceutical industry and its effect on healthcare representatives, including new roles as team members and consultants to healthcare providers.

Instruction: Major topics covered in the course are trends in healthcare delivery, total quality management, benchmarking, consolidation and alliances, changes in the pharmaceutical industry, and the role of the healthcare representative as a team player and consultant. Methods of instruction include self-study with text, audiotape, pre- and post tests, progress checks, course summary, and proctored final examination.

Credit Recommendation: In the upper division baccalaureate category, 3 semester hours in Business Management or Healthcare Administration (11/97).

Business and Strategic Planning for the Healthcare Representative (10C)

Location: Independent self-study by correspondence.

Length: 39 hours (10 weeks) (approximately 36 hours of study time).

Dates: September 1996-Present.

Objective: To provide an overview of business tools and processes, steps critical to project management, and principles of financial decision making that apply to territory management and management of healthcare organizations.

Learning Outcome: Upon successful completion of this course, the student will be able to discuss how to analyze the marketplace, plan strategies, and develop goals; describe the basic steps and tools critical to project management; understand the basic principles underlying financial decisions; discuss financial issues with customers; and write an effective business plan for their territory.

Instruction: Major topics covered in the course are the business planning process, writing a business plan, project management tools, basic principles of accounting, budgeting, and tools for economic evaluation. Methods of instruction include self-study with text, audiotape, pre- and post tests, progress checks, course summary, and proctored final examination.

Credit Recommendation: In the upper division baccalaureate category, 3 semester hours in Business Management or Healthcare Administration (11/97).

Cardiovascular System (6-C)

Location: Throughout the United States.

Length: Self-study.

Dates: January 1988-Present.

Objective: To provide a broad understanding of the mechanisms of the cardiovascular system, pharmacological applications, and disorders of the system and terminology.

Learning Outcome: Upon successful completion of this course, the student will be able to describe the anatomy, physiology, and functions of the cardiovascular system and common disorders of the cardiovascular system, their etiology and symptoms; and describe therapeutic classes of drugs appropriate for cardiovascular disorders.

Instruction: Major topics covered in the course are functions and components of the cardiovascular system, circulation, lymphatic system, cardiovascular system disorders, and related pharmacology and terminology. Methods of instruction include self-study with text, audiotape, pre- and post-tests, progress checks, and proctored final examination.

Credit Recommendation: In the lower division baccalaureate/associate degree category, 2 semester hours in Allied Health, Health Sciences, Human Biology, or Nursing (2/89) (7/94). **NOTE:** Students who complete this course in combination with Digestive, Endocrine, Integumentary, Musculoskeletal, Nervous, Reproductive, Respiratory, Sensory Organs, and Urinary Systems should receive 8 semester hours in Anatomy, 8 semester hours in Physiology, 6 semester hours in Applied Pharmacology, 3 semester hours in Concepts of Disease, and 3 semester hours in Medical Terminology.

Diabetes: Approaches In Disease Management (9B)

Location: Independent self-study by correspondence.

Length: 39 hours (10 weeks) (approximately 36 hours of study time).

Dates: May 1997-Present.

Objective: To provide an overview of the pathophysiology, epidemiology, and treatment of diabetes including general guidelines and elements of diabetes management programs within healthcare systems.

Learning Outcome: Upon successful completion of this course, the student will be able to describe the epidemiology, pathophysiology, causative factors, treatment options, and economic impact of both insulin-dependent diabetes mellitus (IDDM), and non-insulin-dependent diabetes mellitus (NIDDM); discuss current clinical practice guidelines for managing patients with diabetes, including the Diabetes Control and Complications Trial (DCCT); discuss the implementation of diabetes management programs by employers, insurers and healthcare organizations; and describe the types of diabetes management programs being developed by various pharmaceutical companies, including opportunities for healthcare representatives.

Instruction: Major topics covered in the course are types of diabetes, diagnosis of diabetes, treatment of diabetes, economic impact of diabetes, diabetes management guidelines, diabetes management programs, and types of diabetes management services. Methods of instruction include self-study with text, audiotape, pre- and post tests, progress checks, course summary, and proctored final examination.

Credit Recommendation: In the upper division baccalaureate category, 3 semester hours in Health Sciences/Nursing (11/97).

Digestive System (6-H)

Location: Throughout the United States.

Length: Self-study.

Dates: September 1987-Present.

Objective: To provide an understanding of the anatomy of the digestive system and its role in digestion and absorption of food substances for the body's energy and nutrition and related pharmacology.

Learning Outcome: Upon successful completion of this course, the student will be able to describe the anatomy and physiology of the digestive system and its role in conversion of foods to energy and absorbed nutrients, and describe disorders of the digestive system and the pharmacology of drug classes relevant to these disorders and terminology.

Instruction: Major topics covered in the course are the structure and function of the digestive system, the physiology of digestion and absorption, disorders of the system, and the pharmacology of drugs related to digestive system disorders. Methods of instruction include self-study with text, audiotape, pre- and post-test, progress checks, and proctored final examination.

Credit Recommendation: In the lower division baccalaureate/associate degree category, 2 semester hours in Allied Health, Health Sciences, Human Biology, or Nursing (2/89) (7/94). **NOTE:** Students who complete this course in combination with Cardiovascular, Endocrine, Integumentary, Musculoskeletal, Nervous, Reproductive, Respiratory, Sensory Organs, and Urinary Systems should receive 8 semester hours in Anatomy, 8 semester hours in Physiology, 6 semester hours in Applied Pharmacology, 3 semester hours in Concepts of Disease, and 3 semester hours in Medical Terminology.

Endocrine System (6-F)

Location: Throughout the United States.

Length: Self-study.

Dates: May 1988-Present.

Objective: To provide a broad understanding of how the endocrine system influences growth and development, reproduction, homeostasis, and energy production, utilization and storage, the pharmacology related to the system, disease states, and terminology.

Learning Outcome: Upon successful completion of this course, the student will be able to describe the endocrine system (structure and function) and its component parts; describe the hormones of the endocrine system and their roles; and describe common disorders of the system, their diagnosis, and related pharmacology and terminology.

Instruction: Major topics covered in the course are the anatomy and physiology of the endocrine system and its components, disorders of the system, and pharmacology related to the endocrine system. Methods of instruction include self-study with text, audiotape, pre- and post-tests, progress checks, and proctored final examination.

Credit Recommendation: In the lower division baccalaureate/associate degree category, 2 semester hours in Allied Health, Health Sciences, Human Biology, or Nursing (2/89) (7/94). **NOTE:** Students who complete this course in combination with Cardiovascular, Digestive, Integumentary, Musculoskeletal, Nervous, Reproductive, Respiratory, Sensory Organs, and Urinary Systems should receive 8 semester hours in Anatomy, 8 semester hours in Physiology, 6 semester hours in Applied Pharmacology, 3 semester hours in Concepts of Disease, and 3 semester hours in Medical Terminology.

Human Body, Pathology, and Treatment (5-A)

Location: Throughout the United States.

Length: Self-study.

Dates: May 1987-Present.

Objective: To provide basic knowledge and understanding of the body systems and their functions.

Learning Outcome: Upon successful completion of this course, the student will be able to describe basic anatomy and physiology of the human body including body systems and functions; describe in general terms approaches to disease prevention and treatment; and correctly use basic medical terminology in discussions of body systems and pathology.

Instruction: Major topics covered in the course are objectives and concerns of the health profession, basic body chemistry, body cells, tissue systems and defenses, and diagnostic tools and treatment approaches. Methods of instruction include self-study with text, audiotape, pre- and post-tests, progress checks, and proctored final examination.

Credit Recommendation: In the lower division baccalaureate/associate degree category, 3 semester hours in Introductory Human Biology (2/89) (7/94).

Immune System (6-D)

Location: Throughout the United States.

Length: Self-study.

Dates: May 1988-Present.

Objective: To provide general knowledge of the components and functions of the immune system.

Learning Outcome: Upon successful completion of this course, the student will be able to discuss the immune response with respect to cellular interactions in both humoral and cell-mediated responses; discuss disorders related to the immune system including the disease process and methods of treatment; and relate the pharmacology of drugs relevant to immune system disorders to the total concept of the immune system physiology.

Instruction: Major topics covered in the course are production and function of the cells of the immune system, structure and function of antibodies, humoral and cell-mediated immunity, complement, immune response, hypersensitivity, autoimmunity, and immunodeficiency disorders including acquired immune deficiency syndrome, pharmacology of drugs relevant to immune system disorders and the production of immunity, and transplant immunology. Methods of instruction include self-study with text, audiotape, pre- and post-tests, progress checks, and proctored final examination.

Credit Recommendation: In the lower division baccalaureate/associate degree category, 3 semester hours in Basic Immunology (2/89) (7/94).

Integumentary System (6-B)

Location: Throughout the United States.

Length: Self-study.

Dates: September 1987-Present.

Objective: To provide a broad understanding of the anatomy and physiology of the integumentary system and pharmacology disease states and terminology as they relate to the skin.

Learning Outcome: Upon successful completion of this course, the student will be able to describe the anatomy and physiology of the integumentary system; describe common disorders of the system, causes, symptoms, treatments, and terminology.

Instruction: Major topics covered in the course are the anatomy and physiology of the integumentary system, pharmacology of drugs related to skin disorders, disorders of the integumentary system including etiology, symptoms, and treatments. Methods of instruction include self-study with text, audiotape, pre- and post-tests, progress checks, and proctored final examination.

Credit Recommendation: In the lower division baccalaureate/associate degree category, 2 semester hours in Allied Health, Health Sciences, Human Biology, or Nursing (2/89) (7/94). **NOTE:** Students who complete this course in combination with Cardiovascular, Digestive, Endocrine, Musculoskeletal, Nervous, Reproductive, Respiratory, Sensory Organs, and Urinary Systems should receive 8 semester hours in Anatomy, 8 semester hours in Physiology, 6 semester hours in Applied Pharmacology, 3 semester hours in Concepts of Disease, and 3 semester hours in Medical Terminology.

Introduction to Managed Healthcare (formerly Managed Healthcare [7-F]) (5-D)

Location: Throughout the United States.

Length: 45 hours (self-study).

Dates: June 1993-Present.

Objective: To provide a broad understanding of the key elements of managed healthcare in the United States.

Learning Outcome: Upon successful completion of this course, the student will be able to discuss the types of managed healthcare delivery systems; personnel and organizations associated with managed healthcare; role of physicians and hospitals; the effect of managed healthcare on the pharmaceutical industry; and general reimbursement procedures.

Instruction: Major topics covered in the course are definition and history of managed healthcare; types of managed healthcare; public programs; industry and employers use of managed healthcare; changes in medicare reimbursement; roles of physicians, pharmacists, and hospitals in managed care; alternate medical facilities; effect of managed healthcare on pharmacists; and methods of cost control and terminology. Methods of instruction include self-study with text, audiotape, pre- and post-tests, progress checks, and proctored final examination.

Credit Recommendation: In the upper division baccalaureate degree category, 3 semester hours in Managed Healthcare or Healthcare Administration (7/94).

Introduction to Pharmacology (5-B)

Location: Throughout the United States.

Length: Self-study.

Dates: May 1987-Present.

Objective: To provide a broad understanding of basic pharmacology.

Learning Outcome: Upon successful completion of this course, the student will be able to describe basic principles of drug actions and interactions including adverse reactions and factors modifying response; describe actions of drugs by therapeutic classes; and discuss the techniques by which drugs are administered to treat diseases.

Instruction: Major topics covered in the course are basic principles of drug actions and interactions, therapeutic classes of drugs, autonomic nervous system and central nervous system drugs, anti-inflammatory drugs, cardiovascular drugs, antihistamines, hormones, gastrointestinal drugs, and antineoplastic drugs. Methods of instruction include self-study with text, audiotape, pre- and post-tests, progress checks, and proctored final examination.

Credit Recommendation: In the lower division baccalaureate/associate degree category, 3 semester hours in Introduction to Pharmacology (2/89) (7/94).

Musculoskeletal System (6-A)

Location: Throughout the United States.

Length: Self-study.

Dates: September 1987-Present.

Objective: To provide a broad understanding of the anatomy and physiology of the musculoskeletal system, pharmacology as it relates to the system, disease states and terminology.

Learning Outcome: Upon successful completion of this course, the student will be able to describe the anatomy and physiology of the skeletal system, common disorders of the system, and pharmacology of drugs related to the system, as well as describe the anatomy and physiology of the skeletal system, common disorders (and terminology) of the system, and pharmacology of drugs related to the system.

Instruction: Major topics covered in the course are the anatomy and physiology of the musculoskeletal system, disorders of the system, and pharmacology related to the system. Methods of instruction include self-study with text, audiotape, pre- and post-tests, progress checks, and proctored final examination.

Credit Recommendation: In the lower division baccalaureate/associate degree category, 2 semester hours in Allied Health, Health Sciences, Human Biology, or Nursing (2/89) (7/94). **NOTE:** Students who complete this course in combination with Cardiovascular, Digestive, Endocrine, Integumentary, Nervous, Reproductive, Respiratory, Sensory Organs, and Urinary Systems should receive 8 semester hours in Anatomy, 8 semester hours in Physiology, 6 semester hours in Applied Pharmacology, 3 semester hours in Concepts of Disease, and 3 semester hours in Medical Terminology.

Nervous System (6-E)

Location: Throughout the United States.

Length: Self-study.

Dates: September 1988-Present.

Objective: To provide an understanding of the fundamentals of neuroanatomy and neurophysiology.

Learning Outcome: Upon successful completion of this course, the student will be able to describe the anatomy and physiology of the nervous system (central, peripheral, and autonomic); neurologic disorders and their etiology; pharmacology; and terminology related to nervous system disorders.

Instruction: Major topics covered in the course are the anatomy and physiology of the nervous system and its component parts, common disorders of the nervous system, and related pharmacology and terminology. Methods of instruction include self-study with text, audiotape, pre- and post-tests, progress checks, and proctored final examination.

Credit Recommendation: In the lower division baccalaureate/associate degree category, 2 semester hours in Allied Health, Health Sciences, Human Biology, or Nursing (2/89) (7/94). **NOTE:** Students who complete this course in combination with Cardiovascular, Digestive, Endocrine, Integumentary, Musculoskeletal, Reproductive, Respiratory, Sensory Organs, and Urinary Systems should receive 8 semester hours in Anatomy, 8 semester hours in Physiology, and 4 semester hours in Applied Pharmacology.

Outcomes: Measurement, Management and Marketing (7K)

Location: Independent self-study by correspondence.

Length: 39 hours (10 weeks) (approximately 36 hours of study time).

Dates: September 1997-Present.

Objective: To provide an overview of the growing field of outcomes measurement and management, including the tools used for measurement of outcomes and the application of the results of these studies to ensure that quality healthcare is provided throughout healthcare delivery systems. Course provides for the application of business administration to health care.

Learning Outcome: Upon successful completion of this course, the student will be able to discuss how the trend towards outcomes research has evolved and the types of outcomes being measured; discuss how outcomes research is conducted; describe tools used to measure clinical, economic, and humanistic outcomes; describe ways in which providers, including managed care organizations, are coordinating their resources and processes to maximize outcomes; and discuss how outcomes data are being applied in the marketing of healthcare services and products, including the role of the pharmaceutical industry and healthcare representatives in outcomes research and management.

Instruction: Major topics covered in the course are the role of structure, process and outcomes in quality management, data sources for outcomes research, types of outcomes studies, role of outcomes and clinical practice guidelines in disease management, and outcomes in the marketplace including MCO accreditation, the impact of HEDIS on healthcare organizations, and the role of the pharmaceutical industry and the healthcare representative in outcomes management. Methods of instruction include self-study with text, audiotape, pre- and post tests, progress checks, course summary, and proctored final examination.

Credit Recommendation: In the upper division baccalaureate category 3 semester hours or in the graduate category 1 semester hour in Healthcare/Business Administration (11/97). **NOTE:** Graduate credit is only applicable at the introductory level.

Pharmaceutical and Medical Research (7-B)

Location: Throughout the United States.

Length: Self-study.

Dates: January 1989-Present.

Objective: To provide a general knowledge of the pharmaceutical and medical research process.

Learning Outcome: Upon successful completion of this course, the student will be able to identify types of research, institutions, and personnel; discuss the various governmental regulations affecting research with respect to clinical trials, ethics, and cost constraints; and describe the basics of scientific methodology and the statistics of sampling, hypothesis testing, and data analysis.

Instruction: Major topics covered in the course are types of research and research institutions, governmental regulation, clinical trials, research design, methodology and analysis including scientific methodology, data collection and statistical analysis, cost analysis, and ethical constraints. Methods of instruction include self-study with text, audiotape, pre- and post-tests, progress checks, and proctored final examination.

Credit Recommendation: In the upper division baccalaureate degree category, 3 semester hours in Introduction to Research Methodology or Survey of Research Methods (2/89) (7/94).

Pharmacoeconomics (7-G)

Location: Throughout the United States.

Length: 30 hours. (self-study).

Dates: June 1994-Present.

Objective: To provide an overview of the basic principles of pharmacoeconomics and its impact on the pharmaceutical industry.

Learning Outcome: Upon successful completion of this course, the student will be able to discuss the impact of pharmacoeconomics on hospitals, physicians, patients, and society at large; describe the basic structure of a pharmacoeconomic study; and describe and apply the pharmacoeconomic methods of cost effectiveness analysis, cost-utility analysis, cost-benefit analysis, and cost minimization analysis.

Instruction: Major topics covered in the course are the role of third-party payers; the impact of pharmacoeconomic research on hospitals, physicians, patients, and society at large; components of pharmacoeconomic research; and the pharmacoeconomic methods of cost-effectiveness analysis, cost-utility analysis, cost-benefit analysis, and cost minimization analysis. Methods of instruction include self-study with text, audiotape, case studies, pre- and post-tests, progress checks, and proctored final examination.

Credit Recommendation: In the upper division baccalaureate degree category, 2 semester hours in Pharmacoeconomics or Health Economics and Evaluation (7/94).

Reproductive Systems (6-K)

Location: Throughout the United States.

Length: Self-study.

Dates: January 1988-Present.

Objective: To provide a general knowledge of the structure and function of the male and female reproductive systems.

Learning Outcome: Upon successful completion of this course, the student will be able to name and give the function of the organs in the male and female reproductive systems; briefly describe the major disorders of the male and female reproductive systems; relate reproductive disorders to the recommended drug treatments and terminology; and discuss the mechanism of the drug actions.

Instruction: Major topics covered in the course are the anatomy and physiology of the male and female reproductive systems, disorders of the reproductive systems, and methods of diagnosis and pharmacology and terminology relevant to the reproductive systems. Methods of instruction include self-study with text, audiotape, pre- and post-tests, progress checks, and proctored final examination.

Credit Recommendation: In the lower division baccalaureate/associate degree category, 2 semester hours in Allied Health, Health Sciences, Human Biology, or Nursing (2/89) (7/94). **NOTE:** Students who complete this course in combination with Cardiovascular, Digestive, Endocrine, Integumentary, Musculoskeletal, Nervous, Respiratory, Sensory Organs, and Urinary Systems should receive 8 semester hours in Anatomy, 8 semester hours in Physiology, 6 semester hours in Applied Pharmacology, 3 semester hours in Concepts of Disease, and 3 semester hours in Medical Terminology.

Respiratory System (6-I)

Location: Throughout the United States.

Length: Self-study.

Dates: September 1987-Present.

Objective: To provide an understanding of the structure of the respiratory system and its role in oxygen and carbon dioxide exchange.

Learning Outcome: Upon successful completion of this course, the student will be able to describe structure and functions of the respiratory system and describe common disorders of the system, and classes of drugs relevant to treatment of these disorders and terminology.

Instruction: Major topics covered in the course are structure and functions of the respiratory system, mechanics of breathing, gas exchange, disorders of the system, and the pharmacology relating to anti-inflammatory agents, central nervous system drugs, autonomic system drugs, expectorants, and bronchodilators in relation to these disorders. Methods of instruction include self-study with text, audiotape, pre- and post-tests, progress checks, and proctored final examination.

Credit Recommendation: In the lower division baccalaureate/associate degree category, 2 semester hours in Allied Health, Health Sciences, Human Biology, or Nursing (2/89) (7/94). **NOTE:** Students who complete this course in combination with Cardiovascular, Digestive, Endocrine, Integumentary, Musculoskeletal, Nervous, Reproductive, Sensory Organs, and Urinary Systems should receive 8 semester hours in Anatomy, 8 semester hours in Physiology, 6 semester hours in Applied Pharmacology, 3 semester hours in Concepts of Disease, and 3 semester hours in Medical Terminology.

Sensory Organs (6-G)

Location: Throughout the United States.

Length: Self-study.

Dates: September 1988-Present.

Objective: To provide an understanding of the structure and functions of the sensory organs.

Learning Outcome: Upon successful completion of this course, the student will be able to describe the anatomy and physiology of the sensory organs and describe common disorders of the sensory organs and etiology; and diagnosis, pharmacology, and terminology related to disorders.

Instruction: Major topics covered in the course are the receptor functions, vision, hearing and equilibrium, taste, smell, and disorders pharmacology; and terminology related to disorders of the sensory organs. Methods of instruction include self-study with text, audiotape, pre- and post-tests, progress checks, and proctored final examination.

Credit Recommendation: In the lower division baccalaureate/associate degree category, 2 semester hours in Allied Health, Health Sciences, Human Biology, or Nursing (2/89) (7/94). **NOTE:** Students who complete this course in combination with Cardiovascular, Digestive, Endocrine, Integumentary, Musculoskeletal, Nervous, Reproductive, Respiratory, and Urinary Systems should receive 8 semester hours in Anatomy, 8 semester hours in Physiology, 6 semester hours in Applied Pharmacology, 3 semester hours in Concepts of Disease, and 3 semester hours in Medical Terminology.

The Evolving Healthcare Community (7-J) (formerly Healthcare Community [7-D])

Location: Throughout the United States.

Length: Self-study.

Dates: January 1989-May 1996.

Objective: To provide an overview of healthcare providers, funding, and delivery.

Learning Outcome: Upon successful completion of this course, the student will be knowledgeable about the professionals of the healthcare community, their roles, educational backgrounds, and perspectives; be knowledgeable of healthcare funding from the private and public (government) sectors; and be knowledgeable of the healthcare inpatient and outpatient delivery systems.

Instruction: Major topics covered in the course are current issues that affect the relationships between professional groups; the education and development of physicians; types of physicians; a description of the roles of nurses, physician assistants, pharmacists, dentists, and other healthcare professionals; the role of professional associates in the healthcare community; an overview of healthcare funding and private health insurances; a discussion of government programs such as Medicare and Medicaid and recent developments in healthcare delivery; demographics and attitudes of patients; and a description of hospitals and long-term care facilities. Methods of instruction include self-study with text, audiotape, pre- and post-tests, progress checks, and proctored final examination.

Credit Recommendation: In the lower division baccalaureate/associate degree category, 3 semester hours in Allied Health or Health Care Administration (2/89) (7/94).

The Pharmaceutical Industry (7-C)

Location: Throughout the United States.

Length: 15 hours. (self-study).

Dates: January 1989-Present.

Objective: To provide an overview of the modern pharmaceutical industry and a basic knowledge and understanding of the role of pharmacy, pharmaceutical industry, healthcare providers, and regulatory policies in the use of drugs.

Learning Outcome: Upon successful completion of this course, the student will be able to use appropriate terminology to describe and/or define areas of the pharmaceutical industry; the history of pharmacy and the industry; the progression of a new drug product from inception to market; the roles and responsibilities of healthcare providers and patients; and the development of regulatory agencies and policies concerning distribution, sales, safety and efficacy of drug products.

Instruction: Major topics covered in the course are the history of pharmacy and pharmaceutical industry; development and distribution of pharmaceutical products; roles and responsibilities of patients; healthcare providers; and United States government agencies and regulations. Methods of instruction include self-study with text, audiotape, pre- and post-tests, progress checks, and proctored final examination.

Credit Recommendation: In the lower division baccalaureate/associate degree category, 1 semester hour in History of Pharmacy and Pharmaceutical Industry (7/94).

Trends and Issues in Healthcare (7-E)

Location: Throughout the United States.

Length: Self-study.

Dates: September 1988-May 1992.

Objective: To enhance awareness of a variety of current trends and issues in healthcare.

Learning Outcome: Upon successful completion of this course, the student will be able to understand the effects of cost containment on the healthcare industry; have some understanding of technological developments in the medical industry; and become familiar with the changing healthcare delivery system and the medical malpractice crisis.

Instruction: Major topics covered in the course are description of how public support for the medical establishment influenced its growth during the 1960s and 1970s; trends in healthcare are analyzed; a discussion/overview covers the changing healthcare delivery system; the medical malpractice crisis; society's response to epidemic and catastrophic diseases; healthcare on the uninsured and underinsured; transplants and allocations of organs; foregoing or terminating life-sustaining treatments; abortions; Medicare and Medicaid programs; and the percentage of each healthcare dollar that goes toward physician fees and hospital costs.

Methods of instruction include self-study with text, audiotape, pre- and post-tests, progress checks, and final examination.

Credit Recommendation: In the lower division baccalaureate/associate degree category, 2 semester hours in Allied Health or Health Care Administration (2/89).

Urinary System (6-J)

Location: Throughout the United States.

Length: Self-study.

Dates: September 1987-Present.

Objective: To provide general knowledge of the anatomy and physiology of the urinary system.

Learning Outcome: Upon successful completion of this course, the student will be able to identify the organs of the urinary system including the parts of the kidney and nephron; describe the physiology of urine formation including regulation of urine composition; and briefly describe major disorders of the urinary system including methods of diagnosis, treatment, and terminology.

Instruction: Major topics covered in the course are urinary system anatomy, with strong emphasis on the kidney anatomy, physiology of urine formation, disorders of the urinary system, diagnostic procedures, and pharmacology relevant to urinary system disorders. Methods of instruction include self-study with text, audiotape, pre- and post-tests, progress checks, and proctored final examination.

Credit Recommendation: In the lower division baccalaureate/associate degree category, 2 semester hours in Allied Health, Health Sciences, Human Biology, or Nursing (2/89) (7/94). **NOTE:** Students who complete this course in combination with Cardiovascular, Digestive, Endocrine, Integumentary, Musculoskeletal, Nervous, Reproductive, Respiratory, and Sensory Organs Systems should receive 8 semester hours in Anatomy, 8 semester hours in Physiology, 6 semester hours in Applied Pharmacology, 3 semester hours in Concepts of Disease, and 3 semester hours in Medical Terminology.

Charles River Computers

Charles River Computers provides to many companies outsourcing services in local area networking (LAN) management, facilities management (e.g. DEC data centers), software support and management consulting. As examples of some of these services, CRC has set up off-site networks with less than twenty (20) hours notice, and has maintained LAN-based client server networks in six financial centers for one of the world's largest banks.

Today, in the corporate headquarters, CRC maintains the largest library of server and superserver documentation and parts inventory in New York. CRC consultants currently provide user support for large LANs and data centers for financial institutions and insurance companies. This experience has contributed to CRC's innovative approaches and ability to continuously improve and upgrade the full spectrum of support services offered.

CRC's approach to maintaining high service levels is based on a sensitivity and awareness to: business needs of financial institutions, most cost-effective and state-of-the-art software and hardware technologies, and continuing technical education of support and consulting personnel. Because of this emphasis on continuing education, CRC's consultants hold the highest levels of network certification, backed up with experience involving more than twenty years in office and automation and data processing, ten years of PC/networking and eight years of Apple experience.

For more information contact: Director of Technical Education, Charles River Computers, 575 Lexington Avenue, 4th Floor, New York, NY 10022-6102.

Source of official student records: Registry of Credit Recommendations, American Council on Education, One Dupont Circle, Washington, DC 20036-1193.

Additional information about the courses: College Credit Recommendation Service, American Council on Education, One Dupont Circle, Washington, DC 20036-1193.

Advanced Topics in Data Communications (CS501)

Location: Charles River Computers, 575 Lexington Avenue, New York, New York 10022.

Length: 1.5 hours per week for 10 weeks.

Dates: September 1994-Present.

Objective: To provide familiarity with tools to solve business problems in connectivity.

Learning Outcome: Upon successful completion of this course, the student will understand theoretical communications concepts; be able to analyze and develop solutions to data communications problems; be able to analyze and develop solutions to advanced networking problems; understand problem-solving concepts related to multi-platform connectivity; be familiar with principles and usage of Netware and Unixware on the same network.

Instruction: Major topics covered in the course are, imaging, internet, Unix, connectivity, connectivity and communications, setting up and using WWW server, remote access, Netware, high speed switches for networks, transactional processing, and Unixware. Methods of instruction include lectures, discussion, demonstration, video, computers, (LCD), periodic quizzes, feedback from in-class discussion, and a final research project or special project applying knowledge to the workplace.

Credit Recommendation: In the upper division baccalaureate degree category, 2 semester hours in Computer Science, Data Processing, or MIS (10/95).

Advanced Trends in Software Development (CS500)

Location: Charles River Computers, 575 Lexington Avenue, New York, New York 10022.

Length: 1.5 hours per week for 10 weeks.

Dates: September 1994-Present.

Objective: Will provide familiarity with latest technology and software development.

Learning Outcome: Upon successful completion of this course, the student will be familiar with application uses in a multi-user communications environment; able to identify and evaluate appropriate vendor software; familiar with basic use of various software packages; able to select and evaluate appropriate systems for business applications.

Instruction: Major topics covered in the course are Claris, Lotus Notes, SyBase, Unix, PowerBuilder, Visual C++, Windows NT, Apple Scripting, Delphi, and Object Orientation. Methods of instruction include lecture, demonstration, discussion, video, LCD, periodic quizzes, feedback from in-class discussion, and a final research project or special project applying knowledge to the workplace.

Credit Recommendation: In the upper division baccalaureate degree category, 2 semester hours in Computer Science, Data Processing, or MIS (10/95).

Project Management Tools (CS502)

Location: Charles River Computers, 575 Lexington Avenue, New York, New York 10022.

Length: 1.5 hours per week for 10 weeks.

Dates: September 1994-Present.

Objective: To provide tools to facilitate project planning, implementation and management; to provide an introduction to related concepts and software.

Learning Outcome: Upon successful completion of this course, the student will understand basic underlying concepts of planning, coordination and implementation of projects; be able to write clearly, concisely and completely; be familiar with communication tools such as beepers, cellular phones, internet, voice mail and be familiar with technical data communications issues relevant to managing a project.

Instruction: Major topics covered in the course are project management principles, time management, written communication, data security, cross-platform e-mail administration problem management, and transition management (Ethernet). Methods of instruction include lectures, demonstration, videos, computers with LCD, periodic quizzes, feedback from in-class discussion, and a final research project or special project applying knowledge to the workplace.

Credit Recommendation: In the upper division baccalaureate degree category, 2 semester hours in Computer Systems or MIS (10/95).

Christopher Academy and Maitland Montessori School

The Christopher Academy and Maitland Montessori School provides training in the Montessori method. This training consists of the philosophy and theories of Dr. Maria Montessori, as well as how to present the Montessori curriculum and materials to children from 2 1/2-6 years of age.

The courses are delivered by experts in the Montessori method of education and can be taken in various forms.

Source of official student records: Registry of Credit Recommendations, American Council on Education, One Dupont Circle, Washington, DC 20036-1193.

Additional information about the courses: Office of Corporate-Higher Education Programs, Thomas Edison State College, 101 West State Street, CN 545, Trenton, NJ 08625.

Christopher Academy or Maitland Montessori Teacher Training Course in the Montessori Method

Location: Scotch Plains and Westfield, NJ, Maitland & Altamonte Springs, FL.

Length: 10 months (227 hours).

Dates: September 1991-Present.

Objective: To acquaint teachers with the Montessori philosophy and method of education and to prepare them to become qualified as Montessori teachers.

Learning Outcome: Upon successful completion of this course, the teacher will be able to demonstrate an understanding of the philosophy and Montessori education and the growth and development of a child from 2.5 to 6 years of age; implement the Montessori curriculum with appropriate emphasis on the physical, emotional, educational, and cultural needs of children from 2.5 - 6 years old; demonstrate skill in the use of Montessori teaching materials to match the development and learning styles of children; develop a careful arrangement of the student classroom environment; demonstrate program leadership by serving as an advocate for and disseminator of the Montessori movement; and design and evaluate individualized children's curricular materials and resources appropriate for children from various cultural backgrounds and with varying abilities and learning styles.

Instruction: Major topics covered in the course are the qualifications needed to teach in a Montessori school or classroom, the Montessori theory and philosophy, and the use of Montessori methods and materials.

Credit Recommendation: In the upper division baccalaureate degree category, 3 semester hours in Foundations of Early Childhood Education, 3 semester hours in Methods and Materials for Early Childhood Education, and 3 semester hours in Growth and Development of the Young Child, for a total of 9 semester hours (5/95).

Internship

Location: Scotch Plains & Westfield, NJ and Maitland & Altamonte Springs, FL.

Length: 500 hours over 10 months.

Dates: September 1991-Present.

Objective: To have students apply theory and practical knowledge acquired during the course in a classroom with children from 2.5 to 6 years, under a certified Montessori teacher.

Learning Outcome: Upon successful completion of the course, the teacher will become proficient in the use and demonstration of Montessori materials in the classroom; develop observation skills to better meet children's needs; and assume responsibility for the care and preparation of the classroom environment according to the Montessori philosophy.

Instruction: Major topics covered in the course are the opportunity to teach in a Montessori environment and the opportunity to execute the Montessori theory and philosophy through practical application of the materials and curriculum for 2.5 to 6-year old children. The intern is involved in observing, interacting, and communicating with children, the supervising teacher, administrators, parents, and the community.

Credit Recommendation: In the upper division baccalaureate degree category, 9 semester hours in Early Childhood Education Practicum (5/95).

St. Nicholas Montessori Training Course I (Evening Course)

Location: Scotch Plains, NJ.

Length: 9.5 months (includes workshop-60 hours).

Dates: September 1990-August 1991.

Objective: To acquaint teachers with the Montessori philosophy and method of education and to prepare them to become qualified as Montessori teachers.

Learning Outcome: Upon completion of this program, the teacher will be able to discuss the Montessori philosophy of education and the growth and development of a child from birth to 6 years of age; develop a Montessori curriculum, with appropriate stress on all physical, emotional, and educational needs for a child from 0 to 6 years old; and demonstrate skills in the use of Montessori apparatus and activities.

Instruction: Major topics covered in the course are the qualifications needed to teach in a Montessori school or classroom, the Montessori theory and philosophy, and the use of Montessori apparatus.

Credit Recommendation: In the upper division baccalaureate degree category, 6 semester hours in Early Childhood Education (9/88). **NOTE:** This course is offered both a correspondence and an evening classroom course. Both versions require a workshop.

St. Nicholas Montessori Training Course I (Independent Study)

Location: Independent study - Westfield, NJ.

Length: 9-24 months (includes workshop-60 hours).

Dates: July 1986-September 1990.

Objective: To acquaint teachers with the Montessori philosophy and method of education and to prepare them to become qualified as Montessori teachers.

Learning Outcome: Upon completion of this program, the teacher will be able to discuss the Montessori philosophy of education and the growth and development of a child from birth to 6 years of age; develop a Montessori curriculum, with appropriate stress on all physical, emotional, and educational needs for a child from 0 to 6 years old; and demonstrate skills in the use of Montessori apparatus and activities.

Instruction: Major topics covered in the course are the qualifications needed to teach in a Montessori school or classroom, the Montessori theory and philosophy, and the use of Montessori apparatus.

Credit Recommendation: In the upper division baccalaureate degree category, 6 semester hours in Early Childhood Education (9/88). **NOTE:** This course is offered both a correspondence and an evening classroom course. Both versions require a workshop.

St. Nicholas Montessori Training/Christopher Academy or Maitland Montessori

Location: Westfield, NJ and Altamonte Springs, FL.

Length: Independent study.

Dates: September 1991-Present.

Objective: To acquaint teachers with the Montessori philosophy and method of education and to prepare them to become qualified as Montessori teachers.

Learning Outcome: Upon successful completion of the course, the teacher will be able to demonstrate an understanding of the Montessori philosophy of education and the growth and development of a child from 2.5 to 6 years of age; implement the Montessori curriculum with appropriate emphasis on the physical, emotional, educational, and cultural needs of children from 2.5 - 6 years old; demonstrate skill in the use of Montessori teaching materials to match the development and learning styles of children; develop a careful arrangement of the student classroom environment; demonstrate program leadership by serving as an advocate for and disseminator of the Montessori movement; and design and evaluate individualized children's curricular materials and resources appropriate for children from various cultural backgrounds and with varying abilities and learning styles.

Instruction: Major topics covered in the course are the qualifications needed to teach in a Montessori school or classroom, the Montessori theory and philosophy, and the use of Montessori methods and materials. Methods of instruction include correspondence and has an additional 88 hour workshop.

Credit Recommendation: In the upper division baccalaureate degree category, 9 semester hours in Early Childhood Education (5/95).

Chrysler Corporation Advanced Technical Training

Chrysler Corporation Advanced Technical Training (A.T.T.) is a department of Chrysler Corporation's manufacturing organization. The primary responsibility of A.T.T. is to provide technical training programs that improve the skills and productivity of Chrysler employees, specifically those in production, skilled trades, supervisory and engineering positions.

A.T.T. classes are conducted at the Featherstone Road Engineering Center, Auburn Hills, Michigan; Chrysler Technical Center, Auburn Hill, Michigan; and over 30 plant locations in the Chrysler organization. Classrooms are equipped with fully operational trainer units to support each course. Standard industrial equipment and tools are used to increase the value of the laboratory learning experience.

Courses are designed and developed by department task groups, working in conjunction with plant and industry representatives to address the technical training needs of the company. Successful completion of courses is based on a passing test score, completion of all assigned laboratory exercises, and meeting minimum attendance requirements.

Source of official student records: Advanced Technical Training Records Office, Chrysler Corporation, Featherstone Road Engineering Center, 2301 Featherstone Road, Auburn Hills, MI 48326.

Additional information about the courses: College Credit Recommendation Service, American Council on Education, One Dupont Circle, Washington, DC, 20036-1193.

*Advanced Cincinnati Milacron T*3786 (CIM 201)*

Location: Chrysler locations worldwide.

Length: 40 hours (1 week).

Dates: May 1987-Present.

Objective: To develop the student's skills to program, operate, and troubleshoot the T*3786 Cincinnati Milacron Robot.

Learning Outcome: Upon successful completion of this course, the student will be able to program the robot using the teach pendant; match commands with descriptions of functions; and identify wiring schemes for I/O modules.

Instruction: Major topics covered in the course are system operation, programming procedures and commands, installation procedures, and maintenance. Methods of instruction include lecture, and laboratory exercises.

Credit Recommendation: In the lower division baccalaureate/associate degree category, 2 semester hours in Robotics (9/88) (2/94). **NOTE:** To receive credit for this course, students must have successfully completed Industrial Robotics (ROB 101).

Advanced Geometric Dimensioning and Tolerancing for Manufacturing (EGT 102)

Location: UAW Chrysler Technology Training Center.

Length: 40 hours (1 week).

Dates: April 1997-Present.

Objective: To train the students how to identify and apply geometrical characteristics and tolerances as they relate to a part feature.

Learning Outcome: Upon successful completion of this course, the student will be able to verify features, features of size, and features of location.

Instruction: Major topics covered in the course are clearance; transition and/or interference fit; maximum material condition, least material condition, and tolerance zones on internal and external parts; and positional and bonus tolerances. Methods of instructed include lecture, discussion, written exercises, and hands-on labs.

Credit Recommendation: In the vocational certificate category or in the lower division baccalaureate/associate degree category, 2 semester hours in Geometric Dimensioning and Tolerancing (7/97).

Air Logic (ALG 101)

Location: Chrysler locations worldwide.

Length: 40 hours (1 week).

Dates: April 1985-Present.

Objective: To enable the student to set up and troubleshoot air logic systems.

Learning Outcome: Upon successful completion of this course, the student will be able to match circuit functions of air logic components to their symbols; fabricate, operate, and analyze various air logic circuits; and identify basic air logic circuits and the sequence of operation of the system.

Instruction: Major topics covered in the course are the fundamentals of compressed air; power valve symbology; comparison of electrical relays versus pneumatic air logic components and functions; ladder diagrams; and troubleshooting procedures and techniques. Methods of instruction include lecture and laboratory exercises.

Credit Recommendation: In the lower division baccalaureate/associate degree category, 2 semester hours in Pneumatic Logic Controls (9/88) (2/94).

ASEA IRB/90 (ASA 201)

Location: Chrysler locations worldwide.

Length: 40 hours (1 week).

Dates: April 1985-Present.

Objective: To enable the student to set up and troubleshoot the ASEA IRB 90/2 robot.

Learning Outcome: Upon successful completion of this course, the student will be able to demonstrate the ability to safely set up and operate the ASEA IRB-90/2 Robot and S-2 Control; and isolate and correctly diagnose malfunctions between the robot control, weld timer/WC2 panel, and programmable logic controller.

Instruction: Major topics covered in the course are robot specifications, system components/operations, safety, programming procedures, command, maintenance, and troubleshooting. Methods of instruction include lecture, demonstration, and laboratory exercises.

Credit Recommendation: In the lower division baccalaureate/associate degree category, 3 semester hours in Robotics Technology (4/89) (2/94). **NOTE:** To receive credit for this course, student must have successfully completed Industrial Robotics (ROB 101). Credit should not be awarded for both this course and KUKA IR662/100 (KUK 201).

Automotive Brake Systems

Location: Chrysler locations worldwide.

Length: 20 hours.

Dates: August 1986-Present.

Objective: To increase the understanding of automotive brake systems.

Learning Outcome: Upon successful completion of this course, the student will be able to understand the principles of hydraulic brakes; understand the parking brake system; and test and inspect brake system components to determine any problems.

Instruction: Major topics covered in the course are science of hydraulics, brake mechanical system, power booster operation, parking brake operation, and brake service procedures. Methods of instruction include lecture and laboratory.

Credit Recommendation: In the lower division baccalaureate/associate degree category, 1 semester hour in Automotive Technology (4/90) (5/95).

Chassis and Suspension Systems

Location: Chrysler locations worldwide.

Length: 32 hours.

Dates: January 1989-Present.

Objective: To give the student a basic understanding of chassis and suspension systems.

Learning Outcome: Upon successful completion of this course, the student will be able to inspect and diagnose suspension and chassis system problems; understand the operating principles of steering, chassis, and driveline systems; and understand chassis and steering system requirements and service concerns.

Instruction: Major topics covered in the course are suspension systems, chassis systems, steering systems, and alignment procedures. Methods of instruction include lecture and laboratory.

Credit Recommendation: In the lower division baccalaureate/associate degree category, 2 semester hours in Automotive Technology (4/90) (5/95).

Electronic Fuel Injection Systems (PO5 EFI)

Location: Chrysler locations worldwide.

Length: 40 hours (1 or 2 weeks).

Dates: June 1988-Present.

Objective: To provide the student with the basic knowledge to diagnose an improperly functioning vehicle using the latest electronic test equipment.

Learning Outcome: Upon successful completion of this course, the student will be able to identify EFI components and their functions; inspect and diagnose EFI systems using the current scan tool; and have a basic understanding of how the fuel control system, ignition system, and emission systems work together.

Instruction: Major topics covered in the course are the starting system, computers, power/ground systems, ignition systems, throttle body assembly, sensors, EGR system, and charging systems. Methods of instruction include lecture and laboratory exercises.

Credit Recommendation: In the lower division baccalaureate/associate degree category, 2 semester hours in Automotive Technology (4/89) (2/94).

Electronic Transaxle

Location: Chrysler locations worldwide.

Length: 32 hours.

Dates: January 1989-Present.

Objective: To familiarize the student with the operation of the Chrysler A-604 Electronic Transaxle.

Learning Outcome: Upon successful completion of this course, the student will be able to understand the power flow of an A-604 Transaxle; understand the hydraulic and electronic control systems; and be able to understand the diagnostic procedures for the A-604 Transaxle.

Instruction: Major topics covered in the course are mechanical powerflow, hydraulic system, electrical system, and diagnostics. Methods of instruction include lecture and laboratory.

Credit Recommendation: In the lower division baccalaureate/associate degree category, 2 semester hours in Automotive Technology (4/90) (5/95).

Engine Fundamentals (03 EAD)

Location: Chrysler locations worldwide.

Length: 20 hours.

Dates: August 1986-Present.

Objective: To develop an understanding of the operating principles of the internal combustion engine and how the mechanical components of the engine relate to the entire assembly.

Learning Outcome: Upon successful completion of this course, the student will be able to follow the proper procedure for disassembly and assembly of the engine.

Instruction: Major topics covered in the course are basic design of automotive engines; familiarization with engine mechanical components; basic engine systems; valve train operation; lubrication systems; cooling systems; fuel delivery systems; and disassembly, inspection, and assembly of the engine. Methods of instruction include lecture and laboratory.

Credit Recommendation: In the lower division baccalaureate/associate degree category, 1 semester hour in Automotive Technology (5/95).

Engineering Graphics I (EGO 101) (Geometric Dimensioning & Tolerancing for Manufacturing [GDT 100])

Location: Chrysler locations worldwide.

Length: 40 hours (1 week).

Dates: January 1995-Present.

Objective: To train the students how to interpret blueprint drawings used in manufacturing and inspection of parts.

Learning Outcome: Upon successful completion of this course, the student will be able to recognize and sketch part views, apply and interpret symbology, and dimensioning and tolerancing part features in order to provide a more thorough understanding.

Instruction: Major topics covered in the course are sketch part views, symbology, and dimensioning and tolerancing part features. Methods of instruction include lecture, discussion, written exercises and hands-on labs.

Credit Recommendation: In the vocational certificate category, or in the lower division baccalaureate/associate degree category, 2 semester hours (7/97).

Engineering Graphics II (EGT 102) (Advanced Geometric Dimensioning & Tolerancing for Manufacturing)

Location: Chrysler locations worldwide.

Length: 40 hours (1 week).

Dates: January 1995-Present.

Objective: To train the students how to identify and apply geometrical characteristics and tolerances as they relate to a part feature.

Learning Outcome: Upon successful completion of this course, the student will be able to verify Features, Features of size, and Features of Location.

Instruction: Major topics covered in the course are clearance, transition and/or interference fit, Maximum material condition, least material condition, and tolerance zones on internal and external parts, Positional and bonus tolerances. Methods of instruction include lecture, discussion, written exercises and hands-on labs.

Credit Recommendation: In the vocational certificate category, or in the lower division baccalaureate/associate degree category, 2 semester hours (7/97).

Fundamentals of Metallurgy (FWM 200)

Location: UAW Chrysler Technology Training Center

Length: 40 hours (1 week).

Dates: April 1997-Present.

Objective: To provide the student with practical information regarding the manufacture, processing, and use of six important metals that are used in the automotive industry.

Learning Outcome: Upon successful completion of this course, the student will

be able to identify common metals used in auto plants; determine metals repair characteristics for welding or machining; quench and flame harden metals; perform hardness tests; and prepare metal for repair welding procedures.

Instruction: Major topics covered in the course are properties of metals; metal identification; material specifications; crystal structures; effects of plastic deformation and heat treatment; and applications of tool steels, cast irons, stainless steel, copper alloys, and aluminum. Methods of instruction include lecture, discussion, hands-on labs, and instructor demonstrations.

Credit Recommendation: In the lower division baccalaureate/associate degree category, 2 semester hours in Metallurgy (7/97).

Geometric Dimensioning and Tolerancing for Manufacturing (EGO 101)

Location: UAW Chrysler Technology Training Center.

Length: 40 hours (1 week).

Dates: April 1997-Present.

Objective: To train students how to interpret blueprint drawings used in manufacturing and inspection of parts.

Learning Outcome: Upon successful completion of this course, the student will be able to recognize and sketch part views; and apply and interpret symbology, dimensioning, and tolerancing part features in order to provide a more thorough understanding.

Instruction: Major topics covered in the course are sketch part views, symbrology, and dimensioning and tolerancing part features. Methods of instruction include lecture, discussion, written exercises, and hands-on labs.

Credit Recommendation: In the vocational certificate category or in the lower division baccalaureate/associate degree category, 2 semester hours in Blueprint Reading (7/97).

Hydraulic Systems Analysis (HSA 201)

Location: Chrysler locations worldwide.

Length: 40 hours (1 week).

Dates: June 1988-Present.

Objective: To familiarize the student with the various components in a hydraulic system and how they are integrated for system operation.

Learning Outcome: Upon successful completion of this course, the student will be able to match component name with its ANSI symbol; demonstrate proper safety practices; identify characteristics of directional control valves; match common check valve applications with their circuit configuration; and match circuit function of pressure control valves based on drain line and pilot line configuration.

Instruction: Major topics covered in the course are hydraulic systems (input and output devices), control valves, fluids and fluid conditioning, fluid conductors and connectors, and fluid power analysis. Methods of instruction include lecture and demonstration.

Credit Recommendation: In the lower division baccalaureate/associate degree category, 2 semester hours in Fluid Power Technology (4/89) (2/94).

Industrial Electrical Controls (IEC 101)

Location: Chrysler locations worldwide.

Length: 80 hours (2 weeks).

Dates: January 1983-Present.

Objective: To enable the student to repair, maintain, and troubleshoot relay-based machine controls used in manufacturing.

Learning Outcome: Upon successful completion of this course, the student will be able to understand and repair basic components used in relay-based machines including motors and motor control systems; troubleshoot manufacturing systems using relay-based logic controls; and maintain relay-based machines to operate safely under manufacturing conditions.

Instruction: Major topics covered in the course are electrical safety, electrical testing, surge protection switches, relays, solenoids, contactors, AC motors, magnetic motor starters, jogging circuits, circuit breakers, ladder diagrams, preventive maintenance, and troubleshooting control circuits. Methods of instruction include lecture and laboratory.

Credit Recommendation: In the lower division baccalaureate/associate degree category, 4 semester hours in Electrical Control Systems or Electrical Power Technology (9/88) (2/94).

Industrial Electronics (IET 200)

Location: Chrysler locations worldwide.

Length: 200 hours (1 day per week for 25 weeks).

Dates: January 1983-Present.

Objective: To give the student a survey of the basic electronic theory and application of electronics circuits and systems used in industrial electronics controls and processing systems.

Learning Outcome: Upon successful completion of this course, the student will be able to demonstrate the basic knowledge required to effectively troubleshoot and maintain industrial electronic control systems; develop an understanding of basic circuits used in industrial control and logic systems; and develop the proper use of test equipment for proper troubleshooting techniques used in industrial control systems.

Instruction: Major topics covered in the course are a review of DC and AC circuit fundamentals, solid state fundamentals and circuit applications, use of ICs and digital electronics with microprocessors and applications in resistance welding, motor controls, position control systems, and robotics. Methods of instruction include lecture and laboratory.

Credit Recommendation: In the lower division baccalaureate/associate degree category, 8 semester hours in Fundamentals of Industrial Electronics (9/88) (2/94).

Industrial Hydraulic Technology (HYD 101)

Location: Chrysler locations worldwide.

Length: 80 hours (2 weeks).

Dates: January 1983-Present.

Objective: To provide the student with the necessary experience to develop those skills enabling him or her to set up, troubleshoot, and maintain hydraulic systems.

Learning Outcome: Upon successful completion of this course, the student will be able to identify various hydraulic components by their ANSI symbols and function within the hydraulic system; calculate pressures and flows required for simple hydraulic systems; read hydraulic prints; and understand function of system operation.

Instruction: Major topics covered in the course are hydraulic transmission of energy; control of hydraulic energy such as pressure, flow, and direction; and hydraulic energy input and output devices such as motors, cylinders, and safety operations. Methods of instruction include lecture and laboratory.

Credit Recommendation: In the lower division baccalaureate/associate degree

category, 3 semester hours in Basic Hydraulics (9/88) (2/94).

Industrial Pneumatic Technology (PNU 101)

Location: Chrysler locations worldwide.

Length: 40 hours (1 week).

Dates: February 1985-Present.

Objective: To provide the student with the experiences necessary to develop those skills enabling him or her to set up, troubleshoot, and maintain pneumatic systems.

Learning Outcome: Upon successful completion of this course, the student will be able to identify various pneumatic components by their ANSI symbols and functions within the pneumatic system; identify characteristics of directional valves given their ANSI symbols; and identify pneumatic components from prints.

Instruction: Major topics covered in the course are energy transmission using pneumatic systems, control of pneumatic energy, and air preparation. Methods of instruction include lecture and laboratory.

Credit Recommendation: In the lower division baccalaureate/associate degree category, 2 semester hours in Basic Pneumatics (9/88) (2/94).

Industrial Robotics (ROB 101)

Location: Chrysler locations worldwide.

Length: 40 hours (1 week).

Dates: January 1983-Present.

Objective: To introduce the student to robotic technology, hardware devices, and concepts related to industrial devices.

Learning Outcome: Upon successful completion of this course, the student will be able to identify terminology used in robotic applications; identify advantages and disadvantages of various safety devices used in conjunction with robots; and operate a robot using the teach pendant.

Instruction: Major topics covered in the course are robotic classification and operating systems; safety; mechanics of robotics and drive systems; control panels; and programming. Methods of instruction include lecture, demonstration, and laboratory.

Credit Recommendation: In the lower division baccalaureate/associate degree category, 2 semester hours in Manufacturing Engineering or Robotics (9/88) (2/94).

KUKA IR662/100 (KUK 201)

Location: Chrysler locations worldwide.

Length: 80 hours (2 weeks).

Dates: February 1989-Present.

Objective: To enable the student to program, operate, maintain, and troubleshoot the KUKA IR662/100 industrial robot.

Learning Outcome: Upon successful completion of this course, the student will be able to safely operate and modify existing programs and software, perform preventive maintenance tasks, and demonstrate troubleshooting skills on an industrial robot.

Instruction: Major topics covered in the course are robot specifications, system components/operations, safety, programming procedures, commands, maintenance, and troubleshooting. Methods of instruction include lecture, demonstration, and laboratory exercises.

Credit Recommendation: In the lower division baccalaureate/associate degree category, 3 semester hours in Robotics Technology (4/89) (2/94). **NOTE:** Credit should not be awarded for both this course and ASEA IRB-90 (ASA 201).

Microprocessors 6800/6502 (MPU 101)

Location: Chrysler locations worldwide.

Length: 80 hours (2 weeks).

Dates: June 1985-Present.

Objective: To give the student a general understanding of microprocessors including programming and troubleshooting the Motorola 6800/6502.

Learning Outcome: Upon successful completion of this course, the student will be able to understand block diagrams and logic systems used in microprocessors; understand the application of digital logic and programming used in microprocessors; and identify basic troubleshooting techniques used in microprocessors.

Instruction: Major topics covered in the course are number systems used in microprocessors, digital logic, mathematical operation and microprocessor concepts, introduction to programming, memory, program and data storage, and decoding and troubleshooting microprocessor circuits. Methods of instruction include lecture and laboratory.

Credit Recommendation: In the lower division baccalaureate/associate degree category, 4 semester hours in Microprocessors or as an elective in Electronic Systems Technology (9/88) (2/94).

Mig and Flux Cored Arc Welding (WMF 200)

Location: UAW Chrysler Technology Training Center.

Length: 40 hours (1 week).

Dates: April 1997-Present.

Objective: To provide the student with the skills necessary to produce acceptable quality welds on automotive sheet metal and underbody chassis components.

Learning Outcome: Upon successful completion of this course, the student will be able to set-up/adjust production arc welding equipment; weld automotive sheet metal components with both welding processes to Chrysler Engineering processes standards; and inspect completed welds for quality.

Instruction: Major topics covered in the course are the fundamentals of both processes, set up and adjustment of equipment, selection of shielding gases, electrode wire specifications, and variables that affect weld quality and safe practices. Methods of instruction include lecture, discussion, instructor demonstrations, and hands-on lab exercises to enable students to produce quality fillet and groove welds.

Credit Recommendation: In the lower division baccalaureate/associate degree category, 2 semester hours in Welding (GMAW-FCAW) (7/97).

Overview of Mig and Tig Welding Processes (WMT 200)

Location: UAW Chrysler Technology Training Center.

Length: 40 hours (1 week).

Dates: April 1997-Present.

Objective: To provide the student with experience necessary to set up, adjust, and troubleshoot MIG and TIG welding equipment.

Learning Outcome: Upon successful completion of this course, the student will be able to perform welds on mild steel plate materials using the MIG and TIG welding processes; and select the proper filler metals and shielding gases.

Instruction: Major topics covered in the course are the fundamentals of both processes, set up and adjustment of equipment, selection of electrodes and filler metals shielding gases, process variations, and safety. Methods of instruction include lecture, discussion, instructor demonstration, and hands-on lab practice.

Credit Recommendation: In the lower division baccalaureate/associate degree

category, 2 semester hours in Welding (GMAW-GTAW) (7/97).

Pipe and Tube Welding, MIG (PTW 200)

Location: UAW Chrysler Technology Training Center.

Length: 80 hours (2 weeks).

Dates: April 1997-Present.

Objective: To provide the student with skills necessary to produce acceptable quality welds on pipe and tubing.

Learning Outcome: Upon successful completion of this course, the student will be able to prepare, fit, and tack weld pipe joints; weld pipe in all positions using the gas metal arc welding process; and inspect completed welds for quality.

Instruction: Major topics covered in the course are set up and adjustment of MIG equipment for welding pipe; manual techniques to perform quality welds in the 2F, 5F, IGR, 2G, 5G, and fixed positions; and review of prequalified welding procedure of specifications. Methods of instruction include lecture, discussion, instructor demonstrations, and hands-on lab practice.

Credit Recommendation: In the lower division baccalaureate/associate degree category, 3 semester hours in Steel Pipe Welding with GMAW (7/97).

Pipe and Tube Welding, SMAW (PTA 200)

Location: UAW Chrysler Technology Training Center.

Length: 80 hours (2 weeks).

Dates: April 1997-Present.

Objective: To provide the student with skills necessary to produce acceptable quality welds on pipe and tubing.

Learning Outcome: Upon successful completion of this course, the student will be able to prepare, fit, and tack weld pipe joints; weld pipe in all positions using the gas metal arc welding process (STICK); and inspect completed welds for quality.

Instruction: Major topics covered in the course are set up and adjustment of shielded metal arc equipment for welding pipe and manual techniques to perform quality fillet and groove welds in the 2F, 5F, IGR, 2G,and 5G positions. Methods of instruction include lecture, discussion, instructor demonstrations, and hands-on lab practice.

Credit Recommendation: In the lower division baccalaureate/associate degree category, 3 semester hours in Steel Pipe Welding with SMAW (7/97).

Pipe and Tube Welding, TIG (PTT 200)

Location: UAW Chrysler Technology Training Center.

Length: 80 hours (2 weeks).

Dates: April 1997-Present.

Objective: To provide the student with skills necessary to produce acceptable quality welds on pipe and tubing.

Learning Outcome: Upon successful completion of this course, the student will be able to prepare, fit and tack weld pipe joints; weld pipe in all positions using the gas tungsten welding process; and inspect completed welds for quality.

Instruction: Major topics covered in the course are a review of the TIG welding process and electric arc safety; welding codes and specifications; joint designs and variables that affect quality; and manual techniques needed to weld in 1GR, 2G, 5G, and 6G positions. Methods of instruction include lecture, discussion, instructor demonstrations, and hands-on lab practice.

Credit Recommendation: In the lower division baccalaureate/associate degree category, 3 semester hours in Steel Pipe Welding using GTAW (7/97).

PRAB F600 Control (PRB 206)

Location: Chrysler locations worldwide.

Length: 80 hours (2 weeks).

Dates: November 1986-Present.

Objective: To prepare the student to operate, program, and edit programs for the PRAB F600 robot.

Learning Outcome: Upon successful completion of this course, the student will be able to describe the physical components of the PRAB F600 robot, write and execute motion control programs, interactively operate the robot, construct a program controlled I/O device, perform preventive maintenance procedures, and troubleshoot the robot.

Instruction: Major topics covered in the course are general safety, robot movement control, major component description and location, system theory of operation, control operation, basic programming, and maintenance. Methods of instruction include lecture, demonstration, and laboratory exercises.

Credit Recommendation: In the lower division baccalaureate/associate degree category, 3 semester hours in Robotic Technology (4/89) (2/94). **NOTE:** Credit should not be awarded for both this course and PRAB F700 Control (PRB 207).

PRAB F700 Control (PRB 207)

Location: Chrysler locations worldwide.

Length: 80 hours (2 weeks).

Dates: November 1987-Present.

Objective: To prepare the student to operate, program, and edit programs for the PRAB F700 robot.

Learning Outcome: Upon successful completion of this course, the student will be able to describe the physical components of the PRAB F700 robot, write and execute motion control programs, operate the robot, construct a program to control I/O devices, perform preventive maintenance procedures, and troubleshoot the robot.

Instruction: Major topics covered in the course are general safety, robot movement control, major component description and location, system theory of operation, control operation, basic programming, and maintenance. Methods of instruction include lecture, demonstration, and laboratory exercises.

Credit Recommendation: In the lower division baccalaureate/associate degree category, 3 semester hours in Robotic Technology (4/89) (2/94). **NOTE:** Credit should not be awarded for both this course and PRAB F600 Control (PRB 206).

Programmable Controllers PLC-2 Family (BAB 102)

Location: Chrysler locations worldwide.

Length: 40 hours (1 week).

Dates: November 1983-Present.

Objective: To give the student an understanding of the parameters required for installing, operating, and basic troubleshooting the PLC-2 controller, including program editing.

Learning Outcome: Upon successful completion of this course, the student will be able to understand the operations and interfacing parameters of the PLC-2 controller; demonstrate the use and application of the PLC-2 controller in an industrial application; and identify the diagnostic troubleshooting indicators of the PLC-2 controller.

Instruction: Major topics covered in the course are 2/30 processor, cable installations, control functions for PLC-2 controller, logic diagrams, and hardware troubleshooting of PLC-2 controller. Methods of instruction include lecture and laboratory.

Credit Recommendation: In the vocational certificate category, 2 semester hours in Industrial Electrical Controls (9/88) (2/94).

Programmable Controllers PLC-2 Family Advanced Program (AAB 202)

Location: Chrysler locations worldwide.

Length: 40 hours (1 week).

Dates: November 1983-Present.

Objective: To give the student an understanding of the operation and programming of controller (PLC-2).

Learning Outcome: Upon successful completion of this course, the student will be able to input information and data into PLC-2 controller and analyze program operation; program PLC-2 controller to perform and control operation; and edit and troubleshoot program problems regarding the PLC-2.

Instruction: Major topics covered in the course are arithmetic instructions, program control, data transfer and comparison, subroutine and file concepts, sequencing, and block transfer instructions. Methods of instruction include lecture and laboratory.

Credit Recommendation: In the vocational certificate category, 2 semester hours in Industrial Electrical Controls (9/88) (2/94).

Programmable Controllers PLC-3 and PLC 3/10 Advanced Program (AAB 203)

Location: Chrysler locations worldwide.

Length: 40 hours (1 week).

Dates: September 1985-Present.

Objective: To introduce the student to the advanced operation and programming of PLC-3 and PLC-3/10 controllers and the utilization of the advanced instruction set to support machine diagnostics.

Learning Outcome: Upon successful completion of this course, the student will be able to input information and data into the PLC-3 and PLC-3/10 controllers and analyze program operation; program PLC-3 and PLC-3/10 controllers to perform and control operations; and edit and troubleshoot programming problems regarding the PLC-3 and PLC-3/10 controllers.

Instruction: Major topics covered in the course are PLC-3 controller, memory organization, forces, functions and instructions for PLC-3, file concepts and instructions, FIFO, block transfer instructions, and analog input and output usage. Methods of instruction include lecture and laboratory.

Credit Recommendation: In the vocational certificate category, 2 semester hours in Industrial Electrical Controls (9/88) (2/94).

Programmable Controllers PLC-3 and PLC-3/10 (BAB 103)

Location: Chrysler locations worldwide.

Length: 80 hours (2 weeks).

Dates: November 1983-Present.

Objective: To enable the student to understand the parameters required for installation, operation, and basic troubleshooting of the PLC-3 and PLC-3/10 controllers.

Learning Outcome: Upon successful completion of this course, the student will be able to understand the operations and interfacing parameters of the PLC-3 and PLC-3/10 controllers, demonstrate the use and application of the PLC-3 and PLC-3/10 controllers in an industrial application; and identify the diagnostic troubleshooting operations of the PLC-3 and PLC-3/10 controllers.

Instruction: Major topics covered in the course are PLC-3 processor, cable installation, relay ladder diagram conversion, processor mode selection and operation, diagnostic logic for PLC-3 processor, and hardware troubleshooting of PLC-3 and PLC-3/10 systems. Methods of instruction include lecture and laboratory.

Credit Recommendation: In the vocational certificate category, 4 semester hours in Industrial Electrical Controls (9/88) (2/94).

Programmable Controllers PLC-5 Family (BAB 105)

Location: Chrysler locations worldwide.

Length: *Version 1:* 40 hours (1 week); *Version 2:* 80 hours (2 weeks).

Dates: *Version 1:* April 1988-August 1992; *Version 2:* September 1992-Present.

Objective: *Version 1:* To develop the student's skills in the operation of the Allen-Bradley PLC-5/15 family controllers with a 1784-T50 terminal. *Version 2:* To develop skills in the programming and operation of the Allen-Bradley PLC-5/40 and PLC-5/60 programmable controllers.

Learning Outcome: *Version 1:* Upon successful completion of this course, the student will be able to convert a relay logic diagram into a PLC-5/15 program; identify various faults in operation of the controller; and properly set all switches and jumpers. *Version 2:* Upon successful completion of this course, the student will be able to properly install the necessary cabling required by a PLC-5 system, understand various ladder diagram instructions, install I/O sub-systems, identify faulty hardware modules, perform system configuration, and demonstrate proficiency in the use of ICOM software.

Instruction: *Version 1:* Major topics covered in the course are power supplies, processor boards, chassis component identification, introduction to T50 terminal, and programming and introduction to MS DOS. Methods of instruction include lecture and laboratory. *Version 2:* Major topics covered in the course are system installation, configuration, operation, and programming of the Allen-Bradley PLC-5/40 and PLC-5/60 programmable controller. Methods of instruction include lecture and laboratory exercises.

Credit Recommendation: *Version 1:* In the vocational certificate category, 2 semester hours in Industrial Electrical Controls (9/88)(2/94). *Version 2:* In the vocational certificate category, 4 semester hours in Industrial Electrical Controls (2/94).

Programmable Controllers—Modicon 484 (MOD 104)

Location: Chrysler locations worldwide.

Length: 40 hours (1 week).

Dates: November 1983-Present.

Objective: To provide the student with experiences designed to help him or her install, repair, and operate the Modicon 484 programmable controller.

Learning Outcome: Upon successful completion of this course, the student will be able to identify specific hardware and their functions on the Modicon 484 controller; operate the 484 using Modicon software programs; and identify problems indicated by the controller's diagnostic program.

Instruction: Major topics covered in the course are power supplies, processor, system software, I/O hardware, programming, and power distribution. Methods of instruction include lecture and laboratory.

Credit Recommendation: In the vocational certificate category, 2 semester

hours in Industrial Electrical Controls (9/88) (2/94).

Programmable Controllers—Modicon 584 (MOD 105)

Location: Chrysler locations worldwide.

Length: 80 hours (2 weeks).

Dates: September 1985-Present.

Objective: To develop the student's skills in the operation of the Modicon 584 controller with a P190 terminal using user programs.

Learning Outcome: Upon successful completion of this course, the student will be able to properly install all appropriate cables to the 584; properly set all switches and pins; and convert a relay logic diagram into a 584 program.

Instruction: Major topics covered in the course are block diagrams and mainframe hardware and configurations, I/O section hardware, conversion from relay logic to PC logic, Modicon 584 element references, timer instructions, and configuring Modicon 584 system I/O. Methods of instruction include lecture and laboratory.

Credit Recommendation: In the vocational certificate category, 4 semester hours in Industrial Electrical Controls (9/88) (2/94).

Programmable Logic Controllers: Advanced Allen Bradley PLC-5 Family/6200 Software (AAB 205)

Location: UAW Chrysler Technology Training Center.

Length: 40 hours (1 week).

Dates: April 1997-Present.

Objective: To train the students how to program, edit, and troubleshoot Allen Bradley PLC-5 Programmable Logic Controllers.

Learning Outcome: Upon successful completion of this course, the student will be able to enter, edit, and troubleshoot automation systems using the Allen Bradley PLC-5 Programmable Logic Controller.

Instruction: Major topics covered in the course are basic instructions using Allen Bradley 6200 software, hardware, and troubleshooting techniques. Methods of instruction include lecture, discussion, troubleshooting exercises, and hands-on labs.

Credit Recommendation: In the vocational certificate category or in the lower division baccalaureate/associate degree category, 2 semester hours in Industrial/Electrical Controls (7/97).

Programmable Logic Controllers: Advanced Allen Bradley PLC-5 Family/6200 Software (AAB 205)

Location: Chrysler locations worldwide.

Length: 40 hours (1 week).

Dates: January 1995-Present.

Objective: To train the students how to program, edit and troubleshoot Allen Bradley PLC-5 Programmable Logic Controllers.

Learning Outcome: Upon successful completion of this course, the student will be able to enter, edit and troubleshoot automation systems using the Allen Bradley PLC-5 Programmable Logic Controller.

Instruction: Major topics covered in the course are advanced instructions using Allen Bradley 6200 software, hardware and troubleshooting techniques. Methods of instruction include lecture/discussion, troubleshooting exercises and hands-on labs.

Credit Recommendation: In the vocational certificate category, or in the lower division baccalaureate/associate degree category, 2 semester hours in Industrial Electrical Controls (9/88) (2/94) (7/97).

Programmable Logic Controllers: Advanced Allen Bradley PLC-5 Family/ICOM Software (AIC 205)

Location: UAW Chrysler Technology Training Center.

Length: 40 hours (1 week).

Dates: April 1997-Present.

Objective: To train the students how to program, edit, and troubleshoot Allen Bradley PLC-5 Programmable Logic Controllers.

Learning Outcome: Upon successful completion of this course, the student will be able to enter, edit, and troubleshoot automation systems using the Allen Bradley PLC-5 Programmable Logic Controller.

Instruction: Major topics covered in the course are basic instructions using Allen Bradley ICOM software, hardware, and troubleshooting techniques. Methods of instruction include lecture, discussion, troubleshooting exercises, and hands-on labs.

Credit Recommendation: In the vocational certificate category or in the lower division baccalaureate/associate degree category, 2 semester hours in the Industrial/Electrical Controls (7/97).

Programmable Logic Controllers: Advanced Allen Bradley PLC-5 Family/ICOM Software (AIC 205)

Location: Chrysler locations worldwide.

Length: 80 hours (1 week).

Dates: January 1995-Present.

Objective: To train the students how to program edit and troubleshoot Allen Bradley PLC-5 Programmable Logic Controllers.

Learning Outcome: Upon successful completion of this course, the student will be able to enter, edit and troubleshoot automation systems using the Allen Bradley PLC-5 Programmable Logic Controller.

Instruction: Major topics covered in the course are advanced instructions using Allen Bradley ICOM software, hardware and troubleshooting techniques. Methods of instruction include lecture, discussion, troubleshooting exercises and hands-on labs.

Credit Recommendation: In the vocational certificate category, or in the lower division baccalaureate/associate degree category, 2 semester hours in Industrial Electrical Controls (9/88) (2/94) (7/97).

Programmable Logic Controllers: Allen Bradley PLC-5 Family/ICOM Software (BIC 101)

Location: UAW Chrysler Technology Training Center.

Length: 80 hours (2 weeks).

Dates: April 1997-Present.

Objective: To train the students how to program, edit, and troubleshoot Allen Bradley PLC-5 Programmable Logic Controllers.

Learning Outcome: Upon successful completion of this course, the student will be able to enter, edit, and troubleshoot automation systems using the Allen Bradley PLC-5 Programmable Logic Controller.

Instruction: Major topics covered in the course are basic instructions using Allen Bradley ICOM software, hardware, and troubleshooting techniques. Methods of instruction include lecture, discussion, troubleshooting exercises, and hands-on labs.

Credit Recommendation: In the vocational certificate category or in the lower division baccalaureate/associate degree category, 4 semester hours in Industrial/ Electrical Controls (7/97).

Programmable Logic Controllers: Allen Bradley PLC-5 Family/ICOM Software (BIC 101)

Location: Chrysler locations worldwide.

Length: 80 hours (1 week).

Dates: January 1995-Present.

Objective: To train the students how to program edit and troubleshoot Allen Bradley PLC-5 Programmable Logic Controllers.

Learning Outcome: Upon successful completion of this course, the student will be able to enter, edit, and troubleshoot automation systems using the Allen Bradley PLC-5 Programmable Logic Controller.

Instruction: Major topics covered in the course are basic instructions using Allen Bradley ICOM software, hardware and troubleshooting techniques. Methods of instruction include lecture, discussion, troubleshooting exercises and hands-on labs.

Credit Recommendation: In the vocational certificate category, or in the lower division baccalaureate/associate degree category, 4 semester hours in Industrial Electrical Controls (2/94) (7/97).

Qualification/Certification of Welding Skills for Pipe and Tube (TIG and GTAW) (WQT 404)

Location: UAW Chrysler Technology Training Center.

Length: 40 hours (1 week).

Dates: April 1997-Present.

Objective: To provide the student with the opportunity to demonstrate welding skills by completing welder qualification test(s) specified by the American Welding Society, American Society of Mechanical Engineers, and/or the Canadian Welding Bureau.

Learning Outcome: Upon successful completion of this course, the student will be able to receive a welder qualification certificate for passing a visual inspection and passing a guided bend test or fillet break test.

Instruction: Major topics covered in the course are welding codes and qualifications, material preparation, and fit-up. Methods of instruction include lecture, discussion, problem solving, and extensive performance tests that measure the level of skills needed to meet industrial code requirements for welding pipe and tube.

Credit Recommendation: In the lower division baccalaureate/associate degree category, 2 semester hours in Steel Pipe Welding (7/97).

Qualification/Certification of Welding Skills for Sheet Metal, Aluminum (WQT 407)

Location: UAW Chrysler Technology Training Center.

Length: 40 hours (1 week).

Dates: April 1997-Present.

Objective: To provide the student with the opportunity to demonstrate welding skills by completing welder qualification test(s) specified by the American Welding Society, American Society of Mechanical Engineers, and/or the Canadian Welding Bureau.

Learning Outcome: Upon successful completion of this course, the student will be able to receive a welder qualification certificate for passing a visual inspection and passing a guided bend test or fillet break test.

Instruction: Major topics covered in the course are a review of welding codes and specifications, material preparation and joint designs, distortion control, selection of electrodes, filler metals, and shielding gases. Methods of instruction include lecture, discussion, problem solving, and performance testing that measure the level of skills needed to meet American Welding Society (AWS) Sheet Metal Welding Code-D9.1.

Credit Recommendation: In the lower division baccalaureate/associate degree category, 2 semester hours in Aluminum Sheet Metal with GMAW and GTAW (7/97).

Qualification/Certification of Welding Skills for Sheet Metal, Steel, and Stainless (WQT 406)

Location: UAW Chrysler Technology Training Center.

Length: 40 hours (1 week).

Dates: April 1997-Present.

Objective: To provide the student with the opportunity to demonstrate welding skills by completing welder qualification test(s) specified by the American Welding Society, American Society of Mechanical Engineers, and/or the Canadian Welding Bureau.

Learning Outcome: Upon successful completion of this course, the student will be eligible to receive a welder qualification certificate for passing a visual inspection and passing a guided bend test or fillet break test.

Instruction: Major topics covered in the course are a review of welding codes and specifications, material preparation and joint fit-up, distortion control, selection of electrodes, filler metals, and shielding gases. Methods of instruction include lecture, discussion, problem solving exercises, and performance tests that measure the level of skills needed to meet AWS Sheet Metal Welding Code D9.1 requirements.

Credit Recommendation: In the lower division baccalaureate/associate degree category, 2 semester hour in General Welding Qualification (GMAW, FCAW, GTAW, and SMAW) (7/97).

Qualification/Certification of Welding Skills for Steel Pipe (MIG) (GMAW) (WQT 402)

Location: UAW Chrysler Technology Training Center.

Length: 40 hours (1 week).

Dates: April 1997-Present.

Objective: To provide the student with the opportunity to demonstrate welding skills by completing welder qualification test(s) specified by the American Welding Society, American Society of Mechanical Engineers, and/or the Canadian Welding Bureau.

Learning Outcome: Upon successful completion of this course, the student will be able to receive a welder qualification certificate for passing a visual inspection and passing a guided bend test or fillet break test.

Instruction: Major topics covered in the course are welding codes and qualifications, a review of safe practices, material preparation, and fit up of joint details. Methods of instruction include lecture, discussion, problem solving, and extensive performance tests that measure the level of skills needed to meet industrial welding code requirements.

Credit Recommendation: In the lower division baccalaureate/associate degree category, 2 semester hours in Steep Pipe Welding (GMAW) (7/97).

Qualification/Certification of Welding Skills for Steel Pipe (SMAW) (WQT 403)

Location: UAW Chrysler Technology Training Center.

Length: 40 hours (1 week).

Dates: April 1997-Present.

Objective: To provide the student with the opportunity to demonstrate welding skills by completing welder qualification test(s) specified by the American Welding

Society, American Society of Mechanical Engineers, and/or the Canadian Welding Bureau.

Learning Outcome: Upon successful completion of this course, the student will be able to receive a welder qualification certificate for passing a visual inspection and passing a guided bend test or fillet break test.

Instruction: Major topics covered in the course are welding codes and qualifications, a review of safe practice, and material preparation. Methods of instruction include lecture, discussion, problem solving, and extensive performance tests that measure the level of skills needed to meet industrial welding code requirements.

Credit Recommendation: In the lower division baccalaureate/degree category, 2 semester hours in Steel Pipe Welding (GMAW) (7/97).

Qualification/Certification of Welding Skills for Structural Aluminum (WQT 401)

Location: UAW Chrysler Technology Training Center.

Length: 40 hours (1 week).

Dates: April 1997-Present.

Objective: To provide the student with the opportunity to demonstrate welding skills by completing welder qualification test(s) as specified by the American Welding Society, American Society of Mechanical Engineers, and/or the Canadian Welding Bureau.

Learning Outcome: Upon successful completion of this course, the student will be able to receive a welder qualification certificate for passing a visual inspection and passing a guided bend test or fillet break test.

Instruction: Major topics covered in the course are a review of welding procedure specifications, variables that affect weld quality, and preparation of metal coupons for destructive testing. Methods of instruction include lecture, discussion, problem solving exercises, and extensive performance tests that measure the level of skills needed to meet the AWS D1.2 Aluminum Welding Code.

Credit Recommendation: In the lower division baccalaureate/associate degree category, 2 semester hours in Structural Aluminum Welding with GMAW and GTAW (7/97).

Qualification/Certification of Welding Skills for Structural Steel (WQC 400)

Location: UAW Chrysler Technology Training Center.

Length: 40 hours (1 week).

Dates: April 1997-Present.

Objective: To provide the student with the opportunity to demonstrate welding skills by completing welder qualification test(s) as specified by the American Welding Society, American Society of Mechanical Engineers, and/or the Canadian Welding Bureau.

Learning Outcome: Upon successful completion of this course, the student will be able to receive a welder qualification certificate for passing a visual inspection and passing a guided bend test or fillet break test.

Instruction: Major topics covered in the course are a review of welding procedure specifications, variables that affect weld quality, and preparation of metal coupons for destructive testing. Methods of instruction include lecture, discussion, problem solving exercises, and welding performance tests on ASTM A-36 structural steel plate in 2F, 3G, and 4G positions.

Credit Recommendation: In the lower division baccalaureate/associate degree category, 2 semester hours in Structural Steel Welding (7/97).

Qualification/Certification of Welding Skills for Tool and Die (WQT 405)

Location: UAW Chrysler Technology Training Center.

Length: 40 hours (1 week).

Dates: April 1997-Present.

Objective: To provide the student with the opportunity to demonstrate welding skills by completing welder qualification test(s) as specified by the Chrysler Die Engineering process standards.

Learning Outcome: Upon successful completion of this course, the student will be able to receive a welder qualification certificate for passing a visual inspection; passing a cross section and etch test; and passing a die penetrant test inspection.

Instruction: Major topics covered in the course are allowable repairs, problem solving exercises, and acceptable criteria per Die Engineering process standards. Methods of instruction include extensive performance testing to measure the level of skills and competency required to weld tool and die materials.

Credit Recommendation: In the lower division baccalaureate/associate degree category, 2 semester hours in Tool And Die Welding (7/97).

Resistance Welding Technology (RWT 101)

Location: Chrysler locations worldwide.

Length: 40 hours (1 week).

Dates: January 1983-Present.

Objective: To enable the student to set up, maintain, and troubleshoot resistance welding equipment.

Learning Outcome: Upon successful completion of this course, the student will be able to demonstrate the ability to safely set up a welding situation; demonstrate the ability to compensate for factors that affect the welding process; and distinguish the quality of a given weld.

Instruction: Major topics covered in the course are safety, resistance welding, weld quality, weld hardware, weld machines, and troubleshooting. Methods of instruction include lecture and laboratory.

Credit Recommendation: In the lower division baccalaureate/associate degree category, 2 semester hours in Welding Technology (9/88) (2/94).

Structural Steel Welding (WST 200)

Location: UAW Chrysler Technology Training Center.

Length: 40 hours (1 week).

Dates: April 1997-Present.

Objective: To enable the student to produce acceptable quality welds on structural steel using the shielded metal arc and flux-colored arc welding processes.

Learning Outcome: Upon successful completion of this course, the student will be able to prepare structural steel for welding; set up and adjust welding equipment; and weld structural steel in all positions.

Instruction: Major topics covered in the course are material specification, weld joint design, tacking and fit up, filler metal selection and storage of low hydrogen electrodes, set up and adjustment of equipment, and welding techniques. Methods of instruction include lecture, discussion, problem solving exercises, hands-on labs, and an application project.

Credit Recommendation: In the lower division baccalaureate/associate degree

category, 2 semester hours in Welding Structural Steel with SMAW and FCAW (7/97).

Vehicle Automatic Temperature Control Systems

Location: Chrysler locations worldwide.

Length: 32 hours.

Dates: August 1986-Present.

Objective: To provide an understanding of Automotive Automatic Temperature Control Systems.

Learning Outcome: Upon successful completion of this course, the student will be able to understand principles of automatic temperature control systems; perform diagnostic procedures for automatic temperature control systems; and understand component operation of automatic temperature control systems.

Instruction: Major topics covered in the course are the principles of automatic temperature control systems, automatic temperature control diagnostic systems, and component testing. Methods of instruction include lecture and laboratory.

Credit Recommendation: In the lower division baccalaureate/associate degree category, 2 semester hours in Automotive Technology (4/90) (5/95).

Vehicle Electrical/Electronic Systems (PO1 VEE)

Location: Chrysler locations worldwide.

Length: 40 hours (1 or 2 weeks).

Dates: June 1988-Present.

Objective: To provide the student with the basic understanding of automotive electrical systems and related electronic components.

Learning Outcome: Upon successful completion of this course, the student will be able to read wiring diagrams, troubleshoot electrical problems, use test equipment, and have a basic understanding of electrical fundamentals and multiplexing.

Instruction: Major topics covered in the course are the fundamentals of electricity, electronic symbols and wiring diagrams, use of test equipment, diagnostic techniques, and introduction to multiplexing. Methods of instruction include lecture and laboratory exercises.

Credit Recommendation: In the lower division baccalaureate/associate degree category, 2 semester hours in Automotive Technology (4/89) (2/94).

Vehicle Manual Temperature Control Systems (Formerly Vehicle Manual Climate Control Systems)

Location: Chrysler locations worldwide.

Length: 32 hours.

Dates: August 1986-Present.

Objective: To provide an understanding of basic climate control systems.

Learning Outcome: Upon successful completion of this course, the student will be able to understand the basic principles in automotive air conditioning systems; perform diagnosis and troubleshooting of manual climate control systems; and understand climate control component operation.

Instruction: Major topics covered in the course are automotive air conditioning theory and principle, component operation, diagnostic procedures, electrical controls, and climate control system service. Methods of instruction include lecture and laboratory.

Credit Recommendation: In the lower division baccalaureate/associate degree category, 2 semester hours in Automotive Technology (4/90) (5/95).

Weld Controllers (RWC 101)

Location: Chrysler locations worldwide.

Length: 40 hours (1 week).

Dates: March 1984-Present.

Objective: To provide the student with a basic understanding of the installation, programming, editing, and troubleshooting of "Pertron" or "Medar" microprocessor-based WC-2 weld controllers.

Learning Outcome: Upon successful completion of this course, the student will be able to identify component parts and their functions; identify steps to be taken when given the status of diagnostic indicators; and diagnose and isolate a defective part within the weld controller.

Instruction: Major topics covered in the course are safety, functions, hardware, and programming of the "Pertron" and "Medar" WC-2 controllers. Methods of instruction include lecture and laboratory.

Credit Recommendation: In the lower division baccalaureate/associate degree category, 2 semester hours in Welding Technology (9/88) (2/94). **NOTE:** To receive credit for this course, the student must have received credit for Resistance Welding Technology (RWT 101).

Welding Aluminum Alloys (WAA 200)

Location: UAW Chrysler Technology Training Center.

Length: 40 hours (1 week).

Dates: April 1997-Present.

Objective: To provide the student with skills necessary to weld aluminum alloys using recommended welding processes and filler metals.

Learning Outcome: Upon successful completion of this course, the student will be able to select the appropriate welding process for aluminum; select the appropriate filler metal; set up and adjust the welding equipment; and produce acceptable quality welds on aluminum alloys.

Instruction: Major topics covered in the course are aluminum material specifications, selection of welding filler metals, surface preparation prior to welding, shielding gas selection, AC and DC, and DCEN. Methods of instruction include lecture, discussion, problem solving, instructor demonstrations, hands-on labs, and an application project.

Credit Recommendation: In the lower division baccalaureate/associate degree category, 2 semester hours in Welding Aluminum (7/97).

Welding Safety and Overview of Processes (WWP 100)

Location: UAW Chrysler Technology Training Center.

Length: 40 hours (1 week).

Dates: April 1997-Present.

Objective: To provide the student with a general understanding of manual and semi-automatic welding processes used in metal working industries. In addition, the course will prepare the student to safely operate oxy-fuel gas and electric arc welding equipment per Chrysler MTI SMI-116.

Learning Outcome: Upon successful completion of this course, the student will be able to safely set-up and operate oxy-fuel cutting and electric arc welding equipment.

Instruction: Major topics covered in the course are related hazards and safety precautions; proper set up adjustment of oxy-fuel gas and electric arc welding and cutting equipment; and the following welding processes: shielded metal arc, gas metal arc, gas tungsten arc, plasma arc, and oxy-fuel gas cutting. Methods of instruction include lecture, discussion, instructor demonstrations, hands-on lab practices, problem solving, and a performance test.

Credit Recommendation: In the lower division baccalaureate/associate degree category, 2 semester hours in Welding Safety (7/97).

Welding Sheet Metal (WSM 200)

Location: UAW Chrysler Technology Training Center.

Length: 40 hours (1 week).

Dates: April 1997-Present.

Objective: To enable the student to produce acceptable quality welds on sheet metal using the shielded metal arc (STICK), gas metal arc (MIG), and gas tungsten arc welding process (TIG).

Learning Outcome: Upon successful completion of this course, the student will be able to identify the welding processes to use; set up and adjust welding equipment; and weld sheet metal in flat, horizontal, and vertical down welding positions.

Instruction: Major topics covered in the course are material specifications, weld joint designs, techniques for quality welds, process selection, filler metal selection, and distortion control. Methods of instruction include lecture, discussion, instructor demonstrations, and hands-on labs.

Credit Recommendation: In the lower division baccalaureate/associate degree category, 2 semester hours in Sheet Metal Welding using SMAW, GMAW, and GTAW (7/97).

Welding Tool and Die Steels (WTD 200)

Location: UAW Chrysler Technology Training Center.

Length: 40 hours (1 week).

Dates: April 1997-Present.

Objective: To enable the student to successfully repair weld tool and die steels using approved welding processes and procedures.

Learning Outcome: Upon successful completion of this course, the student will be able to identify various tool steels; apply the appropriate preheat; weld repair-worn or broken tools; and apply the appropriate post weld heat treatment.

Instruction: Major topics covered in the course are welding repair procedures for tool steels and cast die materials, material identification, hardness testing, preparation of material surfaces for welding, and preheat and postheat schedules. Methods of instruction include lecture, discussion, problem solving exercises, hands-on labs, and an application project.

Credit Recommendation: In the lower division baccalaureate/associate degree category, 2 semester hours in Tool and Die Welding (7/97).

Chubb Institute

Founded in 1970 by The Chubb Corporation, a Fortune 100 financial services company, The Chubb Institute is an independent subsidiary that provides classroom training in business-oriented computer subjects to the public and industry. The career division provides entry-level business programming and operating training to self-sponsored individuals and to company-sponsored students; the corporate division provides company customers with advanced programming courses for their experienced programmers and introductory computer courses for their non-data processing personnel. The Institute has a traditional approach to training, featuring experienced instructors who also have work experience in the field, a classroom environment to stimulate student/instructor interaction, and a skills oriented curriculum supported by practical workshop exercises.

The Chubb Institute operates three facilities: a main campus in the Parsippany Corporate Center near the intersections of Interstates 80 and 287, a branch campus at Journal Square in Jersey City across from the PATH station and another branch campus, Keystone Campus at Swarthmore, PA. These facilities house a computer center with an IBM mainframe unit for use by both programming and operations students.

The Chubb Institute's entry-level programming and operating curriculum's are approved by the New Jersey Department of Education, approved for veteran's training, and the Institute is accredited by the Accrediting Commission of the National Association of Trade and Technical Schools.

Source of official student records: Registry of Credit Recommendations, American Council on Education, One Dupont Circle, Washington, DC 20036-1193.

Additional information about the courses: Office of Corporate-Higher Education Programs, Thomas Edison State College, 101 West State Street, Trenton, NJ 08608-1176.

Advanced Business Programming Applied Business Programming II (ABP II)

Location: Parsippany, Jersey City and North Brunswick, NJ; Springfield, PA; New York, NY.

Length: 120 hours.

Dates: November 1993-Present.

Objective: To reinforce the structure and operations of relational databases using Microsoft Access to program in a Windows environment using Microsoft Visual BASIC; and to teach effective interviewing and resume writing skills.

Learning Outcome: Upon successful completion of this course, the student will be able to create, design, and use queries, forms, and reports in Access; program business applications using Visual BASIC; and develop job readiness skills.

Instruction: Major topics covered in the course are instruction in the use of Access; and hands-on instruction in the development of Windows-based applications using Visual BASIC. Methods of instruction include lectures, workshops, reading assignments to facilitate learning, simulated technical interviews, oral presentations by the student, and a career counseling workshop.

Credit Recommendation: In the lower division baccalaureate/associate or upper division baccalaureate degree category , 3 semester hours in Visual Basic and 1 semester hour in Database Applications using Access; and in the lower division baccalaureate/associate degree category, 1 semester hour in Career Development Workshop; for a total of 5 semester hours (10/96).

Advanced Operations (Formerly Advanced Labs)

Location: Parsippany, Jersey City, NJ and Springfield, PA.

Length: 105 hours (4 weeks).

Dates: February 1987-August 1994.

Objective: To give the student a working knowledge of VM/CMS and alternate operating systems, and the ability to perform a DOS to OS complete system conversion.

Learning Outcome: Upon successful completion of this course, the student will be able to display a working knowledge of the VM/CMS system, including XEDIT and its various commands; have a fundamental understanding of other manufacturer's operating systems; and perform a system conversion from DOS to OS.

Instruction: Major topics covered in the course are the VM/CMS system, XEDIT is employed throughout the course so the student is completely familiar with its usage, how XEDIT fits into the CMS environment, CMS commands and the operation of DOS/VSE/SP and OS/VS1 under the VM/CMS system, the student is introduced to other manufacturers' equipment, thorough knowledge of DOS/VSE/SP and OS/VS1 enables students to understand that the skills they have acquired are applicable in any data processing environment, and DOS to OS conversion (this reinforces concepts and skills learned about both operating systems and the functional knowledge of what an operating system does while providing added practice in overall system operation).

Credit Recommendation: In the lower division baccalaureate/associate degree category, 3 semester hours in Current Operations Topics (12/89) (6/94).

Advanced Program Design (APD)

Location: Parsippany, Jersey City, NJ and Springfield, PA.

Length: 105 hours (4 weeks).

Dates: April 1992-October 1993.

Objective: To enable the student to code, test and debug a computer program in the assembler language; and provide the student with an understanding of the key logic structures as applied to business applications.

Learning Outcome: Upon successful completion of this course, the student will be able to know and apply fixed point, decimal and logical instructions in the assembler language; design, code, test and debug an assembler program; design solutions to meet business application programming problems; design test data; and apply test data and debugging techniques to business application programs.

Instruction: Major topics covered in the course are a solid base on which other computer languages and concepts may be built, how to design, code, and test assembler language programs, thorough problem analysis, the importance of sound design techniques, input/output concepts, print commands, loop structures, validation routines, elementary table handling techniques, control break logic, advanced table handling techniques, simple match processing, update processing, random updates, testing and debugging techniques, and designing test data. Methods of instruction include lectures, workshops, reading assignments, drills out of class, and a programming project.

Credit Recommendation: In the lower division baccalaureate/associate or upper division baccalaureate degree category, 2 semester hours in Assembler Language and 2 semester hours in Introduction to Programming Design, for a total of 4 semester hours (6/94).

Applications Laboratory (LABS)

Location: Parsippany, Jersey City, NJ and Springfield, PA.

Length: 125 hours (5 weeks).

Dates: January 1974-December 1984.

Objective: To provide a student with Advanced COBOL and Assembler techniques including Structured programming techniques, Program linkage, documentation, file structure, data base concepts and VSAM file processing.

Instruction: Major topics covered in the course consist of lecture and work sessions. Students design, code, test and debug four programs of varying complexity. Other topics covered in the course are Structured Programming Techniques, data base systems, mini computers, Advanced COBOL techniques and Advanced Assembler techniques; program linkage, VSAM file processing, program documentation and computer output to microfilm. In all their projects students are required to write the JCL needed to run the projects. All projects consist of multiple steps and include source library maintenance.

Credit Recommendation: In the upper division baccalaureate category, 3 semester hours in Cobol II and 3 semester hours in Assembler Language II. (When taken after Cobol and Assembler Language, this course provides rich application skills comparable to a second semester in both of these topics (11/83).

Assembler Language

Location: Parsippany, Jersey City, NJ and Springfield, PA.

Length: 105 hours (4 weeks).

Dates: September 1984-March 1992.

Objective: To enable the student to design, code, test and debug a computer program in the Assembler language.

Learning Outcome: Upon successful completion of this course, the student will know and apply fixed point, decimal and logical instructions in the Assembler language. The student will be able to design, code, test and debug a computer program in the Assembler Language.

Instruction: Major topics covered in the course gives the student the opportunity to learn their first programming language in an environment conducive to understanding "how the machine works." Covered are the instructions and concepts needed to give the student the basic skills required of an Assembler language programmer. It provides a solid base on which other computer languages and concepts may build. It is designed so that learning is accomplished by lectures and workshops during class hours and by reading assignments and drills outside of class. The student designs, codes and tests Assembler language applications programs and completes a programming project from design through debugging in the Assembler language.

Credit Recommendation: In the lower division baccalaureate/associate or upper division baccalaureate degree category, 4 semester hours in Assembler Language (12/89). **NOTE:** To earn the credit recommendation, the student must complete the Programming Labs course, in which the student actually develops additional programs in Assembler Language.

Assembler Language (ASM)

Location: Parsippany, Jersey City, NJ and Springfield, PA.

Length: 75 hours (3 weeks).

Dates: January 1974-December 1984.

Objective: To introduce students to fixed-point, decimal, and logical instructions, QSAM I/O macros, and Assembler program structure.

Instruction: Major topics covered in the course are fixed-point, decimal, and logical instructions; Data definition statements; Base registers, entry and return linkage; I/O Macros; EDIT, and TRT instructions. Course also covers: Multiple base registers; Multiple CSECTs; ADCONS, VCONS, LTORG, DSECT; BHX, BXLE; Linkage Editor and Loader functions; Basic dump debugging; Mainline and subroutine structures (BAL, CALL); Functions of the Assembler Translator program; and Workshops are included in this unit with emphasis on coding readable and maintainable assembler programs. Students design, code, test, and debug one program.

Credit Recommendation: In the lower division baccalaureate/associate or upper division baccalaureate degree category, 3 semester hours in Computer Systems or Computer Organization (11/83).

Basic Computer Operations

Location: Parsippany, Jersey City, NJ and Springfield, PA.

Length: 105 hours (4 weeks).

Dates: May 1992-August 1994.

Objective: To provide the student with a full understanding of the role of the mainframe computer in a data processing environment and an operating knowledge of various IBM mainframe devices and peripheral equipment.

Learning Outcome: Upon successful completion of this course, the student will: become familiar with various computer hardware devices, software, and the machine operating system; be introduced to data processing terms and concepts and how they are applied in the DP environment; become familiar with Video Display Terminal (VDT) operations.

Instruction: Major topics covered in the course include the basics of business data processing with emphasis on the role of the operator in running a data center; an introduction to hardware and software, including both business processing and operating systems; data processing terms and concepts are thoroughly defined; the interaction between hardware and software; follow an application system through the data processing center from the original job control language submission through the distribution of printed reports; and develop a basic foundation and hands-on working knowledge of the following computer hardware: central processing unit, direct access storage device, magnetic tape, master console, printer, terminal and control unit. Each student is required to operate this equipment to a standard of efficiency.

Credit Recommendation: In the lower division baccalaureate/associate degree category, 3 semester hours in Introduction to Data Processing and 4 semester hours in Computer Hardware for a cumulative total of 7 semester hours (12/89) (6/94).

Basic Program Design (Intro Concepts)

Location: Parsippany, Jersey City, NJ and Springfield, PA.

Length: 105 hours (4 weeks).

Dates: April 1992-October 1993.

Objective: To provide the student with a realistic view of what programming is and how it fits into the data processing and business environments.

Learning Outcome: Upon successful completion of this course, the student will be able to design, code, and test a simple COBOL program; design more sophisticated programs for coding in the assembler; become familiar with video display terminal operations; and have a realistic view of the position of the computer programmer in the business world.

Instruction: Major topics covered in the course are basics of business computer programming with emphasis on program design; COBOL language; how to design, code, and test a sample program via computer terminals; how a program fits into the applications system; more intricate program design instruction is given as students begin the study of their first programming language, assembler (done in an environment conducive to understanding "how the machine works"); database management, data communications, and operating system concepts; and hardware is reviewed in sufficient detail that students are able to understand the structure, organization, and manipulation of stored data.

Credit Recommendation: In the lower division baccalaureate/associate or upper division baccalaureate degree category, 3 semester hours in Introduction to Computer Programming and 2 semester hours in Assembler Language, for a total of 5 semester hours (6/94).

Basic Program Design (BPD)

Location: Parsippany, Jersey City, NJ and Springfield, PA.

Length: 75 hours (3 weeks).

Dates: January 1974-December 1984.

Objective: To present the most common data processing problems encountered in an applications environment, and teach students how to analyze these problems, design solutions, select appropriate test data, validate the problem solutions, and apply these techniques to the development of a (computer based) system.

Instruction: Major topics covered in the course are methods for problem analysis and program design, flowcharting techniques, and mainline and subroutine logic; and the logic involved in: data validation (single and multiple error analysis), sequence checks (ascending and descending keys), loop structure, master file updates, match programs, control breaks and summary reports, and table handling. Methods of instruction include lecture, about 15 hours of lab, and designing and flowcharting two major problems.

Credit Recommendation: In the lower division baccalaureate/associate or upper division baccalaureate degree category, 3 semester hours in Assembler Language I (11/83). **NOTE:** Student must also complete Programming Fundamentals to earn the credit recommendation. In addition, a student who completes Introduction to Computer Systems, Programming Fundamentals and Basic Program Design will earn 3 semester hours in the lower division baccalaureate/associate degree category in Introduction to Data Processing, and in the upper division baccalaureate category, 1 semester hour in Machine Organization and 3 semester hours in Assembler Language I, for a cumulative total of 7 semester hours.

COBOL

Location: Parsippany, Jersey City, NJ and Springfield, PA.

Length: 100-105 hours (4 weeks).

Dates: September 1984-October 1993.

Objective: To give the student the ability to produce readable and maintainable programs in COBOL code.

Learning Outcome: Upon successful completion of this course, the student will be able to apply ANSI COBOL coding rules; COBOL program structure; define and manipulate data; perform input and output operations.

Instruction: Major topics covered in the course are in-depth coverage of COBOL (the most widely used business programming language), coding rules, data definitions, input/output verbs, arithmetic verbs, sequence control verbs, comparisons, data manipulation, table handling, VSAM concepts, internal sort, linkage section use, and structured design techniques. Students are required to write, code and test COBOL programs.

Credit Recommendation: In the lower division baccalaureate/associate or upper division baccalaureate degree category, 3 semester hours in COBOL I and 3 semester hours in COBOL II for a total of six semester hours (12/89). **NOTE:** To earn the credit recommendation, the student must complete the Programming Labs course, in which the student actually develops additional programs in COBOL.

COBOL Language (COB)

Location: Parsippany, Jersey City, NJ and Springfield, PA.

Length: 75 hours (3 weeks).

Dates: January 1974-December 1984.

Objective: To introduce students to ANS COBOL coding rules, COBOL program structure, data definition and manipulation, input and output operations.

Instruction: Major topics covered in the course are divisions of a COBOL program; arithmetic verbs; I/O verbs; data definitions (77, 88, 01-49); move, if, perform; and table handling; indexing; subscripting; search; sort (using, giving, input procedure, output procedure); program linkage; COBOL listing maps; sequential and VSAM file processing; and coding techniques that produce readable and maintainable COBOL programs. Students design, code, test, and debug a COBOL program that edits the transaction file that is input to the Inventory project. The program produces an edited transaction disk file and a formatted error report.

Credit Recommendation: In the lower division baccalaureate/associate or upper division baccalaureate degree category, 3 semester hours in Cobol I (11/83).

COBOL/COBOL II

Location: Parsippany, Jersey City, NJ and Springfield, PA.

Length: 120 hours (4 weeks).

Dates: November 1993-Present.

Objective: To enable the student to program business problems using the COBOL language.

Learning Outcome: Upon successful completion of this course, the student will be able to understand and use the commands of the COBOL language.

Instruction: Major topics covered in the course are the syntax, structure, and proper use of COBOL and COBOL II (each of the four divisions of the language is covered in sequence with stressed placed on practical examples and real-world standards). Efficient and maintainable code is the unit goal. Methods of instruction include lecture and projects.

Credit Recommendation: In the lower division baccalaureate/associate or upper division baccalaureate degree category, 3 semester hours in COBOL I and 3 semester hours in COBOL II for a total of six semester hours (10/96).

Data Processing Fundamentals (Formerly Data Processing Foundations)

Location: Parsippany, Jersey City and North Brunswick, NJ; Springfield, PA; New York, NY.

Length: 120 hours.

Dates: November 1993-Present.

Objective: To provide the student with an overview of the business computing environment, organization of data, the concepts of records and files, as well as different formats and internal processes of the computer.

Learning Outcome: Upon successful completion of this course, the student will be able to understand the differences and similarities of mainframe and desktop computers; the structure of relational databases versus traditional file organization; identify the components of a computer, as well as perform elementary arithmetic in binary and hexadecimal; and create solutions to standard business problems using flowcharting techniques.

Instruction: Major topics covered in the course are a balanced descriptive treatment of multiple computer topics which include PC topics, microcomputer operating systems, number systems and codes, specific file access, fundamentals of database concepts, and theory of batch design. Methods of instruction include lectures, workshops, and reading assignments to facilitate learning.

Credit Recommendation: In the lower division baccalaureate/associate degree category, 1 semester hour in Data Processing Fundamentals, 2 semester hours in File Organization and Management, and 3 semester hours in Application Program Development-Fundamentals, for a total of 6 semester hours (10/96).

Hardware

Location: Parsippany, Jersey City, NJ and Springfield, PA.

Length: 55 hours.

Dates: February 1987-April 1992.

Objective: To give the student an operating knowledge of various IBM mainframe computer devices and peripheral equipment.

Learning Outcome: Upon successful completion of this course, the student will be able to operate a measurable standard of efficiency, the following computer mainframe devices: Central Processing Unit; Direct Access Storage Devices; Magnetic Tape; Master Console; Printers; Terminals; and Control Devices.

Instruction: Major topics covered in the course are a basic foundation and hands-on working knowledge of the following computer hardware: Central Processing Unit, Direct Access Storage Device, Magnetic Tape, Master Console, Printer, Terminal and Control Unit. Each student is required to operate all of the previously cited equipment to a standard of efficiency. Additionally, the student will understand the concepts of laser printers, mass storage devices, communications devices and card readers.

Credit Recommendation: In the lower division baccalaureate/associate degree category, 4 semester hours in Computer Hardware (12/89).

Intermediate Business Programming (Formerly Applied Business Programming I [ABP I])

Location: Parsippany, Jersey City and North Brunswick, NJ; Springfield, PA; New York, NY.

Length: 120 hours.

Dates: November 1993-Present.

Objective: To understand the foundations of applied database theory using DB2 and to enable students to program business problems using the C language.

Learning Outcome: Upon successful completion of this course, the student will be able to understand the syntax, structure, and major features of the C language; apply database theory by embedding DB2 code into COBOL application programs; and program business applications using the C language.

Instruction: Major topics covered in the course are in-depth instruction in the processing techniques for accessing DB2. SQL is also taught and instruction is given in the C programming language, with students developing an application using this language. Students continue their on-line development project in this unit by utilizing the CICS feature of MicroFocus Workbench to complete their programs. Methods of instruction include lectures, workshops, and reading assignments to facilitate learning.

Credit Recommendation: In the lower division baccalaureate/associate or upper division baccalaureate degree category, 2 semester hours in Database Applications using DB2, and 3 semester hours in C Programming I, for a total of 5 semester hours (10/96).

Introduction to Computer Operations

Location: Parsippany, Jersey City, NJ and Springfield, PA.

Length: 45 hours.

Dates: February 1987-April 1992.

Objective: To provide the student with a full understanding of the role of the mainframe computer in a data processing environment.

Learning Outcome: Upon successful completion of this course, the student will: become familiar with various computer hardware devices, software, and the machine operating system; be introduced to data processing terms and concepts and how they are applied in the DP environment; become familiar with Video Display Terminal (VDT) operations.

Instruction: Major topics covered in the course are the basics of business data processing with emphasis on the role of the operator in running a data center. Students are introduced to hardware and software, including both business processing and operating systems. Data processing terms and concepts are thoroughly defined and students concentrate on learning the interaction between hardware and software. Students follow an application system through the data processing center from the original job control language submission through the distribution of printed reports. Upon completion, students have a realistic picture of what computer operations is and the role of the operator in the data processing environment.

Credit Recommendation: In the lower division baccalaureate/associate degree category, 3 semester hours in Introduction to Data Processing (12/89).

Introduction to Computer Programming (Formerly Introduction to Data Processing)

Location: Parsippany, Jersey City, NJ and Springfield, PA.

Length: *Version 1:* 35 hours (7 days); *Version 2:* 45 hours (9 days).

Dates: *Version 1:* September 1984-September 1985; *Version 2:* October 1985-March 1992.

Objective: To provide the students with a realistic view of what programming is and how it fits into the data processing and business environments.

Learning Outcome: Upon successful completion of this course, the student will: be able to design, code and test a simple COBOL program; become familiar with video display terminal operations; have a realistic view of the position of the computer programmer in the business world.

Instruction: Major topics covered in the course are the basics of business computer programming with emphasis on program design. Students are introduced to a subset of COBOL programming language so they can design, code and test a sample program via computer terminals and understand how a program fits into the applications system. Database management, data communications and operating systems concepts are also introduced. Hardware is reviewed in sufficient detail that students are able to understand the structure, organization and manipulation of stored data.

Credit Recommendation: *Version 1:*In the lower division baccalaureate/associate degree category, 3 semester hours in Introduction to Computer Programming (12/89). **NOTE:** Students must complete Introduction to Data Processing and Logic I & II in order to receive the credit recommendation. *Version 2:* In the lower division baccalaureate/associate degree category, 3 semester hours in Introduction to Computer Programming (12/89).

Introduction to Computer Systems (ICS)

Location: Parsippany, Jersey City, NJ and Springfield, PA.

Length: 23 hours (5 days).

Dates: January 1974-December 1984.

Objective: To provide a thorough introduction to computer systems, computer concepts, programming, and data processing terminology. A basic introduction to binary and hexadecimal number systems is also covered.

Instruction: Major topics covered in the course introduce students to the components of a computer system including: Descriptions of data storage hardware, including disks, drums, tapes, card readers, printers (impact and laser), and MSS; Main storage; Arithmetic/Logic Unit; and Control Unit. Also covered are: Storage addressing (absolute addresses, relative addresses), Binary and hexadecimal number systems (binary and hexadecimal arithmetic), and the steps involved in problem solving. Finally this course treats the differences between logical and physical records, file organizations, record formats, and basic operating system concepts.

Credit Recommendation: In the lower division baccalaureate/associate degree category, if Programming Fundamentals (PRF) is also successfully completed, 3 semester hours in Introduction to Data Processing and in the upper division baccalaureate category, 1 semester hour in Machine Organization (11/83). **NOTE:** No credit recommended if Introduction to Computer Systems taken alone.

Logic (Formerly Logic I & II)

Location: Parsippany, Jersey City, NJ and Springfield, PA.

Length: 65 hours (13 days) for both courses.

Dates: *Version 1:* September 1984-September 1985; *Version 2:* October 1985-March 1992.

Objective: To provide the student with an understanding of basic logic structures as applied to business application programming.

Learning Outcome: Upon successful completion of this course, the student will be able to design solutions to meet business application programming problems; design test data; and apply test and debugging techniques to business application programs.

Instruction: Major topics covered in the course are thorough problem analysis, the importance of sound design techniques, input/output concepts, print commands, loop structures, validation routines, elementary table handling techniques, control break logic, advanced table handling techniques, simple match processing, update processing, random updates, testing and debugging techniques, and designing test data.

Credit Recommendation: *Version 1:* In the lower division baccalaureate/associate or upper division baccalaureate degree category, 2 semester hours in Introduction to Programming Design (12/89). **NOTE:** Students must complete Introduction to Data Processing and Logic I & II to receive the credit recommendation. No credit recommendation for Logic I & II if taken alone. *Version 2:* In the lower division baccalaureate/associate degree category, 2 semester hours in Introduction to Programming Design (12/89).

Multi-Platform Programming

Location: Parsippany, Jersey City and North Brunswick, NJ; Springfield, PA; New York, NY.

Length: 120 hours.

Dates: November 1993-Present.

Objective: To implement the full Program Development Life Cycle using MicroFocus Workbench and to program for an on-line processing environment running under CICS.

Learning Outcome: Upon successful completion of this course, the student will be able to develop and test COBOL programs using MicroFocus Workbench; and design, code, test, and implement an interactive system using CICS and COBOL II.

Instruction: Major topics covered in the course are implementing the full program Development Life-Cycle of designing, writing, testing, and debugging their programs on the mainframe as well as the PC using MicroFocus Workbench. This unit also provides in-depth instruction in programming for an on-line processing environment. Students will code, test, and debug a sample application running under CICS. Methods of instruction include lectures, workshops, and reading assignments to facilitate learning.

Credit Recommendation: In the lower division baccalaureate/associate or upper division baccalaureate degree category, 2 semester hours in MicroFocus Programming Projects, and 2 semester hours in On-Line Development Using CICS, for a total of 4 semester hours (10/96).

Operating Systems Fundamentals (OS/VS)

Location: Parsippany, Jersey City, NJ and Springfield, PA.

Length: 75 hours (3 weeks).

Dates: January 1974-September 1985.

Objective: To introduce students to Operating Systems Fundamentals, MVS JCL, MVS Data Management Utilities, and MVS Debugging using System Dumps.

Instruction: Major topics covered in the course include the functional components of the Operating System are covered with emphasis on the development of conceptual understanding of the job, task, and data management facilities. In the MVS JCL section emphasis is placed on both JCL syntax and coding techniques. The JOB, EXEC, and DD statements and related parameters are covered in-depth as is the use and manipulation of Cataloged Procedures. The Data Management Utilities section presents the IBM Data Management Utilities most often used by applications programmers. Finally in the MVS Debugging section debugging MVS dumps are covered through the use of the Operating System control blocks. Lectures cover task and data management processing and the use of dump information in identifying logic errors.

Credit Recommendation: In the upper division baccalaureate category, 3 semester hours in Operating Systems Fundamentals (11/83).

OS/VS

Location: Parsippany, Jersey City, NJ and Springfield, PA.

Length: 105 hours (4 weeks).

Dates: October 1985-October 1993.

Objective: To give students a fundamental knowledge of the computer's operating system, the use of Job Control Language as interface, and identification and solving of internal and external abnormal ends.

Learning Outcome: Upon successful completion of this course, the student will write job control statements to interface the application program with the machine operating system; utilize various utility programs to perform data manipulation and management functions; use various debugging methods to solve abnormal program ends.

Instruction: Major topics covered in the course include Job Control Language. This part of the course explains the necessity of Job Control Language as a means of interfacing with the computer through its operating system. It comprises both lecture and in-depth workshops to apply learned concepts. Utility Programs: The most widely applied data management service programs are covered in this unit with emphasis on external sort, linkage editor, IDCAMS, IEBGENER and IEBPTPCH. Dumps: This covers more commonly encountered internal and external abends (abnormal program ends), their causes and solutions. Various debugging methods are discussed, i.e., intuitive approach to debugging a dump, searching through a dump to locate appropriate system control blocks, interpreting Job Control Language messages as solutions and using messages and code manuals. During workshops, the student will debug abends, including OC7, OC4, 001, 013, and E37.

Credit Recommendation: In the lower division baccalaureate/associate or upper division baccalaureate degree category, 4 semester hours in Job Control Language and Utilities (12/89).

OS/VS1

Location: Parsippany, Jersey City, NJ and Springfield, PA.

Length: 105 hours (4 weeks).

Dates: February 1987-August 1994.

Objective: To give the student a working knowledge of OS commands and Job Control Language for the OS system.

Learning Outcome: Upon successful completion of this course, the student will display a working knowledge of OS commands and Job Control Language for the OS system. Students will be able to perform various mainframe operations under the OS system in a production environment.

Instruction: Major topics covered in the course are OS/VS1 operating system and compares this system to the DOS system previously learned. The student learns OS commands and Job Control Language and is assigned projects which they test and run. The student operates the equipment in a production environment and learns to check status of jobs, change priorities and troubleshoot both job and system failures. Job Control Language and utility programs are thoroughly reviewed, including messages and errors coverage. The student runs projects in a data center environment and workshops are operated in as close as possible to on-the-job situations.

Credit Recommendation: In the lower division baccalaureate/associate degree category, 4 semester hours in Operating Systems (12/89).

Program Design and Utilities (Formerly Systems Analysis and Design [SAD])

Location: Parsippany, Jersey City and North Brunswick, NJ; Springfield, PA; New York, NY.

Length: 120 hours.

Dates: November 1993-Present.

Objective: To provide the student with in-depth coverage of structured program design that includes arrays, VSAM file processing techniques, and IBM OS/MVS job control language and utilities.

Learning Outcome: Upon successful completion of this course, the student will be able to use flowcharting techniques to solve selected business problems, handle one and two dimensional tables, and diagram random access update logic; use the primary JCL statements in creating a job stream; and implement the IBM utilities IEBGENER, IEFBR12, IDCAMS, and SYNCSORT as well as understand the use of Linkage Editor.

Instruction: Major topics covered in the course are follow-up to Data Processing Fundamentals that carry the application program development effort to a more advanced level; covers the role of JCL in the step-by-step evaluation, scheduling, execution, and final disposition of a processing job. It includes a detailed study of the major parameters of the JOB, EXEC, and DD statements, and gives hands-on experience with vendor utilities programs. Methods of instruction include lectures, workshops, and reading assignments to facilitate learning.

Credit Recommendation: In the lower division baccalaureate/associate degree category, 2 semester hours in Application Program Development-Advanced, 1 semester hour is OS/VS Job Control Language, and 1 semester hour in OS/VS Utilities, for a total of 4 semester hours (10/96).

Programming Fundamentals (PRF)

Location: Parsippany, Jersey City, NJ and Springfield, PA.

Length: 75 hours (3 weeks).

Dates: January 1974-December 1984.

Objective: To provide an in-depth coverage of the principles of program execution, input/output operations, and IBM S/360 - S/370 machine code instructions, and an introduction to IBM machine language instruction set.

Instruction: This course covers machine code programming using fixed point, logical, and decimal instructions, and data formats (fixed-point, zoned, packed, logical). The IBM S/360 - S/370 interrupt handling system in relation to multiprogramming, Task Dispatcher, TCB, and Task status are covered, as well as the relationship between CPU, channels, control units, and devices. Physical I/O and Logical I/O, (CCW, CAW, CSW, I/O Supervisor), characteristics of Sequential, Indexed, Direct and Partitioned Data Sets and tape and disk concepts complete this course. Lecture is used throughout this course with a dozen hours of laboratory work.

Credit Recommendation: When taken with Introduction to Computer Systems in the lower division baccalaureate/associate degree category, 3 semester hours in Introduction to Data Processing; and in the upper division baccalaureate category, 1 semester hour in Machine Organization. When taken with Basic Program Design (BPD) in the lower division baccalaureate/associate degree category or in the upper division baccalaureate degree category, 3 semester hours in Assembly Language I. It is not anticipated that any student would take only Programming Fundamentals, and there is no appropriate credit recommendation for this course if taken alone (11/83) (10/96).

Programming Labs I (Formerly Programming Labs)

Location: Parsippany, Jersey City, NJ and Springfield, PA.

Length: *Version 1:* 150 hours; *Version 2:* 105 hours (4 weeks).

Dates: *Version 1:* September 1984-September 1985; *Version 2:* October 1985-October 1993.

Objective: To give the student the ability to use both Assembly and COBOL languages in the completion and execution of several programming projects.

Learning Outcome: Upon successful completion of this course, the student will be able to design, code, test and debug an entire integrated system of programs and utilities in Assembler and COBOL languages.

Instruction: The student is required to design, code and test an entire integrated system of programs and utilities, including usage of external sort, VSAM, control breaks, match processing, master file update, sub-program linkage and table handling techniques. Programs are written in Assembler and COBOL. The student will write the required Job Control Language to interface the written program with the operating system.

Credit Recommendation: NOTE: There is no independent credit awarded for Programming Labs. It must be taken in combination with Assembler Language and/or COBOL to earn credit (12/89).

VSE (Formerly DOS/VSE/SP)

Location: Parsippany, Jersey City, NJ and Springfield, PA.

Length: 105 hours (4 weeks).

Dates: February 1987-August 1994.

Objective: To provide the student with a working knowledge of the DOS operation system.

Learning Outcome: Upon successful completion of this course, the student will display a working knowledge of DOS libraries, operating concepts, operator commands, Job Control Language, and Entry Control Language, and be able to troubleshoot the DOS operating system in a large mainframe computer.

Instruction: Major topics covered in the course are a working knowledge of DOS libraries, DOS operating system concepts, operator commands, power spooling system, DOS job control language, DOS entry control language, how to operate the DOS system through use of advanced function commands and power commands, full understanding of computer operator duties, know how to interpret and respond to error messages, diagnose hardware and software error conditions, utilize computer equipment to its utmost, how to initial program load of the DOS operating system, and deactivate the DOS operating system. Methods of instruction include assigned projects relative to job control language, job entry control language, and utility programs, which are tested and executed.

Credit Recommendation: In the lower division baccalaureate/associate degree category, 4 semester hours in DOS (12/89) (6/94).

City of Atlanta Water Department

The Atlanta Water Department's training efforts were enhanced in 1988 with the establishment of the Electrical Apprenticeship Program. Building on the success of this program, the Process Control, Maintenance Mechanic, and Water Plant Operator courses were introduced. Each of these courses of study are registered with the U.S. Department of Labor (USDOL), and upon completion students receive a certificate from the USDOL Bureau of Apprenticeship Training.

The purpose of these programs is to educate trade and technical personnel to meet the Water Department objectives to deliver a high quality potable water product and continually improve the manner in which we serve our customers.

Training is accomplished through various media, and is self-paced. Programmed learning using books and videos, as well as lectures, along with on-the-job training are included. Participants come from within the department. Instructors assist students by coordinating all phases of their training during the length of their apprenticeship and are available for continued assistance thereafter.

Source of official student records: Registry of Credit Recommendations, American Council on Education, One Dupont Circle, Washington, DC 20036-1193.

Additional information about the courses: College Credit Recommendation Service, American Council on Education, One Dupont Circle, Washington, DC 20036-1193.

Electrician Apprenticeship Program

Electrician First Year

Location: Atlanta Water Department Training Center.

Length: 200 hours classroom and 1800 hours on-the-job training.

Dates: October 1988-Present.

Objective: Initial year of three year program of classroom and field experience to prepare an apprentice to become a Maintenance Electrician (USDOL) and a Georgia Electrical Contractor II (Non-Restricted License).

Learning Outcome: Upon successful completion of this course, the student will be able to demonstrate knowledge and skills to apply the principles of basic mathematics; the National Electric Code (Chapters 1 & 2); measurement fundamentals; selection and use of hand and power tools; First Aid; CPR; and Industrial Safety in the classroom and during supervised field experience.

Instruction: Major topics covered in the course are basic electric circuits; applied mathematics; measurement fundamentals; blueprint reading; hand and power tools; National Electrical Code; First Aid; CPR; and plant safety. Methods of instruction include audio/visual material, classroom exercises, field experience, observations, and tests.

Credit Recommendation: In the lower division baccalaureate/associate degree category, 2 semester hours in Interpretation of Blueprints and Schematics; 1 semester hour in Basic First Aid and CPR; 2 semester hours in Selection, Use, and Maintenance of Hand and Portable Power Tools; 1 semester hour in Industrial Safety; 1 semester hour in Basic Applied Mathematics; 1 semester hour in Basic Measurement Principles; 2 semester hours in First Year Electrical Construction Laboratory; and 1 semester hour in National Electrical Code for a total of 11 semester hours (11/96).

Electrician Second Year

Location: Atlanta Water Department Training Center.

Length: 200 hours classroom and 1800 hours on-the-job training.

Dates: October 1988-Present.

Objective: Second year of a three year course of study and second year of electrical construction lab to prepare an apprentice to become a Maintenance Electrician (USDOL) and a Georgia Electrical Contractor II (Non-Restricted License).

Learning Outcome: Upon successful completion of this course, the student will be able to demonstrate knowledge, skills and ability to apply the principles of basic DC and AC circuits, electrical motors, controls, protective devices, trouble-shooting, and the National Electrical Code (Chapters 3 & 4).

Instruction: Major topics covered in the course are basic electricity, electrical motors, controls, protective devices, measuring instruments, trouble-shooting and the National Electrical Code. Methods of instruction include audio/visual material, classroom exercises, field experience, observations and tests.

Credit Recommendation: In the lower division baccalaureate/associate degree category, 3 semester hours in Basic AC and DC Circuits; 3 semester hours in Electrical Motors and Controls; 1 semester hour in Electrical Troubleshooting; 1 semester hour in Measuring Instruments; 2 semester hours in 2nd Year Electrical Construction Laboratory; and 1 semester hour in National Electrical Code for a total of 11 semester hours (11/96).

Electrician Third Year

Location: Atlanta Water Department Training Center.

Length: 200 hours classroom and 1800 hours on-the-job training.

Dates: October 1988-Present.

Objective: Third year of a three year course of study and third year of electrical construction lab to prepare an apprentice to become a Maintenance Electrician (USDOL) and a Georgia Electrical Contractor II (Non-Restricted License).

Learning Outcome: Upon successful completion of this course, the student will be able to demonstrate knowledge, skills and ability to apply the principles of basic DC and AC circuits, electrical motors, controls, protective devices, and the National Electrical Code.

Instruction: Major topics covered in the course are basic fundamentals of process controls; programmable logic controllers; residential and commercial wiring; and applied math for electrical applications. Preparation through study and practice tests for the examination required for Georgia Electrical Contractor II License (Non-Restricted.). Methods of instruction include audio/visual material, classroom exercises, field experience, observations, tests, and final examination .

Credit Recommendation: In the lower division baccalaureate/associate degree category, 1 semester hour in Process Control; 1 semester hour in Programmable Logic Controllers; 2 semester hours in Residential and Industrial Wiring; 2 semester hours in Electrical Construction Laboratory; 1 semester hour in Programmable Logic Control Laboratory (Conditional); 3 semester hours in Preparation for Electrical Contractor II License Exam, (Conditional on passing the Electrical Contractor II License Exam), for a total of 10 semester hours (11/96).

Maintenance Mechanic Apprenticeship Program

Maintenance Mechanic First Year

Location: Atlanta Water Department Training Center.

Length: 200 hours classroom and 1800 hours on-the-job training.

Dates: October 1996-Present.

Objective: To provide the initial year of a three-year course of study and field experience to prepare an individual to be a Maintenance Mechanic in an industrial setting.

Learning Outcome: Upon successful completion of this course, the student will be able to perform at a basic level of Maintenance Mechanic. All field and classroom tests must be successfully completed before advancing to more complex subjects, and all first-year program requirements along with instructor recommendation must be successfully completed to advance to the second year of study.

Instruction: Major topics covered in the course are First Aid and CPR; Blueprint and Schematic Diagram Reading; Basic Mathematics; Measurements; Hand and Power Tools; Metal and Non-Metal Materials; Plant Safety and Trouble-shooting Skills. Methods of instruction include classroom exercises, field experience, audio/visual material, reports, observations, quizzes and final examination. Classroom work is primarily self-paced.

Credit Recommendation: In the lower division baccalaureate/associate degree category, 1 semester hour in *Basic First Aid and CPR; *Industrial Safety; *Basic Mathematics; *Measurement Technology; and *Plant Maintenance; and 2 semester hours in *Plan and Schematic Reading and Interpretation; Selection, Use, and Maintenance of Hand and Portable Power Tools; and Manufacturing Technology and Materials Applications (11 hours total) (11/96). **NOTE:** Credits marked with * are also received in Water Treatment Plant Operator Apprenticeship Program.

Maintenance Mechanic Second Year

Location: Atlanta Water Department Second Year.

Length: 200 hours classroom and 1800 hours on-the-job training.

Dates: October 1996-Present.

Objective: To provide the second year of a three-year course of study and field experience to prepare an individual to be a Maintenance Mechanic in an industrial setting.

Learning Outcome: Upon successful completion of this course, the student will be able to perform at a mid-level of Maintenance Mechanic. All field and classroom tests must be successfully completed before advancing to more complex subjects, and all second year program requirements along with instructor recommendation must be successfully completed to advance to the third year of study.

Instruction: Major topics covered in the course are Basic Mechanics; Lubricants; Drive Components; Bearings; Pumps and Piping Systems; Hydraulics and Pneumatics; and Trouble-shooting Skills. Classroom work is primarily self-paced. Methods of instruction include audio/visual material, classroom exercises, field experience , quizzes, observations, and final examination.

Credit Recommendation: In the lower division baccalaureate/associate degree category, 1 semester hour in Basic Physics of Mechanics; 2 semester hours in Machine Maintenance (Lubrication, Bearings, and Drive Components); *3 semester hours in Basic Hydraulics and Pneumatics; 2 semester hours in Hydraulic and Pneumatic Systems Maintenance, for a total of 8 semester hours (11/96). **NOTE:** Credits marked with * are also received in Water Treatment Plant Operator Apprenticeship Program.

Maintenance Mechanic Third Year

Location: Atlanta Water Department Training Center.

Length: 200 hours classroom and 1800 hours on-the-job training.

Dates: October 1996-Present.

Objective: To provide the final year of a three-year course of study and field experience to prepare an individual to be a Maintenance Mechanic in an industrial setting.

Learning Outcome: Upon successful completion of this course, the student will be able to perform at an advanced level of Maintenance Mechanic. All field and classroom tests must be successfully completed before advancing to more complex subjects, and all third year program requirements along with instructor recommendation must be successfully completed to complete program and be classified as a Maintenance Mechanic-Senior.

Instruction: Major topics covered in the course are rigging; equipment installation; mechanical and fluid drive systems; installation and replacement of bearings and shaft seals; pump and pipe-fitting installation and maintenance; tubing and hose systems; and gas and arc welding. Classroom work is primarily self-paced. Methods of instruction include audio/visual material, classroom exercises, field experience , quizzes, observations, and final examination.

Credit Recommendation: In the lower division baccalaureate/associate degree category, 2 semester hours in Industrial Rigging and Equipment Installation; 2 semester hours in Principles and Practices of Gas and Arc Welding; 2 semester hours in Mechanical Systems Maintenance; and 2 semester hours in Installation and Maintenance of Hydraulic Systems, for a total of 8 semester hours (11/96).

Process Control Technician Apprenticeship Program

Process Control First Year

Location: Atlanta Water Department Training Center.

Length: 200 hours classroom and 1800 hours on-the-job training.

Dates: October 1996-Present.

Objective: Initial year of three-year program of classroom and field experience to prepare an apprentice to become a Process Control Technician.

Learning Outcome: Upon successful completion of this course, the student will be able to demonstrate knowledge and skills to apply the principles of Basic Mathematics, Measurement Equipment, Selection and Use of Hand and Power Tools in classroom and supervised field experience. The student will also be able to demonstrate knowledge of First Aid, CPR and Industrial Safety.

Instruction: Major topics covered in the course are Applied Mathematics; Measurement Fundamentals; Blueprint and Schematic Reading; Hand and Power Tools; First Aid; CPR; and Plant Safety. Methods of instruction include audio/visual material, classroom exercises, field experience, observations, and tests.

Credit Recommendation: In the lower division baccalaureate/associate degree category, 2 semester hours in Interpretation of Blueprints and Schematics; 1 semester hour in Basic First Aid and CPR; 2 semester hours in Selection, Use, and Maintenance of Hand and Portable Power Tools; 1 semester hour in Industrial Safety; 1 semester hour in Basic Applied Mathematics; 1 semester hour in Basic Measurement Principles; and 2 semester hours in Application of Process Control Principles, for a total of 10 semester hours (11/96).

Process Control Second Year

Location: Atlanta Water Department Training Center.

Length: 200 hours classroom and 1800 hours on-the-job training.

Dates: October 1996-Present.

Objective: Second year of a three-year program of classroom and field experience to prepare an apprentice to be a Process Control Technician.

Learning Outcome: Upon successful completion of this course, the student will be able to demonstrate knowledge, skills and ability to apply the principles of measuring instruments, basic AC and DC circuit theory, basic electronics, and applied instrumentation laboratory.

Instruction: Major topics covered in the course are basic electricity and electronics; AC and DC theory; measuring instruments; semi-conductors; power supplies; amplifiers; oscillators; logic circuits; and trouble-shooting.

Credit Recommendation: In the lower division baccalaureate/associate degree category, 1 semester hour in Measuring Instruments; 3 semester hours in Basic AC and DC Circuit Theory; 3 semester hours in Basic Electronics; 2 semester hours in Applied Instrumentation Laboratory, for a total of 9 semester hours (11/96).

Process Control Third Year

Location: Atlanta Water Department Training Center.

Length: 200 hours classroom and 1800 hours on-the-job training.

Dates: October 1996-Present.

Objective: Third year of a three-year program of classroom and field experience to prepare an apprentice to become a Process Control Technician.

Learning Outcome: Upon successful completion of this course, the student will be able to demonstrate knowledge, skills and ability to apply the principles of process control, process instrumentation and programmable logic controllers, and demonstrate advanced proficiency in these subjects in the process control environment.

Instruction: Major topics covered in the course are process control; programmable logic controllers; and process instrumentation. Methods of instruction include classroom exercises, field experience, observations, tests, and final examination.

Credit Recommendation: In the lower division baccalaureate/associate degree category, 4 semester hours in Process Instrumentation; 1 semester hour in Programmable Logic Controllers; 1 semester hour in Process Control; 2 semester hours in Process Control Laboratory, for a total of 8 semester hours (11/96).

Water Treatment Plant Operator Apprenticeship Program

Plant Operator First Year

Location: Atlanta Water Department Training Center.

Length: 200 hours classroom and 1800 hours on-the-job training.

Dates: October 1996-Present.

Objective: To provide the first year of a three-year course of study and field experience to prepare an individual to be a Water Treatment Plant Operator and pass the State of Georgia Class III Water Treatment Plant Operator's Test.

Learning Outcome: Upon successful completion of this course, the student will be able to perform at the basic level of a Water Treatment Plant Operator. All field and classroom tests must be successfully completed before advancing to more complex subjects, and all first year program requirements along with instructor's recommendation must be successfully completed to advance to the second year of study.

Instruction: Major topics covered in the course are Basic First Aid and CPR; blueprint and schematic diagram reading and interpretation; basic mathematics; measurements; plant safety and troubleshooting skills; introduction to water technology; and spoken and written communications. Classroom work is primarily self-paced. Methods of instruction include audio/visual material, classroom exercises, field experience, quizzes, observations, reports, and final examination.

Credit Recommendation: In the lower division baccalaureate/associate degree category, *1 semester hour in Basic First Aid and CPR; *2 semester hours in Plan and Schematic Reading and Interpretation; *1 semester hour in Basic Math; *1 semester hour in Measurement Technology; *1 semester hour in Industrial Safety; *1 semester hour in Plant Maintenance; 1 semester hour in Effective Oral Com-munications; 1 semester hour in Effective Written Communications; and 1 semester hour in Basic Water Chemistry, for a total of 10 semester hours (11/96). **NOTE:** Credits marked with * are also received in Maintenance Mechanic Apprenticeship Program.

Plant Operator Second Year

Location: Atlanta Water Department Training Center.

Length: 200 hours classroom and 1800 hours on-the-job training.

Dates: October 1996-Present.

Objective: Second year of a three-year course of study and field experience to be a Water Treatment Plant Operator and pass the State of Georgia Class III Water Treatment Plant Operator Test.

Learning Outcome: Upon successful completion of this course, the student will be able to perform as a mid-level Water Treatment Plant Operator. All field and classroom tests must be successfully completed before advancing to more complex subjects, and all second year program requirements along with instructor's recommendation must be successfully completed to advance to the third year of study.

Instruction: Major topics covered in the course are the operation of pumps and piping systems; basic pneumatics and hydraulics; and introductory water treatment plant operation. Classroom work is primarily self-paced. Methods of instruction include audio/visual material, classroom exercises, field experience, quizzes, observations, reports, and final examination.

Credit Recommendation: In the lower division baccalaureate/associate degree category, *3 semester hours in Basic Hydraulics and Pneumatics; and 6 semester hours in Chemical Engineering Technology, for a total of 9 semester hours (11/96). **NOTE:** Credits marked with * also received in Maintenance Mechanic Apprenticeship Program.

Plant Operator Third Year

Location: Atlanta Water Department Training Center.

Length: 200 hours classroom and 1800 hours on-the-job training.

Dates: October 1996-Present.

Objective: Final year of a three-year course of study and field experience to be a Water Treatment Plant Operator and pass the State of Georgia Class III Water Treatment Plant Operator Test.

Learning Outcome: Upon successful completion of this course, the student will be able to perform as an advanced-level Water Treatment Plant Operator, and will be able to pass the State of Georgia Class III Water Treatment Plant Operator Test. All field and classroom tests must be successfully completed before advancing to more complex subjects, and all third-year program requirement, along with instructor's recommendation, must be successfully completed to complete the program and be classified as a Water Treatment Plant Operator.

Instruction: Major topics covered in the course are water distribution system operation and maintenance, and water treatment plant operation. Classroom work is self-paced. Methods of instruction include audio/visual material, classroom exercises, field experience, quizzes, observations, reports, and final examination.

Credit Recommendation: In the lower division baccalaureate/associate degree category, 6 semester hours in Chemical Engineering Technology; 3 semester hours in Water Distribution System Operation and Maintenance for a total of 9 semester hours (11/96).

City of Oxnard

The City of Oxnard is a full service, general law municipal agency incorporated in 1903. Oversight is provided by an elected Mayor and City Council. The City of Oxnard organization, located in California, supports a population of over 157,000 residents and 900 employees.

The City of Oxnard training program serves as a benchmark and model for other organizations, having been featured in numerous national training and organization development conferences. The City of Oxnard provides its employees and partners in the community with training opportunities through Oxnard University that equips the participants with the needed skills and abilities to meet the changing needs of the public sector. Oxnard University training course work focuses on providing professional and personal skill development to all levels of public sector employees and their community partners in order to assist them in becoming leaders and decision makers. Skills training addresses decision making, facilitation, coaching, performance and development, and process management and improvement issues, etc.

Each year, Oxnard University offers the Oxnard Academy, a series of course work built around the concept of building leadership skills. Over 300 participants, from both the public and private sectors, have taken part in this series annually since 1994.

Source of official student records: Registry of Credit Recommendations, American Council on Education, One Dupont Circle, Washington, DC 20036-1193.

Additional information about the courses: College Credit Recommendation Service, American Council on Education, One Dupont Circle, Washington, DC 20036-1193.

Business Processes

Business Process Analysis and Improvement

Location: Various - City of Oxnard, CA.

Length: 24 hours classroom contact time in four or eight hour segments; six to eight hours independent project preparation time.

Dates: January 1994-Present.

Objective: To identify, price, analyze, measure, evaluate, and improve public services and products; understand pricing public services; analyze programs for providing services and products; and understand the use of Total Quality Management (TQM) and related improvement tools.

Learning Outcome: Upon successful completion of this course, the student will be able to apply pricing, program analysis, and process improvement techniques in the public organization.

Instruction: Major topics covered in the course are basis and techniques for setting prices in the public sector; tools for analysis and evaluation of public programs; process improvement tools including TQM, continuous improvement, and reengineering. Methods of instruction include lecture, discussion, case studies, learner presentations/reports, quizzes, observations, and process improvement projects.

Credit Recommendation: In the vocational certificate category or lower division baccalaureate/associate degree category, 1 semester hour in Business or Public Administration (12/96).

Entrepreneurial Academy

Entrepreneurship

Location: Various - City of Oxnard, CA.

Length: 16 hours classroom contact time in eight hour segments; two to four hours independent project preparation time.

Dates: January 1995-Present.

Objective: To prepare individuals to apply contemporary business and marketing techniques to both private and public sector programs and projects.

Learning Outcome: Upon successful completion of this course, the student will be able to identify the skills and characteristics associated with entrepreneurs; define what entrepreneurial means in both public and private sectors, list benefits of an entrepreneurial approach to profit and nonprofit entities; explain what business they are in and identify internal and external customers as well as additional stakeholders; and develop and initiate a marketing plan that effectively communicates with all stakeholders.

Instruction: Major topics covered in the course are myths, realities, and success factors of entrepreneurialism; changing paradigms; changing nature of government; internal and external customers and other stake holders; marketing principles and practices applied to a customer service approach to doing business; and adding value to both products and services. Methods of instruction include lecture, discussion, classroom exercises, case studies, audio/visual material, learner presentation and reports, quizzes, reports, and observations.

Credit Recommendation: In the vocational certificate category or the lower division baccalaureate/associate degree category, 1 semester hour in Business or Public Administration (12/96).

Oxnard Academy

Leadership and Management

Location: Various - City of Oxnard, CA.

Length: 72 hours classroom contact time in eight hour segments; fifteen to twenty hours independent project preparation time.

Dates: January 1994-Present.

Objective: To provide an understanding of leadership and management; team building; motivating and interpersonal skills and practices; and ethics and ethical practices in both interpersonal and business settings.

Learning Outcome: Upon successful completion of this course, the student will be able to demonstrate leadership and management, apply conflict management skills, develop project management, develop coaching and partnership skills and to demonstrate problem solving and decision making knowledge and skill.

Instruction: Major topics covered in the course are conflict management; coaching; interpersonal skills; managing diversity; motivating skills; problem solving and decision making; leadership; facilitation skills; business ethics; and customer service and relations. Methods of instruction include lecture, discussion, classroom exercises, audio/visual material, learner presentation and reports, home study, quizzes, reports, projects, observations, tests, and papers.

Credit Recommendation: In the vocational certificate category or lower division baccalaureate/associate degree category, 3 semester hours in Business, Management, or Leadership and Interpersonal Skills (12/96).

College for Financial Planning, Inc.

The College of Financial Planning, Inc. (The College) is a for-profit subsidiary of Apollo Group, Inc. The College offers a wide spectrum of self-study educational programs and courses to meet the changing needs of financial services professionals.

The Certified Financial Planner® or CFP® Professional Education Program consists of five separate courses, each of which is followed by a corresponding proctored examination administered on a national basis. Classroom instruction is available through the College's adjunct faculty and affiliated colleges and universities, as well as through select corporations. Individuals who complete the CFP Program learn to recognize existing and potential client problems and to recommend solutions over a broad range of financial circumstances. To qualify for certification by the Certified Financial Planner Board of Standards, Inc. (CFP Board), an independent, nonprofit standards-setting and certification organization, an individual must fulfill certain requirements, including submission of a transcript indicating completion of a financial planning education program that is registered with the CFP Board. In addition, an applicant must successfully complete the CFP Certification Examination administered by the CFP Board, and complete experience and ethics requirements prescribed by the CFP Board.

In 1984, the College developed the Financial Paraplanner Program® to provide administrative and support personnel in financial services with the opportunity to gain knowledge of basic financial planning concepts and skills.

In 1988, the Accredited Tax PreparerSM program was introduced to provide a strong foundation in tax return and compliance work. It was restructured in 1996.

In 1993, the Asset Management Education Program was developed for individuals working in the investment area. In 1996, the course was revised and a designation added, the Accredited Asset Management Specialist (AAMS).

In January1996, the Chartered Mutual Fund Counselor Professional Education Program was introduced to provide specialized education in the characteristics of mutual funds and their selection.

Source of official student records: College for Financial Planning, Inc., 4695 South Monaco Street, Denver, CO 80237.

Additional information about the courses: College Credit Recommendation Service, American Council on Education, One Dupont Circle, Washington, DC 20036-1193.

Asset Management Education Program: For Investment Professionals

Location: Available at various locations nationally and internationally.

Length: One module per month for one year.

Dates: January 1994-Present.

Objective: To provide the investment professional student with practical financial information to better meet client investment needs, and to recognize the best investment solutions for clients while taking into account his or her total financial picture.

Learning Outcome: Upon successful completion of this course, the student will be able to demonstrate knowledge of the asset management and allocation process; investment strategies; risk/return principles; investment issues peculiar to specific client profiles; taxation of investment products; estate planning basics; and regulatory and ethical issues for the investment professional.

Instruction: Major topics covered in the course are the asset management and allocation process, investment strategies, risk/return principles, investment issues peculiar to specific client profiles, taxation of investment products, estate planning basics, and regulatory and ethical issues for the investment professional. Methods of instruction include independent self-study with classroom instruction by some brokerage firms.

Credit Recommendation: In the upper division baccalaureate degree category, 3 semester hours in Finance or Business Administration (1/95).

Foundations in Financial Planning

Location: Available at various locations nationally and internationally.

Length: Approximately 150 to 180 hours of self-study.

Dates: February 1985-Present.

Objective: To introduce the financial planning assistant to financial planning, concepts, and terminology.

Learning Outcome: Upon successful completion of this course, the student will be able to demonstrate adequate communication skills; gather and process data; exhibit the knowledge and skill necessary to construct personal financial statements; and review and analyze information to identify basic strengths and weaknesses in a client's financial situation.

Instruction: Major topics covered in the course are the financial planning process, the time value of money, principles of risk management, life insurance, health insurance, property and liability insurance, investment principles, equity investments, fixed income investments, mutual funds, income tax planning, pension and profit-sharing plans, other retirement plans, principles of estate planning, and estate transfer and planning or estate taxes. Methods of instruction include periodic proctored examinations at various collegiate institutions.

Credit Recommendation: In the lower division baccalaureate/associate degree category, 3 semester hours in Business Administration (2/85) (2/90) (1/95).

Tax Preparer I: Individual Tax Returns

Location: Available at various locations nationally and internationally.

Length: Approximately 200 hours of self-study.

Dates: September 1988-February 1996.

Objective: To provide the student with the tools necessary to efficiently prepare accurate federal income tax returns for individuals.

Learning Outcome: Upon successful completion of this course, the student will be able to prepare individual tax returns.

Instruction: Major topics covered in the course are basic filing considerations, accounting considerations, installment sales, taxpayer employer identification number, changing accounting methods, nonbusiness incomes, adjustments to income, itemized deductions, qualified residence interest after 1987, interest allocation rules, charitable contributions, business income and expenses, like-kind exchanges, farming considerations, in-come tax payments and credits, individual income tax computations, amended returns, claims for refund and tax deficiencies and penalties, running a tax preparation practice, and standards for tax practice. Method of instruction includes supervised self-study.

Credit Recommendation: In the upper division baccalaureate degree category, 3 semester hours in Accounting or Business Administration (2/90) (1/95).

Tax Preparer II: Partnership, Corporation, and Fiduciary Tax Returns

Location: Available at various locations nationally and internationally.

Length: Approximately 200 hours of self-study.

Dates: September 1988-February 1996.

Objective: To provide the student with the tools necessary to efficiently prepare partnership, corporation, and fiduciary tax returns.

Learning Outcome: Upon successful completion of this course, the student will be able to prepare partnership, corporation, and fiduciary tax returns.

Instruction: Major topics covered in the course are computation partnership taxable income (allocation of income and losses, partnership distributions, partnership-partner transactions, and terminations); at-risk and passive activities rules; computation of corporate tax, dividends-paid deduction, dividend distributions, and dividends received by corporate stockholders; corporate alternative minimum tax, collapsible corporations, personal holding companies, and accumulated earnings tax; estate and trust personal exemptions; distributable net income, and distributions to beneficiaries; computation of S corporation taxable income and pass-throughs to shareholders; S stock; worksheet-S corporation shareholder's basis for indebtedness from the S corporation; summary of tax treatment of S corporation distributions to shareholders; election under code section 1368(e)(3) to distribute accumulated earnings and profits in priority order; partnership and corporate formations and liquidations; corporate liquidations and the "General Utilities" rule; simple trusts; complex trusts and estates; and grantor trusts. Method of instruction includes supervised self-study.

Credit Recommendation: In the upper division baccalaureate degree category, 3 semester hours in Accounting or Business Administration (2/90) (1/95).

CERTIFIED FINANCIAL PLANNER®

Professional Education Program (CFP® Program)

Accredited Asset Management Specialist Professional Education Program

Location: Available at various locations nationally.

Length: 15 weeks (96-120 hours).

Dates: June 1996-Present.

Objective: To provide the student, specifically the investment professional, with practical financial information to better meet the investment needs of his or her client; to recognize the best investment solutions for clients while taking into account his or her total financial situation. Completion of the course and other requirements lead to the professional designation, Accredited Asset Management Specialist (AAMS).

Learning Outcome: Upon successful completion of this course, the student will be familiar with the asset management and allocation process, investment strategies, risk/return principles, investment issues peculiar to specific client profiles, taxation of investment products, estate planning basics, and regulatory and ethical issues for the investment professional.

Instruction: Major topics covered in the course are asset management and allocation process, investment strategies, risk/return principles, investment issues peculiar to specific client profiles, taxation of investments, and estate planning basics. Methods of instruction include self-study and classroom instruction.

Credit Recommendation: In the upper division baccalaureate degree category, 3 semester hours in Finance or Business Administration (8/96).

Basic Tax Preparation (Accredited Tax Preparer Program)

Location: Available at various locations nationally.

Length: 180-220 hours (15 weeks).

Dates: February 1996-Present.

Objective: To provide the students, generally the entry-level tax practitioner, with a fundamental understanding of the issues and elements of tax preparation for individuals, partnerships, and corporations. Completion of the course and fulfillment of other professional criteria lead to the professional designation, Accredited Tax Preparer (or ATP).

Learning Outcome: Upon successful completion of this course, the student will gain necessary information to complete Federal income tax returns accurately and properly.

Instruction: Major topics covered in the course are basic filing considerations, income items and concepts for individuals, deductions and expenses, tax credits and payments, partnerships and corporate tax returns, and concerns in running a tax preparation practice. Method of instruction includes independent self-study.

Credit Recommendation: In the upper division baccalaureate degree category, 3 semester hours in Accounting or Business Administration (8/96).

Chartered Mutual Fund Counselor Professional Education Program

Location: Available at various locations nationally.

Length: 72 hours (15 weeks).

Dates: January 1996-Present.

Objective: To provide the student, specifically the investment professional, with a wide range of information on mutual funds and their many applications. Completion of the course and other requirements lead to the professional designation, Chartered Mutual Fund Counselor (CMFC).

Learning Outcome: Upon successful completion of this course, the student will be proficient in the types and characteristics of mutual funds and how they can be used to meet a variety of financial needs for clients.

Instruction: Major topics covered in the course are open- and closed-end funds, risk/return principles, asset allocation strategies, selecting appropriate mutual fund for a client, retirement planning using mutual funds, and ethical conduct of the investment professional. Methods of instruction include independent self-study and/or classroom instruction.

Credit Recommendation: In the upper division baccalaureate degree category, 3 semester hours in Finance, Investments, or Business Administration (8/96).

Estate Planning (CFP V) (Formerly Estate Planning [CFP VI])

Location: Available at various locations nationally and internationally.

Length: Approximately 180 to 210 hours of self-study.

Dates: February 1985-Present.

Objective: To introduce the student to the fundamentals of an estate plan including federal estate and gift taxation as well as specific exclusion and valuation techniques that reduce the size of the gross estate and to enable the student to provide specific estate planning recommendations.

Learning Outcome: Upon successful completion of this course, the student will be able to demonstrate methods of reducing the gross estate through exclusion and valuation techniques; demonstrate a knowledge of the characteristics of wills, intestacy, and the probate process; and show a knowledge of the use of trusts, property ownership forms, and will substitutes.

Instruction: Major topics covered in the course are the estate planning process, gift taxation fundamentals, estate taxation fundamentals, valuation of property in the gross estate, intestacy, the probate process, trusts, ownership of property, annuities, life insurance contracts, lifetime transfers and gifts to minors, unified credit, marital deduction, powers of appointment, charitable trusts, intrafamily business and property transfers, and postmortem planning. The course concludes with a case analysis which requires the student to select appropriate estate planning techniques. Methods of instruction include self-study, group study, or formal class study with proctored national examinations.

Credit Recommendation: In the upper division baccalaureate or graduate degree category, 3 semester hours in Business Administration, Insurance, or Estate Planning (2/90) (3/91) (1/95).

Financial Planning Process and Insurance (CFP I)
(Formerly Insurance Planning (CFP II) and Risk Management [CFP II])

Location: Available at various locations nationally and internationally.

Length: Approximately 150 to 180 hours of self-study.

Dates: *Version 1:* November 1975-May 1994; *Version 2:* June 1994-Present.

Objective: *Version 1:* To provide students with an understanding of risk management and risk analysis including interpreting the insurance contract, coverages provided by property and liability insurance, life and health insurance, group and social insurance, basic insurance taxation, and the business uses of life insurance and to enable the student to demonstrate an understanding of processes associated with the determination of insurance needs and the purchase of insurance products. *Version 2:* To provide a brief summary of the six-stage financial planning process and an introduction to regulations affecting financial planning, to educate students with an understanding of personal risk management and analysis including interpreting the insurance contract, coverages provided by property and liability insurance, life and health insurance, group and social insurance, basic insurance taxation, and the business uses of life insurance and to enable the student to demonstrate; and understanding of processes associated with the determination of insurance needs and the purchase of insurance products.

Learning Outcome: *Version 1:* Upon successful completion of this course, the student will be able to identify a client's risk exposures and select the appropriate risk management techniques in addition to analyzing life insurance by using a 13-step life insurance selection process that utilizes a 10-step needs determination approach. *Version 2:* Upon successful completion of this course, the student will be able to demonstrate knowledge of the financial planning process and will have an introduction to regulation; identify a client's risk exposure; and select the appropriate risk management techniques, in addition to analyzing life insurance by using a 13-step life insurance selection process that utilizes a 10-step needs determination approach.

Instruction: Major topics covered in the course are an introduction to risk management; the fields of insurance; the structure, function, and regulation of the private insurance industry; the insurance contract; homeowner's insurance; health and long-term care insurance; auto insurance; introduction to life insurance; determining life insurance needs; evaluating insurance products; disability income insurance; liability insurance; group life and health insurance; uses of life insurance in business; social insurance and compulsory compensation; and additional cases for analysis. Methods of instruction include self-study, group study, or formal class study with proctored national examinations.

Credit Recommendation: *Versions 1 and 2:* In the upper division baccalaureate degree category, 3 semester hours in Business Administration or Insurance (2/85) (2/90) (1/95).

Fundamentals of Financial Planning (CFP I)
(Formerly Introduction to Financial Planning [CFP I])

Location: Available at various locations nationally and internationally.

Length: Approximately 150 to 180 hours of self-study.

Dates: November 1975-September 1994.

Objective: To present the six-stage financial planning process and an introduction to regulations affecting financial planners, to provide an overview of content areas of program Parts II through VI, to present economic concepts and introduce the time value of money, and to provide the student with basic consumer finance principles, including budgeting and debt management.

Learning Outcome: Upon successful completion of this course, the student will be able to accomplish basic financial tasks, show knowledge of the economic environment; and solve problems using time value of money concepts.

Instruction: Major topics covered in the course are the financial planning process, regulation of financial planners, insurance, investments and financial institutions, individual income tax principles, retirement and estate planning concepts, the time value of money, monetary policy and the business cycle, client data gathering, the construction of personal financial statements, budgeting, and debt management. Methods of instruction include self-study, group study, or formal class study with proctored national examinations.

Credit Recommendation: In the upper division baccalaureate degree category, 3 semester hours in Business Administration or Financial Planning (2/85) (2/90) (1/95).

Income Tax Planning (CFP III)
(Formerly Tax Planning and Management [CFP IV])

Location: Available at various locations nationally and internationally.

Length: Approximately 180 to 210 hours of self-study.

Dates: *Version 1:* November 1975-November 1986; *Version 2:* July 1986-Present.

Objective: To provide the student with an understanding of the fundamentals of individual income tax considerations in selecting a business form, tax planning for the acquisition and disposition of property, tax advantaged investments, tax planning alternatives, tax traps, and personal tax management processes.

Learning Outcome: Upon successful completion of this course, the student will be able to demonstrate a knowledge of the fundamentals of individual income tax including the tax implications of various forms of business, planning for the acquisition and disposition of property, tax advantaged investments, and tax planning for the family.

Instruction: Major topics covered in the course are tax law overview and research, income concepts-basic terminology and tax calculation, sole proprietorships, partnerships, accounting methods, corporations and selecting a business form, basic concepts of property transactions, dispositions of property transactions, basic concepts of tax advantaged investments, selected tax-advantaged investments and the passive activity rules, tax aspects of life insurance, annuities, and securities, intrafamily and charitable transfers, divorce and marital considerations, compensation planning, special tax considerations and computations, and tax traps. Methods of instruction include self-study, group study, or formal class study with proctored national examinations.

Credit Recommendation: *Version 1:* In the upper division baccalaureate degree category, 3 semester hours in Business Administration or Tax Accounting (12/81) (2/85). *Version 2:* In the upper division baccalaureate or graduate degree category, 3 semester hours in Business Administration or Tax Accounting (2/90) (3/91) (1/95).

Investment Planning (CFP II) (Formerly Investment Planning [CFP III] and Investments [CFP III])

Location: Available at various locations nationally and internationally.

Length: Approximately 180 to 210 hours of self-study.

Dates: *Version 1:* November 1975-May 1994; *Version 2:* June 1994-Present.

Objective: *Version 1:* To provide the student with an understanding of the economic and business environment; to provide the fundamentals of investments, including tools and mechanics of investing, security markets, valuation principles, sources of investment risk, and the analysis of corporate financial statements; and to provide a knowledge of valuation techniques, portfolio construction, management process, and asset categories. *Version 2:* To provide the student with an introduction to investment planning; the economic environment, securities markets, risk/return analysis, and tools of investing; and to provide education in portfolio construction and management. Modern portfolio theory is also considered.

Learning Outcome: *Version 1:* Upon successful completion of this course, the student will be able to address the wide variety of investment vehicles that can be included in the client's personal investment portfolio including stocks, bonds, mutual funds, insurance, futures, options, real estate, and real assets; and to recommend investment vehicles appropriate to the client's needs, resources, and financial goals. *Version 2:* Upon successful completion of this course, the student will be able to demonstrate knowledge of the economic environment in which investments are made and the wide variety of investment vehicles that can be included in a client's personal investment portfolio; valuation principles underlying investment theory; and the recommendation of investments appropriate to a client's needs, resources, and financial goals.

Instruction: Major topics covered in the course are the investment environment, security markets, regulation and sources of information; risk/return and tools for analysis; modern portfolio theory; valuation of debt and preferred stock; government securities; valuation of common stock; security selection, options and convertible securities; futures; physical assets and gold; real estate; investment companies; and the economic environment and portfolio construction. Methods of instruction include self-study, group study, or formal class study with proctored examinations.

Credit Recommendation: *Versions 1 and 2:* In the upper division baccalaureate degree category, 3 semester hours in Business Administration or Finance (2/85) (2/90) (1/95).

Retirement Planning and Employee Benefits (CFP IV) (Formerly Retirement Planning and Employee Benefits [CFP V])

Location: Available at various locations nationally and internationally.

Length: Approximately 180 to 210 hours of self-study.

Dates: *Version 1:* November 1975-January 1985; *Version 2:* February 1985-Present.

Objective: To provide the student with an understanding of personal retirement planning, qualified retirement plans, government-sponsored retirement plans, and employee benefits involving group life and medical insurance and related programs including nonqualified deferred compensation.

Learning Outcome: Upon successful completion of this course, the student will be able to identify personal tax-deferred retirement programs available; calculate annual savings needed to reach retirement income goals; and have knowledge of the various forms of insurances, compensation, and other employee benefits.

Instruction: Major topics covered in the course are personal tax-deferred retirement plans; retirement income programming; introduction to qualified retirement plans; contribution-oriented plans; benefit-oriented plans; target benefit plans and other plan design considerations; retirement plan development and maintenance process; distributions from retirement plans; Social Security and Medicare; group, life, health insurance and other employee benefits; nonqualified deferred-compensation plans; and executive compensation. The course concludes with a case study requiring the student to select an appropriate qualified retirement plan for a business owner and to analyze tax implications of employee benefits. Methods of instruction include self-study, group study, or formal class study with proctored national examinations.

Credit Recommendation: *Version 1:* In the upper division baccalaureate degree category, 3 semester hours in Business Administration or Financial Planning (12/81). *Version 2:* In the upper division baccalaureate or graduate degree category, 3 semester hours in Business Administration, Retirement Planning, or Financial Planning (2/90) (3/91) (1/95).

CommandTrain, Inc.

CommandTrain was started in 1984 as a training company with the mission of developing and delivering high quality courses on Computer applications for both engineers and office personnel. The company has done work for Ford Motor Company, 3M Corporation, McDonnell Douglas, and Detroit Edison both at the customers site and at CommandTrain facilities. Courses have been taught throughout the United States, Canada, Mexico, Brazil and England.

The company has grown from one person to a present staff of seven degreed, professional trainers and educators with a total combined experience of more than 100 years. The staff includes a Ph.D. with 20 years in higher education administration and a former professor of mechanical engineering. Each of the staff has a particular area of specialization and each also has a broad range of general technical knowledge and a solid background in education.

The student population has included office workers, UAW union members, engineers, and administrators and courses have been customized to meet the needs of each population.

Courses are developed to meet the needs of the target population based on predetermined objectives and sound educational practices including pre and post tests and surveys to monitor both effectiveness, relevance, and quality of the training. Courses are continually updated to meet the changing needs of students and to reflect the latest software upgrades and revisions.

Source of official student records: Registry of Credit Recommendations, American Council on Education, One Dupont Circle, Washington, DC 20036-1193.

Additional information about the courses: College Credit Recommendation Service, American Council on Education, One Dupont Circle, Washington, DC 20036-1193.

Advanced WordPerfect for Windows

Location: CommandTrain - Dearborn, MI or various on-site locations.

Length: 20 hours (5 weeks).

Dates: January 1986-Present.

Objective: To introduce advanced features of WordPerfect for Windows.

Learning Outcome: Upon successful completion of this course, the student will be able to use advanced WordPerfect for Windows features such as set up and timed backup, dictionary and thesaurus, creation and editing of supplemental documents, font editing, advanced tables and graphics, mailmerge, and macros.

Instruction: Major topics covered in the course are setup and timed backup, dictionary and thesaurus, creation and editing of supplemental documents, font editing, advanced tables and graphics, mailmerge, and macros. Methods of instruction include lecture, laboratory, and an examination.

Credit Recommendation: In the lower division baccalaureate/associate degree category, 1 semester hour in General Education requirements (2/95).

Intermediate AutoCAD

Location: CommandTrain - Dearborn, MI or various on-site locations.

Length: 30 hours (6 weeks).

Dates: January 1988-Present.

Objective: To learn the process for developing and manipulating computer aided drawings using AutoCAD.

Learning Outcome: Upon successful completion of this course, the student will be able to use intermediate AutoCAD commands to create drawings using dimension, duplication, editing, and layering.

Instruction: Major topics covered in the course are intermediate dimensioning and line creating; duplication and editing; creating doughnuts, ellipses, and polygons; and layers. Methods of instruction include lecture, laboratory, and an examination.

Credit Recommendation: In the lower division baccalaureate/associate degree category, 2 semester hours in Industrial Engineering/Information Technology or Mechanical Engineering (2/95).

Intermediate Excel

Location: CommandTrain - Dearborn, MI or various on-site locations.

Length: 24 hours (6 weeks).

Dates: September 1987-Present.

Objective: To expand the concepts of database capabilities including formulas and functions and the utilization of dynamic databases.

Learning Outcome: Upon successful completion of this course, the student will be able to use mathematical, statistical, and financial functions; to create and use complex databases; to relate data between spreadsheets; and to use complex macros and addresses.

Instruction: Major topics covered in the course are complex formulas, related spreadsheets, graphics, macros, database features, debugging spreadsheet, and formula functions. Methods of instruction include lecture, laboratory, and an examination.

Credit Recommendation: In the lower division baccalaureate/associate degree category, 2 semester hours in General Education requirements (2/95).

Introduction to AutoCAD

Location: CommandTrain - Dearborn, MI or various on-site locations.

Length: 30 hours (6 weeks).

Dates: March 1984-Present.

Objective: To introduce the basics of Computer Aided Design.

Learning Outcome: Upon successful completion of this course, the student will be able to use basic AutoCAD commands to create and manipulate lines, arcs, circles, and text objects.

Instruction: Major topics covered in the course are mouse and keyboard functions; file management; on-line help; erase, limits, snap, and grid commands; and absolute, relative, and polar coordinates. Methods of instruction include lecture, laboratory, and an examination.

Credit Recommendation: In the lower division baccalaureate/associate degree category, 2 semester hours in Industrial Engineering/Information Technology or Mechanical Engineering (2/95).

Introduction to Computer Applications (Introduction to Comp)

Location: CommandTrain - Dearborn, MI or various on-site locations.

Length: 15 hours (3 weeks).

Dates: September 1984-Present.

Objective: To introduce the concepts and usage of hardware, operating systems, and application packages.

Learning Outcome: Upon successful completion of this course, the student will be able to use introductory DOS/Windows commands, word processing, spreadsheet, and desktop publishing applications.

Instruction: Major topics covered in the course are DOS, Windows, Word Processing, Spreadsheet application, and desktop Publishing. Methods of instruction include lecture, laboratory, and an examination.

Credit Recommendation: In the lower division baccalaureate/associate degree category, 1 semester hour in Computer Information Systems/Computer Literacy (2/95).

Introduction to Excel

Location: CommandTrain - Dearborn, MI or various on-site locations.

Length: 24 hours (6 weeks).

Dates: June 1987-Present.

Objective: To introduce concepts of spreadsheets including data representation, creation of charts, and elementary database function.

Learning Outcome: Upon successful completion of this course, the student will be able to create and edit a spreadsheet including formatting, formulas, and macros; and to create, edit and extract information from a spreadsheet database.

Instruction: Major topics covered in the course are elementary spreadsheet creation and data editing; formulas and macros; and creation and use of the database. Methods of instruction include lecture, laboratory, and an examination.

Credit Recommendation: In the lower division baccalaureate/associate degree category, 2 semester hours in General Education requirement (2/95).

Introduction to Windows

Location: CommandTrain - Dearborn, MI or various on-site locations.

Length: 16 hours (4 weeks).

Dates: September 1992-Present.

Objective: To introduce the major concepts of Windows including the Program Manager, group windows, icons, and Windows applications.

Learning Outcome: Upon successful completion of this course, the student will be able to create and use groups and launch applications with emphasis on the File Manager, Macro Recorder, and Write and Paintbrush.

Instruction: Major topics covered in the course are Windows, groups and icons, desktop design and customization, launching applications, File Manager, Macro Recorder, and Write and Paintbrush. Methods of instruction include lecture, laboratory, and an examination.

Credit Recommendation: In the lower baccalaureate division/associate degree category, 1 semester hour in General Education requirements (2/95).

Introduction to WordPerfect for Windows

Location: CommandTrain - Dearborn, MI or various on-site locations.

Length: 20 hours (5 weeks).

Dates: January 1986-Present.

Objective: To introduce fundamentals of WordPerfect for Windows.

Learning Outcome: Upon successful completion of this course, the student will be able to create, edit, and format text; and use features such as search and replace, graphics, and the button bar.

Instruction: Major topics covered in the course are Windows WordPerfect screen, document creation and editing; and use of features including graphics and the button bar. Methods of instruction include lecture, laboratory, and an examination.

Credit Recommendation: In the lower division baccalaureate/associate degree category, 1 semester hour in General Education requirements (2/95).

Commerce Bank N.A.

Commerce Bancorp, Inc. headquartered in Cherry Hill, NJ, has three subsidiary banks, Commerce Bank, N.A., Commerce Bank/Pennsylvania, and Commerce Bank/Shore. It is the region's fastest growing, independently locally owned and managed bank with a network of 54 branches spanning Metropolitan Philadelphia to the New Jersey Shore. Throughout 1996, Commerce Bancorp, Inc. will be opening eight new offices across the Greater Delaware Valley. Commerce University, the training department for Commerce Bancorp, Inc., provides the training for all three subsidiaries.

Source of official student records: Registry of Credit Recommendations, American Council on Education, One Dupont Circle, Washington, DC 20036-1193.

Additional information about the courses: Office of Corporate-Higher Education Programs, Thomas Edison State College, 101 West State Street, Trenton, NJ 08608-1176.

Customer Service Representative Level I (RET 1201)

Location: Various locations.

Length: 30 hours (3 days a week/2 weeks), plus 120 hours (4 weeks) field experience.

Dates: January 1994-Present.

Objective: To provide the student with basic bank concepts relevant to personal and business product knowledge, policies, procedures, banking services, and comput er operations necessary to perform the responsibilities of a Customer Service Representative.

Learning Outcome: Upon successful completion of this course, the student will be able to open and service accounts, project a professional and positive image, and speak knowledgeably about the general products and services provided by bank.

Instruction: Major topics covered in the course are product knowledge - personal/business accounts, business types, Money Access Card (MAC), Commerce Check Card, home banking, Deposit Pro, Deluxe and other services; compliance - Regulation CC, Truth in Savings, Right to Financial Privacy Act, and Regulation D; loss prevention/security - new accounts, ID, fraud, robbery; and customer relations. Methods of instruction include lecture, discussion, laboratory experiences, and practice. The classroom portion of the course is followed by a four week field experience at a branch bank where the trainee will serve as a Customer Service Representative. A case study is required after completion of the field experience.

Credit Recommendation: In the lower division baccalaureate/associate degree category, 3 semester hours in Banking/Finance Practicum (field experience) or banking or business elective (4/96).

Customer Service Representative Level II (RET 2200)

Location: Various locations.

Length: 30 hours (3 days a week/2 weeks), plus 120 hours (4 weeks) field experience.

Dates: January 1994-Present.

Objective: To provide the student with concrete knowledge and procedures for safe deposit boxes, Individual Retirement Accounts, consumer loans, Federal Depository Insurance Corporation coverage, attorney accounts, rental security, escrow accounts, bank compliance, and loss prevention/security.

Learning Outcome: Upon successful completion of this course, the student will be able to speak knowledgeably about specific products and services provided by the bank and discuss the State/Federal laws and the bank's policies and procedures governing the bank's projects/services.

Instruction: Major topics covered in the course are product knowledge - safe deposit boxes, Individual Retirement Accounts (IRAs), consumer loans, Federal Depository Insurance Corporation (FDIC), attorney accounts, rental security, and escrow accounts; compliance - money laundering, Federal and State banking regulations; and loss prevention/security - levies, kiting and recent issues in loss prevention and security. Methods of instruction include lecture, discussion, laboratory experience, and practice. The classroom portion of the course is followed by a four-week field experience at a branch bank where the trainee will serve as Customer Service Representative. A case study is required after completion of the field experience.

Credit Recommendation: In the lower division baccalaureate/associate degree category, 3 semester hours in Banking/Finance Practicum (field Experience) or banking or business elective (4/96).

Professional Teller Training Course (RET 1100)

Location: Various locations.

Length: 61 hours (11 days).

Dates: January 1994-Present.

Objective: To provide the students with basic banking knowledge and concepts needed to identify and apply bank policies and procedures for the teller position.

Learning Outcome: Upon successful completion of this course, the student will be able to accurately process basic teller transactions, project a positive and professional image at all times, and reference and use appropriate policies and procedures.

Instruction: Major topics covered in the course are loss prevention and security; robbery, fraud, counterfeiting, identification; cash handling guidelines; drawer limits, coverages and shortages, and cash exchanges; teller compliance; Regulation CC, Community Reinvestment Act, Bank Secrecy Act, Regulation DD, Right to Financial Privacy Act; basic bank product knowledge; and checking, savings and money market accounts, MAC, negotiable instruments, US Savings Bonds, cash advance, treasury tax and loan payments, and night depository. Methods of instruction include classroom discussion, lecture, practice and one day of lab, and a practicum in a branch bank.

Credit Recommendation: In the lower division baccalaureate/associate degree category, 3 semester hours in Banking Elective or Business Elective (4/96).

Commonwealth Edison Company

The Commonwealth Edison Production Training Center is located near Braidwood, Illinois, approximately 65 miles southwest of Chicago, Illinois. This facility opened in late 1982 and houses the Production Training Department staff, including operations, maintenance, technical training, and program development activities. In addition, the Center includes two simulators for LaSalle and Byron/Braidwood plants and is responsible for training approximately 2,000 individuals each year from both fossil and nuclear stations and applicable general office departments.

The Training Center represents a culmination of twenty years of Company efforts to formalize and systematize production training and has as its mission the task of helping to insure the safe, economical, and efficient operation of Commonwealth Edison generating stations by improving human performance. This mission is to be accomplished by controlling the job environment through human factors analysis and design standards and procedures, and by developing the knowledge, skills and attitudes of Design and Operating Area personnel through training.

The Center includes thirty classrooms, several mechanical, electrical, and instrumentation labs, a cafeteria, and a learning resource center. The learning resource center, available to both students and staff, provides access to instructional tapes, reports, and general and specific training books and materials which are certain to be of use to you during your stay.

A tour of the entire facility, including simulators, labs, and the resource center will be provided upon request.

Source of official student records: Registry of Credit Recommendations, American Council on Education, One Dupont Circle, Washington, DC 20036-1193.

Additional information about the courses: College Credit Recommendation Service, American Council on Education, One Dupont Circle, Washington, DC 20036-1193.

Chemistry Technician Generic Initial Training

Location: Wilmington and other off-site locations.

Length: 480 hours (12 weeks).

Dates: January 1983-Present.

Objective: To develop the skills necessary to understand and apply the principles of chemistry and chemical analysis of water, air, and soil samples.

Learning Outcome: Upon successful completion of this course, the student will be able to understand the fundamentals of chemistry as they apply to nuclear power plants and properly collect, analyze, and interpret sample data.

Instruction: Major topics covered in the course are a review of basic mathematics (equation solving, graphing, statistics, and logarithms); basic principles of physics; radioactivity; interaction of radiation with matter; radiation protection and measurements; water treatment techniques (including ion exchange, filtration, chlorination, and reverse osmosis); and chemical analytical techniques (including titrations, gravimetric, gas chromatography ion chromatography, ultra violet/visible light analyses, atomic absorption, and radioactivity determinations). Methods of instruction include lecture, discussion, classroom exercises, audio/visual materials, laboratory practical exercises, and written examinations.

Credit Recommendation: In the lower division baccalaureate/associate degree category, 1 semester hour in Introductory Mathematics, 1 semester hour in Non-Calculus Physics, 3 semester hours in Radiation Protection and Measurement, 2 semester hours in Fundamentals of Chemistry, 1 semester hour in Water Chemistry, 4 semester hours in Analytical Chemistry, and 2 semester hours in Radiochemistry (11/96).

Fundamentals of Radiation Protection

Location: Wilmington and other off-site locations within Illinois.

Length: 560 hours (14 weeks).

Dates: January 1983-Present.

Objective: To develop the skills necessary to understand and apply principles of radiation protection to nuclear power plants.

Learning Outcome: Upon successful completion of this course, the student will be able to understand the fundamentals of radiation protection; measure and estimate external and internal radiation doses; apply principles of exposure control; and comply with applicable rules and regulations.

Instruction: Major topics covered in the course are a review of basic mathematics (equation solving, graphing, and statistics); basic principles of physics; radioactivity; interactions of radiation with matter; instrumentation for monitoring and dosimetry; radiation protection regulations and standards; ALARA; airborne radioactivity; contamination control; radioactive material shipping; radiation protection litigation; and response to emergencies. Methods of instruction include lecture, discussion, classroom exercises, case studies, audio/visual materials, laboratory exercises, and examinations.

Credit Recommendation: In the lower division baccalaureate/associate degree category, 1 semester hour in Non-Calculus Physics and 6 semester hours in Radiation Protection and Measurement in Nuclear Science (Health Physics) (9/94).

Computer Institute

Computer Institute was founded in 1983 to provide computer training to companies and the general public. Our mission is to provide training in the computer field using the latest technologies and maintain the highest quality of instruction for our clients. Computer Institute is affiliated with many software vendors including Microsoft, Lotus, Borland, WordPerfect/ Novell and many other hi-tech organizations and as a solution provider for these companies we are offering quality training in the most optimized period of time.

Computer Institute offers training in more than fifty courses including Certified Novell Engineer (CNE), Microsoft Certified Systems Engineer (MS-CSE), Computer Programming (Unix, C, C++, Visual Basic, Power Builder, Database Design & Programming), Office Automa-tion and many PC-based applications. Our instructors are highly educated in the computer field with many years of practical work experience.

AUTHORIZED COMPUTER INSTITUTE SCHOOL

Computer Institute
7202 Arlington Boulevard, 3rd Floor
Falls Church, VA 22042
Contact: Dr. Agha K. Ghahari
Phone No.: 301-424-0044
Fax No.: 301-424-1693

Source of official student records: Registry of Credit Recommendations, American Council on Education, One Dupont Circle, Washington, DC 20036-1193 or Registrars Office, Computer Institute, Suite 215, 611 Rockville Pike, Rockville MD 20852.

Additional information about the courses: College Credit Recommendation Service, American Council on Education, One Dupont Circle, Washington, DC 20036-1193.

Computer Programming

C Programming

Location: Rockville, MD and Falls Church, VA.

Length: 35 hours, over 5 days.

Dates: January 1988-Present.

Objective: To provide the student with an introduction to basic programming concepts and programming in the C language.

Learning Outcome: Upon successful completion of this course, the student will be able to formulate and solve programming problems using the C programming language.

Instruction: Major topics covered in the course are C variables and constants, operators, expressions and statements, functions, arrays, controlling program flow, and using the C editor. Methods of instruction include instructor-led demonstration and discussion with extensive hands-on work using current computer equipment in the labs.

Credit Recommendation: In the lower division baccalaureate/associate degree category, 2 semester hours in Computer Science, Data Processing, or Computer Information Systems (9/95).

C++ Programming

Location: Rockville, MD and Falls Church, VA.

Length: 35 hours, over 5 days.

Dates: January 1988-Present.

Objective: To provide the student with an introduction to the basic concepts and some advanced features of the C++ object-oriented programming language.

Learning Outcome: Upon successful completion of this course, the student will be able to formulate and solve problems using the C++ programming language, and understand its use for object systems development.

Instruction: Major topics covered in the course are classes and objects, inline and friend functions, arrays, pointers, references, dynamic allocations operators, dynamic memory allocations, and input/ output. Methods of instruction include discussion; and demonstration with extensive hands-on work using current computer equipment in the labs.

Credit Recommendation: In the lower division baccalaureate/associate degree category, 2 semester hours in Computer Science, Data Processing, or Computer Information Systems (9/95).

Database Design and Programming

Location: Rockville, MD and Falls Church, VA.

Length: 35 hours (over 5 days).

Dates: January 1992-Present.

Objective: To provide the student with the skills necessary to utilize FoxPro or Oracle as a database management system programming tool.

Learning Outcome: Upon successful completion of this course, the student will be able to design and program database applications utilizing FoxPro or Oracle including designing, creating, reporting, and querying multiple tables.

Instruction: Major topics covered in the course are DBMS terminology, defining tables, connecting tables, sorting and indexing , creating menus, pop-up controls, and screen building. Methods of instruction include instructor-led demonstrations, discussion, consisting mostly of hands-on organized instruction, and examinations.

Credit Recommendation: In the lower division baccalaureate/associate degree category, 2 semester hours in FoxPro or Oracle as a DBMS Tool in Computer Science, Data Processing, or Computer Information Systems (9/95).

Powerbuilder Programming

Location: Rockville, MD and Falls Church, VA.

Length: 35 hours, over 5 days.

Dates: January 1994-Present.

Objective: To train students in the use of the Powerbuilder programming language.

Learning Outcome: Upon successful completion of this course, the student will understand and be able to apply the techniques necessary for utilizing the Powerbuilder programming language for the Windows environment including designing and using forms, reporting, queries and SQL access.

Instruction: Major topics covered in the course are technology overview, programming concepts, Powerbuilder basics, editing, compiling, running a program, adding controls, menu processing, export & import, dialogue boxes, SQL basics, data filters, libraries, and toolbars. Methods of instruction include instructor-led demonstration, discussion-consisting mainly of hands-on class exercises, organized instruction, and examinations in using the Powerbuilder programming language.

Credit Recommendation: In the lower division baccalaureate/associate degree category, 2 semester hours in Powerbuilder programming in Computer Science, Data Processing or Computer Information Systems (9/95).

UNIX Operating Systems

Location: Rockville, MD and Falls Church, VA.

Length: 21 hours, over 3 days.

Dates: January 1988-Present.

Objective: To train students in the use of the UNIX operating system.

Learning Outcome: Upon successful completion of this course, the student will understand the facilities and capabilities of UNIX including use of the VI editor, file utilities, shell programming, directory structure, input/output processes, and communicating with other users.

Instruction: Major topics covered in the course are accounts & security, login & logout, directory manipulation, standard shell, alternate shells, editing, communicator, vi editor, commands & pipelining, and shell programming basics. Methods of instruction include instructor-led discussion; demonstration, consisting mainly of hands-on class exercises; organized instruction; and examinations in the UNIX operating system.

Credit Recommendation: In the lower division baccalaureate/associate degree category, 1 semester hour in UNIX Programming, Data Processing, or Computer Science (9/95).

Visual Basic

Location: Rockville, MD and Falls Church, VA.

Length: 35 hours (over 5 days).

Dates: January 1992-Present.

Objective: To provide the student with the skills necessary to utilize FoxPro or Oracle as a database management system programming tool.

Learning Outcome: Upon successful completion of this course, the student will be able to design and program Windows applications including dialog boxes and other objects, and the required user interfaces to access data from different database systems, using Visual Basic.

Instruction: Major topics covered in the course are designing and using forms, simple lists, combo lists, check boxes, option boxes, file I/O, arrays, error handling, and OLE. Methods of instruction include instructor-led discussion and hands-on instruction in computer labs presenting Visual Basic techniques and processes as described above, using current up-to-date programming.

Credit Recommendation: In the lower division baccalaureate/associate degree category, 2 semester hours in Visual Basic Programming (9/95).

Microsoft Certified Systems Engineer

Internetworking with TCP/IP Using Windows NT

Location: Rockville, MD and Falls Church, VA.

Length: 14 hours (over 2 days).

Dates: January 1993-Present.

Objective: To provide the student with in-depth coverage of the TCP/IP protocols and their implementation within Windows NT.

Learning Outcome: Upon successful completion of this course, the student will understand the application of the TCP/IP protocols, how it relates to Windows NT communications and how NT utilizes the standard.

Instruction: Major topics covered in the course are TCP/IP basic, IP addressing, subnets routing, NetBios, name resolution, host name resolution, MS-SNMP, performance tuning, optimization, and troubleshooting. Methods of instruction include discussion; demonstration with extensive hands-on work; using current computer equipment in the labs and preparatory MS-CSE examinations.

Credit Recommendation: In the upper division baccalaureate degree category, 1 semester hour in Computer Information Systems, Data Processing, or Computer Science (9/95).

Supporting Microsoft Windows and DOS

Location: Rockville, MD and Falls Church, VA.

Length: 14 hours (over 2 days).

Dates: January 1993-Present.

Objective: This course covers the installation and customization of Windows and the DOS operating system.

Learning Outcome: Upon successful completion of this course, the student will understand Windows and DOS technology, and be able to install and configure both.

Instruction: Major topics covered in the course are DOS and Windows installation, system configuration, memory management and optimization, customization and troubleshooting. Methods of instruction include discussion and demonstration with extensive hands-on work, using current computer equipment in the labs. Preparatory MS-CSE exams are used.

Credit Recommendation: In the lower division baccalaureate/associate degree category, 1 semester hour in Computer Information Systems, Data Processing, or Computer Science (9/95).

Supporting Windows NT

Location: Rockville, MD and Falls Church, VA.

Length: 42 hours (over 6 days).

Dates: January 1993-Present.

Objective: To teach the student about the technology of the Microsoft Windows NT operating system. It includes a component on the system operations and support, and a component on the server technology.

Learning Outcome: Upon successful completion of this course, the student will understand the Windows NT technology, its application and operation, and installation and support issues.

Instruction: Major topics covered in the course are server & workstation technology, installing Windows NT workstation, user rights, file systems & backup, managing resources, the networking environments, protocols, printing, application support, Windows NT server, managing domains, server data protection, TCP/IP, and integrating Novell netware. Methods of instruction include discussion and demonstration with extensive hands-on work, using current computer equipment in the laboratories.

Credit Recommendation: In the lower division baccalaureate/associate degree category, 3 semester hours in Computer Information Systems, Data Processing, or Computer Science (9/95).

Supporting Windows NT Technologies (Formerly Microsoft Systems Management Server)

Location: Rockville, MD and Falls Church, VA.

Length: 28 hours, over 4 days.

Dates: January 1993-Present.

Objective: This course covers the basics of Microsoft Systems Management Server technology, planning, installation, optimization, maintenance and support.

Learning Outcome: Upon successful completion of this course, the student will understand MS Systems Management, Server applications and operation, and know how to plan and install the system for maximum utilization.

Instruction: Major topics covered in the course are MS Systems, Management Server, technology overview, planning, set-up, SMS database management, software distribution, network application management, multiple SMS sites, and troubleshooting SMS. Methods of instruction include discussion, demonstration with extensive hands-on work, using current computer equipment in the laboratories, and preparatory MS-CSE examinations are used.

Credit Recommendation: In the upper division baccalaureate degree category, 2 semester hours in Computer Information

Systems, Data Processing, or Computer Science (9/95).

Novell Certified Netware Engineer

Advanced Netware Administration

Location: Rockville, MD and Falls Church, VA.

Length: 14 hours (over 2 days).

Dates: January 1990-Present.

Objective: To provide students with the knowledge and skills to utilize the advanced planning and management features of Netware.

Learning Outcome: Upon successful completion of this course, the student will understand server management, memory management, performance monitoring, optimization and advanced printing.

Instruction: Major topics covered in the course are server configuration, server management, performance monitoring, server optimization, caching, DOS client management, and printer customization. Methods of instruction include discussion, lecture and hands-on exercises, and example problems. Preparatory CNE exams are also included.

Credit Recommendation: In the upper division baccalaureate degree category, 1 semester hour in Networking, Telecommunications, or Computer Information (9/95).

Netware 3.X to 4.1 Update

Location: Rockville, MD and Falls Church, VA.

Length: 14 hours (over 2 days).

Dates: January 1990-Present.

Objective: to provide the student with the knowledge of Netware migration from 3X to 4.1.

Learning Outcome: Upon successful completion of this course, the student will understand the differences between Netware 3X and 4.1, and understand the migration process.

Instruction: Major topics covered in the course are Network 3x tasks in version 4.1, Netware Directory Services, File system, user environment, menu management, partitioning, synchronization, and troubleshooting. Methods of instruction include discussion, lecture, and hands-on experience in computer laboratories with up-to-date computer equipment.

Credit Recommendation: In the upper division baccalaureate degree category, 1 semester hour in Networking, Telecommunications, or Computer Information (9/95).

Netware Administration

Location: Rockville, MD and Falls Church, VA.

Length: 28 hours, over 4 days.

Dates: January 1990-Present.

Objective: The provide the student with an overview of Novell Netware System Administration from concepts to operation.

Learning Outcome: Upon successful completion of this course, the student will understand Netware technology, planning, implementation, security and operational basics.

Instruction: Major topics covered in the course are microcomputers & DOS, networking basics, servers, security concepts, login & attributes, access rights, netware utilities, network reporting, and network management. Methods of instruction include discussion, lecture, hands-on exercises and example problems, and preparatory CNE examinations.

Credit Recommendation: In the upper division baccalaureate/associate degree category, 2 semester hours in Networking, Telecommunications, Computer Information Systems (9/95).

Netware Design and Implementation

Location: Rockville, MD and Falls Church, VA.

Length: 14 hours, over 2 days.

Dates: January 1990-Present.

Objective: This course will expose the student to the issues, design and implementation of Netware Directory Services.

Learning Outcome: Upon successful completion of this course, the student will understand Netware Directory Services and design issues, partitioning strategies, and creating and implementing NDS.

Instruction: Major topics covered in the course are design issues and approach, NDS directory structure, design, creation and implementation of NDS. Methods of instruction include discussion, lecture, and hands-on exercises and example problems. Preparatory CNE exams are also included.

Credit Recommendation: In the upper division baccalaureate/associate degree category, 1 semester hour in Networking, Telecommunications, or Computer Information (9/95).

Netware Installation and Configuration

Location: Rockville, MD and Falls Church, VA.

Length: 14 hours (over 2 days).

Dates: January 1990-Present.

Objective: To provide students with an overview of Netware design and configuration and implementation issues.

Learning Outcome: Upon successful completion of this course, the student will understand network analysis, design, installation, planning, and implementation issues.

Instruction: Major topics covered in the course are network design issues, hardware and software issues, installation process and procedures, installation options, selection and upgrading. Methods of instruction include discussion, lecture, and hands-on in computer laboratories with up-to-date computer equipment.

Credit Recommendation: In the upper division baccalaureate degree category, 1 semester hour in Networking, Telecommunications, or Computer Information (9/95).

Netware TCP/IP Transport

Location: Rockville, MD and Falls Church, VA.

Length: 14 hours (over 2 days).

Dates: January 1990-Present.

Objective: To teach the student about TCP/IP standards and protocols.

Learning Outcome: Upon successful completion of this course, the student will understand the principles of the TCP/IP standards and protocols, as they apply to Novell netware.

Instruction: Major topics covered in the course are TCP/IP background & development, DOD model, protocol, Netware TCP/IP transport, loading & configuring TCP/IP, internetworking, routing, and IP tunneling. Methods of instruction include discussion, lecture, hands-on exercises and example problems, and preparatory CNE examinations .

Credit Recommendation: In the upper division baccalaureate degree category, 1 semester hour in Networking, Telecommunications, or Computer Information (9/95).

Network Service and Support

Location: Rockville, MD and Falls Church, VA.

Length: 21 hours (over 3 days).

Dates: January 1990-Present.

Objective: To expose the student to the issues, concepts, and practice of supporting a local area network.

Learning Outcome: Upon successful completion of this course, the student will

understand network service and support issues, know some troubleshooting tools & techniques, and be able to troubleshoot & repair typical network problems.

Instruction: Major topics covered in the course are troubleshooting fundamentals, problem prevention, troubleshooting tools, architecture, workstation problems, and printing problems. Methods of instruction include discussion, lecture, hands-on exercises, example problems, and preparatory CNE examinations.

Credit Recommendation: In the upper division baccalaureate degree category, 2 semester hours in Networking, Telecommunications, or Computer Information (9/95).

Networking Technologies

Location: Rockville, MD and Falls Church, VA.

Length: 14 hours, over 2 days.

Dates: January 1990-Present.

Objective: To provide the student with exposure to the concepts of today's networking technology.

Learning Outcome: Upon successful completion of this course, the student will know network concepts and theory and understand the OSI model.

Instruction: Major topics covered in the course are network models and elements, and the OSI model, theory, and implementation. Methods of instruction include discussion, lecture, hands-on exercises, example problems, and preparatory CNE examinations.

Credit Recommendation: In the upper division baccalaureate/associate degree category, 1 semester hour in Networking, Telecommunications, or Computer Information (9/95).

Office Automation Specialist

Office Automation Specialist

Location: Rockville, MD and Falls Church, VA.

Length: 84 hours, over 12 days.

Dates: January 1990-Present.

Objective: To provide the student with the computer knowledge and skills needed in today's changing office environment. Tools such as word processors, spreadsheets, data base systems and presentation applications are covered.

Learning Outcome: Upon successful completion of this course, the student will understand the functions of the most common office tools and be able to utilize micro-computer applications products in an office environment.

Instruction: Major topics covered in the course are DOS, Windows, WordPerfect, Work, Excel, Access, PowerPoint, and the Internet. Methods of instruction include discussion, presentation, and hands-on instruction in computer labs covering the PC applications and processes as described, using current up-to-date equipment.

Credit Recommendation: In the lower division baccalaureate/associate degree category, 4 semester hours in Office Technology Applications or Data Processing (9/95).

Computer Learning Center

Computer Learning Center (CLC) is owned and operated by the Markerdown Corporation. The school has been in operation since 1982 and was purchased from the Airco Educational Services Division of The BOC Group, Inc. in 1987.

CLC is designed to provide quality training responsive to the data processing community. New technology is always explored in an effort to keep all programs up to date and in tune with the needs of employers. CLC is accredited by the Association of Independent Colleges and Schools (AICS).

The administration of the school comprised of five departments: Admissions, Financial Aid, Business, Education, and Placement.

Source of official student records: Registry of Credit Recommendations, American Council on Education, One Dupont Circle, Washington, DC, 20036-1193.

Additional information about the courses: Office of Corporate-Higher Education Programs, Thomas Edison State College, 101 West State Street, Trenton, NJ 08608-1176.

Analog Devices and Circuit Principles (CENT203)

Location: Paramus, NJ.

Length: 200 hours (16 weeks).

Dates: May 1996-Present.

Objective: To teach the student analog devices, operation and application.

Learning Outcome: Upon successful completion of this course, the student will be able to understand the basic semiconductor junction; construct, analyze and troubleshoot various analog circuit configurations utilizing diodes and transistors; understand amplifier classes.

Instruction: Major topic covered in the course is analog devices as they apply to field procedures of an electronic technician. Methods of instruction include lecture in a formal classroom and laboratory experimentation in a modern computer environment. Assignments are given by the instructor for in-school and home study.

Credit Recommendation: In the lower division baccalaureate/associate degree category, 6 semester hours in Electronic Devices and Applications (4/97).

Analog Devices and Circuit Principles (CENT 203/MET 203) (Formerly CET 203-204; DET 203-204) (Formerly Analog Devices and Principles CET 203, DET 203

Location: Paramus, NJ.

Length: 200 hours.

Dates: February 1988-June 1993.

Objective: To teach the student the fundamentals of semiconductor devices and troubleshooting analog circuits.

Learning Outcome: Upon successful completion of this course, the student will be able to understand semiconductor devices and their applications; understand troubleshooting of semiconductor circuits; demonstrate an understanding of junction diode principles by drawing diagrams of a diode in unbiased, forward biased, and reversed biased modes; draw the three configurations for bipolar junction and field effect transistor amplifiers and state the characteristics of each; and demonstrate a basic understanding of the major amplifier classes and their uses.

Instruction: The course reviews composition of material used in electronic operations and states how atomic structure is related to the basic semiconductor junction. It is shown how this junction is formed into the diode and transistor. The various analog circuits utilizing diodes and transistors are constructed, analyzed, and troubleshot in laboratory instruction. Knowledge concerning actual field operations of an electronic technician is applied throughout the course for each subject covered.

Credit Recommendation: In the lower division baccalaureate/associate degree category, 6 semester hours in Electronic Devices and Principles (12/90).

Application Integration Using MS Office (MBA103)

Location: Paramus, NJ.

Length: 225 hours (8 weeks).

Dates: July 1996-Present.

Objective: To teach the student the components of an office suite package.

Learning Outcome: Upon successful completion of this course, the student will be able to understand the fundamentals of word processing (Word); understand the fundamentals of spreadsheets (Excel); create, save, retrieve and print documents using Word and Excel.

Instruction: Major topics covered in the course are Word, Excel, Access and Powerpoint. Methods of instruction include lecture in a formal classroom and laboratory experimentation in a modern computer environment. Assignments are given by the instructor for in school and home study.

Credit Recommendation: In the lower division baccalaureate/associate degree category, 3 semester hours in Microcomputers in Business (4/97).

Application Software and Network Technology (E400)

Location: Paramus, NJ.

Length: 240 hours (8 weeks).

Dates: July 1996-Present.

Objective: To teach students Windows, Microsoft Office, PC Tools, viral detection and introduce Novell Netware.

Learning Outcome: Upon successful completion of this course, the student will be able to use Windows, create icons, use print manager and desktop applications as well as configure printers and manage fonts; install Microsoft Word, Excel, Access and Powerpoint; solve Microsoft Office problems that relate to operator error and corrupted software; manage a system for optimum performance using PC Tools; detect and prevent viral infection of the personal computer; understand Network technologies including layers, synchronous and asynchronous communications, HDLC, SDLC, SNA, gateways and data packets.

Instruction: Major topics covered in the course are Windows, Microsoft Office, PC Tools and viral detection as it pertains to software-related problems encountered in the field. An introduction to Novell Networking end this module to prepare the student for the CNE module. Methods of instruction include lecture in a formal classroom and laboratory experimentation in a modern computer environment. Assignments are given by the instructor for in-school and home study.

Credit Recommendation: In the lower division baccalaureate/associate degree category, 4 semester hours in Microsoft Windows and 2 semester hours in Introduction to Networks (4/97).

AS/400 System Administration (MBS102)

Location: Paramus, NJ.

Length: 225 hours (17 weeks).

Dates: May 1996-Present.

Objective: To teach students basic, intermediate and advanced AS/400 system operation concepts.

Learning Outcome: Upon successful completion of this course, the student will be able to execute CL commands using prompting, position keyboard notation, and menu navigation; backup and restore objects and libraries; Power down and IPL the AS/400.

Instruction: Major topics covered in the course are AS/400 system operations and advanced AS/400 system operations concepts. Methods of instruction include lecture in a formal classroom and laboratory experimentation in a modern computer environment. Assignments are given by the instructor for in-school and home study.

Credit Recommendation: In the lower division baccalaureate/associate degree category, 3 semester hours in Mini-computer Operations (4/97).

AS/400 System Operations (MBS101)

Location: Paramus, NJ.

Length: 100 hours (20 days).

Dates: September 1993-December 1995.

Objective: To enable students to perform system operator functions on the AS/400.

Learning Outcome: Upon successful completion of this course, the student will be able to learn the structure of the CL commands; use the AS/400 menus; use the Save/Restore and system start-up and shut-down commands; work with printer output, sending and receiving messages and use the local device configuration; and use managing devices, status menus and system values.

Instruction: Major topics covered in the course present a comprehensive overview of the OS/400 operating system and attached peripheral devices through lecture and practical hands-on exercises; perform a number of system operator functions including work management functions, object manipulation, save and restore procedures, start-up and shut-down procedures, command interface and menu navigation.

Credit Recommendation: In the lower division baccalaureate/associate degree category, 3 semester hours in AS/400 System Operations (9/93).

AS/400/RPG 400 (DP-200) (Formerly RPG II Programming [DP-200])

Location: Paramus, NJ.

Length: *Version 1:* 100 hours (20 days); *Version 2:* 100 hours (19-23 days).

Dates: *Version 1:* March 1983-February 1991; *Version 2:* March 1991-August 1993.

Objective: *Version 1:* To enable students to understand concepts of RPG II, generate RPG programs, and execute programs. *Version 2:* To enable students to understand concepts of RPG III, generate RPG III programs, and execute programs.

Learning Outcome: *Version 1:* Upon successful completion of this course, the student will be able to understand the concepts of RPG logic flow, indicator usage, arithmetic operations, control levels, compare operations, indexed sequential files, disk storage and retrieval, sort/merge, subroutines, tables, and arrays; transferring information from one file to another using IBM utility programs for listing input and output files; completing a card to print RPG II program using arithmetic operations and report headings; generating sorted input data and complete RPG programs using level breaks for major and minor totals; and completing an RPG II program using indexed sequential input and table look-up. *Version 2:* Upon successful completion of this course, the student will be able to understand the concepts of RPG logic flow, indicator usage, arithmetic operations, control levels, compare operations, disk storage and retrieval, sort/merge and subroutines; transfer information from one file to another using IBM utility programs for listing input and output files; create RPG print program using arithmetic operations and report headings; generate sorted input data and complete RPG programs using level breaks for major and minor totals.

Instruction: *Version 1:* Major topics covered in the course are understanding the concepts of RPG logic flow, indicator usage, arithmetic operations, control levels, compare operations, indexed sequential files, disk storage and retrieval, sort/merge, subroutines, tables, and arrays; transferring information from one file to another using IBM utility programs for listing input and output files; completing a card to print RPG II program using arithmetic operations and report headings; generating sorted input data and complete RPG programs using level breaks for major and minor totals; and completing an RPG II program using indexed sequential input and table look-up. *Version 2:* Major topics covered in the course are understanding the concepts of RPG logic flow, indicator usage, arithmetic operations, control levels, compare operations, disk storage and retrieval, sort/merge and subroutines; transfer information from one file to another using IBM utility programs for listing input and output files; create RPG print program using arithmetic operations and report headings; generate sorted input data and complete RPG programs using level breaks for major and minor totals.

Credit Recommendation: *Version 1:* In the lower division baccalaureate/associate degree category, 3 semester hours in RPG II (2/85). *Version 2:* In the lower division baccalaureate/associate degree category, 3 semester hours in RPG III (5/91).

Assembler Language Coding (CP-301)

Location: Paramus, NJ.

Length: *Version 1:* 200 hours (40 days); *Version 2:* 200 hours (37-45 days).

Dates: April 1983-November 1991.

Objective: To enable students to understand and utilize OS JCL and utilities and to code and debug assembler programs using VSAM and non-VSAM methods.

Learning Outcome: *Version 1:* Upon successful completion of this course, the student will be able to code and run a program by incorporating disk-to-print moves, compares, and headings; using control break, logic, packed decimal instructions, editing techniques and print overflow concept; utilizing OS sort features; executing a sequential updates, using two input files, minor totals, line counters, and output-to-disk concepts; creating an indexed sequential file, using the required Macros; using explicit addressing techniques, and loops; and using three input files, one of which is to be updated based on specifications from a flowchart (maintenance). *Version 2:* Upon successful completion of this course, the student will be able to code and run a program by incorporating disk-to-print moves, compares, and headings; using control break, logic, packed decimal instructions, editing techniques, and, print overflow concept; utilizing OS sort features; executing a sequential update, using two input files, minor totals, line counters, and output-to-disk concepts; using explicit addressing techniques and loops; and using three input files, one of which is to be updated based on specifications from a flowchart (maintenance).

Instruction: Major topics covered in the course are concepts of symbolic language, assembler processing, data representation, standard instruction set, machine format, decimal instructions, defined storage, defined constants, base register, decimal alignment, explicit addressing, table processing, program structure, loop control, closed subroutines, and debugging techniques.

Credit Recommendation: In the lower division baccalaureate/associate degree category, 5 semester hours in Assembler Language or 1 semester hour in OS Job Control Language and Utilities (2/85) (5/91).

Basic Telecommunications and Microprocessor Theory (CET 407, MT 407) (Formerly CET 407-408), Elective I

Location: Paramus, NJ.

Length: 200 hours.

Dates: February 1988-June 1993.

Objective: To teach microprocessor architecture and basic telecommunications theory including fiber optics.

Learning Outcome: Upon successful completion of this course, the student will be able to understand the internal architecture of the microprocessor; explain the arithmetic logic unit and all of the basic registers that make up a microprocessor; explain computer memory including the theory of RAM and ROM, the characteristics of each, and how they are used in the computer; understand several of the most important computer addressing modes and explain why each of the various modes of addressing is necessary; understand how the input/output ports of a computer work; know some of the most important transmission formats such as RS-232 and IEEE-488 and understand when each is used; understand what a UART is and how it works; explain the circuitry and when it is used; explain the theory of microprocessor interrupt including the difference between a maskable and nonmaskable interrupt.

Instruction: Major topics covered in this course are introduction to telecommunication modulation principles, including fiber optics; mircroprocessors and microcomputers; and laboratory experimentation on modulation techniques and microcomputer operations.

Credit Recommendation: In the lower division baccalaureate/associate degree category, 3 semester hours in Survey Basic Telecommunications and 3 semester hours in Survey Microprocessor (12/90).

C Language Programming (CP302)

Location: Paramus, NJ

Length: 225 hours (17 weeks).

Dates: January 1996-December 1995.

Objective: To teach the student C and C++ programming languages.

Learning Outcome: Upon successful completion of this course, the student will be able to understand new C++ programming concepts such as encapsulation, inheritance, and polymorphism; understand the fundamentals of the C programming language such as C data types, looping, making decisions, building arrays, C pointers and structures and other foundation concepts.

Instruction: Major topics covered in the course are to teach the student C and C++ programming languages and their differences and similarities. Methods of instruction include lecture in a formal classroom and laboratory experimentation in a modern computer environment. Assignments are given by the instructor for in-school and home study.

Credit Recommendation: In the lower division baccalaureate/associate degree category, or in the upper division baccalaureate degree category, 4 semester hours in C Programming (4/97).

Computer Architecture and Servicing Techniques (CENT407)

Location: Paramus, NJ.

Length: 200 hours (16 weeks).

Dates: January 1997-Present.

Objective: To teach the students how to build, troubleshoot, and repair a personal computer and its components.

Learning Outcome: Upon successful completion of this course, the student will be able to build and disassemble a personal computer; understand and use MS/PC DOS as it applies to actual personal computer and service problems; troubleshoot and repair disk drives, keyboard, monitors, printers, modems and CPU's; utilize diagnostic software in troubleshooting procedures.

Instruction: Major topics covered in the course are building, troubleshooting, and repairing personal computers and their components. Methods of instruction include lecture in a formal classroom and laboratory experimentation in a modern computer environment. Assignments are given by the instructor for in-school and home study.

Credit Recommendation: In the lower division baccalaureate/associate degree category, or in the upper division baccalaureate degree category, 3 semester hours in MS/PC DOS and 3 semester hours in Personal Computer Servicing (4/97).

Computer Architecture and Servicing Techniques (CENT407)

Location: Paramus, NJ.

Length: 200 hours (40 days).

Dates: July 1993-December 1995.

Objective: To teach microcomputer architecture, software/hardware installation and troubleshooting, and to prepare the student for the ever changing personal computer field.

Learning Outcome: Upon successful completion of this course, the student will be able to understand the internal architectures of various microprocessors found in today's PC's; relate to various types of systems and peripherals in use today, including installation of hardware components and various software packages; diagnose whether a problem is operator error or actual failure of the software/hardware; understand customer relations and the importance of "fixing" the customer first; realize the rapid pace of development and importance of staying current with today's PC technology; and being prepared for the Novell/CNE module with solid understanding of networking technologies and concepts.

Instruction: Major topics covered in the course begin with students assembling their own personal computer, the computer is then used for the remainder of the module in the classroom/lab; become familiar with the disk operating system (DOS), microcomputer failure analysis and troubleshooting techniques are stressed throughout the course, this will allow the student to deal with actual service scenarios regardless of computer architecture or attached peripherals; installation of various peripherals and related software packages occurs throughout the module; preparing students for proper customer relations and situations is continuous from the first day of class; and the module concludes with an overview of networking technologies and concepts to prepare the students for the Novell/CNE module that follows.

Credit Recommendation: In the lower division baccalaureate/associate degree category, 6 semester hours in Microcomputer Architecture and Servicing Techniques (9/93).

Computer Based Accounting IS102

Location: Paramus, NJ.

Length: 100 hours.

Dates: August 1988-June 1993.

Objective: To teach the student basic accounting principles using Lotus 1-2-3 as the software for advanced spreadsheet applications.

Learning Outcome: Upon successful completion of this course, the student will be able to analyze and record business transactions including journals, posting, worksheets, and financial reports; spread journals; banking procedures and control of cash; and payroll preparation, including procedures and taxes. The student will use Lotus 1-2-3 for data selection and computation operations, worksheet operations, advanced range and file operations, importing and exporting, lookup tables, and Macro commands.

Instruction: Major topics covered in the course are a working knowledge of accounting principles and procedures along with advanced Lotus 1-2-3 concepts; accounting and business transactions, trial balances, financial reports, debits, credits, and payroll procedures, including taxes.

Credit Recommendation: In the lower division baccalaureate/associate degree category, 6 semester hours in Accounting with Microcomputer Applications (8/91).

Core IS100

Location: Paramus, NJ.

Length: 200 hours.

Dates: August 1988-July 1993.

Objective: To supply the student with basic hardware and software knowledge; and an understanding of the Disk Operating System, Lotus 1-2-3, word processing concepts, and business communications.

Learning Outcome: Upon successful completion of Business Communications/ Typing Skills, the student will be able to type a minimum of 25 words per minute; demonstrate the basic elements of good writing; understand and apply appropriate letter form; understand and apply types of letters, memos, and reports; and understand and apply oral communication, listening skills, and body language. Upon successful completion of Introduction to Computers/DOS, the student will be able to describe the history and use of computers; demonstrate an understanding of input, processing, output, and storage devices and functions; and understand and proficiently use common DOS commands and custom batch files. Upon successful completion of Introduction to Lotus 1-2-3, the student will be able to understand concepts and applications, including the Lotus worksheet, operators and functions, changing the appearance of the worksheet, print command, copy and move commands, cell reference and calculation, screen and paper graphics. Upon successful completion of Word Processing, the student will be able to understand and apply word processing concepts; creating, saving, and retrieving a document; simple editing functions, and block functions.

Instruction: Major topics covered in the course include a Core Module that is divided into four sections: Introduction to Computers/DOS, Introduction to Word Processing utilizing MultiMate Advantage, Introduction to Lotus 1-2-3, and Business Communications. Introduction to Computers/DOS introduces the student to hardware components and their interrelationships and application and system software concepts. The student obtains proficiency with common DOS commands and demonstrates an understanding of storage devices, file organization, and custom batch files. The Introduction to Word Processing Concepts introduces the student to concepts common to all word processors including creating and saving documents, inserting, deleting, moving and copying text, formatting, spell checking, and printing. The student increases typing skills during this time and demonstrates typing proficiency of 25 words per minute by the end of the course. At the conclusion of Introduction to Lotus 1-2-3 the student can demonstrate proficiency with Lotus, including direct entry into a worksheet from the DOS prompt, keying in labels, values, and editing these entries, and common Lotus 1-2-3 commands. In addition, the student gains proficiency with arithmetic and logical operators and functions, changing the appearance of the worksheet, the print command, the copy and move command with emphasis on their effect on formulas. Cell reference and calculation (recalculation) and screen and paper graphics are also covered.

Credit Recommendation: In the lower division baccalaureate/associate degree category, before August 1991, 3 semester hours in Word Processing and 1 semester hour in Business Communications; in the lower division baccalaureate/associate degree category, after August 1991, 3 semester hours in Introduction to Microcomputers, and 3 semester hours in Word Processing (8/91).

Digital and Microprocessor Concepts (CENT305)

Location: Paramus, NJ.

Length: 200 hours (16 weeks).

Dates: September 1996-Present.

Objective: To teach the student digital and microprocessor concepts.

Learning Outcome: Upon successful completion of this course, the student will be able to: Understand the binary and hexadecimal number systems and their use in digital circuits; Understand how binary logic gates are connected to form encoders, decoders and flip flops and how flip flops are configured to form counters and shift registers; Understand and troubleshoot RAM and ROM and other digital circuits; Understand the basic microprocessor internal architecture including the arithmetic logic unit (ALU), program counter, status register, temporary registers, accumulator and the instruction register.

Instruction: Major topics covered in the course are digital circuits and microprocessor architecture. Methods of instruction include lecture in a formal classroom and laboratory experimentation in a modern computer environment. Assignments are given by the instructor for in-school and home study.

Credit Recommendation: In the lower division baccalaureate/associate degree category, 4 semester hours in Digital Electronics and 2 semester hours in Microprocessors (4/97).

Digital and Microprocessor Concepts (CENT 305)

Location: Paramus, NJ.

Length: 200 hours (40 days).

Dates: July 1993-December 1995.

Objective: To teach students the fundamentals of Digital circuits, microcomputers and fiber optic technology and the techniques of troubleshooting Digital circuits and microcomputer systems.

Learning Outcome: Upon successful completion of this course, the student will be able to trace signals through And, Or, Nand, Nor, Inverter and Exclusive Or gates specifying outputs for given inputs, will produce truth tables for given inputs or outputs; trace signals through various types of flip-flops specifying outputs for given inputs, will produce truth tables for the given inputs/outputs; differentiate between Data, JK, RS, and T flip-flops; state the major characteristics of and differences between the following logic families: RTL, TTL, ECL, CMOS, and Tri-state; demonstrate a working knowledge of digital test equipment via lab exercises and demonstrations; explain microprocessor architecture and operation; understand and apply addressing instructions,, input/output hardware; understand fiber optics technology and its uses in communications; and demonstrate working knowledge of fiber optic tests and measurements via lab exercises.

Instruction: Major topics covered in the course are designed to give the student a clear and well-rounded understanding of digital circuits; binary and hexadecimal number systems and their purpose in digital circuits; how binary logic gates, the building blocks of digital circuits are connected to form encoders, decoders, and flip-flops; how flip-flops are configured to form counters and shift registers; waveform analysis of these circuits and how they are utilized in troubleshooting; arithmetic circuits; RAM and ROM circuits; digital to analog and analog to digital circuits; and troubleshooting of digital circuits.

Credit Recommendation: In the lower division baccalaureate/associate degree category, or in the upper division baccalaureate degree category, 3 semester hours in Digital Electronics: 2 semester hours in Microprocessor/Microcomputers; and 1 semester hour in Fiber Optic Technology (9/93).

Digital Electronics (CET 305, DET 305)
(Formerly CET 305-306; DET 305-306)

Location: Paramus, NJ.

Length: 200 hours.

Dates: February 1988-June 1993.

Objective: To teach the student the fundamentals of digital electronics and the techniques of troubleshooting digital circuits.

Learning Outcome: Upon successful completion of this course, the student will be able to: (1) trace signals through AND, OR, NAND, NOR, INVERTER, and EXCLUSIVE OR gates specifying outputs for given inputs; produce truth tables for given inputs/outputs; (2) trace signals through various types of flip-flops specifying outputs for given inputs; produce truth tables for the given inputs/outputs; (3) differentiate between Data, JK, RS, and T flip-flops; (4) state the major characteristics of and differences between the following logic families: RTL, TTL, ECL, CMOS, and Tristate; (5) demonstrate a working knowledge of digital test equipment via lab exercises and demonstrations.

Instruction: Major topics covered in the course are designed to give the student a clear and well-rounded understanding of digital circuits. Topics include binary and hexadecimal number systems and their purpose in digital circuits; how binary logic gates (the building blocks of digital circuits) are connected to form encoders, decoders, and flip-flops; how flip-flops are configured to form counters and shift registers; waveform analysis of these circuits and how they are utilized in troubleshooting; arithmetic circuits; RAM and ROM circuits; digital to analog and analog to digital circuits.

Credit Recommendation: In the upper division baccalaureate degree category, 4 semester hours in Digital Electronics (12/90).

Disk Operating System and Novell Netware (MBS101)

Location: Paramus, NJ.

Length: 225 hours (8 weeks).

Dates: March 1996-Present.

Objective: To teach the facets of the Disk Operating System (DOS) and Novell Netware Administration.

Learning Outcome: Upon successful completion of this course, the student will be able to apply commonly used file management commands of the Disk Operating System (DOS); use Novell features such as disaster recovery commands, system protection, I/O and batch files; create a structure for a user group, i.e. defining user rights and security levels; configure workstations and printers; troubleshoot, optimize the system, perform back-up operations and create login scripts; manage the print manager, create customized menus and use BACKUP utility.

Instruction: Major topics covered in the course are Disk Operating System (DOS) and Novell Netware. Methods of instruction include lecture in a formal classroom and laboratory experimentation in a modern computer environment. Assignments are given by the instructor for in-school and home study.

Credit Recommendation: In the lower division baccalaureate/associate degree category, 2 semester hours in Networking Technologies and 1 semester hour in Microcomputer Operating System: DOS (4/97).

DOS/Operations (CO-401)

Location: Paramus, NJ.

Length: *Version 1:* 200 hours (40 days); *Version 2:* 200 hours (37-45 days).

Dates: April 1983-February 1994.

Objective: To enable students to operate a large mainframe computer system with a full complement of peripheral devices.

Learning Outcome: Upon completion of the course, the student will be able to respond to DOS console messages with appropriate DOS operator response, work with DOS job control language, diagnose job control errors, and respond with appropriate corrections.

Instruction: Major topics covered in the course are the concepts of DOS Operating Systems, multiprogramming, multiprocessing, data management, task management, queue management, foreground partitions, background partitions, DOS operator commands, DOS utility programs, DOS job control language, spooling, Power II, Power II Operator Commands, Power Job Entry Control Language, and DOS IPL.

Credit Recommendation: In the lower division baccalaureate/associate degree category, 6 semester hours in DOS/Operations (2/85) (5/91).

Electricity Basic Fundamentals of Electronics (E100)

Location: Paramus, NJ.

Length: 240 hours (8 weeks).

Dates: January 1996-Present.

Objective: To teach students the fundamentals of electric circuits.

Learning Outcome: Upon successful completion of this course, the student will be able to perform basic mathematics needed for study of electric circuits; understand Ohms law and power; understand series, parallel and series-parallel circuits; make current, voltage and power calculations; understand the concepts of reactance and A.C. circuits.

Instruction: This course is designed to teach the students the fundamentals of electricity. Methods of instruction include lecture in a formal classroom and laboratory experimentation in a modern computer environment. Assignments are given by the instructor for in-school and home study.

Credit Recommendation: In the lower division baccalaureate/associate degree category, 6 semester hours in Introduction to Electric Circuits for non-Engineering Technology majors (4/97).

Electronics Analog and Digital Concepts (E200)

Location: Paramus, NJ.

Length: 240 hours (8 weeks).

Dates: March 1996-Present.

Objective: To teach analog and digital concepts oriented toward digital computer applications.

Learning Outcome: Upon successful completion of this course, the student will be able to construct, analyze and troubleshoot analog circuits and power supplies; understand the Binary and hexadecimal number systems and their purpose in digital circuits; connect together Binary logic gates to form encoders, decoders and flip flops; configure flip flops to form counters and shift resisters; convert analog to digital and digital to analog.

Instruction: Major topics covered in the course are analog and digital circuit concepts and their applications to computers. Methods of instruction include lecture in a formal classroom and laboratory experimentation in a modern computer environment. Assignments are given by the instructor for in-school and home study.

Credit Recommendation: In the lower division baccalaureate/associate degree category, 3 semester hours in Analog Electronics and 3 semester hours in Digital Electronics (4/97).

Financial Business Applications and Graphics (MBA 101)

Location: Paramus, NJ.

Length: 200 hours (40 days).

Dates: July 1993-December 1995.

Objective: To teach the student basic accounting principles and the fundamentals of business graphics, as well as the proficient use of MS-DOS.

Learning Outcome: Upon successful completion of this course, the student will be able to (in DOS) understand and use common DOS commands for disk and file management and disk organization, understand and use DOS batch files, and understand and use DOS advanced features of redirection; in Accounting Concepts: understand and apply accounting procedures for various types of businesses, analyze and record business transactions including journalizing, posting, worksheets and financial reports, utilize spread journals, apply banking procedures and cash control, prepare payroll, including procedures and taxes; in Business Graphics: understand and create analytical graphics, text charts and organizational charts, develop a slide show, import data from Lotus, and use macros.

Instruction: Major topics covered in the course give the student a working knowledge of DOS commands, accounting principles and procedures, and business graphics; basic and advanced DOS commands for disk and file management as well as batch files; business transactions, trial balances, financial reports, debits, credits and payroll procedures, including taxes; and analytical text and organizational charts are constructed and incorporated into a slide show.

Credit Recommendation: In the lower division baccalaureate/associate degree category, 2 semester hours in DOS, 2 semester hours in Business Graphics (Harvard Graphics); and 3 semester hours in Fundamental Accounting Concepts with Microcomputer Applications (9/93).

Introduction to Computers and Business Applications (CP100)

Location: Paramus, NJ.

Length: 225 hours (17 weeks).

Dates: January 1996-Present.

Objective: To teach basic computer concepts, the Windows graphical operating environment, Microsoft Office and flowcharting.

Learning Outcome: Upon successful completion of this course, the student will be able to understand basic computer concepts and flowcharting methods; utilize Windows graphic user interface (GUI) and accessory programs; create, save, retrieve, modify and format documents and tables using Microsoft Word.

Instruction: Major topics covered in the course are introduction to computers and flowcharting, Windows graphical operating environment and Microsoft Office. Methods of instruction include lecture in a formal classroom and laboratory experimentation in a modern computer environment. Assignments are given by the instructor for in-school and home study.

Credit Recommendation: In the lower division baccalaureate/associate degree category, 3 semester hours in Introduction to Computer Applications (4/97).

Introduction to Computers and Business Applications (MBS100)

Location: Paramus, NJ.

Length: 225 hours (8 weeks).

Dates: January 1996-Present.

Objective: To teach students an introduction to basic computer concepts, the Windows graphic user interface (GUI) and the Microsoft Office package.

Learning Outcome: Upon successful completion of this course, the student will be able to understand basic computer concepts; utilize Windows and accessory programs.

Instruction: Major topics covered in the course are Windows, Word, Excel, Access and Powerpoint. Methods of instruction include lecture in a formal classroom and laboratory experimentation in a modern computer environment. Assignments are given by the instructor for in-school and home study.

Credit Recommendation: In the lower division baccalaureate/associate degree category, 3 semester hours in Microcomputers in Business (4/97).

Introduction to Data Processing (DP-100)

Location: Paramus, NJ.

Length: *Version 1:* 100 hours (20 days); *Version 2:* 100 hours (19-23 days).

Dates: *Version 1:* February 1983-June 1989; *Version 2:* July 1989-August 1993.

Objective: To provide students with an introduction to data processing and to lay the foundation for subsequent computer courses.

Instruction: Major topics covered in the course are an overview of the data processing industry—its history and growth, its application to contemporary society, its terminology, and its possible impact on the future growth of our society; and concepts of components of the computer, internal processing, data formats, access methods; and logic and flowcharting.

Credit Recommendation: *Version 1:* In the lower division baccalaureate/associate degree category, 3 semester hours in Introduction to Data Processing, or 1 semester hour in Job Control Language (2/85). *Version 2:* In the lower division baccalaureate/associate degree category, 4 semester hours in Introduction to Data Processing (5/91).

Introduction to Electricity and Electronics (CENT101)

Location: Paramus, NJ.

Length: 200 hours (16 weeks).

Dates: January 1996-Present.

Objective: To teach the fundamentals of electric circuits to students with no previous knowledge.

Learning Outcome: Upon successful completion of this course, the student will be able to perform basic mathematics needed for the study of electric circuits; calculate resistance, current and voltages in various circuits; understand series circuits and parallel circuits and be able to calculate currents, voltages and power; understand how a capacitor and an inductor work and calculate capacitive and inductive reactance; understand RLC circuits, transformers, and filters.

Instruction: Major topic covered in the course is electricity fundamentals. Methods of instruction include lecture in a formal classroom and laboratory experimentation in a modern computer environment. Assignments are given by the instructor for in-school and home study.

Credit Recommendation: In the lower division baccalaureate/associate degree category, 6 semester hours in Introduction to Electric Circuits for non-Engineering Technology majors (4/97).

Introduction to Electricity and Electronics (CENT101/MET 101) (Formerly CET 101-102; DET 101-102) (Formerly Basic Electricity (CET 101A, DET 101)

Location: Paramus, NJ.

Length: 200 hours.

Dates: February 1988-June 1993.

Objective: To teach the student AC and DC concepts of electricity and fundamental troubleshooting techniques.

Learning Outcome: Upon successful completion of this course, the student will be able to explain, describe, and analyze concepts of electricity and circuits; be familiar with basic electrical lab equipment; state the variations of Ohm's law; manipulate electrical quantities to solve for an unknown using Ohm's law and the power formulas; explain the concepts of inductance and capacitance; list functions of and uses for inductors and capacitors; demonstrate (in writing) an ability to reduce series and parallel inductive or capacitive circuits into a single equivalent; explain what is meant by alternating current, reactance, impedance, resonance, frequency, period, and amplitude.

Instruction: Major topics covered in the course are the fundamentals of electricity to students with no previous knowledge of the subject. Topics covered are: (1) arithmetic as it applies to electrical circuits; Ohm's law and power theory; calculation of resistance; current and voltages in various circuits; series circuits; parallel circuits; calculation of current, voltage drops, and dissipated power; AC circuits; concept of reactance; how a capacitor and an inductor work; calculation of capacitive and inductive reactance; and RLC circuits and basic transformer theory.

Credit Recommendation: In the lower division baccalaureate/associate degree category, 6 semester hours in Introduction to Electric Circuits applicable to Industrial Technology or Electronic Technology (not Electrical Engineering Technology) (12/90).

Introduction to Microcomputers & Applications (MBA100)

Location: Paramus, NJ.

Length: 225 hours (8 weeks).

Dates: January 1996-Present.

Objective: To overview the personal computer, teach Windows graphical user interface (GUI) and Lotus for Windows.

Learning Outcome: Upon successful completion of this course, the student will be able to understand the components of a personal computer; understand the fundamentals of a graphic user interface, accessory programs, and Windows; demonstrate a proficiency of 25 wpm; Perform basic, intermediate, and advanced Lotus commands;

Instruction: Major topics covered in the course are introduction to the Personal Computer, Windows and Lotus. Methods of instruction include lecture in a formal classroom and laboratory experimentation in a modern computer environment. Assignments are given by the instructor for in-school and home study.

Credit Recommendation: In the lower division baccalaureate/associate degree category, 2 semester hours in Microcomputer Spreadsheet Application and 1 semester hour in Windows 3.1. After April 1997, in the lower division baccalaureate/associate degree category, 2 semester hours in Microcomputer Spreadsheet Application and 1 semester hour in Windows '95 (4/97).

Introduction to Microcomputers: Operating Environments and Spreadsheets (MBA 100)

Location: Paramus, NJ.

Length: 200 hours (40 days).

Dates: September 1993-December 1995.

Objective: To supply the student with basic hardware and software knowledge and an understanding of the Windows environment and Lotus 1-2-3.

Learning Outcome: Upon successful completion of this course, the student will be able to in Introduction to Computers: define hardware, software, and the computing cycle and demonstrate an understanding of input, processing, output and storage devices and functions; in Windows 3.1: understand the benefits of a Graphical User Interface, start and end a Windows session, manipulate the desktop, organize programs into meaningful task groups, use the Program Manager, Desktop Accessory Programs and the File Manager; and in Lotus 1-2-3: understand spreadsheet concepts and applications, including the Lotus Worksheet; Operators and Functions, the Classic Menu and the WYSIWYG Menu; Changing the Appearance of the Worksheet; Print Command; Copy and Move Commands; Cell Reference and Calculation; Screen and Paper Graphics; Database Operations; Range and File Operations, and Macros.

Instruction: Major topics covered in the course are divided into three sections: Introduction to Computers, Windows 3.1 and Lotus 1-2-3. Introduction to Computers introduces the student to Hardware components and their interrelationships, and Application and System Software concepts. In the Windows 3.1 component of the course, the student is introduced to the benefits of a Graphical User Interface and gains proficiency starting and ending a Windows session, manipulating the desktop, organizing programs into meaningful task groups, using the Program Managers, using the Desktop Accessory Programs, and using the File Manager. At the conclusion of the Lotus 1-2-3 component, the student will demonstrate proficiency with Lotus including direct entry into a worksheet from the DOS prompt, keying-in labels and values and editing those entries, and common Lotus 1-2-3 commands. In addition, the student gains proficiency with arithmetic and logical operators and functions, changing the appearance of the worksheet, the Print command, the Copy and Move command with emphasis on their effect on formulas; cell reference and calculation (recalculation), screen and paper graphics, database operations, range and file operations, and macros.

Credit Recommendation: In the lower division baccalaureate/associate degree category, 2 semester hours in Introduction to Windows 3.1 and 3 semester hours in Lotus 1-2-3 (9/93).

Introduction to Microcomputers/WordPerfect (MBS 100)

Location: Paramus, NJ.

Length: 100 hours (20 days).

Dates: September 1993-December 1995.

Objective: To give the student a proficient knowledge of WP 5.1.

Learning Outcome: Upon successful completion of this course, the student will be able to understand and apply word processing concepts; create, save and retrieve a document; editing functions; block functions; formatting for printing; search and replace; footnotes/endnotes; file management; speller and thesaurus; sorting and merging; macros; columns; tables of contents; lists and indexes; math; and graphics.

Instruction: Major topics covered in the course are the basic concepts of creating, revising, saving and retrieving documents, revision techniques include changing the font size and appearance, formatting, the search replace feature, spell-check, and using the thesaurus; basic concepts are explored by investigating higher level special features which include sorting, merging, creating and executing macros, text and math columns, generating table of contents, indexes; and incorporating graphics into a file.

Credit Recommendation: In the lower division baccalaureate/associate degree category, 3 semester hours in Word Processing (WordPerfect 5.1) (9/93).

Micro Focus Cobol Programming (CP300)

Location: Paramus, NJ.

Length: 225 hours (17 weeks).

Dates: January 1996-Present.

Objective: To teach the student Micro-Focus Cobol, Customer Control Information System (CICS) and programming languages.

Learning Outcome: Upon successful completion of this course, the student will be able to identify peripheral devices and the roles of data processing professionals they will interact with as programmers; utilize commonly used MS/DOS commands; design, code, debug and test programs utilizing Micro Focus Cobol; understand MVS/JCL concepts and create and edit both ASCII and EBCDIC files; code multiple control break programs that perform internal sorts and programs that use tables in addition to updating both sequential and random accessed data sets.

Instruction: Major topics covered in the course are create, edit, test and debug programs using Micro Focus Cobol and Customer Control Information System (CICS). Methods of instruction include lecture in a formal classroom and laboratory experimentation in a modern computer environment. Assignments are given by the instructor for in-school and home study.

Credit Recommendation: In the upper division baccalaureate degree category, or in the lower division baccalaureate/associate degree category, 4 semester hours in COBOL Programming (4/97).

Microcomputer Troubleshooting (CET 509, MT 407) (Formerly CET 509-510), Elective II

Location: Paramus, NJ.

Length: 200 hours.

Dates: February 1988-June 1993.

Objective: To teach the student microprocessor troubleshooting techniques and introduce students to personal computer operation, maintenance, and repair.

Learning Outcome: Upon successful completion of this course, the student will be able to (1) troubleshoot a microprocessor-based piece of equipment to component level; (2) understand the hardware and software aspects of the operating system for the IBM PC; understand PC peripherals (disk drives, keyboard, monitor, and printers); (3) understand the installation and software setup of a hard disk drive (the student will use partitioning software to initialize, partition, and format a hard disk drive); (4) configure communications software for baud rate, parity, stop-bits, and port address; (5) connect to a host computer through a modem; and upload and download files over telephone lines; and (6) use diagnostic techniques in microcomputer troubleshooting and repair.

Instruction: Major topics covered in the course are microprocessor troubleshooting techniques. The student is shown how the logic probe, signature analyzer, and scope multiplexer are used to troubleshoot a microprocessor-based piece of equipment to component level. The student will also study microprocessor theory to the system level; input/output techniques; memory circuits; MS/PC DOS (Disk Operating System); file maintenance; creation of batch files using the DOS line editor (EDLIN); and how to format a newly installed hard disk drive. The student will deal with actual service problems with real computer equipment including disk drive, keyboard, monitor, printer, and the CPU, using diagnostic software.

Credit Recommendation: In the lower division baccalaureate/associate degree category, 3 semester hours in Microprocessor Troubleshooting and 3 semester hours in Disk Operating Systems (12/90).

Novell Netware with CNE Concentration (E500)

Location: Paramus, NJ.

Length: 240 hours (8 weeks).

Dates: September 1996-Present.

Objective: To teach students installation, operation, administration, and maintenance of a Novell Local Area Network.

Learning Outcome: Upon successful completion of this course, the student will be able to operate a Novell Version 4.1 and 3.1 X Network; install the network software and set up a new network; create new users, issue passwords, write login scripts, create and manage print queues; analyze, troubleshoot and repair the network.

Instruction: Major topics covered in the course are the operational principles of a Novell Area Network, how to install the network software and set up a network, as well as creating new users, passwords and login scripts. Students will be able to analyze, troubleshoot and repair the network. Methods of instruction include lecture in a formal classroom and laboratory experimentation in a modern computer environment. Assignments are given by the instructor for in-school and home study.

Credit Recommendation: In the lower division baccalaureate/associate degree category, 6 semester hours in Network Operations and Maintenance (4/97).

Novell Networking Technology: CNE Preparation (CENT509)

Location: Paramus, NJ.

Length: 200 hours (16 weeks).

Dates: May 1997-Present.

Objective: To teach the principles of a Novell Local Area Network.

Learning Outcome: Upon successful completion of this course, the student will be able to understand operation of Novell Version 3.1 and 4.1 networks; install network software and set up new networks; enable new users, issue passwords, write login scripts, create and use print queues; troubleshoot and repair networks; analyze common network failures to avoid downtime; take CNE exams.

Instruction: Major topic covered in the course are principles of Novell Local Area Networks. Students learn installation, setup, troubleshooting and repair procedures. Methods of instruction include lecture in a formal classroom and laboratory experimentation in a modern computer environment. Assignments are given by the instructor for in-school and home study.

Credit Recommendation: In the upper division baccalaureate degree category, or in the lower division baccalaureate/associate degree category, 6 semester hours in Local Area Network Systems (4/97).

Novell Networking Technology: CNE Preparation (CENT 509)

Location: Paramus, NJ.

Length: 200 hours (40 days).

Dates: July 1993-December 1995.

Objective: To teach students the basics of a Novell Local Area Network, the installation and setting up of a new network and troubleshooting and repair.

Learning Outcome: Upon successful completion of this course, the student will be able to describe, install and operate a Novell Version 2.2 and 3.1 network, including creating new users, issuing passwords, writing login scripts and printing; troubleshoot and repair networks; analyze network statistics; and take the Certified Network Engineer exams.

Instruction: Major topics covered in the course are the principles and network technologies of Novell Local Area Networks, including network structure, internetworking and protocols; Netware Version 2.2 hardware and installation is studied including directory structures, security drive pointers, login scripts, menu creation, printing and performance management; network service and support including cards, cabling, installation, upgrading, troubleshooting, diagnosis, and repair.

Credit Recommendation: In the lower division baccalaureate/associate degree category, 4 semester hours in Networking Technology (9/93).

OS/Operations (CO-400)

Location: Paramus, NJ.

Length: Version 1: 200 hours (37 days); Version 2: 200 hours (37-45 days).

Dates: June 1983-June 1994.

Objective: To enable students to comprehend and execute the IPL process for an IBM OS System.

Learning Outcome: Upon completion of this course, the student will be able to execute and comprehend the IPL process for an IBM OS System; respond to OS console messages with appropriate responses; display techniques used to order and execute work on system and diagnose error messages relative to the operating system and job control language and take appropriate action to rectify errors; understand the internal working of the operating system and the internal logic involved in job processing; understand the use and function of job control language in job processing, and the function of a spooling system; and code and execute IBM utility programs.

Instruction: Major topics covered in the course are the concepts of operating systems, interleaving, multiprogramming, multiprocessing, interrupts, control programs, management routines, reader/interpreter, initiator/terminator, output writers, main storage, virtual storage, partitions, regions, operating commands, spooling, OS job control language, and utility programs.

Credit Recommendation: In the lower division baccalaureate/associate degree category, 3 semester hours in OS/ Operations, or 3 semester hours in OS/Job Control Language and Utilities (2/85) (5/91).

Structured Programming in COBOL (CP-300)

Location: Paramus, NJ.

Length: *Version 1:* 200 hours (40 days); *Version 2:* 200 hours (37-45 days).

Dates: *Version 1:* April 1983-June 1989; *Version 2:* July 1989-December 1995.

Objective: To enable students to comprehend COBOL language in terms of structural and top-down coding techniques.

Instruction: Major topics covered in the course are understanding the concepts of compilers, linkage editors, load module, COBOL coding standards, file processing, indexed sequential file coding standards, control break processing, sort features, table handing, editing input and output, debugging, documentation, IBM 4341 JCL; understanding the flow of an inventory system that has been prepared to comprehensively present the ANSI COBOL instruction set; use ANSI COBOL concepts in flowcharting, coding, testing, debugging, and documenting these problems with emphasis on structured design; code and run a card-to-print program with output headings and page counters; code and run programs that manipulate tables by means of interactive loops, as well as serial and binary searches; code and run a program that sorts an input file and executes control break processing of the output; and master job control language, its syntax and its manipulative concepts relative to job execution; and a general understanding of operating system concepts.

Credit Recommendation: *Version 1:* In the lower division baccalaureate/associate degree category, 5 semester hours in COBOL (2/85). *Version 2:* In the lower division baccalaureate/associate degree category, 3 semester hours in COBOL I and 3 semester hours in COBOL II (5/91).

System Management/Accounting Principles (MBA101)

Location: Paramus, NJ.

Length: 225 hours (8 weeks).

Dates: March 1996-Present.

Objective: To teach fundamental accounting principles and procedures using accounting software, DOS operating system and elements of Novell Netware.

Learning Outcome: Upon successful completion of this course, the student will be able to apply accounting concepts and procedures using an accounting software package; use basic file and disk management commands of the disk operating system (DOS); use advanced features of DOS such as I/O and batch files; apply DOS commands within a networking environment utilizing Novell Netware; manage a network server, add/delete users, create directories, copy files and mapping; utilize Netware utility programs.

Instruction: Major topics covered in the course are accounting concepts, DOS and Novell. Methods of instruction include lecture in a formal classroom and laboratory experimentation in a modern computer environment. Assignments are given by the instructor for in-school and home study.

Credit Recommendation: In the lower division baccalaureate/associate degree category, 3 semester hours in Fundamental Accounting Concepts with Microcomputer Application, 2 semester hours in System Management with Accounting Applications, and 1 semester hour in Microcomputer Operating System: DOS (4/97).

Technical Support (MBS103)

Location: Paramus, NJ.

Length: 225 hours (17 weeks).

Dates: July 1996-Present.

Objective: To teach system maintenance, upkeep, repair and support.

Learning Outcome: Upon successful completion of this course, the student will be able to understand system faults and procedures to deal with these faults in the office; perform system maintenance to act as an intermediary between the applications specialist and the repair specialist; utilize PC tools and diagnostic software; act as a help desk to customers; work with printers to change ribbons, load paper, clear jams, configure printers and proper maintenance.

Instruction: Major topics covered in the course are a basic understanding of system faults and procedures to deal with these faults in an office environment. Methods of instruction include lecture in a formal classroom and laboratory experimentation in a modern computer environment. Assignments are given by the instructor for in-school and home study.

Credit Recommendation: In the lower division baccalaureate/associate degree category, 3 semester hours in PC Maintenance and Repair (4/97).

Using MS DOS and the Personal Computer Maintenance (E300)

Location: Paramus, NJ.

Length: 240 hours (8 weeks).

Dates: May 1996-Present.

Objective: To teach the student to solve both software and hardware problems associated with personal computers.

Learning Outcome: Upon successful completion of this course, the student will be able to identify, analyze, service and repair certain system hardware including keyboards, disk drives, monitors, printers, etc.; assemble their own personal computer; utilize file and disk management commands, text and batch file creation, and editing and advanced DOS features.

Instruction: Major topics covered in the course are system operation, repair and maintenance of PC's including DOS commands and diagnostic software. Methods of instruction include lecture in a formal classroom and laboratory experimentation in a modern computer environment. Assignments are given by the instructor for in-school and home study.

Credit Recommendation: In the lower division baccalaureate/associate degree category, 3 semester hours in Microprocessor Troubleshooting and 3 semester hours in DOS (4/97).

Visual Programming (CP105)

Location: Paramus, NJ

Length: 225 hours (17 weeks).

Dates: January 1996-Present.

Objective: To teach students Visual Basic, Visual FoxPro and Paradox for Windows.

Learning Outcome: Upon successful completion of this course, the student will be able to understand relational database concepts including database design and normalization techniques; utilize the Paradox interface for creating tables, developing queries, syntax of object Pal and building applications; combine programmatic objects, data-aware controls, OLE automation and the crystal reports; use OLE automation to execute methods on an OLE-defined object.

Instruction: Major topics covered in the course are developing programs in the Visual Basic Programming language, developing programs in the Visual Fox Pro Programming language, and developing programs using the Paradox for Windows Object Pal script language. Methods of instruction include lecture in a formal classroom and laboratory experimentation in a modern computer environment. Assignments are given by the instructor for in-school and home study.

Credit Recommendation: In the lower division baccalaureate/associate degree category or in the upper division baccalaureate degree category, 3 semester hours in Fundamentals of Visual Basic and 1 semester hour in Visual Database Applications (4/97).

Word Processing (MBA102)

Location: Paramus, NJ.

Length: 225 hours (8 weeks).

Dates: May 1996-Present.

Objective: To teach word processing applying Word Perfect, while developing business communications skills.

Learning Outcome: Upon successful completion of this course, the student will be able to create, retrieve, and edit documents, spell check, use reveal codes, format documents, footnotes, endnotes, sort/edit, use fonts, and write macros using Word Perfect; create data tables, table of contents, indexes and other manuscript features using Word Perfect; write professional memos and letters; apply professional office practices.

Instruction: Major topics covered in the course are word processing using Word Perfect, business communications and professional office skills. Methods of instruction include lecture in a formal classroom and laboratory experimentation in a modern computer environment. Assignments are given by the instructor for in-school and home study.

Credit Recommendation: In the lower division baccalaureate/associate degree category, 3 semester hour in WordPerfect for Windows and 3 semester hours in Business Communications (4/97).

Word Processing and Novell Network Administration (MBA 102)

Location: Paramus, NJ.

Length: 200 hours (40 days).

Dates: September 1993-December 1995.

Objective: To give the student a proficient knowledge of WP 5.1 and to teach fundamentals of business communications and use of Novell Netware.

Learning Outcome: Upon successful completion of this course, in Word Processing the student will be able to understand and apply word processing concepts; creating, saving, and retrieving a document, editing functions, block functions, formatting for printing, search and replace, footnotes/endnotes, file management, speller and thesaurus, sorting and merging, macros, columns, tables of contents, lists and indexes, math; and graphics.

Instruction: Major topics covered in Word Processing course are the basic concepts of creating, revising, saving, and retrieving documents, revision techniques include changing the font size and appearance, formatting, the search and replace feature, spell-check and using the thesaurus; Basic concepts are explored by investigating higher level special features which include sorting, merging, creating and executing macros, text and math columns, and generating table of contents, indexes and incorporating graphics into a file; the fundamentals of business communications with emphasis given to letter structure, various types of business letters and other documents, and both verbal and nonverbal communications; and in the Novell Netware component of the course, students are exposed to network components and topologies, a file server directory structure and levels of network security and access, learn to use the Filer, Map, and Print Management commands, and the NBackup utility and have experience creating and customizing users' environments; in Business Communications demonstrate the basic elements of good writing, understand appropriate letter structure, create different types of documents, and understand and apply other forms of communication; and in Novell Netware understand and identify the components and topologies of networks, understand a file server's directory structure, use Filer commands, the Map command and Print Management commands, assign levels of security and access to users; create and customize users' environments; and use the NBackup utility.

Credit Recommendation: In the lower division baccalaureate/associate degree category, 3 semester hours in Word Processing (WordPerfect 5.1), 2 semester hours in Novell Netware/Network, and 1 semester hour in Business Communications (9/93).

Word Processing IS101

Location: Paramus, NJ.

Length: 200 hours.

Dates: August 1988-August 1993.

Objective: To give the student a proficient knowledge of WP 5.0 and dBASE III+ and end user's exposure to all of the softwares' capabilities.

Learning Outcome: Upon successful completion of this course, the student will be able to understand and apply word processing concepts: creating, saving and retrieving a document; editing functions; block functions; formatting for printing; search and replace; footnotes/endnotes; file management; speller and thesaurus; sorting and merging; macros; columns;

tables of contents; list and indexes; math; and graphics.

Instruction: Major topics covered in the course are in word processing: the basic concepts of creating, revising, saving, and retrieving documents are covered. Revision techniques include changing the font size and appearance, formatting, the search and replace feature, spellcheck and using the thesaurus; basic concepts are explored by investigating higher level special features. These include sorting, merging, creating and executing macros, text and math columns. Generating table of contents and indexes and incorporating graphics into a file are also taught. In dBASE III+, data base structure is discussed. The Assist Menu and dot commands are used to create files, enter data, and edit existing information. Data base statistics functions, queries and sorting are covered. Generating output, such as reports and labels, is taught. Programs are designed, written, and run.

Credit Recommendation: In the lower division baccalaureate/associate degree category, covering the period of June 1988-July 1991, 1 semester hour in dBASE III+ and 3 semester hours in Word Processing. Covering the period of August 1991-Present, in the lower division baccalaureate/associate degree category, 3 semester hours in Word Processing and 3 semester hours in Using dBASE III+ (8/91).

Computer Learning Centers, Inc. (National)

Computer Learning Centers, Inc. (CLC) is a publicly held corporation that specializes in the preparation of adult students for employment within the computer information and technology fields. CLC, Inc. corporate offices are located in Fairfax, VA. Specialized Associate Degree programs are offered in the following areas; Computer Programming, Computer Applications and Network Administration, Computer Electronics Systems Technology, Computer Science, and Information Technology and Network Support. Diploma programs are offered in the following areas; Computerized Business Systems, Network Engineering and Management, Network Administration, Computer Electronics Technology, Computer Programming, Computer Operations, Client/Server Programming, and Information Technology Support Professional. All CLC, Inc. schools are accredited by the Accrediting Council for Independent Colleges and Schools (ACICS).

AUTHORIZED COMPUTER LEARNING CENTERS, INC. (NATIONAL) SCHOOLS

Computer Learning Centers, Inc. - Anaheim
222 South Harbor Boulevard
Anaheim, CA 92805
Contact: Robert Toren
Phone No.: 714-956-8060
Fax No.: 714-239-6508

Computer Learning Centers, Inc. - Atlanta
2359 Windy Hill Road, #500
Marietta, GA 30067
Contact: Ed Abrams
Phone No.: 770-226-0056
Fax No.: 770-226-0084

Computer Learning Centers, Inc. - Cherry Hill
#2 Executive Campus
Route 70 & Cuthbert Boulevard
Cherry Hill, NJ 08002
Contact: Harry Dotson
Phone No.: 609-663-4270
Fax No.: 609-663-3847

Computer Learning Centers, Inc. - Chicago
200 S. Michigan Avenue
Chicago, IL 60604
Contact: Dee Reynolds
Phone No.: 312-427-2700
Fax No.: 312-427-7099

Computer Learning Centers, Inc. - Dallas
1500 Eastgate Drive, #1610
Garland, TX 75041
Contact: Gerald Brazell
Phone No.: 214-686-6865
Fax No.: 214-681-7549

Computer Learning Centers, Inc. - Fort Worth
305 NE Loop 820, #412
Hurst, TX 76053
Contact: Dewayne Weeks
Phone No.: 817-595-7316
Fax No.: 817-595-7327

Computer Learning Centers, Inc. - Houston
3030 S. Gessner, #295
Houston, TX 77063
Contact: James Garrett
Phone No.: 713-785-6641
Fax No.: 713-785-7544

Computer Learning Centers, Inc. - Laurel
312 Marshall Avenue
Laurel, MD 20707
Contact: Skip Higley
Phone No.: 301-317-3600
Fax No.: 301-317-8431

Computer Learning Centers, Inc. - Los Angeles
3580 Wilshire Boulevard, #100
Los Angeles, CA 90010
Contact: Michael Nielsen
Phone No.: 213-386-6311
Fax No.: 213-384-9744

Computer Learning Centers, Inc. - Manassas
7000 Infantry Ridge Road, #200
Manassas, VA 20109
Contact: Tony Caggiano
Phone No.: 703-392-1415
Fax No.: 703-392-3708

Computer Learning Centers, Inc. - Madison Heights
32500 Concord Drive
Madison Heights, MI 48071
Contact: Myra Dembeic
Phone No.: 810-589-0055
Fax No.: 810-589-0483

Computer Learning Centers, Inc. - Methuen
436 Broadway Village Mall
Methuen, MA 01844
Contact: Mark McGinnis
Phone No.: 978-794-0233
Fax No.: 978-685-6011

Computer Learning Centers, Inc. - Monroeville
777 Penn Center Boulevard, Building 7
Pittsburgh, PA 15235
Contact: Dennis Hirsh
Phone No.: 412-825-5410
Fax No.: 412-825-6119

Computer Learning Centers, Inc. - Northeast Philadelphia
2180 Horning Road, Building A
Philadelphia, PA 19116
Contact: James Tolbert
Phone No.: 215-968-2720
Fax No.: 215-969-2577

Computer Learning Centers, Inc. - Philadelphia
University City Science Center
3600 Market Street
Philadelphia, PA 19104
Contact: Joseph F. Reichard
Phone No.: 215-222-6450
Fax No.: 215-222-4439

Computer Learning Centers, Inc. - Plymouth Meeting
One Plymouth Meeting
Plymouth Meeting, PA 19462
Contact: Alex Tietlebaum
Phone No.: 610-834-0638
Fax No.: 610-834-7521

Computer Learning Centers, Inc. - San Francisco
667 Mission Street
San Francisco, CA 94105
Contact: Jo Ann Meron
Phone No.: 415-495-0800
Fax No.: 415-495-6206

Computer Learning Centers, Inc. - San Jose
111 N. Market Street, #105
San Jose, CA 95113
Contact: Steve Woody
Phone No.: 408-271-3400
Fax No.: 408-271-3434

Computer Learning Centers, Inc. - Schaumburg
920 East Algonquin Road
Schaumburg, IL 60173
Contact: Barbara Nichols
Phone No.: 708-889-0252
Fax No.: 708-889-9487

Computer Learning Centers, Inc. - Somerville
5 Middlesex Avenue
Somerville, MA 02145

Contact: Mark Dugan
Phone No.: 617-776-3500
Fax No.: 617-625-0394

Computer Learning Centers, Inc. - Washington
6295 Edsall Road, #210
Alexandria, VA 22312
Contact: Donald McMullen
Phone No.: 703-823-0300
Fax No.: 703-370-2639

Source of official student records: Registry of Credit Recommendations, American Council on Education, One Dupont Circle, Washington, DC 20036-1193.

Additional information about the courses: College Credit Recommendation Service, American Council on Education, One Dupont Circle, Washington, DC 20036-1193.

Advanced C/UNIX Programming (C/UNIX III) (CP 302)

Location: Various.
Length: 100 hours (4 weeks)
Dates: January 1996-Present.

Objective: To provide the student with further experience in "C" language programming in a UNIX (and optionally, DOS) operating environment, as well as developing larger programs as part of a programming team.

Learning Outcome: Upon successful completion of this course, the student will be able to understand and use the full capability of the "C" programming language; developing large programs in a team environment.

Instruction: Major topics covered in the course are dynamic memory allocation and use of pointers in "C"; use of structures, files, linked lists and tree data structures; development of a large program using a programming team. Methods of instruction include lecture, discussion, classroom exercises, examinations, and laboratory exercises.

Credit Recommendation: In the lower division baccalaureate/associate degree category, 2 semester hours in Computer Science or Application Development (11/95).

Advanced DOS and Hardware (IT 101)

Location: Various.
Length: 100 hours (4 weeks)
Dates: November 1993-Present.

Objective: To provide knowledge of microcomputer desk operating systems and hardware.

Learning Outcome: Upon successful completion of this course, the student will be able to effectively manage files and directories; perform Batch Processing, including Menu Creation; identify all hardware components and upgrade system components; and describe microcomputer technology necessary for LAN Administration.

Instruction: Major topics covered in the course are management of files and directories, batch processing, menu creation, identification of hardware components, and upgrading system components. Methods of instruction include lecture, discussion, classroom exercises, laboratory exercises, and examination.

Credit Recommendation: In the lower division baccalaureate/associate degree category, 3 semester hours in Networking, Microcomputer Systems Administration, Office Technology, Data Processing, or Computer Operations (11/95).

Advanced Windows (OS 100)

Location: Multiple locations.
Length: 100 hours (4 weeks)
Dates: June 1995-Present.

Objective: To provide in-depth study and understanding of the Windows (v 3.11) and Windows for Workgroups (v 3.11) software and to provide detailed learning on the use of Windows for Workgroups in a network setting.

Learning Outcome: Upon successful completion of this course, the student will be able to install and set-up Windows; customize the interface; utilize specialized features such as Terminal and Macros; install and customize Windows applications; access the Windows for Workgroup network; use the Windows management tools; and understand Visual Basic programming.

Instruction: Major topics covered in the course are Windows basics refresher; installing Windows and Windows for Workgroups; data sharing; printing; Terminal; Recorder; Mail; Schedule+; multimedia; installing, configuring and running DOS applications; Windows networking; and Visual Basic programming. Methods of instruction include lecture, discussion, classroom exercises, audio/ visual material, learner presentations/ reports, quizzes, observations, tests, homework, laboratory, and a final examination.

Credit Recommendation: In the lower division baccalaureate/associate degree category, 3 semester hours in Office Technology, Microcomputer Systems Applications, or Microcomputer Operating Systems (10/96).

Application Development and Integration (CP 205)

Location: Multiple locations.
Length: 100 hours (4 weeks)
Dates: January 1997-Present.

Objective: To provide in-depth training and education in the design and development of client-server applications using Visual Basic and Oracle.

Learning Outcome: Upon successful completion of this course, the student will be able to design and implement a client-server application; use Visual Basic; design a graphics user interface; construct client-server tables; create error handling processes; describe the security issues in the client-server application; and create an OLE server and use some third party development tools.

Instruction: Major topics covered in the course are GUI concepts and design, Visual Basic, database concepts, SQL, table construction, ODBC, RDO, OLE servers, on-line help, error handling, applications distribution, data access techniques, security issues and concepts, and system implementation. Methods of instruction include lecture, discussion, classroom exercises, case studies, quizzes, tests, laboratory projects, and a final examination.

Credit Recommendation: In the lower division baccalaureate/associate degree category or upper division baccalaureate degree category, 3 semester hours in Management Information Systems or Computer Science (10/96).

Basic AC/DC Circuits (Basic Electronics) (ET 100)

Location: Various.
Length: 100 hours (4 weeks)
Dates: January 1991-Present.

Objective: To provide basic knowledge of direct and alternating current circuits with special emphasis on troubleshooting.

Learning Outcome: Upon successful completion of this course, the student will be able to analyze basic DC and AC circuits; and use various pieces of electronic test equipment, including volt-ohm-meters, digital multimeters, oscilloscopes, signal generators, and variable power supplies.

Instruction: Major topics covered in the course are atomic structure, metric prefixes, electrical units, resistor color code, direct current and voltage, basic series, parallel and series-parallel circuits, meter measurements, Ohm's Law, basic magnetism, alternating current and voltage, capacitance, inductance, filters and transformers. Methods of instruction include lecture, classroom exercises, audio/visual materials and examinations.

Credit Recommendation: In the lower division baccalaureate/associate degree category, 2 semester hours in Electrical Technology Lecture or 1 semester hour in Electrical Technology Laboratory (11/95).

Business Communications (English: Business Communications) (GE 100)

Location: Various.

Length: 100 hours (4 weeks)

Dates: July 1992-Present.

Objective: To increase competence in communicating with others through use of memos, letters, and oral presentation.

Learning Outcome: Upon successful completion of this course, the student will be able to demonstrate proficiency in English usage, both written and oral, in the business/workplace setting.

Instruction: Major topics covered in the course are vocabulary, grammar, oral presentations and informal communications, nonverbal communications, letters, memo writing and meeting summaries, library usage. Methods of instruction include lecture, discussion, classroom exercises, learner presentations/reports, and examinations.

Credit Recommendation: In the lower division baccalaureate/associate degree category, 3 semester hours in Business Communications, Business Administration, or Office Technology (11/95).

Client-Server Concepts and Architecture (CP 108)

Location: Multiple locations.

Length: 100 hours (4 weeks)

Dates: November 1996-Present.

Objective: To provide the student with a comprehensive introduction to client-server architecture, design, and implementation.

Learning Outcome: Upon successful completion of this course, the student will be able to define client-server systems; evaluate their benefits; describe database models; understand 4GL tools and CASE methodologies; design a relational database management applications; describe the OSE model; evaluate client server protocols; manage network resources; understand software licensing issues; evaluate trends on generating systems; and analyze applications for client-server implementation.

Instruction: Major topics covered in the course are strategic applications in client-server computing; building client-server applications; designing client-server interfaces; designing server process application components; networking in the client-server environment; and middleware and client-server networking management. Methods of instruction include lecture, discussion, classroom exercises, case studies, laboratory assignments, quizzes, observations, tests, laboratory projects, and a final examination.

Credit Recommendation: In the lower division baccalaureate/associate degree category or upper division baccalaureate degree category, 3 semester hours in Computer Science or Management Information Systems (10/96).

COBOL I (CP 101)

Location: Various.

Length: 100 hours (4 weeks)

Dates: January 1987-Present.

Objective: To provide the student knowledge of principles for COBOL programming on a PC.

Learning Outcome: Upon successful completion of this course, the student will be able to write and execute a COBOL program, understand COBOL program divisions, setup work storage section for input and output records, and work with structured code.

Instruction: Major topics covered in the course are principles of structured codes, defining COBOL divisions, using verbs, If statements, numeric editing, usage clause, and working with tables. Methods of instruction include lecture, discussion, classroom exercises, laboratory exercises, programming projects, and examinations.

Credit Recommendation: In the lower division baccalaureate/associate degree category, 3 semester hours in COBOL or Data Processing (11/95).

COBOL II (CP 201)

Location: Various.

Length: 100 hours (4 weeks)

Dates: January 1987-Present.

Objective: To provide the student an introduction to more advanced COBOL concepts to include searches and CICS.

Learning Outcome: Upon successful completion of this course, the student will be able to work effectively with more advanced COBOL concepts, including sorting, table searches, CICS (Customer Information Control Systems).

Instruction: Major topics covered in the course are working with sorts; with the input and output procedures; control breaks; indexed tables and searches; CICS with the Microfocus editor; map processing; passing control in CICS; linkage section and the communications area. Methods of instruction include lecture, classroom exercises, discussion, laboratory exercises, and programming projects.

Credit Recommendation: In the lower division baccalaureate/associate degree category, 3 semester hours in COBOL or Data Processing (11/95).

COBOL III (CP 301)

Location: Various.

Length: 100 hours (4 weeks)

Dates: January 1996-Present.

Objective: To provide knowledge of advanced concepts in designing and coding COBOL programs.

Learning Outcome: Upon successful completion of this course, the student will be able to effectively design and code COBOL programs, using a top-down design.

Instruction: Major topics covered in the course are sorting; control breaks; subprograms; sequential file maintenance; and indexed files. Methods of instruction include lecture, classroom exercises, discussion, laboratory exercises, and programming projects.

Credit Recommendation: In the lower division baccalaureate/associate degree category, 3 semester hours in COBOL or Data Processing (11/95).

Cultural Diversity, Leadership, And Teams in Business (Humanities) (GE 203)

Location: Various.

Length: 100 hours (4 weeks)

Dates: July 1995-Present.

Objective: To explore various cultural origins as a basis to understanding the modern corporation and its influence on societal issues.

Learning Outcome: Upon successful completion of this course, the student will be able to understand the role of both personal and workplace ethics and the nature of prejudice, bias, and discrimination.

Instruction: Major topics covered in the course are culture, prejudice, bias, discrimination, motivation, teaching/training, customer service, leadership, ethics, negotiation, time management, and budgeting. Methods of instruction include lectures, classroom discussions, classroom exercises, report presentations, and examinations.

Credit Recommendation: In the lower division baccalaureate/associate degree category, 3 semester hours in Human Development or Sociology (11/95).

C/UNIX Programming
1. C/UNIX I (CP 102)
2. C/UNIX II (CP 202)

Location: Various.
Length: 200 hours (8 weeks)
Dates: January 1993-Present.
Objective: To provide operating system (UNIX) skills along with "C" language programming capability in both basic and advanced topics.
Learning Outcome: Upon successful completion of these two courses, the student will be able to access the facilities of the UNIX operating system; send and receive electronic mail; and write intermediate to advanced "C" language programs.
Instruction: Major topics covered in the course are UNIX commands, editing functions and file/directory structures; compiling, debugging and executing "C" programs; some advanced data structures in "C"including functions, arrays, structures, pointers and files. Methods of instruction include lecture, discussion, classroom exercises, laboratory exercises, and examinations.
Credit Recommendation: In the lower division baccalaureate/associate degree category, 5 semester hours in Computer Science (4 hours in "C" Language; 1 hour in Operating Systems) (11/95). **NOTE:** Student must successfully complete both parts (CP102, CP202).

Customer Service and Support (IT-104)

Location: Various.
Length: 100 hours (4 weeks)
Dates: February 1997-Present.
Objective: To provide the student with a comprehensive introduction to customer service and support concepts, skills, and methods in a technical environment. The course will also provide the student the opportunity to learn and practice various personal and interpersonal skills including, coaching, team building, and stress management.
Learning Outcome: Upon successful completion of this course, the student will be able to utilize support center terminology and concepts; diagnose and resolve customer problems; document problems and resolutions; manage difficult customers and customers at varying competence levels; and utilize personal and interpersonal skills such as coaching, team building, and stress management in the customer service environment.
Instruction: Major topics covered in the course are support center structure, staffing, and environment; priorities and procedures; tracking data; the use of automation and tools; performance measurement; management of support calls; dealing with difficult customers and customers of varying competence levels; and coaching, team building, and stress management. Methods of instruction include lecture, discussion, classroom exercises and projects, and examination.
Credit Recommendation: In the lower division baccalaureate/associate degree category, 3 semester hours in Special Topics in Computing, Computer Help Center Management, or Customer Service and Support (11/97).

Data Structures Using COBOL (CP 109)

Location: Various.
Length: 100 hours (4 weeks)
Dates: August 1996-Present.
Objective: To provide the student knowledge of principles of data structures using COBOL as a vehicle on a PC.
Learning Outcome: Upon successful completion of this course, the student will be able to identify the three structures used in structured programs; write and execute a structured language program; understand COBOL program divisions; setup work storage section for input and output records; and work with structured code.
Instruction: Major topics covered in the course are principles of structured code, defining COBOL divisions, using verbs, If statements, numeric editing, usage clause, and working with tables. Methods of instruction include lecture, discussion, classroom exercises, and laboratory exercises, programming projects, and an examination.
Credit Recommendation: In the lower division baccalaureate/associate degree category, 3 semester hours in COBOL or Data Processing (2/97).

Database Applications (CA 102)

Location: Various.
Length: 100 hours (4 weeks)
Dates: January 1995-Present.
Objective: To provide an introduction to the concepts and application techniques of a database system.
Learning Outcome: Upon successful completion of this course, the student will be able to employ terminology and explain concepts of database management system; set up design, develop, implement and maintain a database system.
Instruction: Major topics covered in the course are database concepts, design tables, queries, forms, and reports. Methods of instruction include lecture, discussion, laboratory projects and assignments, group projects, examinations, and tutorials.
Credit Recommendation: In the lower division baccalaureate/associate degree category, 3 semester hours in Office Technology, Business Administration, Computer Information Systems, or Data Processing (11/95).

Desktop Systems (OS 102)

Location: Various.
Length: 100 hours (4 weeks)
Dates: February 1997-Present.
Objective: To provide the student with the knowledge and skills to utilize advanced DOS concepts and the Windows 3.1, 3.11 and Windows 95 desktop operating systems.
Learning Outcome: Upon successful completion of this course, the student will be able to apply advanced DOS concepts; understand the basic concepts of Windows 3.1/3.11/ 95; utilize the basic commands of and configure Windows 3.1/3.11/95; use object linking and embedding; and perform file management and print manager functions.
Instruction: Major topics covered in the course are advanced DOS concepts, Windows 3.1/3.11/95 concepts, commands and configuration, file management, print manager, object linking and embedding, and customizing windows. Methods of instruction include lecture, discussion, classroom exercises, laboratory exercises and projects, and examination.
Credit Recommendation: In the lower division baccalaureate/associate degree category, 3 hours in Microcomputer Operating Systems (2 hours lecture and 1 hour lab) (11/97).

Digital Circuit Fundamentals (ET 102)

Location: Various.
Length: 100 hours (4 weeks)
Dates: January 1991-Present.
Objective: To provide knowledge of basic concept of digital integrated circuits.
Learning Outcome: Upon successful completion of this course, the student will be able to demonstrate familiarity with basic logic and arithmetic operations carried out by integrated circuits.

Instruction: Major topics covered in the course are binary based number systems, gates, truth tables vs. circuits, simple arithmetic circuits, and simple sequential circuits. Methods of instruction include lecture, discussion, laboratory exercises, and examinations.

Credit Recommendation: In the lower division baccalaureate/associate degree category, 2 semester hours in Electrical Technology or 1 semester hour in Electric Technology Laboratory (11/95).

Enterprise Networking: Design and Implementation (NT-108) (Internetworking: Design and Implementation)

Location: Various locations.
Length: 100 hours (4 weeks)
Dates: October 1996-Present.

Objective: To provide in-depth study and understanding of the strategies and guidelines to design, analyze, and implement Netware 4 networks.

Learning Outcome: Upon successful completion of this course, the student will be able to identify and sequence all processes in a Netware 4 design and migration project; determine the partition boundaries of the directory tree; create a replica replacement plan for the design; develop an accessibility plan utilizing login scripts, profiles, and directory map objects; devise a migration strategy for clients, servers, and applications; implement an OSI configuration model; and plan and layout an execution schedule.

Instruction: Major topics covered in the course are the design and implementation process; naming standards; designing and organizing the upper and lower layers of the tree; planning network accessibility; NDS partitioning concepts; planning time synchronization; implementing the NDS tree; network hardware; transmission media and connections; networking technologies, concepts and services; and the OSI model and its lower, middle and upper layers. Methods of instruction include lecture, discussion, classroom exercises, audio/visual material, learner presentations, reports, quizzes, tests, observations, homework, laboratory, and midterm and final examinations.

Credit Recommendation: In the upper division baccalaureate degree category, 2 semester hours in Networking, Network Administration, Data Communications, System Security, and 2 semester hours in Networking Laboratory (12/96).

Integrated Applications (CA 103)

Location: Various.
Length: 100 hours (4 weeks)
Dates: January 1995-Present.

Objective: To develop proficiency in using desktop software and to develop team building skills through the use of business simulations.

Learning Outcome: Upon successful completion of this course, the student will be able to demonstrate proficiency in software packages, including professional MS-Office and PC Paintbrush; convert documents from one package to another using dynamic linking; customize applications for business productivity; and demonstrate ability to function as a team member in a business simulation.

Instruction: Major topics covered in the course are reviews of MS-Office applications; presentation software, object linking and embedding, dynamic data exchange, importing files across applications, communication skills, and group evaluations. Methods of instruction include lecture, discussion, group project, laboratory assignments, simulation, and quizzes.

Credit Recommendation: In the lower division baccalaureate/associate degree category, 3 semester hours in Office Technology, Business Administration, or Business Systems (11/95).

Internetworking With TCP/IP (NT 109)

Location: Various.
Length: 100 hours (4 weeks)
Dates: June 1996-Present.

Objective: To provide knowledge of the functions of the OSI model for use as a reference model to categorize industry protocol stacks, and to become knowledgeable of various cabling schemes and transmission media connectors used on networks.

Learning Outcome: Upon successful completion of this course, the student will be able to effectively configure and manage TCP/IP on Netware 4 and Netware 3 servers; assign and manage IP addresses and subnets; and configure Netware servers as IP routers.

Instruction: Major topics covered in the course are network and transport layer functions and protocols; session, presentation, and application layer protocols; IP addresses and subnet masks to IP internetworks; routing protocols; loading TCP/IP on Netware 3 and 4 servers; SNMP agent/manager and TCPCON.NLM; and IP tunneling and troubleshooting. Methods of instruction include lecture, classroom exercises, laboratory exercises, discussion, network projects, and an examination.

Credit Recommendation: In the upper division baccalaureate degree category, 2 semester hours in Networking, Computer Communications, or TCP/IP and 1 semester hour in Networking, Computer Communications, or TCP/IP Laboratory (2/97).

Interpersonal Skills and Social Influences (Social Science) (GE 103)

Location: Various.
Length: 100 hours (4 weeks)
Dates: July 1995-Present.

Objective: To develop interpersonal skills and attitudes in light of societal influences.

Learning Outcome: Upon successful completion of this course, the student will be able to demonstrate improved self-esteem and a productive attitude; overcome obstacles to creative thinking, and understand societal influences on the individual.

Instruction: Major topics covered in the course are self-esteem; mental visualization; human relations and the individual; productivity and the individual; attitude; creative thinking; society and sociology; social groups and organization. Methods of instruction include lecture, discussion, classroom exercises and examinations.

Credit Recommendation: In the lower division baccalaureate/associate degree category, 3 semester hours in Personal Development or Sociology (11/95).

Introduction to Business Mathematics (Statistics) (GE 107)

Location: Various.
Length: 100 hours (4 weeks)
Dates: July 1995-Present.

Objective: To provide basic understanding of statistics and probability.

Learning Outcome: Upon successful completion of this course, the student will be able to understand basic concepts in the field of business statistics; determine from a set of data the mean, mode, median, and range; determine distribution curve skew.

Instruction: Major topics covered in the course are definitions, data collection, data summary, data presentation, probability - joint, conditional, Bayes' Theorem, uniform and binomial distributions, normal and sampling distribution, and estimation. Methods of instruction include lecture, discussion, classroom exercises and examinations.

Credit Recommendation: In the lower division baccalaureate/associate degree category, 2 semester hours in Business Technology (11/95).

Introduction To Computer Programming (CP 110) (CP 100) (Formerly Introduction to Data Processing [CP100])

Location: Various.

Length: 100 hours (4 weeks)

Dates: January 1987-Present.

Objective: To provide knowledge of data processing concepts, hardware, software, numbering systems, and operation of personal computers.

Learning Outcome: Upon successful completion of this course, the student will be able to recognize date formats, describe computer hardware, describe simple operating systems, and create flowcharts.

Instruction: Major topics covered in the course are computer components, operations, and performance; software; flowcharting, number systems and number system conversions; JCL; and CICS. Methods of instruction include lecture, discussion, classroom exercises, laboratory exercises, programming projects and examinations.

Credit Recommendation: In the lower division baccalaureate/associate degree category, 3 semester hours in Data Processing or Computer Programming (11/95).

Introduction to DOS and Windows Operating Systems (NT-101) (Introduction to Networking)

Location: Various locations.

Length: 100 hours (4 weeks)

Dates: May 1995-Present.

Objective: To provide a foundation in microcomputer technology and the MS-DOS, Windows 3.11, and Windows 95 operating systems.

Learning Outcome: Upon successful completion of this course, the student will be able to describe microcomputer and bus architecture; use DOS internal and external commands; use disk management utilities; organize file/directory structure; use file system management commands; automate system operation utilizing batch processing; manage system memory, configuration, and services; install and configure MS Windows for Workgroups and the MS Windows 95 operating system; customize the Windows 3.11 environment and manage the file system; configure peer-to-peer networking; and manage drives, folders, files and common resources in Windows 95.

Instruction: Major topics covered in the course are the MS-DOS, MS Windows 3.11, and MS Windows 95 operating systems; troubleshooting techniques; file management; folders and objects; batch processing; installation and configuration of operating systems; and fundamentals of networking. Methods of instruction include lecture, discussion, classroom exercises, audio/visual material, learner presentations, reports, quizzes, tests, observations, homework, laboratory, and midterm and final examinations.

Credit Recommendation: In the lower division baccalaureate/associate degree category, 3 semester hours in Computer Operating Systems, Data Processing, or Computer Operations (12/96).

Introduction to Information Technology (IT 103)

Location: Various.

Length: 100 hours (4 weeks)

Dates: February 1997-Present.

Objective: To provide the student with the basic concepts and skills in spreadsheet applications using Microsoft Excel and in database applications using Microsoft Access.

Learning Outcome: Upon successful completion of this course, the student will be able to use basic Excel and Access commands; format and document a worksheet; enter labels and formulas; create charts and tables; use the print function; design a database; exchange data between applications; and utilize user options and preferences.

Instruction: Major topics covered in the course are the Excel and Access environments, basic concepts and commands, worksheet planning, formatting and documentation, charts and tables, information exchange, and user options and preferences. Methods of instruction include lecture, discussion, classroom exercises, laboratory exercises and projects, and examination.

Credit Recommendation: In the lower division baccalaureate/associate degree category, 3 semester hours in Computer Information Systems (11/97).

Introduction to Microcomputers (IT 100)

Location: Various.

Length: 100 hours (4 weeks)

Dates: January 1995-Present.

Objective: To provide the student with an introduction to terminology, functions, characteristics, application, and operations of personal computer systems.

Learning Outcome: Upon successful completion of this course, the student will be able to describe components of personal computers and how they work, including input, output, processing and storage cycles; describe concepts of computer information systems, office productivity, software, data communications, and networking; examine MS-DOS operating system and perform basic MS-DOS commands to manage files and disks; work in an MS-DOS environment and use MS-Windows packages and functions.

Instruction: Major topics covered in the course are basic principles of computerized business systems; personal computer hardware and software; general computer information systems, programming languages; and network concepts; MS-DOS commands and MS-Windows utilization. Methods of instruction include lecture, discussion, audio/visual material, laboratory assignments, and quizzes.

Credit Recommendation: In the lower division baccalaureate/associate degree category, 3 semester hours in Office Technology or Microcomputer Systems Administration (11/95).

Introduction to Microprocessor Systems (Microprocessors Hardware and Peripherals I) (ET 103)

Location: Various.

Length: 100 hours (4 weeks)

Dates: January 1996-Present.

Objective: To provide knowledge of a microprocessor assembly language and interface techniques applied to an 80x86 microprocessor system.

Learning Outcome: Upon successful completion of this course, the student will be able to use an 80x86 microprocessor to implement a disk operating system; debug software problems; explain component schematics; replace hardware components; and troubleshoot microprocessor system problems.

Instruction: Major topics covered in the course are microcomputer (80x86) assembly language overview; program segments; addressing modes; BCD and ASCII instructions; 80286 microprocessor; memory interfacing; I/O design; interval timer; interrupt controller; and direct memory access, microprocessor debugging and troubleshooting techniques. Methods of instruction include lecture, discussion, classroom exercises, laboratory exercises, and examinations.

Credit Recommendation: In the lower division baccalaureate/associate degree

category, 2 semester hours in Electrical Technology and 1 semester hour in Electrical Technology Lab (11/95).

Introduction to Spreadsheet and Database Applications (CA-204) (Applications Software II [CA-204])

Location: Various.
Length: 100 hours (4 weeks)
Dates: February 1997-Present.
Objective: To provide the student with the basic concepts and skills in spreadsheet applications using Microsoft Excel and in database applications using Microsoft Access.
Learning Outcome: Upon successful completion of this course, the student will be able to use basic Excel and Access commands; format and document a worksheet; enter labels and formulas; create charts and tables; use the print function; design a database; exchange data between applications; and utilize user options and preferences.
Instruction: Major topics covered in the course are the Excel and Access environments, basic concepts and commands, worksheet planning, formatting and documentation, charts and tables, information exchange, and user options and preferences. Methods of instruction include lecture, discussion, classroom exercises, laboratory exercises and projects, and examination.
Credit Recommendation: In the lower division baccalaureate/associate degree category, 2 semester hours (1 semester hour in Microcomputer Spreadsheets and 1 semester hour in Database Applications) (11/97).

Introduction to Word Processing and the Internet (CA-104) (Applications Software I [CA-104])

Location: Various.
Length: 100 hours (4 weeks)
Dates: February 1997-Present.
Objective: To present students with basic word processing concepts and skills using Microsoft Word, to present fundamental e-mail concepts and configuration options, and to introduce general Internet concepts and activities.
Learning Outcome: Upon successful completion of this course, the student will be able to navigate the Windows Word environment; use basic commands; perform text editing; edit and enhance documents; create tables; conduct paragraph formatting; use multi-page document tools, mail merge, and word processing graphics; understand basic e-mail concepts and user configuration options; and perform Internet activities such as browsing, using search engines, downloading, saving, retrieving, and printing information.
Instruction: Major topics covered in the course are the MS Word environment, commands, and navigation skills; text editing; editing and enhancing documents; tables; paragraph formatting; multi-page document tools; e-mail concepts and user configuration options; and accessing and retrieving information from the Internet. Methods of instruction include lecture, classroom exercises, laboratory exercises and projects, and examination.
Credit Recommendation: In the lower division baccalaureate/associate degree category, 3 semester hours (2 semester hours in Word Processing, Computer Information Systems (CIS), or Office Technology and 1 semester hour in Internet or E-mail) (11/97).

LAN Administration I (NT 100)

Location: Various.
Length: 100 hours (4 weeks)
Dates: November 1993-Present.
Objective: To acquaint students in Local Area Network (LAN) technology, application and administration.
Learning Outcome: Upon successful completion of this course, the student will be able to understand LAN technology and concepts; describe Novell operations and implementation; install Novell Netware and perform basic Novell LAN Administration.
Instruction: Major topics covered in the course are network basics, directory structure, pointers, mapping, basic commands, basic network security, command line utilities, printing services and logon scripts. Methods of instruction include lecture, computer laboratory demonstration, hands-on exercises, assigned readings and classroom discussion.
Credit Recommendation: In the lower division baccalaureate/associate degree category, 3 semester hours in Networking, Office Technology, Computer Information Systems, or Business Technology (11/95).

LAN Administration II (NT 200)

Location: Various.
Length: 100 hours (4 weeks)
Dates: November 1993-Present.
Objective: To provide advanced knowledge of LAN design and administration that builds on LAN Administration I.
Learning Outcome: Upon successful completion of this course, the student will be able to design a basic LAN; install, and manage a NOVELL network; and custom configure the system operations.
Instruction: Major topics covered in the course are specialized netware commands, advanced scripting, menu creation, application selection and implementation and DOS interfacing. Methods of instruction include lecture, computer lab, demonstration, hands-on exercises, assigned readings and classroom discussion.
Credit Recommendation: In the lower division baccalaureate/associate degree category, 3 semester hours in Networking, Business Technology, Computer Information Systems, or Office Technology (11/95).

LAN Maintenance and End-User Support (NT 107)

Location: Various.
Length: 100 hours (4 weeks)
Dates: January 1994-Present.
Objective: To provide students with hands-on experience with network-related hardware and software installation and troubleshooting.
Learning Outcome: Upon successful completion of this course, the student will be able to use research diagnostic tools to solve network problems; install and troubleshoot network cards and cabling; setup and correct various storage devices for network data; and diagnose and correct printing problems.
Instruction: Major topics covered in the course are troubleshooting research tools; configuring, installing, and troubleshooting Ethernet, Token Ring, and Arcnet network adapters and cabling; fixes and patches; server performance bottlenecks; abends and lockups; and third party software to create a data recovery plan. Methods of instruction include lecture, classroom exercises, laboratory exercises, discussion, network projects, and an examination.
Credit Recommendation: In the upper division baccalaureate degree category, 3 semester hours in LAN Maintenance or Networking Laboratory (2/97).

Local Area and Enterprise Networking (Netware 4 Part I NT-105; Netware 4 Part II NT-106)

Location: Various locations.
Length: 200 hours (8 weeks)
Dates: June 1995-Present.
Objective: To provide in-depth study and understanding of the Netware 4 networking system using both the DOS and Windows based network management util-

ities. In addition, to provide detailed learning of data protection techniques such as backup services.

Learning Outcome: Upon successful completion of this course, the student will be able to identify a Netware 4 based network with all components; connect to the network using DOS client software; navigate and search through the NDS and populate the NDS creating user/group and other leaf objects; manage and navigate through the file system mapping drive pointers; structure and manage the file system using file system utilities; implement file system and NDS securities to customize/restrict user access; install, manage and troubleshoot a client workstation; create and debug a DOS based Menu system for users; execute console commands and load NLMs on a Netware 4 server; configure and set up a functional printing environment; implement the advanced NDS issues such as partitioning, replication, time synchronization, and NDS security; manage bindery emulation; merge varying tree structures; and install and configure messaging services.

Instruction: Major topics covered in the course are NDS organization of the network; managing container and leaf objects; file system and NDS security; login scripts and menus; printing; and administering a file server, network management and security. Methods of instruction include lecture, discussion, classroom exercises, audio/visual material, learner presentations, reports, quizzes, tests, homework, laboratory, and midterm and final examinations.

Credit Recommendation: In the upper division baccalaureate degree category, 4 semester hours in Networking, Data Communications, System Security, and 2 semester hours in Networking Laboratory (12/96). **NOTE:** Students must complete both NT-105 and NT-106 to receive the recommended credit.

Microcomputer Applications (IT 102)

Location: Various.

Length: 100 hours (4 weeks)

Dates: January 1987-Present.

Objective: To provide proficiency in application of Microsoft Office Professional for Windows—including MS-Word (V6.0), MS-Excel (V5.0), MS-Access (V2.0), and MS-PowerPoint (V4.0).

Learning Outcome: Upon successful completion of this course, the student will be able to use basic components of MS-Office; create, edit, and format documents using MS-Word 6; use MS-Excel 5 to gather and analyze data, perform calculations, create charts, and make various reports; use MS-Access 2 to manage employee data and information; and use MS-PowerPoint 4 to create presentation charts and enhance written reports and slides for visual presentations.

Instruction: Major topics covered in the course are MS-Word, MS-Access, MS-Excel, and MS-PowerPoint. Methods of instruction include lecture, discussion, audio/visual material, presentations, laboratory exercises, and quizzes.

Credit Recommendation: In the lower division baccalaureate/associate degree category, 3 semester hours in Computer Information Systems, Data Processing, or Office Technology (11/95).

Microcomputer Systems Peripherals (Microprocessors, Hardware and Peripherals II) (ET 203)

Location: Various.

Length: 100 hours (4 weeks)

Dates: January 1996-Present.

Objective: To provide student with an introduction to 32 Bit Microprocessors, including 80386/80486, Intel Pentium and RISC architecture.

Learning Outcome: Upon successful completion of this course, the student will be able to demonstrate basic skills in the use of 32 Bit Microprocessors and peripheral devices.

Instruction: Major topics covered in the course are 32 bit Microprocessors, including 80386/80486; video adapters; graphic programming; serial port uses; disk drives; and memory interfacing. Methods of instruction include lecture, discussion, laboratory exercises, and examination.

Credit Recommendation: In the lower division baccalaureate/associate degree category, 2 semester hours in Electrical Technology, 1 semester hour Electrical Technology Laboratory, or 1 semester hour in Electrical Troubleshooting Laboratory (11/95).

Network Systems (NT-111)

Location: Various.

Length: 100 hours (4 weeks)

Dates: February 1997-Present.

Objective: To provide the student with a foundation and understanding of skills and concepts of both the Novell NetWare and the Microsoft Windows NT operating systems.

Learning Outcome: Upon successful completion of this course, the student will be able to perform basic network applications; install and configure client software; use network directory services; manage files, directories, and servers; implement file system security measures; implement and manage login scripts and network printing; and conduct various system monitoring, diagnostic, and troubleshooting techniques.

Instruction: Major topics covered in the course are basic networking concepts and applications, managing files and directories, file system security, network printing, login scripts, monitoring network resources, client software, and diagnostic problem-solving techniques. Methods of instruction include lecture, discussion, classroom exercises, laboratory exercises and projects, and examination.

Credit Recommendation: In the lower division baccalaureate/associate degree category, 3 semester hours in Local Area Networks or Local Area Network Operating Systems (11/97).

Object Oriented Concepts and Programming in C++ (Object Oriented Programming Concepts) (CP 106)

Location: Various.

Length: 100 hours (4 weeks)

Dates: January 1994-Present.

Objective: To provide object oriented concepts and fundamentals of the C++ language using objects.

Learning Outcome: Upon successful completion of this course, the student will be able to understand object-oriented programming in general and the C++ language (using objects) in particular, and use the C++ language in both the MS-DOS and Windows operating environments.

Instruction: Major topics covered in the course are C++ language constructs; classes; dynamic memory allocation; special functions and data types; overloading, and inheritance. Methods of instruction include lecture, discussion, classroom exercises, examination and laboratory exercises.

Credit Recommendation: In the lower division baccalaureate/associate degree category, 3 semester hours in Computer Science (11/95).

Principles of Accounting (GE 104)

Location: Various.

Length: 100 hours (4 weeks)

Dates: July 1992-Present.

Objective: To provide knowledge of basic accounting principles and practices.

Learning Outcome: Upon successful completion of this course, the student will be able to understand the double-entry philosophy and principles; know how to post debits and credits; understand accounting and financial statements; make journal entries; balance and close journals; and demonstrate knowledge of control mechanisms and specialized topics.

Instruction: Major topics covered in the course are financial statements, managerial statements, accounting principles and practices, GAAP, T-accounts, accounting equation, ledgers, entries, depreciation, inventory management, accounting closing, internal control, mechanisms, and taxes. Methods of instruction include lecture, classroom discussion, homework assignments, quizzes, and tests.

Credit Recommendation: In the lower division baccalaureate/associate degree category, 3 semester hours in Accounting, Business Management, Business Administration, Finance, or Financial Management (11/95).

Problem Solving Tools and Techniques (IT-105)

Location: Various.

Length: 100 hours (4 weeks)

Dates: February 1997-Present.

Objective: To provide the student with a comprehensive introduction to the use of help desk software and an understanding of working with SupportMagic SQL in a technical support center environment.

Learning Outcome: Upon successful completion of this course, the student will be able to open, log, and close a help desk call; assign and forward calls to appropriate individuals or groups; create, modify, and delete service work orders; use query features and work orders to show inventory service history; design and develop a help desk screen; set up an escalation scheme; and use statistical information retrieval features to access external knowledge bases and perform keyword searches.

Instruction: Major topics covered in the course are problem solving tools concepts, basics of SupportMagic SQL, call information maintenance, call assignment, work orders, customizing the work area, statistical information retrieval, and escalation schemes. Methods of instruction include lecture, discussion, classroom exercises, laboratory exercises and projects, and examination.

Credit Recommendation: In the lower division baccalaureate/associate degree category, 3 semester hours in Special Topics in Computing or Computer Problem Diagnosis (11/97).

Relational Database Concepts (CP 104)

Location: Various.

Length: 100 hours (4 weeks)

Dates: January 1996-Present.

Objective: To provide knowledge of past, present, and emerging database concepts and structured query language.

Learning Outcome: Upon successful completion of this course, the student will be able to define the role of database and database applications in contemporary organizations; perform data modeling using entity relational and semantic object models; design and implement a relational database application; design and implement a database dictionary with report application; and use multi-user database processing using a client/server structure.

Instruction: Major topics covered in the course are database history; DBMS; entity, semantic, and relational models; normalization, SQL, Data Language I, CODASYL model, and data dictionaries. Methods of instruction include lecture, classroom discussion, classroom activities, homework, computer lab exercises, quizzes, and exams.

Credit Recommendation: In the upper division baccalaureate degree category, 3 semester hours in Computer Information Systems, MIS, or Networking (11/95).

Solid State Devices (ET 101)

Location: Various.

Length: 100 hours (4 weeks)

Dates: January 1991-Present.

Objective: To provide knowledge of terminology, function, symbology, characteristics, applications and troubleshooting of basic solid state devices.

Learning Outcome: Upon successful completion of this course, the student will be able to use and troubleshoot basic discrete solid state devices.

Instruction: Major topics covered in the course are semiconductor theory; PN junction diodes; rectifier circuits; clipping and clamping circuits; zener diodes; power supplies; bipolar transistors; common emitter, common collector, and common base amplifiers; multistage amplifiers; oscillators; junction field effect transistors; metal oxide semiconductors; unijunction transistors; thyristors; and operational amplifiers. Methods of instruction include lecture, discussion, classroom exercises, audio/visual materials, reports, and examinations.

Credit Recommendation: In the lower division baccalaureate/associate degree category, 2 semester hours in Electrical Technology and 1 semester hour in Electrical Technology Laboratory (11/95).

Spreadsheet Applications I (CA 101)

Location: Various.

Length: 100 hours (4 weeks)

Dates: January 1995-Present.

Objective: To introduce students to Microsoft Excel for Windows as a business productivity tool.

Learning Outcome: Upon successful completion of this course, the student will be able to use Excel as a spreadsheet processing program and use file and printer management.

Instruction: Major topics covered in the course are the basic Excel features open, save, print, close, create, formulas, basic functions, templates, tables & charts, and formatting. Methods of instruction include lecture, discussion, case studies, tutorials, laboratory exercises, and examinations.

Credit Recommendation: In the lower division baccalaureate/associate degree category, 3 semester hours in Microcomputer System Administration, Business Administration, Office Technology, or Accounting (11/95).

Spreadsheet Applications II (CA 201)

Location: Multiple locations.

Length: 100 hours (4 weeks)

Dates: June 1995-Present.

Objective: To understand and learn in-depth use of the advanced features of Microsoft Excel.

Learning Outcome: Upon successful completion of this course, the student will be able to perform "what-if" analysis; use Solver; generate reports; use MS-Query; work with multiple worksheets; use Scenario Manager; use object linking & embedding; design and use macros; and understand the rudiments of Visual Basic.

Instruction: Major topics covered in the course are a review of spreadsheet basics, Goalseek, Solver, Sort, data filtering, Pivot table, external workbook units, Look-up, range names, functions, grouping, Scenario Manager, Visual Basic toolbar, macro creation, debugging and running, user-defined functions, and user prompts. Methods of instruction include lecture, discussion, classroom exercises, case studies, quizzes, observations, tests, laboratory assignments, and a final examination.

Credit Recommendation: In the lower division baccalaureate/associate degree

category, 3 semester hours in Microcomputer System Administration, Office Technology, Accounting, or Business Administration (10/96).

System Analysis and Design I (CP 103)

Location: Various.

Length: 100 hours (4 weeks)

Dates: July 1992-Present.

Objective: To provide the student with a basic understanding of how systems are conceived, constructed, installed and maintained.

Learning Outcome: Upon successful completion of this course, the student will be able to explain concepts, principles and the language of Systems Analysis and Design, and understand how typical system operates.

Instruction: Major topics covered in the course are data flow diagrams; data modeling; decision tables; feasibility analysis; file and database specifications; input/output specifications; network modeling, and process analysis and design. Methods of instruction include lecture; discussions; lab exercises; team exercises, and examinations.

Credit Recommendation: In the lower division baccalaureate/associate degree category, 3 semester hours in Management Information Systems (11/95).

Systems Analysis & Design II (CP 203)

Location: Various.

Length: 100 hours (4 weeks)

Dates: July 1992-Present.

Objective: To provide the student with a comprehensive understanding of systems development and maintenance with emphasis on large database systems and prototyping techniques.

Learning Outcome: Upon successful completion of this course, the student will be able to use feasibility and cost benefit analysis tools and techniques; display competency in fact-finding techniques; design conventional files and controls; design modern computer databases, and use prototyping tools.

Instruction: Major topics covered in the course include process modeling; project repository; project management; prototyping; state transition diagrams; structured techniques; structured program specifications; system flowcharts; systems development life cycle, and terminal dialogue specifications. Methods of instruction include lecture, discussion, classroom exercises, team exercises and lab exercises.

Credit Recommendation: In the lower division baccalaureate/associate degree category, 3 semester hours in Management Information Systems (11/95).

UNIX Administration Program
1. UNIX Administration I (OS 101)
2. UNIX Administration II (OS 201)

Location: Various.

Length: 200 hours (8 weeks)

Dates: April 1993-Present.

Objective: To provide student with experience using a UNIX operating system.

Learning Outcome: Upon successful completion of this course, the student will be able to use a UNIX operating system for administrative tasks including permission, security, using a network; and adding users and peripherals.

Instruction: Major topics covered in the course are UNIX components; use of vi editor; compiling C programs; file permissions; multi-tasking; Bourne shell script; C shell; "History" and "Alias"; system network activities; window modification; file and directory maintenance. Methods of instruction include lecture, classroom exercises, examinations, and laboratory exercises.

Credit Recommendation: In the lower level baccalaureate/associate degree category, 3 semester hours in Business Technology or 1 semester hour in Business Technology Laboratory (11/95). **NOTE:** Must complete both courses to receive credit.

Visual Basic (Application Development Concepts) (CP 105)

Location: Various.

Length: 100 hours (4 weeks)

Dates: January 1996-Present.

Objective: To introduce the students to programming using Microsoft Visual Basic on the IBM PC or IBM compatible computer running Microsoft Windows.

Learning Outcome: Upon successful completion of this course, the student will be able to design programs in Visual Basic; create tables and arrays; use basic file access and graphical processing; and use visual debugging tools.

Instruction: Major topics covered in the course are objects, subprograms, decision logic, repetition, arrays, pointers, sequential file processing, random access processing, graphical processing, and debugging tools. Methods of instruction include lecture, discussion, classroom exercises, laboratory exercises, and exams.

Credit Recommendation: In the lower division baccalaureate/associate degree category, 3 semester hours in Computer Information Systems, MIS, or Computer Science (11/95).

Windows NT Fundamentals (NT 110)

Location: Various.

Length: 100 hours (4 weeks)

Dates: September 1996-Present.

Objective: To provide knowledge of the Microsoft Windows NT operating system at the workstation and server level.

Learning Outcome: Upon successful completion of this course, the student will be able to install and configure the NT workstation as a peer-to-peer node and configure, manage, and troubleshoot Windows NT workstations and servers.

Instruction: Major topics covered in the course are requirements and methods of installation of Windows NT workstation and server; creating, managing, and configuring user/group accounts; NT registry and registry editor; NTFS security; MT networking architecture and protocols; configuring the workstation with TCP/IP and IPX/SPX; diagnostic tools and troubleshooting techniques; using service manager; fault tolerance features; and directory services database synchronization processes. Methods of instruction include lecture, classroom exercises, laboratory exercises, discussion, network projects, and an examination.

Credit Recommendation: In the upper division baccalaureate degree category, 2 semester hours in Networking or Windows NT and 1 semester hour in Networking or Windows NT Laboratory (2/97).

Word Processing and Desktop Publishing (Word Processing Applications II) (CA 200)

Location: Various.

Length: 100 hours (4 weeks)

Dates: January 1995-Present.

Objective: To provide skill in use of Microsoft Word for desktop publishing operations.

Learning Outcome: Upon successful completion of this course, the student will be able to differentiate between word-processing and desktop publishing, describe the elements of graphic arts techniques, format camera-ready copy, and apply the basic elements of graphic design and layout.

Instruction: Major topics covered in the course are importing documents, creating headers and footers, outlining reports, adding tables of contents, column set-ups, mastheads, banner headlines, inserting clip art, and use of graphics. Methods of instruction include lecture, discussion, and laboratory exercises.

Credit Recommendation: In the lower division baccalaureate/associate degree category, 3 semester hours in Office Technology or Business Technology (11/95).

Word Processing Applications (Word Processing Applications I) (CA 100)

Location: Various.

Length: 100 hours (4 weeks)

Dates: January 1995-Present.

Objective: To introduce Microsoft Word for Windows as a business productivity tool for word processing.

Learning Outcome: Upon successful completion of this course, the student will be able to use MS-Word for word processing, file management, printer management, and basic and advanced word processing skills.

Instruction: Major topics covered in the course are Microsoft Word for Windows as a business productivity tool; basic features, advantages, and limitations of Microsoft Word for Windows; most commonly used business document formats including standard resumes, business letters, formal reports, memo layouts, accounting notation, and tabular entry. Methods of instruction include lecture, discussion, learner presentations/reports, examinations, computer laboratory assignments, and classroom and laboratory examinations.

Credit Recommendation: In the lower division baccalaureate/associate degree category, 3 semester hours in Office Technology, Microcomputer Systems Administration, or Business Technology (11/95).

CoreStates New Jersey National Bank

Serving New Jersey families and businesses since 1804, CoreStates New Jersey National Bank (NJNB) is proud of its employees and their commitment to quality customer service. To help employees develop to their fullest potential, the bank offers classes designed to help associates achieve ongoing personal and professional growth, while simultaneously helping NJNB maintain its high level of customer service.

Courses are offered in all areas of banking with concentrations in both consumer bank training and customer service. All instructors are NJNB employees with teaching backgrounds and extensive experience in their subject area. Class size is small, providing students with personal attention and enabling them to develop a thorough understanding of class material.

Source of official student records: Registry of Credit Recommendations, American Council on Education, One Dupont Circle, Washington, DC 20036-1193.

Additional information about the courses: Office of Corporate-Higher Education Programs, Thomas Edison State College, 101 West State Street, Trenton, NJ 08608-1176.

Bank Products/Services

Location: Point Pleasant, Scotch Rd., West Trenton, and Sicklerville, New Jersey.

Length: 65 hours (13 days).

Dates: January 1991-Present.

Objective: To train participants to match customers' needs to the products the bank offers, plus in-depth computer training on methods of accessing all systems required to perform a variety of Retail Banking Services.

Learning Outcome: Upon successful completion of this course, the student will be able to understand the products the bank offers and the methods to match the products to the customers' needs; open accounts; use all of the computer systems accessible in a bank branch and identify the means of accessing and using one or more of them.

Instruction: Methods of instruction include lectures, simulations, field study, lab, drill and practices, multimedia presentation, daily journal discussing learned skills, and a 3-page report relating what they have learned to a banking application.

Credit Recommendation: In the lower division baccalaureate/associate degree category, 3 semester hours in Retail Bank Products and Services or Banking elective (1/94).

Branch Administration/MTP

Location: Scotch Rd., West Trenton, New Jersey.

Length: 262.5 hours (7 weeks).

Dates: April 1988-April 1995.

Objective: To teach students all aspects of managing a bank branch office and functions of its internal departments.

Learning Outcome: Upon successful completion of this course, the student will be able to have a working knowledge of all the functions/responsibilities of both branch and internal departments of the bank; and develop a network of resources for future use on the job.

Instruction: Methods of instruction include field study, comprehensive one-on-one instruction, hands-on experience and required text reading.

Credit Recommendation: In the lower division baccalaureate/associate degree or in the upper division baccalaureate category, 3 semester hours in Banking Management, Banking elective, or Field Experience (3/94).

Business Banking/MTP

Location: Scotch Rd., West Trenton, New Jersey.

Length: 337.5 hours (9 weeks).

Dates: April 1988-April 1995.

Objective: To give students understanding of business operations in banking, including credit policies and procedures, types of lending, and lending functions.

Learning Outcome: Upon successful completion of this course, the student will be able to conduct an interview of a small business customer and know what questions to ask; have a basic knowledge of the bank's business lending products; understand the bank's loan portfolio, cash flow, ratio analysis, and pricing; understand what information is needed to make a business loan decision; know how to perform spreadsheets of company financial statements; and write basic loan proposals.

Instruction: Methods of instruction include a mixture of learning experiences, such as role play, lecture, real time lending decision making, and one-on-one instruction. Writing assignments include an outline for a sample loan interview, discussion of calling skills used by SBB Officers, and preparing a paper identifying a new prospect list based on customer needs.

Credit Recommendation: In the lower division baccalaureate/associate degree or in the upper division baccalaureate category, 3 semester hours in Small Business Banking, or Banking elective, or Field Experience (3/94).

Credit Operations/MTP

Location: Express Loan Center and Lancaster, PA.

Length: 525 hours (14 weeks).

Dates: April 1988-April 1995.

Objective: To develop a mastery of the consumer lending function and competencies in handling consumer loan requests.

Learning Outcome: Upon successful completion of this course, the student will be able to perform the duties/responsibilities of a Customer Service representative working with the Branch Manager; speak with customers, describe loan products, take applications, and follow-up with all required loan documentation; participate in business calls with the Branch Manager; and identify exception issues and be able to complete loan documentation.

Instruction: Methods of instruction include text reading, classroom instruction and lab simulation, and real customer situations, including students handling business calls.

Credit Recommendation: In the upper division baccalaureate category, or in the lower division baccalaureate/associate degree category, 3 semester hours in Banking Credit Operations, or banking elective, or field experience (3/94).

Customer Service/Initial Training

Location: Scotch Rd., West Trenton, NJ.

Length: 219 hours plus 1 week practicum (7 weeks).

Dates: June 1989-Present.

Objective: To provide participants with the skills necessary to answer inquiries and resolve problems relative to bank products and services.

Learning Outcome: Upon successful completion of this course, the student will be able to answer customer inquiries; promote products and related services; demonstrate the steps necessary to investigate and resolve exception situations; process account maintenance and checkbook order requests; and develop interpersonal skills to effectively handle routine and exceptional situations.

Instruction: Methods of instruction include review, lecture, role-plays and hands-on computer utilization. Some sessions include real-time telephone experience responding to customers' inquiries. A one-week practicum is utilized.

Credit Recommendation: In the lower division baccalaureate/associate degree category, 3 semester hours in Customer Relations/Service and 3 semester hours in Banking or Business elective for each course, for a total of 6 credits (1/94).

Introduction to Bank Credit/MTP

Location: Scotch Rd., West Trenton, New Jersey.

Length: 225 hours (6 weeks).

Dates: April 1988-April 1995.

Objective: To prepare management trainees to work as Financial Service Representatives at a branch bank.

Learning Outcome: Upon successful completion of this course, the student will be able to know all consumer loan products to communicate information to customers and cross sell bank products; understand what information is needed to take a complete loan application; know how to apply and comply with federal consumer regulations when handling consumer loan requests; enter loan application on-line using the LAPS System; perform all required credit investigations; read credit bureau and property search reports to understand how the information is used in the credit analysis process; analyze tax returns to calculate income; calculate debt-to-income and loan-to-value ratios; and function as a Financial Service Representative at a branch bank.

Instruction: Methods of instruction include hands-on computer utilization, readings, lectures, one-on-one instruction, and simulations and real time customer interaction.

Credit Recommendation: In the lower division baccalaureate/associate degree or in the upper division baccalaureate category, 3 semester hours in Banking Credit, Banking elective, or Field Experience (3/94).

Management Seminar Phase/MTP

Location: Penn Mutual Building, Philadelphia, PA.

Length: 75 hours (2 weeks).

Dates: April 1988-April 1995.

Objective: To give students a basic knowledge and understanding of the supervisory role of the branch manager.

Learning Outcome: Upon successful completion of this course, the student will be able to develop skills for positive interaction with peers, subordinates, and supervisors with concentration on leadership skills; learn to achieve goals of the organization through others; and develop supervisory and interpersonal skills so that trainees can enter and perform accountable roles.

Instruction: Methods of instruction include classroom training, the submission of a written summary of each management phase, and three application projects which will include feedback from mentor and supervisor.

Credit Recommendation: In the lower division baccalaureate/associate degree or in the upper division baccalaureate category, 3 semester hours in Banking Supervision, or Banking elective, or in Field Experience (3/94).

Teller Training

Location: Point Pleasant, Scotch Rd., West Trenton, and Sicklerville, New Jersey.

Length: 105 hours (14 days).

Dates: May 1993-Present.

Objective: To train individuals in bookkeeping, computer, and interpersonal skills needed to work as an independent teller.

Learning Outcome: Upon successful completion of this course, the student will be able to understand general bank terms; identify and process many different types of basic retail type transactions; serve customers in an efficient and accurate manner; follow procedures to assure compliance with security; use the computer for data processing and interbranch communication; and display interpersonal skills with respect to customer service and co-workers.

Instruction: Methods of instruction include lectures, simulations, field study, lab, drill and practice, multimedia presentation, and an interpersonal relations module . In addition, the student must complete the two-day interpersonal communications course.

Credit Recommendation: In the lower division baccalaureate/associate degree category, 3 semester hours in Introduction to Retail Banking, Banking or Business elective (1/94).

Corporate Educational Services

Corporate Educational Services (CES) provides on-site training and consulting in process and project management, quality deployment, and continuous process improvement. CES delivers general and customized, introductory through advanced programs. To address specific client needs, CES draws upon a network of consultant and instructors with the broad industry experience, in-depth functional knowledge, and proven training abilities to resolve complex quality and productivity issues.

CES training is highly interactive with an emphasis on the practical application of concepts and skills. CES courses incorporate a variety of instructional techniques including examples, exercises and case studies based on actual projects, processes and procedures of the client organization. CES programs range from one-day seminars to multi-week courses.

CES is based in Oakbrook Terrace, Illinois (a suburb of Chicago) with a regional office in Atlanta, Georgia. CES programs are conducted on-site throughout the United States for a rapidly expanding list of client organizations that includes major companies in telecommunications, steel, banking, electronics manufacturing, pharmaceuticals, construction, publishing, and utilities.

Source of official student records: Registry of Credit Recommendations, American Council on Education, One Dupont Circle, Washington, DC 20036-1193 or Operations Manager, Corporate Educational Services, One Tower Lane, Suite 1000, Oakbrook Terrace, IL 60181.

Additional information about the courses: College Credit Recommendation Service, American Council on Education, One Dupont Circle, Washington, DC 20036-1193.

College Algebra

Location: Various on-site locations.

Length: 75 hours (15 weeks).

Dates: September 1993-Present.

Objective: To assist the student in acquiring a thorough knowledge and proficiency in the basic field of algebra.

Learning Outcome: Upon successful completion of this course, the student will be able to understand basic algebra.

Instruction: Major topics covered in the course are fundamental concepts and operations; determinants; functions and graphs; factoring and fractions; systems of linear equations; quadratic equations; numbers, expressions, and order of operations; inequalities; and exponents and radicals. Methods of instruction include lecture, discussion, problem solving, and examinations.

Credit Recommendation: In the lower division baccalaureate/associate degree category, 3 semester hours in General Mathematics (2/94).

Contract and Procurement Management

Location: Various on-site locations.

Length: 40 hours (1 week).

Dates: September 1991-October 1997.

Objective: To examine the process by which goods and services are acquired in the project management environment and the legal issues project managers face. The course also explores the evolution of the contractual relationship from initial formation through completion of the services and/or delivery of the goods or services.

Learning Outcome: Upon successful completion of this course, the student will be able to recognize the need to plan for change; understand the role of the Project Manager in the procurement process; understand basic contract elements; gain an understanding of funding and decision making authority as applied to contract formation and performance; understand bid package preparation and evaluation process; learn how and when to select subcontractor; gain a better understanding of proposal strategy based on a knowledge of procurement regulations; be familiar with proposal terminology and elements, understand what is meant by a win-win approach; understand what it meant by a constructive change, remedy, dispute and arbitration; understand ways to protect the project during the course of performance; learn about the types of warranties and what they mean to project performance; understand the differences between termination for convenience and termination for default and the remedies available to each breached party.

Instruction: Major topics covered in the course are principals of contracting, purchasing, and subcontracting; acquisition process; proposal development; negotiations; contract administration; performance, disputes and arbitration; and terminations, closeouts, and warranties. Methods of instruction include lecture, discussion, simulation, role play, case study, presentations, demonstrations, projects, and examinations.

Credit Recommendation: In the upper division baccalaureate degree category, 3 semester hours in Contract and Procurement Management, elective in General Business, or Industrial and Operations Engineering (10/92).

Elementary Algebra

Location: Various on-site locations.

Length: 75 hours (15 weeks).

Dates: September 1993-Present.

Objective: To provide the student who is unsure of his/her ability in algebra, or who needs an arithmetic refresher before taking more advanced courses in math, with proficiency in the basics of algebra, particularly equations, fractions, exponents, and expression.

Learning Outcome: Upon successful completion of this course, the student will be able to do arithmetic with real numbers, fractions, exponents and radicals; do basic algebraic equations; sketch graphs of fractions; and apply exponential and logarithmic functions.

Instruction: Major topics covered in the course are arithmetic of real numbers, exponent and radicals, equation solving, arithmetic of expressions, factoring, fractions, graphs, and functions. Methods of instruction include lecture, class exercises, and examinations.

Credit Recommendation: In the lower division baccalaureate/associate degree category, 1 semester hour in General Mathematics (2/94).

English Composition-110

Location: Various on-site locations.

Length: 75 hours (15 weeks)

Dates: February 1994-Present.

Objective: To provide the student with practical application of traditional writing skills.

Learning Outcome: Upon successful completion of this course, the student will be able to write well-developed paragraphs, create effective topic sentences, write clear thesis statements, develop a larger and more precise vocabulary, and read and write with awareness of correct spelling of both general and technical words.

Instruction: Major topics covered in the course are vocabulary, diction, dictionary use, definitions, verbs, sentence structure, topic sentences, narrative paragraphs, outlining, plurals, parallelism, critical thinking, paragraph structure, and essay writing. Methods of instruction includes assignments, quizzes, class participation, and laboratory.

Credit Recommendation: In the lower division baccalaureate/associate degree

category, 3 semester hours in English or Speech Communications (2/94).

Introduction to Excel

Location: Various on-site locations.

Length: 15 hours (3 weeks).

Dates: September 1993-Present.

Objective: To introduce the student to spreadsheet applications, design, and usage, and provide the student with a basic understanding of Excel uses and techniques.

Learning Outcome: Upon successful completion of this course, the student will be able to develop a proficiency in Excel, design and use spreadsheets, and develop databases to apply to their daily work.

Instruction: Major topics covered in the course are beginning Excel, worksheets, ranges, functions, absolute references, tool bars, formatting, graphics, printing windows, linking, databases, advanced functions, documents, outlines, templates, reports, charts, and objects. Methods of instruction include assignments, quizzes, exams, class participation, class exercises, and laboratory.

Credit Recommendation: In the lower division baccalaureate/associate degree category, 1 semester hour in Spreadsheet as an elective (2/94).

Introduction to Harvard Graphics

Location: Various on-site locations.

Length: 15 hours (3 weeks).

Dates: September 1993-Present.

Objective: To assist the student in acquiring a basic understanding of Harvard Graphics.

Learning Outcome: Upon successful completion of this course, the student will be able to create text charts, XY charts, and pie charts; learn importing and exporting techniques; and master adding test and graphic objects.

Instruction: Major topics covered in the course are introduction to Harvard Graphics, charting, creating and editing objects; using draw and symbols; creating presentations; and using import/export and templates. Methods of instruction include assignments, quizzes, exams, class participation, class assignments, and laboratory.

Credit Recommendation: In the lower division baccalaureate/associate degree category, 1 semester hour in Graphics as an elective (2/94).

Introduction to Personal Computers

Location: Various on-site locations.

Length: 15 hours (3 weeks).

Dates: September 1993-Present.

Objective: To provide the student with the background needed for using the PC including how to start up and shut down the system; use directories, disks, and drives; and create files.

Learning Outcome: Upon successful completion of this course, the student will be able to understand DOS and the DOS operating systems and do simple problem solving.

Instruction: Major topics covered in the course are understanding hardware, software, booting, DOS commands, directories, disks and drives, file management, screen edits, batch files, advanced commands, memory management, device drives, utilities, and DOS shell. Methods of instruction include assignments, quizzes, in-class assignments, exams, class participation, and laboratory.

Credit Recommendation: In the lower division baccalaureate/associate degree category, 1 semester hour in Computer Science or Computer Information Systems as an elective (2/94).

Introduction to UNIX

Location: Various on-site locations.

Length: 75 hours (15 weeks).

Dates: September 1993-Present.

Objective: To develop the student's education in the fundamentals of UNIX.

Learning Outcome: Upon successful completion of this course, the student will be able to understand and organize the UNIX system files, compile and run various UNIX programs; design, code, document, and run a C program involving complicated logic with multiple conditions; and design, code, document, and run a C program using an array of structures.

Instruction: Major topics covered in the course are an introduction to UNIX basics, UNIX commands, UNIX file structure, commands and standard file communications, screen editor (VI), data retrieve and manipulation, shell programming, and introduction to C programming. Methods of instruction include assignments, quizzes, exams, class participation exams, and laboratory.

Credit Recommendation: In the lower division baccalaureate/associate degree category, 3 semester hours in Computer Information Systems or Computer Science as an elective (2/94).

Introduction to Word for Windows

Location: Various on-site locations.

Length: 15 hours (3 weeks).

Dates: September 1993-Present.

Objective: To provide the student with the basic fundamentals of word processing; specifics on the usage of word for windows software; creating, editing, and printing of documents; and introduction to some of the advanced techniques of Word for Windows.

Learning Outcome: Upon successful completion of this course, the student will be able to apply the principles and techniques learned in this course in the daily workplace environment, and create documents using Word for Windows.

Instruction: Major topics covered in the course are understanding word documents, text processing, formatting, printing, utilities, file management, spreadsheets, headers and footers, and templates. Methods of instruction include assignments, quizzes, exams, class participation, class exercises, and laboratory.

Credit Recommendation: In the lower division baccalaureate/associate degree category, 1 semester hour in Word Processing or Computer Information Systems elective (2/94).

Oral Communications

Location: Various on-site locations.

Length: 75 hours (15 weeks).

Dates: September 1993-Present.

Objective: To introduce the principles of effective public speaking to the student with emphasis on speech preparation including audience analysis, research, outlining, etc. The student will be required to give six speeches during the course.

Learning Outcome: Upon successful completion of this course, the student will have gained proficiency in preparing speeches, particularly outlining and wording a speech with emphasis on speaking to inform and on developing persuasive speech; and delivering speeches in front of groups.

Instruction: Major topics covered in the course are selecting topics; finding materials; supporting the ideas; organizing, outlining, and delivering speeches; and making effective presentations. Methods of instruction include projects, presentations, readings, and examinations.

Credit Recommendation: In the lower division baccalaureate/associate degree category, 3 semester hours in Communications, Business, or General elective (2/94).

Product Cost Analysis

Location: Various on-site locations.

Length: 75 hours (15 weeks).

Dates: February 1994-Present.

Objective: To provide the student with an understanding of the terms, procedures, and analysis techniques used in the cost accounting system, and the ability to apply this understanding in their work environment.

Learning Outcome: Upon successful completion of this course, the student will be able to operate and manage in the manufacturing environment with an understanding of job orders, standard costing, and direct costing; the reporting of each; and the ability to apply to their own work environment.

Instruction: Major topics covered in the course are accounting review, financial and managerial cost accounting, cost terms and concepts, cost behavior and estimating, formulae, contribution margin reporting, job order costing, process costing, accounting for lost units, material and labor costing, factory overhead costing and allocations, standard cost and variance analysis, and variable and gross margin costing. Methods of instruction include lecture, discussion, exercises, videotape, and laboratory.

Credit Recommendation: In the upper division baccalaureate degree category, 3 semester hours in Cost Accounting or Business as an elective (2/94).

Project Cost Management

Location: Various on-site locations.

Length: 40 hours (1 week).

Dates: October 1991-October 1997.

Objective: To provide the students with a basic understanding of project costs, their estimation and tracking.

Learning Outcome: Upon successful completion of this course, the student will be able to perform cost estimating and forecasting; understand budgeting and be able to perform budgeting; know the various cost controls and apply them; understand and use various cost reporting techniques; understand and apply earned value analysis; and understand overhead allocation and cost scheduling.

Instruction: Major topics covered in the course are definitions of project costs and their allocations; time value of money; cash flow estimations; project cost control; and budgeting. Methods of instruction include lecture, discussion, and role play.

Credit Recommendation: In the upper division baccalaureate degree category, 3 semester hours in Financial Management or Cost Management (10/92).

Project Leadership and Team Building

Location: Various on-site locations.

Length: 40 hours (1 week).

Dates: July 1991-October 1997.

Objective: To provide participants with the leadership skills to organize and motivate human resources in a manner that achieves results in complex organizational environments.

Learning Outcome: Upon successful completion of this course, the student will be able to identify and understand various leadership styles; understand why conflicts occur and how to resolve; develop better interpersonal skills and communications; more effectively manage across departmental boundaries; hold more effective meetings; deliver better presentations; and understand how teams work and become a more effective contributing team member.

Instruction: Major topics covered in the course are group behavior, motivation, and transactional analysis; Myers-Briggs; listening skills; leadership; management styles; situational leadership; power; behavior modification; and managing change and conflict. Methods of instruction include lecture, discussion, simulations and role play, case studies, projects, demonstrations, and examinations.

Credit Recommendation: In the upper division baccalaureate degree category, 3 semester hours in Leadership, Project Management, Supervision, or General Management (10/92).

Project Management Systems II

Location: Various on-site locations.

Length: 40 hours (1 week).

Dates: October 1991-October 1997.

Objective: To provide the students with the knowledge and tools to manage projects in a multi discipline environment.

Learning Outcome: Upon successful completion of this course, the student will be able to identify and respond to common errors that occur in the multiple phase duration of a project; sharpen communication techniques and attitudes; integrate planning as the interactive process that is uniquely in the hands of a project manager; gain experience in managing requirements and expectations of sponsors and other project managers; apply tools and techniques to continually reorganize a project for its phases to produce excellent results; negotiate and revise plans to use various mixes of temporary, full-time and part-time resources; and integrate directing and controlling in an action oriented project manager style.

Instruction: Major topics covered in the course are application of a project system to an organization; planning, scheduling, and controlling multiproject programs; program management in a multi-discipline environment; multi-project management; integration of project(s); integrating perspectives of different stake holders. Methods of instruction include lecture, discussion, case study, simulation, role play, presentations, projects, and examinations.

Credit Recommendation: In the upper division baccalaureate degree category, 3 semester hours in Project Management, Entrepreneurship, or General Management (10/92).

Project Management
1. Basic Project Management

Location: Various on-site locations.

Length: 40 hours (1 week).

Dates: March 1991-October 1997.

Objective: To provide the students with a basic understanding and working knowledge of the theories, techniques and tools used in project management.

Learning Outcome: Upon successful completion of this course, the student will be able to understand the terminology, tools, and techniques used in project management; identify and understand the steps required for project management; recognize the snags and pitfalls that might occur and the techniques for handling them.

Instruction: Major topics covered in the course are the project life cycle; project mapping from start to finish; project planning to include scheduling, budgeting and establishing outcomes; and project staffing, tracking and control. Methods of instruction include lecture, discussion, and role play.

Credit Recommendation: In the lower division baccalaureate/associate degree category, 3 semester hours in Project Management or General Management (10/92).

Quality Management and Continuous Improvement Process

Location: Various on-site locations.

Length: 40 hours (1 week).

Dates: November 1991-October 1997.

Objective: To help students understand the nature and principles of quality, how programs of quality control and quality programs are implemented in the workplace.

Learning Outcome: Upon successful completion of this course, the student will be able to understand various quality management diagrams and charts; perform simple probability analysis; interpret quality control charts; perform sampling plans; have a thorough knowledge of Total Quality Management tools; and understand Total Quality Management and Functional Deployment.

Instruction: Major topics covered in the course are Deming's 14 points; cross cultural comparisons of quality in manufacturing; basic statistics-interpretations; Total Quality Management (TQM); quality control; charts and diagrams; sampling; quality awards and reliability; and durability and auditing. Methods of instruction include lecture, discussion, simulative, case study analysis, presentation, readings, and objective and short answer examinations.

Credit Recommendation: In the upper division baccalaureate degree category, 3 semester hours in Quality Management (10/92).

Statistics

Location: Various on-site locations.

Length: 75 hours (15 weeks).

Dates: February 1994-Present.

Objective: To provide the student with an introduction to the basic concepts in probability, descriptive, and inferential statistics.

Learning Outcome: Upon successful completion of this course, the student will be able to apply basic probability and descriptive statistics; fit a curve to data using "least squares"; test elementary hypotheses; perform two-variable regression and correlation; and perform a one-way analysis of variance.

Instruction: Major topics covered in the course are descriptive statistics, frequency distributions (central tendency, dispersion), normal probability distributions, sampling, estimation tests of hypotheses, regression and correlation, and one-way anova. Methods of instruction include lecture, classroom exercises, and examinations.

Credit Recommendation: In the lower division baccalaureate/associate degree category, 3 semester hours in an elective or as a requirement for a non-Calculus Statistics course (2/94).

Trigonometry

Location: Various on-site locations.

Length: 75 hours (15 weeks).

Dates: February 1994-Present.

Objective: To provide the student with a reinforcement of previous mathematics instruction and build on it including the fundamental laws of trigonometry, functions and their graphs, law of sines, cosines, polar coordinates, and De Moivre's theorem.

Learning Outcome: Upon successful completion of this course, the student will be able to find the values of unknown elements of a right triangle; find the six trigonometric ratios of any angle; use the law of sines and the law of cosines; verify trigonometric identities; solve trigonometric equations; identify inverse trigonometric functions and sketch their graphs; and convert a complex number from rectangular to trigonometric, polar, or exponential form and vice versa.

Instruction: Major topics covered in the course are circular trigonometric ratios and functions, trigonometric expression of complex numbers, polar coordinates, systems of equalities and inequalities, and matrices and determinants. Methods of instruction include lecture, discussion, and problem sets.

Credit Recommendation: In the lower division baccalaureate/associate degree category, 2 semester hours in General Mathematics or Introduction to Calculus (2/94).

Credit Union National Association

The Certified Credit Union Executive (CCUE) Program is sponsored by the Credit Union National Association (CUNA). CUNA is the national trade association for over 12,000 credit unions in the United States. The CCUE Program is primarily an independent study program developed by an advisory committee for credit union executives and educators. However, in some localities CCUE courses are also offered by colleges in a conventional classroom format. The CCUE program was initiated in 1975 and is a professional development program for credit union personnel.

To participate in the CCUE Program, a candidate must be actively engaged in the credit union industry and must complete a curriculum of ten independent study courses designed to broaden knowledge and enhance management skills. Successful completion of all ten courses, along with the fulfillment of other academic, experience, affiliation, and ethical requirements, qualifies a candidate for CCUE designation.

Course completion is validated by national examinations prepared by college and university professors and/or program staff, and administered under strict control in colleges and universities in the candidates' home areas. The program is primarily designed for self-study and participants desiring professional assistance may contact the CCUE Staff at CUNA.

Textbooks are either selected by college and university faculty members or prepared by expert consultants. Some review guides are also available for examination preparation.

Source of official student records: Program Assistant, Certified Credit Union Executive Program, CUNA, P.O. Box 431, Madison, WI 53701-0431.

Additional information about the courses: College Credit Recommendation Service, American Council on Education, One Dupont Circle, Washington, DC 20036-1193.

Accounting I (400)

Location: Independent study program.

Length: 15 self-paced lessons. (Formerly 10 self-paced lessons).

Dates: January 1975-May 1991.

Objective: To provide knowledge of basic accounting principles and applications.

Learning Outcome: Upon successful completion of this course, the student will be able to understand accounting principles so that they may be applied to credit union needs.

Instruction: Major topics covered in the course are the areas of financial accounting relevant to external reporting by credit unions; accounting principles, basic accounting cycle, and financial statements; analysis of revenue and expense; analysis of asset, liability, and equity accounts; preparation of financial statements; and present value concepts. This course is a prerequisite for Accounting II. Methods of instruction include self-study utilizing a course syllabus, texts, and an examination.

Credit Recommendation: In the lower division baccalaureate/associate degree category, 3 semester hours in Accounting (6/81) (7/86) (9/91).

Accounting II (1400)
(Accounting II [410])

Location: Independent study program.

Length: 10 self-paced lessons.

Dates: January 1975-May 1987.

Objective: To provide the knowledge of managerial accounting and how it applies to the decision-making process.

Learning Outcome: Upon successful completion of this course, the student will be able to understand the relationship of accounting data to management decisions.

Instruction: Major topics covered in the course are the preparation and use of reports for management decisionmaking; management accounting, cost behavior, cost flows, and capital budgeting; financial statement analysis; measuring performance; planning and control; budgeting; standard costing; internal control; audits; and cost allocations. Methods of instruction include self-study utilizing a course syllabus, texts, and an examination.

Credit Recommendation: In the upper division baccalaureate degree category, 3 semester hours in Managerial Accounting (6/81) (7/86) (9/91). *Prerequisite:* Accounting I.

Business Law (1000)
(Formerly Business Law [10])

Location: Independent study program.

Length: 15 self-paced lessons. (Formerly 10 self-paced lessons).

Dates: *Version 1:* January 1975-June 1986; *Version 2:* July 1986-Present.

Objective: To provide an understanding of business law concepts and terms and to acquaint personnel with the application of these concepts and terms to the operation of credit unions.

Learning Outcome: Upon successful completion of this course, the student will be able to understand basic business law concepts and terms.

Instruction: Major topics covered in the course are a well-rounded study of business law; a working knowledge of legal terminology; social forces and legal rights; contracts, including nature, offer and acceptance, capacity, mutuality and consideration, legality, form and interpretation, transfer of rights, and discharge; agency; commercial paper, including nature, negotiability and transfer, rights of parties, notes, and drafts; bankruptcy; and management of corporations. Methods of instruction include self-study utilizing a course syllabus, a text, a review guide, and an examination.

Credit Recommendation: *Version 1:* In the upper division baccalaureate degree category, 2 semester hours in Business Law I (Contracts and Negotiable Instruments) (6/81). *Version 2:* In the lower division baccalaureate/associate degree or in the upper division baccalaureate degree category, 3 semester hours in Business Law (7/86) (9/91) (5/96).

Credit and Collections (900)
(Formerly Credit and Collections [9])

Location: Independent study program.

Length: 11 self-paced lessons.

Dates: January 1975-Present.

Objective: To develop knowledge of credit granting and collection techniques with application to credit unions.

Learning Outcome: Upon successful completion of this course, the student will be able to understand the basic elements and principles of granting credit and collection techniques.

Instruction: Major topics covered in the course are various aspects of credit; nature and role of credit; types of consumer credit, their management and investigation; basis of credit decision; decision and salesmanship in consumer credit; numerical scoring systems; collection policies, practices, and systems; business and government and international credit functions, and control of credit operations. Methods of instruction include self-study utilizing a course syllabus, a text, a review guide, and an examination.

Credit Recommendation: In the lower division baccalaureate/associate degree category, 2 semester hours in Credit and Collections (6/81) (7/86) (9/91) (5/96).

Credit Union Accounting (1300)

Location: Independent study program.

Length: 13 self-paced lessons.
Dates: September 1990-January 1998.
Objective: To emphasize those areas of financial accounting relevant to external reporting by credit unions.
Learning Outcome: Upon successful completion of this course, the student will be able to define or describe general accounting terms and principles; differentiate between cash and accrual basis accounting; analyze transactions and record their effects; prepare income statements and balance sheets; post closing and year-end entries; and explain control procedures.
Instruction: Major topics covered in the course are accounting principles, recording transactions, preparing financial statements, accounting systems, internal control procedures and reconciliations, accounting for loans and investments, fixed assets and depreciation, the basic accounting cycle and financial statements, analysis of revenue and expense, analysis of asset, liability, and equity accounts, preparation of cash flow statements, and present value concepts. Methods of instruction include self-study utilizing a course syllabus, texts, a workbook and a solutions book, and an examination.
Credit Recommendation: In the lower division baccalaureate/associate degree category, 3 semester hours in Principles of Accounting or Financial Accounting (9/91) (5/96).

Data Processing (1200)

Location: Independent study program.
Length: 15 self-paced lessons.
Dates: December 1985-May 1987.
Objective: To provide students with a comprehensive introduction to the principles of computers and data processing.
Learning Outcome: Upon successful completion of this course, the student will be able to compare the hardware and software components and the input and output devices of manual, personal computer, and data processing systems and describe the differences among microcomputers, minicomputers, and small, medium, and large computer systems; define input, processing, and output, and explain the relationship between data and information; differentiate between temporary and permanent storage, batch and on-line processing, and internal and external storage; describe how software functions and differentiate application from system software; name the technologies used for storage and compare their advantages and disadvantages; and describe common batch data entry devices, types of printers, terminal devices, other input and output devices and their applications, and the tasks performed by special purpose microcomputers.
Instruction: Major topics covered in the course are an overview of computer functions, hardware, software, systems, and how they are integrated in business and credit and credit union settings. Meth-ods of instruction include self-study utilizing a course syllabus, a text, and an examination.
Credit Recommendation: In the lower division baccalaureate/associate degree category, 3 semester hours in Data Processing, Computers, or Information Processing (9/91).

Economics (600) (Formerly Economics, Government, and Business [6])

Location: Independent study program.
Length: 13 self-paced lessons.
Dates: *Version 1:* January 1975-June 1986; *Version 2:* July 1986-November 1991.
Objective: To provide knowledge of general economic principles with special reference to their effect on credit unions.
Learning Outcome: Upon successful completion of this course, the student will be able to understand national economic policies, such as monetary and fiscal policy, and their effect on credit unions and their members.
Instruction: Major topics covered in the course are a systematic study and searching analysis of economic activity; basic economic concepts and national income; pricing, supply, and demand; incomes and living standards; business organization; labor and industrial relations and the economic role of government; national income, savings, investment, and consumption; income determination, business cycles, and forecasting; prices and money, the banking system, and monetary policy; fiscal policy and price determination; pricing and the productive factors, wages, interest, and profits; international trade and finance; and economic problems and alternate economic systems. Methods of instruction include self-study utilizing a course syllabus, texts, a review guide, and an examination.
Credit Recommendation: *Version 1:* In the lower division baccalaureate/associate degree category, 2 semester hours in General Economics (6/81). *Version 2:* In the lower division baccalaureate/associate degree category, 3 semester hours in Economics (7/86) (9/91).

Economics and the Monetary System (1500)

Location: Independent study program.
Length: 15 self-paced lessons.
Dates: March 1991-Present.
Objective: To help students analyze economic activity and understand the structure of financial institutions.
Learning Outcome: Upon successful completion of this course, the student will be able to define basic economic terms and concepts (i.e., macroeconomics, microeconomics, scarcity, supply and demand, diminishing returns, comparative advantage, equilibrium, etc.) and their applications; use the production-possibilities curve; explain the differences between demand and quantity demanded and supply and quantity supplied, diagramming those on appropriate curves, and list the factors of price elasticity of demand and supply; identify the characteristics and functions of commercial banks and non-bank financial institutions and how they are chartered and regulated; list and explain the provisions of major financial legislation; describe the conditions leading to various financial difficulties the legislation remedied; and describe the relationship between real GNP and employment, defining "full employment" and the different kinds of unemployment.
Instruction: Major topics covered in the course are basic macroeconomic concepts and theories such as supply and demand, inflation, GNP, elasticity, and the classic and Keynesian approaches. Upon such a foundation, the course covers issues in money and banking such as money's functions, types of financial institutions, the structure and operations of the Federal Reserve System, open market and money-market operations, the money supply and its impact on prices and employment, monetary and fiscal policies, and the national debt and international trade. Methods of instruction include self-study utilizing a course syllabus, texts, a review guide, and an examination.
Credit Recommendation: In the lower division baccalaureate/associate degree category, 3 semester hours in Economic Principles or 2 semester hours in Macroeconomics and 1 semester hour in Money and Banking or Financial Institutions (9/91) (5/96).

Financial Counseling (800) (Formerly Financial Counseling [8])

Location: Independent study program.
Length: 13 self-paced lessons.
Dates: January 1975-January 1997.
Objective: To provide understanding of the basic elements of personal financial planning and to apply elements of personal

financial planning through the use of a counseling model.

Learning Outcome: Upon successful completion of this course, the student will be able to aid and assist others with their personal financial situation and become more effective in counseling.

Instruction: Major topics covered in the course are family resource management and consumer decision making; consumer credit; family budget components; social security, life insurance, and annuities; savings and investments; estate planning, wills, and trusts; consumer education; forms of financial counseling; foundations of communications with clients; components of financial planning; and investment and taxation fundamentals. Methods of instruction include self-study utilizing a course syllabus, texts, and an examination.

Credit Recommendation: In the lower division baccalaureate/associate degree category, 3 semester hours in Consumer or Personal Finance (6/81) (7/86) (9/91) (5/96).

Financial Management I (1600)

Location: Independent study program.

Length: 18 self-paced lessons.

Dates: March 1991-Present.

Objective: To provide students with an overview of topics critical to the financial well-being of the credit union.

Learning Outcome: Upon successful completion of this course, the student will be able to define the various areas of finance and how they interact; identify the uses and sources of funds, especially in credit unions; identify money's characteristics, functions, and measurements; describe the role and forms of financial intermediaries; list major asset and liability accounts of financial institutions; explain the expansion of the money supply and credit; delineate the structure and functions of the Federal Reserve System and its various tools for affecting the economy; describe inflation and its relationship to interest rates; explain GAP ratios and the SLY principle and their significance; define the balance of payment, foreign exchange market, and exchange rate and its effect on imports and exports; read a foreign exchange rate schedule; and outline how to draw checks on foreign banks.

Instruction: Major topics covered in the course are an introduction to finance and the financial services industry; creation of financial assets; time value of money; capital budgeting; capital structure; ratio analysis; futures and options; international finance; and forecasting and budgeting. Methods of instruction include self-study utilizing a course syllabus, texts, a review guide, and an examination.

Credit Recommendation: In the lower division baccalaureate/associate degree category, 3 semester hours in Principles of Finance (9/91) (5/96). **NOTE:** If student has taken Credit Union Accounting (1300) or a Principles of Accounting course, upper division baccalaureate degree credit should be granted.

Financial Management II (1700)

Location: Independent study.

Length: 13 self-paced lessons.

Dates: January 1994-Present.

Objective: To provide financial management principles and applications which are relevant to the financial management of credit unions.

Learning Outcome: Upon successful completion of this course, the student will be able to understand and apply financial management techniques to the management of credit unions.

Instruction: Major topics covered in the course are financial intermediation; consumer loans and lending policies; liquidity management; investment risk and return; asset and liability management; budgeting and revenue planning; price analysis; price/cost/volume analysis; and basic pricing strategies. Methods of instruction include self-study utilizing a course syllabus, texts, a review guide, and examinations.

Credit Recommendation: In the lower division baccalaureate/associate degree category, 3 semester hours in Management of Financial Institutions (5/96).

Human Resource Management (1800)

Location: Independent study.

Length: 14 self-paced lessons.

Dates: August 1995-Present.

Objective: To provide knowledge of human resource management principles and practices with specific application to credit unions.

Learning Outcome: Upon successful completion of this course, the student will be able to understand managing, through effective planning, policies, and procedures, an organization's human resources.

Instruction: Major topics covered in the course are what human resource management (HRM) is; the human resource manager's role and responsibilities; the HRM environment; HRM laws; HRM policies; job descriptions; recruitment; interviewing and selection; compensation; employee benefits; performance management and appraisal; training and career development; employee rights and discipline; employee health and safety; and labor-management relations. Methods of instruction include self-study utilizing a text, a review guide, and an examination.

Credit Recommendation: In the lower division baccalaureate/associate degree category, 2 semester hours in Human Resource Management or a Business Administration Elective (5/96).

Introduction to Credit Unions (100) (Formerly Foundation and Structure of Credit Unions [1])

Location: Independent study program.

Length: 14 self-paced lessons. (Formerly 15 self-paced lessons).

Dates: January 1975-Present.

Objective: To provide knowledge of the historical origin of credit unions, to broaden understanding of credit union philosophy, and to review credit union organization and working relationships.

Learning Outcome: Upon successful completion of this course, the student will be able to understand the history and philosophy of credit unions, understand the complexities and managerial tasks of credit unions, and operate in an ethical and professional manner.

Instruction: Major topics covered in the course are credit union origins, history, and development; the credit union as a legal entity; development and functioning of board of directors; ethics in the credit union; and credit union relationships and professionalism. Methods of instruction include self-study utilizing a course syllabus, texts, a review guide, and an examination.

Credit Recommendation: In the lower division baccalaureate/associate degree category, 2 semester hours in History and Organization of Credit Unions (6/81) (7/86) (9/91) (5/96).

Management (200) (Formerly Management [2])

Location: Independent study program.

Length: 14 self-paced lessons.

Dates: *Version 1:* January 1975-June 1986; *Version 2:* July 1986-Present.

Objective: To provide knowledge of the fundamentals of management and organizational behavior and the application of this knowledge to the management and operation of credit unions.

Learning Outcome: Upon successful completion of this course, the student will be able to apply the management techniques to running credit unions and supervising employees.

Instruction: Major topics covered in the course are the principles of sound management; the history of management thought, including total quality management; vision and strategy; customer-focused and operational structures; systems thinking; planning; organizing; leadership; communication; delegation and empowerment; control and measurement; problem-solving and decision-making; and evaluation and continuous improvement. Methods of instruction include self-study utilizing a text, a review guide, and an examination.

Credit Recommendation: *Version 1:* In the lower division baccalaureate/associate degree category, 2 semester hours in Principles of Management (6/81). *Version 2:* In the lower division baccalaureate/associate degree category, 3 semester hours in Principles of Management (7/86) (9/91) (5/96).

Marketing (700)
(Formerly Marketing [7])

Location: Independent study program.

Length: 15 self-paced lessons.

Dates: January 1975-Present.

Objective: To further students' knowledge and understanding of how goods and services are marketed with specific attention to marketing techniques related to credit union products and services.

Learning Outcome: Upon successful completion of this course, the student will be able to understand marketing strategy and its effect on credit union managerial decisions.

Instruction: Major topics covered in the course are the facts and principles of marketing; the marketing concept and structure; market research; consumer buying behavior; the differences between products and services; classifications of products; product lines and mixes; the product life cycle; product development and branding; channels of distribution; promotion, methods, and mixes; advertising; publicity; personal selling, salespersons, techniques, and sales promotions; pricing concepts, objectives, and strategies; price setting; strategic marketing planning; preparing and implementing the marketing plan; measuring and evaluating marketing performance; and the marketing audit.

Credit Recommendation: In the lower division baccalaureate/associate degree category, 2 semester hours in Principles of Marketing (6/81) (7/86) (9/91) (5/96).

Money and Banking (1100)

Location: Independent study program.

Length: 15 self-paced lessons.

Dates: December 1985-November 1991.

Objective: To provide students with an understanding about the structure of financial institutions and their role in the financial and economic fields.

Learning Outcome: Upon successful completion of this course, the student will be able to identify the characteristics and functions of money; explain the various definitions of the money supply; identify and distinguish the characteristics and functions of commercial banks and nonbank financial institutions, especially credit unions; describe the various agencies that charter, regulate, and insure the different financial institutions; explain the creation of money and the impact of the reserve requirement on that; list and explain the provisions of major financial legislation, especially their effects on credit unions; describe the structure and functions of the Federal Reserve System; and name and describe the Federal Reserve's five major tools for regulating the money supply and affecting the economy.

Instruction: Major topics covered in the course are the nature and structure of financial institutions, money and its functions, the history and creation of money, the Federal Reserve System, open market operations, changing interest rates, the money supply and its impact on prices and employment, money-market operations, the national debt and the economy, and international economies. Methods of instruction include self-study utilizing a course syllabus, texts, and an examination.

Credit Recommendation: In the lower division baccalaureate/associate degree category, 3 semester hours in Economics, Money and Banking, or Financial Institutions (9/91).

Personnel Administration (300)
(Formerly Office and Personnel Administration [3])

Location: Independent study program.

Length: 12 self-paced lessons.

Dates: January 1975-August 1995.

Objective: To provide knowledge of office administration principles and practices with specific application to credit unions.

Learning Outcome: Upon successful completion of this course, the student will be able to understand office and personnel administration, emphasizing management's authority and responsibility in supervisory situations.

Instruction: Major topics covered in the course are systems and procedures, office layout, records management, information media, supervisory skills, staff development, salary administration, job evaluation, labor relations, performance appraisal and training methods, benefit programs, management's responsibility, and dealing with people. Methods of instruction include self-study utilizing a course syllabus, texts, and an examination.

Credit Recommendation: In the lower division baccalaureate/associate degree category, 2 semester hours in Office and Administrative Management (6/81) (7/86) (9/91).

Risk Management and Insurance (500)
(Formerly Risk Management and Insurance [5])

Location: Independent study program.

Length: 10 self-paced lessons.

Dates: *Version 1:* January 1975-June 1986; *Version 2:* July 1986-Present.

Objective: To provide knowledge of concepts and principles of business insurance and risk management and to provide experience in applying these concepts to credit unions.

Learning Outcome: Upon successful completion of this course, the student will be able to understand the basic ideas, problems, and principles found in various types of modern insurance and other methods of managing risks.

Instruction: Major topics covered in the course are concepts and principles needed to produce and operate a program of risk measurement and control; the concept of risk; the risk management function; risk identification, measurement, management, and control; insurance and noninsurance risk management tools; principles of insurance; the basics of insurance policies; property and liability risk exposures and insurance; personal risk exposures and the uses of life and health insurance; the types of and selection of insurance organizations; and risk management in credit unions. Methods of instruction include self-study utilizing a course syllabus, texts, and an examination.

Credit Recommendation: *Version 1:* In the upper division baccalaureate degree category, 2 semester hours in Business Insurance and Risk Management (6/81). *Version 2:* In the lower division baccalaureate/associate degree or in the upper division baccalaureate degree category, 2 semester hours in Business Insurance and Risk Management (7/86) (9/91) (5/96).

Dale Carnegie & Associates, Inc.

Dale Carnegie Training ® includes the development of effective communication and improved human relations, motivational selling skills, goal-oriented management, personnel development, and improved customer relations. Courses are conducted by licensed sponsors and institutes located throughout the United States and several foreign countries.

Instructors are selected mainly from the executive and managerial ranks. All instructors must complete a formal Instructor Training Conference conducted by a field Instructor Trainer of the Department of Instruction. Upon completion of the Training Conference, potential instructors work with an experienced instructor for one or two cycles of the course. All instructors are evaluated annually by the Department of Instruction.

Records of Dale Carnegie & Associates, Inc. are on file for the period 1959 to date. Local licensees and institutes offering Dale Carnegie Courses maintain their own records. Regular visits by staff members of Dale Carnegie & Associates, Inc., assure that facilities and record-keeping systems are adequate.

Source of official student records: Vice President, Department of Instruction, Dale Carnegie & Associates, Inc., 1475 Franklin Avenue, Garden City, NY 11530.

Additional information about the courses: College Credit Recommendation Service, American Council on Education, One Dupont Circle, Washington, DC 20036-1193.

Leadership Training for Managers (Formerly Dale Carnegie® Management Seminar)

Location: Various locations worldwide.

Length: 18 hours (3 hours per week for 6 weeks plus 9 hours of outside preparation).

Dates: January 1981-Present.

Objective: To provide students with a basic understanding of principles and skills of management.

Learning Outcome: Upon successful completion of this course, the student will be able to apply effectively the principles of management and team building that will enhance their performance as managers.

Instruction: Major topics covered in the course are creative process, planning, organizing, directing, coordinating, delegating, control, decision-making, communicating, motivating, and interpersonal skills. Methods of instruction include lecture, discussion, outside readings, and instructor evaluation of classroom exercises, case studies, and three required papers.

Credit Recommendation: In the upper division baccalaureate degree category, 2 semester hours in Management (4/83) (5/88) (5/94). 2 ELECTIVES PER HOLLY 2/10/00

Oral Communication and Interpersonal Skills (The Dale Carnegie Course® [DCC-1])

Location: Various locations worldwide.

Length: .

Dates: *Version 1:* January 1980-March 1991; *Version 2:* April 1991-Present.

Objective: To enhance student's communications and interpersonal relations skills and to build their self-confidence.

Learning Outcome: Upon successful completion of this course, students will be able to function comfortably and effectively in a conference, work, or social settings where good interpersonal relations are essential; organize and express thoughts clearly; and understand principles of effective public speaking and interpersonal skills.

Instruction: Major topics covered in the course are organization and presentation of ideas, improving memory, setting goals, developing self-confidence, dealing with stress, building positive relationships, problem solving, and interpersonal skills. Methods of instruction include discussion, classroom exercises, outside readings, and instructor and student evaluation of progress.

Credit Recommendation: In the lower division baccalaureate/associate degree category, 3 semester hours in Speech, Communications, or Organizational Behavior (4/83) (5/88) (5/94).

Principles of Salesmanship (The Dale Carnegie® Sales Advantage Program [DCSC-1])

Location: Various locations worldwide.

Length: 42hours (3.5 hours per week for 12 weeks plus 18 hours of outside preparation).

Dates: January 1983-Present.

Objective: To develop an understanding of the generic principles and techniques of sales with emphasis on human relations in the selling process.

Learning Outcome: Upon successful completion of this course, the student will be able to plan sales presentations; communicate effectively with prospective buyers; and stimulate interest of prospective buyers.

Instruction: Major topics covered in the course are organizing and preparing a sales presentation, qualifying prospects, managing time effectively, developing accounts, closing the sale, and prospecting for new clients. Methods of instruction include lecture, discussion, classroom exercises that emphasize participation, written and oral reports that provide instructor/student interaction, and evaluation of progress.

Credit Recommendation: In the lower division baccalaureate/associate degree category, 3 semester hours in the Principles and Practice of Selling (4/83) (5/88) (5/94).

Dana Corporation

Dana Corporation, a multinational company with approximately 28,000 U.S. employees in 86 plants, manufactures and markets proprietary components and systems for the transmission and control of power in the vehicular and industrial markets.

To facilitate a promote-from-within policy, each division of the company sponsors local training, sends people to association, or university-sponsored workshops and seminars, and encourages the use of a tuition refund plan for undergraduate and postgraduate college courses. Personal growth also takes place through active job-rotation programs.

At the corporate level Dana University exists for management development education. Through nearly 140 one-week course offerings annually, Dana University reaches almost half of the company's 5,000 managers each year. Programs are conducted by a full-time central staff and are presented in Toledo, in Dana plant cities, and overseas.

Source of official student records: Dean, Business School, Dana University, Dana Corporation, P.O. Box 1000, Toledo, OH 43697.

Additional information about the courses: College Credit Recommendation Service, American Council on Education, One Dupont Circle, Washington, DC 20036-1193.

Asset Management (Alternative Title: Financial Planning for Business Success)

Location: Toledo, OH; various field locations.

Length: *Version 1:* 48 hours (1 week); *Version 2:* 27 hours (3 days).

Dates: *Version 1:* April 1977-December 1986; *Version 2:* January 1987-Present.

Objective: To provide students with an understanding of financial management and the effect of financial decisions on profit centers in manufacturing organizations.

Learning Outcome: Upon successful completion of this course, the student will be able to understand the effect of input costs such as labor, material, and overhead on the profit and cash flow of the business and understand financial ratios.

Instruction: Major topics covered in the course are the use of a business game to illustrate the effect of cost variables on financial statements and financial ratios. Methods of instruction include lecture, discussion, team activities, and computer-assisted instruction.

Credit Recommendation: *Version 1:* In the lower division baccalaureate/associate degree category, 3 semester hours in Management (4/77) (7/82). *Version 2:* In the lower division baccalaureate/associate degree category, 2 semester hours in Accounting, Business Administration, Finance, or Management (8/89) (10/94).

Business Practices

Location: Toledo, OH; various field locations.

Length: 33 hours (1 week).

Dates: April 1977-June 1982.

Objective: To improve students' skills in written and oral communications and to provide them with an understanding of management relationships and practices.

Instruction: Case studies, written exercises, and films are used extensively along with some lectures in which theory is presented. Specific techniques are discussed for improving skills in preparing written communications, in listening, and in conducting meetings. These are brought together in group discussions, group dynamics exercises, and individual work on a "manager's in-basket" case.

Credit Recommendation: In the lower division baccalaureate/associate degree category, 2 semester hours in Business Communications (4/77) (7/82).

Developing Personal Strengths for Effective Management (Alternative Titles: Fundamentals of Supervision II; How to Develop Your Personal Strengths for More Effective Management) (Formerly Principles of Organizational Behavior)

Location: Toledo, OH; various field locations.

Length: 35 hours (1 week).

Dates: April 1977-Present.

Objective: To strengthen the student's managerial effectiveness through application of principles of organizational behavior.

Learning Outcome: Upon successful completion of this course, the student will be able to demonstrate improved listening habits and skills; apply specific management theories to create a climate where individuals can be motivated to achieve higher levels of performance; and adjust management techniques to account for differences in values, thinking preferences, and work behavior.

Instruction: Major topics covered in the course are self-awareness and positive self-concepts; motivation; listening skills; management of change; and the value of differences in creating an effective organization. Methods of instruction include lecture, discussion, case studies, and role playing.

Credit Recommendation: In the lower division baccalaureate/associate degree category, 2 semester hours in Business Administration or Management (7/82) (8/89) (10/94).

Effective Speaking 114 (Alternative Titles: How to Write and Give a Speech; Speech Workshop)

Location: Toledo, OH; various field locations.

Length: 40 hours (1 week).

Dates: April 1977-Present.

Objective: To provide the student with skills in developing and delivering oral presentations.

Learning Outcome: Upon successful completion of this course, the student will be able to distinguish between impromptu speeches and speeches that inform or persuade; write appropriate introductions and develop the opening, body, and closing of speeches; demonstrate useful platform techniques; and design and use in appropriate ways audiovisual materials and handouts. Methods of evaluation include student/peer critiques of speeches and presentations, along with critiques performed by the instructor.

Instruction: Major topics covered in the course are planning presentations; organization and development of speeches; impromptu, informative, and persuasive speeches; design and use of audiovisual aids and handouts; and platform skills and appearance. Methods of instruction include lecture, discussion, after class preparation, textbooks, videotapes, recording, and critique of student presentations.

Credit Recommendation: In the lower division baccalaureate/associate degree category, 3 semester hours in Communications or Speech (4/77) (7/82) (8/89) (9/94).

Fundamentals of Supervision III

Location: Toledo, OH; various field locations.

Length: 36 hours (1 week).

Dates: April 1977-July 1981.

Objective: To provide first-line supervisors with an understanding of the effects of costs on the financial performance of a manufacturing organization, and labor-management relations and grievance procedures.

Instruction: Cost decision-making theory is examined in the context of burden studies, machine utilization, schedules, inventory costing, and investment concerns. Labor relations theory is reviewed with role playing of labor-management negotiations as they relate to grievance procedures and the arbitration process.

Credit Recommendation: In the lower division baccalaureate/associate degree category, 1 semester hour in Management and 1 semester hour in Labor-Management Relations, for a total of 2 semester hours. (4/77) (7/82).

Intermediate Management

Location: Toledo, OH; various field locations.

Length: 50 hours (1 week).

Dates: April 1977-July 1983.

Objective: To develop the student's skills in the use of management by objectives.

Instruction: Application of management by objectives in a supervisor-subordinate situation, including specific applications, skill building, and critique. Methods of instruction include a case study analysis, using a team approach and applying management by objectives to a plant situation. An in-basket exercise is used in which participants are given the opportunity to establish and implement a system of management by objectives.

Credit Recommendation: In the lower division baccalaureate/associate degree category, 3 semester hours in Management (4/77) (7/82).

Legal Issues for Managers (Law for the Manager)

Location: Toledo, OH; various field locations.

Length: 24 hours (3 days).

Dates: September 1994-Present.

Objective: To provide an awareness of current legal issues that may be encountered by supervisory management.

Learning Outcome: Upon successful completion of this course, the student will be able to identify common legal problems in commercial law.

Instruction: Major topics covered in this course are contracts, employee benefits, creditor rights and bankruptcy, environmental law, risk management, product liability, labor and employment law, international law, intellectual property, and antitrust. Methods of instruction include lecture, discussion, and audio/visual materials.

Credit Recommendation: In the lower division baccalaureate/associate degree category, 1 semester hour in Business Law or Legal Environment of Business (10/94).

Managerial Styles Seminar (Alternative Title: Developing the 9,9 Style of Management)

Location: Toledo, OH; various field locations.

Length: *Version 1:* 50 hours (1 week), 30 hours of preparatory independent study; *Version 2:* 60 hours (1.5 weeks), 30 hours of preparatory independent study; *Version 3:* 60 hours (1 week), plus 40 hours of preparatory independent study.

Dates: *Version 1:* April 1977-July 1989; *Version 2:* April 1977-July 1989; *Version 3:* August 1989-Present.

Objective: To identify and assess managerial behavior based on sound behavioral science principles.

Learning Outcome: Upon successful completion of this course, the student will be able to use the managerial grid as a framework for strengthening managerial behavior; apply conflict-solving skills and the use of critique to enhance team effectiveness; and change personal managerial study to reflect the most effective style for the organization.

Instruction: Major topics covered in the course are the concepts underlying the managerial grid; application of the managerial grid to personal and organizational situations; maintaining intergroup conflict in industry; model for team activity; organizational culture; and personal grid styles. Methods of instruction include pre-course readings, lecture, discussion, team projects, critique of classroom exercises, films, and visual aids.

Credit Recommendation: *Version 1:* In the lower division baccalaureate/associate degree category, 3 semester hours in Management (4/77) (7/82). *Version 2:* In the lower division baccalaureate/associate degree category, 3 semester hours in Management (4/77) (7/82). *Version 3:* In the upper division baccalaureate degree category, 2 semester hours in Business Administration or Management; and in the graduate degree category, 1 semester hour in Management (8/89) (10/94).

Manufacturing Costs and Controls (Alternative Titles: Cost Control for Profit Planning; Product Cost Analysis for Non-financial People)

Location: Toledo, OH; various field locations.

Length: *Version 1:* 48 hours (1 week); *Version 2:* 27 hours (3 days).

Dates: *Version 1:* April 1977-January 1986; *Version 2:* February 1986-Present.

Objective: To provide the student with skill in analyzing cost factors, including human resources, materials, and machines, with emphasis on inventory control.

Learning Outcome: Upon successful completion of this course, the student will be able to identify and analyze the cost elements of a manufactured product and relate concepts of volume and profit relationships to a manufactured product.

Instruction: Major topics covered in the course are cost elements; standard cost systems; volume and profit; manufacturing overhead; and inventory control. Methods of instruction include lecture, discussion, and simulation exercises.

Credit Recommendation: *Version 1:* In the lower division baccalaureate/associate degree category, 3 semester hours in Management (4/77) (7/82). *Version 2:* In the lower division baccalaureate/associate degree category, 2 semester hours in Accounting, Business Administration, or Management (8/89) (10/94).

Positive Leadership

Location: Toledo, OH; various field locations.

Length: 23 hours (3 days).

Dates: July 1990-Present.

Objective: To provide managers/supervisors with an ability to model their understanding of the principles and characteristics of effective leadership.

Learning Outcome: Upon successful completion of this course, the student will be able to understand, recognize, and apply the principles of effective leadership; relate work group goals to corporate goals; empower and facilitate work groups; and take personal responsibility for decision-making.

Instruction: Major topics covered in the course are the principle practices and skills identified as characteristics of successful managers who are meeting such challenges of change as positive leadership, trust, empowerment, competitiveness, and personal responsibility. Methods of instruction include lecture, discussion, classroom exercises, and learner presentations/reports.

Credit Recommendation: In the lower division baccalaureate/associate degree category, 1 semester hour in Supervisory

Management or Organizational Behavior (10/94).

Problem-Solving and Decision-Making

Location: Toledo, OH; various field locations.

Length: 44 hours (1 week).

Dates: April 1977-Present.

Objective: To provide the student with an understanding of how to apply management principles to problem analysis and decision-making, planning, and situation review.

Learning Outcome: Upon successful completion of this course, the student will be able to identify components of complex situations to determine priority sequences; identify causes of problems through observation, analysis, and specific comparisons; determine appropriate courses of action based on setting clear objectives and evaluating alternatives and risks; and effectively conduct meetings to implement problem-solving and decision-making processes.

Instruction: Major topics covered in the course are situation analysis; problem analysis; decision analysis; potential problem avoidance; and procedures for conducting effective meetings. Methods of instruction include lecture, discussion, simulation, case studies, critiques of classroom exercises, and audio/visual aids.

Credit Recommendation: In the lower division baccalaureate/associate degree category, 3 semester hours in Business Administration or Management (7/82) (8/89) (10/94).

Sales Development

Location: Toledo, OH; various field locations.

Length: 40 hours (1 week).

Dates: April 1977-Present.

Objective: To provide the student with a knowledge of sales organizations and their functions and development of sales skills.

Learning Outcome: Upon successful completion of this course, the student will be able to plan and implement a sales call; develop group sales presentations using appropriate audiovisual aids; adapt personal selling style to the buying styles of customers; and perform functions of selling in accordance with laws governing business activities.

Instruction: Major topics covered in the course are the salesperson's responsibilities; individual salesperson's roles in the marketing function; market forecasting; product liability; persuasive sales techniques; and personal styles of salespersons and customers. Methods of instruction include precourse preparation, lecture, discussion, role playing, textbooks, videotapes, out-of-class preparations, and critiques of student presentations.

Credit Recommendation: In the lower division baccalaureate/associate degree category, 3 semester hours in Business Administration, Management, or Marketing (7/82) (8/89) (10/94).

Supervisory Management (Alternative Title: Fundamentals of Supervision I)

Location: Toledo, OH; various field locations.

Length: 34.5 hours (1 week).

Dates: April 1977-Present.

Objective: To develop and improve the supervisory skills of new and experienced managers.

Learning Outcome: Upon successful completion of this course, the student will be able to address supervisory situations in a positive and consistent manner; apply sound management and human relations principles to supervisory situations; and apply appropriate legal concepts to labor-management matters.

Instruction: Major topics covered in the course are job training, positive discipline, motivation and team building, and legal aspects of supervision. Methods of instruction include lecture, discussion, case studies, and video presentations.

Credit Recommendation: In the lower division baccalaureate/associate degree category, 2 semester hours in Business Administration or Management (7/82) (8/89) (10/94).

Data Processing Trainers Business School

For more than a decade DPT has been providing first class training to individuals from all walks of life.

The primary mission is to provide students with the necessary skills to obtain gainful employment upon successful completion.

DPT was founded as a school for main frame programmers, but found that opportunities with proper computer skills existed throughout the corporate arena. Therefore, course development expanded beyond main frame programming. Presently DPT offers programs in the following disciplines: Main Frame Programming; Network Engineering Technology; Client/ Server Programming; Computerized Business Accounting; Business Computer Applications; Medical Office Administration; Computer Servicing and Troubleshooting; and English as a Second Language.

Another key component of DPT's mission is to provide the corporate community with on-going training as needed. DPT will customize and develop training programs so that area corporations are able to maintain quality staff.

Day and evening classes are offered at DPT's Northeast and Center City Philadelphia campuses.

Source of official student records: Registry of Credit Recommendation, American Council on Education, One Dupont Circle, Washington, DC 20036-1193.

Additional information about the courses: College Credit Recommendation Service, American Council on Education, One Dupont Circle, Washington, DC 20036-1193.

1) Introduction to Programming in "C"
2) Advanced Programming in "C" (CSP 650/660)

Location: Philadelphia, PA (2 locations).

Length: 1) 32 hours; 2) 64 hours.

Dates: 1) March 1995-Present; 2) August 1995-Present.

Objective: To teach students how to use the "C" programming language to write programs to solve practical programming problems.

Learning Outcome: Upon successful completion of this course, the student will be able to 1) CSP 650 use the fundamentals of programming in C, currently the programming of choice for business and industry, format input and output, data types, arithmetic, logical operators, structures for decision making and looping in C; 2) CSP 660 use arrays to store large amounts of data, use functions to organize a program and how to use pointers to make a program more efficient, and use data structures to organize tables of data and how to use files to store information.

Instruction: Major topics covered in the introductory course are benefits and advantages of the C programming languages; the steps involved in developing a C program; C variables and data types; formatted 1) Introduction to Programming in "C"; 2) Advanced Programming in "C" input and output; character strings; preprocessor directives; C arithmetic operators, expressions, and statements; the for, while, and do loops; the if, if ... else, and switch decision making structures; an introduction to functions; and an introduction to arrays. The advanced course covers input/output redirection; advanced use of functions; using pointers with variables, arrays, and elements of arrays; string functions; file input/output; storage classes and data structures; and linking a C program with a Visual Basic graphical user interface. The introductory and advanced C programming courses are designed to provide the student with the skills and techniques required to produce professionally written C programs. Methods of instruction include lecture and lab.

Credit Recommendation: In the lower division baccalaureate/associate degree category, 4 semester hours in Introduction to Programming in "C" (1/97). **NOTE:** Student must complete CSP650 and CSP660 to receive the credit recommendation.

Accounting I

Location: Philadelphia, PA.

Length: 78 hours.

Dates: September 1992-Present.

Objective: To enable a student to understand and utilize the basic concepts of accounting in a business environment.

Learning Outcome: Upon successful completion of this course, the student will be able to understand the nature of accounting and its double entry system, understand the importance of internal controls, analyze and classify business transactions, use special ledgers and journals, understand payroll systems, and do accounting for the sole proprietor and the service sector.

Instruction: Major topics covered in the course are introduction to accounting; debits and credits; journalizing, posting and trial balance; worksheets and final reports; adjusting, closing and post closing; sales and cash receipt journals; and purchases and cash payment journals. The course provides a practical foundation in basic accounting. This is achieved through a joint effort of the instructor presenting material and practical applications, giving examples, assigning problems and reviewing them; and the student completing all class exercises, asking questions and reading the textbook. Methods of instruction include lecture, discussion and collaborative learning.

Credit Recommendation: In the upper division baccalaureate degree category or in the lower division baccalaureate/associate degree category, 3 semester hours in Introduction to Accounting I (1/97).

Accounting II

Location: Philadelphia, PA (2 locations).

Length: 78 hours.

Dates: November 1992-Present.

Objective: To enable a student to know, understand and utilize the guidelines set by accounting regulatory authorities in a business environment.

Learning Outcome: Upon successful completion of this course, the student will be able to build upon the basic knowledge from CBA200, understand accounting for bad debts, inventory and fixed assets, understand the underlying concepts of financial accounting, perform accounting cycle for partnerships, corporations, and the merchandising sectors, understand the corporate accounting cycle, and perform reporting and analysis for financial statements.

Instruction: Major topics covered in the course include payroll accounting and employment taxes, financial statements, and the difference between the cash and accrual basis of accounting. This course is a continuation of Accounting I. The students will learn the concepts stated above and demonstrate their level of competency through completed projects and written tests. Instructional methods include lecture, discussion and collaborative learning.

Credit Recommendation: In the upper division baccalaureate degree category or in the lower division baccalaureate/associate degree category, 3 semester hours in Introduction to Accounting II (1/97).

Anatomy and Physiology

Location: Philadelphia, PA (2 locations).

Length: 60 hours.

Dates: May 1994-Present.

Objective: To enable students to understand the basic structure and function of the human body as a whole and the body systems.

Learning Outcome: Upon successful completion of this course, the student will be able to understand the basic structure and functions of the human body, apply the correct medical terminology to basic body structure and functions, and identify cause and effect and types of the most common pathological conditions of body structure and functions.

Instruction: Major topics covered in the course are application of correct medical terminology to basic body structures and functions; and identification of the cause and effect of the most common pathological conditions in the body. This course presents the basic structure and function of the human body as a whole and by body systems. Methods of instruction include lecture, research work and independent study.

Credit Recommendation: In the lower division baccalaureate/associate degree category, 3 semester hours in Anatomy and Physiology (1/97).

Business Communications

Location: Philadelphia, PA (2 locations).

Length: 60 hours.

Dates: September 1992-Present.

Objective: To provide students with the necessary skills and knowledge to communicate effectively in various forms of written and oral communication.

Learning Outcome: Upon successful completion of this course, the student will be able to understand new technological advancements of office equipment utilized in today's office environment, communicate effectively in various forms of written and oral communication, and utilize real world communication concepts that are critical to success in the business environment.

Instruction: Major topics covered in the course include all aspects of communication, including oral, written and nonverbal forms. This course provides students with the necessary skills and knowledge to enhance their overall communication skills in order to assimilate in the office environment. Methods of instruction include group discussions, lectures, collaborative learning and simulation.

Credit Recommendation: In the upper division baccalaureate degree category or in the lower division baccalaureate/associate degree category, 3 semester hours in Business Communications (1/97).

Introduction to Electronics

Location: Philadelphia, PA (2 locations).

Length: 48 hours (5 weeks).

Dates: May 1994-Present.

Objective: To provide students with an understanding of electronic components and principles.

Learning Outcome: Upon successful completion of this course, the student will be able to apply Ohm's laws to solve series and parallel dc and ac circuits, identify electronic components and schematic symbols, understand the operation of capacitors and coils in dc and ac, understand the operation of diode and transistor circuits, and understand the operation of basic digital logic gates.

Instruction: Major topics covered in the course are an introduction to dc and ac electronic principles and components; how to analyze electronic circuits using Ohm's laws; series and parallel circuit rules; introduction to semiconductor and digital logic components and their operation. Methods of instruction include lecture and computer aided instruction.

Credit Recommendation: In the lower division baccalaureate/associate degree category, 3 semester hours in Introduction to Electronics (1/97).

Medical Terminology

Location: Philadelphia, PA (2 locations).

Length: 60 hours.

Dates: May 1994-Present.

Objective: To enable students to understand and use medical language, root words, symbols and abbreviation.

Learning Outcome: Upon successful completion of this course, the student will be able to understand medical language, root words, symbols and abbreviations, and discern the proper use of the medical dictionary and correct pronunciation of medical terms.

Instruction: Major topics covered in the course are the structure of medical terms, word roots, prefixes and suffixes based on a systems approach. Textbook and supplemental material assist students in learning medical terminology through basic knowledge of anatomy and physiology. Disease processes, common medical abbreviation and current testing procedures are also incorporated in the course. Methods of instruction include lecture, independent study and research work.

Credit Recommendation: In the lower division baccalaureate/associate degree category, 3 semester hours in Medical Terminology (1/97).

PC Applications with Windows

Location: Philadelphia, PA (2 locations).

Length: 84 hours.

Dates: June 1994-Present.

Objective: To provide practical skills using the Windows operating environment, and Microsoft Word and Excel applications.

Learning Outcome: Upon successful completion of this course, the student will be able to understand graphical user interfaces and their terminology, navigate a GUI using the mouse, perform basic and advanced tasks in Microsoft Word, and perform basic and advanced tasks in Microsoft Excel.

Instruction: Major topics covered in the course are how to navigate a GUI using a mouse; practical skills using both basic and advanced features in Microsoft Word and Excel application programs. This course introduces the student to the Windows operating environment. Methods of instruction include lecture and lab.

Credit Recommendation: In the lower division baccalaureate/associate degree category, 3 semester hours in PC Applications with Windows (1/97).

Visual Basic (CSP 550)

Location: Philadelphia, PA (2 locations).

Length: 100 hours.

Dates: March 1996-Present.

Objective: To provide the students with the necessary skills to develop client/server, Windows based, production business applications using the object-oriented programming techniques of Microsoft Visual Basic.

Learning Outcome: Upon successful completion of this course, the student will be able to build sophisticated, graphical user applications with access to information stored on databases, understand how to incorporate the use of Microsoft Access and Personal Oracle 7 as the database engine for developing client/server business applications, understand and use all specific commands utilized in Visual Basic application development, and utilize the diverse syntax of Visual Basic to develop practical business applications in a graphical Windows based environment.

Instruction: Major topics covered in the course are the programming techniques of the graphical user interface environment, using Visual Basic to build windows, menus and command buttons; basics of SQL, OLE, DDL, and application debugging. The student will learn and practice the skills necessary to develop and maintain Windows based client/server applications. Methods of instruction include lecture and lab.

Credit Recommendation: In the lower division baccalaureate/associate degree category, 4 semester hours in Visual Basic (1/97).

Datapro Information Technology

Datapro Information Technology (DIT) was established in 1965. DIT's mission is to create and conduct high quality educational and training programs, at an affordable price, that will meet the requirements of students aspiring for professional education in the field of information technology, and to develop skilled manpower for meeting the industry requirements.

For this purpose, DIT offers a range of long-term and short-term (full-time, part-time) courses viz. Masters Diploma in Computer Science, Diploma in Computer Science, PC Architecture and Maintenance, Computerized Financial Accounting, Computer-Aided Design as well as more than 60 short-term courses. Courses include extensive practicals, workshops, and live projects. These courses are offered through 72 locations spread all over India including Bombay, Calcutta, Delhi, Madras, Bangalore, and other major cities. At each location, the courses are offered in a modular format with a choice of seven learning time slots between 8 a.m. and 10 p.m., over 60 subjects and 72 locations. This enables students to effectively learn at their own pace along with their university education or present jobs.

For the corporate sector, covering the government, public, banking and private organizations, PACT (Professional Applied Corporate Training, a division of DIT) conducts tailormade programs covering a wide range of subjects from computer awareness to intensive high-end products state-of-the-art technology workshops and seminars.

All courses are designed by DIT's R&D Center based on analysis of research data, and feedback from industry, universities, faculty and students. The findings are reviewed and discussed at various levels including the Governing Board, the Peer Committee, and the Faculty Group. These groups also include representatives from the universities and the industry. The upgrading of courses, training methodology, and training material is an ongoing process.

The faculty members are selected from leading academic or management institutions after an elaborate process of tests, mocks, and interviews. Besides the initial training, they are also required to periodically attend training programs at the DIT Staff Training Center. The students are evaluated through quizzes, tests, comprehensive final test, and project work.

DIT's systematic approach to training and education has been recognized nationally and internationally. DIT is the authorized training center for Autodesk Inc., Microsoft Corp., GPSS (UK), and Lotus Corp. (UK). DIT also has numerous national recognitions and empanellments to its credit.

DIT provides free placement assistance every year to thousands of its successful students and has a long list of satisfied corporate clients and students.

Source of official student records: Registry of Credit Recommendations, American Council on Education, One Dupont Circle, Washington, DC 20036-1193 or Director - Training, 101 Datapro House, Bandra (West) Bombay 400 050, INDIA.

Additional information about the courses: College Credit Recommendation Service, American Council on Education, One Dupont Circle, Washington, DC 20036-1193.

Advanced dBASE III + (ST.8)

Location: Datapro centers throughout India.

Length: 80 hours (4 weeks).

Dates: July 1985-March 1997.

Objective: To train students to be able to develop commercial, user-friendly applications in dBASE III+.

Learning Outcome: Upon successful completion of this course, the student will be able to effectively use all features in dBASE III+, apply the features in the development of commercial applications; and integrate dBASE III + with other systems such as Lotus 1-2-3.

Instruction: Major topics covered in the course are overview of dBASE III+ fundamentals; programming concepts (files, environment, structure, flow); memory variables, using screen forms; program control commands; data base creation, sorting, indexing, finding records; removing data from data base; dBASE III+ functions; report generation; creating memos; testing and debugging programs; export, import concepts; and efficient programming. Methods of instruction include lecture, discussion, classroom exercises, case studies, problem-solving, computer-assisted videotapes, laboratory, and projects.

Credit Recommendation: In the upper division baccalaureate degree category, 3 semester hours in Computer Science, Computer Information Systems (CIS), Data Processing, or Management Information Systems (3/92).

AutoCAD (ST. 17)

Location: Datapro centers throughout India.

Length: 160 hours (8 weeks).

Dates: July 1985-March 1997.

Objective: To train students in the use of AutoCAD and its functions to produce design drawings.

Learning Outcome: Upon successful completion of this course, the student will be able to design drawings using AutoCAD, store and retrieve drawings, and manipulate drawings.

Instruction: Major topics covered in the course are CAD introduction; basic concepts of AutoCAD; AutoCAD utility commands; entity drawing commands; copying and moving; plotting; isometric drawings; and viewports. Methods of instruction include lecture, discussion, classroom exercises, case studies, problem-solving, computer-assisted videotapes, and laboratory.

Credit Recommendation: In the upper division baccalaureate degree or the graduate degree category, 3 semester hours in Industry and Technology or Engineering Technology (3/92).

BASIC Programming Language (ST.2)

Location: Datapro centers throughout India.

Length: 160 hours (8 weeks).

Dates: July 1985-March 1997.

Objective: To train students to become proficient programmers in the BASIC programming language.

Learning Outcome: Upon successful completion of this course, the student will be able to analyze a given problem; develop an algorithm to solve the problem; and implement the algorithm in BASIC.

Instruction: Major topics covered in the course are introduction to QuickBASIC and the QuickBASIC environment; BASIC syntax; looping statements; branching statements; subprograms; arrays and matrix manipulation; and data files and record processing. Methods of instruction include lecture, discussion, classroom exercises, case studies, and computer-assisted video.

Credit Recommendation: In the lower division baccalaureate/associate degree category, 4 semester hours in BASIC Programming or Data Processing or Computer Information Systems (CIS) or Computer Science (3/92).

C Programming Language (ST.5)

Location: Datapro centers throughout India.

Length: 160 hours (8 weeks).

Dates: July 1985-March 1997.

Objective: To train students to become proficient programmers in the C programming language.

Learning Outcome: Upon successful completion of this course, the student will be able to analyze a given problem; develop an efficient algorithm to solve the problem; and implement the algorithm in C programming.

Instruction: Major topics covered in the course are introduction to QuickCTM and the QuickCTM compiler; C syntax; control statements; C functions; managing data files; pointers; and command line arguments. Methods of instruction include lecture, discussion, classroom exercises, case studies, problem-solving, and computer-assisted videotapes.

Credit Recommendation: In the lower division baccalaureate/associate degree category, 4 semester hours in Computer Science , Computer Information Systems (CIS) or C Programming (3/92).

COBOL (ST.3)

Location: Datapro centers throughout India.

Length: 160 hours (8 weeks).

Dates: July 1985-March 1997.

Objective: To train students to become proficient programmers in the COBOL language.

Learning Outcome: Upon successful completion of this course, the student will be able to analyze a given problem; develop an algorithm to solve the problem; and implement the algorithm in COBOL.

Instruction: Major topics covered in the course are introduction to the COBOL language and its various divisions; COBOL syntax; report generation, sorting, and file updating; and indexed and relative file processing. Methods of instruction include lecture, discussion, classroom exercises, case studies, and problem-solving.

Credit Recommendation: In the lower division baccalaureate/associate degree category, 4 semester hours in Data Processing, Computer Information Systems (CIS), or COBOL Programming (3/92).

Computer Architecture (ST.52, ST.53, ST.55,)

Location: Datapro centers throughout India.

Length: 320 hours (20 hours/week) total; 80 hours, each module.

Dates: July 1985-March 1997.

Objective: To train students to acquire reasonable levels of understanding of computer architecture.

Learning Outcome: Upon successful completion of this course, the student will be knowledgeable about computer fundamentals and organization; hardware components; assembly language programming (8088); and peripherals and interfaces.

Instruction: Major topics covered in the course are hardware components; peripherals and interfaces; assembly language programming; and DOS utilities. Methods of instruction include lecture, discussion, classroom exercises, case studies, problem-solving, computer-assisted videotapes, and laboratory.

Credit Recommendation: In the upper division baccalaureate degree or the graduate degree category, 3 semester hours in Computer Science or Computer Architecture. **NOTE**: The student must successfully complete all four modules to be eligible for the credit recommendation (3/92).

Computer Fundamentals and Software Applications

Location: Datapro centers throughout India.

Length: 320 hours total, 80 hours for each module (20 hours/week); or 400 hours total if optional module ST.10 is completed.

Dates: July 1985-March 1997.

Objective: To introduce the user to the foundational/fundamental concepts in computing and the application and use of word processing, spreadsheets, database management systems (DBMS) concepts, with extensions in the use of Windows.

Learning Outcome: Upon successful completion of this course, the students will be able to explain the basic structure, use, and operation of a computer; apply features of Lotus 1-2-3, appropriate to a given problem or task; design and develop dBASE III+ programs for solving specified problems or tasks; understand and be able to employ word processing technology; and if they complete module ST.10, be able to function within the Windows environment.

Instruction: Major topics covered in the course are computer fundamentals, design and structure, history of computers, software, hardware, operating systems, DOS concepts, PC, mini's, mainframes, Lotus 1-2-3, dBASE III+, and WordStar. If student also completes module ST.10, concepts and use of MS Windows. Methods of instruction include lecture, discussion, classroom exercises, case studies, problem-solving, computer-assisted videotapes, laboratory, and projects.

Credit Recommendation: In the lower division baccalaureate/associate degree category, 3 semester hours in Computer Science, Information Systems, Data Processing, or Information Technology. **NOTE**: Student must successfully complete all four modules (ST.1, ST.6, ST.7, and ST.9) to be eligible for the credit recommendation. If the student has also successfully completed module ST.10 (Windows), then the total credit recommendation is 4 semester hours (3/92).

Data Communications and Local Area Networks (ST.12 and ST.13)

Location: Datapro centers throughout India.

Length: 160 hours (20 hours/week); 80 hours, each module.

Dates: July 1985-March 1997.

Objective: To provide an understanding of data communication system concepts and local area networks (LANs).

Learning Outcome: Upon successful completion of this course, the student will be able to explain the hardware aspects of data communications; understand protocols and standards used in data communications; understand error detection and correction concepts in data communication, as well as network security and controls; understand satellite and other modern-day communication requirements and (if student also completes ST.13 as well as ST.12) understand local area networks, with specific understanding of Novell's Netware.

Instruction: Major topics covered in the course are data communication hardware and concepts; protocols and standards; error detection and correction concepts; network security and controls; TCP/JP, LAN, WAN; satellite and other modern-day communication requirements; LAN (hardware, topology, protocols, evaluation, management, protection, security, and internetworking; and Netware (detailed understanding and use of software). Methods of instruction include lecture, discussion, classroom exercises, case studies, problem-solving, computer-assisted videotapes, laboratory, and projects.

Credit Recommendation: In the upper division baccalaureate degree or the graduate degree category, for successful completion of Module ST.12, 3 semester hours in Computer Science, Computer Information Systems (CIS) or Teleprocessing.

If student also completes Module ST.13, then a total of 4 semester hours (3/92).

Financial Accounting (ST.62)

Location: Datapro centers throughout India.

Length: 80 hours (20 hours/week).

Dates: July 1985-March 1997.

Objective: To make user aware of computerized financial accounting software concepts and to provide operational knowledge of the Microsoft financial accounting package.

Learning Outcome: Upon successful completion of this course, the student will acquire computer-aided "hands on" understanding of basic financial accounting concepts. The Microsoft financial accounting software is designed to give the user a step-by-step walkthrough from the creation of journal and general ledger accounts to the creation of balance and profit and loss statements.

Instruction: Major topics covered in the course are overview of accounting concepts; features and overview of Microsoft financial accounting software package; parameters; codification; accounts receivable; invoicing; general ledger; cash accounts; customer receipts; and journal voucher and financial statements. Methods of instruction include lecture, discussion, classroom exercises, case studies, problem-solving, computer-assisted videotapes, laboratory, and projects.

Credit Recommendation: In the lower division baccalaureate/associate degree category, 1 semester hour in Business Administration or Accounting (3/92).

Maintenance (ST.54)

Location: Datapro centers throughout India.

Length: 48 hours.

Dates: July 1985-March 1997.

Objective: To train students in fault finding in PCs and possible solutions.

Learning Outcome: Upon successful completion of this course, the student will be able to test for faults and find possible solutions to correct them.

Instruction: Major topics covered in the course are troubleshooting (PCs); PC/XT assembly; various peripherals (disk, floppy, pointer, printer); and faults and repair procedures. Methods of instruction include lecture, discussion, classroom exercises, case studies, problem-solving and laboratory. Class is 50 percent theory and 50 percent practical.

Credit Recommendation: In the vocational certificate category, 3 semester hours in Maintenance or Electronic Technology (3/92).

Oracle (ST.14)

Location: Datapro centers throughout India.

Length: 80 hours (4 weeks).

Dates: July 1985-March 1997.

Objective: To provide understanding of relational database concepts using Oracle.

Learning Outcome: Upon successful completion of this course, the student will be able to work with Oracle under DOS/UNIX and develop a data base using Oracle.

Instruction: Major topics covered in the course are introductory data base concepts; introduction to relational data bases; introduction to SQL; introduction to Oracle; data base security and query processing; Oracle utilities; and optimizing system performance. Methods of instruction include lecture, discussion, classroom exercises, case studies, problem-solving, computer-assisted videotapes, and laboratory.

Credit Recommendation: In the upper division baccalaureate degree or the graduate degree category, 3 semester hours in Computer Science, Computer Information Systems (CIS) or Data base Management Systems (3/92).

Pascal Programming Language (ST.4)

Location: Datapro centers throughout India.

Length: 160 hours (8 weeks).

Dates: July 1985-March 1997.

Objective: To train students to become proficient programmers in the Pascal programming language.

Learning Outcome: Upon successful completion of this course, the student will be able to analyze a given problem; develop an efficient algorithm to solve the problem; and implement the algorithm in Pascal.

Instruction: Major topics covered in the course are general structure of a Pascal program; basic control structures; functions and procedures; file processing; recursion; and pointers. Methods of instruction include lecture, discussion, classroom exercises, case studies, problem-solving, and computer-assisted videotapes.

Credit Recommendation: In the lower division baccalaureate/associate degree category, 4 semester hours in Computer Science, Computer Information Systems (CIS), or Pascal Programming (3/92).

Systems Analysis and Design (ST.11 and ST.15)

Location: Datapro centers throughout India.

Length: 240 hours total, 20 hours/week; ST.11=80 hours and ST.15=160 hours.

Dates: January 1989-March 1997 (ST.11); July 1985-March 1997 (ST.15).

Objective: To train students in the formal methodology of analyzing business systems and the use of CASE tools in systems design.

Learning Outcome: Upon successful completion of this course, the student will be able to analyze a business system using the systems development life cycle (SDLC) technique and design user-friendly systems that meet user specifications.

Instruction: Major topics covered in the course are introduction to systems analysis; systems development life cycle; data modeling; data dictionaries; system documentation; software engineering; and introduction to CASE tools and prototyping. Methods of instruction include lecture, discussion, classroom exercises, case studies, problem-solving, computer-assisted videotapes, and laboratory.

Credit Recommendation: In the upper division baccalaureate degree category, 4 semester hours in Computer Science, Computer Information Systems (CIS), or Systems Analysis (3/92).

UNIX (ST.18)

Location: Datapro centers throughout India.

Length: 160 hours (20 hours/week).

Dates: July 1985-March 1997.

Objective: To train students in understanding the UNIX environment.

Learning Outcome: Upon successful completion of this course, the student will be familiar with the UNIX environment.

Instruction: Major topics covered in the course are OS concepts; UNIX overview; UNIX programming environment; file systems; system commands; and shell programming. Methods of instruction include lecture, discussion, classroom exercises, case studies, problem-solving, and laboratory.

Credit Recommendation: In the upper division baccalaureate degree category, 3 semester hours in Computer Science or Computer Information Systems (CIS) (3/92).

Dearborn Financial Institute

Dearborn Financial Institute provides training, textbooks, multimedia materials and administrative services to the financial and business community. The mission of Dearborn Financial Institute is to satisfy the growing and changing global financial information needs of professionals and consumers. Our goal is to offer training that meets the needs of professionals and products of superior value, as well as to provide responsive customer service.

Our training materials and classroom instruction are designed to teach the technical, legal and ethical content necessary to pass licensing examinations, earn continuing education credit and improve professionalism in general. Every year over 20,000 students enroll in at least 16 securities training programs held throughout the country. The history of the securities industry, day-to-day securities operations, ethical issues and pertinent legislation are all explored in depth. Instructors, a full-time answer-phone staff, editors, writers and legal and technical advisors all work toward producing a knowledgeable and successful student.

Source of official student records: Registry of Credit Recommendations, American Council on Education, One Dupont Circle, Washington, DC 20036-1193.

Additional information about the courses: Accreditation Program, Dearborn Financial Institute, 155 N. Wacker Drive, Chicago, IL 60606-1719.

SERIES 26: Investment Company/Variable Contracts Products Principal

Location: Classroom locations throughout the United States or correspondence.

Length: 2 days or self paced

Dates: January 1986-Present.

Objective: To prepare students to pass the NASD (National Association of Securities Dealers) Series 26, which is required of individuals who as principals will supervise individuals soliciting the purchase or sale of redeemable securities (mutual funds) registered under the Investment Company Act of 1940, variable contracts and insurance premium funding programs (variable life) issued by insurance companies.

Learning Outcome: Upon successful completion of this course, the student will be able to identify characteristics of mutual funds; discuss investment company regulations; explain the issuing of investment company securities; understand the management of customer accounts and brokerage office procedures; discuss ethics in the securities industry; describe retirement plans, including qualified and nonqualified plans; identify SEC and NASD rules and regulations; understand record keeping and reporting responsibilities of broker-dealers; discuss customer protection and financial responsibility; and uniform net capital rules.

Instruction: Major topics covered in the course are investment company products, types of customer accounts, brokerage office procedures, retirement planning, securities rules and regulations, recordkeeping and reporting responsibilities, customer protection and financial responsibility and uniform net capital rules. Methods of instruction include lecture, class discussion, homework, review and a final examination. Course requires extensive preparation and homework assignments.

Credit Recommendation: In the upper division baccalaureate degree category, 2 semester hours in Business, Finance, or elective (11/96).

SERIES 65/66: Uniform Investment Adviser Law/Combined State Law Exam

Location: Classroom locations throughout the United States or correspondence.

Length: 1 day or self paced.

Dates: January 1992-Present.

Objective: To prepare students to pass the NASD (National Association of Securities Dealers) Series 65/66 examination, which is required of individuals acting as or soliciting for the service of investment advisers.

Learning Outcome: Upon successful completion of this course, the student will be able to demonstrate an understanding of the regulation of the securities industry, including federal securities laws, the registration of broker-dealers, agents and investment advisers, the registration of securities and fraudulent practices and other prohibitions; describe activities affected by the federal Securities Act of 1933, including the underwriting process, exemptions from the Act, insider trading and securities fraud; describe activities affected by the Investment Advisers Act of 1940, including registration and reporting requirements, advertising, custody of customer funds, enforcement of the act and ethics.

Instruction: Major topics covered in the course are securities markets and regulation, the Securities Act of 1933 and Investment Advisers Act of 1940. Methods of instruction include lecture, class discussion, homework, review and a final examination. Course requires extensive preparation and homework assignments.

Credit Recommendation: In the upper division baccalaureate degree category, 1 semester hour in Business, Finance, or elective (11/96).

SERIES 6: Investment Company/Variable Contracts Representative

Location: Classroom locations throughout the United States or correspondence.

Length: 2.5 days or self paced.

Dates: January 1986-Present.

Objective: To prepare students to pass the NASD (National Association of Securities Dealers) Series 6 examination, which is required of individuals soliciting the purchase or sale of redeemable securities (mutual funds) registered under the Investment Company Act of 1940, variable contracts and insurance premium funding programs (variable life) issued by insurance companies.

Learning Outcome: Upon successful completion of this course, the student will be able to differentiate types of stock and evaluate the risk associated with each; describe the characteristics of bonds; differentiate the kinds of securities; understand the underwriting process; understand and explain the legislation and regulation affecting investment companies; describe mutual funds pricing, taxation and distributions; describe a variable contract; discuss annuities, IRAs and other retirement plans; and understand securities regulation and the role of ethics in the industry.

Instruction: Major topics covered in the course are securities markets and regulation, investment risks, prospectus regulation, investment companies in general, annuities and variable contracts, retirement plans, customer suitability, client accounts, investment recommendations, and brokerage office procedures. Methods of instruction include lecture, class discussion, homework, review, and a final examination. Course requires extensive preparation and homework assignments.

Credit Recommendation: In the upper division baccalaureate degree category, 2 semester hours in Business, Finance, or elective (11/96).

SERIES 7: General Securities Representative

Location: Classroom locations throughout the United States or correspondence.

Length: 5 days or self paced.

Dates: January 1986-Present.

Objective: To prepare students to pass the NASD (National Association of Securities Dealers) Series 7 examination, which is required of individuals soliciting the purchase or sale of corporate, municipal, and U.S. securities, options, direct participation programs, investment company products and variable contracts.

Learning Outcome: Upon successful completion of this course, the student will be able to describe equity securities; understand bonds and differentiate corporate from government bonds; explain the regulation of securities, as well as the underwriting process; understand and describe trading securities, its regulation, exchanges, types of orders and the NASD; define brokerage office procedures; describe the role of economics and analysis in securities; identify ethical issues as they affect securities; understand federal, state and industry rules and regulations; describe retirement planing products; and understand securities tracking procedures.

Instruction: Major topics covered in the course are U.S. government and money-market securities, equity securities, debt securities, municipal securities, options, margin, underwriting, trading securities and settlement, client accounts, equity products, money markets, government bonds, DPPs, investment companies, variable contracts, and retirement plans. Methods of instruction include lecture, class discussion, homework, review, and final examination. Course requires extensive preparation and homework assignments.

Credit Recommendation: In the upper division baccalaureate degree category, 3 semester hours in Business, Finance, or elective (11/96).

Defense Logistics Agency

The Defense Logistics Agency Civilian Personnel Support Office (DCPSO) has been providing training for civilian and military personnel since 1988. DCPSO has four branches each of which is unique in training delivery. The two Columbus, Ohio, locations provide courses in Contracting and Supply Management; the Atlanta, Georgia branch specializes in Production and Quality Management; and the Battle Creek, Michigan branch instructs in the Environmental and Safety areas.

Students are civilian and military personnel employed by the Department of Defense, and occasionally personnel of foreign governments. Courses are taught anywhere in the world that our forces are located. Nearly seventy courses in all are delivered by the staff.

DCPSO continually monitors the quality of all courses taught. Evaluations of materials are done on a continuous basis and revisions are made whenever needed. The teaching staff is selected by subject competence. Staff evaluations are done on a regular basis, and assistance and direction are provided to help all personnel maintain a high professional level. Approximately 50 instructors serve DCPSO at this time. The number of students taught annually runs into the thousands.

Record keeping is done by each branch-keeping track of attendance, performance course completion data and instructor. Certificates are given for course completion indicating title, dates of attendance, location where the course was offered, and instructor's name.

DCPSO provides training to government employees; however, the work is not limited to just delivery. DCPSO also has a development division capable of providing professional training materials for effective instruction to be delivered by other training departments.

The Mission of DCPSO is to proficiently diagnose the causes of human/process problems an to offer creative, effective solutions through training and other means, and to provide exceptionally developed and maintained materials, along with quality instruction which meets the customers' requirements, on time, everywhere and at the lowest level possible price.

To contact the DCPSO Office regarding courses offered, training development or delivery, or other information, call or write the central office at 380 Morrison Road, Columbus, Ohio 43213, 614-692-5935; or contact a DCPSO branch representative in Atlanta, at 404-590-6648 or in Battle Creek, at 616-961-7047.

Source of official student records: Registry of Credit Recommendations, American Council on Education, One Dupont Circle, Washington, DC 20036-1193.

Additional information about the courses: College Credit Recommendation Service, American Council on Education, One Dupont Circle, Washington, DC 20036-1193.

Contract Pricing (CON 104)

Location: Columbus, Ohio and other DoD locations.

Length: 112 hours (3 weeks).

Dates: October 1991-Present.

Objective: To provide entry-level contracting personnel with a solid foundation for the practice of cost analysis, price analysis and negotiating.

Learning Outcome: Upon successful completion of this course, the student will be able to describe the practices of contract pricing, sources and means of acquiring data for cost and price analysis; analyze direct and indirect costs and profit; and apply concepts and methods in exercises that demonstrate cost and profit analysis and negotiation.

Instruction: Major topics covered in the course are a review of the contracting environment's sources of data for cost and price analysis; methods for analyzing direct and indirect costs; methods for performing profit analysis; ethics in contract pricing; and fundamentals of the negotiation process, including essential techniques, strategies, and tactics.

Credit Recommendation: In the upper division baccalaureate degree category, 3 semester hours in Contract Pricing (8/95).

Contracting Fundamentals (CON 101)

Location: Columbus, Ohio and other DoD locations.

Length: 160 hours (4 weeks).

Dates: October 1987-Present.

Objective: To provide students with a survey course in contracting basics as prescribed by the Federal Acquisition Regulation (FAR), statutes, ethics policies, and other pertinent authorities that govern DoD contracting operations.

Learning Outcome: Upon successful completion of this course, the student will be able to describe the regulatory basis for contracting actions and state the importance of such contracting activities, demonstrate an understanding of methods, policies, and procedures in federal government procurement and apply rational decision making with a variety of methods of instruction.

Instruction: Major topics covered in the course are Pre-award and post-award activities from initial receipt of the requirements through contract closure; fundamentals, specifications, purchase requests, competition, solicitation activities, ethics and responsibility, cost and pricing, contract management, quality, and contract closure methods. Methods of instruction include guided study integrated by discussion, exercises and self-help quizzes, explanations of terminology and acronyms, document examples, case studies or scenarios, and performance demonstrated through practice, discussion, and examinations.

Credit Recommendation: In the upper division baccalaureate degree category, 4 semester hours in Contracting Fundamentals (8/95).

DLA Supply Management Course (SUPMGT)

Location: Columbus, Ohio and other DoD locations.

Length: 120 hours (3 weeks).

Dates: October 1986-Present.

Objective: To provide the student with a comprehensive overview and the tools associated with the DLA Inventory Management Program.

Learning Outcome: Upon successful completion of this course, the student will be able to define maximum release quantity; describe the total asset visibility plan; identify and define the three data elements used in demand forecasting; determine when an item is considered to be in excess; describe the purpose of fractionation in relation to stratification; compute reorder point; describe the shelf life program; calculate the average production lead time; describe the various aspects associated with DLA management techniques.

Instruction: Major topics covered in the course are introduction to the automated information systems used in managing wholesale supplies, material obligation validation, inventory adjustments, supply/contracting interface, demand forecasting techniques, and reorder point calculations. Methods of instruction include lecture, case studies, practical exercises, and group participation.

Credit Recommendation: In the upper division baccalaureate degree category, 4

semester hours in Supply Management and Logistics Management (8/95).

Intermediate Contract Pricing (CON 231)

Location: Columbus, Ohio and other DoD locations.

Length: 80 hours (2 weeks).

Dates: October 1994-Present.

Objective: To apply selected quantitative techniques to specific contract pricing situations; critique cost estimates based on a variety of analyses and techniques; determine variances, price adjustment, defining contracts, need for audits, defective cost or pricing, type of contract to use, deficiencies in price realism and use of specialized approaches.

Learning Outcome: Upon successful completion of this course, the student will be able to correctly identify issues and concerns regarding the selection and application of estimating techniques in cost/ price analysis; critique cost estimates based on a variety of analyses and techniques; determine variances; price adjustments; definitization of contracts; need for audits; defetive cost of pricing; type of contract to use; deficiencies in price realism; and use of specialized approaches.

Instruction: Major topics covered in the course are cost estimates based on price index numbers; cost-volume-profit analysis; net present value of leases; statistical analysis; regression analysis; moving averages; improvement curves; work measurement; and production variances.

Credit Recommendation: In the upper division baccalaureate degree category, 3 semester hours in Contract Pricing Problems (8/95).

Intermediate Contracting (CON 211)

Location: Columbus, Ohio and other DoD locations.

Length: 120 hours (3 weeks).

Dates: October 1992-Present.

Objective: To provide a forum for development of decision-making skills and task-related competencies relevant to complex government acquisitions.

Learning Outcome: Upon successful completion of this course, the student will be able to review the procurement request to identify the degree of acquisition planning needed; prepare source lists; evaluate the contractual adequacy of the technical requirements; select the appropriate contract type; and determine the adequacy of funds. Employ evaluation techniques to determine responsibility, competitive range, cost and pricing data, cost accounting standards and source selection to the award of the contract. Recognize and recommend solutions to contract management problems dealing with ethical behavior and determine administrative functions to be transferred to the contract administration office.

Instruction: Major topics covered in the course are Pre-solicitation (need, requirement, and source selection plans); solicitation (terms and conditions); evaluation (of proposals; ensuing discussions); award decisions; post-award activities; and ethics/fraud. Methods of instruction include lecture, case studies, practical exercises and class discussion, individual and group decision-making, and written examinations.

Credit Recommendation: In the upper division baccalaureate degree category, 4 semester hours in Contracting Problems (8/95).

Intermediate Production and Quality Management

Location: Marietta, Georgia and other DoD locations.

Length: 120 hours (3 weeks).

Dates: October 1994-Present.

Objective: To provide students with a broad knowledge and understanding of production and quality assurance processes in an industrial manufacturing environment.

Learning Outcome: Upon successful completion of this course, the student will be able to understand the manufacturing acquisition cycle, production and quality assurance processes, cost estimating and learning curves, contract surveillance, scheduling tools and evaluation of performance, participate in process improvement techniques, and understand and perform simple materials requirement planning (MRP) calculations.

Instruction: Major topics covered in the course are acquisition management; the acquisition life cycle which includes production and quality assurance processes in a manufacturing environment; cost estimating and learning curves; contract surveillance; scheduling; quality assurance and inspection; process improvement techniques; line-of-balance; materials control; manufacturing management; and just-in-time manufacturing. Methods of instruction include lecture, practical exercise, demonstrations and discussions, interactive computer exercises, and video presentations.

Credit Recommendation: In the upper division baccalaureate degree category, 4 semester hours in Production Management (8/95).

Resource Conservation and Recovery Act Facility Compliance (R509)

Location: Battle Creek and other DLA locations.

Length: 32 hours.

Dates: June 1991-Present.

Objective: To provide the student with the skills to manage and operate a Resource Conservation and Recovery Act generator or storage facility in Accordance with 40 CFR 264/265 and/or 262.

Learning Outcome: Upon successful completion of this course, the student will be able to identify hazardous wastes and assign appropriate EPA waste number(s); identify storage facilities at 40 CFR 264/265; verify that land disposal restriction notification forms are correctly and completely prepared; and list the appropriate responses for an emergency.

Instruction: Major topics covered in the course are hazardous waste identification; generator responsibilities; land disposal restrictions; treatment storage disposal facilities and used oil. Methods of instruction include lecture, videotapes, return demonstration, case study, group discussion, and problem solving exercises.

Credit Recommendation: In the lower division baccalaureate/associate degree category, 2 semester hours in Environmental Regulations (8/95).

Statistical Process Control (QA000000S81)

Location: Marietta, Georgia and other DoD locations.

Length: 40 hours (1 week).

Dates: January 1990-Present.

Objective: To provide the student with statistical methods and techniques used to analyze, evaluate, and control manufacturing processes.

Learning Outcome: Upon successful completion of this course, the student will be able to construct, analyze and interpret statistical data in various chart formats; determine the statistical tools needed to analyze a particular process (attribute vs variable charts); determine an out-of-tolerance condition; predict whether a process will yield non-conforming material.

Instruction: Major topics covered in the course are the basic concepts of descriptive statistics; the application of statistical process control (SPC) techniques; interpretation and evaluation of control charts and their relationship to various processes; construction of attribute and variables control charts; calculation of process capability indices (Cp); process performance indices (Cpk); and the estimate of percent nonconforming. Methods of instruction include lecture, reinforced by practical exercises.

Credit Recommendation: In the lower division baccalaureate/associate degree category, 3 semester hours in Manufacturing Quality Control or Quality Control (8/95).

Transportation of Hazardous Materials and Hazardous Waste for DoD (R510)
DCPSO.01 or R510

Location: Battle Creek and other DoD locations.

Length: 40 hours (5 days).

Dates: June 1991-Present.

Objective: To provide the student with the skills and knowledge necessary to comply with the regulatory requirements affecting the highway shipment of hazardous materials and hazardous wastes.

Learning Outcome: Upon successful completion of this course, the student will be able to recognize and classify hazardous material; describe various materials on shipping papers; identify proper packaging for hazardous materials; determine required markings and labels; specify placards required for a loaded vehicle; and comply with emergency response information and training requirements.

Instruction: Major topics covered in the course are codes of federal regulations relating to hazardous materials; hazardous property identification; marking/labeling; shipping papers; uniform hazardous waste manifest; pre-transport requirements. Methods of instruction include lecture demonstration, practical exercises, group projects, and videos.

Credit Recommendation: In the lower division baccalaureate/associate degree category; 2 semester hours in Hazardous Materials Transportation (8/95).

Development Dimensions International

Development Dimensions International, Inc. (DDI), a human resource company founded in 1970, specializes in the research and development of systems designed for organizational diagnosis and evaluation, assessment and selection, training, and performance management.

DDI focuses on enabling senior leaders to clarify their organization's vision and lead by its values, continually improve processes, create and implement effective teams, and build empowered workforces in which individuals and teams are developed to their fullest potential.

To help leaders survive in a rapidly changing work environment, DDI also offers such critical leadership skills as strengthening trust, coaching others to succeed, sustaining team momentum, and developing partnerships. By applying these skills, organizations are better able to respond quickly to technological advances and customer demands, and to consistently maintain a high level of performance.

DDI's skills training is designed for all organizational levels—leaders, middle managers, supervisors, team leaders, team members, and front-line employees. This training addresses sensitive business issues such as selecting the right employees for high-involvement organizations; encouraging innovation, collaboration, and idea generation; creating productive teams; setting performance expectations; coaching for improved performance; identifying and resolving conflict; sustaining continuous improvement, quality, and customer service excellence; and building and fostering high involvement. All DDI training includes and reinforces a set of "Key Principles"—behaviors that help employees at all levels motivate and empower each other.

Headquartered in Pittsburgh, Pennsylvania, DDI has worked with more than 16,000 public and private sector organizations worldwide, including more than 400 of the Fortune 500. DDI training is available in 17 languages and 21 countries through a network of 19 wholly owned national offices.

Source of official student records: Registry of Credit Recommendations, American Council on Education, One Dupont Circle, Washington, DC 20036-1193.

Additional information about the courses: College Credit Recommendation Service, American Council on Education, One Dupont Circle, Washington, DC 20036-1193.

Building Interpersonal Skills

Location: Various sites in North America.

Length: 26 hours; 30 minutes.

Dates: September 1995-Present.

Objective: To provide participants with knowledge and skills (self-empowerment, communication, peer support, and conflict resolution) to contribute to work unit and organizational success.

Learning Outcome: Upon successful completion of this course, the student will be able to communicate more effectively, train, support and influence others, understand the role of trust building; and manage conflict.

Instruction: Major topics covered in the course are team building, interpersonal communications, persuasive communications, training, and conflict management. Methods of instruction include a behavior modeling approach that utilizes lecture and discussion, classroom exercises, audio/visual material, case studies, learner presentations, and skill-building exercises.

Credit Recommendation: In the lower division baccalaureate/associate degree category, 1 semester hour in Applied Supervision or Applied Organizational Behavior (8/95).

Creating Quality and Service Excellence

Location: Various sites in North America.

Length: 18 hours.

Dates: October 1996-Present.

Objective: To provide front-line employees and leaders with the essential knowledge and skills to develop, implement, and sustain continuous improvements; as well as to sustain service excellence on the job and with customers.

Learning Outcome: Upon successful completion of this course, the student will be able to apply a systematic process to problem-solving and continuous improvement; determine and satisfy customer needs; and develop and implement service improvements for the organization.

Instruction: Major topics covered in the course are keys to service, steps to service, extraordinary service opportunities, assessing improvement opportunities, determining causes, targeting improvement ideas, and implementing ongoing improvements. Methods of instruction include lecture, discussion, classroom exercises, case studies, audio/visual material, skill practices/simulation, observations, and reports.

Credit Recommendation: In the lower division baccalaureate/associate degree category, 1 semester hour in Administration, Management, or Supervision (10/96).

Ensuring Team Performance Management Success

Location: Various sites in North America.

Length: 19 hours.

Dates: October 1996-Present.

Objective: To provide employees and front-line leaders with the knowledge and skills necessary to actively contribute to, participate in, and reach agreement in team meetings at work.

Learning Outcome: Upon successful completion of this course, the student will be able to share information and ideas more effectively in meetings; use meetings to solve problems and improve quality; improve commitment and cooperation; and plan and conduct effective meetings.

Instruction: Major topics covered in the course are team performance planning, reviewing team performance, working in teams, participating in meetings, leading effective meetings, and reaching agreement in teams. Methods of instruction include lecture, discussion, classroom exercises, case studies, audio/visual material, and skill practices/simulations.

Credit Recommendation: In the lower division baccalaureate/associate degree category, 1 semester hour in Administration, Management, or Supervision (10/96).

Facilitating Employee Behaviors

Location: Various sites in North America.

Length: 33 hours, 35 minutes.

Dates: September 1995-Present.

Objective: To provide participants with knowledge and skills to facilitate a wide spectrum of employee behaviors including reinforcing effective performance, encouraging greater responsibility, and accepting change. Participants will also develop skills necessary to manage conflict, including complaints and disciplinary issues.

Learning Outcome: Upon successful completion of this course, the student will be able to improve and/or reinforce performance, handle conflict, manage change, and implement effective disciplinary processes.

Instruction: Major topics covered in the course are improving employee performance and work habits, handling conflict, handling complaints, overcoming resistance to change, and conducting effective disciplinary interviews. Methods of instruction include a behavior modeling approach that utilizes lecture and discussion, classroom exercises, audio/visual material, case studies, learner presentations and skill-building exercises.

Credit Recommendation: In the lower division baccalaureate/associate degree category, 1 semester hour in Applied Supervision (8/95). **NOTE:** This is a practitioner oriented applied supervision course.

Fostering Quality and Service for Health Care Professionals

Location: Various sites in North America.

Length: 27 hours.

Dates: September 1995-Present.

Objective: Participants will also develop skills in identifying the health care field with the knowledge and skills necessary to develop, implement, and sustain continuous improvement and service excellence on the job. Participants will also develop skills in identifying and satisfying customer needs.

Learning Outcome: Upon successful completion of this course, the student will be able to apply problem solving and continuous improvement efforts on the job; determine and satisfy customer needs; conduct effective, efficient customer interactions; deal with difficult and emotional customers; suggest customer service improvements; and implement continuous improvement and customer service plans.

Instruction: Major topics covered in the course are customer service interaction, patient/customer feedback, health care trends, and meeting customer needs. Methods of instruction include a behavior modeling approach that utilizes skill-building exercises, role playing, simulations, team-based skill practices, and written actions plans for on-the-job application.

Credit Recommendation: In the upper division baccalaureate degree category, 1 semester hour in Health Care Administration, Quality Management, or Administration (8/95).

Interviewing and Selection Process

Location: Various sites in North America.

Length: 14 hours, 35 minutes (2 day in-class format).

Dates: September 1995-Present.

Objective: To provide participants with knowledge and skills necessary to interview and make optimal hiring decisions.

Learning Outcome: Upon successful completion of this course, the student will be able to maintain effective communications, take thorough interview notes, manage the interview process, evaluate information, and make hiring decisions.

Instruction: Major topics covered in the course are interviewing and communications techniques, data evaluation, and legal considerations. Methods of instruction include a behavior modeling approach that utilizes lecture and discussion, classroom exercises, audio/visual material, case studies, learner presentations, skill-building exercises, and out-of-class activities.

Credit Recommendation: In the lower division baccalaureate/associate degree category, 1 semester hour in Human Resource Management, Administration, or Social Work. **NOTE:** This course duplicates Train-the-Trainer: Interview and Selection Process. Credit should only be granted for one of these courses (8/95).

Maximizing Leadership Skills

Location: Various sites in North America.

Length: 17 hours, 25 minutes.

Dates: September 1995-Present.

Objective: To provide participants with knowledge and skills to effectively delegate, build individual and work unit commitment to change efforts, and facilitate conflict resolution.

Learning Outcome: Upon successful completion of this course, the student will be able to build a more skilled, challenged, motivated, and productive work group; foster trust, collaboration, and teamwork during times of change; recognize and help individuals resolve conflict before it escalates; and plan and facilitate conflict and change discussions.

Instruction: Major topics covered in the course are conflict resolution, adaptation to change, and delegation. Methods of instruction include a behavior modeling approach that utilizes lecture and discussion, classroom exercises, audio/visual material, case studies, learner presentations, and skill-building exercises.

Credit Recommendation: In the upper division baccalaureate degree category, 1 semester hour in Supervision, Business Administration, or Management (8/95).

Performance Planning and Management

Location: Various sites in North America.

Length: 20 hours.

Dates: September 1995-Present.

Objective: To provide participants with knowledge and skills necessary for developing performance plans linked to organizational goals and for promoting open communication and trust in a work unit.

Learning Outcome: Upon successful completion of this course, the student will be able to develop understandable and realistic performance plans related to unit and organizational goals; coach and reinforce team member performance; plan and conduct effective discussions during the performance process; and conduct performance reviews.

Instruction: Major topics covered in the course are performance planning, coaching, performance appraisal, and effective communications. Methods of instruction include a behavior modeling approach that utilizes lecture and discussion, classroom exercises, audio/visual material, case studies, learner presentations, and skill-building exercises.

Credit Recommendation: In the upper division baccalaureate degree category, 1 semester hour in Performance Appraisal, Human Resource Management, or Business Communications (8/95).

Preparing for and Sustaining High Output Performance

Location: Various sites in North America.

Length: 37.15 months.

Dates: September 1995-Present.

Objective: To provide participants with knowledge and skills to develop interpersonal skills, conduct performance planning, coach individuals for success and improvement, and to encourage employee responsibility and involvement.

Learning Outcome: Upon successful completion of this course, the student will be able to apply coaching methods and techniques; integrate organizational, work unit, and individual goals; help individuals identify performance planning tracking methods; implement expectations and progress review discussion plans; and establish and sustain trusting and open working relationships.

Instruction: Major topics covered in the course are leadership, coaching, goal integration, and work unit and individual performance planning and analysis. Methods of instruction include a behavior modeling approach that utilizes lecture and discussion, classroom exercises, audio/visual material, case studies, simulation, learner presentations, and self-assessment.

Credit Recommendation: In the upper division baccalaureate degree category, 2 semester hours in Applied Leadership or Performance Appraisal (8/95).

Preparing for Team Success

Location: Various sites in North America.

Length: 18 hours.

Dates: September 1995-Present.

Objective: To provide participants with the knowledge and skills necessary to actively contribute to, participate in, and reach agreement during team work unit meetings and to develop an awareness of how personal differences contribute to overall team or work unit effectiveness and success.

Learning Outcome: Upon successful completion of this course, the student will be able to reduce conflict; value differences; share information effectively in meetings; use meetings to solve problems and improve quality; improve cooperation and commitment in meetings; diagnose and effectively handle difficult meeting situations; and plan and conduct effective and productive meetings.

Instruction: Major topics covered in the course are stages of team development, working in teams, team building, reaching agreement, and building consensus. Methods of instruction include a behavior modeling approach that utilizes lecture and discussion, classroom exercises, audio/visual material, case studies, learner presentations, and skill-building exercises.

Credit Recommendation: In the lower division baccalaureate/associate degree category, 1 semester hour in Team-Building, Supervision, Group Dynamics, Social Psychology, Group Facilitation, Industrial Psychology, or Industrial Sociology (8/95).

Strategic People Management

Location: Various sites in North America.

Length: 22 hours, 10 minutes.

Dates: September 1995-Present.

Objective: To provide participants with the knowledge and skills necessary to effectively support and coach individuals and to delegate tasks, responsibility, and authority.

Learning Outcome: Upon successful completion of this course, the student will be able to conduct effective development planning, coaching and reinforcing discussions; delegate effectively; and design effective monitoring systems.

Instruction: Major topics covered in the course are coaching and development; and delegating and monitoring. Methods of instruction include a behavior modeling approach that utilizes lecture and discussion, classroom exercises, audio/visual material, case studies, learner presentations, and skill-building exercises.

Credit Recommendation: In the upper division baccalaureate degree category, 1 semester hour in Supervision, Business Administration, Public Administration, or Management (8/95).

Strategic Planning and Decision-Making

Location: Various sites in North America.

Length: 22 hours.

Dates: September 1995-Present.

Objective: To provide participants with knowledge and skills necessary to make sound decisions, solve problems, and develop high-quality plans within organizations.

Learning Outcome: Upon successful completion of this course, the student will be able to improve the quality of decisions; identify causes of significant problems; and use a systematic planning process.

Instruction: Major topics covered in the course are decision making, problem-solving, and performance planning. Methods of instruction include a behavior modeling approach that utilizes lecture and discussion, classroom exercises, audio/visual material, case studies, learner presentations, and skill-building exercises.

Credit Recommendation: In the upper division baccalaureate degree category, 1 semester hour in Strategic Planning, Conflict Resolution (non-quantitative), or Problem Solving in an Organizational Environment (non-quantitative) (8/95).

Strategic Planning, Management, and Leadership

Location: Various sites in North America.

Length: 59 hours.

Dates: September 1995-Present.

Objective: To provide participants with the knowledge and skills necessary to develop and strengthen personal leadership, develop team effectiveness, and promote work unit trust.

Learning Outcome: Upon successful completion of this course, the student will be able to implement a team development plan; encourage initiative from employees, recognize barriers to collaboration, delegate, assume higher level responsibilities with confidence, and initiate an action plan.

Instruction: Major topics covered in the course are coaching, developing, supporting, and empowering individuals; positive modeling; action learning; feedback fundamentals; and building business partnerships. Methods of instruction include a behavior modeling approach that utilizes lecture and discussion, classroom exercises, audio/visual material, case studies, learner presentations, and skill-building exercises.

Credit Recommendation: In the upper division baccalaureate degree category, 3 semester hours in Human Relations, Management, Organizational Development, or Human Resource Management (8/95).

The Role of Leaders in Quality Management and Service

Location: Various sites in North America.

Length: 30 hours.

Dates: September 1995-Present.

Objective: To provide participants with the knowledge and skills to develop, implement, and sustain continuous improvement in management and job-related services.

Learning Outcome: Upon successful completion of this course, the student will be able to apply systematic problem-solving and continuous improvement on the job; develop a continuous improvement action plan; determine and satisfy customer needs; deal effectively with customers; suggest customer service improvements; and implement a customer service plan.

Instruction: Major topics covered in the course are continuous improvement, quality management, customer service, and partnering. Methods of instruction include a behavior modeling approach that utilizes lecture and discussion, classroom exercises, audio/visual material, case studies, learner presentations, skill-building exercises, and written action plans for on-the-job application.

Credit Recommendation: In the upper division baccalaureate degree category, 1 semester hour in Management, Human

Resource Development, or Administration (8/95).

Training Skills for an Empowered Workforce

Location: Various sites in North America.

Length: 32 hours.

Dates: September 1995-Present.

Objective: To provide participants with the knowledge and skills necessary to be an instructor, facilitator, and trainer in a leadership or team-building intervention.

Learning Outcome: Upon successful completion of this course, the student will be able to demonstrate effective presentation skills, i.e., time management, coaching, feedback, and evaluation.

Instruction: Major topics covered in the course are training-the-trainer through a methodology that emphasizes the principles of maintaining or enhancing self-esteem, listening and responding with empathy, asking for help and encouraging involvement. Methods of instruction include a behavior modeling approach that utilizes lecture and discussion, classroom exercises, audio/visual material, case studies, learner presentations and skill-building exercises.

Credit Recommendation: In the upper division baccalaureate degree category, 2 semester hours in Human Resource Development, Supervision, Training and Development, or Educational Techniques and Methods (8/95).

Train-the-Trainer: Interviewing and Selection Process

Location: Various sites in North America.

Length: 34 hours, 40 minutes (4.5 days).

Dates: September 1995-Present.

Objective: To provide participants with knowledge and skills to be a selection administrator, trainer and interviewer.

Learning Outcome: Upon successful completion of this course, the student will be able to perform job analysis; design and conduct interviews; make selection decisions; and train interviewers and interview "coaches".

Instruction: Major topics covered in the course are job analysis, recruiting, interviewing, reference review and verification, selection, training/coaching of interviewers, and legal environment of staffing decisions. Methods of instruction include case studies, learner presentations, role playing, and skill building exercises.

Credit Recommendation: In the upper division baccalaureate degree category, 2 semester hours in Public Administration, Management, or Social Work (8/95). **NOTE:** This course covers topics addressed in Interviewing and Selection Process. Credit should only be granted for one of these courses.

Transformational Leadership

Location: Various sites in North America.

Length: 29 hours, 10 minutes.

Dates: September 1995-Present.

Objective: To provide participants with knowledge and skills necessary to lead and influence others; and to build consensus, solve problems, and reach agreement in a group context.

Learning Outcome: Upon successful completion of this course, the student will be able to demonstrate appropriate group leadership skills; plan and conduct effective staff meetings; lead or participate in group discussions to solve problems, make decisions, and use consensus-building techniques; inspire commitment to organizational vision and values through verbal and nonverbal communication; and implement personal development, organizational leadership, and meeting effectiveness plans.

Instruction: Major topics covered in the course are group dynamics, leadership skills, conducting effective meetings, and consensus-building. Methods of instruction includes a behavior modeling approach that utilizes lecture, discussion, classroom exercises, audio/visual material, case studies, learner presentations, and skill-building exercises.

Credit Recommendation: In the upper division baccalaureate degree category, 1 semester hour in Applied Leadership, Consensus-Building, Team-Building, or Facilitating Meetings (8/95).

Disabled American Veterans

The Disabled American Veterans' (DAV) Structured and Continuing Training Program is designed for use by rehabilitated National Service Officers (NSOs) who have completed a sixteen-month on-the-job training program. The program covers the four important areas of anatomy, pathology, physiology, and Veterans Administration laws. It is a comprehensive course developed for the purpose of enhancing such job-related skills as paralegal and paramedical principles needed to represent veterans before the Department of Veterans' Affairs.

To address those needs, seven key elements were developed for the training program: the DAV Supplement to Veterans Administration (VA) Schedule for Rating Disabilities (SRS), the Supervisor's Training Manual (STM), the National Service Officers' Workbook, videotapes, audiocassettes, and medical charts. Students are taught by tenured National Service Officers with expertise in the subject matter. Training class instructors are monitored by staff members of the national organization.

Students are required to successfully complete each section of the training program. Student progress is monitored at the National Service and Legislative Headquarters. Monitored computer tests are administered after completion of each training module with a final examination upon completion of the course. The director is issued a weekly computer-generated report of the progress of all students. Students who do not master the subject matter, as determined through testing, are rescheduled for additional sessions.

Source of official student records: National Service Director, National Service and Legislative Headquarters, 807 Maine Avenue, S.W., Washington, DC 20024.

Additional information about the courses: College Credit Recommendation Service, American Council on Education, One Dupont Circle, Washington, DC 20036-1193.

Disabled American Veterans (DAV) Continuing Training Program for National Service Officers (NSOs)

Location: Cincinnati, OH; Dallas, TX; and various locations.

Length: 17 self-paced units of instruction (24 to 26 months).

Dates: July 1987-Present.

Objective: To provide an overview of human anatomy and various pathophysiological processes and conditions for use in relation to disability compensation.

Learning Outcome: Upon successful completion of this course, the student will be able to describe the basic structure and function of the major organ systems of the human body; describe pathophysiological and mental conditions commonly encountered in Department of Veterans' Affairs (VA) claimants and define related medical terms; and employ research techniques necessary to evaluate the law, governmental regulations, and court decisions relating to the provision of benefits administered by the Department of Veteran Affairs.

Instruction: Major topics covered in the course are the endocrine system, mental disorders, dental and oral conditions, the hemic and lymphatic system, the skin, the musculoskeletal system, the gynecological system, the genitourinary system, systemic diseases, the digestive system, the respiratory system, the ears, the eyes, the cardiovascular system, organic diseases of the central nervous system, and the application of pathophysiological conditions to specific Department of Veterans' Affairs (VA) compensation and rating systems. Methods of instruction include self-study workbooks, tutorial sessions with supervisor/instructor, videotapes, audiocassettes, and computerized evaluations.

Credit Recommendation: In the lower division baccalaureate/associate degree category, 3 semester hours in Human Anatomy, 2 semester hours in Basic Pathophysiology or Medical Terminology, and 1 semester hour in Administrative Law for Legal Assisting/Paralegal program for a total of 6 semester hours (4/89) (7/94).

Dollar Rent A Car Systems, Inc.

Dollar Rent A Car was founded in 1966 in Los Angeles, where its executive offices remained until August 1994, when Dollar relocated its worldwide headquarters to Tulsa, Oklahoma.

In August 1990, Dollar was acquired by Chrysler, which made it part of its Pentastar Transportation Groups, Inc., along with Thrifty and Snappy in Tulsa. (Snappy sold in 1994). In January 1993, Chrysler-owned General Rent A Car was closed, and non-duplicating rental locations merged with Dollar.

On November 6, 1997, Chrysler Corporation announced that its subsidiary, Dollar Thrifty Automotive Group Inc. (DTAG) formerly Pentastar Transportation Group, Inc. has filed with the United States Securities and Exchange Commission (S.E.C.) a registration statement relating to the issuance and sale in an initial public offering of shares of its common stock. DTAG owns Dollar Rent A Car Systems, Inc. and Thrifty Rent A Car System, Inc.

Today, Dollar Rent A Car has suburban and on-airport locations at all major airports throughout the United States. There are approximately 1000 worldwide locations in 65 countries, including 230 in the U.S.

Led by President and CEO Gary L. Paxton, the Dollar network is comprised of both corporate-owned and operated locations and Dollar Rent A Car licensee operations.

Our purpose is to provide the best personal service and value of all car rental companies to the leisure and discretionary market.

Source of official student records: Registry of Credit Recommendations, American Council on Education, One Dupont Circle, Washington DC 20036-1193.

Additional information about the courses: College Credit Recommendation Service, American Council on Education, One Dupont Circle, Washington, DC 20036-1193.

Customer First! CORE Teams

Location: Various sites throughout the United States and Canada.

Length: 11 hours (1.5 days).

Dates: July 1997-Present.

Objective: To utilize team building materials and videos, the learner will identify steps for team building, relate elements of problem solving, rate performance standards, build communications skills and develop a process for ongoing development.

Learning Outcome: Upon successful completion of this course, the student will be able to participate in teams, solve problems, understand need for positive communication, and analyze means to continue the above named items in a work setting.

Instruction: Major topics covered in the course are team building, problem solving, standards and communications. Methods of instruction include discussion, classroom exercises, role play, and practice sessions.

Credit Recommendation: In the lower division baccalaureate/associate degree category, 1 semester hour in Business Administration (must be taken in combination with Customer First! Frontline Team Building) (12/97).

Customer First! Frontline Team Building

Location: Various sites throughout the United States and Canada.

Length: 7 hours.

Dates: July 1997-Present.

Objective: By utilizing team building materials and videos, the learner/manager will be able to identify steps in team building, relate elements of problem solving, and rate performance standards.

Learning Outcome: Upon successful completion of this course, the student will be able to demonstrate problem solving skills, exhibit performance standards and apply significant team building interactions from the advantage point of management.

Instruction: Major topics covered in the course are problem solving, standards and team building. Methods of instruction include discussion, classroom exercises, role play, and practice sessions.

Credit Recommendation: In the lower division baccalaureate/associate degree category, 1 semester hour in Business Administration (must be taken in combination with Core Team Building) (12/97).

Customer First! Process Leaders Combo

Location: Various sites throughout the United States and Canada.

Length: 21 hours (3 days).

Dates: September 1997-Present.

Objective: To provide an understanding of concepts in leadership, employee development, performance and motivation, communication, conflict management, and quality improvement.

Learning Outcome: Upon successful completion of this course, the student will be able to perform leadership roles in management, employee development and performance, and demonstrate effective communications, conflict management styles, and employee motivation.

Instruction: Major topics covered in the course are coaching, employee development, motivation and performance standards, team building, quality improvement, communication, conflict management and management styles. Methods of instruction include lecture, discussion, classroom exercises, role play, practice sessions and audio/visual.

Credit Recommendation: In the lower division baccalaureate/associate degree category, 1 semester hour in Business Administration (12/97).

Customer First! Process Leaders I

Location: Various sites throughout the United States and Canada.

Length: 21 hours (3 days).

Dates: July 1995-April 1997.

Objective: To provide an understanding of leadership, employee development and employee performance concepts.

Learning Outcome: Upon completion of this course, the student will be able to perform leadership roles in management, employee development and performance.

Instruction: Major topics covered in the course are coaching, employee development and performance standards, team building and quality improvement. Methods of instruction include lecture, discussion, classroom exercises, role playing, practice sessions, and audio/visual materials.

Credit Recommendation: In the lower division baccalaureate/associate degree category, 2 semester hours in Business Administration (when taken in combination with "Customer First! Customer Process II!) (12/97).

Customer First! Process Leaders II

Location: Various sites throughout the United States and Canada.

Length: 14 hours (2 days).

Dates: September 1996-October 1997.

Objective: To provide an understanding of the leadership role in communications conflict management, employee development and motivation.

Learning Outcome: Upon successful completion of this course, the student will be able to demonstrate effective communication, conflict management, alternative management styles, effective employee development and employee motivation.

Instruction: Major topics covered in the course are communication, conflict management, management styles, employee development and employee motivation.

Credit Recommendation: In the lower division baccalaureate/associate degree category, 2 semester hours in Business Administration (when taken in combination with "Customer First! Customer Process I!") (12/97).

Customer First! Service Givers

Location: Various sites throughout the United States and Canada.

Length: 14 hours (2 days).

Dates: November 1995-Present.

Objective: To be able to identify steps to quality service, development, surrounding change and the process of teamwork.

Learning Outcome: Upon successful completion of this course, the student will be able to explain the connection between service and profit, develop a positive service based attitude and relate steps necessary to promote improvement and quality.

Instruction: Major topics include profitability, service, quality, and empowerment/teamwork. Methods of instruction include discussion, classroom exercises, audio/visual material, role playing, and practice lessons.

Credit Recommendation: In the lower division baccalaureate/associate degree category, 1 semester hour in Business Administration (12/97).

Duquesne Light Company

Duquesne Light Company is committed to both fossil and nuclear power generation for meeting the energy needs of its customers. The company recognizes the importance of producing power in a safe and reliable manner and is therefore dedicated to excellence of operation of its facilities. The Duquesne Light Company considers a realistic but effective nuclear training program as the basic foundation to achieve excellence of operation at its nuclear facilities.

It is the intent of the Duquesne Light Company's nuclear training center to train individuals for responsible positions in the operation of its nuclear facilities. It is also the intention of Duquesne Light Company to provide training programs that are properly balanced to meet the training needs of operations and the needs of its customers for safe, reliable, and economical electrical energy.

The nuclear training staff is organized to provide a large part of the training service required for Nuclear Power Division personnel and company support personnel. Job duties are analyzed to ensure that company supervisory personnel engaged in safety-related activities at Duquesne Light Company's nuclear facilities are given required and job-specific training.

In addition, the company is a member of the Institute of Nuclear Power Operations (INPO) and supports its goals and objectives to achieve excellence of operation and training.

Source of official student records: Duquesne Light Company, Nuclear Power Division, P.O. Box 4, Shippingport, PA 15077-0004.

Additional information about the courses: College Credit Recommendation Service, American Council on Education, One Dupont Circle, Washington, DC 20036-1193.

Nuclear Training

Basic Nuclear Physics

Location: Shippingport, PA.

Length: 104 hours (13 days).

Dates: June 1983-October 1991.

Objective: To provide students with the knowledge required to describe the production of energy from the fission process and to apply knowledge of the structure of matter and nuclear processes to other training topics.

Instruction: Major topics covered in the course are atomic structure, nuclear physics, mass defect and binding energy, radioactive decay, decay chain and activity, atomic and nuclear interactions, fission and doppler effect, fission rate and power, neutron production, and neutron generation and criticality. Methods of instruction include lecture/discussion format.

Credit Recommendation: In the lower division baccalaureate/associate degree category, 3 semester hours in Nuclear Engineering/Nuclear Engineering Technology (10/86).

Chemical Analyst Training Program

Location: Beaver Valley Power Station, Shippingport, PA.

Length: 216 hours (6 weeks).

Dates: March 1987-August 1997.

Objective: To enable reactor power plant personnel to perform the in-plant functions of a chemical analyst in a safe, timely, and efficient manner.

Learning Outcome: Upon successful completion of this course, the student will be able to extract reactor plant samples; perform chemistry and radiochemistry analyses; and operate laboratory equipment.

Instruction: Major topics covered in the course are basic chemistry, radiochemistry, corrosion control, water chemistry, laboratory quality assurance and control, instrumentation, and reactor systems.

Credit Recommendation: In the lower division baccalaureate/associate degree category, 4 semester hours in General Chemistry Science or Engineering Technology (8/90).

Chemistry Fundamentals

Location: Beaver Valley Power Station, Shippingport, PA.

Length: 30 hours (1 week).

Dates: November 1981-January 1993.

Objective: To introduce the student to the fundamentals of inorganic chemistry.

Learning Outcome: Upon successful completion of this course, the student will be able to describe the three phases of matter and their properties; understand the Bohr model of the atom and the structure of the periodic table; understand the concepts of atomic and molecular weight and perform calculations relating to the above; understand the ideas of chemical valence of compounds; understand types of molecular bonds; balance chemical formulas, calculate amounts of products, give the amounts of reactants and basic chemical rate of change problems; understand solutions to chemistry and perform calculations on the molarity of solutions boiling point elevation and freezing point depression properties of solutions; and understand basic concepts of electrochemistry.

Instruction: Major topics covered in the course are Bohr model of atom, periodic table, qualitative properties of the phases of matter, atomic and molecular weights, chemical valence, different types of chemical bonds, chemical equations, chemical rate of change, heat of formation, basic solution chemistry, boiling point elevation, freezing point depression, electrochemical calculations, and basic nuclear chemistry. Methods of instruction include lecture and discussion.

Credit Recommendation: In the lower division baccalaureate/associate degree category, 2 semester hours in General Chemistry (1/88).

Chemistry Specialist Initial Training

Location: Beaver Valley Power Station, Shippingport, PA.

Length: 216 hours (4 weeks, plus plant time).

Dates: February 1988-August 1997.

Objective: To provide nuclear power plant chemists with classroom and practical training to be able to perform their daily plant operation analyses efficiently.

Learning Outcome: Upon successful completion of this course, the student will be able to perform chemical analysis; perform radiochemical analysis; use measurement instruments; and interpret the results.

Instruction: Major topics covered in the course are theoretical and practical aspects of nuclear plant systems chemistry, post-accident chemistry, statistics, radiochemistry, and instrumentation.

Credit Recommendation: In the lower baccalaureate/associate degree category, 2 semester hours in General Chemistry, Science, or Engineering Technology (8/90).

Electrical Circuits and Applications
a. Electrical Fundamentals
b. Electrical Practical

Location: Beaver Valley Power Station, Shippingport, PA.

Length: a. 36 hours (14 days); b. 51.6 hours (8 days).

Dates: September 1982-October 1991.

Objective: *Fundamentals:* To provide the student with a knowledge of basic electrical concepts, DC circuits, basic AC concepts and circuits, operation of AC generators, motors and transformers, and basic semiconductor theory and applications. *Practical:* To provide a student with knowledge of power plant circuit breaker operation, electrical schematics, 345 KV and 138 KV switchyards, main generator operation, metering, and protective relaying.

Instruction: *Fundamentals:* Major topics covered in the course are voltage, current, resistance, Kirchoff's laws, bridge circuits, electromagnetism, basic AC concepts, AC circuit analysis, AC generators, 3-phase circuits, instrument transformers, motors, and semiconductors. *Practical:* Major topics covered in the course are symbol review, circuit breakers, 480V/4KV/OCB's and SF6, reading schematics, 345 and 138 KV switchyards, main generator, construction/voltage regulator/parallel operation, metering, and protective relaying. Methods of instruction include lecture and discussion.

Credit Recommendation: In the lower division baccalaureate/associate degree category, 3 semester hours in Survey of Electric Circuits (10/86).

Instructor Development

Location: Beaver Valley Power Station, Shippingport, PA.

Length: 66-106 hours (2 or 3 weeks).

Dates: December 1984-January 1993.

Objective: To provide the student with a knowledge of the Systematic Approach to Training (S.A.T.), including the basics of learning, the adult learning process, course design and development, effective course instruction and implementation, effective evaluation, counseling and tutoring, and supervisory skills. To provide the student with appropriate practice instructional workshops and provide instructions and practice in job task analysis, objective writing, and exam writing and preparation.

Learning Outcome: Upon successful completion of this course, the student will be able to describe factors of learning, including systematic approach to training, the adult learning process, and motivation; construct a training course, including terminal objectives, enabling objectives, and lesson plan format; develop and implement a training program; develop and conduct training program evaluations, counsel, and tutor students; describe effects of attitudes, change, conditioning, motivation, and personnel development; methods of overcoming motivation problems; communication and listening problems; develop proper assertive behavior and methods of dealing with stress; know requirements of goal setting; and provide a practice teaching lesson.

Instruction: Major topics covered in the course are basics of learning, creating learning objectives and lesson plans, implementing a training plan, training planning, methods of counseling, tutoring, and student/teacher interaction. Practicum includes student's preparation and presentation of a one-hour sample lecture. Examinations are used to evaluate performance.

Credit Recommendation: In the upper division baccalaureate degree category, 3 semester hours in Methodology of Teaching Technical Courses (1/88).

Instrumentation and Control Fundamentals

Location: Beaver Valley Power Station, Shippingport, PA.

Length: 120 hours (3 weeks).

Dates: March 1985-January 1993.

Objective: To provide the student with the knowledge of basic sensor concepts, neutron detection methods, and analog and digital process control concepts.

Learning Outcome: Upon successful completion of this course, the student will be able to explain the following: operation of pressure, level, flow, neutron flux; dynamic compensation, signal control modes; relationship of proportional, rate, and reset controllers, basic pneumatic and electronic controllers; basic operational amplifier circuits including summers, multipliers, and comparators. In addition, the student will be able to draw basic logic symbols and application circuits and analyze applications of control circuits.

Instruction: Major topics covered in the course are basic sensors and transducers for measurement of temperature, pressure, fluid level, flow, position, and neutrons; sensor and transducer reliability and failure analysis; and basic process control and control circuits. Methods of instruction include lecture and discussion.

Credit Recommendation: In the lower division baccalaureate/associate degree category, 3 semester hours in Process Instrumentation and Control Fundamentals (1/88).

Materials for Power Plants (Materials for Licensed Operations)

Location: Shippingport, PA.

Length: 44 hours (6 days).

Dates: February 1982-October 1991.

Objective: To provide students with the knowledge needed to relate material selection to plant system limitations; describe the effects of radiation on plant materials; and fully explain the basis for Beaver Valley Power Station Technical Specifications, which are founded on maintaining system/component integrity under physical stress.

Instruction: Major topics covered in the course are properties of metals including physical properties and load-dependent properties; selection of plant materials; testing of materials; fracture and failure modes; linear elastic fracture mechanics; radiation effects on materials; pressurized thermal shock; heatup curve and cooldown curve development; Beaver Valley Power Station Technical Specifications related to materials including generators; and Code of Federal Regulations 10CFR50 (Appendix G and H). Methods of instruction include lecture and discussion.

Credit Recommendation: In the lower division baccalaureate/associate degree category, 1 semester hour in Theory of Nuclear Plant Materials (10/86).

Mitigating Core Damage/Accident Transient Analysis

Location: Beaver Valley Power Station, Shippingport, PA.

Length: 152 hours (19 days).

Dates: January 1984-October 1991.

Objective: To provide the student with the knowledge needed to describe the nuclear power plant response to various transients, the nuclear power plant response to various accidents, and to explain how to mitigate the consequences of various plant transients and accidents.

Instruction: Major topics covered in the course are fundamentals review, power distribution, transient analysis—normal/abnormal, accident analysis—reactivity addition accident/LOCA's miscellaneous, mitigating core damage—post-accident cooling/potentially damaging operating conditions/small break loss of coolant with no high head safety injection/loss of feedwater induced loss of coolant accident/main stream break review/steam generator overfill/loss of all AC, EOP-7/pressurized thermal shock/incore thermocouple maps/vital process instrumentation/instrument qualification and accident response of excore instrumentation/accident response of incore instrumentation/post-accident primary radiochemistry. Methods of instruction include lecture and discussion.

Credit Recommendation: In the upper division baccalaureate degree category, 4

semester hours in Nuclear Engineering (10/86).

Radiation, Radiation Protection, and Radiation Survey (Operator Radiation Safety Training/Radiation Survey Meter Qualifications)

Location: Beaver Valley Power Station, Shippingport, PA.

Length: 120 hours (15 days).

Dates: November 1982-October 1991.

Objective: To provide students with instruction in fundamental radiation protection techniques, regulations, and guidelines governing radiation exposure and radiation survey techniques, and the proper use of radiation survey instruments.

Instruction: Review of basic nuclear concepts, radiation quantities and units, biological effects of radiation, limits, guides and areas, radiation protection techniques, radioactive contamination control, radioactive material control, environmental considerations, and emergency planning. The radiation detection and measurement section covers radiation detection, radiological surveys and portable instrumentation, radiation monitoring system, and radiation accident monitors. Methods of instruction include lecture, discussion and demonstrations.

Credit Recommendation: In the lower division baccalaureate/associate degree category, 3 semester hours in Nuclear Engineering Technology/Health Physics and Radiation Safety Technology (10/86).

Radiation Technician Training Program

Location: Beaver Valley Power Station, Shippingport, PA.

Length: 80 hours (2 weeks).

Dates: June 1981-January 1993.

Objective: To introduce the student to the basic results of nuclear theory.

Learning Outcome: Upon successful completion of this course, the student will be able to perform half-life calculations; understand the ideas of cross-section and ionization and relate these to the range of penetration of radiation in matter; cover the theory of photoelectric, Compton effect, and pair production; develop working knowledge of units of radiation measurement, linear attenuation, and buildup in the case of thick absorbers; perform calculations on neutron penetration and activation; become knowledgeable about the biological hazards of different sources of radiation; and discuss nuclear stability comparing coulombic and nuclear force. Also covered are mass defect theory, nuclear binding energy; nuclear decay rates; units of radiation measurement, and comparison of Co-60 to beta emitter units of activity comparison. Students learn how to perform exposure and dose calculations; discuss biological effectiveness and quality factor; understand definitions of roentgen, rad, rem; and perform conversion calculations.

Instruction: Major topics covered in the course are review of atomic structure, ionization, nuclear cross-section, range and attenuation, biological hazards of radiation sources; the electromagnetic processes associated with ionizing radiation, Compton effect, photoelectric effect, and pair production; neutron attenuation and activation in matter; unit conversions, biological effectiveness calculations, exposure and dose calculations; and quantitative calculations of nuclear decay rates.

Credit Recommendation: In the lower division baccalaureate/associate degree category, 2 semester hours in Basic Nuclear Theory (1/88).

Radiation Technician Training Program: Fundamentals (Phases A, B, C, D)

Location: Beaver Valley Power Station, Shippingport, PA.

Length: 224 hours (5.5 weeks; 74 hours lecture/discussion).

Dates: June 1981-August 1997.

Objective: To provide the radiation technician with instruction in basic mathematics, chemistry, and physics.

Learning Outcome: Upon successful completion of this course, the student will be able to explain and perform basic mathematical operations including algebraic manipulations and calculations with exponents, logarithms, and trigonometric functions; define and explain atomic and nuclear structure, phases of matter, and chemical reactions; and define and explain concepts of motion, energy, and waves.

Instruction: Major topics covered in the course are introductory concepts in mathematics (30 percent), chemistry (40 percent), and physics (30 percent). Methods of instruction include lecture, problem-solving, and discussion.

Credit Recommendation: In the lower division baccalaureate/associate degree category, 1 semester hour in Introductory Mathematics, 2 semester hours in Introductory Chemistry, and 2 semester hours in Noncalculus Physics (8/90). **NOTE:** If Radiation Technician Program: Health Physics (Phase E) is also completed, student should receive 3 semester hours in Noncalculus Physics in the lower division baccalaureate/associate degree category.

Radiation Technician Training Program: Health Physics (Phases E, F, H)

Location: Beaver Valley Power Station, Shippingport, PA.

Length: 126 hours (3 weeks; 90 hours lecture/discussion, 30 hours problem-solving).

Dates: June 1981-August 1997.

Objective: To instruct the radiation technician in the fundamentals of radiation and radiation detection and radiation detection principles/procedures.

Learning Outcome: Upon successful completion of this course, the student will be able to describe nuclear decay processes, interaction of radiation with matter, units of radiation measurement, and radiation detectors and perform and interpret radiation measurements.

Instruction: Major topics covered in the course are nuclear structure radioactive decay, interaction of radiation with matter, radiation quantities and units of measurement, radiation detection, and counting. Methods of instruction include lecture, discussion, and demonstration/hands-on activities.

Credit Recommendation: In the lower division baccalaureate/associate degree category, 3 semester hours in Nuclear Science, Health Physics, or Nuclear Engineering Technology (8/90). **NOTE:** Students who complete this course should not receive credit for the separate listing of Radiation Technician Training Program.

Radiation Technician Training Program: Plant Systems (Phase N)

Location: Beaver Valley Power Station, Shippingport, PA.

Length: 47 hours (7 days).

Dates: June 1981-August 1997.

Objective: To provide radiation technician students with a knowledge of various plant systems.

Learning Outcome: Upon successful completion of this course, the student will be able to state system functions and interactions; list and describe major components; trace flow paths; state set points and parameter values; discuss administrative requirements and technical specifications; and identify associated instrumentation and interpret readouts.

Instruction: Major topics covered in the course are pumps and valves, reactor coolant system, boron recovery, residual heat removal, safety injection system, fuel pool and refueling, incore and excore instrumentation, steam generation, and fire protection. Methods of instruction include classroom presentations.

Credit Recommendation: In the lower division baccalaureate/associate degree category, 3 semester hours in Nuclear Science, Health Physics, or Nuclear Engineering Technology (8/90). **NOTE:** Students who complete this course should not receive credit for the separate listing of Radiation Technician Training Program.

Radiation Technician Training Program: Radioactive Materials Control and Monitoring (Phases I, J, K, L, M)

Location: Beaver Valley Power Station, Shippingport, PA.

Length: 556 hours (14 weeks).

Dates: June 1981-August 1997.

Objective: To introduce students to the control, discharge, and monitoring of radioactive materials.

Learning Outcome: Upon successful completion of this course, the student will be able to perform radiation surveys, air sampling, exposure, and radioactivity control; know the use of anti-"C" clothing, Radiation Worker Practices (RWP), etc. and understand As Low As Reasonably Achievable (ALARA) philosophy and bioassay programs; and describe procedures for handling and disposing of radioactive materials.

Instruction: Major topics covered in the course are radiation survey techniques and exposure control; function and design of gaseous and liquid discharge systems; proper procedures for handling and control of radioactive materials, liquid and gaseous wastes; environmental monitoring; and procedures to react to abnormal conditions. Methods of instruction include classroom/in-plant presentations.

Credit Recommendation: In the lower division baccalaureate/associate degree category, 3 semester hours in Nuclear Reactor Technology or Nuclear Science (8/90).

Reactor Plant Systems

Location: Beaver Valley Power Station, Shippingport, PA.

Length: 960 hours (29 weeks).

Dates: November 1982-January 1993.

Objective: To provide the student with a knowledge of the various reactor plant systems as they apply to a nuclear power plant reactor operator.

Learning Outcome: Upon successful completion of this course, the student will be able to write a description of the function of systems and components, system flow paths, instrumentation and control of each component, and the response of the system to an accident condition and interpret all available indications from systems to determine the plant status and compliance with technical specifications.

Instruction: Major topics covered in the course are lecture, simulation, and on-the-job training. The student covers reactor systems, engineered safeguards, instrumentation, waste disposal, primary cooling, ventilation, primary support, and process computers.

Credit Recommendation: In the lower division baccalaureate/associate degree category, 20 semester hours (15 academic semester hours and 5 on-the-job training semester hours) in Nuclear Engineering Technology (1/88).

Reactor Theory (Reactor Theory for Licensed Operators)

Location: Beaver Valley Power Station, Shippingport, PA.

Length: 160 hours (22 days).

Dates: May 1983-October 1991.

Objective: To provide the student with the knowledge required to describe the neutron life cycle and to predict and explain reactor response.

Instruction: Major topics covered in the course are neutron diffusion, neutron leakage, neutron multiplication, reactivity, period/startup rate, subcritical multiplication, coefficients and reactor control, fission product poisoning, delayed neutrons, transient reactor behavior, reactor startup and shutdown, power distribution, and peaking factors. Methods of instruction include lecture and discussion.

Credit Recommendation: In the lower division baccalaureate/associate degree category, 4 semester hours in Nuclear Engineering Technology (10/86).

Simulator Training For Licensed Nuclear

Location: Beaver Valley Power Station, Shippingport, PA.

Length: 171 hours (3.5 weeks).

Dates: February 1985-January 1993.

Objective: To provide simulator instruction for the student as it applies to a nuclear power plant reactor operator.

Learning Outcome: Upon successful completion of this course, the student will be able to utilize the appropriate controls, indications, and instrumentation to operate each of the systems; use the appropriate indications and instrumentation to assess the plant status; and predict and explain the response of plant parameters during the various evolutions.

Instruction: Major topics covered in the course are lecture and simulator evolutions. The student participates in all phases of simulated reactor operations from shutdown to full power operations, including unusual and accident situations.

Credit Recommendation: In the upper division baccalaureate degree category, 2 semester hours in Nuclear Engineering (1/88).

Thermodynamics for Licensed Operators (2404)

Location: Beaver Valley Power Station, Shippingport, PA.

Length: 183 hours (5 weeks).

Dates: May 1982-January 1989.

Objective: To provide students with an understanding of basic thermodynamic concepts and a survey of heat transfer and fluid flow processes, and heat and energy cycles with applications to nuclear power plant operations.

Instruction: Major topics covered in the course are noncalculus discussions of laws of thermodynamics; the general energy equation; properties of water; methods of heat transfer; fluid statics; fluid mechanics—Bernoulli's principle. Conceptual discussions of compressible and incompressible flow, fluid measurements, pumps, valves, systems; ideal and real gases; cycles—Carnot, Rankine, Rankine Regenerative Reheat, Refrigeration; and reactor thermal and hydraulic limits. Methods of instruction include lecture and discussion.

Credit Recommendation: In the upper division baccalaureate degree category, 3 semester hours in Nuclear Technology (1/84).

Turbine Plant Systems

Location: Beaver Valley Power Station, Shippingport, PA.

Length: 920 hours (28 weeks).

Dates: June 1982-January 1993.

Objective: To provide the student with a knowledge of the various turbine plant systems as they apply to a nuclear power plant reactor operator.

Learning Outcome: Upon successful completion of this course, the student will be able to write the function of the various systems; draw the basic system flow path; describe in detail the operation, control, and location of the major components of the various systems; and explain system procedures.

Instruction: Major topics covered in the course are electrical distribution, steam cycle, turbine-generator, cooling, secondary support, personnel safety, and administrative procedures. Methods of instruction include lecture, simulation, and on-the-job training.

Credit Recommendation: In the lower division baccalaureate/associate degree category, 18 semester hours (13 academic semester hours and 5 on-the-job training semester hours) in Nuclear Engineering Technology (1/88).

DynCorp

DynCorp is a billion dollar, diversified professional and technical services firm. Established in 1946, it is one of the nation's largest employee-owned service companies. We have 23,000 employees and more than 180 operations around the world and in every region of the United States at government installations, research facilities, commercial airports, and company facilities.

Our customers include U.S. and foreign government agencies and clients in the commercial aviation and shipping industries. Services are provided through Strategic Business Units (SBUs) that focus on the federal government, commercial aviation, and advanced technical services.

DynCorp's success is based on a fundamental company value: Be committed to fulfilling the customer's needs, not just meeting requirements but fully understanding and supporting their missions. This commitment to quality drives us to strive continually for improvement, thereby helping our customers better achieve their goals.

Source of official student records: Registry of Credit Recommendations, American Council on Education, One Dupont Circle, Washington, DC 20036-1193.

Additional information about the courses: College Credit Recommendation Service, American Council on Education, One Dupont Circle, Washington, DC 20036-1193.

Design Team/Rollout Workshop (DTRO)
Design Team Workshop (TQM) (DT 400T)

Location: Various sites worldwide.

Length: 40 hours (5 days).

Dates: November 1993-Present.

Objective: To provide students with an organizational structure to develop strategy and support for implementation of a total quality management program.

Learning Outcome: Upon successful completion of this course, the student will be able to produce a comprehensive action plan for developing and implementing his/her organization's total quality management process and be able to confirm that the plan will achieve desired objectives.

Instruction: Major topics covered in the course are TQM and change; overview of TQM, policy management, process management, and teams; quality improvement problem-solving process (the QI Story); purpose of the design team; mission and charter; developing the TQM implementation plan; and a model TQM implementation plan. **NOTE:** Pre-course work includes assessment, locating and reviewing data relating to customer satisfaction/customer needs; business environment; overarching objectives; direction of the organization; charter to the design team from the quality council; and mission/vision/values; this may include a pre-design team assessment done by a third party. Post-course work includes carrying out the action plans for TQM implementation developed during the design team workshop and completing all sections of the implementation plan. Methods of instruction include lecture, classroom exercises, case studies, and visual aids.

Credit Recommendation: In the upper division baccalaureate degree category, 3 semester hours in Management or business elective (4/93).

Managing Quality Improvement (MQ400T)
TQM: Managing Quality Improvement

Location: Various sites worldwide.

Length: 24 hours (3 days).

Dates: April 1991-Present.

Objective: To equip students with the knowledge and skills needed to manage and support a total quality management system. This course focuses on the teams component of the total quality management process.

Learning Outcome: Upon successful completion of this course, the student will be able to understand and plan their management roles in supporting teams; understand and use the five basic principles of quality and the seven statistical tools for problem-solving; and develop a personal action plan to support all team activities for total quality management.

Instruction: Major topics covered in the course are an overview of total quality management; QI tools and QI story; interacting with quality teams; managing results; and action planning. Methods of instruction include lecture, student participation in role-playing and other exercises; and the use of video tapes and overhead slides.

Credit Recommendation: In the upper division baccalaureate degree category, 1 semester hour in Management or business elective (4/93).

Managing Quality Improvement Instructor (MQII)
TQM: Managing Quality Improvement Instructor

Location: Various sites worldwide.

Length: 24 hours (3 days).

Dates: May 1991-Present.

Objective: To provide students with the knowledge and skills necessary to teach and administer Managing Quality Improvement (MQI) courses.

Learning Outcome: Upon successful completion of this course, the student will be able to define expectations and requirements of MQI instructors; prepare course overviews and presentations; teach the MQI course; and demonstrate effective communication skills.

Instruction: Major topics covered in the course are TQM overview; statistical tools used in TQM; overview of components necessary for successful implementation of TQM; and effective instructional skills. Methods of instruction include lecture, skill practice, videotaping, and discussion.

Credit Recommendation: In the upper division baccalaureate degree category, 1 semester hour in Adult Education, Business, Communications, or Human Resource Development (4/93).

Process Management (PM500T)
TQM: Process Management

Location: Various sites worldwide.

Length: 24 hours (3 days).

Dates: December 1992-Present.

Objective: To provide students with a systematic approach to identifying, documenting, prioritizing, and improving key job functions and work processes.

Learning Outcome: Upon successful completion of this course, the student will be able to identify and document key work processes; establish customer requirements; set indicators; begin developing initial process control systems; and monitor and improve performance.

Instruction: Major topics covered in the course are the definition of quality; principles of TQM and process management; building the process control systems; implementing the system; determining and ensuring process stability, capability, and flexibility; and monitoring and improving process control systems. Methods of instruction include lecture, and individual and group skill practice.

Credit Recommendation: In the upper division baccalaureate degree category, 2

semester hours in Management or business elective (4/93).

Process Management Instructor (PM510T)
TQM: Process Management Instructor

Location: Various sites worldwide.
Length: 24 hours (3 days).
Dates: June 1992-Present.
Objective: To provide students with the knowledge and skills necessary to teach and administer the process management course (PM500T).
Learning Outcome: Upon successful completion of this course, the student will be able to teach and administer the process management course effectively and understand the key elements of effective presentations.
Instruction: Major topics covered in the course are defining expectations and requirements of instructors; preparing technical presentations; making presentations; and giving feedback on presentation skills. Methods of instruction include lecture, skill development and practice, and videotaping.
Credit Recommendation: In the upper division baccalaureate degree category, 1 semester hour in Adult Education, Business, Communication, or Human Resource Development (4/93).

QI Team Leader (TL200T)
TQM: Team Leader Training

Location: Various sites worldwide.
Length: 40 hours (5 days).
Dates: June 1990-Present.
Objective: To equip students with the knowledge and skills necessary to lead and maintain quality improvement teams.
Learning Outcome: Upon successful completion of this course, the student will be able to understand team dynamics as related to TQM; comprehend the meaning of TQM and customer satisfaction; exercise appropriate administrative activities in leading teams; and lead teams through the seven step problem-solving process.
Instruction: Major topics covered in the course are the purpose and mechanics of quality improvement processes; principles of TQM; QI story for problem-solving; QC (quality control) tools; and skills needed to build and maintain teams. Methods of instruction include lecture, case study, exercise, video, role-playing, and discussion.
Credit Recommendation: In the upper division baccalaureate degree category, 2 semester hours in Supervision, Management, or business elective (4/93).

QI Team Leader Instructor (TL210T)
TQM: Team Leader Instructor

Location: Various sites worldwide.
Length: 40 hours (5 days).
Dates: March 1990-Present.
Objective: To provide students with instructor training and equip them with the knowledge and skills needed to teach and administer team leader courses.
Learning Outcome: Upon successful completion of this course, the student will be able to effectively teach and administer the team leader course (TL200T) and understand both the technical content and the key elements of effective presentations.
Instruction: Major topics covered in the course are defining expectations and requirements of instructors; preparing presentations; making presentations; technical instruction; group dynamics; and methods for providing feedback of presentation skills. Methods of instruction include lecture, skill practice, and videotaping.
Credit Recommendation: In the upper division baccalaureate degree category, 2 semester hours in Adult Education, Business, Communications, or Human Resource Development (4/93).

QI Team Member (TM100T)
TQM: Team Member Training

Location: Various sites worldwide.
Length: 16 hours (2 days).
Dates: June 1990-Present.
Objective: To provide students with an overview of quality improvement principles, the QI story problem-solving process; and practice in the role of a quality improvement team member.
Learning Outcome: Upon successful completion of this course, the student will be able to understand the basics of quality principles and practices; use quality control tools to reflect factual data; and follow and apply problem-solving principles.
Instruction: Major topics in the course are concepts of total quality management; seven steps in the quality improvement process; cause and effect analysis; tools and techniques for getting started as a team; and use of QI tools such as Pareto charts, histograms, fish bone diagram and line graphs. Methods of instruction include lecture, discussion, classroom exercises, video presentations, and audio visual aids.
Credit Recommendation: In the upper division baccalaureate degree category, 1 semester hour in Management (4/93).

Early Childhood Professional Development Network

The Administration on Children, Youth, and Families of the U.S. Department of Health and Human Services awarded a four-year grant to the Educational Television Endowment of South Carolina, Inc. to demonstrate the effectiveness of professional development training to clusters of Head Start classroom teaching teams through the use of satellite technology. The matching grant has been supported thus far with 7.8 million dollars.

The project was named the Early Childhood Professional Development Network (ECPDN). Geographical areas in which Head Start centers are scattered in small, rural, remote areas or very small in size have been the primary targets for services. For example, individuals working in programs located on Indian reservations, in Alaskan villages, or serving in-stream migrants have received priority to be chosen as participants. With the end of the federal grant in 1995, ECPDN has become a private, not for profit company. Training is now available to all individuals who are interested in early childhood education.

ECPDN has a full-time staff of highly qualified individuals who function as a team to fulfill its mission to deliver the highest quality professional development in an innovative, distance-education model. ECPDN is composed of the Departments of Administration, Curriculum, Production, Higher Education, and Education Services.

The Education Service Department maintains constant contact with students, discussion leaders, and facilitators and it is in that department that all student records are housed. For Student Records information contact: Carolyn S. Dorrell, Executive Director, Early Childhood Professional Development Network, P.O. Box 5574, Columbia, South Carolina 29250-5574, (800) 476-7345, fax (800) 476-9601.

Source of official student records: Registry of Credit Recommendations, American Council on Education, One Dupont Circle, Washington, DC 20036-1193.

Additional information about the courses: College Credit Recommendation Service, American Council on Education, One Dupont Circle, Washington, DC 20036-1193.

Child Guidance Techniques

Location: Various sites utilizing satellite distance education technology.

Length: 15 hours (5 weeks).

Dates: January 1997-Present.

Objective: To provide knowledge and skills in guiding the behavior of preschool children in a group educational setting using developmentally appropriate methods.

Learning Outcome: Upon successful completion of this course, the student will be able to classify the major causes of conflicts between and among children; employ strategies that bring about peaceful resolution of children's conflicts; conduct relevant observations of children's behavior for purposes of analyzing behavior problems; and communicate to colleagues and parents the steps of converting conflicts in preschool settings.

Instruction: Major topics covered in the course are the major causes of conflict in preschool settings with young children, the philosophy of conflict conversion, the observation skills needed to analyze children's behavior, the influence of teacher behavior of children's behavior, and conflict conversion strategies for each type of conflict. Methods of instruction include video observations in classrooms, interviews with experts and classroom teaching staff, graphics, live interactive discussion, and group exercises.

Credit Recommendation: In the vocational certificate category or in the lower division baccalaureate/associate degree category, 1 semester hour in Early Childhood Development or Child Development (1/97).

Foundations in Early Care and Education (Beyond the Horizon: Quality Matters and Best Practices)

Location: Various sites utilizing satellite distance education technology.

Length: 68 hours (6 weeks).

Dates: August 1994-Present.

Objective: To provide culturally relevant training on high quality standards and best practices to Head Start and early childhood staff in pacific territories.

Learning Outcome: Upon successful completion of this course, the student will be able to identify indicators of quality in the classrooms; and implement standards of quality in the areas of health, safety, setting up learning environments, selecting and implementing developmentally appropriate activities in all curriculum areas, work cooperatively with parents, recognize community partnerships, exhibit characteristics of a professional, and recognize role of policy councils and boards.

Instruction: Major topics covered in the course are basic health and safety; learning and young children; indoor and outdoor learning environments; selection and use of purchased and natural materials; curriculum planning; schedules and transitions; curriculum activities in the arts, language, science, math, construction, and physical development; and involvement of parents, building community partnerships, program management, professionalism, policy council, and board relationships. Methods of instruction include video observations in classrooms in all of the pacific territories, interviews with pacific experts and classroom teaching staff, graphics, live interactive discussion, and group exercises.

Credit Recommendation: In the vocational certificate category or in the lower division baccalaureate/associate degree category, 3 semester hours in Early Childhood Development or Child Development (1/97).

Introduction to Early Childhood Education
Early Childhood Education: Quality Matters

Location: Various sites utilizing electronic distance education technology.

Length: 122.5 hours (35 weeks).

Dates: September 1992-Present.

Objective: To provide knowledge and skills needed to work with young children in a manner consistent with developmentally appropriate guidelines.

Learning Outcome: Upon successful completion of this course, the student will be able to develop a safe, healthy, and enriching learning environment that invites learning; advance childrens' affective, cognitive, and psychomotor development; infuse classroom activities with creativity, novelty, and challenge; manage effective and efficient program operation; use appropriate strategies to assess childrens' development; understand and use developmentally appropriate practices throughout the classroom; and establish and maintain partnerships with parents.

Instruction: Major topics covered in the course are an introduction to child development principles, indoor environments, outdoor environments, selecting and making materials, health and nutrition, safety, large motor and movement development and activities, small motor and perceptual development and activities, creativity in the classroom, language development and literacy activities, acquisition of a second language, cognition, discovery and problem solving, children as individuals, peer relationships and developing values, creating a positive classroom environment, child guidance, planning socialization and classroom transitions, parents as partners in Head Start, observing and recording children's behavior, developmental screening and assessment, individualizing the classroom program and lesson planning, parent conferences and home visits, unit teaching and curriculum webs, technology in the classroom, academics in the classroom, inclusion of children with disabilities in the classroom program evaluation, transitions and graduation, building community support systems and families, the early childhood profession, advocacy in early childhood education, career and educational opportunities in early childhood education, and envisioning the future. Methods of instruction include televised lectures, group discussion by telephone conference calls, audio-visual materials, case studies, and a proctored final examination.

Credit Recommendation: In the vocational certificate category or in the lower division baccalaureate/associate degree category, 9 semester hours in Early Childhood Education, Child Development, Curriculum and Instruction, or Teacher Education (9/95).

ECPI College of Technology

ECPI was founded in the Commonwealth of Virginia in 1966 and operates as two separate institutions: ECPI College of Technology in Virginia Beach and Hampton, Virginia, and in Greensboro and Charlotte, North Carolina; and ECPI Technical College in Roanoke and Richmond, Virginia, and Raleigh, North Carolina. ECPI is an independent private technical college offering students the opportunity to quickly earn an Associate of Applied Science degree, diploma, or certificate.

ECPI has developed programs of study that underscore the central role of computer technology in commerce and industry. Graduates are well equipped to meet the requirements for entry-level employment in an increasingly technical economy while providing the foundation for progressive life-long learning.

Programs of instruction are open to applicants who have earned at least a high school diploma or GED. Applicants must call or write ECPI for a personal interview, and admissions testing is required of applicants.

All ECPI courses are developed in close cooperation with industry and business advisory boards to insure that ECPI is providing the education needed for entry-level employment for today's job market. ECPI assists graduates in finding a job in the field in which they were trained.

The faculty at ECPI possesses both academic credentials and job-related experience. Courses include a combination of lecture and laboratory work with additional emphasis on learning and gaining experience and confidence through hands-on training and internships.

ECPI awards Military Merit Scholarships to a limited number of military personnel and their dependents. A limited number of Merit Scholarships are available to graduating high school seniors enrolling in selected programs. These scholarships range from $300 to $3,000. Computer Electronics Technology is offered both during the day and the evening at all ECPI campuses. Networking and System Administration/Computer Programming is offered at both the Richmond and Virginia Beach Campuses with both day and evening schedules.

Source of official student records: Registry of Credit Recommendations, American Council on Education, One Dupont Circle, Washington, DC 20036-1193.

Additional information about the courses: College Credit Recommendation Service, American Council on Education, One Dupont Circle, Washington, DC 20036-1193.

Accounting I (ACC101) (Formerly AC100)

Location: Virginia Beach, VA; Hampton, VA; Richmond, VA; Roanoke, VA; Raleigh, NC; Greensboro, NC; and Charlotte, NC

Length: 48 hours (2.25 hours, 3 nights per week for 7.5 weeks; 2.25 hours, 5 days per week for 5 weeks).

Dates: September 1994-Present.

Objective: To provide students with a thorough introduction to fundamental accounting concepts and principles, including double-entry bookkeeping, the accounting cycle and the preparation of financial statements, emphasizing the sole proprietorship business form.

Learning Outcome: Upon successful completion of this course, the student will be able to define basic accounting terms and describe how to analyze transactions; utilize double entry accounting for the sake of recording business transactions; utilize accounting concepts such as the flow of financial data through an accounting information system by using standardized terms and reports; explain adjusting and closing transactions and how to calculate and record them; describe the cash basis and accrual basis of accounting and how to complete the accounting cycle; and explain the meanings of the term "cash" as it is used in accounting.

Instruction: Major topics covered in the course are basic concepts of accounting; analyzing business transactions; analyzing business transactions using T-Accounts; using the General Journal and the General Ledger; adjustments and the worksheet; and closing entries and the post-closing trial balance. Methods of instruction include lecture, discussion, classroom exercises, quizzes, tests, comprehensive problem, unit tests, and final examination.

Credit Recommendation: In the lower division baccalaureate/associate degree category, 3 semester hours in Accounting (11/96).

Advanced Electronic Circuits (CT297/CET297) Preparation for Certified Electronics Technician Exam (Formerly CT297)

Location: Virginia Beach, VA; Hampton, VA; Roanoke, VA; Richmond, VA; Greensboro, NC; Charlotte, NC; Raleigh, NC.

Length: 48 hours (7.5 weeks at night; and 5 weeks during days).

Dates: September 1994-Present.

Objective: To provide the student with skills in advanced circuit analysis and with troubleshooting techniques needed by the professional technician, including DC circuits, AC circuits, analog electronic circuits, digital circuits, computer circuits, circuit troubleshooting and repair.

Learning Outcome: Upon successful completion of this course, the student will be able to know and understand basic mathematic principles applied in the electronics and computer fields; basic electrical and electronic theories, components and circuits; component nomenclature and basic decibel theory; digital concepts and computer basics; and basic test equipment and measurements.

Instruction: Major topics covered in the course are electronic math; electrical components; electronic components; series and parallel circuits; semi-conductor devices; decibels; digital concepts; computer circuits; test equipment and troubleshooting. Methods of instruction include lecture, classroom exercises, and four unit tests.

Credit Recommendation: In the lower division baccalaureate/associate degree category, 2 semester hours in Advanced Circuit Analysis and Troubleshooting in preparation for the Certified Electronics Technician (CET) Exam (11/96).

Advanced Relational Database Programming and SQL (PRG250) (Advanced Relational Database Programming) (Formerly DP250)

Location: Virginia Beach, VA; and Richmond, VA.

Length: 48 hours (2.5 hours, 3 nights per week for 7.5 weeks, 2.25 hours, 5 days per week for 5 weeks).

Dates: September 1994-Present.

Objective: To reintroduce the student to database design, normalization, and structured query methodology. In addition to learning how to program for a Network, students learn advanced programming concepts and sophisticated I/O interaction. Students complete laboratory assignments and a case study.

Learning Outcome: Upon successful completion of this course, the student will understand how to code, key-in, compile and test SQL programs; be familiar with object-oriented features of the SQL language; understand the relationships of distributed processing centrally held databases and the consequences of file and record locks; the concept of normalization and relational database design; write more sophisticated interactive SQL programs; use advanced compiler options; and build libraries.

Instruction: Major topics covered in the course are database normalization review; SQL programming review; advanced I/O and system integration; working with procedures and functions; data structures and preprocessor; object orientation and advanced functions; SQL networks and object-oriented programming; libraries; and tools. Methods of instruction include lecture, discussion, computer lab exercises, case study, quizzes, unit tests, and a final examination.

Credit Recommendation: In the upper division baccalaureate degree category, 1 semester hour in SQL, Relational Database, Computer Science and 1 semester hour in SQL Lab, Relational Database (11/96).

Advanced Visual Basic Programming (PRG230) (Formerly DP230)

Location: Virginia Beach, VA; and Richmond, VA

Length: 48 hours 2.25 hours, 3 nights per week for 7.5 weeks, 2.25 hours, 5 days per week for 5 weeks).

Dates: September 1994-Present.

Objective: To provide students with an advanced look at the Visual Basic programming language. Emphasizing understanding the application development process from database front ends, MDI applications, OLEs, database development, graphic programming to Windows APIs and DLLs.

Learning Outcome: Upon successful completion of this course, the student will be familiar with how to design the ideal Visual Basic program; understand MDIs and how to use Windows APIs; be familiar with advanced database front ends, Data Management and Data-Driven Programming; develop on-line help; use OLE controls, add-ins and DLLs; and graphical programming and multimedia programming.

Instruction: Major topics covered in the course are an introduction to Advanced Visual Basic; understanding file system controls; understanding MDIs; using Windows API; displaying and printing; using the grid control; SQL; OLE automation, servers and container classes; media control interface; graphics; developing on-line help; networkable applications; OLE controls, add-ins, and 32-bit DLLs; optimizing Visual Basic code; Visual Basic 4.0 versus Visual Basic for applications; and mixed-language development with DLLs. Methods of instruction include lecture, discussion, computer laboratory exercises, case studies, quizzes, unit tests, and a final examination.

Credit Recommendation: In the lower division baccalaureate/associate degree category, 1 semester hour in Computer Science or Programming; 1 semester hour Programming Lab (11/96).

C Programming (PRG160) (Formerly C Programming in a UNIX Environment [DP160])

Location: Virginia Beach, VA; Richmond, VA.

Length: 96 hours (4.5 hours, 3 nights per week for 7.5 weeks; 4.5 hours, 5 days per week for 5 weeks).

Dates: September 1994-Present.

Objective: To provide students with an understanding of C language programming, while also becoming familiar with the UNIX operating system. Students learn about data types, operators and functions of the C language. Students complete laboratory assignments and a case study.

Learning Outcome: Upon successful completion of this course, the student will be able to code, key-in, compile and test C programs; know how to do arithmetic and assignment operations in C; strengthen top-down, structured programming techniques and know how they are applied to C; and know to use and prototype functions.

Instruction: Major topics covered in the course are introduction to C Programming in a UNIX Environment; definition of a program; developing Programs in C; variables and constants; character arrays and strings; preprocessor directives; input and output; math operators and precedence; the IF / ENDIF statement; logical operators; additional operators; the while loop; for loop; switch and go to statements; writing C functions; variable scope; passing values; function return values and prototypes; device and character I/O; character, string and numeric functions; string and numeric functions; array processing; multidimensional arrays; pointers; pointers and arrays; structures; and arrays of structures. Methods of instruction include lecture, discussion, computer lab exercises, case study, quizzes, unit tests, and a final examination.

Credit Recommendation: In the lower division baccalaureate/associate degree category, 3 semester hours in Computer Science or Computer Programming,1 semester hour in Computer Science Lab (11/96).

Career Preparation (CT190/CET190&CIS100) (Formerly CT190)

Location: Virginia Beach, VA; Hampton, VA; Roanoke, VA; Richmond, VA; Greensboro, NC; Charlotte, NC; and Raleigh, NC.

Length: 15 hours (7.5 weeks at night; 5 weeks during days).

Dates: September 1994-Present.

Objective: To prepare students for correct resume development, job interview procedures, dressing for success skills, career planning, and improving job search skills.

Learning Outcome: Upon successful completion of this course, the student will be able to identify personal skills and talents; define success; set career and personal goals; develop effective communication skills; understand resume building; compose personal resume, cover letter, and list of references; establish ways to search and secure a job interview; be prepared for the interview and potential questions; effectively follow-up after the interview.

Instruction: Major topics covered in the course are world of work; expectations of employers; self assessment; goal setting; communication; manners; grooming; dressing for success; locating the right job; resume building and cover letter writing; securing an interview; interview techniques; accepting the job; and packaging and pacing yourself on the job. Methods of instruction include lecture, discussion, classroom exercises, career package project, and exit evaluation.

Credit Recommendation: In the lower division baccalaureate/associate degree category, 1 semester hour in Professional Development or Career Preparation (11/96).

College Composition (ENG101) (Formerly Composition [GE108])

Location: Virginia Beach, VA; Hampton, VA; Richmond, VA; and Roanoke, VA.

Length: 48 hours (7.5 weeks at night; 5 weeks during days).

Dates: September 1994-Present.

Objective: To provide the student with a thorough introduction to college level composition , examine the writing process of understanding audience and purpose, exploring ideas and information, composing, revising, and editing.

Learning Outcome: Upon successful completion of this course, the student will be able to identify and write thesis statements that are restricted, unified, and precise; organize an essay's content into separately developed paragraphs using clearly stated topic sentences; develop essays that are unified, coherent, and sufficiently developed; select appropriate diction; produce clear, emphatic sentences; apply the fundamentals of grammar; define and use correctly the concepts of subject, audience, and purpose to select, narrow, and develop topics; and use effectively the various rhetorical patterns.

Instruction: Major topics covered in the course are the writing process, essay writing, research writing, essay analysis, effective sentences, sentence revision, and punctuation. Methods of instruction include lecture, presentations, writing labs, quizzes, essays, a final examination, and a research paper.

Credit Recommendation: In the lower division baccalaureate/associate degree category, 3 semester hours in Composition, Writing or Business English (11/96).

Communication (SPH150) (Formerly Communications [GE100])

Location: Virginia Beach, VA; Hampton, VA; Richmond, VA; Roanoke, VA; Charlotte, NC; Greensboro, NC; and Raleigh, NC.

Length: 48 hours (7.5 weeks at night; 5 weeks during days).

Dates: September 1994-Present.

Objective: To provide the student with the necessary skills and knowledge for effective interpersonal and group communication in his/her personal, social, and professional endeavors and to examine such timely topics as sexual harassment, multiculturalism, and verbal obscenity.

Learning Outcome: Upon successful completion of this course, the student will be able to define and explain the components of human communications; define communication apprehension and use techniques to overcome it; compare and contrast intrapersonal communication and interpersonal communication; explain the listening process and use techniques for improving listening; define nonverbal communications and explain different ways we communicate nonverbally; define groups and explain differences in groups; develop and present different types of oral presentations; prepare for an interview.

Instruction: Major topics covered in the course are communication theory, interpersonal and intrapersonal communication, group communication, and public speaking. Methods of instruction include lecture, classroom exercises, student presentations, videos, tests, and three presentations.

Credit Recommendation: In the lower division baccalaureate/associate degree category, 3 semester hours in General Communications, Introduction to Speech or Communications (11/96).

Communication Systems (CT285/CET285) (Formerly CT285)

Location: Virginia Beach, VA; Hampton, VA; Roanoke, VA; Richmond, VA; Greensboro, NC; Charlotte, NC; and Raleigh, NC.

Length: 48 hours (7.5 weeks at night; 5 weeks during days).

Dates: September 1994-Present.

Objective: To introduce the student to the fundamentals of analog and digital communications, amplitude, frequency and phase modulation, receiver and transmitter basics, digital communications techniques such as coding, format, protocols and error detection/correction, and modems and the telephone system.

Learning Outcome: Upon successful completion of this course, the student will be able to describe AM and FM communication systems to include the electromagnetic spectrum and the use of decibels as a measurement unit; describe the concept of a digital communications system to include the use of protocols and the key elements required in digital systems; describe digital modulation and testing; describe the telephone system and the handshake signals that must be used by a modem when connecting a computer to the telephone network.

Instruction: Major topics covered in the course are the electro-magnetic spectrum; decibels and noise; amplitude modulation; frequency and phase modulation; digital information; digital communication systems; digital modulation and testing; and the telephone system. Methods of instruction include lecture, discussion, and three unit tests.

Credit Recommendation: In the lower division baccalaureate/associate degree category, 2 semester hours in Electronic Communications (11/96).

Computer Applications (CT125/CET125) (Formerly CT125)

Location: Virginia Beach, VA; Hampton, VA; Roanoke, VA; Richmond, VA; Greensboro, NC; Charlotte, NC; and Raleigh, NC.

Length: 48 hours (7.5 weeks at night; 5 weeks during days).

Dates: September 1994-Present.

Objective: To introduce students to computer concepts, realistic problem-solving using general applications software, and experience using three major microcomputer software applications in word processing, spreadsheets and database management.

Learning Outcome: Upon successful completion of this course, the student will be able to boot a system, and explain the roles that AUTOEXEC.BAT and CONFIG.SYS play in booting; describe the concept of a graphical user interface and know why Microsoft Windows 3.1 is used; start and exit Windows; use the mouse to select menus, commands and icons; start and exit an application; control the size and placement of a window; use Windows' on-line help feature to receive help on any subject; use and recognize group windows and program icons; switch between different application windows and organize application windows, application icons, and group windows; use the File Manager application for many different disk and file maintenance procedures; describe what a computer is and how it processes data; identify and describe the key features of general microcomputer software applications; describe data, how it is processed on the computer, and the need for data management; list the widely used data entry devices and data media; explain the internal operations of a computer system; describe the different types of output which can be obtained from the computer and the different types of devices used for output; describe how auxiliary storage is used to store data and programs for future use.

Instruction: Major topics covered in the course are basic operations; file management; creating documents; formatting documents; advanced editing and multiple files; graphics; columns; tables; template; creating spreadsheets; changing worksheet formats; charting features; creating database tables and forms; database queries and modifications; creating reports and two table queries; and enhancing database applications. Methods of instruction include lecture, discussion, classroom exercises, laboratory exercises, and tests.

Credit Recommendation: In the lower division baccalaureate/associate degree category, 1 semester hour in Microcomputer Applications or 1 semester hour in Microcomputer Lab (11/96). **NOTE:** This course is similar to DP120 Microcomputer

Applications and credit is recommended for either one but not both.

Computer Communications and Networks (CT200/CET200) (Formerly CT200)

Location: Virginia Beach, VA; Hampton, VA; Roanoke, VA; Richmond, VA; Greensboro, NC; Charlotte, NC; and Raleigh, NC.

Length: 96 hours (7.5 weeks at night; 5 weeks during days).

Dates: September 1994-Present.

Objective: To give students an introduction to data communications, local area networks, terminology and fundamental concepts, network hardware and software, Novell NetWare applications, software installation, controlling user accounts, login scripts, trustee rights and network printing.

Learning Outcome: Upon successful completion of this course, the student will be able to describe data communications, data communication networks, and data communication systems; state the purpose and common types of communication media used in data communication networks; understand the benefits of networking; describe the characteristics of a network server system; understand the capabilities of the network supervisor, of groups and of network managers; understand the concepts of network printing; and understand the benefits of using network menus.

Instruction: Major topics covered in the course are communication networks, services, hardware, network basics, Novell NetWare installation, SYSCON, log in scripts, system security, organization and management, workstation customization, network printing, and menus. Methods of instruction include lecture, discussion, classroom exercises, laboratory exercises, and four unit tests, and final examination .

Credit Recommendation: In the upper division baccalaureate degree category, 3 semester hours in Computer Science and 1 semester hour in Networking Lab (11/96).

Computer Peripherals (CT202/CET202) (Formerly CT202)

Location: Virginia Beach, VA; Hampton, VA; Roanoke, VA; Richmond, VA; Greensboro, NC; Charlotte, NC; and Raleigh, NC.

Length: 48 hours (7.5 weeks at night; 5 weeks during days).

Dates: September 1994-Present.

Objective: To give the student an introduction to computer peripheral devices and their internal functions, operation, maintenance, troubleshooting, and repair.

Learning Outcome: Upon successful completion of this course, the student will be able to understand the use and operation of floppy and hard disk drives; demonstrate the ability to disassemble and reassemble floppy and hard disk drives; understand the working theory of other storage devices such as tape drives; understand the internal workings of the PC Keyboard and the methods of cleaning keyboards; demonstrate the ability to disassemble, clean and reassemble the PC's Keyboard using good working procedures; and understand the internal works of an optical scanner and digitizer. Install and configure a scanner system; understand and demonstrate methods of disassembly, cleaning and reassembly of various input devices such as a mouse; discuss the various printer types including maintenance, cleaning and repair of those devices; disassemble, troubleshoot, repair, clean and reassemble various types of printers; discuss the workings of various displays and adapters; understand lecture/demonstration of instructor of monitor devices; understand the concept of various network equipment and topology designs; comprehend modem equipment and how they function; disassemble, clean and repair modem equipment; understand, terminals, music generation, and speech recognition equipment; and use software to load, configure and diagnose systems operation.

Instruction: Major topics covered in the course are introduction to peripherals, disk drives, tape drives and other storage devices, keyboards, optical scanners and digitizers, the mouse, printers, displays, local area networks, modems, terminals and character codes, music and sound generation, speech synthesis and recognition, and interfacing and software. Methods of instruction include lecture, discussion, laboratory exercises, three unit tests and a final project.

Credit Recommendation: In the lower division baccalaureate/associate degree category, 1 semester hour in Computer Repair and 1 semester hour in Computer Repair Lab (11/96).

Critical Thinking (ENG205) (Formerly GE160)

Location: Virginia Beach, VA; Hampton, VA; Richmond, VA; and Roanoke, VA.

Length: 48 hours (7.5 weeks at night; 5 weeks during days).

Dates: September 1994-Present.

Objective: To provide the student with an introduction to two foundational concepts of humanities, critical and creative thinking; to examine the importance of looking at issues from multiple perspectives; and to analyze deductive and inductive logic.

Learning Outcome: Upon successful completion of this course, the student will be able to define critical and creative thinking; explain the value of asking questions in critical thinking and developing questions to examine issues; to explain and use a five-step problem solving method in analyzing conceptual and real life problems and issues; define the concepts and use specific skills that support creative and critical thinking (differences in perceiving, believing, knowing, language systems, concept development, relating and organizing ideas, and distinguishing between reporting, inferring, and judging); and define, analyze, and evaluate deductive and inductive arguments.

Instruction: Major topics covered in the course include thinking, thinking critically, creative thinking, solving problems, perceiving, believing and knowing, language as a system and a tool, forming and applying concepts, relating and organizing, reporting, inferring, judging, constructing arguments, and reasoning critically. Methods of instruction include lecture, classroom exercises, learner presentations, reports, tests, essays, research paper, oral presentation, and final examination.

Credit Recommendation: In the lower division baccalaureate/associate degree category, 3 semester hours in English (11/96).

Customer Relations (CT193/CET193) (Formerly CT193)

Location: Virginia Beach, VA; Hampton, VA; Roanoke, VA; Richmond, VA; Greensboro, NC; Charlotte, NC; and Raleigh, NC.

Length: 30 hours (7.5 weeks at night; 5 weeks during days).

Dates: September 1994-Present.

Objective: To teach the student skills needed by field service technicians in customer relations, understanding people, communication, perception, and self-concept.

Learning Outcome: Upon successful completion of this course, the student will be able to describe the term customer relations; identify the basic behavioral science concepts needed to better understand people; discuss the term communications and how effective communication is an asset to proper customer relations; describe and discuss non-verbal communications; describe how personal perceptions effect relations with customers; state what the causes of defensiveness are and how they can be avoided with customers; discuss why a proper self-concept is important in customer relations; and describe the difference in the terms explaining and persuading.

Instruction: Major topics covered in the course are introduction to customer relations, understanding people, communication, nonverbal communication, perception, defensiveness and self-concept, explaining, persuasion, complaints, and having the last word. Methods of instruction include lecture, discussion, role playing, classroom exercises, quizzes, and three unit tests.

Credit Recommendation: In the lower division baccalaureate/associate degree category, 2 semester hours in Customer Relations (11/96).

Digital Technology (CT146) or Digital Technology I & II (CET149 & CET150) (Formerly Digital Technology [CT146])

Location: Virginia Beach, VA; Hampton, VA; Roanoke, VA; Richmond, VA; Greensboro, NC; Charlotte, NC; Raleigh, NC.

Length: 96 hours (7.5 weeks at night, 5 weeks during days).

Dates: September 1994-Present.

Objective: To provide the student with the basic theory and knowledge of digital logic, computer numbering systems, basic logic gates, digital integrated circuit technology, digital circuits such as flip-flops, counters, registers, arithmetic units, coding circuits, and analysis of digital devices, and circuits using basic test equipment.

Learning Outcome: Upon successful completion of this course, the student will be able to know and understand digital counters, shift registers, arithmetic circuits, memory circuits and analog and digital connection devices; and conduct laboratory experiments using practical, commercially available integrated digital circuits.

Instruction: Major topics covered in the course are numbering systems, binary logic gates, integrated circuit specifications and interfaces, encoders, decoders, seven segment displays, flip-flops, counters, registers, arithmetic units, memories and digital systems, analog to digital converters, digital to analog converters, and troubleshooting. Methods of instruction include lecture, discussion, laboratory exercises, three unit tests, and one performance test.

Credit Recommendation: In the lower division baccalaureate/associate degree category, 5 semester hours in Digital Circuits and Analyses (4 hours lecture, 1 hour lab) (11/96).

Disk Operating System (CT151/CET151) (Formerly CT151)

Location: Virginia Beach, VA; Hampton, VA; Roanoke, VA; Richmond, VA; Greensboro, NC; Charlotte, NC; and Raleigh, NC.

Length: 48 hours (7.5 weeks at night; 5 weeks during days).

Dates: September 1994-Present.

Objective: To provide the student with practical experience in using the disk operating system to manage files, work with hard drives, modify default settings, and determine system requirements.

Learning Outcome: Upon successful completion of this course, the student will be able to describe an operation system; describe the process of executing commands, specifying drives and preparing disks for use; identify commands for managing files, directories, and hard disks; identify commands for using redirection, filters, and pipes; describe concepts of and identify commands for working with text, batch, and system files; and use the DOS shell program for basic operating system tasks.

Instruction: Major topics covered in the course are hardware and software basics, DOS basics, working with disks, creating and displaying files, working with directories, copying files, deleting files, moving files, redirecting input/output and sorting, DOS shell, DOS editor, creating batch files, backup, and other hard disk tasks. Methods of instruction include lecture, discussion, classroom exercises, laboratory exercises, and tests.

Credit Recommendation: In the lower division baccalaureate/associate degree category, 2 semester hours in Microcomputer Applications Lab (11/96). Note: This course is similar to OT135 Introduc-tion to Disk Operating Systems and credit is recommended for either one, but not for both.

Electric Circuits (CT133/CET133) (CT133 Electricity Fundamentals) (Formerly CT133)

Location: Virginia Beach, VA; Hampton, VA; Roanoke, VA; Richmond, VA; Greensboro, NC; Charlotte, NC; and Raleigh, NC.

Length: 96 hours (7.5 weeks at night; 5 weeks during days).

Dates: September 1994-Present.

Objective: To introduce the student to series, parallel and combination circuits; basic concepts of alternating current (AC) theory, including AC signals, capacitors, inductors and transformers; and analysis of DC circuits using basic test equipment and oscilloscopes for basic AC circuit analysis.

Learning Outcome: Upon successful completion of this course, the student will be able to develop an understanding of electrical and electronic circuits; understand the concepts of voltage, current and resistance as they pertain to DC and AC circuits; identify discrete electrical and electronic components as schematic symbols and actual components; identify electrical and electronic component markings; understand the operation of electrical and electronic components as discrete devices and as they operate in complete circuits; and conduct laboratory experiments using electrical and electronic components as discrete devices and in complete circuits.

Instruction: Major topics covered in the course are series circuits; parallel circuits; series-parallel combination circuits; magnetism and electromagnetism; alternating current and voltage; capacitors; inductors; transformers; RC circuits; RL circuits; resonance; and troubleshooting. Methods of instruction include lecture, discussion, classroom exercises, laboratory exercises, three unit tests, and one performance test.

Credit Recommendation: In the lower division baccalaureate/associate degree category, 5 semester hours in DC and AC Circuit Analysis (4 hours lecture and 1 hour lab) (11/96).

Electronics Internship (CT250/CET250) (Formerly CT250)

Location: Virginia Beach, VA; Hampton, VA; Roanoke, VA; Richmond, NC; Greensboro, NC; Charlotte, NC; and Raleigh, NC.

Length: 90 hours (7.5 weeks at night; 5 weeks during days).

Dates: September 1994-Present.

Objective: To provide the student with a school-coordinated work experience in a technical facility setting where skills can be obtained to include, demonstrating knowledge of computer hardware and software, working with others, dressing for the work place, assuming training-related responsibilities, and acquiring constructive employer feedback.

Learning Outcome: Upon successful completion of this course, the student will be able to demonstrate the ability to function independently in a technical facility setting that utilizes computer hardware and software; demonstrate enthusiasm, punctuality, perseverance, dependability, and the ability to follow instructions; show an awareness of business and effective communication skills; maintain excellent attendance; dress professionally; and demonstrate good customer relations skills using appropriate grammar and language.

Instruction: Major topics covered in the course are computer hardware and software experience, and on-the-job experience. Methods of instruction include on-the-job experience in a training-related setting , observations, and reports.

Credit Recommendation: In the lower division baccalaureate/associate degree category, 2 semester hours in Electronics Internship (11/96).

Electronics Technology (CT145) or Electronics Technology I & II (CET147/CET148) (Formerly Electronics Technology [CT145])

Location: Virginia Beach, VA; Hampton, VA; Roanoke, VA; Richmond, VA; Greensboro, NC; Charlotte, NC; and Raleigh, NC.

Length: 96 hours (7.5 weeks at night; 5 weeks during days).

Dates: September 1994-Present.

Objective: To provide the student with the theory and operation of analog electronic devices and circuits such as diodes, transistors, power supplies, basic amplifiers, operational amplifiers, oscillators, integrated circuits, control circuits, regulated power supplies, multi-vibrators, and analysis of electronic circuits using basic test equipment and oscilloscopes.

Learning Outcome: Upon successful completion of this course, the student will be able to recognize, test, and describe the basic operation of diodes, transistors, and power supplies; analyze the operation of the audio amplifier and the operational amplifier; and conduct laboratory experiments with integrated circuits.

Instruction: Major topics covered in the course are semiconductors, diodes, power supplies, transistors, small signal amplifiers, large signal amplifiers, operational amplifiers, oscillators, radio receivers, control devices, and regulated power supplies. Methods of instruction include lecture, discussion, laboratory exercises, four unit tests, and a performance test.

Credit Recommendation: In the lower division baccalaureate/associate degree category, 5 semester hours in Electronic Devices and Circuits (4 hours lecture and1 hour lab) (11/96).

Enterprise Networking or Networking Environment(Cross Platform Connectivity) (DP280)

Location: Virginia Beach, VA; Richmond, VA; Hampton, VA; and Roanoke, VA.

Length: 48 hours (2.25 hours, 3 nights per week for 7.5 weeks; 2.25 hours, 5 days per week for 5 weeks).

Dates: May 1996-Present.

Objective: To introduce students to the wide area enterprise network environment; teach the steps for building a distributed network; and discuss different networking platforms, protocols, and procedures.

Learning Outcome: Upon successful completion of this course, the student will be familiar with the way networks are used in business today and how they have evolved from main-frame based technology; know the characteristics of a successful network in a multi-platform environment; be aware of the various technologies available to the network designer; and be able to discuss security and management issues as they apply to wide area, enterprise networks.

Instruction: Major topics covered in the course are the new enterprise; production-quality enterprise networks; steps toward a network architecture; theory of building distributed networks; and networking platforms, protocols, and management. Methods of instruction include lecture, discussion, classroom exercises, case study, quizzes, unit tests, and a final examination.

Credit Recommendation: In the upper division baccalaureate degree category, 2 semester hours in Networking, Telecommunications or Computer Science (11/96).

Fiber Optic Communications (CT272/CET272) (Formerly CT272)

Location: Virginia Beach, VA; Hampton, VA; Roanoke, VA; Richmond, VA; Greensboro, NC; Charlotte, NC; and Raleigh, NC.

Length: 48 hours (7.5 weeks at night; 5 weeks during days).

Dates: September 1994-Present.

Objective: To introduce the student to the principles of operation and specifications of optoelectronic and laser components, and what the uses are in communication systems, receivers and transmitters.

Learning Outcome: Upon successful completion of this course, the student will be able to define Optoelectronic Terminology; describe semiconductor physics; define and describe Electroluminescence and Electroluminescent devices; describe Photo detection principles; identify and describe laser optics and laser applications; and identify and describe optical fibers, cables, connectors and the fiber optic system.

Instruction: Major topics covered in the course are information transmission; fiber optics as a communication medium and its advantages; theory of light; optical fiber; fiber characteristics; fiber optic cables; sources; detectors; transmitters and receivers; connectors; splices; couplers; fiber optic links; fiber optic cables installation and hardware; fiber optic systems and applications; and test equipment and other equipment. Methods of instruction include lecture, discussion, classroom exercises, and four unit tests.

Credit Recommendation: In the lower division baccalaureate/associate degree category, 2 semester hours in Fiberoptics Communications (11/96).

General Mathematics (MTH101) (Formerly Basic Mathematics (General Mathematics) [GE131])

Location: Virginia Beach, VA; Hampton, VA; Richmond, VA; and Roanoke, VA.

Length: 48 hours (7.5 weeks at night; 5 weeks during days).

Dates: September 1994-Present.

Objective: To provide the student with an introduction to basic arithmetic operations in whole numbers, fractions, decimals, percent, geometric formulae, and with an introduction to signed numbers.

Learning Outcome: Upon successful completion of this course, the student will be able to demonstrate understanding of whole numbers: place value, addition, subtraction, multiplication, division, and solving related word problems; to work with rational numbers: addition and subtraction of like and unlike denominators, mixed fractions and improper fractions, multiplication, division, ratio, and proportion; to recognize decimals as another form of rational numbers and to perform all mathematical operations without the use of a hand-held calculator; to work with percents; to read various types of graphs and to find statistical information from a set of data; to demonstrate a knowledge of integers; and to solve simple algebraic equations.

Instruction: Major topics covered in the course include whole numbers, fractions, decimals, ratios and proportions, percents (to include business applications), statistics, U.S. customary units of measurement, the metric system of measurement, rational numbers, and basic algebra. Methods of instruction include lecture, videos, computer assisted programs, classroom exercises, quizzes, tests, and final examination.

Credit Recommendation: In the lower division baccalaureate/associate degree category, 3 semester hours in Basic Mathematics (11/96).

Industrial Electronics (CT277/CET277) (Formerly CT277)

Location: Virginia Beach, VA; Hampton, VA; Roanoke, VA; Richmond, VA; Greensboro, NC; Charlotte, NC; and Raleigh, NC.

Length: 48 hours (7.5 weeks at night; 5 weeks during days).

Dates: September 1994-Present.

Objective: To provide the student with advanced knowledge of operational amplifiers, linear integrated circuits, motors, switches, transducers, power control circuits, industrial process control, and sequential process control as they apply to industrial control applications.

Learning Outcome: Upon successful completion of this course, the student will be able to describe the circuit operation of instrumentation amplifiers and CDA amplifiers; describe the operation of a relay, including schematic diagrams, logic diagrams and logical connections for relay applications; describe basic motor operations, including DC motor theory and AC motor theory; discuss applications for DC motors, AC motors and the stepper motor; calculate the voltage and current values for Delta and Wye connected three phase power; describe the circuit operation for various power control circuits used in DC and AC motor speed control circuits; describe the properties of light, including fiber optic applications and principles; and describe the parts of a Programmable Logic Controller and the basic structure of instructions used with the PLC.

Instruction: Major topics covered in the course are operational amplifiers; linear integrated circuits; relays; motors; switches; transducers; power control circuits; and industrial process control and sequential process control. Methods of instruction include lecture, discussion, classroom exercises, lab, quizzes, observations, and projects.

Credit Recommendation: In the lower division baccalaureate/associate degree category, 2 semester hours in Industrial Electronics (11/96).

Introduction to Algebra (MTH105) (Formerly Elementary Algebra (Introductory Algebra) [GE137])

Location: Virginia Beach, VA; Hampton, VA; Richmond, VA; and Roanoke, VA.

Length: 48 hours (7.5 weeks at night; 5 weeks during days).

Dates: September 1994-Present.

Objective: To provide the student with an introduction to solving algebraic operations using real numbers, variable expressions, general equations, polynomials, factoring, rational expressions, linear equations, inequalities, radical expressions, and quadratic equations.

Learning Outcome: Upon successful completion of this course, the student will be able to solve problems using real numbers; evaluate and solve variable expressions; solve general equations; add, subtract, divide, and multiply using polynomials; factor; simplify and solve problems using rational expressions; solve and graph linear equations; solve systems of linear equations; solve inequalities; simplify and solve radical expressions; and solve quadratic equations.

Instruction: Major topics covered in the course include real numbers, variable expressions, solving equations, polynomials, factoring, rational expressions, linear equations in two variables, systems of linear equations, inequalities, radical expressions, and quadratic equations. Methods of instruction include lecture, videos, computer assisted programs, and classroom exercises, quizzes, tests, and final examination.

Credit Recommendation: In the lower division baccalaureate/associate degree category, 3 semester hours in Elementary Algebra (11/96).

Introduction to Economics (ECO101) (Formerly Principles of Economics [GE106])

Location: Virginia Beach, VA; Hampton, VA; Richmond, VA; and Roanoke, VA.

Length: 48 hours (7.5 weeks at night; 5 weeks during days).

Dates: September 1994-Present.

Objective: To provide the student with an understanding of the general economic issues and concepts; examine micro-economics by exploring individual market interactions; and the production, distribution, and consumption by individual consumers, firms, and industry.

Learning Outcome: Upon successful completion of this course, the student will be able to identify the economics of personal social choice, use and comprehend the demand schedule and demand curve, identify the basic factors concerning the market structure, and describe and explain the government's role in the nation's economy.

Instruction: Major topics covered in the course are scarcity and economics; law of demand; law of supply; shortages, surpluses, and prices; production, profits, and marginal analysis; competition and monopoly; jobs and wages; market failure and government failure; trade among nations; and an overview of macroeconomics. Methods of instruction include lecture, presentations, videos, tests, reports, and a major project.

Credit Recommendation: In the lower division baccalaureate/associate degree category, 3 semester hours in Economics (11/96).

Introduction to Electronics and Shop Practices (CT103/CT160/CET103/CET160) (CT103/CET103 Introduction to Electronic Mathematics/ CT160/CET160 Principles of Applied Mechanics) (Formerly CT103/CT160)

Location: Virginia Beach, VA; Hampton, VA; Roanoke, VA; Richmond, VA; Greensboro, NC; Charlotte, NC; and Raleigh, NC.

Length: 96 hours (15 weeks at night; 10 weeks during days).

Dates: September 1994-Present.

Objective: To provide the student with the necessary skills required to perform numerical calculations encountered in electricity and electronics, and an understanding of the use of Ohms Law and the three basic power formulas to solve for unknown electrical quantities and to measure these quantities; introduce principles involved in equipment troubleshooting, repair and maintenance; mechanical concepts; applications in mechanical technology; and practice with soldering tools and hand tools.

Learning Outcome: Upon successful completion of this course, the student will be able to add, subtract, multiply and divide a group of fractions and decimal numbers; perform the following mathematical operations on decimal numbers: ratios, rounding off and percentages; add, subtract, multiply and divide a group of signed decimal numbers; determine the absolute value of a group of numbers with square roots and exponents; convert numbers to powers of ten and engineering notation; transpose equations and common electrical and electronic formulas to solve for an unknown quantity; describe the concepts of voltage, current, resistance, and power; solve for any unknown value in the Ohms Law formula or any of the three power formulas using the proper unit of measure; conduct laboratory experiments using electrical and electronic components as discrete devices and in complete circuits; and demonstrate soldering skills, tool use and safety, gear and pulley ratios, and component identification.

Instruction: Major topics covered in the course are fractions, decimals, engineering notation and formula transposition, including a review of trigonometry; the concepts of current flow; resistance; power and voltage; to include the use of Ohms Law and the three basic power formulas; and the measurement of voltage, current, and resistance using basic test equipment; hand tools; soldering; wire splicing; and general shop practices will be covered. Methods of instruction include lecture, discussion, classroom exercises, laboratory exercises, and seven unit tests.

Credit Recommendation: In the lower division baccalaureate/associate degree category, 4 semester hours in Introduction to Electronics and Shop Practices (3 hours in lecture and 1 semester hour in lab) (11/96).

Introduction to Operating Systems (CSA140) (Formerly Introduction to Disk Operating Systems [OT135])

Location: Virginia Beach, VA; Hampton, VA; Richmond, VA; Roanoke, VA; Raleigh, NC; Greensboro, NC; and Charlotte, NC.

Length: 48 hours (2.25 hours, 3 nights per week for 7.5 weeks; 2.25 hours, 5 days per week for 5 weeks).

Dates: May 1996-Present.

Objective: To provide students with an overview of the IBM (Microsoft) DOS operating system, and Windows graphical user interface, including functions, differences between versions, and loading/upgrades; introduces popular hardware and software terminology and buzzwords; and demonstrate how to use the Disk Operating System and Windows.

Learning Outcome: Upon successful completion of this course, the student will be familiar with PC hardware and software basics; know how to boot the system; know how to work with disks, including formatting, viewing contents, and copying data files between disks; know how to name files; know how to create text files; be able to work with directories and paths; be able to copy, move, delete, and undelete files; know how to redirect input and output and sort files; be familiar with batch files; understand parts of a window and understand menus and dialog boxes; use Program Manager, run programs, and switch between applications in a Windows environment; use File Manager to work with files and directories; customize Windows with the Control Panel; and use Print Manager to view the print queue and cancel print jobs.

Instruction: Major topics covered in the course are introduction to disk operating systems; working with disks; creating and displaying files; working with directories; copying, moving, and deleting files; using the DOS editor; creating batch files; introduction to Windows; using the File Manager; using the Print Manager; customizing Windows with the Control Panel; copying material With the Clipboard; and sharing information among applications. Methods of instruction include lecture, discussion, classroom computer laboratory exercises, reports, quizzes, unit tests, and final examination.

Credit Recommendation: In the lower division baccalaureate/associate degree category, 2 semester hours in Computer Science Lab (11/96).

Introduction to Psychology (PSY101) (Formerly Principles of Psychology [GE111])

Location: Virginia Beach, VA; Hampton, VA; Richmond, VA; and Roanoke, VA.

Length: 48 hours (7.5 weeks at night; 5 weeks during days).

Dates: September 1994-Present.

Objective: To provide the student with an introduction to the science of psychology; and examine the areas of motivation, emotion, attitude, personality, states of consciousness, cognition, life span development, different types of therapies, social psychology, and human diversity.

Learning Outcome: Upon successful completion of this course, the student will be able to summarize the goals of psychology; define motive and emotion and explain the roles of stimulus, behavior, and goals in motivation; define personality and distinguish between different theories of personality; define stress and identify sources of stress; define and explain the various states of consciousness; define cognition and explain the role of language; explain the problem solving process; discuss the different stages of life span development; explain the major types of therapies; and define culture and explain cultural differences.

Instruction: Major topics covered in the course include the science of psychology, motivation, emotion, personality, states of consciousness, cognition, life span development, therapies, and social psychology, and human diversity. Methods of instruction include lecture, presentations, videos, classroom exercises, tests, papers, and final examination.

Credit Recommendation: In the lower division baccalaureate/associate degree category, 3 semester hours in Psychology (11/96).

Microcomputer Applications (PRG120) (Formerly DP120)

Location: Virginia Beach, VA; and Richmond, VA.

Length: 48 hours (2.25 hours, 3 nights per week for 7.5 weeks; 2.25 hours, 5 days per week for 5 weeks).

Dates: September 1994-Present.

Objective: To provide students with an introduction to realistic problem-solving using general application software; Microsoft's Windows word processing; spreadsheet; and database applications are covered.

Learning Outcome: Upon successful completion of this course, the student will be able to create, update, save, and print documents; create and update spreadsheets; and create and update database tables and forms and do queries.

Instruction: Major topics covered in the course are an introduction to microcomputer applications; basic Windows operations; File Management in Windows; introducing Microsoft Word 6.0 for Windows; creating documents; formatting documents; advanced editing and multiple files; graphics, columns, templates, and tables; introducing Microsoft Excel 5.0; creating a spreadsheet; changing the worksheet format; modifying the worksheet; using charting features; introducing

Microsoft Access 2.0; creating database tables and forms; database queries and modifications; creating reports and two table queries; and enhancing database applications. Methods of instruction include lecture, discussion, classroom computer laboratory exercises, unit tests, and final examination.

Credit Recommendation: In the lower division baccalaureate/associate degree category, 1 semester hour in Computer Science and 1 semester hour in Computer Science Lab (11/96). **NOTE:** This course is similar to CT125/CET125 Computer Applications and credit is recommended for either one, but not both.

Microcomputer Upgrade and Maintenance (CT201/CET201) (Formerly CT201)

Location: Virginia Beach, VA; Hampton, VA; Roanoke, VA; Richmond, VA; Greensboro, NC; Charlotte, NC; and Raleigh, NC.

Length: 48 hours (7.5 weeks at night; 5 weeks during days).

Dates: September 1994-Present.

Objective: To give students the skills needed to upgrade, maintain and repair personal computers (PC's) using diagnostic software, memory expansion, and hard drive replacement.

Learning Outcome: Upon successful completion of this course, the student will be able to understand the use of operating system commands; understand the working theory of PC components including processors, memory, system boards, power supplies, expansion slots and various other internal components; demonstrate the ability to disassemble and reassemble PC's using various tools and procedures; install and configure PC hardware including hard and floppy drives; install and run various software packages; resolve interrupt conflicts as they occur; and use external diagnostics and proper troubleshooting procedures to repair PC's.

Instruction: Major topics covered in the course are DOS review, disassembly and reassembly procedures, inside the PC, system mapping, preventive maintenance practices, troubleshooting theory, circuit board conflicts (IRQ's and DMA's), power supplies, hard disks, floppy disks, SCSI overview, external devices, and hooking up systems. Methods of instruction include lecture, discussion, laboratory exercises, four unit tests, and a final project.

Credit Recommendation: In the lower division baccalaureate/associate degree category, 2 semester hours in Microcomputer Repair and Maintenance (11/96).

Network Applications Administration (PRG270) (Formerly Network Applications Administration [DP172])

Location: Virginia Beach, VA; Hampton, VA; Richmond, VA; Roanoke, VA; Raleigh, NC; Greensboro, NC; and Charlotte, NC.

Length: 48 hours (2.25 hours, 3 nights per week for 7.5 weeks; 2.25 hours, 5 days per week for 5 weeks).

Dates: May 1996-Present.

Objective: To prepare students for performing the functions of a network administrator, including issues of management, security, procedures and documentation, as well as considerations for managing software applications on the network. The CNA Certification is used as a study guide in order to thoroughly cover all aspects of managing a Novell network.

Learning Outcome: Upon successful completion of this course, the student will be able to perform the functions of a network administrator, including setting up the network and managing the day to day activities of the network; be familiar with the CNA certification and its professional value; be familiar with all of the topics that are covered on the CNA certification exam; and be able to install and run application software on the network.

Instruction: Major topics covered in the course are Microcomputer/DOS fundamentals; NetWare basics:system management; hardware basics; NetWare basics: software basics; Running Applications; NetWare 3.12 directory structure; the NetWare security model and special users accounts; login/password security and login restrictions; access rights and attributes; security command line utilities; Netware 3.12 menu utilities and supervisor utilities; console commands and NetWare loadable modules; Network management strategies; managing the NetWare workstation; user interface; NetWare backup and remote management; NetWare printing; printing setup; printing performance optimization, maintenance, and troubleshooting and customization; NetWare 3.12 performance management; monitoring and optimizing server performance. Methods of instruction include lecture, discussion, classroom exercises, case studies, quizzes, unit tests, and final examination.

Credit Recommendation: In the upper division baccalaureate degree category, 2 semester hours in Networking or Data Communications (11/96).

Network Installation and Administration (Advanced Network Administration) (DP275)

Location: Virginia Beach, VA; Richmond, VA; Hampton, VA; and Roanoke, VA

Length: 48 hours (2.25 hours, 3 nights per week for 7.5 weeks; 2.25 hours, 5 days per week for 5 weeks).

Dates: May 1996-Present.

Objective: To introduce students to the many new features of Novell's NetWare 4 networks and is designed for the student who is already comfortable working in the 3.x environment. The course focuses on the new features and on how to migrate from an existing 3.x network to a 4.x network.

Learning Outcome: Upon successful completion of this course, the student will be able to implement the QuickPath Process to install or migrate a network to NetWare 4; understand the use of NetWare Directory Services (NDS) objects and be able to design an NDS tree; be able to create a migration and installation schedule; be able to discuss security and management issues as they apply to NetWare 4; and be able to perform the day-to-day operations involved in managing a NetWare 4 network.

Instruction: Major topics covered in the course are the QuickPath process and using NDS objects; directory services; partition, replication, and time synchronization; accessing Netware Directory Services; preparing for migration and setting up a pilot system; migrating workstations and servers; print services and utilities; and NDS and security. Methods of instruction include lecture, discussion, classroom exercises, case study, quizzes, unit tests, and final examination.

Credit Recommendation: In the lower division baccalaureate/associate degree category, 1 semester hour in Telecommunications, Networking and 1 semester hour in Telecommunications, Networking Lab (11/96).

Networking and Telecommunications (PRG170) (Formerly DP170)

Location: Virginia Beach, VA; Richmond, VA.

Length: 96 hours (4.5 hours, 3 nights per week for 7.5 weeks; 4.5 hours, 5 days per week for 5 weeks).

Dates: September 1994-Present.

Objective: To give students an understanding of local-area networks, including installation, configuration, and management of a NetWare LAN; and enhancement of the network, such as menus, CD-ROMs, electronic mail, and fax servers .

Learning Outcome: Upon successful completion of this course, the student will be able to describe the benefits of a local-area network and list its components; compare the differences between NetWare versions; describe the various network types, including details regarding architecture and topology; install NetWare 3.12 on the server, and install network interface cards and the NetWare Requester on the workstations; use the MAP command to assign drive letters to server volumes and directories; create users and manage user and group accounts; describe the eight NetWare trustee directory assignments and assign rights to users; create and configure print servers and print queues; create user login scripts, using a variety of commands and variables; use FCONSOLE to manage the network from a workstation; explain the use of NLMs (NetWare Loadable Modules) and use simple console commands; describe and create a network management plan; create, compile, and run a NetWare 3.12 menu script; describe the benefits of using network-based software packages; list the hardware requirements for implementation of CD-ROM sharing; Install and use Basic MHS with FirstMail; describe the use of NetWare with Windows, Windows for Workgroups, OS/2, and Macintosh workstations; and describe the TCP/IP protocol, and discuss its use with NetWare.

Instruction: Major topics covered in the course are introduction to networking and telecommunications; exploring the benefits of networking; understanding the components of a network; introducing NetWare 3.12; choosing the right server hardware; network communications; installing NetWare 3.12; activating workstations; organizing information on a NetWare server; adding users; understanding directory and file rights; managing files; NetWare Security; implementing shared printing; using shared printers; creating login scripts; implementing NetWare Accounting; managing your network from a workstation; using the server console to manage your network; maintaining a healthy network; building menus; sharing software; sharing CD-ROMs; message handling services; third-party enhancements; using Microsoft Windows with NetWare; using Windows for Workgroups with NetWare; NetWare and OS/2; understanding TCP/IP; combining NetWare and TCP/IP; Using LAN WorkPlace for DOS; Using NetWare with the Macintosh; activating Macintosh workstations. Methods of instruction include lecture, discussion, classroom exercises, case study, quizzes, unit tests, and final examination.

Credit Recommendation: In the upper division baccalaureate degree category, 3 semester hours in Networking, Computer Science or Telecommunications (11/96).

Operating Systems Configuration (CT251/CET251) (Formerly CT251)

Location: Virginia Beach, VA; Hampton, VA; Roanoke, VA; Richmond, VA; Greensboro, NC; Charlotte, NC; Raleigh, NC.

Length: 48 hours (7.5 weeks at night, 5 weeks during days).

Dates: September 1994-Present.

Objective: To provide the student with an overview of operating systems other than DOS, including installation, uses, operations, and experience through the application of basic commands used in each operating system.

Learning Outcome: Upon successful completion of this course, the student will be able to compare and contrast the characteristics of different computer operating systems and the DOS-based program named Windows; compare and contrast the hardware requirements of each system; load each system, including disk partitioning, formatting, and setting up a boot manager; customize the computer's hardware configuration to take advantage of the operating system used, and upgrade the computer's hardware and software; demonstrate tasks related to each computer operating system.

Instruction: Major topics covered in the course are Windows installation, Windows basics, file manager, customizing Windows, printers and fonts, applets, controlling applications, networking, troubleshooting, introduction and installation of other operating systems, other operating systems hardware, characteristics, utilities, help files, and troubleshooting. Methods of instruction include lecture, discussion, classroom exercises, laboratory exercises, quizzes, three unit tests and a final examination.

Credit Recommendation: In the lower division baccalaureate/associate degree category, 2 semester hours in Computer Science (1 hour-lecture, 1 hour-lab) (11/96).

Principles of Applied Mechanics (CT160/CET160) (Formerly CT160)

Location: Virginia Beach, VA; Hampton, VA; Roanoke, VA; Richmond, VA; Greensboro, NC; Charlotte, NC; and Raleigh, NC.

Length: 48 hours (7.5 weeks at night; 5 weeks during days).

Dates: September 1994-Present.

Objective: To introduce students to the principles involved in equipment troubleshooting, repair and maintenance, mechanical concepts, applications in mechanical technology, and practice with soldering tools and hand tools.

Learning Outcome: Upon successful completion of this course, the student will be able to demonstrate skill levels learned in basic soldering; identify through a written examination the learned soldering theory; list a selected inventory of basic technician hand tools; identify a selected inventory of basic fasteners and fastening devices; perform a measurement of selected materials using fundamental technician measuring devices; select correct fabricating devices to accomplish a specified repair; given a list of mechanical terminology, identify the appropriate devices found on the training vehicle; with the illustration provided, compute pulley and gear ratio's; given various examples, identify various switches and conditions; and given various examples, identify component level electrical and mechanical devices.

Instruction: Major topics covered in the course are hand tools for soldering, wire splicing, soldering, soldering wire splices, de-soldering, hand tools and fasteners, fastening devices, taking accurate measurements, drilling, tapping, pulley ratios, gear ratios, mechanical terminology, electrical technology. Methods of instruction include lecture, discussion, classroom exercises, laboratory exercises, and three unit tests.

Credit Recommendation: In the vocational certificate category, 2 semester hours in Mechanical Design and Repairs (1 semester hour lecture and 1 semester hour lab (11/96).

Programmable Controllers and Robotics (CT293/CET293) (Formerly CT293)

Location: Virginia Beach, VA; Hampton, VA; Roanoke, VA; Richmond, VA;

Greensboro, NC; Charlotte, NC; and Raleigh, NC.

Length: 48 hours (7.5 weeks at night; 5 weeks during days).

Dates: September 1994-Present.

Objective: To provide the student with an understanding of programming robotics at the system level and the uses of programmable controllers in industrial automation.

Learning Outcome: Upon successful completion of this course, the student will be able to describe the controller components; discuss programming basics as they apply specifically to SLC controllers; discuss the operation of the pocket programmer and how to enter simple programs into memory; recognize and use the various types of instructions for relays, timers, counters, and sequencers; describe how to combine two or more basic instructions, and the keystrokes required to apply the instruction to a specific need; discuss programming editing techniques and on-line data control; describe the controller specifications, system layout, installation and start-up; and discuss controller maintenance and troubleshooting.

Instruction: Major topics covered in the course are introduction to industrial robotics, robot classifications, end-of-arm tooling, automation sensors, robot and controller operation, computer integrated manufacturing, robot programming, human interface training problems, introduction to programmable controllers, equipment overview and programming basics, pocket programmer relay/timer, and sequencer and controller. Methods of instruction include lecture, discussion, classroom exercises, laboratory exercises, and four unit tests.

Credit Recommendation: In the lower division baccalaureate/associate degree category, 1 semester hour in Programmable Controllers and 1 semester hour in Robotics (11/96).

SQL and Relational Database Programming (PRG150) (Relational Database Programming) (Formerly DP150)

Location: Virginia Beach, VA; and Richmond, VA.

Length: 96 hours (4.5 hours, 3 nights per week for 7.5 weeks; 4.5 hours, 5 days per week for 5 weeks).

Dates: September 1994-Present.

Objective: To enable students to develop database programs in FoxPro for Windows, as well as become familiar with general database concepts.

Learning Outcome: Upon successful completion of this course, the student will have an understanding of database concepts that may be applied to any relational database software; have learned uses of FoxPro language in a Windows interface to solve business and technical database management problems; be able to create database fields and memory variables and use them to manipulate data; be able to design, create, maintain, manipulate and retrieve data from database files using the DBF file format; be able to organize data in multiple tables and retrieve the data simultaneously from any of the tables; be able to use the commands and command statements in programs for data manipulation; be able to generate reports from tables.

Instruction: Major topics covered in the course are introduction to database programming with Foxpro; building FoxPro for Windows applications, the business side; introduction to relational databases; normalization of data; the referencing environment; creating and accessing database files; indexing and data ordering; variables and arrays; expressions and functions; control flow; procedures & user-defined functions; windows; input and output; full-screen data editing; Screen Builder; Report Writer and SQL; and menus. Methods of instruction include lecture, discussion, computer lab exercises, case study, quizzes, unit tests, and final examination.

Credit Recommendation: In the upper division baccalaureate degree category, 3 semester hours in Database Concepts or Computer Science (11/96).

Systems Analysis (PRG210) (Formerly DP100)

Location: Virginia Beach, VA; Richmond, VA.

Length: 48 hours 2.5 hours, 3 nights per week for 7.5 weeks; 2.25 hours, 5 days per week for 5 weeks).

Dates: September 1994-Present.

Objective: To give students an understanding of systems analysis and design, stepping them through the System Development Life Cycle (SDLC).

Learning Outcome: Upon successful completion of this course, the student will be able to describe the phases involved in the System Development Life Cycle, and be able to create data dictionaries, data flow diagrams, system flowcharts, file layouts, program flowcharts, and Pert and Gantt charts. Students are assigned a case study where they do the analysis and design of a fictional company.

Instruction: Major topics covered in the course are an introduction to systems analysis; an introduction to system development; preliminary investigation; determining requirements; analyzing requirements; completing the systems analysis phase and considering alternative tools; output design; input design; file concepts; file and database design; software design and completing the systems design phase; project management and costs; programming, testing, and documentation phase; and system implementation and evaluation. Methods of instruction include lecture, discussion, classroom exercises, case study, unit tests, and final examination.

Credit Recommendation: In the upper division baccalaureate degree category, 2 semester hours in IFSM, Computer Science or System Analysis (11/96).

Systems Concepts Practicum (PRG200) (Formerly DP180)

Location: Virginia Beach, VA; and Richmond, VA.

Length: 81 hours (3.5 hours, 3 nights per week for 7.5 weeks; 3.5 hours, 5 days per week for 5 weeks).

Dates: September 1994-Present.

Objective: To give students experience working in a multi-platform environment enhancing existing programs and creating new programs; emphasizing teamwork.

Learning Outcome: Upon successful completion of this course, the student will be able to describe how working in a production environment differs from a school environment; work as a member of a programming team; plan and budget time and resources in accomplishing a large group project; maintain other programmers' programs; demonstrate knowledge of the programming languages learned while in school; and transfer data from one computer system to another. Students participate in programming teams throughout the course.

Instruction: Major topics covered in the course are teamwork; review of programming languages; AS/400 operating system; PC File Transfer. Methods of Instruction include lecture, group projects, case study, quizzes, unit tests, and a final examination.

Credit Recommendation: In the upper division baccalaureate degree category, 2 semester hours in Networking, Telecommunications, Computer Science and 1 semester hour in lab in Networking or Telecommunications Lab (11/96).

Computer Science and 1 semester hour in Case Study Laboratory (11/96).

in Computer Science Programming Lab (11/96).

Theory of Programming (PRG110) (PRG110 Programming Logic) (Formerly DP110)

Location: Virginia Beach, VA; and Richmond, VA.

Length: 48 hours (2.25 hours, 3 nights per week for 7.5 weeks; 2.25 hours, 5 days per week for 5 weeks).

Dates: September 1994-Present.

Objective: To provide students with an introduction to programming concepts and principles, emphasizing the understanding of structured programming techniques using a programming language.

Learning Outcome: Upon successful completion of this course, the student will be able to use good programming strategies; list requirements for creating a program and the entries required to produce a simple input/output program; perform arithmetic operations in a computer program; use the basic IF-THEN-ELSE structure to do comparisons; flowchart and code nested IF statements; and be familiar with processing single and multiple level control break reports.

Instruction: Major topics covered in the course are an introduction to computer programming; planning and problem solving; entering the program; introduction to structured design; input/output operations; arithmetic operations, comparing; conditional statements; control breaks; and data validation. Methods of instruction include lecture, discussion, computer lab projects, case study, unit tests, and final examination.

Credit Recommendation: In the lower division baccalaureate/associate degree category, 1 semester hour in COBOL I, or

Using C++ (Object-Oriented Programming Using C++) (PRG260) (Formerly DP260)

Location: Virginia Beach, VA; and Richmond, VA.

Length: 48 hours (2.25 hours, 3 nights per week for 7.5 weeks; 2.25 hours, 5 days per week for 5 weeks).

Dates: September 1994-Present.

Objective: To introduce the student to a new design methodology; and learn how to program in an Object Oriented manner, students learn advanced programming concepts and sophisticated I/O interaction.

Learning Outcome: Upon successful completion of this course, the student will know the differences between C and C++'s new features; understand how to use a class; be familiar with dynamic allocation of memory; understand static members, friends and arrays of objects; understand the concept of class hierarchy and polymorphism; know how to overload operators and data conversion; and know how to build libraries. Students complete laboratory assignments and a case study.

Instruction: Major topics covered in the course are C++ and new features; using references in C++; using classes in C++; dynamic allocation in C++; static members, friends and arrays of objects; class hierarchy and polymorphism; operator overloading; and data conversion. Methods of instruction include lecture, discussion, computer lab exercises, case study, quizzes, unit tests, and a final examination.

Credit Recommendation: In the lower division baccalaureate/associate degree category, 1 semester hour in Computer Science Programming and 1 semester hour

Visual Basic (PRG130) (Formerly DP130)

Location: Virginia Beach, VA; Richmond, VA.

Length: 48 hours.

Dates: September 1994-Present.

Objective: To provide students with an understanding of the Visual Basic programming language. Emphasis is placed on programming in a graphical environment, as well as on event-driven programming where the programmer gives the user control and responsibility for the flow of the program.

Learning Outcome: Upon successful completion of this course, the student will be able to use Windows 3.1 and control a mouse in a graphical environment; describe requirements for creating a Visual Basic program and the entries required to design a window; attach code to objects and events; use conditional and loop clauses in Visual Basic; use graphic objects and controls; declare and use values and variables; and use arithmetic and string functions.

Instruction: Major topics covered in the course are introduction to Windows; understanding the Visual Basic environment; understanding properties and controls; programming building blocks; mouse movements; keyboard events; menu design; dialog boxes; file system controls and accessing files. Methods of instruction include lecture, discussion, computer laboratory exercises, case study, unit tests, and a final examination.

Credit Recommendation: In the lower division baccalaureate/associate degree category, 2 semester hours in Computer Science (1 hour-lecture, 1 hour-lab) (11/96).

Educational Resources, Inc.

Educational Resources, Inc. (ERI) is a provider of training and educational services in the workplace environment. The company offers skills enhancement instruction to employees with the objective to update skills they already possess and/or to learn new skills. ERI develops educational programs that enable adult learners to improve and advance their on-the-job opportunities.

ERI assesses employee performance levels and designs and delivers specific educational programs that raise the skill level of employees to meet the changing needs of the workplace.

The training and the education services of ERI are available throughout the United States to companies with on-site training programs. Instructors are experienced educators specializing in adult learning. For information about student records please contact: Program Administrator, Educational Resources, Inc., 45064 Underwood Lane, Suite 200, Dulles, VA 20166, Telephone number (703) 904-1800, Fax (703) 904-1856.

Source of official student records: Registry of Credit Recommendations, American Council on Education, One Dupont Circle, Washington, DC 20036-1193.

Additional information about the courses: College Credit Recommendation Service, American Council on Education, One Dupont Circle, Washington, DC 20036-1193.

English (English Grammar)

Location: Various corporate locations throughout the United States.

Length: 36 hours (12 sessions).

Dates: August 1993-Present.

Objective: To provide students with a better command of the fundamentals of English grammar and also improve the students' speaking and writing skills.

Learning Outcome: Upon successful completion of this course, the student will be able to learn the fundamentals of English grammar.

Instruction: Major topics covered in the course are grammar, usage, sentence-building, capitalization, and punctuation. Methods of instruction include self-paced independent study, individual and group instruction, a textbook which allows students to perform and correct their own work at their own pace, and a mid-term and final examination. The instructor may recommend small group sessions to review material or schedule a particular lesson for the entire group. Students will be tested and evaluated throughout the course to ensure that they have mastered each area of study and are proficient and ready to advance to new learning levels.

Credit Recommendation: In the lower division baccalaureate/associate degree category, 3 semester hours in English (10/96).

Introduction to Data Communications and Networking

Location: Offered at various corporate locations throughout the United States.

Length: 48 hours (8 weeks).

Dates: January 1996-Present.

Objective: To expose non-technical students to the growing field of data communications and networking, with an emphasis on applications to telephony.

Learning Outcome: Upon successful completion of this course, the student will be able to understand the terminology of data communications and networking; be familiar with protocols and ASCII codes; show the uses of LANs and WANs; and become familiar with the uses and differences of ISDN and Broad band service.

Instruction: Major topics covered in the course are analog and digital signal characteristics, data communication hardware, protocols, codes, transmission speeds, open system interconnection, communication ports, public switched telephone networks, packet switching, LANs, topologies, WANs, and ISDN/Broad band service. Methods of instruction include lecture, discussion, demonstrations of networks, classroom practical exercises, homework assignments, laboratory modules, pre-test examination, in-class worksheets, quizzes, observations, and final examination.

Credit Recommendation: In the lower division baccalaureate/associate degree category, 3 semester hours in Computer Science or Computer Information Systems (1/98).

Introduction to Digital Logic and Computers

Location: Offered at various corporate locations throughout the United States.

Length: 48 hours (8 weeks).

Dates: November 1995-Present.

Objective: To introduce the non-technical student to the modern world of digital electronics and how simple gates can be combined to make decisions, store data, and compute operations in a binary mathematical system. This develops into the modern microprocessor and its use in today's microcomputers alone with their operating systems and application software.

Learning Outcome: Upon successful completion of this course, the student will be able to understand the hardware of computer systems from the binary numbering system through logic gates, flip flops, counters and registers, and microprocessors; and will be introduced to the software, file, and operating systems used in today's computers.

Instruction: Major topics covered in the course are binary, hexadecimal and octal numbering systems, logic gates, flip flops, binary counters and registers, microprocessors, computer architecture, directory systems, application software, and DOS and UNIX operating systems. Methods of instruction include lecture, discussion, logic circuit and instrument demonstrations, classroom problem sessions, homework assignment, laboratory modules, pretest examination, in-class worksheets, quizzes, observations, and final examination.

Credit Recommendation: In the lower division baccalaureate/associate degree category, 3 semester hours in Fundamentals of Digital Logic and Computers (1/98).

Introduction to Mathematics (Mathematics for Adult Learners)

Location: Various corporate locations throughout the United States.

Length: 96 hours (32 sessions).

Dates: August 1993-Present.

Objective: To develop fundamental skills participants need to master whole numbers, fractions, decimals, percents, measurements, and algebra.

Learning Outcome: Upon successful completion of this course, the student will be able to complete basic operations regarding whole numbers, fractions, decimals, and percents; solve measurement problems involving length, weight, time, and capacity; and complete algebraic equations involving word problems.

Instruction: Major topics covered in the course are whole numbers, fractions, decimals, percents, measurements, and algebra. Problems have real-life applications. Methods of instruction include periodic reviews to determine if students have mastered specific math skills, individual and small group sessions, self-paced independent study, tests, workbook exercises, and a final examination.

Credit Recommendation: In the lower division baccalaureate/associate degree category, 1 semester hour in Introduction to Mathematics (10/96).

Introduction to Technical Mathematics and Electricity and Electronics

Location: Offered at various corporate locations throughout the United States.

Length: 48 hours (8 weeks).

Dates: October 1995-Present.

Objective: To take a student with a limited mathematical background and no previous knowledge of electricity into the field of electricity and electronics with an emphasis on its use in telephony.

Learning Outcome: Upon successful completion of this course, the student will be able to demonstrate the mathematical ability to do problem solving in electronics; and demonstrate knowledge of electricity and electronics form the basic level of electron theory through electric circuits of both direct current and alternating current.

Instruction: Major topics covered in the course are scientific notation, equation solving, graphing, electron theory, electric circuits, Ohm's Law, series and parallel circuits, magnetic fields, inductance, capacitance, timing circuits, reactance, impedance, and introduction to telephony. Methods of instruction include lecture, discussion, circuit and instrument demonstrations, classroom problem sessions, homework assignments, laboratory modules, pre-test examination, observations, in-class worksheets, quizzes, and final examination.

Credit Recommendation: In the lower division baccalaureate/associate degree category, 2 semester hours in Introduction to Electricity and Magnetism (1/98).

Reading Strategies

Location: Various corporate locations throughout the United States.

Length: 72 hours (24 sessions).

Dates: August 1993-Present.

Objective: To provide a systematic presentation of relevant reading materials, exercises, and instruction geared to adult learners.

Learning Outcome: Upon successful completion this course, the student will be able to demonstrate measurably improved comprehension skills and advancement in their reading grade level.

Instruction: Major topics covered in the course are reading topic selections aimed at improving both comprehension and vocabulary, exercises for remediation of ten specific comprehension skills, and reading selections designed specifically for adults whose reading level ranges from grade 2 through grade 13+. Methods of instruction include discussion, classroom exercises, and tests.

Credit Recommendation: In the lower division baccalaureate/associate degree category, 3 semester hours in Reading (10/96).

Educational Services Institute

Educational Services Institute (ESI) was founded in 1981 to provide training and consulting services to government and industry professionals in the fields of public contracting and administration, contract accounting, information systems, and project management. In 1983, we announced the Professional Development Program in Government Contracting which made our courses available to the general public. We later underscored our commitment to educating contracting professionals when we instituted the Master's Certificate in Government Contracting in 1986. Today ESI's Project Management Program is widely considered to be the world's most comprehensive continuing education program for building project management knowledge and skills. Five years later, we initiated the Project Management Professional Development Program to help organizations of all types enhance their ability to compete by developing project management competency.

These two curricula support over 70 different courses and 550 course sessions annually for employees of several major U.S. government agencies and Fortune 500 firms worldwide. Sessions that are open for public enrollment number over 160, with attendance levels of almost 3,500 in 1994. Over 500 professionals have received a Master's Certificate since 1986.

Each of ESI's instructors has a minimum of 10 years' experience in government contracting and/or project management. For most of these individuals, procurement and contract management have been a career-long focus; classroom instruction is both a way of sharing acquired expertise and a vehicle for continuing to develop expertise in a chosen profession. When not teaching, ESI's instructors are busy revising and updating their courses with recent government regulations, court case decisions, articles printed in trade journals, and other publicly-available materials.

Source of official student records: Registry of Credit Recommendations, American Council on Education, One Dupont Circle, Washington, DC 20036-1193 or Office of Transcripts, Educational Services Institute, 2775 South Quincy Street, Suite 500, Arlington, VA 22206-2260.

Additional information about the courses: College Credit Recommendation Service, American Council on Education, One Dupont Circle, Washington, DC 20036-1193.

ADP/Telecommunications (FIP) Contracting in Government Procurement

Location: Various sites nationwide.
Length: 22 hours (4 days).
Dates: September 1987-Present.
Objective: To provide knowledge of rules, regulations, and the process for government acquisition of automated data processing equipment (ADPE).
Learning Outcome: Upon successful completion of this course, the student will be able to explain basic statues of government ADPE acquisition; understand the process of specification development; describe procurement procedures and federal regulations in ADPE acquisition, and conduct an evaluation of ADPE needs and proposals.
Instruction: Major topics covered in the course are sources of acquisition statutes; authority and reviews; defining ADPE; developing specifications; procurement techniques and policies; software procurement; technical evaluation; systems integration contracts; use of GSA sources; contract negotiation and award; contract administration; property rights, and protest procedures. Methods of instruction include lecture, discussion, classroom exercises, readings, and final examination.
Credit Recommendation: In the upper division baccalaureate degree category, 2 semester hours in Procurement Management, Federal Acquisitions, Business Administration, or Public Administration (11/94).

Continuous Improvement and Total Quality Management

Location: Various sites nationwide.
Length: 18 hours (3 days).
Dates: September 1992-Present.
Objective: To explain key elements in successful improvement and quality efforts, and to provide an introduction to quality management.
Learning Outcome: Upon successful completion of this course, the student will be able to describe management technologies for improving quality, increasing productivity, and reducing costs; identify the principles of continuous improvement and the multiple practices that support each of these principles; and demonstrate how streamlining, performance measurement, and commitment to quality are germane to the philosophies of the Continuous Improvement Process (CIP).
Instruction: Major topics covered in the course are the need for CIP; philosophy, principles, and practices of CIP; and tools and techniques of CIP. Methods of instruction include lecture, discussion, classroom exercises, audio/visual material, assessment of case studies and classroom exercises, and final examination.
Credit Recommendation: In the upper division baccalaureate degree category, 1 semester hour in Business Administration, Business Management, or Industrial Management (12/94).

Contract Pricing (Formerly Government Contract Administration and Pricing)

Location: Various sites nationwide.
Length: 22 hours (4 days).
Dates: November 1987-Present.
Objective: To provide knowledge of pricing contracts based on requirements of the *Federal Acquisition Regulation.*
Learning Outcome: Upon successful completion of this course, the student will be able to understand both the seller's and buyer's perspectives on evaluating supplier's proposed price and on establishing final contract price; and use the *Federal Acquisition Regulation* requirements including the concepts of defective pricing, contract cost principles, cost accounting standards, market vs. cost-based pricing, and various certification requirements.
Instruction: Major topics covered in the course are introduction to pricing; government pricing policies; audits; pricing strategies; contract pricing arrangements; Truth in Negotiations Act; cost or price data; cost accounting standards; the estimating system; market-based pricing/price analysis; and cost-based pricing/cost analysis. Methods of instruction include lecture, discussion, classroom exercises, assessment of classroom exercises, and final examination.
Credit Recommendation: In the upper division baccalaureate degree category, 2 semester hours in Procurement Management, Federal Acquisitions, Business Administration, or Public Administration (11/94). **NOTE:** Credit recommendation of 2 semester hours to be awarded only if this course and Operating Practices in Contract Administration are successfully completed.

Contracting for Project Managers

Location: Various sites worldwide.
Length: 28 hours (5 days).

Dates: *Version 1:* June 1994-March 1996; *Version 2:* April 1996-Present.

Objective: *Version 1:* To provide a basic survey of knowledge and skill for project managers to work effectively with contracting personnel. *Version 2:* To provide an understanding and the basic skills necessary for project managers to work effectively with contracting personnel.

Learning Outcome: Upon successful completion of this course, the student will be able to understand contract administration; effectively communicate in dealing with contracting personnel; illustrate proper methods of documentation; and understand dispute resolution and its legal remedies.

Instruction: Major topics covered in the course are the contracting process; objectives and requirements; plans and specifications; contract formation; contract administration; and contract termination. Methods of instruction include lecture, discussion, classroom exercises, case studies, assessment of classroom exercises and case studies, and a final examination.

Credit Recommendation: *Version 1:* In the upper division baccalaureate degree category, or the lower division baccalaureate/associate degree category, 1 semester hour in Acquisition Management, Project Management, or a Business elective (12/94). *Version 2:* In the graduate degree category or upper division baccalaureate degree category, 1 semester hour in Acquisition, Management, Project Management, or a Business elective (3/96). **NOTE:** Students seeking graduate credit must complete pre-course reading assignments, an essay-format final examination, and a research paper.

Contracting with Foreign Governments (Foreign Government Contracting)

Location: Various sites worldwide.

Length: 18 hours (3 days).

Dates: February 1994-Present.

Objective: To teach students how to navigate the myriad, sometimes conflicting, restrictions and requirements with which they must contend in contracting with foreign governments.

Learning Outcome: Upon successful completion of this course, the student will be able to identify and discern the differences between contracting with the U.S. Federal Government and with non-U.S. governments; understand the goals, structure, and scope of the GATT Government Procurement Code; identify the goals, structure, and scope of the European Union Government Procurement Regime; interpret key extraterritorial U.S. laws, including the Foreign Corrupt Practices Act, antiboycott laws, and the export controls and licensing regime; and explicate the framework of the U.S. Foreign Military Sales Program.

Instruction: Major topics covered in the course are government procurement under the GATT and other international agreements, the transfer of defense articles and services to foreign countries, Foreign Corrupt Practices Act, U.S. Antiboycott Law, U.S. Government Assistance in Selling Abroad, procurement by international agencies, and restrictions imposed by foreign governments. Methods of instruction include lecture, case studies, group projects, a final examination, and a final research project for students seeking graduate-level credit.

Credit Recommendation: In the upper division baccalaureate or graduate degree category, 1 semester hour in Purchasing, Government Procurement, or Business (4/95). **NOTE:** Students who seek graduate credit must complete a research project at the end of the course.

Federal Contracting Basics (Formerly Fundamentals of Federal Contracting)

Location: Various sites nationwide.

Length: 28 hours (5 days).

Dates: January 1989-Present.

Objective: To provide an introduction to the organization, content, application, and interpretation of the *Federal Acquisition Regulation* (FAR).

Learning Outcome: Upon successful completion of this course, the student will be able to understand phases of the acquisition process; interpret the *Federal Acquisition Regulation* and other procurement statues and directives; describe the basic methods of federal contracting; and understand competition requirements, contract formats, and cost principles.

Instruction: Major topics covered in the course are introduction to the federal marketplace and acquisition process; contract funding; the FAR system; contracting authority; mandatory sources of supplies and services; competition requirements; methods of contracting; solicitations and the Uniform Contract Format; contract types; contract pricing; and contract administration. Methods of instruction include lecture, discussion, case studies, and final examination.

Credit Recommendation: In the upper division baccalaureate degree category, 2 semester hours in Procurement Management, Federal Acquisitions, Business Administration, or Public Administration (11/94). **NOTE:** Credit recommendation of 2 semester hours to be awarded only if this course, Source Selection in Government Procurement, and Negotiation Strategies and Techniques are all successfully completed.

Global Marketing

Location: Various sites worldwide.

Length: 18 hours (3 days).

Dates: June 1994-Present.

Objective: To provide the skills and knowledge to formulate realistic marketing objectives and focus their resources in the quest to do business in the international marketplace.

Learning Outcome: Upon successful completion of this course, the student will be able to identify and analyze the key economic, social, political, and cultural factors influencing global competition; evaluate relative opportunity and corporate capability in an effort to identify target markets; define market segmentation according to conventional and unconventional criteria; outline research objectives and design an effective, efficient international information gathering system; identify and understand the variables that influence the design and effectiveness of international sourcing and distribution systems; and define and implement the management techniques most effective for controlling and auditing the global marketing process.

Instruction: Major topics covered in the course are going international, motivation and choices; factors influencing global competitiveness; global intermarket segmentation; linking capability with opportunity; international marketing research, culture and social environments, evaluating economic factors, evaluating political and legal factors, developing and implementing the marketing mix; and global marketing management. Methods of instruction include lecture, case studies, group projects, a final examination, and a research paper for candidates seeking graduate-level credit.

Credit Recommendation: In the upper division baccalaureate or graduate degree category, 1 semester hour in Marketing, International Marketing, or Business (4/95). **NOTE:** Students who seek graduate credit must complete a research project at the end of the course.

Global Strategic Planning (Formerly Developing International Business and Financial Plans)

Location: Various sites worldwide.

Length: 18 hours (3 days).
Dates: March 1994-Present.
Objective: To teach how to locate, compile, and analyze the economic, financial, regulatory, cultural, and other data they need to develop an international business or financial plan; and to give guidance in preparing plans that will garner corporate and financial support and provide a solid foundation for their undertakings.
Learning Outcome: Upon successful completion of this course, the student will be able to define the purpose and uses of an international business plan and how it fits into the overall strategic planning process; identify and assess the global forces that impact the potential success of a plan; establish useful international goals, strategies, and controls, and forecast their short-term and long-term effectiveness; define what makes an international business/financial plan credible and persuasive, and implement a plan that exhibits these qualities; and differentiate the structure and goals of a financing plan from those of a general business plan.
Instruction: Major topics covered in the course are framework; planing your plan; situation analysis; information acquisition, mission, and objectives; strategy, implementation plans, sensitivities, contingencies, and audit systems; strategic alliances; and financing plans. Methods of instruction include lecture, case studies, group projects, and a final examination.
Credit Recommendation: In the upper division baccalaureate degree category, 1 semester hour in International Business or Business Management (4/95).

International Contracting

Location: Various sites worldwide.
Length: 22 hours (4 days).
Dates: May 1991-Present.
Objective: To provide a firm understanding of the provisions that govern international contractual relationships and how they differ from those governing domestic ones.
Learning Outcome: Upon successful completion of this course, the student will be able to distinguish the principles of contract law under both common law and civil law systems; identify the impact of key extraterritorial U.S. laws; explicate the provisions of the UN Convention on the international sale of goods and the UNIDROIT principles of international commercial contracts; identify the options available for international dispute resolution; understand the purpose of common and standardized contract clauses and analyze the implementation of those clauses under different legal systems; and describe the use the impact of INCOTERMS.
Instruction: Major topics covered in the course are basic contracting principle, special statutory concerns, treaties and trade agreements, contract formation and drafting, termination and dispute resolution, and shipping. Methods of instruction include lecture, case studies, group projects, and a final examination.
Credit Recommendation: In the upper division baccalaureate or graduate degree category, 1 semester hour in International Business, Law, Contract Administration, or Procurement (4/95). **NOTE:** Students who seek graduate credit must complete a research project at the end of the course.

International Financial Management (Formerly Introduction to International Finance)

Location: Various sites worldwide.
Length: 18 hours (3 days).
Dates: February 1994-Present.
Objective: To increase fluency in the language and tools of international financial management and provide a solid foundation for further research and investigation.
Learning Outcome: Upon successful completion of this course, the student will be able to recognize the historical impact and current structure of the international monetary system; describe the structure and use of the current monetary markets including the spot, forward, futures, and options markets; identify the economic factors that influence exchange rate fluctuation, how to use forecasting services to predict fluctuations; draft bank guarantees, standby letters of credit, performance bonds, and international documentary letters of credit with a thorough understanding of the mechanics, negotiation skills, and legal stipulations that accompany each; and identify, assess, and manage international political and financial risks.
Instruction: Major topics covered in the course are an overview of the international monetary markets and foreign exchange markets; assessing and managing exchange rate risk; and assessing and managing country risk, trade finance, political risk insurance, performance guarantees, and project financing sources. Methods of instruction include lecture, case studies, group projects, and a final examination.
Credit Recommendation: In the upper division baccalaureate degree category, 1 semester hour in Finance, International Business, or as a Business elective (4/95).

International Project Management

Location: Various sites worldwide.
Length: 18 hours (3 days).
Dates: February 1995-Present.
Objective: To teach a systematic approach to managing international projects and minimizing risks in the global marketplace.
Learning Outcome: Upon successful completion of this course, the student will be able to identify the impact of international political, economic, and cultural factors on the project management life cycle; understand the mechanics of the international monetary markets and their impact on project capital budgeting; identify, assess, and manage the risks unique to the international project management arena; delineate the implications of intellectual property laws and disputes for international projects; and build crosscultural communication skills for more effective team management.
Instruction: Major topics covered in the course are globalization of business, project management, international project management life cycle, benefit—cost analysis, capital budgeting, international financial transactions, international finance for large projects, international project management risks, language, cross-cultural communication, international negotiations, labor, international intellectual property laws, international licensing, and export controls. Methods of instruction include lecture, case studies, group projects, and a final examination.
Credit Recommendation: In the upper division baccalaureate degree category, 1 semester hour in International Business or Management (4/95).

Managing Projects in Organizations

Location: Various sites worldwide.
Length: 28 hours (5 days).
Dates: *Version 1:* October 1987-March 1996; *Version 2:* April 1996-Present.
Objective: To provide knowledge and skills in principles and techniques of project management in realistic situations that combine technical, economic, and human resource issues.
Learning Outcome: Upon successful completion of this course, the student will be able to identify the needs-requirements life cycle; set clear project objectives; create cost benefit analyses; use a variety of costing and management control techniques; develop budgets; combine the various resources necessary for project com-

pletion; and apply rapid prototyping in a project environment.

Instruction: Major topics covered in this course are project initiation; planning and control; project execution; project termination; and the use of microcomputers in project management. Methods of instruction include lecture, discussion, classroom exercises, case studies, audio-visual material, assessment of classroom exercises and case studies, and a final examination.

Credit Recommendation: *Version 1:* In the upper division baccalaureate degree category, 2 semester hours in Business Management, Business Administration, Acquisition Management, Project Management, or Industrial Management (12/94). *Version 2:* In the graduate degree category or the upper division baccalaureate degree category, 2 semester hours in Business Management, Business Administration, Acquisition Management, Project Management, or Industrial Management (3/96). **NOTE:** Students seeking graduate credit must complete pre-course reading assignments, an essay-format final examination, and a research paper.

Managing Software Quality (Formerly Software Quality Assurance)

Location: Various sites worldwide.

Length: 18 hours (3 days).

Dates: May 1994-Present.

Objective: To provide knowledge needed to approach software quality assurance (SQA) from a management perspective rather than a technical one, and to provide information on all key SQA issues.

Learning Outcome: Upon successful completion of this course, the student will be able to understand what is meant by all SQA terms, objectives, and techniques; identify the appropriate management and team skills for an SQA group; evaluate and improve skills of an SQA analyst; prepare effective standards and procedures; and manage the various techniques for testing, evaluating, and inspecting software for quality.

Instruction: Major topics covered in the course are organizing for SQA; quality assurance (QA) and software development; QA practices and procedures; software configuration management; the QA competency model; standards, inspections, and walk-throughs; software testing; and launching a corporate SQA program. Methods of instruction include lecture, discussion, classroom exercises, case studies, and final examination.

Credit Recommendation: In the upper division baccalaureate degree category, 1 semester hour in Software Engineering, Information Technology Project Management, Information Systems, Computer Science, or Data Processing (12/94).

Negotiation Strategies and Techniques

Location: Various sites nationwide.

Length: 22 hours (4 days).

Dates: January 1989-Present.

Objective: To provide an introduction to an effective structured system for the negotiation process.

Learning Outcome: Upon successful completion of this course, the student will be able to describe varied negotiating techniques and styles; discuss the characteristics of effective negotiators and competitive and collaborative negotiation strategies; and apply negotiation strategies.

Instruction: Major topics covered in the course are negotiation competencies; preparing for negotiation; conducting the negotiation; influencing the other party; applying your style to the negotiation process; understanding your negotiation strengths; characteristics of an effective negotiator; developing a negotiation strategy; and documenting negotiations. Methods of instruction include lecture, classroom exercises, role playing, audio/visual material, and final examination.

Credit Recommendation: In the upper division baccalaureate degree category, 2 semester hours in Procurement Management, Federal Acquisitions, Business Administration, or Public Administration (11/94). **NOTE:** Credit recommendation of 2 semester hours to be awarded only if this course, Fundamentals of Federal Contracting, and Source Selection in Government Procurement are all successfully completed.

Operating Practices in Contract Administration

Location: Various sites nationwide.

Length: 28 hours (4 days).

Dates: December 1987-Present.

Objective: To provide knowledge of the federal contracting regulations necessary for successful completion of government contracts.

Learning Outcome: Upon successful completion of this course, the student will be able to read and interpret contractual requirements; and recognize impact of pre-contract action, contractual performance requirements, and subcontracting procedures as required by the *Federal Acquisition Regulation.*

Instruction: Major topics covered in the course are contract terms and conditions; inspection, acceptance, and warranties; subcontracting; payment and contract financing; contract costs; administration of government-furnished property; modifications; terminations; options, and contract closeout. Methods of instruction include lecture, discussion, exercises, and final examination.

Credit Recommendation: In the upper division baccalaureate degree category, 2 semester hours in Procurement Management, Federal Acquisitions, Business Administration, or Public Administration (11/94). **NOTE:** Credit recommendation of 2 semester hours to be awarded only if this course and Government Contract Administration and Pricing are successfully completed.

Project Leadership, Management, and Communications

Location: Various sites worldwide.

Length: 28 hours (5 days).

Dates: *Version 1:* November 1990-August 1996; *Version 2:* September 1996-Present.

Objective: To provide knowledge of management and leadership styles, and to develop skill in leading members of a team toward effective problem solving and decision making.

Learning Outcome: *Version 1:* Upon successful completion of this course, the student will be able to recognize leadership styles and rate team members on followership maturity; identify conflicts within a team and facilitate conflict resolution; understand patterns of group behavior and types of motivation; and practice effective communications in negotiation situations. *Version 2:* Upon successful completion of this course, the student will be able to recognize leadership and followership styles in project management; understand team dynamics and group development as they relate to building effective project management teams; assess interpersonal communication styles; identify conflicts within a team and facilitate conflict resolution; use problem-solving steps to analyze and solve problems; and understand the negotiation process.

Instruction: *Version 1:* Major topics covered in the course are leadership and follower behavior; functions of management; team building exercises; and standardized self-assessment instruments on strength/deployment and conflict modes. Methods of instruction include lecture, discussion, classroom exercises, case studies, audio/visual material, assessment of case studies, and a final examination. *Version 2:* Major topics covered in the course are leadership and followership behavior; functions of management; team building; interpersonal communication; negotiation process; conflict management; and problem solving methods. Methods of instruction include lecture, discussion, classroom exercises, case studies, audio/visual material, assessment of classroom exercises and case studies, and a final examination.

Credit Recommendation: *Version 1:* In the lower division baccalaureate/associate degree category, 1 semester hour in Business Administration, Management, or Organizational Behavior (12/94). *Version 2:* In the graduate degree category or the upper division baccalaureate degree category, 2 semester hours in Business Administration, Management, or Organizational Behavior (3/96). **NOTE:** Students seeking graduate credit must complete precourse reading assignments, an essay-format final examination, and a research paper.

Project Management Applications

Location: Various.

Length: 28 hours (5 days).

Dates: *Version 1:* April 1990-March 1996; *Version 2:* April 1996-Present.

Objective: To synthesize and reinforce the knowledge and skills essential to basic project management, and introduce advanced approaches that build upon competencies gained in previous courses.

Learning Outcome: Upon successful completion of this course, the student will be able to apply lessons learned throughout the project management development program; apply a competency model for project managers; explain the process of acquiring competencies; and give and receive feedback on using project manager competencies and project manager functions, including bid and proposal preparation, project plan development, project control, contract management, configuration management, and project closure.

Instruction: *Version 1:* Methods of instruction include lecture, discussion, and simulation exercises. *Version 2:* Methods of instruction include lecture, discussion, classroom exercises, case studies, a final examination, and reports, observations, papers, and a research paper for candidates seeking graduate level credits.

Credit Recommendation: *Version 1:* In the upper division baccalaureate degree category, 2 semester hours in Business Administration, Business Management, Project Management, or Public Administration (12/94). *Version 2:* In the upper division baccalaureate or graduate degree category, 2 semester hours in Business Administration, Business Management, Project Management, or Public Administration (3/96) (6/96). **NOTE:** Students seeking graduate level credit must complete mandatory reading assignments and demonstrate comprehension through daily participation; submit a two (2) page report demonstrating an understanding of daily issues, including an assessment of daily team performance; and write and submit a research paper within three (3) months after completion of this course.

Quality For Project Managers

Location: Various locations worldwide.

Length: 28 hours (5 days).

Dates: September 1996-Present.

Objective: To teach the philosophy and principles of quality management and how to apply them to project management responsibilities.

Learning Outcome: Upon successful completion of this course, the student will be able to identify the proven benefits of quality; describe five common principles underlying quality leadership; use basic continuous process improvement tools and techniques and know when to apply them in project management; and discuss the PMI approach to quality management.

Instruction: Major topics covered in the course are the importance of world class project quality, the five principles of Total Quality Management, continuous improvement tools and techniques, and ISO 9000. Methods of instruction include lecture, discussion, classroom exercises, case studies, audio/visual material, learner presentations/reports, and a final examination.

Credit Recommendation: In the upper division baccalaureate degree or graduate degree category, 2 semester hours in Project Management, Quality Management, or Business Administration (8/96).

Quality for Project Managers

Location: Various locations worldwide.

Length: 18 hours (3 days).

Dates: September 1996-Present.

Objective: To teach the philosophy and principles of quality management and how to apply them to project management responsibilities.

Learning Outcome: Upon successful completion of this course, the student will be able to identify the proven benefits of quality; describe five common principles underlying quality leadership; use basic continuous process improvement tools and techniques, and know when to apply them in project management; and discuss the PMI approach to quality management.

Instruction: Major topics covered in the course are the importance of world class project quality, the five principles of TQM, continuous improvement tools and techniques, and quality teams. Methods of accelerated instruction include lecture, discussion, classroom exercises, case studies, audio/visual material, learner presentations/reports, and a final examination.

Credit Recommendation: In the upper division baccalaureate degree or graduate degree category, 2 semester hours in Project Management, Quality Management, or Business Administration (4/97).

Risk Management

Location: Various sites worldwide.

Length: 28 hours (5 days).

Dates: *Version 1:* July 1990-March 1996; *Version 2:* April 1996-Present.

Objective: *Version 1:* To provide an overview of risk in a project environment, including qualitative and quantitative tools to assess and manage risk, and steps involved in development of a risk assessment and management plan. *Version 2:* To provide an understanding of risk in a project environment, including qualitative and quantitative tools to assess and manage risk, and steps involved in development of a risk assessment and management plan.

Learning Outcome: Upon successful completion of this course, the student will be able to identify basic characteristics of risk, its effects and implications in a project environment; categorize risk events, define the concept of acceptable risk, and evaluate risk in project selection; identify elements of a risk management plan; and identify and apply appropriate risk management tools and techniques for use in projects.

Instruction: Major topics covered in the course are risk management overview, risk types and mitigation strategies, project evaluation and selection, and risk management planning process, tools, and techniques. Methods of instruction include lecture, discussion, classroom exercises, case studies, learner presentations, assessment of case studies and classroom exercises, and a final examination.

Credit Recommendation: *Version 1:* In the upper division baccalaureate degree category, 2 semester hours in Business Administration, Management, Procurement, or Contract Administration (12/94). *Version 2:* In the graduate degree category or in the upper division baccalaureate degree category, 2 semester hours in Business Administration, Management, Procurement, or Contract Administration (3/96). **NOTE:** Students seeking graduate credit must complete pre-course reading assignments, an essay-format final examination, and a research paper.

Scheduling and Cost Control

Location: Various sites worldwide.

Length: 28 hours (5 days).

Dates: *Version 1:* April 1990-March 1996; *Version 2:* April 1996-Present.

Objective: To provide skill in the use of basic project management tools for scheduling and control of major projects.

Learning Outcome: *Version 1:* Upon successful completion of this course, the student will be able to ensure adequate development of a WBS and derivation of project schedules interpreting all subdivisions of work; and prepare estimates, evaluate network logic, and assess progress against the work plan and estimates. *Version 2:* Upon successful completion of this course, the student will be able to identify and apply different scheduling techniques and tools; identify and apply different cost control techniques and tools; evaluate project progress; develop project requirements; build a work breakdown structure; establish and manage cost and schedule baselines; and apply change management practices.

Instruction: *Version 1:* Major topics covered in the course are requirement definition techniques, WBS development, estimating processes, scheduling and network development, progress measurement and projection of outcomes, managing change, and closing out the project. *Version 2:* Major topics covered in the course are project requirements definition; work breakdown structure; estimating, scheduling, project baselining; project monitoring; change management; and project closure.

Credit Recommendation: *Version 1:* In the upper division baccalaureate degree category, 2 semester hours in Business Administration, Project Management, Procurement, or Contract Administration (12/94). *Version 2:* In the graduate degree category or the upper division baccalaureate degree category, 2 semester hours in Business Administration, Project Management, Procurement, or Contract Administration (3/96).

Software Project Management

Location: Various sites nationwide.

Length: 18 hours (3 days).

Dates: February 1994-Present.

Objective: To provide skill in management of software development using proven project management techniques and common sense.

Learning Outcome: Upon successful completion of this course, the student will be able to define a software project's objectives and establish the project's criteria for success; develop a software development project plan; use appropriate estimating tools and techniques; organize a software project; apply modern software management techniques; break a software project into manageable segments, and plan and control the segments; identify when to develop a software testing plan; anticipate and manage documentation requirements in software development; and close out a software development project.

Instruction: Major topics covered in the course are the software process, project team, requirements, project plan, project control, cost estimating, configuration management, testing, documentation, and project close-out. Methods of instruction include lecture, discussion, classroom exercises, case studies, audio/visual material, assessment of case studies and classroom exercises, and final examination.

Credit Recommendation: In the upper division baccalaureate degree category, 1 semester hour in Information Technology Project Management, Software Engineering, Information Systems, Computer Science, or Data Processing (12/94).

Software Risk Management

Location: Various sites nationwide.

Length: 18 hours (3 days).

Dates: November 1994-Present.

Objective: To provide knowledge on how to identify the major sources of risk on a software project, and how to assess and control risk in project situations.

Learning Outcome: Upon successful completion of this course, the student will be able to describe the relationship between risk management and project management; develop and implement a software risk management plan and budget; identify, analyze, prioritize, plan, execute, evaluate, and document software risk; define the range of acceptable risk on a software project, and establish a corporate software risk management assessment program.

Instruction: Major topics covered in the course are the software risk management process; types of software risk and mitigation strategies; software risk management planning; project evaluation and selection; and software risk management tools and techniques. Methods of instruction include lecture, discussion, classroom exercises, case studies, audio/visual material, assessment of case studies, and final examination.

Credit Recommendation: In the upper division baccalaureate degree category, 1 semester hour in Software Engineering, Information Technology Project Management, Information Systems, Computer Science, or Data Processing (12/94).

Source Selection in Government Procurement (Source Selection: The Competitive Proposals Contracting Process)

Location: Various sites nationwide.

Length: 22 hours (4 days).

Dates: October 1987-Present.

Objective: To provide knowledge of source selection regulations, techniques and effective procedures for source selection in government procurement.

Learning Outcome: Upon successful completion of this course, the student will be able to exhibit a working knowledge of the Federal marketplace; describe the methods and organization of the source selection process; prepare and analyze government requests for proposals; and prepare a proposal according to government requirements.

Instruction: Major topics covered in the course are the Federal marketplace, procurement background; introduction to source selection; proposal preparation; and best-and-final-offer discussion. Methods of instruction include lecture, discussion, classroom exercises, case studies, and final examination.

Credit Recommendation: In the upper division baccalaureate degree category, 2 semester hours in Procurement Management, Federal Acquisitions, Business Administration, or Public Administration (11/94). **NOTE:** Credit recommendation of 2 semester hours to be awarded only if this course, Fundamentals of Federal Contracting, and Negotiation Strategies and Techniques are all successfully completed.

Systems Integration and Project Management

Location: Various sites nationwide.

Length: 18 hours (3 days).

Dates: June 1994-Present.

Objective: To provide an overview of planning and managing large, complex, advanced technology projects.

Learning Outcome: Upon successful completion of this course, the student will

be able to understand complexities of systems integration projects and configuration management; and identify key systems integration risks.

Instruction: Major topics covered in the course are system needs; user requirements; system architecture; planning; software management; quality; risk; and legal issues. Methods of instruction include lecture, discussion, classroom exercises, assessment of classroom exercises, and final examination.

Credit Recommendation: In the lower division baccalaureate/associate degree category, 1 semester hour in Acquisition Management, or Project Management (12/94).

Telecommunications Principles for Project Managers

Location: Washington, DC.

Length: 18 hours (3 days).

Dates: August 1994-Present.

Objective: To provide knowledge of fundamental principles underlying voice and data networks, and to enable project managers to handle scheduling, financial, and risk issues related to managing telecommunications projects.

Learning Outcome: Upon successful completion of this course, the student will be able to associate trends in U.S. regulatory policy with international telecommunication issues and future trends; identify key international and national telecommunication standard-setting bodies; compare OCE and TCP/IP standards; understand fundamental principles underlying voice and data communications networks; describe local area network (LAN) typology and the equipment necessary to develop a LAN; identify options in value-added data network offerings; classify a variety of communications types based on capabilities and applications; and discuss pros and cons of implementing integrated services digital networking in the project environment.

Instruction: Major topics covered in this course are the telecommunications industry; importance of standards; voice communications networks; data communications networks; local area networks; communications media; and integrated services digital networks. Methods of instruction include lecture, discussion, classroom exercises, case studies, audio/visual material, and assessment of case studies.

Credit Recommendation: In the upper division baccalaureate degree category, 1 semester hour in Information Technology Project Management, Software Engineering, Information Systems, Data Communication, Computer Science, or Data Processing (12/94).

EG&G Mound Applied Technologies

EG&G Mound Applied Technologies Training and Development (T&ED) has the responsibility of working with Mound's line organizations to identify and meet personnel training needs and is responsible for the quality and conduct of all plant training. Training is developed and conducted in accordance with applicable Department of Energy orders and other Federal regulations and requirements.

EG&G Mound provides training for employees to ensure individuals are properly instructed in performing their duties and have opportunities for personal development and growth in the work environment.

The Training organization establishes training and qualification programs for classroom and on-the-job (OJT) instructors and course developers and ensures that the training staff possess the technical knowledge, experience, and instructional skills for the development of classroom and OJT training; reviews facility, group, or organization training plans; coordinates and assists in the development of all training programs; approves all courses and/or programs prior to the course or program being offered to employees; and in coordination with line management, T&ED may assume technical teaching and course development responsibilities.

Training and Employee Development uses a graded systematic approach in the development and implementation of training programs. The degree of rigor and formality used to develop training programs are adjusted to the hazard potential, risk or complexity of a training need.

Source of official student records: Registry of Credit Recommendations, American Council on Education, One Dupont Circle, Washington, DC 20036-1193.

Additional information about the courses: College Credit Recommendation Service, American Council on Education, One Dupont Circle, Washington, DC 20036-1193.

Advanced WordPerfect (060079)

Location: Miamisburg, OH.

Length: 8 hours (1 day).

Dates: May 1993-Present.

Objective: To use advanced word processing concepts in WordPerfect.

Learning Outcome: Upon successful completion of this course, the student will be able to create and edit parallel columns and tables, import or link with Lotus 1-2-3, use merge features, and create and execute macros.

Instruction: Major topics covered in the course are creating and editing parallel columns; creating, editing, and sorting tables; importing or linking with Lotus 1-2-3; creating a merge document and performing the merge; creating graphic boxes; and creating and executing macros. Methods of instruction include lectures, discussions, visual aids, handouts, and laboratory exercises.

Credit Recommendation: In the lower division baccalaureate/associate degree category, 1 semester hour in WordPerfect if student has completed Introduction to WordPerfect (060076); or 1 semester hour in Software Productivity Tools if student has completed Freelance (060037) (4/94).

Basic Federal Contracting (906019)

Location: Miamisburg, OH.

Length: 16 hours (2 days).

Dates: September 1922-Present.

Objective: To understand the fundamental ways the government obtains its needed supplies and services.

Learning Outcome: Upon successful completion of this course, the student will be able to explain the fundamental concepts of federal contracting; the basic statutes and regulations that govern the acquisition process; the requirements for competition and how to justify exceptions; "responsiveness" and "responsibility; and how to modify a contract.

Instruction: Major topics covered in the course are basic federal contracting; preparing, awarding, and administering socio-economic considerations; sealed bidding; negotiated contracts; contract administration; and claims and remedies. Methods of instruction include lecture, quizzes, and practical examinations.

Credit Recommendation: In the lower division baccalaureate/associate degree category, 1 semester hour in Contracting and Procurement (7/94).

Cost/Price Analysis (906018)

Location: Miamisburg, OH.

Length: 16 hours (2 days).

Dates: September 1992-Present.

Objective: To develop a cost or price analysis that will enable the buyer or contract administrator to negotiate a fair and reasonable price.

Learning Outcome: Upon successful completion of this course, the student will be able to explain the process and objectives of contract pricing; determine the seller's pricing approaches and strategies; determine whether cost data must be certified; establish pre-negotiation price positions including a position on profit or fee; and determine need for audit.

Instruction: Major topics covered in the course are overview of contract pricing, acquisition process and contract pricing, people and contract pricing, cost estimating, price analysis, cost analysis, profit analysis, contract price negotiation, and pricing problems after contract award. Methods of instruction include lecture and case studies.

Credit Recommendation: In the lower division baccalaureate/associate degree category, 1 semester hour in Contracting and Procurement (7/94).

Employee Development Training
1. EEO/AA (090039)
2. American With Disabilities Act (ADA) (990015)

Location: Miamisburg, OH.

Length: 12 hours (2 days).

Dates: 1. January 1994-Present; 2. May 1992-Present.

Objective: To become familiar with the technical assistance manual on the employment provisions of the American With Disabilities Act, ensuring that the affirmative action is a viable program.

Learning Outcome: Upon successful completion of this course, the student will be able to state the consequences of an unsuccessful compliance review; state the types of liabilities that occur from Title VII litigations; define equal opportunity and affirmative action; identify the protected groups (ADA); understand non-discrimination in the hiring process (recruitment, application, pre-employment, testing); and understand "the reasonable accommodation obligation."

Instruction: Major topics covered in the course are analysis of EEO/AA concerns, benefits of making affirmative action plan a "living plan"; legal requirements; non-discrimination in hiring practices, recruitment, pre-employment, and testing. Methods of instruction include lecture, discussion, and exercises.

Credit Recommendation: In the lower division baccalaureate/associate degree category, 1 semester hour in Human Resource Development (7/94). **NOTE**: Both courses must be completed before credit is granted.

Freelance (060037)

Location: Miamisburg, OH.

Length: 8 hours (1 day).

Dates: October 1987-Present.

Objective: To develop graphics including organizational charts, flow charts, graph charts, text charts, and quantitative charts using Freelance software.

Learning Outcome: Upon successful completion of this course, the student will be able to create drawings using text lines, rectangles, and other graphic objects; enhance and edit objects using color, shading, and sizing techniques; create text bar, and organizational charts; enhance existing charts; save and print charts; and import charts from Lotus.

Instruction: Major topics covered in the course are working with a symbol library; creating text, bar, and organizational charts; editing, enhancing, saving, and printing charts; and importing data. Methods of instruction include lecture, discussion, visual aids, handouts, and classroom and laboratory exercises.

Credit Recommendation: In the lower division baccalaureate/associate degree category, 1 semester hour in Software Productivity Tools if student has completed Advanced WordPerfect (060079) (4/94).

Hazardous Waste Worker/Industrial Safety Training
1. Laser Hazard Awareness (080039)
2. Laser Hazard Awareness (080038)
3. Hazard Communication & MSDS Training (070054)
4. Hazard Communication Train-the-Trainer (070052)
5. Hazardous Waste Generator Training Course (070205)

Location: Miamisburg, OH.

Length: 17 hours (3 days).

Dates: *Courses 1 and 2*: November 1990-Present; *Courses 3 and 4:* February 1991-Present; *Course 5:* March 1993-Present.

Objective: To become familiar with and provide hazard communication standards; knowledge of risk assessment, and health and physical hazards of chemicals; and to enable understanding of the liabilities and responsibilities of waste generators under the Resource Conservation and Recovery Act.

Learning Outcome: Upon successful completion of this course, the student will be able to describe the fundamentals of laser operations; explain the hazards of lasers; identify personal protective equipment used with lasers; explain the differences between Class I, 3A, 3B, and 4; demonstrate knowledge of risk assessment; identify physical hazards of chemicals, describe the sources for health hazard determination; and explain the information required on a material safety data sheet.

Instruction: Major topics covered in the course are laser applications, laser operations, laser hazards, electromagnetic spectrum, toxicology, components of hazardous chemical training program, control methods that help reduce risk of chemical discharge and exposure, personal protective equipment, and elements of material safety data sheets. Methods of instruction include lecture, slides, workbooks, quizzes, and tests.

Credit Recommendation: In the lower division baccalaureate/associate degree category, 1 semester hour in Occupational Safety (7/94). **NOTE**: All 5 courses must be completed before any credit is granted.

Introduction to Dbase (060026)

Location: Miamisburg, OH.

Length: 8 hours (1 day).

Dates: February 1985-Present.

Objective: To understand database concepts and to use Dbase III+ as a time saving, organizational tool in the everyday work environment.

Learning Outcome: Upon successful completion of this course, the student will be able to understand database terminology to differentiate between files, records, and fields; create a Dbase III+ database on disk; modify and maintain a Dbase III+ database; and retrieve data from a Dbase III+ database.

Instruction: Major topics covered in the course are database concepts and applicability; database creation, manipulation, and maintenance; and data retrieval. Methods of instruction include lecture, discussion, visual aids, handouts, classroom exercises, and laboratory assignments.

Credit Recommendation: In the lower division baccalaureate/associate degree category, 2 semester hours in Computer Literacy/Office Automation if the student has completed Introduction to PC Hardware (060081), Introduction to DOS (060082), Introduction to Lotus (060027), and Introduction to WordPerfect (060079), or Multimate (060009) (4/94).

Introduction to Lotus (060027)

Location: Miamisburg, OH.

Length: 8 hours (1 day).

Dates: February 1985-Present.

Objective: To become a proficient user of Lotus 1-2-3 as a time saving, organizational tool in the everyday work environment.

Learning Outcome: Upon successful completion of this course, the student will be able to use and explain the Lotus 1-2-3 command menu; retrieve and modify an existing spreadsheet; build a new spreadsheet including labels, values, formulas, and functions; sort and query spreadsheet data; graph (chart) spreadsheet data; print spreadsheets; and define the role of spreadsheet software as a productivity tools.

Instruction: Major topics covered in the course are Lotus 1-2-3 commands, functions, and overview of uses; spreadsheet creation, manipulation, and maintenance; and building graphs and printing spreadsheets. Methods of instruction include lecture, discussion, visual aids, handouts, classroom exercises, and laboratory assignments.

Credit Recommendation: In the lower division baccalaureate/associate degree category, 2 semester hours in Computer Literacy/Office Automation if student has completed Introduction to PC Hardware (060081), Introduction to DOS (060082), Introduction to Dbase (060026), and Introduction to WordPerfect (060079), or Multimate (060009) (4/94).

Introduction to MS DOS (060082)

Location: Miamisburg, OH.

Length: 4 hours (.5 day).

Dates: June 1993-Present.

Objective: To understand the functions of an operating system, DOS commands, and their use in common PC applications.

Learning Outcome: Upon successful completion of this course, the student will be able to understand operating system functions and the use of DOS commands.

Instruction: Major topics covered in the course are an introduction to an operating system; variations of DOS; key DOS files; and directory file, and system maintenance. Methods of instruction include lecture, discussion, and laboratory exercises.

Credit Recommendation: In the lower division baccalaureate/associate degree category, 2 semester hours in Computer Literacy/Office Automation if student has completed Introduction to PC Hardware (060081), Introduction to Dbase (060026), Introduction to Lotus (060027), and Introduction to WordPerfect (060076), or Multimate (060009) (4/94).

Introduction to PC Hardware (060081)

Location: Miamisburg, OH.

Length: 4 hours (.5 day).

Dates: June 1993-Present.

Objective: To understand the major components of a PC, and input/output devices and their functions.

Learning Outcome: Upon successful completion of this course, the student will be able to identify PC components and explain their interrelationships; distinguish between temporary and permanent storage; and understand the functions and uses of expansion cards and slots, serial and parallel ports, keyboards, video monitors, modems, printers, and other input/output devices.

Instruction: Major topics covered in the course are an introduction to hardware and software, expansion cards and slots, temporary and permanent storage, serial and parallel ports, modems, and input/output devices. Methods of instruction include lecture, discussion, and laboratory exercises.

Credit Recommendation: In the lower division baccalaureate/associate degree category, 2 semester hours in Computer Literacy/Office Automation if student has completed Introduction to MS-DOS (060082), Introduction to Dbase (060026), Introduction to Lotus (060027), and Introduction to WordPerfect (060076), or Multimate (060009) (4/94).

Introduction to Performance-Based Training (PBT) (090073)

Location: Miamisburg, OH.

Length: 30 hours, residential (4 days).

Dates: March 1991-Present.

Objective: To provide the knowledge to prepare and conduct performance-based training, and a basic understanding of what is required to develop effective training programs.

Learning Outcome: Upon successful completion of this course, the student will be able to design, develop, and implement curriculum for employee training programs.

Instruction: Major topics covered in the course are needs analysis, job analysis, task analysis, performance-based learning objectives, evaluation measures, training settings, lesson plans, and training materials. Methods of instruction include lecture, discussion, individual and group exercises, and role play.

Credit Recommendation: In the lower division baccalaureate/associate degree category, 2 semester hours in Instruction Methodology (7/94).

Introduction to WordPerfect (060076)

Location: Miamisburg, OH.

Length: 8 hours (1 day).

Dates: September 1991-Present.

Objective: To introduce word processing concepts using WordPerfect commands and menus.

Learning Outcome: Upon successful completion of this course, the student will be able to create, save, and print a document; edit an existing document by copying, moving, inserting, and deleting blocks of text; use reveal codes; format the layout of a document; and convert Multimate documents to WordPerfect.

Instruction: Major topics covered in the course are list files including function keys and pull-down menus; document layouts; document editing including using the speller and thesaurus; and converting Multimate files to WordPerfect. Methods of instruction include lecture, discussion, visual aids, and laboratory exercises.

Credit Recommendation: In the lower division baccalaureate/associate degree category, 1 semester hour in Computer Science if student has completed Advanced WordPerfect (060079); or 2 semester hours in Computer Science if student has completed Introduction to MS-DOS (060082), Introduction to Dbase (060026), Introduction to Lotus (060027), and Introduction to PC Hardware (060081) (4/94).

Multimate (060009)

Location: Miamisburg, OH.

Length: 8 hours (1 day).

Dates: September 1984-Present.

Objective: To introduce various terms and concepts of word processing using Multimate, and to develop skills to format a document.

Learning Outcome: Upon successful completion of this course, the student will be able to create an original document; edit an existing document by copying, moving, inserting, and deleting text; and format and print a document.

Instruction: Major topics covered in the course are using the menu and various options of editing and formatting; paginating a document; using the main and custom dictionary; and saving and printing a document. Methods of instruction include lecture, discussion, visual aids, handouts, and laboratory exercises.

Credit Recommendation: In the lower division baccalaureate/associate degree category, 2 semester hours in Computer Literacy/Office Automation if the student has completed Introduction to MS-DOS (060082), Introduction to Dbase (060026), Introduction to Lotus (060027), and Introduction to PC Hardware (060081) (4/94).

On-the-Job Training (OJT) (090072)

Location: Miamisburg, OH.

Length: 30 hours, residential (4 days).

Dates: October 1990-Present.

Objective: To learn to teach the skills necessary to prepare and conduct on-the-job training.

Learning Outcome: Upon successful completion of this course, the student will have learned the skills necessary to prepare and conduct on-the-job training.

Instruction: Major topics covered in the course are the role of on-the-job training, training needs, training objectives, principles of adult learning, communication techniques, training aids and training materials, and evaluating trainee progress. Methods of instruction include lecture, discussion, individual and group exercises, presentations, and self-paced correspondence.

Credit Recommendation: In the lower division baccalaureate/associate degree category, 1 semester hour in Instructional Methodology (7/94).

Presenting Classroom Instruction (090074)

Location: Miamisburg, OH.

Length: 40 hours (5 days).

Dates: July 1991-Present.

Objective: To develop the basic knowledge and skills required for effectively providing classroom instruction.

Learning Outcome: Upon successful completion of this course, the student will be able to understand the role of the instructor; apply the principles of effective communication and presentation; effectively use instructional aids; evaluate trainee performance; and evaluate course effectiveness.

Instruction: Major topics covered in the course are the role of the instructor, principles of adult learning, principles of performance based training (PBT), effective communication and presentation skills, use of instruction aids, evaluation of trainee performance, and course evaluation. Methods of instruction include lecture, discussion, and taped presentation exercises.

Credit Recommendation: In the lower division baccalaureate/associate degree

category, 2 semester hours in Instructional Methods (7/94).

Radiological Worker/Industrial Hygiene Training
1. Bloodborne Pathogen (Mound Exposure Control Plan) (070123)
2. Bloodborne Pathogen (Generic) (070122)
3. Rad Worker II (035063)

Location: Miamisburg, OH.

Length: 14 hours (2 days).

Dates: *Courses 1 and 2:* August 1992-Present; *Course 3:* November 23, 1993-Present.

Objective: To become familiar with general aspects of Occupational Health and Safety issues attributed to Bloodborne Pathogen and Ionization Radiation.

Learning Outcome: Upon successful completion of Courses 1 and 2, the student will be able to describe bloodborne pathogens; discuss symptoms of bloodborne pathogens; describe how bloodborne pathogens are transmitted and controlled; describe universal precautions, engineering controls, and work practice controls that prevent or reduce exposure to bloodborne pathogens; and describe personal protective equipment that will reduce labels required by OSHA bloodborne pathogen standards and state requirement. Upon successful completion of Course 3, the student will be able to identify potential sources of ionizing radiation; differentiate between non-ionizing and ionizing radiation; define radioactivity and radioactivity half-life; identify physical characteristics, range/shielding, and biological hazards for the four types of ionizing radiation; and identify and manipulate the proper units to measure radiation and radioactivity.

Instruction: Major topics covered in the courses are Bloodborne Pathogen (Mound Exposure Control Plan), Bloodborn Pathogen (Generic), and Radiation Worker II. Methods of instruction include interactive video, trainers from specific work areas, infection control course, registered nurse, and occupational health nurse or physician.

Credit Recommendation: In the lower division baccalaureate/associate degree category, 1 semester hour in Occupational Health (7/94). **NOTE**: All 3 courses listed must be completed before credit is granted.

Root Cause Analysis (090076) (Formerly Root Cause Analysis [909976])

Location: Miamisburg, OH.

Length: 12 hours (2 days).

Dates: August 1991-Present.

Objective: To examine problems using root cause analysis, uncover the causes, and make recommendations for corrective action.

Learning Outcome: Upon successful completion of this course, the student will be able to demonstrate the use of questioning in identification of root cause; use problem analysis techniques to identify immediate cause; identify events and causal factors and be able to construct an event's causal analysis diagram; and identify barrier and controls and geographically display a barrier analysis diagram.

Instruction: Major topics covered in the course are problem analysis, event and causal analysis, barrier analysis, based root cause analysis, and corrective action. Methods of instruction include lecture and discussion (7/94).

Credit Recommendation: In the upper division baccalaureate degree category, 1 semester hour in Decision Processes in Engineering or Business (7/94).

Services Contracting (906020)

Location: Miamisburg, OH.

Length: 16 hours (2 days).

Dates: September 1992-Present.

Objective: To study the types of service contracts, how to select the most appropriate type to use, and how to administer these contracts.

Learning Outcome: Upon successful completion of this course, the student will be able to identify service contracts and their specific subcategory; determine the proper method of buying the needed services; explain the three basic methods to solicit, evaluate, and award service contracts; and explain and apply the rights and obligations of both parties as set forth in various contract clauses.

Instruction: Major topics covered in the course are service contracting, evaluating outside procurement, arriving at a win-win contract, and administering service contracts. Methods of instruction include lecture, case studies, and in-class exercises.

Credit Recommendation: In the lower division baccalaureate/associate degree category, 1 semester hour in Contracting and Procurement (7/94).

Statement of Work (906022)

Location: Miamisburg, OH.

Length: 16 hours (2 days).

Dates: January 1993-Present.

Objective: To study statements of work, specifically how to write them, and how to use them

Learning Outcome: Upon successful completion of this course, the student will be able to understand the reasons for a statement of work; write a clear, cohesive statement of work; understand how a statement of work is a tool used in procurement and related fields; and understand how EG&G Mound and the DOE use a statement of work as a procurement device.

Instruction: Major topics covered in the course are specification writing, preparing quality statements of work, preparing effective technical evaluations, analyzing technical effort, and communicating with vendors. Methods of instruction include lecture and team exercises.

Credit Recommendation: In the lower division baccalaureate/associate degree category, 1 semester hour in Contracting and Procurement (7/94).

Stress Management (090029)

Location: Miamisburg, OH.

Length: 10 hours (2 days).

Dates: February 1986-Present.

Objective: To learn to manage stress in daily life situations by examining attitudes, beliefs, and behaviors; and to develop strategies to reduce stress.

Learning Outcome: Upon successful completion of this course, the student will be able to evaluate their own attitudes and belief systems in order to make positive changes in their life; understand self-help techniques; and recognize the need for professional counseling for stress.

Instruction: Major topics covered in the course are becoming aware of stress, taking stock of your stress levels, managing stress in yourself, solving stress problems, and looking ahead to control stress. Methods of instruction include lecture, discussion, self-assessment tools, reading, exercises, and quizzes.

Credit Recommendation: In the lower division baccalaureate/associate degree category, 1 semester hour in Stress Management/Psychology (7/94).

English Language Institute of America

The English Language Institute is a division of National Learning Systems, Inc., a marketing division of International Correspondence Schools (ICS), the nation's oldest proprietary distance learning institution. The Institute, formerly located in Chicago, IL, has offered the Practical English and the Command of Words program since 1955.

The Institute recognizes that effective communication and a solid understanding of basic mathematical skills are a demand of contemporary business life. The total focus of the Institute is upon the development and delivery of high quality educational products to adults in the business community. Course developers and faculty members, with both practical and theoretical expertise, continually monitor and periodically revise course materials as necessary. Students are usually employees of business and government agencies that approve the course for employee participation. However, individuals can and do take the course independently.

ICS is a world leader in the field of independent learning. Since its founding in 1891, ICS has pioneered in the development of self-paced independent study materials. A charter member of the Distance Education and Training Council, ICS is accredited by the Council and is also licensed by the Pennsylvania Department of Education. The English Language Institute is also a member of the Distance Education and Training Council.

Source of official student records: Registry of Credit Recommendations, American Council on Education, One Dupont Circle, Washington, DC 20036-1193 or Director, Administrative Services, The English Language Institute, 925 Oak Street, Scranton, PA 18515.

Additional information about the courses: College Credit Recommendation Service, American Council on Education, One Dupont Circle, Washington, DC 20036-1193.

Practical English and the Command of Words

Location: Correspondence Program.

Length: Self-study.

Dates: July 1979-Present.

Objective: To provide basic English communication skills.

Learning Outcome: Upon successful completion of this course, the student will be able to communicate more effectively both verbally and in writing.

Instruction: Major topics covered in the course are vocabulary development, pronunciation, grammar and usage, spelling, speech, word meaning, punctuation, sentence structure, paragraph organization, and telephone courtesy. Methods of instruction include self-study, texts, study guides, and a proctored final examination.

Credit Recommendation: In the lower division baccalaureate/associate degree category, 3 semester hours in English as an elective in Grammar and Usage, and in the lower division baccalaureate/associate degree category, 1 semester hour in Business Communication (1/84) (6/94). **NOTE:** In order to receive credit, students must take and successfully pass a final examination developed by the English Language Institute. The final examination can be administered (and monitored) by a company training officer and scored by the Institute or it can be administered, monitored, and scored directly by the Institute.

Real Life Math and the Power of Numbers (Basic Business Math)

Location: Correspondence Program.

Length: Self-study.

Dates: September 1993-Present.

Objective: To provide practical experience in the application of Basic Business Math.

Learning Outcome: Upon successful completion of this course, the student will be able to understand and apply a variety of basic principles of business math used in everyday business situations.

Instruction: Major topics covered in the course are simple and compound interest, payroll calculations and taxes, discounts, product markups and markdowns, loans, basic use of statistics, basic life and property insurance, and depreciation. Methods of instruction include self-study, texts, study guides, and a proctored final examination.

Credit Recommendation: In the vocational certificate category, 3 semester hours as a business elective, or in the lower division baccalaureate/associate degree category, 2 semester hours in Math (6/94). **NOTE:** In order to receive credit, students must take and successfully pass a final examination developed by the English Language Institute. The final examination can be administered (and monitored) by a company training officer and scored by the Institute or it can be administered, monitored, and scored directly by the Institute.

Enhanced Training Opportunities Program, Inc. (ETOP)

ETOP is part of the Employment Security Package negotiated in 1986 between the IBEW and Lucent Technologies (formerly AT&T) which provides EM-3 Council represented employees with education and training opportunities not covered by Lucent Technologies Tuition Assistance Plan.

The objective of ETOP is to make learning experiences available to Lucent employees represented by the IBEW EM-3 Council which help to enhance their occupational skills, provide opportunities for personal and career development, improve communications skills, increase knowledge of state-of-the art technology relevant to the present and future needs of business community, in the event they are affected by Lucent Technologies force reductions.

In late 1987, local ETOP Committees recognized the large need within Lucent Technologies and local job markets for computer skills. This need, and our desire to provide employees with current job qualifying skills in computer technology, gave birth to the idea of establishing on-site Computer Training Centers. These computer Centers have been established at the following seven manufacturing locations: Allentown, PA; Columbus, OH; Denver, CO; Little Rock, AR; Oklahoma City, OK; Omaha, NE; Reading, PA; and Shreveport, LA.

Source of official student records: Registry of Credit Recommendations, American Council on Education, One Dupont Circle, Washington, DC 20036-1193 or Sharon Crowe, ETOP National Office, 1013 Hawthorn Drive, Itasca, IL 60143 (630)-250-9440, (630) 250-9404-Fax.

Additional information about the courses: College Credit Recommendation Service, American Council on Education, One Dupont Circle, Washington, DC 20036-1193.

Introduction to DOS

Location: Various locations throughout the United States.

Length: 20 hours (4 hours a week for 5 weeks or 2 hours a week for 10 weeks).

Dates: May 1988-Present.

Objective: To provide the student with a basic understanding of DOS and its usage related to personal computers.

Learning Outcome: Upon successful completion of this course, the student will be able to perform fundamental DOS commands.

Instruction: Major topics covered in the course are DOS file manipulation commands, MS backup program, MS antivirus program, and basic computer operation. Methods of instruction include lecture, video, hands-on, projects, exercises, and homework.

Credit Recommendation: In the lower division baccalaureate/associate degree category, 1 semester hour in Introduction to DOS (6/95).

Introduction to Lotus 1-2-3

Location: Various locations throughout the United States.

Length: 20 hours (4 hours a week for 5 weeks or 2 hours a week for 10 weeks).

Dates: May 1988-Present.

Objective: To provide introduction to fundamental spreadsheet applications using Lotus 1-2-3.

Learning Outcome: Upon successful completion of this course, the student will be able to enter and edit spreadsheet data; work with spreadsheet formulas; manage spreadsheet files; format the worksheet; and print a worksheet.

Instruction: Major topics covered in the course are an introduction to spreadsheet; file management; cell operations; formulas; printing a spreadsheet; and fundamental graphing. Methods of instruction include lecture, video, hands-on, projects, exercises, and homework.

Credit Recommendation: In the lower division baccalaureate/associate degree category, 1 semester hour in Introduction to Spreadsheet Software or Lotus 1-2-3 (6/95).

Introduction to Microcomputers (COM 101)

Location: Various locations throughout the United States.

Length: 20 hours (4 hours a week for 5 weeks or 2 hours a week for 10 weeks).

Dates: May 1988-Present.

Objective: To provide the student with an introduction to microcomputers.

Learning Outcome: Upon successful completion of this course, the student will be able to demonstrate the fundamentals of operating a microcomputer, demonstrate comprehension of fundamental DOS commands, and experience an introduction to the windows environment.

Instruction: Major topics covered in the course are basic DOS commands, fundamental computer operations, basic definitions system software, and keyboarding/mouse operations. Methods of instruction include lecture, video, hands-on, projects, exercises, and homework.

Credit Recommendation: In the lower division baccalaureate/associate degree category, 1 semester hour in Introduction to Microcomputers (6/95).

Introduction to Microsoft Excel

Location: Various locations throughout the United States.

Length: 20 hours (4 hours a week for 5 weeks or 2 hours a week for 10 weeks).

Dates: May 1988-Present.

Objective: To provide an introduction to fundamental spreadsheet applications using Microsoft Excel.

Learning Outcome: Upon successful completion of this course, the student will be able to create a spreadsheet using Microsoft Excel; save and print a spreadsheet using Microsoft Excel; demonstrate use of fundamental spreadsheet commands and formulas; and create a graph using spreadsheet data, and format a spreadsheet.

Instruction: Major topics covered in the course are basic spreadsheet operations; comprehension of cell operations; basic spreadsheet calculations and formulas and managing files. Methods of instruction include lecture, video, hands-on, projects, exercises, and homework.

Credit Recommendation: In the lower division baccalaureate/associate degree category, 1 semester hour Introduction to Spreadsheet Software or Excel (6/95).

Introduction to Microsoft Word

Location: Various locations throughout the United States.

Length: 20 hours (4 hours a week for 5 weeks or 2 hours a week for 10 weeks).

Dates: May 1988-Present.

Objective: To provide students with an introduction to fundamental word processing applications using Microsoft Word software. Students will feel comfortable using Microsoft Word within a Windows environment.

Learning Outcome: Upon successful completion of this course, the student will be able to create documents in Microsoft Word using fundamental format, save, and print commands.

Instruction: Major topics covered in the course are fundamental word processing terminology; basic text formatting; page set-up; table, header and footer creation; and document save and print. Methods of instruction include lecture, video, hands-on, projects, exercises, and homework.

Credit Recommendation: In the lower division baccalaureate/associate degree category, 1 semester hour in Introduction to Microsoft Word (6/95).

Introduction to Windows

Location: Various locations throughout the United States.

Length: 20 hours (4 hours a week for 5 weeks or 2 hours a week for 10 weeks).

Dates: May 1988-Present.

Objective: To provide the student with an operational knowledge base of the Microsoft Windows program environment.

Learning Outcome: Upon successful completion of this course, the student will be able to install, load, and utilize various MS-Windows applications, and to perform various MS-Windows program commands.

Instruction: Major topics covered in the course are file manipulation, print commands, and desktop formatting in the Microsoft Windows environment. Methods of instruction include lecture, video, hands-on, projects, exercises, and homework.

Credit Recommendation: In the lower division baccalaureate/associate degree category, 1 semester hour in Introduction to Windows (6/95).

Introduction to WordPerfect

Location: Various locations throughout the United States.

Length: 20 hours (4 hours a week for 5 weeks or 2 hours a week for 10 weeks).

Dates: May 1988-Present.

Objective: To provide students with an introduction to fundamental word processing applications using WordPerfect software. Students will feel comfortable using WordPerfect within a DOS environment.

Learning Outcome: Upon successful completion of this course, the student will be able to create documents in WordPerfect using basic format, save, and print commands.

Instruction: Major topics covered in the course are fundamental word processing terminology; text formatting; page setup; table, header and footer creation; and document save and print. Methods of instruction include lecture, video, hands-on, projects, exercises, and homework.

Credit Recommendation: In the lower division baccalaureate/associate degree category, 1 semester hour in WordPerfect (6/95).

Entergy Operations, Inc.

Entergy Corporation is one of the larger investor-owned public utility holding companies in the United States, and the leading electricity supplier in the Middle South region. Headquartered in New Orleans, Entergy serves more than 2.3 million retail customers through its operating companies in Arkansas, Louisiana, Mississippi and Texas. Entergy also provides wholesale electricity off-System to other utilities, and markets its energy expertise worldwide.

Entergy's core business is structured along functional lines and is composed of three System groups: Energy Supply; Transmission, Distribution, and Customer Service; and Entergy Business Support. A fourth group, Entergy Enterprises, Inc. manages the company's consulting services and nonregulated businesses.

Source of official student records: Registry of Credit Recommendations, American Council on Education, One Dupont Circle, Washington, DC 20036-1193.

Additional information about the courses: College Credit Recommendation Service, American Council on Education, One Dupont Circle, Washington, DC 20036-1193.

Administration, Management, Communication and Technical Specifications

Location: Waterford 3 Training Center.

Length: 70 hours (2 weeks).

Dates: January 1986-December 1997.

Objective: To provide the student with an understanding of the administrative procedures and communication methodologies necessary to perform assigned responsibilities in a nuclear power plant and to provide the student with an in-depth understanding of the technical specifications governing the administration and management of a nuclear power plant.

Learning Outcome: Upon successful completion of this course, the student will be able to explain the content and purpose of Title 10 of the Code of Federal Regulations and its impact on nuclear power plants; state and explain technical specifications and their basis for plant systems and operating parameters; explain methods for calculating off site radiation doses and monitoring requirements; and recognize good interpersonal communication and teamwork skills.

Instruction: Major topics covered in the course are a discussion of the Code of Federal Regulations, technical specifications, general administrative procedures, interpersonal communications and teamwork skills. Methods of instruction include lecture and examinations.

Credit Recommendation: In the lower division baccalaureate/associate degree category, 1 semester hour in Supervision (12/92).

Electric Power Distribution

Location: Waterford 3 Training Center.

Length: 30 hours (1 week).

Dates: January 1986-December 1997.

Objective: To provide the student with an understanding of the electric power distribution network at a nuclear generating facility.

Learning Outcome: Upon successful completion of this course, the student will be able to state the purpose of various distribution systems, draw one-line diagrams of various systems, list major components, and state technical specifications or limiting conditions of operation associated with the various distribution systems.

Instruction: Major topics covered in the course are electrical distribution, dc distribution, inverters, low voltage and high voltage distribution systems. Methods of instruction include lecture and examinations.

Credit Recommendation: In the lower division baccalaureate/associate degree category, 1 semester hour in Electrical Technology (12/92).

Emergency Planning and Radiation Protection

Location: Waterford 3 Training Center.

Length: 20 hours (1 week).

Dates: January 1986-December 1997.

Objective: To provide the student with knowledge of emergency planning, emergency preparedness, and the associated topics of environmental monitoring and radiation detection, quantification and protection.

Learning Outcome: Upon successful completion of this course, the student will be able to describe the various emergency plan functions, classifications and actions and explain the differences between these classifications and actions; describe various types of radiation, their effect on man and methods of limiting dose; calculate dose projections; understand relevant parameters in radioactive plume dispersion, and environmental monitoring and movement of dispersed radioactivity.

Instruction: Major topics covered in the course are emergency planning and preparedness concepts, organization and actions, biological effects of ionizing radiation, and methods detecting ionizing radiation. Methods of instruction include lecture and examinations.

Credit Recommendation: In the lower division baccalaureate/associate degree category, 1 semester hour in Radiation Protection Technology (12/92).

Engineered Safeguard Systems

Location: Waterford 3 Training Center.

Length: 110 hours (3 weeks).

Dates: January 1986-December 1997.

Objective: To provide an introduction to nuclear power plant engineered safeguard systems, emphasis placed on design basis for the safeguard systems.

Learning Outcome: Upon successful completion of this course, the student will be able to identify components and instrumentation, describe flow paths, state technical specification limits, and list subsystems interlocks and automatic actuation signals including setpoints for the various systems.

Instruction: Major topics covered in the course are plant protection system, shield building ventilation system, containment spray system, safety injection and shutdown cooling, emergency diesel generators, reactor auxiliary building heating ventilation and air conditioning, and emergency feedwater system. Methods of instruction include lecture, classroom exercises, and examinations.

Credit Recommendation: In the lower division baccalaureate/associate degree category, 3 semester hours in Nuclear Technology (12/92).

Fundamentals of Electrical Theory

Location: Waterford 3 Training Center.

Length: 60 hours (2 weeks).

Dates: January 1986-December 1997.

Objective: To provide the student with the fundamentals of dc and ac electricity, magnetism, generators, and motors.

Learning Outcome: Upon successful completion of this course, the student will be able to describe concepts of electricity, dc and ac circuits, magnetism, and solve simple problems based on these concepts.

Instruction: Major topics covered in the course are Coulomb's law, Ohm's law, dc circuits, Kirchhoff's laws, magnetism, ac circuits, reactance and impedance, generators, and motors. Methods of instruction include lecture, laboratory, in class exercises, and examinations.

Credit Recommendation: In the lower division baccalaureate/associate degree

category, 3 semester hours in Non-Calculus General Physics (12/92).

Main and Auxiliary Feedwater Systems

Location: Waterford 3 Training Center.
Length: 30 hours (1 week).
Dates: January 1986-December 1997.
Objective: To provide the student with an introduction to the main and auxiliary feedwater systems and the associated normal, abnormal and emergency procedures required for successful operation.
Learning Outcome: Upon successful completion of this course, the student will be able to identify, describe and state the primary purpose for the major components of the various systems; list interlocks, controls, instrumentation, and trips available for the major components of the various systems.
Instruction: Major topics covered in the course are the main and auxiliary feedwater systems, feedwater control, feedwater pump and feedwater turbine. Methods of instruction include lecture, in-class exercises and examinations.
Credit Recommendation: In the lower division baccalaureate/associate degree category, 1 semester hour in Nuclear Technology (12/92).

Main and Auxiliary Steam Systems

Location: Waterford 3 Training Center.
Length: 30 hours (1 week).
Dates: January 1986 December 1997.
Objective: To provide the student with an understanding of the main and auxiliary steam systems including all major components, flowpaths, and operating principles.
Learning Outcome: Upon successful completion of this course, the student will be able to identify, describe and state the purpose for the major components of the various systems; draw one line diagram including all major components and system flow paths; identify instrumentation, controls, and setpoints available for the major components of the various systems; and discuss automatic and operator actions associated with the setpoints.
Instruction: Major topics covered in the course are main steam system, auxiliary steam system, condenser air evacuation, and chemical addition system. Methods of instruction include lecture, in-class exercises and examinations.
Credit Recommendation: In the lower division baccalaureate/associate degree category, 1 semester hour in Nuclear Technology (12/92).

Nuclear Power Plant Support Systems

Location: Waterford 3 Training Center.
Length: 67 hours (2 weeks).
Dates: January 1986-December 1997.
Objective: To introduce the student to various systems associated with the operation of a commercial nuclear power plant; emphasis on theory, design basis, components, and operational aspects associated with each system.
Learning Outcome: Upon successful completion of this course, the student will be able to identify components and instrumentation associated with the various systems; identify and apply technical specifications peculiar to the various systems; and summarize design features and draw flow diagrams where applicable.
Instruction: Major topics covered in the course are hydrogen control system integrated with control room, fuel handling building, and turbine building heating ventilation and air conditioning, primary and secondary makeup water systems and degasifier, intake structure, instrument and station air systems, steam generator blowdown system, and fuel pool and turbine building water cooling systems. Methods of instruction include lecture and examinations.
Credit Recommendation: In the lower division baccalaureate/associate degree category, 2 semester hours in Nuclear Technology (12/92).

Nuclear Reactor Accident Analysis

Location: Waterford 3 Training Center.
Length: 120 hours (3 weeks).
Dates: January 1986-December 1997.
Objective: To provide a theoretical understanding of potential nuclear reactor accident scenarios, the ability to predict the behavior of reactor instrumentation in such conditions, and an understanding of the significance of the provided information.
Learning Outcome: Upon successful completion of this course, the student will be able to discuss operation and function of self-powered neutron, and excore detectors, instrumentation qualification, accident progression as a function of radioisotopes present in reactor inventory, radioisotopes present in containment, hydrogen and other noncondensible gases present, core exit thermocouple temperatures; identify safety concerns related to reduced reactor system inventory; discuss accident progression from actual events; and understand plant emergency procedures, and identify appropriate steps given hypothetical plant conditions.
Instruction: Major topics covered in the course are accident analysis relating to incore and excore neutron detectors, instrumentation qualification, reactor inventory, noncondensible gas inventory, core exit thermocouple, radioactivity inventory in the reactor coolant system; and a discussion of most major reactor incidents and plant specific safety analysis. Methods of instruction include lecture.
Credit Recommendation: In the upper division baccalaureate degree category, 2 semester hours in Nuclear Science (12/92).

Pre-Calculus

Location: Waterford 3 Training Center.
Length: 32 hours (1 week).
Dates: January 1986-December 1997.
Objective: To provide the student with an introduction to algebra, logarithms, trigonometry, and the concepts of differential and integral calculus.
Learning Outcome: Upon successful completion of this course, the student will be able to solve linear, quadratic, exponential and logarithmic equations, manipulate algebraic expressions, define and use trigonometric functions, relate the derivative of a function to rates of change and slopes of a graph, and relate the integral of a function to a summation and to the area under a curve.
Instruction: Major topics covered in the course are algebraic expressions, solving and graphing linear, polynomial, exponential, and logarithmic equations, functions, trigonometric functions, and introduction to concepts of differential and integral calculus. Methods of instruction include lecture, classroom exercises, and examinations.
Credit Recommendation: In the lower division baccalaureate/associate degree category, 2 semester hours in Mathematics (Basic Algebra and Trigonometry) (12/92).

Principles of Power Plant Water Chemistry and Material Science

Location: Waterford 3 Training Center.
Length: 19 hours (1 week).
Dates: January 1986-December 1997.
Objective: To provide the student with an understanding of basic principles of water chemistry and materials science.
Learning Outcome: Upon successful completion of this course, the student will

be able to discuss atomic structure, units of concentration, pH, chemical equilibrium, electrochemistry and corrosion; relate stress, strain, and elasticity; and describe material defects and the effects on the properties.

Instruction: Major topics covered in the course are atomic structure, bonding, units of concentration, solutions, ion exchange, electrochemistry, corrosion, water treatment, stress, strain, crystal structure, and crystalline defects. Methods of instruction include lecture and examinations.

Credit Recommendation: In the lower division baccalaureate/associate degree category, 1 semester hour in General Chemistry (12/92).

Reactor Coolant System

Location: Waterford 3 Training Center.

Length: 57 hours (2 weeks).

Dates: January 1986-December 1997.

Objective: To provide the student with an introduction to the reactor coolant system and the associated normal, off-normal and emergency procedures required for normal operations.

Learning Outcome: Upon successful completion of this course, the student will be able to draw system diagrams of the reactor coolant system, the reactor vessel, incore and excore instrumentation systems, reactor regulating system, power cutback system, the boron management system, and the fuel management system; discuss the individual components in each of the above systems, their use and functioning.

Instruction: Major topics covered in the course are a discussion of reactor coolant system flowpath and components, the interrelationship between reactor coolant system components temperature and pressure; nuclear fuel, fuel assemblies, and their characteristics. Methods of instruction include lecture, laboratory, classroom exercises, and examinations.

Credit Recommendation: In the lower division baccalaureate/associate degree category, 2 semester hours in Nuclear Reactor Technology (12/92).

Reactor Engineering

Location: Waterford 3 Training Center.

Length: 55 hours (2 weeks).

Dates: January 1986-December 1997.

Objective: To provide detailed instruction regarding the fundamental principles and advanced theories associated with nuclear engineering.

Learning Outcome: Upon successful completion of this course, the student will be able to discuss radioactive decay, the fission process, the six factor equation and specifics of plant control related to fuel burnup and rodworth; calculate reaction rates for known neutron fluxes, reactor power as a function of time given a known reactor period, and poison inventory as a function of core life.

Instruction: Major topics covered in the course are basic nuclear physics concepts including binding energy, core stability and radioactive decay; the fission process including definitions of fissile, fissionable and fertile material; the six factor equation; neutron kinetics including delayed neutrons and neutron lifetime; critical and subcritical reactors; the approach to criticality; the effect of poisons on reactor operation and plant specific operational aspects relating to reactor engineering. Methods of instruction include lecture and examinations.

Credit Recommendation: In the lower division baccalaureate/associate degree category, 2 semester hours in Reactor Engineering (12/92).

Theory of Instrumentation and Control

Location: Waterford 3 Training Center.

Length: 16 hours (2 days).

Dates: January 1986-December 1997.

Objective: To introduce the student to the fundamentals of instrumentation and control, including the principles of measurement of pressure, liquid level, fluid flow, and temperature.

Learning Outcome: Upon successful completion of this course, the student will be able to describe methods and instruments used to measure pressure, temperature, liquid levels, and fluid flow; explain fundamentals of open and closed loop control systems with pneumatic, hydraulic and electrical actuators.

Instruction: Major topics covered in the course are pressure, temperature, liquid level, and flow sensors, fluid flow fundamentals, Bernoulli's equation, recorders, instrument accuracy and precision, actuators and positioners, open and closed control systems. Methods of instruction include lecture.

Credit Recommendation: In the lower division baccalaureate/associate degree category, 1 semester hour in Instrumentation and Control (12/92).

Thermodynamics, Heat Transfer and Fluid Flow

Location: Waterford 3 Training Center.

Length: 70 hours (2 weeks).

Dates: January 1986-December 1997.

Objective: To introduce the student to fundamental thermodynamic principles and their applications to heat transfer and fluid flow.

Learning Outcome: Upon successful completion of this course, the student will be able to describe and define relevant thermodynamic, fluid dynamics and heat transfer processes and terms; apply simple energy balance, mass balance and Bernoulli equations and knowing inlet and outlet states, calculate work, heat or mass flow in plant components; evaluate heat transfer in specific situations; and discuss effects of various natural processes on plant performance.

Instruction: Major topics covered in the course are basic thermodynamics, plant specific turbine thermodynamics, Bernoulli's equation, pump laws of performance, a discussion of basic heat transfer modes of convection, conduction and radiation; heat generation in a nuclear reactor; heat transfer within fuel rods; valves, pumps and heat exchanges, and a discussion of plant specific thermal limits and core heat removal considerations. Methods of instruction include lecture and problem solving.

Credit Recommendation: In the lower division baccalaureate/associate degree category, 3 semester hours in Thermodynamics (12/92).

Turbine Generator System

Location: Waterford 3 Training Center.

Length: 40 hours (1 week).

Dates: January 1986-December 1997.

Objective: To provide the student with knowledge of the turbine, main generator, exciter, and associated support systems.

Learning Outcome: Upon successful completion of this course, the student will be able to state purposes of the components and systems, describe flowpaths, identify setpoints and operating limits, state technical specifications wherever applicable, and describe appropriate instruments and controls.

Instruction: Major topics covered in the course are main turbine and moisture separator reheater, electro-hydraulic control system, exciter, turbine supervisory equipment, gland sealing steam system, and lube oil functions. Methods of instruction include lecture, classroom exercises, and examinations.

Credit Recommendation: In the lower division baccalaureate/associate degree category, 1 semester hour in Electrical Technology (12/92).

Entergy Operations, Inc., River Bend

River Bend Nuclear Station, a member of Entergy Operations, Inc., began operation in 1985. The purpose of the organization is to produce electricity in a manner that protects the safety and welfare of the employees and the general public. To accomplish this purpose, the organization is charged with the responsibility of providing such scientific, engineering, technical, managerial, and operations' educational and training programs. The mission of training is to promote excellence through high quality thorough, in-depth, and challenging programs and courses. To accomplish this mission, River Bend management is dedicated to supporting a learning environment that encourages innovation, professionalism, teamwork, intellectual curiosity, and high performance.

To build the foundation for the learning environment, the River Bend Nuclear Training Department is responsible for the development and maintenance of educational and training programs that offer a challenging level of knowledge, theory, and concepts. The Operations Training Group is composed of instructors who have extensive knowledge in scientific and engineering areas, and who hold a United States Nuclear Regulatory Commission License or Certification. Additionally, the instructors complete an instructor training program including the following: adult learning and motivational theory, principles of performance-based education, classroom presentation skills, and evaluation methods. Technical and instructional continuing training is an annual requirement.

Courses are designed and developed by qualified instructors who have initial and continuing classes on writing objectives, developing materials, and writing examinations. All instruction is conducted using approved course materials, and a formal revision process is in place to ensure technical accuracy of the materials. Courses at River Bend are systematically evaluated to ensure students' needs and knowledge requirements are met. Course evaluation includes feedback from students, supervisors, upper management, and evaluation specialists. Course examination results are analyzed to ensure objectives are being mastered.

Delivery methods at River Bend employ a variety of presentational techniques to facilitate student involvement in the learning process and to enhance the learning experience. Case studies, participative lectures, demonstrations, scenarios, questioning, and role playing are but a few of the methods used.

The Generation Support Building houses a centralized library of reference and resource materials that support licensing and engineering departments and are available for use by all site employees. Although the materials are primarily site specific documents, the collection also includes approximately four hundred texts that can be checked out by students. In addition, the Administrative Services Department maintains a satellite station in the Training Center where current revisions of plant procedures are kept. Administrative Services also maintains documents and drawing in the plant-referenced simulator. The Training Library also contains approximately five hundred texts that support the education and training programs.

Source of official student records: Registry of Credit Recommendation, American Council on Education, One Dupont Circle, Washington, DC 20036-1193.

Additional information about the courses: College Credit Recommendation Service, American Council on Education, One Dupont Circle, Washington, DC 20036-1193.

Atomic and Nuclear Physics of Reactors (Fundamentals of Classical and Nuclear Physics)

Location: St. Francisville, LA.

Length: 34 hours (2 weeks).

Dates: January 1987-Present.

Objective: To provide the student with an understanding of the fundamental principles of classical and nuclear physics and their applicability to the design and operation of a nuclear power plant.

Learning Outcome: Upon successful completion of this course, the student will be able to understand and describe the concepts of linear and angular motion, forces, work, power, energy, pressure, nuclear reactions, radiation, nuclear power reactor kinetics and operation; and solve problems associated with these concepts.

Instruction: Major topics covered in the course are force, motion, energy, work, power, Newton's Laws, nuclear reactions, radioactivity, fission, interaction of radiation with matter, reaction rates and reactivity coefficients, neutron life cycle, cross section and flux, sub-critical multiplication, fission product poisons, control rod theory and function, and nuclear power reactor kinetics and operation. Methods of instruction include lecture, classroom discussion, visual materials, self-study, and written examinations.

Credit Recommendation: In the lower division baccalaureate/associate degree category, 2 semester hours in Physics (7/97).

Corrosion and Water Chemistry in Nuclear Plant Components (Fundamentals of Chemistry)

Location: St. Francisville, LA.

Length: 31 hours (2 weeks).

Dates: January 1987-Present.

Objective: To provide the student with an understanding of the fundamental principles of chemistry as they apply to the design and operation of a nuclear power plant.

Learning Outcome: Upon successful completion of this course, the student will be able to understand and describe the characteristics of atoms, the periodic table of the elements, principles of chemical bonding, reactions of acids, bases and salts, pH theory and water purity, chemical equilibrium, corrosion, and the effects of temperature and radiation on water chemistry parameters; and solve problems associated with these concepts.

Instruction: Major topics covered in the course are properties of the elements, the periodic table, atomic bonding, chemical reactions, ionization and equilibrium, reactions of acids, bases and salts, corrosion of metals, pH, ion exchange resins and water purity, the effects of dissolved gases, temperature, and radiation on water chemistry parameters. Methods of instruction include lecture, classroom discussion, visual materials, self-study, and written examinations.

Credit Recommendation: In the lower division baccalaureate/associate degree category, 2 semester hours in Chemical Technology (7/97).

Fundamentals of Electrical Science

Location: St. Francisville, LA.

Length: 64 hours (4 weeks).

Dates: January 1987-Present.

Objective: To provide the student with an understanding of the fundamental principles of electrical science and their application to the design and operation of a nuclear power plant.

Learning Outcome: Upon successful completion of this course, the student will be able to understand and describe electrical prints, diagrams and schematics, logic diagrams, electricity, currents, circuits, batteries, generators, motors, transformers, test instruments, wiring schemes and grounding; and solve problems associated with these concepts.

Instruction: Major topics covered in the course are electrical print reading, diagrams and schematics, logic diagrams, electrical theory, alternating and direct current, circuit theory, voltage, Kirchhoff's laws, generators, motors, regulators and resonance, power triangle, three-phase circuits, transformers, test and measuring devices, system components, protection equipment, wiring schemes, and grounding. Methods of instruction include lecture, classroom discussion, visual materials, self-study, and written examinations.

Credit Recommendation: In the lower division baccalaureate/associate degree category, 4 semester hours in Electrical Technology or non-calculus based General Physics (7/97).

Fundamentals of Instrumentation and Control

Location: St. Francisville, LA.
Length: 36 hours (3 weeks).
Dates: January 1987-Present.

Objective: To provide the student with an understanding of the fundamental principles of instrumentation and control and their application to the design and operation of a nuclear power plant.

Learning Outcome: Upon successful completion of this course, the student will be able to understand and describe the operational characteristics of assorted detectors, indicators, sensors, counters, controllers, control systems and control loop diagrams; and solve problems associated with these concepts.

Instruction: Major topics covered in the course are temperature, pressure, level, and flow detectors; position indicators; radiation detection devices; ionization chambers; scintillation counters; neutron instrumentation; controllers and various control systems; and diagrams. Methods of instruction include lecture, classroom discussion, visual materials, self-study, and written examinations.

Credit Recommendation: In the lower division baccalaureate/associate degree category, 2 semester hours in Instrumentation and Control (7/97).

Fundamentals of Material Science

Location: St. Francisville, LA.
Length: 26 hours (2 weeks).
Dates: January 1987-Present.

Objective: To provide the student with an understanding of the fundamental principles of material science and their applicability to the design and operation of a nuclear power plant.

Learning Outcome: Upon successful completion of this course, the student will be able to understand and describe the structure and physical properties of materials, the effects of stress and strain on metals, corrosion and embrittlement, thermal shock and brittle fracture, and the effects of heat and radiation on inorganic/organic materials; and solve problems associated with these concepts.

Instruction: Major topics covered in the course are physical properties of metals; chemical bonding; crystalline structures of metals; imperfections in materials; types of stress and strain; Hooke's Law and Young's Modulus; elasticity; corrosion and embrittlement of metals; thermal shock and brittle fracture; and the effects of temperature, beta, gamma-photon, and neutron radiation on inorganic and organic materials. Methods of instruction include lecture, classroom discussion, visual materials, self-study, and written examinations.

Credit Recommendation: In the lower division baccalaureate/associate degree category, 2 semester hours in Material Science (7/97).

Fundamentals of Mathematics

Location: St. Francisville, LA.
Length: 23 hours (2 weeks).
Dates: January 1987-Present.

Objective: To provide the student with an understanding of the fundamental principles of mathematics and their application in the technical disciplines required for the design and operation of a nuclear power plant.

Learning Outcome: Upon successful completion of this course, the student will be able to understand and use algebra, geometry, trigonometry, statistics, units, and vectors; and perform basis calculations associated with these subjects.

Instruction: Major topics covered in the course are algebra, geometry, trigonometry, statistics, imaginary and complex numbers, introductory calculus, unit systems, and vectors. Methods of instruction include lecture, classroom discussion, visual materials, self-study, and written examinations.

Credit Recommendation: In the lower division baccalaureate/associate degree category, 1 semester hour in Mathematics (Basic Algebra and Trigonometry) (7/97).

Fundamentals of Thermodynamics, Heat Transfer & Fluid Flow

Location: St. Francisville, LA.
Length: 26 hours (2 weeks).
Dates: January 1987-Present.

Objective: To provide the student with an understanding of the fundamental principles of thermodynamics, heat transfer and fluid flow and their application to the design and operation of a nuclear power plant.

Learning Outcome: Upon successful completion of this course, the student will be able to understand and describe the basic principles of thermodynamics, heat transfer, and fluid flow; and solve problems associated with these concepts.

Instruction: Major topics covered in the course are thermodynamic properties, the first and second laws of thermodynamics, compression processes, conduction, convection, radiant and boiling heat transfer, heat generation and decay, heat laminar, and turbulent and two-phase fluid flow. Methods of instruction include lecture, classroom discussion, visual materials, self-study, and written examinations.

Credit Recommendation: In the upper division baccalaureate degree category, 2 semester hours in Mechanical Engineering or Thermal Sciences (7/97). **NOTE:** No credit should be given if 3 credits have already been awarded for the Thermal Sciences (Thermodynamics) course.

Main Generator, Turbine, and Auxiliary Nuclear Plant Systems

Location: St. Francisville, LA.
Length: 22 hours (2 weeks).
Dates: January 1987-Present.

Objective: To provide the student with an understanding of the design and operation of the main generator, turbine, and auxiliary nuclear plants systems.

Learning Outcome: Upon successful completion of this course, the student will be able to understand and describe the design and operation of the main generator, turbine and auxiliary nuclear plant systems, and solve problems associated with these systems.

Instruction: Major topics covered in the course are the main generator, electrohydraulic control system, generator exciter and voltage regulator, turbine monitoring and trips, generator stator cooling water system, generator bus duct cooling system, generator hydrogen seal oil system, generator hydrogen and carbon dioxide system, generator core monitor system, and the main turbine and auxiliaries. Methods of instruction include lecture, classroom discussion, visual materials, self-study, and written examinations.

Credit Recommendation: In the upper division baccalaureate degree category, 3

semester hours in Nuclear or Mechanical Technology (7/97). **NOTE:** Students must complete both this course and Main Steam, Condenser, Feedwater, Circulating Water, and Related Nuclear Plant Systems to receive the credit recommendation.

Main Steam, Condenser, Feedwater, Circulating Water, and Related Nuclear Plant Systems

Location: St. Francisville, LA

Length: 21 hours (2 weeks).

Dates: July 1987-Present.

Objective: To provide the student with an understanding of the design and operation of the main steam, condenser, feedwater, circulating water, and related nuclear plant systems.

Learning Outcome: Upon successful completion of this course, the student will be able to understand and describe the design and operation of the main steam, condenser, feedwater, circulating water, and related nuclear plant systems; and solve problems associated with these systems.

Instruction: Major topics covered in the course are main steam, condenser air removal, feedwater, moisture separator reheater, feedwater heaters, extraction steam, drains, bearing cooling water, condensate makeup, storage and transfer system, condensate system, and feedwater level control. Methods of instruction include lecture, classroom discussion, visual materials, self-study, and written examinations.

Credit Recommendation: In the upper division baccalaureate degree category, 3 semester hours in Nuclear or Mechanical Technology (7/97). **NOTE:** Students must complete both this course and Main Generator, Turbine, and Auxiliary Nuclear Plant Systems to receive the credit recommendation.

Mechanical Systems (Fundamentals of Mechanical Science)

Location: St. Francisville, LA.

Length: 32 hours (2 weeks).

Dates: January 1987-Present.

Objective: To provide the student with an understanding of the fundamental principles of mechanical science and their application to the design and operation of a nuclear power plant.

Learning Outcome: Upon successful completion of this course, the student will be able to understand and utilize engineering fabrication and construction drawings, engineering fluid diagrams, and prints; describe diesel engines and their operation and various types of pumps and valves, valve actuators, compressors, cooling towers, steam traps, demineralizers, and filters and strainers; and diagnose and solve operational problems associated with such equipment.

Instruction: Major topics covered in the course are engineering fluid diagrams; fabrication, construction, and architectural drawings; diesel engine design and operation; heat exchanger types and operation; pump types and operation; valve design and operation; valve actuators; air compressors; hydraulics; cooling towers; demineralizers; steam traps; and filters and strainers. Methods of instruction include lecture, classroom discussion, visual materials, self-study, and written examinations.

Credit Recommendation: In the upper division baccalaureate degree category, 2 semester hours in Mechanical Technology (7/97).

Nuclear Plant Monitoring and Control Systems

Location: St. Francisville, LA.

Length: 19 hours (1 week).

Dates: January 1987-Present.

Objective: To provide the student with an understanding of the design and operation of the Nuclear Plant Monitoring & Control Systems.

Learning Outcome: Upon successful completion of this course, the student will be able to understand and describe the design and operation of the Nuclear Plant Monitoring and Control Systems; and solve problems associated with these systems.

Instruction: Major topics covered in the course are fire detection and prevention, plant process computer, seismic monitoring system, digital radiation monitoring system, meteorological tower, annunciators, Emergency Response Information System, loose parts monitoring, Tamaris temperature scanner, and the Dymac vibration panel. Methods of instruction include lecture, classroom discussion, visual materials, self-study, and written examinations.

Credit Recommendation: In the upper division baccalaureate degree category, 1 semester hour in Nuclear or Mechanical Technology (7/97).

Nuclear Power Plant Components

Location: St. Francisville, LA.

Length: 54 hours (3 weeks).

Dates: January 1987-Present.

Objective: To provide the student with an understanding of the design and operation of the Nuclear Power Plant Components.

Learning Outcome: Upon successful completion of this course, the student will be able to understand and describe the design and operation of the Nuclear Power Plant Components; and solve problems associated with these components.

Instruction: Major topics covered in the course are valves; sensors and detectors; controllers and positioners; pumps; motors and generators; heat exchangers and condensers; demineralizers and ion exchangers; and breakers, relays and disconnects. Methods of instruction include lecture, classroom discussion, visual materials, self-study, and written examinations.

Credit Recommendation: In the lower division baccalaureate/associate degree category, 3 semester hours in Nuclear Technology (7/97).

Nuclear Reactor Theory

Location: St. Francisville, LA.

Length: 55 hours (3 weeks).

Dates: January 1987-Present.

Objective: To provide the student with an understanding of the principles of nuclear reactor theory and their application to the design and operation of a nuclear power plant.

Learning Outcome: Upon successful completion of this course, the student will be able to understand and describe the theory of nuclear reactors including reactor kinetics, neutron production and life cycle, reactivity coefficients, fission products, and operational physics; and solve problems associated with these concepts.

Instruction: Major topics covered in the course are types of neutrons and their sources, life cycles, microscopic and macroscopic cross sections, moderators, reactor kinetics, reactivity coefficients, control rod worth, fission product poisons, fuel depletion and burnable poisons, reactor criticality, and operational physics. Methods of instruction include lecture, classroom discussion, visual materials, self-study, and written examinations.

Credit Recommendation: In the upper division baccalaureate degree category, 3 semester hours in Nuclear Science or Nuclear Engineering (7/97).

Nuclear Reactor Vessel, Internals, and Control Systems

Location: St. Francisville, LA.

Length: 74 hours (4 weeks).

Dates: January 1987-Present.

Objective: To provide the student with an understanding of the design and operation of the Nuclear Reactor Vessel, Internals and Control Systems.

Learning Outcome: Upon successful completion of this course, the student will be able to understand and describe the design and operation of the reactor vessel, internals, and control systems; and solve problems associated with these systems.

Instruction: Major topics covered in the course are the reactor vessel and internals, nuclear fuel, reactor water cleanup system, reactor core isolation cooling, high and low pressure core sprays, residual heat removal, reactor servicing equipment, offgas system, rod control and information system, reactor protection system, leak detection system, high pressure core spray diesel, alternate rod insertion, reactor recirculation system, reactor neutron monitoring systems, control rod drive, and the automatic depressurization system. Methods of instruction include lecture, classroom discussion, visual materials, self-study, and written examinations.

Credit Recommendation: In the upper division baccalaureate degree category, 4 semester hours in Nuclear or Mechanical Technology (7/97).

Nuclear Technical Specifications and Engineering Safeguard Systems

Location: St. Francisville, LA.

Length: 29 hours (2 weeks).

Dates: January 1987-Present.

Objective: To provide the student with an understanding of the Nuclear Technical Specifications and Engineering Safeguard Systems and their applicability to the design and operation of a nuclear power plant.

Learning Outcome: Upon successful completion of this course, the student will be able to understand and describe the applicability of the nuclear technical specifications and the operation of the Engineering Safeguard Systems; and solve problems associated with Safeguard Systems.

Instruction: Major topics covered in the course are penetration valve leakage control, primary containment, containment atmosphere monitoring, standby liquid control, standby gas treatment and standby diesel generators, combustible gas controls, containment and reactor vessel isolation and control system, remote shutdown, and technical specification safety limits. Methods of instruction include lecture, classroom discussion, visual materials, self-study, and written examinations.

Credit Recommendation: In the upper division baccalaureate degree category, 2 semester hours in Nuclear or Mechanical Technology (7/97).

Thermal Sciences (Thermodynamics)

Location: St. Francisville, LA.

Length: 56 hours (3 weeks).

Dates: January 1987-Present.

Objective: To provide the student with an understanding of the principles of thermodynamics and their applicability to the design and operation of a nuclear power plant.

Learning Outcome: Upon successful completion of this course, the student will be able to understand and describe thermodynamic units, properties, laws, cycles, heat transfer processes, and thermal hydraulics; and solve problems associated with these concepts.

Instruction: Major topics covered in the course are thermodynamic units, properties, steam tables, first and second laws, processes, cycles, heat transfer processes and heat exchangers, thermal hydraulics, thermal limits, fluid statics and dynamics, and brittle fracture and vessel thermal stress. Methods of instruction include lecture, classroom discussion, visual materials, self-study, and written examinations.

Credit Recommendation: In the upper division baccalaureate degree category, 3 semester hours in Mechanical Engineering or Thermal Sciences (7/97). **NOTE:** Only 1 additional credit should be given if 2 credits have already been awarded for the Fundamentals of Thermodynamics, Heat Transfer, and Fluid Flow course.

Ventilation and Miscellaneous Nuclear Plant Systems

Location: St. Francisville, LA.

Length: 49 hours (3 weeks).

Dates: January 1987-Present.

Objective: To provide the student with an understanding of the design and operation of the Ventilation & Miscellaneous Nuclear Plant Systems.

Learning Outcome: Upon successful completion of this course, the student well be able to understand and describe the design and operation of the ventilation and miscellaneous nuclear plant systems; and solve problems associated with these systems.

Instruction: Major topics covered in the course are fuel pool cooling and cleanup, fuel storage and handling, reactor plant component cooling water, turbine plant component cooling water, plant air systems, electrical distribution systems, service water system, floor and equipment drains, sewage treatment and domestic water, HVAC for the Reactor Building, Auxiliary Building, Fuel Building, and Control Building. Methods of instruction include lecture, classroom discussion, visual materials, self-study, and written examinations.

Credit Recommendation: In the upper division baccalaureate degree category, 3 semester hours in Nuclear or Mechanical Technology (7/97).

ExecuTrain Corporation

Founded in 1984, ExecuTrain Corporation is one of the nation's leading personal computer training and support companies specializing in educating business professionals about popular software packages. ExecuTrain's philosophy is to serve people by increasing their effectiveness and productivity through quality training and support.

ExecuTrain's corporate headquarters is located in Atlanta, Georgia, with offices in Birmingham and Mobile, Alabama; Phoenix and Tuscon, Arizona; Little Rock, Arkansas; Fresno, Glendale, Long Beach, Los Angeles, Sacramento, San Diego, San Francisco, Santa Anna, Santa Barbara, Ontario, and San Jose, California; Boulder, Colorado Springs, and Denver, Colorado; Fairfield County, Hartford, and New Haven, Connecticut; Washington, DC; Wilmington, Delaware; Orlando, Tampa, Ft. Lauderdale, Miami and Jacksonville, Florida; Boise, Idaho; Chicago and Peoria, Illinois; Indianapolis and Northern Indiana, Indiana; Davenport and Des Moines, Iowa; Wichita, Kansas; Lexington and Louisville, Kentucky; New Orleans and Baton Rouge, Louisiana; Baltimore, Maryland, Boston and Worchester, Massachusetts; Detroit, Lansing, and Grand Rapids, Michigan; Minneapolis, Minnesota; Kansas City and St. Louis, Missouri; Omaha and Lincoln, Nebraska; East Brunswick and Parsipanny, New Jersey; Las Vegas, Nevada; Albuquerque, New Mexico; Providence, Rhode Island; Buffalo, Albany, Rochester, Westchester County, Long Island, and Syracuse, New York; Charlotte, Greensboro, and Raleigh, North Carolina; Cincinnati, Columbus, Cleveland, Toledo, and Dayton, Ohio; Oklahoma City and Tulsa, Oklahoma; Portland, Oregon; Pittsburgh, Allentown, and Philadelphia, Pennsylvania; Columbia, South Carolina; Memphis, Knoxville, and Nashville, Tennessee; Dallas, Houston, Austin, Fort Wayne, and Fort Worth, Texas; Salt Lake City, Utah; Richmond and Virginia Beach, Virginia; Bellevue, Seattle, and Tacoma, Washington; and Madison and Milwaukee, Wisconsin.

Through personalized, thorough instruction, ExecuTrain enables students to quickly and practically apply software capabilities to meet job requirements. Classes are limited to ten students to ensure the requirements are met.

ExecuTrain provides hands-on training at their facilities and at client facilities. Numerous training classes for the beginner, as well as the experienced computer user, are offered in areas that include computer literacy, spreadsheet, data base management, word processing, desktop publishing, graphics, operating system, project management, and integrated software packages.

The training courses are nationally coordinated. All programs, instructors, and course materials undergo thorough pre- and post-testing. Included with all courses are comprehensive, yet easy-to-understand manuals written by ExecuTrain's technical writing department, practice diskettes, and unlimited telephone support.

As a means to ensure up-to-date product knowledge, ExecuTrain may be Microsoft Solution Provider Partners (SP), Lotus Desktop Partner (LDP), members of the Borland Training Connection Program, Software Publishing Platinum Authorized Training Center Program, and WordPerfect Authorized Training Centers.

Source of official student records: Registry of Credit Recommendations, American Council on Education, One Dupont Circle, Washington, DC 20036-1193.

Additional information about the courses: College Credit Recommendation Service, American Council on Education, One Dupont Circle, Washington, DC 20036-1193.

Advanced dBASE: DOS/Windows

Location: Atlanta, GA, and various locations throughout the United States.

Length: 16 hours (2 days).

Dates: September 1989-Present.

Objective: To introduce the advanced features of dBASE including the designing and printing of labels, macros, and the creation and testing of applications.

Learning Outcome: Upon successful completion of this course, the student will be able to design and print labels, create and edit macros, and design and test applications.

Instruction: Major topics covered in the course are labels, macros, applications, and application generator. Methods of instruction include lecture, discussion, classroom exercises, audio/visual material, computer-assisted instruction, and instructor observation and evaluation.

Credit Recommendation: In the lower division baccalaureate/associate degree category, 1 semester hour in Microcomputer Applications (8/89) (6/94). **NOTE:** Student should receive credit for either the DOS version or the Windows version, but not both.

Advanced Lotus 1-2-3: DOS/Windows

Location: Atlanta, GA, and various locations throughout the United States.

Length: 16 hours (2 days).

Dates: September 1989-Present.

Objective: To provide an introduction to the advanced features of Lotus 1-2-3.

Learning Outcome: Upon successful completion of this course, the student will be able to use advanced spreadsheet features, employ advanced @ functions, manage and print three-dimensional files, manage multiple files, use the Backsolver and Solve, and customize and protect the worksheet.

Instruction: Major topics covered in the course are Advanced @ functions, multiple files; Backsolver and Solver, sharing information, and customizing and protecting the worksheet. Methods of instruction include lecture, discussion, classroom exercises, audio/visual material, computer-assisted instruction, and instructor observation and evaluation.

Credit Recommendation: In the lower division baccalaureate/associate degree category, 1 semester hour in Microcomputer Applications (8/89) (6/94). **NOTE:** Student should receive credit for the DOS version or Windows version, but not both.

Advanced Microsoft Excel

Location: Atlanta, GA and various locations throughout the United States.

Length: 16 hours (2 days).

Dates: January 1992-Present.

Objective: To introduce advanced worksheet and database functions of Excel.

Learning Outcome: Upon successful completion of this course, the student will be able to sort and filter data; create and manipulate pivotal tables; use advanced worksheet functions; solve what-if problems; manage, protect, and link worksheets and workbooks; and consolidate information.

Instruction: Major topics covered in the course are sorting and filtering data, pivot tables, advanced worksheet functions, solution of what-if problems, management and protection of workbooks, and linking and consolidation of information. Methods of instruction include lecture, discussion, audio/visual material, computer-assisted instruction, classroom exercises, and instructor observation and evaluation.

Credit Recommendation: In the lower division baccalaureate/associate degree category, 1 semester hour in Microcomputer Applications (6/94).

Advanced Microsoft Word

Location: Atlanta, GA and various locations throughout the United States.

Length: 16 hours (2 days).

Dates: January 1992-Present.

Objective: To introduce advanced features of the Word word processing package.

Learning Outcome: Upon successful completion of this course, the student will be able to use and manipulate autotext entries, bookmarks, fields, styles, outlines, and document accessories; record and run macros; work with templates; customize Word; and transfer information.

Instruction: Major topics covered in the course are autotext entries, bookmarks, fields, styles, macros, templates, outlines, document accessories, information transfer, and customization of Word. Methods of instruction include lecture, discussion, classroom exercises, audio/visual material, computer-assisted instruction , and instructor observation and evaluation.

Credit Recommendation: In the lower division baccalaureate/associate degree category, 1 semester hour in Microcomputer Applications (6/94).

Advanced WordPerfect: DOS/Windows

Location: Atlanta, GA, and various locations throughout the United States.

Length: 16 hours (2 days).

Dates: September 1989-Present.

Objective: To introduce advanced and complex features of WordPerfect word processing package.

Learning Outcome: Upon successful completion of this course, the student will be able to create an index, concordance file, and table of contents; create tables; use macros; and create and edit keyboard layout.

Instruction: Major topics covered in the course are document accessories, working with columns, working with tables, using macros, and editing the keyboard layout. Methods of instruction include lecture, discussion, classroom exercises, audio/visual material, computer-assisted instruction, and instructor observation and evaluation.

Credit Recommendation: In the lower division baccalaureate/associate degree category, 1 semester hour in Microcomputer Applications (8/89) (6/94). **NOTE:** Student should receive credit for the DOS version or the Windows version, but not both.

Beginning dBase and Intermediate dBase: DOS/Windows

Location: Atlanta, GA, and various locations throughout the United States.

Length: 16 hours (2 days).

Dates: September 1989-Present.

Objective: To introduce the concepts of data base management and provide procedures to create, modify, and link data base files to custom reports and forms; and perform query operations.

Learning Outcome: Upon successful completion of this course, the student will be able to explain the underlying concepts of a data base; create, print, edit, and rearrange a data base file and search for specific records in a data base; create customized entry screens and customized forms/reports; understand the concept of query files; create and print labels; understand the concepts of using and relating data bases; employ and use view files; and understand and use file maintenance commands.

Instruction: Major topics covered in the course are an introduction to dBASE (basic commands and editing procedures); creating, working with, and modifying the data base; rearranging and linking data base files; customizing entry forms, query files and Query by Example (QBE) operations; adding/deleting condition boxes and calculated fields; relating data bases, view file (structure and use), and file maintenance procedures. Methods of instruction include lecture, discussion, classroom exercises, audio/visual material, computer-assisted instruction, and instructor observation and evaluation.

Credit Recommendation: In the lower division baccalaureate/associate degree category, 1 semester hour in Microcomputer Applications (8/89) (6/94). **NOTE:** Student must complete both beginning and intermediate levels to receive credit. Student should receive credit for either the DOS version or the Windows version, but not both.

Beginning DOS and Intermediate DOS

Location: Atlanta, GA, and various locations throughout the United States.

Length: 16 hours (2 days).

Dates: September 1989-Present.

Objective: To introduce the basic structure and operation of DOS (Disk Operating System) including working with files, employing a hard disk, organizing subdirectories, utilizing batch files and batch commands, and employing macros.

Learning Outcome: Upon successful completion of this course, the student will be able to understand the necessity of an operating system; identify the key functions performed by DOS; use DOS commands to manage files and create batch files, including menus; understand how to organize and use a hard disk; create and remove subdirectories and understand advanced subdirectory organization; change subdirectories and copy files from one subdirectory to another, and use advanced subdirectory techniques; and backup and restore files on a hard disk.

Instruction: Major topics covered in the course are the basic structure of DOS and why it is needed, working with files, management and use of diskettes, development and use of a backup procedure, introduction to the hard disk, advanced subdirectory organization and techniques, configuring the operating system, creation of batch files, creating menus with batch files, batch file commands, and advanced DOS commands, including macros. Methods of instruction include lecture, discussion, classroom exercises, audio/visual material, computer-assisted instruction, and instructor observation and evaluation.

Credit Recommendation: In the lower division baccalaureate/associate degree category, 1 semester hour in Microcomputer Applications (8/89) (6/94). **NOTE:** Student must complete both beginning and intermediate levels to receive credit.

Beginning Lotus 1-2-3 and Intermediate Lotus 1-2-3: DOS/Windows

Location: Atlanta, GA, and various locations throughout the United States.

Length: 16 hours (2 days).

Dates: September 1989-Present.

Objective: To provide an introduction to Lotus 1-2-3 spreadsheet, data base, and graphics capabilities.

Learning Outcome: Upon successful completion of this course, the student will be able to use the basic commands of spreadsheet analysis; print specified ranges in a spreadsheet; create and print different types of graphs; understand data base management terminology; and use data base commands to manipulate the data base.

Instruction: Major topics covered in the course are working with a spreadsheet, file commands, worksheet commands, @ functions, printing with 1-2-3, graphics with 1-2-3, data base management system, data commands, data base functions, and function keys. Methods of instruction include lecture, discussion, classroom exercises, audio/visual material, computer-assisted instruction, and instructor observation and evaluation.

Credit Recommendation: In the lower division baccalaureate/associate degree category, 1 semester hour in Microcomputer Applications (8/89) (6/94). **NOTE:** Student must complete both beginning and intermediate levels to receive credit. Student should receive credit for either the DOS version or the Windows version, but not both.

Beginning Microsoft Access and Intermediate Microsoft Access

Location: Atlanta, GA and various locations throughout the United States.

Length: 16 hours (2 days).

Dates: January 1992-Present.

Objective: To introduce features of Microsoft Access including basic concepts of a database, database structure, and querying capabilities; and management of relationships, data import/export, and link/embed.

Learning Outcome: Upon successful completion of this course, the student will be able to understand the basic concepts of database structure and operation; create and manage tables, forms, queries, reports, and files; establish and manage relationships among tables; import and export data; work with Form Wizards and Report Wizards; and link and embed objects from other Window applications.

Instruction: Major topics covered in the course are an introduction to the database concepts and structure; working with tables, queries, forms, and reports; querying and managing multiple tables; working with filters; creating mailing labels; managing database objects and files; importing, exporting, and linking data; Form Wizards; and Report Wizards. Methods of instruction include lecture, discussion, classroom exercises, audio/visual material, computer-assisted instruction, and instructor observation and evaluation.

Credit Recommendation: In the lower division baccalaureate/associate degree category, 1 semester hour in Microcomputer Applications (6/94). **NOTE:** Student must complete both beginning and intermediate levels to receive credit.

Beginning Microsoft Excel and Intermediate Microsoft Excel

Location: Atlanta, GA and various locations throughout the United States.

Length: 16 hours (2 days).

Dates: January 1992-Present.

Objective: To provide an introduction to Microsoft Excel spreadsheet, database, and graphics capabilities.

Learning Outcome: Upon successful completion of this course, the student will be able to use the basic commands of spreadsheet analysis; print specified ranges in a spreadsheet; create and print different types of graphs; find, sort, and manage records in a database; use functions to perform calculation and manipulate data; work with Graphic Objects; link and embed objects; and work with slide shows.

Instruction: Major topics covered in the course are enter and change information; save, start, open, close, and manage workbooks; use functions for calculations and data manipulation; search and replace information; enhance worksheet appearance; check spelling; create and print different types of charts with the Chart Wizard; link and embed objects; and create and manage a slide show. Methods of instruction include lecture, discussion, classroom exercises, audio/visual material, computer-assisted instruction , and instructor observation and evaluation.

Credit Recommendation: In the lower division baccalaureate/associate degree category, 1 semester hour in Microcomputer Applications (6/94). **NOTE:** Student must complete both beginning and intermediate levels to receive credit.

Beginning Microsoft PowerPoint and Advanced Microsoft PowerPoint

Location: Atlanta, GA and various locations throughout the United States.

Length: 16 hours (2 days).

Dates: January 1992-Present.

Objective: To introduce the student to the basic and advanced features of the Power Point presentation software package.

Learning Outcome: Upon successful completion of this course, the student will be able to create, edit, format, and spell check a presentation; create and embed charts; create and edit graphic objects; import and insert pictures; and manage a slide show.

Instruction: Major topics covered in the course are creating, editing, and formatting a presentation; creating and editing charts; designing graphic objects; inserting pictures, and managing a slide show. Methods of instruction include lecture, discussion, classroom exercises, audio/visual material, computer-assisted instruction , instructor observation and evaluation.

Credit Recommendation: In the lower division baccalaureate/associate degree category, 1 semester hour in Microcomputer Applications (6/94). **NOTE:** Student must complete both beginning and advanced levels to receive credit.

Beginning Microsoft Windows and Intermediate Microsoft Windows

Location: Atlanta, GA and various locations throughout the United States.

Length: 16 hours (2 days).

Dates: January 1992-Present.

Objective: To introduce basic structure and operation of Windows including managing applications, directories, files, and the operating environment.

Learning Outcome: Upon successful completion of this course, the student will be able to start and run applications; file manager; manage disks; control color, fonts, and printer configurations through control panel; and create and use macros.

Instruction: Major topics covered in the course are basic structure and operation of Windows; running applications from program manager; managing directories and files through file manager; management and use of disks storage; control of operating environment through control panel; and macros. Methods of instruction include lecture, discussion, classroom exercises, audio/visual material, computer-assisted instruction, and instructor observation and evaluation.

Credit Recommendation: In the lower division baccalaureate/associate degree category,1 semester hour in Microcomputer Applications (6/94). **NOTE:** Student must complete both beginning and intermediate levels to receive credit.

Beginning Microsoft Word and Intermediate Microsoft Word

Location: Atlanta, GA and various locations throughout the United States.

Length: 16 hours (2 days).

Dates: January 1992-Present.

Objective: To become familiar with the basic features of the Word word processing package.

Learning Outcome: Upon successful completion of this course, the student will be able to create, edit, check the spelling, format, and print a document; manage page layout; create and format columns and tables; sort text and tables; improve a document using thesaurus and grammar checker; merge documents; and insert pictures and frames.

Instruction: Major topics covered in the course are creating, editing, formatting, printing, and saving a document; special features including merge function; columns and tables; thesaurus and grammar checker; fonts; and graphics. Methods of instruction include lecture, discussion, classroom exercises, audio/visual materials, computer-assisted instruction, and instructor observation and evaluation.

Credit Recommendation: In the lower division baccalaureate/associate degree category,1 semester hour in Microcomputer Applications (6/94). **NOTE:** Student must complete both beginning and intermediate levels to receive credit.

Beginning Paradox and Intermediate Paradox: DOS/Windows

Location: Atlanta, GA, and various locations throughout the United States.

Length: 16 hours (2 days).

Dates: September 1989-Present.

Objective: To introduce the concepts of relational data base management and basic commands of the Paradox software package.

Learning Outcome: Upon successful completion of this course, the student will be able to create, add, modify, view, and edit a table; query one or more tables and rearrange a table; and create customized reports and forms.

Instruction: Major topics covered in the course are an introduction to the concepts of relational data base management systems; commands of the Paradox software package for creating, modifying, editing, viewing, querying, and rearranging tables; and commands for creating customized reports and forms. Methods of instruction include lecture, discussion, classroom exercises, audio/visual material, computer-assisted instruction, and instructor observation and evaluation.

Credit Recommendation: In the lower division baccalaureate/associate degree category, 1 semester hour in Microcomputer Applications (8/89) (6/94). **NOTE:** Student must complete both beginning and intermediate levels to receive credit. Student should receive credit for either the DOS version or the Windows version, but not both.

Beginning WordPerfect and Intermediate Word Perfect: DOS/Windows

Location: Atlanta, GA, and various locations throughout the United States.

Length: 16 hours (2 days).

Dates: September 1989-Present.

Objective: To become familiar with the common uses of the WordPerfect word processing package.

Learning Outcome: Upon successful completion of this course, the student will be able to create, edit, check the spelling, and print a document; change default settings, use merge functions, thesaurus, and line draw features; and create footnotes, change fonts, and insert and edit graphics in a document.

Instruction: Major topics covered in the course are an introduction to WordPerfect; creating, saving, retrieving, and working with a document; and formatting, merge functions, setup menu, document security, fonts, and graphics. Methods of instruction include lecture, discussion, classroom exercises, audio/visual material, computer-assisted instruction, and instructor observation and evaluation.

Credit Recommendation: In the lower division baccalaureate/associate degree category, 1 semester hour in Microcomputer Applications (8/89) (6/94). **NOTE:** Student must complete both beginning and intermediate levels to receive credit. Student should receive credit for either the DOS version or the Windows version, but not both.

Federal Aviation Administration FAA Academy

The Federal Aviation Administration (FAA), a component of the United States Department of Transportation, serves primarily to ensure aviation safety, promote air commerce, and support national security through management of the National Airspace System. Training programs are offered to employees in each of the 9 FAA regions in the United States.

FAA ACADEMY

The FAA Academy was established in the summer of 1959 to administer the agency's technical training programs. FAA personnel must be familiar with current aviation concepts, knowledge, and skills and must also acquire advanced knowledge and skills in order to operate and maintain new equipment as it is developed. Training is provided for air traffic control specialists, engineers, technicians, and pilots. In addition, a wide range of instructor development courses is offered to ensure the efficiency and effectiveness of academy technical instructors.

Source of official student records: Registry of Credit Recommendations, American Council on Education, One Dupont Circle, Washington, DC 20036-1193 or FAA Regional Training Program Management Office (TPMO), Address of the appropriate regional TPMO can be obtained by writing to Aviation Education, 800 Independence Avenue, S.W., Washington, DC 20591-0001.

Additional information about the courses: College Credit Recommendation Service, American Council on Education, One Dupont Circle, Washington, DC 20036-1193.

AIR TRAFFIC TRAINING

Advanced Ada Programming (53024)

Location: FAA Academy, Oklahoma City, OK.

Length: 160 hours (4 weeks).

Dates: September 1990-August 1993.

Objective: To enable the software automation specialists who have software maintenance responsibilities to write and code an Ada program for air traffic and support system operational applications.

Learning Outcome: Upon successful completion of this course, the student will be able to describe the goals and principles of software engineering and the significance of those principles in conjunction with the Ada language; identify terminology and procedures in designing, developing, testing, and verifying software in Ada programming; construct correct Ada language syntax; encode, compile, execute, and correct Ada program units using sound software engineering principles.

Instruction: Major topics covered in the course are lexical elements, sequential/direct I/O commands, file management and maintenance, access types, type objects, dynamic object explicit allocators, task attributes, task type and objects, family of tasks, and an array of objects of tasks.

Credit Recommendation: In the upper division baccalaureate degree category, 4 semester hours in Computer Science or Management Information Systems (10/91).

Advanced Air Traffic Control for International Participants (50003)

Location: FAA Academy, Oklahoma City, OK.

Length: 320 hours.

Dates: January 1972-October 1987.

Objective: To enable students to apply separation standards.

Instruction: Major topics covered in the course are identification of vector and separate aircraft; advisories coordination of air traffic; and emergency assistance. Methods of instruction include lecture, discussion, and practical exercises.

Credit Recommendation: In the lower division baccalaureate/associate degree category, 3 semester hours in Aviation Management (10/82).

Air Traffic Control Screen (50321)

Location: FAA Academy, Oklahoma City, OK.

Length: 366 hours (9 weeks).

Dates: March 1986-March 1992.

Objective: To provide initial screening for enroute and terminal developmental studies students; and includes Air Traffic Control procedures and simulated Air Traffic problems in a synthetic control area.

Learning Outcome: Upon successful completion of this course, the student will be able to identify airspace areas; understand performance characteristics of selected aircraft; identify and understand operation and chart location of navaids; be able to communicate on UHF/VHF radio using proper procedures; and originate and process flight progress strips to control traffic control takeoff, departure, and enroute traffic in a simulated non-radar environment.

Instruction: Major topics covered in the course are national airspace areas and terminology; aircraft performance characteristics (selected); identification and location of navigation aids; communications procedures; flight progress strips; and non-radar air traffic control methods and procedures. Methods of instruction include lecture, classroom exercises, problem solving, and simulation (laboratory).

Credit Recommendation: In the lower division baccalaureate/associate degree category, 3 semester hours in Aviation Science or Aviation Technology (7/92).

Air Traffic Facility Management (50316)

Location: FAA Academy, Oklahoma City, OK.

Length: 80 hours (2 weeks).

Dates: *Version 1:* September 1990-July 1992; *Version 2:* August 1992-September 1997; *Version 3:* October 1997-Present.

Objective: *Version 1:* To provide the student with information, knowledge, and guidance in the administration and management of an air traffic facility. *Version 2:* To enhance air traffic facility managers management skills and knowledge. *Version 3:* To provide the students with information, knowledge, and skills in the administration and management of an air traffic facility.

Learning Outcome: *Version 1:* Upon successful completion of this course, the student will be able to review organizational charts; prepare operational position standards; prepare a policy statement in accordance with orders; describe rules and procedures that govern work weeks, hours of duty, and reporting of attendance; prepare a facility budget; complete the Technical Performance Review; plan and direct facility training ; review accident packages and prepare incident reports; prepare for a facility evaluation; identify FAA human resource management functions; prepare travel authorizations; use time management skills; conduct discipline action; and maintain administrative files. *Version 2:* Upon successful completion of this course, the student will be able to review and describe organizational charts and functions, position descriptions, accident packages; prepare operational position standards and policy statements, incident reports, procurement requests, and travel authorizations and documentation relating to personnel actions. *Version 3:* Upon successful completion of this course, the student will be able to identify the key elements of a policy statement; describe the rules and procedures that govern the establishment or modification of workweeks, hours of duty, and the standards and procedures for the reporting of time and attendance; describe the process necessary to administer a facility budget plan and direct a facility training program; review accident packages and incident reports; describe the Air Traffic Manager's roles and responsibilities; prepare for, participate in, and respond to a facility evaluation; identify and describe FAA human resource management function; prepare travel authorizations and vouchers; identify the requirements for development and maintenance of administrative files; identify the appropriate documentation associated with conduct and discipline, adverse action, appeal, and grievance procedures; use time management skills in accordance with time management principles; describe the Contracting Officer's Technical Representative's responsibilities; and identify and discuss leadership concepts.

Instruction: *Version 1:* Major topics covered in the course are organization; position management; position standards; performance evaluations; human resource management; conduct and discipline; adverse action; contracting officer's responsibility; policy statements; regional response; facility training; facility evaluations; aircraft accidents and incidents; drug testing; budget; procurement; time and attendance; travel PSC-TDY; time management; and facility files. *Version 2:* Major topics covered in the course are air traffic facility documents, human resource management; organizational structure; budgeting and procurement; and accident and incident reports and negotiation. Methods of instruction include lecture, discussion, computers, and videotapes. *Version 3:* Major topics covered in the course are human resource management, labor-management relations to include conduct and discipline, accident and incidents, facility training, procurement, travel and PCS, time and attendance, facility evaluations, and leadership. Methods of instruction include lecture, discussion, audio/visual material, computer-assisted instruction, learner presentations/reports, projects, quizzes, and final examination.

Credit Recommendation: *Version 1:* In the upper division baccalaureate degree category, 3 semester hours in Management or Business Administration (10/91). *Version 2:* In the upper division baccalaureate degree category, 4 semester hours in Air Traffic Facilities Management or 3 semester hours in General Management elective (7/92). *Version 3:* In the upper division baccalaureate degree category, 3 semester hours in Management or Business Administration and 1 semester hour in Personnel Management (7/97).

Airspace and Procedures (50019)

Location: FAA Academy, Oklahoma City, OK.

Length: 104 hours (3 weeks).

Dates: January 1994-Present.

Objective: To teach a full performance level air traffic controller to perform the staff functions of an air traffic procedure specialist.

Learning Outcome: Upon successful completion of this course, the student will be able to describe the coordination and distribution procedures for policy and informational documents; describe the coordination procedures to enhance traffic management procedures and develop new air traffic procedures; perform an airspace review; describe and evaluate the impact of aircraft noise; review and coordinate military operations; and establish terminal control airspace.

Instruction: Major topics covered in the course are policy and information documents, traffic management, airspace review procedures, noise and noise assessment, military operations, terminal control airspace, environmental issues, issuing waivers and notams, NAVAIDS, special use airspace, and IFR operations. Methods of instruction include lecture, classroom exercises, case studies, audio/visual material, laboratory testing, and final examination.

Credit Recommendation: In the upper division baccalaureate degree category, 6 semester hours in Aviation Management, Air Traffic Administration, or Aviation Science (8/94) (7/97).

Airspace Management (50010)

Location: FAA Academy, Oklahoma City, OK.

Length: 56 hours (1 week and 2 days).

Dates: January 1975-September 1994.

Objective: To enable students to develop, review, coordinate, and recommend proposals for the assignment and use of navigable airspace.

Instruction: Major topics covered in the course are location of information, determination and application of procedures, recognition of criteria, designation of special use airspace, and establishment of routes. Methods of instruction include lecture, discussion, and classroom exercises.

Credit Recommendation: In the lower division baccalaureate/associate degree category, 3 semester hours in Aviation Management or Aviation Science (10/82) (10/91).

ARTS IIA for Automation Specialist (53021)

Location: FAA Academy, Oklahoma City, OK.

Length: 408 hours (10 weeks).

Dates: January 1988-September 1995.

Objective: To prepare students to be automation specialists.

Learning Outcome: Upon successful completion of this course, the student will be able to demonstrate an understanding of the operational program (analyze the coding, functions, relationships, etc., of all subprograms.)

Instruction: Major topics covered in the course are computer organization, assembler languages, programming fundamentals, number systems, flow charts, and software maintenance. Methods of instruction include lecture and laboratory.

Credit Recommendation: In the lower division baccalaureate/associate degree category, 6 semester hours in Computer Science or Data Processing (9/90).

ARTS III/A For Automation Specialist (53025)

Location: FAA Academy, Oklahoma City, OK.

Length: 640 hours (16 weeks).

Dates: July 1992-Present.

Objective: To prepare the terminal radar qualified ATC specialist to operate and perform program maintenance of the ARTS III/A system.

Learning Outcome: Upon successful completion of this course, the student will be able to update, maintain, operate, and troubleshoot local/onsite ARTS IIIA systems.

Instruction: Major topics covered in the course are operation and programming of the ARTS IIIA system and specific ARTS IIIE portions and programming. Methods of instruction include lecture, discussion, laboratory exercises, and written examinations.

Credit Recommendation: In the lower division baccalaureate/associate degree category, 5 semester hours in Computer Science or in the upper division baccalaureate degree category, 7 semester hours in

Computer Science, for a total of 12 semester hours (9/93).

Assistant Controller Position Qualification and Certification (55126)

Location: Field facilities throughout the United States.

Length: 80 hours (2 weeks).

Dates: *Version 1:* January 1976-May 1986; *Version 2:* June 1986-Present.

Objective: To qualify the student to perform the full range of assistant controller duties and to obtain certification on all assistant controller positions of operation in an assigned area of specialization.

Learning Outcome: Upon successful completion of this course, the student will be able to demonstrate the ability to receive, process, and deliver flight plan information; effectively communicate and coordinate; enter flight data into the computer directly; coordinate flight processing errors with the FDCS, DSC, or the appropriate controller, as required; service the flight strip printer; and process flight plans manually.

Instruction: Major topics covered in the course are the full range of assistant controller duties. Methods of instruction include on-the-job training.

Credit Recommendation: In the vocational certificate category, 2 semester hours in Aviation Technology (10/82) (5/87) (9/93).

Automated Radar Terminal System (ARTS) IIIA: For Automation Specialists, Phase V (53010)
Air Traffic Control Automated Radar Terminal System
(Formerly ARTS III: A Programmer [53010])

Location: FAA Academy, Oklahoma City, OK.

Length: *Versions 1 and 2:* 272 hours (6 weeks and 4 days); *Version 3:* 248 hours (6 weeks and 1 day).

Dates: *Version 1:* August 1978-May 1982; *Version 2:* June 1982-October 1991; *Version 3:* October 1991-July 1992.

Objective: To prepare students to serve as data system specialists for field support of National Air Traffic Control Automated Radar Terminal systems.

Instruction: Major topics covered in the course are multiprocessing and other principles related to air traffic control automated radar terminal systems. Methods of instruction include lecture and discussion with hands-on laboratory exercises.

Credit Recommendation: *Version 1:* In the lower division baccalaureate/associate degree category, 3 semester hours in Computer Programming or Data Processing. *Version 2: Version 3:* In the upper division baccalaureate degree category, 4 semester hours in Computer/Electronics Technology (10/82) (10/91).

Basic Aviation and Air Traffic (50312)

Location: FAA Academy, Oklahoma City, OK.

Length: 680 hours.

Dates: *Version 1:* January 1972-December 1977; *Version 2:* January 1978-October 1992.

Objective: To provide minority and female students with special aviation and air traffic programs to increase their opportunities for employment in air traffic control.

Instruction: Major topics covered in the course are orientation to aviation, history of civil aviation, and principles of aerodynamics, weather, navigation, and air traffic control. Methods of instruction include lecture and laboratory exercises.

Credit Recommendation: In the lower division baccalaureate/associate degree category, 3 semester hours in Aviation and 3 semester hours in General Education as an elective (10/82) (9/93).

Basic Obstruction Evaluation and Airport/Airspace Analysis (OE/AAA) (12051)

Location: FAA Academy, Oklahoma City, OK.

Length: *Version 1:* 96 hours (3 weeks); *Version 2:* 104 hours (3weeks).

Dates: October 1978-Present.

Objective: *Version 1:* To enable students to understand the basic Federal Aviation Administration responsibilities for local community commercial, non-federal projects that may have an impact on Federal Aviation Administration jurisdiction on airports and in airspace. *Version 2:* To provide training in the protection of the navigable airspace from proposed and existing surface structures, and the proper spacing of airports to ensure visual flight rules (VFR), traffic patterns and instrument flight rules (IFR) procedural compatibility. Heavy emphasis is placed on internal FAA coordination among the Air Traffic, Flight Standards, Airways Facilities, Airports and Aviation Systems services, along with coordination with the military and other aviation interests.

Learning Outcome: Upon successful completion of this course, the student will be able to apply the concepts and determinations of obstruction evaluation (OE) and airport/airspace analysis (AAA) as outlined in FAR 77,91,157, applicable advisory circulars, Public Laws, and FAA orders.

Instruction: *Version 1:* Major topics covered in the course are analysis of projected construction for obstruction and hazard criteria and interpretation of appropriate regulations for analyzing and judging obstruction standards adherence. Methods of instruction include lecture, discussion, and case studies in the form of actual problems taken from Federal Aviation Administration files are the basis of skill application exercises. *Version 2:* Major topics covered in the course are coordination with the various services at the Regional and Headquarters levels, processing proposals under FAR 77, chart and map interpretation and plotting, FAR 77 notice criteria and obstruction standards, the negotiation with proponents process, analyzing obstruction marking and lighting requirements, determining the required circularization of proposals, conducting informal airspace meetings, evaluating aeronautical effect and issuing hazard/no hazard determinations, FAR 157 and AIP airport processing, circularizing and evaluating the aeronautical effect of airport proposals, issuing airport airspace determinations, and utilization of the National Obstruction Evaluation automated program. Methods of instruction include lecture, discussion, classroom exercises, case studies, audio/visual material, computer-assisted instruction, laboratory exercises, reports, and tests.

Credit Recommendation: *Version 1:* In the lower division baccalaureate/associate degree category, 1 semester hour in Aviation Science or in the upper division baccalaureate degree category, 1 semester hour in Management (10/82) (7/92). *Version 2:* In the upper division baccalaureate degree category, 3 semester hours in Aviation Science, Air Ways Management, or Aerospace Technology (7/97). **NOTE:** Students who receive credit for this course should not receive credit for 12050.

Cadre Training for Traffic Management Unit (50403)

Location: FAA Academy, Oklahoma City, OK.

Length: 24 hours (3 days).

Dates: May 1992-Present.

Objective: To train ATC field instructors to teach Course 55139 to other air traffic control specialists.

Learning Outcome: Upon successful completion of this course, the student will be able to use proper instructional techniques to teach the traffic management system course in the field (Course 55139).

Instruction: Major topics covered in the course are the traffic management system; ground delay program; traffic flow management; severe weather management, and instructional techniques including presentation, for future presentation in the field. Methods of instruction include lecture, classroom exercises, end-of-lesson exams, and student presentations.

Credit Recommendation: In the upper division baccalaureate degree category, 1 semester hour in Teacher Training or Instructional Methods (8/94).

En Route Flight Advisory Service (EFAS) (50201)

Location: FAA Academy, Oklahoma City, OK.

Length: 152 hours (3 weeks and 4 days).

Dates: January 1994-Present.

Objective: To translate, interpret, summarize, and assimilate data into a description of the weather in the flight area, and its relationship to specific flight routes.

Learning Outcome: Upon successful completion of this course, the student will be able to translate, interpret, summarize, and assimilate data into a description of the weather in a flight area, and its relationship to special flight rules.

Instruction: Major topics covered in the course are weather, atmosphere, weather products, and identification of hazardous conditions. Methods of instruction include lecture, discussion, classroom exercises, audio/visual material, computer-assisted instruction and laboratory, end of lesson quizzes, and end of course written and practical tests.

Credit Recommendation: In the lower division baccalaureate/associate degree category, 3 semester hours in Aeronautical Science (8/94).

Enroute Phase VII - Preliminary Radar-Associated Radar/Nonradar Duty (55127) (Formerly Preliminary Radar-Associated/Nonradar Control Training and Assistant Controller Duties [55127])

Location: Field facilities throughout the United States.

Length: 320 hours (8 weeks).

Dates: *Version 1:* January 1976-October 1980; *Version 2:* November 1980-Present.

Objective: To familiarize the student with enroute air traffic control.

Learning Outcome: Upon successful completion of this course, the student will identify air traffic control procedures, special military operations, complete phraseology/strip marking exercises, and prepare a detailed map of the assigned area of preparation.

Instruction: Major topics covered in the course are special military operations; letters of agreement; phraseology and strip marking; and a general review of en route air traffic control and the specific assigned area of specialization. Methods of instruction include programmed learning capsules and exercises.

Credit Recommendation: In the vocational certificate category, 2 semester hours in Aviation Technology (5/87) (7/92) (8/95).

Enroute Phase VIII - Radar/Nonradar Controller Training (55128) (Formerly Radar Associated/Nonradar Controller Training [55128])

Location: Field facilities throughout the United States - Air Route Traffic Control Center (ARTCCs).

Length: 240 hours (6 weeks).

Dates: January 1976-Present.

Objective: To enable the student to perform as a radar and nonradar controller.

Learning Outcome: Upon successful completion of this course, the student will be able to record clearances and control information strips, use correct radio format, issue separation clearances, prioritize clearances, and issue altimeter and altitude assignments.

Instruction: Major topics covered in the course are appropriate regulations and procedures and their application to the safe and efficient movement of air traffic, area navigation, radar identification, separation, communications, route and altitude assignment, clearances, departure, arrival, approaches, and holding and emergency procedures. Methods of instruction include lecture, discussion, exercises, and examinations.

Credit Recommendation: In the lower division baccalaureate/associate degree category, 3 semester hours in Aviation Technology (10/82) (7/92) (8/95).

Enroute Radar Initial Qualification Training, Phase 10A (50125) 50124)

Location: FAA Academy, Oklahoma City, OK.

Length: *Version 1:* 250 hours; *Version 2:* 136 hours.

Dates: *Version 1:* April 1980-August 1982; *Version 2:* September 1982-December 1992.

Objective: To teach students the fundamentals, procedures, and techniques of enroute radar air traffic control.

Instruction: Major topics covered in the course are principles, basic concepts, and techniques associated with radar air traffic control. Methods of instruction include lecture, discussion, and supervised laboratory.

Credit Recommendation: In the lower division baccalaureate/associate degree category, 3 semester hours in Aviation Technology (10/82).

Facility Management and Administration for International Participants (50004)

Location: FAA Academy, Oklahoma City, OK.

Length: 120 hours (3 weeks).

Dates: January 1972-Present.

Objective: To enable students to understand and apply basics of management to realistic (case study) problems under staff supervision and critique.

Instruction: Major topics covered in the course are management fundamentals, application of skills evidenced in test question, and case study analyses. Methods of instruction include lecture and discussion; application of materials learned (principles, theories, guidelines) is accomplished individually or in small group environments.

Credit Recommendation: In the upper division baccalaureate degree category, 3 semester hours in Engineering Management or MBA Curricula (10/82) (9/93).

Final Radar Control Position Phase XIII (55133) (Formerly 55130)

Location: Field facilities throughout the United States.

Length: *Version 1:* 60 hours; *Version 2:* 80 clock hours per position.

Dates: *Version 1:* October 1982-August 1985; *Version 2:* September 1985-Present.

Objective: To train personnel to qualify and be certified at the final radar control position full performance level.

Learning Outcome: Upon successful completion of this course, the students will be able to perform the same skills outlined in Phase XII: initial and continued aircraft identification, separation of aircraft in radar and nonradar environments, holding procedures, beacon code assignments, use of correct communication procedures, sequencing of aircraft, handoffs to and from adjacent controller/facilities, recognize and alleviate sector saturation, provide advisory and assistance as needed, detect and report equipment malfunctions, changeover to backup systems, and perform position relief briefing.

Instruction: Major topics covered in the course are full-time instruction on radar procedures for each position including initial and continued aircraft identification; separation in radar and nonradar environments, use of proper communication procedures; sequencing of and handoffs to and from adjacent controller/facilities; advisory and emergency assistance as needed, report system malfunctions and changeover backup systems, and performing position relief briefing. Methods of instruction include laboratory.

Credit Recommendation: *Version 1:* In the vocational certificate category, 3 semester hours in Aviation Technology or Practical Arts (10/82). *Version 2:* In the vocational certificate category, 2 semester hours in Aviation Technology (5/87) (9/93). **NOTE:** Credit should not be granted for both this course and for Phase XII Initial Radar Control Position Qualification and Certification (55132).

Final Radar-Associated/Nonradar Control Position Qualification and Certification (55130)

Location: Field facilities throughout the United States.

Length: 80 hours (18 weeks).

Dates: *Version 1:* January 1976-May 1986; *Version 2:* June 1986-Present.

Objective: To qualify the student to perform the full range of duties and attain certification on all the radar-associated/ nonradar positions of operation in the area of specialization.

Learning Outcome: Upon successful completion of this course, the student will be able to perform independently and under general supervision all duties of a radar-associated/nonradar controller on all the sectors in his or her assigned area of specialization.

Instruction: This phase of training shall be administered in an operational environment, with on-the-job training, as assigned, and supervised by the first-level supervisor.

Credit Recommendation: *Version 1:* In the vocational certificate category, 3 semester hours in Aviation Technology or Practical Arts (10/82) (5/87). *Version 2:* In the vocational certificate category, 2 semester hours in Aviation Technology (9/93).

Flow Management Weather Coordinator (50112/55138)

Location: *50112:* Training at Federal Aviation Administration, Oklahoma City, OK. *55138:* Training at field offices by academy-trained instructors using FAA Academy Lesson Plans.

Length: 64 hours (2 weeks).

Dates: *Version 1:* September 1978-June 1982; *Version 2:* July 1982-Present.

Objective: To train flow controllers and supervisors in current and forecast aviation weather and to teach the use of weather information to promote safe air traffic control.

Instruction: Major topics covered in the course are current and forecast aviation weather. Methods of instruction include lecture, discussion, and supervised laboratory exercises.

Credit Recommendation: In the upper division baccalaureate degree category, 3 semester hours in Meteorology or Aeronautical Sciences (10/82) (9/93).

Fundamentals of Air Traffic Control (50122)

Location: FAA Academy, Oklahoma City, OK.

Length: 120 hours.

Dates: January 1976-December 1992.

Objective: To train personnel to understand factors affecting the operation of aircraft within the national airspace and to relate these factors to the wide variety of aircraft now flying.

Instruction: Major topics covered in the course are principles of flight, aircraft identification and performance, aviation weather, navigation, federal regulations, communication, ATC services, and radar flight assistance service. Methods of instruction include lecture and discussion.

Credit Recommendation: In the lower division baccalaureate/associate degree category, 2 semester hours in Aviation Management (10/82).

Fundamentals of Digital Logic (54004)

Location: FAA Academy, Oklahoma City, OK.

Length: 120 hours (3 weeks).

Dates: July 1982-July 1997.

Objective: To provide students with an understanding of basic digital logic.

Instruction: Major topics covered in the course are basic principles of operation of the microprocessor (6800); basic concepts of programming a microprocessor; and execution of a program, addressing modes and experiments. Methods of instruction include a self-paced course that uses the Heathkit study materials, plus hands-on experience with the Heathkit trainer, and a proctored final examination.

Credit Recommendation: In the lower division baccalaureate/associate degree category, 3 semester hours in Microprocessor or Microcomputer (10/82) (7/92).

Hardware Familiarization and Programming EARTS Software (53133)

Location: FAA Academy, Oklahoma City, OK.

Length: 40 hours (1 week).

Dates: *Version 1:* August 1978-July 1980; *Version 2:* August 1980-Present.

Objective: To provide students with an understanding of the EARTS program and equipment.

Instruction: Major topics covered in the course are associated with EARTS computer hardware and software. Methods of instruction include lecture and discussion technique for two-thirds of the class with one-third devoted to laboratory exercises.

Credit Recommendation: In the lower division baccalaureate/associate degree category, 1 semester hour in Application of Programming (10/82) (9/93).

Initial Qualification (En Route) (50132)

Location: FAA Academy, Oklahoma City, OK.

Length: 608 hours (15 weeks and 1 day).

Dates: July 1992-Present.

Objective: To provide preparation from initial training through entry into en route facility specific and advanced radar associate training.

Learning Outcome: Upon successful completion of this course, the student will be able to give and take hand offs, perform coordination, develop and maintain awareness, enter computer messages at radar position, separate traffic, and work as an effective air traffic control team member.

Instruction: Major topics covered in the course are air traffic control system, aero dynamics, instrumentation, meteorology, radio phraseology, arrival and departure procedures, airspace limitations, basic radar operation, and separation and hand offs. Methods of instruction include lecture, discussion, classroom exercises, audio/visual material, laboratory, and examinations.

Credit Recommendation: In the lower division baccalaureate/associate degree category, 12 semester hours in Aviation Technology (8/94).

Initial Radar Control Position Qualification and Certification - Phase XII (55132)

Location: FAA Academy, Oklahoma City, OK.

Length: 240 hours.

Dates: October 1982-Present.

Objective: To qualify persons to perform certification on radar positions in an area of specialization.

Instruction: Major topics covered in the course are related to initial radar control position. Method of instruction is on-the-job training.

Credit Recommendation: In the vocational certificate category, 3 semester hours in Aviation Technology or Practical Arts (10/82) (9/93).

Initial Radar Position Qualification Certification Phase (55129)

Location: Field facilities throughout the United States.

Length: *Version 1:* 60 hours; *Version 2:* 120 hours (14 weeks).

Dates: *Version 1:* January 1976-May 1986; *Version 2:* June 1986-Present.

Objective: To qualify the student to perform the full range of duties and to attain certification on two radar-associated/nonradar control positions of operation in an area of specialization.

Learning Outcome: Upon successful completion of this course, the student will be able to correctly demonstrate the ability to initiate and accept radar handoffs and point-outs; perform appropriate change-over procedures to transition to and from the primary back-up system; maintain separation using prescribed standards; issue departure clearances; provide beacon code assignments to IFR aircraft; provide assistance to aircraft experiencing inflight emergencies; provide control to aircraft experiencing radio communication failure; employ holding procedures; recognize sector saturation and employ procedures to prevent or alleviate this control problem; provide weather advisories; maintain board management; enter flight data into the computer; effectively communicate over interphone or radio; and apply hijacked aircraft control procedures.

Instruction: Major topics covered in the course are radar-associated/nonradar controller duties on two sectors within an area of specialization. Methods of instruction include on-the-job training and evaluation which provides the student with a realistic but fair standard in demonstrating the ability to handle all control situations anticipated in the assigned area of specialization.

Credit Recommendation: In the vocational certificate category, 3 semester hours in Aviation Technology (10/82) (5/87) (9/93).

Integrated Communications Switching System (ICSS) Spec. Oper. (Litton) (55234)

Location: Field facilities throughout the United States.

Length: 16 hours.

Dates: June 1987-Present.

Objective: To introduce the student to integrated communications switching equipment.

Learning Outcome: Upon successful completion of this course, the student will be able to operate Litton ICSS Type III equipment as part of their duties as a flight service specialist.

Instruction: Major topics covered in the course are intercom, interphone, and radio features, F-9-7; and Automatic Call Distribution System, F-9-8. Methods of instruction include lecture, computer-assisted instruction, learner presentations/reports, and end-of-lesson and end-of-course tests.

Credit Recommendation: In the lower division baccalaureate/associate degree category, 1 semester hour in Telecommunications (7/97).

Integrated Communications Switching System (ICSS) Supervisor Operation Denro- Supv. (55251)

Location: Field facilities throughout the United States.

Length: 28 hours.

Dates: June 1987-Present.

Objective: To introduce the student to integrated communications switching equipment.

Learning Outcome: Upon successful completion of this course, the student will be able to operate Denro ICSS Type III equipment as part of their duties as a flight service supervisor.

Instruction: Major topics covered in the course are System Control Unit, F-9-40; ACD Monitoring, F-9-41; Recording System ACD Prompts and Announcements, F-9-42; and Time Management Information System Plus (TMIS+), F-9-43. Methods of instruction include lecture, computer-assisted instruction, learner presentations/reports, quizzes, and tests.

Credit Recommendation: In the lower division baccalaureate/associate degree category, 2 semester hours in Telecommunications, Training, or Supervision (7/97).

Integrated Communications Switching System (ICSS) Supervisor Operation Denro-Spec. (55250)

Location: FAA Academy, Oklahoma City, OK.

Length: 18 hours.

Dates: June 1987-Present.

Objective: To introduce the student to integrated communications switching equipment.

Learning Outcome: Upon successful completion of this course, the student will be able to operate Denro ICSS Type III equipment as part of their duties as a flight service Specialist.

Instruction: Major topics covered in the course are introduction to ICSS and equipment, F-9-30; interphone, intercom, and radio, F-9-31; and Fast File, PATWAS, TIBS, and ACD, F-9-32. Methods of instruction include lecture, discussion, classroom exercises, interactive computer labs, and end-of-lesson and end-of-course tests.

Credit Recommendation: In the lower division baccalaureate/associate degree category, 1 semester hour in Telecommunications (7/97).

Integrated Communications Switching System (ICSS) Supv. Oper. (Litton) (55235)

Location: Field facilities throughout the United States.

Length: 32 hours.

Dates: June 1987-Present.

Objective: To introduce the student to integrated communications switching equipment.

Learning Outcome: Upon successful completion of this course, the student will be able to operate Litton ICSS Type III equipment as part of their duties as a flight service supervisor.

Instruction: Major topics covered in the course are MRT and RTQC, F-9-9; and Supervisory Aspects of EMIS, ACD, and VRS, F-9-10. Methods of instruction include lecture, presentations, interactive computer labs, and end-of-lesson and end-of-course tests.

Credit Recommendation: In the lower division baccalaureate/associate degree category, 1 semester hour in Telecommunications (7/97).

Introduction to Ada Programming Language (53023)

Location: FAA Academy, Oklahoma City, OK.

Length: 160 hours (4 weeks).

Dates: October 1989-August 1993.

Objective: To enable the student to write/code simple Ada language programs for operational and support systems implementations.

Learning Outcome: Upon successful completion of this course, the student will be able to describe Ada software terminology; recognize, read, understand, construct, and debug Ada language programs; and ascertain and write Ada language syntax.

Instruction: Major topics covered in the course are history and evolution of Ada programming language, Ada syntax and notation, language lexical elements, program units, modular structures, data types and control structures, input and output statements, and program exception. Methods of instruction include lecture and laboratory.

Credit Recommendation: In the lower division baccalaureate/associate degree category, 4 semester hours in Computer Science or Management Information Systems (9/90) (10/91).

Limited Aviation Weather Reporting Station (LAWRS)-METAR (55511)

Location: FAA Academy, Oklahoma City, OK, and field facilities throughout the United States.

Length: 40 hours (1 week).

Dates: March 1996-Present.

Objective: To prepare students to observe, report, and disseminate weather reports.

Learning Outcome: Upon successful completion of this course, the student will be able to identify, evaluate, report, and disseminate each element of a weather report.

Instruction: Major topics covered in the course are administrative requirements, observer responsibilities, types of observations, wind, visibility, runway visual range, weather phenomena, sky conditions, temperature, and dew point pressure. Methods of instruction include lecture, practice exercises, end-of-lesson tests, review tests, and final examination.

Credit Recommendation: In the lower division baccalaureate/associate degree category, 1 semester hour in Aeronautical Science (7/97).

M1FC Flight Service Data Processing System for AUS (53203)

Location: FAA Academy, Oklahoma City, OK.

Length: 288 hours (7.2 weeks).

Dates: October 1992-Present.

Objective: To enable a student to perform the duties and responsibilities of an Automation Specialist (AUS) which includes using the Model 1 Full Capacity Data Processing System.

Learning Outcome: Upon successful completion of this course, the student will be able to administer and execute the course objectives.

Instruction: Major topics covered in the course are Tandem utility programs, system configuration, start-up-diagnostic procedures, database installation/monitoring, exec programming, application software, archiving, event reconstruction, disk drive management, system operation/analysis, and documentation/administration procedures. Methods of instruction include lecture, discussion, computer-assisted instruction, special projects, and final examination.

Credit Recommendation: In the lower division baccalaureate/associate degree category, 3 semester hours in Computer Science and in the upper division baccalaureate degree category, 3 semester hours in Computer Science (7/97).

Model 1 AFSS Specialist Training (55033)

Location: Field facilities throughout the United States.

Length: 81 hours.

Dates: January 1987-Present.

Objective: To teach specialist functions on the Model 1 system.

Learning Outcome: Upon successful completion of this course, the student will be able to utilize all Model 1 specialist functions.

Instruction: Major topics covered in the course are system overview, briefing functions, flight plan functions, message transmission and edit, data base edit, and local alert procedures. Methods of instruction include lecture, classroom exercises, presentations, tests, and final examination.

Credit Recommendation: In the lower division baccalaureate/associate degree category, 2 semester hours in Computer Technology (7/97). **NOTE:** Students who receive credit for Model 1 AFSS Specialist Training (55033) should not receive credit for Model 1 Full Capacity Specialist Training (55034).

Model 1 AFSS Supervisor Training (55035)

Location: Field facilities throughout the United States.

Length: 40 hours.

Dates: January 1987-Present.

Objective: To train the supervisor functions on the Model 1 weather delivery system.

Learning Outcome: Upon successful completion of this course, the student will be able to utilize all Model 1 supervisor functions.

Instruction: Major topics covered in the course are system design, FSAS communication, facility supervisor terminal, and A-COTC/F-COTC. Methods of instruction include lecture, classroom exercises, quizzes, and final examination.

Credit Recommendation: In the lower division baccalaureate/associate degree category, 1 semester hour in Computer Science (7/97).

Model 1 Full Capacity Specialist Training (55034)

Location: Field facilities throughout the United States.

Length: 80 hours.

Dates: January 1990-Present.

Objective: To teach specialist functions on the Model 1 Full Capacity system.

Learning Outcome: Upon successful completion of this course, the student will be able to utilize all Model 1 Full Capacity specialist functions.

Instruction: Major topics covered in the course are system overview, briefing functions, flight plan functions, message transmission and edit, and data base edit. Methods of instruction include lecture, discussion, classroom exercises, end of lesson tests, and an end of course test.

Credit Recommendation: In the lower division baccalaureate/associate degree category, 2 semester hours in Computer Science (7/97). **NOTE:** Students receiving credit for Model 1 Full Capacity Specialist Training (55034) should not receive credit for Model 1 AFSS Specialist Training (55033).

Model 1 Full Capacity Supervisor Training (55036)

Location: Field facilities throughout the United States.

Length: 40 hours.

Dates: January 1990-Present.

Objective: To teach supervisor functions on the Model 1 Full Capacity system.

Learning Outcome: Upon successful completion of this course, the student will be able to utilize all Model 1 full capacity supervisor functions.

Instruction: Major topics covered in the course are M1FC system design, FSAS communication, facility supervisor terminal, system supervisor terminal, FSDPS computer operation terminal console (F-COTC), and position equipment computer terminal console (P-COTC). Methods of instruction include lecture, practice exercises, audio/visual material, end of lesson tests, an end-of-course test, and observations.

Credit Recommendation: In the lower division baccalaureate/associate degree category, 1 semester hour in Computer Science (7/97).

NAS Data Processing Functions (53129)

Location: FAA Academy, Oklahoma City, OK.

Length: 134 hours.

Dates: *Version 1:* October 1978-December 1981; *Version 2:* January 1982-Present.

Objective: To provide students with an understanding of the application of systems analysis to Enroute Operational Computer Program, using already learned computer skills to assemble, execute, and analyze failures of the program. Graduates will have a comprehensive knowledge of the Enroute Operational Computer Program at the completion of this course.

Instruction: Major topics covered in the course are instruction on the IBM 360 system. Methods of instruction include lecture, laboratory, and weekly tests.

Credit Recommendation: In the vocational certificate category, 2 semester hours in Data Entry or Computer Operations (10/82) (9/93).

National AFSS Initial Qualification Training Program (50240) (Formerly National FSS Initial Qualification Program [50230])

Location: FAA Academy, Oklahoma City, OK.

Length: 632 hours (15 weeks).

Dates: November 1991-Present.

Objective: To provide the flight service specialist with the knowledge and skills necessary to perform entry level duties and to enter on-the-job training at their assigned facility.

Learning Outcome: Upon successful completion of this course, the student will be able to collect, interpret, and disseminate weather and aeronautical data and provide weather briefings and other inflight services; describe procedures for handling navigation and communication equipment outages; and copy, analyze, and disseminate flight plan information, flight movement, and control messages and ATC instructions.

Instruction: Major topics in the course are ATC Communications, principles of aerodynamics; aircraft flight controls, aircraft instruments, aircraft categories, aviation hazards, weather analysis and observation, flight plan processing, broadcast and inflight functions, weather equipment and directional finder operations, and search and rescue operations. Methods of instruction lecture, classroom exercises, laboratory, and tests.

Credit Recommendation: In the lower division baccalaureate/associate degree category, 12 semester hours in Aeronautical Sciences (6 Private Pilot Ground, 6 Meteorology) (7/92) (7/97). **NOTE:** Students who receive credit for this course should not receive credit for National Terminal to Flight Service Initial Training Program (50241).

National FSS Initial Qualification Training Program (50230) (Replaced by National AFSS Initial Qualification Training Program [50240])

Location: FAA Academy, Oklahoma City, OK.

Length: 688 hours.

Dates: March 1989-October 1991.

Objective: To provide the flight service specialist with the knowledge and skills necessary to perform entry level duties and to enter on-the-job training at their assigned facility.

Learning Outcome: Upon successful completion of this course, the student will be able to collect, interpret and disseminate weather and aeronautical data and provide weather briefings and other inflight services; describe procedures for handling navigation and communication equipment outages; and copy, analyze and disseminate flight plan information, flight movement and control messages and ATC instructions.

Instruction: Major topics covered in the course are weather analysis and observation; flight plan processing; broadcast and inflight functions; data communications, weather equipment and direction finder operations; and search and rescue procedures. Methods of instruction include lecture, classroom exercises, laboratory, videos, transparencies, written exams and performance evaluation on laboratory exercises.

Credit Recommendation: In the lower division baccalaureate/associate degree category, 9 semester hours in Aeronautical Sciences (7/92) (8/95). **NOTE:** Students should not receive credit for both 50230 and 50240.

National Terminal to Flight Service Initial Training Program (50241)

Location: FAA Academy, Oklahoma City, OK.

Length: 390 hours (10 weeks) or (50 days).

Dates: September 1994-Present.

Objective: To provide the flight service specialist with the knowledge and skills necessary to perform entry level duties and to enter on-the-job training at their assigned facility.

Learning Outcome: Upon successful completion of this course, the student will be able to collect, interpret, and disseminate weather and aeronautical data and provide weather briefings and other inflight services; describe procedures for handling navigation and communication equipment outages; and copy, analyze, and disseminate flight plan information, flight movement, and control messages and ATC instructions.

Instruction: Major topics covered in the course are weather analysis, flight plan processing, broadcast and inflight functions, weather equipment and direction finder operations, and search and rescue procedures. Methods of instruction include lecture, discussion, classroom exercises, audio/visual material, labs, quizzes, and tests.

Credit Recommendation: In the lower division baccalaureate/associate degree

category, 9 semester hours in Aeronautical Sciences (7/97). **NOTE:** Students who receive credit for this course should not receive credit for National AFSS Initial Qualification Training Program (50240).

Nonradar Air Traffic Control (50123)

Location: FAA Academy, Oklahoma City, OK.

Length: 312 hours (8 weeks).

Dates: January 1976-December 1992.

Objective: To train students in the rules and procedures governing the control of air traffic along with the governing theory and principles.

Instruction: Major topics covered in the course are real-time problem-solving, developing and processing flight plans, computation and application of separation standards, performance of correct departure and arrival procedures, and establishment and maintenance of smooth flow control procedures. Methods of instruction include practical exercises.

Credit Recommendation: In the lower division baccalaureate/associate degree category, 6 semester hours in Aeronautical Studies, Aviation Management, or Aviation Technology (10/82).

On-the-Job Training, Final Functional Area Checkout (55104)

Location: Field training from the Federal Aviation Administration Academy, Oklahoma City, OK.

Length: 960 hours (24 weeks).

Dates: *Version 1:* August 1972-September 1975; *Version 2:* October 1975-Present.

Objective: To enable students to apply knowledge obtained in programming courses.

Instruction: Major topics covered in the course are training related to computer programming. Methods of instruction include on-the-job training.

Credit Recommendation: In the vocational certificate category, 5 semester hours in Aviation Technology or Computer Operations (10/82) (9/93).

On-the-Job Training in NAS (55103)

Location: Field training from the Federal Aviation Administration Academy, Oklahoma City, OK.

Length: 720 hours (18 weeks).

Dates: *Version 1:* August 1972-September 1975; *Version 2:* October 1975-Present.

Objective: To provide students with guidelines for on-the-job training at the ARTCC.

Instruction: Major topics covered in the course are NAS adaptation and operations. Methods of instruction include on-the-job training.

Credit Recommendation: In the vocational certificate category, 4 semester hours in Aviation Technology or in the lower division baccalaureate/associate degree category, 2 semester hours in Computer Science or Data Processing (10/82) (9/93).

Pilot Weather Briefing (55206)

Location: FAA Academy, Oklahoma City, OK.

Length: 32 hours.

Dates: September 1989-Present.

Objective: To provide in-depth weather and pilot briefing training on instructional video tapes requiring student interaction and a student/instructor pilot briefing laboratory in order to prepare specialists to become better pilot weather briefers.

Learning Outcome: Upon successful completion of this course, the student will be able to analyze aviation weather and aeronautical information, and communicate weather data in accordance with Flight Services Handbook 7110.10 and Preflight Manual F2-5/1 using a simulated pilot weather briefing laboratory; conduct pilot briefings in accordance with Flight Services Handbook 7110.10 and Operational Position Standards Order 7220.2 using LABS/Model 1 equipment; and document pilot briefings in accordance with Flight Services Handbook 7110.10 and Operational Position Standards Order 7220.2.

Instruction: Major topics covered in the course are an overview, Pilot Briefer's responsibilities and legal obligations, atmospheric conditions and altimetry, wind and circulation, moisture in the atmosphere, clouds and precipitation, air masses and fronts, aviation weather hazards (restrictions to visibility, icing and turbulence, thunderstorms, and density altitude), weather graphics, weather radar, aviation forecasts, aircraft categories and performance, pilot weather reports, weather for soaring and ballooning, and pilot briefing techniques. Methods of instruction include lecture, classroom exercises, audio/visual material, computer-assisted instruction, learner presentations/reports, end-of-lesson tests, and an end-of-course test.

Credit Recommendation: In the lower division baccalaureate/associate degree category, 1 semester hour in Aviation Science or Meteorology (7/97).

Predevelopmental, Phase III Field Environmental Training (55313)

Location: Field facilities throughout the United States.

Length: 324 hours (8 weeks).

Dates: *Version 1:* December 1978-December 1979; *Version 2:* January 1980-October 1992.

Objective: To orient students to actual job tasks and skills, providing job exposure.

Instruction: Major topics covered in the course are actual job tasks and skills including job exposure in the field of Predevelopmental, and Phase III Field Environmental Training. Methods of instruction include on-the-job training.

Credit Recommendation: In the vocational certificate category, 1 semester hour in Aviation Technology or Practical Arts (10/82) (9/93).

Predevelopmental, Phase IV—Option Determination (55314)

Location: Field facilities throughout the United States.

Length: 130 hours.

Dates: June 1979-December 1992.

Objective: To familiarize students with equipment used in daily operations.

Instruction: Major topics covered in the course are the basic operational tasks of any of the major positions within an assigned option. Methods of instruction include on-the-job training.

Credit Recommendation: In the vocational certificate category, 1 semester hour in Aviation Technology or Practical Arts (10/82).

Quality Assurance Program Administration (50314)

Location: FAA Academy, Oklahoma City, OK.

Length: *Version 1:* 52 hours (7.5 weeks); *Version 2:* 48 hours (6 days).

Dates: *Version 1:* December 1990-June 1997; *Version 2:* July 1997-Present.

Objective: To provide instruction to quality assurance officers and specialists on performing facility evaluations, preparing accident and incident packages, performing accident and incident analysis, administering the operational error and deviation elimination program; and utilizing public relations skills.

Learning Outcome: Upon successful completion of this course, the student will be able to apply effective management skills; identify the process for effective communication; perform a facility evaluation in accordance with facility self evaluation guidelines and FAA orders; prepare accident and incident packages in accordance with FAA orders; and administer the FAA's operational error and deviation investigation and reporting program.

Instruction: Major topics covered in the course are time management, communications skills, formal and informal accident packages, accident and incident analysis, operational error and deviation investigation and reporting, and accident notification, information release, and the facility evaluation process. Methods of instruction include lecture, video presentations, interactive computer training, and classroom exercises.

Credit Recommendation: In the upper division baccalaureate degree category, 2 semester hours in Aviation Administration (7/92) (7/97).

Radar Certification Terminal Radar Position/Function (55031) (Formerly Radar Position Certification [55031])

Location: FAA Academy, Oklahoma City, OK.

Length: 200 hours (5 weeks); 80 hours classroom instruction and 120 hours on-the-job-training.

Dates: August 1982-Present.

Objective: To qualify terminal specialists in the performance of the full range of duties necessary for attaining certification in radar and ARTS III-A facilities.

Learning Outcome: Upon successful completion of this course, the student will be qualified for full range of duties in radar and ARTSIII-A facilities.

Instruction: Major topics covered in the course include on-the-job skills needed to qualify for Radar Position Certification. Methods of instruction include lecture, discussion, on-the-job training, and an end-of-lesson test.

Credit Recommendation: In the vocational certificate category, 2 semester hours in Aviation Management or Tower Operation (10/91) (9/93) (8/95).

TAL (Transaction Application Language) Syntax for AUS (Automation Specialists) (54009)

Location: FAA Academy, Oklahoma City, OK.

Length: 200 hours (5 weeks).

Dates: June 1988-Present.

Objective: To provide the flight service automation specialist with the knowledge and skills necessary to perform basic programming duties at their assigned facility.

Learning Outcome: Upon successful completion of this course, the student will be able to interpret, debug, and modify existing TAL programming source code.

Instruction: Major topics covered in the course are program control, data storage methods, debugging tools, TAL programming structure, arithmetic techniques, and data manipulation. Methods of instruction include lecture, discussion, lab exercises, directed correspondence study, observations, tests, and final examination.

Credit Recommendation: In the lower division baccalaureate/associate degree category, 1 semester hour in Computer Sciences (7/97).

Terminal Phase VI Facility Qualification, Flight Data (55026) (Formerly Flight Data [55026])

Location: FAA Academy, Oklahoma City, OK.

Length: 160 hours (4 weeks).

Dates: *Version 1:* January 1976-December 1979; *Version 2:* January 1980-Present.

Objective: To familiarize the student with the scope of airport services and their relation to the Federal Aviation Administration air traffic control.

Learning Outcome: Upon successful completion of this course, the student will be able to demonstrate a working knowledge of tower equipment; flight data requirements; use of forms; special circumstances affecting flight procedures; emergency procedures regarding accidents; and special flight operations and other incidents.

Instruction: Major topics covered in the course are tower equipment, flight data requirements and forms completion procedures, airport specialized circumstances affecting flight procedures and applicable emergency procedures for accidents, special flight operation, and other incidents. Methods of instruction include programmed self-study.

Credit Recommendation: In the vocational certificate category, 2 semester hours in Airport Management (10/82) (10/91) (8/95).

Terminal Phase VII Facility Qualification, Clearance Delivery (55027) (Formerly Phase VII Clearance Delivery [55027])

Location: Field facilities throughout the United States.

Length: Estimated 20 hours (2 days) - Correspondence Course.

Dates: *Version 1:* January 1976-December 1979; *Version 2:* January 1980-Present.

Objective: To provide students with basics related to clearance delivery.

Learning Outcome: Upon successful completion of this course, the student will be able to perform the basic functions as a clearance delivery controller in accordance with accepted FAA air traffic procedures.

Instruction: Major topics covered in the course are introductory Federal Aviation Administration air traffic procedures. Methods of instruction include correspondence instruction.

Credit Recommendation: In the vocational certificate category, 1 semester hour in Air Traffic Control (10/82) (10/91) (8/95).

Terminal Phase VIII Facility Qualification, Ground Control (55028) (Formerly Ground Control [55028])

Location: Field facilities throughout the United States.

Length: 80 hours (2 weeks).

Dates: *Version 1:* January 1976-December 1979; *Version 2:* January 1980-Present.

Objective: To teach the student procedures pertinent to ground control.

Learning Outcome: Upon successful completion of this course, the student will be familiar with basic aircraft operations and their control on the ground.

Instruction: Major topics covered in course are aircraft recognition, airport utilization, console instruments and control procedures. Methods of instruction include programmed self-instruction.

Credit Recommendation: In the vocational certificate category, 2 semester hours in Airport Management (10/82) (10/91) (8/95).

Terminal Phase X Facility Qualification, Local Control (55029) (Formerly Local Control [55029])

Location: Field facilities throughout the United States.

Length: 80 hours (2 weeks).

Dates: *Version 1:* January 1978-December 1979; *Version 2:* January 1980-Present.

Objective: To familiarize the student with airport operating procedures.

Learning Outcome: Upon successful completion of this course, the student will be familiar with aircraft lighting; separation requirements; helicopter and fixed wing aircraft requirements; emergency procedures and weather requirements for local traffic control.

Instruction: Major topics covered in the course are airport lighting; separation minimal; heavy jet and wake turbulence, separation procedure; control procedures, runway use and related information; helicopter aerodynamics; special UFR-fixed wing aircraft and helicopters; emergency procedures and unusual situations; brite qualifications; D Brite; wind effects; and controller-in-charge. Methods of instruction include programmed self-instruction, lesson reviews, and an end-of-phase test.

Credit Recommendation: In the vocational certificate category, 2 semester hours in Airport Management (10/82) (10/91) (8/95).

Terminal Phase X Facility Qualification, Nonradar Control (55030) (Formerly Nonradar Terminal Control [55030])

Location: FAA Academy, Oklahoma City, OK.

Length: 120 hours (3 weeks).

Dates: January 1978-Present.

Objective: To enable the student to apply Federal Aviation Administration established standards to moderately dense aircraft flying traffic.

Learning Outcome: Upon successful completion of this course, the student will be able to identify the requirements for applying vertical separation, describe required longitudinal separation between aircraft in various situations; describe the required vertical separation in various situations; identify requirements for lateral separation; describe required lateral separation in various situations.

Instruction: Major topics covered in the course are maintenance of aircraft clearances in space dimensions, maintenance of accepted discipline levels of proper pre- and post-flight data submitted from aircraft crews and Federal Aviation Administration facilities. Methods of instruction include programmed self-study, lesson reviews, and an end-of-phase test.

Credit Recommendation: In the vocational certificate category, 2 semester hours in Airport Management (10/82) (10/91) (8/95).

Terminal Radar Training (50034)

Location: FAA Academy, Oklahoma City, OK.

Length: 192 hours (4 weeks, 2 days).

Dates: August 1993-Present.

Objective: To prepare students to operate radar approach control in a dual sector, level 4 environment.

Learning Outcome: Upon successful completion of this course, the student will be able to operate radar control positions and solve radar air traffic control problems.

Instruction: Major topics covered in the course are human resource management to include interpersonal communications, airspace, Federal Aviation Regulations, and radar operations. Methods of instruction include lecture, discussion, and laboratory (computer interactive) evaluation.

Credit Recommendation: In the upper division baccalaureate degree category, 5 semester hours in Aeronautical Science (9/93).

Tower Cab Training (50032)

Location: FAA Academy, Oklahoma City, OK.

Length: 456 hours (11.5 weeks).

Dates: June 1992-Present.

Objective: To provide air traffic personnel with skills to function at a level 3 control tower facility.

Learning Outcome: Upon successful completion of this course, the student will be able to operate the flight data, clearance delivery, ground control, and local control positions; and demonstrate the ability to sequence the arriving and departing air traffic.

Instruction: Major topics covered in the course are principles of flight, aircraft types and characteristics, meteorology, navigation, federal aviation regulations, air traffic service, flight assistance service, fundamentals of radar, national airspace system, human factor involved in air traffic control, national weather service visibility certification, and terminal "BRITE" radar qualification. Methods of instruction include discussion, task laboratories, lecture, simulation, block testing, and comprehensive final.

Credit Recommendation: In the lower division baccalaureate/associate degree category, 5 semester hours in Aeronautical Science and 1 hour in Meteorology, for a total of 6 semester hours (9/93).

Traffic Management Coordinator: Specialized Training (50115)

Location: FAA Academy, Oklahoma City, OK.

Length: 64 hours (8 days).

Dates: October 1991-Present.

Objective: To provide the knowledge to identify past, present, and future traffic management systems, programs, orders, document guides, and operational positions of the traffic management system.

Learning Outcome: Upon successful completion of this course, the student will be able to perform required traffic management functions using the traffic management workstation (TMU) computer system and implement/analyze appropriate traffic management programs.

Instruction: Major topics covered in the course are air traffic management systems programs, departure flow management, mission coordinator duties, tower en route control, national route program, severe weather avoidance, arrival flow management, ground delay, en route flow management, delay reporting procedures, and contingency plan procedures. Methods of instruction include lecture, discussion, classroom exercises, audio/visual material, computer-assisted instruction, and written and performance examinations.

Credit Recommendation: In the upper division baccalaureate degree category, 4 semester hours in Aviation Technology (8/94).

Transaction Application Language (TAL) Programming for Air Traffic (53201)

Location: FAA Academy, Oklahoma City, OK.

Length: *Version 1:* 208 hours (5.2 weeks); *Version 2:* 208 hours (5.1 weeks or 26 days).

Dates: July 1989-Present.

Objective: *Version 1:* To enable a student to perform the duties and responsibilities of the Automation Specialist (AUS) who has assigned responsibility for the application software on the Flight Service Automation System (FSAS) or Full Capacity Flight Service Data Processing System (FSDPS) including using the Tandem Guardian Operating System. *Version 2:* To provide the flight service automation specialist with advanced knowledge and skills necessary to perform programming and problem analysis at their assigned facility.

Learning Outcome: *Version 1:* Upon successful completion of this course, the student will be able to execute the main functions and interpret the interrelationships of the modules of the Tandem GUARDIAN Operating System; write, compile, debug, and execute structured (TAL) programs to access disk database files; modify, debug, and execute the program to use Tandem Interprocess Communication techniques; and modify, debug, and execute the program to operate in the Tandem Nonstop mode. *Version 2:* Upon successful completion of this course, the student will be able to design and write TAL programming applications needed to improve operations in the Flight Service Data Processing System; and be more proficient in solving problems that stem from bugs in the existing TAL software.

Instruction: *Version 1:* Major topics covered in the course are TAL syntax, file system management, interprocess communications, nonstop programming techniques, and writing and modifying programs. Methods of instruction include lecture, discussion, laboratory exercises, and written and practical examinations. *Version 2:* Major topics covered in the course are advanced program control, debugging tools, data manipulation, file handling, non-stop processing, and interprocess communication. Methods of instruction include lecture, classroom programming exercises, tests, and programming projects.

Credit Recommendation: *Version 1:* In the upper division baccalaureate degree category, 3 semester hours in Computer Science (9/93). *Version 2:* In the lower division baccalaureate/associate degree category, 3 semester hours in Computer Science (7/97).

Ultra Programming, Terminal Automation Specialists, Phase IV (53003) (Formerly ARTS III for Data Systems Specialist [53003])

Location: FAA Academy, Oklahoma City, OK.

Length: *Versions 1 and 2:* 440 hours (10 weeks); *Version 3:* 240 hours (6 weeks); *Version 4:* 232 hours (4 weeks).

Dates: *Version 1:* March 1972-May 1982; *Version 2:* June 1982-April 1987; *Versions 3 and 4:* May 1987-October 1996.

Objective: To train software automation specialists in the use of the machine and assembly language used by the Univac Ultra 30 computer.

Learning Outcome: Upon successful completion of this course, the student will be able to flowchart, code, debug, and document Ultra 30 computer programs.

Instruction: Major topics covered in the course include instruction in numbering systems, machine code, assembly code, flowcharting, debugging, hardware architecture, subroutines, I/O, and system interrupts.

Credit Recommendation: *Versions 1 and 2:* In the lower division baccalaureate/associate degree category, 7 semester hours in Computer Science and Data Processing. *Version 3:* In the lower division baccalaureate/associate degree category, 4 semester hours in Computer Technology. *Version 4:* In the upper division baccalaureate degree category, 5 credit hours in Computer/Electronics Technology or 4 credit hours in the lower division baccalaureate/associate degree category in Computer Science (10/82) (5/87) (10/91).

Very High Frequency Direction Finder (VDF) (50400)

Location: FAA Academy, Oklahoma City, OK, and field facilities throughout the United States.

Length: 40 hours.

Dates: July 1992-Present.

Objective: To show student how to operate the VDF equipment.

Learning Outcome: Upon successful completion of this course, the student will be able to operate the VDF equipment in the performance of an aircraft orientation.

Instruction: Major topics covered in the course are VDF equipment, VDF simulator/trainer, and VDF procedures. Methods of instruction include lecture, presentations, interactive computer labs, and end-of-lesson and end-of-course tests.

Credit Recommendation: In the vocational certificate category, 1 semester hour in Aviation Technology (7/97). **NOTE:** Students should not receive credit for both Very High Frequency Direction Finder (50400) and Very High Frequency Direction Finder (VDF) (Field Conducted) (55205).

Very High Frequency Direction Finder (VDF) (Field Conducted) (55205)

Location: FAA Academy, Oklahoma City, OK, and field facilities throughout the United States.

Length: 40 hours.

Dates: July 1992-Present.

Objective: To show student how to operate the VDF equipment.

Learning Outcome: Upon successful completion of this course, the student will be able to operate the VDF equipment in the performance of an aircraft orientation.

Instruction: Major topics covered in the course are VDF equipment, VDF simulator/trainer, and VDF procedures. Methods of instruction include lecture, presentations, interactive computer labs, and end-of-lesson and end-of-course tests.

Credit Recommendation: In the vocational certificate category, 1 semester hour in Aviation Technology (7/97). **NOTE:** Students should not receive credit for both Very High Frequency Direction Finder (VDF) (Field Conducted) (55205) and Very High Frequency Direction Finder (50400).

Weather Satellite Data Interpretation (55203)

Location: Field facilities throughout the United States.

Length: 32 hours (4 days).

Dates: January 1994-Present.

Objective: To provide the Flight Service Specialist with the knowledge and skills to interpret weather conditions as portrayed on weather satellite photos.

Learning Outcome: Upon successful completion of this course, the student will be able to use visible and infrared satellite photos to identify the locations as well as the significance to aviation of cloud types, thunderstorms, and general heights of cloud tops; locations of synoptic scale weather systems such as fronts, low pressure centers, jet streams, and hurricanes; phenomena which restrict pilot visibility such as low stratus and fog, haze, dust, and volcanic ash; and mesoscale weather phenomena such as gust fronts, mountain waves, and sea breezes.

Instruction: Major topics covered in the course are weather satellite system operations and the production of visible and infrared photos, satellite photo interpretation of synoptic scale weather systems, weather phenomena which restrict pilot visibility, and mesoscale weather systems. Methods of instruction include lecture, videos, satellite interpretation exercises, end-of-lesson tests, and a certification final examination.

Credit Recommendation: In the lower division baccalaureate/associate degree category, 2 semester hours in Airway Science or Meteorology (7/97). **NOTE:** Credit recommended only for individuals who took 50240 and 50241 prior to April 1988.

AIRPORTS TRAINING

Airport Certification Procedures (06041)

Location: FAA Academy, Oklahoma City, OK.

Length: 152 hours (3 weeks, 4 days).
Dates: January 1995-Present.
Objective: To provide FAA Airport Certification Inspectors with the standards and procedures needed to review applications for Airport Operating Certificates, to conduct inspections related to FAR 139, and to prepare enforcement actions where violations to FAR 139 exist.
Learning Outcome: Upon successful completion of this course, the student will be able to, in accordance with agency regulations, standards, and guidelines, explain the requirements and process for airport certification; identify documents, criteria, and procedures involved in airport inspection; and perform selected inspection activities.
Instruction: Major topics covered in the course are the application of FAR 139 and FAA Advisory Circulars to airport inspections of wildlife, paved/unpaved surfaces, construction, ground vehicle operations, NAVAID protection, personnel, condition reporting, snow/ice control, fueling, marking, signs, lighting, wind indicators, obstructions; and instruction on FAA Form 5010-1 and on FAR 139 enforcement actions and exemptions. Methods of instruction include lecture, discussion, classroom exercises, workshops, and field trips.
Credit Recommendation: In the upper division baccalaureate degree category, 4 semester hours in Airport Management (8/95).

Airport Engineering (06012)

Location: FAA Academy, Oklahoma City, OK.
Length: 36 hours (1 week).
Dates: March 1976-December 1990.
Objective: The course is primarily for airport consultants and airport engineers who need expertise in Federal Aviation Administration regulations affecting airport design, construction standards, and inspection techniques. Course materials in *Pavement Design* and *Airport Lighting and NAVAIDS* will be helpful as prerequisites for this survey course.
Instruction: Major topics covered in the course are subgrade and soil testing; flexible airport paving; rigid airport paving; gradients and drainage; skid-resistant surfacing; airport lighting; runway and edge markings; power requirements; AC and DC; and radio controls. Methods of instruction include lecture using transparencies to support the material.
Credit Recommendation: In the upper division baccalaureate degree category, 2 semester hours in Civil Engineering/General Engineering (10/82).

Airport Management for Internationals (06032)

Location: FAA Academy, Oklahoma City, OK.
Length: 300 hours (8 weeks).
Dates: June 1982-December 1993.
Objective: To provide students with an understanding of terminal and landside operation of an airport, including financial, management, and operation responsibilities.
Instruction: Major topics covered in the course are airport management principles; airport financing; master planning; airport systems; airport sites; airport forecasting; National Airport System plan; runways; airport capacity; airport revenues; fixed based operators; international regulations; airline and ramp operations; airport landing and handling fees; airline and airport regulations; air cargo; and transportation pricing. Methods of instruction include authorities in airport management as guest lecturers, on-site airport visits, and a written examination.
Credit Recommendation: In the lower division baccalaureate/associate degree category, 3 semester hours in Airport Management (elective) (10/82).

Airport Master Planning (06022)

Location: FAA Academy, Oklahoma City, OK.
Length: 36 hours (1 week).
Dates: January 1978-February 1993.
Objective: To prepare airport planners for developing and gaining approval of a master plan for airports from basic utility size to major carrier facilities.
Instruction: Major topics covered in the course are site selection, land use plans, aircraft factors in runway length and capacity, airport layout, noise controls, airspace requirements, environmental assessments and reports, aeronautical activity forecasts, and airport systems plans.
Credit Recommendation: In the lower division baccalaureate/associate degree category, 2 semester hours in Airport Management (elective) (10/82) (9/93).

Airport NAVAIDS and Lighting (06019)

Location: FAA Academy, Oklahoma City, OK.
Length: 36 hours (1 week).
Dates: October 1980-Present.
Objective: This course is designed primarily for airport project managers seeking a basic knowledge in Federal Aviation Administration standards and criteria applicable to NAVAIDS and lighting installed under the AIP program.
Learning Outcome: Upon successful completion of this course, the student will be able to identify the basic standards and criteria applicable to airport marking, lighting, and NAVAIDS.
Instruction: Major topics covered in the course are the basic standards and criteria applicable to airport marking, lighting, and NAVAIDS. Methods of instruction include lecture, discussion, and class problems which demonstrate and clarify the application of selected standards.
Credit Recommendation: In the upper division baccalaureate degree category, 2 semester hours in Civil Engineering or General Engineering (10/82) (9/93).

Airport Pavement Design (06005) (Formerly Airport Paving [06005])

Location: FAA Academy, Oklahoma City, OK.
Length: 76 hours (2 weeks).
Dates: June 1971-Present.
Objective: To provide students with the knowledge necessary to evaluate, design, and construct airport pavements.
Learning Outcome: Upon successful completion of this course, the student will be able to design pavement and overlays using asphalt and concrete in accordance with FAA design methods and industry guidelines.
Instruction: Major topics covered in the course are soil investigation; pavement design (flexible and rigid); surfacing and overlays; pavements for light and heavy aircraft; and pavement evaluation. Methods of instruction include lecture, laboratory, and visits from industry experts. **NOTE:** Knowledge of civil or general engineering is required because of the level of mathematical calculations and graph interpretations. Knowledge of computer operation would be helpful.
Credit Recommendation: In the upper division baccalaureate degree category, 3 semester hours in Civil Engineering or General Engineering (10/82) (9/93).

Introduction to Airport Development (06042) (Formerly AIP Procedures [06025])

Location: FAA Academy, Oklahoma City, OK.
Length: 36 hours (1 week).
Dates: September 1993-Present.

Objective: To provide FAA and non-federal airport personnel with an introduction to airport development programs including a general understanding of the Capital Improvement Program, Airport Improvement Program, and Passenger Facility Charge Program.

Learning Outcome: Upon successful completion of this course, the student will be able to demonstrate a working knowledge of the Airport Improvement Program and Passenger Facility Charge Program and will be able to identify criteria for evaluating airport proposals for funding as well as procedures for fulfilling FAA project responsibilities.

Instruction: Major topics covered in the course are the history of airport development programs, trust fund revenues, project and sponsor eligibility, development program priorities, and Airport Improvement Program grant procedures and assurances. Methods of instruction include lecture and discussion.

Credit Recommendation: In the lower division baccalaureate/associate degree category, 2 semester hours in Airport Management (9/93).

Introduction to NEPA Requirements and Procedures (12000) (Formerly Environmental Assessment [12000])

Location: FAA Academy, Oklahoma City, OK.

Length: 62 hours (8 days).

Dates: May 1976-Present.

Objective: To provide students with a fundamental knowledge of environmental assessment, requirements, and procedures relative to airport development and operation and aircraft operation.

Learning Outcome: Upon successful completion of this course, the student will be able to determine the scope of the environmental assessment required, determine FAA environmental responsibilities, and review and draft portions of an environmental assessment.

Instruction: Major topics covered in the course are legislative mandates; identification of impacts, effects and causes of aircraft noise, air pollution, and wildlife; documentation outlines; processing information; consultation process; public involvement; and legal implications. Methods of instruction include lecture, workshops, and case studies.

Credit Recommendation: In the lower division baccalaureate/associate degree category, 2 semester hours in Airport Management or Environmental Science as an elective (10/82) (9/93).

Land Appraisal and Title Opinion (06028)

Location: FAA Academy, Oklahoma City, OK.

Length: 40 hours (1 week).

Dates: January 1976-July 1997.

Objective: To improve students' understanding of procedures in land acquisition, review sponsor's land appraisal to assure conformance with prescribed procedure, and examine eligibility, allowability, and reasonableness of land costs for land acquisition.

Instruction: Major topics covered in the course are the philosophy, policy, and criteria of Title III of the Uniform Relocation Assistance and Real Estate Property Acquisition Policies Act of 1970; and various appraisal methods and the validity of title opinion.

Credit Recommendation: In the upper division baccalaureate degree category, 2 semester hours in Real Estate (10/82) (7/92).

Project Engineering (06018)

Location: FAA Academy, Oklahoma City, OK.

Length: 80 hours (2 weeks).

Dates: December 1977-December 1993.

Objective: This course is designed for airport engineers who wish to upgrade their knowledge in airport standards, paving, legating, grading, drainage, and general design. In addition, techniques are developed in the area of inspecting and testing.

Instruction: Major topics covered in the course are land acquisition, airport landscaping, soils and testing, airport paving theory (flexible and rigid), joints, overlaps, evaluation, and federal assistance grants. Methods of instruction include an airport paving workshop where students may simulate airport planning and work problems related to airport paving; and a final examination.

Credit Recommendation: In the upper division baccalaureate degree category, 2 semester hours in Civil Engineering or Airport Engineering (10/82).

Recurrent Engineering (06021)

Location: FAA Academy and field locations, Oklahoma City, OK.

Length: 36 hours (1 week).

Dates: January 1977-December 1993.

Objective: The objective of this course is to give practicing engineers an opportunity to update in Federal Aviation Administration design and construction methods and techniques.

Instruction: The same materials are used for this course as are used in *Airport Paving*. The last two days of this course are taught by guest instructors; e.g., a representative from the Bureau of Standards and a representative from the airport engineers area. Subject matter may vary depending on current regulations and techniques.

Credit Recommendation: In the upper division baccalaureate degree category, 1 semester hour in Civil Engineering or General Engineering (10/82). *Prerequisite: Airport Paving* (or equivalent experience).

Relocation Assistance (06027)

Location: FAA Academy, Oklahoma City, OK.

Length: 36 hours (1 week).

Dates: *Version 1:* January 1976-December 1976; *Version 2:* January 1977-July 1997.

Objective: This course is designed for airport personnel who have the responsibility of reviewing and approving the relocation assistance and payments program from an ADAP project; and covers the implementations of the provisions of Title II of the Uniform Relocation Assistance and Real Properties Acquisition Policies Act of 1970 and OST Regulations, Part-5. This training is intended for personnel assigned to positions requiring this knowledge.

Learning Outcome: Upon successful completion of this course, the student will be able to apply the provisions of the Act in simulated problems, assess claims, determine payments, find replacement housing, and determine advisory services to displaced persons in accordance with the Act.

Instruction: Major topics covered in the course are basic philosophy, policies, and criteria of the Uniform Relocation Assistance and Real Property Acquisition Policies Act of 1970. Methods of instruction include 14 hours of lecture and 22 hours of supervised laboratory.

Credit Recommendation: In the upper division baccalaureate degree category, 1 semester hour in Urban Planning, General Business, or Public Administration (10/82) (7/92).

AIRWAY FACILITIES

Advanced Ada Programming Software (43531)

Location: FAA Academy, Oklahoma City, OK.

Length: 160 hours (4 weeks).

Dates: October 1989-May 1996.

Objective: To train the student to design, develop, and test Ada programs.

Learning Outcome: Upon successful completion of this course, the student will be able to design and maintain an Ada program and use reference manuals for the development of Ada programs.

Instruction: Major topics covered in the course are Ada syntax, constructs, and file manipulation. Methods of instruction include lecture, laboratory, and video.

Credit Recommendation: In the lower division baccalaureate/associate degree category, 3 semester hours in Computer Science (9/90).

Air Conditioning (44106)

Location: Correspondence study.

Length: 30 hours (self-paced).

Dates: May 1969-September 1997.

Objective: To teach students introductory principles of air conditioning.

Learning Outcome: Upon successful completion of this course, the student will be able to define basic refrigeration and air conditioning terms; explain the function of major system components using simple diagrams; and use refrigerant tables and charts.

Instruction: Major topics covered in the course are principles of refrigeration, properties of air, and the basic air conditioning system. Method of instruction is by correspondence study.

Credit Recommendation: In the vocational certificate category, 2 semester hours in Air Conditioning or Practical Arts (5/87) (9/93).

Air Route Surveillance Radar (ARSR-3) and Remote Maintenance Monitor (RMM) (40388)

Location: FAA Academy, Oklahoma City, OK.

Length: 560 hours (14 weeks).

Dates: January 1989-Present.

Objective: To teach the student the installation, evaluation, maintenance, certification, or modification of the ARSR-3 system.

Learning Outcome: Upon successful completion of this course, the student will be able to perform a functional analysis on the system; understand system data flow; and perform system alignment, performance analysis, fault diagnosis, and correction.

Instruction: Major topics covered in the course are radar transmitter; digital target extractor; displays; synchronizer; waveguide; antenna, and polarization; and radar receiver. Methods of instruction include lecture, discussion, and laboratory exercises.

Credit Recommendation: In the upper division baccalaureate degree category, 3 semester hours in Communications Electronics and 2 semester hours in Digital Electronics or Electronic Engineering Technology (9/93).

Air Route Surveillance Radar (ARSR-3 and RMM) Update (40385)

Location: FAA Academy, Oklahoma City, OK.

Length: 80 hours (2 weeks).

Dates: August 1988-February 1994.

Objective: To teach the maintenance of the ARSR-3 system.

Learning Outcome: Upon successful completion of this course, the student will be able to install, maintain, certify, and modify the ARSR-3 system.

Instruction: Major topics covered in the course are job-related situations requiring diagnostics, corrective and periodic maintenance activities, block diagram and operation, and electronic circuitry. Methods of instruction include classroom exercises and laboratory.

Credit Recommendation: In the upper division baccalaureate degree category, 3 semester hours in Electronics Technology (9/93).

Air Route Surveillance Radar-3 Three Level Weather Mod (40394)

Location: FAA Academy, Oklahoma City, OK.

Length: 40 hours (1 week).

Dates: June 1993-February 1994.

Objective: To teach personnel responsible for the ARSR-3 system who have completed course 40388, ARSR-3 and RMM, prior to January 1, 1990.

Learning Outcome: Upon successful completion of this course, the student will be able to evaluate, maintain, certify, and repair the Air Route Surveillance Radar System (ARSR-3).

Instruction: Major topics covered in the course are block diagram of the system; its operation, evaluation, and certification procedures; and the maintenance and repair of the system. Methods of instruction include lecture, discussion, and laboratory exercises.

Credit Recommendation: In the upper division baccalaureate degree category, 2 semester hours in Electronics Technology (9/93).

Air Traffic Control Beacon Interrogator (ATCBI)-4 (40335)

Location: FAA Academy, Oklahoma City, OK.

Length: *Version 1:* 96 hours (2.5 weeks).

Dates: *Version 1:* November 1982-June 1992; *Version 2:* July 1992-Present.

Objective: To enable technicians and engineers to maintain, certify, and modify the Air Traffic Beacon Interrogator.

Learning Outcome: Upon successful completion of this course, the student will be able to analyze, diagnose, align, modify, and certify the Air Traffic Beacon Interrogator (ATCBI-4).

Instruction: Major topics covered in the course are systems concepts, pulse mode generator, transmitter receiver, monitors, control circuits, and beacon test set. Methods of instruction include classroom instruction and laboratory sessions to develop skills in systems alignment, systems performance analysis, fault diagnosis, and use of test equipment.

Credit Recommendation: *Version 1:* In the lower division baccalaureate/associate degree category, 2 semester hours in Electronics Technology (11/82). *Version 2:* In the upper division baccalaureate degree category, 2 semester hours in Electronic Technology (7/92).

Air Traffic Control Beacon Interrogator (ATCBI)-5 (CBI) (47706) (Formerly ATC Beacon Indicator (ATCBI) - 5 Transmitter/Receiver Site [40339])

Location: Computer-based and FAA Academy, Oklahoma City, OK.

Length: *Versions 1 and 2:* 80 hours (2 weeks); *Version 3:* 44 CBI units; 9 Advanced Training Aids (ATAs); 6 laboratories (75 hours).

Dates: *Version 1:* January 1982-August 1988; *Version 2:* September 1988-August 1994; *Version 3:* August 1994-Present.

Objective: To train the student to evaluate, modify, maintain, and certify the ATCBI-5 system.

Learning Outcome: Upon successful completion of this course, the student will be able to operate and evaluate the ATCBI-5 system using video and RF test sets and will be able to troubleshoot and correct malfunctions.

Instruction: Major topics covered in the course are system concepts, pulse mode generator, transmitter, receiver, stagger/destagger, control circuits, and test sets. Methods of instruction include lecture and discussion with laboratory activities. Methods of instruction include CBI, ATA, lecture, laboratory, and examinations.

Credit Recommendation: *Version 1:* In the lower division baccalaureate/associate or in the upper division baccalaureate degree category, 2 semester hours in Electronics Technology (11/82). *Version 2:* In the lower division baccalaureate/ associate degree category, 2 semester hours in Electronics Technology (9/88) (9/90) (7/92). *Version 3:* In the lower division baccalaureate/associate degree category, 2 semester hours in Electronics Technology or Avionics Technology (8/95).

Airport Remote Monitoring System (ARMS) for ILS FA-10165/6/8 (CBI) (47202)
(Formerly Airport Remote Monitoring System (ARMS) for ILS FA-10165/6/8 [40270])

Location: Computer-based.

Length: *Version 1:* 80 hours (2 weeks); *Version 2:* 40 hours (1 week) (self-paced).

Dates: *Version 1:* January 1990-December 1993; *Version 2:* January 1994-Present.

Objective: To instruct Airport Remote Monitoring System (ARMS) maintenance personnel to maintain, troubleshoot, and install remote monitoring systems associated with ILS Localizer or ILS Glide Slope.

Learning Outcome: Upon successful completion of this course, the student will be able to state the purpose of ARMS; describe the theory of operation; perform system configuration, maintenance procedures and troubleshooting; and replace circuit card assemblies.

Instruction: Major topics covered in the course are airport layout with ILS, remote monitoring subsystem, battery charger power supply, troubleshooting techniques, and maintenance checks. Methods of instruction include computer-based instruction.

Credit Recommendation: *Version 1:* In the lower division baccalaureate/associate degree category, 2 semester hours in Avionics Technology (9/90). *Version 2:* In the lower division baccalaureate/associate degree category, 1 semester hour in Avionics Technology (8/95).

Airport Surface Detection Equipment (ASDE)-3 Hardware Training (40381)

Location: FAA Academy, Oklahoma, City, OK.

Length: *Version 1:* 160 hours (4 weeks); *Version 2:* 120 hours (3 weeks).

Dates: *Version 1:* March 1992-July 1997; *Version 2:* July 1997-Present.

Objective: To train technicians in the installation, operation, evaluation, modification, and maintenance of the ASDE-3 system.

Learning Outcome: Upon successful completion of this course, the student will be able to perform operational setup; use built in test equipment and maintenance monitoring to perform periodic maintenance; isolate malfunctions; and perform corrective maintenance for the ASDE-3 radar system.

Instruction: *Version 1:* Major topics covered in the course are the Key telephone system; keyboard commands; ASDE-3 features, functions, and characteristics; mini-DCU and maxi-DCU menu mode; function key mode; and command line mode. Methods of instruction include lecture and laboratory. *Version 2:* Major topics covered in the course are ASDE-3 radar familiarization, installation, operation, maintenance, and repair. Methods of instruction include lecture, classroom exercises, and final examination.

Credit Recommendation: *Version 1:* In the upper division baccalaureate degree category, 4 semester hours in Electronics or Electrical Engineering Technology (7/92). *Version 2:* In the upper division baccalaureate degree category, 3 semester hours in Electronics or Electrical Engineering Technology Laboratory (7/97).

Airport Surveillance Radar (ASR) 4/5/6 Transmitter Site-Common Equipment (40342)

Location: FAA Academy, Oklahoma City, OK.

Length: 120 hours (3 weeks).

Dates: *Version 1:* May 1981-June 1992; *Version 2:* July 1992-September 1997.

Objective: To enable students to analyze the ASR-4/5/6 system for correct performance and to diagnose and repair any fault in the system.

Instruction: Major topics covered in the course are circulating trigger loop; modulator; transmitter; receiver; video cancellation; radar control system; power supplies; and video monitoring equipment. Methods of instruction include lecture and laboratory.

Credit Recommendation: *Version 1:* In the lower division baccalaureate/associate degree category, 2 semester hours in Electronics Technology (11/82). *Version 2:* In the upper division baccalaureate degree category, 2 semester hours in Electronic Technology (7/92).

Airport Surveillance Radar (ASR)-7E (40395)

Location: FAA Academy, Oklahoma City, OK.

Length: 200 hours (5 weeks).

Dates: July 1991-Present.

Objective: To train technicians in the operation and maintenance of the ASR-7E Radar System.

Learning Outcome: Upon successful completion of this course, the student will be able to perform and document all periodic maintenance; troubleshoot and isolate malfunctions to the subsystem and component level; and understand ASR-7E system operation and characteristics.

Instruction: Major topics covered in the course are radar system concepts, moving target indicator processing, transmitter and receiver operation, signal timing, antenna beam range, azimuth and video gating, fault diagnostics, test procedures, routine checks and adjustments, and equipment interface cabinets. Methods of instruction include lecture, laboratory, quizzes, tests, and final examination.

Credit Recommendation: In the upper division baccalaureate degree category, 3 semester hours in Electronics Technology or Electrical Engineering Technology (7/92) (7/97).

Airport Surveillance Radar (ASR)-9 (40337)

Location: FAA Academy, Oklahoma City, OK.

Length: 360 hours (9 weeks).

Dates: June 1989-Present.

Objective: To teach preventive and corrective maintenance on the ASR-9 Radar System.

Learning Outcome: Upon successful completion of this course, the student will be able to operate the ASR-9 Radar System; modify the ASR-9 Radar System; and repair the ASR-9 Radar System to contribute to the total air traffic control system.

Instruction: Major topics covered in the course are pulse radar system and its computer control and evaluation subsystem. Fault isolation corrective procedures and certification procedures are covered. Methods of instruction include lecture, laboratory, written examinations, and laboratory work.

Credit Recommendation: In the lower division baccalaureate/associate degree category, 9 semester hours in Electronics Technology, Radar Technician, or Communications Electronics (9/90) (8/95).

Airport Surveillance Radar (ASR)-9 Indicator Site Equipment (SCIP) (40391)

Location: FAA Academy, Oklahoma City, OK.

Length: 80 hours (2 weeks).

Dates: July 1991-Present.

Objective: To train technicians in the maintenance, certification, and modification of the indicator-site equipment of ASR-9 systems.

Learning Outcome: Upon successful completion of this course, the student will be able to perform preventive and corrective maintenance on the ASR-9 remote SCIP equipment.

Instruction: Major topics covered in the course are operation and maintenance of the remote SCIP, modems, and RMS terminal of the ASR-9. Methods of instruction include lecture, classroom exercises, tests, and final examination.

Credit Recommendation: In the lower division baccalaureate/associate degree category, 3 semester hours in Electrical Engineering Technology or Electronics Technology (7/92) (7/97).

Airport Surveillance Radar System (ASR)-8 (40333)

Location: FAA Academy, Oklahoma City, OK.

Length: 240 hours (6 weeks).

Dates: *Version 1:* March 1981-June 1992; *Version 2:* July 1992-Present.

Objective: To train personnel to evaluate radar system operation, isolate defective circuits, take proper corrective measures, use test equipment, and be able to adapt to Airport Surveillance Radar.

Learning Outcome: Upon successful completion of this course, the student will be able to understand principles of operation, detailed circuit analysis, system maintenance, and troubleshooting.

Instruction: Major topics covered in the course are system concepts; system timing; klystron transmitter; normal receivers; video processor; MTI (Moving Target Indicator); STC (Sensitivity Time Controls); remote site equipment; and control systems, with heavy emphasis on troubleshooting. Methods of instruction include lecture, classroom exercises, labs, quizzes, tests, and final examination.

Credit Recommendation: *Version 1:* In the lower division baccalaureate/associate degree category, 4 semester hours in Radar Technology (5/87). *Version 2:* In the upper division baccalaureate degree category, 4 semester hours in Radar Technology or Electronics Technology (7/92).

AN/FPS Series Radars with SSR/DMTI (40399)

Location: FAA Academy, Oklahoma City, OK.

Length: 160 hours (4 weeks).

Dates: August 1988-Present.

Objective: To train field technicians and engineers in the theory and operation of the AN/FPS Radars with the solid state receiver and digital moving target indicator equipment.

Learning Outcome: Upon successful completion of this course, the student will be able to understand basic theory and operation of the AN/FPS radar system with SSR/DMTI equipment; and perform maintenance, troubleshooting, installation, and modification of AN/FPS radar systems with SSR/DMTI equipment.

Instruction: Major topics covered in the course are FPS Transmitter, FPS Common RF and Auxiliary Equipment, and SSR/DMTI and SSR/DMTI Type 2/3. Methods of instruction include lecture, discussion, and laboratory exercises.

Credit Recommendation: In the upper division baccalaureate degree category, 5 semester hours in Electronics or Electrical Engineering Technology (9/93).

AN/GRN-27, Category II Instrument Landing System (ILS) (40232)

Location: FAA Academy, Oklahoma City, OK.

Length: 120 hours (3 weeks).

Dates: October 1982-Present.

Objective: To train technicians to install, maintain, evaluate, and modify the AN/GRN-27 instrument landing system.

Learning Outcome: Upon successful completion of this course, the student will be able to learn the operation and maintenance of AC and DC power systems, localizer/glide slope monitor, control unit, remote control and monitor pad, marker beacon system, antenna system, and localizer transmitter.

Instruction: Major topics covered in the course are the operation down to the component level of the transistor and logic circuit operation, troubleshooting, transistors, receivers, antennas, and power supply on the AN/GRN-27 instrument landing system. Methods of instruction include lecture and laboratory.

Credit Recommendation: In the lower division baccalaureate/associate degree category, 3 semester hours in Electronic Communications (5/87) (9/93).

Approach Lighting System with Flashers (ALSF)-II (Airflo) (40136)

Location: FAA Academy, Oklahoma City, OK.

Length: 120 hours (3 weeks).

Dates: November 1984-Present.

Objective: To train field technicians or engineers in the theory and operation of the Airflo Dual Mode Approach Lighting System.

Learning Outcome: Upon successful completion of this course, the student will be able to understand the theory and operation of the Airflo Type FA-10048 lighting system; and install, operate, modify, troubleshoot, and maintain the Airflo Type FA-10048 lighting system.

Instruction: Major topics covered in the course are system components, system operation, maintenance and troubleshooting, controls, power supplies, and regulators. Methods of instruction include lecture, discussion, and laboratory exercises.

Credit Recommendation: In the upper division baccalaureate degree category, 4 semester hours in Electronics or Electrical Engineering Technology (9/93).

Approach Lighting System with Flashers (ALSF)-II (Godfrey) (40135)

Location: FAA Academy, Oklahoma City, OK.

Length: 120 hours (3 weeks).

Dates: November 1984-Present.

Objective: To train field technicians or engineers in the theory and operation of the Godfrey Dual Mode Approach Lighting System.

Learning Outcome: Upon successful completion of this course, the student will be able to understand the theory and operation of the Godfrey Type FA-9993 lighting system; and install, operate, modify, troubleshoot, and maintain the Godfrey Type FA-9993 lighting system.

Instruction: Major topics covered in the course are system operation, system components, maintenance and troubleshooting, controls, power supplies, and regulators. Methods of instruction include lecture, discussion, and laboratory exercises.

Credit Recommendation: In the upper division baccalaureate degree category, 4 semester hours in Electronics or Electrical Engineering Technology (9/93).

ARSR-1/2 SSR/DMTI Modification (40338)

Location: FAA Academy, Oklahoma City, OK.

Length: 48 hours (1 week and 1 day).

Dates: August 1988-February 1994.

Objective: To train field technicians and engineers in theory and operation of the Solid State Receiver and Digital Moving Target Indicator (SSR/DMTI) equipment.

Learning Outcome: Upon successful completion of this course, the student will be able to understand basic theory and operation of the SSR/DMTI equipment; and perform maintenance, troubleshooting, installation, and modification of SSR/DMTI equipment.

Instruction: Major topics covered in the course are Type I and Type 2/3 Receivers, frequency generation, STC generator, faults, timing, ACP/ARP processor, DMTI processing, video, and power. Methods of instruction include lecture, discussion, and laboratory exercises.

Credit Recommendation: In the upper division baccalaureate degree category, 2 semester hours in Electronics or Electrical Engineering Technology (9/93). **NOTE:** Credit should not be awarded for this course (40338) if credit has been awarded for AN/FPS Radars with SSR/DMTI (40399).

ARSR-3 Military Interface Modification (MIM) (40377)

Location: FAA Academy, Oklahoma City, OK.

Length: 80 hours (2 weeks).

Dates: October 1980-Present.

Objective: To provide students with awareness of the capabilities of the ARSR-3 Military Interface Modification (MIM) and train them how to operate and maintain the system.

Learning Outcome: Upon successful completion of this course, the student will be able to configure the MIM control panel, identify seven major areas of MIM and describe the functions performed by each, physically locate the major components of the MIM, list the inputs and outputs of the MIM to/from the ARSR-3, recognize a failure by observing front panel indications, isolate the faulty card and replace it, and isolate the fault on a card to a component level.

Instruction: Major topics covered in the course are a functional analysis of the MIM systems, operation, overall system data flow, operational analysis of the height finder RADAR, military message processing, sector mapping, and the built-in test equipment. Methods of instruction include lecture, discussion, classroom exercises, and hands-on laboratory.

Credit Recommendation: In the upper division baccalaureate degree category, 2 semester hours in Electronics Engineering Technology or Advanced Radar Techniques (9/93).

ARTCC Power Conditioning Systems (40131)

Location: FAA Academy, Oklahoma City, OK.

Length: 280 hours (7 weeks).

Dates: September 1980-May 1995.

Objective: To make trainee knowledgeable of the installation, operation, and repair of the ARTCC power conditioning system.

Learning Outcome: Upon successful completion of this course, the student will be able to operate the ARTCC power conditioning system operation; recognize system malfunction; and use approved procedures for locating and repairing malfunctions.

Instruction: Major topics covered in the course are electronic testing procedures; digital circuits; linear circuits; operational amplifiers and differential amplifiers; and electromechanical switching. Methods of instruction include lecture and laboratory.

Credit Recommendation: In the lower division baccalaureate/associate degree category, 3 semester hours in Digital Electronics; 3 semester hours in Discrete and Integrated Linear Devices; and 4 semester hours in Test Equipment Operation and Troubleshooting (9/90).

ARTS III-A Systems (42036)

Location: FAA Academy, Oklahoma City, OK.

Length: 240 hours (6 weeks).

Dates: June 1982-April 1992.

Objective: To teach the functional analysis of the Automated Radar Terminal System (ARTS) III-A system.

Learning Outcome: Upon successful completion of this course, the student will be able to write software programs for the ARTS III-A system; understand the system configuration; understand the diagnostic programs; and troubleshoot the hardware and software.

Instruction: Major topics covered in the course are the functional analysis of the entire ARTS III-A radar system, including hardware and software troubleshooting. Methods of instruction include hardware and software training.

Credit Recommendation: In the lower division baccalaureate/associate degree category, 2 semester hours in Computer Programming and 2 semester hours in Electronics Technology (10/91).

Automated Radar Terminal System (ARTS) IIA for Technicians (42042)

Location: FAA Academy, Oklahoma City, OK.

Length: 600 hours (15 weeks).

Dates: January 1987-July 1997.

Objective: To train ARTS II technicians in the operation and maintenance of the ARTS II systems and subsystems.

Learning Outcome: Upon successful completion of this course, the student will be able to describe system operational functions and characteristics, major subassemblies, computer operation and programming, and operating procedures; load and execute operational, utility and diagnostic programs; perform operational and periodic checks to determine proper operation of ARTS II subsystems; analyze and interpret program listings and results; DDAS operation, DEDS operation, IFDS operation, and MTUS operation.

Instruction: Major topics covered in the course are computer operations and programming; computer processor; device controllers; TTY interface; data decoding; program organization; RADS; ban; magnetic tape unit; diagnostic and utility programs; and system evacuation. Methods of instruction include lecture and laboratory.

Credit Recommendation: In the lower division baccalaureate/associate degree category, 12 semester hours in Electronics Technology or Computer Technology, or in the upper division baccalaureate degree category, 6 semester hours in Computer Science (7/92).

Automated Radar Terminal System (ARTS) IIIA Data Acquisition Subsystem (42034)

Location: FAA Academy, Oklahoma City, OK.

Length: 240 hours (6 weeks).

Dates: January 1982-April 1992.

Objective: To enable students to maintain the Automated Radar Terminal System (ARTS) III-A data acquisition subsystem (DAS).

Learning Outcome: Upon successful completion of this course, the student will be able to perform periodic and corrective maintenance of the data acquisition subsystem.

Instruction: Major topics covered in the course are sensor, receiver, and processor (SRAP); peripheral adapter module (PAM); card reader (CR) controller; associated diagnostic and operational software; system and subsystem concepts; interfaces; and troubleshooting. Methods of instruction include lecture and laboratory.

Credit Recommendation: In the lower division baccalaureate/associate degree category, 4 semester hours in Electronics Technology (10/91).

Automated Radar Terminal System (ARTS) IIIA Data Entry and Display Subsystem (DEDS) (42035)

Location: FAA Academy, Oklahoma City, OK.

Length: 120 hours (3 weeks).

Dates: January 1982-Present.

Objective: To train personnel to install, evaluate, modify, and maintain EARTS display; and to diagnose and verify proper operation of ARTS III multiplexed display buffer memory/data entry and display subsystem.

Learning Outcome: Upon successful completion of this course, the student will be able to perform diagnosis and verification of EARTS display; develop skills in equipment routing checks, alignment, and test procedures; and use of test equipment and fault diagnosis.

Instruction: Major topics covered in the course are program description of ARTS III multiplexed display buffer memory (MDBM) and data entry and display subsystem (DEDS); sequence testing; equipment initialization procedures (MDBM, DEDS); basic DEDS display evaluation; MDBM diagnostic program execution procedure; DEDS diagnostic program execution procedure; DEDS display; MDBM program; and program descriptions and flowcharts for MDBM diagnostic program and DEDS diagnostic program. Methods of instruction include lecture and laboratory.

Credit Recommendation: In the lower division baccalaureate/associate degree category, 2 semester hours in Electronics Technology (10/91) (7/97).

Automated Radar Terminal System (ARTS) IIIA Software for Technical Personnel (42037)

Location: FAA Academy, Oklahoma City, OK.

Length: *Version 1:* 160 hours (4 weeks); *Version 2:* 240 hours (6 weeks).

Dates: *Version 1:* June 1983-July 1997; *Version 2:* July 1997-Present.

Objective: To teach programming for the ARTS IIIA system.

Learning Outcome: Upon successful completion of this course, the student will be able to write computer programs for the ARTS IIIA system; understand and modify the diagnostic software; understand the symbolic coding forecasts; code emergency patches; and analyze program discrepancies.

Instruction: Major topics covered in the course are test and maintenance, assembler and builder utility programs, and debug aides. Methods of instruction include laboratory, classroom exercises, and software training for the operation, diagnostic (on-call and off-line), and support programs of the ARTS IIIA system.

Credit Recommendation: *Versions 1 and 2:* In the lower division baccalaureate/associate degree category, 4 semester hours in Computer Programming or Computer Technology (10/91) (7/97).

Automated Radar Tracking System (ARTS)IIA Software for Technical Personnel (42043)

Location: FAA Academy, Oklahoma City, OK.

Length: 200 hours (5 weeks).

Dates: August 1990-July 1997.

Objective: To provide theoretical and practical training on the Automated Radar Terminal Systems (ARTS)IIA operational, diagnostic, and support programming necessary to maintain the ARTS IIA system.

Learning Outcome: Upon successful completion of this course, the student will be able to write programs using the ARTS IIA instruction sets and assembler directives in Omega format; assemble the ARTS IIA assembler program into its final machine coded format; build a library on tape using the program source tape; build an operational program and identify the instruction and data works; determine if a malfunction is hardware or software generated; and correct any software malfunctions.

Instruction: Major topics covered in the course are software that is used for the ARTS IIA computer; software topics include the instruction set, software tools such as editor, loader-links, binary dump and verify, subroutines, flow chart development and diagnostics; ADA basics structure; and to site adapt a complete operational program. Course primarily for system performance specialists. Methods of instruction include lecture, discussion, demonstration, and laboratory.

Credit Recommendation: In the upper division baccalaureate degree category, 4 semester hours in Computer Science or Computer Technology (7/92).

Automatic Fault Log Processor (AFLP) (44022)

Location: Correspondence study via FAA Academy, Oklahoma City, OK.

Length: 80 hours (self-paced).

Dates: April 1996-Present.

Objective: To provide training in the operation of built-in test equipment Automatic Fault Log Processor (AFLP) used to evaluate the ARTS IIIA System.

Learning Outcome: Upon successful completion of this course, the student will be able to operate and evaluate the ARTS IIIA system using the Automatic Fault Log Processor (AFLP).

Instruction: Major topics covered in the course are automatic fault log processor and input/output interface, central processing unit, programmable communications, interface, universal interrupt controller, memory assignments, timing and control, and troubleshooting and diagnostics. Methods of instruction include correspondence study and supervised final examination.

Credit Recommendation: In the vocational certificate category, 2 semester hours in Electronics Technology or Microprocessors Technology (7/97).

Back-Up Emergency Communications (BUEC) System for ARTCC's (CBI) (47501) (Formerly 40028)

Location: Computer-based and FAA Academy, Oklahoma City, OK.

Length: 158 hours (4 weeks) (self-paced).

Dates: *Version 1:* December 1981-September 1983; *Version 2:* October 1983-Present.

Objective: To teach installation, evaluation, and maintenance of Back-Up Emergency Communications Systems at ARTCC locations.

Learning Outcome: Upon successful completion of this course, the student will be able to explain BUEC system operations as well as explain the functions of the blocks inside the system and evaluate operation and perform maintenance on the system.

Instruction: Major topics covered in the course are operation of transceivers operation; selection logic tester; and remote control group operation. Methods of instruction include CBI and laboratory.

Credit Recommendation: In the lower division baccalaureate/associate degree category, 3 semester hours in Electronics Technology (11/82) (8/95). **NOTE:** Credit should not be granted for this course and 47500, 40027, and 40008.

Back-Up Emergency Communications (BUEC) System for Remote Sites (CBI) (47500) (Formerly 40027)

Location: Computer-based and FAA Academy, Oklahoma City, OK.

Length: 120 hours (3 weeks) (self-paced).

Dates: *Version 1:* December 1981-September 1983; *Version 2:* October 1983-Present.

Objective: To teach installation, evaluation, and maintenance of Back-Up Emergency Communications Systems at remote locations.

Learning Outcome: Upon successful completion of this course, the student will be able to explain BUEC System operations as well as explain the functions of the blocks inside the system and evaluate operation and perform maintenance on the system.

Instruction: Major topics covered in the course are operation of transceivers operation, selection logic tester, and remote control group operation. Methods of instruction include CBI and laboratory.

Credit Recommendation: In the lower division baccalaureate/associate degree category, 3 semester hours in Electronics Technology (11/92) (8/95). **NOTE:** Credit should not be granted for this course and 47501, 40028, and 40009.

Basic MultiChannel Theory (44006)

Location: Correspondence study.

Length: 40 hours (1 week) (self-paced).

Dates: August 1981-Present.

Objective: To teach magnetic recording theory, magnetic head operation, digital recording techniques, tape drive systems, and transport systems.

Learning Outcome: Upon successful completion of this course, the student will be able to learn the principles of magnetism, magnetic bias, and equalization as applied to magnetic recording heads; digital recording techniques and tape drive systems (servomechanisms); and tape transport systems and power supplies.

Instruction: Major topics covered in the course are the basic theory of magnetic recording; principles of magnetism, magnetic bias, gaps, azimuth, and skew for tape heads; the theory of tape transport systems and speed control; and digital recording techniques.

Credit Recommendation: In the lower division baccalaureate/associate degree category, 1 semester hour in Electromechanical Technology (5/87) (9/93).

Boilers and Chillers (40132)

Location: FAA Academy, Oklahoma City, OK.

Length: *Version 1:* 160 hours (4 weeks); *Version 2:* 120 hours (15 days).

Dates: *Version 1:* January 1979-July 1994; *Version 2:* August 1994-Present.

Objective: To teach installation, maintenance, and evaluation of boilers and heavy duty air conditioning systems.

Learning Outcome: Upon successful completion of this course, the student will be able to identify the basic operation of boiler and air conditioning units, identify the principle of centrifugal refrigeration units and chillers, and operate and repair the control panel, fuel system, water distribution, water testing, and air distribution system.

Instruction: Major topics covered in the course are the construction, operation, evaluation, and maintenance of boilers and heavy duty air conditioning systems including troubleshooting, water analysis and treatment, safety, centrifugal chillers, motors, control panel, water distribution system, air handling equipment, and auxiliary equipment. Methods of instruction include lecture and laboratory.

Credit Recommendation: In the vocational certificate or lower division baccalaureate/associate degree category, 3 semester hours in Environmental Control Technology or Climate Control Technology/HVAC (5/87) (8/95).

Bright Radar Indicator Tower Equipment (BRITE) 2/4 (40327)

Location: FAA Academy, Oklahoma City, OK.

Length: 120 hours (3 weeks).

Dates: *Version 1:* October 1977-June 1992; *Version 2:* June 1992-May 1995.

Objective: To enable the electronic technician to perform maintenance, testing, and adjustment of Bright Radar Indicator Tower Equipment.

Learning Outcome: Upon successful completion of this course, the student will be able to troubleshoot video systems; use block diagrams to describe system functions; and know theory of operation and maintenance of television systems, including video camera.

Instruction: Major topics covered in the course are theory of operation, maintenance, and troubleshooting of a closed circuit television system. The system is known as the BRITE 2/4 system course and does not include television.

Credit Recommendation: *Version 1:* In the lower division baccalaureate/associate degree category, 2 semester hours in Electronic/Communications Technology (5/87). *Version 2:* In the upper division baccalaureate degree category, 2 semester hours in Electronic Communications Technology (7/92).

C Language Programming (40410)

Location: FAA Academy, Oklahoma City, OK.

Length: 152 hours (4 weeks).

Dates: May 1993-Present.

Objective: To instruct experienced programmers responsible for developing and/or maintaining "C" language programs in writing, reading, modifying, and executing programs in the "C" language.

Learning Outcome: Upon successful completion of this course, the student will be able to write, compile, debug, edit, and run "C" language programs.

Instruction: Major topics covered in the course are "C" language programming including math operations, arrays and strings, loop control, file I/D, sequential and conditional statements, and functions and pointers. Methods of instruction include classroom and laboratory instruction.

Credit Recommendation: In the upper division baccalaureate degree category, 3 semester hours in Computer Science or Computer Programming (9/93).

Cable Fault Analysis and Repair (40121)

Location: FAA Academy, Oklahoma City, OK.

Length: 80 hours (2 weeks).

Dates: April 1985-Present.

Objective: To provide instruction and practice in cable fault location and repair of the fault.

Learning Outcome: Upon successful completion of this course, the student will be able to learn the construction of power cables, including the materials used for the conductor, insulation, and shielding; installation, maintenance, and repair of power cables; and how to test the insulation and locate faults.

Instruction: Major topics covered in the course are installation, maintenance, and evaluation of buried power and control cables; hands-on practice in cable splicing techniques, cable analysis, and cable fault location; and types of cables, insulation, and shielding. Methods of instruction include classroom and laboratory application.

Credit Recommendation: In the vocational certificate category, 2 semester hours in Electrical Power (5/87) (9/93).

CDC/CUE Test Equipment Console (43419)

Location: FAA Academy, Oklahoma City, OK.

Length: 240 hours (6 weeks).

Dates: January 1977-Present.

Objective: To provide the student with the skills necessary to operate, maintain, and test the Test Equipment Console (TEC).

Learning Outcome: Upon successful completion of this course, the student will be able to understand the conversion of numbers from one base to another, such as hexidecimal to binary; write a simple machine language program; understand the use of flowcharts and diagnostic tests; understand the tracing of electronic circuits and logic diagrams; and understand the interfacing of peripherals to data bus (TTY, TTL, and RS 232).

Instruction: Major topics covered in the course are machine language programming of a 16 bit computer, data storage using core and static MOS memory, TTL to RS 232 interfacing, direct and indexed addressing, use of diagnostic software, and peripheral controllers. Methods of instruction include lecture and laboratory.

Credit Recommendation: In the lower division baccalaureate/associate degree category, 4 semester hours in Electronic or Computer Technology (5/87) (9/93).

Central Control Monitoring System (CCMS) (40139)

Location: FAA Academy, Oklahoma City, OK.

Length: 120 hours (3 weeks).

Dates: January 1992-June 1997.

Objective: To train field technicians and engineers in the theory and operation of the CCMS.

Learning Outcome: Upon successful completion of this course, the student will be able to understand the proper operation of CCMS operational programs; diagnostic programs; operation system interrelations and debugging application; and correct program deficiencies, expand system capabilities, verify correct operation, and write system application programs.

Instruction: Major topics covered in the course are software loading; application program patches; software analysis; program revision, modification and operational verification; and data gathering panel and accessories. Methods of instruction include lecture, discussion, and laboratory exercises.

Credit Recommendation: In the lower division baccalaureate/associate degree category, 2 semester hours in Computer Science; or in the upper division baccalaureate degree category, 4 semester hours in Electronics or Electrical Engineering Technology (9/93).

COBOL—Tandem Applications (43498)

Location: FAA Academy, Oklahoma City, OK.

Length: 80 hours (2 weeks).

Dates: January 1986-May 1993.

Objective: To write and use COBOL programs using Tandem computer systems.

Learning Outcome: Upon successful completion of this course, the student will be able to write, debug, and execute COBOL programs using a Tandem computer; manage data bases; and manipulate files.

Instruction: Major topics covered in the course are COBOL syntax; file manipulation; database management; and Tandem computer systems. Methods of instruction include lecture and laboratory.

Credit Recommendation: In the lower division baccalaureate/associate degree category, 2 semester hours in Computer Science or Data Processing (9/90).

Common Digitizer (CD) for FAA/DOD JSS (43517)

Location: FAA Academy, Oklahoma City, OK.

Length: 320 hours (8 weeks).

Dates: December 1983-Present.

Objective: To teach technicians to configure, maintain, troubleshoot, and repair the common digitizer (CD) at the joint service station (JSS) site.

Learning Outcome: Upon successful completion of this course, the student will be able to do preventive maintenance, and troubleshoot and repair the CD equipment to a functional level.

Instruction: Major topics covered in the course are block diagram and system operation, overall system data flow, preventive maintenance procedures, and troubleshooting and repair. Methods of instruction include lecture, discussion, and hands-on laboratory.

Credit Recommendation: In the lower division baccalaureate/associate degree category, 3 semester hours in Electronics Technology (9/93).

Common Digitizer (CD) Model 2C (43492)

Location: FAA Academy, Oklahoma City, OK.

Length: 24 hours (3 days).

Dates: March 1986-Present.

Objective: To teach the routine maintenance, operation and repair of the Common Digitizer (CD) Model C2.

Learning Outcome: Upon successful completion of this course, the student will be able to understand the overall operation, maintenance procedures, fault isolation, and repair of the CD Model C2.

Instruction: Major topics covered in the course are block diagram and overall operation, diagnostic routines and fault isolation, and repair of the unit. Methods of instruction include lecture, discussion, and laboratory exercises.

Credit Recommendation: In the upper division baccalaureate degree category, 1 semester hour in Electronics Technology (9/93).

Common Digitizer (CD) Models 2A/B/D (43488)

Location: FAA Academy, Oklahoma City, OK.

Length: 160 hours (4 weeks).

Dates: March 1988-September 1996.

Objective: To teach the routine maintenance and repair of the Common Digitizer (CD) Models 2A/B/D radar.

Learning Outcome: Upon successful completion of this course, the student will be able to understand the overall operation, maintenance, fault location, and repair of the CD Models 2A/B/D.

Instruction: Major topics covered in the course are block diagram and overall operation, diagnostic routines and fault isolation, and repair of the radar unit. Methods of instruction include lecture, discussion, and laboratory exercises.

Credit Recommendation: In the upper division baccalaureate degree category, 4 semester hours in Electronics Technology (9/93).

Common Principles, AC/DC and Transients (40150)

Location: FAA Academy, Oklahoma City, OK.

Length: 104 hours.

Dates: October 1993-Present.

Objective: To present the fundamental principles of direct and alternating current and transients.

Learning Outcome: Upon successful completion of this course, the student will be able to perform ac/dc and transient analysis on equipment in the field.

Instruction: Major topics covered in the course are circuit analysis using Kirchoff's law, Thevenin's theorem, Norton's theorem, Millman's theorem, LC circuits, and filters and resonance. Methods of instruction include lecture, classroom exercises, quizzes, tests, and final examination.

Credit Recommendation: In the lower division baccalaureate/associate degree category, 3 semester hours in Electronics Technology (7/97). **NOTE:** This course replaces AC/DC and Transients' portion of course 40509.

Common Principles, Antennas and Transmission Lines (40153)

Location: FAA Academy, Oklahoma City, OK.

Length: 104 hours.

Dates: October 1993-Present.

Objective: To train technicians on the theory of antennas and transmission lines.

Learning Outcome: Upon successful completion of this course, the student will be able to analyze antennas and transmission lines in the field environment.

Instruction: Major topics covered in the course are general antenna and transmission line theory including line impedance, line losses, transmitted patterns, multiple antenna patterns, matching, and parasitic suppression. Methods of instruction include lecture and classroom exercises.

Credit Recommendation: In the lower division baccalaureate/associate degree category, 4 semester hours in Electronics Technology (7/97). **NOTE:** This course replaces Antennas and Transmission Lines portion of course 40509.

Common Principles, Digital Logic (40152)

Location: FAA Academy, Oklahoma City, OK.

Length: 96 hours.

Dates: October 1993-Present.

Objective: To train "new hire" electronic technicians the principles of digital electronics.

Learning Outcome: Upon successful completion of this course, the student will be proficient in digital logic analysis on circuitry in the field environment for new assignments within the Airway Facilities technical environment.

Instruction: Major topics covered in the course are number systems and codes, signals, switches, and the basic logic gates (and/or, nand, xor, and xnor); Boolean Algebra and Karnaugh mapping; logic families; flip flops and multivibrators; shift registers; counters; arithmetic circuits; code converters and multiplexers/demultiplexers, and interface circuits (analog-to-digital and digital-to-analog converters). Methods of instruction include lecture, classroom exercises, laboratory assignments, quizzes, tests, and final examination.

Credit Recommendation: In the lower division baccalaureate/associate degree category, 3 semester hours in Electronic Technology or Digital Electronics (7/97). **NOTE:** This course replaces Digital Logic portion of course 40509.

Common Principles for Radar Technicians (40392)

Location: FAA Academy, Oklahoma City, OK.

Length: 400 hours (10 weeks).

Dates: March 1989-Present.

Objective: To teach a general knowledge of common principles of radar circuits and systems theory.

Learning Outcome: Upon successful completion of this course, the student will be able to determine the operational requirements of different types of radar used by the FAA; compute the pulse width, amplitude, shape, and other characteristics of the modulator pulse; measure the attributes of an RF pulse; and adjust the high power amplifier stage (i.e., Klystron, Magnetron, Amplitron).

Instruction: Major topics covered in the course are radar circuit analysis; transmission lines; oscillators used in radar systems; microwave receivers; video amplifiers; video display systems; radar systems; microwave receivers; TWTs; video amplifiers; video display systems; radar systems amplifiers; A-D conversion; servo systems; antenna concepts; and radar system concepts. Methods of instruction include lecture, discussion, and laboratory.

Credit Recommendation: In the lower division baccalaureate/associate degree category, 5 semester hours in Electronics Technology (9/90) (8/95).

Common Principles for VOR/TACAN Technicians (40276)

Location: FAA Academy, Oklahoma City, OK.

Length: 120 hours (3 weeks).

Dates: April 1989-Present.

Objective: To teach procedures of installation, maintenance, and evaluation of the FAA's "state of the art" VOR, TACAN, and DME systems.

Learning Outcome: Upon successful completion of this course, the student will able to perform an analysis of a VOR antenna radiation system; compute RF losses through various components of a TACAN/DME system; and troubleshoot a TACAN/DME receiver to the module level.

Instruction: Major topics covered in the course are VOR principles; antenna and radiation patterns; transmission lines; modulation techniques; magnetic amplifiers; and microwave receiver theory. Methods of instruction include lecture, discussion, classroom exercises, and limited laboratory.

Credit Recommendation: In the lower division baccalaureate/associate degree category, 3 semester hours in Avionics Technology (9/90) (8/95).

Common Principles, Solid State Devices (40151)

Location: FAA Academy, Oklahoma City, OK.

Length: 104 hours.

Dates: October 1993-Present.

Objective: To train "new hire" technicians on the theory and analysis of solid state devices.

Learning Outcome: Upon successful completion of this course, the student will be proficient in solid state device circuit analysis in the field environment within the Airway Facilities technical environment.

Instruction: Major topics covered in the course are ac/dc analysis of PN junction diodes; half-wave recitifiers; clippers, clampers, and bi-polar junction transistor

(BJT's) biasing; transistor modeling, BJT small signal analysis, FET's, operational amplifiers, and differential amplifier integrated circuits; and graphical analysis of S Modeling of solid state devices. Methods of instruction include lecture, classroom exercises, and laboratory assignments.

Credit Recommendation: In the lower division baccalaureate/associate degree category, 4 semester hours in Electronic Technology or Solid State Devices and Circuits (7/97). **NOTE:** This course replaces Solid State Devices portion of course 40509.

Communications Equipment (CBI) (47502)
(Formerly 40029)

Location: Computer-based.

Length: 103 hours (self-paced).

Dates: October 1982-September 1995.

Objective: To prepare personnel for the installation, maintenance, and evaluation of VHF and UHF communication equipment.

Instruction: Major topics covered in the course are mathematics review, theory and operation of solid state VHF and UHF transmitters and receivers, audio control lines, and antennas and transmission lines. Methods of instruction include computer-based and directed instruction.

Credit Recommendation: In the vocational certificate or lower division baccalaureate/associate degree category, 2 semester hours in Electronics Technology (11/82) (9/90).

Communications Operations for MCC Specialists (CBI) (47206)

Location: Computer-Based.

Length: 16 hours (self-paced).

Dates: March 1997-Present.

Objective: To train Air Traffic Systems Specialists to perform communications systems monitoring via MCC.

Learning Outcome: Upon successful completion of this course, the student will be able to perform the following MCC tasks relative to the communications systems: check operational status; verify configuration; acknowledge alarms; and initiate restore or coordination functions, if required.

Instruction: Major topics covered in the course are communication systems and flow within the NAS; ICSS and the NAS, flow of ICSS; remote communications equipment subsystems; RCL integrated into the NAS; and DMN integrated into the NAS. Method of instruction includes CBI: Computer-Based Instruction.

Credit Recommendation: In the lower division baccalaureate/associate degree category, 1 semester hour in Management Information Systems (7/97).

Computer Display Channel (CDC) for Technicians (43426)

Location: FAA Academy, Oklahoma City, OK.

Length: 360 hours (9 weeks).

Dates: January 1975-Present.

Objective: To train technicians to install, provide preventive maintenance, and repair the computer display channel equipment and radar display systems.

Learning Outcome: Upon successful completion of this course, the student will be able to do detailed maintenance and repairs for a CDC display subsystem.

Instruction: Major topics covered in the course are system down to the component level; digital logic, transistor theory, registers, counters, displays, A to D, D to A, CRT circuitry (video amplifiers, etc.), operational amplifiers, keyboard operation, and multiplexing. Methods of instruction include classes and labs on equipment operation and fault isolation.

Credit Recommendation: In the lower division baccalaureate/associate degree category, 10 semester hours in Computer Electronics, Digital Controls, or Digital Electronics (5/87) (9/93).

Computer Display Channel (CDC) Operations (43025)

Location: FAA Academy, Oklahoma City, OK.

Length: 56 hours (7days).

Dates: July 1993-Present.

Objective: To teach the knowledge and skills required to ensure the stability of service of the computer display channel and the computer update equipment.

Learning Outcome: Upon successful completion of this course, the student will be able to reconfigure the CDC and CUE units, and to restore failed units, equipment and interfaces.

Instruction: Major topics covered in the course are the overally block diagram level of operation of the system and the analysis of errors that result in reconfiguration; and the commands and software/hardware relationship. Methods of instruction include lecture, classroom exercises, laboratory, and examinations.

Credit Recommendation: In the lower division baccalaureate/associate degree category, 2 semester hours in Aviation Technology or Computer Operation (8/94).

Computer Display Channel (CDC) Processor (43423)

Location: FAA Academy, Oklahoma City, OK.

Length: *Version 1:* 956 hours (24 weeks); *Version 2:* 720 hours (18 weeks).

Dates: *Version 1:* November 1975-August 1995; *Version 2:* August 1995-Present.

Objective: To teach maintenance of the Computer Display Channel Processor subsystem.

Learning Outcome: Upon successful completion of this course, the student will be able to explain CDC processor operation and use applicable software to test operation of the system.

Instruction: Major topics covered in this course are programming, data strings, central processor, test cart, operational programs, input/output control, high speed filters, refresh memory control, refresh memory input/output control, and configuration and control monitor. Methods of instruction include lecture, laboratory, and evaluation by written examination.

Credit Recommendation: *Version 1:* In the lower division baccalaureate/associate degree or upper division baccalaureate degree category, 14 semester hours in Computer Science or Electronics Technology (11/82) (9/90). *Version 2:* In the lower division baccalaureate/associate degree or upper division baccalaureate degree category, 11 semester hours in Computer Science or Electronics Technology (8/95).

Computer Display Channel (CDC) Software (43451)

Location: FAA Academy, Oklahoma City, OK.

Length: 304 hours (8 weeks).

Dates: March 1984-Present.

Objective: To provide theoretical and practical training necessary to maintain the software used to control the Computer Display Channel Systems.

Learning Outcome: Upon successful completion of this course, the students will have skills in verifying new and revised CDC operational programs; analyzing program discrepancies; coding emergency patches; and maintaining CDC hardware/software integrity.

Instruction: Major topics covered in the course are study of on-line operational programs, test and maintenance programs, and off-line maintenance programs.

Methods of instruction include lecture and laboratory.

Credit Recommendation: In the upper division baccalaureate degree category, 4 semester hours in Computer Science or Computer Technology (5/87) (9/93).

Computer Hardware Fundamentals (40406)

Location: FAA Academy, Oklahoma City, OK.

Length: 120 hours (3 weeks).

Dates: January 1989-November 1994.

Objective: To acquire computer hardware entry-level knowledge and skills.

Learning Outcome: Upon successful completion of this course, the student will be able to execute effective diagnostic techniques for correcting computer and peripheral malfunctions.

Instruction: Major topics covered in the course are micro, mini, and mainframe computers; computer and CPU architecture; power supplies; terminology; hardware/software/firmware; busses; interfacing; and systems integration. Methods of instruction include lecture and laboratory.

Credit Recommendation: In the vocational/technical certificate category, 2 semester hours in Electronics or Electricity (9/90).

Computer Update Equipment (CUE) (43416)

Location: FAA Academy, Oklahoma City, OK.

Length: 152 hours (4 weeks).

Dates: August 1980-Present.

Objective: To train personnel responsible for the maintenance, evaluation, modification, or certification of the Computer Update Equipment.

Learning Outcome: Upon successful completion of this course, the student will be able to learn to make checks, adjustments, and diagnose malfunctions in the CUE system.

Instruction: Major topics covered in the course are the computer display, keyboard multiplexer, console equipment, interface, AC power monitor, and core memory. Methods of instruction include lecture and laboratory.

Credit Recommendation: In the lower division baccalaureate/associate degree category, 3 semester hours in Computer Systems Technology (5/87) (9/93).

Continuous Data Recording System (42025)

Location: FAA Academy, Oklahoma City, OK.

Length: 160 hours (4 weeks).

Dates: January 1979-October 1996.

Objective: To enable students to analyze the CDR system for correct performance and to diagnose and correct any fault that may occur in the CDR system and its interface circuitry.

Instruction: Major topics covered in the course are disk drive units, disk control units, printer control units, printer logic, and printer mechanical unit. Methods of instruction include lecture and laboratory.

Credit Recommendation: In the lower division baccalaureate/associate degree category, 4 semester hours in Electronics Technology (11/82) (10/91).

Data Communications Modem Update (Paradyne) (43537)

Location: FAA Academy, Oklahoma City, OK.

Length: 40 hours (1 week).

Dates: September 1989-Present.

Objective: To teach routine maintenance and checks on the 3450 modem and the 2030 statistical multiplexer.

Learning Outcome: Upon successful completion of this course, the student will be able to describe system operation; locate and identify system subassemblies; strap system; run diagnostics on system with internal and external test equipment; and perform routine maintenance.

Instruction: Major topics covered in the course are system operation; system maintenance; and system troubleshooting. Methods of instruction include classroom instruction, laboratory, examinations, and a multiple choice examination given at the completion of the course.

Credit Recommendation: In the lower division baccalaureate/associate degree category, 1 semester hour in Electronics Technology or Avionics (9/90) (8/95).

Data Communications Modems (Paradyne) (43529)

Location: FAA Academy, Oklahoma City, OK.

Length: 40 hours (1 week).

Dates: April 1987-Present.

Objective: To teach installation, troubleshooting, and routine maintenance of the Paradyne modem.

Learning Outcome: Upon successful completion of this course, the student will be able to troubleshoot equipment; perform routine maintenance on equipment; and install equipment.

Instruction: Major topics covered in the course are system installation; system maintenance; system diagnostics; and system troubleshooting. Methods of instruction include classroom instruction, laboratory, and examinations, multiple choice exams given at the completion of the course.

Credit Recommendation: In the lower division baccalaureate/associate degree category, 1 semester hour in Electronics or Avionics (9/90) (8/95).

Data Processing Subsystem (42027)

Location: FAA Academy, Oklahoma City, OK.

Length: 480 hours (12 weeks).

Dates: March 1982-Present.

Objective: To analyze the data processing system for normal operation.

Learning Outcome: Upon successful completion of this course, the student will be able to analyze, diagnose, and correct faults that may occur in the subsystem or its associated interface circuitry.

Instruction: Major topics covered in the course are input/output processor modification, centralized memory access unit, reconfiguration and fault detection unit, memory, and associated diagnostics and operational software; solid state memory; control indicators; interfacing; simplified operational theory and priority circuits; component descriptions and use in operational sequences; system control interfacing; logic analysis; auxiliary memory descriptions and theory; and diagnostic procedure and execution. Methods of instruction include lecture and laboratory.

Credit Recommendation: In the lower division baccalaureate/associate degree category, 5 semester hours in Computer Science and 5 semester hours in Electronics Technology (11/82) (10/91) (7/97).

Data Receiver Group/IFDS (43417)

Location: FAA Academy, Oklahoma City, OK.

Length: 144 hours (3.5 weeks).

Dates: June 1983-January 1993.

Objective: To train technicians in the operation and maintenance of the Data Receiving and the Inter-Facility Data Set.

Learning Outcome: Upon successful completion of this course, the student will be able to learn the basic operation of each piece of equipment in the Data Receiver Group and the Inter-Facility Data Set and the operation of the overall systems. Students learn to do operational checks, make voltage measurements, and troubleshoot to locate faulty parts.

Instruction: Major topics covered in the course are equipment operation and repair of the Data Receiving Group and the Inter-Facility Data Set, digital logic, counters, registers, number base converters, coders, decoders, processors used in data reception and transmission, operation and troubleshooting, and the CRT, modem, and printer. Methods of instruction include laboratory and hands-on instruction.

Credit Recommendation: In the lower division baccalaureate/associate degree category, 3 semester hours in Electronics or Data Communications (5/87).

DBRITE (40373)

Location: FAA Academy, Oklahoma City, OK.

Length: 80 hours (2 weeks).

Dates: October 1989-July 1997.

Objective: To train technicians in the operation, troubleshooting and maintenance of DBRITE.

Learning Outcome: Upon successful completion of this course, the student will be able to perform troubleshooting, periodic maintenance, and system power up procedures for DBRITE systems.

Instruction: Major topics covered in the course are DBRITE system components and assembly; tower equipment group; fault identification and isolation; functional theory of system components. Methods of instruction include lecture and laboratory.

Credit Recommendation: In the lower division baccalaureate/associate degree category, 2 semester hours in Electronics (7/92).

DBRITE Television Microwave Link (TML) Hardware (40393)

Location: FAA Academy, Oklahoma City, OK.

Length: 40 hours (1 week).

Dates: November 1991-April 1996.

Objective: To train technicians in the installation, maintenance, and certification of the TML system.

Learning Outcome: Upon successful completion of this course, the student will be able to describe TML operating parameters, FM characteristics; DBRITE video, DBRITE transmitter/receiver/repeater terminals and video subsystems; perform routine checks and adjustments; perform power up-down operations, preventive maintenance, normal operating procedures, and fault isolation.

Instruction: Major topics covered in the course are TML system operation; the fault diagnosis; fault isolation; performance analysis; test procedures; use of test equipment; and routine checks and adjustments. Methods of instruction include lecture and laboratory.

Credit Recommendation: In the upper division baccalaureate degree category, 2 semester hours in Electronics or Electrical Engineering Technology (7/92).

DCCR Overview for NAS/NOMs (45601)

Location: FAA Academy, Oklahoma City, OK and Field Facilities Throughout the United States.

Length: 40 hours (1 week).

Dates: June 1996-Present.

Objective: To provide an overall understanding of the DCCR hardware and software operation, and to provide the knowledge and skills necessary to manage the system operation.

Learning Outcome: Upon successful completion of this course, the student will be able to identify system problems and faults to a level sufficient to be competent in providing briefings to other personnel; and have a clear understanding of the procedures required to successfully manage, restore, and recover the system during normal and abnormal operation.

Instruction: Major topics covered in the course are an overview of the major hardware components; the processor subsystem and the display subsystem; an overview of the software changes from the 9020E system to the DCCR system; use of system messages to determine system operational status and to manage, recover, or restore the system; and an overview of the system diagnostics available for system verification and fault analysis. Methods of instruction include lecture and laboratory exercises using messages to manage the system.

Credit Recommendation: In the vocational certificate category, 2 semester hours in Communications Technology (7/97).

Diesel Engine Generators (44102)

Location: Correspondence study.

Length: 45 hours (self-paced) .

Dates: August 1985-Present.

Objective: To teach basic principles, concepts, terminology, and definitions of diesel engine generators and associated control panels.

Learning Outcome: Upon successful completion of this course, the student will be able to describe basic diesel engine operation; understand Bosch, Caterpillar, GMC, Rooso Master, and Cummins PT fuel systems; understand techniques related to a variety of speed governors; trace control signals through the control panel schematics; and understand brushless exciters and voltage regulation.

Instruction: Major topics covered in the course are basic diesel engine operation, fuel systems, governors, and control panels.

Credit Recommendation: In the vocational certificate category, 2 semester hours in Diesel Mechanics (5/87) (9/93).

Digital Techniques (44416)

Location: Correspondence study.

Length: 60 hours (self-paced).

Dates: September 1980-Present.

Objective: To teach the fundamentals of digital electronics.

Learning Outcome: Upon successful completion of this course, the student will be able to understand digital logic circuits and Boolean algebra; know and be able to connect and test digital integrated circuits and logic circuits; and understand the operation of flip-flops, combinational logic circuits, and semiconductor memories.

Instruction: Major topics covered in the course are data conversion; logic circuits; integrated circuits; combinational logic; Boolean algebra; and semiconductor memory. Methods of instruction include self-paced individualized independent study with examinations, laboratory, and a proctored test.

Credit Recommendation: In the lower division baccalaureate/associate degree category, 2 semester hours in Digital Electronics (9/90) (8/95).

Direct Access Radar Channel (DARC) for Engineers (CBI) (47004) (Formerly 43479)

Location: Computer-based.

Length: 40 hours (1 week) (self-paced).

Dates: August 1982-June 1994.

Objective: To prepare engineers and software specialists for the installation, maintenance, and evaluation of the Direct Access Radar Channel equipment.

Instruction: Major topics covered in the course are basic programming data flow, system theory, and error analysis. Methods of instruction include computer-based and directed instruction.

Credit Recommendation: In the upper division baccalaureate/associate degree category, 1 semester hour in Computer Science or Electronics Technology (11/82) (9/90).

Direct Access Radar Channel (DARC) for Technicians (43519) (Formerly 43473)

Location: FAA Academy, Oklahoma City, OK.

Length: *Version 1:* 276 hours (7 weeks); *Version 2:* 360 hours (9 weeks); *Version 3:* 320 hours (8 weeks).

Dates: *Version 1:* July 1978-April 1985; *Version 2:* May 1985-July 1997;*Version 3:* July 1997-Present.

Objective: To prepare students for the responsibility of maintenance of the Direct Access Radar Channel System.

Learning Outcome: Upon successful completion of this course, the student, given TI 6160.9, handouts, and a DARC system, will be able to perform system startups, shutdowns, system performance evaluation, reconfigurations, and examine/change system parameters from appropriate I/0 devices in accordance with procedures in the current program release user's manual and the system handbooks that supplement the user's manual.

Instruction: Major topics covered in the course are National Airspace System/ prime comparison, system operation, system reconfiguration capability, and display generator unit interface equipment. *Versions 1 and 2:* Methods of instruction include lectures, examinations, and laboratory sessions. *Version 3:* Methods of instruction include lectures, classroom exercises, and tests.

Credit Recommendation: *Versions 1, 2, and 3:* In the lower division baccalaureate/associate degree category, 4 semester hours in Electronics Technology (11/82) (9/90) (7/97).

Direct Access Radar Channel (DARC) Operations (43006)

Location: FAA Academy, Oklahoma City, OK.

Length: 40 hours (1 week).

Dates: December 1993-Present.

Objective: To teach the reconfiguration of DARC units and DARC interfaces in accordance with authorized documentation.

Learning Outcome: Upon successful completion of this course, the student will be able to identify the parts and explain their function for the DARC and its interface components and use the commands necessary for operation of the system.

Instruction: Major topics covered in the course are DARC parts and their function, interface units, data flow paths, commands used to operate the system, and operational software. Methods of instruction include lecture, laboratory, and written and practical examinations.

Credit Recommendation: In the lower division baccalaureate/associate degree category, 1 semester hour in Aviation Technology or Computer Operation (8/94).

Direct Access Radar Channel (DARC) Software (43520) (Formerly 43480)

Location: FAA Academy, Oklahoma City, OK.

Length: *Version 1:* 476 hours (12 weeks); *Version 2:* 640 hours (16 weeks).

Dates: *Version 1:* November 1982-April 1985; *Version 2:* May 1985-September 1995.

Objective: To provide Direct Access Radar Channel System performance specialists with theoretical and practical training on the Direct Access Radar Channel operational program and support programs.

Instruction: Major topics covered in the course are operational programs, test and maintenance programs, and diagnostic software. Methods of instruction include classroom instruction, examinations, and laboratory sessions.

Credit Recommendation: In the lower division baccalaureate/associate degree category or in the upper division baccalaureate degree category, 6 semester hours in Electronics Technology or Computer Science (11/82) (9/90).

Display Channel Complex Rehost Hardware (45600)

Location: FAA Academy, Oklahoma City, OK and field facilities throughout the United States.

Length: 152 hours (3 weeks, 4 days).

Dates: June 1996-Present.

Objective: To provide an in-depth understanding of the Display Channel Complex Rehost (DCCR) system hardware, diagnostics, and test facilities to enable the technician to successfully maintain system operation.

Learning Outcome: Upon successful completion of this course, the student will be able to understand the individual hardware components and their function in the system; and perform routine preventative maintenance, system fault isolation to the lowest replaceable unit level, and system restoration procedures after failure based upon knowledge of the system test and diagnostic procedures.

Instruction: Major topics covered in the course are the individual hardware components and their function in the system, routine preventive maintenance, system fault isolation to the lowest replaceable unit level, system restoration procedures, system test and diagnostic procedures, and various procedures for operating and maintaining the system. Methods of instruction include lecture, laboratory exercises, quizzes, and final examination.

Credit Recommendation: In the lower division baccalaureate/associate degree category, 3 semester hours in Computer Systems Technology (7/97).

Distance Measuring Equipment, Models FA-8974/9639 (40258)

Location: FAA Academy, Oklahoma City, OK.

Length: 80 hours (2 weeks).

Dates: January 1979-Present.

Objective: To provide students with a background for installation and maintenance of Distance Measuring Equipment (DME).

Learning Outcome: Upon successful completion of this course, the student will be able to explain transonder signal flow diagrams and the function of the parts within the transponder. The student should also understand the signal generation section of the device as well as be able to install and calibrate the device in the field.

Instruction: Major topics covered in the course are DME theory of operation, test units, transponder analysis, signal flow, monitor, RF generator signal flow analysis, and harm generation and control. Methods of instruction include lecture, laboratory using FA 9639 DME, and evaluation by examination.

Credit Recommendation: In the lower division baccalaureate/associate degree category, 2 semester hours in Electronics Technology (11/82) (9/90) (8/95).

Doppler VHF Omnidirectional Range (DVOR) System (40261)

Location: FAA Academy, Oklahoma City, OK.

Length: 80 hours (2 weeks).
Dates: November 1988-Present.
Objective: To teach the maintenance and repair of the Doppler VOR system.
Learning Outcome: Upon successful completion of this course, the student will be able to place the system in operation; identify the principles of a Doppler radar system; and analyze and do routine and corrective maintenance on the system.
Instruction: Major topics covered in the course are Doppler radar principles; block diagram and system operation; set-up and calibration; and system maintenance and repair. Methods of instruction include lecture and laboratory.
Credit Recommendation: In the lower division baccalaureate/associate degree category, 2 semester hours in Electronics or Avionics (9/90) (8/95).

Electrical Principles (CBI) (47600) (Formerly 40100 and 40135)

Location: Computer-based.
Length: 240 hours (6 weeks) (self-paced).
Dates: *Version 1:* October 1981-January 1983; *Version 2:* February 1983-Present.
Objective: *Version 1:* To teach the basic electrical principles and solid state technology introduction required for future study. *Version 2:* To teach the basics of electricity and the solid state devices related to control of electric generators.
Learning Outcome: Upon successful completion of this course, the student will be able to solve DC circuit problems on paper and in the laboratory; solve AC circuit problems with an algebraic approach and in the laboratory; and describe the operation of basic solid state devices.
Instruction: *Version 1:* Major topics covered in the course are mathematics, transformers, 3-phase power, AC and DC electricity, and power supplies. Methods of instruction include a computer-based and monitored program. *Version 2:* Major topics covered in the course are basic DC and AC circuits and the fundamentals of solid state devices. Methods of instruction include self-paced, computer-aided instruction, including laboratory exercises, with written and practical proctored exams.
Credit Recommendation: *Version 1:* In the vocational certificate or lower division baccalaureate/associate degree category, 4 semester hours in Electronics Technology (11/82). *Version 2:* In the lower division baccalaureate/associate degree category, 4 semester hours in Electrical/Electronics Technology (9/88) (8/95).

Electronic Fundamentals and Engineering Mathematics (44504)

Location: Correspondence study.
Length: 280 hours (7 weeks) (self-paced).
Dates: September 1980-Present.
Objective: To provide the student with math skills applicable to electricity.
Learning Outcome: Upon successful completion of this course, the student will be able to apply basic algebra and trigonometry to solve circuit problems.
Instruction: Major topics covered in the course are Basic Algebra, determants, logarithms, trigonometry, DC circuits and transients, AC theory, and network analyses methods. Methods of instruction include correspondence study.
Credit Recommendation: In the lower division baccalaureate/associate degree category, 5 semester hours in College Algebra or Trigonometry; and 6 semester hours in AC-DC Electricity; a total of 11 semester hours (9/90) (8/95).

Electronic Test Equipment (44511)

Location: Correspondence study.
Length: 120 hours (self-paced).
Dates: October 1989-Present.
Objective: To provide the student with a background in the theory, applications and operation of common test equipment.
Learning Outcome: Upon successful completion of this course, the student will be able to operate and perform tests with a wide variety of electronic test equipment and list and explain the advantages and disadvantages of a wide variety of general purpose test equipment.
Instruction: Major topics covered in the course are analog meters, electronic meters, digital meters, oscilloscopes, frequency measurement, frequency generation, AC and DC bridges, transistor testers, curve tracers, logic analyzers and logic testers. Methods of instruction include correspondence with suggested laboratory exercises if equipment is available.
Credit Recommendation: In the lower division baccalaureate/associate degree category, 3 semester hours in Electronics Technology (9/90) (8/95).

Electronics for FAA Technical Personnel (CBI) (47003) (Formerly 47505)

Location: Computer-based.
Length: 360 hours (9 weeks) (self-paced).
Dates: January 1989-April 1996.
Objective: To teach the concepts, terminology, and analytical techniques of basic electrical and electronic circuits.
Learning Outcome: Upon successful completion of this course, the student will be able to work with signed numbers, powers of ten, and equations that have one unknown; understand, describe, and define direct current, alternating current, and current elements; understand and apply semiconductor principles, power supplies, wave form generators, and oscilloscope fundamentals; apply the binary, decimal, octal, and hexadecimal number systems and logic symbology; and describe the operation of various computer components, arithmetic operations, and computer logic circuits.
Instruction: Major topics covered in the course are safety and first aid; mathematics (basic algebra); direct current and voltage; resistors/series, parallel, and series-parallel; introduction to alternating current; semiconductors and diodes; transistors and bipolar field effect; unijunction and zeners; power supplies; wave form generators; and oscilloscopes. Methods of instruction include computer-assisted instruction.
Credit Recommendation: In the lower division baccalaureate/associate degree category, 9 semester hours in Electronics Technology (9/90) (8/95).

En Route Automated Radar Tracking System (EARTS) (42047)

Location: FAA Academy, Oklahoma City, OK.
Length: 240 hours (6 weeks).
Dates: October 1988-Present.
Objective: To teach the operation, calibration, maintenance, and repair of the En Route Automated Radar Tracking System (EARTS) Radar.
Learning Outcome: Upon successful completion of this course, the student will be able to understand the block diagram and the overall operation, calibration and diagnostic routines for the En Route Automated Radar Tracking System in order to repair it.
Instruction: Major topics covered in the course are block diagram and overall operation, initializing and certification procedures, peripheral evaluation system, and diagnostic routines and repair. Methods of instruction include lecture, discussion, and laboratory.
Credit Recommendation: In the upper division baccalaureate degree category, 4

semester hours in Electronics Technology (9/93).

En Route Automated Radar Tracking System (EARTS) (42021)

Location: FAA Academy, Oklahoma City, OK.

Length: 160 hours (4 weeks).

Dates: March 1982-December 1991.

Objective: To provide technicians and engineers training to analyze normal operation of equipment associated with the EARTS system and diagnose and correct faults within the system, subsystem, or individual modules associated with the interface circuitry.

Instruction: Major topics covered in the course are a study of ULTRA symbolic instruction, EARTS operational program, fault analysis, and system level troubleshooting.

Credit Recommendation: In the lower division baccalaureate/associate degree category, 3 semester hours in Electronics Technology (11/82) (9/90).

En Route Automated Radar Tracking System (EARTS) Data Acquisition Subsystem (DAS) (42046)

Location: FAA Academy, Oklahoma City, OK.

Length: 120 hours (3 weeks).

Dates: January 1991-Present.

Objective: To teach the En Route Automated Radar Tracking System (EARTS) Data Acquisition Subsystem (DAS).

Learning Outcome: Upon successful completion of this course, the student will be able to initialize, operate, adjust, and perform maintenance on the En Route Automated Radar Tracking System (DAS).

Instruction: Major topics covered in the course are block diagram and operation of the system, system calibration and adjustments, and troubleshooting and repair. Methods of instruction include lecture, discussion, and laboratory.

Credit Recommendation: In the upper division baccalaureate degree category, 4 semester hours in Electronics Technology (9/93).

En Route Automated Radar Tracking System (EARTS) Display (43467)

Location: FAA Academy, Oklahoma City, OK.

Length: 112 hours (3 weeks).

Dates: October 1981-Present.

Objective: To train personnel to install, evaluate, modify, and maintain the EARTS display.

Learning Outcome: Upon successful completion of this course, the student will be able to do detailed maintenance and repair for the plan view display of the EARTS.

Instruction: Major topics covered in the course are plan view display operation, routine equipment checks, alignment, test procedures, use of test equipment, and fault diagnosis. Methods of instruction include lecture and laboratory.

Credit Recommendation: In the lower division baccalaureate/associate degree category, 2 semester hours in Electronics Technology (11/82) (9/93).

En Route Radar System with Modification ARSR-1/2 (40383)

Location: FAA Academy, Oklahoma City, OK.

Length: *Version 1:* 80 hours (2 weeks); *Version 2:* 120 hours.

Dates: *Version 1:* January 1982-June 1997; *Version 2:* July 1997-Present.

Objective: *Version 1:* To train students for installation, evaluation, modification, maintenance, or certification of the ARSR-1/2 system. *Version 2:* To teach preventive and corrective maintenance on the ARSR-1/2 Radar.

Learning Outcome: *Version 1:* Upon successful completion of this course, the student will be able to operate and evaluate the ARSR-1/2 system using video and RF test sets; and troubleshoot and correct malfunctions. *Version 2:* Upon successful completion of this course, the student will be able to operate, modify, troubleshoot, and repair the ARSR-1/2 Radar.

Instruction: *Version 1:* Major topics covered in the course are system concepts, pulse mode generator, transmitter, receiver, stagger/de-stagger, SLS/ISLS, monitors, control circuits, and Beacon test sets. Methods of instruction include lecture and discussion with laboratory activities. *Version 2:* Major topics covered in the course are radar concepts, system timing, transmitter operation, and SSR/DMTI monitor and control. Methods of instruction include lecture and classroom exercises in orientation, configuration, alignment, troubleshooting techniques, and final examination.

Credit Recommendation: *Version 1:* In the lower division baccalaureate/associate degree category, 2 semester hours in Electronics Technology (11/82) (9/88) (7/92). *Version 2:* In the lower division baccalaureate/associate degree category, 3 semester hours in Electronics Technology, Radar Technology, or Communications Electronics (7/97).

Engines and Control Panels (40127)

Location: FAA Academy, Oklahoma City, OK.

Length: 200 hours (5 weeks).

Dates: November 1984-Present.

Objective: To provide the student with the knowledge of the operation of a gasoline-diesel electrical power generating system, including the control panel.

Learning Outcome: Upon successful completion of this course, the student will be able to test the system to determine if it is operating properly; determine the faulty component if the system does not operate properly; and replace the faulty component and make the system operational.

Instruction: Major topics covered in the course are the internal combustion engine, the generator, and the control panel for three electrical power generation systems. Methods of instruction include laboratory exercises and lecture.

Credit Recommendation: In the vocational certificate category, 4 semester hours in Automotive, Diesel, or Electrical Technology (5/87) (9/88) (9/93).

Environmental Systems and Controls (40133)

Location: FAA Academy, Oklahoma City, OK.

Length: *Version 1:* 160 hours (4 weeks); *Version 2:* 200 hours (5 weeks).

Dates: *Version 1:* May 1984-March 1993; *Version 2:* April 1993-Present.

Objective: To teach evaluation, calibration, and maintenance of pneumatic control systems used in heating, ventilating, and air conditioning systems.

Learning Outcome: Upon successful completion of this course, the student will be able to identify the basics of air psychrometrics, environmental conditioning processes, and pneumatic control fundamentals; and identify the operation of thermostats, humidistats, methods of transmission of data, system balancing, digital controls, and process controls.

Instruction: Major topics covered in the course are the maintenance, calibration, and operation of pneumatic controls and devices; Johnson, Honeywell, Robertshaw, Barbara-Coleman, and powers systems; properties of psychrometrics and environmental air conditioning; and troubleshooting, calibration, and balancing of systems. Methods of instruction include lecture and laboratory.

Credit Recommendation: In the lower division baccalaureate/associate degree category, 3 semester hours in Environmental Control Technology or Climate Control Technology/HVAC (5/87) (8/95).

Exide Power Conditioning System (PCS) Maintenance (40149)

Location: FAA Academy, Oklahoma City, OK.

Length: 80 hours (2 weeks).

Dates: May 1986-Present.

Objective: To teach students the theory of operation, system operation and evaluation, preventive maintenance procedures, and fault analysis.

Learning Outcome: Upon successful completion of this course, the student will be able to understand system operation, perform system evaluation, perform routine test procedures and adjustments, and isolate faults.

Instruction: Major topics covered in the course are system flow diagrams, principles of operation, and evaluation of system operation (system includes three-phase rectification, SCR inverter bridge, microprocessor diagnostic unit, and logic circuitry). Methods of instruction include lecture, discussion, and laboratory.

Credit Recommendation: In the lower division baccalaureate/associate degree category, 3 semester hours in Electrical or Electronic Technology (9/93).

Exide Uninterruptible Power Supply (40145)

Location: FAA Academy, Oklahoma City, OK.

Length: 80 hours (2 weeks).

Dates: *Version 1:* July 1986-August 1988; *Version 2:* September 1988-Present.

Objective: To teach the student the testing and maintenance of the Exide Uninterruptible Power Supply (UPS).

Learning Outcome: Upon successful completion of this course, the student will be able to test the Exide power supply to determine if it is operating properly and repair the Exide power supply if it is faulty.

Instruction: Major topics covered in the course are overall operation and maintenance of the Exide UPS, including the proper care of the storage batteries. Methods of instruction include laboratory exercises and lecture.

Credit Recommendation: *Version 1:* In the vocational certificate category, 1 semester hour in Electronics Technology (5/87). *Version 2:* In the vocational certificate category, 2 semester hours in Electrical/Electronics Technology (9/88).

Flasher System FA-9989 (44112) (Formerly ADB-ALNACO Flashing Light System [44112])

Location: Correspondence study.

Length: 65 hours (self-paced).

Dates: October 1991-July 1997.

Objective: To prepare the technician to operate and maintain the Flasher System FA-9989 flashing light system utilized in aviation runway approach lighting systems.

Learning Outcome: Upon successful completion of this course, the student will be able to explain the theory of operation of the Flasher System FA-9989 lighting system; describe maintenance procedures to insure proper operation of the system; and perform practical operation and maintenance procedures on the Flasher System FA-9989 flashing light system.

Instruction: Major topics covered in the course are system introduction and orientation; type B master timer operation and maintenance; and type I, II, and III Flasher System FA-9989 flasher operation and maintenance. Methods of instruction include correspondence and on-the-job training under supervision.

Credit Recommendation: In the lower division baccalaureate/associate degree category, 1 semester hour in Electronics (7/92).

Flight Data Input/Output (FDIO) Subsystem, ARTCC (43509)

Location: FAA Academy, Oklahoma City, OK.

Length: 40 hours (1 week).

Dates: January 1988-Present.

Objective: To train field technicians and engineers in the theory and operation of Flight Data Input/Output equipment located at an ARTCC facility.

Learning Outcome: Upon successful completion of this course, the student will be able to understand the theory and operation of ARTCC facility FDIO equipment; and install, maintain, troubleshoot, and modify ARTCC facility FDIO equipment.

Instruction: Major topics covered in the course are system operation, power supply, diagnostics, RFSP, GPI/GPO, bus interfacing, controls, and CCU/PCU/RCU. Methods of instruction include classroom and laboratory exercises.

Credit Recommendation: In the upper division baccalaureate degree category, 2 semester hours in Electronics or Electrical Engineering Technology (9/93).

Flight Data Input/Output (FDIO) Subsystem, ATCT (43518)

Location: FAA Academy, Oklahoma City, OK.

Length: 40 hours (1 week).

Dates: January 1988-April 1996.

Objective: To train field technicians and engineers in the theory and operation of Flight Data Input/Output equipment located at a tower facility.

Learning Outcome: Upon successful completion of this course, the student will be able to understand the theory and operation of a tower facility, and FDIO equipment; and install, maintain, troubleshoot, and modify tower facility FDIO equipment.

Instruction: Major topics covered in the course are system generation, power supply, diagnostics, RFSP, bus interfacing, controls, CRT, and CCU/PCU/RCU. Methods of instruction include classroom and laboratory exercises.

Credit Recommendation: In the upper division baccalaureate degree category, 2 semester hours in Electronics or Electrical Engineering Technology (9/93).

FPS-20 Series SSR/DMTI Modification (40382)

Location: FAA Academy, Oklahoma City, OK.

Length: 48 hours (1 week and 1 day).

Dates: August 1988-Present.

Objective: To train field technicians and engineers in the theory and operation of the FPS-20 Series SSR/DMTI equipment.

Learning Outcome: Upon successful completion of this course, the student will be able to understand basic theory and operation of the FPS-20 radar with SSR/DMTI; and perform maintenance, troubleshooting, installation, and modification of FPS-20 radar with SSR/DMTI equipment.

Instruction: Major topics covered in the course are FPS series transmitter, common RF, and common equipment; and SSR/DMTI equipment. Methods of instruction include lecture, discussion, and laboratory exercises.

Credit Recommendation: In the upper division baccalaureate degree category, 2 semester hours in Electronics or Electrical Engineering Technology (9/93). **NOTE:** Credit should not be awarded for this course (40382) if credit for AN/FPS Radar with SSR/DMTI (40399) has been given.

Full Digital ARTS Display (FDAD) Hardware Maintenance (42051)

Location: FAA Academy, Oklahoma City, OK.

Length: 64 hours (1 week, 3 days).

Dates: August 1995-Present.

Objective: To teach the theory of operation and corrective, periodic maintenance, with EMS precautions, alignment, operation verification, and troubleshooting analysis.

Learning Outcome: Upon successful completion of this course, the student will be able to apply the theory of operation and use this knowledge to perform corrective and periodic maintenance, alignment, operation, verification, and troubleshooting analysis on the Full Digital ARTS Display system.

Instruction: Major topics covered in the course are theory of operation of the WME bus, stroke display controller, stroke display unit, architecture of 68000 chip family, radar processor, graphic processor, and fault analysis. Methods of instruction include lecture and laboratory.

Credit Recommendation: In the lower division baccalaureate/associate degree category, 2 semester hours in Electronics Technology, Radar Systems, or Communications Electronics (7/97).

Glide Slope (Short)-Mark 1D/E/F (CBI) (47703)

Location: Computer-based.

Length: 156 hours (4 weeks) (self-paced).

Dates: July 1984-Present.

Objective: To teach the student the theory of operation and maintenance of the Mark 1D/E/F ILS Glide Slope system.

Learning Outcome: Upon successful completion of this course, the student will be able to explain the block diagram of the system; test and troubleshoot the system; and repair the system to operate correctly.

Instruction: Major topics covered in the course are the power supply, transmitter, antenna, monitor, and localizer systems of the Mark 1D/E/F, system analysis, inspection, and troubleshooting. Methods of instruction include computer-based instruction and on-the-job training.

Credit Recommendation: In the lower division baccalaureate/associate degree category, 2 semester hours in Electronics Technology (5/87) (9/88) (9/93).

High Intensity Approach Lighting System (44114)

Location: Correspondence study.

Length: 128 hours (self-paced).

Dates: March 1992-Present.

Objective: To provide the field technician with proficiency in maintaining and troubleshooting the high-intensity approach lighting system.

Learning Outcome: Upon successful completion of this course, the student will be able to operate and perform preventative and corrective maintenance on the Sylvania Sequenced Flasher system as well as Westinghouse, General Electric, and Heavi-Duty single-phase approach light systems.

Instruction: Major topics covered in the course are overview of high intensity ALS; ALS operation and maintenance; Sylvania Sequenced Flasher system and Westinghouse. General Electric and Heavi-Duty single-phase ALS. Methods of instruction include self-paced correspondence and supervised on-the-job training.

Credit Recommendation: In the vocational certificate category, 2 semester hours in Electronics or in the lower division baccalaureate/associate degree category, 1 semester hour in Electronics (7/92) (7/97).

Host Computer System (HCS) Enhanced Operator Training (43042)

Location: FAA Academy, Oklahoma City, OK.

Length: 144 hours (3 weeks, 3 days).

Dates: July 1989-Present.

Objective: To provide computer operators with problem determination and isolation of HCS hardware, peripheral device and software problems; use of HCS panels, indicators and messages, and virtual machine (VM); and multiple virtual storage (MVS) commands, messages, and utility programs.

Learning Outcome: Upon successful completion of this course, the student will be able to recognize both software and hardware system problems, determine if action is needed and then take the necessary actions to ensure the reliability of the HCS in accordance with commercial and FAA documentation.

Instruction: Major topics covered in the course are Host system components, National Airspace System, Virtual Machine, and Multiple Virtual Storage. Methods of instruction include lecture, discussion, practice labs, and demonstrations.

Credit Recommendation: In the upper division baccalaureate degree category, 6 semester hours in Computer Science (9/93).

Host Computer System (HCS) for Computer Operators (43037)

Location: FAA Academy, Oklahoma City, OK.

Length: 224 hours (5.5 weeks).

Dates: January 1989-Present.

Objective: To instruct AT, AF, and FAATC personnel in Host computer systems hardware; in operations using VM, MVS, JESZ, and support functions; and in performing systems operations.

Learning Outcome: Upon successful completion of this course, the student will be able to instruct Host computer operators in the operation of hardware, computer operations using virtual machine, conversational monitor system, multiple virtual storage, and JESZ support systems operations procedures.

Instruction: Major topics covered in the course are system hardware and software. Methods of instruction include lecture, discussion, and hands-on laboratory.

Credit Recommendation: In the upper division baccalaureate degree category, 8 semester hours in Computer Science (9/93).

Host Computer System (HCS) for SE/ASE (43040)

Location: FAA Academy, Oklahoma City, OK.

Length: 144 hours (3 weeks, 3 days).

Dates: January 1986-Present.

Objective: To instruct personnel in Host computer systems hardware, use of the UM/370 system, and user-specific menu-drive.

Learning Outcome: Upon successful completion of this course, the student will be able to identify the configuration and operation of the HCS hardware; use of the virtual machine 370 system; menu-driven panels; support and primary processor functions; and system operations including system analysis, reconfiguration and verification.

Instruction: Major topics covered in the course are systems hardware, systems software, and system troubleshooting. Methods of instruction include lecture, discussion, and laboratory.

Credit Recommendation: In the upper division baccalaureate degree category, 10

semester hours in Computer Science (9/93).

Host Operations (43014)

Location: FAA Academy, Oklahoma City, OK.

Length: 120 hours (3 weeks).

Dates: June 1993-Present.

Objective: To teach the configuration of HOST, PAMRI, and flight data input/output elements, equipment and interfaces in accordance with existing orders.

Learning Outcome: Upon successful completion of this course, the student will be able to identify and explain the functions, addressing scheme, controls, indicators, and interfacing of the HOST computer system.

Instruction: Major topics covered in the course are the reconfiguration, function, and operational data flow paths of the HOST hardware and software. Methods of instruction include lecture, classroom exercises, and examinations.

Credit Recommendation: In the lower division baccalaureate/associate degree category, 6 semester hours in Computer Operation or Computer Science (8/94).

ICSS Type I, Maintenance (40023) (Formerly Integrated Communications Switching System (ICSS) [40023])

Location: FAA Academy, Oklahoma City, OK.

Length: 40 hours (1 week).

Dates: June 1985-Present.

Objective: To teach the maintenance of the Integrated Communications Switching System (ICSS).

Learning Outcome: Upon successful completion of this course, the student will be able to do routine preventive maintenance of the ICSS system; configure and reconfigure the ICSS system; and repair the system when it fails.

Instruction: Major topics covered in the course are the system parameters; equipment operation; maintenance and repair of the Integrated Communications Switching System; and utilization of hardware and software. Methods of instruction include lecture, demonstration, laboratory, and written examinations.

Credit Recommendation: In the vocational certificate category, 1 semester hour in Electronics Repair (9/90) (8/95).

ICSS Type II, Maintenance (40024) (Formerly Integrated Communications Switching System - Type II [40024])

Location: FAA Academy, Oklahoma City, OK.

Length: 80 hours (2 weeks).

Dates: March 1989-Present.

Objective: To teach preventive and corrective maintenance of the Integrated Communications Switching System (ICSS).

Learning Outcome: Upon successful completion of this course, the student will be able to identify the function of each system component, recognize and repair system malfunctions, and perform and document periodic maintenance.

Instruction: Major topics covered in the course are time division multiplexing; switching equipment; fault display equipment; external interfaces; and power supplies. Methods of instruction include lecture and laboratory.

Credit Recommendation: In the vocational certificate category, 2 semester hours in Electronics Repair (9/90) (8/95).

ILS Capture Effect Glide Slope (CEGS) (CBI) (47708) (Formerly Instrument Landing System (ILS) Capture Effect Glide Slope [40240])

Location: Computer-based and FAA Academy, Oklahoma City, OK.

Length: 23 CBI lessons, 6 Advanced Training Aids, and 5 Resident Lecture/ Laboratory Exercises.

Dates: *Version 1:* February 1975-September 1994; *Version 2:* July 1994-Present.

Objective: To teach operational and maintenance characteristics of a Capture Effect Glide Slope System.

Learning Outcome: Upon successful completion of this course, the student will be able to test system tolerances, perform flight inspection, and adjust and troubleshoot the Capture Effect Glide Slope System.

Instruction: Major topics covered in the course are the uneven effects on glide slope, capture effect principle, CEGS system and specifications, inspection, and troubleshooting methods. Methods of instruction include computer-based instruction, advanced training aids, lecture, and laboratory.

Credit Recommendation: In the lower division baccalaureate/associate degree category, 1 semester hour in Electronics Technology (5/87) (9/88) (8/95).

ILS Operations for MCC Specialists (CBI) (47205)

Location: Computer-Based.

Length: 12 hours (self-paced).

Dates: March 1997-Present.

Objective: To train FAA Air Traffic Systems Specialists to perform ILS monitoring via MCC.

Learning Outcome: Upon successful completion of this course, the student will be able to perform the following MCC tasks relative to the ILS: check operational status; verify configuration; acknowledge alarms; initiate restore or coordination functions, if required; and certify system operation.

Instruction: Major topics covered in the course are basic components of the ILS; functional operation of the equipment that comprise the ILS; FAA required maintenance activities for ILS certification; and resources available to assess, arrange for repair, and log ILS Lowest Repairable Unit (LRU) malfunction to support restoration of the ILS. Method of instruction includes CBI: Computer-Based Instruction.

Credit Recommendation: In the lower division baccalaureate/associate degree category, 1 semester hour in Aviation Science (7/97).

Instrument Landing System (ILS) AIL MK 1B (40236)

Location: FAA Academy, Oklahoma City, OK.

Length: *Version 1:* 40 hours (1 week); *Version 2:* 120 hours (3 weeks).

Dates: *Version 1:* September 1980-August 1989; *Version 2:* September 1989-Present.

Objective: *Version 1:* To teach the theory and operations of an AIL MK 1B Instrument Landing System to the card component level of understanding. *Version 2:* To teach the operation, maintenance, and repair of the Wilcox Instrument Landing System.

Learning Outcome: *Version 1:* Upon successful completion of this course, the student will be able to evaluate and validate Instrument Landing System performance; troubleshoot and correct Instrument Landing System malfunctions; and demonstrate ability to facilitate certain functions assigned to Instrument Landing System facility management. *Version 2:* Upon successful completion of this course, the student will be able to evaluate and validate instrument landing system performance, troubleshoot and correct malfunctions, and demonstrate ability to facilitate ILS facility management.

Instruction: *Version 1:* Major topics covered in the course are transmitters; antenna systems; monitors; central control units; unit status; flight inspections and systems operations; maintenance techniques; systems operations; calibration; and fault diagnosis. Methods of instruction include instructor-led lecture, discussion, and laboratory. *Version 2:* Major topics covered in the course are block diagram and operation; transmitter, antenna system, monitors, central control units and maintenance techniques; and calibration and fault analysis. Methods of instruction include lecture, discussion, and laboratory exercises.

Credit Recommendation: *Version 1:* In the lower division baccalaureate/associate degree category, 3 semester hours in Electronics Technology or Avionics (9/90). *Version 2:* In the lower division baccalaureate/associate degree category, 3 semester hours in Electronics Technology (9/93).

Instrument Landing System (ILS) Concepts (40233)

Location: FAA Academy, Oklahoma City, OK.

Length: *Version 1:* 80 hours (2 weeks); *Version 2:* 120 hours (3 weeks).

Dates: *Version 1:* March 1986-June 1992; *Version 2:* July 1992-Present.

Objective: To teach the basic concepts used in instrument landing systems and to prepare students for equipment courses.

Learning Outcome: Upon successful completion of this course, the student will know the theory of the basic operation of instrument landing systems, fundamentals of antenna systems, amplitude, modulation, glide slope RP and DDM, v-ring RP, ILS waveforms, test equipment, and radiation patterns; and the difference in depth of modulation, proximity effects, and monitor networks.

Instruction: Major topics covered in the course are the basics of installation, evaluation, modification, and maintenance of instrument landing systems in general as well as any one of several instrument landing systems by teaching the basics of modulation, antennas, proximity effects, monitor networks, localizer radiation patterns, and glide slope patterns. Methods of instruction include lecture, discussion, classroom exercises, audio-visual material, and laboratory (shop instruction).

Credit Recommendation: *Version 1:* In the lower division baccalaureate/associate degree category, 2 semester hours in Electronic Communications (5/87). *Version 2:* In the upper division baccalaureate degree category, 2 semester hours in Electronic Communications (7/92).

Instrument Landing System (ILS) Wilcox Mark 1 A/C (40235)

Location: FAA Academy, Oklahoma City, OK.

Length: 120 hours (3 weeks).

Dates: *Version 1:* July 1975-June 1992; *Version 2:* July 1992-Present.

Objective: *Version 1:* To teach technicians to install, do preventive maintenance, and repair the Instrument Landing Systems Equipment (Wilcox Mark 1-A). *Version 2:* To provide an understanding of the overall system operation and performance of the Wilcox ILS Mark I A/C.

Learning Outcome: Upon successful completion of this course, the student will be able to analyze RE transmitter operation; tune and adjust ILS RF circuits including the RF transmitter; glidescope, localizer; oscillator/keyer; identify various circuits and their components; determine system tolerances and adjustments; and describe flight inspection requirements and types.

Instruction: *Version 1:* Major topics covered in the course are the operation of the overall system from a block diagram and functional theory of operation basis; transmitters; oscillator/keyer; modulator; antennas; and monitor. Students receive practice in operation and troubleshooting in lab. One-half of time on instruction and one-half in lab. *Version 2:* Major topics covered in the course are ILS transmitter unit; modulator; antenna system monitor; status unit; status control; oscillator keyer; remote monitor receiver; marker beacon; flight inspection; and overall system operation. Methods of instruction include lecture and laboratory.

Credit Recommendation: *Version 1:* In the lower division baccalaureate/associate degree category, 2 semester hours in Communications Electronics (5/87) (7/92). *Version 2:* In the upper division baccalaureate degree category, 3 semester hours in Electronics Technology, Avionics Science, or Aviation Science (9/93).

Interface Buffer Adaptor and Generator (IBAG) (42024)

Location: FAA Academy, Oklahoma City, OK.

Length: 120 hours (3 weeks).

Dates: *Version 1:* January 1982-December 1987; *Version 2:* January 1988-Present.

Objective: To teach operational theory that will help in operation and maintenance of the Interface Buffer Adaptor and Generator System.

Learning Outcome: Upon successful completion of this course, the student will be able to analyze the Interface Buffer Adaptor and Generator, input/output buffer system; and run various programs to test and troubleshoot the system.

Instruction: Major topics covered in the course are IBAG system analysis; I/O processor buffer; display console interface; micro-execution program; diagnostic programs; logic diagrams; performance analysis; and troubleshooting. Methods of instruction include lecture, laboratory, and written examinations.

Credit Recommendation: In the lower division baccalaureate/associate degree category, 3 semester hours in Engineering Technology or Computer Science (8/95).

Localizer-Mark 1D/E/F (CBI) (47702)

Location: Computer-based.

Length: 156 hours (self-paced).

Dates: July 1984-Present.

Objective: To provide technicians with the skills and knowledge to install, maintain, and modify the Wilcox Mark 1D/E/F Localizer System.

Learning Outcome: Upon successful completion of this course, the student will be able to measure RF power, percent of modulation, and distortion of carrier and sideband; use logic truth tables, block diagrams and schematic diagrams to troubleshoot the system; perform routine maintenance of Localizer; and have the knowledge and skill to perform a complete system alignment and/or adjustment.

Instruction: Major topics covered in the course are the theory of operations, system principles, calibration, and fault analysis of the ILS Localizer. Methods of instruction include practical laboratory experience involving operation, alignment, and maintenance; and computer-based instruction.

Credit Recommendation: In the lower division baccalaureate/associate degree category, 3 semester hours in Communication Electronics (5/87) (9/93).

LORAN-C Maintenance (40269)

Location: FAA Academy, Oklahoma City, OK.

Length: 40 hours (1 week).

Dates: August 1989-April 1993.
Objective: To be capable of maintaining and troubleshooting the LORAN-C.
Learning Outcome: Upon successful completion of this course, the student will be able to perform system operation, preventive maintenance, troubleshooting procedures, and fault isolation.
Instruction: Major topics covered in the course are LORAN-C theory and concepts; theory of receiver, simulator, microprocessor, and power supply; software and firmware theory and applications; and systems interfacing with VORTAC. Methods of instruction include classroom instruction and laboratory.
Credit Recommendation: In the vocational certificate category, 1 semester hour in Electronics or Avionics (9/90).

Low-Level Windshear Alert System (LLWAS), FA-10240 (40274)

Location: FAA Academy, Oklahoma City, OK.
Length: 80 hours (2 weeks).
Dates: June 1986-October 1996.
Objective: To train persons in the installation, operation, preventive maintenance, and troubleshooting of the Enhanced Low Level Windshear Alert System.
Learning Outcome: Upon successful completion of this course, the student will be able to perform system preventive maintenance; and isolate and repair system malfunctions.
Instruction: Major topics covered in the course are wind direction and velocity-generated signals; telemetry; computer-based signal processing; and troubleshooting and use of test equipment. Methods of instruction include lecture and laboratory.
Credit Recommendation: In the vocational certificate category, 2 semester hours in Electronics or Avionics (9/90). **NOTE:** Credit for this course precludes credit for Low Level Windshear Alert (40267).

MALS/RAIL/REIL (44113)

Location: Correspondence study.
Length: 120 hours (self-paced).
Dates: December 1991-Present.
Objective: To provide the technician with the theoretical and practical level of competence to perform system operation, preventive maintenance, and corrective maintenance at the module or board level and to teach the installation, maintenance, or evaluation of runway end identifier lighting (REIL) systems and medium-intensity approach lighting systems (MALS) with runway alignment indicator lights (RAIL) visual landing aid systems.
Learning Outcome: Upon successful completion of this course, the student will be able to operate and perform preventive and corrective maintenance in the Sylvania REIL2; Sylvania REIL (FA9437), Godfrey REIL (FA9628); Multi-electric MALSR (FA8767); Sylvania MALSR (FA8982); SEPCO MALSR (FA9625); Remote-controlled MALSR; and maintain and troubleshoot the REIL/MALS/RAIL systems.
Instruction: Major topics covered in the course are operations, maintenance and troubleshooting, REIL-runway end identifier circuits; REIS-runway end identifier system; MALS/RAIL-medium approach light system (without flasher)/runway alignment indicator light; and MALSR-medium intensity approach lighting system and also Sylvania REIL-2 and Sylvania REIL, Godfrey REIL, overview of MALS/REIL, multi-electric MALSR, Sepco Malsr, and Radio-controlled MALSR. Methods of instruction include correspondence and on-the-job training.
Credit Recommendation: In the vocational certificate category, 3 semester hours in Electrical or Electronic Technology (9/93).

MARK 20 Instrument Landing System (ILS) (40282)

Location: FAA Academy, Oklahoma City, OK.
Length: 120 hours (3 weeks).
Dates: April 1995-August 1996.
Objective: To teach maintenance and troubleshooting on the MARK 20 Instrument Landing System.
Learning Outcome: Upon successful completion of this course, the student will be able to demonstrate mastery of configuring all ILS subsystems for normal operation, perform periodic maintenance, and perform corrective maintenance on the MARK 20 ILS.
Instruction: Major topics covered in the course are the installation, evaluation, and maintenance of the MARK 20 Instru-ment Landing System and the knowledge, skills, and abilities to maintain the ILS Localizer, Glide Slope, and Marker Beacon locally or from a remote point. Methods of instruction include lecture, classroom exercises, laboratory, and an examination.
Credit Recommendation: In the lower division baccalaureate/associate degree category, 2 semester hours in Avionics Technology (8/95). **NOTE:** Replaced by *Mark 20 Instrument Landing System (ILS) (CBI) (47710).*

Mark 20 Instrument Landing System (ILS) (CBI) (47710)

Location: Computer-based and FAA Academy, Oklahoma City Oklahoma.
Length: 88 hours (2 weeks, 1 day) (self-paced).
Dates: June 1996-Present.
Objective: To provide training in preventive and corrective maintenance procedures and flight inspection participation on the Mark 20 ILS facilities.
Learning Outcome: Upon successful completion of this course, the student will be able to set up, operate, modify, repair, test and evaluate the Mark 20 ILS to contribute added safety to the overall air traffic control system.
Instruction: Major topics covered in the course are Mark 20 hardware setup, Mark 20 software control, environmental sensors setup and testing, fault isolation and repair, and flight inspection preparation and procedures. Methods of instruction include Computer-Based Instruction (CBI), laboratory, group discussion, team and individual lab exercises, interactive computer, quizzes, audio/visual material, and laboratory group discussions.
Credit Recommendation: In the lower division baccalaureate/associate degree category, 3 semesters hours in Aviation Science (7/97).

Math for FAA Technical Personnel (CBI) (47002)

Location: Computer-based.
Length: 400 hours (self-paced).
Dates: February 1988-October 1996.
Objective: To teach the fundamentals of mathematics that will allow students to enter the electronic technician courses.
Learning Outcome: Upon successful completion of this course, the student will be able to understand the basic concepts of algebra, trigonometry, geometry and analytic geometry.
Instruction: Major topics covered in the course are algebra, trigonometry, geometry, and precalculus. Methods of instruction include individualized self-paced, computer-assisted instruction.
Credit Recommendation: In the lower division baccalaureate/associate degree

category, 10 semester hours in Mathematics for non majors (9/90) (8/95).

Micro-EARTS Hardware Maintenance (42049)

Location: FAA Academy, Oklahoma City, OK.

Length: 40 hours (1 week).

Dates: October 1996-Present.

Objective: To teach preventive and corrective maintenance on the Micro-EARTS system.

Learning Outcome: Upon successful completion of this course, the student will be able to operate and perform maintenance on the subsystems of the Micro-EARTS system in accordance with system operator's manual.

Instruction: Major topics covered in the course are theory of operation, LRU removal/replacement, operate diagnostic hardware, analysis diagnostic printouts, perform system/subsystem initialization, run diagnostic, remove/replace system/subsystem LRU, and perform LAN troubleshooting analysis. Methods of instruction include lecture, audio/visual material, and laboratory.

Credit Recommendation: In the lower division baccalaureate/associate degree category, 2 semester hours in Computer Technology or Aviation Technology (7/97).

Micro-EARTS Software Maintenance (42048)

Location: FAA Academy, Oklahoma City, OK.

Length: 40 hours (1 week).

Dates: October 1996-Present.

Objective: To teach insertion, retrievals, modifications, and deletion using Micro-EARTS software.

Learning Outcome: Upon successful completion of this course, the student will be able to install an operating system and application software of the Micro-EARTS system in accordance with system operator's manual.

Instruction: Major topics covered in the course are installation of the operating system and application software; configure operational system; analyze displayed data for each subsystem; perform site data insertions, retrievals, modifications, and deletions; analyze reported error conditions and system aborts; generate software corrections/patches; develop, modify, and integrate software modules; and utilize off-line support programs. Methods of instruction include lecture, discussion, and laboratory.

Credit Recommendation: In the lower division baccalaureate/associate degree category, 2 semester hours in Computer Science (7/97).

Microprocessors (44415)

Location: Correspondence study.

Length: 160 hours (self-paced).

Dates: September 1980-November 1996.

Objective: To teach the fundamentals of the microprocessor unit and how to communicate with the microprocessor unit with its own language.

Learning Outcome: Upon successful completion of this course, the student will be able to program a representative microprocessor; interface a representative microprocessor with the "outside world"; describe the internal register structure of the 6800 and 6808 microprocessors; develop a program flowchart to define a problem; and input and output data through a Peripheral Interface Adapter (PIA).

Instruction: Major topics covered in the course are number systems and codes; microcomputer basics; computer arithmetic; introduction to programming; the 6800 microprocessor; interfacing; and microprocessor data sheets. Methods of instruction include independent study, laboratory, and a proctored final examination.

Credit Recommendation: In the lower division baccalaureate/associate degree category, 4 semester hours in Computer Science, Microprocessors, or Digital Electronics Technology (9/90) (8/95).

Mode-S Sensor Maintenance (40398)

Location: FAA Academy, Oklahoma City, OK.

Length: 240 hours (6 weeks).

Dates: January 1992-Present.

Objective: To train field technicians and engineers in the proper maintenance of the Mode Select (Mode-S) Beacon Sensor.

Learning Outcome: Upon successful completion of this course, the student will be able to perform terminal operation major system signal flow, perform test equipment operation, conduct phase alignment of the sensor, perform RTADS operation and data extraction, extract data reduction and data analysis, perform operational certification, conduct electronic troubleshooting, and perform remove and replacement procedures.

Instruction: Major topics covered in the course are Mode Select Beacon System, Data Processing System, signal processor, interrogator, transmitter, diagnostics, troubleshooting, Receiver/RF Test, target generator, and calibration performance monitor equipment. Methods of instruction include lecture, laboratory exercises, and examinations.

Credit Recommendation: In the upper division baccalaureate degree category, 3 semester hours in Aviation Science, Electronics Technology, or Electronics Troubleshooting (9/93).

National Airspace System (NAS) (CBI) (47005) (Formerly Introduction to the National Airspace System (NAS) for New Hires (CBI) [47005])

Location: Computer-based.

Length: 12 hours (self-paced).

Dates: July 1993-Present.

Objective: To teach an overview of the FAA functions within the Department of Transportation.

Learning Outcome: Upon successful completion of this course, the student will be able to explain FAA structure, standards, and certification using the National Airspace System.

Instruction: Major topics covered in the course are FAA organizational structure; DOT organizational structure, standards, and certification; and NAS organization and improvements. Methods of instruction include CBI and examinations.

Credit Recommendation: In the lower division baccalaureate/associate degree category, 1 semester hour in Management or Supervision (8/95).

Nondirectional Beacon (NDB) System (40264)

Location: FAA Academy, Oklahoma City, OK.

Length: 80 hours (2 weeks).

Dates: June 1987-April 1993.

Objective: To perform maintenance on and verification of the nondirectional beacon.

Learning Outcome: Upon successful completion of this course, the student will be able to perform all required maintenance procedures; troubleshoot and repair all system failures; and perform all verification procedures.

Instruction: Major topics covered in the course are remote monitor receiver; transmitter; use of IOT and modem; antenna; and antenna tuning. Methods of instruction include classroom instruction and laboratory.

Credit Recommendation: In the vocational certificate category, 2 semester

hours in Communications Circuits or Antennas (9/90).

Pascal Language Programming (40411)

Location: FAA Academy, Oklahoma City, OK.

Length: 120 hours (3 weeks).

Dates: April 1992-May 1996.

Objective: To instruct experienced programmers responsible for developing and/or maintaining Pascal programs in writing, reading, modifying, and executing programs in the Pascal language.

Learning Outcome: Upon successful completion of this course, the student will be able to write, compile, debug, edit, and run Pascal language programs.

Instruction: Major topics covered in the course are Pascal language programming including arrays and records, pointers, functions, linked lists, and disc I/O. Methods of instruction include classroom and laboratory.

Credit Recommendation: In the upper division baccalaureate degree category, 3 semester hours in Computer Science or Computer Programming (9/93).

Peripheral Adapter Module (PAM) for the ARTS III A System (42045)

Location: FAA Academy, Oklahoma City, OK.

Length: 80 hours (2 weeks).

Dates: January 1971-April 1996.

Objective: To provide technical and engineering personnel with knowledge of modification, evaluation, and corrective and periodic maintenance of the peripheral adapter module for the ARTS III A System.

Learning Outcome: Upon successful completion of this course, the student will be familiar with teletype interface, magnetic tape unit, and inter-facility modem module; troubleshoot system malfunctions using logic circuit diagrams; execute the diagnostic programs; and perform alignment procedures.

Instruction: Major topics covered in the course are teletype interface; magnetic tape unit; and inter-facility modem module. Methods of instruction include lecture, discussion, and hands-on laboratory.

Credit Recommendation: In the upper division baccalaureate degree category, 3 semester hours in Electrical or Electronic Technology (9/93).

PET-2000 Radio Transceiver (44024)

Location: Correspondence study.

Length: 40 hours (self-paced).

Dates: July 1996-Present.

Objective: To provide FAA personnel with detailed information about use and repair of the Motorola PET-2000 Portable Emergency Transceiver.

Learning Outcome: Upon successful completion of this course, the student will know the overall specifications and the intended use of the PET-2000 transceiver; the requirements for and have an understanding of the installation and operation of the equipment; and the requirements for periodic maintenance and repair of the equipment.

Instruction: Major topics covered in the course are an overview of the PET-2000 System including installation, maintenance, and warranty repair. Methods of instruction include self-study with audio-visual material and quizzes. The course is in video tape format supported by a student handbook.

Credit Recommendation: In the vocational certificate category, 2 semester hours in Communications Technology (7/97).

Power Conditioning System for Radar Microwave Link (40122)

Location: FAA Academy, Oklahoma City, OK.

Length: 80 hours (2 weeks).

Dates: June 1977-September 1997.

Objective: To teach installation, operation, evaluation, and repair of PCS/RML systems.

Learning Outcome: Upon successful completion of this course, the student will be able to perform routine maintenance (including calibrations) on the power conditioning system for a radar microwave link.

Instruction: Major topics covered in the course are system concepts, circuit analysis, operation, evaluation, maintenance procedures, troubleshooting, and fault correction down to component level. Methods of instruction include 50% lecture and 50% laboratory.

Credit Recommendation: In the lower division baccalaureate/associate degree category, 2 semester hours in Electronics Technology (11/82) (9/90) (8/95).

Radar Operations for MCC Specialist (CBI) (47207)

Location: Computer-Based.

Length: 52 hours (self-paced).

Dates: March 1997-Present.

Objective: To train FAA Air Traffic Systems Specialists to perform radar systems monitoring via MCC.

Learning Outcome: Upon successful completion of this course, the student will be able to perform the following MCC tasks relative to radar systems: check operational status; verify configuration; acknowledge alarms; initiate restore or coordination functions, if required; and certify system operation.

Instruction: Major topics covered in the course are radar components and concepts, MCC responsibilities associated with the en route ARSR-1/2, MCC responsibilities associated with the en route FPS, MCC responsibilities associated with the ARSR-3/4, MCC responsibilities associated with the ATCBI-3/4/5, MCC responsibilities associated with the MODE S, MCC responsibilities associated with the ASR-4/5/6/7/8/9, MCC responsibilities associated with the ASDE-3, MCC responsibilities associated with the NEXRAD, and MCC responsibilities associated with the TDWR. Method of instruction includes CBI: Computer-Based Instruction.

Credit Recommendation: In the lower division baccalaureate/associate degree category, 3 semester hours in Aviation Science or Management Information Systems (7/97).

Radar Remote Weather Display Systems (RRWDS)-Radar (40379)

Location: FAA Academy, Oklahoma City, OK.

Length: 40 hours (1 week).

Dates: January 1983-July 1996.

Objective: To train site personnel about the internal operation of the RRWDS.

Learning Outcome: Upon successful completion of this course, the student will be responsible of the RRWDS including operation, installation, maintenance, calibration, and fault diagnosis.

Instruction: Major topics covered in the course are system calibration and troubleshooting. Methods of instruction include lecture, discussion, and laboratory exercises.

Credit Recommendation: In the upper division baccalaureate degree category, 1 semester hour in Electrical and Electronics Technology (9/93).

Radar Remote Weather Display Systems (RRWDS)-Remote (40380)

Location: FAA Academy, Oklahoma City, OK.

Length: 80 hours (2 weeks).

Dates: January 1982-July 1996.

Objective: To train field technicians and engineers in the operation and maintenance of the RRWDS.

Learning Outcome: Upon successful completion of this course, the student will be responsible for the RRWDS including operation, installation, maintenance, calibration, and fault diagnosis; identify major system components; and describe system capabilities and major system signal flow.

Instruction: Major topics covered in the course are 8085 and 8086 microprocessors, modems, Data Access Arrangement (DAA), power supply, CRT video generation, and CRT construction and operation. Methods of instruction include lecture, discussion, and laboratory exercises.

Credit Recommendation: In the upper division baccalaureate degree category, 2 semester hours in Electronic or Electronics Engineering Technology (9/93).

Radar System Analysis for Digitized Radars (40310)

Location: FAA Academy, Oklahoma City, OK.

Length: 120 hours (3 weeks).

Dates: September 1993-Present.

Objective: To teach maintenance and optimization of primary and secondary radar data and equipment used to provide all radar services to en route and terminal facilities.

Learning Outcome: Upon successful completion of this course, the student will be able to use a personal computer to evaluate digital radar inputs.

Instruction: Major topics covered in the course are digitized radar and beacon systems, parameters and real time analysis, optimization, and software tools for performance analysis. Methods of instruction include lecture, discussion, classroom exercises, and laboratory exercises.

Credit Recommendation: In the lower division baccalaureate/associate degree category, 3 semester hours in Computer Science, Electronics Technology, or Avionics (9/93).

Radio Communications Link (RCL) Common Equipment (40332)

Location: FAA Academy, Oklahoma City, OK.

Length: 80 hours (2 weeks).

Dates: June 1992-Present.

Objective: To train field technicians and engineers in the operation and maintenance of the RCL common system equipment.

Learning Outcome: Upon successful completion of this course, the student will be able to understand RCL common equipment operation; and perform field maintenance, installation, repair, and modification of the RCL system common equipment.

Instruction: Major topics covered in the course are power plan, FR 8 radio system, DTL 7300 multiplexing system, orderwire/ANMS service channel equipment, and ANMS satellite telemetry unit. Methods of instruction include lecture, discussion, and laboratory exercises.

Credit Recommendation: In the upper division baccalaureate degree category, 3 semester hours in Electronics or Electrical Engineering Technology (9/93).

Radio Communications Link (RCL) Terminal Equipment (40340)

Location: FAA Academy, Oklahoma City, OK.

Length: 80 hours (2 weeks).

Dates: June 1992-Present.

Objective: To train field technicians and engineers in the operation and maintenance of the RCL system terminal equipment.

Learning Outcome: Upon successful completion of this course, the student will be able to understand RCL system terminal equipment; and perform field maintenance, installation, repair, and modification of the RCL system terminal equipment.

Instruction: Major topics covered in the course are Karkar KM9/960 Multiplexing System, Coastcom Channel Bank, Fairchild M505M Microwave Modem, AT&T DSX Cross Connect Panel; Accurate Attenuator Panel; ADC JC4/24M 4 Wire Factfield; MLX Net-work, and RCL Automated Network Management System. Methods of instruction include lecture, discussion, computers, and videos.

Credit Recommendation: In the upper division baccalaureate degree category, 3 semester hours in Electronics or Electrical Engineering Technology (9/93).

Remote Maintenance Monitor (RMM)-Beacon Only (40396)

Location: FAA Academy, Oklahoma City, OK.

Length: 40 hours (1 week).

Dates: January 1992-Present.

Objective: To train electronics technicians who maintain, modify, and certify the Beacon-Only Remote Maintenance Monitoring System (RMMS) to configure the equipment for normal operation.

Learning Outcome: Upon successful completion of this course, the student will be able to configure the Remote Maintenance Monitor equipment for normal operation in accordance with the manufacturers instructions and FAA Handbook Specifications; perform and document all periodic maintenance indicating that the technician has acquired the skills and knowledge necessary to measure and analyze parameters, using assigned test equipment as maintenance aids; and determine whether measured parameters meet specified tolerances.

Instruction: Major topics covered in the course are equipment description; system calibration; RMS central processing unit software; digital and analog interfacing; and system installation maintenance, operation, and troubleshooting. Methods of instruction include lecture and laboratory.

Credit Recommendation: In the lower division baccalaureate/associate degree category, 2 semester hours in Avionics or Electronics Technology (7/92) (7/97).

Remote Radio Control System (RRCS) Maintenance (40280)

Location: FAA Academy, Oklahoma City, OK.

Length: 40 hours (1 week).

Dates: May 1993-Present.

Objective: To teach the installation, evaluation, modification, and maintenance of the Remote Radio Control System.

Learning Outcome: Upon successful completion of this course, the student will be able to identify the theory of operation, perform check out procedures, do operator maintenance, perform maintenance tack procedures, and troubleshoot the RRCS.

Instruction: Major topics covered in the course are block diagram and operation; operation turn-on and shut-down; and unit maintenance, troubleshooting, and repair. Methods of instruction include lecture, discussion, and laboratory exercises.

Credit Recommendation: In the upper division baccalaureate degree category, 2 semester hours in Electronics Technology (9/93).

RRWDS Digitizer (CBI) (47302)

Location: Computer-Based.

Length: 24 hours (self-paced).

Dates: January 1997-Present.

Objective: To teach theory of operation; operating procedures and adjustments; corrective and preventive maintenance on the RRWDS Digitizer.

Learning Outcome: Upon successful completion of this course, the student will be able to operate, adjust/align, and repair the RRWDS digitizer to contribute to the total safe operation of the Air Traffic Control System.

Instruction: Major topics covered in the course are radar interface, video processing, communications system, and built-in-test. Methods of instruction include computer-assisted instruction and Computer-Based Instruction (CBI).

Credit Recommendation: In the lower division baccalaureate/associate degree category, 2 semester hours in Aviation Science (7/97).

Runway Visual Range Equipment Tasker 500 Series (40252)

Location: FAA Academy, Oklahoma City, OK.

Length: *Version 1:* 120 hours (3 weeks); *Version 2:* 80 hours (2 weeks).

Dates: *Version 1:* March 1976-January 1984; *Version 2:* February 1984-July 1997.

Objective: To provide students with an understanding of the installation, evaluation, maintenance, and certification of the Tasker 500 system.

Learning Outcome: Upon successful completion of this course, the student will be able to understand system integration, signal data converter, integrated circuit devices, graphic recorder, functions and sequence of operation, remote programmer, decoding, and remote display operation.

Instruction: Major topics covered in the course are system integration, integrated circuit devices, graphic recorders, functions and sequences of operation, remote programmers, decoding, and remote display operation. Methods of instruction include lecture and laboratory.

Credit Recommendation: In the lower division baccalaureate/associate degree category, 2 semester hours in Electronics Technology (11/82) (5/87) (7/92).

Runway Visual Range (RVR) Equipment, Type FA-7861 (40213) (Formerly Runway Visual Range Equipment (Type FA-7861) [40213])

Location: FAA Academy, Oklahoma City, OK.

Length: 120 hours (3 weeks).

Dates: September 1980-Present.

Objective: To teach the operation, maintenance and repair of the SSR Runway Visual Range system.

Learning Outcome: Upon successful completion of this course, the student will be able to install and make the system operational; do the routine maintenance on the system; and isolate and repair defective parts when corrective maintenance is required.

Instruction: Major topics covered in the course are block diagram; logic boards and encoders; light source and receiver; data analysis; and system maintenance and repair. Methods of instruction include lecture and laboratory.

Credit Recommendation: In the vocational certificate category, 3 semester hours in Electronics or Electromechanical Repair (9/90) (8/95).

Second Generation VORTAC Hardware (CBI) (47701)

Location: Computer-based and FAA Academy, Oklahoma City, OK.

Length: 56 hours (1 week) (self-paced).

Dates: January 1985-Present.

Objective: To teach the theory of operation, diagnostic procedures, fault analysis, and repair of the Second Generation VORTAC/ME.

Learning Outcome: Upon successful completion of this course, the student will be able to configure the system in accordance with manufacturer's instruction book, identify the blocks and understand the overall block diagram of the system, and do routine and corrective maintenance on the system.

Instruction: Major topics covered in the course are block diagram; overall function; calibrate the system; fault analysis; and repair of the system. Methods of instruction include computer-based instruction (96 hours), lecture, hands-on laboratory (56 hours), and a written examination.

Credit Recommendation: In the lower division baccalaureate/associate degree category, 4 semester hours in Electronics Technology or Avionics (9/90) (8/95).

Second Generation VORTAC Overview (CBI) (47008)

Location: Computer-based and FAA Academy, Oklahoma City, OK.

Length: (20 hours) (58 lessons/self-paced).

Dates: March 1995-Present.

Objective: To teach the operation of VOR and TACAN equipment (2nd Generation).

Learning Outcome: Upon successful completion of this course, the student will be able to identify the various subsystems (VOR, Power Supply, TACAN, I/O terminal, and remote monitor control).

Instruction: Major topics covered in the course are an overview; power supply; VOR and TACAN facilities; and CPU I/O terminal and remote monitor subsystems of the VORAC 2nd Generation configuration. Methods of instruction include CBI with written tests.

Credit Recommendation: In the lower division baccalaureate/associate degree category, 1 semester hour in Avionics Technology (8/95).

Semiconductor Devices (44417)

Location: Correspondence study.

Length: 120 hours (3 weeks) (self-paced).

Dates: November 1979-Present.

Objective: To provide training in the areas of semiconductor fundamentals, diodes, zenus, bipolar transistors, FETs, thyristors, ICs, and optoelectronics.

Learning Outcome: Upon successful completion of this course, the student will be able to describe the electrical characteristics of semiconductors; explain how most important semiconductor devices operate; properly handle semiconductor components; and test various semiconductor devices.

Instruction: Major topics covered in the course are the operation and characteristics of the most widely used semiconductor devices. Methods of instruction include a training manual, cassette tapes, and 27 electronics components, eleven experiments, and supervised final examination.

Credit Recommendation: In the lower division baccalaureate/associate degree category, 1 semester hour in Semiconductor Devices (5/87) (9/93).

Sensor Receiver and Processor (SRAP) Automated Radar Tracking System (ARTS) IIIA (42010)

Location: FAA Academy, Oklahoma City, OK.

Length: 160 hours (4 weeks).

Dates: April 1988-July 1997.

Objective: To provide training for Automated Radar Tracking Systems (ARTS) IIIA engineers and technicians who are responsible for periodic and corrective maintenance, modification, evaluation, and fault diagnosis of the SRAP subsystem.

Learning Outcome: Upon successful completion of this course, the student will be able to perform control panel operating procedures and preventive maintenance on the system, detect, troubleshoot, and isolate malfunctions in the SRAP subsystems, remove and replace SRAP assemblies according to the technical manual, and perform adjustments of the power supplies and analog cards according to the technical manual.

Instruction: Major topics covered in the course are a description of the overall RDAS and BDAS block diagrams and interfaces; and explanations of functional operation of the Radar Extractor (REX), Beacon Extractor (BEX), Basic Micro-Controller Concepts, Instructor Repertoire, Instruction Execution, and RMC/BMC firmware. Methods of instruction include lecture and laboratory.

Credit Recommendation: In the lower division baccalaureate/associate degree category, 4 semester hours in Avionics, Aviation Technology, or Electronics Technology (7/92).

Solid-State Direction Finder (DF), Type FA-9964 (40257)

Location: FAA Academy, Oklahoma City, OK.

Length: 80 hours (2 weeks).

Dates: October 1981-Present.

Objective: To teach proper routing performance checks; troubleshooting, and repairs and modifications on the VHF/DF Type FA-9964 equipment.

Learning Outcome: Upon successful completion of this course, the student will be able to perform checks, troubleshoot, repair, and do required modifications.

Instruction: Major topics covered in the course are operational performance checks, bearing display, control assembly, antenna systems, and remote maintenance monitoring systems. Methods of instruction include lecture and laboratory.

Credit Recommendation: In the lower division baccalaureate/associate degree category, 2 semester hours in Electronics Technology (11/82) (9/90) (8/95). **NOTE:** Credit should not be granted both for this course and for (40225 and 40227).

Solid-State Radar Beacon Decoder (CBI) (47011) (Formerly 40397)

Location: Computer-based and FAA Academy, Oklahoma City, OK.

Length: *Version 1:* 40 hours (1 week); *Version 2:* 40 hours (1 week) (self-paced).

Dates: *Version 1:* October 1991-February 1995; *Version 2:* March 1995-Present.

Objective: To teach installation, evaluation, modification, maintenance, and certification of Solid-State Radar Beacon Decoder (SSRBD) equipment.

Learning Outcome: Upon successful completion of this course, the student will be able to align, adjust, and make repairs to the line replacement unit level parts of this system.

Instruction: *Version 1:* Methods of instruction include lecture and laboratory. *Version 2:* Methods of instruction include CBI and laboratory.

Credit Recommendation: In the lower division baccalaureate/associate degree category, 1 semester hour in Aviation Technology or Electronics Technology (7/92) (8/95).

Solid-State Video Mappers (40328)

Location: FAA Academy, Oklahoma City, OK.

Length: 40 hours (1 week).

Dates: July 1982-Present.

Objective: To provide training for electronic technicians on analyzing, installing, evaluating, modifying, maintaining, and certifying solid-state video mappers for the specialized areas within the FAA.

Learning Outcome: Upon successful completion of this course, the student will be proficient in analyzing, installing, evaluating, modifying, maintaining, and certifying the equipment for the airway facilities technical environment.

Instruction: Major topics covered in the course are equipment characteristics, block diagram analysis or map scanners and associated equipment, analysis of simulated malfunctions, system alignment, system performance, fault diagnosis, and use of test equipment. Methods of instruction include lecture, classroom/lab exercises, quizzes, tests, and final examination.

Credit Recommendation: In the lower division baccalaureate/associate degree category, 1 semester hour in Electronics Technology or Avionics Technology (11/82) (9/90) (7/92) (7/97).

Tandem Concepts and Facilities (12007)

Location: FAA Academy, Oklahoma City, OK.

Length: 80 hours (2 weeks).

Dates: October 1988-May 1993.

Objective: To understand the functions of the Tandem hardware and software, and the Guardian operating system.

Learning Outcome: Upon successful completion of this course, the student will be able to utilize command programs supported by the Guardian operating system.

Instruction: Major topics covered in the course are Tandem hardware and software; Guardian operating system; and command interpreter.

Credit Recommendation: In the vocational certificate category, 2 semester hours in Data Processing (9/90).

Tandem Enform (43521)

Location: FAA Academy, Oklahoma City, OK.

Length: 80 hours (2 weeks).

Dates: February 1986-May 1993.

Objective: To train the student to generate, manipulate, and manage the Tandem Enform relational data base.

Learning Outcome: Upon successful completion of this course, the student will be able to generate, manipulate, and manage the Tandem Enform relational data base and generate reports from the Enform data base.

Instruction: Major topics covered in the course are database structures, data manipulation, and report generation. Methods of instruction include lecture and laboratory.

Credit Recommendation: In the lower division baccalaureate/associate degree category, 2 semester hours in Computer Science, Data Processing, or Management Information Systems (9/90).

Tandem Pathway (43522)

Location: FAA Academy, Oklahoma City, OK.

Length: 200 hours (5 weeks).

Dates: January 1986-May 1993.

Objective: To manipulate and manage relational databases using Tandem software products.

Learning Outcome: Upon successful completion of this course, the student will be able to generate and manipulate data bases; use reference materials and manuals; and operate pathway applications including Tandem utilities.

Instruction: Major topics covered in the course are data definition language; pathway support utilities; database management; and pathway systems. Methods of instruction include lecture and laboratory.

Credit Recommendation: In the lower division baccalaureate/associate degree category, 3 semester hours in Data Processing or Management Information Systems (9/90).

Tandem Software (12009)

Location: FAA Academy, Oklahoma City, OK.

Length: 200 hours (5 weeks).

Dates: June 1983-May 1993.

Objective: To teach students to modify and maintain TAI software and to familiarize them with the Guardian operating system.

Learning Outcome: Upon successful completion of this course, the student will be able to develop and maintain TAI programs and to use Tandem reference manuals to write and modify programs.

Instruction: Major topics covered in the course are computer overview, data types, constructs, TAI programming, syntax, and file organizations and operations. Methods of instruction include lecture and laboratory.

Credit Recommendation: In the lower division baccalaureate/associate degree category, 4 semester hours in Computer Science (9/90).

Terminal Doppler Weather Radar (40313)

Location: FAA Academy, Oklahoma City, OK.

Length: 160 hours (4 weeks).

Dates: June 1993-Present.

Objective: To teach operation, preventative maintenance, and repair of a Ter-minal Doppler Weather Radar (TDWR) system.

Learning Outcome: Upon successful completion of this course, the student will be able to explain operation of a TDWR system and perform maintenance and repairs on the system.

Instruction: Major topics covered in the course are the Unix Operating System, Hard disk operations, micro computer software and file operations, computer data, and the TDWR system. Methods of instruction include, lecture, laboratory, and evaluation by written examinations.

Credit Recommendation: In the lower division baccalaureate/associate degree category, 4 semester hours in Electronics Technology or Computer Science (8/95).

VHF Direction Finder (VDF) Maintenance (40271)

Location: FAA Academy, Oklahoma City, OK.

Length: *Version 1:* 80 hours (2 weeks); *Version 2:* 88 hours (11 days).

Dates: *Version 1:* September 1988-August 1995; *Version 2:* August 1995-Present.

Objective: To teach the student to operate, configure, and perform maintenance on the VHF Direction Finder System.

Learning Outcome: Upon successful completion of this course, the student will be able to trace signal flow, identify and locate VDF subsystems, install the VDF system software in the default configuration, perform the VDF antenna/receiver site preventive maintenance, and perform DF and FSS site troubleshooting methods.

Instruction: Major topics covered in the course are VDF systems and functions; RMMC subsystem management functions; preamplifiers/filters; receivers/controllers; antenna maintenance; and switching systems. Methods of instruction include lecture, discussion, laboratory, and evaluation by written tests and laboratory.

Credit Recommendation: *Version 1:* In the lower division baccalaureate/associate degree category, 6 semester hours in Avionics Technology (9/90). *Version 2:* In the lower division baccalaureate/associate degree category, 3 semester hours in Avionics Technology (8/95).

VHF/UHF Doppler Direction Finder (DF) System (40225) (Formerly 40227)

Location: FAA Academy, Oklahoma City, OK.

Length: 160 hours (4 weeks).

Dates: December 1973-April 1993.

Objective: To provide students with an understanding of the installation, evaluation, and maintenance of the FA 5530 Doppler DF system.

Learning Outcome: Upon successful completion of this course, the student will be able to learn the Doppler DF theory; and develop skills in system alignment, preventive and corrective maintenance, and system troubleshooting.

Instruction: Major topics covered in the course are antenna systems, receiver systems, control line frequence slight operation, control system, and data system. Methods of instruction include approximately half classroom participation and half laboratory.

Credit Recommendation: In the lower division baccalaureate/associate degree category, 1 semester hour in Electronics Technology (11/82) (5/87) (7/92).

Visual Approach Slope Indicator (VASI) (CBI) (47606)

Location: Computer-based.

Length: 53 hours (self-paced).

Dates: April 1995-Present.

Objective: To teach maintenance and troubleshooting of the VASI system.

Learning Outcome: Upon successful completion of this course, the student will be able to demonstrate a mastery of the following tasks: describe lamp housing alignment, configuration, and operation; troubleshoot and maintain the LHA assemblies; describe the operation of the VASI; and troubleshoot, maintain, and repair the VASI system.

Instruction: Major topics covered in the course are operational characteristics, assemblies, and subassemblies of the Visual Approach Slope Indicator (VASI) and routine troubleshooting and maintenance of the VASI. Methods of instruction include computer-based instruction and evaluation is by a graded examination.

Credit Recommendation: In the lower division baccalaureate/associate degree category, 1 semester hour in Avionics Technology or Electronics Technology (8/95).

VORTAC/DME Operations for MCC Specialists (CBI) (47204)

Location: Computer-Based.

Length: 17 hours (self-paced).

Dates: March 1997-Present.

Objective: To train FAA Air Traffic Systems Specialists to perform VORTAC/DME System monitoring via MCC.

Learning Outcome: Upon successful completion of this course, the student will be able to perform the following MCC tasks relative to the VORTAC/DME: check operational status; verify configuration; acknowledge alarms; initiate restore or coordination functions, if required; and certify system operation.

Instruction: Major topics covered in the course are purpose, characteristics, and configurations of second generation VORTAC/DME systems; and second generation VORTAC/DME subsystem parameters and certification procedures. Method of Instruction includes CBI: Computer-Based Instruction.

Credit Recommendation: In the lower division baccalaureate/associate degree category, 1 semester hour in Aviation Science (7/97).

AVIATION SECURITY TRAINING

Civil Aviation Security Compliance & Enforcement (70034)

Location: FAA Academy, Oklahoma City, OK.

Length: 40 hours (1 week).

Dates: November 1992-Present.

Objective: To prepare and process an Enforcement Investigative Report (EIR).

Learning Outcome: Upon successful completion of this course, the student will be able to investigate, prepare, and process an Enforcement Investigative Report (EIR) for an alleged regulatory violation by an air carrier, airport, or individual and to demonstrate an understanding of FAA's evolving compliance and enforcement philosophy.

Instruction: Major topics covered in the course are special agent in compliance and enforcement, laws, regulations and directives, evidence, planning and organization of an investigation, interviews, evaluation sanctions, preparing the enforcement investigative report, special problems, adjudications, testifying, and cooperation and coordination. Methods of instruction include lecture, discussion, classroom exercises, case studies, audio visual material, learner presentations/reports, and short answer test items.

Credit Recommendation: In the lower division baccalaureate/associate degree category, 2 semester hours in Fundamentals of Investigation (8/94).

Civil Aviation Security Investigations (70020)

Location: FAA Academy, Oklahoma City, OK.

Length: 76 hours (2 weeks).

Dates: December 1992-Present.

Objective: To develop fundamental skills necessary for special agents to conduct investigations.

Learning Outcome: Upon successful completion of this course, the student will be able to identify citations and cases of varying complexity; gather information and evidence; plan an investigation, conduct interviews; and demonstrate methods of reporting investigations.

Instruction: Major topics covered in the course are role of the investigator, types of investigations, planning the investigation, sources of information, interviewing techniques, gathering evidence and preparing exhibits, obtaining statements, and reports of investigation. Methods of instruction include lecture, discussion, classroom exercises, case studies, audio-visual material, presentations/reports, and written examinations.

Credit Recommendation: In the lower division baccalaureate/associate degree category, 3 semester hours in Criminal Investigation (8/94).

Civil Aviation Security Training (70012) (Formerly [00012])

Location: FAA Academy, Oklahoma City, OK.

Length: 36 hours (1 week).

Dates: January 1993-Present.

Objective: To provide familiarization with the criminal threat to civil aviation and the methods utilized to deter this threat; and to provide an understanding of the respective roles of the FAA and airport security officials in implementing and maintaining appropriate security levels at airports.

Learning Outcome: Upon successful completion of this course, the student will be able to demonstrate a working knowledge of the FAA's Civil Aviation Security Program; identify the criminal threat to aviation; and demonstrate an understanding of the respective roles of the FAA and airport security officials.

Instruction: Major topics covered in the course are principles of protections, passenger screening techniques, legal considerations, airport security, aviation explosives security, terrorism, and crisis management. Methods of instruction include lecture, discussion, classroom exercises, audio visual material, learner presentations/reports, and performance evaluation of group presentations.

Credit Recommendation: In the upper division baccalaureate degree category, 2 semester hours in Security Management (8/94).

Facilities Security Inspection Course (70023)

Location: FAA Academy, Oklahoma City, OK.

Length: 76 hours (9.5 days).

Dates: July 1991-Present.

Objective: To develop skills in applying rules, regulations, policies, and procedures in the conduct of an official Federal Aviation Administration (FAA) facilities inspection to determine vulnerability to breaches of external and internal security.

Learning Outcome: Upon successful completion of this course, the student will be able to conduct an official facilities survey or inspection; to identify records, directives, and other documentation; and complete a physical security analysis in compliance with FAA Orders 1600.6, "Protection of Agency Property" and 1650.7, Civil Aviation Security Program Guidelines."

Instruction: Major topics covered in the course are types of FAA facilities and security considerations, physical security including external and internal access controls, asset control including security for information, communications systems, impress funds, firearms or other controlled items, and equipment or substances. Methods of instruction include lecture, discussion, classroom exercises, case studies, audio visual material, learner presentation/reports, pretest, and examinations.

Credit Recommendation: In the lower division baccalaureate/associate degree category, 3 semester hour in Physical Security, Industrial or Private Security, or Security Administration (8/94).

International Assessments and Inspections (70026)

Location: FAA Academy, Oklahoma City, OK.

Length: 76 hours (2 weeks).

Dates: November 1992-Present.

Objective: To train special agents as team members, and to be able to competently assist the Foreign Assessment Team Leader in conducting Foreign Airport Assessments and Foreign and U.S. Air Carrier Inspections at Foreign Airports in accordance with P.O. 99-83, ICAO Annex 17, Section XV of the ACSSP, Part 129, and Federal Aviation Administration Policy Guidelines.

Learning Outcome: Upon successful completion of this course, the student will be able to use effective techniques in performing investigative and internal security activities; identify internal security functions of the Office of Civil Aviation Security; conduct foreign airport assessments and inspections of U.S. and foreign air carriers in a foreign country; and cite Civil Aviation Security Special Agent responsibilities.

Instruction: Major topics covered in the course are civil aviation security investigations, facilities security inspections, international assessments and inspections, and special agent development programs. Methods of instruction include lecture, discussion, classroom exercises, case studies, audio visual material, learner presentations/reports, and team role playing (scenario).

Credit Recommendation: In the lower division baccalaureate/associate degree category, 2 semester hours in Physical Security and 3 semester hours in Report Writing (8/94).

Special Agent Development Program (70028)

Location: FAA Academy, Oklahoma City, OK,

Length: 116 hours (3 weeks).

Dates: August 1993-Present.

Objective: To provide the fundamental knowledge and skills necessary to perform the duties of Civil Aviation Security Special Agents.

Learning Outcome: Upon successful completion of this course, the student will be able to perform the duties of a civil aviation security Special Agent; perform inspections; and conduct investigations of violations of Federal Aviation Regulations.

Instruction: Major topics covered in the course are airport inspection, communication skills, air carrier inspection, listening skills, interpersonal skills, effective writing techniques, facility security inspection, effective presentation techniques, interviewing techniques, and report writing techniques. Methods of instruction include lecture, discussion, audio visual material, learner presentations/reports, and exams.

Credit Recommendation: In the lower division baccalaureate/associate degree category, 3 semester hours in Physical Security or Principles of Communication (8/94).

LOGISTICS TRAINING

Acquisition for Technical Personnel (07004) (Formerly Procurement for Technical Personnel [07004])

Location: FAA Academy Oklahoma City, Ok, and Field locations.

Length: 40 hours (1 week)

.

Dates: December 1970-October 1995.

Objective: To provide technical and professional personnel with an understanding of the acquisition process while identifying respective roles and responsibilities of both Government and contractor personnel as well as the necessity for coordination and team accomplishment of Government procurements.

Instruction: Major topics covered in the course are the process of acquisition management; the preparation and release of procurement requests; solicitation of contract awards; acquisition management after contract award; statements of work; source selection; contractor responsibility; contract types; nature and scope of contract administration, modification, and termination; acquisition planning; procurement request preparation; describing requirements; and nature and scope of contract administration. Methods of instruction include lecture with practical exercises, case studies, and discussion.

Credit Recommendation: In the lower division baccalaureate/associate degree category, 2 semester hours in Management, Business Administration, or Logistics (10/82) (10/91).

Field Logistics Management (07404)

Location: Self-paced correspondence.

Length: 180 days.

Dates: July 1997-Present.

Objective: To present an overview of field logistics functions.

Learning Outcome: Upon successful completion of this course, the student will be able to identify methods, procedures, and guidelines for performing field level requisitioning and cataloging; shipping, receiving, and storing; local purchasing; property management; warranty; property utilization; screening and disposition; and motor vehicle operations.

Instruction: Major topics covered in the course are data research, acquisition of materiel, receiving/storage, shipping, project and personal property management, reutilization of excess property, and motor vehicle management. Methods of instruction include self-paced instruction, practice exercises, and final examination.

Credit Recommendation: In the lower division baccalaureate/associate degree category, 1 semester hour in Logistics or General Management (7/97). **NOTE:** Credit should not be awarded for both this course and 07009.

Field Logistics Management (07009)

Location: FAA Academy, Oklahoma City, OK, and field locations.

Length: 32 hours (4 days).

Dates: June 1989-Present.

Objective: To provide an overview of field logistics functions with roles and responsibilities addressed in each lesson.

Learning Outcome: Upon successful completion of this course, the student will be able to identify methods, procedures, and guidelines for performing field level requisitioning and cataloging; shipping, receiving, and storing; local purchasing; property management; warranty; property utilization; screening and disposition; and motor vehicle operations.

Instruction: Major topics covered in the course are data research, acquisition of materiel, receiving/storage, shipping, project and personal property management, reutilization of excess property, and motor vehicle management. Methods of instruction include lecture, classroom exercises, computer laboratory practice, observations, and final examination.

Credit Recommendation: In the lower division baccalaureate/associate degree category, 2 semester hours in Logistics or General Business (10/91) (7/97). **NOTE:** Credit should not be awarded for this course (07009) if credit has been awarded for 07404.

National Airspace System (NAS) Facilities and Equipment (F&E) Project Materiel Management (07040)

Location: FAA Academy, Oklahoma City, OK, and field locations.

Length: 32 hours (4 days).

Dates: January 1994-Present.

Objective: To identify the organizational and individual responsibilities, interrelationships, and phases involved in project materiel management utilizing the NAS F&E Project Materiel Management System.

Learning Outcome: Upon successful completion of this course, the student will be able to understand the responsibilities, stages, processes, and procedures for NAS F&E project materiel management.

Instruction: Major topics covered in the course are an overview of the Project Materiel Management System; major events of the initiation, management, and completion stages; project structure; materiel acquisition; project tracking; inventory management; and shipping and receiving. Methods of instruction include lecture, classroom exercises, and final examination.

Credit Recommendation: In the lower division baccalaureate/associate degree category, 1 semester hour in Logistics/Materiel Management (8/94) (7/97).

Personal Property Management (07403)

Location: Correspondence study.

Length: Approximately 24 hours (self-paced).

Dates: February 1997-Present.

Objective: To teach responsibilities, processes, and procedures for in-use personal property management.

Learning Outcome: Upon successful completion of this course, the student will be able to maintain facility master file and data files; perform acquisition actions; maintain PPIMS property records; perform physical inventories; and perform reutilization and disposal procedures.

Instruction: Major topics covered in the course are information systems, acquiring and recording property, reporting exchange and repair (E&R) transactions, transferring in-use personal property, property reutilization and disposition program, lost, damaged, or destroyed property, conducting physical inventories, correcting/reconciling, and property data. Methods of instruction include self-paced instruction, practice exercises, and final examination.

Credit Recommendation: In the lower division baccalaureate/associate degree category, 1 semester hour in Logistics Materiel Management (7/97).

Personal Property Management (07042)

Location: FAA Academy, Oklahoma City, OK, and field locations.

Length: 24 hours (3 days).

Dates: July 1994-Present.

Objective: To provide familiarization with the principles of personal property management and Personal Property In-use Management System (PPIMS) procedures.

Learning Outcome: Upon successful completion of this course, the student will be able to identify accountability criteria; determine the roles and responsibilities and support systems used in personal property management; prepare PPIMS documentation for disposing, recording, changing, and tracking personal property; and conduct physical inventories.

Instruction: Major topics covered in the course are information systems, acquiring and recording property, transferring property, physical inventories, motor vehicle management, property re-utilization/disposal programs; lost/damaged/destroyed property; and exchange and repair of personal property. Methods of instruction include lecture and computer-assisted instruction.

Credit Recommendation: In the upper division baccalaureate degree category, 1 semester hour in Logistics Management (8/94).

Real Estate for Federal Aviation Administration Contracting Officers (07005)

Location: FAA Academy, Oklahoma City, OK.

Length: 72 hours (2 weeks).

Dates: *Version 1:* April 1971-December 1980; *Version 2:* January 1981-April 1992.

Objective: To provide recurrent training for personnel who are responsible for requirements determinations, acquisition, management, utilization, reporting, accountability, and disposal actions relating to the agency real property programs.

Instruction: Major topics covered in the course are agency policy and authority; economic analysis; technical and administrative space requirements; appraisals; acquisition; management; utilization; reporting accountability; and capitalization reporting and disposal. Methods of instruction include classroom discussion, laboratory, and workshop exercises.

Credit Recommendation: In the upper division baccalaureate degree category, 3 semester hours in Real Estate Principles (10/82).

REGULATORY STANDARDS AND COMPLIANCE

Accident Prevention Techniques and Procedures (21506)

Location: FAA Academy, Oklahoma City, OK.

Length: 80 hours (10 days).

Dates: September 1990-Present.

Objective: To prepare job function performance of accident prevention program managers and supervisors.

Learning Outcome: Upon successful completion of this course, the student will be able to prepare and conduct Accident Prevention Program Seminars, prepare annual budgets, prepare and evaluate safety data and accident statistics, and access and initiate procurement procedures.

Instruction: Major topics covered in the course are Accident Prevention Program, procurement, equipment selection, support services, media and public relations, workshop preparation, safety seminars, accident analysis presentation development, audiovisual equipment and operation, physiological factors in accident prevention, and computer graphics. Methods of instruction include lecture, discussion, presentations, and evaluation.

Credit Recommendation: In the lower division baccalaureate/associate degree category, 1 semester hour in Communications (9/93).

Advanced Air Carrier Certification (21629)

Location: FAA Academy, Oklahoma City, OK.

Length: 64 hours (8 days).

Dates: July 1997-Present.

Objective: To train the student to process applications for FAR 135, 9 or less, FAR 135, 10 or more, and FAR 121 air carriers to recognize compliance or noncompliance and to act accordingly.

Learning Outcome: Upon successful completion of this course, the student will be able to process Part 135 and 121 carriers and to determine compliance or noncompliance.

Instruction: Major topics covered in the course are FAA policies and procedures, FAR 121 & 135, hazardous materials, drug abatement, air carrier specific data, and applicant responsibilities. Methods of instruction include lecture, discussion, classroom exercises, audio/visual material, learner presentations/reports, and final examination.

Credit Recommendation: In the lower division baccalaureate/associate degree category, 1 semester hour in Aviation Science (7/97).

Advanced Instrument Approach Procedures Automation (21625)

Location: FAA Academy, Oklahoma City, OK.

Length: 120 hours (3 weeks).

Dates: March 1992-July 1997.

Objective: To emphasize use of automation equipment; skills acquired will enable students to develop, store, and transmit complex approach procedures and perform ancillary tasks.

Learning Outcome: Upon successful completion of this course, the student will be able to utilize computer assisted programs; develop certified final approach segments including circling only; develop complex stepdown fixes associated with final and intermediate segments; develop holding patterns; develop missed approach segments; develop initial and intermediate approach segments; complete appropriate forms and charts; analyze deviations; and correct acceptable procedure.

Instruction: Major topics covered in the course are final approach segments; stepdown procedures; holding patterns; missed approach; forms; and quality control. Methods of instruction include lecture, classroom exercises, and laboratory.

Credit Recommendation: In the upper division baccalaureate degree category, 2 semester hours in Computer Science, Graphics (CAD), or General Technology (7/92).

Air Carrier Airworthiness Advanced Indoctrination (21601)

Location: FAA Academy, Oklahoma City, OK.

Length: 64 hours (1 week, 3 days).

Dates: July 1991-October 1996.

Objective: To train air carrier worthiness (maintenance/avionics) inspectors in the job functions associated with certification and surveillance of FAR Part 121 air carriers.

Learning Outcome: Upon successful completion of this course, the student will

be able to determine and certify FAR Part 121 carrier compliance with certification requirements; evaluate operator MEL, maintenance programs, and management personnel qualifications; approve and issue special flight permits; process aircraft lease agreements; and perform certification tasks in accordance with FARs and directives.

Instruction: Major topics covered in the course are FAR Part 121 operations, leasing, certifications, management personnel evaluations, and airworthiness maintenance programs, minimum equipment lists, and special flight permits.

Credit Recommendation: In the lower division baccalaureate/associate degree category, 3 semester hours in Aviation Technology or Aviation Management (10/91).

Air Carrier Operations Indoctrination (20700)

Location: FAA Academy, Oklahoma City, OK.

Length: 160 hours (4 weeks).

Dates: October 1982-May 1993.

Objective: To provide the student with an introduction for air carrier operations inspector's job functions.

Learning Outcome: Upon successful completion of this course, the student will be able to demonstrate an understanding of flight standards and air carrier mission; and demonstrate skills in performing inspector job functions.

Instruction: Major topics covered in the course are accident prevention, instrument flying rating, aircraft familiarization (Cessna 340-A, 172), test standards, evaluation techniques, qualifications of pilot examiners, V.F.R. maneuvers, cross-country flight planning, conduct of tests, air transport pilot certification, commercial pilot certification, airmen certification, written tests, surveillance/airworthiness, flight instructor certification, and student certification. Methods of instruction include lecture and discussion.

Credit Recommendation: In the upper division baccalaureate degree category, 4 semester hours in Aviation Technology (9/88).

Air Carrier Operations Indoctrination (21607)

Location: FAA Academy, Oklahoma City, OK.

Length: 160 hours (4 weeks).

Dates: October 1982-Present.

Objective: To provide indoctrination for air carrier operations inspectors in the job functions required of this specialty.

Learning Outcome: Upon successful completion of this course, the student will be able to demonstrate an understanding of flight standards and air carrier missions and demonstrate skills in performing inspector job functions.

Instruction: Major topics covered in the course are improving personal relations and effectiveness, inspector job functions, aeromedical training, surveillance, manuals, records, facilities, ramp inspection, certificates, safety, cockpit, and enroute inspections. Methods of instruction include lecture, discussion, audio/visual material, flight simulators, and examinations.

Credit Recommendation: In the upper division baccalaureate degree category, 4 semester hours in Aviation Technology (10/82) (8/95).

Air Carrier Transition (21618)

Location: FAA Academy, Oklahoma City, OK.

Length: 36 hours.

Dates: May 1993-Present.

Objective: To train general aviation airworthiness (maintenance/avionics) inspectors to transition into the air carrier discipline.

Learning Outcome: Upon successful completion of this course, the student will be able to define terms commonly used to distinguish certificate holders, describe legislative milestones pertaining to the air carrier industry, describe an inspector's duties in respect to air carrier operations, distinguish differences between maintenance and inspection programs of air carriers and the general aviation industry, and demonstrate an understanding of applicable federal aviation regulations.

Instruction: Major topics covered in the course are Federal Aviation Regulations, air transportation, and aviation management. Methods of instruction include lecture, classroom exercises, audio/visual material, and an examination.

Credit Recommendation: In the upper division baccalaureate degree category, 1 semester hour in Aviation Management or Aviation Regulatory Environment (8/95).

Airborne Digital Logic Principles (22464)

Location: FAA Academy, Oklahoma City, OK.

Length: 120 hours (3 weeks).

Dates: January 1981-October 1996.

Objective: To instruct basic electronic technicians in basic digital principles and theories.

Learning Outcome: Upon successful completion of this course, the student will be able to perform mathematical operations in binary; understand basic logic elements and analyze logic circuits and Boolean expressions; understand basic solid state device digital circuits; determine correct outputs for D/A and A/D convertors; understand memory devices and operation; understand multivariate operation; understand ARINC 429 characteristics; understand soldering requirements; and understand specialized airborne circuits.

Instruction: Major topics covered in the course are logic gates; De Morgan's theorem flip-flops; counters; registers; data handling; arithmetic circuits; memory; signal conditioning; logic design; soldering requirements; binary mathematics; number systems; and airborne flight inspection systems and equipment. Methods of instruction include lecture and lab.

Credit Recommendation: In the upper division baccalaureate degree category, 4 semester hours in Electronics Technology or Computer Technology (10/91).

Aircraft Certification Indoctrination (21660)

Location: FAA Academy, Oklahoma City, OK.

Length: 64 hours (2 weeks).

Dates: May 1993-Present.

Objective: To familiarize the aircraft certification service employee with the FAA mission and philosophy, relationship with other organizations, and basic regulatory framework.

Learning Outcome: Upon successful completion of this course, the student will be able to understand the relationship and operation of the Aircraft Certification Service and the other organizations of the FAA.

Instruction: Major topics covered in the course are Federal Aviation Administration mission and philosophy, basic regulatory framework, team roles and responsibilities, Federal Aviation Regulations and guidance, type certification, production certification, airworthiness certification, import/export certification, continued operational safety, designees/delegations, current issues, and Federal Aviation Administration/aircraft certification service organizations. Methods of instruction include lecture, discussion, and classroom exercises.

Credit Recommendation: In the lower division baccalaureate/associate degree category, 1 semester hour in Aeronautical Science (9/93).

Aircraft Maintenance Reliability Programs (21813)

Location: FAA Academy, Oklahoma City, OK.

Length: *Version 1:* 80 hours (2 weeks); *Version 2:* 64 hours (8 days).

Dates: *Version 1:* October 1982-June 1997; *Version 2:* July 1997-Present.

Objective: To train airworthiness inspectors to perform evaluation and surveillance of aircraft maintenance reliability or condition-monitoring maintenance programs.

Learning Outcome: Upon successful completion of this course, the student will be able to evaluate aircraft maintenance reliability programs to determine if they meet regulatory guidelines.

Instruction: *Version 1:* Major topics covered in the course are calculations; organizing data; control charts; analysis techniques; electronic data processing; reliability and condition-monitoring maintenance methods; and FARs, handbooks, and circulars, etc., pertaining to reliability and condition-monitoring maintenance programs. Methods of instruction include lectures, workshops, and homework assignments. *Version 2:* Major topics covered in the course are calculations; organizing data; control charts; analysis techniques; reliability and condition-monitoring maintenance methods; and FARs, handbooks, and circulars, etc., pertaining to reliability and condition-monitoring maintenance programs. Methods of instruction include lectures, workshops, and homework assignments, quizzes, and a final course project.

Credit Recommendation: *Version 1:* In the upper division baccalaureate degree category, 3 semester hours in Aviation Maintenance Technology (10/82) (9/91). *Version 2:* In the upper division baccalaureate degree category, 1 semester hour in Aviation Maintenance Technology (7/97).

Airspace System Inspection Pilot (Non-flight) Phase II (21411)

Location: FAA Academy, Oklahoma City, OK.

Length: 216 hours (6 weeks).

Dates: January 1982-July 1997.

Objective: To train pilots in duties associated with flight inspection of navigational aids.

Learning Outcome: Upon successful completion of this course, the student will be able to conduct pilot duties associated with airborne checks of navigational aids used for enroute and terminal applications.

Instruction: Major topics covered in the course are data collection procedures; equipment preparation and calibration; data analysis and interpretation and preparation of flight inspection reports. Methods of instruction include lecture, classroom exercises, and laboratory.

Credit Recommendation: In the upper division baccalaureate degree category, 2 semester hours in Aviation Technology, Aviation Science, or Avionics (7/92).

Airspace System Inspection Technician (Non-flight) Phase II (21412)

Location: FAA Academy, Oklahoma City, OK.

Length: 216 hours (6 weeks).

Dates: January 1982-July 1997.

Objective: To train technicians in the duties associated with flight inspection of navigational aids.

Learning Outcome: Upon successful completion of this course, the student will be able to conduct technician duties associated with airborne checks of navigational aids used for enroute and terminal applications.

Instruction: Major topics covered in the course are data collection procedures; equipment preparation and calibration; data analysis and interpretation; and preparation of flight inspection reports. Methods of instruction include lecture, classroom exercises, and laboratory.

Credit Recommendation: In the upper division baccalaureate degree category, 2 semester hours in Aviation Technology, Aviation Science, or Avionics (7/92).

Airspace Systems Inspection Pilot (21127) Technician (Recurrent) (21128)

Location: FAA Academy, Oklahoma City, OK.

Length: 64 hours (2 weeks).

Dates: June 1990-July 1997.

Objective: To provide flight inspection crews with in-depth knowledge of the automated flight inspection system (AFIS), current equipment changes and procedures related to cockpit avionics.

Learning Outcome: Upon successful completion of this course, the student will be able to operate secure voice unit; recall basic knowledge of AFIS system; understand AFIS system malfunctions; and operate aircraft/equipment to inspect Loran, Kln88, Vortac, ILS, and MLS navigation aids.

Instruction: Major topics covered in the course are AFIS documentation and equipment changes; AFIS enhancements and malfunctions; KLN88, Loran C, Vortac, ILS, MLS check procedures; AFIS recording analysis and methods update. Methods of instruction include lecture, seminar, and simulation.

Credit Recommendation: In the upper division baccalaureate degree category, 1 semester hour in Avionics, Aviation Technology, or Aviation Science (7/92).

Airworthiness Certification (21904)

Location: FAA Academy, Oklahoma City, OK.

Length: 64 hours (1 week, 3 days).

Dates: October 1981-August 1994.

Objective: To provide the manufacturing inspector with classroom studies and laboratory exercises pertaining to airworthiness approvals and enforcement.

Learning Outcome: Upon successful completion of this course, the student will be able to find the specific information needed to provide advice and guidance to the applicant; determine if products/parts meet the requirements for airworthiness approval; determine if the product/part meets the marking requirements; determine that an applicant meets the requirements for the appointment as a representative of the administrator; correctly evaluate applications for airworthiness approval and properly issue the requested approval; properly determine the accuracy of weight and balance data; determine if products/parts conform to the type design; and process/distribute enforcement investigative reports.

Instruction: Major topics covered in the course are regulatory requirements for different types of airworthiness approvals (FAR Part 21), identification and marking (Part 45 and Part 47), domestic/import certification, airworthiness approval tags, export airworthiness approvals, surplus military, and compliance and enforcement. Methods of instruction include lecture and laboratory exercises.

Credit Recommendation: In the lower division baccalaureate/associate degree category, 3 semester hours in Aviation Technology (10/91).

Airworthiness Inspector Cockpit (21406)

Location: FAA Academy, Oklahoma City, OK.

Length: 28 hours (3.5 days).
Dates: January 1988-October 1996.
Objective: To indoctrinate inspectors with no enroute training with required enroute procedures.
Learning Outcome: Upon successful completion of this course, the student will be able to conduct enroute inspections; evaluate air carrier procedures and maintenance programs; determine and impose grounding provisions; identify noncompliance with air carrier's manual and FAR and take appropriate action; and properly document inspection findings.
Instruction: Major topics covered in the course are enroute inspections; grounding provision; ground handling, load manifests, and cargo loading regulations; noncompliance actions; and reporting and recording inspection findings. Methods of instruction include lecture and laboratory.
Credit Recommendation: In the lower division baccalaureate/associate degree category, 2 semester hours in Aviation Management or Aviation Science (10/91).

Airworthiness Inspector Indoctrination (21909)

Location: FAA Academy, Oklahoma City, OK.
Length: 160 hours (4 weeks).
Dates: September 1991-October 1996.
Objective: To provide training on job tasks of airworthiness inspectors, general aviation airworthiness, and air carrier airworthiness.
Learning Outcome: Upon successful completion of this course, the student will be able to determine aircraft conformity to classification, registration, and airworthiness guidelines, practices, and regulations; evaluate compliance with weight and balance, airworthiness directives (AD), and maintenance requirements; certification requirements for standard classification, special classification, and special flight permit; and certification of maintenance technical schools, repair station manned free balloons, mechanics, and FAR 121/125/135 operations.
Instruction: Major topics covered in the course are airworthiness certificates; weight and balance; airworthiness directives; alleviates and repairs; avionics; logbooks; records; inspections; FAR operations; and export approval procedures and certifications. Methods of instruction include lecture, discussion, and classroom exercises.
Credit Recommendation: In the lower division baccalaureate/associate degree category, 6 semester hours in Aviation Technology or Aviation Management (10/91).

Airworthiness Inspector's Repair Station Certification Surveillance (22601)

Location: FAA Academy, Oklahoma City, OK.
Length: 64 hours.
Dates: August 1995-Present.
Objective: To provide the student with the knowledge and expertise necessary to perform the certification of approved foreign and domestic repair stations.
Learning Outcome: Upon successful completion of this course, the student will be able to determine the compliance of foreign and domestic repair stations with pertinent federal aviation regulations and certification standards.
Instruction: Major topics covered in the course are management of foreign and domestic repair stations. Methods of instruction include lecture, classroom exercises, audio/visual material, and learner presentations/reports.
Credit Recommendation: In the upper division baccalaureate degree category, 2 semester hours in Management (8/95).

Allison Convair 580 Maintenance and Inspection (21831)

Location: FAA Academy, Oklahoma City, OK.
Length: 80 hours (2 weeks).
Dates: October 1982-September 1993.
Objective: To familiarize line mechanics and inspectors responsible for maintaining Allison Convair 580 aircraft with required maintenance procedures.
Instruction: Major topics covered in the course are Allison Convair 580 aircraft electrical systems, aircraft bleed system, hydraulic power system, landing gear, brakes, flaps, door and stairs, A/C and pressurization, fuel system, and locating components on the aircraft. Methods of instruction include classroom lecture and study.
Credit Recommendation: In the lower division baccalaureate/associate degree category, 2 semester hours in Aviation Maintenance Technology (10/82). **NOTE:** Credit for this course excludes credit received for 21838 and 21840.

Avionics Certification Procedures (21846)

Location: FAA Academy, Oklahoma City, OK.
Length: 68 hours.
Dates: January 1994-Present.
Objective: To enhance avionics inspector's knowledge and skills in the technical concepts, operational features, approval/installation procedures, and regulatory requirements of avionics systems.
Learning Outcome: Upon successful completion of this course, the student will be able to determine the information needed to issue a routine field approval; issue or deny a routine field approval; monitor and control avionics software changes; and resolve issues relating to air carriers special communications database problems.
Instruction: Major topics covered in the course are Federal Aviation Regulations, Avionics Systems, and Supervisory Management. Methods of instruction include lecture, discussion, classroom exercises, audio-visual material, and an examination.
Credit Recommendation: In the upper division baccalaureate degree category, 2 semester hours in Federal Aviation Regulations and Supervisory Management (8/95).

B-727 Aircraft and JT8D Engine Maintenance and Inspection (21838)

Location: FAA Academy, Oklahoma City, OK.
Length: 120 hours (3 weeks).
Dates: October 1982-September 1993.
Objective: To provide mechanics and inspection and quality control personnel who need a working knowledge of Boeing 727 aircraft systems and the JT8D engine to maintain the airworthiness of the Boeing 727 aircraft.
Instruction: Major topics covered in the course are design features and construction, hydraulic systems, landing gear, brakes and AFT airstairs, flight controls, electrical systems, oxygen and emergency equipment, pneumatic system, air conditioning and pressurization, ice and rain protection, fire detection and control, Pratt and Whitney JT8D power plant, fuel system, and APU. Methods of instruction include lectures and laboratory assignments.
Credit Recommendation: In the lower division baccalaureate/associate degree category, 3 semester hours in Aviation Maintenance Technology (10/82). **NOTE:** Credit for this course excludes credit received for 21840 and 21831.

B-727 Aircraft Systems (21808)

Location: FAA Academy, Oklahoma City, OK.
Length: 80 hours (2 weeks).

Dates: October 1982-September 1993.

Objective: This course is designed to provide the maintenance or electrical/electronics inspectors with a working knowledge of B-727 aircraft systems for the safety/regulatory function.

Instruction: Major topics covered in the course are electrical power, fuel, anti- and de-icing systems, air conditioning and pressurization, hydraulic, landing gear and brake, flight controls, oxygen and emergency equipment, flight instruments, and auto pilot. Methods of instruction include formal classroom lectures, class discussion seminars, supervised lab, and workshop experiences.

Credit Recommendation: In the upper division baccalaureate degree category, 2 semester hours in Aviation Technology (10/82). **NOTE:** Credit for this course excludes credit for 21800, 21806, and 21807.

B-737 Aircraft Systems (21806)

Location: FAA Academy, Oklahoma City, OK.

Length: 80 hours (2 weeks).

Dates: October 1982-September 1993.

Objective: This course is designed to provide the maintenance or electrical/electronics inspector with a working knowledge of Boeing 737 aircraft systems for the safety regulatory function.

Instruction: Major topics covered in the course are electrical power, fuel, anti- and de-icing systems, air conditioning and pressurization, hydraulic, landing gear and brake, flight controls, oxygen and emergency equipment, flight instruments, and auto pilot. Methods of instruction include formal classroom lectures, class discussion and seminars, supervised laboratory and workshop experiences, and homework assignments.

Credit Recommendation: In the upper division baccalaureate degree category, 3 semester hours in Aviation Technology (10/82). **NOTE:** Credit for this course excludes credit for 21800, 21807, and 21808.

BE 300 Flight Control Systems (22477)

Location: FAA Academy, Oklahoma City, OK.

Length: 200 hours.

Dates: May 1989-Present.

Objective: To provide the student with the knowledge and expertise necessary to troubleshoot, repair, and maintain avionics equipment used in the flight inspection fleet.

Learning Outcome: Upon successful completion of this course, the student will be able to identify, troubleshoot, analyze, and repair flight control systems and perform approved technical issuance engineering orders.

Instruction: Major topics covered in the course are advanced solid state avionics. Methods of instruction include lecture, discussion, classroom exercises, audio-visual material, and an examination.

Credit Recommendation: In the upper division baccalaureate degree category, 5 semester hours in Avionics (8/95).

Boeing 727 Inspector Pilot and Flight Engineer Initial Qualification Course (20007)

Location: FAA Academy, Oklahoma City, OK.

Length: 200 hours (5 weeks).

Dates: October 1982-September 1993.

Objective: This course is designed to train air carrier operations inspectors for initial qualification and standardization in Boeing 727 aircraft.

Instruction: Major topics covered in the course are aircraft systems and equipment, limitations, performance, maneuvers, and emergency procedures. Methods of instruction include lectures, pre- and post-flight briefings, and simulator and flight experience.

Credit Recommendation: In the upper division baccalaureate degree category, 7 semester hours in Flight Technology (10/82). **NOTE:** Credit for this course precludes credit for 20006.

Certification and Surveillance of NDT Repair Stations and Facilities (22520)

Location: FAA Academy, Oklahoma City, OK.

Length: 80 hours (2 weeks).

Dates: October 1982-September 1993.

Objective: To familiarize Federal Aviation Administration inspection and engineering personnel with in-depth training in radiographic and eddy current nondestructive testing.

Instruction: Major topics covered in the course are theory and practical application of radiography and eddy current NDT methods and certification and surveillance of NDT repair stations, with emphasis on certification of repair stations to conduct NDT inspections of the Beech 18. Methods of instruction include lecture, laboratory exercises consist of "hands-on" set-up, operation of equipment, and interpretation of results.

Credit Recommendation: In the upper division baccalaureate degree category, 2 semester hours in Aeronautical Engineering (10/82).

Certification Engineering Indoctrination (21604)

Location: FAA Academy, Oklahoma City, OK.

Length: 64 hours (1 week, 3 days).

Dates: August 1990-September 1993.

Objective: To provide new certification engineers with the regulations and directives pertaining to type certification, airworthiness certification, and enforcement.

Learning Outcome: Upon successful completion of this course, the student will be able to assist or understand the procedures for the type certification program; understand the procedure for the airworthiness certification program; investigate and report noncompliance with the regulations; and understand procedure for returning aircraft to service.

Instruction: Major topics covered in the course are FAA history, the various civil aviation acts, the responsibility and organization of FAA, certification procedures, airworthiness approval methods, and enforcement considerations. Methods of instruction include lecture and laboratory.

Credit Recommendation: In the lower division baccalaureate/associate degree category, 3 semester hours in Aviation Technology (10/91).

Compliance and Enforcement (12020)

Location: FAA Academy, Oklahoma City, OK.

Length: 72 hours (1 week, 4 days).

Dates: June 1976-Present.

Objective: To train personnel with direct enforcement duties in the policies, regulations, documentation, and procedures required to satisfy the agency's compliance and enforcement responsibilities.

Learning Outcome: Upon successful completion of this course, the student will be able to investigate, prepare, and process a compliance and enforcement report through the Federal Aviation Administration legal system following federal regulations and national policy guidelines.

Instruction: Major topics covered in the course are the legal system, rules of evidence, investigation, testifying, and report processing. Methods of instruction include lecture, discussion, and workshop.

Credit Recommendation: In the upper division baccalaureate degree category, 3 semester hours in Criminal Justice (9/93).

DC-9 Aircraft Systems (21807)

Location: FAA Academy, Oklahoma City, OK.

Length: 80 hours (2 weeks).

Dates: October 1982-September 1993.

Objective: This course is designed to provide the maintenance or electrical/electronics inspector with a working knowledge of Douglas DC-9 aircraft systems for the safety/regulatory function.

Instruction: Major topics covered in the course are the study of the electrical power system, fuel system, anti- and deicing systems, air conditioning and pressurization systems, hydraulic system, landing gear and brakes, flight controls, oxygen and emergency equipment, flight instruments, and autopilot. Methods of instruction include lectures, class discussions and seminars, supervised laboratory and workshop experiences, and homework assignments.

Credit Recommendation: In the upper division baccalaureate degree category, 3 semester hours in Aviation Technology (10/82). **NOTE:** Credit for this course excludes credit for 21800, 21806, and 21808.

DC-9 Airframe and Powerplant Maintenance and Inspection (21840)

Location: FAA Academy, Oklahoma City, OK.

Length: 120 hours (3 weeks).

Dates: October 1982-September 1993.

Objective: To provide mechanics and inspection personnel with a working knowledge of DC-9 aircraft systems.

Instruction: Major topics covered in the course are the hydraulic power system, landing gear and brake systems, power plants, pneumatic system, air conditioning and pressurization systems, fuel systems, APU, and systems operation in the DC-9 cockpit procedure trainer. Methods of instruction include classroom lecture and study.

Credit Recommendation: In the lower division baccalaureate/associate degree category, 3 semester hours in Aviation Maintenance Technology (10/82). **NOTE:** Credit for this course excludes credit received for 21838 and 21831.

Emergency Evacuation and Survival Equipment (Airworthiness) (21843)

Location: FAA Academy, Oklahoma City, OK.

Length: 36 hours (1 week).

Dates: October 1982-September 1993.

Objective: To provide the airworthiness inspector with an update in the state-of-the-art changes involving emergency equipment on newer aircraft, especially large and wide-bodied jets.

Instruction: Major topics covered in the course are exits, lighting, evacuation slides, flotation equipment, supplemental oxygen, maintenance manual requirements, miscellaneous equipment, and FARs. Methods of instruction include lecture, laboratory, and field training.

Credit Recommendation: In the lower division baccalaureate/associate degree category, 1 semester hour in Aircraft Maintenance Technology (10/82).

Enroute and TERPS Planning and Development (TERPS) (21612)

Location: FAA Academy, Oklahoma City, OK.

Length: 240 hours (6 weeks).

Dates: February 1991-July 1997.

Objective: To train personnel to apply FAA standards for terminal instrument procedures (TERPS), flight procedures and airspace in matters of terminal and enroute instrument flight procedures.

Learning Outcome: Upon successful completion of this course, the student will be able to grasp concepts involved in designing of instrument approach and enroute charts as well as assuring compatibility with the local environment and obstructions. The student will also be familiar with radar (ASR) approaching and MVA charts.

Instruction: Major topics covered in the course are terminal and enroute procedures; plotting procedures using drafting principals; determine reference points (mathematically). Methods of instruction include lecture, laboratory, and discussion.

Credit Recommendation: In the lower division baccalaureate/associate degree category, 1 semester hour in Drafting, 2 semester hours in Aviation Sciences or Aviation Technology, and 1 semester hour in Math (7/92).

Evaluation of Aviation Management Systems (22600)

Location: FAA Academy, Oklahoma City, OK.

Length: 68 hours (1 week, 3.5 days).

Dates: October 1991-Present.

Objective: To teach inspectors a standardized systematic approach for management and analysis during evaluation of aviation companies.

Learning Outcome: Upon successful completion of this course, the student will be able to audit aviation companies' management systems and do a systematic, standard analysis of the management of a company during the evaluation process.

Instruction: Major topics covered in the course are methods used to evaluate effectiveness; types of organizations and organizational principles; general management concepts and system design; methods of charting problem/decision analysis; block and linear responsibilities; and interview techniques. Methods of instruction include lecture and laboratory.

Credit Recommendation: In the lower division baccalaureate/associate degree category, 3 semester hours in Introduction to Management or Organizational Theory (10/91) (9/93).

Evaluation of Aviation Management Systems (22600)

Location: FAA Academy, Oklahoma City, OK.

Length: *Version 1:* 78 hours (2 weeks); *Version 2:* 68 hours (1 week, 3.5 days).

Dates: *Version 1:* October 1982-September 1991; *Version 2:* October 1991-Present.

Objective: To teach inspectors a standardized systematic approach for management and analysis during evaluation of aviation companies.

Learning Outcome: Upon successful completion of this course, the student will be able to audit aviation companies' management systems and do a systematic, standard analysis of the management of a company during the evaluation process.

Instruction: Major topics covered in the course are methods used to evaluate effectiveness; types of organizations and organizational principles; general management concepts and system design; methods of charting problem and decision analysis; block and linear responsibilities; and interview techniques. Methods of instruction include lecture and laboratory.

Credit Recommendation: In the lower division baccalaureate/associate degree category, 3 semester hours in Introduction to Management or Organizational Theory (10/82) (10/91) (9/93).

Federal Aviation Administration Douglas DC-9 Air Carrier Training Unit (20006)

Location: FAA Academy, Oklahoma City, OK.

Length: 168 hours (4 weeks, 1 day).

Dates: October 1982-June 1993.

Objective: This course is designed to train air carrier operations inspectors for initial qualification and standardization in DC-9 aircraft.

Instruction: Major topics covered in the course are aircraft systems and equipment, limitations, performance, maneuvers, and emergency procedures. Methods of instruction include lectures, pre- and post-flight briefings, and simulator and flight experiences.

Credit Recommendation: In the upper division baccalaureate degree category, 6 semester hours in Flight Technology (10/82). **NOTE:** Credit for this course precludes credit for 20007.

Flight Control Systems (22462)

Location: FAA Academy, Oklahoma City, OK.

Length: 240 hours (6 weeks).

Dates: October 1982-October 1987.

Objective: To provide the avionics maintenance technician with the knowledge and ability to perform testing, troubleshooting, repair, and modification of the FCS-105 Flight Control System and the MC-103 Magnetic Compass System.

Instruction: Major topics covered in the course are the theory of flight, logic circuits review, circuit analysis, maintenance, and calibration of the FCS-105 Flight Control System and MC-103 Magnetic Compass System.

Credit Recommendation: In the upper division baccalaureate degree category, 6 semester hours in Avionics (10/82).

FSDO Aviation Clerical (12024)

Location: FAA Academy, Oklahoma City, OK.

Length: 68 hours (1 week, 4 days).

Dates: January 1992-Present.

Objective: To train new clerical and administrative personnel in basic job duties.

Learning Outcome: Upon successful completion of this course, the student will be able to assist in preparation and coordination of various reports and certificates, coordinate projects related to the enforcement information system, provide information for written test examiners and locate information in filing records and the Federal Aviation Administration directives.

Instruction: Major topics covered in the course are correspondence preparation, filing, forms and supplies, written test procedures, and the Privacy Act. Methods of instruction include lecture, discussion, and laboratory.

Credit Recommendation: In the vocational certificate category, 2 semester hours in Office Management (9/93).

Fundamentals of Aircraft Structures for Inspectors (22501)

Location: FAA Academy, Oklahoma City, OK.

Length: 64 hours (1 week, 3 days).

Dates: October 1991-June 1994.

Objective: To instruct manufacturing and maintenance inspectors in structural requirements and principles for aircraft certification.

Learning Outcome: Upon successful completion of this course, the student will be able to determine airframe design and construction features and repairs and alterations that may contribute to unsafe conditions; determine conformity of airframe components and structural test articles with drawings and specifications; and determine the validity of structural test and test plans.

Instruction: Major topics covered in the course are basic mathematics; forces and moments; stress analysis; structural design considerations; detrimental effects on aircraft structures; fasteners and fastening techniques; structural repair; inspection and testing; materials properties and processes; and bonding materials. Methods of instruction include lecture and laboratory.

Credit Recommendation: In the upper division baccalaureate degree category, 3 semester hours in Manufacturing Technology, Materials Science, Mechanical Engineering Technology, or Aviation Technology (10/91).

Fundamentals of Microprocessors (22470)

Location: FAA Academy, Oklahoma City, OK.

Length: 120 hours (3 weeks).

Dates: June 1981-July 1997.

Objective: To provide the student with knowledge of the hardware and software operation of the Intel 8085 microprocessor.

Learning Outcome: Upon successful completion of this course, the student will be able to convert from one number base to another; interpret simple programs written in assembly or machine language; write and debug microprocessor programs; and troubleshoot and repair microprocessor-controlled circuits.

Instruction: Major topics covered in the course are microprocessor fundamentals, introduction to programming, microprocessor system hardware, microprocessor software, and troubleshooting microprocessor systems. Methods of instruction include lecture, laboratory exercises, and written and performance examinations.

Credit Recommendation: In the lower division baccalaureate/associate degree category, 3 semester hours in Microprocessor Technology (9/88) (7/92).

General Aviation Advanced Indoctrination (21603)

Location: FAA Academy, Oklahoma City, OK.

Length: 68 hours (approx. 1.5 weeks).

Dates: October 1991-October 1996.

Objective: To train general aviation (maintenance/avionics) inspectors in the job functions associated with certification and surveillance of FAR Part 135 air carriers.

Learning Outcome: Upon successful completion of this course, the student will be able to determine and certify FAR Part 135 air carriers ten or More Passengers compliance with certification requirements; evaluate operator MEL Maintenance programs, and management personnel qualifications; approve and issue special flight permits; process aircraft lease agreements; and perform certification task in accordance with FAR's and directives.

Instruction: Major topics covered in the course are FAR 135 operations, leasing, certifications, management personnel evaluations, and air worthiness maintenance programs, minimum equipment list, and special flight permits. Methods of instruction include lecture, student presentations, and computer applications.

Credit Recommendation: In the lower division baccalaureate/associate degree category, 2 semester hours in Aircraft Maintenance (10/91).

General Aviation Aircraft Alteration (21811)

Location: FAA Academy, Oklahoma City, OK.

Length: 76 hours (2 weeks).

Dates: October 1982-Present.

Objective: To prepare airworthiness inspectors for the task of approving aircraft alterations and installations.

Instruction: Major topics covered in the course are those areas that may be subject to alteration on general aviation aircraft such as electrical, avionics, propulsion, honeycomb products, fuel and oil, fiberglass and plastics, vacuum, and oxygen system. Methods of instruction include lectures and laboratory experiences.

Credit Recommendation: In the lower division baccalaureate/associate degree

category, 1 semester hour in Aviation Technology (10/82) (9/93).

General Aviation Jet Powerplants (21814)

Location: FAA Academy, Oklahoma City, OK.

Length: 76 hours (2 weeks).

Dates: October 1982-September 1993.

Objective: This course provides a general knowledge of general aviation jet powerplants for general airworthiness inspectors.

Instruction: Major topics covered in the course are turbine powerplant analysis, turbine powerplant regulations, general aviation turbine powerplant familiarization, jet powerplant fuel and oils, powerplant accessories and associated equipment, and maintenance and inspection of turbine powerplants. Methods of instruction include lecture and laboratory.

Credit Recommendation: In the lower division baccalaureate/associate degree category, 3 semester hours in Aviation Maintenance Technology (10/82).

General Purpose Helicopter (21812)

Location: FAA Academy, Oklahoma City, OK.

Length: 80 hours (2 weeks).

Dates: October 1982-September 1993.

Objective: To provide basic knowledge of helicopters for airworthiness inspectors and manufacturing inspectors.

Instruction: Major topics covered in the course are the design, construction, and maintenance of the leading type-certificated helicopters. Methods of instruction include lecture, discussions, and a 2.5-day field trip to an industry site.

Credit Recommendation: In the lower division baccalaureate/associate degree category, 2 semester hours in Aviation Technology (10/82).

Instrument Approach Procedures Automated (IAPA) (21623)

Location: FAA Academy, Oklahoma City, OK.

Length: 64 hours (1 week, 3 days).

Dates: October 1991-October 1996.

Objective: To provide basic knowledge and skill in the use of the instrument approach procedures automated hardware and program protocol.

Learning Outcome: Upon successful completion of this course, the student will be able to identify and use the IAPA hardware; understand the IAPA data base and how it is maintained; understand all available programs; develop and store instrument approach procedures; and understand the procedure file and transmittal file.

Instruction: Major topics covered in the course are IAPA hardware, IAPA data base, users manual, and IAPA programs. Methods of instruction include lecture 20 percent and laboratory with computer application 80 percent.

Credit Recommendation: In the lower division baccalaureate/associate degree category, 2 semester hours in Aviation Technology (10/91).

Introduction to Aircraft Flutter (22504)

Location: FAA Academy, Oklahoma City, OK.

Length: 80 hours (2 weeks).

Dates: October 1982-June 1992.

Objective: To acquaint aerospace engineers with the behavior of aircraft under certain aerodynamic conditions, i.e., aircraft flutter, tubular analysis, flutter prevention, and flight testing.

Instruction: Major topics covered in the course are an introduction to aircraft flutter analysis including aircraft vibration, introduction to flutter, vibration testing, review of mathematics, two- and three-dimensional flutter analysis, tubular analysis, flutter prevention criteria, and flutter flight testing. Methods of instruction include classroom lectures, discussions, seminars, and problem-solving activities covering analyses of flutter reports.

Credit Recommendation: In the upper division baccalaureate degree category, 4 semester hours in Aeronautical Engineering or Mechanical Engineering (10/82) (10/91).

Introduction to Aircraft Vibration (22505)

Location: FAA Academy, Oklahoma City, OK.

Length: 80 hours (4 weeks).

Dates: October 1982-March 1992.

Objective: To provide engineers with an understanding of the theory and application of vibration testing and analysis.

Instruction: Major topics covered in the course are a review of mathematics and mechanics, free and forced-damped systems, unbalance and balancing equipment, absorbers and dampers, vibration equipment and its use, engine and propeller vibration, helicopter vibration, and a complete ground vibration survey on an actual airframe.

Credit Recommendation: In the upper division baccalaureate degree category, 3 semester hours in Aeronautical Engineering (10/82) (10/91).

Introduction to Executive Jet-Powered Aircraft (21816)

Location: FAA Academy, Oklahoma City, OK.

Length: 80 hours (2 weeks).

Dates: October 1982-September 1993.

Objective: To familiarize general aviation inspectors with the basic concepts of the systems and capabilities of small, executive jet aircraft.

Instruction: Major topics covered in the course are executive turbine aircraft design features, high speed airfoil sections, vortex generators, mach trim, other aerodynamic components of executive jet aircraft, and familiarization with the function and operation of representative systems and power plants. Methods of instruction include lectures and workshops.

Credit Recommendation: In the lower division baccalaureate/associate degree category, 2 semester hours in Aviation Maintenance Technology (10/82). **NOTE:** Credit for this course excludes credit received for 21817.

Lear Jet and Sabreliner Aircraft Systems (21817)

Location: FAA Academy, Oklahoma City, OK.

Length: 80 hours (2 weeks).

Dates: October 1982-September 1993.

Objective: To familiarize general aviation airworthiness Inspectors with the systems and components of Lear Jet and Sabreliner aircraft.

Instruction: Major topics covered in the course are aircraft design features, hydraulic systems, environmental control systems, fuel systems, instruments, navigation equipment, weight and balance, and operation limitation. Methods of instruction include lectures and laboratory.

Credit Recommendation: In the lower division baccalaureate/associate degree category, 2 semester hours in Aviation Maintenance Technology (10/82). **NOTE:** Credit for this course excludes credit for 21816.

Loads Analysis for Small Airplanes (22521)

Location: FAA Academy, Oklahoma City, OK.

Length: 76-80 hours (2 weeks).

Dates: October 1982-October 1996.

Objective: To acquaint engineers with the knowledge and procedures involved in the evaluation of loads reports for FAR Part 23 airplanes (small airplanes).

Instruction: Major topics covered in the course are methods of loads analysis, aerodynamics, design data, critical loading conditions, airfoil characteristics, airplane balancing, wing load, and landing loads. Methods of instruction include lecture and laboratory experiences.

Credit Recommendation: In the lower division baccalaureate/associate degree category, 3 semester hours in Aeronautical Engineering (10/82) (10/91).

Maintenance Steering Group (MSG-3) (28403)

Location: FAA Academy, Oklahoma City, OK.

Length: 36 hours (1 week).

Dates: March 1990-July 1997.

Objective: To provide airworthiness inspectors and certification engineers with knowledge of methodology, criteria, techniques and procedures required to utilize the airline/manufacture maintenance program planning document (MSG-3).

Learning Outcome: Upon successful completion of this course, the student will be able to utilize the airline or manufacture maintenance program planning document; demonstrate how an aircraft component can be evaluated using MSG-3; participate as a member of a maintenance review board; evaluate and approve MSG-3 maintenance programs; and provide surveillance of MSG-3 maintenance programs.

Instruction: Major topics covered in the course are maintenance program development; maintenance steering group document development; aircraft evaluation groups; maintenance review boards; MSG-3 logic and analysis. Methods of instruction include lecture, classroom exercises, and videotape.

Credit Recommendation: *Version 1:* In the lower division baccalaureate/associate degree category, 2 semester hours in Aviation Management (10/91). *Version 2:* In the upper division baccalaureate degree category, 1 semester hour in Maintenance Technology or Maintenance Management (7/92).

Manufacturing Inspection Indoctrination (21600)

Location: FAA Academy, Oklahoma City, OK.

Length: 64 hours (1 week, 3 days).

Dates: October 1981-August 1993.

Objective: To provide newly assigned manufacturing inspectors with the regulations and directives pertaining to type certification, original airworthiness certification, and enforcement.

Learning Outcome: Upon successful completion of this course, the student will be able to assist in conducting the type certification program; assist in conducting the production certification program; assist in conducting the original airworthiness certification program; and investigate and report noncompliance with the regulations.

Instruction: Major topics covered in the course are FAA history, Federal Aviation Act, FAA organization and responsibilities, type certification procedures, airworthiness approval methods of materials, parts, processes, and appliances, airworthiness certification procedures, production approvals, and certification compliance and enforcement. Methods of instruction include lecture and laboratory.

Credit Recommendation: In the lower division baccalaureate/associate degree category, 3 semester hours in Aviation Technology or Aviation Management (10/91).

Nondestructive Testing (22502)

Location: FAA Academy, Oklahoma City, OK.

Length: 64-80 hours (1 week and 3 days).

Dates: *Version 1:* October 1982-September 1991; *Version 2:* October 1991-Present.

Objective: To familiarize Federal Aviation Administration inspectors and quality control specialists with types, principles, and procedures for nondestructive testing of aircraft components.

Instruction: Major topics covered in the course are evaluation of nondestructive testing methods, application, limitations, and surveillance of methods. Students will detect metal defects, cracks, changes in material properties, manufacturing voids, mechanical defects, and thickness measurements. Methods of instruction include lectures and laboratory sessions.

Credit Recommendation: *Version 1:* In the upper division baccalaureate degree category, 2 semester hours in Aeronautical Engineering (10/82) (10/91). *Version 2:* In the upper division baccalaureate degree category, 3 semester hours in Aeronautical Engineering, Mechanical Engineering, or Quality Assurance Technology (10/91).

Obstruction Evaluation and Airport/Airspace Analysis (12050)

Location: FAA Academy, Oklahoma City, OK.

Length: 200 hours (5 weeks).

Dates: January 1978-October 1987.

Objective: To enable students to understand responsibilities of the Federal Aviation Administration in integrating commercial construction peripheral to any airport.

Instruction: Major topics covered in the course are analysis and completion of administrative efforts in obstruction/hazard evaluation, skills interpreting and applying Federal Aviation Administration regulations, specifications and associated federal, state, and municipal laws, and regulations and ordinances focusing on safe aircraft operation. Methods of instruction include lecture, discussion activities in a classroom environment as the primary instructional vehicles, and case studies in an individual effort environment with a low student-teacher ratio, i.e., 4:1, is the manner of skill achievement evaluation.

Credit Recommendation: In the lower division baccalaureate/associate degree category, 3 semester hours in Management (10/82). **NOTE:** Students who receive credit for this course should not receive credit for 12051 or 12052.

Omega/Area Navigation Systems (21845)

Location: FAA Academy, Oklahoma City, OK.

Length: *Version 1:* 80 hours (2 weeks); *Version 2:* 76 hours (2 weeks).

Dates: October 1982-October 1987.

Objective: This course is designed for Federal Aviation Administration aviation safety inspectors (avionics) involved in certification, surveillance, and approval of VLF/Omega/RNAU navigation systems.

Instruction: Major topics covered in the course are the characteristics, limitations, and error sources of VLF/Omega/RNAU systems; Federal Aviation Administration regulations; approval procedures; maintenance requirements; and practice problems in conformity inspections. Methods of instruction include lecture and training on Loran "C" and microwave landing systems.

Credit Recommendation: In the upper division baccalaureate degree category, 1 semester hour in Avionics or Electronics (10/82).

Pilot Operations for Engineers (20814)

Location: FAA Academy, Oklahoma City, OK.

Length: 76 hours (approx. 3 weeks).

Dates: September 1985-September 1993.

Objective: To teach engineers the principles of aeronautical knowledge needed by pilots.

Learning Outcome: Upon successful completion of this course, the student will be able to locate and identify major aircraft components; determine performance parameters and limitations; describe navigational aids and flight instruments; describe the functions of the electrical hydraulic, electrical, fuel, pneumatic and auto landing, taxi flight, and other pilot-specific knowledge.

Instruction: Major topics covered in the course are the theory of flight, aircraft operation needed by pilots, and navigation and instrumental flight.

Credit Recommendation: In the lower division baccalaureate/associate degree category, 3 semester hours in Aeronautical Science (10/91).

Professionalism (12030)

Location: FAA Academy, Oklahoma City, OK.

Length: 80 hours (2 weeks).

Dates: February 1991-October 1996.

Objective: To instruct aviation safety inspectors in their professional conduct and responsibilities.

Learning Outcome: Upon successful completion of this course, the students will be able to be more professional in their performance; the aviation safety inspectors will be able to more skillfully communicate and manage conflict with individuals and units within and outside the FAA.

Instruction: Major topics covered in the course are writing skills and oral communications; critical thinking and decision making; professional responsibilities and values; and conflict management skills. Methods of instruction include lecture and laboratory.

Credit Recommendation: In the lower division baccalaureate/associate degree category, 3 semester hours in Business Administration (10/91).

Technical Aviation Training for Attorneys (12031)

Location: FAA Academy, Oklahoma City, OK.

Length: 64 hours (2 weeks).

Dates: September 1991-Present.

Objective: To provide Federal Aviation Administration attorneys who have a limited aviation background with an introduction to aviation technical subject matter.

Learning Outcome: Upon successful completion of this course, the student will be able to demonstrate a rudimentary knowledge of aviation technical subject matter including aerodynamics, meteorology, and air traffic control.

Instruction: Major topics covered in the course are aerodynamics, meteorology, aeronautical charts and navigation, airports, air traffic control, and instrument procedures. Methods of instruction include lecture and laboratory exercises.

Credit Recommendation: In the lower division baccalaureate/associate degree category, 3 semester hours in Aeronautics (9/93).

Type/Production Certification (21903)

Location: FAA Academy, Oklahoma City, OK.

Length: 64 hours (1 week, 3 days).

Dates: October 1981-September 1994.

Objective: To provide the inspector with the requirements and procedures relating to type and production certification.

Learning Outcome: Upon successful completion of this course, the student will be able to develop a plan whereby conformity/compliance inspections will be conducted; determine eligibility, compliance, and conformity of prototype articles; explain applicable regulations for production approvals and provide guidance; evaluate and approve a manufacturer's quality control system; and conduct surveillance activities at a manufacturing facility.

Instruction: Major topics covered in the course are type certificate data sheets, manufacturing inspection relative to quality control, prototype airworthiness certification, supplemental type certification, weight and balance computations, determining compliance/conformity, production certification board members and roles, production certification board audits, production certification approvals, manufacturer supplier surveillance, and laboratory exercises consisting of a preliminary audit conducted by the production board findings. Methods of instruction include lecture and laboratory.

Credit Recommendation: In the lower division baccalaureate/associate degree category, 3 semester hours in Aviation Technology or Quality Assurance (10/91).

TRAINING SUPPORT

Academy Basic Instructor Training (10520) (Formerly Academy Instructor Training (Basic) [10520])

Location: FAA Academy, Oklahoma City, OK.

Length: 128 contact hours.

Dates: *Version 1:* April 1983-February 1992; *Version 2:* March 1992-Present.

Objective: To provide the student with the basic instructional skills to become potential academy instructors.

Learning Outcome: Upon successful completion of this course, the student will have a knowledge of factors affecting learning, leadership, counseling, and equal employment opportunity; and will develop skills in use of training aids, materials, classroom management, human relations practices, and teaching techniques.

Instruction: Major topics covered in the course are oral communication, training aids and materials, classroom management, methods and techniques of instruction, and interpersonal relations. Methods of instruction include lecture, audio/visual material, learner presentations/reports, and an examination.

Credit Recommendation: In the upper division baccalaureate degree category, 3 semester hours in Behavioral Science or Educational Methods (9/88) (10/91) (8/95).

Advanced Instructor Training (10511) (Formerly Academy Instructor Training - Advanced)

Location: FAA Academy, Oklahoma City, OK.

Length: 40 hours (1 week).

Dates: *Version 1:* February 1974-December 1991; *Version 2:* January 1992-Present.

Objective: To improve the experienced instructor's competency in teaching, classroom management, and interpersonal relationships.

Learning Outcome: Upon successful completion of this course, the student will be able to demonstrate creative training techniques and demonstrate skills in managing the learning process.

Instruction: Major topics covered in the course are group dynamics, methods of creative training, and assessing teaching effectiveness. Methods of instruction include lecture, discussion, team activity, case studies, and role playing.

Credit Recommendation: In the upper division baccalaureate degree category, 2 semester hours in Educational Psychology or Educational Methods (8/78) (9/88) (9/93).

Curriculum Development (10512)

Location: FAA Academy, Oklahoma City, OK.

Length: 48 hours (1 week, 1 day).

Dates: November 1972-Present.

Objective: To improve the instructor's competency in curriculum development.

Learning Outcome: Upon successful completion of this course, the student will be able to apply the principles of planning, analyzing, designing, developing, and validating training courses.

Instruction: Major topics covered in the course are training needs assessment, task analysis, course design and development, and validation. Methods of instruction include lecture, discussion, and workshop assignments.

Credit Recommendation: In the upper division baccalaureate degree category, 3 semester hours in Curriculum (8/78) (9/88) (9/93).

Facility Instructor Training (10501)

Location: FAA Academy, Oklahoma City, OK.

Length: 56 hours (1 week, 2 days).

Dates: *Version 1:* June 1977-January 1988; *Version 2:* February 1988-Present.

Objective: To develop the new instructor's understanding of and competency in learning theory, training methods, and classroom management.

Learning Outcome: Upon successful completion of this course, the student will be able to demonstrate an understanding of learning theory, training methods, and classroom management.

Instruction: Major topics covered in the course are planning and conducting training, methods of training, use and preparation of audiovisual aids, classroom management, and lesson plan development. Methods of instruction include lecture, discussion, student participation, and presentations.

Credit Recommendation: In the lower division baccalaureate/associate degree category, 3 semester hours in Behavioral Sciences or Educational Methods (8/78) (9/88) (9/93). **NOTE:** Credit should not be granted both for this course and for Academy Basic Instructor Training (10520).

Instructional Testing (10513)

Location: FAA Academy, Oklahoma City, OK.

Length: *Version 1:* 56 hours (1 week, 2 days); *Version 2:* 32 hours (4 days).

Dates: *Version 1:* November 1976-August 1993; *Version 2:* September 1993-Present.

Objective: To improve the experienced instructor's competency in test construction and administration, particularly criterion-referenced assessment.

Learning Outcome: Upon successful completion of this course, the student will be able to demonstrate skill in test construction and administration; demonstrate an understanding of testing rationale; list and explain the phases of the instructional system process; identify characteristics of effective tests; identify and correct deficiencies in written test items in accordance with course guidelines; and explain and interpret test statistical data to identify test questions for possible deletion or revision.

Instruction: Major topics covered in the course are criteria-referenced evaluation, verbal and motor performance, item analysis, administrative procedures and statistical test analysis; and test item writing and critique. Methods of instruction include lecture, discussion, classroom exercises, audio/visual material, learner presentations/reports, and written tests.

Credit Recommendation: *Version 1:* In the upper division baccalaureate degree category, 3 semester hours in Evaluation or Measurement (9/88) (9/93). *Version 2:* In the upper division baccalaureate degree category, 2 semester hours in Assessment of Instruction, Test Construction, Evaluation, or Measurement (8/94).

Instructor Effectiveness Training (10526)

Location: FAA Academy, Oklahoma City, OK.

Length: 40 hours (1 week).

Dates: May 1993-Present.

Objective: To introduce potential instructors to basic instructional theory, training methodology, and delivery techniques.

Learning Outcome: Upon successful completion of this course, the student will be able to discuss the characteristics of job-centered training; identify qualities of an effective instructor; understand characteristics of adult learners and techniques of motivation; prepare and deliver presentations; and use interactive instruction in the classroom.

Instruction: Major topics covered in the course are learning styles, presentation techniques, interactive learning, and questioning skills. Methods of instruction include lecture, discussion, practice exercises, labs, workshops, and presentations.

Credit Recommendation: In the lower division baccalaureate/associate degree category, 2 semester hours in Instruction or Educational Methods (9/93).

Interactive Video Teletraining (IVT) Skills (10507)

Location: FAA Academy, Oklahoma City, OK.

Length: 40 contact hours.

Dates: *Version 1:* June 1994-February 1995; *Version 2:* March 1995-Present.

Objective: To prepare course developers and instructors to convert portions of resident training to interactive video teletraining.

Learning Outcome: Upon successful completion of this course, the student will be able to identify effective teletraining presentation techniques; design effective visuals; program questions using appropriate software; operate a viewer response system; and adapt and deliver a portion of a traditional classroom lesson to television.

Instruction: Major topics covered in the course are interactive teletraining and development methods, student involvement strategies, effective TV visuals, equipment operation, and computer software application for a viewer response system. Methods of instruction include lecture/discussion from a mock studio, written exercises, role plays, audio-visual presentations, and hands-on applications on camera. Students will also give a final 15-minute presentation on camera.

Credit Recommendation: *Version 1:* In the upper division baccalaureate degree category, 2 semester hours in Communications. *Version 2:* In the upper division baccalaureate degree category, 3 semester hours in Communications (8/95). **NOTE:** Credit should only be granted for on of the two versions.

On-the-Job Training Techniques (14018)

Location: Field facilities throughout the United States (correspondence study).

Length: 15 weeks.

Dates: October 1990-December 1997.

Objective: To teach the skills necessary to prepare and conduct on-the-job training.

Learning Outcome: Upon successful completion of this course, the student will be able to identify individual employee's training needs; select appropriate training techniques to accomplish training objectives; and schedule and conduct on-the-job training.

Instruction: Major topics covered in the course are the role of on-the-job training, training needs, training objectives, training aids and training materials, and evaluating trainee progress. Methods of instruction include self-paced correspondence and tests.

Credit Recommendation: In the vocational certificate category, 1 semester hour in Training (9/90) (7/97).

On-the-Job Training Techniques (10504) (Correspondence Study)

Location: FAA Academy, Oklahoma City, OK.

Length: 40 hours.

Dates: July 1972-Present.

Objective: To provide technical personnel with the knowledge to develop, conduct and evaluate OJT programs.

Learning Outcome: Upon successful completion of this course, the student will be able to develop instructional objectives, identify training needs and requirements, plan and conduct on-the-job training, and develop lesson plans.

Instruction: Major topics covered in the course are methods of evaluation, course development, writing objective and planning. Methods of instruction include lecture, discussion, classroom exercises, audio-visual material, learner presentations/reports, and examination.

Credit Recommendation: In the upper division baccalaureate degree category, 2 semester hours in Education (8/95).

Principles of Instruction (14022) (Correspondence Study)

Location: Field facilities throughout the United States (correspondence study).

Length: 15 weeks.

Dates: October 1990-December 1997.

Objective: To provide students with a basic understanding of what is required to be an effective FAA instructor.

Learning Outcome: Upon successful completion of this course, the student will be able to use various instruction methods; determine which instructional methods should be used to effectively teach the subject matter; and use various instructional aids.

Instruction: Major topics covered in the course are types of instructional methods, traits of a good instructor, and appropriate training aids. Method of instruction includes self-paced correspondence.

Credit Recommendation: In the vocational certificate category, 1 semester hour in Instruction (9/90) (7/97).

Federal Aviation Administration FAA Center for Management Development

The mission of the Federal Aviation Administration's (FAA) Center for Management Development (CMD), established in 1987, is to create a quality learning environment that provides supervisors, managers, and other employees with an understanding of their management responsibilities through appropriate learning opportunities. Students who attend the CMD acquire the knowledge and techniques necessary to improve management skills and behaviors, accomplish program goals, and sustain organizational effectiveness.

Although the CMD courses are attended primarily by FAA employees who come from headquarters, regional locations, and field locations throughout the United States and overseas, they are open to other government workers who wish to update and improve their management skills. In addition to basic and advanced general supervision and management courses, other courses include facilitator training, leadership development, labor-management relations, change management, and team effectiveness. These courses are taught by a highly skilled staff consisting of 43 full-time faculty, all of whom hold masters or doctoral degrees.

The CMD residence courses are delivered centrally at the FAA facility in Palm Coast, Florida, which provides living accommodations for up to 200 people and ensures a private adult/professional retreat for continued learning and improvement. It includes a world-class, outdoor, experiential challenge complex that is designed to foster team building and personal growth. Many of the courses that are offered at the CMD are also delivered at regional training sites. To reach employees who are unable to attend centrally delivered training, the CMD also uses distance learning methods including correspondence study and computer-based instruction.

Source of official student records: Registry of Credit Recommendations, American Council on Education, One Dupont Circle, Washington, DC 20036-1193 or Registrar, FAA Center for Management Development, 4500 Palm Coast Parkway, SE; Palm Coast, FL 32137-8007.

Additional information about the courses: College Credit Recommendation Service, American Council on Education, One Dupont Circle, Washington, DC 20036-1193.

CENTER FOR MANAGEMENT DEVELOPMENT CORRESPONDENCE COURSES

Budgeting and Resource Management (14024)

Location: Field facilities throughout the United States by correspondence.

Length: Approximately 15 weeks (self-paced).

Dates: *Version 1:* June 1980-September 1990; *Version 2:* October 1990-Present.

Objective: To introduce students to the federal budget process, in general and as it applies to the Federal Aviation Administration.

Learning Outcome: Upon successful completion of this course, the student will be able to explain the federal budget process and its background in general terms and explain how the FAA budget cycle coincides with the federal budget process.

Instruction: *Version 1:* Major topics covered in the course are the planning, programming, and budgeting system applied to Federal Aviation Administration resource management. Methods of instruction include self-paced correspondence study. *Version 2:* Major topics covered in the course are basis for budgeting and resource management; relationship of planning, budgeting, and control; the budget cycle and the FAA; evaluation of program effectiveness and efficiency; and key FAA planning process. Methods of instruction include self-paced correspondence.

Credit Recommendation: *Version 1:* In the lower division baccalaureate/associate degree category, 1 semester hour in Management (10/82). *Version 2:* In the vocational certificate category, 1 semester hour in Budgeting (9/90) (8/95).

Building Organizations and Managing Work (14038)

Location: Various sites in the United States.

Length: 12 weeks (self-paced)-Correspondence.

Dates: June 1996-Present.

Objective: To present key aspects of organizational mission and leadership and how supervisors can advance that mission through the everyday work of their group or team.

Learning Outcome: Upon successful completion of this course, the student will be able to understand the significance of an organization's mission statement; use charts or models to represent organizational structures; apply principles of effective organization when evaluating, designing, or redesigning an organizational structure, plan, or schedule and monitor work-related initiatives using a systematic process; identify roles and behaviors in team-based organizations; recognize that the accomplishment of results is the basic test of organizational effectiveness; and prepare a personal action plan for implementing the major concepts addressed in the course.

Instruction: Major topics covered in the course are traditional and contemporary organizational structures, management roles, styles, and principles, planning and scheduling, work analysis and distribution, communicating and managing effectively, and action planning. Methods of instruction include self-paced correspondence study, final examination, and module checks points.

Credit Recommendation: In the lower division baccalaureate/associate degree category, 2 semester hours in Management, Human Resource Management, or Organizational Behavior/Development (8/97).

Clerical/Secretarial Courses
1. Basic Clerical/Secretarial Techniques (14015)
2. Advanced Secretarial Course (14016)

Location: Field facilities throughout the United States.

Length: *Versions 1 and 2:* 15 weeks.

Dates: *Version 1:* October 1980-September 1990; *Version 2:* October 1990-December 1993.

Objective: To provide students with an understanding of the role and functions of clerical workers and an understanding of the effective behaviors of a successful secretary.

Learning Outcome: Upon successful completion of this course, the student will be able to work in a clerical position for the FAA; appreciate the importance of image, interpersonal relationships, and effective written and verbal communications; prepare basic FAA correspondence; understand the importance of public relations; state basic time management strategies; and appreciate the managerial process.

Instruction: *Version 1:* Major topics covered in the course are the responsibilities within the organization of the secretarial position; the needs of the organization personnel lateral to above and below the secretary's job; and executive/upper management needs for secretarial expertise in the management functions. Methods of instruction include correspondence course. *Version 2:* Major topics covered in the course are tasks of a clerk; functions and policies of the FAA; tools for work efficiency; use and preparation of forms and files; personal appearance and habits; public image; verbal and written communications; decision-making; basic concepts of management, motivation, line and staff relationships, and work organization. Methods of instruction include self-paced correspondence.

Credit Recommendation: *Version 1:* In the lower division baccalaureate/associate degree category, 1 semester hour in Administration, Management, or Office Management (10/82). *Version 2:* In the vocational certificate category, 1 semester hour in fundamentals of clerical skills (9/90). **NOTE:** Both courses must be completed before any credit is granted.

Conference/Presentation Techniques 1. Briefing and Presentation Techniques (14010) 2. Conference Techniques in Everyday Management (14000)

Location: Field facilities throughout the United States by correspondence.

Length: *Versions 1 and 2:* Course 1: 15 weeks (self-paced); Course 2: 15 weeks (self-paced); *Version 3:* Approximately 48 hours (5 months) (self-paced).

Dates: *Version 1:* October 1980-September 1990; *Version 2:* October 1990-July 1995; *Version 3:* August 1995-Present.

Objective: *Version 1:* To develop students' oral, communication, and conference organizational competencies. *Version 2:* To develop students' oral, communication, and conference organizational competencies. *Version 3:* To provide participants with an introduction to skills for developing and presenting briefing.

Learning Outcome: *Version 1:* Upon successful completion of this course, the student will be able to determine the objectives of a briefing and plan, develop, and use an outline for its delivery; identify the function of conferences and list their advantages and disadvantages; and identify how the use of conferences and briefings enhances management. *Version 2:* Upon successful completion of this course, the student will be able to determine the objectives of a briefing and plan, develop, and use an outline for its delivery; identify the function of conferences and list their advantages and disadvantages; and identify how the use of conferences and briefings enhances management. *Version 3:* Upon successful completion of this course, the student will be able to determine the objectives of a briefing; prepare preliminary plans; analyze the audience; plan, develop and use an outline for delivery of a briefing; select, prepare and use appropriate visual aids; and arrange facilities and equipment for delivery of effective presentations.

Instruction: *Version 1:* Major topics covered in the course are activities required to provide managerial personnel with information concerning successful presentation skills; and the need for audience analysis, proper visual aids, proper vocabulary selection, and post-presentation analysis. Methods of instruction include home study by correspondence. *Version 2:* Major topics covered in the course are techniques of briefing presentations, basic elements of the communication process, elements of the briefing process, selection and use of training aids, determining proper delivery techniques, preparing a briefing outline, qualifications of the successful conference leader, and brainstorming. Methods of instruction include self-paced correspondence. *Version 3:* Major topics covered in the course are techniques of briefing, presentations, organizing materials, guidelines for determining delivery techniques, and aids. Methods of instruction include self-evaluated assignments and five examinations.

Credit Recommendation: *Version 1:* In the lower division baccalaureate/associate degree category, 2 semester hours in Business Administration or Management (10/82). *Version 2:* In the vocational certificate category, 2 semester hours in Business Administration or Management (9/90). *Version 3:* In the vocational certificate category, 2 semester hours in Business Administration or Management (8/95). **NOTE:** Student must complete both courses for the award of credit.

Effective Discipline in a Changing Workplace (14025)

Location: Various sites in the United States.

Length: 12 weeks (self-paced)-Correspondence.

Dates: June 1996-Present.

Objective: To present the skills and knowledge required for dealing effectively with conduct and discipline issues in the workplace.

Learning Outcome: Upon successful completion of this course, the student will have learned to apply standards of conduct as expressed by laws, rules, and regulations; apply an appropriate penalty to an incident of employee misconduct; apply a formal discipline process to a situation involving employee misconduct; respond appropriately to formal employee appeal and grievance actions; use interpersonal skills to identify discipline and grievance issues; apply discipline and grievance processes under conditions imposed by collective bargaining agreements; and identify the types of employee records that a supervisor may maintain under conditions created by the Privacy Act of 1974.

Instruction: Major topics covered in the course are FAA model of conduct and misconduct, misconduct and discipline, formal discipline process and procedures, grievance and appeal procedures, interpersonal skills in discipline and grievance resolution, and special problems in conduct and discipline. Methods of instruction include self-paced correspondence study, final examination, reports, and tests.

Credit Recommendation: In the lower division baccalaureate/associate degree category, 2 semester hours in Business or Human Resources Management (8/97).

Fundamentals of Supervision (14002)

Location: Field facilities throughout the United States by correspondence.

Length: *Versions 1 and 2:* 12-18 months (self-paced); *Version 3:* 150 hours (6 months) (self-paced).

Dates: *Version 1:* January 1981-September 1990; *Version 2:* October 1990-July 1995; *Version 3:* August 1995-Present.

Objective: *Version 1:* To improve the Federal Aviation Administration (FAA) employee's knowledge of principles of management. *Version 2:* To improve the FAA employee's knowledge of supervisory functions. *Version 3:* To strengthen management and leadership capabilities by presenting an overview of key management skills and concepts.

Learning Outcome: *Version 1:* Upon successful completion of this course, the student will be able to recognize the characteristics of informal groups; identify and understand a supervisor's responsibilities; and understand employee responsibilities in the area of occupational safety and health. *Version 2:* Upon successful completion of this course, the student will be able to recognize the characteristics of informal groups; identify and understand a supervisor's responsibilities; and understand employee responsibilities in the area of occupational safety and health. *Version 3:* Upon successful completion of this course, the student will be able to define, total quality management principles (TQM), identify skills needed for successful supervision, understand several motivational theories, define coaching as a supervisor's primary role, distinguish conflict from anger, refine harassment, and explain affirmative action goals.

Instruction: *Version 1:* Major topics covered in the course are supervisor's responsibilities, leadership, selecting and assigning employees, morale, and job performance. Methods of instruction include self-paced correspondence. *Version 2:* Major topics covered in the course are discipline, management by objectives, report analysis, effective organization of work, and rules and regulations governing EEO and OSHA. Methods of instruction include self-paced correspondence. *Version 3:* Major topics covered in the course are total quality management principles (TQM); leadership, motivation, and self-expression performance management systems; coaching for successful team conflict management strategies; self-managing teams; managing a diverse work force; and successful supervisory principles for designing the future. Methods of instruction include self-directed study, using audio-visual aids, self-evaluated assignments, and four examinations.

Credit Recommendation: *Version 1:* In the lower division baccalaureate/associate degree category, 2 semester hours in Front-line Supervision (10/82). *Version 2:* In the vocational certificate category, 1 semester hour in Basic Supervision (9/90). *Version 3:* In the lower division baccalaureate/associate degree category, 3 semester hours in Supervision (8/95).

Interpersonal Skills for the Leadership Role (14033)

Location: Various sites in the United States.

Length: 12 weeks (self-paced)-Correspondence.

Dates: June 1996-Present.

Objective: To present key aspects of the interpersonal skills most pertinent to the leadership role in the workplace.

Learning Outcome: Upon successful completion of this course, the student will be able to identify shifts in organizational structures and culture occurring in public organizations that are changing the roles of leadership, through self assessment; identify interpersonal skill areas that represent strengths and areas requiring improvement; apply interpersonal skills appropriately in common workplace interactions; analyze workplace scenarios to assess the effectiveness of interactions pertaining to coaching and feedback; demonstrate appropriate leadership behaviors pertaining to conflict management; and formulate an action plan for developing interpersonal skills vital to effective leadership.

Instruction: Major topics covered in the course are the changing role of leadership in the FAA, leadership skills self-assessment, effective communication skills, coaching skills, and managing interpersonal conflict. Methods of instruction include self-paced correspondence study, final examination, reports, and tests.

Credit Recommendation: In the lower division baccalaureate/associate degree category, 2 semester hours in Human Resource Management or Business Electives (8/97).

Management by Objectives (14004)
2. Supervisory Guide (14021)
3. Labor Relations (14028)

Location: Field facilities throughout the United States.

Length: *Versions 1, 2, and 3:* 15 weeks.

Dates: *Version 1:* December 1981-September 1990; *Version 2:* October 1990-September 1995.

Objective: *Version 1:* To provide students with a knowledge of management principles. *Version 2:* Covers the planning and implementing use of the technique "management by objectives"; covers the Blake/Mouton Management Grid to assist the individual in selecting a personal management style; covers the evolution of, and federal response to, organized labor unions as a force in FAA; and grievance procedures are also discussed.

Learning Outcome: Upon successful completion of this course, the student will be able to communicate FAA missions and objectives to co-workers; assist subordinates in developing their individual objectives; define the responsibilities of each employee in terms of results expected; understand Blake/Mouton Management Grid; identify the purpose of the Federal Service Labor-Management Relations statute; and list the basic rights and obligations of employees, labor organizations, and agencies under the law.

Instruction: *Version 1:* Major topics covered in the course are planning and implementing use of the technique "management by objectives"; Blake/Mouton Management Grid to assist the individual in selecting personal management style and its alternatives; the evolution of, and federal response to, organized labor unions as a force in the Federal Aviation Administration; and grievance procedures including arbitration and mediation of labor disputes. *Version 2:* Major topics covered in the course are FAA missions and objectives, setting objectives and measuring results, the Management Grid, dealing with complaints, history of public and federal unionism, structure of Federal Labor Relations Authority, the union campaign—petitions and elections, and issues in negotiations. Methods of instruction include self-paced correspondence course.

Credit Recommendation: *Version 1:* In the lower division baccalaureate/associate degree category, 1 semester hour in Management (10/82). **NOTE:** (1) These three courses serve to fulfill a one semester credit course. (2) Students must have also completed either 14019 or 14026 to receive this credit. *Version 2:* In the vocational certificate category, 3 semester hours in Introduction to Supervision (9/90).

Personnel Management
1. Use and Conservation of Personnel, Money, and Materials (14005)
2. Basic Employment Practices (14029)
3. Position Management and Classification (14030)

Location: FAA Academy, Oklahoma City, OK.

Length: 15 weeks.

Dates: August 1980-September 1995.

Objective: To acquaint the student with the role and functions of position and staff management.

Learning Outcome: Upon successful completion of this course, the student will be able to understand the conservation of money and material with emphasis on effective employee utilization, productivity, and program evaluation; state employment policy, EEO regulations, performance appraisal/awards; forms and processes, grievance and appeals procedures; and appreciate the differences among work positions, employee development strategies, and standards of classification.

Instruction: Major topics covered in the course are FAA Personnel Manual and

Orders; EEO; position management, staffing, and employee development; maintenance of work force; safety and health; and evaluation systems and reports.

Credit Recommendation: In the lower division baccalaureate/associate degree category, 1 semester hour in Fundamentals of Supervision (10/82) (9/90). **NOTE:** (1) Fundamentals of Supervision (14002) must have been completed satisfactorily for this award to be made. (2) All three courses must be completed before any credit is granted.

Program Analysis and Review (14026)

Location: Field facilities throughout the United States by correspondence.

Length: Approximately 15 weeks (self-paced).

Dates: *Version 1:* September 1981-September 1990; *Version 2:* October 1990-Present.

Objective: To give students an understanding of the program manager in a multidisciplinary project.

Learning Outcome: Upon successful completion of this course, the student will be able to set realistic, measurable program objectives; properly allocate resources to the various program activities and monitor their use; and prepare clear, concise reports of program accomplishments.

Instruction: *Version 1:* Major topics covered in the course are integration and management of resources across several distinct skills. Methods of instruction include self-paced correspondence. *Version 2:* Major topics covered in the course are defining objectives, program evaluation, scheduling and controlling, resource management, interpersonal communications, and preparing reports. Methods of instruction include self-paced correspondence.

Credit Recommendation: *Version 1:* In the lower division baccalaureate/associate degree category, 2 semester hours in Business or Management (10/82). *Version 2:* In the vocational certificate category, 1 semester hour in Supervision (9/90) (8/95).

Report Analysis and Consolidation (14027)

Location: FAA Academy, Oklahoma City, OK by correspondence.

Length: Approximately 15 weeks (self-paced).

Dates: October 1990-Present.

Objective: To improve students' analytical ability.

Learning Outcome: Upon successful completion of this course, the student will be able to understand technical report architecture, organization, and presentation; make bar graphs and pie charts; and understand frequency distributions and compute standard deviation.

Instruction: Major topics covered in the course are report purposes, types, and formats; data organization and presentation; statistics and data interpretation; presentation of statistical data; report simplification and consolidation; patterns of report organization; and document collection and analysis. Methods of instruction include self-paced correspondence.

Credit Recommendation: In the vocational certificate category, 2 semester hours in Business Administration or Supervision (9/90) (8/95).

Report Writing
1. Writing Improvement
2. Report Analysis and Consolidation (14014/14027)

Location: FAA Academy, Oklahoma City, OK.

Length: 15 weeks.

Dates: June 1980-October 1987.

Objective: To improve the students' writing ability.

Instruction: Major topics covered in the course are grammar necessary to achieve good writing, organization, and presentation. Methods of instruction include self-paced correspondence.

Credit Recommendation: In the lower division baccalaureate/associate degree category, 2 semester hours in Technical Report Writing (10/82).

Staff Specialist (14019)

Location: Field facilities throughout the United States by correspondence.

Length: Approximately 15 weeks (self-paced).

Dates: *Version 1:* June 1974-March 1982; *Version 2:* April 1982-Present.

Objective: To develop staff skills in studying, analyzing, and recommending alternative solutions to problems for management.

Learning Outcome: Upon successful completion of this course, the student will be able to identify effective techniques of assigning and completing staff work; define the problem and limit the scope of a staff study; and prepare and present a completed staff study.

Instruction: Major topics covered in the course are staff personnel responsibilities and staff report formats necessary to large organizations. Methods of instruction include self-paced study.

Credit Recommendation: *Version 1:* In the lower division baccalaureate/associate degree category, 2 semester hours in Management (10/82) (8/95). *Version 2:* In the lower division baccalaureate/associate degree category, 2 semester hours in Management (10/82) (8/95).

Supervision
1. A Positive Approach to Discipline (14001)
2. Effective Organization of Work (14006)
3. Human Relations in Supervision (14003)

Location: Field facilities throughout the United States.

Length: 15 weeks (self-paced).

Dates: *Version 1:* August 1980-September 1990; *Version 2:* October 1990-September 1995.

Objective: To develop skills and abilities of the supervisor.

Learning Outcome: Upon successful completion of this course, the student will be able to understand the positive approach to discipline; determine and implement appropriate methods for improving organizational culture; and apply the principles of effective organization when evaluating, designing or redesigning an organizational structure.

Instruction: *Version 1:* Major topics covered in the course are organizing and planning of work to be accomplished; determining employee qualifications, training needs for new employees, and effective group communications; employee discipline, dissatisfaction, complaints, and grievances; effective leadership; individual behavior and attitudes of workers; different management styles; and employee counseling. Methods of instruction include directed study and related workshop, 12 hours of group activity, tests, self-evaluation, and peer evaluation. *Version 2:* Major topics covered in the course are human relations and creative discipline; handling dissatisfaction, complaints, and grievances; factors affecting organization; planning, scheduling, and controlling; management and organizational effectiveness; analysis of work and personnel; human relations concepts and counseling; and history of human relations. Methods of instruction include self-paced correspondence.

Credit Recommendation: *Version 1:* In the lower division baccalaureate/associate degree category, 1 semester hour in Front-line Supervision (10/82). **NOTE:** (1) 14002, Fundamentals of Supervision must have been completed satisfactorily for this award to be made. (2) The 1 hour of credit is for successful completion of all three courses. *Version 2:* In the vocational certificate category, 1 semester hour in Front-line Supervision (9/90).

CENTER FOR MANAGEMENT DEVELOPMENT RESIDENT COURSES

Building Effective Agreements (01182)

Location: Various sites in the United States.

Length: 24 hours.

Dates: November 1995-Present.

Objective: To build effective agreements collaboratively and enhance organizational relationships.

Learning Outcome: Upon successful completion of this course, the student will be able to use an interest-based approach to negotiations; use communications skills to support this process; and prepare a plan for negotiations.

Instruction: Major topics covered in the course are conflict resolution, planning for negotiation, effective questioning techniques, handling difficult negotiations, and an interest-based negotiation model and process. Methods of instruction include lecture, discussions, case studies, checklists, debriefing, and feedback.

Credit Recommendation: In the lower division baccalaureate/associate degree category, 1 semester hour in Human Resource Management or Business Elective (8/97).

Change Agent (01553)

Location: Center for Management Development, Federal Aviation Administration, Palm Coast, FL.

Length: 36 hours (1 week).

Dates: December 1993-Present.

Objective: To identify roles and values of change agents, define their ability to assess group/organization development dynamics, and provide feedback related to their observation and assessment.

Learning Outcome: Upon successful completion of this course, the student will be able to accurately assess or diagnose client systems; effectively organize and present complex assessment data; develop increased ability to select and deliver appropriate intervention techniques; manage group dynamics; and analyze interpersonal relationships as related to more effective group performance.

Instruction: Major topics covered in the course are change theory, values clarification, diversity, conflict and group development, problem solving, and intervention design. Methods of instruction include lecture, discussion, classroom exercises, case studies, audio/visual material, computer-assisted instruction, and an examination.

Credit Recommendation: In the upper division baccalaureate degree category, 2 semester hours in Human Resources Management, Organizational Development, or as a Business elective (9/94).

Computer-Based Support for Managerial Decision-Making (01307)

Location: FAA Center for Management Development, Palm Coast, FL.

Length: 60 hours (7.5 days).

Dates: December 1986-August 1992.

Objective: To teach the knowledge and skills necessary to use microcomputers with a view toward optimizing alternatives to meet the criteria for an acceptable solution and support of managerial decision-making.

Learning Outcome: Upon successful completion of this course, the student will be able to use the personal computer and use computer software to make management decisions.

Instruction: Major topics covered in the course are IBM PC and the latest software packages such as Decision Aid, Howard Project Manager, Smart Data Manager, and Symphony. Methods of instruction include lecture (35 percent), hands-on training (55 percent), and case studies.

Credit Recommendation: In the lower division baccalaureate/associate degree category or in the upper division baccalaureate degree category, 3 semester hours in Computer Science, Data Processing, or Management (5/87).

Constructive Communications (Formerly Developing Human Relations Skills [01501])

Location: FAA Center for Management Development, Palm Coast, FL.

Length: *Version 1:* 67 hours (2 weeks), residential; *Version 2:* 60 hours, residential.

Dates: *Version 1:* December 1976-September 1990; *Version 2:* October 1990-December 1991.

Objective: *Version 1:* To provide employees with an understanding of and an opportunity to practice the skills needed for effective conduct of human relations in the organization. *Version 2:* To improve the student's abilities to communicate effectively and acceptably, person to person, with and before a group.

Learning Outcome: Upon successful completion of this course, the student will be able to demonstrate an awareness of self and others; understand the impact of good public relations; influence others by using proven human relations concepts; and identify areas of personal strengths and weaknesses, especially in handling stress and resolving conflict.

Instruction: *Version 1:* Major topics covered in the course are human understanding, self-analysis, listening, stress, group relations, and interpersonal relations. Methods of instruction include individual and group exercises, a practice presentation, and role playing. *Version 2:* Major topics covered in the course are learning and personality; public relations; communication styles; transaction analysis; behavioral concepts; leadership styles; motivation; conflict resolution; handling stress; and effective verbal presentation. Methods of instruction include individual and group exercises, presentations, role playing, and lecture.

Credit Recommendation: *Version 1:* In the lower division baccalaureate/associate degree category or in the upper division baccalaureate degree category, 4 semester hours in General Management or Social Sciences (9/77). *Version 2:* In the lower division baccalaureate/associate degree category, 3 semester hours in General Management or Business Psychology (9/90).

Constructive Discipline (01203)

Location: FAA Center for Management Development, Palm Coast, FL.

Length: 35 hours (1 week); residential.

Dates: October 1975-December 1991.

Objective: To strengthen the ability of managers to maintain organizational discipline in a positive manner.

Learning Outcome: Upon successful completion of this course, the student will be able to describe the role and forms of discipline and explain the means of achieving constructive discipline.

Instruction: Major topics covered in the course are disciplinary principles, disciplinary action, behavior problems, code of ethics, and disciplinary grievances. Methods of instruction include discussion, lecture, films, case studies, and role playing.

Credit Recommendation: In the upper division baccalaureate degree category, 2 semester hours in Management or Public Administration (5/76) (9/90).

Facilitator Training Course

Location: Center for Management Development, Federal Aviation Administration, Palm Coast, FL.

Length: 36 hours (4.5 days).

Dates: July 1992-Present.

Objective: To learn to utilize effective facilitation techniques.

Learning Outcome: Upon successful completion of this course, the student will have an increased awareness of their facilitation skills, strengths, and weaknesses; an ability to perform effective facilitation; be able to monitor and manage group dynamics; an ability to develop open-ended questioning techniques; and an understanding of role changes when involved in a co-facilitation.

Instruction: Major topics covered in the course are valuing diversity, the role of a facilitator, logistics of facilitating, facilitation practices, group dynamics, disruptive behaviors, and co-facilitation. Methods of instruction include lecture, discussion, classroom exercises, case studies, verbal and written feedback, and a self-assessment of filmed facilitation practices.

Credit Recommendation: In the upper division baccalaureate degree category, 2 semester hours in Effective Facilitation Techniques and Practices or as a Business Elective (9/94).

Facilitator's Training Course (01523)

Location: Field facilities throughout the United States.

Length: 68 hours (8.5 days).

Dates: February 1985-Present.

Objective: To prepare the student to function as a facilitator by more directly involving employees in agency goals, resolution of organizational problems, and improvement of work situations.

Learning Outcome: Upon successful completion of this course, the student will be able to identify and explain the major components of QWL and how the program should be initiated and maintained; describe and apply the role of the facilitator in a QWL effort; identify various aspects of human behavior and how they influence organizational effectiveness; determine the need for design and implementation of an organizational evaluation plan; select and apply appropriate group problem-solving techniques; select appropriate data-gathering models and apply appropriate techniques as a facilitator, group leader, or member; and plan, organize, and deliver a recommendation presentation to management.

Instruction: Major topics covered in the course are centered around training individuals to facilitate group problem-solving processes. Methods of instruction include lecture and workshop/experimental learning.

Credit Recommendation: In the upper division baccalaureate degree category, 3 semester hours in Business Administration or Management (5/87) (9/94).

Labor Management Relations - IVT (61205)

Location: Various sites in the United States.

Length: 24 hours.

Dates: April 1997-Present.

Objective: To create effective labor management relations in the workplace through an understanding of the rights and responsibilities as defined by the law, collective bargaining agreements, and executive orders.

Learning Outcome: Upon successful completion of this course, the student will be able to apply knowledge of statutes, executive orders, and collective bargaining agreements to workplace situations; identify various type of problem-solving processes in order to resolve differences between labor and management; understand and apply rights and responsibilities to promote effective, collaborative work relationships; and describe and identify collaborative behaviors.

Instruction: Major topics covered in the course are rights and responsibilities under the law, rights and responsibilities under collective bargaining agreements (contracts), grievances, conduct and discipline, burden of proof and arbitrations, and interest-based bargaining. Methods of instruction include classroom exercises, case studies, audio/visual material, role-playing and telephone, and pre- and post tests.

Credit Recommendation: In the upper division baccalaureate degree category, 2 semester hours in Labor Relations, Law, Management, or Human Resources Management (8/97). **NOTE:** Student should not receive credit for this course and Labor-Management Relations (01205).

Labor-Management Relations (01205)

Location: FAA Center for Management Development, Palm Coast, FL.

Length: *Version 1:* 35 hours (1 week); *Version 2:* 36 hours (1 week).

Dates: *Version 1:* September 1980-July 1995; *Version 2:* August 1995-Present.

Objective: To provide line managers with an in-depth understanding of labor contract administration consistent with Chapter 71 of the Civil Service Reform Act and interpretations and with FAA labor policy and philosophy.

Learning Outcome: Upon successful completion of this course, the student will be able to identify the labor-management relations responsibilities of supervisors/managers and the purpose of the Federal Labor Management Relations statute; understand the role and responsibilities of the supervisor/manager in the collective bargaining process; and identify the statutory criteria for and major components of a grievance procedure.

Instruction: Major topics covered in the course are public sector labor-management relations, the collective bargaining process, negotiating skills and impasse procedures, union-granted exclusive recognition, unfair labor practices, labor agreement administration, and the grievance/arbitration process. Methods of instruction include lecture, films, role playing, and discussion.

Credit Recommendation: *Versions 1 and 2:* In the upper division baccalaureate degree category, 2 semester hours in Labor Relations (9/90) (8/95).

Leadership Development and Labor Relations (01183)

Location: FAA Center for Management Development.

Length: 60 hours.

Dates: November 1995-Present.

Objective: To provide the foundation supervisory knowledge and skills needed by newly selected supervisors and team leaders who work with bargaining unit employees.

Learning Outcome: Upon successful completion of this course, the student will have learned how leadership style impacts job performance, effective use of interpersonal communications skills for creating an environment that promotes trust; coaching skills for resolving performance and conduct issues; and knowledge of workplace policies and programs, management responsibilities in union contract administration, principles of interest-based bargaining, and collaborative problem-solving skills.

Instruction: Major topics covered in the course are supervisory roles and responsibilities, leadership style, and interpersonal skills; coaching and conflict resolution techniques for workplace situations; rights and responsibilities of management and unions as defined by law, contracts, and executive orders; and principles of interest-based communications for building collaborative relationships. Methods of instruction include lecture, discussion, classroom exercises, case studies, learner-presentations, leadership simulations, evaluation of performance on simulations and case studies, and a course summary quiz.

Credit Recommendation: In the upper division baccalaureate degree category, 4 semester hours in Management or Business Elective (8/97). **NOTE:** Students cannot get credit for this course if they also received credit for Leadership Development Program, Phase 1 (01210), Leadership-Management Relations (01205), or Labor Management Relations - IVT (61205).

Leadership Development Program, Phase I (01210)

Location: Center for Management Development.

Length: *Version 1:* 76 hours (2 weeks); *Version 2:* 60 hours (2 weeks); *Version 3:* 36 hours.

Dates: *Version 1:* October 1988-July 1995; *Version 2:* August 1995-December 1996; *Version 3:* January 1997-Present.

Objective: *Version 1:* To train newly selected supervisors in the areas of supervisor qualities, organizational awareness, performance management, personnel issues, and action planning. *Version 2:* To train new supervisors in the areas of effective supervisor qualities and skills; organizational culture dynamics; performance enhancement; personnel, policy, and procedure issues, and designing action plans. *Version 3:* To provide the foundation knowledge and skills needed for new supervisors to become effective leaders.

Learning Outcome: *Version 1:* Upon successful completion of this course, the student will be able to discuss the qualities necessary for a good supervisor to possess; explain the structural organization of the FAA; and explain and use the management performance system. *Version 2:* Upon successful completion of this course, the student will be able to identify and demonstrate the qualities and skills associated with effective supervisors; explain the organizational structure, policies, and culture of the FAA; and explain and demonstrate skills in management leadership performance. *Version 3:* Upon successful completion of this course, the student will have learned how leadership style impacts job performance; effective use of interpersonal, communications skills for creating an environment that promotes trust; coaching skills for resolving performance and conduct issues; knowledge of workplace policies and programs; and communication and partnership skills to resolve an employee conflict situation.

Instruction: *Version 1:* Major topics covered in the course are supervisor qualities and success skills; organizational awareness, presenting change, giving policy briefings, and writing work objectives; performance management, communicating, and documenting; and personnel issues, coaching, and managing conflict. Methods of instruction include lecture, role playing, videotapes, and case studies. *Version 2:* Major topics covered in the course are successful supervisor qualities and skills; organizational culture, facilitating goal attainment, and change; policies, work objectives, and personnel and diversity issues; and coaching, performance reviews, communications, conflict resolution, and documentation of procedures. Methods of instruction include didactic lectures, role playing, case studies, and videotape. *Version 3:* Major topics covered in the course are supervisor competencies, supervisory roles and responsibilities, communicating/coaching, interpersonal style, diversity in the workplace, sexual harassment, and conduct and discipline. Methods of instruction include lecture, discussion, classroom exercises, case studies, audio visual material, readings, evaluation of performance on case studies and simulations, and written knowledge review.

Credit Recommendation: *Version 1:* In the lower division baccalaureate/associate degree category, 3 semester hours in Supervision (9/90). *Version 2:* In the lower division baccalaureate/associate degree category, 3 semester hours in Management or Social Sciences (8/95). *Version 3:* In the lower division baccalaureate/associate degree category, 2 semester hours in Supervision, Management, or Public Administration (8/97).

Leadership Development Program, Phase II (01211) (Formerly Leadership Development II [01211])

Location: FAA Center for Management Development.

Length: *Version 1:* 59 hours (75 days); *Version 2:* 36 hours.

Dates: *Version 1:* March 1991-December 1996; *Version 2:* January 1997-Present.

Objective: *Version 1:* To become self-directed leaders with emphasis on team building and wellness. *Version 2:* To build upon the foundation, knowledge, and skills gained during initial supervisory training. The Leadership Development Program, Phase II, provides an opportunity for participants to engage in a wide range of activities which are designed to challenge current assumptions, increase behavioral options, and provide enhanced leadership skills.

Learning Outcome: *Version 1:* Upon successful completion of this course, the student will be able to recognize the importance of focusing on the team; analyze and solve problems; recognize the importance of flexibility in the work aspect within organizations; and demonstrate enhanced planning and organization skills. *Version 2:* Upon successful completion of this course, the student will be able to create an environment of teamwork and trust in which diversity is valued and in which all are encouraged to contribute fully; model effective leadership habits; manage priorities; and use leadership strategies to identify and take advantage of opportunities in a changing work environment.

Instruction: *Version 1:* Major topics covered in the course are wellness, paradigms, establishing trust, gaining insight, self-direction, and enabling leaders. Methods of instruction include discussion, break out groups, and experiential learning activities. *Version 2:* Major topics covered in the course are applying the basic concepts of dealing with change to the work environment, increasing self-insight, enhancing one's ability to be self directed, and developing additional skills for building productive professional relationships and leading effectively. Methods of instruction include lecture, discussion, classroom exercises, audio/visual material, and evaluation of performance through observations and feedback on targeted areas using 360 degree appraisal.

Credit Recommendation: *Version 1:* In the upper division baccalaureate degree category, 3 semester hours in Leadership, Human Relations, Training, or Public Administration (9/94). *Version 2:* In the upper division baccalaureate degree category, 2 semester hours in Management, Human Resource Management, or Public Administration (8/97).

Managerial Effectiveness (01302)

Location: FAA Center for Management Development, Palm Coast, FL.

Length: 35 hours (1 week); residential.

Dates: December 1972-August 1992.

Objective: To improve the manager's capabilities in a goals-oriented approach to planning and interpersonal relationships.

Instruction: Major topics covered in the course are management philosophy, organizational theory, communications, group processes, and leadership styles. Methods of instruction include lecture, discussion, role playing, and multimedia instruction.

Credit Recommendation: In the upper division baccalaureate degree category, 2 semester hours in Management or Public Administration (5/76). *Prerequisite:* Managerial Initial Course (01300).

Managerial Initial Course (01300)

Location: FAA Center Management Development, Palm Coast, FL.

Length: 75 hours (2 weeks), residential; includes 42 hours of lecture/discussion and 33 hours of classroom exercises .

Dates: July 1975-August 1992.

Objective: To provide managers with the concepts and applications of a systems approach to results-based management.

Instruction: Major topics covered in the course are systems, organization theory, communications, group behavior, management by objectives, evaluation and control, decision-making, and integrating the individual and the organization. Emphasis is on the functions of planning and organizing. Methods of instruction include lecture, discussion, case studies, and role playing.

Credit Recommendation: In the upper division baccalaureate degree category, 4 semester hours in Management or Public Administration (5/76). **NOTE:** The content of this course overlaps to a large extent with that of Management for Program Managers (01509). Credit should not be granted for both courses. *Prerequisite:* Supervisory Initial Course (01200).

Managing Change (01306)

Location: Center for Management Development, Federal Aviation Administration, Palm Coast, FL.

Length: 31 hours (1 week).

Dates: July 1991-Present.

Objective: To reshape perspectives and approach to change as an on-going process.

Learning Outcome: Upon successful completion of this course, the student will be able to establish a baseline self-assessment regarding change; identify personal behavior and attitudes toward the unusual, unexpected, or different; examine the systemic aspects of change; and recognize organization and personal changes.

Instruction: Major topics covered in the course are change as natural and non-threatening, organization change and linkages, the total quality management process, and cultural diversity. Methods of instruction include lecture, discussion, classroom exercises, case studies, and audio-visual materials.

Credit Recommendation: In the upper division baccalaureate degree category, 2 semester hours in Human Resource Management, Organizational Behavior, or Organizational Development (9/94).

Managing Resources and Programs (01155)

Location: FAA Center for Management Development, Palm Coast, Florida and FAA facilities throughout the United States.

Length: 59 hours (2 weeks).

Dates: January 1995-Present.

Objective: To provide the basic skills needed to perform resource management functions on the job and to recognize the criticality of sound resource management.

Learning Outcome: Upon successful completion of this course, the student will be able to develop systems thinking strategies to improve resource planning, acquisition, and usage; apply goal setting and problem solving strategies to accomplish results; perform basic budget formulation and execution tasks; recognize basic staffing considerations and the budgetary implications of actions; promote diversity in the work place for its value as a resource; recognize the importance of information as a resource; apply influence strategies to accomplish resource management goals; and recognize how managerial style may impact organizational performance.

Instruction: Major topics covered in the course are systems thinking, goal setting, problem solving, budget and staffing, influence strategies, information management, and diversity as a competitive advantage. Methods of instruction include lecture, discussion, classroom exercises, computer-assisted instruction, and hands-on laboratory work.

Credit Recommendation: In the upper division baccalaureate category, 3 semester hours in Operations Management (8/95).

Partnership Challenge (05004)

Location: Center for Management Development, Federal Aviation Administration, Palm Coast, FL.

Length: 36 hours (4.5 days).

Dates: May 1994-Present.

Objective: To identify, experience, and commit to and mentor specific ways union and management pairs can build a stronger and more productive partnership.

Learning Outcome: Upon successful completion of this course, the student will be able to value the differences of others; identify mutual values held by both union and management representatives, recognize behavior that impedes or enhances partnership; identify rights and responsibilities of union and management representatives; describe partnership roles of management and unions; resolve work ideas; and identify specific ways to build a stronger partnership.

Instruction: Major topics covered in the course are labor/management role reversal, history of labor/management relationship, rights and responsibilities of labor and management, teamwork skills, interest-based bargaining, and benefits of partnerships. Methods of instruction include lecture, discussion, classroom exercises, case studies, learner presentation/reports, and a final examination.

Credit Recommendation: In the upper division baccalaureate degree category, 2 semester hours in Labor/Management Partnerships or Business elective (9/94).

Performance Improvement and Employee Appraisal (01201)

Location: FAA Center for Management Development, Palm Coast, FL.

Length: 35 hours (1 week); residential.

Dates: August 1972-August 1992.

Objective: To improve the supervisor's understanding and application of FAA approaches to employee performance improvement and appraisal.

Instruction: Major topics covered in the course are performance standards, human relations and communications, employee development programs, the performance appraisal process, and counseling. Methods of instruction include lectures, discussions, and classroom exercises.

Credit Recommendation: In the upper division baccalaureate degree category, 2 semester hours in Management or Public Administration (5/76). *Prerequisite:*

Supervisory Initial Course (01200) or Managerial Initial Course (01300).

Resource Management (01303)

Location: FAA Center for Management Development, Palm Coast, FL.

Length:59 hours (7.5 days); residential.

Dates: March 1976-December 1992.

Objective: To provide the manager with the financial knowledge and skills to manage human, physical, and technical resources effectively.

Learning Outcome: Upon successful completion of this course, the student will be able to demonstrate the ability to interpret and to apply specific principles of resource planning; explain the process by which resources are obtained and programmed for task accomplishment in operating budgets; and use workload experience of staffing standards as an analytical tool in distributing and making optimum use of resources and analyzing operations.

Instruction: Major topics covered in the course are public laws and policies; resource requirements, acquisition and use; congressional budget process; estimates and the budget process; definition, derivation and development of objectives; multiyear programming; forecasting and planning; position management and workload experience; cost analysis; control and evaluation of resources; and management control of fraud, waste, and abuse of resources.

Credit Recommendation: In the upper division baccalaureate degree category, 3 semester hours in Public Administration (5/76) (9/90).

Staff Work, Train-the-Trainer

Location: Center for Management Development, Federal Aviation Administration, Palm Coast, FL.

Length: 40 hours (1 week).

Dates: April 1994-Present.

Objective: To train regional trainers to facilitate the Staff Work Course, train participants in the use of feedback, ensure understanding of staff work content, and sharpen facilitation skills.

Learning Outcome: Upon successful completion of this course, the student will be able to facilitate the staff work course, use feedback mechanism, understand the content of the staff work course and process student work during the course.

Instruction: Major topics covered in the course are facilitator responsibilities; problem solving; written and verbal communication; processing student work; and group dynamics. Methods of instruction include lecture, discussion, classroom exercises, and learner presentations/reports.

Credit Recommendation: In the upper division baccalaureate degree category, 1 semester hour in Educational Methods (9/94).

Strategic Planning Through the Power of Vision (01274)

Location: Center for Management Development, Federal Aviation Administration, Palm Coast, FL.

Length: 40 hours (1 week).

Dates: January 1991-Present.

Objective: To develop a clear personal and professional vision, and articulate it to the organization.

Learning Outcome: Upon successful completion of this course, the student will be able to design and develop professional plans, understand human relations issues, and improve techniques used to evaluate employee performance.

Instruction: Major topics covered in the course are professional development plans, human relations in complex organizations, and job performance. Methods of instruction include group discussion, videos, problem solving, and case studies.

Credit Recommendation: In the upper division baccalaureate category, 2 semester hour in Public Administration, Human Resource Development, or Business (8/95).

Strategies for Experienced Managers

Location: Center for Management Development, Federal Aviation Administration, Palm Coast, FL.

Length: 40 hours (1 week).

Dates: April 1992-Present.

Objective: To learn and practice advanced management techniques and improve managerial effectiveness.

Learning Outcome: Upon successful completion of this course, the student will be able to determine managerial performance, create personnel strategies, resolve organization problems and improve managerial effectiveness.

Instruction: Major topics covered in the course are corporate assessment, management performance evaluation, new organization functions and creative group interaction. Methods of instruction include individual and group discussion, experiential sessions, and evaluation sessions.

Credit Recommendation: In the upper division baccalaureate degree category, 2 semester hours in Public Administration, Personnel, Human Resource Development, Human Resource Management, or Business Administration (9/94).

Supervisor's Course Phase I (01260)

Location: FAA Center for Management Development, Palm Coast, FL.

Length: 99 hours (3 weeks).

Dates: July 1982-August 1992.

Objective: To develop supervisory skills for a new or relatively inexperienced supervisor.

Instruction: Major topics covered in the course are a wide spectrum of critical and primary interactive skills such as counseling; interpersonal skills; performance appraisal; and development, conduct, and discipline.

Credit Recommendation: In the lower division baccalaureate/associate degree category, 5 semester hours in Supervision Management (10/82).

Supervisor's Course Phase II (01226) Interpersonal Behavior In Problem Solving

Location: FAA Center for Management Development, Palm Coast, FL.

Length: 59 hours (2 weeks).

Dates: September 1977-August 1992.

Objective: To develop interpersonal skills in managerial problem-solving.

Instruction: Major topics covered in the course are understanding the interpersonal roles of the supervisor and managerial situations; and skills in interpersonal behavior, problem-solving, and counseling.

Credit Recommendation: In the upper division baccalaureate degree category, 3 semester hours in Supervision Management (10/82).

Supervisory Reinforcement Training

Location: Center for Management Development, Federal Aviation Administration, Palm Coast, FL.

Length: 26.5 hours (3.5 days).

Dates: September 1992-Present.

Objective: To enable FAA supervisors to create a framework for principle-centered leadership.

Learning Outcome: Upon successful completion of this course, the student will be able to recognize their personal preference for a management style, recognize managerial paradigms, write a personal mission statement which clearly states the goals and values upon which it is based, and recognize how to use the diversity of staff to enhance the work environment.

Instruction: Major topics covered in the course are principled-centered leadership through a study of techniques of establishing trust, self-direction enhancing self-awareness, and promoting an attitude of interdependence. Methods of instruction include lecture, discussion, and role-playing.

Credit Recommendation: In the upper division baccalaureate degree category, 2 semester hours in Public Administration or Business Administration (9/94).

Supervisory Skills Enhancement

Location: Center for Management Development, Federal Aviation Administration, Palm Coast, FL.

Length: 34 hours (1 week).

Dates: May 1991-Present.

Objective: To provide supervisory skills training in problem identification/problem solving, planning and organization, direction and motivation, and decisiveness and judgement.

Learning Outcome: Upon successful completion of this course, the student will be able to take responsibility for his/her own effectiveness; demonstrate the ability to plan and organize, understand motivation principles in interaction with others; identify and propose solutions to problems; apply decision skills and understand the importance of judgement in supervisory actions.

Instruction: Major topics covered in the course are executive skill building and enhancement, personal responsibility for individual effectiveness, planning and organization, direction and motivation, problem solving, decisiveness, and judgement. Methods of instruction include lecture, discussion, and case studies.

Credit Recommendation: In the upper division baccalaureate degree category, 2 semester hours in Public Administration or Business Administration (9/94).

Systems Thinking (CNR 01277) (Formerly Creating New Realities [01277])

Location: FAA/CMD, Palm Coast, FL.

Length: 32 hours (5 days).

Dates: March 1995-Present.

Objective: To provide participants with an overview of alternative strategic interventions addressing current organizational issues.

Learning Outcome: Upon successful completion of this course, the student will be able to explain individual assumptions about how organizations work; analyze work situations; analyze and design alternative ways of systematically addressing organizational issues.

Instruction: Major topics covered in the course are personal wellness, organizational learning disabilities, computer-based system simulations, and identifying system variable relationships. Methods of instruction include lecture, classroom exercises, audio-visual materials, simulation and pre-class works.

Credit Recommendation: In the upper division baccalaureate degree category, 2 semester hours in Organizational Development or Management (8/95). **NOTE:** Title of this course was changed in 1996 from "Creating New Realities" to "Systems Thinking."

The Manager's Course, Phase I (MA-I) (01275) (Formerly Establishing an Agenda, MA-I)

Location: Center for Management Development, Federal Aviation Administration, Palm Coast, FL.

Length: 40 hours (1 week).

Dates: January 1991-Present.

Objective: To develop a clear personal and professional vision, and articulate it to the organization.

Learning Outcome: Upon successful completion of this course, the student will be able to design and develop professional plans, understand human relations issues, and improve techniques used to evaluate employee performance.

Instruction: Major topics covered in the course are professional development plans, human relations in complex organizations, and job performance. Methods of instruction include group discussion, videos, problem solving, and case studies.

Credit Recommendation: In the upper division baccalaureate degree category, 2 semester hours in Public Administration, Personnel, Human Resource Development, Human Resource Management, or Business Administration (9/94).

The Manager's Course, Phase II (MA-II) (01276) (Formerly Expanding Your Influence, MA-II)

Location: Center for Management Development, Federal Aviation Administration, Palm Coast, FL.

Length: 64 hours (2 weeks).

Dates: August 1991-Present.

Objective: To learn and demonstrate managerial team work and leadership skills.

Learning Outcome: Upon successful completion of this course, the student will be able to function and work effectively in dynamic group organizations.

Instruction: Major topics covered in this course are group communications, diversity, influence and leadership and implementing organizational plans. Methods of instruction include group discussion, interaction, videos, cases, and assigned team work.

Credit Recommendation: In the upper division baccalaureate degree category, 2 semester hours in Public Administration, Personnel, Human Resource Development-Human Resource Management, or Business Administration (9/94).

Work Group Facilitator's Course (01528)

Location: Field facilities throughout the United States.

Length: 38 hours (5 days).

Dates: June 1983-August 1992.

Objective: To prepare the student to function as a work group facilitator by more directly involving employees in agency goals, resolution of organizational problems, and improvement of work situations.

Learning Outcome: Upon successful completion of this course, the student will be able to identify the role of human relations in the organization, areas of caution, who is responsible for it, and relate the roles and values of individuals and groups and what their similarities and differences are.

Instruction: Major topics covered in the course are group dynamics, group roles and values, group data gathering/problem analyzing/decision-making procedures, and the ability to make an effective presentation to management. Methods of instruction include classroom and workshop activities. This course is designed for individuals who have been selected to become Work Group Facilitators.

Credit Recommendation: In the upper division baccalaureate degree category, 2 semester hours in Business Administration or Management (5/87).

Federal Correctional Institution

The Institution was created in 1932 by an Act of Congress which established The Bureau and authorized the construction of the United States Southwest Reformatory at El Reno, Oklahoma. The institution has under gone 64 years of updating and mission changes to include today's status of a Medium Security Prison and Camp. The Bureau of Prisons is managed by a Central Office in Washington, D.C. with a Director and six Regional Offices across the United States. F.C.I. El Reno is under the South Central Region, Dallas, Texas.

This is a Federal facility which holds court committed felons under the authority of the U.S. Department of Justice as prescribed by Federal laws. Programs are provided for the betterment of one's self and for preparation for release to the community upon completion of sentence. Educational Programs include Mandatory Literacy (certified GED testing center as authorized by the General Educational Testing Center, Washington, DC), ABLE testing, special reading and vocational training programs.

Vocational Training Instructors must meet the requirements of the Office of Personnel Management criteria for each training instructor's position. This would include formal education, experience and knowledge of the subject matter.

Source of official student records: Registry of Credit Recommendations, American Council on Education, One Dupont Circle, Washington, DC 20036-1193.

Additional information about the courses: College Credit Recommendation Service, American Council on Education, One Dupont Circle, Washington, DC 20036-1193.

Vocational Training/Building Trades (VT300)

Location: Federal Correctional Institution (FCI), El Reno, OK.

Length: 800 contact hours, 30 hours/week.

Dates: January 1991-Present.

Objective: To provide the student with basic understanding of the basic language, tools, procedures, and practices of the construction trades so that one could gain marketable skills in a trade related to the construction industry.

Learning Outcome: Upon successful completion of this course, the student will be able to demonstrate how to safely and properly use hand tools, electric hand tools, and power driven machinery; gain skills in developing ideas and sketches into finished products; gain an understanding of the materials and the processes used to fabricate and construct residential buildings, finish flat pours of concrete and proper joints and surfaces; be able to take measurements and transfer these to construction processes; be able to set grades, forms, and prepare sites for casting of concrete; be able to apply finished surfaces to wood and various structures and trim all doors and openings of varied structures; and be able to hang doors and windows in varied structures.

Instruction: Major topics covered in the course are orientation and basic tools; masonry; finishes; tiling; framing; advanced training in trim and cabinetry, doors and windows, cabinets, exterior and interior trims, and desks and chairs; and how to rate using the performance breakdown. Methods of instruction include lecture and classroom discussion, (40%); projects and presentations, (60%); tests; quizzes; projects; daily progress evaluation; notebooks; and a final examination.

Credit Recommendation: In the vocational certificate category or in the lower division baccalaureate/associate degree category, 2 semester hours in Industrial Arts (11/96).

Vocational Training/Meat Processing (VT100)

Location: Federal Correctional Institution (FCI), El Reno, OK.

Length: 500 contact hours, 30 hours/week.

Dates: January 1991-Present.

Objective: To provide the student with the basic skill in the processing of beef for human consumption in a safe and sanitary manner and provide a marketable skill.

Learning Outcome: Upon successful completion of this course, the student will be able to learn the safe and sanitary way to handle live cattle; the safe and sanitary methods of maintaining a slaughter house kill floor; learn the safe and proper methods of using basic knives, saws, sharpeners, hoists, scales, and electric equipment related to the slaughter processes; learn proper and acceptable methods used in managing the disposal of offal, how to handle the processing of carcass, wrapping, packaging, and storage of beef; and learn the procedures used in skinning beef, dressing a carcass, and how to remove the liver and heart from the carcass.

Instruction: Major topics covered in the course are slaughterhouse operations, processing of the carcass (front and hind), working with cold meats, processing frozen chicken and fish, processing cured hams, the meat buyer's, and rating codes. Methods of instruction include lecture; classroom discussion, (40%); projects; presentations; meat judging contest/audio visual, (60%); tests; quizzes; projects; and daily progress evaluation notebooks.

Credit Recommendation: In the vocational certificate category, 3 semester hours in Meat Processing or in the lower division baccalaureate/associate degree category, 3 semester hours in Agriculture (11/96). **NOTE:** To receive credit for this course the student must have a high school diploma or GED.

Vocational Training/Welding (VT200)

Location: Federal Correctional Institution (FCI), El Reno, OK.

Length: 800 contact hours, 30 hours/week.

Dates: January 1991-Present.

Objective: To provide the student with the basic welding procedures, knowledge, and abilities which will provide a marketable skill in the metal fabrication industry.

Learning Outcome: Upon successful completion of this course, the student will be able to set up and operate an oxy-acetylene unit in a safe and proper manner; weld a ripple bead in flat, horizontal, overhead, and vertical positions using a butt joint; bronze weld a butt and fillet joint; set up and operate a oxy-acetylene cutting torch; run weave beads with a shielded metal arc welding unit, weld flat butt welds, flat fillet welds, vertical butt welds, and horizontal and overhead butt welds with the shielded metal arc process; operate safely the gas metal arc equipment; produce flat, horizontal, and vertical butt welds with the gas metal arc processes; produce acceptable fillet beads in flat horizontal and vertical positions with the gas metal arc process; weld aluminum and stainless steel with the gas tungsten arc process; and demonstrate safe and dependable work habits while using metal fabricating tools, equipment, and metal fusing practices.

Instruction: Major topics covered in the course are oxy-acetylene, shielded metal arc, gas metal arc, gas tungsten arc, and rating codes. Methods of instruction include lecture, classroom discussion (40%); projects, presentations, team work (60%); tests; quizzes; projects; and notebooks.

Credit Recommendation: In the vocational certificate category, 3 semester hours in Welding or in the lower division baccalaureate/associate degree category, 3 semester hours in Industrial Arts or Agriculture (11/96).

Federal Market Group

The Federal Market Group/The Federal Market Institute (FMG/FMI) provides a focal-point for those doing business with the United States Government. FMG/FMI provides consulting services and training, conducts research and develops materials for organizations in government and industry, foreign and domestic, to assist them in successfully doing business within the context of the Federal system of government in the United States.

Expertise is provided in subjects such as Program Management, The Federal Procurement Process, Contract Management and Administration, Marketing, Winning Proposals, Pricing, Subcontracts, Negotiations, Statutory/Regulatory Compliance, Performance Improvement, and International Contacting with the U.S. Government.

The Federal Market Group specializes in providing practical in-house consulting services and training for non-procurement professionals such as program and project managers, engineers, scientists, information technology and telecommunications specialists, contracting officer's technical representatives, marketing specialists and senior organization executives.

With offices and personnel strategically located in Atlanta, Denver, Great Britain, Los Angeles and Washington, D.C., FMG/FMI provides cost effective and timely support to its clients worldwide.

FMG/FMI's personnel are engineers, attorneys, accountants, IT/telecommunications experts, program and contract managers who have real-world, hands-on experience in the Federal contracts and program management disciplines in government and industry.

For information about student records contact Federal Market Group, 124 Park Street, SE, Suite 201, Vienna, VA 22180-4654, (703) 242-9650, (703) 242-9652 FAX, 1-800-242-9655, E-mail: FEDMKTGRP@AOL.COM, Web site: www.fedmarketgroup.com.

Source of official student records: Registry of Credit Recommendations, American Council on Education, One Dupont Circle, Washington, DC 20036-1193.

Additional information about the courses: College Credit Recommendation Service, American Council on Education, One Dupont Circle, Washington, DC 20036-1193.

Government Contracting: Contracting Officer's Technical Representative (COTR)

Location: Various locations throughout the country.

Length: 6 days for a total of 40 hours.

Dates: July 1989-Present.

Objective: To provide COTRs basic understanding of how contracting officer's technical representatives (CORTs) operate in the federal acquisition system.

Learning Outcome: Upon successful completion of this course, the student will be able to define and explain the federal government's procurement process; define and clarify the roles and responsibilities of a COTR; create a work breakdown structure(WBS) and statement of work (SOW); develop source selection criteria; effectively monitor a contracts; and implement contract modifications, terms and close-out procedures.

Instruction: Major topics covered in the course are Federal contracting process, Contract formation, Work Breakdown Schedule and Statement of Work, Source Selection and Contract Administration/ Modification/Termination. Methods of instruction include lecture, discussion, classroom exercise, audio/visual material, and a final examination.

Credit Recommendation: In the upper division baccalaureate degree category, 2 semester hours in Business Administration, Management, or Procurement and Acquisition (8/95).

Government Contracting: Subcontracting

Location: Various locations throughout the country.

Length: 27 hours (3 days).

Dates: January 1990-Present.

Objective: To provide understanding of the subcontracting process and statutory and legal requirements of prime or subcontractor in federal government contracting.

Learning Outcome: Upon successful completion of this course, the student will be able to demonstrate understanding of statutory and regulatory foundation including the UCC; contracting principles including the concept of privity; issues of payment, disputes resolution, social policies and pre and post award administration.

Instruction: Major topics covered in the course are federal government contracting, contractual operations, pre-award activities, post-award administration. Methods of instruction include lecture, discussion, case studies, audio/visual material, and final examinations.

Credit Recommendation: In the upper division baccalaureate degree category, 1 semester hour in Business Administration, Management, Marketing, or Procurement and Contracting (8/95).

Managing Contracts for Peak Performance: Contract Administration

Location: Various locations throughout the country.

Length: 32 hours (4 days).

Dates: November 1989-Present.

Objective: To provide the participant with tools and techniques to effect a proactive, problem-avoidance approach to managing government contracts.

Learning Outcome: Upon completion of this course, the student will be able to explain the broad aspects of the federal acquisition environment, and will understand the tools and techniques necessary for the successful completion of federal service contracts.

Instruction: Major topics covered in the course are federal contract management, interpreting federal government contracts, financial aspects of federal contracts, labor compliance, contract modifications, and terminations, and contract closeout. Methods of instruction include lecture, discussion, case studies, classroom exercises and learner presentations.

Credit Recommendation: In the upper division baccalaureate degree category, 1 semester hour in Business Administration, Management, Marketing, or Procurement and Contracting (8/95).

Managing Profitable Government Contracts

Location: Various locations throughout the country.

Length: 16 hours (2 days).

Dates: July 1995-Present.

Objective: To provide understanding of the management of a federal government contract.

Learning Outcome: Upon successful completion of this course, the student will be able to understand the rules of government contracting; identify the roles of government contracting personnel; and understand government contracts and techniques that enhance performance.

Instruction: Major topics covered in the course are contract management, understanding contracts, cost principles, electronic data interface, maximizing performance, government furnished property, and contract modifications. Methods of instruction include lecture, discussion, classroom exercises, audio-visual material, and a final examination.

Credit Recommendation: In the upper division baccalaureate degree category, 1 semester hour in Business Administration, Management, or Procurement and Contracting (8/95). **NOTE**: Both this course and Winning Government Contracts: Marketing and Proposal Management must be completed to qualify for 1 semester hour credit.

Negotiations

Location: Various locations throughout the country.

Length: 16 hours (2 days).

Dates: February 1991-Present.

Objective: To provide a thorough understanding of the fundamentals of principled negotiation techniques.

Learning Outcome: Upon successful completion of this course, the student will be able to demonstrate effective negotiating skills in federal government contracting.

Instruction: Major topics covered in the course are principled negotiations, problem solving, fact finding, effective communications, and planning and conducting a negotiating session. Methods of instruction include lecture, presentations, case studies, and examinations.

Credit Recommendation: In the upper division baccalaureate degree category, 2 semester hours in Business Administration, Management, Marketing, and Procurement and Contracting (8/95). **NOTE**: This course and Contract Management: Source Selection must be completed to qualify for 2 semester hour credits.

Winning Government Contracts: Marketing and Proposal Management.

Location: Various locations throughout the country.

Length: 16 hours (2 days).

Dates: June 1995-Present.

Objective: To provide an overview of the federal government marketplace and understanding of how best to win government contracts.

Learning Outcome: Upon successful completion of this course, the student will be able to demonstrate understanding of the government marketplace, the contracting process, and methods of winning government contracts.

Instruction: Major topics covered in the course are the government marketplace, understanding government contracts, business development and marketing, contract selection, and proposal planning and preparation. Methods of instruction include lecture, presentations, case studies, and a final examination.

Credit Recommendation: In the upper division baccalaureate degree category, 1 semester hour in Business Administration, Management, Marketing, or Procurement and Contracting (8/95). **NOTE**: Both this course and Managing Profitable Government Contracts must be complete to qualify for 1 semester hour credit.

Felde Publications and Programs

Felde Publications and Programs has offered California Department of Real Estate approved college level correspondence courses since 1986. This was the first year in which California law required all prospective salesperson licensees to complete a 45 hour course in Real Estate Principles. Real estate broker applicants were required to complete 8 college level 3 unit (45 hour) courses in order to qualify for the license. Felde Publications has a total of eight 45 hour courses approved by the Department of Real Estate.

Felde Publications and Programs is approved by the California Council for Private Postsecondary and Vocational Education as a private vocational school.

APPRAISAL PROGRAM

A new appraisal license law went into effect on January 1, 1992, requiring all applicants to complete a minimum number of hours of education prior to licensure.

Felde Publications and Programs has been approved by the California Office of Real Estate Appraisers to offer a Prelicense program that consists of two 45 hour correspondence courses. The two prelicense courses are designed to cover specific topics required by the Appraiser Qualification Board and to prepare the applicant to pass the State License Examination. The school also has the OREA's approval for a 56 hour Continuing Education program. This includes the mandated 7 hour course in Uniform Standards of Professional Appraisal Practice and the 4 hour course on Federal State Regulations. The balance of the 45 hours consists of a 3 unit course in Legal Aspects of Real Estate.

All courses have been developed by Thomas E. Felde and are updated each year to reflect all of the latest changed in the law and regulations. Mr. Felde has devoted over 30 years to writing, teaching, and publishing on the subjects of real estate, appraisal, and legal aspects.

Source of official student records: Registry of Credit Recommendations, American Council on Education, One Dupont Circle, Washington, DC 20036-1193.

Additional information about the courses: College Credit Recommendation Service, American Council on Education, One Dupont Circle, Washington, DC 20036-1193.

Elements of California Real Estate Law and Appraisal Regulations (Formerly Continuing Education for Appraiser Licensees)

Location: Independent Study by Correspondence.

Length: 56 hours.

Dates: January 1996-Present.

Objective: To provide the student with an overview of the Uniform Standards for Professional Appraisal Practices (USPAP) and those elements of California law that pertain to real estate.

Learning Outcome: Upon successful completion of this course, the student will be able to demonstrate familiarity with the issues related to the ownership and transfer of real property in California, and the Uniform Standards Professional Appraisal Practice regulations.

Instruction: Major topics covered in the course are nature of real property; ownership of real property; agency law, duties, and liabilities; real estate contracts; litigation and its alternatives; issues in real estate title; real estate financing issues; fair housing laws and landlord/tenant law; USPAP regulations; and federal and California regulations applying to real property. Methods of instruction include correspondence study involving directed text readings, special projects, and a proctored final examination.

Credit Recommendation: In the lower division baccalaureate/associate degree category, 2 semester hours in Real Estate Law or Business Administration (5/97).

First Data Card Services Group

First Data Card Services Group is the world's leading third-party provider of transaction card processing and related card-based services. The company provides credit and debit card processing services for more than 700 financial institutions and retailers who have more than one million merchant locations and over 150 million cardholder accounts. Headquartered in Omaha, Nebraska, First Data Card Services Group also has headquarter locations in Basildon in the United Kingdom and in Sydney, Australia.

First Data Card Services Group is a business unit of First Data Corporation. First Data Corporation (NYSE:FDC) is a provider of high-quality, high-volume information processing and related services to the credit card, consumer funds transfer, teleservices, mutual fund, and receivables management. In 1994, the company had net income of $636 million on revenue of $4.9 billion.

Source of official student records: Registry of Credit Recommendations, American Council on Education, One Dupont Circle, Washington, DC 20036-1193.

Additional information about the courses: College Credit Recommendation Service, American Council on Education, One Dupont Circle, Washington, DC 20036-1193.

Business Communications
1. Effective Business Speaking
2. Advanced Business Speaking

Location: Omaha, NE.

Length: 23 hours (3 days).

Dates: November 1985-Present.

Objective: To examine the role and impact of effective business speaking and delivery of speeches in current business style.

Learning Outcome: Upon successful completion of this course, the student will be able to describe steps necessary for successful presentations; list characteristics of an effective speaker; utilize relaxation techniques as well as deal with anxiety; describe audience factors and strategies for dealing with anxiety and strategies for dealing with audience problems; note types of visual aids; and when and how to use each and deliver a polished speech.

Instruction: Major topics covered in the course are key communication factors; strategies for successful delivery of speeches; audience analysis; utilization of visual aids; body language; use of humor and silence; voice intonation; feedback; and anxiety control. Methods of instruction include video, lecture, visual aids, readings, and handouts.

Credit Recommendation: In the lower division baccalaureate/associate degree category, 1 semester hour in Business Communication (7/93). **NOTE**: Both courses must be taken to receive credit.

Business Writing
(Effective Business Writing)

Location: Omaha, NE.

Length: 23 hours (3 days).

Dates: November 1985-Present.

Objective: To explore the fundamentals of grammar, spelling, and the principles of effective writing.

Learning Outcome: Upon successful completion of this course, the student will be able to write clear, concise letters and memos according to recommended formats, and analyze and evaluate various writing styles.

Instruction: Major topics covered in the course are writing improvement (sentence structure, grammar, and spelling), and proofreading. Methods of instruction include lecture, discussion, and classroom exercises.

Credit Recommendation: In the lower division baccalaureate/associate degree category, 1 semester hour in Business English (7/93).

Conflict Resolution
(Basic Negotiation)

Location: Omaha, NE

Length: 15 hours (2 days).

Dates: November 1985-Present.

Objective: To enable the student to develop his or her own negotiation style and skills.

Learning Outcome: Upon successful completion of this course, the student will be able to identify situations requiring negotiation; select the appropriate negotiation style; plan a negotiation strategy; and execute the negotiation.

Instruction: Major topics covered in the course are current negotiation practices; elements of successful negotiation; pre-negotiation planning; negotiation styles; negotiation tactics; keys to negotiation (communication, fact-finding, planning, and power); and post-negotiation evaluation. Methods of instruction include lectures (with prepared flipcharts), videotapes, written exercises, small group exercises, role playing, and participation in the Negotiation simulation.

Credit Recommendation: In the upper division baccalaureate degree category, 1 semester hour in Management, Communications, or Negotiation (7/93).

Customer Relations
(Customer Satisfaction Strategies)

Location: Omaha, NE.

Length: 15 hours (2 days).

Dates: November 1985-Present.

Objective: To prepare students to effectively manage customer relations and promote customer satisfaction.

Learning Outcome: Upon successful completion of this course, the student will be able to obtain customer information and manage customer dissatisfaction through effective two-way communications.

Instruction: Major topics covered in the course are identification of communication styles; effective use of various communications techniques such as open and closed probes; paraphrasing and acknowledging customer concerns, stating the results the customer can expect; and concluding the conversation. Methods of instruction include lectures (with prepared flipcharts and overheads), audio tapes, video, written exercises, small group activities, and role-plays.

Credit Recommendation: In the upper division baccalaureate degree category, 1 semester hour in Marketing, Sales, or Communications (7/93).

Human Resource Management
(Train the Trainer)

Location: Omaha, NE.

Length: 21 hours (2.5 days).

Dates: November 1985-Present.

Objective: To teach students to design, develop, and deliver an effective training program and enhance their presentation style.

Learning Outcome: Upon successful completion of this course, the student will be able to recall and explain the key principles of adult learning; enhance a training module by applying appropriate design and development techniques; deal with difficult students; promote and handle discussion; present a training module utilizing proven delivery methods; and receive positive feedback on a presentation.

Instruction: Major topics covered in the course are adult learning theory; training objectives; analysis of training needs; design of training for maximum participant comprehension; effective methods, techniques and training aids; teaching styles; barriers to learning; and motivation.

Methods of instruction include video, lecture, visual aids, handouts, and readings.

Credit Recommendation: In the upper division baccalaureate degree category, 2 semester hours in Human Resource Management or Methods of Teaching Adult Learners (7/93).

Human Resource Management 1: Managing Employee Relations 2: Selection Interviewing

Location: Omaha, NE.

Length: 16 hours (2 days).

Dates: November 1985-Present.

Objective: To provide techniques for developing and maintaining a positive work environment.

Learning Outcome: Upon successful completion of this course, the student will be able to state elements of an unlawful employment interview, as well as common pitfalls of an interview; describe problem applicants and strategies for handling; document interviews; demonstrate questioning techniques; describe benefits and problems with good and poor hires, respectively; order the steps of a third party organizational campaign; identify reasons employees join a union; develop strategies for dealing with a third party contact; identify strategies for managing diversity, discrimination, harassment; and define strategies for responding to unlawful personnel issues.

Instruction: Major topics covered in the course are legal implications of EEO, affirmative action and harassment; causes and results of employee unionization; creation of a positive work environment, diverse workforce issues; job descriptions; successful interview practices; and employee orientation. Methods of instruction include lecture, video, visual aids, case studies, handouts, and audiotapes.

Credit Recommendation: In the upper division baccalaureate degree category, 1 semester hour in Human Resource Management (7/93). **NOTE**: Both courses must be taken to receive credit.

Human Resource Management (Developing the High Performance Team)

Location: Omaha, NE.

Length: 16 hours (2 days).

Dates: November 1985-Present.

Objective: To assess individual and work team strengths with developmental opportunities for examining the characteristics and strategies for developing high performance teams.

Learning Outcome: Upon successful completion of this course, the student will be able to identify the benefits that high performance teams provide to the organization; assess team developmental opportunities; practice team building strategies for improvement of team effectiveness; and develop an action plan for work unit application.

Instruction: Major topics covered in the course are team definitions; characteristics; benefits; problems; development; culture; leadership styles and decision making; creativity; and motivation. Methods of instruction include video, lecture, visual aids, handouts, readings, and case studies.

Credit Recommendation: In the upper division baccalaureate degree category, 1 semester hour in Human Resource Management or Methods (7/93).

Introduction to Business Communications (Communicating for Results)

Location: Omaha, NE.

Length: 18 hours (2 days).

Dates: November 1985-Present.

Objective: To emphasize important interpersonal communication skills, including verbal, non-verbal, and listening with a written assessment for self understanding and improvement.

Learning Outcome: Upon successful completion of this course, the student will be able to explain key components of effective communications, a communication model, factors shaping organizational and interpersonal communication problems, as well as message clarity; develop an action plan to overcome communication barriers; practice effective listening skills; and assess types of behaviors that shape personality types and communication styles.

Instruction: Major topics covered in the course are active listening; questioning and paraphrasing techniques; factors causing communication breakdowns; personal communication styles and patterns; and assertive communication skills. Methods of instruction include video, Myers Briggs Type Indicator instrument, handouts, lecture, readings, and audio tapes.

Credit Recommendation: In the lower division baccalaureate/associate degree category, 1 semester hour in Business Communications or Communications (7/93).

Introduction to Project Management

Location: Omaha, NE.

Length: 15 hours (2 days).

Dates: February 1986-Present.

Objective: To teach students to learn and apply tools and techniques for the planning and control of project activities to ensure that goals are achieved on time and within budget.

Learning Outcome: Upon successful completion of this course, the student will be able to explain the benefits of a framework to use for short-term and long-term planning in project management; discuss how team work is affected by project life cycles and critical milestones; and practice developing project plans while emphasizing controls and management skills.

Instruction: Major topics covered in the course are effective project planning steps; techniques for development, implementation, and management of a Project Plan; monitoring a Project Life Cycle; reporting Project Status; and Gantt and PERT charts. Methods of instruction include lecture, discussion, and classroom exercises.

Credit Recommendation: In the upper division baccalaureate degree category, 1 semester hour in Project Management or Advanced Management elective (7/93).

Introduction to Total Quality Management: TQM 1: TQM: Orientation 2: TQM: Problem Solving Process

Location: Omaha, NE.

Length: 17 hours (2.5 days).

Dates: November 1991-Present.

Objective: To provide the historical context of TQM and teach students the basic tools used to identify, analyze, and solve quality-related problems.

Learning Outcome: Upon successful completion of this course, the student will know the key figures in TQM, know the common language of TQM, and be able to describe the function of the tools and techniques used in the TQM problem solving process.

Instruction: Major topics covered in the course are historical figures in TQM; customer satisfaction; performance standards; cost of non-conformance; cost of lost opportunity; situation analysis; brainstorming; TQM tools (Pareto Analysis, Fishbone Diagrams, etc.); solution selection; and presentation to management. Methods of instruction include lectures (with overheads), written exercises, small group problem solving activities, and discussion.

Credit Recommendation: In the upper division baccalaureate degree category, 1 semester hour in Total Quality Management or Advanced Management elective (7/93).

Management Practices
(Basic Management Practices)

Location: Omaha, NE.
Length: 16 hours (2 days).
Dates: February 1987-Present.
Objective: To examine supervisory roles in order to apply specific skills and knowledge to increase job effectiveness and to practice solving typical problems which supervisors and managers encounter.
Learning Outcome: Upon successful completion of this course, the student will be able to solve typical problems encountered by supervisors and managers; improve communication skills through active listening; discover the sources and methods of motivating employees; develop employees using the steps of effective delegation; improve employee performance using the five steps of performance counseling; explore techniques to effectively manage a diverse workforce; and design an action plan to maximize supervisory skills.
Instruction: Major topics covered in the course are communications; motivation; corporate culture; planning, delegation; diverse workforce; and leadership. Methods of instruction include lecture, class discussions; films, videos, and group activities.
Credit Recommendation: In the lower division baccalaureate/associate degree category, 1 semester hour in Principles of Management (7/93).

Stress Management
1: Stress Over Stress: Challenging Life's Demands
2: Success Over Job Stress: Balancing Job Demands

Location: Omaha, NE.
Length: 15 hours (2 days).
Dates: March 1987-Present.
Objective: To provide practical tools to manage stress.
Learning Outcome: Upon successful completion of this course, the student will be able to recognize sources and symptoms of stress; capitalize on positive stress management techniques; and develop an action plan to address and effectively cope with stressors in life and on the job.
Instruction: Major topics covered in the course are sources of stress; conflict resolution; work pressure; balancing life's roles; burn out; life pressures; and assertiveness. Methods of instruction include lecture, discussion, video, and individual and group exercises.
Credit Recommendation: In the lower division baccalaureate/associate degree category, 1 semester hour in Stress Management (7/93). **NOTE**: Both courses must be taken to receive credit.

Supervising for Success
SFSI: Stepping up to Supervisor;
SFSII: Setting Goals and Standards;
SFSIII: Delegating and Coaching;
SFSIV: Counseling and Corrective Action;
SFSV: Appraising Performance;
SFSVI: Promoting Employee Relations;
SFSVII: FDR Human Resources Manual Overview

Location: Omaha, NE.
Length: 32 hours (7.5 days).
Dates: January 1988-Present.
Objective: To provide an overview of the supervisory skills necessary for success in today's corporate environment.
Learning Outcome: Upon successful completion of this course, the student will be able to identify and learn to handle effectively and efficiently a wide variety of supervisory situations.
Instruction: Major topics covered in the course are supervisory skills in seven modules: Module 1: Supervising for Success includes making students aware of the common pitfalls of new supervisors and how to avoid them. Module 2: Setting Goals and Standards develops the student's ability to write clear objectives. Module 3: Delegating and Coaching teaches sound techniques for delegating and effective positive techniques of praising and coaching. Module 4: Counseling and Corrective Action presents a positive approach to re-directing declining performance and delivering "one minute reprimands". Module 5: Appraising Performance addresses how the performance appraisal can be a year-round motivator and provides practice in writing appraisals and performing performance appraisal interviews. Module 6: Promoting Employee Relations develops the understanding of the importance of good employee relations in the company and how Affirmative Action Programs, Equal Employment Opportunities, and nondiscriminatory management practices promote positive employee relations. Module 7: Human Resources Applications links the theories and concepts taught in the previous modules with the human resources policies. Methods of instruction include lecture, discussion, group and individual exercises, and video.
Credit Recommendation: In the lower division baccalaureate/associate degree category, 2 semester hours in Supervision (7/93). **NOTE**: For 1 credit hour Supervising for Success I, II, and III; and 1 additional credit hour for completion of Supervising for Success IV, V, VI, and VII.

Florida Power and Light Company

One of the primary objectives of Florida Power and Light Company's Nuclear Division is to strengthen professionalism, accountability, and knowledge among employees. The strategy to achieve this objective is to build and maintain a working environment for employees that encourages innovation, professionalism and teamwork, and provides opportunities for knowledge enhancement, increasing responsibility, and career advancement.

The Turkey Point nuclear training department is charged with instilling and maintaining education and training that result in personnel who are competent in their performance. In their support of a wide variety of educational activities, a majority of the training organization's effort is in development, delivery, and evaluation of instruction. The courses and programs conducted provide the theory, principles, and concepts necessary to develop an employee's knowledge and skills.

The target audience for training are those plant personnel involved in the areas of operations, maintenance, and technical support. The education and training programs not only provide the learning required to function in current, specific positions in the organization, but also the opportunity for employees to gain additional, advanced knowledge to become eligible for the more demanding positions of leadership and management within the company.

Courses are systematically evaluated to ensure objectives are mastered and student's needs are being met. Course evaluation involves feedback from the students, instructors, supervisors, and evaluation specialists. Course exam results are analyzed to ensure objectives are being mastered.

Instructors at the Turkey Point Nuclear Training Center are categorized into three groups—Operations, Maintenance/ Specialty, and Support. Instructors and developers are assigned to technical programs within these three groups. All groups have instructor qualification requirements according to the following categories: fundamental instructor, fundamental technical instructor, and developer. Instructors are required to complete an initial instructor training program and evaluation as well as annual continuing instructional skills training and technical and instructional evaluations.

Instructors at the St. Lucie Nuclear Training Center are categorized into three groups—Operations, Maintenance, Specialty and Technical. Instructors are assigned to specific programs within these three groups. All groups have instructor qualification requirements according to the following categories: licensed operator instructors, non-licensed operator instructors, and maintenance/technical instructors. Instructors are required to complete an initial instructor training program and evaluation as well as annual continuing instructional skills training and technical and instructional evaluations.

Source of official student records: Administration Services, Turkey Point Nuclear Training Center, Florida Power and Light Company, P.O. Box 029100, Miami, Florida 33102-9100 or Administrative and Services Supervisor, St. Lucie Nuclear Training Center, Florida Power and Light Company, P.O. Box 128, Ft. Pierce, FL 34954-0128.

Additional information about the courses: College Credit Recommendation Service, American Council on Education, One Dupont Circle, Washington, DC 20036-1193.

Administration, Communications, and Supervision

Location: Florida Power and Light, St. Lucie Nuclear Plant.

Length: 36 hours (2 weeks).

Dates: January 1986-April 1997.

Objective: To provide the student with an understanding of the basic principles of effective communication, applicable administrative policies and procedures, and the fundamentals of supervision.

Learning Outcome: Upon successful completion of this course, the student will be able to describe the role, functions, and responsibilities of supervisors, styles of leadership, motivation factors, factors leading to effective communication, and conflict resolution.

Instruction: Major topics covered in the course are effective communication practices; the role, functions and responsibilities of supervisors; styles of leadership; fundamentals of motivation; and effects of stress. Methods of instruction include lecture and self-study.

Credit Recommendation: In the lower division baccalaureate/associate degree category, 2 semester hours in Administration or Management (4/92).

Chemical and Volume Control Systems

Location: Turkey Point Nuclear Plant.

Length: 40 hours (2 weeks).

Dates: January 1985-January 1997.

Objective: To provide the student with an understanding of the theory, design, purpose, and operational characteristics of the chemical and volume control system of a nuclear power plant.

Learning Outcome: Upon successful completion of this course, the student will be able to describe the theory, design, and control of the chemical and volume control system; the use of primary chemistry in controlling the reactor coolant system; the design and operation of the water treatment plant; and function of and design of the compressed gas system.

Instruction: Major topics covered in the course are theory, design, and operation of the chemical and volume control system, radiochemistry of water, control of radiochemical reactions; description of water sampling systems; and compressed gas system. Methods of instruction include lecture and exams.

Credit Recommendation: In the lower division baccalaureate/associate degree category, 1 semester hour in Nuclear Engineering Technology or Nuclear Science (1/92).

Classical Physics

Location: Florida Power and Light, St. Lucie Nuclear Plant.

Length: 40 hours (2 weeks).

Dates: January 1986-April 1997.

Objective: To introduce students to the concepts of linear and angular motion, Newton's laws of motion, momentum, impulse, work, energy, power, and pressure.

Learning Outcome: Upon successful completion of this course, the student will be able to define concepts of linear and angular motion, forces, work, energy, power, pressure, and solve simple problems related to these concepts.

Instruction: Major topics covered in the course are units, dimensional analysis, kinematics, friction, Newton's laws of motion, momentum, impulse work, energy, power, efficiency, angular motion, torques, and mechanical equilibrium. Methods of instruction include lecture, in-class exercises, self-study, and exams.

Credit Recommendation: In the lower division baccalaureate/associate degree category, 2 semester hours in non-calculus General Physics (4/92).

Condensate System

Location: Florida Power & Light, St. Lucie Nuclear Plant.

Length: 52 hours (3 weeks).

Dates: January 1986-April 1997.

Objective: To introduce the student to the plant circulating water, condensate, feedwater, air evacuation and feedwater regulating control systems, associated subsystems, their respective controls, operational characteristics and parameters.

Learning Outcome: Upon successful completion of this course, the student will be able to state the function, design basis, flowpath, parameters, and limitations for the various systems and associated support systems.

Instruction: Major topics covered in the course are circulating water system and associated heaters, condensate and feedwater systems, condensate polisher, feedwater regulating control system. Methods of instruction include lecture, classroom exercises and exams.

Credit Recommendation: In the lower division baccalaureate/associate degree category, 2 semester hours in Nuclear Technology (4/92).

Condensate System

Location: Turkey Point Nuclear Plant.

Length: 70 hours (3 weeks).

Dates: January 1985-January 1997.

Objective: To introduce the student to the liquid phase of power plant steam cycles, support systems, and applied water chemistry. Emphasis is placed upon system design basis and system response to design basis accidents. Several transients are analyzed. Secondary water chemistry, its theory, and application are discussed.

Learning Outcome: Upon successful completion of this course, the student will be able to state the function, design basis, flowpath, parameters, and limitations for the various systems and associated support systems; describe the application, and discuss the theory of secondary water chemistry.

Instruction: Major topics covered in the course are condensate system, feedwater system, and circulating water system including their support systems. Methods of instruction include lecture, classroom exercises, and examinations.

Credit Recommendation: In the lower division baccalaureate/associate degree category, 2 semester hours in Nuclear Technology (1/92).

Fluid Flow

Location: Florida Power and Light, St. Lucie Nuclear Plant.

Length: 28 hours (2 weeks).

Dates: January 1986-April 1997.

Objective: To introduce the student to the fundamental properties of fluids and their behavior under varying conditions of pressure, temperature, and volume. The characteristics of fluid flow in assorted static and dynamic systems using Bernoulli's equation are included.

Learning Outcome: Upon successful completion of this course, the student will be able to describe and calculate pressure change throughout a system due to area and elevation change using Bernoulli's equation; describe and calculate mass flow rate using static and dynamic pressure measurements; and describe and understand pump work and pump characteristics, including not positive suction head.

Instruction: Major topics covered in the course are the concepts of pressure, temperature, volume, density, specific volume, specific gravity, specific weight, and compressibility, an introduction to fluid statics and governing equations, Charles and Gay-Lussac's laws, the ideal gas law and application to several plant systems and Dalton's law, Pascal's law, Bernoulli's equation, and the continuity equation. Various types of pumps and associated pump theory are discussed. Measurement of mass flow rate using a variety of measurement devices is also discussed. Methods of instruction include lecture, self-study, and exams.

Credit Recommendation: In the lower division baccalaureate/associate degree category, 1 semester hour in Engineering Technology (4/92).

Fundamentals of Electrical Science

Location: Florida Power and Light, St. Lucie Nuclear Plant.

Length: 68 hours (4 weeks).

Dates: January 1986-April 1997.

Objective: To provide the student with an introduction to the fundamentals of electrical theory and application necessary for understanding electrical science as it relates to operation at a nuclear generating plant.

Learning Outcome: Upon successful completion of this course, the student will be able to describe concepts of electricity, DC and AC circuits, magnetism, and solve simple problems based on these concepts.

Instruction: Major topics covered in the course are Coulomb's law, Ohm's law, DC circuits, Kirchhoff's laws, capacitance, magnetism, inductance, AC circuits, impedance, transformers, batteries, generators, and motors. Methods of instruction include lecture, classroom exercises, self-study, and exams.

Credit Recommendation: In the lower division baccalaureate/associate degree category, 2 semester hours in non-calculus General Physics (4/92).

Fundamentals of Electrical Theory

Location: Turkey Point Nuclear Plant.

Length: 44 hours (2 weeks).

Dates: January 1987-January 1997.

Objective: To provide an introduction to electrical theory and to facilitate an understanding of the electrical distribution systems and electrical control systems at a nuclear power plant.

Learning Outcome: Upon successful completion of this course, the student will be able to describe and calculate the basic properties of circuits, magnetism, electromagnetism, generators and motors, and read electrical distribution diagrams.

Instruction: Major topics covered in the course are fundamentals of electricity, basic circuit theory, electromagnetism, AC-DC currents, resistors, capacitors, induction, motors and generators, and electrical diagrams. Methods of instruction include lecture, in-class exercises, self-study, and examinations.

Credit Recommendation: In the lower division baccalaureate/associate degree category, 1 semester hour in Electrical Technology or Electrical Engineering (1/92).

Heat Transfer

Location: Florida Power and Light, St. Lucie Nuclear Plant.

Length: 24 hours (2 weeks).

Dates: January 1986-April 1997.

Objective: To introduce the student to the fundamental concepts of heat transfer and to apply these principles to the operations of a nuclear power plant. Heat transfer in different power plant systems is examined in detail.

Learning Outcome: Upon successful completion of this course, the student will be able to describe the three basic modes of heat transfer and understand those modes as they relate to a nuclear power plant, describe temperature profiles to be expected in specific plant heat exchangers and systems, calculate heat transfer in these plant systems given appropriate heat transfer coefficients, calculate heat exchanger duty given fluid inlet and outlet conditions; and describe boiling heat transfer fundamentals and applications to power plant systems.

Instruction: Major topics covered in the course are fundamental concepts of heat transfer as they apply to the operation of a pressurized water reactor nuclear power plant. Topics covered include introduction to conduction, convection and radiation heat transfer; heat transfer in nuclear fuel rods and in the core; boiling heat transfer in the steam generator; and heat exchanger applications. Methods of instruction include lecture, self-study, and exams.

Credit Recommendation: In the lower division baccalaureate/associate degree category, 1 semester hour in Engineering Technology (4/92).

Instrument and Control Theory

Location: Florida Power and Light, St. Lucie Nuclear Plant.

Length: 64 hours (4 weeks).

Dates: January 1986-April 1997.

Objective: To introduce the student to the fundamentals of instrument and control theory including principles of pressure, level, flow, and temperature measurements.

Learning Outcome: Upon successful completion of this course, the student will be able to describe concepts of instrument and control theory and explain the operation of devices used to measure pressure, temperature, liquid level, and fluid flow.

Instruction: Major topics covered in the course are fundamentals of control theory, including open and closed control loops, transmitters, feedback, principles of operation of devices to measure pressure, liquid level, fluid flow and temperature, and reading piping and instrumentation diagrams. Methods of instruction include lecture, self-study, and exams.

Credit Recommendation: In the lower division baccalaureate/associate degree category, 3 semester hours in Instrumentation and Control Technology (4/92).

Instrument and Control Theory

Location: Turkey Point Nuclear Plant.

Length: 44 hours (3 weeks).

Dates: January 1987-January 1997.

Objective: To provide the student with an introduction to the fundamentals of instrument and control theory required for successful measurement and operation procedures at a nuclear generating plant.

Learning Outcome: Upon successful completion of this course, the student will be able to understand various measurement units and conversion techniques; describe devices that measure pressure, temperature, flow, and level; explain the function of logic devices; and identify components on electrical wiring diagrams.

Instruction: Major topics covered in the course are the fundamentals of control theory including measurement, units of measure, and control diagrams; the underlining principles of measurement are introduced, including pressure, temperature, level, and flow; and an introduction to process control theory is presented along with the theory of open and closed loop systems. Methods of instruction include lecture and examinations.

Credit Recommendation: In the vocational certificate category, 2 semester hours in Instrument and Control Technology (1/92).

Introduction to Nuclear Power

Location: Florida Power and Light, St. Lucie Nuclear Plant.

Length: 22 hours (2 weeks).

Dates: January 1986-April 1997.

Objective: To provide the student with a qualitative understanding of the basic principles of controlled nuclear fission, associated nuclear power plant systems and their interrelationships, administrative requirements, and the general considerations of operation of a nuclear generating station.

Learning Outcome: Upon successful completion of this course, the student will be able to discuss Title 10 Code of Federal Regulations, nuclear power plant technical specifications, and the Final Safety Analysis Report and relate the importance of each to the operation of a nuclear generating facility; the relationship of the regulatory and industrial institutions to operation of a nuclear power plant; and the role of reactivity control and neutron multiplication on rector operation.

Instruction: Major topics covered in the course are a qualitative review of nuclear fission, including chain reactions, reaction control, and fundamental reactor theory, and nuclear power plant primary and secondary systems along with their respective control methodologies and associated systems. The applicable Code of Federal Regulations; technical specifications, Final Safety Analysis Report, and the various agencies and organizations that interact with nuclear power generation facilities are also presented. Methods of instruction include lecture, self-study, and exams.

Credit Recommendation: In the lower division baccalaureate/associate degree category, 1 semester hour in Nuclear Technology (4/92).

Introduction to Nuclear Power (Pressurized Water Re)

Location: Turkey Point Nuclear Plant.

Length: 24 hours (2 weeks).

Dates: January 1987-January 1997.

Objective: To provide the student with an overview of the basic principles of controlled nuclear fission, associated nuclear power plant systems and their interrelationships, administrative requirements, and the general considerations of operation of a nuclear generating station.

Learning Outcome: Upon successful completion of this course, the student will be able to identify the purpose and the applicable content of Title 10 Code of Federal Regulations; describe the plant technical specifications and the organizations associated with the nuclear power industry; relate the Final Safety Analysis Report to plant operation; describe basic nuclear processes; and describe and explain primary and secondary plant systems and controls.

Instruction: This course presents an overview of the basic principles of nuclear fission, including chain reactions, reaction control, and fundamental reactor theory. Nuclear power plant primary and secondary systems are discussed along with their respective control methodologies and associated systems. The applicable Code of Federal Regulations, technical specifications, Final Safety Analysis Report, and the various agencies and organizations that interact with nuclear power generating facilities are also presented. Methods of instruction include lecture, self-study, and examinations.

Credit Recommendation: In the vocational certificate category, 1 semester hour in Nuclear Technology (1/92).

Introduction to Physics

Location: Turkey Point Nuclear Plant.

Length: 92 hours (6 weeks).

Dates: January 1987-January 1997.

Objective: To introduce the student to classical physics, the foundation for future nuclear physics, and reactor engineering courses.

Learning Outcome: Upon successful completion of this course, the student will be able to perform precalculus calculations using concepts from classical physics; convert from one unit system to another; perform operations with vectors; and use Newton's Laws of Motion.

Instruction: Major topics covered in the course are units, dimensions, vectors, introductory analytical dynamics, gravitation, and mechanical properties of matter. Methods of instruction include lecture (76 hours), lab (4 hours), and examinations (12 hours).

Credit Recommendation: In the lower division baccalaureate/associate degree

category, 3 semester hours in General Physics (1/92).

Introduction to Reactor Physics

Location: Turkey Point Nuclear Plant.

Length: 52 hours (3 weeks).

Dates: January 1985-January 1997.

Objective: To provide instruction for the fundamentals of reactor physics.

Learning Outcome: Upon successful completion of this course, the student will be able to describe the fundamental properties of matter and energy; determine the structure of an atomic nucleus and the activity of radioactive material; describe nuclear reactions, neutron-induced fission, neutron diffusion theory and neutron slowing down; determine the significance of each quantity in the six-factor equation to criticality, subcriticality, and supercriticality; estimate reactivity changes; and determine causes of transients.

Instruction: Major topics covered in the course are nuclear reactions, neutron physics, reactor physics, reactor kinetics, neutron sources, and reactor theory. Methods of instruction include lecture, classroom exercises, and examinations.

Credit Recommendation: In the lower division baccalaureate/associate degree category, 2 semester hours in Nuclear Technology (1/92).

Main Steam System

Location: Florida Power and Light, St. Lucie Nuclear Plant.

Length: 52 hours (2 weeks).

Dates: January 1986-April 1997.

Objective: To introduce the student to the main steam system, steam generators, and the associated subsystems. Emphasis is placed on design basis and system response under normal and abnormal conditions.

Learning Outcome: Upon successful completion of this course, the student will be able to state functions of components, flowpaths, operating parameters, and limiting conditions; draw one-line diagrams; and explain technical specifications basis for the main steam system and all subsystems.

Instruction: Major topics covered in the course are main steam, auxiliary steam, steam extraction systems and their associated subsystems and components; steam generators; steam generator blowdown system; and blowdown cooling system. Methods of instruction include lecture, classroom exercises, and exams.

Credit Recommendation: In the lower division baccalaureate/associate degree category, 1 semester hour in Nuclear Technology (4/92).

Main Steam System

Location: Turkey Point Nuclear Plant.

Length: 40 hours (2 weeks).

Dates: January 1985-January 1997.

Objective: To introduce the student to the main steam system and the associated subsystems. Emphasis is placed on system design basis and system response to design basis accidents.

Learning Outcome: Upon successful completion of this course, the student will be able to state functions of components, flowpaths, operating parameters, and limiting conditions; draw one-line diagrams; and explain technical specification basis for the main steam system and all subsystems.

Instruction: Major topics covered in the course are the steam generator, steam generator blowdown system, steam generator wet layup, secondary wet layup and feedwater recirculation systems, main and extraction steam, and steam dump system. Methods of instruction include lecture, inclass exercises, and examinations.

Credit Recommendation: In the lower division baccalaureate/associate degree category, 1 semester hour in Nuclear Technology (1/92).

Nuclear Engineering Safeguards

Location: Florida Power and Light, St. Lucie Nuclear Plant.

Length: 184 hours (8 weeks).

Dates: January 1986-April 1997.

Objective: To provide the student with an understanding of the engineered safeguards systems including all major subsystems, flowpaths, components, and operating principles. Normal, off-normal, and emergency operation of these engineered safety features is emphasized.

Learning Outcome: Upon successful completion of this course, the student will be able to identify components, draw flowpaths, state functions, explain system interfaces, explain technical specification bases, limiting conditions for operation, precautions and limitations associated with the operation of the various engineered safeguards systems, and analyze case studies of industry operating experiences.

Instruction: Major topics covered in the course are emergency core cooling, containment heat removal, component cooling water, reactor protection, auxiliary feedwater and auxiliary feedwater actuation systems; plant electrical power distribution and diesel generators; and industry operating experience. Methods of instruction include lecture, classroom exercises, and exams.

Credit Recommendation: In the lower division baccalaureate/associate degree category, 3 semester hours in Nuclear Technology (4/92).

Nuclear Engineering Safeguards

Location: Turkey Point Nuclear Plant.

Length: 84 hours (4 weeks).

Dates: January 1985-January 1997.

Objective: To provide the student with an introduction to nuclear power plant engineered safeguard systems. Emphasis is placed on the design basis of such systems throughout the course.

Learning Outcome: Upon successful completion of this course, the student will be able to identify components; draw flowpaths; state functions; explain system interfaces; and explain technical specification basis for the various engineered safeguard systems.

Instruction: Major topics covered in the course are the components, flowpaths, instrumentation, and controls for the following engineered safeguards systems: emergency core cooling, auxiliary feedwater, containment, emergency diesel generator, component cooling, and reactor protection and safeguard actuation systems. Methods of instruction include lecture, classroom exercises, and examinations.

Credit Recommendation: In the lower division baccalaureate/associate degree category, 2 semester hours in Nuclear Technology (1/92).

Nuclear Reactor Engineering

Location: Florida Power and Light, St. Lucie Nuclear Plant.

Length: 96 hours (5 weeks).

Dates: January 1986-April 1997.

Objective: To introduce the student to the concepts and theories that are the foundation of nuclear reactor engineering. The physics/kinetics associated with nuclear reactor operation and the steady state and transient reactor are presented.

Learning Outcome: Upon successful completion of this course, the student will be able to define and discuss concepts of neutron generation and multiplication and calculate reactivity and its effect on power level; define and discuss negative and positive effects of reactivity; and calculate decay heat and understand its effect on a nuclear reactor.

Instruction: Major topics covered in the course are microscopic and macroscopic cross sections; four-factor equation and reactivity; xenon and samarium poisons; burnable poisons; control rods and rod worth; flux shape and thin interaction, reactivity and reactivity coefficients; point kinetics using an effective neutron generation lifetime; criticality and subcritical multiplication; decay heat and its impact on a nuclear power plant; shutdown margin; burnup; and control rod action. Methods of instruction include lecture, self-study, exams, and laboratory.

Credit Recommendation: In the lower division baccalaureate/associate degree category, 3 semester hours in Nuclear Technology (4/92).

Nuclear Reactor Engineering

Location: Turkey Point Nuclear Plant.

Length: 64 hours (4 weeks).

Dates: January 1985-January 1997.

Objective: To provide an understanding of the fundamental principles of nuclear reactor engineering.

Learning Outcome: Upon successful completion of this course, the student will be able to describe the construction, materials, and design considerations of a nuclear reactor core; calculate reactivity, changes in reactivity and power defect; explain self-shielding, fuel and moderator temperature effects; and core life.

Instruction: Major topics covered in the course are construction of pressurized water reactor cores, reactivity and fuel temperature effects, moderate temperature coefficient, total power defect, fission product poisoning, chemical shim and rod control, shutdown reactivity, and power distribution. Methods of instruction include lecture, self-study, and examinations.

Credit Recommendation: In the lower division baccalaureate/associate degree category, 2 semester hours in Nuclear Technology (1/92).

Nuclear Reactor Physics

Location: Florida Power and Light, St. Lucie Nuclear Plant.

Length: 40 hours (2 weeks).

Dates: January 1986-April 1997.

Objective: To introduce the student to nuclear reactor physics fundamentals. The course covers basic nuclear physics through nuclear reactor kinetics in a qualitative way. The student is expected to apply the principles to several common transients of the operating nuclear reactor.

Learning Outcome: Upon successful completion of this course, the student will be able to discuss the basic structure of the atom, radioactive decay, calculate mass deficit and isotope concentration due to radioactive decay; discuss the common modes of interaction with matter; and calculate neutron cross sections and interaction rates.

Instruction: Major topics covered in the course are basic modern and nuclear physics topics: atomic structure, nuclear stability; decay modes; interactions of radiation with matter; nuclear reactions; neutron physics; neutron life cycle; reactor kinetics; and reactivity. Methods of instruction include lecture, self-study, and exams.

Credit Recommendation: In the lower division baccalaureate/associate degree category, 1 semester hour in Nuclear Science (4/92).

Nuclear Reactor Systems

Location: Florida Power and Light, St. Lucie Nuclear Plant.

Length: 124 hours (5 weeks).

Dates: January 1986-April 1997.

Objective: To provide the student with an understanding of the purpose, design, and operational characteristics of the nuclear reactor systems.

Learning Outcome: Upon successful completion of this course, the student will be able to state functions and operating limitations; identify components and operating parameters; draw simplified diagrams; explain the basis of technical specifications; predict various outcomes; and analyze indications for the various primary systems.

Instruction: Major topics covered in the course are reactor coolant system; reactor vessel and internals; chemical volume and control system; primary sampling system; nuclear instrumentation system; reactor regulating system; and control element drive and display system. Methods of instruction include lecture, classroom exercises, and exams.

Credit Recommendation: In the lower division baccalaureate/associate degree category, 2 semester hours in Nuclear Technology (4/92).

Nuclear Reactor Systems

Location: Turkey Point Nuclear Plant.

Length: 60 hours (3 weeks).

Dates: January 1985-January 1997.

Objective: To provide the student with an understanding of the nuclear reactor coolant system and the associated components, instrumentation, operating procedures, technical specifications, and the basis for technical specifications.

Learning Outcome: Upon successful completion of this course, the student will be able to state functions and operating limitations, identify components and operating parameters, draw simplified diagrams, and explain the basis of the technical specifications for the various primary systems.

Instruction: Major topics covered in the course are the reactor vessel and internals, incore and excore instrumentation, rod control and position indication system, reactor coolant system, pressurizer and relief system, and fuel handling. Methods of instruction include lecture, classroom exercises, and examination.

Credit Recommendation: In the lower division baccalaureate/associate degree category, 1 semester hour in Nuclear Technology (1/92).

Plant Support Systems

Location: Florida Power and Light, St. Lucie Nuclear Plant.

Length: 80 hours (3 weeks).

Dates: January 1986-April 1997.

Objective: To provide the student with an introduction to important support systems that are essential in providing safe operating conditions at a nuclear generating plant.

Learning Outcome: Upon successful completion of this course, the student will be able to describe components, state functions, specify flowpaths, state parameters, and explain the interfacing of the various plant support systems.

Instruction: Major topics covered in the course are water supply systems, air supply systems, plant ventilation systems, and instrument air supply. Methods of instruction include lecture and laboratory.

Credit Recommendation: In the lower division baccalaureate/associate degree category, 1 semester hour in Nuclear Technology (4/92).

Plant Support Systems

Location: Turkey Point Nuclear Plant.

Length: 60 hours (3 weeks).

Dates: January 1985-January 1997.

Objective: To provide the student with an introduction to certain nuclear plant support systems that are essential in providing safe operating conditions at a nuclear generating plant.

Learning Outcome: Upon successful completion of this course, the student will be able to describe components, state functions, specify flowpaths, state parameters, and explain the interfacing of the various plant support systems.

Instruction: Major topics covered in the course are the following support systems: main power distribution; instrument air, 120 volt AC and 125 volt DC, fire and service water, waste disposal, and lube and service water. Methods of instruction include lecture, classroom exercises, and examinations.

Credit Recommendation: In the lower division baccalaureate/associate degree category, 1 semester hour in Nuclear Technology (1/92).

Precalculus

Location: Florida Power and Light, St. Lucie Nuclear Plant.

Length: 100 hours (5 weeks).

Dates: January 1986-April 1997.

Objective: To provide the student with an introduction to basic algebra and trigonometry.

Learning Outcome: Upon successful completion of this course, the student will be able to solve linear, quadratic, exponential, and logarithmic equations; solve systems of linear equations; define trigonometric functions, use trigonometric functions to solve triangles; and graph trigonometric functions.

Instruction: Major topics covered in the course are algebraic expressions; solving and graphing linear, polynomial, exponential, and logarithmic equations; systems of linear equations; vectors; and trigonometric functions and use of trigonometric functions to solve problems involving triangles. Methods of instruction include lecture, self-study, and exams.

Credit Recommendation: In the lower division baccalaureate/associate degree category, 3 semester hours in Mathematics (basic algebra and trigonometry) (4/92).

Precalculus

Location: Turkey Point Nuclear Plant.

Length: 92 hours (5 weeks).

Dates: January 1987-January 1997.

Objective: To provide the student with an introduction to basic algebra and trigonometry.

Learning Outcome: Upon successful completion of this course, the student will be able to solve systems of linear equations, quadratic equations, use the laws of trigonometry to solve right and oblique triangles, and graph trigonometric functions.

Instruction: Major topics covered in the course are logarithms, trigonometry, vectors, introductory algebra, systems of linear equations, quadratic equations, and graphs of functions. Methods of instruction include lecture and examinations.

Credit Recommendation: In the lower division baccalaureate/associate degree category, 3 semester hours in Mathematics (Basic Algebra and Trigonometry) (1/92).

Principles of Chemistry and Materials Science

Location: Florida Power and Light, St. Lucie Nuclear Plant.

Length: 76 hours (4 weeks).

Dates: January 1986-April 1997.

Objective: To provide the student with an understanding of the fundamental principles of inorganic chemistry, physical chemistry, and materials science.

Learning Outcome: Upon successful completion of this course, the student will be able to discuss atomic structure, bonding, the periodic table, compound formation, phase changes, properties of materials, electrochemistry and corrosion, balance chemical equations, and calculate pH.

Instruction: Major topics covered in the course are atomic structure, compounds, bonding, the periodic table, balancing equations, solutions, pH, gas laws, phase changes, specific heats, electrochemistry, corrosion, and mechanical properties of solids. Methods of instruction include lecture and self-study.

Credit Recommendation: In the lower division baccalaureate/associate degree category, 3 semester hours in Chemistry (4/92).

Principles of Chemistry and Materials Science

Location: Turkey Point Nuclear Plant.

Length: 52 hours (3 weeks).

Dates: January 1987-January 1997.

Objective: To provide the student with an understanding of the fundamental principles of inorganic chemistry, physical chemistry, and materials science.

Learning Outcome: Upon successful completion of this course, the student will be able to discuss atomic structure, compound formation, chemical bonding, the periodic table, and ideal gas law; use Dalton's law; calculate the pH; and discuss the properties of metals and neutron effects on metals.

Instruction: Major topics covered in the course are measurements (English, metric system), atomic structure and periodic table, chemical bonds, gas laws, electrolytes and solutions, and fundamentals of material science (metallic bond, defects, deformation, fracture). Methods of instruction include lecture, self-study, and examinations.

Credit Recommendation: In the lower division baccalaureate/associate degree category, 2 semester hours in Chemistry (1/92).

Principles of Radiation Protection

Location: Florida Power and Light, St. Lucie Nuclear Plant.

Length: 56 hours (3 weeks).

Dates: January 1986-April 1997.

Objective: To provide the student with an understanding of radiation, effects on humans, radiation measurement, and radiation protection.

Learning Outcome: Upon successful completion of this course, the student will be able to calculate radiation doses and effects of shielding, explain the operation of radiation detection instruments and operating characteristics, and describe the monitoring of radiation within the nuclear plant.

Instruction: Major topics covered in the course are radiation units, radiation dose, biological effects, principles of operation of radiation detectors, radiation protection, and in-plant monitoring. Methods of instruction include lecture and self-study.

Credit Recommendation: In the lower division baccalaureate/associate degree category, 2 semester hours in Nuclear Science (4/92).

Principles of Radiation Protection

Location: Turkey Point Nuclear Plant.

Length: 28 hours (2 weeks).

Dates: January 1985-January 1997.

Objective: To provide the student with fundamental knowledge of the properties and effects of ionizing radiations and of radiation protection practices.

Learning Outcome: Upon successful completion of this course, the student will have an understanding of physical and biological effects of ionizing radiations; radiation detection and detectors; and radiation standards. Students will be able to detect and suggest control measures for radioactive contamination.

Instruction: Major topics covered in the course are types of ionizing radiation, radiation protection standards, radiation detection and detectors, and interactions of ionizing radiations with matter. Methods of instruction include lecture and examinations.

Credit Recommendation: In the lower division baccalaureate/associate degree category, 1 semester hour in Nuclear Science (1/92).

Solid, Liquid, and Gaseous Waste Systems

Location: Florida Power and Light, St. Lucie Nuclear Plant.
Length: 84 hours (3 weeks).
Dates: January 1986-April 1997.
Objective: To provide the student with a detailed knowledge of the various nuclear power plant solid, liquid, and gaseous waste systems and the nuclear fuel handling system.
Learning Outcome: Upon successful completion of this course, the student will be able to state purposes and functions, describe flowpaths, and describe the design features, associated controls, alarms, and operational parameters and characteristics of the various plant systems.
Instruction: Major topics covered in the course are sewage treatment plant; liquid, solid, and gaseous waste systems; fuel pool cooling and purification; and nuclear fuel handling system. Methods of instruction include lecture, classroom exercises, and exams.
Credit Recommendation: In the lower division baccalaureate/associate degree category, 1 semester hour in Nuclear Technology (4/92).

Thermodynamics

Location: Florida Power and Light, St. Lucie Nuclear Plant.
Length: 36 hours (2 weeks).
Dates: January 1986-April 1997.
Objective: To introduce the student to the first and second laws of thermodynamics and their applications to a power plant steam cycle. The student will be able to apply these principles to future discussions regarding the operation of a nuclear/steam system.
Learning Outcome: Upon successful completion of this course, the student will be able to describe and define the various states and power plant processes of steam/water on a pressure/temperature, temperature water/entropy or enthalpy/entropy or other appropriate diagram, and use the first and second laws of thermodynamics in describing power plant component function and calculating heat load.
Instruction: Major topics covered in the course are basic principles of thermodynamic units and properties, microscopic and macroscopic concepts of temperature and heat, basic principles and processes of pressure-volume-temperature diagrams, steam tables and Mollier diagrams, rudimentary control mass and control volume analysis, and the application of all these concepts to the steam power cycle. Methods of instruction include lecture, self-study, and exams.
Credit Recommendation: In the lower division baccalaureate/associate degree category, 1 semester hour in Engineering Technology (4/92).

Thermodynamics

Location: Turkey Point Nuclear Plant.
Length: 76 hours (4 weeks).
Dates: January 1985-January 1997.
Objective: To introduce the student to the fundamental laws of thermodynamics and their applications to heat transfer and fluid flow. Throughout this course the student will be expected to apply what he or she has learned to the operation of a pressurized water reactor, nuclear/steam power plant.
Learning Outcome: Upon successful completion of this course, the student will be able to describe the basic sequence of energy transfers and energy conversions from the fission of nuclear fuel to the production of electricity within a pressurized water reactor system; apply theory to solve heat transfer and fluid flow problems; identify the major components of the steam generator; and discuss the relationship between thermodynamics and pressurized water reactor efficiency.
Instruction: Major topics covered in the course are thermodynamics, heat transfer, and fluid flow as they apply to steam cycles and electric power production; applying theoretical concepts to actual plant components and systems; and the ability to predict overall plant response to single parameter or component modifications. Methods of instruction include lecture, exercises, and examinations.
Credit Recommendation: In the lower division baccalaureate/associate degree category, 3 semester hours in Nuclear Technology (1/92).

Turbine and Generator

Location: Florida Power and Light, St. Lucie Nuclear Plant.
Length: 48 hours (3 weeks).
Dates: January 1986-April 1997.
Objective: To introduce the student to the main turbine, generator, and associated subsystems with emphasis on design bases, operation, and interrelationships with other plant systems.
Learning Outcome: Upon successful completion of this course, the student will be able to state functions and operating parameters, precautions, limitations, flowpaths, and explain related system interrelationships for the various components of the turbine/generator system.
Instruction: Major topics covered in the course are main turbine, main generator and exciter, compressed gas, and turbine cooling water. Methods of instruction include lecture, classroom exercises, and self-study.
Credit Recommendation: In the lower division baccalaureate/associate degree category, 1 semester hour in Nuclear Technology (4/92).

Turbine and Generator System

Location: Turkey Point Nuclear Plant.
Length: 40 hours (2 weeks).
Dates: January 1985-January 1997.
Objective: To provide the student with an introduction to the components of the turbine/generator system at a nuclear generating plant.
Learning Outcome: Upon successful completion of this course, the student will be able to state functions, operating parameters, precautions and limitations, and flowpaths and explain related system interfaces for the components of the turbine/generator system.
Instruction: Major topics covered in the course are main turbine control; turbine, turbine oil and gland seal system; turbine plant cooling system; and main generator and control system. Methods of instruction include lecture, classroom exercises, and examination.
Credit Recommendation: In the lower division baccalaureate/associate degree category, 1 semester hour in Nuclear Technology (1/92).

General Physics Corporation

General Physics is a high technology training company that assists utility, commercial, and government clients in achieving the maximum effectiveness of their personnel, equipment, and facilities. The Instructional Services Department is responsible for providing instructional services and courses to their clients in addition to providing instructional services internal to General Physics personnel.

The Instructional Services Department of General Physics provides training courses and services that cover a wide range of the skills needed by professional trainers. These courses and services are provided by professional instructors who have extensive experience in all aspects of instructional skills training and related projects. Their experienced instructional technologists and curriculum designers ensure that training programs and materials developed by General Physics incorporate the most advanced instructional technology available.

The primary goal of the Instructional Services Department is to provide an organization's training personnel with the skills to design, develop, and implement performance-based training programs and courses. The Instructional Services Department uses Instructional Systems Design (ISD) model that covers analysis, design, development, implementation, and evaluation for the training curriculum.

Source of official student records: Registry of Credit Recommendations, American Council on Education, One Dupont Circle, Washington, DC 20036-1193 or General Physics Corporation, Instructional Services Department, Department Director, 6700 Alexander Bell Drive, Columbia, MD 21046.

Additional information about the courses: College Credit Recommendation Service, American Council on Education, One Dupont Circle, Washington, DC 20036-1193.

Advanced Instructional Design (H 909)

Location: Columbia, MD, and other regional locations.

Length: 24 hours (3 days).

Dates: January 1990-January 1997.

Objective: To provide knowledge, skills, and practice in concepts and techniques in advanced instructional design.

Learning Outcome: Upon successful completion of this course, the student will be able to design advanced instructional activities using objectives that are appropriate for the various hierarchies of learning.

Instruction: Major topics covered in the course are learning objectives as they relate to a variety of training methods; learning principles; acquisition of knowledge; attitudes and values; and selecting and designing participative learning activities. Methods of instruction include lecture, discussion, small group exercises, and individual projects.

Credit Recommendation: In the upper division baccalaureate degree category, 2 semester hours in Education or Psychology of Learning (1/91).

Basic Instructional Techniques (H 995)

Location: Client sites only.

Length: 40 hours (1 week).

Dates: January 1990-January 1997.

Objective: To provide potential instructors with necessary skills to design and implement an instructional program using materials they develop.

Learning Outcome: Upon successful completion of this course, the student will be able to design, develop, and present instructional materials.

Instruction: Major topics covered in the course are role of the instructor, overview of the instructional system design process, learning process of the adult learner, training analysis, writing objectives, designing lessons, classroom management, instructional methods and presentation skills, training aids, and evaluation. Methods of instruction include lecture, discussion, classroom exercises, and student projects.

Credit Recommendation: In the upper division baccalaureate degree category, 3 semester hours in Educational Methods (1/91).

Designing and Developing Training Programs (H 997)

Location: Columbia, MD, and other regional locations.

Length: 40 hours (1 week).

Dates: January 1990-January 1997.

Objective: To provide detailed information about the instructional system design process as it applies to the analysis and design of classroom and self-study programs.

Learning Outcome: Upon successful completion of this course, the student will be able to design classroom and self-study programs applying the principles of instructional systems design.

Instruction: Major topics covered in the course are principles of instructional design, needs analysis, job and task analysis, writing analysis-based objectives, initial design, instructional analysis, test development, checklist design, lesson design, self-study lesson issues, and evaluation plans and results. Methods of instruction include lecture, discussion, small group exercises, and individual projects.

Credit Recommendation: In the lower division baccalaureate/associate degree category, 3 semester hours in Education or Instructional Design (1/91).

Fundamentals of Classroom Instruction (H 905)

Location: Columbia, MD, and other regional locations.

Length: 40 hours (1 week).

Dates: January 1990-January 1997.

Objective: To provide participants with experience in developing lesson plans and in planning instruction.

Learning Outcome: Upon successful completion of this course, the student will be able to deliver a lesson to satisfy the criteria in the lesson evaluation form; recognize characteristics of good instruction and instructors; explain the importance of each step of the learning process model; describe the function of instructional objectives; distinguish among knowledge, use of knowledge, and psychomotive objectives; describe types of lead-ins that help motivate lesson introduction; identify characteristics of an adult learner; list techniques that can motivate adult learners and gain their respect; describe effective ways to manage self, trainers, and classroom environment; ask and answer questions using proper questioning techniques; describe/plan strategies for presentation and practice of knowledge; explain instructional functions; state value of training aids; list different purposes of training evaluation; describe methods for evaluating trainees during classroom instruction; and state use of a lesson plan before, during, and after instruction.

Instruction: Major topics covered in the course are role of the instructor, learning process, preparing lesson plans, principles of adult learning, dealing with trainee stress and questioning techniques, and managing the classroom, training, and time. Participation manual and textbook are provided. Methods of instruction include lecture, group discussion, videotaped student presentation, and small group exercises.

Credit Recommendation: In the upper division baccalaureate degree category, 3 semester hours or in the graduate degree category, 1 semester hour in Education, Curriculum Design, Adult Education, or Administration and Supervision (1/91).

Fundamentals of Classroom Instruction (H 904)

Location: Columbia, MD, and other regional locations.

Length: 28 hours (3.5 days).

Dates: January 1990-January 1997.

Objective: To enable the student from business or industry, with little or no formal classroom instructional experience, and deliver instruction in his or her area of expertise.

Learning Outcome: Upon successful completion of this course, the student will be able to describe the learning process; introduce lessons effectively with introductory lead-ins; develop instructional objectives; understand the importance of managing self in order to manage training; discuss rationale for managing training; prepare self for teaching; use one or more methods of training aids; and deliver a lesson to satisfy the criteria for a lesson evaluation form.

Instruction: Major topics covered in the course are the learning process, objectives, lesson introductions, classroom management, questioning techniques, instructional methods, training aids, and using lesson plans. Methods of instruction include lecture, discussion, small and large group exercises, and videotaped presentations.

Credit Recommendation: In the upper division baccalaureate degree category, 1 semester hour in Education (1/91). **NOTE**: If taken with Principles of Instructional Design, 3 semester hours in the upper division baccalaureate degree category or 1 semester hour in the graduate degree category in Education should be awarded (1/91).

On-The-Job Training Skills

Location: Columbia, MD, and other regional locations.

Length: *Version 1*: 16 hours (2 days); *Version 2*: 24 hours (3 days).

Dates: January 1990-January 1997.

Objective: To provide first time supervisors with design and implementation skills needed for employee training and evaluation phases of on-the-job training programs.

Learning Outcome: Upon successful completion of this course, the student will be able to demonstrate how to design and implement on-the-job training programs.

Instruction: *Version 1*: Major topics covered in the course are overview of on-the-job training, program design, implementation and evaluation, and general adult learning concept. *Version 2*: Major topics covered in the course are an on-the-job training demonstration and employee evaluation, which is videotaped and critiqued. Methods of instruction include lecture, discussion, and individual participant projects associated with developing on-the-job training and evaluation materials.

Credit Recommendation: *Version 1:* If taken in combination with Principles of Instructional Design, in the lower division baccalaureate/associate degree category, 1 semester hour in Education or Instructional Technology (1/91). *Version 2:* In the lower division baccalaureate/associate degree category, 1 semester hour in Education or Instructional Technology (1/91).

Principles of Instructional Design (H 903)

Location: Columbia, MD, and other regional locations.

Length: 24 hours (3 days).

Dates: January 1990-January 1997.

Objective: To provide the new course developer in business and industry with the knowledge and skills needed to design and deliver courses successfully and effectively.

Learning Outcome: Upon successful completion of this course, the student will be able to discuss the purposes of using the Instructional Systems Development model; write instructional objectives; design and develop effective lesson plans; use training materials with the Instructional Systems Development model; describe the types of training analysis and their value in lesson plan development; and describe different types of training aids and their uses.

Instruction: Major topics covered in the course are the instructional systems development process, analysis, objectives, lesson design and development, training aids, and lesson evaluation and revision. The course is designed for personnel in business and industry who have little experience in training and are responsible for developing instructional materials. Methods of instruction include lecture, discussion, small group exercises, and individual projects.

Credit Recommendation: In the upper division baccalaureate degree category, 2 semester hours, when Task Analysis or Fundamentals of Classroom Instruction (3.5 or 5-day version) is also completed, in Education, Human Resource Development, Human Resource Management, or Instructional Design/Curriculum or in the graduate degree category, 1 semester hour, when Fundamentals of Classroom Instruction (3.5 or 5-day version) is also completed (1/91).

Quality Control of Training

Location: Columbia, MD, and other regional locations.

Length: 16 hours (2 days).

Dates: January 1990-January 1997.

Objective: To provide participants with techniques and methods to assess and evaluate all aspects of training (e.g., systems, media, students, and instructors).

Learning Outcome: Upon successful completion of this course, the student will be able to plan and prepare a systematic approach to evaluate training; conduct a training program analysis; initiate appropriate actions; demonstrate knowledge of several strategies for evaluating training; and link training objectives and goals to output.

Instruction: Major topics covered in the course are training assessment, training systems, and evaluation and quality control. Methods of instruction are lecture, discussion, group exercises, and individual projects.

Credit Recommendation: In the upper division baccalaureate degree category, 1 semester hour in Training Evaluation or Curriculum Evaluation (1/91).

Supervising and Managing Training

Location: Columbia, MD, and other regional locations.

Length: 40 hours (1 week).

Dates: January 1990-January 1997.

Objective: To provide managers and supervisors with an overview of tasks required in maintaining and operating a training system and specific training components within an organization.

Learning Outcome: Upon successful completion of this course, the student will be able to integrate training system programs into larger organizational goals and objectives, and gain a general understanding of training system management and be able to complete higher level courses.

Instruction: Major topics covered in the course are overview of maintaining a training system program within an organization, evaluation, analysis, management, and cost benefit assessment of training components and systems. Course provides only an overview of training programs.

Methods of instruction include lecture, discussion, case studies, and small group and individual exercises.

Credit Recommendation: In the lower division baccalaureate/associate degree category, 2 semester hours in Introduction to Training (1/91).

Task Analysis (Analysis)

Location: Columbia, MD, and other regional locations.

Length: 40 hours (1 week).

Dates: January 1990-January 1997.

Objective: To provide participants with exposure and practice in techniques of task, needs, and job analysis, so they can gather complete and accurate information for use in designing performance-based training.

Learning Outcome: Upon successful completion of this course, the student will be able to conduct a task analysis for use in designing performance-based training and collect data through needs analysis and job analysis that will assist in designing performance-based training programs.

Instruction: Major topics covered in the course are an overview of a performance-based training model, analysis of data collection techniques, roles and responsibilities in analysis, and how to conduct a task analysis, and how to integrate job analysis and needs assessment data in developing job performance objectives and measures. Methods of instruction include lecture, discussion, individual and small group exercises, and student projects.

Credit Recommendation: In the upper division baccalaureate degree category, 3 semester hours or in the graduate degree category, 1 semester hour in Educational Task Analysis, Special Topics in Task Analysis in Education, or School Psychology (1/91).

Test Development: Written and Performance Measures

Location: Columbia, MD, and other regional locations.

Length: 24 hours (3 days).

Dates: January 1990-January 1997.

Objective: To provide practice in using and developing various forms of teacher-made written and performance tests for evaluation of training.

Learning Outcome: Upon successful completion of this course, the student will be able to develop useful written test items and performance tests; develop and conduct objective evaluations of student performance on such instruments; and prepare properly for the administration and scoring of tests.

Instruction: Major topics covered in the course are content sampling, test item design, item analysis, essay question design, performance-based measurement task design, basic concept of test construction and measurement, and evaluating instruments. Methods of instruction include lecture, discussion, and small group exercises.

Credit Recommendation: In the upper division baccalaureate degree category, 2 semester hours in Test Development in Education or Instructional Design when Principles of Instructional Design is completed (1/91).

Graduate School of Banking at Colorado

The Graduate School of Banking at Colorado, established in 1950, provides a program of continuing education and research for practitioners in banking and finance. The student body is composed of bank officers, savings and loan officers, and officials of banking regulatory agencies.

The curriculum emphasizes policy and management problems; it focuses on the tools of bank management and the analytical framework within which general management problems can be recognized and solved. Course offerings are designed and coordinated by the president who works closely with faculty of practicing bankers, academicians, and other professionals. The curriculum is reviewed mainly by the Board of Trustees.

Attendance at three 2-week summer sessions conducted on the campus of the University of Colorado, participation in evening seminar programs, completion of extension work, and a passing grade on exams are required for graduation. Within each of the three course categories students are required to complete core courses and select from a variety of options. The evaluation, however, tests for knowledge in both core and elective areas. For evaluation purposes, courses offered throughout the three years of the program have been grouped together. Thus, students requesting credit must have completed the entire program.

All participants must pass an examination at the end of each annual session. Students also are required to complete three research projects for the first year and three for the second year. Successful completion of the examination and extension work is indicated on the student's record.

The recommendations listed below apply only to those who complete the total program and not to individual courses or sections.

Source of official student records: Registry of Credit Recommendations, American Council on Education, One Dupont Circle, Washington, DC 20036-1193 or Registrar, Graduate School of Banking at Colorado, University of Colorado, Campus Box 411, Boulder, CO 80309.

Additional information about the courses: College Credit Recommendation Service, American Council on Education, One Dupont Circle, Washington, DC 20036-1193.

Bank Lending
1. Agricultural Lending
2. Banking for the Small Business
3. Commercial Lending
4. Consumer Lending
5. Loan Workouts

Location: Graduate School of Banking at Colorado, University of Colorado, Boulder, CO.

Length: *Version 1*: 38 hours (5 days) for students with previous lending experience; 46 hours (1 week) for students with no previous lending experience; *Version 2:* 40 hours (5 days) for students with previous lending experience; 48 hours (1 week) for students with no previous lending experience.

Dates: *Version 1:* August 1988-November 1994; *Version 2:* December 1994-Present.

Objective: To provide an understanding of the basic concepts and practical application of current analytical techniques related to the lending function of a financial institution.

Learning Outcome: Upon successful completion of this course, the student will be able to cover differential credit analysis as it applies to ratios, benchmark, and strategies for borrowing and investing in the agriculture community; identify financial problems through case flow planning, analyzing the smaller companies need for growth; and produce sound loan proposals by using selected ratio concepts emphasizing the characteristics of term and revolving debt, and structuring loans.

Instruction: Major topics covered in the course are financial statement preparation, techniques of credit analysis, loan pricing decisions, short-term versus long-term debt structure, and commercial loan portfolio management. In addition, the student will elect from courses in agricultural lending, consumer lending, loan workouts, and financial analysis. Methods of instruction include lecture, discussion, cases, group processes, and computer simulation.

Credit Recommendation: *Version 1:* In the lower division baccalaureate/associate degree category, 2 semester hours in Bank Lending, Finance, or as a Business elective (4/89). *Version 2:* In the lower division baccalaureate/associate degree category, 3 semester hours in Bank Lending, Finance, or as a Business elective (2/94) (12/94). **NOTE:** In both versions 1 and 2, if student has had no prior experience in lending, the Basic Credit for Non-Lenders is required to earn this credit recommendation.

Management of Financial Institutions
1. Asset/Liability Management I and II
2. Business Condition Analysis
3. Business Law in Banking
4. Economics of Banking
5. Effective Decision Making
6. Financial Analysis
7. Financial Management of Banks
8. Investments and the Money Market
9. BankSim

Location: Graduate School of Banking at Colorado, University of Colorado, Boulder, CO.

Length: *Version 1*: 112 hours (2.5 weeks); *Version 2*: 116.5 hours (2.5 weeks).

Dates: *Version 1:* August 1988-November 1994; *Version 2:* December 1994-Present.

Objective: To explore the management of financial institutions in the context of basic and advanced problems encountered in the banking industry.

Learning Outcome: Upon successful completion of this course, the student will be able to identify and understand asset and liability management, financial reports, and effective managerial techniques; discuss practical methods of management planning and strategy; explain the principles of organization and organizational control; analyze static and dynamic GAP information; manage the bank's portfolio; evaluate different types of banking risk, overall strategic objectives, the role of the Federal Reserve, and legal concepts affecting modern day banking decisions; evaluate use of various liens as security of payment, suretyship, lender liability theories, and bank customer relationships under bankruptcy laws; and have full knowledge of the active operation of a commercial bank through the BankSim class.

Instruction: Major topics covered in the course are the legal aspects of banking, bank regulation, monetary policy, macroeconomics, interest rate behavior, strategic planning, bank investments, asset/liability management, and financial planning. It is recommended that students take the course Electronic Banking. Methods of instruction include lecture, discussion, cases, group processes, and computer simulation.

Credit Recommendation: *Version 1:* In the upper division baccalaureate degree category, 4 semester hours in Bank Management, Finance, or as a Business elective (4/89). *Version 2:* In the upper division baccalaureate degree category, 6 semester hours in Bank Management, Finance, or as a Business elective; or in the graduate degree category, 3 semester hours in Bank Management, Finance, or as a Business elective (2/94) (12/94).

Marketing Management
Version 1:
1. Banking Strategies of the 21st Century
2. Achieving Sustainable Competitive Advantage
3. Marketing Bank Services
4. New Business Development
Version 2:
1. Financial Management of Banks
2. From Manager to Leader: Four Great Lessons
3. Marketing Bank Services
4. Mutual Funds
5. New Business Development

Location: Graduate School of Banking at Colorado, University of Colorado, Boulder, CO.

Length: *Version 1*: 44.5 hours (5 days); *Version 2*: 47 hours (5 days).

Dates: *Version 1:* August 1988-January 1994; *Version 2:* February 1994-Present.

Objective: To provide an understanding of concepts and approaches to marketing management of financial institutions.

Learning Outcome: Upon successful completion of this course, the student will be able to understand the concept of marketing and its importance to the banking industry; discover principles of leadership, goal setting, team building, decision making, and communication; learn how to manage risk-versus-return, maximize shareholder value; review growth of mutual funds and how to retain the customers trust on investing; and have an overview of what must be done for a bank to become more sales business development minded including consultive selling, sales profiling, calling programs, customer relations, and cross selling.

Instruction: Major topics covered in the course are marketing bank services, planning as related to marketing bank services, developing new business, the environment within which marketing occurs, managing human resources, non-bank competitors in financial markets, and issues related to the quality of service. Students are recommended to take the course Quality of Service. Methods of instruction include lecture, discussion, cases, group processes, and computer simulation.

Credit Recommendation: *Version 1:* In the upper division baccalaureate degree category, 2 semester hours in Marketing, Marketing Management, or as a Business elective (4/89). *Version 2:* In the upper division baccalaureate degree category or in the graduate degree category, 3 semester hours in Marketing, Marketing Management, or as a Business elective (2/94) (12/94).

Hacienda La Puente Adult Education

Hacienda La Puente Unified School District Adult Education has been a pioneer in California as well as in the nation in providing a variety of educational and supportive services that seek to break down the barriers which prevent adults from returning to school. Since 1956, this school has sought to offer quality, timely instruction in a broad range of academic and vocational areas.

The Respiratory Therapy Technician Program of Hacienda La Puente Unified School District's Adult Education was established in 1971 and it has been in continuous operation since that time. Hacienda La Puente Adult Education is accredited by the Western Association of Schools and Colleges and the Respiratory Technician Program is fully accredited by Joint Review Committee for Respiratory Therapy Education.

Program Instructors are Registered Respiratory Therapists with many years of clinical experience in the field. In addition they are required to hold teaching certificates from the State of California.

This program is unique in that its format is modified open-entry, open-exit and self-paced allowing the students a great degree of flexibility in the pursuit of a certificate of completion.

The maximum amount of time allowed to complete this 1800 hour course is 20 months following official admittance to the Program. With the self-paced format, however, it is not unusual for students to complete the course of study in 12-16 months.

Graduates will possess the cognitive skills required to comprehend, apply and evaluate information relevant to respiratory care, the psychomotor skills and technical proficiency in all areas necessary to fulfill the role of an entry level practitioner and they will be able to demonstrate individual attitudes and behavior consistent with employer expectations of a respiratory care practitioner. In addition, successful completion of the Program qualifies the graduates to sit for the Certified Respiratory Therapy Technician Examination offered by the National Board of Respiratory Care.

Source of official student records: Registry of Credit Recommendations, American Council on Education, One Dupont Circle, Washington, DC 20036-1193.

Additional information about the courses: College Credit Recommendation Service, American Council on Education, One Dupont Circle, Washington, DC 20036-1193.

Respiratory Therapy Technician Program

Advance Respiratory Care Concepts

Location: La Puente, CA.

Length: 120 hours.

Dates: January 1986-Present.

Objective: To familiarize the student with the principles of mechanical ventilation. The use of positive-end expiratory pressure, special modes of mechanical ventilation, the concepts of weaning and hemodynamic monitoring.

Learning Outcome: Upon successful completion of this course, the student will be able to relate knowledge of cardiopulmonary physiology to mechanical ventilation; explain the principles of mechanical ventilators; perform patient assessment and monitoring; recognize complications associated with mechanical ventilation; describe the principles and procedures for implementing mechanical ventilation; PEEP, IMV, high-frequency ventilation and weaning.

Instruction: Major topics covered in the course are indications, monitoring and weaning for mechanical ventilation; special modes of mechanical ventilation; and hemodynamic monitoring. Methods of instruction include lecture, audio/visual material, independent study with supplemental lectures, video tapes, lab exercises, one on one tutorials , observations, tests, and a final examination.

Credit Recommendation: In the vocational certificate category or in the lower division baccalaureate/associate degree category, 6 semester hours in Advanced Respiratory Care (11/96).

Airway Management

Location: La Puente, CA.

Length: 60 hours.

Dates: January 1986-Present.

Objective: To establish an artificial airway, maintain and remove artificial airways, discuss laryngeal and tracheal complications, and airway maintenance.

Learning Outcome: Upon successful completion of this course, the student will be able to identify steps in intubation and extubation; identify equipment used in establishment and maintenance of airways; discuss airway suctioning and associated hazards; and complications of airway management.

Instruction: Major topics covered in the course are artificial airways and suctioning. Methods of instruction include lecture, audio/visual material, independent study with supplemental lectures, video tapes, lab exercises, one on one tutorials , observations, tests, and a final examination.

Credit Recommendation: In the lower division baccalaureate/associate degree category, 3 semester hours in Airway Management (11/96).

Bronchial Hygiene, Humidity, and Aerosol Therapy

Location: Independent Study/La Puente, CA.

Length: 30 hours(3 lessons and lab).

Dates: January 1986-Present.

Objective: To provide the student with a basic understanding of bronchial hygiene and the utilization of humidity and aerosol therapy to increase mobilization of retained secretions.

Learning Outcome: Upon successful completion of this course, the student will be able to describe normal mucociliary clearance; purposes of aerosol and humidity therapy; and set up various types of humidifies and nebulizers and discuss their clinical applications.

Instruction: Major topics covered in the course are mobilization of retained secretions, humidity and aerosol therapy, humidity and aerosol generators, and hazards of aerosol therapy. Methods of instruction include lecture, audio/visual material, independent study with supplemental lectures, video tapes, lab exercises, one on one tutorials , observations, tests, and a final examination.

Credit Recommendation: In the lower division baccalaureate/associate degree category, 2 semester hours in Humidity and Aerosol Therapy (11/96).

Cardiopulmonary Anatomy and Physiology

Location: Independent Study/La Puente, CA.

Length: 60 hours (3 units of study, plus lab).

Dates: January 1986-Present.

Objective: To provide the student with the necessary knowledge for the development of a basic understanding of the cardiopulmonary systems structure and function.

Learning Outcome: Upon successful completion of this course, the student will be able to describe the structure and function of the respiratory system and cardiovascular system, the normal dynamics of ventilation, and perfusion; describe blood and gas composition; and discuss normal and abnormal ECG's.

Instruction: Major topics covered in the course are pulmonary anatomy and physiology ; cardiovascular anatomy and physiology; physiology of external respiration; and ECG Lab. Methods of instruction include lecture, audio/visual material, computer-assisted instruction and independent study, lecture video tapes, computer programs, lab demonstrations , observations, tests, and a final examination .

Credit Recommendation: In the lower division baccalaureate/associate degree category, 3 semester hours in Cardiopulmonary Anatomy and Physiology (11/96).

Cardiopulmonary Diagnostics

Location: La Puente, CA.

Length: 60 hours.

Dates: January 1986-Present.

Objective: To familiarize the student with the use of arterial blood gases and pulmonary function testing in the evaluation of patients with cardiopulmonary disease; and how to administer tests, results, and interpret values.

Learning Outcome: Upon successful completion of this course, the student will be able to discuss the mechanism of oxygen and carbon dioxide transport; discuss the mechanism of acid-base balance; identify the body buffer systems; list abnormalities of acid-base balance; discuss techniques of blood gas sampling; identify the purpose of pulmonary function testing; and describe devices commonly used in pulmonary function testing.

Instruction: Major topics covered in the course are sampling; interpretation and application of arterial blood gas measurements; application and interpretation of pulmonary function testing. Methods of instruction include self-study, tests, and final examination .

Credit Recommendation: In the vocational certificate category or the lower division baccalaureate/associate degree category, 3 semester hours in General Care Clinical Rotation (11/96).

Critical Care Rotation

Location: La Puente, CA.

Length: 360 hours.

Dates: January 1986-Present.

Objective: To provide experience in the intensive care with respiratory care patients on the ventilator.

Learning Outcome: Upon successful completion of this course, the student will be able to review patient records; collect and evaluate clinical information; assess therapeutic plan; select, assemble, check and correct malfunction of equipment; assure cleanliness of equipment; educate patients; maintain airway; mobilize secretions; assure gas exchange; and assess patient response.

Instruction: Major topics covered in the course are clinical experience managing the intubated patient receiving mechanical ventilation. Methods of instruction include case studies, clinical experience, and observations.

Credit Recommendation: In the vocational certificate category or lower division baccalaureate/associate degree category, 6 semester hours in Cardiopulmonary Therapy (11/96).

Extended Care and Rehabilitation

Location: La Puente, CA.

Length: 40 hours (3 lessons).

Dates: January 1986-Present.

Objective: To provide the student with the necessary knowledge to function in a pulmonary rehabilitation program and provide respiratory care in the home setting.

Learning Outcome: Upon successful completion of this course, the student will be able to demonstrate a knowledge of the definition of pulmonary rehabilitation; discuss the rational for the techniques used in home care; discuss the concerns of the aging population; and describe assessment and rehabilitation of the older COPD patient in the extended care facility.

Instruction: Major topics covered in the course are home care; rehabilitation; and care of the older patient. Methods of instruction include lecture, audio/visual material, discussion, independent study, combined periodic lectures, video tapes, one on one tutorials, tests, and final examination .

Credit Recommendation: In the lower division baccalaureate/associate degree category, 1 semester hour in Extended Care and Pulmonary Rehabilitation (11/96).

General Anatomy and Physiology

Location: La Puente, CA.

Length: 120 hours.

Dates: January 1986-Present.

Objective: To describe the structure and function of cells, tissues, and organs, and to describe the skeletal, muscular, respiratory, circulatory, nervous, digestive, renal, endocrine, and reproductive systems.

Learning Outcome: Upon successful completion of this course, the student will be able to describe function of systems and understand three unifying themes: between physiology and anatomy, the interrelationship amongst the organ systems, and the relationship of each organ system to hemeostasis.

Instruction: Major topics covered in the course are basic chemistry; cells; tissues and membranes; integumentary system; skeletal system; muscular system; nervous system; senses; endocrine system; blood; heart; vascular system; lymphatic system; immunity; respiratory system; digestive system; body temperature and metabolism; urinary system; fluid-electrolyte and acid base balance; reproductive systems; and an introduction to microbiology and human disease. Methods of instruction include lecture, audiovisual material, computer-assisted instruction, bronchoscopy, autopsy, quizzes, and tests.

Credit Recommendation: In the lower division baccalaureate/associate degree category, 4 semester hours in Anatomy and Physiology (11/96).

General Care Clinical Rotation

Location: Area Hospitals/La Puente, CA.

Length: 240 hours.

Dates: January 1986-Present.

Objective: To produce a competent general care respiratory practitioner.

Learning Outcome: Upon successful completion of this course, the student will be able to collect and evaluate clinical information; assess patients therapeutic plan; select, assemble, check and correct malfunction of equipment; maintain airways; mobilize and remove secretions; assure ventilation and oxygenation; assess patient response and modify therapy based on patient response; initiate emergency resuscitation; maintain records; and patient educations.

Instruction: Major topics covered in the course are patient assessment oxygen and gas therapy; humidity and aerosol therapy; chest physiotherapy, IPPB and incentive devices; airway management; pharmacology infection control; and medical records. Methods of instruction include clinical rotation in area hospitals , observations , evaluation of psychomotors skills, and student/patient interaction.

Credit Recommendation: In the lower division baccalaureate/associate degree category, 4 semester hours in General Care Clinical Rotation (11/96).

Lung Expansion Therapy

Location: La Puente, CA.

Length: 60 hours.

Dates: January 1986-Present.

Objective: To familiarize the student with the procedures used in clinical practice to prevent or correct inadequate lung expansion and techniques for assisting the patient with sputum removal .

Learning Outcome: Upon successful completion of this course, the student will be able to discuss the indications, goals, contraindications, and complications of IPPB therapy; list the goals of incentive spirometry; describe the current procedures for performing incentive spirometry and IPPB therapy; list basis, goals, indications, hazards and contraindications for chest physiotherapy; and demonstrate procedure.

Instruction: Major topics covered in the course are IPPB; incentive spirometry; and chest physical therapy and bronchial hygiene. Methods of instruction include lecture, audio/visual material, independent study combined with periodic lectures, video tapes, one on one tutoring, practical labs, observations, tests, and a final examination .

Credit Recommendation: In the vocational certificate category or the lower division baccalaureate/associate degree category, 3 semester hours in General Care Clinical Rotation (11/96).

Medical Gas Therapy

Location: La Puente, CA.

Length: 60 hours (5 lessons and Lab).

Dates: January 1986-Present.

Objective: To provide the student with a basic understanding of Medical Gas Therapy including individual gas properties, delivery devices, indications, hazards, and precautions.

Learning Outcome: Upon successful completion of this course, the student will be able to describe the properties of medical gases including indication for utilization with emphasis on hazards and precautions; and exhibit the ability to assemble, test and properly utilize each device used in medical gas therapy.

Instruction: Major topics covered in the course are gas distribution systems including administrative; controlling and analyzing devices; and practical lab. Methods of instruction include lecture, audio/visual material, independent study combined with periodic lectures, video tapes, one on one tutoring, practical labs, observations, tests, and final examination.

Credit Recommendation: In the lower division baccalaureate/associate degree category, 2 semester hours in Medical Gas Therapy (11/96).

Medical Terminology

Location: La Puente, CA.

Length: 60 hours.

Dates: January 1986-Present.

Objective: To be able to build/interpret medical words from Greek and Latin prefixes, suffixes, word roots and combining forms.

Learning Outcome: Upon successful completion of this course, the student will be able to recognize medical words from the Greek and Latin parts; spell medical words correctly; use a medical dictionary; pronounce medical words correctly; and recall medical abbreviations and their meanings for medical terms and phrases.

Instruction: Major topics covered in the course are Greek, Latin, and English medical terms specific to human morbidity and wellness conditions. Methods of instruction include computer-assisted instruction, and tests.

Credit Recommendation: In the lower division baccalaureate/associate degree category, 2 semester hours in Medical Terminology (11/96).

Microbiology and Infection Control

Location: La Puente, CA.

Length: 40 hours.

Dates: January 1986-Present.

Objective: To describe the field of microbiology, recognize and describe disease causing organisms, identify methods of transmission of infectious organisms, the nature of nosocomial infections, and apply the principles of infection control.

Learning Outcome: Upon successful completion of this course, the student will be able to eliminate sources of pathogens, to control or prevent their spread, and utilize elements of effective surveillance programs to prevent nosocomal infections.

Instruction: Major topics covered in the course are principles of infection control; comparison of sterilization methods; capabilities of various disinfecting agents; levels of disinfection; and classification of microorganisms by cell type. Methods of instruction include lecture, peer tutoring, lab practicals, clinical experience, quizzes, and tests.

Credit Recommendation: In the lower division baccalaureate/associate degree category, 2 semester hours in Infection Control (11/96).

Neonatal

Location: Independent Study/ La Puente, CA.

Length: 40 hours (2 lessons).

Dates: January 1986-Present.

Objective: To provide the student with a basic understanding of normal neonatal development and respiratory therapy intervention in high risk neonates.

Learning Outcome: Upon successful completion of this course, the student will be able to discuss fetal respiratory anatomy and physiology; perform fetal and newborn monitoring and assessment; recognize and identify at risk neonates; identify elements of newborn resuscitation; and discuss neonatal intervention techniques including oxygen therapy, and mechanical ventilation.

Instruction: Major topics covered in the course are neonatal anatomy and physiology; and principles of neonatal care. Methods of instruction include lecture, audio/visual material, computer-assisted instruction, independent study combined with periodic lectures, video tapes, lab practicals, tests, and a final examination .

Credit Recommendation: In the lower division baccalaureate/associate degree category, 2 semester hours in Neonatal Respirating Care (11/96).

Oral Airway Management and CPR

Location: La Puente, CA.

Length: 30 hours.

Dates: January 1986-Present.

Objective: To compare, define, list, describe, and discuss oral airways, manual resusitators, and CPR for infants, children, and adults.

Learning Outcome: Upon successful completion of this course, the student will be able to computer CPR measures for infants, children, and adults; define cardiac arrest and clinical and biological death; list procedures of effective CPR; explain basics of life support measures; describe hazards and common errors of CPR; compare partial and complete airway obstruction; describe airway clearance procedures; discuss the types, indications, placement and hazards of oral airways; and describe the different types of manual resuscitators and application.

Instruction: Major topics covered in the course are oral airways; manual resuscitation; and CPR. Methods of instruction include discussion, classroom exercises, and oral practical exam.

Credit Recommendation: In the vocational certificate category or lower division baccalaureate degree category, 2 semester hours in Oral Airway Management (11/96).

Pathophysiology

Location: La Puente, CA.

Length: 60 hours.

Dates: January 1986-Present.

Objective: To familiarize the student with the more common cardiopulmonary diseases , etiology, pathophysiology, clinical features, and treatment for each disease.

Learning Outcome: Upon successful completion of this course, the student will be able to discuss respiratory diseases; define chronic obstructive, restrictive, and infectious pulmonary disease; describe pulmonary pathology due to trauma; and describe signs, symptoms, diagnostic testing, and management of pulmonary and related disease.

Instruction: Major topics covered in the course are emphysema; bronchitis; cystic fibrosis; asthma; bronchiectasis; pleural disorders; neuromuscular diseases; lung cancer; congestive heart failure; ARD; pneumonia; sleep apnea; tuberculosis; and pneumoconiosis. Methods of instruction include lecture, audio/visual material, computer-assisted instruction, independent study combined with periodic lectures, video tapes, tests, and a final examination.

Credit Recommendation: In the vocational certificate category or lower division baccalaureate/associate degree category, 4 semester hours in Pathophysiology of Respiratory Dz (11/96).

Patient Assessment

Location: La Puente, CA.

Length: 20 hours.

Dates: January 1986-Present.

Objective: To familiarize the student with the process of patient assessment and the skills of physical examination and chest film interpretation.

Learning Outcome: Upon successful completion of this course, the student will be able to describe the procedures for obtaining an accurate and useful history of a hospitalized patient; describe patient observation methods; demonstrate physical assessment of the chest; and explain usefulness of chest roentgenography in patient assessment and describe sputum analysis.

Instruction: Major topics covered in the course are inspection; palpation; percussion and auscultation of the chest; basic interpretation of the chest film; and sputum induction and analysis. Methods of instruction include lecture, audio/visual material, independent study with supplemental lectures, video tapes, lab exercises, one on one tutorials, observations, tests, and a final examination.

Credit Recommendation: In the vocational certificate category or lower division baccalaureate/associate degree category, 1 semester hour in Patient Assessment (11/96).

Pharmacology

Location: La Puente, CA.

Length: 30 hours.

Dates: January 1986-Present.

Objective: Unclear

Learning Outcome: Upon successful completion of this course, the student will be able to recognize and interpret components of a prescription; describe the correct procedures and rules for administering drugs; describe drug indications, contraindictions, and doses; identify routes and methods of drug administration; describe stimulation of bronchodilation and functions of alpha, beta-1 and beta-2 receptors; describe groups of drugs used in respiratory therapy and their intended effects and possible side effects; and discuss the name and function of related drugs commonly used in hospitals.

Instruction: Major topics covered in the course are adrenergic bronchodiltors, anticholinergic bronchodilators, methalxanthines, mucokinetic, wetting agents, antiviral, steroids. Methods of instruction include discussion, self-study, lecture, audio/visual material, on-on-one tutorials, lab exercises, and tests.

Credit Recommendation: In the lower division baccalaureate/associate degree category, 2 semester hours in Pharmacology (11/96).

Hampton Group, Inc.

The Hampton Group, Inc. was founded in 1986 and is dedicated to seminar training and consulting in project management. We also publish our associates' project management textbooks as well as providing a free information resource for project managers on the Internet, *The Projects Manager's Control Tower*, http://www.4pm.com.

We conduct project management training in 4-7 day seminars at our client's site as well as offering our courses on the Internet where students can train at their own pace and on their time schedule. With either delivery mechanism, the courses and learning objectives are identical: to provide practicing managers with the tools and techniques to effectively manage cross-functional corporate projects. All of our courses require advance preparation, homework and written demonstration that the student has mastered the learning objectives. This demonstration is through written exams or case studies where the course concepts and techniques are applied to real world project management situations.

Our faculty are all experienced project managers, who are credentialed to teach graduate level courses in business or project management at accredited U.S. universities. These faculty members also regularly conduct project management consulting assignments with major corporations which continually refines the relevance and "state-of-the-art" nature of our training programs.

Our students hold undergraduate degrees and are mid-career managers in a wide range of functional or technical disciplines who seek to add project management to their skill inventory.

Source of official student records: Registry of Credit Recommendations, American Council on Education, One Dupont Circle, Washington, DC, 20036-1193.

Additional information about the courses: College Credit Recommendation Service, American Council on Education, One Dupont Circle, Washington, DC, 20036-1193.

Managing Complex Projects

Location: Various sites in the United States and on the Internet.

Length: 32 hours (24 lecture and 8 supervised lab).

Dates: June 1994-Present.

Objective: To develop strategic objectives for complex organizational situations, utilize advanced project management software, charts and methods to plan and implement developed goals and to evaluate cost benefit relationships.

Learning Outcome: Upon successful completion of this course, the student will be able to break down broad goals into smaller tasks, strategically analyze situations, develop team leadership, and assess the political and competitive environment.

Instruction: Major topics covered in the course are measuring and quantifying trade-offs relating to risk and costs; measuring project success; team development; and resource allocation. Methods of instruction include lecture, discussion, classroom exercises, case studies, audio/visual material, computer-assisted instruction, learner presentations/reports, papers, test, reports, and a final examination.

Credit Recommendation: In the graduate degree category, 2 semester hours in Project Analysis and Development (11/96).

Managing Project Teams (0009)

Location: Various sites in the United States and on the Internet.

Length: 56 hours (7 full days, or on the Internet 4 months or less).

Dates: June 1993-Present.

Objective: To provide an introduction to the principles and concepts of project management.

Learning Outcome: Upon successful completion of this course, the student will be able to manage small to medium sized projects.

Instruction: Major topics covered in the course are project managers assessment of responsibility, accountability, and authority; acquiring skills in cross-functional management; and matching capability to project requirements. Methods of instruction include lecture, discussion, classroom exercises, audio/visual material, and a final examination.

Credit Recommendation: In the graduate degree category, 3 semester hours in Business Administration, Management, or Industrial or Organizational Psychology (11/96).

Project and Program Management: Matters of Money

Location: Various sites in the United States and on the Internet.

Length: 32 hours (4 days or no more than 4 months on the Internet).

Dates: January 1996-Present.

Objective: To provide an overview of how to select projects based upon financial criteria through the introduction to the concepts of capital budgeting and project investment selection and of how to calculate and use cash flow net present value, profitability index, discounted payback period, internal rates of return and other relevant tools.

Learning Outcome: Upon successful completion of this course, the student will be able to demonstrate a conceptual knowledge and analytical perspectives essential to resource allocation in project-based management and how to use financial and accounting specialists in planning and managing projects.

Instruction: Major topics covered in the course are strategic planning; financial analysis; financial risk analysis; and discounted cash flow. Methods of instruction include lecture, discussion, classroom exercises, case studies, audio/visual material, reports, and a final examination.

Credit Recommendation: In the graduate division degree category, 2 semester hours in Business Administration or Project Management (11/96).

Project and Program Management: Software, People, and Budgets

Location: Various sites in the United States and on the Internet.

Length: 32 hours (24 lecture and 8 supervised lab).

Dates: January 1996-Present.

Objective: To provide an introduction to the principles and concepts of project management utilizing computer software with focus on analyzing business situations, developing project objectives and incorporating personnel, schedules and budgets to achieve and measure defined goals.

Learning Outcome: Upon successful completion of this course, the student will be able to analyze business situations, develop strategies, design and integrate networks, create budgets, and track project performance.

Instruction: Major topics covered in the course are project planning; project software; budgeting; task scheduling and selecting and assigning personnel. Methods of instruction include lecture, discussion, classroom exercises, case studies, audio/visual material, computer-assisted instruction, learner presentations/reports, papers, tests, reports, and a final examination.

Credit Recommendation: In the graduate degree category, 1 semester hour in

Principles and Concepts of Project Management (11/96).

Project Management Certification Course

Location: Various sites in the United States and on the Internet.

Length: 24 hours (8 three hour sessions and no longer than 8 weeks on the Internet).

Dates: January 1996-Present.

Objective: To provide knowledge and integration of the eight major topics in the project management body of knowledge and to prepare students for the project management professional certification exam.

Learning Outcome: Upon successful completion of this course, the student will be able to demonstrate an in-depth understanding of the eight functional areas in project management and their interrelationships.

Instruction: Major topics covered in the course are human resource; contract and procurement; risk, cost, quality, time, scope; and communications management. Methods of instruction include lecture, discussion, tests and a final examination.

Credit Recommendation: In the graduate degree category, 1 semester hour in Business Administration or Project Management (11/96).

Project Management Strategy and Tactics

Location: Various sites in the United States and on the Internet.

Length: 32 hours (24 lecture and 8 supervised lab).

Dates: October 1994-Present.

Objective: To integrate the principles and concepts related to managing complex corporate projects and develop the necessary relationships required with management, politics and consumer demands.

Learning Outcome: Upon successful completion of this course, the student will be able to coordinate people and finances into a workable environment, and integrate techniques to accommodate complex project environments.

Instruction: Major topics covered in the course are cost/benefit analysis, organization change, and resource allocation. Methods of instruction include lecture, discussion, classroom exercises, case studies, audio/visual material, computer-assisted instruction, learner presentations/reports, observations, tests, papers, reports, and a final examination.

Credit Recommendation: In the graduate degree category, 2 semester hours in Project Management Strategy in Business Administration (11/96).

Project Risk Management

Location: Various sites in the United States and on the Internet.

Length: 30 hours (10 weeks or no longer than 4 months maximum on the Internet).

Dates: January 1995-Present.

Objective: To provide knowledge of the tools of identifying, quantifying and mitigating the risks in cross functional corporate projects.

Learning Outcome: Upon successful completion of this course, the student will be able to effectively apply to tools of project risk management.

Instruction: Major topics covered in the course are introduction to risk management; integration and general approach/definitions; risk management goals and methodology/response and documentation; contingency allowances; managing risk of the project environment; computer application of risk; risk management plans; dealing with risk management plans; and dealing with risk management in contracts. Methods of instruction include lecture, discussion, classroom exercises, case studies, learner presentations/reports, papers, reports, and a final examination.

Credit Recommendation: In the graduate degree category, 2 semester hours in Business Administration or Project Management (11/96).

Project-based Organizations (0001)

Location: Various sites in the United States and on the Internet.

Length: 92 hours (32 hours classroom, 60 hours out of class).

Dates: November 1994-Present.

Objective: To provide a set of conceptual skills to facilitate project managers successfully affect large scale change in organizations.

Learning Outcome: Upon successful completion of this course, the student will be able to analyze an organization's strengths and weaknesses for instituting an anticipated change, and to generate a change plan to that analysis.

Instruction: Major topics covered in the course are models of change; force field analysis; diagnosis of change capability; and application of eight transformational levels. Methods of instruction include lecture, discussion, classroom exercises, audio/visual material, papers, class participation, diary assignments, and group presentations.

Credit Recommendation: In the graduate degree category, 2 semester hours in Organizational Behavior, Industrial Psychology, and Introduction to Management (11/96).

Projects That Change Organizations (0008)

Location: Various sites in the United States and on the Internet.

Length: 32 hours (4 days or on Internet-no more than 4 months).

Dates: August 1993-Present.

Objective: To provide a set of conceptual skills to help project managers successfully affect large scale change in organization.

Learning Outcome: Upon successful completion of this course, the student will be able to analyze an organization's strengths and weaknesses in instituting an anticipation change, and to generate a change plan in response to that analysis.

Instruction: Major topics covered in the course are models of change; force field analysis; diagnosis of change capability; and application of eight transformational levels. Methods of instruction include lecture, discussion, classroom exercises, audio/visual material, and papers.

Credit Recommendation: In the graduate degree category, 2 semester hours in Industries Organizations, Business Administrations, or Organizational Psychology (11/96).

Hane Industrial Training

Hane Industrial Training is located in Terre Haute, Indiana, with a regional training center in Indianapolis, Indiana. The company is a leading provider of instructor led, hands-on technical training.

Hane Industrial Training was founded in 1979 by Dr. Craig Hane, a former college professor and a businessman. Dr. Hane has taught mathematics and electronics at Indiana State University and mathematics at Rose-Hulman Institute of Technology. The company has grown considerably since its founding and today has many full time instructors who have delivered dozens of courses to hundreds of clients and thousands of students in industry, the military, public utilities, government agencies, and institutions throughout North America.

Many Hane students are apprentices in various skilled trades. Also, a significant number are cross training from other areas. Students are typically mechanics, millwrights, electricians, electronic technicians, and other skilled workers, or who are in training to become skilled workers. Operators, supervisors, and maintenance managers frequently attend Hane courses too. Engineers take courses from time to time to learn practical, hands-on troubleshooting and repair skills.

Hane offers courses in the following areas: electrical/electronics, industrial motor drives, mechanical, hydraulic/pneumatic, preventive/predictive maintenance, and CNC/PLC troubleshooting, programmer, and operator.

Source of official student records: Registry of Credit Recommendations, American Council on Education, One Dupont Circle, Washington, DC 20036-1193.

Additional information about the courses: College Credit Recommendation Service, American Council on Education, One Dupont Circle, Washington, DC 22036-1193.

Advanced Troubleshooting of the GE-Fanuc Series 15 CNC (380)

Location: Hane clients' facilities or public workshops.

Length: 40 hours (5 days).

Dates: November 1997-Present.

Objective: To train students on how to diagnose problems with the GE-Fanuc Series 15 CNC, and to get it back on line quickly.

Learning Outcome: Upon successful completion of this course, the student will be able to restart by using both the short and long methods; format data; analyze circuit flow; recognize danger areas when working with memory; access key functions; upload and download parts programs; set-up communications between a PC and the CNC; and troubleshoot.

Instruction: Major topics covered in the course are a refresher of keep relays, Basic Machine Interface (BMI), communications between the PC and CNC, deadload, and troubleshooting. Methods of instruction include lecture, discussion, problem solving exercises, and hands-on labs.

Credit Recommendation: In the lower division baccalaureate/associate degree category, 2 semester hours in Industrial Controls (11/97).

Applying Troubleshooting to Industrial Hydraulic Systems (143) (Advanced Troubleshooting Hydraulic Equipment [HYT 300])

Location: Hane clients' facilities or public workshops.

Length: 40 hours (1 week).

Dates: November 1997-Present.

Objective: To provide the students with the ability to troubleshoot industrial hydraulic systems.

Learning Outcome: Upon successful completion of this course, the students will be able to troubleshoot hydraulic systems using prints of the equipment found in their plants; identify the pitfalls of installation procedures; determine why proportional valves fail and how to prevent failure; interpret from schematics the operation of logic and cartridge technology; read and interpret schematics to aid in troubleshooting; and demonstrate an understanding of servo valve technology and how to properly set up various types of servos.

Instruction: Major topics covered in the course are safety, troubleshooting techniques, formulas, directional valves, rectifier circuits, relief valves, check valves, modular stacks, mounting configuration, actuators, proportional valves technology, servo valves, pumps and control technology, logic control forces, filtration, fluid power graphical symbols, fluid power formulas, and definition of terms. Methods of instruction include lecture, discussion, classroom exercises, observations, pretest, lab exercises, and final examination.

Credit Recommendation: In the lower division baccalaureate/associate degree category, 2 semester hours in Fluid Power Technology (11/97).

Basic Operator Training for the GE-Fanuc Series 15 (382)

Location: Hane clients' facilities or public workshops.

Length: 40 hours (5 days).

Dates: November 1997-Present.

Objective: To train all skilled workers responsible for the GE-Fanuc Series 15 CNC how to properly operate this controller.

Learning Outcome: Upon successful completion of this course, the student will be able to select and use the automatic and manual modes of operation of the GE-Fanuc Series 15 CNC and to read a parts program and use signaling commands.

Instruction: Major topics covered in the course are automatic modes such as EDIT, MEM, MDI, and TAPE. Also, manual modes such as JOG, INC, and HND. Signaling commands such as SBK and DRN and optional skip block, axis operation, code systems, programs, and troubleshooting parameters and diagnostics. Methods of instruction include lecture, discussion, problem solving exercises, and hands-on labs.

Credit Recommendation: In the lower division baccalaureate/associate degree category, 2 semester hours in Basic CNC Operations (11/97).

Basic Programmer Training for the GE-Fanuc Series 15 CNC (384)

Location: Hane clients' facilities or public workshops.

Length: 40 hours (5 days).

Dates: November 1997-Present.

Objective: To train all skilled workers responsible for the GE-Fanuc Series 15 CNC how to properly program this controller.

Learning Outcome: Upon successful completion of this course, the student will be able to use, program, and troubleshoot the GE-Fanuc Series 15 CNC.

Instruction: Major topics covered in the course are practical functions and programs, operation, optional block skip, axis operation, code systems, programs, reading and saving programs, and troubleshooting parameters and diagnostics. Methods of instruction include lecture, discussion, problem solving exercises, and hands-on labs.

Credit Recommendation: In the lower division baccalaureate/associate degree

category, 2 semester hours in Industrial Controls (11/97).

Bearing Life Improvement (054)

Location: Hane clients' facilities or public workshops.

Length: 24 hours (5 days).

Dates: November 1997-Present.

Objective: To provide the student with the ability to diagnose the root cause of bearing failure, and to properly repair failed bearings.

Learning Outcome: Upon successful completion of this course, the student will be able to determine proper sizes of shafts and housings; measure straight and tapered shafts; perform mounting and dismounting of bearings; properly lubricate rolling bearings; monitor rolling bearings to prevent catastrophic failure; identify all types of bearing failures and how to prevent future failures; and rework large bearings.

Instruction: Major topics covered in the course are bearing fundamentals, bearing types, bearing seals, bearing shafts and housing fits, bearing mounting and dismounting, bearing lubrication, and bearing failures. Methods of instruction include lecture, discussion, problem solving exercises, and hands-on labs.

Credit Recommendation: In the lower division baccalaureate/associate degree category, 1 semester hour in Bearing Life Improvement or Mechanical Engineering (11/97).

Electrical Controls (203)

Location: Hane clients' facilities or public workshops.

Length: 40 hours (5 days).

Dates: November 1997-Present.

Objective: To provide the student with the knowledge of the fundamentals of electrical and electronic technology, and to train them in basic electrical and electronic troubleshooting and repair procedures.

Learning Outcome: Upon successful completion of this course, the student will be able to work safely with electricity; use instruments to take and calculate electrical readings; read and interpret electrical drawings and ladder diagrams; identify and test electrical components; and understand the basic principles of AC and DC motors.

Instruction: Major topics covered in the course are fundamental concepts, practical applications, units of measurement, circuits, components, circuit parts, ladder diagramming, and AC and DC motors. Methods of instruction include lecture, discussion, problem solving exercises, and hands-on labs.

Credit Recommendation: In the lower division baccalaureate/associate degree category, 2 semester hours in Basic Industrial Electronics or Industrial Electricity (11/97).

Electrical/Electronic Fundamentals for Mechanical Crafts (201)

Location: Hane clients' facilities or public workshops.

Length: 40 hours (5 days).

Dates: November 1997-Present.

Objective: To provide a skilled tradesperson from crafts other than the electrical and electronic crafts with a knowledge of the fundamentals of electrical and electronic technology, and to train them in basic electrical and electronic troubleshooting and repair procedures.

Learning Outcome: Upon successful completion of this course, the student will be able to use a multimeter to make voltage and current readings; read a resister value from three color code; use Ohm's law to calculate voltage drops, current, resistance and power; calculate RC time for resister capacitor circuits; test relays, solenoids, contacters, switches, and motor starters; understand basic principles of AC and DC motors; work safely with electricity; and identify component parts in schematics and ladder diagrams.

Instruction: Major topics covered in the course are fundamental concepts, practical applications, units of measurement, circuits, components, circuit parts, ladder diagramming, and AC and DC motors. Methods of instruction include lecture, discussion, problem solving exercises, and hands-on labs.

Credit Recommendation: In the lower division baccalaureate/associate degree category, 2 semester hours in Electrical/ Electronic Fundamentals (11/97).

Electronics for Material Handling Equipment (130)

Location: Hane clients' facilities or public workshops.

Length: 40 hours (5 days).

Dates: November 1997-Present.

Objective: To provide the student with the ability to troubleshoot and repair electric vehicles, such as, forklifts.

Learning Outcome: Upon successful completion of this course, the student will be to effectively troubleshoot the electrical/electronic controls of electric powered vehicles; read single line drawings; read and interpret control circuit ladder diagrams; identify which circuit components need replaced in a control circuit; understand digital circuits well enough to identify defective components, test components; understand basic principles of DC motors; take voltage and current readings; and use a megger to test motors.

Instruction: Major topics covered in the course are proper use of test equipment, fundamental concepts of electricity, practical applications and calculations, circuits, basic electrical components, single line diagrams, control components, motors, drive train control components, ladder diagrams, and troubleshooting techniques. Methods of instruction include lecture, discussion, problem solving exercises, and hands-on labs.

Credit Recommendation: In the lower division baccalaureate/associate degree category, 2 semester hours in Survey of Electronics Fundamentals (11/97).

Industrial Gear Box Repair (103)

Location: Hane clients' facilities or public workshops.

Length: 40 hours (5 days).

Dates: November 1997-Present.

Objective: To provide the student with the skills required to troubleshoot, align, install, and rebuild gear boxes.

Learning Outcome: Upon successful completion of this course, the student will be able to correctly rebuild gear boxes; troubleshoot failed gear boxes; select the proper gear box; properly install a speed reducer; correctly replace seals and bearings; and correctly set up gear box using shims.

Instruction: Major topics covered in the course are alignment, installation, and rebuilding of gearboxes including worm, helical, herringbone, and spur gear; selection of lubricants; and application of service rating. Methods of instruction include lecture, discussion, problem solving exercises, and hands-on labs.

Credit Recommendation: In the lower division baccalaureate/associate degree category, 2 semester hours in Gear Box Repair or Mechanical Engineering (11/97).

Industrial Rigging (144)

Location: Hane clients' facilities or public workshops.

Length: 40 hours (5 days).

Dates: November 1997-Present.

Objective: To train the student involved in rigging to do so efficiently, and above all, safely.

Learning Outcome: Upon successful completion of this course, the student will be able to inspect various equipment for safety; determine safe load limits; figure balance point of loads; and apply the techniques of a skilled rigger.

Instruction: Major topics covered in the course are how to inspect, select, and safely use hooks, nylon slings, wire rope slings, wire rope, chains, chain slings, hoist chain, metal mesh, and metal mesh slings. Methods of instruction include lecture, discussion, problem solving exercises, and hands-on labs.

Credit Recommendation: In the lower division baccalaureate/associate degree category, 2 semester hours in Industrial Rigging or Mechanical Engineering (11/97).

Troubleshooting AC Motor Drives (165)

Location: Hane clients' facilities or public workshops.

Length: 40 hours (5 days).

Dates: November 1997-Present.

Objective: To provide the student with the skill to set-up, troubleshoot, and repair AC motor drives.

Learning Outcome: Upon successful completion of this course, the student will be able to input parameters into the drive; set-up and get a drive on line; and interpret fault codes and use built-in diagnostics to aid in troubleshooting.

Instruction: Major topics covered in the course are review of electronic basics and consideration of reactive components, AC and DC motors, AC motor drives, power control devices, silicon controlled rectifiers, inverters, AC drive control circuits, and troubleshooting of AC drives. Methods of instruction include lecture, discussion, problem solving exercises, and hands-on labs.

Credit Recommendation: In lower division baccalaureate/associate degree category, 2 semester hours in Electronic Maintenance Troubleshooting AC Motor Drive (11/97).

Troubleshooting Electronics to the Board Level (172)

Location: Hane clients' facilities or public workshops.

Length: 40 hours (5 days).

Dates: November 1997-Present.

Objective: To provide the student with the skill to troubleshoot electronic equipment to the board level.

Learning Outcome: Upon successful completion of this course, the student will be able to use test equipment to identify which board needs replaced or repaired in an electronic system.

Instruction: Major topics covered in the course are basic math, fundamental concepts, circuits, test equipment, solid state switches, op amps, power supplies, digital logic devices, measurement techniques, and troubleshooting. Methods of instruction include lecture, discussion, problem solving exercises, and hands-on labs.

Credit Recommendation: In the lower division baccalaureate/associate degree category, 2 semester hours in Survey of Electronics Fundamentals (11/97).

Troubleshooting Electronics to the Component Level (174)

Location: Hane clients' facilities or public workshops.

Length: 40 hours (5 days).

Dates: November 1997-Present.

Objective: To provide the student with the skills necessary to troubleshoot electronic equipment to the component level.

Learning Outcome: Upon successful completion of this course, the student will be able to identify circuit boards in need of replacement and to use test equipment to identify defective components in a board.

Instruction: Major topics covered in the course are math review, electronic concepts, circuits, semiconductors, op amp circuits, power supplies, digital logic systems, and troubleshooting techniques. Methods of instruction include lecture, discussion, problem solving exercises, and hands-on labs.

Credit Recommendation: In the vocational certificate category, 2 semester hours in Electronic Troubleshooting (11/97).

Troubleshooting Fluid Power Equipment (137)

Location: Hane clients' facilities or public workshops.

Length: 40 hours (5 days).

Dates: November 1997-Present.

Objective: To provide the student with the knowledge of how to effectively and efficiently troubleshoot, repair, and maintain fluid power equipment.

Learning Outcome: Upon successful completion of this course, the student will be able to read pneumatic schematics; identify and understand common hydraulic and pneumatic components; understand common circuit applications; troubleshoot fluid power circuits; perform preventive maintenance; and remove, clean, and replace fluid power components.

Instruction: Major topics covered in the course are basic concepts, compressed air, hydraulics, hydraulic directional control valves, pressure control valves, volume controls, cylinder applications, pumps, and pneumatic power supply systems. Methods of instruction include lecture, discussion, problem solving exercises, and hands-on labs.

Credit Recommendation: In the lower division baccalaureate/associate degree category, 2 semester hours in Survey of Fluid Power (11/97).

Troubleshooting Industrial Hydraulic Equipment (140)

Location: Hane clients' facilities or public workshops.

Length: 40 hours (5 days).

Dates: November 1997-Present.

Objective: To provide the student with the ability to troubleshoot industrial hydraulic equipment.

Learning Outcome: Upon successful completion of this course, the student will be able to read hydraulic schematics; identify and understand common hydraulic components; troubleshoot hydraulic power circuits; perform preventive maintenance on hydraulic systems; and remove, clean, and replace hydraulic power components.

Instruction: Major topics covered in the course are introduction to fluid power and hydraulics, directional control valves, manual overrides, pressure control valves, volume controls, rapid advance, feed speed, and rapid return circuits, cylinder applications, pumps, servo hydraulic systems, and industrial hydraulic circuits and applications. Methods of instruction include lecture, discussion, problem solving exercises, and hands-on labs.

Credit Recommendation: In the vocational certificate or lower division baccalaureate/associate degree category, 2 semester hours in Basic Hydraulics (11/97).

Troubleshooting Pneumatic Controls and Equipment (163)

Location: Hane clients' facilities or public workshops.

Length: 40 hours (5 days).

Dates: November 1997-Present.

Objective: To provide the student with the ability to troubleshoot pneumatic controls and equipment.

Learning Outcome: Upon successful completion of this course, the student will be able to read pneumatic schematics; identify and understand pneumatic components; troubleshoot pneumatic control circuits and programmable logic controllers; read and interpret ladder diagrams; understand common circuit applications; perform preventive maintenance on pneumatic systems; and remove, clean, and replace pneumatic components.

Instruction: Major topics covered in the course are basic concepts, compressed air, cylinders, control valves, volume controls, compressors, plant distribution systems, control circuitry, ladder diagramming, and troubleshooting and repair techniques. Methods of instruction include lecture, discussion, problem solving exercises, and hands-on labs.

Credit Recommendation: In the lower division baccalaureate/associate degree category, 2 semester hours in Mechanical Engineering (11/97).

Troubleshooting with the GE-Fanuc Series 15 CNC (135)

Location: Hane clients' facilities or public workshops.

Length: 40 hours (5 days).

Dates: November 1997-Present.

Objective: To make technicians proficient troubleshooters of problems encountered in the GE-Fanuc Series 15 CNC Controller.

Learning Outcome: Upon successful completion of this course, the student will be able to identify key terms; enter and manipulate data; identify, locate, and trace basic machine interface signals from external sources through the system; sequence program construction and symbols; select and set machine parameters; upload and download parts programs and parameters with a PC; and troubleshoot.

Instruction: Major topics covered in the course are nomenclatures, descriptions, and functional relationships of printed circuit boards, BMI signaling, sequence programming, softkey main menu screens, reading and saving programs, troubleshooting, and parts programming. Methods of instruction include lecture, discussion, problem solving exercises, and hands-on labs.

Credit Recommendation: In the lower division baccalaureate/associate degree category, 2 semester hours in Industrial Controls (11/97).

Vibration Analysis, Alignment, and Balancing (190)

Location: Hane clients' facilities or public workshops.

Length: 40 hours (5 days).

Dates: November 1997-Present.

Objective: To provide the student with the ability to troubleshoot vibration problems encountered in rotating equipment using vibration analysis. Also, they are taught how to properly align and balance rotating equipment.

Learning Outcome: Upon successful completion of this course, the student will be able to diagnose vibration problems, measure phase and vibration; analyze a spectrum; choose transducers; use spike energy; determine resonance; do reverse indicator alignment; compensate for thermal growth; determine balance weight; and perform correct balancing.

Instruction: Major topics covered in the course are basic vibration concepts as they relate to problems with rotating equipment and single channel FFT analysis is emphasized. Also, covers proper alignment procedures and single and dual plane balancing. Methods of instruction include lecture, discussion, problem solving exercises, and hands-on labs.

Credit Recommendation: In the lower division baccalaureate/associate degree category, 2 semester hours in Survey of Vibration Analysis, Alignment, and Balancing or Mechanical Engineering (11/97).

Health Insurance Association of America

The Health Insurance Association of America (HIAA), headquartered in Washington, DC, is a voluntary trade association that represents and promotes the interests of its membership with respect to medical, disability and long-term care insurance, and associated managed care programs. Its members serve the public interest by protecting individuals against the financial burdens of sickness or accidental injury, and by encouraging the effective management of health care expenditures. To fulfill its mission, in part, the Association carries out education programs which enhance understanding of health insurance and managed care programs within the industry and the public at large.

The association has sponsored a formal educational program since 1958. This program currently offers two designations - the Health Insurance Associate (HIA) and the Managed Healthcare Professional (MHP). The Health Insurance Associate curriculum consists of six courses: Fundamentals A and B, Medical Expense, Supplemental, and two electives. The Managed Healthcare Professional consists of six courses: Fundamentals A and B, Managed Care A and B, Medical Expense, and one elective. Electives in Fraud, Disability Income, and Long-Term Care are offered. These courses give the student comprehensive knowledge and understanding of the technical and the socioeconomic aspects of both group and individual health insurance products including disability income, managed care, long-term care, medical expense, and supplemental health insurance.

A comprehensive examination assesses achievement for each course. Students' principal method of preparation for final examinations is through independent study, with on-the-job experience and, in some instances, classroom instruction supplementing this study. HIAA provides self-study materials that candidates can use to prepare for examinations. Course content and examinations are constantly reviewed and updated by persons knowledgeable and active in the various specialties of the health insurance business.

Source of official student records: Registry of Credit Recommendations, American Council on Education, One Dupont Circle, Washington, DC 20036-1193 or Sherry Schlossnagle, Director, Insurance Education Program, Health Insurance Association of America, 555 13th Street, NW, Suite 600 East, Washington, DC 20004-1109.

Additional information about the courses: College Credit Recommendation Service, American Council on Education, One Dupont Circle, Washington, DC 20036-1193.

Disability Income Insurance

Location: Various sites in the United States, Canada, and internationally.

Length: 40 hours (10 weeks).

Dates: February 1996-Present.

Objective: To provide a comprehensive background in disability income insurance.

Learning Outcome: Upon successful completion of this course, the student will be able to explain contracts, premiums, claims, and sales concerns as well as stability and motivation factors and their affect on product language, rate development, underwriting considerations, and claim management.

Instruction: Major topics covered in the course are historical highlights and developments; life insurance versus disability income insurance; stability and motivation; other disability coverage; business insurance, economy and unemployment; contractual provisions and extra benefits; over insurance; sales and marketing; the disability application underwriting tools; substandard underwriting; occupation schedule; administration; claims; actuarial; law department function; product-development process; evaluation of results; reinsurance; governmental disability programs; group disability benefits; disability income future; and managing the disability product line. Methods of instruction include self study with a textbook and study manual, and a final proctored written examination.

Credit Recommendation: In the upper division baccalaureate degree category, 2 semester hours in Health Care Administration, Insurance, Human Resource Management, or Business Administration (10/96).

Fraud: The Hidden Cost of Health Care

Location: Various sites in the United States, Canada, and internationally.

Length: 40 hours (10 weeks).

Dates: August 1996-Present.

Objective: To provide a comprehensive background in health care fraud.

Learning Outcome: Upon successful completion of this course, the student will be able to identify anti-fraud efforts both in government as well as private sectors, understand the basics of criminal investigations and investigative techniques, how automated tools are used in the detection and investigation of fraud, and how fraud occurs in managed care arrangements as well as disability income fraud.

Instruction: Major topics covered in the course are an overview of health care fraud; insurers' anti-fraud efforts; criminal investigations and government anti-fraud efforts; investigative techniques and case preparation; automated tools for detection and investigation; fraud in managed care arrangements; fraud and electronic data interchange; fighting health care fraud in the private sector; and disability income fraud. Methods of instruction include self study with a textbook and study manual, and a final proctored written examination.

Credit Recommendation: In the upper division baccalaureate degree category, 1 semester hour in Health Care Administration, Insurance, or Business Administration (10/96).

Fundamentals of Health Insurance: Part A

Location: Various sites in the United States and internationally.

Length: Approximately 10 weeks — mid-February to mid-May and mid-August to mid-November.

Dates: February 1997-Present.

Objective: To introduce students to the basic concepts underlying group and individual health insurance, both the socioeconomic as well as the technical aspects.

Learning Outcome: Upon successful completion of this course, the student will be able to explain the history of health insurance (particularly in the U.S.), and the background of the insurance industry, as well as describe the various types of health insurance coverages and their evolution. The student will learn the parts of an insurance contract, how marketing and sales are conducted, and understand the principles of underwriting.

Instruction: Major topics covered in the course are the history of health insurance, the insurance industry, various health insurance coverages, marketing and sales of health insurance products, and underwriting health insurance risks. Methods of instruction include self study with a textbook and study manual, and a final proctored written examination.

Credit Recommendation: In the upper division baccalaureate degree category, 2

semester hours in Insurance or Business Administration (11/97).

Fundamentals of Health Insurance:Part B

Location: Various sites in the United States and internationally.

Length: Approximately 10 weeks — mid-February to mid-May and mid-August to mid-November.

Dates: February 1997-Present.

Objective: To introduce students to the basic concepts and socioeconomic aspects of group and individual health insurance.

Learning Outcome: Upon successful completion of this course, the student will be able to explain the basic concepts underlying group and individual health insurance. Students will study managed care and other methods of managing costs and learn how the process of policy issue, renewal, and claims administration operate, as well as how health insurance premiums are set, and how federal and state governments regulate insurance.

Instruction: Major topics covered in the course are managing the cost of health care; policy issue and renewal; claim administration, pricing health insurance products; government regulation; and fraud and abuse. Methods of instruction include self-study with a textbook and study manual, and a final proctored written examination.

Credit Recommendation: In the upper division baccalaureate degree category, 2 semester hours in Insurance or Business Administration (11/97).

Group Life/Health Insurance: Parts A, B, and C

Location: Various locations throughout the United States.

Length: Self-study (approximately 150 hours, including test preparation and testing time).

Dates: *Version 1:* September 1979-August 1989; *Version 2:* September 1989-Present.

Objective: To furnish students with a comprehensive knowledge of the technical and socioeconomic aspects (Parts A and B) as well as the advanced and specialty areas (Part C) of the group life and health insurance business.

Learning Outcome: Upon successful completion of this course, the student will be able to understand the need for life and health insurance and the historical development, structure, and regulation of group life and health insurance business; understand and skillfully and professionally use the fundamentals of group life and health insurance; and understand and explain the role and contribution of the group life and health insurance business in the financing and administration of health care systems and premature death.

Instruction: *Part A:* Major topics covered in the course are the development of group health insurance, analysis of coverages, marketing, underwriting, pricing, and rate making. *Part B:* Major topics covered in the course are the contract, issue and administration, claims, financial analysis of group operations, regulations, and taxation. *Part C:* Major topics covered in the course are design concepts, health care cost containment, funding benefits, flexible benefits, benefits for retirees, group universal life, large case management and rehabilitation, fundamentals of electronic data processing and applications, and industry challenges. Methods of instruction include instructor-directed instruction or self-instruction and supervised examinations. Examinations are given in May and November.

Credit Recommendation: *Version 1:* Parts A and B: In the upper division baccalaureate or graduate degree category, 3 semester hours in Business Administration, or in the upper division baccalaureate or graduate degree category, 2 semester hours in Business Administration or Insurance; and in the lower division baccalaureate/associate degree category, 1 semester hour in Data Processing (5/83). *Version 2:* Parts A and B: In the upper division baccalaureate degree category, 3 semester hours in Business Administration, or in the graduate degree category, 2 semester hours in Business Administration or Health Care Administration. Part C: In the upper division baccalaureate degree category or graduate degree category, 2 semester hours in Business Administration or Health Care Administration (5/88) (9/89).

Individual Health Insurance: Parts A and B

Location: Various locations throughout the United States.

Length: Self-study (approximately 100 hours, including test preparation and testing time).

Dates: May 1968-Present.

Objective: To enable students to have an in-depth understanding of individual health insurance and of the social and economic responsibilities of the industry.

Learning Outcome: Upon successful completion of this course, the student will be able to demonstrate a professional understanding of the need for medical expense and disability insurance; the historical development, structure, and regulation of the individual health insurance business; the fundamentals of individual health insurance; and the role and contribution of the individual health insurance business in the financing and administration of health care systems.

Instruction: *Part A:* Major topics covered in the course are the history and development of health insurance, disability income insurance, medical expense insurance, types of contracts, marketing, underwriting, policy issue, and service. *Part B:* Major topics covered in the course are claims, regulation, pricing, financial reports, investments, and data processing systems. Methods of instruction include self-instruction and supervised examinations. Examinations are given in May and November.

Credit Recommendation: In the upper division baccalaureate degree category, 3 semester hours in Business Administration, Insurance, or Marketing (6/77) (5/83) (5/88) (9/89).

Long-Term Care: Knowing the Risk, Paying the Price (Long-Term Care Insurance)

Location: Various sites in the United States and internationally.

Length: Approximately 10 weeks — mid-February to mid-May and mid-August to mid-November.

Dates: February 1997-Present.

Objective: To provide a comprehensive understanding of long-term care.

Learning Outcome: Upon successful completion of this course, the student will be able to understand long-term care — what it is and what it is not, who needs it, who provides it, and traditional ways of financing it.

Instruction: Major topics covered in the course are what long-term care insurance is, who needs it, who provides it, who pays for it, and how much it costs. The long-term care benefits of government programs are addressed in detail, as well as how long-term care insurance evolved as a product. Various aspects of long-term care marketing, operations, regulation, and supplemental sources of financing are discussed. In addition, consumer issues, emerging trends in long-term care financing, service delivery, and consumer preference and expectations are investigated. Methods of instruction include self-study with a textbook and study manual, and a final proctored written examination.

Credit Recommendation: In the upper division baccalaureate degree category, 2 semester hours in Insurance or Business Administration (11/97).

Long-Term Care: Needs, Costs, and Financing

Location: Various locations throughout the United States.

Length: 40 hours (8 chapters).

Dates: January 1993-Present.

Objective: To provide professionals in financial services, employee benefits, and the insurance field with basic information about current issues in long-term care for individuals and employee groups.

Learning Outcome: Upon successful completion of this course, the student will be able to articulate an appropriate definition of long-term care needs; describe various types of long-term care and available providers; discuss long-term care costs and methods of financing; and discuss the government's role as both provider and regulator of long-term care.

Instruction: Major topics covered in the course are the definition of long-term care need, financing, services, and costs; individual, group, and other kinds of insurance programs and methods of financing; and the government's role as both provider and regulator of long-term care. Methods of instruction include independent study and a proctored final examination.

Credit Recommendation: In the upper division baccalaureate degree category, 1 semester hour in Health Care Administration (elective), Insurance, Business Administration, Human Resource Management, or Financial Planning (11/93).

Managed Care: Integrating the Delivery and Financing of Health Care: Part A

Location: Various sites in the United States, Canada, and internationally.

Length: 40 hours (10 weeks).

Dates: February 1996-Present.

Objective: To provide a comprehensive background in the history, objectives, and theory of managed care as it has developed in the United States.

Learning Outcome: Upon successful completion of this course, the student will be able to explain how and why managed care developed, the various types of managed care organizations, how managed care controls costs, what forms of involvement government has in managed care, and the importance of quality in managed care.

Instruction: Major topics covered in the course are background, history, and theory of managed care; the development of managed care; organization of managed care arrangements; cost control techniques; individuals, employers, and managed care; government involvement in managed care; controlling for quality; and data for quality, cost, and utilization control. Methods of instruction include self study with a textbook and study manual, and a final proctored written examination.

Credit Recommendation: In the in upper division baccalaureate degree category, 3 semester hours in Health Care Administration, Insurance, or Business Administration (10/96). **NOTE:** This course must be taken with Managed Care: Integrating the Delivery and Financing of Health Care: Part B in order to receive 3 semester hours.

Managed Care: Integrating the Delivery and Financing of Health Care: Part B

Location: Various sites in the United States, Canada, and internationally.

Length: 40 hours (10 weeks).

Dates: February 1996-Present.

Objective: To provide a comprehensive background in the delivery and financing of managed care.

Learning Outcome: Upon successful completion of this course, the student will be able to explain how managed care organizations are governed and structured, as well as the overall administration of the network including provider relations, claims, financing, budgeting, rating and have a general understanding of regulations, accreditation, and legal issues.

Instruction: Major topics covered in the course are governance and management structure, selective medical provider contracting; network administration and provider relations; marketing and member services; claims administration; financing, budgeting, and rating; legal issues; accreditation; and regulation. Methods of instruction include self study with a textbook and study manual, and a final proctored written examination.

Credit Recommendation: In the upper division baccalaureate degree category, 3 semester hours in Health Care Administration, Insurance, or Business Administration (10/96). **NOTE:** This course must be taken with Managed Care: Integrating the Delivery and Financing of Health Care: Part A in order to receive 3 semester hours.

Medical Expense Insurance

Location: Various sites in the United States and internationally.

Length: Approximately 10 weeks — mid-February to mid-May and mid-August to mid-November.

Dates: August 1997-Present.

Objective: To provide a comprehensive background and specific information on medical expense insurance.

Learning Outcome: Upon successful completion of this course, the student will be able to understand and discuss the two coverages that provide health insurance to most Americans: group major medical insurance and individual hospital-surgical insurance, as well as the organizational functions and other areas of importance to medical expense products.

Instruction: Major topics covered in the course are group major medical expense insurance and individual hospital-surgical insurance, marketing and selling medical expense insurance, pricing, medical expense contract provisions, underwriting and policy administration, claim administration, and industry issues. Methods of instruction include self-study with a textbook and study manual, and a final proctored written examination.

Credit Recommendation: In the upper division baccalaureate degree category, 2 semester hours in Insurance or Business Administration (11/97).

HoHoKus School of Secretarial and Medical Sciences

The HoHoKus School of Secretarial and Medical Sciences was established in 1968 and is in its third ownership. Although each owner over the past 25 years operated differently, all have had the same goals: to prepare people for the job market in the shortest possible time and to provide an educational opportunity for those individuals who aspire to meet the changing needs of today's business and medical environments. The school's founders recognized the needs of businesses and established the training institution to meet the demand for highly trained workers skilled in modern technology. The current owner adheres to that same philosophy.

Specializing in secretarial and medical assisting courses, our mission is to equip students with the knowledge and skills necessary to attain challenging positions in business, industry and the medical environment. Emphasis is placed on personalized instruction. Our curricula is constantly re-evaluated to assure it meets the changing needs of employers. Training is designed to develop analytical problem solving skills, mature levels of conduct and the attitudes, values and habits required for career advancement. The mission and philosophy of our current staff and administration were developed through studies of the needs of the individual student and surveys of local business entities.

The school's administration and staff consist of a director, assistant director, academic dean, student services coordinator, administrative assistant, high school coordinator, admissions representative, placement director, fifteen instructors, six teaching assistants, and part-time clerical help. The assistant director, administrative assistant and admissions representative are graduates of The HoHoKus School. Consequently, these staff members can view situations from a student's perspective and are often helpful in solving problems. Our placement director has a degree in journalism and is quite effective in communication. Our instructors have a minimum of a bachelor's degree. Several have masters or doctorates. Teaching assistants are former graduates with employment experience.

Source of official student records: Registry of Credit Recommendations, American Council on Education, One Dupont Circle, Washington, DC 20036-1193.

Additional information about the courses: Office of Corporate-Higher Education Programs, Thomas Edison State College, 101 W. State Street, Trenton, NJ 08608-1176.

Advanced Coding (MII4)

Location: Ramsey, New Jersey.

Length: 24 hours (12 weeks).

Dates: January 1994-Present.

Objective: To enable the student to correctly code Diagnosis and Procedures.

Learning Outcome: Upon successful completion of this course, the student will be able to understand the principles behind coding the diagnosis and procedures, correctly code using the ICD book and CPT codes, and apply codes to insurance forms.

Instruction: Major topics covered in the course are the principles of coding procedures and diagnoses, how to apply these principles, and how to correctly code for a variety of specialties. Methods of instruction include lecture, discussion, and exercises.

Credit Recommendation: In the lower division baccalaureate/associate degree category, 2 semester hours in Diagnostic and Procedural Coding (6/96).

Anatomy and Physiology I (Formerly Medical Science I)

Location: Ramsey, NJ.

Length: *Version 1:* 72 hours; *Version 2:* 108 hours.

Dates: *Version 1:* July 1985-March 1993; *Version 2:* April 1993-Present.

Objective: To introduce students to basic human anatomy, physiology, and pathophysiology.

Learning Outcome: *Version 1:* Upon successful completion of this course, the student will be able to explain the fundamental biological and physiological concepts that relate to the structure and function of the body's systems; describe the basic structures of the various cells, tissues, and organs; demonstrate an understanding of how the specific cells, tissues, and organs work; list the various tests and studies that are utilized to evaluate the body's systems; and discuss the major diseases (including the prognosis and treatments) that are associated with deviations from normal structure and function. *Version 2:* Upon successful completion of this course, the student will be able to understand the basic structure and functions of the human body from studying and dissecting animal material; in a laboratory setting, observe human physiology using interactive techniques with other students; explain the fundamental biological and physiological concepts that relate to the structure and function of the body's systems; describe the basic structures of the various cells, tissues, and organs; demonstrate an understanding of how the specific cells, tissues, and organs work; list the various tests and studies that are utilized to evaluate the body's systems; and discuss the major diseases (including prognosis and treatments) that are associated with deviations from normal structure and function.

Instruction: *Version 1:* Major topics covered in the course are utilizing a "systems" approach in teaching the students the basic principles and relationships of body structure (anatomy), function (physiology) and common diseases (pathophysiology); study of blood, lymph, the cardiovascular, lymphatic, respiratory, and digestive systems. *Version 2:* Major topics covered in the course are a "systems" approach in teaching the students the basic principles and relationships of body structure (anatomy), function (physiology) and common diseases (pathophysiology); study of blood, lymph, the cardiovascular, lymphatic, respiratory and digestive systems. Methods of instruction include lecture and laboratory components.

Credit Recommendation: *Version 1:* In the lower division baccalaureate/associate degree category, 3 semester hours in Anatomy and Physiology I (1/93). *Version 2:* In the lower division baccalaureate/associate degree category, 4 semester hours in Anatomy and Physiology I (5/93).

Anatomy and Physiology II (Formerly Medical Science II)

Location: Ramsey, NJ.

Length: *Version 1:* 72 hours; *Version 2:* 108 hours.

Dates: *Version 1:* July 1985-March 1993; *Version 2:* April 1993-Present.

Objective: To introduce the students to basic human anatomy, physiology, and pathophysiology.

Learning Outcome: *Version 1:* Upon successful completion of this course, the student will be able to explain the fundamental biological and physiological concepts that relate to the structure and function of the body's systems; describe the basic structures of the various cells, tissues, and organs; demonstrate an understanding of how the specific cells, tissues, and organs work; list the various tests and studies that are utilized to evaluate the body's systems; and discuss the major diseases (including the prognosis and treatments) that are associated with deviations from normal structure and function. *Version 2:* Upon successful completion of this course, the student will be able to understand the basic structure and functions of the human body from studying and dissecting animal material; in a laboratory setting, observe human physiology using interactive techniques with other students; explain the fundamental biological and physiological concepts that relate to the structure and function of the body's systems; describe the basic structures of the various cells, tissues, and organs; demonstrate an understanding of how the specific cells, tissues, and organs work; list the various tests and studies that are utilized to evaluate the body's systems; and discuss the major diseases (including the prognosis and treatments) that are associated with deviations from normal structure and function.

Instruction: *Version 1:* Major topics covered in the course are utilizing a "systems" approach in teaching students the basic principles and relationships of body structure (anatomy), function (physiology), and common diseases (pathophysiology). *Version 2:* Major topics covered in the course are utilizing a "systems" approach in teaching students the basic principles and relationships of body structure (anatomy), function (physiology), and common diseases (pathophysiology). Methods of instruction include lecture and laboratory components.

Credit Recommendation: *Version 1:* In the lower division baccalaureate/associate degree category, 3 semester hours in Anatomy and Physiology II (1/93). *Version 2:* In the lower division baccalaureate/associate degree category, 4 semester hours in Anatomy and Physiology II (5/93).

Basic Ultrasound - Techniques with Lab (MIII)

Location: Ramsey, New Jersey.

Length: 156 hours (12 weeks).

Dates: January 1994-Present.

Objective: To introduce students to basic ultrasound procedures.

Learning Outcome: Upon successful completion of this course, the student will be able to operate an ultrasound machine; obtain and evaluate an echocardiogram (in gray scale imaging); evaluate the carotid artery with ultrasound and Doppler (in gray scale imaging) imaging; perform a limited ultrasound simulated pelvic exam; and evaluate fetal parameters to include BPD, abdominal, circumference, and femur length.

Instruction: Major topics covered in the course are the principles, concepts, and procedures necessary to perform an ultrasound exam on the cardiovascular and female reproductive systems. Methods of instruction include lecture, discussion, and exercises.

Credit Recommendation: In the lower division baccalaureate/associate degree category, 4 semester hours in Introduction to Ultrasound with emphasis in Echocardiography (6/96).

Business Law

Location: Ramsey, NJ.

Length: 24 hours (3 days).

Dates: October 1985-Present.

Objective: To enable students to become aware of their rights and obligations under the law as private citizens and members of the business community.

Learning Outcome: Upon successful completion of this course, the student will be able to explain and use legal terminology; recognize and discuss crimes and civil wrongs of particular concern to the business community; recognize essential elements of an enforceable contract; understand the law pertaining to possession, title, conveyance, and bailments; identify the differences between agency and employment and the corresponding rights, responsibilities and liabilities; understand warranties, disclaimers, and product liabilities; and understand risk management and emerging areas of law.

Instruction: Major topics include the American System of Law; criminal, tort and administrative law; contracts; agency employment, bailments, commercial paper; and risk management and ethics.

Credit Recommendation: In the lower division baccalaureate/associate degree category, 2 semester hours in Survey of Business Law (1/93).

Business Math

Location: Ramsey, NJ.

Length: 36 hours.

Dates: April 1991-Present.

Objective: To review the basic mathematical processes and their business applications.

Learning Outcome: Upon successful completion of this course, the student will be able to perform arithmetic operations using whole numbers, decimals, fractions and percentages; calculate interest and depreciation and perform banking procedures; and use graphs to report data.

Instruction: Major topics covered in the course are a review of fundamental mathematical processes including fractions, decimals, percentages, interests, discounts, depreciation, retail markup, stocks and bonds, and graphs.

Credit Recommendation: In the lower division baccalaureate/associate degree category, 3 semester hours in Business Math (1/93).

Clinical Lab Procedures

Location: Ramsey, NJ.

Length: 72 hours.

Dates: July 1985-Present.

Objective: To enable students to develop competence in the techniques of laboratory procedures commonly performed in a physician's office.

Learning Outcome: Upon successful completion of this course, the student will be able to explain the elements of an infection and know how to prevent an infection from spreading to other patients as stated by the OSHA guidelines; describe their role in the physical examination of a patient; perform the following procedures according to standards in textbook: discuss the implication of abnormal vital signs; perform and record a patient's height, weight, vision, and hearing tests; perform routine urine tests, understand their implications and record results; perform a venipuncture according to acceptable standards; describe the purpose of doing cultures and correctly perform same; and explain the principles of X-ray.

Instruction: Major topics covered in the course are learning to take blood pressure and check vital signs; laboratory tests such as blood typing, hemoglobin, HCT and blood glucose and routine urinalysis are taught; prepare and analyze specimens using a microscope and centrifuge and accurately chart the results; venipuncture is practiced using prosthesis; receiving training and certification in OSHA regulations, training in the moderate and waived categories of tests as defined by the CLIA 88 regulations; and requirements for training in cultures and Kodak Blood Analyzer and receive certificates that comply with the CLIA regulations.

Credit Recommendation: In the lower division baccalaureate/associate degree category, 3 semester hours in Clinical Lab Procedures (1/93).

College Accounting

Location: Ramsey, NJ.

Length: 48 hours.

Dates: February 1991-Present.

Objective: To prepare students to apply basic accounting fundamentals in service-type businesses.

Learning Outcome: Upon successful completion of this course, the student will be able to perform all the steps in the accounting cycle; use accounting terminology and apply it to general business practices; and prepare payroll registers.

Instruction: Major topics covered in the course are an introduction to basic double-entry accounting, beginning with journalizing through posting to the ledger, financial statements and closing entries.

Credit Recommendation: In the lower division baccalaureate/associate degree category, 3 semester hours in Accounting Fundamentals for Service Industries (1/93).

Communications

Location: Ramsey, NJ.

Length: 24 hours.

Dates: July 1985-Present.

Objective: To improve students' oral communication skills in business.

Learning Outcome: Upon successful completion of this course, the student will be able to counteract barriers to effective communication; recognize non-verbal communications' impact on verbal communications; make effective oral business presentations; effectively and efficiently respond to customer's inquiries and handle complaints with both written and oral communications; and effectively respond to prior communications.

Instruction: Major topics covered in the course are examining the conveyance of thoughts and perceptions in a broad sense; recognition of non-verbal communications and verbal, oral and written communications, and the impact of non-verbal upon the verbal; the processes of communication are examined to enable the student to better understand the aspects of communication and how the resultant knowledge of process is developed within the business realm.

Credit Recommendation: In the lower division baccalaureate/associate degree category, 1 semester hour in Oral Skills in Business (1/93).

English Composition (E103)

Location: Ramsey, New Jersey.

Length: 48 hours.

Dates: June 1994-Present.

Objective: To develop student's writing skills and enhance their ability to critically analyze all written material for readability and effectiveness.

Learning Outcome: Upon successful completion of this course, the student will be able to apply strategies presented in the course to improve writing skills; develop individual strategies for generating ideas on a topic; analyze writings (theirs and others) for readability and effectiveness; organize, write and revise effective essays in the following modes of development: illustration, comparison/contrast, classification, cause and effect, process analysis, definition and argumentation; and improve and apply previously learned grammar skills to their essays.

Instruction: Major topics covered in the course are developing student's writing skills; various types of essays; literary techniques; and brainstorming, prewriting, writing, proof-reading, and revising their creations. Methods of instruction include lecture, discussion, collaborative learning, a research paper, and a variety of personal essays.

Credit Recommendation: In the lower division baccalaureate/associate degree category, 3 semester hours in English Composition I (10/96).

Lotus 1-2-3 Applications

Location: Ramsey, NJ.

Length: 24 hours.

Dates: February 1991-Present.

Objective: To provide students with proficiency in the basic capabilities of Lotus 1-2-3 and their applications.

Learning Outcome: Upon successful completion of this course, the student will be able to design, create, edit, and print spreadsheets utilizing formulas and functions; create graphics from spreadsheet data; and create and use a database.

Instruction: Major topics covered in the course are hands-on approach to Lotus; stressing the importance of spreadsheets for analysis and reporting of data; and basic concepts including labels, formulas, copying and formatting.

Credit Recommendation: In the lower division baccalaureate/associate degree category, 2 semester hours in Lotus 1-2-3 applications (1/93).

Machine Transcription (Medical and Business)

Location: Ramsey, NJ.

Length: 30 hours.

Dates: July 1985-Present.

Objective: To help students become proficient transcribers using a machine transcription unit.

Learning Outcome: Upon successful completion of this course the student will be able to operate a machine transcription unit and produce mailable business communications.

Instruction: Major topics covered are producing mailable copies of business letters, reports and memos from pre-recorded tapes; production and accuracy are stressed.

Credit Recommendation: In the lower division baccalaureate/associate degree category, 2 semester hours in Machine Transcription (1/93).

Management Principles

Location: Ramsey, NJ.

Length: 24 hours.

Dates: July 1985-Present.

Objective: To enable students to understand and practice the principles of effective and efficient supervision of self and others within personal and business settings.

Learning Outcome: Upon successful completion of this course, the student will be able to establish verifiable goals and structure time to effectively and efficiently achieve the goals; recognize and eliminate supervisory mistakes; understand the process and function of private communication, decision making and effective human relations; understand the purpose and process of delegation; and know the law as it pertains to discrimination in the workplace.

Instruction: Major topics teach the means to managing oneself and others and gives insight to the human relations and communications necessary for effective supervision.

Credit Recommendation: In the lower division baccalaureate/associate degree category, 2 semester hours in the Fundamentals of Supervision (1/93).

Medical Front Office Practice

Location: Ramsey, NJ.

Length: 72 hours.

Dates: July 1985-Present.

Objective: To acquaint students with administrative aspects of a medical office.

Learning Outcome: Upon successful completion of this course, the student will be able to apply medical terminology appropriately; prepare and maintain medical records; and understand legal and ethical issues involved in office procedures.

Instruction: Major topics covered in the course are the administrative aspect of a medical office including knowledge of various health care settings, legal and medical issues, and the role of computers in health care; students are trained to complete medical forms, prepare and maintain accounts payable and receivable, schedule appointments and order supplies.

Credit Recommendation: In the lower division baccalaureate/associate degree category, 3 semester hours in Medical Office Practices (1/93).

Medical Specialties Lab Procedures

Location: Ramsey, NJ.
Length: 84 hours.
Dates: July 1985-Present.
Objective: To enable students to develop competence in examination room techniques.
Learning Outcome: Upon successful completion of this course, the student will be able to identify major specialties and describe procedures that are commonly associated with them; discuss the Medical Assistant's role in each specialty; recognize what emergencies can occur in these specialties and how to deal with them; discuss the classification of drugs that are commonly found with the disorders of that specialty; and be certified in EKG's, CPR, and First Aid.
Instruction: Major topics covered in the course are special emphasis on preparing the patient for examination; preparing for sterilization and injection procedures; taking electrocardiograms; and performing first aid and emergency procedures including CPR and caring for supplies and equipment in the physician's office.
Credit Recommendation: In the lower division baccalaureate/associate degree category, 4 semester hours in Medical Specialties Procedures (1/93).

Medical Terminology I, II, III

Location: Ramsey, NJ.
Length: 72 hours.
Dates: July 1985-Present.
Objective: To introduce students to the basic structure of medical words, including prefixes, suffixes, roots, combining forms and the formation of plurals.
Learning Outcome: Upon successful completion of this course, the student will be able to correctly pronounce each medical word; spell each word; breakdown a word into its prefix, root, or suffix; and define medical terms.
Instruction: Major topics covered in the course are emphasizing placement on the correct pronunciation, spelling and definition of medical terms, allowing the student to build a professional vocabulary for working in the medical field.
Credit Recommendation: In the lower division baccalaureate/associate degree category, 3 semester hours in Medical Terminology (1/93).

Non-Invasive Cardiovascular Procedure

Location: Ramsey, New Jersey.
Length: 24 hours (12 weeks).
Dates: January 1995-Present.
Objective: To introduce the student to perform such non-invasive tests as exercise tolerance tests applications of Holter monitors and EKG interpretations.
Learning Outcome: Upon successful completion of this course, the student will be able to prepare patient for an exercise tolerance test, operate exercise tolerance machine, operate a Holter Monitor, and perform basic EKG.
Instruction: Major topics covered in the course are the principles of EKG to exercise tolerance testing and Holter monitoring. Methods of instruction include lecture, discussion, and exercises.
Credit Recommendation: In the lower division baccalaureate/associate degree category, 1 semester hour in Introduction to Non-Invasive Cardiovascular Procedure (6/96).

Patient Process (Formerly Patient Relations Process)

Location: Ramsey, NJ.
Length: *Version 1:* 24 hours; *Version 2:* 24 hours (lecture and 24 hours lab).
Dates: *Version 1:* July 1985-March 1993; *Version 2:* April 1993-Present.
Objective: To recognize the particular needs of a patient who is terminally ill, handicapped, has AIDS or is elderly.
Learning Outcome: Upon successful completion of this course, the student will be able to define peoples' basic needs as described by Maslow; identify the elements of communication; identify how stress and illness can interfere or affect our basic needs and the ability to communicate effectively; identify our pre-existing attitudes towards certain groups of people (the elderly, the handicapped, the AIDS patient); list what resources are available in the community to help our patients meet their basic needs; relate these objectives in a health care setting; and assess an individual's health needs through the use of case studies.
Instruction: Major topics covered in the course stress consideration and understanding along with effective communication techniques and community resources are examined.
Credit Recommendation: *Version 1:* In the lower division baccalaureate/associate degree category, 2 semester hours in Patient Communication Techniques (1/93). *Version 2:* In the lower division baccalaureate/associate degree category, 3 semester hours in Patient Communication Techniques (5/93).

Secretarial Procedures

Location: Ramsey, NJ.
Length: 132 hours.
Dates: July 1985-Present.
Objective: To provide experience in office simulation.
Learning Outcome: Upon successful completion of this course, the student will be able to apply advanced word processing concepts to job assignments of various departments.
Instruction: Major topics covered in the course are providing students with office simulation experience; advanced word processing concepts and set priorities for daily work flow of various departments; and desktop publishing is also incorporated into the simulation.
Credit Recommendation: In the lower division baccalaureate/associate degree category, 3 semester hours in Office Procedures (1/93).

Shorthand I

Location: Ramsey, NJ.
Length: 72 hours.
Dates: October 1986-Present.
Objective: To teach students the basic Gregg alphabet and its derivatives.
Learning Outcome: Upon successful completion of this course, the student will be able to recognize Gregg alphabet and abbreviations; recall and write dictation material; and write Gregg shorthand outlines.
Instruction: Major topics covered in the course include the Gregg alphabet; abbreviated words are taught every other lesson; abbreviated word endings and beginnings; concurrent with the introduction of Gregg symbols is the presentation of business vocabulary, and spelling words and punctuation rules to be applied to the current lesson.
Credit Recommendation: In the lower division baccalaureate/associate degree category, 4 semester hours in Principles of Shorthand (1/93).

Sonographic Anatomy and Physiology (MII2)

Location: Ramsey, New Jersey.
Length: 36 hours (12 weeks).
Dates: October 1995-Present.

Objective: To enable the student to apply the structural knowledge of anatomy to those images in the cardiovascular and reproductive systems imaged with ultrasound.

Learning Outcome: Upon successful completion of this course, the student will be able to relate the physiological functioning of various organs and circulation pathways as they are evaluated by Doppler and recognize the signs of pathophysiology that can be evaluated with ultrasound techniques.

Instruction: Major topics covered in the course are the study of anatomy, physiology, and pathophysiology with emphasis on the cardiovascular and female reproductive signs and circulation pathways which are evaluated with office sonography technique. Methods of instruction include lecture, discussion, and exercises.

Credit Recommendation: In the lower division baccalaureate/associate degree category, 3 semester hours in Cardiovascular Anatomy and Physiology (6/96).

Transcription II/Shorthand III

Location: Ramsey, NJ.

Length: 72 hours.

Dates: October 1986-Present.

Objective: To further reinforce Gregg shorthand principles and increase transcription skills and speed.

Learning Outcome: Upon successful completion of this course, the student will be able to demonstrate sufficient skill in writing and transcribing Gregg shorthand to fulfill standards of marketability; and take dictation at 60 wpm for 3 minutes and produce a mailable document.

Instruction: Major topics covered in the course are taking shorthand at increasing speeds; transcription skills are emphasized through letter placement and office-style dictation; transcription techniques such as developing shortcuts, making corrections and proofreading; and word processing.

Credit Recommendation: In the lower division baccalaureate/associate degree category, 3 semester hours in Gregg Shorthand and Transcription II (1/93).

Transcription I/Shorthand II

Location: Ramsey, NJ.

Length: 72 hours.

Dates: October 1986-Present.

Objective: To reinforce Gregg shorthand principles and develop good transcription skills and speed.

Learning Outcome: Upon successful completion of this course, the student will be able to demonstrate skill in writing and transcribing Gregg shorthand and take dictation at 50 wpm for 3 minutes and produce a mailable document.

Instruction: Major topics covered in the course give students the ability to take Gregg Shorthand at increasing speeds through recall drills of shorthand theory and faster dictation speeds; and transcription skills are developed through grammar, spelling and punctuation practice.d

Credit Recommendation: In the lower division baccalaureate/associate degree category, 3 semester hours in Gregg Shorthand and Transcription I (1/93).

Typing I

Location: Ramsey, NJ.

Length: 96 hours.

Dates: July 1985-Present.

Objective: To acquire basic keyboarding and formatting skills.

Learning Outcome: Upon successful completion of this course, the student will be able to operate a standard keyboard and develop basic speed and accuracy skills and apply the fundamentals of copy arrangement, line lengths or margins, tabs and centering.

Instruction: Major topics covered in the course is an introduction to the keyboard by the touch method; and basic centering, reports, letters, envelopes and tables.

Credit Recommendation: In the lower division baccalaureate/associate degree category, 3 semester hours in Introduction to Typing (1/93).

Typing II

Location: Ramsey, NJ.

Length: 108 hours.

Dates: July 1985-Present.

Objective: To further develop proficiency in formatting skills and speed.

Learning Outcome: Upon successful completion of this course, the student will be able to format more complex letters and reports and increase accuracy and speed.

Instruction: Major topics covered in the course offered continued development of speed and accuracy, applying typing skills on an intermediate level for the preparation of business letters, forms, reports and tabulations.

Credit Recommendation: In the lower division baccalaureate/associate degree category, 3 semester hours in Intermediate Typing (1/93).

Ultrasound Physics

Location: Ramsey, NJ.

Length: 36 hours (12 weeks).

Dates: January 1994-Present.

Objective: To provide students an understanding of how physics relates to ultrasound principles.

Learning Outcome: Upon successful completion of this course, the student will be able to understand the properties of sound waves, understand how ultrasound interacts with tissue, and understand Doppler principles.

Instruction: Major topic covered in the course is the relationship between the principles of sound waves and ultrasound technology. Methods of instruction includes lecture and discussion.

Credit Recommendation: In the lower division baccalaureate/associate degree category, 2 semester hours in Introduction to Ultrasound Physics (6/96).

Word Processing I

Location: Ramsey, NJ.

Length: 96 hours.

Dates: July 1985-Present.

Objective: To provide working knowledge of basic capabilities of WordPerfect 5.1.

Learning Outcome: Upon successful completion of this course, the student will be able to create, edit, save and print new or existing documents.

Instruction: Major topics covered in the course are hands-on experience in WordPerfect 5.1 covering the basic concepts that are applied to creating, editing and printing basic letters and reports.

Credit Recommendation: In the lower division baccalaureate/associate degree category, 3 semester hours in Word Processing I (WordPerfect 5.1) (1/93).

Word Processing II

Location: Ramsey, NJ.

Length: 108 hours.

Dates: July 1985-Present.

Objective: To provide students with more in-depth skills in WordPerfect 5.1.

Learning Outcome: Upon successful completion of this course, the student will be able to increase proficiency in editing letters and reports and use advanced formatting features of WordPerfect 5.1.

Instruction: Major topics covered in the course are Word Processing II hands-on learning of advanced functions and procedures, and master the editing of letters, tabulations, memos, and reports on a production level.

Credit Recommendation: In the lower division baccalaureate/associate degree category, 3 semester hours in Word Processing II (WordPerfect 5.1) (1/93).

Hudson Institute for Teacher Education

The purpose of the Hudson Institute for Teacher Education is to train and certify early childhood teachers in the Montessori method and to provide Montessori schools with qualified personnel for their classrooms. The Hudson Institute for Teacher Education does not discriminate on the basis of race, color, national and ethnic origin in administration of its educational and admissions policies.

Source of official student records: Registry of Credit Recommendations, American Council on Education, One Dupont Circle, Washington, DC 20036-1193.

Additional information about the courses: College Credit Recommendation Service, American Council on Education, One Dupont Circle, Washington, DC 20036-1193.

Teacher Training Course

Location: New Rochelle, NY.

Length: *Version 1:* 200 hours (18 hours/month); *Version 2:* 200-250 hours (20 hours/month).

Dates: September 1991-Present.

Objective: To provide an understanding of Maria Montessori's philosophy of child development and learning and its practical application in the classroom.

Learning Outcome: Upon successful completion of this course, the student will be able to define and describe Montessori concepts, methods, and materials; apply Montessori concepts, methods, and materials in the classroom; provide guidelines for the preparation of a Montessori environment; understand the techniques of observation and of lessons; promote an understanding of uses, purposes, and sequence of materials for mathematical, language, reading, and writing concepts; and promote an understanding of the uses, purposes, and sequence of materials for developing sensorial and practical life concepts.

Instruction: Major topic covered in the course is the Montessori approach and how it pertains to the development of children from birth to age 6, special focus is placed on the educational applications of this approach, especially for children aged 2.5 to 6. Methods of instruction include lectures, readings, discussions, writing assignments, material making, and practicums.

Credit Recommendation: In the lower division baccalaureate/associate degree category, 3 semester hours in Foundations of Montessori Methods of Education, and in the upper division baccalaureate degree category, 6 semester hours in Montessori Curriculum Design and Materials (6/91).

Teacher Training Course: Internship

Location: New Rochelle, NY.

Length: 1000 hours (over 2 semesters); 500 hours per semester.

Dates: September 1991-Present.

Objective: To apply student's theoretical and practical foundation to activities in an actual classroom situation.

Learning Outcome: Upon successful completion of this course, the student will be able to be prepare the classroom environment for Montessori instruction; demonstrate proficiency in the use of the mechanics of Montessori instruction; and recognize and meet children's needs in the classroom.

Instruction: Major topic covered in the course is working with an experienced Montessori teacher while under the supervision of the Internship Coordinator. Methods of instruction include teaching practice, keep a log of all activities, keep subject files, completes all tasks assigned by the Internship Coordinator, and evaluation of teaching success and the quality of written assignments.

Credit Recommendation: *Semester 1:* In the upper division baccalaureate degree category, 3 semester hours in Montessori Internship/Teaching Practice. *Semester 2:* In the upper division baccalaureate degree category, 3 semester hours in Montessori Internship/Teaching Practice. **NOTE:** A total of 6 semester hours should be awarded for successful completion of semesters 1 and 2 (6/91).

I.B.E.W. Local Union 269

Electrical Workers, IBEW Local Union 269 of the International Brotherhood of Electrical Workers represents some 350 construction workers performing various electrical work in the Mercer, Burlington, and Bucks Country areas. A four-year apprenticeship training program includes 210 hours of classroom instruction and 2,000 hours of on-the-job training each year and is administered by Local 269 and the Southern Chapter of the National Electrical Contractors Association. The training enables each apprentice to read blueprints, to work safely with high voltages and to install, repair, and service electrical equipment and controls on residential, commercial, and industrial projects.

Local 269 has its own training facilities adjacent to the Union Offices. The facilities have several classrooms, labs, and demonstration and workshop rooms with a variety of workshops including electrical installation, wire and welding shops. The facilities also have a library with printed materials, overhead transparencies and films. The library is available to apprentices and journeypersons for their personal research. To receive journeyman status, all four years of the program must be completed.

Source of official student records: Registry of Credit Recommendations, American Council on Education, One Dupont Circle, Washington, DC 20036-1193 or Training Director, I.B.E.W. Local 269 J.A.T.C., 676 Whitehead Road, Trenton, NJ 08648.

Additional information about the courses: Office of Corporate-Higher Education, Thomas Edison State College, 101 West State Street, Trenton, NJ 08608-1176.

Effective Foremanship Workshop

Location: I.B.E.W. 269.

Length: 2 days (14-16 hours).

Dates: January 1986-April 1996.

Objective: To teach participants the critical elements necessary to perform effectively in a foreman's position in the electrical contracting industry.

Learning Outcome: Upon successful completion of this course, participants will be able to know and understand a foreman's responsibilities to the employer; understand electrical, architectural, structural and mechanical plans and specs and follow rules dealing with plans and specs; know and understand the rules dealing with the electrical code in effect on the job, including national, state and municipal codes; maintain harmonious working relationships with other trades' contractors and owners' representatives (including the general contractor) on a job and maintain accurate records regarding material, labor and equipment used; schedule and layout work to make the most efficient and uniform use of manpower, tools and equipment on the job an d be able to anticipate any manpower shortages or increases that may occur; supervise employees by enforcing fair standards of workmanship and productivity according to company policy and what the job demands; including: enforcing safety regulations, clear instructions to workers about their tasks; good housekeeping on the job; proper tools and materials available for the work to proceed productively; removing any employee who fails to perform satisfactorily; make sure time cards are filled out properly and on time and according to company policy; be familiar with the labor agreement; maintain good working relationship with a steward if one is assigned to the job by the union; anticipate labor jurisdictional problems and try to discuss with company reps ahead of time if possible; in the event of a labor dispute, keep accurate notes and make reports promptly to proper authorities; correctly deal with material needs through proper requisitioning and oversight, making sure all materials are stored properly to avoid damage or theft; make decisions about the tools and equipment needed for the job and make sure you know proper use and maintenance of tools and equipment and ensure their proper storage while on the job; and keep daily records or a journal on the job, and make sure the notes kept are accurate and authentic. They are necessary for both daily use and for any possible future labor or damage disputes between the company and other contractors on the job.

Instruction: Major topics covered in the course are The Foreman, The Foreman and Company Profit, Developing Leadership and Using It, The Foreman's Technical Know-How, Understanding and Appreciating Business Management and Administrative Procedures, Safety, The Foreman and the Union.

Credit Recommendation: In the lower division baccalaureate/associate degree category, 1 semester hour in Supervision (4/91).

Electrician Apprentice (Inside)

Location: Trenton, NJ.

Length: 4 years (210 clock hours per year of instruction).

Dates: *Version 1:* September 1978-August 1994; *Version 2:* September 1994-Present.

Objective: To prepare apprentices for journeymen status in the electrical construction (inside) industry.

Instruction: *First year:* Major topics covered in the course are principles of direct current, alternating current and electromagnetism; knowledge and application of National Electrical Code requirements pertaining to cable, conduit, and grounding; operation of electric motors; Ohm's law, series circuits, parallel circuits, magnetism, and motors, safety procedures and first aid resuscitation; reading and sketching of evaluation views and plot plans, including symbols and scales used; materials used in the electrical construction industry, such as wires, cables, conduit, conductors, insulation, joints, fasteners, and fuses; under supervision, installation of electrical apparatus such as cables, conduit, tubing, outlet boxes, outlets, fixtures, and securing and holding devices at various job sites; orientation to the apprenticeship form of education and training, the electrical industry, the history of electrical industry, the International Brotherhood of Electrical Workers, local union by-laws, and the history of the operation and contribution of the National Electrical Contractors Association.

Second year: Major topics covered in the course are use and installation of electric meters; National Electrical Code requirements relating to grounding conductors, branch circuits, and transformers; use of algebra and trigonometry in making mathematical calculations; types, construction, winding ratios, functions, and classifications of transformers; operating principles and functions of incandescent lamps, alarms, and refrigeration and air conditioning components; capacitance, inductance; reactance, and RLC circuits; electric motor mechanical drive and load connections; use of architect's blueprints and layouts; use and care of tools of the industry; circuit testing; first aid procedures, including those for electric shock victims; safety rules and practices for the electrical construction industry. Apprentices perform more complex work tasks through a series of six-month job rotations.

Third year: Major topics covered in the course are National Electrical Code requirement for capacitors, electric motors, hazardous locations, and Class I, II, and III installations; use of blueprints pertaining to structural details, floor plan specifications, floor ducts, service entrances, circuits, and rise circuits; electrical wiring and distribution systems; electrical theory pertaining to alternating currents, alternating current motors and transformers, power factor and correction, and primary and secondary connections; analysis of malfunctions and repair of remote controls, protection of devices, and alternating current motor controls. Apprentices apply knowledge by assuming increasingly complex responsibilities and performing increasingly complex tasks in work settings that are rotated each six months.

Fourth year: Major topics covered in the course are knowledge and application of National Electrical Code requirements pertaining to wire closets, junction boxes, and stairway and emergency lighting; metric system conversions; application of rules to radiation exposure, protection, reaction, and other features of nuclear safety; transistor principles and circuits, use of electronic testing equipment; basic rectifier circuits, amplifier circuits, special circuit applications, and transistor use; static control fundamentals, including concepts, circuits, analysis, and applications; alternating current applications in industrial electricity; fundamentals of temperature, pressure, and flow; instrumentation systems; installation and testing of electrical construction materials; use of electrical construction equipment.

Credit Recommendation: *Version 1: First year:* In the lower division baccalaureate/associate degree category, 4 semester hours in Basic Electricity, 1 in National Electrical Code, 1 in Blueprint Reading and Sketching, and 2 in field experience in Electrical Construction, 1 in Technical Mathematics, for a total of 9 semester hours.

Second year: In the lower division baccalaureate/associate degree category, 4 semester hours in Basic Electricity, 5 in field experience in Electrical Construction, 2 in National Electrical Code, 1 in Technical Mathematics, 2 in Blueprint Reading and Sketching, 4 in Electrical Machinery, and 1 in Safety and First Aid for a total of 19 semester hours.

Third year: In the lower division baccalaureate/associate degree category, 4 semester hours in Basic Electricity, 3 in National Electrical Code, 3 in Blueprint Reading and Sketching, 7 in field experience in Electrical Construction, 1 in Technical Mathematics, 2 in A.C. Machinery, 1 in Safety and First Aid for a total of 27 semester hours.

Fourth year: In the lower division baccalaureate/associate degree category, 4 semester hours in Basic Electricity, 1 semester hour in Technical Mathematics, 4 in National Electrical Code, 4 in Blueprint Reading and Sketching, 9 in field experience in Electrical Construction, 2 in Safety and First Aid, 3 in Motor Controls, 3 in Electronics, 4 in Electrical Machinery, 2 in A.C. Machinery for a total of 36 semester hours (1/84) (4/91). **NOTE:** The credit recommendation is cumulative; readers should use the recommendation that corresponds to the number of years completed by the student. *Version 2: First year:* In the lower division baccalaureate/associate degree category, 4 semester hours in Basic Electricity, 1 in National Electrical Code, 1 in Blueprint Reading and Sketching, 2 in field experience in Electrical Construction, and 1 in Technical Mathematics, for a total of 9 semester hours.

Second year: In the lower division baccalaureate/associate degree category, 2 semester hours in Basic Electricity, 3 in field experience in Electrical Construction, 1 in National Electrical Code, 1 in Technical Mathematics, 1 in Blueprint Reading and Sketching, 2 in Electrical Machinery, and 1 in Safety and First Aid for a total of 11 semester hours.

Third year: In the lower division baccalaureate/associate degree category, 1 in National Electrical Code, 1 in Blueprint Reading and Sketching, 2 in field experience in Electrical Construction, 1 in Technical Mathematics, 2 in Motor Controls, 3 in Electrical Machinery, and 2 in Electrical Power for a total of 12 semester hours.

Fourth year: In the lower division baccalaureate/associate degree category, 1 in National Electrical Code, 1 in Blueprint Reading and Sketching, 2 in field experience in Electrical Construction, 1 in Safety and First Aid, 1 in Motor Controls, 2 in Electronics, 1 in Instrumentation Systems and 2 in Industrial Electronics, for a total of 11 semester hours (8/94). **NOTE:** Participants will earn the appropriate credit recommendation based on the time completed in the program (e.g., 1 year-9 semester hours; 2 years-20 semester hours; 3 years-32 semester hours; 4 years-43 semester hours).

Tele-Data and Fiber Optics

Location: Rupert Jahn Trade School.

Length: 109 hours (8 hours per week/over 3 month period).

Dates: *Version 1:* May 1991-August 1994; *Version 2:* September 1994-Present.

Objective: To provide the maximum hands-on training and experience to apprentices or journeymen students in the expanding field of telecommunications.

Instruction: The course is divided into four modulars, Introduction, Data, Telephone, and Fiber Optics. The Introduction Modular covers four areas: voice and data cabling, types of voice and data cabling, methods of termination, and fiber optics. The Telephone Modular covers eight areas: introduction, main distributing frame and closets, pulling station cable-floor cells-overhead, terminating riser cables, terminating station cables in closets, splicing riser cables, terminating different station blocks, and testing. The Data Modular covers seven areas: IBM cabling systems, RS232-twisted pair, coax cables, twin-ax, ethernet, testing and labeling. The Fiber Optics Modular covers the following sixteen points; introduction to fiber optic technology, light guide general information, light wave safety, fiber types and fiber manufacturers, cable types, building and fire code considerations, cable types, building and fire code considerations, cable replacement techniques for LAN, planning and supervising a LAN, installing a Kellems' pulling grip, installing a Kellems' split grip, cable preparation techniques for installing fiber optic connectors, installing ST connectors on multimode fiber; single fiber mechanical splicing techniques, introduction to fiber optic testing, optical time domain reflectometer: principle of operation, optical time domain reflectometer: use and application.

Credit Recommendation: *Version 1:* In the lower division baccalaureate/associate degree category, 3 semester hours in Telecommunications and 1 semester hour in Fiber Optics (4/91). *Version 2:* In the lower division baccalaureate/associate degree category, 4 semester hours in Telecommunications and 2 semester hours in Fiber Optics, for a total of 6 semester hours (8/94).

ICI University

ICI University was founded as the International Correspondence Institute in 1967 by the Division of Foreign Missions of the Assemblies of God. ICI operated in Springfield, Missouri (USA) until 1972 when it moved its international office to Brussels, Belgium. The international office moved to its present location in Irving, Texas (USA) in 1991. In 1993 the name was changed to ICI University to reflect the international nature of its degree programs.

ICI University is a distance learning institution that offers instruction at various levels. ICI has developed evangelism and Christian education courses for preaching the message of Christ, teaching new Christians, and training workers for the local church. For ministerial training ICI University offers an Associate of Arts degree, and two Bachelor's degrees. A Master of Arts degree program was added in 1995.

The purpose of ICI University's academic programs is to train leaders for the various ministries of the church. ICI's courses and programs are suitable for independent study, instruction in school classrooms, and other types of group study. ICI provides courses for a wide variety of needs and goals. ICI University now has offices in more than 130 countries. Educational agreements link ICI University with over 100 schools worldwide who use ICI materials for all or part of their academic programs.

It should be noted that ICI courses and curricula are under constant development. Resident faculty combine their efforts with adjunct or "global" faculty to prepare, teach, revise, and improve the instructional materials. The ICI University faculty hold at least a master's degree and/or long and specific experience in the areas of their expertise. The instructional programs are supported by a world wide program of student services. Outcomes are reviewed by a well-staffed department of Research and Evaluation.

Source of official student records: Registry of Credit Recommendations, American Council on Education, One Dupont Circle, Washington, DC 20036-1193.

Additional information about the courses: College Credit Recommendation Service, American Council on Education, One Dupont Circle, Washington, DC 20036-1193.

BL1013: New Testament Survey

Location: ICIU centers or resident training sites worldwide and home study.

Length: 90-135 study hours (15 lessons).

Dates: October 1988-Present.

Objective: To give the student a panoramic view of the New Testament and an understanding of its messages and personalities and an interpretation of its doctrines.

Learning Outcome: Upon successful completion of this course, the student will be able to do effective biblical studies; gain a better understanding of the message of each New Testament book; see the Christo-centric character of the New Testament; and develop an integrated understanding of the various New Testament books, doctrines, personalities, and problems.

Instruction: Major topics covered in the course are introduction to church history, the Gospels, the records of the early church, and the problems of the early church. Methods of instruction include study guide, textbook, study questions, independent study, self tests, unit progress evaluations, written project, and final examination.

Credit Recommendation: In the lower division baccalaureate/associate degree category, 3 semester hours in Bible, Religion, or Christianity (9/95).

BL1023: Old Testament Survey

Location: ICIU Centers of resident training sites worldwide and home study.

Length: 90-135 study hours (15 lessons).

Dates: September 1985-Present.

Objective: Upon completing this course the student will have an understanding of a range of events from man's creation to the era just prior to the birth of Christ, considered from the historic, prophetic and doctrinal contexts, from a conservative evangelical perspective.

Learning Outcome: Upon successful completion of this course, the student will be able to identify and categorize the Old Testament canon; explain the concept of inspiration as it relates to the authorship, transmission and translation of the test. Summarize and know the significance of what God has revealed in Genesis 1-11; the Abrahamic, Mosaic and Davidic covenants, the exodus, conquest, united and divided kingdoms, exile and restoration. Discuss the values of the poetic and prophetic literature with attention to messianic and eschatological implications. Understand the relationship of the testaments and how the OT is pertinent to our own life and relationship to God.

Instruction: Major topics covered in the course are inspiration, the canon, the creation and fall, the patriarchs, the exodus and birth of the nation of Israel, rise and fall of the kingdom poets and prophets. Methods of instruction include a study guide, textbook, study questions, independent study, self tests, unit progress evaluations, written project, and examination.

Credit Recommendation: In the lower division baccalaureate/associate degree category, 3 semester hours in Bible or Religion (9/95).

BL1032: The Life of Christ

Location: ICIU centers or resident training sites worldwide and home study.

Length: 60-90 study hours (13 lessons).

Dates: November 1992-Present.

Objective: To provide the student with an understanding of the chronological progression and the spiritual significance of the events in the life of Christ.

Learning Outcome: Upon successful completion of this course, the student will be able to summarize Christ's teachings on the kingdom of God and analyze the already but not yet aspects of the Kingdom; explain Christ's purpose in using parables and miracles and discuss His teaching method; discuss the historical background of Palestine and the Jewish religious development that prepared the way for Christ's coming; identify key events in the early life of Christ, His public ministry, and His final days on earth; and distinguish between Christ's early ministry, greater Galilean ministry, later Judean/Perean ministry, and Passion Week.

Instruction: Major topics covered in the course are the historical background; preparation for the ministry; early Judean/Perean ministry and the passion week; the arrest, trial crucifixion, and resurrection; the teachings of Christ; the kingdom of God; the parables of Jesus; and the miracles of Jesus. Methods of instruction include independent-study text, study questions, independent study, self tests, unit progress evaluations, written project, and final examination.

Credit Recommendation: In the lower division baccalaureate/associate degree category, 2 semester hours in Religion, Theology, Bible, or Christianity (9/95).

BL1043: Pentateuch

Location: ICIU Centers or resident training sites worldwide and home study.

Length: 90-135 study hours (14 lessons).

Dates: September 1985-Present.

Objective: Upon completion of the course, the student will have an understanding of the history of the earth from the creation to the establishing of the nation of Israel, including the Decalogue, the Law, and the establishing of the Levitical preisthood, from a conservative evangelical perspective.

Learning Outcome: Upon successful completion of this course, the student will be able to discuss creation as an act of God; discuss man's rebellion, and Gods' redemptive acts; the persevering faith of the Patriarchs; the redemption of Israel; the giving of the law; the wilderness experiences as they are revealed in the Pentateuch; and relate to the student's own experience of God and the world and the student's service for God.

Instruction: Major topics covered in the course are Primeval and patriarchal history, from slavery to freedom, worship and ministry, and Moses' farewell to Israel. Methods of instruction include study guide, textbook, study questions, independent study, self tests, unit progress evaluations, written project, and final examination.

Credit Recommendation: In the upper division baccalaureate degree category, 3 semester hours in Bible or Religion (9/95).

BL1053: Acts

Location: ICIU centers or resident training sites worldwide and home study.

Length: 90-135 study hours (15 lessons).

Dates: October 1988-Present.

Objective: To provide the student with an understanding of the continuing ministry of christ in the world through the Holy Spirit, evidenced through the inception and growth of the church as recounted in Acts.

Learning Outcome: Upon successful completion of this course, the student will be able to demonstrate that one of the major purposes of Acts is to show how the resurrected Christ continued His ministry in the world through the Holy Spirit; demonstrate from the text of Acts why it was written, and relate from personal insight what purposes Acts fulfills today in your life and in your church; identify the main persons and geographical terms used in Acts; trace the geographical and chronological expansion of the gospel from its Jerusalem-Judean base to Rome; and analyze the major reasons for the growth of the church in Acts and apply them to the local church.

Instruction: Major topics covered in the course are; the birth of the Church, persecution and expansion of the Church, the acts of Peter and the beginnings of Gentile Christianity, Paul's first missionary journey and the apostolic decree, evangelization on the Aegean shores, and Paul's planned visit to Rome and unforeseen route. Methods of instruction include study guide, textbook, study questions, independent study, self tests, unit progress evaluations, written project and final examination.

Credit Recommendation: In the lower division baccalaureate/associate degree category, 3 semester hours in Bible, Theology, Religion, or Christianity (9/95).

BL1062: Principles of Biblical Interpretation

Location: ICIU centers or resident training sites worldwide and home study.

Length: 60-90 study hours (13 lessons).

Dates: August 1994-Present.

Objective: To provide the student with an understanding of the guidelines of biblical interpretation.

Learning Outcome: Upon successful completion of this course, the student will be able to describe rules of interpretation associated with each of the six circles of context, justify the need for adhering to rules of interpretation when explaining a biblical text, explain the major systems of Bible interpretation found in Judaism and Christianity, apply rules of interpretation in the study of example passages of scripture, and develop a pattern of personal Bible study based on biblical principles of interpretation.

Instruction: Major topics covered in the course are foundational rules for interpretation, general principles of interpretation, special principles of interpretations, and application of principles of interpretation. Methods of instruction include independent-study text, study questions, independent study, self tests, unit progress evaluations, written project, and final examination.

Credit Recommendation: In the lower division baccalaureate/associate degree category, 2 semester hours in Religion, Christianity, or Bible (9/95).

BL1063: Hermeneutics

Location: ICIU centers or various resident training sites worldwide and home study.

Length: 90-135 hours (15 lessons).

Dates: January 1987-Present.

Objective: To acquaint students with various theories of biblical interpretation and show the superiority of literal interpretation for the evangelical student. Students will apply principles learned to the interpretation of Titus and Habakkuk.

Learning Outcome: Upon successful completion of this course, the student will be able to describe the superiority of literal interpretation over other alternatives and apply these principles to his or her own interpretations of scripture.

Instruction: Major topics covered in the course are major schools of biblical interpretation; validity of literal interpretation; use of biblical reference resources; the doctrine of inerrancy; typological interpretation; prophecy; and devotional use of the Bible. Methods of instruction include study guide, textbooks, study questions, independent study, self tests, unit progress evaluations, written project, and final examination.

Credit Recommendation: In the lower division baccalaureate/associate degree category, 3 semester hours in Bible, Theology, or Religion (12/94).

BL1063: Principles of Biblical Interpretation

Location: ICIU centers or resident training sites worldwide and home study.

Length: 90-135 study hours (13 lessons).

Dates: October 1995-Present.

Objective: To provide the student with an understanding of the guidelines of biblical interpretation.

Learning Outcome: Upon successful completion of this course, the student will be able to describe rules of interpretation associated with each of the six circles of context, justify the need for adhering to rules of interpretation when explaining a biblical text, explain the major systems found in Judaism and Christianity, apply rules of interpretation in the study of example passages of Scripture, and develop a pattern of personal Bible study based on biblical principles of interpretation.

Instruction: Major topics covered in the course are foundation rules for interpretation, general principles of interpretation, special principles of interpretation, and application of principles of interpretation. Methods of instruction include study guide, textbook, study questions, independent study, self tests, unit progress evaluations, written project, and final examination.

Credit Recommendation: In the lower division baccalaureate/associate degree

category, 3 semester hours in Christianity , Bible, or Religion (9/95).

BL1073: Old Testament Historical Books

Location: ICIU Centers or various resident training sites worldwide and home study.

Length: 90-135 study hours (15 lessons).

Dates: November 1985-Present.

Objective: Upon completion of the course, the student will have knowledge of the history of the nation of Israel from its establishment as a nation, through the time of exile, and return and be able to make contemporary application of the material.

Learning Outcome: Upon successful completion of this course the student will be able to understand the background, structure contents and major teaching of each of the historical books; have a chronological understanding of Hebrew history; understand God's redemption purpose in biblical history and particularly Israel's role in that purpose; relate events described in the historical books to other biblical material; increase their ability to study the biblical material and make contemporary application of the biblical texts.

Instruction: Major topics covered in the course are: The nature of biblical history, the period of conquest, the period of judges, the period of monarchy, and the period following the exile. Methods of instruction include study guide, textbook, study questions, independent study, self-tests, unit progress evaluations, written project, and final examination.

Credit Recommendation: In the upper division baccalaureate degree category, 3 semester hours in Bible or Religion (9/95).

BL1083: Galatians and Romans

Location: ICIU centers or various resident training sites worldwide and home study.

Length: 90-135 study hours (14 lessons).

Dates: *Version 1:* January 1992-Present; *Version 2:* October 1995-Present.

Objective: To present to students the historical, literary, and theological background and content of Romans and Galatians, and to analyze Paul's flow of thought in both letters.

Learning Outcome: Upon successful completion of this course, the student will be familiar with the life and ministry of the Apostle Paul as reflected in Romans and Galatians; will be enabled to interpret and apply the teachings of Paul (theological, ecclesiastical, social, and ethical) to contemporary situations, and will understand the significance of Romans and Galatians in Christian history.

Instruction: Major topics covered in the course are the life and ministry of Paul; introductory matters such as dates, recipients, and purpose of the writings; theological issues; the development of Paul's thought and teachings; and the theological, ecclesiastical, and social applications of the two letters for the contemporary situation. Methods of instruction include study guide, textbook, study questions, independent study, self tests, unit progress evaluations, written project, and final examination.

Credit Recommendation: *Version 1:* In the lower division baccalaureate/associate degree category, 3 semester hours in Religion, Theology, or Christianity (12/94). *Version 2:* In the upper division baccalaureate degree category, 3 semester hours in Religion, Theology, or Christianity (9/95).

BL1103: The Gospel of John

Location: ICIU centers or resident training sites worldwide.

Length: 90-135 hours (15 lessons).

Dates: *Version 1:* January 1993-September 1995; *Version 2:* October 1995-Present.

Objective: To introduce students to the historical, literary, theological, and language characteristics and content of the Gospel of John.

Learning Outcome: Upon successful completion of this course, students will be able to interpret the Gospel of John in relation to its historical, literary, theological, and language characteristics and information; and evaluate and apply knowledge gained about John to their individual faith.

Instruction: Major topics covered in the course are authorship, date, vocabulary, literary characteristics, structure, purpose, signs and their significance, and theological themes of the Gospel of John. Methods of instruction include study guide, textbook, study questions, independent study, self tests, unit progress evaluations, written projects, and final examination.

Credit Recommendation: *Version 1:* In the lower division baccalaureate/associate degree category, 3 semester hours in Religion, Theology, or Christianity (12/94). *Version 2:* In the upper division baccalaureate/associate degree category, 3 semester hours in Religion, Theology, or Christianity (9/95).

BL1112: The Corinthian Letters

Location: ICIU centers or resident training sites worldwide and home study.

Length: 60-90 study hours (15 lessons).

Dates: March 1987-Present.

Objective: To provide the student with an understanding of the Corinthian letters, of life in Corinth at the time of the letters and challenges to the Church in that life situation.

Learning Outcome: Upon successful completion of this course, the student will be able to understand Paul's Corinthian correspondence in view of the customs in Corinth and the problems in the church there; identify the main spiritual principles presented by Paul and relate them to situations in life and in church, especially such principles as Christian giving, church ministry, the missionary enterprise of the church, and gifts of the Spirit; recognize areas of Christian life where discipline is needed; and understand and appreciate more deeply the work of the Holy Spirit in the New Testament church and in the church today.

Instruction: Major topics covered in the course are background study of the Corinthian correspondence, Christian and spiritual discipline, church practice, spiritual gifts and applications for the church's ministry in today's world. Methods of instruction include independent-study text, study questions, independent study, self tests, unit progress evaluations, written project, and final examination.

Credit Recommendation: In the upper division baccalaureate degree category, 2 semester hours in Bible, Religion, or Christianity (9/95).

BL1113: Corinthians

Location: ICIU centers or various resident training sites worldwide and home study.

Length: 90-135 study hours (15 lessons).

Dates: March 1984-Present.

Objective: To study the Corinthian correspondence by means of formal exegetical discipline in order to delineate the church's problems and the solutions to those problems.

Learning Outcome: Upon successful completion of this course, the student will be able to apply formal and exegetical methods to the interpretation of Corinthian correspondence and demonstrate that application by interpretation of assigned texts; and apply solutions to the problems of the Corinthian church to the same or similar church problems today.

Instruction: Major topics covered in the course are exegetical methodology; application of exegetical methodology to specified texts; the problems of the Corinthian church and their solutions; and today's church problems and solutions in light of the Corinthian church. Methods of instruction include study guide, textbook, study questions, independent study, self tests, unit progress evaluations, written project, and final examination.

Credit Recommendation: In the upper division baccalaureate degree category, 3 semester hours in Religion, Theology, or Christianity (12/94).

BL1132/3: Themes from the Major Prophets

Location: ICIU centers or resident training sites worldwide and home study.

Length: *Version 1 (BL1132):* 60-90 study hours (15 lessons); *Version 2 (BL1133):* 90-135 study hours (15 lessons).

Dates: *Version 1:* March 1987-Present; *Version 2:* March 1995-Present.

Objective: To provide the student with an understanding of the writings of Isaiah, Jeremiah, and Ezekiel.

Learning Outcome: Upon successful completion of this course, the student will be able to understand more clearly an important and sometimes difficult part of God's Word, describe the similarity between the task of the Old Testament prophet and ministry and service today, explain the importance and meaning of what the prophets were saying to the people of their own time, apply the prophets' message to men and women of the present, and describe how the message of salvation so clearly taught in the New Testament had been a part of God's message in Old Testament times.

Instruction: *Version 1:* Methods of instruction include independent-study text, study questions, independent study, self tests, unit progress evaluations, written project, and final examination. *Version 2:* Methods of instruction include study guide, textbook, study questions, independent study, self tests, unit progress evaluations, written project, and final examination.

Credit Recommendation: *Version 1:* In the upper division baccalaureate degree category, 2 semester hours in Bible, Religion, or Christianity. *Version 2:* In the upper division baccalaureate degree category, 3 semester hours in Bible, Religion, or Christianity (9/95).

BL1163: The Minor Prophets

Location: ICIU centers or resident training sites worldwide and home study.

Length: 90-135 study hours (13 lessons).

Dates: October 1993-Present.

Objective: To provide the student with an understanding of the contributions of the minor prophets from historical, prophetic and doctrinal perspectives.

Learning Outcome: Upon successful completion of this course, the student will be able to state the time of writing, to whom the message was addressed, the historical background and unique characteristics of each of the Minor Prophets; identify the ministry and contribution of each of the minor prophets to his own time and to the Church Age; use the messianic prophecies and their fulfillment in the Gospels to show that Jesus is the Messiah of whom the minor prophets wrote; and discuss the multiple fulfillment of prophecies concerning the Day of the Lord, the outpouring of the Holy Spirit, and other events, including those that will have their complete fulfillment in Christ's millennial kingdom. Methods of instruction include learner presentations, reports, indpendent study, unit evaluations, student project, and final examination.

Instruction: Major topics covered in the course are Obadiah, servant of God; Joel; prophet of Pentecost; Jonah, unwilling missionary; Amos, preacher of holiness; Josea; prophet of love; Micah; prophet of the Messiah; Zephaniah, prophet of universal judgement; Nahum, prophet of Ninveh's doom; Habakkuk, the questioning prophet; Haggai, motivator to build for God; Zechariah, prophet of messianic visions; and Malachi, prophet of revival. Methods of instruction include study guide, textbook, study questions, independent study, unit progress evaluations, self tests, written project, and final examination.

Credit Recommendation: In the upper division baccalaureate degree category, 3 semester hours in Religion, Bible, or Christianity (9/95).

BL1172: A Study in the Book of Hebrews

Location: ICIU centers or resident training sites worldwide and home study.

Length: 60-90 study hours (13 lessons).

Dates: *Version 1:* March 1987-September 1995; *Version 2:* October 1995-Present.

Objective: To provide the student with a clearer understanding of the main themes of the book of Hebrew.

Learning Outcome: Upon successful completion of this course, the student will be able to explain the struggles of the people to whom Hebrews was written and compare it with spiritual problems that exist for some Christians of different religious backgrounds today, understand the relationship between the old covenant and the new and explain how the symbolism in the tabernacle and the sacrificial systems are fulfilled in Christ, and appreciate more deeply the priesthood of Christ and the advantages that He gives by His present ministry.

Instruction: Major topics covered in the course are the best revelation of God's nature, the best revelation of God's love, the best revelation of God's power, Christ the perfect high priest, priesthood of a better order, priesthood with better provisions, priesthood with a perfect sacrifice, call to persevere in faith, examples of living by faith a better way of life and practical instructions for living. Methods of instruction include independent-study text, study questions, independent study, self tests, unit progress evaluations, written project, and final examination.

Credit Recommendation: *Version 1:* In the lower division baccalaureate degree category, 2 semester hours in Religion or Bible. *Version 2:* In the upper division baccalaureate degree category, 2 semester hours in Religion, Bible, or Christianity (9/95).

BL1173: Hebrews

Location: ICIU center or resident training sites worldwide and home study.

Length: 90-135 study hours (14 lessons).

Dates: October 1990-Present.

Objective: An understanding of the exhortations given in the book of Hebrews while gaining an insight to the ministry of Christ as the fulfillment of the Old Covenant.

Learning Outcome: Upon successful completion of this course, the student will be able to relate the Old Testament religion to Christ and to the divine plan of salvation; describe the supremacy of Christ in terms of His person and His atoning and priestly work; identify Old Testament characters, institutions, and events mentioned in the book of Hebrew; understand and appreciate the meaning of salvation;

and explain such basic concepts as faith, salvation, and holiness to non-Christian friends.

Instruction: Major topics covered in the course are; supremacy of the person of Christ, supremacy of the priesthood of Christ; and supremacy of the new and living way. Methods of instruction include study guide, textbook, study questions, independent study, self tests, unit progress evaluations, written project, and final examination.

Credit Recommendation: In the upper division baccalaureate degree category, 3 semester hours in Bible, Religion, or Hebrews (9/95).

BL1182: Genesis

Location: ICIU centers or resident training sites worldwide and home study.

Length: 60-90 study hours (14 lessons).

Dates: September 1985-Present.

Objective: To understand the Genesis record of God's plan of redemption from its beginning promise in Eden to the formation of God's chosen people through whom this plan would be realized.

Learning Outcome: Upon successful completion of this course, the student will be able to answer the arguments of critics about the historical reliability of Genesis; show how the seeming conflict speculative science and the creation account can be resolved; evaluate the historical basis of New Testament doctrines of God's progressive self-revelation, and His purpose in all His dealings with man; identify and draw practical applications from the lives of many people in Genesis; apply the moral and spiritual principle taught in Genesis to their own life; and use illustrative material and other helps from this course in preaching and teaching.

Instruction: Major topics covered in the course are: Genesis and science, creation and fall; antediluvian world; God and his family of faith - Abraham and beginnings of the Israelite — Isaac, Jacob and Joseph. Methods of instruction include independent-study text, study questions, independent study, self tests, unit progress evaluations, written project, and final examination.

Credit Recommendation: In the upper division baccalaureate degree category, 2 semester hours in Bible or Religion (9/95).

BL1212: Daniel and Revelation

Location: ICIU centers or resident training site worldwide and home study.

Length: 60-90 study hours (14 lessons).

Dates: March 1987-Present.

Objective: To provide the student with an understanding of biblical prophecy as recorded in the books of Daniel and Revelation.

Learning Outcome: Upon successful completion of this course, the student will be able to identify major events, terms, time sequences, and personalities referred to in the books of Revelation and Daniel; describe Jesus' messages to the seven churches and explain how they relate to local churches, individuals and to the entire church age; describe the picture of the antichrist prefigured in Daniel and compare and contrast this with the more specific portrayal in Daniel and how this will culminate in the Great Tribulation period and the Battle of Armageddon.

Instruction: Major topics covered in the course are overviews of the books of Daniel and Revelation, personalities and events of both books, and relationship of personalities and events to end-time prophecy. Methods of instruction include independent-study text, study questions, independent study, self tests, unit progress evaluations, written project, and final examination.

Credit Recommendation: In the upper division baccalaureate degree category, 2 semester hours in Bible, Religion, or Christianity (9/95).

BL1244: Greek I

Location: ICIU centers or resident training sites worldwide and home study.

Length: 120-180 study hours (16 lessons).

Dates: October 1985-Present.

Objective: To provide the student with a basic knowledge of Greek grammar for translation of selected portions of the New Testament Greek text into his or her language.

Learning Outcome: Upon successful completion of this course, the student will be able to recognize and recite from memory the endings to greek words that are taught in this course; understand and discuss intelligently those grammatical concepts and constructions that are characteristic of the Greek language; and appreciate the tremendous value that an understanding of the Greek language has as an aid to interpreting the New Testament.

Instruction: Major topics covered in the course are the Greek alphabet and accent, conjugation and declensions of present tense, first and second declensions, declension of masculine nouns, imperfect conjugation of middle and passive voices, and future and aorist conjugation. Methods of instruction include study guide, textbook, audiotapes, study questions, independent study, self tests, unit progress evaluations, written project, and final examination.

Credit Recommendation: In the lower division baccalaureate/associate degree category, 4 semester hours in Language, Greek, or New Testament special studies (9/95).

BL1254: Greek II

Location: ICIU centers or resident training sites worldwide and home study.

Length: 120-180 study hours (17 lessons).

Dates: October 1985-Present.

Objective: To provide the student with a basic knowledge of the elements of syntax and concepts of grammar that are essential to translation and exegesis of the New Testament Greek text.

Learning Outcome: Upon successful completion of this course, the student will be able to recognize (through understanding, recitation, and memorization), the elements of Greek grammar and syntax to translate selected portions of the New Testament.

Instruction: Major topics covered in the course are third declension of nouns; participles; subjective, infinitive, contract and liquid verbs; third declension of nouns and adjectives; numerals; prepositional phrases; pronouns; moods; perfect tense and irregular verbs; and adjectives. Methods of instruction include study guide, textbook, audiotapes, study questions, independent study, self tests, unit progress evaluations, written project, and final examination.

Credit Recommendation: In the lower division baccalaureate/associate degree category, 4 semester hours in Language, Greek, or Religion (9/95).

BL1272: Paul's Letters to Pastors

Location: ICIU centers or resident training sites worldwide and home study.

Length: 60-90 study hours (14 lessons).

Dates: March 1994-Present.

Objective: To provide students with an understanding of the background and content of 1 and 2 Timothy and Titus; to provide an understanding of God's strategy for a healthy church.

Learning Outcome: Upon successful completion of this course the student will be able to discuss the basic outline and content of the pastoral letters, explain how the pastoral letters relate to the rest of the New Testament, describe the basic priorities of the work of a pastor, recognize and avoid errors that are similar to those which existed in the church at the time Paul wrote to Timothy and Titus, explain what the pastoral letters teach about the essential nature of the gospel, and identify what Paul instructed Timothy and Titus teach to the various groupings in their churches.

Instruction: Major topics covered in the course are an introduction to the background and content of the pastoral letters and the ordering of the church, the ministry to the church, the responsibility of the congregation, and the responsibilities of God's ministers. Methods of instruction include independent-study text, study questions, self tests, unit progress evaluations, written project, and final examination.

Credit Recommendation: In the lower division baccalaureate/associate degree category, 2 semester hours in Bible, Religion, or Christianity (9/95).

BL1284: Hebrew I

Location: ICIU centers or resident training sites worldwide and home study.

Length: 120-180 study hours (16 lessons).

Dates: June 1986-Present.

Objective: To provide the student with a basic knowledge of the fundamentals of the Hebrew language and the ability to translate the Hebrew Old Testament text into his or her language.

Learning Outcome: Upon successful completion of this course, the student will be able to describe the basic concepts of Hebrew grammar (including the components of the basic sentence, the function of mood, person number and gender; the construct relation; and the unique nature of the Hebrew verb with its conjugations and their meanings), read and translate simplified prose in biblical Hebrew, and explain certain key concepts connected with Hebrew grammar and vocabulary in order to bring enrichments and inspiration to life.

Instruction: Major topics covered in the course are the pronunciation and formation of Hebrew letters and words, the formation and writing of simple and complex sentences, and the study of the regular and intensive and extensive patterns of the verb. Methods of instruction include study guide, textbook, audiotapes, study questions, independent study, self tests, unit progress evaluations, written project, and final examination.

Credit Recommendation: In the upper division baccalaureate degree category, 4 semester hours in Language, Bible, or Religion (9/95).

BL1294: Hebrew II

Location: ICIU centers or resident training sites worldwide and home study.

Length: 120-180 study hours (16 lessons).

Dates: June 1986-Present.

Objective: To equip the student to read, understand and translate selected passages of narrative prose in the Hebrew Bible.

Learning Outcome: Upon successful completion of this course, the student will be able to read a passage of biblical Hebrew prose with comprehension and without reading difficulty, analyze the relationships within a passage (syntax and morphology) that determine its meaning, and use Hebrew to exegate a passage of Scripture.

Instruction: Major topics covered in the course are the study of verbs not included in BL1284 (Hebrew I), the study of other selected elements of Hebrew grammar, and the application of Hebrew grammar to exegsis. Methods of instruction include study guide, textbook, audiotapes, study questions, independent study, self tests, unit progress evaluations, written project, and final examination.

Credit Recommendation: In the upper division baccalaureate degree category, 4 semester hours in Language, Bible, and Christianity (9/95).

BL5101: Historical Approach to Hermeneutics

Location: ICI University graduate studies centers and resident training sites worldwide and home study.

Length: Approximately 180 contact hours.

Dates: June 1994-Present.

Objective: To provide the student with an awareness of cultural and historic forces that influence biblical interpretation which will help the student recognize forces which influence culture.

Learning Outcome: Upon successful completion of this course, the student will be able to recognize forces at work, forces for change, and currents of thought that impact (and have impacted) the interpretation of Scripture historically, rationally, and scientifically.

Instruction: Major topics covered in the course are two thousand years of biblical interpretation; definition of history, forces at work, currents of thought, and catalysts for change; the development of biblical interpretation in the second century; the development of schools of biblical interpretation; the importance of the fourth and fifth centuries on medieval hermeneutics; background of the Reformation period; from the Reformation and counter-Reformation to the Enlightenment; background of rationalism and scientific thought; rationalism and biblical interpretation; summary of scientific thought; new approaches to biblical interpretation; and trends in present-day biblical interpretation. Methods of instruction include graduate study guide, textbooks, supplemental readings, independent study, questions for reflection or discussion, directed research, written unit assignments, case observation and analysis assignments, and final essay assignment.

Credit Recommendation: In the graduate degree category, 3 semester hours in Religion, Hermeneutics, Christianity, or History of the Bible (7/96).

BL5102: New Testament Exegesis and Criticism

Location: ICI University graduate studies centers and resident training sites worldwide and home study.

Length: Approximately 180 contact hours.

Dates: June 1996-Present.

Objective: To provide the student with knowledge and skills to engage in serious, disciplined exegesis of biblical text with a greater spiritual and intellectual understanding of the meaning that was intended by the author, taking into consideration differences in language, culture, and historical setting.

Learning Outcome: Upon successful completion of this course, the student will be able to employ spiritually and intellectually sound exegetical principles and techniques to exegete and evaluate passages of biblical text in light of historical setting and biblical authority and to distinguish between and assess the validity of criticisms and methods generally accepted by Evangelicals and those not generally accepted by Evangelicals.

Instruction: Major topics covered in the course are background and history of biblical exegesis, the authority of the bible, the "new" hermeneutic, linguistics and philosophy of language, textual analysis, historical analysis, syntactical and verbal analysis, literary analysis, form criticism, redaction criticism and canonical criticism, tradition criticism, approaches to exegesis, and exegesis and expository sermons. Methods of instruction include graduate study guide, textbooks, supplemental readings, independent study, questions for reflection or discussion, directed research, written unit assignments, case observation and analysis assignments, and final essay assignment.

Credit Recommendation: In the graduate degree category, 3 semester hours in Bible, Theology, Religion, or Literary Studies (7/96).

BL5103: The Bible as Literature: Theory and Methodology

Location: ICI University graduate studies centers and resident training sites worldwide and home study.

Length: Approximately 180 contact hours.

Dates: June 1994-Present.

Objective: To equip the student to read and study the Bible more effectively and to recognize literary genres of the Bible and apply the relevant tools of analysis to each genre for interpretation of literary aspects of the Bible.

Learning Outcome: Upon successful completion of this course, the student will be able to defend the Bible as a literary work, recognize of human experiences that make up much biblical content, identify the literary genre(s) of biblical texts, describe unity and structure of biblical texts, and make a complete literary analysis of biblical text.

Instruction: Major topics covered in the course are the literary nature of the Bible, reading and interpreting the Bible as literature, the elements of narrative, hero stories, epic and tragedy, the language of biblical poetry, how to explicate a poem, types of biblical poems, proverb, satire, encomium, drama, visionary literature, New Testament narrative, and further new testament forms. Methods of instruction include graduate study guide, textbooks, supplemental readings, independent study, case studies, learner presentations/reports, directed research, written unit assignments, and final essay assignment.

Credit Recommendation: In the graduate degree category, 3 semester hours in Literature, Bible, Religion, or Theology (7/96).

BL5107: Graduate Greek I

Location: ICI University graduate studies centers and resident training sites worldwide and home study.

Length: Approximately 180 contact hours.

Dates: July 1986-Present.

Objective: To provide the student with a knowledge of the basic elements of *Koine* Greek grammar and syntax and enable the student to read and understand the Greek text of both the New Testament and extrabiblical *Koine* literature with emphasis on reading Greek as it was written by Greek authors and avoiding the English syntactical approach.

Learning Outcome: Upon successful completion of this course, the student will be able to recognize, understand, and discuss grammatical concepts and constructions that are characteristic of *Koine* Greek; appreciate the value of reading with understanding the *Koine* Greek of the New Testament and extrabiblical literature; and understand the importance of knowing *Koine* Greek before exegesis is undertaken.

Instruction: Major topics covered in the course are *Koine* Greek grammar, including the alphabet; verb tenses and their importance, the first two delensions, and other grammatical points. Methods of instruction include graduate study guide, textbooks, audio tapes, study questions, independent study, mentor assistance, self tests, unit progress evaluations, and a proctored 3-hour final examination that includes sight translation of a New Testament and/or extra-neotestament passage.

Credit Recommendation: In the graduate degree category, 3 semester hours in Bible, Religion, or Language Studies (7/96).

BL5108: Graduate Greek II

Location: ICI University graduate studies centers and resident training sites worldwide and home study.

Length: Approximately 180 contact hours.

Dates: July 1986-Present.

Objective: To provide the student with an advanced knowledge of *Koine* Greek grammar and syntax necessary for exegesis of the Greek text of the New Testament as well as extrabiblical materials.

Learning Outcome: Upon successful completion of this course, the student will be able to recognize and use the grammatical concepts and constructions that are characteristic of *Koine* Greek, do advanced exegesis of the Greek text, read with some lexical assistance any portion of the New Testament and extrabiblical writings, and appreciate the *Koine* Greek language.

Instruction: The major topic covered in the course is advanced grammar and vocabulary. Methods of instruction include graduate study guide, textbooks, audio tapes, study questions, mentor assistance, independent study, self tests, unit progress evaluations, and a proctored 3-hour final examination that includes sight translation and exegesis of a New Testament passage and an extrabiblical passage.

Credit Recommendation: In the graduate degree category, 3 semester hours in Bible, Religion, or Language Studies (7/96).

ED5401: Research Methodology

Location: ICI University graduate studies centers and resident training sites worldwide and home study.

Length: Approximately 180 contact hours.

Dates: June 1994-Present.

Objective: To provide the student with skills to conduct effective theological and ministerial research.

Learning Outcome: Upon successful completion of this course, the student will be able to implement research techniques for textual research, qualitative research, and quantitative research and to apply these techniques to problem definition, research, and analysis in ministry.

Instruction: Major topics covered in the course are the nature of research, the instruments of research, identifying the research problem, preparation of the researcher, textual research design methods (historical and exegetical), qualitative research design methods (applied research through observation and evaluation), quantitative research methods and designs, and planning and writing the research proposal. Methods of instruction include graduate study guide, textbooks, supplemental readings, independent study, questions for reflection or discussion, directed research, written unit assignments, case observation and analysis assignments, and final essay assignment.

Credit Recommendation: In the graduate degree category, 3 semester hours in Religion, Research, English (7/96).

GE4012: Basic English

Location: ICIU centers or various resident training sites worldwide and home study.

Length: 60-90 hours of independent study.

Dates: March 1986-Present.

Objective: To provide the student with a basic understanding of the English language including grammar fundamentals, sentence patterns, punctuation, and letter writing.

Learning Outcome: Upon successful completion of this course, the student will be able to write clear and correct letters, both formal and informal; use varying English word order to form different basic sentence patterns; understand the basic grammar fundamentals of eight parts of speech; punctuate written English correctly for clear understanding by the reader; and use mechanics such as capitals, abbreviations, and numbers correctly in his/her writing.

Instruction: Major topics covered in the course are introduction to selected parts of speech, sentence patterns (declarative, interrogative, imperative), punctuation, and letters. Methods of instruction include independent study, exercises, audio material and a final examination.

Credit Recommendation: In the vocational certificate category, 2 semester hours in English (9/95).

GE4013: Introductory English

Location: ICIU centers or various resident training sites worldwide and home study.

Length: 90-135 study hours (15 lessons).

Dates: October 1985-Present.

Objective: To provide the student with an understanding of English grammar.

Learning Outcome: Upon successful completion of this course, the student will be able to identify and use correctly the basic parts of speech; identify and use correctly various kinds of phrases, clauses and sentences; recognize and use standard usage in speaking and writing according to established principles and acceptable usage.

Instruction: Major topics covered in the course are parts of speech, phrases, clauses, sentence structure and punctuation. Methods of instruction include study guide, textbook, study questions, independent study, self tests, unit progress evaluations, written project, and final examination.

Credit Recommendation: In the lower division baccalaureate/associate degree category, 3 semester hours in English (9/95).

GE4022: Writing Better English

Location: ICIU centers or various resident training sites worldwide and home study.

Length: 60-90 study hours (15 lessons).

Dates: October 1995-Present.

Objective: To provide students with a functional understanding of how to organize sentences into effective paragraphs and use them to narrate, describe, explain, or persuade.

Learning Outcome: Upon successful completion of this course, the student will be able to detect stylistic differences in things read; shape writing to a specific audience and purpose for writing; avoid common spelling errors by using some simple spelling rules; identify kinds of verbals, phrases, and clauses and use a variety of them in your writing; recognize several forms which English sentences may take and use them to add variety to writing; state three basic elements of a good paragraph and show an understanding by writing effective paragraphs; state four basic purposes of writing; and know the principles of paraphrase and precis and standard formats of documentation which may be applied in research and report writing.

Instruction: Major topics covered in the course are diction, phrases, clauses, sentence structure, paragraphs, modes (description, narration, exposition, and argument), reports, and library research. Methods of instruction include independent study, text, study questions, independent study, self tests, unit progress evaluations, written project, and final examination.

Credit Recommendation: In the lower division baccalaureate/associate degree category, 2 semester hours in English (9/95).

GE4023: English Composition

Location: ICIU centers or various resident training sites worldwide and home study.

Length: 90-135 study hours (15 lessons).

Dates: October 1995-Present.

Objective: To provide the student with an understanding of how to communicate clearly by writing in the English language at the college level.

Learning Outcome: Upon successful completion of this course, the student will be able to select exact words that are of current, national, and reputable use; write clear, complete sentences; write fully developed paragraphs; apply the appropriate prose forms to fulfill purpose in writing; use to advantage a dictionary and the resources of a library; apply specific guidelines to everyday types of writing; and effectively organize, revise, and proofread writing.

Instruction: Major topics covered in the course are diction, grammatically correct sentences, paragraphs, modes (description, narration, exposition and argument), letters, reports, library research. Methods of instruction include study guide, textbook, study questions, independent study, self tests, unit progress evaluations, written project and final examination.

Credit Recommendation: In the lower division baccalaureate/associate degree category, 3 semester hours in English (9/95).

GE4033: Introduction to Psychology

Location: ICIU centers or various resident training sites worldwide and home study.

Length: 90-135 study hours (15 lessons).

Dates: October 1985-Present.

Objective: To enable the student to gain an understanding of intrinsic values, motivational response techniques, peer relationships, and other psychological concepts as they apply to all aspects of Christian life and service.

Learning Outcome: Upon successful completion of this course, the student will have a foundation of principles upon which to build expertise in the field of psychology; understand the fundamental principles of human behavior as they relate to life experience; demonstrate an appreciation of the teachings of Jesus as He related to people in life experiences; be aware of personal feelings, sensations, perceptions and ways of behaving; and develop an understanding of people by observation, inquiry and the study of the human body.

Instruction: Major topics covered in the course are psychology as a systematic study of human behavior, receiving and using information, adapting to our world, human potential, and applying psychological principles. Methods of instruction include study guide, textbook, audio tapes, study questions, independent study, self tests, unit progress evaluations, written project and final examination.

Credit Recommendation: In the lower division baccalaureate/associate degree category, 3 semester hours in Psychology (9/95).

GE4052: Public Speaking

Location: ICIU centers or various resident training worldwide and home study.

Length: 60-90 study hours (12 lessons).

Dates: October 1985-Present.

Objective: To provide the student with a basic knowledge of the importance of speech in all areas of life and human cultures.

Learning Outcome: Upon successful completion of this course, the student will be able to identify commonly known subjects and topics for speech, recognize purposes for speech, classify communication as verbal or non-verbal, and describe effective listening.

Instruction: Major topics covered in the course are strengths and weaknesses of the speaker, subjects and sources of materials, verbal and non-verbal communication, effective listening, and intercultural communication. Methods of instruction include independent-study text, study questions, learner presentations (tape recorded speeches), independent study, self tests, unit progress evaluations, written project, and final examination.

Credit Recommendation: In the lower division baccalaureate/associate degree category, 2 semester hours in speech (9/95).

GE4053: Public Speaking

Location: ICIU centers or various resident training sites worldwide and home study.

Length: 90-135 study hours (12 lessons).

Dates: October 1985-Present.

Objective: To provide the student with a demonstrated knowledge and awareness of the importance of public speaking in a variety of areas of life and human cultures.

Learning Outcome: Upon successful completion ot his course, the student will be able to explain how a speaker's exploration of personal strengths and weaknesses will help to speak more effectively; identify commonly known subject and topics of speech and purposes for speech as resources of speakers; discover and develop ideas, and use them appropriately as a resource; classify communication between a speaker and the audiences as vocal and nonvocal, describe each of these two ways of communicating, and explain how each of them communicates; describe aspects of effective listening, types of effective discussion, and the relationship between this kind of listening and discussion and explain how the mechanics of modern media work together with the communicative arts of speakers to communicate interculturally.

Instruction: Major topics covered in the course are knowing oneself, resources for speech content, verbal and noverbal communication skills and intercultural communications. Methods of instruction include study guide, textbook, study questions, independent study, learner presentations (tape recorded speeches), self tests, unit progress evaluations, written project, and final examination.

Credit Recommendation: In the lower division baccalaureate/associate degree category, 3 semester hours in Speech (9/95).

GE4064: General Physical Science

Location: ICIU centers or various training sites worldwide and home study.

Length: 120-180 study hours (14 lessons).

Dates: October 1985-Present.

Objective: To provide the student with an expanded understanding of the physical sciences.

Learning Outcome: Upon successful completion of this course, the student will be able to construct an accurate definition of what science is; identify its various branches, distinguish between pure and applied science and technology; demonstrate understanding of the method of science and of the thought processes, procedures, and techniques which support them, and identify their appropriate uses and limitations; demonstrate an understanding of science as a human activity so that he or she will be able to avoid or overcome related prejudices; be aware of and appreciate contributions of scientists of other nations and previous times; know the principles of chemistry and physics as they are expressed in the earth and the universe which surrounds it; show that he or she understands and can apply the scientific principles presented in this course by completing experimental, observational or descriptive activities which illustrate these principles; analyze selected problems and identify conditions necessary to effect a solution; design experiments to determine unknown facts or principles; demonstrate the capacity to think in a constructively critical manner; compare and contrast the teachings of scientists with those of theologians; evaluate the impact of the natural sciences upon selected biblical or theological positions; express appreciation for the physical universe and exercise wise stewardship of the resources God has provided; and identify with those who, throughout the ages, have expressed an awe of the universe and reverence for its Creator.

Instruction: Major topics covered in the course are the nature of science, the nature of matter and energy, the universe and the earth. Methods of instruction include study guide, textbook, lab exercises, study questions, independent study, self tests, unit progress evaluations, written project and final examination.

Credit Recommendation: In the lower division baccalaureate/associate degree category, 4 semester hours in Physical Science (9/95).

GE4073: Introduction to Sociology

Location: ICIU centers of various resident training sites worldwide and home study.

Length: 90-135 study hours (14 lessons).

Dates: October 1985-Present.

Objective: To enable the student to gain an understanding of the nature and scope of sociology and sociological methods and concepts.

Learning Outcome: Upon successful completion of this course, the student will be able to differentiate sociology from other social and natural sciences; explain the aims and scope of socialization as it affects the development of the self; define normative behavior as it relates to cultural life-styles; identify the causes and effects of social structure and social stratification; describe the basic social institutions which regulate social interaction; describe ministerial strategy and impact in the midst of social change; compare and contrast biblical insights with various sociological insights regarding the relationship of self to society; and exhibit spiritual sensitivity in personal ministry.

Instruction: Major topics covered in the course are a scientific discipline, human beings as social beings, the fabric of human society, social organization and social stratification, and social institution and social change. Methods of instruction include study guide, textbook, study questions, independent study, self tests, unit progress evaluations, written project and final examination.

Credit Recommendation: In the lower division baccalaureate/associate degree category, 3 semester hours in Sociology (9/95).

GE4092: People and Their Beliefs

Location: ICIU centers or various resident training sites worldwide and home study.

Length: 60-90 study hours (12 lessons).

Dates: November 1987-Present.

Objective: To provide the student with a basic understanding of the major religions of the world.

Learning Outcome: Upon successful completion of this course, the student will be able to describe the predominant message of the major religions of the world, trace the development of these religions and evaluate their strengths and weaknesses.

Instruction: Major topics covered in the course are Animism, Hinduism, Sikhism, Taoism, Confucianism, Buddhism, Shintoism, Judaism, Islam and Christianity. Methods of instruction include independent-study text, study questions, independent study, self tests, unit progress evaluations, written project, and final examination.

Credit Recommendation: In the lower division baccalaureate/associate degree category, 2 semester hours in Religion or Theology (9/95).

GE4093: World Religions

Location: ICIU centers or various resident training sites worldwide

Length: 90-135 study hours (15 lessons).

Dates: September 1985-Present.

Objective: To enable the student to gain an understanding of the major religions in the world through a survey of Judaism, Christianity and eight non-biblical groups.

Learning Outcome: Upon successful completion of this course, the student will be able to understand world views and belief systems of people of all cultures; trace the origin and historical development of all major religions upon the masses around the world; discuss scriptures and other sources of authority of world religions; and evaluate claims of nonbiblical religions.

Instruction: Major topics covered in the course are West Asian religion, South Asian religions, East Asian religions, and religion and Christianity's challenge. Methods of instruction include study guide, textbook, study questions, independent study, unit progress evaluations, written project and final examination.

Credit Recommendation: In the upper division baccalaureate degree category, 3 semester hours in Religion or Sociology (9/95).

GE4113: Educational Psychology

Location: ICIU centers or various resident training sites worldwide and home study.

Length: 90-135 study hours (14 lessons).

Dates: October 1985-Present.

Objective: Upon completion of the course the student will gain the tools necessary to make the teaching-learning process a more effective part of his work.

Learning Outcome: Upon successful completion of this course, the student will be able to explain the interrelationship of content areas in Educational Psychology; describe how learner and environmental characteristics affect the outcomes of educational experiences; discuss several theories of learning and motivation and their application to educational experiences; apply psychological principles to the design and guidance of educational experiences; and use evaluation and learner assessment procedures to determine the results of educational experiences.

Instruction: Major topics covered in the course are background and perspective of educational psychology, human development, behavioral theories and cognitive strategies, guiding and encouraging learning and evaluation. Methods of instruction include study guide, textbook, study questions, independent study, self tests, unit progress evaluations, written project, and final examination.

Credit Recommendation: In the upper division baccalaureate degree category, 3 semester hours in Psychology (9/95).

GE4122: Fundamentals of Music

Location: ICIU Centers or various resident training sites worldwide and home study.

Length: 60-90 study hours (13 lessons).

Dates: March 1987-Present.

Objective: Upon the completion of the course, the student will have an understanding of melody, musical scale systems, major and minor tonality, rhythm, harmony and the system of musical notation.

Learning Outcome: Upon successful completion of this course, the student will be able to understand basic characteristics of musical sounds and scales; understand and write musical notation; discuss basic elements of music, including melody, rhythm, harmony, chords and tonality; understand basics of developing and conducting a church music program.

Instruction: Major topics covered in the course are; The role of heritage and history in music, melodic concepts and notation, building musical structure and application of music in ministry. Methods of instruction include independent-study text, audio tapes, study questions, indpendent study, self tests, unit progress evaluations, written project, and final examination.

Credit Recommendation: In the lower division baccalaureate/associate degree category, 2 credits in Music (9/95).

GE4153: Principles of Teaching

Location: ICIU centers or various resident training sites worldwide and home study.

Length: 90-135 study hours (13 lessons).

Dates: October 1985-Present.

Objective: To provide the student with an understanding of teaching/learning styles considering a broad range of student ages and cultures.

Learning Outcome: Upon successful completion of this course, the student will be able to write learning goals and indicators of learning; distinguish six levels of learning outcomes; and design evaluation tools to measure learning.

Instruction: Major topics covered in the course are learning goals, indicators, outcomes, planning, and evaluation. Methods of instruction include study guide, textbook, study questions, indpendent study, self tests, unit progress evaluations, written project, and final examination.

Credit Recommendation: In the upper division baccalaureate degree category, 3 semester hours in Education (9/95).

GE4182: Guidelines for Leadership

Location: ICIU centers or various resident training sites worldwide and home study.

Length: 60-90 study hours (13 lessons).

Dates: November 1992-Present.

Objective: To provide the student with a basic knowledge of the practice of Christian leadership.

Learning Outcome: Upon successful completion of this course, the student will be able to describe the characteristics of leadership theories and identify leadership styles of selected prominent Christian leaders.

Instruction: Major topics covered in the course are choosing a leadership style, exercising leadership power, servanthood leadership, biblical leadership and functioning in leadership. Methods of instruction include independent-study text, study questions, independent study, self tests, unit progress evaluations, written project and final examination.

Credit Recommendation: In the upper division baccalaureate degree category, 2 semester hour in Religion, Theology, or Christianity (9/95).

GE4253: Cross Cultural Communications

Location: ICIU centers or various resident training sites worldwide and home study.

Length: 90-135 study hours (13 lessons).

Dates: November 1987-Present.

Objective: To enable the student to determine how communication and culture relate, how to reach people where they are, how different people think and express ideas across cultures and subcultures, and how the thoughts and expressions of people affect their behavior.

Learning Outcome: Upon successful completion of this course the student will be able to define with an emphasis on international and cross-cultural aspects, the process of effective communication; describe some cross-cultural aspects, the process of effective communication; describe some cross-cultural problems that hinder and some cross-cultural conditions that help the process of effective communication; define the term "world view" and describe both similarities and differences among various world views; outline variations within each of six basic value orientations of humanity and give evidence of how individual human cultures maintain specific variations within these orientations.

Instruction: Major topics covered in the course are culture and world views, ways of thinking and expressing ideas, and ways of acting and interacting with other cultures. Methods of instruction include study guide, textbook, study questions, independent study, self tests, unit progress evaluations, written project, and final examination.

Credit Recommendation: In the upper division baccalaureate degree category, 3 semester hours in Sociology or Religion (9/95).

GE4262: Principles of Journalism

Location: ICIU centers or various resident training sites worldwide and home study.

Length: 90-135 study hours (12 lessons).

Dates: October 1985-Present.

Objective: To give the student an understanding of the principles of journalistic writing and their application.

Learning Outcome: Upon successful completion of this course, the student will be able to explain the process of communication; understand the supreme importance of clarity in writing and state rules for clear writing; identify qualities and values of news; describe characteristics of news writing and explain how to accomplish them; relate the inverted pyramid form, 5 Ws and H, Key thought and grammatical form to news leads; prepare for and produce news stories and public relations news releases; define the term "public relations" and state five consecutive steps in the process of achieving good public relations; write a feature article that illustrates differences between feature writing and news writing; and publish an effective church paper that has well-written copy and suitable headlines.

Instruction: Major topics covered in the course are rules for clear writing, characteristics of news writing, public relations, feature writing, and publishing. Methods of instruction include independent-study text, study questions, independent study, self tests, unit process evaluations, written project and final examination.

Credit Recommendation: In the lower division baccalaureate/associate degree category, 3 semester hours in Journalism or English (9/95).

GE4342: The Church: From Pentecost to the Reformation

Location: ICIU centers or various resident training sites worldwide and home study.

Length: 60-90 study hours (12 lessons).

Dates: November 1985-Present.

Objective: To overview or outline the major events and personalities in the history of the Christian church, from the New Testament era up to about 1500 - or the eve of the Protestant Reformation.

Learning Outcome: Upon successful completion of this course, the student will be able to trace and explain the geographic expansion of Christianity throughout its history, to describe and evaluate the major theological movements and controversies of this period, and to appreciate the worldwide nature of the Christian church.

Instruction: Major topics covered in the course are the church during the New Testament and Apostolic eras, major church councils and their decisions, important leaders of this era of church history, growth and development of the Catholic church, and circumstances leading to the Protestant Reformation. Methods of instruction include independent-study text, study questions, independent study, self tests, unit progress evaluations, written project, and final examination.

Credit Recommendation: In the lower division baccalaureate/associate degree category, 2 semester hours in History, Christianity, or Religion (9/95).

GE4343: Church History I

Location: ICIU centers or various resident training sites worldwide and home study.

Length: 90-135 study hours (14 lessons).

Dates: November 1985-Present.

Objective: To help the student understand the major events in the history of the Christian church from New Testament time up to 1517, or the eve of the Protestant Reformation, including major dates, people and events.

Learning Outcome: Upon successful completion of this course, the student will be able to trace in general terms the history of the church up to A.D. 1517, to identify the major events and personalities of this era of church history, to have an appreciation of western culture and the impact which Christianity has had on it, and to analyze and synthesize the data of history.

Instruction: Major topics covered in the course are; The establishment and growth of the early church in New Testament times, the church fathers, the councils of the early church, controversies and schisms in the church, the church and the Roman Empire and Papal supremacy during the middle ages. Methods of instruction include study guide, textbook, audio tapes, study questions, independent study, unit progress evaluations, written project, and final examination.

Credit Recommendation: In the upper division baccalaureate degree category, 3 semester hours in History, Religion, or Christianity (9/95).

GE4352: The Church: From the Reformation to the Present

Location: ICIU centers or various resident training sites worldwide and home study.

Length: 60-90 study hours (14 lessons).

Dates: November 1994-Present.

Objective: To overview or outline the major events and personalities in the history of the Christian church, from the beginning of the Protestant Reformation about A.D. 1500 up to the present time.

Learning Outcome: Upon successful completion of this course, the student will be able to trace and explain the geographic expansion of Christianity during this period, describe and evaluate the major theological movements and controversies of the period, explain the lasting impact which the Protestant Reformation has had on western history and culture, and appreciate the worldwide nature of the Christian church.

Instruction: Major topics covered in the course are personalities and events of the Protestant Reformation, the reaction of the Catholic church to the Reformation, the modern missions movement, the church in the United States, and the spread of the church throughout Africa, Asia and Latin America. Methods of instruction include independent-study text, study questions, independent study, self tests, unit progress evaluations, written project, and final examination.

Credit Recommendation: In the upper division baccalaureate degree category, 2 semester hours in History, Christianity, or Religion (9/95).

LD5301: Foundations for Christian Leadership

Location: ICI University graduate studies centers and resident training sites worldwide and home study.

Length: Approximately 180 contact hours.

Dates: July 1996-Present.

Objective: To provide the student with an understanding of different leadership models that would enable him/her to analyze and evaluate those models and cultural influences in reference to the Christian leadership roles of a specific culture and ministry.

Learning Outcome: Upon successful completion of this course, the student will be able to understand different leadership types; analyze, evaluate, and assess the application of leadership roles in the student's specific culture and ministry; explain cultural influences on Christian leadership; evaluate the importance of spiritual maturity and growth and the role of the Holy Spirit in leadership development; and apply leadership foundations to the student's cultural setting.

Instruction: Major topics covered in the course are leadership theories and definition, leader typology, leader function and introduction to Clinton's schematic for the study of leadership, biblical sources for leadership values, leadership reflection in a biblical perspective, the call and vision of a leader, the leader's self awareness, the Spirit's role in developing leaders, knowing and relating to fellow workers, individual leadership styles, functions of leadership through structures, and the role of leaders responding to power and authority. Methods of instruction include graduate study guide, textbooks, supplemental readings, independent study, questions for reflection or discussion, directed research, written unit assignments, case observation and analysis assignments, and final essay assignment.

Credit Recommendation: In the graduate degree category, 3 semester hours in Religion, Sociology, or Religious Education (7/96).

MN3012: Evangelism Today

Location: ICIU center or various resident training sites worldwide and home study.

Length: 60-90 study hours (15 lessons).

Dates: *Version 1:* February 1977-September 1995; *Version 2:* October 1995-Present.

Objective: To enable the student to gain an understanding of the biblical and theological foundations of effective evangelism, and their application personally and corporately.

Learning Outcome: Upon successful completion of this course, the student will be able to state the biblical principles of evangelism and apply them in their life and ministry; tell people what God says about sin and salvation; use the Bible to help people find and follow Christ; know a wide variety of fields for evangelism and specialized ministries; use the principles, methods and media of effective communication to give people the gospel; develop their abilities in evangelization through practical experience; analyze the needs of their area and cooperate with others in the outreach of the church; cultivate the attitudes and habits that are needed for effective evangelism and be sensitive to the leading of the Spirit.

Instruction: Major topics covered in the course are sources for power in evangelism, the evangelistic message, communicating the message, methods for reaching our world. Methods of instruction include independent-study text, study questions, independent study, self tests, unit progress evaluations, written project, and final examination.

Credit Recommendation: *Version 1:* In the lower division baccalaureate/associate degree category, 2 semester hours in Religion or Practical Ministries. *Version 2:* In the upper division baccalaureate degree category, 2 semester hours in Religion or Practical Ministries (9/95).

MN3023: A Strategy for Church Growth

Location: ICIU centers or various resident training sites worldwide and home study.

Length: 90-135 study hours (15 lessons).

Dates: September 1985-Present.

Objective: To enable the student to identify the principles that underlie the growth of the Church and to make a diagnostic study of a local church.

Learning Outcome: Upon successful completion of this course, the student will be able to critically understand and communicate principles of church growth, both biblically and sociologically; analyze patterns of church growth in different parts of the world; recognize the social structure and cultural features of communities; develop and apply techniques of church growth in parish and cooperative ministry.

Instruction: Major topics covered in the course are; Biblical principles of growth, analysis of church and context, church growth and cooperative ministry. Methods of instruction include study guide, textbook, study questions, indpendent study, self tests, unit progress evaluations, written project and final examination.

Credit Recommendation: In the upper division baccalaureate degree category, 3 semester hours in Religion or Practical Ministries (9/95).

MN3042: Preparing and Preaching Bible Messages

Location: ICIU Centers or various resident training sites worldwide and home study.

Length: 60-90 study hours (14 lessons).

Dates: March 1994-Present.

Objective: To enable the student to gain an understanding of the basic principles of biblical exposition, preaching and communicating the Christ-ian message.

Learning Outcome: Upon successful completion of this course, the student will be able to define and justify the purpose of preaching, its importance as it relates to other aspects of the ministry; establish clear goals in their preaching ministry; become more aware of their own sense of calling and its effect on the urgency of preaching; develop an effective weekly work schedule for sermon preparation; analyze a scripture and determine the best structure or form for a particular sermon; distinguish between topical, textual and expository sermons, determining the appropriate use of each one; create a year's preaching calendar; construct and preach sound biblical sermons.

Instruction: Major topics covered in the course are the place and purpose of preaching, preparing the preacher, sermon preparation, sermon construction, and sermon types. Methods of instruction include independent-study text, study questions, independent study, self tests, unit progress evaluations, written project, and final examination.

Credit Recommendation: In the upper division baccalaureate degree category, 2 semester hours in Practical Ministries, Religion, Communication, or Speech (9/95).

MN3043: Principles of Preaching

Location: ICIU centers or various resident training sites worldwide and home study.

Length: 90-135 study hours (14 lessons).

Dates: January 1991-Present.

Objective: To explore the dynamics of sermon preparation and delivery, including selecting an appropriate biblical text, deciding on a distinctive type of sermon, organizing the sermon outline, and delivering the sermon clearly and concisely.

Learning Outcome: Upon successful completion of this course, the student will be able to distinguish among various preaching terms, define principles of effective sermon building and delivery, and critique an actual sermon correctly in accordance with the principles learned in this course.

Instruction: Major topics covered in the course are the importance of preaching; different types of sermons; the distinctives of topical, textual, and expository sermons; how to structure a sermon; the different elements of a typical sermon; principles of sermon development; and how to deliver a sermon effectively. Methods of instruction include study guide, textbook, audiotapes, critique of two actual sermons, learner presentations (tape recorded sermons), study questions, independent study, self tests, unit progress evaluations, written project, and final examination.

Credit Recommendation: In the lower division baccalaureate/associate degree category, 3 semester hours in Communications, Practical Ministries, or Religion (12/94).

MN3052: The Church's Educational Task

Location: ICIU centers or various training sites worldwide and home study.

Length: 60-90 study hours (12 lessons).

Dates: March 1990-Present.

Objective: To help the student understand the biblical foundation for Christian education and come to appreciate education as an important ministry of the church.

Learning Outcome: Upon successful completion of this course, the student will be able to identify principles and methods for effective teaching of the Bible, to understand how Christian education promotes leadership development, to recognize how different age groups learn and to develop an administration process for creative education in the local church.

Instruction: Major topics covered in the course are the Bible and Christian education, the teaching ministry of Jesus, the teaching-learning process, age-group learning distinctives, and administering an educational program in the local church. Methods of instruction include independent-study text, study questions, independent study, self tests, unit progress evaluations, written project, and final examination.

Credit Recommendation: In the upper division baccalaureate degree category, 2 semester hours in Education or Practical Ministries (9/95).

MN3053: Introduction to Christian Education

Location: ICIU centers or various resident training sites worldwide and home study.

Length: 90-135 study hours (14 lessons).

Dates: November 1987-Present.

Objective: To give the student an understanding of the foundations of Christian education and the process of administering an educational program in the local Church.

Learning Outcome: Upon successful completion of this course, the student will be able to identify the biblical and theological foundations of Christian education, to describe the teaching/learning process, to recognize how different age groups learn, and to explain the responsibilities of the pastor and the director of Christian education in the educational program of the church.

Instruction: Major topics covered in the course are the foundations of Christian education, materials and methods used in Christian education, and the administration of Christian education in the local church. Methods of instruction include study guide, textbook, study questions, independent study, self tests, unit progress evaluations, written project, and final examination.

Credit Recommendation: In the upper division baccalaureate degree category, 3 semester hours in Education or Practical Ministries (9/95).

MN3082: Work of the Pastor

Location: ICIU centers or various training sites worldwide and home study.

Length: 60-90 study hours (14 lessons).

Dates: March 1989-Present.

Objective: To provide participants the opportunity to reflect upon and critically analyze their personal and vocational dimensions of pastoral ministry.

Learning Outcome: Upon successful completion of this course, the student will be able to reflect biblically and critically on the call to ministry and the pastor's preparation; to identify the network of relationships within which the pastor functions; to identify key dimensions of the work of pastoral ministry; to develop a strategic leadership style within the church.

Instruction: Major topics covered in the course are the pastor' preparation; the pastor's relationships; tasks of ministry; elements of strategic leadership. Methods of instruction include independent-study text, study questions, independent study, self tests, case studies, unit progress evaluations, written project, and final examination.

Credit Recommendation: In the lower division baccalaureate/associate degree category, 2 semester hours in Religion or Practical Ministries (9/95).

MN3083: Pastoral Ministries

Location: ICIU centers or various resident training sites worldwide and home study.

Length: 12 lessons (6 months).

Dates: *Version 1:* March 1992-September 1995; *Version 2:* October 1995-Present.

Objective: To focus on the unique role and responsibilities of the minister, including the call to ministry, preparation for service, personal life and ethics, family life and general leadership responsibilities in the church.

Learning Outcome: Upon successful completion of this course, the student will be able to describe the biblical principles which guide the minister's work, understand the preparation needed for functioning as an effective minister, describe the major duties and responsibilities required of the minister.

Instruction: Major topics covered in the course are biblical principles of ministry; the minister's spiritual life, calling, ethics, and family life; principles of leadership for the minister; and the major roles and responsibilities of the minister. Methods of instruction include study guide, textbook, study questions, independent study, self tests, unit progress evaluations, written project, and final examination.

Credit Recommendation: *Version 1:* In the lower division baccalaureate/associate degree category, 3 semester hours Practical Ministries, Bible, or Religion (12/94). *Version 2:* In the upper division baccalaureate degree category, 3 semester hours in Religion, or Practical Ministries (9/95).

MN3092: Church Business

Location: ICIU centers or various training sites worldwide and home study.

Length: 60-90 study hours (15 lessons).

Dates: November 1987-Present.

Objective: To provide the student with any understanding of the principles, procedures, and techniques used in today's business world as they apply to the local church and its leadership.

Learning Outcome: Upon successful completion of this course, the student will be able to locate and interpret the scriptures that form a biblical basis for good management of the local church, the giving of tithes and offerings, and the stewardship of the church's money, facilities and resources; identify the roles and responsibilities of the pastor, board, and officers for the financial management of the local church; define the basic terms, principles and operating procedures associated with church business management; establish a set of recognized procedures for conducting the business of the church in a professional and responsible manner; choose to demonstrate a positive attitude toward the use of business tools and techniques in the work of the church; implement the ideas, procedures and techniques of business management for improving the effectiveness of the business operations of the local church; and apply skills and knowledge in the area of church business management in preparation for a leadership position which involves greater competence and responsibility.

Instruction: Major topics covered in the course are organizing and financing the church for business, accounting for church activities and managing the Church's business. Methods of instruction include independent-study text, study questions, independent study, self tests, unit progress evaluations, written project, and final examination.

Credit Recommendation: In the upper division baccalaureate degree category, 2 semester hours in Business (9/95).

MN3112: Expository Preaching

Location: ICIU centers or various resident training sites worldwide and home study.

Length: 60-90 study hours (13 lessons).

Dates: *Version 1:* November 1988-September 1995; *Version 2:* October 1995-Present.

Objective: To define and prepare expository sermons, building on prior learning of the principles of Biblical Interpretation.

Learning Outcome: Upon successful completion of this course, the student will be able to distinguish between expository preaching and other types of sermons; explain the steps involved in building an expository sermon; relate a sermon passage to its context for proper exposition, and develop expository sermons for preaching.

Instruction: Major topics covered in the course are the definition of expository preaching, the steps in building expository sermons, sermon patterns for variety, proper exposition and how to prepare a preaching plan. Methods of instruction include independent-study text, study questions, independent study, self tests, unit progress evaluations, written project, and final examination.

Credit Recommendation: *Version 1:* In the lower division baccalaureate/associate degree category, 2 semester hours in Bible, Speech, Practical Ministries, or Religion (12/94). *Version 2:* In the upper division baccalaureate degree category, 2 semester hours in Bible, Speech, Practical Ministries, or Religion (9/95).

MN3132: Introduction to Missions

Location: ICIU centers or various resident training sites worldwide and home study.

Length: 60-90 study hours (14 lessons).

Dates: September 1987-Present.

Objective: To give the student an understanding of the biblical basis of missions and outline the challenges and opportunities in Christian missions available to the modern church.

Learning Outcome: Upon successful completion of this course, the student will be able to understand the teaching of the Bible on missions, have a sense of responsibility for the local church to participate in missions, recognize the problems and challenges involved in cross-cultural ministry, and identify the key role of the local church in God's plan for world evangelization.

Instruction: Major topics covered in the course are biblical teachings on missions, the theme of redemption throughout the Bible, missions outreach in the New Testament church, the Holy Spirit's role in missions, modern challenges in world missions and the indigenous church as a goal of missions. Methods of instruction include independent-study text, study questions, independent study, self tests, unit progress evaluations, written project, and final examination

Credit Recommendation: In the upper division baccalaureate degree category, 2 semester hours in Religion or Christianity (9/95).

MN3143: Teaching in the Church

Location: ICIU centers or various resident training sites worldwide and home study.

Length: 90-135 study hours (15 lessons).

Dates: September 1985-Present.

Objective: To help the student understand and apply the principle of effective teaching and learning to his or her teaching ministry in the local church.

Learning Outcome: Upon successful completion of this course, the student will understand the principles of effective and creative teaching, be able to apply the theories of learning to various age groups in the church, and appreciate the central role and ministry of teaching in the church.

Instruction: Major topics covered in the course are the distinctives of Christian teaching, how to teach different age groups, teaching aims and objective, motivating the learner, how people learn, and creative methods of Bible teaching. Methods of instruction include study guide, textbook, study questions, independent study, self tests, unit progress evaluations written project, and final examination.

Credit Recommendation: In the upper division baccalaureate degree category, 3 semester hours in Education (9/95).

MN3152: Christian Counseling

Location: ICIU centers or various resident training sites worldwide and home study.

Length: 60-90 study hours (13 lessons).

Dates: November 1988-Present.

Objective: To provide the student with a basic understanding of the agape therapy approach in counseling.

Learning Outcome: Upon successful completion of this course, the student will be able to explain the basic assumptions and principles of Christian counseling; describe the role that the Christian lay person can have in para-professional counseling in the local church setting; identify and utilize some of the resources available to the Christian counselor; and evaluate personal growth needs as they relate to functioning as a paraprofessional counselor.

Instruction: Major topics covered in the course are an overview of agape therapy, and applying the ministry using agape therapy. Methods of instruction include independent-study text, study questions, independent study, self tests, unit progress evaluations, written project, and final examination.

Credit Recommendation: In the lower division baccalaureate/associate degree category, 2 semester hours in Religion, Christianity, or Pastoral Ministry (9/95).

MN3162: Islam: Introduction and Approach

Location: ICIU centers or various training sites worldwide and home study.

Length: 60-90 study hours (14 lessons).

Dates: February 1992-Present.

Objective: To enable the student to gain an understanding of Islam, its beliefs, practices, status as a world religion, and how to make an effective Christian witness to Muslims.

Learning Outcome: Upon successful completion of this course, the student will be able to describe the essential points of Islamic history, culture and theology; relate to Muslims as fellow human beings whom Christ loves and died for; define the basic vocabulary necessary for evangelizing Muslims; describe the main obstacle Muslims must overcome in order to gain an accurate understanding of Jesus Christ and the gospel message; use practical methods for witnessing to Muslims, both in work and in deed; realize they can be brought into the kingdom of God through love, understanding and the power of the Holy Spirit.

Instruction: Major topics covered in the course are Muhammad and the Qur'an understanding Islam and Muslims, Islam and Christianity, how to approach Muslims with the gospel of Christ. Methods of instruction include the independent-study text, study questions, independent study, self tests, unit progress evaluations, written project, and final examination.

Credit Recommendation: In the upper division baccalaureate degree category, 2 semester hours in World Religions, Applied Anthropology, or Practical Ministry (9/95).

MN3172: The Worship of God

Location: ICIU Centers or various resident training sites worldwide and home study.

Length: 60-90 study hours (13 lessons).

Dates: November 1987-Present.

Objective: To introduce students to the basic elements of Christian worship.

Learning Outcome: Upon successful completion of this course, the student will be able to explain the importance of worship in biblical faith; understand the importance of music in worship lead public worship services; develop strategies for personal worship.

Instruction: Major topics covered in the course are elements of personal worship, relation of doctrine of God to worship, elements of corporate worship. Methods of instruction include independent-study text, study questions, independent study, self tests, unit progress evaluations, written project, and final examination.

Credit Recommendation: In the lower division baccalaureate/associate degree category, 2 semester hours in Religion or Practical Ministries (9/95).

MN3173: Worship: A Biblical Survey

Location: ICIU centers or various training sites worldwide and home study.

Length: 90-135 study hours (13 lessons).

Dates: November 1987-Present.

Objective: To introduce students to the biblical and theological foundations of public worship.

Learning Outcome: Upon successful completion of this course, the student will be able to develop a biblical theology for worship; understand the various dimensions of public worship; discuss the relationships between personal and corporate worship; and provide informed, biblical leadership for public worship.

Instruction: Major topics covered in the course are Biblical theology of worship, elements of public worship, ordinances of the Church, leading public worship. Methods of instruction include study guide, textbook, study questions, independent study, self tests, unit progress evaluations, written project, and final examination.

Credit Recommendation: In the upper division baccalaureate degree category, 3 semester hours in Religion, Bible, or Practical Ministries (9/95).

MN3193: Introduction to Church Music

Location: ICIU centers or various resident training sites worldwide and home study.

Length: 90-135 study hours (13 lessons).

Dates: September 1985-Present.

Objective: To gain a greater understanding of the role of music in church services, evangelism and other ministries.

Learning Outcome: Upon successful completion of this course, the participant will be able to discuss major trends in the historical development of church music; make valid judgements about the value and use of random examples of church music in worship and evangelism; assume leadership in organizing church music activities, relating it to the total program of the church.

Instruction: Major topics include music and the bible, the history of church music, the role of music in the church's ministry and developing a church music program. Methods of instruction include study guide, textbook, audiotapes, study questions, independent study, self tests, unit progress evaluations, written project, and final examination.

Credit Recommendation: In the upper division baccalaureate degree category, 3 semester hours in Religion, Music, or Practical Ministry (9/95).

MN3203: Pastoral Counseling

Location: ICIU centers or various resident training sites worldwide and home study.

Length: 90-135 study hours (14 lessons).

Dates: November 1985-Present.

Objective: To enable the student to gain a greater understanding of the people he or she may be called upon to counsel, the techniques of counseling, and the various forms of counseling.

Learning Outcome: Upon successful completion of this course, the student will be able to summarize the general historical development of counseling; discuss the distinctive role of the minister as counselor; develop familiarity with a variety of forms of counseling and counseling situations; give realistic, comforting counsel to persons who are seriously ill, facing death or experiencing bereavement; use biblical concepts of counseling that will help listeners make wise choices.

Instruction: Major topics covered in the course are the nature and importance of counseling, individual personality, techniques and forms of counseling, and the role of the counselor. Methods of instruction include study guide, textbook, study questions, independent study, self tests, unit progress evaluations, written project, and final examination.

Credit Recommendation: In the upper division baccalaureate degree category, 3 semester hours in Religion or Psychology (9/95).

MN3233: Agape and Human Relations

Location: ICIU centers or various resident training sites worldwide and home study.

Length: 90-135 hours (14 lessons).

Dates: October 1985-Present.

Objective: To provide the student with a basic understanding of how the agape concept is applied to human relationships.

Learning Outcome: Upon successful completion of this course, the student will be able to discuss the meaning of the New Testament concept of agape; develop a biblical model of agape that relates to the basic relationships of life; develop a series of biblical principles based on agape; identify and apply basic agape principles.

Instruction: Major topics covered in the course are basic qualities of human relationships, agape and the leader, principles and techniques in human relations, and making agape work. Methods of instruction include study guide, textbook, study questions, independent study, self tests, case studies, unit progress evaluations, written project, and final examination.

Credit Recommendation: In the lower division baccalaureate/associate degree category, 3 semester hours in Religion or Theology (9/95).

MS5201: The Biblical Theology of Missions

Location: ICI University graduate studies centers and resident training sites worldwide and home study.

Length: Approximately 180 contact hours.

Dates: June 1996-Present.

Objective: To provide the student with an understanding of the mission of God in relation to the kingdom of God in the past, present, and future and the place of the socio-humanitarian ministry of the church in this mission.

Learning Outcome: Upon successful completion of this course, the student will be able to identify and trace God's plan to bless the nations from the Old Testament through the fulfillment of this plan in the New Testament and to interpret biblical literature and contexts in terms of ministry in the church, as well as individual ministry and participation in God's eternal plan, as reflected in the Great Commission.

Instruction: Major topics covered in the course are the methodology of biblical theology and its relevance to missions, mission dei and the kingdom of God, biblical theology in the pentateuch: missions is born, biblical theology in the historical books: the kingdom in missions, biblical theology in the poetical books: life in the kingdom, biblical theology in the prophets: mission dei—judgment and promise, the King declares his mission: biblical theology in the gospels, biblical theology in acts: missions in action, biblical theology in the Pauline Epistles: the spread of missions and the church as the kingdom of God, biblical theology in the general epistles: missions—bringing in the kingdom (closure), biblical theology in the revelation: the triumph of the kingdom, planting the church among the unrelated: ambassadors of the kingdom, and the socio-humanitarian ministry of the church: representing Christ through compassion. Methods of instruction include graduate study guide, textbooks, supplemental readings, independent study, questions for reflection or discussion, directed research, written unit assignments, case observation and analysis assignments, and final essay assignment.

Credit Recommendation: In the graduate degree category, 3 semester hours in Religion, Theology, or Bible (7/96).

MS5202: Strategies for Cross-Cultural Ministry

Location: ICI University graduate studies centers and resident training sites worldwide and home study.

Length: Approximately 180 contact hours.

Dates: July 1996-Present.

Objective: To provide the student with an working understanding of goals, strategies, difficulties, and opposition for ministry in a cross-cultural setting.

Learning Outcome: Upon successful completion of this course, the student will be able to understand and use missiology terminology, church planting methods, and evangelism strategies to propose effective strategies to plant churches; do personal and mass evangelism—including evangelization to the Islamic world; to outline a biblical strategy for transition to a multicultural congregation; and to evaluate the advantages of distance education in a cross-cultural setting.

Instruction: Major topics covered in the course are knowing the meaning of the church and its mission, planting an indigenous church, ministering through the empowerment of pentecost, utilizing the Trinity gifts, communicating via mass evangelism and personal evangelism, communicating cross-culturally, communicating the gospel to the Islamic world, fostering a multicultural congregation, training local leadership, focusing on the missionary family in stress, resolving inter-missionary relationships in conflict, and identifying the role of the sending church. Methods of instruction include graduate study guide, textbooks, supplemental readings, independent study, questions for reflection or discussion, directed research, written unit assignments, case observation and analysis assignments, and final essay assignment.

Credit Recommendation: In the graduate degree category, 3 semester hours in Religion, Bible, Religious Education, Theology, or Sociology (7/96).

MS5204: A History of the Expansion of Christianity

Location: ICI University graduate studies centers and resident training sites worldwide and home study.

Length: Approximately 180 contact hours.

Dates: July 1996-Present.

Objective: To provide the student with an awareness of the missionary effort that was involved in the spread of Christianity and the role of secular world trends and forces-at-work within the church that have impacted, and continue to impact, ministry and evangelization in a specific culture-that of the student.

Learning Outcome: Upon successful completion of this course, the student will be able to identify and analyze contributions of selected individuals, events, and forces at work in Christianity; evaluate the overall impact of monasticism, syncretism, and the establishment of Christianity in the Roman Empire on the spread of Christianity during the Middle Ages; describe the effects of the Reformation and Age of Discovery on missions activity in Europe and the New World; apply lessons for reasons for successes and failures of Christian missions during the nineteenth century to contemporary missions efforts in unreached areas; analyze the impact of religion on the culture of the student; and interpret the rise and spread of Pentecostalism in its historical context and its influence in student's region.

Instruction: Major topics covered in the course are the expansion of Christianity: book of Acts to Edict of Toleration, after Edict of Toleration ca a.d. 100 -311, within and beyond the Roman Empire (a.d. 311-1500), Reformation in the age of discovery and colonization (1500-1814), missions in the great century (1814-1914), expansion to historic churches (1914 to present), and effects of pentecostalism. Methods of instruction include graduate study guide, textbooks, supplemental readings, independent study, questions for reflection or discussion, directed research, written unit assignments, case observation and analysis assignments, and final research project.

Credit Recommendation: In the graduate degree category, 3 semester hours in History, Religion, or Christianity (7/96).

TH2013: The Bible and the Church

Location: ICIU centers or various resident training sites worldwide.

Length: 90-135 study hours (12 lessons).

Dates: January 1987-Present.

Objective: To introduce Christian ministers and workers to an evangelical view of biblical authority and inspiration. In the second half of the course, students are introduced to an evangelical view of the nature, organization, and ministry of the Church.

Learning Outcome: Upon successful completion of this course, the student will be able to describe an evangelical view of biblical authority and inspiration, and the formation of the Protestant canon of Scripture; and define an evangelical view of the church, its organization, and present and future ministries.

Instruction: Major topics covered in the course are the nature of revelation; theories of inspiration; historical, literary, and textual criticism; Old and New Testament canons; universal and local church; church organization; church's inward and outward ministry, and the church as the kingdom community. Methods of instruction include study guide, textbook, study questions, independent study, self tests, unit progress evaluations, written project, and final examination.

Credit Recommendation: In the lower division baccalaureate/associate degree category, 3 semester hours in Bible, Theology, or Religion (12/94).

TH2022: God and Angels

Location: ICIU centers or resident training sites worldwide and home study.

Length: 60-90 study hours (12 lessons).

Dates: March 1992-Present.

Objective: To provide an understanding of the nature of God's plan of redemption and the nature of angels.

Learning Outcome: Upon successful completion of this course, the student will be able to master basic vocabulary for the study of God and angels, explain the various ways of affirming God's existence, present a biblical description of God's nature and qualities, explain the biblical names of god and show how these support the doctrine of the Trinity, and identify and give significance to the teaching on angels.

Instruction: Major topics covered in the course are the nature of God; existence and essence; the nature of God: qualities and names; the Trinity and the works of God; and the existence, nature and activity of angels. Methods of instruction include independent-study text, study questions, independent study, self tests, unit progress evaluations, written project, and final examination.

Credit Recommendation: In the lower division baccalaureate/associate degree category, 2 semester hours in Bible, Religion, Theology, or Christianity (9/95).

TH2023: Theology Proper/Angelology

Location: ICIU centers or resident training sites worldwide and home study.

Length: 90-135 study hours (12 lessons).

Dates: February 1993-Present.

Objective: To provide the student with an understanding of the doctrine of God and angels.

Learning Outcome: Upon successful completion of this course, the student will be able to discuss what theology is and why it is helpful for Christians to have a biblical systematic theology; state Bible-based evidences for existence of God; know main beliefs of nonbiblical philosophies and religions; biblical explanation for essence and attributes of God, persons of Godhead, God's decrees, and their content and purposes; and explain origin of angels/good and evil.

Instruction: Major topics covered in the course are theology and theism, the doctrine of God and the doctrine of angels. Methods of instruction include study guide, textbook, study questions, independent study, self tests, unit progress evaluations, written project, and final examination.

Credit Recommendation: In the lower division baccalaureate/associate degree category, 3 semester hours in Bible, Theology, Religion, or Christianity (9/95).

TH2033: Pneumatology

Location: ICIU centers or various resident training sites worldwide and home study.

Length: 90-135 study hours (16 lessons).

Dates: September 1985-Present.

Objective: To enable the student to gain a greater understanding or the person and work of the Holy Spirit.

Learning Outcome: Upon successful completion of this course, the student will be able to show the personality and work of the Holy Spirit in the scriptures; describe the relationship between the Holy Spirit and Christ; discuss the work of the Spirit in conviction and regeneration, fruits of the Spirit, baptism in the Spirit, and gifts of the Spirit.

Instruction: Major topics covered in the course are The person of the Holy Spirit, the Spirit in the Old Testament, the Holy Spirit and Christ, the Spirit and the Church and the ministries of the Spirit. Methods of instruction include study guide, textbook, study questions, independent study, self tests, unit progress evaluations, written project, and final examination.

Credit Recommendation: In the lower division baccalaureate/associate degree category, 3 semester hours in Religion, Theology, or Christianity (9/95).

TH2043: Christology

Location: ICIU centers or resident training sites worldwide and home study.

Length: 90-135 study hours (12 lessons).

Dates: June 1995-Present.

Objective: To provide the student with an understanding of historical and contemporary view of Jesus and His ministry based on the biblical record.

Learning Outcome: Upon successful completion of this course, the student will be able to comprehend the Old Testament typology/prophecy concerning Christ as this relates to the study of the New Testament; identify some of the leading authors and scholars who have contributed to the field of Christology; relate Christology with other great doctrines of the Bible, including the doctrine of salvation and the doctrine of the Trinity; and recognize the use in teaching or preaching numerous direct references to the person and work of Jesus Christ to be found in the Old Testament historical record.

Instruction: Major topics covered in the course are the reincarnate Christ in Old Testament history, typology and prophecy; the incarnate Christ in the person of Christ, the life of Christ, the suffering, death and resurrection of Christ; and the contemporary and coming Christ in the present work of Christ , the future work of Christ, and Christ in contemporary theology. Methods of instruction include study guide, textbook, study questions, independent study, self tests, unit progress evaluations, written project, and final examination.

Credit Recommendation: In the upper division baccalaureate degree category, 3 semester hours in Bible, Religion, Theology, or Christianity (9/95).

TH2053: Soteriology

Location: ICIU centers or resident training sites worldwide and home study.

Length: 90-135 study hours (12 lessons).

Dates: July 1994-Present.

Objective: To provide the student with an understanding of the doctrine of salvation: the work of Christ in bringing lost man into fellowship with God.

Learning Outcome: Upon successful completion of this course, the student will be able to show the roles of God and man in salvation, put in sequence the logical rather than the experiential steps of salvation, define the biblical and theological terms relating to the doctrines of salvation and understand that precise defining of terms is a necessary background for intelligently proclaiming the truths of salvation, and contrast the method of salvation presented in the Bible with any nonbiblical approach.

Instruction: Major topics covered in the course are preliminary considerations on the background of salvation and God's will in salvation, the activity of man in salvation, the activity of God in salvation, God and man working together in salvation, and the final goal of salvation. Methods of instruction include study guide, textbook, study questions, independent study, unit progress evaluations, written project, and final examination.

Credit Recommendation: In the lower division baccalaureate/associate degree category, 2 semester hours in Bible, Religion, Theology, or Christianity (9/95).

TH2062: Man and Sin

Location: ICIU centers or resident training sites worldwide and home study.

Length: 60-90 study hours (12 lessons).

Dates: July 1994-Present.

Objective: To provide the student with an understanding of the doctrines concerning the origin of man and sin, the nature of man and sin and the effects of the fall.

Learning Outcome: Upon successful completion of this course, the student will be able to summarize biblical teaching concerning human origins, explain nonbiblical views concerning human origins, state basic principles of the biblical doctrine of sin and appreciate the practical implications of the doctrine that humans are created in God's image.

Instruction: Major topics covered in the course are the doctrine of man and the origin, the nature of man, the problem of sin, and related views and issues of the doctrine of man. Methods of instruction include independent-study text, study questions, independent study, self tests, unit progress evaluations, written project and final examination.

Credit Recommendation: In the lower division baccalaureate/associate degree category, 2 semester hours in in Bible, Religion, Theology, and Christianity (9/95).

TH2073: Eschatology

Location: ICIU centers or various resident training sites worldwide and home study.

Length: 90-135 study hours (12 lessons).

Dates: September 1985-Present.

Objective: This course, written from a conservative, evangelical perspective, gives the student a better understanding of the end times and how to interpret the biblical references to the end times.

Learning Outcome: Upon successful completion of this course, the student will be able to identify the apparent order of events associated with the second coming of Christ, to compare and contrast the various theories of the Millennium, and to understand the message, date and authorship of the book of Revelation in the New Testament.

Instruction: Major topics covered in the course are the end times and death, the end times and the coming of Christ, the millennium, the tribulations, and the end times and life everlasting. Methods of instruction include study guide, textbook, study questions, independent study, self tests, unit progress evaluations, written project, and final examination.

Credit Recommendation: In the upper division baccalaureate degree category, 3 semester hours in Bible, Theology, or Christianity (9/95).

TH2093: Old Testament Biblical Theology

Location: ICIU centers or various training site worldwide and home study.

Length: 90-135 study hours (16 lessons).

Dates: September 1985-Present.

Objective: To enable the student to gain a greater understanding of the theological foundations of Christianity based on the Old Testament.

Learning Outcome: Upon successful completion of this course, the student will be able to list the names of God and describe the characteristics of God which each conveys; discuss and choose from among several theories of creation a satisfactory biblical position; understand how man came into being and why he is what he is; identify basic sociological and personal characteristics of mankind and relate them to the teachings of Scripture; explain the doctrine of the Messiah as it applies to His person and work; describe the doctrine of the covenant; appreciate how God's love is perfectly displayed in the covenant and fulfilled by the death and resurrection of Jesus Christ; apply to their life and ministry principles of biblical theology.

Instruction: Major topics covered in the course are major Old Testament doctrines; what the Old Testament teaches about God, creations, man, sin, the Messiah, revelation, inspiration, angels, Satan; the various testaments and covenants, judgement, and life after death; preaching and teaching from the Old Testament. Methods of instruction include study guide, textbook, study questions, independent study, self tests, unit progress evaluations, written project, and final examination.

Credit Recommendation: In the upper division baccalaureate degree category, 3 semester hours in Theology, Religion, or Bible (9/95).

TH2223: Apologetics

Location: ICIU centers or various resident training sites worldwide and home study.

Length: 90-135 study hours (14 lessons).

Dates: September 1985-Present.

Objective: To enable the student to gain a greater knowledge of the differences between faith and knowledge, and the correlation between the two.

Learning Outcome: Upon successful completion of this course, the student will be able to define a proper relationship between faith and reason; distinguish acceptable and unacceptable kinds of doubt; trace a logical line of reasoning for the existence of God; list significant arguments for belief in the deity of Christ and His bodily resurrection from the dead; give reasons why one may trust the Bible as God's authoritative revelation to man; compare the demands of science and Scripture, demonstrating their essential harmony; defend the creationist viewpoint of man's origin in contrast to various evolutionary alternatives; show how a Christian may accept the reality of suffering and evil in this world; give reasons for the validity of Christian experience; apply the material in this course to their ministry by having useful answers to important questions that contemporary men are asking; appreciate God's desire to meet the needs of mankind, including those of the intellect.

Instruction: Major topics covered in the course are God and faith - knowing that God lives; word and faith - knowing that God communicates; experience and faith - knowing that God acts. Methods of instruction include study guide, text book, study questions, independent study, self tests, unit progress evaluations, written project, and final examination.

Credit Recommendation: In the upper division baccalaureate degree category, 3 semester hours in Religion, Practical Ministries, or Philosophy/Logic (9/95).

ICS Learning Systems

ICS Learning Systems, a division of Harcourt Brace and Company, is located in Scranton, Pennsylvania. ICS is a world leader in the field of distance learning. Since its founding in 1891, ICS has pioneered in the the development of self-paced, independent study materials. Its entire business is devoted to the development, marketing, and servicing of vocational, avocational, and degree-level instructional programs. ICS has developed such innovative aids as Dial-A-Question, a toll-free educational assistance system, and Tel-Test, a sophisticated interactive testing device that uses telephone communication between the student and the school. Students are also provided with electronic access to the school via online network connections.

ICS has a permanent faculty of over 20 people plus additional support personnel. The institution has enrolled more than 10 million students.

A charter member of the Distance and Education Training Council (formerly the National Home Study Council), ICS is accredited by the Council and is also licensed by the Pennsylvania State Board of Private Licensed Schools. ICS Center for Degree Studies (CDS) is authorized to grant the ASB and AST Degrees by the Pennsylvania Department of Education. ICS is also a member of the Pennsylvania Association of Two-Year Colleges and the American Association of Collegiate Registrars and Admissions Officers (AACRAO).

Source of official student records: Director, Center for Degree Studies, ICS Learning Systems, 925 Oak Street, Scranton, PA 18515.

Additional information about the courses: College Credit Recommendation Service, American Council on Education, One Dupont Circle, Washington, DC 20036-1193.

AC and DC Motors and Controls

Location: Self-study.

Length: Correspondence Program.

Dates: January 1980-Present.

Objective: To provide an understanding of direct current generators and motors, alternating current motors, and the methods of controlling such equipment.

Learning Outcome: Upon successful completion of this course, the student will be able to understand the construction, operation, rating, and maintenance of different types of AC and DC motors and generators and manual and circuit protective devices.

Instruction: Major topics covered in the course are principles of generator and motor operation; ratings and efficiency; principles of induction motors and synchronous motors; performance and speed control; single-phase motors; principles of motor control system; motor-circuit protective devices; solid-state drive systems; SCRs as AC to DC converters; and installation and maintenance of drive systems. Methods of instruction include self-study, texts, study guides, and a proctored final examination.

Credit Recommendation: In the lower division baccalaureate/associate degree category, 2 semester hours in Electronics Technology (11/84) (4/89) (6/94).

Accounting I

Location: Self-study.

Length: Correspondence Program.

Dates: January 1981-Present.

Objective: To provide the student with basic understanding of the principles of accounting.

Learning Outcome: Upon successful completion of this course, the student will be able to prepare all required procedures in the accounting cycle including the balance sheet and income statement; read and interpret financial reports; record financial transactions; establish a trial balance; make appropriate journal entries; post general ledger and make adjustments; and do payroll calculations.

Instruction: Major topics covered in the course include a review of the nature of accounting; financial reports, including the balance sheet and income statement; recording transactions, the trial balance, journal entries, and posting; adjustments; and cash versus accrual method of accounting; the work sheet; the accounting cycle; accounts and procedures for a merchandising business; and special journals and payroll accounting. Methods of instruction include self study, texts, study guides, and a proctored final examination.

Credit Recommendation: In the lower division baccalaureate/associate degree category, 3 semester hours in Accounting (4/86) (7/90) (9/95).

Accounting II

Location: Self-study.

Length: Correspondence Program.

Dates: January 1981-Present.

Objective: To expand the student's knowledge developed in Accounting I and to explain more detailed uses of accounting techniques.

Learning Outcome: Upon successful completion of this course, the student will be able to prepare and analyze financial statements; present the concepts of assets and liabilities as they apply to business organizations; identify and distinguish several types of fixed assets; establish accounting procedures for current and long-term liabilities; and complete an accounting cycle for a corporation.

Instruction: Major topics covered in this course are an explanation of cash: accounts receivable; notes receivable, investment inventory; nature of fixed assets; accounting for current and long-term liabilities; partnership accounting; and corporate ownership and management. A comprehensive case study dealing with the entire accounting cycle for a merchandising firm operating as a corporation is included. Methods of instruction include self study, texts, study guides, and a proctored final examination.

Credit Recommendation: In the lower baccalaureate/associate degree category, 3 semester hours in Accounting (4/86) (7/90) (9/95).

Advanced Accounting (Formerly Managerial Accounting)

Location: Self-study.

Length: Correspondence Program.

Dates: January 1981-Present.

Objective: To provide an understanding of more complex aspects of accounting theory plus significant opportunity for practice including a computerized business simulation project.

Learning Outcome: Upon successful completion of this course, the student will be able to apply theory and practice issues in income and value measurement and report for multicorporate enterprises and business combinations.

Instruction: Major topics covered in the course are a study of advanced accounting concepts including partnerships, installment sales, consignments, home office and branch combinations, and fund accounting; accounting for the organization; liquidation or incorporation of a partnership; the nature and principles of fund accounting; and elementary consolidated financial statements. Methods of instruction include self-study, texts, study guides, and a proctored final examination.

Credit Recommendation: In the upper division baccalaureate degree category, 3 semester hours in Advanced Accounting (4/86) (7/90) (9/95).

Advanced Business Applications

Location: Self-study.

Length: Correspondence program.

Dates: April 1991-Present.

Objective: To provide the fundamental principles of spreadsheets, database management, word processing, and telecommunications.

Learning Outcome: Upon successful completion of this course, the student will be able to set up and manipulate a spreadsheet, a database, and complete word processing tasks through the use of the McGraw-Hill Integrated Software Package.

Instruction: Major topics covered in the course are fundamental principles of spreadsheets, database management, telecommunications, and application of integrated software. Methods of instruction include self-study, texts, study guides, and a proctored final examination.

Credit Recommendation: In the lower division baccalaureate/associate degree category, 3 semester hours in Management Information Systems or Data Processing (6/94).

Advanced COBOL Programming Techniques

Location: Self-study.

Length: Correspondence program.

Dates: April 1991-Present.

Objective: To provide an overview of the advanced features of COBOL.

Learning Outcome: Upon successful completion of this course, the student will be able to design, develop, code, and debug a structured COBOL program employing advanced features such as file processing and report writing.

Instruction: Major topics covered in the course are an introduction to advanced COBOL, tables, sorting, applications, and interactive processing. Methods of instruction include self-study, texts, study guides, and a proctored final examination.

Credit Recommendation: In the lower division baccalaureate/associate degree category, 3 semester hours in Advanced COBOL (6/94).

Advertising Principles

Location: Self-study.

Length: Correspondence Program.

Dates: *Version 1:* March 1984-August 1995; *Version 2:* September 1995-Present.

Objective: To give the student a general introduction to advertising and its function and role.

Learning Outcome: Upon successful completion of this course, the student will be able to place advertising among the other appropriate marketing functions; describe the steps necessary to build an advertising organization; identify outside specialists; construct an advertising plan; and understand techniques of advertising, the function of advertising, and the role of advertising.

Instruction: Major topics covered in this course are describing the techniques of advertising; the function of advertising in the marketing area; and the role of advertising in the marketplace. Methods of instruction include self study, texts, study guides, and a proctored final examination.

Credit Recommendation: *Version 1:* In the vocational certificate category, 1 semester hour in Marketing (4/86) (7/90). *Version 2:* In the lower division baccalaureate/associate degree category, 3 semester hours in Marketing (9/95).

American Literature

Location: Self-study.

Length: Correspondence Program.

Dates: June 1978-December 1986.

Objective: To provide the student with understanding and appreciation of major authors and forms of writing as found in American Literature — An Introductory Overview.

Instruction: Major topics covered in the course are America's literature evolving into art form from its Puritan beginnings to the twentieth century.

Credit Recommendation: In the lower division baccalaureate/associate degree category, 3 semester hours in American Literature (11/84).

Analytic Geometry and Calculus

Location: Self-study.

Length: Correspondence Program.

Dates: October 1975-Present.

Objective: To provide a basic foundation in analytic geometry and a broad coverage of topics in differential and integral calculus.

Learning Outcome: Upon successful completion of this course, the student will be able to apply principles of analytic geometry and differential and integral calculus.

Instruction: Major topics covered in the course are rectangular coordinates; graphs of linear equations; conic sections; exponential, logarithmic, and trigonometric functions; continuity; limits; derivatives and their applications, including derivatives of implicit functions, parametric equations, and trigonometric, exponential, hyperbolic, and logarithmic functions; integrals and their applications; methods of integration; and polar coordinates. Methods of instruction include self-study, texts, study guides, and a proctored final examination.

Credit Recommendation: In the lower division baccalaureate/associate degree category, 4 semester hours in Analytic Geometry and Calculus (11/84) (4/89) (6/94).

Applications of Industrial Electronics

Location: Self-study.

Length: Correspondence Program.

Dates: January 1982-Present.

Objective: To provide a qualitative understanding of the color TV system, electronic systems applications, and industrial systems troubleshooting techniques.

Learning Outcome: Upon successful completion of this course, the student will be able to qualitatively understand the color TV system, electronic systems applications, and industrial systems troubleshooting techniques.

Instruction: Major topics covered in the course are the color TV system; basic industrial electronic systems application; voltage and frequency controllers; nondestructive test equipment; resistance welding equipment; dielectric and induction heating; and cranes, scales, and materials handling. Advanced troubleshooting; analysis of systems; test equipment applications; safe troubleshooting practices; and troubleshooting industrial systems. Methods of instruction included self-study, texts, study guides, and a proctored final examination.

Credit Recommendation: In the lower division baccalaureate/associate degree category, 3 semester hours in Electronics Technology (11/84) (4/89) (6/94).

Applied Mathematics

Location: Self-study.

Length: Correspondence Program.

Dates: January 1980-Present.

Objective: To provide a foundation in the use of metrics and a working knowledge of the application of certain topics in calculus that are needed in the electronics field of technology.

Learning Outcome: Upon successful completion of this course, the student will be able to use metrics and basic calculus in solving problems encountered in electronics.

Instruction: Major topics covered in the course are the use of metrics; use of calculus in electrical and electronic circuits; graphic differentiation; applications of derivatives and differentials; Kirchhoff's Laws; differentiating circuits; higher order derivatives; maxima and minima;

partial occurrences of maxima and minima; integration; electrical applications of integration; integrating circuits; graphic approach to integration; integrating instruments; polar coordinates; derivatives of trigonometric functions and their applications to electronics; logarithmic and exponential functions; natural logarithms; electrical transients in RC and RL circuits; hyperbolic functions; introduction to partial derivatives of transistor and electron-tube parameters; maxima and minima with partial derivatives; gradients; integration techniques; and application of double integrals to electrical circuits. Methods of instruction include self-study, texts, study guides, and a proctored final examination.

Credit Recommendation: In the lower division baccalaureate/associate degree category, 3 semester hours in Applied Mathematics (11/84) (4/89) (6/94).

Basic Surveying I

Location: Self-study.

Length: Correspondence Program.

Dates: January 1978-Present.

Objective: To introduce the fundamentals of plane surveying including distant measurement, leveling, and transit work.

Learning Outcome: Upon successful completion of this course, the student will be able to work proficiently with various surveying tools and equipment.

Instruction: Major topics covered in the course are principles of taps and accessories; electronic measurements; leveling; use of transit and theodolite; adjustment of instruments; angle measurements; triangulation; trigonometric leveling; balancing traverse; error of sure; and computation of area by latitudes and departures. **NOTE:** Does not include field exercises with surveying instruments. Methods of instruction include self-study, texts, study guides, and a proctored final examination.

Credit Recommendation: In the upper division baccalaureate degree category, 2 semester hours in Basic Surveying I or 1 semester hour in Basic Surveying I when applied to Engineering major (11/84) (4/89) (6/94). **NOTE:** Before credit is awarded, student should have completed a basic surveying lab course or have equivalent field experience.

Basic Surveying II

Location: Self-study.

Length: Correspondence Program.

Dates: January 1980-Present.

Objective: To introduce the principles of highway curve geometry.

Learning Outcome: Upon successful completion of this course, the student will be able to conduct basic surveys that involve a variety of curves: horizontal, vertical, compound, spiral, etc.

Instruction: Major topics covered in the course are tangents and horizontal curves; grades and vertical curves; compound and reverse curves; transition curves; superelevation; field layout of simple, compound, and spiral curves; vertical parabolic curves; and elevations on vertical curves. **NOTE:** Course does not include field exercise with surveying instruments. Methods of instruction include self-study, texts, study guides, and a proctored final examination.

Credit Recommendation: In the upper division baccalaureate degree category, 2 semester hours in Basic Surveying II or 1 semester hour in Basic Surveying II when applied to Engineering major (11/84) (4/89) (6/94).

Basics of the Catering Business

Location: Self-study.

Length: Correspondence Program.

Dates: November 1990-Present.

Objective: To provide the basics in providing catering services to the public.

Learning Outcome: Upon successful completion of this course, the student will be able to list the different kinds of professional catering events and services; describe the proper procedures for transporting and presenting catered foods; construct a buffet layout which utilizes sound traffic management techniques; identify the importance of written contracts and the formulation of a logical approach to charging the client for services rendered; and describe the principles in designing an efficient professional kitchen including the selection of equipment and the stocking of staple items.

Instruction: Major topics covered in the course are the kitchen, storage, production, equipment, costing, and recipes used in providing catering services. Methods of instruction include self-study, texts, study guides, and a proctored final examination.

Credit Recommendation: In the lower division baccalaureate/associate degree category, 2 semester hours in Principles of Catering (6/94). **NOTE:** This is not a lab-based course.

Beverage Operations

Location: Self-study.

Length: Correspondence Program.

Dates: October 1990-Present.

Objective: To introduce the financial, managerial, legal, and practical aspects of providing alcoholic beverage service to the public.

Learning Outcome: Upon completion of this course, the student will be able to describe the developmental history of alcoholic beverages and their service; identify the effects of dram shop laws on beverage service operations; describe the influence of atmosphere, decor, and space ratios on patrons' behavior; explain the total concept approach towards marketing an establishment to a desired target audience; list the key elements of a standard drink recipe; recognize the importance of implementing standard recipes; describe the proper handling, storage, and service techniques for beers, ales, still and sparkling wines, and various types of spirits; demonstrate a knowledge of popular drink ingredients and mixing procedures; and explain techniques for controlling inventory, dealing with problematic patrons, and hiring and retaining dependable and responsible staff members.

Instruction: Major topics covered in the course are the profitability of alcoholic beverages; legal control of alcohol; the types of wine and wine service, malt beverages, and distilled spirits; and the purchase, storage, and control of alcoholic beverages for a profitable operation. Methods of instruction include self-study, texts, study guides, and a proctored final examination.

Credit Recommendation: In the lower division baccalaureate/associate degree category, 2 semester hours in Beverage Management (6/94).

Business Communications Communications/Modern Language Expression

Location: Self-study.

Length: Correspondence Program.

Dates: January 1981-Present.

Objective: To introduce the student to elements of communication necessary for success in business.

Learning Outcome: Upon successful completion of this course, the student will be able to apply principles of grammar to writing samples; list steps to plan and develop effective business letters; understand how to research and prepare formal and informal reports and proposals; identify the key elements of formal and informal proposals; list the steps in research and documentation of material; and understand the mechanics of letter styles and advanced writing techniques.

Instruction: Major topics covered in this course are parts of speech, proper usage, punctuation and capitalization, vocabulary building, and sentence structure; how to address the audience and prepare appropriate effective business letters; how to research, document, and prepare visual aids for presentation of formal and informal reports; development of formal and informal proposals, their purpose, and their scope. Methods of instruction include self study, texts, study guides, and a proctored final examination.

Credit Recommendation: In the lower division baccalaureate/associate degree category, 2 semester hours in Business Communications (4/86) (7/90) (9/95).

Business Computer Systems and Applications

Location: Self-study.

Length: Correspondence Program.

Dates: April 1991-Present.

Objective: To introduce the uses of computers in the business world including inventory and accounting systems.

Learning Outcome: Upon successful completion of this course, the student will have knowledge of the evolution of computers in the business world and awareness of issues surrounding the choice between a manual versus a computerized system.

Instruction: Major topics covered in the course are introduction to computers; components of a computer system; identification of information needs of business; and development of the business plan. Methods of instruction include self-study, texts, study guides, and a proctored final examination.

Credit Recommendation: In the lower division baccalaureate/associate degree category, 2 semester hours in Management Information Systems or Data Processing (6/94).

Business Law I

Location: Self-study.

Length: Correspondence Program.

Dates: *Version 1:* January 1981-June 1995; *Version 2:* July 1995-Present.

Objective: *Version 1:* To introduce the student to the study of law and how it applies to contemporary business. Student will be able to describe and distinguish types of international law; to identify and explain which constitutional amendments affect everyday life; to identify and explain differences in types of contracts; to explain the roles of parties in a contract; and to interpret contractual capacities of minors and insane persons. *Version 2:* To introduce the student to the study of law and how it applies to contemporary business and affects everyday life. Students will be able to explain differences in types of contracts; to explain the roles of parties in a contract; to interpret contractual capacities of minors and insane persons; to explain the nature of an agency relationship and the major characteristics of partnerships and corporations; and to describe and distinguish the types of international law.

Learning Outcome: *Version 1:* Upon successful completion of this course, the student will understand the nature and administration of law, the law of bankruptcy, and commercial paper. *Version 2:* Upon successful completion of this course, the student will understand the nature and administration of law, the central issues of business law, the various forms of business organization, and issues related to international business.

Instruction: *Version 1:* Major topics covered in the course are an introduction to the study of law, its nature, and administration, the law of contracts, bankruptcy, and commercial paper. Method of instruction is self-study. *Version 2:* Major topics covered in the course include the nature and administration of law; the law of contracts; bankruptcy, and commercial paper; torts; real and personal property; organizing and financing a business; and conducting international business. Methods of instruction include self-study, texts, study guides, self administered tests, proctored final comprehensive examination.

Credit Recommendation: *Version 1:* In the lower division baccalaureate/associate degree category, 2 semester hours in Business Law (4/86) (7/90). *Version 2:* In the lower division baccalaureate/associate degree category, 3 semester hours in Business Law (4/86) (7/90) (9/95).

Business Law II

Location: Self-study.

Length: Correspondence Program.

Dates: *Version 1:* January 1981-June 1995; *Version 2:* July 1995-Present.

Objective: To provide the student with an expansion on subjects covered in Business Law I.

Learning Outcome: *Version 1:* Upon successful completion of this course, the student will be able to explain nature of agency relationship and how one can be created; to explain a partnership and major characteristics of a corporation; to explain differences in types of stock and the advantages and disadvantages of each; and to identify significant pieces of legislation affecting laws of trade. The student will have a good understanding of agency, partnership, realty property, corporation, and trade regulations. *Version 2:* Upon successful completion of this course, the student will be able to explain how ethics affect business practices; to explain the Constitution's impact on business; to describe methods of government regulation of business and to identify statutes affecting business and labor; to compare the roles of agents and principals; to examine consumer protection laws; and to identify way to comply with environmental laws and pollution control. The student will have a good understanding of the legal environment of business, including laws and regulations, ethical considerations, procedures, rights, agencies, practices and consumer and environmental protection issues.

Instruction: *Version 1:* Major topics covered include a study of agency, partnerships, real property, and corporations, concluding with an introduction to trade regulations. Methods of instruction include self-study, texts, study guides, self administered tests and proctored final comprehensive examination. *Version 2:* Major topics covered in the course include the relationship between law and ethics; constitutional guarantees that affect business; the role of administrative agencies; labor-management relations; the roles of agents and principals; the regulation of competition, markets, and securities; consumer protection; and environmental law. Methods of instruction include self study, texts, study guides, self administered tests and proctored final comprehensive examination.

Credit Recommendation: *Version 1:* In the lower division baccalaureate/associate degree category, 2 semester hours in Business Law (4/86) (7/90). *Version 2:* In the lower division baccalaureate/associate degree category, 3 semester hours in Business Law II (9/95).

Business Statistics

Location: Self-study.

Length: Correspondence Program.

Dates: *Version 1:* January 1981-August 1995; *Version 2:* September 1995-Present.

Objective: To provide the student with a description of how statistics are applied in the business world and an introduction to basic statistical techniques including visual and statistical description of data, basic probability, sampling, and hypothesis testing.

Learning Outcome: Upon successful completion of this course, the student will be able to describe how statistics are applied in the business world; apply appropriate techniques for visually representing data; define probability; explain the rules that govern discrete and continuous distribution; identify the role of probability sampling in inferential statistics; recognize the relationship between sample size and level of confidence; and apply the binomial, Poisson, standard normal, student's t distribution, and hypothesis testing in business applications.

Instruction: Major topics covered in the course are introduction of business statistics, visual description of data, statistical description of data, basic probability, discrete probability distributions, continuous probability distributions, sampling and sampling distributions, estimation from sample data, and hypothesis tests involving a sample mean or proportion. Methods of instruction include self study, texts, study guides, and a proctored final examination.

Credit Recommendation: *Version 1:* In the lower division baccalaureate/associate degree category, 2 semester hours in Business Math or Business Statistics (4/86) (7/90). *Version 2:* In the lower division baccalaureate/associate degree category, 3 semester hours in Business Statistics (4/86) (7/90) (9/95).

Circuits and Components Testing

Location: Self-study.

Length: Correspondence Program.

Dates: January 1982-Present.

Objective: To provide an understanding of reactive circuits and to perform electrical and electronics measurements experiments by using a measurements trainer.

Learning Outcome: Upon successful completion of this course, the student will be able to understand reactive circuits and to perform basic electrical and electronics measurements.

Instruction: Major topics covered in the course are reactive circuits; resistance, capacitance and inductance; reactance and impedance; resonant circuits; applications of resonant circuits. DC principles experiments; AC principles and components experiments; electrical measurements and instruments experiments; electronic measurements and instruments experiments; reactive circuits experiments; electronic components experiments; and basic electronic circuits experiments. Methods of instruction include self-study, texts, study guides, and a proctored final examination.

Credit Recommendation: In the lower division baccalaureate/associate degree category, 3 semester hours in Electrical/Electronic Technology or Circuits Testing (11/84) (4/89) (6/94).

Communications

Location: Self-study.

Length: Correspondence Program.

Dates: January 1981-Present.

Objective: To introduce the student to elements of communication necessary for success in Business.

Learning Outcome: Upon successful completion of this course, students will be able to apply principles of grammar to writing samples; list steps to plan and develop effective business letters; understand how to research and prepare formal and informal reports and proposals; identify the key elements of formal and informal proposals; list the steps in research and documentation of material; and understand the mechanics of letter styles and advanced writing techniques.

Instruction: Major topics covered in the course are parts of speech, proper usage, punctuation and capitalization, vocabulary building and sentence structure; how to address the audience and prepare appropriate effective business letters; how to research, document and prepare visual aids for presentation of formal and informal reports; development of formal and informal proposals, emphasizing their purpose, and their scope. Methods of instruction include self-study, texts, study guides, and a proctored final examination.

Credit Recommendation: In the lower division baccalaureate/associate degree category, 2 semester hours in Communications (4/89) (6/94) (9/95).

Composition and Rhetoric

Location: Self-study.

Length: Correspondence Program.

Dates: *Version 1:* September 1984-March 1989; *Version 2:* April 1989-Present.

Objective: To provide both theoretical and practical experience in writing.

Learning Outcome: Upon successful completion of this course, the student will be able to write and speak coherently.

Instruction: Major topics covered in the course include practice in expository writing, the application of rhetorical principles, and the writing of a research paper; and a wide variety of readings to stimulate good writing and skill in composition. Methods of instruction include self-study, texts, study guides, and a proctored final examination.

Credit Recommendation: *Version 1:* In the lower division baccalaureate/associate degree category, 2 semester hours in Composition and Rhetoric (11/84). *Version 2:* In the lower division baccalaureate/associate degree category, 3 semester hours in Composition and Rhetoric (4/89) (6/94).

Computer Literacy and Programming in BASIC

Location: Self-study.

Length: Correspondence Program.

Dates: March 1983-Present.

Objective: To provide fundamental computer concepts, flowcharting, and BASIC programming, including graphs, arrays, functions, and file handling techniques.

Learning Outcome: Upon successful completion of this course, the student will be able to understand fundamental computer concepts, flowcharting, and programming using BASIC language.

Instruction: Major topics covered in the course are a general introduction to computers including parts and components, learning extensive programming in BASIC, and the use of microcomputers. Methods of instruction include self-study, texts, study guides, and a proctored final examination.

Credit Recommendation: In the lower division baccalaureate/associate degree category, 3 semester hours in BASIC Programming and 2 semester hours in Computer Literacy (5/84) (4/89) (6/94). **NOTE:** Credit cannot be granted for both this course and Computer Science I and Computer Science II.

Computer Science III (Computer and FORTRAN)

Location: Self-study.

Length: Correspondence Program.

Dates: *Version 1:* January 1982-March 1989; *Version 2:* April 1989-January 1994.

Objective: To provide the student with a fundamental understanding of the FORTRAN IV programming language. Also, an overview of computer application in industry and electronics is provided.

Learning Outcome: Upon successful completion of this course, the student will be able to understand concepts of FORTRAN; write simple FORTRAN programs; and understand how computers are used in industry and electronics.

Instruction: Major topics covered in the course are basic industrial computer systems; computer fundamentals; digital and analog systems; software and programming; computer-aided control systems; interfacing principles; FORTRAN

IV programming; fundamental FORTRAN IV concepts; writing simple FORTRAN program; statement functions; use of magnetic tapes and disks; and review of function and subroutine subprograms.

Credit Recommendation: *Version 1:* In the lower division baccalaureate/associate degree category, 2 semester hours in FORTRAN (11/84). *Version 2:* In the lower division baccalaureate/associate degree category, 3 semester hours in FORTRAN (4/89) (6/94).

Computer Science
1. Computer Science I (Computer Applications and Operations)
2. Computer Science II (BASIC Programming Fundamentals)
3. Computer Science II

Location: Self-study.

Length: Correspondence Program.

Dates: *Version 1:* February 1984-December 1987; *Version 2:* January 1988-Present.

Objective: To provide fundamental computer concepts, flowcharting, and BASIC programming including graphics, arrays, functions, and file handling techniques.

Learning Outcome: Upon successful completion of this course, the student will be able to understand fundamental computer concepts, flowcharting, and date representation; and will learn the BASIC programming language.

Instruction: *Version 1: Course 1:* Major topics covered in the course are Elementary programming and hardware concepts and terminology, data representation, flowcharting, and elementary BASIC programming concepts. Lecture materials emphasize microcomputers. *Course 2:* Major topics covered in the course are comparing and branching; selecting alternative paths; translating two-directional flowcharts into linear programs, using multiple comparisons; subtotaling; internal subroutines; multiple control breaks; defining a table; loading and printing numeric arrays; searching a table; maintaining a data file; alphabetic and numeric sequencing; coding sorts; merging files; formatting lines; columns and references; producing graphics; reverses and output; using pexels; and creating graphs. *Version 2:* Major topics covered in the course are an overall view of the world of computers, the role of software, the principles of programming, structured computer programming, the programming development cycle, a brief view of several programming languages, and an introduction to programming in BASIC. Methods of instruction include correspondence, calls, and examinations.

Credit Recommendation: *Version 1:* In the lower division baccalaureate/associate degree category, 3 semester hours in BASIC Programming and in the lower division baccalaureate/associate degree category, 2 semester hours in Computer Literacy (11/84). *Version 2:* In the lower division baccalaureate/associate degree category, 6 semester hours in BASIC Programming and Computer Literacy (4/89) (6/94). **NOTE:** Both Computer Science I and II must be successfully completed for credit recommendations to apply. Credit cannot be granted for both this course and Programming in BASIC. *Prerequisite:* Computer Science I.

Computer-Aided Drafting and Design

Location: Self-study.

Length: Correspondence program.

Dates: June 1990-Present.

Objective: To introduce the methods of drafting and design as they relate to computer-aided techniques.

Learning Outcome: Upon successful completion of this course, the student will be able to identify common CAD system configuration; describe the operation of CAD system input devices; understand the basic concepts of plotting points and drawing lines, circles, arc segments, and ellipses; understand the basic concepts of how to create and rotate a 3-D model; and identify Basic and Fortran commands related to CAD/CAM graphic software.

Instruction: Major topics covered in the course are CAD system configuration, 3-D CAD/CAM models, modern CAD/CAM equipment in industry, the Mirror ad Window functions, and Basic and fortran commands related to the use of CAM/CAD system graphic software. No extensive use is made of commercially available CAD software packages. Methods of instruction include self-study, texts, study guides, and a proctored final examination.

Credit Recommendation: In the vocational certificate category, 1 semester hour in Mechanical Drawing (6/94).

Computer-Aided Manufacturing

Location: Self-study.

Length: Correspondence program.

Dates: June 1990-Present.

Objective: To introduce the basics of robotics systems and computer numerical controls.

Learning Outcome: Upon successful completion of this course, the student will be able to discuss the history of robotics; identify robotics control system components and peripherals; create robot programs in MAKER, VAL II, RAIL and AML; recognize artificial intelligence and numerical control systems, create robotics motion (linear and angular), identify miscellaneous NC and CNC control functions, identify the characteristics and operation of machine centers, turning centers, and electrical discharge machinery; and be able to discuss the future of machine tool operation.

Instruction: Major topics covered in the course are fundamentals of robot technology such as controls, systems, and components, motion, sensors, machine vision, languages, programming, and robotics economics; CNC technology and programming; simple programming; and machinery centers. Methods of instruction include self-study, texts, study guides, and a proctored final examination.

Credit Recommendation: In the lower division baccalaureate/associate degree category, 1 semester hour in Introduction to Computer-Aided Manufacturing (6/94).

Concrete

Location: Self-study.

Length: Correspondence Program.

Dates: January 1982-Present.

Objective: To provide an understanding of how concrete is produced, tested, and used in the field.

Learning Outcome: Upon successful completion of this course, the student will be able to test and analyze the quality of concrete in the field.

Instruction: Major topics covered in the course are production of concrete; proportioning of concrete mixes; tests for concrete; and field methods in concrete construction. Methods of instruction include self-study, texts, study guides, and a proctored final examination.

Credit Recommendation: In the upper division baccalaureate degree category, 2 semester hours in Civil Engineering Technology (11/84) (4/89) (6/94).

Cost Accounting

Location: Self-study.

Length: Correspondence Program.

Dates: January 1981-Present.

Objective: To provide the student with understanding of cost accounting concepts and the ability to develop timekeeping and payroll reports.

Learning Outcome: Upon successful completion of this course, the student will

be able to explain the necessity for cost information; record entries dealing with raw materials acquisition, labor cost, overhead costs, warehousing, and sales; interpret a job cost system after it is installed; account for work in process in proper terms; use cost data in budgeting and capital planning for various types of manufacturing operations; and use a personal computer to perform various accounting functions.

Instruction: Major topics covered in this course are cost accounting concepts and the interpretation of reports; development of timekeeping and payroll procedures; the setting of overhead rates; accounting for by-products; development of cost analyses; process cost accounting; job-order cost accounting; standard cost; and the use of computers in solving cost accounting problem. Methods of instruction include self study, texts, study guides, and a proctored final examination.

Credit Recommendation: In the upper division baccalaureate degree category, 3 semester hours in Cost Accounting (4/86) (7/90) (9/95).

Directed Project

Location: Self-study.

Length: Correspondence program.

Dates: April 1991-Present.

Objective: To provide the knowledge and skills to apply principles learned throughout the applied computer science program, and to develop a proposal for an electronic automated system.

Learning Outcome: Upon successful completion of this course, the student will be able to apply the principles taught throughout the program by analyzing the present manual system, defining objectives for the new automated system, creating an automated system, and submitting a proposal for review.

Instruction: Major topics covered in the course are assessment and evaluation of the setting; plan, development and design; computerizing patient information; and preparation of final proposal. Methods of instruction include self-study, texts, study guides, and a proctored final examination.

Credit Recommendation: In the lower division baccalaureate/associate degree category, 2 semester hours in Management Information Systems or Data Processing (6/94).

Earthwork

Location: Self-study.

Length: Correspondence Program.

Dates: January 1980-Present.

Objective: To perform earthwork volume computations.

Learning Outcome: Upon successful completion of this course, the student will be able to conduct field and office work in the area of cut-fill calculations, embankment analysis, and grade establishment.

Instruction: Major topics covered in the course are surveys for determining grade; cross-sectioning; earthwork computations; formation of embankments; shrinkage and swell; moving cut to fill; and mass diagrams. Methods of instruction include self-study, texts, study guides, and a proctored final examination.

Credit Recommendation: In the lower division baccalaureate/associate degree category, 1 semester hour in Civil Engineering Technology (11/84) (4/89) (6/94). **NOTE:** Can also apply to Engineering majors.

Economics I

Location: Self-study.

Length: Correspondence Program.

Dates: *Version 1:* January 1981-June 1995; *Version 2:* July 1995-Present.

Objective: *Version 1:* To provide the student with a general survey course that is designed to introduce student to basic concepts of economics. Student will be able to describe a business cycle; to explain importance of the concept of Gross National Product; to list four assumptions concerning consumer behavior; to explain differences between foreign and domestic trade; and to define and give examples of noncompetitive market structures. *Version 2:* To provide the student with basic concepts of macroeconomics; the student will be able to explain the meaning of basic terms and concepts; recognize simple economic equations; describe a business cycle; discuss economic measures; define basic theories; explain how changes effect equilibrium; and explain the differences between foreign and domestic trade.

Learning Outcome: *Version 1:* Upon successful completion of this course, the student will understand macro and micro economic concepts, the economizing problem, and its future implications. *Version 2:* Upon successful completion of this course, the student will understand macroeconomic concepts and how the three sectors of the economy-government, business and households-interact.

Instruction: *Version 1:* Major topics covered in this course include defining the economizing problem, developing it, and exploring its future implications. The course emphasizes economic growth. Macro and micro economic concepts are examined in terms of a discussion of three fundamental economic questions: (1) What is to be produced? (2) Where is it to be produced? and (3) How is it to be produced? *Version 2:* Major topics covered include defining macroeconomics, developing it, and exploring future implications. Macroeconomic concepts are examined in terms of discussion of equilibrium and disequilibrium, countercyclical policies, and the open economy. Methods of instruction include self-study, texts, study guides, and a proctored final examination .

Credit Recommendation: *Versions 1 and 2:* In the lower division baccalaureate/associate degree category, 3 semester hours in Economics (4/86) (7/90) (9/95).

Economics II

Location: Self-study.

Length: Correspondence Program.

Dates: *Version 1:* April 1986-June 1995; *Version 2:* July 1995-Present.

Objective: *Version 1:* To provide the student with an understanding of general concepts of economics and specialized problems such as inequality and poverty. *Version 2:* To provide the student with an understanding of general concepts of mircroeconomics.

Learning Outcome: *Version 1:* Upon successful completion of this course, the student will be able to list and explain some of the reasons for differences in money income received by individuals; to differentiate between the economic growth problems facing more versus less developed countries; to identify and explain major differences between different economic systems; and to identify different kinds of markets. The student will have an expanded understanding of macro and micro economic concepts and will have a knowledge of the economics of inequality and poverty. *Version 2:* Upon successful completion of this course, the student will be able to discuss how decisions made by consumers, business and government affect the microeconomy; to explain demand and supply schedules; to be able to distinguish among the categories of costs and their relationships; to describe the pricing and demand for each of the three factors of production; and to be able to discuss the degrees of competition that prevail among different categories of market models. The student will have an understanding of microeconomic concepts and how these concepts affect the individual consumer, worker, and business and what effect government has on them.

Instruction: *Version 1:* Major topics covered in this course are a continuing study of macro and micro economic concepts. Also includes a discussion of managerial economics. Emphasis is placed on the economics of inequality and poverty. The material is organized to answer two fundamental questions: (1) To whom shall resources be distributed? (2) When will the "poverty amidst plenty" problem be resolved? Methods of instruction include self study, texts, study guides, self administered tests and a proctored final comprehensive examination. *Version 2:* Major topics covered in this course include an overview of microeconomics; an examination of concepts and how they relate to consumer and producer behavior, production and demand for economic resources, industry models, and market structures. Methods of instruction include self study, texts, study guides, self administered tests and a proctored final examination.

Credit Recommendation: *Versions 1 and 2:* In the lower division baccalaureate/associate degree category, 3 semester hours in Economics or Macroeconomics (4/86) (7/90) (9/95).

Electrical Installation Practices

Location: Self-study.

Length: Correspondence Program.

Dates: January 1980-Present.

Objective: To provide a foundation in basic wiring, plus an understanding of the National Electrical Code.

Learning Outcome: Upon successful completion of this course, the student will have a very good understanding of wiring new as well as old work and the rules covered in the National Electrical Code Book.

Instruction: Major topics covered in the course are the review of sizing conduit, conductors, and boxes; review of circuits; testing circuits; running cable; cutting openings; mounting and grounding boxes; preparing cable and installing cable in boxes; wiring commonly used devices; plugs and receptacles; line and extension cords; split-wired and switched receptacles; switch circuits; dimmers; wiring and mounting lampholders and lighting fixtures; use of nipples and hickeys; wiring appliance circuits; wiring doorbell circuits and electric space heaters; conduit bending; raceways; busways; industrial power distribution systems; and definitions and explanation of code. Methods of instruction include self-study, texts, study guides, and a proctored final examination.

Credit Recommendation: In the lower division baccalaureate/associate degree category, 2 semester hours in Electrical Engineering Technology (11/84) (4/89) (6/94).

Electrical Machines

Location: Self-study.

Length: Correspondence Program.

Dates: January 1980-Present.

Objective: To provide the knowledge needed to apply, in industrial settings, fractional-horsepowered motors, direct-current machines, alternators, and alternating-current motors and the knowledge to perform efficiency tests on them.

Learning Outcome: Upon successful completion of this course, the student will be able to define and compute the efficiency of fractional-horsepowered motors, direct-current machines, transformers, synchronous alternating-current machines, and induction machines.

Instruction: Major topics covered in the course are principles and characteristics of DC and AC machines; electrical connections; rating; performance and speed control; thermal overload protection; types of drive systems; efficiency of DC and AC machines; and transformers. Methods of instruction include self-study, texts, study guides, and a proctored final examination.

Credit Recommendation: In the lower division baccalaureate/associate degree category, 3 semester hours in Electrical Engineering Technology (11/84) (4/89) (6/94).

Electrical/Electronic Measurements and Instruments

Location: Self-study.

Length: Correspondence Program.

Dates: January 1982-Present.

Objective: To become familiar with transformers and the various electrical and electronic meters/testing devices that are used in troubleshooting/monitoring circuits.

Learning Outcome: Upon successful completion of this course, the student will be able to understand how various test instruments work and how they are used. The course also provides an introduction to transformers.

Instruction: Major topics covered in the course are transformer fundamentals; electrical measurements and instruments; checking simple circuits; troubleshooting with basic meters; how a voltmeter works; how an ammeter works; AC measuring instruments; miscellaneous electrical measuring instruments; electrical measurements and instruments; electronic quantities and testing principles; multipurpose test instruments; bridge-type instruments; oscilloscopes; component testers; and digital test equipment. Methods of instruction include self-study, texts, study guides, and a proctored final examination.

Credit Recommendation: In the lower division baccalaureate/associate degree category, 1 semester hour in Electrical Engineering Technology (11/84) (4/89) (6/94).

Electronic Circuits

Location: Self-study.

Length: Correspondence Program.

Dates: January 1982-Present.

Objective: To widen the knowledge of electronic circuits and their applications, including an introduction to electronic systems using block diagram techniques; and to provide an introduction to troubleshooting methods and philosophy.

Learning Outcome: Upon successful completion of this course, the student will be able to understand basic troubleshooting methods and philosophy, understand a wider range of circuits, and understand block diagrams of electronic systems.

Instruction: Major topics covered in the course are electronic systems; electronic devices, and amplification; audio and RF circuits; oscillators, feedback and waveform generators; electronic power supply systems; industrial receivers, transmitters, and video systems; servo and control systems; pulse and logic circuits; programmable controllers and microprocessor; troubleshooting electronic equipment and systems; logical troubleshooting methods; instrument selection; measuring techniques; interpreting data and results; use of manufacturers' instructions; and test instruments maintenance. Methods of instruction include self-study, texts, study guides, and a proctored final examination.

Credit Recommendation: In the lower division baccalaureate/associate degree category, 1 semester hour in Electrical/Electronic Technology or Electronic Circuits (11/84) (4/89) (6/94).

Electronic Instrumentation and Control

Location: Self-study.

Length: Correspondence Program.

Dates: January 1982-Present.

Objective: To provide an understanding of the function and use of circuit testing devices, instruments and their control, and electronic circuit applications found within industry.

Learning Outcome: Upon successful completion of this course, the student will

be able to understand the function and use of circuit testing devices, control circuits, and electronic circuit applications found within industry.

Instruction: Major topics covered in the course are automatic testing of electronic devices; electronic instrumentation and control; physical properties and their measurement part 1; physical properties and their measurement part 2; measuring instruments and signal processing; transducers; introduction to control systems; controllers; control system methods; data logging, transmission, and display; control applications; maintenance; and troubleshooting. Industrial electronic circuit applications: interfacing process variables; motor control and servo systems; numeric control systems; programmable controllers; and industrial robots. Methods of instruction include self-study, texts, study guides, and a proctored final examination.

Credit Recommendation: In the lower division baccalaureate/associate degree category, 3 semester hours in Electrical Engineering Technology or Electronics Technology (11/84) (4/89) (6/94).

Engineering Economy

Location: Self-study.

Length: Correspondence Program.

Dates: October 1978-Present.

Objective: To provide a basis for making economic decision in equipment selection or replacement.

Learning Outcome: Upon successful completion of this course, the student will be able to understand the information necessary to make an equipment selection or replacement decision based on economics and various procedures used to make the decision.

Instruction: Major topics covered in the course are cash flow, time value of money, investment methods, use of interest tables, engineering valuation, and canons of ethics for engineers. Methods of instruction include self-study, texts, study guides, and a proctored final examination.

Credit Recommendation: In the lower division baccalaureate/associate degree category, 1 semester hour in Introduction to Engineering Economy (11/84) (4/89) (6/94). *Prerequisite:* Technical Mathematics I.

Engineering Materials

Location: Self-study.

Length: Correspondence Program.

Dates: January 1982-Present.

Objective: To introduce the nature and properties of metallic and nonmetallic materials.

Learning Outcome: Upon successful completion of this course, the student will be able to understand the composition and properties of metallic and nonmetallic materials.

Instruction: Major topics covered in the course are composition and properties of metals, ceramics, concrete, glass, graphite, plastics, and wood. Methods of instruction include self-study, texts, study guides, and a proctored final examination.

Credit Recommendation: In the lower division baccalaureate/associate degree category, 2 semester hours in Engineering Materials or Engineering Technology (11/84) (4/89) (6/94). **NOTE:** Student may receive credit for only 1 of the following courses: Engineering Materials, Technical Materials, or Mechanics of Materials. *Prerequisite:* Technical Science.

Engineering Mechanics

Location: Self-study.

Length: Correspondence Program.

Dates: January 1977-Present.

Objective: To introduce the study of the effect of forces on stationary and moving bodies.

Learning Outcome: Upon successful completion of this course, the student will be able to understand the basic relation between force and energy and stationary or moving bodies.

Instruction: Major topics covered in the course are the scope of engineering mechanics; collinear and concurrent forces; center of gravity of bodies; free body diagrams; characteristics of friction; bodies on level and inclined surfaces; kinematics; translation and rotation; kinetics; force-mass-acceleration method; and collision of two bodies. Methods of instruction include self-study, texts, study guides, and a proctored final examination.

Credit Recommendation: In the lower division baccalaureate/associate degree category, 3 semester hours in Elements of Statics and Dynamics or Engineering Technology (11/84) (4/89) (6/94). *Prerequisite:* Technical Mathematics I and II.

Federal Taxation

Location: Self-study.

Length: Correspondence Program.

Dates: January 1981-Present.

Objective: To provide the student with an understanding of principles of tax laws and simple tax preparation and savings that concentrates on individual tax returns.

Learning Outcome: Upon successful completion of this course, the student will be able to present tax-planning concepts for personal and business decision making and preparation of federal income tax returns; identify deductions and enter them into the proper section of the tax form; calculate gains and losses for both businesses and non-business transactions; and calculate and claim depreciation.

Instruction: Major topics covered in this course are a practical study of government income tax regulations, including a history of the federal income tax and tax savings principles; completion of individual returns; and brief coverage of income tax regulations that apply to partnerships and corporations. Methods of instruction include self-study, texts, study guides, and a proctored final examination.

Credit Recommendation: In the upper division baccalaureate degree category, 3 semester hours in Accounting or Federal Tax Accounting (4/86) (7/90) (9/95).

Fluid Mechanics

Location: Self-study.

Length: Correspondence Program.

Dates: January 1980-Present.

Objective: To introduce the study of fluid flow in open and closed channels.

Learning Outcome: Upon successful completion of this course, the student will be able to assist in the design and analysis of various types of fluid flow in open and closed channels.

Instruction: Major topics covered in the course are properties of materials; intensity of pressure; flow of liquids through pipes, Bernoulli's theorem; resultant forces due to liquid pressure; center of pressure; Chezy-Darcy formula; Hazen-Williams formula; Reynolds number; flow of water in open channels; and rate of discharge through wires. Methods of instruction include self-study, texts, study guides, and a proctored final examination.

Credit Recommendation: In the lower division baccalaureate/associate degree category, 3 semester hours in Introduction to Fluid Mechanics or Engineering Technology (11/84) (4/89) (6/94). *Prerequisite:* Engineering Mechanics.

Fundamentals of Electricity

Location: Self-study.

Length: Correspondence Program.

Dates: January 1982-Present.

Objective: To provide a qualitative approach to basic concepts in AC and DC electricity.

Learning Outcome: Upon successful completion of this course, the student will

be able to understand Ohm's law and basic circuit arrangements, and the student will be familiar with alternators, generators, and transformers.

Instruction: Major topics covered in the course are DC principles: nature of electricity; preventive maintenance; electric cells and batteries; electrical components and Ohm's law; basic circuit arrangements; electrical language and hardware; magnetism and electromagnetism; DC generators. AC principles and components: alternators; transformers; inductance and capacitance; AC circuits; rectification and electronic devices; electric energy distribution; and types of electric circuits. Methods of instruction include self-study, texts, study guides, and a proctored final examination.

Credit Recommendation: In the lower division baccalaureate/associate degree category, 1 semester hour in Electrical Engineering Technology or Electronics Technology (11/84) (4/89) (6/94).

Fundamentals of Electronics

Location: Self-study.

Length: Correspondence Program.

Dates: January 1982-Present.

Objective: To provide a qualitative understanding of various electronic components and how they are used in the various types of electronic circuits.

Learning Outcome: Upon successful completion of this course, the student will be able to recognize typical components and circuits as they appear on a schematic plus have a qualitative understanding of their operation.

Instruction: Major topics covered in the course are electrical components; resistive, capacitive, and inductive components; basic semiconductor components; semiconductor switching devices; special semiconductor devices; rectifiers and electron tubes; switching and connection devices; basic electronic circuits; logic circuits; gating and counting circuits; and pulse digital circuits. Methods of instruction include self-study, texts, study guides, and a proctored final examination.

Credit Recommendation: In the lower division baccalaureate/associate degree category, 3 semester hours in Electrical/ Electronics Technology or Fundamentals of Electronics (11/84) (4/89) (6/94).

General Psychology

Location: Self-study.

Length: Correspondence Program.

Dates: February 1977-December 1986.

Objective: To provide the student with an understanding and familiarity with the basic concepts, theories, and principles of psychology, and to familiarize students with psychological methodologies.

Instruction: Major topics covered in the course are the historical development of scientific psychology, methods of obtaining behavioral data, human development, cognitive processes, awareness, motivation, emotion, personality, normal and abnormal behavior, and interpersonal relations.

Credit Recommendation: In the lower division baccalaureate/associate degree category, 2 semester hours in General Psychology (11/84).

Geodetic Surveying

Location: Self-study.

Length: Correspondence Program.

Dates: January 1980-Present.

Objective: To introduce the advanced topics in land surveying.

Learning Outcome: Upon successful completion of this course, the student will be able to conduct city surveys.

Instruction: Major topics covered in the course are horizontal and vertical control surveys; monuments and markers; triangulation surveys; state plane coordinate systems; methods of projection; construction and maintenance surveys; and subdivision of city blocks into lots. Methods of instruction include self-study, texts, study guides, and a proctored final examination.

Credit Recommendation: In the upper division baccalaureate degree category, 2 semester hours in Land Surveying or Civil Engineering Technology (11/84) (4/89) (6/94).

Highway Construction and Design I

Location: Self-study.

Length: Correspondence Program.

Dates: January 1980-Present.

Objective: To introduce the principles of design and analysis of embankments and subgrades, drainage, highway location, and traffic control facets of highway/ road work.

Learning Outcome: Upon successful completion of this course, the student will be able to compute cuts and fills, estimate the effects of route design on drainage, and select the best possible route for a proposed road.

Instruction: Major topics covered in the course are soil studies, subgrades and drainage, location surveys, selection of route, establishing grade lines, traffic studies, signs, volume and speed studies, and safety appurtenances. Methods of instruction include self-study, texts, study guides, and a proctored final examination.

Credit Recommendation: In the lower division baccalaureate/associate degree category, 2 semester hours in Civil Engineering Technology (11/84) (4/89) (6/94). **NOTE:** Course should not be applied to an Engineering major.

Highway Construction and Design II

Location: Self-study.

Length: Correspondence Program.

Dates: January 1980-Present.

Objective: To continue exposure to the factors involved in highway work in which the student learns about low-cost road surfaces, hard pavements, and the structural design of pipe culverts.

Learning Outcome: Upon successful completion of this course, the student will be able to ascertain the characteristics of various subgrade soils, prepare each soil for service as a roadbed, and design roads paved with concrete or asphalt.

Instruction: Major topics covered in the course are maintenance of untreated surfaces, stabilized soil-bound surfaces, rigid concrete pavements, flexible bituminous pavements, and design of pipe culverts. Methods of instruction include self-study, texts, study guides, and a proctored final examination.

Credit Recommendation: In the lower division baccalaureate/associate degree category, 2 semester hours in Civil Engineering Technology (11/84) (4/89) (6/94). **NOTE:** Course should not be applied to an Engineering major.

Hospitality Accounting

Location: Self-study.

Length: Correspondence Program.

Dates: October 1991-Present.

Objective: To provide the basic principles of financial accounting relevant to the hospitality industry.

Learning Outcome: Upon successful completion of this course, the student will be able to prepare the various documents and perform the various procedures required to complete the accounting cycle and payroll calculations; and identify specific types of financial data relevant to making informed hospitality management decisions.

Instruction: Major topics covered in the course are the nature of accounting and financial reports; balance sheet; income statement; transaction recording; the trial balance; journal entries, posting, adjustments; cash method versus the accrual method of accounting; work sheet; the accounting cycle; accounts and procedures for business; special journals; and payroll accounting as they relate to the hospitality industry. Methods of instruction include self-study, texts, study guides, and a proctored final examination.

Credit Recommendation: In the lower division baccalaureate/associate degree category, 3 semester hours in Accounting (6/94).

Hospitality Engineering Systems

Location: Self-study.

Length: Correspondence Program.

Dates: November 1990-Present.

Objective: To introduce the basic principles of housekeeping and engineering management with emphasis on the proper work methods and the operation of building systems.

Learning Outcome: Upon successful completion of this course, the student will be able to describe the benefits of a sound preventive maintenance program; explain the basic operational principles behind heating, cooling, plumbing, ventilation and electrical systems; identify the sources of food spoilage and food-borne illness transmission; list procedures for the safe handling and storage of food; list the duties of the various housekeeping personnel; describe the procedure for effective room cleaning; and explain the importance of implementing a standardized training program within the housekeeping department.

Instruction: Major topics covered in the course are housekeeping personnel and operations, textiles and fabrics, carpeting, engineering and maintenance, plumbing, heating, ventilating and air treatment, refrigeration, electrical systems, swimming pool maintenance, and sanitation topics. Methods of instruction include self-study, texts, study guides, and a proctored final examination.

Credit Recommendation: In the lower division baccalaureate/associate degree category, 1 semester hour in Housekeeping Management and 1 semester hour in Engineering Management (6/94).

Hospitality Law and Insurance

Location: Self-study.

Length: Correspondence Program.

Dates: January 1992-Present.

Objective: To introduce business law and hospitality application.

Learning Outcome: Upon successful completion of this course, the student will be able to differentiate between the various types of business contracts, explain conditions which must be present in order to establish a valid contract, identify the capacity of minors and mentally disabled persons to enter into a contract, delineate the nature of the inkeeper-guest relationship and discuss the implications of this relationship in terms of third party and supervisory liability, describe the types of contracts which the hotel manager is likely to encounter, and list insurance requirements of the hotel industry.

Instruction: Major topics covered in the course are law of contractual capacity and contractual remedies, legal responsibilities of hospitality personnel, liabilities, legislation, and an overview of insurance. Methods of instruction include self-study, texts, study guides, and a proctored final examination.

Credit Recommendation: In the lower division baccalaureate/associate degree category, 2 semester hours in Business Law (6/94).

Hospitality Marketing/Advertising

Location: Self-study.

Length: Correspondence Program.

Dates: October 1991-Present.

Objective: To introduce the principles involved in marketing and promoting a hospitality operation.

Learning Outcome: Upon successful completion of this course, the student will be able to list the major marketing tools used in the industry; differentiate between the various approaches to market segmentation; identify the various distribution channels for hospitality products and services; compare the value of demographic data to psycho graphic data in terms of performing marketing research; explain the influence which user groups exert over marketing decisions; discriminate between the contributory values of the major marketing tools including advertising, public relations, promotions, collateral materials, packaging, and rate and price strategies; describe the process of developing a strategic placement for hospitality products in relation to market competition; explain the process of market plan formulation; describe the role that forecasting plays in developing future marketing strategies; define the role of marketing research in the formulation of marketing goals; and describe the effects which population, employment, and economic trends have over future marketing efforts.

Instruction: Major topics covered in the course are the techniques and the roles which marketing plays in establishing and maintaining a successful hospitality enterprise and various marketing applications. Methods of instruction include self-study, texts, study guides, and a proctored final examination.

Credit Recommendation: In the lower division baccalaureate/associate degree category, 3 semester hours in Hospitality Marketing (6/94).

Hospitality Purchasing and Storage

Location: Self-study.

Length: Correspondence Program.

Dates: October 1991-Present.

Objective: To introduce the personnel, procedures, and functions of a hospitality purchasing department.

Learning Outcome: Upon successful completion of this course, the student will be able to identify the various positions and organizational structure of the purchasing department; summarize the duties of this department; classify the various markets relevant to the hospitality industry; categorize the various types of buyers; describe the components and purpose of purchasing specifications; explain the organization, functioning, and importance of the receiving department; list the duties of the receiving clerk; detail the proper setup and operation of an efficient storeroom; delineate the implementation of an internal inventory control system; and define the various standards, terminology, specifications, legal requirements and other factors pertinent to the purchasing of meat, poultry, eggs, seafood, dairy products, fresh and processed fruits and vegetables, convenience foods, grocery items, and service and cleaning items.

Instruction: Major topics covered in the course are types of buyers and their functions, the purchasing process, how to prepare and check specifications and where to purchase, receiving procedures, and storage of food and non-food items. Methods of instruction include self-study, texts, study guides, and a proctored final examination.

Credit Recommendation: In the lower division baccalaureate/associate degree category, 3 semester hours in Food Purchasing (6/94).

Human Behavior

Location: Self-study.

Length: Correspondence Program.

Dates: January 1979-Present.

Objective: To introduce the basic concepts, theories, and principles of anthropology, sociology, and psychology as they relate to the business environment.

Learning Outcome: Upon successful completion of this course, the student will be able to recognize cultural, group, and individual behaviors and how they relate to the business environment; distinguish among the differences in the study of anthropology, sociology, and psychology;

and identify man as a cultural, social, and individual being.

Instruction: Major topics covered in the course are selected concepts of anthropology, sociology, and psychology. Methods of instruction include self-study, texts, study guides, and a proctored final examination.

Credit Recommendation: In the lower division baccalaureate/associate degree category, 1 semester hour in Human Behavior (6/94).

Industrial Electrical Systems

Location: Self-study.

Length: Correspondence.

Dates: June 1994-Present.

Objective: To provide the student with a qualitative understanding of Industrial Electrical Systems involving the use of storage batteries, lighting controls, motor controllers, programmable logic controllers and telemetering services.

Learning Outcome: Upon successful completion of this course, the student will be able to understand the different methods of switching in residential and commercial buildings; principles of motor control and symbols; programmable logic controller fundamentals; definition and classification of telemetering and be familiar with many types of storage batteries.

Instruction: Major topics covered in the course are characteristics and applications of storage batteries; lighting control systems; principles of motor control systems; control components; protective devices; solid-state motor drive systems; programmable logic controllers; definition and classification of telemetering systems; transmission of data signals; computations in telemetering; telemetering for automatic control; and electric power systems control. Methods of instruction include self-study, texts, study guides, and a proctored final examination.

Credit Recommendation: In the lower division baccalaureate/associate degree category, 3 semester hours in Electrical/ Electronics Technology (6/94).

Industrial Psychology

Location: Self-study.

Length: Correspondence Program.

Dates: *Version 1:* October 1975-March 1989; *Version 2:* April 1989-Present.

Objective: To provide an awareness of psychological issues relevant to the operation of industrial organizations.

Learning Outcome: Upon successful completion of this course, the student will be able to understand organizational dynamics involving interrelationships of people, processes, and procedures.

Instruction: Major topics covered in the course are the application of psychology to industrial organizations; psychology of attitudes; morale and group processes; supervisory leadership; measuring proficiency; selection and placement; psychological tests; design of jobs and man-machine systems; training in organizations; motivation at work; fatigue; accidents and their prevention; psychological factors in labor turnover; counseling, interviewing, and job contacts; and organizational psychology. Methods of instruction include self-study, texts, study guides, and a proctored final examination.

Credit Recommendation: *Version 1:* In the lower division baccalaureate/associate degree category, 2 semester hours in Management or Psychology (11/84). *Version 2:* In the lower division baccalaureate/associate degree category, 3 semester hours in Industrial Psychology (4/89) (6/94).

Industrial Safety

Location: Self-study.

Length: Correspondence program.

Dates: June 1990-Present.

Objective: To introduce basic safety procedures for an industrial environment including the proper safety procedures for common hand tools and information on personal safety and material handling.

Learning Outcome: Upon successful completion of this course, the student will be able to explain the need for safety practices; list the proper procedures for materials handling; describe the procedures used for operating common hand tools; and describe the most common types of personal injuries and how they can be prevented.

Instruction: Major topics covered in the course are overview of the need for safety awareness in the industrial workplace, specific procedures for handling various materials, operating different kinds of machinery, performing job tasks safely, understanding how the human body is constructed and how it works, learning which parts of the human body are most frequently injured and how to protect them, and survey of the regulations designed to improve industrial safety. Methods of instruction include self-study, texts, study guides, and a proctored final examination.

Credit Recommendation: In the lower division baccalaureate/associate degree category, 2 semester hours in Industrial Engineering Technology (6/94).

Industrial Systems

Location: Self-study.

Length: Correspondence Program.

Dates: January 1980-May 1994.

Objective: To provide a qualitative understanding of industrial systems involving the use of storage batteries, lighting controls, motor controls, and telemetering devices.

Learning Outcome: Upon successful completion of this course, the student will be able to understand the different methods of switching in residential and commercial buildings, principle of motor control and symbols, definition and classification of telemetering, and be familiar with many types of storage batteries.

Instruction: Major topics covered in the course are the characteristics and applications of storage batteries, lighting control systems, principles of motor control systems, control components, protective devices, solid-state motor drive systems, definition and classification of telemetering systems, transmission data signals, computations in telemetering, telemetering for automatic control, and electric power systems control. Methods of instruction include self-study, texts, study guides, and a proctored final examination.

Credit Recommendation: In the lower division baccalaureate/associate degree category, 3 semester hours in Electrical/ Electronics Technology or Industrial Systems (11/84) (4/89).

Intermediate Accounting I

Location: Self-study.

Length: Correspondence Program.

Dates: April 1986-Present.

Objective: To expand on general accounting principles studied in previous courses while providing more detailed knowledge of complex subjects.

Learning Outcome: Upon successful completion of this course, the student will be able to apply accounting theory, concepts, and procedures to financial problems pertaining to stock, investments, and intangibles; explain the objectives of financial statements; describe the basic assumptions of accounting; prepare solutions to practice problems; display compound interest, present value, and annuities in proper fashion; and explain how to account for cash and short-term investments and how to use several methods of accounting for inventory.

Instruction: Major topics covered in the course are contemporary accounting theory; accounting concepts and procedures and their application to financial reporting and intermediate problems pertaining to cash, receivable, inventories, plant and equipment, and investments in securities. Methods of instruction include self-study, texts, study guides, and a proctored final examination.

Credit Recommendation: In the upper division baccalaureate degree category, 3 semester hours in Intermediate Accounting (4/86) (7/90) (9/95).

Intermediate Accounting II

Location: Self-study.

Length: Correspondence Program.

Dates: January 1981-Present.

Objective: To provide the student with an expansion on materials presented in Intermediate Accounting I and to provide deeper understanding of accounting principles.

Learning Outcome: Upon successful completion of this course, the student will be able to prepare reports, including a statement of cash flows; know income tax allocation and future and present value concepts and application; understand and account for current liabilities and bonds payable and retained earnings and dividends; explain the concept of book value earnings and dividends and calculate these earnings; account for long term leases, pensions, and income taxes; make accounting changes and correct errors; and create a statement of cash flows.

Instruction: Major topics covered in this course are a continuation of Intermediate Accounting I; problems pertaining to current and long-term liabilities, stockholders' equity, pensions, and income taxes; financial statement analysis, price-level accounting, and fund and cash flow reporting. Methods of instruction include self-study, texts, study guides, and a proctored final examination.

Credit Recommendation: In the upper division baccalaureate degree category, 3 semester hours in Intermediate Accounting (4/86) (7/90) (9/95).

Introduction to Business

Location: Self-study.

Length: Correspondence Program.

Dates: *Version 1:* January 1981-August 1995; *Version 2:* September 1995-Present.

Objective: To provide the student with a general understanding of the definition of business, how it operates, and how it is managed.

Learning Outcome: Upon successful completion of this course, the student will be able to describe the major division and functions of business; apply attitudinal, motivational, and career information to their roles in these business areas; and have a basic understanding of business - management, finance, production, and marketing.

Instruction: Major topics covered in the course include a study of business and its functions, including management, finance, production, and marketing. This functional study is developed around a framework involving motivation, goal setting, organizational design, and decision-making. Methods of instruction include self-study, texts, study guides, and a proctored final examination.

Credit Recommendation: *Version 1:* In the lower division baccalaureate/associate degree category, 2 semester hours in Business Administration or Management (4/86) (7/90). *Version 2:* In the lower division baccalaureate/associate degree category, 3 semester hours in Business Administration or Management (9/95).

Introduction to COBOL Programming (COBOL Programming)

Location: Self-study.

Length: Correspondence program.

Dates: April 1991-Present.

Objective: To provide an introduction to the overall structure of the COBOL programming language.

Learning Outcome: Upon successful completion of this course, the student will be able to describe the structure of a COBOL program and be able to design, develop, code, and debug a structured program using the COBOL programming language.

Instruction: Major topics covered in the course are introduction to advanced COBOL, data division, procedure division, sequential files, COBOL programming theory, indexed files, and report writing. Methods of instruction include self-study, texts, study guides, and a proctored final examination.

Credit Recommendation: In the lower division baccalaureate/associate degree category, 3 semester hours in COBOL Programming (6/94).

Introduction to Computer Concepts (Business Data Processing)

Location: Self-study.

Length: Correspondence Program.

Dates: January 1981-Present.

Objective: To provide the student with an introduction to fundamental computer concepts.

Learning Outcome: Upon successful completion of this course, the student will be able to identify and draw flowcharting symbols; construct an elementary flowchart; discuss the structured programming methods; discuss the uses of the computers and software; and understand the purpose and uses of computers, software, and structured programming.

Instruction: Major topics covered in the course are a basic introduction of computer fundamentals and a nontechnical introduction into business data processing. Methods of instruction include self-study, texts, study guides, and a proctored final examination.

Credit Recommendation: In the lower division baccalaureate/associate degree category, 3 semester hours in Business Management, Computer Information Systems, or Data Processing (4/86) (7/90) (9/95).

Introduction to Computer Programming

Location: Self-study.

Length: Correspondence program.

Dates: April 1991-Present.

Objective: To introduce programming concepts and methodology with an emphasis placed on the structured approach to programming using pseudo code, structured flowcharts, and a language simulator.

Learning Outcome: Upon successful completion of this course, the student will have knowledge of the program development cycle, beginning skill in creating a structured top down program using the program development cycle, and the language simulator presented in the course materials.

Instruction: Major topics covered in the course are introduction of computer programs, system creation, and tools of system design and development. Methods of instruction include self-study, texts, study guides, and a proctored final examination.

Credit Recommendation: In the lower division baccalaureate/associate degree category, 2 semester hours in Data Processing (6/94).

Introduction to Management Information Systems

Location: Self-study.

Length: Correspondence program.

Dates: April 1991-Present.

Objective: To provide an analysis of management information systems (MIS) for the purpose of planning and decision making, e.g., business operations, control, and planning applications.

Learning Outcome: Upon successful completion of this course, the student will be able to understand the basic components of an information system; its purpose and function in the corporate structure; and the role, function and responsibilities of an MIS manager.

Instruction: Major topics covered in the course are introduction to MIS, the role of MIS in the organization, computing resources for MIS, systems analysis, systems design and program development, system development strategies, managing information resources, and issues in the management of information systems. Methods of instruction include self-study, texts, study guides, and a proctored final examination.

Credit Recommendation: In the lower division baccalaureate/associate degree category, 2 semester hours in Management Information Systems (elective) (6/94).

Introduction to Microprocessors

Location: Self-study.

Length: Correspondence Program.

Dates: January 1983-Present.

Objective: To introduce the fundamentals and uses of computers in business and industry followed by coverage of the basics of microprocessors, their components, theory of operation, and usefulness in industry.

Learning Outcome: Upon successful completion of this course, the student will be able to understand the operation, organization, and typical uses for microprocessors.

Instruction: Major topics covered in this course are an introduction to computers, introduction to microprocessor applications, and microprocessor basics. Methods of instruction include self-study, texts, study guides, and a proctored final examination.

Credit Recommendation: In the lower division baccalaureate/associate degree category, 1 semester hour in Electrical/Electronics Technology or Introduction to Microprocessors (11/84) (4/89) (6/94).

Introduction to Programming in C

Location: Self-study.

Length: Correspondence program.

Dates: April 1991-Present.

Objective: To provide an introduction to the overall structure of the C language.

Learning Outcome: Upon successful completion of this course, the student will be able a describe the structure of a C program and be able to design, develop, code, and debug a structured program using the C language.

Instruction: Major topics covered in the course are a C program overview, variables and data types, input/output, operators, managing data, flow control, functions, arrays and pointers, files, graphics, and programming style. Methods of instruction include independent study, examinations, and laboratory exercises using a PC C compiler. Methods of instruction include self-study, texts, study guides, and a proctored final examination.

Credit Recommendation: In the lower division baccalaureate/associate degree category, 3 semester hours in Programming in C (6/94).

Introduction to Sociology

Location: Self-study.

Length: Correspondence Program.

Dates: July 1977-December 1986.

Objective: To enable the student to interpret sociological theory and to apply the methods used in sociology. The student will also be able to identify and assess basic structures in social life and the process of socialization, social change, deviant behavior, and social control.

Instruction: Major topics covered in the course are an introduction to the fundamental concepts of human society; to the social dimensions of culture, institutions, personality, ecology, and their basic interaction processes; and to social order and social change.

Credit Recommendation: In the lower division baccalaureate/associate degree category, 2 semester hours in Introduction to Sociology (11/84).

Introduction to the Hospitality Industry

Location: Self-study.

Length: Correspondence Program.

Dates: November 1990-Present.

Objective: To introduce the origins and history of the hospitality industry, and the organization and function of the front office and the food and beverage departments; and identify the essential qualities to be successful.

Learning Outcome: Upon successful completion of this course, the student will be able to explain in detail the origin and development of the hospitality industry; identify the roles and functions of various hotel departments and personnel; differentiate between the various styles of restaurant and banquet service; and list the steps required to prepare for and serve guests in a food service establishment.

Instruction: Major topics covered in the course are the origins and history of the hospitality business, front office operations, and dining room and banquet service. Methods of instruction include self-study, texts, study guides, and a proctored final examination.

Credit Recommendation: In the lower division baccalaureate/associate degree category, 1 semester hour in Introduction to Hotel Operations (6/94).

Kinematics

Location: Self-study.

Length: Correspondence Program.

Dates: January 1980-Present.

Objective: To introduce the study of linkages, cams, and gears.

Learning Outcome: Upon successful completion of this course, the student will be able to understand the basic principles of linkages, gears, and cams.

Instruction: Major topics covered in the course are linkages; quick-return mechanisms; kinematics of link mechanisms; spur gearing, worm, and worm gears; gear cutting; use of gear trains; compound gearing; ratchet mechanisms; types and uses of cams; fundamentals of cam motion; and cam profiles. Methods of instruction include self-study, texts, study guides, and a proctored final examination.

Credit Recommendation: In the lower division baccalaureate/associate degree category, 3 semester hours in Kinematics or Engineering Technology (11/84) (4/89) (6/94). *Prerequisite:* Engineering Mechanics.

Land Surveying

Location: Self-study.

Length: Correspondence Program.

Dates: January 1980-Present.

Objective: To introduce boundary surveying computations and the legal aspects of land surveying.

Learning Outcome: Upon successful completion of this course, the student will be able to perform field and office operations in property surveys and resurveys and be knowledgeable in the legal area of surveying.

Instruction: Major topics covered in the course are determination of true meridian, latitudes and longitudes, rectangular system of dividing land, subdivision of townships and sections, identifying and restoring corners, correction of defects in original surveys, and legal descriptions. Methods of instruction include self-study, texts, study guides, and a proctored final examination.

Credit Recommendation: In the upper division baccalaureate degree category, 2 semester hours in Land Surveying I when applied to an Engineering major (11/84) (4/89) (6/94). **NOTE:** To receive credit, student must complete resident lab training or have equivalent laboratory experience.

Linear and Digital Integrated Circuits

Location: Self-study.

Length: Correspondence Program.

Dates: January 1982-Present.

Objective: To provide an understanding of the functions and uses of linear and digital integrated circuits. Also included with this course is a digital trainer. The student performs assigned experiments involving logic circuits, pulse circuits, and linear/ digital IC circuits.

Learning Outcome: Upon successful completion of this course, the student will be able to understand the functions and uses of linear and digital integrated circuits. Completing the experiments will provide experience in handling, using, and testing ICs.

Instruction: Major topics covered in the course are linear and digital integrated circuits, linear and digital circuit principles, integrated circuit techniques, linear integrated circuits, digital integrated circuits, integrated circuit logic systems, troubleshooting linear and digital IC systems, pulse circuits experiments, logic circuits experiments, and linear and digital integrated circuits experiments. Methods of instruction include self-study, texts, study guides, and a proctored final examination.

Credit Recommendation: In the lower division baccalaureate/associate degree category, 3 semester hours in Electrical Engineering or Electrical/Electronics Technology (11/84) (4/89) (6/94).

Machine Design I (Formerly Mechanical Design I)

Location: Self-study.

Length: Correspondence Program.

Dates: *Version 1:* January 1980-December 1985; *Version 2:* January 1986-Present.

Objective: *Version 1:* To introduce the study of material failure theories and analysis of shafts, beams, column, gears, gear trains, belts, clutches, and brakes. *Version 2:* To become familiar with the design of basic machine components.

Learning Outcome: Upon successful completion of this course, the student will be able to understand the information necessary for the successful design of basic machine components and to calculate basic ball and roller bearing loads.

Instruction: *Version 1:* Major topics covered in the course are stress analysis; Mohr's circle; stress-strain relations; torsion; curved beams; deflection analysis; strain energy; column design; statistics in mechanical design; normal distribution; toughness; hardness; strength of machine members; stress concentration; theories of failure; reliability; and notch sensitivity. *Version 2:* Course reviews mechanics and strength of materials; friction and lubrication; bearings; shaft design and seals; fasteners; couplings; keys; retaining rings; welding and weld design; belting; chain drives; hoists and conveyors; and ropes. Methods of instruction include hands-on proficiency of welding and material testing in the resident laboratory at a major university location.

Credit Recommendation: *Versions 1 and 2:* In the lower division baccalaureate/associate degree category, 3 semester hours in Mechanical Design I or Engineering Technology (11/84) (4/89) (6/94). *Prerequisites:* Mechanics of Materials, Manufacturing Processes, Analytic Geometry, and Calculus.

Machine Design II (Formerly Mechanical Design II)

Location: Self-study

Length: Correspondence Program.

Dates: *Version 1:* January 1980-December 1985; *Version 2:* January 1986-Present.

Objective: *Version 1:* To provide continued studies in the design of machine elements based on the principles of material failure theory. *Version 2:* To provide continued studies in the design of machine components based on the principles of force analysis as well as areas of good practice and judgment.

Learning Outcome: Upon successful completion of this course, the student will be able to understand the design of basic machine components as a continued study from Mechanical Design I.

Instruction: *Version 1:* Major topics covered in the course are thread standards; threaded fasteners; bolted and riveted joints; strength of welded joints; design of springs; ball and roller bearings; bearing friction; bearing life; thrust bearings; lubrication of bearings; design of journal bearings; design of spur, helical, worm, and bevel gears; design of power transmission shafts; design of clutches, brakes, couplings, belts, and roller chains. *Version 2:* Major topics covered in the course are brakes; clutches; power screws; gears; cams; spring design; flywheels; miscellaneous machine elements; and power units. Methods of instruction include hands-on proficiency of welding and material testing in the resident laboratory at a major university location.

Credit Recommendation: *Versions 1 and 2:* In the lower division baccalaureate/associate degree category, 3 semester hours in Mechanical Design II or Engineering Technology (11/84) (4/89) (6/94). *Prerequisite:* Mechanical Design I.

Manufacturing Processes

Location: Self-study.

Length: Correspondence Program.

Dates: January 1980-Present.

Objective: To introduce common industrial and manufacturing processes.

Learning Outcome: Upon successful completion of this course, the student will be able to understand the basic concepts and practices of common industrial and manufacturing practices.

Instruction: Major topics covered in the course are cutting tools; machine tools; powder metallurgy; hot and cold working of materials; stamping, drawing, and forming; heat treatment; welding techniques; special forming techniques; electrical and chemical machining; tension, compression, torsion, impact, and hardness testing of materials; nondestructive testing techniques; use of vernier calipers, micrometers, gages, gage blocks, and sine bars; basic numerical control; and numerical control programming. Methods of instruction include self-study, texts, study guides, and a proctored final examination.

Credit Recommendation: In the lower division baccalaureate/associate degree category, 4 semester hours in Manufacturing Processes or Engineering Technology (11/84) (4/89) (6/94). *Prerequisite:* Technical Mathematics I.

Marketing Research

Location: Self-study.

Length: Correspondence Program.

Dates: January 1981-Present.

Objective: To give the student an introduction to techniques of marketing research plus practice in using devices for measuring decision making.

Learning Outcome: Upon successful completion of this course, the student will

be able to identify which market factors can or cannot be controlled; list factors that limit success of market research; to describe key aspects of methods used in market research; perform calculations to determine square root and normal and standard deviation; identify and explain advantages and limitations on uses of secondary research; apply techniques for editing and tabulation; and understand marketing research procedures, sampling, primary and secondary data sources, data analysis, and summary statistics.

Instruction: Major topics covered in this course are the nature and scope of marketing research, including marketing research procedures, sampling and sampling methods, primary and secondary data sources, questionnaire scales, data analysis, and development of summary statistics. Methods of instruction include self-study, texts, study guides, and a proctored final examination.

Credit Recommendation: In the upper division baccalaureate degree category, 2 semester hours in Marketing Research (4/86) (7/90) (9/95).

Math for Business and Finance

Location: Self-study.

Length: Correspondence Program.

Dates: January 1981-Present.

Objective: To provide the student with mathematical skills required in entry level contemporary business positions.

Learning Outcome: Upon successful completion of this course, the student will be able to employ problem-solving skills, calculate percents, discounts, interest, gross profit and loss, net profit and loss and depreciation; identify positive and negative numbers; add, subtract, multiply, and divide algebraic expressions; and understand interest, installment buying, pricing, depreciation, investments, insurance symbols and their application, equations and formulas, and the importance of statistics.

Instruction: Major topics covered in this course are percentages; discounts; interest; present worth; sinking funds; installment buying; the use of symbols and their application; equations and formulas; and the importance of statistics, including table and chart construction. Methods of instruction include self-study, texts, study guides, and a proctored final examination.

Credit Recommendation: In the lower division baccalaureate/associate degree category, 2 semester hours in Business Math (4/86) (7/90) (9/95).

Mechanical Drawing

Location: Self-study.

Length: Correspondence Program.

Dates: January 1985-May 1994.

Objective: To introduce the basics of mechanical drawing.

Learning Outcome: Upon successful completion of this course, the student will be able to prepare geometrical, projection, and introductory mechanical drawings.

Instruction: Major topics covered in the course are drawing equipment; lettering; eight drawing plates; 721, 722, and 723, geometrical drawing problems; 724, projections of simple solids; 725, foreshortened views in projection; 726, common conventions; 727, lifting and test cover; 728, and hanger assembly.

Credit Recommendation: In the vocational certificate category, 1 semester hour in Mechanical Drawing (11/84) (4/89) (6/94).

Mechanics of Materials

Location: Self-study.

Length: Correspondence Program.

Dates: January 1985-Present.

Objective: To enable the student to calculate reactions, stresses, shear and bending moment, deformation and deflection, moment of inertia, section modules, and radius of gyration.

Learning Outcome: Upon successful completion of this course, the student will be able to calculate simple stresses, reactions at beam support, as well as other technical data needed for basic column design.

Instruction: Major topics covered in the course are simple stresses, fixed and moving loads on beams, reactions at beam support, continuous beams, points on inflection, shear and bending moment diagrams, moment of inertia and section modulus, theory of column design, and radius of gyration. Methods of instruction include self-study, texts, study guides, and a proctored final examination.

Credit Recommendation: In the lower division baccalaureate/associate degree category, 2 semester hours in Introduction to Mechanics of Materials or Engineering Technology (11/84) (4/89) (6/94). **NOTE:** Student may receive credit for only 1 of the following courses: Engineering Materials, Technical Materials, or Mechanics of Materials. Credit recommendation is not appropriate for Engineering majors.

Microcomputer and its Applications

Location: Self-study.

Length: Correspondence program.

Dates: April 1991-Present.

Objective: To provide an introduction to the basic uses of the personal computer, reinforced by hands-on use of a PC.

Learning Outcome: Upon successful completion of this course, the student will be able to describe and employ the principles of spreadsheets, database management, word processing, and telecommunications systems.

Instruction: Major topics covered in the course are set-up and operation of a personal computer, fundamental principles of spreadsheets, database management, basic DOS commands, telecommunications, and on-line information service. Methods of instruction include self-study, texts, study guides, and a proctored final examination.

Credit Recommendation: In the lower division baccalaureate/associate degree category, 2 semester hours in Computer Information Systems (6/94).

Microprocessor Applications

Location: Self-study.

Length: Correspondence Program.

Dates: *Version 1:* January 1982-March 1991; *Version 2:* April 1991-Present.

Objective: *Version 1:* To provide an understanding of the functional application of a microprocessor and simple machine language programming, an introduction to microprocessor interfacing, and reinforcement of student learning through the use of a microprocessor trainer. *Version 2:* To provide a basic understanding of the operation and application of a microprocessor, reinforced with hands-on experience.

Learning Outcome: *Version 1:* Upon successful completion of this course, the student will be able to understand the functional application of a microprocessor, simple machine language programming, and basic microprocessor interfacing principles. *Version 2:* Upon successful completion of this course, the student will be able to understand the functional application of a microprocessor, simple machine language programming, and basic microprocessor interfacing principles.

Instruction: *Version 1:* Major topics covered in the course are working with an uncomplicated microprocessor, the MC 6802, part 1; microprocessor programming principles, part 1; working with an uncomplicated microprocessor, the MC 6802, part 2; microprocessor programming principles, part 2; interfacing through serial and parallel ports; troubleshooting microprocessor equipment, part 2; other families of microprocessors; and microprocessor experiments. *Version 2:* Major topics covered in the course are an introduction to a basic microprocessor (Motorola 6800 series); microprocessor programming principles; interfacing through serial and parallel ports; troubleshooting microprocessor equipment; introduction to other families of microprocessors; and microprocessor experiments. Methods of instruction include independent study, examinations, and laboratory experiments using actual microprocessor equipment.

Credit Recommendation: *Versions 1 and 2:* In the lower division baccalaureate/associate degree category, 3 semester hours in Electrical/Electronics Technology or Microprocessor Applications (11/84) (4/89) (6/94).

Nutrition and Menu Planning

Location: Self-study.

Length: Correspondence Program.

Dates: November 1990-Present.

Objective: To provide an introduction to the science of nutrition.

Learning Outcome: Upon successful completion of this course, the student will be able to list the six major nutrients and the types of foods in which they are contained, describe the digestion and absorption of these nutrients, explain the function of the basal metabolism, and define and explain the purpose of RDA's. They should be able to categorize nutrient deficiency and excess symptoms, describe the health hazards posed by obesity, and explain the value of the food exchange system in controlling weight. They should also be able to explain truth-in-menu laws and their influence on menu design, describe the relationship between the design of the menu and the operation's clientele, and develop sound menu procedures in accordance with text guidelines.

Instruction: Major topics covered in the course are the digestive process, identification of the various nutrient groups and their sources, and basic menu planning and design. Methods of instruction include self-study, texts, study guides, and a proctored final examination.

Credit Recommendation: In the lower division baccalaureate/associate degree category, 1 semester hour in Basic Nutrition (6/94).

Operational Analysis

Location: Self-study.

Length: Correspondence program.

Dates: June 1990-Present.

Objective: To provide a background in operation analysis with an emphasis on efficient use of personnel and equipment.

Learning Outcome: Upon successful completion of this course, the student will be able to describe the analysis procedure; explain how to properly select processes and tooling; evaluate working conditions; explain the two common types of plant layout; and be able to describe how motion studies are used.

Instruction: Major topics covered in the course are operation analysis procedures, procedure for effecting operation improvements, selection of process and tooling, working conditions, plant layout, material handling, and motion study. Methods of instruction include self-study, texts, study guides, and a proctored final examination.

Credit Recommendation: In the lower division baccalaureate/associate degree category, 1 semester hour in Industrial Engineering Technology (6/94).

Personal Financial Management

Location: Self-study.

Length: Correspondence Program.

Dates: *Version 1:* March 1984-August 1995; *Version 2:* September 1995-Present.

Objective: To introduce students to concepts of personal financial management, which provides students with general understanding of principles of managing and financing assets; to list and explain concepts of personal financial management and key factors considered in acquisition of assets; and to explain how to use borrowed funds to finance the purchase of assets.

Learning Outcome: Upon successful completion of this course, the student will be able to apply decision-making procedures to realistic problems such as budgets, insurance, and real estate, and security buying.

Instruction: Major topics covered in this course are the fundamental concepts and importance of personal financial management; management of fundamental assets, including how to protect against risk and uncertainty; an in-depth study of estate and retirement planning and investment budgeting. Methods of instruction include self-study, texts, study guides, and a proctored final examination.

Credit Recommendation: *Version 1:* In the lower division baccalaureate/associate degree category, 2 semester hours in Personal Finance (4/86) (7/90). *Version 2:* In the lower division baccalaureate/associate degree category, 3 semester hours in Personal Finance (9/95).

Personnel Management

Location: Self-study.

Length: Correspondence Program.

Dates: April 1986-Present.

Objective: To provide the student with an overview of major concepts in human resources management.

Learning Outcome: Upon successful completion of this course, the student will understand the role of the human resources department in relating to other departments and in the selection, orientation, and training of employees in relation to personnel policies, employee evaluation, benefits, compensation, rights, and legislation; and understand the role of computers in human resources management.

Instruction: Major topics covered in this course are a study of human resources management development; the role of the human resources department in the recruitment, selection, orientation, and training of employees; the work environment; compensation, benefits, safety, and health; employee evaluation programs; labor relations and the effect of unionism on human resources management; international human resources management; and the role of computers in human resources management. Methods of instruction include self-study, texts, study guides, supplements, and a proctored final examination.

Credit Recommendation: In the lower division baccalaureate/associate degree category, 2 semester hours in Management or Human Resource Management (4/86) (7/90) (9/95).

Physical Science

Location: Self-study.

Length: Correspondence Program.

Dates: January 1983-Present.

Objective: To provide a foundation in science by surveying basic aspects of chemistry, mechanics, heat, sound, light, electricity, earth science, and space science.

Learning Outcome: Upon successful completion of this course, the student will be able to apply fundamental principles of chemistry, mechanics, heat, sound, light, electricity, earth science, and space science.

Instruction: Major topics covered in the course are basic concepts of physical science with particular emphasis on mechanics, heat, sound, light, chemistry, electricity, earth science, and space science. Methods of instruction include self-study, texts, study guides, and a proctored final examination.

Credit Recommendation: In the lower division baccalaureate/associate degree category, 3 semester hours in Physical Science (11/84) (4/89) (6/94). **NOTE:** This is a nonlaboratory science course.

Physics

Location: Self-study.

Length: Correspondence Program.

Dates: January 1981-Present.

Objective: To develop technical understanding of heat, electricity, light, and sound.

Learning Outcome: Upon successful completion of this course, the student will be able to understand basic principles of heat, electricity, light, and sound.

Instruction: Major topics covered in the course are nature of heat; transfer of heat; relationship between pressure, volume, temperature; weight of gases and the gas constant; expansion of gases; compression of gases; closed cycles; carnots cycle. Electricity—voltage, current, conductance, and resistance; conductors, insulators, and semiconductors; electric cells and batteries; resistors; switches; parallel, series, and series-parallel circuits; Ohm's Law; electric power; electric energy; analysis of DC circuits; generator and motor action; theory of alternating currents; AC circuits; principle of transformers; AC machines; nature of light; reflection of light; optical mirrors; optical instruments; lasers; relation of sound to wave motion; nature, properties, and sources of sound; functions of the ear; infrasonics and ultrasonics; doppler effect; focusing of sound; absorption of sound; loudness; decibels; and transducers. Methods of instruction include self-study, texts, study guides, and a proctored final examination.

Credit Recommendation: In the lower division baccalaureate/associate degree category, 3 semester hours in Physics (11/84) (4/89) (6/94). **NOTE:** Course does not have lab.

Planning and Control

Location: Self-study.

Length: Correspondence Program.

Dates: January 1980-Present.

Objective: To introduce planning and scheduling of production activities with a focus on volume and quality of production.

Learning Outcome: Upon successful completion of this course, the student will be able to understand the nature of production, including materials handling, acquisitions and forecasting, as well as quality costs and control.

Instruction: Major topics covered in the course are the nature of production control; demand forecasting; economic order quantity; critical-path method; quality costs and their control inspection function; vendor relation; manufacturing planning for quality; quality improvement; fundamentals of materials control; acquisition of materials; storage of materials; control of materials during manufacture; paperwork control; and systems approach to materials control. Methods of instruction include self-study, texts, study guides, and a proctored final examination.

Credit Recommendation: In the lower division baccalaureate/associate degree category, 3 semester hours in Industrial Engineering Technology or Mechanical Engineering Technology (11/84) (4/89) (6/94). *Prerequisite:* Technical Mathematics I.

Plant Facilities

Location: Self-study.

Length: Correspondence Program.

Dates: January 1984-Present.

Objective: To introduce the elements of plant layout and materials handling.

Learning Outcome: Upon successful completion of this course, the student will be able to understand what information is necessary for the development of a plant layout and the procedures and tools used for development and presentation of layouts.

Instruction: Major topics covered in the course are plant layout; definition; scope, importance, advantages, and nature of layout projects; effect of storage, services, and materials handling on plant layout; collection and analysis of data necessary for the development and presentation of layouts; industrial layout; growth planning; manufacturing plant layouts; industrial layout; warehouse design; types of warehouses; use of computer; design factors; alternatives and implementation; materials handling; introduction; sealing equipment; trucks; conveyors; pneumatic systems; bulk handling systems and components; grab attachments; long distance transportation; auxiliary equipment; and specialized components. Methods of instruction include self-study, texts, study guides, and a proctored final examination.

Credit Recommendation: In the lower division baccalaureate/associate degree category, 2 semester hours in Production Facilities Planning or Engineering Technology (11/84) (4/89) (6/94). *Prerequisite:* Technical Mathematics I.

Practical English and the Command of Words

Location: Self-study.

Length: Correspondence Program.

Dates: July 1979-Present.

Objective: To provide basic English communication skills.

Learning Outcome: Upon successful completion of this course, the student will be able to communicate better both verbally and in writing.

Instruction: Major topics covered in the course are vocabulary development, pronunciation, grammar and usage, spelling, speech, word meanings, punctuation, sentence structure, paragraph organization, and telephone courtesy. Methods of instruction include self-study, texts, study guides, and a proctored final examination.

Credit Recommendation: In the lower division baccalaureate/associate degree category, 3 semester hours in English as an elective in Grammar and Usage, and 1 semester hour in Business Communication (1/84) (6/94). **NOTE:** In order to receive credit, students must take and successfully pass a final examination developed by the English Language Institute. The final examination can be administered (and monitored) by a company training officer and scored by the Institute, or it can be administered, monitored, and scored directly by the Institute.

Principles of Finance

Location: Self-study.

Length: Correspondence Program.

Dates: *Version 1:* January 1981-August 1995; *Version 2:* September 1995-Present.

Objective: To introduce the student to money and the role of finance in business organizations.

Learning Outcome: Upon successful completion of this course, the student will understand the role of finance in various business organizations, capital budgets, sources of funds, marketing securities, capital structure, foreign expansion, financial, reorganization of a business firm, and present value analysis.

Instruction: Major topics covered in this course are a history of money; monetary systems; credit; the role of finance in various forms of business organizations; capital budgeting, sources of funds, marketing securities, capital structure, foreign expansion reorganization of a business firm; present value analysis; financial ratio analysis; capital funding; and causes of business failure. Methods of instruction include self-study, texts, study guides, and a proctored final examination.

Credit Recommendation: *Version 1:* In the lower division baccalaureate/associate degree category, 2 semester hours in Principles of Finance (4/86) (7/90). *Version 2:* In the lower division baccalaureate/associate degree category, 3 semester hours in Principles of Finance (9/95).

Principles of Management

Location: Self-study.

Length: Correspondence Program.

Dates: January 1981-Present.

Objective: To introduce the student to basic concepts of management and emphasize the importance of these concepts.

Learning Outcome: Upon successful completion of this course, the student will be able to identify and explain differences between management functions and responsibilities; identify and distinguish basic leadership styles; list procedures for reorganization; provide examples of functions of management; list and describe factors important to controlling cost and simplifying work; and understand the basic management concepts as applied to employee behavior, morale, complaints, grievances, training, and communication.

Instruction: Major topics covered in this course are the importance of management in the business enterprise and concepts such as leadership, functions of management, employee behavior, morale, complaints, and grievances, training, and communications. Methods of instruction include self-study, texts, study guides, and a proctored final examination.

Credit Recommendation: In the upper division baccalaureate degree category, 3 semester hours in Principles of Management or Supervision (4/86) (7/90) (9/95).

Principles of Product Marketing

Location: Self-study.

Length: Correspondence Program.

Dates: *Version 1:* January 1981-August 1995; *Version 2:* September 1995-Present.

Objective: To provide the student with a general understanding of the principles of marketing and product management.

Learning Outcome: Upon successful completion of this course, the student will be able to discriminate between industrial and consumer marketing activities; develop an integrated marketing plan; list and distinguish between internal and external factors involved in introducing new products; list and prioritize the aspects of physical distribution; list factors in site location; and understand the importance of marketing and product management, behavioral science approach, and managing the marketing function.

Instruction: Major topics covered in this course are an introduction to the meaning of marketing and product management; behavioral science approach to marketing; the tools of marketing; and managing the marketing function. Methods of instruction include self-study, texts, study guides, and a proctored final examination.

Credit Recommendation: *Version 1:* In the lower division baccalaureate/associate degree category, 2 semester hours in Marketing or Sales (4/86) (7/90). *Version 2:* In the lower division baccalaureate/associate degree category, 3 semester hours in Marketing or Sales (9/95). **NOTE:** This course has been reevaluated and continues to meet requirements for credit recommendations.

Production Management

Location: Self-study.

Length: Correspondence Program.

Dates: January 1981-Present.

Objective: To introduce the student to the production function with emphasis on plant layout, production planning, and safety.

Learning Outcome: Upon successful completion of this course, the student will be able to define the concept of plant layout and discuss factors that influence plant layout decisions; describe several types of forecasts and apply statistical methods for forecast control; calculate quality costs and controls; discuss advantages and disadvantages of differing types of plant layouts; and understand the production function, including plant layout, production planning, material control production techniques, material inspection, and occupational safety.

Instruction: Major topics covered in the course are an introduction to the production function, including factors affecting plant layout, nature and purpose of production planning, factors in material control, purchasing techniques, materials inspection, analysis of customers' complaints, and occupational safety. Methods of instruction include self-study, texts, study guides, and a proctored final examination.

Credit Recommendation: In the lower division baccalaureate/associate degree category, 2 semester hours in Production Management (4/86) (7/90) (9/95).

Productivity Engineering

Location: Self-study.

Length: Correspondence program.

Dates: June 1990-Present.

Objective: To provide an understanding of Productivity Engineering and how it is used in industry.

Learning Outcome: Upon successful completion of this course, the student will be able to define the concept productivity engineering; discuss factors that affect productivity; describe the components of the productivity cycle; describe the various productivity measurement techniques; calculate total and partial productivities; and discuss the various productivity improvement techniques.

Instruction: Major topics covered in the course are the Productivity Cycle; Measurement, Evaluation, Planning and Improvement; definitions of productivity; factors affecting productivity; productivity engineering and management; productivity measurement at a national level; the need for productivity measurement; the total productivity model; computations in the application of the total productivity model; productivity management using the model; implementing the model; productivity improvement techniques: materials-based, employee-based, task-based; and setting up productivity improvement programs. Methods of instruction include self-study, texts, study guides, and a proctored final examination.

Credit Recommendation: In the upper division baccalaureate degree category, 2 semester hours in Industrial Engineering/Industrial Engineering Technology (6/94). *Prerequisites:* Planning and Control and Engineering Economy.

Programming in BASIC

Location: Self-study.

Length: Correspondence program.

Dates: April 1991-Present.

Objective: To provide an introduction to the overall structure of BASIC programming languages.

Learning Outcome: Upon successful completion of this course, the student will be able to describe the structure of a BASIC program and be able to design, develop, code, and debug a structured program using the BASIC language.

Instruction: Major topics covered in the course are introduction to Quick-BASIC; variables and data types; arithmetic operations; file and sequential file processing; report and screen design; control break processing; table processing and sorting; and chaining, functions, and subprograms. Methods of instruction include self-study, texts, study guides, and a proctored final examination.

Credit Recommendation: In the lower division baccalaureate/associate degree category, 3 semester hours in BASIC Programming (6/94).

Public Relations

Location: Self-study.

Length: Correspondence Program.

Dates: April 1986-Present.

Objective: To provide the student with a general understanding of the role of public relations in contemporary business.

Learning Outcome: Upon successful completion of this course, the student will be able to list differences between corporate reporting and agency reporting relationships; list and define special techniques used in dealing with the press; identify all publics with which public relations departments deal; list and apply techniques for good writing for public relations; and understand the responsibility of the public relations department and dealings with the press, community, employees, and customers.

Instruction: Major topics covered in this course are the evolution of public relations; the organization and responsibility of a public relations department and the importance of communications research. Special emphasis is placed on dealing with the press, government, community, employees, and customers. The course concludes with the techniques of good public relations writing. Methods of instruction include self-study, texts, study guides, and a proctored final examination.

Credit Recommendation: In the lower division baccalaureate/associate degree category, 2 semester hours in Public Affairs, Public Communication, Public Information, or Public Relations (4/86) (7/90) (9/95).

Pulse and Logic Circuits

Location: Self-study.

Length: Correspondence Program.

Dates: January 1982-Present.

Objective: To provide qualitative knowledge of pulse circuits and logic circuits including purpose configuration, applications, and troubleshooting of such circuits.

Learning Outcome: Upon successful completion of this course, the student will be able to qualitatively understand pulse and logic circuits, typical troubleshooting procedures, and applications.

Instruction: Major topics covered in the course include pulse circuits: pulse techniques; pulse generators; waveshaping circuits; timing and synchronization; pulse circuit applications; troubleshooting pulse circuits. Logic circuits: logic circuit fundamentals; introduction to number systems; logic devices and diagrams; logic families; applications of logic circuits; troubleshooting logic circuits. Methods of instruction include self-study, texts, study guides, and a proctored final examination.

Credit Recommendation: In the lower division baccalaureate/associate degree category, 1 semester hour in Electrical/Electronics Technology or Pulse and Logic Circuits (11/84) (4/89) (6/94).

Quantity Food Production

Location: Self-study.

Length: Correspondence Program.

Dates: January 1992-Present.

Objective: To introduce the techniques involved in producing high-quality food in quantity.

Learning Outcome: Upon successful completion of this course, the student will be able to explain the hierarchical structure of a food service operation; describe the proper managerial procedures for drafting position descriptions, hiring and scheduling staff members, and selecting equipment appropriate for the size and scale of the food service operation; demonstrate an understanding of budgeting and cost control methods through the proper use of basic costing, pricing, yield measurement formulas; explain basic concepts relating to the composition and nutritional functions of food; describe the basic principles of heat transference by which the various forms of cookery operate, correctly apply conversion factors and formulas when scaling up a recipe for quantity service; and explain the proper procedures for selecting, handling, storing, and preparing various types of food products.

Instruction: Major topics covered in the course are facilities, tools, equipment, menus, recipes, purchasing, storage, sanitation, safety and cost control; techniques in preparation and service of foods. Methods of instruction include self-study, texts, study guides, and a proctored final examination.

Credit Recommendation: In the lower division baccalaureate/associate degree category, 3 semester hours in Quantity Food Production (6/94). **NOTE:** This is not a lab-based course.

Real Life Math and the Power of Numbers

Location: Self-study.

Length: Correspondence Program.

Dates: September 1993-Present.

Objective: To provide practical experience in the application of Basic Business Math.

Learning Outcome: Upon successful completion of this course, the student will be able to understand and apply a variety of basic principles of business math used in everyday business situations.

Instruction: Major topics covered in the course are simple and compound interest, payroll calculations and taxes, discounts, product markups and markdowns, loans, basic use of statistics, basic life and property insurance, and depreciation. Methods of instruction include self-study, texts, study guides, and a proctored final examination.

Credit Recommendation: In the lower division baccalaureate/associate degree category, 2 semester hours in Math, or in the vocational certificate category, 3 semester hours as a business elective (6/94). **NOTE:** In order to receive credit, students must take and successfully pass a final examination developed by the English Language Institute. The final examination can be administered (and monitored) by a company training officer and scored by the Institute or it can be administered, monitored, and scored directly by the Institute.

Reinforced Concrete Design

Location: Self-study.

Length: Correspondence Program.

Dates: January 1985-Present.

Objective: To enable the student to acquire design ability involving reinforced concrete beams and columns.

Learning Outcome: Upon successful completion of this course, the student will be able to design and detail a variety of reinforced concrete member shapes, one-way slabs, long and short columns- and prestressed beams.

Instruction: Major topics covered in the course are design and analysis of rectangular beams, T-beams, and double-reinforced beams. Methods of instruction include self-study, texts, study guides, and a proctored final examination.

Credit Recommendation: In the lower division baccalaureate/associate degree category, 2 semester hours in Civil Engineering Technology (11/84) (4/89) (6/94).

Retailing

Location: Self-study.

Length: Correspondence Program.

Dates: *Version 1:* January 1983-August 1995; *Version 2:* September 1995-Present.

Objective: To introduce the student to general principles regarding organization of retail stores and sound merchandising.

Learning Outcome: Upon successful completion of this course, the student will be able to list steps in the retail management decision-making process; list and explain key items in retailing; list key elements in the structure of a retail business including pricing policy; and understand the organization of retail stores, merchandising principles, and the management of a successful retail business.

Instruction: Major topics covered in this course are the basics of retailing; management of a successful retail business and merchandising principles. Methods of instruction include self-study, texts, study guides, and a proctored final examination.

Credit Recommendation: *Version 1:* In the vocational certificate category, 2 semester hours in Retail Marketing (4/86) (7/90). *Version 2:* In the lower division baccalaureate/associate degree category, 2 semester hours in Retail Marketing (9/95).

Sales Management

Location: Self-study.

Length: Correspondence Program.

Dates: January 1981-Present.

Objective: To give the student a general introduction to the sales function with emphasis on management of the sales force.

Learning Outcome: Upon successful completion of this course, the student will be able to identify steps necessary for the establishment of a sales organization; list advantages of sales contests; list essential elements in recruiting sales personnel; list key elements of the role of the sales manager; and understand the relation of sales management to other departments, the organization of the sales force, and information on the product and the marketplace.

Instruction: Major topics covered in this course are an analysis of the field of sales management; the relationship between marketing and product development; organization of the sales force; the relationship between the sales organization, other internal departments, and the external community; and the product and the marketplace. Methods of instruction include self-study, texts, study guides, and a proctored final examination.

Credit Recommendation: In the upper division baccalaureate degree category, 2 semester hours in Sales Management (4/86) (7/90) (9/95).

Securities Investments

Location: Self-study.

Length: Correspondence Program.

Dates: January 1981-Present.

Objective: To provide the student with introduction to general principles of investment decision making.

Learning Outcome: Upon successful completion of this course, the student will be able to evaluate securities issued in stock and bond markets; evaluate corporate securities and dividend policies; identify and discuss unique characteristics of various securities; identify steps in the investment decision making process and make investment decisions; and analyze organization and operation of stock and bond markets.

Instruction: Major topics covered in this course are the basic principles underlying investment decisions and a comprehensive study of securities and markets, fundamental and technical analysis, and portfolio selection. Methods of instruction include self-study, texts, study guides, and a proctored final examination.

Credit Recommendation: In the lower division baccalaureate/associate degree category, 3 semester hours in Finance or Securities Investments (4/86) (7/90) (9/95).

Statistical Quality Control

Location: Self-study.

Length: Correspondence program.

Dates: June 1990-Present.

Objective: To give an introduction to Statistical Quality Control.

Learning Outcome: Upon successful completion of this course, the student will be able to identify the objectives of SQC; explain how to use control charts; and describe the theory of probability and some fundamental concepts in acceptance sampling.

Instruction: Major topics covered in the course are *Part 1:* objectives of statistical quality control, Representative Applications; Fundamental Statistical Concepts: Why the Control Chart Works; Examples of a Process in Control: Examples of Processes Out of Control. *Part 2:* Directions for Simple X and R Charts; The Selection of Rational Subgroups; Different Adaptations of the Control Chart for Variables. *Part 3:* Fundamentals of the Theory of Probability; The Control Chart for Fraction Defective; The Control Chart for Defects; Aspects of the Relationship Between Control Charts and Certain Other Statistical Techniques. *Part 4:* Aspects of Specifications and Tolerances; Fundamental Concepts in Acceptance Sampling; Dodge-Roming Type Systems for Acceptance Sampling by Attributes. *Part 5:* Other Types of Systems for Acceptance by Attributes: Acceptance Sampling by Variables; Aspects of Life Testing and Reliability; and Cost Aspects of Quality Decisions. Methods of instruction include self-study, texts, study guides, and a proctored final examination.

Credit Recommendation: In the lower division baccalaureate/associate degree category, 3 semester hours in Industrial Engineering Technology (6/94).

Structural Steel Design

Location: Self-study.

Length: Correspondence Program.

Dates: January 1985-Present.

Objective: To develop capability in the design of steel beams, columns, and connections.

Learning Outcome: Upon successful completion of this course, the student will be able to design and detail rolled steel shapes used in building frames, connections, steel beams and columns, and composite steel/concrete items.

Instruction: Major topics covered in the course are selection of rolled steel shapes for beams and column; allowable unit stresses; design of connections; eccentric loading; and design of column base plates. Methods of instruction include self-study, texts, study guides, and a proctored final examination.

Credit Recommendation: In the lower division baccalaureate/associate degree category, 3 semester hours in Civil Engineering Technology (11/84) (4/89) (6/94). **NOTE:** Course should not be applied to Engineering major.

Structured Systems Analysis

Location: Self-study.

Length: Correspondence program.

Dates: April 1991-Present.

Objective: To provide knowledge of the System Development Life Cycle and the role of the system analyst and project manager with emphasis on documentation, scheduling, monitoring and control.

Learning Outcome: Upon successful completion of this course, the student will be able to understand the basic development of an Information System Life Cycle, and describe the roles of the systems analyst and project manager.

Instruction: Major topics covered in the course are the systems analysis process, definition, documentation, system analysis, and project management. Methods of instruction include self-study, texts, study guides, and a proctored final examination.

Credit Recommendation: In the lower division baccalaureate/associate degree category, 2 semester hours in Management Information Systems (elective) or Data Processing (6/94).

Supervisory Management

Location: Self-study.

Length: Correspondence Program.

Dates: April 1991-Present.

Objective: To further managerial effectiveness by applying the concepts of management through the use of case studies.

Learning Outcome: Upon successful completion of this course, the student will be able to understand the five functions of management; identify and apply managerial skills; improve inter-personal relations and organizational communications; and understand the effective use of a management information system.

Instruction: Major topics covered in the course include decision making, organizing, delegating, group dynamics, motivating, leadership and stress management, and effective use of a management information system. Methods of instruction include self-study, texts, study guides, and a proctored final examination.

Credit Recommendation: In the upper division baccalaureate degree category, 2 semester hours in Principles of Management or Applied Management (6/94).

Survey of Fourth Generation Languages

Location: Self-study.

Length: Correspondence program.

Dates: April 1991-Present.

Objective: To provide an introduction to the concepts defining fourth-generation languages (4GLs).

Learning Outcome: Upon successful completion of this course, the student will be able to describe the characteristics of 4GLs; and demonstrate a proficiency in using them effectively as business problem-solving tools.

Instruction: Major topics covered in the course are the benefits and disadvantages of 4GLs; classifications of 4GL; characteristics of a 4GL; prototypes and the system development life cycle; characteristics benefit and types of prototypes; and planning and managing a prototype project. Methods of instruction include self-study, texts, study guides, and a proctored final examination.

Credit Recommendation: In the lower division baccalaureate/associate degree category, 2 semester hours in Fourth Generation Languages (6/94).

Systems Design

Location: Self-study.

Length: Correspondence program.

Dates: April 1991-Present.

Objective: To provide basic understanding of systems design, role of systems analyst, strategies of software testing, and methods of systems implementation.

Learning Outcome: Upon successful completion of this course, the student will be able to understand the major activities in the design phase, the role of the systems analyst, and the strategies of software testing and system implementation.

Instruction: Major topics covered in the course are introduction to systems development; systems analysis and design; programming, testing, and documentation; implementation, and evaluation. Methods of instruction include self-study, texts, study guides, and a proctored final examination.

Credit Recommendation: In the lower division baccalaureate/associate degree category, 2 semester hours in Management Information Systems or Data Processing (6/94).

Technical Materials

Location: Self-study.

Length: Correspondence Program.

Dates: January 1980-Present.

Objective: To introduce the nature and properties of metallic and nonmetallic elements.

Learning Outcome: Upon successful completion of this course, the student will be able to understand the basic nature and properties of metallic and nonmetallic elements.

Instruction: Major topics covered in the course are the use of metrics; fundamental laws of chemistry; metallic and nonmetallic elements; organic chemistry; unit operations; and composition and properties of materials. Methods of instruction include self-study, texts, study guides, and a proctored final examination.

Credit Recommendation: In the lower division baccalaureate/associate degree category, 3 semester hours in Engineering Materials (including Chemistry) or Engineering Technology (11/84) (4/89) (6/94). **NOTE:** Student may receive credit for only 1 of the following courses: Engineering Materials, Technical Materials, or Mechanics of Materials. *Prerequisite:* Technical Mathematics I.

Technical Mathematics I

Location: Self-study.

Length: Correspondence Program.

Dates: *Version 1:* January 1983-December 1986; *Version 2:* January 1987-Present.

Objective: *Version 1:* To introduce the history of engineering and to provide basic algebra skills necessary to solve technical problems. *Version 2:* To provide the basic algebra skills necessary to solve technical problems.

Learning Outcome: Upon successful completion of this course, the student will be able to solve technical problems involving the use of basic algebra skills.

Instruction: *Version 1:* Overview of the history of engineering; formulas; operations on signed numbers, polynomials, and rational expressions; factoring; solution of linear systems, including the methods of determinants; graphs and graphical solutions of linear and quadratic equations; exponents; radicals; logarithms; imaginary numbers; technical applications are included. *Version 2:* Major topics covered in the course are formulas; operations of signed numbers, polynomials, and rational expressions; factoring; solution of linear systems including the methods of determinants; graphs and graphical solutions of linear quadratic equations; exponents; radicals; logarithms; imaginary numbers; and technical applications. Methods of instruction include independent study, correspondence, telephone assistance, and examinations.

Credit Recommendation: *Versions 1 and 2:* In the lower division baccalaureate/associate degree category, 2 semester hours in Technical Mathematics or Algebra (11/84) (4/89) (6/94). **NOTE:** Course should not be applied to Science or Engineering majors.

Technical Mathematics II

Location: Self-study.

Length: Correspondence Program.

Dates: January 1983-Present.

Objective: To provide a basic knowledge of plane geometry and plane trigonometry.

Learning Outcome: Upon successful completion of this course, the student will be able to understand the basic principles of plane geometry and plane trigonometry.

Instruction: Major topics covered in the course are practical geometry: points, lines, surfaces and angles; perpendicular and parallel lines; triangles; quadrilaterals;

other polygons; the circle, arcs and areas of figures bounded by them; areas and volumes of solids; plane trigonometry: solving a triangle; deriving trigonometric functions; trigonometric and geometric identities; values for the trigonometric functions; using the table of natural trigonometric functions; interpolations; solving the right triangle; solving the right triangle by using logarithms; angles and their measurement; degrees and radians; rectangular coordinates; the trigonometric formulas; finding the values of the functions of angles; reduction formulas; solving the oblique triangle; law of tangents; using half-angle formulas; area of a triangle; radius of an inscribed circle; and radius of a circumscribed circle. Methods of instruction include self-study, texts, study guides, and a proctored final examination.

Credit Recommendation: In the lower division baccalaureate/associate degree category, 2 semester hours in Technical Mathematics or Trigonometry/Plane Geometry (11/84) (4/89) (6/94). **NOTE:** Course should not be applied to Science or Engineering majors.

Technical Science

Location: Self-study.

Length: Correspondence Program.

Dates: January 1982-Present.

Objective: To provide a foundation for the application and use of metrics and to have the student develop an understanding of technical and mathematical aspects of heat, elements of chemistry, and engineering chemistry.

Learning Outcome: Upon successful completion of this course, the student will be able to understand the basic application and use of metrics along with the technical and mathematical aspects of heat, elements of chemistry, and engineering chemistry.

Instruction: Major topics covered in the course are the use of metrics; nature of heat; expansion of gases; carnot's cycle, fundamental laws of chemistry; metallic and nonmetallic elements; organic chemistry and unit operations. Mathematical modeling and problem-solving are used extensively. Methods of instruction include self-study, texts, study guides, and a proctored final examination.

Credit Recommendation: In the lower division baccalaureate/associate degree category, 2 semester hours in Technical Science (11/84) (4/89) (6/94).

Technical Writing

Location: Self-study.

Length: Correspondence program.

Dates: January 1987-Present.

Objective: To provide an understanding of the purposes, types, and structure of informal reports and the methods of communicating in a technical style.

Learning Outcome: Upon successful completion of this course, the student will be able to discuss the purposes, types ad preparation of an informal proposal and report, communicate effectively using a technical style, and prepare an outline and a proposal.

Instruction: Major topics covered in the course are types of reports, proposals, principles of technical style, organizing, outlining, formatting, research and documentation, and writing effective sentences. Methods of instruction include self-study, texts, study guides, and a proctored final examination.

Credit Recommendation: In the lower division baccalaureate/associate degree category, 2 semester hours in Technical Writing (6/94).

Technology Orientation

Location: Self-study.

Length: Correspondence program.

Dates: June 1990-Present.

Objective: To introduce the history of engineering technology and the engineering profession.

Learning Outcome: Upon successful completion of this course, the student will be able to distinguish between the roles of the scientist, engineer, and engineering technician; recognize scientific discovery and engineering inventions and early engineering accomplishments; discuss the "great" giants of the engineering field; identify key areas of contemporary engineering technology; know the engineering and professional technical societies; and know how to seek certification for engineering technicians.

Instruction: Major topics covered in the course are history of engineering technology (modern and ancient), European inventions during the middle ages, engineering and technology development in the U.S., and the growth of technology. Methods of instruction include self-study, texts, study guides, and a proctored final examination.

Credit Recommendation: In the lower division baccalaureate/associate degree category, 1 semester hour in Introduction to Technology (6/94).

Time Study

Location: Self-study.

Length: Correspondence program.

Dates: June 1990-Present.

Objective: To provide an understanding of how time studies are used to evaluate a manufacturing process.

Learning Outcome: Upon successful completion of this course, the student will be able to explain the responsibilities of labor and management in time studies; describe the equipment that is used; explain the basic procedures used; and explain how to analyze the data to evaluate performance.

Instruction: Major topics covered in the course are responsibilities of labor and management, equipment, methodology, rating operator performance, setting standards, derivation and application of standard date, fundamental motion data, and time-formula construction. Methods of instruction include self-study, texts, study guides, and a proctored final examination.

Credit Recommendation: In the lower division baccalaureate/associate degree category, 1 semester hour in Industrial Engineering Technology (6/94).

Tool Design I and II

Location: Self-study.

Length: Correspondence Program.

Dates: *Version 1:* January 1980-December 1986; *Version 2:* January 1987-Present.

Objective: To provide an understanding of the principles of tool planning.

Learning Outcome: Upon successful completion of this course, the student will be able to understand and perform processes associated with tool planning.

Instruction: *Version 1: Course 1.* Single-point, multiple-point, and rotary tools; control of tool wear and failure; types of work-holding devices; power presses; shearing and die-cutting; design of piercing, blanking, and compound dies. *Course 2.* Principles of gaging; types and applications of inspection gages; tools for soldering, brazing, and mechanical joining processes; general considerations in tool design; safety; tool materials; heat-treating; fits and tolerances. *Version 2: Course 1.* Single-point, multiple-point, and rotary tools; control of tool wear and failure; types of work-holding devices; jig and fixture design; power presses; shearing and die-cutting; design of piercing, blanking, and compound dies. *Course 2.* Principles of gaging; types and applications of gages; tools for soldering, brazing, and mechanical joining processes; general considerations in tool design; gage materials; fits and tolerances; fundamentals of numerical control; and overview of CAD in tool design. Methodology for both courses involves hands-on proficiency in material testing procedures and a brief overview of CAD/CAM in the resident laboratory at a major university location.

Credit Recommendation: *Version 1:* In the lower division baccalaureate/associate degree category, 3 semester hours in Introduction to Tool Design or Engineering Technology (11/84). *Prerequisite:* Manufacturing Processes or Production Processes. *Version 2:* In the lower division baccalaureate/associate degree category, 6 semester hours in Tool Design or Engineering Technology (4/89) (6/94). **NOTE:** For credit recommendation to apply, student must complete resident lab training or have equivalent laboratory experience.

Topographic Drawing and Surveying

Location: Self-study.

Length: Correspondence Program.

Dates: *Version 1:* January 1980-March 1989; *Version 2:* April 1989-Present.

Objective: To develop ability in technical drawing by preparing five geometrical drawing plates plus four mapping plates, and the study of topographic surveying.

Learning Outcome: Upon successful completion of this course, the student will be able to prepare drawing and mapping plates and understand principles of topographic surveying.

Instruction: Major topics covered in the course include the use of drafting instruments; azimuths and bearings of lines; topographic symbols and contours; plotting cross sections and profiles; city and village maps; determination of distance by stadia; stadia surveys for locating topography; plane-table surveying; topographic maps; and methods of control. Methods of instruction include self-study, texts, study guides, and a proctored final examination.

Credit Recommendation: *Version 1:* In the upper division baccalaureate degree category, 2 semester hours in Topographic Drawing and Surveying or 1 semester hour when applied to an Engineering major (11/84). *Version 2:* In the lower division baccalaureate/associate degree category, 3 semester hours in Topographic Drawing and Surveying (4/89) (6/94). **NOTE:** For credit recommendation to apply, student must complete resident lab training.

Tourism Process

Location: Self-study.

Length: Correspondence Program.

Dates: November 1990-Present.

Objective: To provide an introduction to the various sectors of the tourism industry, influences on travel, tourism research and marketing, and the role of the travel agent.

Learning Outcome: Upon successful completion of this course, the student will be able to describe the developmental history of the tourism industry; define the terms "tourist" and tourism"; differentiate between the systems of tourism administered by the governments of the United States, Canada, and Great Britain; explain the influence which governments worldwide exert over tourism; describe the role of tourism planning in protecting tourist destinations and attractions; explain the role of marketing research within the scope of tourism development and destination marketing; and identify the steps to be taken in promoting and retaining group meeting and convention business.

Instruction: Major topics covered in the course are introduction to travel and tourism; role of government in tourism; influences in travel; classification of lodging facilities; research, marketing and promotion; and the travel agency. Methods of instruction include self-study, texts, study guides, and a proctored final examination.

Credit Recommendation: In the lower division baccalaureate/associate degree category, 2 semester hours in Introduction to Tourism (6/94).

Illinois Fire Service Institute

The Illinois Fire Service Institute, formerly Firemanship Training, hired the first permanent faculty in 1956. In 1974, legislation created the Illinois Fire Service Institute, the mandated fire academy for the State of Illinois. The Institute is responsible for designing, implementing, and evaluating fire service education and training activities for the Illinois fire service.

The Institute operates a full range of fire training programs including basic training, specialized and technical activities, and weekend programs that fit the needs of the fire service.

The courses offered by the Institute vary in length and location. The courses that require live burning are typically held in Champaign. The remaining programs are taught on campus and in fire training centers throughout the state.

The curriculum for the programs is provided by national standards, state certification programs, and firefighter needs. Curriculum materials are developed by conferring with state certification committees and referencing national standards. The courses are under constant scrutiny to ensure that the information is current and useful to the students. However, not all courses are certified. Successful completion of all of the course evaluation is necessary for the student to become certified. The evaluation section, depending on the program, may require successful completion of a written and skill test to allow the firefighters to challenge the state certification exam.

All student records are entered into a computer according to their personal identification code. Each class the firefighter attends is annotated on their individual record.

Source of official student records: Registry of Credit Recommendations, American Council on Education, One Dupont Circle, Washington, DC 20036-1193 or The Illinois Fire Service Institute, University of Illinois, FSI Building, 11 Gerty Drive, Champaign, Illinois 61820.

Additional information about the courses: College Credit Recommendation Service, American Council on Education, One Dupont Circle, Washington, DC 20036-1193.

Arson Investigation I
(A. Fire Arson Investigation Module I)
(B. Fire Arson Investigation Module II)

Location: University of Illinois or selected off-campus sites.

Length: A. 40 hours (1 week); B. 40 hours (1 week), for a total of 80 hours (2 weeks).

Dates: *Version 1:* October 1982-March 1994; *Version 2:* April 1994-Present.

Objective: To train fire and police personnel in theory and behavior of fire, sources of fire ignition, building construction as it affects fire spread, fire cause and point of origin, indicators of arson, electrical fire causes, vehicle fires, and other related material.

Learning Outcome: Upon successful completion of this course, the student will be able to understand fire/arson investigation, including the chemistry of fire; understand the types of building construction, types of loading and building elements that may increase or decrease fire growth, and understand how to conduct a fire investigation.

Instruction: Major topics covered in the course are fire behavior, building construction, automatic fire detection and supervision system, determining cause and point of origin, accidental fire hazards and causes, incendiary fire causes and indicators, vehicle fires, sketching, appropriate field demonstrations, field interviews, gathering information and evidence, recording facts and observations, recognizing motivations of arsonists, identifying explosives and fires set by explosions, and working within legal guidelines. Methods of instruction include lecture, discussion, practical exercises, and case preparation and presentation.

Credit Recommendation: *Version 1:* In the upper division baccalaureate degree category, 3 semester hours in Criminal Justice, Fire Science, Insurance, or Law Enforcement (10/87) (11/94). *Version 2:* In the upper division baccalaureate degree category, 4 semester hours in Criminal Justice, Fire Science, Insurance, or Law Enforcement (11/94). **NOTE**: To receive credit, student must complete both courses.

Arson Investigation II
(Fire Arson Investigation Module III)

Location: University of Illinois or selected off-campus sites.

Length: 40 hours (1 week).

Dates: *Version 1:* October 1982-February 1994; *Version 2:* March 1994-Present.

Objective: To provide the knowledge and skills required to detect arson patterns and motives in a variety of settings.

Learning Outcome: Upon successful completion of this course, the student will be able to understand intelligence systems, crime laboratory, interview and communications techniques, fatal fires, photography, and arson for profit.

Instruction: Major topics covered in the course are administrative units, intelligence systems, crime laboratory, photography, interviews and communication techniques, fatal fires, and arson for profit. Methods of instruction include lecture, discussion, practical exercises, and examination.

Credit Recommendation: *Version 1:* In the upper division baccalaureate degree category, 1 semester hour in Criminal Justice, Fire Science, Fire Technology, Insurance, or Law Enforcement (10/87) (11/94). *Version 2:* In the upper division baccalaureate degree category, 2 semester hours in Criminal Justice, Fire Science, Fire Technology, Insurance, or Law Enforcement (11/94). *Prerequisite:* Arson Investigation I.

Curriculum and Course Design I
(Fire Service Instructor I)

Location: University of Illinois or selected off-campus sites.

Length: 40 hours (1 week).

Dates: January 1977-Present.

Objective: To provide an understanding of the methods of learning.

Learning Outcome: Upon successful completion of this course, the student will be able to understand techniques related to teaching.

Instruction: Major topics covered in the course are communication, concepts of learning, human relations in the teaching-learning environment, methods of teaching, organizing the learning environment, performance evaluation, records and reports, testing and evaluation, the instructor's role and responsibilities, the lesson plan, the teaching technique, and the use of instructional materials. Methods of instruction include lecture, discussion, role playing, audio/visual aids, and practical exercises.

Credit Recommendation: In the lower division baccalaureate/associate degree category, 3 semester hours in Education Methods of Teaching, Fire Science, or Fire Technology (10/87) (11/94).

Curriculum and Course Design II
(Fire Service Instructor II)

Location: University of Illinois or selected off-campus sites.

Length: 40 hours (1 week).

Dates: January 1977-Present.

Objective: To instruct fire service personnel in developing performance objectives, lesson plans, instructional aids, evaluation systems, references and records, and reports.

Learning Outcome: Upon successful completion of this course, the student will be able to develop performance objectives, lesson plans, instructional aids, evaluation systems, references and records, and reports.

Instruction: Major topics covered in the course are preparation of instructional materials, techniques of testing and evaluation, writing behavioral objectives or performance objectives, lesson plan development, teaching/learning process, methods of instruction, records and reports, and references. Methods of instruction include lecture, discussion, role playing, audio/visual aids, and practical exercises.

Credit Recommendation: In the upper division baccalaureate degree category, 3 semester hours in Education, Fire Science, Fire Technology, or Methods of Teaching (10/87) (11/94). *Prerequisite:* Instructor I or Curriculum and Course Design I.

Curriculum and Course Design III (Instructor III—Advanced Teaching Methods or Fire Service Instructor III—Methods of Instruction)

Location: University of Illinois or selected off-campus sites.

Length: 80 hours (2 weeks).

Dates: January 1985-Present.

Objective: To instruct in advanced methods of curriculum and course design.

Learning Outcome: Upon successful completion of this course, the student will be able to analyze fire service occupations, prepare instructional materials, and understand principles of technical writing and techniques of administering tests and evaluation, and know how to write behavioral objectives.

Instruction: Major topics covered in the course are approaches to training, systems design, developing terminal objectives, instructional techniques, technical writing, course design and sequencing, analysis of evaluation systems (including entire tests, test items, and statistics), course materials development, design and development of instructional aids, the equal opportunity law, and impact of the instructional program and records and reports. Methods of instruction include lecture, discussion, role playing, audio/visual aids, and practical exercises.

Credit Recommendation: In the upper division baccalaureate degree category, 3 semester hours in Education, Fire Science Technology, or Methods of Teaching (10/87) (11/94). *Prerequisite:* Curriculum and Course Design II.

Fire Apparatus Engineer: Pump Operator

Location: University of Illinois or selected off-campus sites.

Length: *Version 1*: 80 hours (2 weeks); *Version 2*: 64 hours (2 week).

Dates: September 1982-Present.

Objective: To provide the necessary background, knowledge, and skills required to perform the duties of a fire apparatus engineer.

Learning Outcome: Upon successful completion of this course, the student will be able to describe the features of a pumper and list the requirements for certification of a fire apparatus with a pump; illustrate and describe the mechanical principles of pumps; list and describe the apparatus systems and pump components; list the types of apparatus records and describe the service and maintenance requirements of a fire apparatus with pump; describe physical properties of water in relationship to its fire extinguishing properties and hydraulic properties; describe water supply systems required for production of fire streams; perform pump operations in simulated fire ground situations; diagnose and describe proper solutions to common problems encountered during pump operations.

Instruction: Major topics covered in the course are the duties of the fire apparatus engineer including demonstrating their understanding of pump operations, fire stream development, and water supply operations in relation to various situations encountered on the ground; and know components of a pumper, the functions of the pump, and the necessary requirements for maintaining and testing of the apparatus. Methods of instruction include lecture, discussion, practical exercises, and classroom instruction (driver training program).

Credit Recommendation: In the lower division baccalaureate/associate degree category, 2 semester hours in Fire Engineering, Fire Science, or Fire Technology (10/87) (11/94).

Fire Department Management I

Location: University of Illinois or selected off-campus sites.

Length: 40 hours (five 8-hour meetings per week or weekends).

Dates: September 1984-Present.

Objective: To introduce the basic principles of management.

Learning Outcome: Upon successful completion of this course, the student will be able to understand basic management principles and concepts; leadership; motivation; organizational culture; concepts of change; giving orders; and the disciplinary process.

Instruction: Major topics covered in the course are role and function of a Fire Officer I, societal and organizational culture, basic management principles, motivation, concepts of leadership, situational leadership, use of power in the leadership role, order giving, discipline, and conflict resolution. Methods of instruction include lecture and discussion.

Credit Recommendation: In the lower division baccalaureate/associate degree category, 3 semester hours in Business Administration, Fire Science, Management, or Public Management (10/87) (11/94).

Fire Department Management II

Location: University of Illinois or selected off-campus sites.

Length: 40 hours (five 8-hour meetings per week or weekends).

Dates: September 1984-Present.

Objective: To provide the skills related to successful management.

Learning Outcome: Upon successful completion of this course, the student will be able to understand basic communication skills; written communications; group dynamics; and conflict resolution.

Instruction: Major topics covered in the course are writing records and reports, nature and structure of a work group, types and functions of small groups, factors affecting group job performance, leadership within a work group, building group cohesion and morale, formal and informal communication channels, communication and self-disclosure patterns in a fire company, and interpersonal and intergroup conflicts. Methods of instruction include lecture, discussion, and classroom exercises.

Credit Recommendation: In the lower division baccalaureate/associate degree category, 3 semester hours in Business Administration, Fire Science, Management, or Public Management (10/87) (11/94).

Fire Department Management III

Location: University of Illinois or selected off-campus sites.

Length: 40 hours (five 8-hour meetings per week or weekends).

Dates: January 1985-Present.

Objective: To provide an understanding of key management techniques.

Learning Outcome: Upon successful completion of this course, the student will be able to understand the functions of risk management; planning and resource management; public finance and budgeting; public relations and the news media; and how to run a meeting.

Instruction: Major topics covered in the course are principles of risk management, budgeting and financial planning, public relations techniques and the news media, principles of public finance, and leadership techniques required to run a meeting. Methods of instruction include lecture, discussion, and classroom exercises.

Credit Recommendation: In the upper division baccalaureate degree category, 3 semester hours in Business Administration, Fire Science, Management, or Public Management (10/87) (11/94).

Fire Department Management IV

Location: University of Illinois or selected off-campus sites.

Length: 40 hours (five 8-hour meetings per week or weekends).

Dates: January 1985-Present.

Objective: To provide negotiation and human relation skills related to successful management.

Learning Outcome: Upon successful completion of this course, the student will be able to understand leadership development; fire officer liability; image development; labor relations; hiring and promotional systems; personnel management; and special topics.

Instruction: Major topics covered in the course are dealing with the media; personnel management; labor relations in the public sector; collective bargaining problems; criminal, civil, and administrative liability; hiring and promotion interviews; job appraisal interview systems; disciplinary hearings; avoiding lawsuits and suspensions; training for leadership; and communication within organizational structures. Methods of instruction include lecture, discussion, classroom exercises, and case studies.

Credit Recommendation: In the upper division baccalaureate degree category, 3 semester hours in Business Administration, Fire Science, Management, or Personnel Management (10/87) (11/94).

Fire Prevention Officer I

Location: University of Illinois or selected off-campus sites.

Length: 240 hours (6 weeks.

Dates: September 1982-June 1994.

Objective: To lead the student to certification at three levels: Fire Investigator I, Fire Prevention Education Officer I, and Fire Inspector I.

Learning Outcome: Upon successful completion of this course, the student will be able to understand the methods and applications of inspection techniques, interpretation and application of fire codes, fire hazards and causes, elements of building construction, and fire protection devices.

Instruction: Major topics covered in the course are inspection techniques, interpretation and application of fire codes, fire hazards and causes, elements of building construction, and fire protection devices. Students must successfully complete this course in order to satisfy requirements for certification as Fire Investigator I, Fire Prevention Education Officer I, and Fire Inspector I. This course is very specialized and covers topics in an in-depth manner. Methods of instruction include lecture, and discussion .

Credit Recommendation: In the lower division baccalaureate/associate degree category, 6 semester hours in Fire Science or Fire Technology (10/87) (11/94).

Fire Prevention Principles (Formerly Fire Prevention Principles I)

Location: University of Illinois or selected off-campus sites.

Length: 40 hours (1 week).

Dates: August 1984-Present.

Objective: To familiarize the company level officer with fire inspection, fire investigation, and public fire safety education.

Learning Outcome: Upon successful completion of this course, the student will be able to understand principles related to fire investigation, public fire safety education, fire prevention, including defining building codes, defining performance codes, defining specification codes, explaining the basis for building codes, identifying the main parts of a building code, identifying the term "standard," identifying the advantages of municipal adoption of model codes, identifying and explaining code terminology, defining the term "ordinance," identifying functions of code enforcement agencies, and identifying various steps in code enforcement.

Instruction: Major topics covered in the course are laws, codes, and ordinances; the Life Safety Code; occupancies; basic building construction; fire hazards and causes; inspection techniques; and basic fire/arson investigation. Methods of instruction include lecture, discussion, classroom exercises, and a final examination.

Credit Recommendation: In the lower division baccalaureate/associate degree category, 3 semester hours in Fire Science or Fire Technology (12/91) (11/94).

Fire Prevention Principles II

Location: University of Illinois or selected off-campus sites.

Length: 40 hours (1 week).

Dates: August 1983-December 1995.

Objective: To provide mid-level fire service managers with advanced knowledge and skills in fire inspection, investigation, and public fire education.

Learning Outcome: Upon successful completion of this course, the student will be able to understand the principles of fire prevention, identify preparations necessary to conduct a fire investigation, describe legal procedures and ramifications of criminal fire investigation, and identify methods and procedures of fire scene photography, fire death investigation, and public fire education.

Instruction: Major topics covered in the course are laws, codes, and ordinances; the life safety code; fire investigation; fire causes; systems and devices; inspection techniques; fire prevention bureau management; plans review; occupancy; and building construction. Methods of instruction include lecture and discussion.

Credit Recommendation: In the lower division baccalaureate/associate degree category, 3 semester hours in Fire Science or Fire Technology (12/91) (11/94).

Hazardous Materials: Chemistry

Location: University of Illinois or selected off-campus sites.

Length: 80 hours (2 weeks).

Dates: April 1986-Present.

Objective: To provide a basic understanding of principles related to organic and inorganic chemistry.

Learning Outcome: Upon successful completion of this course, the student will be able to understand aspects of inorganic and organic chemistry necessary to prepare the hazardous materials first responder or response team member to evaluate a hazardous materials incident scene and initiate appropriate corrective action in accordance with proper safety procedures.

Instruction: Major topics covered in the course are a survey lecture on physical chemistry, chemical formula writing, types of reactions, math review, atomic theory, chemical equations, molecular theory, chemical changes, common organic compounds, incident analysis and mitigation, identification of unknowns, hydrocarbons, and toxicology.

Credit Recommendation: In the lower division baccalaureate/associate degree category, 4 semester hours in Emergency Medical Services, Fire Science, Fire Technology, or Law Enforcement (10/87) (11/94).

Hazardous Materials: Operation

Location: Sites throughout the State of Illinois.

Length: 40 hours (5 days).

Dates: January 1992-Present.

Objective: To provide the knowledge and skills to function at the operations level in hazardous materials situations as defined by NFPA Standard No. 472 and 29CFR.

Learning Outcome: Upon successful completion of this course, the student will be able to identify requirements and actions called for by Federal laws and regulations; identify clues and mechanisms to gather information about products, facilities, containers, and conditions impacting operations; predict hazardous material behavior; select appropriate response objectives and actions including proper protective equipment to be used and basic decontamination procedures; establish scene control and incident management; perform defensive control actions; and evaluate progress toward response objectives. Methods of instruction include lecture, discussion, classroom exercises, audio/visual material, practical demonstration exercises, and final exam.

Instruction: Major topics covered in the course are incident analysis, collecting hazard and response information, predicting behavior of a hazardous material, estimating potential harm, describing response objectives, identifying response options, personal protective equipment, emergency decontamination procedures, establishing and enforcing scene control procedures, incident management system, defensive control actions, and incident progress evaluation.

Credit Recommendation: In the lower division baccalaureate/associate degree category, 1 semester hour in Fire Science, Fire Technology, Emergency Medical Service, Law Enforcement, or Environmental Health and Safety (11/94).

Hazardous Materials: Technician

Location: Sites throughout the State of Illinois.

Length: 80 hours (10 days).

Dates: January 1992-Present.

Objective: To operate as a technical specialist at hazardous substance emergencies as defined by National Fire Protection Association Standard No. 472, U.S. Department of Labor Occupational Safety and Health Administration (OSHA), and U.S. Environmental Protection Agency (USEPA) regulations.

Learning Outcome: Upon successful completion of this course, the student will be able to recognize and identify the presence and characteristics of hazardous substances using generally available references and computer models; and take corrective actions to control, contain, or mitigate hazardous substance releases utilizing personal protective equipment, monitoring equipment, and control or containment procedures or equipment.

Instruction: Major topics covered in the course are hazardous substance classifications and toxicology, personal protective equipment, hazardous substance identification and monitoring instrumentation methods and procedures, containers and containment, incident command and integrated emergency management, psychological stress, and extensive use of simulations and practical exercises. Methods of instruction include lecture, discussion, classroom exercises, case studies, audio/visual material, computer-assisted instruction, practical exercises, and examinations.

Credit Recommendation: In the upper division baccalaureate degree category, 4 semester hours in Fire Science, Fire Technology, Environmental Health and Safety, Emergency Medical Services, or Law Enforcement (11/94).

Tactics and Strategy I

Location: University of Illinois or selected off-campus sites.

Length: 40 hours (1 week).

Dates: October 1982-Present.

Objective: To become familiar with the strategic and tactical information necessary for the officer commanding initial response operations and the responsibilities of engine and truck company officers.

Learning Outcome: Upon successful completion of this course, the student will be able to command basic fire fighting operations of one or two fire fighting companies on a fire emergency scene.

Instruction: Major topics covered in the course are leadership, pre-fire planning, hazardous materials, building construction, fire behavior, basic fire fighting and fire ground decision-making, engine company and water supply operations, truck company operations, and tactical problems and simulation exercises. Methods of instruction include lecture, discussion, classroom exercises, case studies, audio/visual material, and an examination.

Credit Recommendation: In the lower division baccalaureate/associate degree category, 3 semester hours in Fire Science or Fire Technology (12/91) (11/94).

Tactics and Strategy II

Location: University of Illinois or selected off-campus sites.

Length: 40 hours (1 week).

Dates: *Version 1:* October 1982-December 1991; *Version 2:* January 1992-Present.

Objective: To provide the appropriate strategies and tactics for managing or directing fire fighting operations.

Learning Outcome: Upon successful completion of this course, the student will be able to direct multicompany or department fire fighting operations.

Instruction: *Version 1:* Major topics covered in the course are fire ground management, strategic concepts in fire fighting, manpower utilization, hazardous materials, disaster management, and simulated fire problems. Methods of instruction include lecture and practical exercises are used. *Version 2:* Major topics covered in the course are the duties and responsibilities of command officers, critical incident stress, disaster planning and operations, high-rise building emergencies, incident command system, multiple company operations, advanced strategies and tactics, and simulated fire problems. Methods of instruction include lecture, discussion, classroom exercises, case studies, and final examination.

Credit Recommendation: In the lower division baccalaureate/associate degree category, 3 semester hours in Fire Science or Fire Technology (10/87) (11/94).

Independent School of Management

Independent School Management (ISM) is a consulting and service firm committed to the development of cost-effective, efficient management of private-independent schools. Research, on-site consulting, problem analysis, and theory development are all part of its ongoing activities, the results of which are shared in publications, seminars, and workshops.

The Management Institutes are offered in response to the needs of the independent school community. To complement graduate education programs that primarily relate to administrators in the public sector, the ISM workshops are targeted to key administrators of private independent schools. The workshops provide practical information. Techniques, concepts, designs, and theories have been developed and tested by ISM through on-site consultation at hundreds of different types of private-independent schools. Each workshop and seminar takes place under the guidance of men and women with experience in several private-independent schools.

Most of the workshops are operated during the Summer Institute that is held at the Radisson Hotel in Wilmington, Delaware. Other fall and winter workshops are held in Wilmington, Delaware, using hotel facilities.

Source of official student records: Director of Management Institutes, Independent School Management, 1316 North Union Street, Wilmington, DE 19806-2594.

Additional information about the courses: College Credit Recommendation Service, American Council on Education, One Dupont Circle, Washington, DC 20036-1193.

Administering the Small Private-Independent School

Location: Radisson Hotel, Wilmington, DE.

Length: 42 hours (6 days).

Dates: July 1984-August 1990.

Objective: To provide practical information and techniques for administering a small private-independent school with a limited budget and support staff.

Instruction: Major topics covered in the course are general elements of private-independent school administration (role of the head, staffing, working with trustees, business management, curriculum and scheduling, external relations, stress and conflict management, effecting change) from the perspective of a small school headmaster. Methods of instruction include lecture, discussion, and handouts.

Credit Recommendation: In the upper division baccalaureate or graduate degree category, 1 semester hour in School Administration (8/85).

Advanced Business Management for Private-Independent Schools

Location: Radisson Hotel, Wilmington, DE.

Length: 42 hours (6 days).

Dates: July 1985-August 1990.

Objective: To provide independent school managers with advanced training in the areas of financial management, administrative accounting, risk analysis, insurance, property management, budgeting, legal aspects of various decisions, and establishing administrative policies.

Instruction: Methods of instruction include lecture, discussions, handouts, financial and budgeting problems, cases, and readings. Special attention is given to the financial and legal impacts of school decisions on the budgeting process.

Credit Recommendation: In the graduate degree category, 1 semester hour in School Business Management (8/85).

Catholic School Governance: Managing Change

Location: Radisson Hotel, Wilmington, DE.

Length: 21 hours (3 days).

Dates: July 1985-July 1986.

Objective: To provide the emerging lay leadership (trustees and heads) of Catholic schools with understanding and skills for effective governance in times of change.

Instruction: Major topics covered in the course are analyses of the shift from religious to lay leadership and the resulting emergence of advisory and lay governing boards. Addresses questions of philosophy, trust, ownership, super-boards, board responsibility, appointment of heads, finances, and marketing. Methods of instruction include lecture, discussion, handouts, and use of visuals.

Credit Recommendation: In the upper division baccalaureate or graduate degree category, 1 semester hour in Educational Administration (8/85).

Extending Student Counselor's Role in Private-Independent Schools

Location: Radisson Hotel, Wilmington, DE.

Length: 21 hours (3 days).

Dates: July 1985-August 1990.

Objective: To provide counselors in an independent school with additional tools and techniques by which to extend and improve its student assistance programs. The course emphasizes contemporary student distresses and needs, which usually can be favorably affected by early recognition and counselor involvement.

Instruction: Methods of instruction include extensive readings of handouts, lecture on theory and practice of counseling, discussion, shared case evaluations, and early identification of student life problems associated with emotional distress, peer pressures, social isolation, drug use, delinquency, and causes of various disorders (and student suicide). Emphasis is on early problem recognition, evaluation, and counseling.

Credit Recommendation: In the upper division baccalaureate or graduate degree category, 1 semester hour in Counselor Education (8/85).

Fund Raising for Private-Independent Schools

Location: Radisson Hotel, Wilmington, DE.

Length: 21 hours (3 days).

Dates: July 1980-Present.

Objective: To provide private-independent school heads and trustees with an understanding of basic fund-raising methods, operations, and staffing and an appreciation of their appropriate role in overseeing the development program.

Instruction: Major topics covered in the course are an introduction to development, components of the development program, and basic fund-raising techniques for administrators and board members who will oversee development functions in private-independent schools. Methods of instruction include lecture, discussion, display of materials, and handouts.

Credit Recommendation: In the upper division baccalaureate degree category, 1 semester hour in Educational Administration (8/85).

In-Service Workshop for Private-Independent School Headmasters

Location: Radisson Hotel, Wilmington, DE.

Length: *Versions 1 and 2:* 60 hours (11 days).

Dates: July 1982-August 1990.

Objective: To provide experienced private-independent school headmasters with information and techniques for analyzing and managing their schools.

Instruction: Applies models of private-independent school operation and governance to the varied responsibilities of headmasters, including constituent relations, curriculum development, nonacademic programs, personnel management, internal policy, trustee relations, physical plant operations, financial management, and institutional advancement. Methods of instruction include lecture, discussion, and handouts.

Credit Recommendation: In the upper division baccalaureate or graduate degree category, 2 semester hours in Educational Administration (8/85).

Managing the Private-Independent Elementary School

Location: Radisson Hotel, Wilmington, DE.

Length: *Version 1:* 21 hours (3 days); *Version 2:* 42 hours (6 days).

Dates: *Version 1:* July 1980-July 1987; *Version 2:* July 1988-Present.

Objective: To provide information and techniques for operating the elementary division of a private-independent school.

Instruction: Applies concepts of problem solving, communications, testing, leadership, school organization, staffing, and supervision to the management of a private-independent elementary school. Methods of instruction include lecture, discussion, case studies, and handouts.

Credit Recommendation: In the upper division baccalaureate degree category, 1 semester hour in Elementary Education Administration (8/85).

Managing the Private-Independent Middle School

Location: Radisson Hotel, Wilmington, DE.

Length: *Version 1:* 21 hours (3 days); *Version 2:* 42 hours (6 days).

Dates: *Version 1:* July 1981-July 1986; *Version 2:* July 1987-Present.

Objective: To apply selected management techniques to the administration of a middle school division of a private-independent school.

Instruction: Analyzes the needs of early adolescents and the appropriate educational environment for these middle-school students. Attention is given to parent relations, goal setting and planning, staffing, and management techniques. Methods of instruction include lecture, discussion, and handouts.

Credit Recommendation: In the upper division baccalaureate degree category, 1 semester hour in Junior High School Administration (8/85).

Marketing the Private-Independent School: Student Recruitment and Retention

Location: Radisson Hotel, Wilmington, DE.

Length: 42 hours (6 days).

Dates: July 1982-August 1990.

Objective: To provide independent school administrators with the concepts and applications of successful marketing by way of market planning strategy development, promotion, and selling. Well-designed marketing programs lead to successful student recruitment and retention results.

Instruction: Methods of instruction include a review of marketing literature and applications in nonprofit organizations and relevance to school management; lecture and discussions; individualized development of market plans and strategies, case problems and discussions, and implementation of recruiting and retention programs.

Credit Recommendation: In the upper division baccalaureate or graduate degree category, 1 semester hour in School Administration (8/85).

Operating a Private-Independent School Business Office

Location: Radisson Hotel, Wilmington, DE.

Length: 42 hours (6 days).

Dates: July 1977-August 1990.

Objective: To provide an overview of the duties, organization, and management aspects of operating a business office in an independent school and to explore representative topics and problems of finance, budgeting, investment practices, physical plant, taxation, and managerial role of the business officer.

Instruction: Methods of instruction include lecture, discussion, regular handouts, short problems, design of forms, interpreting rules and school policies, and review of representative problems and issues that face the business officer of an independent school.

Credit Recommendation: In the upper division baccalaureate or graduate degree category, 1 semester hour in School Administration (8/85).

Operating the Private-Independent School Development Program—3dd

Location: Radisson Hotel, Wilmington, DE.

Length: 42 hours (6 days).

Dates: July 1979-Present.

Objective: To provide understanding of and techniques for management of a development (fund raising) program.

Instruction: Major topics covered in the course are principal functions of a school development office: long-range planning, annual fund, capital campaign, foundation/corporate solicitation, planned giving, solicitation techniques, and use of computers in development. Methods of instruction include lecture, discussion, handouts, and in-class projects.

Credit Recommendation: In the graduate degree category, 2 semester hours in Financial Resource Development (8/85).

Overview of Business and Financial Management in Private-Independent Schools

Location: Radisson Hotel, Wilmington, DE.

Length: 21 hours (3 days).

Dates: July 1977-August 1990.

Objective: To introduce principles and applications of basic accounting and business and financial management for independent schools and to orient school heads to the operation of a business office.

Instruction: Method of instruction includes lecture and discussion of problems.

Credit Recommendation: In the upper division baccalaureate or graduate degree category, 1 semester hour in School Administration or Leadership (8/85).

Presiding Over the Private-Independent School Board of Trustees

Location: Radisson Hotel, Wilmington, DE.

Length: 21 hours (3 days).

Dates: July 1979-August 1990.

Objective: To review the legal and political setting in which school boards operate, to explore representative board problems and issues, and to provide trustees and board chairpersons with skills for successful board management.

Instruction: Major topics covered in the course are origin and responsibilities of governing boards for private-independent schools, board composition and organization, responsibilities of board presidents and other officers, and behavior of board members. Methods of instruction include seminar, lecture, group discussions, and extensive readings, case problems, simulated board exercises.

Credit Recommendation: In the graduate degree category, 1 semester hour in Educational Administration or Leadership (8/85).

Private-Independent School Curriculum Analysis and Coordination

Location: Ursinus College, Collegeville, PA.

Length: *Version 1:* 21 hours (3 days); *Version 2:* 42 hours (6 days).

Dates: *Version 1:* July 1980-July 1989; *Version 2:* July 1990-Present.

Objective: To provide a framework for analyzing elements of the school environment that affect the curriculum and to provide techniques for scheduling and implementing the school curriculum.

Instruction: Major topics covered in the course are analysis of the community, parents, students, faculty, and school resources and their implications for the school curriculum. Special attention is given to scheduling and implementation of the school curriculum. Methods of instruction include lecture, discussion, and handouts.

Credit Recommendation: In the upper division baccalaureate degree category, 1 semester hour in School Curriculum (8/85). **NOTE:** This credit recommendation will apply if the course goes beyond the personal experience of the instructor by examining insights about curriculum development and evaluation found in the literature of the curriculum field.

Private-Independent School Scheduling: Designs, Process, Techniques

Location: Radisson Hotel, Wilmington, DE.

Length: 42 hours (6 days).

Dates: July 1975-August 1990.

Objective: To provide administrators with the principles and diverse applications of scheduling models to independent school decisions, particularly preregistration and registration, and curricula planning. A variety of scheduling models and designs are introduced along with computer-supported scheduling routines.

Instruction: Methods of instruction include lecture, discussion, handouts, cases, readings, and solving a variety of independent school scheduling problems.

Credit Recommendation: In the upper division baccalaureate or graduate degree category, 1 semester hour in School Administration (8/85).

The Complete Private-Independent School Secretary

Location: Ursinus College, Collegeville, PA.

Length: 21 hours (3 days).

Dates: July 1980-August 1990.

Objective: To improve communication skills of the head's secretary, review office leadership styles, and provide an overview of office management topics and administrative techniques that improve productivity.

Instruction: Methods of instruction include lecture, discussion, current problems, review of office administration principles and practices, and recent developments in word processing and other information handling procedures.

Credit Recommendation: In the vocational certificate category, 1 semester hour in Office Administration or Secretarial Studies (8/85).

The Private-Independent School Admissions Office

Location: Ursinus College, Collegeville, PA.

Length: 21 hours (3 days).

Dates: July 1985-August 1990.

Objective: To provide information on the operation of an independent school admissions office and to relate admissions procedures and techniques to marketing and recruiting concepts.

Instruction: Major topics covered in the course are operations of a private-independent school admissions office, how to interest prospective students, internal procedures for data collection and evaluation, fee structure and financial aids, retention techniques, parent relations, and working with the school head. Methods of instruction include lecture, discussion, and handouts.

Credit Recommendation: In the upper division baccalaureate degree category, 1 semester hour in Student Personnel Administration (8/85).

Women as School Administrators in Private-Independent Schools

Location: Radisson Hotel, Wilmington, DE.

Length: 21 hours (3 days).

Dates: July 1985-August 1990.

Objective: To examine the role and leadership styles of women administrators in independent schools, to improve managerial skills of participants, and to explore professional development options of women executives.

Instruction: Major topics covered in the course are female psychological development, management styles and techniques, conflict resolution, decision making, and collaboration, all within the context of leadership of female administrators. Methods of instruction include seminar, surveys and self-evaluation, critiques from literature, current problems, and conflict resolution.

Credit Recommendation: In the graduate degree category, 1 semester hour in Administration or Leadership (8/85).

Informix Software, Inc.

Informix Software, Inc. is the leading supplier of high-performance, parallel processing database technology for open systems. Informix products also include application development tools for creating client/server production applications, decision support systems, ad-hoc query interfaces, and connectivity software that allows information to be shared transparently from PCs to mainframes within the corporate computing environment. Informix's corporate headquarters are in Menlo Park, California.

Informix offers training on a variety of topics including relational database design, Structured Query Language, database and system administration, and application development at regional facilities across the country. Attending our training courses helps to prepare you for the Informix Certified Professional Program. This program consists of a series of examinations specifically designed for information systems professionals to validate proficiency with Informix technology. Upon successful completion of the required examinations, your product knowledge is certified by Informix. For more information about Informix and our training and certification offerings, please visit our web site at http://www.informix.com or call us at 1-800-529-6999.

AUTHORIZED INFORMIX EDUCATION CENTERS

CHARLOTTE
IKON Office Solutions
8702-A Red Oak Boulevard
Charlotte, NC 28217
Contact: Deborah Wiggins
Phone No.: 704-527-9785
Fax No.: 704-527-9788
Internet: http://www.ikontech.com

CINCINNATI
Knowledge Development Centers
One Financial Way
Suite 305
Cincinnati, OH 45242
Contact: Dana Wells
Phone No.: 513-985-2880
Fax No.: 513-985-2885
Internet: http://www.kdc-cincinnati.com

DETROIT
ZenaComp, Inc.
17197 N. Laurel Park Drive
Suite 281
Livonia, MI 48152
Contact: Steve Ellis
Phone No.: 313-464-9600
Fax No.: 313-464-3730
Internet: http://www.zenacomp.com

EDISON, NJ
Summit Data Group
One Executive Drive
Suite 130
Somerset, NJ 08873
Contact: Dave Kosenko
Phone No.: 732-469-4070
Fax No.: 732-469-5522
Internet: http://www.summitdata.com

LOS ANGELES
Infotec Commercial Systems, Inc.
3100 S. Bundy Drive
Suite 540
Los Angeles, CA 90025
Contact: Meg Christ
Phone No.: 310-442-2204
Fax No.: 310-442-9462
Internet: http://www.infotecweb.com

MEMPHIS
Athena
6401 Poplar Avenue
Memphis, TN 38119
Contact: Mark Lamberth
Phone No.: 901-685-7046
Fax No.: 901-685-7556
Internet: http://www.athenaclc.com

MINNEAPOLIS
Bridge Data
601 Carlson Parkway
Suite 360
Minnetonka, MN 55305
Contact: Chad Vogt
Phone No.: 612-933-3336
Fax No.: 612-449-6320
Internet: http://www.bridgedata.com

ROCHESTER
Actium Corporation
180 WillowBrook Office Park
Fairport, NY 14450
Contact: Mary Thompson
Phone No.: 716-249-2600
Fax No.: 716-249-2650
Internet: http://www.actium.com

SACRAMENTO
Infotec Commercial Systems, Inc.
8950 Calcenter Drive, Building 3
Suite 135
Sacramento, CA 95826
Contact: Mark Vantress
Phone No.: 916-361-6920
Fax No.: 916-361-6931
Internet: http://www.infotecweb.com

SEATTLE, WA
Infotec Commercial Systems, Inc.
2300 130th Avenue NE
Bellevue, WA 98005
Contact: Christie Willms
Phone No.: 425-869-4080
Fax No.: 425-869-4065
Internet: http://www.infotecweb.com

WASHINGTON, DC
FuGEN, Inc.
6001 Montrose Road
Suite 640
Rockville, MD 20852
Contact: April Green
Phone No.: 301-230-1551
Fax No.: 301-230-2903
Internet: http://www.fugen.com

Source of official student records: Registry of Credit Recommendations, American Council on Education, One Dupont Circle, Washington, DC 20036-1193.

Additional information about the courses: College Credit Recommendation Service, American Council on Education, One Dupont Circle, Washington, DC 20036-1193.

INFORMIX-OnLine Dynamic Server Performance Tuning (403)

Location: Various sites in the United States.

Length: 4 days.

Dates: February 1997-Present.

Objective: To provide experienced OnLine Dynamic Server database and systems administrators with practical information on how to improve performance in the OnLine Dynamic Server environment.

Learning Outcome: Upon successful completion of this course, the student will be able to use the onstat, MSI, and oncheck utilities to monitor and tune performance; apply appropriate strategies for optimizing performance of data management tasks such as loading and indexing tables; optimize the creation of referential and integrity constraints; and manage and exploit the parallel database query (PDQ) capabilities of the OnLine Dynamic Server.

Instruction: Major topics covered in the course are monitoring utilities; optimizing load performance, index builds, and update statistics; fragmentation strategies; parallel data query and administration; and tuning client/server and distributed database environments. Methods of instruction include accelerated learning techniques, lecture, hands-on exercises, and the INFORMIX-OnLine Dynamic

Server Performance Tuning examination offered at Sylvan Prometric testing sites across the United States.

Credit Recommendation: In the upper division baccalaureate degree category, or graduate degree category, 2 semester hours in Computer Science, Computer Information Systems, or Management Information Systems (3/97). *Prerequisites:* The Managing and Optimizing INFORMIX-OnLine Dynamic Server Databases and INFORMIX-OnLine Dynamic Server System Administration courses, or equivalent knowledge, and experience using INFORMIX-OnLine Dynamic Server.

INFORMIX-OnLine Dynamic Server System Administration (388)

Location: Various sites in the United States.

Length: 5 days.

Dates: January 1997-Present.

Objective: To teach system administrators administration skills, including how to configure and maintain database servers, using INFORMIX-OnLine Dynamic Server.

Learning Outcome: Upon successful completion of this course, the student will be able to understand the OnLine Dynamic Server multi-threaded architecture; set up client/server connections; configure INFORMIX-OnLine Dynamic Server; set up a multiple residency environment; use OnLine Dynamic Server fault tolerance mechanisms; create and manage transaction logs; perform a system archive using the ontape utility; manage temporary tables and files; and use database utilities.

Instruction: Major topics covered in the course are multi-threaded architecture; server configuration; monitoring utilities; Parallel Database Query (PDQ); mode management and space management; log management; indexing, sorting, and temporary tables; event alarms; and troubleshooting using OnLine Dynamic Server. Methods of instruction include accelerated learning techniques, lecture, hands-on exercises, and the INFORMIX-OnLine Dynamic Server System Administration examination offered at Sylvan Prometric testing sites across the United States.

Credit Recommendation: In the upper division baccalaureate degree category, 2 semester hours in Computer Science, Computer Information Systems, Management Information Systems, or Database Management Systems (3/97). **NOTE:** Students completing both this course and Managing and Optimizing INFORMIX-OnLine Dynamic Server Databases (431) should receive 4 semester hours in the upper division baccalaureate degree category. *Prerequisites:* The Relational Database Design course or equivalent knowledge is required. Knowledge of UNIX System Administration is recommended.

Managing and Optimizing INFORMIX-OnLine Dynamic Server Databases (431)

Location: Various sites in the United States.

Length: 3 days.

Dates: March 1996-Present.

Objective: To teach database administrators and application developers how to create databases, tables, and indexes, and to use features that allow them to control security, maintain data integrity, maintain concurrency control, and improve performance using INFORMIX-OnLine Dynamic Server.

Learning Outcome: Upon successful completion of this course, the student will be able to create databases, tables, and indexes; create fragmented tables and indexes; implement Parallel Database Query (PDQ); create an indexing strategy to improve performance; implement referential and entity integrity; calculate extent sizes; and use database utilities.

Instruction: Major topics covered in the course are INFORMIX-OnLine Dynamic Server terminology, INFORMIX-OnLine Dynamic Server data types, database and table creation, fragmentation, indexing strategies, referential and entity integrity, modes and violation detection, data security, and INFORMIX-OnLine Dynamic Server data movement utilities. Methods of instruction include accelerated learning techniques, lecture, written exercises, and the Managing and Optimizing INFORMIX-OnLine Dynamic Server Databases examination offered at Sylvan Prometric testing sites across the United States.

Credit Recommendation: In the upper division baccalaureate degree category, 2 semester hours in Computer Science, Computer Information Systems, or Management Information Systems (3/97). *Prerequisite:* The Structured Query Language course, or equivalent knowledge, and experience using Informix products.

Relational Database Design (433) (433)

Location: Various sites in the United States.

Length: *Version 1:* 3 days; *Version 2:* 2 days.

Dates: *Version 1:* January 1996-July 1997; *Version 2:* July 1997-Present.

Objective: To provide students without prior database experience an introduction to relational database concepts and terminology.

Learning Outcome: Upon successful completion of this course, the student will be able to describe relational technology and its advantages; understand relational database design concepts and terminology; construct entity-relationship diagrams to model a business enterprise; understand data normalization forms and benefits; apply SQL constructs and referential integrity rules to your data model; and use SQL to create a database, tables, and indexes.

Instruction: Major topics covered in the course are entity-relationship concepts and terminology, entity-relationship diagrams, attribute specifications, data types, normalization, SQL statements for creating a database, data integrity, database schema creation, and data insertion and selection. Methods of instruction include accelerated learning techniques, lecture, hands-on and written exercises, and the Database Fundamentals examination offered at Sylvan Prometric testing centers across the United States.

Credit Recommendation: *Versions 1 and 2:* In the lower division baccalaureate/associate degree category, 2 semester hours in Computer Science, Computer Information Systems, Management Information Systems, or Database Management Systems (3/97) (10/97). **NOTE:** For students completing both Structured Query Language (107) and this course, the credit recommendation is 3 semester hours in the lower baccalaureate/associate degree category.

Structured Query Language (107)

Location: Various sites in the United States.

Length: *Version 1:* 2 days; *Version 2:* 3 days.

Dates: *Version 1:* February 1996-July 1997; *Version 2:* July 1997-Present.

Objective: To teach the Data Manipulation Language (DML) portion of Structured Query Language (SQL), including SELECT, INSERT, UPDATE, and DELETE.

Learning Outcome: Upon successful completion of this course, the student will be able to use SQL data manipulation statements to change the contents of a database; process simple and complex

SELECT statements including outer joins, subqueries, temporary tables, and unions; identify ways to optimize queries; define and use transactions; and understand the importance of concurrency control.

Instruction: Major topics covered in the course are single table SELECT statements; joins; INSERT, UPDATE, DELETE, LOAD, and UNLOAD statements; subqueries; the UNION operator; query optimization; concurrency control; and environment configuration files. Methods of instruction include accelerated learning techniques, lecture, hands-on and written exercises, and the Database Fundamentals examination offered at Sylvan Prometric sites across the United States.

Credit Recommendation: *Versions 1 and 2:* In the lower division baccalaureate/associate degree category, or in the upper division baccalaureate degree category, 1 semester hour in Computer Science, Computer Information Systems, Management Information Systems, or Database Management Systems (3/97) (10/97). **NOTE:** For students completing both Relational Database Design (433) and this course, the credit recommendation is 3 semester hours in the lower division baccalaureate/associate degree category. *Prerequisite:* The Relational Database Design course or equivalent knowledge.

Institute for Nuclear Medical Education

The Institute for Nuclear Medical Education (INME) provides education in the uses of radioactive materials in a medical environment. The school's courses are presented in an itinerant manner at various sites convenient to students.

Courses I through IV are specifically designed to qualify physicians for radioactive material licensure under 10 CFR 35 of the United States Nuclear Regulatory Commission and Agreement States. These courses (I-IV) may also be used by current or potential medical workers to meet the requirements for certification as medical Radiation Safety Officers (RSO). All courses are designed to address advancing technology and to meet continuing education needs of medical radiation workers.

INME is certified by the Colorado Commission on Higher Education (Private Schools Division) and the Accrediting Council for Continuing Education and Training (ACCET), which is listed by the United States Department of Higher Education. Its courses have also been approved for credits by the American Academy of Health Physicists.

The courses described below are arranged in the order of progression, I through VIII.

Source of official student records: Registry of Credit Recommendations, American Council on Education, One Dupont Circle, Washington, DC 20036-1193.

Additional information about the courses: College Credit Recommendation Service, American Council on Education, One Dupont Circle, Washington, DC 20036-1193.

I. Principles of Radiation Physics

Location: Various locations throughout the United States.

Length: 50 hours (4.5 days).

Dates: October 1986-Present.

Objective: To give the student an understanding of the physics of radioactive transformation, the nature of the radiations, the interaction of radiation with matter, radiation dosimetry, and basic principles of radiation protection.

Learning Outcome: Upon successful completion of this course, the student will be able to calculate activity versus time relationships; exposure rate versus distance from a gamma emitter of known activity; and shield thickness to alternate the radiation intensity to any given level.

Instruction: Major topics covered in the course are structure of matter; radioactive transformation; interaction of radiation with matter; radiation exposure and dose units; production of radionuclides; and radiological properties of commonly used radionuclides. Methods of instruction include lecture and discussion.

Credit Recommendation: In the upper division baccalaureate degree category, 3 semester hours in Radiation Physics (8/95). **NOTE:** This course would be suitable for users of radiation sources.

II. Medical Radiation Instrumentation

Location: Various locations throughout the United States.

Length: 50 hours (4.5 days).

Dates: October 1986-Present.

Objective: To give the student an understanding of the structure and principles of radiation detection systems.

Learning Outcome: Upon successful completion of this course, the student will be able to identify types and appropriate application of medical radiation detection systems; understand capabilities and limitation of radiation detection systems; understand and perform calibration of such systems; understand and calculate radiation exposure and dosage; and understand requirements of professional and regulatory documentation.

Instruction: Major topics covered in the course are history of radiation detection; description of principles of detection systems; and clinical aspects of radiation imagery. Methods of instruction include lecture and discussion.

Credit Recommendation: In the upper division baccalaureate degree category, 3 semester hours in Nuclear Science or Nuclear Engineering (8/95).

III. Medical Radiation Protection

Location: Various locations throughout the United States.

Length: 50 hours (4.5 days).

Dates: October 1986-Present.

Objective: To provide the student with an understanding of the biologic effects of radiation on cells, organs, and the total human body. The dose/effect relationship is explained and acute versus chronic exposures are delineated. The acute radiation syndrome and the related clinical conditions are covered along with appropriate federal regulations governing the clinical use of radioactive materials.

Learning Outcome: Upon successful completion of this course, the student will be able to understand the general and specific effects of radiation on living cells, tissues, and organs. Emphasis is placed on the dose/effect relationship, the chronic versus acute dosages and effects, and the overall clinical phenomena described by the acute radiation syndrome. Additionally, the students will understand genetic effects of radiation, the concepts of ALARA (As Low As Reasonably Achievable), and the federal regulations regarding clinical use of radioactive materials.

Instruction: Major topics covered in the course are effects of radiation on cells, tissues, organs, and the whole human body; the acute radiation syndrome and associated clinical conditions; genetic effects of radiation; and federal regulatory guidelines for use of radioactive materials in clinical environments. Methods of instruction include lecture and discussion.

Credit Recommendation: In the upper division baccalaureate degree category, 3 semester hours in Human Radiation Biology (8/95).

IV. Radiopharmaceutical Chemistry (Radiopharmaceuticals and Chemistry)

Location: Various locations throughout the United States.

Length: 50 hours (4.5 days).

Dates: October 1986-Present.

Objective: To provide the student with an in-depth knowledge of the physical, pharmacological, and chemical characteristics of medical radiotracers, their specific applications, and the federal standards that govern their use.

Learning Outcome: Upon successful completion of this course, the student will be able to understand the physical, pharmacological, and chemical characteristics of medical radiotracers, their respective generation, handling, and uses in clinical medicine. Additionally, the student will understand the biological methodologies of transport and systemic distribution of radiotracers and the various governmental regulatory guidelines.

Instruction: Major topics covered in the course are physical, pharmacological, and chemical characteristics of radiotracers; biological methodologies of transport; radiotracer generation and use in clinical environments; and governmental requirements for licensing for possession of radiopharmaceuticals. Method of instruction includes lecture and discussion.

Credit Recommendation: In the upper division baccalaureate degree or the graduate degree category, 3 semester hours in Radiopharmaceutical Chemistry (8/95).

V. Protection Against Biohazards in a Medical Imaging Environment

Location: Various locations throughout the United States.

Length: 24 hours (3 days).

Dates: October 1989-Present.

Objective: To provide the student with an understanding of the biological hazards encountered in a medical imaging environment and the ability to design a risk management program for such hazards.

Learning Outcome: Upon successful completion of this course, the student will be able to understand the biological hazards encountered in a medical imaging environment. Emphasis is placed on the responsibilities of a biological safety officer and associated risk assessment and risk management methodologies.

Instruction: Major topics covered in the course are biological hazards; biological hazards in medical imaging; responsibilities of biological safety officers; risk assessment and risk management; and methodologies for biohazards.

Credit Recommendation: In the upper division baccalaureate degree category, 1 semester hour in Special Topics in Biological Hazards (8/95).

VI. Radiation Safety and Regulatory Compliance

Location: Various locations throughout the United States.

Length: 24 hours (3 days).

Dates: January 1991-Present.

Objective: To give the student an understanding of the bases and regulatory requirements for the safe use of radioisotopes in the practice of nuclear medicine.

Learning Outcome: Upon successful completion of this course, the student will be able to perform quality assurance tests on the instruments used in nuclear medicine practice; record and maintain information required by the nuclear regulatory authorities; perform radiation safety surveys; and comply with radiation safety regulations.

Instruction: Major topics covered in the course are federal and state regulation, documentation requirements, quality assurance, and ALARA (As Low as Reasonably Achievable).

Credit Recommendation: In the upper division baccalaureate degree or the graduate degree degree category, 1 semester hour in Hospital Health Physics (8/95).

VII. Technical Aspects of Nuclear Cardiology

Location: Various locations throughout the United States.

Length: 24 hours (3 days).

Dates: January 1991-Present.

Objective: To give the student an understanding of the principles of the daily operations of a nuclear cardiology facility.

Learning Outcome: Upon successful completion of this course, the student will be able to perform necessary equipment calibrations and maintain required records for radiopharmaceutical quality assurance and personnel radiation dosimetry.

Instruction: Major topics covered in the course are equipment calibration and performance; radiopharmaceutical and quality assurance; and quality control of daily operations. Methods of instruction include lecture and discussion.

Credit Recommendation: In the upper division baccalaureate degree or the graduate degree category, 1 semester hour in Hospital Health Physics (8/95).

VIII. Development and Implementation of Nuclear Cardiology

Location: Various locations throughout the United States.

Length: 24 hours (3 days).

Dates: January 1991-Present.

Objective: To provide the student with an understanding of the specific requirements of a nuclear cardiology facility, its respective organization and design, equipment requirements, and associated performance criteria. Emphasis is also placed on the federal regulations that govern such facilities.

Learning Outcome: Upon successful completion of this course, the student will be able to understand the specific requirements of a nuclear cardiology facility, including its organization, equipment selection, and performance criteria. Additional information is provided on the federal regulations governing the licensing and reporting requirements of such facilities.

Instruction: Major topics covered in the course are nuclear cardiology facility design; nuclear cardiology facility equipment elucidation and selection; nuclear cardiology equipment performance criteria; and the Nuclear Regulatory Commission licensing process for nuclear cardiology facilities.

Credit Recommendation: In the upper division baccalaureate degree or the graduate degree category, 1 semester hour in Special Topics in Nuclear Cardiology (8/95).

Institute of Certified Professional Managers

The Institute of Certified Professional Managers, established in 1974, provides an opportunity for managers to attain the designation of CM (Certified Manager) by achieving passing scores on three examinations. In addition to this independent certification procedure, the Institute seeks to instill a commitment to lifelong learning in the management field through a formal recertification process.

Examinations cover administrative skills, interpersonal skills, and personal skills of managers and are given twice yearly (on the first Saturdays of May and December) at various locations in the United States and abroad. These examinations require demonstration of knowledge of management principles and practices in the areas of leadership, achievement of organizational objectives, motivation of subordinates, and general managerial behavior. Each examination contains 120 multiple-choice questions and takes two hours. All three need not be taken at one time and each may be taken again, if failed.

Since October 1982, preparatory courses appropriate to each of the three examinations have been available through the Institute.

Maintenance of the CM designation requires that proof of continued study in the field of management be presented at five-year intervals.

Source of official student records: Institute of Certified Professional Managers, James Madison University, Harrisonburg, VA 22807.

Additional information about the courses: College Credit Recommendation Service, American Council on Education, One Dupont Circle, Washington, DC 20036-1193.

Administrative Skills for the Manager

Location: Various; materials suitable for self-study, use by study groups, or in a formal course.

Length: Varies with mode of delivery; 20 hours (10 weeks) if a course.

Dates: October 1982-Present.

Objective: To prepare the student for Part II of a standardized examination on administrative skills of effective managers.

Learning Outcome: Upon successful completion of this course, the student will be able to understand legal, economic, and business influences on management; aspects of planning; organizational structure and staffing; control of operations; and the analysis and management of information.

Instruction: Major topics covered in the course are legal, economic, and business influences on management; planning; building organizational staff and structure; controlling; and management and analysis of information. Methods of instruction include study manual, lecture, discussion, and study questions, depending on mode of delivery. A *Leader's Guide*, which includes examples and illustrations, is available to assist individual learners, study group leaders, or instructors of more formal courses.

Credit Recommendation: In the upper division baccalaureate degree category, 1 semester hour in Principles of Management (Administrative Skills of Managers) (8/83) (4/88) (10/93). **NOTE**: Credit should be given only if the student passes the corresponding part of the Professional Managers Certification examination.

Interpersonal Skills for the Manager

Location: Various; materials suitable for self-study, use by study groups, or in a formal course.

Length: Varies with mode of delivery; 20 hours (10 weeks) if a course.

Dates: October 1982-Present.

Objective: To prepare the student for Part III of a standardized examination on interpersonal skills of effective managers.

Learning Outcome: Upon successful completion of this course, the student will be able to understand individual psychology and group dynamics; approaches to leadership that promote loyalty and cooperation; ways to motivate people to maximum potential; the roles of unions in society; and frameworks for human resource planning and management.

Instruction: Major topics covered in the course are management of human resources, understanding individual behavior, group dynamics, motivational theories, leadership, unions, management and communication, conflict causes and resolution, and effective utilization of human resources. Methods of instruction include study manual, lecture, discussion, and study questions depending on mode of delivery. A *Leader's Guide*, which includes examples and illustrations, is available to assist individual learners, study group leaders, or instructors of more formal courses.

Credit Recommendation: In the upper division baccalaureate degree category, 1 semester hour in Principles of Management (Interpersonal Skills of Effective Managers) (8/83) (4/88) (10/93). **NOTE**: Credit should be given only if the student passes the corresponding part of the Professional Managers Certification examination.

Personal Skills for the Manager

Location: Various; materials suitable for self-study, use by study groups, or in a formal course.

Length: Varies with mode of delivery; 20 hours (10 weeks) if a course.

Dates: October 1982-Present.

Objective: To prepare the student for Part I of a standardized examination on personal skills of effective managers.

Learning Outcome: Upon successful completion of this course, the student will be able to understand personal work situations; basic responsibilities of managers in organizations; the manager's role in supervision and achievement of organizational goals; and use key skills of managers (e.g., time management, communication, and delegation of authority).

Instruction: Major topics covered in the course are the manager as a person, a leader, a communicator, and a professional; creativity and change; the manager and time; decision making; delegation; and self-development. Methods of instruction include study manual, lecture, discussion, and study questions, depending on mode of delivery. A *Leader's Guide*, which includes examples and illustrations, is available to assist individual learners, study group leaders, or instructors of more formal courses.

Credit Recommendation: In the upper division baccalaureate degree category, 1 semester hour in Principles of Management (Personal Skills of Managers) (8/83) (4/88) (10/93). **NOTE**: Credit should be given only if the student passes the corresponding part of the Professional Managers Certification examination.

Institute of Certified Travel Agents

In the early 1960s, a nucleus of travel industry leaders recognized the growing need for organized learning in their field. A select group of national American Society of Travel Agents members formed an ad hoc Committee on Attaining Professionalism to study, then formulate a continuing education program for the travel agency sector of the industry. This was the genesis of the Institute of Certified Travel Agents, incorporated in 1964 as a new nonprofit institution with the mission of the pursuit of excellence through continuing education.

The Institute has changed over the years, but its mission has not. In the beginning the Institute was located on the campus of Michigan State University where, under the direction of Dr. Robert W. McIntosh, the education program, initially a series of (correspondence-type) courses, was started. Subsequently, offices were located in Washington, DC, Arlington, Virginia, and since 1974 in the suburban academic community of Wellesley, Massachusetts. The Institute has grown substantially: candidate enrollments have increased steadily; candidates and members are more diverse; the curriculum is richer; and the physical facilities greatly expanded. Yet the goals set by the founding Board back in 1964 are still the goals of the Institute now.

Today the Institute trains women and men for management careers in the travel industry.

While many are travel agency owners, managers, or travel counselors, others are airline sales executives or cruise, hotel, and other executives in the affiliated travel fields. The list also includes travel training directors and travel education curriculum planners.

Through its members, the name of the Institute of Certified Travel Agents and the symbol of accomplishment in the pursuit of excellence—the professional designation CTC (Certified Travel Counselor)—are known and respected throughout the United States.

Source of official student records: Registry of Credit Recommendations, American Council on Education, One Dupont Circle, Washington, DC 20036-1193 or Institute of Certified Travel Agents, 148 Linden Street, P.O. Box 82-56, Wellesley, MA 02181.

Additional information about the courses: Office of Corporate-Higher Education Programs, Thomas Edison State College, 101 West State Street, Trenton, New Jersey 08608-1176.

CTC Travel Management Program

Location: Various locations throughout North America and through independent study.

Length: *Version 1:* 150 hours (approximately), much of the course is self-paced and normally takes a year or more; *Version 2:* 200 hours (approximately), much is individually paced, and normally takes place over the time of a year or more.

Dates: January 1980-Present.

Objective: *Version 1:* To train individuals for management careers in the travel industry. *Version 2:* To provide an educational foundation and framework for a professional career in the travel industry.

Learning Outcome: *Version 1:* Upon successful completion of this program, the student will be able to define their market, create and implement a marketing plan; run an agency as a professional business; successfully manage travel staff; and understand the political, social, and economic implications of tourism. *Version 2:* Upon successful completion of this course, the student will be able to use effective written and oral communicative skills; define the nature of the travel industry and its components and create and implement a business plan; analyze the impact of global events on the travel industry, including political, social and economic issues; identify and emulate the skills of successful sales and service people; and implement effective leadership and management strategies.

Instruction: *Version 1:* Major topics covered in the program are the mastery of a five-part program that includes as one of its parts the Travel Management Project; four courses that provide candidates with a sound foundation in general travel management; a thorough understanding of the functional areas of management as they relate to the travel industry, including accounting, marketing, personnel, and business policy; an understanding of tourism as a social science; an introduction to business; the legal climate; office environment; management accounting; budgets; office risks; an introduction to management theory and practice; the personnel function in the travel industry; human resource development; understanding and managing employees; sales staff development; advanced management topics; marketing theory; market research; developing a marketing plan; advertising and public relations; and the geographic, economic, social, and cultural forces behind destination development. Method of instruction include a four-hour examination that not only tests candidates' knowledge but also their ability to apply that knowledge skillfully and completely to travel industry-related problems is given after completion of each course and a Travel Management Project which gives candidates the opportunity to combine theory and practice, they can do this by writing an original resource paper on an approved topic or by attending one of the Institute's management seminars and writing a substantive paper based on the seminar content. *Version 2:* Major topics covered in the program are the critical professional skills and in-depth industry knowledge they need to succeed in their chosen career and a thorough understanding of business communication skills, sales and marketing strategies, personnel and resource planning, and operations. Methods of instruction include the use of topical articles, case studies, role plays, and group discussions that relate the concepts to practical experiences relevant to the everyday work environment; four of the five required courses end with a comprehensive three-hour examination; and the Communications course requires a 10-20 page research paper and oral presentation.

Credit Recommendation: *Version 1:* In the upper division baccalaureate or lower division baccalaureate/associate degree category, 3 semester hours in Introduction to Travel and Tourism (the content of this course would be found in a social science department as part of the liberal arts program); 3 semester hours in Travel Industry Business Management; 3 semester hours in Travel Industry Marketing; and 3 semester hours in Travel Industry Sales (7/90). **NOTE:** Credit recommendations apply only when the student has completed the entire program and earned the CTC designation. Also, the review team noted that the minimum prerequisite for the CTC designation does not include completion of a college degree. Therefore, no attempt was made to view this academic work as pertaining to the graduate level. However, for any students who have already earned their baccalaureate degree before completion of the CTC designation, this report would not in any way prejudice a graduate school looking at the CTC work as applicable to graduate requirements. *Version 2:* In the upper division baccalaureate degree category or in the lower division baccalaureate/associate degree category, 3 semester hours in Introduction to Travel and Tourism; 3 semester hours in Travel Industry Management; 3 semester hours in Travel Industry Operations; and 3 semester hours in Travel Industry Sales (1/96).

Institute of Financial Education

Founded in 1922, the Institute of Financial Education provides multilevel professional education and training programs for both operations and management personnel of financial institutions. These programs are designed to help employees obtain the knowledge, skills, and attitudes needed for efficient functioning in the various departments of financial institutions.

Programs are delivered through correspondence instruction, in-company training, resident schools, and a network of local chapters throughout the United States. The credit recommendations for the courses listed below apply to the correspondence versions of the courses listed below. Students wishing to apply for credit for a correspondence study course have the option of taking a proctored final examination. Successful completion of the proctored examination is indicated on the student's record.

Students taking the courses listed below may qualify for Institute awarded certification based on seven specific job functions. Each individual award category includes course requirements in at least three categories—technical skills, sales and communication skills, and product knowledge. The current award categories available are Teller, Senior Teller, Financial Counselor, Financial Services Supervisor, Lending Associate, Lending Specialist, and Banking Operations Specialist.

Source of official student records: Registry of Credit Recommendations, American Council on Education, One Dupont Circle, Washington, DC 20036-1193 or Manager of Customer Service, The Institute of Financial Education, 55 West Monroe Street, Suite 2800 , Chicago, IL 60603.

Additional information about the courses: College Credit Recommendation Service, American Council on Education, One Dupont Circle, Washington, DC 20036-1193.

Accounting
1. Accounting Principles for Savings Institutions (004)
2. Accounting Practices for Savings Institutions (005)
(Formerly 1. Savings and Loan Accounting I) (Formerly 2. Savings and Loan Accounting II)

Location: Chapters throughout the United States.

Length: 48 hours (24 weeks).

Dates: July 1979-September 1993.

Objective: To introduce the accounting process in general terms for all employees of savings institutions.

Instruction: Major topics covered in the course are the basic aspects of the accounting process as applied to savings institutions, including the functions of bookkeeping, accounting, and auditing and their interrelationships, the definitions of cash accounting and accrual accounting systems, preparation and analysis of balance sheets, income statements, etc., the internal relationships among the departments of a savings institution as they affect information about transactions and the development of institutional statements, the concept of time value of money, and the specific accounting procedure related to the savings and lending functions. The course also covers the techniques necessary to perform many accounting procedures such as those for savings accounts, mortgage loans, payroll, etc. Methods of instruction include lecture, discussion, and classroom exercises.

Credit Recommendation: In the lower division baccalaureate/associate degree category, 3 semester hours in Accounting for Financial Institutions (7/85)(10/93). **NOTE:** To be eligible for credit, students must take both courses.

Business Math Review (064)

Location: Independent study by correspondence.

Length: 24 hours.

Dates: June 1983-Present.

Objective: To provide the student with a review of basic arithmetic operations as applied to business computational problems.

Learning Outcome: Upon successful completion of this course, the student will be able to reconcile bank statements; perform payroll and interest calculations; compute depreciation using several methods; compute percentage changes in accounts; use present value analysis; and solve co-insurance problems.

Instruction: Major topics covered are account reconciliation, payroll and interest calculations, present value tables, depreciation methods, and mortgage loan amortization. Methods of instruction include independent study by correspondence; or, in formal courses, lecture, discussion, classroom exercises, and final examination.

Credit Recommendation: In the lower division baccalaureate/associate degree category, 2 semester hours in Business Mathematics (7/85) (10/93). **NOTE:** To be eligible for academic credit, students must pass the proctored final examination.

Commercial Banking (081)

Location: Chapters throughout the United States.

Length: 24 hours (12 weeks).

Dates: December 1984-September 1993.

Objective: To provide the student with an examination of the organization, structure, and management of the commercial banking system within a deregulated environment.

Instruction: Major topics covered in the course are the elements of federal and state banking regulation. Explores bank mergers, branch banking, and interstate banking. Describes the components of assets and liability managements and their effect on bank profitability. Presents policies and practices relating to lending, investments, trust services, and international banking. Approved methods of instruction include independent study by correspondence. Also available in formal course.

Credit Recommendation: In the lower division baccalaureate/associate degree category, 1 semester hour in Banking or Finance (7/85) (10/93).

Commercial Law (043 & 044)
1. Commercial Law I (043)
2. Commercial Law II (044)

Location: Chapters throughout the United States.

Length: 48 hours (24 weeks).

Dates: July 1980-July 1991.

Objective: To acquaint the student with general concepts and principles of business law and to enable students to apply legal principles to business problems.

Instruction: Commercial Law I covers contract law and the law of personal and real property, insurance law, bankruptcy, mortgages, and landlord-tenant relationships. Commercial Law II covers commercial paper, partnerships, corporations, security, and secured transactions.

Credit Recommendation: In the lower division baccalaureate/associate degree category, 3 semester hours in General Business or Commercial Law (7/85) (10/93). **NOTE:** To be eligible for credit, student must complete both courses.

Commercial Lending for Savings Institutions (079)

Location: Chapters throughout the United States.

Length: 24 hours (12 weeks).
Dates: January 1983-September 1993.
Objective: To provide students with an introduction to Commercial Lending. The course provides a basic overview of terms, concepts, and techniques related to business lending.
Instruction: Major topics covered in the course are the economic and competitive factors that influence commercial lending, the components of major financial statements, presents an introduction to financial statement analysis, and credit analysis of the potential borrower, and loan administration including bankruptcy proceedings. Methods of Instruction Include lecture, discussion, and case analysis.
Credit Recommendation: In the lower division baccalaureate/associate degree category, 1 semester hour in Commercial Lending or Banking (7/85) (10/93).

Communication Skills for Business: Talking and Listening (066)

Location: Independent study by correspondence; or formal courses at various locations.
Length: 24 hours (12 weeks).
Dates: August 1975-Present.
Objective: To provide an understanding of the basic elements of communication and to introduce the skills necessary to interact in a business world.
Learning Outcome: Upon successful completion of this course, the student will be able to define communication, perception, nonverbal communication, listening, and conflict; analyze techniques of problem solving and effective choice of words; and explain effective listening and purpose of organizational communication skills.
Instruction: Major topics covered in the course are elements of interpersonal communications and discussion skills, speech communication and society, messages and meanings, feedback, nonverbal communication, attention and listening, decision making, barriers and breakdowns, persuasion, conflict, troubled talk, and skill building. Approved methods of instruction include independent study by correspondence. Also available in formal courses, lecture, discussion, small-group interaction, role playing, and final examination.
Credit Recommendation: In the lower division baccalaureate/associate degree category, 1 semester hour in Communications (4/77) (7/85) (10/93). **NOTE:** To be eligible for academic credit, students must pass the proctored final examination.

Consumer Lending (077)

Location: Independent study by correspondence; or, formal courses at various locations.
Length: 20 hours (10 weeks).
Dates: September 1981-Present.
Objective: To provide the student with an introduction to consumer credit and the various types of credit sources, different types of credit, laws and regulations, and the lending process.
Learning Outcome: Upon successful completion of this course, the student will be able to describe various forms of consumer loans; explain major regulations affecting consumer lending and the elements included in consumer loan applications; list the six credit considerations and characteristics of likely borrowers; discuss collection policies and how lenders can be protected from borrower bankruptcy; and know loan processing and underwriting, including the use of collateral.
Instruction: Major topics covered are credit sources, major regulations, credit granting considerations, collection policies, personal bankruptcy, loan processing and underwriting, and the use of collateral. Approved methods of instruction include independent study by correspondence. Also available in formal courses, lecture, discussion, classroom exercises, and final examination.
Credit Recommendation: In the lower division baccalaureate/associate degree category, 1 semester hour in Banking or Finance (7/85) (10/93). **NOTE:** To be eligible for academic credit, students must pass the proctored final examination.

Economics (082)

Location: Chapters throughout the United States.
Length: 24 hours (12 weeks).
Dates: February 1985-September 1993.
Objective: To introduce major economic terminology, concepts, and relationships and to survey the tools available to evaluate fundamental economic behavior.
Instruction: Major topics covered in the course are the basic concepts from both micro- and macro-economics, including supply and demand, competition, monopoly, oligopoly, scarcity and production, production costs, taxation, inflation, and unemployment. Emphasis is also placed on current economic issues such as international trade and monetary policy. The teaching methodology is lecture and discussion.
Credit Recommendation: In the lower division baccalaureate/associate degree category, 1 semester hour in Economics (7/85) (10/93).

Economics (024 & 025)
1. Economics I (024)
2. Economics II (025)

Location: Chapters throughout the United States.
Length: 48 hours (24 weeks).
Dates: September 1973-July 1985.
Objective: To provide students with an understanding of the basic terminology of economics and to familiarize them with the theories of choice, economic motivation, market structure, inflation, and unemployment.
Instruction: Major topics covered in the course are an introduction to supply and demand, scarcity and utilization of economic resources, the price system, and income and expenditure flow. Also covered are goals of full employment and price stability, investment and consumption, money and banking, monetary and fiscal policy, and theories of economic growth. Methods of instruction include lecture, discussion, and classroom exercises.
Credit Recommendation: In the lower division baccalaureate/associate degree category, 3 semester hours in Economics (7/85). **NOTE:** To be eligible for credit, student must complete both courses.

Effective Business Writing (018)

Location: Independent study by correspondence; or, formal courses at various locations.
Length: 24 hours (12 weeks).
Dates: September 1974-Present.
Objective: To provide an understanding of the concepts, form, and style used in writing effective business correspondence and reports.
Learning Outcome: Upon successful completion of this course, the student will be able to describe the three stages of the writing process; write complete, efficient sentences, and emphatic sentences; define readability; format a letter; construct a memo; and write an effective job procedure.
Instruction: Major topics covered in the course are principles of writing, punctuation, sentence structure; types of letters (friendly, bad news, persuasive requests, collection, and goodwill); effective reports; and direct requests. Approved methods of instruction include independent study by correspondence. Also avail-

able in formal courses, lecture, discussion, classroom exercises, and final examination.

Credit Recommendation: In the lower division baccalaureate/associate degree category, 1 semester hour in Business Writing, Business English, or Written Communications (4/77) (7/85) (10/93). **NOTE:** To be eligible for academic credit, students must pass the proctored final examination.

Effective Speaking (019)

Location: Chapters throughout the United States.

Length: 24 hours (12 weeks).

Dates: September 1984-September 1993.

Objective: To introduce fundamental speaking skills and to provide the student with practice to become an effective and confident speaker.

Instruction: Major topics covered in the course are barriers to communication with an audience, controlling stage fright, speech delivery, composing speeches, types of speeches, and group discussion. Students organize, present, and evaluate informative and persuasive speeches and speeches for special occasions.

Credit Recommendation: In the lower division baccalaureate/associate degree category, 2 semester hours in Communications (4/77) (7/85) (10/93).

Essential Business English Skills (017) (Formerly Basic Business English [017])

Location: Independent study by correspondence.

Length: 24 hours.

Dates: July 1982-Present.

Objective: To introduce the student to basic English grammar, spelling, and punctuation as applied to business writing.

Learning Outcome: Upon successful completion of this course, the student will be able to differentiate between complete and incomplete sentences; apply the rules governing punctuation, spelling, and capitalization; proofread material; and revise errors in format, grammar, mechanics, and usage.

Instruction: Major topics covered in the course are components of basic English including sentence structure, spelling, and punctuation; proper use of tense, subject-verb agreement, and analysis of the parts of speech; and punctuation and spelling. Methods of instruction include independent study by correspondence.

Credit Recommendation: In the lower division baccalaureate/associate degree category, 1 semester hour in Basic English (7/85) (10/93). **NOTE:** To be eligible for academic credit, students must pass the proctored final examination.

Financial Institutions (030 & 031) 1.Financial Institutions I (030) 2. Financial Institutions II (031)

Location: Chapters throughout the United States.

Length: 48 hours (24 weeks).

Dates: September 1972-July 1985.

Objective: To provide an understanding of financial agencies and institutions and the process involved in money and credit flow.

Instruction: Major topics covered in the course are financial and monetary institutions and their interrelationships with and influence on money and capital markets and examines corporate financial policies and practices as well as business and consumer finance. Methods of instruction include lecture and discussion. Course is also available through correspondence study.

Credit Recommendation: In the upper division baccalaureate degree category, 3 semester hours in Financial Institutions (4/77).

Financial Statement Analysis (073)

Location: Independent study by correspondence; or, formal courses at various locations.

Length: 24 hours (12 weeks).

Dates: September 1983-Present.

Objective: To introduce the concepts and techniques necessary to analyze financial statements of prospective borrowers.

Learning Outcome: Upon successful completion of this course, the student will be able to create and evaluate a balance sheet, an income statement, a statement of cash flow, use financial ratios; prepare debt evaluation analyses for prospective borrowers, and prepare a financial statement from income tax returns and interviews with prospective borrowers.

Instruction: Major topics covered in the course are the concepts of risk, profitability, solvency, liquidity, and leverage. The analytical techniques for examining income statements and for evaluating liability are studied. Flow-statements, financial ratios, pro forma statements, and cash budgets are explained in relation to financial analysis of business managed by prospective borrowers. Approved methods of instruction include independent study by correspondence. Also available in formal course.

Credit Recommendation: In the lower division baccalaureate/associate degree category, 1 semester hour in Finance (7/85) (10/93). **NOTE:** To be eligible for academic credit, students must pass the proctored final examination.

Housing Construction: Principles and Practices (033)

Location: Chapters throughout the United States.

Length: 24 hours (12 weeks).

Dates: November 1983-December 1988.

Objective: To provide an understanding of basic construction terminology and concepts and the construction techniques used in the production of housing.

Instruction: Major topics covered in the course are materials and construction techniques in all components of the housing structure, including floor, wall, and roof systems, interior and exterior finishes, heat control and insulation, passive heating and cooling, wiring, and plumbing. Lecture and discussion are used.

Credit Recommendation: In the lower division baccalaureate/associate degree category, 1 semester hour in Real Estate or Construction Principles (7/85).

Human Relations in Business (061)

Location: Independent study by correspondence; or, formal courses at various locations.

Length: 24 hours (12 weeks).

Dates: September 1975-Present.

Objective: To provide the student with an introduction to business psychology and personal adjustment.

Learning Outcome: Upon successful completion of this course, the student will be able to define human relations as it applies to an organization; recognize various communication styles and the effect of communication style bias; identify the steps in the motivational cycle and common causes of conflict; and set realistic goals for improving human relationships.

Instruction: Major topics covered in the course are the psychology of work; motivation theory; social interaction; personality development; conflict, frustration, and stress; self-awareness and behavior modification, and group dynamics. Approved methods of instruction include independent study by correspondence. Also available in formal courses, lecture, discussion, classroom exercises, and final examination.

Credit Recommendation: In the lower division baccalaureate/associate degree category, 2 semester hours in General Psychology or Organization Behavior (4/77) (7/85) (10/93). **NOTE:** To be eligible for academic credit, students must pass the proctored final examination.

Human Resources Management (067)

Location: Chapters throughout the United States.

Length: 24 hours (12 weeks).

Dates: August 1984-December 1988.

Objective: To introduce the various aspects of personnel management, including selection, training, and compensation. Emphasis is on the management of human resources in a changing society. The functions of human resources management are treated within the context of the savings institution.

Instruction: Major topics covered in the course are the basic principles of personnel management in a changing society. The selection process is examined as are such functions as training and compensation. The various aspects of the selection decision-making process are studied in light of needs and savings institutions.

Credit Recommendation: In the upper division baccalaureate degree category, 1 semester hour in Management or Personnel Management (7/85).

Income Property Lending (080)

Location: Chapters throughout the United States.

Length: 24 hours (12 weeks).

Dates: June 1983-September 1993.

Objective: To explain the considerations of the mortgage loan officer in negotiating, closing, and administering both construction and permanent loans on income properties.

Instruction: Covers the forms and documentation required for income property lending, project evaluation, borrower analysis, and the processes of loan negotiation, structuring, servicing, problem loan resolution, and loan workouts. Apartment buildings, office buildings, and shopping centers are considered, emphasizing market studies, appraisals, and financial ratios used with borrower and project evaluations. Methods of Instruction Include lecture and discussion.

Credit Recommendation: In the upper division baccalaureate degree category, 1 semester hour in Real Estate or Banking (7/85) (10/93).

Introduction to Electronic Data Processing (053)

Location: Chapters throughout the United States.

Length: 24 hours (12 weeks).

Dates: June 1984-February 1990.

Objective: To introduce the field of electronic data processing through a nontechnical survey of the capabilities of computers as applied to the needs of savings institutions and to familiarize the student with the breadth and depth of computer hardware and software appropriate to data processing needs in the savings field.

Instruction: Major topics covered in the course are (1) the components, capabilities, and limitations of computer systems, (2) the types of processing systems, (3) major developments in computer technology, (4) considerations in developing computer programs, (5) the concept of systems and program flowcharts, (6) the characteristics of storage devices, (7) computer security, and (8) direct applications of computer technology for the savings institution. The teaching methodology used is lecture, discussion, and classroom demonstration.

Credit Recommendation: In the lower division baccalaureate/associate degree category, 1 semester hour in Data Processing or Computer Science (7/85).

Introduction to the Savings Institution Business (060)

Location: Chapters throughout the United States.

Length: 24 hours (12 weeks).

Dates: September 1973-September 1993.

Objective: To provide an introductory understanding of the business world with an emphasis on the role of savings associations in that environment.

Instruction: Major topics covered in the course are forms of business organization, the modern business enterprise, the Federal Reserve and Federal Home Loan Bank systems, introduction to computer technology, securities markets, financial intermediaries, and the savings and investment processes. Emphasized throughout are the history and expansion of savings associations and the role of savings associations in the business community and society. Methods of Instruction Include lecture and discussion. Course is also available through correspondence study.

Credit Recommendation: In the lower division baccalaureate/associate degree category, 1 semester hour in Introduction to Business (4/77) (7/85) (10/93).

Managing Deposit Accounts and Services (009 & 008)
(009)
1. Deposit Account Operations
2. Deposit Accounts and Services (008)
(Formerly Savings Accounts Administration and Savings Accounts)

Location: Independent study by correspondence, or formal courses at various locations.

Length: 48 hours (24 weeks).

Dates: September 1974-Present.

Objective: To provide an understanding of the solicitation, maintenance, and administration of savings funds from a legal perspective.

Learning Outcome: Upon successful completion of this course, the student will be able to know the contractual nature and types of ownership of savings accounts; counsel depositors in deciding which accounts are appropriate to their needs; discuss FDIC deposit insurance; describe the concepts of yield, risk, and return; describe the procedure for handling dormant accounts, accounts of decedents, large currency transaction reports, and use of electronic funds transfers.

Instruction: Major topics covered in the course are analysis of the contractual and legal nature of savings accounts; types of ownership and types of deposit accounts, FDIC deposit insurance, loans secured by deposit accounts, dormant or inactive accounts, accounts of decedents, deposit account terminology, and additional deposit department services. Methods of instruction include independent study by correspondence. Also available in formal courses, lecture, discussion, classroom exercises, and final proctored examination.

Credit Recommendation: In the upper division baccalaureate degree category, 3 semester hours in Business Administration or Finance (4/77) (7/85) (10/93). **NOTE:** To be eligible for 3 semester hours of academic credit, student must complete both Deposit Account Operations and Deposit Accounts and Services, and pass the final examinations in both of these courses.

Marketing for Financial Institutions (063)

Location: Chapters throughout the United States.

Length: 24 hours (12 weeks).
Dates: January 1983-September 1993.
Objective: Provides the student with a basic introduction to marketing and explores applications of these concepts within a financial institution setting. Some of the topics presented in this course include marketing management, pricing, market planning, and marketing research.
Instruction: Major topics covered in the course are the external marketing environment and presents consumer behavior analysis. Identifies primary and secondary sources of market research information. Analyzes pricing decisions and the cost effectiveness of services. Describes the function and use of advertising, public relations, and personal selling within the financial services industry. Methods of Instruction Include lecture, discussion, case studies, and role playing.
Credit Recommendation: In the lower division baccalaureate/associate degree category, 1 semester hour in Financial Institutions Marketing or Banking (7/85) (10/93).

Money and Banking (030) (Formerly Financial Institutions)

Location: Chapters throughout the United States.
Length: 24 hours (12 weeks).
Dates: July 1985-September 1993.
Objective: To provide an understanding of financial agencies and institutions and the processes involved in money and credit flow.
Instruction: Major topics covered in the course are financial and monetary institutions and their interrelationships with and influence on money and capital markets; and corporate financial policies and practices, as well as, business and consumer finance. Methods of instruction include lecture and discussion.
Credit Recommendation: In the upper division baccalaureate degree category, 1 semester hour in Banking Financial Institutions (7/85) (10/93).

Mortgage Loan Servicing (029)

Location: Independent study by correspondence or formal courses at various locations.
Length: 24 hours (12 weeks).
Dates: June 1983-Present.
Objective: To cover the loan servicing function from the time of closing until final payment, focusing on the procedures used in the daily loan servicing operations.
Learning Outcome: Upon successful completion of this course, the student will be able to identify major historical and contemporary changes in loan servicing operations; list procedural steps used in servicing contract changes; compare various mortgage loan programs and describe how each affects loan servicing activities.
Instruction: Major topics covered in the course are organization of the loan servicing department, handling of escrow accounts, processing contract changes, the legal and economic effects of delinquency on the lender, handling of delinquencies, foreclosures, and real estate owned; alternative mortgage programs, FHA and VA loans, and secondary mortgage market activity as they pertain to the mortgage servicing function. Approved methods of instruction include independent study by correspondence. Also available in formal courses, lecture, discussion, classroom exercises, and final examination.
Credit Recommendation: In the lower division baccalaureate/associate degree or vocational certificate categories, 1 semester hour in Banking or Real Estate (7/85) (10/93). **NOTE:** To be eligible for academic credit, students must pass the proctored final examination.

Personal Financial Planning 1. Managing Your Money Today (828) 2. Planning Your Future Finances (829)

Location: Independent study by correspondence.
Length: 1. 12 hours; and 2. 12 hours.
Dates: July 1983-Present.
Objective: To provide the student with a basic introduction to personal money management with emphasis on credit management, insurance coverage, investment decisions, and estate planning.
Learning Outcome: Upon successful completion of this course, the student will be able to prepare and analyze personal financial statements; know advantages and costs of home ownership and the use of personal credit; explain, in general terms, personal income tax matters; describe various types of life, property, and health insurance; know the potential returns and risks of securities investments; and describe the sources of retirement income.
Instruction: Major topics covered in the course are inter-relating money management with personal assets, budgeting, and financial resources and goals; methods of insuring assets; property insurance, liability coverage, auto, health, and life insurance; investments and tax and estate planning; and effective money management strategies. Methods of instruction include independent study by correspondence. Note: The final examination for Personal Financial Planning consists of the final examinations for the two formal courses (828) and (829).
Credit Recommendation: In the lower division baccalaureate/associate degree category, 1 semester hour in Personal Finance (7/85) (10/93). **NOTE:** To be eligible for academic credit, students must complete either Personal Financial Planning by correspondence and pass the two final examinations.

Personal Investments (027)

Location: Chapters throughout the United States.
Length: 24 hours (12 weeks).
Dates: July 1985-September 1993.
Objective: Provides the student with basic techniques, vehicles, and strategies for implementing investment goals in a portfolio context. Explores the basic information needed to aid individual investors so that they can make sound investment decisions.
Instruction: Major topics covered in the course are the economic, market, and price function of different types of investment markets. Evaluates and contrasts the investment characteristics of debt securities, common and preferred stock, mutual funds, real estate, stock options, and commodities. Further applies fundamental and technical analysis to identify the proper timing of an investment decision. Methods of instruction include lecture, discussion, and case studies.
Credit Recommendation: In the upper division baccalaureate degree category, 1 semester hour in Investments (7/85) (10/93).

Principles of Management

Location: Chapters throughout the United States.
Length: 24 hours (12 weeks).
Dates: July 1984-September 1993.
Objective: To introduce the concept of management including planning, leading, organizing, and controlling an enterprise. Emphasis is on the relation of theory to practice as applied to savings institutions. Skills are practiced during applications to real situations.
Instruction: Major topics covered in the course are the fundamental principles of management. Topics covered are planning, and decision-making theory; the relationship among authority, responsibility, and power; the constructive use of conflict; and the benefits of improving productivity. Methods of instruction include

discussion and classroom exercises such as role playing, simulations, and case study analysis.

Credit Recommendation: In the upper division baccalaureate degree category, 1 semester hour in Business Administration or Management (7/85) (10/93).

Real Estate Law
1. Real Estate Law I (006)
2. Real Estate Law II (007)

Location: Independent study by correspondence; or formal courses at various locations.

Length: 48 hours (24 weeks).

Dates: July 1983-Present.

Objective: To provide the student with an introduction to legal principles governing real estate and real estate transactions and to the vocabulary basic to these matters.

Learning Outcome: Upon successful completion of this course, the student will be able to define the concepts of real estate involved in property ownership and transfer including easements, liens, deeds, brokerage, contracts, fraud and deceit; and, describe aspects of real estate closings, escrow, recording mortgages, land use and regulation, environmental law, fair housing law, and types of real estate investment.

Instruction: Major topics covered in Course 1 are the legal concept of land, estates in real property, land descriptions, the law of agency, contracts for the sale of land, deeds, closing the transaction, escrows, evidence of title, insurance, and co-ownership. Major topics covered in Course 2 are real estate financing instruments (use of existing mortgages, purchase money mortgages, wraparounds, and junior mortgages), the due-on-sale clause, installment contracts, ground leases, foreclosure and redemption, land use controls, condominiums, cooperatives, planned unit developments, rehabilitation, landlord-tenant relations, racial discrimination, and taxes. Approved methods of instruction include independent study by correspondence. Also available in formal courses, lecture, discussion, classroom exercises, and final examination.

Credit Recommendation: In the upper division baccalaureate degree category, 3 semester hours in Banking or Real Estate (7/85) (10/93). **NOTE:** To be eligible for credit, student must complete both courses.

Real Estate Principles

Location: Independent study by correspondence; or formal courses at various locations.

Length: 20 hours (10 weeks).

Dates: March 1991-December 1996.

Objective: To provide the participant with a foundation in the legal, economic, and governmental characteristics of real estate and introduce the study of real estate administration by examining the processes involved in making and implementing real estate decisions.

Learning Outcome: Upon successful completion of this course, the participant will be able to identify the factors that influence real estate value, explain property rights and ownership interests, list the elements of a valid real estate contract, explain the three methods of appraising real estate value, identify factors that affect real estate demand, and explain ways of reducing mortgage lending risks.

Instruction: Major topics covered in the course are economic characteristics of real estate, national and regional influences on real estate markets, property rights and ownership interests, real estate brokerage and legal aspects of the broker-client relationship, contracts in real estate transactions, title and legal descriptions, deeds and title closing, basic financial concepts, taxes affecting real estate, sources of real estate credit, real estate financing techniques, valuation of real estate, principles of real property insurance, and residential land use. Methods of instruction include independent study by correspondence; or, in formal courses lecture, discussion, classroom exercises, and final examination.

Credit Recommendation: In the lower division baccalaureate degree category, 1 semester hour in Real Estate Principles (10/93).

Real Estate Principles
1. Real Estate Principles I (015)
2. Real Estate Principles II (016)

Location: Independent study by correspondence; or formal courses at various locations.

Length: 48 hours (24 weeks).

Dates: September 1976-March 1992.

Objective: To provide the student with a foundation in the legal, economic, and governmental aspects of real estate.

Learning Outcome: Upon successful completion of this course, the student will be able to explain the legal, economic, and governmental characteristics of real estate; describe the administrative processes involved in making and implementing real estate decisions; and describe the characteristics of real estate resources, valuation principles, financial institutions and agencies, and mortgage lending.

Instruction: Major topics covered in the course are an examination of principles and practices of real estate relative to the savings association business; a study of real estate administration; the process of making and implementing real estate decisions; evaluation principles, analysis of locations; land us; subdivision and land development; property management; instruments of financing; mortgage lending; and urban and rural development. Methods of instruction include independent study by correspondence, or formal courses, lecture, discussion, classroom exercises, and a final examination.

Credit Recommendation: In the upper division baccalaureate degree category, 3 semester hours in Real Estate Principles (4/77) (7/85) (10/93). **NOTE:** To be eligible for credit, student must complete both courses.

Residential Appraising (013)

Location: Independent study by correspondence; or formal classes in various locations.

Length: 24 hours (12 weeks).

Dates: July 1979-December 1996.

Objective: To provide an introduction to the nature and purposes of residential appraisals, methods of analysis, approaches to value, and the important role played by appraisers.

Learning Outcome: Upon successful completion of this course, the student will be able to understand and describe how appraisers complete the seven basic steps of the evaluation process; identify data sources used by appraisers; prepare an acceptable form report; and explain different approaches to value determination.

Instruction: Major topics covered in the course are appraisal principles and the appraisal process, local economic analysis, housing markets and neighborhood analysis, site analysis, valuation, highest and best use, improvement analysis, the market comparison, cost and gross rent multiplier approaches to value estimation, and preparation of a short-form appraisal. Methods of instruction includes independent study by correspondence; or, in formal courses, lecture, discussion, classroom exercises, and final examination.

Credit Recommendation: In the lower division baccalaureate/associate degree category, 1 semester hour in Real Estate (7/85) (10/93). **NOTE:** To be eligible for academic credit, students must pass the proctored final examination.

Residential Mortgage Lending (011)

Location: Independent study by correspondence; or formal classes in various locations.

Length: 24 hours (12 weeks).

Dates: July 1981-Present.

Objective: To provide the student an overview of the mortgage loan process, including originating, processing, and servicing various types of residential mortgage loans.

Learning Outcome: Upon successful completion of this course, the student will be able to understand and explain key regulations and laws governing the residential mortgage loan process; summarize the routine and special operations of mortgage loan servicing; and describe procedures lenders use to address losses in collections and foreclosures.

Instruction: Major topics covered in the course are the regulations and laws governing residential mortgage lending, analysis of risk and appraisals in residential mortgage lending, the origination, closing, servicing, foreclosure, and workouts of residential mortgage loans, types of loans including FHA/VA loans, and the secondary mortgage market. Approved methods of instruction include independent study by correspondence. Also available in formal courses, lecture, discussion, classroom exercises, and final examination.

Credit Recommendation: In the lower division baccalaureate/associate degree category, 1 semester hour in Banking or Real Estate (7/85) (10/93). **NOTE**: To be eligible for academic credit, students must pass the proctored final examination.

Retirement Plans (816)
1. Individual Retirement Accounts/Keogh Plans (076)
2. NOW Accounts

Location: Chapters throughout the United States.

Length: 24 hours (12 weeks).

Dates: June 1984-December 1988.

Objective: (1) Provides the student with background knowledge of IRA, SEPPs, and Keogh accounts. The course reflects eligibility requirements and contribution limits of the Tax Equity and Fiscal Responsibility Act of 1982. (2) Provides the student with an examination of the history and development of NOW accounts and their legal requirements. Describes the check clearing system, endorsements, and methods of interest calculation.

Instruction: (1) Major topics covered in the course are the major legislation authorizing IRAs and Keogh accounts. Describes the legal relationships created under pension plans and their documentation. Presents tax benefits and penalties, customer eligibility, fiduciary responsibilities, and reporting requirements for retirement accounts. (2) Major topics covered in the course are the elements of NOW accounts and their legal re-quirements. Describes the role of the Fed-eral Reserve, correspondent banks, and the Federal Home Loan Bank in the clearing of NOW drafts. Further explores check processing and the role of NOW account department personnel. Methods of instruction include lecture, discussion, and case studies.

Credit Recommendation: In the vocational certificate category, 1 semester hour in Banking (7/85). **NOTE:** To be eligible for credit, students must complete both courses.

Savings Institution Operations (Formerly Savings Association Operations [062])

Location: Chapters throughout the United States.

Length: 24 hours (12 weeks).

Dates: June 1977-September 1993.

Objective: To introduce the role of savings association in the modern business world with emphasis on theory and practice of internal operations.

Instruction: Major topics covered in the course are the savings function; operations of the savings department; the lending function; operations of the loan department, additional association services; accounting operations; internal auditing, electronic data processing, and other support services; personnel functions and processes; marketing elements and concepts; and management principles in action. Lecture and discussion are used.

Credit Recommendation: In the lower division baccalaureate/associate degree category, 2 semester hours in General Business (4/77) (7/85) (10/93).

Supervisory Personnel Management (047 & 048)
1. Supervisory Personnel Management I: Building Work Relationships (047)
2. Supervisory Personnel Management II: Maximizing your Effectiveness (048)

Location: Independent study by correspondence, or formal courses at various locations.

Length: Independent study (3 lessons covering 10 units in each course); formal courses (20 hours over 10 weeks in each course for a total of 40 hours/20 weeks.

Dates: July 1982-Present.

Objective: To provide new and potential supervisory personnel with the basic knowledge and skills necessary to function as effective supervisors.

Learning Outcome: Upon successful completion of this course, the student will be able to exhibit personal qualities of effective supervisors; describe reasons employees welcome or resist change; describe ways to increase productivity; apply effective interview and listening techniques; develop methods for staff training; describe steps in solving complex problems; conduct employee performance appraisals; recognize and avoid pitfalls in performance appraisal; demonstrate stress and time management skills; and apply techniques of long-range career planning for employees.

Instruction: Major topics covered in the course are managing change; increasing productivity, leadership, and listening skills; influencing group dynamics; delegating decision making; working with authority; motivating and training staff; time management; disciplining employees; dealing with stress; and career development. Approved methods of instruction include independent study by correspondence. Also available in formal courses include lecture, discussion, classroom exercises, case studies, role playing, handouts, and final examination.

Credit Recommendation: In the lower division baccalaureate/associate degree category, 3 semester hours in Management, Personnel, or Supervision (4/77) (7/85) (9/94).

Techniques for Customer Counseling (072)

Location: Independent study by correspondence; or formal classes in various locations.

Length: 24 hours (12 weeks).

Dates: July 1980-June 1997.

Objective: To introduce the student to skills and methods of effective customer counseling with regard to financial matters.

Learning Outcome: Upon successful completion of this course, the student will be able to define financial need, climate, and values; list the four dimensions of interpersonal communications; explain three ways to help customers make good financial decisions; and demonstrate effective interviewing techniques.

Instruction: Major topics covered in the course are counseling and advising techniques; description of how values, beliefs, and attitudes affect the purchase decision; the importance of verbal and nonverbal communication and effective listening skills; and cross-selling techniques useful to a financial counselor. Approved methods of instruction include independent study by correspondence. Also available in formal courses, lecture, discussion, classroom exercises, and final examination.

Credit Recommendation: In the lower division baccalaureate/associate degree category, 1 semester hour in Sales, Banking, or Counseling (7/85) (10/93). **NOTE:** To be eligible for academic credit, students must pass the proctored final examination.

Institute of International Studies

The Perspectives Study Program course was initially developed as the Summer Institute of International Studies, offered in Wheaton IL in 1974. The Institute of International Studies works to develop training opportunities for those who serve in voluntary agencies, especially those focused on developing nations. The course is designed to equip students with the foundation needed to help them effectively and strategically participate in the complex tasks of culturally relevant international development. Students are given understanding and equipped to respond to the biblical challenge to meeting needs including those physical, intellectual, and spiritual needs found in various societies in the world. A textbook was produced for the course in 1981, Perspectives on the World Christian Movement. It is the most widely used text in colleges and graduate schools for students focusing on the Christian mission. Over 100,000 of these volumes have been sold. The text was revised in 1992 and the accompanying Study Guide has been updated as of 1995. Many who serve in voluntary agencies have benefitted from the course, with over 25,000 alumni since its inception. Most students do not intend immediate cross-cultural service, but are able to use the course as a foundation for further training or involvement with internationals locally. Courses are offered by extension in over 60 locations in the U.S. each year, by trained coordinators who bring together a series of expert guest lecturers to present course topics. Information about courses planned is available from the Perspectives National Office.

Source of official student records: Registry of Credit Recommendations, American Council on Education, One Dupont Circle, Washington, DC 20036-1193.

Additional information about the courses: College Credit Recommendation Service, American Council on Education, One Dupont Circle, Washington, DC 20036-1193.

Perspectives on the World Christian Movement

Location: Various locations throughout the United States.

Length: 15 weeks, 3 hours per week, 45 total hours.

Dates: September 1985-Present.

Objective: To provide the student with the necessary perspective for effective participation in the complex task of world evangelization and international development.

Learning Outcome: Upon successful completion of this course, the student will be able to explore new avenues and opportunities available for obedience to God's imperative for involvement in world missions from at home or abroad.

Instruction: Major topics covered in the course are the Biblical rationale and imperative for world evangelization; unique problems and skills involved in communicating the gospel cross-culturally; the expansion of the christian movement across the world from the time of Christ to the present, and the task yet to be accomplished; and the basic components necessary for strategic and intelligent planning in the missionary task of the Church. Methods of instruction include lecture, discussion, audio material, independent study, and examinations.

Credit Recommendation: In the upper division baccalaureate degree category 3 semester hours in Missions, Religion, Bible, Christianity, or Theology (9/95).

Institute of Logistical Management

The Institute of Logistical Management recently celebrated its 70th year of continuous operation, providing specialized education to students interested in pursuing a career in the field of transportation and materials management.

The Institute first opened its doors as an educational institution on September 27, 1923. Mr. George Rottenburg, a rate clerk for the Rock Island Railroad, began the first school ever to teach a curriculum in Transportation management. Originally known as the College of Advanced Traffic, it all started in downtown Chicago. In 1929, a second school was opened in New York City in 1929. This school operated as the Academy of Advanced Traffic for over 57 years. Both schools operated in tandem while servicing over 83,000 students. The large number of Academy and College and now the Institute of Logistical Management graduates help to provide a wonderful pool of qualified graduates that enter into the transportation industry each year. Due to the major changes rendered by the De-regulation of the Transportation Industry in 1980, the names of the Academy and College of Advanced Traffic were changed to The Institute of Logistical Management.

The success of the Institute is due to its ability to build a solid reputation on the concept of practical training, an experienced instructional staff, and development of their own text and workbook materials. This process is carried on today by virtue of materials still being developed by the schools' staff and professionals working within the transportation industry. The purpose is to provide the home study student with suitable experiences that best emulates the kinds of situations and activities that occur within the transportation and materials management departments of the Fortune 500 companies.

It is from this point that the Institute is ready to provide the type of learning required to catapult its students into job demands put upon them as they enter into the next century.

For additional information, contact the Registrar's Office, Institute of Logistical Management, 819 Meetinghouse Road, Cinnaminson, NJ 08077.

Source of official student records: Registry of Credit Recommendations, American Council on Education, One Dupont Circle, Washington, DC 20036-1193.

Additional information about the courses: Office of Corporate-Higher Education Programs, Thomas Edison State College, 101 W. State Street, Trenton, NJ 08608-1176.

Business Logistics Management

Location: Various locations throughout the United States.

Length: 130 hours (Correspondence).

Dates: August 1990-December 1997.

Objective: To give the students an understanding of the role of logistics in a marketing-oriented society and to provide an opportunity for comprehensive analysis and discussion of key contemporary problems in logistics.

Learning Outcome: Upon successful completion of this course, the student will be able to understand the role of logistics in national and multinational business and government activity; understand the characteristics of logistics elements and their interrelationships within individual companies; develop analytical and problem-solving skills necessary to develop solutions for a variety of logistics problems; and learn to recognize areas in which logistics can be improved.

Instruction: Major topics covered in the course are the distribution systems, order entry, materials handling, storage systems, public and private warehousing, distribution center analysis, price and service selection, information retrieval, customer service, techniques of negotiation, and rate structure versus cost of service.

Credit Recommendation: In the lower division baccalaureate/associate degree category, 3 semester hours in Business Logistics Management (9/90).

Business Logistics Principles

Location: Independent Study (National & International).

Length: 150 hours.

Dates: September 1996-Present.

Objective: To give the student an understanding of the role of logistics in business and society and to provide an opportunity for comprehensive analysis of key contemporary problems in logistics.

Learning Outcome: Upon successful completion of this course, the student will be able to understand the role of logistics in national, multinational business and government activity; understand the characteristics of logistics elements and their interrelationships within the supply chain; develop analytical problem solving skills necessary to develop and analyze solutions for a variety of logistical problems; and recognize areas in which logistics can be improved.

Instruction: Major topics covered in the course are the logistics system, supply chain management, inbound logistics, outbound logistics, customer service, inventory management, warehousing, transportation management, operations management, materials handling, order processing, packaging, and organization. Methods of instruction include independent study, course manual, textbooks, projects and proctored exams.

Credit Recommendation: In the lower division baccalaureate/associate degree category, 3 semester hours in Logistics Principles (4/97).

Business Logistics System Analysis

Location: Independent Study (National & International).

Length: 150 hours.

Dates: September 1996-Present.

Objective: To give the student an understanding of today's complex logistics system and an exposure to the decision techniques used to analyze contemporary logistics problems.

Learning Outcome: Upon successful completion of this course, the student will be able to understand the overall logistics system and its interrelated functional areas; develop analytical and problem solving skills necessary for a variety of logistical problems; and learn leading-edge logistics strategies.

Instruction: Major topics covered in the course are supply chain management, channels of description, inventory decision making techniques, transportation management, information systems, network design, facility location, global logistics and logistics strategy. Methods of instruction include independent study, course manual, textbooks, projects and proctored exams.

Credit Recommendation: In the lower division baccalaureate/associate degree category, or in the upper division baccalaureate degree category, 3 semester hours in Logistics System Analysis (4/97).

Export/Import Transportation and Documentation

Location: Various locations throughout the United States.

Length: 300 hours (Correspondence).

Dates: March 1987-December 1997.

Objective: To familiarize the student with the tariff schedules of the U.S. Annotated (TSUSA) and its concept, format, and utilization; to differentiate the types of import entries under U.S. Customs regulations and how they relate to customs entries; to focus on new methods of marketing a company's products overseas; and to develop new techniques and valuations concerning importation concepts and procedures.

Learning Outcome: Upon successful completion of this course, the student will be able to work with and identify most of the terms and language in a policy covering marine insurance; recognize the need for transportation documentation on international shipments and develop familiarity with their preparation and use; develop a practical approach to documentation; and develop a practical application of a complete import and re-export entry.

Instruction: This course provides students with proper techniques in foreign commerce through a proper understanding of the basic tools and terminology, the techniques of import-export, the requirements of governmental agencies, and the method of identifying and entering export markets. This course will thoroughly cover the terms of sale, banking and financial documents, marine insurance, and commercial invoices.

Credit Recommendation: In the lower division baccalaureate/associate degree category, 6 semester hours in Export and Import Transportation and Documentation (9/90).

General Business for Transportation Management

Location: Various locations throughout the United States.

Length: 130 hours (Correspondence).

Dates: January 1989-December 1997.

Objective: To enable business personnel, who desire current knowledge and background on business, to pass the American Society of Traffic and Logistics (AST&L) examination which is given on a yearly basis.

Learning Outcome: Upon successful completion of this course, the student will be able to have up-to-date knowledge on business economics, marketing, finance, and the interaction of government with business. These subjects will enhance the student's success on passing the AST&L examination.

Instruction: This course is designed to provide the student with the broad background in economics, business organization, and finance in connection with the examination given by the American Society of Traffic and Logistics.

Credit Recommendation: In the lower division baccalaureate/associate degree category, 3 semester hours in Survey of Business (9/90).

Global Logistics Management

Location: Independent Study (National & International).

Length: 150 hours.

Dates: February 1997-Present.

Objective: To give students an understanding of the role of logistics in international business; a comprehension of the functional areas involved in global logistics; and an awareness of the various international transportation carriers, intermediaries, and facilities available to the shipper.

Learning Outcome: Upon successful completion of this course, the student will be able to understand the role of logistics in global business; understand the economics and service characteristics of international transportation providers; understand government's role, documentation and terms of sale used in global business; and know the fundamentals of effective management of exporting and importing.

Instruction: Major topics covered in the course are the government's role in global logistics; the global logistics environment; ocean and air transportation; transportation to Canada and Mexico; intermediaries; documentation and insurance; and exporting. Methods of instruction include independent study, course manual, textbooks, case studies, projects, quizzes and proctored exams.

Credit Recommendation: In the upper division baccalaureate degree category, or in the lower division baccalaureate/associate degree category, 3 semester hours in Logistics (4/97).

Hazardous Materials Compliance

Location: Independent Study (National & International).

Length: 135 hours.

Dates: April 1997-Present.

Objective: To enable students to access, know and apply the Department of Transportation requirements on shipping hazardous materials, thereby assuring strict and complete compliance with the federal regulations.

Learning Outcome: Upon successful completion of this course, the student will be able to understand the importance and consequence of adherence to the federal regulations on hazardous materials; demonstrate competence in accessing and using the governing regulations by successful completion of the class work activities and testing; accurately check the required shipping paper information on hazardous materials shipments; and know the current Department of Transportation regulations on hazardous materials.

Instruction: Major topics covered in the course are an overview of Department of Transportation Hazardous Materials Regulations; the Regulatory Authority; the Federal Regulations, hazardous materials shipping pager requirements, packaging requirements. Methods of instruction include independent study, course manual, textbooks, case studies, projects, and proctored exams.

Credit Recommendation: In the upper division baccalaureate degree category, or in the lower division baccalaureate/associate degree category 3 semester hours in Hazardous Materials (4/97).

Industrial Traffic Manager

Location: Various locations throughout the United States.

Length: 130 hours (Correspondence).

Dates: March 1987-December 1997.

Objective: To present business logistics to the student as a total cost and movement concept so coordinated that total costs are minimized while producing the customer service levels desired.

Learning Outcome: Upon successful completion of this course, the student will be able to show how to achieve handling the right quantity at the right place, at the right time, at the right cost, and in good condition; demonstrate the major factors considered in carrier rate making, including the concept of differential pricing; demonstrate the various uses of computer applications in specific situations and the basic criteria required for the selection of the appropriate hardware and software.

Instruction: This course is designed for managers and persons aspiring to advance in transportation, marketing, or materials management with industrial companies or carriers. It provides an extensive overview of transportation and its relationship to the corporate structure.

Credit Recommendation: In the lower division baccalaureate/associate degree category, 3 semester hours in Industrial Traffic Management (9/90). **NOTE:** This credit recommendation applies only if students also complete the course entitled Transportation Law and Regulatory Reform.

Interstate Commerce Law and Practice

Location: Various locations throughout the United States.

Length: 300 hours (Correspondence).

Dates: February 1989-December 1997.

Objective: To enable students to develop the concept of regulation of interstate transportation and establish understanding and knowledge of the Interstate Commerce Commission Act, and to develop the knowledge of practice before the Interstate Commerce Commission.

Learning Outcome: Upon successful completion of this course, the student will be able to take the Interstate Commerce Commission's Examination for Admission to Practice; take Examination No. 4 of the American Society of Transportation and Logistics.

Instruction: This course teaches that although the transportation industry has been deregulated, no substantive changes have taken place in the law that have lessened its power of enforcement. It defines what parties are subject to the act and the extent to which the Interstate Commerce Commission has jurisdiction over transportation.

Credit Recommendation: In the upper division baccalaureate degree category, 3 semester hours in Interstate Commerce Law and Practice (9/90).

Loss and Damage I & II

Location: Various locations throughout the United States.

Length: 300 hours (Correspondence).

Dates: October 1989-December 1997.

Objective: To enable students to become more proficient in working with loss and damage claims, thereby saving the company any lost income through prevention of these situations or through recovery of monies due them.

Learning Outcome: Upon successful completion of this course, the student will be able to demonstrate a knowledge of the many complex legal questions of damage measurement, special damages, consequential damages, bailments, and conversion.

Instruction: This course provides specialized treatment of an important traffic function. It covers the principles of claims and proper procedures to be applied by shippers and carriers in loss, damage, or overcharge situations. The basic laws of carrier liability are explained and illustrated by leading cases.

Credit Recommendation: In the lower division baccalaureate/associate degree category, 3 semester hours in Loss and Damage (9/90). **NOTE:** The student must complete both courses in order to acquire the credit.

The Transportation System

Location: Independent Study (National & International).

Length: 150 hours.

Dates: September 1996-Present.

Objective: To give students an understanding of the role of transportation in business and society, an awareness of the various forms of transportation available to the shipper, and a comprehension of the economic and service characteristics of the different forms of carriage.

Learning Outcome: Upon successful completion of this course, the student will be able to understand the role of transportation in the economy, the demand for transportation, and the role of government; develop an awareness of the economics and service characteristics of basic modes of transportation, as well as, intermodal and special carriers; and develop an economic foundation of the transportation system to permit effective management of a company's transportation process.

Instruction: Major topics covered in the course are transportation in the economy, demand for transportation regulations and public policy, and economic and service characteristics of motor carriers, railroads, air carriers, pipelines, intermodal, special carriers and international transportation. Methods of instruction include independent study, course manual, textbooks, case studies, projects and proctored exams.

Credit Recommendation: In a lower division baccalaureate/associate degree category, 3 semester hours in Introduction to Transportation (4/97).

Transportation Law and Regulatory Reform

Location: Various locations throughout the United States.

Length: 130 hours (Correspondence).

Dates: November 1989-December 1997.

Objective: To provide students with an understanding of the federal transportation regulatory system through knowledge of the Constitution, the Interstate Commerce Commission Act, and the Administrative Procedure Act.

Learning Outcome: Upon successful completion of this course, the student will be able to understand the extent of the jurisdiction of the Interstate Commerce Commission over commerce; analyze and brief statements of cases brought before the Commission; rely upon the causes of actions and determine how the decisions were made; and develop an understanding of the remedies available to the aggrieved party, the penalties for violation of the laws, and how enforcement is achieved.

Credit Recommendation: In the lower division baccalaureate/associate degree category, 3 semester hours in Industrial Traffic Management (9/90). **NOTE:** This credit recommendation applies only if the student also completes Industrial Traffic Management.

Transportation Management

Location: Independent Study (National & International).

Length: 145 hours.

Dates: September 1996-Present.

Objective: To give students an understanding of the transportation management process in business and society; to instill an awareness of the various functions performed by shippers, and to help the student comprehend the decision making skills required to manage today's transportation process.

Learning Outcome: Upon successful completion of this course, the student will be able to understand the transportation management and business logistics processes, including the carrier-shipper interactions and transportation pricing; develop an economic foundation of the cost and service components of transportation pricing, private transportation and carrier operations; and comprehend the managerial implications of carrier negotiations, total quality management and future transportation directions.

Instruction: Major topics covered in the course are business logistics, transportation management, transportation costing and pricing, transportation rate making, carrier negotiations, carrier operations and terminals, private transportation, total quality management and future transportation directions. Methods of instruction include independent study, course manual, textbooks, case studies, projects, and proctored exams.

Credit Recommendation: In a upper division baccalaureate degree category, or in the lower division baccalaureate/associate degree category, 3 semester hours in Transportation Management (4/97).

Transportation Pricing, Theory and Practice I & II

Location: Various locations throughout the United States.

Length: 300 hours (Correspondence).

Dates: March 1989-December 1997.

Objective: *Pricing Theory I:* To introduce the student to carrier pricing schedules and carrier tariffs used by the transportation industry. *Pricing Theory II:* To explore the full scope of the transportation plant and its services as a necessary preliminary to the economic use of the transportation system in the United States.

Learning Outcome: Upon successful completion of the two courses, the student will be able to: *Pricing Theory I:* identify and select the proper carrier whether an ltl, tl, or small shipments carrier to deliver a company's goods; understand the legal principles of contract negotiations and to highlight the basic requirements of a binding, bilateral contract of carriage; prepare the necessary legal documents required by law to record the dealings between shippers and carriers, i.e., the bill of lading and a freight bill or manifest; *Pricing Theory II:* understand the concepts of demurrage, transit privileges, storage, stop-offs, etc.; understand the underlying purpose behind the establishment of the many types of transit services offered by the carrier and learn how to properly price these services; effectively choose a proper household goods carrier, a proper broker, and a third party contractor in order to secure needed services for their respective companies.

Instruction: *Pricing Theory I*: This course teaches fundamental procedures of traffic management from the viewpoint of on-the-job requirements in the field. It provides training and practice in freight classification; tariff interpretation and selection; rate checking techniques; zip code pricing; contracts and negotiations; routing and other elements of every day incidences in the transportation department. *Pricing Theory II*: This course is concerned with more advanced aspects of traffic management techniques of rate construction and tariff compilation. Freight rate relationships are studied by use of the tariff publications which express them. Terminal facilities and switching; demurrage and storage; reconsignment and diversion; transit; and embargoes are similarly treated in this course.

Credit Recommendation: In the lower division baccalaureate/associate degree category, 3 semester hours in Transportation Pricing or 3 semester hours in a Transportation elective (9/90). **NOTE:** The student must complete both courses in order to acquire the credit.

Warehousing

Location: Various locations throughout the United States.

Length: 130 hours (Correspondence).

Dates: March 1987-December 1997.

Objective: To provide the student with a managerial overview of warehousing with a practical-oriented look at how to locate, design, staff, and operate a warehouse.

Learning Outcome: Upon successful completion of this course, the student will be able to differentiate between productivity and performance; identify the elements related to space utilization; develop locations of new warehouses using a grid technique; and identify the different types of bonded warehouses.

Instruction: This course is designed to familiarize the student with the role of the warehousing function and the economy, and its relationship to the transportation function. Details are provided in warehousing operations, inventory control, "Just-In-Time"; layout; the proper uses of storage and handling equipment; packaging; labor and productivity cost controls; and to look at the options of using either a private or public warehouse facility.

Credit Recommendation: In the lower division baccalaureate/associate degree category, 1 semester hour in Warehousing (9/90).

Warehousing Management

Location: Independent Study (National & International).

Length: 130 hours.

Dates: September 1996-Present.

Objective: To provide the student with managerial overview of warehousing and programmatic approach to locate, design, staff, and operate a warehouse.

Learning Outcome: Upon successful completion of this course, the student will be able to differentiate between productivity and performance; identify the elements related to space utilization; develop locations for new warehousing using a grid technique; and Identify the different types of bonded warehousing.

Instruction: Major topics covered in the course are the role of the warehousing function in the economy and its relationship to the logistics function. Major topics covered in the course are:warehousing operations; inventory control; "just in-time" systems; layout; materials handling equipment; packaging, labor and productivity; cost controls, and private vs. public warehousing. Methods of instruction include independent study, course manual, textbooks, projects and proctored exams.

Credit Recommendation: In the upper division baccalaureate degree category, or in the lower division baccalaureate/associate degree category, 2 semester hours in Warehousing (4/97).

Institute of Management and Production

The Institute of Management and Production (IMP) is a Human Resource Development Institution that provides a wide range of management services and training programs to companies and other organizations in both the private and public sectors of the economy.

IMP has, as its primary objective, the improvement of organizational capability with emphasis on the improvement of proficiency, productive performance, and personal growth of people.

IMP works closely with companies to help them to analyze the factors contributing to performance levels and assist them in finding solutions to the problems of low productivity.

Following a formal as well as informal needs assessment of its primary target group—companies in the business community—professional staff of the Institute initiate and develop particular programs for which they identify appropriate instructors. On occasion a particular course may be developed by adjunct faculty and found suitable for implementation in the Institute's program.

The Institute of Management and Production operates its programs and services with full-time professional and administrative staff members. The staff, with the assistance of an adjunct faculty, provide professional training and consultancy services to clients.

Source of official student records: Registry of Credit Recommendations, American Council on Education, One Dupont Circle, Washington, DC 20036-1193 or Program Officer, Institute of Management and Production, 17 Worthington Avenue, Kingston 5, Jamaica, West Indies.

Additional information about the courses: College Credit Recommendation Service, American Council on Education, One Dupont Circle, Washington, DC 20036-1193.

Basic Accounting

Location: Institute of Management and Production, Kingston, Jamaica.

Length: 82 hours (one 3-hour class per week for 27 weeks).

Dates: September 1988-Present.

Objective: To provide an appreciation of the role of accounting within the organization and an understanding of the techniques of collecting and processing accounting data.

Learning Outcome: Upon successful completion of this course, the student will be able to gather and record data in the accounting system, use internal controls to reduce errors, and produce a set of financial statements.

Instruction: Major topics covered in the course are the role of accounting as an information system, creation and maintenance of accounting records, internal control, and financial statements. Methods of instruction include lecture, discussion, and classroom exercises to introduce the role of accounting information for managers, owners, and creditors.

Credit Recommendation: In the lower division baccalaureate/associate degree category, 3 semester hours in Basic Accounting (4/89) (7/94).

Basics of Accounting (Introduction to Financial Management) (Formerly Basics of Accounting and Financial Control [B2]).

Location: Institute of Management and Production, Kingston, Jamaica.

Length: 24 hours (one 3-hour session for 8 weeks).

Dates: January 1980-Present.

Objective: To acquaint nonfinancial staff with the elements of accounting systems and give an understanding of financial statements.

Learning Outcome: Upon successful completion of this course, the student will be able to understand the concepts of double entry bookkeeping; read financial statements; appreciate the role of the accounting department within the firm; and understand the role of the external auditor.

Instruction: Major topics covered in the course are double entry bookkeeping systems, debits, credits, financial statements, and the role of the accounting department in the firm. Methods of instruction include lecture, discussion, and practical exercises.

Credit Recommendation: In the vocational certificate category, 1 semester hour in Basics of Accounting (4/89) (7/94).

Business Administration

Location: Institute of Management and Production, Kingston, Jamaica.

Length: 82 hours (one 3-hour class per week for 27 weeks).

Dates: September 1988-Present.

Objective: To provide a basic understanding of the administration of an organization and an appreciation of basic administrative procedures.

Learning Outcome: Upon successful completion of this course, the student will be able to understand the structure of an organization; construct an organization chart; understand general administrative systems and procedures such as information flow, production control, etc.; understand the importance and application of information technology; measure employee efficiency and conduct a performance review; and have an appreciation for the impact of office design on the organization structure.

Instruction: Major topics covered in the course are organization structures, administrative systems, information technology, performance reviews, and the physical work environment. Methods of instruction include lecture and discussion.

Credit Recommendation: In the lower division baccalaureate/associate degree category, 2 semester hours in Introduction to Business (4/89) (7/94).

Business Administration (Company Administration) (Formerly Management Program)

Location: Institute of Management and Production, Kingston, Jamaica.

Length: 174 contact hours plus field projects.

Dates: May 1984-Present.

Objective: To provide basic tools for monitoring and managing the acquisition and allocation of funds and the production and marketing process within the business enterprise; to give information on the legal requirements of company operation and the legal framework within which companies are formed and operated in Jamaica; and to give basic skills in problem recognition, data collection, and quantitative situation analysis.

Learning Outcome: Upon successful completion of this course, the student will be able to read financial statements and perform basic analyses; appreciate the legal framework within which firms operate; understand the role of marketing in the firm; understand the principles of management in the firm; perform simple statistical analyses of business problems; and understand the role of management information systems.

Instruction: Major topics covered in the course are business finance, business law, production and marketing, management, management information systems, and data interpretation for making decisions. Methods of instruction include lecture, discussion, case studies, and a field project

Credit Recommendation: In the lower division baccalaureate/associate degree category, 5 semester hours in Introduction to Business or 1 semester hour in each of the following areas: Finance, Business Law, Management, Marketing, or Statistics (2/86) (7/94).

Business Communications

Location: Institute of Management and Production, Kingston, Jamaica.

Length: 90 hours (one 3-hour class each week for Module I, 24 hours; for Module II, 26 hours; and for Module III, 18 hours in the first year. For Module IV, 22 hours in the second year.

Dates: September 1992-Present.

Objective: To apply the principles of effective individual and organizational written and verbal communication using the skills of exchanging information, expressing needs and opinions, and accomplishing tasks with minimal conflict and maximum efficiency.

Learning Outcome: Upon successful completion of this course, the student will be able to describe the communication process; analyze the needs, networks, media, dynamics, and problems of organizational communication; use logical thinking, appropriate variables, and correct evaluative criteria in written and verbal communications; prepare a coherent plan for effective communication; write effective business letters, memoranda, reports, proposals and other business documents; interpret verbal and nonverbal, including graphic information; and summarize accurately and efficiently in a variety of business contexts.

Instruction: Major topics covered in the course are the communication process, organizational communication, the individual in the organization, effective listening and speaking, logical thinking, planning for effective communication, written letters and memoranda, interpretation of data and information, summarizing, and writing reports and proposals. Methods of instruction include lecture, class discussions, case studies, simulated business situations, videotape, site visits, and demonstrations.

Credit Recommendation: In the upper division baccalaureate degree category, 6 semester hours in Business Communications or Technical English (7/94).

Business Law

Location: Institute of Management and Production, Kingston, Jamaica.

Length: 70 hours.

Dates: September 1992-Present.

Objective: To provide an understanding of the legal system as it relates to business transactions including elements of contracts, contracts for sale of goods, credit arrangements, law of agency, and law of insurance.

Learning Outcome: Upon successful completion of this course, the student will be able to describe the elements of contracts; set up a contract for the sale of goods; describe credit arrangements; understand the law of agency and law of grievance; and understand laws affecting associations including companies and clubs.

Instruction: Major topics covered in the course are elements of contracts; contracting for sale of goods; law of agency; law of insurance; credit arrangements; and laws affecting associations, companies, and clubs. Methods of instruction include lecture, discussion, case studies, problems, and outside readings.

Credit Recommendation: In the upper division baccalaureate degree category, 4 semester hours in Business Law (7/94).

Caribbean Politics and Society

Location: Institute of Management and Production, Kingston, Jamaica.

Length: 20 hours.

Dates: September 1992-Present.

Objective: To provide the nature of politics and the Caribbean political system.

Learning Outcome: Upon successful completion of this course, the student will be able to define political liberalism versus conservatism; discuss the differences and similarities between the British and American systems of government; understand Caribbean integration and the changing political culture of Jamaica; develop an appreciation for Marxist, liberal, and conservative philosophies; and develop skills in researching global Caribbean politics.

Instruction: Major topics covered in the course are political philosophy, political systems, Caribbean society, Caribbean integration, emerging social and political trends, emergence of the state in Jamaica, constitutional changes, and Jamaican politics. Methods of instruction include lecture, discussion, field trips, outside speakers, tape recordings, examinations, assignments, and a final project.

Credit Recommendation: In the lower division baccalaureate/associate degree category, 1 semester hour in History or Survey of Caribbean History (7/94).

COBOL Programming (IT400) (Formerly COBOL Programming [D5])

Location: Institute of Management and Production, Kingston, Jamaica.

Length: 30 hours with a 20-hour minimum microcomputer laboratory.

Dates: January 1979-Present.

Objective: To provide the student with the tools necessary to code and test programs using COBOL.

Instruction: Major topics covered in the course are language procedure, basic structure analysis, top-down review coding, and testing.

Credit Recommendation: In the lower division baccalaureate/associate degree category, 2 semester hours in Business Administration, Computer Science, or Data Processing (2/86) (7/94). *Prerequisite:* Student must have successfully completed Introduction to Programming (IT210).

Communication

Location: Institute of Management and Production, Kingston, Jamaica.

Length: 82 hours (one 3-hour class per week for 27 weeks).

Dates: September 1988-Present.

Objective: To improve the ability to communicate information in written and oral forms.

Learning Outcome: Upon successful completion of this course, the student will be able to obtain, interpret, select, use, and exchange information; formulate and defend rational arguments; understand the structure and use of communications systems in the organization; and understand the constraints, opportunities, and differing role of individuals within work groups.

Instruction: Major topics covered in the course are informing, persuading, operating communications systems within the organization, and cooperating in the workplace. Methods of instruction include lecture, discussion, simulation, videotaping, audiocassettes, group assignments, role playing, games, use of films, and individual project assignments.

Credit Recommendation: In the lower division baccalaureate/associate degree category, 3 semester hours in Business Communications (4/89) (7/94).

Computer Concepts in Business

Location: Institute of Management and Production, Kingston, Jamaica.

Length: 84 hours (one 3-hour class per week for 28 weeks).

Dates: September 1988-Present.

Objective: To provide the student with an understanding of computer concepts used in the business environment.

Instruction: Major topics covered in the course are computer literacy; history, keyboarding, introduction to personal computers, data processing terminology, hardware and software, and a visit to local data processing installations; system analysis and design: introduction to system analysis, management information system, and organization of a data processing department; and role of system analyst, system programmer, and the electronic office. Methods of instruction include lectures, films, videotapes, a visit to data processing installations, and microcomputer exposures.

Credit Recommendation: In the lower division baccalaureate/associate degree category, 2 semester hours in Computer Information Systems or Data Processing (4/89) (7/94).

Entrepreneurship

Location: Institute of Management and Production, Kingston, Jamaica.

Length: 60 hours.

Dates: September 1992-Present.

Objective: To provide the basics of business management, develop an awareness of entrepreneurship, and prepare the student for starting an enterprise.

Learning Outcome: Upon successful completion of this course, the student will be able to discuss steps for setting up a new business; describe the justification for starting a business; develop a business plan; identify business opportunities; define marketing concepts; price marketing research and competition; and prepare a projected opening day balance sheet.

Instruction: Major topics covered in the course are entrepreneurship, knowledge and skills development for starting a business, accessing funding, ways of dealing with a banker, principle of finance and money management, business plan preparation, and environments that facilitate entrepreneurship. Methods of instruction include lecture, case preparation and discussion, visits to financial institutions, panel discussions, and use of outside guest speakers, essays, and examinations.

Credit Recommendation: In the upper division baccalaureate degree category, 3 semester hours in Entrepreneurship or Small Business Management (7/94).

Ethics in Business

Location: Institute of Management and Production, Kingston, Jamaica.

Length: 20 hours (10/2-hour sessions).

Dates: September 1992-Present.

Objective: To provide an overview of the ethical issues, content, and concerns that occur on a day-to-day basis in the world of business.

Learning Outcome: Upon successful completion of this course, the student will be able to describe the relationship between ethical conduct and business practices; discuss the ethical issues in relation to Jamaican businesses and the global marketplace; and examine ethical practices as they relate to industry, banking, advertising, and the professions.

Instruction: Major topics covered in the course are ethics in industry, business, and Jamaican business; ethical concerns in the conduct of global business; ethics in the professions; and human resource and personnel issues. Methods of instruction include lecture, discussion, videotaped presentations, case studies, outside speakers, and independent research.

Credit Recommendation: In the lower division baccalaureate/associate degree category, 1 semester hour in Ethics, Ethics in Business, Ethical Issues in a Caribbean Context, Caribbean Ethics, or Human Resource Management (7/94).

Financial and Managerial Accounting (Financial Accounting)

Location: Institute of Management and Production, Kingston, Jamaica.

Length: 165 hours.

Dates: January 1992-Present.

Objective: To provide an introduction to essential accounting principles that will prepare students to function at the entry level in the accounting profession or pursue advanced training.

Learning Outcome: Upon successful completion of this course, the student will be able to construct and maintain a set of financial statements; understand differences between accounting and economic income; value long-term assets and liabilities; allocate costs and calculate absorption rates; and conduct cost, volume, profit, and break-even analyses.

Instruction: Major topics covered in the course are the recording process, the accounting cycle, income statements, balance sheets, statement of change in financial position, valuation of assets and liabilities, disclosure requirements, capital expenditure, capital structure, overhead and absorption rates, break-even analysis, and marginal costing. Methods of instruction include lecture and discussion.

Credit Recommendation: In the lower division baccalaureate/associate degree category, 3 semester hours in Financial Accounting and 3 semester hours in Managerial Accounting for a total of 6 semester hours (7/94).

Human Behavior in Organizations

Location: Institute of Management and Production, Kingston, Jamaica.

Length: 60 hours (one 3-hour class per week for 20 weeks).

Dates: September 1992-Present.

Objective: To provide an understanding of human and organizational behavior with an emphasis on organizational and human relationships and strategies for contributing to the positive growth and development of organizations.

Learning Outcome: Upon successful completion of this course, the student will be able to identify types of organizational design considering their advantages and disadvantages; outline factors which shape/influence human behavior; illustrate the reciprocal relationship between the individual and organization; explain and apply two theories of motivation; identify positive and negative behavior affecting an organization; define diagnostic tools for identifying problems, and understand strategies for promoting positive behavior through change or conflict management.

Instruction: Major topics covered in the course are theory, characteristics and designs of organizations, foundations, theories, problems and dynamics of human behavior, organizational behavior, change, processes, conflict, and development. Methods of instruction include lecture, role play, case study, group discussion, readings, oral presentations, and examinations.

Credit Recommendation: In the upper division baccalaureate degree category, 3 semester hours in Business Psychology, Psychology, Organizational Behavior, or Human Resource Management (7/94).

Human Resource Development

Location: Institute of Management and Production, Kingston, Jamaica.

Length: 69 hours, plus 60 hours for specialist area training in training and development or personnel administration.

Dates: *Version 1:* October 1982-July 1995; *Version 2:* July 1995-Present.

Objective: *Version 1:* To provide an understanding of the training function and instruction in the design and evaluation of training programs. *Version 2:* To give students an understanding of the human resource functions as part of management or business and industry.

Learning Outcome: Upon successful completion of this course, the student will be able to identify all the major functions of human resource development in a business and/or industry. The student should become knowledgeable in a specialist area such as training and development or personnel administration.

Instruction: Major topics covered in the course are the organizational environment within the Human Resource Department (HRD) professional functions, overview of the HRD function, manpower planning, assessing HRD needs, and evaluating the human resource environment. Methods of instruction include lecture, discussion, and case studies.

Credit Recommendation: In the upper division baccalaureate degree category, 2 semester hours in Personnel Management (2/86) (7/94).

Introduction to Computer Concepts (Computer Studies)

Location: Institute of Management and Production, Kingston, Jamaica.

Length: 90 hours.

Dates: September 1992-Present.

Objective: To provide an overview of the use of computers in business and also the critical thinking skills to select appropriate software and hardware to address business and industry needs.

Learning Outcome: Upon successful completion of this course, the student will be able to analyze the needs of business and industry for computer support and use the critical thinking skills necessary to assist in the selection of software and hardware to satisfy those computer support needs.

Instruction: Major topics covered in the course are evolution of computers, computer hardware, computer software, computer and communication, systems analysis and design, word processing systems, spreadsheets, and database management systems. Methods of instruction include lecture, discussion, tours of data processing facilities, and work in personal computer laboratory.

Credit Recommendation: In the lower division baccalaureate/associate degree category, 3 semester hours in Introduction to Computer Science or Computer Information Systems (7/94).

Introduction to Management

Location: Institute of Management and Production, Kingston, Jamaica.

Length: 85 hours.

Dates: September 1992-Present.

Objective: To provide an understanding of the principles of management and the knowledge to use those principles on the job.

Learning Outcome: Upon successful completion of this course, the student will be able to describe the fundamentals of management, demonstrate some practical applications of these fundamentals, and conduct a performance appraisal of an employee.

Instruction: Major topics covered in the course are social foundations of management, human relations theory, management functions, and leadership and change. Methods of instruction include lecture, discussion, outside speakers, case studies, and simulations.

Credit Recommendation: In the upper division baccalaureate degree category, 3 semester hours in Principles of Management (7/94).

Labor Relations in Jamaica
1. Collective Bargaining (G3)
2. Industrial Relations, Issues, and Review (G4)
3. Labor Laws in Jamaica (G6)

Location: Institute of Management and Production, Kingston, Jamaica.

Length: 54 hours (3 courses with one 3-hour session for 6 weeks, respectively).

Dates: January 1980-May 1996.

Objective: To give the student an understanding of labor relations in Jamaica.

Instruction: Major topics covered in the course are the history of the union movement in Jamaica, the collective bargaining process, and legislation affecting industrial relations in Jamaica. Methods of instruction include lecture, discussion, and case studies.

Credit Recommendation: In the lower division baccalaureate/associate degree category, 3 semester hours in Labor Relations in Jamaica (4/89) (7/94). **NOTE:** Students must successfully complete all three courses to receive credit.

Marketing

Location: Institute of Management and Production, Kingston, Jamaica.

Length: 80 hours.

Dates: September 1992-Present.

Objective: To provide knowledge of marketing and its applications in business and industry.

Learning Outcome: Upon successful completion of this course, the student will be able to describe the information base of a marketing organization; understand and implement promotional programs and plans to market goods and services; and appreciate the role of international marketing in a global economy.

Instruction: Major topics covered in the course are concepts of marketing, analysis of marketing opportunities, marketing information base, promotional programs for target markets, international marketing, and marketing management. Methods of instruction include lecture, discussion, and case studies and simulations.

Credit Recommendation: In the upper division baccalaureate degree category, 3 semester hours in Principles of Marketing (7/94).

Marketing

Location: Institute of Management and Production, Kingston, Jamaica.

Length: 22 hours (1.5 hours per week for 14 weeks).

Dates: September 1988-Present.

Objective: To provide an overview of marketing elements and concepts with emphasis on formulating a simple marketing plan.

Learning Outcome: Upon successful completion of this course, the student will be able to understand the role of marketing in the firm; analyze marketing opportunities; understand the marketing research function; discuss various pricing strategies; understand the structure of channels of distribution; and understand the advertising and sales function.

Instruction: Major topics covered in the course are the nature of marketing; analysis of marketing opportunities; definition of markets, target market selection, and sales forecasting buying behavior; market research; product and pricing decisions;produce planning, design and development, pricing structures, pricing, and competition; distribution; promotion, advertising, and sales; and organizing and managing marketing strategies. Methods of instruction include lecture, discussion, case studies, and development of a marketing plan.

Credit Recommendation: In the lower division baccalaureate/associate degree

category, 1 semester hour in Marketing as an elective (4/89) (7/94).

Mathematics for Business Analysis and Business Statistics

Location: Institute of Management and Production, Kingston, Jamaica.

Length: 130 hours.

Dates: September 1992-Present.

Objective: To provide the mathematical and statistical tolls necessary for making business decisions.

Learning Outcome: Upon successful completion of this course, the student will be able to solve simple and complex equations; solve problems dealing with matrices; value assets by finding the present value of their cash flows; solve inventory ordering problems; and gather, organize, and analyze data used in the business decision-making process.

Instruction: Major topics covered in the course are solutions to simple and complex equations, functions, matrices, time value of money, capital budgeting, EOQ models, descriptive statistics, probability, sampling and estimation, and simple regression. Methods of instruction include lecture and discussion.

Credit Recommendation: In the lower division baccalaureate/associate degree category, 4 semester hours in Mathematics for Business Analysis and 2 semester hours in Business Statistics (7/94).

Microeconomics and Macroeconomics (Economics)

Location: Institute of Management and Production, Kingston, Jamaica.

Length: 81 hours.

Dates: September 1992-Present.

Objective: To provide an understanding of economics as it relates to individuals and firms as well as an appreciation for the operation of the economy as a whole.

Learning Outcome: Upon successful completion of this course, the student will be able to bring a scientific approach to the analysis of economic issues; understand the impact of the government on the level of economic activity; understand the manner in which scarce resources are allocated; and appreciate the use of marginal concepts in economic decision-making.

Instruction: Major topics covered in the course are price determination, consumer theory, the theory of the firm, national income accounts, income and employment, money and the banking system, fiscal policy, and international economics. Methods of instruction include lecture, discussion, and examinations.

Credit Recommendation: In the lower division baccalaureate/associate degree category, 3 semester hours in Microeconomics and in the lower division baccalaureate/associate degree category, 3 semester hours in Macroeconomics for a total of 6 semester hours (7/94).

Personnel Management 1. Introduction to Personnel Management (G1) 2. Personnel Management: Skills and Techniques (G2)

Location: Institute of Management and Production, Kingston, Jamaica.

Length: 42 hours (1. eight 3-hour sessions; 2. six 3-hour sessions).

Dates: January 1980-May 1996.

Objective: To give the student a basic understanding of the principles of industrial psychology, personnel development, and organization management as they relate to the management of personnel.

Instruction: Major topics covered in the course are the principles of employee recruitment and selection, performance appraisal and training, wage and salary administration, leadership and supervision, employee motivation, communication, and career development. Methods of instruction include lecture and discussion.

Credit Recommendation: In the lower division baccalaureate/associate degree category, 2 semester hours in Personnel Management (4/89) (7/94). **NOTE:** Students must successfully complete both courses to receive credit.

Personnel Management and Industrial Relations (IMP Dip-2) (Formerly Labor Relations in Jamaica: 1. Collective Bargaining [G3], 2. Industrial Relations, Issues, and Review [G4], and Labor Laws in Jamaica [G6]; and Personnel Management: 1. Introduction to Personnel Management [G1], 2. Personnel Management: Skills and Techniques [G2].) (Formerly Personnel Management and Labor Relations)

Location: Institute of Management and Production, Kingston, Jamaica.

Length: 78 hours.

Dates: January 1980-Present.

Objective: To provide personnel managers, industrial relations officers, and senior supervisors with a basic understanding of personnel management, administration, and industrial relations.

Learning Outcome: Upon successful completion of this course, the student will be able to conduct program appraisals; conduct interviews; orient new employees; plan training programs; communicate more effectively; assist in the development of career planning; discuss the development of the trade union movement in Jamaica; describe the types and stages of collective bargaining and the basic legislation affecting industrial relations practices in Jamaica.

Instruction: Major topics covered in the course are personnel development and organizational management; recruitment and selection; industrial psychology; performance appraisal and training; wage and salary administration; leadership and supervision; motivation; communication; and manpower development. Methods of instruction include lecture, discussion, and practical activities.

Credit Recommendation: In the lower division baccalaureate/associate degree category, 2 semester hours in Personnel Management and 2 semester hours in Labor Relations in Jamaica (7/94).

Principles of Public Relations

Location: Institute of Management and Production, Kingston, Jamaica.

Length: *Version 1:* 22 hours (1.5 hours per week for 14 weeks); *Version 2:* 96 hours (3 hours per week).

Dates: *Version 1:* September 1989-June 1994; *Version 2:* July 1994-Present.

Objective: To provide an appreciation for the principles of public relations and exposure to specific public relations activities.

Learning Outcome: Upon successful completion of this course, the student will be able to understand basic principles or techniques of public relations; discuss how these principles can be applied; assess the use of mass media; write news and feature articles; make effective presentations; and plan meetings and conferences.

Instruction: Major topics in the course are development of public relations programs, speech writing techniques, print publications, and written and oral communications skills. Methods of instruction include lecture, panel discussions, tours, oral and written assignments, and a special project.

Credit Recommendation: *Version 1:* In the lower division baccalaureate/associate degree category, 1 semester hour in Public Relations. *Version 2:* In the lower division baccalaureate/associate degree category, 3 semester hours in Principles of Public Relations (4/89) (7/94).

Principles of Supervision
1. Fundamentals of Supervisory Practice
2. Supervisory Management—Part I
3. Supervisory Management—Part II

Location: Institute of Management and Production, Kingston, Jamaica.

Length: 72 hours.

Dates: September 1988-Present.

Objective: *Course 1:* To provide the basic management principles with applications to work situations. *Course 2:* To provide advanced supervisory management principles with emphasis on individual differences, personality and behavior, discipline, communication improvement, job satisfaction, and self-actualization by guiding and developing the employee. *Course 3:* To provide an overview of the principles involved in the supervision of people by exploring the scientific yet sensitive approach to the supervision of Jamaican employees.

Learning Outcome: Upon successful completion of *Course 1:* the student will be able to describe basic management principles and how they apply to local business and industries; *Course 2:* the student will be able to identify and adapt the qualities of leadership, understand what makes people different and what causes frustration of employees, identify barriers to communication, handle grievances, and counsel and motivate employees; *Course 3:* the student will be able to describe the basic requirements of supervision and apply them to their own on-the-job circumstance.

Instruction: Major topics covered in *Course 1:* are the nature of management, planning, organizing, controlling, standard/appraisal, communications, motivation, and decision-making; *Course 2:* attributes of effective supervision, elements of effective leadership in business, and differences between leadership and management; and *Course 3:* case studies exploring leadership, management, and human relations. Methods of instruction include lecture, discussion, and case studies.

Credit Recommendation: In the lower division baccalaureate/associate degree category, 3 semester hours in Supervision (4/89)(7/94). **NOTE:** Students must successfully complete all three courses to receive credit.

Systems Analysis and Design
1. Fundamentals of Systems Analysis (D3)
2. Systems Analysis (D4)

Location: Institute of Management and Production, Kingston, Jamaica.

Length: 48 hours (eight 3-hour sessions for both Course 1 and 2).

Dates: January 1979-Present.

Objective: To provide the student with the fundamental knowledge and skills to use the techniques and concepts of systems analysis and design.

Instruction: *Course 1:* Major topics covered in the course are an introduction to the role of systems analysis including information gathering, information analysis, data capture, input-output design, system specification, implementation, feasibility study, appraisal of hardware with regard to systems needs, and presentation of findings. *Course 2:* Major topics covered in the course are the process of systems development, systems design process, file concepts and structures, timing, systems testing, data control, systems security and recovery, documentation, and transaction processing. *Courses 1 and 2:* Methods of instruction include lecture and discussion.

Credit Recommendation: In the lower division baccalaureate/associate degree category, 3 semester hours in Business Administration, Computer Science, or Data Processing (2/86) (7/94).

The World Around Us

Location: Institute of Management and Production, Kingston, Jamaica.

Length: 20 hours.

Dates: September 1992-Present.

Objective: To develop an awareness, understanding, and appreciation of aspects of the physical, human, and economic environment.

Learning Outcome: Upon successful completion of this course, the student will be able to understand measurements and movements of the earth and ecosystems; relate environmental relationships; begin to develop an appreciation for population growth, distribution, urbanization, and population problems; and understand and appreciate the need for conservation and the development of human resources.

Instruction: Major topics covered in the course are early civilization, ecosystems, the Jamaican ecosystem, development, under-development; poverty, environment, measurement and movement of the earth. Methods of instruction include lecture, discussion, group projects, handouts, practical exercises, and a research project.

Credit Recommendation: In the lower division baccalaureate/associate degree category, 1 semester hour in Social Studies or Geography (7/94).

Institute of Management Sciences

The Institute of Management Sciences (IMS), incorporated in January 1992, is a nonprofit, self-supporting, higher education institution, governed by a Board appointed by the Trustees. The expressed mission of the Institute is "to make a valid and meaningful contribution to the development of Postsecondary Education in Jamaica which will be achieved by offering a consistently high level of educational programs suited to both the specific and general needs of the business community." IMS has membership in several professional organizations such as the Private Sector Organization of Jamaica, the Professional Societies Association of Jamaica, the Jamaica Association of Training and Development, the Jamaica Computer Society, and the Joint Committee on Tertiary Education (JCTE). Furthermore, in 1997, a formal alliance has been established with the University of New Orleans (UNO), a highly reputable U.S. Institution, to offer the Executive MBA and B.Sc. Programs in Jamaica. The Institute seeks to enhance educational and employment opportunities for a better quality of life for Jamaicans who reside in both rural and urban communities. The majority of participants are mid-professionals seeking quality education that is consistent with their individual lifestyle, and all have a common need for convenient, affordable, and practical educational programs. They are adults who wish to upgrade their skills in industry or commerce, prepare for a new field of employment, or fulfill personal goals.

The Business Program Faculty boasts a distinguished team of lecturers, educators, researchers, and practicing managers, with a reputable track record of success. It is a diverse and adjunct faculty which brings together a wide variety of management and business skills. Course development is usually initiated through the IMS Academic Council which is composed of full-time administrative, professional, and adjunct faculty staff members. The Council is therefore mandated to exercise authority over the implementation, effectiveness, and quality of the Institute's programs and educational policies. Programs have been designed so as to develop new and Contemporary Management Skills; the application of these skills to actual organizational problems; enabling individual focus and integrating the functional business areas. All courses are conducted in Kingston, but a few are generally offered at other regional centers in Mandeville, Ocho Rios, and Montego Bay.

The Institute offers six one year diploma programs in: Management Studies, Computer Studies and Management, Accounting and Financial Management, Hotel Management and Hospitality, Marketing and Sales Management, and a two year Associate of Science degree program in Business Administration.

Source of official student records: Registry of Credit Recommendations, American Council on Education, One Dupont Circle, Washington, DC 20036 or Department of Studies, Institute of Management Sciences, 34 Old Hope Road, Kingston5, Jamaica, West Indies.

Additional information about the courses: College Credit Recommendation Service, American Council on Education, One Dupont Circle, Washington, DC 20036.

Associate Degree Program

Introduction to Management (PMT 102) (Principles of Management)

Location: Kingston, Jamaica.
Length: 30 hours (10 weeks).
Dates: February 1993-Present.
Objective: To identify the principal functions of management and provide an overview of the processes encompassed by these functions.
Learning Outcome: Upon successful completion of this course, the student will be able to be aware of an organization's resources, structure, processes, and culture; and identify actions to improve efficiency in the organization.
Instruction: Major topics covered in the course are management levels; the planning, organizing, directing, motivation, and control functions; planning tools; communication; and the human resource process. Methods of instruction include lecture, student presentations, an end-of-term examination, and a written student project.
Credit Recommendation: In the lower division baccalaureate/associate degree category, 2 semester hours in Business Administration or Introduction to Management (2/97).

Personnel Management (PSM 203)

Location: Kingston, Jamaica.
Length: 30 hours (10 weeks).
Dates: July 1995-Present.
Objective: To provide exposure to the critical issues which affect the management of the enterprise's human resources.
Learning Outcome: Upon successful completion of this course, the student will be able to explain the role of the human resource practitioner; differentiate between line and staff responsibilities in human resource management; understand planning, staffing, and compensation issues for personnel; and contrast Jamaican personnel and industrial relations practices to those in North American and Europe.
Instruction: Major topics covered in the course are the role of human resource management, organizational design, manpower planning and recruiting, training, salary administration, and industrial relations in the Caribbean. Methods of in-struction include lecture, discussion, classroom exercises, and an end-of-term examination.
Credit Recommendation: In the lower division baccalaureate/associate degree category, 2 semester hours in Personnel Management or Business Administration (2/97).

Principles of Macroeconomics (ECN 200)

Location: Kingston, Jamaica.
Length: 30 hours (10 weeks).
Dates: June 1993-Present.
Objective: To provide students with a basic knowledge of macro-economics, an understanding of some of the economic issues that face society and knowledge of some of the analytical tools used in the discipline.
Learning Outcome: Upon successful completion of this course, the student will be able to define the terms used in national income determination; understand what fiscal and monetary policy are and the role each plays in the economy; and understand international economics as it relates to Jamaica.
Instruction: Major topics covered in the course are national income accounting, income and employment equilibrium, fiscal policy, the budget, taxation, banking system in the Unite States and Jamaica, inflation, and international economics. Methods of instruction include lecture, classroom exercises, and course tests.
Credit Recommendation: In the lower division baccalaureate/associate degree category, 2 semester hours in Macroeconomics (2/97).

Public Speaking and Communication (SCL 208)

Location: Kingston, Jamaica.

Length: 30 hours (10 weeks).
Dates: January 1994-Present.
Objective: To understand public speaking fundamentals, and to effectively demonstrate, assess, and critique oral communication patterns.
Learning Outcome: Upon successful completion of this course, the student will be able to understand the fundamental elements of speech communication and effective skills in the delivery of oral presentations.
Instruction: Major topics covered in the course are the definition of communication and rationale, types of speech communication, and elements of effective speech communication. Methods of instruction include lecture, discussion, classroom exercises, quizzes, papers, and final examinations.
Credit Recommendation: In the lower division baccalaureate/associate degree category, 1 semester hour in Speech or Introduction to Communication (2/97).

Use of English

Location: Kingston, Jamaica.
Length: 25 hours (10 weeks).
Dates: October 1996-Present.
Objective: To understand the nature, characteristics, and function of language, its value, appropriateness, and use in daily living (both English and Jamaican/Creole); and to develop and expand English language skills both oral and written.
Learning Outcome: Upon successful completion of this course, the student will be able to have knowledge of a variety of writing styles and their appropriate use; and demonstrate an understanding of basic literal, interpretive, analytical, and evaluative skills, and their application.
Instruction: Major topics covered in the course are elements of English Language including parts of speech, grammatical rules, sentence structure, and the application of grammatical rules to written and oral communication. Methods of instruction include lecture, discussion, classroom exercises, audio/visual material, quizzes, and examinations.
Credit Recommendation: In the vocational certificate category, 2 semester hours in Introduction to English (2/97).

Diploma Program

Accounting Fundamentals (ACT 101/102) (Principles of Accounting I & II)

Location: Kingston, Jamaica.
Length: 30 hours (10 weeks each) total 60 hours.
Dates: June 1993-Present.
Objective: To provide the fundamentals of accounting, to gain an understanding of financial statements, and to analyze the financial position of a company by using financial ratios.
Learning Outcome: Upon successful completion of this course, the student will be able to understand the principles of accounting of profit and nonprofit organizations; understand the techniques of double-entry bookkeeping; reconcile a bank statement; and make entries for partnership accounts.
Instruction: Major topics covered in the course are accounting concepts, double-entry bookkeeping, bank reconciliation, depreciation, preparing financial statements, and entries on partnership accounts. Methods of instruction include lecture and classroom exercises.
Credit Recommendation: In the lower division baccalaureate/associate degree category, 3 semester hours in Introduction to Accounting or Accounting Fundamentals (2/97). **NOTE:** Students must complete both ACT 101 & 102 to receive this credit.

Cost and Management Accounts

Location: Kingston, Jamaica.
Length: 25 hours (10 weeks).
Dates: June 1992-Present.
Objective: To gain an understanding of basic bookkeeping and accounting fundamentals.
Learning Outcome: Upon successful completion of this course, the student will be able to manage and control various costs and expenses on the job and in their personal lives; prepare income statements and balance sheets; identify the types of costs; and calculate a break-even point.
Instruction: Major topics covered in the course are variable and fixed costs, direct and indirect costs, break-even analysis, budgeting, and starting a business. Methods of instruction include lecture, learner presentations, and audio/visual material.
Credit Recommendation: In the vocational certificate category, 1 semester hour in Bookkeeping or Fundamental Accounting (2/97).

Economics in Business

Location: Kingston, Jamaica.
Length: 25 hours (10 weeks).
Dates: January 1992-Present.
Objective: To provide a basic understanding of economic concepts as it relates to individuals and businesses.
Learning Outcome: Upon successful completion of this course, the student will be able to discuss economics as it relates to monetary and fiscal policies; explain the balance of payments concept; explain the effects of inflation and unemployment on the economy; discuss the effect of comparative advantage as a business or country; and understand the components of GDP.
Instruction: Major topics covered in the course are supply and demand, production costs, marginal analysis, equilibrium, market structure—monopoly, competition, GNP, GDP, fiscal policy, supply-side economics, international trade, and inflation. Methods of instruction include lecture, classroom exercises, quizzes, a team presentation, and final examination.
Credit Recommendation: In the vocational certificate category, 1 semester hour in Economics (2/97).

Insurance Data Management Association

Insurance Data Management Association (IDMA) is a non-profit professional association dedicated to increasing the level of professionalism among insurance data managers. More than eighty insurance organizations are represented by nearly six hundred members. In addition to a eight-course curriculum, successful completion of which leads to designation as a Certified Insurance Data Manager (CIDM), completion of only the four IDMA-designed courses leads to designation as an Associate Insurance Data Manager (AIDM). Additionally, the Association sponsors technical seminars, conducts meetings and forums for pertinent topics, produces analysis packages for special state data requests and publishes opinion papers and a monthly bulletin.

In addition to the four IDMA-designed courses, the IDMA curriculum incorporates selected courses from other curricula: four courses from the American Institute for Chartered Property Casualty Underwriters (CPCU) program, or four courses from the Life Office Management Association (LOMA) curriculum of the Life Management Institute, or selected courses from the Casualty Actuarial Society (CAS) curriculum. Curriculum activities are coordinated by the Education Committee and advised by an Academic Advisory Committee. Courses are designed to facilitate self-study and performance is tested in examinations administered twice yearly.

The courses offered by the Insurance Data Management Association are not presented in any required sequence. A student may begin with any one of the four courses in the sequence; hence, each course must contain all the background information a student might need to complete the course successfully. As a result, there is a certain level of content overlap among the courses. The credit recommendations that are made for each course are firm. However, if a student has completed several of these courses, a college might want to examine the student's degree program to determine if there is any overlap in the cumulative total of the credit recommendations that are appropriate for that particular student.

Source of official student records: Director, Insurance Data Management Association, 85 John Street, New York, NY 10038.

Additional information about the courses: College Credit Recommendation Service, American Council on Education, One Dupont Circle, Washington, DC 20036-1193.

Data Administration

Location: Independent study.

Length: 150 hours (15 weeks).

Dates: August 1987-Present.

Objective: To provide students with a perspective on data management to enhance their effectiveness as data managers.

Learning Outcome: Upon successful completion of this course, the student will be able to appreciate the importance of information to company success; understand that data is an important company resource; understand data based management systems and the need to develop appropriate new systems.

Instruction: Major topics covered in this course are data evolution reengineering; migration & ownership; designing data; approaches to data modeling; data administration responsibilities; computer files; database approach; navigational databases; relational tools; data base design and data dictionaries; data management; relational design methodology; beginning the logical data model; data integrity/attributes; normalization & domains; and completing the logical model. Methods of instruction include an independent study to prepare for a 3 hour, 100 item examination.

Credit Recommendation: In the graduate degree or upper division baccalaureate degree category, 3 semester hours in Management or Business Elective (4/88) (9/95). **NOTE:** This course is particularly applicable to computer systems or business degree programs.

Insurance Accounting and Data Quality (IDMA 2)

Location: Independent study.

Length: 160 hours (16 weeks).

Dates: August 1989-December 1994.

Objective: To provide the student with an understanding of the accounting practices of the insurance industry and how data quality issues affect an organization.

Learning Outcome: Upon successful completion of the course, the student should be able to understand and interpret accounting reports and information and to understand the interface with non-accounting data management functions in the insurance industry; understand data quality issues well enough to participate in planning a quality control program; be able to participate in or coordinate a statistical examination by either the company or state insurance department; and understand the statistical data monitoring system as a quality control tool.

Instruction: Major topics include accounting and data management functions; products of accounting and the system involved; overview and very detailed exploration of data quality issues; quality control from set up to maintenance to emergency/contingency responses; statistical examinations; and state-mandated statistical data monitoring system.

Credit Recommendation: In the upper division baccalaureate degree category, 3 semester hours in Insurance Accounting and Data Quality or Business elective (4/90) (9/95).

Insurance Data Collection and Statistical Reporting (IDMA 1)

Location: Independent Study.

Length: 150 hours (15 weeks).

Dates: December 1988-Present.

Objective: To provide students with an understanding of the sources of insurance statistical data in the companies and methods of and reasons for reporting.

Learning Outcome: Upon successful completion of the course, the student should understand the need for effective insurance information systems in sufficient detail to explain and advocate a position in organizational policy-making meetings; comprehend the history, purpose, and functions of insurance-related statistical organizations sufficiently to determine their effectiveness in serving the needs of a given company; and possess a usable knowledge of the uses and limitations of data and how they can be used by governments or organizations to affect the insurance industry.

Instruction: Major topics include descriptions and history of insurance information systems; descriptions of automation techniques and results; standards and guidelines; cycles; objectives and specific departmental needs within the company; statistical reporting to agents; specific characteristics of agent reporting; responding to special state data requests; and ratemaking data and systems. Methods of instruction include independent study to prepare for a 3 hour, 100 item examination.

Credit Recommendation: In the upper division baccalaureate degree category, 3 semester hours in Information Systems

Management, Insurance or Business elective (9/95).

Insurance Data Quality (IDMA 2-Revised)

Location: Independent study.
Length: 160 hours (16 weeks).
Dates: January 1995-Present.
Objective: To provide knowledge of methods of assessing data quality, techniques of assuring high quality, current affairs/issues and initiatives relevant to insurance data quality assurance.
Learning Outcome: Upon successful completion of this course, the student will be able to understand data quality issues and have sufficient competency to participate in planning an organizational quality strategy; comprehend change, control, and recovery of data programs, sampling, audit procedures, requirements for in-house, bureau/agency, or regulatory audits; plan procedures, techniques, scheduling for cost-efficient responses; and interpret results of audits for the good of the organization.
Instruction: Major topics covered in the course are data quality in statistical reporting; history and definition of quality; quality strategies; change process; methodology and tools; quality costs; data quality in an automated environment; introduction to sampling and other statistical examinations. Methods of instruction include independent study to prepare for a 3 hour, 100 item examination.
Credit Recommendation: In the upper division baccalaureate degree category, 3 semester hours in Information Management Systems, Insurance, or Business elective (9/95).

Systems Development and Project Management (IDMA 3)

Location: Independent Study.
Length: 150 hours (15 weeks).
Dates: September 1994-Present.
Objective: To provide knowledge and skills needed for developing specifications for information systems and managing related projects.
Learning Outcome: Upon successful completion of this course, the student will be able to lead or participate in strategic planning and management systems projects; state specifications and develop systems using new technology; integrate business goals that use personnel more efficiently and use feedback to redesign the system and the organization.
Instruction: Major topics covered in this course are the system development process; integrating business and systems issues and managing in a team environment; planning for change; business process redesign; system development; quality and project management; managing for productivity; system and project management education. Methods of instruction include independent study to prepare for a 3 hour, 100 item examination.
Credit Recommendation: In the upper division baccalaureate degree category or graduate degree category 3 semester hours in Information Systems Management, Computer Information Systems or Insurance (9/95).

Insurance Educational Association

The Insurance Educational Association (IEA) is a voluntary, nonprofit corporation, organized for the purpose of meeting the needs of people for education in the fields of risk and insurance.

The IEA management provides students with the preparation necessary for professional certification for careers in insurance, risk management, and employee benefits. In addition, it provides continuing education for persons employed within these industries.

Courses offered may lead to preparation for national examinations offered by The American Institute for Property and Liability Underwriters/Insurance Institute of America and the International Foundation of Employee Benefit Plans in its Certified Employee Benefit Specialist program. Students successfully completing national examinations in these programs may apply to these organizations, which are listed elsewhere in this *National Guide*, to receive appropriate academic credit recommendations. To be eligible for credit, students should have received at least a grade of "C".

Other specialized, technical classes are offered and may apply toward the IEA's certificate programs. These include (1) Commercial Multiple Line Insurance and (2) Workers' Compensation Claims.

The IEA offers a professional designation in claims. The Workers' Compensation Claims Professional (WCCP) designation is conferred by the IEA to students completing eight college level courses, which includes CA-10 through CA-14, CA15, CA17, and CA20; listed in the American Council on Education's *National Guide*.

The IEA offers a professional designation program in disability management. The Certified Professional in Disability Management (CODM) is conferred following the completion of three college level courses, CPDM1, Introduction to Disability Management; CPDM2, Disability Case Management-The Medical and Administrative Components; and CPDM3, Disability Management Imple-mentation. Please contact the IEA regarding submission for college credit.

The association provides seminars, workshops, self-instructional courses, and special programs in all aspects of insurance, from basic introductory courses to advanced technical and managerial studies.

Source of official student records: Registry of Credit Recommendations, American Council on Education, One Dupont Circle, Washington, DC 20036-1193 or Northern California: Insurance Educational Association, 100 California Street, Suite 1100, San Francisco, California 94111. Southern California: Insurance Educational Association, 1201 Dove Street, Suite 570, Newport Beach, California 92660.

Additional information about the courses: College Credit Recommendation Service, American Council on Education, One Dupont Circle, Washington, DC 20036-1193.

NOTE: To be eligible for credit, students should receive at least a grade of "C."

Advanced Issues in Workers Compensation (CA-20)

Location: Various locations throughout California.

Length: 35 hours.

Dates: January 1993-Present.

Objective: To provide the student with a broader understanding of the impact their claims decisions have on the self insured employer, insurance company, reinsurance company, captive and society as a whole.

Learning Outcome: Upon successful completion of this course, the student will be able to monitor and evaluate the risks, costs, financing and payout of workers' Compensation claims and their impact on the involved parties.

Instruction: Major topics covered in the course are self-insurance; reinsurance; structured settlements; experience and retrospective rating; civil law; risk management and integrated benefit programs. Methods of instruction include lecture, discussion, classroom exercises, audio/visual material.

Credit Recommendation: In the upper division baccalaureate degree category, 2 semester hours in Insurance, Risk Management, or Business Administration (8/95).

Medical Coordination of Workers' Compensation Claims (Formerly Medical Management of Workers' Compensation Claims [CA12])

Location: Various locations throughout California.

Length: 30 hours (12 weeks).

Dates: *Version 1:* September 1974-May 1990; *Version 2:* June 1990-Present.

Objective: To provide students with the ability to recognize and define medical word roots, prefixes, suffixes, and related disease and surgical terms; and to assist in the interpretation of medical reports on the industrial injured worker.

Learning Outcome: Upon successful completion of this course, students will gain a thorough understanding of the medical specialties required in most workers' compensation claims scenarios. In addition, students will be able to explain and define frequently used medical terms in the workers' compensation claims community.

Instruction: Major topics covered in the course are an introduction to medical language, anatomy, and physiology. This course prepares the student to understand and process workers' compensation medical claims and understand the management of medical claims. Methods of instruction include discussion and a series of lectures by medical injury specialists.

Credit Recommendation: *Version 1:* In the upper division baccalaureate degree category, 1 semester hour in Insurance or Medical Technology (5/78) (3/84). *Version 2:* In the lower division baccalaureate/associate degree category, 2 semester hours in Insurance or Medical Technology (6/90) (4/91) (8/95).

Medical Terminology and Case Management (OR-13)

Location: Various locations throughout Oregon.

Length: 30 hours (12 weeks).

Dates: January 1989-Present.

Objective: To provide students with the ability to recognize and define medical word roots, prefixes, suffixes and related disease and surgical terms; and to assist in the interpretation of medical reports on the injured worker.

Learning Outcome: Upon successful completion of this course, the student will be able to learn effective use of independent medical examinations, communication with medical professionals, common diagnostic procedures and surgeries, and current trends in medical rehabilitation.

Instruction: Major topics covered in the course are basic anatomy, medical terminology, communicating with medical examinations, chronic pain control, and the effective use of medical case managers. Methods of instruction include lecture and discussion.

Credit Recommendation: In the upper division baccalaureate degree category, 2

semester hours in Insurance or Medical Terminology (8/95).

Permanent Disability Rating - Advanced (CA-15)

Location: Throughout California.

Length: 225 hours (9 weeks).

Dates: January 1984-Present.

Objective: To provide the experienced claims individual with the ability to interpret actual medical reports and interpret usual language of unscheduled ratings.

Learning Outcome: Upon successful completion of this course, the student will be able to recognize and calculate disability factors and apply results to appropriate rating formulas.

Instruction: Major topics covered in the course are an overview of the fine points of training including concepts, terms and procedures; subjective add-ons; bilateral; ambidextrous; pyramiding; overlapping and other multiple disabilities; and work on utilization of information outside of the schedule, including administrative protocols for physicians, case law, and other resources. Methods of instruction include lecture and discussion.

Credit Recommendation: In the upper division baccalaureate degree category, 1 semester hour in Insurance or Workers' Compensation (8/95).

Preparation for Litigation (OR-12)

Location: Various locations throughout Oregon.

Length: 30 hours (12 weeks).

Dates: January 1989-Present.

Objective: To prepare for the litigation process with respect to the Oregon Workers' Compensation statutory laws, rules and related issues.

Learning Outcome: Upon successful completion of this course, the student will be able to prepare a workers' compensation claim in anticipation of litigation and effectively participate in the presentation of the case.

Instruction: Major topics covered in the course are factual and legal investigation techniques, negotiation skills, settlement strategies, structured settlements, and preparation for testimony. Methods of instruction include lecture, discussion, classroom exercises, and audio/visual material.

Credit Recommendation: In the upper division baccalaureate degree category, 2 semester hours in Insurance, Health, Business Administration, or Political Science (8/95).

Principles of Case Management - Advanced (OR-11)

Location: Various locations throughout Oregon.

Length: 30 hours (12 weeks).

Dates: November 1989-Present.

Objective: To provide an indepth review of the Oregon workers' compensation statutory law, rules/regulations, and some case law as it applies to the daily task of claims handling.

Learning Outcome: Upon successful completion of this course, the student will be able to develop a claims handling process which will help to apply the statutory law, state and rules at the appropriate time the claim matures.

Instruction: Major topics covered in the course are practical application of case management; time management and communication skills; cost effective use of vendors; investigation and subrosa methods; technical resource development; medical case management techniques; and early return-to-work programs, timely claims closures, negotiation techniques, vocational rehabilitation, and working with managed care organizations. Methods of instruction include lecture, discussion, audio/visual material, and examinations.

Credit Recommendation: In the upper division baccalaureate degree category, 2 semester hours in Insurance or Workers' Compensation (8/95).

The Labor Code and Current Case Law (CA-17)

Location: Various locations throughout California.

Length: 30 hours (12 weeks).

Dates: January 1984-Present.

Objective: To provide a thorough review and discussion of all sections of the labor code and current case law applicable to workers' compensation laws in the state of California.

Learning Outcome: Upon successful completion of this course, the student will be able to recognize and understand the impact of current case law on workers' compensation claims and to analyze or "brief" a legal decision.

Instruction: Major topics covered in the course are the role of the Department of Industrial Relations, employment contracts, legal definition of terms, compensation insurance, and disability indemnity. Methods of instruction include lecture, discussion, classroom exercises, and audio/visual material.

Credit Recommendation: In the upper division baccalaureate degree category, 2 semester hours in Insurance or Labor Law (8/95).

Workers' Compensation Claims Advanced (CA11)

Location: Various locations throughout California.

Length: 30 hours (12 weeks).

Dates: February 1975-Present.

Objective: To provide coverage at an advanced level of current case law involved with employment, injury, and permanent disability.

Learning Outcome: Upon successful completion of this course, students will learn the same basic subject matter as contained in CA-10, Basic Worker's Compensation Claims, however, CA-11 is attended to provide greater technical detail than CA-10. Additionally, CA-11 focuses on underlying concepts of the California Workers' Compensation scheme. Students will learn in this advanced course current case law governing employment, injury, earnings, permanent disability, and medical control. Present practices and procedures of the Workers' Compensation Appeals practices and procedures of the Workers' Compensation Appeals Board (WCAP) are reviewed. Legal research and some material is presented to the student to enable them to evaluate claims issues and the appropriate statutory law that applies to their claims situation. CA-11 is the last course taken in the IEA certificate series (CA-10 through CA-14). Completing CA-11 will allow the student to handle a workers' compensation claims file from beginning to closure.

Instruction: Major topics covered in this course are Functioning of the Workers' Compensation Appeals Board, analysis of current case law concerning compensable injuries; and degree of disability and rehabilitation. Methods of instruction include lecture and discussion.

Credit Recommendation: In the upper division baccalaureate degree category, 2 semester hours in Insurance or Business Administration (5/78) (3/84) (6/90) (4/91) (8/95).

Workers' Compensation Claims Basic (CA10)

Location: Various locations throughout California.

Length: 30 hours (12 weeks).

Dates: September 1974-Present.

Objective: To provide an introduction to the history of worker's compensation policy forms and endorsements; injury; medical claim disability; vocational rehabilitation; and the Worker's Compensation Appeal Board.

Learning Outcome: Upon successful completion of this course, student will have a broad understanding of the California Workers' Compensation Statutory Law. Additionally, students will learn the basic language and jargon along with the basic components of the California Workers' Compensation system. Students will understand the definition of an employee, employer and independent contractor, circumstances of injury with emphasis on criteria for AOE/COE issues; benefits provided in statues of limitation enforcement; medical control of workers' compensation claims, and the use of medical specialists are reviewed.

Instruction: Major topics covered in this course are workers' compensation insurance claims adjusting, investigation required to determine application of the law and its interpretation; payment of benefits; and subrogation. Methods of instruction include lecture, and discussion.

Credit Recommendation: In the upper division baccalaureate degree category, 2 semester hours in Insurance or Business Administration (5/78) (3/84) (4/91) (8/95).

Workers' Compensation Rehabilitation (CA14)

Location: Various locations throughout California.

Length: 30 hours (12 weeks).

Dates: September 1977-Present.

Objective: To provide an understanding of the administration of the Workers' Compensation Rehabilitation program as outlined in the Rules and Regulations.

Learning Outcome: Upon successful completion of this course, students will have a thorough understanding of the basic purpose of rehabilitation within workers' compensation and an indepth understanding of current statues, rules and analysis of a law, administration of benefits and methods for meeting legal requirements. Students will have a thorough understanding of the process they must follow in managing an injured worker seeking rehabilitation benefits under California Workers' Compensation statutory law.

Instruction: Major topics covered in the course are history and concept, organization and authority, due process, qualifying the injured worker, role of the rehabilitation representative, evaluation, and testing and plan maintenance. Methods of instruction include lecture and discussion.

Credit Recommendation: In the upper division baccalaureate degree category, 2 semester hours in Health Care Administration, Insurance, or Business Administration (6/78) (3/84) (6/90) (8/95).

Workers' Compensation Statutory Overview (OR-10)

Location: Various locations in Oregon.

Length: 30 hours (over 12 weeks).

Dates: January 1989-Present.

Objective: To provide an overview of the basic principles of workers' compensation. The focus is on Oregon's workers compensation history from the beginnings through the major reform in 1990 and the impact these changes have had in the workers' compensation system.

Learning Outcome: Upon successful completion of this course, the student will be able to make a compensability decision, manage a workers' compensation claim to closure and determine when to pay time loss and how to establish reserves.

Instruction: Major topics covered in the course are history of workers compensation, determining compensability of injury claims, and medical rules and medical management closures, and claims settlement practices. Methods of instruction include lecture, discussion, quizzes, and examination.

Credit Recommendation: In the upper division baccalaureate degree category, 2 semester hours in Insurance or Workers' Compensation (8/95).

Workers' Compensation: Permanent Disability Rating (CA13)

Location: Various locations throughout California.

Length: 30 hours (12 weeks).

Dates: *Version 1:* September 1974-May 1990; *Version 2:* June 1990-Present.

Objective: To recognize and calculate disability factors and apply results to appropriate rating formulas.

Learning Outcome: Upon successful completion of this course, students will be able to understand permanent disability rating of scheduled disabilities. Students will understand the rating process, contents and use of the permanent disability rating schedule, relevant rating terminology, anatomical terms, medical descriptions and measurements, and the objective and subjective mechanics of rating disabilities. Students will be able to calculate the dollar value of any single injury suffered by an injured worker.

Instruction: Major topics covered in this course are the mechanics of rating and the interpretation of medical reports including multiple disabilities, bilateral and ambidextrous disabilities, and subsequent injuries fund.

Credit Recommendation: *Version 1:* In the upper division baccalaureate degree category, 1 semester hour in Insurance (3/84). *Version 2:* In the lower division baccalaureate/associate degree category, 2 semester hours in Insurance and Business Administration (6/90) (4/91) (8/95).

Interagency Training Center

The Interagency Training Center (ITC) was established in 1968 to provide a wide range of highly complex technical training courses to employees of the United States government military, justice system, law enforcement, and intelligence community agencies. The ITC is governed by its trainees sponsoring organizations.

Source of official student records: Registrar, Interagency Training Center, 10530 Riverview Road, Fort Washington, MD 20744-5821.

Additional information about the courses: College Credit Recommendation Service, American Council on Education, One Dupont Circle, Washington, DC 20036-1193.

Communications Technology Fundamentals (ITC 22)

Location: Interagency Training Center, Ft. Washington, MD.

Length: 280 hours (8 weeks).

Dates: June 1987-Present.

Objective: To provide the student with the knowledge of basic physical, electrical, electronic, and optical concepts relative to communications technology; and to provide the student with hands-on experience in the operation of basic tools and instrumentation used in modern communications systems.

Learning Outcome: Upon successful completion of this course, the student will be able to fully participate as a junior team member in the installation, testing, maintenance and repair of specialized communications systems.

Instruction: Major topics covered in the course are basic RF theory and telephony, in addition to the tools and techniques necessary to perform specialized communications work. Methods of instruction include lecture, discussion, classroom exercises, case studies, audio/visual material, laboratory, and laboratory exercises. Methods of evaluating learning outcomes include quizzes, final examination, reports, and observations.

Credit Recommendation: In the lower division baccalaureate/associate degree category, 4 semester hours in Engineering Technology (7/92) (10/97). *Prerequisite*: a background in Associate of Art (or Sciences), Electronic Technology degree (AAGT or ASET), or equivalent military or trade school training.

Internal Revenue Service

The Internal Revenue Service (IRS) is part of the United States Department of the Treasury, a federal government agency. The IRS training and development organization is known as Corporate Education. There are three schools within Corporate Education responsible for designing, developing and delivering the training to all IRS employees; School of Taxation, School of Professional Development and the School of Information Technology.

The following information pertains to the school where the courses have received college credit recommendation:

SCHOOL OF TAXATION

The overall objective of the School of Taxation is to prepare Internal Revenue Service (IRS) employees to accomplish the IRS mission and to achieve the organization's goals. This involves not only tax law, accounting, auditing standards, and interacting with people, but also the policies, procedures, and administrative practices for which the employee will be ultimately responsible. The program is designed to give the employee both the skills and knowledge necessary to do his or her job properly.

The training program incorporates both formal classroom training and on-the-job training, as well as computer-based training and self-study training. Training policy is established by Corporate Education in a cooperative effort between the appropriate functional division and Corporate Education. The policy is formalized in the Internal Revenue Manual (IRM). Most formal classroom training is conducted and monitored by the education branch office. Continuing professional education courses and on-the-job training phases are handled by the local district function and monitored by local district training. Training facilities are designed to provide IRS instructors and participants with an optimal environment for learning.

Potential instructors must be members of an Instructor Cadre. To become a member, the employee must apply and compete with fellow employees. Technical expertise, instructor potential, communication skills, and educational background are all considerations. After being selected for the Instructor Cadre, an employee must successfully complete a Basic Instructor Training Course (BITC).

Courses are generally developed by a task force consisting of experienced employees from across the country. They are reviewed for accuracy by technical experts and periodically updated.

Certification of course completion is based on test scores, class participation, and performance on technical problems. If an instructor is unable to certify that a student met the objectives, a recommendation is forwarded to the appropriate function indicating where the student did not meet the objectives.

Paper records are kept of student progress during each class. At the end of each class, a training recommendation as to the successful completion of the course is made in quadruplicate. One copy is given to the student, one copy to the student's manager, one copy to the local district training office, and one copy is kept by the education branch office. In addition, a computerized record of course completion is made. A hard copy is forwarded to the employee's personnel folder. Detailed records are kept for one year. A record of successful completion is kept in the employee's official personnel folder until three years after the employee leaves the IRS.

SCHOOL OF PROFESSIONAL DEVELOPMENT

The General Leadership Institute has the primary responsibility of designing, developing and delivering management training to IRS employees. The General Leadership Institute is committed to providing the highest quality training using the latest training methods, new technology, highly skilled faculty, and the most current information. The Institute supports diversity, valuing and developing all employees to their fullest potential.

Partnerships have been developed with corporations, universities/colleges, government agencies and non profit organizations to ensure the integrity and quality of the leadership training program.

To become a member of the internal adjunct faculty, potential candidates must submit a resume that clearly indicates the level of education and experience required to teach a particular course. Selected candidates are required to successfully complete a train-the-trainer workshop and teach at least one class successfully to be considered members of the adjunct faculty. A continuing education requirement of varying hours are required annually to remain a member of the adjunct faculty. Instructors are evaluated annually based on the performance standards established for each course in the leadership curriculum. Contract instructors are contracted through a procurement process.

The instructional design system used to ensure that the curriculum is a quality product is the Training and Development Quality Assurance System (TDQAS). This process monitors and tracks the successful implementation of the curriculum to ensure that the customer receives the appropriate knowledge and skills to perform successful in his or her job.

The Kirkpatrick level of evaluation model is used to measure the successful implementation of the curriculum. the evaluation process is constantly reviewed to ensure consistency and relevancy in the course design and participant job performance. All participants must pass the course test and attend the required number of hours to successfully pass the course.

The 21 education branch offices located throughout the service, input and access the training administration system known as the Automated Corporate Education System (ACES) to obtain information of participants' successful completion of the course objectives, number of hours, total costs, etc.

Remedial action is taken to ensure that participants complete all required course requirements before being certified as completing the course successfully.

Source of official student records: The Director, General Leadership Institute, should be contacted for information on the appropriate office to contact regarding student records at: Internal Revenue Service, General Leadership Institute, 300 South Riverside Plaza, MS 1650CH, Chicago, IL 60606.

Additional information about the courses: College Credit Recommendation Service, American Council on Education, One Dupont Circle, Washington, DC 20036-1193.

Revenue Agent Training: Phase 2 (3140d)

Location: All IRS District/Regional Training Centers.

Length: 210 hours (28 days).

Dates: September 1984-February 1995.

Objective: To enable the student to properly examine complex individual and business tax returns.

Learning Outcome: Upon successful completion of this course, the student will be able to examine and audit complex individual and business returns; use tax law researching techniques on a more advanced scale; and do report writing covering complex individual returns.

Instruction: Major topics covered in the course are Schedule C, profit or loss from a business, accounting methods, cost of goods sold and inventory methods, depreciation, depletion, bad debts, investment tax credits, individual net operating losses, individual capital gains and losses, sale or disposition of property, Section 1231 assets, estate, gift, and excise tax returns, examination and auditing techniques, including indirect methods of determining income, contributions of appreciated property, and advance report writing.

Credit Recommendation: In the upper division baccalaureate degree category, 3 semester hours in Business Income Tax (2/90). **NOTE:** All students must complete 24 semester hours in accounting and normally have a baccalaureate degree before beginning this course.

Revenue Agent Training: Phase 3 (3140e)

Location: All IRS District/Regional Training Centers.

Length: 157 hours (21 days).

Dates: March 1985-February 1995.

Objective: To enable the student to properly examine corporate tax returns, including subchapter S corporations.

Learning Outcome: Upon successful completion of this course, the student will be able to examine and audit corporate tax returns, including those for subchapter S corporations; use tax law researching techniques applied to corporations; and write reports covering corporate returns.

Instruction: Major topics covered in the course are earnings and profits, dividends, reasonable compensation, corporate NOLs and carryovers, transactions between related parties, corporate employee plans, penalties including personal holding company and accumulated earnings (Sec. 531 IRC), S corporation election, operations, distributions and terminations, TEFRA tax law changes (subchapter S corporations), and balance sheet examinations.

Credit Recommendation: In the graduate degree category, 2 semester hours in Corporate Income Tax I (2/90). **NOTE:** All students must complete 24 semester hours in accounting and Revenue Agent Training—Phase 2 before beginning the course. Students normally have a baccalaureate degree or above.

Revenue Agent Training: Phase 4 (3140g)

Location: All IRS District/Regional Training Centers.

Length: 112 hours (14 days).

Dates: December 1985-February 1995.

Objective: To enable the student to properly examine a 1065 Partnership return.

Learning Outcome: Upon successful completion of this course, the student will be able to examine and audit a 1065 Partnership tax return; use tax researching techniques applied to the partnership's return; and write reports covering the partnership's and partners' returns.

Instruction: Major topics covered in the course are formation of partnerships, transactions between partnerships and partners, transfer of partners' interest and the effect on the new partner and the partnership, transfer of a partner's interest and the effect on the selling partner, effect of liquidating distributions, payment to a retiring partner, family partnerships and miscellaneous provisions, overview of TEFRA, and tax penalties including Section 6700 and 7408 IRC.

Credit Recommendation: In the graduate degree category, 2 semester hours in Partnership Income Tax (2/90). **NOTE:** All students must complete 24 semester hours of accounting and Revenue Agent Training—Phase 3 before beginning this course. Students normally have a baccalaureate degree or above.

Revenue Agent Training: Phase 5 (3140j)

Location: All IRS District/Regional Training Centers.

Length: 135 hours (18 days).

Dates: January 1988-February 1995.

Objective: To provide the student with advanced technical aspects of corporate taxation.

Learning Outcome: Upon successful completion of this course, the student will be able to examine and audit complex corporate returns; use advanced techniques of researching complex tax law issues related to corporations; and write reports covering advanced, complex issues on corporate returns.

Instruction: Major topics covered in the course are Schedules M-1 and M-2 and a review of earnings and profits; distributions in kind; preferred stock bailouts; Section 302 and other redemptions; Section 482 allocations; complete liquidations, which include Sections 331, 332, 333, 337, and 338; collapsible corporations, consolidations including Regulation 1.1502, corporate reorganizations Section 368 (a)1(a)-(a)1(g), and corporate tax attributes.

Credit Recommendation: In the graduate degree category, 2 semester hours in Corporate Income Tax II (2/90). **NOTE:** All students must complete 24 semester hours of accounting and Revenue Agent Training—Phase 4 before beginning this course. Students normally have a baccalaureate degree or above.

Tax Auditor Classroom Training: Phase 1 (3167b)

Location: All IRS District/Regional Training Centers.

Length: 180 hours (24 days).

Dates: January 1986-February 1995.

Objective: To prepare the student to effectively conduct examinations of nonbusiness individual tax returns.

Learning Outcome: Upon successful completion of this course, the student will be able to conduct audits of individual income tax returns through an acquired knowledge of the new tax laws.

Instruction: Course prepares the student to perform the job of tax auditor. Phase 1 covers exemptions, any expense item that may fall within the category of an itemized deduction, tax credits, tax computations, and preparation of workpapers. In addition, there are detailed sessions related to other auditing skills, including researching tax law and issues, taxpayer relations, interviewing taxpayers, communication skills, fraud and bribery awareness, and auditor responsibilities. There is a detailed case study problem that takes the student from a pre-examination analysis to the issuing of a completed report of tax adjustments. This case study is designed around tasks performed by an auditor in the course of a routine audit.

Credit Recommendation: In the lower division baccalaureate/associate degree category, 3 semester hours in Income Tax I (2/90).

Tax Auditor Classroom Training: Phase 2 (3167d)

Location: All IRS District/Regional Training Centers.

Length: 142 hours (19 days).

Dates: June 1986-February 1995.

Objective: To train the student to effectively conduct examinations of nonbusiness individual tax returns.

Learning Outcome: Upon successful completion of this course, the student will be further trained in the skills of auditing individual income tax returns. The emphasis is on the more complex tax laws and regulations that an auditor will encounter.

Instruction: Major topics covered in the course are the reporting of capital gains and losses on Schedule D, the principles of nonrecognition of gains and losses, exclusions from income, travel outside the United States, depreciation recapture, and repossessions. There is also a case study problem that is designed to develop the student's auditing skills, by requiring the student to interview a supposed taxpayer, make a determination based on the facts gathered, and write a report proposing adjustments. In addition, there are detailed sessions related to other auditing skills, which include researching tax law through the use of the Prentice-Hall material, illegal tax protesters, and introductions to corporations and tax shelter issues.

Credit Recommendation: In the lower division baccalaureate/associate degree category, 2 semester hours in Income Tax II (2/90).

Tax Auditor Classroom Training: Phase 3 (3167g)

Location: All IRS District/Regional Training Centers.

Length: 105 hours (14 days).

Dates: January 1984-February 1995.

Objective: To train the student to be able to conduct examinations of business returns and complex issues.

Learning Outcome: Upon successful completion of this course, the student will be further trained in the skills of auditing. The emphasis is on complex issues that could appear on individual income tax returns, as well as methods of detecting unreported income.

Instruction: Major topics covered in the course are net operating losses and the sale of a business. Much time is spent on techniques related to the auditing of income and possible unreported income on the part of the taxpayer. In addition, there are six auditing technique problems that simulate actual audits of taxpayers. They require the student to develop pre-audit plans based on a set of facts and to write reports proposing adjustments. These auditing technique problems cover "Direct Examinations of Books and Records," "Individual Net Operating Losses," "Cash Transactions," "Bank Deposits Analysis," "Source and Application of Funds," and a "Conclusion of Indirect Methods" in detecting unreported income.

Credit Recommendation: In the lower division baccalaureate/associate degree category, 2 semester hours in Income Tax III (2/90).

Taxpayer Service Specialist Training: Phase 1 (3032a)

Location: All IRS District/Regional Training Centers.

Length: 142 hours (19 days).

Dates: February 1980-February 1995.

Objective: To prepare the student Taxpayer Service Specialist to provide service to taxpayers in complex tax law issues generally affecting the individual taxpayer.

Learning Outcome: Upon successful completion of this course, the student will be able to provide answers to questions from taxpayers about individual income tax law as it applies to filing an individual tax return.

Instruction: Course provides a study of individual income tax law, including stock transactions, passive activity losses, alternative minimum tax, and related subjects.

Credit Recommendation: In the lower division baccalaureate/associate degree category, 2 semester hours in Introduction to Income Tax (2/90).

Leadership Studies Institute

Leadership Development Series I: Communications Skills (9697), Interest-Based Problem Solving (9860) and Managing Work (9677)

Location: All IRS District/Regional Service Center Offices.

Length: 64 hours (course [9697], 24 hours; course [9860], 16 hours; course [9677], 24 hours).

Dates: July 1995-Present.

Objective: To introduce entry-level managers to the fundamentals of supervision.

Learning Outcome: Upon successful completion of these courses, the student will be able to apply communication skills which foster effective relationships with staff, employees and customers, apply interest based problem solving process and understand the basic competencies and attributes necessary to be an effective leader.

Instruction: Major topics covered in these courses are active listening, communication styles, managerial communications, cross-cultural communication, presentation, and meeting skills, interest-based problem solving process, overcoming barriers, situational leadership, goal setting, planning, delegating and empowering employees. Methods of instruction include lecture, large and small group discussion, video-taping, exercises/case studies, role-playing, and pre and post-testing.

Credit Recommendation: In the lower division baccalaureate/associate degree category, 2 semester hours in Introduction to Supervision (10/96).

Leadership Development Series II: Facilitative Leadership (9647), Leading in a Changing Environment, (9681) Leadership Focus (9620), and Leading Empowered Work Groups (9652)

Location: All IRS District/Regional Service Center Offices.

Length: 96 hours (course [9647], 24 hours; course [9681], 16 hours; course [9620], 24 hours; course [9652], 32 hours).

Dates: January 1992-Present.

Objective: To develop leadership skills of entry-level managers.

Learning Outcome: Upon successful completion of these courses, the student will be able to understand and apply facilitation skills; understand the nature of change and change management strategies; understand different leadership styles; assess and develop his/her leadership skills; and understand group dynamics and collaborative leadership.

Instruction: Major topics covered in these courses are leadership facilitation as it relates to achieving results, improving process, work relationships, and decision making; the nature, impact and context of change, leadership in a changing environment, and the transitional model; leadership skills, leadership styles, communication, motivation and group skills, group dynamic principles, empowering leadership to clarify group and organizational goals. Methods of instruction include lecture, discussion, classroom exercises, case studies, audio/visual materials, and pre or post-testing.

Credit Recommendation: In the lower division baccalaureate/associate degree category, 3 semester hours in Leadership Development (10/96).

International Association of Fire Fighters

The International Association of Fire Fighters (IAFF) is an AFL-CIO affiliated labor union representing 225,000 professional fire fighters and emergency response personnel in the United States and Canada. One of the oldest public employee unions in America, the IAFF was formed in 1918. IAFF members protect more than 85 percent of the lives and property and are the largest providers of pre-hospital emergency medical care in the United States.

The mission of the IAFF Hazardous Materials Training Department is to provide emergency response personnel with high quality training that will enable them to recognize dangers posed by hazardous materials and take appropriate precautions to protect themselves when those dangers are observed.

In an effort to educate those emergency responders responsible for hazardous materials incidents, the Hazardous Materials Training Department of the International Association of Fire Fighters develops, markets, conducts, and evaluates some of the most comprehensive training programs available today.

IAFF's training materials and direct training programs have attracted fire fighters and emergency medical personnel from a wide array of fire service organizations around the globe. IAFF's flexibility provides training where emergency responders work, accommodating their shifts so that departments incur a minimum of overtime while their employees are trained. Moreover, the IAFF has never charged for training. This flexible, free of charge approach enables personnel who respond together, to train together.

Source of official student records: Registry of Credit Recommendations, American Council on Education, One Dupont Circle, Washington, DC 20036-1193.

Additional information about the courses: College Credit Recommendation Service, American Council on Education, One Dupont Circle, Washington, DC 20036-1193.

Hazardous Materials Response for Confined Space Operations

Location: Requested locations throughout the United States.

Length: 24 hours (3 days).

Dates: January 1996-Present.

Objective: To learn to recognize a confined space; to increase first responder knowledge of the nature of the hazards of confined spaces; to influence first responder attitudes toward health and safety when faced with a confined space incident; and to teach appropriate skills in responding to confined space incidents.

Learning Outcome: Upon successful completion of this course, the student will be able to identify at least five examples of hazardous confined spaces; describe the requirements of the permit space entry program and its components; describe procedures for routine confined space entry and identify three categories of confined space workers; and list key provisions of the OSHA confined space standard that apply to rescuers.

Instruction: Major topics covered in the course are confined space regulation and pre-incident planning; the hazards associated with confined spaces; ventilation of confined spaces, and proper rescue equipment and procedures pertaining to confined spaces; emergency trench operations and the confined space management system; pre-incident planning; ventilation; selecting protective clothing; trench and excavation; rescue; the general responsibilities of an Incident Commander and the usage of the Incident Command system at a confined space incident; and a safe approach to managing confined space incidents according to the incident management system used in jurisdictions of Incident Commanders. Methods of instruction include lecture, discussion, classroom and table-top exercises, quizzes, hands-on development of course topics, and a pre and post -test.

Credit Recommendation: In the lower division baccalaureate/associate or upper division baccalaureate degree category, 1 semester hour in Fire Science, Emergency Medical Technology, Administration of Justice, Police Science, Health Technologies, Public Administration, Health and Safety Management, or Industrial Management (7/97).

Hazardous Materials Training for First Responder Operations

Location: Requested locations throughout the United States.

Length: 24 hours (3 days).

Dates: July 1995-Present.

Objective: To address and reinforce health and safety issues of the First Responder in hazardous materials incidents in order to: raise First Responder knowledge of the type, nature, and physiological effects of hazardous materials; instill new First Responder attitudes toward health & safety; and identify safe behaviors in responding to hazardous materials incidents.

Learning Outcome: Upon successful completion of this course, the student will understand the basic strategies to safeguard their health and safety when their work involves potential exposure to hazardous materials; and possess and prove competency in skills needed for detecting the presence of hazardous substances, consulting references for additional information, and implementing work practices that will minimize the possibility of contamination to self, others, and property.

Instruction: Major topics covered in the course are responses to "Common Alarms" and the potential for exposure to hazardous materials; the health & safety of the First Responder; the routes of chemical exposure; the various effects of exposures; preventative strategies; medical surveillance; recognition and identification of the types of hazardous materials, their container shapes and sizes, characteristics of common hazardous materials, and familiarization of reference materials and marking systems to help identify unknown hazardous materials; basic chemistry; personal protective clothing; scene management; and preincident planning. Methods of instruction include lecture, discussion, classroom and table-top exercises, quizzes, hands-on development of course topics, and a pre and post -test.

Credit Recommendation: In the lower division baccalaureate/associate or upper division baccalaureate degree category, 1 semester hour in Fire Science, Emergency Medical Technology, Administration of Justice, Police Science, Health Technologies, or Public Administration (7/97).

Training for Hazardous Materials Response: Operations Refresher/Radiation

Location: Requested locations throughout the United States.

Length: 24 hours (3 days).

Dates: July 1997-Present.

Objective: To provide training in the initial response and control of radiation - related emergencies as well as a refresher of operations training for emergency responders who are currently trained to the *National Fire Protection Association (NFPA) Standard for Professional Competence of Responders to Hazardous Materials (NFPA 472).*

Learning Outcome: Upon successful completion of this course, the student will be able to recognize the hazard associated with radiation-related emergencies and how the location of the incident may indicate the type and quantity of hazards present.

Instruction: Major topics covered in the course are review of hazardous materials e.g., types of alarms, health & safety, general precautions, and medical surveillance; recognition and detection; basic chemistry; introduction to radioactive materials; packaging, transportation, and storage of radioactive materials; radiation emergencies; scene management; and pre-incident planning. Methods of instruction include lecture, discussion, classroom and table-top exercises, quizzes, hands-on development of course topics, and a pre and post-test.

Credit Recommendation: In the lower division baccalaureate/associate or upper division baccalaureate degree category, 1 semester hour in Fire Science, Health Technologies, Health and Safety Management, Transportation Manage-ment, Administration of Justice, or Police Science (7/97).

International Association of Machinists and Aerospace Workers

William W. Winpisinger Education And Technology Center was established in 1980 and is located on 72 acres in Hollywood, Maryland. The school was built by workers for workers and is designed to meet the complete range of educational needs of over 500,000 members of the International Association of Machinist's and Aerospace Workers located in the United States, Canada, Puerto Rico and the Republic of Panama. Providing over 76 diverse week-long courses per year, the members can study and learn in an atmosphere undisturbed by the daily pressures and demands of the workplace.

Source of official student records: Registry of Credit Recommendations, American Council on Education, One Dupont Circle, Washington, DC 20036-1193.

Additional information about the courses: College Credit Recommendation Service, American Council on Education, One Dupont Circle, Washington, DC 20036-1193.

Advanced Leadership

Location: Hollywood, MD; William W. Winpisinger Education and Technology Center.

Length: 42 hours (1 week).

Dates: January 1993-Present.

Objective: To develop team building, planning, and communication skills for union leaders.

Learning Outcome: Upon successful completion of this course, the student will be able to identify and develop their own leadership style; build solidarity and motivation in the workplace to help resolve problems; identify differences between static and innovative organizations; use planning as a change vehicle; understand current economic policies, trends, and systems and how they impact labor, management, and living standards; utilize more effective workplace communications; and develop an understanding of how technology affects the workers, workplace, the union, and society.

Instruction: Major topics covered in the course are group dynamics, workplace communications, technology and change, economics for union leaders, and Internet research. Methods of instruction include films, lectures, discussions, brainstorming, exercises, computer lab, and group presentations.

Credit Recommendation: In the lower division baccalaureate/associate degree category, 2 semester hours in Business Administration and Management, Communications, Labor Studies, or Organizational Behavior (1/98).

Arbitration

Location: Hollywood, MD.

Length: 27.75 hours (1 week).

Dates: January 1993-Present.

Objective: To develop basic knowledge and skills for grievance arbitration procedures.

Learning Outcome: Upon successful completion of this course, the student will be able to demonstrate a basic understanding of arbitration procedures and techniques; research the merits of a case; examine witnesses and evidence; write position papers and briefs; and represent the interests of unions and their members in arbitration proceedings.

Instruction: Major topics covered in the course are arbitration procedures; researching merits of the case; theory of the case; hearing conduct; preparation of witnesses and evidence; and the Duty of Fair Representation, position papers, and briefs. Methods of instruction include lecture, discussion, classroom exercises, computer lab, video, and arbitration simulations.

Credit Recommendation: In the lower division baccalaureate/associate or upper division baccalaureate degree category, 2 semester hours in Industrial Relations, Labor Studies, Human Resource Management, or Business Administration (1/98).

Collective Bargaining

Location: Hollywood, MD.

Length: 34.25 hours (1 week).

Dates: January 1993-Present.

Objective: To develop the knowledge and skills necessary for effective collective bargaining.

Learning Outcome: Upon successful completion of this course, the student will be able to demonstrate a basic understanding of collective bargaining principles and techniques; and demonstrate basic skills through contract costing, retrieving company and financial information, and preparing for negotiations.

Instruction: Major topics covered in the course are collective bargaining and the law, bargaining strategies, group dynamics, researching the company, and costing a contract. Methods of instruction include lecture, discussion, role play, classroom exercises, computer lab, video, and collective bargaining simulation.

Credit Recommendation: In the lower division baccalaureate/associate or upper division baccalaureate degree category, 2 semester hours in Industrial Relations, Labor Studies, Human Resource Management, or Business Administration (1/98).

Labor Leadership I (Leadership I)

Location: Hollywood, MD.

Length: 42.5 hours (1 week).

Dates: January 1993-Present.

Objective: To develop an understanding of the fundamentals of trade unionism and the basic laws and operations of the International Association of Machinists and Aerospace Workers.

Learning Outcome: Upon successful completion of this course, the student will be able to identify the roots of the North American labor movement and its influence on the development of labor law, involvement in government, and the growth of the North American economy; understand the role and responsibilities of the union steward; identify the organizational structure of the IAM, the duties of the various officers, and the elements of a local lodge meeting; describe the basic structure of the United States and Canadian governments and ways to facilitate activism on a local level; and define collective bargaining, the types of collective bargaining relationships, and the elements of a collective bargaining agreement.

Instruction: Major topics covered in the course are Labor History, collective bargaining, role of the steward, government and politics, and lodge administration/structures and services. Methods of instruction include films, lectures, discussions, brainstorming, exercises, computer lab, and field trip.

Credit Recommendation: In the lower division baccalaureate/associate degree category, 1 semester hour in Business Administration, Business Management, Labor Studies, Human Resource Management, or Industrial Relations (1/98).

Labor Leadership II (Leadership II)

Location: Hollywood, MD.

Length: 41.75 hours (1 week).

Dates: January 1993-Present.

Objective: To develop knowledge and skills to prepare participants to assume a leadership role in a labor organization.

Learning Outcome: Upon successful completion of these classes, the student will be able to understand labor law and the process of contract negotiations; "Cost-out" a collective bargaining agreement; understand technology and manage workplace change; administer and enforce the collective bargaining agreement; understand the importance of the legislative process on the labor movement; and demonstrate appropriate lobbying techniques.

Instruction: Major topics covered in the course are researching an employer; costing a contract; Collective Bargaining Law; contract administration and enforcement; legislative process and lobbying techniques; and technology and workplace change. Methods of instruction include films, lectures, discussions, brainstorming, exercises, computer lab, field trip, concert, and examination.

Credit Recommendation: In the lower division baccalaureate/associate degree category, 2 semester hours in Business Administration, Business Management, Labor Studies, Human Resource Management, or Industrial Relations (1/98). **NOTE:** Labor Leadership I must be completed before this credit can apply.

Strategies for Change (Strategic Planning)

Location: Hollywood, MD; Placid Harbor Education and Technology Center.

Length: 31.75 hours (1 week).

Dates: November 1995-Present.

Objective: To critically explore organizational change and learning theories to plan and develop strategies for change.

Learning Outcome: Upon successful completion of this course, the student will be able to understand the importance of strategic thinking; assess the current state of their organization; and design a strategic change plan.

Instruction: Major topics covered in the course are organizational learning theory, leadership styles, facilitation skills, communications, change process, environmental scanning, force field analysis, and organizational structure. Methods of instruction include lecture, discussion, classroom exercises, video, computer lab, and presentations.

Credit Recommendation: In the upper division baccalaureate degree category, 2 semester hours in Organizational Behavior, Labor Studies, Business Administration and Management, or Industrial Relations (1/98).

Train-the-Trainer

Location: Hollywood, MD; William W. Winpisinger Education and Technology Center

Length: 40 hours (1 week).

Dates: January 1993-Present.

Objective: To develop the knowledge and skills necessary to effectively train adult learners.

Learning Outcome: Upon successful completion of this course, the student will be able to demonstrate a basic understanding of adult learning principles; develop materials and pedagogy for adult learners; develop effective lesson plan; and teach a 30 minute segment on steward training.

Instruction: Major topics covered in the course are adult learning principles, lesson plan development, and introduction to instructional media. Methods of instruction include lecture, discussion, classroom exercises, computer lab, video, and training presentations.

Credit Recommendation: In the lower division baccalaureate/associate or upper division baccalaureate degree category, 2 semester hours in Industrial Relations, Labor Studies, Human Resource Management, or Business Administration (1/98).

International Hearing Society

The Audioprosthology Educational Program was initiated by the American Conference of Audioprosthology (ACA). Responsibility of offering the program was assumed by the International Hearing Society (IHS) in 1994. The IHS continues to offer the program and to provide an educational opportunity for those individuals who engage in the hearing instrument dispensing vocation (sales) and assure that they practice professionally, skillfully, and ethically. Proof of high school diploma or GED is a prerequisite for enrollment.

The educational program of IHS contains five courses, structured to conform to a semester hour basis common to universities. The core faculty is made up of individuals with extensive knowledge and experience in the academic and/or business world. It is the core faculty's responsibility to teach the courses in the IHS program, make suggestions about the use of outside faculty, and periodically review the curriculum. The faculty is also responsible for curriculum revision in light of new knowledge and methodology.

Source of official student records: Registry of Credit Recommendations, American Council on Education, One Dupont Circle, Washington, DC 20036-1193 or ACA Administrator 55 Twin Oaks Ave., Suite A-1, Lebanon, OR 97355.

Additional information about the courses: College Credit Recommendation Service, American Council on Education, One Dupont Circle, Washington, DC 20036-1193.

Audioprosthology 301: Hearing Science (Formerly Program in Audioprosthology)

Location: Various locations throughout the United States.

Length: 45 contact hours (15 hours for three weekends).

Dates: July 1994-Present.

Objective: To develop understanding of the physics of sound, anatomy, physiology, and neurology of the human auditory system and principles of psycho acoustics.

Learning Outcome: Upon successful completion of this course, the student will be able to apply the principles of sound to the actual measurement of acoustic signals; measure psycho acoustic perception of signals; and recognize anatomical structures and their interaction and contribution to the perception of sound.

Instruction: Major topics covered in the course are sound propagation, components, and measurement; anatomical structures and the physiological process involved in hearing; and psycho acoustic assessment. Methods of instruction include lecture, discussion, audiovisual material, and written examination.

Credit Recommendation: In the upper division baccalaureate degree category, 3 semester hours in Introduction to Hearing Science (7/94).

Audioprosthology 302: Introduction to Audioprosthology Management (Formerly Program in Audioprosthology)

Location: Various locations throughout the United States.

Length: 45 contact hours (15 hours for 3 weekends).

Dates: July 1994-Present.

Objective: To understand management strategies as they relate to patient needs, marketing approaches, and legal aspects of business practices.

Learning Outcome: Upon successful completion of this course, the student will be able to emulate workable management strategies to ensure effective patient care and effective business practices.

Instruction: Major topics covered in the course are the basics of communication, awareness of self, value clarification, marketing strategies, analysis of buyers behavior, products and pricing, promotion, advertising, selling, computerized accounting and records systems, American judicial system, malpractice, corporations, partnerships, sole proprietorship, and employee/employer liability. Methods of instruction include lecture, discussion, classroom exercises, case studies, audiovisual material, and written examination.

Credit Recommendation: In the upper division baccalaureate degree category, 3 semester hours in Introduction to Audioprosthology Management (7/94).

Audioprosthology 401: Audiology (Formerly Program in Audioprosthology)

Location: Various locations throughout the United States.

Length: 45 contact hours (15 hours for 3 weekends).

Dates: July 1994-Present.

Objective: To understand the principles of pure tone and speech audiometry; speech science; and the principle and application of amplification.

Learning Outcome: Upon successful completion of this course, the student will be able to perform basic audiometric examination and interpretation of results; perform basic hearing aid evaluation; and understand amplification testing selection and fitting of hearing aids.

Instruction: Major topics covered in the course are basic audiometric assessment science, basic hearing aid evaluation, and basic hearing aid selection. Methods of instruction include lecture, discussion, practicum (6 hours) reading, and written examination.

Credit Recommendation: In the upper division baccalaureate degree category, 3 semester hours in Introduction to Audiology (7/94).

Audioprosthology 402: Rehabilitation (formerly Program in Audioprosthology)

Location: Various locations throughout the U.S.

Length: 45 contact hours (15 hours for 3 weekends).

Dates: July 1994-Present.

Objective: To understand the terminology and classification disorders as they relate to hearing impairment, to understand aural rehabilitation, recognize patient behavior and/or symptoms that warrant referral, to have knowledge of the selection and fitting of hearing aids and assistive listing devices.

Learning Outcome: Upon successful completion of this course, the student will have knowledge of language of speech and development related to hearing impairment; knowledge of how loss of hearing affects speech and language development; will be able to recognize disorders of communication of the hearing impaired; be able to apply principles of aural rehabilitation in the fitting and adaptation of amplification devices for the hearing impaired; and know electroacoustic function of hearing aids and earmold acoustics.

Instruction: Major topics covered in the course are phonetics and speech/language development as they relate to the hearing impaired, etiology and classification of communication disorders, processes of communication, strategies in aural rehabilitation, laws governing rights of the hearing impaired, earmold acoustics, and electro acoustic characteristics of hearing aids. Methods of instruction include lecture, discussion, audio visual material, practicum, and written examination.

Credit Recommendation: In the upper division baccalaureate degree category, 3

semester hours in Introduction to Aural Rehabilitation (7/94).

Audioprosthology 403: Practicum (Formerly Program in Audioprosthology)

Location: Various locations throughout the United States.

Length: 135 hours supervised hours.

Dates: January 1988-Present.

Objective: To increase clinical skills in assessing hearing impairment for purposes of amplification.

Learning Outcome: Upon successful completion of this course, the student will be able to demonstrate a level of competency in basic audiometric evaluation, selection, fitting and evaluation of amplification.

Instruction: Major topics covered in the course are hearing testing and the selection and fitting of amplification. Methods of instruction include practicum, review of audiometric results, and supervisor's reports.

Credit Recommendation: In the upper division baccalaureate degree category, 3

International Union of Operating Engineers

The International Union of Operating Engineers is a 360,000-member AFL-CIO affiliated craft union with jurisdiction over heavy equipment operators and mechanics, surveyors, stationary engineers, and petrochemical refinery workers.

Source of official student records: General Secretary-Treasurer, International Union of Operating Engineers, 1125 17th Street, N.W., Washington, DC 20036.

Additional information about the courses: College Credit Recommendation Service, American Council on Education, One Dupont Circle, Washington, DC 20036-1193.

Hazardous Waste Materials Training

Location: U.S. Mine Safety and Health Academy, Beckley, WV.

Length: 80 hours (2 weeks).

Dates: January 1988-August 1993.

Objective: To train instructors for locals to give courses in proper procedures and personnel protection with emphasis on hazardous waste disposal sites.

Learning Outcome: Upon successful completion of this course, the student will be able to understand the legal and biological limits on exposure to hazardous materials; instruct others on the potential dangers and proper amelioration procedures when working at hazardous waste disposal sites; and train workers in the use of personnel protective equipment.

Instruction: Major topics covered in the course are basic concepts in industrial hygiene, toxicology, hazard identification, the use of material safety data sheets, monitoring equipment, respirators and self-contained breathing apparatus, other personnel protective equipment and clothing, techniques of site remediation, decontamination, and emergency response procedures.

Credit Recommendation: In the lower division baccalaureate/associate degree category, 3 semester hours in Environmental Engineering or Waste Management (8/88).

Interop Graduate Institute

The Interop Graduate Institute was developed by Interop, a division of Softbank Forums, which is a leading producer of education-rich, interactive technology forums that include conferences, expositions, Web sites, and university-level technical courses. The Interop Graduate Institute was formed to provide a rigorous, high-quality, graduate-level program that gives networking professionals the fundamental understanding they need as they plan, install, assess, and manage computer networks. The program covers technologies for computer networking, internetworking, and distributed computing. In addition to giving the scientific and engineering principles behind each technology, the courses provide perspective on their importance and use.

The Institute curriculum was developed by a committee of experts that include Heads of Computer Science Departments at well-known universities and leading networking researchers; all members hold a Ph.D. in Computer Science or Engineering. Institute courses are written by leading authorities, who hold a Ph.D. and have published research papers in the area of networking; courses are reviewed and approved by the curriculum committee. Some course offerings are taught by instructors other than course authors. Such instructors also hold an advanced degree in Computer Science or Engineering, and have worked in a university or research laboratory.

Institute courses are offered several times each year at various sites. The times and locations of each offering can be found on the web site (www.interop.com/igi). Each course begins with an intensive week of lecture and hands-on laboratory experience followed by six to eight weeks of independent study and additional work. During the independent study period, students access the IGI Lab facilities over the Internet.

To earn credit, a student must successfully complete assignments and pass an examination (some courses substitute a large project for an exam); an audit option is available for anyone who only attends lectures.

Source of official student records: Registry of Credit Recommendations, American Council on Education, One Dupont Circle, Washington, DC 20036-1193.

Additional information about the courses: College Credit Recommendation Service, American Council on Education, One Dupont Circle, Washington, DC 20036-1193.

C501: Networking Technologies

Location: Various sites in the United States.

Length: 40 hours (1 week onsite followed by 6-8 weeks of independent study).

Dates: July 1997-Present.

Objective: To provide an in-depth understanding of the scientific and engineering principles behind networking technologies, how the technologies operate, and their capabilities and limitations.

Learning Outcome: Upon successful completion of this course, the student will be able to understand the principles and properties behind many networking technologies and apply this knowledge when assessing and evaluating networking products and/or protocols.

Instruction: Major topics covered in the course are signal theory, physical media, and bit transmission; modems, data link protocols, shared-media, and media access; Local and Wide Area Networks; telecommunication networks; and specific technologies such as Ethernet, Token Ring, and ATM. Methods of instruction include lectures, discussions, lab experiments, lab exercises, quizzes, and final examination.

Credit Recommendation: In the graduate degree category, 3 semester hours in Telecommunications, Information Systems, Electrical Engineering, or Computer Science (6/97).

C502: Network Interconnection and Internetworking

Location: Various sites in the United States.

Length: 40 hours (1 week onsite followed by 6-8 weeks of independent study).

Dates: July 1997-Present.

Objective: To provide an understanding of the principles and concepts behind technologies that allow interconnection of homogeneous and heterogeneous networks.

Learning Outcome: Upon successful completion of this course, the student will be able to understand the basic techniques for the interconnection of networks, addressing, specific technologies such as bridging, switching, and routing, and protocols related to network interconnection and route propagation; evaluate simple network architectures to determine appropriate interconnection technologies and develop appropriate addressing architectures; and analyze and debug routing configurations.

Instruction: Major topics covered in the course are interconnection technologies, LAN/WAN addressing, Internet addressing, address binding, packet forwarding, packet switching, and implementation techniques. Methods of instruction include lectures, class exercises, interactive lab sessions, an independent project, objective quizzes, lab exercises, independent project evaluation, and final examination.

Credit Recommendation: In the graduate degree category, 3 semester hours in Telecommunications, Electrical Engineering, or Computer Science (6/97).

C503: Network Protocols and Protocol Design

Location: Various sites in the United States.

Length: 40 hours (1 week onsite followed by 6-8 weeks of independent study).

Dates: July 1997-Present.

Objective: To provide an in-depth understanding of the protocols that computers use when they communicate across networks and internets, emphasizing the elements of good protocol design; and to explain the fundamental techniques protocols use to solve the problems of loss, reordering, congestion, and duplication.

Learning Outcome: Upon successful completion of this course, the student will be able to understand the concepts of sound protocol design; and complete a significant programming assignment that demonstrates they can apply the protocol design techniques discussed in class.

Instruction: Major topics covered in the course are network protocols and protocol design; protocol layering; problems protocols solve including: loss, reordering, corruption, congestion, and duplication; techniques such as framing, checksumming, sliding window, slow start, and adaptive retransmission; and focus on the transport layer, but cover other layers. Methods of instruction include lectures, discussions, lab experiments, lab exercises, quizzes, written homework, programming assignments, and final examination.

Credit Recommendation: In the graduate degree category, 3 semester hours in Electrical Engineering or Computer Science (6/97).

C504: Distributed Programming and Applications

Location: Various sites in the United States.

Length: 40 hours (1 week onsite followed by 6-8 weeks of independent study).

Dates: July 1997-Present.

Objective: To understand the mechanisms used in distributed programs and services; explain the internals of several key distributed services; compare distributed systems: performance, cost, scalability, reliability, and security; and write and analyze distributed applications using Java and Internet tools.

Learning Outcome: Upon successful completion of this course, the student will be able to write concurrent and parallel programs; send RPC messages over a network; build a client/server application; understand the design criteria of name services; evaluate the internals of distributed files systems; understand distributed shared memory and mobile code; evaluate reliability mechanisms; and decompose a security protocol.

Instruction: Major topics covered in the course are client/server paradigm, socket API, middle-ware (e.g., RPC and COBRA), building a server, multithread server execution, protection and authorization, and example applications. Methods of instruction include lectures, class discussions, lab experiments, in-class participation, programming assignments, and final examination.

Credit Recommendation: In the graduate degree category, 3 semester hours in Electrical Engineering or Computer Science (6/97).

C551: Internet Measurement, Analysis, and Modeling

Location: Various sites in the United States.

Length: 40 hours (1 week onsite followed by 6-8 weeks of independent study).

Dates: July 1997-Present.

Objective: To understand the scientific principles underlying sound network measurement and what has been learned about the Internet by applying them.

Learning Outcome: Upon successful completion of this course, the student will be able to develop critical thinking regarding what has purportedly been measured; understand techniques for calibrating measurement, basic statistical analysis of measurement data, the different factors contributing to network performance, the measured behavior of different Internet applications, end-to-end Internet path properties, and the significance of fractal traffic models; and undertake sound, measurement-based analysis of network performance.

Instruction: Major topics covered in the course are why Internet measurement is complex, use of packet filters for measurement, assessing transport performance and behavior, basic statistics for network traffic analysis, what is known about Internet applications and traffic, and the ``fractal revolution'' in network modeling. Methods of instruction include lecture, interactive lab sessions, class discussion, individual consultation with an instructor, and a comprehensive network measurement project.

Credit Recommendation: In the graduate degree category, 3 semester hours in Telecommunications, Information Systems, Electrical Engineering, or Computer Science (6/97).

C552: Network and Protocol Support For Multimedia Applications

Location: Various sites in the United States.

Length: 40 hours (1 week onsite followed by 6-8 weeks of independent study).

Dates: July 1997-Present.

Objective: To explain digital audio and video as a new computer data type and how these data types may be communicated in real-time across the Internet.

Learning Outcome: Upon successful completion of this course, the student will be able to understand how audio and video are represented in computer systems, how these data types may be compressed, and learn the most common compression standards; know how multimedia data streams may be transmitted across the Internet; know how multicasting works; know how one can ameliorate the effects of congestion on real-time streams; and know how proposals for the evolution of the Internet into an integrated services network aim to support multimedia traffic.

Instruction: Major topics covered in the course are multimedia applications; user and application performance (``quality-of-service'') requirements; audio and video coding and compression technologies; multicast routing techniques and algorithms; the MBONE multicast backbone; real-time transport protocol RTP; videoconferencing; application-level protocols for best-effort real-time communication; and integrated services architecture for the Internet, RSVP, packet scheduling, and ATM. Methods of instruction include lectures, directed classroom discussion, interactive lab sessions, objective quizzes, a comprehensive programming project, and written comprehensive final examination.

Credit Recommendation: In the graduate degree category, 3 semester hours in Telecommunications, Information Systems, Electrical Engineering, or Computer Science (6/97).

IWCC Training In Communications

IWCC Training In Communications delivers communications programs at client sites worldwide to meet identified training needs. We are in business to make a positive difference in the way people communicate with employees, co-workers and customers. IWCC specializes in two areas of communications training; writing skills and presentations skills.

IWCC offers workshops on writing letters, recommendation reports, progress reports, audit reports, feasibility studies or proposals. Participants learn practical skills for writing clear, well-organized documents that are reader-focused.

IWCC's presentation skills workshops target professionals who deliver presentations to groups. Participants learn techniques for developing content, using visuals, handling audience interaction, and using effective delivery skills.

The Effective Business Communications program combines a three-day Writing Business Letters and Reports course with a two-day Presenting To Groups course. IWCC's Effective Technical Communications program includes a three-day Writing Technical Letters and Reports course and a two-day Technical Presentations course. The Effective Sales Communications program combines a three-day Writing Sales Letters and Proposals course with a two-day Selling On Your Feet course.

Pre-, post- and follow-up assessments measure the effectiveness of training and ensure that new skills are transferred back to the job. IWCC workshops are led by professional workshop leaders located in major cities across North America. Alternatively, we can train your trainers to deliver our programs under license.

Source of official student records: Registry of Credit Recommendations, American Council on Education, One Dupont Circle, Washington, DC 20036-1193.

Additional information about the courses: College Credit Recommendation Service, American Council on Education, One Dupont Circle, Washington, DC 20036-1193.

Business Communications

Presenting To Groups

Location: Client sites worldwide.

Length: 16 hours (2 days).

Dates: January 1988-Present.

Objective: To provide skills in preparing and delivering compelling and informative business presentations.

Learning Outcome: Upon successful completion of this course, the student will be able to make presentations that are informative and audience-directed, thoroughly and efficiently prepared, and competently and confidently delivered.

Instruction: Major topics covered in the course are audience/client analysis, objective setting, openings, closings, visual aids, delivery skills, and audience interaction. Methods of instruction include lecture, discussion, classroom presentations, and instructor and peer assessment of presentations.

Credit Recommendation: In the lower division baccalaureate/associate degree category, 2 semester hours in Speech or Communications (10/95). **NOTE:** Both this course and Writing Business Letters and Reports must be completed to receive 2 semester hours of credit. If 2 semester hours are awarded for these two courses, no additional credit should be awarded for either the Technical or Sales Communications programs.

Writing Business Letters and Reports

Location: Client sites worldwide.

Length: 21 hours (3 days).

Dates: January 1988-Present.

Objective: To provide skills in writing clear business letters and well-organized reports.

Learning Outcome: Upon successful completion of this course, the student will be able to write easily understood letters and reports that can be read quickly; assess and edit their own writing; and write more economically and confidently.

Instruction: Major topics covered in the course are writing style, paragraphing, tone, voice, making content decisions, early and well-supported recommendations, and helpful headings. Methods of instruction include lecture, discussion, classroom writing exercises, and instructor and peer assessment of business writing assignments.

Credit Recommendation: In the lower division baccalaureate/associate degree category, 2 semester hours in English, Business, Communications, or Writing (10/95). **NOTE:** Both this course and Presenting To Groups must be completed to receive 2 semester hours of credit. If 2 semester hours are awarded for these two courses, no additional credit should be awarded for either the Technical or Sales Communications programs.

Sales Communications

Selling On Your Feet

Location: Client sites worldwide.

Length: 16 hours (2 days).

Dates: February 1995-Present.

Objective: To provide skills in preparing and delivering customer-focused sales or business development presentations.

Learning Outcome: Upon successful completion of this course, the student will be able to relate product benefits to customer buying objectives in sales presentations that are thoroughly and efficiently prepared and persuasively delivered.

Instruction: Major topics covered in the course are customer analysis, competitor analysis, openings, closings, visual aids, delivery skills, and handling audience questions and problematic interactions. Methods of instruction include lecture, discussion, classroom presentations, and instructor and peer assessment of sales presentations.

Credit Recommendation: In the lower division baccalaureate/associate degree category, 2 semester hours in Speech or Communications (10/95). **NOTE:** Both this course and Writing Sales Letters and Proposals must be completed to receive 2 semester hours of credit. If 2 semester hours are awarded for these 2 courses, no additional credit should be awarded for either the Business or Technical Communications programs.

Writing Sales Letters and Proposals

Location: Client sites worldwide.

Length: 21 hours (3 days).

Dates: January 1988-Present.

Objective: To provide skills in writing effective sales letters and customer-focused proposals.

Learning Outcome: Upon successful completion of this course, the student will be able to write letters that strengthen customer relations and proposals that win business; assess and edit their own writing; and write more economically and confidently.

Instruction: Major topics covered in the course are writing style, paragraphing, tone, voice, and making content decisions; stating customer needs; and emphasizing product benefits. Methods of instruction include lecture, discussion, classroom writing exercises, and instruction and peer assessment of letter and proposal writing tasks.

Credit Recommendation: In the lower division baccalaureate/associate degree category, 2 semester hours in English, Business, Communications, or Writing (10/95). **NOTE:** Both this course and Selling On Your Feet must be completed to receive 2 semester hours of credit. If 2 semester hours are awarded for these 2 courses, no additional credit should be awarded for either the Business or Technical Communications programs.

Technical Communications

Technical Presentations

Location: Client sites worldwide.

Length: 16 hours (2 days).

Dates: October 1994-Present.

Objective: To provide skills in preparing and delivering informative technical or scientific presentations.

Learning Outcome: Upon successful completion of this course, the student will be able to make technical presentations that communicate complex information clearly and concisely; that are thoroughly and efficiently prepared; and are professionally delivered.

Instruction: Major topics covered in the course are audience/client analysis, objective setting, openings, closings, visual aids, delivery skills, and audience interaction. Methods of instruction include lecture, discussion, classroom presentations, and instructor and peer assessment of technical presentations.

Credit Recommendation: In the lower division baccalaureate/associate degree category, 2 semester hours in Speech or Communications (10/95). **NOTE:** Both this course and Writing Technical Letters and Reports must be completed to receive 2 semester hours of credit. If 2 semester hours are awarded for these 2 courses, no additional credit should be awarded for either the Business or Sales Communications programs.

Writing Technical Letters and Reports

Location: Client sites worldwide.

Length: 21 hours (3 days).

Dates: January 1988-Present.

Objective: To provide skills in writing clear and well-organized, reader-focused technical letters and reports.

Learning Outcome: Upon successful completion of this course, the student will be able to write easily-understood technical communications for non-technical readers; assess and edit their own writing; and write more economically and confidently.

Instruction: Major topics covered in the course are writing style, paragraphing, tone, making content decisions, making technical data understandable and effectively using graphs, statistics, and visuals. Methods of instruction include lecture, discussion, classroom writing exercises, and instructor and peer assessment of technical writing assignments.

Credit Recommendation: In the lower division baccalaureate/associate degree category, 2 semester hours in English, Business, Communications, or Writing (10/95). **NOTE:** Both this course and Technical Presentations must be completed to receive 2 semester hours of credit. If 2 semester hours are awarded for these 2 courses, no additional credit should be awarded for either the Business or Sales Communications programs.

Jamaican Institute of Management

The Jamaican Institute of Management (JIM) is an independent nonprofit, nonpolitical membership organization, established in 1967 by a group of businessmen to promote professional management and raise the standard of management in Jamaica.

The institute is dedicated to promoting the better management of enterprises in both private and public sectors in Jamaica. It is an institute for persons and organizations concerned with and interested in management, and is the oldest management development institution in the country.

The institute maintains classroom facilities at its head office and in rented quarters, in near proximity in the capital city of Kingston. In addition, the same courses are now being offered in regional capitals in Mandeville and Montego Bay, approximately 70-150 miles away, respectively.

The courses are of uniform quality in all respects at all locations, including course duration, content, and selection of faculty staff.

Courses are usually initiated by the faculties based on perceived need of the business community (or special needs survey), then examined by the Board of Studies, reviewed by the Programmes Advisory Committee for appropriateness, and recommended to the Executive Committee for approval.

An instructor's performance is progressively assessed by a faculty of professionals and academic staff (with a faculty head) reporting to the Board of Studies established to assist the Executive Director in the formulation of policies affecting management training and in the maintenance of good standards in all aspects of course and student performance.

Source of official student records: Assistant Director, Program Research and Development, Jamaican Institute of Management, 15 Hillcrest Avenue, Kingston 6, Jamaica, West Indies.

Additional information about the courses: College Credit Recommendation Service, American Council on Education, One Dupont Circle, Washington, DC 20036-1193.

Financial Management and Advanced Financial Management (Formerly Diploma in Financial Management)

Location: Financial and Accounting College of Training, Kingston, Jamaica.

Length: 210 hours (36 weeks).

Dates: January 1984-Present.

Objective: To provide an understanding of the concepts of financial management as it relates to the business firm.

Learning Outcome: Upon successful completion of this course, the student will be able to critically examine the role of the selected finance personnel (financial controller, treasurer, etc.); allocate and manage effectively the working capital of a firm; select, examine, and decide on different methods of financing and investing; use statistical techniques in budgeting judiciously and monitoring risks; analyze and evaluate financial reports, and prepare an appraisal of the performance of a business; develop and implement a good information system and procedure in the financial management of a business; conduct feasibility studies for an organization; plan and organize maintenance and control of a business site; and select and install systems in a data processing department.

Instruction: Major topics covered in the course are financial planning and control, valuation and capital budgeting, cost of capital, and theory of capital structure. Methods of instruction include lecture, discussion, and projects.

Credit Recommendation: In the upper division baccalaureate degree category, 3 semester hours in Principles of Financial Management and 3 semester hours in Advanced Financial Management for a total of 6 semester hours (2/86) (7/94).

Human Resource Management (Formerly Personnel Management and Industrial Relations; and Diploma in Personnel Management)

Location: Jamaican Institute of Management, Kingston, Jamaica.

Length: 210 hours (36 weeks).

Dates: January 1985-Present.

Objective: To provide a sound knowledge of human resource management approaches and techniques in business and industry.

Learning Outcome: Upon successful completion of this course, the student will be able to demonstrate knowledge of the human relations management role in Jamaican business and industry; conduct employment interviews and performance appraisals; handle grievances; and conduct career counseling.

Instruction: Major topics covered in the course are management and the personnel manager, functions of personnel, personnel policies, organizational behavior, industrial relations, training and development, and interviewing techniques. Methods of instruction include lecture, discussion, case studies, simulation exercises, and special job-related projects.

Credit Recommendation: In the upper division baccalaureate degree category, 4 semester hours in Personnel Management and 2 semester hours in Industrial Relations in the West Indies (2/86) (7/94).

Introduction to Business and Principles of Management (Diploma in Management Studies)

Location: Financial and Accounting College of Training, Kingston, Jamaica.

Length: 210 hours (36 weeks).

Dates: January 1984-Present.

Objective: To provide training in the theoretical and practical aspects of management.

Learning Outcome: Upon successful completion of this course, the student will be able to plan, organize, implement, and evaluate managerial strategies; effectively use the available human resources to efficiently manage an enterprise; modify and adjust plans to suit prevailing economic variables including fiscal and monetary measures implemented by the government; use knowledge of supply and demand and other parameters to determine levels of production and maximize the use of the factors of production; produce, interpret, and utilize a variety of methods of statistical representation; apply knowledge gained on information technology and the use of computers in a business environment; organize and manage a data processing department; critically examine and evaluate accounting procedures in a business; examine corporate reports and help make decisions on investments; and apply knowledge of business law in the management of a business.

Instruction: Major topics covered in the course are principles of management, principles of economics, quantitative aspects of management, computer management, managerial finance and accounting, organizational behavior, and business law. Methods of instruction include lecture, discussion, and individual projects.

Credit Recommendation: In the lower division baccalaureate/associate degree category, 3 semester hours in Introduction to Business and in the upper division baccalaureate degree category, 3 semester hours in Principles of Management (2/86) (7/94).

Principles of Management (Formerly Certificate in Management Studies)

Location: Financial and Accounting College of Training, Kingston, Jamaica.

Length: 150 hours (25 weeks; two 3-hour meetings per week)

Dates: January 1984-July 1994.

Objective: To introduce the nature, scope, and functions of management and to relate that knowledge to certain specialized, job-related skills.

Instruction: Major topics covered in the course are management principles; basics of accounting and internal control; statistics for business managers; introductory personnel management; and leadership skills. Methods of instruction include lecture and discussion, programmed instruction, film presentations, case studies, games, and simulation exercises

Credit Recommendation: In the vocational certificate category, 4 semester hours in Principles of Management (2/86) (7/94).

Principles of Marketing and Marketing Management (Diploma in Marketing)

Location: Financial and Accounting College of Training, Kingston, Jamaica.

Length: 225 hours (39 weeks).

Dates: January 1984-Present.

Objective: To provide a sound knowledge and understanding of key principles and applications of marketing mix strategies.

Learning Outcome: Upon successful completion of this course, the student will be able to describe the basic fundamentals of marketing and demonstrate some practical applications of marketing in the Jamaican business environment.

Instruction: Major topics covered in the course are principles and practices of marketing, quantitative aspects of marketing, marketing behavior systems, planning the marketing effort, principles of export marketing, and organizational behavior. Methods of instruction include lecture, discussion, case studies, film presentations, and project assignment.

Credit Recommendation: In the upper division baccalaureate degree category, 3 semester hours in Principles of Marketing and 3 semester hours in Marketing Management (2/86) (7/94).

Principles of Public Relations I and II (Formerly Diploma in Public Relations)

Location: Jamaican Institute of Management, Kingston, Jamaica.

Length: 210 hours (36 weeks).

Dates: January 1990-Present.

Objective: To provide familiarization with the wide and varied scope of public relations; and to provide an appreciation of the function of public relations in the Jamaican society.

Learning Outcome: Upon successful completion of this course, the student will be able to discuss the historical development of public relations; examine public relations and mass media; write news releases; do copy editing; interact with companies and the public; interact with journalists; develop video recordings and slide productions; and simulate news conferences.

Instruction: Major topics covered in the course are introduction to public relations, communications theory, public affairs issues, public relations practices, management principles, and public relations planning and programming. Methods of instruction include lecture, discussion, case studies, guest lectures, film presentations, simulations of exercises, field visits, and special projects.

Credit Recommendation: In the graduate degree category, 6 semester hours in Public Relations in the Caribbean, Customer Relations, Public Relations for Managers, or Multicultural Studies—Public Relations (7/94).

Principles of Supervision (Formerly Certificate in Supervision)

Location: Jamaican Management Institute, Kingston, Jamaica.

Length: 150 hours (25 weeks; two 3-hour meetings per week).

Dates: January 1984-July 1994.

Objective: To introduce basic supervisory skills.

Instruction: Methods of instruction include lecture and discussion.

Credit Recommendation: In the vocational certificate category, 4 semester hours in Principles of Supervision (2/86) (7/94).

JR Electronics And Pneumatics, Corp.

The JR Electronics and Pneumatics Corporation has served the industry in Puerto Rico and Latin America introducing the most up to date automation technology of the market. Developing and im-proving the production processes throughout the Didactic training Center, providing professional teaching to technicians and/or engineers of the industry. Our Educational mission is based on the development of highly professional individuals to fulfill the changing needs of the industry. Through our specialized seminars, students develop the necessary skills and know-how needed to work with most modern technical equipment. Our classrooms are equipped with state-of-the-art technology for pneumatic and electronic together with our dynamic teaching faculty.

Source of official student records: Registry of Credit Recommendations, American Council on Education, One Dupont Circle, Washington, DC 20036-1193.

Additional information about the courses: College Credit Recommendation Service, American Council on Education, One Dupont Circle, Washington, DC 20036-1193.

A) Omrom PLC; B) Basic Allen Bradley SLC 500 PLC; C) Intermediate Allen Bradley SLC 500 PLC

Location: 829 Campo Rico Avenue Country Club, Río Piedras, P.R. 00924.

Length: *Courses A, B, and C:*24 hours.

Dates: August 1996-Present.

Objective: To introduce the student to the fundamentals of programmable logic controllers.

Learning Outcome: Upon successful completion of this course, the student will be able to apply the principles of programmable logic controllers PLC to the use of Omron And Allen Bradley SLC500 PLC.

Instruction: Major topics covered in the course are ladder diagrams, concepts of programming, timers, shift registers, use of computer to program a PLC, batch process analysis, and troubleshooting. Methods of instruction include lecture lab exercises, quizzes, and observations.

Credit Recommendation: In the lower division baccalaureate/associate degree category, 3 semester hours in Principles of Program Control Logic using OMROM and Allen Bradley PLC's (8/97).

A) Process & Temperature Control; B) Sensors; C) Pneumatic Principles & Controls; D) Advance Controls

Location: 829 Campo Rico Avenue Country Club, Río Piedras, P.R. 00924.

Length: *Courses A and B:* 16 hours; *Courses C and D:* 24 hours.

Dates: August 1996-Present.

Objective: To provide the student with the fundamentals of sensors, process and temperature controls and their integration into the use of pneumatic and PLC technology.

Learning Outcome: Upon successful completion of this course, the student will be able to assemble and test typical pneumatic systems; be familiar with various process, temperature controls, and sensor technologies; and combine PLC devices with pneumatic circuit controls.

Instruction: Major topics covered in the course are sensors, control theory, application analysis, temperature measuring methods, fuzzy logic, control interfaces and communication, pneumatic circuit diagrams, vacuum applications, pneumatic electrical interfaces, ladder logic diagrams, and PLC programming concepts. Methods of instruction include lecture, laboratory exercises, quizzes, and observations.

Credit Recommendation: In the lower division baccalaureate/associate degree category, 3 semester hours in Principles of Industrial Control Devices and 1 semester hour in Industrial Control Laboratory (8/97).

Kepner-Tregoe, Inc.

Kepner-Tregoe is an international leader in the quest to improve individual, group, and organizational effectiveness through the creation and dissemination of new approaches to strategic and operational decision making.

Founded over 35 years ago by Dr. Charles H. Kepner and Dr. Benjamin B. Tregoe, the company now conducts business in 44 countries and its programs and services are available in 14 languages. To date, thousands of organizations worldwide have benefited from Kepner-Tregoe's results-oriented services and programs which are focuses on four distinct areas: Skill Development, Strategic Decision Making, Organizational Improvement, and Diagnosis and Evaluation. These services can be provided on a stand-alone basis or in combination to help an organization reach its goals.

Source of official student records: Registry of Credit Recommendations, American Council on Education, One Dupont Circle, Washington, DC 20036-1193.

Additional information about the courses: Office of Corporate-Higher Education Programs, Thomas Edison State College, 101 West State Street, Trenton, NJ 08608-1176.

Analytic Troubleshooting Workshop

Location: Various locations throughout North America.

Length: 40 hours (5 days).

Dates: August 1992-July 1997.

Objective: To teach participants who work in production environments how to find the cause of problems, then take action to fix them.

Learning Outcome: Upon successful completion of this course, the student will be able to use a systematic approach to analyze problems, avoid future problems and handle complex issues; identify the highest priority problem and focus on it; describe a problem in specific terms and find the true cause; verify hunches by checking the facts to avoid unnecessary fixes; choose a fix or other action which best solves the problem; avoid recurring problems by finding the root cause; maximize efforts by looking for other places to use the results of the troubleshooting; and recognize that a fix is a change which may cause future problems and consider what might go wrong with any fix before doing it.

Instruction: Major topics covered in the course are teaching participants to sort out complex situations, separate problems from decisions or actions, then set priorities to choose what to work on first. Next, possible causes are identified and tested to see if they explain the problem description. Participants learn to consider objectives, alternatives and risks to help them select or recommend a fix. Troubleshooters learn to anticipate the problems the fix could create, think ahead and avoid future problems and plan contingent action. Students must complete a project as part of a class requirement to gain the credit recommendation.

Credit Recommendation: In the lower division baccalaureate/associate degree category, 3 semester hours in General Business elective or Decision Making Process (7/92).

Apex

Location: Various locations around the country and select locations worldwide.

Length: 52-60 hours (1 week).

Dates: July 1981-December 1982.

Objective: To improve the managerial skills of persons in manufacturing or the service industry (banks, etc.).

Instruction: Major topics covered in the course are situations appraisal, problem analysis, decision analysis, and potential problem analysis. Prework, lectures, and in-class participation are used. Course also includes a constant testing for understanding and further honing of management skills, application of management skills, and planning for their future use.

Credit Recommendation: In the upper division baccalaureate or graduate degree category, 3 semester hours in Business Administration, Management, or Public Administration (7/81) (7/92).

Course 1: Engineering the Performance System
Course 2: Advanced Engineering the Performance System

Location: Worldwide locations.

Length: 19 hours (3 days).

Dates: August 1995-Present.

Objective: *Courses 1 and 2:* To enable the student to analyze human behavior to improve and maintain on the job performance.

Learning Outcome: *Courses 1 and 2:* Upon successful completion of these courses, the student will be able to learn a performance system model that helps explain why people perform the way they do; understand the five components of performance systems and how they are related; use questioning techniques to analyze each component of a given performance system and identify areas for improvement; examine the role of the individual Performer in the system; experience the effects of Consequences and Feedback in shaping employee behavior on the job; practice the elements of coaching and learn how to use them to optimize performance on a day-to-day basis; work with team members in a Consultation Group to apply proven, research-based tools to real, on-the-job performance issues; and plan for ongoing use of these skills to achieve continuous performance improvement.

Instruction: *Course 1:* Major topics covered in the course are how to identify, analyze, and correct deficiencies in the system that influences performance and coaching and communication tools to help them work more effectively with others to plan for performance and provide useful feedback. *Course 2:* Major topics covered in the course are the same as in Course 1. Methods of instruction include written critiques and a post course project, (e.g., case analysis relevant to course material covered.)

Credit Recommendation: *Course 1:* In the upper division baccalaureate degree category, 1 semester hour in Organizational Behavior (12/95). *Course 2:* In the upper division baccalaureate degree category, 2 semester hours in Organizational Behavior (12/95).

Fulcrum

Location: Various locations around the country and select locations worldwide.

Length: 26 hours (3 days).

Dates: July 1981-January 1989.

Objective: To enable participants (office workers and middle management) to improve their managerial skills.

Instruction: Major topics covered in the course are situation appraisal problem analysis, decision analysis, and potential problem analysis. Prework, lectures, and in-class participation are used. Course also includes a constant testing for understanding and further honing of management skills, application of management skills, and planning for their future use.

Credit Recommendation: In the lower division baccalaureate/associate degree category, 2 semester hours in Business Administration or Management (7/81) (4/87) (7/92).

Genco

Location: Various locations around the country and select locations worldwide.

Length: 52-60 hours (1 week).

Dates: July 1981-January 1989.

Objective: To improve the managerial skills of persons at the middle-management level.

Instruction: Major topics covered in the course are situation appraisal, problem analysis, decision analysis, and potential problem analysis. Methods of instruction include prework, lectures, and in-class participation. Course also includes a constant testing for understanding and further honing of management skills, application of management skills, and planning for their future use.

Credit Recommendation: In the upper division baccalaureate degree category, 3 semester hours in Business Administration or Management (7/81) (4/87) (7/92).

Government Management Seminar (GMS)

Location: Various locations around the country and select locations worldwide.

Length: 52-60 hours (1 week).

Dates: July 1981-December 1985.

Objective: To improve managerial skills of government workers.

Instruction: Major topics covered in the course are situation appraisal, problem analysis, decision analysis, and potential problem analysis. Methods of instruction include prework, lectures, and in-class participation. Course also includes a constant testing for understanding and further honing of management skills, application of management skills, and planning for their future use.

Credit Recommendation: In the upper division baccalaureate degree category, 3 semester hours in Management or Public Administration (7/81) (7/92).

Managing Involvement (Formerly Telos)

Location: Various locations around the country and select locations worldwide.

Length: *Version 1:* 22 hours (2.5 days); *Version 2:* 8 hours.

Dates: *Version 1:* July 1981-December 1990; *Version 2:* January 1991-July 1997.

Objective: *Version 1:* To enable participants (top and middle management) to improve their managerial skills by using common sense approach to decide when and how to involve others in resolving a concern. *Version 2:* To present students with a model of the managing involvement program for selecting the leadership to effectively resolve the specific issue at hand.

Instruction: Major topics covered in the course are situational appraisal and managerial leadership behavior. Prework, lecture, and in-class participation are used. Course also includes a constant testing for understanding and further honing of management skills, application of managerial skills, and planning for their use.

Credit Recommendation: *Version 1:* In the upper division baccalaureate degree category, 1 semester hour in Business Administration or Management (7/81) (4/87). *Version 2:* This course carries no credit as a standalone course; but if taken in combination with "Problem Solving and Decision Making, 3 semester hours in the upper division baccalaureate degree category in Business Administration or Management will be granted (7/92).

Problem Analysis/Decision Analysis (PADA)

Location: Various locations around the country and select locations worldwide.

Length: 40 hours (5 days).

Dates: November 1993-Present.

Objective: To learn a step-by-step process by analysis to organize information; uses judgment and experience to solve complex problems and make prudent decisions; and also learns necessary analytical techniques.

Learning Outcome: Upon successful completion of this course, the student will be able to understand the basic steps, refinements and appropriate application of Situation Appraisal, Problem Analysis, Decision Analysis and Potential Problem Analysis; question incisively to access relevant information; interact more effectively as a team through use of a common approach; recognize when participation and/or involvement is needed to create commitment or enhance the quality of both analysis and outcomes; build awareness of techniques for managing conflict and reaching group consensus; and use statistical tools to gather and process information for problem analysis.

Instruction: Major topics covered in the course are five components of the problem solving and decision making methods. Situation Appraisal which teaches participants to look at the whole picture by identifying and evaluating overall concerns and the concerns are broken into manageable issues and prioritized. A plan is developed for the effective resolution of the issues, including what analysis is required and who needs to be involved. Problem Analysis in which participants learn to resolve problems by first defining the problem in detail and possible causes are identified and tested to verify true cause before taking action. Decision Analysis which teaches a decision-making procedure that is applicable when the choice between alternatives is unclear and participants learn to clarify the purpose of the decision, form clear objectives, evaluate alternatives and assess risks of possible alternatives. Potential Problem Analysis and Opportunity Analysis where the participant learns to focus on a future plan to anticipate potential problems and maximize potential opportunities; and special emphasis is given to statistical tools with assigned evening readings.

Credit Recommendation: In the upper division baccalaureate degree category, 3 semester hours in Business Administration or Management (12/93).

Problem Solving and Decision Making (PSDM)

Location: Various locations around the country and select locations worldwide.

Length: *Version 1:* 36 hours (3 days); *Version 2:* 52 hours (5 days: 3 days PSDM and 2 days of application).

Dates: *Version 1:* July 1981-August 1987; *Version 2:* September 1987-July 1997.

Objective: *Version 1:* To enable participants to improve their managerial skills. *Version 2:* To learn a step-by-step process that organizes information, judgement and experience to solve complex problems and make prudent decisions.

Learning Outcome: Upon successful completion of this course, the student will be able to understand the basic steps and appropriate application of Situation Appraisal, Problem Analysis, Decision Analysis and Potential Problem Analysis; question incisively to access relevant information; interact more effectively as a team through use of a common approach; recognize when participation is needed to create commitment or enhance the quality of a solution; and understand techniques for managing conflict and reaching group consensus.

Instruction: *Version 1:* Major topics covered in the course are situation appraisal, problem analysis, decision analysis, and potential problem analysis. Prework, lecture, and in-class participation are used. Course also includes a constant testing for understanding and further honing of management skills, application of management skills, and planning for their future use. *Version 2:* Major topics covered in the course are the five components of the Problem Solving and Decision Making method are covered in this course. They are: Situation Appraisal-this method teaches participants to look at the whole picture by identifying and evaluating overall concerns. The concerns are broken into manageable issues and prioritized. A plan is developed for the effective resolution of the issues, including what analysis is required and who needs to be involved. Problem Analysis-participants learn to resolve problems by first defining the problem in detail. Possible causes are identified and tested to verify true cause before taking action. Decision Analysis-teaches a decision making procedure that is applicable when the choice between alternatives is unclear. Participants learn to clarify the purpose of the decision and form clear objectives. Potential Problem Analysis and Opportunity Analysis-through this process the participant learns to focus on a future plan to anticipate potential problems and maximize potential opportunities.

Credit Recommendation: *Version 1:* In the upper division baccalaureate degree category, 2 semester hours in Business Administration or Management (7/81) (4/87). *Version 2:* In the upper division baccalaureate degree category, 2 semester hours in Business Administration or Principles of Management or Management elective (7/92).

Project Management

Location: Various locations around the country and select locations worldwide.

Length: 21 hours (3 days).

Dates: August 1986-July 1997.

Objective: To develop an understanding and application of principles of Project Management for engineers and administrators.

Learning Outcome: Upon successful completion of this course, the student will be able to understand project management, define the key components of a project and determine the parameters; comprehend the stages of project management; apply the techniques and conceptual tools through the various stages; understand how to monitor, control, evaluate and close-out an on-going project.

Instruction: Major topics covered in the course are the three phases of project management—project definition, project planning, and project implementation. Course teaches techniques for setting project objectives, developing a work breakdown structure, allocating resources, and developing a project plan. The program covers technical tools such as network diagramming and human management techniques. Participants practice these techniques and case situations and then apply them to their own projects during the program.

Credit Recommendation: In the upper division baccalaureate degree category, 1 semester hour in Project Management, Business Administration, or Management (4/87) (7/92).

Vertex

Location: Various locations around the country and select locations worldwide.

Length: 52-60 hours (4.5 days).

Dates: July 1981-December 1984.

Objective: To improve managerial skills of persons in sales and marketing.

Instruction: Major topics covered in the course are situation appraisal, problem analysis. Prework, lectures, and in-class participation are used. Course also includes a constant testing for understanding and further honing of management skills, application of management skills, and planning for their future use.

Credit Recommendation: In the upper division baccalaureate degree category, 3 semester hours in Business Administration or Management (7/81) (7/92).

Knight-Ridder, Inc.

Knight-Ridder, Inc. is a worldwide information and communications company engaged in newspaper publishing, business news and information services, electronic retrieval services, news, graphics, and photo services, cable television, and newsprint manufacturing.

With 32 daily newspapers, it is the second largest newspaper company in the United States in terms of newspaper circulation (4.8 million, Sunday; 3.8 million, daily) and total revenues ($3 billion). Knight-Ridder's various information services reach more than 100 million people daily in 100 countries.

From 1984 to 1995, Knight-Ridder newspapers were honored to receive 36 Pulitzer Prizes, journalism's highest award—the greatest number received by any newspaper organization.

Knight-Ridder, Inc. offers many professional/management development courses to its employees to help them accelerate their professional and executive careers. These courses are offered under the auspices of the Knight-Ridder Institute of Training, located in Miami, Florida.

Source of official student records: Training Department, Knight-Ridder, Inc., 1 Herald Plaza, Miami, FL 33132.

Additional information about the courses: College Credit Recommendation Service, American Council on Education, One Dupont Circle, Washington, DC 20036-1193.

Advertising Sales Management

Location: Miami, FL.

Length: 40 hours (1 week); residential; 8 hours precourse work.

Dates: November 1979-December 1992.

Objective: To assist new sales managers in the development of managerial objectives, attitudes, and skills.

Instruction: Major topics covered in the course are learning managerial responsibilities in relation to selection and evaluation of new employees, acquisition of leadership skills, techniques for training and evaluating staff, development of selling by objectives programs, and how to utilize market research to determine consumer behavior. Participants also learn to correlate media strategy and decisions and the role of planning in advertising management. Methods of Instruction Include lecture, discussion, case studies, and practical exercises.

Credit Recommendation: In the lower division baccalaureate/associate degree category or in the upper division baccalaureate degree category, 3 semester hours in Marketing Management (8/82) (12/88).

Career Planning and Counseling

Location: Miami, FL.

Length: 40 hours (1 week); residential; 4 hours precourse work.

Dates: March 1982-January 1988.

Objective: To identify skills and clarify values and objectives of managers, editors, and supervisors with the formulation of individual plans of action for professional growth. Participants are assisted in managing nonpromotable employees through counseling, motivation, and techniques in redirecting subordinates.

Instruction: Major topics covered in the course are the elements of an effective career plan, an approach to planning a career, and overcoming career development problems. Participants develop an understanding of nonpromotability and techniques to revitalize static careers. Methods of instruction include lectures, discussion, skills inventories, exercises in value clarification, texts, and films.

Credit Recommendation: In the lower division baccalaureate/associate degree category, 2 semester hours in Career Planning and 1 semester hour in Personnel Administration (8/82).

Circulation Management

Location: Miami, FL.

Length: 40 hours (1 week); residential; 4 hours of precourse work.

Dates: June 1973-December 1992.

Objective: To assist circulation managers and managers from other departments in developing key marketing-management skills.

Instruction: Major topics covered in the course are the management cycle; problem-solving; consumer information systems; marketing; and promotion problems are addressed. In-basket exercises and case studies are used to develop skills in applying appropriate management techniques to the solution of problems and improvement of operations of the circulation department.

Credit Recommendation: In the lower division baccalaureate/associate degree category, 3 semester hours in Marketing Management (9/77) (8/82) (12/88).

Effective Human Relations

Location: Miami, FL.

Length: 40 hours (1 week); residential; 4 hours of precourse work.

Dates: June 1971-January 1988.

Objective: To provide managers with understanding, information, and skills in human relations within the organization.

Instruction: Major topics covered in the course are varieties of managerial styles and behavior; motivation theories; and means to develop effective relations with subordinates, peers, and supervisors in an organization. Methods of Instruction Include individual and team exercises, videotaped role play, case studies, and audiovisuals.

Credit Recommendation: In the lower division baccalaureate/associate degree category or in the upper division baccalaureate degree category, 3 semester hours in Supervision (9/77) (8/82).

Effective Newspaper Design and Graphics Editing

Location: Miami, FL.

Length: 40 hours (1 week); residential; 2 to 4 hours of precourse work.

Dates: October 1978-January 1989.

Objective: To develop the creative and technical skills of newspaper layout editors, picture editors, and design editors.

Instruction: Major topics covered in the course are hands-on experience in the organization, packaging, and layout of a newspaper. Course includes news hole efficiency, instant-art capabilities, type selection, tools of the trade, graphic capabilities of computer editing systems, redesign and prototype development, news-art department coordination, and photo, art, and graphics editing. Methods of Instruction Include lectures, discussions, hands-on kits for individual and team exercises, slides, and other visual aids.

Credit Recommendation: In the lower division baccalaureate/associate degree category, 3 semester hours in Newspaper Design and Graphics Editing (8/82) (12/88).

Finance for Non-Financial Executives (formerly Financial Management for Non-Financial Executives)

Location: Miami, FL.

Length: 40 hours (1 week); residential.

Dates: September 1972-December 1992.

Objective: To familiarize participants with the vocabulary and concepts of finance and accounting and to provide ability to interpret and analyze financial reports as a basis for decision-making.

Instruction: Major topics covered in the course are basic financial vocabulary;

analysis of transactions; recording and summarizing of accounting information; generally accepted accounting principles; financial reports; ratio analysis; cost and profit relationships; capital budgeting; ROI; and the auditing and treasurer functions are covered. Methods of Instruction Include lecture, discussion, case studies, and practical exercises.

Credit Recommendation: In the lower division baccalaureate/associate degree category or in the upper division baccalaureate degree category, 3 semester hours in Financial Management (2/78) (8/82) (12/88).

Improving Personnel Selection

Location: Miami, FL.

Length: 40 hours (1 week); residential.

Dates: March 1975-December 1993.

Objective: To provide line supervisors with interviewing, testing, and selection techniques.

Instruction: Major topics covered in the course are preparation for and conduct of the interview; reference checks; test administration; making the selection decision; and equal employment considerations are covered. Methods of Instruction Include lecture and emphasizes role playing, which is videotaped and critiqued.

Credit Recommendation: In the upper division baccalaureate degree category, 3 semester hours in Business Administration, General Management, or Personnel Administration (9/77) (8/82) (12/88).

Interpersonal and Organizational Communications

Location: Miami, FL.

Length: 40 hours (1 week); residential; 4 hours of precourse work.

Dates: February 1972-January 1988.

Objective: To provide line managers with information and experiences to increase their understanding and effectiveness in verbal and nonverbal communications.

Instruction: Major topics covered in the course are one-on-one communications between a manager and individuals with whom he or she works. Specific interview situations relate to employment (hiring and exit), counseling, disciplining, and appraisal. Methods of Instruction Include case studies, team exercises, role playing and critique, and audiovisual aids.

Credit Recommendation: In the lower division baccalaureate/associate degree category, 2 semester hours in Communications or General Management (9/77) (8/82).

Knight-Ridder Supervisory Training

Location: Miami, FL.

Length: 40 hours (1 week); residential; 8 hours of precourse work.

Dates: September 1977-January 1988.

Objective: To develop the skills of experienced personnel directors, trainers, and department heads in education and training methodology.

Instruction: Major topics covered in the course are techniques of instruction, such as lecture, audiovisual, role playing, and case study. Selected current management topics are examined. Methodology emphasizes practical exercises.

Credit Recommendation: In the upper division baccalaureate degree category, 3 semester hours in Educational Methodology or Personnel Administration (9/77) (8/82).

Making Effective Presentations

Location: Miami, FL.

Length: 40 hours (1 week); residential.

Dates: August 1976-December 1993.

Objective: To provide principles and practices of oral communication to top level supervisors.

Instruction: Major topics covered in the course are the communication process, preparing informal and formal presentations, presenting technical information, and the use of visual aids and effective presentation techniques. Managers acquire understanding of principles through self instruction materials and case studies. Skills are developed by making presentations, which are videotaped and critiqued.

Credit Recommendation: In the lower division baccalaureate/associate degree category or in the upper division baccalaureate degree category, 3 semester hours in Communications or Speech (9/77) (8/82) (12/88).

Managing for Commitment (Formerly Effective Management Skills)

Location: Miami, FL.

Length: 40 hours (1 week); residential; 6 hours of precourse work.

Dates: October 1978-December 1992.

Objective: To develop effective management skills for new managers and editors.

Learning Outcome: Upon successful completion of this course, the student will be able to define the "process" school of management; understand and apply the management functions, including planning, organizing, directing, and controlling; and apply motivation and teamwork skills to the organizational environment.

Instruction: Major topics covered in the course are the management process; management functions, including planning, organizing, directing, and controlling; leadership versus management; management by objectives; the communication process; visionary leadership; motivation and group behavior; and the control process. Methods of Instruction Include lectures, case studies, self-assessment inventories, role playing, business games, team exercises, and audiovisuals.

Credit Recommendation: In the lower division baccalaureate/associate degree category or in the upper division/baccalaureate degree category, 3 semester hours in Principles of Management (8/82) (12/88).

Marketing (Classified: The Action Approach)

Location: Miami, FL.

Length: 40 hours (1 week); residential; 6 hours of precourse work.

Dates: March 1975-January 1989.

Objective: To provide sales, advertising, and management training to managers and supervisors of classified advertising departments.

Instruction: Major topics covered in the course are the role of the classified manager, selecting and training sales people, measuring and evaluating their performance, the "positive selling" approach, creative copywriting, and sales incentives programs. Instructional methods include lectures, in-basket exercises, role playing, and workshops.

Credit Recommendation: In the lower division baccalaureate/associate degree category or in the upper division baccalaureate degree category, 3 semester hours in Marketing (9/77) (8/82) (12/88).

Newspaper Production Techniques (Formerly Modern Newspaper Production)

Location: Miami, FL.

Length: 40 hours (1 week); residential.

Dates: April 1971-December 1993.

Objective: To provide an understanding of the integrated systems employed in newspaper production including direct experience with techniques, tools, and equipment.

Instruction: Major topics covered in the course are ad service and editorial composition, engraving, stereotype, press-room, and mailroom. Methods of Instruction Include some lecture but emphasis is on hands-on experience and tutoring by staff in each department.

Credit Recommendation: In the lower division baccalaureate/associate degree category, 2 semester hours in General Business Administration, or in the upper division baccalaureate degree category, 2 semester hours in Graphics, Industrial Arts, or Journalism (2/78) (8/82) (12/88).

Newsroom Management

Location: Miami, FL.

Length: 40 hours (1 week); residential; 2 or 3 hours precourse work.

Dates: October 1979-December 1993.

Objective: To meet the managerial needs of the newly promoted editor as well as reporters about to make the transition into management.

Instruction: Major topics covered in the course are how to apply successful managerial techniques and managerial skills to the newsroom environment of the 1990s. the role of the editor, styles of leadership, and methods of evaluating employees and potential employees, and examines how to analyze and resolve interpersonal problems, and budget planning. Methods of Instruction Include lectures, discussion, individual and team exercises, and audiovisuals.

Credit Recommendation: In the lower division baccalaureate/associate degree category, or in the upper division baccalaureate degree category, 3 semester hours in Newsroom Management (8/82) (12/88).

Organization and Team Development

Location: Miami, FL.

Length: 40 hours (1 week); residential; 3 hours of precourse work.

Dates: March 1977-December 1991.

Objective: To provide editors, general managers, and division directors with an understanding of individual and group behavior.

Learning Outcome: Upon successful completion of this course, the student will be able to understand how different management styles influence behavior; identify factors that influence individual and team behavior; develop organizational consensus; and identify aspects of effective management and leadership.

Instruction: Major topics covered in the course are the forces influencing individual and team behavior, communication techniques, theories of leadership and motivation, self-analysis and evaluation, and planning strategies for change. Methods of Instruction Include lectures, individual and team exercises, case studies, films, and other visual aids.

Credit Recommendation: In the lower division baccalaureate/associate degree category or in the upper division baccalaureate degree category, 3 semester hours in General Management or Organizational Behavior (8/82) (12/88).

Problem-Solving and Decision-Making

Location: Miami, FL.

Length: 40 hours (1 week); residential; 3 hours of precourse work and a minimum of 8 hours.

Dates: March 1971-December 1991.

Objective: To provide the manager with skills used in rational problem analysis, problem-solving, and decision-making.

Learning Outcome: Upon successful completion of this course, the student will be able to determine the appropriate method to analyze and verify the cause of a specific organizational problem; establish criteria for decision-making; and develop specific planning skills for decision-making.

Instruction: Major topics covered in the course are a systematic and logical approach to information gathering and analysis, problem-solving, cause analysis, decision-making, plan analysis, and situation review. Methods of instruction include small group discussion and case studies. A film series is also used.

Credit Recommendation: In the lower division baccalaureate/associate degree category or in the upper division baccalaureate degree category, 3 semester hours in General Management (9/77) (8/82) (12/88).

Training, Developing, and Evaluating Your Employees

Location: Miami, FL.

Length: 40 hours (1 week); residential; 4 hours of precourse work.

Dates: December 1972-January 1989.

Objective: To develop in managers the skills needed to evaluate employee performance and to provide needed training and development.

Instruction: Major topics covered in the course are programmed instruction, films, case studies, and role playing are used to teach supervisory techniques for observing and evaluating performance, determining development needs, conducting development interviews, and on-the-job training.

Credit Recommendation: In the lower division baccalaureate/associate degree category, 2 semester hours in General Management (9/77) (8/82) (12/88).

Laborers-AGC

The Laborers-AGC Education and Training Fund is a nonprofit, jointly administered labor-management trust fund created pursuant to Section 302 of the Taft-Hartley Act. The parties to the fund are the Laborers' International Union of North America, AFL-CIO (LIUNA) and the Associated General Contractors of America (AGC). Laborers-AGC acts as an umbrella organization to provide primary support for sixty-nine affiliated funds engaged in training Construction Craft Laborers in construction and environmental remediation laborers across the United States and Canada.

The purpose of training and education is to improve and expand the competitive position of employers and union laborers. Laborers' training funds provide comprehensive education and training opportunities to individuals at all levels throughout their careers. Emphasis is placed on pride, dignity, and commitment to the trade. Training and education further the labor-management partnership and enhance individual and organizational recognition, security, and productivity.

Source of official student records: Registry of Credit Recommendations, American Council on Education, One Dupont Circle, Washington, DC 20036-1193.

Additional information about the courses: College Credit Recommendation Service, American Council on Education, One Dupont Circle, Washington, DC 20036-1193.

Asbestos Abatement Worker Course (ASB.W.)

Location: Local training fund programs affiliated with Laborers-AGC.

Length: 39 hours (5 days).

Dates: October 1987-Present.

Objective: To provide workers with information on asbestos hazards, engineering controls, protective equipment, procedures and technology of abatement; and with information on how to become certified under federal, state, or local regulations to gain access to the workplace.

Learning Outcome: Upon successful completion of this course, the student will be able to recognize the hazards of asbestos; know the regulations governing asbestos abatement operations; perform asbestos abatement tasks; and know the worker's rights referent to asbestos work.

Instruction: Major topics covered in the course are asbestos and its uses; health effects of asbestos; medical monitoring; legal rights; personal protective equipment; safe working practices; engineering controls; negative pressure worksite systems; preparation and decontamination; abatement techniques; air monitoring; and hazard communication. Methods of instruction include lecture, discussion, role playing, problem solving, classroom exercises, and hands-on experience.

Credit Recommendation: In the lower division baccalaureate/associate degree category, 2 semester hours in Industrial or Environmental Technology (6/93).

Environmental Remediation Worker Course

Location: Local training fund programs affiliated with Laborers-AGC.

Length: 104 hours (3 weeks).

Dates: July 1992-Present.

Objective: To provide classroom and performance-based training to environmental remediation workers.

Learning Outcome: Upon successful completion of this course, the student will be able to identify appropriate hazards categories, definitions, and regulations; list rights and responsibilities for workers and employers; understand radiation sources and health effects and be able to use appropriate radiation detectors and regulations; identify protective clothing and their uses; and identify appropriate emergency responses.

Instruction: Major topics covered in the course are hazard recognition; hazard communication; environmental laws and regulations; basic chemistry; health effects; personal protective equipment; radiation protection; decontamination; health and safety, emergency response, and confined space entry. Methods of instruction include lecture, discussion, exercises, laboratory, and hands-on experience.

Credit Recommendation: In the lower division baccalaureate/associate degree category, 3 semester hours in Environmental Science (6/93).

Hazardous Waste Operations Course (HAZ.O)

Location: Local training fund programs affiliated with Laborers-AGC.

Length: 45 hours (1 week).

Dates: April 1991-Present.

Objective: To prepare individuals such as local union representatives, contractor personnel, federal, state, and local compliance officers and others monitoring hazardous substance cleanup activities to recognize hazards and operate safely on hazardous substance cleanup sites.

Learning Outcome: Upon successful completion of this course, the student will be able to monitor hazardous substance cleanup activities and operate safely on hazardous substance cleanup sites.

Instruction: Major topics covered in the course are hazard recognition and identification; hazard communication regulations; health effects; legal rights; personal protective equipment; decontamination; site safety and health plans; hazardous waste handling, storage, and transportation; sampling techniques and air monitoring; and Superfund community relations. Methods of instruction include lecture, discussion, demonstration, classroom exercises, and practical exercises.

Credit Recommendation: In the upper division baccalaureate degree category, 2 semester hours in Environmental Science or Industrial Health and Safety (6/93).

Hazardous Waste Worker Course (HAZ.W)

Location: Local training fund programs affiliated with Laborers-AGC.

Length: 80 hours (2 weeks).

Dates: March 1988-Present.

Objective: To prepare workers to recognize hazards and safely perform job tasks on hazardous waste cleanup sites.

Learning Outcome: Upon successful completion of this course, the student will be able to recognize hazards and work safely on hazardous waste sites.

Instruction: Major topics covered in the course are hazard recognition and identification; hazard communication regulations; health effects; legal rights; personal protective equipment; decontamination; site safety and health plans; hazardous waste handling, storage and transportation; sampling techniques and air monitoring; and Superfund community relations. Methods of instruction include lecture, discussion, demonstration, classroom exercises, and practical exercises.

Credit Recommendation: In the lower division baccalaureate/associate degree category, 3 semester hours in Environmental Technology (6/93).

Lead Abatement Worker Course (LEAD.W.)

Location: Local training fund programs affiliated with Laborers-AGC.

Length: 40 hours (5 days).

Dates: January 1991-Present.

Objective: To provide information on identifying and evaluating building lead hazards and the abatement methods for its safe removal within applicable regulations.

Learning Outcome: Upon successful completion of this course, the student will know the hazards and regulations for lead removal operations, and the procedures and technologies to perform safe lead abatement work.

Instruction: Major topics covered in the course are lead and its uses; regulations and worker rights; health effects of lead; personal protective equipment; work practices at lead abatement sites; disposal methods; hazard communication; and inspections and reports. Methods of instruction include lecture, discussion, role playing, problem solving, and hands-on exercises.

Credit Recommendation: In the lower division baccalaureate/associate degree category, 2 semester hours in Industrial or Environmental Technology (6/93).

Radiation Worker II (RAD.W.) Radiation Worker Course (Formerly Radiation Worker Course [RAD.W])

Location: Local training fund programs affiliated with Laborers-AGC.

Length: 24 hours (3 days).

Dates: March 1992-Present.

Objective: To introduce the basic concepts of ionizing radiation and its attending hazards, use of instruments, survey techniques, and control measures.

Learning Outcome: Upon successful completion of this course, the student will be able to work safely in areas controlled for radiological purposes by applying measures to reduce exposure to ionizing radiation.

Instruction: Major topics covered in the course are radiation and its properties; sources of radiation exposure; health effects of radiation; control measures; radiological posting; personal protective equipment; radiation detection instruments; personal dosimetry; emergency response; and quality assurance. Methods of instruction include classroom lecture, discussion, classroom exercises, laboratory, and hands-on experience.

Credit Recommendation: In the lower division baccalaureate/associate degree category, 1 semester hour in Radiation Science, Environmental Science, or Industrial Hygiene (6/93).

Land Rover University

Land Rover, located in Solihull, England, is the world's only exclusive manufacturer of four-wheel drive vehicles. A small division of the Rover Group, Land Rover produces approximately 100,000 vehicles annually. Land Rover products were first imported to North America in 1949, appealing primarily to an agricultural and industrial market. With the recent growth in the popularity of sport utility vehicles, Land Rover has changed marketing thrust to meet the needs of an upscale market interested in safe, all-weather, around-town family transportation and had gained the reputation for manufacturing three of the world's best sport utility vehicles--Range Rover, Discovery, and Defender.

Land Rover University, the training arm of Land Rover North America, Inc., is dedicated to the recruitment and continuous development of everyone within the Land Rover family in North America, believing that a business's only true appreciating asset is its people. Land Rover University courses are held at a variety of venues throughout North America, with Technician training offered at four sites: Eastern Training Campus (Lanham, Maryland), Western Training Campus (Aliso Viejo, California), Central Training Campus (Triton College, River Grove, Illinois), and Canadian Training Campus (Mississauga, Ontario). Classes are conducted in modern facilities dedicated to training. Technicians use Land Rover approved tools and procedures in all hands-on situations. Instructors stress on-the-job safety and use all industry recommended procedures and equipment applicable to a particular job. In all courses, learning, not speed, is the objective.

Courses for technicians are developed as part of an effort to support the product by conveying the information and teaching the skills necessary to provide the finest owner experiences in the auto industry.

Source of official student records: Registry of Credit Recommendations, American Council on Education, One Dupont Circle, Washington, DC 20036-1193.

Additional information about the courses: College Credit Recommendation Service, American Council on Education, One Dupont Circle, Washington, DC 20036-1193.

Axles, Swivels, and Differentials (TT54.1)

Location: Four sites of Land Rover University: Lanham, MD, Aliso Viejo, CA, River Grove, IL, Mississauga, Ontario.

Length: 16 hours (2 days).

Dates: May 1995-Present.

Objective: To provide the student with the knowledge and skills necessary to successfully use a micrometer, diagnose, repair, and/or adjust sport utility vehicle steering swivels, differential units and other axle components.

Learning Outcome: Upon successful completion of this course, the student will be able to measure parts with SAE and metric micrometers; overhaul all axle components; measure part movements with SAE and metric dial indicators; dismantle, inspect, diagnose, repair and reassemble a differential.

Instruction: Major topics covered in the course are precision measuring devices, front axle and steering arrangements, final drive assemblies, service update bulletins. Methods of instruction include 25% lecture; 35% discussion; 40% classroom/lab exercises, competency demonstrations, and a final examination.

Credit Recommendation: In the vocational certificate category or the lower division baccalaureate/associate degree category, 1 semester hour in Automotive Technology (11/96).

Chassis Systems (TT57.3)

Location: Four sites of Land Rover University: Lanham, MD, Aliso Viejo, CA, River Grove, IL, Mississauga, Ontario.

Length: 16 hours (2 days).

Dates: April 1995-Present.

Objective: To provide the student with the knowledge and skills to diagnose and service chassis systems.

Learning Outcome: Upon completion of this course, the student will be able to understand operation, diagnosis, and service of sport utility vehicle chassis, brakes, and steering suspension systems; and be able to diagnose and accomplish basic maintenance and repairs on these systems

Instruction: Major topics covered in the course are basic brake systems, antilock brake systems, traction control systems, steering/brake/suspension systems, and electronic air suspension systems. Methods of instruction include 20% lecture; 20% discussion; 60% classroom/lab exercises, competency demonstration, and a final examination.

Credit Recommendation: In the vocational certificate category or lower division baccalaureate/associate degree category, 1 semester hour in Introduction to Automotive Technology (11/96).

Electrical Troubleshooting I (TT86.3)

Location: Four sites of Land Rover University: Lanham, MD, Aliso Viejo, CA, River Grove, IL, Mississauga, Ontario.

Length: 16 hours (2 days).

Dates: April 1995-Present.

Objective: To provide the student with an introduction to the principles of automotive electrical, electricity systems; and an introduction to the fundamentals of operation and troubleshooting procedures of automotive electrical systems.

Learning Outcome: Upon successful completion of this course, the student will be able to demonstrate the principles of test and diagnosis of some major systems using wire diagrams and test equipment.

Instruction: Major topics covered in the course are introduction to electrical circuits, test equipment, basic battery starting and charging systems operations, construction and diagnosis, introduction to wire schematics, symbols and their interpretations. Methods of instruction include 30% lecture; 30% discussion; 40% classroom/lab exercises, quizzes, observations, and a final examination.

Credit Recommendation: In the vocational certificate category, one semester hour in Automotive Technology (11/96).

Electrical Troubleshooting II (TT86.46) (Prerequisite Electrical Troubleshooting I TT86.3)

Location: Four sites of Land Rover University: Lanham, MD, Aliso Viejo, CA, River Grove, IL, Mississauga, Ontario.

Length: 16 hours (2 days).

Dates: May 1995-Present.

Objective: To provide the student with an introduction to electrical troubleshooting using diagnostic test equipment and electrical troubleshooting manuals.

Learning Outcome: Upon successful completion of this course, the student will be able to use an electrical troubleshooting manual to apply learned diagnosis processes to hands-on vehicle diagnostics using current level test equipment.

Instruction: Major topics covered in the course are Review of basic theory and circuit devices, semiconductors, computers, oscilloscope, and its use as a diagnostic tool using wave forms. Methods of instruction include 30% lecture; 35% discussion; 45% classroom/lab exercises, quizzes, observations, and final examinations.

Credit Recommendation: In the vocational certificate category, 1 semester hour in Automotive Technology (11/96).

Engine Management Systems (TT19.2)

Location: Four sites of Land Rover University: Lanham, MD, Aliso Viejo, CA, River Grove, IL, Mississauga, Ontario

Length: 16 hours (2 days).

Dates: April 1995-Present.

Objective: To acquaint the students with modern engine control systems and enable them to apply relevant SAE standards in diagnosing and servicing these systems.

Learning Outcome: Upon successful completion of this course, the student will be able to demonstrate a knowledge of the critical balance between engine performance, fuel economy and emissions; demonstrate familiarity with basic engine management systems and components; diagnostic trouble codes, connector form and location; demonstrate familiarity with relevant automotive terms and acronyms.

Instruction: Major topics covered in the course are fuel injection systems, ignition system, emissions control system, onboard computer systems, generic engine management system, and on-board diagnostics system, use of computer diagnostic equipment (TestBook). Methods of instruction include 25% lecture, 30% discussion and 45% classroom/lab exercises, quizzes, and final examination.

Credit Recommendation: In the vocational certificate category or the lower division baccalaureate/associate degree category, 1 semester hour in Introduction to Engine Management (11/96).

HVAC/Climate Control Systems in Sport Utility Vehicles (TT80.1)

Location: Four sites of Land Rover University: Lanham, MD, Aliso Viejo, CA, River Grove, IL, Mississauga, Ontario.

Length: 16 hours (2 days).

Dates: July 1995-Present.

Objective: To provide the student with a basic knowledge of the HVAC/climate control systems in sports utility vehicles.

Learning Outcome: Upon successful completion of this course, the student will be able to demonstrate a knowledge of HVAC/Climate control theory, various sports utility vehicle systems and their components, the Testbook diagnosis of HVAC/Climate control systems and electrical system components as well as the approved evacuation/recharge procedures.

Instruction: Major topics covered in the course are basic heating, venting, air conditioning and climate control theory; TestBook diagnosis of climate control systems, HVAC electrical systems diagnosis, air conditioning system diagnosis and evacuation/recharge procedures. Methods of instruction include lecture, discussion, classroom demonstrations, AV material, quizzes, observations, and a final examination.

Credit Recommendation: In the vocational certificate category or the lower division baccalaureate/associate degree category, 1 semester hour in Introductory HVAC (11/96).

Manual Transmission Overhaul (TT37.2)

Location: Four sites of Land Rover University: Lanham, MD, Aliso Viejo, CA, River Grove, IL, Mississauga, Ontario.

Length: 16 hours (2 days).

Dates: May 1995-Present.

Objective: To provide an introduction to manual transmission overhaul procedures, repair and diagnosis.

Learning Outcome: Upon successful completion of this course, the student will be able to demonstrate a basic familiarity with manual transmission overhaul.

Instruction: Major topics covered in the course are measurement, component identification, overhaul procedures, and Technical Service Bulletin use. Methods of instruction include 25% lecture; 35% discussion; 40% classroom/lab exercises, observations and quizzes.

Credit Recommendation: In the vocational certificate category, 1 semester hour in Automotive Technology (11/96).

Transfer Gearbox Overhaul (TT37.1)

Location: Four sites of Land Rover University: Lanham, MD, Aliso Viejo, CA, River Grove, IL, Mississauga, Ontario

Length: 16 hours (2 days).

Dates: March 1996-Present.

Objective: To provide the student with the necessary skills and knowledge to diagnose and overhaul transfer gearboxes in sports utility vehicles.

Learning Outcome: Upon successful completion of this course, the student will be able to demonstrate a knowledge of mechanical and electrical design functions, the technical information necessary to overhaul transfer gearboxes; and be able to demonstrate diagnostic, measurement, and overhaul procedures for the listed gearboxes.

Instruction: Major topics covered in the course are mechanical and electrical functions of transfer gear boxes, diagnostic procedures, precision measurement, and overhaul procedures. Methods of instruction include 40% lecture; 20% discussion; 40% classroom/lab exercises, quizzes, final examination, and observations.

Credit Recommendation: In the vocational certificate category or lower division baccalaureate/associate degree category, 1 semester hour in Mechanical Automotive Gearboxes (11/96).

V-8 Engine Overhaul (TT12.1)

Location: Four sites of Land Rover University: Lanham, MD, Aliso Viejo, CA, River Grove, IL, Mississauga, Ontario.

Length: 16 hours (2 days).

Dates: May 1995-Present.

Objective: To provide an introduction to engine overhaul procedures, disassembly, repair, and reassembly.

Learning Outcome: Upon successful completion of this course, the student will be able to demonstrate basic familiarity with engine overhaul, procedures, and measurement.

Instruction: Major topics covered in the course are Technical Service Bulletin use, and measurement and overhaul procedures. Methods of instruction include 35% lecture, 20% discussion, 45% classroom/lab exercises, observations, and a quiz.

Credit Recommendation: In the vocational certificate category, 1 semester hour in Automotive Technology (11/96).

Language Connect University

Language Connect University (LCU) was launched in January 1997, as a program of Syracuse Language Systems in Syracuse, NY. Enrolled LCU students enjoy the unique learning combination of a flexible, self-paced, multimedia curriculum and structure and attention from experienced foreign language teachers, specifically trained to provide instruction via the Internet.

After completion of the course, LCU students will receive a certificate acknowledging that they have developed the fundamental vocabulary and comprehension necessary to meet everyday needs in a Spanish-speaking environment.

The mission of Language Connect University is to provide a top-quality, interactive online language program, incorporating powerful multimedia software, the latest Internet technology and the traditional aspect of student-instructor interaction. As the acknowledged leader in foreign language software production, Syracuse Language Systems' LCU provides individualized expert instruction to the non-traditional student whose busy life precludes specific class schedules required by traditional education programs, and who desires personalized instructor interaction not found in current self-study products.

The course is designed to allow students to choose both the location and the pace at which they develop their language skills during a 12 to 16-week period of study. Our instructors are available via a variety of methods to provide lesson help, suggest remedial material as needed and answer other questions regarding Spanish study. Information about individual student records is available from LCU, by writing to the Coordinator of Student Services, Language Connect University, Syracuse Language Systems, 5790 Widewaters Parkway, Syracuse, NY 13214-2845.

Source of official student records: Registry of Credit Recommendations, American Council on Education, One Dupont Circle, Washington, DC 20036-1193.

Additional information about the courses: College Credit Recommendation Service, American Council on Education, One Dupont Circle, Washington, DC 20036-1193.

Spanish I

Location: Distance education course, based in Syracuse, NY, available worldwide through the Internet.

Length: 80-140 hours (approximately) (12-16 weeks) 12 lessons.

Dates: January 1997-Present.

Objective: To enable students to communicate effectively in Spanish at an elementary level and provide the foundation for further study of the language.

Learning Outcome: Upon successful completion of this course, the student will be able to participate in and understand conversations with native Spanish speakers in situations such as social gatherings, dining out, shopping, travel, and medical emergencies; read and understand authentic Spanish texts dealing with these same topics; and students who complete the optional language enrichment component of the course will become much more culturally aware about the Spanish speaking world.

Instruction: Major topics covered in the course are subject pronouns; the present and present- progressive tenses of commonly-used regular, irregular, and reflexive verbs; the preterit tense of commonly-used irregular verbs; negation; prepositions; expressing likes and dislikes; possession, direct, and indirect object pronouns; making comparisons; giving directions, commands, and asking questions; and discussing time, numbers, and weather. Methods of instruction include a structured sequence of multimedia lessons, exercises, quizzes, and exams incorporating listening and reading comprehension; speaking practice featuring a record/playback function and interactive speech recognition, allowing for instant feedback on pronunciation; written grammatical explanations, skill-reinforcing games, and instructor feedback offering individualized assistance and suggested materials for remediation; guided, culturally-authentic excursions into the Spanish-speaking world via the World Wide Web; and a moderated, electronic newsletter (listserv) providing an open forum for faculty/peer interaction.

Credit Recommendation: In the lower division baccalaureate/associate degree category, 4 semester hours in Spanish I (10/97).

Language Matters, Inc.

Language Matters, Incorporated (LMI) provides state-of-the-art information and quality education with regard to the use of spoken, signed, and cued languages. Through research, curriculum design, material development, and educational opportunities, LMI aims to distinguish and promote the use of language where Deaf, hard-of-hearing, and hearing people interact.

One way that this is accomplished is through the CUED LANGUAGE TRANSLITERATOR (CLT) PROFESSIONAL EDUCATION SERIES, which has served interpreters, transliterators, trainers, teachers, and educational administrators nationwide since 1988. Through a cumulative knowledge and skill building program, the CLT PROFESSIONAL EDUCATION SERIES provides educational opportunities to both novice and experienced interpreters and transliterators who facilitate linguistic and cultural communication between Deaf, hard-of-hearing, and hearing people.

Language Matters, Inc.'s CLT PROFESSIONAL EDUCATION SERIES is especially designed to meet the educational needs of transliterators who do not have access to state-of-the-art training in local or regional transliterator education programs. These courses are also appropriate for a variety of other professionals, as well as consumers of transliterating services.

The CLT PROFESSIONAL EDUCATION SERIES has been sponsored by colleges and universities in every region of the country, including, Galludet University in Washington, D.C., the National Technical Institute for the Deaf in New York, the University of Southern Maine, and California State Univeristy at Northridge.

Each Language Matters, Inc. course or module is taught by two (2) instructors. Each instructor is a nationally certified cued language-spoken language transliterator and is trained in at least two specialty areas found in a given course or module. This allows for two or more class activities to be conducted simultaneously and provides a greater opportunity for participants to receive individualized attention. This provides a more effective and cohesive educational experience.

For more information about Language Matters, Inc.'s educational programs, contact Lauren Tribby, Coordinator of Professional Development at: P.O. Box 3326, Silver Spring, Maryland 20918 or call (301) 439-5766 or Fax (301) 439-0830.

Source of official student records: Registry of Credit Recommendations, American Council on Education, One Dupont Circle, Washington, DC, 20036-1193 or Lauren Tribby, Coordinator of Professional Development, P.O. Box 3326, Silver Spring, MD, 20918 or call (301) 439-5766 or Fax (301) 439-0830.

Additional information about the courses: College Credit Recommendation Service, American Council on Education, One Dupont Circle, Washington, DC 20036-1193.

Cued Language Transliteration Advanced I: Self Assessment II

Location: Washington, DC and various locations nationwide.

Length: 15 hours (2 days).

Dates: February 1996-Present.

Objective: To provide students with an opportunity to learn specific skill areas, which will be targeted, discussed, and analyzed using a videotaped sample of the transliterator's work. Instructors will provide feedback and assist in the self-analysis process.

Learning Outcome: Upon successful completion of this course, the student will be able to recognize relevant topics in the analysis of spoken-to-cued and cued-to-spoken transliteration skills; apply self-assessment skills to rehearsed performance; apply assessment skills to integrated performance of both modeled transliteration and self assessment; identify and discuss a range of performance skills; conduct an in-depth analysis of their cued English to spoken English transliteration skills; conduct an in-depth analysis of their spoken English to cued English transliteration skills; and identify areas of strength and improvement for integrated performance (not isolated assessments).

Instruction: Major topics covered in the course are expressive and receptive fluency; expressive and receptive prosody and demeanor; distinguishing speakers; integrated AES; integrated transphonation; analysis of multiple tasks; and transcription as a tool for analysis. Methods of instruction include lecture, discussion, classroom exercises, teamwork, and a final examination.

Credit Recommendation: In the upper division baccalaureate or graduate degree category, 1 semester hour in Audiology and Speech Pathology, Communication, Communication Science, Education, Linguistics, Interpretation, or Speech and Hearing (12/96). **NOTE:** Depending upon the educational background of students, credit may be given at the undergraduate or graduate degree level because of the uniqueness of course content. This is consistent with the issuance of credit in college courses in signed language interpretation.

Cued Language Transliteration Intermediate I-A: Skills Development III

Location: Washington, DC and various locations nationwide.

Length: 15 hours (2 days).

Dates: November 1990-Present.

Objective: To give students a more advanced understanding of the skills required of a professional transliterator, and an opportunity to develop those skills.

Learning Outcome: Upon successful completion of this course, the student will be able to distinguish among transphonation, transliteration and interpretation; conduct a basic phonemic analysis of accents, dialects and foreign languages; identify at least three techniques for distinguishing multiple speaker; comprehend cued poetry; comprehend and transliterate from native cuers; conduct self-analyses of receptive skills, paraphrasing skills, etc; describe and demonstrate techniques for increasing expressive fluency; describe techniques for conveying non-linguistic environmental information; explain human perception and its relevance on prioritizing; describe five features relevant to logistical issues for transliterators; identify impact of consumer background on transliterator services; identify impact of transliterator services on consumer development/perception.

Instruction: Major topics covered in the course are overviews of psychology of perception; logistics; human development; audiology; deaf and hard of hearing human characteristics; language development; introductory articulatory phonetics; introduction to prioritizing; introduction to applied auditory environmental stimuli (AES); introductory intralingual skills development; introductory cued-to-spoken transliteration; and applied receptive skills (poetry). Methods of instruction include lecture, discussion, language lab exercises, team work, a video taped performance assessment, and a written examination.

Credit Recommendation: In the upper division baccalaureate or graduate degree category, 1 semester hour in Audiology and Speech Pathology, Communication, Communication Science, Education, Linguistics, Interpretation, or Speech and Hearing (12/92) (12/96). **NOTE:** Depending upon the educational background of students, credit may be given at the undergraduate or graduate degree level because of the uniqueness of course content. This is consistent with the issuance of credit in college courses in signed language interpretation. Students who successfully complete Cued Language Transliteration Intermediate I-A, I-B, and I-C may receive 3 semester hours for one course in Cued Language Transliteration Intermediate I.

Cued Language Transliteration Intermediate I-B: Receptive IV and Transphonation IV

Location: Washington, DC and various locations nationwide.

Length: 15 hours.

Dates: November 1990-Present.

Objective: To give students an understanding of how cued-to-spoken transliterating functions, how it impacts upon consumers, what isolated skills are required to perform multiple tasks without cognitive overload, and of how spoken and cued language articulatory phonetics are related to the provision of sociolinguistic information.

Learning Outcome: Upon successful completion of this course, the student will be able to comprehend common cuing derivations, perform decalage; identify component skills involved in cued-to-spoken transliteration; identify and engage in tasks designed to improve understanding of native and non-native English cuers; identify phonetic attributes of cued and spoken English; perform basic analyses and transcriptions of dialectal variation; analyze, transcribe and cue European-based foreign languages; and describe and engage in developmental exercises geared to improving component skills involved in transphonation of accents, dialects, and foreign languages.

Instruction: Major topics covered in the course are sociolinguistics; receptive language development; cognition; transphonation; receptive cuing skills; and developmental learning techniques. Methods of instruction include lecture, discussion, classroom exercises, team work, language lab work, and a final examination.

Credit Recommendation: In the upper division baccalaureate or graduate degree category, 1 semester hour in Audiology and Speech Pathology, Communication, Communication Science, Education, Linguistics, Interpretation, or Speech and Hearing (12/96). **NOTE:** Depending upon the educational background of students, credit may be given at the undergraduate or graduate degree level because of the uniqueness of course content. This is consistent with the issuance of credit in college courses in signed language interpretation. Students who successfully complete Cued Language Transliteration Intermediate I-A, I-B, and I-C may receive 3 semester hours for one course in Cued Language Transliteration Intermediate I.

Cued Language Transliteration Intermediate I-C: Auditory Environmental Stimuli and Information Chunking IV

Location: Washington, DC and various locations nationwide.

Length: 15 hours (2 days).

Dates: May 1994-Present.

Objective: To give students an understanding of the processes involved in providing sociolinguistic and cultural access to hearing mainstream environments, of the skills required for this, and of relevant skill building exercises.

Learning Outcome: Upon successful completion of this course, the student will be able to explain schema and memory; identify basic factors influencing prioritizing decisions; describe ranking strategies; identify text structures and functions; identify subordinate and superordinate categories; describe developmental activities for building long-term memory; shadow linguistic and non-linguistic acoustic information with lag; explain the relevance of specific intralingual skills to transliteration tasks.

Instruction: Major topics covered in the course are anthropology; cognition; sociolinguistics; English composition; and intralingual skills for transliterators. Methods of instruction include lecture, discussion, classroom exercises, teamwork, language lab exercises, and a final examination.

Credit Recommendation: In the upper division baccalaureate or graduate degree category, 1 semester hour in Audiology and Speech Pathology, Communication, Communication Science, Education, Linguistics, Interpretation, or Speech and Hearing (12/96). **NOTE:** Depending upon the educational background of students, credit may be given at the undergraduate or graduate degree level because of the uniqueness of course content. This is consistent with the issuance of credit in college courses in signed language interpretation. Students who successfully complete Cued Language Transliteration Intermediate I-A, I-B, and I-C may receive 3 semester hours for one course in Cued Language Transliteration Intermediate I.

Cued Language Transliteration Intermediate II-A: Silent Workshop & Transphonation V

Location: Washington, DC and various locations nationwide.

Length: 15 hours (2 days).

Dates: February 1995-Present.

Objective: To give students an understanding of natural cued language acquisition relevant for receptive skills, and to provide a more advanced understanding of the sociolinguistic issues related to transphonation of accents, dialects, and foreign languages.

Learning Outcome: Upon successful completion of this course, the student will be able to distinguish between dialect and language; identify language attitudes; analyze non-European languages; transcribe non-European accents; cue non-European languages; discuss American dialects and their causes; identify social and other factors influencing language variation; identify and describe transphonation skill building activities; identify and describe receptive skill building activities; develop strategies for comprehending cued discourse; make appropriate predictions about upcoming cued discourse (within a constrained context).

Instruction: Major topics covered in the course are linguistics, applied sociolinguistics; dialectology; anthropology; receptive language development; and transphonation. Methods of instruction include lecture, discussion, videotape; classroom exercises, teamwork, language lab exercises, and a final examination.

Credit Recommendation: In the upper division baccalaureate or graduate degree category, 1 semester hour in Audiology and Speech Pathology, Communication, Communication Science, Education, Linguistics, Interpretation, or Speech and Hearing (12/96). **NOTE:** Depending upon the educational background of students, credit may be given at the undergraduate or graduate degree level because of the uniqueness of course content. This is consistent with the issuance of credit in college courses in signed language interpretation. Students who successfully complete Cued Language Transliteration Intermediate II-A, II-B, and II-C may receive 3 semester hours for one course in Cued Language Transliteration Intermediate II.

Cued Language Transliteration Intermediate II-B: Ethical Decision Making II & Cued Interaction

Location: Washington, DC and various locations nationwide.

Length: 15 hours (2 days).

Dates: February 1995-Present.

Objective: To give students an opportunity to develop a more advanced ability to engage in ethical decision making as it applies to the cued-spoken language transliteration profession, and to develop expressive and receptive skills via immersion in cued English discourse.

Learning Outcome: Upon successful completion of this course, the student will be able to discuss specific ethical issues that apply to particular transliteration situations; analyze and resolve fundamental ethical considerations; explain and apply the Code of Conduct to ethical decisions; recognize the fundamental premises underlying the professional Code of Conduct; comprehend cued messages in immersion settings; recognize and identify strategies for improving comprehension during discourse; recognize and identify strategies for improving receptive skills in general; demonstrate the ability to apply supportive clarification techniques while cuing spontaneous discourse; and comprehend the cued discourse of a variety of non-native cuers.

Instruction: Major topics covered in the course are intermediate interpreter ethics and professional responsibility; substantive issues in interpreter ethics including confidentiality, equal access, consumer education; intermediate ethical decision making; human social development; cued language development; and natural language development. Methods of instruction include lecture, discussion, classroom exercises, teamwork, a quiz, and a written examination.

Credit Recommendation: In the upper division baccalaureate or graduate degree category, 1 semester hour in Audiology and Speech Pathology, Communication, Communication Science, Education, Linguistics, Interpretation, or Speech and Hearing (12/96). **NOTE:** Depending upon the educational background of students, credit may be given at the undergraduate or graduate degree level because of the uniqueness of course content. This is consistent with the issuance of credit in college courses in signed language interpretation. Students who successfully complete Cued Language Transliteration Intermediate II-A, II-B, and II-C may receive 3 semester hours for one course in Cued Language Transliteration Intermediate II.

Cued Language Transliteration Intermediate II-C: Mock Evaluation & Self Assessment I

Location: Washington, DC and various locations nationwide.

Length: 15 hours (2 days).

Dates: April 1995-Present.

Objective: To provide students with the opportunity to understand the processes and standards involved in assessing and rating professional transliterator competencies, and to evaluate their own skills in keeping with these processes and standards of practice.

Learning Outcome: Upon successful completion of this course, the student will be able to describe the process of transliterator performance assessments; identify relevant features of transliteration for analysis; identify modeled transliterator strengths; identify modeled transliterator weaknesses; analyze his/her own performance and identify strengths and weaknesses; identify an appropriate professional development plan based on self-analysis.

Instruction: Major topics covered in the course are transliterator performance assessment processes; transliterator performance assessment preparation; transliterator performance assessment rating criteria for a variety of tasks including transphonation, voicing, and expressive fluency assessment; and self/peer critique. Methods of instruction include lecture, discussion, classroom exercises, teamwork, and a final examination.

Credit Recommendation: In the upper division baccalaureate or graduate degree category, 1 semester hour in Audiology and Speech Pathology, Communication, Communication Science, Education, Linguistics, Interpretation, or Speech and Hearing (12/96). **NOTE:** Depending upon the educational background of students, credit may be given at the undergraduate or graduate degree level because of the uniqueness of course content. This is consistent with the issuance of credit in college courses in signed language interpretation. Students who successfully complete Cued Language Transliteration Intermediate II-A, II-B, and II-C may receive 3 semester hours for one course in Cued Language Transliteration Intermediate II.

Introduction to Cued Language-Spoken Language Transliteration A: Educational Interpreting Defined and Skills Development I

Location: Washington, DC and various locations nationwide.

Length: 15 hours (2 days).

Dates: November 1987-Present.

Objective: To give students an understanding of how the practice of transliteration is regulated, how it impacts upon consumers, how it compares with related services, and what skills are required to practice in the profession.

Learning Outcome: Upon successful completion of this course, the student will be able to describe why mainstreaming is a linguistic issue in the education of deaf children; define mainstreaming and distinguish between inclusive and exclusive practices; understand the Code of Ethics and Code of Conduct; understand the basic linguistic structures of signed languages, spoken languages, cued languages, and sign-coded systems; and discuss the differences between signed-spoken language interpreting and cued-spoken language transliteration processes and outcomes. In addition, the student will be able to identify and describe at least ten different skills associated with the practice of transliteration as well as some appropriate activities for increasing these skills.

Instruction: Major topics covered in the course are introduction to linguistics; general interpreter ethics and professional responsibility; substantive issues in interpreter ethics, confidentiality, equal access, consumer education; introduction to ethical decision making; introductory sociolinguistics; introduction to the identification and analysis of linguistics and environmental information; and introductory human social development. Methods of instruction include: lecture, discussion, classroom exercises, teamwork, presentations, and two written examinations.

Credit Recommendation: In the upper division baccalaureate or graduate degree category, 1 semester hour in Audiology and Speech Pathology, Communication, Communication Science, Education, Linguistics, Interpretation, or Speech and Hearing (12/96). **NOTE:** Depending upon the educational background of students, credit may be given at the undergraduate or graduate degree level because of the uniqueness of course content. This is consistent with the issuance of credit in college courses in signed language interpretation. Students who successfully complete Introduction to Cued Language-Spoken Language Transliteration A, B, and C may receive 3 semester hours in one course: Introduction to Cued Language-Spoken Language Transliteration.

Introduction to Cued Language-Spoken Language Transliteration B: Skills Development II

Location: Washington, DC and various locations nationwide.

Length: 15 hours (2 days).

Dates: September 1991-Present.

Objective: To provide students with in-depth development of transliterator skills, and an opportunity to discuss the application of those skills in real-life professional settings.

Learning Outcome: Upon successful completion of this course, the student will be able to identify and describe at least ten common cuing errors; identify the pertinent components in receiving cued discourse; cueread stories and answer related questions with 80% accuracy; identify and describe two strategies for condensing information; explain appropriate circumstances for their use and implications for their misuse; discuss the application of these skills and their relevance to equal access services.

Instruction: Major topics covered in the course are expressive cued language development, receptive cued language development; linguistics; phonetics and phonology; introduction to information processing and text analysis; ethical decision making; identification and analysis of linguistic and environmental information; and introductory human social development. Methods of instruction include lecture, discussion, classroom exercises, teamwork, audiotape exercises, quizzes, and a final examination.

Credit Recommendation: In the upper division baccalaureate or graduate degree category, 1 semester hour in Audiology and Speech Pathology, Communication, Communication Science, Education, Linguistics, Interpretation, or Speech and Hearing (12/96). **NOTE:** Depending upon the educational background of students, credit may be given at the undergraduate or graduate degree level because of the uniqueness of course content. This is consistent with the issuance of credit in college courses in signed language interpretation. Students who successfully complete Introduction to Cued Language-Spoken Language Transliteration A, B, and C may receive 3 semester hours in one course: Introduction to Cued Language-Spoken Language Transliteration.

Introduction to Cued Language-Spoken Language Transliteration C: Ethical Decision Making I

Location: Washington, DC and various locations nationwide.

Length: 15 hours (2 days).

Dates: March 1993-Present.

Objective: To provide students with a heightened awareness of personal and professional ethical issues and the consequences of potential conflicts between the two in the transliteration profession.

Learning Outcome: Upon successful completion of this course, the student will be able to distinguish between personal and professional ethics, explain why ethics are a part of the field of transliteration, describe the Code of Conduct and Code of Ethics, explain the consequences for unethical conduct, discuss ethical issues such as confidentiality and equal access; demonstrate an ability to determine ethical or unethical practices in specific transliteration (or transliteration related) situations.

Instruction: Major topics covered in the course are professional transliterator codes, professional ethics, introduction to general ethical issues, substantive issues in transliterator ethics, ethics in conflict, ethical decision making, professional ethics and test-taking strategies. Methods of instruction include lecture, small and large group discussion, classroom exercises, team work, quizzes, and final examination.

Credit Recommendation: In the upper division baccalaureate or graduate degree category, 1 semester hour in Audiology and Speech Pathology, Communication, Communication Science, Education, Linguistics, Interpretation, or Speech and Hearing (12/96). **NOTE:** Depending upon the educational background of students, credit may be given at the undergraduate or graduate degree level because of the uniqueness of course content. This is consistent with the issuance of credit in college courses in signed language interpretation. Students who successfully complete Introduction to Cued Language-Spoken Language Transliteration A, B, and C may receive 3 semester hours for one course in Introduction to Cued Language-Spoken Language Transliteration.

Learning International, Inc.

Learning International pioneered sales training using principles of behavioral psychology in the 1960's. Today, Learning International continues to offer skills-based training for people who are directly involved with their company's customers. It began as Basic Systems, became Xerox Learning Systems, and was subsequently bought by The Times Mirror Company and given its current name in 1985.

Our program development process involves research, instructional design and rigorous testing by our permanent staff and cadre of external experts. Both standard and customized products meet strict standards. Drawing upon the work of Baldwin, Bandura, Gagne, Ford, McClelland, Neisser, and others, Learning International has created a learning model which ensures a standard of effectiveness, reliability and educational integrity while maximizing student retention rates and knowledge transfer.

Our training staff is chosen, developed and managed by a team dedicated to the ongoing quality of our course implementation and each instructor undergoes a thorough training program. Measurement and feedback mechanisms are in place to ensure consistent, high quality instruction and continuous improvement of our products, based upon student and instructor input and periodic product developer review.

Student populations come from diverse industries and locations around the country and include a wide variety of job titles and professional qualifications. The typical student for the courses listed here will be involved in sales or sales management. Courses are conducted in one of several ways; at the customer's site, at an appropriate public location, or in one of the Learning International's facilities. In each case, care is taken that the environment be conducive to learning and that both student and instructor are comfortable with the arrangement.

Contact Customer Service Manager, Learning International, P.O. Box 10211, Stamford, CT 06904.

Source of official student records: Registry of Credit Recommendations, American Council on Education, One Dupont Circle, Washington, DC 20036-1193.

Additional information about the courses: College Credit Recommendation Service, American Council on Education, One Dupont Circle, Washington, DC 20036-1193.

Account Development Strategies

Location: Throughout the United States.

Length: 14 hours (2 days).

Dates: January 1986-Present.

Objective: This program presents a total process that salespeople can use to build account relationships and better compete in today's challenging marketplace.

Learning Outcome: Upon successful completion of this course, the student will be able to recognize and respond to organizational and personal needs of customers; build more long-term relationships with their accounts; plan a probing strategy to uncover needs and problem solve effectively; analyze and assess factors affecting their accounts; formulate account strategies and plans appropriate to each situation.

Instruction: Major topics covered in the course are account presentations activity, introductory and concluding activities. Needs and relationships, tactical probing, and planning are presented in a sequence designed to build step-by-step to the account presentation activity, where students demonstrate mastery of the overall account development model.

Credit Recommendation: In the lower division baccalaureate/associate degree category, 1 semester hour in Marketing or Business Administration (7/95).

Breakthrough Sales Strategies

Location: Throughout the United States.

Length: 14 hours (2 days).

Dates: January 1995-Present.

Objective: To provide the process which helps salespeople to think strategically and plan practical solutions when dealing with difficult, high risk or important account situations.

Learning Outcome: Upon successful completion of this course, the student will be able to understand the differences in types of sales opportunities establishing an overall picture of the sales opportunities; use strategies and tactics to create desired sales relationship and outcomes; and conduct a self assessment and identify ways to improve sales performance.

Instruction: Major topics covered in the course are the selling environment, customer relationship process, key roles of a salesperson, the types of sales opportunity, information gathering skills, comfort-zone self assessment, and application of concepts to personal sales opportunities. Students are encouraged to integrate the skills and knowledge they've acquired and transfer it to their individual sales processes. Final activities include group and peer review and development of individual best practices.

Credit Recommendation: In the upper division baccalaureate degree category, 1 semester hour in Salesmanship, Marketing Elective, or Business Administration (7/95).

Focused Interviewing

Location: Throughout the United States.

Length: 14 hours (2 days).

Dates: January 1986-Present.

Objective: To provide a model for planning, conducting and evaluating within the current legal guidelines.

Learning Outcome: Upon successful completion of this course, the student will be able to analyze open positions; describe job requirements; assess candidates qualifications; determine focus areas and formulate questions; conduct a focused interview; be aware of personal biases, legal issues, and nonverbal cues; process information received by checking its usefulness as evidence; evaluate results of the interview including preparation of summary ratings and rankings for each candidate; and select the best candidate(s).

Instruction: Major topics covered in the course are planning, conducting and evaluating interviews; combining concepts and skills in a way which follows the logical sequence of an interview. Students develop a job profile and prepare for an interview, learn to open the interview, gather and process information, close the interview, identify useful evidence, assess applicants, and make a hiring decision.

Credit Recommendation: In the upper division baccalaureate degree or lower division baccalaureate/associate degree category, 1 semester hour in Human Resources or Management (7/95).

Interpersonal Managing Skills

Location: Locations through the United States.

Length: 21 hours (3 days).

Dates: January 1986-Present.

Objective: To promote and sustain better communications and greater motivation resulting in improvements in performance and productivity.

Learning Outcome: Upon successful completion of this course, the student will be able to provide recognition for successful performance of others; actively seek and take into account the ideas and opinions of others; redirect the inefficient or inadequate efforts of others; encourage useful contributions from others; and deal with conflicts between individual goals and organizational priorities in ways that ensure differences are resolved as productively as possible.

Instruction: Major topics covered in the course are clarifying and confirming, constructive criticism, discussion skills, managing differences and crediting. Students learn when and how to use each skill and gain experience using them.

Credit Recommendation: In the lower division baccalaureate/associate degree category, 1 semester hour in Management, Organizational Behavior, or Business Administration (7/95).

Professional Sales Coaching

Location: Throughout the United States.

Length: 16 hours (2 day).

Dates: January 1986-Present.

Objective: To improve the coaching skills of sales managers.

Learning Outcome: Upon successful completion of this course, the student will be able to observe and evaluate sales call performance, plan for and conduct structured coaching conversations to improve sales performance, and create and implement a development action plan.

Instruction: Major topics covered in the course are the framework, communication skills and planning tools that affect coaching relationships.

Credit Recommendation: In the upper division baccalaureate degree or lower division baccalaureate/associate degree category, 1 semester hour in Sales Management. (7/95).

Professional Sales Negotiations

Location: Locations throughout the United States.

Length: 21 hours (3 days).

Dates: January 1989-Present.

Objective: To understand, plan, and conduct effective sales negotiations.

Learning Outcome: Upon successful completion of this course, the student will be able to differentiate between selling and negotiating; decide how to plan and when to begin negotiating; know the different phases of negotiation and carry out the skill steps for each phase; utilize four alternative approaches to resolve a difference; judge the success of a negotiation.

Instruction: Major topics covered in the course are understanding, planning, and conducting negotiations. Students gain a conceptual framework for reaching mutually satisfying sales agreements; develop a keen awareness of the elements of negotiation and planning; and gain confidence and ability to conduct profitable sales agreements. Methods of instruction include reading, video models and recognition exercises, group discussions, connections exercises, single-skill practice exercises, mini role plays and full role plays

Credit Recommendation: In the upper division baccalaureate degree or lower division baccalaureate/associate degree category, 1 semester hour in Marketing Elective or Business Administration (7/95).

Professional Selling Skills

Location: Throughout the United States.

Length: 21 hours (3 days).

Dates: January 1986-Present.

Objective: To introduce students to basic selling skills.

Learning Outcome: Upon successful completion of this course, the student will be able to conduct effective sales calls which lead to long-term business relationships; develop clear, complete, mutual understanding of their customer's needs; effectively communicate product information and benefits; and effectively close a sales commitment.

Instruction: Major topics covered in the course are the overall selling process, key skills that are used on every sales call, and skills and strategies for managing challenging sales call situations. Methods of instruction include video introductions and examples, reading and written exercises, experiential activities, connections exercises, and practice (including single-skill practice, cumulative-skill "respond-in-role" practice, role plays, write-your-own role play).

Credit Recommendation: In the lower division baccalaureate/associate degree category, 1 semester hour in Business Administration or Marketing (7/95).

Professional Telephone Selling Skills

Location: Throughout the United States.

Length: 21 hours (3 days).

Dates: January 1986-Present.

Objective: To learn to sell effectively over the telephone.

Learning Outcome: Upon successful completion of this course, the student will be able to open a call; qualify and begin dialogue with prospect; recognize and use various questioning techniques; uncover and confirm customer needs; explain features and benefits to support customer's need(s); identify and handle customer attitudes; recognize buying signals and gain customer commitment; close the sale.

Instruction: Major topics covered in the course are the concept of selling to customer needs, the telephone sales process, skills necessary to handle the "ideal" sale, and overcoming selling obstacles. Methods of instruction include hands-on practice.

Credit Recommendation: In the lower division baccalaureate/associate degree category, 1 semester hour in Marketing Communication, or Telecommunications (7/95).

Learning Tree International

Learning Tree International is an advanced technology training company. We do not sell hardware, software, publications, or consulting services. Our focus is on providing high quality training, and education is our *only* business. Our company mission statement reads as follows:

We are the finest Technology Education company in the world.

Our mission is to develop and deliver throughout the world a broad range of high quality educational services in rapidly changing and growing technologies.

Our services provide technical professionals and managers with skills and knowledge that significantly enhance their on-the-job productivity.

We judge our success through our ability to supply the highest quality service, achieve a steady growth in revenue and profit, and provide our personnel with the opportunity for individual satisfaction and pride of contribution.

Learning Tree International was founded based on one vital concept: Technology emerges at a much faster rate than industry can easily absorb and use it, thus creating an "implementation gap." This gap is measured by taking the difference in what is actually achievable with current technology and what is currently being achieved. With this concept in mind, we are dedicated to providing the continuing education in advanced technology required to bridge this implementation gap.

Our dedication to education means that we stay 100% focused on achieving educational goals. Our focus on providing high-quality training has been recognized by tens of thousands of organizations from around the world. The result has been 20 years of steady growth to the point that our company has now trained more than 450,000 technical professionals and managers and has developed an experienced staff of over 250 employees plus 500 expert instructors.

Most of our courses are 4 days in length with an examination at the end of the fourth day. Courses are offered at our Education Centers throughout the world (Washington DC, Los Angeles, Boston, New York, London, Ottawa, Paris, Stockholm, Tokyo, Toronto), as well as customer sites. We currently offer our courses at various hotel sites, including, but not limited to, the following cities: San Diego, San Francisco, Dallas, Chicago, Orlando, Edinburgh, Dublin, Oslo, Barcelona, Lisbon, Rome, Berlin, Munich, and Helsinki.

Each Learning Tree Instructor is a technical expert who spends the majority of the year working in industry with the technology being taught in our course. This ensures that participants learn practical, real-world knowledge and skills.

AUTHORIZED LEARNING TREE INTERNATIONAL FRANCHISES:

Learning Tree International - USA
1805 Library Street
Reston, VA 22090
Contact: Linda Trude
Phone: 703-709-9119
Fax: 703-471-4732

Learning Tree International - USA
1801 Rockville Pike
Rockville, MD 20852
Contact: Dennis Coleman
Phone: 301-230-0388
Fax: 212-230-9345

Learning Tree International - USA
1177 Avenue of the Americas
New York, NY 10063
Contact: Laura Romanowski
Phone: 212-302-6226
Fax: 212-302-6240

Learning Tree International - USA
5 Burlington Woods Drive
Burlington, MA 01903
Contact: Judy Patterson
Phone: 617-221-4653
Fax: 617-229-1339

Learning Tree International - USA
6053 West Century Boulevard
Suite 150
Los Angeles, CA 90045
Contact: Tomeiko Pollard
Phone: 310-342-2150
Fax: 310-410-2952

Learning Tree International - Canada
1223 Michael Street North
Suite 110
Gloucester, Ontario K1J 7T2 Canada
Contact: Bernadette Coady
Phone: 613-748-7520
Fax: 613-748-0479

Learning Tree International - Canada
Eaton Centre
250 Yonge Street, 27th Floor
Toronto, Ontario M5B 2L7 Canada
Contact: Jackie Taylor
Phone: 416-971-4390
Fax: 416-971-4389

Source of official student records: Registry of Credit Recommendations, American Council on Education, One Dupont Circle, Washington, DC 20036-1193 or General Manager, Learning Tree International, 1831 Michael Faraday Drive, Reston, VA 20190.

Additional information about the courses: College Credit Recommendation Service, American Council on Education, One Dupont Circle, Washington, DC 20036-1193.

Ada Object-Oriented Programming: Hands-On (335)

Location: Worldwide.
Length: 24 hours (4 days).
Dates: March 1995-March 1996.
Objective: To provide knowledge and skills needed to analyze requirements, design, and test Ada programs.
Learning Outcome: Upon successful completion of this course, the student will be able to analyze requirements and create object-oriented designs; make full use of object-oriented programming in Ada 95; build adaptable software using type extension; develop interface classes to encapsulate external bindings; and use object-oriented programming style.
Instruction: Major topics covered in the course are an introduction to Ada; an Ada overview; extensible data types; object-oriented software development; parallel and distributed systems; building systems with Ada 95; and Ada 95 and the evolution of software engineering. Methods of instruction include lecture, discussion, laboratory exercises, and a final examination.
Credit Recommendation: In the upper division baccalaureate degree category, 2 semester hours in Information Systems Management or Data Processing (4/95).

Advanced PC Software Configuration, Troubleshooting, and Data Recovery (150)

Location: Worldwide.
Length: 24 hours (4 days).
Dates: March 1993-Present.
Objective: To provide the student with the tools and techniques for maximizing the performance of PC operating systems software, troubleshooting the problems that accompany complex configurations, and recovering lost data and files.
Learning Outcome: Upon successful completion of this course, the student will be able to recover lost files and directories; revive nonbootable floppies and hard disks; rescue damaged application program files (Lotus 1-2-3, etc.); detect, isolate and contain damage from virus pro-

grams; benefit from the new features of DOS 6.x; relocate selected routines to high memory to increase DOS memory space; resolve memory-management conflicts; and configure Windows for maximum performance.

Instruction: Major topics covered in the course are basic concepts of data recovery, disk drives, recovering files and directories, surviving hard disk drive disasters, solutions to common disk problems; protecting data, disk optimization techniques, DOS 6.0, maximizing memory usage with DOS 6.x, advanced memory-management programs, and optimizing Windows performance. Methods of instruction include lecture, discussion, laboratory exercises, out-of-class activities, and examination.

Credit Recommendation: In the lower division baccalaureate/associate degree category, 2 semester hours in Data Communications, Data Processing, Information Systems Management, or Computer Science (3/94).

Application Development Workshop: Applying Object-Oriented Methods (421)

Location: Worldwide.

Length: 24 hours (4 days).

Dates: July 1994-September 1997.

Objective: To provide knowledge and skills to apply object-oriented software development to real-world business problems.

Learning Outcome: Upon successful completion of this course, the student will be able to develop object models for business applications; structure requirements systematically; work in teams on object-oriented analysis and design; validate designs for completeness, consistency, and accuracy with checklists; use tools to generate object models and code frameworks; and build and test applications by adapting reusable components.

Instruction: Major topics covered in the course are object-oriented technology, analysis, design, and implementation. Methods of instruction include lecture, discussion, audio/visual material, and graded application development team project.

Credit Recommendation: In the upper division baccalaureate degree category, 2 semester hours in Computer Science (8/94).

Building a Data Warehouse: Hands-On (229)

Location: Worldwide.

Length: 24 hours (4 days).

Dates: June 1996-Present.

Objective: To provide students the knowledge and skills needed to design and build a Data Warehouse.

Learning Outcome: Upon successful completion of this course, the student will be able to identify and translate requirements into a Data Warehouse design; implement data structures for a Data Warehouse environment; develop and query a Data Warehouse using Oracle; employ On-Line Analytical Processing (OLAP) tools; and optimize Data Warehouse performance.

Instruction: Major topics covered in this course are an introduction to data warehousing; the Data Warehouse approach; guidelines for implementing a Data Warehouse; building and populating Data Warehouse; query performance considerations; Data Warehouse applications; On-Line Analytical Processing (OLAP); optimization; and operational and maintenance issues. Methods of instruction include lecture, discussion, audio/visual material, hands-on exercises, and a multiple-choice one-hour proctored final examination.

Credit Recommendation: In the lower division baccalaureate/associate degree category, 2 semester hours in Computer Information Systems (CIS) or Data Processing (6/96).

Building Office 97 Internet Applications: Hands-On (308) (Developing Applications Using Visual Basic and Microsoft Office) (Formerly Integrating Microsoft Office Applications[308])

Location: Worldwide.

Length: 24 hours (4 days).

Dates: July 1995-Present.

Objective: To provide students with the knowledge and skills needed to build Windows applications with Visual Basic integrating the features and functions of Microsoft Office.

Learning Outcome: Upon successful completion of this course, the student will be able to develop Windows applications in Visual Basic that exploit the Microsoft Office Suite, connect your Visual Basic front-end with other Windows programs using OLE 2, link and embed objects between Word, Excel, Access, and PowerPoint files, take full advantage of OLE automation, select the best combination of development tools and applications for the job, and exploit the power and ease of use of the new Visual Basic 4.0 features.

Instruction: Major topics covered in the course are introduction to Visual Basic/Microsoft Office integration, creating an integration solution, picking the best office tools, automating office applications with objects and OLE 2, Visual Basic development, integrating the office, communications via Microsoft Office, and future trends in integrated solutions. Methods of instruction include lecture, discussion, laboratory exercises, and an one-hour, multiple-choice, proctored final examination.

Credit Recommendation: In the lower division baccalaureate/associate degree category, 2 semester hours in Business Information Systems, Computer Information Systems, or Data Processing (2/96).

Building Oracle and Web Server Applications: Hands-On (238)

Location: Worldwide.

Length: 24 hours (4 days).

Dates: May 1997-Present.

Objective: To provide knowledge and skill needed to develop and manage Oracle-based Web application, and to implement effective Web pages.

Learning Outcome: Upon successful completion of this course, the student will be able to build dynamic Web sites that are integrated with Oracle7 databases; configure and manage the Oracle WebServer environment; build static web pages using HTML; design and construct web applications to query and update Oracle7 databases; and exploit the PL/SQL Web Toolkit to generate dynamic HTML pages.

Instruction: Major topics covered in the course are Internet and the World Wide Web, WebServers, configuring the Oracle WebServer, developing HTML web pages, using PL/SQL, generating web pages with PL/SQL Web Toolkit, building web applications, extending webserver capability and security, and optimization. Methods of instruction include lecture, discussion, classroom exercises, audio/visual material, and examination.

Credit Recommendation: In the upper division baccalaureate degree category, 1 semester hour in Management Information Systems or Computer Science (8/97).

Business Process Re-Engineering (381)

Location: Worldwide.

Length: 24 hours (4 days).

Dates: July 1994-Present.

Objective: To provide knowledge and skills needed to implement Business Process Re-engineering (BPR).

Learning Outcome: Upon successful completion of this course, the student will be able to select, organize, and implement a business re-engineering project; redesign business processes by analyzing customer values, workflows, and structures; organize an effective re-engineering team; identify information technologies which will enable performance improvement; select and use software tools that support re-engineering activities; apply a structured approach to business process re-engineering; and develop a strategy for implementing re-engineered processes.

Instruction: Major topics covered in this course include an introduction to business process re-engineering, the re-engineering team, identification and analysis of core business processes, redesign of business processes, and implementation of the re-engineered process. Methods of instruction include lecture, discussion, classroom exercises, case studies, audio/visual material, and final examination.

Credit Recommendation: In the graduate degree category, 2 semester hours in Information Systems Management (8/94).

C++ Hands-On Object-Oriented Programming (337) (Formerly C++ Object-Oriented Programming [337])

Location: Worldwide.

Length: 24 hours (4 days).

Dates: May 1993-Present.

Objective: To provide student with the ability to write C++ object-oriented programs.

Learning Outcome: Upon successful completion of this course, the student will be able to use C++ classes for encapsulation; use good C++ programming style for programs that are reliable, efficient, and reusable; build extensible class libraries; manage storage using constructors and destructors and control the aliasing of heap storage; use Borland C++ integrated environment; and convert existing C programs into C++ object-oriented routines.

Instruction: Major topics covered in the course are introduction to object-oriented programming, wading into a better C, types-references and constants, dynamic storage management, advanced C++ functions and operators, inheritance and derived classes, C++ libraries, object-oriented design, the C++ landscape, the hands-on programming environment, and C++ examples. Methods of instruction include lecture, discussion, laboratory exercises, and examination.

Credit Recommendation: In the lower division baccalaureate/associate degree category or in the upper division baccalaureate degree category, 2 semester hours in Computer Science, Information Systems Management, or Data Processing (1/94).

C++ Object-Oriented Programming for Business Applications (437)

Location: Worldwide.

Length: 24 hours (4 days).

Dates: July 1994-Present.

Objective: To provide the principles underlying object-oriented programming using C++.

Learning Outcome: Upon successful completion of this course, the student will be able to create object-oriented business programs using C++ environments and tools; exploit commercial software libraries; make use of C++'s classes for encapsulation; manage storage with constructors and destructors; convert existing C programs into C++ object-oriented routines; and practice good C++ programming style.

Instruction: Major topics covered in this course are an introduction to object-oriented programming, C versus C++, types-references and constants, dynamic storage management, advanced functions and operators, inheritance and derived classes, C++ libraries, object-oriented design, and the C++ landscape. Methods of instruction include lecture, discussion, classroom exercises, audio/visual materials, and final examination.

Credit Recommendation: In the upper division baccalaureate degree category, 3 semester hours in Computer Science or Information Systems (8/94).

C Programming (338) (Formerly C Programming Hands-On Workshop)

Location: Worldwide.

Length: 24 hours (4 days).

Dates: August 1992-Present.

Objective: To provide student with the knowledge required to write, compile, and execute structured ANSI C programs.

Learning Outcome: Upon successful completion of this course, the student will be able to read and maintain existing C programs, write new programs in ANSI C, define and use functions and modules in C, declare and use base and derived variable of different types, use C's control constructs to write loops and branches, interface C programs with hardware and operating systems and other programming languages, use dynamic memory allocation to manage flexible data structures, and use the C preprocessor and standard C library functions.

Instruction: Major topics covered in the course are C and our development environment; building blocks of C programs; base types, pointers, and arrays; control flow and functions; structures and graphs; program organization; hardware and operating systems; the C preprocessor; the standard C library; "K&R" C, C++, and Objective C; suggested readings; C reference charts; frequently asked questions; miscellaneous tricky situations; recursive programming; and make, lint, and other development tools. Methods of instruction include lecture, discussion, laboratory exercises, and examination.

Credit Recommendation: In the lower division baccalaureate/associate degree category or in the upper division baccalaureate degree category, 2 semester hours in Computer Science, Information Systems Management, or Data Processing (1/94).

C Programming for Business Applications (438)

Location: Worldwide.

Length: 24 hours (4 days).

Dates: May 1994-September 1997.

Objective: To provide the knowledge needed to make the successful transition from the traditional business programming languages to C programming.

Learning Outcome: Upon successful completion of this course, the student will be able to write, compile, and execute ANSI C programs; make full use of C's programming features; develop programs using standard C library functions; use software tools for C development; read and write complex data structure descriptions; and convert COBOL applications into C.

Instruction: Major topics covered in the course are C and the development environment; the building blocks of C programs; base types, pointers, and arrays; control flow and functions; structures and graphs; program organization; operating systems; tools and libraries; and "K&R" C and C++. Methods of instruction include lecture, discussion, laboratory exercises, and examination.

Credit Recommendation: In the upper division baccalaureate degree category, 2 semester hours in Computer Science,

Information Systems Management, or Data Processing (6/94).

Cisco Routers: A Comprehensive Hands-On Introduction (466)

Location: Worldwide.

Length: 24 hours (4 days).

Dates: February 1997-Present.

Objective: To provide students with a comprehensive introduction to deploying Cisco routers in an internetworked environment. Students will gain the fundamental knowledge and skills needed to install, configure and troubleshoot Cisco routers.

Learning Outcome: Upon successful completion of this course, the student will be able to successfully install and configure Cisco routers to build multiprotocol internetworks; create Cisco router configuration files from scratch; configure IP and IPX routing protocols; troubleshoot IP/IPX routing problems using Cisco's Debug commands; perform software and hardware upgrades; and effectively manage and maintain Cisco routes with SNMP.

Instruction: Major topics covered in the course are an overview of Cisco router architectures, internetworking with TCP/IP, IP routing protocols, using Novell routing, using serial interfaces, using transparent bridging, maintenance and upgrade procedures, troubleshooting your Cisco network, and managing your router with SNMP. Methods of instruction include lecture, discussion, classroom exercises, audio/visual material, and final examination.

Credit Recommendation: In the lower division baccalaureate/associate degree category, 2 semester hours in Computer Information Systems (4/97).

Client Server Systems: Analysis and Design (389)
(Formerly Client/Server System Design and Configuration)

Location: Worldwide.

Length: 24 hours (4 days).

Dates: January 1994-Present.

Objective: To provide the student with the knowledge needed to design and configure client/server computing systems.

Learning Outcome: Upon successful completion of this course, the student will be able to analyze and design new client/server systems; integrate legacy systems using middleware facilities to achieve a common client environment, integrate components to achieve interoperability; apply interface standards to achieve flexibility, portability and scalability; and select data access technologies.

Instruction: Major topics covered in the course are base technologies and frameworks; blueprints for client/server; distributed services—directories, files and data, and miscellaneous; building your client/server blueprint; and future trends in client/server design. Methods of instruction include lecture, discussion, classroom exercises, and examination.

Credit Recommendation: In the lower division baccalaureate/associate degree category or upper division baccalaureate degree category, 2 semester hours in Computer Science, Data Processing, Data Communications, or Information Systems Management (3/94).

COM and ActiveX Programming with C++: Hands-on (406)

Location: Various sites in the United States.

Length: 24 hours (4 days).

Dates: December 1997-Present.

Objective: To provide students with the skills to use C++ to develop software components taking advantage of COM, DCOM, and ActiveX.

Learning Outcome: Upon successful completion of this course, the student will be able to design and build reusable software components using Microsoft's Component Object Model (COM); implement scalable client/server systems using COM standards; take advantage of transparent remoting features of distributed COM (DCOM); build COM objects and ActiveX controls with the active template library (ATL); control applications via automation; and apply COM and ActiveX to Internet and Internet programming.

Instruction: Major topics covered in the course are component object model fundamentals, practical applications of COM, distributed objects, developing component software, the active template library (ATL), ActiveX code components, creating ActiveX controls, and building an application out of components. Methods of instruction include lecture, discussion, classroom exercises, audio-visual material, module tests and final examination.

Credit Recommendation: In the upper division baccalaureate degree category, 2 semester hours (1 semester hour in Information Systems, and 1 semester hour in Information Systems laboratory) (2/98).

Computer Network Architectures and Protocols (355)

Location: Worldwide.

Length: 24 hours (4 days).

Dates: August 1993-Present.

Objective: To provide students the detailed knowledge required to work in computer networking projects by expanding the knowledge of the concepts, terminology, and acronyms of networks.

Learning Outcome: Upon successful completion of this course the student will be able to understand the Open Systems Interconnection (OSI) reference mode; understand the similarities and differences between the standard networking protocols; evaluate available hardware and software components and implement layered network protocols; and use gateways between Local and Wide Area Networks and control networks to ensure reliability and security.

Instruction: Major topics covered in the course are an in-depth working knowledge of layered network architectures, protocols, standards, and hardware/software components. Emphasis is on the practical aspects of packet-switched network design and implementation, utilizing existing and evolving protocol standards. Methods of instruction include lecture, discussion, hands-on exercises, out-of-class activities, and an examination.

Credit Recommendation: In the upper division baccalaureate degree category or in the lower division baccalaureate/associate degree category, 2 semester hours in Information Systems Management, Data Processing, or Computer Science (12/93).

Configuring Cisco Routers: Advanced Hands-On Workshop (481)

Location: Worldwide.

Length: 24 hours (4 days).

Dates: April 1997-Present.

Objective: To provide the knowledge and skills required to master the advanced features of Cisco router configuration, including protocol prioritization, route redistribution, network security and VLSM.

Learning Outcome: Upon successful completion of this course, the student will be able to optimize Cisco router configuration for large and complex multiprotocol internetworks; manage congestion in IP and IPX networks; deploy scalable routing protocols, OSPF, NLSP, EIGRP and BGP; conserve network addresses with variable length submet masking (VLSM); construct access control lists (ACLs) for network security; implement advanced features such as bandwidth-on-demand; and apply advanced troubleshooting techniques.

Instruction: Major topics covered in the course are internetworking review, implementing large IP Networks, linking autonomous systems, supporting other protocols, wide area networks, building multiprotocol networks, enhanced IGRP, troubleshooting, and bridging. Methods of instruction include lecture, discussion, classroom exercises, audio/visual material, and examination.

Credit Recommendation: In the upper division baccalaureate degree category, 1 semester hour in Computer Technology or Networks (8/97).

Data Network Design and Performance Optimization (453)

Location: Worldwide.

Length: 24 hours (4 days).

Dates: December 1996-Present.

Objective: To provide students with skills needed to design new, scalable networks or optimize existing networks.

Learning Outcome: Upon successful completion of this course, the student will be able to identify business requirements and traffic performance criteria for your organization; design scalable networks based on bandwidth, delay, and growth criteria; use measurement and simulation techniques to validate network performance; assess the impact of applications on network performance; select the best LAN/WAN technologies based on application requirements; and maintain high availability for network services by building in resilience.

Instruction: Major topics covered in the course are introduction to network design, application performance objectives, LAN technologies, WAN infrastructure design, topologies and segmentation, planning network layer addressing and routing, strategies for fault tolerance, logical and physical design, network management and operations, other network services, and security considerations. Methods of instruction include lecture, discussion, classroom exercises, audio/visual material, and final examination.

Credit Recommendation: In the lower division baccalaureate/associate degree category, 2 semester hours in Computer Information Systems, Data Communications, or Computer Science (4/97).

DB2 for Client/Server: Hands-On Introduction (223)

Location: Worldwide.

Length: 24 hours (4 days).

Dates: September 1996-September 1997.

Objective: To provide student with hands-on experience needed to design and implement distributed DB2 applications in a multiplatform networked environment.

Learning Outcome: Upon successful completion of this course, the student will be able to build high-performance DB2 distributed database applications; code efficient and accurate SQL queries; create stored procedures and triggers; implement object-oriented features including UDT's and UDF's; access data stored on remote platforms; connect desktop applications to DB2 data via ODBC within client/server systems; and access legacy databases from a client/server environment.

Instruction: Major topics covered in the course are fundamental concepts; the building blocks of DB2; data access using SQL; application data access; data integrity; remote data access; database performance and tuning; advanced features of DB2; and database management system issues. Methods of instruction include lecture, discussion, classroom exercises, audio/ visual material, classroom exercises, observations, and a final examination.

Credit Recommendation: In the lower division baccalaureate/associate degree category, 2 semester hours (1 semester hour in Computer Science or Information Systems and 1 semester hour in Computer Science Laboratory or Information Systems Laboratory) (10/96).

Deploying Internet and Intranet Firewalls: Hands-On (488)

Location: Worldwide.

Length: 24 hours (4 days).

Dates: March 1997-Present.

Objective: To provide students with skills to evaluate the leading firewall approaches and determine the best firewall implementation for their security needs. Students will design, configure, and test a firewall.

Learning Outcome: Upon successful completion of this course, the student will be able to build a firewall to defend your network from external attack; match the appropriate firewall architecture to your security needs; audit networks to detect attacks; "harden" windows NT and UNIX for use as part of a firewall; determine the strengths and functionality of popular firewall approaches; and configure and test a firewall.

Instruction: Major topics covered in the course are introduction to security and firewalls, formulating and maintaining a security policy, attack methods and testing, packet filters, circuit-level gateways, application proxies, preparing for the firewall installation, essentials of computer auditing for firewall system, securing systems for use in a firewall environment, hardening windows NT and UNIX systems for use in firewalls, firewall topologies, and the gauntlet internet firewall. Methods of instruction include lecture, discussion, classroom exercises, audio/ visual material, and final examination.

Credit Recommendation: In the upper division baccalaureate degree category, 2 semester hours in Computer Information Systems, Computer Security, or Data Communications (4/97).

Deploying T1 and T3 Services (277)

Location: Various sites in the United States.

Length: 18 hours (3 days).

Dates: September 1997-Present.

Objective: To provide students with the knowledge and skills necessary to understand T1 and T3 interconnect services, how they are applied, what performance options are available, and how to evaluate and best utilize T1/T3 services for communication needs.

Learning Outcome: Upon successful completion of this course the student will be able to evaluate and deploy T-carrier services (T1 and T3); compare T1 and T3 systems to other alternative WAN technologies; maximize the benefits of properly configured T-carrier networks; combine voice and data onto a single T1 with fractional rate services; manage and control a T-carrier network; and use T-carrier networks to access the Internet and virtual private networks.

Instruction: Major topics covered in the course include an introduction to T-carrier services, equipment and media for T1, framing, multiplexing, modulation, and coding, fractional T1, high-speed digital services, developing T-carrier networks, T1 and the Internet, and assessing the need for T-carrier services, and alternative high-speed transmission services. Methods of instruction include lecture, discussion, classroom exercises, audio-visual material, module tests and final examination.

Credit Recommendation: In the lower division baccalaureate/associate degree category, 1 semester hour in Data Communications and Networking, Computer Information Systems or Computer Science (2/98).

Designing An Intranet: Hands-On (475) (Formerly Building an Intranet: A Hands-On Workshop [475])

Location: Worldwide.

Length: 24 hours (4 days).

Dates: November 1996-Present.

Objective: To provide students with skills and knowledge needed to successfully manage the development of intranet services. Students will gain experience using the latest development tools, authorizing web documents, and integrating database and workgroup access for their Intranet.

Learning Outcome: Upon successful completion of this course, the student will be able to build a common interface to a range of different information technologies; develop and manage an intranet web site; use tools to simplify creation and updating of web content; expand intranet services by adding client-side processing, implement on-the-fly publishing form a database; secure your intranet against unauthorized access; and integrate internet servers on the corporate intranet.

Instruction: Major topics covered in the course are intranet overview, the web as enable technology, web publishing, site management and support, integrating database applications, integrating workgroup applications, and integrating communication services and putting it all together. Methods of instruction include lecture, discussion, classroom exercises, audio/visual material, and final examination.

Credit Recommendation: In the lower division baccalaureate/associate degree category, 2 semester hours (1 semester hour in Computer Information Systems or Data Communications and 1 semester hour in Computer Information Systems or Data Communications Lab) (4/97).

Developing a Website: Hands-On (470) (Internet/Intranet Web Site Development) (Formerly World Wide Web Development [470])

Location: Worldwide.

Length: 24 hours (4 days).

Dates: April 1996-Present.

Objective: To provide students with the knowledge needed to create, publish, and maintain a World Wide Web site.

Learning Outcome: Upon successful completion of this course, the student will be able to install, configure, and maintain an Intra- or Internet Web server; develop and publish Web pages using HyperText Markup Language (HTML); utilize CGI scripting; interface the Web to a DBMS; include multi-media effects; and process secure transactions and manage a Web site.

Instruction: Major topics covered in the course are an introduction to the World Wide Web; Hypertext Markup Language (HTML) and HTML extensions; understanding the Web Server; common gateway interface; interfacing to a database; Web administration; and the future of the Web. Methods of instruction include lecture, discussion, classroom exercises, audio/visual material, hands-on exercises, and an one-hour, multiple-choice, proctored final examination.

Credit Recommendation: In the lower division baccalaureate/associate degree category, 2 semester hours in Computer Science, Computer Information Systems, Software Engineering, or Data Processing (6/96).

Developing Applications with PowerBuilder 5 and Oracle7 (239) (Developing Applications with PowerBuilder 5 and Oracle7: Hands-On)

Location: Worldwide.

Length: 24 hours (4 days).

Dates: June 1996-Present.

Objective: To provide students the knowledge and skills necessary to design, develop and implement large-scale client/server applications using the combined PowerBuilder 5 and Oracle7 environments.

Learning Outcome: Upon successful completion of this course, the student will be able to design and develop combined PowerBuilder 5/Oracle7 applications; evaluate strengths and weaknesses of alternative implementation strategies; write PL/SQL procedures; design and enforce data integrity requirements; apply Oracle security methods; and avoid common Oracle and PowerBuilder design mistakes.

Instruction: Major topics covered in the course are an introduction to the client/server environment; PowerBuilder and Oracle development; SQL; building windows and menus; creating and working with tables; PowerScript; Oracle stored procedures; Windows 95 development; Oracle security; record keeping and transaction logging; and security and reporting. Methods of instruction include lecture, discussion, audio/visual material, hands-on exercises, and a multiple-choice one-hour proctored final examination.

Credit Recommendation: In the lower division baccalaureate/associate degree category, 2 semester hours in Computer Science, Computer Information Systems, or Data Processing (6/96).

Developing Client/Server Applications: Hands-On (386) (Formerly Building Client/Server Applications [386])

Location: Worldwide.

Length: 24 hours (4 days).

Dates: March 1994-Present.

Objective: To provide the student with knowledge and skills to develop client/server applications using visual development tools.

Learning Outcome: Upon successful completion of this course, the student will be able to build successful client/server applications with visual development tools; use rapid prototyping techniques to discover unstated user requirements; use the common user access standard to define application screens; use middleware to access databases; test and maintain client/server applications; and understand the expected evolution of client/server development tools and technology.

Instruction: Major topics covered in the course are client/server system fundamentals, the application development process, GUI design, user requirements and database development, building the application window, building data window objects, enhancing database access, menus, testing and maintaining client/server applications, tools for client/server development, and future trends in client/server development. Methods of instruction include lecture, discussion, laboratory exercises, out-of-class activities, and examination.

Credit Recommendation: In the lower division baccalaureate/associate degree category or in the upper division baccalaureate degree category, 2 semester hours in Computer Science, Data Processing, Data Communications, or Information Systems Management (3/94).

Developing SQL Queries for Oracle 7: Hands-On (234) (Formerly Advanced SQL Queries [234])

Location: Worldwide.

Length: 12 hours (2 days).

Dates: April 1995-Present.

Objective: To provide knowledge and skills for developing complex SQL queries.

Learning Outcome: Upon successful completion of this course, the student will be able to formulate complex database queries with SQL and SQL*Plus; apply the full range of complex query types; select the best query method for each application; and test queries completely and optimize their performance.

Instruction: Major topics covered in the course are SQL overview; groupings and functions; querying multiple tables; nested queries; views and temporary tables; and SQL*Plus. Methods of instruction include lecture, discussion, laboratory exercises, and a final examination.

Credit Recommendation: In the lower division baccalaureate/associate degree category, both this course and Oracle7 for Application Developers (232) must be completed to receive 2 semester hours in Information Systems Management or Data Processing; or this course, Oracle7 for Application Developers (232), and Tuning Oracle7 Applications (233) must all be completed to receive 3 semester hours in Information Systems Management or Data Processing (4/95).

Developing SQL Server Applications with Visual Basic 5: Hands On (227)

Location: Worldwide.

Length: 24 hours (4 days).

Dates: July 1997-Present.

Objective: To provide practical experience using advanced SQL server and Visual Basic programming techniques to build working database applications.

Learning Outcome: Upon successful completion of this course, the student will be able to build DB2 distributed database applications; code efficient and accurate SQL queries; create stored procedures and triggers; implement object-oriented features including UDT's and UDF's; access data stored on remote platforms; connect desktop applications to DB2 data via ODBC within client/server systems; and access legacy databases from a client/server environment.

Instruction: Major topics covered in the course are jump-starting SQL server and VB, data retrieval, maintaining data, SQL server-based programs, building business servers, and working with Microsoft transaction servers. Methods of instruction include lecture, discussion, classroom exercises, audio/visual material, and examination.

Credit Recommendation: In the lower division baccalaureate/associate degree category, 2 semester hours in Management Information Systems or Data Processing (8/97).

Distributed Programming Using DCE: Workshop (383)

Location: Worldwide.

Length: 24 hours (4 days).

Dates: May 1994-May 1996.

Objective: To provide an understanding of distributed programming using DCE (Distributed Computing Environment.)

Learning Outcome: Upon successful completion of this course, the student will be able to access DCE services across the in-class LAN; use the DCE transport, RPC and security mechanisms, develop protable client/server programs; and utilize threads for performance.

Instruction: Major topics covered in the course are DCE services and development tools, distributed programming concepts, using remote procedure calls, advanced RPC topics, DCE security, multithreaded programming, models of distributed programming, and DCE in the marketplace. Methods of instruction include lecture, discussion, laboratory exercises, and examination.

Credit Recommendation: In the upper division baccalaureate degree category, 2 semester hours in Computer Science, Information Systems Management, or Data Processing (6/94).

Distributing Data in Client/Server Systems (385)

Location: Worldwide.

Length: 24 hours (4 days).

Dates: January 1994-Present.

Objective: To provide the student with knowledge for organizing, managing, and accessing data in a client/server system.

Learning Outcome: Upon successful completion of this course, the student will be able to organize, manage and access data in a client/server architecture; integrate data from multiple sources onto a single data server; segment and replicate data onto multiple data servers; evaluate various approaches to distributed database management; migrate a mainframe database to an alternative platform; and use commitment, concurrency, and control strategies for distributed databases.

Instruction: Major topics covered in the course are an introduction to data management and client/server computing; data server principles, pragmatics and internals; organizing and managing databases, both single and multiple servers; standards and benchmarks; and an overview of popular data servers. Methods of instruction include lecture, discussion, classroom exercises, out-of-class activities, and examination.

Credit Recommendation: In the lower division baccalaureate/associate degree category or in the upper division baccalaureate degree category, 2 semester hours in Computer Science, Data Processing, Data Communications, or Information Systems Management (3/94).

Effective Communication Skills for IT Professionals (292)

Location: Worldwide.

Length: 18 hours (3 days).

Dates: December 1996-Present.

Objective: To provide students with specific tools and techniques for improving listening skills, delivering effective messages and bridging different communication styles.

Learning Outcome: Upon successful completion of this course, the student will be able to sharpen verbal communication skills to improve clarity and conciseness; pave the way for positive interactions by building rapport, trust, and credibility; read the "emotional content" accompanying messages; anticipate and avoid coon misunderstandings; and diffuse difference that can lead to conflict and adapt to your medium: meetings, conversations, e-mail, phone calls, and print.

Instruction: Major topics covered in the course are process of communicating, communication patterns, establishing collaborative relationships, creating effective messages, listening skills, openness in communications, communication styles and orientations, bridging the gap, and self-development plan. Methods of instruction include lecture, discussion, classroom exercises, audio/visual materials, and final examination.

Credit Recommendation: In the lower division baccalaureate/associate degree category, 1 semester hour in Business Communications (4/97).

Ethernet (Hands-On High-Performance Ethernet: Switched, Fast, and Traditional) (452)

Location: Worldwide.

Length: 24 hours (4 days).

Dates: October 1996-Present.

Objective: To provide students with practical skills and knowledge required to evaluate and implement the latest Ethernet technologies to meet the needs of their organization.

Learning Outcome: Upon successful completion of this course, the student will be able to install and configure the latest Ethernet technologies; analyze the Ethernet protocol and its impact on network performance; segment an existing network with bridges and switches to reduce LAN congestion; use switches for collapsed backbones and high-speed server connections; implement fast Ethernet: 100BASE-T4, 100BASE-TX, and 1200BASE-FX; and organize our LAN infrastructure to meet changing demands.

Instruction: Major topics covered in the course are fundamentals of Ethernet/IEEE 802.3, Ethernet media and adapter cards, security and performance issues, extending the life of your 10 Mbp Ethernet, enhancing your 10-Mbps Ethernet, 100 Mbps fast Ethernet, and building and managing enterprise Ethernet. Methods of instruction include lecture, discussion, classroom exercises, audio/visual material, and final examination.

Credit Recommendation: In the lower division baccalaureate/associate degree category, 2 semester hours in Computer Information Systems or Data Communications (4/97).

Exploiting the New Features of Oracle 8 (495)

Location: Various sites in the United States.

Length: 30 hours (5 days).

Dates: November 1997-Present.

Objective: To provide students with the knowledge and skills to evaluate and utilize new features Oracle8.

Learning Outcome: Upon successful completion of this course the student will be able to: utilize the new features of Oracle8; build partitioned tables to manage VLDBs; implement object-relational extensions; use object views to ease the migration from relational to object-relational technology; utilize user-defined object types and Oracle8 collection types; store and manage large objects (LOBs) and utilize deferred constraints and queuing for index-only tables.

Instruction: Major topics covered in the course include the Oracle architecture, object related features, utilizing PL/SQL and SQL enhancements, working with large objects (LOBs), partitioning tables and indexes, backup and recovery, tuning for performance, and migrating to Oracle.

Credit Recommendation: In the lower division baccalaureate/associate degree category, 2 semester hours in Computer Information Systems or Computer Science (2/98).

Fast LAN Technologies (259)

Location: Worldwide.

Length: 24 hours (4 days).

Dates: August 1995-Present.

Objective: To provide students with the knowledge about the latest fast LAN products and services, and how to select the right solution for their organization.

Learning Outcome: Upon successful completion of this course, the student will be able to evaluate and select 100+ Mbit/s solutions including Fast Ethernet, FDDI, ATM, and 100 VG-AnyLAN; resolve complex LAN performance and management issues; support multimedia applications including video conferencing and distance learning, assess the benefits and risks of implementing virtual LANs, exploit the scalability and manageability of intelligent hubs, and position your organization to migrate to the latest high-speed network technology.

Instruction: Major topics covered in the course are Fast LANs, Fast Ethernet and 100 VG-AnyLAN, FDDI (Fiber-Distributed Data Interface), CDDI (Copper-Distributed Data Interface) and FDDI Extensions, Switched LANs, Switching and Multiplexing, ATM (Asynchronous Transfer Mode), Implementing Local Area ATM Networks, Architectural Options and Network Upgrading, and Fast LAN Interconnect Services. Methods of instruction include lecture, discussion, case studies, and an one-hour proctored final examination.

Credit Recommendation: In the upper division baccalaureate degree category, 2 semester hours in Computer Information Systems, Business Information Systems, or Telecommunications (2/96).

Hands-on Advanced C++ Programming (397)
C++ Libraries, Tools, and Advanced Programming Techniques

Location: Worldwide.

Length: 24 hours (4 days).

Dates: May 1994-Present.

Objective: To provide knowledge of C++ libraries and expand knowledge of C++ programming methods.

Learning Outcome: Upon successful completion of this course, the student will be able to develop efficient, reusable and portable C++ libraries; use the latest draft standard C++ extensions, take advantage of the standard C++ code library, including the standard template library (STL); implement fault-tolerant programs using exceptions, exploit advance C++ development libraries; and increase C++ program quality and efficiency with idioms and patterns.

Instruction: Major topics covered in the course are advanced C++ features, the draft standard C++ library; the object-oriented development process; applications libraries, achieving code reusability; and object-oriented development standards and tools. Methods of instruction include lecture, discussion, laboratory exercises, and examination.

Credit Recommendation: In the upper division baccalaureate degree category, 2 semester hours in Computer Science, Information Systems Management, or Data Processing (6/94).

Hands-On C Advanced Programming (339)
(Formerly Advanced C Programming [339])
(Formerly C Advanced Programming: Techniques and Data Structures)

Location: Worldwide.

Length: 24 hours (4 days).

Dates: November 1992-Present.

Objective: To provide student with the ability to generate reliable, portable, and maintainable software using C language.

Learning Outcome: Upon successful completion of this course, the student will be able to structure, modify, and debug large, multimodule C programs; select and customize advanced data structures; code complex algorithms efficiently and easily in C; program modern windows I/O environment; exploit advanced techniques and C development tools; and create and exploit reliable modules and libraries.

Instruction: Major topics covered in the course are C development environment, ANSI C language and review of advanced features, data-driven programming; object-oriented programming (OOP) in C; indexed data structures; modern input/output techniques; and concurrent and real-time programming in C. Methods of instruction include lecture, discussion, laboratory exercises, and examination.

Credit Recommendation: In the lower division baccalaureate/associate degree category or in the upper division baccalaureate degree category, 2 semester hours in Computer Science, Information Systems Management, or Data Processing (1/94).

Hands-on Datacomm and WAN Troubleshooting(356)
(Formerly Datacomm and WAN Troubleshooting 356)

Location: Worldwide.

Length: 24 hours (4 days).

Dates: August 1993-April 1998.

Objective: To provide students with a systematic approach to troubleshooting and familiarity with the Electronic Industries Association (EIA-232) Interface.

Learning Outcome: Upon successful completion of this course the student will be able to gain extensive hands-on experience using protocol analyzers, programmable data test sets, breakout boxes and custom-built modem hardware to detect and identify real-world faults; configure and troubleshoot the EIA-232 interfaces and modems and employ loop back and bit error ratio tests to isolate local and remote faults; and effectively diagnose failures in terminals, modems, and analog lines, as well as troubleshoot hardware and software protocol problems.

Instruction: Major topics covered in the course are the full range of skills and techniques needed for Datacomm and Wide Area Network troubleshooting; protocol analyzers; breakout boxes and hand-held data test sets to detect and identify problems; configuring and troubleshooting RS-232 interfaces and modems; loopback and bit error ratio tests; and diagnosing failures in terminals, modems, and analog lines. Methods of instruction include lecture, discussion, hands-on exercises, out-of-class activities, and an examination.

Credit Recommendation: In the lower division baccalaureate/associate or upper division baccalaureate degree category, 2 semester hours in Information Systems Management, Data Processing, or Computer Science (12/93).

Hands-On Delphi: Object-Oriented Applications Development (402)

Location: Worldwide.

Length: 24 hours (4 days).

Dates: December 1996-Present.

Objective: To provide students with practical Delphi skills needed to develop stand alone and client/server applications quickly and easily.

Learning Outcome: Upon successful completion of this course, the student will be able to use Delphi to rapidly develop client/server and stand alone Windows solutions; scale a local database application to a client/server architecture using Delphi; save development time by building reusable objects and custom controls; incorporate multimedia functionality into applications with Delphi; integrate off-the-shelf applications using OLE automation; and create Web-enabled applications with Delphi.

Instruction: Major topics covered in the course are an introduction to Delphi, object Pascal, Delphi component palette, database controls, database programming, reporting, advanced Delphi programming, program design, and an window API. Methods of instruction include lecture, discussion, classroom exercises, audio/visual material, and final examination.

Credit Recommendation: In the lower division baccalaureate/associate degree category, 2 semester hours in Computer Information Systems or Computer Applications(4/97).

Hands-On Internetworking with TCP/IP (467) (Formerly Internetworking with TCP/IP [467])

Location: Worldwide.

Length: 24 hours (4 days).

Dates: August 1994-Present.

Objective: To provide knowledge to design, build, configure, and manage TCP/IP internetworks.

Learning Outcome: Upon successful completion of this course, the student will be able to design, build, configure, and manage TCP/IP internetworks; properly implement subnets to avoid ongoing maintenance headaches; set up mail for text, graphics, audio, and video; configure IP routers and troubleshoot a wide range of routing problems; accomplish the challenging setup of important services such as DNS and BOOTP; and apply a structured methodology for troubleshooting TCP/IP internetworks.

Instruction: Major topics covered in the course include an IP review and configuring your system, the domain name system (DNS) and the Berkeley name domain (BIND) software, mail protocols and interfaces, routing and routing protocols, IP and troubleshooting routers, performance implication of internetworking components (IP) applications and protocols, additional protocols and applications, and SNMP and the future. Methods of instruction include lecture, discussion, classroom exercises, audio/visual materials, and final examination.

Credit Recommendation: In the upper division baccalaureate degree category, 2 semester hours in Data Communications or Computer Science (8/94).

Hands-On IntranetWare: Netware 4.x Administration (264) (Formerly NetWare 4.x Administration [264])

Location: Worldwide.

Length: 24 hours (4 days).

Dates: November 1993-Present.

Objective: To provide the student with the ability to administer NetWare 4.x.

Learning Outcome: Upon successful completion of this course, the student will be able to create and manage NetWare Directory Service database; create a workable directory structure; create new users and file systems directories on the network server; implement an efficient security structure; setup network printing; review the system backup process; and create effective system automation using batch files, login scripts, profile scripts, and menus.

Instruction: Major topics covered in the course are introduction to NetWare 4.x and NetWare Directory Services, accessing NDS resources, NetWare 4.x file system, NetWare file system security, NetWare directory services security, customizing the user environment, managing NetWare servers, NetWare applications, and Network data protection. Methods of instruction include lecture, discussion, laboratory exercises, and examination.

Credit Recommendation: In the lower division baccalaureate/associate degree category or in the upper division baccalaureate degree category, 2 semester hours in Data Communication, Data Processing, Information System Management, or Computer Science (1/94).

Hands-On IntranetWare: NetWare 4.x Advanced Administration (265) (Formerly NetWare 4.x Advanced Administration [265])

Location: Worldwide.

Length: 18 hours (3 days).

Dates: November 1993-Present.

Objective: To provide knowledge needed to administer 4.0 NetWare.

Learning Outcome: Upon successful completion of this course, the student will be able to plan and manage complex NDS trees; manage and configure workstation VLMs; perform advanced print server setup and customization; configure and tune resources to enhance performance; and use auditing to enhance security.

Instruction: Major topics covered in the course are the NDS tree; security; partitions and replicas; client software; managing the server; optimizing the network; auditing; printing; and SBACKUP. Methods of instruction include lecture, discussion, laboratory exercises, and examination.

Credit Recommendation: In the upper division baccalaureate degree category, 1 semester hour in Data Communications, Computer Science, Information Systems Management, or Data Processing (6/94).

Hands-On IntranetWare: NetWare 4.x Installation and Configuration (266) (Formerly NetWare 4.x Installation and Configuration [266])

Location: Worldwide.

Length: 12 hours (2 days).

Dates: December 1993-Present.

Objective: To provide the student with the knowledge required to install and configure NetWare 4.x.

Learning Outcome: Upon successful completion of this course, the student will be able to manipulate the NetWare Directory Services tree and practice NDS object security, upgrade from NetWare 3.11 to 4.x, install client NetWare drivers (VLMs), configure NetWare 4.x print services, backup NetWare 4.x, and use the auditing functions.

Instruction: Major topics covered in the course are workshop structures; NetWare 4.x installation workshops; workstation/client NetWare 4.x files; managing the NDS tree, context and script files; NetWare 4.x security; printing under NetWare 4.x; backing up NetWare; and NetWare 4.x console commands. Methods of instruction include lecture, discussion, laboratory exercises, and examination.

Credit Recommendation: In the lower division baccalaureate/associate degree category or in the upper division baccalaureate degree category, 1 semester hour in Data Communications, Data Processing, Information Systems Management, or Computer Science (1/94).

Hands-On IntranetWare: Updating from NetWare 3.x to NetWare 4.x (263)
(Formerly Updating from NetWare 3.x to NetWare 4.x [263])

Location: Worldwide.

Length: 18 hours (3 days).

Dates: November 1993-Present.

Objective: To provide the student with the knowledge required to update networks to enhance NetWare 4.x features.

Learning Outcome: Upon successful completion of this course, the student will be able to identify new features of NetWare 4.x, understand the NetWare Directory Service (NDS), use Netware 4.x tools to manage the NDS tree, and use NDS object security.

Instruction: Major topics covered in the course are NetWare 4.x overview and directory services; managing NDS objectives; timer services; NetWare 4.x workstation setup and client tools, printing enhancements, auditing, installation and upgrading; backup services; and new console management. Methods of instruction include lecture, discussion, laboratory exercises, and examination.

Credit Recommendation: In the lower division baccalaureate/associate degree category or in the upper division baccalaureate degree category, 1 semester hour in Data Communications, Data Processing, Information Systems Management, or Computer Science (1/94).

Hands-On Introduction to C++ for Non-C Programmers (327)
(Formerly Introduction to C++ for Non-C Programmers [327])

Location: Worldwide.

Length: 24 hours (4-days).

Dates: July 1996-Present.

Objective: To provide students with the understanding of key object-oriented programming concepts and valuable hands-on experience developing C++ programs.

Learning Outcome: Upon successful completion of this course, the student will be able to create, compile and run C++ programs; define and use C++ classes—the basic units of reliable, reusable code; read and understand basic C++ syntax; declare, use and distinguish variables, constants arrays, pointers and references; write functions, decisions and loops; use standard input and output functions and operators; and derive new classes from existing classes with inheritance.

Instruction: Major topics covered in the course are C++ and our development environment; the main function and standard output; evolution of programming paradigms; variables, calculations, and loops; standard input, decisions, and logic; functions, references, and constants; arrays, pointers, and strings; C++ classes; overloading, friends, and inline functions; inheritance; dynamic memory allocation; linked data structures; and C++ tools and libraries. Methods of instruction include lecture, discussion, classroom exercises, audio/visual materials, observations, and a final examination.

Credit Recommendation: In the lower division baccalaureate/associate degree category, 2 semester hours (1 semester hour in Computer Science or Information Systems and 1 semester hour in Computer Science Laboratory or Information Systems Laboratory) (10/96).

Hands-on Introduction to TCP/IP (367)
(Formerly TCP/IP Internetworking; Hands-On TCP/IP Internetworking [467])

Location: Worldwide.

Length: 24 hours (4 days).

Dates: August 1993-Present.

Objective: To give students an understanding of TCP/IP functionality including: layering concepts, components of networks, and physical transport services.

Learning Outcome: Upon successful completion of this course the student will be able to be familiar with TCP/IP applications (including TELNET, FTP, NFS, Berkeley utilities, DNS, SNMP); use a protocol analyzer to study, decode, and troubleshoot TCP/IP protocols and applications; understand all IP functionality and support on different physical networks; configure and troubleshoot IP routers, examine IP routing protocols, and use ICMP in network troubleshooting; implement and manage internets using TCP/IP protocols, solve connectivity problems using major TCP/IP applications, migrate from TCP/IP to OSI, and optimize and fine-tune TCP/IP networks; and avoid common internetworking problems, troubleshoot TCP/IP related problems, and evaluate vendor-specific implementations and extensions.

Instruction: This course provides 4 days of guidance from an expert and hands-on experience on a classroom network. This enables students to design, implement, configure and maintain networks based on TCP/IP and to add TCP/IP applications and protocols to existing networks.

Methods of instruction include lecture, discussion, hands-on exercises, out-of-class activities, and an examination.

Credit Recommendation: In the upper division baccalaureate degree category or in the lower division baccalaureate/associate degree category, 2 semester hours in Information Systems Management, Data Processing, or Computer Science (12/93).

Hands-On Java Programming (471)
(Formerly Java Programming: Hands-On [471])

Location: Worldwide.

Length: 24 hours (4 days).

Dates: April 1996-Present.

Objective: To provide students the knowledge and skills necessary to design, create, and implement programs using the Java programming language.

Learning Outcome: Upon successful completion of this course, the student will be able to design, write, and execute JAVA programs; create Web-sites with embedded JAVA applets; create World-Wide Web applications using JAVA class libraries; build JAVA-based object-oriented applications; develop GUI's with JAVA tools; and use JAVA built-up security safeguards.

Instruction: Major topics covered in the course are an introduction to JAVA programming; overview of the World-Wide Web; HTML basics; object-oriented design concepts; JAVA syntax and statements; classes, interfaces, and packages; threading and synchronization; file I/O; pipes, files and directories; TCP/IP networking; blending with native C code; and client/server and portable applications. Methods of instruction include lecture, discussion, audio/visual material, hands-on exercises, and a multiple-choice one-hour proctored final examination.

Credit Recommendation: In the lower division baccalaureate/associate degree category, 2 semester hours in Computer Science, Computer Information Systems, or Data Processing (6/96).

Hands-On Lan Troubleshooting (254) (Formerly LAN Troubleshooting with Protocol Analyzer Workshops [254]) (Formerly LAN Troubleshooting with Ethernet Workshops; LAN Troubleshooting with Hands-On Ethernet Workshops)

Location: Worldwide.

Length: 24 hours (4 days).

Dates: August 1993-Present.

Objective: To teach students a systematic approach to troubleshooting and provide them with an understanding of how LANs operate, configure and test LAN cards, solve capacity overload problems, and use LAN protocol analyzer.

Learning Outcome: Upon successful completion of this course the student will be able to use Time Domain Reflectometers (TDR) to find cable faults, and select management tools and procedures for a LAN; find faults in LAN cabling and connectors, test LAN interface cards on and off the network, and use troubleshooting tools and equipment to detect errors such as collisions, short packets and bad CRCs; and monitor, store and decode complex LAN protocols, measure and interpret traffic levels with bridges, monitor, store and decode complex LAN protocols; and troubleshoot a small network.

Instruction: Major topics covered in the course are a hands-on working knowledge of the latest tools and techniques needed to identify and cure LAN faults; procedures to prevent faults from occurring; and the practical knowledge and hands-on experience required to install, troubleshoot, and maintain LANs. Methods of instruction include lecture, discussion, hands-on exercises, out-of-class activities, and an examination.

Credit Recommendation: In the upper division baccalaureate degree category or in the lower division baccalaureate/associate degree category, 2 semester hours in Information Systems Management, Data Processing, or Computer Science (12/93).

Hands-On Macintosh Configuration and Troubleshooting (135) (Formerly Macintosh Configuration and Troubleshooting [135])

Location: Worldwide.

Length: 24 hours (4 days).

Dates: May 1993-Present.

Objective: To provide the student with knowledge of the complete Macintosh system, and to develop the skills needed to support Macintosh hardware and system software.

Learning Outcome: Upon successful completion of this course, the student will be able to safely disassemble and reassemble a complete system; upgrade and configure memory; configure your system with extensions, control panels, printer and video drivers, fonts, and other system resources; troubleshoot start-up conflicts and interpret error messages; organize and optimize the hard disk; recover crashed disks and lost data; prevent, detect and eradicate viruses; and set up an AppleTalk network.

Instruction: Major topics covered in the course are an introduction to the Macintosh; Macintosh hardware, technology, maintenance, and troubleshooting; disk optimization and data recovery with Norton Utilities; software troubleshooting; networks and communication; and trends in Macintosh hardware and software architecture. Methods of instruction include lecture, discussion, laboratory exercises, and examination.

Credit Recommendation: In the lower division baccalaureate/associate degree category, 2 semester hours in Data Communications, Data Processing, Information Systems Management, or Computer Science (3/94).

Hands-On Microsoft Access (307)

Location: Worldwide.

Length: 24 hours (4 days).

Dates: February 1995-Present.

Objective: To understand database concepts and technology, and how to use Microsoft Access to create a system.

Learning Outcome: Upon successful completion of this course, the student will be able to understand database terminology, know how to create a database using Access, develop queries and reports, do programming in the macro language, use Access basic to do Rapid Application development, and use Object Linking and Embedding (OLE) to develop cross-application systems.

Instruction: Major topics covered in the course are database overview, design, objects, entering data, queries and reports, SQL, Macro programming, OLE, and future developments. Methods of instruction include hands-on practical experience, lecture, hand-out material, and examination.

Credit Recommendation: In the lower division baccalaureate/associate degree category, 2 semester hours in Data Processing, Information Systems Management or Computer Science (6/95).

Hands-On Microsoft Exchange (157) (Formerly Microsoft Exchange: Hands-On [157])

Location: Worldwide.

Length: 24 hours (4-days).

Dates: July 1996-Present.

Objective: To provide students with the knowledge and skills needed to install and configure Exchange, integrate it with or migrate from existing E-mail systems and provide additional capabilities such as work-group computing.

Learning Outcome: Upon successful completion of this course, the student will be able to design and implement a Microsoft exchange infrastructure; provide single-seat administration of an exchange organization hierarchy; present users with a single view to global data via the universal inbox; maximize personal productivity with forms, views and exchange assistants; secure data storage and message transfer; and install connectors and gateways to foreign mail systems and the internet.

Instruction: Major topics covered in the course are an introduction to exchange; organizing and securing data; maximizing productivity; supporting users on the move; planning considerations; single-site administration; connecting beyond a single site and putting it all together; and implementing and exchange message system. Methods of instruction include lecture, discussion, classroom exercises, audio/visual material, quizzes, observations, and a final examination.

Credit Recommendation: In the lower division baccalaureate/associate degree category, 2 semester hours in Microcomputer Applications Laboratory (10/96).

Hands-On Microsoft SQL Server System Administration (226) (Formerly Hands-On Microsoft SQL Server 6 System Administration [226])

Location: Worldwide.

Length: 24 hours (4 days).
Dates: February 1996-Present.
Objective: To provide students with the knowledge and skills to install, configure, and use Microsoft SQL Server 6.
Learning Outcome: Upon successful completion of this course, the student will be able to apply the key features of SQL Server 6; create devices, databases tables, and views; retrieve and maintain data using Transact-SQL; write procedures to enhance performance and security; maintain database integrity; and build server-side components of client/server applications.
Instruction: Major topics covered in the course are an introduction to client/server architecture; SQL server setup and installation, physical device management, managing databases, alerts and scheduling, database backup and recovery, managing SQL server security, replication, troubleshooting, integrating SQL servers with external systems, and SQL distributed management framework. Methods of instruction include lecture, discussion, audio/visual material, hands-on exercises, and an one-hour, multiple-choice, proctored final examination.
Credit Recommendation: In the lower division baccalaureate/associate degree category, 2 semester hours in Computer Information Systems (CIS) or Data Processing (6/96).

Hands-On Microsoft Systems Management Server (156) (Formerly Introduction to the Microsoft Systems Management Server [156])

Location: Worldwide.
Length: 24 hours (4 days), plus a one hour proctored examination.
Dates: February 1996-Present.
Objective: To provide students with the knowledge and skills needed to install, configure, and use Microsoft SMS within your environment.
Learning Outcome: Upon successful completion of this course, the student will be able to install and use systems management server (SMS) to create enterprise solutions, utilize SMS as a help desk tool, install Windows NT system services and monitor performance, execute SQL queries against SMS inventory for strategic business planning, plan and administer distributed SMS sites, and use SMS to control an enterprise network using client auditing software distribution and remote troubleshooting.
Instruction: Major topics covered in the course are an introduction to Systems Management Server (SMS) and BackOffice; enterprise administration with Systems Management Server; installing Systems Management Server; working with inventory collection; using SMS as a help-desk tool; creating software distribution packages; implementing SMS jobs; distributing shared network applications; administering the SMS database; adding SMS sites; SMS diagnostics and extensions; and SMS, BackOffice, and the future. Methods of instruction include lecture, discussion, laboratory exercises, and a multiple-choice final examination.
Credit Recommendation: In the lower division baccalaureate/associate degree category, 2 semester hours in Computer Information Systems, Data Processing, or Business Information Systems (6/96).

Hands-On NetWare Service and Support (269) (Formerly NetWare Service and Support [269])

Location: Worldwide.
Length: 24 hours (4 days).
Dates: August 1993-Present.
Objective: To provide student with the ability to install and upgrade NetWare file server operating systems and troubleshoot common problems using diagnostic tools.
Learning Outcome: Upon successful completion of this course, the student will be able to configure and install network hardware; install and configure NetWare file servers, workstations, and routers (internal and external); understand IPX routing; configure diskless workstations; use common NetWare troubleshooting techniques; and use NetWare management, support, diagnostic, and repair tools.
Instruction: Major topics covered in the course are NetWare architecture; installing and diagnosing network adapters; network boards and cabling standards; network workstation support; file-server subsystems; installing a NetWare 2.x and 3.x file server; upgrading NetWare and installing diskless workstations; NetWare routers and diskless workstations; and troubleshooting, diagnosing, and repairing NetWare tools. Methods of instruction include lectures, discussion, laboratory exercises, and examination.
Credit Recommendation: In the lower division baccalaureate/associate degree category or in the upper division baccalaureate degree category, 2 semester hours in Data Communications, Data Processing, Information Systems Management, or Computer Science (1/94).

Hands-On PC Configuration and Troubleshooting (145) (Formerly PC Configuration and Troubleshooting [145])

Location: Worldwide.
Length: 24 hours (4 days).
Dates: September 1992-Present.
Objective: To provide the student with the knowledge required to repair or reconfigure a PC, install upgrades, expand memory, or increase disk capacity.
Learning Outcome: Upon successful completion of this course, the student will be able to safely disassemble and reassemble a complete PC system; install and configure the motherboard and adapter cards; fix PC hardware and software problems; install, configure, and format floppy and hard disks; use Power-On Self-Test (POST) and advanced diagnostics; configure and troubleshoot interrupt request jumpers on adapter cards; and expand memory beyond 640K.
Instruction: Major topics covered in the course are the IBM PC family and components; the motherboard; the power supply; preventive maintenance and a troubleshooting strategy for PC's; the keyboard; display adapters; expanding and troubleshooting memory; diskette drives; hard disk drives; troubleshooting software problems; and serial and parallel ports. Methods of instruction include lecture, discussion, laboratory exercises, out-of-class activities, and examination.
Credit Recommendation: In the lower division baccalaureate/associate degree category, 2 semester hours in Data Communications, Data Processing, Information Systems Management, or Computer Science (3/94).

Hands-On PC Networking (253) (Formerly PC Networking [253])

Location: Worldwide.
Length: 24 hours (4 days).
Dates: August 1993-Present.
Objective: To teach students the key LAN concepts and technologies and to articulate the international and industry standards.
Learning Outcome: Upon successful completion of this course the student will be able to use Novell NetWare, Microsoft Windows for Workgroups and Microsoft Windows 95; run NetWare and Windows 95 concurrently on the same network, install and run network applications on PC LANs; optimize network performance,

share and control the use of peripherals, software and data, and choose an appropriate LAN operating system; and have a working knowledge of network DOS, OS/2, UNIX, and MacIntosh PCs.

Instruction: Major topics covered in the course are the best way to learn about PC networks, under the guidance of an expert instructor in lab intensive training, practical knowledge, and hands-on experience required to install and use the PC networks successfully. Methods of instruction include lecture, discussion, hands-on exercises, out-of-class activities, and an examination.

Credit Recommendation: In the upper division baccalaureate degree category or in the lower division baccalaureate/associate degree category, 2 semester hours in Information Systems Management, Data Processing, or Computer Science (12/93).

Hands-On PowerBuilder (309) (Formerly Introduction to PowerBuilder [309])

Location: Worldwide.

Length: 24 hours (4 days).

Dates: June 1995-Present.

Objective: To provide students with the knowledge and skills to utilize the capabilities of PowerBuilder.

Learning Outcome: Upon successful completion of this course, the student will be able to take advantage of the features and capabilities of PowerBuilder, use PowerBuilder as a front-end to RDBMSs and file based systems, build Windows and associate controls using the Windows painter, create user-defined events with PowerScript, reduce development time by using inheritance and user objects, use DataWindows to modify data from Back-End RDBMSs, and use PowerBuilder to develop client/server applications.

Instruction: Major topics covered in the course are the fundamentals of PowerBuilder; configuring the environment; Window Painter; working with DataWindows; using the PowerScript language; using the menu printer; the Database Painter; DataWindows; structure, user objects, and the debugger; more DataWindows; and deploying the system. Methods of instruction include lecture, discussion, laboratory exercises, audio/visual material, and an one-hour, multiple-choice, proctored final examination.

Credit Recommendation: In the lower division baccalaureate/associate degree category, 2 semester hours in Computer Science, Data Processing, Computer Information Systems, or Business Information Systems (2/96).

Hands-On Project Management: Skills for Success (296) (Formerly Project Management: Skills for Success [296])

Location: Worldwide.

Length: 24 hours (4 days).

Dates: May 1993-Present.

Objective: To provide knowledge needed to organize, plan, schedule, monitor, and control projects.

Learning Outcome: Upon successful completion of this course, the student will be able to produce a project plan with a high-win expectation; plan projects using a clear 6-step method; fully define a project manager job; develop "accountability contracts" for your subordinates; recognize and practice the leadership skills needed to run a project; use PC based & manual tools for planning, scheduling, and budgeting; and implement monitoring tools and controls to keep in command of a project.

Instruction: Major topics covered in the course are project management fundamentals; laying the foundations for success; defining project objectives; structuring the project; estimating time and resources; scheduling the project; finalizing the plan; establishing tracking and control systems; running the project; and people, projects, and project management skills for success. Methods of instruction include lecture, discussion, laboratory exercises, role-playing, and examination.

Credit Recommendation: In the upper division baccalaureate degree category, 2 semester hours in Information Systems Management, Software Engineering, Computer Science, or Data Processing (6/94).

Hands-On SNMP: From Workgroup to Enterprise Networks (464) (Formerly SNMP: From Workgroup to Enterprise Networks [464]) (Formerly Hands-On SNMP: From Workgroup to Enterprise Networks)

Location: Worldwide.

Length: 24 hours (4 days).

Dates: November 1993-Present.

Objective: To teach students to handle networks with multiple management domains and diagnose and troubleshoot network faults using SNMP.

Learning Outcome: Upon successful completion of this course the student will be able to learn the basics of managing a Novell network; practice using MIB-II, RMON, and other MIBs; analyze SNMP protocol structure and encoding; manage hubs, bridges, routers and systems using SNMP; interpret and customize Management Information Bases (MIBs); manage networks ranging from small PC networks to Enterprise-wide WANs; and effectively compare network manager platforms including SunNet Manager, OpenView and NetView.

Instruction: Major topics covered in the course are a thorough understanding of SNMP's capabilities and limitations and the essential skills and knowledge needed to effectively monitor and control multi-vendor networks using SNMP tools. Methods of instruction include lecture, discussion, hands-on exercises, out-of-class activities, and an examination.

Credit Recommendation: In the upper division baccalaureate degree category or in the lower division baccalaureate/associate degree category, 2 semester hours in Information Systems Management, Data Processing, or Computer Science (12/93).

Hands-On TCP/IP Internetworking on Windows NT (154) (Formerly Introduction to TCP/IP Internetworking on Windows NT [154])

Location: Worldwide.

Length: 24 hours (4 days).

Dates: December 1995-Present.

Objective: To provide students the knowledge and skills needed to install, configure, and optimize a TCP/IP internetwork on Windows NT.

Learning Outcome: Upon successful completion of this course, the student will be able to define the requirements for implementing internetworks, select suitable IP addresses & subnet masks, install & troubleshoot TCP/IP on Windows NT, resolve domain and NetBIOS names using DNS and WINS, configure TCP/IP automatically with DHCP; correctly locate WINS and SHCP servers on multiple subnets; and tune TCP/IP settings via the registry.

Instruction: Major topics covered in the course are Windows NT networking; internetworking primer; IP addresses and subnet masks; troubleshooting and tuning TCP/IP on Windows NT; address and name resolution; name resolution with WINS; automatic configuration with DHCP; routing on Windows NT; and interoperability. Methods of instruction include lecture, discussion, laboratory exercises, and a multiple-choice final examination.

Credit Recommendation: In the lower division baccalaureate/associate degree

category, 2 semester hours in Business Information Systems, Computer Information Systems, or Telecommunications (2/96).

Hands-On TCP/IP Programming (363) (Formerly UNIX Network Programming [363]) (Formerly UNIX Client/Server Programming)

Location: Worldwide.

Length: 24 hours (4 days).

Dates: July 1992-Present.

Objective: To provide student with the ability to configure a UNIX network, exploit end user UNIX network tools, and examine network activity and status.

Learning Outcome: Upon successful completion of this course, the student will be able to exploit end user UNIX network tools across a LAN; use the UNIX IPC mechanisms; access TCP/IP transport services from programs; develop client/server applications using sockets and TLI; develop client/server applications using Remote Procedure Calls (RPCs); examine network activity and debug client/server applications; and get help via electronic mail, archives, and news services.

Instruction: Major topics covered in this course include client/server concepts and benefits; distributed programming under UNIX; end user network utilities; underlying protocols; UNIX network services; writing clients and servers; distributed programming using RPC; talking to the outside world; survival UNIX. Methods of instruction include lecture, discussion, laboratory exercises, and examination.

Credit Recommendation: In the lower division baccalaureate/associate degree category or in the upper division baccalaureate degree category, 2 semester hours in Computer Science, Data Communications, Information Systems Management, or Data Processing (1/94).

Hands-On UNIX Programming (333) (Formerly UNIX Programming [333]) (Formerly Exploiting the UNIX Programming Interface)

Location: Worldwide.

Length: 24 hours (4 days).

Dates: May 1992-Present.

Objective: To provide student with the ability to apply UNIX system calls and library functions for writing systems and applications in C.

Learning Outcome: Upon successful completion of this course, the student will be able to write distributed applications using the UNIX networking tools; write and install a simple device driver in the UNIX kernel; write UNIX client/server programs and portable, open applications; initiate, control, and communicate between UNIX processes; and use configuration and version control systems to maintain large software projects.

Instruction: Major topics covered in the course are UNIX manuals, system calls, and library functions; files and the file system; process information and signals; introduction to networks and communication facilities; interprocess communication and distributed processing; and introduction to UNIX device drivers; using the UNIX software development tools. Methods of instruction include lecture, discussion, laboratory exercises, and examination.

Credit Recommendation: In the lower division baccalaureate/associate degree category or in the upper division baccalaureate degree category, 2 semester hours in Computer Science, Information Systems Management, or Data Processing (1/94).

Hands-On UNIX Tools and Utilities (396) (Formerly UNIX Tools and Utilities [396]) (Formerly UNIX Tools and Utilities [Hands-on Workshop])

Location: Worldwide.

Length: 24 hours (4 days).

Dates: May 1994-Present.

Objective: To provide knowledge and techniques needed to use standard and third-party UNIX tools and utilities, and to adapt the UNIX environment to individual needs.

Learning Outcome: Upon successful completion of this course, the student will be able to build and use UNIX tools and utilities; customize a user environment; employ standard and programmable editors and text filters to manipulate text and data; build shell scripts to automate routine tasks; augment and extend standard utilities with third-party software; and achieve significant productivity gains by matching the mix of tools to the task at hand.

Instruction: Major topics covered in the course are a UNIX and software tools overview; editing text in UNIX; searching text with regular expressions; filtering text; restructuring data with Awk; shell scripts without shell shock; other shells and scripting languages; climbing the file system tree; programs for controlling file production; and producing and disseminating documentation. Methods of instruction include lecture, discussion, laboratory exercises, and examination.

Credit Recommendation: In the upper division baccalaureate degree category, 2 semester hours in Computer Science, Information Systems Management, or Data Processing (6/94).

Hands-On Visual Basic 5 (304) (Formerly Visual Basic [304])

Location: Worldwide.

Length: 24 hours (4 days).

Dates: August 1994-Present.

Objective: To provide the knowledge and skills required to utilize the features and capabilities of Visual Basic.

Learning Outcome: Upon successful completion of this course, the student will be able to use Visual Basic to develop Windows applications quickly and effectively; prototype event-driven Windows programs; access database information with the new ODBC Data Control; create GUI front-ends for client/server applications; use OLE 2 and Visual Basic for Applications (VBA) to integrate Windows programs; and extend Visual Basic with powerful custom controls (VBXs).

Instruction: Major topics covered in the course include an introduction to Visual Basic; forms and basic controls; advanced controls and properties; variables, constants, and operators; program control; menus and dialog boxes; databases and OLE 2; and MDI, API, and VBA. Methods of instruction include lecture, discussion, audio/visual material, classroom exercises, computer aided instruction, and final examination.

Credit Recommendation: In the lower division baccalaureate degree category, 1 semester hour in Data Processing (8/94).

Hands-On Visual C++: Windows Programming with Microsoft Foundation Classes for C Programmers (301) (Formerly Visual C++: Windows Programming with Microsoft Foundation Classes [301]) (Formerly Visual C++)

Location: Worldwide.

Length: 24 hours (4 days).

Dates: May 1994-Present.

Objective: To provide knowledge and skills to use Visual C++ in the Windows programming environment.

Learning Outcome: Upon successful completion of this course, the student will

be able to use Visual C++ to quickly and effectively develop 16-and 32-Bit Windows applications; exploit the Microsoft Foundation Class (MFC) Library and application framework; automate repetitive tasks with AppWizard and ClassWizard; access databases with ODBC; and construct OLE 2 full-server applications with visual in-place editing.

Instruction: Major topics covered in the course are the Document/View architecture; implementing the user interface; Open Database Connectivity (ODBC); and Object Linking and Embedding (OLE). Methods of instruction include lecture, discussion, audio/visual material, computer-assisted instruction, extensive classroom exercises, and final examination.

Credit Recommendation: In the upper division baccalaureate degree category, 2 semester hours in Computer Science (8/94).

Hands-On Visual J++ (476) (Formerly Visual J++: A Hands-On Workshop [476])

Location: Worldwide.

Length: 24 hours (4 days).

Dates: November 1996-Present.

Objective: To provide students with in-depth knowledge and skills needed to use Visual J++ and achieve significant gains in programming quality and productivity.

Learning Outcome: Upon successful completion of this course, the student will be able to write, compile, and execute cross-platform Java programs in Visual J++; build applets and component object model (COM) objects using wizards and utilities; troubleshoot applications using the visual debugger with datatips; integrate Java with COM and ActiveX technologies; and use Visual J++ to enhanced Internet and intranet applets and windows applications.

Instruction: Major topics covered in the course are introduction to Java programming with Visual J++; Java primer; object-oriented concepts in Java: object-oriented programming in Java; COM and ActiveX; integrating COM and Java; the abstract window toolkit; event handling, menus, and dialogs; and code signing. Methods of instruction include lecture, discussion, classroom exercises, audio/visual material, and final examination.

Credit Recommendation: In the lower division baccalaureate/associate degree category, 2 semester hours in Computer Science or Computer Information Systems Lab (4/97).

Hands-On Wide Area Network Troubleshooting (456)

Location: Worldwide.

Length: 24 hours (4 days).

Dates: July 1995-Present.

Objective: To provide students with a comprehensive set of skills, tools and techniques that dramatically reduces the tie to troubleshoot WANs, including the latest high-speed dial modems, network protocols and interfaces.

Learning Outcome: Upon successful completion of this course, the student will be able to use protocol analyzers, breakout boxes, hand-held test sets, and other equipment; quickly diagnose failures in modems, multiplexers, and terminals; rapidly troubleshoot hardware and software protocol problems; configure and troubleshoot EIA-232, V.24/V.28, and V.35 interfaces; configure and test V.32 bis, V.34 (28.8/33.6 kbit/s), and fax modems; and employ loopback and bit error ratio tests to isolate local and remote faults.

Instruction: Major topics covered in the course are data communications concepts; testing interfaces and links; analyzing character-oriented protocols; advanced RS-232/V.24 techniques and other interface standards; dial modems: basic and advanced; PC communications; error correction, data compression, and flow control; modern multiplexers; decoding bit-oriented protocols; and implementing ISDN and putting it all together. Methods of instruction include lecture, discussion, classroom exercises, audio/visual material, and final examination.

Credit Recommendation: In the lower division baccalaureate/associate degree category, 2 semester hours in Data Communications or Computer Information Systems (4/97).

Hands-on Windows 95 Support and Networking (153) Hands-On Windows 95 Introduction to Windows 95

Location: Worldwide.

Length: 30 hours (5 days).

Dates: March 1995-Present.

Objective: To provide knowledge and skills to successfully implement Windows 95.

Learning Outcome: Upon successful completion of this course,, the student will be able to install and configure Windows 95 for optimum use; navigate the Windows 95 user interface; establish network resource sharing and network security; integrate Windows 95 Workgroups with NetWare and Windows NT; remotely administer user profiles, passwords and the registry; and establish user and machine system policies.

Instruction: Major topics covered in the course are getting started with Windows 95; working with Windows 95; network resources and security; system components and configuration; system management; and Windows 95 networking and remote access. Methods of instruction include lecture, discussion, laboratory exercises, and a final examination.

Credit Recommendation: In the lower division baccalaureate/associate degree category, 2 semester hours in Information Systems Management or Data Processing (4/95).

Hands-on Windows NT Workstation and Server (155) (Formerly Windows NT)

Location: Worldwide.

Length: 30 hours (5 days).

Dates: June 1993-Present.

Objective: To provide the student with knowledge of Windows NT components and capabilities.

Learning Outcome: Upon successful completion of this course, the student will be able to install and configure Windows NT; run Win32, Windows 3.x, DOS and OS/2 applications; use Windows NT's built-in networking capabilities; evaluate internetworking capabilities including TCP/IP; implement Windows NT user and filesystem security; monitor Windows NT performance; and compare Windows NT to existing operating system.

Instruction: Major topics covered in the course are an introduction to Windows NT; installing and exploring Windows NT; Windows NT subsystems; managing Kernel resources; Windows NT filesystem and file security, user management, networking, and system maintenance; building Win32 applications; and evaluating Windows NT. Methods of instruction include lecture, discussion, laboratory exercises, out-of-class activities, and examination.

Credit Recommendation: In the lower division baccalaureate/associate degree category or in the upper division baccalaureate degree category, 2 semester hours in Data Communications, Data Processing,

Information Systems Management, or Computer Science (3/94).

Hands-On X Window System Programming (331) (Formerly X Window System Programming [331]) (Formerly X Window System Programming:Hands-On Workshop)

Location: Worldwide.
Length: 24 hours (4 days).
Dates: March 1993-Present.
Objective: To provide student with the ability to design and implement X Window System applications.
Learning Outcome: Upon successful completion of this course, the student will be able to exploit the event-processing and error-handling capabilities; create bit mapped graphics applications with color; interact with the Window Manager and communicate between X applications; and use Athena, Motif, and X toolkits and the Xlib Procedural Interface and X toolkits.
Instruction: Major topics covered in the course are X development environment; and fundamentals of Xlib programming, graphics in X, toolkits, and motif. Methods of instruction include lecture, discussion, laboratory exercises, and examination.
Credit Recommendation: In the lower division baccalaureate/associate degree category or in the upper division baccalaureate degree category, 2 semester hours in Computer Science, Information Systems Management, or Data Processing (1/94).

Hands-On X.25 (362) (Formerly X.25 [362]) (Formerly Hands-On X.25)

Location: Worldwide.
Length: 24 hours (4 days).
Dates: August 1993-Present.
Objective: To provide students familiarity with the X.25 packets down to the bit level and an understanding of the X.25 procedures, features and limitations.
Learning Outcome: Upon successful completion of this course the student will be able to set up and run an X.25 network and verify X.25 connectivity and performance; understand all facets of X.25, the dominant standard for wide area packet-switched networking; allow them to function within all major networking architectures (including SNA, DECnet and TCP/IP.); and ask the appropriate questions of their suppliers in this environment.
Instruction: Major topics covered in the course are development of the practical expertise needed to design, procure and use private X.25 networks and to take full advantage of public data network services. Methods of instruction include lecture, discussion, hands-on exercises, out-of-class activities, and an examination.
Credit Recommendation: In the upper division baccalaureate degree category or in the lower division baccalaureate/associate degree category, 2 semester hours in Information Systems Management, Data Processing, or Computer Science (12/93).

Hands-On: Microsoft Internet Information Server (163)

Location: Worldwide.
Length: 24 hours (4 days).
Dates: June 1997-Present.
Objective: To provide knowledge and skill needed to provide Internet and intranet services with Internet Information Server (IIS).
Learning Outcome: Upon successful completion of this course, the student will be able to install, configure, and manage Microsoft's Internet Information Server (IIS)3.x; generate web content "on the fly" using ILS's active server features; configure Internet Database Connector (IDC) to publish SQL server data on the web; provide comprehensive web site search capabilities with the MS Index Server; exploit the MS Proxy Server to enhance site security and performance; and extend IIS's functionality using Microsoft Commercial Internet System (MCIS).
Instruction: Major topics covered in the course are an introduction to Internet Information Server, FTP service, WWW service, managing static WWW content, managing index server, security, proxy server, DNS and virtual servers performance tuning and optimization, crystal reports for IIS, netshow, and Internet commerce. Methods of instruction include lecture, discussion, classroom exercises, audio/visual material, and examinations.
Credit Recommendation: In the upper division baccalaureate degree category, 1 semester hour in Management Information System or Computer Science (8/97).

High Speed Wide Area Networks (379) (Formerly High-Speed Networks)

Location: Worldwide.
Length: 24 hours (4 days).
Dates: October 1993-Present.
Objective: To give students an understanding of high-speed networks that will proliferate in the future and teach them to evaluate high-speed network technology to make the best choice for their business.
Learning Outcome: Upon successful completion of this course the student will be able to select the high-speed MAN and WAN services that meet your LAN-to-LAN interconnection requirements; evaluate the suitability of frame relay, FDDI, SMDS and ATM; apply high-speed transmission technologies, including SONET, SDH and leased fiber; prepare your enterprise to take advantage of B-ISDN and ATM; unleash the multimedia power of high-speed networks; and evaluate high-speed networking products and Customer Premises Equipment (CPE).
Instruction: This course provides the latest network concepts, products, services and growth potential which enable participants to choose the best high-speed network technology for their needs. Methods of instruction include lecture, discussion, hands-on exercises, out-of-class activities, and an examination.
Credit Recommendation: In the upper division baccalaureate degree category or in the lower division baccalaureate/associate degree category, 2 semester hours in Information Systems Management, Data Processing, or Computer Science (12/93).

Identifying and Confirming User Requirements (315)

Location: Worldwide.
Length: 24 hours (4 days).
Dates: June 1993-Present.
Objective: To provide the student with methods, techniques, and strategies to identify user requirements and close the gap between users and developers.
Learning Outcome: Upon successful completion of this course, the student will be able to use a step-by-step user requirements definition framework; conduct effective, information-gathering interviews with users and managers; translate an opportunity into functional goals; profile and understand the users and their environment; evaluate work flow and perform gap analysis; obtain user participation and confirmation; and anticipate changes and hit the moving target.
Instruction: Major topics covered in the course are information gathering skills (methods, techniques, and effective interviewing); opportunity appraisal and definition; organization profiles, requirements, and guidelines; work flow analysis; user participation; deriving a scenario; target requirements documents; development and confirmation strategies; and managing the process. Methods of instruction include lecture, discussion, classroom workshops/exercises, out-of-class activities, and examination.

Credit Recommendation: In the lower division baccalaureate/associate degree category or in the upper division baccalaureate degree category, 2 semester hours in Data Processing, Information Systems Management, or Computer Science (3/94).

Implementing ATM (279)

Location: Various sites in the United States.

Length: 18 hours (3 days).

Dates: June 1997-Present.

Objective: To provide students with a foundation in ATM and related technologies, evaluate and select appropriate ATM products and services, and plan the integration of ATM into an enterprise network.

Learning Outcome: Upon successful completion of this course, the student will be able to apply Asynchronous Transfer Mode (ATM) in an enterprise; integrate ATM into an existing LAN at the desktop, departmental or backbone level; choose the appropriate ATM service for WAN needs; support TCP/IP and other protocols in an ATM environment; control and manage an ATM network; and take advantage of the multimedia capabilities and scalability of ATM.

Instruction: Major topics covered in this course are networking essentials, ATM fundamentals, cell relay, adapting traffic to ATM, signaling, deploying ATM in the LAN, using ATM in the WAN, and managing ATM networks. Methods of instruction include lecture, discussion, classroom exercises, audio-visual material, module tests and final examination.

Credit Recommendation: In the lower division baccalaureate/associate degree category, 1 semester hour in Data Communications and Networking, Computer Information Systems or Computer Science (2/98).

Implementing Computer Telephone Integration (376)

Location: Worldwide.

Length: 24 hours (4 days).

Dates: July 1997-Present.

Objective: To provide the knowledge and skills to evaluate the major CTI tools and technology available today, and to select and implement the system best suited to an organization.

Learning Outcome: Upon successful completion of this course, the student will be able to evaluate and select CTI applications appropriate for your organization; ask the right questions of your hardware and software CTI vendors; identify requirements and design your CTI system; apply telephone integration and automation to desktop and call cent applications; implement voice, image, and video messaging and response systems; and incorporate the Internet with your CTI systems.

Instruction: Major topics covered in the course are an introduction to CTI, telephony essentials, computer essentials, network essentials, enabling integration, voice processing, media processing, hardware CTI components, merged systems, CTI supply and system implementation, and applying CTI. Methods of instruction include lecture, discussion, classroom exercises, audio/visual material, and examination.

Credit Recommendation: In the lower division baccalaureate/associate degree category, 2 semester hours in Information Systems Management, Data Processing, or Computer Technology (8/97).

Implementing Fiber-Optic Communication (440) (Formerly Introduction to Fiber Optic Communications)

Location: Worldwide.

Length: 24 hours (4 days).

Dates: June 1993-Present.

Objective: To provide an introduction to the fiber optic communication field with emphasis on practical applications of fiber to design and construct communications systems and networks.

Learning Outcome: Upon successful completion of this course, the student will be able to apply fiber optics in data, voice, or TV networks; design fiber-optic systems using "take-home" software; test, troubleshoot, and maintain fiber-optic systems; specify optical fiber, transmitters, and receivers; and evaluate third-party solutions to fiber-optic needs.

Instruction: Major topics covered in the course are fundamentals of optical fiber, cables and installation techniques, optical transmitters and receivers, link design and multiplexing, testing and safety standards, FDDI and LANs, wide area fiber networks, and future trends and product review. Methods of instruction include lecture, discussion, classroom exercises, case study, role-playing, problem solving, computer demonstration, and examination.

Credit Recommendation: In the upper division baccalaureate degree category, 2 semester hours in Data Communications, Computer Science, Information Systems Management, Data Processing, or Computer Operations (6/94).

Implementing High-Performance Cabling Systems (258)

Location: Worldwide.

Length: 24 hours (4 days).

Dates: June 1994-Present.

Objective: To provide knowledge needed to plan, cost, design, install, and maintain a state-of-the-art cabling system.

Learning Outcome: Upon successful completion of this course, the student will be able to define clear user requirements for installing new and upgrading existing LAN and telecommunications cabling systems; develop an implementation plan including task breakdowns and investment analysis; select fiber and copper cable components; design, install and test a system; manage and maintain a cable plant; certify a cabling system performance to 100 Mbits/second and beyond; and ensure secure implementations.

Instruction: Major topics covered in the course are the case for structuring and cabling applications, signaling concepts, and terminology; evaluation of transmission media; standards; preinstallation design consideration; LAN component design; an overview of major cabling system vendors; fiber-optic cable plant design; the copper cable plant; and cable plant installation and testing. Methods of instruction include lecture, discussion, classroom exercises, case studies, role-playing, problem-solving, and examination.

Credit Recommendation: In the upper division baccalaureate degree category, 2 semester hours in Data Communications, Computer Science, Information Systems Management, Data Processing, or Computer Operations (6/94).

Implementing ISDN Data Networks: Hands-On (374) (Hands-On ISDN for Data Communications) (Formerly ISDN Data Communications [374])

Location: Worldwide.

Length: 24 hours (4 days).

Dates: May 1996-Present.

Objective: To provide students the knowledge and skills to design, configure, install, and apply ISDN technology in a computer network.

Learning Outcome: Upon successful completion of this course, the student will be able to specify the ISDN equipment and services most appropriate to meet needs;

implement a cost-effective telecommuting and remote connectivity network; evaluate video conferencing, remote access, and control software; install and configure ISDN bridges, routers, and terminal adapters; and apply effective management and security measures in an ISDN environment.

Instruction: Major topics covered in the course are an introduction to ISDN; using ISDN terminal adapters; deploying ISDN bridges; BRA and PRA methods; TCP/IP over ISDN; system security; Internet access via ISDN; video applications; ordering and installing ISDN; and future networking trends. Methods of instruction include lecture, discussion, classroom exercises, audio/visual material, hands-on exercises, and a multiple-choice one-hour proctored final examination.

Credit Recommendation: In the lower division baccalaureate/associate degree category, 2 semester hours in Data Communications, Data Processing, Information Systems Management, or Computer Science (6/96).

Implementing Microsoft SNA Server 3: Hands-On (164)

Location: Worldwide.

Length: 24 hours (4 days).

Dates: July 1997-Present.

Objective: To provide practical experience integrating and managing SNA server as part of a robust, secure and fault-tolerant SNA network.

Learning Outcome: Upon successful completion of this course, the student will be able to integrate client/server and IBM host systems using SNA Server 3; plan for a robust and secure implementation of SNA Server; configure SNA Server for hierarchical an peer-to-peer models; provide terminal and printer access to IBM host systems; troubleshoot and optimize SNA Server; create a fault-tolerant environment with third-part tools; and evaluate Web-to-host integration.

Instruction: Major topics covered in the course are an introduction and overview, installing SNA Server, configuring SNA Server, troubleshooting and optimization, security in an SNA environment, and developing a plan for an SNA Server implementation. Methods of instruction include lecture, discussion, classroom exercises, audio/visual material, and examinations.

Credit Recommendation: In the upper division baccalaureate degree category, 1 semester hour in Management Information System or Computer Science (8/97).

Implementing Windows NT Security: Hands-On (162)

Location: Worldwide.

Length: 24 hours (4 days).

Dates: February 1997-Present.

Objective: To provide students the knowledge and skills needed to maintain the integrity, authenticity, availability and privacy of their data.

Learning Outcome: Upon successful completion of this course, the student will be able to implement and maintain data and systems security for a Windows NT environment; comply with C2 security certification; construct Access Control Lists (ACLs) for users and applications; evaluate and select a Windows NT-based firewall for their environment; configure security with Microsoft's Internet Information Server (IIS) 2.0; and secure Windows NT in Intranet and Internet environments.

Instruction: Major topics covered in the course are introduction to Windows NT security, Windows NT C2 certification, administering Windows NT security, internals of Access Control Lists (ACLs), auditing security, securing intranet and internet environments, and the evolution of Windows NT security. Methods of instruction include lecture, discussion, classroom exercises, audio/visual material, and final examination.

Credit Recommendation: In the upper division baccalaureate degree category, 1 semester hour in Computer Science, Computer Information Systems, or Computer Security Lab (4/97).

Influence Skills (294) (Formerly Influence Skills: Getting Results Without Direct Authority [294])

Location: Worldwide.

Length: 24 hours (4 days).

Dates: January 1993-Present.

Objective: To provide ability to achieve goals through influence when they do not have direct authority.

Learning Outcome: Upon successful completion of this course, the student will be able to achieve goals by instilling trust and cooperation; convince others to buy into decisions; deal effectively with "difficult" people; use knowledge and competence rather than position and status to influence others; create a climate that promotes commitment; and improve your ability to overcome resistance and inertia in others.

Instruction: Major topics covered in the course are the characteristics of influence; the influence process; communicating effectively; practicing leadership; establishing and maintaining trust; networking for results; using influence strategies; Microcomputer Applications Development (MAD); and the self-development guide. Methods of instruction include lectures, discussion, classroom exercises, role-playing, case studies, and examination.

Credit Recommendation: In the upper division baccalaureate degree category, 2 semester hours in Information Systems Management or Management elective (6/94).

Integrating Microsoft Office 97 (208)

Location: Various sites in the United States.

Length: 24 hours (4 days).

Dates: April 1997-Present.

Objective: To provide students with the knowledge and skills needed to integrate and automate the functions of the Office 97 application suite.

Learning Outcome: Upon successful completion of this course the student will be able to improve business productivity through Microsoft Office 97 automation and integration capabilities; effectively exchange data among Office 97 applications; publish and access data between Office 97 and an Internet; record and design macros to automate processes; use Outlook as a central communications interface; and use the scheduling capabilities of Office 97.

Instruction: Major topics covered in the course are an overview of Office 97, centralizing communications with Outlook, integrating Office 97 applications, Web publishing with Office 97, automating Office 97 functions, and moving towards Activex automation.

Credit Recommendation: In the lower division baccalaureate/associate degree category, 2 semester hours (1 semester hour in Information Systems and 1 semester hour in Information Systems laboratory). (2/98).

Internet and System Security: Attacks and Countermeasures (468) (Formerly Survey of Internet and Computer Security Issues [468])

Location: Worldwide.

Length: 24 hours (4 days).

Dates: August 1995-Present.

Objective: To provide students with an introduction to computer security and the skills to analyze risks to a system and the knowledge to implement a workable security policy to protect assets from potential intrusion, damage or theft.

Learning Outcome: Upon successful completion of this course, the student will be able to analyze exposure to security threats from outside and inside the organization; manage the additional risks introduced to an organization via the Internet; reduce susceptibility to an attack by deploying firewalls, data encryption and decryption, and other countermeasures; evaluate tools and techniques for performing security audits; and develop a comprehensive security policy to protect your organization's systems and data.

Instruction: Major topics covered in the course are an introduction to the Internet and system security; authenticity vs. masquerade; privacy vs. interception; integrity vs. modification; availability vs. interruption; developing security policy; and encryption, audit, and firewall tools. Methods of instruction include lecture, discussion, classroom exercises, and an one-hour, multiple-choice, proctored final examination.

Credit Recommendation: In the lower division baccalaureate/associate degree category or upper division baccalaureate degree category, 2 semester hours in Business Information Systems, Computer Information Systems, or Data Processing (2/96).

IntranetWare: NetWare 4.x Design and Implementation (268) (Hands-On Netware 4.x Design and Implementation) (Formerly NetWare 4.x Design and Implementation [268])

Location: Worldwide.

Length: 12 hours (2 days), plus a one hour proctored examination.

Dates: December 1995-Present.

Objective: To provide students with the knowledge to successfully design and implement a NetWare 4.x network.

Learning Outcome: Upon successful completion of this course, the student will be able to design and implement NetWare Directory Services (NDS), create a project team, estimate the scope of a NetWare 4 implementation, identify critical components of a migration strategy, use proven design and implementation guidelines, and develop a successful implementation plan.

Instruction: Major topics covered in the course are an introduction to NetWare 4 project design and implementation, designing the directory tree, partitioning and replication strategies, planning a time-synchronization strategy, creating an accessibility plan, and developing a migration strategy. Methods of instruction include lecture, discussion, Novell application notes, and multiple-choice interim and final examinations.

Credit Recommendation: In the lower division baccalaureate/associate degree category, 1 semester hour in Computer Science, Business Information Systems, Computer Information Systems, Data Processing, or Telecommunications (2/96).

Introduction to Client/Server Computing (369) (Formerly Introduction to Client/Server Systems)

Location: Worldwide.

Length: 24 hours (4 days).

Dates: April 1993-Present.

Objective: To provide the student with an introduction to client/server computing from architecture and application design to system performance and support.

Learning Outcome: Upon successful completion of this course, the student will be able to evaluate the benefits of a client/server approach vs. traditional data processing; migrate legacy applications to client/server; compare major client/server architectures; adapt software design methods to the client/server model; apply the client/server model to distributed databases; test and tune client/server applications; and manage a cooperative processing environment.

Instruction: Major topics covered in the course are attributes of client/server systems, client/server architecture, designing successful client/server applications, interprocess communication, implementing client/server applications, distributive computing environment and the client/server model, vendors and visions, supporting the system, and emerging trends in client/server computing. Methods of instruction include lecture, discussion, case studies, exercises, videotape, out-of-class activities, and examination.

Credit Recommendation: In the lower division baccalaureate/associate degree category or in the upper division baccalaureate degree category, 2 semester hours in Data Communications, Data Processing, Information Systems Management, or Computer Science (3/94).

Introduction to Datacomm and Networks (350)

Location: Worldwide.

Length: 24 hours (4 days).

Dates: August 1993-Present.

Objective: To introduce students to data communications and networking. Students will gain an understanding of the terminology and concepts, along with the hardware and software aspects of data communications and networking.

Learning Outcome: Upon successful completion of this course the student will be able to utilize existing protocols and standards, and gain an understanding of how packet-switching networks and Local Area Networks function; link computers to mini and mainframe computers; understand how the basic networking components work, and how they're put together to implement a system; and apply their skills and knowledge in a large, organization-wide internet featuring Token Ring LAN, an Ethernet LAN, and FDDI LAN, bridges, routers, gateways, an X.25 wide-area network, PC-to-mainframe connection.

Instruction: Major topics covered in the course are a comprehensive technical foundation in the Datacomm and networks concepts that underlie LANs, WANs, and internetworked systems; how Datacomm and network components work and how they're integrated to implement a system; and the key protocols and standards, including OSI and TCP/IP. Methods of instruction include lecture, discussion, hands-on exercises, out-of-class activities, and an examination.

Credit Recommendation: In the lower division baccalaureate/associate degree category, 2 semester hours in Information Systems Management, Data Processing, or Computer Science (12/93).

Introduction to Internetworking: Bridges and Routers (364) (Formerly Internetworking: Bridges and Routers [364]) (Formerly Internetworking: Bridges, Routers and Gateways)

Location: Worldwide.

Length: 24 hours (4 days).

Dates: August 1993-Present.

Objective: To provide the student with a basic understanding of the operations of bridges routers and gateways.

Learning Outcome: Upon successful completion of this course the student will be able to identify when and how to use bridges and routers; design multiprotocol internetworks using TCP/IP and IPX/SPX; develop practical multivendor management solutions using SNMP; evaluate products for speed and functionality; define WAN requirements and select appropriate technologies, and design scalable networks that can support increasing demands for services.

Instruction: Major topics covered in the course are all aspects of internetworking using bridges and routers. Emphasis is on a series of workshops which enable participants to design solutions to typical internetworking problems. Methods of instruction include lecture, discussion, hands-on exercises, out-of-class activities, and an examination.

Credit Recommendation: In the upper division baccalaureate degree category or in the lower division baccalaureate/associate degree category, 2 semester hours in Information Systems Management, Data Processing, or Computer Science (12/93).

Introduction to Object Technology (215)

Location: Worldwide.

Length: 24 hours (4 days).

Dates: March 1997-Present.

Objective: To teach students how to apply object technology, and to choose the most appropriate methodologies and languages. Through in-class demonstrations of major modeling tools, students gain insight into the best practices and trade-offs of object-oriented development.

Learning Outcome: Upon successful completion of this course, the student will be able to apply the core object concepts of inheritance, encapsulation, and polymorphism; select and apply key components and tools of object technology; compare leading object-oriented languages, including C++ and Java; evaluate visual development tools for developing object-oriented applications; sorter objects in traditional and object-oriented databases; make use of component object technologies, e.g. ActiveX/DCOM, CORBA, and Web applets; and develop strategies for applying object technology in your workplace.

Instruction: Major topics covered in the course are what is object technology, object modeling, programming with objects - 1: Java, visual development environments, programming with objects - 2: C++, storing objects, component-based software, and applying object technology. Methods of instruction include lecture, discussion, classroom exercises, audio/visual material, and final examination.

Credit Recommendation: In the lower division baccalaureate/associate degree category, 2 semester hours in Computer Information Systems or Computer Science (4/97).

Introduction to Open Systems (360) (Formerly Implementing Open Systems)

Location: Worldwide.

Length: 24 hours (4 days).

Dates: April 1993-Present.

Objective: To provide student with the ability to understand the technical attributes of open systems including identifying the key components, vendors, and standards.

Learning Outcome: Upon successful completion of this course, the student will be able to understand the technical attributes of open systems; identify the key components, vendors, and standards; determine open system requirements and assess the technical and business aspect; develop an open systems strategy for an organization; assess the risks and analyze the costs; and plan and implement a successful migration to open systems.

Instruction: Major topics covered in the course include attributes, components, architectures, operating systems, networking, user interface, software development, data management, security, and management of an Open System. Methods of instruction include lecture, discussion, laboratory exercises, case studies, computer-assisted videos, and examination.

Credit Recommendation: In the lower division baccalaureate/associate degree category or in the upper division baccalaureate degree category, 2 semester hours in Computer Science, Data Communications, Information Systems Management, and Data Processing (1/94).

Introduction to Programming: Hands-On (325) (Formerly Introduction to Programming: A Hands-On Workshop [325])

Location: Worldwide.

Length: 24 hours (4 days).

Dates: June 1997-Present.

Objective: To provide a basic hands-on introduction to programming, including both conceptual background as well as hands-on experience with writing, compiling and debugging programs in C/C++.

Learning Outcome: Upon successful completion of this course, the student will be able to implement the software development process from problem definition to final product; understand and use the basic components of a programming language; package code into functions to enable reuse; identify and correct different types of programming bugs; evaluate the performance of your programs; and produce clear, easy-to-maintain code.

Instruction: Major topics covered in the course are an overview of computers both conceptual background as well as hands-on experience with writing, compiling, and debugging programs in C/C++. Methods of instruction include lecture, classroom exercises, audio/visual material, and a project.

Credit Recommendation: In the lower division baccalaureate/associate degree category, 1 semester hour in Data Processing (8/97).

Introduction to the Internet and Intranets for Business: Hands-On (469) (Hands-On Internet for Business Applications) (Formerly Introduction to Business on the Internet [469])

Location: Worldwide.

Length: 24 hours (4 days).

Dates: February 1995-Present.

Objective: To provide knowledge and skills needed to utilize Internet resources and services for business.

Learning Outcome: Upon successful completion of this course, the student will be able to choose and implement the Internet connection options as appropriate to needs; install and configure Internet access tools, communicate text and data worldwide; locate and retrieve information using FTP, Telnet, Archie, Gopher and World Wide Web; establish an on-line information service; protect internal networks and data from unauthorized intrusion via the Internet; exploit the full range of Internet resources and services; and apply Internet for business purposes.

Instruction: Major topics covered in the course are an introduction to the Internet; business applications; configuring basic and advanced client services; client tools for Internet access; business security issues and strategies; configuring basic and advanced server services; Internet connectivity alternatives; and future of the Internet. Methods of instruction include lecture, discussion, laboratory exercises, and a final examination.

Credit Recommendation: In the lower division baccalaureate/associate degree category, 2 semester hours in Information

Systems Management or Data Processing. (4/95).

Introduction to Visual InterDev: Hands-On (408)

Location: Various sites in the United States.

Length: 24 hours (4 days).

Dates: November 1997-Present.

Objective: To provide students the knowledge and skills necessary to create and manage websites with Visual InterDev.

Learning Outcome: Upon successful completion of this course the student will be able to utilize Microsoft's Visual InterDev to create and manage active Web sites; create active server pages using the JScript and VBScript languages; incorporate dynamic HTML, sound, and video into Web applications; connect Web applications to any ODBC data source; deploy Java applets and ActiveX components with Wizard; and create applications that integrate with Office 97.

Instruction: Major topics covered in the course are Web development fundamentals, introducing Visual InterDev, enhancing pages with active service technology, putting data in applications, creating an active browser interface, integrating rich content and external applications. Methods of instruction include lecture, discussion, classroom exercises, audio-visual material, module tests and final examination.

Credit Recommendation: In the lower division baccalaureate/associate degree category, 2 semester hours (1 semester hour in Information Systems and 1 semester hour in Information Systems laboratory) (2/98).

IP Routing with OSPF and BGP: Hands-On (465) (Formerly Multiprotocol Routing: Hands-On [465])

Location: Worldwide.

Length: 24 hours (4-days).

Dates: July 1996-Present.

Objective: To provide students with the key operational concepts behind each of the major routing protocols, and experience in designing and building resilient internetworks.

Learning Outcome: Upon successful completion of this course, the student will be able to design and build resilient multiprotocol internetworks using routers; configure router parameters in detail; deploy OSPF to optimize net performance; configure your routers for use as a firewall; troubleshoot and correct router-based faults on large-scale internetworks; and implement collaborative computing with the MBONE.

Instruction: Major topics covered in the course are an introduction to routing; distance vector routing; introduction to OSPF; OSPF design techniques; routers as firewalls; non-IP routing protocols; multicast; and selecting a routing protocol. Methods of instruction include lecture, discussion, classroom exercises, audio/visual material, observations, and a final examination.

Credit Recommendation: In the lower division baccalaureate/associate degree category, 2 semester hours in Computer Science or Information Systems (10/96).

ISDN for Telecommunications (359) (Formerly Introduction to ISDN [359])

Location: Worldwide.

Length: 24 hours (4 days).

Dates: August 1993-Present.

Objective: To teach students the fundamental concepts of ISDN and enable them to compare and contrast ISDN with existing technologies.

Learning Outcome: Upon successful completion of this course the student will be able to understand how ISDN really works; assess the value of ISDN services, plan for the installation of ISDN systems and evaluate the success of existing systems; effectively choose between ISDN and competitive technologies; understand the value of ISDN to the organization; and plan the evolution of voice, data, and LAN systems towards ISDN.

Instruction: Major topics covered in the course are a comprehensive technical introduction to ISDN based on the CCITT Blue Book recommendations and how to plan and install ISDN facilities in their own organization. Methods of instruction include lecture, discussion, hands-on exercises, out-of-class activities, and an examination.

Credit Recommendation: In the upper division baccalaureate degree category or in the lower division baccalaureate/associate degree category, 2 semester hours in Information Systems Management, Data Processing, or Computer Science (12/93).

Java for Enterprise Systems Development: Hands-On (472) (Formerly Advanced Java Programming Tools and Techniques: Hands-On [472])

Location: Worldwide.

Length: 24 hours (4 days).

Dates: September 1996-Present.

Objective: To provide students with practical experience using advanced Java tools and techniques to build content-rich client/server applications.

Learning Outcome: Upon successful completion of this course, the student will be able to use advanced Java programming to build applets and cross-platform client/server applications, develop flexible database applications using Java DataBase Connectivity (JDBC), create socket programs to enable network connectivity, streamline development with a Java Integrated Development Environment (IDE), design effective distributed applications with Java, and employ Java client/server techniques to provide internet and intranet solutions.

Instruction: Major topics covered in the course are what is in the Java APIs?; using a Java Integrated Development Environment (IDE); client/server and distributed systems; introducing JDBC; applying JDBC; advanced Abstract Windows Toolkit (AWT); using sockets to communicate in Java; and RMI and other future technologies. Methods of instruction include lecture, discussion, classroom exercises, audio/visual material, observations, and a final examination.

Credit Recommendation: In the lower division baccalaureate/associate degree category, 2 semester hours (1 semester hour in Computer Science or Information Systems and 1 semester hour in Computer Science Laboratory or Information Systems Laboratory) (10/96).

Java for Multimedia Applications Development (477)

Location: Worldwide.

Length: 24 hours (4 days).

Dates: June 1997-Present.

Objective: To provide the skills to use the JAVA APIs to develop multimedia applications and enhance JAVA applets with interactivity, graphics animation, sound, and professional GUI design.

Learning Outcome: Upon successful completion of this course, the student will be able to enhance JAVA applets and stand-alone applications with multimedia capabilities; create professional graphical user interfaces (GUIs) using JAVA APIs; use third party tools for rapid GUI development; animate and transform 2-D objects using JAVA animation; render images to enhance application interfaces; and apply an incremental design methodology to develop industrial-strength multimedia applications.

Instruction: Major topics covered in the course are an overview of multimedia; GUI design and implementation; model view control (MVC) architecture; 2-D drawing: graphics, fonts, and colors; image processing; animation and sound; application software; and future APIs. Methods of instruction include lecture, discussion, classroom exercises, audio/visual material, and examination.

Credit Recommendation: In the lower division baccalaureate/associate degree category, 2 semester hours in Management Information Systems or Data Processing (8/97).

KornShell Programming (434)

Location: Worldwide.

Length: 24 hours (4 days).

Dates: August 1997-Present.

Objective: To provide the skills necessary to write advanced, robust shell scripts to extend the user environment and automate complex system administrative tasks.

Learning Outcome: Upon successful completion of this course, the student will be able to write KornShell scripts to improve the productivity and usefulness of a UNIX system; exploit advanced shell language features to improve development speed and runtime efficiency; customize and extend the user environment with shell scripts and functions; use shell scripts in combination with other UNIX tools; apply debugging techniques; and defend shell scripts against security attacks.

Instruction: Major topics covered in the course are basic shell programming skills, command execution, variables, functions, arithmetic, shell I/O, process handling, production quality programming, and interactive programming. Methods of instruction include lecture, discussion, classroom exercises, audio/visual material, and examination.

Credit Recommendation: In the lower division baccalaureate/associate degree category, 2 semester hours in Computer Science or Management Information (8/97).

Local Area Networks: Implementation and Configuration (352)

Location: Worldwide.

Length: 24 1/4 hours (4 days).

Dates: August 1993-Present.

Objective: To provide students with an understanding of basic LAN technology, architecture and protocols.

Learning Outcome: Upon successful completion of this course the student will be able to analyze multiple LAN environments, select appropriate LAN technology based on application requirements, configure LANs to interconnect computing resources of their organizations; evolve from work area LANs to Enterprise Wide Networks; understand the LAN architecture; use their knowledge as they configure, interconnect and implement LAN technology at their job sites; and determine design trade-offs in configurations and also properly use LANs for downsizing and interoperability.

Instruction: Major topics covered in the course are the fundamental knowledge needed to design, configure, and implement LANs; integration of available software and hardware elements; and a solid understanding of network architectures and protocols. Methods of instruction include lecture, discussion, hands-on exercises, out-of-class activities, and an examination.

Credit Recommendation: In the lower division baccalaureate/associate degree category, 2 semester hours in Information Systems Management, Data Processing, or Computer Science (12/93).

Lotus Domino Web Site Development: Hands-On (182)

Location: Various sites in the United States.

Length: 24 hours (4 days).

Dates: April 1997-Present.

Objective: To provide knowledge and skills needed to build and manage dynamic, high-performance Web sites using Lotus Domino.

Learning Outcome: Upon successful completion of this course, the student will be able to design and develop a Lotus Domino Web site for intranet and Internet use; install and configure the Domino Web server; add interactive content using advanced Domino development tools; implement secure electronic business transactions with workflow applications; publish existing Notes databases and integrate legacy data with your Web site; implement Domino security features; and enhance the site with Domino add-ins.

Instruction: Major topics covered in this course include Domino and the Web, implementing the Domino server, creating a Web Site with Domino, exploiting Dominoís advanced features, securing and managing the site, the Domino add-ins, and future directions. Methods of instruction include lecture, discussion, classroom exercises, audio-visual material, module tests and final examination.

Credit Recommendation: In the lower division baccalaureate/associate degree category, 2 semester hours (1 semester hour in Information Systems, and 1 semester hour in Information Systems laboratory) (2/98).

Lotus Notes and Domino System Administration: Hands-On (181) (Formerly Lotus Notes R4 System Administration: Hands-On [181])

Location: Worldwide.

Length: 24 hours (4 days).

Dates: June 1996-Present.

Objective: To provide students the knowledge and skills to plan, install, configure and manage a network of Lotus Notes servers and workstations.

Learning Outcome: Upon successful completion of this course, the student will be able to install, configure, and manage Lotus Notes networks; administer information replication and mail routing; design and implement a security policy; integrate Notes with other corporate mail systems and the World Wide Web; and support enterprisewide workgroup infrastructure.

Instruction: Major topics covered in the course are Lotus Notes overview and system administration, client features, Notes networking, Notes server, database, encryption, electronic signatures, security, access control modeling, Notes mail, e-mail gateways, server monitoring, event logging, remote users, Internet services, Notes Internet security, and Notes administration role and function. Methods of instruction include lecture, discussion, audio/visual material, hands-on exercises, and a multiple-choice one-hour proctored final examination.

Credit Recommendation: In the lower division baccalaureate/associate degree category, 2 semester hours in Computer Information Systems or Data Processing (6/96).

Lotus Notes and Domino: A Comprehensive Hands-On Introduction (179) (Formerly Lotus Notes R4.5: A Comprehensive Hands-On Introduction [179])

Location: Worldwide.

Length: 24 hours (4 days).

Dates: July 1997-Present.

Objective: To provide an understanding of Lotus Notes and its common applications in the business world.

Learning Outcome: Upon successful completion of this course, the student will

be able to evaluate the capabilities, major features, and potential benefits of Lotus Notes\R4.5.; navigate the Notes client and server user interfaces; appraise the Lotus Notes security model for your project's needs; examine the structure of a working Notes application to determine its adaptability; assess impact of Domino Internet/Intranet solutions on Notes application design; and deploy Lotus Notes in your organization.

Instruction: Major topics covered in the course are what are Lotus Notes?, components of Lotus Notes, notes-based business applications, maintaining security, integration with other data sources, and connecting to the Internet/Intranet. Methods of instruction include lecture, discussion, classroom exercises, audio/visual material, and examination.

Credit Recommendation: In the lower division baccalaureate/associate degree category, 2 semester hours in Management Information Systems or Data Processing (8/97).

Lotus Notes Application Development: Hands-On (180) (Hands-On Lotus Notes Application Development) (Formerly Introduction to Lotus Notes Application Development [180])

Location: Worldwide.

Length: 24 hours (4 days), plus a one hour examination.

Dates: February 1996-Present.

Objective: To provide students with the knowledge and skills to design and develop a wide range of effective workgroup solutions, using Lotus Notes development software.

Learning Outcome: Upon successful completion of this course, the student will be able to build collaborative Client/Server Groupware applications that fully exploit advanced Lotus Notes features and capabilities; design effective documents, forms, and views; use send and shared-model workflows; create and customize notes applications and templates; automate processes with advanced programming techniques, macros, and formulas; and deploy access control list (ACL)-based security for your Notes applications.

Instruction: Major topics included in the course are an introduction to Lotus Notes; designing Notes documents; working with views, folders, and navigators; advanced topics in Lotus Notes; programming in LotusScript; deploying applications; database planning and design; and development tools for Lotus Notes. Methods of instruction include lecture, discussion, laboratory exercises, and a multiple-choice final examination.

Credit Recommendation: In the lower division baccalaureate/associate degree category, 2 semester hours in Computer Information Systems, Data Processing, or Information Systems Management (2/96).

Management Skills for IT Technical Managers (290) (Formerly Skills for Technical Managers [290]) (Formerly Effective Skills for Technical Managers)

Location: Worldwide.

Length: 24 hours (4 days).

Dates: August 1992-Present.

Objective: To provide knowledge needed to be a successful manager in a technical environment.

Learning Outcome: Upon successful completion of this course, the student will be able to develop the vision and skills that result in real team commitment; build and lead empowered and motivated project teams; delegate tasks and authority while maintaining control; communicate effectively at all levels; plan, organize and control complex projects; manage time effectively; and become a skilled and effective leader.

Instruction: Major topics covered in the course are the manager's job, down-in-the-trenches look at motivation, tools to analyze management/leadership style, techniques for success, and communication skills. Methods of instruction include lecture, discussion, classroom exercises, case studies, videotape, and examination.

Credit Recommendation: In the upper division baccalaureate degree category, 2 semester hours in Information Systems Management, Data Processing, or Computer Science (6/94).

Managing and Supporting Client/Server Systems (394)

Location: Worldwide.

Length: 24 hours (4 days).

Dates: October 1996-Present.

Objective: To provide students with a comprehensive, multifaceted understanding of client/server management and support issues. Students learn the methods and strategies needed to optimally define, implement, maintain and enhance real-world client/server environments.

Learning Outcome: Upon successful completion of this course, the student will be able to develop and implement an integrated client/server systems management program; choose among the many client/server management architectures; manage the support, integration, and expansion of diverse networks, communications, and operating system environments; apply a structured framework to assess your existing client/server environment; and plan organizational and training strategies to ensure the successful achievement of the organization's client/server goals.

Instruction: Major topics covered in the course are managing and supporting client/server systems: introduction and overview, managing client/server communications, software management, managing the data, managing the systems, managing the people, and working with the vendors. Methods of instruction include lecture, discussion, classroom exercises, audio/visual material, and final examination.

Credit Recommendation: In the lower division baccalaureate/associate degree category, 2 semester hours in Computer Information Systems or Data Communications (4/97).

Microsoft Access Programming: Hands-On (407)

Location: Worldwide.

Length: 24 hours (4-days).

Dates: September 1996-Present.

Objective: To provide students with a thorough working knowledge of Access programming techniques. During extensive hands-on exercises, students will gain practical experience writing Access programs that utilize advanced features such as DAO, VBA, and OLE Automation.

Learning Outcome: Upon successful completion of this course, the student will be able to program Microsoft access applications for client/server databases using VBA; achieve source code portability across access applications; exploit the power of Data Access Objects (DAO) and new error handling techniques; maintain data integrity using transaction processing techniques; implement security to control database accessibility; and integrate access into multi-tier database environments using OLE technology

Instruction: Major topics covered in the course are an introduction to the access programming environment; VBA for Access 95; Access queries and SQL; manipulating the database with data access objects; replication; securing the database; access and client/server computing; using access with Microsoft applications; and rolling out your application. Methods of instruction include lecture, discussion, classroom exercises, audio/visual material, observations, and a final examination.

Credit Recommendation: In the lower division baccalaureate/associate degree category, 2 semester hours (1 semester hour in Computer Science or Information Systems; and 1 semester hour in Computer Science Laboratory or Information Systems Laboratory) (10/96).

Microsoft (Exchange 5 Server Administration: Hands-On (167)

Location: Various sites in the United States.

Length: 24 hours (4 days).

Dates: August 1997-Present.

Objective: To provide the students with the knowledge and skills for configuring and managing the key concepts of Microsoft Exchange 5 Server.

Learning Outcome: Upon successful completion of this course, the student will be able to: implement and administer single and multi-server Exchange organizations; install and configure Microsoft Exchange 5 Server; configure inter-site connectors including site, X.400 and Internet Connector; set up and connect the Internet Mail Service (IMS); monitor, manage the Exchange infrastructure; and manage the Active Server Components for Internet access.

Instruction: Major topics covered in this course are Exchange server installation, Exchange architecture, Exchange connectors, planning your Exchange network, configuring public folders, managing the Exchange Environment, troubleshooting Exchange, and Exchange server and the Internet connection. Methods of instruction include lecture, discussion, classroom exercises, audio-visual material, module tests and final examination.

Credit Recommendation: In the lower division baccalaureate/associate degree category, 2 semester hours (1 semester hour in Information Systems, and 1 semester hour in Information Systems laboratory) (2/98).

Microsoft Exchange Applications Development: Hands-On (168)

Location: Worldwide.

Length: 24 hours (4 days).

Dates: March 1997-Present.

Objective: To provide students hands-on experience developing and implementing custom applications that integrate exchange functions with the personal and workgroup productivity tools of MS Office.

Learning Outcome: Upon successful completion of this course, the student will be able to design and program Microsoft Exchange applications tailored to their organization; construct and implement custom exchange forms with the Forms Designer; integrate messaging into custom applications using MAPI objects & controls; manage data through OLE DB and ActiveX Data Objects (ADO); utilize ActiveX technology to integrate MS Office applications with exchange; and incorporate workgroup support in Intranet and Internet environments using Visual Basic 5

Instruction: Major topics covered in the course are Microsoft exchange components, exchange folders, exchange forms design, extending forms with visual basic, Office 97 and Outlook 97, messaging application programming interface (MAPI), advanced forms and ActiveX controls, database connectivity, and transition to the new technologies. Methods of instruction include lecture, discussion, classroom exercises, audio/visual material, and final examination.

Credit Recommendation: In the lower division baccalaureate/associate degree category, 2 semester hours (1 semester hour in Computer Information Systems and 1 semester hour in Computer Information Systems Lab) (4/97).

Microsoft SQL Server: A Comprehensive Hands-On Introduction (225) (Formerly Introduction to Microsoft SQL Server [225])

Location: Worldwide.

Length: 24 hours (4 days), plus a one hour proctored examination.

Dates: February 1996-Present.

Objective: To provide students with the knowledge and skills to use Microsoft SQL Server 6.

Learning Outcome: Upon successful completion of this course, the student will be able to apply the key features of SQL Server 6; create devices, databases tables, and views; retrieve and maintain data using Transact-SQL; write stored procedures to enhance performance and security; query and modify data with scrollable cursors; maintain database integrity; analyze and improve query performance; and build server-side components of client/server applications.

Instruction: Major topics covered in the course are fundamental concepts; SQL server database design; data retrieval; advanced SQL; programming with Transact-SQL; modifying data; cursors; writing stored procedures; maintaining database integrity; techniques and tips for improving performance; and beyond SQL. Methods of instruction include lecture, discussion, laboratory exercises, and a multiple-choice final examination.

Credit Recommendation: In the lower division baccalaureate/associate degree category, 2 semester hours in Computer Information Systems (CIS), Business Information Systems, or Data Processing (2/96).

Mitigating to IPv6: Hands-On (463)

Location: Worldwide.

Length: 24 hours (4 days).

Dates: July 1997-Present.

Objective: Experienced Internet working professionals gain the knowledge and skills they need to implement IPv6 and migrate existing networks to the new protocol.

Learning Outcome: Upon successful completion of this course, the student will be able to migrate your existing TPC/IP environment to IPv6, and the Next Generation protocol; use auto-configuration techniques to manage Internet and Intranet address space; deploy IPv6 routing protocols including RIPv6 and OSPF; set up and manage IPv6 security systems; and use dual stacking to support co-existence and migration.

Instruction: Major topics covered in the course are an introduction to IPv6, the Ipv6 protocol, plug and play with IPv6, Internet working with IPv6, IPv6 across different media, IPv6 security mechanisms, impact on other protocols, name services, migrating from IPv4 to IPv6, IPv6 in special situations, IPv6 glossary, and Ipv6 multicast assignments. Methods of instruction include lecture, discussion, classroom exercises, audio/visual material, and examination.

Credit Recommendation: In the lower division baccalaureate/associate degree category, 2 semester hours in Computer Technology, Management Information Systems, or Data Processing (8/97).

Mobile Communications and Wireless Networks (378) (Formerly Wireless Networks and Mobile Communications[378]) (Formerly Wireless Networks)

Location: Worldwide.

Length: 24 hours (4 days).

Dates: August 1994-Present.

Objective: To provide a technical foundation in wireless products, services, and applications development.

Learning Outcome: Upon successful completion of this course, the student will be able to evaluate, specify, plan, and design wireless networks for voice, data, and images; select among competing wireless technologies and standards; and identify the specific wireless products, services, and service providers needed to implement an application.

Instruction: Major topics covered in the course are wireless system basics, fixed wireless services, cellular basics, digital cellular, private wireless services, mobile data services, global services, and personal communication technology. Methods of instruction include lecture, discussion, audio/visual material, and final examination.

Credit Recommendation: In the upper division baccalaureate degree category, 2 semester hours in Computer Science, Data Communications, or Information Systems Management (8/94).

Modern Software Systems Analysis and Design (422)

Location: Worldwide.

Length: 24 hours (4 days).

Dates: June 1994-September 1997.

Objective: To provide a comprehensive set of current, proven methods for the analysis and design of software systems.

Learning Outcome: Upon successful completion of this course, the student will be able to apply systematic techniques for analyzing business requirements; create data models; use structured analysis and design techniques; use object modeling; and evaluate CASE tools.

Instruction: Major topics covered include an overview of analysis and design; analyzing data requirements and designing data; analyzing and designing processes; object-modeling techniques; quality during analysis and design; and methods and tools for analysis and design. Methods of instruction include lecture, discussion, classroom exercises, and examination.

Credit Recommendation: In the upper division baccalaureate degree category, 2 semester hours in Computer Science, Software Engineering, Information Systems Management, or Data Processing (6/94).

Multivendor Networking (361)

Location: Worldwide.

Length: 24 hours (4 days).

Dates: August 1993-Present.

Objective: To teach students the terminology of multivendor integration. They will examine the competing and complementary standards available.

Learning Outcome: Upon successful completion of this course the student will be able to understand the physical components and how to select and evaluate components for integration; understand the interoperability of applications and services and network management issues involved in integration; examine the integration of network operating systems; design multivendor and multiplatform networks; develop strategies for multivendor network management, integrate terminal networks with emerging LAN Peer networks; and choose a Peer protocol strategy, as well as evaluate downsizing and cooperative system solutions for the organization.

Instruction: Major topics covered in the course are practical information and guidance needed to plan and implement effective multivendor networks and emphasis on the implications and considerations involved in selecting different networking strategies. Methods of instruction include lecture, discussion, hands-on exercises, out-of-class activities, and an examination.

Credit Recommendation: In the upper division baccalaureate degree category or in the lower division baccalaureate/associate degree category, 2 semester hours in Information Systems Management, Data Processing, or Computer Science (12/93).

Negotiating Skills for Technical Managers and Professionals (295) (Negotiating Skills for Technical Managers and Professionals: Achieving the Results you Want)

Location: Worldwide.

Length: 24 hours (4 days).

Dates: February 1995-May 1996.

Objective: To provide knowledge and skills to be a competent negotiator.

Learning Outcome: Upon successful completion of this course, the student will be able to use a structured process to persuade and negotiate the desired results; exploit strengths and values of negotiators to develop effective negotiations; recognize and respond confidently to the tactics used by others; avoid the mistakes that lead to deadlocks, breakdowns, or win-lose outcomes; and reach closure and implement agreements.

Instruction: Major topics covered in the course are laying the groundwork; taking personality factors into account; setting negotiation goals and understanding the needs of the other party; negotiating in teams; opening moves (questioning and probing and making your proposal); bargaining (trading concessions and responding to tactics and closing); and making it stick (implementing the agreement). Methods of instruction include lecture, discussion, role playing, and a final examination.

Credit Recommendation: In the upper division baccalaureate degree category, 2 semester hours in Information Systems Management, Business Administration, or Management (4/95).

Netscape SuiteSpot Servers for Internet/Internet Development (485)

Location: Worldwide.

Length: 24 hours (4 days).

Dates: August 1997-Present.

Objective: To provide the knowledge and skills needed to design and manage a Netscape-based intranet and Internet Web site.

Learning Outcome: Upon successful completion of this course, the student will be able to implement and maintain Intranet and Internet services using the Netscape SuiteSpot Servers; install and configure the Netscape Enterprise Web Server and related server products; utilize the Proxy Server to maximize throughput and enhance security; implement advanced mail and news services; establish security and access restrictions; enable catalog and keyword search capabilities; and develop dynamic content using LiveWire Pro.

Instruction: Major topics covered in the course are an introduction to the SuiteSpot Architecture, visual HTML editing, the Enterprise Web Server, the Proxy Server, messaging and collaboration services, the Catalog Server, creating application in JavaScript, integrating databases with JavaScript, and additional technologies. Methods of instruction include lecture, discussion, classroom exercises, audio/visual material, and examination.

Credit Recommendation: In the lower division baccalaureate/associate degree category, 2 semester hours in Management Information Systems or Business Information Systems (8/97).

NetWare 3.x Administration (261) (Formerly Hands-On Netware 3.x System Management)

Location: Worldwide.

Length: 19 hours (3 days).

Dates: August 1993-January 1997.

Objective: To provide students an understanding of NetWare Client/Server architecture and NetWare shell fundamentals, and to prepare them for the NetWare System Manager CNE Exam.

Learning Outcome: Upon successful completion of this course the student will be able to identify components of the NetWare file system and implement Network drive mappings; create and manage NetWare user accounts, workgroup manager, write login scripts for users, perform server management and configure Novell menus and NetWare print services; use SYSCON to create and configure user accounts, implement effective network security; install applications, use the Novell menu utility, and implement effective network backup strategies; perform remote management using RCONSOLE and network management NLMs; and pass the NetWare 3.x System Manager CNE exam.

Instruction: Major topics covered in the course are the skills needed to configure, optimize, administer, and maintain a NetWare 3.x based network and how to apply each and every concept using the central class server in the extensive hands-on workshops. Methods of instruction include lecture, discussion, hands-on exercises, out-of-class activities, and an examination.

Credit Recommendation: In the upper division baccalaureate degree category or in the lower division baccalaureate/associate degree category, 1 semester hour in Information Systems Management, Data Processing, or Computer Science (12/93).

NetWare 3.x Advanced Administration (262) (Formerly NetWare 3.x Advanced System Management)

Location: Worldwide.

Length: 13 hours (2 days).

Dates: August 1993-January 1997.

Objective: To provide the student with knowledge required to configure and tune server resources to enhance server performance.

Learning Outcome: Upon successful completion of this course, the student will be able to configure and tune server resources to enhance performance; manually start the server; configure the netware DOS requester and VLMS; configure multiple protocol support and name space support; and implement strategies to customize advanced print server setup.

Instruction: Major topics covered in the course are protocol and OS support, remote management facility, advanced printing, managing performance, network maintenance, SBACKUP, and NetWare name service. Methods of instruction include lecture, discussion, laboratory exercises, and examination.

Credit Recommendation: In the lower division baccalaureate/associate degree category or in the upper division baccalaureate degree category, 1 semester hour in Data Communications, Data Processing, Information Systems Management, or Computer Science (1/94).

NetWare 3.x Installation and Configuration (267) (Hands-On NetWare 3.x Installation and Configuration)

Location: Worldwide.

Length: 12 hours (2 days).

Dates: September 1994-May 1996.

Objective: To provide students with the knowledge and skills to install and configure NetWare 3.x.

Learning Outcome: Upon successful completion of this course, the student will be able to install NetWare 3.x Server; install NetWare Client; configure NetWare 3.x Server; and manage NetWare 3.x Server.

Instruction: Major topics covered in the course are installing NetWare 3.x file server (concepts); installing and upgrading to a NetWare 3.12 server; upgrading NetWare 2.2 to 3.12; NetWare DOS client; NetWare 3.x server configuration; strategies in defining a NetWare 3.x environment; and optimizing and troubleshooting the NetWare 3.x server. Methods of instruction include lecture, discussion, laboratory exercises, and a final examination.

Credit Recommendation: In the lower division baccalaureate/associate degree category, 1 semester hour in Information Systems Management or Data Processing (4/95).

NetWare Network File System (NFS) (272)

Location: Worldwide.

Length: 13.5 hours (2 days).

Dates: September 1993-March 1996.

Objective: To provide the student with the ability to install and configure NFS on a NetWare server and perform NFS administration on NetWare servers.

Learning Outcome: Upon successful completion of this course, the student will be able to understand UNIX basics and to troubleshoot NetWare NFS problems, install and configure NetWare NFS, use UNIX-to-NetWare print services and NetWare-to-UNIX print services, and configure FTP servers.

Instruction: Major topics covered in the course are introduction to NFS and UNIX; NetWare NFS; network printing; and FTP server, SBACKUP, and XCONSOLE. Methods of instruction include lecture, discussion, laboratory exercises, and examination.

Credit Recommendation: In the lower division baccalaureate/associate degree category or in the upper division baccalaureate degree category, 1 semester hour in Data Communications, Data Processing, Information Systems Management, or Computer Science (1/94).

NetWare to Windows NT Integration and Migration: Hands-On (159) (NetWare to Windows NT Integration and Migration: Hands-On) (Formerly NetWare to Windows NT Integration and Migration [159])

Location: Worldwide.

Length: 24 hours (4 days).

Dates: February 1996-Present.

Objective: To provide students with the necessary internetworking knowledge and experience to integrate Windows NT into an existing NetWare environment or to migrate completely to the Windows NT platform.

Learning Outcome: Upon successful completion of this course, the student will be able to differentiate between NetWare and Windows and Windows NT architecture; integrate NetWare and NT, migrate from NetWare to NT; connect NetWare clients to NT servers; access a NetWare server via a NTS gateway; and implement a NT print gateway, file and print services.

Instruction: Major topics covered in the course are an overview of NetWare and Windows NT architecture; integrating NetWare clients to Windows NT servers and NT workstations with NetWare clients to emulating NetWare services on a NT server; managing server access, file system security, and printing; optimizing protocols; and planning migration processes. Methods of instruction include lecture, discussion, audio/visual material, classroom and hands-on exercises, and an one-hour, multiple-choice, proctored final examination.

Credit Recommendation: In the lower division baccalaureate/associate degree category, 2 semester hours in Data Communications, Data Processing, Information Systems Management, or Computer Science (6/96).

Network Planning, Support, and Management (353)

Location: Worldwide.

Length: 24 hours (4 days).
Dates: August 1990-September 1997.
Objective: To provide skills needed to design and manage communications networks in today's rapidly changing network technology.
Learning Outcome: Upon successful completion of this course, the student will be able to manage the planning, installation and upgrade of a network; design and size the network to meet quality of service requirements; evaluate network performance and availability; and select effective network monitoring and control equipment and software.
Instruction: Major topics covered include elements of network planning, support, and management; planning the network project; networking options; sizing your network; reliability and availability; network security control; human issues; user support; and installation and operation. Methods of instruction include lecture, discussion, case studies, role-playing, and examination.
Credit Recommendation: In the upper division baccalaureate degree category, 2 semester hours in Data Communications, Information Systems Management, Computer Science, or Data Processing (6/94).

Networking Technologies: Comprehensive Introduction (270) (Formerly Networking Technologies [270])

Location: Worldwide.
Length: 18 hours (3 days).
Dates: July 1993-Present.
Objective: To provide the student with an overview of the data communications environment including a strong emphasis on LANs and the NetWare network operating system.
Learning Outcome: Upon successful completion of this course, the student will be able to describe data communications models, protocols, standards, and standards organizations; identify the characteristics of a synchronous and synchronous communications and baseband and broadband signaling; and identify the media types, characteristics, and costs.
Instruction: Major topics covered in the course are data communications in the computing environment; data communications standards, models, and protocols; signals, media, and transmission technologies; channel access technologies; higher level protocols; inter-networking with bridges, routers, and gateways; and the future of networking. Methods of instruction include lecture, discussion, laboratory exercises, and examination.
Credit Recommendation: In the lower division baccalaureate/associate degree category or in the upper division baccalaureate category, 1 semester hour in Data Communications, Data Processing, Information Systems Management, or Computer Science (1/94).

Object-Oriented Analysis and Design (323)

Location: Worldwide.
Length: 24 hours (4 days).
Dates: May 1993-Present.
Objective: To provide student with an understanding of the concepts and techniques of object-oriented analysis and design.
Learning Outcome: Upon successful completion of this course, the student will be able to analyze requirements documents and identify key objects; exploit inheritance and reusability; determine attributes, methods and associations for object classes; optimize data and behavioral models and be able to expand the analysis into a full design; and convert the full design into a language implementation.
Instruction: Major topics covered in the course are Object-oriented: What does it mean?; object modeling; event modeling; class hierarchy; refining the model; object-oriented design; object-oriented construction. Methods of instruction include lecture, discussion, laboratory exercises, case studies, and examination.
Credit Recommendation: In the lower division baccalaureate/associate degree category or in the upper division baccalaureate degree category, 2 semester hours in Information Systems Management, Data Processing, or Computer Science (1/94).

Object-Oriented Methods for Business Applications (423)

Location: Worldwide.
Length: 24 hours (4 days).
Dates: June 1994-September 1997.
Objective: To provide knowledge of object-oriented analysis and design methods.
Learning Outcome: Upon successful completion of this course, the student will be able to analyze business system requirements using object-oriented methods; identify key objects and classify them hierarchically; determine object attributes and methods at each level of the hierarchy; expand the model into a full design; and prepare and present the design to managers, users, and programmers.
Instruction: Major topics covered in the course are basic object-oriented concepts; object modeling; event modeling; class hierarchy; refining the model; object-oriented design; object oriented construction; and benefits of object-oriented approach. Methods of instruction include lecture, discussion, classroom exercises, and examination.
Credit Recommendation: In the upper division baccalaureate degree category, 2 semester hours in Computer Science, Software Engineering, Information Systems Management, or Data Processing (6/94).

Optimizing SQL Server Database and Application Performance: Hands-On (228)

Location: Worldwide.
Length: 24 hours (4 days).
Dates: May 1997-Present.
Objective: To provide an introduction to design high-performance SQL Server databases and applications, techniques for preventing performance problems, and a methodology for analyzing and resolving performance-related problems when they do occur.
Learning Outcome: Upon successful completion of this course, the student will be able to implement high-performance SQL server databases and applications; configure SQL server and windows NT; create appropriate indexes for multiple query types; write intelligent SQL queries; analyze performance problems using SQL server tools; reduce deadlock and contention with optimistic concurrency; and administer databases for performance in both OLTP and DSS applications.
Instruction: Major topics covered in the course are fundamental concepts, QL server architecture and internals, configuring SQL server for optimal performance, optimizing application performance, handling special case systems, and administering high-performance databases. Methods of instruction include lecture, discussion, classroom exercises, audio/visual materials, and examination.
Credit Recommendation: In the upper division baccalaureate degree category, 1 semester hour in Management Information System or Computer Science (8/97).

Oracle Developer/2000 Forms: Hands-On (235)

Location: Worldwide.
Length: 24 hours (4 days).
Dates: June 1995-January 1997.
Objective: To provide students the knowledge and skills to use Oracle/2000 Forms to develop Oracle7 applications.

Learning Outcome: Upon successful completion of this course, the student will be able to use Developer/2000 forms to develop Oracle7 applications; navigate the Forms design interface; apply graphical user interface (GUI) design principles using Forms; post SQL*Forms 3 applications; and use PL/SQL programming.

Instruction: Major topics covered in the course are basic Developer/2000 Forms concepts, basic Forms techniques, basic menu techniques, graphical user interface (GUI) design, advanced Forms techniques, customizing Forms processing and migrating Forms, and related packages. Methods of instruction include lecture, discussion, audio/visual material, hands-on exercises, and an one-hour, multiple-choice, proctored final examination.

Credit Recommendation: In the lower division baccalaureate/associate degree category, 2 semester hours in Computer Information Systems or Data Processing (6/96).

Oracle Developer/2000 Reports (237) (Formerly Oracle Reports: Hands-On)

Location: Worldwide.

Length: 12 hours (2 days).

Dates: April 1995-January 1997.

Objective: To provide knowledge and skills needed to create effective business reports.

Learning Outcome: Upon successful completion of this course, the student will be able to use Developer/2000 Reports to quickly build effective business reports; create tabular, master-detail, form letter and matrix reports; design reports for maximum readability and impact; build reports in a wide range of environments and processing modes; and extend functionality through PL/SQL.

Instruction: Major topics covered in the course are getting started with Oracle Reports; report layout; computations and summaries; parameters; advanced report layouts; triggers; external objects; Oracle reports product components; and guidelines for report design. Methods of instruction include lecture, discussion, laboratory exercises, and a final examination.

Credit Recommendation: In the lower division baccalaureate/associate degree category, both this course and Introduction to Oracle7 (230) must be completed to receive 3 semester hours in Information Systems Management or Data Processing (4/95).

Oracle Developer/2000: Hands-On (236)

Location: Worldwide.

Length: 30 hours (5 days).

Dates: January 1997-Present.

Objective: To provide students with indepth knowledge of the features and capabilities of the Developer/2000 components as well as a overview of graphical user interface design.

Learning Outcome: Upon successful completion of this course, the student will be able to use Developer/2000 to develop Oracle7 applications quickly and easily; apply effective graphical user interface (GUI) design principles; develop forms and menus and enhance their functionality using triggers and PI/SQL; create tabular, master-detail, and matrix reports; define chart items and graphical displays; and integrate forms, reports, and graphs into a client/server application.

Instruction: Major topics covered in the course are Developer/2000 concepts, basic forms techniques, basic menu techniques, effective GUI design, advanced forms techniques, customizing forms processing, basic reports techniques, report layout, report runtime parameters, advanced report techniques, oracle graphics, and building applications. Methods of instruction include lecture, discussion, classroom exercises, audio/visual material, and final examination.

Credit Recommendation: In the lower division baccalaureate/associate degree category, 2 semester hours (1 semester hour in Computer Information Systems or Computer Science and Computer Information Systems or Computer Science Lab) (4/97).

Oracle7 for Application Developers: Hands-On (232 (Formerly Oracle7 for Application Developers [232])

Location: Worldwide.

Length: 18 hours (3 days).

Dates: January 1995-Present.

Objective: To provide knowledge and skills needed to write Oracle7 applications.

Learning Outcome: Upon successful completion of this course, the student will be able to use Oracle7's architecture to create powerful, efficient applications; estimate storage requirements accurately; ensure data integrity and implement data security; produce scalable applications; reduce development time by using best practices; and diagnose and correct problems in Oracle7 applications.

Instruction: Major topics covered in the course are Oracle7 features; transaction processing; using Oracle7 to enforce business rules; enforcing security; indexes and clusters; Oracle7 architecture; database storage; and the development process. Methods of instruction include lecture, discussion, laboratory exercises, and a final examination.

Credit Recommendation: In the lower division baccalaureate degree category, 1 semester hour; or, if this course and Tuning Oracle7 Applications(233) are both completed, 2 semester hours are recommended; or, if this course and Advanced SQL Queries (234) are both completed, 2 semester hours are recommended; or, if this course, Tuning Oracle7 Applications(233), and Advanced SQL Queries (234) are all completed, 3 semester hours are recommended. All credit recommendations are in Information Systems Management or Data Processing (4/95).

Oracle7 for Database Administrators: Hands-On (231) (Oracle7 for Database Administrators: Hands-On) (Formerly Introduction to Database Administration Using Oracle7 [231])

Location: Worldwide.

Length: 30 hours (5 days).

Dates: February 1995-Present.

Objective: To provide knowledge and skills to administer Oracle7 databases in both stand alone and client/server environments.

Learning Outcome: Upon successful completion of this course, the student will be able to perform the role and functions of a database administrator; specify system configuration, directory structure, and database options while installing Oracle7; successfully create, maintain, and support Oracle7 databases; manage disk space and memory utilization; manage user privileges and resources; maintain database security in Oracle7; implement effective backup and restore procedures for Oracle7 databases; and identify and correct transaction processing related performance problems.

Instruction: Major topics covered in the course are Oracle7 architecture; starting and stopping the database; Oracle installation; creating a database; managing space; managing users and resources; maintaining security; backup and recovery; transaction processing and concurrency; and Oracle performance tuning. Methods of instruction include lecture, discussion, laboratory exercises, and a final examination.

Credit Recommendation: In the lower division baccalaureate/associate degree category, 2 semester hours in Information Systems Management or Data Processing (4/95).

Oracle7: A Comprehensive Hands-On Introduction (230) (Formerly Introduction to Oracle7 [230])

Location: Worldwide.

Length: 30 hours (5 days).

Dates: February 1995-Present.

Objective: To provide knowledge and skills needed to develop database applications using Oracle7 and basic Oracle tools.

Learning Outcome: Upon successful completion of this course, the student will be able to understand relational database concepts and be able to create, modify, and use an Oracle database; use PL/SQL for Oracle 7; create tables and indexes; write reports using SQL* Plus; and use the Developer/2000 Forms tool to create a GUI interface.

Instruction: Major topics covered in the course are introduction to Oracle; using SQL to retrieve, report and manage data; define organization and integrity; enforce security; improve performance; usage of PL/SQL; Oracle forms; and application tools. Methods of instruction include lecture, discussion, laboratory exercises, and a final examination.

Credit Recommendation: In the lower division baccalaureate/associate degree category, 2 semester hours in Information Systems Management (4/95).

Oracle8 Database Administration (491)

Location: Various sites in the United States.

Length: 30 hours (5 days).

Dates: October 1997-Present.

Objective: To provide students with the knowledge and skills necessary to set up and configure Oracle8 databases, control and administer user accounts, monitor and optimize database storage and protect the database with appropriate backup and recovery strategies.

Learning Outcome: Upon successful completion of this course, the student will be able to configure and manage Oracle8 databases; understand the Oracle8 architecture; manage users and accounts by specifying privileges and roles; perform effective storage management to maximize space usage and performance; implement Oracle8 partitions to manage large tables; and select appropriate Oracle8 backup and recovery options, including the use of Recovery Manager.

Instruction: Major topics covered in the course are introduction to the Oracle database environment, building an Oracle8 database, controlling disk storage, managing users and resources, partitioning to support very large databases (VLDBS), backup and recovery, and fundamental tuning techniques.

Credit Recommendation: In the lower division baccalaureate/associate degree category or in the upper division baccalaureate degree category, 2 semester hours in Computer Information Systems or Computer Science (2/98).

Oracle8 for Application Development and Tuning (492)

Location: Various sites in the United States.

Length: 30 hours (5 days).

Dates: November 1997-Present.

Objective: To provide students with the knowledge and skills necessary to create Oracle8 database applications, provide security for the applications and the databases and tune them for optimal performance.

Learning Outcome: Upon successful completion of this course, the student will be able to design and implement efficient Oracle8 database applications; use Oracle8 datatypes and techniques in application design; load external data using SQL *Loader; ensure data integrity and security; perform debugging and implement error handling; enhance performance with parallel operations; and tune the applications for optimal performance.

Instruction: Major topics covered in the course are an introduction to the application environment, preparing the database, maintaining data integrity, PL/SQL programming techniques, Oracle8 PL/SQL extensions, improving query performance, and tuning the application.

Credit Recommendation: In the lower division baccalaureate/associate degree category or in the upper division baccalaureate degree category, 2 semester hours in Computer Information Systems or Computer Science (2/98).

Oracle8: A Comprehensive Hands-on Introduction (490)

Location: Various sites in the United States.

Length: 30 hours (5 days).

Dates: October 1997-Present.

Objective: To provide students with the introductory knowledge and skills to understand and function in an Oracle8 environment, to utilize Oracle8 features and design, develop and use databases based on Oracle8 technology.

Learning Outcome: Upon successful completion of this course, the student will be able to implement Oracle8 databases; use Oracles8's object capabilities to create efficient reusable code; utilize SQL to retrieve and manipulate data; enforce data integrity and establish security; write structured PL/SQL code with packages and triggers; use indexes to improve performance; and employ methods, VARRAYs and nested tables.

Instruction: Major topics covered in the course include an introduction to Oracle technology, accessing and updating data with SQL, designing the database schema, creating objects, data integrity, data security and performance, using the PL/SQ language, and advanced PL/SQL features. Methods of instruction include lecture, discussion, classroom exercises, audio-visual material, module tests and final examination.

Credit Recommendation: In the lower division baccalaureate/associate degree category, 2 semester hours in Computer Information Systems or Computer Science (2/98).

OS/2 Warp: A Comprehensive Hands-On Workshop (332) (Formerly OS/2 [332])

Location: Worldwide.

Length: 24 hours (4 days).

Dates: July 1992-Present.

Objective: To provide the student with the knowledge to configure, use, and support OS/2 and its applications.

Learning Outcome: Upon successful completion of this course, the student will be able to navigate with ease through the OS/2 workplace shell; use REXX to build custom workplace shell desktops; understand and tune Config.Sys for optimal performance and reliability; repair damaged file systems and INI files; diagnose and resolve trap errors; use templates, objects and settings notebooks; install printer drivers and fonts; make DOS and Windows Applications work under OS/2; and cut and paste between DOS, Windows, and OS/2 applications.

Instruction: Major topics covered in the course are the introduction to OS/2 features and the workplace shell, multitasking and session management, memory management and protection, OS/2 LAN fundamentals, structure of OS/2, extended services, OS/2 requirements and installation, and advanced and future features of OS/2. Methods of instruction include lecture, discussion, laboratory exercises, out-of-class activities, and examination.

Credit Recommendation: In the lower division baccalaureate/associate degree category or in the upper division baccalaureate degree category, 2 semester hours in Data Processing, Information Systems Management, or Computer Science (3/94).

Perl Programming: Hands-On (431)

Location: Worldwide.

Length: 18 hours (3 days).

Dates: August 1997-Present.

Objective: To provide knowledge and skills needed to integrate Perl scripts to apply the built-in functions of the language, and as the standard Perl library into operating system and application environments.

Learning Outcome: Upon successful completion of this course, the student will be able to quickly create effective, reusable Perl scripts; master Perl 5's many small operators; structure code with subroutines, built-in functions, and packages; exploit Perl's sockets and database capabilities to create client/server scripts; build administration scripts for UNIX and Win32 platforms; and integrate CGI Perl scripts with Web server software.

Instruction: Major topics covered in the course are Introduction to Perl, Perl syntax fundamentals, patterns matching and operators, looping, decisions & flow control, subroutines, modules and functions, Perl and object orientation, interprocess, communication, databases, and the Internet. Methods of instruction include lecture, discussion, classroom exercises, audio/visual material, and examination.

Credit Recommendation: In the lower division baccalaureate/associate degree category, 1 semester hour in Computer Science, Management Information Systems, or Data Processing (8/97).

Porting Applications from UNIX to Windows NT: Hands-on (399)

Location: Various sites in the United States.

Length: 24 hours (4 days).

Dates: March 1997-Present.

Objective: To provide students with the knowledge and skills needed to port UNIX applications to the 32-bt Windows NT environment.

Learning Outcome: Upon successful completion of this course, the student will be able to establish a development environment for porting and maintaining UNIX/NT applications; port simple UNIX code directly using a Windows NT POSIX subsystem; select the Windows NT APIs best suited to replace existing UXIX-specified calls; adapt X Window GUI applications to the Win32 windowing model; achieve cross-platform code capability using third-party tools and libraries; and give ported UNIX applications the Windows NT look and feel.

Instruction: Major topics covered in the course are an introduction and overview, mapping UNIX processes to Windows NT, interprocess communications, migrating background processes, transferring a GUI from UNIX to NT, using third-party tools for cross-platform compatibility, file systems and security. Methods of instruction include lecture, discussion, classroom exercises, audio-visual material, module tests and final examination.

Credit Recommendation: In the lower division baccalaureate/associate degree category, 2 semester hours (1 semester hour in Information Systems and 1 semester hour in Information Systems laboratory) (2/98).

Practical Software Testing Methods (316)
Formerly Software Testing and Validation

Location: Worldwide.

Length: 24 hours (4 days).

Dates: May 1994-Present.

Objective: To provide knowledge of various software testing and validation techniques.

Learning Outcome: Upon successful completion of this course, the student will be able to implement testing strategies for software projects; integrate testing into the development life cycles; select and apply the major approaches for testing and validation; write test plans, cases, scripts and reports; and conform to relevant industry, military and international standards.

Instruction: Major topics covered in the course are an introduction to software testing and validation; the inspection process; test techniques; unit testing; integration testing; system testing; user acceptance testing; maintenance and regression testing; and establishing test planning. Methods of instruction include lecture, discussion, and examination.

Credit Recommendation: In the upper division baccalaureate degree category, 2 semester hours in Computer Science, Software Engineering, Information Systems Management, or Data Processing (6/94).

Programming ActiveX with Microsoft Foundation Classes: Hands-On (398) (Formerly Hands-On Advanced Windows Programming with Microsoft Foundation Classes [398])

Location: Worldwide.

Length: 24 hours (4 days).

Dates: February 1996-Present.

Objective: To provide students the knowledge of Windows 95 and NT user interface and Object-Linking and Embedding (OLE) technologies.

Learning Outcome: Upon successful completion of this course, the student will be able to understand the Windows 95 and Windows NT user interface; incorporate OLE into Windows 95 and NT applications; create and interconnect OLE servers and OLE containers; and use programmatic control of OLE objects via OLE automation, and OLE custom controls (OCXA).

Instruction: Major topics covered in the course are Windows 95 user interface, programming the Windows 95 user interface components, the Component Object Model (COM), Object-Linking and Embedding (OLE), OLE automation servers and clients, and OLE Custom Controls (OCX) and OCX containers. Methods of instruction include lecture, discussion, audio/visual material, hands-on exercises, and an one-hour, multiple-choice, proctored final examination.

Credit Recommendation: In the lower division baccalaureate/associate degree category, 2 semester hours in Computer Science, Computer Information Systems, or Data Processing (6/96).

Relational Databases—Design, Tools, and Techniques (382)

Location: Worldwide.

Length: 24 hours (4 days).

Dates: May 1993-Present.

Objective: To enable student to understand, design, and use relational databases and commercial relational database management systems.

Learning Outcome: Upon successful completion of this course, the student will be able to distinguish between relational and traditional databases; develop a data model to describe an application's data; design a relational database using data modeling and normalization; use SQL to access data in a relational database; work with a relational database in a client/server environment; and evaluate the strengths and weaknesses of RDMSs.

Instruction: Major topics covered in the course are the database basic concepts; relational theory; logical and physical database design; using a relational (SQL) DBMS; DBMS implementation techniques; databases in a client/server architecture; distributed databases; selecting a DBMS; and products, trends, and futures. Methods of instruction include lecture, discussion, classroom exercises, case studies, videotape, out-of-class activities, and examination.

Credit Recommendation: In the lower division baccalaureate/associate degree category or in the upper division baccalaureate degree category, 2 semester hours in Computer Science, Data Processing, or Information Systems Management (3/94).

Software Configuration Management (342)

Location: Worldwide.

Length: 24 hours (4 days).

Dates: December 1993-Present.

Objective: To provide the student with knowledge of software configuration management, techniques, and tools that facilitate project completion in an orderly, accurate, and timely manner.

Learning Outcome: Upon successful completion of this course, the student will be able to identify and implement configuration management (CM) activities and techniques; determine the level of CM needed for each software product; define roles for CM team members; make use of automated tools to support CM activities; and start and sustain continuous CM process improvement.

Instruction: Major topics covered in the course are an introduction to configuration management; the identification function; the control function; the status accounting function; the configuration audit function; the version and release management function; organizing the software configuration management (SCM) team and the CCB (configuration control board); preparing and updating an SCM plan; and software packages to assist SCM. Methods of instruction include lecture, discussion, classroom exercises/case studies, out-of-class activities, and examination.

Credit Recommendation: In the upper division baccalaureate degree category, 2 semester hours in Data Processing, Information Systems Management, or Computer Science (3/94).

Software Project Planning and Management (340) (Formerly Software Project Management Tools and Techniques)

Location: Worldwide.

Length: 24 hours (4 days).

Dates: May 1993-Present.

Objective: To provide the student with techniques and tools for software project management.

Learning Outcome: Upon successful completion of this course, the student will be able to manage software-development projects; select and adapt a development model to suit your needs; build quality into every step of the process; increase productivity and cut costs; produce reasonable estimates; convert documentation from hindrance to help; and select and use selected current management-support tools.

Instruction: Major topics covered in the course are process-driven project management; a project-planning process; definition design, build, and integration phases; system test; documentation; estimating; and people management. Methods of instruction include lecture, discussion, classroom exercises, out-of-class activities, videotape, and examination.

Credit Recommendation: In the upper division baccalaureate degree category, 2 semester hours in Data Processing, Information Systems Management, or Computer Science (3/94).

Software Quality Assurance (312) Formerly Software Quality Assurance and Testing

Location: Worldwide.

Length: 24 hours (4 days).

Dates: April 1993-Present.

Objective: To provide the student with skills needed to implement effective quality assurance and testing processes for each phase of the software development life cycle.

Learning Outcome: Upon successful completion of this course, the student will be able to verify and validate software quality at each phase of development; design test scenarios and cases to ensure accurate testing; develop an integration test and build plan; select appropriate hardware and software for test support; use configuration management to support quality assurance, quality control, and testing; and validate final products and gain acceptance from the user.

Instruction: Major topics covered in the course are an introduction to quality and testing, key skills, quality and testing during requirements development, quality design and code, unit testing, integration testing, system integration and acceptance testing, and testing during maintenance. Methods of instruction include lecture, discussion, classroom exercises, out-of-class activities, and examination.

Credit Recommendation: In the lower division baccalaureate/associate degree category or in the upper division baccalaureate degree category, 2 semester hours in Data Communications, Data Processing, Information Systems Management, or Computer Science (3/94).

Software Systems Analysis and Design (322)

Location: Worldwide.

Length: 24 hours (4 days).

Dates: May 1993-Present.

Objective: To provide student with the skills to use systematic techniques for analyzing requirements and creating data models for data designs.

Learning Outcome: Upon successful completion of this course, the student will be able to apply systematic techniques for analyzing requirements; create data models for high-quality data designs; apply structured analysis (SA) and design techniques to produce process models of the software system; use object modeling to enable reuse of existing software; choose a successful problem-solving approach that produces high-quality, testable designs; and evaluate a range of CASE tools.

Instruction: Major topics covered in the course are the overview of analysis and design, analyzing data requirements and designing data, analyzing and designing processes, object-modeling techniques, quality during analysis and design, and methods and tools for analysis and design. Methods of instruction include lecture, discussion, laboratory exercises, case studies, and examinations.

Credit Recommendation: In the lower division baccalaureate/associate degree category or in the upper division baccalaureate degree category, 2 semester hours in Information Systems Management, Data Processing, or Computer Science (1/94).

Specifying System Requirements (317) (Formerly Specifying and Managing Software Requirements [317])

Location: Worldwide.

Length: 24 hours (4 days).

Dates: May 1994-Present.

Objective: To provide knowledge of practical methods for specifying and managing software requirements that meet user needs while accommodating changes throughout the life cycle.

Learning Outcome: Upon successful completion of this course, the student will be able to develop accurate specifications from higher-level requirements, goals and constraints; manage evolving requirements; make use of automated tools for requirements traceability and management control; use requirements as the basis for updating project cost and schedule estimates; apply these methods to small, medium, and large software projects.

Instruction: Major topics covered in the course are an introduction to software requirements; analyzing requirements; documenting the requirements; managing the requirements development process; involving developers and users; building a framework for change; and the role of standards. Methods of instruction include lecture, discussion, case studies, role-playing, and examination.

Credit Recommendation: In the upper division baccalaureate degree category, 2 semester hours in Information Systems Management, Data Processing, or Computer Science (6/94).

SQL (387)

Location: Worldwide.

Length: 24 hours (4 days).

Dates: January 1993-September 1997.

Objective: To provide the student with the knowledge to use and manipulate SQL-based relational databases.

Learning Outcome: Upon successful completion of this course, the student will be able to develop SQL queries to retrieve the exact data desired; add, update, and delete data in the database; create views for both simplicity and security; build tables and indexes for efficient storage and access of data; and take full advantage of an SQL-based RDBMs capabilities.

Instruction: Major topics covered in the course are an introduction to SQL and relational database technology; querying a relational database; more advanced queries; using a relational database; designing, building, and managing a relational database; and developing database applications. Methods of instruction include lecture, discussion, laboratory exercises, out-of-class activities, and examination.

Credit Recommendation: In the lower division baccalaureate/associate degree category or in the upper division baccalaureate degree category, 2 semester hours in Computer Science, Data Processing, or Information Systems Management (3/94).

Sybase SQL Server: A Comprehensive Hands-on Introduction (220) (Formerly Introduction to Sybase; Sybase System 10: A Comprehensive Introduction)

Location: Worldwide.

Length: 30 hours (5 days).

Dates: December 1994-Present.

Objective: To provide knowledge and skills to develop and use client/server databases and to use Sybase SQL Server 10.

Learning Outcome: Upon successful completion of this course, the student will be able to fully utilize the capabilities of Sybase SQL Server; retrieve and maintain data using SQL; write stored procedures to enhance performance; maintain database integrity using declarative statements and triggers; handle resource contention problems with transaction management; and build high-performance Sybase client/server applications.

Instruction: Major topics covered in the course are data retrieval; use of Transact SQL; programming; adding, modifying, and deleting data; transaction management; security; and Sybase tools. Methods of instruction include lecture, discussion, laboratory exercises, and a final examination.

Credit Recommendation: In the lower division baccalaureate/associate degree category, 2 semester hours in Information Systems Management or Data Processing (4/95).

Systems Engineering (348)

Location: Worldwide.

Length: 24 hours (4 days).

Dates: May 1993-January 1997.

Objective: To provide knowledge of the techniques needed to lead and control development and integration of hardware and software systems for large and small projects.

Learning Outcome: Upon successful completion of this course, the student will be able to apply an interdisciplinary team approach to system development; coordinate technical and programmatic issues with project managers; translate objectives into system requirements; formulate a system architecture and partition requirements; perform trade-off analysis; allocate requirements to system elements; develop system test strategies and plans; and control in-process changes.

Instruction: Major topics covered in the course are a systems engineering overview; the system life cycle; generic life cycle activities; developing the conceptual design; developing system requirements; developing a system design; implementation coordination; and system integration, testing, and delivery. Methods of instruction include lecture, discussion, classroom exercises, case studies, role-playing, problem-solving, and examination.

Credit Recommendation: In the upper division baccalaureate degree category, 2 semester hours in Computer Science, Information Systems Management, or Data Processing (6/94).

TCP/IP for NetWare (271)

Location: Worldwide.

Length: 13 hours (2 days).

Dates: September 1993-Present.

Objective: To provide the student with the ability to install and configure TCP/IP on a NetWare server.

Learning Outcome: Upon successful completion of this course, the student will be able to understand layering concepts in TCP/IP networks, mechanisms, and address resolution protocols for TCP/IP networks; configure TCP/IP protocol stack on a NetWare server; understand IP routing and tunneling issues; configure NetWareIP routers and manage routing tables; manage NetWare networks using SNMP; configure IP tunneling for IPX networks; use TCP/IP to inter networking UNIX and NetWare; manage NetWare servers with TCPCON; and use TCP/IP applications on a NetWare server.

Instruction: Major topics covered in the course are introduction to TCP/IP networks and protocol architectures, TCP/IP for NetWare, inter-networking with TCP/IP, and management of TCP/IP networks. Methods of instruction include lecture, discussion, laboratory exercises, and examination.

Credit Recommendation: In the lower division baccalaureate/associate degree category or in the upper division baccalaureate degree category, 1 semester hour in Data Communications, Data Processing, Information Systems Management, or Computer Science (1/94).

Teambuilding Skills for IT Professionals (293)

Location: Worldwide.

Length: 18 hours (3 days).

Dates: December 1996-Present.

Objective: To provide students with practical tools and insight to significantly improve your teambuilding skills. Through a series if interrelated workshops, case studies, and the discussions, you will learn techniques to help you function effectively as an IT professional in a team environment.

Learning Outcome: Upon successful completion of this course, the student will be able to lead and contribute to successful and productive teams; focus team members on a project's success - and keep them focused; maximize the contribution of part-time team members; manage teams with a broad range of skills and personalities; work effectively with teams spread across wide geographic areas; and keep the team's goals aligned with the goals for the organization.

Instruction: Major topics covered in the course are team fundamentals, basics of team effectiveness, vision and expectations, teamwork in the real world, and realities of people working together. Methods of instruction include lecture, discussion, classroom exercises, audio/visual material, and final examination.

Credit Recommendation: In the lower division baccalaureate/associate degree category, 1 semester hour in Business Communications (4/97).

Telecommunications and Wide Area Networking (373) (Formerly Wide Area Networking and Telecommunications)

Location: Worldwide.

Length: 24 hours (4 days).

Dates: November 1993-Present.

Objective: To teach students about data, voice and multimedia applications.

Learning Outcome: Upon successful completion of this course the student will be able to understand the fundamentals of WAN communications; apply analog and digital technologies appropriately and learn how to select PABX size, features and options; understand the options and trade-offs in data communications; understand WAN terminology, international standards, present. and future WAN applications, and apply their knowledge to solve practical problems; relate fundamental data and voice concepts to real world Wide Area Networking; understand current and future WAN/Telecom technologies; effectively select analog and digital transmission, options for cost, performance and reliability; evaluate cost saving approaches including frame relay, ATM, V.fast, and voice/video/data compression; and become familiar with open standards such as ISDN, X.25, T1/E1, V.32bis and V.42bis.

Instruction: Major topics covered in the course are demystification of the complexities of converging telecom and WAN technologies, services and standards; how to evaluate an organization's wide area data and telecom needs; develop a strategy that achieves the optimum balance between cost, security and performance; and how to form networks of any size to interconnect their companies resources. Methods of instruction include lecture, discussion, hands-on exercises, out-of-class activities, and an examination.

Credit Recommendation: In the lower division baccalaureate/associate degree category, 2 semester hours in Information Systems Management, Data Processing, or Computer Science (12/93).

Tuning Oracle7 Applications (233) (Tuning Oracle7 Applications: Hands-On)

Location: Worldwide.

Length: 12 hours (2 days).

Dates: February 1995-Present.

Objective: To provide skills needed to tune Oracle7 applications and programs.

Learning Outcome: Upon successful completion of this course, the student will be able to speed up applications by using a structured tuning methodology; exploit the full features of both cost- and rule-based optimizers; size tables and indexes to reduce space and increase performance; develop effective indexing strategies to efficiently retrieve data; and use Oracle performance tools to dramatically improve performance and efficiency.

Instruction: Major topics covered in the course are Oracle tuning overview; indexes and clusters; using the Oracle optimizer; space optimization; tuning program units; and optimizing applications in client/server systems. Methods of instruction include lecture, discussion, laboratory exercises, and a final examination.

Credit Recommendation: In the lower division baccalaureate/associate degree category, both this course and Oracle7 for Application Developers (232) must be completed to receive 2 semester hours credit in Information Systems Management or Data Processing; or this course, Oracle7 for Application Developers (232), and Advanced SQL Queries (234) must all be completed to receive 3 semester hours in Information Systems Management or Data Processing (4/95).

UNIX and Windows NT Integration: Hands-On (158)

Location: Worldwide.

Length: 24 hours (4-days).

Dates: July 1996-Present.

Objective: To provide students with the skills and practical experience needed to provide seamless access to network resources.

Learning Outcome: Upon successful completion of this course, the student will be able to integrate Windows NT and UNIX networks to access enterprisewide resources; define the requirements for heterogeneous network operations; configure compatible network protocols including TCP/IP, NFS and FTP; enable transparent UNIX and Windows NT file access using NFS and SMB; implement bi-directional printing; establish integrated naming services using DNS and WINS; and administer Windows NT and UNIX in an integrated environment.

Instruction: Major topics covered in the course are UNIX and NT platforms comparison; integrating UNIX and Windows NT; communication protocols for internetworking; system and user administration; multiplatform printing; file systems and multiplatform access; IP address and name resolution; application support and porting; and Windows NT and the internet. Methods of instruction include lecture, discussion, classroom exercises, audio/visual material, quizzes, observations, and a final examination.

Credit Recommendation: In the lower division baccalaureate/associate degree category, 2 semester hours (1 semester hour in Computer Science or Information Systems and 1 semester hour in Computer Science Laboratory or Information Systems Laboratory) (10/96).

UNIX Server Administration: Hands-On (436) (Hands-On UNIX Server Administration)

Location: Worldwide.

Length: 24 hours (4 days).

Dates: June 1996-Present.

Objective: To introduce students to UNIX server administration, and to provide them the knowledge and skills necessary to setup a UNIX server, and implement a TCP/IP network and internetwork services on a UNIX platforms.

Learning Outcome: Upon successful completion of this course, the student will

be able to design and install a UNIX-based network; setup and configure a UNIX server; configure it to server UNIX and non-UNIX systems via TCP/IP and other protocols; manage resources among UNIX servers; manage system-wide backup and recovery processes; optimize the UNIX server performance; and plan basic security measures.

Instruction: Major topics covered in the course are the planning server and network setup; client/server architecture; TCP/IP; disk and file management; server backup and recovery; printing; e-mail; X-terminal; PC-to-mainframe connectivity; performance monitoring and management; optimization; and kernel configuration. Methods of instruction include lecture, discussion, audio/visual material, hands-on classroom exercises, and a multiple-choice one-hour proctored final examination.

Credit Recommendation: In the lower division baccalaureate/associate degree category, 2 semester hours in Computer Information Systems, Data Processing, or Computer Science (6/96).

UNIX System and Network Security: Hands-On (433)

Location: Worldwide.

Length: 24 hours (4 days).

Dates: July 1997-Present.

Objective: To provide knowledge and skills needed to establish security for UNIX platforms. Through a series of practical hands-on exercises, learn to use tools and utilities to assess vulnerabilities, detect configurations that threaten security, and provide effective access controls.

Learning Outcome: Upon successful completion of this course, the student will be able to secure UNIX systems from internal and external threats; establish authenticated access to local and remote resources; avoid potential security loopholes by limiting superuser privileges; protect UNIX files systems by setting modes of directories, data files, and executables; configure tools and utilities to minimize exposure and detect intrusions; and tackle security problems by swapping out insecure software components.

Instruction: Major topics covered in the course are UNIX and security, accounts and authentication, superuser privileges, local and network filesystems, processes and program execution, internal network services, and external network services. Methods of instruction include lecture, discussion, classroom exercises, audio/visual material, and examination.

Credit Recommendation: In the upper division baccalaureate degree category, 1 semester hour in Management Information System or Computer Science (8/97).

UNIX System and Networking (366)

Location: Worldwide.

Length: 24 hours (4 days).

Dates: December 1992-May 1996.

Objective: To provide student with knowledge required to administer a UNIX system.

Learning Outcome: Upon successful completion of this course, the student will be able to understand system administrator duties, responsibilities, and context; set up and delete user accounts; install software packages and system upgrades; choose appropriate backup strategies; configure local network printers; prepare for and recover from system crashes; audit security risks and monitor violations; provide X Windows-based logins; configure distributed file system servers and clients; and use tools to monitor system and network performance.

Instruction: Major topics covered in the course are system administration overview and fundamentals; procedures; local user services; network services; security; crashes, panics, and living through them; and performance monitoring, tuning, and debugging. Methods of instruction include lecture, discussion, laboratory exercises, and examination.

Credit Recommendation: In the lower division baccalaureate/associate degree category or in the upper division baccalaureate degree category, 2 semester hours in Computer Science, Data Communications, Information Systems Management, or Data Processing (1/94).

UNIX Workstation Administration: Hands-On (435) (Formerly UNIX Workstation Administration [435])

Location: Worldwide.

Length: 24 hours (4 days).

Dates: June 1996-Present.

Objective: To introduce students to UNIX workstation administration, and provide them the knowledge and skills necessary to setup a local UNIX workstation, and install and configure system and application software.

Learning Outcome: Upon successful completion of this course, the student will be able to install and configure UNIX on a workstation; manage UNIX system resources; install UNIX system and application software; manage system backup and recovery methods under UNIX; and access the UNIX server resources, including printing and file sharing.

Instruction: Major topics covered in the course are UNIX workstation basics; installation and configuration; disk and memory subsystems; file management; boot-up and shut-down; user accounts and user management; UNIX client networking; system backup and recovery; software installation; X-windows system; workstation security, access, encryption, and monitoring; and kernel configuration. Methods of instruction include lecture, discussion, audio/visual material, hands-on classroom exercises, and a multiple-choice one-hour proctored final examination.

Credit Recommendation: In the lower division baccalaureate/associate degree category, 2 semester hours in Computer Science, Computer Information Systems, or Data Processing (6/96).

UNIX: A Hands-On Introduction (336) (Formerly UNIX Operating Systems [336]) (Formerly UNIX Hands-On Workshop)

Location: Worldwide.

Length: 24 hours (4 days).

Dates: May 1993-Present.

Objective: To provide student with the ability to use UNIX-based systems.

Learning Outcome: Upon successful completion of this course, the student will be able to read the UNIX reference manual and on-line documentation and store information in files and control file access; execute commands using the UNIX shells and combine filter commands into pipelines for flexible data processing; and write and run shell programs, send and receive electronic mail, create and remove user accounts, and perform backups and other system administration functions.

Instruction: Major topics covered in the course are UNIX past and present; commands, files, and filters; the UNIX file system; using the UNIX shells; X Window system applications; UNIX shell and filter programming; the UNIX programming environment; and local and network communication; system administration issues. Methods of instruction include lecture, discussion, laboratory exercises, and examination.

Credit Recommendation: In the lower division baccalaureate/associate degree category or in the upper division baccalaureate degree category, 2 semester hours in

Computer Science, Information Systems Management, or Data Processing (1/94).

Utilizing Frame Relay Networks (278)

Location: Various sites in the United States.

Length: 18 hours (3 days).

Dates: December 1997-Present.

Objective: To provide students with the knowledge and skills necessary to understand frame relay principles and the implementation of this technology in enterprise networks.

Learning Outcome: Upon successful completion of this course, the student will be able to utilize frame relay for data, voice and video traffic; design and build private frame relay networks; interface to public frame relay networks; configure virtual circuits to meet the needs of network applications; optimize throughput using CIR and congestion control and optimize the use of frame relay bandwidth on demand concepts.

Instruction: Major topics covered in this course include introduction to frame relay, key frame relay concepts and features, evaluating frame relay, frame relay standardization, signaling and network functions, monitoring and controlling frame relay traffic, frame relay inter-working, managing frame relay networks, and frame relay enhancements. Methods of instruction include lecture, discussion, classroom exercises, audio-visual material, module tests and final examination.

Credit Recommendation: In the lower division baccalaureate/associate degree category, 1 semester hour in Data Communication and Networking, Computer Information Systems or Computer Science (2/98).

Visual Basic 5 and Active X for Enterprise Applications: Hands-On (404) (Formerly Visual Basic 4 for Enterprise Applications [404]) (Hands-On Visual Basic 4 for Enterprise Applications)

Location: Worldwide.

Length: 24 hours (4 days), plus a one hour proctored examination.

Dates: October 1995-Present.

Objective: To provide students with the knowledge and skills to develop Visual Basic applications that query databases and function as OLE automation servers.

Learning Outcome: Upon successful completion of this course, the student will be able to fully exploit the advanced features of Visual Basic 4, including OLE custom controls (OCX) and Windows 95 features; develop flexible database applications using data access objects (DAO) and the new remote data objects (RDO); create OLE automation servers in Visual Basic and control applications across the network using remote automation; employ object-oriented techniques in Visual Basic to build reusable classes; and select the appropriate database access strategy for your environment.

Instruction: Major topics covered in the course are what's new in Visual Basic 4, the Microsoft jet database engine, data access objects, ODBC (the database connectivity solution), remote data objects, and creating OLE automation servers. Methods of instruction include lecture, discussion, laboratory exercises, and a multiple-choice final examination.

Credit Recommendation: In the lower division baccalaureate/associate degree category, 2 semester hours in Computer Science, Data Processing, Computer Information Systems, or Business Information Systems (2/96).

Visual FoxPro Applications Development (405)

Location: Worldwide.

Length: 24 hours (4 days).

Dates: August 1997-Present.

Objective: To provide the knowledge needed to develop database applications using Visual FoxPro. Students will also learn to migrate legacy FoxPro applications to Visual FoxPro's object-oriented programming environment.

Learning Outcome: Upon successful completion of this course, the student will be able to develop robust database applications using Visual FoxPro (VFP) 5; migrate FoxPro legacy applications to VFP; design high-performance databases; program in an integrated database development system; use powerful object-oriented and event-driven technology provided by VFP; exploit VFP Wizard for rapid application development; utilize ActiveX controls to increase Internet functionality; and publish VFP on the Internet.

Instruction: Major topics covered in the course are an overview, exploring and customizing the Visual FoxPro interface, building the database, creating forms, programming FoxPro, querying VFP, database programming, object-oriented programming with Visual FoxPro, putting it all together-application development with VFP, using VFP with ActiveX, OLE, and the Internet. Methods of instruction include lecture, discussion, classroom exercises, audio/visual material, and examination.

Credit Recommendation: In the lower division baccalaureate/associate degree category, 2 semester hours in Computer Science, Management Information Systems, or Data Processing (8/97).

Visual InterDev for Enterprise Applications: Hands-On (409)

Location: Various sites in the United States.

Length: 24 hours (4 days).

Dates: November 1997-Present.

Objective: To provide students with the knowledge and skills needed to use Visual InterDev to create expertise-wide business applications to access new and legacy databases. Students will learn to extend database applications to incorporate business logic.

Learning Outcome: Upon successful completion of this course, the student will be able to create Web-based client/server applications with Visual InterDev; integrate database technologies such as OLE DB, ADO & ADC into applications; connect to multiple data sources; access data with tables and stored procedures; add business logic to Web applications using tools such as Visual Basic and Visual J++; manage team-based development efforts; and utilize MS Transaction Server to manage distributed transactions.

Instruction: Major topics covered in this course are planning Web applications, developing interactive Web pages, storing information in databases, building dynamic, intelligent Web-based applications, and implementing applications.

Credit Recommendation: In the lower division baccalaureate/associate degree category, 2 semester hours (1 semester hour in Information Systems and 1 semester hour in Information Systems laboratory) (2/98).

Win32 GUI Programming (300) (Formerly Windows Programming [300]) (Formerly Hands On Windows Programming)

Location: Worldwide.

Length: 24 hours (4 days).

Dates: July 1992-Present.

Objective: To provide student with the ability to write programs that port between Windows 3.x and Win32.

Learning Outcome: Upon successful completion of this course, the student will be able to tune and use Windows and its

Software Development Kit (SDK); handle input from keyboard, mouse, timers and windows; create and use graphics resources, dialogs and menus; manage memory and write Dynamic Link Libraries; and use multivendor resources and program design tools.

Instruction: Major topics covered in the course are Windows and the Windows toolkits; Windows programming first steps; managing input to Windows programs; menus and controls; graphics and the GDI; text, fonts, and bitmaps; accelerators and dialogs; effective use of memory; advanced techniques; and Windows into the future. Methods of instruction include lecture, discussion, laboratory exercises, and examination.

Credit Recommendation: In the lower division baccalaureate/associate degree category or in the upper division baccalaureate degree category, 2 semester hours in Information Systems Management, Data Processing, or Computer Science (1/94).

Win32 Systems and Network Programming: Hands-On (302) (Formerly Windows NT Systems & Application Programming) (Formerly Client Server and Systems Programming for Windows [302]) (Formerly Win32 Programming) (Formerly Hands-On Windows NT Systems & Application Programming)

Location: Worldwide.

Length: 24 hours (4 days).

Dates: May 1993-Present.

Objective: To provide student with the ability to use the Windows NT Application Programming Interfaces to develop 32-bit applications.

Learning Outcome: Upon successful completion of this course, the student will be able to exploit the Win32 Software Development Kit (SDK) and its tools; write simple Windows GUI applications in C using message crackers; take advantage of Windows NT multitasking and multithreading in programs; use console character I/O as well as GUI I/O; employ object, file, and network security in programs; and write network client/server applications with a variety of network APIs.

Instruction: Major topics covered in the course are Windows NT architecture and components, Windows NT Software Development Kit, Windows programming with the Win32 API; Dynamic link libraries for Windows NT; processes and threads, interprocess communication, network programming, and input/output and security subsystems. Methods of instruction include lecture, discussion, laboratory exercises, and examination.

Credit Recommendation: In the lower division baccalaureate/associate degree category or in the upper division baccalaureate degree category, 2 semester hours in Information Systems Management, Data Processing, or Computer Science (1/94).

Windows 3.1 (152) (Formerly Windows 3.1)(Hands-On Windows)

Location: Worldwide.

Length: 24 hours (4 days).

Dates: May 1993-Present.

Objective: To provide the student with knowledge of Windows 3.1.

Learning Outcome: Upon successful completion of this course, the student will be able to install and upgrade Windows 3.1 correctly; customize and tune Windows for optimum performance; optimize the running of DOS applications under Windows; resolve memory conflicts; edit INI files with confidence; increase Windows functionality with third-party utilities; configure fonts for the screen and printers; and troubleshoot Windows problems.

Instruction: Major topics covered in the course are introduction to Windows; starting Windows and applications; customizing the desktop; installing Windows, ports, printers, and fonts; application integration and data exchange; Windows and PC memory; running DOS applications; application builders; tuning for performance; designing and creating hypertext help; networking Windows; and multimedia and the future. Methods of instruction include lecture, discussion, classroom activities, out-of-class activities, and examination.

Credit Recommendation: In the lower division baccalaureate/associate degree or in the upper division baccalaureate degree category, 2 semester hours in Data Communications, Data Processing, Information Systems Management, or Computer Science (3/94).

Windows 95/NT/3.11 Multiplatform Networking: Hands-On (151) (Formerly Windows Networking: Hands-On [151])

Location: Worldwide.

Length: 24 hours (4-days).

Dates: July 1996-Present.

Objective: To provide students with the knowledge and skills needed to configure and manage Windows-based networks.

Learning Outcome: Upon successful completion of this course, the student will be able to integrate windows clients with NetWare, Windows NT server and UNIX services; configure shared windows applications to run across the network; develop and execute installation procedures for windows clients; plan, implement and configure access to printers, modems, fax and e-mail services; manage workstations using system policies and remote administration tools; and connect windows networks to the internet.

Instruction: Major topics covered in the course are an introduction to Windows networking; network clients and user authentication; installation and supporting clients; workstation management; resource management; network services; and integrating internet and intranet. Methods of instruction include lecture, discussion, classroom exercises, audio/visual material, quizzes, observations, and a final examination.

Credit Recommendation: In the lower division baccalaureate/associate degree category, 2 semester hours (1 semester hour in Computer Science or Information Systems, and 1 semester hour in Computer Science Laboratory or Information Systems Laboratory) (10/96).

Windows NT 4 Workstation and Server: Hands-On (455)

Location: Worldwide.

Length: 30 hours (5 days).

Dates: October 1996-Present.

Objective: To provide students with comprehensive and practical knowledge of Windows NT components and capabilities and develop the skills needed to implement and configure Windows NT 4.0.

Learning Outcome: Upon successful completion of this course, the student will be able to plan the correct Windows NT 4.0 implementation for your environment; establish trusted and trusting domains; recover from a domain controller failure; configure local and global users and groups; implement system policies to control machine and user environments; establish local and network resource security; and configure and use Windows NTs built-in network capabilities.

Instruction: Major topics covered in the course are introduction to Windows NT; system configuration and support; managing workstation user accounts and groups; files, file system security, and printing; domains; installing a Windows NT network; domain controllers and trust relationships; network interoperability; and troubleshooting and optimization.

Methods of instruction include lecture, discussion, classroom exercises, audio/visual material, and final examination.

Credit Recommendation: In the lower division baccalaureate/associate degree category, 2 semester hours in Computer Information Systems or Data Communications (4/97).

Windows NT Optimization and Troubleshooting: Hands-On (160)

Location: Worldwide.

Length: 30 hours (5-days).

Dates: September 1996-Present.

Objective: To provide students with high-level knowledge and advanced skills needed to optimize and troubleshoot Windows NT.

Learning Outcome: Upon successful completion of this course, the student will be able to utilize advanced tools and techniques to effectively support Windows NT; optimize application, operating system and network performance; employ advanced troubleshooting methods and strategies; diagnose and repair Windows NT problems; implement a fault-tolerant Windows NT network; and apply capacity planning techniques to determine hardware and software needs.

Instruction: Major topics covered in the course are Windows NT architecture, security, and file system; Windows NT resource kit; introduction to the performance monitor; leveraging the performance monitor; additional troubleshooting and optimization tools; advanced troubleshooting; and enterprise technologies. Methods of instruction include lecture, discussion, classroom exercises, audio/visual material, exercises, observations, and a final examination.

Credit Recommendation: In the lower division baccalaureate/associate degree category, 2 semester hours in Microcomputer Applications (10/96).

Windows Open Services Architecture: Hands-On (400)

Location: Worldwide.

Length: 18 hours (3 days).

Dates: March 1996-Present.

Objective: To provide students with the knowledge and skills needed to develop Open Windows applications.

Learning Outcome: Upon successful completion of this course, the student will be able to create scalable database systems using Open Database Connectivity (ODBC); use Object Linking and Embedding (OLE) to develop reuseable software components; utilize Messaging Application Programming Interface (MAPI) to design work group applications; and develop effective user interfaces.

Instruction: Major topics covered in the course are an Introduction to Windows Open Systems Architecture (WOSA); capabilities of Win 32 architecture, Open Database Connectivity (ODBC); integrating applications with OLE; communicating using MAPI; user interface guidelines; and cross-platform connectivity. Methods of instruction include lecture, discussion, laboratory exercises, and an one-hour, multiple-choice, proctored final examination.

Credit Recommendation: In the lower division baccalaureate/associate degree category, 1 semester hour in Data Processing or Computer Information Systems (6/96).

Windows Programming with Visual C++ and MFC for C++ Programmers (403)

Location: Various sites in the United States.

Length: 24 hours (4 days).

Dates: November 1997-Present.

Objective: To provide students with the knowledge to create Window applications using Visual C++, MFC and AFX.

Learning Outcome: Upon successful completion of this course, the student will be able to generate Windows Applications build upon MFC and the Application Framework (AFX); understand the MFC's document/view architecture; employ ClassWizard to generate message and command handling functions; rapidly create user interfaces using dialog boxes, graphics, form views and controls; integrate ActiveX controls and exploit ODBC to access databases.

Instruction: Major topics covered in the course are an introduction and overview; MFC's Document/View architecture; editing application resources, dialog box templates, forms and controls; open database connectivity (ODCBC); working with ActiveX controls. Methods of instruction include lecture, discussion, classroom exercises, audio-visual material, module tests and final examination.

Credit Recommendation: In the lower division baccalaureate/associate degree category, 2 semester hours (1 semester hour in Computer Science or Information Systems and 1 semester hour in Computer Science Laboratory or Information Systems (2/98).

Lockheed Martin Utility Services, Inc.

Lockheed Martin Utility Services, Inc., serves as the operating contractor for the United States Enrichment Corporation at the Portsmouth Gaseous Diffusion Plant, located in Piketon, Ohio. The purpose of the plant is to increase the concentration of the U-235 isotope by separating it from the U-238 isotope. The Portsmouth plant ships enriched uranium product to fuel assembly fabricators for use in nuclear reactors of both domestic and foreign electric utility customers. The Portsmouth plant has a workforce of approximately 2,400 employees.

On March 3, 1997, the Portsmouth plant transitioned to regulation by the Nuclear Regulatory Commission. This transition was required by the Energy Policy Act of 1992, which laid the groundwork for the future privatization of the domestic uranium enrichment business. The Portsmouth plant is also under the regulatory requirements of other state and federal agencies.

The mission of the Protective Force is to protect Department of Energy and the United States Enrichment Corporation security interests from theft, sabotage, and other hostile acts that may cause adverse impact on national security or the health and safety of the public; and to protect life and property. In order to fulfill their mission, the Protective Forces administers and manages and extensive training program.

Source of official student records: Registry of Credit Recommendations, American Council on Education, One Dupont Circle, Washington, DC 20036-1193.

Additional information about the courses: College Credit Recommendation Service, American Council on Education, One Dupont Circle, Washington, DC 20036-1193.

Arrest Authority (PFT02.28)
STRESS (PFT03.36.01)
Limited Scope Performance Tests (PFT02.14)
Crime Scene and Evidence Preservation (PFT01.15)
Use of Force/Deadly Force (PFT01.13)
Demonstration/Riot Control (PFT02.06)
Vehicle Stop Tactics (PFT02.05)
Tactical Familiarization (PFT02.08)
Communications (PFT02.10)
Aberrant Behavior (PFT06.02)
First Aid/CPR (PFT02.17)
Bloodborne Pathogens (MAN02.50.01)
Fire Protection (PFT02.19)
Weapons Maintenance/Cleaning (PFT03.01.02)
Range Rules and Firearms Safety (PFT03.22) (PFT03.22)

Location: Piketon, Ohio.

Length: 45 hours.

Dates: January 1986-Present.

Objective: To provide the student with knowledge of police patrol operations.

Learning Outcome: Upon successful completion of these courses, the student will be able to demonstrate a knowledge of the basic principles, concepts, and strategies of police patrol operations.

Instruction: Major topics covered in these courses are the use of force/deadly force, arrest authority, crime scene and evidence preservation, demonstration/riot control, vehicle stop tactics, tactical familiarization, first aid/CPR, bloodborne pathogens, fire protection, weapons maintenance/cleaning, and range rules and firearms safety. Methods of instruction include lecture, discussion, cases studies, role-playing exercises, computer assisted instruction, and examinations.

Credit Recommendation: In the lower division baccalaureate/associate degree category, 3 semester hours in Police Patrol Operations (11/96). **NOTE:** Student must complete all courses to receive the credit.

Lucent Technologies Customer Training & Information Products

Lucent Technologies Customer Training & Information Products is a division of the AT&T Corporate Education and Training organization. Lucent Technologies Customer Training & Information Products' mission is "To provide human performance solutions for users of information technology worldwide." Its motto is "Helping people excel." Lucent Technologies Customer Training & Information Products' training facilities are spread throughout the United States with headquarters in Dublin, Ohio.

Lucent Technologies Customer Training & Information Products develops and maintains its own training materials. All materials are developed using a systematic approach to assure that training objectives are met efficiently and effectively. In total, over 450 courses are offered in a wide range of telecommunications topics, including network engineering, installation, operation, administration, and maintenance of complex systems.

Delivery media techniques include lecture-led, hands-on, electronic training systems (ETS), and distance learning (audio and video). Instructors must meet stringent certification procedures to assure a consistently high level of performance. Student satisfaction levels and comments are monitored continually.

Source of official student records: Registry of Credit Recommendations, American Council on Education, One Dupont Circle, Washington, DC 20036-1193 or Telessentials Product Manager, Lucent Technologies Customer Training & Information Products, 5151 Blazer Memorial Parkway, Dublin, Ohio 43017

Additional information about the courses: College Credit Recommendation Service, American Council on Education, One Dupont Circle, Washington, DC 20036-1193.

Analog and Digital Concepts (TC 1602)

Location: Various AT&T and licensed customer locations.

Length: Self-paced, computer managed multimedia (appr. 6 hours).

Dates: December 1990-Present.

Objective: To provide an understanding of analog and digital electrical signals, bid and baud rates, modulation, multiplexing techniques, analog and digital conversion and distributive processing.

Learning Outcome: Upon successful completion of this course, the student will be able to describe the characteristics of analog and digital signals, modulation principles, analog to digital conversion, and multiplexing.

Instruction: Major topics covered in the course are analog and digital electrical signals, bit and baud rates, modulation and multiplexing, and distributive processing. Methods of instruction include competency based instruction using computer managed modules with a workbook and videotape.

Credit Recommendation: In the lower division baccalaureate/associate degree category, 3 semester hours in Telecommunications (12/91). **NOTE**: In order to receive credit, students must successfully complete TC1601 through TC1607.

Communication Basics (TC1601)

Location: Various AT&T and licensed customer locations.

Length: Self-paced, computer managed multimedia (appr. 11 hours).

Dates: December 1990-Present.

Objective: To provide an understanding of telecommunications basics.

Learning Outcome: Upon successful completion of this course, the student will be able to define communications; identify four characteristics of waveforms; describe the evolution of transmission media from open telephone wires to modern systems; compare air and wire as mediums; and identify four functions computers perform and the hardware devices that perform each function.

Instruction: Major topics covered in this course are components of the communication process; using electrical signals for communication; evolution of telecommunications; telephony concepts of the 1960s and 1970s; public switched telephone network; and basic computer terminology. Methods of instruction include competency based instruction using computer managed modules with a workbook and videotape.

Credit Recommendation: In the lower division baccalaureate/associate degree category, 3 semester hours in Telecommunications (12/91). **NOTE**: In order to receive credit, students must successfully complete TC1601 through TC1607.

Communications Networks (TC1605)

Location: Various AT&T and licensed customer locations.

Length: Self-paced, computer managed multimedia (appr. 11 hours).

Dates: December 1990-Present.

Objective: To provide an introduction to networks and to explore interfaces and protocols.

Learning Outcome: Upon successful completion of this course, the student will be able to discriminate between public and private networks; understand the role of the Public Switched Telephone Network; define the terms "standard" and "protocol;" identify examples of switched and dedicated services; differentiate between circuit switching and packet switching; and identify fundamental LAN concepts and terminology.

Instruction: Major topics covered in the course are voice, data and signaling networks; LANs, MANs, and WANs; components of the Public Switched Network, protocols and interfaces; the Public Packet Data Network; and cellular mobile networks. Methods of instruction include competency based instruction using computer managed modules with a workbook and videotape.

Credit Recommendation: In the lower division baccalaureate/associate degree category, 3 semester hours in Telecommunications (12/91). **NOTE**: In order to receive credit, students must successfully complete TC1601 through TC1607.

ISDN Fundamentals (TC1606)

Location: Various AT&T and licensed customer locations.

Length: Self-paced computer managed multimedia (appr. 10 hours).

Dates: December 1990-Present.

Objective: To provide the student with an introduction to the fundamental concepts of ISDN.

Learning Outcome: Upon successful completion of this course, the student will be able to define ISDN and its relationship to various protocols and standards, understand basic principles as applied to the customer premise equipment (CPE), describe signal transmission in the ISDN system, understand the methods of call processing for ISDN, and describe the present and future applications of ISDN.

Instruction: Major topics covered in the course are ISDN definitions, protocols, evolution, and future applications; customer premises equipment for ISDN service; ISDN signal transmission; ISDN call processing. Methods of instruction include competency based instruction using computer managed modules with a workbook and videotape.

Credit Recommendation: In the lower division baccalaureate/associate degree category, 3 semester hours in Telecommunications (12/91). **NOTE**: In order to receive credit, students must successfully complete TC1601 through TC1607.

Operations Systems (TC1607)

Location: Various AT&T and licensed customer locations.

Length: Self-paced, computer managed multimedia (appr. 4 hours).

Dates: December 1990-Present.

Objective: To provide the student with a knowledge of the customer and network related operations required for telephone company operations.

Learning Outcome: Upon successful completion of this course, the student will be able to describe various telephone company operating systems, understand various computerized operations support systems, and describe the various specialized centers in operations.

Instruction: Major topics covered in the course are operations system functions, computerized operations support systems, and operations systems applications. Methods of instruction include competency based instruction using computer managed modules with a workbook and videotape.

Credit Recommendation: In the lower division baccalaureate/associate degree category, 3 semester hours in Telecommunications (12/91). **NOTE**: In order to receive credit, students must successfully complete TC1601 through TC1607.

Switching (TC1604)

Location: Various AT&T and licensed customer locations.

Length: Self-paced, computer managed multimedia (appr. 6 hours).

Dates: December 1990-Present.

Objective: To provide students with an overview of central office switching techniques.

Learning Outcome: Upon successful completion of this course, the student will be able to define, identify and describe functions and components of analog and digital switching systems (ESS); describe how an interoffice call is processed; and describe the evolution applications and classes of signaling.

Instruction: Major topics covered in the course are switching and signaling concepts and techniques concentrating on central office applications. Methods of instruction include competency based instruction using computer managed modules with a workbook and videotape.

Credit Recommendation: In the lower division baccalaureate/associate degree category, 3 semester hours in Telecommunications (12/91). **NOTE**: In order to receive credit, students must successfully complete TC1601 through TC1607.

Transmission (TC1603)

Location: Various AT&T and licensed customer locations.

Length: Self-paced, computer managed multimedia (appr. 6 hours).

Dates: December 1990-Present.

Objective: To provide an understanding of the various types of transmission signals, facilities, rates and media.

Learning Outcome: Upon successful completion of this course, the student will be able to define impairment and identify the three major categories, define and contrast transmission facility and carrier system, describe the function of regenerators; describe intersymbol interference; describe an open wire circuit, describe the nature of microwaves, describe the characteristics and sources of lightwaves.

Instruction: Major topics covered in the course are transmission concepts and definitions, transmission impairments, wire transmission facilities, using microwave for transmission, and fiber transmission facilities. Methods of instruction include competency based instruction using computer managed modules with a workbook and videotape.

Credit Recommendation: In the lower division baccalaureate/associate degree category, 3 semester hours in Telecommunications (12/91). **NOTE**: In order to receive credit, students must successfully complete this course and TC1601, TC1602 and TC1604 through TC1607.

Lucent Technologies, Inc., Business Communications Systems Education & Training

Lucent Technologies BCS Education & Training (E&T) provides a great breadth of services to BCS and its customers. The core services include competency modeling, need analysis, and training development and delivery. In addition, BCS E&T provides change management facilitation services, performance consulting, broadcast television service and industry specific professional programs. Currently, these programs are offered in seven different Lucent Technologies training locations nationwide, at requested customer sites and globally at Lucent Technologies Centers of Excellence.

Educational and Professional Programs are developed specifically for professionals in a variety of fields. The Telecommunications Manager Certificate Program is offered to telecommunications professionals, regardless of their telecommunications supplier, looking for the legitimacy of a Certificate in Telecommunica-tions Management. The program is co-sponsored by University College of the University of Denver. A comprehensive Capstone Project is offered as the culminating activity to this program.

Source of official student records: Registry of Credit Recommendations, American Council on Education, One Dupont Circle, Washington, DC 20036-1193.

Additional information about the courses: Office of Corporate-Higher Education Programs, Thomas Edison State College, 101 West State Street, Trenton, NJ 08608-1176.

Delighting the Internal Customer (TCM1001)

Location: Atlanta, Georgia; Beltsville, Maryland; Chicago, Illinois; Dallas, Texas; Englewood, Colorado; Pasadena, California; Valhalla, New York; and special customer arranged sites.

Length: 24 hours (3 days).

Dates: January 1997-Present.

Objective: To help telecommunications professionals assess their customers' current level of satisfaction with the service provided them and learn how to build a customer service plan for becoming a more effective results-oriented catalyst in their respective companies.

Learning Outcome: Upon successful completion of this course, the student will be able to articulate the benefits of providing superior internal customer service; assess their current departmental and individual performance in delivering superior customer service; implement a department customer service improvement process plan; implement an individual customer service improvement process plan; better serve internal customers; and use problem resolution skills and techniques to more effectively deal with difficult situations.

Instruction: Major topics covered in the course are how to create win-win relationships with the internal customers their department serves; ability to assess their customers' current level of satisfaction with the service provided by their department; how to build a customer service plan for becoming a more effective catalyst for results in their respective companies; step-by-step techniques for providing superior service at both the departmental and the individual level in simple " how to" language; how to maximize customer satisfaction and support their organization while enhancing their own career and potential for success. Methods of instruction include classroom discussion and lecture, simulation, independent study, and collaborative learning. An end of course project is part of the course.

Credit Recommendation: In the lower division baccalaureate/associate degree category or in the upper division baccalaureate degree category, 2 semester hours in Business Communications or Marketing (5/97).

Meeting Business Objectives Through Technology Planning (TCM1004)

Location: Various training locations nationwide.

Length: 24 hours (3 days).

Dates: July 1996-Present.

Objective: To provide the telecommunications manager with a working-level knowledge of how to construct and gain acceptance for a Technology Plan in support of business needs.

Learning Outcome: Upon successful completion of this course, the student will be able to describe typical technology characteristics of an organization and explain the benefits of technology planning; define and discuss company business plans, technology plans, and communications architectures; explain the Technology Planning Process which is composed of (1) data gathering, (2) analysis, (3) requirements definition and justification, (4) management review, (5) options development and selection, (6) design, and (7) implementation; and explore methods of gaining acceptance of the Technology Plan by upper management and integrating the Technology Plan into the business planning process.

Instruction: Major topics covered in the course are conceptual and practical knowledge in the process of developing technology plans, the content of the company business plans for use as one of the drivers in the Technology Planning process, and the knowledge and tools needed to develop the technology plan and through that to become a proactive member of the corporate management team.

Credit Recommendation: In the lower division baccalaureate/associate degree category, 2 semester hours in Telecommunications Management or Information Systems Management (1/96).

Minimizing Risk: Business Recovery and Security (TCM2003)

Location: Atlanta, Georgia; Beltsville, Maryland; Chicago, Illinois; Dallas, Texas; Englewood, Colorado; Pasadena, California; Valhalla, New York; and special customer arranged sites.

Length: 24 hours (3 days).

Dates: January 1997-Present.

Objective: To provide the student with an understanding of the critical need for business recovery planning in a crisis situation and the ways to prevent toll fraud from having a major negative impact on their business.

Learning Outcome: Upon successful completion of this course, the student will be able to analyze the needs of their company relative to crisis recovery; build a business case for a crisis recovery plan; identify crisis recovery options and their associated costs; define "telephone fraud" and its associated costs; identify signs that toll fraud is occurring/has occurred; and analyze the methods hackers use to gain access to their telecommunications systems.

Instruction: Major topics covered in the course are: (Part I) step-by-step techniques for constructing and maintaining plans to safeguard their company against the potentially catastrophic effects of disaster and toll fraud; how to analyze their company's unique needs for business recovery; how to build a business case, how to investigate options and cost, and how to select the option most closely suited to their company's unique needs. (Part

II) how toll fraud occurs; how to spot early warning signs of potential fraud; how to develop plans to protect their company against it; and practical actions to take if they discover toll fraud. Methods of instruction include classroom discussion and lecture, simulation, independent study, and collaborative learning.

Credit Recommendation: In the lower division baccalaureate/associate degree category or in the upper division baccalaureate degree category, 2 semester hours in Strategic Planning or Security Management (5/97).

Premises Distribution System Management for the TCM (TCM2004)

Location: Various training locations nationwide.

Length: 24 hours (3 days), plus precourse readings.

Dates: July 1996-Present.

Objective: To provide the telecommunications manager with knowledge of the technology and standards needed to manage the analysis, planning, design, procurement, implementation, and maintenance of communications media in the office, building, and campus environments.

Learning Outcome: Upon successful completion of this course, the student will be able to define the function and purpose of telecommunications standards and explain the pros and cons of adopting them; discuss the background and makeup of the standards organizations and the relationships among them; delineate and describe the major, relevant standards that support premises distribution systems and explain their value to the TCM; define structured distribution systems and explain the costs and benefits associated with following the structured distribution system model; define and describe the individual subsystems of a structured distribution system; describe the types of media used in communications systems, showing examples and discussing the advantages and disadvantages of each; discuss communications applications (voice, data, video, multimedia, security, and sensor) in terms of the type of media used to support them; discuss communications infrastructure concepts, the importance of using vendor independent design and the critical nature of standard adherence to grounding and bonding requirements; explain purpose, benefits, and process of communications infrastructure planning; examine the management and maintenance of the premises distribution system with emphasis on standards and regulatory code considerations, documentations, management software packages, cable designation schemes, voice and data integration, system certification, and long-term operations costs; and explain and discuss the phases of the system selection process.

Instruction: Major topics covered in the course are an understanding of the many functions and nuances of premises distribution systems in support of business needs; the development of the manager of the telecommunications organization, a comprehensive understanding of the issues of strategic planning to develop support within senior management for proper long-range decisions, specifying business needs and procuring/implementing the system, knowledge of standards, structured distribution systems, management techniques, communications media, and requirements analysis and specification. Methods of instruction include lecture and discussion.

Credit Recommendation: In the lower division baccalaureate/associate degree category, 2 semester hours in Telecommunications Management or Information Systems Management (1/96).

Understanding and Managing Enterprise Data Networks (TCM2001)

Location: Various training locations nationwide.

Length: 24 hours (3 days), plus precourse readings.

Dates: July 1996-Present.

Objective: To provide students with an understanding of Public LAN Internetworking including topics such as: Frame Relay, SMDS, ATM, Commercial Internet Services, Public Network FDDI, and private lines and emerging alternatives.

Learning Outcome: Upon successful completion of this course, the student will be able to list the components of local area networks and wide area networks; define, compare, and contrast differences within LAN technologies; compare and contrast the three fast packet technologies (Frame Relay, SMDS, ATM) and demonstrate a working knowledge of these technologies; define and demonstrate a working knowledge of the client server environment, including hardware/software, types of servers utilized, and the various communication protocols inherent within the C/S environment; and use the Internet, its open protocol (TCP/IP) and worldwide WEB browsers.

Instruction: Major topics covered in the course are a working-level knowledge of how LAN internetworks are created utilizing bridges and routers; how technologies are being trialed and used in public networks for facilitating Wide Area Networks (WANs) and Local Area Networks (LANs); how customer routers are used as access devices into Frame Relay and SMDS networks; and an overview that looks at the "whys" of WAN services from a carrier and then looks at three of the highest-speed virtual-networks connectivity plans that are presently offered: Frame Relay, SMDS, and ATM.

Credit Recommendation: In the lower division baccalaureate/associate degree category, 2 semester hours in Telecommunications Management or Information Systems Management (1/96).

Lucent Technologies, Inc., Learning and Performance Center

The Learning and Performance Center is the new learning arm of Lucent Technologies that brings together technical, business, and manufacturing programs under one learning leader. It combines parts of what used to be the AT&T School of Business, the Technical Education Center, Learning Services, and the Network Systems manufacturing training organizations.

Functioning now under one umbrella known as the Lucent Technologies Learning and Performance Center (LPC), the focus of the organization will be on improving the performance of Lucent employees, and ultimately their organizations, in key strategic areas such as software, wireless technology, global business management, sales, diversity, leadership, product/project management, and manufacturing.

Courses range from the basic overview to the highly technical. Classes are taught in modern facilities that include fully equipped classrooms, caserooms, and computer rooms. The faculty has been recruited from academia as well as business and industry. Many have advanced degrees and are recognized for their contributions and expertise in their field, thereby ensuring high quality in course content and instructional techniques. Primary training facilities are located at Piscataway and Holmdel, New Jersey; and Lisle, Illinois. Supplemental locations in cities across the country and internationally are available.

Source of official student records: Registry of Credit Recommendations, American Council on Education, One Dupont Circle, Washington, DC 20036-1193.

Additional information about the courses: Office of Corporate-Higher Education Programs, Thomas Edison State College, 101 West State Street, Trenton, NJ 08608-1176.

Accelerated Microsoft Project for Windows (IE1693)

Location: Piscataway, NJ and various other locations nationwide.

Length: 24 hours (3 days).

Dates: July 1996-Present.

Objective: To teach participants to use Microsoft Project 4.0 to effectively create and manage single and multiple project schedules using accepted project management principles.

Learning Outcome: Upon successful completion of this course, the student will be able to create a new project; enter task and resource information for the project; organize the project in outline form; display various views of project information; analyze and adjust schedules, resources, and costs as the project progresses; preview and print views for the project; preview and print reports on the project; create master project to subproject relationships; combine multiple projects; share a common resource pool between projects; analyze resource conflicts between multi-project assignments; and customize Microsoft Project filters, reports, tables, and tool bars.

Instruction: Major topics covered in the course are customization of Microsoft Project is introduced by creating custom views, tables, filters, reports and tool bars; the principles of sharing customized objects among projects; and project management principles along with their application in Microsoft Project.

Credit Recommendation: In the lower division baccalaureate/associate degree category or in the upper division baccalaureate degree category, 2 semester hours in Microsoft Projects for Windows I & II (6/95).

Active Communicating: Professional Presence and Creativity (MD6411)

Location: Somerset, NJ and other School of Business sites.

Length: 21 hours (3 days).

Dates: July 1990-Present.

Objective: To develop more conscious and competent communication within a business environment.

Learning Outcome: Upon successful completion of this course, the student will be able to understand the relationship between language and its expression through the voice and the body; improve interpersonal communication skills, including listening, sensitivity to others and team building skills; improve presentation skills, including use of voice, body and the ability to think quickly under pressure; and develop a more self-confident overall communication style.

Instruction: Methods of instruction include the use of theater-based exercises to bring to awareness and improve the various components which determine effective communication, such as voice use; concentration; creativity and imagination; timing; listening; body awareness; sensitivity to others; pacing; memory; ability to improvise; emotional expressiveness and self-confidence in speaking. Course readings, lectures and discussions relate the exercises to the interpersonal communication dynamics of the workplace and how individuals can make a contribution towards their improvement.

Credit Recommendation: In the lower division baccalaureate/associate degree category, 1 semester hour in Oral Business Communication (6/94).

Activity Based Management: Fundamentals and Applications (FE0203)

Location: Somerset, NJ and Atlanta, GA.

Length: 16 hours (2 days).

Dates: July 1996-Present.

Objective: To learn to improve your organization's profitability, productivity and operational processes through a hands-on introduction to Activity-Based Costing/ Activity-Based Management.

Learning Outcome: Upon successful completion of this course, the student will be able to understand the concepts, applications and importance of ABC and ABM; understand how ABC/ABM can help your organization increase profitability and productivity, improve business processes and enrich decision making; learn the tools and techniques necessary to design and implement an ABC/ABM project within your organization; learn how ABC/ABM has been applied within AT&T; and locate experienced internal and external re-sources to help you implement an ABM project.

Instruction: Major topics covered in the course are the need for ABC/ABM, ABC/ABM as the foundation for increasing profitability and productivity, improving business processes and highlighting opportunities, ABC and ABM concepts and techniques, managing and implementing a successful ABC/ABM project, and ABC/ABM in AT&T. A comprehensive paper is required as part of this course.

Credit Recommendation: In the upper division baccalaureate degree category or in the graduate degree category, 1 semester hour in Production/Operations Management (7/95).

Advanced Finance Concepts (FM1000) (Formerly Fundamental Concepts in Financial Management [FM1000])

Location: Somerset, NJ and other AT&T locations.

Length: 24 hours (3 days).

Dates: March 1994-Present.

Objective: To give managers an understanding of basic financial skills and concepts.

Learning Outcome: Upon successful completion of this course, the student will be able to analyze and positively impact corporate results; understand differences in financial policies; apply basic financial concepts, such as risk, reward, and the time value of money; and understand capital markets and the implications of bond and stock financing.

Instruction: Major topics covered in the course are designed to give students an understanding of basic non-accounting oriented financial skills and concepts, through the analysis of various case studies. The course includes time value of money, budgeting and planning, working capital management, financial markets, bond and stock valuation, capital structure, risk and return, and capital budgeting. Methods of instruction include lecture and discussions. An appropriate graduate level research project is submitted as part of the course requirements.

Credit Recommendation: In the upper division baccalaureate degree category or in the graduate degree category, 2 semester hours in Fundamental Concepts in Financial Management (6/94).

Advanced Microsoft Project for Windows (IE1692)

Location: Piscataway, NJ and various other locations nationwide.

Length: 14 hours (92 days).

Dates: July 1996-Present.

Objective: To teach those students who have mastered the essential functions, features, commands, and keystrokes of Microsoft Project for Windows 4.0 to manage their projects.

Learning Outcome: Upon successful completion of this course, the student will be able to exchange information with other products; build a resource pool which can be shared by multiple projects; manage Master Project/Subproject relationships; resolve resource conflicts and over-allocation in a multiple project environment; control file access and update protection by managing file security; and understand macro syntax.

Instruction: Major topics covered in the course are an advanced level course for those who have mastered the essential functions, features, commands, and keystrokes of Microsoft Project for Windows to manage their projects.

Credit Recommendation: In the lower division baccalaureate/associate degree category or in the upper division baccalaureate degree category, 1 semester hour in Microsoft Project for Windows II (6/95).

Applied Quality Principles in Computer Systems (IE1954) (Formerly Applied Quality Principles for Systems Developers (Process Quality Management Improvement) [IE1954])

Location: Piscataway, NJ and other AT&T locations.

Length: *Version 1:* 18 hours (3 days); *Version 2:* 21 hours (3 days).

Dates: *Version 1:* September 1988-December 1993; *Version 2:* January 1994-Present.

Objective: *Version 1:* To apply the seven-step PQMI methodology to manage and improve work processes. *Version 2:* To focus on the qualitative approaches used by project managers to ensure that projects meet quality and cost requirements.

Learning Outcome: *Version 1:* Upon successful completion of this course, the student will be able to apply the customer-supplier model to computer system development and operational work processes; apply the seven-step PQMI methodology to manage and improve work processes; construct a block diagram (high-level flowchart) of a selected work process; conduct a customer needs analysis; define and establish measurements based on customer requirements; construct a micro (task-level) flowchart, including decision points; perform a cause-and-effect analysis and construct a cause-and-effect diagram; and construct X (X-bar) and R (Range) variables control charts. *Version 2:* Upon successful completion of this course, the student will be able to demonstrate a knowledge of basic quality concepts; use quality in the system development process; and use tools and techniques in the use of quality in the process management.

Instruction: *Version 1:* Major topics covered in the course are concepts of quality management and improvement, as well as the benefits and results of a quality-oriented process. Emphasis is placed on recognizing the importance of the customer/supplier model and on consistently meeting the needs and expectations of immediate, intermediate, and end customers. Participants are introduced to the seven-step PQMI quality process and learn how to systematically apply it by means of a relevant case study for system developers. *Version 2:* Major topics covered in the course are the qualitative and quantitative approaches used by project managers to ensure that projects and ongoing operations meet quality requirements as well as cost and schedule demands. Practical tools and techniques are introduced to help manage and improve quality in the development and operation of computer systems.

Credit Recommendation: *Version 1:* In the upper division baccalaureate degree category, 1 semester hour in Management Information/Quality Systems (7/90). *Version 2:* In the graduate degree category, 1 semester hour in Applied Quality Principles (6/95).

Applied Quality Principles in System Development (Quality Improvement Cycle) (IE1952)

Location: Piscataway, NJ, and other AT&T locations.

Length: 18 hours (3 days).

Dates: May 1988-December 1991.

Objective: To provide participants with tools and techniques for quality improvement in the management development and operations of computer systems.

Learning Outcome: Upon successful completion of this course, the student will be able to create a system products map; perform simple Statistical Process Control measurements; create and analyze X-bar and R control charts; create and analyze a work process micro-flowchart; perform a Pareto analysis and create a Pareto diagram; and create and analyze a cause-and-effect diagram.

Instruction: Major topics covered in the course are concepts of quality improvement, including a common definition of quality, as well as the benefits and results of a quality-oriented process. Emphasis is placed on recognizing the importance of the customer/supplier model and on meeting the needs and expectations of immediate, intermediate, and end customers; also participants are introduced to a step-by-step quality process and learn how to systematically apply it by the use of a case study.

Credit Recommendation: In the upper division baccalaureate degree category, 1 semester hour in Business Administration (7/90).

Auditing Standards and Principles (FE0660)

Location: AT&T locations worldwide.

Length: 46 hours (5 days).

Dates: April 1994-July 1996.

Objective: To provide managers with the skills and background to effectively perform an audit to operational review.

Learning Outcome: Upon successful completion of this course, the student will

be able to prepare for an audit by identifying resources needed; document the audit program using flowchart work operations; identify controls, recognize objectives; design audit tests; conduct pre-audit fieldwork by applying statistical sampling techniques; conduct field interviews; review work operations and documentation; analyze results of test actions by summarizing and analyzing audit test results; evaluate controls and determine significance of findings; communicate results to management; perform exit interviews; write audit reports; conduct post audit reviews; and organize audit documentation in accordance with standards.

Instruction: Major topics covered in the course are construction of a flowchart of the audit/review subject; a basic understanding of controls and how they relate to the business environment; how to recognize the objectives of an audited operation and determine if controls are adequate; and identify and document the key controls of a business operation. Methods of instruction include lectures, discussions, exercises, and a case study.

Credit Recommendation: In the graduate degree category, 3 semester hours in Auditing Standards & Principles (12/94).

Basic Negotiations: Negotiating to Yes (MS6420) (Formerly Negotiation to Yes [MS6420])

Location: Worldwide.

Length: 16 hours (2 days).

Dates: July 1996-Present.

Objective: To provide managers with a method of negotiating with integrity and a way to reach satisfying agreements while maintaining the relationship.

Learning Outcome: Upon successful completion of this course, the student will be able to have a conceptual framework for understanding negotiations, a language and a process to use before, during, and after negotiation; apply a simple strategy for negotiating that enables them to pursue their interests without giving in or getting into confrontation; and follow a preparation procedure that covers a crucial step in negotiation.

Instruction: Major topics covered in the course are the techniques to successfully implement the process, using personal application; the negotiating process; and win-win negotiation strategy and tactics. An appropriate graduate level project is included as part of the course requirement. Methods of instruction include lecture, experiential exercises, discussion, and video tapes.

Credit Recommendation: In the graduate degree category, 1 semester hour in Negotiations (10/91) (5/96).

Benchmarking Workshop (CQ1016) (Formerly Benchmarking Techniques, [CQ1016]; Seminar in Benchmarking [CQ1016])

Location: AT&T locations nationwide.

Length: 16 hours (2 days).

Dates: July 1996-Present.

Objective: To understand the benchmarking process, its underlying concepts, and how it can lead to superior performance; and apply benchmarking techniques to specific work situations.

Learning Outcome: Upon successful completion of this course, the student will be able to effectively benchmark a function within an organization; determine which companies to benchmark against based upon the needs of your organization; and assess competition and refocus business strategies and goals.

Instruction: Major topics covered in the course are a detailed step-by-step blueprint to benchmarking; concepts, cases, and job applications in critical areas of the benchmarking process; and how to incorporate benchmarking into your strategic quality planning and quality improvement processes. An appropriate graduate level project is included as part of the course requirement.

Credit Recommendation: In the graduate degree category, 1 semester hour in Strategic Quality Management (8/91) (5/96).

Business and Marketing Plans: Design and Implementation (SA4600) (Formerly Marketing and Business Plans: Design and Implementation (SA4600))

Location: Sommerset, NJ and other AT&T Locations.

Length: *Version 1:* 16 hours plus lab; *Version 2:* 24 hours (3 days).

Dates: *Version 1:* June 1989-December 1994; *Version 2:* July 1996-Present.

Objective: To teach students how to design and build a marketing plan.

Learning Outcome: Upon successful completion of this course, the student will be able to develop a business definition and demonstrate bridging to other strategic decisions such as organizational/functional strategies; and understand the analytical techniques required to determine appropriate goals and strategic alternatives, e.g., market opportunities, cost dynamics, scale and experience effects, and portfolio analysis.

Instruction: Major topics covered in the course are how to develop and fine-tune market/business plans that translate corporate goals into effective marketplace behaviors; and how to improve skills in the planning, design, and evaluation of strategic and tactical plans of the organization. An appropriate graduate level project is included as part of the course requirement. Methods of instruction include case studies, lectures, group discussions, and practice exercises.

Credit Recommendation: In the graduate degree category, 2 semester hours in Marketing (8/91) (5/96).

Business Case Fundamentals (LBF002L) (Formerly Fundamentals of Business Decisions [LBF002L])

Location: Piscataway, NJ and other locations nationwide.

Length: 16 hours (2 days).

Dates: July 1996-Present.

Objective: To teach managers a method to analyze R&D projects and techniques to prioritize and maximize the productivity of the R&D portfolio.

Learning Outcome: Upon successful completion of this course, the student will be able to assess probabilities of technical success and market performance; calculate expected R&D value and expenditure; and combine the risk and value characteristics of individual projects to show the risk and value of the R&D portfolio.

Instruction: Major topics covered in the course are decision and risk analysis techniques to improve R&D productivity. R&D project analysis methods are explained and R&D productivity is measured. A system to prioritize R&D projects is developed to maximize the productivity of the R&D portfolio. During the seminar, a methodology will be introduced which uses influence diagrams, decision trees, probability assessment and cash flow analysis to combine technical, regulatory and market uncertainties in computing expected R&D value versus expenditure.

Credit Recommendation: In the upper division baccalaureate degree category, 1 semester hour in Improving R&D Productivity-Case Method (6/94).

Business Case: Advanced Decision Making and Risk Analysis (LBF450L)

Location: Piscataway, NJ and other locations nationwide.

Length: 40 hours (5 days).

Dates: July 1996-Present.

Objective: To teach managers the capability of preparing business cases for AT&T's most complex, high-risk ventures.

Learning Outcome: Upon successful completion of this course, the student will be able to use a variety of issue-raising approaches to examine industry structure, customer value, and competitive position; determine the appropriate membership of the decision board, project team, and subject matter experts; use a variety of strategy-generation techniques to create a wide range of alternative strategies; use the influence diagram to structure uncertainty and talk at, rather than around, the real issues; build complex cash flow models using the AIM system; assess ranges of uncertainty and probability distributions on continuous and discrete variables, recognizing dependence where appropriate; use decision tree and influence diagram software to compute the probability distributions on NPV, the value of perfect and imperfect control; communicate business case results and recommendations; and develop functional support plans, milestones and responsibility assignments, and a tracking system.

Instruction: Major topics covered in the course are in-depth decision and risk analysis training, building on the techniques learned in the prerequisite courses. Advanced business case techniques are applied to unique, complex, high-risk ventures. An appropriate graduate level project is required as part of the course for students to earn the credit recommendation.

Credit Recommendation: In the upper division baccalaureate degree category or in the graduate degree category, 2 semester hours in Advanced Decision Making and Risk Analysis (7/95).

Business Case: Business Strategy and Risk Analysis (FE0445)

Location: AT&T locations throughout the United States.

Length: 16 hours (2 days).

Dates: July 1996-Present.

Objective: To build on the basic skills developed in the course entitled "Business Case: Decision Making and Financial Analysis" and provide an overview of the AT&T Business Case Process.

Learning Outcome: Upon successful completion of this course, students will be able to understand decision quality principles and use AT&T's Business Case Process to develop quality business cases; "frame" a business case properly to raise all pertinent issues, get the participation of appropriate decision makers and staff, consider all the alternatives, and identify questions to be addressed; "analyze" various alternatives, including evaluation of information and control, to gain insight into sources of value and risk; "connect" the results of the business case to the business plan that addresses functional support, budgeting, and implementation.

Instruction: Major topics covered in the course are the AT&T Business Case Process and the principles of decision quality embedded in the process stages to build quality business cases from discovery to implementation. General instruction is given in 1) techniques for issue raising, taking into consideration the dynamics of industry structure, customer value, and competitive position; 2) techniques for creating a wide range of alternative strategies; 3) techniques for structuring and assessing uncertainty; 4) techniques for comparing and communicating opportunity versus risk; and 5) techniques for getting a shared commitment to the recommendation. Through a case study combining R&D, manufacturing and marketing decisions, participants develop a business case using the techniques taught in the course.

Credit Recommendation: In the upper division baccalaureate degree category, 1 semester hour in Strategic Planning or Analysis (12/90) (7/95).

Business Case: Decision Making and Financial Analysis (FE0400)

Location: AT&T locations throughout the United States.

Length: 24 hours (3 days).

Dates: *Version 1:* March 1990-February 1993; *Version 2:* March 1993-Present.

Objective: To teach students basic decision-making and financial analysis skills required in developing business cases and prepare them to analyze routine projects.

Learning Outcome: Upon successful completion of this course, students will be able to systematically identify decisions and critical issues in business cases; build a cash flow model, using the AT&T Investment Modeling Software (AIM) System; correctly use discounted cash flow analysis, NPV, IRR, and MOI; assess ranges of uncertainty on important variables; and conduct sensitivity analysis and present results.

Instruction: Major topics covered in the course are a systematic process to define the decision, how to identify important questions, model cash flows, assess uncertainty and risk, and conduct and interpret sensitivity analysis. These topics are integrated via two investment cases: the first, a simple tutorial example; and the second, and a potential multimillion dollar investment in cost reduction. An application project is required as part of the course for students to earn the credit recommendation.

Credit Recommendation: *Version 1:* In the upper division baccalaureate degree category, 1 semester hour in Financial Analysis (12/90). *Version 2:* In the upper division baccalaureate degree category or in the graduate degree category, 2 semester hours in Decision Making and Financial Analysis (7/95).

Business Writing (MS6520)

Location: Somerset, NJ and other AT&T locations.

Length: 24 hours (3 days).

Dates: January 1985-April 1997.

Objective: To apply the principles of contemporary business writing to the writing of letters, memos, and reports.

Learning Outcome: Upon successful completion of this course, the student will be able to apply principles of contemporary business writing to letters; set and use appropriate style in letters, reports, and memos; and use proper guidelines in writing for the signature of another person.

Instruction: Major topics covered in the course are submitting writing samples to the instructor who will critique them and give specific feedback where improvement is needed. They will also study and practice writing actual letters, memos, other documents from the AT&T environment; use a standard reference and style guide to create new documents and improve documents that were written previously.

Credit Recommendation: In the lower division baccalaureate/associate degree category, 2 semester hours in Business Communications (4/92).

Communication Workshop (MS6410)

Location: Throughout the continental United States and global locations.

Length: 21 hours (3 days).

Dates: July 1996-September 1997.

Objective: To provide the principles upon which communications are based for the student to gain knowledge and insight to communicate more effectively.

Learning Outcome: Upon successful completion of this course, the student will be able to achieve more powerful results in communication situations; use the style option that best adapts to others' styles; apply key patterns of assertiveness behavior; resolve conflict situations constructively; listen actively; and clarify both verbal and nonverbal messages.

Instruction: Major topics covered in the course are improving the students' effectiveness as managers by increasing their understanding of how their communications styles impact others' styles; how to help them develop assertiveness techniques they can use to identify and achieve their objectives as well as help them assess their conflict management skills; and sharpening the students' abilities to listen actively to verbal messages, to interpret nonverbal messages, and to clarify the intended meaning of both.

Credit Recommendation: In the lower division baccalaureate/associate degree category, or in the upper division baccalaureate degree category, 1 semester hour in Communications (12/90) (12/95).

Competitive Intelligence: Analyzing and Collecting Competitive Information (ME2022)

Location: Somerset, NJ and other AT&T locations.

Length: 21 hours (3 days).

Dates: March 1994-Present.

Objective: To have a better understanding of how to collect relevant information and effectively use it on your competitors.

Learning Outcome: Upon successful completion of this course the student will be able to gather, analyze and integrate competitive information, apply a systematic framework for developing a competitor analysis, better utilize the competitive information available within AT&T.

Instruction: Major topics covered in the course are an overview of competitor and competitive analysis, with an emphasis on those aspects of product development and marketing that are competitor driven. Students will explore how competitive information affects marketing and the product decision. They will learn how competitive analysis is done, who does it, and the role of a R&D professional. Methods of instruction include lectures and guided class discussions based on competitive analysis activities.

Credit Recommendation: In the upper division baccalaureate degree category, 2 semester hours in Competitive Intelligence (6/94).

Cost of Quality Workshop (LQM302L) [Quality Control Techniques I]

Location: Piscataway, NJ and other locations nationwide.

Length: 8 hours.

Dates: July 1996-August 1996.

Objective: To assist students in understanding data analysis as it relates to quality costs in ongoing processes.

Learning Outcome: Upon successful completion of this course, the student will be able to use Cost of Quality techniques within the context of ongoing process management; define Cost of Quality and describe the Cost of Quality identification process; identify Cost of Quality work plan, conduct data collection, and analyze Cost of Quality data.

Instruction: This course provides a hands-on application of the AT&T Cost of Quality (COQ) Guidelines. Participants will use a case to learn the COQ concepts, identify, analyze, and use data to learn how to reduce process costs. Students will gain an in-depth knowledge of the Cost of Quality Guidelines and long term cost reductions when implementing Quality initiatives.

Credit Recommendation: In the upper division baccalaureate degree category, 1 semester hour in Quality Control Techniques (8/91). **NOTE**: The credit recommendation only applies to those students who successfully complete an Implementation project or plan to be assessed by the instructor.

Creating Business Value: Workshop on EVA, CVA, and PVA (FE2020)

Location: Somerset, NJ and other AT&T locations.

Length: 16 hours (2 days).

Dates: September 1993-Present.

Objective: To teach managers techniques to create and/or improve value in three key business dimensions - customers, people and shareholders.

Learning Outcome: Upon successful completion of this course the student will be able to choose actions, behaviors and decisions that best satisfy customers, employees and shareholders - short-term and long-term, promote innovation and develop win-win supplier relationships, implement a business impact plan, to initiate a process of continuous value creation in various aspects of your job.

Instruction: Major topics covered in the course are specific techniques to be used to create or improve value in three key business dimensions - customers, people and shareholders - and connect value concepts and measures such as Economic Value Added (EVA) with specific actions, behaviors, and decisions to improve or create value in the job.

Credit Recommendation: In the upper division baccalaureate degree category, 1 semester hour in Business Value Concepts (6/94).

Cross-Cultural Effectiveness (GM1075) (Intercultural Training Seminar [GM1075]))

Location: Somerset, NJ and other AT&T locations.

Length: 16 hours (2 days).

Dates: *Version 1:* January 1989-September 1992; *Version 2:* October 1992-Present.

Objective: *Version 1:* To enable participants to develop strategies for success when working with people from other cultures. *Version 2:* To make the student aware of how cross-cultural factors impact his/her effectiveness and success when working with people from other cultures.

Learning Outcome: *Version 1:* Upon successful completion of this course, the student will be able to identify the role that cultural factors play in interpersonal interaction; identify the traits and skills necessary for success overseas; identify American values, assumptions and stereotypes and contrast these with those of other cultures; recognize potential intercultural adjustment problems and identify steps for reducing the stress and anxiety associated with working in a new culture. *Version 2:* Upon successful completion of this course, the student will be able to identify the cultural factors which facilitate or inhibit interaction; and identify specific situations where misunderstandings are likely to occur and develop a strategy to prevent these misunderstandings

Instruction: *Version 1:* Major topics covered in the course are a variety of learning strategies to facilitate instruction. Methods of instruction include simulations, videotapes, self assessments, lecturettes, group discussions, and workshops using the very latest cross-cultural research and training techniques to enable the participants to develop strategies for success when working with people from other cultures. *Version 2:* Major topics covered in the course are designed for those who require an intensive examination of the impact of cross-cultural factors on their effectiveness and success when working with people from other cultures. It includes globalization, cultural values, language insights, critical incidents, four dimensions of national cultures. Methods of instruction include case study, group role plays, lecture, and discussion. An appropriate graduate level research project is submitted as part of the course requirements.

Credit Recommendation: *Version 1:* In the upper division baccalaureate degree category, 1 semester hour in Intercultural Education or Business elective (8/91). **NOTE:** The credit recommendation applies only to those students who successfully complete a major project on intercultural issues to be assessed by the instructor. *Version 2:* In the graduate degree category, 1 semester hour in International Business (12/93).

Customer Service Calling Skills Workshop (LSS020L)

Location: Locations worldwide.

Length: 8 hours (1 day).

Dates: July 1996-August 1997.

Objective: To provide participants with the tools and techniques to enable them to gain a competitive advantage in the marketplace, elevating their companies to world class status as they differentiate themselves by delivering quality customer service.

Learning Outcome: Upon successful completion of this course, the student will be able to create a win-win partnership with customers, delight customers by anticipating their needs; soothe irate customers with specific proven techniques; and build rapport and create goodwill for future sales.

Instruction: This course will help participants communicate effectively with their customers, becoming service leaders who are capable of handling diverse and demanding customers and situations with poise and confidence. Agents will become CEO's of customer care after attending this course. They will gain practice with techniques to delight their customers and build relationships.

Credit Recommendation: In the upper division baccalaureate degree category, 1 semester hour in Sales (7/95). **NOTE:** Student must also complete LSS010L to earn the credit recommendation.

Data Requirements Analysis & Modeling (IE 2533)

Location: Piscataway, NJ and other AT&T locations.

Length: 35 hours (5 days).

Dates: July 1996-Present.

Objective: To learn and apply the principles and concepts needed to formulate an entity-relationship model for a business; and gain a full set of practical skills in all aspects of entity modeling.

Learning Outcome: Upon successful completion of this course, the student will be able to appreciate the purpose and the work involved in each state of the business system life cycle; explain the difference between requirements analysis and system engineering; describe the purpose of business requirements analysis, the different types of analysis activities involved and the relationships between these activities; identify valid entity types and relationship types for a given business scope; construct a detailed entity-relationship diagram (ERD), and make appropriate adjustments to improve the data model; understand the principles of normalization and the subsequent impact on the formation of entity types and the assignment of data elements to the entity types; assign data elements to the correct entity type based on the principles of normalization; explain the purpose and need for logical access path diagrams; and create basic logical access path diagrams for given business functions.

Instruction: Major topics covered in the course are going beyond the theory and teaches the practical application of entity modeling, self-assessment skills are developed for entity modeling (data requirements) products, a full set of practical skills in all aspects of entity modeling is gained, how to find the business's most vital objects that are the basis of object-oriented design, and develop the key skills and foundations that leverage organizational investment in CASE tools, and what an entity model illustrates about a business. Methods of instruction include a top-down, business resource-driven approach and self-assessment and practical exercises.

Credit Recommendation: In the lower division baccalaureate/associate degree category or upper division baccalaureate degree category, 2 semester hours in Organizational Analysis (9/94).

Doing Business With...(Specific Country/Region) (LBG07XL)

Location: Piscataway, NJ and other locations nationwide.

Length: 14 hours (2 days).

Dates: July 1996-April 1997.

Objective: To enable participants to feel more comfortable with cultural differences and to work and interact more effectively with the people of a specific country.

Learning Outcome: Upon successful completion of this course, the student will be able to understand key concepts of cultural behavior and the role of culture in shaping perceptions, thoughts and behavior; explore aspects of doing business with a specific country such as protocol, presentations, expectations at meetings, management styles, decision-making, work attitudes and motivation, skill transfer, boss-subordinate relations, role of business women, business entertaining and executive gift-giving; learn verbal and nonverbal communication skills for more effective communications and negotiations; identify critical points on the job where misunderstandings could occur using a problem-solving model; discuss strategies and tactics for handling these situations more effectively; gain a better understanding of the people, country and customs, as well as an understanding of the underlying political issues; and learn a few important language phrases.

Instruction: This course is designed for AT&T employees who need to understand, communicate, and interface successfully with their counterparts in a targeted country. Training will focus on cultural differences and how these impact work effectiveness. A research paper on the country studied is required for students to complete the course.

Credit Recommendation: In the lower division baccalaureate/associate degree category, 1 semester hour in Socio-cultural Aspects of Business (4/92).

Effective Strategies for Launching New Services (LMB010L)

Location: Piscataway, NJ and other locations nationwide.

Length: 16 hours.

Dates: July 1996-August 1996.

Objective: To provide AT&T managers with the skills to source, screen and evaluate new product/service ideas.

Learning Outcome: Upon successful completion of this course, the student will be able to understand the issues faced in the concept, design and development phases of the product life cycle; apply the Product Management Process during the early phases of the product life cycle; and evaluate and screen new product ideas.

Instruction: Major topic covered in the course is providing product managers with the tools to maximize their effectiveness in the search for additional sources of revenue for their products and services. Through a combination of lectures and case studies they explore methods to improve their success rate and reduce their costs.

Credit Recommendation: In the upper division baccalaureate degree category, 2 semester hours in Advanced Marketing or Business elective (8/91).

Facilitation Workshop (MS6460)

Location: All AT&T regional and international training centers and business units.

Length: 24 hours (3 days).

Dates: June 1988-Present.

Objective: To train people to facilitate quality teams.

Learning Outcome: Upon successful completion of this course the student will be able to effectively provide feedback to groups and/or individuals; recognize key indices of a team's growth and development and the actions needed to move the group forward at each stage of their development; select appropriate data gathering tools and instruments for assessing team/group development; and identify your strengths and weaknesses as a facilitator.

Instruction: Major topics covered in the course are those skills necessary to effectively facilitate groups through experiential, knowledge-based, practice, and self-awareness exercises. These experiences will involve: group and team growth and development; leadership; facilitation and intervention styles; data gathering; conflict resolution; and questioning and processing techniques.

Credit Recommendation: In the upper division baccalaureate degree category, 2 semester hours in Group Dynamics (6/94).

Finance for the Non-Finance Manager (FE0120)

Location: Somerset, NJ and other locations throughout the world.

Length: 24 hours (3 days).

Dates: July 1994-Present.

Objective: To teach both general and finance managers to use financial concepts and techniques to improve the management and profitability of their business.

Learning Outcome: Upon successful completion of this course, the student will be able to understand financial statements and utilize financial statement information to improve business performance; understand EVA concepts; apply contribution margin and break-even analysis to manage for profitability; perform activity-based costing techniques to increase profitability, productivity, and operational processes; and utilize capital budgeting and net present value analysis to accept projects that add value to the corporation.

Instruction: Major topics covered in the course are fundamentals of financial management; GAAP principles; three basic financial statement analysis; management accounting; contribution margins breakevens; time value of money; and capital budgeting. Methods of instruction include lecture, classroom exercises, and a comprehensive case study.

Credit Recommendation: In the upper division baccalaureate degree category or in the graduate degree category, 2 semester hours in Financial Management (12/94).

Financial Applications Using Excel (FM2030)

Location: Somerset, NJ and Lisle, IL.

Length: 16 hours (2 days).

Dates: July 1996-Present.

Objective: To learn to develop and utilize spreadsheets for many different financial applications, and to use sophisticated spreadsheeting techniques.

Learning Outcome: Upon successful completion of this course, the student will be able to more productively create and utilize spreadsheet programs for financial analysis; create spreadsheets to analyze financial statements, perform financial forecasts and sensitivity analyses, evaluate projects using NPV, and assess product profitability and others; utilize sophisticated spreadsheeting methods, including linking, graphing, and macros; and learn to unlock the power of EXCEL, Version 5.

Instruction: Major topics covered in the course are applications for EVA analysis; financial statement analysis; ratio analysis; financial forecasting; NPV analysis; sensitivity/what if analysis; variance analysis; pricing and break-even analysis and budgeting; and techniques for graphing, linking spreadsheets, macros, and exporting data to documents.

Credit Recommendation: In the upper division baccalaureate degree category, 1 semester hour in Financial Analysis Using Excel (12/95).

Financial Leadership Program (Module III): Taxation, Treasury, and Financial Services

Location: Basking Ridge, NJ.

Length: 75 hours (over 12 weeks).

Dates: July 1996-July 1996.

Objective: To provide students with an understanding of taxation, cash and risk management, international finance, and credit and capital management.

Learning Outcome: Upon successful completion of this course, the student will be able to demonstrate understanding of taxation issues; demonstrate understanding of key treasury functions; demonstrate knowledge of discounted cash flow analysis and the time value of money; recognize the role of Wall Street analysis, investment banks, commercial banks, and agencies; understand risk management in the area of property and casualty risks; demonstrate knowledge of the use of short term borrowing and derivatives; cash management; demonstrate understanding of managing foreign exchange exposure; understand the nature of the credit and financing industries and their associated risk; and demonstrate understanding of the concept of securitization.

Instruction: Major topics covered in the course are taxation and tax accounting; corporate finance; investment management; and cash and credit management; economics of financial services; financial services risk management; and financial services accounting. The course is delivered in three segments: Taxation 10 sessions, Treasury 9 sessions, and Financial Services 9 sessions. Methods of instruction include lecture, dialogue, team projects, homework precourse reading, and examinations.

Credit Recommendation: In the graduate degree category, 4 semester hours in Selected Topics in Financial Management: Taxation, Treasury and Financial Services, or Finance elective (5/96).

Financial Leadership Program (Module IV): Business Analysis and Decision Support

Location: Basking Ridge, NJ.

Length: 80 hours (2 weeks).

Dates: July 1996-July 1996.

Objective: To provide participants with the skills to perform financial analysis and support business decision making.

Learning Outcome: Upon successful completion of the course, the student will be able to demonstrate ability to perform financial statement analysis to support business decision making; demonstrate understanding of cost and managerial accounting for management planning and control, performance measurement, and process improvement; demonstrate knowledge of foreign exchange risk and financing; and demonstrate understanding of financial implications of common business events and decisions (PC simulation).

Instruction: Major topics covered in the course are financial statement analysis; managerial accounting issues; managing a corporation for a one-year cycle; and practicing the financial implications of business events and decisions. The class participant teams are joined by experienced marketing or manufacturing managers. Methods of instruction include problem-solving, case studies, and a PC simulation.

Credit Recommendation: In the graduate degree category, 4 semester hours in Financial Analysis and Business Decision-Making, Accounting elective, or Finance elective (5/96).

Financial Leadership Program: (Module I) Accounting and Reporting

Location: Basking Ridge, NJ.

Length: 72 hours (over 12 weeks).

Dates: July 1996-July 1996.

Objective: To provide participants with the skills to successfully perform in an accounting or reporting function in the CFO organization.

Learning Outcome: Upon successful completion of this course, the student will be able to apply appropriate accounting skills to specific business processes; demonstrate knowledge of the effects of regulatory, economic, legal, and political events on accounting and reporting policies and processes; understand the role the CFO community plays in supporting business decisions; appropriately respond to external shareholders and agencies; recognize the need for appropriate controls and technology to insure the welfare of corporate assets and information; and understand contemporary financial issues and their impact upon the corporation.

Instruction: Major topics covered in the course are supporting business opportunities; performance evaluation; current finance issues; control issues; and accounting for specific business processes. Methods of instruction include lecture, dialogue, team assignments and in-class presentations, precourse reading, homework, quizzes, and examinations.

Credit Recommendation: In the graduate degree category, 4 semester hours in Accounting and Financial Reporting or Accounting elective (5/96).

Financial Leadership Program: (Module II): Managing Risk

Location: Basking Ridge, NJ.

Length: 67 hours (over 12 weeks).

Dates: July 1996-July 1996.

Objective: To provide participants with the skills to successfully perform in a risk or internal control function and to demonstrate knowledge of the importance of risk management for all managers.

Learning Outcome: Upon successful completion of this course, the student will be able to apply appropriate risk assessment activities to business functions; understand internal control objectives; apply knowledge of the audit process to a case study; and understand the role of financial security within the greater corporate community.

Instruction: Major topics covered in the course are control theory and audit process methodology and application related to the following significant business processes; information management, financial reporting, billing, payments, and security and network reliability. An on-site visit to observe control activities is completed and documented. Methods of instruction include lecture, dialogue, team and individual assignments, precourse reading, flowcharting, case study analysis, quizzes, and examinations.

Credit Recommendation: In the graduate degree category, 4 semester hours in Internal Auditing and Control or Accounting elective (5/96).

Financial Statement Analysis (FE0200)

Location: Somerset, NJ and other AT&T locations.

Length: 16 hours (2 days).

Dates: April 1994-Present.

Objective: To give managers an understanding of financial statements and reports.

Learning Outcome: Upon successful completion of this course the student will be able to understand accounting and financial statement principles, processes and influences; analyze a variety of financial statements; analyze corporate performance and financial conditions using ratios; read and understand AT&T financial reports.

Instruction: Major topics covered in the course are financial statements and reports including an analysis of various case studies.

Credit Recommendation: In the upper division baccalaureate degree category, 1 semester hour in Financial Statement Analysis (6/94).

Function Analysis Workshop (IE 2535)

Location: Piscataway, NJ and other AT&T locations.

Length: 32 hours (5 days).

Dates: June 1991-Present.

Objective: To learn and apply the principles, concepts, and skills needed to bound, partition and home-in on specific, logical, functional needs.

Learning Outcome: Upon successful completion of this course, the student will be able to explain the purpose and results of business requirements analysis; describe, contrast and list the basic specification components of each of the six building blocks of even and function analysis; explain the purpose, the work involved, and the products that are created in each of the major activities in event and function analysis; describe what an analysis scope represents; discover and validate interfaces for a given scope of analysis; explain the significance and characteristics of processes; identify and differentiate various types of business events for a given analysis scope, allocate the events to processes and functions; subdivide a process for a given scope of analysis into appropriately shaped/sized business functions; apply the criteria to ensure that the business functions are leveled to elementary; explain the purpose, the relevant supporting analysis work products, and the principles which apply to analysis data flow diagrams; and build an analysis data flow diagram, given relevant event and function analysis products.

Instruction: Major topics covered in this course teach the basic skills and knowledge needed to perform event and function analysis. Case study activities include bounding the business scope, recognizing and correlating business events, interfaces and processes, decomposing functions to the elementary level, and defining function precedence via data flow diagrams; and function analysis techniques (as they would be applied to new system development, prior to a solution being determined or designed) are also covered.

Credit Recommendation: In the upper division baccalaureate degree category, 2 semester hours in Organizational Processes (9/94).

Function Point Workshop (IE1660)

Location: Piscataway, NJ and other Lucent locations.

Length: 16 hours (2 days).

Dates: July 1996-Present.

Objective: To enable participants to estimate the development time of a system or application.

Learning Outcome: Upon successful completion of this course, the student will be able to recognize the components necessary for a function point analysis; perform a function point analysis on a new and continuing development application; complete all the worksheets, forms and calculations necessary to achieve an accurate function point count for each application; and apply the 4.0 methodology based on instructor-led examples and more comprehensive case exercises.

Instruction: Major topics covered in the course are a methodology of measurement which is used to estimate the development time of a system, application, or project; and measure the productivity and quality of such applications. Methods of instruction include classroom discussion, lecture, and lab.

Credit Recommendation: In the upper division baccalaureate degree category, 1 semester hour in Business Administration or Computer Information Systems (7/90) (10/96). **NOTE**: To receive the credit recommendation, an examination must be given and passed by the student.

Fundamental Legal Concepts of Global Procurement (GP1020)

Location: All AT&T training locations in the U.S.

Length: 16 hours (2 days).

Dates: June 1994-December 1996.

Objective: To prepare the student to practice up-to-date skills as they relate to the ever-changing legal concept of Global Procurement.

Learning Outcome: Upon successful completion of this course, the student will be able to understand terminology and specifications of UCC; understand the basics and usage of contracts; define major clauses, e.g., warranty, insurance; understand intellectual property; and execute a model contract.

Instruction: Major topics covered in the course are the elements of contracts and their applicability to global business practice.

Credit Recommendation: In the upper division baccalaureate degree category, 1 semester hour in Fundamentals of Global Contracts Law (7/95).

Fundamentals of Marketing (SA4060) (Formerly Fundamentals of Modern Marketing (SA4060))

Location: AT&T locations nationwide.

Length: *Version 1:* 36 hours (1 week); *Version 2:* 24 hours (3 days); *Version 3:* 16 hours (2 days).

Dates: *Version 1:* January 1983-December 1990; *Version 2:* January 1991-December 1995: *Version 3:* July 1996-Present.

Objective: To provide new marketing personnel and those from related areas with the principles and concepts which they will need to manage effectively in their new environment.

Learning Outcome: Upon successful completion of this course, the student will be able to identify and describe the challenges, activities and institutions involved in managing marketing process; analyze the dynamic relationship between marketing and its environment; identify and explain the major elements of the marketing program; and develop a strategic approach for capitalizing on marketing opportunities.

Instruction: Major topics covered in the course are a general overview of the marketing process as it relates to service marketing, and an overview of those marketing principles needed to function effectively in Lucent's new marketing environment. Methods of instruction include case studies, guest lectures, and relevant current literature.

Credit Recommendation: *Versions 1 and 2:* In the upper division baccalaureate degree category, 2 semester hours in Introduction to Marketing (9/84) (8/91). *Version 3:* In the upper division baccalaureate degree category, 1 semester hour in Fundamentals of Marketing (5/96).

Fundamentals of Marketing Research (ME 0955)

Location: Somerset, NJ, and other AT&T locations throughout the country.

Length: *Version 1:* 40 hours (5 days); *Version 2:* 24 hours (3 days).

Dates: *Version 1:* January 1986-April 1993; *Version 2:* May 1993-Present.

Objective: *Version 1:* To acquaint students with methodologies of marketing research and measurement. *Version 2:* To give participants an overview of all aspects of marketing research.

Learning Outcome: *Version 1:* Upon successful completion of this course, the student will be able to list the considerations in selecting appropriate research strategies; recognize the various data collection techniques and identify the strengths and weaknesses of each; describe the basic data analysis procedures and their proper application; translate marketing research findings into management recommendations regarding applications to forecasting, market segmentation, and product innovation decision making; and effectively organize and communicate marketing research findings and recommendations. *Version 2:* Upon successful completion of this course, the student will be able to identify and solve common marketing research design problems and describe the basic analysis procedures and their proper application and translate marketing research findings into management recommendations. An appropriate graduate level research project is submitted as part of the course requirements.

Instruction: *Version 1:* Major topics covered in the course are an introduction to marketing research for individuals conducting research projects, managing the marketing research function, or making decisions based on study results. *Version 2:* Major topics covered in the course are an end-to-end overview of the marketing research process from research problem definition and design through sampling, survey methods, and data analysis; and how to choose the right marketing research design to meet objectives and avoid common marketing research problems. Methods of instruction include lecture and objectives.

Credit Recommendation: *Version 1:* In the upper division baccalaureate degree category, 3 semester hours in Fundamentals of Marketing Research or in the graduate degree category, 2 semester hours (11/86) (8/91). *Version 2:* In the graduate degree category, 2 semester hours in Fundamentals of Marketing Research (12/93).

Fundamentals of New Product Development (ME2010) (Formerly ME2003)

Location: Somerset, NJ. and other AT&T locations.

Length: 16 hours.

Dates: June 1989-August 1996.

Objective: To provide AT&T managers with the skills to source, screen and evaluate new product/service ideas.

Learning Outcome: Upon successful completion of this course, the student will be able to understand the issues faced in the concept, design, and development phases of the product life cycle; apply the Product Management Process during the early phases of the product life cycle; and evaluate and screen new product ideas.

Instruction: Major topics covered in the course provide product managers with the tools to maximize their effectiveness in the search for additional sources of revenue for their products and services; and examine the steps involved in developing an overall new business strategy and learning how to write a Product Innovation Charter (PIC). Methods of instruction include through lectures and case studies exploring methods to improve their success rate and reduce their costs.

Credit Recommendation: In the upper division baccalaureate degree category, 2

semester hours in Advanced Marketing or Business elective (8/91).

Fundamentals of Purchasing (PR5051)

Location: All AT&T training locations in the U.S.

Length: 24 hours (3 days).

Dates: July 1996-Present.

Objective: To provide a broad-based overview of the responsibilities and tools of purchasing management.

Learning Outcome: Upon successful completion of this course, the student will be able to understand the procurement environment, manage procurement personnel, manage cost and price analysis inventory, select and manage suppliers, understand competitive bidding and negotiation, and understand financial and value analysis.

Instruction: Major topics covered in the course are concepts, including opportunities and challenges of purchasing; managing purchasing responsibilities; legal concepts of purchasing; analytical tools for purchasers; sources of supply, bidding, and negotiation; introduction to contracts; code of conduct; standard clauses; and supplier quality management. Methods of instruction include classroom instruction and an appropriate graduate level project is required to earn the graduate credit recommendation.

Credit Recommendation: In the upper division baccalaureate degree category, 2 semester hours in Purchasing Management or in the graduate degree category, 1 semester hour in Purchasing Management (12/95).

Fundamentals of the UNIX Operating System for Programmers (UC1080)

Location: Piscataway, NJ and other Lucent locations.

Length: *Version 1:* 24 hours; *Version 2:* 32 hours (1 week).

Dates: *Version 1:* January 1987-December 1993; *Version 2:* July 1996-Present.

Objective: To introduce programmers to the fundamentals of the UNIX Operating System.

Learning Outcome: Upon successful completion of this course, the student will be able to use the UNIX System User's Manual to locate commands by name or description and recognize syntax conventions; use the UNIX system's basic commands; communicate with other users of the system; create lists and manipulate files and directories; use the UNIX system full screen editor -"vi"; use file generation characters; and name features included in the UNIX system.

Instruction: Major topics covered in the course are basic UNIX operating system characteristics; accessing a UNIX system; the Shell command language architecture; the hierarchical file system; the UNIX system full screen editor - "vi"; Interuser communications; using the UNIX system documentation; and a summary of the UNIX system features. Methods of instruction include classroom discussion, lecture, and lab.

Credit Recommendation: *Version 1:* In the lower division baccalaureate/associate degree category, 1 semester hour in UNIX Fundamentals, Computer Science, or Data Processing (7/90) **NOTE**: If a student has taken UC1070, this course duplicates the information and no credit will be given. *Version 2:* In the upper division baccalaureate degree category, 1 semester hour in Computer Information Systems (lecture) and 1 semester hour in Computer Information Systems (lab), for a total of 2 semester hours (10/96). **NOTE**: To receive the credit recommendation, an examination must be given and passed by the student.

Fundamentals of UNIX Operating System for Users (UC1070)

Location: Piscataway, NJ and other Lucent locations.

Length: *Version 1:* 30 hours; *Version 2:* 40 hours (1 week).

Dates: *Version 1:* January 1987 February 1993; *Version 2:* July 1996-Present.

Objective: To provide users with an introduction to the fundamentals of UNIX Operating Systems.

Learning Outcome: Upon successful completion of this course, the student will be able to gain access (logon) to the UNIX system; send and manage UNIX system mail; control the input and output of commands; use redirection and pipelining; use the UNIX System V User reference manual to obtain information about new commands; locate and use files on the UNIX file system; use the "vi" editor to create and change text files; crete a profile file to customize one's login environment; and print the contents of text files and directories.

Instruction: Major topics covered in the course are the file system hierarchy; commonly used UNIX system commands; the UNIX system editor - "vi"; shell programming; and communicating with and transferring files to other UNIX systems. Methods of instruction include class lectures and hands-on exercises.

Credit Recommendation: In the lower division baccalaureate/associate degree category, 2 semester hours in UNIX Fundamentals, Computer Science, or Data Processing (7/90) (10/96). **NOTE**: If student has already completed UC1080, then student will receive only 1 semester hour because of content overlap. To receive the credit recommendation, an examination must be given and passed by the student.

Global Business Fundamentals (GM1000) (Formerly Elements of Global Business (GM1000))

Location: AT&T locations worldwide.

Length: 16 hours (2 days).

Dates: July 1996-Present.

Objective: To give participants a general understanding of global business, touching on finance, marketing, competition, and cultural difference issues.

Learning Outcome: Upon successful completion of this course, the student will be able to develop skills and attitudes needed to be effective in a global business environment; identify factors such as income, populations, market potential, and competition that will influence global strategy development; understand the development stages of a global business; understand the implication of global competition and the globalization of industries; identify company winners and losers in global competition and the lessons and implications for your LOB; and formulate a market entry strategy for AT&T in a large, high potential developing country.

Instruction: Major topics covered in the course are competition, finance, marketing, cross-cultural communications, product management, and international and global business issues essential to succeed in the global marketplace. Methods of instruction include lecture, discussion, and a graduate level research project.

Credit Recommendation: In the graduate degree category, 1 semester hour in International Business (12/94).

Human Factors in Computer Systems (IE1002)

Location: Piscataway, NJ and other Lucent locations.

Length: 95 hours (15 days over 3 months).

Dates: July 1996-Present.

Objective: To provide the base education needed to perform Human Factors activities.

Learning Outcome: Upon successful completion of this course, the student will be able to make and support Human Factors decisions and recommendations; conduct research in the various subtopics within Human Factors; perform various analysis techniques required to produce HF products; analyze error rates and costs; design dialog, command language, codes, and error messages; critique the effectiveness of various forms of user documentation for specific use; evaluate screens and forms and make recommendations for improvements; conduct experiments to evaluate problem situations; and apply ergonomic principles to work station design.

Instruction: Major topics covered in the course are basic human information processing principles and how to apply the results to design activities. Methods of instruction include experiments, and testing.

Credit Recommendation: In the graduate degree category, 3 semester hours in Industrial Engineering, Computer Science, or Computer Information Systems (7/85) (7/90) (10/96). **NOTE**: To receive the credit recommendation, an examination must be given and passed by the student.

Human Factors Usability Design Strategies (IE1001)

Location: Piscataway, NJ and other Lucent locations.

Length: 24.25 hours.

Dates: July 1996-Present.

Objective: To teach system developers the issues and problems affecting the usability of computer systems.

Learning Outcome: Upon successful completion of this course, the student will be able to identify how and when human factors methods and techniques can be applied throughout the development cycle to increase the accuracy, speed, and acceptance of systems; demonstrate the cost benefits of greater usability in systems and conduct cost/benefit analyses; and design systems which conform to users' psychological, physical and physiological requirements and limits, based on human factors research.

Instruction: Major topics covered in the course are identification of human performance problems and issues related to user documentation, training, and help systems; hardware ergonomics issues and the effect of the physical environment on human performance in systems; demonstrates how to conduct simple human factors tests and studies for evaluating and measuring human performance of individual system functions; and identifies sources of information for further study and research. Methods of instruction include lecture and collaborative learning formats.

Credit Recommendation: In the upper division baccalaureate degree category, 1 semester hour in Systems (7/90) (10/96). **NOTE**: To receive the credit recommendation, an examination must be given and passed by the student.

Human Performance Engineering (IE1004)

Location: Piscataway, NJ, and other AT&T locations.

Length: 28 hours (4 days).

Dates: September 1982-December 1985.

Objective: To introduce the participant to the principles and techniques of human factors issues in the design and selection of work procedures, work stations, control panels, and office layout.

Learning Outcome: Upon successful completion of this course, the student will be able to discuss the evolution of the human performance engineering field; discuss human factor considerations within each phase of the system development process; identify factors affecting human performance; use anthropometric data charts; and develop a preliminary design for a manual work station and office layout using human factor principles.

Credit Recommendation: In the upper division baccalaureate degree category, 1 semester hour in Business Administration or Industrial Engineering (7/85).

Information Mapping, Structured Writing (IE1202)

Location: Piscataway, NJ and other Lucent locations.

Length: *Version 1:* 24 hours; *Version 2:* 18 hours.

Dates: *Version 1:* June 1980-December 1995; *Version 2:* July 1996-Present.

Objective: To teach participants to use this systematic method (Information Mapping) which makes writing simple, clear, more efficient and more effective.

Learning Outcome: Upon successful completion of this course, the student will be able to describe Information Mapping Structured Writing; write and edit a training unit according to the course standards; write and edit basic and supplementary types of maps; identify good applications of the structured writing methods; and survey other aspects of this approach, i.e., memos and reports.

Instruction: Major topics covered in the course are a modular way of organizing and presenting written materials and a carefully-structured format combining simple graphics and words. Methods of instruction include classroom discussion, lecture, and collaborative learning.

Credit Recommendation: *Version 1:* In the lower division baccalaureate/associate degree category, 2 semester hours in Business or Managerial Communications (7/85) (7/90). *Version 2:* In the upper division baccalaureate degree category, 1 semester hour in Business or Managerial Communications (10/96). **NOTE**: To receive the credit recommendation, an examination must be given and passed by the student.

Instructional Design and Development Workshop (TD0930) (Formerly Course QL0303)

Location: Morristown, NJ and other AT&T locations throughout the country.

Length: *Version 1:* 40 hours (5 days); *Version 2:* 32 hours (4 days).

Dates: *Version 1:* October 1984-June 1988; *Version 2:* July 1988-Present.

Objective: *Version 1:* To provide the new course developer with the knowledge and skills needed to design courses successfully and effectively. *Version 2:* To enable employees to demonstrate effective skills to design and develop courses that reflect sound learner-centered instructional principles and methods that support learning and retention.

Learning Outcome: *Version 1:* Upon successful completion of this course, the student will be able to describe techniques to determine performance problems; gather and analyze data about job tasks; determine what skills and knowledge should be taught; choose the instructional strategies, methods and media for the course; describe the balanced instruction technique; and describe learning styles and how they relate to the instructional design and development process. *Version 2:* Upon successful completion of this course, the student will be able to identify the major phases of the systematic training development model, as well as the purpose and outputs of each phase; identify the major cost and time variables associated with course development; demonstrate methods for determining performance problems and opportunities; demonstrate methods for performing task analysis and skill, knowledge derivation; demonstrate how to derive and write performance related objectives and test items; define and develop learning strategies and methods appropriate for different learning outcomes; and demonstrate techniques for evaluating course materials.

Instruction: *Version 1:* Major topics covered in the course are the fundamental principles of instructional design, as presented in a four (4) step model; practical application of the model and its underlying principles are as students design and develop a training package; and students will study task analysis, needs analysis and job analysis. Methods of instruction include precourse materials two weeks prior to the class and must be completed before class begins. No prior teaching experience is required. *Version 2:* Major topics covered in the course are fundamental principles of instructional design; practical application of the systematic development process and its underlying principles are emphasized and practiced.

Credit Recommendation: *Version 1:* In the upper division baccalaureate degree category, 3 semester hours in Instructional Design and Development (for those students who do not already possess a baccalaureate degree) or in the graduate degree category, 3 semester hours in Instructional Design and Development (for those students who already possess a baccalaureate degree or above) or (1/87). *Version 2:* In the upper division baccalaureate degree category, 3 semester hours in Instructional Design and Development (7/93).

Instructor Skills Practicum (TD0910)

Location: Morristown, NJ and other AT&T locations throughout the country.

Length: 24 hours (3 days).

Dates: February 1991-June 1997.

Objective: To enable subject competent employees to demonstrate effective teaching skills reflecting appropriate learning principles, instructional methods and techniques that facilitate learning.

Learning Outcome: Upon successful completion of this course, the student will be able to identify and practice using principles of learning and the application of adult learning theory; describe and demonstrate classroom motivational strategies to ensure interesting and challenging instructional delivery; practice introducing, managing, and debriefing group and team exercises; demonstrate effective questioning techniques, experiential learning strategies and proper use of instructional media; and describe how to deal with disruptive student behaviors and classroom conflicts.

Instruction: Major topics covered in the course are an intensive three-day workshop designed to help students develop instructional delivery skills through practice; students are encouraged to take risks,incorporate new teaching strategies and skills into their teaching repertoires, and then receive precise and constructive feedback on performance from a skilled master trainer as well as "instructor" peers. Methods of instruction include structured videotaped practice sessions.

Credit Recommendation: In the upper division baccalaureate degree category, 2 semester hours in Instructor Skills Methods (7/93).

Instructor Training Workshop (TD0911) (Formerly Basic Instructor Skills (QL0101-A)

Location: Morristown, NJ and other AT&T locations throughout the country.

Length: *Version 1:* 28 hours (4 days); *Version 2:* 40 hours (5 days).

Dates: *Version 1:* September 1985-June 1988; *Version 2:* July 1988-Present.

Objective: To enable subject competent employees to demonstrate effective teaching skills reflecting appropriate learning principles, instructional methods and techniques that facilitate learning.

Learning Outcome: *Version 1:* Upon successful completion of this course, the student will be able to describe the four learning styles and implications of those styles for instructing; explain the 3-step intervention process for handling problem situations in the classroom; explain the ARCS model of motivation and major strategies for stimulating desire to learn; demonstrate effective techniques for giving and receiving feedback; and demonstrate the effective use of questioning skills and presentation skills as major tools for enhancing learning. *Version 2:* Upon successful completion of this course, the student will be able to identify and apply sound learner-centered principles of instruction that support learning; describe and demonstrate classroom motivational strategies to ensure interesting and challenging instructional delivery; identify instructional factors that promote (and hinder) student interaction and learning; identify and apply classroom delivery behaviors that support and enhance instructor credibility; describe instructor preparation strategies; demonstrate effective questioning techniques, experiential learning strategies and proper use of instructional media; and describe how to deal with disruptive student behaviors and classroom conflicts.

Instruction: *Version 1:* Major topics covered in the course are various concepts and skills for effective stand-up instruction and participative student-centered lecture; and the 3-step intervention process and uses the ARCS model of motivation. Methods of instruction include students preparing and delivering two 20-minute balanced instruction lectures, instructor observation, an instructor skills inventory and quizzes. *Version 2:* Major topics covered in the course are learning principles, instructional methods, and techniques that facilitate learning; and also practice in the planning and delivery of instructional sessions to demonstrate newly acquired skills.

Credit Recommendation: *Version 1:* In the upper division baccalaureate degree category, 2 semester hours in Basic Instructor Skills (1/87). *Version 2:* In the upper division baccalaureate degree category, 3 semester hours in Basic Instructor Skills (7/93).

Integrated Marketing and Financial Strategies (SA4500) (Formerly Financial Applications in Marketing Achieving Customer and Investor Satisfaction)

Location: Somerset Seminars Center, Somerset, NJ.

Length: *Version 1:* 21 hours (3 days); *Version 2:* 24 hours (3 days).

Dates: *Version 1:* October 1985-February 1993; *Version 2:* March 1993-Present.

Objective: *Version 1:* To acquaint students with the role of financial analysis in marketing. *Version 2:* To use financial and market measures to evaluate strategic and tactical marketing alternatives and make decisions, and to understand the bottom line impact of these decisions.

Learning Outcome: Upon successful completion of this course, the student will be able to use an integrated spreadsheet program to model the costs and benefits of specific programs; translate your marketing strategies into specific tactics and objectives; for example, awareness, CVA, repeat consumption, and market volume share; and accurately measure the impact of your marketing decisions using specific financial and marketing metrics, including variable contribution/margin, EVA, market share, and net present value.

Instruction: Major topics covered in the course are strategic alternatives in the areas of promotion, price, and distribution as related to the marketing of products and services; the role of financial analysis in the control of marketing mix decisions; how to assess the bottom-line impact of your strategic and tactical marketing decisions; a review the financial and market measure used to determine the impact decisions have; and learn to calculate the costs and benefits of alternative marketing strategies and tactics. An appropriate graduate level project is included as part of the course requirement for students to earn credit recommendation.

Credit Recommendation: *Version 1:* In the upper division baccalaureate degree category or in the graduate degree category, 1 semester hour in Marketing (11/85). *Version 2:* In the upper division baccalaureate degree category or in the graduate degree category, 1 semester hour in Integrated Marketing Strategies (7/95). **NOTE:** An appropriate graduate level project is included as part of the course requirement for students to earn credit recommendation.

Introduction to Accounting (FE0100)

Location: AT&T locations throughout the United States.

Length: 21 hours (3 days).

Dates: July 1996-Present.

Objective: To teach students the basic principles of accounting and the six-step accounting process.

Learning Outcome: Upon successful completion of this course, students will be able to explain basic accounting concepts; define the accounting process; match AT&T main accounts to the appropriate categories on AT&T financial reports; describe the balance sheet equation; record written financial transactions in T-accounts, journal entries, and post and balance ledger accounts; prepare trial balance worksheet; perform closing process; and develop financial statements.

Instruction: Major topics covered in the course include an introduction to T-accounts, discussion of recording financial transactions, posting and balancing worksheets, and culminates with the preparation of financial statements.

Credit Recommendation: In the upper division baccalaureate degree category, 1 semester hour in Introduction to Accounting (12/90) (7/95).

Introduction to Basic Statistics (SE6000)
(Formerly Basic Statistics [SE6000])

Location: AT&T locations nationwide.

Length: 21 hours (3 days).

Dates: July 1996-July 1996.

Objective: To provide the student with an understanding of basic statistics; to improve the quality of communication between AT&T statisticians and their clients.

Learning Outcome: Upon successful completion of this course, the student will be able to apply statistics in daily work environments to improve productivity; use statistics to improve data gathering and evaluation techniques; and use statistical terminology with subject matter experts to bridge the communication gap.

Instruction: Major topics covered in the course are probability and statistics at the most basic level; measures of central tendency (mean, median, mode); measures of variability (variance, standard deviation); random variables; continuous and discrete probability distributions; binomial distribution and normal distribution; concepts of sampling distributions; confidence intervals; sampling theory; language of statistics and how to communicate effectively with statisticians.

Credit Recommendation: In the upper division baccalaureate degree category, 2 semester hours in Statistics (8/91) (5/96).

Introduction to Budgeting Workshop (LBF108L)

Location: Piscataway, NJ and other locations nationwide.

Length: 16 hours (2 days).

Dates: July 1996-Present.

Objective: To learn the purpose and principles of budgeting and how to develop, implement and manage a budget in AT&T.

Learning Outcome: Upon successful completion of this course, the student will be able to understand the budgeting process; develop, implement, and manage a budget for your business unit using a spreadsheet or budget software program; pinpoint budget variances, analyze budget vs. actual results and recommend solutions to problems; and use a budget as a managerial tool to achieve corporate/business unit objectives, improve profitability and cash flow.

Instruction: Major topics covered in the course are the principles of budgeting, the structure of a budgeting report, master budget and operational/financial budgets, how to evaluate financial results, budget preparation and capital assets, how to manage a budget, variances: Budget vs. Actual, and recommend solutions. Students will apply the concepts in hands-on exercises using a manual spreadsheet and AT&T sample budget forms.

Credit Recommendation: In the upper division baccalaureate degree category, 1 semester hour in Financial Management: Budgeting (12/95).

Introduction to Finance (FE0101)

Location: Somerset, NJ, and other AT&T regional facilities.

Length: 16 hours (2 days).

Dates: July 1996-Present.

Objective: To introduce basic financial concepts, including the components of financial statements by allowing the student to construct his/ her personal financial position and cash flow statement.

Learning Outcome: Upon successful completion of this course, the student will be able to use data from personal experience and the Balance Sheet Equation, identify an asset and its component parts and the two categories of liabilities; given interest tables and the "Rule of 72," describe the concept Time Value of Money; provided with cash expenditures data and the categories of revenues and expenses, accurately develop a pro forma cash flow statement; given examples of financial statements and their components, identify and describe the elements of a corporate financial statement; use personal financial concepts developed in the program, correctly relate the concepts developed in a financial environment; and using financial reports and ratios, interpret the reports using ratios to make financial decisions.

Instruction: This course is for students with little or no background in finance. Students will learn the concept of compound interest and apply it to the theory of time value of money. They will also learn how to apply personal financial concepts to corporate finance to better understand the components of financial reports and analysis. Other topics include Wall Street, income tax, and financing a business.

Credit Recommendation: In the upper division baccalaureate degree category, 1 semester hour in Introduction to Finance (12/90) (7/95).

Introduction to Manufacturing SPC (MF3405)
(Formerly Introduction to SPC)

Location: Various locations.

Length: 36 hours (5 days).

Dates: *Version 1:* June 1988-December 1992: *Version 2:* July 1996-Present.

Objective: To teach statistical process control techniques for use in manufacturing environments.

Learning Outcome: Upon successful completion of this course, the student will be able to use scatter plots, frequency distributions, cause and effect diagrams, pareto and box-and-whisker charts and defect concentration; calculate the centerline and control limits for variables and attributes control charts, plot the charts, identify out-of-control conditions; know when to apply attributes or variables control charts; calculate the coefficient of correlation, the coefficient determination, and the regression equation for a set of data; use analysis f means and test of hypotheses to compare groups of data; and discuss the applications of statistically designed experiments.

Instruction: Major topics covered in the course are an overview of statistical process control methods for manufacturing professionals; the application of statistical tools to control a process and how to assess changes in process; and how to use SQC Troubleshooter to analyze data. The course is presented on a level suitable for engineers. Methods of instruction include classroom discussion, lecture, and simulation.

Credit Recommendation: *Version 1:* In the upper division baccalaureate degree category, 3 semester hours in Statistical Methods for Quality Control or Statistical Quality Control (10/91). *Version 2:* In the upper division baccalaureate degree category, 2 semester hours in Statistical Methods for Quality Control or Statistical Quality Control (10/96). **NOTE**: To earn the credit recommendation, students must successfully complete the specified examination, or an independent project utilizing appropriate statistical process control techniques.

Introduction to Project Management (MS6310)

Location: AT&T locations throughout the United States.

Length: 24 hours (3 days).

Dates: *Version 1:* January 1988-December 1992; *Version 2:* January 1993-Present.

Objective: *Version 1:* To provide participants with the basic concepts, techniques, and tools to plan, schedule, organize, implement, and control projects. *Version 2:* To provide concepts, tools, and techniques to plan, schedule, organize and implement projects to enable students to better manage projects instead of projects managing them.

Learning Outcome: *Version 1:* Upon successful completion of this course, the student will be able to define project management and its phases in terms of an information systems model; describe the characteristics of effective project managers and team members; plan, organize, monitor, and control a project using a work breakdown structure and an analysis of critical and high-risk factors; use several scheduling techniques, develop an activity network diagram, and calculate the critical path and slack for activities; describe the uses of project management personal computer software and the types of outputs that can be generated for all phases of a project; and describe how team building, managing differences, and personal style can affect team and interpersonal effectiveness and the strategies that can be used to improve them. *Version 2:* Upon successful completion of this course, the student will be able to develop a step-by-step process to plan, organize, monitor and control a project; determine the life cycle of a project and what must be done at each stage; identify the characteristics, roles and responsibilities of the project manager; and to introduce and provide practical application of the principles and concepts of the Project Management Institute Body of Knowledge (PMBOK).

Instruction: *Version 1:* Major topics covered in the course are a number of behavioral and organizational issues associated with projects. These topics can help both project team members and team leaders to get the right expected level of quality. *Version 2:* Major topics covered in the course are designed for students managing projects or members of a project team. It includes project management, project planning, scheduling and budget, monitoring and controlling, using PC software for project management, and project teams. Methods of instruction include lecture and discussion.

Credit Recommendation: *Version 1:* In the upper division baccalaureate degree category, 1 semester hour in Introduction to Project Management (12/90). *Version 2:* In the upper division baccalaureate degree category, 2 semester hours in Project Management (12/93).

Leadership for the Future: a Principle-Centered Leadership-Based Model (MD7603) (Formerly Leadership for the Future [MD7603])

Location: Worldwide with AT&T/Lucent Technologies.

Length: 32 hours (4 days).

Dates: July 1996-Present.

Objective: To stimulate personal and organizational development, increase the levels of trust in the workplace and create an awareness around leadership development.

Learning Outcome: Major topics covered in the course are the critical role of all managers and how they can positively impact their organization, mission, and strategy by exercising judgment; initiative and leadership behaviors; and the concepts of "Principle-Centered Leadership", this approach translates into greater organizational unity, interpersonal flexibility, and personal productivity. Students also need to submit an application project.

Instruction: Upon successful completion of this course, the student will be able to identify the principles through which lasting and effective leadership is developed, and assess how their current behaviors relate to these principles; state how applying these principles foster the development of the Dimension of Leadership; develop unity in their organization or work team around a commonly shared mission and values; establish a foundation around mission and values as a way of productively preparing the work team/organization for change; cultivate trust, strength, and desire in work group members to be proactive and take risks; manage interpersonal conflicts in a courageous yet collaborative manner; maximize group members' individual contribution while nurturing their personal satisfaction and development; and develop plans for assessing their progress, as well as a work group's progress, towards fulfilling the mission of the organization.

Credit Recommendation: In the lower division baccalaureate/associate degree or in the upper division baccalaureate degree category, 2 semester hours in Leadership Principles, Management, or Human Resources (12/90) (5/96).

Leading Performance Improvement Teams (MQ6012) (Formerly Quality Improvement Team Leader Workshop [MQ6012])

Location: Somerset, NJ and other AT&T locations.

Length: 24 hours (3 days).

Dates: February 1992-April 1997.

Objective: To give quality improvement team leaders a practical workshop dealing with the issues they will face as a team facilitator.

Learning Outcome: Upon successful completion of this course, the student will be able to lead a quality improvement team using QIC, QIS, or PQMI methodology; and acquire the facilitation skills needed to manage effectively in a team oriented improvement process.

Instruction: Major topics covered in the course are practical workshops using exercises and role plays to establish facilitation skills essential to success as a team leader. Methods of instruction include role plays and an application project at the graduate level to complete the course.

Credit Recommendation: In the graduate degree category, 2 semester hours in Group Dynamics (4/92).

Managing Conflict (LBL431L) (Formerly Managing Conflict and Differences [MS6431])

Location: Somerset, NJ and other AT&T locations.

Length: 16 hours (2 days).

Dates: January 1992-April 1997.

Objective: To provide a framework for identifying, surfacing, clarifying and resolving systematic and interpersonal types of conflict.

Learning Outcome: Upon successful completion of this course, the student will be able to apply a framework for identifying, surfacing, clarifying and resolving systematic conflict; and increase your set of behaviors to use in conflict to avoid getting stuck, losing altogether or annihilating your "adversary."

Instruction: Major topics covered in the course are interpersonal and organizational conflict presentation, experiential exercises, small group discussion, and practice sessions; summary of feedback on their current conflict style from co-workers of their choice; feedback will be basis of an action plan for back-on-the-job application of the new behaviors learned in the workshop; and students must submit a graduate level research project to earn the graduate credit recommendation.

Credit Recommendation: In the graduate degree category, 1 semester hour in Conflict Management (4/92).

Managing Emerging Technologies (IE1623)

Location: Piscataway, NJ and various other locations nationwide.

Length: 12 hours (2 days).

Dates: January 1994-Present.

Objective: To identify recent advances in the information technology industry, the organizational dynamics of their adoption and their impact on Project Management.

Learning Outcome: Upon successful completion of this course, the student will be able to understand and manage the organizational issues of emerging technology adoption; recognize and evaluate emerging technologies; understand and manage the effect of technical issues on system development; building the system right; understand the management of a project when emerging technologies are involved; and plan for implementing new technologies and management philosophies.

Instruction: Major topics covered in the course are identifying recent advances in the information technology industry and their impact on organizations and project management and future technologies and their impact on current usage are defined, including their effect on the project life cycle.

Credit Recommendation: In the graduate degree category, 1 semester hour in Managing Change (6/95). **NOTE:** In order for the student to receive this credit recommendation the student must also complete IE1620.

Managing Human Performance in the Information Systems Environment (IE1103)

Location: Piscataway, NJ and other AT&T locations.

Length: 12 hours (2 days).

Dates: December 1986-October 1991.

Objective: To help managers clearly define and troubleshoot performance concerns in their work teams.

Learning Outcome: Upon successful completion of this course, the student will be able to identify the components of an effective human performance systems and recognize deficiencies; effectively troubleshoot and develop solutions to performance problems; and apply performance analysis to current job concerns and plan for future effective performance systems.

Instruction: Major topic covered in this course is a model for identifying factors in the workplace that influence human performance. In addition, it gives the manager practice in using tools to describe these factors specifically in individual situations and diagnose why people behave the way they do. The workshop also covers ways managers can improve the performance of individuals and teams.

Credit Recommendation: In the upper division baccalaureate degree category, 1 semester hour in Management or Business Administration (7/90).

Managing People and Performance (MD7601) (Formerly Managing People's Performance)

Location: AT&T locations worldwide.

Length: 32 hours (4 days).

Dates: *Version 1:* January 1988-June 1994; *Version 2:* July 1994-Present.

Objective: To provide managers with the ability to assess and enhance their management skills and to emphasize achieving results through people.

Learning Outcome: Upon successful completion of this course, students will be able to understand the roles/responsibilities of the first- and second-level managers; receive feedback from subordinates on management skills and develop personal development plans; implement the Management Practices that positively affect the work group climate; become familiar with the work group development process; conduct effective goal setting and performance appraisal sessions; analyze performance problems and establish developmental plans for improved work performance; and utilize the supportive roles of corporate resource organizations.

Instruction: Major topics covered in the course are an intensive, comprehensive workshop provides managers with the ability to assess and enhance their management skills and emphasizes achieving results through people; how to identify and examine practices, communication style and leadership behavior, and practice handling typical work situations; and how to develop specific plans to assist them in achieving personal and organizational effectiveness.

Credit Recommendation: *Version 1:* In the lower division baccalaureate/associate degree category, 1 semester hour in Managing People and Performance (12/90). *Version 2:* In the lower division baccalaureate/associate degree category, 2 semester hours in Management (7/95).

Managing Policy Deployment (CQ8056)

Location: Somerset, NJ and other locations throughout the country.

Length: 16 hours (2 days).

Dates: May 1991-Present.

Objective: To prepare Quality Professionals to facilitate the implementation and assist with the ongoing management of Policy Deployment within their organization.

Learning Outcome: Upon successful completion of this course, the student will be able to introduce Policy Deployment within their organization, facilitate the integration of Policy Deployment with other Quality Initiatives, support the preparation of a plan for implementation and ongoing management of Policy Deployment, and guide the alignment of resources and activities required to support Policy Deployment.

Instruction: Major topics covered in the course introduces the Policy Deployment process, how it works, its benefits, the tools that support the process and the Quality Manager's role. Through a case study exercise, participants will gain experience in developing an organizational vision and breakthrough objectives. The link between Policy Deployment, Business Planning and other Quality programs is reviewed. Participants will gain a complete understanding of how Policy Deployment can be employed to increase business success.

Credit Recommendation: In the upper division baccalaureate degree category, 1 semester hour in Business Policy (10/91) (10/96).

Managing Product Profitability (FE0895)

Location: Locations throughout the U.S.

Length: 16 hours (2 days).

Dates: July 1996-Present.

Objective: To improve participants' financial and planning skills and help ensure profitable management of products and services.

Learning Outcome: Upon successful completion of this course, students will be able to define, calculate, and manage profitability at all levels (i.e., corporate, business unit, program/function); read and comprehend basic financial statements; analyze an AT&T report card to determine key ratios and information required to measure profit margins; and demonstrate improved planning and financial skills and use these skills to manage products, services, or functions for greater profitability.

Instruction: Major topics covered in the course are the continuing pressure to reduce costs and stimulate revenue; financial and planning skills, and helps to ensure profitable management of products and services; profitability calculation and management methods; managerial accounting techniques; analysis of marketing decisions; and how to analyze decisions to determine cost vs. revenue and overall impact on financial results. An application project is part of the course requirement for students to earn the credit recommendation.

Credit Recommendation: In the upper division baccalaureate degree category, 1 semester hour in Product Management (12/90) (7/95).

Managing the Software End Game (LCS103L)

Location: Locations worldwide.

Length: 16 hours (2 days).

Dates: March 1997-Present.

Objective: To provide insight and strategies into analyzing, planning, organizing, monitoring and controlling the Software End Game so that the project remains on schedule, with budget, and meets quality requirements during this crucial, time sensitive period.

Learning Outcome: Upon successful completion of this course, the student will be able to understand and analyze the Software End Game to determine the feasibility of stakeholders requirements; utilize analysis data and information to effectively plan the Software End Game; understand and apply a Change management strategy within the Software End Game with the goal of managing and controlling the introduction of change requests; utilize a simple formula to assess, at any time within the Software End Game, whether the project is on schedule and will know what actions can and should be taken if the project is found to be behind schedule.

Instruction: Major topics covered in the course are use strategies to analyze, plan, organize, monitor and control the Software End Game. Methods of instruction include discussion, lecture and collaborative learning. An appropriate graduate level research project is included as part of the course requirement for each student who seeks the credit recommendation.

Credit Recommendation: In the graduate degree category, 1 semester hour in Software Engineering or Software Management (11/97).

Managing the Virtual Workplace (LBB206L)

Location: Piscataway, NJ and other locations nationwide.

Length: 7 hours (1 day).

Dates: July 1996-Present.

Objective: To provide managers with an understanding of the issues associated with managing remote workers and how to supervise for success and maintain teamwork and synergy with associates working in a remote environment.

Learning Outcome: Upon successful completion of this course, the student will be able to identify the major concerns of Virtual Workplace managers and the adjustments they might need to make to effectively supervise remotely; apply the principles and tools of performance management to enhance productivity and create the necessary results-oriented mindsets; identify techniques for establishing and maintaining trust with virtual workers as well as fostering location independent teamwork; plan for the resources, policies and procedures and monitoring program that you will need to support virtual workers.

Instruction: For managers of remote workers, the challenges are particularly pronounced. How do you manage people when they are physically out of sight? How do you measure productivity if you can't see the work as it is being completed? How do you maintain an atmosphere of trust and productivity, not just with people outside the traditional office, but also with those remaining? The answers lie in a need to manage by results and output rather than hours worked, activity level or personal style. This program combines a variety of interactive and diagnostic exercises with practical guidelines you can use to make this important paradigm shift.

Credit Recommendation: In the lower division baccalaureate/associate degree category, 1 semester hour in Telecommunication Management (12/95). **NOTE:** To earn this credit recommendation, student must complete this course and one of the following courses: LBB000L or LBB205L.

Manufacturing Leadership Program (MF3000)

Location: Somerset, NJ.

Length: *Version 1:* 168 hours (4 weeks); *Version 2:* 128 hours (3 weeks).

Dates: *Version 1:* April 1987-August 1996; *Version 2:* July 1996-Present.

Objective: To educate influential manufacturing managers in current topics of technologic and managerial techniques needed to insure Lucent Technologies as a world class competitor.

Learning Outcome: Upon successful completion of this course, the student will be able to implement many changes using leading-edge processes; impart leadership skills to change and establish a culture that promotes organizational effectiveness and commitment; understand latest technologic systems and future trends; benchmark your operation; and meet with classmates in future reviews to share experiences.

Instruction: Major topics covered in the course are how to increase your abilities to manage technological change; and how to implement the manufacturing strategy. Methods of instruction includes classroom work utilizing state-of-the-art learning methods: manufacturing systems simulation, business simulations, case studies, and "hands-on" laboratories; and discussions led by external and internal corporate executives, leading business consultants, and prominent university faculty. Each session of the Manufacturing Leadership Program offers a sound practical approach that translates today's critical leadership and management trends into learnable concepts and skills. An appropriate graduate level project is included as part of the course requirement.

Credit Recommendation: In the graduate degree category, 5 semester hours in Manufacturing Management (10/91) (5/96).

Marketing Communications (ME0885)

Location: Various AT&T locations throughout the U.S.

Length: 16 hours (2 days).

Dates: July 1996-Present.

Objective: To learn how to plan and manage advertising, public relations, and general communications plans to meet tight budgets and achieve profitability.

Learning Outcome: Upon successful completion of this course, the student will be able to understand the relationship of marketing communications to business goals and objectives; understand the key steps in the marketing communications process; understand the management of the marketing communications process from strategic development through execution; and gain experience in the application of the marketing communications process to situations related to the student's real business needs.

Instruction: Major topics covered in the course are the various communications tools and tactics used to reach business and consumer markets, then develop an integrated marketing communications plan to support your umbrella market strategy and numerous marketing approaches, such as public relations, trade shows, logos and design, and direct marketing.

Credit Recommendation: In the upper division baccalaureate degree category, 1 semester hour in Marketing Promotions (7/95).

Microsoft Windows Programming (IE3180)

Location: All AT&T training locations.

Length: 35 hours (5 days).

Dates: July 1996-April 1997.

Objective: To teach the skills and knowledge necessary to create an application that runs in the Windows environment.

Learning Outcome: Upon successful completion of this course, the student will be able to know how to implement the text and visual editors of the Microsoft C++ workbench, understand Windows Architecture, know message processing in the Windows event-driven environment, and implement resources such as icons, cursors, menus, accelerators and dialog boxes.

Instruction: Major topics covered in the course include a hands-on computer lab course which teaches students how to create a basic application that displays a window. As the course progresses, increasing functionality is added to the application, such as menus, dialog boxes and text. At course end, students will be able to recognize and apply the basic elements of the windows application programming interface (API). They will know how to use the Windows messaging system and basic memory management techniques, implement basic user interface objects, and create basic windows-based applications.

Credit Recommendation: In the upper division baccalaureate degree category, 1 semester hour in Computer Information Systems (lecture) and 1 semester hour in Computer Information Systems (lab), for a total of 2 semester hours (10/96).

Mini-MBA in Competitive Advantage (ME2050) (Formerly Understanding Your Customers, Markets, & Competitors [RB1011]; Establishing Your Business Focus [RB1012]; Maximizing Value of Resources: How to Leverage [RB1013]; and Ensuring Business Results: How to Read & Monitor Vital Signs of Your Business [RB1014])

Location: All AT&T locations nationwide.

Length: 64 hours (8 days, two 4 day sessions a month apart).

Dates: July 1996-Present.

Objective: To address the concepts of identifying, enhancing, and implementing your competitive advantage through direct application to your business.

Learning Outcome: Upon successful completion of this course, the student will be able to develop a situation analysis to understand your customers, markets, and competitors in developing your point of competitive advantage; identify a strategic direction to establish long-term direction and focus while identifying and gaining alignment among key stakeholders, determine a resourcing plan to maximize the value of your resources while focusing on continuous improvement and innovation; and create a vital sign system to ensure business success in marketplace execution.

Instruction: Major topics covered in the course are integrating advanced business concepts by leveraging your business' core competencies; using your energy to align your customers, resources, and stakeholders; and the key concepts brought to life through real examples, multi-media presentations, and in-class case studies, but more importantly, provides actual application directly to your business with expert consulting to guide your work. Methods of instruction include multi-media presentations, in-class case studies, and an appropriate graduate level research project for those students seeking to earn the graduate credit recommendation.

Credit Recommendation: In the upper division baccalaureate degree category, 4 semester hours in Strategic Management; or in the graduate degree category, 3 semester hours in Strategic Management (12/95).

Mini-MBA in Finance (FM3000)

Location: Somerset, NJ and other locations throughout the world.

Length: 64 hours over 8 days (over a 6 week period).

Dates: June 1994-March 1997.

Objective: To provide participants with a good working understanding of the key concepts in financial management and how to apply them to improve business performance and increase shareholder value.

Learning Outcome: Upon successful completion of this course, the student will be able to analyze financial statements to improve business results; utilize management accounting principles to improve business operations; manage cash flow and working capital; manage foreign exchange risk; and select among various budgeting techniques to project decisions.

Instruction: Major topics covered in the course are precourse assignment covering accounting fundamentals and time value of money; the knowledge to make financial decisions considering all aspects from time value of money to global finance; and how to interpret financial statements. Methods of instruction include lecture, coursework, and exercises.

Credit Recommendation: In the graduate degree category, 4 semester hours in Finance or in the upper division baccalaureate degree category, 6 semester hours in Finance (12/94).

Mini-MBA in General Management (LBM025L)

Location: Piscataway, NJ and other locations worldwide.

Length: 64 hours (8 days).

Dates: July 1996-April 1997.

Objective: To expose students to the main ideas, techniques and paradigms taught in traditional two-year MBA programs.

Learning Outcome: Upon successful completion of this course, the student will be able to make more efficient day-to-day business decisions, identify strategies and tactics to use to be a more effective manager, apply various frameworks to decisions and issues he/she faces, and analyze how his/her decisions affect other people and other organizations.

Instruction: Major topics covered in the course are all the elements in a typical MBA program, including marketing, strategy, research, finance, forecasting, organizational behavior, ethics and the global marketplace. Methods of instruction include discussion, lecture, case studies, and guest speakers. An appropriate graduate level research project is submitted as part of the course requirements.

Credit Recommendation: In the upper division baccalaureate degree category, 2 semester hours in Marketing, 1 semester hour in Business Strategy, 1 semester hour in Global Economics, 1 semester hour in Finance, 1 semester hour in Forecasting and Statistics, 1 semester hour in Organizational Behavior and 1 semester hour in Decision-Making, for a total of 8 semester hours; or in the graduate degree category, 2 semester hours in General Management and 2 semester hours in Marketing for a total of 4 semester hours (12/93).

Mini-MBA in Global Business (GM3000)

Location: Somerset, NJ and other AT&T locations.

Length: 64 hours (8 days).

Dates: November 1994-Present.

Objective: To expose students to various functional aspects of global business from the strategic point of view.

Learning Outcome: Upon successful completion of this course the student will be able to appreciate and understand the similarities and differences in global markets; develop skills and knowledge to effectively compete in global markets; develop a global strategy for products and services; and identify and measure various financial aspects of global business, including exchange rate risk.

Instruction: Major topics covered in the course are the various environmental aspects of global business. The topics included are: economic and socio-cultural, international organizational behavior, global finance and accounting, and multinational marketing strategies.

Credit Recommendation: In the graduate degree category, 4 semester hours in Advanced Global Management (6/94).

Mini-MBA in Global Technology (ME2035)

Location: AT&T locations through U.S. and the international marketplace.

Length: 64 hours (8 days).

Dates: July 1996-Present.

Objective: To gain new insights into the dynamics of the evolving global market technology, the course will analyze the ways in which globalization and regionalization have affected strategic attitudes and practices towards the development and diffusion of technology.

Learning Outcome: Upon successful completion of this course, the student will be able to learn a strategic prospective on the Global Management of Technology, understand how technology (hardware & software) can be harnessed to meet both long term and short term corporate marketing and profit objectives, forecast technological changes by understanding the dynamics of technological change; understand the alternative perspectives on cross-border movement through technological transfer and joint ventures; and understand the new challenges to global management of technology including time-based competition and managing cross-cultural teams.

Instruction: This course is designed to provide AT&T with a strategic perspective on the Global Management of Technology, highlighting those ways in which technology-hardware and software-can be harnessed to meet both short and long-term corporate marketing and profit objectives. Along with providing new insight into the dynamics of the evolving global market technology, the course will analyze the ways in which globalization and regionalization have affected strategic attitudes and practices towards the development and diffusion of technology. A comprehensive application project is part of the course requirement for students to earn the credit recommendation.

Credit Recommendation: In the upper division baccalaureate degree category or in the graduate degree category, 4 semester hours in Strategic Global Marketing (7/95).

Mini-MBA in Management of Information (IM2025)

Location: AT&T locations worldwide.

Length: 64 hours (8 days over a 6-8 week period).

Dates: May 1994-Present.

Objective: To provide managers with a working knowledge and skills for managing information in the life cycle process.

Learning Outcome: Upon successful completion of this course, the student will be able to develop a management process for creating and/or collecting quality data and information in the corporate environment; enhance techniques for analyzing information systems; identify the expanding world of management information and its impact on business; develop strategic, tactical, and operational views of data information and knowledge; and apply content of knowledge, information, and data management processes to the business environment.

Instruction: Major topics covered in the course are an overview of the data and information life cycle. Methods of instruction include lecture, discussion, and classroom exercises.

Credit Recommendation: In the graduate degree category, 4 semester hours in Management of Information or in the upper division baccalaureate degree category, 6 semester hours in Management of Information (12/94).

Negotiationing Across Borders (GM1070) (Formerly Cross-Cultural Business Negotiations and Communications [GM1070])

Location: Somerset, NJ and other AT&T locations.

Length: 14 hours (2 days).

Dates: January 1989-April 1997.

Objective: To develop cultural sensitivity and techniques for negotiating and communicating with other cultures effectively.

Learning Outcome: Upon successful completion of this course, the student will be able to appreciate the overall context of an international business negotiation; recognize, with the self-awareness gained from role-plays and videotape feedback, how you and your American colleagues generally conduct business negotiations; anticipate common negotiating styles and practices in diverse regions and countries such as China, France, Japan, Mexico, Nigeria, and Saudi Arabia; and apply within this context, the skills and insights essential for you and other individuals to negotiate effectively.

Instruction: Major topics covered in the course are negotiating skills individuals need in international and cross-cultural business settings; complex context of international business negotiations, determinants of negotiation outcomes, cultural aspects of negotiation, and three skill areas (preparing, communicating, and problem-solving). **NOTE**: A graduate level project is required to complete this course.

Credit Recommendation: In the graduate degree category, 1 semester hour in International Business Negotiations (4/92).

Overview of Global Finance (LBG104L)

Location: Piscataway, NJ.

Length: 21 hours (3 days).

Dates: July 1996-Present.

Objective: To explain to participants the global financial issues involved in doing business internationally.

Learning Outcome: Upon successful completion of this course, the student will be able to understand the workings of the foreign exchange markets and the impact of macro-economic policy on exchange rates; relate AT&T's international operating agreements to the foreign exchange risks faced by the company; identify and measure the various types of foreign exchange risks and explain the pros and cons of the foreign exchange risk management tools available in the market; develop a strategy for currency of invoice selection in the case of accounts receivable, accounts payable, and short-term financing; describe the institutional structure of the international financial system and the benefits of the various financial instruments offered; and identify the critical differences in the foreign versus domestic direct investment decision.

Instruction: Major topic covered in the course is the world of global financial issues. The objective of the course is to enhance participants' abilities to incorporate various facets of international finance into their pricing, sourcing, and sales decisions.

The program also addresses the issues of AT&T's international operating agreements and discusses the foreign exchange risk management and global financing issues associated with such agreements. An appropriate graduate level project is included as part of the course requirement for students to earn the credit recommendation.

Credit Recommendation: In the graduate degree category or in the upper division baccalaureate degree category, 2 semester hours in Global Finance (7/95).

Performance Analysis Workshop (IE1102)

Location: Piscataway, NJ and other AT&T locations.

Length: 18 hours (3 days).

Dates: June 1978-October 1991.

Objective: To increase the effectiveness and scope of the organization by adapting performance analysis strategies, worth analysis techniques, and the systems approach to training.

Learning Outcome: Upon successful completion of this course, participants should be able to apply performance analysis strategies to organizational and individual performance problems; recommend and implement non-training solutions such as feedback systems, incentive systems, and job engineering for appropriate non-training problems; and conduct a worth analysis of training problems (a comparison of the value of solving the problems to the cost of training solutions).

Credit Recommendation: In the upper division baccalaureate degree category, 1 semester hour in Business Administration or Industrial Engineering (7/85) (7/90).

Presentation Techniques (MS6515)

Location: Throughout the continental United States and global locations.

Length: 21 hours (3 days).

Dates: July 1996-Present.

Objective: To incorporate effective platform skills, both vocal and physical delivery, into a presentation.

Learning Outcome: Upon successful completion of this course, students should be able to incorporate effective platform skills into a presentation (platform skills in this sense would encompass both vocal and physical delivery); analyze an audience and understand how it will relate to the presentation; utilize patterns of organization and methods of preparation, including the Monroe Motivated Sequence; effectively handle question and answer sessions; and integrate visual aids into a presentation.

Instruction: Major topics covered in the course are how to master the skills needed to plan, structure, and deliver oral presentations; delivering numerous presentations, most of which are videotaped for playback critique; and how to deliver convincing presentations with confidence, credibility, and personal impact.

Credit Recommendation: In the lower division baccalaureate/associate degree category, 1 semester hour in Presentation Techniques or Business Communications (12/90) (12/95).

Pricing Your Products or Services (ME2009)

Location: Somerset, NJ and other AT&T locations.

Length: 16 hours (2 days).

Dates: May 1993-Present.

Objective: To teach students how to develop effective pricing strategies and tactics.

Learning Outcome: Upon successful completion of this course, the student will be able to make intelligent pricing decisions; develop pricing strategies, and tactics; analyze what impact costs, demand, customers, and competitors have on price; determine how marketing research can be used to help establish price; avoid pricing traps; and establish realistic pricing objectives.

Instruction: Major topics covered in the course provide students with techniques to develop effective pricing strategies and tactics for both new and existing products and services. Topics include pricing research, upward and downward price limits, the role of cost in pricing decisions, pricing analysis, pricing objectives, pricing strategies, and tactics. Methods of instruction include discussion and lecture. An appropriate graduate level research project is submitted as part of the course requirements.

Credit Recommendation: In the upper division baccalaureate degree category, 2 semester hours in Marketing elective, or in the graduate degree category, 1 semester hour in Marketing elective (12/93).

Process Quality Management and Improvement (CQ1004) (Version 2 of Managing and Improving Processes with Quality [CQ1004])

Location: Somerset, NJ and other locations around the world based on customer needs.

Length: 16 hours (2 days) plus extensive independent study/project.

Dates: July 1994-Present.

Objective: To prepare students to use a proven approach to managing and improving process performance to become the supplier of choice by consistently delivering superior value as measured against customer requirements.

Learning Outcome: Upon successful completion of this course, the student will be able to understand and apply the basics of process management and improvement; explain the role and importance of customer requirements in PQMI; and construct a block diagram of a business process and interpret basic data display tools such as histograms, control charts, and trend lines.

Instruction: Major topics covered in the course are PQMI's seven step approach to process management; diagramming and mapping the process; identifying customer requirements and translating them into effective measures; gathering and using data; objectives for improvement; and roles of process management and quality improvement teams. Methods of instruction include lecture, discussion, case studies, and exercises.

Credit Recommendation: In the upper division baccalaureate degree category, 2 semester hours in Process Quality Management and Improvement (12/94).

Product Logistics Management (ME2007)

Location: AT&T locations nationwide.

Length: 32 hours (4 days).

Dates: July 1996-Present.

Objective: To acquire the tools and techniques to forecast, control, and manage inventory successfully.

Learning Outcome: Upon successful completion of this course, the student will be able to understand the pluses and minuses of various distribution strategies; use a variety of analytical tools and techniques to solve logistics problems; develop a physical distribution plan for products; and assess the impact of transportation costs, carrying costs, order processing costs, and warehousing costs in a physical distribution strategy.

Instruction: Major topics covered in this course are the linkages and information flows necessary between marketing, manufacturing, finance, and data systems to ensure the optimal, cost-effective provisioning of products to meet customer needs; and the integration of distribution-related activities including: inventory management, customer service, order processing, and production planning. An appropriate graduate level project is included as part of the course requirement. Methods of instruction include case study analysis, 18 hours of pre-course readings and case problems, and a paper which is submitted to the instructor following completion of class time.

Credit Recommendation: In the graduate degree category, 2 semester hours in Physical Distribution Management or Business Logistics (8/91) (5/96).

Product Management Concepts (ME2001)

Location: AT&T locations nationwide.

Length: 40 hours (5 days).

Dates: July 1996-Present.

Objective: To provide managers with the purposes and techniques of product management.

Learning Outcome: Upon successful completion of this course, the student will be able to understand the key marketing, management and strategic issues product managers face; identify strategies and tactics to use in meeting market and financial goals; apply various pricing, life cycle and product portfolio models to the products; and lead or participate in a more effective product team.

Instruction: Major topics covered in the course are the key concepts pertaining to the planning, developing, and marketing of existing and new products; competitive analysis; environmental analysis; and market research, segmentation and forecasting. An appropriate graduate level project is included as part of the course requirement.

Credit Recommendation: In the graduate degree category, 3 semester hours in Product Planning and Management, Applied Marketing Management, Advanced Marketing, or Strategic Marketing (11/86) (8/91) (5/96).

Project Contract-Procurement Management (IE1622)

Location: Piscataway, NJ and various locations nationwide.

Length: 26 hours (4 days).

Dates: January 1994-Present.

Objective: To enable project managers to positively impact quality, cost and schedule of any project through the tools of contract development and procurement management process.

Learning Outcome: Upon successful completion of this course, the student will be able to understand the role the Project Manager has in the Contract and Procurement processes; appreciate the interrelationships of the skills of Contracts knowledge, Procurement, Marketing and Negotiations. Also, how this interrelationship is an important element in project success; understand the role Needs Identification play in the proposal process; understand the Basic Elements of Contracts and the factors to consider in the proposal process; understand the components to review when determining a Make or Buy decision; develop a Bid Package; and appreciate the importance of preparation in the Negotiations process.

Instruction: Major topics covered in the course are the process by which goods and services are acquired in project management environments and the legal issues project managers face; and the evolution of the contractual relationship from initial formation through completion of the services and delivery of goods.

Credit Recommendation: In the graduate degree category, 2 semester hours in Procurement Management (6/95).

Project Cost Management: Estimating, Budgeting and Controlling (IE1621)

Location: Piscataway, NJ and various locations nationwide.

Length: 26 hours (4 days).

Dates: January 1994-Present.

Objective: To provide a broad overview of the differing perspectives of cost within a project, various financial techniques and the factors influencing cost data.

Learning Outcome: Upon successful completion of this course, the student will be able to identify types of costs in your industry and others, and classify them by direct, indirect, and overhead categories; recognize sources of cost problems and develop ways to minimize them; understand financial and cost accounting terminology and know how it is used in your projects; review cash flow estimations and financial projections for reasonableness; and understand various methods of estimating, budgeting, and monitoring and the appropriate situations for their use.

Instruction: Major topics covered in the course are a broad overview of the differing perspectives of cost within a project and an organization, various financial techniques, and the factors influencing cost data and control methods.

Credit Recommendation: In the graduate degree category, 2 semester hours in Capital Budgeting (6/95).

Project Management Essentials (IE1602)

Location: Piscataway, NJ and various locations nationwide.

Length: *Version 1:* 18 hours (3 days); *Version 2:* 21.5 hours (3 days).

Dates: *Version 1:* November 1979-December 1993; *Version 2:* January 1994-Present.

Objective: *Version 1:* To provide the student with detailed conceptual knowledge of the project management process. *Version 2:* To introduce the participant to the principles, methods, and tools of project management.

Learning Outcome: Upon successful completion of this course, the student will be able to define a project, list the important characteristics of any project, define the primary functions of project management, describe the relationship between the project management process and any product development process, and list the project management roles and their major responsibilities.

Instruction: *Version 1:* Major topics covered in the course are the characteristics of a complex systems project and the important aspects of the structure, environment, and vocabulary of project management. Methods of instruction include lecture, discussion, and workshops. *Version 2:* Major topics covered in the course are the principles, methods, and tools of project management; and project management techniques and methods discussed from the standpoint of the manager who must plan, schedule, organize, and control nonroutine activities to achieve schedule, budget, and performance objectives. Methods of instruction include lecture, discussion, and classroom exercises. An appropriate graduate level research project is included as part of the course requirement for each student who seeks the credit recommendation.

Credit Recommendation: *Version 1:* In the upper division baccalaureate degree category, 3 semester hours in Business Administration or Management (5/80) (7/85) (7/90). **NOTE:** Students must complete both courses to receive credit for Introductory Project Management. This course was previously evaluated in combination with "Project Management Workshop" IE1604. They were organized as two courses under the title, "Introductory Project Management," and received one credit recommendation. *Version 2:* In the graduate degree category, 1 semester hour in Principles of Project Management I (6/95).

Project Management Experience and Practice (LCS100L)

Location: Locations worldwide.

Length: 48 hours (6 days).

Dates: July 1996-Present.

Objective: To provide experienced software managers with an experience that will enhance their project management capabilities.

Learning Outcome: Upon successful completion of this course, the student will be able to describe a common approach to project management as used in Lucent Technologies; identify key project management methods for managing software development projects; apply proven management methods to planning and executing a project; and negotiate with project stakeholders to achieve project objectives.

Instruction: Major topics covered in the course are project planning, project management audits, negotiating schedules, scope budget, estimation, risk management, organization and teambuilding, monitoring and control, changing customer requirements, managing external partners and vendors, multiple location/organization projects, avoiding common pitfalls, and successfully completing projects. Methods of instruction include lecture, lab, simulation and computer-aided instruction. An appropriate graduate level research project is included as part of the course requirement for each student who seeks the credit recommendation.

Credit Recommendation: In the graduate degree category, 3 semester hours in Project Management (11/97).

Project Management Scheduling and Analysis Software Tools (LCS101H)

Location: Locations worldwide.

Length: 24 hours (3 days).

Dates: August 1996-Present.

Objective: To effectively create and manage project schedules using accepted project management principles. Students are introduced to 'Risk+" and 'WBS Chart for Project'. Students are encouraged to bring samples from their work projects.

Learning Outcome: Upon successful completion of this course, the student will be able to create a new project, enter task and resource information for the project, organize the project in outline form, display various views of project information, analyze and adjust schedules, resources and costs as the project progresses; preview and print view for the project.

Instruction: Major topics covered in the course are using data entry screens, view screens, preference setting and dialog boxes, understanding work breakdown structure and task outline features to group project tasks, learning resource management capabilities for more realistic, resource constrained scheduling of projects, understanding tracking and control features to ensure project completion within budget, producing project reports, managing file security, using dynamic data exchange/object linking and embedding to build a status report, customizing Microsoft Project for Windows, using the organizer to share customized objects. Methods of instruction include lecture and lab. An appropriate graduate level research project is included as part of the course requirement for each student who seeks the credit recommendation.

Credit Recommendation: In the graduate degree category, 1 semester hour in Project Management (11/97).

Project Management Using Microsoft Project for Windows (IE1691)

Location: Piscataway, NJ and various locations nationwide.

Length: 14 hours (2 days).

Dates: July 1996-Present.

Objective: To provide students hands-on exercises with the latest version of Microsoft Project for Windows 4.0.

Learning Outcome: Upon successful completion of this course, the student will be able to enter and access data, view screens, set preferences, and use dialog boxes; breakdown the structure and outline features to group project tasks; prepare resource management capabilities for more realistic resource constrained scheduling of projects; use the table, filter, tool bar, and sorting capabilities including customization; and use track and control features to ensure project completion within budget.

Instruction: Major topics covered in the course are a hands-on exercises with the latest version of Microsoft Project for Windows 4.0; the major functions and features of the software and how to use them to plan, organize, control, and report progress; and how to use the software to effectively create and manage project schedules using accepted project management principles.

Credit Recommendation: In the lower division baccalaureate/associate degree category or in the upper division baccalaureate degree category, 1 semester hour in Microsoft Projects for Windows I (6/95).

Project Management Workshop (IE1604)

Location: Piscataway, NJ and various locations nationwide.

Length: *Version 1:* 34 hours (5 days); *Version 2:* 38 hours (5 days).

Dates: *Version 1:* November 1979-December 1993; *Version 2:* January 1994-Present.

Objective: *Version 1:* To provide the student with the detailed conceptual knowledge of the project management process. *Version 2:* To provide the exposure to the project management functions of planning, organizing, and controlling using computer-based simulation.

Learning Outcome: Upon successful completion of this course, the student will be able to produce Network and Gantt charts; identify Gantt charts, critical path methods, and work breakdown structures; and recognize the terms: slack, CPM, concurrent activity, bar chart, and network.

Instruction: *Version 1:* Major topics covered in the course are the characteristics of a complex systems project and the important aspects of the structure, environment, and vocabulary of project management. Methods of instruction include lecture, discussion, and workshops. *Version 2:* Major topics covered in the course are practicing the project management functions of planning, organizing, and controlling; scheduling and cost-control techniques; and the skills required to project manage a non-trivial development project. Methods of instruction include computer-based simulators to exercise the skills required to project manage a non-trivial development project. An appropriate graduate level research project is included as part of the course requirement for each student who seeks the credit recommendation.

Credit Recommendation: *Version 1:* In the upper division baccalaureate degree category, 3 semester hours in Business Administration or Management (5/80) (7/85) (7/90). **NOTE:** Students must complete both modules to receive credit for Introductory Project Management. This course was previously evaluated in combination with "Project Management Essentials" IE1602. They were organized as two courses under the title, "Introductory Project Management," and received one credit recommendation, i.e., both courses had to be taken to gain the credit. *Version 2:* In the graduate degree category, 2 semester hours in Principles of Project Management II (6/95).

Project Quality Management (IE1624)

Location: Piscataway, NJ and various locations nationwide.

Length: 35 hours (5 days).

Dates: January 1994-Present.

Objective: To provide students with a focus on both the qualitative and quantitative approaches used by project managers to ensure that project and ongoing operations meet quality requirements as well as cost and schedule demands.

Learning Outcome: Upon successful completion of this course, the student will be able to demonstrate a knowledge of basic quality concepts; use quality in the system development process; and apply quality tools and techniques in the process management.

Instruction: Major topics covered in the course are the qualitative and quantitative approaches used by project managers to ensure that project and ongoing operations meet quality requirements as well as cost and schedule demands; and the use of continuous process improvement techniques as a means of improving productivity and performance within an organization. An appropriate graduate level research project is included as part of the course requirement for each student who seeks the credit recommendation.

Credit Recommendation: In the graduate degree category, 2 semester hours in Quality Management (6/95).

Project Risk Management (IE1625)

Location: Piscataway, NJ and various locations nationwide.

Length: 35 hours (5 days).

Dates: January 1994-Present.

Objective: To enable a student to understand risk management, identify project risks and develop strategies which significantly reduce them or take steps to avoid them.

Learning Outcome: Upon successful completion of this course, the student will be able to define risk in a project environment; understand the project manager's role in managing risk; define the role of risk in project selection; recognize external and internal forces that cause risk on the project; develop a method of identifying risks and dependencies; apply statistical methods in quantifying risk; understand risk tolerance of individuals; identify methods of mitigating risk; develop techniques for developing contingency plans; control risk throughout the project life cycle; and prepare for the Project Risk Management portion of the PMP exam.

Instruction: Major topics covered in the course are integrating risk and estimating technologies that have been established to ensure optimum project decision making and the study of ways a project manager can identify, analyze, quantify, mitigate, and plan contingencies and manage risks in projects. All projects involve a degree of uncertainty due to factors both internal and external to the company. By their nature, projects are more risky than ongoing operations.

Credit Recommendation: In the graduate degree category, 2 semester hours in Principles of Risk Management (6/95).

Project Team Leadership: Human Resources and Communications (IE1620)

Location: Piscataway, NJ and various locations nationwide.

Length: 32.5 hours (5 days).

Dates: January 1994-Present.

Objective: To prepare the student for leading teams to successfully complete a technical project.

Learning Outcome: Upon successful completion of this course, the student will be able to identify student's and others' interpersonal styles and use in motivating and goal setting; understand the characteristics of people and processes on a Systems Project Team; demonstrate interpersonal skills to involve team members in win-win solutions to conflict; identify student's own strengths as they relate to team building and project management; define and demonstrate behavioral and leadership styles for team and project management; identify and demonstrate group leadership and communication skills; list project management roles and major responsibilities; use negotiation and delegation to aid in reaching group goals; demonstrate understanding of group dynamics and group process; and demonstrate knowledge of appropriate strategies for balancing participation, correcting confusion, and bringing team goals to closure.

Instruction: Major topics covered in the course are the leadership skills required of project managers to organize and motivate people in a manner that achieves results in complex organizational environments. Methods of instruction include class discussions, case studies, and simulations.

Credit Recommendation: In the graduate degree category, 2 semester hours in Organizational Behavior (6/95).

Quality Improvement Cycle Process (LQM103L)

Location: Locations nationwide.

Length: 16 hours.

Dates: July 1996-August 1996.

Objective: To move Quality Improvement Cycle (QIC) teams forward in current problem solving methodologies.

Learning Outcome: Upon successful completion of this course, the student will be able to understand the roles and responsibilities of QIC teams in the context of AT&T Total Quality Approach; describe the purpose of the Quality Improvement Cycle and apply the method; and learn and apply the tools associated to each step of the Quality Improvement Cycle.

Instruction: Major topic covered in the course is an understanding of the Quality Improvement Cycle. Team members will use the tools and learn the steps of this powerful problem solving methodology.

Credit Recommendation: In the upper division baccalaureate degree category, 1 semester hour in Quantitative Methods (8/91). **NOTE:** The credit recommendation applies only to those students who successfully complete an Application Project using selected tools taught in the course and assessed by the instructor.

Rapid Prototyping (LCS201L)

Location: Piscataway, NJ; Atlanta, GA.

Length: 18 hours (3 days).

Dates: July 1996-Present.

Objective: To enable a student to understand, develop and evaluate software prototypes.

Learning Outcome: Upon successful completion of this course, the student will be able to know when to begin prototyping, and when to stop; know how to select appropriate prototyping software; and know how to use two popular prototyping packages.

Instruction: Major topic covered in the course is software prototyping, i.e., the development of computer system models. These models can simulate both system functionality and the user interface.

The course demonstrates how prototyping can be used in the design and development of software products; then, using "hands-on" exercises, participants create, modify, evaluate and test many different types of prototypes. Several case problems are presented and participants use PC-based prototyping tools to complete the prototyping exercises.

Credit Recommendation: In the upper division baccalaureate degree category, or in the graduate degree category, 1 semester hour in Software Prototyping (9/94).

R&D Business Cases to Improve R&D Productivity (FE8002)

Location: Somerset, NJ and other AT&T locations.

Length: 16 hours (2 days).

Dates: November 1994-Present.

Objective: To teach managers a method to analyze R&D projects and techniques to prioritize and maximize the productivity of the R&D portfolio.

Learning Outcome: Upon successful completion of this course, the student will be able to assess probabilities of technical success and market performance; calculate expected R&D value and expenditure; and combine the risk and value characteristics of individual projects to show the risk and value of the R&D portfolio.

Instruction: Major topics covered in the course are decision and risk analysis techniques to improve R&D productivity. R&D project analysis methods are explained and R&D productivity is measured. A system to prioritize R&D projects is developed to maximize the productivity of the R&D portfolio. During the seminar, a methodology will be introduced which uses influence diagrams, decision trees, probability assessment and cash flow analysis to combine technical, regulatory and market uncertainties in computing expected R&D value versus expenditure.

Credit Recommendation: In the upper division baccalaureate degree category, 1 semester hour in Improving R&D Productivity-Case Method (6/94).

Sales Calling Skills Workshop (LSS010L)

Location: Locations worldwide.

Length: 8 hours (1 day).

Dates: July 1996-August 1997.

Objective: To position participants to be able to increase sales, qualify leads and utilize effective sales call process, establishing long-term customer relationships.

Learning Outcome: Upon successful completion of this course, the student will be able to maximize bottom line results by effective listening to customers; respond to customer objections and learn to deal effectively and efficiently with resistance; effectively manage customer contacts from start to finish and close the sale.

Instruction: This course will help enable participants to recognize that the goal is not simply winning sales but rather winning customers, as long term partners. Sales agents will learn how to qualify leads, reach decision makers, uncover and use benefits oriented presentations to gain sales.

Credit Recommendation: In the upper division baccalaureate degree category, 1 semester hour in Sales (7/95). **NOTE:** Student must also complete LSS020 to earn the credit recommendation.

Sales Skills Application Workshop (LSS050L)

Location: Piscataway, NJ and various locations nationwide.

Length: 24 hours (3 days).

Dates: July 1996-August 1997.

Objective: To improve confidence in face-to-face selling situations; increase ability to productively control the tone, flow and outcome of sales calls; and enhance ability to build partnerships.

Learning Outcome: Upon successful completion of this course, the student will be able to implement a structured approach for conducting sales calls; tailors his/her approach to specific selling situations; and develop sales relationships based on understanding client needs.

Instruction: Major topic covered in the course is face-to-face selling skills for students involved in selling and those who want to learn skills for effective management of sales situations. It includes sales call planning, presenting solutions, handling objections, and closing the sale. Methodology includes videotaped role play, lecture and discussion.

Credit Recommendation: In the lower division baccalaureate/associate degree category, 1 semester hour in Sales Management (12/93).

Software Cost/Risk Management (LCS102L)

Location: Locations worldwide.

Length: 28 hours (4 days).

Dates: August 1997-Present.

Objective: To develop a cost estimate for a software project, develop a cost performance baseline, perform a variance analysis for a current project, identify project risks, develop contingency plans, and prepare Monte Carlo simulation estimates for cost and duration. Students will see a demonstration of the CHECKPOINT estimating software package and a demo of RISK+, a simulation package for project duration and cost estimating.

Learning Outcome: Upon successful completion of this course, the student will be able to explain how project cost management fits into overall project management; use various techniques for estimating project costs; define direct cost, indirect cost and capital, and know how to apply them to a project; describe the process of establishing a project budget; define and use Project Cost Control Processes; establish time and cost reporting processes to manage project status; define risk in a project environment; identify project risk events; apply probabilistic methods in quantifying risk; and develop appropriate responses to project risks.

Instruction: Major topics covered in the course are types and techniques of estimating, ranges and confidence limits in estimating, staffing peaks and budget cuts, contingency funding, cost control and the control loop, rules of thumb for controlling costs, variance analysis, project risk identification, applying probabilistic methods, Monte Carlo simulation, risk response, mitigation, contingency planning, change management and risk. Methods of instruction include discussion, lecture, lab, case studies and tests. An appropriate graduate level research project is included as part of the course requirement for each student who seeks the credit recommendation.

Credit Recommendation: In the graduate degree category, 1 semester hour in Software Engineering (11/97).

Software Quality Management Using Software Process Assessment (SPA) (LCS105L)

Location: Locations worldwide.

Length: 24 hours (3 days).

Dates: July 1997-Present.

Objective: To equip students with the knowledge to accelerate improvements in their organization. This should result in both improvement of their SPS results and improvement in the business' interval, defect, and cost performance.

Learning Outcome: Upon successful completion of this course, the student will be able to explain the urgency for Lucent Technologies to become a world-class software development organization and the role of the Software Leadership Council (SLC) in getting us there; describe the Lucent Technologies Software Process Assessment (SPA) methodology which combines the Software Engineering Institute (SEI) and Software Productivity Research (SPR) models; cite industry data and examples to demonstrate that the organization that follows Best-in-Class quality management practices achieves superior business results; describe the SEI Software Capability Maturity Model; apply understanding of Best-in-Class quality management practices in a case study to help achieve goals such as lower defect levels, shorter intervals, and higher customer satisfaction with software products; explain how the SEI and SPR models complement each other by comparing and contrasting similarities and differences; and describe how to approach improvement once you have your SPA results.

Instruction: Major topics covered in the course are role of Software Leader-ship Council (SLC), Software Process Assessment (SPA), Software Producti-vity Research (SPR), SEI Software Capability Maturity Model, quality management practices. Methods of instruction include lecture and practi-cum. An appropriate graduate level research project is included as part of the course requirement for each student who seeks the credit recommendation.

Credit Recommendation: In the graduate degree category, 1 semester hour in Software Engineering (11/97).

SPC for Process Management (CQ1009)

Location: Piscataway, NJ and other AT&T locations.

Length: 36 hours (5 days).

Dates: May 1990-October 1996.

Objective: To teach statistical process control techniques for use in service and administrative environments.

Learning Outcome: Upon successful completion of this course, the student will be able to collect data that can be analyzed to help improve customer satisfaction, use histograms and Pareto analysis to determine the types of problems occurring in the process, perform process capability studies, construct and analyze various control charts to monitor process performance over time, use scatterplots and analysis of means (ANOM) to detect causes of problems, and apply some quality consulting "tips" to help lead co-workers toward continuous quality improvement.

Instruction: Major topics covered in the course are statistical process control to those working in a service or administrative function; how and when to collect useful data and several graphical and statistical tools for analyzing the data, SQC Troubleshooter, and analysis of real-life service examples and problems.

Credit Recommendation: In the upper division baccalaureate degree category, 2 semester hours in Statistical Quality Control (for non-technical managers) (10/91). **NOTE:** Credit recommendation applies only to those students who also successfully complete an independent project applying several of the identified statistics procedures.

Strategic Marketing for Maximum Profitability (ME0872)

Location: Somerset, NJ and other AT&T locations worldwide.

Length: 24 hours plus lab.

Dates: *Version 1:* September 1990-June 1996; *Version 2:* July 1996-Present.

Objective: To teach students how to utilize the latest theories and practices in Strategic Marketing.

Learning Outcome: Upon successful completion of this course, the student will be able to develop and implement directly job applicable SBU oriented strategic and tactical marketing strategies; strategically protect and win market share; formulate an umbrella marketing strategy; optimally manage the marketing mix through all stages of the product/service life cycle to maximize profits; implement strategies to increase revenue/profits from a current market base; construct and write a short range and long range marketing plan for a business case; participate in developing and implementing an SBU market information system, designing focus groups, writing questionnaires, collecting data, interpreting research findings, and presenting results to management for Lucent actionable marketing decision making; analyze SBU's micro and macro environment; identify whether a product/service should be marketed as a market leader, challenger or nicher and how to implement the strategy; and apply seminar material to the international market.

Instruction: Major topics covered in the course are strategic marketing; formulating an umbrella marketing strategy; developing and implementing an SBU market information system; analyzing an SBU's micro and macro environment; strategically targeting market segments; market analysis and demand; constructing a short-range tactical marketing plan for a business case; constructing a long-range marketing plan for a business case; strategic marketing for market leader SBU's and challenger SBUs; market strategies to protect and win back market share; developing and implementing tactical marketing decisions; developing and implementing long range marketing decisions; strategic marketing formula for success; strategies for new product/service development; strategic marketing for new products/services; strategic marketing for mature products/services; customer focused strategic pricing; strategic marketing communications and promotion; strategic channel marketing; identifying and strategically marketing to business and consumer innovators; international strategic marketing; apply seminar material to the international market; strategic marketing customer focus; and quality application. Students are required to complete a graduate level project related to Strategic Marketing at the end of the course.

Credit Recommendation: *Version 1:* In the graduate degree category, 3 semester hours in Strategic Marketing (8/91). *Version 2:* In the graduate degree category, 2 semester hours in Marketing (5/96).

Strategies for Competing Globally (GM1020)

Location: AT&T locations worldwide.

Length: *Version 1:* 21 hours (3 days); *Version 2:* 16 hours (2 days).

Dates: *Version 1:* April 1990-January 1995; *Version 2:* February 1995-Present.

Objective: *Version 1:* To help participants identify the elements involved in formulating successful global strategies and describe AT&T's current approach/position. *Version 2:* To provide participants a conceptual framework for strategic competitive analysis and planning.

Learning Outcome: *Version 1:* Upon successful completion of this course, the student will be able to understand the major trends, variables, and factors (external and internal) that have an impact on global competitive advantage—in general and with reference to AT&T's businesses; analyze foreign buying behavior, with emphasis on market research and information acquisition; understand how to use concepts, methodologies, and market information to formulate strategies and courses of action that will improve AT&T's competitive position; discuss product/service planning, including sourcing, offshore manufacturing, countertrade agreements, market segmentation, pricing policies, and international sales management; and understand AT&T's current global presence, competitive position, and stated competitive strategy. *Version 2:* Upon successful completion of this course, the student will be able to evaluate major trends, including internal and external variables that impact global competition with reference to AT&T's businesses; use concepts, methodologies and market information to formulate strategies and courses of action that will improve competitive position; and understand and discuss AT&T's global business strategy.

Instruction: *Version 1:* Major topics covered in the course are an in-depth discussion of the competitive forces AT&T is facing in global markets and a comprehensive and integrated framework for analyzing and interpreting relevant competitive information and for designing effective global strategies. Methods of instruction include lectures, exercises, and discussions centering on vital aspects of competitive strategic planning in a global context. *Version 2:* Major topics covered in the course are a conceptual framework for strategic competitive analysis and planning, competitive analysis and strategic positioning for success in the telecommunications market, global structure and strategy, global presence, competitive position, and competitive strategy. Meth-ods of instruction include lectures, exercises, and discussions centering on vital aspects of competitive strategic planning in a global context.

Credit Recommendation: *Version 1:* In the graduate degree category, 2 semester hours in International Business Strategies (12/90). *Version 2:* In the upper division baccalaureate degree category or in the graduate degree category, 1 semester hour in Global Business Strategies (7/95). **NOTE:** An appropriate graduate level project is included as part of the course requirement for students to earn the credit recommendation.

Supplier Quality Management (CQ9001)

Location: U.S. and locations globally.

Length: 16 hours (2 days).

Dates: February 1994-Present.

Objective: To provide guidelines to assist organizations in helping their suppliers deliver customer-focused value.

Learning Outcome: Upon successful completion of this course, the student will be able to develop a supply strategy for managing suppliers in support of business goals; determine the appropriate type of rel,ationship to develop with suppliers; and monitor and improve supplier performance to achieve business goals.

Instruction: Major topics covered in the course are developing a supply strategy, selecting and qualifying suppliers, and monitoring and improving their performance based on the desired relationship identified for specific suppliers. This course links supplier relationships to a customer-focused business plan designed to produce superior value through continuous improvement of performance in the supply channels.

Credit Recommendation: In the graduate degree category, 1 semester hour in Supplier Quality Management (6/94).

Targeting Your Markets for Today's Changing Environment: Tools for the External and Internal Markets (SA4070) (Formerly Market Segmentation for Customer Value [SA4070]; Targeting Your Customer: Segmenting Markets for Profitability [SA4070]; Market Segmentation/Buyer Behavior [SA4070])

Location: Somerset, NJ and various other AT&T locations.

Length: *Version 1:* 34 hours (4 days); *Version 2:* 24 hours (3 days); *Version 3:* 16 hours (2 days).

Dates: *Version 1:* January 1980-December 1990; *Version 2:* January 1991-December 1993; *Version 3:* July 1996-Present.

Objective: To teach participants the core elements of the market segmentation process and the criteria used to assess potential alternative market segments.

Learning Outcome: Upon successful completion of this course, the student will be able to review the concepts of market segmentation; explore the importance of micro marketing or niche marketing in today's marketplace; and analyze the relationship between customer behavior and segmenting in the market.

Instruction: Major topics covered in the course are market segmentation concepts, the interrelationship between customer behavior and segmentation, and how to implement a market segmentation strategy to achieve profitability.

Credit Recommendation: *Versions 1 and 2:* In the upper division baccalaureate degree category, 2 semester hours in Marketing (9/80) (11/85) (8/91). *Version 3:* In the upper division baccalaureate degree category, 1 semester hour in Marketing (5/96).

Team Collaboration Skills (MS6480)

Location: U.S. and locations globally.

Length: 16 hours (2 days).

Dates: June 1993-Present.

Objective: To help students gain insights into their own strengths as a team member. In addition, they will learn to influence their interpersonal and team relationships toward shared power, joint problem-solving and mutual accountability.

Learning Outcome: Upon successful completion of this course, the student will be able to assess his/her unique strengths in promoting the work of a team; develop techniques for strengthening team communication; recognize the task and relationship roles team members must play and how to provide those roles when they are missing; and practice collaboration in generating ideas, solving problems and making decisions.

Instruction: Major topics covered in the course are how student can maximize their potential to contribute to their team. In addition students will learn to interact more collaboratively with individuals and teams and to identify and act on opportunities for them to contribute from their own natural strengths. Students will learn to influence their interpersonal and team relationships toward shared power, joint problem-solving and mutual accountability. A post-course paper is required to complete this course.

Credit Recommendation: In the lower division baccalaureate/associate degree category, 1 semester hour in Team Collaboration Skills (6/94).

The Scheuing Method (PR5001)

Location: AT&T training locations in the U.S.

Length: 40 hours (5 days).

Dates: July 1996-Present.

Objective: To prepare the student to pass the Certified Purchasing Manager (CPM) examination.

Learning Outcome: Upon successful completion of this course, the student will be able to pass the CPM examination from having studied major topics such as reading and interpreting questions; administrative aspects of the purchasing department; personnel issues; updates on exam content; and suggestions for preparation.

Instruction: Major topics covered in the course are a lecture presentation with videos on the Purchasing function; gaining a better understanding of preparation techniques for completing exam requirements; reviewing the organizational functions of Purchasing; understanding the continuing education function of Purchasing. An appropriate graduate level project is included as part of the course requirement for students to earn the credit recommendation.

Credit Recommendation: In the upper division baccalaureate degree category or in the graduate degree category, 3 semester hours in Purchasing Management (7/95).

The Telecommuting and Virtual Workplace Seminar (VO2000)

Location: Open/General Enrollment: Somerset, NJ; Atlanta, GA; Chicago, IL; and Pleasanton, CA. Suitcased/On-site Delivery: Internationally.

Length: 7 hours (1 day).

Dates: July 1996-Present.

Objective: To establish a foundation by which participants can understand the trends, issues, opportunities, and challenges associated with implementing non-traditional work environments such as telecommuting, satellite officing, and hoteling.

Learning Outcome: Upon successful completion of this course, the student will be able to define the key concepts associated with alternative work arrangements, recognize the driving forces and the many benefits of non-traditional work environments, and understand the human factor issues associated with non-traditional work environments.

Instruction: Major topics covered in the course are an overview of the issues and trends driving businesses to explore a variety of non-traditional work arrangements such as telecommuting, satellite officing, hoteling, and the virtual office and how these trends affect business and operational results; and a step-by-step process that enables one to assess whether or not a non-traditional work environment is appropriate for the individual and/or organization.

Credit Recommendation: In the lower division baccalaureate/associate degree category, 1 semester hour in Telecommunication Management (12/95). **NOTE:** To earn this credit recommendation, the student must complete this course and one of the following courses: Working in the Virtual Workplace (VO2005) or Managing in the Virtual Workplace (VO2006).

Tools and Process Overview (CQ1015) (Quality Control Techniques II)

Location: AT&T locations nationwide.

Length: 16 hours.

Dates: October 1989-December 1994.

Objective: To move Quality Improvement Cycle (QIC) teams forward in current problem solving methodologies.

Learning Outcome: Upon successful completion of this course, the student will be able to understand the roles and responsibilities of QIC teams in the context of AT&T Total Quality Approach; describe the purpose of the Quality Improvement Cycle and apply the method; and learn and apply the tools associated to each step of the Quality Improvement Cycle.

Instruction: Major topics covered in the course are an understanding of the Quality Improvement Cycle; and team members will use the tools and learn steps of this powerful problem solving methodology.

Credit Recommendation: In the upper division baccalaureate degree category, 1 semester hour in Quantitative Methods (8/91). **NOTE:** The credit recommendation applies only to those students who successfully complete an Application Project using selected tools taught in the course and assessed by the instructor.

Understanding UNIX System Files & Processes (LCU300L)

Location: Piscataway, NJ and other Lucent locations.

Length: 40 hours (1 week).

Dates: July 1996-December 1996.

Objective: To enable programmers and administrators to identify and make use of many system resources.

Learning Outcome: Upon successful completion of this course, the student will be able to describe the division of UNIX system memory among the kernel and the user processes; describe a UNIX system process and its attributes; use various commands for effective management of files and processes; and compare efficient versus inefficient usage of system resources in UNIX system programming or administration.

Instruction: Major topic covered in the course is the necessary background information about the internal operations of the UNIX system to enable the UNIX system programmers and administrators to identify and make efficient use of the many important system resources. Commands that increase human efficiency in the management of UNIX system files and processes are also examined.

Credit Recommendation: In the upper division baccalaureate degree category, 2 semester hours in Topics in Computer Science (11/96).

UNIX System for Programmers (LCU101H) (Formerly Fundamentals of the UNIX Operating System for Programmers)

Location: Piscataway, NJ and other Lucent locations.

Length: 32 hours (1 week).

Dates: July 1996-December 1996.

Objective: To introduce programmers to the fundamentals of the UNIX Operating System.

Learning Outcome: Upon successful completion of this course, the student will be able to use the UNIX System User's

Manual to locate commands by name or description and recognize syntax conventions; use the UNIX system's basic commands; communicate with other users of the system; create, list and manipulate files and directories; use the UNIX system full screen editor - "vi"; use file generation characters; and name features included in the UNIX system.

Instruction: Major topics covered in the course are basic UNIX operating system characteristics; assessing a UNIX system; the Shell command language architecture; the hierarchical file system; the UNIX system full screen editor-"vi"; Interuser communications; using the UNIX system documentation; a summary of the UNIX system features. Instructional methods include classroom discussion, lecture and lab. **NOTE:** To receive the credit recommendation, an examination must be given and passed by the student.

Credit Recommendation: In the upper division baccalaureate degree category, 1 semester hour in Computer Information Systems (lecture) and 1 semester hour in Computer Information Systems (lab), for a total of 2 semester hours (11/96).

UNIX System Resource Efficiencies (IE5004)

Location: Piscataway, NJ and other Lucent locations.

Length: *Version 1:* 30 hours (5 days); *Version 2:* 40 hours (1 week).

Dates: *Version 1:* December 1987-January 1995; *Version 2:* July 1996-Present.

Objective: To enable programmers and administrators to identify and make use of many system resources.

Learning Outcome: Upon successful completion of this course, the student will be able to describe the division of UNIX system memory among the kernel and the user processes; describe a UNIX system process and its attributes; use various commands for effective management of files and processes; and compare efficient versus inefficient usage of system resources in UNIX system programming or administration.

Instruction: Major topics covered in the course are the internal operations of the UNIX system to enable the user to identify and make efficient use of the many important system resources and commands that increase human efficiency in the management of UNIX system files and processes.

Credit Recommendation: *Version 1:* In the lower division baccalaureate/associate degree category, 1 semester hour in Topics in Computer Science (7/90). *Version 2:* In the upper division baccalaureate degree category, 2 semester hours in Topics in Computer Science (10/96).

Using the Business Case Process in Sales (LBF455L)

Location: Piscataway, NJ and other locations nationwide.

Length: 16 hours (2 days).

Dates: July 1996-Present.

Objective: To teach marketing and sales personnel how to use the business case process in preparing sales presentations from their customer's perspective.

Learning Outcome: Upon successful completion of this course, the student will be able to understand the business investment decision making process; utilize this investment process to understand and address customer needs at each step of the investment process; identify and create value for the customer; frame the customer sales opportunity; perform a value analysis; use a business case format to present the value analysis to the customer.

Instruction: This course is designed for marketing and sales personnel to use the business case format in their sales presentation. This workshop will teach students to develop business cases from the customer's perspective. Included are also: how to frame the customer sales opportunity and perform a value analysis, including economic value added (EVA).

Credit Recommendation: In the upper division baccalaureate degree category, 1 semester hour in Sales Analysis-Case Method (6/94).

Visual Basic Programming (IE 3190)

Location: Piscataway, NJ; Cincinnati, OH; Herndon, VA; Alpharetta, GA; Altamonte Springs, FL; Kansas City, MO.

Length: 30 hours (5 days).

Dates: June 1993-Present.

Objective: To enable the student to effectively design and implement a graphical user interface using Visual Basic.

Learning Outcome: Upon successful completion of this course, the student will be able to explain the function of individual components of the Visual Basic environment; use Visual Basic Controls to interactively exchange information with users; code Visual Basic statements, methods and function calls within Event and General Procedures; create and access application data files; use the Data Control to access databases; and use dynamic data exchange facilities for cross applications communication.

Instruction: Major topics covered in the course provide the students with the skills and knowledge necessary to develop Microsoft Windows based applications. Methods of instruction include lectures, on-line demonstrations, and extensive hands-on exercises. Students develop an application using multiple Visual Basic controls.

Credit Recommendation: In the lower division baccalaureate/associate degree category, 2 semester hours in Visual Basic Programming (9/94).

Voice of the Customer (CQ1020)

Location: Somerset, NJ and other AT&T locations.

Length: 15 hours (2 days).

Dates: April 1993-Present.

Objective: To prepare students to utilize the Voice of the Customer" approach in decision making, the development of measurements and managing business improvements.

Learning Outcome: Upon successful completion of this course, the student will be able to develop measures of customer satisfaction, service standards and process requirements that are linked to customer needs; identify and manage critical Moments of Truth when customers form their opinions about your products and services; and identify and measure gaps between current performance and key measures and target performance needed to satisfy customers.

Instruction: Major topics covered in the course are designed for students making business decisions and want the Voice of the Customer represented in those decisions. It includes VOC framework, customer information processes, managing moments of truth, family of measures, and customer driven improvement strategies. Methods of instruction include lecture and discussions. An appropriate graduate level research project is submitted as part of the course requirements.

Credit Recommendation: In the upper division baccalaureate degree category, 2 semester hours in Marketing or General Business (12/93).

Working in the Virtual Workplace (VO2005)

Location: Open/General Enrollments: Somerset, NJ; Atlanta, GA; Chicago, IL; and Pleasanton, CA. Suitcased/On-site Delivery: Internationally.

Length: 7 hours (1 day).

Dates: July 1996-Present.

Objective: To provide participants with an understanding of how to achieve success and maintain communication with customers, managers, and peers while working in a remote environment.

Learning Outcome: Upon successful completion of this course, the student will be able to describe the key success factors for working in the Virtual Workplace/ Telecommuting; identify techniques for maintaining effective communications with customers, team members, and management; and apply key principles of performance management to enhance productivity and effectiveness in attaining business objectives when working remotely.

Instruction: Major topics covered in the course are practical tools, techniques, job aids, and hands-on practice to maximize their ability to effectively overcome the following challenges: How to manage time effectively and efficiently?; How to maintain effective communication with customers, suppliers, managers, and peers?; How to ensure that "out of sight" does not turn into "out of mind?"; and How to ensure consistent levels of performance?

Credit Recommendation: In the lower division baccalaureate/associate degree category, 1 semester hour in Telecommunication Management (12/95). **NOTE:** To earn this credit recommendation, the student must complete this course and one of the following: The Telecommuting and Virtual Workplace Seminar (VO2000) or Managing in the Virtual Workplace (VO2006).

Writing Winning Sales Proposals (LSS277L)

Location: Piscataway, NJ and other locations nationwide.

Length: 16 hours (2 days).

Dates: July 1996-Present.

Objective: To improve the quality of the sales process by focusing on producing a winning proposal of better quality, in less time, and at less cost.

Learning Outcome: Upon successful completion of this course, the student will be able to improve success rate by eliminating proposal efforts he/she has little chance of winning; improve his/her win percentage in those proposal efforts consistent with corporate and office objectives through effective proposal planning and writing.

Instruction: This course is for students working on proposals. It includes client evaluation, selecting winning proposals, analyzing opportunities, planning the proposals and writing the proposal. Methods of instruction include lecture and discussions.

Credit Recommendation: In the lower division baccalaureate/associate degree category, 1 semester hour in Business Writing (12/93).

Written Communications (MS6522)

Location: Piscataway, NJ and other locations nationwide.

Length: 40 hours (5 days).

Dates: July 1996-April 1997.

Objective: To apply the principles of contemporary business writing to the writing of letters, memos and reports.

Learning Outcome: Upon successful completion of this course, the student will be able to set and meet objectives for each writing task; apply principles of contemporary writing; choose and use the most effective format and style.

Instruction: Major topics covered in the course are a full review of functional grammar and business style. It will provide a basic foundation for business writing, including letters, memos and reports. Students will submit writing samples which will be critiqued in detail by the instructor. Individually and as a member of the group, students will study actual AT&T documents and rewrite them according to the principals of style and usage explained and demonstrated in class. They will apply the principles of basic grammar and punctuation to numerous examples of actual business writing.

Credit Recommendation: In the upper division baccalaureate category, 3 semester hours in Written Communications (4/92).

Lucent Technologies, Inc., Technical Services Company

Our San Antonio, Texas training organization is part of the Lucent Technologies Services and Technical Services Company Inc. which are headquartered in Greensboro, North Carolina, and is a wholy owned subsidiary of New Jersey based Lucent Technologies which was one of the three companies that AT&T created. The organization encompasses four divisions—Education services, Communication Services, Information Protection Services, and Business Development Services—with our primary business emphasis on training and consulting for the Federal Government.

We began operations in San Antonio, Texas in 1989. Our first training customer was the U.S. Air Force under the Standard Multi-user Small Computer Requirements Contract (SMSCRC). This endeavor consisted of training for System V Release 3 and 4 UNIX on the AT&T 3B2 computers. Since that time we have expanded our training operations into two facilities—the Training Center and the Training Center Annex where classified courses can be taught. These facilities house a total of six fully equipped classrooms that can be configured to teach any of our current courses, or new courses developed, based on customer needs. Our training cadre encompasses both DOX and UNIX operating system platforms and includes 140 instructor led courses and 32 videos. We offer programs for users spanning from basic concepts such as Introduction to DOX or UNIX Fundamentals to more advanced topics such as system and network administration.

We use the Instructional System Development (ISD) model as a guide for all curriculum development and instructor presentations. This process incorporates a continuous validation process which includes students, instructors, developers, and managers. We also use an instructor training precess which utilizes our own train the trainer course materials. All of our instructors are required to complete a vigorous training program that allows them to be certified at one of four instructor levels: professional, lead, senior and master instructor. Additionally, they must complete a course certification process to be certified to teach specific courses.

Our instructors also have the technical expertise to develop and modify courses. They perform technical writing and class preparation which promotes a delivery of professional instruction that customers have grown to expect from this company.

Source of official student records: Registry of Credit Recommendations, American Council on Education, One Dupont Circle, Washington, DC 20036-1193.

Additional information about the courses: Office of Corporate-Higher Education Programs, Thomas Edison State College, 101 West State Street, Trenton, NJ 08608-1176.

C2 Security Training (SA5002)

Location: San Antonio, TX and other locations.

Length: 16 hours (2 days).

Dates: July 1996-Present.

Objective: To enable students to perform basic system security administration on a C2 level secure system.

Learning Outcome: Upon successful completion of this course, the student will be able to understand operation system security and Discretionary Access controls; perform security administration using the System Administration Menu (SAM) on a C2 system; and use the Security Audit Trail (SAT) to monitor system usage.

Instruction: Major topics covered in the course are discretionary access controls; System Administration Menu (SAM); C2 password features; text editors, terminal, and device security features; and Security Audit Trail (SAT). Methods of instruction include classroom discussion, lecture, lab, and simulation.

Credit Recommendation: In the lower division baccalaureate/associate degree category, 2 semester hours in Principles of UNIX Security (9/96). **NOTE**: Students must also complete Information Protection Network UNIX Fundamentals (SA50-23BN) to receive a total of 2 semester hours for the credit recommendation.

Communications and Network Management (SA3007)

Location: San Antonio, TX and other locations.

Length: 40 hours (5 days).

Dates: July 1996-Present.

Objective: To enable students to administer network software, configure network hardware, and manage networks.

Learning Outcome: Upon the successful completion of this course, the student will be able to understand basic networking terminologies, definitions and concepts; perform the installation of hardware and software for a network; monitor a network; and troubleshoot networks.

Instruction: Major topics covered in the course are standard network configurations; concepts and environment concerns; and installation verification. Methods of instruction include classroom discussion, lecture, and lab.

Credit Recommendation: In the lower division baccalaureate/associate degree category, 2 semester hours in Principles of Local Area Networks (9/96). **NOTE**: Students must also complete Network Administration Training (SA3002) to receive a total of 2 semester hours for the credit recommendation.

HP-UX System Administration: Advanced 10.x (SA1012)

Location: San Antonio, TX and other locations.

Length: 40 hours (5 days).

Dates: July 1996-Present.

Objective: To acquire system operation and administration skills, including hardware capabilities, system performance and tuning, system debugging and system security.

Learning Outcome: Upon successful completion of this course, the student will be able to establish and maintain system security; perform disk management; perform process and memory management; modify the kernel; and load/reload the operating system.

Instruction: Major topics covered in the course are discretionary access controls; disk process and memory management; graphical environment management; system trouble shooting; and system kernel maintenance. Methods of instruction include classroom discussion, lecture, and lab.

Credit Recommendation: In the lower division baccalaureate/associate degree category, 2 semester hours in HP-UX Systems Administration (9/96). **NOTE**: Students must also complete HP-UX System Administration: Basic 10.x (SA1011) to receive a total of 2 semester hours for the credit recommendation.

HP-UX System Administration: Advanced 9.x (SA1003)

Location: San Antonio, TX and other locations.

Length: 40 hours (5 days).

Dates: July 1996-Present.

Objective: To introduce students to the operation and administration of the HP-UX system through the use of menus and shell access.

Learning Outcome: Upon successful completion of this course, the student will be able to understand system components; demonstrate system security; perform system management; perform system diagnositics; and monitor system performance.

Instruction: Major topics covered in the course are security features; discretionary access control; system management tools; system diagnositics; and debugging skills. Methods of instruction include classroom discussion, lecture, and lab.

Credit Recommendation: In the lower division baccalaureate/associate degree category, 2 semester hours in HP-UX System Administration (9/96). **NOTE**: Students must also complete HP-UX System Administration: Basic 9.x (SA102) to receive a total of 2 semester hours for the credit recommendation.

HP-UX System Administration: Basic 10.x (SA1011)

Location: San Antonio, TX and other locations.

Length: 32 hours (4 days).

Dates: July 1996-Present.

Objective: To provide hands-on training in the operation and administration of HP 9000 super-minicomputers and network servers using HP-UX 10.x.

Learning Outcome: Upon successful completion of this course, the student will be able to explain different platform architectures; explain the system boot process; perform disk management; explain file system theory and create a file system; and perform user administration.

Instruction: Major topics covered in the course are hands-on training in the operations and administration of HP superminicomputers and network servers using HP-UX 10.x. Methods of instruction include classroom discussion, lecture, and lab.

Credit Recommendation: In the lower division baccalaureate/associate degree category, 2 semester hours in HP-UX Systems Administration 10.x (9/96). **NOTE**: Students must also complete HP-UX System Administration: Advanced 10.x (SA1012) to receive a total of 2 semester hours for the credit recommendation.

HP-UX System Administration: Basic 9.x (SA1002)

Location: San Antonio, TX and other locations.

Length: 32 hours (4 days).

Dates: July 1996-Present.

Objective: To provide hands-on training in the operation and administration of super-minicomputers and network servers using HP-UX.

Learning Outcome: Upon successful completion of this course, the student will be able to understand system components and capabilities; demonstrate security features; explain file system theory; develop chronological routines; monitor system efficiency; and recover from a catastrophic event.

Instruction: Major topics covered in the course are hands-on training in the operation and administration of HP 9000 super-mini computers and network servers using HP-UX. Methods of instruction include classroom discussion, lecture, and lab.

Credit Recommendation: In the lower division baccalaureate/associate degree category, 2 semester hours in HP-UX Systems Administration (9/96). **NOTE**: Students must also complete HP-UX System Administration: Advanced 9.x (SA1003) to receive a total of 2 semester hours for the credit recommendation.

Information Protection Network Management and Advanced Security Tools (SA5028BN)

Location: San Antonio, TX and other locations.

Length: 144 hours (18 days).

Dates: July 1996-Present.

Objective: To enable students to establish a Firewall for the internal network, perform system, network and security administration, and troubleshoot and take action to resolve simple network problems.

Learning Outcome: Upon successful completion of this course, the student will be able to understand Local Area Networks, INTERNET definitions and concepts; understand and perform LAN configuration, management and security; understand and configure the Network Management System Hardware/Software; understand and use the HP Open View Network Node Manager; and understand and use Firewalls.

Instruction: Major topics covered in the course are LAN concepts and system security tools on the HJ platform; physical and logical topologies of LANs; bridges, gateways, and routers; hardware and software components; and control and maintenance of the LAN system. Methods of instruction include classroom discussion, lecture, and lab.

Credit Recommendation: In the lower division baccalaureate/associate degree or in the upper division baccalaureate degree category, 4 semester hours in Network Management (9/96).

Information Protection Network System Administration (SA5025BN)

Location: San Antonio, TX and other locations.

Length: 80 hours (10 days).

Dates: July 1996-Present.

Objective: To enable students to perform system and security administration tasks for the Hewlett Packard HP9000 series of computers using the HP-UX operation system.

Learning Outcome: Upon successful completion of this course, the student will be able to understand system components and software capabilities; demonstrate security features and file system management; demonstrate practical system administration skills; develop chronological utility routines to aid in task control and administrative functions; and perform system diagnostics and monitor system efficiency.

Instruction: Major topics covered in the course are system components, optimization and diagnostics; shell commands and text editing; file system, disk and device management; and backup and recovery. Methods of instruction include classroom discussion, lecture, and lab.

Credit Recommendation: In the lower division baccalaureate/associate degree category, 2 semester hours in Fundamentals of LAN Administration (9/96).

Information Protection Network System Administration and System Security Tools (SA5026BN)

Location: San Antonio, TX and other locations.

Length: 120 hours (15 days).

Dates: July 1996-Present.

Objective: To enable students to perform system and security administration tasks for the Hewlett Packard HP9000 series of computers using the HP-UX operating system and various Information Protection System Security Tools.

Learning Outcome: Upon successful completion of this course, the student will be able to understand the HP-UX operating system, system components and capabilities; understand and demonstrate the purpose and use of the Information Protection Network Security; perform system management and demonstrate practical system administration skills; monitor system usage and use the various software network tools available to perform this function; and perform system diagnostics.

Instruction: Major topics covered in the course are hands-on training in system and security administration of the Hewlett Packard HP9000 series of computers using the HP-UX operating system; C2 security; text editing; shell commands; user management; disk management; file system management; device management; system performance and tuning; and system trouble shooting and catastrophic recovery techniques performance. Students will use knowledge gained as a system administrator to install, configure, and use Information Protection System Security Tools on the UNIX platform. Methods of instruction include classroom discussion, lecture, and lab.

Credit Recommendation: In the lower division baccalaureate/associate degree category, 3 semester hours in Network System and Security Administration (9/96).

Information Protection Network UNIX Fundamentals (SA5023BN)

Location: San Antonio, TX and other locations.

Length: 40 hours (5 days).

Dates: July 1996-Present.

Objective: To introduce students to fundamental security guidelines, and the UNIX Operating System on an Information Protection Network.

Learning Outcome: Upon the successful completion of this course, the student will be able to understand the overview of Information Protection awareness requirements and locate Information Protection reference information; identify the UNIX file and directory structure, perform basic commands, and use fundamental shell programming techniques; manage and print standard text files; communicate with others on the system and use process control utilities; explain Information Protection Network risk management and understand how to identify Communication Security requirements; and understand the current and future initiatives for securing Information Protection Systems.

Instruction: Major topics covered in the course are Security Awareness, Training, and Education (SATE); UNIX file and directory structures; base operating commands, shell commands and process control utilities; text files and text editors; and risk management and current and future initiatives. Methods of instruction include classroom discussion, lecture, and lab.

Credit Recommendation: In the lower division baccalaureate/associate degree category, 2 semester hours in Principles of UNIX Security (9/96). **NOTE**: Students must also complete C2 Security Training (SA5002) to receive a total of 2 semester hours for the credit recommendation.

Information Protection Network Management and System Security Tools (SA5027BN)

Location: San Antonio, TX and other locations.

Length: 144 hours (18 days).

Dates: July 1996-Present.

Objective: To enable students to monitor network events, perform network administration and hardware configuration, configure and control a secure system, and troubleshoot simple problems for the Hewlett Packard HP9000 series of computers using the UP-UX operating system and various Information Protection System Security Tools.

Learning Outcome: Upon successful completion of this course, the student will be able to understand Local Area Networks; INTERNET definitions and concepts; understand and perform LAN configuration; understand and configure the Network Management System Hardware/Software; understand and use the HP Open View Network Node Manager; and understand and use the Information Protection System Security Tools.

Instruction: Major topics covered in the course are LAN concepts and system security tools on the HP platform; physical and logical topologies of LANs; bridges, gateways, and routers; hardware and software components; and control and maintenance of the LAN system. Methods of instruction include classroom discussion, lecture, and lab.

Credit Recommendation: In the lower division baccalaureate/associate degree or in the upper division baccalaureate degree category, 4 semester hours in Network Management (9/96).

Information System Security Key Management (SA5007)

Location: San Antonio, TX and other locations.

Length: 80 hours (10 days).

Dates: July 1996-Present.

Objective: To enable students to install, configure, and use the hardware and software needed to manage, distribute, and generate electronic cryptographic key within the Department of Defense and federal government.

Learning Outcome: Upon successful completion of this course, the student will be able to understand the Electronic Key Management Systems (EKMS) platform; perform functions using the Data Transfer Device; demonstrate basic SCO UNIX system administration; perform security audit trail administration; perform electronic Communications Security (COMSEC) account functions using local COMSEC management Software (LCMS); and demonstrate EKMS contingency planning.

Instruction: Major topics covered in the course are SCO UNIX fundamentals and basic system administration; data transfer device operations; local management device and key processor setup and operations; and local communications security management software fundamentals. Methods of instruction include classroom discussion, lecture, and lab.

Credit Recommendation: In the lower division baccalaureate/associate degree category, 2 semester hours in Fundamentals of Security Key Management (9/96).

Network Administration Training (SA3002)

Location: San Antonio, TX and other locations.

Length: 24 hours (3 days).

Dates: July 1996-Present.

Objective: To enable students to administer network software and configure network hardware.

Learning Outcome: Upon the successful completion of this course, the student will be able to understand communications hardware and software; understand LAN networking concepts and definitions; understand LANs and the Internet; install and configure a LAN; perform LAN management; and implement network security.

Instruction: Major topics covered in the course are a comprehensive introduction to important LAN concepts and how they are applied; LAN topologies; component connectivity; hardware and software components; and control and maintenance of the system. Methods of instruction include classroom discussion, lecture, and lab.

Credit Recommendation: In the lower division baccalaureate/associate degree category, 2 semester hours in Principles of Local Area Networks (9/96). **NOTE**: Students must also complete Communications and Network Management (SA3007) to receive a total of 2 semester hours for the credit recommendation.

SCO System Administration: Advanced (SA1004)

Location: San Antonio, TX and other locations.
Length: 24 hours (3 days).
Dates: July 1996-Present.
Objective: To enable students to perform system operation and administration tasks in the intelligent workstation environment through the use of menus and shell access.
Learning Outcome: Upon successful completion of this course, the student will be able to perform advanced system administration tasks; perform system accounting routines and functions; and demonstrate system performance management.
Instruction: Major topics covered in the course are system components; advanced system administration tasks; system accounting; basic system diagnostics; and performance management. Methods of instruction include classroom discussion, lecture, and lab.
Credit Recommendation: In the lower division baccalaureate/associate degree category, 2 semester hours in Introduction to Systems Administration (9/96). **NOTE**: Students also must complete SCO System Administration: Basic (SA1001) to receive a total of 2 semester hours for the credit recommendation.

SCO System Administration: Basic (SA1001)

Location: San Antonio, TX and other locations.
Length: 40 hours (5 days).
Dates: July 1996-Present.
Objective: To enable students to perform system administration functions on an Open Desktop (ODT) Intelligent Workstation.
Learning Outcome: Upon successful completion of this course, the student will be able to understand the role of system administration; understand system components; demonstrate system operation skills; and demonstrate process control utilities.
Instruction: Major topics covered in the course are an administration plan; system components; hardware devices; system installation; security; communications; login process; file management; menu-driven system administration; and system backup and recovery. Methods of instruction include classroom discussion, lecture, and lab.
Credit Recommendation: In the lower division baccalaureate/associate degree category, 2 semester hours in Introduction to Systems Administration (9/96). **NOTE**: Student also must complete SCO System Administration: Advanced (SA1004) to receive a total of 2 semester hours for the credit recommendation.

Solaris System Administration: Advanced (SA1010)

Location: San Antonio, TX and other locations.
Length: 40 hours (5 days).
Dates: July 1996-Present.
Objective: To enable students to perform systems administration and the basic duties of a Solaris network system administrator.
Learning Outcome: Upon successful completion of this course, the student will be able to identify standard network configurations; understand network software, concepts and environment concerns; and show an understanding of installation verification.
Instruction: Major topics covered in the course are standard network configurations and concepts, and installation verification. Methods of instruction include classroom discussion, lecture, and lab.
Credit Recommendation: In the lower division baccalaureate/associate degree category, 2 semester hours in Solaris Systems Administration (9/96). **NOTE**: Students also must complete Solaris Systems Administration: Basic (SA1009) to receive a total of 2 semester hours for the credit recommendation.

Solaris System Administration: Basic (SA1009)

Location: San Antonio, TX and other locations.
Length: 40 hours (5 days).
Dates: July 1996-Present.
Objective: To teach students how to perform the basic duties of a Solaris client/server system administrator.
Learning Outcome: Upon successful completion of this course, the student will be able to perform basic user management; automate administrative functions; and perform basic system administrative functions.
Instruction: Major topics covered in the course are structure and maintenance of UNIX file systems; device configuration; UNIX shells; OpenWindows GUI; user management; system security; system printing service; and system installation. Methods of instruction include classroom discussion, lecture, and lab.
Credit Recommendation: In the lower division baccalaureate/associate degree category, 2 semester hours in Solaris Systems Administration (9/96). **NOTE**: Students also must complete Solaris System Administration: Advanced (SA1010) to receive a total of 2 semester hours for the credit recommendation.

UNIX Operating System: Advanced 10.x (SA1014)

Location: San Antonio, TX and other locations.
Length: 24 hours (3 days).
Dates: July 1996-Present.
Objective: To help students acquire operating system skills, including advanced editing, commands, environment variables and shell programming.
Learning Outcome: Upon successful completion of this course, the student will be able to explain the file system and directory structure; manage standard text files; modify the shell environment; use process control utilities; and write shell script programs.
Instruction: Major topics covered in the course are file and directory structure, text files, shell features, process control, and shell procedures. Methods of instruction include classroom discussion, lecture, and lab.
Credit Recommendation: In the lower division baccalaureate/associate degree category, 2 semester hours in Fundamentals of UNIX 10.x (9/96). **NOTE**: Students also must complete UNIX Operating System: Basic (SA1013) to receive a total of 2 semester hours for the credit recommendation.

UNIX Operating System: Basic 10.x (SA1013)

Location: San Antonio, TX and other locations.
Length: 16 hours (2 days).
Dates: July 1996-Present.
Objective: To enable students to perform basic work station operations on HP-UX and Open Desktop (ODT) systems.
Learning Outcome: Upon successful completion of this course, the student will be able to identify the file and directory structure; use system reference information; utilize basic shell commands; use process control utilities; and perform basic text editing using the UNIX "vi" editor.
Instruction: Major topics covered in the course are file and directory structure; system reference information; shell proce-

dures and programming fundamentals; process control; and text editors. Methods of instruction include classroom discussion, lecture, and lab.

Credit Recommendation: In the lower division baccalaureate/associate degree category, 2 semester hours in Fundamentals of UNIX 10.x (9/96). **NOTE**: Student must also complete UNIX Operating System: Advanced 10.x (SA 1014) to receive a total of 2 semester hours for the credit recommendation.

Maalot New York - A Division of the Zaidner Institute

The Neve Yerushalayim College was founded in 1970 to offer women with a limited background in Jewish studies an intensive education with an appreciation of the Land of Israel and its history. Its subsequent development has seen the introduction of additional academic programs designed to meet the changing needs of contemporary Jewish women.

The Zaidner Institute, formerly known as Ma'alot Yerushalayim College, was established in Jerusalem in 1984 as an affiliate school of Neve Yerushalayim College. The institute provides a post-high school, college level, career-oriented education. The student body consists of young Jewish women with substantial prior Judaic and secular education, as well as women adult learners.

Zaidner's mission is to provide young women in Israel the opportunity of pursuing advanced Jewish studies, while at the same time, achieving a level of secular education enabling entry into the job markets of both Israel and the United States. Zaidner also seeks to meet the needs of adult women who must balance their desire for educationally valid study with family obligations.

At the time of its first class in 1984, Ma'alot offered courses in Computer Science and Business, in addition to Judaic Studies. From 1985, a fourth area of study, Education/Psychology, was offered. In 1995, a program in graphic arts was introduced. An integrated set of courses in Speech Pathology was made available in Fall 1996. These courses are designed to enable students to satisfy the prerequisites for admission to the University of North Texas graduate program in Speech Pathology which will be offered at Neve Yerushalayim College beginning with the Spring 1998 term.

Students matriculating to accredited institutions of higher learning have been able to receive college credits for some, if not all, of their Zaidner course work. Currently, students who choose to earn a college diploma may select from seven available tracks developed to articulate with degree programs offered through Thomas A. Edison State College of New Jersey. There are Baccalaureate degrees with specializations in: Art, Business Administration, Computer Science, Humanities, Liberal Studies, Psychology and Social Sciences.

For all courses taught at the Zaidner Institute, the hours listed are each a full 60 minutes of instruction, not the academic hour of 45-50 minutes.

Source of official student records: Registry of Credit Recommendations, American Council on Education, One Dupont Circle, Washington, DC 20036-1193.

Additional information about the courses: College Credit Recommendation Service, American Council on Education, One Dupont Circle, Washington, DC 20036-1193.

Analysis of Hebrew Scriptures: Exodus (REL 230)
Analysis of Hebrew Scriptures: Genesis (REL 220)
College Algebra (MAT 101)
Ethics of the Fathers (PHI 250)
Introduction to Computers (CMP 101)
Introduction to Sociology (SOC 101)
Introduction to Statistics (MAT 201)
Megillot II: Song of Songs, Ecclesiastes, Lamentations (REL 365)
Philosophy of Jewish Education (PHI 245)
Programming C++ (CMP 250)
Proverbs (REL 350)
Psychological Foundations of Education (PSY 260)
Sociology of Education (SOC 210)
Studies in Jewish Law: Dietary Law (REL 110)
Studies in Jewish Law: Economics and Business Relationships (REL 310)
Survey of Biblical Themes (REL 385)
Survey of Exceptional Children (PSY 310)
Topics in Jewish Philosophy (PHI 485)

"For complete information about the courses see Zaidner Institute."

Maryland Fire and Rescue Institute

The Maryland Fire and Rescue Institute of the University of Maryland at College Park was initiated in 1928 to meet the need for formalized fire service training. The Institute's role has been expanded through legislative action to be the state's comprehensive training and education system for emergency services.

The central administration facilities and training academy are located at the flagship campus in College Park with six regional offices and four satellite training academies positioned around the state. Forty eight full-time faculty/staff, and 350 part-time field instructors serve more that 20,700 students per year acquiring 490,000 student hours of course work.

Programs cover a wide-span ranging from basic firefighter training to upper level management with specialization in areas including emergency medical services, hazardous materials, and many other contemporary subjects. The Institute provides education and training to career and volunteer fire service students as well as industrial and commercial clients seeking professional level instruction which meets state and federal regulations.

Many of the Institute's developmental courses lead to certification under the National Fire Protection Association Professional Qualifications Standards. All courses are developed by a professional team meeting contemporary standards and are subject to regular review and enhancement. Testing procedure and examination validity is consistent with current educational and legal requirements of the University of Maryland.

Source of official student records: Registry of Credit Recommendations, American Council on Education, One Dupont Circle, Washington, DC 20036-1193.

Additional information about the courses: College Credit Recommendation Service, American Council on Education, One Dupont Circle, Washington, DC 20036-1193.

Aerial Apparatus Operator (AAOT-CO)
(Formerly Truck Company Operations [TCO])

Location: Maryland Fire and Rescue Institute Training Centers; Maryland Emergency Services Organizations' Facilities.

Length: 24 hours (8 weeks).

Dates: July 1982-Present.

Objective: To provide the knowledge and skills to operate a fire department aerial ladder truck and associated equipment.

Learning Outcome: Upon successful completion of this course, the student will be able to safely and effectively operate an aerial ladder truck at a fire or emergency scene. (National Fire Protection Association standard 1002, Fire Department Vehicle Driver/Operator Professional Qualifications, 1993 edition, Chapters 4 and 5).

Instruction: Major topics covered in the course are truck company operations, tool requirements, terminology, techniques of spotting, stabilizing, working angles, loading, extreme operating conditions, raising and lowering, controls and valves, hydraulic systems, water tower operations, standpipe operations, ladders, safety rules, maintenance, and testing. Methods of instruction include lecture, discussion, classroom exercises, audio/visual material, practical exercises, graded practical exercises, and a final examination.

Credit Recommendation: In the vocational certificate category, 1 semester hour in Fire Science Technology (11/94).

Basic Life Support and Hazardous Materials Response (BLSNFA)
(Basic Life Support and Hazardous Materials Response [R246])

Location: Maryland Fire and Rescue Institute Training Centers; Maryland Emergency Services Organizations' Facilities.

Length: 14 hours (2 days).

Dates: October 1994-Present.

Objective: To provide an overview of critical concerns for emergency medical responders at hazardous material incidents, including toxicological aspects associated with hazardous material incident response.

Learning Outcome: Upon successful completion of this course, the student will be able to successfully identify potential problems and safety concerns (responders and victims) from videotaped incidents; define hazardous materials and indications of their presence including respiratory, dermal, and systemic toxicology and ingestion injuries; describe decontamination processes and equipment; describe level of protective clothing and protective equipment and its use; define standard of care; understand federal laws relating to hazardous material response; and identify the process and techniques for assessing responder's condition.

Instruction: Major topics covered in the course are safety issues for EMS-hazardous material response teams, managing contaminated victims, decontaminating and treatment procedures at basic life support level, transportation and receiving facilities, and compliance/ understanding of federal regulations regarding hazardous material response. Methods of instruction include lecture, discussion, classroom exercises, audio/visual material, graded participation and projects, and a final examination.

Credit Recommendation: In the lower division baccalaureate/associate degree, or in the upper division baccalaureate degree category, 1 semester hour in Fire Science, Public Administration, Emergency Medical Services, or Community Health (2/95).

Building Construction: Non-Combustible and Fire Resistive (BCNCNFA)
(Building Construction: Non-Combustible and Fire Resistive [F150])

Location: Maryland Fire and Rescue Institute Training Centers, Maryland Emergency Services Organizations' Facilities.

Length: 16 hours (2 days).

Dates: July 1983-Present.

Objective: To enable the student to cite key features of noncombustible or fire-resistive buildings that affect emergency operations. Fire and life safety concerns that exist in non-combustible and fire-resistive structures are studied.

Instruction: Major topics covered in the course are the key features of non-combustible and fire-resistive structures that affect emergency operations; fire behaviors of steel and concrete are presented so that the effect of their presence in non-combustible or fire-resistive structures may be better anticipated; basic principles that apply to the spread of fire, products of combustion in structures, and special problems with interior finishes and building elements are discussed; testing methods for materials are covered; and the unique problems of conducting emergency operations in buildings under construction are studied. Methods of instruction include lecture, discussion, and simulation exercises.

Credit Recommendation: In the lower division baccalaureate/associate degree

category, 1 semester hour in Construction Technology or Fire Science (8/86) (2/95).

Building Construction: Principles—Wood and Ordinary Construction (BCOCNFA)
(Building Construction: Principles-Wood and Ordinary Construction [F100])

Location: Maryland Fire and Rescue Institute Training Centers, Maryland Emergency Services Organizations' Facilities.

Length: 16 hours (2 days).

Dates: July 1982-Present.

Objective: To enable the student to recognize construction types, design, alteration consequences, materials used, and their influence on the building's reaction to fire. In a tactical situation construction features and resultant potential hazards to firefighters are studied.

Instruction: Major topics covered in the course are information of how the construction type, alterations, design, and materials influence a building's reaction to fire; the principle of "fireground" reading of a building and the value of relevant advance information about buildings are explained; building stability and resistance to fire; special hazards to firefighters and construction elements; and the determination of likely paths of fire extension. Methods of instruction include lecture, discussion, and simulation exercises.

Credit Recommendation: In the lower division baccalaureate/associate degree category, 1 semester hour in Construction Technology or Fire Science (8/86) (2/95).

Emergency Care Basic: EMT/A (ECB)
(Formerly Emergency Care Basic: EMT/A)

Location: Maryland Fire and Rescue Institute Training Centers; Maryland Emergency Services Organizations' Facilities.

Length: 95 hours (16 weeks).

Dates: July 1989-July 1996.

Objective: To provide the necessary knowledge and skills to perform emergency medical care in a pre-hospital environment at the basic life support level.

Learning Outcome: Upon successful completion of this course, the student will be able to assess, recognize, and manage medical and trauma signs and symptoms in patients of emergency situations; to determine and use appropriate equipment for patient management and care; to communicate and work with other emergency services personnel in the care, transport, and transfer of patients; and to maintain patient and department records.

Instruction: Major topics covered in the course are legal aspects of emergency care, infection control, patient assessment, respiratory system, oxygen adjuncts and delivery, CPR, bleeding control and management of soft tissue injuries, musculoskeletal injuries and management, spinal immobilization, pediatric and obstetric emergencies, crisis intervention, multiple casualty and triage management, ambulance operations and EMS systems. Methods of instruction include lecture, discussion, classroom exercises, audio/visual material, skills practical scenarios, quizzes, midterm and final exams, and graded practical skills.

Credit Recommendation: In the vocational certificate category or in the lower division baccalaureate/associate degree category, 3 semester hours in Emergency Medical Services Technology or Public Administration (11/94).

Emergency Medical Services Officer (EMSO1)

Location: Maryland Fire and Rescue Institute Training Centers; Maryland Emergency Services Organizations' Facilities.

Length: 48 hours.

Dates: September 1996-Present.

Objective: To provide students with entry-level training in company/departmental emergency medical services operations and administration at the first-line supervisory level.

Learning Outcome: Upon successful completion of this course, the student will be able to effectively manage human resources, community/public relations; EMS company/departmental organization and administration, including budgets, reports, and incident pre-planning; and public EMS education, safety, and emergency services delivery.

Instruction: Major topics covered in the course are the role of the EMS officer, facing compliance and accountability issues of the 21st century, recognizing and managing cultural diversity, safety/wellness, TQM, interfacing with the community and media at large, functional leadership, supervising EMS company/departmental operations, effective communications, introduction to EMS operations, incident management system(s), and managing multiple casualty incidents. Methods of instruction include lecture, discussion, classroom exercises, case studies, audio/visual material, preceptorship program, observations, tests, and examinations and completion of required skills.

Credit Recommendation: In the lower division baccalaureate/associate or upper division baccalaureate degree category, 3 semester hours in Emergency Medical Services Administration, Management, Fire Science, Emergency Management, or Public Administration (9/96).

Emergency Medical Technician-Basic (EMTB)

Location: Maryland Fire and Rescue Institute Training Centers; Maryland Emergency Services Organizations' Facilities.

Length: 125 hours.

Dates: July 1995-Present.

Objective: To provide students with the necessary knowledge and skills to perform emergency medical care in a pre-hospital environment at the basic life support level.

Learning Outcome: Upon successful completion of this course, the student will be able to recognize, assess, and manage medical and trauma signs and symptoms in patients of emergency situations; determine and use appropriate equipment for patient management and care; communicate and work with other emergency service personnel in the care, transport, and transfer of patients; and maintain patient and department records.

Instruction: Major topics covered in the course are legal aspects of emergency care, infection control, patient assessment, respiratory system, oxygen adjuncts and delivery, CPR, AED, bleeding control and management of soft tissue injuries, musculoskeletal injuries and management, spinal immobilization, pediatric and obstetric emergencies, crisis intervention, multiple casualty and triage management, ambulance operations, and EMS systems. Methods of instruction include lecture, discussion, classroom exercises case studies, audio/visual material, skills practical scenarios, quizzes, a graded practical examination, practical skill evaluations, and mid-term and final examinations.

Credit Recommendation: In the vocational certificate or lower division baccalaureate/associate degree category, 6 semester hours in Emergency Medical Technology, Fire Science, or Public Administration (9/96).

Fire Command I (FCI)

Location: Maryland Fire and Rescue Institute Training Centers; Maryland Emergency Services Organizations' Facilities.

Length: 27 hours (4 weeks).
Dates: April 1985-June 1997.
Objective: To provide the student with the knowledge and skills of basic fireground command including basics of strategy and tactics at the company level.
Learning Outcome: Upon successful completion of this course, the student will be able to describe the many aspects of fireground command; factors affecting command operations, such as building construction, fire protection systems, collapse, safety, and communications; and initial response within the concept of "operational success."
Instruction: Major topics covered in the course are fundamentals of command, fire and smoke spread, cause of fire, collapse, fire suppression systems, time considerations, rescue, safety, communications, standard operating procedures, staging, hoseline selection, truck company operations, size-up, decision making, company responsibilities, decision sequence, critique, and simulation activities. Methods of instruction include lecture, discussion, classroom exercises, audio/visual material, learner presentations/reports, simulations, quizzes, classroom exercises, homework, and a final exam.
Credit Recommendation: In the vocational certificate category or lower division baccalaureate/associate degree category, 1 semester hour in Fire Science Technology or Public Administration (11/94).

Fire Officer I: Company Level Operations (FOTI)

Location: Maryland Fire and Rescue Institute Training Centers; Maryland Emergency Services Organizations' Facilities.
Length: 60 hours (10 weeks).
Dates: January 1994-Present.
Objective: To provide entry level training in company operations and administration at the first line supervisory level.
Learning Outcome: Upon successful completion of this course, the student will be able to find ways to effectively manage human resources; community/public relations; fire department organization and administration, including budgets, reports, and planning; fire inspection, investigation, and public education; emergency service delivery; and safety. (National Fire Protection Association 1021 standard, Fire Officer Professional Qualifications, 1992 edition, Chapter 2).
Instruction: Major topics covered in the course are the role of the fire officer, fire officer's responsibility in facing compliance and accountability, recognition and managing cultural diversity, safety and wellness of fire, quality management within the organizational structure, community awareness, public relations, fire safety education, functional leadership, problem solving, performance appraisal, building construction, fire cause determination, effective communication skills, and incident command system with strategy and tactics. Methods of instruction include lecture, discussion, classroom exercises, case studies, audio/visual material, learner presentations/reports, preceptorship program, quizzes, a final examination, and completion of required skills and preceptorship program.
Credit Recommendation: In the vocational certificate category or in the lower division baccalaureate/associate degree category, 4 semester hours in Fire Science Technology, Emergency Medical Service Technology, Emergency Management, or Public Administration (11/94).

Fire Officer II: Strategies for the Success of Company Level Officers (FOTII)

Location: Maryland Fire and Rescue Institute Training Centers; Maryland Emergency Services Organizations' Facilities.
Length: 42 hours (7 weeks).
Dates: July 1994-Present.
Objective: To provide the student with training in company operations and administration that enhances the entry level company officer training course.
Learning Outcome: Upon successful completion of this course, the student will be able to effectively manage human resources; community/public relations; fire department organization and administration, including budgets, reports, and planning; fire inspection, investigation, public education, and emergency service delivery; and safety. (National Fire Protection Association 1021 standard, Fire Officer Professional Qualifications 1992 edition, Chapter 3).
Instruction: Major topics covered in the course are human resource management, managing affirmative action, government agencies, supervisor and subordinate interaction, the budgetary process, information management systems, health and safety, fire safety inspection, public fire education, specialized fire protection equipment, organizational communications, strategic planning, and tactics. Methods of instruction include lecture, discussion, classroom exercises, case studies, audio/visual material, learner presentations/reports, quizzes, final written examination, and skills checkoff list.
Credit Recommendation: In the lower division baccalaureate/associate degree category, or the upper division baccalaureate degree category, 3 semester hours in Fire Science Technology, Emergency Medical Service Technology, Emergency Management, or Public Administration (11/94).

Firefighter Health and Safety: Program Implementation and Management (FHSNFA) (Firefighter Health and Safety: Program Implementation and Management [F128])

Location: Maryland Fire and Rescue Institute Training Centers, Maryland Emergency Services Organizations' Facilities.
Length: 16 hours (two 8-hour days).
Dates: May 1986-Present.
Objective: To provide the student with an understanding of general health and safety guidelines and practices needed by firefighters.
Learning Outcome: Upon successful completion of this course, the student will be able to identify and analyze firefighter health and safety concerns; determine the components of an effective department health and safety program; and understand the steps and process necessary to design and implement such a program.
Instruction: Major topics covered in the course are safety as an attitude, developing a health and safety program, laws, standards and regulations, health maintenance and physical fitness, stress, emergency scene safety, and safety investigation.
Credit Recommendation: In the lower division baccalaureate/associate degree category, or in the upper division baccalaureate degree category, 2 semester hours in Engineering, Fire Science Industrial, Health Promotion, Health Safety, or Occupational Safety (12/88) (2/93).

Firefighter I (FFI)

Location: Maryland Fire and Rescue Institute Training Centers; Maryland Emergency Services Organizations' Facilities.
Length: 93 hours (15 weeks).
Dates: July 1993-Present.
Objective: To provide students with the knowledge and skills to safely and effectively perform basic firefighting operations as part of a firefighting team.

Learning Outcome: Upon successful completion of this course, the student will be able to understand and apply the principles of fire behavior; building construction; water distribution systems; fixed fire protection systems; ventilation; hose streams; fire prevention; and inspections, ladders, and rescue techniques. (National Fire Protection Association standard 1001, Fire Fighter Professional Qualifications, 1992 edition, Chapter 3).

Instruction: Major topics covered in the course are the Fire Department Organization, communications, incident command system, ropes and knots, fire behavior, safety, fire prevention, personal protective equipment, fire extinguishers, respiratory protection, ventilation, hoselines, forcible entry, search and rescue procedures, and ladder and sprinkler systems. Methods of instruction include lecture, discussion, classroom exercises, audio/visual material, graded practical exercises, midterm and final exams; series of practical exams; and skills checkoff and home work assignments which are all evaluated by the instructor for satisfactory completion. Minimum passing score on midterm and final exams of 70%; 100% satisfactory completion of required skills and satisfactory evaluation by instructor.

Credit Recommendation: In the vocational certificate category or in the lower division baccalaureate/associate degree category, 3 semester hours in Fire Science Technology (11/94).

Firefighter II (FFII)

Location: Maryland Fire and Rescue Institute Training Centers; Maryland Emergency Services Organizations' Facilities.

Length: 57 hours (9-15 weeks).

Dates: January 1994-Present.

Objective: To provide the knowledge and skills needed to become a journeyman firefighter.

Learning Outcome: Upon successful completion of this course, the student will be able to understand and apply the principles of fire behavior, building construction, water distribution systems, fixed fire protection systems, ventilation, hose streams, fire prevention, inspections, ladders, and rescue techniques. (National Fire Protection Association standard 1001, Fire Fighter Professional Qualifications, 1992 edition, Chapter 4).

Instruction: Major topics covered in the course are incident command, building construction, ventilation, water distribution, hose streams, fixed fire protection systems, fire prevention, inspection preplanning, ladders, and rescue procedures. Methods of instruction include lecture, discussion, classroom exercises, audio/visual material, practical skills graded, and a final exam.

Credit Recommendation: In the vocational certificate category or in the lower division baccalaureate/associate degree category, 2 semester hours in Fire Science Technology (11/94).

Firefighter Safety and Survival: Company Officer's Responsibility (FSSNFA) (Firefighter Safety and Survival: Company Officer's Responsibility [F125])

Location: Maryland Fire and Rescue Institute Training Centers, Maryland Emergency Services Organizations' Facilities.

Length: 16 hours (2 days).

Dates: June 1985-Present.

Objective: To provide the student with an appreciation of the seriousness of the firefighter injury and death problems and to provide an awareness of techniques for reducing injuries and deaths.

Learning Outcome: Upon successful completion of this course, the student will be able to understand the causes of injury and death; understand the behavior problems and attitudes that are addressed; identify health and fitness programs related to injury and death; identify hazardous situations found in training; identify and correct fire station hazards; identify and resolve hazards responding to and return ing from a fire; identify and enforce procedures to improve incident scene safety; and identify safety and survival tips.

Instruction: Major topics covered in the course are an explanation of firefighter injuries and deaths; firefighter health and fitness, safety in training, station and response preparation safety, incident safety, post-incident safety, and survival tips.

Credit Recommendation: In the lower division baccalaureate/associate degree category, 1 semester hour in Fire Administration, Fire Management, or Fire Science (12/88) (2/93).

Fireground Operations I: Engine Company Functions (FGOI)

Location: Maryland Fire and Rescue Institute Training Centers; Maryland Emergency Services Organizations' Facilities.

Length: 24 hours (8 weeks).

Dates: July 1985-Present.

Objective: To provide the student with the fundamental principles of engine company operations and how they can be integrated during fireground operations.

Learning Outcome: Upon successful completion of this course, the student will be able to describe the functions and responsibilities of the engine company and demonstrate the use of nozzles, a hose, hydrants, foam, and testing equipment during practical evolutions.

Instruction: Major topics covered in the course are functions and responsibilities of the engine company; construction and operation of nozzles; positioning and utilizing the engine; utilizing hydrants, pilot gauge and foam; size-up; emergency response considerations; initial fireground operation; and selecting and placing attack and supply lines. Methods of instruction include lecture, discussion, audio/visual material, practical skills exercise, final written examination, and required assignments.

Credit Recommendation: In the vocational certificate category, 1 semester hour in Fire Science Technology (11/94).

First Responder Basic (FRB)

Location: Maryland Fire and Rescue Institute Training Centers; Maryland Emergency Services Organizations' Facilities.

Length: 42 hours (7 weeks).

Dates: July 1988-Present.

Objective: To provide skills necessary to begin, at the emergency location, assessment and care for injured or ill patients.

Learning Outcome: Upon successful completion of this course, the student will be able to provide immediate medical care to critically ill or injured patients until personnel with advanced training arrive, and to assist those personnel.

Instruction: Major topics covered in the course are an introduction to the EMS system, legal aspects of care, equipment, tools, and supplies; general anatomy and patient assessment; respiratory system, resuscitation, and CPR; aids to resuscitation and oxygen administration; management of bleeding, shock, and soft tissue injuries; management of fractures and spinal injuries; environmental emergencies and care of burns; care of special patients including obstetric, pediatric, and elderly; special incidents including triage, water accidents, and gaining access to and moving patients. Methods of instruction include lecture; discussion; classroom exercises; audio/visual material; skills, written, and practical exams; and graded skill evaluations.

Credit Recommendation: In the vocational certificate category or in the lower division baccalaureate/associate degree category, 2 semester hours in Emergency Medical Service Technology or Fire Science Technology (11/94). **NOTE:** Credit should not be awarded for this course and Emergency Care Basic EMT/A.

Hazardous Materials Incident Analysis (HMIANFA) (Hazardous Materials Incident Analysis [F410])

Location: Maryland Fire and Rescue Institute Training Centers, Maryland Emergency Services Organizations' Facilities.

Length: 12 hours (2 days) or in 8 modules.

Dates: June 1981-November 1994.

Objective: To provide the student with the knowledge required for effective analysis of a hazardous materials incident.

Learning Outcome: Upon successful completion of this course, the student will be able to categorize hazardous materials, their storage, and transportation; recognize presence of hazardous materials and the likely behavior of such materials; estimate likely harmful emergency outcomes related to hazardous materials; and select appropriate action related to hazardous materials situations.

Instruction: Major topics covered in the course are the definition of hazardous materials, hazardous materials emergencies and their outcomes, potentially dangerous assumptions, estimating likely harm, events analysis, and characteristics and behavior of hazardous materials. Methods of instruction Include lecture, discussion, classroom exercises, case studies, audiovisual aids, and examinations.

Credit Recommendation: In the lower division baccalaureate/associate degree category, 1 semester hour in Fire Science (11/89).

Hazardous Materials Operations (HMO)

Location: Maryland Fire and Rescue Institute Training Centers; Maryland Emergency Services Organizations' Facilities.

Length: 24 hours.

Dates: September 1995-Present.

Objective: To provide the student with the knowledge and skills to perform hazardous materials first response.

Learning Outcome: Upon successful completion of this course, the student will be able to analyze a hazardous materials incident, plan an initial response, implement the response, and evaluate the progress of the actions taken.

Instruction: Major topics covered in the course are firefighter safety, regulations and standards, chemistry, recognition and identifications, DOT guidebook, site management, container behavior, defensive control measures, personal protective equipment, and decontamination. Methods of instruction include lecture, discussion, classroom exercises, audio/visual material, practical exercises, quizzes, observations, written examinations, and a final examination.

Credit Recommendation: In the vocational certificate or lower division baccalaureate/associate degree category, 1 semester hour in EMS Technology, Fire Sciences, or Emergency Management (9/96).

Health and Safety Officer (HSONFA) (Health and Safety Officer [W720])

Location: Maryland Fire and Rescue Institute Training Centers; Maryland Emergency Services Organizations' Facilities.

Length: 14 hours (2 days).

Dates: July 1994-Present.

Objective: To examine the health and safety officer's role in identifying, evaluating, and implementing policy and procedure that affect the safety and health of emergency responders.

Learning Outcome: Upon successful completion of this course, the student will be able to understand the role of the health and safety officer in both emergency and nonemergency situations.

Instruction: Major topics covered in the course are the role of the health and safety officer; the laws, standards, and regulations; health maintenance; accident investigation; and post incident evaluation. Methods of instruction include lecture, discussion, classroom exercises, case studies, audio/visual material, learner presentations/reports, end of the course testing, and graded individual and group activities throughout the course.

Credit Recommendation: In the lower division baccalaureate/associate degree category or in the upper division baccalaureate degree category, 1 semester hour in Occupational Health and Safety, Fire Science, or Emergency Management (2/95).

Incident Command System (ICSNFA) (Incident Command System [F200])

Location: Maryland Fire and Rescue Institute Training Centers, Maryland Emergency Services Organizations' Facilities.

Length: 16 hours (two days).

Dates: May 1988-Present.

Objective: To allow the student to demonstrate the need for an organized approach to managing emergency incidents, to identify the laws and standards requiring this approach, to identify the elements of an emergency response system, and to assess department capabilities for implementing such a system.

Learning Outcome: Upon successful completion of this course, the student will be able to demonstrate the need for an organized approach to emergency incidents; identify the laws and standards requiring this approach; identify the elements of an effective system; and evaluate his or her department capabilities.

Instruction: Major topics covered in the course are the need for organized incident management; the laws and standards requiring same; the components of such a system; relationship between business management and incident management; the NFA model of such a system; and other examples of incident management systems.

Credit Recommendation: In the lower division baccalaureate/associate degree category, 1 semester hour in Administration, Fire Science, or Management (12/88) (2/93). **NOTE:** Credit for Fire Command Operations should not be awarded if credit is awarded for this course.

Incident Safety Officer (ISONFA) (Incident Safety Officer [W719])

Location: Maryland Fire and Rescue Institute Training Centers; Maryland Emergency Services Organizations' Facilities.

Length: 16 hours (2 days).

Dates: February 1995-Present.

Objective: To provide understanding of the safety officer's role at emergency response situations, with specific emphasis on the role of the safety officer in the Incident Command System.

Learning Outcome: Upon successful completion of this course, the student will be able to provide the Company Officer with the skills to function effectively as a Safety Officer at emergency incidents.

Instruction: Major topics covered in the course are the role of the Safety Officer; regulations, standards, and policies; record keeping and documentation; and risk management and communications. Methods of instruction include lecture, discussion, classroom exercises, case studies, audio/visual material, and a final examination.

Credit Recommendation: In the lower division baccalaureate/associate degree category or in the upper division baccalaureate degree category, 1 semester hour in Occupational Health and Safety or Fire Science (2/95).

Infection Control for Emergency Response Personnel: The Supervisor's Role and Responsibilities (ICERPNFA) (Infection Control for Emergency Response Personnel: The Supervisor's Role and Responsibilities [W250])

Location: Maryland Fire and Rescue Institute Training Centers, Maryland Emergency Services Organizations' Facilities.

Length: 12 hours (2 days).

Dates: December 1990-March 1996.

Objective: To enable supervisory fire and EMS personnel to ensure infection control in the work environment by providing the knowledge and skills required to conduct training, monitor compliance with OSHA (CFR SS190.1030), and serve as a role model for positive behaviors and attitudes.

Learning Outcome: Upon successful completion of this course, students will be able to ensure infection control in their work environment by providing the knowledge and skills required to conduct training, monitor compliance, and serve as a role model for positive behaviors and attitudes.

Instruction: This course is designed to meet the needs of fire service officers and emergency medical service first-line supervisors in order to improve the knowledge and protection of the individual and department/station personnel from the full range of infectious diseases spread through occupational or other exposure. The training stresses protection of the individual and department/station from the full range of infectious diseases spread through occupational or other exposures. Appropriate target audiences for the course include career and volunteer firefighters and allied professionals. Private sector and public sector third service emergency health care providers will also benefit from this instruction. Training will be compatible with NFPA standards and all applicable federal regulations. The importance of the supervisor as a role model is emphasized throughout the course. To highlight, the student prepares a personal plan for developing and demonstrating constructive behaviors and attitudes. Motivating students to practice infection control in all aspects of the job is also stressed. The sequencing of instruction follows the basic progression of an emergency incident—pre-response, on-scene, and post-response. Major topics covered in the course are brisk exposure, modes of transmission, health maintenance personal protective equipment, scene management post-exposures, and post-response and station issues. Methods of instruction include lecture, classroom exercises, group projects, and final exam.

Credit Recommendation: In the lower division baccalaureate/associate degree category, 1 semester hour in Fire Science or Health Care Administration and Public Health (3/91).

Initial Response to Hazardous Materials Incidents-Basic Concepts (IRHMIBC) (Initial Response to Hazardous Materials Incidents-Basic Concepts [F700])

Location: Maryland Fire and Rescue Institute Training Centers, Maryland Emergency Services Organizations' Facilities.

Length: 16 hours (2 days).

Dates: March 1990-February 1997.

Objective: To provide the first responder at a hazardous materials incident basic concepts and techniques for appropriate behavior before, during, and after the incident. The course defines hazardous materials and describes roles, responsibilities, and risks associated with the incident.

Learning Outcome: Upon successful completion of this course, the student will be able to define hazardous materials and describe associated risks to personal safety; explain the roles, responsibilities, and limitations of first responders in hazardous materials incidents; implement appropriate behaviors before, during, and after a hazardous materials incident; identify the presence and potential dangers of hazardous materials in different emergency situations; identify local, state, and federal resources appropriate to emergency and nonemergency situations; and describe basic concepts and techniques of site management and scene setup, to include the proper use of personal protective equipment and decontamination.

Instruction: Major topics covered in the course are introduction; regulations and standards; personal safety; toxicology; site management and scene set-up; personal protective equipment; decontamination; and resources. Methods of instruction include lecture/discussion, classroom exercises, case studies, role playing, and problem-solving (facilitated by instructor and performed by student).

Credit Recommendation: In the lower division baccalaureate/associate degree category, 1 semester hour in Fire Science (2/92).

Initial Response to Hazardous Materials Incidents-Concept Implementation (IRHMICI) (Initial Response to Hazardous Materials Incidents-Concept Implementation [F808])

Location: Maryland Fire and Rescue Institute Training Centers, Maryland Emergency Services Organizations' Facilities.

Length: 16 hours (2 days).

Dates: August 1992-Present.

Objective: To give the first responder an understanding of the basic steps of a systematic process for a safe and appropriate response to hazardous materials incidents, it will identify the types, uses, and sources of information needed to recognize and identify the hazard; and identify basic options, requirements, and limitations of the methods used to control, contain, or confine a hazardous materials incident.

Learning Outcome: Upon successful completion of this course, the student will be able to respond to hazardous materials incidents as a first-responder, and mitigate damage and dangers involving hazardous materials spills.

Instruction: Major topics covered in the course are estimating the potential course and harm of the incident; determine strategic goals; assess tactical options; plan and implement actions; and evaluate and review. Methods of instruction include lecture, two examinations, and two presentations.

Credit Recommendation: In the upper division baccalaureate degree category, 1 semester hour in Fire Science, Applied Science, Physical Science, or General Science (2/93).

Leadership and Supervision (LS)

Location: Maryland Fire and Rescue Institute Training Centers; Maryland Emergency Services Organizations' Facilities.

Length: 18 hours (6 weeks).

Dates: July 1983-June 1997.

Objective: To provide the student with the skills necessary to effectively utilize leadership principles and to communicate successfully in written and verbal forms.

Learning Outcome: Upon successful completion of this course, the student will be able to describe the fundamentals and skills of leadership; the roles and characteristics of effective leaders; the methods of improving individual and group effectiveness; and apply the principles of effective communication.

Instruction: Major topics covered in the course are the principles and methods of leadership group process; subordinate behavior; communication process; and listening skills and other processes. Methods of instruction include lecture, discussion, classroom exercises, case studies, audio/visual material, learner presentations/reports, quizzes, and a final exam.

Credit Recommendation: In the vocation certificate category or lower division baccalaureate/associate degree category, 1 semester hour in Fire Science Technology, Public Administration, Emergency Management, or Emergency Medical Service Technology (11/94).

Leadership I: Strategies for Company Success (LISFCSNFA) (Leadership I: Strategies for Company Success [F803])

Location: Maryland Fire and Rescue Institute Training Centers, Maryland Emergency Services Organizations' Facilities.

Length: 12 hours (2 days) or in four 3-hour modules.

Dates: April 1989-Present.

Objective: To provide the student with leadership skills of mid-level managers, especially fire company officers.

Learning Outcome: Upon successful completion of this course, the student will be able to apply appropriate decision-making styles to given situations; outline critical steps in problem-solving methods; identify services provided by a "typical" fire company and the resources needed to provide these services; understand the relationship between resources and services provided by a fire company; and describe the requirements involved in running effective meetings.

Instruction: Major topics covered in the course are decision-making, problem-solving, brainstorming, and meeting management. Methods of instruction Include lecture, discussion, audiovisual aids, and examinations.

Credit Recommendation: In the lower division baccalaureate/associate degree category, 1 semester hour in Business Administration, Fire Science, Public Administration, or Urban/Regional Planning (11/89) (2/95).

Leadership II: Strategies for Personal Success (LIISFPSNFA) (Leadership II: Strategies for Personal Success [F804])

Location: Maryland Fire and Rescue Institute Training Centers, Maryland Emergency Services Organizations' Facilities.

Length: 12 hours (2 days) or in four 3-hour modules.

Dates: April 1989-Present.

Objective: To provide the student with an understanding of leadership skills and tasks associated with management of multiple roles of managers, ethics, abuse of power, and personal creativity.

Learning Outcome: Upon successful completion of this course, the student will be able to identify typical roles and responsibilities of a commanding officer; identify, define, and analyze the role of creativity and innovation in fire service organizations; identify the sources and limits of different types of power; and make appropriate decisions involving ethical issues.

Instruction: Major topics covered in the course are ethics, role conflict, fostering creativity and innovation, and power. Methods of instruction Include lecture, discussion, audiovisual aids, role playing, and examinations.

Credit Recommendation: In the lower division baccalaureate/associate degree category, 1 semester hour in Business Administration, Fire Science, Public Administration, or Urban/Regional Planning (11/89) (2/95).

Leadership III: Strategies for Supervisory Success (LIIISFSSNF) (Leadership III: Strategies for Supervisory Success [F805])

Location: Maryland Fire and Rescue Institute Training Centers, Maryland Emergency Services Organizations' Facilities.

Length: 12 hours (2 days) or in four 3-hour modules.

Dates: April 1987-Present.

Objective: To provide the student with an understanding of basic leadership skills related to supervision of personnel.

Learning Outcome: Upon successful completion of this course, the student will be able to describe the relationship between development level and leadership style; identify benefits derived from effective delegation and barriers that prevent it; recognize similarities that characterize effective coaches and effective leaders; and use discipline to correct improper employee behavior.

Instruction: Major topics covered in the course are situational leadership, delegation, coaching, and discipline. Methods of instruction include lecture, discussion, audiovisual aids, small group activity, and examinations.

Credit Recommendation: In the lower division baccalaureate/associate degree category, 1 semester hour in Business Administration, Fire Science, Public Administration, or Urban/Regional Planning (11/89) (2/95).

Managing Company Tactical Operations: Decision Making (MCTODNFA) (Managing Company Tactical Operations: Decision Making)

Location: Maryland Fire and Rescue Institute Training Centers, Maryland Emergency Services Organizations' Facilities.

Length: 12 hours (2 days).

Dates: May 1991-Present.

Objective: To provide a framework for effective structural firefighting decision making and tactical organization.

Learning Outcome: Upon successful completion of this course, the student will be able to apply a systematic approach for developing basic fireground strategies and implementing tactical plans; and implement a basic incident command system for structural fire fighting.

Instruction: Major topics covered in the course are the command sequence: size-up, developing an action plan, implementing an action plan, and introduction to incident command. Methods of instruction include lecture, 35 mm slides, instructor-monitored individual and group activities, and written examination.

Credit Recommendation: In the lower division baccalaureate/associate degree category, 1 semester hour in Fire

Science/Technology or Fire Administration (2/93).

Managing Company Tactical Operations: Preparation (MCTOPN-FA)
(Managing Company Tactical Operations: Preparation)

Location: Maryland Fire and Rescue Institute Training Centers, Maryland Emergency Services Organizations' Facilities.

Length: 12 hours (2 days).

Dates: May 1991-Present.

Objective: To provide the new or prospective fire officer with the basic knowledge and skills necessary to manage one or more fire companies in structural fire fighting operations.

Learning Outcome: Upon successful completion of this course, the student will be able to understand the company officers' principal roles and responsibilities in preparing the company to engage in tactical fire fighting operations.

Instruction: Major topics covered in the course are the roles and responsibilities of the fire company officer; personal readiness; company readiness; departmental readiness; operational communications; building construction and fire behavior; and preincident preparation (prefire planning). Methods of instruction include lecture, 33 mm slides, instructor-monitored individual and group activities, and written examination.

Credit Recommendation: In the lower division baccalaureate/associate degree category, 1 semester hour in Fire Science/Technology or Fire Administration (2/93).

Managing Company Tactical Operations: Tactics (MCTOTNFA)
(Managing Company Tactical Operations: Tactics [F870])

Location: Maryland Fire and Rescue Institute Training Centers, Maryland Emergency Services Organizations' Facilities.

Length: 12 hours (2 days).

Dates: May 1991-Present.

Objective: To provide senior or acting company officers with the knowledge and skills needed to effectively accomplish assigned tactics at a structural fire emergency.

Learning Outcome: Upon successful completion of this course, the student will be able to explain the purpose and use of the Communications Model and the Quick Access Prefire Plan in tactical operations at fire incidents; define the relationship between incident priorities, strategy, tactics, and implementation in the command sequence; select the appropriate strategic mode, based on consideration of risk/benefit and available resources; describe the six steps required to implement the Tactical Action Model; and list the factors on which apparatus placement is based.

Instruction: Major topics covered in the course are introduction to managing company tactical operations; ventilation and rescue; fire confinement and extinguishment; water supply and exposure protection; salvage, overhaul, and support activities; and private dwelling simulations. Methods of instruction include lecture, discussion, classroom exercises, audio-visual aides, and final examination.

Credit Recommendation: In the lower division baccalaureate/associate degree category, 1 semester hour in Fire Technology or Administration (2/94).

Methods of Instruction Level I: Teaching Techniques (ITI)

Location: Maryland Fire and Rescue Institute Training Centers; Maryland Emergency Services Organizations' Facilities.

Length: 30 hours (5 weeks).

Dates: January 1992-Present.

Objective: To teach instructors and trainers how to organize and teach a course effectively, using existing lesson plans.

Learning Outcome: Upon successful completion of this course, the student will be able to make an effective classroom presentation based on appropriate lesson plans.

Instruction: Major topics covered in the course are an overview of instructor and student profiles; communicating methods; learning theories; learning environment; instructional materials and media usage; legal aspects of education; student records and reports; and participation in group activities and presentations. Methods of instruction include lecture, discussion, classroom exercises, case studies, audio/visual material, learner presentations/reports, exams, written tests, quizzes, and presentations.

Credit Recommendation: In the vocational certificate category or in the lower division baccalaureate/associate degree category, 2 semester hours in Fire Science Technology, Public Administration, or Adult Education (11/94). **NOTE:** Credit should not be granted for both Methods of Instruction Level II and this course because the content of Methods of Instruction Level I is repeated in the Level II course.

Methods of Instruction Level II: Teaching and Program Development Techniques (ITII)
(Formerly Methods of Instruction Level II: Teaching and Program Development Techniques)

Location: Maryland Fire and Rescue Institute Training Centers; Maryland Emergency Services Organizations' Facilities.

Length: 54 hours (9 weeks).

Dates: January 1992-Present.

Objective: To prepare the student to use instructional methodologies that address various learning styles and teaching methods and to plan and develop lessons and programs for the purpose of delivering instruction.

Learning Outcome: Upon successful completion of this course, the student will be able to describe and define instructional terms; use reference materials; use various instructional methods and techniques; use instructional materials and aids; evaluate learning; maintain training records and reports; describe concepts of learning; use communications methods and skills; and be aware of instructor rolls and responsibilities. (National Fire Protection Association 1041 standard, Fire Service Instructor Professional Qualifications, 1992 edition, Chapter 2).

Instruction: Major topics covered in the course are the development process; task analysis; developing goals and objectives; course development and lesson outline; developing instructional materials; instructional techniques; lesson preparation and delivery; evaluation process and methods; student records and reports; and participation in group activities and presentations. Methods of instruction include lecture, discussion, classroom exercises, case studies, audio/visual material, learner presentations/reports, research paper preparation and presentation, tests, presentations, and a research paper.

Credit Recommendation: In the lower division baccalaureate/associate degree category or in the upper division baccalaureate degree category, 3 semester hours in Fire Science Technology, Public Administration, or Adult Education (11/94). **NOTE:** Credit should not be granted for both Methods of Instruction Level I and this course because the content of Methods of Instruction I is repeated in the Level II course.

Personal Effectiveness (FSSIPEN-FA)
(Personal Effectiveness [F310])
(Fire Service Supervisor: Personal)

Location: Maryland Fire and Rescue Institute Training Centers, Maryland Emergency Services Organizations' Facilities.

Length: 16 hours (2 days).

Dates: August 1983-January 1992.

Objective: To provide fire service managers and supervisors with basic supervisory skills and techniques that will improve their personal effectiveness as key leaders.

Instruction: Major topics covered in the course are basic skills and techniques that will assist the individual in improving his/her personal effectiveness; management culture, leadership managerial style, and personal performance; time management; stress management; and personal professional development planning.

Credit Recommendation: In the upper division baccalaureate degree category, 1 semester hour in Business Management, Behavioral Science, Fire Science, Prin--ciples of Management, or Supervision (8/86).

Pump Operator (PO)
(Formerly Pumps [P])

Location: Maryland Fire and Rescue Institute Training Centers; Maryland Emergency Services Organizations' Facilities.

Length: 30 hours (7 weeks).

Dates: July 1984-Present.

Objective: To provide students with the basic knowledge and skills needed to operate fire department pumping apparatus.

Learning Outcome: Upon successful completion of this course, the student will be able to determine how much water is flowing; give the nozzles in service, the available pressure, and available hoselines; and calculate pressures needed for a supply pumper, relay pumper, and attack pumper. (National Fire Protection Association Standard 1002, Fire Department Vehicle Driver/Operator Professional Qualifications, Chapter 3).

Instruction: Major topics covered in the course are basic terminology, water supply, water pressure and gauges, hydraulics, positive displacement props, centrifugal pumps, pump power supply systems, relief valves, pressure governors, primers, water sources, and maintenance. Methods of instruction include lecture, discussion, classroom exercises, audio/visual material, graded practical exercises, and a final examination.

Credit Recommendation: In the vocational certificate category or in the lower division baccalaureate/associate degree category, 1 semester hour in Fire Science Technology (11/94).

Rescue Technician (RTR)

Location: Maryland Fire and Rescue Institute Training Centers; Maryland Emergency Services Organizations' Facilities.

Length: 60 hours.

Dates: October 1995-Present.

Objective: To provide the student with the fundamental principles of rescue to safely perform skills required at an auto accident, forcible entry situation, or land rescue.

Learning Outcome: Upon successful completion of this course, the student will be able to describe the principles and hazards of rescue and demonstrate the use of tools and equipment to properly and safely perform auto extrication, rudimentary rigging, ladder rescue, forcible entry operations, and overland rappelling.

Instruction: Major topics covered in the course are victim removal and transfer, vehicle extrication, hand and power tools, vehicle stabilization, gaining access to vehicles, ropes and knots, rigging, overland rappelling, ladders, and forcible entry. Methods of instruction include lecture, discussion, classroom exercises, audio/visual material, practical exercises, graded practical exercises, quizzes, observations, and written and practical examinations.

Credit Recommendation: In the vocational certificate or lower division baccalaureate/associate degree category, 3 semester hours in Fire Science, EMS Technology, or Emergency Management (9/96).

Rescue Technician

Location: Maryland Fire and Rescue Institute Training Centers; Maryland Emergency Services Organizations' Facilities.

Length: 45 hours (7 weeks).

Dates: April 1989-June 1996.

Objective: To provide the student with the fundamental principles of rescue to safely perform skills required at an auto accident, forcible entry situation, or land rescue.

Learning Outcome: Upon successful completion of this course, the student will be able to describe the principles and hazards of rescue and demonstrate the use of tools and equipment to properly and safely perform auto extrication, rudimentary rigging, ladder rescue, forcible entry operations, and overland rappelling.

Instruction: Major topics covered in the course are victim removal and transfer, vehicle extrication, hand and power tools, vehicle stabilization, gaining access to vehicles, ropes and knots, rigging, overland rappelling, ladders, and forcible entry. Methods of instruction include lecture, discussion, classroom exercises, audio/visual material, practical exercises, graded practical exercises, and written and practical examinations.

Credit Recommendation: In the vocational certificate category, 1 semester hour in Fire Science Technology or Emergency Medical Service Technology (11/94).

Team Effectiveness (FSSITENFA)
(Team Effectiveness [F320])
(Fire Service Supervisor: Team)

Location: Maryland Fire and Rescue Institute Training Centers, Maryland Emergency Services Organizations' Facilities.

Length: 16 hours (2 days).

Dates: November 1983-January 1992.

Objective: To introduce fire service managers and supervisors to basic skills and techniques that will improve their ability to relate to others in the work environment. Service managers will be expected to incorporate the principles of team building in their daily jobs.

Instruction: Major topics covered in the course are the team leader's needs of fire service supervisors and program managers; manager's interpersonal skills, motivation, interpersonal communications, counseling, group dynamics, and conflict resolution. Methods of instruction include lecture, discussion, media, and student activities.

Credit Recommendation: In the upper division baccalaureate degree category, 1 semester hour in Behavioral Science, Business Management, Fire Science, Principles of Management or Supervision (8/86).

Truck Company Fireground Operations (TCFO)
(Formerly Fireground Operations II: Truck Company Functions [FGOII])

Location: Maryland Fire and Rescue Institute Training Centers; Maryland Emergency Services Organizations' Facilities.

Length: 24 hours (8 weeks).

Dates: March 1983-Present.

Objective: To provide the student with the fundamental principles of truck company operations and how they are integrated during fireground operations.

Learning Outcome: Upon successful completion of this course, the student will be able to demonstrate forcible entry, search and rescue, ventilation, salvage, overhaul, and ladders.

Instruction: Major topics covered in the course are the function and responsibilities of the truck company; forced entry, ground ladder use, techniques and procedures for locating victims, techniques for removal of smoke and gases, salvage operations, checking for fire extension, procedures for overhauling, building construction, utility control, and electrical and lighting the fireground. Methods of instruction include lecture, discussion, audio-visual material, practice skill exercises, final exam, and required assignments.

Credit Recommendation: In the vocational certificate category, 1 semester hour in Fire Science Technology (11/94).

Massachusetts Bankers Association, Inc.

The Massachusetts Bankers Association (MBA) is a trade association that represents 220 mutual savings banks, stock savings banks, and commercial banks in Massachusetts, with assets totaling $212 billion. The MBA staff is organized in seven departments: Education and Management Development, Finance and Administration, Legislative and Regulatory Affairs, Public Affairs and Marketing, Research and Planning, Member Services, and Trust. The Massachusetts School of Financial Studies (MSFS) was founded in 1961 as the School of Savings Banking. The name was changed in 1984 to reflect the program's increased emphasis on financial and management studies.

The Massachusetts School of Financial Studies is located at the Center for Executive Education, Babson College, Wellesley, Massachusetts. The center's facilities include lecture theaters, which feature audiovisual equipment and small break-out rooms that surround the lecture theaters. Students can be divided into small groups for discussion, problem-solving, and case study activities.

The director of Education and Management Development is advised by an Education and Management Development Committee composed of senior bank executives. The committee meets four times annually to discuss additions to the curriculum, program quality, and admissions and standards. Programs are changed and revised in response to industry trends and changes as well as proposed introduction of a subject of importance to the industry. During this process, consultants are used as resources in revision and development.

The MSFS selects faculty from leading academic, government, business, and financial organizations. An advanced degree or significant experience (over five years) in a specialty is required. The prospective faculty member is interviewed by the director of Education and Management Development, qualifications are weighed carefully, and recommendations from peers and students are considered for a faculty position. MSFS instructors are evaluated frequently and systematically. A faculty member is present during all class presentations, and students complete an evaluation for each segment of the program. The information is evaluated by the director, who then counsels the instructor.

Source of official student records: Ms. Kathleen E. Jones, Senior Vice President and Director of Education and Management Development, Massachusetts Bankers Association, 73 Tremont Street, Suite 306, Boston, MA 02108-3906.

Additional information about the courses: College Credit Recommendation Service, American Council on Education, One Dupont Circle, Washington, DC 20036-1193.

MSFS: Business Policy

Location: Babson College Center for Executive Education, Wellesley, MA.

Length: 315 hours (due to the integrated nature of the material).

Dates: April 1982-Present.

Objective: To develop in the student an understanding of financial management problems in banks and to expose them to a wide range of operating decisions.

Learning Outcome: Upon successful completion of this course, the student will be able to understand vocabulary and basic concepts of strategic planning; use a simulation model for strategic planning; and understand the relationship between corporate culture and successful creation and implementation of a plan.

Instruction: Major topics covered in the course are operational and strategic long-range planning; definition of objectives, goals, and strategies; use of simulation modeling and cases to develop decision-making skills; and alternative perspectives of strategic planning. Methods of instruction include lecture, discussion, cases, simulation modeling, and small-group processes.

Credit Recommendation: In the upper division baccalaureate degree category, 3 semester hours in Business Policy, Economics, or General Business (2/89) (5/94). **NOTE:** Credit awarded only on completion of the full one-year program.

MSFS: Human Resource Management

Location: Babson College Center for Executive Education, Wellesley, MA.

Length: 315 hours (due to the integrated nature of the material).

Dates: April 1982-Present.

Objective: To instruct students in the concepts and techniques necessary to understand and manage employees in an organization.

Learning Outcome: Upon successful completion of this course, the student will be able to demonstrate communication and career planning skills; analyze the dynamics of human behavior and conflict resolution in the workplace; and describe and explain management styles and the role of human resources management in an organization.

Instruction: Major topics covered in the course are business communication, recruitment, staffing and training, human relations and motivation, and salary and benefits administration. Methods of instruction include lecture, discussion, cases, simulation modeling, and small-group processes.

Credit Recommendation: In the upper division baccalaureate degree category, 3 semester hours in General Business or Human Resource Management (2/89) (5/94). **NOTE:** Credit awarded only on completion of the full one-year program.

MSFS: Investments/Financial Analysis

Location: Babson College Center for Executive Education, Wellesley, MA.

Length: 315 hours (due to the integrated nature of the material).

Dates: *Version 1:* April 1982-March 1994; *Version 2:* April 1994-Present.

Objective: To provide students with a basic understanding of the principles of investments with special emphasis on money and capital markets, investment instruments, interest rate forecasting, portfolio policy with specific attention to bank investments; and to instruct students in the financial analysis of a bank and the evaluation of a bank's performance.

Learning Outcome: Upon successful completion of this course, the student will be able to identify and explain investment characteristics, objectives, and risks; describe, calculate, and compare yields on various investments; explain the function and importance of investments in banking; and apply techniques of financial analysis to the performance of a bank.

Instruction: Major topics covered in the course are an introduction to risk and return, investment mathematics including yield calculations and present value analysis, money and capital market securities, bank asset liability-asset management, and the application of tools and techniques to analyze a bank's financial performance. Methods of instruction include lecture, discussion, cases, simulation modeling, and small-group processes.

Credit Recommendation: *Version 1:* In the upper division baccalaureate degree category, 3 semester hours in Business, Economics, or Finance (2/89). *Version 2:* In the upper division baccalaureate degree category or in the graduate degree category, 3 semester hours in Business, Economics, or Finance (5/94). **NOTE:**

Credit awarded only on completion of the full one-year program.

MSFS: Lending Fundamentals

Location: Babson College Center for Executive Education, Wellesley, MA.

Length: 315 hours (due to the integrated nature of the material).

Dates: *Version 1:* April 1982-March 1994; *Version 2:* April 1994-Present.

Objective: To provide students with an understanding of the fundamentals of residential real estate, commercial lending, and the philosophy and implementation of fair lending practices.

Learning Outcome: Upon successful completion of this course, the student will be able to identify and describe the properties of residential mortgages; conduct preliminary financial analysis of residential and commercial borrowers; describe and explain the workings of the secondary market for residential mortgages; and describe the role of a fair lending policy and the steps necessary to successfully implement fair lending.

Instruction: Major topics covered in the course are for residential real estate are lending, pricing, and profitability of the mortgage product; first mortgage products; second mortgages and secured equity lines of credit; and secondary mortgage market including underwriting, types of sales, servicing, and profit analysis. Major topics covered in the course for commercial lending are the analysis of credit risk, secured and unsecured loans, lines of credit, term loans, revolving credit agreements, and letters of credit. Major topics covered in the course for fair lending are a description of fair lending policy, the benefits to customer and lender, key pitfalls to avoid in executing fair lending, and ways to measure the success of a fair lending program. Methods of instruction include lecture, discussion, cases, simulation modeling, and small-group processes.

Credit Recommendation: *Version 1:* In the upper division baccalaureate degree category, 3 semester hours in Business, Economics, or Finance (2/89). *Version 2:* In the upper division baccalaureate degree category, 3 semester hours in Business, Economics, or Finance or in the graduate degree category, 2 semester hours in Business, Economics, or Finance (5/94). **NOTE:** Credit awarded only on completion of the full one-year program.

MSFS: Management Topics

Location: Babson College Center for Executive Education, Wellesley, MA.

Length: 315 hours (due to the integrated nature of the material).

Dates: *Version 1:* April 1982-March 1994; *Version 2:* April 1994-Present.

Objective: To instruct students in the concepts, techniques, and current issues in managing an organization.

Learning Outcome: Upon successful completion of this course, the student will be able to prepare long and short term strategic plans for the organization; build an organizational structure focused on quality management practices and customer satisfaction; manage corporate change in uncertain economies; institute corporate policies to insure ethical practice and regulatory compliance; analyze the traditional management functions of planning, organizing, leading, and controlling; and analyze and implement styles of management and effective communication skills.

Instruction: Major topics covered in the course are strategic planning, decision making, delegating, stockholder relations, ethics, styles of management, total quality management, leadership styles, ethical decision making, managing change, and stress management. Methods of instruction include lecture, discussion, cases, simulation modeling, and small-group processes.

Credit Recommendation: *Version 1:* In the upper division baccalaureate degree category, 3 semester hours in General Business or Management (2/89). *Version 2:* In the upper division baccalaureate degree category or in the graduate degree category, 3 semester hours in General Business or Management (5/94). **NOTE:** Credit awarded only on completion of the full one-year program.

MSFS: Marketing of Financial Services

Location: Babson College Center for Executive Education, Wellesley, MA.

Length: 315 hours (due to the integrated nature of the material).

Dates: April 1982-Present.

Objective: To provide students with an understanding of the marketing function of a financial institution and the steps necessary to develop and implement marketing strategy.

Learning Outcome: Upon successful completion of this course, the student will be able to identify and describe market research and its uses; explain product development, pricing, and management; and describe the role of marketing in advertising and public relations.

Instruction: Major topics covered in the course are marketing promotion, pricing, product and market research, marketing strategy, product profitability analysis, and new product entry strategies. Methods of instruction include lecture, discussion, cases, simulation modeling, and small-group processes.

Credit Recommendation: In the upper division baccalaureate degree category, 3 semester hours in Marketing or as a Business elective (2/89) (5/94). **NOTE:** Credit awarded only on completion of the full one-year program.

McDonald's Corporation

The McDonald's Corporation provides training for its management personnel at the restaurant level, at Regional Training Departments, and Hamburger University. The courses offered are designed to improve the skills and knowledge of management personnel in the McDonald's Corporation. This includes specific on-the-job training as well as comprehensive skills and knowledge involved in restaurant management and food service equipment for various levels of management personnel.

Course delivery is carried out by McDonald's Corporation instructional and corporate staff within Hamburger University and at Regional Training Departments.

All McDonald's training courses are systematically designed and offered at either Hamburger University or at Regional Training Departments.

Classrooms, audiovisual support, and other student/instructor facilities have been designed to ensure an effective learning environment.

In addition to the training offered to management personnel, specialized training for home office staff is provided at the corporate headquarters in Oak Brook.

Source of official student records: Dean, Hamburger University, Ronald Lane, Oak Brook, IL 60521.

Additional information about the courses: College Credit Recommendation Service, American Council on Education, One Dupont Circle, Washington, DC 20036-1193.

Additional contact person is Sue McNaham at 630/623-7185.

Advanced Operations (AOC)

Location: Hamburger University, Oak Brook, IL.

Length: *Versions 1 and 2:* 70 hours (2 weeks); *Version 3:* 74.75 hours (2 weeks); *Version 4:* 42 hours (5.5 days).

Dates: *Version 1:* January 1974-December 1983; *Version 2:* January 1984-November 1990; *Version 3:* December 1990-December 1996; *Version 4:* January 1997-Present.

Objective: *Versions 1 and 2:* To provide managers with a knowledge of restaurant management and food service equipment. *Versions 3 and 4:* To provide managers with advanced knowledge, competence, and skills in the operation of a food service unit.

Learning Outcome: Upon successful completion of this course, the student will be able to work effectively with restaurant personnel, suppliers, and customers; staff and retain restaurant personnel in a culturally diverse workforce; and manage all facets of the restaurant operation.

Instruction: *Versions 1 and 2:* Major topics covered in the course are personnel management, skill development and equipment operation, maintenance, and troubleshooting. Methods of instruction include individual lessons prepared around specific objectives augmented by audio/visual presentations, lecture, discussion, workshops, and testing. *Version 3:* Major topics covered in the course are interpersonal skills, human relations skills, personnel management skills, operation management skills, equipment management skills, cost control, administrative management, and marketing. *Version 4:* Major topics covered in the course are effective people practices including delegation, communications, and teambuilding; profit management including balancing customer satisfaction and profit improvement; staffing and retention including turnover issues; and market share including analyzing demographics and identifying appropriate sales strategies. Methods of instruction include lecture, discussion, classroom exercises, case studies, audio-visual materials, observations, and tests.

Credit Recommendation: *Version 1:* In the lower division baccalaureate/associate degree category, 2 semester hours in Food Service Equipment and in the upper division baccalaureate degree category, 2 semester hours in Personnel Management (10/80). *Version 2:* In the lower division baccalaureate/associate degree category, 1 semester hour in Food Service Equipment, or in the upper division baccalaureate degree category, 3 semester hours in Restaurant Management (7/85). *Prerequisites for Versions 1 and 2:* Basic Operations, Intermediate Operations, Regional Equipment Classes (formerly Applied Equipment), and Management Development I, II, and III. *Version 3:* In the upper division baccalaureate degree category, 3 semester hours in Restaurant/Food Service Management (12/90). *Prerequisites:* Management Development Program I-III, Basic Operations Course, Basic Management Course, Intermediate Operations Course, and Regional Equipment Classes (formerly Applied Equipment). *Version 4:* In the upper division baccalaureate degree category, 3 semester hours in Restaurant/Food Service Management or Business Management (10/97). *Prerequisites:* Management Development Program, Basic Operations Course, Basic Management Course, and Intermediate Operations Course.

Advanced Restaurant Management

Location: Hamburger University, Oak Brook, IL.

Length: 35 hours (1 week).

Dates: *Version 1:* December 1977-December 1983; *Version 2:* January 1984-December 1990.

Objective: To strengthen students' decision-making ability in a variety of complex operational situations in restaurants.

Instruction: Major topics covered in the course are advanced management techniques, operational procedures, profits, cost and pricing, local store marketing, and personnel administration. Methods of instruction include lecture and discussion.

Credit Recommendation: *Version 1:* In the upper division baccalaureate degree category, 2 semester hours in Seminar in Restaurant Management and Finance (10/80). *Version 2:* In the upper division baccalaureate degree category, 2 semester hours in General Management (7/85).

Area Supervisor's Class—McOpCo (Formerly Supervisory Management Skills)

Location: Hamburger University, Oak Brook, IL.

Length: *Versions 1 and 2:* 40 hours (1 week); *Version 3:* 31.75 hours (5 days).

Dates: *Version 1:* September 1975-February 1982; *Version 2:* March 1982-February 1991; *Version 3:* March 1991-Present.

Objective: To prepare students to successfully manage multi-unit food service operations.

Learning Outcome: Upon successful completion of this course, the student will be able to describe the responsibilities of supervising multiple restaurants; prioritize activities; and plan time to accomplish objectives.

Instruction: *Version 1:* Major topics covered in the course are personnel and food service management. Methods of instruction include lecture and discussion. *Version 2:* Major topics covered in the course are the responsibilities of a multi-restaurant supervisor, labor relations, personnel management, leadership, accounting, security, operational procedures, and time management. *Version 3:* Major topics covered in the course are building sales; leadership; effective restaurant visits (human resources management, accounting, and operational procedures); profitability; and calendar management. Methods of instruction include lecture, discussion, classroom exercises, and field visits.

Credit Recommendation: *Version 1:* In the lower division baccalaureate/associate degree category, 1 semester hour in Food Service Management and 1 semester hour in Personnel Management (10/80). *Versions 2 and 3:* In the upper division baccalaureate degree category, 2 semester hours in Supervision or Management (7/85) (12/90) (10/97). *Prerequisites for Version 2:* Management Development Program I-IV, Basic Operations Course, Basic Management Course, Intermediate Operations Course, Regional Equipment Classes [formerly Applied Equipment], Advanced Operations Course, and Area Supervisor's Development Program. *Prerequisite for Version 3:* Area Supervisor's Development Program—McOpCo.

Area Supervisor's Development Program—McOpCo (Formerly Area Supervisor's Development Program [Volume I])

Location: McDonald's Regional Training Centers.

Length: *Versions 1 and 2:* 120 hours (3 months); *Version 3:* 224-268 hours (60-90 days).

Dates: *Version 1:* January 1980-November 1990; *Version 2:* December 1990-February 1991; *Version 3:* March 1991-Present.

Objective: *Versions 1 and 2:* To prepare the newly promoted area supervisor to assume mid-management responsibilities in multi-restaurant supervision and to make a smooth transition from restaurant operations. *Version 3:* To provide the student with a supervised, self-paced introduction to multi-unit restaurant management.

Learning Outcome: *Version 3:* Upon successful completion of this course, the student (in a multiple store environment) will be able to orient new managers to achieve consistency; analyze profit and loss statements; recruit and retain management personnel; and effectively manage time in the face of multiple demands.

Instruction: *Versions 1 and 2:* Major topics covered in the course are personal development, transition from store to region, orientation, supervision, profit and loss, field operations, and human resources. Method of instruction is self-paced. *Version 3:* Major topics covered in the course are managing change; time management, management of development, and training, and quantitative decision making. Methods of instruction include case studies, directed readings in a self-paced program, and assessment is through supervisor review.

Credit Recommendation: *Version 1:* In the lower division baccalaureate/associate degree category, 2 semester hours in Cooperative Education (10/80) (7/85). *Version 2:* In the upper division baccalaureate degree category, 2 semester hours in Multi-unit Restaurant Management (12/90). *Version 3:* In the lower division baccalaureate/associate degree category or the upper division baccalaureate degree category, 2 semester hours in Restaurant Management (10/97).

Basic Management Course (BMC)

Location: McDonald's Regional Training Centers.

Length: *Version 1:* 27 hours (4 days); *Version 2:* 27 hours (3.5 days).

Dates: *Version 1:* January 1990-June 1990; *Version 2:* July 1990-Present.

Objective: To provide basic managerial and supervisory skills that result in good business practices in the operation of a restaurant.

Learning Outcome: *Version 1:* Upon successful completion of this course, the student will be able to observe and gather facts; analyze information; and act and communicate according to established policies. *Version 2:* Upon successful completion of this course, the student will be able to exhibit effective leadership skills and attitudes; interview, hire, and counsel staff; handle special situations; and trouble shoot small equipment.

Instruction: *Version 1:* Major topics covered in the course are human relations, functional management, and basic leadership skills. *Version 2:* Major topics covered in the course are human relations, functional management, basic leadership skills, and maintaining and trouble shooting small equipment. Methods of instruction include lecture, participant involvement, interactive problem-solving, small-group techniques, skill-building activities, observation, pre- and post-tests, and post-class action plan.

Credit Recommendation: *Versions 1 and 2:* In the lower division baccalaureate/associate degree category, 2 semester hours in Human Resource Management (12/90) (10/97). *Prerequisites for Version 1:* Basic Operations Course, Management Development Program I, and Modules 1 and 2 of Management Development Program II. *Prerequisites for Version 2:* Basic Operations Course and required Management Development Program modules.

Basic Operations Course (BOC)

Location: *Versions 1 and 2:* Hamburger University, Oak Brook, IL; McDonald's Regional Training Centers; *Version 3:* McDonald's Regional Training Centers; *Version 4:* McDonald's Regional Training Centers.

Length: *Versions 1 and 2:* 38.25 hours (1 week); *Version 3:* 33.5 hours (1 week); *Version 4:* 36 hours (4 days).

Dates: *Versions 1 and 2:* January 1979-February 1989; *Version 3:* March 1989-July 1992; *Version 4:* August 1992-Present.

Objective: *Versions 1 and 2:* To augment and complete management trainees' individualized instruction in basic operational functions of restaurant management. *Version 3:* To reinforce and augment the management trainee's individualized instruction in the basic functions of restaurant management. *Version 4:* To provide students with the knowledge and skills necessary to effectively manage shifts.

Learning Outcome: *Versions 1, 2, and 3:* Upon successful completion of this course, the student will be able to manage a restaurant during non-peak shifts. *Version 4:* Upon successful completion of this course, the student will be able to demonstrate effective communication; maintain food safety; manage a crew to deliver quality products in an atmosphere of Total Customer Satisfaction; and to understand state and federal law, and McDonald's shift and security policies.

Instruction: *Version 1:* Major topics covered in the course are raw products, equipment operations, finished quality, other areas covering production, personnel, maintenance, and general operation. Methods of instruction include lecture-discussion workshops, and testing. *Version 2:* Major topics covered in the course are raw products, production and quality control, communications, time management, training, service, security, personnel, and maintenance. Methods of instruction include lectures, discussions, and demonstrations. *Version 3:* Major topics covered in the course are communication, training, raw finished product quality, service, sanitation, managing people, floor control, security, and managing change. Methods of instruction include lecture, discussion, demonstration, group activities, and an applied management laboratory. *Version 4:* Major topics covered in the course are communication, training, food safety and sanitation, product quality, customer satisfaction, floor management, and security. Methods of instruction include lecture, discussion, classroom exercises, "hands-on" lab experience, observation, tests, a final examination, and post class action plans.

Credit Recommendation: *Versions 1, 2, 3, and 4:* In the lower division baccalaureate/associate degree category, 2 semester hours in Food Service Management (10/80) (7/85) (12/90) (10/97). *Prerequisite for Versions 2 and 3:* Management Development Program I.

Business Consultant Development Program (includes Financial Skills CBT course)

Location: McDonald's Regional Training Centers.

Length: 77-93 hours (self-paced over 60-90 days).

Dates: June 1996-Present.

Objective: To provide the student with the basic skills and knowledge needed to begin consulting with franchised business operators.

Learning Outcome: Upon successful completion of this course, the student will be able to describe the responsibilities and roles of the business consultant in meeting established standards; explain the relationship between the corporate and operator goals; develop a base of regional resources, establish efficient calendar, time management, and information retrieval techniques; develop an effective and flexible business planning process; analyze and monitor financial data to improve a business's financial position; and to communicate more effectively in writing.

Instruction: Major topics covered in the course are the roles and responsibilities of the business consultant, identifying regional resources, organizing time and files, consulting activities and skills, business planning, financial data, building market share, and written communication. Methods of instruction include computer-based instruction, case studies, classroom exercises, assigned reading, and peer, supervisor, and operator observation and feedback.

Credit Recommendation: In the upper division baccalaureate degree category, 3 semester hours in Business Administration or Hospitality Administration (10/97).

Business Consultants Course

Location: Hamburger University, Oak Brook, IL.

Length: 33.5 hours (5 days).

Dates: December 1996-Present.

Objective: To prepare students to effectively provide business operators with consulting services in the areas of sales, financial and reinvestment matters, planning and corporate strategies.

Learning Outcome: Upon successful completion of this course, the student will be able to develop an effective consulting relationship with business operators to assist in improving their businesses.

Instruction: Major topics covered in the course are understanding the operator's perspective; running a business; building relationships; committing to mutual goals; preparing for improvement; providing support; assessing the relationship; and planning and organizing. Methods of instruction include lecture, discussion, case studies, role play, observation, peer evaluations and critiques of role plays.

Credit Recommendation: In the upper division baccalaureate degree category, 2 semester hours in Business Administration or Hospitality Administration (10/97).

Coaching Workshop

Location: Hamburger University, Oak Brook, IL.

Length: 15 hours (2 days).

Dates: January 1996-Present.

Objective: To provide students with the skills to be effective coaches when working with employees in performance development, counseling or career advising.

Learning Outcome: Upon successful completion of this course, the student will be able to demonstrate increased proficiency in core coaching skills.

Instruction: Major topics covered in the course are the coaching model including skills and behaviors; building trust; questioning; empathetic listening; receiving feedback; assessing interaction; involving the employee and developing and practicing a coaching plan. Methods of instruction include lecture, discussion, classroom exercises and observation.

Credit Recommendation: In the lower division baccalaureate/associate degree category, 1 semester hour in Supervision (10/97).

Department Heads Course

Location: Hamburger University, Oak Brook, IL.

Length: 18.5 hours (3 days).

Dates: March 1996-Present.

Objective: To provide students with basic skills in managing change, teaching, and team assessment within the organization.

Learning Outcome: Upon successful completion of this course, the student will be able to differentiate between coaching and managing or supervising; demonstrate increased proficiency in empathetic listening, building trust, giving and receiving feedback and questioning for discovery; enhance performance using effective coaching skills.

Instruction: Major topics covered in the course are managing change; coaching; and team development. Methods of instruction include lecture, discussion, case studies, role plays and observation.

Credit Recommendation: In the upper division baccalaureate degree category, 1 semester hour in Restaurant Management, Food Service Management or Management (10/97).

Field Consultants' Class

Location: Hamburger University, Oak Brook, IL.

Length: 30 hours (1 week).

Dates: December 1975-October 1996.

Objective: To analyze the operational level of the restaurant and to provide professional advice, methods, and direction to owners and operators in the areas of sales, financial, and reinvestment matters.

Instruction: Major topics covered in the course are owner/operator expectations, strategies of effective consultation, and financial concepts. Methods of instruction include discussion and lecture. Prerequisite: Advanced Operations within the past 3 years.

Credit Recommendation: In the upper division baccalaureate degree category, 2 semester hours in Food Service Management (10/80) (7/85) (12/90) (10/97).

Field Consultant's Development Program

Location: McDonald's Regional Offices.

Length: 120 hours (3 months).

Dates: *Version 1:* February 1981-May 1989; *Version 2:* June 1989-Present.

Objective: To prepare the newly promoted field consultant to assume the responsibilities of a business management consultant representing the mutual interests of the independent operators and the parent company.

Learning Outcome: Upon successful completion of this course, the student will be able to perform effectively as a business consultant to independent operators.

Instruction: *Version 1:* Under the direction of the field service managers, the field consultant is introduced to the various functions and supporting personnel relative to the conduct of the position. Covers licensing, consultations with owner operators, financial reviews, and specialized departmental orientations. *Version 2:* Major topics covered in the course are affirmative action, field process, test products and equipment, licensing, finance, and department operations. Methods of instruction include self-paced instruction.

Credit Recommendation: *Version 1:* In the lower division baccalaureate/associate degree category, 2 semester hours in Cooperative Education in Restaurant Management (7/85). *Version 2:* In the upper division baccalaureate degree category, 2 semester hours in Restaurant Management (12/90).

Intermediate Operations Course (IOC)

Location: Hamburger University, Oak Brook, IL; McDonald's Regional Training Centers.

Length: *Version 1:* 25 hours (3 days); *Version 2:* 35 hours (5 days); *Version 3:* 28 hours (4 days).

Dates: *Version 1:* August 1978-August 1982; *Version 2:* September 1982-May 1992; *Version 3:* June 1993-Present.

Objective: *Versions 1 and 2:* To analyze and reinforce the second assistant's instruction in the successful operation of a restaurant; *Version 3:* To provide students with the knowledge and skills needed to analyze and optimize the proper operation and profitability of a restaurant.

Learning Outcome: *Version 3:* Upon successful completion of this course, the student will be able to identify and solve problems in a restaurant; describe, analyze and address the factors that influence food and labor cost controls; and plan and manage crew training.

Instruction: *Versions 1 and 2:* Major topics covered in the course are personnel skills in orientation and training, knowledge of equipment function and maintenance, scheduling, and record keeping. Methods of instruction include individual lessons prepared around specific objectives, audiovisual presentations, lecture-discussions workshops, and testing. Prerequisites: Basic Operations plus three months' experience in management training and completion of the McDonald's Management Development Program II. *Version 3:* Major topics covered in the course are managing for improved performance including food and labor cost controls; and crew training. Methods of evaluation include observation, final examination and post-class action plans. Prerequisites, Basic Operations Course, Basic Management Course and required Management Development Program modules.

Credit Recommendation: *Version 1:* In the lower division baccalaureate/associate degree category, 1 semester hour in Food Service Management (10/80). *Versions 2 and 3:* In the lower division baccalaureate/associate degree category, 2 semester hours in Food Service Management (7/85) (12/90) (10/97).

Management Development Program (MDP) and Management Development Program Vol. IV (MDP IV) (Formerly Management Development Program I, II, III and IV; and 1. Management Development Program I, II, III, and IV and 2. Registered Applicants Program I and II).

Location: *Version 1:* Hamburger University, Oak Brook, IL; McDonald's Regional Training Centers *Version 2:* Hamburger University, Oak Brook, IL; McDonald's Regional Training Centers *Version 3:* McDonald's Regional Training Centers. *Version 4:* In-Restaurant.

Length: *Version 1:* Approximately 6 months to 2 years; *Version 2:* 1 to 2 years; *Version 3:* 2 to 4 years (self-paced); *Version 4:* 1-3 years (MDP - self-paced) and 9-12 months (MDP IV - self-paced).

Dates: *Version 1:* September 1977-February 1985; *Version 2:* March 1985-April 1990; *Version 3:* May 1990-February 1997; *Version 4:* March 1997-Present.

Objective: *Versions 1, 2 and 3:* To prepare students to assume the responsibilities of food service management by providing experience carrying out the functions of the trainee, second assistant, first assistant, and store manager/owner-operator. *Version 4:* To provide the student with the knowledge and skills needed to fulfill the responsibilities of a restaurant manager (MDP) and to effectively manage a restaurant by using all aspects of restaurant control and executing objective-based plans and routines (MDP IV).

Learning Outcome: *Versions 1, 2, and 3:* Upon successful completion of this course, the student will be able to carry out assigned responsibilities of the trainee (MDP I), second assistant (MDP II), first assistant (MDP III), and restaurant manager (MDP IV). *Version 4:* Upon successful completion of this course, the student will be able to demonstrate knowledge of management responsibilities in all aspects and areas of a restaurant (MDP); and the student will be able to perform necessary administrative functions and develop and execute practical plans in order to assume management of a restaurant (MDP IV).

Instruction: *Version 1:* Major topics covered in the course are basic food service operations, basic management functions and applications, and advanced management control. The trainee's performance is evaluated by supervisory personnel according to established performance objectives. On-the-job training is used. *Version 2:* Major topics covered in the course are basic food service operations, basic management functions and applications, and advanced management control. The trainee's performance is evaluated by supervisory personnel according to established performance objectives. On-the-job training is used. *Version 3:* Major topics covered in the course are basic food service operations, basic human resource management, advanced management functions and applications, and restaurant planning and control. *Version 4:* Major topics covered in the course are 24 (MDP) modules addressing three management areas of managing the restaurant, leadership, and managing the business; Methods of instruction include AV material, assigned readings, in-store activities, tests, observations and supervisor evaluations.

Credit Recommendation: *Version 1:* In the lower division baccalaureate/associate degree category, 6 semester hours in Cooperative Education/Coordinated Internship of a food service program (10/80) (7/85). *Version 2:* In the lower division baccalaureate/associate degree category, 6 semester hours in Cooperative Education/Coordinated Internship of a food service program (10/80) (7/85). *Version 3:* In the lower division baccalaureate/associate degree category, 6 semester hours in Cooperative Education/ Coordinated Internship in Restaurant/Food Service Management (12/90). **NOTE:** Students may receive the credit for either the Management Development Program or the Registered Applicant Program but not both. Students must complete the entire Management Development Program to receive credit recommendations. *Version 4:* In the lower division baccalaureate/ associate degree category, 6 semester hours in Cooperative Education/ Coordinated Internship in Hospitality Management. **NOTE:** Students must complete all 24 MDP modules to receive credit for the Management Development Program (MDP) (10/97).

Management Development Program, Vol IV (MDP IV)

Location: McDonald's Regional Training Centers.

Length: Self-paced over 36-52 weeks.

Dates: March 1997-Present.

Objective: To provide the participant with the knowledge and skills needed to effectively manage a restaurant by using all aspects of restaurant control and executing objective-based plans and routines.

Learning Outcome: Upon successful completion of this course, the student will be able to perform the necessary administrative functions, develop and execute practical plans in order to assume management of a restaurant.

Instruction: Major topics covered in the course are management transition, assuming control, and taking charge of a restaurant. Methods of instruction include AV material, assigned readings and in-store activities, observations and supervisor evaluations.

Credit Recommendation: In the upper division baccalaureate degree category, 2 semester hours in Restaurant Management (10/97).

Meeting Facilitation Skills

Location: Hamburger University, Oak Brook, IL.

Length: 14 hours (2 days).

Dates: March 1995-Present.

Objective: To provide students with tools and techniques to effectively plan and conduct meetings and follow-up on meeting results.

Learning Outcome: Upon successful completion of this course, the participant will be able to sequence the steps of the Facilitation model; construct an agenda; understand group processing techniques that achieve synergy; apply techniques to manage creativity and conflict.

Instruction: Major topics covered in the course are keys to successful meetings: leading a successful meeting; improving meetings; and handling difficult meetings. Methods of instruction include lecture, discussion, classroom exercises, case studies, role play, quizzes, reports and demonstrations.

Credit Recommendation: In the upper division baccalaureate degree category, 1 semester hour in Hotel, Restaurant, Institution Management, Management, or Human Resource Development (10/97).

Operations Consultants Course-Training

Location: Hamburger University, Oak Brook, IL.

Length: 33.25 hours (5 days).

Dates: October 1997-Present.

Objective: To provide students with the skills needed to effectively present training courses, and to consult restaurants in addressing training needs.

Learning Outcome: Upon successful completion of this course, the student will be able to demonstrate effective presentation skills, effective class management skills, and basic facilitation skills.

Instruction: Major topics covered in the course are classroom management, presentation skills, facilitation skills, and training development process. Methods of instruction include lecture, discussion, classroom exercises, video taping, critique of videos, and peer feedback.

Credit Recommendation: In the upper division baccalaureate degree category, 2 semester hours in Educational Methodology or Training Development (10/97). *Prerequisite:* Operations Consultant Development Program.

Operations Consultants Development Program-Training

Location: McDonald's Regional Training Centers.

Length: 140-215 hours self paced over 90-120 days.

Dates: November 1991-Present.

Objective: To provide students with the knowledge and skills needed to conduct classroom training and meet the administrative responsibilities of a training consultant, thereby preparing the student for the Operations Consultant Training Course.

Learning Outcome: Upon successful completion of this course, the student will be able to describe the responsibilities of a training consultant; understand training concepts and adult learning principles, classroom management and testing; understand and apply instructional methods; demonstrate presentation skills; and consult regarding identifying training needs.

Instruction: Major topics covered in the course are classroom instruction skills, presentation skills and consulting skills. Methods of instruction include assigned reading, on-the job activities, classroom exercises, observation, feedback from peers, and required completion of all exercises.

Credit Recommendation: In the upper division baccalaureate degree category, 3 semester hours in Educational Methodology or Training Development (10/97).

Operations Manager's Class (Formerly Operations Department Head's Class)

Location: Hamburger University, Oak Brook, IL.

Length: 34 hours (1 week).

Dates: April 1980-February 1996.

Objective: To provide mid-level managers with advanced training in the areas of food service leadership and operational decision-making.

Instruction: Major topics covered in the course are personnel and performance appraisal, leadership, problem analysis, decision-making, marketing analysis, owner/operator relations, and building construction. Methods of instruction include lecture and case studies.

Credit Recommendation: In the upper division baccalaureate degree category, 2 semester hours in Advanced Food Service Management (10/80) (7/85) (12/90) (10/97).

Presentation Skills I and II

Location: Hamburger University, Oak Brook, IL.

Length: 15 hours (2 days).

Dates: January 1978-October 1997.

Objective: To identify techniques necessary for successful oral communication.

Instruction: Major topics covered in the course are an emphasis on the use of eye contact, gestures, voice and emotion; managing distracter and distractions; responding to questions; and the major tasks of a facilitator. Methods of instruction include student practice sessions, videotape feedback, instructor critiques, lectures and workshops.

Credit Recommendation: In the lower division baccalaureate/associate degree category, 1 semester hour in Oral Communication or Public Speaking (10/80) (7/85) (12/90) (10/97).

Regional Equipment Classes (Formerly Applied Equipment)

Location: *Version 1:* Hamburger University, Oak Brook, IL; McDonald's Regional Training Centers *Version 2:* McDonald's Regional Training Centers.

Length: *Version 1:* 62.5 hours (32.5 hours of classwork in one week and 30 hours of laboratory work in 30-90 days); *Version 2:* 30 hours (6 days).

Dates: *Version 1:* August 1980-December 1990; *Version 2:* January 1991-Present.

Objective: *Version 1:* To provide knowledge and skill in working with all components of food-service equipment, including equipment parts identification, basic operations, calibration, preventive maintenance, and troubleshooting. *Version 2:* To provide knowledge and skill in performing basic calibrations on restaurant equipment, manage planned maintenance, and perform simple troubleshooting activities.

Learning Outcome: Upon successful completion of this course, the student will be able to perform basic calibration of equipment, manage planned maintenance, and perform simple troubleshooting activities on restaurant equipment.

Instruction: *Version 1:* Major topic covered in the course is key information on the operation and repair of equipment with emphasis on theory of systems as well as practical applications. After the classroom experience, students must complete a workbook that is designed to enrich and personalize their experience in their restaurant. A combination of classroom lecture and laboratory (in-store) hands-on instruction is used. *Version 2:* Major topics covered in this course are calibration, planned maintenance, troubleshooting of beverage-dispensing equipment, gas grills, electric clam shell grills, gas and electric fryers, and HVAC systems. Methods of instruction include lecture, demonstration, and self-paced laboratory experiences.

Credit Recommendation: *Version 1:* In the lower division baccalaureate/associate degree category, 3 semester hours in Food Service Equipment Engineering (10/80) (7/85). *Version 2:* In the lower division baccalaureate/associate degree category, 3 semester hours in Food Equipment and Maintenance (12/90). **NOTE:** This is the fourth course in a five-course sequence in Food Management Training.*Prerequisites:* Basic and Intermediate Operations plus Management Development I and II and 3 months of III.

Training Consultants Course
1. Training Consultant Development Program
2. Training Consultants Course
(Formerly 1. Training Consultant's Development; 2. Training Consultants)

Location: *Version 1:* Hamburger University, Oak Brook, IL; McDonald's Regional Training Centers; *Version 2: Course 1*: McDonald's Regional Training Centers; *Course 2:* Hamburger University.

Length: *Version 1: Course 1*: Self-paced, approximately 20-25 hours; *Course 2:* Classroom, 31 hours (1 week); *Version 2: Course 1*: self-paced, 20-25 hours; *Course 2*: 36 hours.

Dates: April 1977-Present.

Objective: *Version 1:* To instruct training consultants in presentation skills and to develop an understanding of the conceptual framework in which training activities take place. *Version 2:* To instruct training consultants in presentation and facilitation skills, and to develop an understanding of the conceptual framework in which training activities take place.

Learning Outcome: Upon successful completion of this course, the student will be able to provide information and demonstrate effective use of presentation and facilitation skills.

Instruction: *Version 1:* Major topics covered in the course are individual presentation skills and a general exposure to the areas of verifying training needs, appropriate training methods, effective use of visual aids, lesson plan preparation, and testing. Methods of instruction in Course 1 include lecture and discussion in a pace set by the student. Methods of instruction in Course 2 emphasize practice teaching exercises. *Version 2:* Major topics covered in the course are classroom management, presentation skills, facilitation skills, and training development process. Method of instruction in Course 1 is self-paced. Methods of instruction in Course 2 include lecture, practice teaching, and group activities.

Credit Recommendation: In the upper division baccalaureate degree category, 3 semester hours in Educational Methodology or Training Development (10/80) (7/85) (12/90) (10/97).

Medical Legal Consulting Institute, Inc.

Established in 1982, the Medical-Legal Consulting Institute, Inc. provides distance education in the field of legal nurse consulting in a certificate of completion. Upon successful completion of a proctored certification exam, the student obtains a CLNC^{CM} Certification.

The mission of the Institute is to positively impact the legal and healthcare systems; to promote high standards of quality and professionalism in practice of legal nurse consulting; and to inspire excellence in consulting through education.

The Institute Leader is Vickie L. Milazzo, RN, MSN, JD, who has been a successful legal nurse consultant since 1982. Most of the distance education courses are personally taught by Ms. Milazzo, the pioneer in the field, and are designed to teach her proven step-by-step approach for developing a successful practice as a legal nurse consultant.

Students learn exactly what they need to know to be successful as consultants. They also benefit from Ms. Milazzo's years of experience and vast know-how - including both practices to emulate and mistakes to avoid in order to expedite their personal success timetable.

Our courses are designed to allow students to study at their own pace in the comfort of their own home. The Medical-Legal Consulting Institute consultants are available Monday-Friday 8:30 a.m.-5:30 p.m. central time to assist students and answer questions regarding the course of instruction and the practice of legal nurse consulting. Students can call our toll-free number for assistance.

All our programs are nationally approved for nursing continuing education. The CLNC^{CM} Certification Program is approved for 90 contact hours. Medical-Legal Consulting Institute, Inc., Provider #97-0712-B, has been awarded Provider Status by the Texas Nurses Association, which is accredited by the American Nurses Credentialing Center (ANCC). This approval meets Type 1 criteria for mandatory continuing education requirements towards re-licensure as established by the Board of Nurse Ex-aminers for the State of Texas. This program is also approved by the California Board of Registered Nursing, Provider #9643 for 75 contact hours.

Source of official student records: Registry of Credit Recommendations, American Council on Education, One Dupont Circle, Washington, DC 20036-1193.

Additional information about the courses: College Credit Recommendation Service, American Council on Education, One Dupont Circle, Washington, DC 20036-1193.

CLNC^{CM} Certification Program

Location: Independent study by correspondence.

Length: Approximately 75 hours of independent study.

Dates: January 1998-Present.

Objective: To provide the student with the skills and knowledge for starting a successful business as a legal consultant and achieving certification as a Certified Legal Nurse Consultant^{CM} (CLNC^{CM}).

Learning Outcome: Upon successful completion of this course, the student will be able to identify roles, services and scope of practice of the legal nurse consultant; perform the functions of a legal nurse consultant, demonstrate how to professionally interact with attorneys and manage a legal nurse consulting practice.

Instruction: Major topics covered in the course are role of the legal nurse consultant; screening medical-related cases; Standards of Care; report writing; detection of tampering; library research; marketing strategies; negotiating contracts; role of the expert witness; theories of liability; personal injury; products liability; environmental and workers' compensation cases; alternative dispute resolution; tort reform; successful interview techniques; managed-care litigation; legal and ethical issues; and federal acts. Methods of instruction include taped or on-site lecture, audio/video material, computer-assisted instruction, case studies, quizzes, and proctored final exam.

Credit Recommendation: In the lower division baccalaureate/associate degree category, 3 semester hours in Marketing, Management or Business (1/98).

Mercantile Stores, Inc.

Mercantile Stores Company, Inc., is a retail corporation comprised of 104 fine department stores, concentrated in the Midwestern and Southeastern regions of the United States. In 1990, Mercantile committed to providing educational courses to all associates, beginning with management. Also in 1990, Mercantile began relocating corporate headquarters from New York City to Cincinnati, Ohio.

Mercantile Stores University (MSU) is housed in a 30,000 square foot facility which was completed in September 1992. It includes an auditorium and various sized classrooms. Educational courses range from management skills, to financial skills, to technical skills. MSU's goal is to optimize management performance by offering specific skill-based education. MSU designs coursework based on needs assessments, consumer feedback, and surveys of associates and customers.

MSU uses both internal subject matter experts and outside resources to develop course material. The facilitation team has a wide range of experience in the retail industry and within the company, which supports addressing student needs and current business trends.

Classes are kept small (22 students or less) to insure individual instruction and foster an interactive environment for all participants. Carefully planned and supervised experiential activities support learning transferal techniques to emphasize course material.

MSU's programs are designed to provide basic theories and to support management plans, strategies, and goals. MSU offers courses targeted at skills which speak to current corporate direction and culture.

Source of official student records: Registry of Credit Recommendations, American Council on Education, One Dupont Circle, Washington, DC 20036-1193.

Additional information about the courses: College Credit Recommendation Service, American Council on Education, One Dupont Circle, Washington, DC 20036-1193.

Business Analysis and Application I (Formerly Basic Finance for Profit I)

Location: Mercantile Stores University, Fairfield, OH and remote sites.

Length: 40 hours (1 week).

Dates: March 1992-October 1994.

Objective: To familiarize students with the concepts of retail math, and to relate these concepts to forecasting sales and strategy.

Learning Outcome: Upon successful completion of this course, the student will be able to understand retail math and financial retail formulas; and understand retail business forecasting and the need for strategy.

Instruction: Major topics covered in the course are retail math, retail financial forms, forecasting sales, and strategy. Methods of instruction include lecture, discussion, and classroom exercises.

Credit Recommendation: In the lower division baccalaureate/associate degree category, 2 semester hours in Retail Merchandising (8/93).

Business Analysis and Application II

Location: Mercantile Stores University, Fairfield, OH and remote sites.

Length: 40 hours (1 week).

Dates: July 1993-October 1994.

Objective: To understand performance measure including profit margins and return on investment; and to develop a business plan and measure its performance.

Learning Outcome: Upon successful completion of this course, the student will be able to calculate gross margins, return on investment, and inventory turnovers; measure vendor performance and profitability; develop a business plan to include a forecast of sales; understand demographics, inventory requirements, and strategy; and build a team for success.

Instruction: Major topics covered in the course are math (mark up, mark down, gross margins, inventory turnover); gross margin return on investment; sales and business planning; strategic planning; and team building. Methods of instruction include lecture; discussion; and classroom exercises to include case studies, role playing, and problem solving with computer interaction.

Credit Recommendation: In the upper division baccalaureate degree category, 2 semester hours in Business Management (8/93).

Leadership I

Location: Mercantile Stores University, Fairfield, OH and remote sites.

Length: 40 hours (1 week).

Dates: March 1992-October 1994.

Objective: To develop basic managerial and leadership skills that will form the foundation for continued management development.

Learning Outcome: Upon successful completion of this course, the student will be able to understand the role of leadership in business success; apply basic principles of leadership and motivation to work-related problems; and improve core leadership skills.

Instruction: Major topics covered in the course are leadership fundamentals, communication principles, team work as a management philosophy, introduction to problem solving, performance appraisal, empowerment, associate motivation, and team management. Methods of instruction include lecture, discussion, individual exercises, video presentation, small group exercises, and outdoor education experiences.

Credit Recommendation: In the lower division baccalaureate/associate degree category, 2 semester hours in Human Relations or Supervision (8/93).

Leadership II

Location: Mercantile Stores University, Fairfield, OH and remote sites.

Length: 40 hours (1 week).

Dates: July 1992-Present.

Objective: To build on the basics of leadership by focusing on redevelopment of central leadership understandings and skills.

Learning Outcome: Upon successful completion of this course, the student will be able to communicate more effectively with subordinates, peers, superiors, and customers; conduct more effective meetings; use effective interviewing techniques; improve content of performance reviews; and improve decision-making skills.

Instruction: Major topics covered in the course are interpersonal communication, written and oral communication skills, problem solving, performance appraisal process, Americans With Disabilities Act, and interviewing skills. Methods of instruction include lecture, discussion, individual exercises, group exercises, videos, role-playing, and outdoor education experiences.

Credit Recommendation: In the lower division baccalaureate/associate degree category, 2 semester hours in Human Relations or Supervision (8/93).

Negotiations

Location: Mercantile Stores University Business School, Fairfield, OH and remote sites.

Length: 40 hours (1 week).

Dates: June 1993-Present.

Objective: To recognize the benefits of building strong vendor partnerships, anticipate and resolve vendor conflicts, assess vendor relationships in terms of corporate goals, and develop a short- and long-term strategy for managing and maintaining vendor partnerships.

Learning Outcome: Upon successful completion of this course, the student will be able to pre-plan vendor negotiation; establish short range and long range negotiation goals and objectives; practice effective negotiation skills; develop "win-win" negotiation solutions; understand and practice alternative negotiation roles; complete integrated vendor programs; interpret body language of vendors; avoid legal negotiation pitfalls; and complete post planning negotiation summary.

Instruction: Major topics covered in the course are vendor relations, buyer/vendor conflict resolution, reading body language, goals and objectives development, tactical planning, personal styles of negotiation, pre and post negotiation planning, negotiation roles, negotiation skills, "win-win" strategy development, vendor programs, and legal aspects of negotiations. Methods of instruction include lecture, discussion, role playing, small group dynamics, mini case studies, written exercises, videotapes, overheads, videotaped skill practices for self-critique, and outdoor education experiences.

Credit Recommendation: In the upper division baccalaureate degree category, 2 semester hours in Retail or Retail/Vendor Negotiation (8/93).

Progressive Leadership Leadership III

Location: Mercantile Stores University, Fairfield, OH and remote sites.

Length: 40 hours (1 week).

Dates: August 1993-October 1996.

Objective: To build on the content of Leadership I and Leadership II; and to build a more sophisticated understanding of leadership and the skills necessary to exercise it.

Learning Outcome: Upon successful completion of this course, the student will be able to communicate complex materials to others effectively through presentations; manage conflict for constructive results; systematically approach and solve problems; improve time management skills and better manage in a diverse workforce.

Instruction: Major topics covered in the course are effective communication through presentations, problem definition and problem solving, conflict management, business ethics, and time management. Methods of instruction include lecture, discussion, individual exercises, video presentations, case analyses, role playing, and group exercises.

Credit Recommendation: In the upper division baccalaureate degree category, 2 semester hours in Organizational Behavior (8/93).

World Class Customer Service

Location: Mercantile Stores University Business School, Fairfield, OH and remote sites.

Length: 40 hours (1 week).

Dates: February 1993-Present.

Objective: To develop a total quality service plan including defining the customer, store standards, service goal, setting, delivery, and measurement.

Learning Outcome: Upon successful completion of this course, the student will be able to define quality service; meet customer expectations; handle customer complaints; learn the elements of service; and develop a complete quality service plan.

Instruction: Major topics covered in the course are customer service definition, quality service planning, setting service goals, the service environment, handling complaints and problems, and service delivery. Methods of instruction include lecture, discussion, written team project, and role playing.

Credit Recommendation: In the lower division baccalaureate/associate degree category, 2 semester hours in Retailing (8/93).

Metropolitan Technical Institute

Founded on May 18, 1966, by Mr. Frank Gergelyi, Metropolitan Technical Institute is an independent private institute that provides training in electronics to the public and industry.

Due to changes in technology throughout the years, Metropolitan Technical Institute introduced the following new courses: *Day Division:* Electronics Engineering Technology Program, Electronic Technology Program, Computer Science Program, and the Service Technician Course; *Evening Division:* Linear Integrated Circuits, Digital and Microprocessors, Interfacing and Robotics, and Data Communications Course.

Metropolitan Technical Institute has a practically oriented approach to training, featuring experienced instructors who combine work experience in the field with quality teaching in a classroom environment to stimulate student/instructor interaction. The program is supported by two fully equipped electronic laboratories and an in-house Digital Equipment Corporation computer with 15 terminals available for use by the faculty and students.

Metropolitan Technical Institute is approved by the New Jersey Department of Education, the Veterans Administration, the New Jersey Rehabilitation Commission, the U.S. Immigration and Naturalization Service for foreign students, the National Association of Trade and Technical Schools (NATTS), and the Accrediting Commission of Career Schools and Colleges of Technology (ACCSCT).

Source of official student records: Registry of Credit Recommendations, American Council on Education, One Dupont Circle, Washington, DC 20036-1193.

Additional information about the courses: Office of Corporate-Higher Education Programs, Thomas Edison State College, 101 West State Street, Trenton, NJ 08608-1176.

BASIC Programming (CS-213; CS-213L)

Location: Fairfield, NJ.

Length: 105 hours (21 weeks).

Dates: April 1979-August 1994.

Objective: To provide the student with an overview of computer systems and their operation, and to teach them general programming techniques with specific training in BASIC.

Learning Outcome: Upon successful completion of this course, the student will be able to understand the concepts and terminology of computer systems; design, code, and debug programs written in BASIC; and understand and use the various operating system commands.

Instruction: Major topics covered in the course are an introduction to computer fundamentals; computer hardware components and organization; applications software; data organization and file structure; an introduction to the BASIC language; structured programming techniques including data structures; and data manipulation and file processing, including sorting, sequential and virtual files, and an introduction to the text editor. Methods of instruction include lecture, discussion, and over 40 hours of hands-on laboratory work in which experiments are performed in BASIC using a DEC-PDP-11 time-sharing computer. The laboratory exercises stress the development of engineering and business-oriented application programs.

Credit Recommendation: In the lower division baccalaureate/associate degree category, 3 semester hours in BASIC (4/89) (2/95).

Calculus I (TM-211)

Location: Fairfield, NJ.

Length: 105 hours (21 weeks).

Dates: April 1979-August 1994.

Objective: To develop new methods and skills in problem solving and the capability to apply calculus to electrical circuits and electronics.

Learning Outcome: Upon successful completion of this course, the student will be able to find slopes and the instantaneous rate of change of linear and nonlinear equations; determine limits and continuity of functions; differentiate linear and nonlinear equations, trigonometric functions, and logarithms; find maxima/minima and inflection points by first and second derivative test; evaluate definite and indefinite integrals including trigonometric and logarithmic integrals; evaluate areas under/between the curve; evaluate volumes generated by rotation of curve; graph linear and nonlinear equations; and apply calculus to electrical circuit problems such as series RLC circuits.

Instruction: Major topics covered in the course are differential and integral calculus; limits and continuity; derivatives of functions; rational expressions; integrals and logarithms; implicit differentials; maxima/minima (graph and derivative); indefinite and definite; the area under the curve and between curves; and fundamental theorems of calculus. Methods of instruction include lecture, discussion, and classroom exercises.

Credit Recommendation: In the lower division baccalaureate/associate degree category, 4 semester hours in Technical Calculus (4/89).

Communication Electronics (ET-211, ET-211L)

Location: Fairfield, NJ.

Length: 114 hours (23 weeks).

Dates: April 1979-August 1994.

Objective: To study the operation of different communication circuits, such as power amplifiers, oscillators, tuned amplifiers, modulation, and demodulation.

Learning Outcome: Upon successful completion of this course, the student will be able to analyze, repair, or redesign communication circuits according to the specifications or needs of a particular system.

Instruction: Major topics covered in the course are power amplifier circuits; tuned amplifier modulation; sine wave oscillators; amplitude modulation; frequency modulation; pulse modulation and sampling; demodulation circuits; and deflection systems. Methods of instruction include lecture, discussion, and classroom exercises.

Credit Recommendation: In the lower division baccalaureate/associate degree category, 3 semester hours in Introductory Communications Electronics (4/89).

Digital Computer Programming (CS-212; CS-212L)
2. Integrated Digital Electronics

Location: Fairfield, NJ.

Length: 1. 80 hours (8 weeks); 2. 228 hours (16 weeks).

Dates: April 1979-August 1994.

Objective: (1) To gain an understanding of BASIC programming and to learn the fundamental concepts of digital logic. (2) To provide the student with a theoretical and practical background in digital circuitry and to prepare for the microprocessor course.

Learning Outcome: (1) Upon successful completion of this course, the student will be able to write simple programs in BASIC and understand the basics of digital circuits. (2) Upon completion of this course, students will be able to understand the operation of various types of digital components and circuits, design various combinational and sequential logic circuits, understand the operation of the individual components used in microprocessor-based systems, and construct and troubleshoot digital circuits.

Instruction: (1) Major topics covered in the course are introduction to BASIC; BASIC statements; introductory digital concepts; logic circuit analysis, using Boolean algebra; logic circuit design; and number systems and codes. (2) Major topics covered in the course are digital systems; discrete and integrated circuitry; integrated circuit logic gates; comparator circuitry; digital codes, decoders and encoders; random access memories; digital communications; and multivibrator circuitry. Methods of instruction include lecture, discussion, and classroom exercises.

Credit Recommendation: In the lower division baccalaureate/associate degree category, 4 semester hours in Introductory Digital Electronics (4/89) (2/95).

Electric Circuits II (ET-121; ET-121L)

Location: Fairfield, NJ.

Length: *Version 1:* 240 hours (24 weeks); *Version 2:* 225 hours (24 weeks).

Dates: *Version 1:* April 1979-August 1994; *Version 2:* September 1994-Present.

Objective: To develop a basic understanding of how electrical devices are connected in circuits and how to analyze such circuits in AC Lab; to study the types of calculations and formulas used in the AC theory, to learn to set up circuits from circuit diagrams and to take accurate measurements.

Learning Outcome: Upon successful completion of this course, the student will be able to analyze AC electric circuits and do some simple designing of circuits; recognize components, set up circuits, and use AC power sources and measuring devices in laboratory.

Instruction: Major topics covered in the course are AC time domain; frequency domain; impedances and admittances; AC Ohm's law; AC series circuit analysis; AC parallel circuit analysis; series-parallel circuits; AC network theory; and AC bridges.

Credit Recommendation: In the lower division baccalaureate/associate degree category, 4 semester hours in AC Circuits II (4/89) (2/95).

Electric Courses
1. Electric Circuits (ET-111; ET-111L)
2. Electric and Magnetic Devices (ET-112; ET-112L)

Location: Fairfield, NJ.

Length: *Version 1:* 1. 216 hours (24 weeks); 2. 144 hours (24 weeks); *Version 2:* 1. 225 hours (24 weeks); 2. 135 hours (24 weeks).

Dates: *Version 1:* April 1979-August 1994; *Version 2:* September 1994-Present.

Objective: (1) To develop a basic understanding of how electrical devices are connected in circuits and how to analyze such circuits from circuit diagrams and to take accurate measurements. (2) To study basic concepts and relationships in electric and magnetic devices.

Learning Outcome: (1) Upon successful completion of this course, the student will be able to analyze DC electric circuits and do some simple designing of circuits and recognize components, set up circuits, and use many DC power sources and measuring devices in laboratory. (2) Upon successful completion of this course, the student will be able to use electrical and magnetic concepts and understand units and their relationships in the applications of electronics.

Instruction: (1) Major topics covered in the course are an introduction to electronics; Ohm's Law; power equations; introduction to circuit analysis; series circuit analysis; parallel circuit analysis; series-parallel circuitry; DC network theory; and DC bridges. (2) Major topics covered in the course are electrical concepts; units and scientific notation; atomic structure of matter; electric charge and physics of electricity; resistance calculations; magnetism; inductance; transformers; and capacitance. Methods of instruction include lecture, discussion, and laboratory exercises.

Credit Recommendation: In the lower division baccalaureate/associate degree category, 4 semester hours in DC Circuits (4/89) (2/95).

Electronic Amplifiers (ET-211, ET-211L)

Location: Fairfield, NJ.

Length: 225 hours (24 weeks).

Dates: September 1994-Present.

Objective: To provide the student with the ability to do a Q point analysis of an amplifier; perform an AC analysis of a single stage or multi-stage amplifier and determine its voltage gain, current gain, input impedance, output impedance and frequency response.

Learning Outcome: Upon successful completion of the course, the student will be able to understand various methods of using transistors in amplifier circuits and apply DC biasing voltages that will allow the circuit to operate effectively as an amplifier.

Instruction: Major topics covered in the course are transistor amplifiers operation, AC and DC load lines, small signal transistor model, common base amplifier analysis, common emitter amplifier, cascaded amplifier, FET amplifier analysis, common source amplifier, small signal FET model, and FET as a variable resistor.

Credit Recommendation: In the lower division baccalaureate/associate degree category, 3 semester hours in Electronic Amplifiers or Electronic Circuits (2/95).

Electronics Courses
1. Electronic Amplifiers (ET-211; ET-211L)
2. Electronics (ET-123; ET-123L)
3. Semiconductors Materials and Devices (ET-122; ET-122L)

Location: Fairfield, NJ.

Length: 1. 114 hours (24 weeks); 2. 40 hours (8 weeks); 3. 74 hours (16 weeks).

Dates: April 1979-August 1994.

Objective: (1) To provide the student with the ability to do a Q point analysis of an amplifier; perform an AC analysis of a single-stage or multistage amplifier and determine its voltage gain, current gain, input impedance, output impedance, and frequency response. (2) To give the student an understanding of various methods of using transistors in amplifier circuits and to apply DC biasing voltages that will allow the circuit to operate effectively as an amplifier. (3) To present the student with the basic principles of semiconductor materials and devices and an understanding of their operation and applications.

Learning Outcome: Upon successful completion of this course, the student will be able to (1) repair or redesign amplifier circuits using analysis and troubleshooting techniques; (2) become familiar with all transistor DC biasing circuits from the elementary to sophisticated—their disadvantages and merits; (3) and apply semiconductor devices in electronic circuits such as rectifiers, detectors, voltage reference circuits and amplifiers, and to troubleshoot.

Instruction: (1) Major topics covered in the course are transistor amplifier operation, AC and DC load lines, small signal transistor model, common base amplifier analysis, common emitter amplifier, cascaded amplifiers, FET amplifier analysis, common source amplifier, small signal FET model, and FET as a variable resistor. (2) Major topics covered in the course are transistor biasing, transistor operation, design of DC bias circuits, and transistors as amplifiers. (3) Major topics covered in the course are the physics of materials; PN junction; additional semiconductor devices; and transistors.

Credit Recommendation: In the lower division baccalaureate/associate degree category, 4 semester hours in Semiconductor Devices and Circuits (4/89).

Electronics Instrumentation ((ET-212; ET-212)

Location: Fairfield, NJ.

Length: *Version 1:* 114 hours (9 weeks); *Version 2:* 75 hours (9 weeks).

Dates: *Version 1:* April 1979-August 1994; *Version 2:* September 1994-Present.

Objective: *Version 1:* To familiarize students with transient operation of RC and RL circuits activated by pulse inputs, wave-shaping circuits, passive filter circuits, and the study of various transducers and circuits involving use of transducers. *Version 2:* To develop an understanding of the transient operation of RC and RL circuits activated by pulse input, wave shaping circuits, passive filter circuits and the various transducers and circuits involving transducers.

Learning Outcome: *Versions 1 and 2:* Upon successful completion of the course, the student will be able to test, modify, and implement different wave shaping circuits and transducers in instrumentation equipment.

Instruction: *Versions 1 and 2:* Major topics covered in the course are waveshaping circuits and decibel gain; clippers and clampers; transducers; photo diodes; applications of photo resisters; difference amplifier; and AC and DC analysis of a difference amplifier.

Credit Recommendation: *Versions 1 and 2:* In the lower division baccalaureate/associate degree category, 3 semester hours in Opto Electronic Devices (4/89) (2/95).

FORTRAN
1. FORTRAN and Assembly (PDP-11)
2. Programming Lab (CS-223; CS-223L)

Location: Fairfield, NJ.

Length: 105 hours (21 weeks).

Dates: April 1979-August 1994.

Objective: To provide the student with an understanding of computer operations at the machine level and to make them proficient in FORTRAN and PDP-11 assembly language programming.

Learning Outcome: Upon successful completion of this course, the student will be able to understand how the computer operates at the machine level and interacts with the operating system; design, code, and debug programs written in FORTRAN; design, code, and debug programs written in MACRO-11 assembly language; and understand how to use and write diagnostic test software.

Instruction: Major topics covered in the course are introduction to FORTRAN; FORTRAN statements; structured programming techniques in FORTRAN; FORTRAN programming process; introduction to assembly language; MACRO-II assembler control; assembly language programming techniques; and diagnostic programming.

Credit Recommendation: In the lower division baccalaureate/associate degree category, 3 semester hours in FORTRAN and Assembly Language (4/89).

Integrated Digital Electronics (CS-212, CS-212L)

Location: Fairfield, NJ.

Length: 210 hours (24 weeks).

Dates: September 1994-Present.

Objective: To provide the student with a theoretical and practical background in digital circuitry and to prepare for the microprocessor course.

Learning Outcome: Upon successful completion of this course, the student will be able to understand the operation of various types of digital components and circuits, design various types of combinational and sequential logic circuits, understand the operation of the individual components used in microprocessor-based systems, and construct and troubleshoot digital circuits.

Instruction: Major topics covered in the course are digital systems; discrete and integrated circuitry, integrated circuit logic gates; comparator circuitry; digital codes, decoders and encoders; random access memories; digital communications; and multivibrator circuitry.

Credit Recommendation: In the lower division baccalaureate/associate degree category, 4 semester hours in Introductory Digital Electronics (2/95).

Introduction to Computers and Programming (CS-121)

Location: Fairfield, NJ.

Length: 75 hours (9 weeks).

Dates: August 1994-Present.

Objective: To introduce the concepts of Digital Logic and BASIC Programming.

Learning Outcome: Upon successful completion of this course, the student will be able to understand the operation of various types of digital components and circuits; design various types of simple combinational and sequential logic circuits; understand the operation of the individual components used in microprocessor-based systems; understand the operation of the individual components used in microprocessor-based systems; construct and troubleshoot digital circuitry; and write simple programs in BASIC and understand the basics of digital circuits.

Instruction: Major topics covered in the course are Introduction to BASIC; BASIC statements; introductory digital concepts; logic circuit analysis; using boolean algebra; logic circuit design; number system and codes; digital systems; discrete and integrated circuitry; integrated circuit logic gates; comparator circuitry; digital codes; decoders and encoders; random access memories; digital communications; and multivibrator circuitry.

Credit Recommendation: In the lower division baccalaureate/associate degree category, 2 semester hours in Introduction to Computers and Programming (2/95).

Linear Integrated Circuits (ET-222; ET-222L)

Location: Fairfield, NJ.

Length: 225 hours (24 weeks).

Dates: April 1979-Present.

Objective: To teach the student the application, analysis and design of circuits involving the use of operational amplifiers and linear integrated circuits.

Learning Outcome: Upon successful completion of this course, the student will be able to understand op-amp operator; analyze, repair, design circuit applications of op-amps and linear integrated circuits.

Instruction: Major topics covered in the course are OP-AMP as an open loop amplifier; inverting amplifier; other OP-AMP circuits; integrators and differentiators; comparators with positive feedback; 555 timer; DA and AD converters; and integrated voltage regulations.

Credit Recommendation: In the lower division baccalaureate/associate degree category, 4 semester hours in Linear Integrated Circuits (4/89) (2/95).

Microprocessor (CS-221; CS-221L)
1. Microprocessor Hardware (CS-222; CS-222L)
2. Microprocessor Software (CS-221; CS-221L)

Location: Fairfield, NJ.

Length: *Version 1:* 1 and 2. 114 hours (12 weeks); *Version 2:* 1 and 2. 75 hours (12 weeks).

Dates: *Version 1:* April 1979-August 1994; *Version 2:* September 1994-Present.

Objective: *Versions 1 and 2:* To provide the student with an in-depth theoretical and practical background in microprocessor hardware and software and to cover the basic system concepts.

Learning Outcome: *Versions 1 and 2:* (1) Upon successful completion of this course, the student will be able to understand the operation of a microprocessor from a hardware viewpoint; understand the operation of various support chips used in microprocessor circuits; analyze a micro-based system schematic and design a simple system; and relate the knowledge of a micro-based system to larger systems. (2) Upon successful completion of this course, the student will be able to understand the operation of a microprocessor from a software viewpoint; write assembly language programs for the 6800 microprocessor; understand the role of software in a micro-based system; and relate the knowledge of micro-based software to that found in large systems.

Instruction: *Versions 1 and 2:* (1) Major topics covered in the course are input-output ports; interfacing microprocessor to a CRT; programmable interface adapters and interrupts. (2) Major topics covered in the course are advantages of using microprocessor-based products; software; assembly language coding; comparison of commercial MPUs; microcomputer memory organization; the 6800 instruction set; addressing modes; structured programming techniques; and subroutines.

Credit Recommendation: *Versions 1 and 2:* In the lower division baccalaureate/associate degree category, 4 semester hours in Microprocessors (4/89) (2/95).

Physics I and II (PHY-221)

Location: Fairfield, NJ.

Length: *Version 1:* 105 hours (21 weeks); *Version 2:* 90 hours (21 weeks).

Dates: *Version 1:* April 1979-August 1994; *Version 2:* September 1994-Present.

Objective: To understand the position and motion of matter in space and the effect of forces on bodies.

Learning Outcome: Upon successful completion of this course, the student will be able to express physical relationships quantitatively and to calculate resultant forces; determine linear and circular velocities, and determine linear and circular accelerations.

Instruction: Major topics covered in the course are vector mechanics; translational equilibrium; rotational equilibrium; accelerated motion; Newton's Second Law of Motion; work, energy, and power; impulse and momentum; and uniform circular motion.

Credit Recommendation: In the lower division baccalaureate/associate degree category, 3 semester hours in Physics I and II (4/89) (2/95).

Pulse Circuits (CS-211; CS-211L)

Location: Fairfield, NJ.

Length: *Version 1:* 117 hours (8 weeks); *Version 2:* 75 hours (8 weeks).

Dates: *Version 1:* April 1979-August 1994; *Version 2:* September 1994-Present.

Objective: To familiarize the student with the application, design, and analysis of transistor switching circuits, as well as applications and analysis of RC and RL circuits, stressing transient response to step inputs.

Learning Outcome: Upon successful completion of this course, the student will be able to test, modify, and implement pulse inputs and outputs according to specific design requirements.

Instruction: Major topics covered in the course are pulse waveforms; introduction to transient analysis; RC circuit transient operation; and the transistor as a switch.

Credit Recommendation: *Version 1:* In the lower division baccalaureate/associate degree category, 3 semester hours in Pulse Circuits (4/89). *Version 2:* In the lower division baccalaureate/associate degree category, 2 semester hours in Pulse Circuits (2/95).

Semiconductor Devices
1. Introduction to Electronics (ET-123; ET-123L)
2. Semiconductor Materials and Devices (ET-122; ET-122L)

Location: Fairfield, NJ.

Length: 75 hours (12 weeks).

Dates: September 1994-Present.

Objective: 1. To provide the student with an understanding of various methods of biasing transistors used in amplifier circuits. 2. To provide the student with an understanding of the basic principles of semiconductor materials and devices and their operations and applications.

Learning Outcome: 1. Upon successful completion of this course, the student will become familiar with transistor DC biasing circuits from the most elementary to the more sophisticated-their advantages and merits. 2. Upon successful completion of this course, the student will be able to use semiconductor devices in electronic circuits such as rectifiers, detectors, voltage reference circuits and amplifiers and to troubleshoot devices in different types of circuits.

Instruction: 1. Major topics covered in the course are transistor biasing, transistor operations, design of DC bias circuits and transistors as amplifiers. 2. Major topics covered in the course are physics of materials, PN junctions, additional semiconductor devices and transistors.

Credit Recommendation: In the lower division baccalaureate/associate degree category, 2 semester hours in Semiconductor Devices and Circuits (2/95).

Technical Mathematics (TM-121)

Location: Fairfield, NJ.

Length: *Version 1:* 148 hours (15 weeks); *Version 2:* 135 hours (15 weeks).

Dates: *Version 1:* April 1979-August 1994; *Version 2:* September 1994-Present.

Objective: To develop a proficiency in technical mathematics needed in calculations and applied problems.

Learning Outcome: Upon successful completion of this course, the student will be able to perform standard calculator computations used in problem solving; apply the problem solving techniques of algebra, trigonometry, and geometry to applications of DC and AC analysis; and eliminate often observed mistaken concepts of how to perform algebraic, geometric, and trigonometric solutions.

Instruction: Major topics covered in the course are factoring polynomials; solving quadratic equations; the quadratic formula; simplifying radicals; conjugating and solving fractional and radical equations; logarithms with application including growth and decay; complex numbers; Demoivre's theorem; trigonometric functions and identities; laws of sines and cosines; solutions of trigonometric equations; and applications.

Credit Recommendation: In the lower division baccalaureate/associate degree category, 3 semester hours in College Algebra and Trigonometry II (4/89) (2/95).

Technical Mathematics (TM-111)

Location: Fairfield, NJ.

Length: *Version 1:* 228 hours (23 weeks); *Version 2:* 210 hours (24 weeks).

Dates: *Version 1:* April 1979-August 1994; *Version 2:* September 1994-Present.

Objective: To develop a proficiency in technical mathematics needed in calculations and applied problem solving related to the field of electronics.

Learning Outcome: Upon successful completion of this course, the student will be able to perform standard calculator computations used in problem solving; and apply problem solving techniques of algebra, trigonometry, and geometry to applications in DC circuit analysis.

Instruction: Major topics covered in the course are operations of polynomials; solution of linear equations; solving systems of equations; matrices and determinants; ratios; proportion; direct, indirect, and joint variation; trigonometry functions and inverse functions; degree and radian measure; simple programming; and use of calculators and programmable calculators.

Credit Recommendation: In the lower division baccalaureate/associate degree category, 3 semester hours in College Algebra and Trigonometry I (4/89) (2/95).

National Academy of Railroad Sciences Burlington Northern Santa Fe Railroad

The National Academy of Railroad Sciences provides entry-level and ongoing training in railroad operations including customer service, dispatching, maintenance of way, mechanical, signal systems, system electrical, telecommunications, and train, yard, and engine service to the railroad industry. Located on the campus of Johnson County Community College since 1988, the Academy is part of Burlington Northern Santa Fe Railroad's operations organization.

Instructors are practitioners in their crafts, trained in effective instructional techniques through the Academy's Master Instructor Certification program. To support its belief that "hand-on" learning is essential in effective technical training, the Academy has furnished state-of-the-art laboratories, simulators, and media-equipped classrooms to provide optimal environments for study and practice. The Academy takes some of its courses into the field to serve operations personnel where they work and can tailor training to meet organizations' unique requirements.

The Academy also supports Johnson County Community College's program leading to the Associate of Science degree in Railroad Operations. Students may elect technical training in dispatching, conductor service, mechanical, and other emphases at the Academy to complete their degrees.

Source of official student records: Registry of Credit Recommendations, American Council on Education, One Dupont Circle, Washington, DC 20036-1193.

Additional information about the courses: College Credit Recommendation Service, American Council on Education, One Dupont Circle, Washington, DC 20036-1193.

Apprentice Locomotive Engineer Training (02)

Location: Overland Park, KS.
Length: 240 hours (6 weeks).
Dates: January 1995-Present.

Objective: To train, certify, and promote locomotive engineers within the guidelines and requirements set forth in FRA 49 CFR, Part 240.

Learning Outcome: Upon successful completion of this course, the student will be able to demonstrate safe and effective train handling methods in a TS-3 locomotive simulator run, demonstrate ability to operate air brakes safely and effectively in a TS-3 simulated run, demonstrate knowledge of locomotive mechanical and electrical basics in a laboratory setting, and demonstrate knowledge of operating and safety rules and their application in a TS-3 simulated run.

Instruction: Major topics covered in the course are train handling methods, air brake operations, and freight car and locomotive mechanical and electrical principles and operating rules and regulations. Methods of instruction include lecture, discussion, classroom exercises, computer assisted instruction, simulation, and audio visual based formats.

Credit Recommendation: In the lower division baccalaureate/associate degree category, 6 semester hours in Railroad Operations, Engineering Technology, Transportation, or Industrial Technology (9/95).

Apprentice Yardmaster Training (09)

Location: Overland Park, KS.
Length: 160 hours (4 weeks).
Dates: January 1995-Present.

Objective: To provide students and employees promoted to yardmaster positions, with knowledge of and skills in safely overseeing the prompt and efficient movement of cars and the safe make up of trains.

Learning Outcome: Upon successful completion of this course, the student will be able to demonstrate proficiency in managing yard operations, safety, computer skills, hazardous materials handling, special instructions, mechanical skills, train makeup, and problem resolution.

Instruction: Major topics covered in the course are computer operations, communications, switching strategies and yardmaster operations. Methods of instruction include lecture, discussion, classroom exercises, computer assisted instruction, simulation, and audio-visual based formats.

Credit Recommendation: In the lower division baccalaureate/associate degree category, 4 semester hours in Railroad Operations, Engineering Technology, Transportation Technology, or Management/Supervisory Technology (9/95).

Conductor Promotion (11)

Location: Overland Park, KS.
Length: 120 hours (3 weeks).
Dates: January 1995-Present.

Objective: To provide the student with the basic knowledge to safely operate, supervise, and administer over-the-road freight trains as a conductor.

Learning Outcome: Upon successful completion of this course, the student will be able to apply the General Code of Operating Rules to his/her performance as a railroad conductor and demonstrate a knowledge of safe railroad practices.

Instruction: Major topics covered in the course are railroad operating rules, conductor job duties and general railroad operations. Instruction is also provided in hazardous material handling, administrative documentation, special and freight car mechanics. Methods of instruction include lecture, computer assisted instruction, and audio visual based formats.

Credit Recommendation: In the lower division baccalaureate/associate degree category, 3 semester hours in Railroad Operations, Engineering Technology, or Supervision/Management (9/95). **NOTE:** A student may receive credit only for this course or Operating Rules, but not for both.

Conductor Update (12)

Location: Overland Park, KS.
Length: 40 hours (1 week).
Dates: January 1995-Present.

Objective: To provide the experienced conductor with current knowledge of safe and effective over-the-road freight train operations.

Learning Outcome: Upon successful completion of this course, the student will be able to apply the General Code of Operating Rules to his/her performance as a railroad conductor, outline the full responsibilities of a conductor, and administer first aid and CPR.

Instruction: Major topics covered in the course are railroad operating rules, train equipment, car air brakes, hazardous material handling, freight car mechanics, first aid and CPR. Methods of instruction include via lecture, computer assisted instruction, and audio visual based formats.

Credit Recommendation: In the lower division baccalaureate/associate degree category, 1 semester hour in Railroad Operations, Engineering Technology, or Supervision/Management (9/95). **NOTE:** A student may receive credit only for this course or Conductor Promotion, but not for both.

Designated Supervisor of Locomotive Engineer Training (04)

Location: Overland Park, KS.

Length: 36 hours (1 week).
Dates: January 1992-Present.
Objective: To train and qualify designated supervisors of locomotive engineers as required by FRA 49 CFR, Part 240 and to upgrade their supervisory skills.
Learning Outcome: Upon successful completion of this course, the student will be able to demonstrate safe and effective train handling and personnel supervision and will have knowledge of locomotive mechanical and electrical principles.
Instruction: Major topics covered in the course are train handling methods, air brake operations, and freight car and locomotive mechanical and electrical principles. Methods of instruction include lecture, discussion, classroom exercises, computer assisted instruction, simulation, and audio visual based formats.
Credit Recommendation: In the lower division baccalaureate/associate degree category, 1 semester hour in Railroad Operations, Engineering Technology, Transportation Technology, or Management/Supervisory Technology (9/95).

Journeyman Yardmaster Training (10)

Location: Overland Park, KS.
Length: 40 hours (1week).
Dates: January 1995-Present.
Objective: To provide students, experienced journeyman yardmasters, with advanced knowledge of and skills in management, safety, computer operations and communications.
Learning Outcome: Upon successful completion of this course, the student will demonstrate proficiency in managing yard operations, safety, computer skills, hazardous materials handling, special instructions, mechanical skills train makeup, and problem resolution.
Instruction: Major topics covered in the course are management and safety skills as applied to experienced yardmasters, computer operations, technical communications, yard management and hazardous material handling. Methods of instruction include lecture, discussion, classroom exercises, computer assisted instruction, simulation, and audio visual based formats.
Credit Recommendation: In the lower division baccalaureate/associate degree category, 1 semester hour in Railroad Operations, Engineering Technology, Transportation Technology, or Management/Supervisory Technology (9/95).

Locomotive Engineer Recertification Training (03)

Location: Overland Park, KS.
Length: 40 hours (1 week).
Dates: January 1992-Present.
Objective: To upgrade and recertify locomotive engineers (journeyman, designated supervisors, service continuation) to the standards set forth in FRA 49 CFR, Part 240.
Learning Outcome: Upon successful completion of this course, the student will demonstrate safe and effective train handling, air brake utilization, and locomotive mechanical and electrical principles. Designated supervisors will also demonstrate knowledge of FRA Locomotive Engineer Certification Regulations.
Instruction: Major topics covered in the course are train handling methods, air brake operations, freight car and locomotive mechanical and electrical principles, operating rules and regulations, and GCOR. Methods of instruction include lecture, discussion, classroom exercises, computer assisted instruction, simulation and audio visual based formats.
Credit Recommendation: In the lower division baccalaureate/associate degree category, 1 semester hour in Railroad Operations, Engineering Technology, or Transportation Technology (9/95).

Operating Rules (01)

Location: Overland Park, KS.
Length: 80 hours.
Dates: January 1995-Present.
Objective: To provide the student with a thorough knowledge of operating rules and procedures applicable to railroad industry yardmasters, dispatchers, conductors or locomotive engineers.
Learning Outcome: Upon successful completion of this course, the student will be able to apply the operating rules and procedures to his/her work on the railroad.
Instruction: Major topics covered in the course are the General Code of Operating Rules and associated procedures, including safety, timetables, signals, movement of trains and engines, switches, block systems rules, and track bulletins. Methods of instruction include lecture, discussion, classroom exercises, and computer assisted instruction, and audio visual based formats.
Credit Recommendation: In the lower division baccalaureate/associate degree category, 2 semester hours in Railroad Operations or Engineering Technology (9/95). **NOTE:** A student may receive credit only for this course or Conductor Promotion, but not for both.

Suburban Train Operations (05)

Location: Overland Park, Kansas and Cicero, Illinois.
Length: 40 hours (1 week).
Dates: January 1992-December 1997.
Objective: To provide students, engineers in suburban passenger train service, with knowledge of and skills in effectively operating suburban locomotive equipment.
Learning Outcome: Upon successful completion of this course, the student will demonstrate safe and effective suburban train handling methods, operate air brakes safely and effectively, and understand suburban locomotive mechanical and electrical basics and suburban operating and safety rules and their application.
Instruction: Major topics covered in the course are suburban train handling methods, air brake operation, locomotive and freight car mechanical and electrical principles, and operating rules and their application. Methods of instruction include lecture, discussion, classroom exercises, computer assisted instruction, simulation, and audio visual based formats.
Credit Recommendation: In the lower division baccalaureate/associate degree category, 1 semester hour in Railroad Operations, Engineering Technology, or Transportation Technology (9/95).

National Association Medical Staff Services

The NAMSS Institute is the continuing education division of the National Association Medical Staff Services (NAMSS). The Institute provides educational resources to medical staff and provider credentialing professionals at all levels of the healthcare industry.

The quality of patient care at a healthcare facility is a direct reflection of the skills and training of the professionals who administer the care. The competence of those professionals is the primary concern of the Medical Staff Services Professional and Provider Credentialing Specialists—they are the individuals who research and monitor the credentials and backgrounds of physicians and other healthcare providers.

In June 1993, a five-course independent study program titled *Medical Staff Organization Management* was developed to facilitate learning opportunities for individuals interested in the field. Also in 1992, the NAMSS Institute was formed; its mission: to help increase educational opportunities for healthcare professionals so they could achieve greater success in the changing organizational structure of the healthcare industry.

The goals and objectives of the Institute were developed by the NAMSS Education Council and Board of Directors, based on research of industry trends and needs for advanced study in a convenient format. Learning outcomes of each course are reviewed annually by the NAMSS Education Council and to keep course materials current, input is sought from NAMSS representatives to the Joint Commission on Accreditation of Healthcare Organizations (JCAHO), the National Committee for Quality Assurance (NCQA), the American Hospital Association, and the American Medical Association.

The five self-paced correspondence courses are designed to give students a better understanding of management theories and practices, medical terminology, healthcare finance, the industry shift toward managed care, ever-changing healthcare accreditation and regulatory standards, and healthcare legal issues impacting practitioners.

The Institute staff have extensive backgrounds in higher education administration, as well as the medical staff services profession. Their goal is to develop and provide up-to-date educational materials of the highest quality to help students meet the challenges of the rapidly changing healthcare arena.

Source of official student records: Registry of Credit Recommendations, American Council on Education, One Dupont Circle, Washington, DC 20036-1193.

Additional information about the courses: College Credit Recommendation Service, American Council on Education, One Dupont Circle, Washington, DC 20036-1193.

Medical Staff Organization Management

Module I: Medical Staff Office Administration (Formerly Administration and Management)

Location: Various locations throughout the United States.

Length: Independent study.

Dates: June 1993-Present.

Objective: To provide the medical staff services professional with an introduction to management, its functions, and terminology with a special emphasis upon communications and meetings.

Learning Outcome: Upon successful completion of this course, the student will be able to define management and its functions; list the steps in the problem solving process; understand the importance of the decision-making process; be cognizant of the differing approaches to file management; and be aware of the basics of organizing meetings, as well as the fundamentals of meeting minutes and parliamentary procedures.

Instruction: Major topics covered in the course are an overview of management and its functions; basics of office information management and record keeping; written communications; organizing meetings; basics of parliamentary procedure and medical staff service ethics. Methods of instruction include self-study of printed material and a proctored final examination.

Credit Recommendation: In the lower division baccalaureate/associate degree category, 2 semester hours in Office Administration and Management, Medical Records Administration, or Public Administration (1/96).

Module II: Medical Terminology

Location: Various locations throughout the United States.

Length: Independent study.

Dates: June 1993-Present.

Objective: To provide knowledge of medical terminology necessary for use in the credentialing process of physician and reappointment applications; when writing section/department meeting minutes, and in credentialing for new procedures.

Learning Outcome: Upon successful completion of this course, the student will be able to use a medical dictionary as a reference tool for determining correct spelling and definition of medical terms; change spellings of medical terms from singular to plural; identify and define word elements, combining forms and medical terms; analyze terms to determine meaning; recognize the body functions of each body system, and identify and define typical diseases and the terms associated with typical signs and symptoms.

Instruction: Major topics covered in the course are use of the medical dictionary; spelling and pronunciation rules; basic concepts of word analyses; terminology of the gastrointestinal system, urinary system, reproductive systems, nervous system, cardiovascular system, blood and lymphatics, respiratory system, integumentary system, endocrine system, special senses, and abbreviations. Methods of instruction include self-study of printed material and a proctored final examination.

Credit Recommendation: In the lower division baccalaureate/associate degree category, 3 semester hours in Medical Terminology (1/96).

Module III: An Overview of Medical Staff Organization (Formerly Principles of Medical Staff Organization)

Location: Various locations throughout the United States.

Length: Independent study.

Dates: June 1993-Present.

Objective: To provide an overview of the principles of medical staff organization (MSO), including the areas where the MSO intersects with the hospital organization, as well as the various roles played by medical staff members and committees in hospital operations.

Learning Outcome: Upon successful completion of this course, the student will be able to describe the organizational responsibilities of the medical staff including interactions with the governing body and the CEO; the components of the medical staff organizational structure, including the types of documents that guide actions of members of the medical staff; the roles of the individuals in leadership positions in medical staff organizations; and the sources of patient care revenue. The medical staff services professional will also become familiar with the organizations affecting the MSO, particularly those that are sources of regulation.

Instruction: Major topics covered in the course are the role of the medical staff in the hospital organization; medical staff organization structures; medical staff leaders; healthcare finance; and an overview of external bodies affecting medical staff organizations. Methods of instruction include self-study of printed material and a proctored final examination.

Credit Recommendation: In the lower division baccalaureate/associate degree category, 2 semester hours in Health Care Administration (1/96).

Module IV: Overview of Healthcare Accreditation (Formerly Accreditation Knowledge)

Location: Various locations throughout the United States.

Length: Independent study.

Dates: June 1993-Present.

Objective: To provide a basic familiarity with the regulatory agencies found in today's healthcare industry; an overview of the standards of the Joint Commission on Accreditation of Healthcare Organizations (JCAHO), the National Committee for Quality Assurance (NCQA), and other agencies that accredit or regulate healthcare facilities and/or managed healthcare organizations.

Learning Outcome: Upon successful completion of this course, the student will be able to understand JCAHO, NCQA, and other pertinent standards relative to medical staff appointment, credentialing, classification, and reappointment/appraisal; delineate procedures for awarding and evaluating clinical privileges; identify information resources for standards of ethical practice, outline activities designed to evaluate quality and appropriateness of care; list various requirements for, and objectives of continuing medical education; identify the requirements for hospital programs designed to assess and improve the quality of patient care; and describe the requirements for an approved cancer program, and identify the purpose and function of the Institutional Review Board.

Instruction: Major topics covered in the course are medical staff membership and privileges; review and monitoring of medical staff practice and functions as identified by JCAHO; medical staff participation in continuing education; hospital quality management; cancer programs; and institution review boards. Methods of instruction include self-study of printed material and a proctored final examination.

Credit Recommendation: In the lower division baccalaureate/associate degree category, 1 semester hour in Health Science or Health Care Administration (1/96).

Module V: Basic Elements of Medical Staff Law (Formerly Medical Staff Law)

Location: Various locations throughout the United States.

Length: Independent study.

Dates: June 1993-Present.

Objective: To provide an overview of the legal principles that guide healthcare providers.

Learning Outcome: Upon successful completion of this course, the student will be able to list major elements of the U.S. legal system; define terms associated with healthcare law; describe basic concepts of tort law; list common areas of liability for healthcare providers; describe characteristics of due process as they apply to medical staff activities, and describe legal aspects of medical records.

Instruction: Major topics covered in the course are the American legal system; tort law; hospital liability; practitioners' liability; and medical records, and the legal aspects of peer review. Methods of instruction include self study of printed material and a proctored final examination.

Credit Recommendation: In the lower division baccalaureate/associate degree category, 1 semester hour in Health Science or Health Care Administration (1/96).

National Association of Independent Fee Appraisers

The National Association of Independent Fee Appraisers was founded in 1961 as a nonprofit, professional society of real estate appraisers and is incorporated under the laws of the state of Arizona.

Today the association has chapters throughout the United States and Canada, and continues to grow not only in number, but also in stature.

The association's objective is to raise the standards of the profession, gain recognition for "its members as qualified appraisers and promote fellowship among the appraisers. This further affords reasonable assurance to the public of the professional skill, integrity, and responsibility of the membership.

Members of the association include full time professional real estate appraisers and others in related fields such as real estate, banking, building construction, governmental agencies and savings, and loan associations.

Source of official student records: National Association of Independent Fee Appraisers, 7501 Murdoch Avenue, St. Louis, Mo 63119.

Additional information about the courses: College Credit Recommendation Service, American Council on Education, One Dupont Circle, Washington, DC 20036-1193.

Farm, Ranch, and Rural Appraisal

Location: Various locations throughout the United States.

Length: 21 hours (3 days).

Dates: February 1980-March 1990.

Objective: To train individuals in the principles and procedures of farm, ranch, and rural appraisal.

Instruction: This course is designed to make participants aware of the reasons for conclusions of value and to present a method of writing an acceptable farm appraisal. Students learn about effectively using data sources, inspecting of the farm, three approaches to value, case studies, and report writing.

Credit Recommendation: In the lower division baccalaureate/associate degree or the upper division baccalaureate degree category, 1 semester hour in Farm, Ranch and Rural Appraisal (3/85).

Income Property Appraising

Location: Various locations throughout the United States.

Length: 24 hours (3 days classroom, plus extended independent studies).

Dates: April 1976-March 1990.

Objective: To train individuals in the principles and procedures of income property appraising.

Instruction: Major topics covered in this course are three approaches to value and when to apply them, processing and analyzing income, capitalization, rate development, compound interest, techniques of capitalization, and case studies. This course is designed to give participants an understanding of the forces that create and affect value and to provide the techniques and methods to process income into value. In addition to the classroom hours, there is an extended independent study culminating in a detailed narrative income property appraisal report.

Credit Recommendation: In the lower division baccalaureate/associate degree or the upper division baccalaureate degree category, 3 semester hours in Income Property Appraisal (3/85). **NOTE:** To be eligible for the credit recommendation students must submit a narrative appraisal report on an income-producing property and attain the Senior Member IFAS designation.

Principles of Residential Real Estate Appraising

Location: Various locations throughout the United States.

Length: 24 hours (3 days classroom, plus independent study).

Dates: October 1975-March 1990.

Objective: To train individuals in the principles and procedures of residential real estate appraising.

Instruction: Major topics covered in the course are the elements involved in residential appraising. Topics include value, definition and kinds, forces and factors that influence value, principles and construction. The appraisal process is divided into identifying the problem, gathering data, approach to value, and correlation and final value. In addition to the classroom hours, there is an extended independent study culminating in a detailed narrative residential appraisal report.

Credit Recommendation: In the lower division baccalaureate/associate degree or the upper division baccalaureate degree category, 3 semester hours in the Principles of Real Estate Appraising (3/85). **NOTE:** To be eligible for the credit recommendation students must submit a narrative residential appraisal report and attain the member IFA designation.

National Association of Power Engineers Educational Foundation

The National Association of Power Engineers Educational Foundation (NAPEEF) is a non-profit organization founded in 1991. The mission of NAPEEF is to promote the professional competence of engineers through continuing education. It is the education foundation of the District of Columbia Chapter (#1) of the National Association of Power Engineers (NAPE), which was founded in 1882. The Chapter has been offering education programs since 1970, and it is the largest program in the national association. NAPEEF is accredited by the National Institute of Uniform Licensing of Power Engineers (NIULPE).

Eleven hundred students, at both entry and advanced levels, are registered each year in NAPEEF courses. Most students take courses at the Power Engineering Education Center located at 5707 Seminary Road, Falls Church, VA where simulators and demonstration equipment are located. Courses are presented using lecture, videos, handouts, field trips, equipment demonstrations, and hands-on exercises. Courses also are provided on-site at local offices of national corporations when requested.

Instructors are individuals with professional experience and competence, academic background, appropriate licenses, and prior experience with the NAPEEF and the NIULPE educational philosophies. Applications for instructor positions are reviewed by NAPEEF's staff and a committee of the Board, which consists of experienced, licensed power engineers, many of whom are or have been national board members of NAPE and NIULPE. This committee also guides the course development process.

Source of official student records: Registry of Credit Recommendations, American Council on Education, One Dupont Circle, Washington, DC 20036-1193.

Additional information about the courses: College Credit Recommendation Service, American Council on Education, One Dupont Circle, Washington, DC 20036-1193.

Advanced Technical Knowledge For 1st Class Steam Plant Maintenance and Operation (1st Class Steam)

Location: Various locations throughout the United States.

Length: 60 hours (20 weeks).

Dates: September 1986-Present.

Objective: To investigate communication and relationships in creating a productive work environment.

Learning Outcome: Upon successful completion of this course, the student will be able to understand the importance of communication and methods of communicating effectively in organizations; identify and analyze facilitating and hindering forces in effective communications; practice developing and delivering effective interpersonal communications; understand theory and practice team-building, conflict resolution, and problem solving; understand how communication and organizational cultures relate to one another; and understand the role of verbal and nonverbal messages and how to use them effectively.

Instruction: Major topics covered in the course are the communication process and media, team building, and conflict resolution. Methods of instruction include discussion, classroom exercises, lecture, audio/visual material, role play, classroom participation, homework assignments, and a summary paper.

Credit Recommendation: In the upper division baccalaureate degree category, 3 semester hours in Organizational Communication or Business Administration (8/96).

Air Conditioning and Refrigeration I

Location: Power Engineering Education Center, Falls Church, VA and Carr America Training Center, Washington, DC.

Length: 60 hours (20 weeks).

Dates: January 1991-Present.

Objective: To provide the student with an entry-level understanding of the basic refrigeration system, components, and theory; and to provide knowledge about the basic tools and equipment used in service, installation, and maintenance of air conditioning and refrigeration equipment.

Learning Outcome: Upon successful completion of this course, the student will be able to describe the basic refrigeration cycle and its components (evaporators, condensers, compressors); theory of heat, matter, energy, and refrigerants; and how to safely use wiring diagrams and tools for troubleshooting, recovery, and brazing.

Instruction: Major topics covered in the course are policies of the National Association of Power Engineers Education Foundation (NAPEEF), theory of air conditioning and refrigeration, energy and matter, refrigeration and refrigerants, evaporators and the refrigeration system, condensers, compressors, expansion devices, general safety practices, tolls and equipment, troubleshooting, recovery, brazing and soldering, basic electricity, and wiring diagrams. Methods of instruction include lecture, videos, "hands-on" demonstrations, drawings, field trip, quizzes, projects, and examinations.

Credit Recommendation: In the vocational certificate or lower division baccalaureate/associate degree category, 3 semester hours in Fundamentals of Air Conditioning and Refrigeration Technology (12/97).

Air Conditioning and Refrigeration II - Diagnostics and Analysis

Location: Power Engineering Education Center, Falls Church, VA and Carr America Training Center, Washington, DC.

Length: 60 hours (20 weeks).

Dates: September 1994-Present.

Objective: To provide knowledge about the step by step methods of analyzing why the electrical and mechanical components of an air conditioning and refrigeration system are inefficient or will not run, and the solutions to increase efficiency and make a system operational.

Learning Outcome: Upon successful completion of the course, the student will be able to troubleshoot refrigeration systems, including all components and accessories, using a variety of troubleshooting techniques such as pressure and temperatures, heat loads, schematics and diagrams.

Instruction: Major topics covered in the course are troubleshooting, compressors, metering devices, valves, temperature and pressure, water treatment, cleaning coils, air handlers, commercial systems, heat loads, schematics and wire diagrams. Methods of instruction include lecture, "hands-on" demonstrations, field trip, schematics, diagrams, quizzes and examinations.

Credit Recommendation: In the vocational certificate or lower division baccalaureate/associate degree category, 3 semester hours in Comfort Cooling Systems or Intermediate Air Conditioning Systems (12/97).

Air Conditioning and Refrigeration III - Operations and Management

Location: Power Engineering Education Center, Falls Church, VA.

Length: 60 hours (20 weeks).

Dates: January 1996-Present.

Objective: To provide knowledge of the operations and maintenance of large, integrated air conditioning and refrigeration systems, commercial chiller plants of all types, operation and maintenance of all types of compressors, and absorption plants.

Learning Outcome: Upon successful completion of this course, the student will have an understanding of the operation and maintenance of chiller plants of all types, compressors, absorption plants, cooling towers, water chemistry, and energy management.

Instruction: Major topics covered in the course are cooling towers, water treatment, evaporators, load calculations, chillers, thermal storage, heat pumps, variable air volume, energy management, EPA regulations, PM systems, Hazmat materials. Methods of instruction include lecture with handouts, drawings and overheads, field trips, quizzes, mid term, and final examinations.

Credit Recommendation: In the vocational certificate or lower division baccalaureate/associate degree category, 3 semester hours in Commercial Air Conditioning and Refrigeration Operations and Management (12/97).

Basic Principles of Low Pressure Boilers (Low Pressure Boilers)

Location: Power Engineering Education Center, Falls Church, VA and Carr America Training Center, Washington, DC.

Length: 60 hours (20 weeks).

Dates: January 1989-Present.

Objective: To provide basic knowledge of principles of boiler operation, fittings, accessories, water treatment, and safety in a beginners class for those who have one year or less experience.

Learning Outcome: Upon successful completion of the course, students will able to work with boilers and all related equipment; comprehend and be able to describe theory and practical applications to boiler operations; work safely with boilers and related equipment; and describe for other engineers safety principles.

Instruction: Major topics covered in the course are engineering principles, computations of horse power, BTUs (British training Units), volumes, coefficients of expansion, fuels and combustion, draft control, fitting and accessories, water treatment, hot water systems, cooling systems, drawings, diagrams, pumps, safety operation and steam turbines. Methods of instruction include lecture, classroom exercises, "hands-on" demonstrations, field trips, lab shop wor, quizzes, midterm, and final examination.

Credit Recommendation: In the vocational certificate or lower division baccalaureate/associate degree category, 3 semester hours in Basic Principles of Low Pressure Boilers (12/97).

Heat Pumps

Location: Power Engineering Education Center, Falls Church, VA.

Length: 30 hours (10 weeks).

Dates: September 1991-Present.

Objective: To provide knowledge or an understanding and "hands on" instruction about the heat pump operation cycle, components, efficiency, supplemental heat, service and troubleshooting and wiring diagrams.

Learning Outcome: Upon successful completion of the course, the student will be able to describe and explain the operation of heat pumps, including the cooling, heating, and defrost modes and emergency heating operations; how to charge a heat pump; and how to troubleshoot and diagnose problems and make necessary repairs.

Instruction: Major topics covered in the course are heat pump cycle and efficiency, compressors and motor controls, refrigerant controls, reversing valves, air and water coils, defrosting cycles, supplemental heat, service, trouble shooting, and wiring diagrams. Methods of instruction include lecture, discussion, "hands-on" demonstrations, lab assignments, tests, quizzes, in-class projects, and final examination.

Credit Recommendation: In the vocational certificate or lower division baccalaureate/associate degree category, 2 semester hours in Heat Pumps (12/97).

Pneumatic Controls

Location: Power Engineering Education Center, Fall Church, VA and Carr America Training Center, Washington, DC.

Length: 60 hours (20 weeks).

Dates: January 1989-Present.

Objective: To provide students with HVAC experience knowledge of the fundamentals of pneumatic controls as components of equipment maintained by building engineers and hands on experience with calibration.

Learning Outcome: Upon successful completion of the course, students will be able understand the terminology of pneumatics and to describe and explain the operation of pneumatic controls, including basic system operations, maintenance, calibration, service, system application and energy conversation.

Instruction: Major topics covered in the course are air supply systems, compressors, dryers, pressure reducing stations, thermostats, calibration, schematics, control applications and devices, relays, switches, receiver controllers, HVAC systems, special systems. Methods of instruction include lecture, discussion, calibration labs, assignments from text, quizzes, midterm, and final examination.

Credit Recommendation: In the vocational certificate or lower division baccalaureate/associate degree category, 3 semester hours in Pneumatics (12/97).

Principles and Practices of High Pressure Steam Boilers (3rd Class Steam)

Location: Power Engineering Education Center, Falls Church, VA and Carr America Training Center, Washington, DC.

Length: 60 hours (20 weeks).

Dates: January 1989-Present.

Objective: To provide knowledge beyond a basic steam/low pressure course, related to steam boilers and accessories, operational theories, and practices by which engineers can ensure safe and efficient steam plant operation.

Learning Outcome: Upon successful completion of this second level steam course, students who have had the basic steam course and/or steam experience will demonstrate knowledge and skills in all aspects of boilers, including accessories, fuels, water treatment, electrical systems, and efficient and safe plant operation.

Instruction: Major topics covered in the course are design and operation of high pressure steam, boilers and auxiliaries, combustion fuels, draft, introduction to air conditioning and auxiliaries, water treatment systems, turbines, steam management, computation of pressures and volumes, electricity, and general safety and maintenance procedures. Methods of instruction used are lecture, discussion, hands-on demonstrations, lab experience, videos, drawings, field trips, quizzes, midterm, and final examination.

Credit Recommendation: In the vocational certificate or lower division baccalaureate/associate degree category, 3 semester hours in Principles and Practices of High Pressure Steam Boilers (12/97).

National Association of Securities Dealers, Inc.

The National Association of Securities Dealers, Inc. (NASD), is the primary organization of the securities industry and is responsible for regulating the over-the-counter securities market. The NASD was established by the 1938 Maloney Act amendments to the Securities Exchange Act of 1934. The principle behind the legislation is that of cooperative regulation by which voluntary associations of broker-dealers regulate themselves under the oversight of the Securities and Exchange Commission. The NASD is the only securities association to have been established under the legislation. Today, its membership comprises approximately 90 percent of the nation's broker-dealers. The NASD, in addition to enforcing federal securities laws as well as the broader ethical requirements of its own rules which obligate members to observe high standards of commercial honor, also operates a nationwide electronic "stockmarket" for OTC securities called "NASDAQ."

To ensure that its staff has the necessary knowledge, the NASD developed its own training/education program for its regulatory personnel. The program stresses subjects dealing with the various types and forms of securities products, financial and operational analysis, and securities laws and the rules and regulations thereunder.

The NASD's training program has two objectives. The first is to enable a participant to master the major aspects of federal securities laws and disciplines relating to the investment banking and securities business and to demonstrate that knowledge by on-site inspections of the business of investment bankers and securities broker-dealers. The second objective is to enable a participant to learn how to analyze the financial and operational systems of the investment community and to demonstrate that knowledge by capital analyses and operational audits.

Source of official student records: National Association of Securities Dealers, Inc., 9513 Key West Avenue, Rockville, MD 20850.

Additional information about the courses: College Credit Recommendation Service, American Council on Education, One Dupont Circle, Washington, DC 20036-1193.

Cornerstone Program
1. Investments and/or Brokerage Accounting
2. Securities, Regulation, Law, and Self-Regulation

Location: *Version 1:* Washington, DC;*Version 2:* Washington, DC; *Version 3:* Rockville, MD, New York, NY, Philadelphia, PA, Washington, DC, Cleveland, OH; Chicago, IL, Kansas City, MO, New Orleans, LA, Atlanta, GA, Dallas, TX, Denver, CO, Seattle, WA, San Francisco, CA, and Los Angeles, CA.

Length: *Version 1:* 210 hours (6 weeks), plus a pre-phase component; *Version 2:* 140 hours (4 weeks), plus a pre-phase component; *Version 3:* 140 hours (CBT and classroom training over 6-10 months).

Dates: *Version 1:* July 1975-December 1993; *Version 2:* January 1994-July 1995; *Version 3:* August 1995-Present.

Objective: *Versions 1 and 2:* To enable a participant to master the major aspects of federal securities laws and disciplines relating to the investment banking and securities business and to demonstrate that knowledge by examining the business of investment bankers or securities broker-dealers. *Version 3:* To provide participants with a fundamental understanding of brokerage operations, the examination process, securities laws; and SEC rules and regulations.

Learning Outcome: *Version 3:* Upon successful completion of this course, the student will be able to perform the essential job functions of an examiner, conducting routine and cause examinations for member firms of the NASD.

Instruction: *Versions 1 and 2:* Major topics covered in the course are comparisons of the auction and negotiated markets and the exchange specialist and over-the-counter market making systems; investment banking and the capital formation process; and operations of a securities firm. Course also covers the Securities Act of 1933, Securities Exchange Act of 1934, and the elements of discovering and proving a market manipulation. A detailed explanation of securities products and the federal regulations governing them is provided on such instruments as options, municipal securities, government-guaranteed mortgaged-backed securities, direct participation programs (e.g., real estate syndications, oil and gas programs, cattle-feeding programs), and commodity futures, investment banking, and secondary market making. Emphasis is placed on broker-dealer operations and their specialized accounting systems, Federal Reserve System credit regulations and margin rules, coupled with the exhaustive analysis of financial and capital data, and operational audits. Methods of instruction include lecture, discussions, and classroom exercises. *Version 3:* Major topics covered in the course are those shown in *Versions 1 and 2*, as well as an examiner's workshop which includes actual case documents, the procedure for conducting interviews, making determinations, and discussing advanced investigative and sales practices issues; and mentor training. Methods of instruction include self-directed instruction, print-based and computer-based; mentoring and on-the-job activities; instructor-led classroom discussion; case studies; and examinations.

Credit Recommendation: *Versions 1 and 2:* In the upper division baccalaureate degree category or in the graduate degree category, 3 semester hours in Investments and/or Brokerage Accounting and Operation. In the upper division baccalaureate degree category or in the graduate degree category, 3 semester hours in Securities, Regulation, and Law, for a total of 6 hours (7/81). **NOTE:** Participants must complete both Phases I and II in order to receive credit (7/87). *Version 3:* In the upper division baccalaureate degree category, 6 semester hours in Securities Regulation and Law or General Business; or in the graduate degree category, 3 semester hours in Securities Regulation and Law or General Business (11/95).

National Certified Public Manager Consortium

The purpose of the National Certified Public Manager (CPM) Consortium is to accredit Certified Public Manager programs by promoting high standards, facilitating program development, encouraging innovation and developing linkages with programs and organizations with similar concerns. The CPM Consortium is made up of two representatives from each member state and two representatives from the American Academy of Certified Public Managers.

The first Certified Public Manager Program was developed in Georgia in March, 1976. Since that time 16 states and the USDA Graduate School, Washington, DC, have received full accreditation from the National Certified Public Manager Consortium to award the Certificate of Public Management.

Participants in the program are employees of state, local, and city governments, employees from federal government, and employees from non-profit organizations.

Instructors are practitioners and academicians experience in management and public administration. The instructors are trained in educational techniques thus assuring the highest quality in training and education.

Source of official student records: Registry of Credit Recommendations, American Council on Education, One Dupont Circle, Washington, DC 20036-1193.

Additional information about the courses: College Credit Recommendation Service, American Council on Education, One Dupont Circle, Washington, DC 20036-1193.

Alabama Certified Public Management Program

Location: Various sites in the State of Alabama.

Length: 248 hours.

Dates: March 1991-Present.

Objective: To develop effective public management skills.

Learning Outcome: Upon successful completion of this course, the student will be able to demonstrate effective management skills including communication, problem solving, behavior modification, teamwork, employee interviewing, performance appraisal, employee discipline, conflict resolution, and time management.

Instruction: Major topics covered in the course are the basics of management and personnel policies and procedures, management practices related to effective leadership, interpersonal skills and group dynamics, and communication. Methods of instruction include lecture, discussion, classroom exercises, case studies, audio/visual material, projects, tests, and examinations.

Credit Recommendation: In the upper division baccalaureate degree category, 15 semester hours, or in the graduate degree category, 9 semester hours in Public Administration, Management, or Human Relations (3/97).

Arkansas Certified Public Management Program

Location: University of Arkansas Little Rock.

Length: 288 hours.

Dates: March 1991-Present.

Objective: To develop public management skills.

Learning Outcome: Upon successful completion of this course, the student will be able to demonstrate effective administrative, management, and human resource skills including communication, problem solving, behavior modification, teamwork, performance review, positive discipline, conflict resolution, and time management; and understand the state legislative process.

Instruction: Major topics covered in the course are the basics of management and personnel policies and procedures, management practices related to effective leadership, continuous process improvement including interpersonal skills and group dynamics, speech and written communication, budgetary process and the budget system, the legislative process, administrative law, ethics, human resources, improving productivity, leadership, management communication, Management Development Planning Seminar, media and public relations, political process, presentation skills, program planning and evaluation, statistics in government, and stress management. Methods of instruction include lecture, classroom exercises, case studies, audio/visual material, written examinations, and designing and presenting a project plan to the agency supervisor that addresses how to improve the efficiency and effectiveness of agency operations.

Credit Recommendation: In the upper division baccalaureate degree category, 9 semester hours, or in the graduate degree category, 6 semesters hours in Public Administration, Management or Human Relations (3/97).

Kansas Certified Public Management Program

Location: Topeka and Wichita, Kansas.

Length: 300 hours.

Dates: January 1993-Present.

Objective: To develop effective public management skills.

Learning Outcome: Upon successful completion of this course, the student will be able to demonstrate effective administrative, management, and human resource skills including communication, problem solving, behavior modification, teamwork, performance review, positive discipline, conflict resolution, and time management; and understand the state legislative process.

Instruction: Major topics covered in the course are the basics of management and personnel policies and procedures, management practices related to effective leadership, continuous process improvement including interpersonal skills and group dynamics, speech and written communication, budgetary process and the budget system, and the legislative process. Methods of instruction include lecture, discussion, classroom exercises, case studies, audio/visual material, learner presentations/reports, projects, presentations, and examinations.

Credit Recommendation: In the upper division baccalaureate degree category, 15 semester hours, or in the graduate degree category, 9 semester hours in Public Administration, Management, or Human Relations (3/97).

Mississippi Certified Public Management Program

Location: Various sites in the State of Mississippi.

Length: 300 hours.

Dates: March 1991-Present.

Objective: To develop effective public management skills.

Learning Outcome: Upon successful completion of this course, the student will be able to demonstrate effective administrative, management, and human resource skills including communication, problem solving, behavior modification, teamwork, performance review, positive discipline, conflict resolution, and time management; and understand the state legislative process.

Instruction: Major topics covered in the course are the basics of management and personnel policies and procedures, management practices related to effective leadership, continuous process improvement including interpersonal skills and group dynamics, speech and written communication, budgetary process and the budget system, the legislative process, personal styles, ethics in government, concepts of management, leadership, managing for results, interpersonal communication, delegation, performance measurement and evaluation, budgeting in Mississippi, the legislative process, leadership and group dynamics, motivation, coaching, counseling and performance appraisal, creative problem solving and decision making, management of organizational conflict, assessing management practices, organizational climate, managing organizational pressures, strategic management, organizational communications, organizational change, legal liability of the public manager, and innovation and excellence in the public sector. Methods of instruction include lecture, discussion, classroom experiential exercises, assessment instruments, study questions, videos, case studies, projects, presentations, objective examinations, individual and group presentations, papers, reading abstracts, and job-related project proposal evaluation.

Credit Recommendation: In the upper division baccalaureate degree category, 15 semester hours, or in the graduate degree category, 9 semester hours in Public Administration, Management, or Human Relations (3/97).

Oklahoma Certified Public Management Program

Location: Various sites in the State of Oklahoma.

Length: 300 hours.

Dates: March 1991-Present.

Objective: To develop effective public management skills.

Learning Outcome: Upon successful completion of this course, the student will be able to demonstrate effective administrative, management, and human resource skills including communication, problem solving, behavior modification, teamwork, performance review, positive discipline, conflict resolution, and time management; and understand the state legislative process.

Instruction: Major topics covered in the course are the basics of management and personnel policies and procedures, management practices related to effective leadership, continuous process improvement including interpersonal skills and group dynamics, speech and written communication, budgetary process and the budget system, the legislative process, challenges of supervision, delegation, writing, time management, Certified Public Manager orientation, effective communication, sexual harassment, performance appraisal in state government, progressive discipline, on-job-training, Management 2000, applied leadership, conducting group meetings, effective negotiation, conflict management, motivating for performance, problem solving skills, ethics in public management, administrative law, personnel policies and practices, public speaking and effective presentations, management, policy analysis, program evaluation, systems management, facilitator training, capstone, and Executive Development Seminar. Methods of instruction include case studies, lecture, small group discussions, large group discussions, presentations, simulation exercises, team assignments, classroom exercises, audio-visual material, applied written projects, objective and multiple choice questions, individual and group exercises and presentations, completion of 4 projects, and use of case studies.

Credit Recommendation: In the upper division baccalaureate degree category, 15 semester hours, or in the graduate degree category, 9 semester hours in Public Administration, Management, or Human Relations (3/97).

Utah Certified Public Management Program

Location: Various sites in the State of Utah.

Length: 300 hours.

Dates: January 1991-Present.

Objective: To develop effective public management skills.

Learning Outcome: Upon successful completion of this course, the student will be able to demonstrate effective administrative, management, and human resource skills including communication, problem solving, behavior modification, teamwork, performance review, positive discipline, conflict resolution, and time management; and understand the state legislative process.

Instruction: Major topics covered in the course are the basics of management and personnel policies and procedures, management practices related to effective leadership, continuous process improvement including interpersonal skills and group dynamics, speech and written communication, budgetary process and the budget system, the legislative process, organizational dynamics, team development, diversity management, meeting management, decision making, problem solving, communication and presentation, leadership dynamics, employee work contracting, conflict management, training, ethics, risk management, advanced leadership, advanced team processes, organizational culture and climate, advanced communication, customer and customer service, managing and improving work processes, financial management, future planning, human resource management, risk management and liability avoidance, how agencies work in state government, and administrative law. Methods of instruction include lecture, discussion, classroom experiential exercises, case studies, audio-visual material, pre-tests, projects, essay, objective and multiple choice tests, oral examinations, completion of projects, and final examinations.

Credit Recommendation: In the upper division baccalaureate degree category, 15 semester hours, or in the graduate degree category, 9 semester hours in Public Administration, Management, or Human Relations (3/97).

Wisconsin Certified Public Management Program

Location: Various sites in the State of Wisconsin.

Length: 304 hours (Phase 1: 73 hours; Phase 2: 108 hours; Phase 3: 123 hours).

Dates: March 1991-Present.

Objective: To develop effective public management skills.

Learning Outcome: Upon successful completion of this course, the student will be able to demonstrate effective management skills including strategic planning, financial planning, decision-making, supervision, leadership, team building, employment interviewing, performance appraisal, employee discipline, quality concepts, communication, media relations, customer/client relations, information management, conflict management, risk management, and project management.

Instruction: Major topics covered in the course are the basics of management and personnel policies and procedures, management practices related to effective leadership, interpersonal skills and group dynamics, and communications. Methods of instruction include lecture, discussion, classroom exercises, case studies, audio-visual material, computer-assisted instruction, learner presentation/reports, simulation, projects, tests, and examinations.

Credit Recommendation: In the upper division baccalaureate degree category, 15 semester hours; or in the graduate degree category, 9 semester hours in Public Administration, Management, or Human Relations (3/97).

National Child Care Association

The National Child Care Association was founded in 1987 to serve the needs of the private, licensed child care community and working families nationwide. NCCA is guided by a Board of Directors representing each of the organization's state association members.

Because the National Child Care Association is vitally concerned with the availability of quality, affordable care for children, we see an important element of our mission to be the encouragement of and provision of valuable, job-related educational opportunities for program staff. A number of important studies have shown that well-trained staff can impact the quality of an early childhood program more than nearly any other factor. That is why NCCA is dedicated to professional development and education initiatives.

The National Administrator Credential course is designed for directors and managers of child care and preschool programs. Other education programs offered by the National Child Care Association include a credential for teachers and short workshops for both directors and staff.

Instructors for the National Administrator Credential have appropriate education credentials and are specifically trained to teach this course by the National Child Care Association. All instructors have hands-on experience in adult education. Courses offered in most states through a network of NCCA member state associations.

Source of official student records: Registry of Credit Recommendations, American Council on Education, One Dupont Circle, Washington, DC 20036-1193 or the National Care Association, 1029 Railroad Street, Conyers, GA 30207.

Additional information about the courses: College Credit Recommendation Service, American Council on Education, One Dupont Circle, Washington, DC 20036-1193.

National Administrator Credential

Location: Various states nationwide.

Length: 40 hours (5 days).

Dates: February 1995-Present.

Objective: To equip administrators of child care programs or prospective administrators with the skills and competencies necessary to effectively manage a child care facility.

Learning Outcome: Upon successful completion of this course, the student will be to demonstrate the mastery of the objective; develop and maintain an effective child care organization; effectively market the program; supervise and develop personnel; understand the legal aspects of child care; develop and maintain the facility; develop good community relations; and manage the program's finances.

Instruction: Major topics covered in the course are planning and developing programs, administrative systems, marketing, personnel management, facility management, laws and regulations, community relations, financial management, and director self-development. Methods of instruction include lecture, discussion, classroom exercises, audio-visual material, learner presentations, reports, quizzes, observations, out-of-class exercises, and a final examination.

Credit Recommendation: In the lower division baccalaureate/associate degree category, 3 semester hours in Education (1/97).

National Cryptologic School

The National Cryptologic School operates under the Government Employees Training Act and applicable Department of Defense directives. It provides training in cryptology and related activities to military and civilian personnel of the U.S. Government. The school is organized into three departments: Cryptologic Skills Department, Technology and Skills Department, and Leadership and Support Department.

Source of official student records: Registrar, National Cryptologic School, Fort George G. Meade, MD 20755-6000, ATTN: E11.

Additional information about the courses: College Credit Recommendation Service, American Council on Education, One Dupont Circle, Washington, DC 20036-1193.

LANGUAGE DEPARTMENT

The Language Department is one of several departments in the Language and Analysis Faculty. It provides training in different languages to those in language-associated jobs. Linguistics courses are listed first, followed by courses arranged alphabetically by title under the Language (Arabic, Chinese, Hebrew, etc.).

Foreign Language Testing (ED-Q04) (Writing Foreign Language/Area Studies Test Items)

Location: National Cryptologic School, Ft. Meade, MD.

Length: 16 hours (2 days).

Dates: March 1988-July 1992.

Objective: Systematic development of test items for foreign language and target studies.

Learning Outcome: Upon successful completion of this course, the student will be able to produce valid and reliable test items, recognize invalid test items, and evaluate test items.

Instruction: Major topics covered in the course are principles of testing, test item typologies, and validity and reliability. Methods of instruction include lecture, discussion, demonstration and problem solving.

Credit Recommendation: In the upper division baccalaureate degree category, 1 semester hour in Applied Linguistics or Foreign Language Education (8/91).

Introduction to Linguistic Theory (LG-130)

Location: National Cryptologic School, Ft. Meade, MD.

Length: 48 hours (6 weeks).

Dates: July 1972-September 1996.

Objective: To introduce the basic principles of linguistic analysis in the areas of phonetics, morphology, syntax, semantics, and pragmatics; and application of these principles to text processing.

Learning Outcome: Upon successful completion of this course, the student will be able to identify what features other than language affect the meaning of sentences and texts (e.g. indirect speech, speaker/writer intent); identify features that affect how we understand spoken discourse and process texts; analyze the syntax and semantics of sentences; apply principles of work formation and inflection; and apply a basic knowledge of articulatory phonetics to an analysis of differences in this area.

Instruction: Major topics covered in the course are the principles of phonetics, phonemics, morphology, and syntax; analysis of the principles underlying different writing systems; and exercises in various forms of linguistic analysis including establishment of phonemic status, determining distribution and conditioning of allophones, segmentation of utterances into morphemes, determining distribution and conditioning of allomorphs and morphophonemic changes, IC analysis, and descriptions of syntactic features (emphasis is both synchronic and diachronic.) Methods of instruction include lecture, discussion, classroom exercises, learner presentations/reports, and evaluation.

Credit Recommendation: In the lower division baccalaureate/associate degree category, 3 semester hours in Linguistics (3/80) (10/85) (9/94).

Linguistics (ED-031)
1. Foreign Language Methodology: Course Design (ED-Q03)
2. Foreign Language Methodology: Reading and Listening
(Writing Foreign Language/Area Studies Course Documentation) (Teaching Foreign Language Reading and Listening)

Location: National Cryptologic School, Ft. Meade, MD.

Length: *Course 1:* 16 hours (2 days); *Course 2:* 16 hours (2 days).

Dates: March 1988-August 1996.

Objective: *Course 1:* Development and design of course training standards and outlines. *Course 2:* Development and use of techniques to teach reading and listening in a variety of foreign languages to adult learners.

Learning Outcome: *Course 1:* Upon successful completion of the course, the student will be able to develop foreign language course content according to NCS Administrative Instruction I-2; sequence course materials and instructional strategies; develop tasks and outcomes; and develop criteria for measuring student progress. *Course 2:* Upon successful completion of the course, the student will be able to develop appropriate reading and listening comprehension activities for suitable foreign language texts, and demonstrate understanding of theoretical principles of the teaching of reading and listening comprehension.

Instruction: *Course 1:* Major topics covered in the course are review of NCS Administra-tive Instruction I-2; training standards; and scope and sequence of materials and instructional techniques. *Course 2* : Major topics covered in the course are textual analysis; previewing, prediction, scanning, skimming, lexical recovery, paraphrasing, and gisting; and testing techniques. Methods of instruction include lecture, discussion, demonstration; problem-solving; and independent project development.

Credit Recommendation: In the upper division baccalaureate degree category, 2 semester hours in Linguistics (8/91). **NOTE:** Both courses must be taken to receive the credit recommendation

Linguistics Analysis of Foreign Language Texts for Comprehension (LG-140) (Applied Cryptologic Linguistics)

Location: National Cryptologic School, Ft. Meade, MD.

Length: 20 hours (5 days).

Dates: March 1988-Present.

Objective: To provide the student with application of principles of linguistic analysis to foreign language texts.

Learning Outcome: Upon successful completion of this course, the student will be able to analyze foreign language texts for meaning, degarble corrupt text, transcribe oral texts accurately, and use structural and lexical cues to make texts readable.

Instruction: Major topics covered in the course are gisting, degarbling, transcription, and structural and lexical analysis. Methods of instruction include lecture, discussion, classroom exercises, problem-solving, group activities, and group and individual projects.

Credit Recommendation: In the upper division baccalaureate degree category, 1 semester hour in Linguistics or Foreign Language (8/91) (9/96).

Technical Aspects of Translation (LG-240)
(Translation Techniques)

Location: National Cryptologic School, Ft. Meade, MD.

Length: 30 hours (10 days).

Dates: March 1988-Present.

Objective: To teach the student acquisition and development of skills and techniques for translating foreign language texts into English.

Learning Outcome: Upon successful completion of this course, the student will be able to understand the content of a foreign language text, demonstrate an understanding of tools and processes necessary to produce an accurate (language and content) translation of a 2 to 2+ level text, and demonstrate the ability to identify and correct translation errors in an inaccurate translation of a 2+ to 3 level text.

Instruction: Major topics covered in the course are text organization, information retrieval, cohesion and coherence, paraphrase, and criterion-referenced evaluation. Methods of instruction include lecture, discussion, classroom exercises, translation exercises, group activities, problem-solving, and an independent project.

Credit Recommendation: In the upper division baccalaureate degree category, 1 semester hour in any of the Foreign Languages (8/91) (9/96).

Workshop or Colloquium on Computer-Assisted Instruction (ED-120)
(Area Studies & Language Instruction Go High Tech-ALIGHT)

Location: National Cryptologic School, Ft. Meade, MD.

Length: 64 hours (2 one-hour meetings per week).

Dates: March 1988-August 1996.

Objective: Development of tools and skills for the design, development, and implementation of computer-assisted teaching and learning.

Learning Outcome: Upon successful completion of this course, the student will be able to incorporate computers in instructional programs, adapt computer software to instruction and learning, and develop computer-assisted materials.

Instruction: Major topics covered in the course are principles of computer literacy, computer-assisted instructional design, machine translation techniques, introduction to artificial intelligence, and text processing by machine. Methods of instruction include lecture, discussion, demonstration, and manipulation of menu-driven software.

Credit Recommendation: In the upper division baccalaureate degree category, 3 semester hours in Applied Linguistics or Educational Technology (8/91).

Arabic

Arabic Syria Course (AA-111)
(Formerly Levantine Arabic Course)

Location: National Cryptologic School, Ft. Meade, MD.

Length: 320 hours.

Dates: April 1985-Present.

Objective: To enable the student to comprehend Interagency Language Roundtable (ILR) level 2 aural and graphic texts in Levantine; answer questions about everyday topics in Levantine; and gist ILR level 2 Levantine texts in Arabic or English.

Learning Outcome: Upon successful completion of this course, the student will be able to listen and read proficiently at the ILR level 2, and demonstrate limited speaking competence.

Instruction: Major topics covered in the course are the Levantine Arabic spoken dialect, and be familiar with everyday topics. Methods of instruction include lecture, discussion, classroom exercises, and audio/visual material.

Credit Recommendation: In the upper division baccalaureate degree category, 6 semester hours in Arabic (6/87) (9/94). **NOTE:** Student must have completed Basic Modern Standard Arabic (AA-10-A) or its equivalent, and have a proven ILR level 2 in listening to receive this credit.

Basic Modern Standard Arabic (AA-15A)

Location: National Cryptologic School, Ft. Meade, MD.

Length: 1,880 hours (47 weeks).

Dates: November 1983-December 1989.

Objective: To provide a thorough knowledge of the basic grammatical features of modern standard Arabic and to provide a moderately broad familiarity with newspaper vocabulary and skills in listening comprehension, transcription, and translation into English.

Learning Outcome: Upon successful completion of this course, the student will be able to write a summary in English of an Arabic text at the L2 Level; translate a text into good English; write a summary of a voice recording in Modern Standard Arabic at L2 Level (news segment); transcribe a news segment in Arabic script; and conjugate verbs in all forms.

Instruction: Major topics covered in the course are grammatical structures, listening and reading for understanding, and six weeks of transcription and translation of Arabic operational material. This course is the equivalent of three years of intensive study (five hours weekly) with strong emphasis on military and political vocabulary.

Credit Recommendation: In the lower division baccalaureate/associate degree category or in the upper division baccalaureate degree category, 32 semester hours in Modern Standard Arabic (6/87).

Basic Modern Standard Arabic (AA-10A)
Course 1: Basic Modern Standard Arabic
Course 2: Intermediate Modern Standard Arabic

Location: National Cryptologic School, Ft. Meade, MD.

Length: *Version 1:* 1,520 hours (38 weeks), classroom and self-study included; *Course 1:* 1010 hours (25 weeks); *Course 2:* 510 hours (13 weeks); *Version 2:* 1,880 hours (47 weeks).

Dates: *Version 1:* July 1974-April 1984; *Version 2:* May 1984-Present.

Objective: To provide a thorough knowledge of the basic grammatical features of Modern Standard Arabic and to provide a moderately broad familiarity with newspaper vocabulary and skills in listening comprehension, transcription, and translation into English.

Learning Outcome: Upon successful completion of this course, the student will be able to write a summary in English of an Arabic text at the L2 Level; translate a text in good English; write a summary of a voice recording in Modern Standard Arabic at L2 Level (news segment); transcribe a news segment in Arabic script; and conjugate verbs in all forms.

Instruction: Major topics covered in the course are grammatical structures, and listening and reading for understanding. This course is the equivalent of three years of intensive study (five hours weekly) with strong emphasis on military and political vocabulary. Methods of instruction include lecture, discussion, classroom exercises, and audio/visual material.

Credit Recommendation: *Versions 1 and 2: Course 1:* In the lower division baccalaureate/associate degree category, 20 semester hours in Basic Modern Standard Arabic. *Course 2:* In the upper division baccalaureate degree category, 10 semester hours in Intermediate Modern Standard Arabic (3/80) (10/85) (9/94).

Intermediate Arabic Structure (AA-201)
(Formerly Arabic Morphology)

Location: National Cryptologic School, Ft. Meade, MD.

Length: 160 hours (4 weeks, 8 hours per day).

Dates: January 1985-Present.

Objective: To provide a comprehensive, detailed study of Arabic grammar at the intermediate level, using Arabic grammar terms; to provide the ability to recognize and "read through" errors in an Arabic text; and to provide knowledge to use sophisticated lexical aids.

Learning Outcome: Upon successful completion of this course, the student will be able to provide diacritical marks for an unvoweled Arabic text (L3 Level); correct grammatical errors; conjugate verbs in the past, present, and imperative tenses; and poise sentences (L3 Level).

Instruction: Major topics covered in the course are mechanics needed to deal with more sophisticated written and recorded materials. This course is de-signed for students who have already ac-quired a basic foundation in Arabic vocabulary and grammar, i.e., they have taken the "Basic Modern Standard Arabic" courses (AA-10A or AA-15A) or the equivalent. Methods of instruction include lecture, discussion, and classroom exercises.

Credit Recommendation: In the upper division baccalaureate degree category, 4 semester hours in Modern Standard Arabic (6/87) (9/94).

Chinese

Advanced Newspaper/Broadcast Chinese (CI-243)
(Formerly Newspaper/Broadcast Chinese I [CI-103])
(Formerly Newspaper Chinese [CI-103])

Location: National Cryptologic School, Ft. Meade, MD.

Length: 480 hours (12 weeks).

Dates: December 1970-Present.

Objective: To comprehend and translate articles of general interest from major newspapers of the People's Republic of China, Taiwan, and Hong Kong; to comprehend, transcribe in characters, and translate broadcasts of news items from Voice of America and shortwave radio broadcasts from the People's Republic of China and Taiwan; to enable the student to read, translate, and gist non-technical newspaper articles in Chinese of level 2+ to level 3 difficulty into English with the help of dictionaries; and to listen, translate, and summarize news broadcasts ranging from level 2+ to level 3 difficulty into English with the help of dictionaries.

Learning Outcome: Upon successful completion of this course, the student will be able to read and translate newspaper articles from the People's Republic of China, Taiwan, and Hong Kong; analyze the grammatical structure of complex sentences characteristic of such articles; give the official English translations for terms drawn from current PRC jargon; identify the key sentences and items of an article; and read, listen, and understand newspaper articles and new broadcasts ranging in difficulty from level 2+ to level 3. Transcribing can come at a later stage because it presents a greater challenge than reading/speaking.

Instruction: Major topics covered in the course are complex grammatical structures, low frequency function words, current PRC jargon and acronyms, newspaper articles, news broadcasts, taped radio news programs, and difficulties encountered in translations. Methods of instruction include lecture, discussion, classroom exercises, case studies, audio/visual material, computer-assisted instruction, presentation of news/articles by native speakers of Chinese, quizzes, observations, tests, papers, reports, and a final examination.

Credit Recommendation: In the upper division baccalaureate degree category, 10 semester hours in Chinese (Mandarin) (3/80) (10/85) (8/91) (9/96).

Advanced Readings in Chinese (CI-244)
(Formerly Intermediate Readings in Chinese [CI-244])
(Formerly Newspaper/Broadcast Chinese II [C-141])
(Formerly Advanced Newspaper Chinese [CI-104])

Location: National Cryptologic School, Ft. Meade, MD.

Length: 480 hours (12 weeks).

Dates: December 1970-Present.

Objective: To enable the student to read printed materials with Level 2+ to Level 3 difficulty in the areas of political, economic, social, and technical Chinese and to gist/translate the content into English with the help of dictionaries.

Learning Outcome: Upon successful completion of this course, the student will be able to comprehend and translate newspaper articles, journal articles, and editorials on many topics; analyze the grammatical structure of a complex sentence; translate common Chinese sayings; and identify the main ideas of a text.

Instruction: Major topics covered in the course are complex grammatical structures; idiomatic expressions and sayings; and basic vocabulary characteristic of social, political, economic, scientific, and technical Chinese. Methods of instruction include the translation of texts, discussion of their content, structure and vocabulary, and exercises and examinations that test translation.

Credit Recommendation: In the upper division baccalaureate degree category, 10 semester hours in Chinese (Mandarin) (3/80) (10/85) (8/91) (9/96).

Culture and Civilization
(Formerly Advanced Readings in Chinese [CI-344])

Location: National Cryptologic School, Ft. Meade, MD.

Length: 240 hours (6 weeks).

Dates: December 1986-August 1996.

Objective: To enable the student to read and translate passages from classical Chinese literature, 20th century Chinese prose and essays written for educated Chinese readers, and to read short contemporary passages in handwritten cursive style.

Learning Outcome: Upon successful completion of this course, the student will be able to read and translate classical texts and modern texts written in standard Mandarin and in forms of Mandarin with dialect-influenced grammatical structures and vocabulary; give colloquial Chinese equivalents for classical function words; give the approximate western dates of the dynasties; state the main philosophy of major Chinese schools of thought; read cursive Chinese; and construct cohesive and coherent Chinese sentences.

Instruction: Major topics covered in the course are slang, dialect-influenced Mandarin, the basic structures, function words and vocabulary of classical Chinese, handwritten cursive script, and major historical and philosophical trends in

China. Methods of instruction include reading and translating printed and written texts, discussion, and watching training videotapes

Credit Recommendation: In the upper division baccalaureate degree category, 5 semester hours in Chinese (Mandarin) (8/91).

Intermediate Chinese (CI-152) (Formerly Chinese Refresher II [CI-152]) (Formerly Basic Chinese Structure II [CI-102]) (Formerly Basic Structure of Written Chinese [CI-102])

Location: National Cryptologic School, Ft. Meade, MD.

Length: 480 hours (12 weeks).

Dates: December 1970-Present.

Objective: To enable the student with the aid of dictionaries to read with comprehension and translate newspaper articles written for the general reader in nontechnical Chinese ranging in difficulty from level 2 to 2+ into English and to understand, transcribe, and translate Chinese radio broadcasts of news items of current general interest.

Learning Outcome: Upon successful completion of this course, the student will be able to read and translate authentic 2/2+ Chinese texts; analyze the grammatical structure of sentences and the structure of words found in such texts; answer questions on their content in Chinese or English; understand authentic level 2/2+ Chinese language radio broadcasts; and identify the important ideas in those broadcasts, transcribe them into traditional and simplified characters, and translate them and answer questions about their content in either Chinese or English.

Instruction: Major topics covered in the course are the major grammatical structures of the standard language; a wide range of vocabulary characteristic of authentic nontechnical texts and broadcasts; and the structure of words utilizing readings from Chinese culture, history, government, politics, social systems, and diplomatic correspondence. Methods of instruction include lecture; discussion; case studies; audio/visual material; computer-assisted instruction; learner presentation/reports; observations; papers; the introduction of grammar and vocabulary through reading texts and listening to tapes; field trips; practice through the use of written and oral exercises; and evaluation by examinations and quizzes that test translation and transcription skills, comprehension, and the knowledge of important vocabulary items and major grammatical structures; and a final examination.

Credit Recommendation: In the upper division baccalaureate degree category, 10 semester hours in Chinese (Mandarin) (3/80) (10/85) (8/91) (9/96).

French

Basic French Refresher - Reading (FE-151)

Location: National Cryptologic School, Ft. Meade, MD.

Length: 80 hours (2 weeks).

Dates: May 1991-August 1996.

Objective: To enable students who have had formal academic training in French at the elementary level to gain Level 2/2+ (intermediate) proficiency in reading journalistic French texts for understanding.

Learning Outcome: Upon successful completion of this course, the student will be able to read texts from current journalistic francophone materials and to provide a brief written summary in English with 90% accuracy in critical information.

Instruction: Major topics covered in the course are reading and translation of contemporary journalistic francophone texts with an emphasis on political, military, economic, social, and cultural current issues. Methods of instruction include self-paced reading and summarizing of each article and instructor-led review and critique of a student's work. This is a pass/fail course based on the students' ability to summarize Level 2 intermediate journalistic French texts with 90% accuracy.

Credit Recommendation: In the lower division baccalaureate/associate degree category, 2 semester hours in French (8/91).

French Basic Refresher - Transcription (FE-153)

Location: National Cryptologic School, Ft. Meade, MD.

Length: 80 hours (2 weeks).

Dates: June 1988-August 1996.

Objective: To enable students who have had formal academic training in French at the elementary level to regain competency in transcribing French Level 2 (intermediate) texts.

Learning Outcome: Upon successful completion of this course, the student will be able to produce a highly accurate transcription (85% accuracy) in French of a Level 2 text of aural French information.

Instruction: Major topic covered in the course is transcription of aural materials on government, political, economic, and contemporary cultural issues. Methods of instruction include instructor-led and facilitated instruction, work at the student's own pace, and exit on a pass/fail basis.

Credit Recommendation: In the lower division baccalaureate/associate degree category, 2 semester hours in French (8/91).

French Basic Refresher - Translation (FE-152)

Location: National Cryptologic School, Ft. Meade, MD.

Length: 80 hours (2 weeks).

Dates: March 1987-Present.

Objective: To enable students who have had formal academic training in French at the elementary level to gain Level 2/2+ (intermediate) proficiency in translating journalistic French texts into English.

Learning Outcome: Upon successful completion of this course, the student will be able to translate texts from current journalistic francophone materials into English using a dictionary with 85% accuracy.

Instruction: Major topic covered in the course is translation of current journalistic francophone texts on political, military, economic, and cultural subjects. Methods of instruction include lecture, discussion, classroom exercises, instructor-led and facilitated instruction, individual counseling, quizzes, and self-paced translation exercises.

Credit Recommendation: In the lower division baccalaureate/associate degree category, 2 semester hours in French (8/91) (9/96).

Intermediate French Translation (FE-270)

Location: National Cryptologic School, Ft. Meade, MD.

Length: 128 hours (8 weeks, two 8-hour sessions per week).

Dates: February 1985-Present.

Objective: To enable students to progress from Level 2 to Intermediate Level 3 in French to English translation skills.

Learning Outcome: Upon successful completion of this course, students will be able to translate at 85% accuracy, a text of about 500 level 3 French words into English with the use of a dictionary.

Instruction: Major topics covered in the course include review of general principles of grammar and syntax; most common categories of translation difficulties;

proper use of a dictionary; and proofreading skills. Methods of instruction include classroom exercises, audio/visual material, computer-assisted instruction, pre-test, mid-term exercise, and final examination.

Credit Recommendation: In the upper division baccalaureate degree category, 3 semester hours in Intermediate French Translation (6/87) (9/94).

Rapid Survey of French Structure (FE-022)

Location: National Cryptologic School, Ft. Meade, MD.

Length: 192 hours (8 weeks).

Dates: September 1988-August 1996.

Objective: To acquaint students experienced in related languages with French language structures, to develop Level 2 (intermediate) competency in translating, transcribing, and summarizing journalistic francophone texts.

Learning Outcome: Upon successful completion of this course, the student will be able to demonstrate comprehension of Level 2 (intermediate) journalistic francophone texts (90% accuracy), translate such texts (80% accuracy) using a dictionary, and transcribe similar recorded texts (70% accuracy).

Instruction: Major topics covered in the course are phonological, morphological, and grammatical structures and vocabulary building. Methods of instruction include instructor-led and facilitated instruction using current articles from French journalistic publications, aural materials, or grammar reference texts; practice in reading, writing, and listening in French; frequent quizzes; written translations; class discussion; and a final examination (70% mastery level).

Credit Recommendation: In the lower division baccalaureate/associate degree category, 8 semester hours in French (8/91).

German

German for Reading Knowledge (GR-145)
(Formerly Basic German Reading)

Location: National Cryptologic School, Ft. Meade, MD.

Length: 144 hours (6 weeks).

Dates: June 1986-December 1994.

Objective: To enable students who have had formal academic German training to refresh their skills in reading the language for understanding.

Learning Outcome: Upon successful completion of this course, the student will be able to demonstrate developed reading and comprehension skills through exposure to periodical articles with different styles and different purposes in the German language.

Instruction: Major topics covered in the course are reading German for understanding; and synthesizing and writing summary statements, without the use of a dictionary, using topics taken from international, local, and general news items in German newspapers and magazines. Methods of instruction include lecture, discussion, classroom exercises, and evaluation of a series of written summaries of German texts in which students must provide 90% of the critical information.

Credit Recommendation: In the upper division baccalaureate degree category, 6 semester hours in German for Reading Knowledge (6/87) (9/94).

Intermediate German Grammar (GR-205)

Location: National Cryptologic School, Ft. Meade, MD.

Length: *Version 1:* 120 hours (5 weeks); *Version 2:* 192 hours (8 weeks).

Dates: *Version 1:* August 1988-December 1991; *Version 2:* January 1992-Present.

Objective: To provide the student with a systematic grammar review as preparation for German-English translations.

Learning Outcome: Upon successful completion of this course, the student will be able to read fluently at an intermediate level and demonstrate an excellent understanding of all aspects of German grammar.

Instruction: Major topics covered in the course are grammar review, German to English translation, and limited oral and English to German exercises. Methods of instruction include lecture, classroom exercises, quizzes, tests, oral exercises, and dictation.

Credit Recommendation: *Version 1:* In the lower division baccalaureate/associate degree category, 3 semester hours in Intermediate German Grammar (8/91). *Version 2:* In the lower division baccalaureate/associate degree category, 4 semester hours in Intermediate German (9/96).

Intermediate German Review (GR-153)
(Formerly German Refresher Maintenance Course)

Location: National Cryptologic School, Ft. Meade, MD.

Length: *Version 1:* 220 hours (6 weeks); *Version 2:* 240 hours.

Dates: *Version 1:* August 1985-May 1987; *Version 2:* June 1987-Present.

Objective: To enable students to raise their language to a Level 2 capacity. This course is for students who have lost their previous language proficiency through a long period of non-language use.

Learning Outcome: Upon successful completion of this course, the student will be able to read, translate, transcribe, listen, and understand beyond the Level 2 training in this language.

Instruction: Major topics covered in the course are grammar, translation, and transcription components offered in a formal environment which allow students to work at their own pace. Methods of instruction include lecture, discussion, classroom exercises, audio/visual materials, quizzes, and tests.

Credit Recommendation: *Versions 1 and 2:* In the upper division baccalaureate degree category, 12 semester hours in Intermediate German Review (6/87) (9/94).

Intermediate German Translation (GR-270)

Location: National Cryptologic School, Ft. Meade, MD.

Length: 120 hours (5 weeks).

Dates: September 1989-Present.

Objective: To produce German-English translations from general sources with 95% accuracy.

Learning Outcome: Upon successful completion of this course, the student will be able to read German at a 2+ or 3 level, recognize and understand principles of German grammar, and translate effectively German to English.

Instruction: Major topics covered in the course are various topics from the German press. Methods of instruction include classroom exercises, out of class translations exercises, in class translations, and tests.

Credit Recommendation: In the lower division baccalaureate/associate degree category, 3 semester hours in German (8/91) (9/96).

Introduction to German (GR-010)

Location: National Cryptologic School, Ft. Meade, MD.

Length: 120 hours.

Dates: March 1986-Present.

Objective: To provide the student with a basic knowledge of German grammar for comprehending and summarizing information from short authentic texts.

Learning Outcome: Upon successful completion of this course, the students, using given texts, will be able to answer questions derived from the text with an 80% level of accuracy.

Instruction: Major topics covered in the course are sound systems and basic grammar in the German language. Methods of instruction include lecture, discussion, classroom exercises, audio/visual materials, and a final examination.

Credit Recommendation: In the lower division baccalaureate/associate degree category, 6-8 semester hours in German (6/87) (9/94).

Introductory German (GR-020)

Location: National Cryptologic School, Ft. Meade, MD.

Length: *Version 1:* 96 hours (6 weeks); *Version 2:* 192 hours (8 weeks).

Dates: *Version 1:* January 1989-March 1993; *Version 2:* April 1993-Present.

Objective: *Version 1:* To recognize specific linguistic items and prepare general summaries with 80% accuracy. *Version 2:* To provide a rapid structural survey of German so as to enable students who have a high language aptitude or considerable experience in related languages to read and translate the standard, nontechnical, Level 2 written language with the aid of a dictionary.

Learning Outcome: Upon successful completion of this course, the student will be able to work with limited passive vocabulary, use a dictionary to translate, and show familiarity with basic German grammar.

Instruction: Major topic covered in the course is German grammar. Methods of instruction include lecture, classroom exercises, tests, and evaluative quizzes.

Credit Recommendation: *Version 1:* In the lower division baccalaureate/associate degree category, 3 semester hours in Introductory German (8/91). *Version 2:* In the lower division baccalaureate/associate degree category, 4 semester hours in German (9/96).

Hebrew

Basic Hebrew Refresher (HB-150)

Location: National Cryptologic School, Ft. Meade, MD.

Length: 320 hours (40 hours per week for 8 weeks).

Dates: *Version 1:* January 1977-July 1991; *Version 2:* August 1991-Present.

Objective: To give the student competency in understanding spoken and written Hebrew on an elementary-intermediate level.

Instruction: Major topics covered in the course are a review of basic grammar and vocabulary, with particular emphasis on reading, translation, and transcription. Course content emphasis is on military and political affairs.

Credit Recommendation: *Version 1:* In the lower division baccalaureate/associate degree category, 6 semester hours in Hebrew (10/85). *Version 2:* In the lower division baccalaureate/associate degree or upper division baccalaureate degree category, 8 semester hours in Elementary-Intermediate Hebrew (8/91). **NOTE:** This course overlaps with HB-153. A student should not receive credit for both courses. This course conforms to an intermediate university-level course.

Basic Modern Standard Hebrew (HB-10A)
(Formerly Basic Modern Standard Hebrew ([IU-10A])
Course 1: Basic Modern Standard Hebrew
Course 2: Intermediate Modern Standard Hebrew

Location: National Cryptologic School, Ft. Meade, MD.

Length: 1,880 hours (47 weeks); classroom and self-study included. *Course 1:* 1,200 hours (30 weeks); *Course 2:* 600 hours (15 weeks).

Dates: October 1974-August 1991.

Objective: To provide a thorough knowledge of Hebrew grammar and the ability to read newspaper articles of moderate difficulty.

Instruction: Major topics covered in the course are broad knowledge of political and military vocabulary and the acquisition of listening, speaking, transcription, and translation skills. This course corresponds to completion of an advanced intermediate college program.

Credit Recommendation: *Course 1:* In the lower division baccalaureate/associate degree category, 20 semester hours in Basic Modern Standard Hebrew. *Course 2:* In the upper division baccalaureate degree category, 10 semester hours in Intermediate Modern Standard Hebrew (3/80) (10/85).

Hebrew Refresher/Maintenance (HB-153)

Location: National Cryptologic School, Ft. Meade, MD.

Length: 240 hours (6 weeks).

Dates: January 1987-August 1996.

Objective: To reinforce basic skills in grammar, reading, and listening comprehension.

Learning Outcome: Upon successful completion of this course, the student will be able to read and translate modern Hebrew material on an elementary-intermediate level and understand aural material such as TV programs on an elementary-intermediate level.

Instruction: Major topics covered in the course are review of grammar; reading articles in modern Hebrew, especially newspapers; aural comprehension; and translation. Methods of instruction include lecture, class exercises, and interactive video/computer-assisted instruction.

Credit Recommendation: In the lower division baccalaureate/associate or in the upper division baccalaureate degree category, 6 semester hours in Elementary-Intermediate Hebrew (8/91). **NOTE:** This course overlaps with HB-150. A student should not receive credit for both courses. This course conforms to an intermediate university-level course.

Intermediate Hebrew Reading Comprehension (HB-240)
(Formerly Basic Hebrew Reading Comprehension [HB-240])

Location: National Cryptologic School, Ft. Meade, MD.

Length: 320 hours (8 weeks).

Dates: *Version 1:* January 1984-June 1991; *Version 2:* August 1991-Present.

Objective: To enable the student to comprehend written Hebrew on topics of current political and military interest of intermediate difficulty.

Learning Outcome: Upon successful completion of this course, the student will be able to comprehend middle level newspaper or journal articles with proficiency in asking and responding to questions.

Instruction: Major topics covered in the course are reading and translating intermediate level of difficulty Hebrew texts that are primarily drawn from newspaper articles. Methods of instruction include discussion, classroom exercises, computer-assisted instruction, quizzes, and tests.

Credit Recommendation: *Version 1:* In the lower division baccalaureate/associate degree category, 6 semester hours in Intermediate Hebrew (10/85). *Version 2:* In the upper division baccalaureate degree category, 8 semester hours in Intermediate

Hebrew (8/91). **NOTE:** This course conforms to an intermediate university-level course.

Intermediate Hebrew Refresher (HB-200)

Location: National Cryptologic School, Fort Meade, MD.

Length: 480 hours (40 hours per week for 12 weeks).

Dates: *Version 1:* January 1977-July 1991; *Version 2:* August 1991-August 1996.

Objective: To enable the student to comprehend spoken and written modern Hebrew, specifically news broadcasts, newspapers, military communications, and similar technical material of an advanced level.

Instruction: Major topics covered in the course are the analysis of advanced Hebrew texts drawn primarily from Israeli journals, magazines, newspapers, and news broadcasts.

Credit Recommendation: *Version 1:* In the upper division baccalaureate degree category, 9 semester hours in Advanced Hebrew (10/85). *Version 2:* In the upper division baccalaureate degree category, 12 semester hours in Intermediate Hebrew Grammar and Comprehension (8/91). **NOTE:** This course overlaps with HB-201. Students should not receive credit for both courses. This course conforms to an intermediate university-level course.

Intermediate Hebrew Structure (HB-201)

Location: National Cryptologic School, Ft. Meade, MD.

Length: 160 hours (4 weeks).

Dates: January 1989-Present.

Objective: To comprehend spoken and written Hebrew of a technical nature at the intermediate level.

Learning Outcome: Upon successful completion of this course, the student will be able to transcribe short news broadcasts of an elementary to intermediate level and answer semantic and grammatical questions on military, political, and economic texts.

Instruction: Major topics covered in the course are review of morphology and syntax; emphasis on weak and guttural verbs; acquisition of high frequency idioms and specialized vocabulary; and transcription of recorded newspaper articles. Methods of instruction include classroom exercises, audio/visual material, computer-assisted instruction, tests, and a final examination.

Credit Recommendation: In the upper division baccalaureate degree category, 4 semester hours in Intermediate Hebrew Grammar and Comprehension (8/91) (9/96). **NOTE:** This course overlaps with HB-200. Students should not receive credit for both courses. This course conforms to an intermediate university-level course.

Intermediate Hebrew Structure (Intermediate Hebrew [IU-250]) (Formerly HB-250)

Location: National Cryptologic School, Ft. Meade, MD.

Length: 1,200 hours (30 weeks); classroom and self-study included.

Dates: November 1975-October 1985.

Objective: To provide students who have one year of prior experience in intensive Hebrew with further study of the language.

Instruction: Major topics covered in the course are an intensive review of materials covered in Basic Modern Standard Hebrew and strengthens the basic skills of speaking, understanding, reading, and writing. This course corresponds to an intensive advanced intermediate-level college course emphasizing military and political vocabulary.

Credit Recommendation: In the upper division baccalaureate degree category, 16 semester hours in Intermediate Hebrew (3/80) (10/85) (8/91). **NOTE:** This course conforms to an intermediate university-level course.

Intermediate Hebrew Transcription (HB-220)

Location: National Cryptologic School, Ft. Meade, MD.

Length: 320 hours (8 weeks).

Dates: September 1986-Present.

Objective: To transcribe radio or television broadcasts or other recordings of a military or diplomatic nature.

Learning Outcome: Upon successful completion of this course, the student will be able to transcribe and comprehend actual broadcasts and similar communications on an intermediate level.

Instruction: Major topics covered in the course are listening comprehension and aural training, transcribing and translating, gisting the contents, and searching for specific information. Methods of instruction include classroom exercises, audio/visual material, computer-assisted instruction, and tests.

Credit Recommendation: In the upper division baccalaureate degree category, 6 semester hours in Hebrew Listening Comprehension and Transcription (8/91) (9/96). **NOTE:** This course conforms to an intermediate university-level course.

Intermediate Hebrew Translation (HB-271) (Formerly [HB-270])

Location: National Cryptologic School, Ft. Meade, MD.

Length: 320 hours (8 weeks).

Dates: May 1987-Present.

Objective: To enable a student to translate a short text on military, political, economic, and related subjects.

Learning Outcome: Upon successful completion of this course, the student will be able to translate short, intermediate-level texts (newspapers, periodicals) dealing with military, political, economic, and technical subjects.

Instruction: Major topics covered in the course are paraphrasing, translating, gisting, skimming for main idea, and comparing Hebrew and English forms of expression. Methods of instruction include classroom exercises, quizzes, and tests.

Credit Recommendation: In the upper division baccalaureate degree category, 6 semester hours in Hebrew Transcription (8/91) (9/96). **NOTE:** This course conforms to an intermediate university-level course.

Iraqi

Arabic Iraqi (AA-112) (Formerly Basic Colloquial Iraqi Arabic AA-112)

Location: National Cryptologic School, Ft. Meade, MD.

Length: 320 hours.

Dates: March 1986-Present.

Objective: To enable the student to comprehend Interagency Language Roundtable (ILR) level 2 aural and graphic texts in Iraqi Arabic, answer questions about everyday topics in Iraqi Arabic; and gist Iraqi texts in Arabic or English.

Learning Outcome: Upon successful completion this course, the student will have been exposed to the Arabic spoken dialect and be familiar with everyday topics.

Instruction: Major topics covered in the course are extensive drill practice in the phonology, morphology, and syntax of the Iraqi Arabic dialect; and primary concentration on reading, writing, and translating a wide range of situational dialogues, texts, and proverbial expressions. Methods of instruction include lecture, discussion, classroom exercises, and audio/visual material.

Credit Recommendation: In the upper division baccalaureate degree category, 8 semester hours in the Arabic Language (10/87) (9/94). **NOTE:** This course presupposes completion of Basic Modern Standard Arabic (AA-10A) or its equivalent and a proven ILR level 2 in listening.

Italian

Basic Italian (IA-10A)

Location: National Cryptologic School, Ft. Meade, MD.

Length: *Version 1:* 720 hours (18 weeks), classroom and self-study included; *Version 2:* 640 hours (20 weeks), classroom and self-study included.

Dates: *Version 1:* January 1985-July 1991; *Version 2:* August 1991-Present.

Objective: To enable the student with little or no knowledge of the language to perform with proficiency in the basic skills of listening, speaking, reading, and writing.

Instruction: Major topics covered in the course are comprehensive presentation of grammar, vocabulary, writing system, and phonology. Methods of instruction include extensive use of texts, supplementary native materials and accompanying tapes, and intensive aural-oral drilling.

Credit Recommendation: *Version 1:* In the lower division baccalaureate/associate degree category, 10-12 semester hours in Italian (10/85). *Version 2:* In the lower division baccalaureate/associate degree category, 10 semester hours in Italian (8/91). **NOTE:** Transcriptions and native text readings go beyond first year Italian level of difficulty.

Basic Italian Transcription (IA-120)

Location: National Cryptologic School, Ft. Meade, MD.

Length: *Version 1:* 192 hours (8 weeks); *Version 2:* 192 hours (12 weeks).

Dates: *Version 1:* February 1987-February 1992; *Version 2:* March 1992-Present.

Objective: To enable students, with some formal training in Italian, to develop Level 2+ competency in classifying and evaluating information contained in native texts; writing gists; and transcribing clear, to relatively clear, audio quality materials consisting of selected spoken Italian texts which present Italian speakers from various age, regional, and social groups.

Learning Outcome: *Version 1:* Upon successful completion of this course, the student will be able to transcribe Level 2+ voice recordings of personal, general, and semitechnical materials with 60-100% accuracy. *Version 2:* Upon successful completion of this course, the student will be able to provide a gist in English accounting fro 85% of the information when given a three-five minute cut of authentic Level 2 Italian audio material of relatively clear quality and provide a verbatim transcript of an entire text with 85% accuracy when given a three to five minute cut of authentic Level 2 Italian audio material of relatively clear audio quality.

Instruction: Major topics covered in the course are phonetics; grammar; conversation; oral practice; listening comprehension; and aural cloze exercises utilizing cultural, political, and literary writings and news items to raise the student's competency to Level 2+ in transcription and translation of Italian voice recordings. Methods of instruction include lecture, laboratory practice, audio/visual material, learner presentations/reports, instructor-led and facilitated exercises, examinations, quizzes, a mid-term test, transcriptions to determine whether a student has achieved Level 2+ competency (60% mastery level required), and a final examination.

Credit Recommendation: *Version 1:* In the lower division baccalaureate/associate degree category, 3-4 semester hours in Italian (8/91). *Version 2:* In the lower division baccalaureate/associate degree category, 4 semester hours in Italian (9/96). *Prerequisite:* Basic knowledge of Italian.

Intermediate Italian Transcription (IA-220)

Location: National Cryptologic School, Ft. Meade, MD.

Length: 192 hours (8 weeks).

Dates: *Version 1:* March 1989-August 1996; *Version 2:* September 1996-Present.

Objective: To enable students with prior knowledge of Italian to achieve Level 3 proficiency in Italian voice transcription.

Learning Outcome: *Version 1:* Upon successful completion of this course, the student will be able to transcribe Level 3 recordings of personal, general, and semitechnical materials with 60-100% accuracy. *Version 2:* Upon successful completion of this course, the student will be able to transcribe Level 3 recordings of personal, general, and semi-technical materials with 85-100% accuracy.

Instruction: Major topics covered in the course are transcription from video discs, written exercises, gist, scanning, cloze exercises, and paraphrasing designed to raise the student's competency to Level 3 in transcription and translation of Italian voice recordings. *Version 1:* Methods of instruction include instructor-led, facilitated exercises, and examinations to determine whether a student has achieved Level 3 competency (60% mastery level required). *Version 2:* Methods of instruction include lecture, discussion, classroom exercises, audio/visual material, learner presentations/reports, laboratory practice, quizzes, tests, and a final examination (85% mastery level required).

Credit Recommendation: *Version 1:* In the lower division baccalaureate/associate degree category, 3-4 semester hours in Italian (8/91). *Version 2:* In the upper division baccalaureate degree category, 4 semester hours in Italian (9/96).

Intermediate Italian Translation (IA-270)

Location: National Cryptologic School, Ft. Meade, MD.

Length: 128 hours (8 weeks, classroom and self-study included).

Dates: March 1986-Present.

Objective: To enable Level 2 Italian students to improve Italian to English translation skills to a Level 3 proficiency.

Learning Outcome: Upon successful completion of this course, the student will be able to translate Level 3 materials dealing with social, cultural, military, political, economic, technological, and scientific subjects.

Instruction: Major topics covered in the course are translation of news, advertisements, and short articles published in the Italian press; and review of formal and informal vocabulary. Methods of instruction include lecture, discussion, classroom exercises, and computer-assisted instruction.

Credit Recommendation: In the lower division baccalaureate/associate degree category, 3 semester hours in Italian (6/87) (9/94).

Rapid Survey of Italian Structure (IA-020)

Location: National Cryptologic School, Ft. Meade, MD.

Length: 192 hours.

Dates: July 1984-Present.

Objective: To enable a student with translation proficiency in a foreign language to acquire Level 2 translating skills in Italian.

Learning Outcome: Upon successful completion of this course, the student will be able to read and translate Level 2 materials from Italian to English with the aid of a dictionary.

Instruction: Major topics covered in the course are reading and translation, from Italian to English, of news printed in the daily/weekly Italian press as well as other short texts of contemporary interest. Methods of instruction include classroom exercises, audio/visual material, learner presentation/reports, quizzes, a mid-term examination, and a final examination.

Credit Recommendation: In the lower division baccalaureate/associate degree category, 3 semester hours in Italian (6/87) (9/94). **NOTE:** Level to be determined by placement examination.

Japanese

Advanced Japanese Reading (JP-340)

Location: National Cryptologic School, Ft. Meade, MD.

Length: 192 hours (8 weeks).

Dates: August 1986-August 1996.

Objective: To enable the student to read and translate technical Japanese at the 3/3+ level.

Learning Outcome: Upon successful completion of this course, the student will be able to scan and translate articles from a range of sources on political, diplomatic, economic, financial, military, and commercial topics.

Instruction: Major topics covered in the course are recent Japanese writings on current events, social science, and technology.

Credit Recommendation: In the upper division baccalaureate degree category, 3 semester hours in Advanced Japanese (8/91).

Basic Japanese Level I (JP-101) (Formerly Basic Japanese Structure [JP-101])

Location: National Cryptologic School, Ft. Meade, MD.

Length: 480 hours (12 weeks).

Dates: April 1975-Present.

Objective: To develop basic skills in listening, speaking, reading, and writing, with structural points introduced inductively.

Learning Outcome: Upon successful completion of this course, the student will be able to recite a basic Japanese passage and read and provide written responses to basic Japanese passages.

Instruction: Major topics covered in the course are the development of basic Japanese language skills, using intensive training in listening, speaking, reading, and writing. Methods of instruction include lecture, discussion, classroom exercises, case studies, observations, tests, quizzes, papers, and a final examination.

Credit Recommendation: In the lower division baccalaureate/associate degree or in the upper division baccalaureate degree category, 10 semester hours in Japanese (3/80) (10/85) (8/91) (9/96).

Basic Japanese Level II (JP-102) (Formerly Basic Japanese Structure [JP-102])

Location: National Cryptologic School, Ft. Meade, MD.

Length: 480 hours (12 weeks).

Dates: April 1975-Present.

Objective: Starting at 101 level, to continue developing skills in listening, speaking, reading, and writing, with structural points learned inductively.

Learning Outcome: Upon successful completion of this course, the student will be able to read, and recite passages in a basic Japanese text and will be able to respond in grammatically correct written Japanese to basic Japanese passages.

Instruction: Major topics covered in the course are the development of Japanese language skills beyond the 101 level, using intensive training in listening, speaking, reading, and writing. Methods of instruction include extensive use of text, supplementary materials and accompanying tapes, quizzes, and mid-term and final examinations.

Credit Recommendation: In the lower division baccalaureate/associate degree category or in the upper division baccalaureate degree category, 10 semester hours in Japanese (3/80) (10/85) (8/91) (9/96).

Basic Japanese Level III (JP-103) (Formerly Basic Japanese Structure [JP-103])

Location: National Cryptologic School, Ft. Meade, MD.

Length: 480 hours (12 weeks).

Dates: April 1975-Present.

Objective: Starting at 102 level, to continue developing skills in listening, speaking, reading, and writing, with structural points learned inductively, and to develop proficiency in major sentence patterns.

Learning Outcome: Upon successful completion of this course, the student will be able to read and demonstrate comprehension of Japanese questions and will be able to carry a Japanese conversation.

Instruction: Major topics covered in the course are the development of Japanese language skills beyond the 102 level, using intensive training in listening, speaking, reading, and writing. Methods of instruction include extensive use of text, supplementary materials, and accompanying tapes; translation skills are emphasized; quizzes; a mid-term; and a final examination.

Credit Recommendation: In the lower division baccalaureate/associate degree category or in the upper division baccalaureate degree category, 10 semester hours in Japanese (3/80) (10/85) (8/91) (9/96).

Basic Japanese Level IV (JP-104) (Formerly Basic Japanese Structure [JP-104])

Location: National Cryptologic School, Ft. Meade, MD.

Length: 480 hours (12 weeks).

Dates: April 1975-Present.

Objective: Starting at 103 level, to continue developing translation and comprehension skills, achieving proficiency in all major sentence patterns.

Learning Outcome: Upon successful completion of this course, the student will be able to read Japanese and to carry a conversation in a specific FSI area such as economics, politics or commerce.

Instruction: Major topic covered in the course is the development of Japanese language skills beyond the 103 level, using intensive training in listening, speaking, reading, and writing. Methods of instruction include extensive use of text, supplementary materials, and accompanying tapes; translation skills for newspaper and journal articles emphasized; quizzes; a mid-term examination; and a final examination.

Credit Recommendation: In the lower division baccalaureate/associate degree category or in the upper division baccalaureate degree category, 10 semester hours in Japanese (3/80) (10/85) (8/91) (9/96).

Basic Japanese Reading (JP-145)

Location: National Cryptologic School, Ft. Meade, MD.

Length: 192-224 hours (8 weeks).

Dates: January 1989-Present.

Objective: To teach the student to read and translate non-technical Japanese at the 2/2+ level using a dictionary.

Learning Outcome: Upon successful completion of this course, the student will be able to scan for general comprehension newspaper and magazine articles at the 2/2+ level and to translate such articles into English with the aid of a dictionary.

Instruction: Major topics covered in the course are existing Japanese style, grammar, and vocabulary. Methods of instruction include lecture, discussion, classroom exercises, case studies, and examinations.

Credit Recommendation: In the upper division baccalaureate degree category, 3 semester hours in Advanced Japanese (8/91) (9/96).

Intermediate Japanese Reading (JP-240)

Location: National Cryptologic School, Ft. Meade, MD.

Length: 192 hours (8 weeks).

Dates: January 1985-August 1996.

Objective: To teach the student to read and translate with the aid of a dictionary, technical and semi-technical Japanese ranging from colloquial to formal in style at the 2+/3 level.

Learning Outcome: Upon successful completion of this course, the student will be able to translate articles from Japanese newspapers, books, and journals devoted to a wide variety of topics.

Instruction: Major topics covered in the course are technical and semi-technical Japanese vocabulary and style.

Credit Recommendation: In the upper division baccalaureate degree category, 3 semester hours in Advanced Japanese (8/91).

Introduction to Classical Japanese Forms (JP-280)

Location: National Cryptologic School, Ft. Meade, MD.

Length: 120 hours (5 weeks).

Dates: January 1989-August 1996.

Objective: To familiarize students with classical Japanese style.

Learning Outcome: Upon successful completion of this course, the student will be able to analyze classical Japanese forms and translate them, using dictionaries and other working aids.

Instruction: Major topics covered in the course are classical Japanese structure and vocabulary.

Credit Recommendation: In the upper division baccalaureate degree category, 3 semester hours in Classical Japanese (8/91).

Korean

Basic Korean Reading Translation (KR-140)

Location: National Cryptologic School, Ft. Meade, MD.

Length: 120 hours (5 weeks).

Dates: *Version 1:* October 1984-August 1996; *Version 2:* September 1996-Present.

Objective: To enable students to translate, with the help of a dictionary, a Level 2/2+ passage from a non-technical Korean publication.

Learning Outcome: Upon successful completion of this course, the student will be able to scan for general understanding a Level 2/2+ article from a Korean magazine; translate with help of a dictionary a Level 2/2+ non-technical article; and determine the Korean readings of Chinese characters.

Instruction: *Versions 1 and 2:* Major topics covered in the course are written Korean style, grammar, and vocabulary and use of Chinese characters in written Korean. Versions and methods of instruction include lecture, classroom exercises, learner presentations and reports, and quizzes.

Credit Recommendation: *Version 1:* In the upper division baccalaureate degree category, 3 semester hours in Advanced Korean (8/91). *Version 2:* In the lower division baccalaureate/associate degree category, 3 semester hours in Korean (9/96).

Basic Korean Refresher Course (KR-150)

Location: National Cryptologic School, Ft. Meade, MD.

Length: *Version 1:* 360 hours (15 weeks); *Version 2:* 480 hours (12 weeks) (consists of Basic Korean Refresher Course, Part 1 [KR151] and Basic Korean Refresher Course, Part 2 [KR 152]).

Dates: *Version 1:* June 1985-April 1995; *Version 2:* May 1995-Present.

Objective: To enable students who have had one year prior Korean language learning experience, but who have lost broad-base language competency, to regain that competency so that they are able to translate and transcribe Level 2 materials.

Learning Outcome: Upon successful completion of this course, the student will be able to translate and transcribe Level 2 selections.

Instruction: Major topic covered in the course is enhancing functional Korean competence by reviewing basic grammar and vocabulary with particular emphasis on translation, transcription, and reading. Methods of instruction include lecture, classroom exercises, audio/visual material, learner presentations/reports, tests, and a final examination.

Credit Recommendation: *Version 1:* In the upper division baccalaureate degree category, 7 semester hours in Basic Korean Refresher Course (6/87) (9/94). *Version 2:* In the upper division baccalaureate degree category, 8 semester hours in Basic Korean Refresher Course (9/96). **NOTE:** Credit cannot be received for both this course, KR 150 and either KR 151 (Basic Korean Refresher, Part 1) or KR 152 (Basic Korean Refresher, Part 2).

Basic Korean Refresher Course, Part 1 (KR-151)

Location: National Cryptologic School, Ft. Meade, MD.

Length: 240 hours (6 weeks).

Dates: February 1996-Present.

Objective: To enable students who have had one year prior basic Korean language learning experience, but who have lost broad-base language competency, to regain that competency so that they are able to translate and transcribe Level 1+ materials. This course is prerequisite to KR-152; designed to be taken in sequence with KR-152.

Learning Outcome: Upon successful completion of this course, the student will be able to translate and transcribe Level 1+ selections.

Instruction: Major topics covered in the course are enhancing functional Korean competence by reviewing basic grammar and vocabulary with particular emphasis on translation, transcription, and reading. Methods of instruction include lecture, discussion, classroom exercises, audio-visual material, tests, and a final examination.

Credit Recommendation: In the upper division baccalaureate degree category, 4 semester hours in Basic Korean Refresher Course (9/96). **NOTE:** Credit cannot be received for both KR-150 (Basic Korean Refresher Course) and this course KR 151.

Basic Korean Refresher Course, Part 2 (KR-152)

Location: National Cryptologic School, Ft. Meade, MD.

Length: 240 hours (6 weeks).
Dates: February 1996-Present.
Objective: To enable students who have had one year or more prior basic Korean language learning experience, but who have lost broad-base language competency, to regain that competency so that they are able to translate and transcribe Level 2 materials. Designed to be a follow-up course to KR 151, this course will enable students to gain additional active reading vocabulary and competency to locate and understand the main ideas and details written for the general reader.
Learning Outcome: Upon successful completion of this course, the student will be able to translate and transcribe Level 2 selections.
Instruction: Major topics covered in the course are enhancing functional Korean competence by reviewing basic grammar and vocabulary with particular emphasis on translation, transcription, and reading. Methods of instruction include lecture, discussion, classroom exercises, audio-visual material, tests, and a final examination.
Credit Recommendation: In the upper division baccalaureate degree category, 4 semester hours in Basic Korean Refresher Course (9/96). **NOTE:** Credit cannot be received for both KR-150 (Basic Korean Refresher Course) and this course KR 152.

Basic Korean Structure I (KR-101) (Formerly Basic Korean Structure [KR-101])

Location: National Cryptologic School, Ft. Meade, MD.
Length: 480 hours (12 weeks); classroom instruction and self-study included.
Dates: October 1979-September 1996.
Objective: To provide students who have no language background in Korean with a knowledge of basic vocabulary, structure, and simple Chinese characters of the language in order to conduct a simple conversation on a familiar topic and to read.
Instruction: Major topics covered in the course are an introduction to the phonology, morphology, syntax, and writing systems of Korean orthography "Hangu'l"; simple Chinese characters; and development of basic skills in speaking and reading. Method of instruction includes the audiolingual approach.
Credit Recommendation: In the lower division baccalaureate/associate degree category or in the upper division baccalaureate degree category, 10 semester hours in Korean (3/80) (10/85) (8/91).

Basic Korean Structure II (KR-102) (Formerly Basic Korean Structure [KR-102])

Location: National Cryptologic School, Ft. Meade, MD.
Length: 480 hours (12 weeks), classroom instruction and self-study.
Dates: January 1979-September 1996.
Objective: To provide students possessing a basic understanding of Korean (101 level), additional training in listening, speaking, and reading. Translation skills are emphasized. Additional Chinese characters are introduced.
Instruction: Major topics covered in the course are development of Korean language skills using the intensive model with emphasis on translation skills. Methods of instruction include the audiolingual mode with accompanying text.
Credit Recommendation: In the lower division baccalaureate/associate degree or in the upper division baccalaureate degree category, 10 semester hours in Korean (10/85) (8/91).

Basic Korean Structure III (KR-103) (Formerly Basic Korean Structure [KR-103])

Location: National Cryptologic School, Fort Meade, MD.
Length: 480 hours (8 hours per day, 5 days per week, 12 weeks), classroom instruction and self-study.
Dates: January 1979-September 1996.
Objective: To provide the student with continued skill development in the Korean language beyond the 102 level. Translation skills are emphasized. Additional Chinese characters are introduced.
Instruction: Major topics covered in the course are development of Korean language skills beyond 102 level using intensive training in listening and translating and Intermediate level Chinese characters.
Credit Recommendation: In the lower division baccalaureate/associate degree category or in the upper division baccalaureate degree category, 10 semester hours in Korean (10/85) (8/91).

Basic Korean Structure IV (KR-104) (Formerly Basic Korean Structure [KR-104])

Location: National Cryptologic School, Fort Meade, MD.
Length: 480 hours (8 hours per day, 5 days per week, 12 weeks), classroom instruction and self-study.
Dates: January 1979-September 1996.
Objective: To provide the student with continued development of language ability starting at 103 level, and to develop skill in reading, translating, and transcribing colloquial Korean. Additional Chinese characters are introduced.
Instruction: Major topics covered in the course are development of Korean language skills beyond 103 level using intensive training in primarily reading, translating, and transcribing of colloquial Korean; study of grammatical topics, including post positions, verbalizers, and style levels; and advanced level Chinese characters. Methods of instruction include extensive use of texts and supplemental materials.
Credit Recommendation: In the lower division baccalaureate/associate degree category or in the upper division baccalaureate degree category, 10 semester hours in Korean (10/85) (8/91).

Intermediate Korean Reading Translation (KR-245)

Location: National Cryptologic School, Ft. Meade, MD.
Length: 120 hours (5 weeks).
Dates: January 1985-Present.
Objective: To teach students to read Level 2+/3 Korean texts.
Learning Outcome: Upon successful completion of this course, the student will be able to scan for general understanding a Level 2/3+ Korean text, and translate, using dictionaries, such a text into English.
Instruction: Major topics covered in the course are various writing styles and vocabulary found in North and South Korean publications (such as, essays, magazines, geographic publications, and various fields including history). Methods of instruction include classroom exercises, audio/visual material, learner presentations/reports, and a final examination.
Credit Recommendation: In the upper division baccalaureate degree category, 3 semester hours in Advanced Korean or Sociology (8/91) (9/96).

Korean Readings in Politics and Economics (KR-270)

Location: National Cryptologic School, Ft. Meade, MD.
Length: 168 hours (7 weeks).
Dates: March 1987-Present.

Objective: To enable students to read and translate Korean publications on political and economic topics.

Learning Outcome: Upon successful completion of this course, the student will be able to read with general understanding of Korean articles on politics, economics, diplomacy, and current events and to translate such articles into English using dictionaries.

Instruction: Major topic covered in the course is timely publications on current events in South Korea. Methods of instruction include lecture and discussion.

Credit Recommendation: In the upper division baccalaureate degree category, 3 semester hours in Asian Studies or Korean Studies (8/91) (9/96).

Korean Readings in Science and Technology (KR-340) (Formerly Advanced Korean Reading Translation)

Location: National Cryptologic School, Ft. Meade, MD.

Length: 120 hours (5 weeks).

Dates: May 1989-Present.

Objective: To teach students to read scientific and technical articles written in Korean.

Learning Outcome: Upon successful completion of this course, the student will be able to translate technical and scientific articles at the 3/3+ level into English with the aid of dictionaries.

Instruction: Major topics covered in the course are style and vocabulary found in technical Korean writing. Methods of instruction include lecture, discussion, translation exercises, and examinations.

Credit Recommendation: In the upper division baccalaureate degree category, 3 semester hours in Technical Korean (8/91) (9/96).

Newspaper Korean (KR-160)

Location: National Cryptologic School, Ft. Meade, MD.

Length: 120 hours (5 weeks).

Dates: October 1984-Present.

Objective: To teach students to read and translate 2/2+ articles from Korean newspapers and journals.

Learning Outcome: Upon successful completion of this course, the student will be able to scan for general content a 2/2+ level newspaper article and translate with the help of a dictionary at 2/2+ level a newspaper or journal article.

Instruction: Major topics covered in the course are styles and vocabulary of North and South Korean newspapers, especially when covering politics, trade, diplomacy, and military and cultural affairs. Methods of instruction include lecture, discussion, audio/visual material, learner presentations/reports, and quizzes. **NOTE:** Students must receive a grade of 75 or better on all required reports and tests.

Credit Recommendation: In the upper division baccalaureate degree category, 3 semester hours in Advanced Korean or Korean Studies (8/91) (9/96).

Workshop on Hanmun (KR-280) (Formerly Korean Character Workshop)

Location: National Cryptologic School, Ft. Meade, MD.

Length: 288 hours (12 weeks).

Dates: October 1986-Present.

Objective: To familiarize students with 900 basic Chinese characters and enable them to use a Chinese-Korean dictionary.

Learning Outcome: Upon successful completion of this course, the student will be able to recognize 900 basic Chinese characters, read them accurately, and look up more difficult characters in a Chinese-Korean dictionary.

Instruction: Major topics covered in the course are the structure of Chinese characters and the use of Chinese characters in Korean-language texts. Methods of instruction include lecture, classroom exercises, quizzes, and tests.

Credit Recommendation: In the upper division baccalaureate degree category, 3 semester hours in Advanced Korean (8/91) (9/96). **NOTE:** Students should not receive credit if student has already received credit for KR-140 or KR-245.

Persian

Basic Intensive Modern Persian (PR-10A)

Location: National Cryptologic School, Ft. Meade, MD.

Length: 1,520 hours (38 weeks).

Dates: October 1984-Present.

Objective: To enable students to read, understand, and translate Persian into English at a second year (Level 2+) capability.

Learning Outcome: Upon successful completion of this course, the student will be able to read and translate written Persian at Level 2+; comprehend formal and colloquial spoken Persian at Level 2+; and speak and write communications in Persian at Level 2 or near Level 2.

Instruction: Major topics covered in the course are intensive exposure to Persian grammar, vocabulary, pronunciation/speaking, and writing/reading. Methods of instruction include lecture, discussion, classroom exercises, audio/visual material, and a final examination.

Credit Recommendation: In the lower division baccalaureate/associate degree category, 16 semester hours in Elementary Persian; and in the upper division/baccalaureate degree category, 16 semester hours in Intermediate Persion (11/89) (9/94).

Portuguese

Basic Portuguese (PT-10A)

Location: National Cryptologic School, Fort Meade, MD.

Length: *Version 1:* 880 hours (22 weeks); *Version 2:* 800 hours (20 weeks).

Dates: *Version 1:* January 1985-November 1990; *Version 2:* December 1990-Present.

Objective: To develop student's listening and reading skills and ability to write and speak short sentences in Portuguese as used in Brazil.

Learning Outcome: Upon successful completion of this course, the student will be able to understand oral Portuguese such as simple conversations and short news and announcements over the radio and on television; and, read simple texts of easy reading newspapers.

Instruction: Major topics covered in the course are Portuguese texts of local, national, and international interest; Brazilian usage of the Portuguese language; numbers, adjectives, nouns, and articles; and extensive survey of Portuguese structure. Methods of instruction include lecture, discussion, classroom exercises, audio/visual material, and computer-assisted instruction.

Credit Recommendation: *Version 1:* In the lower division baccalaureate/associate degree category, 14 semester hours in Portuguese (10/85) (9/94). *Version 2:* In the lower division baccalaureate/associate degree category, 14 semester hours in Portuguese (10/85) (9/94).

Basic Portuguese Refresher Translation (PT-152)

Location: National Cryptologic School, Ft. Meade, MD.

Length: 80 hours (2 weeks, 5 days per week, 8 hours per day).

Dates: July 1985-January 1990.

Objective: To enable students with formal academic training in Portuguese to regain competency in translating intermediate-level Portuguese texts from Portuguese into English.

Learning Outcome: Upon successful completion of this course, the student will be able to read authentic Portuguese language texts and write a translation from Portuguese into English with 70% accuracy.

Instruction: Major topics covered in the course are readings on social, economic, and political issues in Portuguese language newspapers and magazines. Methods of instruction include instructor-led lectures and discussion; a variety of classroom exercises performed by the student and facilitated by the instructor; and some use of computer-assisted and videotaped programs and materials.

Credit Recommendation: In the lower division baccalaureate/associate degree category, 2 semester hours in Basic Portuguese (8/91).

Basic Portuguese Transcription (PT-120)

Location: National Cryptologic School, Ft. Meade, MD.

Length: 192 hours (24 days).

Dates: July 1986-Present.

Objective: To enable the students with formal academic training in Portuguese at the intermediate level to transcribe and translate intermediate-level Portuguese texts from Portuguese into English.

Learning Outcome: Upon successful completion of this course, the student will be able to listen to authentic intermediate Portuguese language texts and write a verbatim transcription and translation of the texts from Portuguese into English with 70% accuracy.

Instruction: Major topics covered in the course are oral radio and television broadcasts on social, economic, political, and cultural issues. Methods of instruction include instructor-led lectures and discussions, a variety of classroom exercises performed by the student and facilitated by the instructor, some use of computer-assisted and videotaped programs and materials, quizzes, translations from Portuguese to English, and a final examination.

Credit Recommendation: In the lower division baccalaureate/associate degree category, 3 semester hours in Basic Portuguese Transcription (6/87) (8/91) (9/96).

Introductory Portuguese (PT-010)

Location: National Cryptologic School, Ft. Meade, MD.

Length: 120 hours (3 weeks).

Dates: March 1989-Present.

Objective: To enable students with no formal academic training in Portuguese to identify Portuguese language texts from other language texts and write summaries and gists in clear journalistic English.

Learning Outcome: Upon successful completion of this course, the student will be able to identify authentic Portuguese language texts and write, in clear journalistic English, a gist of the texts with 70% accuracy.

Instruction: Major topics covered in the course are an overview of the basic grammar and sound system of the Portuguese language through the use of readings on social, economic, political, and cultural issues taken from Portuguese language newspapers, magazines, fliers, brochures, posters, and billboards. Methods of instruction include instructor-led lectures and discussions; a variety of classroom exercises performed by the student and facilitated by the instructor; and some use of computer-assisted and videotaped programs and materials; quizzes, and a final examination.

Credit Recommendation: In the lower division baccalaureate/associate degree category, 3-4 semester hours in Introductory Portuguese (8/91) (9/96). **NOTE:** The credit-granting academic institution should make the decision based on the number of credits given to its first semester introductory course.

Portuguese for Spanish Linguists (PT-021)

Location: National Cryptologic School, Ft. Meade, MD.

Length: 144 hours (9 weeks, two 8-hour meetings per week).

Dates: July 1984-October 1987.

Objective: To use effectively the student's knowledge of Spanish, emphasizing the similarities of the two languages, as well as the contrasts between them.

Learning Outcome: Upon successful completion of this course, the student will be able to read and fully understand Level 2 texts from Brazilian magazines, such as *Veja* and *Visao*, and newspapers such as *O Globo*, considered the best written texts in the current Brazilian press. The student will learn grammar in a practical way: by reading the selected texts after a brief introduction on the main characteristics of a given grammatical situation. The Spanish formation mastered by the student serves as a foundation for the contrasts, comparisons, and similarities between the two languages.

Instruction: Major topics covered in the course are the reading and understanding of Brazilian news and advertising in a global comprehension of the language. The grammar is reviewed with the presentation of the texts. Designed for students who already know Spanish.

Credit Recommendation: In the lower division baccalaureate/associate degree category, 4 semester hours in Portuguese (6/87). **NOTE:** Credit should not be granted for both this course and Rapid Survey of Portuguese (PT-020).

Rapid Survey of Portuguese (PT-020)

Location: National Cryptologic School, Ft. Meade, MD.

Length: 192 hours (12 weeks, two 8-hour meetings per week).

Dates: July 1984-August 1987.

Objective: To use effectively the student's knowledge of Spanish, emphasizing the similarities of the two languages, as well as the contrasts between them.

Learning Outcome: Upon successful completion of this course, the student will be able to read and fully understand Level 2 texts from Brazilian magazines, such as *Veja* and *Visao*, and newspapers such as *O Globo*, considered the best written texts in the current Brazilian press. The student will learn grammar in a practical way: by reading the selected texts after a brief introduction on the main characteristics of a given grammatical situation. The Spanish formation mastered by the student serves as a foundation for the contrasts, comparisons, and similarities between the two languages.

Instruction: Major topics covered in the course are the reading and understanding of Brazilian news and advertising in a global comprehension of the language. The grammar is reviewed along with the presentation of texts.

Credit Recommendation: In the lower division baccalaureate/associate degree category, 6 semester hours in Portuguese (6/87). **NOTE:** Credit should not be granted for both this course and Portuguese for Spanish Linguistics (PT-021).

Russian

Accelerated Intermediate Intensive Russian (RS-151) (Formerly Basic Russian Refresher [RS-151])

Location: National Cryptologic School, Ft. Meade, MD.

Length: 224 hours (14 weeks); two full-day sessions per week; classroom instruction and self-study.

Dates: April 1975-December 1981.

Objective: To provide students who have one year of prior experience in Russian with further study of the language.

Instruction: Major topics covered in the course are the four basic skills of speaking, understanding, reading, and writing. Method of instruction includes the audiolingual approach. This course is the equivalent of a one-year intensive intermediate Russian course in an accelerated form.

Credit Recommendation: In the lower division baccalaureate/associate degree category, 10 semester hours in Russian (5/76) (11/82). **NOTE:** If this course is completed after Russian 105 or Russian 110, credit should be reduced. This course has been reevaluated and continues to meet the requirements for credit recommendations.

Advanced Russian Conversation and Composition I (RU-310) (Formerly Intermediate Russian Seminar [RS-260])

Location: National Cryptologic School, Ft. Meade, MD.

Length: 160 hours (10 weeks); two full-day sessions per week; classroom instruction and self-study.

Dates: December 1972-Present.

Objective: To provide students the opportunity to improve speaking and writing skills by reading, discussing, and writing about selected topics from the Russian press, television, and films.

Learning Outcome: Upon successful completion of this course, the student will be able to speak and write in Russian on a range of topics at an L3 proficiency (advanced level).

Instruction: Major topics covered in the course are Russian conversation and composition, stylistics, and idiomatic usage. Methods of instruction include discussion, audio/visual material, learner presentation/reports, and evaluation of presentations and compositions. This course corresponds to a fourth-year Russian conversation and composition course.

Credit Recommendation: In the upper division baccalaureate degree category, 3 semester hours in Russian (5/76) (11/82) (11/89) (9/94).

Advanced Russian Conversation and Composition II (RU-311) (Formerly Advanced Russian Seminar [RS-360])

Location: National Cryptologic School, Ft. Meade, MD.

Length: 160 hours (10 weeks); two full-day sessions per week; classroom instruction and self-study.

Dates: September 1971-June 1984.

Objective: To enable students to perfect speaking skills, aural comprehension, and understanding of selected grammar problems and to express themselves in writing.

Instruction: Major topics covered in the course are stylistics and idiomatic usage. This course is a continuation of RU-310 at the fourth-year level.

Credit Recommendation: In the upper division baccalaureate degree category, 3 semester hours in Russian (5/76) (11/82).

Advanced Russian Reading (RU-240) (Formerly Basic Russian Reading [RS-140])

Location: National Cryptologic School, Ft. Meade, MD.

Length: 112 hours (7 weeks).

Dates: September 1974-December 1980.

Objective: To enable students who have an intermediate knowledge of Russian to acquire further skills in reading Russian periodicals.

Instruction: Major topics covered in the course are reading and abstracting technical texts and primary Soviet sources. Corresponds to one semester of a third-year nonintensive Russian course.

Credit Recommendation: In the upper division baccalaureate degree category, 3 semester hours in Russian (5/76) (11/82). *Prerequisite:* Intermediate Russian or equivalent.

Advanced Russian Translation (RU-270) (Formerly Russian Translation Techniques [RU-270]; and Intermediate Russian Translation [RS-200])

Location: National Cryptologic School, Ft. Meade, MD.

Length: *Version 1:* 192 hours (12 weeks), two full-day sessions/week, classroom instruction and self-study included; *Version 2:* 128 hours (8 weeks), two full-day sessions/week; *Version 3:* 160 hours (10 weeks), 2 full-day sessions/week.

Dates: *Version 1:* January 1976-December 1976; *Version 2:* January 1977-December 1980; *Version 3:* January 1981-Present.

Objective: To translate articles from the Russian press on themes ranging from political and economic to military and technical.

Learning Outcome: Upon successful completion of this course, the student will be able to use translation techniques to produce idiomatic, stylistically correct translations.

Instruction: Major topics covered in the course are word order, relative clauses and participles, phrases with generic words, elimination of genitive case strings, false friends, difficulties arising from cultural differences, and course projects. Methods of instruction include lecture, discussion, classroom exercises, and graded translations.

Credit Recommendation: *Versions 1, 2 and 3:* In the upper division baccalaureate degree category, 3 semester hours in Russian (5/76) (11/82) (11/89) (9/94).

Basic Russian Structure (RU-101) (Formerly Russian Structure I [RU-101])

Location: National Cryptologic School, Ft. Meade, MD.

Length: *Version 1:* 225 hours (15 weeks), classroom instruction and self-study included; *Version 2:* 280 hours (14 weeks).

Dates: January 1973-Present.

Objective: To provide students who have no background in Russian with a knowledge of the basic vocabulary and structure of the language.

Learning Outcome: Upon successful completion of this course, the student will be able to pronounce Russian with reasonable accuracy; speak and comprehend the language on a basic level; and read expository prose of moderate difficulty.

Instruction: Major topics covered in the course are verbal aspect and tense; reflexive verbs; imperatives; verbs of motion; forms and functions of the six cases; declension of nouns, pronouns, and adjectives; comparatives, and superlatives; time expression; numbers; and use of short adjectives. Methods of instruction include lecture, discussion, classroom exercises, audio/visual material, and graded translation exercises.

Credit Recommendation: *Version 1:* In the lower division baccalaureate/associate degree category, 6 semester hours in Russian (5/76) (11/82) (11/89) (9/94). **NOTE:** If credit is awarded for Intensive Basic and Intermediate Russion (RU-15A), do not award credit for this course because it duplicates Phase I of RU-15A. *Version 2:* In the lower division baccalaureate/associate degree category, 6 semester hours in Russian (5/76) (11/82) (11/89) (9/94). **NOTE:** If credit is awarded for Intensive Basic and Intermediate Russion (RU-15A), do not award credit for this course because it duplicates Phase I of RU-15A.

Intensive Basic and Intermediate Russian (RU-15A)
(Comprehensive Russian [RU-15A])

Location: National Cryptologic School, Ft. Meade, MD.

Length: *Version 1:* 2,240 hours (58 weeks); *Version 2:* 2,080 hours (52 weeks).

Dates: *Version 1:* January 1973-October 1991; *Version 2:* November 1991-Present.

Objective: To bring the student, in the shortest possible time, to the level of fluency generally acquired in two years of language study.

Learning Outcome: Upon successful completion of this course, the student will be able to read authentic Russian materials of a journalistic nature; and understand Russian news broadcasts and speak at L2 (intermediate level) with an active vocabulary of approximately 2000 words.

Instruction: Major topics covered in the course are basic Russian grammar with emphasis on regularities, and introduces a basic vocabulary of approximately 650 words; a review of grammar while introducing more complex topics such as participles, prefixed verbs of motion, and declension of numerals with emphasis on grammatical exceptions; language usage with students reading authentic texts at the 2/2+ level and practicing manipulating structures and rephrasing texts while giving attention to Russian phraseology and idioms; and listening skills, especially transcription. Methods of instruction include lecture, discussion, classroom exercises, audio/visual material, learner presentation/reports, and tests. This course, structured in 4 phases, is the equivalent of a two-year basic and intermediate intensive Russian program.

Credit Recommendation: *Version 1:* In the lower division baccalaureate/associate degree category, 22 semester hours in Russian (5/76) (11/82) (11/89) (9/94). **NOTE:** If student has been awarded credit for Basic Russian Structure RU-101, credit for this course should be reduced because RU-101 duplicates Phase I of this course. *Version 2*: In the lower division baccalaureate/associate degree category, 22 semester hours in Russian (5/76) (11/82) (11/89) (9/94). **NOTE:** If student has been awarded credit for Basic Russian Structure RU-101, credit for this course should be reduced because RU-101 duplicates Phase I of this course.

Intermediate Russian (RU-102)
(Formerly Intermediate Russian Structure)

Location: National Cryptologic School, Ft. Meade, MD.

Length: *Version 1:* 240 hours (16 weeks, part-time); *Version 2:* 400 hours (10 weeks, full-time).

Dates: *Version 1:* September 1975-June 1987; *Version 2:* July 1987-Present.

Objective: To provide students who have a basic knowledge of Russian with further language development emphasizing reading.

Learning Outcome: Upon successful completion of this course, the student will be able to read newspapers with a dictionary; engage in limited conversations with reasonable pronunciation accuracy; accurately transcribe approximately 85% of material dictated in Russian; and with 85% accuracy at the 2 level, read and/or translate a Russian text, comprehend spoken Russian, and respond orally in Russian to specific situations.

Instruction: Major topics covered by this course are grammar review, reading strategies, conversation skills, and introductory transcription. Methods of instruction include lecture, discussion, classroom exercises, case studies, audio/visual material, evaluation of translations, limited English-Russian translation, and written examinations including Russian-English translations, grammar items, and transcription.

Credit Recommendation: In the lower division baccalaureate/associate degree category, 9 semester hours in Russian (11/82) (11/89) (9/94). **NOTE:** Credit should not be awarded for both this course and Intermediate Russian Structure (RU 201). *Prerequisites*: Russian Structure I or one year of college-level Russian. Satisfactory completion of a basic Russian language course plus a minimum score of 75% of the RU-102 Intermediate Russian Pre-Test, or a minimum of 26 correct answers on the Russian Intermediate Placement Test, or instructor approval.

Intermediate Russian Structure (RU-201)
(Formerly Intermediate Russian Structure I [RU-201])
(Formerly Basic Russian Refresher [RS-150])

Location: National Cryptologic School, Ft. Meade, MD.

Length: 400 hours (10 weeks).

Dates: January 1971-Present.

Objective: To provide increased proficiency in speaking, understanding, reading, and writing nontechnical Russian.

Learning Outcome: Upon successful completion of this course, the student will be able to read and comprehend most L2 nontechnical writing in Russian newspapers, magazines, and news broadcasts; demonstrate increased aural comprehension and speaking skills; and use an expanded active and passive vocabulary.

Instruction: Major topics covered in the course are a survey of Russian grammar, word formation and problematic lexicology, readings from Russian press, Russian Films, and television broadcasts. Methods of instruction include lecture, discussion, classroom exercises, computer-assisted instruction, and examinations.

Credit Recommendation: In the lower division baccalaureate/associate degree category, 9 semester hours in Russian (5/76) (11/82) (11/89) (9/94). **NOTE:** Credit should not be awarded for both this course and Intermediate Russian (RU-102).

Intermediate Spoken Russian (RU-210)
(Formerly Basic Colloquial Russian [RS-110])

Location: National Cryptologic School, Ft. Meade, MD.

Length: 160 hours (10 weeks).

Dates: *Version 1:* March 1974-December 1975; *Version 2:* April 1991-Present.

Objective: To enable students who have a basic knowledge of Russian to acquire further skills in spoken Russian.

Instruction: Major topics covered in the course are aural comprehension and oral production. Method of instruction includes an audiolingual approach. This course corresponds to the first semester of a second-year, nonintensive Russian course.

Credit Recommendation: In the lower division baccalaureate/associate degree

category, 3 semester hours in Russian (5/76) (11/82).

Linguistic Analysis of Russian (RU-230)
(Formerly Russian Linguistics [RU-230])

Location: National Cryptologic School, Ft. Meade, MD.

Length: *Version 1:* 128 hours (8 weeks); *Version 2:* 96 hours (8 weeks).

Dates: *Version 1:* April 1976-January 1987; *Version 2:* February 1987-Present.

Objective: To familiarize the student with the basic principles of the phonological and morphological structure of contemporary standard Russian.

Learning Outcome: Upon successful completion of this course, the student will be able to carry out the phonetic transcription of a Russian word or phrase; identify the actual lexical item(s) with 70% accuracy; analyze the relationship between Russian orthography, sound, and meaning; understand the phonological differences between informal speech and standard literary Russian; and apply principles of Russian declension and conjugation and the corresponding stress patterns.

Instruction: Major topics covered in the course are orthography, articulatory phonetics, phonemics, stressed and unstressed vowels, phonological analysis of colloquial speech, morphology, and morphophonemics. Methods of instruction include lecture, discussion, classroom exercises, audio/visual material, and examinations.

Credit Recommendation: *Versions 1: and 2*: In the upper division baccalaureate degree category, 3 semester hours in Russian Linguistics (5/76) (11/82) (11/89) (9/94).

Problems in Russian Lexicology (RU-285)

Location: National Cryptologic School, Ft. Meade, MD.

Length: 128 hours (8 weeks).

Dates: June 1989-Present.

Objective: To comprehend and use standard and non-standard Russian vocabulary.

Learning Outcome: Upon successful completion of this course, the student will be able to maximize comprehension of written Russian recognition of linguistic variants and nuances or connotations connected with usage and will have the ability to draw cultural inferences from texts.

Instruction: Major topics covered in the course are analysis of vocabulary, analysis of usage and effect on meaning, and analysis of links between language and culture. Methods of instruction include lecture, discussion, class exercises, audio/visual material, one-on-one mentoring on items of specific interest, written quizzes, observations, oral quizzes, and a final examination.

Credit Recommendation: In the upper division baccalaureate degree category, 3 semester hours in Russian Language or Russian Linguistics (8/91) (9/96).

Reading in the Soviet Press (RU-245)

Location: National Cryptologic School, Ft. Meade, MD.

Length: 96 hours (6 weeks, 2 days per week, 8 hours per day).

Dates: September 1990-August 1996.

Objective: To give the student the skills to read, understand, and translate specialized military texts from the Soviet press.

Learning Outcome: Upon successful completion of this course, the student will be able to work with materials found in the Soviet military press.

Instruction: Major topics covered in the course are reading, analyzing, translating Soviet military press materials and building up general and special Russian vocabulary. Methods of instruction include lecture, discussion, and class exercises.

Credit Recommendation: In the upper division baccalaureate degree category, 3 semester hours in Russian (8/91).

Reading Russian (RU-111)

Location: National Cryptologic School, Ft. Meade, MD.

Length: 16 weeks (5 days per week, 3 hours per day).

Dates: June 1990-August 1996.

Objective: To teach students reading/translation skills sufficient to work with everyday Russian texts.

Learning Outcome: Upon successful completion of this course, the student will be able to read and translate into English Russian texts related to everyday life topics.

Instruction: Major topics covered in the course are mastering the Russian alphabet for reading and writing; learning the basic (1,000 words) Russian vocabulary; and understanding the basics of Russian grammar.

Credit Recommendation: In the lower division baccalaureate/associate degree category, 3 semester hours in Russian (8/91).

Russian Textual Analysis I (RU-202)

Location: National Cryptologic School, Ft. Meade, MD.

Length: 240 hours (8 hours/day, 3 days/week, 10 weeks).

Dates: January 1980-Present.

Objective: To develop reading skills and text processing strategies, enable comprehension of straightforward, nontechnical writing that appears in Russian emigre periodicals; and increase aural comprehension and speaking skills.

Learning Outcome: Upon successful completion of this course, the student will be able to restore 75% of the missing items in an L2+ text in standard written Russian from which markers of category, function, or relationship are missing; demonstrate 75% comprehension and render a full translation into English of a Russion L2+ text in a Russian newspaper or magazine with minimum use of lexical aids; discuss the general topic and demonstrate L2+ speaking proficiency with full grasp of content, cultural, and linguistic features of an L2+ Russian text; demonstrate 75% comprehension of a 3-minute Russian language news broadcast; and restore 75% of missing lexical and grammatical markers in a written transcription of the broadcast.

Instruction: Major topics covered in the course are grammar, reading, listening comprehension, and conversation; aspects of Russian syntax and textual phenomena such as lexical, referential, and conjunctive cohesion; translation techniques; and analysis of material from Russian press and television. Methods of instruction include lecture, discussion, classroom exercises, learner presentations/reports, quizzes, and a final examination.

Credit Recommendation: In the upper division baccalaureate degree category, 5 semester hours in Russian (11/82) (11/89) (9/94).

Russian Textual Analysis II (RU-203)
(Formerly Intermediate Russian Translation [RS-200])

Location: National Cryptologic School, Ft. Meade, MD.

Length: *Version 1:* 128 hours (8 weeks, two full-day sessions/week); *Version 2:* 160 hours (8 hours/day, 2 days/week, 10 weeks).

Dates: *Version 1:* October 1974-September 1981; *Version 2:* October 1981-Present.

Objective: To read standard Russian texts on several stylistic levels, to be prepared for advanced courses in translation, to apply textual analysis techniques to reading Russian texts on various stylistic levels, and to perform controlled translations of Russian texts with minimal loss of information.

Learning Outcome: Upon successful completion of this course, the student will be able to use translation techniques to produce idiomatic, stylistically correct translations.

Instruction: Major topics covered in the course are a survey of certain aspects of Russian syntax; textual phenomena such as word order, cohesion, deletion, and ellipsis; techniques of translation; and materials from current Russian press. Methods of instruction include lecture, discussion, classroom exercises, and examinations.

Credit Recommendation: *Version 1:* In the upper division baccalaureate degree category, 1 semester hour in Russian (5/76). *Version 2:* In the upper division baccalaureate degree category, 3 semester hours in Russian (11/82) (11/89) (9/94).

Workshop in Colloquial Russian (RU-380)

Location: National Cryptologic School, Ft. Meade, MD.

Length: 10 weeks (2 days per week, 8 hours per day).

Dates: June 1984-August 1996.

Objective: To develop skill and oral and written comprehension of colloquial Russian conversational patterns and reproduce, if necessary.

Learning Outcome: Upon successful completion of this course, the student will be able to understand colloquial Russian conversational nuances; recognize deviations of colloquial speech from standard literacy forms or word orders and supply standard alternatives; reproduce colloquialisms in conversation/oral presentation; and analyze written texts for maximum comprehension of nuances of colloquial usage.

Instruction: Major topics covered in the course are word order; pronunciation/intonation; word formation; and practical use of language skills. Methods of instruction include lecture, discussion, and classroom exercises.

Credit Recommendation: In the upper division baccalaureate degree or the graduate degree category, 3 semester hours in Russian (8/91).

Workshop in Russian Stylistics (RU-280)

Location: National Cryptologic School, Ft. Meade, MD.

Length: 160 hours (10 weeks, 2 full-day sessions/week); classroom instruction and self-study.

Dates: *Version 1:* March 1974-July 1991; *Version 2:* August 1991-Present.

Objective: To enable students to understand colloquial Russian in its spoken and written form.

Learning Outcome: Upon successful completion of this course, the student will be able to understand the use of particles in authentic Russian texts and employ them with accuracy in spoken Russian; and converse on a wide range of subjects relating to contemporary Russian life.

Instruction: Major topics covered in the course are the meaning and uses of particles in their relationship to word order and intonation; analysis of compound and complex sentences as well as sentence types, e.g. declarative, interrogative, exhortative, exclamatory, and negative; and focus on the semantics of synonyms, antonyms, verbal prefixes and motion verbs. Methods of instruction include lecture, discussion, classroom exercises, audio/visual material, learner presentations/reports, and evaluation of presentations and translations.

Credit Recommendation: *Version 1:* In the upper division baccalaureate degree category, 1 semester hour in Russian (11/82) (11/89). *Version 2:* In the upper division baccalaureate degree category, 3 semester hours in Russian (8/91) (9/94).

Spanish

Basic Spanish Structure (SN-100) (Formerly Basic to Intermediate Spanish Language Course I and II [SN-100])

Location: National Cryptologic School, Fort Meade, MD.

Length: 240 hours (6 weeks, 5 days per week).

Dates: April 1983-October 1987.

Objective: To develop the student's reading comprehension and listening skills based on grammatical sequences. Emphasis is on vocabulary, translations, and transcription.

Instruction: Major topics covered in the course are developing reading comprehension and listening skills, vocabulary, military and radio terminology, translation, and transcription. Methods of instruction include graded presentation of grammar; individualized instruction; extensive use of text, periodicals, and tapes; frequent quizzes; and diagnostic tests.

Credit Recommendation: In the lower division baccalaureate/associate degree category, 12-16 hours in Spanish (10/85). **NOTE:** This course covers basic to intermediate college level Spanish (12 to 16 semester hours or four college semesters).

Basic Spanish Translation (SN-170) or Spanish Refresher Course Translation (SN-152)

Location: National Cryptologic School, Ft. Meade, MD.

Length: *Version 1: Course 1:* SN-152: 80 hours (2 weeks, 8 hours a day); *Course 2:* SN-170: 128 hours (16 days); *Version 2:* 128 hours (16 days).

Dates: June 1987-Present.

Objective: To enable students who have had formal academic training in the Spanish language to develop their skills in translating intermediate-level Spanish texts from Spanish to English at level 2/2+.

Learning Outcome: Upon successful completion of this course, the student will be able to read a text from a current Latin American or Spanish newspaper or magazine and write a translation from Spanish to English.

Instruction: Major topics covered in the course are translation of current newspaper and magazine articles on government, military, and political subjects while students have an opportunity to work at their own pace. Methods of instruction include lecture, discussion, classroom exercises, and final examination.

Credit Recommendation: In the lower division baccalaureate/associate degree category, 2 semester hours in Spanish (6/87) (9/94). **NOTE:** Credit may be granted for one of these courses but not both.

Intermediate Spanish Grammar (SN-200) (Formerly Advanced Intermediate Spanish Structure)

Location: National Cryptologic School, Ft. Meade, MD.

Length: *Version 1:* 128 hours (5 weeks); *Version 2:* 192 hours (6.5 weeks).

Dates: *Version 1:* September 1986-January 1992; *Version 2:* March 1992-Present.

Objective: To raise students' grammar skills from Level 2/2+ (upper intermediate) to Level 3 (advanced) and to enable students to comprehend and translate Level 2+ Spanish texts.

Learning Outcome: Upon successful completion of this course, the student will be able to demonstrate the ability to comprehend and translate Level 2+ Spanish texts by scoring an average of at least 60% on the comprehensive post-assessment exam and course exams.

Instruction: Major topics covered in the course are Spanish grammar, morphology, and syntax with a special emphasis on the subjunctive mood. Methods of instruction include lecture, classroom exercises, instructor-led and facilitated instruction using a grammar textbook and supplementary journalistic Spanish texts, quizzes, tests, and a final examination. Exit is by course and post-assessment examinations at 60% average score.

Credit Recommendation: *Version 1:* In the upper division baccalaureate degree category, 6 semester hours in Spanish (8/91). *Version 2:* In the upper division baccalaureate degree category, 8 semester hours in Spanish (9/96).

Intermediate Spanish Reading Comprehension (SN-240)

Location: National Cryptologic School, Ft. Meade, MD.

Length: 120 hours (5 weeks, three 8-hour meetings per week).

Dates: July 1989-December 1993.

Objective: To enable students with formal academic training in Spanish at the intermediate level to enhance reading competency at the intermediate level and move to the advanced level in reading the language for understanding.

Learning Outcome: Upon successful completion of this course, the student will be able to read and write a summary in English of authentic intermediate to advanced level Spanish language texts, without the use of a dictionary, with 90% accuracy.

Instruction: Major topic covered in the course is readings about social, economic, and political issues in Spanish language newspapers and magazines. Methods of instruction include instructor-led lectures and discussions; a variety of classroom exercises performed by the student and facilitated by the instructor and some use of computer-assisted and videotaped programs and materials.

Credit Recommendation: In the upper division baccalaureate degree category, 3 semester hours in Spanish (8/91).

Intermediate Spanish Structure (SN-103)
(Basic Spanish Structure)

Location: National Cryptologic School, Ft. Meade, MD.

Length: 192 hours (12 weeks).

Dates: September 1989-Present.

Objective: To raise students' grammar skills from Level 1+/2 (upper elementary) to Level 2/2+ (upper intermediate) and to enable students to understand and produce written Spanish at level 2/2+.

Learning Outcome: Upon successful completion of this course, the student will be able to demonstrate an understanding of major Spanish grammar concepts by scoring at least 60% on the comprehensive post-assessment exam and course exams.

Instruction: Major topics covered in the course are Spanish grammar, morphology, and syntax. Methods of instruction include instructor-led lectures and exercises facilitated by instructor using a grammar textbook and supplementary journalistic Spanish texts, discussion, classroom exercises, quizzes, tests, and a final examination. Exit is by course and post-assessment examinations at 60% average score.

Credit Recommendation: In the lower division baccalaureate/associate degree category, 8 semester hours in Spanish or Foreign Languages (8/91) (9/96).

Intermediate Spanish Translation (SN-270)

Location: National Cryptologic School, Ft. Meade, MD.

Length: 128 hours (8 weeks, 16 hours per week).

Dates: February 1985-Present.

Objective: To assist Spanish translators in improving their ability in translating Spanish to English from Level 2+ to Level 3.

Learning Outcome: Upon successful completion of this course, the student will be able to analyze and translate relatively complex texts on political, economical, military, and scientific topics from authentic sources written in Spanish.

Instruction: Major topics covered in the course are a text of semitechnical subject matter in Spanish which the student will write an English translation using general and technical reference sources. Methods of instruction include lecture, discussion, classroom exercises, evaluation, and final examination.

Credit Recommendation: In the upper division baccalaureate degree category, 4 semester hours in Spanish (6/87) (9/94).

Introductory Spanish (SN-010)

Location: National Cryptologic School, Ft. Meade, MD.

Length: 128 hours (8 weeks).

Dates: May 1986-Present.

Objective: To enable students with no formal academic training in Spanish to identify Spanish language texts from other language texts and write summaries and gists in clear journalistic English.

Learning Outcome: Upon successful completion of this course, the student will be able to identify authentic Spanish language texts and write, in clear journalistic English, a gist of the texts with 70% accuracy.

Instruction: Major topics covered in the course are an overview of the grammar and phonetic system of the Spanish language through readings about social, economic, and political issues in Spanish language newspapers and magazines. Methods of instruction include instructor-led lectures and discussions; a variety of classroom exercises performed by the student and facilitated by the instructor, some use of computer-assisted and videotaped programs and materials, quizzes, test, and a final examination.

Credit Recommendation: In the lower division baccalaureate/associate degree category, 3-4 semester hours in Spanish (8/91) (9/96). **NOTE:** The credit-granting academic institution should make the decision based on the number of credits given to its first-semester introductory course.

Rapid Survey of Spanish (SN-020)

Location: National Cryptologic School, Ft. Meade, MD.

Length: 192 hours (8 weeks).

Dates: August 1986-Present.

Objective: To enable students with formal academic training in other related languages to develop an intermediate level competency in translating Spanish to English.

Learning Outcome: Upon successful completion of this course, the student will be able to demonstrate comprehension of Level 2 (intermediate) journalistic Spanish-language texts (90% accuracy); to translate such texts (80% accuracy) using a dictionary; and to transcribe similar recorded texts (70% accuracy).

Instruction: Major topic covered in the course is the comprehension of authentic texts about social, economic, and political issues in Spanish language newspapers, magazines, and audio/video tapes. Methods of instruction include instructor-led lectures and discussion, a variety of classroom exercises performed by the student and facilitated by the instructor, some use of videotaped programs and materials, quizzes, and tests.

Credit Recommendation: In the lower division baccalaureate/associate degree category, 8 semester hours in Spanish or Foreign Languages (8/91) (9/96). **NOTE:** Credit should not be granted for both this course and Introductory Spanish (SN-010).

Spanish Refresher Course (SN-154) (Basic Spanish Refresher)

Location: National Cryptologic School, Ft. Meade, MD.

Length: 240 hours (6 weeks).

Dates: February 1986-Present.

Objective: To provide basic knowledge of the Spanish language with the opportunity to further develop basic skills in listening, speaking, reading, and writing to an intermediate level.

Learning Outcome: Upon successful completion of this course, the student will be able to comprehend the written Level 2 language of newspapers or magazine articles on personal, government, military, or commercial documents; write basic information items; and understand basic oral communication.

Instruction: Major topics covered in the course are a review of basic grammar and vocabulary with special emphasis on reading, translation, and transcription; extensive listening practice and grammatical quizzes; and use of periodicals and video materials. Methods of instruction include lecture, discussion, classroom exercises, audio/visual material, and quizzes.

Credit Recommendation: In the lower division baccalaureate/associate degree category, 6 semester hours in Spanish (6/87) (9/94).

Spanish Refresher Course: Reading (SN-151) (Formerly Basic Spanish Refresher - Reading)

Location: National Cryptologic School, Ft. Meade, MD.

Length: 80 hours (2 weeks, 8 hours a day).

Dates: August 1982-Present.

Objective: To enable students who have had formal academic training to refresh their skills in reading the Spanish language for understanding to Level 2+.

Learning Outcome: Upon successful completion of this course, the student will be able to read a text from a current Latin American or Spanish newspaper or magazine, understand military, political, or technical articles, and write a summary or gist.

Instruction: Major topics covered in the course are reading current newspaper and magazine articles on government, military, and political subjects at the student's own pace with materials graded on the intermediate level. Methods of instruction include discussion, classroom exercises, learner presentation/reports, and final examination.

Credit Recommendation: In the lower division baccalaureate/associate degree category, 2 semester hours in Spanish (6/87) (9/94).

Spanish Refresher Course: Transcription (SN-153) (Formerly Basic Spanish Refresher - Transcription)

Location: National Cryptologic School, Ft. Meade, MD.

Length: 80 hours (2 weeks, 8 hours a day).

Dates: August 1982-Present.

Objective: To enable students who have had formal academic training in Spanish to refresh their ability to transcribe intermediate Spanish Level 2 text material.

Learning Outcome: Upon successful completion of this course, the student will be able to produce a verbatim transcription in Spanish from a text of aural Spanish information.

Instruction: Major topics covered in the course are transcription of currently taped radio and audio materials on government, military, and political issues with students working at their own pace. Methods of instruction include discussion, classroom exercises, audio/visual material, and transcriptions that are graded and compiled for a final evaluation.

Credit Recommendation: In the lower division baccalaureate/associate degree category, 2 semester hours in Spanish (6/87) (9/94).

Thai

Beginning and Intermediate Thai (TI-112) (Formerly Basic Thai Language)

Location: National Cryptologic School, Ft. Meade, MD.

Length: 1,120 hours (28 weeks, 5 days per week, 8 hours per day).

Dates: January 1988-August 1996.

Objective: To be able to communicate effectively with native speakers in work and social settings. The emphasis of the course is spoken proficiency at the 1+ to 2 level. Reading is developed to a proficiency level of 2, including brief informational items from Thai newspapers. Writing proficiency is at the 1 level.

Learning Outcome: Upon successful completion of this course, the student will be able to use Thai competently in most professional and social situations, as well as to meet everyday personal needs. The ability to read will be limited to gathering basic information such as reading, signs, menus, and simple newspaper items and advertisements. Writing skill will be minimal—taking notes and answering questions, for the most part.

Instruction: Major topics covered in the course are the equivalent of a (two-year) beginning and intermediate course in Thai. It develops the four basic skills—listening, speaking, reading, and writing—as well as facility in translation. A modified audiolingual approach is used. Topics in the first level of the course are social formulae and survival situations. Later, reading and discussion topics include culture, communication, education, agriculture, health, industry, government, and the judicial system. Newspaper readings cover topics of current national and international importance.

Credit Recommendation: In the lower division baccalaureate/associate degree category, 20 semester hours in Thai (8/91).

Beginning Intermediate and Advanced Thai (TI-10A) (Formerly Basic Thai)

Location: National Cryptologic School, Ft. Meade, MD.

Length: 1,520 hours (38 weeks, 5 days per week, 8 hours per day).

Dates: October 1984-August 1996.

Objective: To be able to communicate effectively with native speakers in work and social settings, as in Basic Thai course TI-112. The difference here is that the students will have more exposure to outside readings. Proficiency levels of 2 in speaking and reading are expected.

Learning Outcome: Upon successful completion of this course, the student will be able to use Thai competently in most professional and social situations, as well as to meet everyday personal needs. The ability to read will extend to gathering information from newspapers on current events and national and international issues, but will not be strong enough to read editorials. Writing skills will extend to producing brief statements, summaries, and bio-data.

Instruction: Major topics covered in the course are equivalent to beginning, intermediate, and advanced Thai. It is essentially an extension or addition of advanced materials concentrating on readings from newspaper articles beyond the level of TI-112. Topics deal with current events, particularly those of political importance.

Credit Recommendation: In the lower division baccalaureate/associate degree category, 20 semester hours or in the upper division baccalaureate degree category, 6 semester hours in Thai, a total of 26 hours (8/91).

Turkish

Basic Modern Turkish (TR-10A)

Location: National Cryptologic School, Ft. Meade, MD.

Length: *Version 1:* 1,200 hours (30 weeks); *Version 2:* 1,880 hours; classroom.

Dates: *Version 1:* December 1975-April 1984; *Version 2:* May 1984-Present.

Objective: To provide knowledge of and fluency in using the grammatical structures of Turkish; and to expand acquisition of vocabulary used in Turkish newspapers.

Learning Outcome: Upon successful completion of this course, the student will be able to comprehend Turkish at considerably higher levels in both written and spoken forms; and exercise speaking skills at moderately high levels.

Instruction: Major topics covered in the course are phonology, morphology, and syntax of the Turkish language; vocabulary development; and readings from various printed media on political, social, and economic topics. Methods of instruction include lecture, discussion, classroom exercises, audio/visual material, learner presentations/reports, and final examination.

Credit Recommendation: In the lower division baccalaureate/associate degree category or in the upper division baccalaureate degree category, 20 semester hours in Turkish (3/80) (10/85) (9/94).

COMPUTER SOFTWARE AND OPERATIONS DIVISION

The Computer Software and Operations Division is one of several departments in the Science and Technology Department. It provides training for computer operators and programmers as well as systems analysts, engineers, and mathematicians.

Access 95 Development (70551, 70552, 70553)

Location: Computer-based.

Length: Self-paced.

Dates: October 1996-Present.

Objective: To improve application development skills to use advanced features such as Visual Basic for application and data access objects.

Learning Outcome: Upon successful completion of this course, the student will be able to apply OLE Automation and OLE Controls, create add-in, work with forms, implement security for applications, synchronize data, and manage related client/server issues.

Instruction: Major topics covered in the course are introduction to VB Programming, providing functionality to forms and reports, Programming Objects, trapping and preventing errors, working with Records, communicating with other applications, working with Windows DLL, working with add-ins, optimizing and application performance, and client/server application development. Methods of instruction include materials available on CD-ROM, network, or intranet for self-study.

Credit Recommendation: In the lower division baccalaureate/associate degree category, 1 semester hour in Computer Science or Computer Information Systems (5/97). **NOTE:** Student must complete 3 modules to receive credit.

Advanced ELINT Collection and Analysis (EA-380)

Location: National Cryptologic School, Ft. Meade, MD.

Length: 400 hours (10 weeks).

Dates: September 1996-Present.

Objective: To identify various types of modulated signals, interpret various ways that signal information can be transmitted and received, describe the characteristics of one-way microwave transmission, and analyze information to define and describe electronic intelligence (ELINT) signals and systems.

Learning Outcome: Upon successful completion of this course, the student will be able to describe signal transmission, reception, and characteristics of an electronic signal; analyze and perform measurements on commonly used RF and microwave signals; and use signal generators and electronic measurement equipment.

Instruction: Major topics covered in the course are review of mathematical analysis techniques, noise and filters, microwave propagation; different types of modulation techniques, antenna types and characteristics, microwave receivers, continuous pulse and doppler radars, electronically scanned radars, millimeter wave and optical waves, digitized signals, and target tracking radar. Methods of instruction include lecture, discussion, classroom exercises, learner presentations, quizzes, reports, papers, and a final examination.

Credit Recommendation: In the lower division baccalaureate/associate degree category, 3 semester hours in Telecommunications or Electronics Engineering Technology (9/96).

ALGOL Programming (MP-243)

Location: National Cryptologic School, Ft. Meade, MD.

Length: 45 hours (5 weeks).

Dates: *Version 1:* August 1969-October 1989; *Version 2:* November 1989-Present.

Objective: To provide an understanding of the ALGOL programming language and to teach the student to program in ALGOL.

Instruction: Major topics covered in the course are origins of the ALGOL language, writing, and debugging of at least four ALGOL programs and presentation of various programming techniques useful in solving selected problems. Methods of instruction include lecture, discussion, and computer usage.

Credit Recommendation: *Version 1:* In the upper division baccalaureate degree category, 2 semester hours in Computer Science (11/75) (12/80). *Version 2:* In the lower division baccalaureate/associate degree category, 2 semester hours in Computer Engineering or Computer Science (9/94). *Prerequisite:* Mechanics of Algebra (MA-012) or college-level algebra and demonstrated competency in another programming language.

Antenna Fundamentals (EA-171)

Location: National Cryptologic School, Ft. Meade, MD.

Length: 30 hours (4 weeks).

Dates: January 1986-Present.

Objective: To provide the student with knowledge of antenna fundamentals, specifications, design, and application of simple antenna systems, and antenna terminology.

Learning Outcome: Upon successful completion of this course, the student will be able to identify antennas, demonstrate correct use of antenna terminology, estimate application and performance parameters of antennas, and solve equations.

Instruction: Major topics covered in the course are concepts and functions of antennas; antenna fundamentals and definitions; basic concepts of the antenna in transmission and reception applications; simple antenna elements (electrically small dipoles, the half wave dipole, antennas above ground plane, and small loop antennas); and principles of arrays, wire antennas, broadband antennas, and aperture antennas. Methods of instruction include lecture, discussion, classroom exercises, and an examination.

Credit Recommendation: In the vocational certificate category, 1 semester hour in Telecommunications or Electronics Technology (8/91) (9/96).

AN/TNH-25 Recorder Maintenance (EM-305)

Location: National Cryptologic School, Ft. Meade, MD.

Length: *Version 1:* 40 hours (1 week); *Version 2:* 48 hours (1.5 weeks).

Dates: November 1982-August 1992.

Objective: To provide the student with the knowledge necessary to operate and perform preventive and corrective maintenance on the AN/TNH-25 recorder/reproducer.

Learning Outcome: Upon successful completion of this course, the student will be able to operate the AN/TNH-25 recorder/reproducer and perform preventive and corrective maintenance to the LRU level on the AN/TNH-25 recorder/reproducer.

Instruction: Major topics covered in the course are function of controls and indicators, functional theory of operation, test and alignment procedures, LRU failure analysis, preventive maintenance procedures, fault isolation, and corrective maintenance. Methods of instruction include lecture, discussion, laboratory exercises, and an examination.

Credit Recommendation: In the vocational certificate category, 1 semester hour in Digital Electronic Equipment Maintenance (8/91). **NOTE:** This course and one other in the EM series must be completed to receive 1 credit.

APL Programming (MP-188)

Location: National Cryptologic School, Ft. Meade, MD.

Length: 40 hours (5 weeks).

Dates: November 1973-December 1985.

Objective: To teach the student the APL programming language.

Instruction: Major topics covered in the course are the ability to use APL as an effective tool for the solution of operational problems and syntax and semantics of APL commands and operators used in selected quantitative problems. Methods of instruction include lectures, discussion, and the use of interactive computer terminals.

Credit Recommendation: In the upper division baccalaureate degree category, 2 semester hours in Computational or Quantitative Research Methods (11/75) (12/80). *Prerequisite:* Mechanics of Algebra (MA-012) or college-level algebra.

Architectures for Secure Systems (ND-385) (Formerly Architecture for Secure Systems [IN-385] and [CP-530])

Location: National Cryptologic School, Ft. Meade, MD.

Length: 40 hours (1 week).

Dates: July 1989-August 1996.

Objective: To provide the student with an understanding of basic architectural features necessary to support design and implementation of secure computer systems.

Learning Outcome: Upon successful completion of this course, the student will be able to describe design and implementation concepts of various protection mechanisms for secure computer systems and compare architectures of various systems with respect to the requirements of DOD and Trusted Computer System Evaluation Criteria (TCSEC).

Instruction: Major topics covered in the course are architectural features required to support secure computer systems; study of trusted computer systems for purposes of design and implementation; case studies of secure system architectures; and future trends in security architecture. Methods of instruction include lecture, discussion, practical group exercises and a final examination.

Credit Recommendation: In the upper division baccalaureate degree category, 1 semester hour in Computer Science or Computer Security (8/91).

Burroughs B6700/7000 Advanced Technical Skills (MP-1H6) (Formerly Burroughs B6700 Advanced Technical Skills [MP-1H6])

Location: National Cryptologic School, Ft. Meade, MD.

Length: 70 hours (2 weeks).

Dates: July 1974-November 1987.

Objective: To provide the experienced operator with an in-depth understanding from an operational viewpoint of the internal functions of the Burroughs B6700 MCP Operating System software.

Instruction: Major topics covered in the course provide an in-depth study of the concepts and facilities of the Burroughs B6700 MCP Operating System and the use of its job control statements; emphasis is on data management and system utilities.

Credit Recommendation: In the lower division baccalaureate/associate degree category, 2 semester hours in Data Processing (9/77) (11/82) (11/89). *Prerequisite:* Burroughs B6700 Systems Software (MP-1H5) and FORTRAN for Operators (MP-166).

Burroughs B6700/7000 Systems Software (MP-1H5) (Formerly Burroughs B6700 Systems Software [MP-1H5])

Location: National Cryptologic School, Ft. Meade, MD.

Length: 35 hours (1 week).

Dates: July 1973-November 1987.

Objective: To enhance the apprentice operator's ability to interact with the Burroughs B6700 Operating System software.

Instruction: Major topics covered in the course are system reconfiguration, initialization memory control, work flow language and management, input/output subsystem, operator MCP communications, and data communication.

Credit Recommendation: In the lower division baccalaureate/associate degree category, 1 semester hour in Data Processing (9/77) (11/82) (11/89). *Prerequisite:* Introduction to Computer Systems Operations (MP-154).

C Programming Language (MP-220)

Location: National Cryptologic School, Ft. Meade, MD.

Length: 72 hours (3 hours a day, 3 days per week for 8 weeks).

Dates: October 1982-Present.

Objective: To provide an understanding of the C computer programming language.

Learning Outcome: Upon successful completion of this course, the student will be able to demonstrate an understanding of the C programming language; develop stand-alone C structured programs; and demonstrate an understanding of basic UNIX system calls.

Instruction: Major topics covered in the course are data types, control flow, functions, program structure, storage classes, expression evaluation, arrays and pointers, standard portable library, and UNIX system calls. Methods of instruction include lecture, classroom exercises, audio/visual material, outside assignments, and examinations.

Credit Recommendation: In the lower division baccalaureate/associate degree category, 3 semester hours in Management Information Systems, Computer Engineering, Computer Science, or Electrical Engineering (11/89) (9/94).

C++ Programming with MFC 4.0 Library Version 2 (70611, 70612) 70613, 70614, 70615

Location: Computer-based.

Length: Self-paced.

Dates: October 1996-Present.

Objective: To introduce concepts necessary for developing application using Microsoft Visual C++ 4.0.

Learning Outcome: Upon successful completion of this course, the student will be able to develop applications using Visual C++.

Instruction: Major topics covered in the course are fundamentals of windows architecture, MFC fundamentals and architecture, building an application framework using Visual C++, implementing user interfaces, outputting simple text and graphics, document/view architecture and component gallery, dialog boxes, command routing and update command handling, storing and retrieving data, implementing ODBC support in MFC, programming in MFC, and registry and MFC platform issues. Methods of instruction include materials available on CD-ROM, network, or intranet for self-study.

Credit Recommendation: In the lower division baccalaureate/associate degree category, 2 semester hours in Programming (5/97). **NOTE:** Student must complete 5 of 5 modules to receive credit. Also 2 hours credit maximum for Version 1 and Version 2.

C++ Programming with MFC Class 4.0 Library (70612-70613)

Location: Computer-based.

Length: Self-paced.

Dates: June 1996-Present.

Objective: To introduce C++ Programming with Microsoft Foundation Class 4.0 Library.

Learning Outcome: Upon successful completion of this course, the student will be able to discuss how to use Microsoft Visual C++ with Microsoft Foundation Class 4.0.

Instruction: Major topics covered in the course are fundamentals of Windows Architecture, MFC fundamentals and implementing user interfaces, outputting simple text and graphics, Document/View architecture and Component gallery, dialog boxes, command routing and update command handling, storing and retrieving. Methods of instruction include course materials available on CD-Rom for self-study, and tests.

Credit Recommendation: In the lower division baccalaureate/associate degree category, 1 semester hour in Programming (9/96). **NOTE:** Students must complete 3 of 3 modules to receive credit.

C Series (12688)

Location: Computer-based.

Length: Self-paced.

Dates: May 1996-Present.

Objective: To introduce the C programming language.

Learning Outcome: Upon successful completion of this course, the student will be able to use C to develop applications.

Instruction: Major topics covered in the course are to define the basic elements of the language, including fundamental types, constants, operators, statements and functions; understand the key concepts of pointers and arrays, structures, unions, type conversations and scope and linkage; utilize machine-level programming in C, C memory management, and C and C++ preprocessor directives; and understand ANSI C and other widely used C function libraries. Methods of instruction include course materials available on CD-Rom for self-study, and tests.

Credit Recommendation: In the lower division baccalaureate/associate degree category, 1 semester hour in Programming (9/96).

C/C++ Series (11678)

Location: Computer-based.

Length: Self-paced.

Dates: March 1996-Present.

Objective: To introduce C++.

Learning Outcome: Upon successful completion of this course, the student will be able to use C++ to develop applications.

Instruction: Major topics covered in the course are to compare the features that are common to C++ and C, understand the C++ and understand details that are essential for writing solid C++ programs. Methods of instruction include course materials available on CD-Rom for self-study, and tests.

Credit Recommendation: In the lower division baccalaureate/associate degree category, 1 semester hour in Programming (9/96).

CDC NOS Advanced Technical Skills (MP-1P6) (Formerly CDC 6600 Series Advanced Technical Skills)

Location: National Cryptologic School, Ft. Meade, MD.

Length: 35-40 hours (1 week).

Dates: July 1971-December 1994.

Objective: To provide the experienced operator with an in-depth understanding from an operational viewpoint of the internal functions of the CDC 6600 SCOPE Operating System software.

Instruction: Major topics covered in the course are an in-depth study of the concepts and facilities of the CDC 6600 SCOPE Operating System and the use of job control statements. Method of instruction includes computer-aided instruction (CAI).

Credit Recommendation: In the lower division baccalaureate/associate degree category, 1 semester hour in Data Processing (9/77) (11/82) (11/89) (9/94). *Prerequisite:* FORTRAN for Operators (MP-166) and CDC 6600 Series System Software (MP-1B5).

CDC NOS Operating System Hardware (MP-1P5) (Formerly CDC 6600 Series System Software)

Location: National Cryptologic School, Ft. Meade, MD.

Length: 35-40 hours (1 week).

Dates: July 1970-December 1994.

Objective: To enhance the apprentice operator's ability to interact with the CDC 6600 SCOPE Operating Series software.

Instruction: Major topics covered in the course provide an overview of the concepts and facilities of the CDC 6600 SCOPE Operating System and the use of its job control statements. Method of instruction includes computer-aided instruction (CAI).

Credit Recommendation: In the lower division baccalaureate/associate degree category, 1 semester hour in Data Processing (9/77) (11/82) (11/89) (9/94). *Prerequisite:* Introduction to Computer Systems Operations (MP-154).

CICS/ESA 4.1 Programming (11947, 11949)

Location: Computer-based.

Length: Self-paced.

Dates: December 1996-Present.

Objective: To design, code, and use BMS maps and page building.

Learning Outcome: Upon successful completion of this course, the student will be able to design, code, and use BMS; and discuss program structure, control, and commands to use the Execution Diagnostic Facility (EDF).

Instruction: Major topics covered in the course are introduction to designing and coding MNS Maps, using BMS Maps, program structure and control, file handling commands, temporary storage and transient data, and execution diagnostic facility. Methods of instruction include student guide and computer-based instruction for self-study.

Credit Recommendation: In the lower division baccalaureate/associate degree category, 1 semester hour in Computer Science or Computer Information Systems (5/97). **NOTE:** Students must complete 2 of 2 modules to receive credit.

COBOL for MVS and VM (11954, 12009, 11955) 11980

Location: Computer-based.

Length: Self-paced.

Dates: September 1996-Present.

Objective: To introduce COBOL programming for MVS and VM.

Learning Outcome: Upon successful completion of this course, the student will be able to write COBOL programs and use COBTEST as a debugging tool.

Instruction: Major topics covered in the course are introduction to programming fundamentals, defining data fields and data types, defining data and structuring the Procedure Division, initializing data fields and editing numeric data, writing a report program, performing arithmetic operations, coding alternative processing, presenting data and records, combining repetitive statement, control break processing, file handling, sorting, performing setup and displaying panels, and running a COBTEST session. Methods of instruction include student guide and computer-based instruction for self-study.

Credit Recommendation: In the lower division baccalaureate/associate degree category, 2 semester hours in COBOL Programming (5/97). **NOTE:** Students must complete 4 of 4 modules to receive credit.

COBOL Programming (MP-230)

Location: National Cryptologic School, Ft. Meade, MD.

Length: 72 hours (8 weeks).

Dates: August 1969-September 1987.

Objective: To teach students to write, debug, and document computer programs in COBOL compiler language.

Instruction: Major topics covered in the course are the mechanics of COBOL, use and syntactic aspects of the COBOL language, punctuation and coding sheet rules, data structure, types of data items, file and record description entries, use of I/O, arithmetic, data manipulation, switching and linkage verbs, arithmetic and conditional expressions, defining tables with emphasis on retrieval methods, and writing and debugging of at least three COBOL programs. Method of instruction is self-paced program instruction approach with access to instructor when needed.

Credit Recommendation: In the lower division baccalaureate/associate degree category, 3 semester hours in Data Processing (11/75) (12/80) (11/89). *Prerequisite:* Introduction to Computer Science (MP-160) or equivalent.

Computer Graphics (MP-413)

Location: National Cryptologic School, Ft. Meade, MD.

Length: *Version 1:* 48 hours (2 hours per day, 2 days per week for 12 weeks); *Version 2:* 96 hours (4 hours a day for 6 weeks).

Dates: March 1985-December 1994.

Objective: To enable the student to prepare graphic applications programs using the Professional Hierarchical Interactive Graphic System (PHIGS), an emerging ANSI standard.

Learning Outcome: Upon successful completion of this course, the student will be able to code, compile, debug, and execute graphics applications programs of moderate difficulty; understand three-dimensional concepts and hidden-surface and hidden-line concepts; and design a user interface.

Instruction: Major topics covered in the course are graphics systems, output primitives, attributes of output primitives, two- and three-dimensional transformations, hidden-surfaces and hidden-lines, and user interface design. Methods of instruction include lecture, classroom exercises, demonstrations, and laboratory exercises.

Credit Recommendation: In the upper division baccalaureate degree category, 3 semester hours in Computer Engineering, Computer Science, or Electrical Engineering (11/89) (9/94).

Computer Hardware Organization (MP-410) (Formerly Modern Computer Architecture [MP-410])

Location: National Cryptologic School, Ft. Meade, MD.

Length: 40-48 hours (5 weeks).

Dates: September 1973-Present.

Objective: To provide an introduction to hardware computer system design, organization, and operation.

Learning Outcome: Upon successful completion of this course, the student will be able to express the terminology used by computer hardware designers; communicate with computer engineers; design on a small scale, some computer sub-system circuits such as counters, decoders, encoders, and adders; and understand the concepts of arithmetic-logic units, control units, and memory circuits.

Instruction: Major topics covered in the course are Boolean algebra, hardware circuitry, elementary digital computer design, subcomponent design, high-speed arithmetic techniques, implementation of arithmetic operations, control operations, input/output operation, and storage techniques. Methods of instruction include lecture, discussion, classroom exercises, learner/presentation reports, homework, and design projects.

Credit Recommendation: In the lower division baccalaureate/associate degree category, 3 semester hours in Management Information Systems or Data Processing (11/75) (12/80) (11/89) (9/94). *Prerequisite:* Successful completion of an assembly language programming course.

Computer Protection (MP-404)

Location: National Cryptologic School, Ft. Meade, MD.

Length: *Version 1:* 40 hours (2 hours per day, 2 days per week for 10 weeks); *Version 2:* 60 hours (10 weeks).

Dates: *Version 1:* July 1985-February 1991; *Version 2:* March 1991-August 1996.

Objective: *Version 1:* To provide the computer professional with a knowledge of computer security theory and applications. *Version 2:* To provide the student with an understanding of computer security theory and application.

Learning Outcome: *Version 1:* Upon successful completion of this course, the student will be able to understand the hierarchical guidelines for developing trusted computer systems; understand password management; and formally specify and verify trusted computing systems. *Version 2:* Upon successful completion of this course, the student will be able to demonstrate understanding of hierarchical guidelines for developing trusted computer systems; understand password management; specify and verify trusted computer systems; and demonstrate ability to design a mock system.

Instruction: *Version 1:* Major topics covered in the course are risk assessment and vulnerabilities, physical environment, access controls, and incidental and intentional threats. Methods of instruction include lecture, classroom exercises, demonstrations, and laboratory exercises. *Version 2:* Major topics covered in the course are risk assessment and vulnerabilities; physical environment and access controls; incidental and intentional threats; formal specifications, verifications, and models; security of information storage and transmission; and encryption and architectural security considerations. Methods of instruction include lecture, discussion, laboratory exercises, course paper, and examinations.

Credit Recommendation: *Version 1:* In the lower division baccalaureate/associate degree category, 2 semester hours in Computer Science or Computer Security (11/89). *Version 2:* In the upper division baccalaureate degree category, 3 semester hours in Computer Science, Management Information Systems, or Computer Security (8/91).

CRAY (UNICOS) Advanced Technical Skills (MP-1K6) (Formerly Phase VI CDC 7600 System (IDA) Advanced Technical Skills)

Location: National Cryptologic School, Ft. Meade, MD.

Length: 35-40 hours (1 week).

Dates: *Version 1:* July 1972-August 1994; *Version 2:* September 1994-Present.

Objective: To provide the experienced operator with an in-depth understanding from an operational viewpoint of the internal functions of the CDC 7600 IDA Operating System software.

Instruction: Major topics covered in the course include an in-depth study of the concepts and facilities of the CDC 7600 IDA operating system and the use of its job control statements. Methods of instruction include computer-assisted instruction (CAI).

Credit Recommendation: *Version 1:* In the lower division baccalaureate/associate degree category, 1 semester hour in Data Processing (9/77) (11/82) (11/89) *Version 2:* In the vocational certificate category, 1 semester hour in Data Processing (9/94). *Prerequisite:* FORTRAN for Operators (MP-166) and Phase V CDC 7600 System (IDA) Software Concepts (MP-1K5).

CV-3440 Telephone Converter-Digitizer Maintenance (EM-130)

Location: National Cryptologic School, Ft. Meade, MD.

Length: 40 hours (1 week).

Dates: October 1976-September 1994.

Objective: To provide the student with the ability to perform limited maintenance on the CV-3440 Telephone Converter Digitizer to the lowest replaceable unit level.

Learning Outcome: Upon successful completion of this course, the student will be able to perform limited maintenance on the CV-3440 Telephone Converter Digitizer.

Instruction: Major topics covered in the course are decibel principles; signaling concepts; characteristics, configurations, and options of the CV-3440; block diagram analysis; detailed logic diagram analysis; alignment; and troubleshooting. Methods of instruction include lecture, discussion, laboratory exercises, and an examination.

Credit Recommendation: In the vocational certificate category, 1 semester hour in Digital Electronics Equipment Maintenance (8/91). **NOTE:** This course and one other EM series must be completed in order to receive 1 credit.

Database Design (MP-479)

Location: National Cryptologic School, Ft. Meade, MD.

Length: 60 hours (10 weeks).

Dates: January 1991-Present.

Objective: To provide the student with the understanding of theory and techniques involved in the relational database design process.

Learning Outcome: Upon successful completion of this course, the student will be able to design databases tailored to user requirements.

Instruction: Major topics covered in the course are conceptual database design (entity-relationship, diagram development, and manipulation into normal form); logical database design (techniques for translating ER diagrams into relational data model schema and algorithms for normalizing relational schema); and physical database design (overview of physical database design considerations). Methods of instruction include lecture, discussion, classroom projects, optional homework, and examinations.

Credit Recommendation: In the upper division baccalaureate degree category, 3 semester hours in Computer and Information Sciences or Management Information Systems (8/91) (9/96).

DB2 SQL (12018, 12299) 12300, 12302

Location: Computer-based.

Length: Self-paced.

Dates: January 1997-Present.

Objective: To develop code using SQL.

Learning Outcome: Upon successful completion of this course, the student will be able to code, retrieve, and manipulate embedded SQL statements and prepare a VS/COBOL program using SQL statements.

Instruction: Major topics covered in the course are introduction to embedding SQL statements, preparing programs for execution, data definition language (DDL), data control language (DCL), basic SELECT statements, advanced SELECT statements, selection from multiple tables, and writing embedded SQL and CICS, JCL, and CICS/DB2 interface. Methods of instruction include student guide and computer-based instruction for self-study.

Credit Recommendation: In the lower division baccalaureate/associate degree category, 1 semester hour in Computer Science or Computer Information Systems (5/97). **NOTE:** Students must complete 4 of 4 modules to receive credit.

Fiber Optic Theory and Maintenance Techniques (EM-523)

Location: National Cryptologic School, Ft. Meade, MD.

Length: 40 hours (1 week).

Dates: January 1991-Present.

Objective: To provide knowledge and skills necessary to install and test fiber optic systems.

Learning Outcome: Upon successful completion of this course, the student will be able to install, maintain, and test fiber optic systems using proper safety equipment and procedures to meet specific installation criteria.

Instruction: Major topics covered in the course are safety procedures, single and multimode optic connector assembly, splicing of light guide fibers, CSL (cleave-sleeve-leave) splicing, rotary mechanical splicing, and fusion splicing. Methods of instruction include classroom exercises, observations, and tested practical application exercises.

Credit Recommendation: In the vocational certificate category, 2 semester hours in Electronics Engineering Technology or Telecommunications (9/96). **NOTE:** Since this course includes topics taught in TC-C02 (CBT), credit can be given for EM 523 or TC C02, but not for both courses.

Fiber Optic Transmission Theory (CBT) (TC-C02)

Location: National Cryptologic School, Ft. Meade, MD and other DoD locations.

Length: 16 hours (self-paced).

Dates: January 1991-Present.

Objective: To introduce students to fiber optic transmission including optical waveguide theory, optical fibers and cables, terminals and system layout, and fiber optic testing.

Learning Outcome: Upon successful completion of this course, the student will be able to define optical terms related to transmission of light waves; identify fiber optic materials such as cables and connectors; observe safety precautions when working with fiber optic cable; differentiate between various types of optical sources such as LEDs and lasers; identify various components of a fiber optic system; and test components.

Instruction: Major topics covered in the course are fiber optical waveguide theory, optical fibers and cables, optical terminals and system layout, and fiber optic testing. Methods of instruction is audio/visual material, Computer-Based-Training (CBT), a course manual, and a final examination.

Credit Recommendation: In the vocational certificate category, 1 semester hour in Fiber Optics or Telecommunications (9/96).

FORTRAN Programming (MP-227)

Location: National Cryptologic School, Ft. Meade, MD.

Length: 45 hours (5 weeks).

Dates: December 1974-Present.

Objective: To write programs in structured FORTRAN.

Instruction: Major topics covered in the course are a detailed examination of the structured programming constructs, specifically, their implementation in FORTRAN; writing and debugging of at least four FORTRAN programs; and presentation of various programming techniques useful in the efficient solution of frequently encountered problems. Methods of instruction include lecture, discussion, and computer usage.

Credit Recommendation: In the lower division baccalaureate/associate degree category, 2 semester hours in Data Processing or Management Information Systems (11/75) (12/80) (11/89) (9/94). *Prerequisite:* Introduction to Computing or equivalent.

Fundamentals of Digital Signal Processing (EA-181)

Location: National Cryptologic School, Ft. Meade, MD.

Length: 60 hours (10 weeks).

Dates: *Version 1:* January 1985-August 1996; *Version 2:* September 1996-Present.

Objective: To provide the student with an understanding of mathematics associated with digital signal processing.

Learning Outcome: Upon successful completion of this course, the student will be able to specify properties of digital systems and discuss ramifications; translate descriptions of linear difference equations into spectral properties of the networks that implement them; construct algorithms to perform Fast Fourier Transforms/Chirp Z Transforms and determine the computational savings resulting from their use; design and implement a variety of useful digital filter designs; and use discrete transforms and the discrete spectral domain to demodulate a variety of keyed signals.

Instruction: Major topics covered in the course are discrete time functions, convolution and correlation, Z transforms, transfer functions, discrete Fourier transform, fast Fourier transform, FIR digital filters, and IIR digital filters. Methods of instruction include lecture, discussion, homework assignments, and an examination.

Credit Recommendation: *Version 1:* In the vocational certificate category, 2 semester hours in Electrical Engineering Technology (8/91). *Version 2:* In the lower division baccalaureate/associate degree category or the upper division baccalaureate degree category, 2 semester hours in Electrical or Electronic Engineering Technology (9/96).

Fundamentals of Optics and Lasers (EA-179)

Location: National Cryptologic School, Ft. Meade, MD.

Length: 36 hours (4 weeks).

Dates: September 1981-September 1996.

Objective: To provide the student with the knowledge of fiber optic and laser theory, applications, and optical processing techniques.

Learning Outcome: Upon successful completion of this course, the student will be able to define and illustrate terms used in physical optics; discuss types of lasers and their modulation techniques; discuss lasers as communication systems, radars, and hologram sources; and define and illustrate terms used in optical fiber transmission.

Instruction: Major topics covered in the course are reflection, refraction, dispersion, diffraction, color, polarization, lasers and laser application, infrared, electrooptics, holograph, and fiber optics and optical processing. Methods of instruction include lecture, discussion, classroom exercises, and examination.

Credit Recommendation: In the vocational certificate category, 1 semester hour in Electrical Engineering Technology or Applied Physics (8/91).

Fundamentals of Radar (EA-165)

Location: National Cryptologic School, Ft. Meade, MD.

Length: *Version 1:* 45 hours (5 weeks); *Version 2:* 80 hours, CBT (self-based).

Dates: *Version 1:* September 1981-August 1996; *Version 2:* September 1996-March 1997.

Objective: *Version 1:* To provide the student with knowledge of principles of radar technology and the applications and characteristics of modern radar systems at a technical level. *Version 2:* To provide the student with the fundamentals of radar technology including unique types of modulation techniques and collection of data.

Learning Outcome: *Version 1:* Upon successful completion of this course, the student will be able to demonstrate technical knowledge of radar systems, their characteristics, applications, and solve radar equation codes. *Version 2:* Upon successful completion of this course, the student will be able to identify various types of modulated signals; describe the working of complete radar system; and execute collection operations.

Instruction: *Version 1:* Major topics covered in the course are introduction to radar, the radar range equation, pulsed radar, CW radar, MTI and pulsed Doppler, modulation techniques, ECM/ECCM, over-the-horizon detection scanning techniques, and antennas and radar applications. Methods of instruction include lecture, discussion, field trip, and an examination. *Version 2:* Major topics covered in the course are mathematical concepts of radar systems, waveform analysis, modulation techniques, radar components, range equations, scan types, radar characteristics, CW & FM-CW radar, radar applications, and basic operational concepts of data collection and detection scanning techniques. Methods of instruction include audio-visual material, computer-assisted instruction, and reference books.

Credit Recommendation: *Version 1:* In the vocational certificate category, 1 semester hour in Radar Technology (8/91). *Version 2:* In the lower division baccalaureate/associate degree category, 2 semester hours in Telecommunications or Electronics Engineering Technology (9/96).

Fundamentals of Radio Wave Propagation (EA-172)

Location: National Cryptologic School, Ft. Meade, MD.

Length: 27 hours (3 weeks).

Dates: September 1981-Present.

Objective: To provide the student with the knowledge of electromagnetic wave propagation and the effects various media have on wave propagation.

Learning Outcome: Upon successful completion of this course, the student will be able to predict and identify effects of ionospheric variations, troposphere, frequencies, antennas, and transmission media on radio wave propagation.

Instruction: Major topics covered in the course are the nature of radio waves, the atmosphere, radio wave properties, atmospheric effects on radio waves, radio frequency bands and their applications, antennas, and propagation loss calculations. Methods of instruction include lecture, discussion, classroom demonstrations, and an examination.

Credit Recommendation: In the vocational certificate category, 1 semester hour in Radio Communication Technology or Electronics Technology (8/91) (9/96).

Fundamentals of Relational Databases (MP-275)

Location: National Cryptologic School, Ft. Meade, MD.

Length: 45 hours (5 weeks).

Dates: February 1991-Present.

Objective: To provide the student with the knowledge of database systems for database designers and application developers.

Learning Outcome: Upon successful completion of this course, the student will be able to understand basic, underlying concepts and terminology of data base management systems with primary emphasis on the relational model.

Instruction: Major topics covered in the course are theory of relational databases and principles of relational database design; data modeling (entity-relationship); normalization; and structured query language concepts. Methods of instruction include lecture, discussion, laboratory exercises, homework assignments, projects, and an examination.

Credit Recommendation: In the lower division baccalaureate/associate degree category, 2 semester hours; or in the upper division (elective) baccalaureate degree category, 2 semester hours; or in the upper division baccalaureate (for CIS or MIS majors) degree category, 1 semester hour in Computer and Information Sciences or Management Information Systems (8/91) (9/96).

Fundamentals of Spread Spectrum (EA-161)

Location: National Cryptologic School, Ft. Meade, MD.

Length: *Version 1:* 27 hours (3 weeks); *Versions 2 and 3:* 33 hours (11 classes, 2-3 hours per week).

Dates: *Versions 1 and 2:* September 1981-August 1996; *Version 3:* September 1996-Present.

Objective: To provide the student with knowledge of spread spectrum modulation techniques.

Learning Outcome: Upon successful completion of this course, the student will be able to sketch and label block diagrams for several spread spectrum modulation techniques and perform calculations relative to parameters associated with spread spectrum modulation techniques as applied to communication systems problems.

Instruction: *Version 1:* Major topics covered in the course are basic spread spectrum system elements; frequency hopping; time hopping; and direct sequence signals. Methods of instruction include lecture, discussion, laboratory exercises, and an examination. *Versions 2 and 3:* Major topics covered in the course include frequency hopping; time hopping; direct sequence; hybrid modulation types; synchronization and acquisition; processing gain; jamming margin; spreading codes; gold codes; error correcting codes; and correlation. Methods of instruction include lecture, discussion, homework exercises, guest speakers, laboratory tours, and examinations.

Credit Recommendation: *Versions 1 and 2:* In the vocational certificate category, 1 semester hour in Electrical Engineering Technology (8/91). *Version 3:* In the lower division baccalaureate/ associate degree category, 1 semester hour in Electrical or Electronic Engineering Technology (9/96).

Fundamentals of TECHELINT (EA-279)

Location: National Cryptologic School, Ft. Meade, MD.

Length: 120 hours, CBT (self-paced).

Dates: September 1996-Present.

Objective: To enhance the existing skills of personnel performing the duties of technicians and operators at Electronic Intelligence (ELINT) collection sites or analysis centers.

Learning Outcome: Upon successful completion of this course, the student will be able to apply proper collection procedures to pre-detection, routine, new, or unusual electronic intelligence signals; perform amplitude, time, and frequency measurements of ELINT signals; and identify capabilities and limitations of equipment for analysis of ELINT signals.

Instruction: Major topics covered in the course are mathematical concepts of radar systems, waveform analysis, modulation techniques, radar components, range equations, scan types, radar characteristics, applications using various types of radars, data collection operations and analysis, safety procedures, signal processing equipment, and signal sources and signal analysis techniques using scan and pulse analysis. Methods of instruction include computer-assisted instruction and reference books.

Credit Recommendation: In the lower division baccalaureate/associate degree category, 3 semester hours in Telecommunications or Electronics Engineering Technology (9/96). **NOTE:** Credit can be given for EA-172 or EA-165, but not both.

General DB2 Version 4 Track (12016, 12017, 12065)

Location: Computer-based.

Length: Self-paced.

Dates: August 1997-Present.

Objective: To introduce concepts, terminology, structural components, and facilities associated with the DB2 release 4 environment including: QMF, Utilities, and Operating Techniques.

Learning Outcome: Upon successful completion of this course, the student will be able to explain the concepts, terminology, structural components, and facilities associated with the DB2 release 4 environment including: QMF, Utilities, and Operating Techniques.

Instruction: Major topics covered in the course are DB2 Objects, the system environment and SQL, programming environment and SQL and application cycle, referential integrity and distributed processing; getting started in QMF, query processing in SQL and QBE, formatting reports, executing and monitoring DB2 Utilities, database preventive maintenance, maintaining database integrity; starting monitoring and stopping DB2, and controlling DB2 subsystem connections. Methods of instruction include student guide and computer-based instruction for self-study.

Credit Recommendation: In the lower division baccalaureate/associate degree category, 1 semester hour in Computer Science or Computer Information Systems (5/97). **NOTE:** Student must complete modules 12016 and at least another module (12017 or 12065) to receive credit.

General Programming Techniques (MP-430)

Location: National Cryptologic School, Ft. Meade, MD.

Length: 60 hours (12 weeks).

Dates: June 1974-Present.

Objective: To provide a background in the use of advanced general techniques in programming.

Learning Outcome: Upon successful completion of this course, the student will be able to demonstrate an understanding of the various techniques available in developing modular, structured, modifiable, and maintainable software; select and implement the appropriate algorithm to solve various types of programming problems; understand data management techniques including data structures, file structures, data compression, data communications, and dynamic storage; and understand linear and dynamic programming techniques and various sorting and searching methods.

Instruction: Major topics covered in the course are top-down design, structured programming, sorting, table look-up techniques, dynamic programming, data structures, dynamic storage allocation, character strings, data compression, and profiling. Methods of instruction include lecture, discussion, laboratory, computer-assisted instruction, and a group project.

Credit Recommendation: In the upper division baccalaureate degree category, 3 semester hours in Computer Science (11/75) (12/80) (11/89) (9/94). *Prerequisites:* Introduction to Computing or equivalent; FORTRAN Programming (MP-227) or equivalent; and Introduction to Computer Science Mathematics (MA-400) or equivalent.

IBM 360 System Software (OS) (MP-1D5)

Location: National Cryptologic School, Ft. Meade, MD.

Length: 40 hours (5 days).

Dates: July 1971-September 1975.

Objective: To introduce the student to technical concepts of OS/360.

Instruction: Major topics covered in the course are reviews 360 hardware features relevant to OS operations; explains the operating system components and their interrelationships, including interrupt systems, principles of multiprogramming and Job Control Language (JCL), critical OS utilities and Recovery Management Support functions. Instruction by lecture and discussion.

Credit Recommendation: In the vocational certificate category, 2 semester hours in Data Processing; or in the lower division baccalaureate/associate degree category, 1 semester hour in Data Processing (11/75) (12/80) (11/89). *Prerequisite:* IBM 360 (MP-1A4) or equivalent.

IBM 370 MVS Advanced Technical Skills (MP-156)

Location: National Cryptologic School, Ft. Meade, MD.

Length: 70 hours (2 weeks).

Dates: *Version 1:* July 1976-August 1994; *Version 2:* September 1994-Present.

Objective: To provide the experienced operator with an in-depth understanding from an operational viewpoint of the internal functions of the 370 MVS Operating System software.

Learning Outcome: Upon successful completion of this course, the student will be able to understand in-depth, MVS statement structure, syntax, and job organization; understand DSAD and storage access methods in detail; know major MVS utility calls and uses; and read and analyze ABEND dumps.

Instruction: Major topics covered in the course are the concepts and facilities of the 370 MVS Operating System and the use of its job control statements; emphasis on data management operations (including VSAM); system utilities; and 3850 Mass Storage System. Methods of instruction include quizzes and examination.

Credit Recommendation: *Version 1:* In the lower division baccalaureate/associate degree category, 2 semester hours in Data Processing (9/77) (11/82) (11/89). *Version 2:* In the vocational certificate category, 2 semester hours in Data Processing (9/94). *Prerequisite:* FORTRAN for Operators (MP-166) and Introduction to the 370 MVS Operating System (MP-1S5).

IBM 370 MVS Operating System (MP-1S5)

Location: National Cryptologic School, Ft. Meade, MD.

Length: 35-40 hours (1 week).

Dates: *Version 1:* July 1976-August 1994; *Version 2:* September 1994-Present.

Objective: To enhance the apprentice operator's ability to interact with the 370 Operating System software.

Learning Outcome: Upon successful completion of this course, the student will be able to understand IBM 370 hardware; MVS operation system; remote job entry subsystem; teleprocessing environment; job control language; and storage access methods.

Instruction: Major topics covered in the course are an overview of the concepts and facilities of the 370 MVS Operating System and the use of its job control statements and introduction to data management (including VSAM). Methods of instruction include self-paced study in a learning center.

Credit Recommendation: *Version 1:* In the lower division baccalaureate/associate degree category, 2 semester hours in Data Processing (9/77) (11/82) (11/89). *Version 2:* In the vocational certificate category, 2 semester hours in Data Processing (9/94). *Prerequisite:* Introduction to Computer Systems Operations (MP-154).

IBM Assembly Language Programming (MP-335) (Formerly IBM 370 Programming [MP-335])

Location: National Cryptologic School, Ft. Meade, MD.

Length: 100 hours (5 weeks).

Dates: July 1974-June 1988.

Objective: To teach the student programming in the IBM 370 assembler language.

Instruction: Major topics covered in the course are the standard instruction set; how to write instructions in both the symbolic and explicit forms; how to use macros involving QSAM access; how to make use of debugging aids, which include the dump macros and an interpretation of an OS hexadecimal dump; and how to write a structured program using IBM macros and the subroutine linkages between assembly language and FORTRAN programs. Methods of instruction include lecture, discussion, laboratory, and computer usage.

Credit Recommendation: In the lower division baccalaureate/associate degree category, 3 semester hours in Data Processing (11/75) (12/80) (11/89). *Prerequisite:* FORTRAN Programming (MP-227) or equivalent.

IBM Job Control Language (MP-368) (Formerly IBM 370 Job Control Language [MP-268])

Location: National Cryptologic School, Ft. Meade, MD.

Length: 54 hours (6 days).

Dates: *Version 1:* November 1969-December 1975; *Version 2:* January 1976-Present.

Objective: *Version 1:* To teach the preparation of control statements for the S360/OS. *MP-368* Version 2: To provide an introduction to Job Control Language (JCL) and enable the use JCL to effectively manage the execution of jobs.

Learning Outcome: Upon successful completion of this course, the student will be able to enter jobs into the IBM operating system; control the system's processing of jobs; and request the resources needed to run jobs.

Instruction: *Version 1:* Major topics covered in the course are discussion of syntax of job control language required to perform the elementary functions of job, task, and data management. *MP-368 Version 2:* Major topics covered in the course are substantially the same as Version 1 but use the IBM-370 computer, which replaced the IBM-360 computer. Methods of instruction include lecture, discussion, laboratory, and computer usage.

Credit Recommendation: *Version 1:* In the lower division baccalaureate/associate degree category, 1 semester hour in Data Processing; or in the vocational certificate category, 2 semester hours in Data Processing (11/75) (12/80) (11/89) (9/94). *Version 2:* In the lower division baccalaureate/associate degree category, 1 semester hour in Data Processing; or in the vocational certificate category, 2 semester hours in Data Processing (11/75) (12/80) (11/89) (9/94).

IBM OS/390 MVS/ESA5.x, Job Control Language (JCL) (12196, 12225)

Location: Computer-based.

Length: Self-paced.

Dates: July 1996-Present.

Objective: To introduce job submission, job control language, and interpreting JCL listing for error conditions and use advanced JCL coding for creating and accessing generation data groups (GDG).

Learning Outcome: Upon successful completion of this course, the student will be able to identify basic JCL components; interpret syntax notation used with JCL; code the most commonly used keyword parameters of the job statement; identify and use the PARM parameter; and code a referback between job steps and producers.

Instruction: Major topics covered in the course are introduction to coding JCL to create jobs and apply advanced JCL features. Methods of instruction include student guide, computer based instruction for self-study, and a text.

Credit Recommendation: In the lower division baccalaureate/associate degree category, 1 semester hour in Computer Science or Computer Information Systems (5/97). **NOTE:** Students must complete 1 of 2 modules to receive credit.

IBM OS/390 MVS/ESA5.x, Operations and Job Entry System 2 (JES2)

Location: Computer-based.

Length: Self-paced.

Dates: May 1997-Present.

Objective: To introduce tasks applicable to running the IBM OS/390 operating system and Job Entry System 2 (JES2).

Learning Outcome: Upon successful completion of this course, the student will be able to develop knowledge and skill to run the master console; load and shut down the operating system; and run JES2.

Instruction: Major topics covered in the course are introduction to understand the IPL process and the steps necessary to activate the system, perform a standalone dump, control syslog and SMF data output, compose MVS commands to control the operating system and identify which manuals are required for assistance, compose JES 2 command to control the submission, starting and control of batch jobs, and identify which manuals are required for assistance. Methods of instruction include student guide, computer based instruction for self-study, and a text.

Credit Recommendation: In the lower division baccalaureate/associate degree category, 1 semester hour in Computer Science or Computer Information Systems (5/97). **NOTE:** Students must complete at least 1 of the 2 modules for credit.

IBM OS/390 MVS/ESA5.x, Production and Development Tools (12227, 12228, 12231) 12232, 12301, 12330

Location: Computer-based.

Length: Self-paced.

Dates: November 1996-Present.

Objective: To introduce ISPF features used for programming, editing, compiling, linking, and testing programs with a COBOL orientation.

Learning Outcome: Upon successful completion of this course, the student will be able to display and edit databases; program using Restructured Extended Executor Language (REXX) for MVS; use ISPF dialogue manager; and select and execute utility programs.

Instruction: Major topics covered in the course are ISPF production and development tools, REXX programming, and selecting and executing utility programs. Methods of instruction include student guide, computer based instruction for self-study, and a text.

Credit Recommendation: In the lower division baccalaureate/associate degree category, 3 semester hours in Computer Science or Computer Information Systems (5/97). **NOTE:** Students must complete 6 of 6 modules to receive credit.

Implementing Microsoft Exchange Server (71361, 71362, 71363)

Location: Computer-based.

Length: Self-paced.

Dates: November 1996-Present.

Objective: To implement Microsoft Exchange in a single-site environment.

Learning Outcome: Upon successful completion of this course, the student will be able to install, configure, troubleshoot, and support Microsoft Exchange.

Instruction: Major topics covered in the course are fundamentals of Microsoft Exchange, designing an exchange organization, installing server and client, directory service, administration of mail related tasks, administration of message recipients and optional services, and migration to a Microsoft Exchange organization. Methods of instruction include materials available on CD-ROM, network, or intranet for self-study.

Credit Recommendation: In the lower division baccalaureate/associate degree category, 1 semester hour in Computer Science or Computer Information Systems (5/97). **NOTE:** Students must complete 3 of 3 modules to receive credit.

Information Transmission and Coding Basics (EA-182)

Location: National Cryptologic School, Ft. Meade, MD.

Length: *Version 1:* 27 hours (3 weeks); *Version 2:* 33 hours (11 classes, 2-3 hours per week).

Dates: January 1985-Present.

Objective: To provide the student with knowledge of information transmission through a communication system and the principles of algebraic coding used to represent that information.

Learning Outcome: *Version 1:* Upon successful completion of this course, the student will be able to explain the basic concepts of information transmission and algebraic coding; calculate the maximum amount of information a system can transmit successfully in a specified amount of time; and calculate the maximum signal information capacity given the characteristics of the information system. *Version 2:* Upon successful completion of this course, the student will be able to explain the basic concepts on information theory and describe the advantages and implementations of a variety of algebraic coding schemes.

Instruction: *Version 1:* Major topics covered in the course are communication fundamentals, applications of information theory, digital and binary concepts, channel capacity, noise, pulse-code modulation, Delta modulation, error-correcting coding, generation and resolution of coding schemes, efficiency and redundancy of specific codes, and application of coding schemes to communications problems. Methods of instruction include lecture, discussion, classroom exercises, and examination. *Version 2:* Major topics covered in the course are a review of communication fundamentals including SNR and BER; present material on entropy; information content; channel capacity; error-detecting codes; error correcting; block codes; hamming codes; variable-length codes; Hoffman codes; convolution codes; sequential decoding; and Viterbi decoding. Methods of instruction include lecture, discussion, homework exercises, guest speakers, lab tours, and examinations.

Credit Recommendation: *Versions 1 and 2:* In the vocational certificate category, 1 semester hour in Engineering Technology (8/91) (9/96).

INFOSEC Evaluation Using Formal Methods (IN-565) (Formerly [IN-565])

Location: National Cryptologic School, Ft. Meade, MD.

Length: 40 hours (1 week).

Dates: September 1990-September 1996.

Objective: To provide the student with an understanding of how to interpret design specifications and verification requirements in the Trusted Computer System Evaluation Criteria and how to evaluate evidence alleged to satisfy those requirements for A1 evaluations.

Learning Outcome: Upon successful completion of this course, the student will be able to identify A1 design specification and verification requirements; distinguish between acceptable and unacceptable evidence in evaluations; define types of covert channels and methods of analysis; and conduct and organize A1 verification evaluation activities.

Instruction: Major topics covered in the course are A1 requirements and evaluation process, formal model, formal top level specification (FTLS), descriptive top level specification (DTLS). and specification-to-code correspondence. Examples will cover how verification can be used with cryptographic Communications Security (COMSEC) products. Methods of instruction include lecture, discussion, classroom exercises and examination.

Credit Recommendation: In the upper division baccalaureate degree category, 1 semester hour in Computer and Information Science (8/91).

Interface Design (MP-328)

Location: National Cryptologic School, Ft. Meade, MD.

Length: *Version 1*: 36 hours (3 weeks): *Version 2*: 18 hours (15 weeks).

Dates: August 1990-August 1996.

Objective: To provide the student with the understanding of the guidelines and fundamental principles behind user interface design.

Learning Outcome: Upon successful completion of this course, the student will be able to design an effective user interface.

Instruction: Major topics covered in the course are software development and design; cognitive psychology in UI design; general design guidelines; basic interaction styles; writing effective error and status messages; hardcopy and softcopy documentation; on-line HELP; screen layout and design; relationship of object-oriented design to UP; comparison of MOTIF and OpenLook style specifications; window systems and managers; X programming environment, toolkits, and widget sets. Methods of instruction include lecture, discussion, classroom exercises, and an examination.

Credit Recommendation: In the lower division baccalaureate/associate degree category, 2 semester hours in Computer Science, Engineering or Information Systems Management (8/91).

Intermediate Technical ELINT Analysis (EA-280)

Location: National Cryptologic School, Ft. Meade, MD.

Length: 240 hours (6 weeks).

Dates: September 1996-Present.

Objective: To provide the student with necessary knowledge and skills to obtain accurate detailed signal measurements and parametric values from live, simulated, and/or magnetic recordings of electronic intelligence (ELINT) signals and prepare written reports based on their findings.

Learning Outcome: Upon successful completion of this course, the student will be able to perform technical ELINT analysis in a laboratory environment; and use analog generator, measurement, and display equipment like a dual-beam oscilloscope, frequency counter, fiber optics visicorder, digital signal analyzers, vectorscope, pulse stretcher, and signal monitors.

Instruction: Major topics covered in the course are an introduction to analog measurement instruments, scans, modulation types, and intrapulse modulation; signal analysis techniques; and report writing. Methods of instruction include lecture, learner presentations and reports, laboratory exercises, demonstrations, tests, laboratory examinations, and a final examination.

Credit Recommendation: In the lower division baccalaureate/associate degree category, 2 semester hours in Electronics Engineering Technology (9/96).

Interpretation of Computer Program (MP-434)

Location: National Cryptologic School, Ft. Meade, MD.

Length: 160 hours (4 weeks).

Dates: September 1989-August 1991.

Objective: To provide the student with the understanding of the process of designing and building software.

Learning Outcome: Upon successful completion of this course, the student will be able to design and write efficient computer programs.

Instruction: Major topics covered in the course are introduction to LISP; black box abstraction; data abstraction; metalinguistic abstraction; modularity; data objects and computational objects; data-directed programming; object-oriented programming; streams; pattern matching; programming language design; logic programming; and register-level programming. Methods of instruction include lectures, discussion, laboratory exercises, out-of-class exercises, and examinations.

Credit Recommendation: In the upper division baccalaureate degree category, 3 semester hours in Computer Science or Information Systems Management (8/91).

Introduction to Artificial Intelligence (MP-450)

Location: National Cryptologic School, Ft. Meade, MD.

Length: 60 hours (10 weeks).

Dates: January 1991-April 1995.

Objective: To provide the student with the knowledge of the design of computer systems that exhibit the characteristics associated with intelligence in human behavior.

Learning Outcome: Upon successful completion of this course, the student will be able to recognize different search algorithms, heuristic algorithm, chaining techniques, expert systems, and neural networks, and understand AI, and use LISP programming language.

Instruction: Major topics covered in the course are basic problem-solving methods (heuristic search, forward/backward reasoning, means-ends analysis, etc.); knowledge representation; expert systems; neural networks; and natural language understanding. Methods of instruction include lecture, discussion, classroom exercises, laboratory exercises, homework projects, and examinations.

Credit Recommendation: In the lower division baccalaureate/associate degree category, 2 semester hours in Computer and Information Sciences or Management Information Systems or in the upper division baccalaureate degree category, 2 semester hours non-Computer and Information Sciences or Management Information Systems majors (8/91). **NOTE:** At the upper division, credit granted only for non-CIS or MIS majors.

Introduction to C Programming (MP-160) (Introduction to Computing with C [MP-160])

Location: National Cryptologic School, Ft. Meade, MD; Anne Arundel Community College at Arundel Center North, Anne Arundel, MD.

Length: *Versions 1, 2, and 3:* 60 hours (6 weeks); *Version 4:* 80 hours (8 weeks).

Dates: *Version 1:* June 1966-October 1985; *Version 2:* November 1985-December 1989; *Version 3:* January 1990-April 1996; *Version 4:* May 1996-Present.

Objective: *Version 1:* To introduce underlying concepts in computing and to provide a base for programming language courses. *Version 2:* To introduce underlying concepts in computing and to provide a base for programming language courses. *Version 3:* To provide understanding of basic concepts of computer science using a high-level programming language (C). *Version 4:* To introduce techniques and principles utilized in computer programming using the C programming language.

Learning Outcome: Upon successful completion of this course, the student will be able to create well-documented programs using loops, arrays, and multiple functions emphasizing concepts of structured programming such as modularity and top-down design.

Instruction: *Version 1:* Major topics covered in the course are general consideration of computer history, number systems, con *Version 2:* Major topics covered in the course are general consideration of computer history, number systems, con *Version 3:* Major topics covered in the course are overview of program environment; introduction to Quick C; variables and data types; operators; input/output; control structures; arrays; and functions. *Version 4:* Major topics covered in the course are psuedocode, software development cycle, data types, and operators using printf and scanf, loop structures, and array structures and functions with parameters. Methods of instruction include lecture, discussion, classroom exercises, out-of-class assignments, laboratory exercises, and examinations.

Credit Recommendation: *Version 1:* In the lower division baccalaureate/associate degree category, 2 semester hours in Computer Science (11/75) (12/80). *Version 2:* In the lower division baccalaureate/associate degree category, 2 semester hours in Computer Science or Data Processing (11/89). *Version 3:* In the lower division baccalaureate/associate degree category, 3 semester hours in Computer Science, Computer Engineering, Data Processing, or Information Systems (8/91). *Version 4:* In the lower division baccalaureate/associate degree category or in the upper division baccalaureate degree category, 3 semester hours in Computer Information Systems, Computer Science, or Data Processing (9/96).

Introduction to Computer Networks (MP-414)

Location: National Cryptologic School, Ft. Meade, MD.

Length: 60 hours (2.5 hours/day, 2 days/week for 12 weeks).

Dates: December 1988-Present.

Objective: To provide the computer professional with a basic knowledge of computer communications and network concepts.

Learning Outcome: Upon successful completion of this course, the student will be able to understand data communications, networking, and local area networks and understand high speed LANs (local area networks).

Instruction: Major topics covered in the course are data transmission and encoding, multiplexing, communication networking techniques, packet switching, LAN topologies, protocols, security briefing, and network management briefing. Methods of instruction include lecture, tests, term papers, and article reviews.

Credit Recommendation: In the upper division baccalaureate degree category, 3 semester hours in Computer Engineering or Computer Science (11/89) (9/94).

Introduction to Computer Systems Operations (MP-154)

Location: National Cryptologic School, Ft. Meade, MD.

Length: *Version 1:* 70 hours (2 weeks); *Version 2:* 40 hours (5 days).

Dates: *Version 1:* June 1973-October 1989; *Version 2:* November 1989-Present.

Objective: *Version 1:* To provide an introduction to data processing terminology and methodology. *Version 2:* To provide the student with the knowledge of data processing terminology and methodology.

Learning Outcome: Upon successful completion of this course, the student will be able to serve as an apprentice operator on any NSA/CSS computer system.

Instruction: *Version 1:* Major topics covered in the course are computer history, numbering systems, components of digital computers, characteristics of assemblers and compilers, characteristics of I/O devices, and operating systems. Programming, specific types of business applications, and punch card processing are not emphasized. *Version 2:* Major topics covered in the course are computer history; numbering systems; components of digital computers; characteristics of memory, the ALU, and I/O devices; instruction and execution cycles; and advanced computer features. Methods of instruction include lecture, discussion, classroom exercises, and examinations.

Credit Recommendation: *Version 1:* In the lower division baccalaureate/associate degree category, 2 semester hours in Data Processing (9/77) (11/82) (11/89). *Version 2:* In the lower division baccalaureate/associate degree category, 2 semester hours in Data Processing (8/91).

Introduction to Network Communications with Microsoft TCP/IP for Windows NT 3.5x (80201-80202-70417) 70418

Location: Computer-based.

Length: Self-paced.

Dates: May 1996-Present.

Objective: To introduce the concepts and terminology of computer network communications and the features of TCP/IP for Windows NT 3.5x.

Learning Outcome: Upon successful completion of this course, the student will be able to explain the concepts of computer network communications, identify the features of TCP/IP, and explain how to install and configure an FTP server.

Instruction: Major topics covered in the course are terms and concepts of computer network communications; components of TCP/IP network; installing and configuring an FTP server. Methods of instruction include course materials available on CD-Rom for self-study, and tests.

Credit Recommendation: In the lower division baccalaureate/associate degree category, 1 semester hour in Telecommunications (9/96). **NOTE:** Students must complete 4 of 4 modules to receive credit.

Introduction to Satellites (EA-164)

Location: National Cryptologic School, Ft. Meade, MD.

Length: 39 hours (4 weeks).

Dates: March 1981-Present.

Objective: To provide the student with the knowledge of satellites, orbits, and orbital maneuvers and perturbations.

Learning Outcome: Upon successful completion of this course, the student will be able to use correctly terminology of satellites and orbits; determine orbital elements, coordinate systems and ephemerides; and determine the effect of orbital perturbations.

Instruction: Major topics covered in the course are basic physics of satellites and orbits, orbit perturbations, orbital elements, coordinate systems and ephemerides, orbital launch and maneuvers, and satellite subsystems. Methods of instruction include lecture, discussion, audiovisual aids, and an examination.

Credit Recommendation: In the vocational certificate category, 1 semester hour in Satellite Systems and Orbits (8/91) (9/96). **NOTE:** Credit cannot be earned for both this course and EC-250.

Introduction to Software Verification (IN-576) (Formerly [CP-550])

Location: National Cryptologic School, Ft. Meade, MD.

Length: 120 hours (3 weeks).

Dates: August 1987-August 1994.

Objective: To provide the student with an understanding of state-of-the-art verification techniques and practices.

Learning Outcome: Upon successful completion of this course, the student will be able to read, write, and execute basic specifications; understand first-order logic and verification systems; and develop and prove properties of formal specification.

Instruction: Major topics covered in the course are propositional logic predicate calculus; proving program correctness, and using two agency-endorsed formal verification tools (FDM and GYPSY). Methods of instruction include lecture, discussion, computer laboratory, practical exercises, and a final exam at the end of each week.

Credit Recommendation: In the upper division baccalaureate degree category, 2 semester hours in Computer Science or Computer Security (8/91).

Introduction to the UNIX Operating System (MP 318-C Shell Programming, MP 319-Bourne Shell Programming, MP 322-UNIX Software Tools, and MP 323-UNIX System Calls)

Location: National Cryptologic School, Ft. Meade, MD.

Length: *Version 1:* 112 hours (2 weeks, 4 days); *Version 2:* 120 to 128 hours (4 to 6 weeks).

Dates: *Version 1:* August 1989-August 1994; *Version 2:* September 1994-Present.

Objective: To provide in-depth information on specific features of the UNIX operating system.

Learning Outcome: Upon successful completion of this course, the student will be able to write shell programs with system calls and understand UNIX tools including SCSS, MAKE, AR, etc.

Instruction: Major topics covered in the course are file system layout, system calls, make files, shell variables, control constructs, interrupt handling and debugging, and other shell tools. Methods of instruction include lecture, in-class exercises, outside assignments, and examinations.

Credit Recommendation: *Version 1:* In the lower division baccalaureate/associate degree category, 2 semester hours in Computer Engineering, Computer Science, or Electrical Engineering (11/89). *Version 2:* In the lower division baccalaureate/associate degree category, 3 semester hours in Computer Science or Management Information Systems (9/94). **NOTE:** Student must complete MP-322 and MP-323 and either MP-318 or MP-319.

Introduction to WHIPPOORWILL Analysis (EA-105)

Location: National Cryptologic School, Ft. Meade, MD.

Length: 72 hours (2 weeks).

Dates: August 1990-December 1992.

Objective: To provide the student with an introductory knowledge of digital signals analysis fundamentals in preparation for training in the WHIPPOORWILL system.

Learning Outcome: Upon successful completion of this course, the student will know basic definitions and mathematics of digital signal processes; understand basic principles of digitization and digital filters; and understand basic organization and function of computers.

Instruction: Major topics covered in the course are computer hardware/software, theory and types of digitization, system throughput, digital filtering, and basic mathematics used for digital analysis. Methods of instruction include lecture, discussion, laboratory exercises, and examination.

Credit Recommendation: In the vocational certificate category, 1 semester hour in Digital Signals Analysis (8/91).

LNR-70 Microwave Receiver Maintenance (EM-522)

Location: National Cryptologic School, Ft. Meade, MD.

Length: 40 hours (1 week).

Dates: July 1989-August 1996.

Objective: To provide the student with the knowledge necessary to perform preventive and corrective maintenance on the LNR-70 microwave receiver.

Learning Outcome: Upon successful completion of this course, the student will be able to perform preventive and corrective maintenance to the LRU level on the LNR-70 microwave receiver.

Instruction: Major topics covered in the course are function of controls and indicators, functional theory of operation, test and alignment procedures, LRU failure analysis, preventive maintenance procedures, and fault isolation and corrective maintenance. Methods of instruction include lecture, discussion, laboratory exercises, and an examination.

Credit Recommendation: In the vocational certificate category, 1 semester hour in Digital Electronics Maintenance (8/91). **NOTE:** This course and one more in the EM series must be completed to receive 1 credit.

Mathematics for SIGINT (EA-183) (Introduction to Technical Mathematics)

Location: National Cryptologic School, Ft. Meade, MD.

Length: 48 hours (2 weeks; also as self-paced course).

Dates: *Version 1:* July 1982-August 1996; *Version 2:* September 1996-Present.

Objective: To provide the student with the knowledge of basic technical mathematics associated with signals technology.

Learning Outcome: Upon successful completion of this course, the student will be able to solve mathematical problems using basic algebraic methods; apply basic trigonometric and logarithmic methods to solve problems in power level calculations; and translate numbers into different number systems.

Instruction: Major topics covered in the course are arithmetic and signed numbers, exponents, scientific notation, graphs, introduction to algebra, introduction to trigonometry, vectors, logarithms, decibels, and number systems. Methods of instruction include lecture, discussion, classroom exercises, an examination, or as self-paced course.

Credit Recommendation: *Version 1:* In the vocational certificate category, or in the lower division baccalaureate/associate degree category, 1 semester hour in Engineering Technology (8/91). *Version 2:* In the lower division baccalaureate/associate degree category, 1 semester hour in Technical Mathematics (9/96).

Microsoft SQL Server 6.0 System Administration and Database Design 70471-70472-70473-70475-70476-70477

Location: Computer-based.

Length: Self-paced.

Dates: April 1996-Present.

Objective: To identify system administration tasks that can be performed using Microsoft SQL Server 6.0 and provide a basic understanding of database design, simple data transfer and manipulation.

Learning Outcome: Upon successful completion of this course, the student will be able to understand the process by which Microsoft SQL 6.0 client/server systems interact and the fundamentals of database design and system components of SQL Server 6.0.

Instruction: Major topics covered in the course are installation techniques for the server and client; identify the process of automatic and custom synchronization; understanding of client/server database designs; management of disk space; table creation; different methods of data retrieval and manipulation, and the creation of views and indexes and their use. Methods of instruction include course materials available on CD-Rom for self-study, and tests.

Credit Recommendation: In the lower division baccalaureate/associate or upper division baccalaureate degree category, 1 semester hour in System Administration or Database Design (9/96). **NOTE:** Students must complete 6 of 6 modules to receive credit.

Microsoft Visual C++ Series (11676)

Location: Computer-based.

Length: Self-paced.

Dates: May 1996-Present.

Objective: To introduce Windows programming using Visual C++ and Microsoft Foundation Class.

Learning Outcome: Upon successful completion of this course, the students will be able to understand the essentials of Microsoft Visual C++ for developing Windows-based applications and identify features of Microsoft Foundation Class and the graphic tools of Visual C++.

Instruction: Major topics covered in the course are introduction of object, class program structure, inheritance, information hiding, identify, polymorphism, interface, analysis, associations and standards. Methods of instruction include course materials available on CD-Rom for self-study, and tests.

Credit Recommendation: In the upper division baccalaureate degree category, 1 semester hour in Programming (9/96).

Microsoft Windows 3.x 11144-11145-11569-11657-11712-11756-11829

Location: Computer-based.

Length: Self-paced.

Dates: December 1992-Present.

Objective: To introduce the fundamental applications of Microsoft Windows 3.x.

Learning Outcome: Upon successful completion of this course, the student will be able to perform basic Microsoft applications in Windows, Word 6.0, Excel 5.0, and either PowerPoint 4.0 or Access 2.0 and be able to apply skills to individual work.

Instruction: Major topics covered in the course are basic applications in Word 6.0 (development of basic document), Excel 5.0 (identification of fundamental features), PowerPoint 4.0 (screen elements and nativation) and/or Access 2.0 (fundamentals of a database). Methods of instruction include course materials available on CD-Rom for self-study, and tests.

Credit Recommendation: In the lower division baccalaureate/associate degree category, 1 semester hour in Computer Applications (9/96). **NOTE:** Students must complete 6 or 7 modules (electives included) to receive credit.

Microsoft Windows 95-Advanced 70012-70022-70032-70091

Location: Computer-based.

Length: Self-paced.

Dates: February 1996-Present.

Objective: To improve the basic understanding of Windows 95 and introduce advanced features of Windows 95.

Learning Outcome: Upon successful completion of this course, the student will be able to apply advanced Windows 95 applications using Word for 95 and Excel for 95 and understand the Windows 95 Office Integration environment.

Instruction: Major topics covered in the course are desktop customization, time savers, communications and networks, remote computing, import and export of text and data, data query and mapping. Methods of instruction include course materials available on CD-Rom for self-study, and tests.

Credit Recommendation: In the lower division baccalaureate/associate degree category, 1 semester hour in Computer Applications (9/96). **NOTE:** Students must complete 4 of 4 modules to receive credit.

Microsoft Windows 95-Fundamentals 70011-70021-70031-70041-70051-70061-70071-70081

Location: Computer-based.

Length: Self-paced.

Dates: August 1995-Present.

Objective: To introduce the basic features of Microsoft Windows 95 through completion of 6 of 8 modules involving Word for 95, Excel for 95, PowerPoint for 95, and Access for 95.

Learning Outcome: Upon successful completion of this course, the student will be able to use the basic features of Windows 95 applications software and demonstrate mastery of fundamental vocabulary of Windows 95 applications.

Instruction: Major topics covered in the course are fundamentals of Windows 95, Word, Excel, PowerPoint, and Access for Windows 95 and a basic knowledge of Scheduler+ and Microsoft Project. Methods of instruction include course materials available on CD-Rom for self-study, and tests.

Credit Recommendation: In the lower division baccalaureate/associate degree category, 1 semester hour in Computer Applications (9/96). **NOTE:** Students must complete 6 of 8 modules (electives included) to receive credit.

Microsoft Windows NT 4.0 Track 71410, 71411, 71412, 71413

Location: Computer-based.

Length: Self-paced.

Dates: January 1997-Present.

Objective: To present the concept involved in installing, configuring, customizing, and supporting Microsoft Windows NT Server 4.0.

Learning Outcome: Upon successful completion of this course, the student will be able to install, configure, customize, optimize, network, integrate, and troubleshoot Windows NT 4.0.

Instruction: Major topics covered in the course are introduction to Microsoft Windows, installing NT Server, configuring NT environment, user profiles and system policies, managing user and group accounts, managing file systems, fault tolerance, applications supported by the NT server, NT-based networking environment, network protocols, configuration, NT networking services, NT features, functions and tools related to server and workstation, security, subsystems, Kernel mode components, and remote access service (RAS) and telephony application programming interface (TAPI). Methods of instruction include materials available on CD-ROM, network, and intranet for self-study.

Credit Recommendation: In the lower division baccalaureate/associate degree category, 1 semester hour in Computer Science or Computer Information Systems (5/97). **NOTE:** Students must complete 4 of 4 modules to receive credit.

Model 204 File Manager (MP-385)

Location: National Cryptologic School, Ft. Meade, MD.

Length: 64 hours (4 hours a day, 2 days per week for 8 weeks).

Dates: July 1989-December 1994.

Objective: To provide the file manager with the information and skills needed to create, load, and maintain Model 204 data files.

Learning Outcome: Upon successful completion of this course, the student will be able to create and load database files; read Model 204 dumps; and maintain database files.

Instruction: Major topics covered in the course are basic file structures, tables, file attributes, creation of files, file space calculation, data dictionary, file integrity, job control language, introduction to indexed file access methods (IFAM), security, and recovery. Methods of instruction include lectures, classroom exercises, laboratory exercises, and outside assignments.

Credit Recommendation: In the lower division baccalaureate/associate degree category, 3 semester hours in Data Processing (11/89) (9/94).

Model 204 Information Retrieval Language (MP-185)

Location: National Cryptologic School, Ft. Meade, MD.

Length: 54 hours (6 weeks).

Dates: *Version 1:* June 1973-August 1994; *Version 2:* September 1994-Present.

Objective: To explain and demonstrate instructions for utilizing retrieval capabilities of the CCA Model 204 System.

Learning Outcome: Upon successful completion of this course, the student will be able to understand Model 204 database design; know the program language structure and syntax, program in the Model 204 language; and know the program loopery and process control techniques in the Model 204 language.

Instruction: Major topics covered in the course are general use of the Model 204 remote terminal; system control commands, including sign-on procedures and opening and closing files; retrieving stored information; outputting retrieved information in the format desired; performing arithmetic or conditional operations with stored information; updating or deleting old information; storing new information; and using the editor and functions. Methods of instruction include lecture, discussion, laboratory, and computer usage.

Credit Recommendation: *Version 1:* In the lower division baccalaureate/associate degree category or in the vocational certificate category, 2 semester hours in Data Processing (11/75) (12/80) (11/89). *Version 2:* In the vocational certificate category, 2 semester hours in Data Processing (9/94).

Model Interpretation (IN-575) (Formerly [CP-540])

Location: National Cryptologic School, Ft. Meade, MD.

Length: 40 hours (1 week).

Dates: August 1987-November 1994.

Objective: To provide the student with an understanding of the interpretation and application of formal computer security models.

Learning Outcome: Upon successful completion of this course, the student will be able to interpret and apply rules of formal security policy models and compare rules to a system's software to ensure compliance with formal security models.

Instruction: Major topics covered in the course are real-life examples, mathematics, and terminology of models; security and use of formal models; Bell and LaPadula model; Multics interpretation, SCOMP, XENIX; Bell's Network Model; transition security; non-interference; Military Message Model; integrity (denial of service); Brewer-Nash Chinese Wall model and its implementation in Bell-LaPadula format. Methods of instruction include lecture, discussion, classroom and out-of-class exercises, group project, and an examination.

Credit Recommendation: In the upper division baccalaureate degree category, 1 semester hour in Computer Science or Computer Engineering (8/91).

Modern Computer Architecture (MP-411)

Location: National Cryptologic School, Ft. Meade, MD.

Length: 48 hours (12 weeks).

Dates: April 1991-Present.

Objective: To provide the student with an understanding of the concepts of computer design including emphasis on various subsystems.

Learning Outcome: Upon successful completion of this course, the student will be able to perform comparative evaluation of alternative computer architectures as related to various hardware and operating system design operations.

Instruction: Major topics covered in the course are organization of modern computers with particular emphasis on large mainframe computers; computer organization; micro code (RISC v. VISC); bus structures; interrupt vectors; memory (RAM) organizations; instruction decoding and execution; and roles of instruction pipelines and cache. Methods of instruction include lecture, discussion, design projects, homework, and examinations.

Credit Recommendation: In the upper division baccalaureate degree category, 3 semester hours in Computer and Information Sciences (8/91) (9/96).

Modulation Methods (EA-162)

Location: National Cryptologic School, Ft. Meade, MD.

Length: 39 hours (5 weeks).

Dates: September 1981-August 1996.

Objective: To provide the student with an elementary understanding of methods of modulation and demodulation employed by analog and digital electrical communications.

Learning Outcome: Upon successful completion of this course, the student will be able to understand fundamentals of how communications systems modulate and demodulate, code, and decode and define technical terms employed in the description and use of communications equipment.

Instruction: Major topics covered in the course are fundamentals of modulation concepts, amplitude modulation, angle modulation, noise in signals, pulse amplitude modulation, pulse time modulation, digital modulation, data communication, frequency shift keying, phase shift keying, M-condition signals, and comparative analysis of modulations. Methods of instruction include lecture, discussion, and examinations.

Credit Recommendation: In the vocational certificate category, 1 semester hour in Radio Communication Technology or Electronic Technology (8/91).

Multichannel Crypto Controller (MC3) Maintenance (EM-114)

Location: National Cryptologic School, Ft. Meade, MD.

Length: 32 hours (4 days).

Dates: November 1986-July 1994.

Objective: To provide the student with the ability to operate and perform LRU maintenance on the Multichannel Crypto Controller.

Learning Outcome: Upon successful completion of this course, the student will be able to perform installation, set-up configuration parameters using a control terminal, and preventive and corrective maintenance to the LRU level on the MC3.

Instruction: Major topics covered in the course are technical characteristics, MC3 compatibility and installations, front panel operations, parameters and passwords, commands, programming block diagram, programming calculations, control terminal operation, signal analysis, and troubleshooting. Methods of instruction include lecture, laboratory exercises, and an examination.

Credit Recommendation: In the vocational certificate category, 1 semester hour in Digital Electronics Equipment Maintenance (8/91). **NOTE:** This course and one other EM series course must be completed in order to receive 1 credit.

Multiplexing Technology (EA-168)

Location: National Cryptologic School, Ft. Meade, MD.

Length: 35 hours (4 weeks).

Dates: *Version 1:* January 1981-August 1996; *Version 2:* September 1996-Present.

Objective: To provide the student with an understanding of characteristics, limitations, and applications of multiplexing technology.

Learning Outcome: Upon successful completion of this course, the student will be able to define terms and concepts of multiplexing technology, demonstrate technical knowledge of multiplexing technology characteristics and applications, and solve calculations.

Instruction: Major topics covered in the course are multiplexing, frequency and frequency management, CW and pulse signals and filters, frequency division multiplexing carrier systems, time division multiplexing carrier systems, code division multiplexing, and demultiplexing techniques. Methods of instruction include lecture, discussion, and examinations.

Credit Recommendation: *Version 1:* In the vocational certificate category, 1 semester hour in Electronics Technology (8/91). *Version 2:* In the vocational certificate category, 2 semester hours in Electronics Technology (9/96).

MVS/ESA 5.2 Debug and Analyze Program Problems (12329)

Location: Computer-based.

Length: Self-paced.

Dates: January 1997-Present.

Objective: To introduce concepts for debugging and analyzing program problems.

Learning Outcome: Upon successful completion of this course, the student will be able to locate errors in a dump to pinpoint logic and I/O errors.

Instruction: Major topics covered in the course are dump and debug concepts, program logic errors, I/O error debugging, additional I/O errors, and on-line debugging with IPCS. Methods of instruction include student guide and computer-based instruction for self-study.

Credit Recommendation: In the lower division baccalaureate/associate degree category, 1 semester hour in Computer Science or Computer Information Systems (5/97).

National Computer Security Course (CP-330-331) (Formerly CY-330/CY-331)

Location: National Cryptologic School, Ft. Meade, MD.

Length: 40 hours (1 week).

Dates: June 1984-September 1993.

Objective: To provide the student with a knowledge of global computer security issues, computer systems, and network security in the federal government.

Learning Outcome: Upon successful completion of this course, the student will be able to demonstrate sensitivity to the necessity of computer security; demonstrate basic understanding of computer security by applying security concepts in the workplace; recognize need for total systems planning; and understand DOD and other federal government computer security information.

Instruction: Major topics covered in the course are concepts and principles of computer security; policy development and procedural implementation in the workplace; technical evaluation of computer systems and network security; and assessment of vulnerabilities of computer systems. Methods of instruction include lecture, discussion, and classroom exercises.

Credit Recommendation: In the upper division baccalaureate degree category, 1 semester hour in Computer Science (8/91).

National INFOSEC Cadre Course (CS-230)

Location: National Cryptologic School, Ft. Meade, MD.

Length: 40 hours (1 week).

Dates: January 1986-September 1993.

Objective: To provide the student with the knowledge and skill required to be an INFOSEC instructor.

Learning Outcome: Upon successful completion of this course, the student will be able to conduct INFOSEC courses and develop other individuals as instructors.

Instruction: Major topics covered in the course are instructor training, INFOSEC overview, threat to U.S. communications, human threat, computer security overview, malicious codes, transmission security, audio penetration, INFOSEC cover and deception, foreign COMSEC tempest, COMSEC historical perspective, operation security, and COMSEC applications. Methods of instruction include lecture, discussion, videotapes, class presentations, and examinations.

Credit Recommendation: In the lower division baccalaureate/associate degree category, 1 semester hour in Political Science, Public Administration, or Public Affairs (8/91).

Network Technology Workshop (NT-250)

Location: National Cryptologic School, Ft. Meade, MD.

Length: 80 hours (2 weeks).

Dates: August 1996-Present.

Objective: To teach digital and analog communications maintenance technicians how to install and maintain local area networks and to differentiate between different LAN topologies and connectivity protocols.

Learning Outcome: Upon successful completion of this course, the student will be able to demonstrate an understanding of the trouble-shooting methods applied to local area networks (LANS), wide area networks (WANS), and internetworks.

Instruction: Major topics covered in the course are different network topologies and protocols; standards; network devices; network applications; TCP, UDP, and IP protocols; message and routing protocols; and ethernet FDDI and ring connectivity concepts. Methods of instruction include lecture, discussion, classroom exercises, and laboratory experiences.

Credit Recommendation: In the lower division baccalaureate/associate degree category, 3 semester hours in Data Communications, Computer Information Systems, or Computer Science (9/96).

Networking Essentials (70421, 70422, 70423)

Location: Computer-based.

Length: Self-paced.

Dates: November 1996-Present.

Objective: To introduce the concepts and terminology for local area and wide area networks.

Learning Outcome: Upon successful completion of this course, the student will be able to understand current networking technology for local and wide area networks.

Instruction: Major topics covered in the course are network operating system terms and definition, architectures and protocols, data transmission, network communication, standards, operating system, peripherals, and applications. Methods of instruction include materials available on CD-ROM and network or intranet for self-study.

Credit Recommendation: In the lower division baccalaureate/associate degree category, 1 semester hour in Computer Science or Computer Information Systems (5/97). **NOTE:** Students must complete 3 of 3 modules to receive credit.

Novell GroupWise 4 Administration

Location: Computer-based.

Length: Self-paced.

Dates: June 1996-Present.

Objective: To familiarize students with Novell GroupWise Administration and asynchronous gateways.

Learning Outcome: Upon successful completion of this course, the student will be able to explain the procedures to set up and maintain single and multiple post office systems; and explain how to manage async gateways.

Instruction: Major topics covered in the course are installing GroupWise to primary domains; administering single post offices and clients; working with multiple domains and post offices; and understanding async gateways and GroupWise remote. Methods of instruction include course materials available on CD-Rom for self-study, and tests.

Credit Recommendation: In the lower division baccalaureate/associate degree category, 1 semester hour in Network Administration (9/96).

Novell NetWare 4.1 Implementation and Administration 80301-80302-80311-80312-80401-80501

Location: Computer-based.

Length: Self-paced.

Dates: June 1996-Present.

Objective: To present the concepts involved in implementing and administrating Novell NetWare 4.1.

Learning Outcome: Upon successful completion of this course, the student will be able to explain to process involved in installing, upgrading, and configuring Novell NetWare 4.1.

Instruction: Major topics covered in the course are installing NetWare 4.1.; upgrading 3.1x to NetWare 4.1.; configuring a NetWare environment; and managing NetWare 4.1 server. Methods of instruction include course materials available on CD-Rom for self-study, and tests.

Credit Recommendation: In the lower division baccalaureate/associate degree category, 1 semester hour in System Administration (9/96). **NOTE:** Students must complete 6 of 6 modules to receive credit.

Novell NetWare 4.11 Administration 81301, 81302, 81303, 81311, 81312, 81313

Location: Computer-based.

Length: Self-paced.

Dates: February 1997-Present.

Objective: To administer performance tuning with Novell IntraNetWare 4.11.

Learning Outcome: Upon successful completion of this course, the student will be able to perform tasks associated with daily administration; do performance tuning for the network server; and design NetWare directory services (NDS) structure trees.

Instruction: Major topics covered in the course are server startup procedures, file configurations, network concepts, directory tree structures (DTS), client network support, map network and search drives, security, integrating and managing NetWare 3 servers, and configuration of the NetWare 4 servers for diverse clients. Methods of instruction include materials available on CD-ROM, network, or intranet for self-study.

Credit Recommendation: In the lower division baccalaureate/associate degree category, 2 semester hours in Computer Science or Computer Information Systems

(5/97). **NOTE:** Students must complete 6 of 6 modules to receive credit.

Novell NetWare 4.11 Installation, Service and Support 80211, 80212, 80213, 80214, 81401, 81402

Location: Computer-based.

Length: Self-paced.

Dates: February 1997-Present.

Objective: To install, configure, service and support Novell NetWare (intranet) version 4.11.

Learning Outcome: Upon successful completion of this course, the student will be able to explain the process of installation, configuration, troubleshooting, and supporting a Novell IntraNetWare 4.11.

Instruction: Major topics covered in the course are installing NetWare 4.11, upgrading 3.5x to NetWare 4.11, configuring in a NetWare environment, troubleshooting NetWare problems using the Micro House Technical Library, use Network Support Encyclopedia Professional (NSE Pro) volume, manage cabling and network boards, and identify steps involved in installing network boards and hard disks. Methods of instruction include computer-based training and testing.

Credit Recommendation: In the lower division baccalaureate/associate degree category, 2 semester hours in Computer Science or Computer Information Systems (5/97). **NOTE:**Must complete 6 of 6 modules to receive credit.

Object COBOL Series (11981)

Location: Computer-based.

Length: Self-paced.

Dates: May 1996-Present.

Objective: To introduce key concepts of object technology and its extension to COBOL language.

Learning Outcome: Upon successful completion of this course, the student will be able to understand object-oriented concepts and structure of object COBOL language.

Instruction: Major topics covered in the course are introduction of object, class program structure, inheritance, information hiding, identity, polymorphism, interface, analysis, associations, and standards. Methods of instruction include course materials available on CD-Rom for self-study, and tests.

Credit Recommendation: In the upper division baccalaureate degree category, 1 semester hour in Computer Science or Computer Information Systems (9/96).

Object-Oriented Development

Location: Computer-based.

Length: Self-paced.

Dates: April 1996-Present.

Objective: To introduce the basic concepts of object technology, define objects, introduce CRC, OMT and Booch notations, and dynamic modeling.

Learning Outcome: Upon successful completion of this course, the student will be able to understand the role of object technology in software development, the concepts of inheritance, polymorphism, representation of object, and classes, and representation of problems with CC, OMT and Booch notations, and dynamic modeling.

Instruction: Major topics covered in the course are basics of object technology, object-oriented life cycle; class responsibility collaboration (CRC) technique to identify objects, object-modeling techniques (OMT) and Booch notation, association and entertainment relations, inheritance, polymorphism, object-identify, and dynamic modeling. Methods of instruction include course materials available on CD-Rom for self-study, and tests.

Credit Recommendation: In the upper division baccalaureate degree category, 1 semester hour in Computer Science or Computer Information Systems (9/96). **NOTE:** Students must complete 3 of 3 modules to receive credit.

OLE Series (11982)

Location: Computer-based.

Length: Self-paced.

Dates: May 1996-Present.

Objective: To introduce rationale behind OLE, Windows Object Structured Storage Model, and Uniform Data Transfer technology.

Learning Outcome: Upon successful completion of this course, the student will be able to understand rationale behind OLE, concept of Windows object, component object model, structured storage model, and architecture of compound documents.

Instruction: Major topics covered in the course are rationale for use of Visual C++ environment, tools; MFC concepts, basics of drawing and painting; core MFC classes supporting Windows-based applications; and recognizing issues related to Visual C++ programming and the MFC. Methods of instruction include course materials available on CD-Rom for self-study, and tests.

Credit Recommendation: In the lower division baccalaureate/associate degree category, 1 semester hour in Microcomputer Applications (9/96).

Operating System Security Concepts (ND-272) (Formerly Operating System Security Analysis (IN-272) and Operating System Concepts [CP-420])

Location: National Cryptologic School, Ft. Meade, MD.

Length: 40 hours (1 week).

Dates: *Version 1 (CP-420):* February 1989-December 1995; *Version 2 (IN-272):* January 1996-Present.

Objective: *Version 1:* To provide the student with an understanding of various operating systems concepts and terminology in computer security mechanisms. *Version 2:* To provide the student with an understanding of various operating systems concepts and terminology in order to assess system security functionality and assurance.

Learning Outcome: *Version 1:* Upon successful completion of this course, the student will be able to understand basic computer operating system terminology, concepts, and principles and identify basic functions, architecture, structures, and processes; describe common methods for implementing I/O file systems; define how memory management works, virtual memory, and common methods of I/O file systems implementation; and explain typical threats and vulnerabilities to operating system security and countermeasures to combat them. *Version 2:* Upon successful completion of this course, the student will be able to read and comprehend a set of computer security requirements, select documentation on a given computer system, and analyze the system and decide if it complies with the specific security requirements.

Instruction: *Version 1:* Major topics covered in the course are operations systems services, operating system structures, processes, memory management, input/output, and file systems. Methods of instruction include lecture, discussion, group exercises, written assignments, and a final examination. *Version 2:* Major topics covered in the course are common criteria security requirements, management security issues, process management security, memory management security issues, security support service, network security, security assurance, and operational security. Methods of instruction include lecture, discussion, group exercises, written assignments, and a final examination.

Credit Recommendation: *Version 1:* In the upper division baccalaureate degree category, 1 semester hour in Computer Science or Operating Systems (8/91). *Version 2:* In the lower division baccalaureate/associate degree category or in the upper division baccalaureate degree category, 1 semester hour in Computer Information Systems, Data Processing, or Computer Science (9/96).

Operational Computer Security (ND225) (Formerly Operational Computer Security (CP-202))

Location: National Cryptologic School, Ft. Meade, MD.

Length: 40 hours (2 weeks).

Dates: August 1987-Present.

Objective: To provide the student with issues of computer security.

Learning Outcome: Upon successful completion of this course, the student will be able to identify the threats and vulnerabilities applicable to a computer system or network, identify the risks, implement procedures to counter threats and vulnerabilities, foster computer security awareness, and work with management to develop computer security policies.

Instruction: Major topics covered in the course are operational computer security concepts including computer system and network threats, vulnerabilities, and risks; development and implementation of computer security procedures including access control, information labeling, auditing, password management, and risk assessment; and COMPUSEC tools such as computer security manuals, guidelines, and policies. Methods of instruction include lecture, discussion, case studies, audio/visual material, articles, and homework assignments.

Credit Recommendation: In the vocational certificate category, 2 semester hours in Management Information Systems, Computer Operations, or Data Processing (11/89) (9/94).

Operator Technology for Satellite Communications (EC-250)

Location: National Cryptologic School, Ft. Meade, MD.

Length: *Version 1:* 175 hours (5 weeks); *Version 2:* 280 hours (7 weeks).

Dates: *Version 1:* April 1989-August 1996; *Version 2:* September 1996-Present.

Objective: To provide the student with the knowledge required to identify, describe, or define terms and concepts used by collection operators working at satellite communication sites.

Learning Outcome: Upon successful completion of this course, the student will be able to operate unique collection subsystems; identify mission-associated signals and parameters; describe how collection system components affect signal processing; identify modulation types and recognize abnormalities; identify and describe procedures for formatting reports; and define the function and mission of major COMSATs and signal analysis.

Instruction: Major topics covered in the course are waveforms and different types of modulation, satellite functions and orbits, satellite communication systems, COMSAT systems, dual-beam oscilloscope, electronic counter, oscillator, frequency comparison technique, recorder, signal modification, visicorder, fiberoptics, intensity modulation, sonagraph, spectrum analyzer, 446A Mini-Ubiquitous discriminator, FSK and PSK demodulators, tunable demodulator, spectrum analyzer, up and down conversion, collection management and tasking, intercept procedures, and reporting procedures. Methods of instruction include lecture, discussion, laboratory exercises, and theory and laboratory examinations.

Credit Recommendation: *Version 1:* In the vocational certificate category, 3 semester hours in Electronic Engineering Technology (8/91). *Version 2:* In the lower division baccalaureate/associate degree category, 3 semester hours in Electronics Engineering Technology or Telecommunications Technology (9/96). **NOTE:** Credit cannot be awarded for this course and EA-164, EA-178, and EA-200. This course covers the material in the three shorter courses.

Oracle 7 Administration and Programming 11838-11839-11841-11842-11843

Location: Computer-based.

Length: Self-paced.

Dates: March 1995-Present.

Objective: To introduce Oracle 7 administration and programming.

Learning Outcome: Upon successful completion of this course, the student will be able to explain how to perform basic and advanced administrative tasks and Oracle 7; complete tasks associated with application development; manage database objects; and manipulate data.

Instruction: Major topics covered in the course are introduction to Oracle 7; introduction to PL/SQL programming; making queries; and manipulating data. Methods of instruction include course materials available on CD-Rom for self-study, and tests.

Credit Recommendation: In the lower division baccalaureate/associate degree category, 1 semester hour in Database (9/96). **NOTE:** Students must complete 5 of 5 modules to receive credit.

Parallel Processing Architecture and Programming (MP-466)

Location: National Cryptologic School, Ft. Meade, MD.

Length: 40-45 hours (9 weeks).

Dates: July 1991-March 1995.

Objective: To provide the student with the knowledge of advanced concepts for parallel processing architecture and parallel programming techniques.

Learning Outcome: Upon successful completion of this course, the student will be familiar with various contemporary parallel processing architectures; make decisions on which architecture is best suited for a particular computing problem; and write efficient parallel processing programs.

Instruction: Major topics covered in the course are multiple processor architectural designs (SIMD, MIMD, Mesh, Hypercube, Bit Serial); data flow and control; software considerations (synchronization, data structures, task partitioning, performance measurements, languages, compilers, etc.). Methods of instruction include lecture, discussion, classroom projects, optional homework, and examinations.

Credit Recommendation: In the upper division baccalaureate degree category, 2 semester hours in Computer and Information Sciences (8/91) (9/96).

PDP-11 Programming (MP-375) (Formerly PDP-11 Programming [MP-377])

Location: National Cryptologic School, Ft. Meade, MD.

Length: *MP-375 Version 1:* 120 hours (3 weeks); *MP-377 Version 2:* 200 hours (5 weeks).

Dates: *Version 1:* November 1973-April 1976; *Version 2:* May 1977-June 1986.

Objective: To teach students to write and execute assembly language programs using the PDP-11 instruction set.

Instruction: *Version 1:* Covers communications with the DOS operating system using monitor commands and programmed request (I/O), editing of source language programs, debugging and modifying programs using ODT subsystem, and managing and manipulating files using PDP. Instruction by lecture, discussion, laboratory, and computer usage. *Version 2:* Additional instruction on the operation of the computer, using a specific operating system to support requirements for PDP-11 operations.

Credit Recommendation: *Version 1:* In the vocational certificate category, 6 semester hours in Data Processing; or in the lower division baccalaureate/associate degree category, 3 semester hours in Data Processing (11/75) (12/80) (11/89) (9/94). *Version 2:* In the vocational certificate category, 6 semester hours in Data Processing; or in the lower division baccalaureate/associate degree category, 3 semester hours in Data Processing (11/75) (12/80) (11/89) (9/94). *Prerequisite:* Competence in an assembly language.

Phase V CDC 7600 System (IDA) Software Concepts (MP-1K5)

Location: National Cryptologic School, Ft. Meade, MD.

Length: 35 hours (1 week).

Dates: *Version 1:* July 1971-August 1994; *Version 2:* September 1994-Present.

Objective: To enhance the apprentice operator's ability to interact with the CDC 7600 IDA Operating System software.

Learning Outcome: Upon successful completion of this course, the student will be able to control Data Cybex-170 and CRAY X-MC hardware and software basic operations; operate the standard system software; and provide basic problem identification, analysis, and resolution recommendations.

Instruction: Major topics covered in the course are an overview of the concepts and facilities of the CDC 7600 IDA Operating System and the use of its job control statements. Methods of instruction include computer-aided instruction (primary method) (CAI).

Credit Recommendation: *Version 1:* In the lower division baccalaureate/associate degree category, 1 semester hour in Data Processing (9/77) (11/82) (11/89). *Version 2:* In the vocational certificate category, 1 semester hour in Data Processing (9/94). *Prerequisite:* Introduction to Computer Systems Operations (MP-154).

PL/1 Programming (MP-242)

Location: National Cryptologic School, Ft. Meade, MD.

Length: 72 hours (8 weeks).

Dates: October 1969-April 1995.

Objective: To teach the student to write, debug, and document programs in the PL/1 compiler language.

Instruction: Major topics covered in the course are an ex*f*ation of PL/1, writing and debugging at least four PL/1 programs, class discussion of various sample programs, and presentation of various programming techniques useful in the efficient solution of frequently encountered problems. Methods of instruction include lecture, discussion, and computer usage.

Credit Recommendation: In the lower division baccalaureate/associate degree category, 3 semester hours in Data Processing (11/75) (12/80) (11/89) (9/94). *Prerequisite:* College-level algebra course or Mechanics of Algebra (MA-012) and demonstrated competency in another programming language.

PowerBuilder 4.0

Location: Computer-based.

Length: Self-paced.

Dates: October 1994-Present.

Objective: To provide an introduction to PowerBuilder 4.0 and understand how to build applications within a Windows environment.

Learning Outcome: Upon successful completion of this course, the student will be able to identify and describe the major features used to build applications within a Windows environment.

Instruction: Major topics covered in the course are introduction to PowerBuilder 4.0; application development; building windows and controls; writing script for windows and controls; retrieving data using alternate presentation styles; transaction management; Data Window mechanisms and techniques; reporting; dynamic Data Windows and dynamic SQL. Methods of instruction include course materials available on CD-Rom for self-study, and tests.

Credit Recommendation: In the lower division baccalaureate/associate degree category, 1 semester hour in PowerBuilder 4.0 (9/96). **NOTE:** Students must complete 2 of 2 modules to receive credit.

Program Construction and Verification (MP-470)

Location: National Cryptologic School, Ft. Meade, MD.

Length: 72 hours (12 weeks).

Dates: September 1990-January 1993.

Objective: To provide the student with a review of the logical functions, develop the concept of "program construction that is probably correct" and illustrate with examples.

Learning Outcome: Upon successful completion of this course, the student will be able to implement a large class of (specified) programs in such a way that the programs are shown to be (mathematically proved) correct (consistent with) the specifications (of the programs).

Instruction: Major topics covered in the course are propositional calculus, predicate calculus, verification, and program construction. Methods of instruction include lecture plus midterm and final examinations.

Credit Recommendation: In the upper division baccalaureate degree category, 3 semester hours in Computer Science (10/91).

Programming for Operators (MP-166) (Formerly FORTRAN for Operators [MP-166])

Location: National Cryptologic School, Ft. Meade, MD.

Length: 40 hours (1 week).

Dates: January 1971-August 1992.

Objective: To familiarize computer operators with the FORTRAN language.

Instruction: Major topics covered in the course are an introduction to the basic features of FORTRAN and the programming environment; concepts of FORTRAN commands, including input/output instructions; data manipulation; and data structure. Methods of instruction include lecture, laboratory, and computer usage. *Prerequisite:* Familiarity at the operator's level with a specific computer system's operation.

Credit Recommendation: In the vocational certificate category, 2 semester hours in Data Processing or in the lower division baccalaureate/associate degree category, 1 semester hour in Data Processing (11/75) (12/80) (11/89).

Programming in X (MP-428)

Location: National Cryptologic School, Ft. Meade, MD.

Length: *Version 1:* 60 hours (6 weeks); *Versions 2 and 3:* 72 hours (7 weeks).

Dates: *Versions 1 and 2:* September 1990-Present; *Version 3:* September 1996-Present.

Objective: To provide the student with the understanding of the general concepts and programming practices associated with the X programming language.

Learning Outcome: Upon successful completion of this course, the student will

be able to design and implement an X-language application.

Instruction: Major topics covered in the course are general concepts of X; windows and drawing; events; advanced graphics; color and resources; and toolkits and intrinsics. *Versions 1 and 2:* Methods of instruction include lectures, discussion, classroom and laboratory exercises, an out-of-class project, and examinations. *Version 3:* Methods of instruction include lectures, discussion, classroom and laboratory exercises, an out-of-class project, examinations, and in-class mid-term and final examinations.

Credit Recommendation: *Versions 1 and 2:* In the lower division baccalaureate/associate degree category, 2 semester hours in Computer Science, Computer Engineering, Data Processing, or Information Systems Management (8/91). *Version 3:* In the lower division baccalaureate/associate degree category, or in the upper division baccalaureate degree category, 3 semester hours in Computer Science, Computer Information Systems, or Data Processing (9/96).

Programming Language Logic and Automated Proofs (MP-472)

Location: National Cryptologic School, Ft. Meade, MD.

Length: 72 hours (12 weeks).

Dates: September 1990-January 1992.

Objective: To provide the student with an understanding of how program verification can be mechanized and the use of such a mechanical tool that implements the mechanization.

Learning Outcome: Upon successful completion of this course, the student will have the ability to design, implement, and use simple mechanical (computer-based) tools for program verification.

Instruction: Methods of instruction include lecture, tests (midterm and final), and assigned homework.

Credit Recommendation: In the upper division baccalaureate degree category, 3 semester hours in Computer and Information Sciences (10/91).

Satellite Communications Systems (EA-178)

Location: National Cryptologic School, Ft. Meade, MD.

Length: *Version 1:* 30 hours (4 weeks); *Versions 2 and 3:* 45 hours (5 weeks).

Dates: *Versions 1 and 2:* September 1981-August 1996; *Version 3:* September 1996-Present.

Objective: To provide the student with knowledge of concepts and technology unique to satellite communications.

Learning Outcome: Upon successful completion of this course, the student will be able to define the terms commonly used in satellite communications; identify specific satellite communications frequency bands; know the relationship of antenna gain, frequency, and diameter; distinguish between different multiple access techniques; and identify difference noise sources and interference.

Instruction: Major topics covered in the course are history of satellite communications and models of satellite systems, including earth terminals, channels, spacecraft and spacecraft subsystems, analog and digital systems, and link protection. Methods of instruction include lecture, discussion, homework assignments, and an examination.

Credit Recommendation: *Versions 1 and 2:* In the vocational certificate category, 1 semester hour in Electrical Engineering Technology or Applied Physics (8/91). *Version 3:* In the lower division baccalaureate/associate degree category, 2 semester hours in Electrical or Electronic Engineering or Telecommunications Technology (9/96). **NOTE:** Credit cannot be earned for this course and for EC-250.

Secure Data Network Architecture
1. Secure Data Network Architecture (CP-533)
2. Advanced Secure Data Network Architecture (CP-535)
(Course 1 Formerly [CP-580])
(Course 2 Formerly [CP-585])

Location: National Cryptologic School, Ft. Meade, MD.

Length: *Course 1:* 16 hours (2 days); *Course 2:* 24 hours (3 days).

Dates: August 1990-May 1995.

Objective: To provide the student with an understanding of basic networking and protocol concepts and issues required to build secure computer systems.

Learning Outcome: Upon successful completion of this course, the student will be able to understand current network architecture and protocol issues associated with developing and implementing secure networks and to understand why and how security is designed into protocols.

Instruction: Major topics covered in the course are network security architecture and protocols; advanced network security terminology and concepts; Open Systems Interconnection Model (OSI); Government OSI Profile (GOSIP); Integrated Services Digital Network (ISDN); and network security design factors and security issues related to protocols. Methods of instruction include lecture, discussion, practical exercises, and examinations.

Credit Recommendation: In the upper division baccalaureate degree category, 1 semester hour in Computer Science or Computer Security (8/91). **NOTE:** Both courses must be completed to receive credit recommendation.

Shift Register Generator Sequences (EA-163)

Location: National Cryptologic School, Ft. Meade, MD.

Length: *Version 1:* 27 hours (3 weeks); *Versions 2 and 3:* 33 hours (2-3 hours per week).

Dates: *Versions 1 and 2:* September 1981-August 1996; *Version 3:* September 1996-Present.

Objective: *Version 1:* To provide the student with knowledge of methods of generation, characteristics, and applications of pseudo-random sequences to communications and radar problems. *Versions 2 and 3:* To provide the student with knowledge of the generation, description, properties, recovery techniques, and applications of linear recursive sequences, and to include spread spectrum, coding, and radar.

Learning Outcome: *Version 1:* Upon successful completion of this course, the student will be able to use terminology of pseudo-random sequences, shift register-generated sequences, and resolve the generating polynomial for simple sequences. *Versions 2 and 3:* Upon successful completion of this course, the student will be able to demonstrate some basic knowledge regarding linear recursive sequences and their applications; perform some basic sequence analysis and synthesis techniques in order to identify a sequence; recover missing bits; and produce more of the sequence.

Instruction: *Version 1:* Major topics covered in the course are mathematics of shift registers, deterministic properties of pseudo-random sequences, sequence lengths, polynomials and the shift register, methods of resolving the generating polynomial, and application of PN sequences as used for improved radar resolution. Methods of instruction include lecture, discussion, classroom exercises, and an examination. *Versions 2 and 3:* Major topics covered in the course are mathematics of linear shift registers; correlation of shift register sequences, determining sequence lengths; polynomial and bit notation; maximal-length sequences; gold codes; simple generator recovery techniques, and some applications. The applications include using shift registers to generate spread spectrum spreading codes, generate the parity bits and error syndrome for block codes; and perform radar pulse encoding. Methods of instruction include lecture, discussion, homework exercises, and examinations.

Credit Recommendation: *Versions 1 and 2:* In the vocational certificate category, 1 semester hour in Electrical Engineering Technology (8/91). *Version 3:* In the lower division baccalaureate/associate degree category, 1 semester hour in Electrical or Electronics Engineering Technology (9/96).

SIGINT Instrumentation and Measurement Techniques (EA-200)

Location: National Cryptologic School, Ft. Meade, MD.

Length: 200 hours (5 weeks).

Dates: April 1989-Present.

Objective: To provide the student with the knowledge of SIGINT equipment operation and analysis techniques with emphasis on characteristics, operations, and utilization of equipment.

Learning Outcome: Upon successful completion of this course, the student will be able to use specific analysis equipment to perform amplitude, frequency, phase, and time measurements of simulated signals and recognize limitations and capabilities of specific analysis equipment.

Instruction: Major topics covered in the course are theory and application of analysis equipment, to include oscilloscopes, filters, magnetic tape recorders, spectrum analyzers, synthesizers, counters, cameras, frequency converters, discriminators, demodulators, and function generators. Methods of instruction include lecture, discussion, laboratory exercises, and an examination.

Credit Recommendation: In the vocational certificate category, 3 semester hours in Electronic Technology (8/91) (9/96). **NOTE:** Credit cannot be earned for this course and for EC-250.

Spectrum Analysis (EA-166)

Location: National Cryptologic School, Ft. Meade, MD.

Length: 30 hours (4 weeks).

Dates: *Version 1:* May 1980-August 1996; *Version 2:* September 1996-Present.

Objective: To provide the student with an understanding and interpretation of frequency domain spectral characteristics.

Learning Outcome: Upon successful completion of this course, the student will be able to explain the concept of signal representation by employing Fourier series and Fourier transforms; apply basic spectral techniques to analyze a signal; and convert frequency domain signal representation to time domain representation.

Instruction: Major topics covered in the course are introduction to spectra, Fourier series, Fourier transforms, spectral analysis of linear systems, spectral characteristics of discrete signals, and spectrum analysis. Methods of instruction include lecture, discussion, classroom exercises, and an examination.

Credit Recommendation: *Version 1:* In the vocational certificate category, 1 semester hour in Electrical Engineering Technology (8/91). *Version 2:* In the lower division baccalaureate/associate degree category, 1 semester hour in Electrical or Electronic Technology (9/96).

Supporting Windows 95 (70312-70313)

Location: Computer-based.

Length: Self-paced.

Dates: November 1995-Present.

Objective: To present the skills to implement and support Microsoft Windows 95.

Learning Outcome: Upon successful completion of this course, the student will be able to describe the features of the Windows 95 networking architecture and explain the steps involved in setting up and supporting Windows 95.

Instruction: Major topics covered in the course are installing and configuring Windows 95 and troubleshooting. Methods of instruction include course materials available on CD-Rom for self-study, and tests.

Credit Recommendation: In the lower division baccalaureate/associate degree category, 1 semester hour in Systems Administration (9/96). **NOTE:** Students must complete 3 of 3 modules to receive credit.

Sybase System 10.01 11658-11659-11661-11662-11663

Location: Computer-based.

Length: Self-paced.

Dates: June 1994-Present.

Objective: To provide an overview of the Sybase System 10 architecture.

Learning Outcome: Upon successful completion of this course, the student will be able to understand the basic architecture of the Sybase System 10; explain basic T-SQL programming tasks; demonstrate the administration of Sybase System 10 in a client/server environment, the monitoring and tuning of the SQL server for performance improvements and the management of remote servers.

Instruction: Major topics covered in the course are introduction to Sybase System 10 architecture; Sybase Server; introduction to server programming, writing stored procedures; writing triggers; managing transactions and locking; cursors; T-SQL programming; performing queries and manipulating data; basic and advanced topics in system administration. Methods of instruction include course materials available on CD-Rom for self-study, and tests.

Credit Recommendation: In the lower division baccalaureate/associate degree or upper division baccalaureate degree category, 1 semester hour in Database Design (9/96). **NOTE:** Students must complete 5 of 5 modules to receive credit.

Systems Software (MP-420) (Formerly Introduction to Computer Software [MP-420])

Location: National Cryptologic School, Ft. Meade, MD.

Length: 60 hours (2.5 hour/day, 2 days/week, for 12 weeks).

Dates: *Version 1:* September 1973-August 1994; *Version 2:* September 1994-Present.

Objective: To provide an introduction to the field of general systems programming and an understanding of how operating systems and compilers are constructed and implemented.

Learning Outcome: Upon successful completion of this course, the student will be able to understand the function and operation of operating system software; how various programming languages function and are used; programming structure general design, development, and implementation; performance measurement methology; and file and database system accessing.

Instruction: Major topics covered in the course are a detailed discussion and investigation of the nature and characteristics of systems programs, systems design, structural programming, optimization, language utility, microprogramming, compilers, and operating systems. Methods of instruction include lecture and discussion.

Credit Recommendation: *Version 1:* In the upper division baccalaureate degree category or in the graduate degree category, 3 semester hours in Computer Science or Data Processing (11/75) (12/80)

(11/89). *Version 2:* In the upper division baccalaureate degree category, 3 semester hours in Computer Science or Data Processing (9/94). *Prerequisites:* Compiler Level Programming Language and College Level Math (MA-400).

TCP/IP for MVS (12322, 12323)

Location: Computer-based.

Length: Self-paced.

Dates: June 1996-Present.

Objective: To introduce concepts of TCP/IP for MVS.

Learning Outcome: Upon successful completion of this course, the student will be able to install and implement TCP/IP for MVS.

Instruction: Major topics covered in the course are concepts of TCP/IP, TELNET, differences between TELNET and TN370, connection to the mainframe from the IP network, CLAW devices, installing and customizing the product, interfacing TCP/IP to CICS, using IMS interfaces for TCP/IP, and set up NETVIEW interfaces for TCP/IP. Methods of instruction include student guide and computer-based instruction for self-study.

Credit Recommendation: In the lower division baccalaureate/associate degree category, 1 semester hour in Computer Science or Computer Information Systems (5/97). **NOTE:** Students must complete 2 of 2 modules to receive credit.

Theoretical Foundations for Trusted Information Systems (IN-375) (Formerly [CP-520])

Location: National Cryptologic School, Ft. Meade, MD.

Length: 2 days.

Dates: June 1989-August 1996.

Objective: To provide the student with the knowledge of fundamental concepts of computer security models.

Learning Outcome: Upon successful completion of this course, the student will be able to identify and describe problems in computer security using mathematical and logical concepts; develop a formal model for computer security; and demonstrate that the model is consistent with its axioms.

Instruction: Major topics covered in the course are classic Bell LaPadula (BLP) model, access control, information flow and non-interference models, integrity, database and event-based models, concurrence, network models, and the take-grant model. Methods of instruction include lectures, guest speakers, discussion, written assignments, and examinations.

Credit Recommendation: In the upper division baccalaureate degree category, 1 semester hour in Computer Science or Computer Security (8/91).

Trusted Systems Criteria and Concepts (ND-172) (Formerly Trusted Systems and Criteria Concepts [CP-510])

Location: National Cryptologic School, Ft. Meade, MD.

Length: *Version 1:* 40 hours (1 week); *Version 2:* 32 hours (4 days).

Dates: *Version 1:* January 1990-June 1996; *Version 2:* July 1996-Present.

Objective: *Version 1:* To provide the student with an understanding of principles, concepts, and technology of the DOD Trusted Computer Systems Evaluation Criteria (TCSEC) and related topics of trusted system evaluations and accreditation. *Version 2:* To provide the student with an understanding of principles, concepts, technology and other related topics of trusted systems evaluations and accreditation and an understanding of the DoD TCSEC (Trusted Computer Systems Evaluation Criteria.)

Learning Outcome: *Version 1:* Upon successful completion of this course, the student will be able to demonstrate an understanding of the computer security problem, technical aspects of trusted systems technology, and DOD criteria and standards; use and interpret the TCSEC; and apply the NCSC and NRL guidelines to determine significant characteristics of each TCSEC class to given operational environments. *Version 2:* Upon successful completion of this course, the student will be able to apply COMPUSEC principles to building, installing, using, or analyzing a computer system; construct simple protection profiles out of the common criteria; and analyze other protection profiles.

Instruction: *Version 1:* Major topics covered in the course are principles, concepts, and technology of TCSEC; principles of trusted systems; and mandatory and discretionary access controls, user accountability, identification and authentication, security/architectures, and security models. Methods of instruction include lecture, discussion, laboratory exercises, and examinations. *Version 2:* Major topics covered in the course are principles of trusted systems; mandatory and discretionary access controls, user accountability, identification and authentication, security/architectures, and security models; and the principles, concepts, and technology of TCSEC and common criteria for Information Technology Security Evaluation (CCITSE). Methods of instruction include lecture, discussion, laboratory exercises, and examinations.

Credit Recommendation: *Version 1:* In the upper division baccalaureate degree category, 1 semester hour in Computer Science or Computer Security (8/91). *Version 2:* In the lower division baccalaureate/associate degree category or in the upper division baccalaureate degree category, 1 semester hour in Computer Information Systems, Data Processing, or Computer Science (9/96).

UNISYS A-Series Software; UNISYS A-Series Advanced Technical Skills (MP-1U5; MP-1U6) (Formerly UNISYS A-Series Computer Operations)

Location: National Cryptologic School, Linthicum, MD.

Length: 80 hours (2 weeks).

Dates: October 1989-September 1992.

Objective: To develop a complete understanding of the UNISYS A-Series computer software and its interaction with the hardware for computer operations personnel.

Learning Outcome: Upon successful completion of this course, the student will be able to use system software with hardware interaction to fully implement the UNISYS A-Series computer; employ system utilities for job implementation; and employ databases, tapes, and disks to support a variety of jobs.

Instruction: Major topics covered in the course are number conversions from one base to another, stack concepts, file attributes, cold start procedures, communications, queues and scheduling, memory management, system initialization, library maintenance, print subsystem, and disk subsystem. Methods of instruction include lecture, classroom exercises, demonstrations, and laboratory.

Credit Recommendation: In the lower division baccalaureate/associate degree category, 2 semester hours in Computer Operations (11/89).

UNIVAC 1100 Advanced Training Skills (MP-1E6) (Formerly Univac 1108 Advanced Technical Skills [MP-1E6])

Location: National Cryptologic School, Ft. Meade, MD.

Length: 35 hours (1 week).

Dates: July 1973-July 1993.

Objective: To provide the experienced operator with an in-depth understanding from an operational viewpoint of the internal functions of the UNIVAC 1108 EXEC 8 Operating System software.

Instruction: Major topics covered in the course are an in-depth study of the concepts and facilities of the UNIVAC 1108 EXEC 8 Operating System and the use of its job control language. Method of instruction includes computer-aided instruction (CAI).

Credit Recommendation: In the lower division baccalaureate/associate degree category, 1 semester hour in Data Processing (9/77) (11/82) (11/89). *Prerequisite:* FORTRAN for Operators (MP-166) and UNIVAC 1108 Systems Software (MP-1E5).

UNIVAC 1100 Systems Software (MP-1E5) (Formerly UNIVAC 1108 Systems Software [MP-1E5])

Location: National Cryptologic School, Ft. Meade, MD.

Length: 35 hours (1 week).

Dates: July 1972-July 1993.

Objective: To enhance the apprentice operator's ability to interact with the UNIVAC 1108 EXEC 8 Operating System software.

Instruction: Major topics covered in the course are an overview of the concepts and facilities of the UNIVAC 1108 EXEC 8 Operating System and the use of its job control statements. Method of instruction includes computer-aided instruction (CAI).

Credit Recommendation: In the lower division baccalaureate/associate degree category, 1 semester hour in Data Processing (9/77) (11/82) (11/89). *Prerequisite:* Introduction to Computer Systems Operations (MP-154).

UNIVAC 494 Advanced Technical Skills (MP-1C6)

Location: National Cryptologic School, Ft. Meade, MD.

Length: 35 hours (1 week).

Dates: July 1972-June 1983.

Objective: To provide the experienced operator with an in-depth understanding from an operational viewpoint of the internal functions of the UNIVAC 494 Operating System software.

Instruction: Major topics covered in the course are an in-depth study of the concepts and facilities of the UNIVAC 494 Operating System and the use of its job control statements; programming techniques; machine language instructions; input and output conventions; program segmentation; FORTRAN programming; file control; debugging aids; file standards; and communications.

Credit Recommendation: In the lower division baccalaureate/associate degree category, 1 semester hour in Data Processing (9/77) (11/82) (11/89). *Prerequisite:* FORTRAN for Operators (MP-166) and UNIVAC 494 System Software (MP-1C5).

UNIVAC 494 HOLDER System Software (MP-1G5)

Location: National Cryptologic School, Ft. Meade, MD.

Length: 35 hours (1 week).

Dates: July 1975-June 1988.

Objective: To enhance the apprentice operator's ability to interact with the UNIVAC 494 Real Time Interrupt Processing executive software.

Instruction: Major topics covered in the course are an overview of the concepts and facilities of the UNIVAC 494 Real Time Interrupt Processing Executive Operating System and the use of its job control statements.

Credit Recommendation: In the lower division baccalaureate/associate degree category, 1 semester hour in Data Processing (9/77) (11/82) (11/89). *Prerequisite:* Introduction to Computer Systems Operations (MP-154).

UNIVAC 494 RYE System Software (MP-1C5)

Location: National Cryptologic School, Ft. Meade, MD.

Length: 35 hours (1 week).

Dates: July 1971-July 1983.

Objective: To enhance the apprentice operator's ability to interact with the UNIVAC 494 Operating System software.

Instruction: Major topics covered in the course are an overview of the concepts and facilities of the UNIVAC 494 Operating System and the use of its job control statements to schedule, prioritize, log, and monitor system operation.

Credit Recommendation: In the lower division baccalaureate/associate degree category, 1 semester hour in Data Processing (9/77) (11/82). *Prerequisite:* Introduction to Computer Systems Operations (MP-154).

Visual Basic 4.0 (70592-70593)

Location: Computer-based.

Length: Self-paced.

Dates: February 1996-Present.

Objective: To introduce applications development, instructional technology, terminology and the design of custom business applications.

Learning Outcome: Upon successful completion of this course, the student will be able to create fundamental Visual Basic projects, comprehend the necessary code to write using multiple forms and controls, and understand the design, and implementation of custom business applications using Visual Basic 4.0.

Instruction: Major topics covered in the course are writing code in Visual Basic, manipulating external databases, understanding the use of a dynamic link library and the use of OLE applications. Methods of instruction include course materials available on CD-Rom for self-study, and tests.

Credit Recommendation: In the lower division baccalaureate/associate degree category, 1 semester hour in Programming (9/96).

Windows NT 3.5x Support Fundamentals and Server 70401-70402-70403-70411-70412-70413

Location: Computer-based.

Length: Self-paced.

Dates: November 1995-Present.

Objective: To present an overview of Windows NT client and server.

Learning Outcome: Upon successful completion of this course, the student will be able to explain the processes involved in installing and setting up Windows NT Server and clients.

Instruction: Major topics covered in the course are getting started with Windows NT; setting up Windows NT Client software; setting up Windows NT Workstation; and troubleshooting. Methods of instruction include course materials available on CD-Rom for self-study, and tests.

Credit Recommendation: In the lower division baccalaureate/associate degree category, 1 semester hour in System Administration (9/96). **NOTE:** Students must complete 6 of 6 modules to receive credit.

WJ-8615 UHF/VHF Receiver Maintenance (EM-525)

Location: National Cryptologic School, Ft. Meade, MD.

Length: 32 hours (1 week).

Dates: July 1989-August 1996.

Objective: To provide the student with the knowledge necessary to perform preventive and corrective maintenance on the WJ-8615 UHF/VHF Receiver.

Learning Outcome: Upon successful completion of this course, the student will be able to perform preventive and corrective maintenance to the LRU level on the WJ-8615 UHF/VHF Receiver.

Instruction: Major topics covered in the course are function of controls and indicators, functional theory of operation, test and alignment procedures, LRU failure analysis, preventive maintenance procedures, fault isolation, and corrective maintenance. Methods of instruction include lecture, discussion, laboratory exercises, and an examination.

Credit Recommendation: In the vocational certificate category, 1 semester hour in Digital Electronics Maintenance (8/91). **NOTE:** This course and one other in the EM series must be completed to receive 1 credit.

WJ-8618 UHF/VHF Receiver Maintenance (EM-524)

Location: National Cryptologic School, Ft. Meade, MD.

Length: 48 hours (1 week).

Dates: July 1989-August 1996.

Objective: To provide the student with the knowledge necessary to perform preventive and corrective maintenance on the WJ-8618 UHF/VHF Receiver.

Learning Outcome: Upon successful completion of this course, the student will be able to perform preventive and corrective maintenance to the LRU level on the WJ-8618 UHF/VHF Receiver.

Instruction: Major topics covered in the course are function of controls and indicators, functional theory of operation, test and alignment procedures, LRU failure analysis, preventive maintenance procedures, fault isolation, and corrective maintenance. Methods of instruction include lecture, discussion, laboratory exercises, and an examination.

Credit Recommendation: In the vocational certificate category, 1 semester hour in Digital Electronics Maintenance (8/91). **NOTE:** This course and one other in the EM series must be completed to receive 1 credit.

WJ-8718/16 HF Receiver Maintenance (EM-210)

Location: National Cryptologic School, Ft. Meade, MD.

Length: 40 hours (1 week).

Dates: September 1985-August 1996.

Objective: To provide the student with the ability to perform corrective and preventive maintenance on the WJ-8718/16 Receiver.

Learning Outcome: Upon successful completion of this course, the student will be able to perform corrective and preventive maintenance to the LRU level on the WJ-8718/16 HF Receiver.

Instruction: Major topics covered in the course are receiver characteristics, functional theory of operation, test and alignment procedures, LRU failure analysis, preventive maintenance procedures, fault isolation, and corrective maintenance. Methods of instruction include lecture, discussion, laboratory exercises, and an examination.

Credit Recommendation: In the vocational certificate category, 1 semester hour in Digital Electronics Maintenance (8/91). **NOTE:** This course and one other EM series course must be completed in order to receive 1 credit.

WJ-8718/16 HF Receiver Maintenance (EM-210)

Location: National Cryptologic School, Ft. Meade, MD.

Length: 40 hours (1 week).

Dates: September 1985-August 1996.

Objective: To provide the student with the ability to perform corrective and preventive maintenance on the WJ-8718/16 Receiver.

Learning Outcome: Upon successful completion of this course, the student will be able to perform corrective and preventive maintenance to the LRU level in the WJ-8718/16 HF Receiver.

Instruction: Major topics covered in the course are receiver characteristics, functional theory of operation, test and alignment procedures, LRU failure analysis, preventive maintenance procedures, fault isolation and corrective maintenance. Methods of instruction include lecture, discussion, laboratory exercises and examination.

Credit Recommendation: In the vocational certificate category, 1 semester hour in Digital Electronics Maintenance. (8/91). **NOTE:** This course and one other EM series course must be completed in order to receive one credit.

WJ-9518AE-9 Demodulator Maintenance (EM-526)

Location: National Cryptologic School, Ft. Meade, MD.

Length: 32 hours (1 week).

Dates: July 1989-September 1994.

Objective: To provide the student with the knowledge necessary to perform preventive and corrective maintenance on the WJ-9518AE-9 Demodulator.

Learning Outcome: Upon successful completion of this course, the student will be able to perform preventive and corrective maintenance to the LRU level on the WJ-9518AE-9 Demodulator.

Instruction: Major topics covered in the course are function of controls and indicators, functional theory of operation, test and alignment procedures, LRU failure analysis, preventive maintenance procedures, fault isolation, and corrective maintenance. Methods of instruction include lecture, discussion, laboratory exercises, and an examination.

Credit Recommendation: In the vocational certificate category, 1 semester hour in Digital Electronics Maintenance (8/91). **NOTE:** This course and one other EM series course must be completed in order to receive 1 credit.

WJ-9518BE-9 Demodulator LRU Maintenance (EM-527)

Location: National Cryptologic School, Ft. Meade, MD.

Length: 40 hours (1 week).

Dates: July 1989-August 1996.

Objective: To provide the student with the knowledge necessary to perform corrective and preventive maintenance on the WJ-9518BE-9 Demodulator.

Learning Outcome: Upon successful completion of this course, the student will be able to perform maintenance at the LRU level on the WJ-9518BE-9 Demodulator.

Instruction: Major topics covered in the course are function of controls and indicators, functional theory of operation, test and alignment procedures, LRU failure analysis, preventive maintenance procedures, fault isolation, and corrective maintenance. Methods of instruction include lecture, discussion, laboratory exercises, and an examination.

Credit Recommendation: In the vocational certificate category, 1 semester hour in Digital Electronics Maintenance (8/91). **NOTE:** This course and one other EM series course must be completed in order to receive 1 credit.

MANAGEMENT EDUCATION DEPARTMENT

The Management Education Department is a department of the Cryptologic Management Faculty. It provides supervisory, managerial, and executive management education to all levels of management at the National Cryptologic School. It is also responsible for providing functional management training to meet agency needs.

Active Learning Techniques (ED-218)

Location: National Cryptologic School, Ft. Meade, MD.

Length: 16 hours (2 days).

Dates: May 1995-Present.

Learning Outcome: Upon successful completion of this course, the student will be able to demonstrate how to design and present different interactive techniques and how to select the best strategy for presenting specific content to a particular target audience.

Instruction: Major topics covered in the course are icebreakers, openers, instructional games, data presentation/review techniques, demonstrations, and feedback. Methods of instruction include lecture, classroom exercises, demonstrations, performance evaluation of criterion exercises, group discussions, and peer review using checklists.

Credit Recommendation: In the upper division baccalaureate degree or graduate degree category, 1 semester hour in Communication, Education, Psychology, or Human Resource Development (9/96).

Advanced Project Management (MR-S55)

Location: National Cryptologic School, Ft. Meade, MD.

Length: 32 hours (4 days).

Dates: October 1986-September 1996.

Objective: To provide the student with knowledge of project management functions of planning, organizing, scheduling, directing, motivating, and controlling projects.

Learning Outcome: Upon successful completion of this course, the student will be able to manage projects effectively; describe life cycle phases of project; design and price out work breakdown structures; and prepare multiple schedules for status reporting.

Instruction: Major topics covered in the course are benefits of project management; interfacing with management; working with the customer; tailoring project management to needs; planning begins with realistic objectives; project manager as an effective leader; power and authority; project plan; pricing and estimating methodologies; fixed manpower dile; life cycle costing; project management control cycle; earned value and accomplishment monitoring; trend analysis; configuration control; project report technique; conflicts; replanning and problem-solving; and project termination-variable to success. Methods of instruction include lectures, class exercises, case studies, and open discussion (textbook, student workbook, and vugraphs).

Credit Recommendation: In the upper division baccalaureate degree category, 2 semester hours in Systems Management, Project Management, or Engineering Management (8/91).

Analysis and Design for Real-Time Systems (MR-S1B)

Location: National Cryptologic School, Ft. Meade, MD.

Length: 40 hours (5 days).

Dates: January 1988-August 1996.

Objective: To design and analyze real-time systems.

Learning Outcome: Upon successful completion of this course, the student will be able to design and evaluate real-time systems.

Instruction: Major topics covered in the course are modeling; abstraction techniques; flow diagrams; structured analysis; conventions; verification; and testing.

Credit Recommendation: In the graduate degree category, 1 semester hour in System Analysis or Computer Science (8/91).

Analysis of C/SSR Data (MR-484)

Location: National Cryptologic School, Ft. Meade, MD.

Length: *Version 1:* 24 hours (3 days); *Version 2:* 32 hours (4 days).

Dates: *Version 1:* October 1986-September 1993; *Version 2:* October 1993-August 1996.

Objective: To reinforce the concepts of contractor performance measurement and offer an introduction to advanced data analysis techniques.

Learning Outcome: Upon successful completion of this course, the student will be able to describe several systematic techniques of reviewing performance data, evaluate effects of the data on baselines, estimates at completion, choice of earned value methods, and application of management reserve. Understand the use of microcomputer-based analysis support tools in performing the tasks of managing and monitoring contractor performance.

Instruction: Major topics covered in the course are measuring performance to the baseline; extracting meaningful information from reports; generating estimates at completion; and forecasting techniques. A workshop approach is used to provide maximum student participation. Methods of instruction include lecture, discussion, class exercises and case study.

Credit Recommendation: In the upper division baccalaureate degree category, 1 semester hour in Quantitative Analysis (8/91).

Behavioral Sciences Concepts and Applications in Management (MC-120)
(Cryptologic Management for Supervisors [MC-120])

Location: *Version 1:* National Cryptologic School, Ft. Meade, MD *Version 2:* Field only.

Length: 70 hours (2 weeks).

Dates: *Version 1:* September 1969-August 1994; *Version 2:* September 1994-Present.

Objective: To enable students to increase their effectiveness as first-line supervisors through knowledge of behavioral sciences and their applications to management.

Learning Outcome: Upon successful completion of this course, the student will know and be able to apply techniques of interpersonal communication and conflict resolution; exhibit a knowledge of performance appraisal; understand the various leadership styles and their appropriate uses; and know motivational theories and applications.

Instruction: Major topics covered in the course are interpersonal communications and conflict resolution, performance appraisal and counseling, leadership styles and group behavior, management of personnel, and motivational theories and applications. Methods of instruction include lecture, discussion, classroom exercises, case studies, and group exercises.

Credit Recommendation: *Version 1:* In the upper division baccalaureate degree category, 2 semester hours in Business Administration or Management (9/76) (11/82) (11/89). *Version 2:* In the upper division baccalaureate degree category, 2 semester hours in Business Administration, Management, or Organizational Behavior (9/94). **NOTE:** A substantial portion of the material covered in this course is covered in MC-210. Therefore, credit should not be granted for MC-210 if it is granted for Behavioral Sciences Concepts and Applications in Management.

Briefing Skills (EG-243)

Location: National Cryptologic School, Ft. Meade, MD.

Length: 24 hours (3 weeks).

Dates: October 1986-Present.

Objective: To provide students with skills to prepare, deliver, and evaluate oral and written briefings.

Learning Outcome: Upon successful completion of this course, the student will be able to prepare, present, and evaluate briefings.

Instruction: Major topics covered in the course are platform presentation, preparation of briefing materials, audiovisual equipment, and effective verbal and physical techniques during presentation. Methods of instruction include lecture, discussion, classroom exercises, audio/ visual material, computer-assisted instruction, presentations/briefings, observations, and reports.

Credit Recommendation: In the lower division baccalaureate/associate degree category, 1 semester hour in Communications, Business/Executive Communications, or Training (8/91) (9/96).

CBT Authoring-TENCORE (EDE-50)

Location: National Cryptologic School, Ft. Meade, MD.

Length: 80 hours (2 weeks).

Dates: May 1989-August 1996.

Objective: To provide CBT course developers the knowledge and skills needed to use the authoring language TENCORE to design computer training that is effective for adult learners.

Learning Outcome: Upon successful completion of this course, the student will be able to use TENCORE integrated editing to write and deliver a lesson; use the TENCORE Computer Managed Instruction (CMI) function to create tests in support of the lesson; and use the TENCORE producer to write and deliver a lesson.

Instruction: Major topics covered in the course are TENCORE language terms, conventions and notation; displaying text; conditional and selective command mechanism; mouse input and windowing techniques; item analysis data; the response models; and the image editor. Methods of instruction include both instructor and student use of computers. Instructor also uses projection system.

Credit Recommendation: In the upper division baccalaureate degree category, 3 semester hours in Computer Instruction, Business Administration, Business Management, or Media (8/91).

Classroom Technology Management (RESPONDEX) (ED-201)

Location: National Cryptologic School, Ft. Meade, MD.

Length: 32 hours (4 days).

Dates: July 1990-August 1996.

Objective: To provide experienced instructors with the knowledge and skills needed to develop and present lessons using the RESPONDEX systems.

Learning Outcome: Upon successful completion of this course, the student will be able to design, develop, and teach lessons using the classroom technology management system (RESPONDEX).

Instruction: Major topics covered in the course are individual/group mode on RESPONDEX; creating a presentation; and utility program. Methods of instruction include lecture, demonstration, and performance, and use of computer and projection system by both students and instructor.

Credit Recommendation: In the upper division baccalaureate degree category, 2 semester hours in Computer Technology, Business Administration, Business Management, or Instructional Technology (8/91).

Clerical Orientation (OS-052) (Formerly Clerical Introduction [OS-051] or [OS-050])

Location: National Cryptologic School, Ft. Meade, MD.

Length: 32 hours (4 days).

Dates: June 1971-Present.

Objective: To enable the employee to upgrade clerical skills.

Learning Outcome: Upon successful completion of this course, the student will be able to perform various clerical procedures including preparation of forms, mail processing, proofreading, and managing paperwork flow.

Instruction: Major topics covered in the course are an introduction to clerical procedures including filing, drafts, proofreading, and use of office machines; mail management; and managing paperwork flow. Methods of instruction include lecture, discussion, classroom exercises, and practical exercises.

Credit Recommendation: In the lower division baccalaureate/associate degree category, 1 semester hour in Secretarial Science (9/76) (11/82) (11/89) (9/94).

Conducting On-The-Job Training (ED-125)

Location: National Cryptologic School, Ft. Meade, MD.

Length: *Version 1:* 40 hours (5 days); *Version 2:* 32 hours (4 days).

Dates: *Version 1:* October 1987-December 1993; *Version 2:* January 1994-Present.

Objective: To enable first-line supervisors and section leaders to develop the knowledge and skills necessary to design and conduct on-the-job training (OJT) in a work environment.

Learning Outcome: Upon successful completion of this course, the student will be able to analyze and accommodate trainer learning styles; evaluate work situations; write a job description and sample task listing; complete a task detailing form; construct a job aid; use OJT methods and know how to apply the methods; and develop good counseling and coaching skills, i.e., listening, feedback, and self-assessment skills.

Instruction: Major topics covered in the course are training adult learners, task analysis, use of job aids, OJT training methods, and counseling and coaching trainees. Methods of evaluation include self evaluation, case studies, written exercises, and two project presentations.

Credit Recommendation: *Versions 1 and 2:* In the upper division baccalaureate degree category, 2 semester hours in Education, Psychology of Learning, Manpower and Planning, or Human Resource Development (8/91) (9/96).

Contractor Performance Measurement (MR-479)

Location: National Cryptologic School, Ft. Meade, MD.

Length: 40 hours (5 days).

Dates: October 1986-August 1996.

Objective: To introduce the student to contractor performance measurement regulations and requirements and to explore the concepts of cost/schedule management of major programs and of determining earned value, estimates at completion, and baseline management using appropriate techniques as presented in the course.

Learning Outcome: Upon successful completion of this course, the student will be able to monitor contractor performance.

Instruction: Major topics covered in the course are earned value concepts; earned value techniques; current status analytical techniques; estimates at completion; baseline management; charting analysis; and lessons learned.

Credit Recommendation: In the upper division baccalaureate degree category, 1

semester hour in Contracting, Purchasing, or Applied Management (8/91).

Course Manager's Procedures (ED-116)

Location: National Cryptologic School, Ft. Meade, MD.

Length: *Version 1:* 24 hours (3 days); *Version 2:* 16 hours (2 days).

Dates: *Version 1:* February 1991-December 1993; *Version 2:* January 1994-Present.

Objective: To provide knowledge and skills to fulfill all responsibilities of running a course, including managing, selecting, and doing a final course evaluation. The manager oversees all details, course documentation, selection of teaching techniques, and provides feedback to the instructor.

Learning Outcome: Upon successful completion of this course, the student will be able to manage all types of training; learn how to hire consultants; evaluate commercial training proposals; monitor enrollments and schedules; and give feedback to contractors and guest speakers.

Instruction: *Version 1:* Major topics covered in the course are manager responsibilities; administrative responsibilities; principles of adult learning, principles of instructional design, providing support to the students; writing course objectives; documenting the course; giving feedback; and PR and CORS. Methods of instruction include self-evaluation exercise, case studies, written scenarios, written exercises, and role play. *Version 2:* Major topics covered in the course are course management effectiveness factors; mentoring the instructor; organizing and planning for a course; visiting instructors, speakers and adjunct faculty; and PR and COR. Methods of instruction include self-evaluation exercise, case studies, written scenarios and exercises, and role play.

Credit Recommendation: *Version 1:* In the upper division baccalaureate degree category, 2 semester hours in Educational Methodology (8/91). *Version 2:* In the upper division baccalaureate degree category, 1 semester hour in Educational Methodology (9/96).

Cryptologic Instructor Training (ED-108)

Location: National Cryptologic School, Ft. Meade, MD.

Length: 80 hours; 20 outside.

Dates: January 1989-December 1995.

Objective: To provide an experienced subject matter expert with the tools needed to assess training needs, develop objectives, design exercises and tests, select appropriate instructional strategies, select and design instructional support materials and media, accommodate the needs of adult learners with varying learning styles, and develop and present instructionally sound lessons.

Learning Outcome: Upon successful completion of this course, the student will be able to accommodate different learning styles; develop strategies for training adults; develop objectives and tests; and manage challenging instructional situations; design media, support materials, and lesson plans; present a five-minute introduction, a ten-minute Socratic lesson, and a 45-minute lesson using all skills learned in the course.

Instruction: Major topics covered in the course are adult learning and learning styles, presentation and delivery techniques, instructional design, organizing content, developing objectives, questioning techniques, creating videoshow lesson support, technology and media use, defining effective teaching, managing challenging situations, developing support materials, using instructional games, demonstration-performance, case studies, role playing, brainstorming, and active lecture strategies. Methods of instruction include lecture, discussion, case studies, role plays, instructional games, active lectures, and demonstration/performance. One day of computer training is included where the instructor uses a computer and a projection system while students use computers to design visual lessons.

Credit Recommendation: In the graduate degree category, 3 semester hours in Adult Education (8/91) (5/92).

Cryptologic Management for Managers (MC-210)

Location: National Cryptologic School, Ft. Meade, MD.

Length: 80 hours (2 weeks).

Dates: September 1973-June 1985.

Objective: To enable mid-level managers to broaden their knowledge of modern management concepts, philosophy, and techniques as well as of behavioral science.

Instruction: Major topics covered in the course are the components of the management process, organization theory, motivation, job enrichment, management by objectives, network theory and analysis, transactional analysis, and organizational development. Methods of instruction include lecture, discussion, case studies, and practical exercises.

Credit Recommendation: In the upper division baccalaureate degree category or in the graduate degree category, 3 semester hours in Business Administration or Management (9/76) (11/82). **NOTE:** A substantial portion of the material presented in this course is covered in Behavioral Sciences Concepts and Applications in Management. Therefore, credit should not be granted for Behavioral Sciences Concepts and Applications in Management if it is granted for MC-210. This course has been reevaluated and continues to meet the requirements for credit recommendations.

Cryptologic Training Methods (ED-103)

Location: National Cryptologic School, Ft. Meade, MD.

Length: 24 hours (3 days).

Dates: June 1995-Present.

Objective: To provide an overview of National Cryptologic School instructional and course development philosophy to those individuals seeking to become education and training professionals in other than a platform instructor position.

Learning Outcome: Upon successful completion of this course, the student will be able to demonstrate how to meet the needs of the adult learner; understand the Instructional System Design (ISD) process; organize content in the NCS lesson plan format; develop methods that increase retention (including effective presentation skills and questioning techniques); select appropriate media and support materials; and better deal with problem trainees.

Instruction: Major topics covered in the course are adult learning, Instructional System Design, content organization in the NCS lesson plan format, NCS instructions and regulations related to training and platform methods that enhance retention, presentation skills, questioning technique, use of media and support materials, and problem trainees. Methods of instruction include lecture, discussion, role playing, criteria exercises, performance evaluation of criteria exercises, group discussion, and peer review using checklists.

Credit Recommendation: In the upper division baccalaureate degree category, 1 semester hour in Adult Education, Business Communication, or Behavioral Science (9/96).

Decision Analysis (MR-S33)

Location: National Cryptologic School, Ft. Meade, MD.

Length: 24 hours (3 days).
Dates: October 1986-September 1996.
Objective: To solve decision problems.
Learning Outcome: Upon successful completion of this course, the student will be able to analyze and apply decision analysis rules and models to problems.
Instruction: Major topics covered in the course are concepts; uncertainty; benefits/cost analysis; and computer applications. Methods of instruction include lecture, discussion, class exercises, and case studies.
Credit Recommendation: In the graduate degree category, 1 semester hour in Decision Science, Managerial Decision Analysis, or Management Science (8/91).

Defense Contracts Management for Technical Personnel (MT-420)

Location: National Cryptologic School, Ft. Meade, MD.
Length: 40 hours (1 week).
Dates: October 1986-Present.
Objective: To provide technical personnel with an overview of the statutory and procedural requirements associated with basic contracting functions and pre-award and post-award segments of the contracting process.
Learning Outcome: Upon successful completion of this course, the student will be able to understand and interact as a team member in the acquisition process; to address the requirements determination by identifying scope of needs; appreciate the respective roles of technical and contracting personnel; and appreciate and adhere to the pertinent public policy guidelines by all three branches of the government.
Instruction: Major topics covered in the course are planning for the specific acquisition, statement of work, and preparation of purchase requests and solicitations document (IFB and RFP). Methods of instruction include lectures, case studies, and open discussion.
Credit Recommendation: In the upper division baccalaureate degree category, 3 semester hours in Business Administration, Business Management, Business Law, or Paralegal Studies (8/91) (9/94).

Defense Small Purchases (MT-431)

Location: National Cryptologic School, Ft. Meade, MD.
Length: 80 hours (2 weeks).
Dates: January 1989-August 1996.
Objective: To determine material availability; use FSSPG; monitor progress on order; apply contract administration factors when warranted; and choose the best and most effective method of making small purchases.
Learning Outcome: Upon successful completion of this course, the student will be able to know small purchase procedures from FAR; basic statutes, and authorities for, governing procurement and understanding of the FAR; and students will know the techniques for government purchasing costing up to $25,000.
Instruction: Major topics covered in the course are standards of conduct; regulations; acquisition authority and responsibility; government sources of supply; administrative matters; purchase request review; pre-solicitation consideration; clauses/provision; solicitation procedures; price-related factors; price evaluation; determination of responsibility; Blanket Purchase Agreement (BPA); purchase order/delivery order; imprest fund/SF 44; services; construction; and small purchase administration. Methods of instruction include lectures, case studies, and open discussions.
Credit Recommendation: In the upper division baccalaureate degree category, 1 semester hour in Contracting Procurement, Acquisition/Contract Field, Small Purchase Administration, or Contract Management (8/91).

Designing Computer-Based Training (ED-243)

Location: National Cryptologic School, Ft. Meade, MD.
Length: 40 hours (5 days).
Dates: June 1990-January 1995.
Objective: To provide experienced platform instructors and course developers with tools needed to design CBT with emphasis on learning design and development strategies.
Learning Outcome: Upon successful completion of this course, the student will be able to develop instructionally sound CBT (Computer-Based Training); use the TENCORE producer authoring system; and design, develop, and code an actual CBT lesson.
Instruction: Major topics covered in the course are definitions of CBT, CAT, and CMI; CBT design/development cycles; and evaluation phase. Methods of instruction include a computer and projection system.
Credit Recommendation: In the upper division baccalaureate degree category, 2 semester hours in Business Administration, Business Management, Instructional Technology, Adult Education, or Training (8/91).

Designing Interactive Video Instruction (EDE-09)

Location: National Cryptologic School, Ft. Meade, MD.
Length: 40 hours (5 days).
Dates: September 1989-August 1990.
Objective: To provide knowledge and skills needed for designing interactive training programs that use video, CBJ, visuals, touch screens, and panels, hype text, etc. Designers will aim to learn strategies for and actually do multimedia flowcharting and design.
Learning Outcome: Upon successful completion of this course, the student will be able to construct flow charts and story boards that contain examples of each type of multimedia, include exercises for each of the five types of content, and use instrumentational strategies that support examples.
Instruction: Major topics covered in the course are systematic approaches for instructional design, learning outcomes, types of learning outcomes, and sequence of learning outcome; construction of institutional strategies; analysis of strategies; description of applications; advantages of authorizing systems, instructional messages, strategies as flowcharts, story board frames; and development of project plans. Methods of instruction include lecture, discussion, classroom exercises, case studies, role playing, and problem-solving.
Credit Recommendation: In the upper division baccalaureate degree category, 2 semester hours in Educational Technology, Media Technology, or Methods of Instruction (8/91).

Developing Case Studies (ED-222)

Location: National Cryptologic School, Ft. Meade, MD.
Length: 32 hours (4 days).
Dates: May 1996-Present.
Objective: To provide a training professional with the skills to successfully develop and facilitate case studies.
Learning Outcome: Upon successful completion of this course, the student will be able to define case studies; identify the critical parts of the case and design them with the adult learner in mind, explain full/partial case studies; construct and evaluate a case plan; and explain learning styles and questioning techniques to effectively facilitate a case study.
Instruction: Major topics covered in the course are an overview of the case

study method, types of case studies, case plans, evaluating performance, and facilitating case studies. Methods of instruction include lecture, discussion, classroom exercises, case studies, learner presentations and reports, and case study projects.

Credit Recommendation: In the upper division baccalaureate degree category, 2 semester hours in Instructional Design, Methods of Teaching, or Human Resource Development (9/96).

Developing Objectives and Tests (ED-170)

Location: National Cryptologic School, Ft. Meade, MD.

Length: *Version 1:* 40 hours (5 days); *Version 2:* 24 hours (3 days).

Dates: *Version 1:* January 1990-September 1995; *Version 2:* October 1995-Present.

Objective: *Version 1:* To provide instructors with the tools needed to apply the rules of performance agreement, item construction, and validation to produce a test that matches a set of formal performance objectives. *Version 2:* To provide instructors with the tools needed to conduct a job task analysis and to apply the rules of performance agreement, item construction, and validation to produce a test that matches a set of formal performance objectives.

Learning Outcome: Upon successful completion of this course, the student will be able to perform a task/content analysis; to construct formal performance objectives for the subordinate skills identified in the analysis; and to use the formal performance objectives to construct and evaluate assessment instruments, a performance test and items in a written test.

Instruction: *Version 1:* Major topics covered in the course are performance agreements; item construction; and validation of performance-based tests. Methods of instruction include lecture, classroom exercises, case studies, and instructional games. *Version 2:* Major topics covered in the course are conducting a job task analysis, constructing formal performance objectives, constructing assessment instruments, and evaluating assessment instruments. Methods of instruction include lecture, discussion, classroom exercises, scenarios, projects, and gallery presentation with peer and instructor feedback.

Credit Recommendation: *Version 1:* In the upper division baccalaureate degree category, 2 semester hours in Instruction Planning and Design or Needs Assessment (Education Methods or Human Resource Development) (8/91). *Version 2:* In the upper division baccalaureate degree category, 1 semester hour in Needs Assessment or Instruction Planning and Design (9/96). *Prerequisite:* Course ED-125.

Distance Learning Teaching Methods (ED-205)

Location: National Cryptologic School, Ft. Meade, MD.

Length: 24 hours (3 days).

Dates: December 1991-Present.

Objective: To provide instructors with knowledge and skills needed to teach or manage a course(s) presented via the NCS's Distance Leaning Network.

Learning Outcome: Upon successful completion of this course, the student will be able to create and deliver lessons in two-way audio and video in a distance learning environment; use equipment utilized in a distance learning delivery system; develop lesson plans, graphics, and student handouts; discuss and evaluate distance learning presentations; and develop a checklist.

Instruction: Major topics covered in the course are distance learning facility and networking; organizing and developing lessons; designing graphics and handouts, and network protocols. Methods of instruction include lecture, discussion, classroom exercises, audio/visual material, computer-assisted instruction, learner reports, and group and individual presentations.

Credit Recommendation: In the upper division baccalaureate degree category, 2 semester hours in Distance Education or Human Resource Development (9/96).

Effective Agency Writing I (EG-055) (Formerly Introductory Writing [EG-022])

Location: National Cryptologic School, Ft. Meade, MD.

Length: *Version 1:* 48 hours (8 weeks); *Version 2:* 36 hours (6 weeks).

Dates: October 1986-Present.

Objective: To teach grammatical and structural rules and paragraph development.

Learning Outcome: Upon successful completion of this course, the student will be able to recognize and correct mechanical and grammatical errors in writing and practice proper sentence structure, punctuation, word choice, and paragraph development.

Instruction: Major topics covered in the course are the parts of speech, sentence structure, phrases and their functions, clauses, form, punctuation, and development of sentences and paragraphs. Methods of instruction include lecture; discussion; classroom exercises; quizzes; review of written paragraphs, memoranda, and personal summaries; and a final examination.

Credit Recommendation: In the vocational certificate category, 1 semester hour in English or Writing (8/91) (9/96).

Effective Agency Writing II (EG-155) (Formerly Expository Writing [EG-122])

Location: National Cryptologic School, Ft. Meade, MD.

Length: 48 hours (8 weeks).

Dates: *Version 1:* October 1986-October 1991; *Version 2:* November 1991-Present.

Objective: *Version 1:* To teach sentence and paragraph development. *Version 2:* To teach sentence and paragraph development, essay writing, and research skills.

Learning Outcome: *Version 1:* Upon successful completion of this course, the student will be able to recognize and correct common writing problems and to write more effectively in an organizational environment. *Version 2:* Upon successful completion of this course, the student will be able to recognize and correct common writing problems and write effective paragraphs, essays, and research papers.

Instruction: *Version 1:* Major topics covered in the course are grammar and common problems; abuses to avoid, including jargon and federalese; and strengths to develop, including clarity and persuasiveness. *Version 2:* Major topics covered in the course are grammar and common writing problems; abuses to avoid, including jargon and federalese; clarity and tone; paragraph and essay development; and research skills. Methods of instruction include lecture, discussion, classroom exercises, quizzes, papers, and a final examination.

Credit Recommendation: *Version 1:* In the lower division baccalaureate/associate degree category, 2 semester hours in English composition, English writing, Communications, Business writing, or Journalism. *Version 2:* In the lower division baccalaureate/associate degree category, 3 semester hours in English composition, English writing, or Communications (8/91) (5/92) (9/96).

Government Contract Law (MT-424)

Location: National Cryptologic School, Ft. Meade, MD.

Length: 80 hours (64 in class; 18 outside).

Dates: October 1986-August 1996.

Objective: To provide experienced contracting personnel knowledge of government contract law and how it pertains to the procurement field.

Learning Outcome: Upon successful completion of this course, the student will be able to understand the essential elements of a contract; compare governmental and commercial contracting processes and remedies; and participate in the contract disputes procedure.

Instruction: Major topics covered in the course are contract elements; general contract principles and authoring; modification of contracts; equitable adjustment; disputes procedure; patents and data; labor law; and remedies of the government. Methods of instruction include lecture, case studies, and a student presentation.

Credit Recommendation: In the graduate degree category, 3 semester hours in Business Administration or Business Management (8/91).

ILS Elements and Applications (MR-430)

Location: National Cryptologic School, Ft. Meade, MD.

Length: 80 hours (2 weeks).

Dates: October 1986-August 1996.

Objective: To teach integrated logistics support management.

Learning Outcome: Upon successful completion of this course, the student will be able to prepare a draft preliminary ILSP for acquisition.

Instruction: Major topics covered in the course are ILS elements; maintenance and support concept development; logistics support analysis (LSA); technical data; the MEILSR process; logistics aspects of a purchase description and contract data requirement list (CDRL); cost of support; ILS planning conference; configuration management and quality assurance; and program execution.

Credit Recommendation: In the graduate degree category, 1 semester hour in Logistics, Governmental Contract Logistics, or Contracting (8/91).

Information Mapping: Developing Procedures, Policies, and Documentation (EG-236) (Formerly Information Mapping: Developing Procedures, Policies, and Documentation (ED-236))

Location: National Cryptologic School, Ft. Meade, MD.

Length: 24 hours (3 days).

Dates: November 1992-Present.

Objective: To transfer the analytical and organization skills of the information mapping writing method to the design and development of technical documents or training materials.

Learning Outcome: Upon successful completion of this course, the student will be able to design and develop job aids, course handouts, and reference materials that are complete, accurate, accessible, and effective.

Instruction: Major topics covered in the course are mapping for the seven basic information types (procedures, processes, structures, concepts, policies, facts, and classifications), managing the size of the message, gathering information and drafting key blocks; and sequencing and completing the draft. Methods of instruction include lecture, discussion, classroom exercises, case studies, audio/visual material, and projects.

Credit Recommendation: In the upper division baccalaureate degree category, 1 semester hour in Business Communication, Technical Writing, Management, Education, or Instructional Methods (9/96).

Instructional Design and Cognitive Psychology (ED-180)

Location: National Cryptologic School, Ft. Meade, MD.

Length: *Version 1:* 40 hours (5 days), 20 hours outside work; *Version 2:* 64 hours (8 days), 30 hours outside work.

Dates: *Version 1:* February 1990-June 1991; *Version 2:* June 1991-Present.

Objective: To teach experienced platform instructors and curriculum specialists the knowledge and skills needed to incorporate cognitive psychology research data into the instructional design process.

Learning Outcome: Upon successful completion of this course, the student will be able to make use of psychology of learning and instruction methods that support human information process; evaluate existing lesson to identify strengths and weaknesses in terms of human information processing; and develop short lessons for evaluation and revision using instructional strategies associated with cognitive learning.

Instruction: Major topics covered in the course are ISD process, job and task analysis, instructional methods media selection, designing instruction for working memory, evaluating instructional effectiveness, and designing instruction for long-term memory evaluation. Methods of instruction include lecture, discussion, classroom exercise, case studies, role playing, problem-solving, and computer-assisted/videotape.

Credit Recommendation: *Version 1:* In the graduate degree category, 2 semester hours in Cognitive Psychology, Educational Psychology, Psychology of Learning, Educational Methodology, or Instructional Psychology (8/91). *Version 2:* In the graduate degree category, 4 semester hours in Cognitive Psychology, Educational Psychology, Psychology of Learning, Educational Methodology, or Instructional Psychology (8/91) (5/92).

Instructional Media-VIDEOSHOW (ED-203)

Location: National Cryptologic School, Ft. Meade, MD.

Length: 24 hours (3 days).

Dates: November 1989-July 1996.

Objective: To provide instructors and support personnel the knowledge and skills needed to create graphics.

Learning Outcome: Upon successful completion of this course, the student will be able to create an original video show presentation from scratch, containing pictures and slides, bar, pie, or diagram chart.

Instruction: Major topics covered in the course are video show picture formats, word charts, diagrams, pie charts, bar charts, and graphs. Methods of instruction include computer-based (computers and projection system used by both instructor and students).

Credit Recommendation: In the upper division baccalaureate degree category, 1 semester hour in Instructional Technology or Adult Education (8/91).

Instructional Programs Development (ED-181)

Location: National Cryptologic School, Ft. Meade, MD.

Length: 40 hours (1 week).

Dates: March 1996-Present.

Objective: To provide fundamental skills needed to plan, organize, and produce training courses by applying a systematic approach to instructional engineering and development.

Learning Outcome: Upon successful completion of this course, the student will be able to give instruction in the four basic principles underlying training programs and demonstrate how to use the Instructional System Design (ISD) process for systematic planning of training.

Instruction: Major topics covered in this course are how to do a job analysis including, classification of skills on a performance matrix and utilization of information mapping techniques; write lesson outlines; learning objectives; formal training manuals; design practice exercises and job aids; identify cost effective delivery of media; and evaluate sources of training. Methods of instruction include lecture, discussion, classroom exercises, precourse readings, quizzes, and a final project.

Credit Recommendation: In the graduate degree category, 3 semester hours in Educational Psychology, Psychology of Learning, Educational Methodology, or Human Resource Development (9/96).

Instructor Training Curriculum (ITC) (ED-001-007)

Location: National Cryptologic School, Ft. Meade, MD.

Length: 29 hours (1 week).

Dates: September 1989-December 1995.

Objective: To familiarize students with the basic teaching theories, skills, and techniques for effective classroom instruction.

Learning Outcome: Upon successful completion of this course, the student will be able to identify six major instructor responsibilities; apply learning theory; analyze an audience before and during a course; design course and development; use delivery skills in communication and teaching methodologies; handle challenging situations; test development; and evaluate course effectiveness.

Instruction: Major topics covered in the course are course and design development learning theory, analyzing the audience, delivery skills, responding to challenging situations, test development, and evaluating course effectiveness. Methods of instruction include computer-assisted/videotaped with video disk simulation; CBT testing; and a final written examination.

Credit Recommendation: In the upper division baccalaureate degree category, 2 semester hours in Educational Methods, Instruction, Methods of Teaching, or Adult Education (8/91).

Integrative Leadership Skills (MD-300)
(Formerly Critical Management Skills [MD-300])
(Formerly Integrative Management and Leadership Skills for Mid-Level Leaders [MD-300])

Location: National Cryptologic School, Ft. Meade, MD.

Length: *Version 1:* 136 hours (3 weeks); *Version 2:* 120 hours (2.5 weeks); *Version 3:* 80 hours (2 non consecutive weeks).

Dates: *Version 1:* January 1989-August 1994; *Version 2:* June 1993-Present.

Objective: *Versions 1 and 2:* To enable mid-level managers to broaden their knowledge and skills of modern management concepts, philosophy, and techniques by using an individual management development plan. *Version 3:* To enable mid-level leaders to broaden their knowledge of and skills in leadership concepts, philosophy, and techniques.

Learning Outcome: *Versions 1 and 2:* Upon successful completion of this course, the student will be able to identify internal and external components of their environment, increase their awareness and sensitivity, broaden perspective on managerial issues, recognize their personal leadership tendencies and select avenues for future development, demonstrate an understanding of current management practices, and assess needs for self-development activities. *Version 3:* Upon successful completion of this course, the student will be able to effectively meet the mission and human resource challenges created by a rapidly changing NSA environment whether they are leaders from the managerial or technical fields.

Instruction: *Versions 1 and 2:* Major topics covered in the course are the managerial environment, ethics, communication skills, leadership, organizational development, planning tools, problem-solving/decision-making, conflict management/negotiation, managing change, stress management, employee selection, team building, organizational culture and design, and leading the empowered workforce. Methods of instruction include lecture, group exercises, discussion, classroom exercises, case studies, use of Management Excellence Inventory (U.S. Office of Personnel Management), and case presentations. *Version 3:* Major topics covered in the course are communications, conflict management, the Malcolm Baldridge Award, Groupthink, creativity, diversity, EEO, vision, and a "senior perspective" on leadership. Methods of instruction include lecture, discussion, class exercises, situational skills practices, student activities, presentations, and the development of an action plan.

Credit Recommendation: *Versions 1 and 2:* In the upper division baccalaureate degree category, 6 semester hours in Behavioral Science or Managerial Science, and in the graduate degree category, 3 semester hours in Behavioral Science or Managerial Science (11/89) (9/94). *Version 3:* In the upper division baccalaureate degree category or the graduate degree category, 6 semester hours in Behavior Science or Managerial Science (9/96).

Introduction to Computer Based Training (CBT) (EDE-11)

Location: National Cryptologic School, Ft. Meade, MD.

Length: 24 hours (3 days plus 15 hours of computer-based training).

Dates: September 1989-Present.

Objective: To provide managers and novice platform instructors an overview of the CBT development process and indicate when CBT is a cost-effective alternative.

Learning Outcome: Upon successful completion of this course, the student will be able to use an authoring software package for personal computers and design, create, and run a module of tutorial computer-assisted instruction.

Instruction: Major topics covered in the course are CBT terms and concepts, CBT hardware options, sequencing alternatives, and introduction to teaching frames. Methods of instruction include computers to develop CBT programs, writing a unit objective, and designing a unit test based on specific content supplied by the instructor.

Credit Recommendation: In the lower division baccalaureate/associate degree category, 2 semester hours in Computer Technology, Business Management, or Instructional Technology (8/91) (9/96).

Introduction to Cost Estimation and Life Cycle Cost (MR-S84)

Location: National Cryptologic School, Ft. Meade, MD.

Length: *Version 1:* 32 hours (4 days); *Version 2:* 40 hours (5 days).

Dates: *Version 1:* October 1986-July 1993; *Version 2:* August 1993-Present.

Objective: To introduce the student to life cycle cost management and the fundamentals of cost estimating.

Learning Outcome: Upon successful completion of this course, the student will be able to understand life cycle cost management, cost estimating, and the problems associated with it.

Instruction: Major topics covered in the course are R&D production and O&M costs; cost breakdown structures; cost estimates and budgeting; cost estimating techniques (analogy, parametric, engineering) with an emphasis on parametric, cost/quality relationships; cost analysis and trade-off studies; cost/risk relationships; and an overview of the cost models used at NSA and the procedures to be followed to get cost estimating support. Methods of instruction include lecture, discussion, and classroom exercises.

Credit Recommendation: In the upper division baccalaureate degree category, 1 semester hour in Managerial and Cost Accounting or Project Management (8/91).

Introduction to Counseling Techniques (MC-122) (Formerly MO-300)

Location: National Cryptologic School, Ft. Meade, MD.

Length: 40 hours (5 days).

Dates: March 1989-August 1996.

Objective: To examine current counseling style and basic preferences for collecting information and processing it in a counseling environment.

Learning Outcome: Upon successful completion of this course, the student will be able to explore and develop skills in self-awareness, message sending, listening, receiving, and feedback to apply to counseling; develop counseling style and basic preference for collecting information; and show skills and techniques regarding climate, listening, feeling, attending skills; questioning; managing conflict; problem-solving; and interviewing.

Instruction: Major topics covered in the course are Meyers-Briggs type indicator; listening skills; audiotaped counseling session; feedback; nonverbal communication skills; paraphrasing/questions skills; verbal communication skills; structuring the counseling session; assertiveness training; audiotape critiquing; related problem-solving skills; professional ethics; and evaluation of counseling video. Methods of instruction include active lecture, discussion, classroom exercises, case studies, role playing, problem-solving, and videotape critiquing.

Credit Recommendation: In the upper division baccalaureate degree category, 1 semester hour in Counseling or Supervision (8/91).

Introduction to Management (MC-107) (Crypotologic Management) (Formerly Cryptologic Management for Interns [MC-107])

Location: National Cryptologic School, Ft. Meade, MD.

Length: 35 hours (1 week).

Dates: March 1975-August 1979.

Objective: To enable new supervisors to develop interpersonal administrative skills to improve job performance.

Instruction: Major topics covered in the course are the functions of supervision, styles of leadership, personnel practices, interpersonal communications, motivation, performance appraisal and counseling, decision-making and problem-solving. Methods of instruction include lecture, discussion, case studies, and group exercises.

Credit Recommendation: In the lower division baccalaureate/associate degree category, 2 semester hours in Business Administration or Management (9/76) (11/82). **NOTE:** Credit should be granted for this course or for MC-105, but not for both. *Prerequisites:* Assigned to a supervisory position; completion of Cryptologic Management for Managers (MC-210) and Cryptologic Management for Supervisors (MC-120); voluntary participation.

Introduction to Supervision (MC-105)

Location: National Cryptologic School, Ft. Meade, MD.

Length: 35 hours (1 week).

Dates: September 1970-October 1989.

Objective: To enable new supervisors to develop interpersonal and administrative skills to improve their job performance.

Instruction: Major topics covered in the course are the functions of supervision, styles of leadership, personnel practices, interpersonal communications, motivation, performance appraisal and counseling, and decision-making and problem-solving. Methods of instruction include lecture, discussion, case studies, and group exercises.

Credit Recommendation: In the lower division baccalaureate/associate degree category, 2 semester hours in Business Administration or Management (9/76) (11/82) (11/89). **NOTE:** Credit should be granted for this course or for Introduction to Management (MC-107), but not for both. Additionally, a substantial portion of the material in this course is covered in MC-120. This course has been reevaluated and continues to meet the requirements for credit recommendations.

Introduction to Systems Acquisitions (MR-460)

Location: National Cryptologic School, Ft. Meade, MD.

Length: *Version 1:* 40 hours (5 days); *Version 2:* 32 hours (4 days).

Dates: *Version 1:* October 1986-September 1993; *Version 2:* October 1993-August 1996.

Objective: To introduce an overview of acquisition process with emphasis on program activities.

Learning Outcome: Upon successful completion of this course, the student will be able to work in, and understand, the NSA system acquisition process.

Instruction: Major topics covered in the course are acquisition environment and players; systems acquisition life cycle planning (with emphasis on engineering perspective); integrated logistic support aspects; contracting and performance measurement aspects; and acquisition execution. Methods of instruction include lecture, discussion, and classroom exercises.

Credit Recommendation: In the graduate degree category, 1 semester hour in Project Management or Production/Project Management (8/91).

Management Courses 1. Critical Management Skills (MD-300) 2. The Managerial Environment (MD-30A)

Location: National Cryptologic School, Ft. Meade, MD.

Length: *Course 1:* 88 hours (11 days); *Course 2:* 40 hours (5 days).

Dates: April 1986-January 1989.

Objective: To enable mid-level managers to broaden their knowledge and skills of modern management concepts, philosophy, and techniques by using individual management development plan.

Learning Outcome: Upon successful completion of this course, the student will be able to identify internal and external components of their environment, increase their awareness and sensitivity, and broaden perspective on managerial issues; recognize their personal leadership tendencies and select avenues for future development; and demonstrate an understanding of current management practices; and assess present staff needs of self-development activities.

Instruction: Major topics covered in the course are communication skills, leadership, organizational development, planning and forecasting, problem-solving/decision-making, conflict management/negotiation, managing change, stress/time management, employee selection, and team building. Methods of Instruction Include lecture, group exercises, discussion, case studies, use of Management Excellence Inventory (U.S. Office of

Personnel Management), case presentations, and written examination.

Credit Recommendation: In the upper division baccalaureate degree category, 6 semester hours in Behavioral Science or Managerial Science, and in the graduate degree category, 3 semester hours in Behavioral Science or Managerial Science (8/91). **NOTE:** These two courses duplicate the course content of the stand-alone course Critical Management Skills (MD-300).

Management of Defense Acquisition Contracts-Basic (MT-425)

Location: National Cryptologic School, Ft. Meade, MD.

Length: 160 hours (4 weeks).

Dates: October 1986-August 1996.

Objective: To provide detailed understanding of information regarding military contracting procedures and applicable statutes including FAR, DFARS, and other directives and court decisions.

Learning Outcome: Upon successful completion of this course, the student will be able to recognize constitutional and statutory authority in support of military acquisitions; understand basic terminology used throughout FAR and DFARS; and understand the major methods of contracting (formal advertising and negotiation).

Instruction: Major topics covered in the course are legal authority for federal acquisition, e.g., Constitution Art.I, 8 statutes, e.g., ASPA of 1947; 10 USC 2304; general FAR and DFARS purposes and policies; construction contracting; competition; terminations; and disputes and appeals. Methods of instruction include lecture, discussion, viewgraphs, and class exercises.

Credit Recommendation: In the graduate degree category, 3 semester hours in Contract or Acquisition Management (8/91).

Managerial Grid Seminar (MG-240)

Location: National Cryptologic School, Ft. Meade, MD.

Length: 50 hours (5.5 days); residential; 30 hours preparatory independent study.

Dates: January 1967-May 1987.

Objective: To enable managers to understand and apply the management grid concept.

Instruction: Major topics covered in the course are an introduction to the managerial grid and clarification of the grid concept, with special emphasis on application of grid techniques. Method of instruction includes extensive use of practical exercises.

Credit Recommendation: In the upper division baccalaureate degree category, 2 semester hours, or in the graduate degree category, 1 semester hour, in Business Administration or Management (9/76).

Mind Tools (ED-182)

Location: National Cryptologic School, Ft. Meade, MD.

Length: 16 hours (2 days).

Dates: June 1996-Present.

Objective: To teach students how to apply human information processing and learning theory to the design, development, and delivery of training.

Learning Outcome: Upon successful completion of this course, the student will be able to apply research-based instructional principles; use the latest techniques for instructional development; and apply problem-solving skills.

Instruction: Major topics covered in the course are an overview of human information-working memory; how to avoid cognitive overload; and design practice exercises for learning, problem-solving, and analytic skills. Methods of instruction include lecture, discussion, classroom exercises, quizzes, peer review, and checklists.

Credit Recommendation: In the graduate degree category, 1 semester hour in Cognitive Psychology, Educational Psychology, Psychology of Learning, Educational Methodology, or Human Resource Development (9/96).

Minimum Essential Integrated Logistics Support (ILS) Requirements (MEILSR) (MR-S21)

Location: National Cryptologic School, Ft. Meade, MD.

Length: 24 hours (3 days).

Dates: October 1986-August 1996.

Objective: To understand and participate in the minimum essential integrated logistics support process.

Learning Outcome: Upon successful completion of this course, the student will be able to apply rules on minimum essential ILS on both a system level and a equipment level.

Instruction: Major topics covered in the course are acquisition process, maintenance and support, and regulation. Methods of instruction include lecture and practical exercises.

Credit Recommendation: In the graduate degree category, 1 semester hour in Industrial Management or Industrial Engineering (8/91). *Prerequisite:* MR-430.

Organizational Problem Solving for Executives (MC-320) (Formerly Executive-Level Problem Analysis and Decision Making Seminar[MG-320])

Location: National Cryptologic School, Ft. Meade, MD.

Length: 50 hours (5.5 days); residential; 30 hours preparatory independent study.

Dates: July 1969-September 1982.

Objective: To enable executive-level managers to improve their ability to integrate the concepts of problem-solving and decision-making with those of the communication process.

Instruction: Major topics covered in the course are communication, planning, and problem-solving; concept integration; quantitative decision- making; problem diagnosis and means-ends analyses; and group process and individual approaches. Methods of instruction include extensive use of case studies and practical exercises.

Credit Recommendation: In the upper division baccalaureate degree category or in the graduate degree category, 3 semester hours in Management (9/76) (11/82). **NOTE:** Credit should be granted for this course or for MG-230, but not for both.

Organizational Problem Solving for Managers (MC-230) (Formerly Manager-Level Decision Making Seminar [MG-320])

Location: National Cryptologic School, Ft. Meade, MD; San Angelo, TX.

Length: 50 hours (5.5 days); residential; 30 hours preparatory independent study.

Dates: December 1970-December 1986.

Objective: To enable mid-level managers to improve their ability to integrate the concepts of problem- solving and decision-making with those of the communication process.

Instruction: Major topics covered in the course are communication, planning, and problem-solving; concept integration; total systems integration; problem diagnosis and means-ends analyses; and group process and individual approaches. Methods of instruction include extensive use of case studies and practical exercises.

Credit Recommendation: In the upper division baccalaureate degree category or in the graduate degree category, 3 semester hours in Management (9/76) (11/82).

NOTE: Credit should be granted for this course or for MG-320, but not for both.

Resource Management in Systems Acquisition (MR-457)

Location: National Cryptologic School, Ft. Meade, MD.

Length: 40 hours (5 days).

Dates: September 1989-September 1996.

Objective: To provide the student with a working knowledge and the management skills needed to participate in the planning, programming, budgeting, and execution cycle within the systems acquisition process.

Learning Outcome: Upon successful completion of this course, the student will be able to develop skills in planning, programming, budgeting, and execution cycle, and identify, analyze, evaluate, and resolve resource-related tasks, problems, and issues.

Instruction: Major topics covered in the course are introduction to resource management, NSA Systems Acquisition, NSAC 25-5 Planning and Decision Documentation; PPBS and Resource Management; DOD and NSA Planning, DOD programming and Budgeting, CRP/CSP and TCP Program Budget Development; CCP-Consolidated Crypto-logic Program, Manpower Management; Cost Estimating/ Life Cycle Costing; Decision Analysis; Case Study; PBS1/ PBRG; Congressional Budget Process; Financial Plan (FIN-PLAN); Plan Develop-ment; FINPLAN-Case Study; Contracting Planning and Solicitation; and Purchase Request (PR) Development and Review. Methods of instruction include lecture, class exercises, case studies, and open discussion.

Credit Recommendation: In the upper division baccalaureate degree category, 2 semester hours in Marketing, Procurement, Contracting, or Systems Acquisition (8/91).

Software Acquisition Management (MR-600)

Location: National Cryptologic School, Ft. Meade, MD.

Length: 40 hours (5 days).

Dates: October 1986-April 1995.

Objective: To teach software acquisition management.

Learning Outcome: Upon successful completion of this course, the student will be able to understand and manage the software acquisition process.

Instruction: Major topics covered in the course are rules and guidance, policies, design, test, acceptance, and maintenance.

Credit Recommendation: In the graduate degree category, 1 semester hour in Logistics, Purchasing, Business Marketing, Acquisition Management, or Computer Science (8/91).

Software Cost Estimation (MR-S16)

Location: National Cryptologic School, Ft. Meade, MD.

Length: 40 hours (5 days).

Dates: October 1986-September 1997.

Objective: To survey estimation procedures for software costs.

Learning Outcome: Upon successful completion of this course, the student will be able to understand the software life cycle; identify cost estimation methods; and estimate software cost.

Instruction: Major topics covered in the course are life cycles, estimation method, and parameters. Methods of instruction include lecture and discussion.

Credit Recommendation: In the graduate degree category, 1 semester hour in Industrial Engineering, Cost Analysis, or Managerial Accounting (8/91).

Software Project Management (MR-S19)

Location: National Cryptologic School, Ft. Meade, MD.

Length: *Version 1:* 24 hours (3 days); *Version 2:* 40 hours (5 days).

Dates: *Version 1:* October 1986-September 1991; *Version 2:* October 1991-Present.

Objective: To provide students with introduction to theories and techniques of software management.

Learning Outcome: Upon successful completion of this course, the student will be able to manage software projects effectively in an organizational setting.

Instruction: Major topics covered in the course are project management principles; planning tools and techniques; software development plans; work breakdown schedules; risk analysis; organizing; and staff and team building. Methods of instruction include lecture, discussion, and classroom exercises.

Credit Recommendation: In the graduate degree category, 1 semester hour in Management, Industrial Engineering, or Computer Science (8/91).

Software Quality Assurance (MR-S89)

Location: National Cryptologic School, Ft. Meade, MD.

Length: 24 hours (3 days).

Dates: October 1986-September 1994.

Objective: To introduce the student to the process of assuring quality in software development projects and to provide the student with techniques for measuring and assuring software quality.

Learning Outcome: Upon successful completion of this course, the student will be able to perform software quality analysis.

Instruction: Major topics covered in the course are quality control; quality testing; quality engineering; how to implement a software QA program; and how to specify quality requirements in contracts, critique QA plans and proposals, and manage quality-related aspects of software developments. Methods of instruction include lecture, discussion, case studies, and exercises.

Credit Recommendation: In the graduate degree category, 1 semester hour in Project Management, Operations Management, Production/Project Management in Business Administration, or Public Administration (8/91).

Software Requirements Analysis (MR-S04)

Location: National Cryptologic School, Ft. Meade, MD.

Length: 40 hours (5 days).

Dates: October 1986-July 1994.

Objective: To improve understanding of software requirement.

Learning Outcome: Upon successful completion of this course, the student will be able to specify software requirement for analysis.

Instruction: Major topics covered in the course are functional requirements, real-time analysis, Petri-Nets, and guidelines. Methods of instruction include lecture, discussion, and case study exercises.

Credit Recommendation: In the graduate degree category, 1 semester hour in Operation Research or Computer Science (8/91).

Software Structured Analysis and Design (MR-S15)

Location: National Cryptologic School, Ft. Meade, MD.

Length: 40 hours (5 days).

Dates: October 1986-March 1994.

Objective: To introduce structured analysis and design of software.

Learning Outcome: Upon successful completion of this course, the student will be able to do basic structural design of software.

Instruction: Major topics covered in the course are terminology, flow diagrams, notation, convention, logic models, tree structure, design language, and evaluation. Methods of instruction include lecture, discussion, case studies, and exercises.

Credit Recommendation: In the graduate degree category, 1 semester hour in Programming Computer Science or Software Design (8/91).

Software Structured Testing (MR-S07)

Location: National Cryptologic School, Ft. Meade, MD.

Length: 24 hours (3 days).

Dates: October 1986-August 1994.

Objective: To improve knowledge of software testing.

Learning Outcome: Upon successful completion of this course, the student will be able to develop structured software tests.

Instruction: Major topics covered in the course are flowchart notation, complexity, integration, and test tools. Methods of instruction include lecture, discussion, case studies, and exercises.

Credit Recommendation: In the graduate degree category, 1 semester hour in Computer Science, Programming, or Software Testing (8/91).

The Congressional Process
1. The Congressional Hearing Process (XT-371)
2. Judiciary, Media, and Interest Groups (XT-323)
3. The Presidency and the Executive Branch (XT-320)
4. The Congress (XT-312)

Location: National Cryptologic School, Ft. Meade, MD.

Length: *Course 1:* 26 hours (4 days); *Course 2: Version 1:* 24 hours (3 days); *Version 2:* 32 hours (4 days); *Course 3:* 18 hours (2.5 days); *Course 4:* 18 hours (2.5 days).

Dates: *Course 1:* October 1983-Present; *Course 2: Version 1:* June 1983-August 1989; *Version 2:* August 1989-August 1996; *Course 3:* May 1982-Present; *Course 4:* September 1981-Present.

Objective: To provide executives with an appreciation of the broad governmental environment in which public agencies operate.

Learning Outcome: Upon successful completion of this course, the student will be able to demonstrate a broad understanding of the federal government's organizational structure and processes by effectively preparing for interfaces with executive branch, congressional, judicial, media, and special interest entities. These offerings are designed to broaden the perspectives of the students with respect to the external environment.

Instruction: Major topics covered in the course are executive branch structure and process; congressional branch structure and process; judicial structure and process; and media and interest groups as players in governmental processes.

Credit Recommendation: In the graduate degree category, 3 semester hours in Governmental Relations, Public Administration, or Political Process (8/91). **NOTE:** To receive credit, student must complete 3 of 4 courses.

Training Methods for Cryptologic Instructors (ED-101)
(Formerly Training Methods for Adjunct Faculty [ED 101])

Location: National Cryptologic School, Ft. Meade, MD.

Length: 40 hours (5 days).

Dates: December 1988-Present.

Objective: To provide experienced subject matter experts with an overview of training methods and methodologies needed to develop objectives, design correlating exercises, and select appropriate instructional strategies.

Learning Outcome: Upon successful completion of this course, the student will be able to analyze and meet the instructional needs of the adult learner; organize and sequence content in the NCS lesson plan format; and display presentation skills, effective platform methods, and questioning techniques.

Instruction: Major topics covered in the course are andragogy, applying adult learning and adult learning styles, Instructional System Design (ISD), writing objectives, presentation techniques, organizing content, training methods, media, and support materials. Methods of instruction include lecture, instruction and classroom role-playing for problem-solving, student practice exercises, criterion exercises, performance evaluation, self evaluation, and peer-based evaluation.

Credit Recommendation: In the graduate degree category, 3 semester hours in Adult Education, Business Communications, or Behavior Science (8/91) (9/96).

Training Needs Analysis and Assessment (ED-190)

Location: National Cryptologic School, Ft. Meade, MD.

Length: 24 hours (3 days).

Dates: *Version 1:* March 1991-November 1994; *Version 2:* December 1994-Present.

Objective: To provide knowledge and skills for assessing training needs and to recommend appropriate training intervention.

Learning Outcome: *Version 1:* Upon successful completion of this course, the student will be able to conduct a needs assessment; prepare recommendations for starting an instructional system; and define evaluation and explain where it fits in the training needs assessment process. *Version 2:* Upon successful completion of this course, the student will be able to state why needs assessment is the first stage of the Instructional Systems Design (ISD) process and describe specific steps, tools, and techniques for conducting needs assessments.

Instruction: Major topics covered in the course are the purpose of a needs assessment; systematic approach; and defining five stages: needs assessment, thinking about it, how to do it, how to use it, and evaluation. Methods of instruction include classroom exercises, written exercises, case studies, and role play.

Credit Recommendation: In the graduate degree category, 2 semester hours in Instructional Design, Methods of Teaching, Adult Education, or Human Resource Development (8/91) (9/96).

Transactional Analysis (MG-255)

Location: National Cryptologic School, Ft. Meade, MD.

Length: 28 hours (2 weeks); two full-day sessions per week; 8 hours preparatory independent study.

Dates: October 1975-October 1976.

Objective: To enable managers to improve management skills through interpersonal communications.

Instruction: Major topics covered in the course are the definition of ego states, application of ego states in interpersonal communications, and role of transactional analysis. Methods of instruction include lecture, discussion, and practical exercises.

Credit Recommendation: In the upper division baccalaureate degree category, 1 semester hour in Behavioral Science or Communication (9/76) (11/82).

Writing Workshop (EG-322)

Location: National Cryptologic School, Ft. Meade, MD.

Length: 36 hours (6 weeks).

Dates: October 1986-September 1992.

Objective: To teach the principles of good writing and editing skills.

Learning Outcome: Upon successful completion of this course, the student will be able to write and edit clearly, critically, and in plain English.

Instruction: Major topics covered in the course are audience analysis, voice, draft interaction to final form, letters, memos, jargon, and style.

Credit Recommendation: In the upper division baccalaureate degree category, 1 semester hour in English, Writing, or Journalism (8/91).

MATHEMATICS DEPARTMENT

Combinatorial Mathematics (MA-414)

Location: National Cryptologic School, Fort Meade, MD.

Length: 48 hours (6 hours per week for 8 weeks).

Dates: January 1975-Present.

Objective: To introduce advanced principles of combinatorial theory and illustrate a wide range of current and potential applications.

Learning Outcome: Upon successful completion of this course, the student will be able to perform a wide array of advanced combinatorial manipulations and solve most classical conbinatorial identities.

Instruction: Major topics covered in the course are techniques of enumeration, generating functions and recursions, Mobus inversion in partially order set, fast transformations, systems of distinct representatives, lating squares, finite geometries, Hadamard matrices, block design and difference sets, and code design. Methods of instruction include lecture, exercises, advanced problems, and examinations.

Credit Recommendation: In the graduate degree category, 3 semester hours in Advanced Operations Research (I.E. or E.E.), Artificial Intelligence, or Mathematics (special topics) (10/85) (9/94).

Fourier Analysis (MA-302) (Formerly Fourier Analysis)

Location: National Cryptologic School, Fort Meade, MD.

Dates: January 1975-July 1990.

Objective: To provide students with an extensive coverage of Fourier analysis and advanced coverage of select Fourier analysis applications in engineering and physics.

Instruction: Major topics covered in the course are an overview of the many applications of the Fourier transformation and its many forms, continuous, discrete, multidimensional, and optical transformations and review of complex variable theory, Residue Theorem, Cauchy-Schwartz, and Rumann-Lebesgue Lemma. Methods of instruction include lecture; discussion; exercises; (unsolved) problems; research on present, real-world applications; and problem-solving.

Credit Recommendation: In the graduate degree category, 3 semester hours in Applied Mathematics, Electrical Engineering Applications of Fourier Analysis, or Physics (10/85).

Intermediate Algebra (MA-111)

Location: National Cryptologic School, Ft. Meade, MD.

Length: 100 hours (12 weeks maximum); self-paced.

Dates: June 1983-Present.

Objective: To develop the algebra skills necessary for precalculus.

Learning Outcome: Upon successful completion of this course, the student will be able to perform basic algebraic manipulations necessary for precalculus.

Instruction: Major topics covered in the course are rational, real, and complex numbers, laws for manipulating numbers, properties of exponents, solving linear equations, graphing linear functions, polynomials, quadratic equations, solving radical equations, and fractional equations. Methods of instruction include self-paced lecture material problems, discussions, exercises, and an examination.

Credit Recommendation: In the lower division baccalaureate/associate degree category, 3 semester hours in College Algebra (11/89) (9/94).

Introduction to Astrodynamics (MA 500)

Location: National Cryptologic School, Fort Meade, MD.

Length: 48 hours (6 hours per week for 8 weeks).

Dates: January 1975-Present.

Objective: To introduce students to the concepts and applications of astrodynamics.

Learning Outcome: Upon successful completion of this course, the student will be able to numerically integrate various equations of motion; determine classical orbits; and do guidance and space navigation problems.

Instruction: Major topics covered in the course are coordinating systems and time scales and references; two-body problems; perturbations, special and general; powered flight; and orbit determination and tracking. Methods of instruction include lecture, discussion, exercises, and projects.

Credit Recommendation: In the graduate degree category, 3 semester hours in Astronomy, Geophysics, Mathematical Modeling, or Operations Research (10/85) (9/94).

Introduction to Computer Science Math (MA 400)

Location: National Cryptologic School, Fort Meade, MD.

Length: 60 hours (6 hours per week for 10 weeks).

Dates: July 1976-Present.

Objective: To provide mathematical knowledge and skills beyond college and intermediate algebra, with which to proceed into math-related computer coursework and applications, and statistics.

Learning Outcome: Upon successful completion of this course, the student will be able to perform most basic algebraic manipulations necessary for introductory courses in computer science.

Instruction: Major topics covered in the course are problems in the topical areas of linear functions, arrays and matrices, polynomial functions, exponential and logarithmic functions, logic tables, and Boolean algebra. Methods of instruction include lecture, exercises, and a final examination.

Credit Recommendation: In the lower division baccalaureate/associate degree category, 3 semester hours in Finite Mathematics or Precalculus Math (10/85) (9/94).

Mathematical Statistics (MA 146)

Location: National Cryptologic School, Fort Meade, MD.

Length: 60 hours (6 hours per week for 10 weeks).

Dates: January 1975-April 1990.

Objective: To provide students with an advanced coverage of statistics utilizing calculus-based mathematics (integral calculus required).

Instruction: Major topics covered in the course are the nature of statistical methods; elementary sampling theory for one variable; correlation, regression, and theoretical frequency distributions for studying these; general principles for hypothesis testing and estimation; testing goodness of fit; small sample distributions; and cryptologic examples and exercises. Course stresses both theory and cryptologic applications.

Credit Recommendation: In the upper division baccalaureate or graduate degree category, 2 semester hours in Economics, Math Statistics, or M.B.A. Stat/ Quantitative Applications (10/85).

Probability and Statistics (MA 144) (Formerly Social Sciences Statistics) (Formerly Economics/Business Administration Statistics)

Location: National Cryptologic School, Fort Meade, MD.

Length: *Version 1:* 72 hours (12 weeks); *Version 2:* 48 hours (8 weeks).

Dates: *Version 1:* July 1976-August 1994; *Version 2:* September 1994-Present.

Objective: To provide an introduction and overview of the theory and applications of probability, descriptive statistics, and statistical testing.

Learning Outcome: Upon successful completion of this course, the student will be able to analyze, interpret, and present data using elementary statistical techniques.

Instruction: Major topics covered in the course are over permutations; combinations; probability rules; Bayes rule; descriptive statistics; binomial, Poisson, and normal distributions; point and interval estimation; sampling; hypothesis testing; Student t-distribution, chi-square, regression, and correlation analysis; and non-parametric statistics. Methods of instruction include lecture, exercises, problems, and examinations.

Credit Recommendation: *Version 1:* In the lower division baccalaureate/associate degree category, 3 semester hours in Business Administration or Economics (10/85). *Version 2:* In the lower division baccalaureate/associate degree category, 2 semester hours in Business Administration or Economics (9/94).

Probability Theory (MA 145)

Location: National Cryptologic School, Fort Meade, MD.

Length: 60 hours (6 hours per week for 10 weeks).

Dates: January 1975-February 1990.

Objective: To provide students with an advanced coverage of probability theory utilizing calculus-based mathematics (integral calculus required).

Instruction: Major topics covered in the course are probability theory as a study of mathematical models of random phenomena; basic probability theory; random variables; independence and dependence; Markov chains; numerical-valued random phenomena; mean and variance of a probability law; normal, Poisson, and related probability laws; and cryptologic examples and exercises.

Credit Recommendation: In the upper division baccalaureate or graduate degree category, 2 semester hours in Economics, M.B.A. Stat/Quantitative Applications, or Math Statistics (10/85).

National Education Training Group

National Education Training Group (NETG) has a 27-year history of providing information technology professionals with high quality, interactive training solutions. Today, NETG's interactive multimedia training includes titles in such key areas as Client/Server and networking, end-user computing and management and professional development. With partnerships with leading providers in the information technology industry, including Microsoft and Novell, NETG is able to provide Anytime Anywhere Learning to meet strict certification examination guidelines and the core skills requirements for today's "technology worker".

NETG's courses are designed using only the best instructional design practices. These efforts ensure students engage in a learning experience focused on attaining skills that can be practiced in a simulated application environment and verified through mastery testing-before they return to work environment. By providing courses that teach the way adults learn, NETG is able to help students overcome the barriers of limited time and resources to take training. Each course offers intuitive navigation icons, hands-on exercises, and mastery test exercises that provide first class self-paced and self-directed learning.

NETG's courses are delivered using a wide host of technology platforms. This "delivery flexibility" allows every organization to gain further value in the investment in hardware by providing training deployable over CD-Rom equipped workstations, Local and Wide Area Networks (LAN/WAN) and standard workstations without CD-Rom capability. With the growth in Internet and corporate intranet technologies, NETG is developing strategies that can leverage technology for virtual access to skills when and where they are needed most.

To receive additional information about NETG, please call 1-800-265-1900. To obtain information about NETG by mail, write to NETG-1751 Diehl Road; Suite 200, Naperville, IL 60563.

AUTHORIZED NATIONAL EDUCATION TRAINING GROUP SITE

Georgia-Pacific/PSC
133 Peachtree Street, 24th Floor
Atlanta, GA 30303
Contact: Niki P. Cook, Director
Performance Support and Executive Development
Phone No.: 404-652-6431
Fax No.: 404-654-4826
E-mail: NPCOOK@GAPAC.COM

Source of official student records: Registry of Credit Recommendations, American Council on Education, One Dupont Circle, Washington, DC 20036-1193.

Additional information about the courses: College Credit Recommendation Service, American Council on Education, One Dupont Circle, Washington, DC 20036-1193.

Access 95 Development (70551, 70552, 70553)

Location: Computer-based.
Length: Self-paced.
Dates: October 1996-Present.

Objective: To improve application development skills to use advanced features such as Visual Basic for application and data access objects.

Learning Outcome: Upon successful completion of this course, the student will be able to apply OLE Automation and OLE Controls, create add-in, work with forms, implement security for applications, synchronize data, and manage related client/server issues.

Instruction: Major topics covered in the course are introduction to VB Programming, providing functionality to forms and reports, Programming Objects, trapping and preventing errors, working with Records, communicating with other applications, working with Windows DLL, working with add-ins, optimizing and application performance, and client/server application development. Methods of instruction include materials available on CD-ROM, network, or intranet for self-study.

Credit Recommendation: In the lower division baccalaureate/associate degree category, 1 semester hour in Computer Science or Computer Information Systems (5/97). **NOTE:** Student must complete 3 of 3 modules to receive credit.

C++ Programming with MFC 4.0 Library Version 2 (70611, 70612, 70613, 70614, 70615)

Location: Computer-based.
Length: Self-paced.
Dates: October 1996-Present.

Objective: To introduce concepts necessary for developing applications using Microsoft Visual C++ 4.0.

Learning Outcome: Upon successful completion of this course, the student will be able to develop applications using Visual C++.

Instruction: Major topics covered in the course are fundamentals of windows architecture, MFC fundamentals and architecture, building an application framework using Visual C++, implementing user interfaces, outputting simple text and graphics, document/view architecture and component gallery, dialog boxes, command routing and update command handling, storing and retrieving data, implementing ODBC support in MFC, programming in MFC, and registry and MFC platform issues. Methods of instruction include materials available on CD-ROM, network, or intranet for self-study.

Credit Recommendation: In the lower division baccalaureate/associate degree category, 2 semester hours in Programming (5/97). **NOTE:** Student must complete 5 of 5 modules to receive credit. Also 2 hours credit maximum for Version 1 and Version 2.

C++ Programming with MFC Class 4.0 Library (70611-70612-70613)

Location: Computer-based.
Length: Self-paced.
Dates: June 1996-Present.

Objective: To introduce C++ Programming with Microsoft Foundation Class 4.0 Library.

Learning Outcome: Upon successful completion of this course, the student will be able to discuss how to use Microsoft Visual C++ with Microsoft Foundation Class 4.0.

Instruction: Major topics covered in the course are fundamentals of Windows Architecture, MFC fundamentals and implementing user interfaces, outputting simple text and graphics, Document/View architecture and Component gallery, dialog boxes, command routing and update command handling, storing and retrieving. Methods of instruction include course materials available on CD-Rom for self-study, and tests.

Credit Recommendation: In the lower division baccalaureate/associate degree category, 1 semester hour in Programming (9/96). **NOTE:** Students must complete 3 of 3 modules to receive credit.

C Series (12688)

Location: Computer-based.
Length: Self-paced.
Dates: May 1996-Present.

Objective: To introduce the C programming language.

Learning Outcome: Upon successful completion of this course, the student will be able to use C to develop applications.

Instruction: Major topics covered in the course are to define the basic elements of the language, including fundamental types, constants, operators, statements and functions; understand the key concepts of pointers and arrays, structures, unions, type conversations and scope and linkage; utilize machine-level programming in C, C memory management, and C and C++ preprocessor directives; and understand ANSI C and other widely used C function libraries. Methods of instruction include course materials available on CD-Rom for self-study, and tests.

Credit Recommendation: In the lower division baccalaureate/associate degree category, 1 semester hour in Programming (9/96).

C/C++ Series (11678)

Location: Computer-based.

Length: Self-paced.

Dates: March 1996-Present.

Objective: To introduce C++.

Learning Outcome: Upon successful completion of this course, the student will be able to use C++ to develop applications.

Instruction: Major topics covered in the course are to compare the features that are common to C++ and C, understand the C++ and understand details that are essential for writing solid C++ programs. Methods of instruction include course materials available on CD-Rom for self-study, and tests.

Credit Recommendation: In the lower division baccalaureate/associate degree category, 1 semester hour in Programming (9/96).

CICS/ESA 4.1 Programming (11947, 11949)

Location: Computer-based.

Length: Self-paced.

Dates: December 1996-Present.

Objective: To design, code, and use BMS maps and page building.

Learning Outcome: Upon successful completion of this course, the student will be able to design, code, and use BMS; and discuss program structure, control, and commands to use the Execution Diagnostic Facility (EDF).

Instruction: Major topics covered in the course are introduction to designing and coding MNS Maps, using BMS Maps, program structure and control, file handling commands, temporary storage and transient data, and execution diagnostic facility. Methods of instruction include student guide and computer-based instruction for self-study.

Credit Recommendation: In the lower division baccalaureate/associate degree category, 1 semester hour in Computer Science or Computer Information Systems (5/97). **NOTE:** Students must complete 2 of 2 modules to receive credit.

COBOL for MVS and VM (11954, 12009, 11955, 11980)

Location: Computer-based.

Length: Self-paced.

Dates: September 1996-Present.

Objective: To introduce COBOL programming for MVS and VM.

Learning Outcome: Upon successful completion of this course, the student will be able to write COBOL programs and use COBTEST as a debugging tool.

Instruction: Major topics covered in the course are introduction to programming fundamentals, defining data fields and data types, defining data and structuring the Procedure Division, initializing data fields and editing numeric data, writing a report program, performing arithmetic operations, coding alternative processing, presenting data and records, combining repetitive statement, control break processing, file handling, sorting, performing setup and displaying panels, and running a COBTEST session. Methods of instruction include student guide and computer-based instruction for self-study.

Credit Recommendation: In the lower division baccalaureate/associate degree category, 2 semester hours in COBOL Programming (5/97). **NOTE:** Students must complete 4 of 4 modules to receive credit.

DB2 SQL (12018, 12299, 12300, 12302)

Location: Computer-based.

Length: Self-paced.

Dates: January 1997-Present.

Objective: To develop code using SQL.

Learning Outcome: Upon successful completion of this course, the student will be able to code, retrieve, and manipulate embedded SQL statements and prepare a VS/COBOL program using SQL statements.

Instruction: Major topics covered in the course are introduction to embedding SQL statements, preparing programs for execution, data definition language (DDL), data control language (DCL), basic SELECT statements, advanced SELECT statements, selection from multiple tables, and writing embedded SQL and CICS, JCL, and CICS/DB2 interface. Methods of instruction include student guide and computer-based instruction for self-study.

Credit Recommendation: In the lower division baccalaureate/associate degree category, 1 semester hour in Computer Science or Computer Information Systems (5/97). **NOTE:** Students must complete 4 of 4 modules to receive credit.

General DB2 Version 4 Track (12016, 12017, 12065)

Location: Computer-based.

Length: Self-paced.

Dates: August 1997-Present.

Objective: To introduce concepts, terminology, structural components, and facilities associated with the DB2 release 4 environment including: QMF, Utilities, and Operating Techniques.

Learning Outcome: Upon successful completion of this course, the student will be able to explain the concepts, terminology, structural components, and facilities associated with the DB2 release 4 environment including: QMF, Utilities, and Operating Techniques.

Instruction: Major topics covered in the course are DB2 Objects, the system environment and SQL, programming environment and SQL and application cycle, referential integrity and distributed processing; getting started in QMF, query processing in SQL and QBE, formatting reports, executing and monitoring DB2 Utilities, database preventive maintenance, maintaining database integrity; starting monitoring and stopping DB2, and controlling DB2 subsystem connections. Methods of instruction include student guide and computer-based instruction for self-study.

Credit Recommendation: In the lower division baccalaureate/associate degree category, 1 semester hour in Computer Science or Computer Information Systems (5/97). **NOTE:** Student must complete modules number 12016 and at least another module (12017 or 12065) to receive credit.

IBM OS/390 MVS/ESA5.x, Job Control Language (JCL) (12196, 12225)

Location: Computer-based.

Length: Self-paced.

Dates: July 1996-Present.

Objective: To introduce job submission, job control language, and interpreting

JCL listing for error conditions and use advanced JCL coding for creating and accessing generation data groups (GDG).

Learning Outcome: Upon successful completion of this course, the student will be able to identify basic JCL components; interpret syntax notation used wit JCL; code the most commonly used keyword parameters of the job statement; identify and use the PARM parameter; and code a referback between job steps and producers.

Instruction: Major topics covered in the course are introduction to coding JCL to create jobs and apply advanced JCL features. Methods of instruction include student guide, computer based instruction for self-study, and a text.

Credit Recommendation: In the lower division baccalaureate/associate degree category, 1 semester hour in Computer Science or Computer Information Systems (5/97). **NOTE:** Students must complete 1 of 2 modules to receive credit.

IBM OS/390 MVS/ESA5.x, Operations and Job Entry System 2 (JES2) Operations (12324, 12325)

Location: Computer-based.

Length: Self-paced.

Dates: May 1997-Present.

Objective: To introduce tasks applicable to running the IBM OS/390 operating system and Job Entry System 2 (JES2).

Learning Outcome: Upon successful completion of this course, the student will be able to develop knowledge and skill to run the master console; load and shut down the operating system; and run JES2.

Instruction: Major topics covered in the course are introduction to understand the IPL process and the steps necessary to activate the system, perform a standalone dump, control syslog and SMF data output, compose MVS commands to control the operating system and identify which manuals are required for assistance, compose JES 2 command to control the submission, starting and control of batch jobs, and identify which manuals are required for assistance. Methods of instruction include student guide, computer based instruction for self-study, and a text.

Credit Recommendation: In the lower division baccalaureate/associate degree category, 1 semester hour in Computer Science or Computer Information Systems (5/97). **NOTE:** Students must complete at least 1 of the 2 modules for credit.

IBM OS/390 MVS/ESA5.x, Production and Development Tools (12227, 12228, 12231, 12232, 12301, 12330)

Location: Computer-based.

Length: Self-paced.

Dates: November 1996-Present.

Objective: To introduce ISPF features used for programming, editing, compiling, linking, and testing programs with a COBOL orientation.

Learning Outcome: Upon successful completion of this course, the student will be able to display and edit databases; program using Restructured Extended Executor Language (REXX) for MVS; use ISPF dialogue manager; and select and execute utility programs.

Instruction: Major topics covered in the course are ISPF production and development tools, REXX programming, and selecting and executing utility programs. Methods of instruction include student guide, computer based instruction for self-study, and a text.

Credit Recommendation: In the lower baccalaureate/associate degree category, 3 semester hours in Computer Science or Computer Information Systems (5/97). **NOTE:** Students must complete 6 of 6 modules to receive credit.

Implementing Microsoft Exchange Server (71361, 71362, 71363)

Location: Computer-based.

Length: Self-paced.

Dates: November 1996-Present.

Objective: To implement Microsoft Exchange in a single-site environment.

Learning Outcome: Upon successful completion of this course, the student will be able to install, configure, troubleshoot, and support Microsoft Exchange.

Instruction: Major topics covered in the course are fundamentals of Microsoft Exchange, designing an exchange organization, installing server and client, directory service, administration of mail related tasks, administration of message recipients and optional services, and migration to a Microsoft Exchange organization. Methods of instruction include materials available on CD-ROM, network, or intranet for self-study.

Credit Recommendation: In the lower division baccalaureate/associate degree category, 1 semester hour in Computer Science or Computer Information Systems (5/97). **NOTE:** Students must complete 3 of 3 modules to receive credit.

Introduction to Network Communications with Microsoft TCP/IP for Windows NT 3.5x (80201-80202-70417-70418)

Location: Computer-based.

Length: Self-paced.

Dates: May 1996-Present.

Objective: To introduce the concepts and terminology of computer network communications and the features of TCP/IP for Windows NT 3.5x.

Learning Outcome: Upon successful completion of this course, the student will be able to explain the concepts of computer network communications, identify the features of TCP/IP, and explain how to install and configure an FTP server.

Instruction: Major topics covered in the course are terms and concepts of computer network communications; components of TCP/IP network; installing and configuring an FTP server. Methods of instruction include course materials available on CD-Rom for self-study, and tests.

Credit Recommendation: In the lower division baccalaureate/associate degree category, 1 semester hour in Telecommunications (9/96). **NOTE:** Students must complete 4 of 4 modules to receive credit.

Microsoft SQL Server 6.0 System Administration and Database Design (70471-70472-70473-70475-70476-70477)

Location: Computer-based.

Length: Self-paced.

Dates: April 1996-Present.

Objective: To identify system administration tasks that can be performed using Microsoft SQL Server 6.0 and provide a basic understanding of database design, simple data transfer and manipulation.

Learning Outcome: Upon successful completion of this course, the student will be able to understand the process by which Microsoft SQL 6.0 client/server systems interact and the fundamentals of database design and system components of SQL Server 6.0.

Instruction: Major topics covered in the course are installation techniques for the server and client; identify the process of automatic and custom synchronization; understanding of client/server database designs; management of disk space; table creation; different methods of data retrieval and manipulation, and the creation of views and indexes and their use.

Methods of instruction include course materials available on CD-Rom for self-study, and tests.

Credit Recommendation: In the lower division baccalaureate/associate or upper division baccalaureate degree category, 1 semester hour in System Administration or Database Design (9/96). **NOTE:** Students must complete 6 of 6 modules to receive credit.

Microsoft Visual C++ Series (11676)

Location: Computer-based.

Length: Self-paced.

Dates: May 1996-Present.

Objective: To introduce Windows programming using Visual C++ and Microsoft Foundation Class.

Learning Outcome: Upon successful completion of this course, the student will be able to understand the essentials of Microsoft Visual C++ for developing Windows-based applications and identify features of Microsoft Foundation Class and the graphic tools of Visual C++.

Instruction: Major topics covered in the course are introduction of object, class program structure, inheritance, information hiding, identify, polymorphism, interface, analysis,associations and standards. Methods of instruction include course materials available on CD-Rom for self-study, and tests.

Credit Recommendation: In the upper division baccalaureate degree category, 1 semester hour in Programming (9/96).

Microsoft Windows 3.x (11144-11145-11569-11657-11712-11756-11829)

Location: Computer-based.

Length: Self-paced.

Dates: December 1992-Present.

Objective: To introduce the fundamental applications of Microsoft Windows 3.x.

Learning Outcome: Upon successful completion of this course, the student will be able to perform basic Microsoft applications in Windows, Word 6.0, Excel 5.0, and either PowerPoint 4.0 or Access 2.0 and be able to apply skills to individual work.

Instruction: Major topics covered in the course are basic applications in Word 6.0 (development of basic document), Excel 5.0 (identification of fundamental features), PowerPoint 4.0 (screen elements and navigation) and/or Access 2.0 (fundamentals of a database). Methods of instruction include course materials available on CD-Rom for self-study, and tests.

Credit Recommendation: In the lower division baccalaureate/associate degree category, 1 semester hour in Computer Applications (9/96). **NOTE**: Students must complete 6 or 7 modules (electives included) to receive credit.

Microsoft Windows 95-Advanced (70012-70022-70032-70091)

Location: Computer-based.

Length: Self-paced.

Dates: February 1996-Present.

Objective: To improve the basic understanding of Windows 95 and introduce advanced features of Windows 95.

Learning Outcome: Upon successful completion of this course, the student will be able to apply advanced Windows 95 applications using Word for 95 and Excel for 95 and understand the Windows 95 Office Integration environment.

Instruction: Major topics covered in the course are desktop customization, time savers, communications and networks, remote computing, import and export of text and data, data query and mapping. Methods of instruction include course materials available on CD-Rom for self-study, and tests.

Credit Recommendation: In the lower division baccalaureate/associate degree category, 1 semester hour in Computer Applications (9/96). **NOTE:** Students must complete 4 of 4 modules to receive credit.

Microsoft Windows 95-Fundamentals (70011-70021-70031-70041-70051-70061-70071-70081)

Location: Computer-based.

Length: Self-paced.

Dates: August 1995-Present.

Objective: To introduce the basic features of Microsoft Windows 95 through completion of 6 of 8 modules involving Word for 95, Excel for 95, PowerPoint for 95, and Access for 95.

Learning Outcome: Upon successful completion of this course, the student will be able to use the basic features of Windows 95 applications software and demonstrate mastery of fundamental vocabulary of Windows 95 applications.

Instruction: Major topics covered in the course are fundamentals of Windows 95, Word, Excel, PowerPoint, and Access for Windows 95 and a basic knowledge of Scheduler+ and Microsoft Project. Methods of Instruction include course materials available on CD-Rom for self-study, and tests.

Credit Recommendation: In the lower division baccalaureate/associate degree category, 1 semester hour in Computer Applications (9/96). **NOTE**: Students must complete 6 of 8 modules (electives included) to receive credit.

Microsoft Windows NT 4.0 Track (71410, 71411, 71412, 71413)

Location: Computer-based.

Length: Self-paced.

Dates: January 1997-Present.

Objective: To present the concept involved in installing, configuring, customizing, and supporting Microsoft Windows NT Server 4.0.

Learning Outcome: Upon successful completion of this course, the student will be able to install, configure, customize, optimize, network, integrate, and troubleshoot Windows NT 4.0.

Instruction: Major topics covered in the course are introduction to Microsoft Windows, installing NT Server, configuring NT environment, user profiles and system policies, managing user and group accounts, managing file systems, fault tolerance, applications supported by the NT server, NT-based networking environment, network protocols configuration, NT networking services, NT features, functions and tools related to server and workstation, security, subsystems, Kernel mode components, and remote access service (RAS) and telephony application programming interface (TAPI). Methods of instruction include materials available on CD-ROM, network, and intranet for self-study.

Credit Recommendation: In the lower division baccalaureate/associate degree category, 1 semester hour in Computer Science or Computer Information Systems (5/97). **NOTE:** Students must complete 4 of 4 modules to receive credit.

MVS/ESA 5.2 Debug and Analyze Program Problems (12329)

Location: Computer-based.

Length: Self-paced.

Dates: January 1997-Present.

Objective: To introduce concepts for debugging and analyzing program problems.

Learning Outcome: Upon successful completion of this course, the student will be able to locate errors in a dump to pinpoint logic and I/O errors.

Instruction: Major topics covered in the course are dump and debug concepts, program logic errors, I/O error debugging, additional I/O errors, and on-line debugging with IPCS. Methods of instruction include student guide and computer-based instruction for self-study.

Credit Recommendation: In the lower division baccalaureate/associate degree category, 1 semester hour in Computer Science or Computer Information Systems (5/97).

Networking Essentials (70421, 70422, 70423)

Location: Computer-based.

Length: Self-paced.

Dates: November 1996-Present.

Objective: To introduce the concepts and terminology for local area and wide area networks.

Learning Outcome: Upon successful completion of this course, the student will be able to understand current networking technology for local and wide area networks.

Instruction: Major topics covered in the course are network operating system terms and definition, architectures and protocols, data transmission, network communication, standards, operating system, peripherals, and applications. Methods of instruction include materials available on CD-ROM and network or intranet for self-study.

Credit Recommendation: In the lower division baccalaureate/associate degree category, 1 semester hour in Computer Science or Computer Information Systems (5/97). **NOTE:** Students must complete 3 of 3 modules to receive credit.

Novell GroupWise 4 Administration (80601-80602-80701)

Location: Computer-based.

Length: Self-paced.

Dates: June 1996-Present.

Objective: To familiarize students with Novell GroupWise Administration and asynchronous gateways.

Learning Outcome: Upon successful completion of this course, the student will be able to explain the procedures to set up and maintain single and multiple post office systems; and explain how to manage async gateways.

Instruction: Major topics covered in the course are installing GroupWise to primary domains; administering single post offices and clients; working with multiple domains and post offices; and understanding async gateways and GroupWise remote. Methods of instruction include course materials available on CD-Rom for self-study, and tests.

Credit Recommendation: In the lower division baccalaureate/associate degree category, 1 semester hour in Network Administration (9/96).

Novell NetWare 4.1 Implementation and Administration (80301-80302-80311-80312-80401-80501)

Location: Computer-based.

Length: Self-paced.

Dates: June 1996-Present.

Objective: To present the concepts involved in implementing and administrating Novell NetWare 4.1.

Learning Outcome: Upon successful completion of this course, the student will be able to explain the process involved in installing, upgrading, and configuring Novell NetWare 4.1.

Instruction: Major topics covered in the course are installing NetWare 4.1; upgrading 3.1x to NetWare 4.1; configuring a NetWare environment; and managing NetWare 4.1 server. Methods of instruction include course materials available on CD-Rom for self-study, and tests.

Credit Recommendation: In the lower division baccalaureate/associate degree category, 1 semester hour in System Administration (9/96). **NOTE:** Students must complete 6 of 6 modules to receive credit.

Novell NetWare 4.11 Administration (81301, 81302, 81303, 81311, 81312, 81313)

Location: Computer-based.

Length: Self-paced.

Dates: February 1997-Present.

Objective: To administer performance tuning with Novell IntraNetWare 4.11.

Learning Outcome: Upon successful completion of this course, the student will be able to perform tasks associated with daily administration; do performance tuning for the network server; and design NetWare directory services (NDS) structure trees.

Instruction: Major topics covered in the course are server startup procedures, file configurations, network concepts, directory tree structures (DTS), client network support, map network and search drives, security, integrating and managing NetWare 3 servers, and configuration of the NetWare 4 servers for diverse clients. Methods of instruction include materials available on CD-ROM, network, or intranet for self-study.

Credit Recommendation: In the lower division baccalaureate/associate degree category, 2 semester hours in Computer Science or Computer Information Systems (5/97). **NOTE:** Students must complete 6 of 6 modules to receive credit.

Novell NetWare 4.11 Installation, Service and Support (80211, 80212, 80213, 80214, 81401, 81402)

Location: Computer-based.

Length: Self-paced.

Dates: February 1997-Present.

Objective: To install, configure, service and support Novell NetWare (intranet) version 4.11.

Learning Outcome: Upon successful completion of this course, the student will be able to explain the process of installation, configuration, troubleshooting, and supporting a Novell IntraNetWare 4.11.

Instruction: Major topics covered in the course are installing NetWare 4.11, upgrading 3.5x to NetWare 4.11, configuring in a NetWare environment, troubleshooting NetWare problems using Micro House Technical Library, use Network Support Encyclopedia Professional (NSE Pro) volume, manage cabling and network boards, and identify steps involved in installing network boards and hard disks. Methods of instruction include computer-based training and testing.

Credit Recommendation: In the lower division baccalaureate/associate degree category, 2 semester hours in Computer Science or Computer Information Systems (5/97). **NOTE:** Must complete 6 of 6 modules to receive credit.

Object COBOL Series (11981)

Location: Computer-based.

Length: Self-paced.

Dates: May 1996-Present.

Objective: To introduce key concepts of object technology and its extension to COBOL language.

Learning Outcome: Upon successful completion of this course, the student will be able to understand object-oriented concepts and structure of object COBOL language.

Instruction: Major topics covered in the course are introduction of object, class program structure, inheritance, information hiding, identity, polymorphism, interface, analysis, associations and standards. Methods of instruction include course materials available on CD-Rom for self-study, and tests.

Credit Recommendation: In the upper division baccalaureate degree category, 1

semester hour in Computer Science or Computer Information Systems (9/96).

Object-Oriented Development (11677-12653-12654)

Location: Computer-based.
Length: Self-paced.
Dates: April 1996-Present.
Objective: To introduce the basic concepts of object technology, define objects, introduce CRC, OMT and Booch notations, and dynamic modeling.
Learning Outcome: Upon successful completion of this course, the student will be able to understand the role of object technology in software development, the concepts of inheritance, polymorphism, representation of object, and classes, and representation of problems with CC, OMT and Booch notations, and dynamic modeling.
Instruction: Major topics covered in the course are basics of object technology, object-oriented life cycle; class responsibility collaboration (CRC) technique to identify objects, object-modeling techniques (OMT) and Booch notation, association and entertainment relations, inheritance, polymorphism, object-identify; and dynamic modeling. Methods of instruction include course materials available on CD-Rom for self-study, and tests.
Credit Recommendation: In the upper division baccalaureate degree category, 1 semester hour in Computer Science or Computer Information Systems (9/96). **NOTE:** Students must complete 3 of 3 modules to receive credit.

OLE Series (11982)

Location: Computer-based.
Length: Self-paced.
Dates: May 1996-Present.
Objective: To introduce rationale behind OLE, Windows Object Structured Storage Model, and Uniform Data Transfer technology.
Learning Outcome: Upon successful completion of this course, the student will be able to understand rationale behind OLE, concept of Windows object, component object model, structured storage model, and architecture of compound documents.
Instruction: Major topics covered in the course are rationale for use of Visual C++ environment, tools; MFC concepts, basics of drawing and painting; core MFC classes supporting Windows-based applications; and recognizing issues related to Visual C++ programming and the MFC. Methods of instruction include course materials available on CD-Rom for self-study, and tests.
Credit Recommendation: In the lower division baccalaureate/associate degree category, 1 semester hour in Microcomputer Applications (9/96).

Oracle 7 Administration and Programming (11838-11839-11841-11842-11843)

Location: Computer-based.
Length: Self-paced.
Dates: March 1995-Present.
Objective: To introduce Oracle 7 administration and programming.
Learning Outcome: Upon successful completion of this course, the student will be able to explain how to perform basic and advanced administrative tasks and Oracle 7; complete tasks associated with application development; manage database objects; and manipulate data.
Instruction: Major topics covered in the course are introduction to Oracle 7; introduction to PL/SQL programming; making queries; and manipulating data. Methods of instruction include course materials available on CD-Rom for self-study, and tests.
Credit Recommendation: In the lower division baccalaureate/associate degree category, 1 semester hour in Database (9/96). **NOTE:** Students must complete 5 of 5 modules to receive credit.

PowerBuilder 4.0 (11831-12083)

Location: Computer-based.
Length: Self-paced.
Dates: October 1994-Present.
Objective: To provide an introduction to PowerBuilder 4.0 and understand how to build applications within a Windows environment.
Learning Outcome: Upon successful completion of this course, the student will be able to identify and describe the major features used to build applications within a Windows environment.
Instruction: Major topics covered in the course are introduction to PowerBuilder 4.0; application development; building windows and controls; writing script for windows and controls; retrieving data using alternate presentation styles; transaction management; Data Window mechanisms and techniques; reporting; dynamic Data Windows and dynamic SQL. Methods of Instruction include course materials available on CD-Rom for self-study, and tests.
Credit Recommendation: In the lower division baccalaureate/associate degree category, 1 semester hour in Power Builder 4.0 (9/96). **NOTE:** Students must complete 2 of 2 modules to receive credit.

Supporting Windows 95 (70311-70312-70313)

Location: Computer-based.
Length: Self-paced.
Dates: November 1995-Present.
Objective: To present the skills to implement and support Microsoft Windows 95.
Learning Outcome: Upon successful completion of this course, the student will be able to describe the features of the Windows 95 networking architecture and explain the steps involved in setting up and supporting Windows 95.
Instruction: Major topics covered in the course are installing and configuring Windows 95 and troubleshooting. Methods of instruction include course materials available on CD-Rom for self-study, and tests.
Credit Recommendation: In the lower division baccalaureate/associate degree category, 1 semester hour in Systems Administration (9/96). **NOTE:** Students must complete 3 of 3 modules to receive credit.

Sybase System 10.01 (11658-11659-11661-11662-11663)

Location: Computer-based.
Length: Self-paced.
Dates: June 1994-Present.
Objective: To provide an overview of the Sybase System 10 architecture.
Learning Outcome: Upon successful completion of this course, the student will be able to understand the basic architecture of the Sybase System 10; explain basic T-SQL programming tasks; demonstrate the administration of Sybase System 10 in a client/server environment, the monitoring and tuning of the SQL server for performance improvements and the management of remote servers.
Instruction: Major topics covered in the course are introduction to Sybase System 10 architecture; Sybase Server; introduction to server programming, writing stored procedures; writing triggers; managing transactions and locking; cursors; T-SQL programming; performing queries and manipulating data; basic and advanced topics in system administration. Methods of instruction include course materials available on CD-Rom for self-study, and tests.
Credit Recommendation: In the lower division baccalaureate/associate degree or

upper division baccalaureate degree category, 1 semester hour in Database Design (9/96). **NOTE:** Students must complete 5 of 5 modules to receive credit.

TCP/IP for MVS (12322, 12323)

Location: Computer-based.
Length: Self-paced.
Dates: June 1996-Present.
Objective: To introduce concepts of TCP/IP for MVS.
Learning Outcome: Upon successful completion of this course, the student will be able to install and implement TCP/IP for MVS.
Instruction: Major topics covered in the course are concepts of TCP/IP, TELNET, differences between TELNET and TN370, connection to the mainframe from the IP network, CLAW devices, installing and customizing the product, interfacing TCP/IP to CICS, using IMS interfaces for TCP/IP, and set up NETVIEW interfaces for TCP/IP. Methods of instruction include student guide and computer-based instruction for self-study.
Credit Recommendation: In the lower division baccalaureate/associate degree category, 1 semester hour in Computer Science or Computer Information Systems (5/97). **NOTE:** Students must complete 2 of 2 modules to receive credit.

Visual Basic 4.0 (70591-70592-70593)

Location: Computer-based.
Length: Self-paced.
Dates: February 1996-Present.
Objective: To introduce applications development, instructional technology, terminology and the design of custom business applications.
Learning Outcome: Upon successful completion of this course, the student will be able to create fundamental Visual Basic projects, comprehend the necessary code to write using multiple forms and controls, and understand the design, and implementation of custom business applications using Visual Basic 4.0.
Instruction: Major topics covered in the course are writing code in Visual Basic, manipulating external databases, understanding the use of a dynamic link library and the use of OLE applications. Methods of instruction include course materials available on CD-Rom for self-study, and tests.
Credit Recommendation: In the lower division baccalaureate/associate degree category, 1 semester hour in Programming (9/96).

Windows NT 3.5x Support Fundamentals and Server (70401-70402-70403-70411-70412-70413)

Location: Computer-based.
Length: Self-paced.
Dates: November 1995-Present.
Objective: To present an overview of Windows NT client and server.
Learning Outcome: Upon successful completion of this course, the student will be able to explain the processes involved in installing and setting up Windows NT Server and clients.
Instruction: Major topics covered in the course are getting started with Windows NT; setting up Windows NT Client software; setting up Windows NT Workstation; and troubleshooting. Methods of instruction include course materials available on CD-Rom for self-study, and tests.
Credit Recommendation: In the lower division baccalaureate/associate degree category, 1 semester hour in System Administration (9/96). **NOTE:** Students must complete 6 of 6 modules to receive credit.

National Emergency Training Center (EMI)

The National Emergency Training Center (NETC) is a training facility where training opportunities are offered in fire prevention and control and emergency management through the National Fire Academy and the Emergency Management Institute. Situated on a 107-acre campus near historic Gettysburg, the two institutions maintain 19 fully equipped classrooms and can accommodate up to 1,000 students with housing for over 540.

The training institutions develop and deliver training sponsored by the program offices in the Federal Emergency Management Agency (FEMA). NETC provides cost-effective, safe facilities that maximize student comfort and educational resources.

Source of official student records: Office of Admissions and Registration, National Emergency Training Center, 18625 South Seton Avenue, Emmitsburg, MD 21727.

Additional information about the courses: College Credit Recommendation Service, American Council on Education, One Dupont Circle, Washington, DC 20036-1193.

Emergency Management Institute

Training activities, which consist of courses, workshops, seminars, conferences, teleconferences, and exercises, are conducted throughout the United States. EMI's curriculum addresses all phases of emergency management, mitigation, preparedness, response and recovery, and applies emergency management concepts and experiential information to hazards ranging from earthquakes to hazardous materials to nuclear attack.

Advanced Radiological Accident Assessment (E349)

Location: Emmitsburg, MD.

Length: 30 hours (1 week).

Dates: August 1988-Present.

Objective: To provide the students, who are state and local technical personnel with the knowledge and skills necessary to assist in decision making that will protect the public during and after nuclear power plant accidents.

Learning Outcome: Upon successful completion of this course, the student will be able to evaluate release characteristics by recognizing the complexity of a nuclear incident; understand the relative doses, response levels, and action required to adequately protect the public; and use computer assistance, data gathering, and evaluation techniques necessary to protect the public and the food chain.

Instruction: Major topics covered in the course include release characteristics; data collection, federal guidelines and the us of computer-based programs to help assess and predict the impact of a nuclear incident. Methods of instruction include lecture, discussion, and group activities and exercises.

Credit Recommendation: In the upper division baccalaureate or graduate degree category, 2 semester hours in Public Health or Radiological Safety (10/89) (9/95). **NOTE:** (E350) Radiological Accident Assessment is a prerequisite for this course.

Basic Skills for Emergency Program Managers Course 1: Module 1: Leadership and Influence (G-240) Module 2: Decision making and Problem solving (G-241) Module 3: Effective Communications (G-242) Course 2: Module 4: Creative Financing (G-243)

Location: State Offices of Emergency Management Nationwide.

Length: *Course 1: Module 1:* 20 hours (3 days); *Module 2:* 8 hours (1 day); *Module 3:* 24 hours (3 days); *Course 2: Module 4:* 16 hours (2 days).

Dates: *Course 1:* November 1981-Present; *Course 2:* November 1982-January 1996.

Objective: *Course 1: Module 1:* To provide students with concepts of leadership, influence, power relationships and conflict mediation in the community setting. *Module 2:* To provide students with concepts of various decision-making and problem solving processes and the ability to apply these in the emergency management setting. *Module 3:* To provide students with concepts of communication and presentation skills in the community setting. *Course 2: Module 4:* To provide students with skills in effective budget planning, budget presentation to community budget authorities, and determination of alternative funding sources and mechanisms.

Learning Outcome: *Course 1: Module 1:* Upon successful completion of this course, the student will be able to determine personal values, influence style, leadership style, and power bases as they apply to interpersonal relations and group dynamics. *Module 2:* Upon successful completion of this course, the student will be able to draw conclusions regarding individual and the group decision making process. *Module 3:* Upon successful completion of this course, the student will be able to identify and utilize both verbal and nonverbal communications techniques in developing a structured presentation. *Course 2: Module 4:* Upon successful completion of this course, the student will be able to list and describe basic emergency management creative financing concepts; describe standard elements of proposals and utilize them in a team development process; and evaluate creative financing activities and apply them in development of a community plan.

Instruction: *Course 1: Module 1:* Major topics covered areorganizational behavior; conflict management; interpersonal relations; and group dynamics in an emergency setting. Methods of instruction include lectures, discussions, and exercises. *Module 2:* Major topics covered are decision making process and theory as applied in emergency situations. Methods of instruction include lectures, discussions, and case study. *Module 3:* Major topics covered are communication issues for emergency managers; the communication cycle; nonverbal communication; and public speaking. Methods of instruction include lectures, discussions, and exercises. *Course 2: Module 4:* Major topics covered are public budgeting; grantsmanship, and financial planning for emergency managers. Methods of instruction include lectures and exercises.

Credit Recommendation: *Course 1:* In the lower division baccalaureate/associate degree category, 3 semester hours in Emergency Management or Public Administration. *Course 2:* In the lower division baccalaureate/associate degree category, 1 semester hour in Public Administration (Fund-Raising or Grantsmanship) or Emergency Management (3/84) (6/88) (5/93).

Course Development

Location: National Emergency Training Center, Emmitsburg, MD.

Length: 30 hours (4 days).

Dates: February 1997-Present.

Objective: To provide the student with the knowledge, skills, and tools necessary to develop course materials and deliver training to individuals involved in emergency management training.

Learning Outcome: Upon successful completion of this course, the student will

be able to plan and manage the course development process, including development, revision, and delivery of course materials, such as instructor guides, student manuals, job aids, and visual displays.

Instruction: Major topics covered in the course are developing instructor guides, visual displays, and student manuals; determining materials, time and funding; managing the development process; and coordinating changes and revisions.

Credit Recommendation: In the upper division baccalaureate degree category, 2 semester hours in Education, Adult Education and Training, or Human Resource Management (11/97).

Course Evaluation

Location: National Emergency Training Center, Emmitsburg, MD.

Length: 34 hours (4 days).

Dates: March 1997-Present.

Objective: To provide the student with practical experience in the selection, development, and analysis of evaluation methods and instruments.

Learning Outcome: Upon successful completion of this course, the student will be able to identify the purpose of various methods; select the appropriate evaluation method for a particular situation; develop evaluation instruments; analyze and interpret the data provided by the various evaluation instruments; and recommend a plan of action for a course and/or instruction based on evaluation data.

Instruction: Majors topics covered in the course are design and development of course evaluations; conducting course evaluations; analyzing the results of evaluations; and interpreting evaluation results.

Credit Recommendation: In the upper division baccalaureate degree category, 2 semester hours in Education, Adult Education and Training, or Human Resource Management (11/97).

Earthquakes: A Teacher's Package for K-6 (Train-the-Trainer) (E436)

Location: Emmitsburg, MD.

Length: 30 hours (4 days).

Dates: *Version 1:* August 1990-November 1996; *Version 2:* December 1996-Present.

Objective: To train elementary school teachers in the curriculum presented in "Earthquakes: A Teacher's Package for K-6." These teachers will, in turn, present this material to their colleagues in their own schools.

Learning Outcome: Upon successful completion of this course, these teachers will be acquainted with all elements of the Earthquake course and able to train their colleagues in the teaching of this topic.

Instruction: Major topics covered in the course are understanding why earthquakes occur; understanding the results of earthquake; and earthquakes and safety and survival. The course includes a series of projects to be ultimately presented to elementary school children through which they can learn more about earthquakes. Elements of language arts, science, social studies, and art are included in the curriculum. These train-the-trainers are also given additional background knowledge in earthquake phenomena. Methods of instruction include lecture, discussion, and classroom exercises.

Credit Recommendation: *Version 1:* In the graduate degree category, 1 semester hour in Science Education (11/91). *Version 2:* In the upper division baccalaureate or graduate degree category, 1 semester hour in Education or Science (12/96).

Electromagnetic Pulse Inspection (EMP) and Maintenance (E351)

Location: Emmitsburg, MD.

Length: 24 hours (3.5 days).

Dates: January 1990-March 1995.

Objective: To provide the student with the knowledge and skills needed to perform inspection and maintenance on EMP protection devices.

Learning Outcome: Upon successful completion of this course, the student will be able to understand importance of EMP protection program in continuance of communications, life support, and other emergency systems; conduct inspections, determine needed changes; perform maintenance operations; and understand criticality of frequent inspection and maintenance.

Instruction: Major topics covered in the course are overview of EMP; nature and effects of EMP; principles of protection; FEMA EMP protection program; and inspection and maintenance procedures. Methods of instruction include lecture, discussion, classroom exercises, and examinations.

Credit Recommendation: In the lower division baccalaureate/associate degree category, 1 semester hour in Electronics, Communications Technology, or Emergency Management (3/91).

Emergency Operations Center (EOC) Management and Operations (G275)

Location: Various.

Length: 24 hours (3 days).

Dates: November 1994-Present.

Objective: To provide students with the knowledge to effectively design, configure and operate an Emergency Operations Center.

Learning Outcome: Upon successful completion of this course, the student will be able to organize and staff an EOC; design the layout of an EOC; maintain cooperation and communication in the EOC; develop EOC standard operating procedures; conduct exercises and briefings; recognize and resolve operational problems and establish and deactivate the EOC.

Instruction: Major topics covered in this course are EOC design and layout considerations; financing the EOC; creating job aids; conducting exercises and evaluations of the EOC; maintaining communication and cooperation in the EOC and organization and staffing of the EOC. Methods of instruction include lecture, discussion, classroom exercises, audio-visual material, case studies and a series of classroom group exercises, used to assess student proficiency and successful completion of the course.

Credit Recommendation: In the lower division baccalaureate/associate degree category, 2 semester hours in Emergency Management or Management (9/95).

Emergency Planning Course (G235)

Location: State Offices of Emergency Management nationwide.

Length: 27 hours (4.5 days of classroom instruction and post-class practicum)

Dates: October 1982-Present.

Objective: To provide students with advanced competency in planning skills for emergency situations.

Learning Outcome: Upon successful completion of this course, the student will be able to establish a planning framework for emergency management; develop an emergency planning strategy and integrate principles of group processes, team building, and decision-making; and evaluate the adequacy of existing plans.

Instruction: Major topics covered in the course are needs assessment (hazard/vulnerability analysis) techniques, comprehensive planning, action planning and organization development in the emergency planning process. Methods of instruction include lectures, discussions, and individual and group activities including pre- and post-class projects.

Credit Recommendation: In the upper division baccalaureate degree category, 2 semester hours in Public Administration (planning) or Emergency Management (3/84) (6/88) (5/93).

Executive Development for Emergency Program Managers (E215)

Location: State Offices of Emergency Management Nationwide.

Length: 78 hours (2 weeks).

Dates: January 1985-August 1992.

Objective: To provide the participant with in-depth knowledge about executive management and leadership skills for helping the manager plan and implement a good emergency response.

Learning Outcome: Upon successful completion of this course, students will be aware of legal issues in the local emergency management system; develop a strategic management plan for their jurisdiction; assess the current status of their emergency management system; formulate techniques for long-range planning and strategies; and develop alternative marketing approaches for involving the community in planning and carrying out emergency management goals.

Instruction: Major topics covered in the course are legal issues, strategic management, executive skills, community involvement, and stress management. Methods of instruction include lecture and discussion.

Credit Recommendation: In the upper division baccalaureate degree category, 3 semester hours in Administrative Principles of Management (6/88) (5/93).

Exercise Design (G120)

Location: Emmitsburg, MD and State Offices of Emergency Management nationwide.

Length: *Version 1:* 21 hours (3 days); *Version 2:* 21 hours (3 days)—includes 5-8 hours of independent study prior to classroom instruction.

Dates: *Version 1:* May 1984-June 1995; *Version 2:* July 1995-Present.

Objective: To enable students to design a comprehensive community exercise program with emphasis on tabletop, functional, and full-scale exercises.

Learning Outcome: Upon successful completion of this course, the student will be able to identify the characteristics of various emergency preparedness exercises; demonstrate the ability to develop, conduct, evaluate, and provide recommendations for follow-up action on various emergency preparedness exercises; identify resources for exercise enhancement; and define the role of emergency managers in increasing community support for community preparedness through emergency exercises.

Instruction: Major topics covered in the course are an overview and information for developing tabletop exercises, functional exercises, and full-scale exercises; along with a discussion on how to identify and obtain resources to enhance such exercises. Methods of instruction include lecture, discussion, audio-visual material, and classroom exercises.

Credit Recommendation: In the lower division baccalaureate/associate degree category, 1 semester hour in Emergency Management or Public Administration (11/91) (12/96). *Prerequisite:* Independent Study Orientation.

Exercise Design (Train-the-Trainer) (E440)

Location: Various sites.

Length: 32 hours (4.5 days).

Dates: April 1984-April 1995.

Objective: To provide the student with the knowledge of techniques and methods for presenting the Exercise Design course to emergency program managers at state and local government levels.

Learning Outcome: Upon successful completion of this course, the student will be able to fulfill the role of course manager and successfully teach all units of the Exercise Design course.

Instruction: Major topics covered in the course are exercise overview; community exercise programs; tabletop exercise development; functional exercise overview; functional exercise development; exercise instructions; full-scale exercise overview; and resources for exercise enhancement. Methods of instruction include lecture, discussion, and classroom exercises.

Credit Recommendation: In the upper division baccalaureate degree category, 2 semester hours in Emergency Management or Public Administration (3/91). **NOTE:** Students who receive credit for this course should not receive credit for Exercise Design.

Exercise Evaluation (G130)

Location: Emmitsburg, MD and various field locations.

Length: 14 hours (2 days).

Dates: May 1992-Present.

Objective: To understand the need for exercise evaluation and the organization, phases, and skills required in exercise evaluation.

Learning Outcome: Upon successful completion of this course, the student will be able to see the need for a systematic approach to exercise evaluation; identify and organize an effective exercise evaluation team; summarize components of exercise evaluation; demonstrate key post-exercise activities; and identify key tasks in three phases in exercise evaluation.

Instruction: Major topics covered in the course are systematic exercise evaluation; evaluation team leader; evaluation packages; evaluator selection; observing and documenting; achieving objectives; post-exercise meetings; and written reports. Methods of instruction include lecture, discussions, classroom exercises, and evaluation by instructor.

Credit Recommendation: In the lower division baccalaureate/associate degree category, 1 semester hour in Emergency Management or Public Administration (8/86) (5/93).

Fundamentals Course for Radiological Monitors (G320)

Location: *Version 1:* Emergency Management Institute field locations *Version 2:* Various sites nationwide. *Version 3:* Various sites nationwide.

Length: *Versions 1 and 2:* 8-12 hours (1-2 days); *Version 3:* 8 hours (1 day).

Dates: *Version 1:* November 1984-February 1991; *Version 2:* March 1991-September 1993; *Version 3:* October 1993-Present.

Objective: *Version 1:* To provide participants with appropriate knowledge and skills related to monitoring radiation and performing as a member of a radiological response team. *Version 2:* To provide participants with knowledge of immediate protective actions in response to contamination resulting from radiological materials or radioactive fallout. *Version 3:* To provide participants with appropriate knowledge and skills related to monitoring radiation and performing as a member of a radiological response team.

Learning Outcome: *Version 2:* Upon successful completion of this course, the student will be able to use radiation detection instruments; understand limitations of radiation detection instruments; take immediate protective actions; and notify response teams. *Version 3:* Upon successful completion of this course, the student will be able to use, care for, and accurately read civil defense radiation detection instruments; identify and report radiation exposure rates; identify signs, labels, and placards which indicate radioactive materials that may be present; locate radioactive materials in order to prevent spread of contamination; and list basic biological effects of radiation and list protective action used to limit exposure and spread of contamination.

Instruction: *Version 1:* Major topics covered in the course are an overview of radiological emergencies, radiation fundamentals; biological effects and risks; radiological monitoring instruments; exposure and contamination control techniques; on-scene assessment techniques; and special nuclear attack considerations. Methods of instruction include lecture, discussion, classroom exercises, and written examinations. *Version 2:* Major topics covered in the course are an overview of radiological emergencies, radiation fundamentals; biological effects and risks; radiological monitoring instruments; exposure and contamination control techniques; on-scene assessment techniques; and special nuclear attack considerations. Methods of instruction include lecture, discussion, classroom exercises, and written examinations. *Version 3:* Major topics covered in the course are an overview of radiological protection and hazards; review of radiological emergency management; radiological instruments and radiological incidents; and assessment and protective actions. Methods of instruction include lecture, discussion, classroom exercises, case studies, and computer-assisted VT/TV.

Credit Recommendation: *Version 1:* In the lower division baccalaureate/associate degree category, 3 semester hours in Radiological Science (8/85). **NOTE:** In order to receive credit, students must complete both Fundamentals Course for Radiological Monitors (G320) and Fundamentals Course for Radiological Response Teams (G326). *Version 2:* In the lower division baccalaureate/associate degree category, 2 semester hours in Radiological Science (3/91). **NOTE:** If student only completes Fundamentals Course for Radiological Monitors (G320), only 1 credit should be awarded. *Version 3:* In the vocational certificate or lower division baccalaureate/associate degree category, 2 semester hours in Radiation Safety (9/95). **NOTE:** To qualify for 2 semester hours both Fundamentals Course for Radiological Monitors (G320) and Fundamentals Course for Radiological Response Teams (G326) must be completed.

Fundamentals Course for Radiological Officers (G323) (Formerly Fundamentals Course for Radiological Defense Officers)

Location: Various sites.

Length: 24 hours (3 days).

Dates: November 1984-Present.

Objective: To provide the student with the knowledge and skills needed by state and local radiological officers to implement initial protective actions in a radiological emergency, and application of planning and management principles to planning and administration of radiological protection systems.

Learning Outcome: Upon successful completion of this course, the student will be able to describe examples of radiological emergencies and of relevant emergency response systems; apply biological concepts of radiation exposure to radiological operations and evaluate capabilities and limitations of radiological instruments; develop and evaluate plans for radiological emergencies and evaluate nuclear threat preparedness; and communicate with technical and nontechnical personnel.

Instruction: Major topics covered in the course are review of RRT; special considerations of nuclear terrorism; basic concepts of radiation and biological effects; radiological instrumentation; managing a radiological protection system; radiological response planning and state radiological protection systems. Methods of instruction include lecture, discussion, classroom exercises, and final examination.

Credit Recommendation: In the upper division baccalaureate degree category, 2 semester hours in Radiological Sciences or Emergency Management (8/85) (3/91) (9/95).

Fundamentals Course for Radiological Response Teams (G326)

Location: *Version 1:* Emergency Management Institute field locations *Version 2:* Various sites nationwide. *Version 3:* Various sites nationwide.

Length: *Versions 1 and 2:* 32 hours (5 days); *Version 3:* 24 hours (3 days).

Dates: *Version 1:* November 1984-February 1991; *Version 2:* March 1991-September 1993; *Version 3:* October 1993-Present.

Objective: *Version 1:* To provide participants with appropriate knowledge and skills related to monitoring radiation and performing as a member of a radiological response team. *Version 2:* To provide participants with an understanding of radiation protection concepts and techniques of radiological monitoring and response. *Version 3:* To qualify participants as radiological response team members.

Learning Outcome: *Version 2:* Upon successful completion of this course, the student will be able to identify radiological emergencies and assess risk associated with such incidents; demonstrate appropriate monitoring techniques and communicate appropriate radiological information; describe response team's role and perform necessary tasks for effective exposure control, including evacuation and shelter preparation; apply radiation fundamentals, including radiation protection, detection, and biological effects of tasks to response teams; operate and troubleshoot radiological instruments; and apply skills to both wartime and peacetime radiation hazards. *Version 3:* Upon successful completion of this course, the student will be able to classify the roles and responsibilities of each component of the radiological protection system; explain the radiation characteristics of commonly shipped radionuclides and the hazards involved; specify the factors that will affect biological response to radiation and describe the risk in various types of radiation incidents; use the table response of radiation monitoring instruments to normalize risk quantities of radionuclides and demonstrate knowledge of radiological instruments; and use the fallout exposure rate prediction tables.

Instruction: *Version 1:* Major topics covered in the course are an overview of radiological emergencies, radiation fundamentals; biological effects and risks; radiological monitoring instruments; exposure and contamination control techniques; on-scene assessment techniques; and special nuclear attack considerations. Methods of instruction include lecture, discussion, classroom exercises, and written examinations. *Version 2:* Major topics covered in the course are radiological emergencies and the radiological defense system; radiation fundamentals; biological effects and risks; radiological monitoring assessment; and state radiological defense programs and systems. Methods of instruction include lecture, discussion, audiovisual aids, classroom exercises, and written examinations. *Version 3:* Major topics covered in the course are a review of basic concepts; radiological response team operations; practical radiation physics for radiological response teams; effects and risks of radiation; exposure control; contamination control and decontamination; and nuclear terrorism radiation accident. Methods of instruction include lecture, discussion, classroom exercises, case studies, and computer-assisted VT/TV.

Credit Recommendation: *Version 1:* In the lower division baccalaureate/associate degree category, 3 semester hours in

Radiological Science (8/85). **NOTE:** In order to receive credit, students must complete both Fundamentals Course for Radiological Monitors (G320) and Fundamentals Course for Radiological Response Teams (G326). *Version 2:* In the lower division baccalaureate/associate degree category, 2 semester hours in Radiological Science (3/91). **NOTE:** If student only completes Fundamentals Course for Radiological Response Teams (G326), only 1 credit should be awarded. *Version 3:* In the vocational certificate or lower division baccalaureate/associate degree category, 2 semester hours in Radiation Safety (9/95). **NOTE:** To qualify for 2 semester hours both Fundamentals Course for Radiological Monitors (G320) and Fundamentals Course for Radiological Response Team (G326) must be completed. *Prerequisite*: G320.

Hazardous Materials Contingency Planning (G311)

Location: Field locations, assigned and scheduled by each state.

Length: *Version 1:* 29 hours (5 days); *Version 2:* 35 hours (4.5 days).

Dates: *Version 1:* January 1986-September 1989; *Version 2:* October 1989-Present.

Objective: *Version 1:* To provide the student with advanced competency, knowledge, and skills in hazardous materials planning and response techniques. *Version 2:* To provide the students, as emergency management personnel with the skills and knowledge to develop a community-based planning capability for hazardous materials, address the full spectrum of hazardous materials planning concerns, and to integrate hazardous materials planning into the overall community emergency planning process.

Learning Outcome: *Version 1:* Upon successful completion of this course, the student will be able to list and discuss basic techniques necessary to hazardous materials planning and response and to critique and develop hazardous materials plans that will pass review criteria. *Version 2:* Upon successful completion of this course, the student will be able to develop a new plan or review an existing hazardous materials contingency plan using the planning process, techniques and terminology established by the local emergency planning committee and by applicable federal and state laws and regulations.

Instruction: *Version 1:* Major topics covered in the course are hazardous materials hazard vulnerability; assessment of resources; development of hazardous materials contingency plan; and development of fixed site hazardous materials contingency plan. Methods of instruction include lecture, discussion, exercises, and individual and group activity. *Version 2:* Major topics covered in this course are the planning process; federal requirements; community awareness; marketing the local emergency planning committee concept; hazard analysis; capability and the assessment, planning implementation and evaluation of a contingency plan. Methods of instruction include lecture, discussion, group activity and student exercises.

Credit Recommendation: *Version 1:* In the upper division baccalaureate or graduate degree category, 2 semester hours in Emergency Management, Public Administration, or Radiological Sciences (8/86) (10/89). *Version 2:* In the upper division baccalaureate degree category or the graduate degree category, 2 semester hours in Emergency Management or Public Administration (9/95).

Instructional Design (E603)

Location: Emmitsburg, MD.

Length: 34 hours (4.5 days).

Dates: September 1996-Present.

Objective: To provide the student with the knowledge, skills, and tools necessary to conduct instructional design processes in order to develop effective and useful training.

Learning Outcome: Upon successful completion of this course, the student will be able to identify the elements of an instructional design plan, understand instructional models, appropriate data sources and collection techniques, and understand behavior for effective learning.

Instruction: Major topics covered in the course are instructional design modules; task analysis; instructional analysis; writing performance objectives; instructional strategy; and course evaluation. Methods of instruction include lecture, small group discussions, classroom exercises, and audio-visual material.

Credit Recommendation: In the upper division baccalaureate degree category, 2 semester hours in Education, Public Administration, and Emergency Management (12/96).

Introduction to Emergency Management (G230)

Location: State Offices of Emergency Management Nationwide.

Length: 27 hours (4.5 days, 23 hours lecture and discussion, and 4 hours of workshop).

Dates: April 1983-Present.

Objective: To describe elements of an integrated emergency management system, necessity for emergency management teamwork and the identification of hazards and hazard sources, all of which lead to a community emergency management strategy.

Learning Outcome: Upon successful completion of this course, the student will be able to identify hazards and draw conclusions regarding scope, importance, and implications to the community; describe operational elements of a comprehensive emergency management system; and identify fundamental organizational characteristics and the relationship between individual and group behavior.

Instruction: Major topics covered in the course are community needs assessment for emergency management; systems approach to emergency management; community organization development; and management planning for community emergencies. Methods of instruction include lecture and discussion.

Credit Recommendation: In the lower division baccalaureate/associate degree category, 2 semester hours in Emergency Management or Public Administration (3/84) (6/88) (5/93).

Management and Supervision of Training (E225)

Location: Emergency Management Institute, Emmitsburg, MD.

Length: 30 hours (4.5 days).

Dates: November 1993-Present.

Objective: To provide FEMA training managers with the knowledge and skills to effectively analyze training needs and design develop, plan, manage and evaluate training courses.

Learning Outcome: Upon successful completion of the course, participants will be able to analyze & prioritize methods and oversee the training process.

Instruction: Major topics covered in the course are analyzing state training needs; designing training (adult learning principles, developing plans of instruction, writing learning objectives, training content, training methods, selecting training media); developing and reviewing training materials, producing training materials; planning training - marketing training, selecting training sites, selecting and preparing presenter; managing training; evaluating training. Methods of instruction include lecture, small group exercises, audio tape, video tape, job aids, precourse readings, and knowledge/skill assessment tool.

Credit Recommendation: In the upper division baccalaureate degree category, 2 semester hours in Human Resource Management or Adult Education (9/95).

Methods and Techniques of Adult Learning (E204)

Location: Emergency Management Institute, Emmitsburg, MD, and State Offices of Emergency Management nationwide.

Length: 32.5 hours (4 days).

Dates: August 1987-August 1993.

Objective: To familiarize experienced emergency management trainers with adult learning theory with reference to adult learning techniques, media usage, presentation topics, and training techniques.

Learning Outcome: Upon successful completion of this course, the student will be able to provide students with a series of alternative techniques to present information in the most efficient and effective method; know something about classroom environment for learning; carry out appropriate communications principles and techniques; and plan and perform a team teaching activity that incorporates one or more instructional techniques.

Instruction: Major topics covered in the course are introduction and overview, presentation, media usage, practical applications, and evaluation. Methods of instruction include lecture and discussion.

Credit Recommendation: In the upper division baccalaureate degree category, 2 semester hours in Education, Educational Methods, Extension Education, Psychology of Learning, or Training Methods (6/88).

Microcomputer Applications in Emergency Management (E230)

Location: Emmitsburg, MD.

Length: 37 hours (4.5 days).

Dates: June 1985-September 1993.

Objective: To provide the student with the skills needed to develop an information management strategic plan, determining the requirements, researching and evaluating design alternatives, and implementing the system; and introduce state and local emergency managers to ways in which a microcomputer system can be used to facilitate emergency management functions.

Learning Outcome: Upon successful completion of this course, the student will be able to understand how microcomputer hardware and software can be used by emergency managers; identify the microcomputer management skills required to become a more effective emergency manager; identify information which comprises an emergency management information system and how it may be used by emergency managers on state and local levels; identify the components of the Life Cycle of an Information Management System; plan and develop an Information Management System strategic plan; manage and utilize available resources; and establish regular and emergency procedures for operation and maintenance of data, hardware, and software.

Instruction: Major topics covered in the course are management overview; application of microcomputers to emergency management; word processing software application; evaluation of alternative hardware and software; communications; data base management; and spreadsheet software applications. Methods of instruction include lecture, discussion, and laboratory exercises.

Credit Recommendation: In the upper division baccalaureate or graduate degree category, 3 semester hours in Emergency Management, Public Administration, or Computer Science (8/86) (3/91).

Natural Hazards Mitigation and Recovery (E319) (Formerly Natural Hazards Mitigations [Inland] [E306] and Natural Hazards Recovery [Coastal] [E313])

Location: Emmitsburg, MD.

Length: 32 hours (4.5 days).

Dates: March 1990-May 1995.

Objective: To give the student the understanding of mitigation and recovery planning and skill in relating natural hazards mitigation processes to disaster recovery planning.

Learning Outcome: Upon successful completion of this course, the student will be able to describe phases of emergency management and relate them to hazard mitigation; identify features, benefits, costs, and consequences of mitigation strategies and approaches; identify process of implementing and integrating risk assessment, hazard mitigation, and disaster recovery plans; and apply knowledge and skills of hazard mitigation and disaster recovery.

Instruction: Major topics covered in the course are components of emergency management; hazard mitigation; disaster recovery; relationship of mitigation and recovery; hazard assessment, risk perception, vulnerability, and risk communication; hazard mitigation concepts, strategies, planning, conflicts, and resources. Methods of instruction include lecture, discussion, and classroom exercises.

Credit Recommendation: In the upper division baccalaureate degree category, 2 semester hours in Emergency Planning, Public Administration, Environmental Management, or Resource Economics (3/91).

Natural Hazards Mitigation (Inland) (E306)

Location: National Emergency Training Center, Emmitsburg, MD.

Length: 30 hours (4.5 days).

Dates: November 1987-July 1988.

Objective: To introduce concepts and skills of mitigation planning for application in general community planning processes.

Learning Outcome: Upon successful completion of this course, the student will be able to apply knowledge and skills to the local context of mitigation planning processes, legal and liability issues, hazards assessment, and implementation strategies.

Instruction: Major topics covered in the course are local context of mitigation planning, hazards assessment, legal issues in mitigation, implementation strategies, and action steps. Methods of instruction include lecture, exercises, and case study.

Credit Recommendation: In the upper division baccalaureate degree category, 1 semester hour in Emergency Management (6/88).

Natural Hazards Recovery (Coastal) (E313)

Location: National Emergency Training Center, Emmitsburg, MD.

Length: 30 hours (4.5 days).

Dates: November 1987-July 1988.

Objective: To provide information on disaster recovery, planning techniques, political and community context of disaster recovery, post-disaster mitigation planning, community planning, and implementation assessment techniques.

Learning Outcome: Upon successful completion of this course, the student will be able to apply a working knowledge of effective approaches, tools and techniques to initiate pre-disaster recovery planning in their communities; and relate disaster recovery planning to mitigation and general community planning.

Instruction: Major topics covered in the course are disaster recovery planning, recovery organizing priorities, community infrastructure recovery, state and federal assistance, land use planning, and building codes in post-disaster mitigation. Methods of instruction include lecture and exercises.

Credit Recommendation: In the upper division baccalaureate degree category, 1 semester hour in Emergency Management (6/88).

Performance and Needs Assessment (E602)

Location: EMI, Emmitsburg, MD.

Length: 4.5 days or 30 hours.

Dates: October 1995-Present.

Objective: To provide students with the knowledge, skills, and abilities to develop a plan for conducting a needs assessment, practice various techniques and tools of needs assessment and analyze data and communicate results.

Learning Outcome: Upon successful completion of this course, the student will be able to understand the importance of needs assessment, develop a detailed plan for needs assessment based on performance problems in their community, select and use analysis techniques to accomplish a needs assessment to communicate results.

Instruction: Major topics covered in the course are analyzing performance problems; basic concepts for needs assessment; developing techniques and tools for performance and needs assessment; and planning needs assessment. Methods of instruction include lecture, discussion, classroom exercises, case studies, audiovisual material, and learner presentations.

Credit Recommendation: In the upper division baccalaureate/associate degree, 2 semester hours in Education, Public Administration, or Emergency Management (12/96).

Radiological Accident Assessment (E350)

Location: Emergency Management Institute, Emmitsburg, MD.

Length: 30 hours (1 week).

Dates: June 1985-Present.

Objective: This course is designed for individuals who have, or will have, responsibilities for helping to assess the radiological consequences to the public following an accidental release of radioactivity from a nuclear facility. It will provide knowledge and skills required to make recommendations to public officials to minimize the hazards to the public.

Learning Outcome: Upon successful completion of this course, the student will be able to assess the off-site radiological consequences to the public following a release of radioactivity from a nuclear facility; make recommendations to public officials concerning minimizing the hazards of a release of radioactivity; and identify factors affecting the movement of radioactivity.

Instruction: Major topics covered in the course are accident classification and protective action decision-making, projection methods, off-site monitoring, and meteorology. Methods of instruction include lecture, discussion, and exercises.

Credit Recommendation: In the upper division baccalaureate or graduate degree category, 2 semester hours in Public Health or Radiological Science (8/85) (10/89) (9/95).

Radiological Emergency Preparedness Exercise Evaluation (E304)

Location: Emergency Management Institute, Emmitsburg, MD, and various field locations.

Length: 31 hours (4.5 days).

Dates: September 1986-Present.

Objective: To provide the student with the skills and knowledge necessary to effectively evaluate a radiological emergency preparedness exercise to determine the response capabilities of off-site response organizations.

Learning Outcome: Upon successful completion of this course, the student will be able to determine the process, procedures, and personnel necessary in a REP exercise; and determine the organization facilities and operation required in a REP exercise.

Instruction: Major topics covered in the course are the purpose and process and methods of the evaluation; and the role of the evaluator. Exercise evaluation skills should be improved by participating in this activity. Methods of instruction include laboratory exercises, field study, and case studies-major exercise involvement.

Credit Recommendation: In the upper division baccalaureate or graduate degree category, 2 semester hours in Public Administration or Radiological Safety (10/89) (9/95).

Radiological Emergency Preparedness Planning (E340)

Location: Emergency Management Institute, Emmitsburg, MD.

Length: *Version 1:* 34 hours (1 week); *Version 2:* 31 hours (4.5 days).

Dates: *Version 1:* January 1985-March 1989; *Version 2:* April 1989-Present.

Objective: *Version 1:* To provide federal, state, local, and private industry radiological planners with federal guidance for planning around nuclear power generating stations. *Version 2:* To provide local, state or federal personnel or utility company personnel with the knowledge and skills needed for planning for an off-site nuclear accident, focusing on both the federal regulatory and public policy issues.

Learning Outcome: Upon successful completion of this course, the student will be able to describe the technical and regulatory requirements of radiological emergency planning, apply the criteria in developing a plan, determine the plans adequacy, and describe the federal process of reviewing and approving such plans.

Instruction: *Version 1:* Major topics covered in the course are basic principles and procedures of nuclear physics, map reading, environmental sampling, radiological area control, respiratory protection, field instrument techniques, personnel and equipment anti-contamination, and hotline procedures and personnel monitoring. Methods of instruction include lectures, discussions, and exercises. *Version 2:* Major topics covered in the course are regulations regarding radiological emergency planning, plan design, planning criteria and plan approval. Methods of instruction include lectures, discussion, group discussions and activity and exercises.

Credit Recommendation: In the upper division baccalaureate degree category, 2 semester hours in Public Administration or Radiological Safety (8/85) (10/89) (9/95).

Radiological Emergency Response Operations

Location: Mt. Weather, Berryville, VA.

Length: 44 hours (5.5 days).

Dates: October 1994-Present.

Objective: To provide students with the ability to respond as a member of a radiological response team to a variety of incidents and perform initial assessment, establish on-site communication and implement appropriate response options to safely and effectively control emergency situations involving radioactive materials.

Learning Outcome: Upon successful completion of this course, the student will be able to conduct a site safety briefing; describe potential safety hazards; develop a radiological field response plan; conduct a field survey; perform an on-scene radiological assessment of an accident site; conduct appropriate monitoring to designate control zones; and perform exposure, contamination and decontamination procedures.

Instruction: Major topics covered in the course are planning principles for radiation accidents; emergency organizational structure and responsibilities; radiological emergency response procedures; protective actions; site safety practices; exposure assessment and control; decontamination procedures and monitoring principles and practices and personal protective equipment. Methods of instruction include lecture, discussion, classroom practical exercises and case studies. Demonstration of skills through a series of practical exercises and proficiency tests.

Credit Recommendation: In the upper division baccalaureate degree category, 3 semester hours in Radiological Safety (9/95). *Prerequisites:* (IS-301) Radiological Emergency Response Independent Study, (G326) Fundamentals course for Radiological Response Teams, and (G320) Fundamentals Course for Radiological Monitors.

Radiological Emergency Response Operations (E301)

Location: Mt. Weather, Berryville, VA.

Length: 44 hours (5.5 days).

Dates: October 1994-Present.

Objective: To provide students with the ability to respond as a member of a radiological response team to a variety of incidents and perform initial assessment, establish on-site communication and implement appropriate response options to safely and effectively control emergency situations involving radioactive materials.

Learning Outcome: Upon successful completion of this course the student will be able to conduct a site safety briefing; describe potential safety hazards; develop a radiological field response plan; conduct a field survey; perform an on-scene radiological assessment of an accident site; conduct appropriate monitoring to designate control zones; and perform exposure, contamination and decontamination procedures.

Instruction: Major topics covered in the course are planning principles for radiation accidents; emergency organizational structure and responsibilities; radiological emergency response procedures; protective actions; site safety practices; exposure assessment and control; decontamination procedures and monitoring principles and practices and personal protective equipment. Methods of instruction include lecture, discussion, classroom practical exercises and case studies. Demonstration of skills through a series of practical exercises and proficiency tests.

Credit Recommendation: In the upper division baccalaureate degree category, 3 semester hours in Radiological Safety (9/95). *Prerequisites:* (IS-301) Radiological Emergency Response Independent Study, (G326) Fundamentals course for Radiological Response Teams, and (G320) Fundamentals Course for Radiological Monitors.

Radiological Emergency Response Operations (E301) (Formerly Radiological Emergency Response)

Location: Las Vegas, NV, test site.

Length: 44 hours (5.5 days).

Dates: *Version 1:* August 1985-October 1989; *Version 2:* October 1991-October 1994.

Objective: To provide persons assigned to state and local radiological emergency response teams with "hands-on" experience in simulated radiation accidents.

Learning Outcome: Upon successful completion of this course, the student will be able to appropriately respond to and handle a radiological emergency situation.

Instruction: Major topics covered in the course are exercises in basic principles and procedures of nuclear physics, map reading, environmental sampling, radiological area control, respiratory protection, field instrument techniques, personnel and equipment anti-contamination, and hotline procedures and personnel monitoring. Methods of instruction include lectures, discussions, use of videotapes, and exercises.

Credit Recommendation: In the upper division baccalaureate degree category, 3 semester hours in Radiological Sciences or related programs (8/85) (10/89) (9/95).

Radiological Instructors III (Train the Trainer) (E425) (Formerly Train the Trainer for Radiological Instructors III [E425])

Location: Emergency Management Institute, Emmitsburg, MD.

Length: 35 hours (1 week).

Dates: May 1984-December 1989.

Objective: To qualify trainers as Radiological Instructor III to teach the "Fundamentals Course for Radiological Response Teams," the "Fundamentals Course for Radiological Officers," and the "Radiological Monitor Instructor Course."

Instruction: Major topics covered in this course are "Fundamentals Course for Radiological Response Teams," "Fundamentals Course for Radiological Officers," and the "Radiological Monitor Instructor Course." Methods of instruction include lectures, discussions, and workshops.

Credit Recommendation: In the upper division baccalaureate degree category, 2 semester hours in Radiological Science or Education (8/85) (9/95).

Radiological Monitors Instructor (Part 1) (G340)

Location: State offices of Emergency Management Institute nationwide.

Length: 24 hours (3 days).

Dates: August 1985-Present.

Objective: To provide qualified instructors with knowledge and skills necessary to teach the "Fundamentals Course for Radiological Monitors."

Learning Outcome: Upon successful completion of this course, the student will be able to demonstrate instructional skills in presenting any segment of the Fundamentals Course for Radiological Monitors. They must demonstrate knowledge, skills, and abilities to manage, deliver, and evaluate the FCRM class.

Instruction: Major topics covered in the course are student recruitment and scheduling; instructional techniques and methodology; expedient radiological training; source handling techniques; and student teaching. Methods of instruction include lecture, discussion, and exercises.

Credit Recommendation: In the lower division baccalaureate/associate degree category, 2 semester hours in Radiological Science Education (8/85) (11/91) (12/96).

Radiological Series (Train-the-Trainer) (E425)

Location: Various sites.

Length: 30 hours (4.5 days).

Dates: June 1990-Present.

Objective: To provide the student with the knowledge and skills to plan, administer, teach, and evaluate field offerings of FEMA's Radiological Training Series.

Learning Outcome: Upon successful completion of this course, the student will be able to effectively teach courses in the Radiological Training Series and explain the rationale for each course; consider specific audience needs and concerns in conducting a field course; exhibit knowledge of radiological hazards, protection systems; identify current issues in radiological preparedness; and understand TD 100 Management Plan for the training series.

Instruction: Major topics covered in the course are adult education methodology; review of courses in the Radiological Training Series; and review of FCRRT and FCRM course and microteaching assignments. Methods of instruction include lecture, discussion, and micro-teaching activities.

Credit Recommendation: In the upper division baccalaureate degree category, 2 semester hours in Radiological Science, Education, or Educational Technology (3/91) (9/95).

Resource Management Course (G276)

Location: Various states.

Length: 12.5 hours.

Dates: April 1995-Present.

Objective: To provide resource management coordinators with the knowledge and skills needed to perform resource management functions within the overall framework of an emergency operations center.

Learning Outcome: Upon successful completion of this course, students will be able to implement and activate a resource management system during an emergency; manage the coordination of resources during an emergency.

Instruction: Major topics covered in the course are resource needs assessment and analysis; developing standard operating procedures; evaluation of SOP's; and implementing the Resource Management System. Methods of instruction include lecture, discussion, classroom exercises, audio-visual material, computer-assisted instruction, evaluation - quizzes, projects - exercises.

Credit Recommendation: In the lower division baccalaureate/associate degree category, 1 semester hour in Management (9/95).

State Radiological Defense Officer Management Workshop (E390) (Formerly State Radiological Officer Management)

Location: Emmitsburg, MD.

Length: 30 hours (4.5 days).

Dates: February 1985-June 1992.

Objective: To provide the student with the knowledge and skills needed by radiological protection officers to develop and manage an integrated state radiological protective system.

Learning Outcome: Upon successful completion of this course, the student will be able to develop, manage, and evaluate state and local RADEF systems.

Instruction: Major topics covered in the course are radiological defense preparedness overview, applying management principles to RADEF programs and systems; planning and organizing comprehensive RADEF programs; staffing and equipping a RADEF system; RADEF training requirements and resources; exercising and evaluating a RADEF system; radiological intelligence gathering, processing, and reporting; administering state RADEF programs; and professional development of state RDOs. Methods of instruction include lecture, discussion, audiovisual aids, and classroom exercises.

Credit Recommendation: In the upper division baccalaureate degree category, 2 semester hours in Public Administration or Emergency Management (8/85) (3/91) (9/95).

Telecommunication and Warning Systems (E367)

Location: Emmitsburg, MD.

Length: 26 hours (4.5 days).

Dates: February 1989-May 1995.

Objective: To provide the student with an understanding of telecommunications and warning systems technology and its role in emergency management.

Learning Outcome: Upon successful completion of this course, the student will be able to define telecommunications alerting and warning elements and their relationship to emergency management; define and identify warning systems and their warning technical capabilities and uses in emergency management; develop plans for federal and state requirements of emergency management and emergency operations.

Instruction: Major topics covered in the course are telecommunications and warning systems; systems management; staffing; external resources management; systems analysis, assessment, and design; acquisition; installation and acceptance testing; inventory control; and preventive maintenance. Methods of instruction include lecture, discussion, and classroom activities.

Credit Recommendation: In the lower division baccalaureate/associate degree category, 1 semester hour in Public Administration, Emergency Management, Systems Engineering, or Communications Management (12/96).

National Emergency Training Center (NFA)

The National Emergency Training Center (NETC), Emmitsburg, Maryland, is operated by the Federal Emergency Management Agency (FEMA). It provides training opportunities in fire and prevention control and emergency management at the National Fire Academy and the Emergency Management Institute respectively. Situated on a 107-acre campus near historic Gettysburg, Pennsylvania, the two institutions maintain 16 fully equipped classrooms and various learning laboratories as well as dining facilities and dormitories for over 450 students.

Both institutions develop and deliver state-of-the-art training programs sponsored by the program offices in FEMA.

Source of official student records: Office of Admissions and Registration, National Emergency Training Center, 18625 South Seton Avenue, Emmitsburg, MD 21727.

Additional information about the courses: College Credit Recommendation Service, American Council on Education, One Dupont Circle, Washington, DC 20036-1193.

National Fire Academy

The Academy offers specialized training courses primarily to mid-level and senior-level fire service or emergency medical service officers, to training instructors in both of these services and to their counterparts in allied professions. The Academy offers its courses in a concentrated, residential setting conducive to intense, shared learning.

Advanced Fire Safety (R341) (Formerly Management or Administration of Public Fire Education)

Location: Emmitsburg, MD.

Length: 80 hours (2 weeks).

Dates: October 1984-May 1989.

Objective: To provide the student with the necessary knowledge and skill to formulate and administer a public education program in fire prevention.

Learning Outcome: Upon successful completion of this course, the student will be able to create an education package which includes a planning process for fire safety; demonstrate selecting appropriate instructional strategies related to task analysis; and create a criterion-referenced test with three types of questions.

Instruction: Major topics covered in the course are sharing with other participants one program, program element, audiovisual element, or other public education from home-based public education program and applying accepted principles of statistical and cost-benefit analyses.

Credit Recommendation: In the lower division baccalaureate/associate degree category, 2 semester hours in Educational Administration, Fire Administration, or Introductory Management (3/83) (12/88).

Advanced Leadership Issues in Emergency Medical Services (R151)

Location: Emmitsburg, MD.

Length: 80 hours (2 weeks).

Dates: November 1994-Present.

Objective: To provide knowledge of current and emerging management practices as they relate to emergency medical service organizations.

Learning Outcome: Upon successful completion of this course, the student will be able to display skills and knowledge to effectively fill position as mid-and upper-level managers in an emergency medical service delivery organization.

Instruction: Major topics covered in the course are leadership, management, networking/political influence, human resources, relationship with the medical director, and customer service. Methods of instruction include lecture, discussion, classroom exercises, case studies, audio/visual material, and a final examination.

Credit Recommendation: In the upper division baccalaureate or graduate degree category, 3 semester hours in Emergency Medical Service, Fire Science, Public Administration, or Health Care Administration (2/95). **NOTE:** Students seeking graduate level credit must complete the ALIEMS research paper requirement.

Advanced Life Support Response to Hazardous Materials Incidents (R247)

Location: Emmitsburg, MD.

Length: 80 hours.

Dates: May 1995-Present.

Objective: To enable advanced life support personnel to recognize the dangers associated with hazardous material and to effectively provide treatment techniques to those affected by hazardous material exposure.

Learning Outcome: Upon successful completion of this course, the student will be able to recognize the dangers associated with hazardous material; respond in an appropriate manner to hazardous material medical emergencies using advanced life support techniques to prevent death and human suffering; and understand the proper pharmacology and the effects of toxic materials to citizen and fire/rescue personnel.

Instruction: Major topics covered in the course are defining the standards of care for hazardous material medical emergencies, chemistry of hazardous material, general principles of toxicology and pharmacology, understanding of physiologic systems and cellular function, and the effects of hazardous material and recommended strategies for treatment. Methods of instruction include lecture, discussion, classroom exercises, audio/visual material, computer-assisted instruction, quizzes, observations, and a final examination.

Credit Recommendation: *Version 1:* In the upper division baccalaureate degree category, 3 semester hours in Fire Science, Health Care Administration, Public Health, General Science, Emergency Medical Service, or Chemistry (7/96). *Version 2:* In the upper division baccalaureate degree category, 3 semester hours in Fire Science, Health Care Administration, Public Health, General Science, Emergency Medical Service, or Chemistry or in the graduate degree category, 3 semester hours in Industrial Hygiene Laboratory, Environmental Science Laboratory, or Public Health Laboratory (7/97).

Applied Research Projects

Location: Independent study.

Length: Self-paced.

Dates: October 1995-Present.

Objective: To allow students to investigate a key issue or problem identified as being important to their fire service organization.

Learning Outcome: Upon successful completion of this course, the student will be able to reach conclusions and offer recommendations which contribute to the improvement of their organization.

Instruction: Major topics covered in the course are the research format including title page, abstract, table of contents, introduction, background and significance, literature review, procedures, results, discussion, recommendations, references, and appendices. Methods of instruction include independent study, research, and preparing a research paper.

Credit Recommendation: In the upper division baccalaureate degree category or graduate degree category, 3 semester hours in Fire Science, Fire Administration, or Public Administration (7/96). **NOTE:** In order to receive the credit recommendation a participant must receive an evaluation score of 3.0 (on a 4.0 scale) on all four research papers.

Arson Detection (R200)

Location: Emmitsburg, MD.

Length: 36.5 hours (1 week).

Dates: July 1978-September 1985.

Objective: To provide students with a basic understanding of arson motivation to enable them to relate types of fires to certain individuals and groups. To provide overviews of evidence-collection procedures and of legal requirements governing fire-scene searches. To suggest the proper demeanor for courtroom testimony.

Instruction: Major topics covered in the course are method of determining the point of origin of a fire, what indicators to search for at the fire scene, and how to evaluate fire-scene conditions to determine the fire's probable cause. Students are taught to interpret the visual indicators that make possible a preliminary determination of cause of death when fatalities are associated with fires, and learn the procedures to follow in such cases. Discriminating between accidental and incendiary fire causes, handling operations at the fire scene, collecting and preserving evidence, and recording information for support of later arson investigations are also covered. This course is not designed to fill the more advanced needs of the fire investigator. Methods of instruction include lecture, discussion, and media techniques are used.

Credit Recommendation: In the lower division baccalaureate/associate degree category, 2 semester hours in Criminal Justice, Fire Science, Insurance, or Investigation (6/81).

Arson Detection for First Responders (F201)

Location: National Emergency Training Center, National Fire Academy, Emmitsburg, Md. and other sites around the nation.

Length: 12.5 hours.

Dates: July 1996-Present.

Objective: To provide a clear definition of the role of the initial responder organizations; to provide essential knowledge to enable them to recognize the potential of an intentionally-set fire; to preserve evidence; and to properly report the information to appropriate officials.

Learning Outcome: Upon successful completion of this course, the student will be able to recognize the indicators of an intentionally-set fire; preserve evidence; and report the information to an appropriate official.

Instruction: Major topics covered in the course are fire behavior, critical observations of the first responder, fire cause, scene security and evidence preservation, legal considerations, and reporting of findings. Methods of instruction include lecture, discussion, classroom exercises, and case studies.

Credit Recommendation: In the vocational certificate category or lower division baccalaureate/associate degree category, 1 semester hour in Fire Science (7/97).

Basic Life Support and Hazardous Materials Response (R246)

Location: Host sites throughout the United States.

Length: 14 hours (2 days).

Dates: October 1994-Present.

Objective: To provide an overview of critical concerns for emergency medical responders at hazardous material incidents, including toxicological aspects associated with hazardous material incident response.

Learning Outcome: Upon successful completion of this course, the student will be able to successfully identify potential problems and safety concerns (responders and victims) from videotaped incidents; define hazardous materials and indications of their presence including respiratory, dermal and systemic toxicology and ingestion injuries; describe decontamination processes and equipment; describe level of protective clothing and protective equipment and its use; define standard of care; and understand federal laws relating to hazardous material response and identify processes and techniques for assessing a responders' condition.

Instruction: Major topics covered in the course are safety issues for EMS hazardous material response teams; managing contaminated victims; decontaminating and treatment procedures at basic life support level; transportation and receiving facilities; and compliance/understanding of federal regulations regarding hazardous material response. Methods of instruction include lecture, discussion, classroom exercises, audio/visual material, graded participation and projects, and a final examination.

Credit Recommendation: In the lower division baccalaureate/associate degree category or upper division baccalaureate degree category, 1 semester hour in Fire Science, Public Administration, Emergency Medical Services, or Community Health (2/95).

Building Construction: Non-Combustible and Fire-Resistive (F150)

Location: Host sites throughout the United States.

Length: 16 hours (2 days).

Dates: July 1983-June 1992.

Objective: To enable the student to cite key features of non-combustible or fire-resistive buildings that affect emergency operations. Fire and life safety concerns that exist in non-combustible and fire-resistive structures are studied.

Instruction: Major topics covered in the course are the key features of non-combustible and fire-resistive that affect emergency operations; fire behaviors of steel and concrete are presented so that the effect of their presence in non-combustible and fire-resistive structures may be better anticipated; basic principles that apply to the spread of fire, products of combustion in structures, and special problems with interior finishes and building elements; testing methods for materials; and the unique problems of conducting emergency operations in buildings under construction. Methods of instruction include lecture, discussion, and simulation exercises.

Credit Recommendation: In the lower division baccalaureate/associate degree category, 1 semester hour in Construction Technology or Fire Science (8/86) (2/95).

Building Construction: Principles-Wood and Ordinary Construction (F100)

Location: Host sites throughout the United States.

Length: 16 hours (2 days).

Dates: July 1982-June 1992.

Objective: To enable the student to recognize construction types, design, alteration consequences, materials used, and their influence on the building's reaction to fire. In a tactical situation construction features and resultant potential hazards to firefighters are studied.

Instruction: Major topics covered in the course are information about how the construction type, alterations, design and materials influence building's reaction to fire; the principle of fireground reading of a building; the value of relevant advance information about buildings are explained; building stability and resistance to fire; special hazards to firefighters and construction elements; and how to determine the likely paths of fire extension. Methods of instruction include lecture, discussion, and simulation exercises.

Credit Recommendation: In the lower division baccalaureate/associate degree category, 1 semester hour in Construction Technology of Fire Science (8/86) (2/95).

Chemistry of Hazardous Materials (R234/R239) (R234 On Campus/R239 Off Campus) (Formerly Hazardous Materials I)

Location: Emmitsburg, MD, and host sites throughout the United States.

Length: *Versions 1 and 2:* 80 hours plus tutorials (2 weeks); *Version 3:* 95 hours (2 weeks).

Dates: *Version 1:* January 1981-February 1983; *Version 2:* March 1983-November 1988; *Version 3:* December 1988-Present.

Objective: To provide students with a sound understanding of the basic chemistry of hazardous materials, key properties of important hazardous materials products, and significant storage and handling requirements for hazardous materials in their normal environment.

Learning Outcome: Upon completion of this course, the student will be able to identify the inherent hazards (toxicity, flammability, reactivity) of chemicals from the name, the formula, and the structure; and deduce worse case synergistic reactions in the event of a release.

Instruction: *Versions 1 and 2:* Major topics covered in the course are basic knowledge required to evaluate potential hazards and behaviors of materials considered dangerous. Emphasis is on the underlying reasons for recommended handling of hazardous materials, with the hope this knowledge will lead to improved decision-making and safer operations and handling for fire officers who may be involved in hazardous-material incidents or in the inspection of occupancies, vehicles, watercraft, or aircraft containing hazardous materials. Methods of instruction include lecture, discussion, laboratory, and workshops. *Version 3:* Major topic covered in the course is an increased emphasis is placed on the chemistry of hazardous materials.

Credit Recommendation: *Version 1:* In the lower division baccalaureate/associate degree category, 2 semester hours in Fire Science Chemistry, General Science, or Physical Science (6/81). *Version 2:* In the lower division baccalaureate/associate degree category, 3 semester hours in Fire Science Chemistry, General Science, or Physical Science (3/83). *Version 3:* In the upper division baccalaureate degree category, 4 semester hours in Fire Science, Fire Technology, Chemistry, General Science, or Physical Science (12/88) (2/94).

Chemistry of Hazardous Materials: Instructor's Program, Level I (R239) (Formerly Instructor's Program Level I—Chemistry of Hazardous Materials [R239])

Location: Emmitsburg, MD, and host sites throughout the United States.

Length: 80 hours (2 weeks).

Dates: February 1988-Present.

Objective: To enable the student to instruct in the area of hazardous materials. Particular attention is directed toward the chemistry of the various types of materials such as acids, salts, plastics, and petroleum products of various kinds. The course has two primary objectives: methodology of instruction in hazardous materials and the chemical and physical problems associated with hazardous materials.

Learning Outcome: Upon successful completion of this course, the student will be able to teach the course, Chemistry of Hazardous Materials.

Instruction: Major topics covered in the course are basic chemistry; elements; the use of the periodic table, as well as an understanding of the combination of elements into complex compounds; various kinds of salts; organic compounds and their properties are explained and investigated; Cryogenics, liquids, and gasses; and fuels and the handling of incidents involving fuels. Methods of instruction include lecture, discussion, workshop, quizzes, videotapes, and a final examination.

Credit Recommendation: In the upper division baccalaureate degree category, 3 semester hours in Applied Chemistry, Educational Methodology, Fire Science, Fire Technology, Fire Prevention Chemistry, Physical Science, Science, Industrial Safety, or Teaching Methods (12/88) (2/93) (2/94). **NOTE:** Credit for this course should not be awarded if the student has received credit for Chemistry of Hazardous Materials (R239), and Fire Service Instructor's Methodology (R113).

Code Management: A Systems Approach (R101)

Location: Emmitsburg, MD.

Length: 68 hours (2 weeks).

Dates: August 1988-February 1997.

Objective: To develop the student's awareness of code management functions as an integrated system and to enhance management skills in areas of system analysis, knowledge of codes, code development and adoption, code management, and evaluation of code functions.

Learning Outcome: Upon successful completion of this course, the student will have knowledge of analyzing specific codes systems; be able to apply and evaluate knowledge of code systems; and role play a comprehensive code adoption hearing.

Instruction: Major topics covered in the course are system analysis, data collection, risk analysis, codes, codes in the United States, fire in America, general scope of codes, scope of building codes, fire codes, model consensus codes, code groups, standards, appeals process, application of codes, code development research, new technology, data analysis, and adopting effective laws.

Credit Recommendation: In the upper division baccalaureate or graduate degree category, 3 semester hours in Administrative Law, Decision Making, Legal Environment of Management as Business, Management, Policy Development, or Policy Formation (12/88) (2/92).

Command and Control of Fire Department Operations at Multi-Alarm Incidents (R304) (Formerly Command and Control of Fire Department Operations [R304])

Location: Emmitsburg, MD.

Length: 63 hours (2 weeks).

Dates: February 1986-Present.

Objective: To enable the student to command greater alarm emergencies utilizing the Incident Command System and to provide the student with applicable techniques, skills, and information to implement command and control applications during significant emergencies.

Learning Outcome: Upon successful completion of this course, the student will be able to apply effective command and control techniques for major multi-alarm incidents while demonstrating proficiency in utilizing the Incident Command System.

Instruction: Major topics covered in the course are the command officer's responsibilities in conducting major operations involving multi-alarm units; emphasis is on rapid fireground decision making, advanced incident command, command and control, safety, personnel accountability and communications. Methods of instruction include through intensive simulation, the student learns to recognize critical cues specific to various types of complex emergencies and to decide on proper command and control procedures to bring these emergencies to closure. The scenario used to simulate multi-hazard operations include multi-family, hotel, high-rise and commercial occupancies as well as large shopping malls, railroad incidents, and wildland fires.

Credit Recommendation: *Version 1:* In the upper division baccalaureate degree category, 3 semester hours in Fire Science (8/86) (2/92). *Version 2:* In the lower division baccalaureate/associate or upper division baccalaureate degree category, 3 semester hours in Fire Science or Emergency Management (7/97).

Command and Control of Fire Department Operations at Natural and Man-Made Disasters

Location: Emmitsburg, MD.

Length: 54 hours.

Dates: April 1995-December 1997.

Objective: To provide rescue fire commanders the requisite knowledge, skills, and attributes to successfully command fire department operations at large-scale natural or man-made disasters, such as an earthquake, hurricane, tornado, flood, or civil unrest.

Learning Outcome: Upon successful completion of this course, the student will be able to address the magnitude of damage and problems in commanding fire department operations at large-scale disasters, utilize the incident command system, understand hazard planning, review interagency coordination and resource issues, use communication systems and counter measures, and understand strategic decision-making in disaster situations.

Instruction: Major topics covered in the course are fire and rescue department operations at natural and man-made disasters; hazards of hurricanes, blizzards, floods, earthquakes, tornadoes, and civil unrest; the primary focus is the field or operational component of the fire department's response to such incidents, emphasis on command and control and on the interrelationship of the operational function to disaster preparedness; mitigation; response; and recovery. Methods of instruction include lecture, discussion, classroom exercises, case studies, audio/visual material, computer-assisted instruction, presentations, and reports.

Credit Recommendation: In the upper division baccalaureate degree category, 3 semester hours in Emergency Management, Environmental Science, or Fire Science (7/96).

Command and Control of Fire Department Operations at Natural and Man-Made Disasters (R308) (Formerly Command and Control of Fire Department Operations at Catastrophic Disasters [R308] or Command and Control of Fire Department Operations at Earthquake and Other Catastrophic Disasters [R308])

Location: Emmitsburg, MD.

Length: 65 hours (2 weeks).

Dates: April 1986-February 1997.

Objective: To provide fire commanders and emergency control officers with the necessary knowledge, skills, and attitudes for commanding fire department field operations during a large-scale natural or man-made disaster such as an earthquake, hurricane, tornado, or flood.

Instruction: Major topics covered in the course are fire and rescue department operations at natural and man-made catastrophic disasters; hazards of hurricanes, blizzards, civil disturbances, acts of terrorism, hazardous materials releases, tornadoes, and floods; the primary focus is the field or operational component of the fire department's response to such incidents, emphasis on command and control and on the interrelationship of the operational function to disaster preparedness, mitigation, response and recovery. Methods of instruction include highly interactive, scenario-based simulation in the advanced application of principles of incident command, command and control, the interface of the ICS and EOC, the use of the Integrated Emergency Management System, evacuation and sheltering, and communications.

Credit Recommendation: In the upper division baccalaureate degree category, 3 semester hours in Emergency Management, Environmental Science, or Fire Science (8/86) (2/92).

Command and Control of Fire Department Operations at Target Hazards (R314) (Formerly Command and Control of Fire Department Operations at Target Hazards)

Location: Emmitsburg, MD.

Length: 80 hours.

Dates: July 1996-Present.

Objective: To increase the incident commander's ability to integrate both fire and community resources to address specific target hazards using proper emergency incident command and control techniques.

Learning Outcome: Upon successful completion of this course, the student will be able to develop a target hazard profile; complete a comprehensive sign-up; use recognition primed decision-making techniques; utilize the incident command system; identify resources needed to mutate target hazards; demonstrate how to identify and reduce the community risk at target hazards; and identify the response scenarios to specific target hazard occupancies.

Instruction: Major topics covered in the course are comprehension, sizeup, recognition, primary decisionmaking, post-incident analysis, incident command system, pre-incident planning, command staff and communications, resources and documentation, and mitigation procedures. Methods of instruction include lecture, discussion, classroom exercises, case studies, and audio/visual material.

Credit Recommendation: In the upper division baccalaureate degree category, 3 semester hours in Emergency Management , Fire Administration, Fire Technology, or Public Administration (7/96).

Community Education Leadership (R343) (N816)

Location: Emmitsburg, Maryland.

Length: *Version 1:* 45 hours (9 days); *Version 2:* 32 hours (6 days).

Dates: June 1996-Present.

Objective: To provide students the essential tools and skills to enhance their organization's public education function. The course is designed for students who have coordination or total program responsibility for public education in their organization.

Learning Outcome: Upon successful completion of this course, the student will be able to enhance their prevention and public education efforts; apply some new methods and techniques in this discipline; increase their community contacts; better utilize their own organization to support public education; become more personally charged as a leader in the field of public education; better plan for community education programs; maximize resources and markets to support community education; and better identify community risks issues and apply sound prevention interventions.

Instruction: Major topics covered in the course are leadership in community safety education; gaining internal support for community education; coalition development and maintenance; analyzing people, messages, and media; planning for community risks; evaluating community education and sharing results; funding and resources strategies in prevention education; and community risk issues and prevention interventions. Methods of instruction include lectures; discussions; videos; individual, small, and large group activities; an individual project, and four examinations.

Credit Recommendation: *Version 1:* In the lower division baccalaureate/associate or upper division baccalaureate degree category, 3 semester hours in Adult Education, Public Health, Public Administration, General Education, or Safety Studies (7/97). *Version 2:* In the lower division baccalaureate/associate or upper division baccalaureate degree category, 2 semester hours in Adult Education, Public Health, Public Administration, General Education, or Safety Studies (7/97).

Community Fire Defenses: Challenges and Solutions (F800)

Location: Emmitsburg, MD.

Length: 16 hours (2 days).

Dates: November 1983-December 1989.

Objective: To enable students to use a workable problem-solving process for analyzing risk and addressing community fire protection.

Instruction: Major topics covered in the course are training in analyzing data, identifying problems, formulating objectives, analyzing casual factors, developing selection criteria, identifying alternative solutions, developing implementation strategies, and designing an evaluation plan. Methods of instruction include lecture, discussion, media, and application activities are used.

Credit Recommendation: In the lower division baccalaureate/associate degree category, 1 semester hour in Fire Science (8/85).

Developing Fire and Life Safety Strategies (R352)

Location: Emmitsburg, MD.

Length: *Version 1:* 79 hours (10 days); *Version 2:* 53 hours.

Dates: January 1990-Present.

Objective: *Version 1:* To enable students to use effective strategies to plan, develop, implement, and evaluate life safety programs in local communities through demonstration of research, a local community injury project, assessments of various materials, programs and strategies, and discussions or group work in class learning activities. *Version 2:* To examine the latest strategies for developing and promoting fire and life safety education programs in local communities includes fire prevention as an injury control issue, prevention education as a community-driven process, prevention as a way to form strong community-based programs, and dynamic leadership to successfully integrate these themes.

Learning Outcome: Upon successful completion of this course, students will be able to profile their community injury causes; provide an injury-control model; identify similarities and differences between home and simulated communities; develop a problem statement; compile a comprehensive plan for that problem; describe program delivery; develop an injury intervention planning document; develop an evaluation plan; and prepare an executive summary.

Instruction: *Versions 1 and 2:* Major topics covered in this course are injury and injury prevention, community involvement, identifying the problem and population, fire prevention and injury control strategies, educational strategies, community strategies, evaluation techniques, and program analysis. *Version 1:* Methods of instruction include lecture, discussion, learning activities, audio/visual materials, and a group project. *Version 2:* Methods of instruction include lecture, discussion, classroom exercises, case studies, audio/visual material, reports, exercises, observations, and class activities.

Credit Recommendation: *Versions 1 and 2:* In the upper division baccalaureate degree category, 3 semester hours in Adult Education, Fire Science, General Education, Public Health, or Safety Studies (3/91) (10/91) (7/96).

Emergency Medical Service and Administration: An Overview (F500)

Location: Emmitsburg, MD, and host sites throughout the United States.

Length: 16 hours (2 days).

Dates: April 1981-December 1987.

Objective: To provide students with an overview of the skills needed to design and manage an emergency medical services organization unit.

Instruction: The EMS administration course provides the fire and rescue service manager with an overview of the issues associated with the development of an EMS program. Specific topics include resources and constraints to system development impact of EMS on capital and operation costs of the fire department mechanisms for medical control and quality assurance, sources of support, implementation, and administration of EMS service, and legal implications of EMS. Individual and group activities provide opportunities for interaction among participants. Methods of instruction include lecture, discussion, and media techniques are used.

Credit Recommendation: In the lower division baccalaureate/associate degree category, 1 semester hour in Emergency Management, Fire Science, Health Safety, or Public Administration (8/85).

Executive Analysis of Fire Service Operations in Emergency Management (R311) (Formerly Strategic Analysis of Fire Department Operations R-306)

Location: Emmitsburg, MD.

Length: 74 hours (2 weeks).

Dates: August 1994-Present.

Objective: To prepare senior staff officers in the administrative functions necessary to effectively manage the operational component of a fire and rescue department.

Learning Outcome: Upon successful completion of this course, the student will be able to effectively develop plans for and manage the operational component of a fire and rescue department; and exercise executive-level command at large-scale emergency incidents using the Incident Command System.

Instruction: Major topics covered in the course are risk assessment, incident documentation, media/political considerations, standards, legal mandates, emergency operations, and use of the Integrated Emergency Management System. Methods of instruction include lecture, discussion, classroom exercises, case studies, audio-visual material, computer-assisted instruction, and a final examination.

Credit Recommendation: In the lower division baccalaureate/associate degree category or upper division baccalaureate degree category, 3 semester hours in Fire Science, Public Administration, or Emergency Management (2/95).

Executive Development (R123) (Formerly Senior Executive Development) (Formerly Fire Executive Development III [R123])

Location: Emmitsburg, MD.

Length: *Version 1:* 76.5 hours (2 weeks); *Version 2:* 65 hours (2 weeks).

Dates: *Version 1:* January 1980-July 1990; *Version 2:* August 1990-Present.

Objective: *Version 1:* To enable students to identify the role and responsibilities of the fire executive and current and future challenges affecting that role and to provide students with a knowledge of the effective use of management concepts and techniques as well as current issues in management. *Version 2:* To assist managers in becoming senior executives; to provide effective management and leadership strategies; and to enhance team building skills and use of action research.

Learning Outcome: Upon successful completion of this course, the student will be able to contribute to the development of approaches to address contemporary fire services' managerial issues, deal with current challenges to fire safety leadership, and contribute to policy development and implementation in a changing environment; develop synergistic teambased approaches to action-based solutions; formulate problem-solving strategies; effectively and efficiently employ ethical, creative, and management-of-change approaches to dynamic situations, and produce a well researched and communicated study/project report to demonstrate the understanding of complex issues/problems facing contemporary fire executives.

Instruction: *Version 1:* Major topics covered in the course are an opportunity for senior-level fire executives to expand their managerial approaches and improve the effectiveness of their organizations by applying current theories of management. Subject areas include the emerging role and responsibilities of executives, future trends in American communities, policy formulation and planning, legal dimensions of the fire service, management of human and physical resources, personnel management, and fire department effectiveness and productivity. Students are generally senior-level fire officers, state fire marshals, and assistant state fire marshals. Methods of instruction include lecture and discussion. *Version 2:* Major topics covered in the course are contemporary fire service issues in a framework of team development and consensus decision-making. Course enhances the executives' ability to effectively and efficiently lead within a dynamic and complex organization by enhancing development of teams and the application of action research. Major topics covered in the course are introduction, team building, project development, research, and problem-solving; following and leadership ethics; creativity and innovation; marketing in the public sector; organizational change and development; outside preparation; elected official and city managers; legal aspects of fire protection; service equality; and research project report. Methods of instruction include lecture, case studies, group experiential learning activities, discussion, presentations, and use of audiovisual aids.

Credit Recommendation: *Version 1:* In the upper division baccalaureate degree category, 4 semester hours or in the graduate degree category, 3 semester hours in Business Administration, Fire Science Management, or Public Administration (6/81)(7/86). *Version 2:* In the upper division baccalaureate degree category, or in the graduate degree category, 3 semester hours in Public Management, Organizational Behavior, Management, or Fire Science (10/91). **NOTE:** Students who receive graduate credit for this course must complete the research project.

Executive Leadership (R125) (Formerly Strategic Analysis of Executive Leadership [R125])

Location: Emmitsburg, MD.

Length: *Version 1:* 72 hours (2 weeks); *Versions 2 and 3:* 77 hours (2 weeks).

Dates: *Version 1:* July 1987-April 1990; *Version 2:* May 1990-February 1995; *Version 3*: March 1995-Present.

Objective: To develop the ability to conceptualize and employ the key processes used by effective executive-level managers.

Learning Outcome: *Version 1:* Upon successful completion of this course, the executive fire officer will be able to conceptualize and employ the key processes used by executive-level managers. *Versions 2 and 3:* Upon successful completion of this course, the student will be able to participate in individual and group class learning activities; develop analysis and synthesis of case studies; participate in class discussions; complete advanced assignments in reading, written activity, mock negotiation, instrumentation, and self-assessment.

Instruction: *Version 1:* This course includes an examination of contemporary public sector and fire service issues using a case study approach to enhance the ability to perform at the executive level. Social and behavioral frameworks are provided for application to administration of fire programs. *Versions 2 and 3:* Major topics covered in the course are the management process; developing self as a leader; managing multiple roles; developing influence skills; fostering creativity and innovation; assessing organization culture; developing decision-making skills; networking planning for change; labor relations evaluation; and analysis development plan. Methods of instruction include lecture, discussions, case analysis, group projects, instrumentation, and personal self-assessment plan.

Credit Recommendation: *Version 1:* In the graduate degree category, 3 semester hours in Business Management, Human Resource Management, Organizational Behavior, Public Management, or Supervision (7/87). *Version 2:* In the upper division baccalaureate degree categories, or in the graduate degree category, 3 semester hours in Organization Behavior, Management, Leadership Management, or Public Management (3/91). *Version 3*: In the upper degree baccalaureate or graduate degree category, 3 semester hours in Organizational Behavior, Management, Leadership Management, or Public Administration (7/96).

Executive Planning (R506) (Formerly Executive Information Planning [R506])

Location: Emmitsburg, MD.

Length: 72 hours (2 weeks).

Dates: May 1993-Present.

Objective: To prepare fire department senior managers to be proactive in planning for and implementing change.

Learning Outcome: Upon successful completion of this course, the student will be able to shape the fire department's future to insure it is responsive to its environment; plan and prepare for the future through effective and efficient management of information; and, anticipate services that fire departments will need to provide their stakeholders and customers.

Instruction: Major topics covered in the course are an overview of executive planning issues, project leadership and management, strategic planning, system analysis, acquisition processes, and implementation and evaluation of projects. Methods of instruction include lecture, discussion, classroom exercises, audio visual aides, and examinations.

Credit Recommendation: In the upper division baccalaureate degree category, 3 semester hours in Fire Service Administration, Public Administration, or Management (2/94).

Fire Cause Determination for Company Officers (R811) (N809)

Location: Emmitsburg, MD.

Length: 36 hours (6 days).

Dates: August 1994-Present.

Objective: To provide fire department company officers basic information on principal aspects of fire origin and cause determination.

Learning Outcome: Upon successful completion of this course, the student will be able to make observations and gather information that will assist in identifying areas of fire origin, identify causes of common fires, and assess the need for additional assistance, in a manner consistent with the principles of fire behavior and building construction.

Instruction: Major topics covered in the course are initial observations, information and data collection, fire behavior, scene security, determination of origin and cause, incendiary and accidental fire causes, vehicle fires, fatal fires, legal aspects, and fire exercises, case studies, audiovisual materials, and successfully passing a comprehensive written examination with a score of 70% or greater.

Credit Recommendation: In the lower division baccalaureate/associate degree or upper division baccalaureate degree category, 2 semester hours in Fire Science or Arson Investigation (2/95).

Fire Command Operations (R801) (N807)

Location: Emmitsburg, MD.

Length: *Version 1:* 35 hours (1 week); *Version 2:* 48 hours (1 week).

Dates: *Version 1:* July 1988-January 1993; *Version 2:* February 1993-Present.

Objective: To develop the student's skills, technique, and knowledge for managing and directing operations at emergency sites.

Learning Outcome: Upon successful completion of this course, the student will be able to apply the "Incident Command System" in organizing emergency procedures at various kinds of sites and under varying types of conditions and situations; coordinate the activities of multiple skill units; and provide a concentrated effort at effecting solutions in emergency situations.

Instruction: *Version 1:* Major topics covered in the course are problem identification, planning, pre-planning, intra-agency coordination, incident identification, management, and strategic planning. *Version 2:* Major topics covered in the course are fire command, mutual aid, command sequence, incident command system fire behavior in buildings, preincident preparation, tactical unit operations, and incident organization. Methods of instruction include lecture, discussion, classroom exercises, and an examination.

Credit Recommendation: *Version 1:* In the upper division baccalaureate degree category, 2 semester hours in Fire Science, Fire Technology, Human Resource Management, Occupational Health and Safety, or Public Management. *Version 2:* In the upper division baccalaureate degree category, 3 semester hours in Fire Science, Fire Technology, Human Resource Management, Occupational Health and Safety, or Public Management (12/88) (2/93) (2/94). **NOTE:** Credit for Incident Command Systems should not be awarded if credit is awarded for this course.

Fire Inspection Principles (R220) (N219) (Formerly Fire Prevention Specialist I)

Location: Emmitsburg, MD.

Length: *Version 1:* 57 hours (2 weeks); *Version 2:* 61 hours (2 weeks).

Dates: *Version 1:* July 1980-April 1991; *Version 2:* May 1991-June 1997;*Version 3:* July 1997-Present.

Objective: To provide student with the fundamental knowledge, skills, and attitudes to conduct both basic and intermediate level fire safety inspections effectively and confidently.

Learning Outcome: Upon successful completion of this course, the student will be able to explain the code enforcement system; perform fire inspector's role professionally; recognize potential hazards of fire spread; analyze construction types and building systems; describe human behavior in fire situations; explain codes and standards; evaluate fire safety of a structure; verify level of safety; identify hazardous materials or processes; identify methods of mitigating hazards; identify special hazard suppression systems; and verify operation of sprinkler systems and alarm detection systems.

Instruction: Major topics covered in the course are participant's role in code enforcement; fire and codes and their relationship; general fire safety; life safety; hazardous materials and processes; special hazards; and fire protection systems and equipment. Methods of instruction include lecture, audiovisuals (film, overhead transparencies, photographs, and diagrams), learning activity assignments, discussion, and group presentations.

Credit Recommendation: *Versions 1 and 2:* In the lower division baccalaureate/associate degree category, 3 semester hours in Fire Science, Industrial Safety, or Insurance (6/81) (7/86) (2/92). *Version 3:* In the vocational certificate category or lower division baccalaureate/associate degree category, 3 semester hours in Fire Science, Industrial Safety, or Insurance (7/97).

Fire Risk Analysis: A Systems Approach (F700)

Location: Emmitsburg, MD, and host sites throughout the United States.

Length: 16 hours (2 days).

Dates: July 1984-November 1989.

Objective: To enable fire service managers to identify the needs and capabilities of community fire defense systems through the application of systematic risk analysis techniques.

Instruction: This course examines community fire defenses as a system and provides fire service managers with a system concept to identify and measure risk level and the level of protection provided by existing resources. Topics in the course include problem identification, community fire protection systems models, risk analysis, effectiveness, and efficiency considerations. Methods of instruction include lecture, discussion, and media techniques are used.

Credit Recommendation: In the lower division baccalaureate/associate degree category, 1 semester hour in Administration, Fire Science, or Management (8/85).

Fire Service Communications (R107) Version 1: (Formerly Executive Development II/Leadership and Communications) Version 2: (Formerly Fire Service Leadership Communications (R106)

Location: Host sites throughout the United States.

Length: *Version 1:* 93.5 hours (3 weeks); *Version 2:* 80 hours (2 weeks).

Dates: *Version 1:* November 1981-September 1988; *Version 2:* October 1988-Present.

Objective: *Version 1:* To develop mid-level fire service managers' understanding of leadership styles and situations when each is most effective and to increase managers' skills and knowledge in the areas of supervisory skills, personal counseling, motivation, and communication skills, both oral and written. *Version 2:* To develop student oral and written skills and communications knowledge with particular emphasis upon the job-related work environment or context.

Learning Outcome: Upon successful completion of this course, the student will be able to demonstrate by performance and on tests, effective written and verbal communications on fire or hazardous material topics.

Instruction: *Version 1:* Major topics covered in the course are analyzing leadership styles; developing an individual's effectiveness in oral and written communication; focusing on three managerial techniques—leader match training, the behavioral modeling approach, and goal setting; and using effective written and oral communication skills within the framework of leadership skills and their importance to effectiveness management. Methods of instruction include lecture and discussion. *Version 2:* Major topics covered in the course are the main elements of writing; self-assessment of writing; verbal communications such as planning, delivery, and evaluation; and the role of communication in effective organizational management. Methods of instruction include lecture, video, computer-aided writing evaluation, producing demo videos, verbal reports and team presentations.

Credit Recommendation: *Version 1:* In the upper division baccalaureate degree category, 3 semester hours in Business Administration, Fire Science, Management, or Public Administration (1/81) (7/86) (2/92). *Version 2:* In the upper division baccalaureate degree category, 3 semester hours in Communications, Business Communications, English, English Composition, Speech, Fire Science, Business Management, or Public Administration (2/93).

Fire Service Course Design (R114) (Formerly Fire Service Course Development)

Location: Emmitsburg, MD.

Length: *Version 1:* 68 hours (2 weeks); *Versions 2 and 3:* 67.5 hours (2 weeks).

Dates: *Version 1:* May 1980-December 1988; *Versions 2 and 3:* January 1989-Present.

Objective: *Version 1:* To teach trainers how to design courses that are tailored to meet specific objectives. *Version 2:* To provide the student with the knowledge and skills required to design effective courses that can be used by other instructors. *Version 3:* To help emergency service personnel design and deliver courses to meet local needs.

Learning Outcome: Upon successful completion of this course, the student will be able to identify components of effective course design and apply course development techniques to the design and creation of training courses.

Instruction: *Version 1:* This course prepares fire service personnel to design and develop curricula. It identifies the components of a typical training program and provides trainers with the necessary planning, research, writing, and evaluation skills to design and successfully implement a training program. A systematic process is used; learning principles and design criteria are considered. Functioning as members of project groups, students design and develop a course and lesson plans. Students are not expected to deliver a similar course in their jurisdictions. Methods of instruction include lecture, discussion, and laboratories are used. *Version 2:* Major topics covered in the course are instructional design components, needs assessment, audience analysis, task analysis, writing course goals and objectives, developing content outlines, evaluation plan and methods, determining instructional methods and media, developing instructor guides and student manuals, and administering and marketing courses. Methods of instruction include lecture, discussion, student projects, tests, audiovisual aids, and examinations. *Version 3:* Major topics covered in the course are instructional design components, needs assessment, audience, analysis, task analysis, written course goals, and objectives, developing content outlines, evaluation plan and methods, determining instructional methods, developing instructor guides and student manuals, and administering and marketing courses. Methods of instruction include lecture, discussion, classroom exercises, reports, graded class activities, and a final examination.

Credit Recommendation: *Version 1:* In the upper division baccalaureate degree category, 3 semester hours in Education or Fire Science (6/81) (7/86). *Prerequisite:* Fire Service Instructional Methodology or equivalent course. *Version 2:* In the upper division baccalaureate degree category, 3 semester hours in Curriculum Development or Instructional Design (11/89) (3/91). *Prerequisite:* Fire Service Instructional Methodology or equivalent 40-hour course. *Version 3:* In the upper division baccalaureate degree category or in the graduate degree category, 3 semester hours in Education, Public Service Programs, or Fire Science (7/96).

Fire Service Financial Management (R333)

Location: Emmitsburg, MD.

Length: *Version 1:* 74 hours (2 weeks); *Version 2:* 81 hours (2 weeks).

Dates: *Version 1:* January 1986-April 1988; *Version 2:* May 1988-Present.

Objective: *Version 1:* To provide fire service managers with the necessary techniques to effectively identify, prepare, justify, and manage the components of an operating budget. Steps of typical budget preparation cycles are identified, and the interrelationships of each step in the cycle and the result of each step are analyzed. *Version 2:* To develop the capability of the student to manage a fire department financial program, to include the planning for and design of the financial system as well as budget preparation, justification, and administration.

Learning Outcome: Upon successful completion of this course, the student will be able to design and develop the fire department financial system; design, develop, present, and justify the budget; and administer the fire department financial system.

Instruction: *Version 1:* This course will assist fire service managers in planning and managing their fire department's fiscal program. The course will lead the participants through a cyclical process of effectively identifying, preparing, and justifying the components of a budget, including assessing budgetary needs, developing long-range financial revenues, understanding the technical and political aspects of preparing a budget, administering a budget, managing revenues, and evaluating the efficiency and effectiveness of funded programs. Methods of instruction include lecture, discussion, and simulation exercises are used. *Version 2:* Major topics covered in the course are the financial management cycle to include system design, budget preparation, budget justification, and budget administration.

Credit Recommendation: In the upper division baccalaureate degree category, 3 semester hours in Business Administration, Fire Science, or Public Administration (8/86) (12/88) (2/92) (7/97).

Fire Service Information Management (R502) (Formerly Fire Service Information Management)

Location: Emmitsburg, MD.

Length: *Version 1:* 57 hours (2 weeks); *Version 2:* 80 hours (2 weeks).

Dates: *Version 1:* October 1984-February 1991; *Version 2:* March 1991-May 1993.

Objective: To provide students with the appropriate theory, information, and technical requirement to enable them to effectively design, acquire, and implement a multi-use information system suitable for a local fire service agency.

Instruction: *Version 1:* The course is intended to provide fire service personnel with background and necessary information required to develop, plan, and acquire an operating information system. A variety of teaching methods, such as lectures, discussion, case study, and simulation, are used. The course is planning oriented with emphasis on the decision-making process required to rent or purchase an information system. Group and individual projects are discussed and graded. *Version 2:* Major topics covered in the course are determining informational needs; information management systems; decision-making and managing with information management systems; designing and procurement of end-user system; and implementation and monitoring system performance. Methods of instruction include lecture, individual and group projects, and case studies.

Credit Recommendation: *Version 1:* In the upper division baccalaureate degree category, 2 semester hours in Business or Engineering Administration, Fire Science, or Management (9/85). *Version 2:* In the upper division baccalaureate degree category, 3 semester hours in Business or Engineering Administration, Fire Science, or Management (3/91).

Fire Service Instructional Methodology (R113) (Formerly Educational Methodology)

Location: Emmitsburg, MD.

Length: *Version 1:* 64 hours (2 weeks); *Version 2:* 73 hours (2 weeks).

Dates: *Version 1:* January 1980-January 1989; *Version 2:* February 1989-Present.

Objective: *Version 1:* To teach fire service instructors and trainers how to organize and teach a lesson or course effectively. *Version 2:* To provide the student with skills required for effective instruction.

Learning Outcome: Upon successful completion of this course, the student will be able to make effective classroom presentations based on appropriate lesson plans; select and correctly employ instructional methods, classroom activities, media, and evaluation techniques; and apply adult learning principles and effectively manage the classroom environment.

Instruction: *Version 1:* Major topics covered in the course are educational concepts necessary to train prospective trainers. The first stage of the course delivers specific information about student-trainers' objectives, teaching strategies, instructional aids and media, lesson planning, and testing. Students engage in applied performance activities to demonstrate understanding of concepts. The second stage requires students to design instructional approaches, create instructional materials, and demonstrate training deliveries for peer and instructor evaluation. In addition, students are provided with opportunities to refine the techniques they will apply as trainers. Methods of instruction include lecture, discussion, and media techniques are used. *Version 2:* Major topics covered in the course are qualities of effective instruction, instructional communication techniques, audience assessment, instructional objectives, lesson planning, evaluation techniques, instructional methods and activities, use of media, adult learning principles, and classroom management. Methods of Instruction Include lecture, discussion, student teaching demonstrations, audiovisual aids, student manual, and examinations.

Credit Recommendation: *Version 1:* In the upper division baccalaureate degree category, 3 semester hours in Education or Fire Science (6/81) (7/86). *Version 2:* In the upper division baccalaureate degree category, 3 semester hours in Classroom Instruction or Teaching Methods (11/89)(2/95).

Fire Service Organizational Theory (R331) (Executive Development II: Middle Management I) (Formerly Executive Development for Middle Management I)

Location: Emmitsburg, MD.

Length: 75.5 hours (2 weeks).

Dates: July 1981-September 1985.

Objective: To enable students to develop and improve skills of mid-level responsibilities.

Instruction: Major topics covered in the course are strategic and operational planning, financing, budgeting, resource allocation, fire-loss analysis, risk-level clarification, and public relations. It is designed to provide present or future mid-level fire service managers with an understanding of current management functions and their practical application in daily problem-solving. Workshop exercises, case studies, force-field analysis, lecture, and discussion are used.

Credit Recommendation: In the upper division baccalaureate degree category, 3 semester hours in Business Administration, Fire Science, Management, or Public Administration (6/81).

Fire Service Planning for the 21st Century-VIP (R802) (N808) (Formerly Community Fire Protection: Master Planning [R802])

Location: Emmitsburg, MD, and host sites throughout the United States.

Length: *Version 1:* 40 hours (1 week); *Version 2:* 53 hours (1 week).

Dates: *Version 1:* July 1988-April 1989; *Version 2:* May 1989-Present.

Objective: To develop and provide students with the planning skills necessary from a technical and political standpoint to effectively plan a local fire program.

Learning Outcome: Upon successful completion of this course, the student will be able to evaluate the community needs associated with risk of fire; select and evaluate the most efficient system in developing community fire protection programs; and define and design a fire and life safety system for a community.

Instruction: Major topics covered in the course are planning strategy; analysis of current systems including risk, developing solutions, and action plans to be implemented; and evaluating the various problems associated with community fire planning. Methods of instruction include lecture, discussion, classroom exercises, and critique of classroom presentations.

Credit Recommendation: In the upper division baccalaureate degree category, 2 semester hours in Administration, Fire Science, Fire Technology, Management, or Public Administration (12/88) (2/93) (2/94).

Fire Service Supervision: Personal Effectiveness (F310) (Formerly Personal Effectiveness)

Location: Emmitsburg, MD, and state fire-training academies.

Length: 16 hours (2 days).

Dates: August 1983-January 1992

Objective: To provide fire service managers and supervisors with basic supervisory skills and techniques that will improve their personal effectiveness as key leaders.

Instruction: Major topics covered in the course are the basic skills and techniques that will assist an individual in improving his or her personal effectiveness, management culture, leadership managerial style and personal performance, time management, stress management, and personal professional development planning.

Credit Recommendation: In the upper division baccalaureate degree category, 1 semester hour in Business Management, Behavioral Science, Fire Science, Principles of Management, or Supervision (8/86).

Fire/Arson Investigation (R205) (Formerly Arson Investigation)

Location: Emmitsburg, MD.

Length: *Version 1:* 90 hours (3 weeks); *Version 2:* 80 hours (2 weeks); *Version 3:* 63.5 hours (2 weeks).

Dates: *Version 1:* January 1978-August 1985; *Version 2:* September 1985-June 1994; *Version 3:* July 1994-Present.

Objective: *Version 1:* To enable students to conduct legal investigations of fires that occur in their jurisdictions. *Version 2:* To enable students to properly identify the origin and cause of a fire, conduct a technically and legally proper scene and follow-up investigation, and properly pursue the case throughout the judicial system. *Version 3:* To provide students with the knowledge and skills necessary to develop an understanding of the scientific principles of fire dynamics, ensure a systematic approach to proper scene investigation and documentation, conduct a systematic origin-and-cause investigation, and facilitate a thorough followup investigation and case presentation.

Learning Outcome: *Version 3:* Upon successful completion of this course, the student will be able to identify and explain fire behavior and characteristics of fire growth and development; differentiate between accidental and incendiary fire causes to accurately determine origin and cause; evaluate scenes where explosions have occurred to identify the characteristics and indicators of incidents where explosives have been used; use accepted practices for the proper collection, preservation, and interpretation of physical evidence; recognize legal constraints related to fire scene investigation and evidence collection; and prepare reports and documentation of incident investigation of case presentation.

Instruction: *Version 1:* Major topics covered in the course are training for personnel primarily responsible for the investigation of fire-related incidents. It is an in-depth course dealing with methods and techniques of conducting a legal investigation into all aspects of fire. The course deals with fire investigation and prosecution of arson. Students will be able to determine the origin and cause of a fire and prepare the necessary forms, sketches, and reports an investigation requires. The identity of common motives encountered in fire investigations and collection and preservation of evidence that may be used to prove some fact or occurrence are covered. The course includes both classroom and application, where knowledge and experience are acquired from observation of actual building-burning, scene examinations, and case development. Methods of instruction include lecture, discussion, and media techniques are used. *Version 2:* Major topics covered in the course are training in fire investigation. The course is a rigorous treatment in which objectives are accomplished through concentrated effort in the classroom and laboratory. It identifies recommended methods for conducting legal fire investigations that culminate, when appropriate, in prosecution for arson. Emphasis is given to determining origin and cause of the fire as well as motivation of the firesetter. Details of investigation, insurance, fire protection systems, types of fires, incendiary devices, legal aspects, interviews, evidence collection and information management are provided. Methods of instruction include lecture, discussion, media, laboratory work, and application activities are used. *Version 3:* Major topics covered in the course are chemistry and physics of fire, building construction, fire causes, determining point of origin, automobile and fatal fires, collection and preservation of evidence, motives, legal considerations, report writing, interviews and interrogations, and explosives and incendiary devices. Methods of instruction include lecture, discussion, classroom exercises, case studies, audio/visual material, a final written examination, and satisfactory completion of simulated burn activities.

Credit Recommendation: *Version 1:* In the lower division baccalaureate/associate degree category, 4 semester hours in Criminal Justice, Fire Science, Insurance, or Investigation (6/81). *Version 2:* In the upper division baccalaureate or graduate degree category, 3 semester hours in Arson Investigation, Criminal Justice, Fire Science, or Insurance (7/86) (2/92). *Version 3:* In the vocational certificate category, in the lower division baccalaureate/associate degree category, or in the upper division baccalaureate degree category, 3 semester hours in Fire Science, Criminal Justice, or Fire and Arson Investigation (2/95).

Firefighter Safety and Survival: Company Officer's Responsibility (F125)

Location: Emmitsburg, MD, and host sites throughout the United States.

Length: 16 hours (two 8-hour days).

Dates: June 1985-January 1992.

Objective: To provide the student with an appreciation of the seriousness of the firefighter injury and death problems and to provide an awareness of techniques for reducing injuries and deaths.

Learning Outcome: Upon successful completion of this course, the student will be able to understand the causes of injury and death; understand the behavior problems and attitudes that are addressed; identify health and fitness programs related to injury and death; identify hazardous situations found in training; identify and correct five station hazards; identify and resolve hazards responding to and returning from a fire; identify and enforce procedures to improve incident scene safety; and identify safety and survival tips.

Instruction: Major topics covered in the course are an explanation of firefighter injuries and deaths; firefighter health and fitness, safety in training, station and response preparation safety, incident safety, post-incident safety, and survival tips.

Credit Recommendation: In the lower division baccalaureate/associate degree category, 1 semester hour in Fire Administration, Fire Management, or Fire Science (12/88) (2/93).

Hazardous Materials Incident Analysis (F410)

Location: Various locations.

Length: 12 or (2 days) or in 8 modules.

Dates: June 1981-November 1994.

Objective: To provide the student with the knowledge required for effective analysis of a hazardous materials incident.

Learning Outcome: Upon successful completion of this course, the student will be able to categorize hazardous materials, their storage, and transportation; recognize the presence of hazardous materials and the likely behavior of such materials; estimate likely harmful emergency outcomes related to hazardous materials; and select appropriate action related to hazardous materials situations.

Instruction: Major topics covered in the course are the definition of hazardous materials, hazardous materials emergencies and their outcomes, potentially dangerous assumptions, estimating likely harm, events analysis, and characteristics and behavior of hazardous materials. Methods of instruction include lecture, discussion, classroom exercises, case studies, audio/visual aids, and examination.

Credit Recommendation: In the lower division baccalaureate/associate degree category, 1 semester hour in Fire Science (11/89) (2/95).

Hazardous Materials Incident Management (R243) (N248)

Location: Emmitsburg, MD.

Length: 48 hours plus tutorials (6 days).

Dates: August 1993-Present.

Objective: To provide knowledge and skill to effectively plan, manage, and conclude a hazardous material or environmental emergency incident within legal and strategic parameters.

Learning Outcome: Upon successful completion of this course, the student will be able to identify liability in hazardous materials response; identify legal requirements under state and federal laws, regulations, and standards; identify and apply the appropriate management strategies necessary to successfully mitigate a hazardous materials incident; and, using strategies that conform to federal requirements, respond to a variety of hazardous materials incident scenarios.

Instruction: Major topics covered in the course are liability issues under state law, planning, training response personnel, resources, facility reports and plans, stress and leadership, the Gedaper process, incident command system, hazardous materials modules, incident planning and documentation, emergency operations interaction within an incident command system, incident recovery, and termination. Methods of instruction include lecture, discussions, library research, individual and group presentations, videos, and media exercises.

Credit Recommendation: In the upper division baccalaureate degree or graduate degree category, 3 semester hours in Public Safety, Fire Administration, or Public Administration (2/94).

Hazardous Materials Operating Site Practices (R229)

Location: Emmitsburg, MD, and host sites throughout the United States.

Length: 80 hours (9 days, 2 weeks) plus evening individual instruction.

Dates: November 1992-Present.

Objective: To address systematic issues in bringing a hazardous materials incident safely to conclusion. The course integrates knowledge about hazardous materials chemistry, storage, transportation, and potential release scenarios with information about local hazardous materials incident plans and response systems.

Learning Outcome: Upon successful completion of this course, the student will be able to serve on a fire service hazardous materials response team or as a hazardous materials company officer; and help identify product characteristics which will help determine initial worst case scenarios (crucial relationships with public media and state/local officials are emphasized.)

Instruction: Major topics covered in the course are Federal Laws, NFPA Stds and processes dealing with on-site hazardous waste incidents; physical properties, terms, and identification references used; environmental threats, conditions influenced by hazardous waste incidents; methods of containment, analysis, site surveys, and incident estimating techniques; and setting hazardous materials goals, tactical objectives, media relatives, and state/local planning and response. Methods of instruction include lectures, individual projects, group presentation, and examinations.

Credit Recommendation: In the upper division baccalaureate degree category, 4 semester hours in General Science, Physical Science, Fire Science, or Applied Science (2/93).

Hazardous Materials Operating Site Practices: Instructor's Program (R404)

Location: Emmitsburg, MD.

Length: 80 hours (2 weeks).

Dates: January 1993-Present.

Objective: To examine advanced and supplemental Hazardous Materials subject matter, and prepare candidate instructors for an anticipated teaching assignment.

Learning Outcome: Upon successful completion of this course, the student will be able to effectively teach the Hazardous Materials course sponsored by the National Fire Academy to related education and training organizations.

Instruction: Major topics covered in the course are advanced Hazardous Materials knowledge, particularly of critical incidents; HM Information Management Systems (HMIS); preparation of classroom materials, lesson plans, and media; and teach classroom modules in HM, adult education psychology, and motivation. Methods of instruction include lecture, discussion, library research, individual and group presentations, videos, media exercises, and extensive testing with high-passing grades required.

Credit Recommendation: In the upper division baccalaureate degree category, 3 semester hours in Fire Science, Fire Technology, Vocational Education, MAT (Master's teaching), Public Administration, or Applied Chemistry (2/94).

Hazardous Materials Tactical Considerations (R235) (Formerly Hazardous Materials II)

Location: Emmitsburg, MD.

Length: *Version 1:* 60 hours (2 weeks); *Version 2:* 79 hours (2 weeks).

Dates: January 1981-December 1989.

Objective: To provide students with knowledge and skills to evaluate and manage properly incidents involving hazardous materials.

Instruction: Prepares fire officers and other emergency personnel to command an incident involving hazardous materials. Physical handling of the materials rather than the chemical properties of the materials is emphasized. The discussion of chemical properties will be adequate for understanding the reasons for specific handling of the materials under various conditions and circumstances. Evaluative capabilities will be enhanced by the study of carrier and labeling requirements and other available information. Methods of instruction include lecture, discussion, laboratory, workshop, and evening classes.

Credit Recommendation: *Version 1:* In the lower division baccalaureate/associate degree category, 2 semester hours in Engineering, Fire Science Chemistry, General Science, or Physical Science (6/81). *Version 2:* In the lower division baccalaureate/associate degree category, 3 semester hours in Engineering, Fire Science Chemistry, General Science, or Physical Science (7/86).

Hazardous Substance Specialist (R237) (Formerly Hazardous Materials Substance Specialist)

Location: Emmitsburg, MD.

Length: 120 hours (3 weeks).

Dates: March 1985-September 1987.

Objective: To give students an understanding of the basic chemistry of hazardous materials, key properties of hazardous material products, and the proper measures for the safe control of hazardous materials. Students will also learn about specific codes, standards, and regulations of fire protection safety.

Instruction: Hazardous Substance Specialist is designed to meet the needs of those fire service individuals who will be responsible for code compliance and fire prevention, specifically in the area of hazardous materials. The first 2 weeks of the course are heavily oriented to chemistry of hazardous materials to provide the student with a basic knowledge of the compatibility of products considered to be hazardous. The third week involves the student with the study of the appropriate National Fire Protection Agency (NFPA) codes and right-to-know laws dealing with the storage and handling of hazardous materials. Methods of instruction include lecture, discussion, and media techniques are used.

Credit Recommendation: In the lower division baccalaureate/associate degree category, 3 semester hours in Engineering, Fire Science Chemistry, General Science, or Physical Science (8/85).

Health and Safety Officer (W720)

Location: Emmitsburg, MD.

Length: 14 hours (2 days).

Dates: July 1994-Present.

Objective: To examine the health and safety officer's role in identifying, evaluating, and implementing policy and procedure that affect the safety and health of emergency responders.

Learning Outcome: Upon successful completion of this course, the student will be able to understand the role of the health and safety officer in both emergency and nonemergency situations.

Instruction: Major topics covered in the course are the role of the health and safety officer; the laws, standards, and regulations; health maintenance; accident investigation; and post incident evaluation. Methods of instruction include lecture, discussion, classroom exercises, case studies, audio/visual material, learner presentations/reports, end of the course testing, and graded individual and group activities throughout the course.

Credit Recommendation: In the lower division baccalaureate/associate degree or upper division baccalaureate degree category, 1 semester hour in Occupational Health and Safety or Fire Science (2/95).

Incident Command Systems for Emergency Medical Services (F160)

Location: Emmitsburg, MD.

Length: 18 hours.

Dates: October 1995-Present.

Objective: To enable emergency medical service (EMS) personnel to effectively understand and participate in the incident command system (ICS) at all stages of an emergency incident.

Learning Outcome: Upon successful completion of this course, the student will be able to identify and use an organized approach to the management of EMS incidents; understand and use proper communications, transfer of command, and emergency incident organization and command techniques; and understand the interpersonal skills and proper safety strategies necessary for Incident Command Systems.

Instruction: Major topics covered in the course are incident command responsibilities and organization, incident command communications, response organization, incident command system, and incident demobilization and termination. Methods of instruction include lecture, discussion, classroom exercises, audio/visual material, observations, and a final examination.

Credit Recommendation: In the vocational certificate or lower division baccalaureate/associate degree category, 1 semester hour in Fire Science or Fire Administration (7/96).

Incident Safety Officer (W719)

Location: Host sites throughout the United States.

Length: 16 hours (2 days).

Dates: February 1995-Present.

Objective: To provide an understanding of the safety officer's role at emergency response situations, with specific emphasis on the role of the safety officer in the Incident Command System.

Learning Outcome: Upon successful completion of this course, the student will be able to provide the Company Officer with the skills to function effectively as a Safety Officer at emergency incidents.

Instruction: Major topics covered in the course are the role of the Safety Officer; regulations, standards, and policies; record keeping and documentation; and risk management and communications. Methods of instruction include lecture, discussion, classroom exercises, case studies, audio/visual material, and a final examination.

Credit Recommendation: In the lower division baccalaureate/associate degree or upper division baccalaureate degree category, 1 semester hour in Occupational Health and Safety or Fire Science (2/95).

Infection Control for Emergency Response Personnel: The Supervisor's Role and Responsibilities (W250)

Location: Emmitsburg, MD, and host sites throughout the United States.

Length: 12 hours (2 days).

Dates: December 1990-March 1996.

Objective: To enable supervisory fire and EMS personnel to ensure infection control in the work environment by providing the knowledge and skills required to conduct training, monitor compliance with OSHA (CFR SS190.1030), and serve as a role model for positive behaviors and attitudes.

Learning Outcome: Upon successful completion of this course, the student will be able to ensure infection control in their work environment by providing the knowledge and skills required to conduct training, monitor compliance, and serve as a role model for positive behaviors and attitudes.

Instruction: Major topics covered in the course are how to protect the individual and department/station personnel from the full range of infectious diseases spread through occupational or other exposures, brisk exposure, modes of transmission, health maintenance personal protective equipment, scene management post-exposures, post-response and station issues, and the importance of the supervisor as a role model. Appropriate target audiences for the course include career and volunteer firefighters, allied professionals, and private and public sector third service emergency health care providers. Methods of instruction include lecture, classroom exercises, group projects, a personal plan for developing and demonstrating constructive behaviors and attitudes, and a final examination.

Credit Recommendation: In the lower division baccalaureate/associate degree category, 1 semester hour in Fire Science or Health Care Administration and Public Health (3/91).

Initial Fire Investigation (R216) (N216)

Location: Host sites throughout the United States.

Length: 40 hours.

Dates: December 1995-Present.

Objective: To provide the new fire investigator with the basic concepts of fire origin and cause origin and provide the information needed to assist in the process of fire investigation.

Learning Outcome: Upon successful completion of this course, the student will be able to appreciate the nature and behavior of fire; recognize signs of fire spread; and identify and locate the kinds of fire-scene evidence that will help establish origin and cause.

Instruction: Major topics covered in the course are fire behavior, building construction and systems, fire scene evaluation, collection and preservation of evidence, interview techniques, and report writing and legal consideration of fire investigation. Methods of instruction include lecture, discussion, classroom exercises, case studies, audio/visual material, quizzes, reports, and a final examination.

Credit Recommendation: In the lower division baccalaureate/associate degree category or upper division baccalaureate degree category, 3 semester hours in

Criminal Justice, Fire Science, Insurance, or Investigation (7/96).

Initial Response to Hazardous Materials Incidents-Basic Concepts (F809)
(Formerly Initial Response to Hazardous Materials Incidents-Basic Concepts [F700])

Location: Emmitsburg, MD, and host sites throughout the United States.

Length: 16 hours (2 days).

Dates: March 1990-February 1997.

Objective: To provide the first responder at a hazardous materials incident basic concepts and techniques for appropriate behavior before, during, and after the incident. The course defines hazardous materials and describes roles, responsibilities, and risks associated with the incident.

Learning Outcome: Upon successful completion of this course, the student will be able to define hazardous materials and describe associated risks to personal safety; explain the roles, responsibilities, and limitations of first responders in hazardous materials incidents; implement appropriate behaviors before, during, and after a hazardous materials incident; identify the presence and potential dangers of hazardous materials in different emergency situations; identify local, state, and federal resources appropriate to emergency and nonemergency situations; and describe basic concepts and techniques of site management and scene setup, to include the proper use of personal protective equipment and decontamination.

Instruction: Major topics covered in the course are introduction; regulations and standards; personal safety; toxicology; site management and scene set-up; personal protective equipment; decontamination; and resources. Methods of instruction include lecture/discussion, classroom exercises, case studies, role playing, and problem-solving (facilitated by instructor and performed by student).

Credit Recommendation: In the lower division baccalaureate/associate degree category, 1 semester hour in Fire Science (2/92).

Initial Response to Hazardous Materials Incidents-Concept Implementation (F808)

Location: Emmitsburg, MD and host sites throughout the United States.

Length: 16 hours (2 days).

Dates: August 1992-Present.

Objective: To give the first responder an understanding of the basic steps of a systematic process for a safe and appropriate response to hazardous materials incidents, it will identify the types, uses, and sources of information needed to recognize and identify the hazard; identify basic options, requirements, and limitations of the methods used to control, contain, or confine a hazardous materials incident.

Learning Outcome: Upon successful completion of this course, the student will be able to respond to hazardous materials incidents as a first-responder, and mitigate damage and dangers involving hazardous materials spills.

Instruction: Major topics covered in the course are estimating the potential course and harm of the incident; determine strategic goals; assess tactical options; plan and implement actions; and evaluate and review. Methods of instruction include lecture, two examinations, and two presentations.

Credit Recommendation: In the upper division baccalaureate degree category, 1 semester hour in Fire Science, Applied Science, Physical Science, or General Science (2/93).

Interpersonal Dynamics in Fire Service Organizations (R332)
(Formerly Executive Development for Middle Management II)

Location: Emmitsburg, MD.

Length: 73.5 hours (2 weeks).

Dates: October 1981-February 1997.

Objective: To enable students to enhance development of personal, interpersonal, and group behavior skills and to enable students to identify, describe, and explain the concepts and techniques involved in effective human resource development and utilization especially as they pertain to managerial productivity.

Instruction: Major topics covered in the course are leadership styles, conflict resolution, counseling, team building, delegation, personnel management, stress management, and interpersonal relationships. Course is designed to provide present or future mid-level fire service managers with the basic knowledge and skills required to become effective human resource managers. Methods of instruction include workshop exercises, case studies, force-field analysis, lecture, and discussion are used.

Credit Recommendation: In the upper division baccalaureate degree category, 3 semester hours in Business Administration, Fire Science, Management, or Public Administration (6/81) (7/86) (2/92).

Introduction to Fire Prevention Inspection: Principles and Practices (R222)
Fire Prevention Specialist II

Location: Host sites throughout the United States.

Length: 24 hours (number of days vary).

Dates: July 1995-December 1997.

Objective: To provide an introduction to fire inspection principles and practices that illustrate the complexity of today's building designs and systems and their potential impact on life, the environment, and property. (For firefighter with responsibility for conducting fire and life safety inspection.)

Learning Outcome: Upon successful completion of this course, the student will be able describe how fire prevention inspection can affect fire cause and spread; explain role of codes and standards in inspection process; recognize fire hazards and hazardous materials and processes; identify basic types of construction, building subsystems, and their functions; identify classifications of occupancy and major life safety concerns of each; identify fire protection systems, devices, and procedures to validate readiness including water distribution systems.

Instruction: Major topics covered in the course are fire behavior and prevention; common fire hazards; building construction and occupancy type; fire detection systems; life safety systems; and inspection practices and procedures. Methods of instruction include lecture, discussion, classroom exercises, case studies, audio-visual material, computer-assisted instruction, learner presentations/reports, written exam, student participation, group activities, and group presentations.

Credit Recommendation: In the lower division baccalaureate/associate degree or upper division baccalaureate degree category, 1 semester hour in Fire Science or Insurance (2/95).

Introduction to Fire Safety Education (R115)

Location: Emmitsburg, MD.

Length: 89 hours (2 weeks).

Dates: October 1985-September 1989.

Objective: To enable the student to identify fire/burn problems, design and implement information and education programs, and evaluate their effects.

Instruction: The course is designed as an introduction to the concepts and techniques of fire safety information and education. Students learn the five-step planning process for public fire safety education programs. Appropriate media channel selection for the message and effective delivery are facilitated through student presentations and experience in a media workshop. Data acquisition, strategic information and education planning, product development, delivery, and evaluation are used to improve communication skills and foster effective fire service education. The course involves extensive student participation in learning activities and presentations, followed by videotape feedback.

Credit Recommendation: In the upper division baccalaureate degree category, 3 semester hours in Fire Science (8/86).

Leadership and Incident Command/Communications Course (R301)
(Formerly Incident Command I)

Location: Emmitsburg, MD.

Length: 56 hours (2 weeks).

Dates: July 1981-September 1984.

Objective: To provide students with an understanding of the principles of fire-site management and basic familiarization with tactics and strategies associated with fire-control methods and accepted fire fighting practices.

Instruction: Major topics covered in the course are basic fire fighting considerations of initial fire-site operations and fire fighting methods for typical occupancies. It is geared to a three-company response with two pumping units and ladder operations. Role play, simulation, and case studies are used.

Credit Recommendation: In the upper division baccalaureate degree category, 2 semester hours in Fire Science (6/81).

Leadership I: Strategies for Company Success (F803)

Location: Host sites throughout the United States.

Length: 12 hours (2 days) or in four 3-hour modules.

Dates: April 1989-Present.

Objective: To provide the student with leadership skills of mid-level managers, especially fire company officers.

Learning Outcome: Upon successful completion of this course, the student will be able to apply appropriate decision-making styles to given situations; outline critical steps in problem-solving methods; identify services provided by a "typical" fire company and the resources needed to provide these services; understand the relationship between resources and services provided by a fire company; and describe the requirements involved in running effective meetings.

Instruction: Major topics covered in the course are decision-making, problem-solving, brainstorming, and meeting management. Methods of instruction include lecture, discussion, audiovisual aids, and examinations.

Credit Recommendation: In the lower division baccalaureate/associate degree category, 1 semester hour in Business Administration, Fire Science, Public Administration, or Urban/Regional Planning (11/89) (2/95) (7/97).

Leadership II: Strategies for Personal Success (F804)

Location: Host sites throughout the United States.

Length: 12 hours (2 days) or in four 3-hour modules.

Dates: April 1989-Present.

Objective: To provide the student with an understanding of leadership skills and tasks associated with management of multiple roles of managers, ethics, abuse of power, and personal creativity.

Learning Outcome: Upon successful completion of this course, the student will be able to identify typical roles and responsibilities of a commanding officer; identify, define, and analyze the role of creativity and innovation in fire service organizations; identify the sources and limits of different types of power; and make appropriate decisions involving ethical issues.

Instruction: Major topics covered in the course are ethics, role conflict, fostering creativity and innovation, and power. Methods of instruction include lecture, discussion, audiovisual aids, role playing, and examinations.

Credit Recommendation: In the lower division baccalaureate/associate degree category, 1 semester hour in Business Administration, Fire Science, Public Administration, or Urban/Regional Planning (11/89) (2/95) (7/97).

Leadership III: Strategies for Supervisory Success (F805)

Location: Host sites throughout the United States.

Length: 12 hours (2 days) or in four 3-hour modules.

Dates: April 1987-Present.

Objective: To provide the student with an understanding of basic leadership skills related to supervision of personnel.

Learning Outcome: Upon successful completion of this course, the student will be able to describe the relationship between development level and leadership style; identify benefits derived from effective delegation and barriers that prevent it; recognize similarities that characterize effective coaches and effective leaders; and use discipline to correct improper employee behavior.

Instruction: Major topics covered in the course are situational leadership, delegation, coaching, and discipline. Methods of instruction include lecture, discussion, audiovisual aids, small group activity, and examinations.

Credit Recommendation: In the lower division baccalaureate/associate degree category, 1 semester hour in Business Administration, Fire Science, Public Administration, or Urban/Regional Planning (11/89) (2/95) (7/97).

Management For Arson Prevention and Control (R207)

Location: National Emergency Training Center, National Fire Academy, Emmitsburg, Md.

Length: 63 hours (9 days).

Dates: December 1996-Present.

Objective: To enable the student to demonstrate knowledge of innovative concepts and practical skills for managing a synergistic response to arson prevention and control.

Learning Outcome: Upon successful completion of this course, the student will be able to define their arson problem and apply a range of concepts and skills to aid in the prevention and control of arson within their jurisdiction.

Instruction: Major topics covered in the course are problem identification, management skills, the investigation process, intra- and interagency cooperation, juvenile firesetting, public education and awareness, and training. Methods of instruction include an assortment of building block activities (activities will provide specifics (such as statistics and skills) and will revolve around a simulated community); videos; lectures designed to provide a foundation for development of a comprehensive Arson Prevention and Control Plan (AP&CP); presenting, discussing, and justifying their portion of the Arson Prevention and Control Plan; using the information from their own communities to independently author an AP&CP Executive Summary; role play, demonstration, discussion, writing, brainstorming, and case study analysis.

Credit Recommendation: In the lower division baccalaureate/associate or upper division baccalaureate degree category, 3 semester hours in Fire Science, Fire Management, Police Administration, or Public Administration (7/97).

Management of Emergency Medical Services (R150) (Management of Emergency Medical Services for the Fire Service)

Location: Emmitsburg, MD.

Length: *Version 1:* 61 hours (2 weeks); *Version 2:* 80 hours (2 weeks).

Dates: *Version 1:* January 1981-March 1994; *Version 2:* April 1994-Present.

Objective: *Version 1:* To help upgrade the fire service manager's skills and knowledge in planning, implementing, and evaluating an emergency medical service program within the fire department. The course emphasizes the manager's role with the fire department, although the system management functions are also considered. *Version 2:* To provide training on knowledge, skills, and abilities required for first-line management of EMS personnel, operations, and equipment. Also provides forum for exchange of ideas of current and future EMS issues.

Learning Outcome: *Version 2:* Upon successful completion of this course, the student will be able to demonstrate leadership skills required of a front-line EMS manager based on peer/supervisor expectations; demonstrate organizational planning, and time management essential to front-line EMS personnel; collection and analysis of data skills required of front-line EMS personnel; demonstrate management of legal and ethical issues required of first-line EMS managers; and demonstrate communications skills required of first-line EMS managers.

Instruction: *Version 1:* Major topics covered in the course are a structured process of applying contemporary management skills and practices to the challenges of EMS delivery; the EMS delivery process as a business with the special focus on financial management, human resource development, system diagnosis, resource management, and stress management; and EMS issues such as communicable disease transmission and prevention, mass casualty incident planning, and critical incident stress. Methods of instruction include lecture, discussion, research groups, and a research paper. *Version 2:* Major topics covered in the course are leadership/management skills, management of human resources, management of EMS system resources (nonpersonnel), interactions with external organizations, and current management issues in EMS. Methods of instruction include lecture, classroom exercises, case studies, computer-assisted instruction, learner presentations/reports, end test/objective, assessment student in small group activities (simulated actual events), and requiring decisionmaking.

Credit Recommendation: *Version 1:* In the upper division baccalaureate degree category, 3 semester hours in Engineering Administration, Fire Science, or Health Care Administration (6/81) (7/86) (2/92). *Version 2:* In the lower division baccalaureate/associate degree category or upper division baccalaureate degree category, 3 semester hours in Fire Science, Health Care Administrator, Community Health Public Administrator, or Emergency Medical Services (2/95).

Management of Fire Prevention Programs (R225)

Location: Emmitsburg, Maryland.

Length: 58 hours (10 days).

Dates: August 1985-Present.

Objective: To give fire prevention managers the requisite knowledge and skills to plan and execute fire prevention functions effectively in the communities, given a finite amount of resources.

Learning Outcome: Upon successful completion of this course, the student will be able to plan and organize for current and future needs of a respective department or jurisdiction and formulate and manage ideas, concepts, and techniques that a fire prevention organization can use to structure and administer to ultimately reduce life and property losses from unfriendly fires.

Instruction: Major topics covered in the course are effective and efficient fire prevention program leadership and management principles; structures of fire prevention organizations; legal and legislative considerations; education, engineering, and enforcement approaches; successful promotion of fire prevention practices; and making it all work back home. Methods of instruction include instructor-led lectures and discussions; small and large workgroup presentations; a case-study; role-playing; and computer-aided, videotaped, and TV instruction.

Credit Recommendation: *Version 1:* In the upper division baccalaureate degree category, 3 semester hours in Fire Science, Public Administration, or Management (7/97). *Version 2:* In the lower division baccalaureate/associate or upper division baccalaureate degree category, 3 semester hours in Fire Science, Public Administration, or Management (7/97).

Management of Fire Prevention Programs (R225)

Location: Emmitsburg, MD.

Length: 72 hours (2 weeks).

Dates: August 1985-July 1996.

Objective: To enable fire prevention managers to plan and execute effective fire prevention functions in their communities.

Instruction: Major topics covered in the course are contemporary issues in the management of fire prevention functions. Top level fire managers address present day and potential challenges in fire prevention. Topics include effective management principles, leadership styles, structure of the fire prevention bureau, technical skills of the fire prevention manager, promoting fire prevention, and the law in fire prevention. Modern management literature is integrated with fire prevention concepts. Methods of instruction include lecture, discussion, and student activities are used.

Credit Recommendation: In the upper division baccalaureate degree category, 3 semester hours in Fire Science, Public Administration, or Principles of Management (8/86) (2/92).

Managing Company Tactical Operations: Decision Making (F450) (Formerly Managing Company Tactical Operations: Decision Making)

Location: Emmitsburg, MD, and host sites throughout the United States.

Length: 12 hours (2 days).

Dates: May 1991-Present.

Objective: To provide a framework for effective structural firefighting decision making and tactical organization.

Learning Outcome: Upon successful completion of this course, the student will be able to apply a systematic approach for developing basic fireground strategies and implementing tactical plans; and implement a basic incident command system for structural firefighting.

Instruction: Major topics covered in the course are the command sequence: size-up, developing an action plan, implementing an action plan, and introduction to incident command. Methods of instruction include lecture, 35 mm slides, instructor-monitored individual and group activities, and a written examination.

Credit Recommendation: In the lower division baccalaureate/associate degree category, 1 semester hour in Fire Science/Technology or Fire Administration (2/93).

Managing Company Tactical Operations: Preparation (F375) (Formerly Managing Company Tactical Operations: Preparation)

Location: Emmitsburg, MD, and host sites throughout the United States.

Length: 12 hours (2 days).

Dates: May 1991-Present.

Objective: To provide the new or prospective fire officer with the basic knowledge and skills necessary to manage one or more fire companies in structural firefighting operations.

Learning Outcome: Upon successful completion of this course, the student will be able to understand the company officer's principal roles and responsibilities in preparing the company to engage in tactical firefighting operations.

Instruction: Major topics covered in the course are the roles and responsibilities of the fire company officer, personal readiness, company readiness, departmental readiness, operational communications, building construction and fire behavior, and preincident preparation (prefire planning). Methods of instruction include lecture, 33 mm slides, instructor-monitored individual and group activities, and a written examination.

Credit Recommendation: In the lower division baccalaureate/associate degree category, 1 semester hour in Fire Science/Technology or Fire Administration (2/93).

Managing Company Tactical Operations: Tactics (R870)

Location: Emmitsburg, MD, and host sites throughout the United States.

Length: 12 hours (2 days).

Dates: May 1991-Present.

Objective: To provide senior or acting company officers with the knowledge and skills needed to effectively accomplish assigned tactics at a structural fire emergency.

Learning Outcome: Upon successful completion of this course, the student will be able to explain the purpose and use of the Communications Model and the Quick Access Prefire Plan in tactical operations at fire incidents; define the relationship between incident priorities, strategy, tactics, and implementation in the command sequence; select the appropriate strategic mode, based on consideration of risk, benefit, and available resources; describe the six steps required to implement the Tactical Action Model; and list the factors on which apparatus placement is based.

Instruction: Major topics covered in the course are an introduction to managing company tactical operations; ventilation and rescue; fire confinement and extinguishment; water supply and exposure protection; salvage, overhaul, and support activities; and private dwelling simulations. Methods of instruction include lecture, discussion, classroom exercises, audio/visual aides, and a final examination.

Credit Recommendation: In the lower division baccalaureate/associate degree category, 1 semester hour in Fire Technology or Administration (2/94).

Managing the Code Process (R101) (Formerly Codes and Ordinances)

Location: Emmitsburg, MD.

Length: 69 hours (2 weeks).

Dates: July 1981-June 1985.

Objective: To enable students to develop, apply, and enforce codes properly upon return to their local jurisdictions. To help students understand the principles, history, function, development, and application of codes and ordinances, as well as understand administrative procedures, working relationships, with various segments of the community, and legal implications related to codes and ordinances.

Instruction: Major topics covered in the course are an introduction to fire building codes; development, adoption, and implementation of fire building codes; and the code-revision process. The course is designed to meet the professional needs of code administrators and enforcers who must be familiar with the development, application, and enforcement of the codes. Code-development background and the general need for codes and ordinances are also explored. Methods of instruction include lecture, discussion, and classroom exercises are used.

Credit Recommendation: In the lower division baccalaureate/associate degree category, 3 semester hours in Business Law or Fire Science (6/81).

National Fire Incident Reporting System Program Management (R499)

Location: Emmitsburg, MD.

Length: 35 hours (2 weeks).

Dates: August 1994-Present.

Objective: To teach promotion, support, and management of data collection, processing, and analysis as it pertains to fire department and other information management programs.

Learning Outcome: Upon successful completion of this course, the student will be able to motivate and encourage the use of standardized data collection, recognize the importance of changing data into information, and to shape the future of the fire service and the fire service's response to community needs.

Instruction: Major topics covered in the course are data management, introduction, documenting the incident, managing data, operating the data system, quality control, and data analysis and presentation. Methods of instruction include lecture, classroom exercises, audio/visual material, computer-assisted instruction, learner presentations/reports, and self-evaluation at end of each module and a final examination.

Credit Recommendation: In the lower division baccalaureate/associate degree or upper division baccalaureate degree category, 2 semester hours in Fire Science, Information Management, or Public Administration (2/95).

Organizational Theory in Practice (R331)

Location: Emmitsburg, MD.

Length: 58 hours (9 days).

Dates: February 1991-March 1996.

Objective: To interpret and apply the theoretical basis for organizational practices.

Learning Outcome: Upon successful completion of this course, the student will be able to analyze the process of theory development and relate it to practice; explain how theory changes over time in response to the environment; critically analyze literature to determine whether the argument or theory is valid; become familiar with the general development of organizational theory; recognize theories in an organization; look at organizations, their missions, cultures, and the environment they operate in; consider the internal and external forces that influence what we do and how we do it; relate the importance of planning to a successful organization; understand various planning techniques; identify and effectively determine methods to enhance decision making in their organizations; select and effectively use communication systems appropriate to their organizations; select effective leadership styles for each group or situation within the organization; determine the most effective control systems for their departments; formulate performance-based evaluation criteria; use the results of their class projects in solving the identified problem; and identify practical tips on how to remain current on organizational theory and practice.

Instruction: Major topics covered in the course are development or organizational theory; organizations; planning; decision-making; organizational communication; leadership and supervision; and control and evaluation. Methods of instruction include lecture, discussion, learning activities, audiovisual materials, a group project, and individual written project.

Credit Recommendation: In the upper division baccalaureate degree category, 3 semester hours in Organizational Behavior, Fire Science Management, or Public Administration (3/91). **NOTE:** Students must complete a 6-month project before receiving the credit recommendations.

Planning for a Hazardous Materials Incident (R236) (Formerly Hazardous Materials III)

Location: Emmitsburg, MD.

Length: 55.5 hours (2 weeks). Approximately three-fourths lecture, and one-fourth laboratory.

Dates: May 1980-April 1984.

Objective: To prepare students to plan for and manage a hazardous materials incident. Major subject areas include the community's potential for disaster, government and private sector capability and assistance, interagency relations, command organization, emergency response teams, and preparation of operational guidelines for the management of hazardous-materials programs.

Instruction: Major topics covered in the course are the community's potential for disaster, government and private sector capability and assistance, interagency relations, command organization, emergency response teams, and preparation of a hazardous-materials-incident management manual. For senior-level fire and rescue officers who may have planning and operational responsibility. Other participants may be selected from allied professions with similar command and planning responsibilities. Methods of instruction include lecture, discussion, laboratory, and workshop are used.

Credit Recommendation: In the lower division baccalaureate/associate degree category, 3 semester hours in Engineering, Fire Science Chemistry, General Science, or Physical Science (6/81).

Plans Review for Inspectors (R102) (Formerly Overview of Plans Review for Inspectors)

Location: Emmitsburg, MD.

Length: *Version 1:* 66 hours (2 weeks); 30 hours lecture, 10 hours discussion, 26 hours lab; *Version 2:* 74 hours (2 weeks); 30 hours lecture, 10 hours discussion, 8 hours classroom, and 26 hours lab.

Dates: *Version 1:* October 1982-November 1988; *Version 2:* December 1988-December 1994.

Objective: *Version 1:* To introduce the student to plan review systems confirming compliance with applicable codes and standards and to develop a report identifying at least five positive and five negative elements of the student's local plan review system along with recommended changes. *Version 2:* To develop the student's understanding of plan review systems confirming compliance with applicable codes and standards and provide an understanding of architect/designer submitted drawings.

Learning Outcome: Upon successful completion of this course, the student will be able to evaluate a set of construction documents for compliance with applicable codes and standards; and develop the skills and attitude required to make his or her unit effective in the plans review process.

Instruction: *Version 1:* Major topic covered in the course is an overview of a systematic checklist approach to verifying that a complete set of construction documents complies with applicable codes. Also introduces applicable standards for the design of sprinkler, standpipe, fire alarm and detection systems, and fire pump installation. Methods of instruction include lecture, discussion, and laboratory exercises are used. *Version 2:* Major topics covered in the course are centered around providing knowledge and developing attitudes helpful in establishing a competent review organization. The course also deals with the "how-to's" of reviewing construction documents.

Credit Recommendation: *Version 1:* In the lower division baccalaureate/associate degree category, 2 semester hours in Fire Engineering, Fire Science, or Fire Technology, or in the upper division baccalaureate degree category, 2 semester hours in Environmental Science, Fire Administration, or Management (3/83). *Version 2:* In the lower division baccalaureate/associate degree category, 3 semester hours in Fire Engineering, Fire Science, or Fire Technology or in the upper division baccalaureate degree category, 3 semester hours in Environmental Science or Fire Administration (12/88) (2/95).

Presenting Effective Public Education Programs (R116/R117) (R116 On Campus; R117 or N116 Off Campus)

Location: Emmitsburg, MD, and host sites throughout the United States.

Length: 35 hours plus tutorials (5 days).

Dates: July 1993-Present.

Objective: To provide public safety educators with the knowledge and skills to apply various learning strategies and presentation techniques in order to make effective deliveries of a community safety education program.

Learning Outcome: Upon successful completion of this course, the student will be able to demonstrate presentation skills for delivering a community safety education program; understand learning strategies appropriate for adults and children; evaluate the delivery of a program and its impact on reducing the identified safety problem; network effectively with various persons and organizations who are in a position of supporting the delivery of a safety program; and analyze neighborhoods for the purpose of confirming an existing community safety problem.

Instruction: Major topics covered in the course are life safety education and the public educator, community analysis, networking strategies, educational principles, choosing the best fire and life safety program, evaluation of impact of course on students and the community, and effective instruction and presentation techniques. Methods of instruction include lecture, discussion, classroom exercises, visual aids, and a final examination.

Credit Recommendation: In the upper division baccalaureate degree category, 2 semester hours in Fire Administration, Fire Science, Fire Technology, or Educational Methods (2/94).

Principles of Fire Protection: Structures and Systems (R222) (Formerly Principles of Fire Protection: Structures and Systems [R226])

Location: Emmitsbury, MD.

Length: 74 hours (2 weeks).

Dates: November 1993-Present.

Objective: To provide advanced knowledge, skills and attitudes regarding fire and life safety inspections, perspective of codes, and standards being enforced in students' jurisdiction.

Learning Outcome: Upon successful completion of this course, the student will be able to conduct fire safety inspection including level of fire and life safety in buildings; understand principles of automatic sprinkler systems, fire alarm and detection systems and specialized extinguisher systems; and understand and apply acceptance and testing criteria for fire protection systems.

Instruction: Major topics covered in the course are legal environment, plans review, identifying and using resources; dealing with the public, industry, and agencies; conducting inspections; and testing, maintenance, inspection of fire protection systems and equipment. Methods of instruction include lecture, discussion, classroom exercises, computer-assisted instruction, learner presentations/reports, role playing (small group activities, group project, and oral lab exams), and a midterm and final examination. (Oral exam in wet and dry labs).

Credit Recommendation: In the upper division baccalaureate degree category or lower division baccalaureate/associate degree category, 3 semester hours in Fire Science, Insurance of Investigation (2/95).

Public Fire Education Specialist (R340)
(Formerly Public Information)

Location: Emmitsburg, MD.

Length: 33.3 hours (1 week).

Dates: February 1980-April 1985.

Objective: To assist students in the design, development, and presentation of fire safety education programs. Students learn communication skills needed to construct public relations programs, speeches, public service announcements, and news releases and the instructional skills needed to construct behavioral objectives and educational programs and activities.

Instruction: Major topics covered in the course are the design, development, and delivery of public fire safety education and public relations programs in the community. Students increase their communication skills in speaking, writing, and use of media; apply behavioral objectives; utilize evaluation techniques; and match instructional methodology to the learner. Topics include high-risk attitudes, behavior, and environments and related public education programs. Methods of instruction include lecture, discussion, and media techniques are used.

Credit Recommendation: In the lower division baccalaureate/associate degree category, 2 semester hours in Communications, Fire Science, or Public Information (6/81).

Strategic Analysis of Community Risk Reduction (R309)
(Formerly Strategic Analysis of Fire Prevention Programs R309 or R310)

Location: Emmitsburg, MD.

Length: *Version 1:* 51 hours; *Version 2:* 72 hours.

Dates: May 1994-Present.

Objective: To provide the student with information to implement community-wide risk reduction activities.

Learning Outcome: Upon successful completion of this course, the student will be able to develop and implement an integrated program of engineering, pubic policy, and education programs to reduce risks within an emergency service organization and within the community itself.

Instruction: Major topics covered in the course are the history of fire prevention, strategic planning, introduction to risk, education and behavior change, and program design and evaluation. *Version 1:* Methods of instruction include lecture, discussion, classroom exercises, case studies, and learner presentation/reports. *Version 2:* Methods of instruction include lecture, discussion, classroom exercises, case studies, learner presentations/reports, reports, observations, papers, and a final examination.

Credit Recommendation: *Version 1:* In the lower division baccalaureate/associate degree or upper division baccalaureate degree, 3 semester hours in Community Development, Occupational Health and Safety, or Fire Science (2/95). *Version 2:* In the lower division baccalaureate/associate degree category or upper division baccalaureate degree category, 3 semester hours in Community Development, Public Administration, Urban Planning, Emergency Management, Occupational Health and Safety, or Fire Science (7/96).

Strategic Analysis of Fire Department Operations (R306)

Location: Emmitsburg, MD.

Length: *Version 1:* 67 hours (2 weeks); *Version 2:* 60 hours (2 weeks).

Dates: *Version 1:* November 1984-December 1989; *Version 2:* January 1990-June 1994.

Objective: To provide the students with an understanding of strategic management principles relevant to command of incidents involving major fire and property loss.

Learning Outcome: Upon successful completion of this course, the student will be able to understand principles of strategic management and apply strategic management principles to the analysis, evaluation, and control of incidents involving major property loss resulting from fires.

Instruction: *Version 1:* Course prepares the student with managerial principles through course studies and supportive material and instruction that enable the (learner) student to understand, analyze, manage, control, and evaluate incidents involving major life and property loss. Methods of instruction include lecture, discussion, media techniques, and student activities are used. *Version 2:* Major topics covered in the course are strategy and tactics, command preplanning, interagency cooperation, incident management systems, large area incidents, tank farms, hazardous materials, conflagrations, civil disturbances, aircraft crash, penal institutions, health care institutions, natural disasters, public assemblies, and brush fires. Methods of Instruction Include lecture, discussion, audiovisual aids, computer-assisted instruction, and examinations. A team research paper is required prior to the end of the course.

Credit Recommendation: *Version 1:* In the upper division baccalaureate degree category, 3 semester hours in Business Administration, Fire Science, Management, or Public Administration (8/85). *Version 2:* In the graduate degree category, or in the upper division baccalaureate degree category, 3 semester hours in Fire Science Management or Public Administration (11/89) (2/95).

Strategic Management of Change (R130)

Location: Emmitsburg, MD.

Length: 10 days.

Dates: March 1996-Present.

Objective: To provide the knowledge, skills, and abilities on change management required of executive-level managers in fire and emergency services organizations.

Learning Outcome: Upon successful completion of this course, the student will be able to demonstrate change management skills and knowledge; demonstrate knowledge and understanding of the Change Management Model; demonstrate the skills and knowledge required to manage and lead change; demonstrate an understanding of the personal aspects of change management; and synthesize and assimilate change management concepts.

Instruction: Major topics covered in the course are an introduction to change management, the Change Management Model, managing and leading change using the Change Management Model, and the personal aspects of change management. Methods of instruction include lecture, discussion, classroom exercises, case studies, simulations, audio/visual material, learner presentations, reports (daily logs), a mid-term test, and a final examination.

Credit Recommendation: In the upper division baccalaureate degree category or graduate degree category, 3 semester hours in Business Administration, Fire Science, Public Administration, or Management (7/96).

Tactical Operations for Company Officers I (F801) (TOCO I)

Location: Emmitsburg, MD.

Length: 16 hours (two 8-hour days).

Dates: April 1988-November 1989.

Objective: To provide the student with basic knowledge of tactics and incident command techniques necessary to effectively manage and direct company-level tactical operations.

Learning Outcome: Upon successful completion of this course, the student will be able to know the multiple roles of the company officer; know the techniques for gathering and developing incident information; know the methods for utilizing strategic information; and know the organization and management of incident resources and the appreciation of the incident command system at the company level.

Instruction: Major topics covered in the course are multiple roles of the company officer, techniques for gathering and developing incident information, the organization and management of incident resources; application of the incident command system at the company level; and using strategic information.

Credit Recommendation: In the lower division baccalaureate/associate degree category, or in the upper division baccalaureate degree category, 2 semester hours in Fire Science or Strategic Planning (12/88).

Tactical Operations for Company Officers II (F802) (TOCO II)

Location: Emmitsburg, MD.

Length: 16 hours (two 8-hour days).

Dates: April 1988-November 1989.

Objective: To provide the student with the basic knowledge and tactics and incident command techniques necessary to effectively manage and direct company-level tactical operations.

Learning Outcome: Upon successful completion of this course, the student will be able to learn the responsibilities of the company officer to provide for safety of firefighters; know the five basic categories of apparatus placement; demonstrate and explain proper apparatus placement to accomplish the specific tactical objectives; know use of entry techniques as essential to facilitate all other tactical operations; and review the common obstructions encountered in entry operations and the methods used to gain entry.

Instruction: Major topics covered in the course are introduction, apparatus placement, entry, water supply, hose lines, salvage, utility control and overhaul, laddering, ventilation, search and rescue, tactical operations (basic incidents), and tactical operations (complex incidents).

Credit Recommendation: In the lower division baccalaureate/associate degree category, 2 semester hours in Emergency Management, Fire Science, or Strategic Management, or in the upper division baccalaureate degree category, 1 semester hour in Emergency Management, Fire Science, or Strategic Management (12/88).

Team Effectiveness (F320) (Fire Service Supervision: Team)

Location: Emmitsburg, MD, and state fire training academies.

Length: 16 hours (2 days).

Dates: November 1983-January 1992.

Objective: To introduce fire service managers and supervisors to basic skills and techniques that will improve their ability to relate to others in the work environment. Service managers will be expected to incorporate the principles of team building in their daily jobs.

Instruction: Major topics covered in the course are a manager's interpersonal skills, motivation, interpersonal communications, counseling, group dynamics, and conflict resolution. Methods of instruction include lecture, discussion, media, and student activities.

Credit Recommendation: In the upper division baccalaureate degree category, 1 semester hour in Behavioral Science, Business Management, Fire Science, Principles of Management, or Supervision (8/86).

Training Program Management (R342)

Location: Emmitsburg, Maryland.

Length: 52 hours (9 days).

Dates: August 1995-Present.

Objective: To apply leadership philosophy to the Training Division in a fire/EMS organization.

Learning Outcome: Upon successful completion of this course, the student will be able to utilize various tools and skills to lead and manage an entire training program; either establish and/or enhance the following functions within their training division: implement various technologies in their division; be aware of various legal issues in training; adopt a variety of techniques in financial/personnel management; manage the functions of design; delivery, development, and evaluation of training; and market the training division within and outside their organization.

Instruction: Major topics covered in the course are leadership in training, implementing technologies, legal issues, managing the needs assessment process, financial management, evaluation, personnel management, managing design and development, managing delivery, marketing for training, and individual projects. Methods of instruction include lecture, discussion, large and small group activities, individual activities, an individual project, and comprehensive examination.

Credit Recommendation: In the upper division baccalaureate degree category, 3 semester hours in Education, Public Administration, Fire Service, Manage-ment, or Human Resource Management (7/97).

Use of Microcomputers For Fire Service Management (R500)

Location: Emmitsburg, MD.

Length: 86 hours (2 weeks).

Dates: October 1982-September 1987.

Objective: To familiarize the student with the application of low-cost microcomputer technology to the management of fire service and EMS organizations.

Instruction: Major topics covered in the course are decision support systems, data collection, analysis and reporting, and organizational implications. "Hands-on" experience with microcomputer hardware and commercial software is available in a microcomputer laboratory. Methods of instruction include lecture, demonstrations, and group projects to introduce the student to microcomputer applications in fire service and EMS organizations.

Credit Recommendation: In the lower division baccalaureate/associate degree category, 2 semester hours in Emergency

Medicine, Fire Administration, Fire Management, or Fire Science (3/83).

VIP: Leadership and Administration (R810)

Location: Emmitsburg, MD and throughout the United States.

Length: 51 hours (6 days).

Dates: January 1994-Present.

Objective: To provide skills needed by volunteer emergency senior officers to enhance community emergency services through effective leadership and administration.

Learning Outcome: Upon successful completion of this course, the student will be able to demonstrate understanding of the role of managing, human resources in a volunteer emergency service organization.

Instruction: Major topics covered in the course are human resources including development recruitment, retention, leadership, change management, financial management, and legal issues. Methods of instruction include lecture, discussion, classroom exercises, case studies, audio/visual material, learner presentations/reports, and a midterm and final examination.

Credit Recommendation: In the lower division baccalaureate/associate degree or upper division baccalaureate degree category, 3 semester hours in Fire Science, Public Administration, or Management (2/95).

Wildland/Urban Interface Fire Protection: A National Problem with Local Solutions (R600)

Location: Self-study course.

Length: Self-paced (approximately 32 hours).

Dates: November 1988-Present.

Objective: To increase the student's level of understanding of the wildland/urban interface problem and to provide effective and defensible strategies and solutions in protecting the interfaces of people and their environment. The interface between rural/urban and developed/undeveloped areas is of particular concern.

Learning Outcome: Upon successful completion of this course, the student will be able to assess the interface problem associated with fire and develop solutions; establish the relationship between fire and regulation; and develop programs on enforcement, public education, and maintaining community support.

Instruction: Major topics covered in the course are the wildland/urban interface, assessing local wildland/urban interface, protection solutions/options, building and maintaining support; and building an action plan. Methods of instruction include self-study with final examination.

Credit Recommendation: In the lower division baccalaureate/associate degree category, 1 semester hour in Civil Engineering, Environmental Management, Range Management, Urban and Regional Planning, or Urban Policy (12/88) (2/94).

National Institute for Paralegal Arts and Sciences

Established in 1976, National Institute for Paralegal Arts and Sciences (NIPAS) is an accredited, attorney and paralegal instructed, distance education institute which provides paralegal diploma, certificate, and degree programs with national application. NIPAS is accredited by the Accrediting Commission of the Distance Education and Training Council (DETC).

Upon completion of the 920 clock hour #1001 Paralegal Diploma Program or the 1440 clock hour Paralegal Specialized Associate's Degree (PSAD) Program, students may sit for the Certified Legal Assistant (CLA) Examination, sponsored by the National Association of Legal Assistants (NALA). Students with prior academic or work experience in the legal field are eligible for tuition and transfer credit into the PSAD Program which consists of (11) foundation level paralegal courses, (4) legal specialty courses, (3) office technology courses, and (3) general knowledge courses.

The mission of National Institute for Paralegal Arts and Sciences (NIPAS) is to provide paralegal training to busy adults. As specialists in this field and in distance education, we understand the special needs of adult learners and offer programs which nurture their talents and experience. Our expert staff focuses on motivating students toward success.

The skills our students learn to be successful as distance education students are the exact skills needed to be effective paralegals—organization, self-reliance, motivation, the desire to learn, the will to succeed, and the ability to solve problems and make decisions.

Our programs and services are designed to allow students to set their own pace toward graduation. The attorney and paralegal instructors are always available on a toll-free "homework hot line" to assist with lesson help or to provide information on the paralegal profession. If you wish to receive information about your student record from NIPAS, please write the Registrar's Office, National Institute for Paralegal Arts and Sciences, 164 West Royal Palm Road, Boca Raton, FL 33432.

Source of official student records: Registry of Credit Recommendations, American Council on Education, One Dupont Circle, Washington, DC 20036-1193.

Additional information about the courses: College Credit Recommendation Service, American Council on Education, One Dupont Circle, Washington, DC 20036-1193.

Paralegal Specialized Associate's Degree Program

American History to 1877

Location: Independent study by correspondence.

Length: Approximately 72 hours of independent study.

Dates: January 1994-Present.

Objective: To give students an understanding of early American history and the formation of the American legal system through 1877.

Learning Outcome: Upon successful completion of this course, the student will be able to explain the derivation of the American legal system, including specific historical events that contributed to the current state of the American Legal system since 1877.

Instruction: Major topics covered in the course are the discovery of the Americas, Spanish and English migration to the new colonies, early colonial economy and government, clashes between colonists and native tribes, the Age of Reason in the 18th century and its colonial impact, the French and Indian War, Great Britain's control and taxation of the colonists, the Revolutionary War, the formation of a new nation and the Constitution, early American politics, the Supreme Court, the Era of Good Feelings, the two-party system of government, early industrialization and development, the Dred-Scott decision, slavery and civil war, the Fifteenth Amendment to the Constitution, and Reconstruction. Methods of instruction include supplemental reading, quizzes, mandatory projects, practical projects, a mid-term and final examination for self-evaluation, and a proctored mid-term and final examination.

Credit Recommendation: In the lower division baccalaureate/associate degree category, 3 semester hours in American History (1/96).

Billing, Bookkeeping, Law Office Management

Location: Independent study by correspondence.

Length: Approximately 72 hours of independent study.

Dates: January 1994-Present.

Objective: To help students attain the knowledge and skills related to law office operations in the areas of billing, bookkeeping, and law office management.

Learning Outcome: Upon successful completion of this course, the student will be able to discuss the importance of an attorney-client agreement; prepare new case memos; list different types of law office fee structures; discuss the differences and similarities between attorney, paralegal, and law firm hours; use daily record log sheets and tickler systems; understand docketing; handle client billing matters; perform basic law firm accounting and bookkeeping duties; describe various forms of law office practices; hire and train law firm personnel; analyze law firm automation and computer hardware and software needs; manage client files; organize a law firm library; write a law office procedures manual; and understand the basic elements of law marketing.

Instruction: Major topics covered in the course are billing (structure of fees, billable hours, timekeeping records, generating billable hours, client billing, disbursements, collection of fees, role of the American Bar Association and state bar associations); bookkeeping (types of bookkeeping and accounting, accounts receivable, accounts payable, monthly and yearly reports and statements, types of bank accounts, preparing the payroll, client ledger cards); and law office management (office management concepts and techniques, how to write procedures, managing personnel, law office design, law office machines and computers, records management, law library, legal fees, and marketing). Methods of instruction include self-evaluation quizzes, a placement skills project, a reference form file project, and a proctored final examination.

Credit Recommendation: In the lower division baccalaureate/associate degree category, 3 semester hours in Introduction to Law Office Management (1/96). **NOTE:** To receive credit for this course, students must pass a proctored examination which is given at the completion of the five courses in the second part of this program.

Business Mathematics for Colleges

Location: Independent study by correspondence.

Length: Approximately 72 hours of independent study.

Dates: August 1996-Present.

Objective: To teach students the skills necessary to perform the most common mathematical calculations used in the business environment.

Learning Outcome: Upon successful completion of this course, the student will be able to perform basic mathematical functions, including addition, subtraction, multiplication, and division and to apply those functions related to the paralegal practice.

Instruction: Major topics covered in the course are fundamental processes, word problems and equations, weights and measurements, fractions, decimals, bank records, percents in business, payroll records, simple interest, commissions, notes and interest variables, federal income tax, life and health insurance, property and auto insurance, and international business. Methods of instruction include supplemental reading, assignments for self-evaluation, and a proctored mid-term and final examination.

Credit Recommendation: In the lower division baccalaureate/associate degree category, 2 semester hours in Business Math (8/96).

Business Organizations

Location: Independent study by correspondence.

Length: Approximately 72 hours of independent study.

Dates: January 1994-Present.

Objective: To help students attain a knowledge of the various types of business organizations, understand the advantages and disadvantages of each, and how they are formed, operated, and terminated.

Learning Outcome: Upon successful completion of this course, the student will be able to understand how to form a sole proprietorship, its advantages and disadvantages; know how sole proprietorships are taxed and what licenses and permits may be required; distinguish among different types of partnerships; draft a partnership agreement; distinguish various advantages and disadvantages of a partnership; discuss the difference between a general partnership and limited liability partnership; locate corporate laws in his or her state related to forming a corporation; explain the requirements for forming a corporation; draft Articles of Incorporation and By-Laws; distinguish among the different types of stock; explain the advantages and disadvantages of incorporating; discuss various government regulations related to the regulation of business; and perform various other duties required of paralegals who assist attorneys in corporate matters.

Instruction: Major topics covered in the course are sole proprietorships, general partnership, limited partnerships, types of corporations, aspects of corporations, other forms of businesses, and legal research related to business organizations. Methods of instruction include self-evaluation quizzes, a placement skills project, a reference form file project, and a proctored final examination.

Credit Recommendation: In the lower division baccalaureate/associate degree category, 3 semester hours in Business Associations, Business Law II, or Business Units (1/96). **NOTE:** To receive credit for this course, students must pass a proctored examination which is given at the completion of the five courses in the second part of this program.

Civil Litigation, Torts, and Administrative Law

Location: Independent study by correspondence.

Length: Approximately 72 hours of independent study.

Dates: January 1994-Present.

Objective: To help students develop an understanding of the differing forms of civil actions in American law in order to assist attorneys with a wide range of related litigation duties and to understand the role, responsibilities, and limitations of the paralegal within administrative law.

Learning Outcome: Upon successful completion of this course, the student will be able to demonstrate knowledge of various tort actions; explain aspects of personal injury law such as products liability, strict liability, wrongful death, and wrongful life; distinguish among the court systems; understand the components of case management; distinguish among different types of motions; draft various pleadings used in civil litigation; describe the different parts of a motion, explain the various stages of discovery; describe pre-trial and post-trial procedures; explain the steps in a trial; know how to use the Federal (and state) Rules of Civil Procedure; and discuss various types of defenses.

Instruction: Major topics covered in the course are civil litigation, torts and personal injury law, and the history of administrative law, administrative hearings, and the role of the paralegal in administrative law. Methods of instruction include self-evaluation quizzes, a placement skills project, a reference form file project, and a proctored final examination.

Credit Recommendation: In the lower division baccalaureate/associate degree category, 1 semester hour in Civil Litigation, 1 semester hour in Torts, and 1 semester hour in Administrative Law (1/96). **NOTE:** To receive credit for this course, students must pass a proctored examination which is given at the completion of the five courses in the second part of this program.

Computer Basics for the Law Office

Location: Independent study by correspondence.

Length: Approximately 48 hours of independent study.

Dates: January 1994-Present.

Objective: To teach students the skills necessary to perform law office computer tasks.

Learning Outcome: Upon successful completion of this course, the student will be able to understand the history of computers and how paralegals use computers in their work.

Instruction: Major topics covered in the course are introduction to computer use in law; computer hardware and software; document processing; database management systems; litigation support; spreadsheet software; time, billing, and accounting; data communications; computer-assisted research; and advanced computer hardware and software topics. Methods of instruction include supplemental reading, self-evaluation review questions, and a proctored mid-term and final examination.

Credit Recommendation: In the lower division baccalaureate/associate degree category, 2 semester hours in Computer Literacy and Basic Programming (1/96).

Contracts

Location: Independent study by correspondence.

Length: Approximately 72 hours of independent study.

Dates: January 1994-Present.

Objective: To help students develop an understanding of the elements a contract as well as the different classifications and types of contracts; to prepare students to draft contracts and to assist clients in preparing documents that have contractual significance; to teach students to perform legal research related to contract litigation and assist attorneys in bringing or defending breach of contract lawsuits.

Learning Outcome: Upon successful completion of this course, the student will be able to understand legal terminology associated with contract law; discuss the four basic elements of a contract; list types of contracts; discuss the three basic parts of contract formation; understand the concept of promise in a contract; discuss various ways a contract can be breached;

understand ways a contract can be modified; list several ways that extinguish a party's duty to perform; understand how a contract can be assigned to a third party and discuss novation; distinguish types of damages; understand the different kinds of warranties; discuss the various ways a contract can be discharged; understand the basic procedures in a small claims court; discuss the basic concepts of the Uniform Commercial Code, Statute of Frauds, and the Statute of Limitations; draft a basic contract and interpret the elements of a contract; locate contract law and cases in his or her state; know the requirements for forming a contract; discuss various governmental regulations related to contracts; and understand and perform the duties of paralegals who assist attorneys in contract matters.

Instruction: Major topics covered in the course are the elements of a contract, classifications and types of contracts, contract formation, promises, breach of contract, defenses to breach of contract law suits, modifications, conditions, performance, contracts involving more than two parties, remedies, warranties, discharge of contracts, contract law litigation, the Uniform Commercial Code, the Statute of Frauds, the Statute of Limitations, legal research for contracts, legal writing, legal forms related to contract, and the role of the paralegal in contract law. Methods of instruction include self-evaluation quizzes, a placement skills project, a reference form file project, and a proctored mid-term and final examination.

Credit Recommendation: In the lower division baccalaureate/associate degree category, 3 semester hours in Business Law I or Legal Environment (1/96). **NOTE:** To receive credit for this course, students must pass a proctored examination which is given at the completion of the first six courses in this program.

Criminal Law Process

Location: Independent study by correspondence.

Length: Approximately 72 hours of independent study.

Dates: January 1994-Present.

Objective: To help students attain an understanding of the criminal law process and elements and types of crimes; introductory knowledge about legal research strategies; and a familiarity with the legal forms that pertain to the criminal law process.

Learning Outcome: Upon successful completion of this course, the student will be able to distinguish between detention and arrests; enumerate the Miranda Warnings, discuss Sixth Amendment rights; explain the booking procedure; distinguish between indictments and information; identify discovery evidence; explain plea negotiations; describe pre-sentencing investigation; list and explain several types of crimes; explain criminal capacity; name defenses and punishments for a crime; explain how laws are made on the state and federal levels; list basic steps in legal research, differentiate between case law, regulations and statutes; explain the difference between legal publications, treatises, and other legal sources; list legal publications; use the uniform system of citing cases; explain the Shepard System of cross referencing cases; and recognize and explain various legal forms used in the criminal law process.

Instruction: Major topics covered in the course are detention, the right to remain silent, booking, bail, attorneys, arraignment, indictments, plea negotiations, sentencing, elements of crimes, elements for the commission of a crime, mens rea, actus reus, prohibited acts, causation, corpus delicti, probable cause, types of crimes, preparatory crimes, persons capable of committing a crime, parties to crimes, defenses, limitations, cases, introductory legal research procedures, and legal forms. Methods of instruction include self-evaluation quizzes, a placement skills project, a reference form file project, and a proctored mid-term and final examination.

Credit Recommendation: In the lower division baccalaureate/associate degree category, 3 semester hours in Criminal Law (1/96). **NOTE:** To receive credit for this course, students must pass a proctored examination which is given at the completion of the first six courses in this program.

Debtor/Creditor Relations and Bankruptcy

Location: Independent study by correspondence.

Length: Approximately 72 hours of independent study.

Dates: January 1994-Present.

Objective: To develop an understanding of debtors' and creditors' rights as well as the uniform law governing the collection of debts; an understanding of what legally can and cannot be done in the collection process; and a familiarity with Chapters 7, 11, and 13 on bankruptcy proceedings.

Learning Outcome: Upon successful completion of this course, the student will be able to demonstrate knowledge of debtor/creditor laws in his or her state; demonstrate an understanding of federal debtor/creditor law; assist an attorney in the collection of a debt; work within the guidelines of the Fair Debt Collection Practices Act; understand how the court system operates as a means to collect debts; demonstrate knowledge of the Federal Wage Garnishment Act; assist in matters related to creditors' remedies before a judgment; obtain a judgment lien; discuss bankruptcy proceedings and alternatives to bankruptcy; locate bankruptcy codes and bankruptcy courts in his or her jurisdiction; and demonstrate an understanding of the differences and similarities of Chapters 7, 11, and 13 bankruptcy proceedings.

Instruction: Major topics covered in the course are debtor/creditor laws, the Fair Debt Collection Practices Act, the Fair Debt Credit Reporting Act, the collection process, the Federal Wage Garnishment Act, Writ of Attachment, creditors' remedies before judgment, the Uniform Fraudulent conveyance Act, Writ of Execution, quasi-contract, quantum merit, and exempt property, bankruptcy proceedings, the Bankruptcy Code, alternatives to bankruptcy, and bankruptcy proceedings in Chapters 7, 11, and 13. Methods of instruction include self-evaluation quizzes, a placement skills project, a reference form file project, and a proctored mid-term and final examination.

Credit Recommendation: In the lower division baccalaureate/associate degree category, 3 semester hours in Bankruptcy, Bankruptcy and Alternatives, or Introduction to Bankruptcy (1/96). **NOTE:** To receive credit for this course, students must pass a proctored examination which is given at the completion of the first six courses in this program.

Ethics

Location: Independent study by correspondence.

Length: Approximately 72 hours of independent study.

Dates: January 1994-Present.

Objective: To give students an understanding of how the practice of law is regulated and to develop a heightened sense of ethical awareness for application in the paralegal profession.

Learning Outcome: Upon successful completion of this course, the student will be able to explain why ethics are a part of our legal system; describe the sources of American legal ethics; explain the consequences attorneys and paralegals face for unethical conduct; discuss ethical issues such as sexual harassment, whistle blowing, and cultural diversity; understand and explain the importance of client confidentiality; demonstrate an understanding of conflict of interest issues; understand what actions are considered to be the unauthorized practice of law; explain historical and public interest reasons for the regulations regarding law firm advertising and solicitation, understand what zealous representation means and why it should be avoided; demonstrate an understanding of the ethical considerations related to client competence; discuss fact specific ethical issues in specialized practices; and demonstrate the ability to determine unethical practices in specific situations.

Instruction: Major topics covered in the course are legal ethics and professional responsibility; introduction to legal ethics; general ethical issues; substantive issues in paralegal ethics - confidentiality, conflict of interest, and unauthorized practice of law; advertising and solicitation; zealous representation; handling client funds; competence; ethical issues in specialized practices; and paralegal principles and practices. Methods of instruction include self-evaluation quizzes, a placement skills project, a reference form file project, and a proctored final examination.

Credit Recommendation: In the lower division baccalaureate/associate degree category, 3 semester hours in Legal Ethics, Legal Ethics and Professional Responsibility, or Legal Ethics for Paralegals (1/96). **NOTE:** To receive credit for this course, students must pass a proctored examination which is given at the completion of the five courses in the second part of this program.

Family Law

Location: Independent study by correspondence.

Length: Approximately 72 hours of independent study.

Dates: January 1994-Present.

Objective: To give students an overview of the family in American law and the many variables that affect family law such as divorce, child support, custody, adoption, child abuse, and alimony.

Learning Outcome: Upon successful completion of this course, the student will be able to understand and explain the concepts of marriage and divorce and how disputes are settled in our American legal system; describe attorney and paralegal roles in the family law process; define the "marriage relationship" and explain how it can be terminated; discuss the rights of children and women in family law issues; define annulment; explain the procedures related to ante-nuptial, post-nuptial, and separation agreements; discuss alternatives to marriage; and explain how property settlements, alimony, and child support issues are resolved.

Instruction: Major topics covered in the course are family law and the paralegal; ethics and family law; family law in historical perspective; current issues in family law; marriage as a contract; annulment; ante-nuptial, post-nuptial, and separation agreements; husband and wife as partners, cohabitation and marriage alternatives; breaking the contract; property settlements, and spousal support; child support; and child custody and adoption. Methods of instruction include self-evaluation exercises, a placement skills project, a reference form file project, and a proctored final examination.

Credit Recommendation: In the lower division baccalaureate/associate degree category, 3 semester hours in Introduction to Family Law or Domestic Relations (1/96). **NOTE:** To receive credit for this course, students must pass a proctored examination which is given at the completion of the five courses in the second part of this program.

Interviewing, Investigation, the American Legal System

Location: Independent study by correspondence.

Length: Approximately 72 hours of independent study.

Dates: January 1994-Present.

Objective: To help students develop interviewing, investigations, and evidence gathering skills necessary to the litigation process and attain an understanding of the American legal system, the U.S. court system, and the U.S. Constitution.

Learning Outcome: Upon successful completion of this course, the student will be able to understand the ethical aspects and responsibilities of legal interviewing, communicate effectively in client and witness interviews, prepare for and perform various types of interviews, handle unique interview situations, prepare a comprehensive post-interview memorandum, develop and execute a plan for the gathering of case evidence, identify and locate witnesses, understand the history and background of the U.S. Constitution, and explain the sources of law in the U.S.

Instruction: Major topics covered in the course are ethical aspects of interviewing, types of interviews, types of clients and witnesses, interview preparation techniques, the interview environment, questioning techniques, listening techniques, unique interview situations, interview memoranda, investigative techniques, evidence, identifying and locating witnesses, the background of the U.S. Constitution and amendments to the Constitution, the structure of the U.S. government, types of courts in the U.S. court system, the federal court structure, the state court structure, and sources of law in the U.S. Methods of instruction include self-evaluation quizzes, a placement skills project, a reference form file project, and a proctored mid-term and final examination.

Credit Recommendation: In the lower division baccalaureate/associate degree category, 2 semester hours in Legal Investigations or Case Preparation/Interviewing Techniques, and in the lower division baccalaureate/associate degree category, 1 semester hour in American Jurisprudence or American Legal System (1/96). **NOTE:** To receive credit for this course, students must pass a proctored examination which is given at the completion of the first six courses in this program.

Keyboarding

Location: Independent study by correspondence.

Length: Approximately 48 hours of independent study.

Dates: January 1994-Present.

Objective: To provide students with effective keyboarding skills.

Learning Outcome: Upon successful completion of this course, the student will be able to key the alphabet and numeric keys by touch using proper techniques; perform basic format functions; format basic letters, memoranda, reports, and tables; and apply quality management concepts to document production.

Instruction: Major topics covered in the course are keyboard basics, letter keyreaches, copy formatting techniques, and figure keyreaches; symbol keyreaches; block letter format; error correction; modified block format with notations; memos; simple reports; outlines; enumerations; tables; vertical centering; business letters; resumes; correspondent measurement; report measurement; and table measurement. Methods of instruction include supplemental reading, practice lessons, and a proctored mid-term and final examination.

Credit Recommendation: In the lower division baccalaureate/associate degree category, 2 semester hours in Keyboarding (1/96).

Law Office Management Specialty

Location: Independent study by correspondence.

Length: Approximately 72 hours of independent study.

Dates: January 1994-Present.

Objective: To give students the knowledge and skills needed to assume administrative positions in a legal environment or any work environment which requires office management skills.

Learning Outcome: Upon successful completion of this course, the student will be able to understand the importance and general functions of the law office manager; recognize the various forms of a law practice; distinguish between private law practice and corporate law practice; and explain the types of specialty law firms and levels of management within an organization.

Instruction: Major topics covered in the course are forms of law practice, law office personnel, ethics, law office procedures manual, personnel management, law office design, law office automation, records management, time management, law library development, legal fees, law firm marketing, and professionalism. Methods of instruction include self-evaluation quizzes, mandatory projects, practical projects, and a proctored mid-term and final examination.

Credit Recommendation: In the upper division baccalaureate category, 3 semester hours in Law Office Management (1/96).

Legal Communications for Paralegals (English Composition)

Location: Independent study by correspondence.

Length: Approximately 72 hours of independent study.

Dates: January 1994-Present.

Objective: To assist students in developing skills necessary to prepare legal documents for clients, internal memoranda of law, documents, and legal briefs.

Learning Outcome: Upon successful completion of this course, the student will be able to understand basic sentence grammar and use it effectively in the paralegal profession.

Instruction: Major topics covered in the course are grammar, vocabulary building, sentence structure, letter writing, and thesis writing; elements of logical thinking as they pertain to written communication, including, inductive and deductive reasoning, fallacies, slanting, syllogisms, equivocation; and editing and proofreading. Methods of instruction include supplemental reading, quizzes, mandatory projects, practical projects, a mid-term and final examination for self-evaluation, and a proctored mid-term and final examination.

Credit Recommendation: In the lower division baccalaureate/associate degree category, 3 semester hours in Legal Communications for Paralegals or Business Communications (1/96).

Legal Research Speciality

Location: Independent study by correspondence.

Length: Approximately 96 hours of independent study.

Dates: January 1994-Present.

Objective: To give students an understanding of the skills needed to find the legal rules that apply to cases and to analyze and communicate those findings in writing.

Learning Outcome: Upon successful completion of this course, the student will be able to explain the history of our common law system; define case law and how it is reported; and explain how computerized legal research works and what services are currently available.

Instruction: Major topics covered in the course are characteristics of American law, the goal of legal research, primary authority, case reporters, published opinions, finding and updating case law, statutes, constitutions, administrative laws, secondary authority, digests, legal periodicals, A.L.R. annotations, legal encyclopedias, looseleaf services, legislative history, model jury instructions, restatements of the law, legal textbooks and rules of court, legal research strategies, critical thinking, deductive reasoning, case analysis, legal writing techniques, types of documents, and memoranda. Methods of instruction include self-evaluation quizzes, a placement skills project, a reference form file project, a honors project, and a proctored mid-term and final examination.

Credit Recommendation: In the lower division baccalaureate/associate degree category, 3 semester hours in Legal Research or Legal Research Analysis (1/96).

Litigation Assistantship Specialty

Location: Independent study by correspondence.

Length: Approximately 96 hours of independent study.

Dates: January 1994-Present.

Objective: To give students the knowledge and skills needed to assist attorneys who specialize in civil litigation, particularly related to the mastery of duties related to trial preparation.

Learning Outcome: Upon successful completion of this course, the student will be able to understand the prerequisites for filing a lawsuit including determining the proper jurisdiction over the subject matter, the location in which the action should be filed, and how to serve the client.

Instruction: Major topics covered in the course are jurisdiction over the subject matter, venue, jurisdiction over the person, pleadings, complaints, file management, discovery and devices, termination to litigation prior to trial, the trial process, post-trial motions, depositions, interrogatories, expert witnesses, trial readiness procedures, and settlement procedures. Methods of instruction include supplemental reading, mandatory projects, alternative projects, a placement skills project, and a proctored mid-term and final examination.

Credit Recommendation: In the upper division baccalaureate category, 3 semester hours in Litigation or Civil Procedure (1/96).

Paralegalism Today

Location: Independent study by correspondence.

Length: Approximately 24 hours of independent study.

Dates: December 1995-Present.

Objective: To orient students about the paralegal profession by providing an overview of the current issues, trends, employment options, and networking strategies related to the profession.

Learning Outcome: Upon successful completion of this course, the student will be able to begin planning a job search strategy at the start of their studies; and evaluate their office-related computer and business skills.

Instruction: Major topics covered in the course are a history of the paralegal profession, a "paralegal" definition, paralegal duties, paralegal skills and attributes, career growth issues, professional ethics, paralegal licensing and certification, types of employers, legal specialty areas and related employment information, law firm structure, professional image, effective cover letters and resumes, networking strategies, paralegal associations, and computer skills. Methods of instruction include self-evaluation quizzes, and a proctored mid-term and final examination.

Credit Recommendation: In the lower division baccalaureate/associate degree category, 1 semester hour in Introduction to Paralegalism (1/96). **NOTE:** To receive credit for this course, students must pass a proctored examination which is given at the completion of the first six courses in this program.

Real Estate Law Specialty

Location: Independent study by correspondence.

Length: Approximately 96 hours of independent study.

Dates: January 1994-Present.

Objective: To attain knowledge and skills to assist attorneys by handling a wide range of functions within the field of real estate law, advance in a current job, or to use real estate knowledge to handle personal or business needs.

Learning Outcome: Upon successful completion of this course, the student will be able to distinguish between real property and personal property; explain how personal property becomes fixtures; and list the four general property rights and give a brief description of each.

Instruction: Major topics covered in the course are ownership interests in real estate; types of ownership; specific rights and interests; transfer interests in real property; special aspects of real estate such as easements, adverse possession, and real covenants; governmental regulations; leases; condominiums and cooperatives; real estate ownership and taxes; real estate transactions; title to real property; mortgages and alternative financing; deeds; and closings. Methods of instruction include self-evaluation quizzes, mandatory projects, practical projects, honors projects, and a proctored mid-term and final examination.

Credit Recommendation: In the lower division baccalaureate/associate degree category, 3 semester hours in Introduction to Real Estate or Real Estate (Real Property) Transactions (1/96).

Wills, Trusts, and Estate Planning

Location: Independent study by correspondence.

Length: Approximately 72 hours of independent study.

Dates: January 1994-Present.

Objective: To help students develop an understanding of estate planning and administration and to attain the skills necessary to draft wills and trusts, collect and valuate assets, maintain records, prepare drafts for tax returns, and perform legal research tasks associated with estate planning.

Learning Outcome: Upon successful completion of this course, the student will be able to discuss the basic types of wills and the specific elements of a will; discuss ways to modify and validate a will; explain the roles and responsibilities of the personal representative/executor and administrator; list several ways a will can be revoked; describe how a will can be contested; draft a will; discuss the requirements for the formation of a trust; discuss the ways an estate can be settled; distinguish between testate and intestate estates; understand the Uniform Probate Code; prepare probate documents; perform accounting procedures related to estate planning; explain the duties and responsibilities of guardians; research probate law in his or her state; and discuss governmental regulations related to probate law.

Instruction: Major topics covered in the course are the formation of a will; contents of a standard will; types of wills; modifications of wills; personal representatives; revocations of wills; contesting a will; intestacy; the formation and classification of trusts; reversions, remainders, and termination of trusts; types of probate proceedings contesting probate administration; probate estate taxation; tax returns; classification of guardians, duties and responsibilities of guardians; and legal research and writing related to wills, trusts, and estate planning. Methods of instruction include self-evaluation quizzes, a placement skills project, a reference form file project, and a proctored mid-term and final examination.

Credit Recommendation: In the lower division baccalaureate/associate degree category, 3 semester hours in Administration of Estates, Decedent Estates, or Wills and Trusts (1/96). **NOTE:** To receive credit for this course, students must pass a proctored examination which is given at the completion of the first six courses in this program.

Word Processing, WordPerfect 6.0 for Windows

Location: Independent study by correspondence.

Length: Approximately 48 hours of independent study.

Dates: January 1994-Present.

Objective: To teach students effective word processing skills using WordPerfect 6.0 for Windows.

Learning Outcome: Upon successful completion of this course, the student will be able to understand basic computer hardware and software; the function of the computer; computer memory and network basics; and how to apply that understanding to the full use of WordPerfect 6.0 for Windows.

Instruction: Major topics covered in the course are computer and word processing basics; file and directory management; help resources; speller options; document formatting techniques; editing techniques; printing techniques; addressing envelopes; WordPerfect bars; outline techniques; thesaurus; sorting; paper sizes; tables; macros; columns; graphics; merging; headers, footers, and endnotes; and tables and graphics. Methods of instruction include supplemental reading, lessons, projects, and a proctored mid-term and final examination.

Credit Recommendation: In the lower division baccalaureate/associate degree category, 2 semester hours in Introduction to Computers, Computer Literacy, or Word Processing (1/96).

National Institute of Nutritional Education

The National Institute of Nutritional Education (NINE) is the oldest distance education program in nutrition sciences in the United States, and the only institution offering the professional *Certified Nutritionist (CNR)* designation. NINE's mission is to increase awareness and motivation for quality living through distance education courses in contemporary nutrition.

NINE was established in 1980 in response to the natural foods industry's need for a nutrition education program based on the health-wellness model—a natural approach to good health emphasizing diet, exercise, lifestyle changes, and alternative medicine. The program has grown to include professional health care practitioners, their assistants, non-health care professionals, members of the natural products industry, and individuals practicing recognized alternative therapies.

There are six courses in the CN program. These courses were developed by experts in the fields of nutrition, medicine, and alternative medicine, and they are reviewed every six months for review and updating.

Courses are delivered through distance education and are available anywhere in the United States. Students work through the program at their own pace, taking up to five months to complete each course and up to 30 months to complete the program. The course study guide explains what to do each step of the way, but when help is needed students can call the toll-free Help Hotline. Student progress is monitored through quizzes, which are submitted at the end of each course section. Quizzes are ungraded, but instructors provide feedback. The course grade is based on a proctored final examination. In the last two courses of the program, students gain practical experience through a nutrition counseling practicum.

Instructors have or are working on graduate degrees, have completed the six-course program and are committed to healthy lifestyles.

Source of official student records: Registry of Credit Recommendations, American Council on Education, One Dupont Circle, Washington, DC 20036-1193.

Additional information about the courses: College Credit Recommendation Service, American Council on Education, One Dupont Circle, Washington, DC 20036-1193.

Nutritional Counseling Five: Professional Aspects of Counseling (NC-5)

Location: Throughout the United States (through distance education; administration is in Aurora, Colorado).

Length: Self paced (approximately 148 hours of work must be completed within 2.5 to 5 months).

Dates: February 1986-Present.

Objective: To provide students with communications skills and counseling tools and techniques for working with clients, including interviewing, assessing, planning, executing plans, dealing with special problems, keeping records, termination, and follow-up.

Learning Outcome: Upon successful completion of this course, the student will be able to describe the effective use of interviewing skills; select and apply appropriate strategies for dealing with specific nutrition problems; use tools and techniques to monitor and evaluate both counselor and client behavior and progress; adapt counseling strategies to changing situations; and explain how nutrition relates to the prevention and management of major chronic diseases.

Instruction: Major topics covered in the course are definition of counseling, Client-Centered Therapy, Behavioral Counseling, Reality Therapy, Rational-Emotive Therapy, Transactional Analysis, malnutrition, nutritional health failure, undernutrition, over-nutrition, deficiency states, imbalances, and the relationship of nutrition to the prevention and management of major diseases. Methods of instruction include required and optional readings, a nutritional counseling practicum, quizzes are used to monitor student progress in the course (they are not graded but students receive feedback on them), a practicum journal, and a proctored final examination. Each item on the final examination corresponds directly to a learning objective from the course.

Credit Recommendation: In the lower division baccalaureate/associate or upper division baccalaureate degree category, 3 semester hours in Dietary Management (11/96). **NOTE:** Only students who have completed two years of a Nutrition and Food Science program at the college level, or its equivalent, would be eligible for upper division baccalaureate credit.

Nutritional Counseling One: Health and Wellness Survey (NC-1)

Location: Throughout the United States (through distance education; administration is in Aurora, Colorado).

Length: Self paced (approximately 144 hours of work must be completed within 2.5 to 5 months).

Dates: October 1986-Present.

Objective: To provide students with a solid understanding of general health concepts applied to the holistic approach to health and wellness.

Learning Outcome: Upon successful completion of this course, the student will be able to describe the medical, environmental, and holistic/wellness models of health, and discuss the strengths and weaknesses of each; explain the role of diet, fitness, and a low-stress environment as major components of the holistic health philosophy, and discuss how each can overcome inadequacies of the traditional health care system; describe how healthy lifestyle habits can reduce the chances of contracting a disease or illness, lessen the seriousness of an affliction, and shorten its duration; describe the uses and abuses of drugs, alcohol, and nicotine, and explain how knowledge of these substances can help people improve their health and lifestyle habits; explain how heart problems, cancer, and environmental hazards affect personal health; and describe lifestyle habits that minimize these risks.

Instruction: Major topics covered in the course are models of health (with emphasis on the holistic health model); roles of diet and fitness in health; understanding and preventing disease; drugs, nicotine, and alcohol; and making healthy choices, including being a wise health care consumer, exploring alternative medicines, and preventing accidents. Methods of instruction include required and optional readings, vocabulary review, study questions, questionnaires, exercises, case studies, quizzes are used to monitor student progress in the course (they are not graded but students receive feedback on them), and a proctored final examination. Each item on the final examination corresponds directly to a learning objective from the course.

Credit Recommendation: In the lower division baccalaureate/associate degree category, 3 semester hours in Health Education or Health and Wellness (11/96).

Nutritional Counseling Six: Practice Management, Ethics, Legal Aspects, and Case Studies (NC-6) (Practice Management, Ethics, Legal Aspects, and Case Studies)

Location: Throughout the United States (through distance education; administration is in Aurora, Colorado).

Length: Self paced (approximately 145 hours of work must be completed within 2.5 to 5 months).

Dates: October 1986-Present.

Objective: To provide students with a process of assessing and managing individual people who have problems that can be completely or partially resolved through nutrition, examples or case studies.

Learning Outcome: Upon successful completion of this course, the student will be able to cite examples showing how diet and diet supplementation play a major role in preventing illness and achieving optimum health; cite examples showing how diet and carefully chosen supplementation can be effective treatments for many problems that are usually treated with drugs or surgery; explain how standard health history formats are developed and list the additional questions that people who are interested in nutritional biochemistry should ask their doctors; describe the nutrition assessment process; discuss the interaction of drugs with foods and nutrients; define nutrition intervention, and list and describe the steps involved; and discuss the role of record-keeping in nutritional counseling, and explain why it is important to maintain up-to-date, accurate information.

Instruction: Major topics covered in the course are preventative nutrition and preventative medicine, food sensitivity, folic acid, biochemical laboratory tests, digestion, enzymes, nutrient absorption, molecular disease, serum lipids, prostaglandins, marine oils, nutritional assessment process, nutrition intervention, nutritional services—implementing, evaluating, and monitoring. Methods of instruction include required and optional readings, case studies, a nutritional counseling practicum, quizzes are used to monitor student progress in the course (they are not graded but students receive feedback on them), a practicum journal, and a proctored final examination. Each item on the final examination corresponds directly to a learning objective from the course.

Credit Recommendation: In the lower division baccalaureate/associate or upper division baccalaureate degree category, 3 semester hours in Practice Management (11/96). **NOTE:** Only students who have completed two years of a Nutrition and Food Science program at the college level, or its equivalent, would be eligible for upper division baccalaureate credit.

Nutritional Counseling Three: Normal Nutrition (NC-3)

Location: Throughout the United States (through distance education; administration is in Aurora, Colorado).

Length: Self paced (approximately 183.5 hours of work must be completed within 2.5 to 5 months).

Dates: June 1986-Present.

Objective: To help students understand the critical relationship between the cells of our bodies and the foods we eat—how the body handles the nutrients it receives from foods, how nutrition influences peoples' lives, and how nutrition and illness are related.

Learning Outcome: Upon successful completion of this course, the student will be able to explain how food is transformed into nutrients for use by the body and how these nutrients are absorbed and distributed to the various cells of the body; describe the chemical structures of carbohydrates, lipids, and proteins, and explain how they are used in the body; list sources, functions, uses, deficiencies, toxicities, and dosages of fat-soluble and water-soluble vitamins; list sources, functions, uses, deficiencies, toxicities, and dosages of the macro- and micro-minerals; and explain normal nutrition concepts such as maintenance of proper body weight, nutrition for the various life stages, and special concerns such as the nutritional needs of pregnant women, nursing mothers, and infants.

Instruction: Major topics covered in the course are nutrition and the digestive process, metabolism, the micronutrients, and normal nutrition in the various life stages. Methods of instruction include required and optional readings, vocabulary review, study questions, questionnaires, exercises in the publisher's study guide, computerized diet analysis, case studies, quizzes are used to monitor student progress in the course (they are not graded but students receive feedback on them), and a proctored final examination. Each item on the final examination corresponds directly to a learning objective from the course.

Credit Recommendation: In the lower division baccalaureate/associate degree category, 3 semester hours in Nutrition or Elements of Nutrition (11/96).

Nutritional Counseling Two: Anatomy and Physiology (NC-2)

Location: Throughout the United States (through distance education; administration is in Aurora, Colorado).

Length: Self paced (approximately 148 hours of work must be completed within 2.5 to 5 months).

Dates: February 1986-Present.

Objective: To provide students with a firm foundation in human anatomy and physiology so that they can grasp the complex, vital relationship between the eleven body systems, diet, and health.

Learning Outcome: Upon successful completion of this course, the student will be able to define the terminology and concepts that are basic to the field of anatomy and physiology; list and describe the human body's structural levels of organization; list and describe the eleven major organ systems in the body and the organs that make up these systems; and describe how each system functions, and discuss factors that affect the health of each system.

Instruction: Major topics covered in the course are general body structure and function and the specific organ systems: skin, bone, muscle, nervous, endocrine, circulation, lymphatic, respiratory, digestive, urinary, and reproductive. Methods of instruction include required and optional readings, vocabulary review, study questions, questionnaires, exercises in the publisher's study guide, case studies (clinical applications), quizzes are used to monitor student progress in the course (they are not graded but students receive feedback on them), and a proctored final examination. Each item on the final examination corresponds directly to a learning objective from the course.

Credit Recommendation: In the lower division baccalaureate/associate degree category, 3 semester hours in Biology or Life Sciences (11/96).

National Joint Apprenticeship and Training Committee for the Electrical Industry

The National Joint Apprenticeship and Training Committee for the Electrical Industry (NJATC) is headquartered in Upper Marlboro, Maryland. The program is administered by an Executive Director appointed by the NJATC Executive Committee. Curriculum development, production, and distribution is done by the National office. Additionally, the NJATC develops National Standards, Operational Procedures and curriculum for local implementation. Workshops are conducted by the NJATC on a national, regional, and local level to ensure that national policies and curricula are understood, implemented, and properly utilized. Additionally, the NJATC conducts an annual training Institute which is presented at a major university specializing in educator development. This full week of college level professional is dedicated to the development of instructional skills, technological awareness, curriculum enhancement and a superior educational system. The Institute is designed to be an accumulative four year educational experience for all instructors teaching in the NJATC's programs. A full-time staff comprised of curriculum specialists, technical writers, clerical, and secretarial profession als and other personnel is maintained to accomplish this mission.

The five year inside apprenticeship program consists of a course of study designed to instruct the student in electrical theory, design, installation, and maintenance of electrical systems providing power, light, heat, air-conditioning, refrigeration, control, communication, monitorization, and automation to residential, commercial, and industrial markets.

Source of official student records: Registry of Credit Recommendations, American Council on Education, One Dupont Circle, Washington, DC 20036-1193.

Additional information about the courses: College Credit Recommendation Service, American Council on Education, One Dupont Circle, Washington, DC 20036-1193.

NJATC Apprentice Inside Wiremen 1st Year Course

Location: Various locations throughout the U.S.

Length: *Version 1:*130 hours and 2,000 hours field cooperative experience (1 year); *Version 2:* 180 hours (minimum) and 2,000 hours field cooperative experience (1 year).

Dates: *Version 1:* December 1982-October 1997; *Version 2:* November 1997-Present.

Objective: Initial year of a five year course of study and field experience to prepare an apprentice for Journeyman Inside Wireman status in the electrical construction (inside) industry.

Learning Outcome: Upon successful completion of this course, the student will be able to demonstrate knowledge, skills, and abilities to apply the principles of basic electricity, National Electrical Codes, engineering reading, drawing and sketching, and mathematics in classroom instruction, demonstration, and supervised field experience; complete all NJATC examinations (written, demonstration, and field competency) with a passing grade. All field and classroom performance tests must be completed to the mastery level necessary to advance to more complex learning and field work; and complete all first year program required to advance and instructor recommendation to advance to next phase of the five year program.

Instruction: Major topics covered in the course are DC electricity, National Electrical Code, engineering drawing, reading and sketching, units and measurements, geometry, algebraic equations, ratios, powers, roots, basic trigonometry, electrical construction materials and methods, electrical construction field experience. Methods of instruction include lecture, discussion, demonstration, and audiovisual and field cooperative training.

Credit Recommendation: *Version 1:* In the lower division baccalaureate/associate degree category, 2 semester hours in Basic Electricity, 1 semester hour in National Electrical Code, 1 semester hour in Blueprint Reading and Sketching, 2 semester hours in Field Experience in Electrical Construction, 1 semester hour in Technical Math for a total of 7 semester hours (12/92). *Version 2:* In the lower division baccalaureate/associate degree category, 1 semester hour in DC Circuits Lab, 1 semester hour in Electrical Construction Lab 1, 1 semester hour in National Electrical Code Theory, 1 semester hour in Electrical Construction Field Experience I for a total of 4 semester hours (11/97).

NJATC Apprentice Inside Wiremen 2nd Year Course

Location: Various locations throughout the U.S.

Length: *Version 1:* 160 hours (minimum) and 2,000 hours field cooperative experience (1 year); *Version 2:* 180 hours(minimum) and 2,000 hours field cooperative experience (1 year).

Dates: *Version 1:* December 1982-October 1997; *Version 2:* November 1997-Present.

Objective: Second year of apprentice development for Journeyman Inside Wireman status in the electrical construction (inside) industry.

Learning Outcome: Upon successful completion of this course, the student will be able to further mastery of knowledge, skills, and abilities to apply the principles of basic electricity, National Electrical Codes, engineering drawing, reading and sketching, Mathematics, and electrical construction materials and methods in classroom instruction, demonstration, and supervised field experience, complete all NJATC examinations (written, demonstration, and field competency) with a passing grade. All field and classroom performance tests must be completed to the mastery level necessary to advance to more complex learning and field work; and complete all second year program requirements and instructor recommendation to advance to next phase of the five year program.

Instruction: Major topics covered in the course include AC resistive, inductive, capacitive and 3 phase circuits, introduction to oscilloscopes and multimeters, R-C, R-L, R-L-C circuits, single and 3 phase transformer circuits, vector algebra, engineering drawing, reading and sketching, and electrical construction materials and methods, and electrical construction field experience. Methods of instruction include lecture, discussion, demonstration, audiovisual, laboratory, and field cooperative training.

Credit Recommendation: *Version 1:* In the lower division baccalaureate/associate degree category, 2 semester hours in Basic Electricity, 1 semester hour in National Electrical Code, 1 semester hour in Blueprint Reading and Sketching, 2 semester hours in Field Experience II in Electrical Construction, 1 semester hour in Electrical Construction Materials and

Methods, 2 semester hour in Technical Math for a total of 9 semester hours (12/92).*Version 2:* In the lower division baccalaureate/associate degree category, 4 semester hours in AC-DC Circuits (cumulative of years 1 & 2), 2 semester hours in Engineering Drawing (cumulative of years 1 & 2), 1 semester hour in Electrical Construction Lab II, 1 semester hour in A-C Circuits Lab, 1 semester hours in Electrical Construction Field Experience II for a total of 9 hours (11/97).

NJATC Apprentice Inside Wiremen 3rd Year Course

Location: Various locations throughout the U.S.

Length: *Version 1:* 160 hours (minimum) and 2,000 hours field cooperative experience (1 year); *Version 2:* 180 hours (minimum) and 2,000 hours field cooperative experience (1 year).

Dates: *Version 1:* December 1982-October 1997; *Version 2:* November 1997-Present.

Objective: Third year of apprentice development for Journeyman Inside Wireman status in the electrical construction (inside) industry.

Learning Outcome: Upon successful completion of this course, the student will be able to demonstrate mastery of principles of electronic devices, National Electrical Codes, engineering drawing, reading and sketching, and mathematics in classroom, demonstration and supervised field experience; demonstrate competency in skills and abilities in motor controls, electrical machinery, and industrial safety practices in classroom and field experience environment; and complete all NJATC examinations (written, demonstration, and field competency) with a passing grade. All field and classroom performance tests must be completed to the mastery level necessary to advance to more complex learning and field work; complete all third year program requirements and instructor recommendation to advance to next phase of the five year program.

Instruction: Major topics covered in the course are diodes, transistors, timers and grounding systems, overcurrent protection and load calculations, National Electrical Code, and field experience in electrical construction. Methods of instruction include lecture, discussion, demonstration, audiovisual, laboratory, and field cooperative training.

Credit Recommendation: *Version 1*: In the lower division baccalaureate/associate degree category, 2 semester hours in Basic Electricity, 1 semester hour in Blueprint Reading and Sketching, 2 semester hours in Field Experience in Electrical Construction, 2 semester hours in Motor Controls, 3 semester hours in Electrical Machinery, 1 semester hour in Industrial Safety Practices for a total of 11 semester hours (12/92). *Version 2*: In the lower division baccalaureate/associate degree category, 3 semester hours in Industrial Electronics, 1 semester hour in Basic Electronics Lab, 1 semester hour in Electrical Circuit Fault Analysis, 2 semester hours in Industrial Safety (cumulative of years 1, 2 & 3), 3 semester hours in College Algebra (cumulative of years 1,2, & 3), 2 semester hours in Electrical Construction Field Experience III for a total of 12 semester hours (11/97).

NJATC Apprentice Inside Wiremen 4th Year Course

Location: Various locations throughout the U.S.

Length: *Version 1:* 160 hours (minimum) and 2,000 hours field cooperative experience (1 year); *Version 2:* 180 hours (minimum) and 2,000 hours field cooperative experience (1 year).

Dates: *Version 1:* December 1982-October 1997; *Version 2:* November 1997-Present.

Objective: Fourth year of apprentice development for Journeyman Inside Wireman status in the electrical construction (inside) industry.

Learning Outcome: Upon successful completion of this course, the student will be able to demonstrate mastery of knowledge, skills, and abilities in motor controls, electronics and industrial electronics in classroom demonstration and supervised field experience, complete all NJATC examinations (written, demonstration, and field competency) with a passing grade. All field and classroom performance tests must be completed to the mastery level to advance to more complex learning and field work; and complete all fourth year program requirements and instructor recommendation to advance to next phase of the five year program.

Instruction: Major topics covered in the course are AC and DC motors, starters, motor controllers, control transformers, resonance, filters, power factor correction, basic digital logic circuits, fiber optic and opto-electronic theory and applications, and field experience in electrical construction. Methods of instruction include lecture, discussion, demonstration, audiovisual, laboratory, and field cooperative training.

Credit Recommendation: *Version 1:* In the lower division baccalaureate/associate degree category, 3 semester hours in Electronics, 3 semester hours in Industrial Electronics, 2 semester hours in Motor Controls, 2 semester hours in Field Experience in Electrical Construction, 1 semester hour in HVAC for a total of 11 semester hours (12/92). *Version 2*: In the lower division baccalaureate/associate degree category, 4 semester hours in AC and DC Motors, 1 semester hour in Motor Control Lab, 2 semester hours in Motor Control Circuits, 3 semester hours in Digital Electronic Fundamentals, 2 semester hours in Electrical Construction Field Experience IV, 1 semester hour in Digital Electronic Lab for a total of 13 semester hours (11/97).

NJATC Apprentice Inside Wiremen 5th Year Course

Location: Various locations throughout the U.S.

Length: *Version 1:* 160 hours (minimum) and 2,000 hours field cooperative experience (1 year); *Version 2:* 180 hours(minimum) and 2,000 hours field cooperative experience (1 year).

Dates: *Version 1:* December 1982-October 1997; *Version 2:* November 1997-Present.

Objective: Fifth and final year of apprentice development for Journeyman Inside Wireman status in the electrical construction (inside) industry.

Learning Outcome: Upon successful completion of this course, the student will be able to demonstrate complete mastery of knowledge, skills, and abilities in use of National Electrical Codes, instrumentation and testing techniques and equipment, and industrial electronics in classroom instruction, demonstration, and supervised field experience, and complete all NJATC examinations (written, demonstration, and field competency) with a passing grade. All field and classroom performance tests must be completed to the mastery level to complete program requirements for Journeyman Inside Wireman; complete all fifth year program requirements and instructor recommendation to achieve the designation as Journeyman Inside Wireman in the electrical construction (inside) industry.

Instruction: Major topics covered in the course are security and fire alarm systems, sensors, instrumentation setup and calibration, theory of flow, pressure, level, temperature, pneumatics, telephone wiring, high voltage safety and testing, heating, ventilating, air conditioning

(HVAC) theory, controls and troubleshooting, and uninterruptible power supplies. Methods of instruction include lecture, discussion, demonstration, audio-visual, laboratory, and field cooperative training.

Credit Recommendation: *Version 1:* In the lower division baccalaureate/associate degree category, 1 semester hour in National Electrical Code, 3 semester hours in Instrumentation and Testing, 3 semester hours in Industrial Electronics, 2 semester hours in Field Experience in Electrical Construction for a total of 9 semester hours (12/92). *Version 2:* In the lower division baccalaureate/associate degree category, 3 semester hours in Instrumentation and Testing, 3 semester hours in Industrial Electronics II, 1 semester hour in Electronic Instrumentation Lab, 1 semester hour in Electro-mechanical Troubleshooting, 4 semester hours in Basic Physics (cumulative of years 1-5)for a total of 12 semester hours (11/97).

NJATC Apprentice Lineman 1st Year Course

Location: Various IBEW locals throughout the U.S.

Length: 160 hours (9 months) classroom and 2,000 hours (1 year) field cooperative experience.

Dates: November 1984-Present.

Objective: First year of a three year program of study and field experience for Journeyman Lineman status in the electrical construction (outside) industry.

Learning Outcome: Upon successful completion of this course, the student will be able to apply the principles of technical mathematics, basic electricity, electrical safety and first aid, perform outside electrical construction activities under supervision, and meet OSHA safety and CPR certification requirements.

Instruction: Major topics covered in the course are technical mathematics, basic AC/DC electricity, electrical safety, OSHA safety program, CPR, and field experience in electrical construction with heavy equipment. Methods of instruction include lecture, discussion, audio/visual materials, and classroom and laboratory exercises.

Credit Recommendation: In the lower division baccalaureate/associate degree category, 3 semester hours in Technical Math, 2 semester hours in Industrial Safety and First Aid, 3 semester hours in Basic (AC/DC) Electricity, and 2 semester hours in Electrical Construction Laboratory for a total of 10 semester hours (12/94).

NJATC Apprentice Lineman 2nd Year Course

Location: Various IBEW locals throughout the U.S.

Length: 160 hours (9 months) classroom and 2,000 hours (1 year) field cooperative experience.

Dates: November 1984-Present.

Objective: Second year of a three year program of study and field experience for Journeyman Lineman status in the electrical construction (outside) industry.

Learning Outcome: Upon successful completion of this course, the student will be able to apply the principles of AC electrical circuitry to the use of transformers in single phase and three phase circuits; read power/electrical schematics and construction plans; follow high voltage safety procedures; and perform high voltage installation of electrical components.

Instruction: Major topics covered in the course are AC circuits, including inductance, three phase connections, polarity, and distribution circuits; electrical schematics and site plan drawing reading; high voltage safety; and high voltage installation procedures. Methods of instruction include lecture, discussion, audio/visual materials, and classroom and laboratory exercises.

Credit Recommendation: In the lower division baccalaureate/associate degree category, 3 semester hours in AC Circuits, 2 semester hours in High Voltage Circuits Laboratory, 2 semester hours in Industrial High Voltage Safety, 2 semester hours in Construction/Electrical Reading, and 2 semester hours in Technical Math for a total of 11 semester hours (12/94).

NJATC Apprentice Lineman 3rd Year Course

Location: Various IBEW locals throughout the U.S.

Length: 160 hours (9 months) classroom and 2,000 hours (1 year) field cooperative experience.

Dates: November 1984-Present.

Objective: Third year of a three year program of study and field experience for Journeyman Lineman status in the electrical construction (outside) industry.

Learning Outcome: Upon successful completion of this course, the student will be able to apply AC circuit theory toward use in power AC installations; use metering to troubleshoot power electrical circuits; exhibit knowledge of power switching circuits; understand residential circuits; and perform live wire maintenance.

Instruction: Major topics covered in the course are advanced transformer connections; high voltage testing; fault currents; live line maintenance; cable splicing; oil circuit breakers; circuit metering; watthour meter use; fusing; and substations. Methods of instruction include lecture, discussion, audio/visual materials, and classroom and laboratory exercises.

Credit Recommendation: In the lower division baccalaureate/associate degree category, 2 semester hours in Power Electrical Measurements Methods, 3 semester hours in Electrical Troubleshooting (Power) Theory; 2 semester hours in Electrical Troubleshooting (Power) Laboratory, and 2 semester hours in AC Circuits (Power) Laboratory for a total of 9 semester hours (12/94).

National Management Association

The National Management Association is one of the oldest and largest organizations espousing management as a profession and the personal and professional development of the manager. Founded in the early nineteen hundreds at the Dayton Engineering Laboratories Company by the famous inventor, Charles Kettering, it became the National Association of Foremen in 1925. In 1957 the name was changed to the National Management Association.

The NMA has affiliated chapters throughout the U.S.A. The organization is committed to bringing its members the latest state of the art thinking in management training through its professional development course materials. To enhance managerial interactions, all course materials are prepared with a complete discussion leader guide to be used in a group discussion learning format.

Source of official student records: National Management Association, Professional Development Division, 2210 Arbor Boulevard, Dayton, OH 45439.

Additional information about the courses: College Credit Recommendation Service, American Council on Education, One Dupont Circle, Washington, DC 20036-1193.

Supervisory and Management Skills Program
Course 5: Developing Employee Performance
Course 6: Challenge of a New Employee
Course 7: Coaching and Counseling
(Formerly First Line Supervisor Program)

Location: Nationwide.

Length: 42 hours (2 hours per week for 21 weeks); 3 hours precourse work.

Dates: July 1982-Present.

Objective: To provide participants with an introduction to contemporary principles and practices of hiring, developing, and maintaining productive employees.

Instruction: Major topics covered in the course are hiring, orientation, and training of new employees; the development and implementation of personnel management systems; and the role of counseling as a corrective strategy. Methods of instruction include videotape cases, classroom discussion, individual/ team exercises, readings, and tests.

Credit Recommendation: In the lower division baccalaureate/associate degree category, 2 semester hours in Personnel Management (8/83).

Supervisory and Management Skills Program
Course 3: Communication Skills
Course 4: Interpersonal Relationship Skills
(Formerly First Line Supervisor Program)

Location: Nationwide.

Length: 28 hours (14 weeks); 2 hours of precourse work.

Dates: July 1981-Present.

Objective: To provide the supervisor with knowledge and skills in order to increase his understanding and effectiveness in communicating both verbally and nonverbally.

Learning Outcome: Upon successful completion of this course, the student will be able to resolve communication problems, develop oral and listening skills, read and write effectively, conduct meetings and presentations, handle conflicts and interpersonal relationships, work effectively with groups, and build effective working relationships with subordinates, peers, and supervisors.

Instruction: Major topics in the course are the basics of communication and working with people, oral and written communication, handling meetings and conferences, and dealing with written and oral communication in an organization. Methods of instruction include discussion, classroom exercises, case studies, team exercises, role playing and critiques, audio/visual materials, learner presentations/reports, tests, quizzes, and a final examination.

Credit Recommendation: In the lower division baccalaureate/associate degree category, 2 semester hours in Business Communications, Communications, Human Behavior, or Interpersonal Dynamics (8/83) (12/96).

Supervisory and Management Skills Program
Course 9: Business Concepts
Course 10: Law for the Layman
(Formerly First Line Supervisor Program)

Location: Nationwide.

Length: 28 hours (14 weeks); 2 hours of precourse work.

Dates: January 1983-Present.

Objective: To provide supervisors with an understanding and working knowledge of business, legal concepts, and practices.

Instruction: Major topics covered in the course are economic systems, management information systems, financial management systems, quality and productivity, the changing business world, employee and employment law, and government regulations. Methods of instruction include lecture, discussion, videotapes, and case studies.

Credit Recommendation: In the lower division baccalaureate/associate degree category, 2 semester hours in Contemporary Business Issues (8/83).

Supervisory and Management Skills Program
Course 1: Introduction to Supervision
Course 2: Management Principles
Course 8: Leadership Development
(Formerly First Line Supervisor Program)

Location: Nationwide.

Length: 42 hours (21 weeks); 2 hours of precourse work.

Dates: September 1980-Present.

Objective: To develop an understanding of the supervisor's role within the organization or environment, to develop an understanding of the basic principles of management, and to develop an understanding of supervisory leadership.

Instruction: Major topics covered in the course are the supervisory setting and the role of the supervisor as leader, problem solver, and person. The principles course treats the organization as a system within which the classic management functions of planning, organizing, directing, and controlling are examined. The leadership course considers the environment of the supervisor and his interpersonal and organizational role. Methods of instruction include videotapes, lectures, role playing, quizzes, situational problems, and reading assignments.

Credit Recommendation: In the lower division baccalaureate/associate degree category, 3 semester hours in Management and Supervision (8/83).

National Mine Health and Safety Academy

The mission of the National Mine Health and Safety Academy of the U.S. Department of Labor is to provide education and training services in support of the Mine Safety and Health Administration's effort to reduce accidents and improve health conditions in the nation's mines and mineral industries.

The Academy provides a wide range of education and training for Coal and Metal/Nonmetal mine inspectors and other technical specialists required to enforce the provisions of the Federal Mine Safety and Health Act of 1977. Training is also offered, on safety and health and management subjects, to selected mine employees, and qualified mining students to enhance their knowledge of and compliance with the 1977 Act.

Source of official student records: Student Services Coordinator, National Mine Health and Safety Academy, P.O. Box 1166, Beckley, WV 25802-1166.

Additional information about the courses: College Credit Recommendation Service, American Council on Education, One Dupont Circle, Washington, DC 20036-1193.

Accident Analysis and Problem Identification

Location: National Mine Health and Safety Academy, Beckley, WV.

Length: 28 hours (1 week).

Dates: October 1985-April 1991.

Objective: To survey new accident prevention techniques and their solutions by group problem solving exercises and conceptual overview of the results.

Instruction: Major topics covered in the course are logic of technique, customizing solutions, physical barrier analysis, human barrier analysis, planned inquiry, on-site concerns, optimizing resources used in analyzing accidents and gathering field data. Methods of instruction include lecture, discussion, classroom exercises, case studies, and problem solving.

Credit Recommendation: In the lower division baccalaureate/associate degree category, 2 semester hours in Accident Prevention and Safety (4/86).

Accident Prevention in the Mining Industry

Location: National Mine Health and Safety Academy, Beckley, WV.

Length: 35 hours (5 days).

Dates: September 1980-April 1991.

Objective: To teach accident prevention with emphasis on mine safety.

Instruction: Major topics covered in the course are accident investigation and analysis, job safety analysis, behavioral aspects of accident prevention, and related methodology. Methods of instruction include lecture, discussion, and classroom exercises.

Credit Recommendation: In the lower division baccalaureate/associate degree category, 2 semester hours in Accident Prevention and Safety (4/86).

Accident Prevention Techniques

Location: National Mine Health and Safety Academy, Beckley, WV and at various coal and metal/nonmetal mine sites throughout the United States.

Length: 21 hours (3 days).

Dates: May 1980-April 1991.

Objective: To teach general accident prevention with emphasis on mine safety.

Instruction: Major topics covered in the course are accident/incident analysis, analyzing performance problems, communications and effective safety, safety awareness, motivation, managing stress, job safety analysis, job observation, accident investigation and mine safety program rating procedures. Methods of instruction include lecture, discussion, and classroom exercises.

Credit Recommendation: In the lower division baccalaureate/associate degree category, 1 semester hour in Accident Prevention and Safety (4/86).

Applied Communication Techniques

Location: National Mine Health and Safety Academy, Beckley, WV.

Length: 56 hours (2 weeks).

Dates: December 1983-April 1991.

Objective: To provide the participant training in listening skills, interviewing, conducting pre-inspection conferences, case-study problem solving, and the presentation of evidence in court in situations involving mine safety violations.

Instruction: Major topics covered in the course are the communication skills needed by an inspector in order to conduct inspection conferences and make courtroom appearances. Methods of instruction include lecture, discussion, case-studies, problem-solving, video-tapes, and extensive role playing.

Credit Recommendation: In the upper division baccalaureate degree category, 3 semester hours in Interviewing or Interviewing and Interrogation Procedures (4/86).

Coal Mine Dust Control

Location: National Mine Health and Safety Academy, Beckley, WV.

Length: 28 hours (4 days).

Dates: September 1985-April 1991.

Objective: To present the various techniques useful for dust control emphasizing the current technology.

Instruction: Major topics covered in the course are problems associated with coal mine dust control; suppression techniques, social-medical problems associated with coal mine dust control, and problems arising from specific mining techniques as applied to coal mine dust management. Methods of instruction include lecture, discussion, laboratory exercises and workshops.

Credit Recommendation: In the upper division baccalaureate degree category, 2 semester hours in Mine Atmosphere and Detection Instruments (4/86).

Coal Mine Explosion Prevention

Location: National Mine Health and Safety Academy, Beckley, WV.

Length: 28 hours (4 days).

Dates: February 1983-April 1991.

Objective: To learn to recognize, evaluate and control explosion hazards in coal mines.

Instruction: Major topics covered in the course are historical background; study of methane, coal dust, and ignition sources; sealing and ventilation, explosives use, and characteristics; and inspection and preventive measures.

Credit Recommendation: In the upper division baccalaureate degree category, 2 semester hours in Mine Safety (4/86).

Coal Preparation

Location: National Mine Health and Safety Academy, Beckley, WV.

Length: 56 hours (8 days).

Dates: June 1986-April 1991.

Objective: To enable employees and industry personnel to recognize and understand the function of the individual processes of coal preparation and the hazards associated with each.

Instruction: Major topics covered in the course are chemical properties of coal, electrical properties of coal, physical properties of coal, mechanical sampling, laboratory determination, uses of coal, mine property data collection, screening, dense medium process and hydraulic separation, fine coal benefication, dry concretation, mechanical dewatering, thermal drying, dust control, coal storage, unit train loading, barge and ship loading, waste disposal, noise control, fire protection. Methods of instruction include lecture, discussion, computer assisted instruction, video tape and field trips.

Credit Recommendation: In the upper division baccalaureate degree category, 3 semester hours in Coal Preparation (4/86).

Communication Skills I or Communication, Interpersonal, Small Group

Location: National Mine Health and Safety Academy, Beckley, WV and other mine sites.

Length: 28 hours (4 days).

Dates: April 1981-April 1991.

Objective: To provide participants an opportunity to learn and practice the effective use of interpersonal, intrapersonal, and small group communication skills.

Instruction: Major topics covered in the course are barriers to communication, listening skills, group problem solving, verbal and nonverbal communication; small group communications, values conflict resolution, and a review of the effects of stress. Methods of instruction include discussion, mini-lectures, experiential activities, practice teaching, role playing, and problem solving.

Credit Recommendation: In the lower division baccalaureate/associate degree category, 2 semester hours in Communication, Helping Skills, or Interpersonal Relations (4/86).

Courtroom Procedures

Location: National Mine Health and Safety Academy, Beckley, WV.

Length: 28 hours (4 days).

Dates: July 1986-April 1991.

Objective: To prepare the journey man coal mine inspector for appearances in court.

Instruction: Major topics covered in the course are listening skills, interviewing, role of the inspector, importance of note making, the role of the commission and courts, elements in a citation, evidence in hearings, and understanding the procedures in preparing to testifying in court. Methods of instruction include lecture, discussion, case studies, problem solving, and extensive role playing.

Credit Recommendation: In the lower division baccalaureate/associate degree category, 2 semester hours in Court Room Procedures or Trial Practices. **NOTE:** Credit should not be awarded for both this course and the Applied Communication Techniques course (4/86).

Effective Writing

Location: National Mine Health and Safety Academy, Beckley, WV.

Length: 28 hours (4 days).

Dates: November 1978-April 1991.

Objective: To understand the techniques for effective, simple and logical writing.

Instruction: Major topics covered in the course are elements of grammar, mechanics of writing, report writing, effective sentences, effective paragraphs, and the various aspects of effective writing. Methods of instruction include lecture, discussion, films, and writing exercises.

Credit Recommendation: In the lower division baccalaureate/associate degree category, 1 semester hour in Business Communication (4/86).

Electrical Permissibility

Location: National Mine Health and Safety Academy, Beckley, WV.

Length: 16 hours (3 days).

Dates: June 1976-April 1991.

Objective: To provide an understanding of permissibility locations where permissible equipment is required.

Instruction: Major topics covered in the course are concepts and application of permissibility, component requirements, tables and specifications, inspection activities, explosion proof electrical compartments, audible warning devices, and citation description. Methods of instruction include lectures, classroom discussions, and laboratory exercises.

Credit Recommendation: In the lower division baccalaureate/associate degree category, 1 semester hour in Electrical Permissibility (4/86).

Electricity and Permissibility for the Non-Electrical Inspector

Location: National Mine Health and Safety Academy, Beckley, WV.

Length: 28 hours (4 days).

Dates: March 1983-April 1991.

Objective: To review the basic principles of electricity; to show how the principles are applied in coal mining.

Instruction: Major topics covered in the course are voltage, current and resistance and how to calculate these in electrical circuits, single and thru-phase circuits, grounding, overload protection, checking methane, monitors and permissibility of electrical face equipment, electrical shock and physiological consequences. Methods of instruction include lecture, discussion, and laboratory experiences.

Credit Recommendation: In the lower division baccalaureate/associate degree category, 2 semester hours in Mine Electricity and Permissibility (4/86).

First Responder

Location: National Mine Health and Safety Academy, Beckley, WV.

Length: 40 hours (1 week).

Dates: March 1983-April 1991.

Objective: To provide training in emergency care services rendered to victims of accidents and illness from those who are apt to be the first responding to an accident.

Instruction: Major topics covered in the course are the roles and responsibilities of the first responder, the human body, patient examination, CPR, injuries to organs and extremities, heart attack, emergency childbirth, skull and chest injuries, poisons and drugs, triage, and burns. Methods of instruction include lecture, discussion, and laboratory instruction.

Credit Recommendation: In the lower division baccalaureate/associate degree category, 2 semester hours in Health Education or CPR (4/86).

General Math or Introduction to Algebra

Location: National Mine Health and Safety Academy, Beckley, WV.

Length: 35 hours (1 week).

Dates: September 1985-April 1991.

Objective: To review math skills to qualify students to take advanced math courses.

Instruction: Major topics covered in the course are a review of basic mathematics, experiences in practical applications, new vocabulary that applies to the material, problem-solving, operations with real numbers, exponents, radicals, polynomials, algebraic fractions, functions and graphing with exponential and logarithmic functions. Methods of instruction include lecture and classroom exercises.

Credit Recommendation: In the lower division baccalaureate/associate degree category, 2 semester hours in General Mathematics (4/86).

Hazardous Materials

Location: National Mine Health and Safety Academy, Beckley, WV.

Length: 40 hours (1 week).

Dates: March 1982-April 1991.

Objective: To introduce the student to the problems of hazardous materials and hazardous waste disposal.

Instruction: Major topics covered in the course are hazard recognition and evaluation; physical controls and identification during manufacture, storage, and handling; and personal protective equipment. Methods of instruction include lecture, discussion and laboratory exercises.

Credit Recommendation: In the upper division baccalaureate degree category, 3 semester hours in Hazardous Materials (4/86).

Health Hazards in Mining

Location: National Mine Health and Safety Academy, Beckley, WV.

Length: 35 hours (1 week).

Dates: October 1983-April 1991.

Objective: To understand the basic principles of industrial hygiene and the diverse fields that this specialty encompasses.

Instruction: Major topics covered in the course are fundamental concepts of industrial hygiene, health hazards associated with the respiratory system, occupational skin disorders, particulates exposure, hearing impairment, industrial dermatoses, documentation of exposure, industrial noise, ventilation and protective equipment. Methods of instruction include lecture, discussion, and laboratory exercises.

Credit Recommendation: In the upper division baccalaureate degree category, 3 semester hours in Health Hazards in Mining (4/86).

Hoisting: Mine Elevators

Location: National Mine Health and Safety Academy, Beckley, WV.

Length: 21 hours (3 days).

Dates: April 1980-April 1991.

Objective: To acquaint the student with the requirements of the ANSI A17.1 1984 and A17.2 1985 codes relative to elevator installation, inspection and maintenance.

Instruction: Major topics covered in the course are drum, brakes, cage attachments, surry area; field trip to inspect gear driven and gearless hoists; study of American National Standards Institute code requirements on installation, maintenance, testing and inspection. Methods of instruction include lecture, discussion and field trips.

Credit Recommendation: In the upper division baccalaureate degree category, 1 semester hour in Mine Hoist Operations (4/86).

Human Factors Engineering

Location: National Mine Health and Safety Academy, Beckley, WV.

Length: 28 hours (4 days).

Dates: December 1981-April 1991.

Objective: To be acquainted with concepts that enable the student to recognize, evaluate and control human factors engineering problems in the mining industry.

Instruction: Major topics covered in the course are perceived mining needs in the human factors engineering field, primary goals of human factors and accidents, population stereotypes, design and operation of mining machines, decreasing the mine machine human factors problems, mine machine control, human factors in mine machine designs, training miners on the mine machine system, human lag time, and use of signals. Methods of instruction include lecture, discussion, and laboratory exercises.

Credit Recommendation: In the upper division baccalaureate degree category, 2 semester hours in Human Factors Engineering (4/86).

Instructor Training

Location: National Mine Health and Safety Academy, Beckley, WV.

Length: 21 hours (3 days).

Dates: March 1983-April 1991.

Objective: To provide instructors with the fundamentals of curriculum design, evaluation techniques, and instructional strategies.

Instruction: Major topics covered in the course are the development of behavioral objectives, development of criterion tests, planning of instructional activities, development of lesson plans, and development and use of audiovisuals. Methods of instruction include lecture, discussion, and videotaped presentations.

Credit Recommendation: In the lower division baccalaureate/associate degree category, 1 semester hour in Teaching Methods (4/86).

Introduction to Mining

Location: National Mine Health and Safety Academy, Beckley, WV.

Length: 21 hours (3 days).

Dates: March 1981-April 1991.

Objective: To provide the participant with a general understanding of mining history, development, systems terminology, procedures, methods, and health and safety activities.

Instruction: Major topics covered in the course are introduction to mining, history-geology-exploration in mining, environmental factors, survey and mapping, mining methods, hoisting-haulage, coal preparation, mineral processing, health and safety activities. Methods of instruction include lecture, discussion, laboratory exercises, and field trips.

Credit Recommendation: In the lower division baccalaureate/associate degree category, 1 semester hour in Introduction to Mining (4/86).

Man, Machine, and the Environment

Location: National Mine Health and Safety Academy, Beckley, WV.

Length: 35 hours (1 week).

Dates: July 1981-April 1991.

Objective: To acquaint the student with the basic principles used by human factor engineering in the design of mining systems.

Instruction: Major topics covered in the course are industry "population stereotypes," early studies of human factors engineering, survey of human factors in underground bituminous coal mining, improving the safety and quality of consumer products, effects of sound and noise, work stations for operators, restrictions of detents on component controls, and residual energy. Methods of instruction include lecture, discussion, and laboratory exercises.

Credit Recommendation: In the upper division baccalaureate degree category, 2 semester hours in Man, Machines and the Environment in the Mining Industry (4/86).

Mine Disaster Procedures

Location: National Mine Health and Safety Academy, Beckley, WV.

Length: 28 hours (1 week).

Dates: March 1981-April 1991.

Objective: To identify the types of rescue equipment, procedures for their use, and methods for mine rescue.

Instruction: Major topics covered in the course are principles of mine rescue, mine emergency operations, history of disaster prevention activities, mine gasses, detection instruments, respiratory protection, rescue team activities, tactical procedures, map exercises and mine emergency operations system.

Credit Recommendation: In the lower division baccalaureate/associate degree

category, 2 semester hours in Mine Disaster Procedures (4/86).

Mine Electricity: Metal/Nonmetal Mines

Location: National Mine Health and Safety Academy, Beckley, WV.

Length: 56 hours (8 days).

Dates: February 1982-April 1991.

Objective: To provide inspectors with an understanding of electricity and the electrical standards in 30 CFR for use in their inspection activities.

Instruction: Major topics covered in the course are basic electrical terms and circuits; transformers and connections; systems grounding; electrical substations and related equipment; circuit breakers; substation perimeter fencing requirements; permissibility and permissibility standards; and inspection procedures to ascertain compliance with standards. Methods of instruction include lecture, discussion, and laboratory exercises.

Credit Recommendation: In the lower division baccalaureate/associate degree category, 3 semester hours in Mine Electricity (4/86).

Mine Haulage and Transportation

Location: National Mine Health and Safety Academy, Beckley, WV.

Length: 35 hours (1 week).

Dates: March 1982-April 1991.

Objective: To introduce the student to the various systems used for haulage and transportation of product, supplies and personnel in surface and underground mining.

Instruction: Major topics covered in the course are the recognition and the evaluation of hazardous conditions relating to surface and underground haulage, knowledge of hoisting systems, wire rope technology, static load safety factors, inspection techniques, inspection procedures for conveyor belt-roller type slippage switch. Methods of instruction include lecture, discussion, and laboratory exercises.

Credit Recommendation: In the upper division baccalaureate degree category, 2 semester hours in Mine Haulage and Transportation (4/86).

Mine Safety and Health Legislation

Location: National Mine Health and Safety Academy, Beckley, WV.

Length: 35 hours (1 week).

Dates: November 1982-April 1991.

Objective: To acquaint the student in the history of Mine Safety and Health Legislation in the United States.

Instruction: Major topics covered in the course are the functions of the Bureau of Mines and its functions and limitations, mine safety and health 1910 to present, Mine Safety and Health Act of 1977 and reasons for its establishment, problems of miner's pneumonconiosis, and extent of mine disasters. Methods of instruction include lecture, discussion, classroom exercises and library research.

Credit Recommendation: In the upper division baccalaureate degree category, 2 semester hours in Mine Safety and Health Legislation (4/86).

Philosophical Concepts of Mine Safety and Health

Location: National Mine Health and Safety Academy, Beckley, WV.

Length: 35 hours (1 week).

Dates: December 1981-April 1991.

Objective: To provide the student with the opportunity to explore and discuss various factors which have had impact upon the philosophy of health and safety in the industrial environment.

Instruction: Major topics covered in the course are social factors which influence one's philosophy, the effects of organized labor upon the philosophy of health and safety in the workplace, Federal laws pertaining to health and safety, and comparison of foreign countries' philosophies on health and safety. Methods of instruction include lecture and discussion.

Credit Recommendation: In the upper division baccalaureate degree category, 3 semester hours in Philosophical Concepts of Mine Safety and Health (4/86).

Public Speaking and Briefing Techniques

Location: National Mine Health and Safety Academy, Beckley, WV and selected MSHA field locations.

Length: 28 hours (4 days).

Dates: June 1984-April 1991.

Objective: To provide public speaking and briefing skills techniques, knowledge, and workshop practice to increase job effectiveness.

Instruction: Major topics covered in the course are public speaking fears, public communication objectives, speaking effectively, preparing a speech, planning a speech, speaking aids, conducting question and answer sessions, and communications by voice and action. Methods of instruction include lecture, discussion, classroom exercises, role playing, films, and videotapes.

Credit Recommendation: In the lower division baccalaureate/associate degree category, 2 semester hours in Speech, or Public Speaking (4/86).

Research Applications in Occupational Education

Location: National Mine Health and Safety Academy, Beckley, WV.

Length: 40 hours (1 week).

Dates: September 1983-April 1991.

Objective: A study of methodology, application, analysis, and synthesis of research in occupational education.

Instruction: Major topics covered in the course are a review of current occupational studies, clustered by areas, with attention to statistical techniques, data collecting, data handling and the audience and impact of particular projects and research organizations. Methods of instruction include lecture, discussion, and library exercises.

Credit Recommendation: In the upper division baccalaureate degree category, 2 semester hours in Research Application in Occupational Education (4/86).

Resident IV Industrial Hygiene II

Location: National Mine Health and Safety Academy, Beckley, WV.

Length: 56 hours (2 weeks).

Dates: March 1984-April 1991.

Objective: To understand instrumentation and documentation principles of industrial hygiene.

Instruction: Major topics covered in the course are industrial noise, ionizing radiation, non-ionizing radiation, temperature extremes, ergonomics, biological hazards, industrial toxicology and levels of exposure to determine compliance with applicable regulations. Methods of instruction include lecture, discussion, and classroom exercises.

Credit Recommendation: In the upper division baccalaureate degree category, 3 semester hours in Industrial Hygiene (4/86).

Roof Control for the Specialist

Location: National Mine Health and Safety Academy, Beckley, WV.

Length: 28 hours (4 days).

Dates: June 1977-April 1991.

Objective: To train inspectors to recognize and minimize the hazards created by roof and rib conditions.

Instruction: Major topics covered in the course are basic geology as it relates to coal bearing and nearby strata, effects of water and temperature on rock, rock stresses, poisson effect; roof control methods and procedures, roof bolting systems and trusses; laboratory and test procedures to evaluate anchorage; and inspection procedures. Methods of instruction include lecture, discussion, films, and laboratory exercises.

Credit Recommendation: In the lower division baccalaureate/associate degree category, 2 semester hours in Roof and Rib Control (4/86).

Stress: Its Implications in Health and Safety

Location: National Mine Health and Safety Academy, Beckley, WV.

Length: 40 hours (1 week).

Dates: November 1984-April 1991.

Objective: To introduce the student to the problems of stress in the work environment.

Instruction: Major topics covered in the course are the sources of stress, physiological effects of stress, psychological effects of stress, relaxation techniques, stress management, and the financial implications of stress in industry. Methods of instruction include lecture, discussion, and laboratory exercises.

Credit Recommendation: In the upper division baccalaureate degree category, 3 semester hours in Stress and Its Impact on Safety and Health in Mining (4/86).

Substance Abuse or Alcohol and Drug Abuse

Location: National Mine Health and Safety Academy, Beckley, WV and in the field.

Length: 28 hours (4 days).

Dates: February 1983-April 1991.

Objective: To explore the history of the rise of the chemical dependency problem in society and its impact on the individual and industry.

Instruction: Major topics covered in the course are the history of drug culture development, identification of licit and illicit substances in the workplace, the physiological effects of drugs on the human body and mind, signs and symptoms of a chemical substance abuser, legality of pre-employment drug screening, search and seizure, the financial impact on the industrial setting, and the role of and employee assistance program. Methods of instruction include lecture, discussion, case studies, and labor.

Credit Recommendation: In the lower division baccalaureate/associate degree category, 2 semester hours in Alcohol and Drug Abuse, Substance Abuse, Alcohol and Health, or Drug Abuse (4/86).

System Safety Engineering

Location: National Mine Health and Safety Academy, Beckley, WV.

Length: 28 hours (4 days).

Dates: August 1978-April 1991.

Objective: To acquaint the student with established system safety engineering concepts and techniques and the ability to apply those techniques in the analysis of safety hazards.

Instruction: Major topics covered in the course are the basic components of a "system," system characteristics that constitute a measure of "system effectiveness," methods that may be used to gain understanding of system operations, five phases in the system life cycle model, qualitative and quantitative evaluation of system safety engineering, Job Safety Analysis, and Fault Free Analysis. Methods of instruction include lecture, discussion, and case studies.

Credit Recommendation: In the upper division baccalaureate degree category, 2 semester hours in System Safety Engineering in the Mining Industry (4/86).

Ventilation

Location: National Mine Health and Safety Academy, Beckley, WV.

Length: 28 hours (4 days).

Dates: February 1983-April 1991.

Objective: To review the principles of coal mine ventilation and applicable ventilation regulations.

Instruction: Major topics covered in the course are mine gases, abandoned areas, sealed areas, air velocity measurements, face ventilation, longwalls, rock dusting, job areas, ventilation plans, calculation of face liberation, and leakage. Methods of instruction include lecture, discussion, and laboratory exercises.

Credit Recommendation: In the lower division baccalaureate/associate degree category, 2 semester hours in Coal Mine Ventilation (4/86).

National Registry of Radiation Protection Technologists (NRRPT)

The NRRPT evolved from the need for improved training programs and certification of radiation protection technicians. Under guidance from the American Board of Health Physics, a committee of industry technologists studied the feasibility of a registration and recommended to the board that the technologists registration program be implemented.

Since its inception the NRRPT has registered more than 3,000 technologists throughout the country from many industry facilities and each year more and more interest is expressed. Due to this interest, training programs are being upgraded to accommodate candidates, and as a result, the level of competence is being raised nationwide within the industry.

The increased presence of RPT's in the Health Physics community is adding to the credibility of competent radiation protection, which is in demand by both regulatory agencies and the general public.

Source of official student records: Registry of Credit Recommendations, American Council on Education, One Dupont Circle, Washington, DC 20036-1193.

Additional information about the courses: Office of Corporate-Higher Education Programs, Thomas Edison State College, 101 West State Street, Trenton, NJ 08608-1176.

National Registry of Radiation Protection Technologists

Location: Various locations throughout the U.S.

Length: Independent study.

Dates: November 1978-Present.

Objective: To promote technical competence in the radiation protection field at the operational level by establishing a standard of excellence for the radiation protection technologist.

Learning Outcome: Upon successful completion of this course, the student will be able to have achieved an established standard of excellence for the radiation protection technologist; demonstrate competency of readiation protection practices to assure compliance with the various standards and regulations, specifically: evaluate radiological hazard in a variety of situations; safely ship (transport) radioactive materials; conduct data reduction and calculations; follow/conduct technical SOPs; apply regulations; understand function of and operate readiation survey and monitoring equipment; know methods of protecting people from radiation exposure; understand the origin, characteristics and interaction of various types of radiation; and recognize and respond to radiological emergencies.

Instruction: Major topics covered in the Registry are an introduction to atomic and nuclear physics; natural and artificial radioactivity; decay schemes; nuclear reactions including fission and fusion; interaction of radiation with matter; radiation quantities and units; shielding; biological effects of radiation; radiation protection standards and regulations; principles of radiation detection and detection devices; counting systems and assay of alpha, beta, and gamma emitters; survey and monitoring equipment; external radiation exposure and protection techniques; radiation safety and control; accelerator and reactor health physics; medical radiation physics; an introduction to radiation protection, including radiation sources, radiation dose, and dose measurement; radiation exposure; radiation protection techniques; monitoring methods and instruments; contamination control and waste storage; facility design; hazards analysis and applied health physics techniques for the safe handling and control of radioactive material; and laboratory and field practices and techniques in radiation protection. Each applicant also has applied work experience as a health physics technician at a government agency or laboratory, military, or a radiation facility of some industry, hospital, or education and research institution.

Credit Recommendation: In the lower division baccalaureate/associate degree category, 6 semester hours in Introduction to Radiological Science; in the upper division baccalaureate degree category, 8 semester hours in Radiation Detection and Measurement; in the upper division baccalaureate degree category, 8 semester hours in Radiation Protection and Control; and in the upper division baccalaureate degree category, 8 semester hours in Applied Health Physics Internship (11/88) (8/94). **NOTE:** Prior to sitting for the Registry, applicants must be high school graduates and have at least 5 years qualified experience in the field of radiation protection. Students prepare for the Registry through independent study. They must have supervisor and professional recommendations as conditions for qualifying for the Registry. For those students who already possess a baccalaureate degree, these upper level baccalaureate credit recommendations can be considered for graduate credit.

National Training Fund for the Sheet Metal and Air Conditioning Industry

The National Training Fund for the Sheet Metal and Air Conditioning Industry (NTF) is a joint labor-management trust fund created in 1971 between the Sheet Metal Workers' International Association (SMWIA) and Sheet Metal and Air Conditioning Workers' International Association (SMANCA). NTF's mission is to develop training curriculum, educational support, and instructor training for the Sheet Metal and Air Conditioning Industry. Students are enrolled in local apprenticeship programs sponsored by the local labor-management Joint Apprenticeship Training Committee.

Instructors are journeyperson sheet metal workers who participate in a five year instructor training program administered by the NTF and Ohio State University. This program ensures the highest in quality training and education for those in the apprenticeship program. NTF's materials and programs are only available to local Joint Apprenticeship Training Committees in the United States and Canada.

Source of official student records: Registry of Credit Recommendations, American Council on Education, One Dupont Circle, Washington, DC 20036-1193.

Additional information about the courses: College Credit Recommendation Service, American Council on Education, One Dupont Circle, Washington, DC 20036-1193.

National Training Fund Sheet Metal and Air Conditioning Apprentice Curriculum

Location: Various sites in the United States and Canada.

Length: 720 hours (4-5 years) plus supervised practical experience.

Dates: September 1985-Present.

Objective: To provide knowledge and skills required of sheet metal journeypersons in fabricating and installing sheet metal products in heating and air conditioning systems and architectural applications.

Learning Outcome: Upon successful completion of this course, the student will be able to calculate related mathematic applications; calculate air movement and capacities; calculate heating and air conditioning loads; design, layout patterns, and assemble sheet metal components; define characteristics of different sheet metals and fibrous ductwork and their uses; install and test ductwork and architectural sheet metal; use sheet metal tools and power equipment in an efficient and safe manner; explain principles of electric motors and controls; explain basic principles of air conditioning, test and balance circulation systems; and explain and demonstrate safe use of the various welding methods.

Instruction: Major topics covered in the course are communication skills; personal relations within the industry; air movements and duct capacities; use of computers in sheet metal work; system design and layout; pattern development; various duct shapes; electric motors, circuits, and controls; applied mathematics; heating and air conditioning loads; use of fibrous materials and sheet metals; installation, testing, and balance of circulation systems; joining and fastening materials; safe use of sheet metal tools, machines, and power equipment; environmental and hazmat safety; principles of air conditioning; emergency procedures; and modern techniques of gas and electric welding, and basic metallurgy. Methods of instruction include lecture, discussion, audio visual materials, unit quizzes, and yearly final examinations.

Credit Recommendation: In the vocational certificate or the lower division baccalaureate/associate degree category, 2 semester hours in Applied Mathematics; 1 semester hour in Basic Electricity; 5 semester hours in Building Components; 3 semester hours in Environmental Health and Safety; 2 semester hours in Human Relations in the Workplace; 12 semester hours in HVAC Installation and Service; 1 semester hour in HVAC Tools and Equipment; 6 semester hours in Sheet Metal Layout and Fabrication; and 16 semester hours in Technical Drawing and Blueprint Reading for a total of 48 semester hours (2/95).

National Weather Service Training Center

The National Weather Service, an agency within the National Oceanic and Atmospheric Administration (NOAA) and the U.S. Department of Commerce, established the Training Center to provide residence courses in meteorology, electronics, management, and supervision for employees. Limited space is made available to personnel of other U.S. government agencies and to foreign countries that have cooperative weather program agreements with the United States. The Center also administers a correspondence program for National Weather Service employees.

Source of official student records: Student Coordinator, National Weather Service Training Center, 617 Hardesty, Kansas City, MO 64124.

Additional information about the courses: College Credit Recommendation Service, American Council on Education, One Dupont Circle, Washington, DC 20036-1193.

Air Pollution Meteorology (APMO1)

Location: National Weather Service Training Center, Kansas City, MO.

Length: 64 hours (2 weeks).

Dates: May 1975-November 1979.

Objective: To enable professional meteorologists to serve as air pollution specialists.

Instruction: Major topics covered in the course are forecasting the atmosphere's ability to transport and dilute emitted pollutants, recognition of pending atmospheric stagnation, sources and hazards of various pollutants, Briggs plume rise equations, and atmospheric dispersion equations.

Credit Recommendation: In the upper division baccalaureate degree category or in the graduate degree category, 2 semester hours in Meteorology (10/77).

ART-Automatic Radio Theodolite System (J-12-03)

Location: National Weather Service Training Center, Kansas City, MO.

Length: 96 hours (12 days).

Dates: May 1984-Present.

Objective: Upon successful completion of this course, the student will be able to provide electronics technicians with the knowledge and skills required to align, calibrate, and maintain the ART system and associated ground equipment.

Learning Outcome: Upon successful completion of this course, the student will be able to understand the operation of the ART system including troubleshooting and maintenance.

Instruction: Major topics covered in the course are principles of tracking active targets of conical scanning; system operation and diagnostic evaluation of subsystems; alignment; calibration; and troubleshooting and repair of ART systems. Methods of instruction include lecture, demonstrations, laboratory exercises, and examinations.

Credit Recommendation: In the lower division baccalaureate/associate degree category, 2 semester hours in Electronic Systems (11/85) (7/93). **NOTE:** This course is essentially identical to GMD RAWIN System J-10-03 and WBRT-RAWIN System J-11-03; credit should be awarded for no more than one of these courses.

ASOS Maintenance (S-09-03)

Location: National Weather Service Training Center, Kansas City, MO.

Length: 104 hours (13 working days).

Dates: October 1993-Present.

Objective: To provide the knowledge and skills necessary to calibrate and perform preventive and corrective maintenance on the ASOS system including the associated sensors.

Learning Outcome: Upon successful completion of this course, the student will be able to describe the overall ASOS system including underlying algorithms and both operational and diagnostic levels of communications software; use diagnostic firmware and built-in test equipment to monitor system operation and detect failed sensors or assemblies; perform preventive maintenance and sensor alignments; and remove and replace failed assemblies.

Instruction: Major topics covered in the course are system configuration, operation, algorithms, monitoring and diagnostic procedures, and maintenance tot he field replaceable unit level; and sensor characteristics and maintenance. Methods of instruction include lecture, laboratory with ASOS installation, and examinations.

Credit Recommendation: In the lower division baccalaureate/associate degree category, 3 semester hours in Digital and Electronic Systems Maintenance (6/94).

Automated Surface Observer System: Maintenance Level II, Specialist (ASOS-II S-08-02)

Location: National Weather Service Training Center, Kansas City, MO.

Length: 104 hours (1 week, 3 days).

Dates: February 1992-July 1993.

Objective: To provide comprehensive knowledge and training to upper level engineers and electronics technicians who provide maintenance and technical support for the AMOS II.

Learning Outcome: Upon successful completion of this course, the student will be able to provide maintenance and technical support to first level technicians in solving non-routine maintenance and diagnostic tests on an automated surface observing system.

Instruction: Major topics covered in the course are organization and use of system manuals, hands-on use of advanced diagnostic firmware for serving; sensors, built in test equipment, preventive maintenance, diagnostic system checks, remote monitoring, flow chart signal logic, algorithm processing, system, interconnections, and data acquisition processing. Methods of instruction include lecture, demonstrations, and hands-on experience with an ASOS installation.

Credit Recommendation: In the lower division baccalaureate/associate degree category, 4 semester hours in Meteorological Instrumentation, Instrumentation laboratory, or Physical Laboratory Science elective (7/93).

Automated Surface Observing System: Technician Series (ASOS-I S-07-01)

Location: National Weather Training Center, Kansas City, MO.

Length: 64 hours (1 week, 3 days).

Dates: January 1992-August 1993.

Objective: To provide NWS Field Automated Surface Observing technicians with the knowledge and skills necessary to service field replacement units.

Learning Outcome: Upon successful completion of this course, the student will be able to inspect, provide routine maintenance on an ASOS including sensors; utilize built in test instruments; remove and replace failed assemblies; operate diagnostic procedures for remote monitors; installation of field equipment; and trouble shooting.

Instruction: Major topics covered in the course are organization and content of system manuals; use of diagnostic firmware; testing replacement sensors; use of built-in test equipment; schedule preventive maintenance; diagnostic tests on remote monitors; and maintenance and alignment of sensors. Methods of instruction include lecture, demonstrations, hands-on laboratory, practice with an ASOS installation, and examination.

Credit Recommendation: In the vocational certificate category, 2 semester hours in Electronic Maintenance (7/93).

Automatic Meteorological Observing System (AMOS S-02-02)

Location: National Weather Service Training Center, Kansas City, MO.

Length: 64 hours (8 days).

Dates: January 1972-Present.

Objective: To provide electronic technicians with the knowledge, skills and techniques required to install, calibrate and maintain AMOS III systems.

Learning Outcome: Upon successful completion of this course, the student will understand the total operation of AMOS III system including its calibration, fault detection, and maintenance.

Instruction: Major topics covered in the course are detailed study of all the circuit and electromechanical components including teletype, coding and output; automatic programming; sensors, pulse connectors, and coders. Methods of instruction include lecture, laboratory, exercises, equipment manuals, instruction manuals, handouts, and examinations.

Credit Recommendation: In the lower division baccalaureate/associate degree category, 2 semester hours in Digital Equipment Diagnostics and Repair (8/80) (11/85) (7/93).

Automation of Field Operations and Services (AFOS II A & B)

Location: National Weather Service Training Center, Kansas City, MO.

Length: *Version 1:* 264 hours (33 working days); *Version 2:* 280 hours (35 working days).

Dates: *Version 1:* May 1978-October 1985; *Version 2:* November 1985-September 1991.

Objective: To supplement knowledge gained from the AFOS I course, M-04-04, with a more in-depth study of each subsystem in the nationally distributed computer communications system. Emphasis is given to diagnostic and troubleshooting procedures. Graduates should be able to repair independently 80 percent of malfunctions and give phone advice to less experienced electronics technicians.

Instruction: Major topics covered in the course are each subsystem of the AFOS system down to chip level. Detailed subsystem schematics, as well as system software, are studied. Advanced diagnostic and troubleshooting procedures are covered and practiced in a coordinate laboratory.

Credit Recommendation: In the in the lower division baccalaureate/associate degree category or upper division baccalaureate degree, 4 semester hours in Digital Equipment, Computer Equipment Diagnostics and Repair, Advanced Digital or Computer Circuitry (8/80) (11/85). **NOTE:** Students who complete the course should be extremely well versed in digital electronics, computer circuitry, and computer system diagnostics and troubleshooting. *Prerequisite:* Automation of Field Operations and Services AFOS I M-04-04.

Automation of Field Operations and Services (AFOS I)

Location: National Weather Service Training Center, Kansas City, MO.

Length: *Version 1:* 144 hours (18 working days); *Version 2:* 184 hours (23 working days).

Dates: *Version 1:* May 1978-October 1985; *Version 2:* November 1985-September 1991.

Objective: To prepare experienced electronics technicians to activate newly installed AFOS systems and to run quality assurance tests on the equipment, and to enable technicians to diagnose trouble to board level 50 percent of the time and 80 percent of the time with phone advice from a systems specialist.

Instruction: Major topic covered in the course is an overview of the national computer distributed system with protocol for information transfer within the system. Also covers the real time disk operating system used in AFOS; computer architecture with emphasis on diagnostic and troubleshooting procedures; subsystems including the disk controller and drive; synchronous and asynchronous modems; graphics display module; printer/plotter; alphanumeric display module; and systems interface modules. Methods of instruction include lecture, laboratory work, extensive use of audiovisual materials, and testing.

Credit Recommendation: In the lower division baccalaureate/associate degree category, 4 semester hours in Computer System Maintenance and Repair (8/80) (11/85). *Prerequisites:* Solid State and Digital Logic Y-02-03, or its equivalent, and Computer Technology Y-03-01.

Automation of Field Operations and Services (AFOS-Z) Systems Management (M-11-01)

Location: National Weather Training Center, Kansas City, MO.

Length: 40 hours (5 days).

Dates: May 1992-Present.

Objective: To provide AFOS System Z managers with the knowledge and skills necessary to maintain the system site specification software, back up software, identify and recover from specific software failures, provide students with an overview of other hardware and software relationship within System Z.

Learning Outcome: Upon successful completion of this course, the student will be able to understand the various displays and messages which provide information on the operational integrity of the system; understand and follow the procedures necessary to utilize and reconfigure system Z in an operational setting; make routine changes to software; repair system; and software failures.

Instruction: Major topics covered in the course are AFOS communication data handling, command line interpreter (CLI), RDOS Disk/file structure, preparing and maintaining disks, analyzing failures in and repair of system software, software backup, and recovery. Methods of instruction include lecture, laboratory, problem solving exercises, operating handbooks, handouts, and examination.

Credit Recommendation: In the lower division baccalaureate/associate degree category, 1 semester hour in Computer Software, Software Applications, or Computer Science elective (7/93).

Automation of Forecasting Observations, and Services (AFOS-System Z, Maintenance) (M-09-06)

Location: National Weather Service Training Center, Kansas City, MO.

Length: 104 hours (13 working days).

Dates: October 1991-Present.

Objective: To provide electronic technicians with the knowledge and skills necessary to align and maintain the hardware associated with System Z computer installations including an overview of the hardware and software within the system; and to understand the techniques necessary to initialize and reconfigure System Z in an operational setting.

Learning Outcome: Upon successful completion of this course, the student will be able to understand the AFOS communications network; identify and locate AFOS hardware according to standard nomenclature; demonstrate the use of all test equipment used in troubleshooting of AFOS; understand the function, and be able to maintain the modules associated with the AFOS system.

Instruction: Major topics covered in the course are System Z physical configuration, corrective and preventive maintenance procedures and techniques, system degradation techniques, use of diagnostic resources and programs, maintenance aids, component removal and replacement procedures, and alignment of all subsystems. Methods of instruction include lecture, laboratory, problem solving exercises, videotapes, and examination.

Credit Recommendation: In the lower division baccalaureate/associate degree category, 4 semester hours in Computer System Maintenance or Computer Science elective (7/93).

Basic Operational Hydrology (HYD01)

Location: National Weather Service Training Center, Kansas City, MO.

Length: 60 hours (10 working days).

Dates: September 1993-November 1996.

Objective: To prepare the student to use basic hydrologic principles, precipitation and related data from various sources, and basic hydrologic modeling concepts to develop hydrologic forecasts and other products.

Learning Outcome: Upon successful completion of this course, the student will be able to use precipitation and other relevant data with appropriate hydrologic principles and models to develop hydrologic forecasts, flash flood guidance, and other related hydrologic products.

Instruction: Major topics covered in the course are basic hydrometeorology, precipitation forecasts, precipitation estimates from gage and radar data, basic rainfall-runoff processes, runoff prediction, hydrographs and river routing, rating curves, and use of hydrologic models. Methods of instruction include lecture, exercises, and examinations.

Credit Recommendation: In the upper division baccalaureate degree category or in the graduate degree category, 3 semester hours in Hydrology or Hydrometeorology (6/94). **NOTE:** Students may be awarded credit for either Basic Operational Hydrology (HYD01) or Flash Flood Forecasting (FFF01), but not both.

Computer Technology (Y-03-01)

Location: National Weather Service Training Center, Kansas City, MO.

Length: *Version 1:* 40 hours (5 days); *Version 2:* 32 hours (4 days).

Dates: *Version 1:* May 1978-October 1985; *Version 2:* November 1985-September 1991.

Objective: To introduce minicomputer systems architecture; to develop skills in interpreting and running short programs using the NOVA computer instruction set; and to demonstrate how to boot-up the system's operating system software from disk.

Instruction: Major topics covered in the course are minicomputer systems architecture and programming using the NOVA computer instruction set. Students should become familiar with short programs that use peripheral devices. Students are also introduced to the use of canned diagnostic programs. Methods of instruction include lecture/discussion and laboratory work.

Credit Recommendation: In the lower division baccalaureate/associate degree category, 1 semester hour in Computers (8/80) (11/85). **NOTE:** Course is too specialized to be substituted for by the usual computer programming course found in lower division technical programs.

Data Communications II (B-18-02)

Location: National Weather Service Training Center, Kansas City, MO.

Length: 48 hours (8 working days).

Dates: October 1993-Present.

Objective: To provide in-depth knowledge of data communications including modern digital systems.

Learning Outcome: Upon successful completion of this course, the student will be able to isolate faults or verify proper system operation by using appropriate data communications test equipment.

Instruction: Major topics covered in the course are data terminals, transmission channels, asynchronous and synchronous modems/interfaces, multiplexing, satellite communications, protocols, LANS, packet networks, and ISDN. Methods of instruction include lecture and discussion.

Credit Recommendation: In the upper division baccalaureate degree category or in the graduate degree category, 3 semester hours in Computer Science, Data Communications, or Telecommunications (6/94).

Device for Automatic Remote Data Collection (DARDC)

Location: National Weather Service Training Center, Kansas City, MO.

Length: 64 hours (8 working days).

Dates: July 1972-December 1984.

Objective: To enable students to install, operate, and localize trouble to block or card level using visual and audio outputs from the DARDC to a TTY or DARDC test set. (A DARDC is a device that measures wind speed, direction, temperature, dew point, and precipitation at a remote site and forwards the data over telephone lines or by radio transmission to a central point.)

Instruction: Major topics covered in the course are a system overview, including the actual DARDC unit, telephone coupler, solar panel, battery charger, DARDC simulator, and test set; reviews basic digital COS/MOS circuitry, including gates, flip-flops, shift registers, four-bit adders, A/D converters, phase-locked loop, parity generator/checker, voltage comparator, voltage-to-frequency converters, and the ASCII code; treats in detail the proper installation and operation of each major component of the system; and emphasizes diagnostic and troubleshooting procedures to board level. Methods of instruction include lecture, laboratory work, and out-of-class problem-solving.

Credit Recommendation: In the lower division baccalaureate/associate degree category, 2 semester hours in Digital Equipment Diagnostics and Repair (8/80) (11/85). *Prerequisite:* Solid State Electronics and Digital Logic course Y-02-03.

Digital Video Integrator Processor: Logicon DVIP (R-13-02)

Location: National Weather Service Training Center, Kansas City, MO.

Length: 64 hours (8 working days).

Dates: May 1978-October 1979.

Objective: To teach qualified electronics technicians the methods of improving accuracy of radar displays through digital quantitizing of data and the circuit theory needed to accomplish this work.

Instruction: Major topics covered in the course are logic diagrams; linear and digital modules; and various digital operations, such as integration, division, and addition, are studied. Although applied to specific equipment, the concepts covered have many other applications.

Credit Recommendation: In the upper division baccalaureate degree category, 2 semester hours in Digital Systems (8/80) (11/85). **NOTE:** Credit should not be given if it has been awarded for WSR (Weather Service Radar)-57/DVIP Radar

System R-08-06 or WSR (Weather Service Radar) 74C Radar System R-12-04.

ESA Development: Electronic Systems Analysis (A-01-03)

Location: National Weather Service Training Center, Kansas City, MO.

Length: 120 hours (15 working days).

Dates: November 1993-March 1995.

Objective: To enable National Weather Service electronic systems analyst to function as a team leader and first line supervisor.

Learning Outcome: Upon successful completion of this course, the student will be able to manage and direct proper employment of physical resources and personnel necessary to ensure availability of an array of weather sensors, data communication links, online computers, and the WSR-88D weather radar system; understand basic labor management relations; perform necessary objective standards; and possess ability to train subordinate personnel.

Instruction: Major topics covered in the course are labor management relations, basic principles of supervision, software and hardware management of computerized radar, and data communications systems and proper maintenance procedures. Methods of instruction include lecture and laboratory exercises.

Credit Recommendation: In the lower division baccalaureate/associate degree category, 1 semester hour in Principles of Supervision and 3 semester hours in Computer Systems (6/94).

Flash Flood Forecasting (FFF-01)

Location: National Weather Service Training Center, Kansas City, MO.

Length: 64 hours (2 weeks).

Dates: *Version 1:* July 1978-September 1990; *Version 2:* October 1990-Present.

Objective: To enable the professional meteorologist to predict the likelihood and characteristics of flash floods.

Learning Outcome: Upon successful completion of this course, the student will be able to deal effectively with the flash flood phenomenon through the use of specialized techniques and forecasting tools; and enable the hydrometeorologist to furnish applicable guidance concerning their incidence.

Instruction: Major topics covered in the course are flash flood hydrology and meteorology, climatology, uses of radar and satellite data in forecasting, and flash flood planning and preparedness. Methods of instruction include lecture, demonstrations, case studies, and examination.

Credit Recommendation: *Version 1:* In the upper division baccalaureate degree category or in the graduate degree category, 2 semester hours in Hydrology or Meteorology (7/79). *Version 2:* In the upper division baccalaureate or graduate degree category, 3 semester hours in Hydrometeorology (7/93).

Forecasters' Development (FDC02)

Location: National Weather Service Training Center, Kansas City, MO.

Length: 78 hours (13 working days).

Dates: October 1987-Present.

Objective: To provide the professional meteorological intern with the practical knowledge and skills needed to function as a professional forecaster at a weather forecast office, and to provide a base knowledge of hydrology and meteorology as used at the weather forecast office.

Learning Outcome: Upon successful completion of this course, the student will be able to utilize meteorological data from sources such as digital radars, satellites, UHF wind profilers, lightening sensors; issue accurate forecasts and warnings of severe weather; and utilize properly the computer-aided, gridded analysis.

Instruction: Major topics covered in the course are weather radar, satellite data, wind profilers, lightening sensors, use of applied dynamics/gridded data mesoanalysis, stability indices, thunderstorm outflows, aviation forecasts, isentropic analysis, warning procedures, and hydrological forecasts. Methods of instruction include lecture and laboratory exercises.

Credit Recommendation: In the upper division baccalaureate degree category or in the graduate degree category, 4 semester hours in Forecasting or Synoptic Meteorology (6/94).

Fundamentals of Meteorology (FOM01) (Formerly Basic Meteorology)

Location: Honolulu, HI.

Length: 184 hours (5 weeks).

Dates: February 1973-February 1976.

Objective: To qualify meteorological technicians to deliver weather briefings to pilots.

Instruction: Methods of instruction include lectures and practical exercises in basic meteorology, reading forecasts, and communication techniques in providing weather briefings to pilots. Also includes instruction in elementary aeronautics.

Credit Recommendation: In the lower division baccalaureate/associate degree category, 3 semester hours in Meteorology (10/77) (8/82).

GMD: Ground Meteorological Device RAWIN System (J-10-03)

Location: National Weather Service Training Center, Kansas City, MO.

Length: 104 hours (13 working days).

Dates: January 1960-September 1986.

Objective: To provide electronics technicians with the skills required to install, align, calibrate, and maintain the GMD-1 RAWIN system and associated ground equipment.

Instruction: Major topics covered in the course are upper air sounding systems, radiosonde operation, principles of tracking active targets by conical scanning, frequency-to-voltage conversion, null-balance recording systems, and alignment, calibration, troubleshooting, and repair of GMD-1 systems. Methods of instruction include lecture and laboratory exercises.

Credit Recommendation: In the lower division baccalaureate/associate degree category, 2 semester hours in Electronic Systems (8/80) (11/85). **NOTE:** This course is essentially identical to WBRT (Weather Bureau Radio Theodolite) RAWIN System J-11-03; therefore, credit should not be awarded for both this course and WBRT.

Hydrometeorological Techniques (HMT02)

Location: National Weather Service Training Center, Kansas City, MO.

Length: 48 hours (8 working days).

Dates: April 1993-January 1997.

Objective: To provide the experienced meteorological technician with awareness of, and the ability to utilize data from, various meteorological sources; and to assist in the analysis of possible flooding conditions and issuance of needed warnings.

Learning Outcome: Upon successful completion of this course, the student will be able to utilize satellite imagery, weather radar data, automated surface observing systems, automated field observing systems, normal and emergency telephone, fax and computer transmission systems; and to assist in the analysis of rainfall and possible flooding conditions.

Instruction: Major topics covered in the course are the duties of the hydrometeorological technician; the purpose of the hydrological service, data communication systems, various meteorological sensor systems, and river stage forecasting; and methods of issuance of flooding conditions. Methods of instruction include lecture and problem solving.

Credit Recommendation: In the upper division baccalaureate degree category, 2 semester hours in Hydrometeorology (6/94).

Instructor Training (ITT01)

Location: National Weather Service Training Center, Kansas City, MO.

Length: 72 hours (9 days).

Dates: January 1974-September 1984.

Objective: To prepare effective instructors for training programs.

Learning Outcome: Upon successful completion of this course, the student will be able to analyze student learning processes, teaching methods, and course material; prepare effective courses and course materials; and conduct instruction using appropriate methods.

Instruction: Major topics covered in the course are psychology of learning; motivation; instructional stages, methods, and techniques; instructor personality and characteristics; training aids; communication, speech techniques, and voice development; and test construction. Methods of instruction include lecture, discussion, group critique of student instructional presentations, out-of-class assignments, and evaluation of student's teaching ability, and examinations.

Credit Recommendation: In the lower division baccalaureate/associate degree category or in the upper division baccalaureate degree category, 1 semester hour in Education or Human Resource Development (2/77) (4/82) (7/88).

Integrated Circuits and Application Concepts (Y-02-03) (Formerly Solid State and Digital Logic Y-02-03)

Location: National Weather Service Training Center, Kansas City, MO.

Length: 104 hours (13 working days).

Dates: June 1975-February 1986.

Objective: To provide electronics technicians with a basic understanding of integrated circuits and computer logic.

Instruction: Major topics covered in the course are in the digital portion are number systems, Boolean algebra, logic elements, logic trees, and various kinds of flip-flops in counting and register circuits. The linear portion covers the basics of integrated operational amplifiers and some of their applications. Half of the course is devoted to lecture/discussion and half to laboratory work. This course has been offered as a self-paced personal computer course since August 1983.

Credit Recommendation: In the lower division baccalaureate/associate degree category, 3 semester hours in Linear and Digital Electronics (8/80) (11/85).

Introduction to Meteorology (BMT01) Basic Meteorological Technician

Location: National Weather Service Training Center, Kansas City, MO.

Length: 304 hours (8 weeks).

Dates: April 1974-January 1978.

Objective: To qualify the student to enter the meteorological technician/observer job series.

Instruction: Major topics covered in the course are instruction in basic English (oral and written skills), basic mathematics, and geography. Course does not require knowledge of calculus. Methods of instruction include lecture, hands-on training, and practical sessions in basic meteorology, weather code interpretation, instrument operation and observation, communication equipment operation, and weather station operation.

Credit Recommendation: In the lower division baccalaureate/associate degree category, 4 semester hours in Meteorology (3 hours lecture and 1 hour laboratory) (10/77).

MAR Management (MGT02)

Location: National Weather Service Training Center, Kansas City, MO.

Length: 80 hours (10 working days).

Dates: May 1993-December 1996.

Objective: To provide knowledge regarding currently emphasized managerial topics and to enhance supervisory skills of upper level managers.

Learning Outcome: Upon successful completion of this course, the student will be able to understand the impact of managerial style on communications, motivation, and employee involvement; understand the importance of compliance with regulations and policies regarding sexual harassment and EEO; and use group dynamics effectively in team building and making group decisions.

Instruction: Major topics covered in the course are EEO and sexual harassment; management values and styles; employee involvement; and motivation, group decision making, labor-management relations, and media relations. Methods of instruction include lecture, discussion, problem-solving, classroom exercises, case studies, and laboratory.

Credit Recommendation: In the upper division baccalaureate degree category or in the graduate degree category, 3 semester hours in Personnel Administration, Public Administration, or Public Management (6/94).

Microprocessor: Fundamental Concepts and Applications (Y-04-02)

Location: National Weather Service Training Center, Kansas City, MO.

Length: 56 hours (7 working days).

Dates: July 1979-October 1987.

Objective: To introduce experienced electronics technicians to this "state-of-the-art" technology to enable them to use both software and hardware in a variety of ways. Graduates should be able to apply this knowledge in operating microprocessor-based equipment in the National Weather Service.

Instruction: Major topic covered in the course is the Z80A microprocessor. Computer architecture, the Z80A instruction set, CP/M operating system, basic 80 language and program development and debugging, arithmetic routines, timing loops, I/O programming and interfacing, and using the microcomputer for real-time applications. There is introduction to CP/M assembly languages, register change and *call* instruction sets, and the generation of short assembly language programs. Block diagrams are used with microcomputers for laboratory practice.

Credit Recommendation: In the upper division baccalaureate degree category, 3 semester hours in Introduction to Microcomputers (8/80) (11/85). *Prerequisite:* A digital electronics background.

NOAA Weather Radio (B422/B222) (Formerly VHF Weather Warning System [B422/B220D] B-16-03)

Location: National Weather Service Training Center, Kansas City, MO.

Length: 104 hours (13 working days).

Dates: September 1977-September 1986.

Objective: To teach well-qualified electronics technicians to install, maintain, and monitor the technical operations of the VHF weather warning systems.

Instruction: Major topics covered in the course are basics and applied studies of magnetic-tape recording systems, control logic, and the theory and use of VHF transmitters, their control circuitry and diagnostic methods. Methods of instruction include lecture, discussion, and laboratory exercises.

Credit Recommendation: In the lower division baccalaureate/associate degree category, 3 semester hours in Radio Systems (8/80) (11/85).

NWS Engineering Fundamentals (X-03-02)

Location: National Weather Service Training Center, Kansas City, MO.

Length: 64 hours (8 working days).

Dates: December 1991-August 1997.

Objective: To provide newly hired electronic technicians with knowledge and training on the use of engineering references, PC maintenance and troubleshooting, PC configuration and operating procedures, and information generation procedures and practices.

Learning Outcome: Upon successful completion of this course, the student will be able to demonstrate proficiency with the operation and safety procedures associated with PCs; understand system assemblies and subassemblies; demonstrate knowledge of DOS commands and their applications; demonstrate working knowledge of software and select computer languages; use of NWS engineering handbooks; and understand the Engineering Management Report System (EMRS).

Instruction: Major topics covered in the course are engineering management structure, updating and use of engineering handbooks, the Engineering Management Report System (EMRS), PC maintenance, DOS and other program software applications, introduction to data communications, and the Consolidated Logistics System (CLS). Methods of instruction include lecture, laboratory, exercises, problem solving, operating manuals, handouts, and examination.

Credit Recommendation: In the lower division baccalaureate/associate degree category, 2 semester hours in Introduction to Computers (7/93).

Radar Meteorology (RAD06)

Location: National Weather Service Training Center, Kansas City, MO.

Length: 104 hours (3 weeks).

Dates: October 1987-September 1994.

Objective: To give students the necessary basic knowledge and skills to operate and disseminate "correct" conventional and Doppler radar weather information.

Learning Outcome: Upon successful completion of this course, the student will be able to understand basic weather radar systems, obtain and analyze radar data, properly utilize the NWS radar code, and disseminate data in standard format.

Instruction: Major topics covered in the course are theory and practical operation of weather radars, radio wave propagation, interpretation of radar images, measurement techniques, and methods of dissemination of radar information. Methods of instruction include lecture, demonstrations, exercises, operation of radar equipment at NWSTC, WRT-78 radar simulator, and examination.

Credit Recommendation: In the upper division baccalaureate degree category, 3 semesters hours in Radar Meteorology, Meteorology, or Science elective (6/83) (7/88) (7/93).

Radar Meteorology (RAD05) (Formerly RAD01, RAD02, LWR01)

Location: National Weather Service Training Center, Kansas City, MO.

Length: 144 hours (4 weeks).

Dates: October 1983-September 1987.

Objective: To enable the student to apply radar principles and theory to the practical operation of National Weather Service meteorological radars, to operate these radars at an acceptable level of competence and to interpret and disseminate accurate radar data.

Instruction: Major topics covered in the course are theory and operation of weather surveillance radars used by the National Weather Service, mathematical and physical principles in radar, radar physics, radio wave propagation, interpretation of radar scope depictions, measurement techniques, integration and analysis, and dissemination of radar information.

Credit Recommendation: In the upper division baccalaureate degree category, 3 semester hours in Meteorology (6/83).

Radar Meteorology Users (RAD07)

Location: National Weather Service Training Center, Kansas City, MO.

Length: 64 hours (8 days).

Dates: December 1980-January 1993.

Objective: To enable the student to apply radar theory and principles to the interpretation of data from Doppler and conventional weather radars.

Learning Outcome: Upon successful completion of this course, the student will be able to interpret conventional and Doppler radar displays; distinguish displays of various radars; utilize the NWS radar code; and apply contemporary models to interpret displays of thunder storms, tornados, flash floods, and hurricanes.

Instruction: Major topics covered in the course are comparative study of weather radars, decoding techniques, and the interpretation of radar displays in terms of various weather phenomena. Methods of instruction include lecture, discussion, laboratory, practical exercises, problem solving, and examination.

Credit Recommendation: In the upper division baccalaureate degree category, 2 semester hours in Radar Meteorology, or Laboratory Science elective (7/88) (7/93).

Radar Meteorology: A Short Course (RAD03) (Formerly [RSC01])

Location: National Weather Service Training Center, Kansas City, MO.

Length: 104 hours (3 weeks).

Dates: November 1977-March 1984.

Objective: To enable the student to apply radar principles and theory to the practical operation of weather radars and to interpret and disseminate accurate radar data.

Instruction: Major topics covered in the course are radar principles; interpretation of radar scope depictions; measurement techniques; integration and analysis; and the dissemination of radar information.

Credit Recommendation: In the upper division baccalaureate degree category, 3 semester hours in Meteorology (10/77) (4/82). *Prerequisite:* Mathematics through trigonometry and one year of college physics.

Radar Meteorology: WSR-57 (RAD01)

Location: National Weather Service Training Center, Kansas City, MO.

Length: 144 hours (4 weeks).

Dates: January 1972-September 1983.

Objective: To enable the student to apply radar principles and theory to the practical operation of the WSR-57, to operate the WSR-57 at an acceptable level of competence, and to interpret and disseminate accurate radar data.

Instruction: Major topics covered in the course are theory and operation of the primary weather surveillance radar used by the National Weather Service, basic mathematical and physical principles in radar, radar principles, radio wave propagation, interpretation of radar scope depictions, measurement techniques, integration and analysis, and the dissemination of radar information.

Credit Recommendation: In the upper division baccalaureate degree category, 3 semester hours in Meteorology (10/77).

Radar Meteorology: WSR-74 (RAD02) (Formerly [LWR01])

Location: National Weather Service Training Center, Kansas City, MO.

Length: 144 hours (4 weeks).

Dates: December 1974-September 1983.

Objective: To enable the student to apply radar principles and theory to the practical operation of the WSR-74, to operate the WSR-74 at an acceptable level of competence, and to interpret and disseminate accurate radar data.

Instruction: Major topics covered in the course are theory and operation of the local warning surveillance radar used by the National Weather Service, mathematical and physical principles in radar, radar principles, radio wave propagation, interpretation of radar scope depictions, measurement techniques, integration and analysis, and dissemination of radar information.

Credit Recommendation: In the upper division baccalaureate degree category, 3 semester hours in Meteorology (10/77).

RAMOS Circuit Operation (S-03-02)

Location: National Weather Service Training Center, Kansas City, MO.

Length: 64 hours (8 days).

Dates: *Version 1:* August 1977-December 1987; *Version 2:* January 1988-Present.

Objective: To provide electronics technicians experienced in digital logic the knowledge and skills necessary to install, calibrate, and maintain the RAMOS system.

Learning Outcome: Upon successful completion of this course, the student will be able to understand the complete Remote Automated Meteorological Observing System (RAMOS) circuit operation including fault locations and proper adjustments, maintenance, and installation.

Instruction: Major topics covered in the course are a detailed study of all module block diagrams and mechanical components of the RAMOS system including the process of programming base and field stations. Methods of instruction include lecture, laboratory exercises supplemented by equipment manuals, instruction manuals, hand out materials, and examination.

Credit Recommendation: *Version 1:* In the lower division baccalaureate/associate degree category, 2 semester hours in Solid State Electronics (8/80) (11/85). *Version 2:* In the lower division baccalaureate/associate degree category, 2 semester hours in Electronic System Operations and Analysis (7/93).

Satellite Weather Information System (SWIS) Maintenance (M-10-02)

Location: National Weather Service Training Center, Kansas City, MO.

Length: 80 hours (two weeks).

Dates: August 1987-June 1994.

Objective: To provide the AFOS (Automation of Field Operations and Services) electronic technician with a functional understanding of the Satellite Weather Information System (SWIS) operation and maintenance activities and procedures.

Learning Outcome: Upon successful completion of this course, the student will be able to trace signal flow through complex digital equipment; observe and troubleshoot circuits that receive satellite images; run diagnostic tests on the disc storage system that provides time-lapse images to the AFOS installation; and employ a PC-based monitor program to diagnose processor failures.

Instruction: Major topics covered in the course are overview of the SWIS design and operation, GOES satellite imagery storage system, processor-system interface, fault detection and isolation, disk subsystems, SWIS-AFOS interface system, and power supply layout. Methods of instruction include lecture, discussion, laboratory, and hands-on practice on a SWIS installation. (10 class room days, 20 hours class, 60 in assignments, 40 in laboratory).

Credit Recommendation: In the lower division baccalaureate/associate degree category, 2 semester hours in Electronic Maintenance or Physical Science elective (7/93).

SOO-DOH Training Techniques (ITT02)

Location: National Weather Service Training Center, Kansas City, MO.

Length: 24 hours (4 working days).

Dates: July 1993-September 1996.

Objective: To provide the Science and Operations Officer and (SOO) and Development and Operations Officer (DOH) with the basic tools needed to conduct an on-station training program.

Learning Outcome: Upon successful completion of this course, the student will be able to define training objectives for his/her on-station training program; select effective training methods; evaluate scheduling alternatives; use a variety of presentation techniques; and evaluate the effectiveness of local training efforts.

Instruction: Major topics covered in the course are principles of adult learning, definition of training objectives, preparation of training materials, methods of presentation, mentoring, and scheduling and evaluating training. Methods of instruction include lecture, discussion, case studies, role-playing, classroom exercises, and student project and presentation.

Credit Recommendation: In the upper division baccalaureate degree category or in the graduate degree category, 1 semester hour in Industrial Education, Training and Development, Organizational Behavior, Human Resource Development, or related fields (6/94).

Station Management and Supervision (MGT-01)

Location: National Weather Service Training Center, Kansas City, MO.

Length: 104 hours (3 weeks).

Dates: January 1978-February 1995.

Objective: To improve knowledge of management principles and to provide students with supervisory skills for beginning and middle level managers.

Learning Outcome: Upon successful completion of this course, the student will be able to supervise the work of subordinate employees; perform personnel actions; demonstrate leadership abilities; and perform various administrative functions associated with management of a weather station.

Instruction: Major topics covered in the course are management theory and principles; supervision, leadership and managerial functions and activities; and communication. Methods of instruction include lecture, discussion, problem solving, case studies, classroom exercises, written assignments, and examinations.

Credit Recommendation: In the upper division baccalaureate degree category, 4 semester hours in Personnel Administration, Public Administration, or Public Management, or in the graduate degree category, 3 semester hours in Personnel Administration, Public Administration, or Public Management (8/82) (7/88) (7/93).

Surface Instruments Maintenance Training (SIMT)

Location: National Weather Service Training Center, Kansas City, MO.

Length: 160 hours (20 working days).

Dates: December 1972-September 1988.

Objective: To provide experienced electronics technicians with the skills necessary to install, calibrate, and maintain the surface measurement equipment used by the National Weather Service.

Instruction: Covers basic principles of servo positioning systems, digital logic for common data recorders, digital decoding, temperature, wind speed, and direction, dew point, precipitation recorders, cloud height indicators, and radiation recorders. Methods of instruction include lecture, discussion, and laboratories.

Credit Recommendation: In the upper division baccalaureate degree category, 3 semester hours in Meteorological Instrumentation (8/80) (11/85).

System Z, Analysis Techniques (M-10-06)

Location: National Weather Service Training Center, Kansas City, MO.

Length: 104 hours (13 days).

Dates: April 1992-Present.

Objective: To provide electronic technicians with advanced knowledge and training on System Z (updated communications and data handling computer system) with emphasis on diagnostic performance including hardware, software, and communications.

Learning Outcome: Upon successful completion of this course, the student will be able to perform System Z data base management functions including setup; edit async directories; identify critical files; create procedures; operate all system backups, and analyze and repair defective subsystems.

Instruction: Major topics covered in the course are in-depth study of System Z including topics of operations; hardware, diagnostic and operational software, and database management techniques; communications; backup; recovery; and reconfiguration procedures. Methods of instruction include lecture, laboratory, problem solving exercises, equipment books, manuals, instructors handouts, and exams. (15 class, 15 laboratory, 10 outside preparation).

Credit Recommendation: In the upper division baccalaureate degree category, 4 semester hours in Database Management or Computer Science elective (7/93).

Upper Air Minicomputer (M-03-06)

Location: National Weather Service Training Center, Kansas City, MO.

Length: 240 hours (30 working days).

Dates: February 1978-February 1985.

Objective: To discuss in detail the subsystems of the Model 3610 upper air minicomputer system including NOVA minicomputer, paper-tape reader, paper-tape punch, keyboard, printer, link mag tape transport, and T.I. Silent-700 data terminal, and to enable students to use diagnostic programming, static testing, schematics, and oscilloscope to trace malfunctions to chip level.

Instruction: Major topics covered in the course are an overview of the upper air minicomputer; review of Boolean algebra; basic digital building blocks including BCD counters, shift registers, binary-to-octal decoders; NOVA architecture and instruction set; use of diagnostic routines; use of oscilloscope in isolating computer troubles to chip level; and peripherals and peripheral control cards. Methods of instruction for half of the course include lecture/discussion and half laboratory work.

Credit Recommendation: In the lower division baccalaureate/associate degree category, 5 semester hours in Computer and Digital Equipment Diagnostics and Repair (8/80) (11/85).

Upper Air Observations (UAO01)

Location: National Weather Service Training Center, Kansas City, MO.

Length: 224 hours (6 weeks).

Dates: December 1974-April 1984.

Objective: To enable meteorological technicians to take, record, and disseminate rawinsonde observations.

Instruction: Major topics covered in the course are flight equipment preparation, balloon release, instrument tracking, and data reduction by computer methods. Also includes interpolation and extrapolation techniques, encoding and decoding data, selecting mandatory and significant levels, and operation of communications equipment. Course does not require knowledge of calculus.

Credit Recommendation: In the lower division baccalaureate/associate degree category, 2 semester hours in Meteorological Instrumentation Laboratory (10/77) (4/82).

WBRT: Weather Bureau Radio Theodolite RAWIN System (J-11-03)

Location: National Weather Service Training Center, Kansas City, MO.

Length: 104 hours (13 working days).

Dates: January 1960-November 1985.

Objective: To provide electronics technicians with the knowledge and skills required to install, align, calibrate, and maintain the WBRT RAWIN system.

Instruction: Major topics covered in the course are upper air sounding systems; radiosonde operations; principles of tracking active targets by conical scanning; frequency-to-voltage conversion; null-balance recording systems; and alignment, calibration, troubleshooting, and repair of WBRT systems. Methods of instruction include lecture and laboratory exercises.

Credit Recommendation: In the lower division baccalaureate/associate degree category, 2 semester hours in Electronics Systems (8/80). **NOTE:** This course is essentially identical to GMD (Ground Meteorological Device) RAWIN System J-10-03; therefore, credit should not be awarded for both this course and GMD RAWIN System J-10-03.

Weather Bureau Radar Remote 1 and 2 (R-05-03)

Location: National Weather Service Training Center, Kansas City, MO.

Length: 136 hours (17 working days).

Dates: May 1969-November 1983.

Objective: To provide electronics technicians with the knowledge and skills required to install, activate, align, and maintain the Weather Bureau Radar Remoting (WBRR) systems.

Instruction: Major topics covered in the course are slow-scan-video remoting techniques; vidicon and iatron operation; FM data transmission by telephone lines; and the theory and mechanics of operation, alignment, troubleshooting, and repair of the WBRR radar remoting units. Methods of instruction include lecture and laboratory exercises.

Credit Recommendation: In the lower division baccalaureate/associate degree category, 3 semester hours in Electronics Systems (8/80).

Weather Bureau Radar Remote Recorder: WBRR-4 and RRM Models (R-06-02)

Location: National Weather Service Training Center, Kansas City, MO.

Length: 80 hours (10 working days).

Dates: May 1969-November 1983.

Objective: To provide electronics technicians with the knowledge and skills required to install, activate, align, and maintain the WBRR-4 facsimile recorder.

Instruction: Major topics covered in the course are AM and FM demodulation circuitry; facsimile transmission; recording principles; servo systems; logic circuits; and alignment, troubleshooting, and repair of the WBRR-4 and RRM recorders. Methods of instruction include lecture and laboratory exercises.

Credit Recommendation: In the lower division baccalaureate/associate degree category, 2 semester hours in Electronics Systems (8/80).

Weather Service Operations (WSO-02)

Location: National Weather Service Training Center, Kansas City, MO.

Length: 104 hours (3 weeks).

Dates: *Version 1:* October 1988-January 1991; *Version 2:* February 1991-Present.

Objective: To increase NWS specialists understanding and ability to use the wide range of product and services of the organization, and knowledge for communicating weather information.

Learning Outcome: Upon successful completion of this course, the student will be able to utilize effectively NWS products; have knowledge of services; and effective means of communicating information about NWS.

Instruction: Major topics covered in the course are oral and written communications, preparation of local forecasts and related weather information, flash flood warnings, aviation weather, hurricanes, winter and severe local storms, and public warnings. Methods of instruction include lecture, laboratory, exercises, case studies, and examinations.

Credit Recommendation: *Version 1:* In the upper division baccalaureate degree category, 3 semester hours in Synoptic Meteorology (7/88). *Version 2:* In the upper division baccalaureate degree category, 1 semester hour in Communications and 3 semester hours in Synoptic Meteorology, or Physical Science elective (7/93).

Weather Service Operations (WSO01)

Location: National Weather Service Training Center, Kansas City, MO.

Length: 144 hours (4 weeks).

Dates: May 1970-October 1988.

Objective: To increase the Weather Service Specialist's ability to use all National Weather Service products and programs and to improve his or her ability to communicate weather information.

Instruction: Methods of instruction include lectures and practical exercises in three major subject areas: oral and written communications, preparation of adapted local forecasts from National Meteorological Center Guidance products, and special topics. The communications area covers preparation of weather reports and pilot briefings through videotaped student presentations. Special topics include flash flood warnings, hydrology, aviation weather, hurricanes, winter storms, and severe local storms. This course is equivalent to a first course in synoptic meteorology.

Credit Recommendation: In the lower division baccalaureate/associate degree category, 1 semester hour in Communications, and in the upper division baccalaureate degree category, 3 semester hours in Meteorology (10/77) (4/82).

Weather Service Radar: WSR-57/DVIP (R-08-06)

Location: National Weather Service Training Center, Kansas City, MO.

Length: 240 hours (30 days).

Dates: September 1959-August 1994.

Objective: To enable qualified electronics technicians to install, calibrate, maintain, and monitor the operation of the complete WSR-57 weather radar including the digital video integrator processor system.

Learning Outcome: Upon successful completion of this course, the student will be able to understand radar circuit theory and systems; calibration; troubleshooting techniques; and circuits.

Instruction: Major topics covered in the course are radar systems in general, with emphasis on the WSR-57. Detailed study is made of the electronic circuitry, electromechanical components, microwave techniques, power measurements, integrated circuits, and the digital video integrator processor.

Credit Recommendation: In the upper division baccalaureate degree category, 4 semester hours in Radar Systems, or 2 semester hours in Digital Systems (8/80) (11/85) (7/93). **NOTE:** Students may be awarded credit for either Weather Service Radar (R-08-06), or Radar System (R-12-04), but not both.

Weather Surveillance Radar: 1988 Doppler (WSR-88D)

Location: Norman, OK.

Length: *Version 1:* 160 hours (20 days); *Version 2:* 144 hours (18 days) (after 10/93).

Dates: October 1991-Present.

Objective: To enable the student to apply Doppler radar theory and principles for maximum operational use of the Weather Surveillance Radar-1988 Doppler; describe capabilities and limitations of WSR-88D products; interpret WSR-88D products; and apply information gleaned from these products in performing operational duties of meteorologists, forecasters, hydrologists, and air traffic controllers.

Learning Outcome: Upon successful completion of this course, the student will be able to make critical, life-saving decisions using the WSR-88D to meet the agency's mission; serve as a hydrometeorologist at a WSR-88D radar installation; make skillful efficient decisions regarding severe and nonsevere weather situations, issue weather and flood advisories, and advise associated personnel relative to proper analysis of weather radar data.

Instruction: Major topics covered in the course are radar fundamentals; description of radar parameters such as power, beam width, pulse length, and scanning strategies; propagation of electromagnetic waves under various meteorological conditions; actual and radial velocity vectors; radar errors including beam intercept errors, range folding, and velocity dealiasing; processing procedures for radar return signals; determinations of velocity profiles under various conditions; application of convective storm structure and methodology to use algorithms that derive the desired radar products; and criteria needed to issue severe and nonsevere weather forecasts and flooding forecasts. Methods of instruction include lecture, participation, and laboratory exercises.

Credit Recommendation: In the upper division baccalaureate degree category, 6 semester hours in Applied Radar Meteorology; or in the graduate degree category, 4 semester hours in Applied Radar Meteorology (11/93). **NOTE:** Student should receive credit at only one level.

Writing and Broadcast Seminar (WBS01)

Location: National Weather Service Training Center, Kansas City, MO.

Length: 28 hours (4 working days).

Dates: September 1993-November 1996.

Objective: To become familiar with word choice, writing, and speaking skills important to presenting frequently technical weather information in laymen's terms to the general public with an emphasis on presentation through radio and television; and to provide weather service personnel with more awareness of how today's news media operate with suggestions on how to make the relationship with the media more productive.

Learning Outcome: Upon successful completion of this course, the student will be able to condense and simplify information developed by meteorologists into more conversational language for distribution to broadcast outlets in written form, or to record that information for broadcast on NOAA radio or other outlets; to respond to the needs of news media, particularly in emergency situations; and to suggest weather service-related story ideas to the media.

Instruction: Major topics covered in the course are elements of news writing, particularly for broadcast with the primary focus on applying those elements to weather information; introduction to developing one's on-air delivery skills; and establishing and maintaining good relations with the news media. Methods of instruction include lecture, in-studio delivery of weather information, and writing labs.

Credit Recommendation: In the lower division baccalaureate/associate degree category, 1 semester hour in Communications (6/94).

WSR-88D Maintenance (R-40-06) (WSR-88D)

Location: National Weather Service Training Center, Kansas City, MO.

Length: 240 hours (six weeks).

Dates: January 1992-Present.

Objective: To acquire the knowledge, skills, and ability to perform complete WSR-88D radar system maintenance on and off-line.

Learning Outcome: Upon successful completion of this course, the student will be able to demonstrate knowledge about the WSR-88D radar system including transmitters, receivers, data acquisition, communications, displays; and be able to analyze, diagnose and repair system problems.

Instruction: Major topics covered in the course are system configuration, information processing, data transmission, information displays, and malfunction analysis and repair. Methods of instruction include lecture, laboratory, problem solving exercises, and examination.

Credit Recommendation: In the lower division baccalaureate/associate degree category, 4 semester hours in Computer Systems Operations or Radar Systems Maintenance (7/93).

WSR-88D Management Overview (R-43-02)

Location: National Weather Service Training Center, Kansas City, MO.

Length: 24 hours (3 days).

Dates: April 1993-Present.

Objective: To provide knowledge of radar systems, data acquisition, transmission, display, maintenance overview, and specific operational requirements for the WSR-88D weather radar.

Learning Outcome: Upon successful completion of this course, the student will be able to demonstrate general systems management knowledge of the WSR-88D weather radar, and understand general operations and diagnostic procedures for it.

Instruction: Major topics covered in the course are management overview, background and fundamentals of radar, operational requirements, basic maintenance, and understanding the load and run software requirements of the WSR-88D. Methods of instruction include lecture, laboratory, fundamental text, evaluation, and examinations.

Credit Recommendation: In the lower division baccalaureate/associate degree category, 1 semester hour in Computer Systems Management (7/93).

WSR-88D Principal User Position (PUP) Maintenance (R-41-02)

Location: National Weather Service Training Center, Kansas City, MO.

Length: 80 hours (2 weeks).

Dates: May 1992-Present.

Objective: To familiarize students with WSR-88D system; and the ability to power down and activate the WSR-88D PUP, and perform on-line system diagnostics.

Learning Outcome: Upon successful completion of this course, the student will be able to demonstrate on-line diagnostics of the WSR-88D system, and replace LRU components.

Instruction: Major topics covered in the course are WSR-88D system familiarity, and on-line diagnostic software. Methods of instruction include lecture, laboratory, text, manuals, and examinations.

Credit Recommendation: In the vocational certificate category, 2 semester hours in Computer Operations (7/93).

WSR: Weather Service Radar-74C Radar System (WSR-74C) (R-12-04)

Location: National Weather Service Training Center, Kansas City, MO.

Length: 160 hours (20 days).

Dates: December 1976-August 1994.

Objective: To provide electronics technicians with the knowledge and skills needed to activate, calibrate, and maintain the WSR-74C meteorological radar system and the associated Digital Video Integrator and Processor (DVIP).

Learning Outcome: Upon successful completion of this course, the student will be able to understand radar circuit theory and systems operations; calibration; troubleshooting; and systems level repairs.

Instruction: Major topics covered in the course are radar system principles, WSR-74C characteristics, subsystem details and theory of operation; alignment, calibration, troubleshooting, and repair techniques; integrated circuits, functioning, and maintenance of the DVIP. Methods of instruction include lecture and laboratory sessions.

Credit Recommendation: In the upper division baccalaureate degree category, 2 semester hours in Radar Systems and 2 semester hours in Digital Systems (8/80) (11/85) (7/93). **NOTE:** Credit may be awarded for this course, Radar System (R-12-04), or Weather Service Radar (R-08-06), but not both.

Naval Center for Acquisition Training Office

The Navy Acquisition Management Training Office (NAMTO) was established to provide worldwide acquisition training to the Navy's contracting and procurement personnel. The mission of the entity is to eliminate the inadequacies in quality, substance, and availability of acquisition training. To accomplish this objective, the program provides current, state-of-the-art instruction as prescribed in the certified acquisition and procurement courses of the Defense Management Education Training (DMET) manual and the DOD Civilian Career Program for Contracting and Acquisition Personnel (DOD Directive 1430.10-M-1.). The program also provides management advisory services and technical assistance for Navy operating officials in promoting current, cost-effective, and economical contracting practices.

NAMTO was established in October 1985 under the provision of the Navy's Buy Our Spares Smart (BOSS) program and Weinberger's 10-point initiatives. The program's concept was reemphasized under the President's Blue Ribbon Commission (Packard Commission) on Defense Management. NAMTO, located at NSC Norfolk, is supported by COMNAVSUPSYSCOM'S Contract Management Division with authority delegated by the Assistant Secretary of the Navy for Shipbuilding and Logistics ASN(S&L).

Source of official student records: U.S. Navy Acquisition Management Training Office, Naval Supply Center, Norfolk, VA 23512-5000.

Additional information about the courses: College Credit Recommendation Service, American Council on Education, One Dupont Circle, Washington, DC 20036-1193.

Advanced Skills in Research and Instructional Methodologies

Location: Various locations worldwide.

Length: 40 hours (1 week).

Dates: June 1993-Present.

Objective: To learn needs assessment, effective classroom leadership, and criterion referenced test construction.

Learning Outcome: Upon successful completion of this course, the student will be able to construct and utilize appropriate needs assessment methods; plan and conduct effective classroom exercises; and write and evaluate criterion-referenced tests.

Instruction: Major topics covered in the course are survey methods; analysis and reporting techniques; facilitation techniques and group dynamics; criterion-referenced test development; formatting; piloting; and evaluating criterion-referenced tests. Methods of instruction in-clude lecture, discussion, audiovisual aids, out of class assignments, and classroom exercises.

Credit Recommendation: In the upper division baccalaureate degree category, 2 semester hours in Educational Methods or Adult and Continuing Education (4/93).

Automation of Procurement and Accounting Data Entry (APADE) Part 1: Input Clerk's Course Part 2: Buyer's Course

Location: Various locations throughout the country.

Length: *Part 1:* 18 hours (3 days); *Part 2:* 42 hours (7 days); Part 1 is a prerequisite to Part 2.

Dates: April 1986-November 1991.

Objective: *Part 1:* To obtain skill in use of APADE system for requisition input and inquiry. *Part 2:* To obtain skill in use of APADE system for the entire procurement process.

Learning Outcome: *Part 1:* Upon successful completion of this course, the student will be able to use procurement computing systems to enter requisitions and perform an inquiry using a procurement computer system. *Part 2:* Upon successful completion of this course, the student will be able to update requisitions, process a pre-award, process a contract award, and process an award subclining, and exchange data through an on-line automated data based system.

Instruction: *Part 1:* Major topics covered in the course are introduction to personal computers and requisition input and inquiry. *Part 2:* Major topics covered in the course are requisition update, pre-award, awards, subclining, and data exchange. Method of instruction includes lecture, discussion, practice exercises, and examinations.

Credit Recommendation: *Part 1:* In the lower division baccalaureate/associate degree category, 1 semester hour in Computer Science, Data Processing, or Procurement and Contracting (3/88). *Part 2:* In the lower division baccalaureate/ associate degree category, 2 semester hours in Computer Science, Data Processing, or Procurement and Contracting (3/88).

Basic Contract Administration (AQ 501) (Formerly Basic Contract Administration)

Location: Various locations worldwide.

Length: 90 hours (3 weeks).

Dates: October 1987-November 1991.

Objective: To provide the student with an understanding of the basic principles of government contracting administration and development of a philosophy of contract administration.

Learning Outcome: Upon successful completion of this course, the student will have knowledge of advantages and disadvantages of various contracts, areas of application, and limitations under various conditions; understand the lines of authority and responsibility associated with contracts under applicable federal acquisition regulations; understand quality assurance, including inspection and application warranties; and understand the role of finance, subcontracting, negotiation, and remedies associated with contract administration.

Instruction: Major topics covered in the course are the acquisition process, funding, ethics in contract evaluation, types of contracts, profit, property, quality assurance, contract modification, negotiation, remedies, financing, and the role of subcontractors. Methods of instruction include lecture, discussion, case studies, and examinations.

Credit Recommendation: In the upper division baccalaureate or graduate degree category, 3 semester hours in Business Administration, Logistics and Materials Management, or Procurement and Contracting (3/88).

Becoming a More Effective Instructor (ED 401) (Formerly ED301)

Location: Various locations worldwide.

Length: *Version 1*: 24 hours (3 days); *Version 2*: 40 hours (5 days).

Dates: *Version 1:* September 1986-December 1992; *Version 2:* January 1993-Present.

Objective: To design and deliver effective instruction to adult learners.

Learning Outcome: Upon the successful completion of this course, the student will be able to recognize and develop "master-teaching" techniques; write appropriate course objectives; understand characteristics of adult learners; skillfully present course content; and manage the learning environment.

Instruction: Major topics covered in the course are effective teaching; competency-based education; lesson plan organization; classroom presentation skills; verbal and nonverbal communication; and characteristics of adult and traditional learners. Methods of instruction include lecture, classroom exercises, examination, and out of class assignments.

Credit Recommendation: *Version 1:* In the upper division baccalaureate degree category, 1 semester hour in Methods of Adult Education (11/86). *Version 2:* In the upper division baccalaureate degree category, 2 semester hours in Educational Methods or Adult and Continuing Education (4/93).

Configuration Management (AMEC-12)

Location: Resident, on-site.

Length: 40 hours (1 week).

Dates: November 1984-Present.

Objective: To explain and describe configuration management requirements and techniques.

Learning Outcome: Upon successful completion of this course, the participant will be able to design, develop, implement, and operate a CM program; apply correct CM procedures and policies; and understand basic elements of CM.

Instruction: Major topics covered in the course are CM policies, procedures and applications with DOD, Army, and Army Material Command; system life cycle model; basic elements of CM; CM software and future trends; planning and operating a CM program; and configuration identification, status accounting, control, and audits. Methods of instruction include lecture, practical exercises, and case studies.

Credit Recommendation: In the upper division baccalaureate degree category, 3 semester hours in Business Management or Organizational Design (3/92).

Contract Pricing (CON 104) (Formerly QMT-170)

Location: Various locations worldwide.

Length: 84 hours (2 weeks, 4 days).

Dates: January 1993-Present.

Objective: To introduce the student to the goals and basic principles of cost and price analysis, and to provide a solid foundation for obtaining their cost/price objectives through the practice of negotiating simulated cases.

Learning Outcome: Upon successful completion of this course, the student will be able to apply their knowledge of cost development and pricing theory in the analysis of the contractors' proposal and in the development of negotiation objectives; prepare for negotiations by identifying the fundamentals of effective negotiations and practicing/observing different negotiation styles.

Instruction: Major topics covered in the course are the role of the specialist in evaluating bids and proposals; analyzing cost and price estimates by applying quantitive techniques; making price related decisions; analyzing elements of costs in the development of pre-negotiation objectives; accounting for differences in proposed costs and the Government's estimates computing cost of money and a fair and reasonable profit; developing effective approaches and styles for negotiating contracts, modifications, and terminations. Methods of instruction include lecture, classroom discussion, out-of-class readings and problem solving assignments, examinations, and qualitative review.

Credit Recommendation: In the upper division baccalaureate degree category, 3 semester hours in Acquisition Contracting, Purchasing, or Business Management elective (4/93).

Contracting Fundamentals (Formerly Management of Defense Acquisition Contracts Basic (AQ 301) and formerly [MD-001-86])

Location: Various locations worldwide.

Length: 120 hours (4 weeks).

Dates: January 1986-November 1992.

Objective: To give the student an introduction and expansion of basic knowledge and skills of government contracts management.

Learning Outcome: Upon the successful completion of this course, the student will have knowledge of basic contracting functions, responsibilities, and techniques in solving operational problems of contract management; develop acquisition strategy; apply applicable federal regulations; and make sound judgements for timely delivery of quality and products at a reasonable price.

Instruction: Major topics covered in the course are fundamental concepts of contracting; appropriations and funding competition requirements; specifications; contractor qualifications; solicitations; sealed bidding; types of contracts; pricing policies and techniques; negotiation; quality assurance; contract administration and modifications; contract termination; protests; disputes and appeals; and contract closeout. Methods of instruction include lecture, classroom discussion, weekly examinations, and out of class readings.

Credit Recommendation: In the lower division baccalaureate/associate degree or upper division baccalaureate degree category, 3 semester hours in Acquisitions Contracting or Business Management (11/86) (4/93).

Defense Contract Negotiation Workshop (AQ302) (Formerly Defense Contract Negotiation Workshop [NG-004-86])

Location: Various locations worldwide.

Length: 40 hours (1 week).

Dates: January 1986-November 1992.

Objective: To provide the student with knowledge of negotiation issues, strategies and tactics, and application of this knowledge in negotiation sessions.

Learning Outcome: Upon the successful completion of this course, the student will be able to identify the elements of effective negotiations; recognize and use negotiation strategies and tactics; and prepare for negotiation sessions.

Instruction: Major topics covered in the course are techniques for negotiating prime contracts; contract modifications; and contract terminations. Methods of instruction include lecture, discussion, out-of-class readings, case studies, and group exercises.

Credit Recommendation: In the lower division baccalaureate/associate degree category, 1 semester hour in Acquisitions Contracting, Business Management, or Personnel Administration (11/86) (4/93).

Defense Cost and Price Analysis (ACQ 302) (Formerly Defense Cost and Price Analysis [NG-004-86])

Location: Various locations worldwide.

Length: 80 hours (2 weeks).

Dates: January 1986-November 1992.

Objective: To give the student basic understanding of cost and price relationships and of relevant policies, tools, and techniques and application of this knowledge to contract pricing.

Learning Outcome: Upon the successful completion of this course, the student will have knowledge of cost and price theory and an ability to appropriately apply this knowledge in cost/price analysis of contractor proposals.

Instruction: Major topics covered in the course are pricing; cost estimates and analysis; cost projection; effects of learning rates on costs; and the role of buyers in evaluating bid proposals, including profit analysis, depreciation, and legal implications. Methods of instruction include lecture, classroom discussion, out-of-class readings, problem solving assignments, and examinations.

Credit Recommendation: In the lower division baccalaureate/associate degree category, 3 semester hours in Acquisition Contracting or Business Management (11/86) (4/93).

Developing the Effective Contemporary Manager

Location: Various locations worldwide.

Length: 76 hours (2 weeks).

Dates: May 1993-Present.

Objective: To exercise managerial skills necessitated by contemporary organization demands and the dynamic managerial environment.

Learning Outcome: Upon successful completion of this course, the student will be able to utilize effective communication and facilitation skills; use appropriate motivation strategies; manage conflict; use qualitative and quantitative data for decision making; use time management techniques; prepare and present briefs and reports; and apply ethical principles to managerial and employee conduct.

Instruction: Major topics covered in the course are organizational communication; motivation; ethics; leadership and facilitation; conflict management; qualitative and quantitative methods for decisions; time management; and presentation skills. Methods of instruction include lecture, discussion, audiovisual aids, classroom exercises, case studies, student presentations; out of class assignments, and examinations.

Credit Recommendation: In the upper division baccalaureate degree category, 3 semester hours in Business Administration or Management (4/93).

Economic Analysis and Decision Making (7A-F10)

Location: AMEC, Rock Island, IL, and other sites.

Length: 80 hours (2 weeks).

Dates: January 1984-Present.

Objective: To provide the skills necessary to perform an economic analysis to assist in long-term resource allocation decisions.

Learning Outcome: Upon successful completion of this course, the participant will be able to describe the steps in economic analysis process; recognize the impact of uncertainty on the decision-making process; relate to the theory of interest rates to the timing and value of cash flows; identify the benefits that are to be received by adoption of a particular course of action; and perform satisfactory economic analysis.

Instruction: Major topics covered in the course are cost estimating techniques; time value of money; methods for comparison of alternatives; benefit identification and quantification; and cost benefit analysis. Methods of instruction include lecture, case study, practical exercises, and student presentation.

Credit Recommendation: In the upper division baccalaureate degree category, 3 semester hours in Economics or Finance (3/92). **NOTE:** Credit for course is excluded if credit is given for AMEC 153 or AMEC 149.

Fundamentals of Procurement Planning

Location: Various locations worldwide.

Length: 35 hours (1 week).

Dates: October 1993-Present.

Objective: To learn basic elements of procurement planning from the users' point of view to assure desired quality of product and/or service.

Learning Outcome: Upon successful completion of this course, the student will be able to apply basic knowledge of factors and steps involved in developing a procurement plan from inception of a purchase specification and request, and critique specifications and methods of procurement to the preparation of a procurement plan.

Instruction: Major topics covered in the course are acquisition process review; funding; specification critique; analysis of service requirements; supplier competition; evaluation factors for contract award; methods of procurement; and preparation of a procurement plan. Methods of instruction include lecture, discussion, examinations, practical in-class exercises, and out-of-class readings.

Credit Recommendation: In the lower division baccalaureate/associate degree category, 1 semester hour in Planning or Business Administration elective (4/93).

Government Contract Law (CON 201) (Formerly Government Contracting Law [AQ 503])

Location: Various locations worldwide.

Length: 80 hours (2 weeks).

Dates: October 1987-Present.

Objective: To provide the student with the knowledge and understanding of the legal aspects of government contracting.

Learning Outcome: Upon successful completion of this course, the student will be able to identify legislation relevant to contracting law; understand basic legal principles and sources of contracting law; interpret contract language, include modifications, terminations, remedies, and awards; recognize the major elements of contracting, procurement, bid procedures, subcontracting, and funding; and recognize the need to seek professional legal advice.

Instruction: Major topics covered in the course are contract formation and modification; essential elements of a contract; specifications and inspection acceptances, equitable adjustments; labor law; and termination for default and convenience. Methods of instruction include lecture, classroom discussion, case studies, video and computer-assisted instruction, and examinations.

Credit Recommendation: In the upper division baccalaureate or graduate degree category, 3 semester hours in Commercial or Business Contract Law (11/86) (4/93).

Intermediate Post-Award Contracting (CON 221) (Formerly Advanced Contract Administration [AQ 502])

Location: Various locations worldwide.

Length: 68 hours (2 weeks).

Dates: January 1986-Present.

Objective: To apply quality assurance techniques to contract management, including articulation with outside agencies and cost analysis.

Learning Outcome: Upon successful completion of this course, the student will be able to apply quality assurance techniques to contract administration; articulate contract administration services with outside agencies; understand importance of overhead expenses; compute value ratios; and understand the key labor laws and environmental laws affecting governmental acquisition.

Instruction: Major topics covered in the course are standard of conduct; contract modifications; subcontract management; cost and pricing; government property control; contract financing; contract termination; labor relations; and environmental laws. Methods of instruction include lecture, discussion, audiovisual aids, practice exercises, and examinations.

Credit Recommendation: In the upper division baccalaureate or graduate degree category, 3 semester hours in Business Administration, Logistics and Material

Management, or Procurement (3/88) (4/93).

Intermediate Pre-Award Contracting (Formerly Management of Defense Acquisition Contracts Advanced (AQ 401) and [MDA-002-86])

Location: Various locations worldwide.
Length: 112 hours (14 days).
Dates: February 1986-Present.
Objective: To reinforce and extend the student's basic contract formulation and contract management knowledge and skills and application of theoretical concepts to acquisition planning.
Learning Outcome: Upon the successful completion of this course, the student will be able to develop an acquisition strategy and acquire or develop information needed for sound procurement decisions; evaluate offers and awards in appropriately applying contractual mechanisms; and identify and solve problems associated with acquisitions contracting.
Instruction: Major topics covered in the course are Acquisition Planning; Contract Type selection; Sealed Bids; Competitive Negotiations and numerous other pre and post award processes. Methods of instruction include lecture, classroom discussion, out-of-class assignments, case studies, student presentations, panels, group problem solving, individual exercises, and examinations.
Credit Recommendation: In the lower division baccalaureate/associate degree or upper division baccalaureate degree category, 3 semester hours in Contracting or Business Management (11/86) (4/93).

Management Development Seminar (MG 201) (Formerly Management Development Seminar)

Location: Various locations worldwide.
Length: 40 hours (1 week).
Dates: August 1987-November 1991.
Objective: To provide the student with the understanding and application of basic management concepts.
Learning Outcome: Upon successful completion of this course, the student will be able to define and apply components of the communication process; define objectives for an organizational unit; apply principles of time management; recognize types of conflict and apply resolution techniques; apply problem-solving techniques to work-related situations; and utilize team-building techniques in group situations.
Instruction: Major topics covered in the course are managerial communications, goal setting, time management, confrontation and conflict resolution, problem-solving, and team building. Methods of instruction include lecture, discussion, case studies, use of teaching aids, examinations, and self-evaluation exercises.
Credit Recommendation: In the lower division baccalaureate/associate degree category, 2 semester hours in Business Administration or Management (3/88).

Management of Managers (MG 501) (Formerly Management of Managers [MGM-006-86])

Location: Various locations worldwide.
Length: 80 hours (2 weeks).
Dates: October 1986-November 1991.
Objective: To provide the student with an understanding of alternate modes of behavior appropriate for the supervision of subordinate managers.
Learning Outcome: Upon the successful completion of this course, the student will have knowledge of personnel management techniques and skill in application of this knowledge, and an understanding of a manager's role in human resource development.
Instruction: Major topics of covered in the course are competencies and role of managers; communication; motivation; goal setting; coaching; delegating; time management; problem-solving; preparing presentations; stress management; situational leadership; and adapting to change. Methods of instruction include lecture-discussion, out-of-class readings, demonstrations, role playing, video presentations, and individual and group exercises.
Credit Recommendation: In the upper division baccalaureate or graduate degree category, 3 semester hours in Business and Personnel Management or Human Resource Development (11/86).

Management Statistics (7E-F15C)

Location: On-site.
Length: 80 hours (1 year to complete).
Dates: July 1982-Present.
Objective: To provide the participant with the basic statistical methods, techniques, and tools used in the collection, analysis, evaluation, interpretation, and presentation of data to aid in the decision-making processes of the federal government.
Learning Outcome: Upon successful completion of this course, the participant will be able to understand basic statistical measures and methods and the analysis, interpretation, and evaluation of statistical data, and define the role of statistics in management.
Instruction: Major topics covered in the course are graphical data presentation; measures of central tendency; frequency distributions; normal curves; statistical sampling and estimation; correlation and regression; and hypothesis testing. Methods of instruction include correspondence.
Credit Recommendation: In the upper division baccalaureate degree category, 3 semester hours in Business Management Statistics or Economics (3/92).

Principles and Applications of Value Engineering (8D-F27)

Location: Resident Campus, Rock Island, IL. On-site location.
Length: 40 hours (1 week).
Dates: May 1982-Present.
Objective: To provide the basic principles and techniques of value engineering.
Learning Outcome: Upon successful completion of this course, the participant will be able to find innovative alternatives to current functions; evaluate functionality, cost, and worth; understand the impact of finishes, tolerances, materials, and processes on cost; explain where and how value engineering can be applied; organize a value engineering study; establish a value engineering program; and estimate costs for proposed changes to parts and processes.
Instruction: Major topics covered in the course are introduction to value engineering; creativity; value engineering methodology; cost estimating and value comparisons; applications of value engineering; information sources; value engineering studies and change proposal; value engineering in contracts; requirements for value engineering; and value engineering project. Methods of instruction include lecture, practical exercises, and examinations.
Credit Recommendation: In the upper division baccalaureate degree category, 3 semester hours in Principles of Value Engineering (3/92).

Problem Solving Techniques for Quality Improvement (AMEC 197)

Location: Resident; on-site.
Length: 24 hours (3 days).
Dates: September 1991-Present.
Objective: To provide students with methods and techniques of problem solving applicable to work processes and continuous quality improvement.
Learning Outcome: Upon successful completion of this course, the student will be able to understand the need and role of technical problem analysis and solution for continuous improvement; identify opportunities for improvement; select appropriate

techniques for each; use Pareto, histograms, and scattergrams; and understand basic statistical process control.

Instruction: Major topics covered in the course are concepts of continuous improvement; cause and effect analysis and brainstorming; variation, frequency distributions and charts; calculation of basic sample statistics; introduction to statistical process control; process analysis and flow charting. Methods of instruction include lecture, case studies, and examinations.

Credit Recommendation: In the upper division baccalaureate degree category, 2 semester hours in Quality Management (3/92).

Reliability and Maintainability Testing (8A-F27)

Location: Resident; on-site.

Length: 80 hours (2 weeks).

Dates: December 1982-Present.

Objective: To provide students with a working knowledge of applied statistical methods used to assure R&M of products based on DOD standard tests.

Learning Outcome: Upon successful completion of this course, the student will be able to describe importance of R&M testing and methods selection; describe and apply classical measures of probability and descriptive statistics; understand and apply discrete and continuous probability distribution models; perform goodness-of-fit tests; compute single-and double-sided confidence statements; discuss nonparametric inspection by attributes; and apply stratified sampling techniques and failure simulation methods.

Instruction: Major topics covered in the course are review of basic probability and applied statistics; hypothesis testing and parameter estimation; tests for underlying distribution; exponential distribution reliability testing; non-exponential R&M testing; and nonparametric R&M testing. Methods of instruction include lecture, practical exercises, and examinations.

Credit Recommendation: In the upper division baccalaureate degree or in the graduate degree category, 4 semester hours in Reliability Theory and Techniques (3/92). **NOTE:** Based upon student having bachelor's degree.

Statistical Process Control (8D-F44)

Location: Resident; on-site.

Length: 40 hours (1 week).

Dates: March 1986-Present.

Objective: To provide students with a working knowledge on development, application, interpretation, and evaluation of statistical process control methods and techniques.

Learning Outcome: Upon successful completion of this course, the student will be able to understand the fundamental concepts of variability and capability; construct a control chart by calculating the centerline and limits; apply basic techniques of variables control; and analyze and evaluate process performance.

Instruction: Major topics covered in the course are need and objectives of SPC; frequency distributions and histograms; normal curve and estimation; sampling distribution and data collection; sources of variation and types of charts; and calculation of control chart limits. Methods of instruction include lecture, practical exercises, and examinations.

Credit Recommendation: In the upper division baccalaureate degree category, 2 semester hours in Statistical Process Control (3/92).

Statistical Process Control for Short Runs (AMEC-215)

Location: Resident; on-site.

Length: 40 hours (1 week).

Dates: January 1991-Present.

Objective: To provide students with a working knowledge of SPC application to low volume, job shop production processes.

Learning Outcome: Upon successful completion of this course, the student will be able to review basic concepts of SPC; define short run production; identify differences and similarities with standard SPC methodology; and modify standards and procedures to accommodate short runs.

Instruction: Major topics covered in the course are X-bar and R-charts; normal distribution; nominal, moving, and adjusted limits; and pre-control techniques. Methods of instruction include lecture, exercises, and examinations.

Credit Recommendation: In the upper division baccalaureate degree category, 1 semester hour in Statistical Process Control (3/92).

Statistical Quality Control (8D-F23)

Location: Resident; on-site.

Length: 80 hours (2 weeks).

Dates: February 1983-Present.

Objective: To provide students with a working knowledge of basic statistical techniques to evaluate process control and acceptance sampling plans.

Learning Outcome: Upon successful completion of this course, the student will be able to apply fundamentals of probability to quality acceptance inspection; compute and interpret statistical estimates; apply basic techniques of statistical process control for variables inspection and for attributes inspection; and identify and apply sampling inspection methods by attributes and by variables.

Instruction: Major topics covered in the course are statistical and probabilistic concepts; quality control methods; process control techniques; process capability analysis; and selection and evaluation of acceptance sampling plans. Methods of instruction include lecture, practical exercises, and examinations.

Credit Recommendation: In the upper division baccalaureate degree category, 3 semester hours in Statistical Quality Control (3/92).

Technical Data Package Development/Preparation (AMEC-13)

Location: Resident Campus, Rock Island, IL; on-site at various locations.

Length: 80 hours (2 weeks).

Dates: June 1984-Present.

Objective: To provide a detailed explanation and description of the requirements and responsibilities for the development and preparation of technical data packages used for procurement and production.

Learning Outcome: Upon successful completion of this course, the participant will be able to prepare a complete data package for procurement or production; determine the appropriate quality, reliability, and maintainability requirements; determine the adequacy of the technical data for competitive procurement; determine criteria for selection of contractors and vendors; and plan the steps necessary for assembling the technical data.

Instruction: Major topics covered in the course are introduction to technical data package development; acquisition of the technical data package; preparation of the technical data package; quality assurance provisions; review and proofing of the technical data package; maintenance and improvement of the technical data package; and transmission of the technical data package. Methods of instruction include lecture, practical exercises, demonstrations, and examinations.

Credit Recommendation: In the graduate degree category, 3 semester hours in Management of Technical Procurement (3/92).

New Horizons Computer Learning Centers, Inc.

New Horizons Computer Learning Centers Inc., headquartered in Santa Ana, California, is the largest worldwide Computer Training IntegratorSM, providing customer-focused computer training choices to meet the needs of over 1.5 million students each year. Founded in 1982, New Horizons is both an operator and franchisor of computer learning centers that offer top-quality computer training in multiple delivery methods and formats. With more than 200 centers in 24 countries, 1,100 instructors and 375,000 classes a year, New Horizons trains more people than any other computer training company.

New Horizons is committed to helping businesses develop a more skilled and productive workforce—one that gets the most out of its computers, and keeps pace with the rapid and complex technological changes taking place in operating systems and software development. New Horizons provides customers with integrated cost-effective solutions that are grounded in the uncompromising quality of training delivered by knowledgeable and enthusiastic instructors. By integrating cutting-edge technology and customized courseware with flexible learning options, corporate customers and individuals receive the most comprehensive learning experience.

A telephone help desk is offered 24-hours-a-day, 365-days-a-year to provide free post-class support to each New Horizon's student. Flexible schedules for open enrollment; on-site training; private, evening, and weekend classes; give customers more options to tailor their training needs. New Horizons also offers an unconditional Learning Guarantee with free repeat class privileges for up to six months. Pre- and post-assessment testing determines the skill set of the student and the level of qualification - beginner, intermediate, or advanced - to ensure that each student begins at the right level and learns the content of the course.

The New Horizon's Web site (www.newhorizons.com) provides complete course schedules, news, fast facts, and online registration for more than 125,000 classes, as well as course outlines, technical training, and certification updates - all in an easy-to-navigate format.

As the world's largest Computer Training Integrator, New Horizons Computer Learning Centers provides customer-focused computer training choices in multiple formats and delivery methods, offering businesses and individuals top-quality computer training that is tailored to meet their specific needs - when and how they want it.

New Horizon's corporate headquarters is in Santa Ana, California, with offices in Calgary, AB; Birmingham, Huntsville, and Mobile, AL; Tempe and Tucson, AZ; Sherwood (Little Rock), AR; Vancouver, BC; Bakersfield, Burbank, Chico, Colton, Fairfield, Irvine, Culver City (Los Angeles), Redding, Rosamond, Sacra-mento, San Diego, San Francisco, San Jose, Santa Ana, Santa Barbara, Stockton, Walnut Creek, and Westlake Village (Thousand Oaks), CA; Aurora, Boulder, Colorado Springs, Denver, and Wheat Ridge (Golden), CO; Trumbull (Fairfield County) and Windsor (Hartford), CT; Clearwater (Tampa Bay), Ft. Lauderdale, Jacksonville, Miami, Maitland (Orlando), and Pensacola, FL; Atlanta and Marietta, GA; Boise, ID; Chicago, IL; Carmel (Indianapolis), IN; Hiawatha (Cedar Rapids) and Clive (Des Moines), IA; Wichita, KS; Lexington and Louisville, KY; Baton Rouge, Lafayette, Metairie (New Orleans), and Shreveport, LA; Baltimore and Bethesda, MD; Boston, Burlington, and Westborough, MA; Detroit, East Lansing, Grand Rapids, Livonia, Southfield, and Troy, MI; Brooklyn Center, Minneapolis, Richfield, and St. Paul, MN; Ridgeland (Biloxi), and Ridgeland (Jackson), MS; Overland Park (Kansas City) and St. Louis, MO; Lincoln, and Omaha, NE; Concord, and Nashua, NH; Iselin and Voorhees, NJ; Albuquer-que and Santa Fe, NM; Commack (Long Island), New York, and Pittsford (Roch-ester), NY; Charlotte, Greensboro, and Raleigh-Durham, NC; Cincinnati, Dublin (Columbus), Fairborn (Dayton), and Independence (Cleveland), OH; Oklahoma City and Tulsa, OK; Toronto, ON; Beaverton (Portland), Eugene, Medford, and Salem, OR; Bethlehem (Allentown), Cannonsburgh (Pittsburgh), and King of Prussia (Phil-=adelphia), PA; Montreal, PQ; Cranston (Providence), RI; Columbia and Greenville, SC; Chattanooga, Jackson, Memphis, and Nashville, TN; Austin, Corpus Christi, Dallas, Fort Worth, Houston, Pharr, and San Antonio, TX; Salt Lake City, UT; McLean, VA (Washington DC) and Richmond, VA; Seattle, Spokane, and Vancouver, WA; Washington DC; and Appleton (Green Bay), Madison, Sheboygan, and Wauwatosa (Milwaukee), WI.

Source of official student records: Registry of Credit Recommendations, American Council on Education, One Dupont Circle, Washington, DC 20036-1193.

Additional information about the courses: College Credit Recommendation Service, American Council on Education, One Dupont Circle, Washington, DC 20036-1193.

Advanced Access 2.0

Location: Various sites in the United States.

Length: 7 hours (1 day).

Dates: July 1994-Present.

Objective: To provide advanced knowledge of Access 2.0 features needed to create macros and use modules.

Learning Outcome: Upon successful completion of this course, the student will be able to run a macro; create a macro; use the DoMenuItem action; add a macro shortcut; make a macro button; construct decision-making macros; run a macro from a macro; explore the module window; use Access basic help; use the immediate window; edit module syntax; set a breakpoint; use a module function in a form; write user-defined functions; use if-then-else statements; use select case-end select statements; use for-next loops; use do-while loop statements; use access SQL statements; use the menu builder; run a macro from an event; and add a graph to a form.

Instruction: Major topics covered in the course advanced macros, Access modules, writing in Access basic, and power Access techniques. Methods of instruction include lecture, discussion, classroom exercises, observations, self-check module review, and final examination.

Credit Recommendation: In the lower division baccalaureate/associate degree category, 1 semester hour in Microcomputer Applications (8/97). **NOTE:** Student must successful complete both Intermediate Access and Advanced Access to receive credit for this course. Students receiving credit for Access 2.0 courses are ineligible to receive credit for Access 7.0 or Access 97 courses.

Advanced Access 7.0

Location: Various sites in the United States.

Length: 7 hours (1 day).

Dates: February 1996-Present.

Objective: To provide advanced knowledge of Access 7.0 features needed to create macros and use modules.

Learning Outcome: Upon successful completion of this course, the student will be able to run a macro; create a macro; create autokey macros; use the domenuitem action; reference object properties; create decision-making macros; run macros at startup; synchronize forms to same record; run macros in macros; assign macros to events; create a macro button; explore access SQL; write a SQL statement; assign SQL statements to objects; use the menu builder; create a crosstab query; use charts; explore the module windows; use the debug window; edit Visual Basic code; write user-defined functions; use if-then-else statements; use select case...end select statements; and use a module function in a form.

Instruction: Major topics covered in the course are macros, control extensions, power accessing techniques, and accessing modules. Methods of instruction include lecture, discussion, classroom exercises, observations, self-check module review, and final examination.

Credit Recommendation: In the lower division baccalaureate/associate degree category, 1 semester hour in Microcomputer Applications (8/97). **NOTE:** Student must successful complete both Intermediate Access and Advanced Access to receive credit for this course. Students receiving credit for Access 7.0 courses are ineligible to receive credit for Access 2.0 or Access 97 courses.

Advanced Access 97 for Windows 95

Location: Various sites in the United States.

Length: 7 hours (1 day).

Dates: January 1997-Present.

Objective: To provide advanced knowledge of Access 97 for Windows 95 features needed to create macros and modules.

Learning Outcome: Upon successful completion of this course, the student will be able to run a macro; create a macro; create autokey macros; use the runcommand action; reference object properties; create decision-making macros; run macros at startup; synchronize forms to same record; run macros in macros; assign macros to events; create a macro button; explore access SQL; write a SQL statement; assign SQL statements to objects; create a crosstab query; use charts; explore the module window; use the debug window; edit Visual Basic code; write user-defined functions; use if-then-else statements; use select case...end select statements; and use a module function in a form.

Instruction: Major topics covered in the course are how to use macros, control extensions, power Access techniques, and accessing modules. Methods of instruction include lecture, discussion, classroom exercises, observations, self-check module review, and final examination.

Credit Recommendation: In the lower division baccalaureate/associate degree category, 1 semester hour in Microcomputer Applications (8/97). **NOTE:** Student must successful complete both Intermediate Access and Advanced Access to receive credit for this course. Students receiving credit for Access 97 courses are ineligible to receive credit for Access 2.0 or Access 7.0 courses.

Advanced Corel WordPerfect 7.0 for Windows 95

Location: Various sites in the United States.

Length: 7 hours (1 day).

Dates: August 1996-Present.

Objective: To provide advanced level skills training in WordPerfect 7.0 including styles, graphics, formulas, and macros.

Learning Outcome: Upon successful completion of this course, the student will be able to create and apply a character style; create a paragraph style; apply and redefine styles; work with outlines; add drop caps; use textart; create a text box; insert an image; wrap text around an image; draw in WordPerfect; create a watermark; import a spreadsheet from QuattroPro; format a spreadsheet; calculate in a table; chart a table; create a quickmacro; record a macro; edit a macro; and create a template.

Instruction: Major topics covered in the course are using styles, introduction to graphics, tables and formulas, and macros and templates. Methods of instruction include lecture, discussion, classroom exercises, observations, self-check module review, and final examination.

Credit Recommendation: In the lower division baccalaureate/associate degree category, 1 semester hour in Microcomputer Applications (8/97). **NOTE:** Students must successfully complete Beginning and Intermediate WordPerfect 7.0 for Windows 95, Beginning and Advanced WordPerfect 7.0 for Windows 95, or Intermediate and Advanced WordPerfect 7.0 for Windows 95 to receive this credit recommendation. Students receiving credit for WordPerfect 7.0 courses are ineligible to receive credit for WordPerfect 6.1 courses.

Advanced Excel 5.0

Location: Various sites in the United States.

Length: 7 hours (1 day).

Dates: February 1994-Present.

Objective: To provide more sophisticated knowledge of Excel 5.0 spreadsheet skills with an emphasis on built-in functions, tables, subroutines, and other advanced features.

Learning Outcome: Upon successful completion of this course, the student will be able to employ trend analysis; use Goal Seek; determine frequency distribution; use the scenario manager; audit a spreadsheet; use data validation; use the if function; nest if functions; combine logical functions; use HLOOKUP; use VLOOKUP; create an one-input table; create a two-input table; create a function procedure; use an application object; control procedure flow; write a subroutine; create a celltip; create a custom menu; create a custom toolbar; add custom tools; modify the environment; use workgroup features; and create an HTML spreadsheet.

Instruction: Major topics covered in the course are the use of If logic, advanced data management, user-define functions and customization, lookup and data tables, array functions and conditional functions, and create advanced macros. Methods of instruction include lecture, discussion, classroom exercises, observations, self-check module review, and final examination.

Credit Recommendation: In the lower division baccalaureate/associate degree category, 1 semester hour in Microcomputer Applications (8/97). **NOTE:** Student must successfully complete two or the following three: Beginning Excel 5.0, Intermediate Excel 5.0, and/or Advanced Excel 5.0. Students receiving credit for Excel 5.0 courses are ineligible to receive credit for Excel 7.0 and Excel 97 courses.

Advanced Excel 7.0

Location: Various sites in the United States.

Length: 7 hours (1 day).

Dates: August 1995-Present.

Objective: To provide more sophisticated Excel 7.0 spreadsheet skills with an emphasis on built-in functions, tables, subroutines, and other advanced features.

Learning Outcome: Upon successful completion of this course, the student will be able to employ trend analysis; use Goal Seek; determine frequency distribution; use the scenario manager; use the if function; nest if functions; combine logical functions; use HLOOKUP; use VLOOKUP; create an one-input table; create a two-input table; create a function procedure; use an application object; control procedure flow; write a subroutine; create a celltip; add menu options; create a custom toolbar; add custom tools; and modify the environment.

Instruction: Major topics covered in the course are the use of If logic, advanced data management, user-defined functions and customization, using if logic, advanced data management, user-defined functions, and customizing Excel. Methods of include lecture, discussion, classroom exercises, observations, self-check module review, and final examination.

Credit Recommendation: In the lower division baccalaureate/associate degree category, 1 semester hour in Microcomputer Applications (8/97). **NOTE:** Student must successfully complete two or the following three: Beginning Excel 7.0, Intermediate Excel 7.0, and/or Advanced Excel 7.0. Students receiving credit for Excel 7.0 courses are ineligible to receive credit for Excel 5.0 and Excel 97 courses.

Advanced Excel 97 for Windows 95

Location: Various sites in the United States.

Length: 7 hours (1 day).

Dates: December 1996-Present.

Objective: To provide more sophisticated Excel 97 spreadsheet skills with an emphasis on built-in functions, tables, subroutines, and other advanced features.

Learning Outcome: Upon successful completion of this course, the student will be able to employ trend analysis; use Goal Seek; determine frequency distribution; use scenario manager; audit a spreadsheet; use data validation; use the if function; nest if functions; combine logical functions; use HLOOKUP; use VLOOKUP; create an one-input table; create a two-input table; create a function procedure; use an application object; control procedure flow; write a subroutine; create a celltip; create a custom menu; create a custom toolbar; add custom tools; modify the environment; use workgroup features; and create an html spreadsheet.

Instruction: Major topics covered in the course are the use of If logic, advanced data management, user-defined functions, and customization. Methods of instruction include lecture, discussion, classroom exercises, observations, self-check module review, and final examination.

Credit Recommendation: In the lower division baccalaureate/associate degree category, 1 semester hour in Microcomputer Applications (8/97). **NOTE:** Student must successfully complete two or the following three: Beginning Excel 97 for Windows 95, Intermediate Excel 97 for Windows 95, and/or Advanced Excel 97 for Windows 95. Students receiving credit for Excel 97 courses are ineligible to receive credit for Excel 5.0 and Excel 7.0 courses.

Advanced FrontPage 97 for Windows 95

Location: Various sites in the United States.

Length: 7 hours (1 day).

Dates: January 1997-Present.

Objective: To provide sophisticated knowledge of the FrontPage 97 for Windows 95 application's expertise web page authoring tools skills needed to create forms, webbots, and other advanced resource tools.

Learning Outcome: Upon successful completion of this course, the student will be able to use the frames wizard to create a frame set; set a default target frame; use target frames and image maps; put frame sets inside a frame; display links in different frames; use a form wizard to create a form; add features to a form; add boxes and buttons; use forms with frames and tables; explore form handlers; create interactive pages; create a search form; create a discussion group; assign other webbot components; configure editors; fine tune pages with text editors; insert a script; use the script wizard; and publish your web.

Instruction: Major topics covered in the course are frames, creating forms, webbots, and advanced resource use. Methods of instruction include lecture, discussion, classroom exercises, observations, self-check module review, and final examination.

Credit Recommendation: In the lower division baccalaureate/associate degree category, 1 semester hour in Microcomputer Applications (8/97). **NOTE:** Student must successfully complete two or the following three: Beginning FrontPage 97 for Windows 95, Intermediate FrontPage 97 for Windows 95, and/or Advanced FrontPage 97 for Windows 95.

Advanced Windows 95

Location: Various sites in the United States.

Length: 7 hours (1 day).

Dates: June 1995-Present.

Objective: To explore advanced Windows 95 operations including advanced files system operations and customize environment settings.

Learning Outcome: Upon successful completion of this course, the student will be able to use Scandisk; use Backup; modify the Recycle bin properties; use long filenames; create a user profile; optimize the taskbar; optimize the start menu; use the briefcase; use Disk Defragmenter; manage virtual memory; check system performance; use the command prompt; use a troubleshooter; explore the Registry Editor; create a startup disk; and troubleshoot startup.

Instruction: Major topics covered in the course are protecting data, customizing the Windows 95 interface, optimizing system performance, and troubleshooting startup and the registry. Methods of instruction include lecture, discussion, classroom exercises, self-check module review, and final examination.

Credit Recommendation: In the lower division baccalaureate/associate degree category, 1 semester hour in Microcomputer Applications (8/97). **NOTE:** Student must successfully complete two or the following three: Beginning, Intermediate, or Advanced Windows 95.

Advanced Word 6.0 for Windows 95

Location: Various sites in the United States.

Length: 7 hours (1 day).

Dates: January 1994-Present.

Objective: To provide advanced level skills training in Microsoft Word 6.0 including styles, graphics, formulas, and macros.

Learning Outcome: Upon successful completion of this course, the student will be able to create and apply a character style; create a paragraph style; apply styles; redefine a paragraph style; use the organizer; create an outline; define styles with outline mode; use the drawing toolbar; add a graphic; insert sophisticated headers and footers; use frames and captions; apply borders and shading; set drop caps; place a worksheet in a report; format a table; calculate in a table; chart a table; record a simple macro; use fill-in macros; edit a macro; and create a template.

Instruction: Major topics covered in the course are advanced editing tools, columns and tables, mail merging, and introduction to desktop publishing. Methods of instruction include lecture, discussion, classroom exercises, observations, self-check module review, and final examination.

Credit Recommendation: In the lower division baccalaureate/associate degree category, 1 semester hour in Microcomputer Applications (8/97). **NOTE:** Student must successfully complete two or the following three: Beginning, Intermediate, or Advanced Word 6.0 for Windows 95. Students receiving credit for Word 6.0

courses are ineligible to receive credit for Word 97 and Word 7.0 courses.

Advanced Word 7.0

Location: Various sites in the United States.

Length: 7 hours (1 day).

Dates: October 1995-Present.

Objective: To provide advanced level skills training in Microsoft Word 7.0 including styles, graphics, formulas, and macros.

Learning Outcome: Upon successful completion of this course, the student will be able to create and apply a character style; create a paragraph style; apply and redefine styles; work with outlines; use the organizer; section a document; add drop caps; use the drawing toolbar; insert a picture; use WordArt; add frames and captions; create a watermark; create a spreadsheet in Excel; link a spreadsheet; import and format a spreadsheet; calculate in a table; chart a table; record a macro; create a template; attach a fill-in macro; and edit a macro.

Instruction: Major topics covered in the course are styles, graphics, advanced table features, macros, using styles, sections and graphics, tables and formulas, and macros and templates. Methods of instruction include lecture, discussion, classroom exercises, observations, self-check module review, and final examination.

Credit Recommendation: In the lower division baccalaureate/associate degree category, 1 semester hour in Microcomputer Applications (8/97). **NOTE:** Student must successfully complete two or the following three: Beginning, Intermediate, or Advanced Word 7.0. Students receiving credit for Word 7.0 courses are ineligible to receive credit for Word 97 and Word 6.0 courses.

Advanced Word 97 for Windows 95

Location: Various sites in the United States.

Length: 7 hours (1 day).

Dates: January 1997-Present.

Objective: To provide advanced level skills training in Microsoft Word 97 including styles, graphics, formulas, and macros.

Learning Outcome: Upon successful completion of this course, the student will be able to create and apply a character style; create a paragraph style; apply and redefine styles; work with outlines; use the organizer; create a master document; route documents; insert comments and track changes to a document; section a document; add drop caps; use the drawing toolbar; insert a picture; use WordArt; create a watermark; create a hyperlink; create a spreadsheet in Excel; link a spreadsheet; import and format a spreadsheet; calculate in a table; chart a table; create a form; record a macro; create a template; attach a fill-in macro; and edit a macro.

Instruction: Major topics covered in the course are using styles, workgroup editing, sections and graphics, tables and formulas, and macros and templates. Methods of instruction include lecture, discussion, classroom exercises, observations, self-check module review, and final examination.

Credit Recommendation: In the lower division baccalaureate/associate degree category, 1 semester hour in Microcomputer Applications (8/97). **NOTE:** Student must successfully complete two or the following three: Beginning, Intermediate, or Advanced Word 97 for Windows 95. Students receiving credit for Word 97 courses are ineligible to receive credit for Word 6.0 and Word 7.0 courses.

Advanced WordPerfect 6.1 for Windows

Location: Various sites in the United States.

Length: 7 hours (1 day).

Dates: March 1995-Present.

Objective: To provide advanced level skills training in WordPerfect 6.1 including styles, graphics, formulas, and macros.

Learning Outcome: Upon successful completion of this course, the student will be able to create a apply a character style; create a paragraph style; apply and redefine a paragraph style; copy styles between documents; work with outlines; use WordPerfect draw; add drop caps; add graphics; create a text box; use textart; create a watermark; import a spreadsheet; apply advanced formatting to a table; calculate in a table; chart a table; create a template; set initial codes; edit a template; record a simple macro; and assign a macro to a button.

Instruction: Major topics covered in the course are WordPerfect styles, introduction to graphics, tables and formats, and macros and templates. Methods of instruction include lecture, discussion, classroom exercises, observations, self-check module review, and final examination.

Credit Recommendation: In the lower division baccalaureate/associate degree category, 1 semester hour in Microcomputer Applications (8/97). **NOTE:** Students must successfully complete Beginning and Intermediate WordPerfect 6.1 for Windows, Beginning and Advanced WordPerfect 6.1 for Windows, or Intermediate and Advanced WordPerfect 6.1 for Windows to receive this credit recommendation. Students receiving credit for WordPerfect 6.1 courses are ineligible to receive credit for WordPerfect 7.0 courses.

Beginning Access 2.0

Location: Various sites in the United States.

Length: 14 hours (2 days).

Dates: May 1994-Present.

Objective: To provide basic knowledge of Access 2.0 features needed to create and manage databases.

Learning Outcome: Upon successful completion of this course, the student will be able to navigate the screen; view operating modes; access help; use cue cards; use a table wizard; design a table; enter data; modify the datasheet; edit field attributes; filter/sort; set value limits; use default values; create required fields; change format properties; use input masks; use a form wizard; design a form; modify controls; use calculated fields; create a select query; sort data; use multiple criteria: ands; use multiple criteria: ors; create a calculation query; use an action query; use a query wizard; export to Excel; import an Excel worksheet; export to a text file; import to a text file; import a Foxpro file; import an Access object; normalize data; establish simple relationships; create a complex relational database; use the relationships window; use the report wizards; lay out a report; use calculated fields; and create mailing labels.

Instruction: Major topics covered in the course are Access relational database concepts, report creation, providing a foundation for database management, accessing Access, table design, fields and formats, form design, searching and sorting, import and export data, data relations, and report creation. Methods of instruction include lecture, discussion, classroom exercises, observations, self-check module review, and final examination.

Credit Recommendation: In the lower division baccalaureate/associate degree category, 1 semester hour in Microcomputer Applications (8/97). **NOTE:** Students receiving credit for Access 2.0 courses are ineligible to receive credit for Access 97 or Access 7.0 courses.

Beginning Access 7.0

Location: Various sites in the United States.

Length: 14 hours (2 days).
Dates: October 1995-Present.
Objective: To provide basic knowledge of Access 7.0 features needed to create and manage databases.
Learning Outcome: Upon successful completion of this course, the student will be able to navigate the screen; get on-line help; view operating modes; understand object properties; create a database file; use a table wizard; design a table; enter and delete data; format the datasheet; filter and sort tables; edit field attributes; set value limits; use default values; create required fields; change format properties; use input masks; explore forms; use a form wizard; design a form; modify display attributes; modify form controls; change tab order; use calculated fields; create a select query; sort data; use multiple criteria: ands/ors; create a calculation query; use an action query; use a query wizard; create a parameter query; export to Excel; import an Excel worksheet; export to a text file; import to a text file; import a Paradox file; import an Access object; use analyzing tools; normalize data; and establish simple relationships.
Instruction: Major topics covered in the course are relational database concepts, providing a foundation for database management, accessing Access, table design, fields and formats, form design, searching and sorting, import and export data, data relations, and report creation. Methods of instruction include lecture, discussion, classroom exercises, observations, self-check module review, and final examination.
Credit Recommendation: In the lower division baccalaureate/associate degree category, 1 semester hour in Microcomputer Applications (8/97). **NOTE:** Students receiving credit for Access 7.0 courses are ineligible to receive credit for Access 97 or Access 2.0 courses.

Beginning Access 97 for Windows 95
Location: Various sites in the United States.
Length: 14 hours (2 days).
Dates: January 1997-Present.
Objective: To provide basic knowledge of the Access 97 for Windows 95 features needed to create and manage databases.
Learning Outcome: Upon successful completion of this course, the student will be able to navigate the screen; get on-line help; view operating modes; understand object properties; create a database file; use a table wizard; design a table; enter and delete data; format the datasheet; filter and sort tables; create hyperlinks; edit field attributes; set value limits; use default values; create required fields; change format properties; use input masks; explore forms; use a form wizard; design a form; modify display attributes; modify form controls; change tab order; use calculated fields; create a select query; sort data; use multiple criteria: ands/ors; create a calculation query; use an action query; use a query wizard; create a parameter query; export to Excel; import an Excel worksheet; export to a text file; import to a text file; import a Dbase file; and import an Access object.
Instruction: Major topics covered in the course are accessing Access, table design, fields and formats, form design, searching and sorting, import and export data, data relations, and report creation. Methods of instruction include lecture, discussion, classroom exercises, self-check module review, and final examination.
Credit Recommendation: In the lower division baccalaureate/associate degree category, 1 semester hour in Microcomputer Applications (8/97). **NOTE:** Students receiving credit for Access 97 courses are ineligible to receive credit for Access 2.0 or Access 7.0 courses.

Beginning Corel WordPerfect 7.0 for Windows 95
Location: Various sites in the United States.
Length: 7 hours (1 day).
Dates: June 1996-Present.
Objective: To provide beginning level skills training in WordPerfect 7.0 including fundamentals, creating, editing, and printing.
Learning Outcome: Upon successful completion of this course, the student will be able to create and save a document; tour the WordPerfect windows; select and navigate through text; work with multiple documents; get help; manage files; use spell-as-you-go; use quickcorrect; undo and redo actions; use built-in styles; use an expert; set up the page; shift text; format text; format paragraphs; use quickmenus; set tab stops; insert tab leaders; work with reveal codes; use the thesaurus; find and replace text; create headers and footers; check spelling and grammar; and preview and print a document.
Instruction: Major topics covered in the course are WordPerfect basics, automatic formatting, editing and formatting, and the final product. Methods of instruction include lecture, discussion, classroom exercises, observations, self-check module review, and final examination.
Credit Recommendation: In the lower division baccalaureate/associate degree category, 1 semester hour in Microcomputer Applications (8/97). **NOTE:** Students must successfully complete Beginning and Intermediate Corel WordPerfect 7.0 for Windows 95, Begin-ning and Advanced Corel WordPerfect 7.0 for Windows 95, or Intermediate and Advanced Corel WordPerfect 7.0 for Windows 95 to receive this credit recommendation. Students receiving credit for WordPerfect 7.0 courses are ineligible to receive credit for WordPerfect 6.1 courses.

Beginning Excel 5.0
Location: Various sites in the United States.
Length: 7 hours (1 day).
Dates: October 1993-Present.
Objective: To explore the basic features of Excel 5.0 in order to create, modify, print worksheets, and create charts.
Learning Outcome: Upon successful completion of this course, the student will be able to navigate a workbook; explore the Excel menus; select multiple cells; create a spreadsheet; save a workbook; use the toolbars; edit the spreadsheet; use Help; write math statements; use the function Wizard; use Autosum; use the fill commands; create absolute references; format numbers; use Autoformat; use the drawing toolbar; check spelling; orient a printout; alter print margins; center a printout; create headers and footers; scale the print area; print the document; use Chartwizard; insert a chart sheet; change chart types; modify a chart; and rotate a chart.
Instruction: Major topics covered in the course Excel basics, formulas and formats, preview and print, and charts. Methods of instruction include lecture, discussion, classroom exercises, observations, self-check module review, and final examination.
Credit Recommendation: In the lower division baccalaureate/associate degree category, 1 semester hour in Microcomputer Applications (8/97). **NOTE:** Student must successfully complete two or the following three: Beginning Excel 5.0, Intermediate Excel 5.0, and/or Advanced Excel 5.0. Students receiving credit for Excel 5.0 courses are ineligible to receive credit for Excel 97 and Excel 7.0 courses.

Beginning Excel 7.0
Location: Various sites in the United States.
Length: 7 hours (1 day).
Dates: August 1995-Present.

Objective: To explore the basic features of Excel 7.0 in order to create, modify, print worksheets, and create charts.

Learning Outcome: Upon successful completion of this course, the student will be able to navigate Excel; explore the menus; select multiple cells; create and save a spreadsheet; use the toolbars; edit the spreadsheet; use a template; use help; create a formula; use the function wizard; use autosum; use the fill commands; create absolute references; format values; use autoformat; check spelling; orient the document; adjust the margins; center the printout; create headers and footers; scale the print area; print the document; use chartwizard; insert a chart sheet; explore chart types; modify a chart; rotate a chart; create a pie chart; and create a map.

Instruction: Major topics covered in the course are using the Excel screen, mouse controls, various worksheet creation and formatting commands, file saving, file retrieving, printing and graphics, Excel basics, formulas and formats, preview and print, and charts and maps. Methods of instruction include lecture, discussion, classroom exercises, observations, self-check module review, and final examination.

Credit Recommendation: In the lower division baccalaureate/associate degree category, 1 semester hour in Microcomputer Applications (8/97). **NOTE:** Student must successfully complete two or the following three: Beginning Excel 7.0, Intermediate Excel 7.0, and/or Advanced Excel 7.0. Students receiving credit for Excel 7.0 courses are ineligible to receive credit for Excel 97 and Excel 5.0 courses.

Beginning Excel 97 for Windows 95

Location: Various sites in the United States.

Length: 7 hours (1 day).

Dates: December 1996-Present.

Objective: To explore the basic features of Excel 97 in order to create, modify, print worksheets, and create charts.

Learning Outcome: Upon successful completion of this course, the student will be able to navigate the screen; get on-line help; view operating modes; understand object properties; create a database file; use a table wizard; design a table; enter and delete data; format the datasheet; filter and sort tables; edit field attributes; set value limits; use default values; create required fields; change format properties; use input masks; explore forms; use a form wizard; design a form; modify display attributes; modify form controls; change tab order; use calculated fields; create a select query; sort data; use multiple criteria: ands/ors; create a calculation query; use an action query; use a query wizard; create a parameter query; export to Excel; import an Excel worksheet; export to a text file; import to a text file; import a paradox file; import an access object; use analyzing tools; normalize data; establish simple relationships; create a complex relational database; use the relationships windows; explore referential integrity; use the reports wizard; lay out a report; modify display attributes; use calculated fields; print a report; and create mailing labels.

Instruction: Major topics covered in the course are Excel basics, formulas and formats, preview and print, and charts and maps. Methods of instruction include lecture, discussion, classroom exercises, observations, self-check module review, and final examination.

Credit Recommendation: In the lower division baccalaureate/associate degree category, 1 semester hour in Microcomputer Applications (8/97). **NOTE:** Student must successfully complete two or the following three: Beginning Excel 97 for Windows 95, Intermediate Excel 97 for Windows 95, and/or Advanced Excel 97 for Windows 95. Students receiving credit for Excel 97 courses are ineligible to receive credit for Excel 7.0 and Excel 5.0 courses.

Beginning FrontPage 97 for Windows 95

Location: Various sites in the United States.

Length: 7 hours (1 day).

Dates: September 1996-Present.

Objective: To provide basic knowledge of the FrontPage 97 for Windows 95 application's foundation web page authoring tools skills needed to create and manage a web page.

Learning Outcome: Upon successful completion of this course, the student will be able to use a page template; create a web document; use spell check and thesaurus; view and edit HTML code; create a bookmark; create a hyperlink to a new page; create an interdocument hyperlink; create an external hyperlink; create an image hyperlink; verify hyperlinks; create a new web; import pages to a web; add a web to a web; export web pages; delegate web design tasks; create headings and align text; insert special characters and text files; set font styles and formats; define background images; insert inline graphics; and define graphic alternatives.

Instruction: Major topics covered in the course are creating and using hyperlinks, web creation and management, beginning text, and graphic use. Methods of instruction include lecture, discussion, classroom exercises, observations, self-check module review, and final examination.

Credit Recommendation: In the lower division baccalaureate/associate degree category, 1 semester hour in Microcomputer Applications (8/97). **NOTE:** Student must successfully complete two or the following three: Beginning FrontPage 97 for Windows 95, Intermediate FrontPage 97 for Windows 95, and/or Advanced FrontPage 97 for Windows 95.

Beginning PowerPoint 4.0

Location: Various sites in the United States.

Length: 7 hours (1 day).

Dates: April 1994-Present.

Objective: To explore the basic features of PowerPoint 4.0 in order to create presentations using graphics and formatted text.

Learning Outcome: Upon successful completion of this course, the student will be able to plan a presentation; use menus; use toolbars; work with a wizard; explore the elements of a slide; change views; save and open a file; get help; use the drawing tools; add special effects to objects; insert label text; insert clip art; insert outline text; format text; insert tabs and indents; find and replace; spell check; and run a slide show.

Instruction: Major topics covered in the course are presentation basics, presentation and file management, drawing and graphics, formatting text, and checking the final presentation. Methods of instruction include lecture, discussion, classroom exercises, self-check module review, and final examination.

Credit Recommendation: In the lower division baccalaureate/associate degree category, 1 semester hour in Microcomputer Applications (8/97). **NOTE:** Student must successfully complete both Beginning and Intermediate PowerPoint 4.0 to receive this credit recommendation. Students receiving credit for PowerPoint 4.0 courses are ineligible to receive credit for PowerPoint 7.0 and PowerPoint 97 courses.

Beginning PowerPoint 7.0

Location: Various sites in the United States.

Length: 7 hours (1 day).

Dates: August 1995-Present.

Objective: To explore the basic features of PowerPoint 7.0 in order to create presentations using graphics and formatted text.

Learning Outcome: Upon successful completion of this course, the student will be able to use the autocontent wizard; explore PowerPoint; get help; use the slide sorter view; create a new slide show; edit slides; use the outline view; use AutoCorrect; create an organization chart; use the drawing tools; change object attributes; insert and modify clip art; create a slide master; spell check; use the style checker; add transitions to a slide show; rehearse a slide show; find and replace text; and create and print speaker's notes.

Instruction: Major topics covered in the course are PowerPoint basics, working with slides, drawing and graphics, and putting the finishing touches on a presentation. Methods of instruction include lecture, discussion, classroom exercises, self-check module review, and final examination.

Credit Recommendation: In the lower division baccalaureate/associate degree category, 1 semester hour in Microcomputer Applications (8/97). **NOTE:** Student must successfully complete both Beginning and Intermediate PowerPoint 7.0 to receive this credit recommendation. Students receiving credit for PowerPoint 7.0 courses are ineligible to receive credit for PowerPoint 97 and PowerPoint 4.0 courses.

Beginning PowerPoint 97 for Windows 95

Location: Various sites in the United States.

Length: 7 hours (1 day).

Dates: December 1996-Present.

Objective: To explore the basic features of PowerPoint 97 in order to create presentations using graphics and formatted text.

Learning Outcome: Upon successful completion of this course, the student will be able to use the autocontent wizard; explore PowerPoint; get help; use the slide sorter view; create a new slide show; edit slides; use the outline view; use AutoCorrect; create an organization chart; use the drawing tools; change object attributes; insert and modify clip art; create a slide master; spell check; use the style checker; add transitions to a slide show; rehearse a slide show; find and replace text; create and print speaker's notes; and export and print.

Instruction: Major topics covered in the course are PowerPoint basics, work with slides, drawing and graphics, and the finishing touches. Methods of instruction include lecture, discussion, classroom exercises, self-check module review, and final examination.

Credit Recommendation: In the lower division baccalaureate/associate degree category, 1 semester hour in Microcomputer Applications (8/97). **NOTE:** Student must successfully complete both Beginning and Intermediate PowerPoint 97 for Windows 95 to receive this credit recommendation. Students receiving credit for PowerPoint 97 courses are ineligible to receive credit for PowerPoint 7.0 and PowerPoint 4.0 courses.

Beginning Project 4.0

Location: Various sites in the United States.

Length: 14 hours (2 days).

Dates: February 1995-Present.

Objective: To explore the beginning features of Project 4.0 in order to manage a project including scheduling, charting, and resource management.

Learning Outcome: Upon successful completion of this course, the student will be able to explore the Project 4.0 environment; use help; enter data; set the standard calendar; set and remove constraints; create and assign a resource; set the start date; set working hours; enter and link tasks; designate milestones; allocate resources; use the resource graph; create a report; add a task; level resources; define summary tasks; use multiple resource units; create a baseline; set actual dates; update the project; print the project; modify the master project; sort resources; link resources; modify imported calendar options; delay a resource assignment; split a resource assignment; link tasks; save the workspace; customize the gantt chart; create a bar style; add menu options; create a custom toolbar; use the organizer; graph the data; anchor the object; update the object; and add a text box.

Instruction: Major topics covered in the course are planning tasks, allocating resources, costing, tracking and reporting using Gantt charts, Pert charts, reports, subprojects, introduction to Project, building a project schedule, managing tasks and resources, baselines, actual dates, printing, managing a master project, managing a subproject, customizing Microsoft Project, and drawing and linking objects. Methods of instruction include lecture, discussion, classroom exercises, self-check module review, and final examination.

Credit Recommendation: In the lower division baccalaureate/associate degree category, 1 semester hour in Microcomputer Applications (8/97). **NOTE:** Students receiving credit for Beginning Project 4.0 are ineligible to receive credit for Beginning Project 4.1.

Beginning Project 4.1

Location: Various sites in the United States.

Length: 14 hours (2 days).

Dates: March 1996-Present.

Objective: To explore the beginning features of Project 4.1 in order to manage a project including scheduling, charting, and resource management.

Learning Outcome: Upon successful completion of this course, the student will be able to explore the Project 4.1 environment; explore the views; use help; set the standard calendar; change default settings; enter tasks; edit tasks; organize tasks; outline tasks; set the project start date; set durations; link tasks; build relationships; use lag time; set constraints; create a resource pool; create a resource calendar; assign resources; level resources; assign task priority; share resources; sort resources; create a subproject; link projects; save a workspace; protect files; save a baseline; enter actual data; enter actual costs; create a report; print a report; customize the gantt chart; modify tables; create a custom toolbar; add menu commands; use the organizer; use the drawing toolbar; create a chart; edit a chart; and anchor a chart.

Instruction: Major topics covered in the course are project basics, managing tasks, time management, resource management, multiple projects, tracking and reports, customization and graphics. Methods of instruction include lecture, discussion, classroom exercises, self-check module review, and final examination.

Credit Recommendation: In the lower division baccalaureate/associate degree category, 1 semester hour in Microcomputer Applications (8/97). **NOTE:** Students receiving credit for Beginning Project 4.1 are ineligible to receive credit for Beginning Project 4.0.

Beginning Windows 95

Location: Various sites in the United States.

Length: 7 hours (1 day).

Dates: April 1995-Present.

Objective: To explore basic Windows 95 operations including how to launch programs, manage files, and use folders.

Learning Outcome: Upon successful completion of this course, the student will be able to use the mouse; explore menus; use the taskbar; manipulate windows; use a property sheet; get help; use exact matches; use quick view; use regular expressions; specify a folder; perform a text search; save a search; access the Explorer; format a diskette; use the view menu; create folders; copy and move files; work with folders; use the hierarchy system; use open/save as options; create shortcuts; and use the recycle bin.

Instruction: Major topics covered in the course are Windows 95 basics: the mouse, menus, taskbar, manipulating windows, and property sheets; using find; the Windows Explorer; and file management. Methods of instruction include lecture, discussion, classroom exercises, self-check module review, and final examination.

Credit Recommendation: In the lower division baccalaureate/associate degree category, 1 semester hour in Microcomputer Applications (8/97). **NOTE:** Student must successfully complete two or the following three: Beginning, Intermediate, or Advanced Windows 95.

Beginning Word 6.0 for Windows 95

Location: Various sites in the United States.

Length: 7 hours (1 day).

Dates: November 1993-Present.

Objective: To provide beginning level skills training in Microsoft Word 6.0 including fundamentals, creating, editing, and printing.

Learning Outcome: Upon successful completion of this course, the student will be able to tour the Word window; create and save a document; select and edit text; use undo and redo; use AutoCorrect; manage multiple documents; use help; manipulate the toolbars; cut, copy, paste, and move text; format text; use format painter; use autoformat; study guide; place tab stops; use decimal tabs; insert dot leaders; insert line leaders; transfer tab formatting; use find file; apply advanced formatting; explore views; check grammar and spelling; use the thesaurus; find and replace text; create headers and footers; and view and print a document.

Instruction: Major topics covered in the course are learn to edit, formatting, saving and printing a document, Word basics, editing and formatting, working with tabs, and the final product. Methods of instruction include lecture, discussion, classroom exercises, observations, self-check module review, and final examination.

Credit Recommendation: In the lower division baccalaureate/associate degree category, 1 semester hour in Microcomputer Applications (8/97). **NOTE:** Student must successfully complete two or the following three: Beginning, Intermediate, or Advanced Word 6.0 for Windows 95. Students receiving credit for Word 6.0 courses are ineligible to receive credit for Word 97 and Word 7.0 courses.

Beginning Word 7.0

Location: Various sites in the United States.

Length: 7 hours (1 day).

Dates: August 1995-Present.

Objective: To provide beginning level skills training in Microsoft Word 7.0 including fundamentals, creating, editing, and printing.

Learning Outcome: Upon successful completion of this course, the student will be able to create and save documents; tour the Word window; select and edit text; work with multiple documents; get help; manage files; use spell it; use AutoCorrect; apply autoformatting; undo and redo actions; use a wizard; set up the page; shift text; format text; format paragraphs; use format painter; set tab stops; insert tab leaders; use the thesaurus; find and replace text; create headers and footers; check spelling and grammar; and preview and print a document.

Instruction: Major topics covered in the course are editing, formatting, saving and printing a document, Word basics, automatic formatting, and the final product. Methods of instruction include lecture, discussion, classroom exercises, observations, self-check module review, and final examination.

Credit Recommendation: In the lower division baccalaureate/associate degree category, 1 semester hour in Microcomputer Applications (8/97). **NOTE:** Student must successfully complete two or the following three: Beginning, Intermediate, or Advanced Word 7.0. Students receiving credit for Word 7.0 courses are ineligible to receive credit for Word 6.0 and Word 97 courses.

Beginning Word 97 for Windows 95

Location: Various sites in the United States.

Length: 7 hours (1 day).

Dates: December 1996-Present.

Objective: To provide beginning level skills training in Microsoft Word 97 including fundamentals, creating, editing, and printing.

Learning Outcome: Upon successful completion of this course, the student will be able to create and save documents; tour the Word window; select and navigate text; work with multiple documents; get help; manage files; use spell it; use AutoCorrect; apply autoformatting; undo and redo actions; use a wizard; set up the page; shift text; format text; format paragraphs; use format painter; set tab stops; insert tab leaders; use the thesaurus; find and replace text; create headers and footers; check spelling and grammar; create passwords; create a document summary; and preview and print a document.

Instruction: Major topics covered in the course are Word basics, automatic formatting, editing and formatting, and the final product. Methods of instruction include lecture, discussion, classroom exercises, observations, self-check module review, and final examination.

Credit Recommendation: In the lower division baccalaureate/associate degree category, 1 semester hour in Microcomputer Applications (8/97). **NOTE:** Student must successfully complete two or the following three: Beginning, Intermediate, or Advanced Word 97 for Windows 95. Students receiving credit for Word 97 courses are ineligible to receive credit for Word 6.0 and Word 7.0 courses.

Beginning WordPerfect 6.1 for Windows

Location: Various sites in the United States.

Length: 7 hours (1 day).

Dates: March 1995-Present.

Objective: To provide beginning level skills training in WordPerfect 6.1. including fundamentals, creating, editing, and printing.

Learning Outcome: Upon successful completion of this course, the student will be able to tour the WordPerfect window; create and save a document; select and edit text; use undo and redo; use quickcorrect; manage multiple documents; manage files; use help; manipulate the toolbars; cut, copy, paste, and move text; format text; use quickformat; place tabs; use decimal tabs; insert dot leaders; insert line leaders; transfer tab formatting; use quick finder; apply advanced formatting; explore the views; use spell checker, grammatik, and thesaurus; find and replace text; create headers and footers; use the make it fit expert; and print a document.

Instruction: Major topics covered in the course are WordPerfect basics, editing and formatting, working with tabs, and the final product (finishing touches). Methods of instruction include lecture, discussion, classroom exercises, self-check module review, and final examination.

Credit Recommendation: In the lower division baccalaureate/associate degree category, 1 semester hour in Microcomputer Applications (8/97). **NOTE:** Students must successfully complete Beginning and Intermediate WordPerfect 6.1 for Windows, Beginning and Advanced WordPerfect 6.1 for Windows, or Intermediate and Advanced WordPerfect 6.1 for Windows to receive this credit recommendation. Students receiving credit for WordPerfect 6.1 courses are ineligible to receive credit for WordPerfect 7.0 courses.

Intermediate Access 2.0

Location: Various sites in the United States.

Length: 7 hours (1 day).

Dates: July 1994-Present.

Objective: To provide more sophisticated knowledge of Access 2.0 features needed to create advanced queries, reports, forms, and tables.

Learning Outcome: Upon successful completion of this course, the student will be able to make a multitable query; create an equi-join; make outer joins; create a theta join; explore referential integrity; use action queries; attach a table; delete an attached table; attach a Foxpro table; use the if function; cascade updates and deletes; use headers and footers; insert graphics; change tab order; make combo boxes; make a subform; group data; use summary controls; create a multicolumn report; and make subreports.

Instruction: Major topics covered in the course are advanced Access queries, custom forms, powerful table, advanced queries, power table use, customizing forms, and formatting reports. Methods of instruction include lecture, discussion, classroom exercises, observations, self-check module review, and final examination.

Credit Recommendation: In the lower division baccalaureate/associate degree category, 1 semester hour in Microcomputer Applications (8/97). **NOTE:** Student must successful complete both Intermediate Access and Advanced Access to receive credit for this course. Students receiving credit for Access 2.0 courses are ineligible to receive credit for Access 7.0 or Access 97 courses.

Intermediate Access 7.0 for Windows 95

Location: Various sites in the United States.

Length: 7 hours (1 day).

Dates: January 1996-Present.

Objective: To provide more sophisticated knowledge of Access 7.0 features needed to create advanced queries, reports, forms, and tables.

Learning Outcome: Upon successful completion of this course, the student will be able to make multitable queries; create equi-joins; create outer joins; use action queries; use referential integrity; use multitable queries; link and unlink a table; modify table properties; create combo boxes; create lookup tables; insert graphics in fields; insert graphics; employ display controls; create grouped controls; modify form properties; use the DLOOKUP function; use the if function; make a subform; create multitable reports; use graphics in reports; create report templates; create autoform entries; group data; and use summary controls.

Instruction: Major topics covered in the course are Access queries, custom forms, table techniques, advanced queries, power table use, customizing forms, and formatting reports. Methods of instruction include lecture, discussion, classroom exercises, observations, self-check module review, and final examination.

Credit Recommendation: In the lower division baccalaureate/associate degree category, 1 semester hour in Microcomputer Applications (8/97). **NOTE:** Student must successful complete both Intermediate Access and Advanced Access to receive credit for this course. Students receiving credit for Access 7.0 courses are ineligible to receive credit for Access 2.0 or Access 97 courses.

Intermediate Access 97 for Windows 95

Location: Various sites in the United States.

Length: 7 hours (1 day).

Dates: January 1997-Present.

Objective: To provide more sophisticated knowledge of Access 97 for Windows 95 features needed to create advanced queries, reports, forms, and tables.

Learning Outcome: Upon successful completion of this course, the student will be able to make multitable queries; create equi-joins; create outer joins; use action queries; use referential integrity; use multitable queries; link and unlink a table; modify table properties; create combo boxes; create lookup tables; insert graphics in fields; insert graphics; employ display controls; create grouped controls; modify form properties; use the DLOOKUP function; use the if function; make a subform; create multitable reports; use graphics in reports; create report templates; create autoform entries; group data; and use summary controls.

Instruction: Major topics covered in the course are advanced Access queries, custom forms, table techniques, advanced queries, power table use, customizing forms, and formatting reports. Methods of instruction include lecture, discussion, classroom exercises, observations, self-check module review, test your understanding exercises, and final examination.

Credit Recommendation: In the lower division baccalaureate/associate degree category, 1 semester hour in Microcomputer Applications (8/97). **NOTE:** Student must successful complete both Intermediate Access and Advanced Access to receive credit for this course. Students receiving credit for Access 97 courses are ineligible to receive credit for Access 2.0 or Access 7.0 courses.

Intermediate Corel WordPerfect 7.0 for Windows 95

Location: Various sites in the United States.

Length: 7 hours (1 day).

Dates: August 1996-Present.

Objective: To provide intermediate level skills training in WordPerfect 7.0 including advanced editing, columns, tables, and merging.

Learning Outcome: Upon successful completion of this course, the student will be able to manipulate toolbars; use abbreviations; use WordPerfect characters; apply bullets and numbering; insert a comment; create multiple columns; modify columns; create and format a table; use speedformat; create footnotes and endnotes; use bookmarks and quickmarks; create a cross-reference; build an index; create a table of contents; create a data source; create a form file; sort records; select records; use WordPerfect fields; and print labels and envelopes.

Instruction: Major topics covered in the course are advanced editing tools, columns and tables, use the reference tools, and mail merging. Methods of instruction include lecture, discussion, classroom exercises, observations, self-check module review, and final examination.

Credit Recommendation: In the lower division baccalaureate/associate degree category, 1 semester hour in Microcomputer Applications (8/97). **NOTE:** Students must successfully complete Beginning and Intermediate WordPerfect 7.0 for Windows 95, Beginning and Advanced WordPerfect 7.0 for Windows 95, or Intermediate and Advanced WordPerfect 7.0 for Windows 95 to receive this credit recommendation. Students receiving credit for WordPerfect 7.0 courses are ineligible to receive credit for WordPerfect 6.1 courses.

Intermediate Excel 5.0

Location: Various sites in the United States.

Length: 7 hours (1 day).

Dates: November 1993-Present.

Objective: To provide more sophisticated knowledge of Excel 5.0 spreadsheet skills with an emphasis on database operations, print tables, worksheet operations, and macros.

Learning Outcome: Upon successful completion of this course, the student will be able to create a database; sort a database; perform multiple sorts; use the data form; locate records; delete records; use autofilter; use compound criteria; extract unique records; use database functions; create a pivot table; import and export data; formula-link worksheets; command-link worksheets; use a name range; link workbook files; consolidate worksheets; assign passwords; protect cells and objects; outline a worksheet; create report views; record a macro; debug a macro; edit a macro; and create a macro button.

Instruction: Major topics covered in the course are database basics, database management, linking, protecting, and macros. Methods of instruction include lecture, discussion, classroom exercises, observations, self-check module review, and final examination.

Credit Recommendation: In the lower division baccalaureate/associate degree category, 1 semester hour in Microcomputer Applications (8/97). **NOTE:** Student must successfully complete two or the following three: Beginning Excel 5.0, Intermediate Excel 5.0, and/or Advanced Excel 5.0. Students receiving credit for Excel 5.0 courses are ineligible to receive credit for Excel 97 and Excel 7.0 courses.

Intermediate Excel 7.0

Location: Various sites in the United States.

Length: 7 hours (1 day).

Dates: August 1995-Present.

Objective: To provide more sophisticated Excel 7.0 spreadsheet skills with an emphasis on database operations, pivot tables, worksheet operations, and macros.

Learning Outcome: Upon successful completion of this course, the student will be able to create a database; sort a database; perform multiple sorts; use the data form; locate records; delete records; use autofilter; use compound criteria; extract unique records; use database functions; create a pivot table; formula-link worksheets; command-link worksheets; name a cell range; link workbook files; consolidate worksheets; assign a password; protect cells and objects; outline a worksheet; create report views; record a macro; debug a macro; edit a macro; and create a macro button.

Instruction: Major topics covered in the course database basics, database management, linking, protecting, and macros. Methods of instruction include lecture, discussion, classroom exercises, observations, self-check module review, and final examination.

Credit Recommendation: In the lower division baccalaureate/associate degree category, 1 semester hour in Microcomputer Applications (8/97). **NOTE:** Student must successfully complete two or the following three: Beginning Excel 7.0, Intermediate Excel 7.0, and/or Advanced Excel 7.0. Students receiving credit for Excel 7.0 courses are ineligible to receive credit for Excel 97 and Excel 5.0 courses.

Intermediate Excel 97 for Windows 95

Location: Various sites in the United States.

Length: 7 hours (1 day).

Dates: December 1996-Present.

Objective: To provide more sophisticated Excel 97 spreadsheet skills with an emphasis on database operations, pivot tables, worksheet operations, and macros.

Learning Outcome: Upon successful completion of this course, the student will be able to extract unique records; use database functions; create a pivot table; import and export data; formula-link worksheets; command-link worksheets; use a name range; link workbook files; consolidate worksheets; assign a password; protect cells and objects; outline a worksheet; create report views; record a macro; debug a macro; edit a macro; and create a macro button.

Instruction: Major topics covered in the course are database basics, database management, linking and protecting, and visual basic. Methods of instruction include lecture, discussion, classroom exercises, observations, self-check module review, and final examination.

Credit Recommendation: In the lower division baccalaureate/associate degree category, 1 semester hour in Microcomputer Applications (8/97). **NOTE:** Student must successfully complete two or the following three: Beginning Excel 97 for Windows 95, Intermediate Excel 97 for Windows 95, and/or Advanced Excel 97 for Windows 95. Students receiving credit for Excel 97 courses are ineligible to receive credit for Excel 7.0 and Excel 5.0 courses.

Intermediate FrontPage 97 for Windows 95

Location: Various sites in the United States.

Length: 7 hours (1 day).

Dates: October 1996-Present.

Objective: To provide more sophisticated knowledge of the FrontPage 97 for Windows 95 application's progressive web page authoring tools skills needed to use advanced design tools.

Learning Outcome: Upon successful completion of this course, the student will be able to use comments; make a page template; customize page appearance; configure page variables; create navigation tools; convert graphic types; use transparent and interlaced images; use .gif animation; create a hotspot; create overlapping hotspots; create a bulleted list; create a numbered list; create nested lists; create a table; format table cells; embed a table; insert an image into a table; explore microsoft image composer; create a marquee; insert a video; insert background sounds; and insert a Java applet.

Instruction: Major topics covered in the course are design tips, intermediate graphic use, list and tables, and create and use special effects. Methods of instruction include lecture, discussion, classroom exercises, observations, self-check module review, and final examination.

Credit Recommendation: In the lower division baccalaureate/associate degree category, 1 semester hour in Microcomputer Applications (8/97). **NOTE:** Student must successfully complete two or the following three: Beginning FrontPage 97 for Windows 95, Intermediate FrontPage 97 for Windows 95, and/or Advanced FrontPage 97 for Windows 95.

Intermediate Microsoft Word 97 for Windows 95

Location: Various sites in the United States.

Length: 7 hours (1 day).

Dates: December 1996-Present.

Objective: To provide intermediate level skill training in Microsoft Word 97 including advanced editing, columns, tables, and merging.

Learning Outcome: Upon successful completion of this course, the student will be able to manipulate toolbars; use autotext; add special symbols; apply bullets and numbering; apply multiple columns;

modify columns; create and format a table; use table autoformat; create footnotes and endnotes; use bookmarks; create a cross-reference; build an index; create a table of contents; create a source document; create a main document; sort records; query records; use word fields; and print labels and envelopes.

Instruction: Major topics covered in the course are advanced editing tools, columns and tables, use of the reference tools, and mail merging. Methods of instruction include lecture, discussion, classroom exercises, observations, self-check module review, and final examination.

Credit Recommendation: In the lower division baccalaureate/associate degree category, 1 semester hour in Microcomputer Applications (8/97). **NOTE:** Student must successfully complete two or the following three: Beginning, Intermediate, or Advanced Word 97 for Windows 95. Students receiving credit for Word 97 courses are ineligible to receive credit for Word 6.0 and Word 7.0 courses.

Intermediate PowerPoint 4.0

Location: Various sites in the United States.

Length: 7 hours (1 day).

Dates: June 1995-Present.

Objective: To explore the features of Intermediate PowerPoint 4.0 in order to change the appearance of text and graphics in slide show presentations.

Learning Outcome: Upon successful completion of this course, the student will be able to import a spreadsheet; create a graph; rotate a graph; ungroup and regroup objects; create an organizational chart; use WordArt; use the autocontent wizard; change text; modify borders; change the color scheme; set transitions; set timings; create a build slide; hide a slide; print handouts and notes pages; create a drill-down icon; add a black slide; and run a presentation.

Instruction: Major topics covered in the course are advanced graphic techniques, working with templates and wizards, using special effects, and the final presentation. Methods of instruction include lecture, discussion, classroom exercises, self-check module review, and final examination.

Credit Recommendation: In the lower division baccalaureate/associate degree category, 1 semester hour in Microcomputer Applications (8/97). **NOTE:** Student must successfully complete both Beginning and Intermediate PowerPoint 4.0 to receive this credit recommendation. Students receiving credit for PowerPoint 4.0 courses are ineligible to receive credit for PowerPoint 7.0 and PowerPoint 97 courses.

Intermediate PowerPoint 7.0 for Windows 95

Location: Various sites in the United States.

Length: 7 hours (1 day).

Dates: September 1995-Present.

Objective: To explore the features of PowerPoint 7.0 in order to embed a spreadsheet, change the appearance of graphics and text, create a design template, and create and print a handout.

Learning Outcome: Upon successful completion of this course, the student will be able to insert an Excel spreadsheet; insert an x-y data chart; edit an x-y chart; recolor a chart; change text attributes; split text to a new slide; fit text into shapes; use WordArt; insert a Word table; create a custom background; create a color scheme; create a design template; create a presentation template; apply animation effects; use the slide navigator; play a slide show; create and print a handout; and use the "pack and go" wizard.

Instruction: Major topics covered in the course are data charts, advanced text formatting, working with templates, and advanced slide shows. Methods of instruction include lecture, discussion, classroom exercises, self-check module review, and final examination.

Credit Recommendation: In the lower division baccalaureate/associate degree category, 1 semester hour in Microcom-puter Applications (8/97). **NOTE:** Stu-dent must successfully complete both Be-ginning and Intermediate PowerPoint 7.0 to receive this credit recommendation. Students receiving credit for PowerPoint 7.0 courses are ineligible to receive credit for PowerPoint 4.0 and PowerPoint 97 courses.

Intermediate PowerPoint 97 for Windows 95

Location: Various sites in the United States.

Length: 7 hours (1 day).

Dates: February 1997-Present.

Objective: To explore the features of Intermediate PowerPoint 97 to change the appearance of text and graphics in slide show presentations.

Learning Outcome: Upon successful completion of this course, the student will be able to insert an Excel spreadsheet; insert an x-y data chart; edit an x-y data chart; recolor a chart; change text attributes; split text to a new slide; fit text into shapes; use WordArt; insert a Word table; export to another application; work with tabs; create a background; create a color scheme; create a design template; create a presentation template; apply movie and sound effects; apply animation effects; use the slide navigator; play a slide show; create and print handouts; use the "pack and go" wizard; and use presentation conferencing.

Instruction: Major topics covered in the course are data charts, advanced text formatting, working with templates, and advanced slide shows. Methods of instruction include lecture, discussion, classroom exercises, self-check module review, and final examination.

Credit Recommendation: In the lower division baccalaureate/associate degree category, 1 semester hour in Microcomputer Applications (8/97). **NOTE:** Student must successfully complete both Beginning and Intermediate PowerPoint 97 for Windows 95 to receive this credit recommendation. Students receiving credit for PowerPoint 97 courses are ineligible to receive credit for PowerPoint 7.0 and PowerPoint 4.0 courses.

Intermediate Windows 95

Location: Various sites in the United States.

Length: 7 hours (1 day).

Dates: May 1995-Present.

Objective: To explore intermediate Windows 95 operations including how to customize the appearance of windows, use accessories, multi-tasking, and embed OLE objects.

Learning Outcome: Upon successful completion of this course, the student will be able to adjust the mouse and keyboard; set the date and time; adjust the display; customize the start menu; use Notepad; use Paint; create a Wordpad document; format a Wordpad document; use the Calculator; use the character map; use preemptive multitasking; understand font types; remove and restore fonts; install a printer driver; use drag and drop printing; manage print jobs; create a link; update links; embed an object; and edit an embedded object.

Instruction: Major topics covered in the course are modifying the Windows environment, multitasking, fonts and printing, and object linking and embedding. Methods of instruction include lecture, discussion, classroom exercises, self-check module review, and final examination.

Credit Recommendation: In the lower division baccalaureate/associate degree category, 1 semester hour in Microcom-puter Applications (8/97). **NOTE:** Stu-dent must successfully complete two or the following three: Beginning, Intermediate, or Advanced Windows 95.

Intermediate Word 6.0 for Windows 95

Location: Various sites in the United States.

Length: 7 hours (1 day).

Dates: November 1993-Present.

Objective: To provide intermediate level skills training in Microsoft Word 6.0 including advanced editing, columns, table merging, and desktop publishing.

Learning Outcome: Upon successful completion of this course, the student will be able to work with wizards; use autotext; add special symbols; apply bullets and numbering; use spike; apply multiple columns; modify columns; create and format a table; use table autoformat; create a source document; create a main document; sort records; query records; use word fields; print labels; print envelopes; create footnotes and endnotes; use bookmarks; create a cross-reference; build an index; and create a table of contents.

Instruction: Major topics covered in the course are mail-merging, outlining, table of contents, indexing, footnotes, and boilerplates. Methods of instruction include lecture, discussion, classroom exercises, observations, self-check module review, and final examination.

Credit Recommendation: In the lower division baccalaureate/associate degree category, 1 semester hour in Microcomputer Applications (8/97). **NOTE:** Student must successfully complete two or the following three: Beginning, Intermediate, or Advanced Word 6.0 for Windows 95. Students receiving credit for Word 6.0 courses are ineligible to receive credit for Word 97 and Word 7.0 courses.

Intermediate Word 7.0

Location: Various sites in the United States.

Length: 7 hours (1 day).

Dates: August 1995-Present.

Objective: To provide intermediate level skill training in Microsoft Word 7.0 including advanced editing, columns, tables, and merging.

Learning Outcome: Upon successful completion of this course, the student will be able to manipulate toolbars; use autotext; add special symbols; apply bullets and numbering; apply multiple columns; modify columns; create and format a table; use table autoformat; create footnotes and endnotes; use bookmarks; create a cross-reference; build an index; create a table of contents; create a source document; create a main document; sort records; query records; use word fields; and print labels and envelopes.

Instruction: Major topics covered in the course are advanced editing tools, columns and tables, use of the reference tools, and mail merging. Methods of instruction include lecture, discussion, classroom exercises, observations, self-check module review, and final examination.

Credit Recommendation: In the lower division baccalaureate/associate degree category, 1 semester hour in Microcomputer Applications (8/97). **NOTE:** Student must successfully complete two or the following three: Beginning, Intermediate, or Advanced Word 7.0. Students receiving credit for Word 7.0 courses are ineligible to receive credit for Word 97 and Word 6.0 courses.

Intermediate WordPerfect 6.1 for Windows

Location: Various sites in the United States.

Length: 7 hours (1 day).

Dates: March 1995-Present.

Objective: To provide intermediate level skills training in WordPerfect 6.1 including advanced editing, columns, tables, and publishing features.

Learning Outcome: Upon successful completion of this course, the student will be able to use a document expert; create a quicklist; use abbreviations; use WordPerfect characters; apply bullets and numbering; use reveal codes; use append and undelete; create multiple columns; modify columns; keep text together; create and format a table; use a table expert; create a data file; create a form file; sort records; select records/specify merge conditions; merge labels; merge to envelopes; create footnotes and endnotes; use bookmarks and quickmarks; create a cross-reference; build an index; and create a table of contents.

Instruction: Major topics covered in the course are advanced editing tools, columns and tables, mail merging, and introduction to desktop publishing. Methods of instruction include lecture, discussion, classroom exercises, observations, self-check module review, and final examination.

Credit Recommendation: In the lower division baccalaureate/associate degree category, 1 semester hour in Microcomputer Applications (8/97). **NOTE:** Students must successfully complete Beginning and Intermediate WordPerfect 6.1 for Windows, Beginning and Advanced WordPerfect 6.1 for Windows, or Intermediate and Advanced WordPerfect 6.1 for Windows to receive this credit recommendation. Students receiving credit for WordPerfect 6.1 courses are ineligible to receive credit for WordPerfect 7.0 courses.

New Jersey Association of Realtors

Established in 1970 by the New Jersey Association of Realtors, the New Jersey Realtors' Institute was designed and developed to satisfy the need for a more comprehensive and more fully effective learning experience in all phases of a real estate transaction.

The New Jersey Realtors' Institute remains as the single, most exciting innovation in today's New Jersey real estate industry. It serves as the most widely emulated model for real estate programs in the nation. The New Jersey Realtors' Institute is a door to a broadening of knowledge, an increase in productivity, and an evaluation of the standards of New Jersey's real estate industry.

The very foundation of the real estate profession rests on the desire to keep abreast of the changes occurring in the concept and handling of real property. Though not a cure-all, it has been proven that the curriculum and excellent instruction in the Realtors' Institute have enabled the student to become a more competent professional, render greater and broader service, and develop greater earning potential.

Source of official student records: Registry of Credit Recommendations, American Council on Education, One Dupont Circle, Washington, DC 20036-1193.

Additional information about the courses: Office of Corporate-Higher Education Programs, Thomas Edison State College, 101 West State Street, Trenton, NJ 08608-1176.

Graduate Realtors Institute (GRI)

Location: Various locations throughout New Jersey.

Length: 30 hours (4 days).

Dates: *Version 1:* September 1974-December 1990; *Version 2:* January 1991-February 1996.

Objective: To prepare Realtors and Realtor Associates to function effectively in the real estate brokerage business.

Instruction: Major topics covered in the ten sessions of the course are organized real estate industries and ethics; urban development; legal environment of real estate; construction and energy; prospecting for listings and market analysis; real estate contracts; financing; qualifying the buyer, showing the property, and obtaining and presenting the offer; career management; and brokerage I.

Credit Recommendation: *Version 1:* In the lower division baccalaureate/associate degree category, 4 semester hours in Principles and Practices of Real Estate when GRI II and III are also completed (12/93). **NOTE:** Credit recommendation does not apply for any single course. *Version 2:* In the lower division baccalaureate/associate degree category, 6 semester hours in Principles and Practices of Real Estate when GRI II and III are also completed (12/83) (2/91). **NOTE:** Credit recommendation does not apply for any single course.

Graduate Realtors Institute (GRI) Course II

Location: Various locations throughout New Jersey.

Length: 30 hours (4 days).

Dates: *Version 1:* September 1974-December 1990; *Version 2:* January 1991-February 1996.

Objective: To prepare Realtors and Realtor Associates to function effectively in the real estate brokerage business.

Instruction: Major topics covered in the ten sessions of the course are brokerage II; communication; economic analysis; real property taxation and tax appeals; residential subdivisions; condominiums; real estate counseling; advertising and marketing; court decision workshop; and land use and its impact on the industry.

Credit Recommendation: *Version 1:* In the lower division baccalaureate/associate degree category, 4 semester hours in Principles and Practices of Real Estate when GRI I and III are also completed (12/83). **NOTE:** Credit recommendation does not apply for any single course. *Version 2:* In the lower division baccalaureate/associate degree category, 6 semester hours in Principles and Practices of Real Estate when GRI I and III are also completed (12/83) (2/91). **NOTE:** Credit recommendation does not apply for any single course.

Graduate Realtors Institute (GRI) Course III

Location: Various locations throughout New Jersey.

Length: 30 hours (4 days).

Dates: *Version 1:* September 1974-December 1990; *Version 2:* January 1991-February 1996.

Objective: To prepare Realtors and Realtor Associates to function effectively in the real estate brokerage business.

Instruction: Major topics covered in the ten sessions of the course are Investment real estate (characteristics and risks); estimating cash flow; appraisal; taxation and real estate investment; financing (other than residential); industrial and commercial real estate; managing investment property; managing broker operations; real estate syndication; and leases.

Credit Recommendation: *Version 1:* In the lower division baccalaureate/associate degree category, 4 semester hours in Principles and Practices of Real Estate when GRI I and II are also completed (12/83). **NOTE:** Credit recommendation does not apply for any single course. *Version 2:* In the lower division baccalaureate/associate degree category, 6 semester hours in Principles and Practices of Real Estate when GRI I and II are also completed (12/83) (2/91). **NOTE:** Credit recommendation does not apply for any single course.

Graduate Realtors Institute (GRI) Course IV

Location: Various locations throughout New Jersey.

Length: 30 hours (4 days).

Dates: *Version 1:* August 1971-December 1990; *Version 2:* January 1991-February 1996.

Objective: To prepare Realtor Associates to function effectively as brokers and to qualify for the New Jersey brokers license examination.

Instruction: Major topics covered in the course are laws-rules-regulations; interest in realty; how title is held; real estate contracts; liens; leases; mortgages-financing; deeds and legal descriptions; voluntary and involuntary alienation; settlement procedures and settlement sheets; mathematics-broker level; discrimination-investment; and Real Estate Commission rules and regulations.

Credit Recommendation: *Version 1:* In the lower division baccalaureate/associate degree category, an additional 2 semester hours in Principles and Practices of Real Estate for those who have already completed GRI I, II, and III. Therefore, completion of GRI I, II, III, and IV yields a cumulative total of 6 semester hours (12/83). *Version 2:* In the lower division baccalaureate/associate degree category, an additional 2 semester hours in Principles and Practices of Real Estate for those who have already completed GRI I, II, and III. Therefore, completion of GRI I, II, III, and IV yields a cumulative total of 8 semester hours (12/83) (2/91).

New Jersey Council for the Humanities

The New Jersey Council for the Humanities (NJCH), a state affiliate of the National Endowment for the Humanities, is an independent non-profit organization that was founded in 1972 to enrich the lives of the citizens of New Jersey and stimulate inquiry and thought through public humanities programs.

NJCH supports the NJ Teacher Institute, which began in 1994. The Institute in 1995-97 will consist of two annual series of five week-long, intellectually challenging, residential seminars for educators and offer follow-up activities designed to promote professional development at the local level: a humanities grant program for teacher-directed, in-service training (Teachers' Grant Fund); a Content Resources Guide; and a Directory of Professional Development Resources in New Jersey.

The seminars, open to all New Jersey K-12 teachers and administrators, will be based on interdisciplinary academic subjects in the Humanities aligned with content standards in History, English, Civics, and the Arts.

Source of official student records: Registry of Credit Recommendations, American Council on Education, One Dupont Circle, Washington, DC 20036-1193.

Additional information about the courses: Office of Corporate-Higher Education Programs, Thomas Edison State College, 101 West State Street, Trenton, NJ 08608-1176 .

Holding Up Half the World: Women and the Community

Location: Locations throughout New Jersey.

Length: 60 hours (6 days).

Dates: November 1995-Present.

Objective: To introduce K through 12 New Jersey teachers to the rich field of women's studies.

Learning Outcome: Upon successful completion of this course, the student will be able to develop a critical awareness of gender roles in American Society, understand the history of women's struggle for political, economic, and social equality, and understand basic tenets of feminist theory.

Instruction: Major topics covered in the course are the ways in which women's studies has shifted women's lives and voices to the center of scholarship. Methods of instruction include lectures, group discussions, writing workshops, film screenings and commentaries, and assigned readings.

Credit Recommendation: In the graduate degree category, 3 semester hours in Women's Studies, Sociology, or History (11/95). **NOTE:** Students must read all assigned readings, participate in course discussions, and submit a graduate level paper as part of the course requirement.

Individual and Community in America

Location: Locations throughout New Jersey.

Length: 60 hours (6 days).

Dates: May 1995-Present.

Objective: To introduce K through 12 New Jersey teachers to the political and social philosophies that have shaped American civilization.

Learning Outcome: Upon successful completion of this course, the student will be able to identify major currents in American intellectual thought, understand American theories of self and society and recognize their influence on the design of our Constitution and modern political practice, and understand current academic discussions about "identity politics" and the problems of forging a common civic spirit in American society.

Instruction: Major topics covered in the course are the relation between individualism and community in America, an overview of individualism and communitarianism in American history and culture, and an examination of community and individualism in relation to race, class, ethnicity and sexual orientation, locality, neighborhood, and citizenship in an age of mass media and mass politics. Methods of instruction include lectures, group discussions, writing workshops, film viewings and commentaries, and a field trip.

Credit Recommendation: In the graduate degree category, 3 semester hours in American Studies, Sociology, or Political Science (11/95). **NOTE:** Student must submit a graduate level paper as part of the course requirement.

New Jersey's History: The Barrel Tapped at Both Ends

Location: Locations throughout New Jersey.

Length: 60 hours (6 days).

Dates: October 1995-July 1996.

Objective: To provide K through 12 New Jersey teachers with an overview of New Jersey's economic, political, and cultural past.

Learning Outcome: Upon successful completion of this course, the student will be able to understand the impact of nineteenth century industrialism on New Jersey, understand racial, ethnic, gender, immigrant, and class conflicts in New Jersey history, and understand New Jerseyians' attempt to re-invent their past and create a vision of their state's future.

Instruction: Major topics covered in the course are the impact of nineteenth century industrialism on New Jersey; racial, ethnic, gender, immigrant, and class conflicts in New Jersey history; and why New Jerseyans decided to re-invent their past and create a vision for their state's future. Methods of instruction include lectures, group discussion, writing workshops, film screening and commentaries, and a field trip to Trenton and Atlantic City.

Credit Recommendation: In the graduate degree category, 3 semester hours in History, American Studies, or Political Science (11/95). **NOTE:** Students must read all of the assigned readings, participate in course discussions, and submit a graduate level paper as part of the course requirement.

Religious Diversity in America

Location: Locations throughout New Jersey.

Length: 60 hours (6 days).

Dates: August 1995-Present.

Objective: To introduce K through 12 New Jersey teachers to the history of American religion and its impact on contemporary cultural conflicts.

Learning Outcome: Upon successful completion of this course, the student will be able to understand the religious roots of cultural conflicts in American society, understand the similarities and differences between major world religions, and grasp the basic principles of interreligious dialogue.

Instruction: Major topics covered in the course are an exploration of history from a cultural and sociological perspective and an exploration of how the many different religious traditions which came to these shores adapted to the American dream or challenged them. Methods of instruction include readings, lectures, group discussions, film viewings, writing workshops, and artistic performances.

Credit Recommendation: In the graduate degree category, 3 semester hours in Religion, History, or Sociology (11/95). **NOTE:** Student must submit a graduate level paper as part of the course requirement.

Worlds Apart: American Cities and Suburbs in Comparative Perspective

Location: Locations throughout New Jersey.

Length: 60 hours (6 days).

Dates: June 1995-Present.

Objective: To introduce K through 12 New Jersey teachers to the history of American cities, the growth of suburbanization and the economic and cultural consequences of federal land use and transportation policy.

Learning Outcome: Upon successful completion of this course, the student will be able to understand, in general terms, the economic and cultural forces that caused the rapid growth of suburbanization in the 19th and 20th centuries, understand the impact of suburbanization on civic life and race relations in the United States, and understand how federal land use and transportation policies have supported the suburban ideal in the United States.

Instruction: Major topics covered in the course are an exploration of the relation between very different types of areas and the reasons why the United States has become residentially and spatially different from the rest of the world. Methods of instruction include lectures, group discussions, writing workshops, film viewings and commentaries, and two field trips.

Credit Recommendation: In the graduate degree category, 3 semester hours in Geography and Urban Studies, History, or Political Science (11/95). **NOTE:** Student must submit a graduate level paper as part of the course requirement.

New Jersey Department of Personnel, Human Resource Development Institute

The Human Resource Development Institute within the New Jersey Department of Personnel provides training and education to all levels of government employees. The Department provides practical instruction to meet the ever-increasing demands of governmental organizations.

Since 1960, those training opportunities have been available to address everyday technical, management, maintenance, and clerical concerns of managers and executives.

Course offerings include clerical skills training, communications, health and safety, and management and labor relations. In addition to these courses, tailor-made programs are available throughout the State.

Source of official student records: Registry of Credit Recommendations, American Council on Education, One Dupont Circle, Washington, DC 20036-1193.

Additional information about the courses: Office of Corporate-Higher Education Programs, Thomas Edison State College, 101 West State Street, Trenton, New Jersey 08608-1176.

COURSES ORIGINALLY EVALUATED UNDER NEW JERSEY DEPT. OF HUMAN SERVICES

The following courses were originally conducted through the New Jersey Department of Human Services, Office of Manpower Planning, Development and Training. All their training programs were consolidated under the Department of Personnel, Human Resources Development Institute in 1993.

Executive Development Seminar (Follow-Up)

Location: Various locations in New Jersey.

Length: 23 hours (3 days).

Dates: October 1981-December 1983.

Objective: To enable students to apply the most recent managerial concepts and theories, as well as plan, organize, and control operating units and make better use of available human resources.

Instruction: Major topics covered in the course are dynamics of organizational trust, team building, leadership effectiveness, and stress. Methods of instruction include lecturettes, audiovisual aids, handout materials, experiential group activities/discussions, role-play simulations, case studies/participant presentations with feedback, individual inventories, and dialogue with instructor.

Credit Recommendation: In the graduate degree category, 1 semester hour in Management Development Seminar (10/81). **NOTE:** This course was previously listed under the NJ Department of Human Services.

Executive Development Seminar (Basic)

Location: Various locations in New Jersey.

Length: 45 hours (5 days, 3 evenings).

Dates: October 1981-December 1983.

Objective: To enable students to evaluate their own leadership styles and make modifications in their own operating units and to use concepts that will be results oriented within their own operating units.

Instruction: Major topics covered in the course are management techniques, cohesion, managerial practice, human response development, planning, organizing, directing, communication, motivation, and organizational change. Methods of instruction include lecturettes, audiovisual aids, hand-out materials, experiential group activities/discussions, role-play simulations, case studies/participant presentations with feedback, individual inventories, and dialogue with instructor.

Credit Recommendation: In the graduate degree category, 3 semester hours in Management Development, Organizational Behavior, Organization Development and Change, or Team Building (10/81). **NOTE:** This course was previously listed under the NJ Department of Human Services.

Gerontology Training Series

Location: Various Department of Human Services locations in New Jersey.

Length: 36 hours (in class) and supervised application in practical settings.

Dates: September 1983-June 1991.

Objective: To prepare staff members (ranging from direct care workers to physicians to CEOs) to address the holistic needs of the elderly and the problems they encounter when providing services to the elderly.

Learning Outcome: Upon successful completion of this course, the student will be able to identify and describe principles of gerontology and techniques of care for the institutionalized elderly; express positive attitudes about the institutionalized elderly; apply knowledge and skills learned in training to on-the-job situations; and better understand the relationship between institution and community and focus upon ways to use outside resources.

Instruction: Major topics covered in the course are 12 modules covering a wide range of areas in the field of aging. It includes ways the staff can address the needs of the elderly, stressing quality of life and prevention strategies. Topics include normal aging process, common problems of aging, and the effects of institutionalization. Knowledge of gerontology is coupled with approaches to promote individuality, independence, and respect.

Credit Recommendation: In the upper division baccalaureate degree category, 3 semester hours in Gerontological Studies or Human Services. If participant already possesses a baccalaureate degree and successfully completes a "research paper" read by a qualified independent assessor, then on the graduate level, 3 semester hours in Gerontological Studies or Human Services (8/87). **NOTE:** This course was previously listed under the NJ Department of Human Services.

Management II Basic (Mid-level Management)

Location: Various locations in New Jersey.

Length: 30 hours (1 week).

Dates: October 1981-June 1991.

Objective: To enable the student to develop a sound management system and solve management problems.

Instruction: Major topics covered in the course are the application of the management functions of planning, organizing, directing, and controlling, and their relations to decision-making. Methods of instruction include lecturettes, audiovisual aids, handout materials, experiential group activities/discussions, role-play simulations, case studies/participant presentations with feedback, individual inventories, and dialogue with instructor.

Credit Recommendation: In the upper division baccalaureate degree category, 2 semester hours in basic Principles of Su=pervision (10/81) (3/87). **NOTE:** This course material is no longer included by most colleges as part of their business major, but is still applicable, as appropriate, to any other degree program or as business electives. This course was previously listed under the NJ Department of Human Services.

Management III Basic (Supervisory Level)

Location: Various locations in New Jersey.

Length: 30 hours (1 week).

Dates: October 1981-June 1991.

Objective: To enable the student to perform the tasks of a supervisor (i.e., planning, control, organization, problem solving, and decision-making).

Instruction: Major topics covered in the course are the role of the supervisor, leadership style and application, planning, problem-solving and decision-making, group dynamics, time management, communication styles, and assertive supervision. Methods of instruction include lecturettes, audiovisual aids, handout materials, experiential group activities/discussions, role-play simulations, case studies/ participant presentations with feedback, individual inventories, and dialogue with instructor.

Credit Recommendation: In the upper division baccalaureate degree category, 2 semester hours in Basic Principles of Supervision (10/81) (3/87). **NOTE:** This course material is no longer included by most colleges as part of their business major, but is still applicable, as appropriate, to any other degree program or as a business elective. This course was previously listed under the NJ Department of Human Services.

Prediction and Prevention of Aggressive Behavior in the System (CRPI)

Location: Various Department of Human Services locations in New Jersey.

Length: *Version 1:* 40 hours (5 days); *Version 2:* 32 hours (4 days).

Dates: *Version 1:* June 1980-May 1985; *Version 2:* June 1985-October 1994.

Objective: To develop skills in predicting and preventing "acting out" client behavior. This course is designed for all staff who provide services to clients in a residential setting.

Instruction: Major topics covered in the course are specific skills in nonphysical client control and also emphasizes verbal communication skills. Methods of instruction include interactive lectures; self-instruction multimedia learning modes such as work books, videotapes, and slide-tapes; role playing; and field observation.

Credit Recommendation: In the upper division baccalaureate degree category, 2 semester hours in Counseling, Special Education, Rehabilitation, or Human Services (6/82) (8/87). **NOTE:** This course was previously listed under the NJ Department of Human Services.

Psychiatric Rehabilitation Practitioner Training (M882)

Location: Greystone Park, NJ.

Length: *Version 1:* 148 hours (21 days); *Version 2:* 84 hours (12 days).

Dates: *Version 1:* April 1984-April 1986; *Version 2:* April 1986-June 1991.

Objective: To provide necessary skills in psychiatric rehabilitation to enable staff to work more effectively with resident clients.

Learning Outcome: Upon successful completion of this course, the trainee should be able to conduct the functional and resource assessment; determine skill intervention and set time frames; direct skills teaching; use interviewing techniques; and make skill-language translations.

Instruction: Major topics covered in the course are an overview of psychiatric rehabilitation methods, including the goals of psychiatric rehab, the three phases of psychiatric rehab, and a comparison between physical and psychiatric rehabilitation. Each of the three phases (diagnostic, planning, and intervention) is then studied in more detail.

Credit Recommendation: In the lower division baccalaureate/associate degree category, 3 semester hours in Psychiatric Rehabilitation Training Development or Human Service elective (not a core course) (12/87). **NOTE:** This course was previously listed under the NJ Department of Human Services.

Psychiatric Rehabilitation Trainer Development (M-883)

Location: Greystone Park, NJ.

Length: 70 hours (3-month supervised internship).

Dates: September 1983-June 1991.

Objective: To enable trainees to present the Psychiatric Rehabilitation Practitioner Training course to other staff members.

Learning Outcome: Upon successful completion of this course, the student will be able to deliver the complete psychiatric rehabilitation program to practitioners; modify programs to suit learners' needs; and facilitate implementation of psychiatric rehabilitation into clinical areas of hospital.

Instruction: This course involves a two-week classroom component followed by a three-month supervised internship. Topics included in the classroom section are platform skills, methods of presentation, use of media, lesson planning and intervention strategies for the difficult learner. In the internship, students actually present training course under supervision of senior trainer.

Credit Recommendation: In the lower division baccalaureate/associate degree category, 2 semester hours in Applied Training Procedures (12/87). **NOTE:** This course was previously listed under the NJ Department of Human Services.

Special Management Topics
1. Management "B" - Management by Objectives/Standards of Performance
2. Management "C" - Interviewing and Counseling
3. Management "D" - Motivation/Communication
4. Management "E" - Performance Appraisal/Standards
5. Management "F" - Problem Solving/Decision Making
6. Management "G" - Transactional Analysis
7. Management "H" - Employee Relations and Grievance Handling
8. Management "I" - Equal Employment Opportunity
9. Management "J" - Assertiveness Training
10. Management "K" - Stress Management
11. Management "L" - Team Building/Group Dynamics
12. Women in Management

Location: Various locations in New Jersey.

Length: 12 hours (2 days) for each Management course "B" through "L;" 18 hours (3 days).

Dates: October 1981-June 1991.

Objective: To enable students to:

1. Identify organizational and individual objectives and determine the procedures necessary to achieve them and to write and use objectives in formulating decisions and policies for the organization.

2. Extract pertinent information for interviewing situations and deal effectively with a variety of job-related situations that necessitate good rapport and communication skills.

3. Develop and sustain an organizational environment that will motivate employees and to apply a variety of motivational techniques to improve the organizational climate of the work unit.

4. Improve the work unit's performance by increasing knowledge of, approaches to, and techniques for performance appraisal and to write standards in the context of MBO theories and the Performance Assessment Review (PAR).

5. Identify and analyze the causes of problems and to develop appropriate options for resolving problems.

6. Improve the organizational climate and the flow of communications through a greater understanding of interpersonal relations and to analyze interpersonal problems and examine relationships among members of the work unit.

7. Recognize the role and responsibilities of the supervisor in the equitable disposition of grievances and handle situations before they become grievable issues.

8. Cite EEO legislation, identify discrimination on the job, and interview and counsel employees in compliance with EEO regulations.

9. Define and distinguish assertive, passive, and aggressive behavior and identify verbal and nonverbal components of these behaviors.

10. Recognize clues that trigger counterproductive stress and learn to use stress creatively and to change negative perceptions.

11. Effectively use techniques to deal with change and resistance through team building, and develop sharply defined objectives as a team leader.

12. To enable participants to understand the nature and scope of some internal, interpersonal, and structural barriers to advancement that women face and to develop strategies using personal strengths and abilities to overcome barriers to advancement.

Instruction: Major topics covered in the course are:

1. Goal and objective clarification, setting standards, utilizing time-management techniques, and relating standards to organizational goals.

2. Communication theory, counseling employees, listening skills, and role-play exercises.

3. Motivation concepts, change, verbal and nonverbal modalities, and listening and feedback.

4. Instructional techniques to enhance skills and improve organizational effectiveness.

5. Problem analysis and decision-making.

6. Transactional analysis as a management tool, and analyzing transactions and improving interpersonal communications.

7. Handling of grievances, unionism, and role playing.

8. EEO legislation, regulation, and guidelines; discrimination complaint process; and interviewing and counseling skills.

9. Basic human rights, assertion, and communication skills.

10. Defining stress, sources of stress, self-motivation, and tension levels.

11. Team building and group dynamics.

12. Covers the nature and scope of traditional socialization, communication and self-assessment, time-management skills, managing change, problem-solving and decision-making, leadership, assertion techniques, conflict resolution, and career pathing and planning. Methods of instruction include lecturettes, audiovisual aids, handout materials, experiential group activities/discussions, role-play simulations, case studies/participant presentations with feedback, individual inventories, and dialogue with instructor.

Credit Recommendation: In the upper division baccalaureate degree category, 2 semester hours in Management Development (10/81) (3/87). **NOTE:** This credit recommendation applies for successful completion of any three of these courses. Four credits should be awarded for completion of any six of the courses. This course was previously listed under the NJ Department of Human Services.

Training for Trainers - Crisis Recognition, Prevention, and Intervention (Formerly Delivering Crisis Management Prevention Program, or Train the Trainers)

Location: Various Department of Human Services locations in New Jersey.

Length: *Version 1:* 120 hours (15 days); *Version 2:* 96 hours (12 days).

Dates: *Version 1:* May 1980-May 1985; *Version 2:* June 1985-Present.

Objective: To develop trainer's competence in delivering training in verbal, nonintrusive, nonphysical control to predict and prevent "acting out" client behavior.

Instruction: Major topics covered in the course are training strategies including behavioral rehearsal, communications skills, and methods of presentations. Teaches specific skills in nonphysical client control.

Credit Recommendation: In the upper division baccalaureate degree category, 5 semester hours in Special Education, Rehabilitation, or Human Services (6/82) (8/87). **NOTE:** This course was previously listed under the NJ Department of Human Services.

NEW JERSEY CERTIFIED PUBLIC MANAGER PROGRAM

The New Jersey Certified Public Manager Program and the companion Certified Public Manager-Law Enforcement Program are specialized training and management development programs for the supervisors and managers of New Jersey government and the law enforcement community. The Program's purpose is to provide practical "hands-on" training for those levels of employees, supervisors, and managers whose actions impact upon the delivery of services and the smooth operation of New Jersey government at both the State and local levels.

The Certified Public Manager and Law Enforcement Programs are designed to give a supervisor or manager, at any level in an organization, the basic skills necessary to perform well in an ever-changing environment. The Programs do not pretend to produce a "finished product." There is no closure to the Programs; they are well-founded framework upon which the open-minded and serious supervisory or managerial practitioner can continue to build throughout his or her career.

The areas covered in the Programs are deliberately limited to allow time to treat comprehensively that material considered essential. The classroom sessions are heavily supported by practice exercises in the application of the concepts. The desired outcome is not only to impart information, but to allow for the practical application of the theories through outside readings, relevant case studies, and projects. Supervisors complete the Program only after substantial "hands-on" practice necessary to apply the theory.

Leading and Directing (Level 1 of CPM Program)

Location: Trenton, NJ, and other locations throughout the state.

Length: 30 hours (6 hour sessions over 5 weeks).

Dates: February 1983-Present.

Objective: To present managers (supervisors) with theory and techniques of successful management.

Learning Outcome: Upon successful completion of this course, the student will be able to have a more effective understanding of the six managerial functions; the role of the supervisor; motivation, its theory and reinforcement; leadership, its theory and styles; and discipline, traditional approval, and preventative techniques.

Instruction: Major topics covered in the course are the individual manager's role, strengths, and weaknesses as they relate to various managerial functions and the one-on-one relationship of leading and directing others. Methods of instruction include a written examination and presentation of an in-class practicum. (To complete the course, students must pass a written examination and present an in-class practicum relating a theory from class to their practicum situation.)

Credit Recommendation: In the upper division baccalaureate degree category, with completion of Levels 2 and 3, 3 semester hours in Organizational Behavior and 3 semester hours in Human Resources Management or Management in the Public Sector (11/86) (3/96).

Management Functions in State Government (Level 4 of CPM Program)

Location: Trenton, NJ, and other locations throughout the state.

Length: 39 hours (6 hour sessions over 6.5 weeks).

Dates: October 1983-Present.

Objective: To extend the manager's concern from the individual employee and the employee group to the overall organization.

Learning Outcome: Upon successful completion of this course, the student will be able to have a more effective understanding of the role of management in government; organizational systems and structures; public personnel and motivation; decision-making theory, structure and styles; management budget process; budget development and planning; and the context of public management in a political (interest group) environment.

Instruction: Major topics covered in the course are an introduction to relevant theories and models of administrative theory and organization, as well as major issues facing local, state, and federal governments and key modules focusing on developing skills of the public manager as an effective problem-solver. Methods of instruction include written examinations and a research paper. (Successful completion of a graduate level application project is required to earn the graduate level credit recommendation.)

Credit Recommendation: In the upper division baccalaureate degree or graduate degree category, 3 semester hours in Public Administration (11/86) (3/96). *Prerequisite:* Successful completion of Levels 1, 2 and 3 of the CPM Program.

Managerial Tools for Today's Executive (Level 5 of CPM Program)

Location: Trenton, NJ, and other locations throughout the state.

Length: 72 hours (6 hour sessions over 12 weeks).

Dates: January 1984-Present.

Objective: To prepare managers to make sound fiscal and policy decisions in an ever-changing environment.

Learning Outcome: Upon successful completion of this course, the student will be able to have a more effective understanding of administrative law; analytical skills; capital budgeting; the New Jersey budget process; and an executive's use of computing and microcomputing.

Instruction: Major topics covered in the course are the tools needed by managers to make decisions which have an organizational impact; public finance; an integrated overview of the computer as a managerial tool, and administrative law. Methods of instruction include the use of computers by managers, written examinations, and a written project. (Successful completion of a graduate level application project is required to earn the graduate level credit recommendation.)

Credit Recommendation: In the upper division baccalaureate degree or graduate degree category, 3 semester hours in Introduction to Microcomputers for Managers or Management Information Systems in the Public Sector (not a computer science course), 2 semester hours in Public Finances, and 1 semester hour in Administrative Law (11/86) (3/96). *Prerequisite:* Successful completion of Level 4 of the CPM Program.

Organizational and Human Resources Development (Level 6 of CPM Program)

Location: Trenton, NJ, and other locations throughout the state.

Length: 39 hours (6 hour sessions over 6.5 weeks).

Dates: May 1984-Present.

Objective: To prepare managers to produce and guide effective change within their organization.

Learning Outcome: Upon successful completion of this course, the student will be able to have a more effective understanding of techniques of organizational development; productivity and employee participation; participatory techniques for organization units; and strategies for placement change.

Instruction: Major topics covered in the course are the manager's role in managing change within the organization and an in-depth look at organizational development and team building. Methods of instruction include written examinations and an out-of-class project. (Successful completion of a graduate level application project is required to earn the graduate level credit recommendation.)

Credit Recommendation: In the upper division baccalaureate degree or graduate degree category, 3 semester hours in Organizational Development or Organizational Change and Development (11/86) (3/96). *Prerequisite:* Successful completion of Level 5 of the CPM Program.

Organizing (Level 2 of CPM Program)

Location: Trenton, NJ, and other locations throughout the state.

Length: 30 hours (6 hour sessions over 5 weeks).

Dates: February 1983-Present.

Objective: To explore and develop the manager's role in developing high performance work groups.

Learning Outcome: Upon successful completion of this course, the student will be able to have a more effective understanding of leading a diverse workforce; group dynamics and team building; delegation and time management; performance planning & constructive feedback; and coaching the poor performer.

Instruction: Major topics covered in the course are the topics introduced in Level 1 by further examining their relevance to the managerial function of organizing. The overall focus of this level is on the manager's role in developing high performance work groups in a practicum situation. Methods of instruction include a written examination and presentation of an in-class practicum. (To complete the course students must pass a written examination and present an in-class practicum relating a theory from class to their practicum situation.)

Credit Recommendation: In the upper division baccalaureate degree category, with successful completion of Levels 1 and 3, 3 semester hours in Organizational Behavior and 3 semester hours in Human Resources Management or Management in the Public Sector (11/86) (3/96). *Prereq-*

uisite: Successful completion of Level 1 of CPM Program.

Planning (Level 3 of CPM Program)

Location: Trenton, NJ, and other locations throughout the state.

Length: 30 hours (6 hour sessions over 5 weeks).

Dates: February 1983-Present.

Objective: To enable managers to study and utilize the skills necessary to manage the planning function.

Learning Outcome: Upon successful completion of this course, the student will be able to have a more effective understanding of managing conflict; discipline; process improvement; problem solving; and decision making.

Instruction: Major topics covered in the course are an opportunity to learn about and experiment with the skills and strategies necessary to manage the planning function. It is the experience for participants who will be eligible for the Certificate in Supervisory Management. Methods of instruction include working with a problem-solving model, working with a decision-making model, determining and writing statements, performance planning, and the appraisal interview. (To complete the course, students must pass a written examination and present an in-class practicum relating a theory from class to their practicum situation.)

Credit Recommendation: In the upper division baccalaureate degree category, with successful completion of Levels 1 and 2, 3 semester hours in Organizational Behavior and 3 semester hours in Human Resources Management or Management in the Public Sector (11/86) (3/96).

STATE CORE LEADERSHIP PROGRAM

State Core Leadership Program

Location: State of New Jersey.

Length: 34 hours (8 weeks).

Dates: March 1996-Present.

Objective: To provide upper level State managers and administrators with state-of-the-art approaches to Leadership, Customer Service and Diversity Management, and application of these approaches within their State organizations.

Learning Outcome: Upon successful completion of this course, the student will be able to state the difference between traditional and emerging forms of government leadership; identify the manager's role as a leader within this new environment; identify 3 ways to lead change and support innovation consistent with their organization's emerging vision; identify 3 critical skills necessary to develop, encourage and support teamwork at the worksite; identify, challenge and replace those mental models which serve as obstacles to building a learning organization; identify 3 areas within their Department's organization structure and operations which need to be addressed in order to support improved internal and external customer service that are related to the Department's mission and in alignment with the primary identified needs of their customers; identify 3 strategies for enhancing the working relationships within the multi-cultural environment of their Department; and identify and explain the steps involved in systems problem solving and apply these steps to case studies and the student's own organization.

Instruction: Major topics covered in the course are 3 days of training in State Government Leadership, 1 day of training in Leading a Diverse Workforce, 1 day of training in Leading a Customer Service organization, and a 4-hour Post-Training Consultation and Evaluation Session conducted by the HRDI Customer Service Consultant for that Department. Methods of instruction include discussion, small group exercises, and personal action plans and projects. (Successful completion of a graduate level application project is required to earn the credit recommendation.)

Credit Recommendation: In the graduate degree category, 2 semester hours in Executive Leadership (3/96). *Prerequisite:* Each trainee must complete a leadership assessment tool, the results of which will be used in the Leadership component of the Program.

SUPPORT SPECIALIST PROGRAM

The following courses were originally conducted through the New Jersey Department of Human Services, Office of Manpower Planning, Development and Training. This office of the Department of Human Services has been abolished and all their training programs consolidated under the Department of Personnel, Human Resource Development Institute.

Support Specialist Program

Location: New Jersey Department of Personnel, Human Resources Training Center, Princeton, New Jersey, and other locations throughout New Jersey.

Length: *Version 1:* 108 hours (18 days); *Version 2:* 90 hours (15 days).

Dates: *Version 1:* May 1986-July 1991; *Version 2:* September 1991-October 1994.

Objective: To enable support staff in state government to understand and to participate effectively with the team concept in contemporary management and with the technological changes in the contemporary office.

Learning Outcome: Upon successful completion of this program, the participants will have increased job skills and knowledge, especially in an overall understanding of the structure of state government and the structure of the new technological office. Participants will also develop the ability to apply the principles of effective communications and will develop an understanding of the team concept for an effective work environment.

Instruction: This course is conceptually based rather than skills based and is offered to employees whose job is to support supervisors, managers, and executives in government. The program is divided into three sections, with each section building on the previous section to form an integrated whole. The course includes oral presentations, written examinations, and outside projects. Topics covered in the program include the role and function of a support specialist, the organization of state government, work simplification, problem-solving and decision-making, communication and presentation skills, the meaning and role of management, and effective team membership. The major areas covered by this program are leadership; communication, especially verbal skills; motivation; and elements of management and supervision.

Credit Recommendation: *Version 1:* In the lower division baccalaureate/associate degree category, 6 semester hours (which can be applied as 6 semester hours in any one of the following subjects, or 3 semester hours in one subject and another 3 semester hours in another of the subjects) in Principles of Administrative Support, Office Administration, Public Administration elective, or Business elective (8/89). **NOTE:** Credit recommendation is based on successful completion of Sections 1, 2, and 3. There is no credit recommendation for individual sections of the program. *Version 2:* In the lower division baccalaureate/associate degree category, 6 semester hours (which can be applied as 6 semester hours in any one of the following subjects, or 3 semester hours in one subject and another 3 semester hours in another of the subjects) in Principles of Administrative Support, Office Administration, Public Administration elective, or Business elective (8/89). **NOTE:** Credit recommendation is based on successful completion of Sections 1, 2, and 3. There is no credit recommendation for individual sections of the program.

New Mexico State Fire Academy

The New Mexico State Fire Academy (NMSFA) was established in 1989 to deliver training to emergency service personnel. NMSFA is a "State of the Art" education institution with a variety of courses. They range from basic to advanced and Firefighter to Management. These courses are held at the Fire Academy campus and host sites throughout New Mexico.

Courses, seminars, and other training activities are evaluated on a continual basis. Input into this evaluation process comes from students and faculty feedback; poor student performance; new technology; new methods of instruction; and how effective is the training meeting the needs of the fire service. New courses are being added to improve the NMSFA curriculum.

Faculty members at NMSFA have a variety of education levels and backgrounds in fire related fields. Because of the ever changing nature of the fire environment, the faculty is encouraged to attend courses to improve their knowledge.

Student performance is evaluated by a series of quizzes, module examinations, and comprehensive final examinations for each of the courses being offered.

Source of official student records: Registry of Credit Recommendations, American Council on Education, One Dupont Circle, Washington, DC 20036-1193 or Director of Training, New Mexico State Fire Academy, P.O. Box 239, Socorro, New Mexico 87801.

Additional information about the courses: College Credit Recommendation Service, American Council on Education, One Dupont Circle, Washington, DC 20036-1193.

Building Construction: Non-Combustible and Fire Resistive (F150)

Location: Socorro, NM and host sites throughout New Mexico.

Length: 16 hours (2 days).

Dates: January 1989-Present.

Objective: To enable the student to cite key features of non-combustible or fire resistive buildings that affect emergency operations; and fire and life safety concerns that exist in non-combustible and fire-resistive structures.

Instruction: Major topics covered in the course links the key features of non-combustible and fire-resistive structures that affect emergency operations; the fire behaviors of steel and concrete are presented so that the effect of their presence in non-combustible or fire resistive structures may be better anticipated; basic principles that apply to the spread of fire, products of combustion in structures, and special problems with interior finishes and building elements; testing methods for materials; and the unique lecture, discussion, and simulation exercises.

Credit Recommendation: In the lower division baccalaureate/associate degree category, 1 semester hour in Construction Technology or Fire Science (8/86) (2/95).

Building Construction: Principles of Wood and Ordinary Construction (F100)

Location: Socorro, NM and host sites throughout New Mexico.

Length: 16 hours (2 days).

Dates: January 1989-Present.

Objective: To enable the student to recognize construction types, design, alteration consequences, materials used, and their influence on the building's reaction to fire; and in a tactical situation construction features and resultant potential hazards to firefighters.

Instruction: Major topics covered in the course provide information of how the construction type, alterations, design, and materials influence a building's reaction to fire; the principle of "fireground" reading of a building and the value of relevant advance information about buildings; major areas of study include building stability and resistance to fire, special hazards to firefighters and construction elements, and the determination of likely paths of fire extension. Methods of instruction include lecture, discussion, and simulation exercises.

Credit Recommendation: In the lower division baccalaureate/associate degree category, 1 semester hour in Construction Technology or Fire Science (8/86) (2/95).

Firefighter Health and Safety: Program Implementation and Management (F128)

Location: Socorro, NM and host sites throughout New Mexico.

Length: 16 hours (two 8-hour days).

Dates: January 1989-December 1993.

Objective: To provide the student with an understanding of general health and safety guidelines and practices needed by firefighters.

Learning Outcome: Upon successful completion of this course, the student will be able to identify and analyze firefighter health and safety concerns; determine the components of an effective department health and safety program; and understand the steps and process necessary to design and implement such a program.

Instruction: Major topics covered in the course are safety as an attitude, developing a health and safety program; laws; standards and regulations; health maintenance and physical fitness; stress; emergency scene safety; and safety investigation.

Credit Recommendation: In the lower division baccalaureate/associate degree category or in the upper division baccalaureate degree category, 2 semester hours in Engineering (Industrial), Fire Science, Health Promotion, Health Safety, or Occupational Safety (12/88).

Firefighter Safety and Survival: Company Officer's Responsibility (F125)

Location: Socorro, NM and host sites throughout New Mexico.

Length: 16 hours (two 8-hour days).

Dates: January 1989-Present.

Objective: To provide the student with an appreciation of the seriousness of the firefighter injury and death problems and to provide an awareness of techniques for reducing injuries and deaths.

Learning Outcome: Upon successful completion of this course, the student will be able to understand the causes of injury and death; understand the behavior problems and attitudes that are addressed; identify health and fitness programs related to injury and death; identify hazardous situations found in training; identify and correct five station hazards; identify and resolve hazards responding to and returning from a fire; identify and enforce procedures to improve incident scene safety; and identify safety and survival tips.

Instruction: Major topics covered in the course are an explanation of firefighter injuries and deaths; firefighter health and fitness; safety in training, station and response preparation safety; incident safety; post-incident safety; and survival tips.

Credit Recommendation: In the lower division baccalaureate/associate degree category, 1 semester hour in Fire Administration, Fire Management, or Fire Science (12/88) (2/93).

Hazardous Materials Incident Analysis (F410)

Location: Socorro, NM and host sites throughout New Mexico.

Length: 12 hours (2 days) or in 8 modules.

Dates: January 1989-November 1994.

Objective: To provide the student with the knowledge required for effective analysis of a hazardous materials incident.

Learning Outcome: Upon successful completion of this course, the student will be able to categorize hazardous materials, their storage, and transportation; recognize presence of hazardous materials and the likely behavior of such materials; estimate likely harmful emergency outcomes related to hazardous materials; and select appropriate action related to hazardous materials situations.

Instruction: Major topics covered in the course are the definition of hazardous materials, hazardous materials emergencies and their outcomes; potentially dangerous assumptions; estimating likely harm; events analysis; and characteristics and behavior of hazardous materials. Methods of instruction include lecture, discussion, classroom exercises, case studies, audiovisual aids, and examinations.

Credit Recommendation: In the lower division baccalaureate/associate degree category, 1 semester hour Fire Science (11/89).

Incident Command System (F200)

Location: Socorro, NM and host sites throughout New Mexico.

Length: 16 hours (two 8-hour days).

Dates: January 1989-December 1993.

Objective: To allow the student to demonstrate the need for an organized approach to managing emergency incidents, to identify the laws and standards requiring this approach, to identify the elements of an emergency response system, and to assess department capabilities for implementing such a system.

Learning Outcome: Upon successful completion of this course, the student will be able to demonstrate the need for an organized approach to emergency incidents; identify the laws and standards requiring this approach; identify the elements of an effective system; and evaluate his or her department capabilities.

Instruction: Major topics covered in the course are the need for organized incident management; the laws and standards requiring same; the components of such a system; relationship between business management and incident management; the NFA model of such a system; and other examples of incident management systems.

Credit Recommendation: In the lower division baccalaureate/associate degree category, 1 semester hour in Administration, Fire Science, or Management (12/88). **NOTE:** Credit for Fire Commands Operations should not be awarded if credit is awarded for this course.

Infection Control for Emergency Response Personnel (W250)

Location: Socorro, NM and host sites throughout New Mexico.

Length: 12 hours (2 days).

Dates: December 1990-March 1996.

Objective: To enable supervisory fire and EMS personnel to ensure infection control in the work environment by providing the knowledge and skills required to conduct training, monitor compliance with OSHA (CFRSS190.1030), and serve as a role model for positive behaviors and attitudes.

Learning Outcome: Upon successful completion of this course, the student will be able to ensure infection control in their work environment by providing the knowledge and skills required to conduct training, monitor compliance, and serve as a role model for positive behaviors and attitudes.

Instruction: Major topics covered in the course are designed to meet the needs of fire service officers and emergency medical service first-line supervisors in order to improve the knowledge and protection of the individual and department/station personnel from the full range of infectious diseases spread through occupational or other exposure; the training stresses protection of the individual and department/station from the full range of infectious diseases spread through occupational and other exposures; appropriate target audiences for the course include career and volunteer firefighters and allied professionals; private sector and public sector third service emergency health care providers will also benefit from this instruction Training will be compatible with NFPA standards and all applicable federal regulations; the importance of the supervisor as a role model is emphasized throughout the course; to highlight, the student prepares a personal plan for developing and demonstrating constructive behaviors and attitudes; motivating students to practice infection control in all aspects of the job; the sequencing of instruction follows the basic progression of an emergency incident—pre-response, on-scene, and post-response; other topics include brisk exposure, modes of transmission, health maintenance, personal protective equipment, scene management post-exposures, and post-response and station issues. Methods of instruction include lecture, classroom exercises, group projects, and final exam.

Credit Recommendation: In the lower division baccalaureate/associate degree category, 1 semester hour in Fire Science, Health Care Administration, or Public Health (3/91).

Initial Response to Hazardous Materials Incidents: Basic Course

Location: Socorro, NM and other sites throughout New Mexico.

Length: 16 hours (2 days).

Dates: January 1989-February 1997.

Objective: To provide the first responder at a hazardous materials incident basic concepts and techniques for appropriate behavior before, during, and after the incident; defines hazardous materials and describes roles, responsibilities, and risks associated with the incident.

Learning Outcome: Upon successful completion of this course, the student will be able to define hazardous materials and describe associated risks to personal safety; explain the roles, responsibilities, and limitations of first responders in hazardous materials incidents; implement appropriate behaviors before, during, and after a hazardous materials in different emergency situations; identify local, state, and federal resources appropriate to emergency and nonemergency situations; and describe basic concepts and techniques of site management and scene setup, to include the proper use of personal protective equipment and decontamination.

Instruction: Major topics covered in the course are introduction; regulations and standards; personal safety; toxicology; site management and scene set-up; personal protective equipment; decontamination; and resources. Methods of instruction include lecture, discussion, classroom exercises, case studies, role playing, and problem-solving (facilitated by instructor and performed by student).

Credit Recommendation: In the lower division baccalaureate/associate degree category, 1 semester hour in Fire Science (2/92).

New York State Academy of Fire Science

The Senator Frederick L. Warder New York State Academy of Fire Science (NYSAFS), established in 1971, is the residential training facility of New York State's Department of State, Office of Fire Prevention and Control. The objectives of the academy programs are: To develop fire administrators, fire commanders, skilled instructors, and technical personnel; to provide a permanent facility staffed with skilled personnel employing modern training techniques, and utilizing a physical plant which will make it possible to create realistic fire conditions and develop fire command programs; to offer curricula to meet the full range of training needs of the fire services in New York State, particularly for leaders and technicians; and to conduct cooperative programs to share talents, facilities, and ideas with all public, private, educational and industrial agencies active in public administration and public safety in the state.

Courses, seminars and other training activities are evaluated on a continual basis. Input into this evaluation process comes from student and faculty feedback, student performance, new technology, new method of instruction, and how effective the training is in meeting the needs of the fire service. Courses are always under revision and new courses are developed as the need arises.

Instructors are practitioners in the field, trained in educational techniques thus assuring the highest quality in training and education. Courses are presently conducted at the campus in Montour Falls, but will soon be offered at a new annex located at Camp Smith, Peekskill, NY.

Student performance is evaluated by a series of quizzes, and comprehensive final examinations for each of the courses being offered.

Courses are offered in these subject areas: Instructor Development, Fire Prevention/Code Enforcement, Officer Development, Health and Safety, Dispatcher Training, Fire Suppression/Rescue Operations, Equipment Maintenance, Fire/Arson Investigation, and Hazardous Materials.

For student record information contact: Director, New York State Academy of Fire Science, P.O. Box 811, Montour Falls, NY 14865.

Source of official student records: Registry of Credit Recommendations, American Council on Education, One Dupont Circle, Washington, DC 20036-1193.

Additional information about the courses: College Credit Recommendation Service, American Council on Education, One Dupont Circle, Washington, DC 20036-1193.

Building Construction for Fire Suppression Forces: Non-Combustible and Fire Resistive

Location: New York State Academy of Fire Science.

Length: 16 hours (2 days).

Dates: May 1985-Present.

Objective: To enable the student to cite key features of non-combustible or fire-resistive buildings that affect emergency operations. Fire and life safety concerns that exist in non-combustible and fire-resistive structures are studied.

Instruction: Major topics covered in the course are the key features of non-combustible and fire-resistive structures that affect emergency operations; fire behaviors of steel and concrete are presented so that the effect of their presence in non-combustible and fire-resistive structures may be better anticipated; basic principles that apply to the spread of fire, products of combustion in structures, and special problems with interior finishes and building elements; testing methods for materials; and the unique problems of conducting emergency operations in buildings under construction. Methods of instruction include lecture, discussion, and simulation exercises.

Credit Recommendation: In the lower division baccalaureate/associate degree category, 1 semester hour in Construction Technology or Fire Science (2/95).

Building Construction for Fire Suppression Forces: Principles of Wood and Ordinary Construction

Location: New York State Academy of Fire Science.

Length: 16 hours (2 days).

Dates: February 1985-Present.

Objective: To enable the student to recognize construction types, design, alteration consequences, materials used, and their influence on the building's reaction to fire. In a tactical situation, construction features and resultant potential hazards to firefighters are studied.

Instruction: Major topics covered in the course are information about how the construction type, alterations, design, and materials influence a building's reaction to fire; the principle of "fireground" reading of a building; the value of relevant advance information about buildings; building stability and resistance to fire; special hazards to firefighters and construction elements; and how to determine the likely paths of fire extension. Methods of instruction include lecture, discussion, and simulation exercises.

Credit Recommendation: In the lower division baccalaureate/associate degree category, 1 semester hour in Construction Technology or Fire Science (2/95).

Chemistry of Hazardous Materials

Location: New York State Academy of Fire Science.

Length: 80 hours (10 days).

Dates: February 1989-Present.

Objective: To provide students with a sound understanding of the basic chemistry of hazardous materials, key properties of important hazardous materials products, and significant storage and handling requirements for hazardous materials in their normal environment.

Learning Outcome: Upon successful completion of the course, the student will be able to identify the inherent hazards (toxicity, flammability, reactivity) of chemicals from the name, the formula, and the structure, and deduce worse case synergistic reaction in the event of a release.

Instruction: Major topics covered in the course are basic knowledge required to evaluate potential hazards and behaviors of materials considered dangerous. Emphasis is on the underlying reasons for recommended handling of hazardous materials, with the hope this knowledge will lead to improved decision-making and safer operations and handling for fire officers who may be involved in hazardous material incidents or in the inspection of occupancies, vehicles, water craft, or aircraft containing hazardous materials. Methods of instruction include lecture, discussion, laboratory, and workshops.

Credit Recommendation: In the lower division baccalaureate/associate degree category, 3 semester hours in Fire Science, Chemistry, General Science, or Physical Science (2/94).

Community Fire Protection: Master Planning

Location: New York State Academy of Fire Science.

Length: 53 hours (1 week).

Dates: July 1996-Present.

Objective: To develop and provide students with the planning skills necessary from a technical and political standpoint to effectively plan a local fire program.

Learning Outcome: Upon successful completion of this course, the student will be able to evaluate the community needs associated with risk of fire; select and evaluate the most efficient system in developing community fire protection programs; and define and design a fire and life safety system for a community.

Instruction: Major topics covered in the course are planning strategy; analysis of current systems including risk, developing solutions, and action plans to be implemented; and evaluating the various problems associated with community fire planning. Methods of instruction include lecture, discussion, classroom exercises, and critique of classroom presentations.

Credit Recommendation: In the upper division baccalaureate degree category, 2 semester hours in Administration, Fire Science, Fire Technology, Management, or Public Administration (2/94).

Fire Command Operations

Location: New York State Academy of Fire Science.

Length: 48 hours (1 week).

Dates: May 1993-Present.

Objective: To develop the student's skills, technique, and knowledge for managing and directing operations at emergency sites.

Learning Outcome: Upon successful completion of this course, the student will be able to apply the "Incident Command System" in organizing emergency procedures at various kinds of sites and under varying types of conditions and situations; coordinate the activities of multiple skills units; and provide a concentrated effort at effecting solutions in emergency situations.

Instruction: Major topics covered in the course are fire command, mutual aid, command sequence, incident command system, fire behavior in buildings, preincident preparation, tactical unit operations, and incident organization. Methods of instruction include lecture, discussion, classroom exercises, and an examination.

Credit Recommendation: In the upper division baccalaureate degree category, 3 semester hours in Fire Science, Fire Technology, Human Resource Management, Occupational Health and Safety, or Public Management (2/94). **NOTE:** Credit for Incident Command Systems should not be awarded if credit is awarded for this course.

Fire Inspection Principles

Location: New York State Academy of Fire Science.

Length: 61 hours (2 weeks).

Dates: August 1997-October 1997.

Objective: To provide students with the fundamental knowledge, skills, and attitudes to conduct basic fire safety inspections effectively and confidently.

Learning Outcome: Upon successful completion of this course, the student will be able to explain the code enforcement system; perform fire inspector's role professionally; recognize potential hazards of fire spread; analyze construction types and building systems; describe human behavior in fire situations; explain codes and standards; evaluate fire safety of structure, verify level of safety; identify hazardous materials or processes; identify methods of mitigating hazards; identify special hazard suppression systems; and verify operations of sprinkler systems and alarm detection systems.

Instruction: Major topics covered in the course are participant's role in code enforcement; fire and codes and their relationship; general fire safety; life safety; hazardous materials and processes; special hazards; and fire protection systems and equipment. Methods of instruction include lecture, audio visuals (film, overhead transparencies, photographs, and diagrams), learning activity assignments, discussion, and group presentations.

Credit Recommendation: In lower division baccalaureate/associate degree category, 3 semester hours in Fire Science, Industrial Safety, or Insurance (2/92).

Health and Safety Officer

Location: New York State Academy of Fire Science.

Length: 14 hours (2 days).

Dates: June 1995-Present.

Objective: To examine the health and safety officer's role in identifying, evaluating, and implementing policy and procedure that affect the safety and health of emergency responders.

Learning Outcome: Upon successful completion of this course, the student will be able to understand the role of the health and safety officer in both emergency and non-emergency situations.

Instruction: Major topics covered in the course are the role of the health and safety officer, the laws, standards, and regulations; health maintenance; accident investigation; and post incident evaluation. Methods of instruction include lecture, discussion, classroom exercises, case studies, audio visual material, learner presentation/reports, end of the course testing, and graded individual and group activities throughout the course.

Credit Recommendation: In the lower division baccalaureate/associate degree or upper division baccalaureate degree category, 1 semester hour in Occupational Health and Safety, or Fire Science (2/95).

Incident Safety Officer

Location: New York State Academy of Fire Science.

Length: 16 hours (2 days).

Dates: May 1995-Present.

Objective: To provide an understanding of the safety officer's role at emergency response situations, with specific emphasis on the role of the safety officer in the Incident Command System.

Learning Outcome: Upon successful completion of this course, the student will be able to provide the Company Officer with the skills to function effectively as a Safety Officer at emergency incidents.

Instruction: Major topics covered in the course are the role of the Safety Officer; regulations, standards and policies; record keeping and documentation; risk management and communications. Methods of instruction include lecture, discussion, classroom exercises, case studies, audio/visual material, and a final examination.

Credit Recommendation: In the lower division baccalaureate/associate degree or upper division baccalaureate degree category, 1 semester hour in Occupational Health and Safety or Fire Science (2/95).

Infection Control for Emergency Response Personnel: The Supervisor's Role and Responsibility

Location: New York State Academy of Fire Science.

Length: 12 hours (2 days).

Dates: April 1992-March 1996.

Objective: To enable supervisory fire and EMS personnel to ensure infection control in the work environment by providing the knowledge and skills required to conduct training, monitor compliance with OSHA (SFR SS190.1030), and serve as a role model for positive behaviors and attitudes.

Learning Outcome: Upon successful completion of this course, the student will be able to ensure infection control in their work environment by providing the knowledge and skills required to conduct training, monitor compliance, and serve as a role model for positive behaviors and attitudes.

Instruction: Major topics covered in the course are how to protect the individual and department/station personnel from the full range of infectious diseases spread through occupational or other exposures, brisk exposure, modes of transmission, health maintenance personal protective equipment, scene management post-exposures, post-response and station issues, and the importance of the supervisor as a role model. Appropriate target audiences for the course include career and volunteer firefighters, allied professionals, and private and public sector third service emergency health care providers. Methods of instruction include lecture, classroom exercise, group projects, a personal plan for developing and demonstrating constructive behaviors and attitudes, and a final examination.

Credit Recommendation: In the lower division baccalaureate/associate degree category, 1 semester hour in Fire Science or Health Care Administration and Public Health (3/91).

Leadership I: Strategies for Company Success

Location: New York State Academy of Fire Science.

Length: 12 hours (2 days).

Dates: October 1989-Present.

Objective: To provide the student with leadership skills of mid-level managers, especially fire company officers.

Learning Outcome: Upon successful completion of this course, the student will be able to apply appropriate decision-making styles to given situations, outline critical steps in problem-solving methods, identify services provided by a "typical" fire company and the resources needed to provide these services, understand the relationship between resources and services provided by a fire company, and describe the requirements involved in running effective meetings.

Instruction: Major topics covered in the course are decision-making, problem-solving, brainstorming, and meeting management. Methods of instruction include lecture, discussion, audio visual aids, and examinations.

Credit Recommendation: In the lower division baccalaureate/associate degree category, 1 semester hour in Business Administration, Fire Science, Public Administration, or Urban/Regional Plan-ning (2/95).

Leadership II: Strategies for Personal Success

Location: New York State Academy of Fire Science.

Length: 12 hours (2 days).

Dates: January 1990-Present.

Objective: To provide the student with an understanding of leadership skills and tasks associated with management of multiple roles of managers, ethics, abuse of power, and personal creativity.

Learning Outcome: Upon successful completion of this course, the student will be able to identify typical roles and responsibilities of a commanding officer; identify, define, and analyze the role of creativity and innovation in fire service organizations; identify the sources and limits of different types of power; and make appropriate decisions involving ethical issues.

Instruction: Major topics covered in the course are ethics, role conflict, fostering creativity and innovation, and power. Methods of instruction include lecture, discussion, audio visual aids, role playing, and examinations.

Credit Recommendation: In the lower division baccalaureate/associate degree category, 1 semester hour in Business Administration, Fire Science, Public Administration, or Urban/Regional Plan-ning (2/95).

Leadership III: Strategies for Supervisory Success

Location: New York State Academy of Fire Science.

Length: 12 hours (2 days).

Dates: April 1990-Present.

Objective: To provide the student with an understanding of basic leadership skills related to supervision of personnel.

Learning Outcome: Upon successful completion of this course, the student will be able to describe the relationship between development level and leadership style, identify benefits derived from effective delegation and barriers that prevent it, recognize similarities that characterize effective coaches and effective leaders, and use discipline to correct improper employee behavior.

Instruction: Major topics covered in the course are situational leadership, delegation, coaching, and discipline. Methods of instruction include lecture, discussion, audio visual aids, small group activity, and examinations.

Credit Recommendation: In the lower division baccalaureate/associate degree category, 1 semester hour in Business Administration, Fire Science, Public Administration, or Urban/Regional Planning (2/95).

Managing Company Tactical Operations: Decision Making

Location: New York State Academy of Fire Science.

Length: 12 hours (2 days).

Dates: January 1992-Present.

Objective: To provide a framework for effective structural firefighting decision-making and tactical organization.

Learning Outcome: Upon successful completion of this course, the student will be able to apply a systematic approach for developing basic fireground strategies and implementing tactical plans; and implement a basic incident command system for structural firefighting.

Instruction: Major topics covered in the course are the command sequence, size-up, developing an action plan, implementing an action plan, and introduction to incident command. Methods for instruction include lecture, 35 mm slides, instructor-monitored individual and group activities, and a written examination.

Credit Recommendation: In the lower division baccalaureate/associate degree category, 1 semester hour in Fire Science/ Technology or Fire Administration (2/93).

Managing Company Tactical Operations: Preparation

Location: New York State Academy of Fire Science.

Length: 12 hours (2 days).

Dates: October 1991-Present.

Objective: To provide the new or prospective fire officer with the basic knowledge and skills necessary to manage one or more fire companies in structural firefighting operations.

Learning Outcome: Upon successful completion of this course, the student will be able to understand the company officer's principal roles and responsibilities in preparing the company to engage in tactical firefighting operations.

Instruction: Major topics covered in the course are the roles and responsibilities of the fire company officer, personal readiness, company readiness, departmental readiness, operational communications, building construction and fire behavior, and preincident preparation (prefire planning). Methods of instruction include lecture, 35 mm slides, instructor-monitored individual and group activities, and written examination.

Credit Recommendation: In the lower division baccalaureate/associate degree

category, 1 semester hour in Fire Science/Technology or Fire Administration (2/93).

Managing Company Tactical Operations: Tactics

Location: New York State Academy of Fire Science.

Length: 12 hours (2 days).

Dates: September 1994-Present.

Objective: To provide senior or acting company officers with the knowledge and skills needed to effectively accomplish assigned tactics at a structural fire emergency.

Learning Outcome: Upon successful completion of this course, the student will be able to explain the purpose and use of the Communications Model and the Quick Access Prefire Plan in tactical operations at fire incidents; define the relationship between incident priorities, strategy, tactics, and implementation in the command sequence; select the appropriate strategic mode, based on consideration of risk, benefit, and available resources; describe the six steps required to implement the Tactical Action Model; and list the factors on which apparatus placement is based.

Instruction: Major topics covered in this course are an introduction to managing company tactical operations; ventilation and rescue; fire confinement and extinguishment; water supply and exposure protection; salvage, overhaul, and support activities; and private dwelling simulations. Methods of instruction include lecture, discussion, classroom exercises, audio visual aids, and a final examination.

Credit Recommendation: In the lower division baccalaureate/associate degree category, 1 semester hour in Fire Technology or Administration (2/94).

Presenting Effective Public Education Programs

Location: New York State Academy of Fire Science.

Length: 35 hours (5 days).

Dates: May 1994-Present.

Objective: To provide public safety educators with the knowledge and skills to apply various learning strategies and presentation techniques in order to make effective deliveries of a community safety education program.

Learning Outcome: Upon successful completion of this course, the student will be able to demonstrate presentation skills for delivering a community safety education program; understand learning strategies appropriate for adults and children; evaluate the delivery of a program and its impact on reducing the identified safety problem; network effectively with various persons and organizations who are in a position of supporting the delivery of a safety program; and analyze neighborhoods for the purpose of confirming an existing community safety problem.

Instruction: Major topics covered in the course are life safety education and the public educator, community analysis, networking strategies, educational principles, choosing the best fire and life safety program, evaluation of impact of course on students and the community, and effective instruction and presentation techniques. Methods of instruction include lecture, discussion, classroom exercises, visual aids, and a final examination.

Credit Recommendation: In the upper division baccalaureate degree category, 2 semester hours in Fire Administration, Fire Science, Fire Technology, or Educational Methods (2/94).

NIIT Ltd.

Established in 1981, NIIT offers IT and training solutions to over 1,000 global clients and operates from over 150 locations world-wide including operations in Singapore, Bangkok, Jakarta, Atlanta, New Jersey, London, Tokyo, and all major cities in India.

The Instructional Software Group develops Instructional Software for clients such as IBM, the World Bank, and the Education Development Center (EDC). The Software Engineering Groups develop application software for global clients like Sun Microsystems and NETG Applied Learning on state-of-the-art software platforms. The entire international operations have received two ISO 9001 certifications from BVQI, UK under the rigorous and exclusive *TICK IT* scheme.

The Software Solutions Group markets and supports world-leading software products such as Sybase, Powerbuilder, Pilot Lightship, Excelerator, Harvard Graphics, and Harvard Project Manager. The Engineering and Geomatics Group offers a range of software products and services which include training, consultancy, turnkey solutions, and systems integration for Computer-Aided Design (CAD), both mechanical and electronic and Geographic Information Systems.

The Business Solutions Group caters to the needs of system integration of the manufacturing and financial sector. It provides IT solutions to the corporate sector by providing consultancy, IT planning, design, and implementation of Executive Information Systems for top management. It also develops and implements customized application software.

The Multimedia Technologies Group develops and markets multimedia edutainment products and configures multimedia solutions for schools.

At the core is the R&D Group which drives all NIIT businesses. The R&D Group comprises Instructional Research Division (IRD) which continually refines the curriculum and the development methodology; Computer Applications Research Division (CARD) which focuses on man-machine interface, Artificial Intelligence, Expert Systems, multimedia, and neural networks; Advanced Technologies Division (ATD) which researches front-runner technologies such as Graphical User Interface, Object-Oriented Development, and Open Systems; and the Institute for Research in Information Sciences (IRIS) which provides research support services.

The Global Education and Training Group has been the pioneer of computer training in India, and offers education and training in information technology across the globe. Education and training at NIIT include short introductory programs, career programs, career upgrade programs, and end-user programs.

The career programs not only impart advanced computer knowledge and skills and prepare learners for emerging technologies but help them to explore their creativity and to develop professional attributes. The integrated education concept is designed to inculcate the professional skills required for effective communication, technical articulation, information search and analysis, reasoning, problem-solving, and team building. This is done through NIIT's Mind Room, equipped with a multi-node Local Area Network and multimedia delivery systems. The focus is on drawing out and developing latent personal and professional attributes, on learning to learn, and on integration of skills. Hands-on projects ensure a strong focus on application development. Self-paced practice is facilitated by Computerdromes through Technology Based Learning.

The Instructional Research & Development Division designs these courses and continually refines NIIT's development methodology based on current trends, research findings, feedback from students, and changing market requirements. The courses are reviewed by research and validation teams and are subjected to a pilot-phase.

Student performance is evaluated by a series of quizzes, module tests, projects, seminars, information search and analysis skills exercises, and comprehensive final examinations.

At the core of NIIT's quality in education and training is its staff of over 1,500 IT professionals. Faculty members at NIIT have formal qualifications in computer science and MIS. They are selected from leading management and academic institutions. Every year, NIIT provides 15 person days of training to each of its faculty members at the School for Employee Education and Development (SEED), an in-house training facility of NIIT. The performance of faculty members is reviewed and feedback given on a regular basis.

NIIT has trained over 400,000 students and working professionals at over 150 training centers world-wide.

Source of official student records: Registry of Credit Recommendations, American Council on Education, One Dupont Circle, Washington, DC 20036-1193 or Head, Education Planning Group, NIIT, NIIT House, C-125 Okhla Phase I, New Delhi 110 020, India.

Additional information about the courses: College Credit Recommendation Service, American Council on Education, One Dupont Circle, Washington, DC 20036-1193.

Advanced Diploma in Software Technology and Systems Management

Location: Various locations throughout India.

Length: 114 hours (26 weeks).

Dates: June 1993-Present.

Objective: To prepare the student to write programs in the UNIX environment using object oriented programming techniques.

Learning Outcome: Upon successful completion of this course, the student will be able to build applications using the C++ object oriented programming language and to perform systems administrator functions required to support a UNIX system.

Instruction: Major topics covered in the course are advanced UNIX system security; UNIX internals and utilities such as stream editor, source code control, file system options, system calls, and device drivers; C++ object oriented programming including OOPS concepts, object oriented modeling, data abstraction, encapsulation, and inheritance; and design methodology for object oriented systems including design tools, life cycle planning, complex hierarchies, and independent subsystems and physical implementation. Methods of instruction include lecture, practical exercises, various CBT modules, self-paced learning, reading assignments, laboratory practice, and examinations.

Credit Recommendation: In the lower division baccalaureate/associate degree category, 5 semester hours, and in the upper division baccalaureate degree category, 4 semester hours in Computer Science, Computer Information Systems, or Data Processing (11/95). **NOTE:** The student must successfully complete both the Certificate Program in Computer Applications and the Honors Diploma in Software Technology and Systems Management before taking this course.

Advanced Diploma in Systems Management (ASM)

Location: Various locations offered by NIIT in India.

Length: 624 hours (104 weeks); three 2-hour meetings per week, including 66 project hours.

Dates: June 1989-Present.

Objective: To prepare students to enter the real world as computer professionals in EDP possessing skills in programming (dBASE, COBOL, UNIX shell, C) analysis and design as well as state-of-the-art environments (DBMS, Expert Systems, CASE tools).

Instruction: Major topics covered in the first section 1 are a basic overview of computers, which includes a brief history, an overview of computer hardware, software and applications, and various types of computer systems (centralized, decentralized and distributed). Programming Logic and Techniques covers problem-solving techniques using flowcharts. COBOL exposure relates to ANSI COBOL and its use in commercial data processing and includes complex report generation, data entry through screen section and validations, table handling and indexed file maintenance.

Major topics covered in section 2 are the data base management system (dBASE III+) as a complete programming language and spreadsheets as a tool for MIS. Specific applications areas like financial accounting, inventory control, payroll and production planning and control are covered from both data processing and MIS perspectives. Tools for structured systems analysis and design such as data flow diagrams, structure charts, and data dictionaries are covered along with relevant analysis and design concepts including all stages from initial development, through testing and finally handing over to external users.

Major topics covered in section 3 are operating system concepts with specific reference to UNIX where shell programming skills are imparted. Subsequently two streams are provided either for C or UNIFY. The C program covers detailed application programming as well as systems programming ending with the construction of a DBMS in C using linked lists. The UNIFY program covers basic DBMS concepts and applications development in the UNIFY DBMS environment.

Major topics covered in section 4 are data base design and construction. SYBASE and FOCUS DBMS products are used to construct hierarchical, network, and relational data bases. There is also an emphasis on fourth generation languages such as FOCUS and SQL. Finally, various DBMS products are compared. The section also deals with CASE tools and enables learners to build Expert Systems.

Methods of instruction include lectures, practical exercises, self-paced learning, student/instructor consultation sessions, reading assignments in NIIT-prepared text, booklets, and extensive program development, compiling and execution on inhouse computers, as well as a major project that will allow the student to demonstrate mastery of all the course components.

Credit Recommendation: In the lower division baccalaureate/associate degree category, 3 semester hours in Introduction to Computers; in the upper division baccalaureate or graduate degree category, 4 semester hours in COBOL Programming; in the lower division baccalaureate/associate degree category, 3 semester hours in Computer Programming; and in the upper division baccalaureate degree category, 3 semester hours in Advanced Computer Programming Applications. In the graduate degree category, 2 semester hours in UNIX; in the graduate degree category, 3 semester hours in "C" Programming; in the graduate degree category, 2 semester hours in Advanced "C"; in the graduate degree category, 1 semester hour in Data Structures; and in the graduate degree category, 1 semester hour in Computer Applications; in the graduate degree category, 1 semester hour in Computer Aided Software Engineering (CASE); in the graduate degree category, 2 semester hours in Expert Systems; in the graduate degree category, 1 semester hour in Fourth Generation Languages; in the graduate degree category, 8 semester hours in Database Design and Implementation (4/91) (11/95). **NOTE:** Students who receive total credit for this course should not receive credit for COBOL Programming and Application (Certificate in COBOL Programming [CCP]), Computer-Based Business Systems (Diploma in Systems Management [DSM], or Honors Diploma in Systems Management [HSM].

Certificate Program in Computer Applications

Location: Various locations throughout India.

Length: 108 hours (26 weeks).

Dates: June 1993-Present.

Objective: To prepare the student with sufficient computing skills to understand the functions and use of microcomputers in the business environment.

Learning Outcome: Upon successful completion of this course, the student will be able to demonstrate a working knowledge of microcomputers; basic knowledge of PC computing systems; and will have exposure to PC applications including spreadsheets, databases, and word processors.

Instruction: Major topics covered in the course are computer overview and computer concepts, the DOS operating system, microcomputer data bases using FOXBASE Plus, creating and manipulating spreadsheets, utilizing a word processor to enter and format text, introduction to business graphics, and local area network concepts and GUI interfaces based on Microsoft Windows. Methods of instruction include lectures, practical exercises, various CBT exercises, self-paced learning, reading assignments, laboratory practice, and examinations.

Credit Recommendation: In the lower division baccalaureate/associate degree category, 8 semester hours in Computer Science, Computer Information Systems, or Data Processing (11/95).

COBOL Programming and Application
Certificate in COBOL Programming [CCP]

Location: Various locations offered by NIIT in India.

Length: 150 hours (25 weeks); three 2-hour meetings per week, including an 8-hour project.

Dates: April 1986-Present.

Objective: To train students to become proficient COBOL programmers.

Learning Outcome: Upon successful completion of this course, the student will be able to understand the workings of a computer system; break a problem down into its composite parts and then structure the problem into flowchart form; and write COBOL programs for varied case studies.

Instruction: Major topics covered in the course are a basic overview of computers that includes a brief history, an overview of computer hardware, software and applications, and various types of computer systems ((centralized, decentralized, and distributed). Programming Logic and Techniques covers problem-solving techniques using flowcharts. COBOL exposure relates to ANSI COBOL and its use in commercial data processing and includes complex report generation, data entry through screen section and validations, table handling, and indexed file maintenance. Methods of instruction include lectures, practical exercises, self-paced learning, student/instructor consultation sessions, reading assignments in NIIT-prepared text, booklets, and extensive program development, compiling, and execution on in-house computers.

Credit Recommendation: In the lower division baccalaureate/associate degree category, 1 semester hour in Introduction to Computers and in the upper division baccalaureate or graduate degree category, 4 semester hours in COBOL Programming and Applications (3/89) (11/95).

Diploma in Systems Management (DSM)

Location: Various locations offered by NIIT in India.

Length: 312 hours (52 weeks); three 2-hour meetings per week, including a 48-hour project.

Dates: April 1986-Present.

Objective: To provide the student with the skills and experience to support computer-based problem solving.

Learning Outcome: Upon successful completion of this course, the student will be able to understand the workings of a computer system; break a problem down into its composite parts and then structure the problem into flowchart form; write COBOL programs for varied case studies; use micro database and spreadsheet programs; and use basic concepts to analyze and interpret problems into a logical format useful for structuring computer programs.

Instruction: Major topics covered in the *first section* of the course are a basic overview of computers that includes a brief history; an overview of computer hardware, software, and applications; and various types of computer systems (centralized, decentralized, and distributed). Programming Logic and Techniques covers problem-solving techniques using flowcharts. COBOL Exposure relates to ANSI COBOL and its use in commercial data processing and includes complex report generation, data entry through screen section and validations, table handling, and indexed file maintenance. Major topics covered in the *second section* covers the database management system (dBAse III+) as a complete programming language and spreadsheets as a tool for MIS. Specific applications areas such as financial accounting, inventory control, payroll, and production planning and control are covered from both data processing and MIS perspectives. Tools for structured systems analysis and design such as data flow diagrams, structure charts, and data dictionaries are covered along with relevant analysis and design concepts, including all stages from initial development through testing and the final handing over to external users. Coverage also includes procedures to select and appraise the quality and usage of small computer systems. Methods of instruction include lectures, practical exercises, self-paced learning, student/instructor consultation sessions, reading assignments in NIIT-prepared text, booklets, and extensive program development, compiling, and execution on in-house computers. A major project is also accomplished that will allow the student to demonstrate his/her mastery of all the course components.

Credit Recommendation: In the lower division baccalaureate/associate degree category, 3 semester hours in Introduction to Computers; in the upper division baccalaureate or graduate degree category, 4 semester hours in COBOL Programming; in the lower division baccalaureate/associate degree category, 3 semester hours in Computer Programming; and in the upper division baccalaureate degree category, 3 semester hours in Advanced Computer Programming Applications (3/89) (11/95). **NOTE:** Students who receive total credit for this course should not receive credit for COBOL Programming and Application (Certificate in COBOL Programming [CCP]).

Honors Diploma in Software Technology and Systems Management

Location: Various locations throughout India.

Length: 127 hours (26 weeks).

Dates: June 1993-Present.

Objective: To prepare the student to perform basic systems analysis in the DOS and UNIX environments.

Learning Outcome: Upon successful completion of the course, the student will be able to understand the systems development process as it relates to the DOS and UNIX platforms and use the C programming language to program business applications and system utilities.

Instruction: Major topics covered in the course are UNIX as an operating system and as a programming language using shell scripts; C programming, including the use of pointers, memory allocation, linked lists, and interrupts; data structures with a focus on developing skills for writing utilities and I/O functions, and library development; introduction to systems analysis and design; and using FOXPRO to develop simple single-user PC applications. Methods of instruction include lectures, practical exercises, various CBT modules, self-paced learning, reading assignments, laboratory practice, and examinations.

Credit Recommendation: In the lower division baccalaureate/associate degree category, 6 semester hours, and in the upper division baccalaureate degree category, 3 semester hours in the area of Computer Science, Computer Information Systems, or Data Processing (11/95). **NOTE:** The student must successfully complete the Certificate Program in Computer Applications before taking this course.

Honors Diploma in Systems Management (HSM)

Location: Various locations offered by NIIT in India.

Length: 468 hours (78 weeks); 3 two-hour meetings per week, including 66 project hours.

Dates: June 1988-Present.

Objective: To familiarize students to work in the UNIX operating systems environment, and to write "C" programs in both UNIX and DOS environments. The main objective is to prepare students for the "Applications Programming" environment which is a rapidly growing market. The "Applications Orientation" should be clearly distinguished, especially in regard to comparisons with similar courses in "computer science and engineering" streams whose objectives must necessarily be wider in perspective and include systems programming and R&D programming competence as possible options. Here the focus is clearly "applications" in business.

Learning Outcome: Upon successful completion of the course, the student will be able to have the knowledge and skills required to work in UNIX and DOS environments, using COBOL or "C" in writing "applications programs" for varied business environments; and apart from competency in actual machine handling and computer language usage, students are exposed to "real world" problems.

Instruction: Major topics covered in Section One of the course are a basic overview of computers which includes a brief history; an overview of computer hardware, software, and applications; and various types of computer systems (centralized, decentralized, and distributed). Programming Logic and Techniques covers problem-solving techniques using flowcharts. COBOL exposure relates to ANSI COBOL and its use in commercial data processing and includes complex report generation, data entry through screen section and validations, table handling, and indexed file maintenance. Major topics covered in Section Two of the course are the database management system (dBase III+) as a complete programming language and spreadsheets as a tool for MIS. Specific applications areas such as financial accounting, inventory control, payroll, and production planning and control are covered from both data processing and MIS perspectives. Tools for structured systems analysis and design such as data flow diagrams, structure charts, and data dictionaries are covered along with relevant analysis and design concepts including all stages from initial development, through testing and finally handing over to external users. Major topics covered in Section Three of the course are operating system concepts with specific reference to UNIX where shell programming skills are imparted. Subsequently two streams are provided either for "C" or UNIFY. The "C" program covers detailed application programming as well as systems programming ending with the construction of a DBMS in "C" using linked lists. The UNIFY program covers basic DBMS concepts and applications development in the UNIFY DBMS environment. Methods of instruction include lectures, practical exercises, self-paced learning, student/instructor consultation sessions, reading assignments in NIIT prepared text, booklets, and extensive program development, compiling and execution on in-house computers, as well as a major project which will allow the student to demonstrate his/her mastery of all the course components.

Credit Recommendation: In the lower division baccalaureate/associate degree category, 3 semester hours in Introduction to Computers; in the upper division baccalaureate or graduate degree category, 4 semester hours in COBOL Programming; in the lower division baccalaureate/associate degree category, 3 semester hours in Computer Programming; and in the upper division baccalaureate degree category, 3 semester hours in Advanced Computer Programming Applications. In the lower division baccalaureate/associate degree category, 3 semester hours in UNIX and Database Management Systems (UNIFY) or 3 semester hours in UNIX and "C" Programming (3/89) (11/95). **NOTE:** Students who receive total credit for this course should not receive credit for COBOL Programming and Application (Certificate in COBOL Programming [CCP]) or Computer-Based Business Systems (Diploma in Systems Management [DSM]).

Professional Diploma in Software Technology and Systems Management

Location: Various locations throughout India.

Length: 160 hours (26 weeks).

Dates: June 1993-Present.

Objective: To prepare the student to create application programs in the DBMS environment with a perspective of developing goal oriented systems.

Learning Outcome: Upon successful completion of this course, the student will be able to design and build applications in a DBMS environment, be able to compare and contrast various DBMS systems, understand the concepts of expert systems, CASE tools, and various fourth generation languages.

Instruction: Major topics covered in the course are the development of expert systems, inference engines and interface to a data base; CASE tools for generating graphics, reports, code and documentation; 4GL prototyping, interactive screen formats, report generation, and 4GL comparisons; use of RDMS concepts for OLTP systems; and a technical comparison of various DBMS systems. Methods of instruction include lectures, practical exercises, various CBT modules, self-paced learning, reading assignments, laboratory practice, and examinations.

Credit Recommendation: In the lower division baccalaureate/associate degree category, 3 semester hours, and in the upper division baccalaureate degree category, 5 semester hours, and in graduate degree category, 4 semester hours in Computer Science, Computer Information Systems, or Data Processing (11/95). **NOTE:** The student must successfully complete the Certificate Program in Computer Applications, the Honors Diploma in Software Technology and Systems Management, and the Advanced Diploma in Software Technology and Systems Management before taking this course.

Professional Practice I

Location: Various locations throughout India.

Length: 390 hours (26 weeks).

Dates: June 1993-Present.

Objective: To prepare students for careers in computer applications by exposing them to a comprehensive work place experience.

Learning Outcome: Upon successful completion of this course, the student will be able to extend his/her knowledge, intellectual abilities and skills to permit analysis and solution of real world problems.

Instruction: Major topics covered in the course are all aspects of the system development life cycle. Methods of instruction include the assignment of real world computer application projects that the student must complete to the satisfaction of his/her mentor.

Credit Recommendation: In the graduate degree category, 8 semester hours in Computer Science, Computer Information Systems, or Data Processing (11/95).

Professional Practice II

Location: Various locations throughout India.

Length: 390 hours (26 weeks).

Dates: June 1993-Present.

Objective: To prepare students for careers in computer applications by exposing them to a comprehensive work place experience.

Learning Outcome: Upon successful completion of this course, the student will be able to extend his/her knowledge, intellectual abilities and skills to permit analysis and solution of real world problems.

Instruction: Major topics covered in the course are all aspects of the system development life cycle. Methods of instruction include the assignment of real world computer application projects that the student must complete to the satisfaction of his/her mentor.

Credit Recommendation: In the graduate degree category, 8 semester hours in Computer Science, Computer Information Systems, or Data Processing (11/95).

Noblefields School of Real Estate

Noblefields School of Real Estate was originally started in 1985 by Ms. Noble Fields who is sole proprietor. The school has been approved to operate in the State of California by the State of California Council for Private Postsecondary and Vocational Education. In January of 1998, there will be a transition from the Council to the Bureau for Private Postsecondary and Vocational Education. Noblefields School of Real Estate offers approved homestudy license qualification, and Continuing Education Courses for both real estate licensee, and the appraiser licensee. Noblefields School of Real Estate is the only downtown San Francisco location where transportation is excellent for the outlining bay area counties to connect to the Bay Area Rapid Transit System (BART).

Noblefields School of Real Estate offers approved courses for live instruction for students requiring residential instruction for mandatory classes by Office of the Real Estate Appraisers.

The official records of all students are located on site at the 870 Market Street Suite 623, San Francisco, CA. Noble Fields is the Director and constantly works with American Council on Education and other organizations of higher learning for educational needs and current information. A toll free number is provided for all students: 1-888-80 NOBLE.

Source of official student records: Registry of Credit Recommendations, American Council on Education, One Dupont Circle, Washington, DC 20036-1193.

Additional information about the courses: College Credit Recommendation Service, American Council on Education, One Dupont Circle, Washington, DC 20036-1193.

Elements of California Real Estate Law (Formerly California Real Estate Law/Legal Aspects of Real Estate)

Location: Independent study by correspondence.

Length: 45 hours.

Dates: January 1991-Present.

Objective: To provide the student with an overview of those elements of California law that pertain to real estate.

Learning Outcome: Upon successful completion of this course, the student will be able to demonstrate familiarity with the issues related to the ownership and transfer of real property in California.

Instruction: Major topics covered in the course are the nature of real property; ownership of real property; agency law, duties, and liabilities; real estate contracts, litigation and its alternatives; issues in real estate title; real estate financing issues; fair housing laws; and landlord/tenant law. Methods of instruction include correspondence study involving directed text readings, special projects, and a proctored final examination.

Credit Recommendation: In the lower division baccalaureate/associate degree category, 2 semester hours in Real Estate Law or Business Administration (5/97).

NRI Schools/A Division of The McGraw-Hill Companies

NRI Schools, established in 1914 and acquired by The McGraw-Hill Companies in 1968, is now part of the McGraw-Hill Continuing Education Center. Located in Washington, DC, NRI Schools offer diploma, certificate, and degree programs through distance education to individuals, industry, and government. NRI Schools' mission is to provide quality instruction to adult learners and to facilitate academic success and the realization of individual goals through guided independent study. NRI Schools' course offerings range from diploma courses in computer programming, networking, bookkeeping, and writing to AAS degree programs in accounting and business management. Our staff of educators and subject matter specialists provide resources and guidance through a mix of traditional, mastery learning, and high-technology techniques. Most courses are broken down into learning modules made up of step-by-step lessons and hands-on projects. Degree programs often use McGraw-Hill college textbooks supplemented by detailed, custom-published study guides. Qualified instructors are proactive in contacting students for tutoring sessions, and the school's exclusive Online Connection makes it possible for students to talk to their instructors, download additional resources, attend online seminars, and even order items from the NRI Bookstore. Lesson examinations may be submitted by mail or through a 24-hour TeleGrading hotline. Degree programs require a proctored examination for each semester, administered at a place and time convenient for the student. Answers to administrative questions are available 24 hours a day through NRI Schools' TeleService hotline. Upon request, graduates of NRI Schools' programs receive letters of recommendation, tips on resume writing, and career advice. NRI Schools are licensed by the DC Licensure Commission and accredited by the Accrediting Commission of the Distance Education and Training Council. In addition, many employee tuition assistance plans cover the cost of NRI Schools' programs.

Source of official student records: Registry of Credit Recommendations, American Council on Education, One Dupont Circle, Washington, DC 20036-1193.

Additional information about the courses: College Credit Recommendation Service, American Council on Education, One Dupont Circle, Washington, DC 20036-1193.

Business Communication (EN101)

Location: Distance Education.

Length: 135 hours (correspondence).

Dates: June 1996-Present.

Objective: To teach oral and written communication techniques and to provide an overview of effective organizational strategies.

Learning Outcome: Upon successful completion of this course, the student will be able to apply the fundamentals of grammar and usage and improve skills in listening, speaking, writing, interviewing, resume writing, and communicating interculturally.

Instruction: Major topics covered in the course are business communication, communicating interculturally, interviewing, listening, writing resumes, conducting meetings, and oral presentations. Methods of instruction include self-test questions, lesson examinations, proctored examinations, and interaction with the instructor by mail, fax, phone, e-mail, and a final project.

Credit Recommendation: In the lower division baccalaureate/associate degree category, 3 semester hours in Business Communication or Business English (9/96).

Business Communication II (EN102)

Location: Distance Education.

Length: 135 hours (correspondence).

Dates: December 1996-Present.

Objective: To teach students to write effective business reports, proposals, persuasive messages and requests. This course includes case studies on well-known companies.

Learning Outcome: Upon successful completion of this course, the student will be able to plan messages according to message purpose, formulate well-organized messages, organize direct requests, create positive messages, create short reports that contain accurate information, follow a five-step process for planning long reports, and prepare and assemble formal reports and proposals.

Instruction: Major topics covered in the course are planning and composing business messages, revising messages, writing letters, memos and other brief messages, writing routine, good-news, and goodwill messages, writing bad-news messages, writing persuasive messages and reports and proposals. Methods of instruction include college textbooks with accompanying study guides, self-test questions, case studies, project, proctored final examination, and interaction with the instructor by mail, fax, phone, and e-mail.

Credit Recommendation: In the lower division baccalaureate/associate degree category, 3 semester hours in Business Communication (11/96).

Business Law I (LA101)

Location: Distance Education.

Length: 135 hours (Correspondence).

Dates: December 1996-Present.

Objective: To introduce the various legal aspects of the business environment, including the court system, judicial process, contract and tort law, product and service liabilities, and international business law. The case briefing system is used and precedent-setting cases are incorporated into the material.

Learning Outcome: Upon successful completion of this course, the student will be able to define types of law, describe how the American litigation system works, discuss the nature of the judicial process, compare and contrast the different types of business organizational forms, discuss the implications of contract and tort law on businesses, identify the basic theories and defenses of product liability, and indicate how international business transactions require a knowledge of international law.

Instruction: Major topics covered in the course are an introduction to law, courts and litigation, alternative dispute resolution systems, the Constitution, the regulatory process, ethics and self-regulation, forms of business organizations, contract law, torts, products and service liability, and international business transactions. Methods of instruction include college textbooks with accompanying study guides, self-test questions, case studies, six multiple-choice exams, a final project, a proctored final examination, and interaction with the instructor by mail, fax, phone, and e-mail.

Credit Recommendation: In the lower division baccalaureate/associate degree category, 3 semester hours in Business Law (11/96).

Business Law II (LA 102)

Location: Distance Education.

Length: 135 hours (correspondence).

Dates: November 1997-Present.

Objective: To introduce the legislation related to governmental regulation of business activities, including an overview of the criminal law system, antitrust law, environmental laws, discrimination laws, the labor-management relationship, and investor protection legislation.

Learning Outcome: Upon successful completion of this course, the student will be able to identify and explain basic terms and procedures of criminal law, including Constitutional rights; discuss the concepts of antitrust law, the Sherman Act and other laws that support it; indicate how and why government regulates itself and business; describe legislation that protects against discrimination and employment practices that may be challenged; explain types of legislation affecting the labor-management relationship; and specify how securities laws regulate the sale and purchase of securities.

Instruction: Major topics covered in the course are criminal law and business; antitrust law and the Sherman Act; environmental protection and pollution control; discrimination and other employment issues; the labor-management relationship; and investor protection. Methods of instruction include self-test questions, lesson examinations, proctored final examination, and interaction with the instructor by mail, fax, phone, and E-mail.

Credit Recommendation: In the lower division baccalaureate/associate degree category, 3 semester hours in Business Law (11/97).

Business Management I (MG101)

Location: Distance Education.

Length: 135 hours (correspondence).

Dates: June 1996-Present.

Objective: To introduce the four major functions of management, to teach management techniques of planning and organizing, and to learn goal setting, strategy, innovation and change, decision-making, organizational design, and human resource management.

Learning Outcome: Upon successful completion of this course, the student will be able to describe the four functions of management, including planning, organizing, leading, and controlling; identify the skills managers need; describe the methods used by organizations to manage environments; explain the nature of organizational culture; outline the planning process; and outline the human resources management process.

Instruction: Major topics covered in the course are the functions of management, managerial skills, organizational culture, planning process, change and innovation, the decision-making process, and the human resources management process. Methods of instruction include college textbooks with accompanying study guides, self-test questions, case studies, lesson examinations, a final project, a proctored examination, and interaction with the instructor by mail, fax, phone, and e-mail.

Credit Recommendation: In the lower division baccalaureate/associate degree category, 3 semester hours in Business Management (9/96).

Business Management II (MG102)

Location: Distance Education.

Length: 135 hours (correspondence).

Dates: December 1996-Present.

Objective: To explore the remaining two major functions of management-leading and controlling, which were not covered in detail in Business Management I. Leadership, managerial communications, group dynamics, managerial control techniques, operations management, and information systems are covered.

Learning Outcome: Upon successful completion of this course, the student will be able to explain the leading and controlling functions of management; identify specific leadership traits, behaviors, and influential situational factors; discuss the foundations and stages of group development; evaluate managerial approaches to controls; define operations management; identify the roles information systems play; and discuss the social responsibilities and ethical demands involved in managing a business.

Instruction: Major topics covered in the course are motivation, leadership, managerial communication, managing groups, controlling the organization, operations management, information systems for managers, social responsibility and ethics, and international management. Methods of instruction include college textbooks with accompanying study guides, self-test questions, multiple choice examinations, a project, a proctored examination and interaction with the instructor by mail, fax, phone and e-mail.

Credit Recommendation: In the lower division baccalaureate/associate degree category, 3 semester hours in Business Management (11/96).

Business Math (BU110)

Location: Distance Education.

Length: 135 hours (correspondence).

Dates: June 1996-Present.

Objective: To teach basic mathematics as applied to computing interest, taxes, annuity problems, and simple statistical measures.

Learning Outcome: Upon successful completion of this course, the student will be able to compute interest for negotiable instruments, credit cards, and determine the annual percentage rate; be able to reconcile a checking account balance; compute simple statistical measures; and solve annuity problems.

Instruction: Major topics covered in the course are whole number rounding, bank account reconciliation, discounting notes, credit card interest, finding the annual percentage rate, mortgage payments, property taxes, present value of an annuity, basic statistics, and graphs. Methods of instruction include self-test questions, lesson examinations, a proctored examination, and interaction with the instructor by mail, fax, phone, and e-mail.

Credit Recommendation: In the lower division baccalaureate/associate degree category, 3 semester hours in Business Mathematics (9/96).

College Survival Skills (HE 105)

Location: Distance Education

Length: 135 hours (correspondence).

Dates: November 1997-Present.

Objective: To learn the techniques and understand the essential skills for effective and efficient completion of courses found in a distance learning environment.

Learning Outcome: Upon successful completion of this course, the student will be able to apply effective techniques in improving reading, studying, note-taking, previewing a book or article, identifying main ideas, taking tests, minimizing anxiety and stress, conducting library research, making oral presentation reports, and to clearly and concisely write.

Instruction: Major topics covered in the course are goal-setting, time management, study skills, note-taking, reading, test-preparation, preparing reports, and making oral presentations. Methods of instruction include self-test questions, lesson examinations, proctored final examination, and interaction with the instructor by mail, fax, phone, and E-mail.

Credit Recommendation: In the lower division baccalaureate/associate degree category, 2 semester hours in General Education or Interdisciplinary Studies (11/97).

Computerized Accounting (AC210)

Location: Distance Education.

Length: 135 hours (correspondence).

Dates: June 1996-Present.

Objective: To perform computerized accounting for a sole proprietorship.

Learning Outcome: Upon successful completion of this course, the student will be able to use a computerized accounting program to account for the transactions of a sole proprietorship, including preparation of financial statements, budgets, and payroll and tax records.

Instruction: Major topics covered in the course are setting up the general ledger, accounts receivable and payable, payroll and tax records, inventory management, preparation of financial statements, budgeting, and forecasting. Methods of instruction include computer-assisted instruction, learner presentation/reports, and hands-on exercises with Peachtree Accounting for Windows.

Credit Recommendation: In the lower division baccalaureate/associate degree category, 2 semester hours in Computerized Accounting (9/96).

Entrepreneurship (MG210)

Location: Distance Education.

Length: 135 hours (correspondence).

Dates: June 1996-Present.

Objective: To teach the ins and outs of opening a business.

Learning Outcome: Upon successful completion of this course, the student will be able to keep accurate business records; write a business and marketing plan; identify effective advertising, marketing, and public relations efforts; and evaluate the business.

Instruction: Major topics covered in the course are business reports and records, the business plan, developing a marketing plan, advertising, managing time, and charting the growth of a business. Methods of instruction include self-test questions, lesson examinations, a proctored examination, and interaction with the instructor by mail, fax, phone, and e-mail.

Credit Recommendation: In the lower division baccalaureate/associate degree category, 3 semester hours in Entrepreneurship or Small Business Management (11/96).

Marketing (MK 101)

Location: Distance Education

Length: 135 hours (correspondence).

Dates: November 1997-Present.

Objective: To provide the student with a general understanding of marketing principles in today's environment and enable the student to learn the techniques of marketing planning, consumer versus business markets, and all the strategies involved in marketing, research, developing a product or service, distribution, promoting and pricing.

Learning Outcome: Upon successful completion of this course, the student will be able to define the role of product and services marketing in the individual organization and the American and world economy, explain the critical nature of the customer-oriented approach, market segmentation and target markets, explain the concepts of marketing product, price, placement, and promotion and identify marketing career opportunities.

Instruction: Major topics covered in the course are the field of marketing; the dynamic marketing environment; strategic marketing planning; consumer markets and buying behavior; business markets and buying behavior; market segmentation and target-market strategies; product planning and development; product-mix strategies; brands, packaging, and other product features; services marketing by for-profit and nonprofit organizations; price determination; pricing strategies; channels of distribution; retailing; wholesaling and physical distribution; promotional programs; personal selling and sales management; advertising, sales promotion, and public relations. Methods of instruction include self-test questions, lesson examinations, proctored final examination, and interaction with the instructor by mail, fax, phone, or E-mail.

Credit Recommendation: In the lower division baccalaureate/associate degree category, 3 semester hours in Business Administration or Marketing (11/97).

Microsoft Word for Windows 95 (CS110)

Location: Distance Education.

Length: 135 hours (correspondence).

Dates: June 1996-Present.

Objective: To teach basic skills for a word processing program, including opening and closing documents, basic editing, saving work, working with several documents at once, macros, templates, formatting, and creating table, footnotes, and endnotes.

Learning Outcome: Upon successful completion of this course, the student will be able to explain basic editing and formatting skills in Word for Windows 95; show how to work with multiple documents; demonstrate fundamental commands; use Word's writing tools; and utilize features such as creating tables, footnotes, endnotes, templates, and styles.

Instruction: Major topics covered in the course are Microsoft Word fundamentals, formatting documents, moving beyond the basics, advanced features, special Word features, and working with MS-Word for Windows 95. Methods of instruction include six customized lesson manuals published expressly for use in *Microsoft Word for Windows 95,* hands-on exercises with *Microsoft Word for Windows 95* software, self-test questions, lesson examinations, a proctored examination, and interaction with the instructor by mail, fax, phone, and e-mail.

Credit Recommendation: In the vocational certificate category, 3 semester hours in Data Processing (9/96).

Personal and Professional Success (HE112)

Location: Distance Education.

Length: 135 hours (correspondence).

Dates: June 1996-Present.

Objective: To understand the skills required to achieve personal and professional goals in the changing workplace.

Learning Outcome: Upon successful completion of this course, the student will be able to practice good time management skills, understand stress, practice effective decision-making skills, and apply techniques for negotiating and resolving conflicts.

Instruction: Major topics covered in the course are time management, stress management, decision-making negotiations and conflict resolutions, the creative process, and motivation. Methods of instruction include self-test questions, lesson examinations, a proctored examination, and interaction with the instructor by mail, fax, phone, and e-mail.

Credit Recommendation: In the lower division baccalaureate/associate degree category, 3 semester hours in Professional/Personal Development (11/96).

Principles of Accounting I (AC101)

Location: Distance Education.

Length: 135 hours (correspondence).

Dates: June 1996-Present.

Objective: To learn accounting for a sole proprietorship, including journal entries and the preparation of financial statements.

Learning Outcome: Upon successful completion of this course, the student will be able to record business transactions, prepare balance sheets and income statements, calculate depreciation, and be familiar with internal control of assets.

Instruction: Major topics covered in the course are accounting equations, double-entry accounting, cash basis, accrual basis, preparation of balance sheets and income statements, internal control, depreciation, receivables, and merchandise inventory. Methods of instruction include self-test questions, lesson examinations, a proctored examination, and interaction with the instructor by mail, fax, phone, and e-mail.

Credit Recommendation: In the lower division baccalaureate/associate degree category, 3 semester hours in Accounting I (11/96).

Principles of Accounting II (AC102)

Location: Distance Education.

Length: 135 hours (correspondence).

Dates: December 1996-Present.

Objective: To understand generally accepted accounting principles as it relates to partnerships and corporations. Emphasis is on corporate accounting and stockholder equity issues along with cash flow statements and techniques of financial statement analysis.

Learning Outcome: Upon successful completion of this course, the student will be able to calculate and prepare the necessary journal entries for payroll, related employer and employee taxes, prepare journal entries for international transactions, prepare financial statements for partnerships and corporations, list the advantages and disadvantages of the partnership and corporate form of business ownership, account for the admission, withdrawal or death of a partner, prepare journal entries to record the issuance of stocks and bonds, and prepare the stockholder's equity section of a balance sheet and statement of retained earnings.

Instruction: Major topics covered in the course are payroll, generally accepted accounting principles, partnerships, corporations, retained earnings and corporate income, long-term liabilities, corporate investments and consolidations, cash flows and financial statement analysis. Methods of instruction include multiple choice exams, a project, a proctored final examination and interaction with the instructor by mail, fax, phone, and e-mail.

Credit Recommendation: In the lower division baccalaureate/associate degree category, 3 semester hours in Accounting (11/96).

Research Methods in Education (SO 110)

Location: Distance Education.

Length: 135 hours (correspondence).

Dates: November 1997-Present.

Objective: To introduce research and its relevance to the students' business and personal lives, familiarizing students with research processes and techniques, identifying sources of data, differentiating between qualitative and quantitative data, calculating probabilities, and using basic statistics.

Learning Outcome: Upon successful completion of this course, the student will be able to apply the scientific method to research situations; develop hypotheses, test hypotheses, identify the different types of studies and the relevant place for each; realize the ethical and moral problems presented by research; determine the best source of information to use in which situation; locate the information required to perform research; distinguish the difference between qualitative and quantitative research; apply sampling techniques; and determine probability.

Instruction: Major topics covered in the course are the fundamentals of research, finding and communicating information, qualitative and quantitative research, surveys and questionnaires, and quantitative data analysis. Methods of instruction include self-test questions, lesson examinations, proctored final examination, and interaction with the instructor by mail fax, phone, and E-mail.

Credit Recommendation: In the lower division baccalaureate/associate degree category, 3 semester hours in General Education (11/97).

Offshore Sailing School, Ltd.

The Offshore Sailing School is headquartered in Ft. Myers, Florida. Five resort locations, two New York area locations and one Chicago location are managed from the headquarters. The school provides instruction in sailing for those people visiting the resort locations. Boats used by the school are Colgate 26's, designed specifically for training, 27 and modern cruising boats such as Beneteaus and Hunters.

All instructors are U.S. Sailing Certified. The instructional staff undergoes periodic review which includes a student evaluation and performance review by the operations manager. Prospective instructors are required to pass a written examination before they are included as Offshore Sailing instructors.

Course development is handled by the office in Ft. Myers. In general, courses are developed by the management with input from the Training Committee of the United States Sailing Association, the governing body of sailing.

Source of official student records: Operations Manager, Offshore Sailing School, 16731 McGregor Boulevard,Suite 110, Ft. Myers, FL 33908.

Additional information about the courses: College Credit Recommendation Service, American Council on Education, One Dupont Circle, Washington, DC 20036-1193.

Bareboat Cruising Preparation

Location: Jersey City, NJ; Captiva Island, FL; Chicago, IL; and Stamford, CT.

Length: 26 hours (20 hours (5 days), 6 hours optional [Saturday and Sunday]).

Dates: January 1975-Present.

Objective: To give the student the ability to operate larger chartered cruising sailboats without assistance of a professional captain and crew.

Learning Outcome: Upon successful completion of this course, the student will be able to conduct his/her own sailboat charter on a mid-size sailboat with confidence gained from additional training in marine diesels, AC and DC power, and related mid-size sailboat components and characteristics.

Instruction: Major topics covered in the course are electrical power, diesel engines, docking, deck layout, underway procedures, sails, lights, VHF, seamanship, cruising tips, anchoring, galley, and navigation. Methods of instruction include lecture, audio/visual material, on-water training, informal tests, observed performance, and optional completion of U.S. Sailing, Basic Cruising, and Bareboat Cruising Certifica-tion Tests (fee charged).

Credit Recommendation: In the lower division baccalaureate/associate degree category, 1 semester hour in Sailing (9/85) (2/96). *Prerequisite:* Learn to Sail or equivalent experience.

Learn to Sail

Location: Jersey City, NJ; Barnegat Bay, NJ; Captiva Island, FL; Tortola, British Virgin Islands; Stamford, CT; Newport, RI; St. Petersburg, FL; and Chicago, IL.

Length: 26 hours (20 hours (5 days), 6 hours optional [Saturday and Sunday]).

Dates: January 1975-Present.

Objective: To provide the student with knowledge of basic sailing terms, theory, and equipment; ability to prepare and equip a boat for sailing; and ability to sail a boat in a safe and seamanlike manner.

Learning Outcome: Upon successful completion of this course, the student will be able to utilize the basic skills learned in lectures and aboard actual sailboats to safely and correctly sail a boat alone by knowing how to handle the rigging and be familiar with sailing nomenclature; wind and weather effects; mooring, anchoring, and docking techniques; rules of the road; and man overboard and grounding recovery techniques.

Instruction: Major topics covered in the course are weather adjustments, types of boats, nomenclature, theory, technique, knots, boating safety, running rigging, standing rigging, seamanship, knowing and using sails, knowing the wind and how to use it, mooring, man overboard, sailboat care, balance, stability, rules of the road, anchoring, docking, navigation, compass, and running aground. Methods of instruction include lecture, audio/visual material, on-water sailing, informal tests, observed performance on the water, and performance on U.S. Sailing and Basic Keelboat Certification Test.

Credit Recommendation: In the lower division baccalaureate/associate degree category, 1 semester hour in Sailing (9/85) (2/96).

Performance Sailing (Formerly Advanced Sailing or Sailing and Cruising)

Location: Jersey City, NJ; Captiva Island, FL.

Length: 26 hours (20 hours (5 days, 6 hours optional [Saturday and Sunday]).

Dates: January 1982-Present.

Objective: To provide the student with an understanding of advanced sailing theory and techniques; an ability to cope with emergency situations; skill in applying advanced sailing and cruising techniques; and an ability to sail solo in a small cruising sailboat.

Learning Outcome: Upon successful completion of this course, the student will be able to sail solo with the added confidence of knowing how to use sails to maximum advantage, particularly the spinnaker in downwind sailing and use emergency procedures to offset problems relating to inoperable or damaged rigging/gear.

Instruction: Major topics covered in the course are sail characteristics, shape, and control; advanced sailboat handling; spinnaker handling; underway repairs; emergency procedures; piloting; radiotelephone operation; cruising tips; distress signals; collisions and navigation; and anchoring procedures. Methods of in-struction include lecture, audio/visual material, on-water sailing, informal tests, observed performance, and performance on U.S. Sailing and Basic Cruising Certification Tests.

Credit Recommendation: In the lower division baccalaureate/associate degree category, 1 semester hour in Sailing (9/85) (2/96). *Prerequisite:* Learn to Sail or equivalent experience.

Sailboat Racing

Location: Captiva Island, FL.

Length: 26 hours (1 week)

Dates: January 1975-Present.

Objective: To reinforce the student's understanding of basic seamanship and preparation for racing; to give the student knowledge of advanced seamanship; and to teach him or her to apply seamanship knowledge and skills under actual racing conditions and appreciate sailboat racing as a participatory sport.

Learning Outcome: Upon successful completion of this course, the student will be able to apply the additional sail controlling and boat handling techniques learned in this course to sailboat racing by the rules to become a more effective racing sailor.

Instruction: Major topics covered in the course are sail control, racing rules, tactics, racing starts, spinnaker work, boat preparation, current, time, starting rules, helmsmanship, windshifts, luffing, lay lines, mark roundings,and finishing. Methods of instruction include lecture, audio/visual material, on-water sailing, and performance observation during course and at two-day regatta at the end of the course.

Credit Recommendation: In the lower division baccalaureate/associate degree category, 1 semester hour in Sailing (9/85) (2/96). *Prerequisite:* Learn to Sail or equivalent experience.

Omaha Public Power District

Omaha Public Power District (OPPD) is one of the largest publicly owned electric utilities in the United States. It was organized as a poli tical subdivision of the state of Nebraska in 1946. OPPD provides electric service in the City of Omaha, Nebraska, and adjacent territory. The service area is approximately 5,000 square miles, with an estimated population of 600,000. Omaha, with an estimated population of 335,000 within the corporate limits, is the largest city in the state of Nebraska and is the only community among the 48 cities and villages served by the district with a population of more than 40,000.

The training organization of the Nuclear Operations Division develops and delivers performance-based training to all personnel assigned to the Fort Calhoun Nuclear Power Station located in Washington County, Nebraska. In April 1988, the training programs were accredited and OPPD was installed as a full member of the National Academy for Nuclear Training.

Source of official student records: Supervisor, Training Support, c/o Omaha Public Power District, Fort Calhoun Nuclear Power Station, 444 South 16th Street Mall, Omaha, NE 68102-2247.

Additional information about the courses: College Credit Recommendation Service, American Council on Education, One Dupont Circle, Washington, DC 20036-1193.

Airborne Radioactivity Monitoring and Control (ACEHP 88-06)

Location: Omaha Public Power District, Fort Calhoun Nuclear Station.

Length: *Version 1*: 42 hours (6 weeks); *Version 2*: 60 hours (6 weeks).

Dates: *Version 1:* January 1988-October 1994; *Version 2:* November 1994-Present.

Objective: To provide instruction on airborne radioactivity hazards, monitoring, and control including bioassay techniques, engineering controls, and respiratory protection measures.

Learning Outcome: Upon successful completion of this course, the student will be able to describe the typical sources, causes, sample collection, and analysis of airborne radioactivity; apply respiratory protection principles and perform calculations of body burden based upon different determinations of uptake quantity; and explain regulations as they relate to control of airborne radioactivity.

Instruction: Major topics covered in the course are collection and analysis of airborne contaminants, sources and causes of airborne radioactivity, the use of different types of respiratory equipment, and regulations associated with respiratory programs. Methods of instruction include lecture.

Credit Recommendation: *Version 1:* In the lower division baccalaureate/associate degree category, 2 semester hours in Radiation Protection Technology (7/88) (11/94) *Version 2:* In the lower division baccalaureate/associate degree category, 3 semester hours in Radiation Protection Technology (11/94).

Algebra (ACEOPS 88-07)

Location: Omaha Public Power District, Fort Calhoun Nuclear Station.

Length: *Version 1*: 40 hours (1 week); *Version 2*: 40 hours (6 weeks).

Dates: July 1985-Present.

Objective: To provide the student with the ability to solve algebraic equations and to understand exponents, logarithms, and graphs.

Learning Outcome: Upon successful completion of this course, the student will be able to describe the construction of a cartesian coordinate system; graph relationships with respect to a cartesian coordinate system; solve for unknowns of a second degree equation; solve algebraic word problems; work with exponents, powers, radicals, logarithms, and scientific notation; and plot functions on semi-log and log-log scales.

Instruction: Major topics covered in the course are fractions, exponentials, powers, radicals, scientific notation, common and natural logarithms, algebraic operations, algebraic equations, systems of equations, matrices, algebraic word problems, and functions and graphs. Methods of instruction include lecture and problem-solving.

Credit Recommendation: In the lower division baccalaureate/associate degree category, 2 semester hours in Mathematics (7/88) (11/94).

Applied Calculus (ACEOPS 88-05)

Location: Omaha Public Power District, Fort Calhoun Nuclear Station.

Length: *Version 1*: 40 hours (1 week); *Version 2*: 40 (6 weeks).

Dates: January 1987-Present.

Objective: To provide the student with a knowledge of the basic concepts in and ability to solve problems using differential and integral calculus as it applies to a nuclear power plant reactor operator.

Learning Outcome: Upon successful completion of this course, the student will be able to calculate the limit of a function; list the properties of limits and apply them to the solution of problems involving limits; determine if a function is continuous at a point; define and evaluate the derivative of a function; define and evaluate the integral of a function; and use the concept of rate of change to solve rate problems that involve multiple additive rates.

Instruction: Major topics covered in the course are limits, continuity, differentiation, integration; and applications to radioactive decay problems, equilibrium equation for fission products, and the first and second kinetics equations. Methods of instruction include lecture, discussion, and problem-solving.

Credit Recommendation: In the lower division baccalaureate/associate degree category, 2 semester hours in Mathematics (7/88) (11/94).

Applied Thermodynamics (ACEOPS 88-02)

Location: Omaha Public Power District, Fort Calhoun Nuclear Station.

Length: *Version 1*: 60 hours (1.5 weeks); *Version 2*: 60 hours (6 weeks).

Dates: January 1987-Present.

Objective: To provide the student with a quantitative and qualitative understanding of thermodynamics, heat transfer, and fluid-flow phenomena.

Learning Outcome: Upon successful completion of this course, the student will be able to apply and understand the basic laws of thermodynamics; apply fluid statics, hydraulics, and pressure measurements; and understand basic heat transfer phenomena.

Instruction: Major topics covered in the course are the first and second laws of thermodynamics, heat transfer principles, and reactor core heat generation and removal. Methods of instruction include lecture and classroom exercises.

Credit Recommendation: In the lower division baccalaureate/associate degree category, 2 semester hours in Applied Sciences/Mechanical Engineering (7/88) (11/94).

Basic Concepts of Mechanics, Heat, Electricity and Atomic Physics (ACEOPS 88-14)

Location: Omaha Public Power District, Fort Calhoun Nuclear Station.

Length: *Version 1*: 42 hours (1 week); *Version 2*: 42 (6 weeks).

Dates: January 1986-Present.

Objective: To provide a survey of various topics in mechanics, heat, electricity, and atomic physics.

Learning Outcome: Upon successful completion of this course, the student will be able to define terms and list units; state laws and explain concepts; and perform calculations and solve problems for a variety of topics related to mechanics, heat, electricity, and atomic physics.

Instruction: Major topics covered in the course are systems of units: English-metric, mass, force, work, energy, power, Newton's laws, electric charge, Coulomb's law, electric fields, temperature, heat, heat transfer, specific heat, enthalpy, entropy, electrostatic potential, atomic structure, nuclear structure, isotopes, mass energy conversion, mass defect, binding energy, fuels: fissile, fissionable, fertile; nuclear interactions and reactions; radioactive decay and types of radiation; and the chart of nuclides. Methods of instruction include illustrated lecture, discussion, and problem-solving.

Credit Recommendation: In the lower division baccalaureate/associate degree category, 2 semester hours in Physics (7/88) (11/94).

Basic Electronics (ACE I&C 88-02)

Location: Omaha Public Power District, Fort Calhoun Nuclear Station, and also North Omaha and Nebraska City Plants.

Length: 64 hours (8 weeks).

Dates: January 1988-Present.

Objective: To provide the student with an understanding of electronic circuits and operation.

Learning Outcome: Upon successful completion of this course, the student will be able to apply Kirchoff's voltage and current laws; understand basic operational amplifier circuits; and understand transistor biasing and small-signal analysis.

Instruction: Major topics covered in the course are electrical circuits and theory, Kirchoff's voltage and current laws, semiconductor principles, semiconductor diode applications and circuits, transistor amplifiers and oscillators, specialized electronic devices (tunnels, UTTs, SCRs, etc.), and operational amplifiers and circuits. Methods of instruction include lecture, classroom exercises, and video.

Credit Recommendation: In the lower division baccalaureate/associate degree category, 2 semester hours in Basic Electronics/Electrical Engineering (7/88) (11/94). **NOTE:** If this course and Electrical Circuits, Machinery, and Instruments (ACEOPS 88-04) are taken, then a total of 4 semester hours is awarded in Electrical Technology/Engineering.

Basic Mathematics (ACEEM 88-01) or (ACEHP 88-07)

Location: Omaha Public Power District, Fort Calhoun Nuclear Station.

Length: *Version 1*: 30 hours (five 6-hour meetings); *Version 2*: 36 hours (6 weeks).

Dates: January 1988-Present.

Objective: To provide the student with a review of basic algebra, trigonometry and vectors commonly used in electrical circuits and applications.

Learning Outcome: Upon successful completion of this course, the student will be able to solve linear equations; use trig-functions in solving right triangles; and do vector addition.

Instruction: Major topics covered in the course are the Pythagorean theorem, sines and cosines, point-slope formula of a straight line and vector addition. Methods of instruction include lecture and classroom exercises.

Credit Recommendation: In the vocational certificate category, 2 semester hours in Basic Mathematics (7/88) (11/94).

Dosimetry and Contamination Control (ACEHP 88-08)

Location: Omaha Public Power District, Fort Calhoun Nuclear Station.

Length: 49 hours (7 days).

Dates: January 1988-July 1989.

Objective: To provide instruction on internal and external radiation dosimetry including contamination control.

Learning Outcome: Upon successful completion of this course, the student will be able to specify the principles of operation of dosimetry instruments; apply basic concepts of internal dosimetry; and explain the principles of contamination control.

Instruction: Major topics covered in the course are instruction on self-reading; thermoluminescent, alarming and remote readout dosimeters; fundamental internal dosimetry; general decontamination techniques; and typical contamination control devices. Methods of instruction include lecture.

Credit Recommendation: In the lower division baccalaureate/associate degree category, 2 semester hours in Radiation Protection Technology (7/88) (11/94).

Electrical Circuits Lab (ACEEM 88-02)

Location: Omaha Public Power District, Ft. Calhoun Nuclear Station.

Length: 106 hours (7 weeks).

Dates: January 1988-Present.

Objective: To provide the student with the ability to demonstrate analytical and practical applications of basic electrical circuits.

Learning Outcome: Upon successful completion of this course, the student will be able to use an oscilloscope effectively; use a digital multimeter; and connect, test, evaluate, and troubleshoot basic electrical circuits.

Instruction: Major topics covered in the course are electrical symbols and abbreviations, electronic power supplies, Ohm's law, Kirchoff's law, Thevenin and Norton's theorems, maximum power transfer, reading electrical diagrams, three-phase circuits, vectors and phasors, electronic and transistor fundamentals, and amplifiers. Methods of instruction include lecture, laboratory, and classroom exercises.

Credit Recommendation: In the lower division baccalaureate/associate degree category, 3 semester hours in Basic Electrical Circuits/Electrical Engineering (7/88) (11/94).

Electrical Circuits, Machinery, and Instruments (ACEOPS 88-04)

Location: Omaha Public Power District, Fort Calhoun Nuclear Station.

Length: *Version 1*: 80 hours (2 weeks); *Version 2*: 63 hours (6 weeks).

Dates: July 1985-Present.

Objective: To provide the student with a knowledge of basic electrical concepts, AC and DC circuits, AC generators, motors, transformers and control instrumentation.

Learning Outcome: Upon successful completion of this course, the student will be able to describe, define, and calculate the basic properties of electrical circuits, devices, and control instruments.

Instruction: Major topics covered in the course are current and voltage laws, AC and DC circuit analysis, power factor, AC and DC motors and generators, and rectifiers; phase relationships in resistive, inductive, and capacitive circuits, RLC series and parallel circuit analysis, and circuit time constants; and applications and control systems and control instrumentation. Methods of instruction include illustrated lecture, discussion, problem-solving, and plant tour.

Credit Recommendation: In the lower division baccalaureate/associate degree category, 3 semester hours in Electrical Technology/Electrical Engineering (7/88) (11/94). **NOTE:** If both this course and Basic Electronics (ACE I&C 88-02) are taken, then a total of 4 semester hours is awarded in Electrical Technology/ Engineering.

Electronics Lab (ACEEM 88-04)

Location: Omaha Public Power District, Fort Calhoun Nuclear Station.

Length: *Version 1*: 125 hours (8 weeks); *Version 2*: 82 hours 2 weeks).

Dates: *Version 1:* January 1988-February 1994; *Version 2:* March 1994-Present.

Objective: To establish a broad base knowledge in understanding the operation of power electronics.

Learning Outcome: Upon successful completion of this course, the student will be able to construct and test power and advanced analog circuits.

Instruction: Major topics covered in the course are power electronics, industrial electronics, and instrumentation. Methods of instruction include lecture, classroom exercises, video, and laboratory.

Credit Recommendation: *Version 1:* In the lower division baccalaureate/associate degree category, 3 semester hours in Basic Electronics/Electrical Engineering (7/88). *Version 2:* In the lower division baccalaureate/associate degree category, 2 semester hours in Basic Electronics or Electrical Engineering (11/94).

Environmental Radioactivity and Accident Evaluation (ACEHP 88-05)

Location: Omaha Public Power District, Fort Calhoun Nuclear Station.

Length: 23 hours (3 months).

Dates: January 1988-Present.

Objective: To provide instruction on environmental radioactivity and accident analysis as they apply to a radiation protection technician.

Learning Outcome: Upon successful completion of this course, the student will be able to describe environmental considerations associated with the operation of a nuclear power plant; discuss radiological incident responses; and apply basic principles of incident and accident evaluation.

Instruction: Major topics covered in the course are site selection, land and water food cycles, environmental monitoring, health physics, incident responses, and classes of accidents considered in FSARs. Methods of instruction include lecture and examination.

Credit Recommendation: In the lower division baccalaureate/associate degree category, 1 semester hour in Radiation Science or Environmental Chemistry (7/88) (11/94).

Fundamentals of Digital Electronics (ACE I&C 88-03)

Location: Omaha Public Power District, Fort Calhoun Nuclear Station, North Omaha and Nebraska City plants.

Length: 96 hours (12 weeks).

Dates: January 1988-Present.

Objective: To provide the student with a fundamental understanding of digital electronics and displays.

Learning Outcome: Upon successful completion of this course, the student will be able to understand the basic structure of various number systems (binary, octal, hexidecimal, etc.); identify and describe the function of AND, NOT, NAND, OR, NOR, etc.; and identify and describe the operation of various digital circuits (two-line to four-line decoders, multiplexers, etc.).

Instruction: Major topics covered in the course are number system and digital codes, digital logic and technology, digital circuits (ANDs, ORs, NORs, decoders, etc.), digital displays, digital bus concepts, and power supplies. Methods of instruction include lecture, classroom exercises, video, and laboratory.

Credit Recommendation: In the lower division baccalaureate/associate degree category, 3 semester hours in Basic Electronics/Electrical Engineering (7/88) (11/94).

General Chemistry (ACECH 88-01) (Formerly Chemistry Lecture)

Location: Omaha Public Power District, Fort Calhoun Nuclear Station.

Length: 98 hours (3 months).

Dates: January 1988-Present.

Objective: To provide a thorough foundation in the principles of General Chemistry.

Learning Outcome: Upon successful completion of this course, the student will be able to discuss atomic structure; compound formation and chemical reactions; discuss the fundamental concepts of gases, acids, bases and salts; and electrical properties of solutions.

Instruction: Major topics covered in the course are pH, atomic structure, properties of gases, compounds, chemical reactions, acids and bases, solutions, and specific power plant chemistry. Methods of instruction include lecture.

Credit Recommendation: In the lower division baccalaureate/associate degree category, 3 semester hours in General Chemistry (7/88) (11/94).

Health Physics Fundamentals (ACEHP 88-02)

Location: Omaha Public Power District, Fort Calhoun Nuclear Station.

Length: *Version 1*: 40 hours (3 months); *Version 2*: 68 hours (3 months).

Dates: *Version 1:* January 1988-December 1990; *Version 2:* January 1991-Present.

Objective: To provide instruction in the principles of Health Physics.

Learning Outcome: Upon successful completion of this course, the student will be able to define basic terms used in radiation protection programs; describe radiation sources and doses; apply basic principles of radioactive decay; and describe the neutron activation process.

Instruction: Major topics covered in the course are basic nuclear terminology, data references, radiation sources, radioactive decay, introduction to radiation, and radiation interactions with matter. Methods of instruction include lecture and examinations.

Credit Recommendation: *Version 1:* In the lower division baccalaureate/associate degree category, 1 semester hour in Radiation Protection Technology (7/88). *Version 2:* In the lower division baccalaureate/associate degree category, 3 semester hours in Health Physics (11/94).

Introduction to Management Skills (ACEOPS 88-09)

Location: Omaha Public Power District, Ft. Calhoun Nuclear Station.

Length: 30 hours (4 days).

Dates: January 1987-December 1990.

Objective: To provide the student with the skills needed to communicate effectively, plan projects, delegate authority, and manage.

Learning Outcome: Upon successful completion of this course, the student will be able to organize and prepare effective oral and written business communications; identify/set goals and delegate responsibilities; and determine what, when, and how to coach/counsel others.

Instruction: Major topics covered in the course are how to manage one's boss, rate one's self, set priorities; guidelines for effective delegation and the ABCs of management; improving below-average performance; and self-assessment profiles and motivation. Methods of instruction include lecture and classroom exercises.

Credit Recommendation: In the lower division baccalaureate/associate degree category, 1 semester hour in Personnel Management (7/88) (11/94). **NOTE:** Credit should not be awarded for both this course and Introduction to Personnel Management (ACEOPS 88-08) .

Introduction to Nuclear Physics and Power Reactors (ACEHP 88-01)

Location: Omaha Public Power District, Fort Calhoun Nuclear Station.

Length: *Version 1*: 36 hours (1 week); *Version 2*: 72 hours (3 weeks).

Dates: *Version 1:* January 1988-October 1994; *Version 2:* November 1994-Present.

Objective: To provide instruction in basic nuclear and reactor care concepts and an overview of power reactor designs and operation.

Learning Outcome: Upon successful completion of this course, the student will be able to explain the way in which an atom is constructed; discuss sources of radioactivity; explain radiation interaction with matter; discuss the origin of radionuclides; and discuss the design of different power reactors.

Instruction: Major topics covered in the course are basic math and science, basic atomic nature of matter, man-made and natural radioactivity, types of radiation, reactor core components, major reactor primary and secondary components, and control systems used in a pressurized water reactor. Methods of instruction include lecture.

Credit Recommendation: *Version 1:* In the lower division baccalaureate/associate degree category, 1 semester hour in Radiation Protection Technology (7/88) (11/94) *Version 2:* In the lower division baccalaureate/associate degree category, 3 semester hours in Radiation Protection Technology (11/94).

Introduction to Personnel Management (ACEOPS 88-08)

Location: Omaha Public Power District, Fort Calhoun Nuclear Station.

Length: 16 hours (3 days).

Dates: January 1987-October 1994.

Objective: To provide the student with the skills needed to communicate effectively, plan projects, delegate authority, and manage.

Learning Outcome: Upon successful completion of this course, the student will be able to organize and prepare effective oral and written business communications; identify/set goals and delegate responsibilities; and determine what, when, and how to coach/counsel others.

Instruction: Major topics covered in the course are how to manage one's boss, rate one's self, and set priorities; guidelines for effective delegation; the ABCs of management; improving below-average performance; and self-assessment profiles and motivation. Methods of instruction include lecture and classroom exercises.

Credit Recommendation: In the lower division baccalaureate/associate degree category, 1 semester hour in Personnel Management (7/88) (11/94). **NOTE:** Credit should not be awarded for both this course and Introduction to Management Skills (ACEOPS 88-09).

Introduction to Thermodynamics (ACEOPS 88-03)

Location: Omaha Public Power District, Fort Calhoun Nuclear Station.

Length: *Version 1*: 81 hours (6 weeks); *Version 2*: 37 hours (6 weeks).

Dates: *Version 1:* January 1985-December 1992; *Version 2:* January 1993-Present.

Objective: To provide an overview of the basic concepts of thermodynamics, heat transfer, and fluid-flow phenomena.

Learning Outcome: Upon successful completion of this course, the student will be able to understand international units associated with fluid mechanics and thermodynamics; understand the first and second laws of thermodynamics; and understand the principles behind turbine generator design and operation.

Instruction: Major topics covered in the course are the steam power cycle, heat at work, steam and turbine generation, pumps and fluid flow, reactor fuel and core design, and valve principles. Methods of instruction include lecture, video, and classroom exercises.

Credit Recommendation: *Version 1:* In the vocational certificate category, 3 semester hours in Fluid Mechanics/ Thermodynamics (7/88) (11/94). *Version 2:* In the vocational certificate category, 2 semester hours in Fluid Mechanics/ Thermodynamics (11/94).

Motors, Generators, and Transformers (ACEEM 88-03)

Location: Omaha Public Power District, Fort Calhoun Nuclear Station.

Length: 71 hours (4 weeks).

Dates: January 1988-Present.

Objective: To provide a fundamental knowledge of motor, generator, and transformer theory, application and maintenance.

Learning Outcome: Upon successful completion of this course, the student will be able to perform transformer, generator, and motor maintenance and connect transformers, generators, and motors in various configurations.

Instruction: Major topics covered in the course are single-phase motor principles, three-phase AC induction motor principles, DC motors/generators, electromagnetic induction, transformer principles and operations, AC Generator maintenance and instrument transformers. Methods of instruction include lecture, laboratory, and classroom exercises.

Credit Recommendation: In the vocational certificate category, 3 semester hours in Electrical Power Technology (7/88) (11/94).

Process Measurement Fundamentals (ACE I&C 88-01)

Location: Omaha Public Power District, Fort Calhoun Nuclear Station, North Omaha and Nebraska City plants.

Length: 72 hours (9 weeks).

Dates: July 1987-Present.

Objective: To review the instruments and measurement techniques used to determine temperature, pressure, and liquid level.

Learning Outcome: Upon successful completion of this course, the student will be able to use level, fluid flow, temperature, pressure instruments and simple instrumentation systems.

Instruction: Major topics covered in the course are unit conversion, constructing and plotting of graphs, pressure measurements, liquid level measurements, fluid-flow measurements and temperature measurements. Methods of instruction include lecture, videos, demonstration, and problem sessions.

Credit Recommendation: In the vocational certificate category, 2 semester hours in Basic Process Measurements/ Industrial Processes (7/88) (11/94).

Radiation Biology and Radiation Exposure Control (ACEHP 88-04) (Formerly Radiation Biology and Exposure Control [ACEHP 88-04])

Location: Omaha Public Power District, Fort Calhoun Nuclear Station.

Length: *Version 1*: 34 hours (3 months); *Version 2*: 32 hours (3 months).
Dates: *Version 1:* January 1988-November 1994; *Version 2:* December 1994-Present.
Objective: To provide instruction on radiation biology and radiation exposure as they apply to a radiation protection technician.
Learning Outcome: Upon successful completion of this course, the student will be able to describe the biological effects of ionizing radiation and perform basic calculations associated with radiation exposure reduction.
Instruction: Major topics covered in the course are cell structure, cell radiosensitivity, scope of regulatory guides 8.13 and 8.29, linear energy transfer, quality factor, exposure rates from radiation sources, ALARA considerations, and radiation shielding.
Credit Recommendation: *Version 1:* In the lower division baccalaureate/associate degree category, 1 semester hour in Radiation Protection Technology (7/88). *Version 2:* In the lower division baccalaureate/associate degree category, 2 semester hours in Radiation Biology and Radiation Exposure Control (11/94).

Radiation Measurements, Calculations, and Material Handling (ACEHP 88-03)

Location: Omaha Public Power District, Fort Calhoun Nuclear Station.
Length: *Version 1*: 27 hours 6 weeks); *Version 2*: 80 hours (6 weeks) .
Dates: *Version 1:* January 1988-October 1994; *Version 2:* November 1994-Present.
Objective: To provide instruction on radiation measurement, instrument operating characteristics, calculation methods, counting statistics, and handling radioactive material.
Learning Outcome: Upon successful completion of this course, the student will be able to explain the principles of radiation detection and measurement; calculate various sample activity concentrations; identify characteristics and preoperational testing methods for survey and count room instruments; identify and calculate statistical variations for count room instruments; and describe regulations associated with receipt and shipment of radioactive material.
Instruction: Major topics covered in the course are methods for measuring different types of radiation; calculating parameters that affect sample activity and volume; design characteristics for specific survey instruments; calculate statistical variations for count room instruments; and proper classification, packaging, and shipping of radioactive materials. Methods of instruction include lecture.
Credit Recommendation: *Version 1:* In the lower division baccalaureate/associate degree category, 1 semester hour in Radiation Protection Technology (7/88) (11/94) *Version 2:* In the lower division baccalaureate/associate degree category, 4 semester hours in Radiation Protection Technology (11/94).

Radiation Protection and Detection (ACEOPS 88-11)

Location: Omaha Public Power District, Fort Calhoun Nuclear Station.
Length: 36 hours (5 days).
Dates: January 1986-December 1992.
Objective: To provide instruction in the fundamentals of radiation protection and detection for a nuclear power plant operator.
Learning Outcome: Upon successful completion of this course, the student will be able to explain the construction and operation of various types of radiation detectors; discuss radiation spectroscopy; discuss principles of nuclear physics; explain federal and OPPD limits and guidelines for radiation exposures; and explain radiation protection techniques for external and internal exposure.
Instruction: Major topics covered in the course are gas-filled detectors, scintillation, semiconductor self-powered, portable radiation monitors, area monitors, radioactive decay, radiation interaction with matter, units of measurements, biological effects, exposure guidelines, and techniques for radiation protection. Methods of instruction include lecture.
Credit Recommendation: In the lower division baccalaureate/associate degree category, 1 semester hour in Nuclear Engineering Technology (7/88) (11/94).

Radiochemistry I (ACECH 88-02)

Location: Omaha Public Power District, Fort Calhoun Nuclear Station.
Length: *Version 1*: 51 hours (1.5 weeks); *Version 2*: 48 hours (1.5 weeks).
Dates: *Version 1:* January 1988-December 1991; *Version 2:* January 1991-Present.
Objective: To provide instruction on radiochemistry fundamentals.
Learning Outcome: Upon successful completion of this course, the student will be able to discuss the fundamentals of radiochemistry, radioactive decay, and the fundamental concepts associated with reactor plant chemistry.
Instruction: Major topics covered in the course are rate of radioactive decay, interaction of radiation with matter, sources of reactor coolant radiation, effects of power level and time at power on radioactivity production, counting instrumentation, and liquid scintillation counting techniques. Methods of instruction include lecture, laboratory experiments, and examinations.
Credit Recommendation: In the upper division baccalaureate degree category, 2 semester hours in Radiochemistry (7/88) (11/94).

Radiochemistry II (ACECH 88-03)

Location: Omaha Public Power District, Fort Calhoun Nuclear Station.
Length: *Version 1*: 66 hours (3 months); *Version 2*: 56 hours (3 months).
Dates: *Version 1:* January 1988-December 1991; *Version 2:* January 1991-Present.
Objective: To provide instruction on advanced radiochemistry.
Learning Outcome: Upon successful completion of this course, the student will be able to discuss the basic techniques associated with MCA calibration; discuss the basic concepts associated with counting instrumentation; discuss the fission product releases; and describe the parameters used to evaluate primary and secondary leakage.
Instruction: Major topics covered in the course are gamma ray spectrometry, defective fuel and core damage, primary to secondary leakage and steam generator tube rupture, borated water problems, and toxic gas monitors. Methods of instruction include lecture, laboratory, and examination.
Credit Recommendation: *Version 1:* In the upper division baccalaureate degree category, 3 semester hours in Chemistry (7/88) (11/94). *Version 2:* In the upper division baccalaureate degree category, 2 semester hours in Advanced Radiochemistry. (11/94).

Radiological Protection (ACEOPS 88-10)

Location: Omaha Public Power District, Ft. Calhoun Nuclear Station.
Length: 44 hours (6 days).
Dates: January 1987-December 1992.
Objective: To provide instruction in radiological protection.
Learning Outcome: Upon successful completion of this course, the student will

be able to discuss basic principles of nuclear physics; learn biological effects and risks; explain federal and OPPD limits and guidelines for radiation exposures; and explain basic radiological protection techniques.

Instruction: Major topics covered in the course are radioactive decay, radiation interaction with matter, units of measurement, biological effects, radiation protection manual, shielding, contamination, and respiratory protection. Methods of instruction include lecture.

Credit Recommendation: In the lower division baccalaureate/associate degree category, 1 semester hour in Nuclear Engineering Technology (7/88) (11/94).

Reactor Theory and Core Physics (ACEOPS 88-01)

Location: Omaha Public Power District, Fort Calhoun Nuclear Station.

Length: *Version 1*: 136 hours (3 months); *Version 2*: 68 hours (3 months).

Dates: *Version 1:* January 1987-December 1992; *Version 2:* January 1992-Present.

Objective: To provide the student with information on the properties of neutrons, the static and dynamic behavior of the reactor and the flux characteristics and coefficients of the reactor.

Learning Outcome: Upon successful completion of this course, the student will be able to describe, define, list, or calculate various neutron processes (i.e., slowing down, diffusion); radial and axial flux and power distribution; reactivity effects of various coefficients on reactivity; six-factor formula; static and dynamic behavior of reactor and power ranges and the behavior of the reactor in different power ranges as reactivity changes.

Instruction: Major topics covered in the course are neutron slowing down, thermal diffusion of neutrons, cross sections, flux profiles; neutron life-cycle and the six-factor formula, criticality determination, various reactor parameter variation effects on criticality, reactivity changes; power ranges, sources of reactor neutrons, delayed neutrons, reactor dynamics, startup rate, reactor response to reactivity change, power decrease effects, shutdown effects, decay heat; fast and thermal flux spatial variation effects on power distribution; and research reactor experiments. Methods of instruction include illustrated lecture, discussion, problem-solving, and experimentation with a research reactor.

Credit Recommendation: *Version 1:* In the lower division baccalaureate/associate degree category, 6 semester hours in Nuclear Engineering/Nuclear Technology (7/88) *Version 2:* In the lower division baccalaureate/associate degree category, 3 semester hours in Nuclear Engineering/Nuclear Technology (11/94).

Trigonometry (ACEOPS 88-06)

Location: Omaha Public Power District, Fort Calhoun Nuclear Station.

Length: 40 hours (3 months).

Dates: January 1986-Present.

Objective: To provide the student with an understanding of the trigonometric functions, graphing of the functions, and trigonometric identities, with an emphasis on right triangle trigonometry and vector analysis.

Learning Outcome: Upon successful completion of this course, the student will be able to use trigonometric relationships and concepts to graph the functions and solve for unknowns; use trigonometric tables; use trigonometric identities to solve for unknown values; convert from radians to degrees and vice versa; and use vector analysis to determine resultant vectors with the proper magnitude and direction.

Instruction: Major topics covered in the course are the wrapping function, properties of the trigonometric functions, graphs of the trigonometric functions, fundamental identities, trigonometric formulas, inverse trigonometric functions, right triangle trigonometry, law of sines and law of cosines, vectors and trigonometry, vector addition, and scalar product. Methods of instruction include lecture and problem-solving.

Credit Recommendation: In the lower division baccalaureate/associate degree category, 2 semester hours in Mathematics (7/88) (11/94).

Water and Corrosion Chemistry (Formerly Chemistry; Basic Concepts of Water Chemistry [ACEOPS 88-13])

Location: Omaha Public Power District, Fort Calhoun Nuclear Station.

Length: *Version 1*: 70 hours (2 weeks); *Version 2*: 70 hours (6 weeks).

Dates: January 1987-Present.

Objective: To provide the student with instruction in fundamental water chemistry as it applies to a nuclear power plant.

Learning Outcome: Upon successful completion of this course, the student will be able to define and/or discuss concepts and principles and perform basic analyses in fundamental chemistry with emphasis on applications in water chemistry and water treatment for the performance and safety of a nuclear power reactor.

Instruction: Major topics covered in the course are chemistry fundamentals, corrosion and corrosion control, water treatment quality and purity, physical and chemical methods for removal of water impurities, and general chemistry techniques used in water chemistry analysis. Methods of instruction include lecture, discussion, and laboratory.

Credit Recommendation: In the lower division baccalaureate/associate degree category, 3 semester hours in Water and Corrosion Chemistry (7/88) (11/94).

Omega Institute

Since 1980, Omega Institute has provided paralegal/legal assistant training for the greater Philadelphia and southern New Jersey regions. The paralegal program was evaluated and granted credit recommendations through the Program on Noncollegiate Sponsored Instruction (PONSI) in 1988. Recently, additional programs including Business, Allied Health, and Hospitality and Tourism have also been evaluated and granted credit recommendations through PONSI. These programs consist of 450 hours to 900 hours of classroom instruction. Daytime classes are held Monday through Friday from 9:00 AM to 3:00 PM and evening classes are held Monday, Wednesday, and Thursday from 6:00 PM to 10:00 PM.

Omega Institute is accredited as a Business School by the Accrediting Council for Independent Colleges and Schools (ACICS). The Medical Assistant Program is accredited by the Accrediting Bureau of Health Education Schools (ABHES). Omega Institute is a member of the Career College Association (CCA).

Omega Institute is approved as a private business school by the New Jersey Department of Education. It is approved for training of veterans and their eligible dependents and for training of JTPA, REACH, Workforce Development Program, Vocational Rehabilitation and Trade Act participants.

Source of official student records: Registry of Credit Recommendations, American Council on Education, One Dupont Circle, Washington, DC 20036-1193.

Additional information about the courses: Office of Corporate-Higher Education Programs, Thomas Edison State College, 101 West State Street, Trenton, NJ 08608-1176.

Administrative Law (202)

Location: Pennsauken, NJ.

Length: 23 hours (1.5 weeks).

Dates: May 1993-Present.

Objective: To introduce students to the purposes and functions of selected governmental administrative agencies.

Learning Outcome: Upon successful completion of this course, the student will be able to understand the purposes, powers, functions, and limitations of administrative agencies; utilize the forms used within administrative agencies; assume the duties and responsibilities of paralegals within administrative agencies; and understand the application of the Administrative Procedure Act.

Instruction: Major topics covered in the course are an overview of various federal and state administrative agencies, workings of these agencies and the forms used within them, and utilization of paralegals within these agencies. Focus is on the nature of administrative agencies, their proceedings, hearings, findings, and the function of the paralegal as advocate within in contrast and relation to Private Law. Methods of instruction include regular written exercises, and a final examination.

Credit Recommendation: In the lower division baccalaureate/associate degree category, 2 semester hours in Administrative Law (12/93) (12/96).

Air Travel (402)

Location: Pennsauken, NJ.

Length: 10 hours (3 days).

Dates: September 1986-Present.

Objective: To familiarize the students with interline agreements, fares, classes of service, fare restrictions, city/airport codes, airline codes, inflight services, deregulation, types of airlines, airport security and check-ins, and other personal liability of airlines.

Learning Outcome: Upon successful completion of this course the student will be able to differentiate between types of airlines and aircraft; decode and encode major cities and airlines by memory; demonstrate telephone reservation procedures; learn and utilize the uses of the Travel Planner, N.A. Edition; interpret travel restrictions for:

Instruction: Major topics covered in the course are interline agreements, fares, classes of service, fare restrictions, city/airport codes, airline codes, inflight services, deregulations, types of airlines, airport security and check-ins, and other personal liability of airlines.

Credit Recommendation: In the lower division baccalaureate/associate degree category, 3 semester hours in Reservation and Ticketing, only if students complete a combination of 3 courses: #402, either #405 or #442, and #406 (11/93).

Airlines Reservations Computer Systems (405)

Location: Pennsauken, NJ.

Length: 130 hours (22.5 days).

Dates: September 1986-January 1994.

Objective: To provide hands-on experience on a major airline reservation system, taking them from the basics through advanced techniques.

Learning Outcome: Upon successful completion of this course the student will be able to demonstrate proficiency on a microcomputer: access and interpret fares, display and interpret flight schedules, make optional entries for accessing availability, display availability and fares simultaneously , sell air space; create Passenger Name Records (PNR), use the START (Special Traveler Account Record) systems, initialize the ticket printer, modify itineraries, and PNRs. request Automatic seat assignment, obtain queue count display hotel index, determine room types and rates, obtain hotel availability; display and work with car rental availability; and understand the method for Total Access and Multi-Access functions, use Direct Reference System.

Instruction: Major topics covered in the course are intensive training through hands-on experience on the travel industry's most important tool. Through access to major reservations systems, students will expand their knowledge concerning all aspects of air and land travel services. Instruction carries the student from the basics through advanced techniques.

Credit Recommendation: In the lower division baccalaureate/associate degree category, 3 semester hours in Reservation and Ticketing, only if students complete a combination of 3 courses: #402, either #405 or #442, and #406 (11/93).

Business Aspects of Travel (407)

Location: Pennsauken, NJ.

Length: 25 hours (8 days).

Dates: September 1991-January 1994

Objective: To provide an overview of a travel office business.

Learning Outcome: Upon successful completion of this course the student will be able to learn to follow directions, establish priorities, budget time; organize work station, using standard procedures and formats, filing and retrieving documents; and make decisions concerning procedural problems.

Instruction: Major topics covered in the course are an overview of a travel agency's office procedures. It includes making arrangements for air travel, train and cruise reservations, hotel and motel accommodations, and car rentals. As the student moves from one job to another, he/she will recognize the continuity and interrelationship of the work done by travel agencies.

Credit Recommendation: In the lower division baccalaureate/associate degree category, 3 semester hours in General Tourism, only if students complete a combination of 3 courses: #407, #409, and #434 (11/93).

Business Communications (326,327,328)

Location: Pennsauken, NJ.
Length: 75 hours (25 days).
Dates: June 1988-Present.
Objective: To instruct students in effective written and oral communication skills useful in a business and professional setting.
Learning Outcome: Upon successful completion of this course the student will be able to understand the process of communication within an organization and be able to identify and solve common business communication problems and plan, draft and revise letters, memos and reports.
Instruction: Major topics covered in the course are to build and develop effective written and oral communication skills which can be applied within the business environment. Extensive practice is provided utilizing various forms of writing appropriate for use by all levels of management. Emphasis is placed on letters, memos, proposals, reports, formal research projects and graphics. Techniques of oral business presentations are also included.
Credit Recommendation: In the lower division baccalaureate/associate degree category, 3 semester hours in Business Communications (11/93).

Business Mathematics (329,330,331)

Location: Pennsauken, NJ.
Length: 75 hours (25 days).
Dates: October 1990-Present.
Objective: To help students gain a higher level of competence in using business math and develop their application skills and problem solving techniques in business activities.
Learning Outcome: Upon successful completion of this course the student will be able to perform basic math functions including using fractions, decimals and percents and understand and apply business math in the areas of discounts, markups, interest, insurance, annuities, bonds, and business statistics.
Instruction: Major topics covered in the course are a review of basic math functions as fractions, decimals, percents. Emphasis is placed on understanding and applying discounts, markups, interest, insurance, stocks, bonds, annuities and statistics in areas common to most business enterprises. In addition, applications in accounting as payroll, bank reconciliations, inventories, depreciation financial statement analysis, and records management are also included.
Credit Recommendation: In the lower division baccalaureate/associate degree category, 3 semester hours in Business Math (11/93).

Business Office Procedures (332)

Location: Pennsauken, NJ.
Length: 75 hours (25 days).
Dates: April 1990-Present.
Objective: To prepare management support personnel for work in a business office using recognized office procedures and practices.
Learning Outcome: Upon successful completion of this course the student will be able to learn and develop general office skills as organization, planning, decision making, verbal and written communication, and qualities as flexibility, initiative, loyalty, confidentiality and dependability and understand and develop human relation skills in a culturally diverse work environment.
Instruction: Major topics covered in the course are instruction on office practices and procedures, technological information, office equipment usage, time management and resume preparation. Students will be expected to develop sound strategies for working in this environment utilizing textbook information in case studies and discussion groups.
Credit Recommendation: In the lower division baccalaureate/associate degree category, 3 semester hours in Business Office Procedures (11/93).

Civil Litigation (207)

Location: Pennsauken, NJ.
Length: 36 hours (2.4 weeks).
Dates: May 1993-Present.
Objective: To introduce students to civil court rules and procedures.
Learning Outcome: Upon successful completion of this course, the student will be able to identify various courts and their functions; describe the rules and procedures of various courts; and assist a lawyer in preparing for a civil trial by preparing pleadings, interrogatories, depositions, and other discovery requests.
Instruction: Major topics covered in the course are examining the functions and processes of our judicial system and the role of a legal assistant in the law with emphasis on the canons of ethics of the American Bar Association and the National Association of Legal Assistants. This course analyzes civil court rules and filing requirements. Methods of instruction include regular written exercises, and a final examination.
Credit Recommendation: In the lower division baccalaureate/associate degree category, 2 semester hours in Civil Litigation or Civil Procedure (12/93) (12/96).

Civil Litigation Practice a. Judgments, Executions and Remedies (204) b. Civil Litigation (207)

Location: Pennsauken, NJ.
Length: *Version 1*: a. 35 hours (6 days), b. 50 hours (8 days); *Version 2*: a. 26 hours (9 days), b. 36 hours (12 days).
Dates: *Version 1:* January 1984-March 1991; *Version 2:* April 1991-April 1993.
Objective: a. To present a summary of debtor/creditor law; b. To introduce students to civil court procedures.
Instruction: a. The first portion of this course summarizes the areas of debtor/creditor law and examines creditor's rights in attachment, garnishment, replevin, receivership, and execution sales, followed by an overview of secured transactions covering creditors with special rights. The second portion of this course is devoted to bankruptcy practice and covers in detail the law and procedures for processing a Chapter 7, Chapter 11, or Chapter 13 bankruptcy petition together with creditor's and bankrupt's rights and defenses. In the final portion of this course, students are exposed to a review of the basic systems and procedures used in legal systems and offices with special emphasis on alternative forms of filing systems, organization of work schedules, and management of office personnel.
b. This course examines the functions and processes of our judicial system and the role of a legal assistant in the law with emphasis on the canons of ethics of the American Bar Association and the Nation-al Association of Legal Assistants. This area analyzes civil court procedure rules and filing requirements. In addition to regular written exercises, the students must pass a midterm and a final examination in both a and b.
Credit Recommendation: In the lower division baccalaureate/associate degree category, 4 semester hours in Civil Litigation Practice (6/86) (11/88) (4/93).

Clinical Procedures and Sterilization (606)

Location: Pennsauken, NJ.
Length: 40-45 hours (15 days).

Dates: January 1983-Present.

Objective: To teach the student to assist the physician in the clinical assessment, treatment and preparation of the patient.

Learning Outcome: Upon successful completion of this course the student will be able to list the precautions when handling body fluids in compliance with OSHA regulations; name the sites for taking temperatures and give normals for each site; describe the process by which sterilization is accomplished; and discuss the warning signs of inflammation.

Instruction: This course is a study of the techniques involved in assisting the physician in the preparation of the patient for routine examination and treatment. The student also learns the techniques essential to sterilization of instruments and equipment. Emphasis is on the development of clinical skills essential to effective performance of these functions.

Credit Recommendation: In the lower division baccalaureate/associate degree category, 3 semester hours in Clinical Procedures and Sterilization (11/93).

Computer Technology (1001)

Location: Pennsauken, NJ.

Length: 75 hours (3 hours/day over 5 weeks).

Dates: February 1994-Present.

Objective: To introduce the business student to the fundamentals of the computer, its components, and all related peripheral devices along with the operating system.

Learning Outcome: Upon successful completion of this course, the student will be able to identify all major components of the computer; identify all internal boards and drives of computer; properly set up a computer and install the DOS; install and configure printers to computer systems; install and configure popular applications software programs; perform basic maintenance on the computer system; use the Disk Operating System to perform basic function; perform preventative maintenance on the system.

Instruction: Major topics covered in this course are basic training in computer terminology, operation, hardware, and software.

Credit Recommendation: In the lower division baccalaureate/associate degree category, 4 semester hours in MIS, or Computer Operations, or Data Communications, or Computer Science (7/94).

Constitutional Law and Governmental Agencies
a. Administrative Law (202)
b. Public Rights and Remedies (206)

Location: Pennsauken, NJ.

Length: *Version 1*: a. 25 hours (4 days), b. 25 hours (4 days); *Version 2*: a. 23 hours (4 days), b. 20 hours (4 days).

Dates: *Version 1:* January 1984-March 1991; *Version 2:* April 1991-December 1993.

Objective: a. To introduce students to the purpose and function of various governmental administrative agencies; b. To introduce students to the area of basic constitutional rights.

Instruction: a. Major topics covered in this course include an overview of various federal and state administrative agencies, working of these agencies and the forms used within them, and utilization of paralegals within the government agencies. Stress is on the nature of administrative agencies, their proceedings, hearings, findings, and function of the paralegal as advocate within public law in contrast and relation to private law.

b. Major topics covered in this course include a study of the basic constitutional rights, focusing on such contemporary issues as civil rights, welfare rights, tenant and housing rights, fair/equal employment rights and consumer rights. In addition to regular written exercises, the students must pass a midterm and a final examination in both a and b.

Credit Recommendation: In the lower division baccalaureate/associate degree category, 3 semester hours in Constitutional Law and Governmental Agencies (6/86) (11/88) (4/93).

Contract Law (205)

Location: Pennsauken, NJ.

Length: *Version 1*: 35 hours (6 days); *Version 2*: 39 hours (2.6 weeks).

Dates: *Version 1:* January 1984-March 1991; *Version 2:* April 1991-Present.

Objective: To provide students with an overview of contract and commercial law.

Learning Outcome: Upon successful completion of this course, the student will be able to determine the existence of a valid contract, including whether there has been an offer and acceptance, consideration, legal capacity, and a legal purpose; understand defenses to contract formation or enforceability, including the statute of frauds; and learn about the Uniform Commercial Code and its relation to the common law of contracts.

Instruction: Major topics covered in the course are an overview of the field of commercial law, with emphasis on the formation of contracts, including a discussion of offer and acceptance, consideration, the statute of frauds, the capacity to contract, third-party beneficiaries, parole evidence, breach of contract, remedies, Uniform Commercial Code, and basic contract drafting experience. Methods of instructions include written exercises and a final examination.

Credit Recommendation: In the lower division baccalaureate/associate degree category, 2 semester hours in Contract Law or Commercial Law (6/86) (4/93) (12/96).

Corporate Law (203)

Location: Pennsauken, NJ.

Length: *Version 1*: 40 hours (7 days); *Version 2*: 26 hours (1.7 weeks).

Dates: *Version 1:* January 1984-March 1991; *Version 2:* April 1991-Present.

Objective: To provide an overview of business organizations or corporate law and enable students to assist with preparing legal documents in this field.

Learning Outcome: Upon successful completion of this course, the student will be able to identify the types of business organizations, including sole proprietorship, partnership, and corporation, limited liability partnership, and limited liability company; understand the formation, operation, and dissolution of the various forms of business organizations; prepare and understand basic legal documents connected with business organizations; and understand how profits and losses of various forms of business organizations are shared.

Instruction: Major topics covered in this course are the basic documents and principles associated with various forms of business, including sole proprietorship, partnership, and corporation; the formation, operation, and dissolution of these forms of business; how to prepare the basic legal documents connected with this field of law including, but not limited to, documents necessary for incorporation, amendments to a corporate charter, bylaws, director's meetings and minutes, stock certificates, corporate resolutions, and fictitious name applications; and partnership agreements. Methods of instruction include written exercises and a final examination.

Credit Recommendation: In the lower division baccalaureate/associate degree

category, 2 semester hours in Business Organizations or Corporate Law (6/86) (11/88) (4/93) (12/96).

dBase (351)

Location: Pennsauken, NJ.
Length: 75 hours.
Dates: January 1991-August 1994.
Objective: To introduce students to database concepts and skills.
Learning Outcome: Upon successful completion of this course, the student will be able to design and operate a database; list and describe the file processing operation provided by file managers; create reports with databases; and gain practical understanding of the uses of a DBMS by learning and applying the fundamentals of dBASE III Plus.
Instruction: Major topics covered in the course are the concepts of a database including file management, reporting; and programming.
Credit Recommendation: In the lower division baccalaureate/associate degree category, 3 semester hours in Database Management (4/93).

DeskTop Publishing (1340)

Location: Pennsauken, NJ.
Length: 75 hours (25 days).
Dates: September 1990-Present.
Objective: To provide a basic understanding of word processing software used to perform desktop publishing.
Learning Outcome: Upon successful completion of this course the student will be able to operate a desktop publishing program using fundamental techniques acquired through the course including creating, printing and saving files, editing, formatting, blocking, defining, executing macros, using styles, using tables; and layout and design advertising, promotional and other organization planning/management products using desktop publishing techniques, including: creating graphic lines, using graphics, designing display pages and cards, resumes, letterheads, presentations, flyers, forms, floor plans and calendars, certificates and catalog pages, programs, and newsletters.
Instruction: Major topics covered in the course are desktop publishing techniques currently used in business organizations. Instructional information, techniques and supplemental materials will focus on reinforcement of newly introduced concepts through practical application, i.e., by immediately and repetitiously using basic techniques, alone and in combination with others, to build desktop publishing skills for use in business, other professional organizations and government offices. Methods of instruction include self-instruction with assistance from lab personnel when complex procedures and/or concepts are encountered.
Credit Recommendation: In the lower division baccalaureate/associate degree category, 3 semester hours in DeskTop Publishing (11/93).

Domestic Relations (210)

Location: Pennsauken, NJ.
Length: *Version 1*: 32 hours (6 days); *Version 2*: 35 hours (2.3 weeks).
Dates: *Version 1:* January 1984-March 1991; *Version 2:* April 1991-Present.
Objective: To present an overview of the legal issues involved in domestic relations.
Learning Outcome: Upon successful completion of this course, the student will be able to understand the requirements for a valid marriage; identify family issues involving marriage, divorce, separation, annulment, alimony, and the equitable distribution of assets; understand court proceedings and procedures as they relate to domestic relations issues; and learn about parental rights and obligations, including the legitimacy of children, custody, and adoption.
Instruction: Major topics covered in the course are the law of domestic relations, including marriage, annulment, separation, divorce, alimony, legitimacy of children, custody, and adoption; how to obtain basic divorce information while working under the supervision of a lawyer; and how to use data to pursue successful completion of divorce. Methods of instruction include written exercises and a final examination.
Credit Recommendation: In the lower division baccalaureate/associate degree category, 2 semester hours in Domestic Relations or Family Law (6/86) (11/88) (4/93) (12/96).

Electrocardiography Procedures (EKG) (609)

Location: Pennsauken, NJ.
Length: 45-60 hours (20 days).
Dates: January 1983-Present.
Objective: To prepare the student in proper EKG techniques and to identify normal and abnormal cardiac conduction patterns.
Learning Outcome: Upon successful completion of this course the student will be able to explain the polarity of the myocardial cells in the active and resting stages; define Einthovens triangle; discuss normal sinus rhythm and arrhythmias; list and explain the functions of the heart's normal electrical pathway; and demonstrate the proper technique in the performance of an EKG.
Instruction: Major topics covered in the course are the anatomy of the heart and blood flow through the heart, as well as the conduction system, how it relates to the EKG pattern in both normal and abnormal conditions and the proper technique to acquire an accurate graph.
Credit Recommendation: In the lower division baccalaureate/associate degree category, 1 semester hour in First Aid (11/93).

Estates and Trusts (209)

Location: Pennsauken, NJ.
Length: *Version 1*: 35 hours (6 days); *Version 2*: 45 hours (3 weeks).
Dates: *Version 1:* January 1984-March 1991; *Version 2:* April 1991-Present.
Objective: To present an introduction to estate planning and the probate court system .
Learning Outcome: Upon successful completion of this course, the student will be able to describe the nature of property and its forms of ownership; understand the administration of estates, including methods of settlement, the distribution of assets, inheritance and estate taxes, and estate planning tools and techniques; and understand the various documents necessary to do an estate plan, including wills and trusts.
Instruction: Major topics covered in the course are study of the New Jersey probate procedures and the administration of estates, including methods of settlement , inheritance, and estate; gift taxes; estate planning and a review of the tools and techniques applicable thereto; and preparation of will and trust documents. Methods of instruction include written exercises and a final examination.
Credit Recommendation: *Version 1:* In the lower division baccalaureate/associate degree category, 2 semester hours in Estates and Trusts (6/86) (11/88). *Version 2:* In the lower division baccalaureate/associate degree category, 3 semester hours in Estates and Trusts (4/93).

First Aid (610)

Location: Pennsauken, NJ.
Length: 15-25 hours (5 days).
Dates: January 1983-Present.
Objective: To equip students with a basic knowledge of first aid and CPR.
Learning Outcome: Upon successful completion of this course, the student will

be able to explain how to give immediate first aid for shocks and burns; perform RACE FOR LIFE/CPR; and discuss how to keep seizure victims from harm.

Instruction: Major topics covered in this course are immediate and temporary care of accident victims, CPR, and the Heimlich Maneuver.

Credit Recommendation: In the lower division baccalaureate/associate degree category, 1 semester hour in First Aid (11/94).

Front Office Management (420)

Location: Pennsauken, NJ.

Length: 75 hours (25 days).

Dates: September 1991-Present.

Objective: To explain the effects of the front office on the overall operation of a hotel or motel and works step-by-step through the front office guest cycle.

Learning Outcome: Upon successful completion of this course the student will be able to identify clerical functions, e.g., maintain guest ledger/folio balances, post transactions, collect payment, maintain the work station, prepare room status reports, prepare shift deposits, verify payment authorization, maintain/secure keys; describe handling reservations, e.g., take room reservations, cancel room reservations, change/modify room reservations, preblock special room requests, maintain room reservation log/system; identify Guest Service Functions, e.g., preregister arrivals with special room needs, greet guests, resolve/refer guest complaints/

Instruction: Major topics covered in the course are the effects of the front office on the overall operation of a hotel and works step-by-step through the front office guest cycle. It features information on today's front office computer technology, yield management, and reservation systems, and discusses how guests' concerns shape management strategies and front office procedures. This is an AH&MA Educational Institute certificate course.

Credit Recommendation: In the lower division baccalaureate/associate degree category, 3 semester hours in Front Office Management (11/93).

Fundamentals of Anatomy and Physiology (603)

Location: Pennsauken, NJ.

Length: 70 hours (23 days).

Dates: January 1983-Present.

Objective: To provide the student with an understanding of how the human body is put together and how it functions in health and disease states.

Learning Outcome: Upon successful completion of this course the student will be able to explain the difference between organic and inorganic compounds; describe body directions, surfaces and planes; list the functions of the skeletal system; and explain the anatomy and functions of veins and arteries.

Instruction: Major topics covered in the course are anatomy, physiology and pathology. Emphasis is on the structure and functions of the body systems. Included is instruction in the principles of the biological and physical sciences that lay a foundation for the understanding of the normal body processes and abnormal states and conditions of the body.

Credit Recommendation: In the lower division baccalaureate/associate degree category, 3 semester hours in Fundamentals of Anatomy and Physiology (11/93).

Geography (400)

Location: Pennsauken, NJ.

Length: 60 hours (20 days).

Dates: September 1991-Present.

Objective: To provide the student with a thorough foundation in geography as it relates to travel and tourism. It presents the world as a wide variety of destinations, and provides a natural bridge to other areas of product knowledge vital to adequate preparation for a career in travel and tourism.

Learning Outcome: Upon successful completion of this course the student will be able to read a map using longitude and latitude and use an atlas; identify destination resources; identify the continents, countries, major rivers, mountains, and bodies of water of the world; be familiar with the tourism areas from this destination; identify major cities (airports) in the world; and identify major tourist attractions in the world.

Instruction: Major topic covered in the course is geography from a travel industry perspective. It treats geography as something the travel industry sells, matching clients to destinations. Through the use of videos, maps and lectures, students will work with and discuss major tourist areas of the world.

Credit Recommendation: In the lower division baccalaureate/associate degree category, 3 semester hours in Destination Geography or Tourism Geography, only if students complete a combination of 2 courses: #400 and #403 (11/93).

Hospitality Computer Systems (436)

Location: Pennsauken, NJ.

Length: 75 hours (25 days).

Dates: September 1991-Present.

Objective: To provide students with a basic understanding of the hospitality's computer systems through text and hands-on experience.

Learning Outcome: Upon successful completion of this course the student will be able to identify the most common front office components of a property management system (PMS) and some of the computer systems that can interface with a PMS, and describe the functions performed by front office PMS modules, such as an in-house reservations module, rooms, management module, guest account module, and general management module; describe the process of selecting and implementing a computer system at a hospitality operation, the basic functions performed by generic applications software, such as word processing, electronic spreadsheet analysis, and database management packages; and identify and explain the function of files maintained by the modules of a PMS back office package, including accounts receivable, accounts payable, payroll, and financial reporting; also identify the functions of common PMS interfaces which include point-of-sale systems, call accounting systems, energy management systems, electronic locking systems, and guest-operated devices; and identify and explain the function of files maintained by food service management applications, such as recipe management, precosting and postcosting, sales analysis, menu management, and back office accounting applications.

Instruction: Major topics covered in the course are computer applications for all hospitality functional areas. It examines reservations for all hospitality functional areas. It also examines reservations and other features of hotel property management systems, service and management applications of food and beverage systems, and the management of information systems. This is an AH&MA Educational Institute certificate course.

Credit Recommendation: In the lower division baccalaureate/associate degree category, 3 semester hours in Hospitality Computer Systems (11/93).

Hospitality Law (432)

Location: Pennsauken, NJ.

Length: 75 hours (25 days).

Dates: September 1991-Present.

Objective: To provide students with a basic understanding of the laws and regulations affecting the hospitality industry.

Learning Outcome: Upon successful completion of this course the student will be able to describe the hotelkeeper's legal rights and responsibilities and the implications of the major laws affecting hotel operations, particularly those related to public health and safety, alcoholic beverages, food service, and copyrighting of music and TV programs; describe the hotel's legal obligations to receive a guest, his duties related to the protection and care of guests, tenants, and others; procedures to follow in the event of a guest's death; describe the rights and responsibilities of a hotelkeeper with regard to employees; e.g., employee unions, the Immigration Reform and Control Act of 1986, polygraph tests, discrimination in employment, OSHA regulations, state and federal laws, and their requirements, affecting employment; identify the major items that should be included in a written contract between a hotel/motel and its convection or group travel clients; and identify the hotelkeeper's responsibilities for the lost or damage to the property of guests and non-guests, responsibilities with regard to fire safety.

Instruction: Major topics covered in the course are the legal considerations of hospitality property management in straightforward, understandable terms. It explores important legislation affecting hospitality operations and helps students learn to recognize legal pitfalls before they become problems. Includes comprehensive sections on food and beverage laws. This is an AH&MA Educational Institute certificate course.

Credit Recommendation: In the lower division baccalaureate/associate degree category, 3 semester hours in Hospitality Law (11/93).

Hospitality Supervision (431)

Location: Pennsauken, NJ.

Length: 75 hours (25 days).

Dates: September 1991-Present.

Objective: To teach the qualities needed for the role of the supervisor in hospitality operations so they can be an effective supervisor.

Learning Outcome: Upon successful completion of this course the student will be able to describe the role of the supervisor and the management; understand the importance of effective verbal and nonverbal communication; learn and utilize techniques to develop and improve recruitment and selection skills, to develop and improve skills in orienting and training, to develop and enhance evaluating and coaching skills; understand the importance of managing productivity and controlling labor costs, special supervisory concerns, including the labor shortage, Equal Employment Opportunity laws, sexual harassment, the supervisor's legal role, safety and security, supervising a multicultural workforce, substance abuse, and working with employee unions; apply techniques in team-building, manage conflict, and manage time effectively understand strategies designed to increase employee motivation.

Instruction: Major topic covered in the course is managing people from the hospitality supervisor's viewpoint. Includes techniques for increasing productivity and controlling labor costs, time management, and managing change. It also stresses effective communication and explains the responsibilities of a supervisor in a lodging or food service operation. It helps students understand to motivate employees and resolve conflicts with staff, guests, and other departments. This is an AH&MA Educational Institute certificate course.

Credit Recommendation: In the lower division baccalaureate/associate degree category, 3 semester hours in Hospitality Supervision (11/93).

Human Relations (1342)

Location: Pennsauken, NJ.

Length: 75 hours (3 hours/day over 5 weeks).

Dates: January 1994-Present.

Objective: To help students understand and apply theories and concepts of human relations in an organizational environment.

Learning Outcome: Upon successful completion of this course, the student will be able to understand and apply basic precepts and principle of human relations in a business setting; understand how human relations are influenced by communication styles, group dynamics, organizational values, and leadership techniques; demonstrate appropriate resume writing and interviewing techniques.

Instruction: Major topics covered in this course are concepts of human behavior in an organizational environment; skill building for personal and professional application; communication styles; organizational values; group dynamics; motivation and reinforcement; conflict management and team building; job search and interviewing skills.

Credit Recommendation: In the lower division baccalaureate/associate degree category, 3 semester hours in Human Relations or Organizational Behavior (7/94).

International Travel (403)

Location: Pennsauken, NJ.

Length: 15 hours (5 days).

Dates: September 1986-Present.

Objective: To teach students the international travel markets covering all major areas of the world.

Learning Outcome: Upon successful completion of this course the student will be able to identify the IATA Traffic Conference Areas; summarize the basic international air fare construction techniques of maximum permitted mileage, excess mileage, higher intermediate points, sector mileage, add-ons, and fare construction units; calculate elapsed flying times; summarize international travel regulations for passport and visa, health certificates, and custom regulations; and calculate exchange rates.

Instruction: Major topics covered in the course are the international travel markets covering all major areas of the world. International travel will include IATA, IATAN, international air fares, regulations on international travel and foreign currencies.

Credit Recommendation: In the lower division baccalaureate/associate degree category, 3 semester hours in Destination Geography or Tourism Geography, only if students complete a combination of 2 courses: #400 and #403 (11/93).

Introduction to Business Organization (352)

Location: Pennsauken, NJ.

Length: 75 hours (25 days).

Dates: September 1990-Present.

Objective: To introduce students to the structures, processes and operational environments of business organizations.

Learning Outcome: Upon successful completion of this course the student will be able to identify and understand business environment variables, components and phenomena; conduct fundamental business planning activities through a business function approach; manage a component of a business operation through a computer simulation; and use appropriate business vocabulary.

Instruction: Major topics covered in the course are business organization and management in contemporary society and the future direction of business organization and commerce as well. Throughout the course, students will be exposed to the concepts and ideas which are fundamental to an understanding of business environments, organization and management. Instruction will focus on providing an understanding of organization and management theory as well as fundamental matters underlying business organization and activities: including social and demographic trends affecting business, technological developments, small business organization, business management, as well as social issues, ethical/social responsibilities of business organizations to the community and society. In addition the course will explore the business environment, various business structures, management processes/systems, human resources, marketing, computer information, finance, legal and tax environments, and career options in business. The learning process will be an interplay of lecture, text assignments, class discussions and presentations, computer simulations and exercises to test skill development.

Credit Recommendation: In the lower division baccalaureate/associate degree category, 3 semester hours in Introduction to Business (11/93).

Introduction to Medical Assisting (601)

Location: Pennsauken, NJ.

Length: 15-20 hours (6.5 days).

Dates: January 1983-Present.

Objective: To introduce the student to the role and functions of a professional Medical Assistant.

Learning Outcome: Upon successful completion of this course the student will be able to list the professional organizations which certify Medical Assistants; define the most commonly used medical abbreviations; understand and explain the various medical specialities; discuss the history of medicine as it applies to the Medical Assistant; and explain the importance of continuing education.

Instruction: Major topics covered in the course are an overview of the Medical Assistant profession and is designed to give the student an introduction to the skills and responsibilities required as a member of the health care team. A brief history of medicine and important medical contributions are discussed as well as disciplines of various medical specialities.

Credit Recommendation: In the lower division baccalaureate/associate degree category, 1 semester hour in Introduction to Medical Assisting (11/93). **NOTE**: This course also includes a 10-hour version, which is not eligible for credit recommendation.

Introduction to the Hospitality Industry (440)

Location: Pennsauken, NJ.

Length: 75 hours (25 days).

Dates: September 1991-Present.

Objective: To explain the complex interrelationships involved in the business, and to stress the variety of career opportunities available.

Learning Outcome: Upon successful completion of this course the student will be able to describe the scope of the travel and tourism industry and its economic impact on the local, national, and international levels; evaluate and discuss several major factors, developments, and trends which have affected lodging and food service operations in recent years and which will continue to affect the industry in the future; compare and contrast the effects on the industry of franchising, management contracts, referral organizations, independent and chain ownership, and condominium growth; identify the general classifications of hotels and describe the most distinctive features of each; and identify the common divisions or functional areas of hotel organization rooms, food and beverage, engineering, marketing and sales, accounting, human resources, and security and explain the responsibilities and activities of each.

Instruction: Major topics covered in the course are the industry's most current trends, practices, and statistics. It gives students an international perspective on the travel and tourism industry and a comprehensive look at each department in lodging and food service operations. Insights from leading industry professionals expose students to the real-life issues hospitality managers face daily. The course highlights career opportunities and predicts the future of the industry. This is an AH&MA Educational Institute certificate course.

Credit Recommendation: In the lower division baccalaureate/associate degree category, 3 semester hours in Introduction to Hospitality Industry (11/93).

Judgements: Executions and Remedies (204)

Location: Pennsauken, NJ.

Length: 26 hours (1.8 weeks).

Dates: May 1993-Present.

Objective: To present a summary of debtor/creditor law.

Learning Outcome: Upon successful completion of this course, the student will be able to understand the rights and obligations of debtors and creditors; understand the kinds of Bankruptcy, including Chapters 7, 11, and 13; and understand alternative forms of filing systems, organization of work schedules, and management of office personnel.

Instruction: Major topics covered in the course are summarizing the areas of debtor/creditor law and examines creditor's rights in attachment, garnishment, replevin, receivership, and execution sales, followed by an overview of secured transactions covering creditors with special rights. The second portion of this course is devoted to bankruptcy practice and covers in detail the law and procedures for processing a Chapter 7, Chapter 11, or Chapter 13 bankruptcy petition together with creditor's and bankrupt's rights and defenses. In the final portion of this course, students are exposed to a review of the basic systems and procedures used in legal systems and offices with special emphasis on alternative forms of filing systems, organization of work schedules and management of office personnel. In addition to regular written exercises, the students must pass a midterm and a final examination.

Credit Recommendation: In the lower division baccalaureate/associate degree category, 2 semester hours in Judgements: Executions and Remedies, Bankruptcy Law or Debtor and Creditor Relations (12/93) (12/96).

Land and Sea Accommodations and Services (404)

Location: Pennsauken, NJ.

Length: 50 hours (17 days).

Dates: September 1986-Present.

Objective: To familiarize the student with researching and booking all types of land/sea accommodations, through hands-on experience.

Learning Outcome: Upon successful completion of this course the student will be able to learn and utilize various types of Amtrak Accommodations, the differences between domestic and international rail service, restrictions that apply to a Eurailpass and requirements for renting a car (domestic and International); identify the four benefits of cruising, explain what is included in the cost of a cruise, disadvantages of cruising, identify the four factors that determine the cost of a cruise, and differentiate among cruise ships, yachts, freighters and ferries; distinguish among the types of properties, identify the factors that affect the price of a room, describe meal plans, identify hotel reference guides, display the importance of yield management; learn and utilize the various components of a typical tour package, identify three types of tours, identify the benefits of tours to the client and the agent, explain the responsibility and liability of a tour operator; and through hands-on experience, book reservations for train travel, auto rentals, cruises, hotels and tour packages.

Instruction: Major topics covered in the course are reference materials and methods used to book reservations for cruises, hotels, automobiles, tours and charters. It also gives students hands-on activities regarding documentation, cost calculations, payment procedures and confirmation of these services.

Credit Recommendation: In the lower division baccalaureate/associate degree category, 3 semester hours in Travel and Tourism (11/93).

Legal Office Procedures (333)

Location: Pennsauken, NJ.

Length: 75 hours (25 days).

Dates: August 1993-Present.

Objective: To prepare management support personnel for work in a law office setting utilizing various law office practices.

Learning Outcome: Upon successful completion of this course the student will be able to learn general office duties as calendaring, mail and telephone procedures, records management, ordering supplies of the law office assistant; prepare general legal forms, documents and report cases in areas of bankruptcies, property settlements, wills, estates, civil and criminal matters; use basic legal terminology correctly; understand various court systems, utilize the law library, conduct basic research, and plan and organize business meetings; and use various equipment skillfully, such as the facsimile machine and computer, dictaphone machine through the use of cassette tapes and be able to transcribe handwritten materials.

Instruction: Major topics covered in the course are law office duties, preparing general legal documents, the court system, civil and criminal litigation and other court actions. Emphasis is placed on concepts of working in a legal environment and applying the information for class projects.

Credit Recommendation: In the lower division baccalaureate/associate degree category, 3 semester hours in Legal Office Procedures (11/93).

Legal Problem Solving: Analysis, Research, and Writing (217)

Location: Pennsauken, NJ.

Length: 75 hours (3 hours/day over 5 weeks).

Dates: March 1994-December 1996.

Objective: To provide further understanding of legal research, tools and methodology to achieve the objectives of the supervising attorney.

Learning Outcome: Upon successful completion of this course, the student will be able to apply legal research methodologies to resolve client's legal problems effectively and efficiently; draft appropriate legal documents for filing and/or completion of various transactions; further understand legal analysis and research methods; understand court practices, trial, and appellate preparations; and respond to briefs.

Instruction: Major topics covered in this course include writing skills; computer-assisted legal research techniques; and formulation of searches utilizing search planners found in software packages.

Credit Recommendation: In the lower division baccalaureate/associate degree category, 3 semester hours in Legal Research Writing II (7/94).

Legal Research and Writing (208)

Location: Pennsauken, NJ.

Length: *Version 1*: 35 hours (6 days); *Version 2*: 95 hours (3 weeks); *Version 3*: 105 hours (3.5 weeks).

Dates: *Version 1:* January 1984-March 1991; *Version 2:* April 1991-March 1996; *Version 3:* April 1996-Present.

Objective: To present an introduction to methods of legal research and writing.

Learning Outcome: Upon successful completion of this course, the student will be able to perform legal research by analyzing cases, statutes, and other appropriate sources; understand how to read, digest, and dissect case law, as well as how to write case citations; write legal memorandums and participate in legal problem solving; and understand how to utilize the computer in conducting legal research.

Instruction: Major topics covered in the course are an introduction to legal research methods utilizing primary sources, secondary materials, and related finding tools; examination of and instruction on the use of a law library, legal terminology, the structure and citation of court opinions, and the writing of legal memoranda and briefs; and the development of legal writing techniques and skills. Methods of instruction include written exercises and two graded memoranda.

Credit Recommendation: *Version 1:* In the lower division baccalaureate/associate degree category, 2 semester hours in Legal Research and Writing (6/86) (11/88). *Versions 2 and 3:* In the lower division baccalaureate/associate degree category, 4 semester hours in Legal Research and Writing or Legal Methods (4/93) (12/96).

Legal Support Specialist Internship (220) (Formerly Advanced Paralegal Internship)

Location: Pennsauken, NJ.

Length: 225 hours (10 weeks).

Dates: September 1994-December 1996.

Objective: To provide an opportunity to define and gain additional skills and proficiency in an actual office environment.

Learning Outcome: Upon successful completion of this course, the student will be able to explain the Internship program and workings of a paralegal or related office; apply knowledge of substantive legal fields to resolve legal problems of actual clients; and apply legal procedures to achieve clients' objectives efficiently and effectively.

Instruction: The Internship is a continuation of the curriculum program designed to give the students practical training and experience. The internship program evaluates students in all areas of professional performance.

Credit Recommendation: In the lower division baccalaureate/associate degree category, 4 semester hours in Internship of field experience (7/94).

Managing Service in Food and Beverage Operations (1550)

Location: Pennsauken, NJ.

Length: 75 hours (25 days).

Dates: September 1991-Present.

Objective: To provide thorough knowledge of the procedures necessary to plan for and manage effectively the delivery of food and beverage products to guests in outlets ranging from employee cafeterias and coffee shops to room service, banquet areas, and high-check average gourmet dining rooms.

Learning Outcome: Upon successful completion of this course the student will be able to identify types of commercial food service facilities, three levels of management, typical production and service personnel, and a typical organization for a large restaurant; learn and utilize the steps in the management process; learn and utilize the importance of nutrition, the nutritional responsibilities of institutional and commercial food service managers, advantages of standard recipes, serving alcohol with care; describe kitchen design factors, factors in food and beverage equipment selection; and describe operating ratios.

Instruction: Major topics covered in the course are every facet of hospitality food and beverage management—from coffee shops to room service, dining rooms, banquets, cafeterias, employee food service, catering, clubs and shows, and more. This course includes ideas for efficient planning, management, and delivery of service. This is an AH&MA Educational Institute certificate course.

Credit Recommendation: In the lower division baccalaureate/associate degree category, 3 semester hours in Food and Beverage Management (11/93).

Medical Laboratory Theory and Application (612)

Location: Pennsauken, NJ.

Length: 120-150 hours (25 days).

Dates: January 1983-Present.

Objective: To introduce the student to the clinical laboratory, its disciplines, and the importance of accurate diagnostic testing.

Learning Outcome: Upon successful completion of this course the student will be able to list and apply the steps involved in testing biological specimens in accordance with OSHA regulations; explain the importance of advance patient preparation for the collection of laboratory specimens; identify and define the categories of laboratory tests based on function; and explain the purpose of quality control and methods of quality control employed.

Instruction: Major topics covered in the course are to instruct the student in the principles and clinical application of various tests that assist in the diagnosis of pathologic conditions, help confirm a clinical diagnosis and obtain information regarding a patient's condition.

Credit Recommendation: In the lower division baccalaureate/associate degree category, 4 semester hours in Medical Laboratory Theory and Applications for the 150-hour version of this course; 3 semester hours in Medical Laboratory Theory and Applications for the 120-hour version of this course (11/93) (11/94).

Medical Law (614)

Location: Pennsauken, NJ.

Length: 15 hours (5 days).

Dates: January 1983-Present.

Objective: To provide medical assistants with a basic knowledge of law, applicable to the medical office.

Learning Outcome: Upon successful completion of this course the student will be able to explain the importance of law and ethics in the practice of medicine; identify requirements for a physician to be licensed; describe office procedures for administering and dispensing medication; and explain the legal relationship of the physician and patient.

Instruction: Major topics covered in the course are the study of legal aspects of the patient/physician relationship stressing laws of negligence, malpractice and consents.

Credit Recommendation: In the lower division baccalaureate/associate degree category, 3 semester hours in Medical Office Procedures (11/93).

Medical Office Procedures (611)

Location: Pennsauken, NJ.

Length: 45-60 hours (20 days).

Dates: January 1983-Present.

Objective: To prepare the student for front desk responsibilities in a medical facility.

Learning Outcome: Upon successful completion of this course, the student will be able to explain the process by which the pegboard system of accounting is accomplished; list the steps for preplanning of long distance telephone calls; discuss the information needed from the patient to establish his file; discuss the procedure for processing insurance forms; demonstrate proper telephone technique.

Instruction: Major topics covered in this course are proper use of the telephone, and setting priorities and making decisions to effectively function in an office setting. Methods of instruction include role playing, discussion, and simulated office situations.

Credit Recommendation: In the lower division baccalaureate/associate degree category, 3 semester hours in Medical Office Procedures (11/94).

Medical Terminology (602)

Location: Pennsauken, NJ.

Length: 75 hours (25 days).

Dates: January 1983-Present.

Objective: To introduce the student to the medical language.

Learning Outcome: Upon successful completion of this course the student will be able to discuss word roots, combining forms, prefixes and suffixes of the medical language; list the meanings of major pathological conditions affecting the heart and blood vessels; discuss the origins of medical terms; and explain rules for pronunciation of medical terms.

Instruction: Major topics covered in the course are the development of medical vocabulary used in practice with emphasis on prefixes, suffixes, root words and combining forms. Physiologic and anatomic terms referring to body systems are also covered.

Credit Recommendation: In the lower division baccalaureate/associate degree category, 3 semester hours in Medical Terminology (11/93).

Meeting Planning (434)

Location: Pennsauken, NJ.

Length: 75 hours (25 days).

Dates: September 1991-Present.

Objective: To provide students with a basic understanding of planning, managing, and servicing meetings and conventions.

Learning Outcome: Upon successful completion of this course the student will be able to identify the importance of the meetings market, detailing types of meetings, the role of the professional meeting planner and the role of the lodging industry; describe the miscellaneous markets; planning, managing, and conducting a meeting from the meeting planner's perspective; and how to develop a marketing plan for group business; identify the sales/marketing department organization, identifying typical positions and organizational structures. Identify sales tools and explain their use; and identify meeting functions: banquets, special events, audiovisual aids used in the meeting environment, and exhibits, trade shows, and other ancillary activities.

Instruction: Major topics covered in the course are both the meeting planner's and convention service manager's perspectives to help students understand the meeting requirements of various market segments. It covers the countless details that make or break conventions and meetings, and outlines techniques for reaching target markets and making the sale. This is an AH&MA Educational Institute certificate course.

Credit Recommendation: In the lower division baccalaureate/associate degree

category, 3 semester hours in Meeting Planning for students in the Hotel Management Program; 3 semester hours in General Tourism for students in the Hospitality and Tourism, and Travel Careers Programs, only if students complete a combination of 3 courses: #352, #409 and #434 (11/93).

Paralegal Internship (214)

Location: Pennsauken, NJ.

Length: 150 hours (5 weeks).

Dates: September 1994-December 1996.

Objective: To provide an opportunity to define and gain additional skills and proficiency in an actual office environment.

Learning Outcome: Upon successful completion of this course, the student will be able to explain the Internship program and workings of a paralegal or related office; apply knowledge of substantive legal fields to resolve legal problems of actual clients; and apply legal procedures to achieve clients' objectives efficiently and effectively.

Instruction: The Internship is a continuation of the curriculum program designed to give the students practical training and experience. The internship program evaluates students in all areas of professional performance.

Credit Recommendation: In the lower division baccalaureate/associate degree category, 3 semester hours in Internship or field experience (7/94).

Phlebotomist in the Health Care System (901-907)

Location: Pennsauken, NJ.

Length: 60 hours (15 days).

Dates: January 1983-Present.

Objective: To provide the students with theoretical information and instruction in phlebotomy procedures and techniques.

Learning Outcome: Upon successful completion of this course the student will be able to discuss the various departments within the health care setting, the level of care given in each department, the organizational structure in the clinical laboratory and the phlebotomist's role as a member of the laboratory team; explain the major body systems and their functions, the components of blood and their functions, and the laboratory's assessment of the circulatory system; understand and explain the types of laboratory specimens used for testing the various anticoagulants in the vacutainer system, venous and microcollection equipment needed for blood collection, and the interference of drugs and other substances in blood; discuss preparation for blood collection, physiological factors that affect patient's laboratory test results, proper patient identification and labeling of his/her specimen tubes, correct equipment for the blood draw, and how to deal with complications that may result from blood collection; understand and explain the methods for infection control, modes of bacterial transmission, specific isolation techniques used to protect the patient and staff, correct procedures for handling and labeling biohazardous material and the OSHA requirements for disposal of equipment used for obtaining specimens; discuss the communication cycles within the laboratory and outside of the laboratory, procedure manuals, function of the laboratory computer system, proper usage of requisition forms and specimen labels, various transport systems and reporting mechanisms; and explain quality assurance guidelines for specimen collection and processing, record keeping, proficiency testing and day to day quality control, protocols for quality blood culture collection, laboratory safety rules and personal safety.

Instruction: Major topics covered in the course are to provide theoretical and practical instruction in phlebotomy with emphasis on laboratory information systems, quality assurance, routine and special laboratory specimen collection in accordance with OSHA Regulations, the terminology of phlebotomy and an overview of anatomy and physiology with special attention to the circulatory system.

Credit Recommendation: In the lower division baccalaureate/associate degree category, 3 semester hours in Phlebotomy (11/93).

Public Rights and Remedies (206)

Location: Pennsauken, NJ.

Length: 20 hours (1.4 weeks).

Dates: May 1993-Present.

Objective: To introduce students to the U.S. Constitutional and its legal implications.

Learning Outcome: Upon successful completion of this course, the student will be able to understand basic constitutional rights; understand the separation of powers into the judicial, executive, and legislative branches of government; and understand the Bill of Rights and the role of amendments.

Instruction: Major topics covered in the course are a study of the basic constitutional rights, focusing on such contemporary issues as civil rights, welfare rights, tenant and housing rights, fair/equal employment rights and consumer rights. Methods of instruction include regular written exercises and a final examination.

Credit Recommendation: In the lower division baccalaureate/associate degree category, 2 semester hours in Public Rights and Remedies or Constitutional Law (12/93) (12/96).

Real and Personal Property (211)

Location: Pennsauken, NJ.

Length: *Version 1*: 43 hours (7 days); *Version 2*: 28 hours (1.8 weeks).

Dates: *Version 1:* January 1984-March 1991; *Version 2:* April 1991-Present.

Objective: To present an overview of real and personal property.

Learning Outcome: Upon successful completion of this course, the student will be able to distinguish between real property and personal property; understand the nature of interests in property; and understand the legal means of acquiring and transferring ownership of interests in property.

Instruction: Major topics covered in the course are surveys the types and ways of owning real and personal property, with an emphasis on estates in land, future interest, concurrent and marital estates, easements and covenants; various interests in property and how they are created, including liens, mortgages, and the methods for transferring title to land. Methods of instruction include written exercises and a final examination.

Credit Recommendation: In the lower division baccalaureate/associate degree category, 2 semester hours in Real and Personal Property (6/86) (11/88) (4/93) (12/96).

Reservations, OAG, and Ticketing (406)

Location: Pennsauken, NJ.

Length: 65 hours (22 days).

Dates: September 1991-Present.

Objective: To provide the student with thorough knowledge of the reservation procedure, using the OAGs, and being able to complete all the various forms of ARC documents, along with the Settlement Authorization form.

Learning Outcome: Upon successful completion of this course the student will be able to learn and utilize the NAOAG and WWOAG; the most common city/airport codes; complete the following ARC documents: 2 & 4 flight tickets, Universal Charge form, Refund and Exchange Notice, Tour Orders, and MCOs; complete a reservation; have knowledge of agency operation: the role of the area bank and the procedure of completing the sales report; and have knowledge of agency accounting system.

Instruction: Major topics covered in the course are the principles of the NAOAG and the WWOAG, creating a reservation and writing tickets. Ticketing procedures will be taught for standard ARC tickets, MCOs, prepaid tickets, tour orders, refunds and exchanges. Money management, including the sales report is also included.

Credit Recommendation: In the lower division baccalaureate/associate degree category, 3 semester hours in Reservations and Ticketing. **NOTE:** Give credit only if students complete a combination of 3 courses: (402), either (405) or (442), and (406) (11/93).

SABRE (442)

Location: Pennsauken, NJ.

Length: 75 hours (25 days).

Dates: February 1994-Present.

Objective: To provide hands-on experience on a major airline reservation system, taking them from the basics through advanced techniques.

Learning Outcome: Upon successful completion of this course the student will be able to demonstrate proficiency on a microcomputer: access and interpret fares, display and interpret flight schedules, make optional entries for accessing availability, display availability and fares simultaneously, sell air space; create Passenger Name Records (PNR), use the STARS (Special Traveler Account Record) systems, initialize the ticket printer, modify itineraries and PNRs, request automatic seat assignment, obtain queue count; display hotel index, determine room types and rates, obtain hotel availability; display and work with car rental availability; and understand the method for Total Access and Multi-Access functions, use Direct Reference System.

Instruction: Major topics covered in the course are intensive training through hands-on experience on the travel industry's most important tool. Through access to major reservations systems, students will expand their knowledge concerning all aspects of air and land travel services. Instruction carries the student from the basics through advanced techniques.

Credit Recommendation: In the lower division baccalaureate/associate degree category, 3 semester hours in Reservation and Ticketing. **NOTE:** Give credit only if students complete a combination of 3 courses: (402), either (405) or (442), and (406) (11/93).

Sales and Marketing (409)

Location: Pennsauken, NJ.

Length: 25 hours (7 days).

Dates: September 1986-Present.

Objective: To familiarize the students with the principles of selling and identify the various steps involved in marketing.

Learning Outcome: Upon successful completion of this course the student will be able to identify the principles of selling travel, qualifying the client, and closing the sale; describe the difference between inside and outside sales, and customized sales: incentive travel, group travel, handicapped travelers; explain follow up sales procedures: Clients' change of plans, emergency situations, travel insurance, steps involved in reissues, importance of a client profile, and written and oral contracts; identify the steps involved in marketing, differentiate between sales and marketing, analyze market segmentation; and describe the relationship between the travel agent and a supplier, relate the importance of service to the travel industry, and the importance of the agency image.

Instruction: Major topics covered in the course are the principles of selling, the difference between inside and outside sales. It will define the different types of customized sales: incentive travel, group travel, business clients, and handicapped travelers. It will compare the difference between a written and an oral contract, handling complaints, identify the various steps involved in marketing, agency image and types of marketing strategies.

Credit Recommendation: In the lower division baccalaureate/associate degree category, 3 semester hours in General Tourism. **NOTE:** Give credit only if students complete a combination of 3 courses: (352), (409) and (434) (11/93).

Spreadsheets (350)

Location: Pennsauken, NJ.

Length: 75 hours.

Dates: January 1988-Present.

Objective: To provide students with a functional understanding of spreadsheets and their applications.

Learning Outcome: Upon successful completion of this course, the student will be able to understand operating system concepts frequently used in micro-computer applications; and understand fundamental, intermediate and advanced techniques for development, design and alteration of spreadsheets.

Instruction: Major topics covered in the course are the use of spreadsheets in business; emphasis is placed on profit and loss models, "what if" projections and budgeting; and Lotus 1-2-3 application package to demonstrate the use of the spreadsheet concept and functions.

Credit Recommendation: In the lower division baccalaureate/associate degree category, 3 semester hours in Spreadsheets (4/93).

Torts (213)

Location: Pennsauken, NJ.

Length: *Version 1*: 40 hours (7 days); *Version 2*: 27 hours (1.8 weeks).

Dates: *Version 1:* January 1984-March 1991; *Version 2:* April 1991-Present.

Objective: To familiarize students with the provisions of tort law and products liability.

Learning Outcome: Upon successful completion of this course, the student will be able to identify the commission of a tortious act and distinguish the types of international and unintentional torts; understand the law of negligence and its defenses; and understand other tort concepts, including strict liability, nuisance, products liability, pollution, and premises liability.

Instruction: Major topics covered in the course are intentional torts such as battery, assault, false imprisonment, conversion and emotional distress, as well as negligence and its defenses; strict liability; nuisance; misrepresentation; defamation; invasion of privacy; trespass; and New Jersey no-fault law. Methods of instruction include written exercises and a final examination.

Credit Recommendation: In the lower division baccalaureate/associate degree category, 2 semester hours in Tort Law (6/86) (11/88) (4/93) (12/96).

Typing I (301)

Location: Pennsauken, NJ.

Length: 75 hours.

Dates: January 1985-Present.

Objective: To stress proper keyboarding techniques and introduce basic business formatting.

Learning Outcome: Upon successful completion of this course, the student will be able to demonstrate a minimum speed of 20 wpm on a 5-minute timed writing with no more than 5 mistakes; and operate a standard keyboard and develop basic speed and accuracy skills, using proper techniques.

Instruction: Major topics covered in the course are the opportunity to develop effective keyboard skills and master a minimum speed of 20 wpm for 5 minutes.

Credit Recommendation: In the lower division baccalaureate/associate degree category, 2 semester hours in Beginning Typing (4/93).

Typing II (302)

Location: Pennsauken, NJ.

Length: 75 hours.

Dates: January 1985-Present.

Objective: To develop speed and accuracy in addition to practical application of skills in typing letters, business forms, tables and reports.

Learning Outcome: Upon successful completion of this course, the student will be able to demonstrate a minimum speed of 30 wpm on a 5-minute timed writing with no more than 5 mistakes; and continue improvement of speed and accuracy using proper stroking techniques.

Instruction: Major topics covered in the course involve continuing the process of improving keyboarding skills while applying them to more detailed typing applications.

Credit Recommendation: In the lower division baccalaureate/associate degree category, 1 semester hour in Beginning Typing and 1 semester hour in Intermediate Typing, for a total of 2 semester hours (4/93).

Typing III (303)

Location: Cinnaminson, NJ.

Length: 75 hours.

Dates: January 1985-Present.

Objective: To develop speed, accuracy, and proofreading techniques.

Learning Outcome: Upon successful completion of this course, the student will be able to demonstrate a minimum speed of 40 wpm on a 5-minute timed writing with no more than 5 errors; and improve speed and accuracy through the use of proper stroking techniques.

Instruction: Major topics covered in the course are developing students' keyboarding skills and their ability to prepare more advanced typing projects.

Credit Recommendation: In the lower division baccalaureate/associate degree category, 2 semester hours in Intermediate Typing (4/93). **NOTE**: If Typing I, II, and III are completed, the student will earn 3 semester hours in Beginning Typing and 3 semester hours in Intermediate Typing, for a total of six semester hours.

Word Processing #310 (310) (Formerly Word Processing: WordPerfect 5.1 (310)

Location: Pennsauken, NJ.

Length: 75 hours.

Dates: April 1990-Present.

Objective: To provide the student with a functional understanding of the word processing program, WordPerfect 5.1.

Learning Outcome: Upon successful completion of this course, the student will be able to understand the fundamentals of word processing using WordPerfect 5.1 program; and use WordPerfect 5.1 to design and produce business documents.

Instruction: Major topics covered in the course are designed to train students to use word processing software; use the basic software functions including document saving, retrieving, formatting, numeric sorting, spell checking, creating, and deleting files.

Credit Recommendation: In the lower division baccalaureate/associate degree category, 3 semester hours in Word Processing using WordPerfect 5.1 (4/93).

Word Processing #311 (311) (Formerly Word Processing: First Choice (311)

Location: Pennsauken, NJ.

Length: 75 hours.

Dates: January 1993-Present.

Objective: To train students to use computer hardware as well as software to perform basic business computer applications such as Word Processing, database, and spreadsheet using integrated software.

Learning Outcome: Upon successful completion of this course, the student will be able to demonstrate an understanding of the concepts of DOS, word processing, spreadsheets, and database; create, revise, store, retrieve and print documents, spreadsheets and databases; and integrate word processing, and database and spreadsheets.

Instruction: Major topics covered in the course include instruction on how to use computer hardware and software to perform word processing, spreadsheet, database, and integration functions.

Credit Recommendation: In the lower division baccalaureate/associate degree category, 3 semester hours in Integrated Business Computer Applications (4/93).

OmniTech® Consulting Group, Inc.

OmniTech® Consulting Group, Inc. is a custom marketing/management consulting firm specializing in developing training for global 1000 companies in areas ranging from business basics to strategy formation— including customized courses in strategic management, finance, budgeting, channel and supplier management, new product development, and sales. Founded in 1985 and headquartered in Chicago, the firm's training mission and approach is linked to "hands-on" learning and a comprehensive understanding of competitive marketing and the business applications related to traditional and emerging technologies.

OmniTech instructors have extensive experience working across a broad spectrum of industries, with particular emphasis on telecommunications, information technology, and financial services. Company staffers are premiere trainers of finance, information technology, and telecommunications within the United States, having developed and taught hundreds of courses to professionals at companies such as AT&T, Ameritech, BellSouth, Colgate-Palmolive, Digital, First Chicago, Motorola, Northern Telecom, Reebok, U.S. West, Unisys, Warner-Lambert, and others. International courses have been taught in Europe, Russia, and Latin America. Instructors are deep subject matter experts in their field who combine industry expertise with extensive classroom experience. All courses are customized to the specific needs of each business.

OmniTech also offers customized courses covering a variety of business needs including high-technology solution selling, effective technical marketing, high-technology quality control, and business leadership. Courses can be conducted on any site, or via electronic or multimedia. For more information about OmniTech courses, contact: OmniTech Consulting Group, Inc., 1 North Franklin Street, Chicago, IL 60606-3401, phone: 312-696-0070, fax: 312-696-0100.

Source of official student records: Registry of Credit Recommendations, American Council on Education, One Dupont Circle, Washington, DC 20036-1193.

Additional information about the courses: College Credit Recommendation Service, American Council on Education, One Dupont Circle, Washington, DC 20036-1193.

Choosing and Managing Your Telecom Supplies

Location: Locations throughout the nation.

Length: 24 hours (3 days).

Dates: October 1985-Present.

Objective: To enable students to effectively solicit, select, and manage their suppliers of telecommunications products and services.

Learning Outcome: Upon successful completion of this course, the student will be able to effectively plan and manage the RFP, RFI and RFQ process resulting in an appropriately written RFX; select a telecom supplier based on numerous evaluation, criteria and dimensions; negotiate fair contracts and working agreements with selected suppliers; resolve conflicts between the supplier and customer, and between multiple suppliers; and develop review and feedback mechanisms and reward programs to drive desired supplier behavior and incent the supplier to provide superior performance.

Instruction: Major topics covered in the course are guidelines, skills, techniques and tools to help managers select and manage their telecommunications suppliers with emphasis on communication - specifically mutual understanding, expectation building, and frequent feedback - as the key to creating successful supplier partnerships. Methods of instruction include lecture, discussion, simulation, case study, testing and role playing.

Credit Recommendation: In the lower division baccalaureate/associate degree or the upper division baccalaureate degree category, 1 semester hour in Management, Business Administration, Public Administration, or Marketing (9/95).

Finance and Budgets for the TCM

Location: Locations throughout the nation.

Length: 32 hours (4 days).

Dates: October 1995-Present.

Objective: To enable the student to effectively review and manage operating budgets, and prepare and evaluate financial evaluations for decision making purposes.

Learning Outcome: Upon successful completion of this course, the student will be able to read and evaluate corporate financial statements in order to manage financial performance and cash flow; build payback, ROI, DCF and IRR analyses to assess the long-term impact of proposed projects; make prudent business decisions based on best case, worst case and most likely case assumptions; and build and manage expense and capital budgets.

Instruction: Major topics covered in the course are accounting principles, financial statements, ratios, managing cash flow, NPV, IRR, budgeting process, and building and managing a budget. Methods of instruction include pre-course review, lecture, discussion, exercises, and exams.

Credit Recommendation: In the lower division baccalaureate/associate degree or the upper division baccalaureate degree category, 2 semester hours in Fundamentals of Finance (9/95).

On-Site Inspection Agency

The On-Site Inspection Agency is the nation's prime implementer of arms control operations worldwide. OSIA provides US policy makers with arms control treaties implementation expertise, compliance information, and related services to advance US national security. OSIA organizes, trains, equips, and provides infrastructure support to lead and conduct inspections, audits, and monitoring and assisting in international activities in which the US is involved; assists preparations for national compliance; escorts foreign entities conducting arms control activities at US facilities; and provides linguistic and technical expertise to a broad spectrum of international, security, cooperation, and negotiation activities.

Source of official student records: Registry of Credit Recommendations, American Council on Education, One Dupont Circle, Washington, DC 20036-1193.

Additional information about the courses: College Credit Recommendation Service, American Council on Education, One Dupont Circle, Washington, DC 20036-1193.

International Treaty Administration: Chemical Weapons (Chemical Weapons Treaty Orientation)

Location: Various sites in the United States.

Length: 19 hours (3.3 days).

Dates: January 1997-Present.

Objective: To provide inspectors and escorts a working knowledge of the Chemical Weapons Treaty, On-Site Inspection Agency (OSIA) operations procedures and operating environment.

Learning Outcome: Upon successful completion of this course, the student will be able to demonstrate an ability to use and locate information in the Chemical Weapons Treaty; understand OSIA site preparation guidelines; and operate an in environment to accomplish their treaty related missions.

Instruction: Major topics covered in the course are the many aspects of the Chemical Weapons Convention (CWC), to include a CWC overview, an interagency overview, escort procedures and experiences, and U.S. Developmental Production and Storage Facilities. Methods of instruction include lecture, discussion, audio-visual materials, and an examination.

Credit Recommendation: In the upper division baccalaureate degree category, 1 semester hour in International Treaty Administration: Chemical Weapons (2/97).

International Treaty Administration: Conventional Forces In Europe Treaty (CFE) (Conventional Forces In Europe Treaty)

Location: McLean, VA.

Length: 21 hours, 55 minutes (3.5 days).

Dates: May 1995-Present.

Objective: To provide inspectors and escorts a working knowledge of the Conventional Forces in Europe Treaty, On-Site Inspection Agency (OSIA) operations procedures, and operating environment.

Learning Outcome: Upon successful completion of this course, the student will be able to demonstrate an ability to use and locate information in the CFE Treaty; understand OSIA site preparation guidelines; and operate in an environment to accomplish their treaty related missions.

Instruction: Major topics covered in the course are CFE treaty background and overview, summary of treaty provisions, verification, information exchange, inspection and mission timelines, escort procedures, planning, preparation and conduct of CFE Inspections, and Treaty update. Methods of instruction include lecture, practical exercises and presentations, discussion, and audio-visual material.

Credit Recommendation: In the upper division baccalaureate degree category, 1 semester hour in International Treaty Administration: Conventional Forces in Europe Treaty (2/97).

International Treaty Administration: Open Skies (Open Skies Treaty Orientation Course)

Location: McLean, VA.

Length: 15 hours (2 days).

Dates: September 1993-Present.

Objective: To familiarize personnel with the administration of the Open Skies Treaty.

Learning Outcome: Upon successful completion of this course, the student will be able to demonstrate an ability to use and locate information in the Open Skies Treaty; understand the operational procedures and restrictions, and operate in an environment under which this Treaty is executed.

Instruction: Major topics covered in the course are operational requirements and restrictions associated with the Open Skies Treaty. Detailed analysis of the Treaty, and articles and decisions are used to illustrate the operational environment under which this Treaty is executed. Methods of instruction include lecture and group discussion. Group discussion presents an opportunity for individuals to demonstrate hands on knowledge of locating and interpreting the operational requirements of the Treaty.

Credit Recommendation: In the upper division baccalaureate degree category, 1 semester hour in International Treaty Administration: Open Skies (2/97).

International Treaty Administration: Strategic Arms Reduction Treaty and Intermediate Range Nuclear Forces Treaty (Strategic Arms Reduction Treaty and Intermediate Range Nuclear Forces Treaty) (START/INF) Course

Location: McLean, VA.

Length: 31 hours (5 days).

Dates: April 1996-Present.

Objective: To provide inspectors and escorts a working knowledge of the Strategic Arms Reduction Treaty (START) and Intermediate Range Nuclear Forces (INF) Treaty, OSIA operations and procedures, site preparation guidelines, and operating environment to accomplish their treaty related missions.

Learning Outcome: Upon successful completion of this course, the student will be able to demonstrate an ability to use and locate information in the START Treaty; understand the operations procedures and site preparation guidelines; and operate in an environment to accomplish their treaty related missions.

Instruction: Major topics covered in the course are Treaty protocols for: notifications, inspections, conversions, and elimination; history of START; START II; and INF. Methods of instruction include lecture, practical exercises working in small groups, and mock inspection.

Credit Recommendation: In the graduate degree category, 2 semester hours in International Treaty Administration: Strategic Arms Reduction Treaty and Intermediate Range Nuclear Forces Treaty (4/97).

Pacific Bell

Pacific Bell is a public utility located in California with 64,000 employees. The training department is composed of two districts responsible to an assistant vice president of employee placement and training, a unit of the company's human resources department. The company offers employee referral and educational assistance through the Tuition Aid Office.

Courses are systematically designed in accordance with the Pacific Bell Training Development Guidelines. Instructors are full-time Pacific Bell employees selected for their subject matter expertise and teaching skills. Classroom facilities, audiovisual support, and other needs have been designed to ensure an effective learning environment.

Source of official student records: Registry of Credit Recommendations, American Council on Education, One Dupont Circle, Washington, DC 20036-1193 or Pacific Bell Training Department, Tuition Aid Office, 2600 Camino Ramon, Room 2N400-L, San Ramon, CA 94583 .

Additional information about the courses: College Credit Recommendation Service, American Council on Education, One Dupont Circle, Washington, DC 20036-1193.

Account Team Selling Skills (42191)

Location: Various locations throughout California.

Length: 32 hours (4 days).

Dates: October 1991-Present.

Objective: To instruct personnel in basic sales skills, including preparatory financial analysis and systems theory.

Learning Outcome: Upon successful completion of this course, the student will be able to demonstrate an understanding of the 11 step selling process; secure appointments with important decision makers in client organizations; gather all data to develop and sell solutions; and utilize positioning, proposal, presentation and cost justification skills to close more sales for the business unit.

Instruction: Major topics covered in the course are financial calculations, sales planning and preparation, cost justification, and conducting a system study. Methods of instruction include lecture, case studies, and role playing.

Credit Recommendation: In the upper division baccalaureate degree category, 2 semester hours in Marketing or Sales (6/92).

Achieving Extraordinary Customer Relations (65005)

Location: Various locations throughout California.

Length: 16 hours (2 days).

Dates: March 1990-Present.

Objective: To recognize the benefits that come from providing positive experiences for customers and learn specific behaviors that will make customer contacts positive instead of negative.

Learning Outcome: Upon successful completion of this course, the student will be able to identify six types of customer behaviors; deal with difficult customers and handle these stressful contacts; identify barriers to listening and discover ways to eliminate the barriers; and respond to verbal attacks in a positive manner and turn the contact into a positive experience.

Instruction: Major topics covered in the course are identifying customers-internal and external, reducing stress, building rapport, creating positive outcomes, and building positive customer relations. Methods of instruction include role play, lecture, and discussion.

Credit Recommendation: In the lower division baccalaureate/associate degree category, 1 semester hour in Customer Relations or Business elective (6/92).

Active Communicating, Stage II (20579)

Location: Various locations throughout California.

Length: 60 hours (8 days).

Dates: January 1992-Present.

Objective: To provide students with strategies to enhance their interpersonal skills and become more effective and efficient in the leadership roles as it relates to reaching the organization's goals.

Learning Outcome: Upon successful completion of this course, the student will understand how attitudes are communicated both verbally and nonverbally, understand cross cultural symbols and diversity when communicating and understand the origins of leadership and communication as it relates to effective communicating.

Instruction: Major topics covered in the course are principles of communicating, communication barriers, motivating others through active listening, cross cultural symbols and diversity and leadership effectiveness and communications. Methods of instruction include lecture, discussion, case studies, role playing, and written assignments.

Credit Recommendation: In the upper division baccalaureate degree category, 3 semester hours in Communication or Speech Communication (6/92).

Active Communicating: Maintaining Customer Focus (20399C) (Formerly Active Communicating: Professional Presence and Creativity [20399])

Location: Various locations throughout California.

Length: *Version 1:* 21 hours (3 days); *Version 2:* 15 hours (2 days).

Dates: *Version 1:* July 1990-May 1996; *Version 2:* June 1996-Present.

Objective: *Version 1:* To use drama-based techniques, this course develops the student's ability to think clearly under pressure, listen accurately, show sensitivity to others, demonstrate verbal dexterity, and convey a self-confident "presence." *Version 2:* To use drama-based techniques within a Paulo Freirean philosophy of transformative education in order to develop the student's interpersonal communication ability to be more sensitive to customers.

Learning Outcome: *Version 1:* Upon successful completion of this course, the student will be able to understand the relevance to the corporate professional of the actor's skills development process; understand the relationship between language and its expression through the voice and the body; improve interpersonal communication skills, including voice, body use, and quick thinking; and develop a more self-confident overall communication style. *Version 2:* Upon successful completion of this course, the student will be able to understand the relevance and application of a theater-based skills development process to everyday customer communication; understand communication as a process involving thought, emotion, and physical and vocal expression that varies according to social context; refine customer interaction skills to include awareness, listening, timing, and relationship building; improve presentation skills (with the customer as receiver) in vocal and physical expressiveness, and in the ability to think effectively under pressure; and develop a more self-confident and reflective style of interpersonal communication.

Instruction: *Version 1:* Major topics covered in the course are voice and body usage; concentration and memory; creativity, imagination, and communication; timing and listening; improvisation; and self-confidence. Methods of instruction include lecture, discussion, performance exercises, and written assignments. *Version 2:* Major topics covered in the course are voice and body usage, concentration and memory, creativity and imagination, listening and feedback, authenticity and empathy, flexibility, and self-confidence. Methods of instruction include lecture, discussion, performance exercises, learner presentations/reports, written assignments, individual and dyadic oral presentations throughout the course, and a reflective written assignment at course conclusion.

Credit Recommendation: *Version 1:* In the upper division baccalaureate degree category, 1 semester hour in Speech or Communications (11/90). *Version 2:* In the upper division baccalaureate degree category, 1 semester hour in Communication or Speech (6/96).

Advanced Network Design (42313)

Location: Dublin, Los Angeles, and Oakland.

Length: 32 hours (4 days).

Dates: January 1989-Present.

Objective: To provide systems design consultants with the skill and knowledge to design complex data networks by using computer-based tools.

Learning Outcome: Upon successful completion of this course, the student will be able to identify specific network design criteria; price alternatives for private line data communication; use the MND's software to calculate response time and other performance-modeling tasks; use MND to design and price a credible and accurate network; and identify factors that affect response time.

Instruction: Major topics covered in the course are accepted methods of data gathering; understanding design criteria, i.e., terms, statistics, and theories used in design tools; hands-on experience with the PC-based design tool "Connections"; and knowledge of data network designs.

Credit Recommendation: In the upper division baccalaureate degree category, 2 semester hours in Telecommunications or Information Science (11/90).

Affirmative Action (01005)

Location: Various locations throughout California.

Length: *Version 1:* 16 hours (2 days); *Version 2:* 8 hours (1 day).

Dates: *Version 1:* January 1985-June 1992; *Version 2:* July 1992-Present.

Objective: To enable students to understand EEO and Affirmative Action, explore their own issues and concerns relative to the topic, and clarify their role in EEO/Affirmative Action programs.

Learning Outcome: Upon successful completion of this course, the student will be able to understand the legal and historical background of EEO/Affirmative Action, define what discrimination and reverse discrimination are, demonstrate how Affirmative Action benefits all employees, understand the organization's commitment to EEO/AA, and understand their role in Affirmative Action and how it relates to their own career development.

Instruction: Major topics covered in the course are in the course are legal aspects of EEO/AA, developing Affirmative Action plans and objectives, perceptions of discrimination, reverse discrimination, the older employee, the additionally challenged, selection decisions, defining sexual harassment, problem resolution, and the future of Affirmative Action. Methods of instruction include lecture, discussion, and videotapes.

Credit Recommendation: *Version 1:* In the upper division baccalaureate degree category, 1 semester hour in Affirmative Action (11/86). *Version 2:* In the lower division baccalaureate/associate degree category, 1 semester hour in Supervision or Management (6/92). **NOTE**: Student must take both Affirmative Action (01005) and New Management Seminar (01055) to receive credit recommendation given in

Authentic Leadership: Leading in the 21st Century (20855)

Location: San Ramon, Pacific Grove, Marshall, and Stanford, CA.

Length: 118 hours (8 days).

Dates: October 1994-Present.

Objective: To provide knowledge of the different paradigms of leadership and to take the participants through a learning process by which they identify their authentic leadership, the kind of leadership required during the turbulent times in which we live.

Learning Outcome: Upon successful completion of this course, the student will be able to identify their beliefs (values) about leadership, assess the effectiveness of their leadership behavior, develop personal leadership vision, and create specific strategies appropriate to the environment in which they lead.

Instruction: Major topics covered in the course are the evolution of organizational form, paradigms of leadership, leadership orientations, psychological and cognitive processing orientations, problem-solving frameworks and applications, women and the glass ceiling, chaos theory, active communication theory, and practice, vision, and values. Methods of instruction include lecture, journaling, story telling, group theater, simulations, slides, speakers, a puppet show, structured observation, art projects, presentations, written assignments, and discussions.

Credit Recommendation: In the graduate degree category, 3 semester hours in Business Administration or Management (8/96).

Basic Business Writing (01010A)

Location: Various locations throughout California.

Length: 16 hours (2 days).

Dates: October 1991-Present.

Objective: To introduce the student to basic business writing skills and techniques.

Learning Outcome: Upon successful completion of this course, the student will be able to organize ideas effectively, write "reader centered" documents, apply guidelines for writing memos and letters, and revise writing for clarity and conciseness.

Instruction: Major topics covered in the course are assessing oral and written communication; recognizing effective writing, writing the first draft, revising, and grammar. Methods of instruction include group discussions, individual and group exercises, questioning and appropriate response evaluation and instructor feedback on student writing.

Credit Recommendation: In the lower division baccalaureate/associate degree category, 1 semester hour in Business Writing or Business Communications (6/92).

Basic Negotiation Skills (41427)

Location: Various locations throughout California.

Length: 18 hours.

Dates: January 1989-July 1996.

Objective: To provide the student with the essential tools of negotiations and the techniques for applying the basic steps needed for successful negotiation.

Learning Outcome: Upon successful completion of this course, the student will be able to acknowledge the importance of time, information, and power in any negotiation; successfully prepare and apply negotiation techniques; identify and avoid common negotiation mistakes; and understand the factors involved in developing a win/win attitude.

Instruction: Major topics covered in the course are essential skills of negotiation; negotiating strategies; steps involved in successful negotiations; and differences between win/win attitudes and win/lose attitudes. Methods of instruction include examination, projects, presentations, and role play.

Credit Recommendation: In the lower division baccalaureate/associate degree category, 1 semester hour in Management (11/90).

Basic Network Design and Applications (42009) *Basic Network Design Foundations (42007)* *(Formerly Basic Network Design (02257 or 02257A and B])*

Location: Sacramento, Los Angeles, San Diego, and Oakland, CA.

Length: 24 hours (3 days).

Dates: March 1987-July 1996.

Objective: To provide the student with a thorough understanding of data collection, design terminology and criteria, and computer-based design tools.

Learning Outcome: Upon successful completion of this course, the student will have a thorough understanding of data collection (how-to and interpretation); have a thorough understanding of design terminology and criteria; effectively use data and design criteria with computer-based design tools, i.e., SWAT, RDF/FEX optimizer; understand effect on design output if certain design criteria are changed; and be able to incorporate design output into proposal form for customers.

Instruction: Major topics covered in the course are theory, general terminology used in network design including definition, conversions, and traffic characteristics. Methods of instruction include computer-based training (CBT) and leader-led.

Credit Recommendation: In the lower division baccalaureate/associate degree category, 1 semester hour in Computer Information Systems, Data Processing, or Telecommunications (8/87) (6/92).

Beginning WordPerfect (1427A); Intermediate Word Perfect (1427B); Advanced WordPerfect (1427C)

Location: Various locations throughout California.

Length: 21 hours (3 days).

Dates: August 1984-Present.

Objective: To provide the student with a solid introduction to the word processing program, WordPerfect, by emphasizing those skills and concepts most used in the business world.

Learning Outcome: Upon successful completion of this course, the student will be able to use a personal computer to create, edit, and print documents.

Instruction: Major topics covered in the course are a comprehensive three-part series of classes consisting of beginning, intermediate, and advanced topics in the word processing program, Word Perfect; and editing, printing, and merge techniques, as well as formatting features. Methods of instruction include lecture and laboratory experience.

Credit Recommendation: In the lower division baccalaureate/associate degree category, 1 semester hour in Business Administration, Data Processing, or Management Information Systems (8/87) (6/92). **NOTE:** Students should be granted credit in only one word processing course (i.e. Multimate, Displaywrite, Wordstar, etc).

Business and Selling Skills *1. Business Functions (45061) or (65812)* *2. Consultative Selling Workshop (45060) or (65800)*

Location: Various locations throughout California.

Length: 1. 40 hours (5 days); 2. 8 hours (1 day).

Dates: March 1990-July 1996.

Objective: 1. To introduce the trainee to various business functions. 2. To introduce the trainee to the concepts of consultative selling and how its utilization will benefit the customer.

Learning Outcome: Upon successful completion of Course 1, the student will be able to gather information about a customer's business and make product recommendations, understand the interdependence of the functional areas of business, and understand basic business fundamentals. Upon successful completion of Course 2, the student will be able to respond to an opening statement, state a five-step transition statement, ask three fact-finding questions to uncover needs, offer solutions, and adopt proper follow-up procedures.

Instruction: Major topics covered in Course 1. are the fundamental areas of business—marketing, operations, and administration; finance; and basic business concepts. Major topics covered in Course 2 are the characteristics of a consultant, types of consultative selling in today's marketplace, and the positive aspects of a consultative salesperson. Methods of instruction include case studies, group exercises, and role play.

Credit Recommendation: 1. In the vocational certificate category, 2 semester hours in General Business or Introduction to Business (11/90). 1. and 2.: If students take 45060 and 45061, 3 semester hours in Introduction to Business or General Business should be awarded in the vocational certificate area (11/90). **NOTE:** No credit should be awarded for completion of only Course 2, Consultative Selling Workshop (45060).

Business Fundamentals (42163)

Location: Various locations throughout California.

Length: 16 hours (2 days).

Dates: March 1989-July 1996.

Objective: To provide familiarization with basic business concepts and terms used in small- and medium-sized businesses surveying marketing, operations, administration, and finance.

Learning Outcome: Upon successful completion of this course, the student will be able to describe basic business fundamentals, understand the interdependence of functional business areas, and facilitate better communications through utilization of business terminology.

Instruction: Major topics covered in the course are financial terms and concepts; ratio analysis, sources, and uses of funds; operations, decisions, and management; capacity, inventory management, research and development, and leverage; marketing share vs. size; and marketing segmentation, research, and mix strategy. Methods of instruction include lecture, discussion, role play, and feedback.

Credit Recommendation: In the lower division baccalaureate/associate degree category, 1 semester hour in General Business (11/90).

C Library Calls (59874-S)

Location: San Ramon, Oakland, and Los Angeles, CA.

Length: 32 hours (4 days).

Dates: January 1992-Present.

Objective: To enable the student to become fully productive in C programming application development environment by introducing the student to the C pre-processor, standard I/O library functions, environment library routines, and portability topics.

Learning Outcome: Upon successful completion of this course, the student will be able to use the typedef and preprocessor commands, describe the UNIX I/O library functions, describe the UNIX environment functions, and describe the characteristics of portable "C" code.

Instruction: Major topics covered in the course are structures and pointers, standard C library, the standard I/O routines, UNIX-specific library routines, the UNIX system interface, and the X window system. Methods of instruction include lecture, text readings, board work, overhead transparencies, handouts, and class projects.

Credit Recommendation: In the upper division baccalaureate degree category, 2 semester hours in Information Systems (5/94).

Cable Repair - Fault Locating (06215)

Location: Various training locations throughout California and Nevada.

Length: 40 hours (1 week).

Dates: January 1981-July 1996.

Objective: To train the student to understand the application of various test sets to the cable fault locating process and to locate any fault within the capability of the selected test set.

Instruction: Major topics covered in the course are electrical measurement to fault, tracing of the tone to fault, application of high voltage, sectionalizing and uses of volt-ohmmeter, open fault locator, open-split locator, and various fault locators. Methods of instruction include nine independent units supported by printed materials and audiocassette tapes with significant hands-on application of 15 cable fault location test sets.

Credit Recommendation: In the vocational certificate category, 1 semester hour in Electronics Technology (8/85).

Career Life Planning Workshop (19201)

Location: Various locations throughout California.

Length: 16 hours (2 days).

Dates: March 1989-Present.

Objective: To provide the students with the skills to identify and understand their individual strengths, limitations, and personal values as it relates to the career development process.

Learning Outcome: Upon successful completion of this course, the student will be able to understand and clearly respond to the following questions: Who Am I? in terms of life stage development issues; What are my skills and talents? functional, adaptive, and work-related skills; Where do I want to make my contributions? values clarification (personal and occupational); and What options are available? goal setting and implementation strategies.

Instruction: Major topics covered in the course are Life stage development, skills identification, values clarification, personality and occupation development, goal setting strategies, and developing an action plan. Methods of instruction include lecture, classroom discussion, interest inventories, self-awareness exercises and written exercises assessing outcomes.

Credit Recommendation: In the lower division baccalaureate/associate degree category, 1 semester hour in Career Exploration or Career Planning (6/92).

Coaching Applications (01043)

Location: Various locations throughout California.

Length: 16 hours (2 days).

Dates: October 1988-July 1996.

Objective: To enhance the coaching skills of supervising managers so they feel confident coaching difficult situations.

Learning Outcome: Upon successful completion of this course, the student will be able to deal with situations that can be difficult, uncomfortable, and out of the ordinary; more readily meet changing needs of business; and meet the diverse situations of human relations faced on the job.

Instruction: Major topics covered in the course are object, ground rules, identifying the coaching opportunity, what makes this individual tick, advanced planning process, and closing the coaching interaction. Methods of instruction include lecture, discussion, laboratory-classroom exercises, simulations, and problem-solving.

Credit Recommendation: In the lower division baccalaureate/associate degree category, 1 semester hour in Supervision (11/90). **NOTE:** When 01043, 01033, and 01044 are all completed, the credit recommendation would be 3 semester hours in Supervision.

Coaching Performance (01033)

Location: Various locations throughout California.

Length: 16 hours (2 days).

Dates: October 1988-Present.

Objective: To introduce managers to appropriate techniques that can be used during coaching interactions that are relative to an individual's performance. Managers will be able to recognize the difference between observing behavior and drawing inferences.

Learning Outcome: Upon successful completion of this course, the student will be able to coach to motivate, coach performance problems, coach marginal performers, and coach high performers.

Instruction: Major topics covered in the course are pre-course, review, expectations, observing and recording performance, and coaching motivational problems. Methods of instruction include lecture, discussion, exercises, and role playing.

Credit Recommendation: In the lower division baccalaureate/associate degree category, 1 semester hour in Supervision (11/90). **NOTE:** When 01043, 01033, and 01044 are all completed, the credit recommendation would be 3 semester hours in Supervision.

Coaching Skills (01044)

Location: Various locations throughout California.

Length: 16 hours (2 days).

Dates: October 1988-July 1996.

Objective: To provide managers with the skills necessary to plan and conduct coaching interactions, recognize the differences in learning styles, and determine the best approach for optimizing individual performance.

Learning Outcome: Upon successful completion of this course, the student will be able to plan and conduct meaningful coaching interactions, enhance the quality of the interactions, and recognize coaching developmental areas in themselves and others.

Instruction: Major topics covered in the course are defining coaching and when to coach, identifying coaching benefits and factors that influence the process including modeling principles, define communications and identify factors that influence the process, and increase the understanding of the relationship between the company's business plan and the manager's ever-increasing role as coach for making valued contributions. Methods of instruction include lecture, discussion, laboratory/classroom participation in exercises, simulations, and problem-solving.

Credit Recommendation: In the lower division baccalaureate/associate degree category, 1 semester hour in Supervision (11/90). **NOTE:** When 01043, 01033, and 01044 are all completed, the credit recommendation would be 3 semester hours in Supervision.

COBOL II Basic Programming (59680)

Location: San Ramon, CA.

Length: 120 hours (3 weeks).

Dates: July 1989-Present.

Objective: To provide students with the knowledge and basic skills that will enable them to successfully code, compile, link, and execute programs written in COBOL II.

Learning Outcome: Upon successful completion of this course, the student will be able to correctly use VS COBOL II Structured Programming Standards, correctly use Systems Technology Programming Standards, and use the major features of the COBOL II language in solving business problems.

Instruction: Major topics covered in the course are division, paragraphs, and structure; data descriptions; verbs; conditions; compiler directives; and job management/monitoring. Methods of instruction include lecture, discussion, and laboratory exercises.

Credit Recommendation: In the lower division baccalaureate/associate degree category, 3 semester hours in Data Processing, Computer Information Systems, Computer Science, or Management Information Systems (11/90).

COBOL II Sort/Merge (59683)

Location: San Ramon, CA.

Length: 32 hours (4 days).

Dates: October 1989-Present.

Objective: To instruct students in the COBOL II Sort/Merge facility.

Learning Outcome: Upon successful completion of this course, the student will be able to invoke the COBOL sort/merge facility to sort data files on one or more data fields with pre and post sort processing.

Instruction: Major topics covered in the course are sort/merge concepts; standalone and COBOL sort; necessary JCL and COBOL statements to accomplish the sort. Methods of instruction include lecture and laboratory exercise.

Credit Recommendation: In the lower division baccalaureate/associate degree category, 1 semester hour in Computer Science or Computer Information System (6/92).

COBOL II Subprograms (59746)

Location: San Ramon, CA.

Length: 32 hours (4 days).

Dates: October 1989-Present.

Objective: To instruct students in the essentials of COBOL to COBOL subroutine calls.

Learning Outcome: Upon successful completion of this course, the student will be able to code COBOL subprogram calling sequence, code COBOL subprograms, and understand the parameter passing convention.

Instruction: Major topics covered in the course are subprogram concepts/ advantages, calling conventions, and essential COBOL statements and JCL to accomplish a COBOL subroutine call. Methods of instruction include lecture and laboratory exercise.

Credit Recommendation: In the lower division baccalaureate/associate degree category, 1 semester hour in Computer Science or Computer Information System (6/92).

COBOL II Tables (59682)

Location: San Ramon, CA.

Length: 40 hours (1 week).

Dates: September 1989-Present.

Objective: To provide students with the knowledge necessary to process tables using indexes and subscripts on one-dimension and multidimension tables.

Learning Outcome: Upon successful completion of this course, the student will be able to code table definitions, initialize/load tables, and search a table in sequence by using a binary search.

Instruction: Major topics covered in the course are one-level tables using indexes, multi-level tables using indexes, table manipulation through the use of subscripts, and differences in COBOL II. Methods of instruction include lecture, discussion, and laboratory exercises.

Credit Recommendation: In the upper division baccalaureate degree category, 3 semester hours in Data Processing, Computer Information Systems, or Management Information Systems (11/90).

Computer Systems Concepts (02262)

Location: Los Angeles and Oakland, CA.

Length: 40 hours (5 days).

Dates: November 1986-Present.

Objective: To provide the student with an understanding of computer hardware, operating systems, and systems software.

Learning Outcome: Upon successful completion of this course, the student will have an understanding of hardware processing, transactions, and characteristics of operating systems; estimate sizing requirements, develop and cost detailed computer configurations, and evaluate the effectiveness of current computer systems at the mainframe and minicomputer level.

Instruction: Major topics covered in the course are the detailed operation of computer hardware, operating systems, and systems software; hardware at the mainframe, minicomputer, and microcomputer levels; specific operating systems covered include MVS, VM, VMS, and DOS; systems analysis includes hardware and system sizing as well as system evaluation; performance monitoring, tuning, and capacity in the context of current computer operations. Methods of instruction include homework assignments in addition to reading include hardware comparison, operating system evaluation, minicomputer sizing and configuration analysis, and mainframe performance analysis. Course prerequisite includes coursework in data processing, telecommunications, and computer programming.

Credit Recommendation: In the upper division baccalaureate degree category, 3 semester hours in Computer Science or Computer Information Systems, or in the graduate degree category, 2 semester hours in Management (11/86) (5/94).

Contract Negotiations and Agreements (Formerly Win-Win Negotiations [42180])

Location: Various locations throughout California.

Length: 16 hours (2 days).

Dates: August 1990-July 1996.

Objective: To acquaint students with win-win negotiations in agreements and contracts.

Learning Outcome: Upon successful completion of this course, the student will be able to establish win-win plans, develop win-win relationships, form win-win agreements, and perform win-win maintenance.

Instruction: Major topics covered in the course are situational assessment, defining "own" needs, anticipating wants of other party, identifying common ground, and developing win-win solutions. Methods of instruction include lecture, participation, and role playing.

Credit Recommendation: In the upper division baccalaureate degree category, 1 semester hour in Marketing, Management, Human Resources Management, or Business elective (11/90).

Course Developer Competencies (01244)

Location: Oakland, CA.

Length: 80 hours (2 weeks).

Dates: July 1991-Present.

Objective: To provide the students with the basic skills and knowledge needed to develop instructional courses or lesson materials.

Learning Outcome: Upon successful completion of the course, the student will be able to analyze, design, develop, and implement a training solution through practical application and use of a Training Development Guidelines (TDG) Reference binder.

Instruction: Major topics covered in the course are introduction to adult learning theory; analysis of needs, tasks, and audience; design of job aids, training objectives, course or lesson plans; developing instructor, student, and support materials; field testing and implementing the course and evaluating the training. Methods of instruction include lecture, discussion, and exercises.

Credit Recommendation: In the upper division baccalaureate degree category, 3 semester hours in Education or Course Development (6/92) (8/96).

Data Communications Institute (42700)

Location: Dublin, CA.

Length: 320 hours (8 weeks).

Dates: September 1989-Present.

Objective: To develop skills that will permit students to become consultants in the areas of information technology and data communications.

Learning Outcome: Upon successful completion of the course, the student will be able to make critical judgements concerning information technology and data communications and verbally express related topics through a rigid oral examination.

Instruction: Major topics covered in the course are computer architecture, operating systems and programming; OSI reference model-layers 1 through 7; X.25 and packet switching, ISDN and integrated information transport, local area networks and network management. Methods of instruction include lecture, discussion, workshops, and laboratory exercises.

Credit Recommendation: In the upper division baccalaureate degree category, 18 semester hours in Computer Science, Computer Information Systems, or Telecommunications (6/92) (8/96).

Data Modeling Workshop Series (59930A-59930H)

Location: San Ramon, CA.

Length: 56 hours (8 days).

Dates: October 1996-Present.

Objective: To give the student the academic grounding necessary to be a competent data modeler.

Learning Outcome: Upon successful completion of this course, the student will be able to construct and thoroughly document a normalized data model of moderate complexity in response to a business problem statement, understand how to integrate models, and demonstrate how to participate in the translation to a physical database.

Instruction: Major topics covered in the course are Entity/Relationship Basics I, Entity/Relationship Basics II, entity/relationship data modeling, identifiers and dependencies, documentation and standards, normalization, abstraction, model integration and refinement; and logical to physical translation. Methods of instruction include lecture, exercises, overhead slides, charts, group participation, and presentations.

Credit Recommendation: In the lower division baccalaureate/associate degree category, 3 semester hours in Business or Information Systems (8/96).

Data Modeling Workshop Series (59930A-59930L) (12 Workshops)

Location: San Ramon, CA.

Length: 72 hours (6 days).

Dates: January 1988-Present.

Objective: To acquaint students with the basics and applications of relational databases.

Learning Outcome: Upon successful completion of this course, the student will be able to define what a data model is, draw entity/relation diagrams, and design relational databases.

Instruction: Major topics covered in the course are entity relationship models, identifiers and dependencies, normalization, abstraction, transaction analysis, and logical to physical conversion. Methods of instruction include lecture and laboratory exercises.

Credit Recommendation: In the lower division baccalaureate/associate degree category, 3 semester hours in Computer Science and Computer Information System (6/92).

Data Processing/Data Communications (45503) (Formerly [02024])

Location: Oakland and Los Angeles, CA.

Length: 36 hours (1 week).

Dates: July 1981-July 1988.

Objective: To enable students to develop knowledge needed to identify and solve customer DP/DC system problems.

Instruction: Major topics covered in the course are technological applications in a manual environment, data processing, data communications, a simple batch system, and a complex distributed application information system. Methods of instruction include case exercises, multiple applications to reinforce concepts, and home assignments.

Credit Recommendation: In the upper division baccalaureate degree category, 3 semester hours in Business Administration, Computer Science, or Data Processing (11/84).

DCE Use and Testing (51584)

Location: Various locations in California and Nevada.

Length: 24 hours (3 days).

Dates: January 1989-July 1996.

Objective: To provide the student with a basic understanding of what data communications is and how it works.

Learning Outcome: Upon successful completion of this course, the student will be able to understand the function of data communications equipment, understand and use vocabulary associated with this equipment, and test various types of data communications equipment.

Instruction: Major topics covered in the course are common terminology, modem operation and testing, data service unit operation and testing, and data communications equipment synchronous and asynchronous operations. Methods of instruction include lecture, discussion, and laboratory exercises.

Credit Recommendation: In the upper division baccalaureate degree category, 1 semester hour in Computer Science or Telecommunications (11/90).

Dymaxion Laboratory I: The Big Picture (Experiment in Individual Initiative) (90001)
Dymaxion Laboratory II: Synergetic Principles (90002)

Location: Various locations throughout California.

Length: 16 hours (2 days).

Dates: *Dymaxion Laboratory 1:* August 1987-Present; *Dymaxion Laboratory 2:* December 1988-Present.

Objective: To enhance the participant's capacity to make an impact in the world through greater "comprehensive anticipatory" problem-solving skills.

Learning Outcome: Upon successful completion of this course, the student will be able to apply Fuller's "big picture" philosophy of problem-solving and comprehending change; observe and apply principles such as synergy, trimtab, precession, and tensequrity to problems in social dynamics, marketing, human relations, and education; and approach the dynamics of our changing "global village" with an increased experience of their ability to create change in the the world through their own initiative.

Instruction: Major topics covered in the course are an introduction to Fuller's life, work, and fundamental problem-solving strategies; application of principles such as synergy, trimtab, synergetic advantage, precession, and tensequrity; and assessment of global trends and needs. Methods of instruction include videotape, presentations, discussion, demonstration, and problem-solving exercises.

Credit Recommendation: In the upper division baccalaureate degree category, 1 semester hour in Design, Engineering, Philosophy, Business, or Management (11/90) (6/92).

Dymaxion Laboratory III: Design Science (90003)
Dymaxion Laboratory IV: Making the World Work (90004)

Location: Various locations throughout California.

Length: 16 hours (2 days).

Dates: *Dymaxion Laboratory III:* December 1990-Present; *Dymaxion Laboratory IV:* January 1991-Present.

Objective: To examine R. Buckminster Fuller's life and work, with specific attention to his methodologies, principles, self-disciplines, and strategies for developing the individual's ability to make impactful initiatives in his/her own life and work.

Learning Outcome: Upon successful completion of this course, the student will be able to recognize and apply Comprehensive Anticipatory Design Science principles and observe and apply principles such as gestation rates, macrocomprehensive to micro-incisive, artifacts, change as normal, and critical path planning.

Instruction: Major topics covered in the course are reforming the environment, not the people; synergetic advantage; navigation; precession; and gestation rates and more with less. Methods of instruction include lecture, discussion, workshop, laboratories, and videotape.

Credit Recommendation: In the upper division baccalaureate degree category, 1 semester hour in Design, Engineering, Philosophy, Business, or Management (6/92).

EDP Concepts for Business (42267, 02267, 65271))

Location: Various locations throughout California.

Length: 19 hours (2 days).

Dates: July 1987-Present.

Objective: To provide the student with an understanding of the basic elements of data processing.

Learning Outcome: Upon successful completion of this course, the student will recognize the definition of data processing, identify the primary purpose of CPU, identify hardware elements of a data processing system, and identify the functions of the CPU components.

Instruction: Major topics covered in the course are computer components, computer terminology, and definitions, programs, purpose and definition, major types of programs, program components, and system development basics.

Credit Recommendation: In the lower division baccalaureate/associate degree category, 1 semester hour in Business Administration or Data Processing (8/87) (6/92).

Effective Business Presentations (42211)

Location: Various locations throughout California.

Length: 24 hours (3 days).

Dates: November 1987-Present.

Objective: To help managers improve communication skills and to improve the managers' ability to plan, develop, and deliver effective and professional presentations.

Learning Outcome: Upon successful completion of this course, the student will be able to organize content in a logical, persuasive way; illustrate the content effectively; and deliver the message in a professional manner.

Instruction: Major topics covered in the course are basics of effective business presentations, understanding communication problems, how to animate presentations, making a presentation to inform and to persuade, and using visual aids effectively. Methods of instruction include lecture, discussion, classroom exercises, simulations, videotaping, and feedback.

Credit Recommendation: In the lower division baccalaureate/associate degree category, 1 semester hour in Speech or Communication (11/90) (8/96).

Effective Business Systems Selling (42145)

Location: Various locations throughout California.

Length: 32 hours (4 days).

Dates: December 1988-Present.

Objective: To learn selling techniques that will aid in sales of business systems.

Learning Outcome: Upon successful completion of this course, the student will be able to demonstrate an understanding of consultative selling and customer business problems; manage successful telephone and premises sales calls from pre-call planning to closing the sale; and prepare a pre-call plan for approaching customers, including positioning objectives and tactics.

Instruction: Major topics covered in the course are sales funnel, positioning techniques, value added selling, overcoming objections, and closing strategies. Methods of instruction include lecture, videotapes, and role playing.

Credit Recommendation: In the lower division baccalaureate/associate degree category, 2 semester hours in Sales (6/92).

Effective Business Writing (01048)

Location: Various locations throughout California.

Length: 16 hours (2 days).

Dates: November 1989-Present.

Objective: To teach participants to apply a useful, repeatable writing process that will improve their effectiveness and efficiency in writing letters, memos, reports, and documents.

Learning Outcome: Upon successful completion of this course, the student will be able to define the writing task and purpose, identify the reading audience and its priorities, write a rough first draft, and revise a draft copy.

Instruction: Major topics covered in the course are planning the writing task, identifying your readers, brainstorming the content, organizing first drafts, and writing first drafts. Methods of instruction include examinations, projects, and presentation.

Credit Recommendation: In the lower division baccalaureate/associate degree category, 1 semester hour in Business Writing or Business Communications (6/92).

Effective Team Building (Formerly Team Effectiveness [42170])

Location: Various locations throughout California.

Length: 24 hours (3 days).

Dates: February 1989-Present.

Objective: To measure the effectiveness of team development and uncover the environmental needs of team members.

Learning Outcome: Upon successful completion of this course, the student will be able to communicate individual expectations, understand the stages of team development and behavioral patterns, prioritize activities, and design procedures for accomplishing performance goals.

Instruction: Major topics covered in the course are goal clarity and conflict, interrelating with team members, clarifying roles, stages of team development, and the mature team. Methods of instruction include examinations, projects, and presentations.

Credit Recommendation: In the lower division baccalaureate/associate degree category, 1 semester hour in Management (11/90).

ESS 1/1A SCC Trunk Tester (05617)

Location: Oakland, Pasadena, Sacramento, and Tustin, CA.

Length: 58 hours (8 days).

Dates: January 1985-Present.

Objective: To enable students to acquire the skills and knowledge necessary to perform the following tasks in the Switching Control Center (SCC)—trunking and facilities, interoffice signaling, transmission, trunk orders, trunk testing, administration, and full maintenance.

Learning Outcome: Upon successful completion of this course, the student will be able to perform the trunk maintenance function in a Switching Control Center (SCC) or duties in the field, perform basic trunk maintenance common to any stored program control switching system, and perform trunk testing details specific to 1/1A ESS.

Instruction: Major topics covered in the course are the Switching Control Center (SCC); trunk workstation; SCC procedures as they apply to trunk installation/maintenance functions; how to perform basic trunk testing, trunk installation, and trunk field maintenance. Method of instruction includes self-paced instruction.

Credit Recommendation: In the lower division baccalaureate/associate degree category, 2 semester hours in Electronics Technology (8/85) (11/90).

ESS and Minicomputer Fundamentals (05600) (Formerly ESS Introduction [05600])

Location: Tustin, Oakland, Pasadena, and Sacramento, CA.

Length: 112 hours (14 days).

Dates: January 1984-July 1996.

Objective: To provide the fundamental knowledge and skills prerequisite to stored program switching systems using minicomputer fundamentals.

Learning Outcome: Upon successful completion of this course, the student will be able to define and understand ESS switch and minicomputer fundamentals, understand intermediate computer concepts and system configurations, become familiar with general digital concepts, and learn to interpret controls and measurements of signal measurement devices.

Instruction: Major topics covered in the course are basic and intermediate computer concepts; call processing; number systems; diodes and transistors; electrostatic discharge; hardware familiarization; and schematics, Belpac, BSPs, and ESS communication buses. Methods of instruction include the instructional workbench delivery system using the UNIX operating system and unit tests for each module.

Credit Recommendation: In the lower division baccalaureate/associate degree category, 2 semester hours in Electronics Technology (11/90).

Essentials of Data Communications (05739-S)

Location: Various training locations throughout California.

Length: 48 hours (over three months).

Dates: January 1993-Present.

Objective: To provide students with a comprehensive overview of data communications technology covering a thorough introduction of basic concepts, fundamental principles, and terminology used in the design, operation, and maintenance of teleprocessing and data communications systems.

Learning Outcome: Upon successful completion of this course, the student will be able to take advanced technology courses; understand the technology underlying the most advanced products and services; and understand data communications basics, development, and trends in the field to be followed.

Instruction: Major topics covered in the course are components and concepts, networking, protocol basics, data transports, modems and modulation, analog transmission, digital transmission, OSI and protocols, LAN and protocol conversions, protocols and architectures, new and emerging technology and digital services, and network management. Methods of instruction include lectures and instructor feedback.

Credit Recommendation: In the upper division baccalaureate degree category, 3 semester hours in Telecommunications (5/94).

Ethics Plus (01054)

Location: Various locations throughout California.

Length: 16 hours (2 days).

Dates: October 1989-Present.

Objective: To provide tools for identifying, clarifying and resolving ethical issues, and building and maintaining a more ethical work environment.

Learning Outcome: Upon successful completion of this course, the student will be able to demonstrate a clear understanding of business ethics, relate conduct to principles, values and standards, examine common personal and corporate values, and identify and clarify ethical issues in business situations.

Instruction: Major topics covered in the course are the meaning of business ethics, personal and corporate values, ethical goal setting, roadblocks to ethical behavior, implications of ethical decision making, and personal responsibility. Methods of instruction include lecture, discussion, class participation, case studies, laboratory exercises, role playing, and presentations.

Credit Recommendation: In the upper division baccalaureate degree category, 1 semester hour in Business Ethics or Business elective (6/92).

Every Agents' Guide to Consultative Sales (65056)

Location: Various Pacific Bell Learning Centers and client locations.

Length: 15.25 hours (2 days).

Dates: December 1995-Present.

Objective: To teach the steps of the sales process and demonstrate their knowledge through role play and to take customer calls on job using their new skills which include the four steps of the sales call process (the sales funnel), product families, and product/consultative selling.

Learning Outcome: Upon successful completion of this course, the student will be able to demonstrate via role play and customer contact calls their skills in consultative selling.

Instruction: Major topics covered in the course are sales experience, reality of consultative sales, and sales funnel. Methods of instruction include lectures, group discussion, written quiz, group, individual/team roleplays, and an on-the-job session taking customer calls.

Credit Recommendation: In the lower division baccalaureate/associate degree

category, 1 semester hour in Business Marketing (8/96).

Fiber Optics: Sales (42165, 02165) or Technical (42166, 02166)

Location: Various locations throughout California.

Length: 16 hours (2 days).

Dates: July 1987-Present.

Objective: To provide the student with an understanding of fiber optics systems and light transmission theory.

Learning Outcome: Upon successful completion of this course, the student will be able to identify and understand fundamentals of fiber optics technology.

Instruction: Major topics covered in the course are fundamentals of fiber optics technology, performance characteristics such as speed error rates, fiber optics systems including transmitters and multiplexers, comparison with other types of transmission systems, applications, Pacific Bell fiber systems, and fiber optics capabilities and performance. Method of instruction is computer-based training.

Credit Recommendation: In the lower division baccalaureate/associate degree category, 1 semester hour in Data Processing or Telecommunications (8/87) (6/92). **NOTE:** Students may receive credit for Fiber Optics (Sales) or Fiber Optics (Technical), but not both.

Financial Effectiveness Seminar (01068)

Location: Various locations throughout California.

Length: 16 hours (2 days).

Dates: January 1989-Present.

Objective: To provide theory and mechanics of financial analysis, and capital investment decision making as outlined in the context of the general business matrix.

Learning Outcome: Upon successful completion of this course, the student will be able to identify how different industries and potential competitors will be formulating their financial strategies, recognize the linkages between financial performance and a corporation's ability to effectively compete, and determine how shareholder value is created.

Instruction: Major topics covered in the course are the importance of cash in financial management; fundamentals of capital budgeting; financial statements; keys to monitoring cash flow; industry analysis, strategy, and execution; and using ratios to evaluate financial performance. Methods of instruction include examinations, projects, presentations, and interactive exercises.

Credit Recommendation: In the lower division baccalaureate/associate degree category, 1 semester hour in Introduction to Finance or Business elective (6/92).

Financial Selling Strategies (42195)

Location: Various locations throughout California.

Length: *Version 1:* 32 hours (4 days); *Version 2:* 18 hours (2 days).

Dates: *Version 1:* January 1986-June 1993; *Version 2:* July 1993-Present.

Objective: *Versions 1 and 2:* To improve sales team effectiveness by integrating financial theory and selling skills into the sales process, augmented by the hands-on use of computer models to compare systems costs.

Learning Outcome: *Versions 1 and 2:* Upon successful completion of this course, the student will be able to demonstrate knowledge of financial concepts and their role in the client's decision-making process; use computer models to calculate net present value and rate of return for systems, determining the most financially viable choice for the customer; apply basic financial fundamentals to quantify client business problems; and convert benefits to hard dollar recommendations.

Instruction: *Version 1:* Major topics covered in the course are the selling process; financial management; financial analysis; team contacts; financial modeling; and taxation. Methods of instruction include lecture, discussion, projects, role play, feedback, and examinations. *Version 2:* Major topics covered in the course are sales skills with a financial focus, financial management, financial analysis, team contacts, financial modeling, and taxation. Methods of instruction include lecture, discussion, projects, role play, feedback, and examinations.

Credit Recommendation: *Version 1:* In the upper division baccalaureate degree category, 2 semester hours in Professional Selling or Business electives (11/90) *Version 2:* In the upper division baccalaureate degree category, 1 semester hour in Business Administration, Finance, Accounting, or Business elective (5/94).

Fundamentals of Computer Operations (50001A)

Location: San Ramon, Concord, Anaheim, San Diego, CA.

Length: 16 hours (2 days).

Dates: January 1988-July 1996.

Objective: To introduce students to basic data processing terminology and equipment.

Learning Outcome: Upon successful completion of this course, the student will be able to distinguish the role of hardware and software, name different hardware components, distinguish between the different types of software and the role of each, and define fundamental hardware operations.

Instruction: Major topics covered in the course are definition of data processing, hardware-components/functions types of software, programming languages, operating systems, data storage, and data representation. Methods of instruction include lecture and computer-based learning.

Credit Recommendation: In the lower division baccalaureate/associate degree category, 1 semester hour in Computer Science or Computer Information System (6/92).

Fundamentals of Data Communication (51551)

Location: San Diego and San Ramon, CA.

Length: 32 hours (4 days).

Dates: September 1984-Present.

Objective: To explain how data communications systems and their hardware and software components work as well as data communication concepts.

Learning Outcome: Upon successful completion of this course, the student will be able to understand the basic principles of data communications, develop hands-on skills on formulating their own code and protocol for data transmission, and perform basic testing and troubleshooting as they build data circuits with circuit troubles inserted.

Instruction: Major topics covered in the course are transmission modes; binary and hexadecimal conversions; protocol; analog and digital transmission; circuit paths and components; morse, baudot, ASCII, and EBCDIC codes; VRC, LRC, and CRC; asynchronous transmission; and synchronous transmission. Methods of instruction include lecture and laboratory.

Credit Recommendation: In the lower division baccalaureate/associate degree category, 2 semester hours in Telecommunications (11/90).

High Gain Listening (01059)

Location: Various locations throughout California.

Length: 16 hours (2 days).

Dates: August 1990-Present.
Objective: To improve listening skills.
Learning Outcome: Upon successful completion of this course, the student will be able to define listening, discuss listening blocks and building rapport with others, phrase open-ended questions, paraphrase for clarification, and state techniques for capturing key points during a conversation.
Instruction: Major topics covered in the course are benefits of good listening, cost of poor listening, subjectivity of listening, filtering systems, listener responsibilities, listening blocks, listening readiness, open communication, reflection of content and feelings, listening for results and mind mapping. Methods of instruction include lecture, discussion, role play, and group exercises.
Credit Recommendation: In the lower division baccalaureate/associate degree category, 1 semester hour in Effective Communication in Business (5/94).

High Impact Presenting (01095)

Location: Various locations throughout California.
Length: 16 hours (2 days).
Dates: April 1993-Present.
Objective: To deliver an effective planned and unplanned presentation.
Learning Outcome: Upon successful completion of this course, the student will be able to focus on improvement of delivery techniques; enhance gestures, movement, posture, and eye communication during presentations; prepare a preliminary plan; select resource materials; organize materials; use audio and visual media materials; flow chart a presentation; and develop confidence in delivering a speech.
Instruction: Major topics covered in the course are common fears of presentations, presentation format, six steps in preparing a presentation, delivery techniques, audio and visual media, handling questions, descriptive language, and unplanned presentations. Methods of instruction include discussion and planned and unplanned speeches.
Credit Recommendation: In the lower division baccalaureate/associate degree category, 1 semester hour in Business Communications, Business Speech, Salesmanship, or Speech (5/94).

Improving Performance (01009)

Location: Various locations throughout California.
Length: 16 hours (2 days).
Dates: April 1986-July 1996.
Objective: To provide students with an understanding of the performance appraisal process and to develop the skills necessary to set performance standards and conduct performance reviews.
Learning Outcome: Upon successful completion of this course, the student will be able to determine measurable job standards; prepare for and plan strategies for conducting appraisal interviews; guide an appraisal discussion using the skills of listening, questioning, handling conflict, negotiating, and reaching resolution; and set performance objectives that relate to employee needs.
Instruction: Major topics covered in the course are performance appraisal skills, performance standards, identifying job parts, setting objectives, formal performance appraisals, coaching, developing action plans, solving problems, and documenting past performance.
Credit Recommendation: In the upper division baccalaureate degree category, 1 semester hour in Performance Appraisal (11/86).

Influence: Collaborating for Results (01029)
(Formerly Influence Management)

Location: Various locations throughout California.
Length: 24 hours (3 days).
Dates: September 1984-Present.
Objective: To improve the manager's ability to work with and through others.
Learning Outcome: Upon successful completion of this course, the student will be able to have an awareness of the influence process, plan for improvement in performing high priority influence practices, improve influence practices and tactics to allow them to implement their plan, develop a system for tracking the progress of their plan, and have a plan for involving others in their improvement efforts.
Instruction: Major topics covered in the course are identification of the manager's influence environment, conflict anticipation and management in working relationships, methods of enhancing rapport in the work group, and the effective use of influence to make high-quality decisions. Methods of instruction include a pre-course computerized feedback on the participant's influence skills as compared to the top managers in the Fortune 500 companies, lectures, audiovisual materials, group exercises, and role playing.
Credit Recommendation: In the upper division baccalaureate degree category, 1 semester hour in Organizational Behavior or Supervisory Management (11/86) (6/92).

Information Mapping (01267)

Location: Various locations throughout California.
Length: 40 hours (1 week).
Dates: June 1980-Present.
Objective: To improve student's ability to write business documents (e.g., user manuals, technical reference manuals, methods and procedures) utilizing a format that helps the reader understand the information.
Instruction: Major topics covered in the course are a structured format to write business documents and organize large or complex information into manageable units that are easy to read and understand. Methods of instruction include self-paced written materials with some instructor-led discussion and group activities.
Credit Recommendation: In the upper division baccalaureate degree category, 2 semester hours in Principles of Information Mapping (8/85) (11/90).

Information Transport Technologies (45525)

Location: Los Angeles and Oakland, CA.
Length: 30 hours (4 days).
Dates: September 1989-July 1996.
Objective: To provide participants with an understanding of telecommunications networks.
Learning Outcome: Upon successful completion of this course, the student will be able to describe the types and characteristics of voice and data information carrying systems, their benefits, and limitations; define basic principles of signal propagation, modulation, analog/digital modulations, and transmission performance; and describe the switching hierarchy and switching principles.
Instruction: Major topics covered in the course are a overview of switching technology, transmission media and carrier systems transmission impairments, data transmission and digital transmission media, digital networks, and ISDN.
Credit Recommendation: In the vocational certificate or lower division baccalaureate/associate degree or upper division baccalaureate degree category, 2 sem-

ester hours in Telecommunications Technology (6/92).

Instructor Competencies Module I (01226), Module 2 (01227) (Formerly Trainer Skills Workshop [01245])

Location: Various training locations throughout California.

Length: 64 hours (8 days).

Dates: May 1982-July 1996.

Objective: To provide the student with teaching skills essential for effective industrial training.

Learning Outcome: Upon successful completion of this course, the students will be able to identify learning characteristics and styles, utilize various instructional methods, assess their own instructor skills and set learning goals for their professional development, and create an effective learning climate.

Instruction: Major topics covered in the course are the philosophy of adult education, adult learning characteristics and styles, instructional methods, creating effective learning climates, and ethical considerations in training. Methods of instruction include lecture, discussion, and class presentations using various instructional methods.

Credit Recommendation: In the upper division baccalaureate degree category, 3 semester hours in Instructional Design or Education (11/84) (11/90) (8/96).

Internetworking with TCP/IP (51830)

Location: Various training locations throughout California.

Length: 16 hours (2 days).

Dates: July 1993-Present.

Objective: To enable the student to use TCP/IP, related protocols, and applications and internetworking services; prepares the student to discuss architecture and nomenclature of the TCP/IP model; and, while being able to describe the protocols in each layer, explain the use of TCP/IP protocol suite and LAN/WAN technology.

Learning Outcome: Upon successful completion of this course, the student will be able to use TCP/IP to plan and integrate TCP/IP network elements in a network and provide effective and efficient internetworking; and understand the IP routing methods, client/server paradigm, Simple Network Management Protocol (SNMP), and related services and applications.

Instruction: Major topics covered in the course are mechanism and protocols of the Network Interface Layer; gateways, internet protocols (IP), Transmission Control (TCP), User Datagram Protocol (UDP), and Network Management Protocol (SNMP), and related services and applications.

Credit Recommendation: In the lower division baccalaureate/associate degree category, 1 semester hour in Information Systems or Computer Information Systems (5/94).

Introduction to Basic Accounting (02264)

Location: San Francisco, CA.

Length: 18.3 hours (3 days).

Dates: September 1986-July 1996.

Objective: To give the student a general background in basic accounting that assists the student in understanding and using financial statements.

Learning Outcome: Upon successful completion of this course, the student will understand the basic language and concepts of financial accounting, be able to prepare basic financial statements, and use basic analytical tools to interpret financial statements.

Instruction: Major topics covered in the course are basic accounting principles and definitions, journal entries, the general ledger, income statements, and balance sheets. Methods of instruction include examinations, projects, and presentation.

Credit Recommendation: In the lower division baccalaureate/associate degree category, 1 semester hour in Introduction to Accounting (8/87) (6/92).

Introduction to C++ Part I (59881-S)

Location: San Ramon, Oakland, and Los Angeles, CA.

Length: 32 hours (4 days).

Dates: January 1991-Present.

Objective: To provide the student in-depth coverage of data/code encapsulation and how C++ implements it. (This is a second course in computer fundamentals.)

Learning Outcome: Upon successful completion of this course, the student will be able to analyze and perform high level object-oriented C++ software design and have experience using C++ to implement object-oriented software.

Instruction: Major topics covered in the course are C++ data types, C++ expressions and statements, overloaded and template functions, the C++ class, class member functions, class templates, class derivation and inheritance, object-oriented programming, and object-oriented design. Methods of instruction include text readings, lecture, classroom discussion, classroom and laboratory activities, and instructor feedback.

Credit Recommendation: In the upper division baccalaureate degree category, 2 semester hours in Computer Science (5/94).

Introduction to C++ Part II (59987)

Location: San Ramon, Oakland, and Los Angeles, CA.

Length: 32 hours (4 days).

Dates: January 1993-Present.

Objective: To emphasize a number of advanced features of C++ and to increase proficiency in analysis and design of C++ software.

Learning Outcome: Upon successful completion of this course, the student will be able to analyze and design C++ software with greater proficiency, specifically, design and implement effective classes and hierarchies, customize memory allocation and de-allocation, use templates to write generic classes and functions, use multiple inheritance, use pointers to functions, use pointers to members, understand type conversions, and resolve calls to overloaded functions.

Instruction: Major topics covered in the course are designing and implementing effective classes and hierarchies, customizing memory allocation and de-allocations using templates to write generic classes and functions, handling exceptional cases, using multiple inheritance effectively, advanced uses of inheritance, using tape conversions resolving calls to overloaded functions, and solving common problems with C++. Methods of instruction include text readings, lectures, classroom discussion, classroom activities, laboratory activities, and instructor feedback.

Credit Recommendation: In the upper division baccalaureate degree category, 2 semester hours in Computer Science or Information Systems (5/94).

Introduction to C Programming (59787-S)

Location: San Ramon, Oakland, and Los Angeles, CA.

Length: 40 hours (1 week).

Dates: January 1992-Present.

Objective: To introduce the student the C programming fundamentals and applications and an understanding of arrays, pointers, structures, and the ability to design new languages using finite state automations and Backus-Naur Form notations.

Learning Outcome: Upon successful completion of this course, the student will

be able to master reading and writing of ANSI/C programs; learn principles and techniques of scanning, parsing, and semantic analysis; and write a complete multi-file application while becoming exposed to the design and specification of formal language grammars.

Instruction: Major topics covered in the course are compiler basics, DOS/ Windows, and environments; control structures, arrays, and functions; and Inter-file communications and programming techniques. Methods of instruction include lecture, classroom discussion and activities, lab exercises, and instructor feedback.

Credit Recommendation: In the lower division baccalaureate/associate degree category, 3 semester hours in Information Systems (5/94).

Introduction to C Programming (59787)

Location: Oakland, CA.

Length: 40 hours (5 days).

Dates: May 1984-Present.

Objective: To provide the student with the ability to use the basic structure and syntax of C language to design, code test, and execute programs.

Learning Outcome: Upon successful completion of this course, the student will be able to describe how an application program interfaces with the UNIX system; discuss the basic structure and syntax of the C programming language; design programs using arrays, pointers, and structured programming concepts; handle file control via storage management and I/O processing; design and code C programs in a UNIX environment; and compile and execute C programs.

Instruction: Major topics covered in the course are structure of the language, declaration of variables, arithmetic processing, logical constructs, loop exit instructions, array processing, pointer processing, functions other than main, structure variable processing, storage management, I/O processing, executing commands from programs, and compilation and executing.

Credit Recommendation: In the lower division baccalaureate/associate degree category, 2 semester hours in Computer Science or Data Processing (8/87).

Introduction to Management and Supervision (45900-A) (Manager Initial Training)

Location: Sacramento, Oakland, Pasadena, Los Angeles, Tustin, and San Diego, CA.

Length: 64 hours (8 eight-hour days).

Dates: January 1988-Present.

Objective: To prepare the manager for his or her role by studying the principles of effective job management and practicing the related skills.

Learning Outcome: Upon successful completion of this course, the student will be able to provide quality customer service, coach and develop subordinates toward effective performance, and use the skills necessary for effective supervision.

Instruction: Major topics covered in the course are coaching and development, learning and demonstrating the different feedback techniques, conducting a monitoring session, demonstrating a coaching session, professionalism, effective communication, group meetings, goal setting, establishing daily priorities, and payroll. Methods of instruction include lecture, group discussion, role playing, and quizzes.

Credit Recommendation: In the vocational certificate category, or in the lower division baccalaureate/associate degree category, 3 semester hours in Principles of Supervision or Management and Supervision (9/88).

Introduction to UNIX Internals (59786)

Location: San Ramon, Oakland, and Los Angeles, CA.

Length: 32 hours (4 days).

Dates: January 1992-Present.

Objective: To guide the student in understanding the concept of operating system processes and how they differ from programs; and to aid the student in understanding UNIX operating system's basic components and how they interrelate.

Learning Outcome: Upon successful completion of this course, the student will be able to state the functions of the kernal; state the functions of the shell; explain the interaction of the hardware, the kernal, and the shell; understand the basic nature of the tree structure beginning with the route directory; identify UNIX system file types; and describe the procedures involved in the login process.

Instruction: Major topics covered in the course are the overview of the operating system, the dev directory, the login process, customizing the system, file system concepts and construction file system networking, communications tools, and monitoring system performance. Methods of instruction include lecture, text readings, classroom discussion, projects, lab exercises, and instructor feedback.

Credit Recommendation: In the upper division baccalaureate degree category, 2 semester hours in Information Systems or Computer Information Systems (5/94).

Introduction to UNIX System Administration I (59000-S)

Location: San Ramon, Oakland, and Los Angeles, CA.

Length: 32 hours (4 days).

Dates: January 1994-July 1996.

Objective: To enable the student to focus on the inner workings of most Von Neumann computing architectures so as to enable effective UNIX systems administration; and introduces the student to a balanced coverage between computer hardware/software architecture and the day-to-day tasks of the systems administration function.

Learning Outcome: Upon successful completion of this course, the student will be able to understand the basic concepts of UNIX System V administration concepts; basic components of the UNIX operating system: hardware, kernel, shell, and how these three components interrelate; and the terms and concepts related to strong storage devices.

Instruction: Major topics covered in the course are an overview of the operating system, customizing the system, file system concepts, file system construction, managing stored data, networking, and communication tools. Methods of instruction include lecture, board work, class projects, lab exercises, instructor feedback, classroom discussion, and activities.

Credit Recommendation: In the upper division baccalaureate degree category, 2 semester hours in Information Systems (5/94).

ISDN Technology Protocols (42243)

Location: Dublin, CA.

Length: 36-38 hours (1 week).

Dates: December 1990-Present.

Objective: To provide the student with an understanding of ISDN, its architecture, and its network and switching applications.

Learning Outcome: Upon successful completion of this course, the student will be able to understand and discuss integrated systems distributed network (ISDN) and its applications.

Instruction: Major topics covered in the course are ISDN architecture, transmission protocols, basic applications, ISDN capabilities, and Pacific Bell ISDN offerings. Methods of instruction include lecture, discussion, and workshops.

Credit Recommendation: In the upper division baccalaureate degree category, 2 semester hours in Telecommunications or Telecommunications Management (6/92).

Job Aid Analysis and Design (1265) Development of Instructional Materials (1207)

Location: Various training locations throughout California.

Length: 76 hours (2 weeks).

Dates: December 1982-July 1996.

Objective: To prepare a trainer to determine which behavior should be job aided, design and construct job aids, and apply appropriate training course design to produce both lecture and self-instructing training courses.

Learning Outcome: Upon successful completion of this course, the student will be able to perform job aid analysis, select formats for job aids, construct job aids, develop a module plan, and predict and match learning problems with selected teaching strategies.

Instruction: Major topics covered in the course are performing job aid analysis, selecting appropriate formats, editing written materials, determining performance characteristics, selecting teaching strategies, sequencing modules, deciding simulation, and media. Methods of instruction include lecture, discussion workshop, and laboratory activities.

Credit Recommendation: In the upper division baccalaureate degree category, 3 semester hours in Curriculum Design (11/84) (11/90). **NOTE:** Both courses must be taken to receive credit recommendation.

Managing Professional Growth (01012)

Location: Various locations throughout California.

Length: 16 hours (2 days).

Dates: April 1986-Present.

Objective: To guide the participants toward an understanding of personal values and individual strengths and weaknesses as they relate to career development.

Learning Outcome: Upon successful completion of this course, the students will be able to identify personal values; assess their own strengths and weaknesses; identify skills required to perform a job; and prepare a framework for career development.

Instruction: Major topics covered in the course are value clarification, development of a personal definition of job satisfaction, identification of special talents, description of development needs, and individualized development strategy. Methods of instruction include a pre-workshop assignment completed by both the participant and manager as well as lecture, classroom exercises, and discussion.

Credit Recommendation: In the upper division baccalaureate degree category, 1 semester hour in Performance Appraisal (11/86) (6/92).

Managing Skills Development Series (42327, 42331-340 or) [Formerly Management Skill Development Series (42327 or 42327P)]

Location: Various locations throughout California.

Length: 20-40 hours (interactive video).

Dates: July 1987-Present.

Objective: To develop or improve the management skills of managers in the ten skill areas listed in the instruction section, and to develop or enhance the student's managerial skills.

Learning Outcome: Upon successful completion of this course, the student will be able to use basic management skills required for an effective supervisor.

Instruction: Major topics covered in the course are Organization and Planning; Control and Follow-up; Decisiveness; Decisionmaking; Perception; Interpersonal Relations; Leadership; Flexibility; Oral Communication; and Written Communication. Methods of instruction are interactive video through the use of computer software and student workbooks.

Credit Recommendation: In the lower division baccalaureate/associate degree category, 2 semester hours in Introduction to Management (8/87)(6/92).

Managing the Goal Setting Process (42171)

Location: Various locations throughout California.

Length: 24 hours (3 days).

Dates: August 1989-July 1996.

Objective: To provide managers with the skills necessary to effectively facilitate an approach for establishing attainable goals for employees, personal and professional development.

Learning Outcome: Upon successful completion of this course, the students will be able to recognize the levels of goal setting and how goals affect both the planning and the appraisal process; determine work motivators for self and others, identify values, and relate their job satisfaction and career plans; and minimize conflict through an understanding of differences in values and value systems.

Instruction: Major topics covered in the course are introduction of the goal-setting process; identifying the steps involved in goal setting; the concept of work motivates needs; the concept of value systems; and motivational skills. Methods of instruction include lecture, discussion, laboratory classroom exercises, simulation, and problem-solving.

Credit Recommendation: In the lower division baccalaureate/associate degree category, 1 semester hour in Management (11/90).

Marketing Concepts and Principles (42244A)

Location: Various locations throughout California.

Length: 16 hours (2 days).

Dates: January 1986-Present.

Objective: To provide an overview of the key components of marketing.

Learning Outcome: Upon successful completion of the course, the student will be able to discuss strategic marketing planning with customers, apply the principles presented in lecture to account planning and understand the marketing process as it applies to business.

Instruction: Major topics covered in the course are competitive analysis, target markets and marketing mix variables, strategic planning, and product life cycles. Methods of instruction include discussion and workbooks.

Credit Recommendation: In the lower division baccalaureate/associate degree category, 1 semester hour in Marketing (6/92).

Marketing Residence Service Representative Basic-RASC (02321-A) (Billing Group - Residence)

Location: Various locations throughout California.

Length: 240 hours (6 weeks).

Dates: September 1984-June 1990.

Objective: To provide training to non-management personnel in performing service representative functions.

Instruction: Major topics covered in the course are training in handling customer questions and complaints and collection and adjustments of overdue bills in a professional manner. Methods of Instruction Include self-paced learning under an instructor's guidance and student application practice sessions.

Credit Recommendation: In the lower division baccalaureate/associate degree category, 3 semester hours in Customer Relations (8/85).

Microcomputer Fundamentals (1400)

Location: Los Angeles, Oakland, Pasadena, Sacramento, San Diego, San Francisco, San Jose, San Ramon, and Tustin, CA.

Length: 21 hours (3 days).

Dates: August 1984-July 1996.

Objective: To enable the student to identify, connect, and use microcomputers including peripheral equipment and to learn to use various software programs including word processing, spreadsheet, and communications.

Learning Outcome: Upon successful completion of this course, the student will be able to identify major hardware and software components of a microcomputer; work with files and directories; and understand the basic capabilities of word processing, spreadsheet, data base, and communication software packages.

Instruction: Major topics covered in the course are hardware basics, software basics; DOS basics; files and directories; formatting disks; word processing basics; communications basics; data base basics; and spreadsheet basics. Methods of instruction include lecture, video classroom discussion, and hands-on activities.

Credit Recommendation: In the lower division baccalaureate/associate degree category, 2 semester hours in Data Processing, Computer Information Systems, or Management Information Systems (11/90).

Motivating Toward Peak Performance (45135) (Formerly Motivating for Extraordinary Service)

Location: Various locations throughout California.

Length: 16 hours (2 days).

Dates: June 1992-Present.

Objective: To introduce the student to the role and responsibilities of leadership including performance coaching, motivation, evaluation, and problem solving.

Learning Outcome: Upon successful completion of this course, the student will be able to describe the role of coach as a motivator; create and communicate specific, measurable performance and behavior standards; deliver effective, constructive feedback; match responsibilities and rewards considering human needs; understand the impact of altering expectations to improve employee performance; identify and evaluate job situation problems; determine how and when to take action to resolve problems; and utilize strategies for creating mutually agreed-upon goals.

Instruction: Major topics covered in the course are constructive feedback, behavioral and non-behavioral standards, the eight-step coaching model, behaviors relating to job standards, effective and ineffective behaviors for problem solving, and motivational factors. Methods of instruction include lecture, discussion, role play, and video presentation.

Credit Recommendation: In the lower division baccalaureate/associate degree category, 1 semester hour in Business Management (5/94).

Network Architectures (42610 and 42611) (Formerly IBM's SNA and Critical Software Technologies and IBM vs. DEC: Comparative Network Architecture)

Location: Los Angeles and San Francisco, CA.

Length: 74 hours (2 weeks).

Dates: May 1992-Present.

Objective: To provide the student with knowledge of hardware, software, and communications technologies used in IBM and Digital processors and networking components.

Learning Outcome: Upon successful completion of the course, the student will be able to discuss IBM and Digital hardware, software, and communications products; understand how IBM and Digital architectures compare to that of the OSI model; identify the major components of an SNA network; and describe the SNA layers construction.

Instruction: Major topics covered in the course are IBM's mainframes, distributed processors, desktop computers and networking products and Digital's processors and networking components. Methods of instruction include lecture and discussion.

Credit Recommendation: In the upper division baccalaureate degree category, 3 semester hours in Information Systems, Computer Science, Telecommunications, and Telecommunications Management (6/92). NOTE: Both 42611 and 42610 must be completed to receive the credit.

New Manager Seminar (01055)

Location: Various locations throughout California.

Length: 16 hours (2 days).

Dates: July 1992-Present.

Objective: To enhance the students ability to deal with key business issues of the 1990's.

Learning Outcome: Upon successful completion of the course, the student will be able to identify and deal effectively with individuals and groups from a management perspective, and be exposed to managing the firm in a global economy.

Instruction: Major topics covered in the course are ethics, regulations, public policy, and networking. Methods of instruction include lecture, discussion, case studies, and laboratory exercises.

Credit Recommendation: In the lower division baccalaureate/associate degree category, 1 semester hour in Supervision or Management elective (6/92). **NOTE**: Students must take both Affirmative Action (01005) and New Management Seminar (01055) to receive credit recommendation.

One ESS Central Processor and Programming Fundamentals (05620)

Location: Various training locations throughout California.

Length: 123 hours (3 weeks).

Dates: June 1984-May 1990.

Objective: To provide the student with the skills necessary to characterize data failures in No. 1 Electronic Switching Systems Program Store or Call Store memory systems and to interpret program instructions and apply software diagnostic tactics in locating system hardware failures.

Instruction: Major topics covered in the course are the operation, maintenance, and repair of an advanced-level ESS control unit, including logic circuit analysis; block diagram and timing analysis; address operations; computer system operations; memory addressing (32K and 8K); program instruction codes; core memory operations; program diagnostics; troubleshooting procedures; and repair methods. Methods of instruction include self-paced instruction and practical exercises.

Credit Recommendation: In the lower division baccalaureate/associate degree category, 3 semester hours in Computer Systems or Logic Circuit Fundamentals (8/85).

OS/VS/JCL (59678) (Formerly Introduction to JCL [52142] [JCL 1])

Location: Various locations throughout California.

Length: 24 hours (3 days).

Dates: April 1985-Present.

Objective: To provide students with the necessary skills to write the job control statements required to process a basic one-step job.

Learning Outcome: Upon successful completion of this course, the student will know the purpose of JCL and be able to explain how it is used in the computer operations environment.

Instruction: The course is divided into fourteen units. Included in these units are need for JCL in an IBM environment; relationships between hardware and software; syntax for formatting JCL statements; and a criterion test for the course.

Credit Recommendation: In the lower division baccalaureate/associate degree category, 2 semester hours in Computer Science, Data Processing, or Management Information Systems (8/87) (11/90).

Paradox Users Series: Introduction to Paradox (1425); Using Paradox (1425A); Applying Paradox (1425B)

Location: Various locations throughout California.

Length: 21 hours (3 days).

Dates: August 1984-Present.

Objective: To familiarize students with the relational data base program called Paradox. This course takes the beginning data base user from introductory through advanced levels of Paradox.

Learning Outcome: Upon successful completion of this course, the student will be able to understand the concepts of relational data bases; enter, update, edit, and delete database information; query and sort the data base; format and print reports and tables; customize forms; and design a summary report.

Instruction: Major topics covered in the course are database concepts, definitions, and terminology used by Paradox. Covers the creation, addition, editing, and deletion of files. It also covers data manipulation functions, how to create tables, Paradox querying abilities, customized forms and data summary. Methods of instruction include classroom lectures and personal computer usage.

Credit Recommendation: In the lower division baccalaureate/associate degree category, 1 semester hour in Business Administration, Data Processing, or Management Information Systems (8/87) (6/92).

Personal Computing (42011 or 42011P) (Introduction to Personal Computing)

Location: Various business marketing locations throughout California.

Length: 5-15 hours (interactive video).

Dates: June 1987-July 1996.

Objective: To provide students with an understanding of the types of computers and their components, computer assembly, and basic operation.

Learning Outcome: Upon successful completion of this course, the student will gain a basic understanding of microcomputers and their use. It should make the student more confident and comfortable in operating a microcomputer.

Instruction: Major topics covered in the course are computer types, computer components, computer assembly, data entry, editing, and computer selection. Methods of instruction include interactive video and workbook assignment.

Credit Recommendation: In the lower division baccalaureate/associate degree category, 1 semester hour in Business Administration or Data Processing (8/87) (6/92).

Physical Concepts of Communications (45548)

Location: San Francisco and Los Angeles, CA.

Length: 40 hours (1 week).

Dates: January 1987-Present.

Objective: To provide the student with a basic understanding of electricity, signals, circuits, and electronics as used in communications systems.

Learning Outcome: Upon successful completion of the course, the student will be able to define terms and concepts used in electricity, electronics, circuits and their components.

Instruction: Major topics covered in the course are basic atomic structure; electricity, sound, and light; basic electronic circuits and components. Methods of instruction include lecture, discussion, lab, and some individual assignments.

Credit Recommendation: In the lower division baccalaureate/associate degree category, 3 semester hours in Electronics (6/92).

1. Planning Controlling the Work (1064)
2. Managing Performance (1063)
3. Taking Charge of Time (1007)

Location: Various training locations throughout California.

Length: 40 hours (1 week).

Dates: January 1981-December 1988.

Objective: *Course 1:* To introduce the student to strategies of control and their impact on motivation and to enable the student to plan and monitor work more effectively. *Course 2:* To teach the student a process that will help him or her plan, conduct, and follow up discussions with employees. *Course 3:* To enable the student to evaluate use of time and apply scientific time management techniques to job activities.

Instruction: *Course 1* Major topics covered in the course are the types and categories of control strategies, theories of planning, and an 8-step process of planning and monitoring and its application to specific case studies. *Course 2* Major topics covered in the course are setting specific and measurable performance standards, a work-related discussion process, communication skills, and a process for coaching and counseling employee performance. *Course 3:* Major topics covered in the course are the evaluation and processing of time management techniques and includes choosing five techniques that will increase personal effectiveness and efficiency. Methods of instruction include lecture, discussion, workshop, lab, and audio-visual aids.

Credit Recommendation: In the lower division baccalaureate/associate degree category, 2 semester hours in Employee Development (11/84).

Positive Sales Skills (42139)

Location: Various locations throughout California.

Length: 32 hours (4 days).

Dates: December 1988-Present.

Objective: To teach the consultative sales approach.

Learning Outcome: Upon successful completion of the course, the student will be able to design applications to solve customer's business problems, gather data, handle objections, close the sale, and provide proper follow-up procedures.

Instruction: Major topics covered in the course are determining customer needs, making positive recommendations, selling the recommendation, how to handle objections and methods of closing the sale. Methods of instruction include lecture, group discussion, videotapes, workbook, and partnership activities.

Credit Recommendation: In the lower division baccalaureate/associate degree category, 2 semester hours in Sales or Business elective (6/92). **NOTE:** Duplicate credit cannot be given for the following courses: 45139, 45073, 45074, or 45024.

Positive Sales Skills: Consultant Specialist (45074)

Location: Various locations throughout California.

Length: 16 hours (2 days).

Dates: February 1992-August 1996.

Objective: To teach sales skills to Residence Service Representatives.

Learning Outcome: Upon successful completion of the course, the student will be able to determine customer needs, make a positive recommendation, answer objections, close the sale and use proper follow-up procedures.

Instruction: Major topics covered in the course are the positive sales approach, listening, and asking questions; determining customer needs, answering objections and making a positive recommendation. Methods of instruction include lecture, workbook, role play, and a written test.

Credit Recommendation: In the lower division baccalaureate/associate degree category, 1 semester hour in Sales or Business elective (6/92). **NOTE:** Duplicate credit cannot be given for the following courses: 45074, 45139, 45073, or 45024.

Positive Sales Skills: Continuation Training (45073)

Location: Various locations throughout California.

Length: 32 hours (4 days).

Dates: September 1991-Present.

Objective: To teach the consultative sales process to Business Service Representatives.

Learning Outcome: Upon successful completion of the course, the student will be able to determine customer needs, answer objections, make a positive recommendation, close the sale, and use proper follow-up procedures.

Instruction: Major topics covered in the course are the positive sales approach, listening and answering questions, determining customer needs, answering objections, and making a positive recommendation. Methods of instruction include lecture, workbook, role play, and written test.

Credit Recommendation: In the lower division baccalaureate/associate degree category, 2 semester hours in Sales or Business elective (6/92). **NOTE:** Duplicate credit cannot be given for the following courses: 45073, 45139, 45074, or 45024.

Positive Sales Skills: Initial Training (45024) or (65610)

Location: Various locations throughout California.

Length: 32 hours (4 days).

Dates: February 1989-Present.

Objective: To teach the positive sales approach, questions, techniques, making an effective presentation, answering objections, and closing the sale.

Learning Outcome: Upon successful completion of this course, the student will be able to determine customer needs, make a presentation, answer objections, and close the sale.

Instruction: Major topics covered in the course are positive sales approach; listening and asking questions; determining customer needs; making a positive recommendation; answering objections; and closing the sale. Methods of instruction include lecture, discussion, workshop, and classroom exercise.

Credit Recommendation: In the lower division baccalaureate/associate degree category, 2 semester hours in Sales (11/90).

Principles of Digital Technology (05703) (Formerly 25050)

Location: Various training locations throughout California and Nevada.

Length: 40 hours (1 week) .

Dates: *Version 1:* April 1981-October 1990; *Version 2:* November 1990-Present.

Objective: To enable the student to interpret, identify, and describe the digital technology currently in use, the evolution of the technology, and the methods for management of the technology.

Learning Outcome: Upon successful completion of this course, the student will be able to describe coding and pulse code modulation processes and system components, identify the major functions of digital channels and channel banks, and describe the design and operations of PCM time division switching systems and ISDN.

Instruction: Major topics covered in the course are digital technology used in the communications network and basic digital theory and terminology. Methods of instruction include lecture, discussion, a workshop, and classroom exercises.

Credit Recommendation: *Version 1:* In the upper division baccalaureate degree category, 2 semester hours in Information Science or Telecommunications (11/84). *Version 2:* In the lower division baccalaureate/associate degree category, 2 semester hours in Information Science or Telecommunications (11/90).

Principles of Engineering Economy and Economic Alternative Selection for Outside Plant (EASOP) (03361)

Location: Various training locations throughout California.

Length: 24-40 hours (1 week).

Dates: March 1981-Present.

Objective: To provide the student with the basic skills and knowledge to complete an economic study using manual, engineering, and computer-based analysis techniques.

Learning Outcome: Upon successful completion of this course, the student will be able to relate basic concepts of accounting and finance to the cash flows associated with an outside plant project; convert cash flows into their equivalent values at different times using time value of money principles; explain the effect of inflation on the cost of capital; and evaluate the modified rate of return and discounted payback period of alternative plans.

Instruction: Major topics covered in the course are cash flows; time value of money; developing alternatives; cost study indicators; NPV calculations; PWE calculations;and recommending a plan. Methods of instruction include laboratory exercises and self-paced instruction.

Credit Recommendation: In the lower division baccalaureate/associate degree category, 1 semester hour in Engineering Economics (11/90).

Producing Results with Others (01269A)

Location: Various locations throughout California.

Length: 16 hours (2 days).

Dates: April 1987-Present.

Objective: To enable the student to establish more productive relationships in the work environment and develop new understanding of behavior of others and how others perceive you.

Learning Outcome: Upon successful completion of this course, the student will be able to acknowledge the importance of versatility when dealing with others; recognize the difference between productive and nonproductive tension and to anticipate and modify behavior in order to minimize communications mistakes; select and use behavior that will help others feel more comfortable; and develop strategies for dealing with unsatisfactory relationships.

Instruction: Major topics covered in the course are basics of behavior; social style models, profiles, and concepts; and skill building. Methods of instruction include lecture, discussion, laboratory, classroom exercises, simulations, problem solving, etc.

Credit Recommendation: In the lower division baccalaureate/associate degree category, 1 semester hour in Supervision (11/90).

Quality Skills Appreciation (06031)

Location: Various locations throughout California.

Length: 18 hours (2 days).

Dates: January 1992-Present.

Objective: To gain an appreciation for the quality improvement process and what is required to coach, guide, and role model the quality principles.

Learning Outcome: Upon successful completion of the course, the student will be able to understand the basic concepts underlying costs of quality, appropriately apply the following quality tools; affinity diagram, bar chart, brainstorming, checksheet, fishbone diagram, flow chart, histogram, multivoting, Pareto Chart, run chart, scatter diagram, and stratification.

Instruction: Major topics covered in the course are customer requirements; suppliers and supplier specifications; identifying current work process; identifying how, where, and what to improve; establishing and verifying cause and effect; revising the work process and establish measurements; conducting small scale tests of the revised process; and evaluating test results. Methods of instruction include lecture and discussion, group exercises, and team exercises.

Credit Recommendation: In the lower division baccalaureate/associate degree category, 1 semester hour in Quality Control (6/92).

Residence Marketing Center Consultative Sales Skills (42103)

Location: Various Pacific Bell Learning Centers and client locations.

Length: 15.25 hours (2 days).

Dates: February 1995-Present.

Objective: To teach the steps of the sales process and demonstrate their knowledge through role play and to take calls on the job using their new skills which include the four steps of the sales call process (sales funnel), product families, and product/consultative selling.

Learning Outcome: Upon successful completion of this course, the student will be able to demonstrate via role play and customer contact calls their skills in consultative selling.

Instruction: Major topics covered in the course are sales experience, reality of consultative sales, and sales funnel. Methods of instruction include lectures, group discussion, written quiz, group, and individual/team role play with instructor feedback and coaching.

Credit Recommendation: In the lower division baccalaureate/associate degree category, 1 semester hour in Business Marketing (8/96).

Risk Taking for Professional Development (01049)

Location: Various locations throughout California.

Length: 16 hours (2 days).

Dates: December 1988-July 1996.

Objective: To teach managers about the factors that control their risk taking and development.

Learning Outcome: Upon successful completion of this course, the student will be able to plan a strategy around a risk situation; learn what factors are present in risk situations; and learn how to control risk.

Instruction: Major topics covered in the course are survey of risk taking; project analysis; influences on risk taking and development; strategies for development; attribution theory; sort feedback; goal setting. Methods of instruction include lecture, discussion, exercises, and self-assessment.

Credit Recommendation: In the lower division baccalaureate/associate degree category, 1 semester hour in General Business or Management (11/90).

SCC Trunk Tester (05617)

Location: Oakland, Pasadena, Sacramento, and Tustin, CA.

Length: 58 hours (8 days).

Dates: January 1985-July 1996.

Objective: To enable students upon completion of the course to acquire the skills and knowledge necessary to perform the following tasks in the switching control center: trunking and facilities, interoffice signaling, transmission, trunk orders, trunk testing, administration, and full maintenance.

Instruction: Major topics covered in the course are the switching control center (SCC) and trunk workstation as well as SCC procedures as they apply to the trunk installation/maintenance function. This course will enable the student to perform basic trunk testing, trunk installation, and trunk field maintenance. Methods of Instruction Include self-paced instruction.

Credit Recommendation: In the lower division baccalaureate/associate degree category, 2 semester hours in Electronics Technology (8/85).

Seven Habits of Highly Effective People

Location: Various locations throughout California.

Length: 16 hours (2 days).

Dates: February 1994-Present.

Objective: To empower people and their organizations to enhance their performance capability through the application of the seven habits and how they directly correlate with effective and efficient leadership.

Learning Outcome: Upon successful completion of this course, the student will be able to identify each habit in a meaningful way and know how to maximize its effectiveness; choose responses to various situations rather than react in a predictable or predetermined way; become more proactive and innovation oriented; manage interpersonal conflict through collaboration; bridge the gap between knowing what to do and deciding to do it; and assess current behavior in relation to the seven habits.

Instruction: Major topics covered in the course are definitions and implications of each habit, effectiveness and efficiency, how to get the most benefit from the seven habits, paradigm shifting, and how the seven habits relate to each other. Methods of instruction include lecture, class discussion, individual and group presentations, and case studies.

Credit Recommendation: In the lower division baccalaureate/associate degree category, 1 semester hour in Management, Organizational Behavior, or Business elective (5/94).

Shell-Part I (59733)

Location: San Ramon, CA.

Length: 24 hours (3 days).

Dates: January 1989-Present.

Objective: To instruct students in UNIX shell programming.

Learning Outcome: Upon successful completion of the course, the student will know what shell is and how it relates to the other parts of UNIX, program in shell.

Instruction: Major topics covered in the course are the shell environment; files; I/O redirection and pipes; shell commands. Methods of instruction include lecture and laboratory exercise.

Credit Recommendation: In the lower division baccalaureate/associate degree category, 1 semester hour in Computer Science (6/92).

Signalling System Seven/Common Channel Signalling Overview (05638)

Location: Various training locations throughout California.

Length: 16 hours (2 days).

Dates: November 1986-July 1996.

Objective: To acquaint students with the concepts of Common Channel Signaling, specifically SS7, and to familiarize them with the implications to Pacific Bell.

Learning Outcome: Upon successful completion of this course, the student will be able to understand network features; understand SS7 protocol used in CCS; be familiar with Pacific Bell's SS7 network and services; and understand network architecture and services (general).

Instruction: Major topics covered in the course are system overview; network features; SS7 protocol; network architecture; the Pacific Bell SS7 network; switching system modifications; and the Intelligent Network. Methods of instruction include lecture, discussion, and lab.

Credit Recommendation: In the lower division baccalaureate/associate degree category, 1 semester hour in Telecommunications (11/90).

Sold on Selling (45087)

Location: Various locations throughout California.

Length: 32 hours (4 days).

Dates: November 1990-Present.

Objective: To provide managers with a sales development system they can follow to help Service Representatives improve their sales skills and the consultative sales skills they need to model desired behavior and coach for improvement.

Learning Outcome: Upon successful completion of the course, the student will be able to work with Service Rep-resentatives to establish personal sales goals; develop techniques to foster teaming and peer coaching among Service Representatives; allocate management time; coach sales performance; motivate sales people and conduct sales meetings.

Instruction: Major topics covered in the course are sales leadership; communication, expectation, motivation; how to improve sales skills; coaching; conducting sales meetings; sales skills, sales attitudes, and sales integrity. Methods of instruction include lecture, discussion, and role play.

Credit Recommendation: In the upper division baccalaureate degree category, 2 semester hours in Sales Management or Business elective (6/92).

System Design Consultant Communication Skills (02138)

Location: Various training locations throughout California and Nevada.

Length: 24 hours (3 days).

Dates: October 1982-December 1988.

Objective: To teach the student effective communication skills in a technical environment, with the client and other members of the marketing team through consideration of basic communication models and techniques and the design and development of technical reports, sales proposals, and presentations.

Instruction: Major topics covered in the course are communications concepts and techniques, proposal strategies, understanding one's audience, presentation style and techniques, effective use of language and English skills, and managing and rehearsing presentations.

Credit Recommendation: In the upper division baccalaureate degree category, 2 semester hours in Business Communications (11/84).

System Development Life Cycle: A Technical Sales Approach: Part A and Part B (42277A and 42277B)

Location: Client's site.

Length: *Part A:* 4 hours (self-paced); *Part B:* 8.5 hour workshop.

Dates: *Part A:* September 1995-Present; *Part B:* October 1996-Present.

Objective: To reinforce and familiarize student with the specific eight step sales process called the System Development Life Cycle or SDLC; and to reinforce familiarity with SDLC and its role in the sales/analysis process.

Learning Outcome: Upon successful completion of this course, the student will be able to use phases of SDLC in a case work environment and to practically apply the concepts of SDLC to customer scenarios.

Instruction: Major topics covered in the course are an overview of the SDLC process, pre SDLC consulting, project management, systems analysis and design, and the eight phase SDLC used by Pacific Bell sales professionals. Methods of instruction include reading material, role-playing, group exercises, presentations, and tests.

Credit Recommendation: In the upper division baccalaureate degree category, 1 semester hour in Marketing or Business Administration (8/96).

Systems Analysis and Design (42256) (Formerly Systems Analysis and Design [02256])

Location: Los Angeles and Oakland, CA.

Length: *Version 1:* 40 hours (5 days); *Version 2:* 28 hours (3.5 days).

Dates: *Version 1:* October 1986-October 1990; *Version 2:* November 1990-Present.

Objective: To provide the student with an understanding of the system design lifecycle as a methodology, and analysis and design skill.

Learning Outcome: Upon successful completion of this course, the student will be able to identify solutions and alternatives, collect data, interview, define problems, prepare and support proposals, and oversee installations and operations.

Instruction: Major topics covered in the course are methods of data collection; problem definition; analysis; systems planning; design in support of proposal preparation, and followup, installation, and operations; post-implementation review; techniques for tracking progress in analysis and design; and techniques for evaluating situations. Methods of instruction include examples and case studies.

Credit Recommendation: *Version 1:* In the upper division baccalaureate degree category, 3 semester hours in Computer Information Systems (11/86). **NOTE:** No graduate credit; students do not have prerequisites to suggest graduate. Text material is at undergraduate level. *Version 2:* In the lower division baccalaureate/associate degree category, 2 semester hours in Computer Science, Data Processing, or Management Information Systems (11/90).

Telecommunications Fundamentals (05733)

Location: Various locations throughout California.

Length: 28 hours (4 days).

Dates: March 1988-Present.
Objective: To provide the student with an understanding of the functions and interrelationships of the major components of a telephone communications network.
Learning Outcome: Upon successful completion of the course, the student will be able to describe a telephone network and the major components comprising it, describe the elements required for signal transmission, describe the function and use of an interconnecting network, and understand the different types of switching (analog vs. digital).
Instruction: Major topics covered in the course are terminology, network theory, network component functions, switching theory basics, and switching applications. Methods of instruction include lecture and discussion.
Credit Recommendation: In the lower division baccalaureate/associate degree category, 2 semester hours in Telecommunications, Information Systems, or Telecommunications Management (6/92) (8/96).

Telemarketing Concepts and Sales Process (02145-A)

Location: Oakland and Los Angeles, CA.
Length: 24 hours (3 days).
Dates: January 1985-September 1988.
Objective: To provide students with skills required to understand telecommunications marketing, which can assist potential customers of the company's product and services.
Instruction: Covers telecommunications technology as a marketing tool in a well-organized marketing program. Marketing strategies, the sales process, and information gathering are included. Methods of Instruction Include lectures and customer-led discussions as well as classroom exercises and problem-solving.
Credit Recommendation: In the lower division baccalaureate/associate degree category, 1 semester hour in Marketing Seminar (8/85).

The Versatile Organization (42000 or 42000P) (Formerly Social Styles/Interpersonal Skills)

Location: Various locations throughout California.
Length: 8-13 hours (interactive video).
Dates: November 1986-July 1996.
Objective: To enable students to observe behavioral characteristics of customers/managers/subordinates in a nonjudgemental way and from those observations be able to be versatile in meeting the expectations of people different or same as themselves.
Learning Outcome: Upon successful completion of this course, the student will be able to discriminate degrees of assertiveness and responsiveness in people based on their behavior, so as to classify them in one of four social types; identify the need and expectations of each social style; and design and implement appropriate strategies for interacting with each style.
Instruction: Major topics covered in the course are the idea that behavior reflects preferred styles for interacting with others; how to observe behavioral characteristics in a nonjudgemental way and to develop appropriate interpersonal skills for versatility dealing with the different styles. The course is self-paced and utilizes interactive video. Methods of instruction include interactive video, computer simulation games, lecture, discussion, and group activities.
Credit Recommendation: In the lower division baccalaureate/associate degree category, 1 semester hour in Interpersonal Skills (8/87) (6/92).

Trends in Communications Technology (42153)

Location: Various locations throughout California.
Length: 40 hours (1 week).
Dates: January 1989-Present.
Objective: To provide the student with an understanding of the basic functionality, terminology, and topologies of data communications networks.
Learning Outcome: Upon successful completion of this course, the student will be able to identify the major components of computer systems and describe their function; evaluate the characteristics of circuit and packet switched networks; identify the layers of the OSI reference model; and assess the market within the information systems environment.
Instruction: Major topics covered in the course are computer systems; network technology; circuit switching; packet switching; and the OSI reference model. Methods of instruction include lecture.
Credit Recommendation: In the upper division baccalaureate degree category, 2 semester hours in Information Systems or Telecommunications (6/92).

Understanding Career Change and Resiliency (19206) Resume Writing (19203) Interviewing Preparation Workshop (19204)

Location: Various locations throughout California.
Length: 16 hours (2 days) for combined courses.
Dates: December 1993-Present.
Objective: To understand the stages of forced change, the career change model, and resiliency; to identify appropriate resume information and to demonstrate the knowledge to draft a resume; and to increase the awareness of skills necessary for successful job networking and interviewing.
Learning Outcome: Upon successful completion of this course, the student will understand the psychological impact of change; understand resiliency as a process of managing change; develop an action plan; gain the necessary knowledge and skills to draft a resume and cover letter; and identify, practice and critique interviewing skills and strategies for job hiring opportunities and career changes.
Instruction: Major topics covered in the course are models for understanding the impact of change and acquiring resiliency; and identification of the purpose, forms and components of a resume, highlighting the qualifications and integrating the data, references, and cover letter. Methods of instruction include projects, presentations, role playing, and examinations.
Credit Recommendation: In the lower division baccalaureate/associate degree category, 1 semester hour in Career Counseling or Business elective (5/94). **NOTE:** All three parts must be successfully completed for course credit.

Utilities (Survey of IBM Utilities Progress) (52139)

Location: Concord, Hayward, San Ramon, and San Diego, CA.
Length: 20 hours (2.5 days).
Dates: June 1984-July 1996.
Objective: To teach computer systems operators the purpose and use of utilities progress and the utilities manual.
Learning Outcome: Upon successful completion of this course, the student will be able to describe the purpose of utility programs; identify the type of utility program; and use a utilities manual.

Instruction: Major topics covered in the course are the IBM utility manual, the more commonly used utilities, and techniques for copying from one storage medium to another.

Credit Recommendation: In the lower division baccalaureate/associate degree category, 1 semester hour in Computer Science, Data Processing, or Management Information Systems (9/88).

Windows, Word for Windows Modules 1 and 2 (1488A, 1489A, 1489B)

Location: Various locations throughout California.

Length: 21 hours (3 days).

Dates: April 1991-Present.

Objective: To introduce students to Microsoft Windows 3.0 and to Versions 1.1 and 2.0 of the Wordprocessor Microsoft Word for Windows.

Learning Outcome: Upon successful completion of the course, the student will be able to start Windows; work with the program manager; use paintbrush, and other Window accessories; understand intermediate and advanced word processing concepts and be able to use these concepts to create, edit, and store documents using Microsoft Word.

Instruction: Major topics covered in the course are multiple Windows; common Windows elements; combining documents, creating headers and footers; use of macros; how to find and organize programs and data on disks and create, copy, move, rename, and delete files. Methods of instruction include lecture, discussion, and laboratory exercises.

Credit Recommendation: In the lower division baccalaureate/associate degree category, 1 semester hour in Business Data Processing or Computer Information Systems (8/87) (6/92). **NOTE**: Students should be granted credit in only one word processing course (i.e. Multimate, Displaywrite, Wordstar, etc.).

Writing Management Reports (01266)

Location: Various training locations throughout California.

Length: 24 hours (3 days).

Dates: November 1984-Present.

Objective: To enable managers to write reports more effectively, applying the basic principles of information mapping.

Learning Outcome: Upon successful completion of this course, the student will be able to use research-based principles; utilize information mapping hierarchy; sequence and write the initial draft; edit sentences; format specifications; and write final paper.

Instruction: Major topics covered in the course are basic principles of information mapping writing methods and writing of memos and reports that involve how the mind processes information. Methods of instruction include lecture, discussion, and student exercises.

Credit Recommendation: In the upper division baccalaureate degree category, 1 semester hour in Management Report Writing (8/85) (11/90).

PADI International, Inc.

PADI International, Inc. is a professional organization whose activities center around the training of scuba divers and scuba diving instructors. PADI's goal is to promote the training and education of the general public in the proper techniques of participating in recreational underwater activities and the advancement of those activities.

As a professional association, PADI has four types of members: (1) supervisory, (2) instructional, (3) retail, and (4) resorts. PADI members in a supervisory category include PADI Divemasters and Assistant Instructors. These members have completed courses allowing them to perform limited teaching activities and primarily act as supervisory personnel during diving instructional activities conducted by fully qualified PADI Instructors. PADI members belonging to the instructional category include PADI Underwater Instructors, Open Water Scuba Instructors, Master Instructors, and Course Directors (instructor trainers). These members have completed specific qualification programs allowing them to teach the general public how to scuba dive and, in the case of the Course Directors, train instructors. Professional retail dive stores and dive resorts whose business it is to sell scuba equipment and provide instruction, equipment rentals, equipment repair, take people diving and other related services may also become members.

PADI is international in scope with service offices located in Australia, Canada, Switzerland, Japan, New Zealand, Norway, Singapore, Sweden, the United Kingdom and the United States. PADI Worldwide (corporate headquarters) is located in California, United States. PADI Offices serve more than 80,000 individual professional members and more than 3,000 dive centers and resorts in more than 175 countries. To serve the needs of divers worldwide, translations of PADI education materials are available in more than 20 languages.

The PADI method of diving instruction is based on progressive training in the classroom, pool, and open water.

Instructor ethics, teaching methods, and course equipment are monitored by PADI to uphold PADI training standards. Records are required to be maintained on all courses conducted under the sanction of PADI.

PADI does not "select" its teaching staff *per se*. Rather, qualified individuals must complete training programs specific to the type of PADI courses they wish to teach. Experienced scuba divers who wish to become PADI Instructors must successfully complete a series of instructor preparation and evaluation courses.

All PADI courses are developed in terms of demonstrable student performance. PADI course materials employ the concepts of mastery learning based on student-centered objectives and the curriculum is performance-based rather than time-based.

Students are not certified as PADI divers until all cognitive and motor-skills performance objectives are mastered. Students who have not demonstrated an acceptable level of performance typically matriculate to another course or begin remedial training with the instructor until all cognitive or motor-skill performance objectives are met.

Student records are kept at two levels: (1) PADI members are required to maintain records of the students in their courses, and (2) PADI headquarters maintains records of students receiving course completion documents.

Source of official student records: Registry of Credit Recommendations, American Council on Education, One Dupont Circle, Washington, DC 20036-1193 or PADI International, Inc., Office of Academic Transcripts, 1251 E. Dyer Road, Suite 100, Santa Ana, CA 92705-5605.

Additional information about the courses: College Credit Recommendation Service, American Council on Education, One Dupont Circle, Washington, DC 20036-1193.

Advanced Open Water Diver

Location: Various locations throughout the United States and internationally, including PADI Affiliated Dive Centers and Resorts.

Length: 23 hours (flexible modular schedule).

Dates: January 1980-Present.

Objective: To provide advanced training that will expand the student's open water diving capabilities.

Learning Outcome: Upon successful completion of this course, the student will be able to demonstrate ability to navigate underwater, demonstrate skills for night diving, and demonstrate proper deep-diving procedures.

Instruction: Major topics covered in the course are underwater phenomena, the body and diving, diving procedures, the diving environment, and deep diving. Methods of instruction include unit lectures, demonstrations, and evaluation through written and performance testing.

Credit Recommendation: In the lower division baccalaureate/associate degree category, 1 semester hour in Recreation or Physical Education (3/87) (5/94).

Course Director Training Course (Formerly Director Training Course)

Location: Various locations throughout the United States and internationally, including PADI Affiliated Dive Centers and Resorts.

Length: 90 hours (flexible modular schedule).

Dates: March 1985-Present.

Objective: To teach qualified individuals how to teach the PADI Instructor Development Course, PADI Instructor Orientation Course and PADI Instructor Level Continuing Education courses.

Learning Outcome: Upon successful completion of this course, the student will be able to conduct all IDC training sessions per PADI manual; present teaching topics from PADI Open Water Diver Course and IDC Curriculum; demonstrate quality skills during teaching; demonstrate comprehensive understanding of PADI standards and procedures such as IDC, IOC, IE, OWSI, including all status upgrades.

Instruction: Major topics covered in the course are PADI manual; PADI standards and procedures such as IDC, IOC, IC, OWSI. Methods of instruction include lecture, demonstrations, confined and open water dive experiences, and evaluation through written and performance testing, teaching presentations, and professional attitude development.

Credit Recommendation: In the upper division baccalaureate degree category, 3 semester hours in Physical Education, Recreation, or Education (5/94).

Deep Diver

Location: Various locations throughout the United States and internationally, including PADI Affiliated Dive Centers and Resorts.

Length: 24 hours (flexible modular schedule).

Dates: June 1988-Present.

Objective: To familiarize divers with the skills, knowledge, planning, organization, procedures, techniques, problems, hazards, and enjoyment of diving between depths of 60 and 130 feet.

Learning Outcome: Upon successful completion of this course, the student will be familiar with the planning, organization, procedures, techniques, and hazards of deep diving; possess the knowledge of risk factors and decompression tables including safety stops and emergency decompression procedures; be familiar with special equipment descent lines and buoyancy-control considerations; understand procedures for flying after diving and high-altitude diving; and be familiar with recompression chambers.

Instruction: Major topics covered in the course are the knowledge of deep diving activities and objectives, deep diving equipment, techniques for deep diving, medical hazards of deep diving including nitrogen narcosis and decompressions sickness, dive conditions evaluation to 130 foot depths, and deep diving navigation techniques and marine life. Methods of instruction include lecture, discussion, and lab exercises including open water dive experiences.

Credit Recommendation: In the lower division baccalaureate/associate degree category, 1 semester hour in Physical Education or Recreation (5/94).

Divemaster

Location: Various locations throughout the United States and internationally, including PADI Affiliated Dive Centers and Resorts.

Length: 50 hours (flexible modular schedule).

Dates: January 1985-Present.

Objective: To provide certified rescue divers with the knowledge and skills to organize, conduct, and supervise recreational diving activities.

Learning Outcome: Upon successful completion of this course, the student will be able to plan safe and successful dives, including boat dives; supervise students in training; supervise deep and specialized diving; and demonstrate first aid and CPR procedures.

Instruction: Major topics covered in the course are the role of the divemaster, dive planning, dive management and control, how to supervise students in training, boat diving supervision and control, deep-diving supervision, and supervision of specialized diving activities. Methods of instruction include unit lectures, demonstrations, and evaluation through written and performance testing.

Credit Recommendation: In the lower division baccalaureate/associate degree category, 2 semester hours in Recreation or Physical Education (3/87) (5/94).

Instructor Development

Location: Various locations throughout the United States and internationally, including PADI Affiliated Dive Centers and Resorts.

Length: 57.5 hours (flexible modular schedule).

Dates: August 1984-Present.

Objective: To provide certified PADI Divemasters and Assistant Instructors the knowledge and skills necessary to teach recreational scuba diving.

Learning Outcome: Upon successful completion of this course, the student will be able to demonstrate competence in teaching methodology, and familiarity with the entire PADI instructional system.

Instruction: Major topics covered in the course are a diving industry overview, overview and analysis of all PADI courses, lesson planning and delivery, teaching and using the PADI dive tables, techniques for teaching in a pool environment, open water problem-solving, opportunities for the professional diving instructor, noninstructional duties, PADI standards and procedures, the PADI continuing education system, and marketing and promotion for the professional instructor. Methods of instruction include lecture, discussion, demonstration, unit lectures with audiovisual materials, and classroom exercises. Pool sessions allow students to demonstrate teaching proficiency. Open water allows students to demonstrate teaching proficiency.

Credit Recommendation: In the upper division baccalaureate degree category, 2 semester hours in Physical Education, Recreation, or Education (3/87) (5/94).

Night Diver

Location: Various locations throughout the United States and internationally, including PADI Affiliated Dive Centers and Resorts.

Length: 24 hours (flexible modular schedule).

Dates: June 1988-Present.

Objective: To provide skills, knowledge, planning, organization, procedures, techniques, hazards, and enjoyment of night diving.

Learning Outcome: Upon successful completion of this course, the student will have mastered objectives from nocturnal aquatic life; night diving equipment; planning night dives; and special night diving situations, techniques, communication, and navigation.

Instruction: Major topics covered in the course are planning, hazards, buoyancy control, navigation, communications, aquatic life, and equipment. Methods of instruction include lecture, demonstrations, cognitive learning, and lab including open water dive experiences.

Credit Recommendation: In the lower division baccalaureate/associate degree category, 1 semester hour in Physical Education or Recreation (5/94).

Open Water Diver

Location: Various locations throughout the United States and internationally, including PADI Affiliated Dive Centers and Resorts.

Length: 30 hours (flexible modular schedule).

Dates: January 1978-Present.

Objective: To provide students with the necessary entry-level knowledge and skills to scuba dive.

Learning Outcome: Upon successful completion of this course, the student will be able to engage in beginning recreational scuba diving activities in local aquatic environments without direct or indirect supervision by a certified diving instructor.

Instruction: Major topics covered in the course are adapting to the underwater world, underwater communications, dive planning; diving equipment; boat diving; health for diving; dive tables; marine life identification; the underwater environment; skill development in a confined water (e.g., pool) situation; and practical application of acquired skills in an open water environment (e.g., ocean, lake, spring, quarry). Methods of instruction include unit lectures with audiovisual materials, demonstrations, discussions, and evaluation through written unit quizzes and final exam.

Credit Recommendation: In the lower division baccalaureate/associate degree category, 1 semester hour in Recreation or Physical Education (3/87) (5/94).

Rescue Diver

Location: Various locations throughout the United States and internationally, including PADI Affiliated Dive Centers and Resorts.

Length: 25 hours (flexible modular schedule).

Dates: January 1984-Present.

Objective: To become knowledgeable in recognizing signs and symptoms of aquatic stress and potential rescue situations as related to scuba diving and to become competent in scuba diving rescue and emergency procedures.

Learning Outcome: Upon successful completion of this course, the student will

be able to demonstrate knowledge of the physiology and psychology of scuba-related rescue situations; the skills of effecting a scuba-related rescue; and the application of emergency procedures.

Instruction: Major topics covered in the course are first aid for diving maladies, first aid for marine injuries, emergency procedures, rescue equipment, panic syndrome, distress recognition, self-rescue, rescue entries and approaches, use of extensions and floats, assists, transporting, submerged diver rescue, missing diver procedures, in-water artificial respiration, equipment considerations, rescue exits and accident recording and reporting. Methods of instruction include unit lectures, demonstrations, and evaluation through written and performance testing.

Credit Recommendation: In the lower division baccalaureate/associate degree category, 1 semester hour in Recreation or Physical Education (3/87) (5/94).

Paychex, Inc.

Thomas Golisano founded Paychex in Rochester, NY in 1971 with one employee and forty clients. It started as a single operation and expanded through franchise agreements and joint ventures until the company consolidated in 1979. In 1983, Paychex went public. Today, the company has over 4,500 employees nationwide, operates in over 100 locations, and serves approximately 262,000 clients. The organization's purpose is service. Paychex is a national payroll processing and payroll tax preparation company for small to medium-sized businesses. While payroll is the core business, the company also provides human resources products and services, including Section 125 cafeteria plans, 401(k) recordkeeping services, employee handbooks, and insurance services. The organization's goals are financial performance, employee development, and exceptional customer service.

The organization's dedication to employee development is most clearly seen through the Paychex Training and Development Center. Our mission is to create and develop partnerships with the leaders of the organization to facilitate success by listening to and anticipating the organization's goals. The training and Development Center impacts the professional development of all Paychex employees through programs which development product, technical, sales, customer service, management, and career planning skills.

The organization's courses are developed, revised, and implemented by the staff of approximately 40 employees within the Training and Development Center. Courses are delivered in a classroom setting at the Paychex Corporate Headquarters in Rochester, NY. Trainers come to the organization with extensive backgrounds in education, training, and instructional design as well as expertise in the main subject areas of sales, customer service, management, and/or computer systems. All participants in our programs are current Paychex employees and most are newly hired into the organization, with the exception of the multi-level management development programs.

Within the Paychex Training and Development Center, our goal is simple....to help others to reach theirs.

Source of official student records: Registry of Credit Recommendations, American Council on Education, One Dupont Circle, Washington, DC 200036-1193.

Additional information about the courses: College Credit Recommendation Service, American Council on Education, One Dupont Circle, Washington, DC 20036-1193.

Advanced Computer Systems Training

Location: Paychex Training and Development Center, Rochester, NY.

Length: 40 hours (5 days).

Dates: August 1995-Present.

Objective: To provide more in depth, advanced technical systems operations competency.

Learning Outcome: Upon successful completion of this course, the student will be able to solve problems and make effective decisions related to the payrun process; evaluate scripts; write reports using IQ; demonstrate advanced backup procedures; explain the purpose of testbase and how one is created; identify the components of a new release; explain business continuity procedures; and explain the daemon processes that control our system.

Instruction: Major topics covered in the course are system review, daemons, programming standards, script comprehension, print environment, new releases and transmits, inspecting the payrun, testbase, Intelligent Query (IQ), solutions and exercises, quarter-end processing, case studies, backups/file restores, business continuity, response center overview, and communication. Methods of instruction include lecture, discussion, classroom exercises, audio-visual material, participant reaction to training program, homework assignments, quizzes, role play, demonstrations, and final examination.

Credit Recommendation: In the lower division baccalaureate/associate degree category, 2 semester hours in Computer Operations (11/97).

Advanced Training Program for Payroll Sales Representatives

Location: Paychex Training and Development Center, Rochester, NY.

Length: 40 hours (1 week).

Dates: March 1997-Present.

Objective: To provide technical knowledge of 401(K) product information, employee management systems, business solutions, and the importance of value selling.

Learning Outcome: Upon successful completion of this course, the student will be able to demonstrate and apply the knowledge of 401 (k) products and their application to payroll and tax payment services; apply advanced sales techniques and finalize a verbal agenda; apply and design career planning; utilize motivation techniques; and identify the major changes in the Paychex business culture and the payroll processing business.

Instruction: Major topics covered in the course are 401(k) product information, Employee Management System products, Paychex Business Solutions products, Section 125 Premium Only Plan, internal coaching, restaurant payrolls, personality profiling, setting a verbal agenda, SPIN selling techniques, General Ledger/ Accounting Principles, SPIN Application, exercise, role play exercises, group breakout sessions, electronic network services, getting to the next level of sales, CPA development, value selling, applying Covey's Seven Habits, and career planning and motivation. Methods of instruction include lecture, discussion, classroom exercises, case studies, audio-visual material, participant presentations, role play exercises, formal role play demonstrations, and evaluation of learner reaction is completed at the conclusion of the course.

Credit Recommendation: In the lower division baccalaureate/associate degree category, 1 semester hour in Payroll Applications or Business Applications (11/97).

Computer Systems Training

Location: Paychex Training and Development Center, Rochester, NY.

Length: 40 hours (5 days).

Dates: September 1996-Present.

Objective: To provide Introductory systems operations competency.

Learning Outcome: Upon successful completion of this course, the student will be able to log on to a system and execute the basic functions of the payroll process; write in Intelligent Query (IQ) procedure; run the quarter-end process determine what backups are required and do the system backup; use the UNIX operating system.

Instruction: Major topics covered in the course are introduction to payroll, payrun, UNIX, data integrity, Intelligent Query(IQ), weekly/monthly processing, system ethics, computer room organization, branch output reports, system backups, business continuity, response center presentation, and communication. Methods of instruction include lecture, discussion, classroom exercises, audio-visual material, participant reaction to training program, homework assignments, quizzes, role play, demonstrations, and final examination.

Credit Recommendation: In the lower division baccalaureate/associate degree

category, 1 semester hour in Computer Operations (11/97).

Foundations for Service Excellence

Location: Paychex Training and Development Center, Rochester, NY.

Length: 40 hours (5 days).

Dates: January 1996-Present.

Objective: To provide participants with internal and external service strategies, training skills, customer service training techniques, and a basic philosophy of the company on which to build their own successful service strategies.

Learning Outcome: Upon successful completion of this course, the student will be able to describe the Paychex philosophy surrounding our belief in quality client service as one of our primary company goals; create an action plan for implementing new service initiatives into their own branch or department based on the tools and techniques discussed during the week; prepare a lesson plan complete with learner objectives and deliver training on an upcoming session in their branch or department; and utilize new tools and job aids for improving service to customers through effective communication, cooperation, service recovery, problem-solving, and partnering within the Paychex organization.

Instruction: Major topics covered in the course are blueprints for a service culture, the Disney approach to quality service, communication for service excellence, the Paychex Service Exchange, customers as partners, the nature of service, service recovery/problem solving, training adult learners, cooperative learning, creative training techniques, action planning, situational leadership and points of power, and networking. Methods of instruction include instructor presentation, class discussion (instructor facilitated, participant centered), video and written case study, hands-on class activities, field experience, a post-course implementation project, homework assignments, role play demonstrations, evaluation of learner reaction, and evaluation of job performance change through manager observation for 45 days after course ends (minimum 40 hours to complete).

Credit Recommendation: In the lower division baccalaureate/associate or upper division baccalaureate degree category, 2 semester hours in Introduction to Business, Introduction to Management, or Introduction to Quality Control (11/97).

Human Resource Services Sales Training

Location: Paychex Training and Development Center, Rochester, NY.

Length: 120 hours (3 weeks).

Dates: June 1996-Present.

Objective: To provide knowledge of the Human Resource Sales position and the product and sales skills needed to begin a successful career at Paychex.

Learning Outcome: Upon successful completion of this course, the student will be able to explain and demonstrate job expectations; be well versed in all Human Resource products and services; apply successful sales/service techniques; be oriented to the Paychex business culture; and perform their jobs well using the tools to succeed.

Instruction: Major topics covered in the course are Human Resource sales organization, introduction to retirement planning, 401(k), plan administration requirements, Paychex 401(k) recordkeeping service, sales consultant, guidebook, case submission, presentation format, enrollment process, payroll, Paychex financial overview, output reports, introduction to GIANT, health care, concerns in business, Section 125, additional requirements for FSA option, case submission, operations responsibilities, personality profiling, Employee Management System, pricing structure and examples, Employee Handbook Starter Kit, EMS sales application objection handling, HRS Sales Application, telemarketing training, sales cycle comparison, goal setting, and telemarketing day-offsite. Methods of instruction include lecture, discussion, classroom exercises, case studies, audio/visual material, participant presentations, role playing, homework assignments, quizzes, final examination, formal role play demonstrations, and evaluation of learner reaction is completed at the conclusion of the course.

Credit Recommendation: In the lower division baccalaureate/associate or upper division baccalaureate degree category, 3 semester hours in Sales Management or Selling (11/97).

Level 1: Paychex Management Essentials

Location: Paychex Training and Development Center, Rochester, NY.

Length: 40 hours (5 days).

Dates: January 1996-Present.

Objective: To provide first time managers and supervisors in branch, sales, and corporate positions with a management model emphasizing the classic components of planning, organizing, controlling, motivating, communicating, and training and the basic management tools, skills, and interpretations to function within the Paychex culture and the industry.

Learning Outcome: Upon successful completion of this course, the student will be able to identify strategic issues; relate those issues to the Paychex profit and loss statement; determine tactical resolutions and action plans; develop team members in new tasks; delegate tasks to experienced team members; prioritize tasks for accomplishment; and recruit, interview, and select to ensure team continuity.

Instruction: Major topics covered in the course are behavior-based and probing questions, selection process, employee orientation process, situational leadership model, situational leadership, video case study, management theory, trust and its role in management, effective listening techniques harassment prevention problem solving session, performance management, employee counseling and termination, and time management. Methods of instruction include lecture, multi-media presentations, self-awareness tests, interactive exercises, role playing, guest appearances by senior level managers, a post-course implementation project, homework assignments, role play demonstrations, evaluation of learner reaction, and evaluation of job performance change through manager observation for 45 days after course ends (minimum 40 hours to complete).

Credit Recommendation: In the lower division baccalaureate/associate or upper division baccalaureate degree category, 2 semester hours in Business Management or Business Administration (11/97).

Level 2.5: The Developing Paychex Client Services Manager

Location: Paychex Training and Development Center, Rochester, NY.

Length: 46 hours (1 week).

Dates: April 1997-Present.

Objective: To provide participants with the opportunity to focus and develop the leadership skills and business behaviors necessary to successfully run a Paychex branch office.

Learning Outcome: Upon successful completion of this course, the student will be able to demonstrate skills necessary to determine if production or budget is on target or if adjustments are needed; demonstrate fundamental management skills in a professional working environment; effectively communicate with managers of all segments of culture to assist in leading a multi-cultural workforce; develop team members in order to grow operationally as well as professionally promotable; network and connect with corporate staff members as resources and develop working relationships; prepare and present a ten minute professional speech; and demonstrate cost benefit analysis skills to present enhancements and changes within their operations.

Instruction: Major topics covered in the course are process evaluation, sales skills, marketplace research, effective meeting skills, influence skills, leadership and role models, Situational Leadership Review, employee development and coaching, setting expectations and giving feedback, Human Resource Roundtable, Paychex budget process and location, speech and business, case preparation, business behaviors, company ethics/culture, Human Resources Roundtable, and corporate networking. Methods of instruction include instructor presentation, class discussion (instructor facilitated-participant centered), video and written case study, hands-on class activities, field experience, a post-course implementation project, homework assignments, role play demonstrations, evaluation of learner reaction, and evaluation of job performance change through Manager observation for 45 days after course ends (minimum 40 hours to complete).

Credit Recommendation: In the lower division baccalaureate/associate or upper division baccalaureate degree category, 2 semester hours in Introduction to Management, Leadership, or Sales Management (11/97).

Level 2: The Developing Paychex Manager

Location: Paychex Training and Development Center, Rochester, NY.

Length: 43.5 hours (5 days).

Dates: January 1997-Present.

Objective: To develop manager's awareness of budgets and cash flow and techniques for meaningful information gathering to strengthen decision making and develop a higher level of understanding of high litigation costs resulting from hiring or termination errors.

Learning Outcome: Upon successful completion of this course, the student will be able to identify issues related to the Paychex profit and loss statement; determine tactical resolutions and action plans; develop their teams to higher levels of productivity and solidarity; facilitate their plans in highly effective ways; and apply labor laws impacting hiring and terminations.

Instruction: Major topics covered in the course are concept of professional manager, recruiting and managing top performers, motivation and turnover, overview of operations, key business indicators, fiscal management, benchmarking for quality, action plans for continuous, improvement, management by objective's, employee development, developing information and feedback through surveys, Myers Briggs Type Indicators, identifying skill sets, Human Resources Workshop on interviewing, Situational Leadership Model for groups, effective coaching techniques, leadership grid, Paychex leadership ethic, company culture, human resources issues and answers, facilitation skills, and business behaviors. Methods of instruction include instructor presentation, class discussion (instructor facilitated, participant centered), video and written case study, hands-on class activities, evaluation of learner reaction, homework assignments, in-class assignments, presentations, and evaluation of job performance change through Manager observation for 45 days after course ends (minimum 40 hours to complete).

Credit Recommendation: In the lower division baccalaureate/associate or upper division baccalaureate degree category, 1 semester hour in Business Management (11/97).

Level 2: The Developing Paychex Sales Manager

Location: Paychex Training and Development Center, Rochester, NY.

Length: 40.25 hours (1 week).

Dates: January 1996-Present.

Objective: To teach participants how to apply the Situational Leadership Model as a coaching tool for developing disillusioned or plateaued Sales Representatives and to develop an awareness of time and territory management, to develop interviewing skills, and to develop a higher level of understanding of high litigation costs from hiring or termination errors.

Learning Outcome: Upon successful completion of this course, the student will be able to become highly effective interviewers; coach their Sales Representatives to higher levels of performance; reorganize a sales territory; and determine conflict resolution styles.

Instruction: Major topics covered in the course are concept of professional manager, recruiting and managing top performers, motivation and turnover, resume review techniques and interviewing questions, live video interviews and critiques, Myers Briggs Type Indicators, fiscal year action plans, identifying skill sets and employee, development plans, review of Situational Leadership Model, effective coaching techniques, managing conflict and partnership relationships, leadership grid, sales closing, techniques, case study on territory determination, analyzing performance problems, and human resources issues and answers. Methods of instruction include instructor presentation, class discussion (instructor facilitated-participant centered), video and written case study, hands-on class activities, a post-course implementation project, homework assignments, role play demonstrations, evaluation of learner reaction, and evaluation of job performance change through manager observation for 45 days after course ends (minimum 40 hours to complete).

Credit Recommendation: In the lower division baccalaureate/associate or upper division baccalaureate degree category, 1 semester hour in Business Management (11/97).

Level 2: The Developing Paychex Supervisor

Location: Paychex Training and Development Center, Rochester, NY.

Length: 40 hours (5 days).

Dates: November 1996-Present.

Objective: To build upon the objectives of Level 1: Paychex Management Essentials, expanding the Situational Leadership Model to groups and teams. To develop the supervisor's awareness of budgets and cash flow, techniques for meaningful information gathering strengthen decision making and client service, and develop a higher level of understanding of high litigation costs resulting from hiring or termination errors.

Learning Outcome: Upon successful completion of this course, the student will be able to identify elements related to Paychex profit and loss statements; determine resolutions and action plans; develop their teams to higher levels of productivity and solidarity; facilitate their plans in highly effective ways; and apply labor laws impacting interviewing and terminations.

Instruction: Major topics covered in the course are definition of management, key business indicators and fiscal management, benchmarking, tactical objectives, employee development plans, Myers-Briggs Type Indicator, organizing resources, behavior-based questioning, human resource issues and answers, networking, Situational Leadership Model for groups, team development - case study and application, the Paychex culture, business behaviors, and best practices. Methods of instruction include instructor presentation, class discussion (instructor facilitated, participant centered), video and written case studies, guest speaker-led discussions, hands-on class activities, a post-course implementation project, homework assignments, role play demonstrations, evaluation of learner reaction, and a behavioral evaluation through manager observation for 45 days after course ends (minimum 40 hours to complete).

Credit Recommendation: In the lower division baccalaureate/associate or upper division baccalaureate degree category, 1 semester hour in Business Management, Business Administration, or Supervision (11/97).

Level 3: Innovative Leadership Skills

Location: Paychex Training and Development Center, Rochester, NY.

Length: 33.75 hours (4 days).

Dates: April 1994-Present.

Objective: To provide an advanced leadership program focusing on success factors critical for Paychex' continued growth, to provide continued professional study for experienced managers in an ever-changing environment.

Learning Outcome: Upon successful completion of this course, the student will be able to identify strategic issues and develop planning skills as an integral part of problem solving and decision making; identify Key Business Indicators which quickly diagnose the profitability or viability of a branch/department; relate those to the Paychex profit and loss statement; determine tactical resolutions and action plans; be able to facilitate change; and understand personal influence strategies which are used by successful managers at Paychex.

Instruction: Major topics covered in the course are outdoor ropes experience and debriefing, state of branch/district, non-verbal communications, resisting change, paradigms, creativity, developing strategic and tactical objectives, change management, relating change, management to Situational Leadership, networking, personal influence strategies, best practices, and ropes experience. Methods of instruction include instructor presentation, class discussion (instructor facilitated-participant centered), written case study, hands-on class activities, evaluation of learner reaction, homework assignments, in-class assignments, presentations, and evaluation of job performance change through Manager observation for 45 days after course ends (minimum 40 hours to complete).

Credit Recommendation: In the lower division baccalaureate/associate or upper division baccalaureate degree category, 3 semester hours in Business Management, Leadership, or Supervision (11/97).

Major Market Service Training

Location: Paychex Training and Development Center, Rochester, NY.

Length: 80 hours (2 weeks).

Dates: May 1997-Present.

Objective: To provide qualified participants with extensive knowledge of payroll and tax payment law. In addition, participants learn how to effective and efficiently navigate and process client payroll through the Preview Payroll software program.

Learning Outcome: Upon successful completion of this course, the student will be able to explain and demonstrate job expectations; be well versed in all Major Market products and services; apply successful sales and service techniques; be oriented to the Paychex business culture; perform their jobs well using the tools to succeed.

Instruction: Major topics covered in the course are introduction to major market services and preview payroll, system information, function keys and system structure employee entry, begin new pay period, payroll entry, output reports report writer, company set up, conversion and interface overview Human Resources integration, installations, train communication software DOS version, and train communication software Windows version, presentation skills training, and client training role playing. Methods of instruction include lecture, discussion, classroom exercises, case studies, audio/visual material, participant presentations, computer-assisted instruction, homework assignments, final examination, role play demonstrations, and evaluation of learner reaction is completed at the conclusion of the course.

Credit Recommendation: In the lower division baccalaureate/associate degree category, 1 semester hour in Computer Application or Sales Communications (11/97).

Paychex Business Solutions Product & Sales Training

Location: Rochester, NY.

Length: 96 hours (2.5 weeks).

Dates: January 1997-Present.

Objective: To provide knowledge of payroll, Benefit Time Reports, Workers' Compensation reports, health insurance, and Sales Service Skills in prospecting tips, fact gathering, and final risk analysis.

Learning Outcome: Upon successful completion of this course, the student will be able to recognize the sales force, products, Benefit Time Reports, applications to payroll, PBS reports, and 401(k) plans; utilize presentation techniques; and present various payroll packets.

Instruction: Major topics covered in the course are sales force and products, organizational information, benefit time and reporting, workers compensation and reporting, payroll and PBS reports, Section 125, 401(k), health insurance, COBRA, human resources, PBS Payroll System, corporate networking, prospecting, PBS/HRS sales/conversion process, implementation plan, fact gathering meeting, the proposal process and system, closing meeting, client contact meeting, orientation meeting, Paylink overview, consultant Guide Book, sales (prospecting tips, fact gathering tips, proposal generation, presentation tips, closing meeting tips, final risk analysis), and sales/CSR. Methods of instruction include lecture, discussion, classroom exercises, audio/visual material, computer-assisted instruction, learner presentations/reports, homework assignments, quizzes, and final examination.

Credit Recommendation: In the lower division baccalaureate/associate degree category, 3 semester hours in Business Solutions, Business Problems, or Sales Techniques (11/97).

Paylink Specialist Training

Location: Paychex Training and Development Center, Rochester, NY.

Length: 40.25 hours (5 days).

Dates: February 1998-Present.

Objective: To provide a basic understanding of preferences, security applications, retrieve and process files, selections, audit reports, and close and send files, and using data exports.

Learning Outcome: Upon successful completion of this course, the student will be able to import conversion or simple ASCII interface in Paylink (an automated payroll system) in DOS and Windows formats; operate modems; and download processing, troubleshooting, and set-up procedures.

Instruction: Major topics covered in the course are Advanced Paylink applications; payroll entry; system configuration;

import basics and advanced import for Paylink; memory management; modem/communication networks; and client set-up, directory, structures, and troubleshooting. Methods of instruction include lecture, discussion, classroom exercises, case studies, audio-visual material, participant presentations, computer-assisted instruction, homework assignments, final examination, role play demonstrations, and evaluation of learner reaction is completed at the conclusion of the course.

Credit Recommendation: In the lower division baccalaureate/associate degree category, 1 semester hour in Payroll Applications/Business Applications (11/97).

Payroll Sales Training

Location: Paychex Training and Development Center, District office

Length: 40 hours (1 week) in district, 80 hours (2 weeks) in Rochester, 80 hours (2 weeks) in district, 80 hours (2 weeks) in Rochester.

Dates: June 1996-Present.

Objective: To provide an understanding of payroll tax payments, tax liability, ancillary products and services, sales presentation and telemarketing practices, and field applications and provide a knowledge of field applications, output reports, general accounting principles, sales presentation analysis, selling value and discounting, and expecting referrals.

Learning Outcome: Upon successful completion of this course, the student will be able to complete federal withholdings and social security; process new client payrolls and voluntary adjustments; practice sales presentations; handle objections; complete a telemarketing exercise offsite; review field applications; complete output reports; post to General Ledger; perform a sales presentation analysis; and incorporate competitive selling principles.

Instruction: Major topics covered in the course are Payroll Sales Product Training 1, introduction to payroll, federal tax liability, FUTA, adjustments, new client processing, direct deposit, tax pay, output reports, Electronic Federal Tax Payment System, and year end reporting; Payroll Sales Product Training 2, restaurant payrolls, TEFRA/TRAC, output reports, new load workshop, Paylink, Section 125 Premium Only Plan, third party sick pay/disability, general accounting, principles, general ledger posting, Scenario Workshop, and Expecting Referrals Workshop; Payroll Sales Skills Training 1, goal setting and business plans, time and territory management, prospecting, the sales presentation, end user, CPA, sales binder presentation, techniques, SPIN sales techniques, competition objection handling/video, and telemarketing; and Payroll Sales Skills Training 2, effective follow-up/video, guest CPA presentation, accountant development, sales presentation analysis/SPIN competitive selling, Human Resource Services Overview, selling value and discounting, national sales support networking, guest sales representative, and Expecting Referrals Workshop. Methods of instruction include lecture, discussion, classroom exercises, case studies, audio/visual material, role play exercises, quizzes, final examination, and formal role play demonstrations.

Credit Recommendation: *Payroll Sales Training 1:* In the lower division baccalaureate/associate degree category, 4 semester hours Payroll Applications; and *Payroll Sales Training 2:* In the lower division baccalaureate/associate degree category, 4 semester hours in Sales, Business Sales, Sales Techniques, Case Studies in Marketing, or Introduction to Marketing (for a total credit recommendation of 8 semester hours) (11/97).

Payroll Specialist Training

Location: Rochester, NY.

Length: 80 hours (2 weeks).

Dates: April 1997-Present.

Objective: To provide and understanding of the History of Paychex, product lines, Client Alert Tracers, the payroll system, Federal Liability, Third Party Sick Pay, and managing appointment schedules.

Learning Outcome: Upon successful completion of this course, the student will be able to respond to client questions; handle payroll errors; identify the four components of federal income withholding taxes; and identify the components of the payroll system.

Instruction: Major topics covered in the course are a review of the introduction to payroll including, payroll check definitions, statutory deductions, Federal Income Withholding Tax, payroll taxes, and exempt compensation; payroll taking including, distributed earnings, correcting vouchers, voucher calculation, terminations, on-line reports system/X Term Browser; output reports including, per pay period, optional, quarterly, federal tax liability, Federal Unemployment Tax, adjustments and category codes new client processing, client/employee master screens, ancillary products and services, direct deposit, and tax pay; business discussions with executive management; restaurant payrolls; quarter end; stress management; corporate networking; and appointment schedule management. Methods of instruction include lecture, discussion, classroom exercises, computer-assisted instruction, homework assignments, quizzes, and final examinations.

Credit Recommendation: In the lower division baccalaureate/associate degree category, 3 semester hours in Payroll Applications or Business/Accounting Applications (11/97).

Peachbottom Atomic Power Station

PECO Energy Company's Nuclear Training Group provides its nuclear personnel with educational opportunities to improve their scientific and engineering levels of expertise, as well as their technical knowledge and skills to ensure the safe and economical operation of the Peach Bottom Atomic Power Plant and the Limerick Generating Station.

Drawing upon the combined expertise of a cadre of experienced educators and technical personnel, the Nuclear Training Groups have developed a wide range of technical, engineering, management, and operations programs, which provide guidance for the Nuclear Group training activities within the company.

Source of official student records: Registry of Credit Recommendations, American Council on Education, One Dupont Circle, Washington, DC 20036-1193 or Director of Training, Peach Bottom Atomic Power Station, 1848 Lay Road, Delta, PA 17314; Director of Training, Limerick Training Center, 341 Longview Road, Linfield, PA 19468 .

Additional information about the courses: College Credit Recommendation Service, American Council on Education, One Dupont Circle, Washington, DC 20036-1193.

Accident and Transient Analysis

Location: Peach Bottom Training Center, Delta, PA, and Limerick Training Center, Linfield, PA.

Length: 42 hours.

Dates: September 1981-Present.

Objective: To provide instruction on accident and transient analysis as it applies to reactor operations personnel.

Learning Outcome: Upon successful completion of this course, the student will be able to describe adverse affects of various transients; discuss safety actions required during various transients; discuss the function of systems that mitigate core damage during various transients, and discuss instrument responses during various transients.

Instruction: Major topics covered in the course are transient and accident analysis, core cooling, potentially damaging operating condition, recognizing core damage, core damage migration and various hazards. Methods of instruction include lecture, simulation training, and discussion.

Credit Recommendation: In the lower division baccalaureate/associate degree category, 1 semester hour in Nuclear Engineering Technology (5/90) (12/95). **NOTE:** Students must complete Reactor Operator Training or Generic Fundamentals/LOT to receive credit.

Advanced Nuclear Power Plant Systems NESP-ASYS-01 through 08

Location: Peach Bottom Training Center, Delta, PA, and Limerick Training Center, Linfield, PA.

Length: 288 hours (8 weeks).

Dates: February 1994-Present.

Objective: To give the student an in-depth knowledge of the operation of Nuclear Power Plant Systems.

Learning Outcome: Upon successful completion of this course, the student will be able to state design bases of studied systems, describe function, operation and flow path for the systems, understand response to transients, and use the plant Technical Specifications to recognize conditions of non-compliance and appropriate corrective actions.

Instruction: Major topics covered in the course are eight modules (each module covers a particular critical plant system, the first two modules provide an overview to plant systems, the remaining six cover main generator and auxiliary systems, reactor control support systems, nuclear instrumentation, containment systems, plant systems, and balance of plant), system operations, interlocks, control room indications, system interrelations, use of station prints and references, and application of plant technical specifications. Methods of instruction include lecture, discussion, and simulator training.

Credit Recommendation: In the lower division baccalaureate/associate degree category, 3 semester hours in Nuclear Energy Technology (12/95). **NOTE:** Basic Nuclear Power Plant Systems is a course prerequisite. Students may not also obtain credit for Reactor Safety Systems or Reactor Support Systems.

Basic Nuclear Physics

Location: Peach Bottom Training Center, Delta, PA and Limerick Training Center, Linfield, PA.

Length: 41.5 hours.

Dates: August 1981-Present.

Objective: To provide the student with knowledge to describe nuclear processes and the production of energy from nuclear fission.

Learning Outcome: Upon successful completion of this course, the student will be able to describe atomic and nuclear structure and understand nuclear processes including decay, fission, and reaction energies.

Instruction: Major topics covered in the course are atomic structure, mass defect and binding energy, nuclear fission and energy production, radioactive decay and radiation, and interactions of radiation and matter. Methods of instruction include lecture.

Credit Recommendation: In the lower division baccalaureate/associate degree category, 2 semester hours in Nuclear Engineering Technology (5/90) (12/95). **NOTE:** Students must complete Reactor Operator Training or Generic Fundamentals/LOT to receive credit.

Basic Nuclear Power Plant Systems/NESP-OSYS

Location: Peach Bottom Training Center, Delta, PA, and Limerick Training Center, Linfield, PA.

Length: 120 hours (3 weeks).

Dates: October 1989-Present.

Objective: To provide the student with knowledge of the fundamentals of the major components of a nuclear power plant.

Learning Outcome: Upon successful completion of this course, the student will be able to describe the purpose and operation of major components of a nuclear power plant.

Instruction: Major topics covered in the course are boiling water steam loop; reactor vessel construction; instrumentation; fuel and control rods; control systems; protection systems; reactor water cleanup; containment and support systems; ventilation; pressure relief; condensate and feedwater systems; main generator and auxiliary systems. Methods of instruction include lecture and examinations.

Credit Recommendation: In the lower division baccalaureate/associate degree category, 3 semester hours in Nuclear Engineering Technology (12/95).

Chemistry/NSP 2.0

Location: Peach Bottom Training Center, Delta, PA, and Limerick Training Center, Linfield, PA.

Length: 920 hours (23 weeks).

Dates: December 1985-Present.

Objective: To provide the student with instruction in chemistry fundamentals, requirements and analysis methods as related to power plant water chemistry.

Learning Outcome: Upon successful completion of this course, the student will be able to demonstrate competency in the performance of analytical methods related to water chemistry and radiochemistry associated with the operation of nuclear power plants, demonstrate the ability to comply with various standards and regulations involving water chemistry and effluent releases, perform functions and analyses necessary to determine and maintain reactor water chemistry, determine the extent of core damage, and perform offsite dose calculations required during accident conditions.

Instruction: Major topics covered in the course are chemistry fundamentals, analysis techniques and instrumentation, and chemistry as applied to nuclear power plant operation. Methods of instruction include lecture, classroom exercises, and on-the-job training. Methods of instruction include quizzes, examinations, and on-the-job training evaluations.

Credit Recommendation: In the lower division baccalaureate/associate degree category, 5 semester hours in General Chemistry, in the upper division baccalaureate degree category, 3 semester hours in Radiochemistry, 4 semester hours in Analytical Chemistry or Instrument Analysis (12/95).

Electrical Fundamentals

Location: Peach Bottom Training Center, Delta, PA, and Limerick Training Center, Linfield, PA.

Length: *Version 1:* 146 hours (106 hours lectures, discussions, exams; 40 hours on-the-job training); *Version 2:* 414 hours (11 weeks).

Dates: *Version 1:* August 1981-May 1992; *Version 2:* June 1992-Present.

Objective: *Version 1:* To provide the student with a basic understanding of AC circuit fundamentals, DC circuit theory, and an introduction to nuclear plant power generation. *Version 2:* To provide student with a basic understanding of AC and DC circuits; basic AC and DC machines; and high voltage distribution systems; and auxiliary power systems.

Learning Outcome: *Version 1:* Upon successful completion of this course, the student will be able to describe atomic structure and discuss electron shells and valence electrons; define and explain basic electricity and magnetism laws; apply Ohm's and Kirchhoff's laws; describe electrical circuit components; and explain magnetism and topics related to transformers, motors, generators, and circuit breakers. *Version 2:* Upon successful completion of this course, the student will be able to explain AC and DC circuits and transformer circuits; AC and DC motor and generator operation; power plant and distribution circuits including 13 KV equipment operation; protection circuits; and electrical safety and precautions.

Instruction: *Version 1:* Major topics covered in the course are principles of electricity; the structure of matter; Coulomb's law; electric field phenomena; current, voltage, resistance, and Ohm's law; also included is an introduction to AC and DC circuit analysis; and principles of magnetism including molecular theory of magnetism, magnetic flux, inductance, and applications in electrical devices. Methods of instruction include lectures, discussions, and on-the-job training. *Version 2:* Major topics of covered in the course are an introduction to DC and AC circuit analysis; principles of magnetism and transformers; AC and DC motors and generators. Also covered are power plant equipment including electrical components, protective equipment, diesel auxiliary equipment, instrument and control systems, substation system, and 13 KV and 480 V distribution. Methods of instruction include lecture, discussion, classroom exercises, simulator and OJT.

Credit Recommendation: *Version 1:* In the lower division baccalaureate/associate degree category, 3 semester hours in Electrical Technology (5/90). *Version 2:* In the lower division baccalaureate/associate degree category, 3 semester hours in AC-DC circuits, 3 semester hours in AC-DC Motors and Generators, or 1 semester hour in Nuclear Technology Laboratory (12/95). **NOTE:** Students must complete Reactor Operator Training or Generic Fundamentals/LOT to receive credit.

Electro-Hydraulic Control Logic (Formerly Process Instrumentation and Control)

Location: Peach Bottom Training Center, Delta, PA, and Limerick Training Center, Linfield, PA.

Length: 47 hours (2 weeks).

Dates: June 1992-Present.

Objective: To provide students with knowledge of Electro-Hydraulic Control Systems.

Learning Outcome: Upon successful completion of this course, the student will be able to explain basic Electro-Hydraulic Control Logic and its application to nuclear power plants.

Instruction: Major topics covered in the course are EHC logic components; cause/effect applications in a reactor facility; and malfunction analysis of EHC in Nuclear Power Plant. Methods of instruction include lecture, an examination, and laboratory exercises.

Credit Recommendation: In the lower division baccalaureate/associate degree category, 1 semester hour in Nuclear Technology Laboratory (12/95).

Health Physics

Location: Peach Bottom Training Center, Delta, PA and Limerick Training Center, Linfield, PA.

Length: 48 hours.

Dates: September 1981-Present.

Objective: To provide introduction to health physics, radiation protection, and radioactive material handling procedures.

Learning Outcome: Upon successful completion of this course, the student will be able to discuss properties and biological effects of radiation, radiation exposure limit, and methods of limiting exposure; define units of exposure; and understand procedures for handling radioactive materials and waste.

Instruction: Major topics covered in the course are radioactive decay, shielding, biological effects of radiation, dosimetry, shielding, radioactive material handling, and waste disposal. Methods of instruction include lecture, discussion, and laboratory.

Credit Recommendation: In the lower division baccalaureate/associate degree category, 1 semester hour in Nuclear Science or Health Physics (5/90) (12/95). **NOTE:** Students must complete Reactor Operator Training or Generic Fundamentals/LOT to receive credit.

Health Physics Technician

Location: Peach Bottom Training Center, Delta, PA, and Limerick Training Center, Linfield, PA.

Length: 208 hours (28 classroom/laboratory, 180 of supervised on-the-job training).

Dates: June 1992-Present.

Objective: To provide the student with instruction in health physics, radiation management, contamination control, and radioactive material handling techniques and procedures.

Learning Outcome: Upon successful completion of this course, the student will have demonstrated competency in health physics and radiation protection practices, thereby assuring compliance with various standards and regulatory requirements. Specifically, the student will have demonstrated the ability to operate radiation detection instrumentation, evaluate data to determine personnel protection requirements, perform radiation/contamination surveys, properly control radioactive material, and respond to emergency situations involving radiation/contamination.

Instruction: Major topics covered in the course are science and mathematical background skills, radiation decay, shielding, biological effects of radiation, dosi-metry, instrumentation, contamination and airborne surveys, radioactive material control, decontamination techniques and administrative requirements. Methods of instruction include lecture, classroom ex-ercises, comprehensive on-the-job experience, supervised on-the-job training, quizzes, unit examinations, and final examinations.

Credit Recommendation: In the upper division baccalaureate degree category or in the lower division baccalaureate/associate degree category, 3 semester hours in Health Physics (12/95).

Heat Transfer and Fluid Flow

Location: Peach Bottom Training Center, Delta, PA, and Limerick Training Center, Linfield, PA.

Length: *Version 1:* 61 hours; *Version 2:* 94 hours (69 hours of lecture, 25 hours of simulation).

Dates: September 1981-Present.

Objective: To introduce students to heat transfer, fluid flow, and their application to heat exchangers.

Learning Outcome: Upon successful completion of this course, the student will be able to define and discuss Bernoulli's equation, laminar and turbulent fluid flow, fluid friction, pressure measurements, and the principles of operation of pumps and valves. They will be able to describe heat transfer and heat exchangers; and understand heat generation, heat flow, and heat distribution in a boiling water reactor.

Instruction: Major topics covered in the course are fluid statics and dynamics, Bernoulli's equation, laminar and turbulent flow, pumps and valves, heat transfer in fluids, heat exchangers, and heat generation and distribution in a boiling water reactor. Methods of instruction include lecture, discussion, and laboratory.

Credit Recommendation: In the lower division baccalaureate/associate degree category, 2 semester hours in Nuclear Engineering Technology (5/90) (12/95). **NOTE:** Students must complete Reactor Operator Training or Generic Fundamentals/LOT to receive credit.

Integrated Nuclear Power Plant Operation NESP/IPO

Location: Peach Bottom Training Center, Delta, PA, and Limerick Training Center, Linfield, PA.

Length: 160 hours (4 weeks).

Dates: June 1994-Present.

Objective: To provide an understanding of plant operating procedures, the Technical Specifications and the integrated operation of plant systems.

Learning Outcome: Upon successful completion of this course, the student will learn how to use Technical Specifications and plant procedures to determine if reactor or fuel integrity has been compromised for any given plant scenario. The student will understand appropriate corrective actions and the implementation of Special Event Plant Procedures.

Instruction: Major topics covered in the course are operational transients, off-normal conditions, transient response, special event procedures, and general plant procedures. Methods of instruction include lecture, discussion, and simulation training. A major portion of the course involves the use of the plant simulator.

Credit Recommendation: In the lower division baccalaureate/associate degree category, 2 semester hours in Nuclear Engineering Technology (12/95). **NOTE:** Basic Nuclear Power Plant Systems is a course prerequisite. Credit may also be obtained for Advanced Nuclear Power Plant Systems. A student may not also receive credit for Reactor Safety Systems or Reactor Support Systems.

Introduction to Reactor Engineering (Reactor Engineering I and II)

Location: Peach Bottom Training Center, Delta, PA and Limerick Training Center, Linfield, PA.

Length: 97 hours.

Dates: September 1981-Present.

Objective: To provide students with instruction on the fundamentals of reactor physics and an introduction to reactor engineering concepts.

Learning Outcome: Upon successful completion of this course, the student will be able to define neutron moderation and behavior; discuss neutron kinetics; define effective multiplication factor and criticality; describe reactor coefficients; and describe reactor control and flux shape.

Instruction: Major topics covered in the course are neutron thermalization, moderators, four- and six-factor formulas, multiplication factors, reactivity, neutron sources, subcritical multiplication, prompt and delayed neutrons, reactor period, void coefficient, Doppler coefficient, burnable poisons and control rods, fusion product poisoning, decay heat, and fuel properties and design. Methods of instruction include lecture, discussion, and simulator training.

Credit Recommendation: In the lower division baccalaureate/associate degree category, 2 semester hours in Nuclear Engineering Technology (5/90) (12/95). **NOTE:** Students must complete Reactor Operator Training or Generic Fundamentals/LOT to receive credit.

Normal, Abnormal, and Reactor Operational Procedures

Location: Peach Bottom Training Center, Delta, PA, and Limerick Training Center, Linfield, PA.

Length: *Version 1:* 133 hours; *Version 2:* 97 hours.

Dates: *Version 1:* June 1981-May 1992; *Version 2:* June 1992-Present.

Objective: To provide instruction on normal, abnormal, and reactor operational procedures as they apply to reactor operations personnel.

Learning Outcome: Upon successful completion of this course, the student will be able to state the purpose for the various procedures; categorize certain procedures and state immediate operator actions; give bases for various procedures; demonstrate ability to use various procedures; and show where and how diagnostic methods are applied.

Instruction: Major topics covered in the course are procedures for emergency planning, operational transients, off-normal, various trips, and special events. Diagnostic skills are developed as applied to the various procedures. Methods of instruction include lecture and discussion.

Credit Recommendation: *Version 1:* In the upper division baccalaureate degree category, 3 semester hours in Nuclear Plant Management (5/90). *Version 2:* In the upper division baccalaureate degree category, 2 semester hours in Nuclear Plant Management (12/95). **NOTE:** Students must complete Reactor Operator Training or Generic Fundamentals/LOT to receive credit.

Process Instrumentation and Control

Location: Peach Bottom Atomic Center, Delta, PA, and Limerick Training Center, Linfield, PA.

Length: 68 hours (32 hours lecture; 40 hours on-the-job training).

Dates: November 1984-June 1992.

Objective: To provide the student with instruction on basic instrumentation and measurement devices and an understanding of process control as applied to a nuclear generating facility.

Learning Outcome: Upon successful completion of this course, the student will be able to explain basic logic elements such as "and", or, "not" gates, coincidence, time delay, and memory units; describe various plant control and measurement instruments; and identify components on diagrams.

Instruction: Major topics covered in the course are instrument and control fundamentals, measurement devices, process control fundamentals, and process loop diagrams. Methods of instruction include lecture, discussion, and on-the-job training.

Credit Recommendation: In the lower division baccalaureate/associate degree category, 2 semester hours in Electrical Technology (5/90) (12/95). **NOTE:** Students must complete Reactor Operator Training or Generic Fundamentals/LOT to receive credit.

Radiation Detection Principles and Neutron Monitoring Instruments

Location: Peach Bottom Training Center, Delta, PA, and Limerick Training Center, Linfield, PA.

Length: *Version 1:* 67.5 hours; *Version 2:* 83 hours (3 weeks).

Dates: *Version 1:* September 1981-May 1992; *Version 2:* June 1992-Present.

Objective: To introduce students to the fundamentals of radiation detection and measurement.

Learning Outcome: Upon successful completion of this course, the student will be able to discuss the principles of operation of radiation detectors and counters and understand monitoring of process radiation and of associated systems and areas.

Instruction: *Version 1:* Methods of instruction include lecture, discussion, and laboratory. *Version 2:* Methods of instruction include lecture, simulation, and on-the-job training.

Credit Recommendation: *Version 1:* In the lower division baccalaureate/associate degree category, 1 semester hour in Nuclear Engineering Technology or Radiation Protection Technology (5/90). *Version 2:* In the lower division baccalaureate/associate degree category, 2 semester hours in Nuclear Engineering Technology (12/95). **NOTE:** Students must complete Reactor Operator Training or Generic Fundamentals/LOT to receive credit.

Reactor Operation Technical Specifications

Location: Peach Bottom Training Center, Delta, PA, and Limerick Training Center, Linfield, PA.

Length: *Version 1:* 72 hours; *Version 2:* 109 hours (4 weeks).

Dates: *Version 1:* September 1981-May 1992; *Version 2:* June 1992-Present.

Objective: To provide instruction on technical specifications, administrative procedures, and controls as they apply to reactor operations personnel.

Learning Outcome: Upon successful completion of this course, the student will be able to state the purposes and define terms in administrative procedures and controls; state purposes for, state bases for, list various limits, set points, and conditions for safety limits and limiting safety system settings; and identify areas of noncompliance and necessary actions where applicable.

Instruction: Major topics covered in the course are administrative procedures; introduction to technical specifications and related definitions; technical specification safety limits, limiting safety systems, the systems that perform reactor water cleanup main steam and pressure relief, drywell chilled water, containment atmosphere control, steam supply shutoff, and post-accident sampling. Also covered are primary and secondary containment and drywell and reactor enclosure ventilation. Methods of instruction include lecture, discussion, and laboratory.

Credit Recommendation: In the upper division baccalaureate degree category, 2 semester hours in Nuclear Plant Management (5/90) (12/95). **NOTE:** Students must complete Reactor Operator Training or Generic Fundamentals/LOT to receive credit.

Reactor Safety Systems

Location: Peach Bottom Training Center, Delta, PA, and Limerick Training Center, Linfield, PA.

Length: *Version 1:* 93 hours; *Version 2:* 134 hours (5 weeks).

Dates: *Version 1:* September 1981-May 1992; *Version 2:* June 1992-Present.

Objective: To familiarize the student with plant reactor safety system function and components and to provide an introduction to system operational aspects and their effect on safe plant operation.

Learning Outcome: Upon successful completion of this course, the student will be able to list or state the purpose of each of the various systems; state various system parameters and list set points; identify, discuss, and explain the function of the various systems components; describe interrelationship between various systems; and identify trips and technical specification noncompliance and the appropriate operator actions.

Instruction: *Version 1:* Major topics covered in the course are the systems that provide reactor protection, standby liquid control, automatic depressurization, high pressure coolant injection, core spray, residual heat removal, and emergency service water and loss of coolant water accident scenario. Methods of instruction include lecture, discussion, and laboratory. *Version 2:* Major topics covered in the course are the systems that provide reactor protection, standby liquid control, automatic depressurization, high pressure coolant injection, core spray, residual heat removal, and emergency service water and loss of coolant water accident scenario, standby liquid control, reactor water cleanup, reactor core isolation, and core spray system. Methods of instruction include lecture, discussion, and laboratory.

Credit Recommendation: *Version 1:* In the lower division baccalaureate/associate degree category, 2 semester hours in Nuclear Engineering Technology (5/90). *Version 2:* In the lower division baccalaureate/associate degree category, 3 semester hours in Nuclear Engineering Technology (12/95). **NOTE:** Students must complete Reactor Operator Training or Generic Fundamentals/LOT to receive credit.

Reactor Support Systems

Location: Peach Bottom Training Center, Delta, PA, and Limerick Training Center, Linfield, PA.

Length: *Version 1:* 72 hours; *Version 2:* 152 hours (4 weeks).

Dates: *Version 1:* September 1981-May 1992; *Version 2:* June 1992-Present.

Objective: To familiarize the student with various nuclear reactor support systems, their operational characteristics, and their impact on safe plant operations.

Learning Outcome: Upon successful completion of this course, the student will be able to identify, discuss, and explain the function of various systems components; identify technical specifications noncompliance associated with various systems and determine appropriate action; and state various systems parameters and list set points.

Instruction: *Version 1:* Major topics covered in the course are the systems that perform reactor water cleanup, main steam and pressure relief, drywell chilled water, containment atmosphere control, steam supply shutoff, and post-accident sampling, primary and secondary containment, and drywell and reactor enclosure ventilation. Methods of instruction include lecture, discussion, and laboratory. *Version 2:* Major topics covered in the course are the systems that perform reactor water cleanup, main steam and pressure relief, drywell chilled water, containment atmosphere control, steam supply shutoff, and post-accident sampling, primary and secondary containment, drywell and reactor enclosure ventilation, reactor water cleanup, primary containment, containment atmosphere control and dilution, and residual heat removal. Methods of instruction include lecture, discussion, and laboratory.

Credit Recommendation: *Version 1:* In the lower division baccalaureate/associate degree category, 1 semester hour in Nuclear Engineering Technology (5/90). *Version 2:* In the lower division baccalaureate/associate degree category, 3 semester hours in Nuclear Engineering Technology (12/95). **NOTE:** Students must complete Reactor Operator Training or Generic Fundamentals/LOT to receive credit.

Thermodynamics I

Location: Peach Bottom Training Center, Delta, PA, and Limerick Training Center, Linfield, PA.

Length: *Version 1:* 189 hours; *Version 2:* 76 hours (26 hours lecture/discussion; 10 hours simulation, 40 hours on-the-job training).

Dates: *Version 1:* August 1981-May 1992; *Version 2:* June 1992-Present.

Objective: To provide the student with instruction in energy, phase changes, and the first law of thermodynamics.

Learning Outcome: Upon successful completion of this course, the student will be able to define and interpret thermodynamic quantities such as energy, entropy enthalpy, phase changes, and the first law of thermodynamics and determine thermodynamic quantities using steam tables, Mollier diagrams, and phase diagrams.

Instruction: Major topics covered in the course are work, energy, and power; phases of matter and phase changes; and first law of thermodynamics. Methods of instruction include lecture, laboratory work, and discussion.

Credit Recommendation: *Version 1:* In the upper division baccalaureate degree category, 3 semester hours in Nuclear Engineering Technology, Physics, or Chemistry (5/90). *Version 2:* In the upper division baccalaureate degree category, 1 semester hour in Nuclear Engineering Technology, Physics, or Chemistry (12/95).

Thermodynamics II

Location: Peach Bottom Training Center, Delta, PA, and Limerick Training Center, Linfield, PA.

Length: *Version 1:* 51 hours; *Version 2:* 80 hours (40 hours lecture/discussion; 40 hours on-the-job training).

Dates: *Version 1:* August 1981-May 1992; *Version 2:* June 1992-Present.

Objective: To provide the student with an understanding of the second law of thermodynamics and applications to Rankine and Carnot cycles.

Learning Outcome: Upon successful completion of this course, the student will be able to interpret the thermodynamic factors affecting the efficiencies of heat engines; calculate efficiencies of the Rankine and Carnot cycles; and describe the operation of heat exchangers.

Instruction: Major topics covered in the course are heat exchangers, second law of thermodynamics, heat engine efficiency, the Rankine and Carnot cycles, and plant efficiency. Methods of instruction include lecture, discussion, and laboratory work.

Credit Recommendation: In the upper division baccalaureate degree category, 1 semester hour in Nuclear Engineering Technology, Physics, or Chemistry (5/90) (12/95).

Water Chemistry and Material Science

Location: Peach Bottom Training Center, Delta, PA, and Limerick Training Center, Linfield, PA.

Length: *Version 1:* 20 hours; *Version 2:* 48 hours (2 weeks).

Dates: *Version 1:* September 1981-May 1992; *Version 2:* June 1992-Present.

Objective: To introduce students to fundamentals of water chemistry and material strength and corrosion.

Learning Outcome: Upon successful completion of this course, the student will be able to discuss chemical properties that affect the quality of reactor cooling water, water conditioning and the corrosion of metals and describe factors relating to strength of materials.

Instruction: Major topics covered in the course are fundamentals of water quality; basic chemical analyses; physical and chemical methods of improving water quality; corrosion; materials stress, strain, and failure. Methods of instruction include lecture, discussion, and laboratory.

Credit Recommendation: *Version 1:* In the lower division baccalaureate/associate degree category, 1 semester hour in Chemistry (5/90). *Version 2:* In the lower division baccalaureate/associate degree category, 2 semester hours in Water Chemistry or Chemistry (12/95).

Pennsylvania School of Muscle Therapy, Ltd.

The Pennsylvania School of Muscle Therapy, Ltd., founded in 1980, is dedicated to providing superior education in the science and art of massage therapy. The school's mission is "to educate and train dedicated individuals to provide professional quality massage therapy in order to promote the health and well-being of humanity while bringing due recognition to the art and science of massage." To fulfill this, PSMT offers a variety of courses to meet the needs of both the beginner and the professional bodyworker.

PSMT basic course offerings include Swedish Massage, Anatomy and Physiology, and Pathology. Taken together, these three basic courses comprise a complete educational program for prospective bodyworkers. It is the first COMTAA-accredited program in the tri-state area. Successful program graduates attain full status as professional massage therapists and automatically qualify for full active membership in the American Massage Therapy Association and Associated Bodywork and Massage Professionals. In addition to the theory and practice of massage, anatomy and physiology, and pathology, subjects studied in the basic course program include sports massage, business and professional ethics, hydrotherapy, CPR, and first aid. PSMT also offers a course in Shiatsu for those wishing to learn the basics of Oriental Massage. This course satisfies the requirements for licensing in New York State.

PSMT offers several advanced courses for experienced bodyworkers who wish to increase their hands-on skills and deepen their knowledge of the sciences. These include Pfrimmer Deep Muscle Therapy®, Advanced Techniques, Advanced Anatomy and Physiology, Kinesiology, and Orthopedic Assessment. PSMT is one of only two schools in the world to offer training in Pfrimmer Deep Muscle Therapy.

All courses are taught by experienced professionals who are well established in the field and trained in educational techniques, ensuring the highest quality training and education. Courses are conducted in a pleasant, serene learning environment in Wayne, Pennsylvania, a suburb of Philadelphia. A variety of class times provides PSMT students with choice and flexibility to meet their diverse scheduling needs.

Source of official student records: Registry of Credit Recommendations, American Council on Education, One Dupont Circle, Washington, DC 20036-1193.

Additional information about the courses: College Credit Recommendation Service, American Council on Education, One Dupont Circle, Washington, DC 20036-1193.

Anatomy and Physiology II (8)
(Advanced Anatomy and Physiology)

Location: Wayne, PA.

Length: 72 hours (24 days).

Dates: June 1994-Present.

Objective: To provide the student with continued study of human anatomy and physiology with significant emphasis on the musculoskeletal and nervous systems.

Learning Outcome: Upon successful completion of this course, the student will be able to identify and describe human anatomical structures, explain the functions of the organ systems, and describe the major physiological processes.

Instruction: Major topics covered in the course are the anatomy and physiology of the cardiovascular, respiratory, digestive, endocrine, nervous systems, the physiology of the organ systems with emphasis placed on the study of the anatomy and physiology of the musculoskeletal and nervous systems. Methods of instruction include lectures and demonstrations but exclude conventional laboratory exercises.

Credit Recommendation: In the lower division baccalaureate/associate degree category, 3 semester hours in Anatomy and Physiology (8/96).

Basic Orthopedic Assessment (11)
(Understanding and Responding to Orthopedic Complaints for the Massage Therapist)

Location: Wayne, PA.

Length: 40 hours (7 days).

Dates: June 1996-Present.

Objective: To instruct students in elementary physical assessment procedures for musculoskeletal dysfunction.

Learning Outcome: Upon successful completion of this course, the student will be able to identify and describe basic causes of musculoskeletal dysfunction and to apply and interpret basic musculoskeletal assessment tests.

Instruction: Major topics covered in the course are musculoskeletal conditions and soft tissue assessment. Methods of instruction include lectures, demonstrations, video presentations, and lab work.

Credit Recommendation: In the lower division baccalaureate/associate degree category, 2 semester hours in Orthopedic Assessment (8/96).

Evaluation and Correction of the Muscular System Through Massage Therapy (3)
(Evaluation and Correction of the Muscular System Through Advanced Techniques)

Location: Wayne, PA.

Length: 40 hours (5 days).

Dates: February 1985-Present.

Objective: To instruct graduates of the Pfrimmer Deep Muscle Therapy® course and other experienced body workers to develop and refine the skills of palpation and correction of difficult muscle problems.

Learning Outcome: Upon successful completion of this course, the student will be able to prepare a written evaluation and treatment plan for clients, muscular and joint irregularities, perform both a quick and an extended structural balancing on a client, perform muscular and joint corrective troubleshooting, and perform remedial neck, back and abdominal exercises for the client/therapist.

Instruction: Major topics covered in the course are plumb line and movement evaluation, joint ROM evaluation, table evaluations, hands-on evaluation and correction with myofascial release, and evaluating and correcting tissue tension with Gentle Fascial Release®. Methods of in-struction include lectures, team work, role plays, presentations, and hands-on demonstrations.

Credit Recommendation: In the lower division baccalaureate/associate degree category, 1 semester hour in Massage (8/96).

Introduction to Kinesiology (10)
(Science of Kinesiology)

Location: Wayne, PA.

Length: 60 hours (10 days).

Dates: June 1996-Present.

Objective: To provide an introduction to the scientific study of human movement.

Learning Outcome: Upon successful completion of this course, the student will be able to explain the basic principles of the laws of motion; describe the body structures that produce and regulate human motion; explain the physiological and mechanical processes involved in skeletal muscle function; and identify the movements that are available at the major synovial joints and how these movements are controlled.

Instruction: Major topics covered in the course are the entire musculoskeletal system, muscle contraction, and biomechanics. This course excludes the study of gait or movement analysis, but includes an in-depth study of muscle and joint function. Methods of instruction include lectures, demonstrations, lab work, video presentations, and overhead presentations.

Credit Recommendation: In the lower division baccalaureate/associate degree category, 3 semester hours in Introduction to Kinesiology (8/96).

Theory and Practice of Pfrimmer Deep Muscle Therapy (2) (Pfrimmer Deep Muscle Therapy®)

Location: Wayne, PA.

Length: 80 hours (10 days).

Dates: April 1982-Present.

Objective: To provide the student with the theoretical background and basic skills to perform Pfrimmer Deep Muscle Therapy.

Learning Outcome: Upon successful completion of this course, the student will be able to administer a full body Pfrimmer Deep Muscle Therapy® session, palpate and identify major anatomical structures, explain the history, purpose, rationale, application to specific muscular conditions and contraindications of basic PDMT, and consider the sources/causes of muscular damage.

Instruction: Major topics covered in the course are the basic hands-on technique work for Pfrimmer Deep Muscle Therapy, the Pfrimmer corrective approach for 50 common conditions, how Pfrimmer supports each of the body systems, and professionalism. Methods of instruction include lectures, demonstrations, role plays, skills practice, critical thinking group discussions, problem solving scenarios, and outreach clinic.

Credit Recommendation: In the upper division baccalaureate category, 3 semester hours in the Theory and Practice of Pfrimmer Deep Muscle Therapy (8/96).

Theory and Practice of Shiatsu (9) (Shiatsu)

Location: Wayne, PA.

Length: 108 hours (24 days).

Dates: June 1994-Present.

Objective: To help students develop their understanding of meridian theory and Shiatsu techniques.

Learning Outcome: Upon successful completion of this course, the student will be able to administer a professional quality Shiatsu massage, discuss and explain Shiatsu theory, list and explain the contraindications to Shiatsu, and demonstrate proficiency in meridian point locations, palming, thumbing, and Hara assessment.

Instruction: Major topics covered in the course are Shiatsu theory, acupressure, assessment, hands-on practice, palming, thumbing, five-elements theory, body mechanics, patterns of K1, Jitsu, and Kyo in treatment, energy, point location, meridian location, treatment planning and assessment. Methods of instruction include lectures, supervised demonstrations, and practice.

Credit Recommendation: In the lower division baccalaureate/associate degree category, 3 semester hours in the Theory and Practice of Shiatsu (8/96).

Full Curriculum Swedish Massage

Anatomy and Physiology I (6) (Anatomy and Physiology)

Location: Wayne, PA.

Length: 102 hours (34 days).

Dates: January 1986-Present.

Objective: To provide the student with basic knowledge of the systems, organs, and tissues of the human body, stressing the integration of anatomical structure and function.

Learning Outcome: Upon successful completion of this course, the student will be able to identify and describe all major anatomical structures of the human body, explain the basic functions of the organs and organ systems, and describe the major physiological processes of the human body.

Instruction: Major topics covered in the course are defining anatomy and physiology; anatomical relationships and the body systems:skeletal system; muscular system; body chemistry; cardiovascular system; lymphatic system; respiratory system; digestive system; metabolism; urinary system; endocrine system; integumentary system; and reproductive system. Methods of instruction include lectures, discussion and classroom exercises but exclude conventional laboratory exercises.

Credit Recommendation: In the lower division baccalaureate/associate degree category, 4 semester hours in Anatomy and Physiology (8/96).

Pathology (7)

Location: Wayne, PA.

Length: 85 hours (34 lessons).

Dates: January 1986-Present.

Objective: To introduce students to the study of pathology of the musculoskeletal system and specifically as applied to massage therapy.

Learning Outcome: Upon successful completion of this course, the student will be able to list the basic causes and effects of diseases, demonstrate knowledge of common musculoskeletal and systemic conditions, demonstrate knowledge of various conditions for which massage can be beneficial, and list the contraindications of massage.

Instruction: Major topics covered in the course are pathological theories, structural bone and joint disorders, stress management, nutrition, disorders of specific organ systems, endangerment zones, and indications and contraindications for massage. Methods of instruction include lectures, team work, and hands-on demonstrations.

Credit Recommendation: In the lower division baccalaureate/associate degree category, 3 semester hours in Pathology (8/96).

Theory and Practice of Massage (Swedish Massage)

Location: Wayne, PA.

Length: 334 hours (71 days).

Dates: January 1986-Present.

Objective: To provide the student with knowledge and skill in the art and science of massage.

Learning Outcome: Upon successful completion of this course, the student will be able to administer therapeutic, Swedish, sports massage, and myofascial release; describe the benefits and effects of massage; identify contraindications to massage; apply hydrotherapy; discuss professional, ethical, and legal issues; and discuss the history of massage.

Instruction: Major topics covered in the course are therapeutic massage techniques, Swedish Massage techniques, myofascial release, sports massage, seated massage, benefits and effects of massage, contraindications for massage, hygiene, massage related therapies, hydrotherapy, CPR and first aid, muscle tracing, palpation, professional responsibilities, professional ethics, legal issues, history of massage, and business practices. Methods of instruction include lectures, projects, presentations, video presentations, massage technique demonstrations, field trips, and outreach programs.

Credit Recommendation: In the lower division baccalaureate/associate degree category, 10 semester hours in the Theory and Practice of Massage (8/96).

PJA School

The PJA School provides a Paralegal Including Computer Applications Program designed to educate students for employment as entry level paralegals, as well as a Para-Accountant Specialist Program designed to educate students for employment as entry level para-accountants. Paralegals are skilled paraprofessionals who assist attorneys, while para-accountants are skilled paraprofessionals who assist certified public accountants.

The Paralegal Including Computer Applications Program and the Para-Accountant Specialist Program each entail 600 classroom hours.

The Programs are divided into the areas of study marked below. Courses labeled "P" are contained in the Paralegal Including Computer Applications Program, while courses with a "P-A" are contained in the Para-Accountant Specialist Program.

The PJA School's educational objective is to give students the skills that will allow them to work as entry-level para-professionals. This entails imparting legal theory, presenting practical skills, and giving background enrichment.

The Programs have been licensed by the Pennsylvania Department of Education Board of Private Licensed Schools and accredited by the Accrediting Commission of Career Schools and Colleges of Technology.

The PJA School employs a faculty of practicing attorneys and certified public accountants. The faculty is evaluated by students at the end of each class.

The PJA School conducts extensive evaluations of its students. These evaluations consist both of periodic examinations and written assignments. These evaluations are designed to test the student's retention of theory and terminology as well as to monitor the student's practical skills.

Source of official student records: Director of Admissions, The PJA School, 7900 West Chester Pike, Upper Darby, PA 19082.

Additional information about the courses: College Credit Recommendation Service, American Council on Education, One Dupont Circle, Washington, DC 20036-1193.

Advanced Financial Accounting (P-A 106)

Location: Upper Darby, PA.

Length: 90 hours.

Dates: *Version 1:* October 1991-December 1994; *Version 2:* January 1995-Present.

Objective: To provide the students with a knowledge of the generally accepted accounting principles, systems, and procedures applicable to the asset, liability, and equity accounts and income determination.

Learning Outcome: Upon successful completion of this course, the student will be able to demonstrate a working knowledge of the procedures, methods, and systems necessary to properly account for the major asset, liability, and equity accounts and know how they are affected by generally accepted accounting principles; use the practical skills acquired during the program to maintain the integrity of the accounting system; demonstrate knowledge of the importance of maintaining proper inventories, identifying the major inventory valuation methods (specific identification, LIFO, FIFO, and weighted average), and the periodic and perpetual inventory systems; identify the differences in the area of equity based upon the type of business organization - sole proprietors, partnerships, or corporations; apply the tools of financial analysis (horizontal, vertical, trend, and to monitor an organization's performance); and understand the methods used to prepare a statement of cash flow (direct and indirect) and how to use the information contained in the statement.

Instruction: Major topics covered in the course are cash and accounts receivable, inventory valuation methods, disposal of plant assets, intangible and natural resources, securities investments, bonds, income taxes, leases, pensions, equity accounting, statement of cash flows, and financial statement analysis. Methods of instruction include lecture, discussion, classroom exercises, case studies, and examinations.

Credit Recommendation: In the lower division baccalaureate/associate degree category, 2 semester hours in Financial Accounting or Accounting Elective and in the upper division baccalaureate degree category, 4 semester hours in Intermediate Accounting (6 hours total) (9/95).

Auditing (P-A 110)

Location: Upper Darby, PA.

Length: 45 hours.

Dates: *Version 1:* October 1991-December 1994; *Version 2:* January 1995-Present.

Objective: To provide the student with an understanding of the generally accepted auditing standards and procedures used for examination and attestation of the accuracy and reliability of financial statements.

Learning Outcome: Upon successful completion of this course, the student shall have an understanding of accepted auditing standards. The student will be aware of the various audit perspectives - financial, operational and compliance, that are performed by internal and external auditors. The student will possess the practical tools needed to gather sufficient substantive evidential matter and to evaluate internal controls.

Instruction: Major topics covered in the course are the practical tools needed to gather sufficient substantive evidential matter; how to evaluate internal controls; working paper techniques; and how to perform a mock audit. Methods of instruction include lecture, discussion, classroom exercises and a mock audit.

Credit Recommendation: In the upper division baccalaureate degree category, 3 semester hours in Auditing (9/95).

Automated Accounting (P-A 105)

Location: Upper Darby, PA.

Length: 90 hours.

Dates: October 1993-Present.

Objective: To introduce the student to a computerized accounting environment and how the accounting cycle using a manual accounting system differs from the accounting process using a computerized system.

Learning Outcome: Upon successful completion of this course, the student will be able to operate in a computerized accounting environment; understand the various types of automated accounting systems (full featured, modular, basic, and complete) and how they compare to manual systems; and operate the Peachtree Complete III Program, version 5.0 and One-Write Plus.

Instruction: Major topics covered in the course are how and why automated accounting systems are selected, and training on the One-Write Plus and Peachtree Complete III Accounting Programs. Methods of instruction include lecture, discussion, and laboratory exercises.

Credit Recommendation: In the lower division baccalaureate/associate degree category, 3 semester hours in Automated Accounting (10/94). **NOTE:** This recommendation applies after successful completion of this course and Computer Spreadsheets in Accounting; no credit is recommended if this course is taken alone.

Business Entities (P102) (Formerly Business Entities)

Location: Upper Darby, PA.

Length: *Version 1:* 35 hours (5-12 weeks); *Version 2:* 42 hours (6-12 weeks).

Dates: *Version 1:* January 1982-December 1994; *Version 2:* January 1995-Present.

Objective: To give students both basic knowledge of business organizations and skills to assist in their operation.

Learning Outcome: Upon successful completion of this course, the student will be able to read and interpret a Partnership Agreement with a minimum of assistance; draft a Pennsylvania Articles of Incorporation and Registry Statement without assistance; identify the nature of a business by examining its structure, financing, and extent of government control; give a comprehensive overview of corporate management and financing; and identify different methods for corporate takeover, different mechanisms for combining corporations, the major functions of the Securities Exchange Commission, the classic common law and SEC fiduciary duties, and the dynamics of corporate dissolution and liquidation.

Instruction: Major topics covered in the course are knowledge of the various types of Pennsylvania business forms from sole proprietorships through partnerships to corporations; corporate forms; and drafting of appropriate documents. Methods of instruction include lecture and discussion.

Credit Recommendation: In the lower division baccalaureate/associate degree category or in the upper division baccalaureate degree category, 3 semester hours in Business Entities (5/86) (10/94).

Civil Litigation (P101)
(Formerly Civil Litigation)

Location: Upper Darby, PA.

Length: *Version 1:* 42 hours (5-12 weeks); *Version 2:* 45 hours (6-12 weeks).

Dates: *Version 1:* January 1982-December 1994; *Version 2:* January 1995-Present.

Objective: To give the student comprehensive instruction on the theories and practical application of Pennsylvania and federal procedural law with a view toward the student obtaining skills to provide independent litigation support.

Learning Outcome: Upon successful completion of this course, the student will be able to identify the court system to which the Pennsylvania, New Jersey, or Federal Court belong and the level of the court; identify a hypothetical dispute as a contract or tort situation and be able to analyze the relative merits of both sides' cases; draft a Pennsylvania or Federal Court Civil Complaint; answer a Civil Complaint; prepare or answer a Request for Production of Documents or Interrogatories with minimal supervision by an attorney; prepare a Notice of Deposition or Subpoena without error; digest a deposition with minimal attorney supervision; prepare settlement papers without mistakes; maintain files and a reminder or "tickler" system without errors; prepare without assistance a Pennsylvania Motion or Answer to Motion; and identify the purpose and sequence of civil trial states.

Instruction: Major topics covered in the course are the essentials of handling a lawsuit; the Pennsylvania and Federal Court systems, and a background of substantive law; and how to handle a lawsuit from beginning to end, including filing pleadings and handling discovery. Methods of instruction include lecture and discussion.

Credit Recommendation: In the lower division baccalaureate/associate or in the upper division baccalaureate degree category, 3 semester hours in Civil Litigation (5/86) (10/94).

Computer Spreadsheets in Accounting (P-A 103)

Location: Upper Darby, PA.

Length: 60 hours.

Dates: October 1991-Present.

Objective: To give the student the ability to utilize the power of a computer spreadsheet program, including planning and constructing worksheets, creating and printing graphs, utilizing Lotus database capabilities, and developing and using macros.

Learning Outcome: Upon successful completion of this course, the student will be able to plan, construct, and document worksheets; create and print graphs; utilize Lotus database capabilities; develop and use macros; proficiently use Lotus 1-2-3, Version 2.2; and be knowledgeable of Quattro Pro, Version 3.0.

Instruction: Major topics covered in the course are Lotus 1-2-3; how to plan, construct, and document worksheets; creating and printing graphs; utilizing the Lotus database capabilities; and Quattro Pro. Methods of instruction include lecture, discussion, and laboratory exercises.

Credit Recommendation: In the lower division baccalaureate/associate degree category, 3 semester hours in Automated Accounting (10/94). **NOTE:** This recommendation applies after successful completion of this course and Automated Accounting; no credit is recommended if this course is taken alone.

Computers for the Paralegal I (P 403 A)

Location: Upper Darby, PA.

Length: 25 hours (6-12 weeks).

Dates: October 1993-Present.

Objective: To give the student the ability to perform the computer-related functions common in modern legal organizations.

Learning Outcome: Upon successful completion of this course, the student will be able to demonstrate the basic skills required to generate documents using WordPerfect, and perform computer-assisted legal research using a system such as Lexis or Westlaw.

Instruction: Major topics covered in the course are the knowledge and skills required to use a computer in a legal setting; creating, editing, and printing documents in WordPerfect 5.1, including employing basic skills such as moving the cursor, inserting, deleting, and enhancing text, plus intermediate skills such as using margins, indents, tabs, justification, and line spacing; how to use the search and replace commands, Speller, and Thesaurus; researching law using Westlaw and Lexis; and how to use Lotus 1-2-3 and a computerized database in a law firm setting. Methods of instruction include lecture, discussion, and laboratory exercises.

Credit Recommendation: In the lower division baccalaureate/associate degree category, 3 semester hours in Computing for the Paralegal (10/94). **NOTE:** Credit should be given only if this course and Computers for the Paralegal II (P 403 B) have both successfully been completed.

Computers for the Paralegal II (P 403 B)

Location: Upper Darby, PA.

Length: 25 hours (6-12 weeks).

Dates: October 1993-Present.

Objective: To give the student the ability to perform the computer-assisted functions common in modern legal organizations.

Learning Outcome: Upon successful completion of this course, the student will be able to demonstrate a fundamental ability to work with Lotus 1-2-3, and attain a basic ability to utilize a data program common to the law firm of today.

Instruction: Major topics covered in the course are the knowledge and skills required to use a computer in a legal setting; creating, editing, and printing documents in WordPerfect 5.1, including employing basic skills such as moving the cursor, inserting, deleting, and enhancing text, plus intermediate skills such as using margins, indents, tabs, justification, and line spacing; how to use the search and replace commands, Speller, and Thesaurus; researching law using Westlaw and Lexis; and how to use Lotus 1-2-3 and a computerized database in a law firm setting. Methods of instruction include lecture, discussion, and laboratory exercises.

Credit Recommendation: In the lower division baccalaureate/associate degree category, 3 semester hours in Computing for the Paralegal (10/94). **NOTE:** Credit should be given only if this course and Computers for the Paralegal I (P 403 A) have both successfully been completed.

Creditor's and Debtor's Rights (P204)

Location: Upper Darby, PA.

Length: 12 hours (6-12 weeks).

Dates: January 1987-Present.

Objective: To give the student an overview of issues and skills involved in the legal relationship between creditors and debtors, with emphasis placed on collection lawsuits, secured transactions, and bankruptcy procedures.

Learning Outcome: Upon successful completion of this course, the student will be able to handle a client during a collection action, determine the business status of the debtor, draft the collection complaint, monitor the action, and execute the judgment; create and perfect a security interest loan; assist in the preparation of a Bankruptcy Petition, Plan, and Statement; and prepare a Proof of Claim Form and a Petition for Relief from Automatic Stay.

Instruction: Major topics covered in the course are legal rights and obligations of creditors and debtors; collection actions; secured transactions; and bankruptcy law and the appropriate documents. Methods of instruction include lecture, discussion, and classroom exercises.

Credit Recommendation: In the lower division baccalaureate/associate degree category, 1 semester hour in Creditors and Debtors (10/94).

Criminal Law (P201) (Formerly Criminal Law)

Location: Upper Darby, PA.

Length: 42 hours (6-12 weeks).

Dates: January 1982-Present.

Objective: To acquaint students with the definitions of various crimes, the nature of the criminal process and the area of Constitutional criminal law.

Learning Outcome: Upon successful completion of this course, the student will be able to identify the crimes committed when faced with the description of a criminal act; describe the criminal process and its various stages; identify areas of Constitutional misconduct when given the description of a certain activity by the police or the judiciary; and draft an Entry of Appearance, Petition for a Change of Venue, or Petition to Suppress Evidence.

Instruction: Major topics covered in the course are the essentials of the criminal system—both substantive criminal law and criminal procedure; Constitutional considerations; and the drafting of papers. Methods of instruction include lecture and discussion.

Credit Recommendation: In the lower division baccalaureate/associate degree category, 3 semester hours in Criminal Procedures (5/86) (10/94).

Domestic Relations (P202) (Formerly Domestic Relations)

Location: Upper Darby, PA.

Length: *Version 1:* 36 hours (5-12 weeks); *Version 2:* 33 hours (6-12 weeks).

Dates: *Version 1:* January 1982-December 1994; *Version 2:* January 1995-Present.

Objective: To acquaint the student with major areas of family law and to give the student the skills to deal with these areas.

Learning Outcome: Upon successful completion of this course, the student will be able to indicate the statutory requirements for marriage and the requirements for a valid prenuptial agreement to a client contemplating marriage; identify and describe the various mechanisms for the enforcement of support when dealing with a divorced spouse; describe the adoption procedure and draft an Adoption Petition when working with prospective adoptive parents; describe the divorce procedure to the clients when working with divorcing clients; and draft divorce complaints, answers, motions, and related documents.

Instruction: Major topics covered in the course are family law—the judicial resolution of disputes and questions involving the family, including divorce, separation, support, custody, and adoption in Pennsylvania court systems; and how to handle a divorce case from beginning to end. Methods of instruction include lecture and discussion.

Credit Recommendation: *Version 1:* In the upper division baccalaureate or graduate degree category, 3 semester hours in Domestic Relations (5/86). *Version 2:* In the upper division baccalaureate or graduate degree category, 2 semester hours in Domestic Relations or an elective in Legal Studies (10/94).

Federal Income Taxes: Business (P-A 108)

Location: Upper Darby, PA.

Length: 30 hours.

Dates: October 1991-Present.

Objective: To teach the student income taxes a business organization is subject to at the federal level.

Learning Outcome: Upon successful completion of this course, the student will be able to demonstrate knowledge of the taxes a business organization is subject to at the federal level; recognize the different forms and schedules required by corporations, partnerships, and sole proprietors in order to report federal income taxes; and demonstrate knowledge of the importance of tax planning.

Instruction: Major topics covered in the course are the taxes a business organization is subject to at the federal level, and the common forms and schedules required for corporations, partnerships, and sole proprietors. Methods of instruction include lecture, discussion, and classroom exercises.

Credit Recommendation: In the lower division baccalaureate/associate degree category, 2 semester hours in Federal Income Taxes in Business (10/94).

Financial Accounting (P-A 101)

Location: Upper Darby, PA.

Length: 60 hours.

Dates: October 1991-Present.

Objective: To provide the student with a brief introduction to the accounting environment, an overview of business organization forms, and the importance of the accounting cycle required for business management and legal recordkeeping.

Learning Outcome: Upon successful completion of this course, the student will be able to demonstrate a working knowledge of the accounting environment and define the accounting environment; describe the different areas of accounting and the fundamental principles and concepts of accounting; know the business organizations forms and why one form may be chosen over another; understand the many methods of classifying a business for tax purposes; understand the basic fundamental concepts and principles of accounting; handle the entire accounting cycle including recording transactions in the proper journals (general, sales, purchases, cash receipts, and cash disbursements); post ledgers (accounts receivable and accounts payable); prepare a working trial balance; make adjusting entries; summarize the information into financial statements; prepare closing entries; prepare a post closing trial balance; make opening entries; and journalize reversing entries.

Instruction: Major topics covered in the course are the fundamental concepts and principles of accounting; completing the accounting cycle; journalizing, posting, balancing, and adjusting entries; financial statements; and closing, opening, and reversing entries. Methods of instruction include lecture, discussion, and classroom exercises.

Credit Recommendation: In the lower division baccalaureate/associate degree category, 3 semester hours in Financial Accounting (10/94).

Individual Income Taxes (P-A 109)

Location: Upper Darby, PA.

Length: 60 hours.

Dates: October 1993-Present.

Objective: To teach the student basic Federal Income Tax including a review of significant job related forms.

Learning Outcome: Upon successful completion of this course, the student will be able to recognize taxable revenue and allowable deductions, and prepare the approved reporting forms.

Instruction: Major topics covered in the course are preparation of the major forms commonly used to report and pay individual income taxes manually and by computer. Methods of instruction include lecture, discussion, and classroom exercises.

Credit Recommendation: In the lower division baccalaureate/associate degree category, 2 semester hours in Individual Income Taxes (10/94). **NOTE:** An abbreviated version is being used since October 1991.

Legal Drafting I (P 301A)

Location: Upper Darby, PA.

Length: 25 hours (6-12 weeks).

Dates: October 1993-Present.

Objective: To give the student more extensive skills in drafting the types of documents that are commonly assigned to entry level paralegals.

Learning Outcome: Upon successful completion of this course, the student will be able to prepare basic pleadings and discovery papers involved in civil litigation; master the technique of creating fundamental documents connected with the formulation of partnerships and corporations; create wills, codicils, and other basic paperwork involved in the planning and administration of estates; and master the art of outlining cases and preparing memoranda based on the outlines.

Instruction: Major topics covered in the course are perfection of practical skills used by paralegals; and additional document drafting. Methods of instruction include lecture, discussion, and classroom exercises.

Credit Recommendation: In the lower division baccalaureate/associate degree category, 4 semester hours in Legal Drafting I (10/94).

Legal Drafting II (P 301B)

Location: Upper Darby, PA.

Length: 25 hours (6-12 weeks).

Dates: October 1993-Present.

Objective: To give the student more extensive skills in drafting the types of documents that are commonly assigned to entry level paralegals.

Learning Outcome: Upon successful completion of this course, the student will be able to prepare fundamental papers connected with divorce and adoption; draft the basic documents pertaining to the sale and leasing of real estate; master the art of creating basic court filings in the criminal justice process; and prepare fundamental paperwork in collection actions, secured transactions, and bankruptcies.

Instruction: Major topics covered in the course are preparation of fundamental paperwork for divorce, adoption, collection actions, secured transactions, and bankruptcies; drafting of basic documents pertaining to selling and leasing real estate; and the art of creating basic court filings in the criminal justice process. Methods of instruction include lecture, discussion, and classroom exercises.

Credit Recommendation: In the lower division baccalaureate/associate degree category, 4 semester hours in Legal Drafting II (10/94).

Legal Research (P104) (Formerly Legal Research)

Location: Upper Darby, PA.

Length: *Version 1:* 60 hours (5-12 weeks); *Version 2:* 45 hours (6-12 weeks).

Dates: *Version 1:* January 1982-December 1994; *Version 2:* January 1995-Present.

Objective: To give students basic research skills in how to read cases and statutes, how to write memoranda of law, how to find the law, and how to update the law.

Learning Outcome: Upon successful completion of this course, the student will be able to read a case opinion, construct an outline of the opinion, and convert the outline into a written memorandum of law; find a case on a certain legal topic in a Law Encyclopedia or Digest, to find a certain statute in a Statute Book, to find a certain rule of court in a Rule Book, and to find a certain legal form in a Form Book; and Shepardize a case.

Instruction: Major topics covered in the course are valuable skills to be used to find and analyzing law, how to use the law library and the books in it, reading cases, and Shepardization. Methods of instruction include lecture and discussion.

Credit Recommendation: *Version 1:* In the lower division baccalaureate/associate degree category, 2 semester hours in Legal Research or an elective in Legal Studies (5/86). *Version 2:* In the lower division baccalaureate/associate degree category, 3 semester hours in Legal Research or an elective in Legal Studies (10/94).

Legal Research Shop (P401)

Location: Upper Darby, PA.

Length: 25 hours (6-12 weeks).

Dates: October 1993-Present.

Objective: To give the student additional skills in the area of finding the law, reading the law, and creating outlines and memoranda of the law.

Learning Outcome: Upon successful completion of this course, the student will be able to find the law, read the law, and write the law using skills which exceed those acquired in the basic Legal Research Course; demonstrate perfection of skills in using research tools such as digests, law encyclopedias, statute books, form books, and annotations; and demonstrate perfection of skills used to read and write cases.

Instruction: Major topics covered in the course are proficiency in finding and updating statutes, cases, and secondary sources of law, and intense practice work in law finding skills. Methods of instruction include lecture, discussion, and classroom exercises.

Credit Recommendation: In the lower division baccalaureate/associate degree category, 1 semester hour in Legal Drafting I (10/94).

Managerial Accounting (P-A 107)

Location: Upper Darby, PA.

Length: 45 hours.

Dates: *Version 1:* January 1991-December 1994; *Version 2:* January 1995-Present.

Objective: To provide the student with managerial accounting skills that are useful in all areas of accounting and business analysis to provide business management recommendations.

Learning Outcome: Upon successful completion of this course, the student will be able to demonstrate managerial accounting skills that are useful in control and decision-making; understand manufacturing environments and be knowledgeable of the various product costing methods (job cost, process cost, and standard cost); and use the tools of managerial accounting, such as, responsibility accounting, cost-profit-volume analysis, differential analysis, and budgeting in a variety of settings.

Instruction: Major topics covered in the course are managerial accounting tools such as responsibility accounting, cost-profit-volume analysis, differential analysis, budgeting and manufacturing cost accounting. Methods of instruction include lecture, discussion, classroom exercises and discussion.

Credit Recommendation: In the lower division baccalaureate/associate degree category, 3 semester hours in Managerial Accounting (10/94) (9/95).

Para-Accountant's Senior Project

Location: Upper Darby, PA.

Length: 90 Hours (including 18 hours preparing Senior Project).

Dates: January 1995-Present.

Objective: To have the student demonstrate accounting knowledge and ability by completing a significant independent project.

Learning Outcome: Upon successful completion of this course, the student must demonstrate the ability to make the transition from the knowledge of accounting skills to their application. A final portfolio and detailed employment plan are developed. Selected project topics include developing a small business plan, estate and gift tax returns, or family tax planning.

Instruction: Major topics covered in the course are computerized accounting applications, portfolio preparation and completion of an independent research paper. Methods of instruction include lecture, discussion, classroom exercises, case studies, computer-assisted instruction and reports.

Credit Recommendation: In the lower division baccalaureate/associate degree category, 2 semester hours in Independent Accounting Study Project (9/95).

Payroll and Payroll Taxes (P-A 104)

Location: Upper Darby, PA.

Length: 15 hours.

Dates: October 1991-Present.

Objective: To teach the student how to prepare a payroll, and how to maintain the proper payroll records to comply with the payroll tax laws.

Learning Outcome: Upon successful completion of this course, the student will be able to prepare a payroll; maintain proper payroll records; comply with the payroll tax laws with regard to payment and reporting; recognize manual systems, payroll services, and computerized systems; and determine the differences between independent contractors and employees.

Instruction: Major topics covered in the course are maintaining proper payroll records; complying with payroll tax laws; and manual and computerized payroll systems. Methods of instruction include lecture, discussion, and classroom exercises.

Credit Recommendation: In the lower division baccalaureate/associate degree category, 1 semester hour in Payroll and Payroll Taxes (10/94).

Real Property (P203)
(Formerly Real Property)

Location: Upper Darby, PA.

Length: *Version 1:* 36 hours (5-12 weeks); *Version 2:* 33 hours (6-12 weeks).

Dates: *Version 1:* January 1982-December 1994; *Version 2:* January 1995-Present.

Objective: To give students both knowledge and skills in real estate law.

Learning Outcome: Upon successful completion of this course, the student will be able to identify and describe such different types of land ownership as fee simple, life estate, cooperative and condominium, joint tenancy, tenancy-in-common, and tenancy by the entireties; draft an exclusive sales brokerage agreement, a buyer's financial information form, a buyer's estimated settlement costs form, and a seller's estimated proceeds form; draft an agreement of sale, a mortgage, a mortgage note, a deed, and a settlement sheet; draft a landlord-tenant complaint and a form lease; and describe such land use control mechanisms as zoning, easements, restrictive covenants, and reciprocal negative easements.

Instruction: Major topics covered in the course are real estate law; the basic roots of English and American property law; and deeds, mortgages, leases, and contracts in Pennsylvania legal practice. Methods of instruction include lecture and discussions.

Credit Recommendation: *Version 1:* In the lower division baccalaureate/associate degree category, 3 semester hours in Fundamentals of Real Estate (5/86). *Version 2:* In the lower division baccalaureate/associate degree category, 2 semester hours in Fundamentals of Real Estate (10/94).

Wills and Estates (P103)
(Formerly Wills and Estates)

Location: Upper Darby, PA.

Length: *Version 1:* 36 hours (5-12 weeks); *Version 2:* 45 hours (6-12 weeks).

Dates: *Version 1:* January 1982-December 1994; *Version 2:* January 1995-Present.

Objective: To give students both knowledge of probate issues and the skills to deal with probate problems.

Learning Outcome: Upon successful completion of this course, the student will be able to list the steps in the probate of both testate and intestate estates and assist the attorney in the handling of these steps; draft a simple will, self-proved will affidavits, and codicils without assistance; and distinguish among different types of insurance policies, trusts and estates arising from status without assistance.

Instruction: Major topics covered in the course are how to handle an estate from the filing of initial papers to the final distribution of assets; drafting documents; and how to interview executors and administrators. Methods of instruction include lecture and discussion.

Credit Recommendation: In the lower division baccalaureate/associate degree category, 3 semester hours in Wills and Estates or as an elective in Legal Studies (5/86) (10/94).

Word Processing for Para-Accountants (P-A 102)

Location: Upper Darby, PA.

Length: 30 hours.

Dates: October 1991-Present.

Objective: To improve the student's ability to communicate effectively and efficiently in the Para-Accounting field utilizing WordPerfect 5.1.

Learning Outcome: Upon successful completion of this course, the student will be able to take a hands on, task oriented approach to writing memos, letters, preparing a resume, and designing forms;

and use the word processing features of WordPerfect 5.1, including moving, blocking, importing, linking, tab alignments, columns, tables, and math.

Instruction: Major topics covered in the course are training Para-Accountants to use word processing effectively to perform their duties, and learning how to use the features of WordPerfect 5.1. Methods of instruction include lecture, discussion, and laboratory exercises.

Credit Recommendation: In the lower division baccalaureate/associate degree category, 2 semester hours in Word Processing for the Para-Accountant (10/94).

Positive Child Development Training, Inc.

In 1993, after many years of teaching in the Early Childhood field, Dr. Diana Pope came to the realization that obtaining adequate training for child care providers was very difficult for those who could not afford or did not desire a college degree. Positive Child Development Training, Inc. (PCDT) was organized by Dr. Pope and a board of educators and child care professionals as a tax exempt corporation designed to provide an affordable and field intensive training program for child care providers.

PCDT offers a number of training courses: the 6 hour child care orientation course mandated by the state of Kentucky; various individual topic workshops; and the120 training hour nationally accepted CDA course, plus its renewal component. These classes are offered on a regular schedule at our training facility in Lexington. Dr. Pope and the PCDT Board review all course materials and developments biannually in order to keep the training and delivery of the competencies required at a current level. Dr. Pope, who is PCDT's primary trainer and President of the Corporation, attends a number of Early Childhood symposiums and training workshops each year to keep up to date in the discipline. In addition, she is a member of the Kentucky Early Childhood Advisory Council and Kentucky Institute for Early Childhood Professional Development.

Dr. Pope received her B.A. in early childhood education, M.A. in family studies with an early childhood emphasis, and her Ed.D in Early and Middle Childhood Education. In addition, she received a life time teaching certificate for Kindergarten through 6th grade. Dr. Pope has taught in the discipline at a number of institutions of higher learning. She is also a certified CDA advisor and field representative; one of the founders of Unlimited Potential, Inc., an early childhood training agency; and has been a featured speaker at several conferences, including the National Association of the Education of Young Children.

Source of official student records: Registry of Credit Recommendations, American Council on Education, One Dupont Circle, Washington, DC 20036-1193.

Additional information about the courses: College Credit Recommendation Service, American Council on Education, One Dupont Circle, Washington, DC 20036-1193.

Early Childhood Education 100: Introduction to Early Childhood Education

Location: Lexington, KY.

Length: 40 hours (8 meetings).

Dates: December 1997-Present.

Objective: To familiarize students with the field of professional child care and the CDA Competency Goals.

Learning Outcome: Upon successful completion of this course, the student will be able to demonstrate professionalism in his/her attitude and actions and demonstrate knowledge and skill in the creation of learning environments, program management, and working with families.

Instruction: Major topics covered in the course are early childhood philosophy, goals, and ethical practices; roles of the teacher; professional organizations/journals; advocacy; historical roots; licensing; assessment; observations; productive family involvement; early childhood facilities and settings; and schedules, transitions, record keeping, and activity planning. Methods of instruction include lecture, audio/visual material, discussion, in-class projects, oral reports, tests, quizzes, projects, and final examinations.

Credit Recommendation: In the vocational certificate category or the lower division baccalaureate/associate degree category, 9 semester hours in Early Childhood Education (12/97). **NOTE:** ECE 100, ECE 150, and ECE 200 must all be successfully completed for this credit recommendation to apply. If all three courses have not been taken and successfully completed, the student should not receive any credit.

Early Childhood Education 150: Child Development

Location: Lexington, KY.

Length: 40 hours (8 meetings).

Dates: December 1997-Present.

Objective: To provide an overview of children's development (physical, cognitive, language, creative, social and emotional); and to explore best current practices in fostering each area of development.

Learning Outcome: Upon successful completion of this course, the student will be able to use techniques that promote each area of a young child's development.

Instruction: Major topics covered in the course are the characteristics of child development from birth through age 5; course identifies how the teacher can foster current best practices; and particular attention is given to physical, cognitive, language/literacy, social and emotional development, and creativity. Methods of instruction include lecture, audio/visual material, group discussion, in-class projects, child observations, tests, quizzes, projects, and final examinations.

Credit Recommendation: In the vocational certificate category or the lower division baccalaureate/associate degree category, 9 semester hours in Early Childhood Education (12/97). **NOTE:** ECE 100, ECE 150, and ECE 200 must all be successfully completed for this credit recommendation to apply. If all three courses have not been taken and successfully completed, the student should not receive any credit.

Early Childhood Education 200: CDA Practicum

Location: Lexington, KY.

Length: 40 hours (8 meetings).

Dates: December 1997-Present.

Objective: As the final course in the three-course child development series, the practicum will assist students in demonstrating proficiency in best practices as set forth in the CDA Competency Goals.

Learning Outcome: Upon successful completion of this course, the student will be able to demonstrate successful techniques when working with young children and develop a resource portfolio.

Instruction: Major topics covered in the course are practical application of the establishment of a safe, healthy learning environment; the advancement of physical and intellectual competence; support of social and emotional development; provision of positive guidance; establishment of positive and productive relationships with families; endurance of a well-run purposeful program responsive to participant needs; and a commitment to professionalism. Methods of instruction include lecture, audio/visual material, discussion, portfolio preparation, observations, conferences, and oral reports.

Credit Recommendation: In the vocational certificate category or the lower division baccalaureate/associate degree category, 9 semester hours in Early Childhood Education (12/97). **NOTE:** ECE 100, ECE 150, and ECE 200 must all be successfully completed for this credit recommendation to apply. If all three courses have not been taken and successfully completed, the student should not receive any credit.

Early Childhood Education 256: Guidance Techniques for Young Children

Location: Lexington, KY.

Length: 40 hours (8 meetings).

Dates: December 1997-Present.

Objective: To provide knowledge of the variety of guidance techniques available to professionals in the field of early childhood education.

Learning Outcome: Upon successful completion of this course, the student will be able to assess guidance needs and provide and maintain appropriate guidance within the classroom.

Instruction: Major topics covered in the course are direct and indirect guidance techniques; prosocial behavior and social esteem; understanding and dealing with chronic behaviors; routines and scheduling; and working with staff and parents. Methods of instruction include lecture, audio/visual materials, discussion, in-class projects, observations, oral reports, tests, quizzes, projects, and final examinations.

Credit Recommendation: In the lower division baccalaureate/associate degree category, 3 semester hours in Early Childhood Education (12/97).

Early Childhood Education 260: Early Childhood Curriculum

Location: Lexington, KY.

Length: 40 hours (8 meetings).

Dates: December 1997-Present.

Objective: To examine infant, toddler, and preschool curriculum approaches and applications to create developmentally appropriate practices and activities.

Learning Outcome: Upon successful completion of this course, the student will be able to evaluate and select appropriate curriculum for use in the classroom; and produce a portfolio of developmentally appropriate activities (infant through preschool) in the areas of physical, social, emotional, and cognitive development.

Instruction: Major topics covered in the course are examination and evaluation of curriculum approaches; curriculum development considerations; and application of developmentally appropriate activities to support children's (0-5) physical, social, emotional, and cognitive growth. Methods of instruction include lecture, audio/visual materials, discussion, in-class projects, classroom observations, oral reports, tests, quizzes, projects, and final examinations.

Credit Recommendation: In the lower division baccalaureate/associate degree category or the upper division baccalaureate degree category, 3 semester hours in Early Childhood Education (12/97).

Productivity Point International

Productivity Point International provides integrated computer software training and support services to the corporate market. PPI's more than 110 state-of-the-art training centers throughout North America serve the needs of both computer users and information technology professionals in subjects such as end-user applications, local area networks, application development, system migrations and client/server computing.

PPI offers results-oriented training in more than 500 seminar topics, created by a staff of experienced curriculum developers, and delivered by more than 1,000 professional instructors.

Since launching its franchising operations in 1990, PPI has trained more than three million students from thousands of companies. PPI specializes in designing and delivering customized solutions that fulfill its clients' specific computer training needs. Its roster of blue-chip clients includes leaders in manufacturing, financial and other information-intensive industries, as well as government institutions.

PPI offers a unique, proprietary methodology—Productivity Plan—which integrates the software training process, products and services under an umbrella of strategic planning. This consultative methodology delivers a customized productivity solution for people who use software as an integral part of their jobs. ProductivityPlan consists of three components: DISCOVERY (needs analysis and skills assessment), DESIGN (training plans, products and support services) and DELIVERY (implementation and evaluation).

PPI has developed proprietary, objective evaluation and measurement techniques that quantify the results of Productivity Plan and the return on investment. PPI's evaluation system also provides a formal method of channeling feedback into the ongoing Discovery process, delivering a "closed loop" process that lets the client company refine its software productivity solution through time. These results yield a number of important benefits: more cost-effective use of training dollars; improved skill retention and transfer to the job; better employee time-utilization; and increased on-the-job productivity.

Source of official student records: Registry of Credit Recommendations, American Council on Education, One Dupont Circle, Washington, DC 20036-1193.

Additional information about the courses: College Credit Recommendation Service, American Council on Education, One Dupont Circle, Washington, DC 20036-1193.

Access 2.0 for Windows Advanced

Location: Various locations throughout North America.

Length: 14 hours (2 days).

Dates: August 1994-Present.

Objective: To explore capabilities most requested by administrative and executive users, advanced query techniques, validity checks, custom forms, and exporting and importing data; focusing on advanced reporting techniques, graphing data, writing basic macros, analyzing the database, and selecting multi-user settings.

Learning Outcome: Upon successful completion of this course, the student will be able to change query join types; use calculations, summaries, crosstabs, and parameters in queries; apply validity checks to Access fields; export and import data using spreadsheet and text files; create multi-table forms and place advanced controls such as list and combo boxes; create multi-table reports and enhance report design with calculations and grouping; create customized graphs of selected data; create macros to automate common database tasks; analyze the database; and select multi-user settings.

Instruction: Major topics covered in the course are advanced query techniques, advanced editing techniques, creating advanced forms, exporting and importing data, advanced reporting techniques, graphing data, creating basic macros, automating forms with macros and exploring advanced features. Methods of instruction include lecture, interactive demonstrations, instructor-led exercises, independent exercises, discussions, audio-visual material, and pre- and post class tests.

Credit Recommendation: In the lower division baccalaureate/associate degree category, 1 semester hour in Microcomputer Applications (8/96). **NOTE**: Student should receive credit for completion of one Advanced Access course; either Access 2.0 for Windows Advanced, Access 7.0 for Windows 95 Advanced, or Access 97 for Windows 95/NT 4.0 Advanced.

Access 2.0 for Windows Introduction

Location: Various locations throughout North America.

Length: 14 hours (2 days).

Dates: August 1994-Present.

Objective: To explore viewing, editing, creating, and querying single and multiple tables, as well as using many operators in Access queries and creating and modifying custom reports.

Learning Outcome: Upon successful completion of this course, the student will be able to view and locate records; add, edit, and delete records; design and modify tables using Table Wizards; create a new database table using most field types; create and execute a variety of queries on a single table and multiple tables; use calculations in queries; design and modify forms using the Form Wizards; design and modify reports using the Report Wizards; create mailing labels; and print reports.

Instruction: Major topics covered in the course are exploring Access, working with tables, working with records in a table, creating a database and using table wizards, designing tables, creating simple queries, creating advanced queries, creating basic forms, customizing forms, creating basic reports and customizing reports. Methods of instruction include lecture, interactive demonstrations, instructor-led exercises, independent exercises, discussions, audio-visual material, and pre- and post class tests.

Credit Recommendation: In the lower division baccalaureate/associate degree category, 1 semester hour in Microcomputer Applications (8/96). **NOTE**: Student should receive credit for completion of one Introduction Access course; either Access 2.0 for Windows Introduction, Access 7.0 for Windows 95 Introduction, or Access 97 for Windows 95/NT 4.0 Introduction.

Access 7.0 for Windows 95 Advanced

Location: Various locations throughout North America.

Length: 14 hours (2 days).

Dates: December 1995-Present.

Objective: To explore advanced query techniques; creating crosstab, action and parameter queries; working with relations, key fields, and indexes; using field properties; creating and customizing forms; using advanced reporting techniques; adding charts to forms and reports; and exporting and importing data.

Learning Outcome: Upon successful completion of this course, the student will be able to specify complex criteria in a query; perform calculations in queries; create a multi-table query; create crosstab, action, and parameter queries; define permanent relationships between tables; specify key fields and define indexes; use field properties to customize fields and validate data; create custom forms to improve data entry; create forms and reports based on multiple tables; use a query as the basis for a report; create a summary report; create and customize a chart on a form or report; export, import, and link data in a variety of formats and customize the Access environment.

Instruction: Major topics covered in the course are exploring advanced query techniques, creating crosstabs, action, and parameter queries; working with relationships, key fields and indexes; using field properties to customize fields; creating custom forms; creating advanced reports; adding charts to forms and reports; exporting and importing data and customizing access. Methods of instruction include lecture, interactive demonstrations, instructor-led exercises, independent exercises, discussions, audio-visual material, and pre- and post class tests.

Credit Recommendation: In the lower division baccalaureate/associate degree category, 1 semester hour in Microcomputer Applications (8/96). **NOTE**: Student should receive credit for completion of one Advanced Access course; either Access 2.0 for Windows Advanced, Access 7.0 for Windows 95 Advanced, or Access 97 for Windows 95/NT 4.0 Advanced.

Access 7.0 for Windows 95 Introduction

Location: Various locations throughout North America.

Length: 14 hours (2 days).

Dates: December 1995-Present.

Objective: To explore designing a database; creating, viewing, and editing and relating tables; creating queries based on single and multiple tables; designing custom data entry forms; and creating, customizing, and printing reports and labels.

Learning Outcome: Upon successful completion of this course, the student will be able to start Access and identify components of the interface; access the various types of Help; add, edit, locate, and delete table records; use the Spell Checker to check for spelling errors in a table; design and created databases; design, create, and modify tables; sort, filter, and query data in a table; create queries based on multiple tables; establish permanent relationships between tables; design, customize, and use forms; design, customize, and print reports; and create mailing labels.

Instruction: Major topics covered in the course are exploring Access, working with tables, working with records, designing and creating a database, designing and creating tables, sorting, filtering, and querying data, creating advanced queries, creating and using basic forms, creating basic reports and labels and customizing a report. Methods of instruction include lecture, interactive demonstrations, instructor-led exercises, independent exercises, discussions, audio-visual material, and pre- and post class tests.

Credit Recommendation: In the lower division baccalaureate/associate degree category, 1 semester hour in Microcomputer Applications(8/96). **NOTE**: Student should receive credit for completion of one Introduction Access course; either Access 2.0 for Windows Introduction, Access 7.0 for Windows 95 Introduction, or Access 97 for Windows 95/NT 4.0 Introduction.

Access 97 for Windows 95/NT 4.0 Advanced

Location: Various locations throughout North America.

Length: 14 hours (2 days).

Dates: March 1997-Present.

Objective: To explore advanced query techniques, creating crosstab, action, and parameter queries, working with relationships, key fields, and indexes, creating custom forms, creating advanced forms, adding charts to forms, creating advanced reports, creating a document for the Web, creating and using hyperlinks, exporting, importing, and linking data.

Learning Outcome: Upon successful completion of this course, the student will be able to review basic query techniques; specify complex criteria in a query; perform calculations in a query; create a multi-table query; create crosstab, action, and parameter queries; define permanent relationships between tables and enforced referential integrity; specify key fields and indexes; customize fields and validate data using field properties; create custom forms to improve data entry; add a chart to a form or report using the chart wizard; create a report based on a query; create summary reports and perform calculations within a report; edit, enhance, and customize a chart using Microsoft graph; create a document for the web; create and use hyperlinks; export access data to different file formats; and import and link data from other applications.

Instruction: Major topics covered in the course are reviewing basic query techniques; exploring advanced query techniques; creating cross tab, action, and parameter queries; working with relationships, key fields, and indexes; using properties to customize fields; creating custom forms; creating advanced forms; creating advanced reports; and working with external data. Methods of instruction include lecture, interactive demonstrations, instructor-led exercises, independent exercises, discussions, audio-visual material, pre- and post-class tests, final examination, observation, and hands-on classroom exercises.

Credit Recommendation: In the lower division baccalaureate/associate degree category, 1 semester hour in Microcomputer Application (8/97). **NOTE:** Student should receive credit for completion of only one Advanced Access course either Access 2.0 for Windows Advanced, Access 7.0 for Windows 95 Advanced, or Access 97 for Windows 95/NT 4.0 Advanced.

Access 97 for Windows 95/NT 4.0 Introduction

Location: Various locations throughout North America.

Length: 14 hours (2 days).

Dates: January 1997-Present.

Objective: To explore designing a database, creating, viewing, editing and relating tables, sorting and filtering data, creating queries based on single and multiple tables, designing and using custom data entry forms, and creating/printing reports and labels.

Learning Outcome: Upon successful completion of this course, the student will be able to define database concepts and key features of Access; start Access and identify the components of the interface; use the various types of Help available; add, edit, locate, and delete table records; use the Spell Checker to check for spelling errors in a table; create and open databases; design, create, and modify tables; sort and filter data using a variety of techniques; create basic queries, as well as queries based upon multiple tables; establish permanent relationships between tables; and design and customize data entry forms, reports, and mailing labels.

Instruction: Major topics covered in the course are exploring Access, working with tables, working with records, designing and creating tables, modifying the design of tables, sorting and filtering data, querying data, creating advanced queries, creating and using basic forms, and creating basic reports and labels. Methods of instruction include lecture, interactive demonstrations, instructor-led exercises, independent exercises, discussions, audio-visual material, pre- and post-class tests, final examination, observations, and hand-on classroom exercises.

Credit Recommendation: In the lower division baccalaureate/associate category, 1 semester hour in Microcomputer Applications (8/97). **NOTE:** Student should receive credit for completion of only one Introduction Access course either Access 2.0 for Windows Introduction, Access 7.0 for Windows 95 Introduction, or Access 97 for Windows 95/NT 4.0 Introduction.

Excel 5.0 for Windows and Macintosh Advanced

Location: Various locations throughout North America.

Length: 7 hours (1 day).

Dates: October 1994-Present.

Objective: To explore concepts and offer hands-on practice in creating custom Excel toolbars, auditing, annotating, and applying advanced worksheet analysis techniques as well as linking, protecting, and consolidating information and creating outlines; procedures for creating and using worksheets as databases and searching, finding, extracting, and presenting information using advanced database techniques are also covered; and analyzing worksheets using advanced techniques involving Goal Seek, Scenarios, and logical functions.

Learning Outcome: Upon successful completion of this course, the student will be able to create custom toolbars; analyze worksheets using features including the Info window, notes, Goal Seek, and Scenarios; use advanced logical functions including, IF, VLOOKUP, and HLOOKUP; consolidate and protect information; link files; create outlines, and use a variety of database techniques to query, search, extract, and present information.

Instruction: Major topics covered in the course are customizing toolbars, analyzing worksheets, using advanced functions, applying file techniques, creating and manipulating database information and presenting database information. Methods of instruction include lecture, interactive demonstrations, instructor-led exercises, independent exercises, discussions, audio-visual material and pre- and post class tests.

Credit Recommendation: In the lower division baccalaureate/associate degree category, 1 semester hour in Microcomputer Applications for successful completion of any two of the following three: Excel 5.0 for Windows and Macintosh Introduction, Excel 5.0 for Windows and Macintosh Intermediate, and/or Excel 5.0 for Windows and Macintosh Advanced (8/96). **NOTE**: Student should receive credit for completion of Excel 5.0, Excel 7.0 or Excel 97 courses.

Excel 5.0 for Windows and Macintosh Intermediate

Location: Various locations throughout North America.

Length: 7 hours (1 day).

Dates: October 1994-Present.

Objective: To explore worksheet and chart capabilities in Excel, including special Toolbars; statistical, financial, date and time functions; multiple workbooks, windows, titles, and views; use formatting features including fonts and styles, and create graphic objects to enhance documents; covers chart tools and ChartWizard to create embedded charts and separate chart documents; change chart types and formats, and add and modify chart objects.

Learning Outcome: Upon successful completion of this course, the student will be able to review worksheet concepts; use tools in the four Toolbars; work with multiple windows and documents; use special worksheet features to lock and freeze titles; create and use range names; use statistical and financial functions in formulas; use functions to time and date a report; create and use styles; create and modify charts for a workbook, and print worksheets and charts.

Instruction: Major topics covered in the course are reviewing Excel basics, using workbooks and multiple windows, using worksheet commands, using functions, enhancing a worksheet and constructing charts. Methods of instruction include lecture, interactive demonstrations, instructor-led exercises, independent exercises, discussions, audio-visual material, and pre- and post class tests.

Credit Recommendation: In the lower division baccalaureate/associate degree category, 1 semester hour in Microcomputer Applications for successful completion of any two of the following three: Excel 5.0 for Windows and Macintosh Introduction, Excel 5.0 for Windows and Macintosh Intermediate, and/or Excel 5.0 for Windows and Macintosh Advanced (8/96). **NOTE**: Student should receive credit for completion of Excel 5.0, Excel 7.0 or Excel 97 courses.

Excel 5.0 for Windows and Macintosh Introduction

Location: Various locations throughout North America.

Length: 7 hours (1 day).

Dates: October 1994-Present.

Objective: To explore spreadsheets using Excel 5.0, with an emphasis on features like the toolbar; drag and drop; shortcut menus; and automatic commands such as AutoFormat, AutoFill, and AutoSum; creating worksheets containing constant values and formulas, then modifying the contents and appearance of these worksheets and printing them.

Learning Outcome: Upon successful completion of this course, the student will be able to enter and change constant values; save and retrieve Excel files; enter both simple formulas and functions by typing, pointing, and using AutoSum and the Paste command; study concepts including the mathematical order of operations, and absolute and relative cell references; use other features like shortcut menus; AutoFill, drag and drop; and commands such as copy, cut, clear, and paste; use the standard Toolbar and menu commands to change selections with number formats, cell alignments, fonts, cell borders, and patterns; change worksheet appearance with AutoFormat by inserting, deleting, and changing the size of columns/rows; preview and print entire and partial worksheets with new margins, headers and footers, gridlines, and column headings.

Instruction: Major topics covered in the course are exploring Excel 5.0, entering constant values, working with files, changing cell contents, entering formulas, using help, copying and moving, changing cell appearance, changing worksheet appearance and printing worksheets. Methods of instruction include lecture, interactive demonstrations, instructor-led exercises, independent exercises, discussions, audio-visual material, and pre- and post class tests.

Credit Recommendation: In the lower division baccalaureate/associate degree category, 1 semester hour in Microcomputer Applications for successful completion of any two of the following three: Excel 5.0 for Windows and Macintosh Introduction, Excel 5.0 for Windows and Macintosh Intermediate, and/or Excel 5.0 for Windows and Macintosh Advanced (8/96). **NOTE**: Student should receive credit for completion of Excel 5.0, Excel 7.0 or Excel 97 courses.

Excel 7.0 for Windows 95 Advanced

Location: Various locations throughout North America.

Length: 7 hours (1 day).

Dates: December 1995-Present.

Objective: To explore concepts and offers hands-on practice in creating custom Excel toolbars, auditing, annotating, and applying advanced worksheet analysis techniques as well as linking, protecting, and consolidating information and creating outlines; creating and using worksheets as databases and searching, finding, extracting, and presenting information using advanced database techniques are also covered; analyzing worksheets using advanced techniques involving Goal Seek, Scenarios, and logical functions.

Learning Outcome: Upon successful completion of this course, the student will be able to create custom toolbars; analyze worksheets using Auditing routines, Info window, Notes, Goal Seek, and Scenarios; use advanced logical functions including, IF, VLOOKUP, and HLOOKUP; consolidate and protect information, linked files, and create outlines; use a variety of database techniques to query, search, extract, and present information.

Instruction: Major topics covered in the course are customizing Excel, analyzing worksheets, using advanced functions, applying file techniques, working with spreadsheets as database lists and presenting database information using database functions, subtotals and grand totals and analyzing information with pivot tables. Methods of instruction include lecture, interactive demonstrations, instructor-led exercises, independent exercises, discussions, audio-visual material and pre- and post class tests.

Credit Recommendation: In the lower division baccalaureate/associate degree category, 1 semester hour in Microcomputer Applications for successful completion of any two of the following three: Excel 7.0 for Windows 95 Introduction, Excel 7.0 for Windows 95 Intermediate, and/or Excel 7.0 for Windows 95 Advanced (8/96). **NOTE**: Student should receive credit for completion of Excel 5.0, Excel 7.0 or Excel 97 courses.

Excel 7.0 for Windows 95 Intermediate

Location: Various locations throughout North America.

Length: 7 hours (1 day).

Dates: December 1995-Present.

Objective: To explore worksheet and chart capabilities in Excel, including special toolbars; financial functions, multiple workbooks, windows, titles, and views; use formatting features including fonts and styles, and create graphic objects to enhance documents; use chart tools and the ChartWizard to create both embedded charts and separate chart documents by changing chart types and formats, and adding and modifying chart objects.

Learning Outcome: Upon successful completion of this course, the student will be able to review worksheet concepts; move and copy data; print worksheets and charts; work with multiple windows and documents; use special worksheet features to lock and freeze titles; create and use range names; use financial functions in formulas; create and used styles and templates; create and modify charts for a workbook; map data; and modify map elements.

Instruction: Major topics covered in the course are reviewing Excel basics, creating and using multiple sheet files, managing workbooks, using functions, enhancing a worksheet and creating charts and maps. Methods of instruction include lecture, interactive demonstrations, instructor-led exercises, independent exercises, discussions, audio-visual material, and pre- and post class tests.

Credit Recommendation: In the lower division baccalaureate/associate degree category, 1 semester hour in Microcomputer Applications for successful completion of any two of the following three: Excel 7.0 for Windows 95 Introduction, Excel 7.0 for Windows 95 Intermediate, and/or Excel 7.0 for Windows 95 Advanced (8/96). **NOTE**: Student should receive credit for completion of Excel 5.0, Excel 7.0 or Excel 97 courses.

Excel 7.0 for Windows 95 Introduction

Location: Various locations throughout North America.

Length: 7 hours (1 day).

Dates: December 1995-Present.

Objective: To explore Excel 7.0 for Windows 95, creating worksheets containing constant values and formulas, then modifying the contents and appearance of these worksheets and printing them; emphasis on features like the toolbar; drag and drop; shortcut menus; and automatic commands such as AutoFill, AutoSum, AutoCalculate, AutoComplete, and AutoFormat.

Learning Outcome: Upon successful completion of this course, the student will be able to examine the new look and features of Excel 7.0 for Windows 95; enter and change constant values; save and retrieve Excel files; enter both simple formulas and formulas with functions by typing, pointing, and using AutoSum and AutoCalculate; study concepts including the mathematical order of operations, and absolute and relative cell references; use other features like shortcut menus, AutoFill, drag and drop, AutoComplete and commands such as copy, cut, clear, and paste; use the toolbars and menu commands to change selections with number formats, cell alignments, fonts, cell borders, and patterns; use the Spell Check and AutoCorrect features; change worksheet appearance with AutoFormat and by inserting, deleting, and changing the size of columns/rows; preview and print entire and partial worksheets with new margins, headers and footers, gridlines, and column headings.

Instruction: Major topics covered in the course are exploring Excel 7.0, creating a worksheet, entering constant values, working with files, changing cell contents, entering formulas, using help, copying and moving, changing cell appearance, changing worksheet appearance and printing worksheets. Methods of instruction include lecture, interactive demonstrations, instructor-led exercises, independent exercises, discussions, audio-visual material, and pre- and post class tests.

Credit Recommendation: In the lower division baccalaureate/associate degree category, 1 semester hour in Microcomputer Applications for successful completion of any two of the following three: Excel 7.0 for Windows 95 Introduction, Excel 7.0 for Windows 95 Intermediate, and/or Excel 7.0 for Windows 95 Advanced (8/96). **NOTE**: Student should receive credit for completion of Excel 5.0, Excel 7.0 or Excel 97 courses.

Excel 97 for Windows 95/NT 4.0 Advanced

Location: Various locations throughout North America.

Length: 7 hours.

Dates: April 1997-Present.

Objective: To explore several of the advanced tools that Excel provides for analyzing and summarizing data to include special features, built-in functions, and Internet access

Learning Outcome: Upon successful completion of this course, the student will be able to analyze a worksheet using auditing tools; use the Goal Seek tool to complete a calculation; create and report several worksheet scenarios; use date and time functions and numeric functions in a worksheet; create formulas using a variety of functions, link worksheet data, protect files, worksheets, and cells; track changes to a shared file; sort a data list and use a data form to edit and review data; set data validation rules on a data list; filter a data list using the Autofilter tool; summarize a data list using subtotals and grand totals; summarize a data list using pivot tables; and explore Excel's Internet features.

Instruction: Major topics covered in the course are reviewing Excel basics, working with workbook sheets, managing the workbook display, using named ranges, creating charts and enhancing a worksheet, and using special features and built-in functions. Methods of instruction include lecture, interactive demonstrations, instructor-led exercises, independent exercises, discussions, audio-visual material, pre- and post-class tests, final examination, observations, and hands-on classroom exercises.

Credit Recommendation: In the lower division baccalaureate/associate degree category, 1 semester hour in Microcomputer Applications for successful completion of this course and one of the following: Excel 97 for Windows 95/NT 4.0 Introduction or Excel 97 for Windows 95/NT 4.0 Intermediate (8/97). **NOTE:** Student should receive credit for successful completion of only one of following either Excel 5.0 for Windows and Macintosh, Excel 7.0 for Windows 95, or Excel 97 for Windows 95/NT 4.0 courses.

Excel 97 for Windows 95/NT 4.0 Intermediate

Location: Various locations throughout North America.

Length: 7 hours.

Dates: February 1997-Present.

Objective: To explore the basic worksheet and chart capabilities in Excel 1997.

Learning Outcome: Upon successful completion of this course, the student will be able to employ worksheet concepts; move and copy data; print worksheets and charts; work with multiple windows and documents; manage multiple sheet workbooks; use special worksheet features to lock and freeze titles; create and apply custom views; create and use range names; create and use styles and templates; create and modify charts for a workbook; and add graphic objects using the drawing toolbar.

Instruction: Major topics covered in the course are reviewing Excel basics, working with workbook sheets, managing the workbook display, using named ranges, creating charts, and enhancing a worksheet. Methods of instruction include lecture, interactive demonstrations, instructor-led exercises, independent exercises, discussions, audio-visual material, pre- and post-class tests, final examination, observations, and hands-on classroom exercises.

Credit Recommendation: In the lower division baccalaureate/associate degree category, 1 semester hour in Microcomputer Applications for successful completion of this course and one of the following: Excel 97 for Windows 95/NT 4.0 Introduction or Excel 97 for Windows 95/NT 4.0 Advanced (8/97). **NOTE:** Students should receive credit for completion of only one of the following either Excel 5.0 for Windows and Macintosh , Excel 7.0 for Windows 95, or Excel 97 for Windows 95/NT 4.0 courses.

Excel 97 for Windows 95/NT 4.0 Introduction

Location: Various locations throughout North America.

Length: 7 hours.

Dates: January 1997-Present.

Objective: To explore the creation, modification, and printing of worksheets with an emphasis on features such as the toolbar, drag and drop, shortcut menus, and automatic commands.

Learning Outcome: Upon successful completion of this course, the student will be able to examine the new look and features of Excel 97 for Windows 95; enter and change constant values; save and retrieve Excel files; enter both simple formulas and formulas with functions by typing, pointing, and using Autosum and Autocalculate; understand concepts including the mathematical order of operations, and absolute and relative cell references; use other features such as shortcut menus, Autofill, drag and drop, Autocomplete, and commands such as copy, cut, clear, and paste; use the toolbars and menu commands to change selections with number formats, cell alignments, fonts, cell borders, and patterns; use the spell check and Autocorrect features; change worksheet appearance with autoformat, insert, delete, and change the size of columns/rows; and preview and print entire and partial worksheets with new margins, headers and footers, gridlines, and column headings.

Instruction: Major topics covered in the course are exploring Excel 97, creating a worksheet, editing techniques, entering formulas, moving and copying data, changing cell appearance, changing worksheet appearance, and printing worksheets. Methods of instruction include lecture, interactive demonstrations, instructor-led exercises, independent exercises, discussions, audio-visual material, pre- and post-class tests, final examination, observations, and hands-on classroom exercises.

Credit Recommendation: In the lower division baccalaureate/associate degree category, 1 semester hour in Microcomputer Applications for successful completion of this course and one of the following: Excel 97 for Windows 95/NT 4.0 Intermediate or Excel 97 for Windows 95/NT 4.0 Advanced (8/97). **NOTE:** Students should receive credit for completion of only one of the following either Excel 5.0 for Windows and Macintosh, Excel 7.0 for Windows 95, or Excel 97 for Windows 95/NT 4.0 courses.

PowerPoint 4.0 for Windows and Macintosh Advanced

Location: Various locations throughout North America.

Length: 7 hours (1 day).

Dates: August 1994-Present.

Objective: To explore advanced techniques used in presentation graphics to customize PowerPoint, design and create custom templates and color schemes, and apply special presentation graphic effects; techniques involved in importing and exporting data between PowerPoint and other applications.

Learning Outcome: Upon successful completion of this course, the student will be able customized PowerPoint by changing the default fonts and template; design custom color schemes; design and create a custom template, color scheme, and multiple-template presentation; add charts, graphs, and organizations charts to presentations; create a build-slide, branch presentations, and rehearse presentation timings; apply presentation transitions and other special effects; and import and export data.

Instruction: Major topics covered in the course are customizing PowerPoint, designing color schemes, designing templates, graphing data, creating organizational charts, applying advanced slide show techniques, sharing information and managing files. Methods of instruction include lecture, interactive demonstrations, instructor-led exercises, independent exercises, discussions, audio-visual material, and pre- and post class tests.

Credit Recommendation: In the lower division baccalaureate/associate degree category, 1 semester hour in Microcomputer Applications (8/96). **NOTE**: Student must complete both PowerPoint 4.0 for Windows and Macintosh Introduction and PowerPoint 4.0 for Windows and Macintosh Advanced courses to receive credit. Student should receive credit for

PowerPoint 4.0, PowerPoint 7.0, or PowerPoint 97 courses.

PowerPoint 4.0 for Windows and Macintosh Introduction

Location: Various locations throughout North America.

Length: 7 hours (1 day).

Dates: August 1994-Present.

Objective: To explore presentation graphics concepts needed to plan, compose, and create complete presentations.

Learning Outcome: Upon successful completion of this course, the student will be able to use Wizards to create presentations and format existing presentations; use Masters and Templates to give presentations consistent design formats; edit and revise presentations by manipulating text, graphics, and slides to achieve the desired effect; create a variety of objects using drawing tools; add graphics text and Clip Art objects to presentations; produce a self-running PC based presentation, and save and print a presentation, handouts, and notes pages.

Instruction: Major topics covered in the course are exploring the PowerPoint environment, working with presentations, working with slides, working with text, working with objects, creating outlines and notes pages, working with masters and templates and working with slide shows. Methods of instruction include lecture, interactive demonstrations, instructor-led exercises, independent exercises, discussions, audio-visual material, and pre- and post class tests.

Credit Recommendation: In the lower division baccalaureate/associate degree category, 1 semester hour in Microcomputer Applications (8/96). **NOTE**: Student must complete both PowerPoint 4.0 for Windows and Macintosh Introduction and PowerPoint 4.0for Windows and Macintosh Advanced courses to receive credit. Student should receive credit for PowerPoint 4.0, PowerPoint 7.0, or Powerpoint 97 courses.

PowerPoint 7.0 for Windows 95 Advanced

Location: Various locations throughout North America.

Length: 7 hours (1 day).

Dates: December 1995-Present.

Objective: To explore advanced text formatting features, drawing techniques and charting; create tables and organization charts; work with and customize color palettes and templates, and share data with other applications; use advanced slide show features, including branching, animation setting, the Slide Meter, and the Meeting Minder.

Learning Outcome: Upon successful completion of this course, the student will be able to format text with advanced tools; use advanced techniques to modify and manipulate graphics objects; use advanced graphing techniques and create and enhance custom graphs, combination charts, and pie charts; create and modify tables and organization charts; work with and customize color palettes and templates; create a slide show with special effects and annotation.

Instruction: Major topics covered in the course are advanced text formatting, advanced drawing techniques, advanced charting, working with organization charts and tables, working with color schemes, customizing templates and advanced slide show techniques. Methods of instruction include lecture, interactive demonstrations, instructor-led exercises, independent exercises, discussions, audio-visual material, and pre- and post class tests.

Credit Recommendation: In the lower division baccalaureate/associate degree category, 1 semester hour in Microcomputer Applications (8/96). **NOTE**: Student must complete both PowerPoint 7.0 for Windows 95 Introduction and PowerPoint 7.0 for Windows 95 Advanced courses to receive credit. Student should receive credit for PowerPoint 4.0, PowerPoint 7.0, or PowerPoint 97 courses.

PowerPoint 7.0 for Windows 95 Introduction

Location: Various locations throughout North America.

Length: 7 hours (1 day).

Dates: December 1995-Present.

Objective: To explore creating a presentation from scratch, applying a template, choosing slide layouts, and working with placeholders; adding clip art, objects, and charts to a presentation; running a slide show and formatting a presentation for printing.

Learning Outcome: Upon successful completion of this course, the student will be able to review presentation components, explore the PowerPoint 7.0 environment, and discuss how to plan a presentation; use toolbars, menus, and the status bar to create and revise a presentation; use Outline view to work with presentation slides and text; select, edit, and format text; check presentation spelling; add graphics objects to a presentation; create charts for a presentation; copy, delete, and move presentation slides; set print options and print a slide, an outline, handouts, and speaker notes; rehearse a slide show and add transitions and builds.

Instruction: Major topics covered in the course are exploring the PowerPoint environment, creating a presentation, working with text, working in outline view, working with slides, working with objects, working with graphs, and finalizing and printing a presentation. Methods of instruction include lecture, interactive demonstrations, instructor-led exercises, independent exercises, discussions, audio-visual material, and pre- and post class tests.

Credit Recommendation: In the lower division baccalaureate/associate degree category, 1 semester hour in Microcomputer Applications for Windows 95 (8/96). **NOTE**: Student must complete both PowerPoint 7.0 for Windows 95 Introduction and PowerPoint 7.0 for Windows 95 Advanced courses to receive credit. Student should receive credit for PowerPoint 4.0, PowerPoint 7.0, or PowerPoint 97 courses.

PowerPoint 97 for Windows 95/NT 4.0 Advanced

Location: Various locations throughout North America.

Length: 7 hours.

Dates: April 1997-Present.

Objective: To work with advanced text formatting features, drawing techniques, and charting. This course also explores creating tables and organization charts. It examines how to work with and customize color palettes and templates, and share data with other applications. It also includes learning how to use advanced slide show features, including branching, animation setting, the Slide Meter, presentation conferencing, and the Meeting Minder.

Learning Outcome: Upon successful completion of this course, the student will be able to format text with advanced tools; use advanced techniques to modify and manipulate graphic objects; use advanced graphing techniques; create and enhance custom graphs, combination charts, and pie charts; create and modify tables and organization charts; work with and customize color palettes and templates; and create a slide show with special effects and annotation.

Instruction: Major topics covered in the course are advanced text formatting, advanced drawing techniques, advanced charting, working with organization charts and tables, working with color schemes, customizing templates, and advanced slide show techniques. Methods of instruction include lecture, interactive demonstrations, instructor-led exercises, independent exercises, discussions, audio-visual material, pre- and post-class tests, final examination, observations, and hands-on classroom exercises.

Credit Recommendation: In the lower division baccalaureate/associate degree category, 1 semester hour in Microcomputer Applications for successful completion of both PowerPoint 97 for Windows 95/NT 4.0 Introduction and PowerPoint 97 for Windows 95/NT 4.0 Advanced (8/97). **NOTE:** Students should receive credit for completion of only one of the following either PowerPoint 4.0 for Windows and Macintosh, PowerPoint 7.0 for Windows 95, or PowerPoint 97 for Windows 95/NT 4.0 courses.

PowerPoint 97 for Windows 95/NT 4.0 Introduction

Location: Various locations throughout North America.

Length: 7 hours.

Dates: January 1997-Present.

Objective: To explore the basics of creating a presentation, applying a template, choosing slide layouts, and working with placeholders. This course also includes adding clip art, objects, and charts to a presentation that also covers running a slide show and formatting a presentation for printing.

Learning Outcome: Upon successful completion of this course, the student will be able to review presentation components; explore the PowerPoint 1997 environment; plan a presentation; use toolbars, menus, and the status bar to create and revise a presentation; use outline view to work with presentation slides and text; select, edit, and format text; check presentation spelling; add graphics and objects to a presentation; create charts for a presentation; copy, delete, and move presentation slides; set print options and print a slide, an outline, and speaker notes; rehearse a slide show; and add transitions and builds.

Instruction: Major topics covered in the course are exploring the PowerPoint environment, creating a presentation, working with text, working in outline view, working with slides, working with objects, working with graphs, and finalizing and printing a presentation. Methods of instruction include lecture, interactive demonstrations, instructor-led exercises, independent exercises, discussions, audio-visual material, pre- and post-class tests, final examination, observations, and hands-on classroom exercises.

Credit Recommendation: In the lower division baccalaureate/associate degree category, 1 semester hour in Microcomputer Applications for completion of both PowerPoint 97 for Windows 95/NT 4.0 Introduction and PowerPoint 97 for Windows 95/NT 4.0 Advanced (8/97). **NOTE:** Students should receive credit for completion of only one of the following either PowerPoint for Windows and Macintosh, PowerPoint 7.0 for Windows 95, or PowerPoint 97 for Windows 95/NT 4.0 courses.

Project 4.0 for Windows and Macintosh Introduction

Location: Various locations throughout North America.

Length: 14 hours (2 days).

Dates: August 1994-Present.

Objective: To explore Microsoft Project for Windows and Macintosh from two perspectives as a project reviewer and as a project creator; also explores the basic commands for reviewing, building, and revising project plans; reporting project progress and tasks; and tracking costs.

Learning Outcome: Upon successful completion of this course, the student will be able to review existing project plans using various views; plan, design, and create new projects; create, modify, and use standard and custom views; enter and report information about project tasks and assigned resources; analyze and examine projects from various perspectives; update and track project progress; generate reports to communicate project plan components.

Instruction: Major topics covered in the course are introducing project management, exploring Microsoft Project, planning a project, defining the tasks, entering resources and costs, auditing the project, tracking work on the project, using and enhancing views and printing views and reports. Methods of instruction include lecture, interactive demonstrations, instructor-led exercises, independent exercises, discussions, audio-visual material, and pre- and post class tests.

Credit Recommendation: In the lower division baccalaureate/associate degree category, 1 semester hour in Computer Information Systems, Management Information Systems, or Microcomputer Applications (8/96). **NOTE**: Student should receive credit for PowerPoint 4.0, PowerPoint7.0 Power Project 4.1 courses, but not both.

Project 4.1 for Windows 95 Introduction

Location: Various locations throughout North America.

Length: 14 hours (2 days).

Dates: December 1995-Present.

Objective: To explore the tools that Project 4.1 for Windows provides for creating and managing projects; planning a project, customizing calendars, building a workplan outline, creating dependency links, and defining resources as well as assigning resources to tasks; managing resource allocation, setting a baseline for a project, tracking progress on a project; formatting views; and printing.

Learning Outcome: Upon successful completion of this course, the student will be able to create and save a new project file; define and outline a project task list; create and modify task dependency links; define a resource pool and assign resources to various tasks; explore several methods for managing resource work; set a baseline for a project; track actual progress on a project and reschedule incomplete work; format a Gantt Chart view, include task bars, timescales, and text attributes and preview and print views and reports.

Instruction: Major topics covered in the course are introducing project management, exploring Microsoft Project, planning a project, defining and outlining tasks, creating task dependencies, defining and assigning resources, managing resource allocations, finalizing the project plan, tracking work on the project and enhancing views and printing. Methods of instruction include lecture, interactive demonstrations, instructor-led exercises, independent exercises, discussions, audio-visual material, and pre- and post class tests.

Credit Recommendation: In the lower division baccalaureate/associate degree category, 1 semester hour in Computer Information Systems, Management Information Systems, or Microcomputer Applications (8/96). **NOTE**: Student should receive credit for either Project 4.1 or Project 4.0 courses, but not both.

Word 6.0 for Windows Desktop Publishing

Location: Various locations throughout North America.

Length: 7 hours (1 day).

Dates: August 1994-Present.

Objective: To explore advanced features of Word for Windows which enhance the professionalism and communicability of documents.

Learning Outcome: Upon successful completion of this course, the student will be able to identify concepts and methods used in desktop publishing; manage and apply different fonts and font enhancements within documents; insert special symbols such as copyright or trademark symbols into a document; create a drop cap for the first letter in a paragraph; create and manage text columns; use styles to create faster and more consistent formatting within and between documents; create borders, shading, and graphics in a document; automatically generate a table of contents and index; and use a master document to organize long documents.

Instruction: Major topics covered in the course are using Word for desktop publishing, working with type and spacing, working with the page layout, using styles for consistency and efficiency, enhancing a document with borders and graphics and creating a table of contents, index and master documents. Methods of instruction include lecture, interactive demonstrations, instructor-led exercises, independent exercises, discussions, audio-visual material, and pre- and post class tests.

Credit Recommendation: In the lower division baccalaureate/associate degree category, 1 semester hour in Microcomputer Applications for successful completion of any two of the following three: Word 6.0 for Windows Introduction, Word 6.0 for Windows Productivity, and/or Word 6.0 for Windows Desktop Publishing (8/96). **NOTE**: Student should receive credit for Word 6.0, Word 7.0, or Word 97 courses.

Word 6.0 for Windows Introduction

Location: Various locations throughout North America.

Length: 7 hours (1 day).

Dates: August 1994-Present.

Objective: To explore the basics of document preparation, including entering and enhancing text, checking the spelling, and previewing and printing documents; saving documents; opening existing documents; and modifying documents.

Learning Outcome: Upon successful completion of this course, the student will be able to create a simple business document using manual formatting and Wizards; enhance the appearance and readability of documents using features such as center, indent, underline, boldface, and various fonts; edit and revise documents quickly and easily by inserting, deleting, copying, and moving blocks of text; use the AutoCorrect feature;

Instruction: Major topics covered in the course are using the shortcut menu, toolbars and rulers, getting online help, creating a document, editing a document, improving the accuracy of documents, formatting lines and paragraphs, formatting pages and printing a document. Methods of instruction include lecture, interactive demonstrations, instructor-led exercises, independent exercises, discussions, audio-visual material, and pre- and post class tests.

Credit Recommendation: In the lower division baccalaureate/associate degree category, 1 semester hour in Microcomputer Applications for successful completion of any two of the following three: Word 6.0 for Windows Introduction, Word 6.0 for Windows Productivity, and/or Word 6.0 for Windows Desktop Publishing (8/96). **NOTE**: Student should receive credit for Word 6.0, Word 7.0, or Word 97 courses.

Word 6.0 for Windows Productivity

Location: Various locations throughout North America.

Length: 7 hours (1 day).

Dates: August 1994-Present.

Objective: To explore techniques for producing multi-page documents including using templates and Wizards; creating tables, creating and using custom forms; creating and using macros, and AutoText, and using mail merge.

Learning Outcome: Upon successful completion of this course, the student will be able to control the Windows environment to display and edit more than one document; create documents using Wizards and templates; create a template; create tables; perform simple calculations in tables; use tables to create custom forms; automate repetitive tasks using macros and AutoText; customize the Word environment by changing the options; modify or create a Toolbar; adding macros to the Toolbars or menus; prepare form letters; envelopes, and labels; and use the Merge feature.

Instruction: Major topics covered in the course are reviewing document formatting, producing documents quickly, organizing data with tables, customizing word and automating tasks, producing documents with merge and managing documents on disk. Methods of instruction include lecture, interactive demonstrations, instructor-led exercises, independent exercises, discussions, audio-visual material, and pre- and post class tests.

Credit Recommendation: In the lower division baccalaureate/associate degree category, 1 semester hour in Microcomputer Applications for successful completion of any two of the following three: Word 6.0 for Windows Introduction, Word 6.0 for Windows Productivity, and/or Word 6.0 for Windows Desktop Publishing (8/96). **NOTE**: Student should receive credit for Word 6.0, Word 7.0, or Word 97 courses.

Word 7.0 for Windows 95 Advanced

Location: Various locations throughout North America.

Length: 7 hours (1 day).

Dates: November 1995-Present.

Objective: To explore applying special effects and inserting graphics; creating and editing templates; creating complex documents; creating, running, and editing simple macros; and embedding and linking objects.

Learning Outcome: Upon successful completion of this course, the student will be able to created a text box and a frame; insert a graphic; insert text enhanced with WordArt; insert Drop Caps; use borders and shading; create a new template; create a form with fill-in fields; create a master document with subdocuments; generate a table of contents; create, run, and edit a simple macro; and embed and link OLE objects.

Instruction: Major topics covered in the course are applying special graphics effects, designing templates, designing outline forms, working with complex documents, automating tasks using macros and sharing information. Methods of instruction include lecture, interactive demonstrations, instructor-led exercises, independent exercises, discussions, audio-visual material, and pre- and post class tests.

Credit Recommendation: In the lower division baccalaureate/associate degree category, 1 semester hour in Microcomputer Applications for successful completion of any two of the following three: Word 7.0 for Windows 95 Introduction, Word 7.0 for Windows 95 Intermediate, and/or Word 7.0 for Windows 95 Advanced (8/96). **NOTE**: Student should receive credit for Word 6.0, Word 7.0, or Word 97 courses.

Word 7.0 for Windows 95 Intermediate

Location: Various locations throughout North America.

Length: 7 hours (1 day).

Dates: November 1995-Present.

Objective: To explore setting up defaults for the working environment; creating and using styles; creating, modifying, and enhancing tables; merging form letters, envelopes, and labels with lists; and using formatting techniques for multi-page documents, columns, and outlines.

Learning Outcome: Upon successful completion of this course, the student will be able to apply and modify styles; create new styles; create tables and modify their structure; enhance tables with borders and shading; create a merge document and Data Source File; create a merge envelope and label; create headers and footers; use multiple columns; insert section breaks; create an outline and insert a graphic.

Instruction: Major topics covered in the course are setting up the environment, working with styles, creating tables, exploring merging, advanced merging techniques, and applying formatting techniques. Methods of instruction include lecture, interactive demonstrations, instructor-led exercises, independent exercises, discussions, audio-visual material, and pre- and post class tests.

Credit Recommendation: In the lower division baccalaureate/associate degree category, 1 semester hour in Microcomputer Applications for successful completion of any two of the following three: Word 7.0 for Windows 95 Introduction, Word 7.0 for Windows 95 Intermediate, and/or Word 7.0 for Windows 95 Advanced (8/96). **NOTE**: Student should receive credit for Word 6.0, Word 7.0, or Word 97 courses.

Word 7.0 for Windows 95 Introduction

Location: Various locations throughout North America.

Length: 7 hours (1 day).

Dates: November 1995-Present.

Objective: To explore the basics of creating and editing letters and other professional documents; focusing on using Word for Windows 95 ease-of-use features to effectively create, edit, format, save, and print business documents.

Learning Outcome: Upon successful completion of this course, the student will be able to open Word for Windows 95 and examine the components of the screen;

Instruction: Major topics covered in the course are exploring Word for Windows 95, creating a document, editing a document, formatting text, formatting pages and paragraphs, previewing and printing a document and creating an envelope. Methods of instruction include lecture, interactive demonstrations, instructor-led exercises, independent exercises, discussions, audio-visual material, and pre- and post class tests.

Credit Recommendation: In the lower division baccalaureate/associate degree category, 1 semester hour in Microcomputer Applications for successful completion of any two of the following three: Word 7.0 for Windows 95 Introduction, Word 7.0 for Windows 95 Intermediate, and/or Word 7.0 for Windows 95 Advanced (8/96). **NOTE**: Student should receive credit for Word 6.0, Word 7.0, or Word 97 courses.

Word 97 for Windows 95/NT 4.0 Advanced

Location: Various locations throughout North America.

Length: 7 hours.

Dates: April 1997-Present.

Objective: To explore the more advanced features of Word 1997 including designing templates and on-line forms, working with long documents and master documents that have tables of contents and index, and creating HTML documents that can be used on the World Wide Web.

Learning Outcome: Upon successful completion of this course, the student will be able to create a chart; create newspaper columns; design and use a template; create a long document with alternating headers and footers, a table of contents, cross references, footnotes, endnotes, and an index; create a master document; create and edit a macro; create multiple versions of a document; track changes in a revised document; create and use an on-line form; save a document as an HTML file and format it; and preview the HTML file.

Instruction: Major topics covered in the course are using charts, using newspaper columns, designing templates, working with complex documents, automating tasks using macros, tracking changes, designing on-line forms, and creating HTML files. Methods of instruction include lecture, interactive demonstrations, instructor-led exercises, independent exercises, discussions, audio-visual material, pre- and post-class tests, final examination, observations, and hands-on classroom exercises.

Credit Recommendation: In the lower division baccalaureate/associate degree category, 1 semester hour in Microcomputer Applications for successful completion of this course and one of the following: Word 97 for Windows 95/NT 4.0 Introduction or Word 97 for Windows 95/NT 4.0 Intermediate (8/97). **NOTE:** Students should receive credit for successful completion of only one of the following either Word 6.0, Word 7.0, or Word 97 courses.

Word 97 for Windows 95/NT 4.0 Intermediate

Location: Various locations throughout North America

Length: 7 hours.

Dates: February 1997-Present.

Objective: To explore some of the more sophisticated features of Word 1997 such as using styles, creating tables, and mail merge.

Learning Outcome: Upon successful completion of this course, the student will be able to create, modify, delete, and apply styles; create and delete tables; enter and sort data in a table; modify the table structure; enhance the table with borders and shading; include calculations in a table; import and create a new worksheet; create a main document and data source file and merged them; edit and sort the data source file; create merged envelopes and labels; create a merged catalog; create headers and footers; number pages; create sections; hyphenate text; sort text; create an outline; insert, size, and move a graphic; draw lines, rectangles, ellipses, and Autoshapes; create 3D effects; and create WordArt.

Instruction: Major topics covered in the course are setting up the environment, working with styles and templates, creating tables, exploring merging, using advanced merging techniques, applying formatting techniques, and using graphics and office art. Methods of instruction include lecture, interactive demonstrations, instructor-led exercises, independent exercises, discussions, audio-visual material, pre- and post-class tests, final examination, observations, and hands-on classroom exercises.

Credit Recommendation: In the lower division baccalaureate/associate degree category, 1 semester hour in Microcomputer Applications for successful completion of this course and one of the following: Word 97 for Windows 95/NT 4.0 Introduction or Word 97 for Windows 95/NT 4.0 Advanced (8/97). **NOTE:** Students should receive credit for successful completion of only one of the following courses: Word 6.0, Word 7.0, or Word 97.

Word 97 for Windows 95/NT 4.0 Introduction

Location: Various locations throughout North America.

Length: 7 hours.

Dates: January 1997-Present.

Objective: To explore the basics of creating, editing, formatting, saving, and print business documents.

Learning Outcome: Upon successful completion of this course, the student will be able to open and examine the components of the screen; create, edit, and save a new document; execute commands using the menu, the toolbars, and the shortcut menus; insert a date and time in a document; save and close a document; work with page breaks in a multiple page document; use find and replace to quickly update a document; correct a document with Automatic Spell Checking, the Spelling dialog box, AutoCorrect, and Grammar Checking; use Autotext entries; enhance a document by adding attributes, changing font and font size; apply special characters, adding shading and borders; use the Highlighter to highlight text; change page margins and page orientation for a document; adjust paragraph settings such as tabs, indentation, alignment, line spacing, and text flow options; create numbered and bulleted lists; apply word styles to paragraphs; and print a letter document along with envelopes and mailing labels.

Instruction: Major topics covered in the course are exploring the Word environment, creating a document, editing a document, formatting text, formatting pages and paragraphs, and previewing and printing a document. Methods of instruction include lecture, interactive demonstrations, instructor-led exercises, independent exercises, discussions, audio-visual material, pre- and post-class tests, final examination, observations, and hands-on classroom exercises.

Credit Recommendation: In the lower division baccalaureate/associate degree category, 1 semester hour in Microcom-puter Applications for successful completion of this course and one of the following: Word 97 for Windows 95/NT 4.0 Intermediate or Word 97 for Windows 95/NT 4.0 Advanced (8/97). **NOTE:** Students should receive credit for successful completion of only one of the following either Word 6.0, Word 7.0, or Word 97 courses.

Professionals for Technology, Inc.

Professionals for Technology, Inc., Florida Seminar Institute (Pro-Tech) are World Class experienced professionals providing Consulting Services, Education and Training from the Operator to the Executive Boardroom. The company was founded in 1984 by Peter L. Grieco, Jr., President and CEO. Our focus is on providing high-quality public and in-house training. We want to assist people/companies in implementing solutions which will enable them to compete in a world market place. Our services will help in achieving World Class status, the employee involvement process, inventory management, the elimination of waste, improving total quality and lowering total quality cost.

Education is a necessary cornerstone of any company's continuous improvement plan. Pro-Tech concentrates its efforts on improving the professional capability of all levels and phases of a company's operations. Our training is tailored to meet the specific needs of each business/individual.

All of our courses are taught by a staff of full-time, qualified experts who have gained their experience as top level executives in a wide range of industries; many of them have advanced degrees. Our staff is always gaining a working knowledge of the latest in technology and real world examples by continually providing consulting expertise for our Fortune 500 clients.

Pro-Techs' courses were developed inhouse by our personnel and are taught internationally and across the United States. Each course includes classroom instruction, as well as a workbook and textbook to use as reference materials on the job. These are supplemented with classroom exercises and actual workshops. These courses are offered at client sites and publicly in such cities as: Dallas, Chicago, San Diego, Santa Clara, Pittsburgh, Saddlebrook, Milwaukee, Ft. Lauderdale and many more.

Our courses are primarily attended by presidents, vice presidents, upper and middle level management and professionals in the following areas: purchasing, quality, engineering, human resources, manufacturing, and accounting. Each attendee must pass a classroom test in order to successfully complete our programs. Our goal is to allow the technology transfer to be utilized by individuals who will make the transfer part of their corporate culture. If you would like to receive information about your student record from Pro-Tech, please write to Sarah Worel, Professionals for Technology, Inc., Florida Seminar Institute, 3109 45th Street #100, West Palm Beach, FL 33407.

Source of official student records: Registry of Credit Recommendation, American Council on Education, One Dupont Circle, Washington, DC 20036-1193.

Additional information about the courses: College Credit Recommendation Service, American Council on Education, One Dupont Circle, Washington, DC 20036-1193.

Executive Purchasing (PS133)

Location: Various U.S. and International locations.

Length: 37.5 hours (5 days).

Dates: January 1995-Present.

Objective: To assist individuals and companies in learning strategic planning and the role of purchasing in order to promote the success of the organization.

Learning Outcome: Upon successful completion of this course, the student will be able to develop plans for purchasing; use strategies for competitive purchasing; do centralized and decentralized purchasing; apply decision-making techniques to the organization; use problem-solving tools and applications for purchasing; establish supplier partnerships and purchasing agreements; know the ethics in procurement; understand financial analysis as it applies to purchasing; and develop a purchasing professional team.

Instruction: Major topics covered in the course are the procurement role in strategic planning; decision making techniques; establishing supplier partnerships; legal issues in purchasing, quality, and engineering; and developing purchasing professionals. Methods of instruction include lecture, discussion, and case studies.

Credit Recommendation: In the upper division baccalaureate degree category, 2 semester hours in Business Administration (6/96).

Maintenance Management and Total Preventative Maintenance (MFG117)

Location: Various U.S. and International locations.

Length: 15 hours (2 days).

Dates: January 1995-Present.

Objective: To assist individuals and companies in identifying and using the latest management philosophies to identify and deal with problems, Just-In-Time/ Total Quality Control, and Predictive/ Preventive Maintenance concepts.

Learning Outcome: Upon successful completion of this course, the student will be able to use management philosophies in their respective environments, recognize how they affect the overall manufacturing organization, and apply them to the interaction within the maintenance department; understand how systems and concepts can be applied to maintenance, and identify the four major phases: Concepts, Implementation, Execution, Planning and Scheduling; and apply the criteria for successful team selection, the establishment of goals, Performance Measurements, and the steps required to assure the total team commitment necessary for success.

Instruction: Major topics covered in the course are identification of maintenance problems before they happen, measuring maintenance performance and managing repair costs, management of failure loss reporting and productivity of maintenance, maintenance policy, procedures and processes, and eliminating breakdowns and emergency repairs. Methods of instruction include lecture, classroom exercises, and case studies.

Credit Recommendation: In the lower division baccalaureate/associate degree category, 1 semester hour in Supervision or Business Elective (6/96).

Negotiations: How to Win Every Time (PS115)

Location: Various U.S. and International locations.

Length: 15 hours (2 days).

Dates: January 1995-Present.

Objective: To take students through a five-step process of effective negotiation to demonstrate that successful negotiators plan and know how to create, assess, and tradeoff alternatives. Course sessions reinforce how to apply negotiation to any encountered situation.

Learning Outcome: Upon successful completion of this course, the student will be able to recognize why almost everything is negotiable, how supplier selection can improve negotiations, how to control power, time, and information, and effective techniques for establishing long-term relations; identify negotiating styles; negotiate in the international marketplace; set and meet negotiating targets; focus planning to accomplish company objectives; meet the change in purchasing's role; plan for partnerships that promote win/win relationships; know the five steps to negotiations for success; identify and deal with risk; know the different types of negotiations; and know how and when to use proper tactics in negotiations.

Instruction: Major topics covered in the course are win/win partnerships, effective negotiation techniques, preparing and planning for the negotiation process, types of negotiations, practical negotiating tactics, saving money, interface requirements, and getting to an agreement. Methods of instruction include lecture, discussion, and case studies.

Credit Recommendation: In the upper division baccalaureate degree category, 1 semester hour in Business Administration (6/96).

Statistical Process Control (QM114)

Location: Various U.S. and International locations.

Length: 22.5 hours (3 days).

Dates: January 1995-Present.

Objective: To assist individuals and companies in maintaining a manufacturing process that is in control. Concepts and skills will result in improved quality, assured consistency, reduced lead-time, assurance of optimum scheduling, and increased customer satisfaction.

Learning Outcome: Upon successful completion of this course, the student will be able to use practical methods to statistically measure the quality of machines and processes; discover real manufacturing problems; compile data so it gives an accurate and clear picture of the manufacturing process, with total quality versus total costs; know when and how to use the three major probability distributions employed in manufacturing; identify and prevent potential problems; use the four major types of sampling and which is best for a company; know the smallest sampling size that will give reliable data; and use methods for training a work force in Statistical Process Control.

Instruction: Major topics covered in the course are Statistical Process Control as a system for preventing defects; the process of data collection and analysis to provide warning of possible problems; how to improve quality and assure consistency; statistical concepts; problem analysis; and data collection and analysis. Methods of instruction include lecture, discussion, classroom exercises, and case studies.

Credit Recommendation: In the upper division baccalaureate degree category, 1 semester hour in Business Administration or Engineering Management (6/96).

Supplier Certification: The Path to Excellence (QM115)

Location: Various U.S. and International locations.

Length: 15 hours (2 days).

Dates: January 1995-Present.

Objective: To assist individuals and companies in learning the importance of Supplier Certification and to implement the criteria and the process for success.

Learning Outcome: Upon successful completion of this course, the student will be able to determine how Total Quality Management and Supplier Certification work together to create a company on the cutting edge; demonstrate knowledge of thirty-two practical and proven supplier selection criteria and ten essential steps to implement a successful program; understand how to measure the results of Supplier Certification on size, inventory, company culture, and profits; demonstrate how to measure the cost of quality and inventory; and understand how to apply the five tools and techniques critical to the continuous improvement process.

Instruction: Major topics covered in the course are guidelines, checklists, and questionnaires to assist the student in implementing a Supplier Certification program and how an effective Supplier Certification Program interfaces with the manufacturing technique of Just-In-Time to bring about Total Quality Control of the production process. Methods of instruction include lecture, discussion, and case studies.

Credit Recommendation: In the upper division baccalaureate degree category, 1 semester hour in Business Administration or Engineering Management (6/96).

Supply Management (PS131)

Location: Various U.S. and International locations.

Length: 15 hours (2 days).

Dates: January 1995-Present.

Objective: To assist individuals and companies in understanding their roles to play in the JIT/World Class business environment.

Learning Outcome: Upon successful completion of this course, the student will be able to explore concepts and trends in purchasing, determine what Supply Management is, conduct a purchasing audit, select supplier partners as a basis for win/win relationships, know the requirements/applications of total quality control, define supplier certification, know the "how to's" of integrating financial objectives into the supply management process, know about paper less purchasing and associated technology, control transportation costs, and know the importance and applications of ethics in business.

Instruction: Major topics covered in the course are purchasing organization concepts, managing the function, supplier selection and relationship, total quality control, financial objectives, paper less purchasing, performance measures, transportation, ethics in purchasing, and forecasting. Methods of instruction include lecture, discussion, and case studies.

Credit Recommendation: In the upper division baccalaureate degree category, 1 semester hour in Business Administration (6/96).

Total Cycle Time Management (WC130)

Location: Various U.S. and International locations.

Length: 15 hours (2 days).

Dates: January 1995-Present.

Objective: To assist individuals and companies in learning and use of Total Cycle Time Management as one of the most highly leveraged strategies for competitive advantage. It's purpose is to position a company to respond to changes in the marketplace in an ever decreasing time frame, also driven by the three variables of competitiveness: quality, price/cost, and dependability.

Learning Outcome: Upon successful completion of this course, the student will be able to reduce cycle time, and Work-In Process; orient management teams to Total Cycle Time Management (TCTM); construct a model of business; know the principles to apply for factory layout; know the critical success factors in product and process design; know how the Japanese develop new products twice as fast as American and European competitors, and how to integrate product planning, product design, process planning, and process control.

Instruction: Major topics covered in the course are establishing a Cycle Time Management model, managing Cycle Time in manufacturing, managing the supplier and administration cycle time, techniques and examples of application, and maintaining a continuous improvement process. Methods of instruction include lecture, discussion, and case studies.

Credit Recommendation: In the upper division baccalaureate degree category, 1 semester hour in Business Administration or Engineering Management (6/96).

Total Quality Management (QM117)

Location: Various U.S. and International locations.

Length: 15 hours (2 days).

Dates: January 1995-Present.

Objective: To assist individuals and companies in knowing and applying Total Quality Management. An effective Total Quality Management process requires total involvement at every level with the organization, from senior management to the lowest level employee. Everyone in the organization must have an awareness of how Total Quality can be applied to their daily activities.

Learning Outcome: Upon successful completion of this course, the student will be able to implement and manage the TQM process, know how TQM impacts every functional area within the organization, change the corporate culture - making TQM a standard practice, use the TQM process as a competitive tool, solve problems and make the right decisions, and develop and install performance measurements and assess customer satisfaction.

Instruction: Major topics covered in the course are Total Quality Management as both a philosophy and a methodology of business operations; structured policies and operating procedures to guide employees in their improvement efforts; the costs of nonconformance and the accompanying costs; and practical methods are identified for carrying out Total Quality Management. Methods of instruction include lecture, discussion, classroom exercises, and case studies.

Credit Recommendation: In the upper division baccalaureate degree category, 1 semester hour in Business Administration or Engineering Management (6/96).

Public Education Institute

Public Education Institute is a nonprofit organization dedicated to provide a non-partisan forum for the discussion of issues in elementary and secondary education and to offer opportunities for interested citizens to expand their knowledge of how the public education system functions.

The institute is governed by a twelve-member volunteer board. Other members represent business, civic, and educational institutions.

A major concern of the institute is to improve the involvement and effectiveness of parents in the public schools. The course described here addresses that concern. Parent volunteers are the course participants.

Source of official student records: Registry of Credit Recommendations, American Council on Education, One Dupont Circle, Washington, DC 20036-1193.

Additional information about the courses: Office of Corporate-Higher Education Programs, Thomas Edison State College, 101 W. State Street, Trenton, NJ 08608-1176.

Public Policy and Public Schools

Location: Various Urban New Jersey School Districts.

Length: *Version 1:* 120 hours (30 weeks); *Versions 2 and 3:* 80 hours (24 weeks).

Dates: *Version 1:* September 1982-June 1984; *Version 2:* September 1984-December 1991; *Version 3:* January 1992-January 1997.

Objective: To increase the awareness and involvement in issues of decision-making in public education to enhance the effectiveness of parents and other interested parties.

Learning Outcome: Upon completion of this course, the student will be able to identify, analyze, and evaluate issues surrounding or involved in distribution of power and decision making, equity, resource provision, control, and innovation; enhance an advocacy role with respect to issues of public education; and increase student capabilities to apply knowledge and participate effectively in public policy and decision making in public education.

Instruction: Parent volunteers are the course participants. The instructor-led course uses simulations, presentations, and reading and writing assignments to cover federal, state, and local legislative and fiscal policies including school budgets; school district organization; discipline; curriculum; testing; effective schools research; parent roles and family roles; and communication in schools. Parent volunteers and other interested parties are the course participants.

Credit Recommendation: *Version 1:* In the lower division baccalaureate/associate degree category, 3 semester hours in Political Science/Public Policy, 3 semester hours in Educational Psychology or Tests and Measurements, and 3 semester hours in Communications or Introductory Speech. *Version 2:* In the lower division baccalaureate/associate degree category, 3 semester hours in Political Science or Public Policy and 3 semester hours in Introductory Speech or Communications (5/85). **NOTE:** This course is taught in a very integrated manner over a full term of 24 weeks. If a student completes only one half of the course (12 weeks), 3 semester hours in either Political Science/Public Policy or Introductory Speech/ Communications. In the first half of the course there is an extensive communications component but the content is primarily Public Policy. A total of 3 semester hours should be awarded, but it could properly be given in either discipline. *Version 3:* In the lower division baccalaureate/associate degree category, 3 semester hours in Political Science or Public Policy, and 3 semester hours in Decision-Making in Public Education, or elective in Education, for a total of 6 semester hours (5/85) (1/92). **NOTE:** This course is taught in a very integrated manner over a full term of 24 weeks. If a student completes only one-half of the course (12 weeks), 3 semester hours in Political Science/Public Policy.

Public Service Electric & Gas

The Personnel Development Department of Human Resources is devoted to improving the skills of PSE&G employees, increasing individual and team performance on the job and facilitating the personnel growth and development of PSE&G employees.

The Personnel Development Department will accomplish this mission through the following strategies: provide appropriate training opportunities at all employees' levels; act as the corporate resource for increasing productivity through improved performance appraisal systems; disseminate information about training and development opportunities and related services throughout the company; and encourage ongoing relationships with academic and professional institutions to keep abreast of current trends in the field of Training and Development.

Training at PSE&G is viewed as a continuing process to assure high quality performance on the part of the entire work force at all levels of the organization.

Prior to participation in any program, it is important that participants and their supervisors clarify together the specific objectives for attendance at any given workshop. This process allows the individuals to approach their training experience with a clear set of learning goals.

Source of official student records: Registry of Credit Recommendations, American Council on Education, One Dupont Circle, Washington, DC 20063-1193.

Additional information about the courses: Office of Corporate-Higher Education Programs, Thomas Edison State College, 101 West State Street, Trenton, NJ 08608-1176.

Oral Presentation Skills

Location: Various PSE&G locations throughout New Jersey.

Length: 16 hours (2 days).

Dates: August 1983-August 1993.

Objective: To improve the verbal and nonverbal skills necessary for formal presentations and group discussions.

Learning Outcome: Upon successful completion of this course, the student will be able to control nervousness and turn it from a negative destructive force into a positive constructive force; recognize and eliminate restraining inhibitions; use five forms of evidence for maximum persuasion; prepare effective visual aids and use them to achieve action and understanding; control a question and answer session with group; and design, plan, and present a written script.

Instruction: Major topics covered in the course are specific techniques for improving oral presentation skills. Areas such as audience analysis, preparation, delivery, relaxation, and confidence building will be covered. Participants will be required to make several oral presentations to demonstrate acquired skills to the satisfaction of class instructor. Videotape will be used to define individual strengths and weaknesses.

Credit Recommendation: In the lower division baccalaureate/associate degree category, 1 semester hour in Speech Workshop (8/88).

Supervisory Training Program (Part 1 and 2)

Location: Salem and Newark, NJ.

Length: *Part 1:* 30 hours (5 days) separated by 3 months; *Part 2:* 12 hours (2 days).

Dates: March 1983-August 1993.

Objective: To provide first-line supervisors with the skills necessary to manage work, people, and self.

Learning Outcome: Upon successful completion of this course, the student will be able to manage themselves and others and do the supervisor's job more effectively; implement decisions; manage time better; gain consensus, support, and communicate effectively; listen effectively and solve problems, including sensitive personnel situations (e.g., performance appraisal, alcoholism, and drugs); implement a behavioral performance model of supervision; delegate; and schedule work fairly and realistically.

Instruction: Major topics covered in the course are basic management skills and clarifies the major roles and responsibilities of a supervisor. Through various activities, participants will learn the methods that help motivate employees to achieve and maintain high performance levels. In addition, the workshop clarifies the many regulations and procedures that affect a supervisor's job.

Credit Recommendation: In the lower division baccalaureate/associate degree category, 3 semester hours in Principles and Practices of Supervision (8/88).

Systematic Analysis of Ideas

Location: Various PSE&G locations throughout New Jersey.

Length: 30 hours (5 days).

Dates: August 1978-August 1993.

Objective: To teach participants how to prepare and present persuasive recommendations.

Learning Outcome: Upon successful completion of this course, the student will be able to determine the other person's real, but often hidden, objectives and goals and relate their idea, plan, or recommendation to those objectives; generate interest for their idea or recommendation when dealing with complacent, self-satisfied people; organize and present ideas and recommendations concisely and answer questions and objections in advance; calm emotion and more effectively handle confrontation; handle and express themselves in strenuous and difficult situations; and handle objections, such as "We've always done it that way."

Instruction: Major topic covered in the course is the required behavior that must exist between two people if successful communication is to take place. The course also prepares a speaker to analyze, organize, and think from a listener's point of view, so that this behavior can be maintained when the listener is being persuaded to make a change. There is a sequence of communication that must be used if a person is willing to change behavior. If the sequence is not used, the person may resist change. The course examines both logical and emotional elements of communication, and discusses when to use each one most effectively.

Credit Recommendation: In the lower division baccalaureate/associate degree category, 2 semester hours in Persuasive Communications (8/88).

QualPro

QualPro is a privately held process improvement consulting firm dedicated to teaching clients to develop, maintain, and manage self-sufficient process improvement programs. The company was founded in 1982 and has provided consulting, training, implementation assistance, and technical support to more than 500 national and international companies.

QualPro's process improvement training is based on a philosophy of continuous improvement, a non-technical approach to practical statistical techniques, and an emphasis on data-based decision making. Training includes the development of a customized implementation strategy; a focus on internal and external points of view; line managed process improvement; employee involvement through the productive use of teams; and an emphasis on quick results, measurable returns on investment, and continuing success.

All courses are taught by a staff of experienced, full-time, and extensively-trained process improvement experts, most with advanced degrees. Each of these instructors actively consults with various companies and thus has up-to-the-minute knowledge of specific needs and advances within the quality improvement industry. Their consulting work also helps the instructors bring a wealth of practical experience into the QualPro classrooms.

QualPro's process improvement courses were developed by QualPro's personnel and are taught publicly in Knoxville, TN, and in-house at client's facilities. Advanced courses require attendance in a prerequisite basic course. Basic courses require a rudimentary understanding of mathematical concepts and the ability to use a calculator to add, subtract, multiply, divide, and find a square root. All coursework includes classroom instruction and exercises using actual workplace examples. Content is technically-oriented and is taught through industry and function-specific training manuals that are continually revised to reflect updated information and examples. Successful completion of each course is based on a passing test score and/or project.

QualPro courses are primarily attended by managers and professional workers actively involved in developing or managing process improvement programs. Courses are open to all individuals who wish to learn practical statistical process improvement methods, to update their skills in those areas, to prepare for a different field of employment, or to fulfill personal goals.

Source of official student records: Registry of Credit Recommendations, American Council on Education, One Dupont Circle, Washington, DC 20036-1193.

Additional information about the courses: College Credit Recommendation Service, American Council on Education, One Dupont Circle, Washington, DC 20036-1193.

Advanced Multivariable Testing Techniques (12) (Formerly Advanced Experimental Design Methods [12])

Location: Several major U.S. cities and client locations.

Length: 28 hours (4 days).

Dates: January 1993-Present.

Objective: To teach advanced experimental design methods and the theory on which experimental design techniques are based.

Learning Outcome: Upon successful completion of this course, the student will be able to differentiate between fractional factorial and Plackett-Burman families of experimental design, understand how to best block a nested design, perform analysis of variance (ANOVA) for more than two levels, perform analysis of means (ANOM) for more than two levels, derive the expected mean square, analyze nested designs, analyze reflected designs, calculate sample size for percent defective response, experiment with mixtures, and work with confounding schemes.

Instruction: Major topics covered in the course are a review of basic experimental design, analysis of variance procedures for more than two levels, contacts and paired comparisons of means, design concepts—completely randomized, randomized complete block nested, fixed and random factors—expected mean squares, blocking in 2 factorials, fractional factorials of 2 designs, introduction to blocking of 3 designs, review of Plackett-Burman versus Taguchi, evolutionary operations (EVOP), response surface designs, introduction to mixture designs, and review of pitfalls in application. Methods of instruction include lecture, overheads, discussion, exercises, case studies, and examination.

Credit Recommendation: In the upper division baccalaureate/associate degree category, 2 semester hours in Quality Management or Statistics (4/93). *Prerequisites*: Student must have attended a QualPro basic course and a QualPro basic experimental design course.

Advanced Process Improvement Techniques (11) (Formerly Advanced Statistical Quality Improvement Techniques [11])

Location: Several major U.S. cities and client locations.

Length: 28 hours (4 days).

Dates: January 1993-Present.

Objective: To enhance basic quality control techniques and teach the application of more specialized and advanced techniques to processes.

Learning Outcome: Upon successful completion of this course, the student will be able to calculate limits, plot data, analyze multivariate control charts, calculate T2 (squared) to analyze special causes, list best methods for analyzing standard deviation, calculate standard deviation using various methods, perform the Kolmogorov-Smirnov test for normality, perform analysis of variance (ANOVA), perform analysis of means (ANOM), calculate and analyze Duncan's multiple range test, evaluate average run length (ARL) to real and false signals, and understand the effects of over- or underadjustment.

Instruction: Major topics covered in the course are evaluation of uncertainties associated with control chart decisions, adequacy of measurement systems, use of control charts for custom or specialty products, normal distribution of process data, judging when and how to make process adjustments, using autocorrelated data in quality improvement, and using average run length. Methods of instruction include lecture, overheads, discussion, exercises, case studies, and examination.

Credit Recommendation: In the upper division baccalaureate degree category, 2 semester hours in Quality Management or Statistics (4/93). *Prerequisite*: Student must have attended a QualPro basic course.

Companywide Quality Function Deployment (21)

Location: Several major U.S. cities and client locations.

Length: 21 hours (3 days).

Dates: January 1993-Present.

Objective: To teach the Quality Function Deployment (QFD) concept which integrates marketing, product/service development, production, and sales so that the products or services provided meet the customers' wants, needs, and expectations.

Learning Outcome: Upon successful completion of this course, the student will be able to understand the basic categories of customer need, complete Product Planning Matrix, understand how to collect customer need data and translate into design requirements, prepare affinity diagram, complete relationship and interaction tables, rank design requirements, complete Part/Component Matrix, understand role and purpose of Process Planning and Production Planning Matrix, understand how to carry the voice of the customer through each matrix, understand what activities take place during production planning, and understand what is meant by the "Right Product."

Instruction: Major topics covered in the course are Quality Function Deployment (QFD), the four Matrix Macabe Approach, understanding customer needs, and application of QFD to specific projects. Methods of instruction include lecture, overheads, discussion, exercises, case studies, presentations, and examination.

Credit Recommendation: In the lower division baccalaureate/associate degree category, 1 semester hour in Quality Management (4/93).

Customer Satisfaction Survey Techniques for Assessing Product and Service Quality (28)

Location: Several major U.S. cities and client locations.

Length: 28 hours (4 days).

Dates: January 1993-Present.

Objective: To teach survey design and sampling techniques with a particular emphasis upon customer satisfaction as a quality dimension.

Learning Outcome: Upon successful completion of this course, the student will be able to design surveys, develop sampling and data gathering plans, and analyze acquired survey data.

Instruction: Major topics covered in the course are fundamentals of sampling; sampling errors; systematic, cluster, and stratified sampling; response rates; data collection methods; and descriptive statistics from results. Methods of instruction include lecture, overheads, discussion, exercises, case studies, and examination.

Credit Recommendation: In the upper division baccalaureate/associate degree category, 1 semester hour in Survey Research, Marketing Research or Management Research, or Opinion Surveys (4/93).

Development of a Process Improvement Training Program for the Work Force (07) (Formerly Development of a Quality Improvement Training Program for the Work Force [07])

Location: Several major U.S. cities and client locations.

Length: 28 hours (4 days).

Dates: January 1993-Present.

Objective: To teach how to design and implement an effective continuous quality improvement training program.

Learning Outcome: Upon successful completion of this course, the student will be able to adapt the principles of effective adult learning to the design, development, and presentation of a successful process improvement training program. The student will learn the varied aspects of training program planning from training materials to training attendees, will know how to choose the proper methods for effective process improvement training, and will learn and refine effective delivery techniques for process improvement training.

Instruction: Major topics covered in the course are the design, development, and presentation of an effective continuous quality improvement training program with specific emphasis on curriculum design, training methods, training materials, instructor skills, and evaluation of training results. Methods of instruction include lecture, overheads, discussion, exercises, student presentation, and evaluation.

Credit Recommendation: In the lower division baccalaureate/associate degree category, 2 semester hours in Training or Teacher Education (4/93). *Prerequisite*: Student must have attended a QualPro basic course.

Development of a Supplier Process Improvement Process (13) (Formerly Development of a Supplier Quality Improvement Process [13])

Location: Several major U.S. cities and client locations.

Length: 28 hours (4 days).

Dates: January 1993-Present.

Objective: To teach valuable techniques for developing an effective relationship with suppliers in order to receive quality goods.

Learning Outcome: Upon successful completion of this course, the student will be able to assess the consequences of input variability, evaluate supplier performance, and establish a supplier quality control process.

Instruction: Major topics covered in the course are problems, benefits, and barriers to single sourcing; how to implement a supplier quality improvement process; and how to monitor suppliers for certification. Methods of instruction include lecture, overheads, discussion, exercises, case studies, and examination.

Credit Recommendation: In the lower division baccalaureate/associate degree category, 2 semester hours in Purchasing, Industrial Buy/Purchasing, Industrial Marketing (buying), Manufacturing Management, or Business/Industrial Management elective (4/93). *Prerequisite*: Student must have attended a QualPro basic course.

Excellence Through Quality

Location: Southwestern Bell Telephone Company locations.

Length: 12 hours (1.5 days).

Dates: June 1992-Present.

Objective: To teach basic techniques of statistical quality control, and provide the fundamental background for continuous quality improvement.

Learning Outcome: Upon successful completion of this course, the student will be able to understand and apply basic concepts of quality management; understand importance of customer focus; state Shewhart's concept of process improvement; calculate descriptive statistics; construct and apply run charts, fishbone diagrams, flowcharts, histograms, and Pareto charts; interpret control charts and scatter diagrams; understand QualPro's Eight-Step Procedure for Improving a Process; and understand brainstorming processes.

Instruction: Major topics covered in the course are quality improvement in the telecommunications industry; basic principles of continuous quality improvement; construct, interpret, and monitor control charts; and major reasons to improve a process. Methods of instruction include lecture, in-class demonstrations, exercises, and problem solving.

Credit Recommendation: In the lower division baccalaureate/associate degree category, 1 semester hour in General Business or Quality Management (4/93).

Finding Special Causes of Uncontrolled Variation (16)

Location: Client locations.

Length: 21 hours (3 days).

Dates: January 1993-Present.

Objective: To teach problem solving techniques.

Learning Outcome: Upon successful completion of this course, the student will be able to use good questioning and listening skills, gather and organize pertinent facts to test possible causes before taking action, apply diagnostic techniques to determine root causes efficiently, and interpret control charts.

Instruction: Major topics covered in the course are questioning skills, data gathering, interpreting control charts, and defining problems. Methods of instruction include lecture, overheads, discussion, exercises, case studies, and examination.

Credit Recommendation: In the lower division baccalaureate/associate degree category, 1 semester hour in Problem Solving Techniques (4/93). *Prerequisite*: Student must have attended a QualPro basic course.

Improving Measurement Systems (15) (Formerly Statistical Methods for Improving Measurement Systems [15])

Location: Several major U.S. cities and client locations.

Length: 28 hours (4 days).

Dates: January 1993-Present.

Objective: To teach methods for evaluating, controlling, and improving measurement systems.

Learning Outcome: Upon successful completion of this course, the student will be able to state the definition of precision and accuracy, determine adequacy of measurement instrument discrimination, assess precision and accuracy for a measurement system, compare two measurement systems, calculate percent of specification and percent of total variation for measurement system, and improve a measurement system.

Instruction: Major topics covered in the course are how to assess precision and accuracy, how to compare two measurement systems, measurement capability on production samples, how to apply measurement capability studies, gauge discrimination, attributes measurements, rational subgrouping for measurement control, how to use production and measurement control charts together, the use of standards, design of experiments in measurement system improvement, interlaboratory comparisons, and preliminary scoping for measurement studies. Methods of instruction are lecture, overheads, discussion, exercises, case studies, and examination.

Credit Recommendation: In the lower division baccalaureate/associate degree category, 2 semester hours in Applied Statistics (4/93). *Prerequisite*: Student must have attended a QualPro basic course.

Introduction to Process Improvement: Public and In-House (06) (Formerly Improving Competitive Advantage: Public and In-House [06])

Location: Several major U.S. cities and client locations.

Length: 21 hours (3 days) at major U.S. cities or 14 hours (2 days) at client locations.

Dates: January 1993-Present.

Objective: To serve as a springboard for quality improvement with emphasis on fundamentals of quality improvement and the refinement of a companywide action plan.

Learning Outcome: Upon successful completion of this course, the student will be able to describe the continuous improvement process, demonstrate an elementary knowledge of basic statistical tools, appreciate the potential of experimental design, and develop an action plan for the first phase of quality improvement.

Instruction: Major topics covered in the course are the role of quality, statistical and systems thinking, definitions, tools and measurement of quality and process improvement, and use and selection of basic control charts. Methods of instruction include lecture, overheads, discussion, video, exercises, case studies, and examination.

Credit Recommendation: In the vocational certificate category, 1 semester hour in Business Mathematics (4/93).

Management of Process Improvement (23) (Formerly Management of the Quality Improvement Process [23])

Location: Client locations.

Length: 28 hours (4 days).

Dates: January 1993-Present.

Objective: To teach effective management of continuous quality improvement. Focus is on the management skills and appropriate activities necessary to sustain the proper application of statistical methods.

Learning Outcome: Upon successful completion of this course, the student will be able to establish practical foundations for "good management" of process improvement, exploit the "leadership tie" between process management and the management of continuous process improvement, assign responsibility and delegate authority for process improvement, manage teamwork in the line organization to optimize the continuous improvement effort, and conduct extensive work with case studies to learn the techniques that must be both used and managed.

Instruction: Major topics covered in the course are historical overview of management theorists, tools and skills necessary for effective management of continuous quality improvement, resource allocation, coordination and teamwork important to sustaining the application of statistical methods, and types of leaders. Methods of instruction include lecture, overheads, discussion, case studies, and examination.

Credit Recommendation: In the lower division baccalaureate/associate degree category, 2 semester hours in Management or Quality Management (4/93). *Prerequisite*: Student must have attended a QualPro basic course.

Managing Improvement and Competitive Advantage (Formerly Managing Improvement and Competitive Advantage: RQC Stage III)

Location: Knoxville, TN.

Length: 38 hours (1 week) and outside independent study.

Dates: January 1993-Present.

Objective: To teach the history, development stages and philosophy of the quality movement, examine a variety of pio neering works, and explore current directions in quality theory and practice.

Learning Outcome: Upon successful completion of this course, the student will be able to understand historical roots and theoretical foundations of quality management, and demonstrate knowledge about contemporary issues and problems.

Instruction: Major topics covered in the course are original works of Shewhart and others, interactive discussion based on field experience and quality management knowledge, current issues, alternative futures, student projects and reports, and Technical Guidance review. Methods of instruction include lecture, overheads, discussion, intense study of classic books in field, research, formal reports with technical guidance review and evaluation, student presentations, and examination.

Credit Recommendation: In the graduate degree category, 1 semester hour in TQM, Management Seminar, or Special Topics in TQM (4/93). *Prerequisite:*

Student must be in either the Resident Quality Consultant or the Process Improvement Specialist Program.

Multivariable Testing Techniques for Manufacturing Processes (03) (Formerly Experimental Design Techniques for Existing Manufacturing Processes [03])

Location: Several major U.S. cities and client locations.

Length: 28 hours (4 days).

Dates: January 1993-Present.

Objective: To teach the fundamental concepts of experimental design.

Learning Outcome: Upon successful completion of this course, the student will know the advantages of factorial experimental design over one-factor-at-a-time experiments; know the importance of randomizing experimental runs; know how to calculate effects and interactions of factors; know how to analyze factorials, fractional factorials, and Plackett-Burman designs in order to identify factors which significantly affect either the average or the variation; know how to assess curvature; know how to plot interactions; and know when to use repeats, replicates, and reflection.

Instruction: Major topics covered in the course are fundamental concepts of experimental design, optimum strategies and procedures for applying experimental design to existing processes, case studies from various industries, evolutionary operations (EVOP), response surface methodology, and multi-level designs. Methods of instruction include lecture, overheads, discussion, exercises, case studies, and examination.

Credit Recommendation: In the lower division baccalaureate/associate degree category, 2 semester hours in Quality Management or Statistics (4/93). *Prerequisite*: Student must have attended a QualPro basic course.

Multivariable Testing Techniques for Research and Development Processes (04) (Formerly Statistical Methods for Improving Research and Development Performance [04])

Location: Several major U.S. cities and client locations.

Length: 28 hours (4 days).

Dates: January 1993-Present.

Objective: To teach an understanding of new processes; how to design them efficiently and correctly; how to alter them to meet changing design requirements; how to identify key process variables during the process development stage; and how to determine the potential effects of and relationships between these variables.

Learning Outcome: Upon successful completion of this course, the student will know the advantages of factorial experimental design over one-factor-at-a-time experiments; know the importance of randomizing experimental runs; know how to calculate effects and interactions of factors; know how to analyze factorials, fractional factorials, and Plackett-Burman designs in order to identify factors which significantly affect either the average or the variation; know how to assess curvature; know how to plot interactions; and know when to use repeats, replicates, and reflection and where, when, and how to use Quality Function Deployment (QFD).

Instruction: Major topics covered in the course are fundamental concepts of experimental design, optimum strategies and procedures for applying experimental design to existing processes, new process and new product development, and the practical management of experimental design. Methods of instruction include lecture, overheads, discussion, exercises, case studies, and examination.

Credit Recommendation: In the lower division baccalaureate/associate degree category, 2 semester hours in Quality Management or Statistics (4/93). *Prerequisite*: Student must have attended a QualPro basic course.

Multivariable Testing Techniques for Service Processes (33) (Formerly Experimental Design Techniques for Service Processes [33])

Location: Several major U.S. cities and client locations.

Length: 28 hours (4 days).

Dates: January 1993-Present.

Objective: To teach the fundamentals of experimental design as a research technique, and their applications in service industries.

Learning Outcome: Upon successful completion of this course, the student will know the advantages of factorial experimental design over one-factor-at-a-time experiments; know the importance of randomizing experimental runs; know how to calculate effects and interactions of factors; know how to analyze factorials, fractional factorials, and Plackett-Burman designs in order to identify factors which significantly affect either the average or the variation; know how to assess curvature; understand the use of replication in studies including overtime, computer applications and data analysis presentation.

Instruction: Major topics covered in the course are fundamental concepts and applications of experimental design and procedures for applying experimental designs to existing processes and multilevel designs. Methods of instruction include lecture, overheads, discussion, exercises, case studies, and examination.

Credit Recommendation: In the lower division baccalaureate/associate degree category, 2 semester hours in Quality Management, Applied Statistics, Services/Non-Profit Management, Marketing, or Marketing Research elective (4/93). *Prerequisite*: Student must have attended a QualPro basic course.

Multivariate Methods for Process Improvement (Formerly Multivariate Methods and Survey Sampling for Process Improvement: RQC Stage II)

Location: Knoxville, TN.

Length: 38 hours (1 week).

Dates: January 1993-Present.

Objective: To teach multivariate analysis topics and computer applications.

Learning Outcome: Upon successful completion of this course, the student will be able to recognize conditions where multivariate analysis might be appropriately applied, and demonstrate successful software applications with computer results.

Instruction: Major topics covered in the course are multivariate regression analysis, discriminate analysis, cluster analysis, and principal component analysis. Methods of instruction include lecture, overheads, discussion, video, exercises, computer laboratory, and examination.

Credit Recommendation: In the graduate degree category, 3 semester hours in Industrial Engineering/Management, Operations Management, Marketing Research, or Applied Statistics (4/93). **NOTE**: Student must complete RQC Stage I to receive credit. *Prerequisite*: Student must be in either the Resident Quality Consultant Program or the Process Improvement Specialist Program.

Process Improvement for Architecture, Engineering, and Construction Processes (24) (Formerly Basic Statistical Quality Improvement Techniques for the Architecture, Engineering, and Construction Industries [24])

Location: Client locations.

Length: 28 hours (4 days).

Dates: January 1993-Present.

Objective: To present methods to break down a project into major subprocesses, and show the application of statistical methods to measure these parts and enhance performance of the overall system.

Learning Outcome: Upon successful completion of this course, the student will be able to improve nonrecurring projects continuously, use simple tools to identify common elements within all projects, apply measures to improve project execution, and demonstrate assessment and evaluation of the overall project.

Instruction: Major topics covered in the course are statistical quality control, systems focus, variation, quality measurement, and control charts in project management. Methods of instruction include lecture, overheads, discussion, video, exercises, case studies, and examination.

Credit Recommendation: In the lower division baccalaureate/associate degree category, 2 semester hours in Quality Management, Manufacturing Management, or Statistics (4/93).

Process Improvement for Chemical Processes (08) *(Formerly Basic Statistical Quality Improvement Techniques for the Chemical Industry [08])*

Location: Several major U.S. cities and client locations.

Length: 28 hours (4 days).

Dates: January 1993-Present.

Objective: To teach the basic techniques of statistical quality control and provide training in the basic principles of continuous improvement.

Learning Outcome: Upon successful completion of this course, the student will be able to state the differences between the types of variation, calculate and understand capability indices, select the correct control chart, calculate control limits, plot data for standard statistical data, perform tests for non-randomness on control charts, analyze measurement precision and accuracy, and understand autocorrelation.

Instruction: Major topics covered in the course are the status of quality im-provement in the chemical industry, how to apply quality improvement techniques to continuous and batch process in the chemical industry, how to monitor and control key product characteristics, how to identify and prioritize systems that need improvement, techniques to recognize excessive sampling, and methods for continuous improvement in customized batch processes. Methods of instruction include lecture, overheads, discussion, video, exercises, case studies, and examination.

Credit Recommendation: In the lower division baccalaureate/associate degree category, 2 semester hours in Quality Management or Statistics (4/93).

Process Improvement for Electronics Processes (09) *(Formerly Basic Statistical Quality Improvement Techniques for the Electronics Industry [09])*

Location: Client locations.

Length: 28 hours (4 days).

Dates: January 1993-Present.

Objective: To teach the basic techniques of statistical quality control and provide training in the basic principles of continuous improvement.

Learning Outcome: Upon successful completion of this course, the student will be able to differentiate between the types of variation, calculate and understand capability indices, select the correct control chart, calculate control limits, plot data, perform tests for non-randomness on control charts, analyze measurement precision and accuracy, and understand autocorrelation.

Instruction: Major topics covered in the course are the status of quality improvement in the electronics industry, techniques for pass/fail and visual measurements, how to identify and prioritize systems that need improvement, how to monitor and control key product characteristics, how to identify major causes of product defects, methods for determining optimum economic sampling, quality improvement techniques for complex process flows such as digital semiconductor manufacturing and assembly, and how to handle hypersensitivity caused by extremely large group sizes. Methods of instruction include lecture, overheads, discussion, video, exercises, case studies, and examination.

Credit Recommendation: In the lower division baccalaureate/associate degree category, 2 semester hours in Quality Management or Statistics (4/93).

Process Improvement for Health Care Processes (20) *(Formerly Basic Statistical Quality Improvement Techniques for the Health Care Industry [20])*

Location: Several major U.S. cities and client locations.

Length: 28 hours (4 days).

Dates: January 1993-Present.

Objective: To teach the basic techniques of problem solving and statistical quality control applicable to the health care industry.

Learning Outcome: Upon successful completion of this course, the student will be able to compute basic statistics, interpret statistical results, and demonstrate applications in a health care setting with a quality perspective.

Instruction: Major topics covered in the course are statistical quality control, systems focus, variation, control charts, and experimental design. Methods of instruction include lecture, overheads, discussion, video, exercises, case studies, and examination.

Credit Recommendation: In the lower division baccalaureate/associate degree category, 2 semester hours in Statistics, Business Statistics, Quality Management, or Biometrics (Nursing, Health Care) (4/93).

Process Improvement for Maintenance Processes (14) *(Formerly Basic Statistical Quality Improvement Techniques for Maintenance Processes [14])*

Location: Several major U.S. cities and client locations.

Length: 28 hours (4 days).

Dates: January 1993-Present.

Objective: To teach the fundamentals of using statistical tools to evaluate and improve maintenance systems.

Learning Outcome: Upon successful completion of this course, the student will be able to understand variation and its effect on maintenance systems, use statistical quality control techniques to define and analyze maintenance processes, reduce shutdown costs and assess reliability, and assess performance and consistency in maintenance processes.

Instruction: Major topics covered in the course are statistical quality control, systems focus, variation, quality measurement, and using control charts. Methods of instruction include lecture, overheads, discussion, video, exercises, case studies, and examination.

Credit Recommendation: In the lower division baccalaureate/associate degree category, 2 semester hours in Quality Management or Statistics (4/93).

Process Improvement for Manufacturing Processes (01) *(Formerly Basic Statistical Quality Improvement Techniques for Manufacturing Processes [01])*

Location: Several major U.S. cities and client locations.

Length: 28 hours (4 days).

Dates: January 1993-Present.

Objective: To teach the basic techniques of statistical quality control and provide training in the basic principles of continuous improvement.

Learning Outcome: Upon successful completion of this course, the student will be able to state the differences between the types of variation, calculate and understand capability indices, select the correct control charts, calculate control limits, plot data for established statistical measures, perform tests for non-randomness on control charts, analyze measurement precision and accuracy, and understand autocorrelation.

Instruction: Major topics covered in the course are the status of quality improvement in manufacturing processes, basic principles of continuous quality improvement and how they relate to manufacturing process improvement, how to identify and prioritize systems that need improvement, how to monitor and control key product characteristics, and how to identify major causes of product defects. Methods of instruction include lecture, overheads, discussion, video, exercises, case studies, and examination.

Credit Recommendation: In the lower division baccalaureate/associate degree category, 2 semester hours in Quality Management or Statistics (4/93).

Process Improvement for Marketing and Sales Processes (05) (Formerly Basic Statistical Quality Improvement Techniques for Marketing and Sales Processes [05])

Location: Several major U.S. cities and client locations.

Length: 28 hours (4 days).

Dates: January 1993-Present.

Objective: To teach a step-by-step approach for applying statistical quality control techniques to the marketing, sales, and customer service departments.

Learning Outcome: Upon successful completion of this course, the student will be able to compute basic statistics, interpret computed results, and demonstrate applications in a sales and marketing quality perspective.

Instruction: Major topics covered in the course are statistical quality control, systems focus, variation, sampling, time series, control charts, surveys, and experimental design. Methods of instruction include lecture, overheads, discussion, video, exercises, case studies, and examination.

Credit Recommendation: In the lower division baccalaureate/associate degree category, 2 semester hours in Statistics, Business Statistics, or Quality Management (4/93).

Process Improvement for Metallurgical Processes (10) (Formerly Basic Statistical Quality Improvement Techniques for Metallurgical Processes [10])

Location: Client locations.

Length: 28 hours (4 days).

Dates: January 1993-Present.

Objective: To teach the basic techniques of statistical quality control and provide training in the basic principles of continuous improvement.

Learning Outcome: Upon successful completion of this course, the student will be able to state the differences between the types of variation, calculate and understand capability indices, select the correct control chart, calculate control limits, plot data, perform tests for non-randomness on control charts, analyze measurement precision and accuracy, and understand autocorrelation.

Instruction: Major topics covered in the course are the status of quality improvement in the metals industry; how to identify and prioritize systems that need improvement; how to monitor and control key product characteristics; how to identify and prioritize systems that need improvement; how to identify major causes of product defects; and how to apply statistical techniques to hybrid, continuous, and batch processes. Methods of instruction include lecture, overheads, discussion, video, exercises, case studies, and examination.

Credit Recommendation: In the lower division baccalaureate/associate degree category, 2 semester hours in Quality Management or Statistics (4/93).

Process Improvement for Paper Processes (18) (Formerly Basic Statistical Quality Improvement Techniques for the Paper Industry [18])

Location: Several major U.S. cities and client locations.

Length: 28 hours (4 days).

Dates: January 1993-Present.

Objective: To teach the basic techniques of statistical quality control and provide training in the basic principles of continuous improvement.

Learning Outcome: Upon successful completion of this course, the student will be able to state the differences between the types of variation, calculate and understand capability indices, select the correct control chart, calculate control limits, plot data, perform tests for non-randomness on control charts, analyze measurement precision and accuracy, and understand autocorrelation.

Instruction: Major topics covered in the course are the status of quality improvement in the paper industry; how to monitor and control continuous processes; how to identify and prioritize systems that need improvement; how to identify major causes of product defects; how to improve paper processes from the wood yard, through the digesters and the paper machines to the converter; techniques to recognize excessive sampling; and charting techniques for short production runs. Methods of instruction include lecture, overheads, discussion, video, exercises, case studies, and examination.

Credit Recommendation: In the lower division baccalaureate/associate degree category, 2 semester hours in Quality Management or Statistics (4/93).

Process Improvement for Service and Administrative Processes (02) (Formerly Basic Statistical Quality Improvement Techniques for Service and Administrative Processes [02])

Location: Several major U.S. cities and client locations.

Length: 28 hours (4 days).

Dates: January 1993-Present.

Objective: To teach the basic techniques of problem solving and statistical quality control applicable to service companies.

Learning Outcome: Upon successful completion of this course, the student will be able to view service as a system; identify and prioritize systems that need improvement; monitor and control key measures such as costs, time to invoice, and computer downtime; identify major causes of problems such as billing errors; and calculate and understand capability indices.

Instruction: Major topics covered in the course are statistical quality control, systems focus, variation, quality measurement, and using control charts. Methods of instruction include lecture, overheads, discussion, video, exercises, case studies, and examination.

Credit Recommendation: In the lower division baccalaureate/associate degree

category, 2 semester hours in Quality Management or Statistics (4/93).

Process Improvement for Telecommunications Processes (27) (Formerly Basic Statistical Quality Improvement Techniques for the Telecommunications Industry [27])

Location: Several major U.S. cities and client locations.

Length: 28 hours (4 days).

Dates: January 1993-Present.

Objective: To teach the basic techniques of problem solving and statistical quality control applicable to the telecommunications industry.

Learning Outcome: Upon successful completion of this course, the student will be able to compute basic statistics, interpret statistical results, and demonstrate applications in a telecommunications setting with a quality perspective.

Instruction: Major topics covered in the course are the status of quality improvement in the telecommunications industry, identifying major causes of service outages, monitoring computer down time, reducing response time to customer service requests, and statistical techniques for measuring and managing quality assurance. Methods of instruction include lecture, overheads, discussion, video, exercises, case studies, and examination.

Credit Recommendation: In the lower division baccalaureate/associate degree category, 2 semester hours in Quality Management or Statistics (4/93).

Process Improvement for the Apparel and Textile Industries (19) (Formerly Basic Statistical Quality Improvement Techniques for the Apparel and Textile Industries [19])

Location: Several major U.S. cities and client locations.

Length: 28 hours (4 days).

Dates: January 1993-Present.

Objective: To teach the basic techniques of statistical quality control and provide training in the basic principles of continuous improvement.

Learning Outcome: Upon successful completion of this course, the student will be able to state the differences between the types of variation, calculate and understand capability indices, select the correct control chart, calculate control limits, plot data, perform tests for non-randomness on control charts, analyze measurement precision and accuracy, and understand autocorrelation.

Instruction: Major topics covered in the course are the status of quality im-provement in the apparel and textile industries, how to monitor and control key product characteristics, how to identify major causes of product defects, how to sample multiposition processes, special techniques for monitoring and controlling fabric point count, measurement assessment for destructive tests and visual tests, and charting aesthetic and subjective measurements. Methods of instruction include lecture, overheads, discussion, video, exercises, case studies, and examination.

Credit Recommendation: In the lower division baccalaureate/associate degree category, 2 semester hours in Quality Management or Statistics (4/93).

Process Improvement Methods for Managers in Manufacturing Industries (25) (Formerly Quality Improvement Methods for Managers in Manufacturing Industries [25])

Location: Client locations.

Length: 35 hours (5 days).

Dates: January 1993-Present.

Objective: To review continuous quality improvement theory and tools, introducing advanced process improvement techniques such as survey sampling, experimental design, regression, multivariate control charts, and analysis for management of improvement.

Learning Outcome: Upon successful completion of this course, the student will be able to understand the strategic role of quality improvement; plan and organize for quality; know the continuous improvement philosophy; understand basic statistical tools; use control charts; interpret basic statistical charts; and manage improvement.

Instruction: Major topics covered in the course are history of the quality movement, process improvement, measurement of quality with simple process improvement tools, basic statistical tests, control charts, variables control charts, attributes control charts, measurement improvement, and experimental design in manufacturing industries. Methods of instruction include lecture, overheads, discussion, video, exercises, case studies, and examination.

Credit Recommendation: In the lower division baccalaureate/associate degree category, 2 semester hours in Math (Basic Statistics) (4/93).

Process Improvement Methods for Managers in Service Industries (26) (Formerly Quality Improvement Methods for Managers in Service Industries [26])

Location: Client locations.

Length: 35 hours (5 days).

Dates: January 1993-Present.

Objective: To review continuous quality improvement theory and tools, introducing advanced process improvement techniques, such as survey sampling, experimental design, regression, multivariate control charts, and analysis for management of improvement.

Learning Outcome: Upon successful completion of this course, the student will be able to understand the strategic role of quality improvement; plan and organize for quality; know the continuous improvement philosophy; understand basic statistical tools; use control charts; interpret basic statistical charts; and manage improvement.

Instruction: Major topics covered in the course are history of the quality movement, process improvement, measurement of quality with simple process improvement tools, basic statistical tests, control charts, variables control charts, attributes control charts, measurement improvement, and experimental design in service industries. Methods of instruction include lecture, overheads, discussion, video, exercises, case studies, and examination

Credit Recommendation: In the lower division baccalaureate/associate degree category, 2 semester hours in Math (Basic Statistics) (4/93).

Regression Analysis for Process Improvement (Formerly Regression Analysis for Process Improvement: RQC Stage I)

Location: Knoxville, TN.

Length: 38 hours (1 week).

Dates: January 1993-Present.

Objective: To teach intermediate and advanced regression and correlation analysis topics, including computer applications options and routines.

Learning Outcome: Upon successful completion of this course, the student will be able to enter and evaluate data for regression and correlation analysis; and demonstrate computer applications proficiency on advanced and applied problems in continuous quality improvement.

Instruction: Major topics covered in the course are data evaluation prior to regression and correlation analysis, simple regression and correlation, multiple regression, computations by forward, backward, and stepwise selection procedures, R2 (squared), F statistic, and evaluation of computer-generated results. Methods of instruction include lecture, overheads, discussion, individual and group problems, computer exercises and software applications, and examination.

Credit Recommendation: In the graduate degree category, 3 semester hours in Industrial Engineering Statistics, Applied Regression Topics, Operations Research or Operations Management, Quantitative Analysis (4/93). **NOTE**: Student must complete RQC Stage II to receive credit. *Prerequisite*: Student must be in either the Resident Quality Consultant Program or the Process Improvement Specialist Program.

The Team Process for Process Improvement (22) (Formerly The Team Process for Quality Improvement [22])

Location: Several major U.S. cities and client locations.

Length: 28 hours (4 days).

Dates: January 1993-Present.

Objective: To teach participants to work with a process that will minimize risks, and maximize effectiveness using teamwork in the line organization to implement continuous quality improvement.

Learning Outcome: Upon successful completion of this course, the student will be able to select team members for continuing improvement, assign team improvement projects, conduct results-oriented meetings, resolve conflicts, and select appropriate statistical techniques for evaluation of each stage in the process.

Instruction: The major topic covered in the course is the team process, which includes getting started, working together, and reaching agreement. Methods of instruction include lecture, overheads, discussion, exercises, projects, group presentations for peer review, and examination.

Credit Recommendation: In the lower division baccalaureate/associate degree category, 2 semester hours in Organizational Management (4/93). *Prerequisite:* Student must have attended a QualPro basic course.

Qualtec Institute for Competitive Advantage

As the quality improvement process developed and quantifiable positive results were achieved in the 1980's, Qualtec Quality Services, Inc. found itself in a position of leadership in the quality arena. A consulting and training organization formed in 1985, Qualtec Quality Services, Inc. (QQS), and its team of total quality management practitioners provides access to the experiences and expertise of Florida Power & Light Company, winner of the coveted Deming Prize in 1989.

QQS provides clients with products and services that are unique in two ways. One, these products and services are developed from areas of proven expertise and performance. Two, they are specifically designed to meet individual customer's needs. QQS serves many diverse clients, including utilities, manufacturing and service organizations, universities, and governmental organizations, both domestic and international. To each of its clients, QQS offers the same benefit-cost effective resources and strategies to enhance the customer's business performance and competitive advantage.

Training is recognized as an integral part of Total Quality. However, QQS' management realized that a more formal approach to designing, developing, delivering, and evaluating training would enhance an already successful program. In 1988, a decision was made to develop an infrastructure for training and development through formation of the Qualtec Institute for Competitive Advantage, formalize the Institute as a non-degree granting proprietary school, and seek accreditation in September of 1990. Certification by the American Council on Education was received in 1993.

A curriculum of Total Quality Management and related courses is offered to client organizations. Quality of instruction is controlled by a staff of experts.

Source of official student records: Registry of Credit Recommendations, American Council on Education, One Dupont Circle, Washington, DC 20036-1193.

Additional information about the courses: College Credit Recommendation Service, American Council on Education, One Dupont Circle, Washington, DC 20036-1193.

Benchmarking Workshop (B2000T) (Quest for the Best: The Benchmarking Workshop)

Location: Various locations nationally and internationally.

Length: 16 hours (2 days).

Dates: August 1991-Present.

Objective: To teach students the concepts underlying successful implementation of benchmarking, focusing on critical elements of the process and its role in implementation.

Learning Outcome: Upon successful completion of this course, the student will be able to select benchmarking projects and teams; review and support benchmarking activities; and take an active role in implementation.

Instruction: Major topics covered in the course are principles of benchmarking; the benchmarking process; and case study analysis. Methods of instruction include lecture, group discussion, and case study.

Credit Recommendation: In the upper division baccalaureate degree category, 1 semester hour in Human Resources or Business elective (4/93).

Benchmarking Workshop Instructor (B2010T)

Location: Various locations nationally and internationally.

Length: 16 hours (2 days).

Dates: May 1988-Present.

Objective: To provide students with the knowledge and skills necessary to teach and administer benchmarking courses.

Learning Outcome: Upon successful completion of this course, the student will be able to prepare lesson plans and technical presentations; teach the benchmarking course; and evaluate feedback on presentation skills.

Instruction: Major topics covered in the course are principles of benchmarking; the benchmarking process; case study analysis; and presentation techniques. Methods of instruction include lecture, discussion, and videotaping.

Credit Recommendation: In the upper division baccalaureate degree category, 1 semester hour in Adult Education, Business, Communication, or Human Resource Development (4/93).

Danger in the Comfort Zone (DC100T)

Location: Various locations nationally and internationally.

Length: 16 hours (2 days).

Dates: September 1994-July 1995.

Objective: To provide a hands-on workshop to introduce the concepts inherent in the psychologies of entitlement, fear, and earning in the workplace and the strategies for moving the organization into earning.

Learning Outcome: Upon successful completion of this course, the student will be able to understand the interrelationship between the psychologies of entitlement, fear, and earning; the psychology of entitlement and its real cost in terms of lost performance, innovation, and creative thinking; tools for moving from a psychology of entitlement to a psychology of earning; and discuss the earning curve.

Instruction: Major topics covered in the course are the lethargy of entitlement; paralysis of fear; the energy of earning; moving away from entitlement, fear; maintaining creative energy of earning; and empowering an organization. (The workshop in based on Bardwick's book, Danger in the Comfort Zone.) Methods of instruction include lecture, classroom exercises, case studies, audio/visual materials, and role playing.

Credit Recommendation: In the upper division baccalaureate degree category, 1 semester hour in Organizational Culture Change or Management elective (10/94).

Design Team Workshop: TQM (DT400T)

Location: Various locations nationally and internationally.

Length: 40 hours (5 days) (3 to 5 days pre/post-course work).

Dates: July 1988-Present.

Objective: To provide students with an organizational structure to develop strategy and support for implementation of a total quality management program.

Learning Outcome: Upon successful completion of this course, the student will be able to produce a comprehensive action plan for developing and implementing his/her organization's total quality management process and be able to confirm that the plan will achieve desired objectives.

Instruction: Major topics covered in the course are TQM and change; overview of TQM, policy management, process management, and teams; quality improvement problem-solving process (the QI Story); purpose of the design team; mission and charter; developing the TQM implementation plan; and a model TQM implementation plan. **NOTE:** Pre-course work includes assessment, locating and reviewing data relating to customer satisfaction/customer needs; business environment; overarching objectives; direction of the organization; charter to the design team from the quality council; and mission/vision/values; this may include a predesign team assessment done by a third party. Post-course work includes carrying out the action plans for TQM implementation developed during the design team workshop and completing all sections of the implementation plan. Methods of instruction include lecture, classroom exercises, case studies, and visual aids.

Credit Recommendation: In the upper division baccalaureate degree category, 3 semester hours in Management or Business elective (4/93).

Instructor in New Quality Techniques (Seven New QC Tools Instructor)

Location: Various locations nationally and internationally.

Length: 16 hours (2 days).

Dates: July 1994-Present.

Objective: To provide quality control tools instructors with the knowledge and skills to teach and administer the course in new quality control tools.

Learning Outcome: Upon successful completion of this course, the student will be able to prepare lesson plans, do presentations, and obtain certification by classroom teaching under the guidance of a Qualtec Quality Services Master Instructor.

Instruction: Major topics covered in the course are the seven new quality control tools including their objectives and use; relationship between the new tools and the seven basic quality control tools, affinity diagrams, relations diagram, systematic diagrams, matrix diagrams for multi-variable thinking, matrix data analysis, process decision charts, and arrow diagrams. Methods of instruction include lecture, discussion, classroom case studies, audio/visual materials, learner presentations, and critique/feedback.

Credit Recommendation: In the upper division baccalaureate degree category, 1 semester hour in Education, Management, or as a Business elective (10/94).

ISO 9000 Auditor/Lead Auditor Training (19100T)

Location: Various locations nationally and internationally.

Length: 40 hours (5 days).

Dates: January 1992-Present.

Objective: To provide practical and comprehensive knowledge to perform audits and assessments of quality management systems.

Learning Outcome: Upon successful completion of this course, the student will be able to conduct external assessments and audits of contractors and suppliers; will be aware of the third-party certification process; know the principles and concepts of quality management, quality assurance, and quality audits, know corrective action requirements; and pass the examination for registered lead auditor.

Instruction: Major topics covered in the course are quality management standards and principles, quality system audits, documentation and reward requirements, and auditor and lead auditor qualifications. Methods of instruction include lecture, discussion, classroom exercises, case studies, audio/visual materials, and learner presentations.

Credit Recommendation: In the upper division baccalaureate degree category, 3 semester hours in Quality Management, Operations Management, or as a Business elective (10/94).

ISO 9000 Quality System Implementation Instructor (I9010T)

Location: Various locations nationally and internationally.

Length: 24 hours (3 days).

Dates: January 1993-Present.

Objective: To provide students with the knowledge and skills necessary to track and administer the ISO 9000 Quality System Implementation Workshop.

Learning Outcome: Upon successful completion of this course, the student will be able to teach and administer the ISO 9000 Quality System Implementation course.

Instruction: Major topics covered in the course are implementation strategies; preparation for practice presentations; auditing strategies; presentations; and feedback. Methods of instruction include lecture, discussion, videos, critique/feedback, and presentation.

Credit Recommendation: In the upper division baccalaureate degree category, 1 semester hour in Personnel, Training, Adult Education in Business, Education, or Public Administration (4/93).

ISO 9000 Quality System Implementation Team Workshop (I9300T)

Location: Various locations nationally and internationally.

Length: 16 hours (2 days).

Dates: January 1992-Present.

Objective: To teach students the team functions and roles in TQM that are a fundamental part of the organization and continuous improvement process defined by ISO 9000 standards.

Learning Outcome: Upon successful completion of this course, the student will be able to understand the functions and activities of QM teams and demonstrate the ability to serve effectively in a variety of roles and assignments consistent with ISO 9000 standards.

Instruction: Major topics covered in the course are linkage of ISO 9000 and TQM; ISO 9000 standards in greater depth of information and understanding; and interpretation of ISO standards in order to document and audit the ISO 9000 Quality System. Methods of instruction include lecture, discussion, videos, scenario analysis, studies and reports, case study, and presentations.

Credit Recommendation: In the upper division baccalaureate degree category, 1 semester hour in Manufacturing Management, or elective in Quality Management or Public Administration (4/93).

ISO 9000 Quality System Implementation Team Workshop Instructor Training (I9310T)

Location: Various locations nationally and internationally.

Length: 16 hours (2 days).

Dates: January 1993-Present.

Objective: To provide students with the knowledge and skills necessary to track and administer the ISO 9000 Quality System Implementation Team Workshop.

Learning Outcome: Upon successful completion of this course, the student will be able to teach and administer the ISO 9000 Quality System Implementation Team course.

Instruction: Major topics covered in the course are the definition of expectations of participant and requirements of future instructors; course overviews and presentation techniques; lesson plan preparation and presenting; feedback of presentation skills; complete practice presentations; and plan for first time teaching. Methods of instruction include lecture, discussion, videos, critique/feedback, and presentation.

Credit Recommendation: In the upper division baccalaureate degree category, 1 semester hour in Adult Education, Training, Business, or TQM elective (4/93).

ISO 9000 Quality System Implementation Workshop (I9000T)

Location: Various locations nationally and internationally.

Length: 24 hours (3 days).
Dates: April 1992-Present.
Objective: To provide students with the knowledge, skills, and tools needed to prepare their organizations for ISO 9000 registration.
Learning Outcome: Upon successful completion of this course, the student will be able to understand the forces driving manufacturing and service organizations toward ISO 9000; how the ISO 9000 quality system fits into the broader process of Total Quality Management; the role of executive management in structuring and supporting an ISO 9000 quality system; a step-by-step implementation plan for ISO 9000 registration; knowledge and skills to perform an internal self-assessment of their organization against the ISO 9000 standard; and a model ISO 9000 documentation package.
Instruction: Major topics covered in the course are TQM overview; TQM-ISO linkage; interpretation of ISO elements; implementation challenges; quality documentation; internal auditing; and corrective action. Methods of instruction include lecture, discussion, videos, action planning, and case study.
Credit Recommendation: In the lower division baccalaureate/associate degree category, 1 semester hour in Quality Production, Operations Management, or Business elective (4/93).

Key Business Process Planning (KB100T)

Location: Various locations nationally and internationally.
Length: *Module I*: 16 hours (2 days); *Module II:* 16 hours (2 days).
Dates: January 1994-Present.
Objective: To define key process planning structure and develop a macro key process flowchart.
Learning Outcome: Upon successful completion of this course, the student will be able to understand key business process planning, prioritize processes, map processes, and develop action plans.
Instruction: Major topics covered in the course are the establishment, deployment, and review of process planning. Methods of instruction include lecture and classroom exercises.
Credit Recommendation: In the lower division baccalaureate/associate degree category, 2 semester hours in Productions Operations Management or as a Business elective (10/94). **NOTE**: One semester hour of credit is recommended for each module.

Planning and Implementing: TQM (EB100T)

Location: Various locations nationally and internationally.
Length: 24 hours (3 days).
Dates: January 1990-Present.
Objective: To provide students with an understanding of an integrated TQM model and how it works in a smaller company.
Learning Outcome: Upon successful completion of this course, the student will be able to understand how TQM works in a small company, set objectives and produce an implementation plan. (Recommended for small business CEO's or directors.)
Instruction: Major topics covered in the course are TQM overview; problem solving process; QC tools and techniques; visioning; setting objectives; and planning for TQM. Methods of instruction include lecture, exercises, videotapes, and developing the plan.
Credit Recommendation: In the upper division baccalaureate degree category, 1 semester hour in Small Business Studies, Quality Management, or Business elective (4/93).

Quality Function Deployment (QF400T)

Location: Various locations nationally and internationally.
Length: 16 hours (2 days).
Dates: July 1992-Present.
Objective: To teach students how to use customer input and deploy that input through design, development, and delivery to the customer.
Learning Outcome: Upon successful completion of this course, the student will be able to use quality function deployment; and to design or redesign a service or product based on customer input.
Instruction: Major topics covered in the course are overview of quality function deployment; designing products and services; the voice of the customer; planning and deployment process; and implementation and action planning. Methods of instruction include lecture, discussion, case studies, and class activities.
Credit Recommendation: In the upper division baccalaureate degree category, 1 semester hour in Business elective or Management (4/93).

Quality Function Deployment Instructor (QF410T)

Location: Various locations nationally and internationally.
Length: 24 hours (3 days).
Dates: November 1993-Present.
Objective: To provide prospective instructors with the knowledge and skills to teach and administer the course in quality function deployment with certification by classroom teaching under guidance of a Qualtec Institute Master instructor.
Learning Outcome: Upon successful completion of this course, the prospective instructor will be able to teach the students to understand the role of quality function deployment in total quality management (TQM); identify customer requirements for new service or bundles of processes; develop a plan for the delivery system of the new services; and select the necessary resources including considerations of cost, technology, and reliability.
Instruction: Major topics covered in the course are the relationship of total quality management (TQM), identification of customer requirements, team uses of specific tools and techniques, service planning, delivery process planning, material planning, operation planning, and aligning new services with existing processes to plan for continuous improvement. Methods of instruction include lecture, discussion, classroom exercises, case studies, audio/visual materials, and learner presentations with critiques.
Credit Recommendation: In the upper division baccalaureate degree category, 1 semester hour in Quality Management, Education, or as a Business elective (10/94).

Quality Improvement Story Workshop (QI100T)

Location: Various locations nationally and internationally.
Length: 16 hours (2 days).
Dates: September 1994-Present.
Objective: To provide an understanding of the quality improvement process including appropriate tools and techniques and application of the process to work data.
Learning Outcome: Upon successful completion of this course, the student will be able to understand the quality improvement process; know its tools and techniques such as brainstorming and quality control tools; and apply the tools and techniques to determine the reason for

improvement, the current situation, and analysis of root causes.

Instruction: Major topics covered in the course are quality indicators; steps in the quality improvement problem-solving process; tool and techniques including brainstorming and statistical quality control charts; and applications of the steps in a practical exercise. Methods of instruction include lecture, discussion, classroom exercises, case studies, audio/visual materials, and group reports on team projects.

Credit Recommendation: In the lower division baccalaureate/associate degree category, 1 semester hour Quality Management or as a Business elective (10/94).

Quality in Daily Work Instructor: TQM (QD710T)

Location: Various locations nationally and internationally.

Length: 24 hours (3 days).

Dates: January 1991-Present.

Objective: To provide students with the knowledge and skills necessary to teach and administer the QIDW course (QD700T).

Learning Outcome: Upon successful completion of this course, the student will be able to effectively teach and administer the QIDW course and understand the key elements of effective presentations.

Instruction: Major topics covered in the course are defining expectations and requirements of instructors; preparing technical presentations; making presentations; and giving feedback on presentation skills. Methods of instruction include lecture, skill development and practice, and videotaping.

Credit Recommendation: In the upper division baccalaureate degree category, 1 semester hour in Adult Education, Business, Communication, or Human Resource Development (4/93). **NOTE:** Students who receive credit for Process Management Instructor (PM510T) should not receive credit for this course.

Quality in Daily Work: TQM (QD700T)

Location: Various locations nationally and internationally.

Length: 24 hours (3 days).

Dates: January 1990-Present.

Objective: To provide students with a systematic approach to identifying and improving key job functions and work processes.

Learning Outcome: Upon successful completion of this course, the student will be able to identify key work processes and customer needs; develop quality indicators; build the process control system; and monitor and improve process performance.

Instruction: Major topics covered in the course are defining quality and TQM; choosing quality indicators; building the process system; developing an action plan; and reviewing and improving systems. Methods of instruction include lecture and individual and group skill practice.

Credit Recommendation: In the upper division baccalaureate degree category, 1 semester hour in Management or Business elective (4/93). **NOTE:** Students who receive credit for Process Management (PM500T) should not receive credit for this course.

Reengineering Workshop

Location: Various locations nationally and internationally.

Length: 32 hours (4 days).

Dates: March 1994-Present.

Objective: To conduct a reengineering project.

Learning Outcome: Upon successful completion of this course, the student will be able to achieve an understanding of the reengineering process and perform as a member of a reengineering team.

Instruction: Major topics covered in the course are the reengineering process flowchart, developing strategies for process innovation, creating the new process design, piloting the redesign process, and transitioning the organization to the redesigned process. Methods of instruction include lecture, classroom exercises and video-tapes.

Credit Recommendation: In the lower division baccalaureate/associate degree category, 2 semester hours in Change Management (10/94).

Statistical Tools and Techniques (SC800T)

Location: Various locations nationally and internationally.

Length: 32 hours (4 days).

Dates: March 1989-Present.

Objective: To teach students the basic concepts and computations of descriptive statistics, and their applications in the quality improvement process.

Learning Outcome: Upon successful completion of this course, the student will be able to collect and analyze data; do basic computations accurately; interpret data; and present business information in an objective and statistically acceptable fashion.

Instruction: Major topics covered in the course are frequency distributions and their characteristics; measures of central tendency and variation including S and R; histograms and control charts; presentation and interpretation of problem and survey data; sampling; basic inference; sample proportions; flow charting the decision and statistical process; scatter diagrams; elementary correlation; and regression. Methods of instruction include problem solving, computations and discussion, lectures, assigned exercises, examinations, videos, supplemental text and assigned readings, and flowchart exercises.

Credit Recommendation: In the lower division baccalaureate/associate degree category, 2 semester hours in Business, Economic Statistics, or Statistics for the Social Sciences (4/93).

Statistical Tools and Techniques Instructor (SC801T)

Location: Various locations nationally and internationally.

Length: 40 hours (5 days).

Dates: January 1992-Present.

Objective: To provide students with the skills to teach the concepts of descriptive statistics and their application to the quality improvement process.

Learning Outcome: Upon successful completion of this course, the student will be able to teach and administer the Statistical Tools and Techniques course with an in-depth understanding of the key elements of basic statistics.

Instruction: Major topics covered in the course are methods of teaching data analysis, frequency distributions, scatter diagrams, control charts, capability analysis, and other statistical applications. Methods of instruction include lecture, skill development and practice, discussion, videotaping, observation, and critique.

Credit Recommendation: In the lower division baccalaureate/associate degree category, 2 semester hours in Adult Education, Communications, or Human Resources Development (4/93).

Systems Approach to Training: Enhanced Training Techniques (TE950T)

Location: Various locations nationally and internationally.

Length: 24 hours (3 days).

Dates: June 1989-Present.

Objective: To train students in classroom presentation skills.

Learning Outcome: Upon successful completion of this course, the student will

be able to understand the impact of a variety of instructional aids; demonstrate effective use of instructional aids; recognize and demonstrate effective presentation skills; and prepare and deliver presentations.

Instruction: Major topics covered in the course are preparation and effective use of instructional aids; platform skills and presentation skills; skills practice; and evaluation of presentations. Methods of instruction include lecture, classroom exercises, presentations, and videotaping.

Credit Recommendation: In the upper division baccalaureate degree category, 1 semester hour in Methods in Teaching or Education elective (4/93). **NOTE:** This course may also be considered as part of the curriculum for a certificate in Instructional Technology which is recommended for 7 semester hours.

Systems Approach to Training: Fundamentals of On-the-Job Training (TE960T)

Location: Various locations nationally and internationally.

Length: 24 hours (3 days).

Dates: June 1989-Present.

Objective: To prepare students to conduct on-the-job training programs.

Learning Outcome: Upon successful completion of this course, the student will be able to distinguish between the appropriate uses of classroom and on-the-job (OJT) instruction and the advantages and disadvantages of OJT; distinguish between the three basic instructional methods used in OJT; identify key practices that influence OJT; conduct a demonstration of OJT; and conduct an effective performance evaluation.

Instruction: Major topics covered in the course are OJT requirements, key terms and concepts; conducting a comprehensive demonstration/practice; applying principles of adult learning to on-the-job training; and conducting an effective performance evaluation. Methods of instruction include lecture, discussion, classroom exercises, role-playing, and videos.

Credit Recommendation: In the upper division baccalaureate degree category, 1 semester hour in Methods of Teaching, Human Resources, or as an Education elective (4/93). **NOTE:** This course may also be considered as part of the curriculum for a certificate in Instructional Technology which has been recommended for a total of 7 semester hours.

Systems Approach to Training: Post Training Evaluation (TE970T)

Location: Various locations nationally and internationally.

Length: 24 hours (3 days).

Dates: June 1989-Present.

Objective: To prepare students to develop instruments; evaluate training after it has occurred; and analyze and use the results to assess application and impact of training.

Learning Outcome: Upon successful completion of this course, the student will be able to develop post-training questionnaires; analyze results of post training data; prepare charts and graphs to show results; determine strengths and weaknesses of training using results; and prepare a written technical report.

Instruction: Major topics covered in the course are analysis of post-training data; development of questionnaires/survey instruments; analysis of survey data; conducting follow-up interviews; and the preparation of technical reports. Methods of instruction include lecture, discussion, and exercises.

Credit Recommendation: In the upper division baccalaureate degree category, 1 semester hour in Methods of Teaching or Education elective (4/93). **NOTE:** This course may also be considered as part of the curriculum for a certificate in Instructional Technology which has been recommended for a total of 7 semester hours.

Systems Approach to Training: Systems Approach to Needs, Job, and Task Analysis (TE910T)

Location: Various locations nationally and internationally.

Length: 40 hours (5 days).

Dates: June 1989-Present.

Objective: To prepare students in the application of a systems approach to training as it relates to all phases of analysis-needs, job, and task.

Learning Outcome: Upon successful completion of this course, the student will be able to conduct training needs analysis and job analysis; collect and analyze data; select and analyze critical tasks; write performance objectives and criterion tests; and prepare a work plan and report, all in preparation for the program design phase.

Instruction: Major topics covered in the course are needs analysis; job analysis; job survey; task analysis; skill and knowledge analysis; and resource selection. Methods of instruction include lecture, discussion, and class exercises.

Credit Recommendation: In the upper division baccalaureate degree category, 1 semester hour in Methods in Teaching or as an Education elective (4/93). *Prerequisite:* Since materials generated in this course may be used in the course, Training Design (TE920T), it is recommended that this course, Systems Approach, be a prerequisite course. **NOTE:** This course may also be considered as part of the curriculum for a certificate in Instructional Technology which has been recommended for a total of 7 semester hours.

Systems Approach to Training: Training Materials Development (TE930T)

Location: Various locations nationally and internationally.

Length: 40 hours (5 days).

Dates: June 1989-Present.

Objective: To prepare students in the development of high-quality training materials.

Learning Outcome: Upon successful completion of this course, the student will be able to develop supporting text material and self-tests; prepare course performance objectives; develop course modules and other training materials; and prepare course control documents. (Recommended for instructors, analysts, and instructional technologists.)

Instruction: Major topics covered in the course are supporting text material; self-testing; course modules and other materials; performance objectives and task performance aids, and course control documents. Methods of instruction include lecture and class exercises.

Credit Recommendation: In the upper division baccalaureate degree category, 1 semester hour in Methods in Teaching or Education elective (4/93). **NOTE:** This course may also be considered as part of the curriculum for a certificate in Instructional Technology which has been recommended for a total of 7 semester hours.

Systems Approach to Training: Training Program Design (TE920T)

Location: Various locations nationally and internationally.

Length: 32 hours (4 days).

Dates: September 1989-Present.

Objective: To prepare students to design courses and training programs using a systems approach.

Learning Outcome: Upon successful completion of this course, the student will

be able to use information from task analysis worksheets for program design; select appropriate instructional methods and media; and develop a course map and training map. (Recommended for instructors, analysts, and instructional technologists.)

Instruction: Major topics covered in the course are preparation of target populations and training setting descriptions; selection of instructional methods and media; development of course maps; and development of training maps. Methods of instruction include lecture and classroom exercises.

Credit Recommendation: In the upper division baccalaureate degree category, 1 semester hour in Methods in Teaching or Education elective. (4/93). **NOTE:** This course may be considered as part of the curriculum for a certificate in Instructional Technology which has been recommended for a total of 7 semester hours.

Test Development (TE940T)

Location: Various locations nationally and internationally.

Length: 40 hours (5 days).

Dates: June 1989-Present.

Objective: To prepare students to develop test items and tests from content and in good form.

Learning Outcome: Upon successful completion of this course, the student will be able to devise test development information from resources; develop multiple-choice and matching test items; develop arrangement, identification, and completion test items; develop long-and short-answer test items; construct post-test analysis; develop, analyze, and revise job performance measures; and develop tests from the items. (Recommended for instructors, test developers, and instructional technologists.)

Instruction: Major topics covered in the course are developing test items from materials; developing various types of testing, including multiple choice, short answer, long answer, and matching; and analyzing and revising performance tests. Methods of instruction include lecture and classroom exercises.

Credit Recommendation: In the upper division baccalaureate degree category, 1 semester hour in Methods in Teaching or Education elective (4/93). **NOTE:** This course may also be considered as part of the curriculum for a certificate in Instructional Technology which has been recommended for a total of 7 semester hours.

TQM: Facilitator Skills Instructor Training (FL310T)

Location: Various locations nationally and internationally.

Length: 32 hours (4 days).

Dates: July 1987-Present.

Objective: To provide students with knowledge and skills necessary to teach and administer the TQM facilitator courses.

Learning Outcome: Upon successful completion of this course, the student will be able to conduct classes in facilitator skills; define expectations of students and requirements of future instructors; and understand the role of the facilitator in team development, group dynamics, and the TQM continuous improvement process.

Instruction: Major topics covered in the course are facilitator overview; facilitator skills; coordinator role; communicator role; teacher, coach, and promoter roles; and facilitator instructor skills. Methods of instruction include lecture, videotaping, discussions, group exercises, and peer review.

Credit Recommendation: In the upper division baccalaureate degree category, 2 semester hours in Business Communications or Human Resource Development (4/93).

TQM: Facilitator Skills Training (FL300T)

Location: Various locations nationally and internationally.

Length: 32 hours (4 days).

Dates: July 1987-Present.

Objective: To provide students with the information and practice necessary to facilitate quality improvement team activities.

Learning Outcome: Upon successful completion of this course, the student will be able to understand the five roles of the facilitator in teams; demonstrate the group dynamic skills necessary to guide QI teams in activities; and establish the facilitator-teams-management relationship.

Instruction: Major topics covered in the course are TQM concepts; facilitator role in group activities; overview of adult learning; skills as a coordinator, communicator, teacher, coach, and promoter; and other effective facilitation skills. Methods of instruction include lecture, videos, group activities, discussion, and role playing.

Credit Recommendation: In the upper division baccalaureate degree category, 2 semester hours in Business elective, Supervision, or Management Leadership (4/93).

TQM: Managing Quality Improvement (MQ400T)

Location: Various locations nationally and internationally.

Length: 24 hours (3 days).

Dates: July 1987-Present.

Objective: To equip students with the knowledge and skills needed to manage and support a total quality management system. This course focuses on the teams component of the total quality management process.

Learning Outcome: Upon successful completion of this course, the student will be able to understand and plan their management roles in supporting teams; understand and use the four basic principles of quality; and the seven statistical tools for problem solving; and develop a personal action plan to support all team activities for total quality management.

Instruction: Major topics covered in the course are an overview of total quality management; QC tools and QI story; interacting with quality teams; managing results; and action planning. Methods of instruction include lecture, student participation in role-playing and other exercises; and use of video tapes and overhead slides.

Credit Recommendation: In the upper division baccalaureate degree category, 1 semester hour in Management or Business elective (4/93).

TQM: Managing Quality Improvement Instructor (MQ410T)

Location: Various locations nationally and internationally.

Length: 24-40 hours (3-5 days).

Dates: July 1987-Present.

Objective: To provide students with the knowledge and skills necessary to teach and administer Managing Quality Improvement (MQI) courses.

Learning Outcome: Upon successful completion of this course, the student will be able to define expectations and requirements of MQI instructors; prepare course overviews and presentations; teach the MQI course; and demonstrate effective communication skills.

Instruction: Major topics covered in the course are TQM overview; statistical tools used in TQM; overview of components necessary for successful implementation of TQM; and effective instructional skills. Methods of instruction include lecture, skill practice, videotaping, and discussion.

Credit Recommendation: In the upper division baccalaureate degree category, 1 semester hour in Adult Education, Business, Communications, or Human Resource Development (4/93).

TQM: Managing the Supplier Quality Improvement Process (V1700T)

Location: Various locations nationally and internationally.

Length: 16 hours (2 days).

Dates: September 1992-Present.

Objective: To teach students the detailed implementation steps to evaluate and improve the organization's internal procurement process and to provide instruction for guiding the quality improvement process.

Learning Outcome: Upon successful completion of this course, the student will be able to understand internal procurement, supplier relationships in a TQM organization, and will demonstrate the ability to perform effectively in management of suppliers.

Instruction: Major topics covered in the course are quality improvement process (QIP); supplier quality improvement process (SQIP); internal procurement; quality assessment of suppliers; benefit cost analysis; Plan, Do, Check, Act (PDCA) process; flow charting the purchasing decision; and continuous nature of supplier quality management. Methods of instruction include lecture, discussion, problem solving, case studies, projects for evaluation, presentation, and peer review of reports.

Credit Recommendation: In the upper division baccalaureate degree category, 1 semester hour in Purchasing/Buying, Manufacturing Management in Business, or elective in Industrial Marketing, Manufacturing Management or Public Administration (4/93). **NOTE:** If this course is taken, credit should not also be granted for Quality Supplier Process (VI900T).

TQM: Policy Management for Managers (PM200T)

Location: Various locations nationally and internationally.

Length: 16 hours (2 days).

Dates: January 1992-Present.

Objective: To teach students deployment, implementation, and review policy with particular emphasis on priority areas in the organization and the continuous nature of the process.

Learning Outcome: Upon successful completion of this course, the student will be able to understand and demonstrate proficiency in the deployment implementation and review of policy decisions.

Instruction: Major topics covered in the course are the purpose and function of management; deployment and implementation of policy; and management review. Methods of instruction include lecture, case studies, peer review, and group activity.

Credit Recommendation: In the upper division baccalaureate degree category, 1 semester hour in Organizational Behavior, Quality Management in Business, or Public Administration (4/93).

TQM: Process Management (PM500T) (Process Management)

Location: Various locations nationally and internationally.

Length: 24 hours (3 days).

Dates: November 1992-Present.

Objective: To provide students with a systematic approach to identifying, documenting, prioritizing, and improving key job functions and work processes.

Learning Outcome: Upon successful completion of this course, the student will be able to identify and document key work processes; establish customer requirements; set indicators; begin developing initial process control systems; and monitor and improve performance.

Instruction: Major topics covered in the course are the definition of quality; principles of TQM and process management; building process control systems; implementing the system; determining and ensuring process stability, capability, and flexibility; and monitoring and improving process control systems. Methods of instruction include lecture, and individual and group skill practice.

Credit Recommendation: In the upper division baccalaureate degree category, 2 semester hours in Management or Business elective (4/93). **NOTE:** Students who receive credit for Quality in Daily Work (QD700T) should not receive credit for this course.

TQM: Process Management Instructor (PM510T)

Location: Various locations nationally and internationally.

Length: 24 hours (3 days).

Dates: January 1993-Present.

Objective: To provide students with the knowledge and skills necessary to teach and administer the process management course (PM500T).

Learning Outcome: Upon successful completion of this course, the student will be able to teach and administer the process management course effectively and understand the key elements of effective presentations.

Instruction: Major topics covered in the course are defining expectations and requirements of instructors; preparing technical presentations; making presentations; and giving feedback on presentation skills. Methods of instruction include lecture, skill development and practice, and videotaping.

Credit Recommendation: In the upper division baccalaureate degree category, 1 semester hour in Adult Education, Business, Communication, or Human Resource Development (4/93). **NOTE:** Students who receive credit for Quality in Daily Work Instructor (QD710T) should not receive credit for this course.

TQM: Quality Council Policy Management (QC500T)

Location: Various locations nationally and internationally.

Length: 20 hours (2.5 days).

Dates: March 1992-Present.

Objective: To provide the students with the knowledge and skills to set the vision and assess current business status; to set parameters, key policy components, and execute responsibilities required to achieve a policy management system.

Learning Outcome: Upon successful completion of this course, the student will be able to understand TQM and its components; differentiate between policy management and other business planning processes; understand the importance of a mission and vision; select critical success factors in greatest need for improvement; prioritize activities; and establish communication plans and implementation schedule.

Instruction: Major topics covered in the course are policy management overview; mission/vision; critical success factors; breakthrough objectives; priority activities; and implementation plan. Methods of instruction include lecture, hands-on activities, and discussion.

Credit Recommendation: In the upper division baccalaureate degree category, 1

semester hour in Quality Management or Business elective (4/93).

TQM: Quality Council Workshop (QC600T)

Location: Various locations nationally and internationally.

Length: 16 hours (2 days).

Dates: June 1989-Present.

Objective: To teach students an organizational structure for Total Quality Management and develop executive leadership skills for leading the implementation of TQM in the organization.

Learning Outcome: Upon successful completion of this course, the student will be able to understand successful strategies for implementing TQM and the role the Quality Council plays as leaders of the process. (Recommended for senior management.)

Instruction: Major topics covered in the course are overview of TQM; results to be expected of a TQM implementation; detailed implementation strategies; and role of the Quality Council. Methods of instruction include lecture, discussion, reports, evaluation, team projects, presentations, and role playing in actual business situations under current conditions.

Credit Recommendation: In the upper division baccalaureate degree category, 1 semester hour Business or Public Administration, or as an elective in Management, Executive Development, Administration, Quality Management (4/93).

TQM: Quality Improvement Turbo Team Workshop (TT200T)

Location: Various locations nationally and internationally.

Length: 24-40 hours (3-5 days).

Dates: June 1992-Present.

Objective: To equip students with the knowledge and skills in team problem solving to achieve maximum results in a short period of time on high priority improvement opportunities.

Learning Outcome: Upon successful completion of this course, the student will be able to demonstrate measurable progress in using QC tools and techniques to solve problems and understand how their team activities contribute to the overall objectives of their organization.

Instruction: Major topics covered in the course are problem area identification; quality control tools and the seven-step quality improvement process; brainstorming; and root cause analysis. Methods of instruction include lecture, discussion, problem solving, and practice on their own QI story as a case study.

Credit Recommendation: In the upper division baccalaureate degree category, 2 semester hours in Management or Quality Control (4/93).

TQM: Quality Management Core Process Planning (CP100T)

Location: Various locations nationally and internationally.

Length: 16 hours (2 days).

Dates: October 1992-Present.

Objective: To provide students with a macro view of core process planning and process management as part of a total quality management system.

Learning Outcome: Upon successful completion of this course, the student will be able to understand concepts of total quality management and its relationship to process planning; understand the role of the processing planning team and member/leader relationships; develop macro core processing flowcharts; and develop an action plan for data collection, indicator development, and appropriate documentation. (Recommended for upper level executives.)

Instruction: Major topics covered in the course are process team roles and group dynamics; flowcharting (quality and process indicators); and development of macro process control charts and action plans. Methods of instruction include lecture, practice, and student participation in group activities.

Credit Recommendation: In the upper division baccalaureate degree category, 1 semester hour in Manufacturing, Management, or Business elective (4/93).

TQM: Seven New Quality Control Tools (QC100T)

Location: Various locations nationally and internationally.

Length: 16 hours (2 days).

Dates: October 1992-Present.

Objective: To provide students with an understanding of the seven new quality control tools; with application to quality planning and improvement and use for improved communication of company objectives; and other verbal data.

Learning Outcome: Upon successful completion of this course, the student will be able to describe the seven new quality control (QC) tools; basic uses and applications; understand the relationship of the new QC tools to the basic QC tools; apply the new QC tools (individually and in combination) to quality planning and improvement activities; and use the new QC tools for improved communication of company objectives and qualitative information.

Instruction: Major topics covered in the course are definition of seven new QC tools; discussion and use of affinity, relations, systematic, matrix, and arrow diagrams; and discussion and use of matrix data analysis and the process decision and program chart. Methods of instruction include lecture, discussion, and exercises.

Credit Recommendation: In the upper division baccalaureate degree category, 1 semester hour in Business Management (4/93).

TQM: Steering Committee Deployment (SCD00T) (Steering Committee Deployment Workshop)

Location: Various locations nationally and internationally.

Length: 16 hours (2 days).

Dates: June 1992-Present.

Objective: To train students to identify priority activity indicators, targets, and deployment models for policy management.

Learning Outcome: Upon successful completion of this course, the student will be able to understand policy management and its components; reach consensus on priority activities; establish indicators and targets for priority activities; understand data collection and analysis techniques; deployment of plans into the organization; and formalize action plans.

Instruction: Major topics include policy management overview; setting priorities, activities and indicators; targets and "catchball"; and action planning. Methods of instruction include lecture, hands-on activity, and discussion.

Credit Recommendation: In the upper division baccalaureate degree category, 1 semester hour in Management or Business elective (4/93).

TQM: Supplier Quality Improvement Process (V1600T)

Location: Various locations nationally and internationally.

Length: 16 hours (2 days).

Dates: September 1992-Present.

Objective: To teach students the particulars of the total quality management process applied to buying, purchasing, and working with suppliers, including their role in implementing certification Phase I of the Quality Supplier Process.

Learning Outcome: Upon successful completion of this course, the student will be able to understand the full spectrum of purchasing and buying Quality Management company-supplier issues, and demonstrate the ability to perform effectively in daily operation with quality suppliers.

Instruction: Major topics covered in the course are Quality Improvement Process (QIP); Supplier Quality Improve-ment Process (SQIP); internal procurement; quality assessment of suppliers; benefit cost analysis; PDCA process; flowcharting the purchasing decision; and continuous nature of supplier quality management. Methods of instruction include lecture, discussion, case studies, problem solving, projects for evaluation, presentations, and peer review of reports.

Credit Recommendation: In the upper division baccalaureate degree category, 1 semester hour Purchasing/Buying, Industrial Marketing elective, Manufacturing Management in Business, or Public Administration (4/93). **NOTE:** No credit should be given for this course if Managing the Supplier Process (VI700T) is also taken.

TQM: Team Leader (TL200T) (Team Leader Training)

Location: Various locations nationally and internationally.

Length: 40 hours (5 days).

Dates: May 1986-Present.

Objective: To equip students with the knowledge and skills necessary to lead and maintain quality improvement teams.

Learning Outcome: Upon successful completion of this course, the student will be able to understand team dynamics as related to TQM; comprehend the meaning of TQM and customer satisfaction; exercise appropriate administrative activities in leading teams; and lead teams through the seven-step problem solving process.

Instruction: Major topics covered in the course are purpose and mechanics of quality improvement processes; principles of TQM; QI story for problem solving; QC (quality control) tools; and skills needed to build and maintain teams. Methods of instruction included lecture, case study, exercise, video, role playing, and discussion.

Credit Recommendation: In the upper division baccalaureate degree category, 2 semester hours in Supervision, Management, or Business elective (4/93).

TQM: Team Leader Instructor (TL210T)

Location: Various locations nationally and internationally.

Length: 40 hours (5 days).

Dates: August 1986-Present.

Objective: To provide students with instructor training and equip them with the knowledge and skills needed to teach and administer team leader courses.

Learning Outcome: Upon successful completion of this course, the student will be able to effectively teach and administer the team leader course (TL200T) and understand both the technical content and the key elements of effective presentations.

Instruction: Major topics covered in the course are defining expectations and requirements of instructors; preparing presentations; making presentations; technical instruction, group dynamics; and methods for providing feedback or presentation skills. Methods of instruction include lecture, skill practice, and videotaping.

Credit Recommendation: In the upper division baccalaureate degree category, 2 semester hours in Adult Education, Business Communications, or Human Resource Development (4/93).

TQM: Team Member Training (TM100T)

Location: Various locations nationally and internationally.

Length: 16 hours (2 days).

Dates: May 1988-Present.

Objective: To provide students with an overview of quality improvement principles, the QI story problem solving process, and practice in the role of a quality improvement team member.

Learning Outcome: Upon successful completion of this course, the student will be able to understand the basics of quality principles and practices; use quality control tools to reflect factual data; and follow and apply problem solving principles.

Instruction: Major topics covered in this course are concepts of total quality management; seven steps in the quality improvement process; cause and effect analysis; tools and techniques for getting started as a team; and use of QC tools such as Pareto charts, histograms, fish bone diagrams and line graphs. Methods of instruction include lecture, discussion, classroom exercises, video presentations, and audio visual aids.

Credit Recommendation: In the upper division baccalaureate degree category, 1 semester hour in Management (4/93).

TQM: Voice of the Business (VB500T)

Location: Various locations nationally and internationally.

Length: 16 hours (2 days).

Dates: January 1992-Present.

Objective: To teach students to identify and analyze strategic factors of organization decisions and planning units, the participation and valid concerns of internal stake holders and external publics (other than customers) with particular emphasis on the quality management program.

Learning Outcome: Upon successful completion of this course, the student will be able to demonstrate proficiency in acquiring, analyzing and presenting relevant data and concerns into the quality planning process from employees, unions, suppliers and external public constituencies and stake holders (other than customers).

Instruction: Major topics covered in the course are identification of stakeholders in the organization and their needs; identification and prioritization of emerging issues for the organization; business elements that address stakeholder needs and emerging issues; and setting business indicators. Methods of instruction include lecture, case problems, individual and team projects, presentations and team review, independent study, and research projects.

Credit Recommendation: In the upper division baccalaureate degree category, 1 semester hour Planning, Policy Formation, Management in Business, or Public Administration (4/93).

TQM: Voice of the Customer (VC500T)

Location: Various locations nationally and internationally.

Length: 16 hours (2 days).

Dates: January 1992-Present.

Objective: To teach students the management system of continuously improving customer satisfaction and objective means of measuring, reporting, and evaluating customer feedback into organizational policy making.

Learning Outcome: Upon successful completion of this course, the student will

be able to demonstrate an understanding and an ability to conduct customer studies; evaluate results; and utilize feedback to adjust or change organizational plans and programs.

Instruction: Major topics covered in the course are customer requirements; needs assessment matrix; customer evaluation; segments; TQM elements that can be documented through customer analysis; consumer surveys; and monitoring the customer information system. Methods of instruction include lecture, discussion, consumer problems, cases, designing surveys, analyzing results, and reporting to TQM committees and boards.

Credit Recommendation: In the upper division baccalaureate degree category, 1 semester hour as an elective in Management, Marketing Research, Consumer Behavior in Business, or Public Administration (4/93).

Recovery Assistance Program Training, Inc.

Recovery Assistance Program Training was designed to help a person respond to the substance abuse issues of our society. We established a comprehensive education/training program that provides all the certified hours of recovery counselor education required to apply toward certification as a Certified Alcoholism Counselor, Certified Drug Counselor, or Certified Substance Abuse Counselor in any of 46 states.

The Recovery Assistance Program is fully accredited by Boards of Counselor Certification throughout the United States and provides a person with all hours and education topics required in the process of professional certification for substance abuse recovery counselors. Most conveniently, all of this education is provided at any one of the many RAPT locations. Using one evening each week and one full Saturday per month, RAPT offers students the opportunity to get their education in one location, comprehensively. At the time of this publication RAPT courses were being State Certified and offered in California, Illinois, Washington, DC, Maryland, Delaware, Pennsylvania, New Jersey, Massachusetts, and New York.

Source of official student records: Registry of Credit Recommendations, American Council on Education, One Dupont Circle, Washington, DC 20036-1193.

Additional information about the courses: Office of Corporate-Higher Education Programs, Thomas Edison State College, 101 West State Street, Trenton, NJ 08608-1176.

Addiction and Its Effects

Location: Multiple locations throughout the United States.

Length: 45 hours (1-2 weeks).

Dates: September 1991-Present.

Objective: To provide students with knowledge of how the brain, central nervous system, respiratory and cardiac systems of the body function normally in comparison to how they are affected by substance use/abuse.

Learning Outcome: Upon successful completion of this course, the student will be able to apply classification system of drug pharmacology; understand drug abuse and gain intensive knowledge of particular drugs, such as alcohol, cocaine, heroine, nicotine, caffeine, and hallucinogens; and know the potential for drug dependency and toxicity.

Instruction: Major topics covered in the course draw special attention to issues related to the development of Fetal Alcohol Syndrome, and the effects of psychoactive substances on HIV infected clients.

Credit Recommendation: In the upper division baccalaureate degree category, 3 semester hours in Affects of Substances (5/95).

Case Management II

Location: Multiple locations throughout the United States.

Length: 45 hours (1-2 weeks).

Dates: September 1993-Present.

Objective: To provide students with in-depth knowledge and skills in substance abuse counseling and modalities of treatment.

Learning Outcome: Upon successful completion of this course, the student will be able to obtain and maintain information about community resources and services through establishing contact with other service providers; match community resources with client needs and provide education for the client about self-help groups, i.e., explain to the client all appropriate assessments, test results, goals, objectives, rules and obligations of the programs; consult with supervisors, counselors, professionals, and/or service providers by discussing one's own cases resulting in comprehensive quality care for the client; and participate as a team member by presenting cases, providing input into other's cases and advocate for their client's interest by negotiating plans to resolve client's problems.

Instruction: Major topics covered in this course involve case review. The class work is "people" oriented, utilizing current issues and questions to introduce students to the practical real life case management.

Credit Recommendation: In the upper division baccalaureate degree category, 3 semester hours in Advanced Case Management (5/95).

Case Management of Substance Abuse Clients (The Recovery Process)

Location: Multiple locations throughout the United States.

Length: 45 hours (1-2 weeks).

Dates: September 1991-Present.

Objective: To learn the requirements and means for collecting client data, assessing client illness and constructing a treatment plan. To give students an understanding of how recovery begins with appropriate data collection, record keeping, treatment planning, and subsequent assessment.

Learning Outcome: Upon successful completion of this course, the student will be able to use interviewing techniques for gathering relevant information on the client's status and history; find various sources of information exclusive of the client and evaluate this information to validate the client's information in order to give a complete history; design a treatment plan with the client; determine the client's appropriateness and eligibility for admission or referral to a range of programs by assessing the match between client's needs and program target populations and services; and write a diagnostic summary based on the results of separate assessments performed by the counselor or multidisciplinary team.

Instruction: Major topics covered in the course are a wide range of practical material, using actual client data collection forms and diagnostic tests. The course is designed to prepare students for in-take procedures, screening, and assessment. Exams are provided through role play and practicums.

Credit Recommendation: In the upper division baccalaureate degree category, 3 semester hours in Case Management of Substance Abuse Clients (5/95).

Counseling Individual Substance Abusing Client (Individual Counseling)

Location: Multiple locations throughout the United States.

Length: 45 hours (1-2 weeks).

Dates: September 1991-Present.

Objective: To educate students in the basic psychology and dynamics of substance abuse recovery techniques.

Learning Outcome: Upon successful completion of this course, the student will be able to establish rapport and trust with client, family members, and community support systems; understand various counseling theories and approaches relevant to alcohol and other drugs of abuse; understand continuum of care, evaluation techniques to determine treatment effectiveness, knowledge and communication processes and use of feedback; understand behavior patterns, and progressive states of alcohol and other drug abuse/dependencies; provide individual counseling using relevant and current client data with an appropriate therapeutic approach to meet the client's needs, problems, strengths and weaknesses to promote the client's recovery process; recognize transference and counter transference; evaluate the client's progress, interpret client issues, give feedback to the client and promote growth through periodic review of client's treatment goals and accomplishments; and provide current and accurate information and education to the client through written materials, peer support and other educational methods in order to prevent initiation of relapse or progress of disease of dependencies.

Instruction: Major topics covered in the course are the following intervention techniques; psychodynamics', individual psychotherapy, motivational counseling and self analysis. The course also includes client self-examination, counselor role, assessment skills and professional ethics.

Credit Recommendation: In the upper division baccalaureate degree category, 3 semester hours in Counseling Substance Abuse Clients (5/95).

Family Counseling for Substance Abusing Clients (Family Counseling)

Location: Multiple locations throughout the United States.

Length: 45 hours (1-2 weeks).

Dates: September 1991-Present.

Objective: To give the counselor assessment skills in addition to include the family dynamics as a facet of the addiction process.

Learning Outcome: Upon successful completion of this course, the student will be able to assist the client in understanding the role of the family in client's addiction; acquaint the client with the dynamics of chemically dependent families which result in maintaining client's addiction; gain the skill to intervene and treat the family along with the client; introduce family therapy as a specialized technique in treating the client; be aware of the special needs of adolescent substance abusers as they mature; be acquainted with the special needs of substance abusing single parent families, especially the substance abusing single parent mothers; and gain the skills to teach parents how to prevent substance abuse in their families through the use of knowledge gained in the Family Counseling course.

Instruction: Major topics covered in the course are cognitive, conceptual and applied knowledge for counselors to be able to work with and educate chemically dependent families in order to help the family move through stages of recovery. The course will enable the student to identify chemically dependent families and interventions by way of family systems therapy.

Credit Recommendation: In the upper division baccalaureate degree category, 3 semester hours in Introduction of Family Counseling for Substance Abuse (5/95).

Individual Counseling

Location: Multiple locations throughout the United States.

Length: 60 hours (1-2 weeks).

Dates: September 1991-Present.

Objective: To educate the participants in the theory and techniques of client motivation in the process of recovery, and guiding them through the complete continuum of services to recovery.

Learning Outcome: Upon successful completion of this course, the student will be able to know the various drug and alcohol treatment modalities and understand networking as a dynamic process, i.e. learning how to educate the community to treatment issues, outcomes, and availability; understand the need for chemical abusers to learn problem solving skills to solve problems and to teach them these techniques; understand substance abuse in relation to cultural differences; understand how alcohol and drug use differs in various diverse cultures; know the counselor code of ethics and its application to cases; identify Mentally Impaired Chemical Abuser (MICA); and understand crisis theory, its recognition and intervention.

Instruction: Major topics covered in the course are all areas of human development in the individual. These include self-understanding, origin and expression of human emotions, sexual development, spiritual development, grief and loss, and crisis. The course also includes the definition and establishment of a therapeutic relationship. Confidentiality issues, as required by law, are detailed.

Credit Recommendation: In the upper division baccalaureate degree category, 3 semester hours in Individual Counseling for Substance Abuse (5/95).

Inspiration in Recovery

Location: Multiple locations throughout the United States.

Length: 45 hours (1 week).

Dates: September 1991-Present.

Objective: To educate participants in human spirituality (emotional, moral, intellectual, etc.) and how these elements are involved in the process of human maturation. Particular emphasis is placed on the developmental nature of the human conscience and how the consciousness of the human individual motivates human relationships and behavior.

Learning Outcome: Upon successful completion of the course, the student will be able to know how spirituality is presented in the language and theory of twelve step recovery; understand the developmental nature of human spirituality; know how to apply the twelve step program to his/her life experience; know the theory and techniques of spiritual guidance and application of the processes of journaling, meditation and artistic expression and their effect on treatment; interpret the addicted client's spiritual journey and educate the client in using course materials in the self-reflective process of change; and know the developmental milestones as it pertains to spirituality and the methods to educate the client in using this knowledge for treatment success.

Instruction: Major topics covered in the course are the natural process of human psychospiritual development from the perspective of the Twelve Steps Recovery process. It also presents the Faith Development theories and techniques of James W. Fowler. The effects of the addiction upon spiritual development/deterioration are particularly emphasized and included in the continuum of recovery.

Credit Recommendation: In the upper division baccalaureate degree category, 3 semester hours in Philosophy of Religion (5/95).

Prevention

Location: Multiple locations throughout the United States.

Length: 45 hours (1 week).

Dates: September 1991-Present.

Objective: To provide the students with knowledge in Human Developmental theories and techniques to instill healthy life coping skills in people in order to prevent the use and abuse of addicting substances.

Learning Outcome: Upon successful completion of this course, the student will be able to know the rationale, theory, and techniques of chemical dependence prevention with individuals, schools, communities and college campus programs; know that education about chemical substance abuse prevention is the single most effective tool available to reduce the incidents and severity of chemical abuse among individuals; know the important theories and techniques for peer interactions in substance abuse prevention; know the role of education in prevention; know the behaviors which indicate an individual's developing problem with chemical use; and identify groups significant to each individual. Enable people to recognize individual differences among group members so that individuals can function collaboratively and functionally within a group and other social milieus to prevent substance abuse.

Instruction: Major topics covered in the course are the definition of prevention, training in prevention theories, study of community prevention programs, tools for designing prevention programs and evaluating program effectiveness. It also contains case studies and information on school based programs, community awareness programs, family intervention strategies and prevention through employee assistance programs.

Credit Recommendation: In the upper division baccalaureate degree category, 3 semester hours in Social Psychology or Social Work (5/95).

Special Populations

Location: Multiple locations throughout the United States.

Length: 45 hours (1 week).

Dates: September 1993-Present.

Objective: To sensitize students to the particular needs, stresses and problems necessary to serve clients from groups with unique, social, psychological and treatment needs.

Learning Outcome: Upon successful completion of this course, the student will be able to identify the needs of special populations; know the variety of effective methodologies used in treatment of special populations; know the supportive services necessary for rehabilitation and recovery for this population; know the theories necessary to serve these populations; and know special populations, information and personal knowledge (shared through presentations made by members of the population being studied) for the purpose of making students aware of the issue of multicultural differences in substance abuse, including but not limited to MICA clients, minorities and other special population groups.

Instruction: Major topics covered in the course focus on the various means for finding healthy strategies to ward off substance abuse relapses. Classes will include learning theories through role play.

Credit Recommendation: In the upper division baccalaureate degree category, 3 semester hours in Special Populations in Sociology or in Social Work (5/95).

Special Problems

Location: Multiple locations throughout the United States.

Length: 45 hours (1 week).

Dates: September 1993-Present.

Objective: To teach students to apply techniques for assisting substance abusers in recovery to cope with crisis, stress, sexual abuse, grief, anger and relapse issues.

Learning Outcome: Upon successful completion of this course, the student will be able to know the differences found in various populations and know how they affect assessment and response treatment; know life issues including the stages of grief and grief resolution and knowledge of the dynamics of relapse to clients; develop an understanding of client defense mechanisms; have knowledge of the treatment processes to include establishment of objectives, stages, and techniques for working with clients with special problems; know the intervention methods to assist the client in life crisis situations; and know the correlation between alcohol and other drug abuse/dependence and specific problems, such as mood disorders, anxiety disorders and schizophrenia.

Instruction: Major topics covered in the course are focused on the various means for finding healthy strategies to ward off substance abuse relapses. Classes will include learning theories through role play.

Credit Recommendation: In the upper division baccalaureate degree category, 3 semester hours in Social Work or Sociology or Health Sciences (5/95).

Substance Abuse, Addiction, and Group Counseling (Group Counseling)

Location: Multiple locations throughout the United States.

Length: 45 hours (1 week).

Dates: September 1991-Present.

Objective: To provide students with knowledge and technique in group analysis and therapy. Emphasis is placed on the comprehension of therapeutic factors in groups.

Learning Outcome: Upon successful completion of this course, the student will be able to know the general principles and stages of group counseling treatment; know the techniques and methodology of treatment through group counseling; understand and know the gender differences in substance abuse patterns and problems as they relate to group counseling; identify the special needs of addicted individuals in groups; and know the skills necessary for group supervision.

Instruction: Major topics covered in this course provide study of the general principles of different types of groups in operation, details of the characteristics and transitional processes of group formation, and the cohesiveness theory of functioning. Effective group supervision is integral to this course.

Credit Recommendation: In the upper division baccalaureate degree category, 3 semester hours in Group Counseling for Substance Abuse (5/95).

Substance Abusing Client Education

Location: Multiple locations throughout the United States.

Length: 45 hours (1 week).

Dates: September 1993-Present.

Objective: To train professional substance abuse recovery counselors in knowledge and skills necessary to give clients an understanding of the need to undergo learning processes in various areas of life (health and hygiene, vocational skills, life coping skills, etc.) that were impeded because of active addiction.

Learning Outcome: Upon successful completion of this course, the student will be able to measure through testing, interviews and personal observation the client's skills for employment, personal relationships, family environment, social integration, stress management, and substance abuse recovery maintenance; know and apply the skill for individualizing treatment plans according to the results of the skills testing; know the resources available for client education and how to do networking with various sources in order to effectuate client education and rehabilitation; familiarize clients with the continuum of educational, social, legal, medical, vocational and support services available to assist them in their recovery; learn the processes integral to reviewing, evaluating and revising treatment plan to further client progress in programs of client education; and research and connect client to those educational services that will continue to support client's recovery after termination of formal therapeutic relationship.

Instruction: Major topics covered in the course are the continuum of services necessary for the rehabilitation of the substance abuse client; including analysis of client status, procedures necessary for rehabilitation for networking with supportive organizations and incorporating the client into society.

Credit Recommendation: In the upper division baccalaureate degree category, 3 semester hours in Social Work or Psychology or Sociology (5/95).

RETS Institute

RETS Institute is owned and operated by M. Eastwick Colleges, Incorporated. Radio Electronics Television Schools (RETS) was established in 1935 in Detroit, Michigan. THe New Jersey school was located in Newark when the first resident students enrolled in 1957. To accommodate increasing enrollments, the school moved to River Road in Kearny in 1964 and to its present location in 1967. In 1968, the school became known a RETS Electronics School. It was acquired by National Education Corporation in 1978 and in 1979 was made part of the Technical schools group. In 1983, the name was changed to National Education Center—RETS Campus. In 1995, the school was acquired by M. Eastwick Colleges, Inc. The name of the school was changed to RETS Institute.

The facility is located on 2 1/2 acres and occupies approximately 22,000 square feet containing 13 classrooms designed for theory and laboratory instruction, 8 administrative offices, bookstore, faculty room, full-service cafeteria, student services/resources center and restrooms.

RETS Institute currently offers training courses in Electronics Technology and Business Office Operations.

This institute, the facilities it occupies, and the equipment it uses comply with all federal, state, and local ordinances, and regulations, including those related to fire safety, building safety, and health.

Source of official student records: Registry of Credit Recommendations, American Council on Education, One Dupont Circle, Washington, DC 20036-1193.

Additional information about the courses: Office of Corporate-Higher Education Programs, Thomas Edison State College, 101 West State Street, Trenton, NJ 08608-1176.

Analog/Digital Principles - Analog/Digital Laboratory (ET131Q-ELL132)

Location: Nutley, New Jersey.

Length: 120 hours-lecture/120 hours-lab.

Dates: April 1985-Present.

Objective: To provide students with an appreciation and understanding of integrated circuits.

Learning Outcome: Upon successful completion of this course, the student will be able to understand the theory and operation of digital circuits; understand and apply Boolean Algebra and Karnaugh Mapping; understand the theory of A/D and D/A conversions; understand the theory and operation of differential amplifiers; understand the theory and application of operational amplifiers; understand theory and application of other integrated circuits such as rectifiers, filters, oscillators and timing circuits; use simulation software.

Instruction: Major topics covered in Analog are differential amplifiers, operational amplifiers, rectifiers, filters, function generators, timing circuits, and phase lock loops. Major topics covered in Digital are logic gates and truth tables, gate circuits, tri-state logic, mux/demux, flip-flops, counters and registers; and various number systems. Methods of instruction include formal classroom lectures and hands-on laboratory experiences.

Credit Recommendation: In the lower division baccalaureate/associate degree category, 6 semester hours in Integrated Circuits and 2 semester hours in Integrated Circuits Lab in Electronics Technology (7/97). **NOTE:** Students must complete Analog/Digital Principles ET131Q and Analog/Digital Laboratory ELL132 to receive the credit recommendation.

Applied Mathematics I (MAA113)

Location: Nutley, New Jersey.

Length: 36 hours.

Dates: April 1985-Present.

Objective: To provide students with the mathematical skills necessary to analyze basic AC and DC circuits.

Learning Outcome: Upon successful completion of this course, the student will be able to solve basic algebraic equations; Solve basic trigonometric equations.

Instruction: Major topics covered in the course are algebraic fundamentals, scientific notation, simultaneous equations, introduction to trigonometry, trigonometric functions and vectors. Methods of instruction include formal classroom lectures.

Credit Recommendation: In the lower division baccalaureate/associate degree category, 2 semester hours in Elements of Algebra and Trigonometry (7/97).

Applied Mathematics II (MAA123)

Location: Nutley, New Jersey.

Length: 24 hours .

Dates: April 1985-Present.

Objective: To provide students with the mathematical skills necessary to analyze active electronic circuits.

Learning Outcome: Upon successful completion of this course, the student will be able to solve basic logarithmic equations; Use logarithms to calculate the gain and attenuation of electronic circuits;

Instruction: Major topics covered in the course are logarithms, decibels and their applications. Methods of instruction include formal classroom lectures.

Credit Recommendation: In the lower division baccalaureate/associate degree category, 1 semester hour in Elements of Algebra (7/97).

Basic Electricity and Electronics (ET111N)

Length: 84 hours-lecture/120 hours-lab.

Dates: April 1985-Present.

Objective: To provide students with the skills they need to analyze DC and AC circuits.

Learning Outcome: Upon successful completion of this course, the student will be able to understand the theory of operation of DC/AC series and parallel circuits; Identify electronic parts and be able to read schematics; Be proficient in assembly, disassembly, wiring, and soldering; Use laboratory test equipment such as multimeter, oscilloscope, and function generator; Troubleshoot defects.

Instruction: Major topics covered in the course are DC and AC circuits. These courses place emphasis on mathematics as it applies to electronic technology. Methods of instruction include formal classroom lectures and hands-on laboratory experiences.

Credit Recommendation: In the lower division baccalaureate/associate degree category, 3 semester hours in AC Circuits, 3 semester hours in DC Circuits, 1 semester hour in AC Circuit Lab, and 1 semester hour in DC Circuit Lab in Electronics Technology, for a total of 8 semester hours (7/97). **NOTE:** Students must complete Basic Electricity and Electronics ET111N and Basic Electronics Laboratory EL-112N to receive the credit recommendation.

Delighting the Internal Customer (TCM1001)

Location: Atlanta, Georgia; Beltsville, Maryland; Chicago, Illinois; Dallas, Texas; Englewood, Colorado; Pasadena, California; Valhalla, New York; and special customer arranged sites.

Length: 24 hours (3 days).

Dates: January 1997-Present.

Objective: To help telecommunications professionals assess their customers' current level of satisfaction with the service provided them and learn how to build a customer service plan for becoming a more effective results-oriented catalyst in their respective companies.

Learning Outcome: Upon successful completion of this course, the student will be able to articulate the benefits of providing superior internal customer service; Assess their current departmental and individual performance in delivering superior customer service; Implement a department customer service improvement process plan; Implement an individual customer service improvement process plan; Better serve internal customers; Use problem resolution skills and techniques to more effectively deal with difficult situations.

Instruction: Major topics covered in the course are how to create win-win relationships with the internal customers their department serves; ability to assess their customers' current level of satisfaction with the service provided by their department; how to build a customer service plan for becoming a more effective catalyst for results in their respective companies; step-by-step techniques for providing superior service at both the departmental and the individual level in simple " how to" language; how to maximize customer satisfaction and support their organization while enhancing their own career and potential for success. Methods of instruction include classroom discussion and lecture, simulation, independent study, and collaborative learning. An end of course project is part of the course.

Credit Recommendation: In the upper division baccalaureate degree category or in the lower division baccalaureate/associate degree category, 2 semester hours in Business Communications or Marketing (5/97).

Digital Circuits and Devices - Electronics Laboratory (EET241-EL242N)

Location: Nutley, New Jersey.

Length: 96 hours-lecture/120 hours-lab.

Dates: April 1985-Present.

Objective: To provide students with the skills they need to analyze and construct digital circuits.

Learning Outcome: Upon successful completion of this course, the student will be able to Understand the theory and operations of digital circuits; Understand and apply Boolean algebra; Understand the theory of A/D and D/A conversions; Understand and use computer simulation software for digital circuitry.

Instruction: Major topics covered in the course are logic gates and truth tables, Boolean algebra, Karnaugh mapping, tri-state logic, multiplexers, flip-flops, registers, counters, A/D and D/A, and number systems; also, computer analysis and simulation of digital circuits. Methods of instruction include formal classroom lectures and hands-on laboratory experiences.

Credit Recommendation: In the lower division baccalaureate/associate degree category, 6 semester hours in Digital Electronics and 2 semester hours in Digital Electronics Lab in Electronics Technology (7/97). **NOTE:** Students must complete Digital Circuits and Devices EET241 and Electronics Laboratory EL242N to receive the credit recommendation.

Electronics Principles - Electronics Principles Laboratory (ET111Q-ELL112)

Location: Nutley, New Jersey.

Length: 120 hours-lecture/120 hours-lab.

Dates: April 1985-Present.

Objective: To provide students with the skills they need to analyze DC and AC circuits.

Learning Outcome: Upon successful completion of this course, the student will be able to understand the theory of operation of DC/AC series and parallel circuits; Identify electronic parts and be able to read schematics; Be proficient in assembly, disassembly, wiring, and soldering; Use laboratory test equipment such as multimeter, oscilloscope, and function generator; Troubleshoot defects.

Instruction: Major topics covered in the course are DC and AC circuits. These courses place emphasis on mathematics as it applies to electronic technology. Methods of instruction include formal classroom lectures and hands-on laboratory experiences.

Credit Recommendation: In the lower division baccalaureate/associate degree category, 3 semester hours in AC Circuits, 3 semester hours in DC Circuits, 1 semester hour in AC Circuit Lab, and 1 semester hour in DC Circuit Lab in Electronics Technology (7/97). **NOTE:** Students must complete Electronics Principles ET111Q and Electronics Principles Laboratory ELL112 to receive the credit recommendation.

English Communications (ET243)

Location: Nutley, New Jersey.

Length: 24 hours.

Dates: April 1985-Present.

Objective: To provide students with the skills needed to make oral technical presentations and write business memoranda.

Learning Outcome: Upon successful completion of this course, the student will be able to make an oral technical presentation; Write business memoranda and letters.

Instruction: Major topics covered in the course are developing, organizing, and making oral presentations; and writing, editing and proofreading memos and letters. Methods of instruction include formal classroom lectures and student speeches.

Credit Recommendation: In the lower division baccalaureate/associate degree category, 1 semester hour in Oral Communications (7/97).

Industrial Electronics Technology - Industrial Electronics Laboratory (TE274-EL275N)

Location: Nutley, New Jersey.

Length: 96 hours-lecture/120 hours-lab.

Dates: April 1985-Present.

Objective: To provide students with the skills necessary to apply electronics to the industrial environment.

Learning Outcome: Upon successful completion of this course, the student will be able to understand the theory and operation of vacuum tubes; Use electronics to control motors; Understand the operation of magnetic amplifiers; Understand modulation techniques; Demonstrate the applications of electronics to robotics; Explain the operation of television.

Instruction: Major topics covered in the course are vacuum tubes, television, circuitry, magnetic amplifiers, and programmable logic controllers. Methods of instruction include formal classroom lectures and hands-on laboratory experiences.

Credit Recommendation: In the lower division baccalaureate/associate degree category, 6 semester hours in Industrial Electronics and 2 semester hours in Industrial Electronics Lab in Electronics Technology (7/97). **NOTE:** Students must complete Industrial Electronics Technology TE274 and Industrial Electronics Laboratory EL275N to receive the credit recommendation.

Microelectronics: Devices and Applications - Electronics Laboratory (TE131-EL132N)

Location: Nutley, New Jersey.

Length: 96 hours-lecture/120 hours-lab.

Dates: April 1985-Present.

Objective: To provide students with an appreciation and understanding of integrated circuits.

Learning Outcome: Upon successful completion of this course, the student will be able to understand the theory and operation of differential amplifiers; Understand the theory and application of operational amplifiers; Understand theory and application of other integrated circuits such as rectifiers, filters, oscillators and timing circuits; Use simulation software.

Instruction: Major topics covered in the course are differential amplifiers, operational amplifiers, rectifiers, filters, function generators, timing circuits, and phase lock loops. Methods of instruction include formal classroom lectures and hands-on laboratory experiences.

Credit Recommendation: In the lower division baccalaureate/associate degree category, 6 semester hours in Integrated Circuits and 2 semester hours in Integrated Circuits Lab in Electronics Technology (7/97). **NOTE:** Students must complete Microelectronics: Devices and Applications TE131 and Electronics Laboratory EL132N to receive the credit recommendation,.

Microprocessor/Computer Technology - Electronics Laboratory (ET251-EL252N)

Location: Nutley, New Jersey.

Length: 120 hours-lecture/120 hours-lab.

Dates: January 1997-Present.

Objective: To provide students with an understanding of the basic characteristics and functions of a microprocessor and the use of microprocessors in control applications and microcomputers.

Learning Outcome: Upon successful completion of this course, the student will be able to describe the purpose, architecture, and application of a microprocessor; Explain RAM, ROM, ALU, registers, I/O; Understand bus organization; Use the instructional set to program microprocessor functions; Identify all component parts of a PC; Assemble and disassemble a microcomputer from component parts; Configure system, install application software in a PC; Use the PC to control external devices such as a robotic arm; Understand the hardware aspects of computer networking.

Instruction: Major topics covered in the course are microprocessor architecture, registers, ALU, clocking, RAM, ROM, bus organization, machine language programming. Instruction sets, I/O, PC, component parts, drives, software applications, robotic arms and LAN. Methods of instruction include formal classroom lectures and hands-on laboratory experiences.

Credit Recommendation: In the lower division baccalaureate/associate degree category, 6 semester hours in Microprocessor Systems and 2 semester hours in Microprocessor Systems lab in Electronics Technology (7/97). **NOTE:** Students must complete Microprocessor/ Computer Technology ET251 and Elec-tronics Laboratory EL252N to receive the credit recommendation.

Microprocessor/Computer Theory - Microprocessor/Computer Laboratory (ET241Q-ELL242)

Location: Nutley, New Jersey.

Length: 120 hours-lecture/120 hours-lab.

Dates: January 1997-Present.

Objective: To provide students with an understanding of the basic characteristics and functions of a microprocessor and the use of microprocessors in control applications and microcomputers.

Learning Outcome: Upon successful completion of this course, the student will be able to describe the purpose, architecture, and application of a microprocessor; Explain RAM, ROM, ALU, registers, I/O; Understand bus organization; Use the instructional set to program microprocessor functions; Identify all component parts of a PC; Assemble and disassemble a microcomputer from component parts; Configure system, install application software in a PC; Use the PC to control external devices such as a robotic arm; Understand the hardware aspects of computer networking.

Instruction: Major topics covered in the course are microprocessor architecture, registers, ALU, clocking, RAM, ROM, bus organization, machine language programming, Instruction sets, I/O, PC, component parts, drives, software applications, robotic arms and LAN. Methods of instruction include formal classroom lectures and hands-on laboratory experiences.

Credit Recommendation: In the lower division baccalaureate/associate degree category, 6 semester hours in Microprocessor Systems and 2 semester hours in Microprocessor Systems lab in Electronics Technology (7/97). **NOTE:** Students must complete Microprocessor/Computer Theory ET241Q and Microprocessor/ Computer Laboratory ELL242 to receive the credit recommendation.

Minimizing Risk: Business Recovery and Security (TCM2003)

Location: Atlanta, Georgia; Beltsville, Maryland; Chicago, Illinois; Dallas, Texas; Englewood, Colorado; Pasadena, California; Valhalla, New York; and special customer arranged sites.

Length: 24 hours (3 days).

Dates: January 1997-Present.

Objective: To provide the student with an understanding of the critical need for business recovery planning in a crisis situation and the ways to prevent toll fraud from having a major negative impact on their business.

Learning Outcome: Upon successful completion of this course, the student will be able to analyze the needs of their company relative to crisis recovery; Build a business case for a crisis recovery plan; Identify crisis recovery options and their associated costs.

Instruction: Major topics covered in the course are: (Part I) step-by-step techniques for constructing and maintaining plans to safeguard their company against the potentially catastrophic effects of disaster and toll fraud; how to analyze their company's unique needs for business recovery; how to build a business case, how to investigate options and cost, and how to select the option most closely suited to their company's unique needs. (Part II) how toll fraud occurs; how to spot early warning signs of potential fraud; how to develop plans to protect their company against it; and practical actions to take if they discover toll fraud. Methods of instruction include classroom discussion and lecture, simulation, independent study, and collaborative learning.

Credit Recommendation: In the upper division baccalaureate degree category or in the lower division baccalaureate/associate degree category, 2 semester hours in Strategic Planning or Security Management (5/97).

Professional Career Development (ET269)

Location: Nutley, New Jersey.

Length: 24 hours.

Dates: April 1985-Present.

Objective: To provide students with the written and verbal skills to obtain employment.

Learning Outcome: Upon successful completion of this course, the student will be able to write a professional resume and cover letter; Successfully participate in an interview.

Instruction: Major topics covered in the course are writing a resume and a cover letter; how to prepare for, conduct, and follow up an interview and techniques for a job search. Methods of instruction include formal classroom lectures and mock interviews.

Credit Recommendation: In the lower division baccalaureate/associate degree category, 1 semester hour in Business Communications (7/97).

Semiconductor Circuits/Devices Theory - Semiconductor Circuits/Devices Laboratory (ET121Q-EL122N)

Location: Nutley, New Jersey.

Length: 120 hours-lecture/120 hours-lab.

Dates: April 1985-Present.

Objective: To provide students with the skills they need to understand and analyze semiconductor devices and circuits.

Learning Outcome: Upon successful completion of this course, the student will be able to understand the theory of operation of semiconductor devices including diodes, transistors and other solid state devices; Be able to use semiconductor devices in circuits; Use test equipment to measure input/output responses of amplifiers; Troubleshoot defects in these circuits.

Instruction: Major topics covered in the courses are solid state devices such as diodes and transistors and their use in circuits with resistors and capacitors. Study how circuits such as rectifiers, amplifiers and oscillators control current in electrical circuits. Methods of instruction include formal classroom lectures and hands-on laboratory experiences.

Credit Recommendation: In the lower division baccalaureate/associate degree category, 6 semester hours in Semiconductor electronics, and 2 semester hours in Semiconductor laboratory in Electronics Technology (7/97). **NOTE:** Students must complete Semiconductor Circuits/Devices Theory ET121Q and Semiconductor Circuits/Devices Laboratory EL122N to receive the credit recommendation.

Semiconductors: Circuits and Devices - Electronics Laboratory (EET121-LE122)

Location: Nutley, New Jersey.

Length: 96 hours-lecture/96 hours-lab.

Dates: April 1985-Present.

Objective: To provide students with the skills they need to understand and analyze semiconductor devices and circuits.

Learning Outcome: Upon successful completion of this course, the student will be able to understand the theory of operation of semiconductor devices including diodes, transistors and other solid state devices; Be able to use semiconductor devices in circuits; Use test equipment to measure input/output responses of amplifiers; Troubleshoot defects in these circuits.

Instruction: Major topics covered in the courses are solid state devices such as diodes and transistors and their use in circuits with resistors and capacitors. Study how circuits such as rectifiers, amplifiers and oscillators control current in electrical circuits. Methods of instruction include formal classroom lectures and hands-on laboratory experiences.

Credit Recommendation: In the lower division baccalaureate/associate degree category, 6 semester hours in Semiconductor electronics in Electronics Tech-nology and 2 semester hours in semiconductor laboratory in Electronics Technology (7/97). **NOTE:** Students must complete Semiconductors: Circuits and Devices EET121 and Electronics Laboratory LE122 to receive the credit recommendation.

Technical Drawing (TE124C)

Location: Nutley, New Jersey.

Length: 24 hours .

Dates: April 1985-Present.

Objective: To provide students with necessary skills to draw schematic diagrams and develop printed circuits.

Learning Outcome: Upon successful completion of this course, the student will be able to read and draw schematic diagrams; Layout printed circuit boards.

Instruction: Major topics covered in the course are electronic symbols, lines and lettering, block diagrams, schematic diagrams, and printed circuits. Methods of instruction include formal classroom lectures and hands-on laboratory experiences.

Credit Recommendation: In the lower division baccalaureate/associate degree category, 1 semester hour in Electronic Drafting (7/97).

Technical Writing (ET133)

Location: Nutley, New Jersey.

Length: 24 hours.

Dates: April 1985-Present.

Objective: To provide students with the skills they need to write and present a technical report.

Learning Outcome: Upon successful completion of this course, the student will be able to write a technical report; Make a brief technical presentation.

Instruction: Major topics covered in the course are writing sentences, writing paragraphs, developing an outline, writing a formal report, making a presentation, and writing inter-office memorandums. Methods of instruction include formal classroom lectures.

Credit Recommendation: In the lower division baccalaureate/associate degree category, 1 semester hour in Technical Writing (7/97).

Safeguards and Security Central Training Academy

The Department of Energy (DOE) Safeguards and Security Central Training Academy (S&SCTA) was established, in 1984, to enable DOE to provide efficient and effective standardized training for the DOE complex. The S&SCTA provides training in multiple disciplines, to include: tactical and firearms training, behavioral sciences, management and instructional training, safeguards and technical security training and materials control and accountability. By providing standardized training and development of standardized training programs and materials through a central location, the DOE ensures consistency and efficiency, as well as quality in job training.

The S&SCTA is divided into five training departments, each with courses designed for a specific target audience. Program Planning and Management is designed for personnel who assess, review and verify a site's ability to protect its assigned assets through vulnerability assessments, performance testing of systems, security inspections, and information management. Protection Program Operations is for personnel who respond to security incidents, conduct self-defense, tactical and firearms training, crisis negotiators, armorers, and live fire range managers. Materials Control and Accountability is for personnel who are nuclear materials handlers, accountants, custodians, controllers, inspectors, and auditors. Personnel Security and Training Development is for those who conduct investigations for security clearances and for management/supervisory and instructor training. Information and Technical Security is designed for information handlers, computer security specialists, and site security managers.

The vehicle for delivery of training falls within one of these categories: Training at the S&SCTA; Mobile Training Teams; Site Certification; and Distance Learning Training.

The S&SCTACTA's staff members are experienced security and nuclear materials specialists, supplemented by an adjunct faculty with experience in highly specialized disciplines, including counterterrorism, tactical response, crisis negotiations, nuclear material control and accountability, physical security and information and operations security. The staff profiles and the evolution of the training programs, to meet the needs of safeguards and security requirements as well as those of the students, ensure the most accurate and state-of-the-art training is available for the DOE.

Source of official student records: Registry of Credit Recommendations, American Council on Education, One Dupont Circle, Washington, DC 20036-1193.

Additional information about the courses: College Credit Recommendation Service, American Council on Education, One Dupont Circle, Washington, DC 20036-1193.

Introduction to Basic Survey-Correspondence Course (PHY-128D)

Location: CTA, Albuquerque, NM.

Length: 20 hours (self-study).

Dates: July 1997-Present.

Objective: To cover the basic elements required to develop, implement, and analyze safeguards and security surveys. These elements are planning, conduct and post survey activities. The primary objective of this course is the standardization and accomplishment of professional, comprehensive, site specific, compliance-oriented, and performance oriented surveys.

Learning Outcome: Upon successful completion of this course, the student will have a basic understanding of the survey process and terminology for attendance in the Basic Survey course ((PHY-130).

Instruction: Major topics covered in the course are an introduction to basic survey, team member responsibilities, survey data collection, conducting interviews, performance testing, post survey activities, facility ratings, and final report development. Methods of instruction include self-study correspondence, review questions, and final examination.

Credit Recommendation: In the lower division baccalaureate/associate degree category or in the upper division baccalaureate degree category, 2 semester hours in Principles of Management (8/97).

Introduction to MC&A Measurement Programs (MCA-104D)

Location: CTA, Albuquerque, NM.

Length: 24 hours (self-paced).

Dates: May 1997-Present.

Objective: To provide students with basic knowledge about MC&A measurement programs. The elements of measurement programs, the generic measurement process, and the role of measurements in MC&A are described. The basic DOE requirements and guidance for measurements are addressed and introduces students to the properties of nuclear materials relevant to nuclear material measurements, and the metrology and statistics concepts and terminology used in measurement activities.

Learning Outcome: Upon successful completion of this course, the student will be able to understand the rationale for and elements of measurement programs, be sufficiently familiar with the physical and chemical properties of nuclear materials to understand measurement principles; and understand the basic elements of three types of measurement methods used in MC&A.

Instruction: Major topics covered in the course are measurement programs, process measurements, nondestructive analysis, destructive analysis, statistical concepts and terminology, measurement error and uncertainty, calibration of measurement systems, and the MC&A measurement and measurement control programs. Methods of instruction include self-study correspondence, written examinations, and exercises.

Credit Recommendation: In the lower division baccalaureate/associate degree category, 1 semester hour in Physical Sciences (8/97).

Supervisor Development Program-Interactive Television (MIT-200D)

Location: CTA, Albuquerque, NM.

Length: 16 hours (4 days).

Dates: April 1996-Present.

Objective: To provide participants with an insight into the role of supervisors and the organizational environments within which they must function. The program covers areas including human resources development, communication, human behavior, labor relations, and leadership.

Learning Outcome: Upon successful completion of this course, the student will be able to understand the need for effective supervisory responsibilities and accurate interpretation of DOE policies and programs.

Instruction: Major topics covered in the course are social challenges, training, keys to effective writing, developing reading skills, human relations and motivation, group process, dealing with difficult people, problem solving and decision making, and situational leadership II. Methods of instruction include lecture, discussions, problem solving, group activities, class participation, group involvement, individual assignments, and written evaluations.

Credit Recommendation: In the lower division baccalaureate/associate degree

category, 2 semester hours in Principles of Supervision (8/97).

Vulnerability Assessment Fundamentals-Interactive Television (CTA-140D)

Location: CTA, Albuquerque, NM.
Length: 33.5 hours (5 days).
Dates: September 1996-Present.
Objective: To prepare newly assigned vulnerability assessment personnel to function as members of vulnerability assessment teams and give the participants an introduction of the fundamentals of the safeguards and security vulnerability assessment process to prepare them to participate in the development, review, and/or verification of vulnerability assessments.
Learning Outcome: Upon successful completion of this course, the student will be able to identify the critical steps in the vulnerability assessment process; understand the philosophy, concepts, and terminology associated with the process; and apply the knowledge and skills learned.
Instruction: Major topics covered in the course are insider analysis, quantifying effectiveness assessments, outsider analysis, and upgrades analysis. Methods of instruction include lecture, discussions, problem solving, group activities, examination, written examinations, and small group projects.
Credit Recommendation: In the upper division baccalaureate degree category, 2 semester hours in Security Administration, Criminal Justice, Law Enforcement, or Private Security. *Prerequisite:* Successful completion of Vulnerability Assessment Overview-Interactive Television (CTA-139D) (8/97).

Curriculum Development and Instruction

1. Basic Instructor Training (MIT-111)
2. Curriculum Development (MIT 210)
(Introduction to the Instructional Systems Development Process)

Location: S&SCTA, Albuquerque, NM.
Length: 1. 40 hours (5 days); 2. 32 hours (4 days).
Dates: 1. January 1985-Present; 2. October 1990-Present
Objective: To train students in the basic teaching tools needed to provide effective training and develop an effective curriculum.
Learning Outcome: Upon successful completion of this course, the student will be able to explain and demonstrate the use of the Instructional Systems Developmental model for curriculum construction, and develop course and lesson objectives; prepare lesson plans; develop effective training aids; and present formally structured lessons.
Instruction: Major topics covered in the course are management of adult learning; standardized approach to curriculum development; communications; instructional goals and objectives; lesson plans; teaching aids; classroom environments; and evaluation. Methods of instruction include lecture, student presentations, and projects.
Credit Recommendation: In the upper division baccalaureate degree category, 3 semester hours in Education or Training and Learning Technologies (10/93). **NOTE:** Both courses must be taken to receive credit.

Introduction to Job Analysis (MIT-119D)

Location: On or Off-campus distance education.
Length: Self-paced correspondence course.
Dates: January 1996-Present.
Objective: To provide students with a basic understanding of the job analysis process and the background to describe job analysis techniques and application.
Learning Outcome: Upon successful completion of this course, the student will be able to define job analysis terminology, describe the job analysis process, identify the uses of job analyses, list job analysis techniques, identify how training recommendations are determined, and identify and describe the components of a job analysis report.
Instruction: Major topics covered in the course are job analysis terminology, benefits of job analysis, fundamentals of job analysis techniques, planning for a job analysis, and job analysis products. Methods of instruction include independent study and exercises.
Credit Recommendation: In the upper division baccalaureate degree category, 1 semester hour in Human Resource Management or Training and Learning Technologies (1/96).

Job Analysis (MIT-120)

Location: S&SCTA, Albuquerque, NM.
Length: 40 hours (5 days).
Dates: June 1988-Present.
Objective: To focus on Job Task Analysis (JTA), process and procedures, and emphasizing basic knowledge and skills required to initiate and conduct a JTA.
Learning Outcome: Upon successful completion of this course, the student will be able to develop a draft JTA; write task statements; develop a task inventory questionnaire; prioritize tasks and subtasks; and apply the JTA process to an instructional systems development process and job descriptions.
Instruction: Major topics covered in the course are JTA process, task statements, task inventory, questionnaires, prioritization of tasks, reports, presentation skills, and job descriptions. Methods of instruction include lecture, discussion, demonstration, and software application.
Credit Recommendation: In the upper division baccalaureate degree category, 3 semester hours in Human Resource Management or Training and Learning Technologies (10/93) (12/95). *Prerequisite:* Introduction to Job Analysis (correspondence course).

Information Security

Classified Matter Protection and Control I (ISC-221)

Location: S&SCTA, Albuquerque, NM.
Length: 23 hours (3 days).
Dates: October 1992-Present.
Objective: To provide the student with the requisite knowledge and skills to identify and utilize appropriate resources needed to implement a classified matter protection program.
Learning Outcome: Upon successful completion of this course, the student will be able to demonstrate the technical knowledge and skills required to develop, implement, and oversee an information protection program; and evaluate such programs.
Instruction: Major topics covered in the course are the skills needed for both the implementation and evaluation of the classified matter protection and control programs including the generation, preparation, physical protection, storage, accountability, transmission, reproduction, destruction, unaccounted for matter, self assessments, infractions and violations; and the relationships between protecting

classified matter and other safeguards and security programs. Methods of instruction include lecture, discussion, and problem-solving.

Credit Recommendation: In the upper division baccalaureate degree category, 1 semester hour in Criminal Justice, Law Enforcement, Business Administration, International Business, Personnel Administration, Private Security, or Records Management (5/94). **NOTE:** Prerequisite is Classified Matter Protection and Control Correspondence Course.

Classified Matter Protection and Control II (ISC-321)

Location: S&SCTA, Albuquerque, NM.

Length: 29 hours (4 days).

Dates: August 1993-Present.

Objective: To provide the student with the knowledge and skills requisite to the identification and usage of appropriate resources needed to implement a classified matter protection program.

Learning Outcome: Upon successful completion of this course, the student will demonstrate the technical knowledge and skills required to develop, implement, and manage an information protection program; evaluate such programs; and conduct inquiries into compromised information and/or unaccounted for classified matter.

Instruction: Major topics covered in the course are the skills needed for both the implementation and evaluation of the classified matter protection and control program including generation preparation, physical protection, storage, accountability, transmission, reproduction, destruction, unaccounted for matter, self assessments, and infractions and violations; and the relationships between protecting classified matter and other information and security programs. Methods of instruction include lecture, discussion, and problem-solving.

Credit Recommendation: In the upper division baccalaureate degree category, 2 semester hours in Criminal Justice, Law Enforcement, Business Administration, International Business Personnel Administration, Private Security, or Records Management (5/94). *Prerequisite:* Classified Matter Protection and Control I.

Foreign Ownership, Control, or Influence (PPM-151)

Location: S&SCTA, Albuquerque, NM.

Length: 23 hours (3 days).

Dates: November 1993-Present.

Objective: To provide the student with the methods and procedures to be used by business and governments to protect sensitive information.

Learning Outcome: Upon successful completion of this course, the student will be able to determine the existence of a threat to sensitive or classified information due to the foreign ownership, control, or influence of an associated company.

Instruction: Major topics covered in the course are governmental policies, orders, and regulations implementing the foreign ownership, control, or influence program; responsibilities and authorities in implementing the foreign ownership, control or influence program; the phases of the foreign ownership, control, or influence process; the types of business structures; criteria to be considered for determining whether companies or individuals are under foreign ownership, control, or Influence. Methods of instruction include lecture, discussion, and problem-solving.

Credit Recommendation: In the upper division baccalaureate degree category, 1 semester hour in Criminal Justice, Law Enforcement, Business Administration, Personnel Administration, Private Security, or Records Management (5/94).

Operations Security (ISC-241)

Location: S&SCTA, Albuquerque, NM.

Length: 28 hours (4 days).

Dates: February 1988-Present.

Objective: To provide personnel with the knowledge and skills necessary to protect sensitive information and interests from compromise by disrupting or defeating an adversary's ability to exploit operational weaknesses.

Learning Outcome: Upon successful completion of this course, the student will be able to identify sensitive information and other activities which require protection, analyze threats to these activities/information by determining potential adversaries, analyze vulnerabilities and weaknesses which may be exploited, perform risk assessments, develop and apply appropriate countermeasures, identify requirements for planning and implementing a protection program, and describe methods of evaluating these programs.

Instruction: Major topics covered in the course are protection program resources, policies, and training that deny unauthorized individuals or governments access to sensitive information. Emphasis is placed on the identification of exploitable sources of information that are available to an adversary and on countermeasures for denying access to this information. Methods of instruction include lecture, discussion, classroom exercises, and a final examination.

Credit Recommendation: In the upper division baccalaureate degree category, 2 semester hours in Industrial Security, and in the lower division baccalaureate/associate degree category, 2 semester hours in Principles of Management (6/96).

Unauthorized Disclosure (ISC-301)

Location: S&SCTA, Albuquerque, NM.

Length: 24 hours (3.5 days).

Dates: November 1993-Present.

Objective: To provide the requisite technical knowledge and skills to conduct inquiries into unauthorized disclosures of classified information and/or violations of law within established legal parameters.

Learning Outcome: Upon successful completion of this course, the student will be able to apply Fourth Amendment Rights and requirements to actions associated with inquiries/investigations of violations of law; identify elements of the Tort Claims Act associated with such inquiries/investigations; plan and conduct a non-custodial interview; and develop written reports based upon interview statements, records reviews, and physical searches.

Instruction: Major topics covered in the course are legal parameters associated with inquiries/investigations to include Fourth Amendment Rights and requirements (color of law, law of agency, exclusionary rule, privacy expectations, probable cause, search and seizure, consent searches, warrantless inspections), Tort Claims Act, False Claims Act, Obstruction of Justice (18 USC 1505, 1512, & 1513); interface with other security and counterespionage programs within the Department of Energy; and practical skills associated with inquiries and investigations (e.g. interviewing, conducting physical searches, and reviewing records). Methods of instruction include lecture, discussion, classroom exercises, case studies, learner presentations/reports, observations, reports, and a final examination.

Credit Recommendation: In the upper division baccalaureate degree category, 2 semester hours in Special Problems in Criminal Justice (6/96).

MATERIALS CONTROL AND ACCOUNTABILITY

Basics of Material Control and Accountability Measurements (MCA-140)

Location: S&SCTA, Albuquerque, NM.

Length: 32 hours (4 days).

Dates: April 1993-Present.

Objective: To provide initial knowledge and skills needed to use Nuclear Material Control and Accountability measurements or preparing for more advanced Material Control and Accountability training.

Learning Outcome: Upon successful completion of this course, the student will be able to understand the fundamental reasons for making Material Control and Accountability measurements; have a basic understanding of the types, applications, and limitations of Material Control and Accountability measurements; have an appreciation of the measurement process, and the errors inherent in measurement data; and be prepared for additional site-specific Material Control and Accountability measurement training or for more advanced measurement courses.

Instruction: Major topics covered in the course are reasons for making Material Control and Accountability measurements and the generic measurement process; an overview of the nuclear materials measurements techniques including destructive analysis, non-destructive analysis, and process measurements; and the variability of measurements and measurement control. Methods of instruction include lecture, discussion, and problem-solving.

Credit Recommendation: In the lower division baccalaureate/associate degree category, 3 semester hours in Nuclear Material Management, Physics, or Chemistry (5/94). *Prerequisites:* Introduction to MCA Measurement Programs, Introduction to Nuclear Materials and Nuclear Control Accountability (MCA-101D), and MCA-104D.

Basics of Nuclear Material Accountability (MCA-110)

Location: S&SCTA, Albuquerque, NM.

Length: 35 hours (4 days).

Dates: November 1993-Present.

Objective: To provide initial knowledge and skills to begin work in the nuclear materials accountability field.

Learning Outcome: Upon successful completion of this course, the student will be able to understand fundamental knowledge of accounting systems as they relate to Material Control and Accountability; concepts of Generally Accepted Accounting Principles (GAAP) as they relate to nuclear material accounting; inventory requirements and conduct of physical inventories; the effect of measurement uncertainties on inventory differences; and statistical tools and data analysis techniques associated with inventory differences.

Instruction: Major topics covered in the course are Generally Accepted Accounting Principles (GAAP), accounting systems, calculations of accountability values, external and internal transactions, inventory requirements, physical inventories, measurement uncertainties, and reporting principles. Methods of instruction include lecture, discussion, and problem-solving.

Credit Recommendation: In the lower division baccalaureate/associate degree category, 3 semester hours in Nuclear Technology or Materials Management (5/94). *Prerequisite:* Introduction to Nuclear Materials and Nuclear Control Accountability (MCA-101D).

Basics of Nuclear Materials Control (MCA-120)

Location: S&SCTA, Albuquerque, NM.

Length: 28 hours (3.5 days).

Dates: May 1993-Present.

Objective: To provide fundamental information on Nuclear Materials Control. This course will provide knowledge and skills to personnel working in or interfacing with Nuclear Materials Control Programs to assure that consistency and standardization will be implemented throughout the Department of Energy Complex.

Learning Outcome: Upon successful completion of this course, the student will be able to understand the requirements concerning nuclear control issues including the requirements concerning access control, surveillance, containment, and detection/assessment of the different nuclear material categories.

Instruction: Major topics covered in the course are basic elements of materials control programs, including administrative control, access controls, materials surveillance, materials containment, and detection/assessment mechanisms; also presented are specific Materials Control policy requirements and guidance for implementing these elements. Methods of instruction include lecture, discussion, and problem-solving.

Credit Recommendation: In the vocational certificate category, 2 semester hours in Materials Management (5/94). *Prerequisite:* Introduction to Nuclear Materials and Nuclear Control Accountability (MCA-101D).

Introduction to Nuclear Materials and Nuclear Materials Control Accountability (MCA-101D)

Location: On or Off-Campus Distance Education.

Length: Self-paced computer-based training.

Dates: January 1995-Present.

Objective: To provide familiarization with the fundamentals of materials control and accountability policy and systems operations.

Learning Outcome: Upon successful completion of this course, the student will be able to understand information about nuclear materials within the complex that includes categorization and attractiveness levels; basic requirements of the materials control and accountability program; and information about related areas of accountability, measurement, and control.

Instruction: Major topics covered in the course are isotopes and special nuclear materials, threat guidance, nuclear materials, accountancy including measurements and measurement control, nuclear materials control, and the graded safeguards concept. Methods of instruction include computer-assisted instruction, involving practice problems and tests.

Credit Recommendation: In the lower division baccalaureate/associate degree category, 2 semester hours in Nuclear Technology (1/95).

Introduction to Nuclear Materials Control and Accountability (MCA-101)

Location: S&SCTA, Albuquerque, NM.

Length: 24 hours (3 days).

Dates: August 1993-April 1997.

Objective: To provide familiarization with the fundamentals of materials control and accountability policy and system operations.

Learning Outcome: Upon successful completion of this course, the student will be able to understand information about nuclear materials within the complex that includes categorization and safeguards; basic requirements of the materials control and accountability program; and information about related areas of accountability, measurement, and control.

Instruction: Major topics covered in the course are isotopes and special nuclear materials, threat guidance, nuclear materials, accountability including measurements and measurement control, nuclear materials control, and the graded safeguards concept. Methods of instruction include lecture, discussion, and problem-solving.

Credit Recommendation: In the lower division baccalaureate/associate degree category, 2 semester hours in Nuclear Technology (5/94).

Introduction to Performance Testing for Materials and Control Accountability (MCA-153)

Location: S&SCTA, Albuquerque, NM.

Length: 32 hours (4 days).

Dates: October 1993-Present.

Objective: To provide knowledge and skills to plan, conduct, evaluate, and document Material Control and Accountability performance tests.

Learning Outcome: Upon successful completion of this course, the student will be able to understand the policy, standards, and responsibilities for the conduct of Material Control and Accountability performance tests; recognize detection elements and how to determine critical system elements; develop performance test plans and scenarios for program elements; understand the process for conducting tests; collect data and information; evaluate the information and draw conclusions; identify possible facility impacts; and report test results.

Instruction: Major topics covered in the course are an overview of Material Control and Accountability components that can prevent, deter, or detect nuclear material loss (detection elements); and an overview of the process of planning conducting, and evaluating performance tests of Material Control and Accountability components. Methods of instruction include lecture, discussion, and problem-solving.

Credit Recommendation: In the lower division baccalaureate/associate degree category, 2 semester hours in Nuclear Technology or Auditing (5/94). *Prerequisite:* Introduction to Nuclear Materials and Nuclear Control Accountability (MCA-101D).

Material Control and Accountability Survey Procedures (MCA-150)

Location: S&SCTA, Albuquerque, NM.

Length: 40 hours (5 days).

Dates: September 1993-Present.

Objective: To provide knowledge and skills to function as team members during the conduct of compliance and performance-based Material Control and Accountability surveys, audits, and assessments; and includes basic techniques to review functional areas of the Material Control and Accountability program.

Learning Outcome: Upon successful completion of this course, the student will be able to understand the purpose, regulations, responsibilities, and techniques for Material Control and Accountability surveys; difference in using a compliance approach and a performance approach when conducting surveys; program administration features of a Material Control and Accountability program and the basic activities for surveying these features; and process of validating and analyzing survey data, preparing a report, and closing out the survey.

Instruction: Major topics covered in the course are the planning and conducting Material Control and Accountability surveys; examining various survey techniques for both compliance and performance reviews of Material Control and Accountability systems; and Material Control and Accountability program administration, materials accounting, measurements inventories, and material control programs. Methods of instruction include lecture, discussion, and problem-solving.

Credit Recommendation: In the lower division baccalaureate/associate degree category, 2 semester hours in Auditing (5/94). *Prerequisites:* PHY-128D and Introduction to Nuclear Materials and Nuclear Control Accountability (MCA-101D).

Nuclear Materials Management Safeguards Systems (MCA-112)

Location: S&SCTA, Albuquerque, NM.

Length: 32 hours (4 days).

Dates: December 1990-Present.

Objective: To provide the necessary understanding and skills to use the Nuclear Material Management and Safeguards System.

Learning Outcome: Upon successful completion of this course, the student will be able to understand relationships between source documents and data processing forms; the use of the Nuclear Materials Management Safeguards System contractor reference manual and other reference tools; procedures necessary for proper documentation; various Nuclear Materials Management Safeguards System report products; and other specialized topics.

Instruction: Major topics covered in the course are the content of the facility-supplied information to the Nuclear Materials Management Safeguards System, the proper documentation for the typical types of nuclear materials transfer activity, tools to assist with interpreting the requirements, and the usefulness of the Nuclear Materials Management Safeguards System report products to the nuclear materials accounting organization. Methods of instruction include lecture, discussion, and problem-solving.

Credit Recommendation: In the vocational certificate category, 3 semester hours in Accounting or Materials Management (5/94). *Prerequisite:* Introduction to Nuclear Materials and Nuclear Control Accountability (MCA-101D).

Sampling Plans for Material Control and Accountability (MCA-132)

Location: S&SCTA, Albuquerque, NM.

Length: 40 hours (5 days).

Dates: May 1993-Present.

Objective: To provide background with which to participate as a member of a team that writes and executes Material Control and Accountability statistical sampling plans.

Learning Outcome: Upon successful completion of this course, the student will be able to understand the statistical concepts and calculations for developing and executing a statistical sampling plan with specific reference to inventories of nuclear materials.

Instruction: Major topics covered in the course are the fundamentals of developing and executing a statistical sampling plans in order to equip the students to be knowledgeable members of statistical sampling plan development and execution teams for inventories of nuclear materials. Methods of instruction include lecture, discussion, and problem-solving.

Credit Recommendation: In the lower division baccalaureate/associate degree category or in the upper division baccalaureate degree category, 2 semester hours in Mathematics or Statistics (5/94). *Prerequisite:* Introduction to Nuclear Materials and Nuclear Control Accountability (MCA-101D).

Statistical Concepts in Material Control and Accountability (MCA-130)

Location: S&SCTA, Albuquerque, NM.
Length: 21 hours (3 days).
Dates: July 1993-Present.
Objective: To provide an understanding of basic statistical concepts as they apply to the field of Material Control and Accountability.
Learning Outcome: Upon successful completion of this course, the student will be able to understand enough statistical vocabulary to communicate effectively with statisticians and to understand statistical technology and concepts in the Material Control and Accountability orders, guidance, reports, and standards and criteria, etc; application of a number of elementary statistical techniques and concepts; how statistical technology is applied to Material Control and Accountability problems; and which particular statistical techniques apply to specific areas of Material Control and Accountability.
Instruction: Major topics covered in the course are an overview of statistical applications in nuclear materials control and accountability, designed to provide nonstatisticians with a general understanding of how statistics are applied to Material Control and Accountability. Methods of instruction include lecture, discussion, and problem-solving.
Credit Recommendation: In the lower division baccalaureate/associate degree category, 2 semester hours in Mathematics or Statistics (5/94). *Prerequisite:* Introduction to Nuclear Materials and Nuclear Control Accountability (MCA-101D).

Tamper Indicating Devices (MCA-121)
Location: S&SCTA, Albuquerque, NM.
Length: 24 hours (3 days).
Dates: July 1994-Present.
Objective: To train administrators, trainers, and custodians to implement proper Tamper Indicating Devices programs.
Learning Outcome: Upon successful completion of this course, the student will be able to understand the purpose, use and program objectives of a Tamper Indicating Device Program. Students will also understand how to establish and maintain Tamper Indicating Device program from acquisition to disposal, and administrative and documentation requirements needed for such a program.
Instruction: Major topics covered in this course are to provide training for administrators, applicators, custodians, trainers, and auditors in the requirements and techniques for proper conduct of a Tamper Indicating Device Program. The course covers policy and requirements including Tamper Indicating Device selection, acquisition, storage, authorization for use, utilization, accountability, destruction, records, verification and inspection, and response actions. Methods of instruction include lecture, discussion, and problem-solving.
Credit Recommendation: In the vocational certificate category, 1 semester hour in Material Control, or Industrial Security (5/94). *Prerequisite:* Introduction to Nuclear Materials and Nuclear Control Accountability (MCA-101D).

Personnel Security

Administrative Review Hearing Procedures (PER-300)
Location: S&SCTA, Albuquerque, NM.
Length: 29 hours (3.5 days).
Dates: June 1989-Present.
Objective: To provide the analytical skills to evaluate personnel security cases for presentation in an administrative review hearing.
Learning Outcome: Upon successful completion of this course, the student will be able to comprehend the relationship between the requirements of National Security, Personnel Security, and the eligibility of employees for access to classified information.
Instruction: Major topics covered in the course are administrative review process; preparing the expert witness resume; hearing preparation; testifying in hearings; and issues in national security. Methods of instruction include lecture, instructor-led discussion, classroom exercises, case studies, role-playing, problem solving (facilitated by instructor; performed by student); computer-assisted/videotaped laboratory (shop instruction); and other evaluation.
Credit Recommendation: In the lower division baccalaureate/associate degree category, 1 semester hour in Legal Studies, Paralegal Studies, or Pre-Law (10/93).

Advanced Personnel Security Training (PER-200)
Location: S&SCTA, Albuquerque, NM.
Length: 28 hours (3.5 days).
Dates: July 1992-Present.
Objective: To understand the underlying issues of derogatory behavior and interviewing skills for security specialists.
Learning Outcome: Upon successful completion of this course, the student will be able to apply adjudicative criteria to a given complex personnel security situation and demonstrate the skills necessary to conduct a complex personnel security interview with an applicant who may possibly be deceitful.
Instruction: Major topics covered in the course are counterintelligence issues; financial concerns; substance abuse; abnormal behavior reformation and rehabilitation issues; and advanced interview techniques. Methods of instruction include discussion-demonstration combined with individual/group involvement through exercises, case studies, and problem solving activities.
Credit Recommendation: In the lower division baccalaureate/associate degree category, 1 semester hour in Counseling or General Psychology (10/93).

Personnel Security Assistant Training (PER-110)
Location: S&SCTA, Albuquerque, NM.
Length: 24 hours (3 days).
Dates: August 1993-Present.
Objective: To provide students with an overview of skills in pre-screening and post-investigation screening of security clearance case files and analyzing cases for derogatory information and reporting the results.
Learning Outcome: Upon successful completion of this course, the student will be able to understand the interdependent relationship among various components of a personnel security program; apply criteria for determining access by employees to classified information; and analyze derogatory information contained within personnel security cases.
Instruction: Major topics covered in the course are personnel security issues, pre-screening requests for security clearances, post-investigating screening of security clearance case files, analyzing derogatory information, reporting results, and adjudicating personnel security cases. Methods of instruction include discussion, demonstration combined with individual group involvement through exercises, case studies, and problem solving activities.
Credit Recommendation: In the lower division baccalaureate/associate degree category, 1 semester hour in Industrial

Security, Office Technology, or Security Management (10/93).

Personnel Security Specialist Adjudication Training (PER-101)

Location: S&SCTA, Albuquerque, NM.

Length: 76 hours (9.5 days).

Dates: October 1992-Present.

Objective: To understand the duties and responsibilities of a personnel security analyst with emphasis on processing initial and subsequent personnel security clearances.

Learning Outcome: Upon successful completion of this course, the student will be able to comprehend the purpose and role of the specialist in the personnel security program; understand the relationship between potentially derogatory information and an employee's eligibility for access to classified information; apply skills necessary to screen effectively; and evaluate information found in personnel security case files.

Instruction: Major topics covered in the course are introduction to personnel security; counterintelligence issues a changing threat to the environment, human behavior, adjudicating personnel security cases; pre-screening requests for security clearances; post-investigation screening of security case files; analyzing derogatory information and reporting results; applying other fact-finding techniques; and the personnel security interview. Methods of instruction include discussion, demonstration combined with student involvement through exercises, case studies, role playing, problem solving, and individual group presentations.

Credit Recommendation: In the lower division baccalaureate/associate degree category, 3 semester hours in Criminal Justice, Legal Studies, or Paralegal Studies (10/93).

Security Education Coordinators Training (CTA-110)

Location: S&SCTA, Albuquerque, NM.

Length: 36 hours (4.5 days).

Dates: January 1990-Present.

Objective: To acquaint students with the fundamentals of preparing, conducting, and presenting security education programs.

Learning Outcome: Upon successful completion of this course, the student will be able to demonstrate through the development and presentation of an instructional lesson, the ability to apply presentation techniques and use various training aids in administering a security education program.

Instruction: Major topics covered in the course are the administration of security education program, the preparation and delivery of lessons and the skills needed to develop newsletters, posters, and audiovisual enhancements for instruction. Methods of instruction include lecture, case studies, role playing, problem solving, computer assisted videotape, and laboratory.

Credit Recommendation: In the vocational certificate category, 1 semester hour in Communications (10/93).

Planning and Management

Basic Surveys (PHY-130)

Location: S&SCTA, Albuquerque, NM.

Length: 40 hours (5 days).

Dates: November 1993-Present.

Objective: To prepare personnel to function as members of designated Safeguards and Security survey or self-assessment teams leading to identification of deficient security practices and procedures.

Learning Outcome: Upon successful completion of this course, the student will be able to compare surveys and self-assessments, identify research techniques and requirements for survey planning, describe the components of a survey plan, identify the activities associated with conducting a survey, and develop survey findings based upon identified safeguards and security deficiencies.

Instruction: Major topics covered in the course are data collection, interview techniques, materials/inventory control, and security survey planning and conduct. Methods of instruction include lecture, discussion, classroom exercises, case studies, audio/visual material, learner presentations/reports, observations, and practical exercises.

Credit Recommendation: In the lower division baccalaureate/associate degree category, 3 semester hours in Security Practicum (6/96). *Prerequisite:* Introduction to Basic Survey Correspondence Course.

Facility Survey Team Leader (PHY-230)

Location: S&SCTA, Albuquerque, NM.

Length: 41.5 hours (5 days).

Dates: November 1993-Present.

Objective: To provide methods and procedures to successfully plan and direct evaluation and assessment activities within the public and private sector.

Learning Outcome: Upon successful completion of this course, the student will be able to demonstrate the step-by-step procedures for planning an assessment/evaluation, organize and direct the activities of an evaluation team, conduct meetings and briefings, analyze records and data for accuracy and compliance, conduct performance testing, inspect and evaluate for compliance with specific requirements, manage and direct the conduct of the evaluation to include qualitative and quantitative ratings, and prepare and present an evaluation report.

Instruction: Major topics covered in the course are the leader's role and activities relative to survey planning, conduct, and post-survey actions as well as specific skills necessary to develop and lead a team. Methods of instruction include presentation skills, techniques to conduct effective meetings, and report writing requirements, and techniques.

Credit Recommendation: In the upper division baccalaureate degree category or graduate degree category, 3 semester hours in Security Management, Business Administration, Business Management, Criminal Justice, or Law Enforcement (5/94).

Introduction to Leadership (MIT-101) (Leadership Development Program)

Location: S&SCTA, Albuquerque, NM.

Length: 32 hours (4 days).

Dates: January 1993-Present.

Objective: To provide students with introductory leadership knowledge and skills necessary to function in an initial supervisory capacity.

Learning Outcome: Upon successful completion of this course, the student will be able to list initial supervisory responsibilities; explain the importance of effective communication; understand the basic principles of security organizational management; and demonstrate the need for personnel recognition and evaluation systems.

Instruction: Major topics covered in the course are leadership skills and knowledge including leadership styles, effective communication, motivation, time management and principles of evaluation. Methods of instruction include lecture, discussion, case studies, role play, problem solving, computer-assisted videotape, laboratory, and guided discussion.

Credit Recommendation: In the lower division baccalaureate/associate degree category, 1 semester hour in Instructional Training, Management, or Public Administration (10/93).

Introduction to Management (MIT-300)
(Management Development Program)

Location: S&SCTA, Albuquerque, NM.

Length: 32 hours (4 days).

Dates: September 1988-Present.

Objective: To provide students with an understanding of managerial roles and responsibilities.

Learning Outcome: Upon successful completion of this course, the student will be able to recognize current trends in managing an organization; understand the impact of a corporate culture, conflict and change; explain the effect of union and non-union environments on handling grievances; and state the strategies for planning.

Instruction: Major topics covered in the course are dealing with conflict, organization changes, individual and group communications, management functions and skills, grievances and discipline methodologies, and liability issues for the manager. Methods of instruction include lecture, discussion, group projects, and case studies.

Credit Recommendation: In the upper division baccalaureate degree category, 2 semester hours in Principles of Management or Introduction to Management (10/93).

Principles and Techniques of Supervision (MIT-200)
(Supervisor Development Program)

Location: S&SCTA, Albuquerque, NM.

Length: 36 hours (4.5 days).

Dates: June 1987-Present.

Objective: To provide each student with a working knowledge of the principles and techniques of supervision.

Learning Outcome: Upon successful completion of this course, the student will be able to demonstrate an understanding of the supervisory role as a learner; explain the importance of understanding human behavior; describe the principles of labor relations; list the basic components of good communications; and demonstrate an understanding of performance appraisal and evaluation.

Instruction: Major topics covered in the course are human relations; writing, reading, and speaking skills; performance appraisal and evaluation; labor management relations; and situational leadership. Methods of instruction include lecture, case studies, role play, problem solving, computer exercises, and guided discussion.

Credit Recommendation: In the lower division baccalaureate/associate degree category, 2 semester hours in Introduction to Supervision, Principles of Supervision, or Public Administration (10/93).

Vulnerability Assessment Fundamentals (CTA-140)

Location: S&SCTA, Albuquerque, NM.

Length: 33.5 hours (5 days).

Dates: August 1992-Present.

Objective: To provide an introduction to the fundamental philosophy and concepts of assessing vulnerabilities to national security interests and/or corporate assets.

Learning Outcome: Upon successful completion of this course, the student will be able to identify the critical steps in the vulnerability assessment process; understand the philosophy, concepts, and terminology associated with the process; and be able to apply the knowledge and skills learned as a productive member of an asset vulnerability assessment team.

Instruction: Major topics covered in the course are an introduction to the concept of risk, determination, and utilizing the conditional risk equation of the site's ability to defend against threats; and risk management and planning techniques which provide the tools required to make decisions for possible upgrading of the existing safeguards, and security system. Methods of instruction include lecture, discussion, and problem-solving.

Credit Recommendation: In the upper division baccalaureate degree category, 2 semester hours in Criminal Justice, Law Enforcement, Private Security, Business Administration, or Management (5/94).

Protection Program Operations

Armorer Certification
1. Basic Armorer Certification (LFR-102)
2. Advanced Armorer Certification (LFR-103)

Location: S&SCTA, Albuquerque, NM.

Length: 1. 80 hours (2 weeks); 2. 40 hours (1 week).

Dates: 1. February 1988-Present; 2. August 1988-Present.

Objective: 1. and 2.: To provide the student with the knowledge and skills necessary to maintain, diagnose, repair, and modify standard duty and sophisticated advanced weapons systems.

Learning Outcome: 1. and 2.: Upon successful completion of this course, the student will be able to describe characteristics and uses; diagnose malfunctions; disassemble and repair weapons; adjust sights, and generally maintain weapons.

Instruction: 1. and 2.: Major topics covered in the course are inspection, maintenance, and repair of weaponry; and weaponry nomenclature. Methods of instruction include lecture, classroom exercises, audio/visual material, learner practical exercises, and a written examination.

Credit Recommendation: In the lower division baccalaureate/associate degree category, 5 semester hours in Police Weapons or General Gunsmithing (4/95). **NOTE:** Both Basic and Advanced must be taken to receive credit.

Bomb Threat Management (PFT-302)

Location: S&SCTA, Albuquerque, NM.

Length: 30 hours (4 days).

Dates: June 1992-Present.

Objective: To familiarize the student with various explosives and explosive devices, and planning for and managing a bomb threat incident.

Learning Outcome: Upon successful completion of this course, the student will be able to demonstrate knowledge and understanding of explosives, demonstrate knowledge and understanding of explosive threat management, and establish or design search and control measures.

Instruction: Major topics covered in the course are managing bomb threats, identifications of explosive devices, site management and search techniques, basic physics, and chemistry of explosives. Methods of instruction include lecture, discussion, classroom exercises, case studies, audio/visual material, written examinations, and practical graded exercises.

Credit Recommendation: In the upper division baccalaureate degree category, 2 semester hours in Explosive Materials and

Devices or Critical Incident Management (4/95).

Intermediate Force Instructor Certification (PFT-403)

Location: S&SCTA, Albuquerque, NM.

Length: 80 hours (2 weeks).

Dates: August 1987-Present.

Objective: To provide instruction in weaponless self-defense.

Learning Outcome: Upon successful completion of this course, the student will be able to demonstrate competence in empty hand techniques including control holds, pressure points and take downs, demonstrate baton techniques, arrest and handcuffing procedures, and principles of psychomotor skills instruction.

Instruction: Major topics covered in the course are knowledge and application of the use of force continuum, mechanics of arrest, restraint, and control of a violator. Methods of instruction include lecture, discussion, classroom exercises, case studies, role playing, problem solving, computer-assisted/video-taped instruction, laboratory, written and performance examinations, projects, and presentations.

Credit Recommendation: In the lower division baccalaureate/associate degree category, 3 semester hours in Defensive Tactics and Pressure Point Control or Arrest Control Procedures (4/95).

Introduction to Physical Security Systems (PHY-100)

Location: S&SCTA, Albuquerque, NM.

Length: 36 hours (4.5 days).

Dates: February 1993-Present.

Objective: To teach the student the roles of hardware and technology as they integrate with physical security systems.

Learning Outcome: Upon successful completion of this course, the student will be able to test, operate, and maintain physical security equipment and conduct a systematic system analysis of intrusion vulnerability.

Instruction: Major topics covered in the course are philosophy of physical security systems and exterior/interior sensors and their design operation and vulnerabilities. Methods of instruction include lecture, classroom exercises, audio/visual material, computer-assisted instruction, a written test, exercise evaluations, and performance reviews.

Credit Recommendation: In the lower division baccalaureate/associate degree category, 2 semester hours in Asset Protection, Physical Security, Security Systems, or Security Technology (4/95).

Introduction to Physical Security Systems Correspondence Course (PHY-100D)

Location: S&SCTA, Albuquerque, NM.

Length: Self-paced independent study.

Dates: January 1993-Present.

Objective: To provide student with the background on Physical Security Systems and their relationship to organizational operating procedures.

Learning Outcome: Upon successful completion of this course, the student will be able to demonstrate a basic understanding of all segments of an integrated physical security system.

Instruction: Major topics covered in the course are interior and exterior physical security systems, including access controls, cctv, threat definition, target identification, and basic system design and communications linkages. Also covered are the roles of hardware and technology as they integrate with the roles of protective forces and procedures. Methods of instruction include independent study and a self-paced workbook.

Credit Recommendation: In the vocational certificate category, 2 semester hours in Security Systems (6/96).

Precision Rifle Forward Observer Team (PFT-320)

Location: S&SCTA, Albuquerque, NM; and various other sites.

Length: 97 hours (2 weeks).

Dates: June 1988-Present.

Objective: To provide instruction in precision weaponry, with special emphasis on special response team training (SRT).

Learning Outcome: Upon successful completion of this course, the student will be able to serve as a member of a special response team as both a precision marksman and observer.

Instruction: Major topics covered in the course are firearms safety rules, precision rifle team operations, and range qualifications. Methods of instruction include lecture, classroom exercises, audio/visual material, range exercises, written tests, and special response team exercises.

Credit Recommendation: In the lower division baccalaureate/associate degree category, 2 semester hours in Police Weapons or as an elective (4/95).

Range Officer Program (PFT-303)

Location: S&SCTA, Albuquerque, NM.

Length: 28 hours.

Dates: June 1990-Present.

Objective: To provide the student with the knowledge to safely conduct qualification courses for the rifle, pistol, and shotgun in a live-fire range environment.

Learning Outcome: Upon successful completion of this course, the student will be able to understand the techniques of safely commanding a firing line at a firing range.

Instruction: Major topics covered in the course are basic firearms safety, range safety, range operations, range commands, target scoring, and recognition of aberrant behavior. Methods of instruction include lecture, discussion, classroom exercises, computer-assisted instruction, practical experience on a firing range, a written examination, evaluation of individual presentations, and performance-based checklists.

Credit Recommendation: In the lower division baccalaureate/associate degree category, 1 semester hour in Firearms Safety (4/95).

Security Police Officer Leadership (PFT-301)

Location: S&SCTA, Albuquerque, NM.

Length: 37 hours (1 week).

Dates: April 1993-Present.

Objective: To provide the student with the fundamentals necessary to plan, prepare, brief operational orders, and command security police officers.

Learning Outcome: Upon successful completion of this course, the student will be able to understand the concepts of leadership and demonstrate the principles of planning, briefing, and operational factors during a protective force response.

Instruction: Major topics covered in the course are leadership, belief systems and norms, goal identification, problem solving, motivation, and planning. Methods of instruction include lecture, discussion, classroom exercises, audio/visual material, learner presentation/reports, written examinations, and classroom and field exercises.

Credit Recommendation: In the lower division baccalaureate/associate degree category, 2 semester hours in Police Supervision (4/95).

SBC Center for Learning

The SBC Center for Learning serves the educational needs of various business units of its parent corporation, SBC Communications, Inc. The Center for Learning serves employees across the United States, Mexico, South America, the United Kingdom, and France representing all facets of the telecommunications industry, such as landline, wireless, internet, publications, cable television, technology research, voice messaging, and international holdings. The company provides curricula that includes marketing, sales, customer contact, information services, engineering, supervision, administration, technical, safety, and leadership development. Course materials are delivered in a variety of methods including instructor led, distance learning, virtual reality, interactive video, and audio/video tape.

The Center for Learning's campus headquarters is located in Irving, Texas with additional campus facilities located in Missouri, Arkansas, Texas, Oklahoma, and Kansas. Other training sites include Chicago, Baltimore/Washington, Boston, and Syracuse.

Source of official student records: Registry of Credit Recommendations, American Council on Education, One Dupont Circle, Washington, DC 20036-1193 or SBC Center for Learning, 6301 Colwell Boulevard, Irving, Texas 75039-3199.

Additional information about the courses: College Credit Recommendation Service, American Council on Education, One Dupont Circle, Washington, DC 20036-1193.

Account Inquiry Initial Training (Formerly Account Inquiry Center)

Location: Arkansas, Kansas, Missouri, Oklahoma, and Texas.

Length: *Version 1:* 352 hours (9 weeks); *Version 2:* 414 hours (10.4 weeks).

Dates: *Version 1:* January 1979-October 1992; *Version 2:* November 1992-Present.

Objective: To provide the student with initial training as service representative.

Learning Outcome: Upon successful completion of this course, the student will be able to use effective interpersonal skills and knowledge to represent the company to the customer; handle credit, billing, and collection procedures; and suggest services to meet customer needs.

Instruction: Major topics covered in the course are communication skills, credit procedures, billing and collection procedures, customer accounts, and customer relations. Methods of instruction include lecture, multiple experiential methods, and on-the-job training.

Credit Recommendation: *Version 1:* In the lower division baccalaureate/associate degree category, 2 semester hours in Customer Relations, or in the vocational certificate category, 3 semester hours in a vocational/technical curriculum (7/88). *Version 2:* In the lower division baccalaureate/associate degree category, 3 semester hours in Customer Relations, or in the vocational certificate category, 3 semester hours in a vocational/technical curriculum (10/93).

Advanced Instructor Skills Workshop

Location: Irving, TX.

Length: 40 hours (5 days).

Dates: May 1983-May 1994.

Objective: To provide the student with an increased understanding and development of advanced skills through practice in areas of teaching and methods of learning.

Learning Outcome: Upon successful completion of this course, the student will be able to generate meaningful involvement with his or her students; receive feedback on advanced instructor skills; provide solutions for common problems encountered in a classroom situation; design and deliver independent lessons; and focus on the key issues and ideas within his or her discipline.

Instruction: Major topics covered in the course are multiple methodologies of instruction and learning, stress management, intervention skills, learning styles, evaluation, group development, motivation, and humor in the classroom.

Credit Recommendation: In the upper division baccalaureate degree category, 2 semester hours in Instructional Methodology (5/89). **NOTE:** This course is the practicum for Training Skills Workshop.

Advanced Interaction Management (0226)

Location: Missouri, Arkansas, Texas, Oklahoma, Kansas and selected other locations.

Length: 16 hours (2 days).

Dates: January 1990-Present.

Objective: To build upon the basic skills developed in Interaction Management and learn advanced skills related to delegation, conflict management, and management of change.

Learning Outcome: Upon successful completion of this course, the student will be able to understand and effectively utilize delegation skills; utilize and understand basic conflict resolution skills & management of change.

Instruction: Major topics covered in the course are how to introduce change to a work group, overcome resistance to change, utilize conflict resolution skills, identify and overcome causes of conflict in the workplace and how to delegate. Methods of instruction include lecture, discussion, videos, classroom exercises, case studies, role playing, and guided group discussion.

Credit Recommendation: In the lower division baccalaureate/associate degree category, 1 semester hour in Supervisory Management (9/92) (9/94). *Prerequisite:* Interaction Management.

All-In-One (D-958, D-958.1, D-958.4, D-958.5)

Location: Southwestern Bell at St. Louis, San Antonio, Mission, Topeka, Wichita, and Oklahoma City.

Length: 48 hours (6 days).

Dates: March 1988-April 1995.

Objective: To teach students to operate personal productivity software including word processors, and time and task management software tools.

Learning Outcome: Upon successful completion of this course, the student will be able to operate electronic message, desk management, and word processing software, and create and modify complex documents using word processing programs.

Instruction: Major topics include word processing operations and techniques, time management operations and techniques, and electronic message techniques. Methods of instruction include lecture, laboratory, computer-assisted instruction, and videos.

Credit Recommendation: In the lower division baccalaureate/associate degree category, 2 semester hours in Data Processing or Office Systems Technology (4/90).

Application Development Using Visual Basic (1551)

Location: ISCTE, St. Louis, MO.

Length: 20 hours (5 weeks).

Dates: July 1994-Present.

Objective: To provide knowledge of the major programming constructs for the Visual Basic programming language.

Learning Outcome: Upon successful completion of this course, the student will be able to program at the intermediate level in the Visual Basic language.

Instruction: Major topics covered in the course are the Visual Basic environment, controls and events, variables and the Basic language, multiple forms, sub procedures, functions and frames, arrays, file I/O, error handling and debugging, menus, database access, and advanced features. Methods of instruction include lecture, presentations, demonstration, and computer examples and a final project.

Credit Recommendation: In the lower division baccalaureate/associate degree category, 2 semester hours in Computer Science, Computer Information Systems, or Management Information Systems (11/97).

Applied Creativity

Location: Various locations in the United States and Great Britain.

Length: 16 hours (2 days).

Dates: January 1995 to Present.

Objective: Participants will become familiar with how to think and manage in a creative and dynamic manner.

Learning Outcome: Upon successful completion of this course, the student will be able to identify basic and advanced creative management techniques; develop strategies to generate new ideas and utilize creative strategies to reduce costs associated with risk taking.

Instruction: Major topics covered in the course are nature of creative concepts; creative attitudes, traits and beliefs and the creative thinking process.

Credit Recommendation: In the lower division baccalaureate/associate degree category, 1 hour in Management (9/95).

Assembler Language and Case Study (ISC/TE I4050L and I4050C or L4051L and L4051C)

Location: Southwestern Bell, One Bell Center, St. Louis, MO.

Length: 160 hours (20 days).

Dates: January 1982-April 1995.

Objective: The course teaches students to write programs in assembler language coding and teaches program structure, together with design methodologies and applications.

Learning Outcome: Upon successful completion of this course, the student will be able to design, code, assemble, and execute assembler language programs; perform arithmetic operations, data manipulation, and condition-testing in assembler language; and structure programs using branch-and-link connections; and use Get and Put macros.

Instruction: Major topics covered in the course are Introduction to Assembler and Fundamentals of Assembler Language Coding; Data Representation; Decimal Arithmetic; Testing; Edit Program Logic; Report Program Logic; Programming Submodules; using Sequential Files and Table Programming Logic; and Case Problem. Methods of instruction include lecture, discussion, classroom exercises, and linear video.

Credit Recommendation: In the lower division baccalaureate/associate degree category, 3 semester hours in Data Processing, Computer Information Systems, Management Information Systems, or Computer Science (4/90). **NOTE:** All course numbers listed in course title must be completed to receive the credit recommendation.

Assistant Manager Job Design

Location: Dallas, TX.

Length: 40 hours (1 week).

Dates: January 1980-July 1993.

Objective: To train the student how to function as first-level managers of customer services with specific job activities and procedures.

Learning Outcome: Upon successful completion of this course, the student will be able to practice the procedures inherent in the job of supervisor of customer services, and integrate policies, procedures, and regulations to achieve departmental objectives.

Instruction: Major topics covered in the course are location of reference material, training employees, safety, meetings, employee privacy, reports and logs, procedures, customer screening, employee absence control, credit management, scheduling, discipline, performance appraisal, and management/union relations. Methods of instruction include lecture and multiple experiential methods.

Credit Recommendation: In the lower division baccalaureate/associate degree category, 2 semester hours in Introduction to Supervision (7/88).

Attached Processor Maintenance (515.4) (3B20 Processor Operation and Maintenance and 1A-APS Maintenance)

Location: Advanced Education Center, Irving, TX.

Length: 71 hours (2 weeks).

Dates: January 1983-March 1994.

Objective: To teach the student to maintain an attached computer processor.

Learning Outcome: Upon successful completion of this course, the student will be able to understand the circuiting of a large attached computer processor; correct malfunctions in a large attached computer processor; and analyze diagnostic information from an attached computer processor to determine problem areas.

Instruction: Major topics covered in the course are troubleshooting on an attached computer processor supplementing a telephone switching CPU. Methods of instruction include self-paced instruction.

Credit Recommendation: In the lower division baccalaureate/associate degree category, 2 semester hours in Electronics (3/89). **NOTE:** This course combined with 1/1A ESS Peripheral Maintenance (515.1) and 1/A ESS Processor Maintenance (515.2) comprise course 1/1A ESS Peri-pheral/Processor Maintenance (515.0) for 5 semester hours. Credit should be awarded for either this sequence of courses or for course 515.0, but not both.

Basic JCL (3031)

Location: Various locations in the United States and Great Britain.

Length: 24 hours.

Dates: January 1996-Present.

Objective: To provide the basic knowledge necessary to successfully run jobs in an IBM MVS mainframe environment.

Learning Outcome: Upon completion of this course, the student will be able to code JOB, EXEC, and DD statements along with their associated parameters.

Instruction: Major topics covered in the course are general Job Control Language concepts and syntax rules for the successful execution of programs and procedures in batch mode. Methods of instruction include lecture, discussion, and written and online exercises.

Credit Recommendation: In the lower division baccalaureate/associate degree category, 1 semester hour in Data Processing or Computer Information Systems (11/97).

Beyond Customer Expectations (0221)

Location: Missouri, Arkansas, Texas, Oklahoma, Kansas, and other selected locations.

Length: 16 hours (2 days).

Dates: January 1991-Present.

Objective: To provide an understanding of the principles and value of providing effective customer service.

Learning Outcome: Upon successful completion of this course, the student will be able to improve customer satisfaction by raising quality; increase efficiency in handling customer transactions; and manage dissatisfied customers.

Instruction: Major topics covered in the course are key principles of effective customer service and enhancing customer service interactions. Methods of instruction include lecture, discussion, cases, and videotape.

Credit Recommendation: In the vocational certificate category, 1 semester hour in General Business (9/91) (9/94). **NOTE:** One hour of credit is recommended for either Beyond Customer Expectations or Supporting Service Excellence but not both.

Cable Repair: Fault Locating (D-401)

Location: Houston, TX; Oklahoma City, OK; and St. Louis, MO.

Length: 32 hours (4 days).

Dates: February 1985-Present.

Objective: To teach students how to locate a fault on an underground or aerial cable.

Learning Outcome: Upon successful completion of this course, the student will be able to determine the starting point, test set choice and data analysis method necessary to clear a cable fault; operate various fault locating test sets; and locate faults in cables and locate and stake the path of a buried cable.

Instruction: Major topics covered in the course is how to locate faults on underground and aerial cables using standard test equipment. Methods of instruction include self-paced, individualized programmed instruction.

Credit Recommendation: In the vocational certificate category, 1 semester hour in Telecommunications (7/88) (10/93).

COBOL Language and Case Study (ISC/TE I4050L and I4050C or L4051L and L4051C)

Location: Southwestern Bell, One Bell Center, St. Louis, MO.

Length: 160 hours (20 days).

Dates: January 1982-April 1995.

Objective: The course teaches students to write programs in COBOL and emphasizes report preparation, table processing, and sorting.

Learning Outcome: Upon successful completion of this course, the student will be able to describe the margins, punctuation, sections and paragraphs; code the Identification, Environment, Data, and Procedure Divisions; compile and execute COBOL programs; and test and debug COBOL programs.

Instruction: Major topics include COBOL II language syntax, program structure and logic, compiling and executing, data representation and movement; file declaration; record I/O; and table programming and logic. Methods of instruction include lecture, discussion, and classroom exercises.

Credit Recommendation: In the lower division baccalaureate/associate degree category, 3 semester hours in Data Processing, Computer Information Systems, Management Information Systems, or Computer Science (4/90). **NOTE:** All course numbers listed in course title must be completed to receive the credit recommendation.

Collections Professional's Workshop (0222)

Location: Missouri, Arkansas, Texas, Oklahoma, Kansas, and other selected locations.

Length: 24 hours (3 days).

Dates: January 1991-Present.

Objective: To provide an overview of current and effective collection practices.

Learning Outcome: Upon successful completion of this course, the student will be able to see how collections affect profitability; increase ability to approach customers and raise the issue of a past due account; develop effective collections/negotiations skills; and use effective organization skills.

Instruction: Major topics covered in the course are collections and profitability; communication and listening skills; collection negotiation skills; organization skills; and legal issues. Methods of instruction include lecture, cases, role play, and videotape.

Credit Recommendation: In the vocational certificate category, 1 semester hour in General Business (9/91) (9/94).

Communispond Effective Presentation Skills (CEPS)

Location: St. Louis, MO; Irving, TX; Houston, TX; San Antonio, TX.

Length: 16 hours (2 days).

Dates: December 1984-January 1994.

Objective: To help the student improve presentation skills, avoid nervousness, organize subject matter, develop visualization and visual aids, field questions, and control dialog.

Learning Outcome: Upon successful completion of this course, the student will be able to make oral presentations with relative ease; organize materials and physical arrangements; and control a discussion.

Instruction: Major topics covered in the course are physical skills in presentation; organization and visualization of content material; delivery of oral presentations with visual aids; and stimulation of questions and discussion. Methods of instruction include oral presentations, exercises, and group discussions.

Credit Recommendation: In the vocational certificate category, 1 semester hour in Oral Presentations or Speech (1/89).

Computer Architecture (DQ 301/302)

Location: Advanced Education System, Irving, TX.

Length: 32 hours (4 days).

Dates: October 1988-October 1995.

Objective: To introduce open systems interconnection (OSI) and its function in the corporate networking market.

Learning Outcome: Upon successful completion of this course, the student will be able to describe the design alternatives available to an architect in structuring a computer network; explain the concept of layering and the importance of design transparency; delineate carefully the responsibilities of each layer in an open architecture; and enumerate emerging standards at the various layers of the model.

Instruction: Major topics covered in the course are network architectures, OSI layers, and network architecture trends. Methods of instruction include lecture, discussion, and case study.

Credit Recommendation: In the upper division baccalaureate degree category, 2 semester hours in Telecommunications or Computer Science (10/90).

Computer CPU and Peripheral Maintenance (515.0) (1/1A ESS Peripheral/Processor Maintenance)

Location: Advanced Education System, Irving, TX.

Length: 215 hours (5.5 weeks).

Dates: January 1983-March 1994.

Objective: To teach the student to maintain computer hardware, including a large CPU and specialized telephone peripheral equipment.

Learning Outcome: Upon successful completion of this course, the student will

be able to diagnose, analyze, and correct malfunctions on specialized switching computer peripherals, telephone switching CPUs, and attached processors to telephone switching computers.

Instruction: Course provides hands-on training in troubleshooting phone trunk lines, peripheral control units, digital carriers, analog CPU hardware (1 and 1A switching computer), and attached processor. Methods of instruction include self-paced instruction.

Credit Recommendation: In the lower division baccalaureate/associate degree category, 5 semester hours in Electronics (3/89). **NOTE:** This course combined with courses 1/1A ESS Peripheral Maintenance (515.1), 1/A ESS Processor Maintenance (515.2), and 3B20 Processor Operation and Maintenance and 1A-APS Mainten-ance (515.4) comprise a course sequence for 5 semester hours. Credit should be awarded for either this sequence or this course, but not both.

Computer CPU Maintenance (515.2) (1A ESS Processor Maintenance)

Location: Advanced Education System, Irving, TX.

Length: 32 hours (4 days).

Dates: January 1983-March 1994.

Objective: To teach students to maintain a large telephone switching CPU.

Learning Outcome: Upon successful completion of this course, the student will be able to interpret and react to CPU interrupts, retrieve and analyze self-diagnostic information from the CPU, and recover the system from a malfunction.

Instruction: Major topics covered in the course are troubleshooting a large switching CPU, including CPU interrupts, deferral fault recognition, and system recovery. Methods of instruction include self-paced instruction.

Credit Recommendation: In the lower division baccalaureate/associate degree category, 1 semester hour in Electronics (3/89). **NOTE:** This course combined with Specialized Computer Peripheral Maintenance (515.1) and 1A-APS Maintenance (515.4) comprise course Computer CPU and Peripheral Maintenance (515.0) for 5 semester hours. Credit should be awarded for either this sequence of courses or for course 515.0, but not both.

Computer Systems (DQ 102, 103) MIS-Software Development (DQ 402)

Location: Advanced Education System, Irving, TX.

Length: 48 hours (6 days).

Dates: October 1988-October 1995.

Objective: To introduce and survey computer hardware, software, applications, and the MIS organization.

Learning Outcome: Upon successful completion of this course, the student will be able to describe the architecture of a typical computing system; identify the principal system software components and describe their functions; describe several typical MIS environments; read and modify simple application programs written in BASIC; explain each step of software design process; and identify different methods of software design.

Instruction: Major topics covered in the course are computer history, programming, operations, operating systems, microcomputers, software design, and MIS organization structure. Methods of instruction include lecture and discussion.

Credit Recommendation: In the lower division baccalaureate/associate degree category, 3 semester hours in Computer/ Information Systems (10/90).

Constructive Contention

Location: Various locations in the United States and Great Britain.

Length: 20 hours (25 days).

Dates: January 1995-Present.

Objective: To provide the student with basic knowledge about how to effectively handle differences and disagreements in the workplace.

Learning Outcome: Upon successful completion of this course, the student will be able to develop conflict resolution skills understand styles of conflict resolution; and identify and overcome barriers to organizational effectiveness.

Instruction: Major topics covered in the course are principles of conflict resolution; personal conflict resolution styles and practical issues concerning conflict management. Methods of instruction include lecture, discussion, and case study.

Credit Recommendation: In the lower division baccalaureate/associate degree category, 1 hour in Management (9/95).

Consultative Selling

Location: Irving, TX, and St. Louis, MO.

Length: 24 hours (3 days).

Dates: December 1988-May 1994.

Objective: To provide the student with the preparation of a customer and product analysis in order to create an effective sales presentation.

Learning Outcome: Upon successful completion of this course, the student will be able to analyze a client's business and identify opportunities and approaches; develop a sales plan and a personal network; and maintain a team orientation in consultative selling.

Instruction: Major topics covered in the course are the review of the sales procedure and the sales process, development of client qualifications, and identification of opportunities; understanding the client's business and trends in the client's industry; and sales plan development and personal networking.

Credit Recommendation: In the upper division baccalaureate degree category, 2 semester hours in Sales Management (5/89). *Prerequisite:* Sales Strategies and Tactics-Management (SST-M) or Sales Strategies and Tactics-Account Executives.

1. Corporate Grammar
2. Power Writing

Location: St. Louis, MO; Dallas, TX; and other Southwestern Bell locations.

Length: *Versions 1 and 2:* 8 hours (1 day)

Dates: *Versions 1 and 2:* July 1993-Present

Objective: *Version 1:* To learn how to use the basic principles of grammar in written communication. *Version 2:* To provide express and organize ideas in various forms of written communication.

Learning Outcome: *Version 1:* Upon successful completion of this course, the student will be able to identify and correct grammatical errors; improve individual writing skills, and avoid common errors in usage. *Version 2:* Upon successful completion of this course, the student will be able to identify objectives and the purpose of writing; control tone, direction, and message of written communication; and effectively appeal to the interests of the reader.

Instruction: *Version 1:* Major topics covered in the course are verb agreement, use of nouns and pronouns, placement and use of modifiers, punctuation, capitalization, prepositions, and transitions. *Version 2:* Major topics covered in the course are analysis of writing skills, establishing objectives, controlling tone and readability, and structuring letters and memos. Methods of instruction for both courses include lecture and classroom exercises.

Credit Recommendation: In the lower division baccalaureate/associate degree category, 1 semester hour in Business

Writing only when Corporate Grammar and Power Writing are taken (9/93) (9/94).

Creating High Performance Teams

Location: Management Development Training Centers in Arkansas, Kansas, Missouri, Oklahoma, Texas, plus suitcased throughout Texas.

Length: 24 hours (3 days).

Dates: October 1988-March 1994.

Objective: To provide the student with the skills to create a highly productive, efficiently functioning work group.

Learning Outcome: Upon successful completion of this course, the student will be able to create an environment for participative leadership, shared responsibility, purposeful activity, effective communication, future orientation, and effective use of human resources.

Instruction: Major topics covered in the course are the high performance team, the role of the manager, participative/authoritative leadership, goal setting and high performance, defining and creating high performance teams, power, shared responsibility, managerial responsibility, two-way communication, apathy, team on task, barriers to creativity, and action planning.

Credit Recommendation: In the upper division baccalaureate degree category, 1 semester hour in Organization Behavior, or in the upper division baccalaureate degree category, 3 semester hours in Organization Behavior if taken in conjunction with Positive Discipline and Situational Leadership (5/89).

Data Communications

Location: Irving, TX and various locations.

Length: 24 hours (3 days).

Dates: May 1990-December 1996.

Objective: To introduce the terminology and concepts of computers and data communications system.

Learning Outcome: Upon successful completion of this course, the student will be able to explain the basic concepts and capabilities of computers and data communications systems, using appropriate terminology; identify the components of a data communications network and specify their functions; describe the methods of data transport; and discuss trends affecting the industry.

Instruction: Major topics covered in the course are computers; hardware and software; terminal equipment; data transmission; data communications networks; protocols and standards; and applications. Methods of instruction include lecture, discussion, and group exercise.

Credit Recommendation: In the lower division baccalaureate/associate degree category, 1 semester hour in Marketing/Telecommunications (12/91).

Data Communications Technology (1025)

Location: Advanced Education System, Irving, TX.

Length: 80 hours (2 weeks).

Dates: November 1988-March 1994.

Objective: To provide students with a comprehensive understanding of data communication fundamentals.

Learning Outcome: Upon successful completion of this course, the student will be able to install and maintain various types of modems and data service units; convert from one numbering system to another; use a data line monitor to observe and analyze data; understand modulation and mulitplexing schemes; and understand various data communications protocols.

Instruction: Major topics covered in the course are analog and digital transmission requirements, numbering systems, data codes and error checking schemes, elements of digital logic, modulation and multiplexing, and transmission protocols. Methods of instruction include lecture, discussion, and laboratory exercises.

Credit Recommendation: In the lower division baccalaureate/associate degree category, 3 semester hours in Computer Science, Electronics Technology, or Telecommunications (3/89).

Data Link Laboratory (DQ 201)

Location: Advanced Education System, Irving, TX.

Length: 24 hours (3 days).

Dates: October 1988-October 1995.

Objective: To provide an in-depth exposure to data communications.

Learning Outcome: Upon successful completion of this course, the student will be able to describe the function of all interface circuits in the most common DTE-DCE physical layer protocols; differentiate among various data link protocols; and explain how noise and distortion affect link error rates and link speed.

Instruction: Major topics covered in the course are physical layer and asynchronous, binary, and bit-oriented protocols. Method of instruction includes laboratory exercises.

Credit Recommendation: In the upper division baccalaureate degree category, 1 semester hour in Engineering or Computer Science (10/90).

DB2 Application Development and Database Administration (5530)

Location: St. Louis, MO.

Length: 29.5 hours (5 days).

Dates: June 1989-Present.

Objective: To prepare the student to create and maintain DB2 objects such as tables, table spaces, indexes, views, and covers the structure of the DB2 catalog tables, DB2 security facilities, and DB2 utilities.

Learning Outcome: Upon successful completion of this course, the student will be able to create and drop DB2 objects; establish referential integrity between related DB2 tables; describe alternatives for loading tables; understand how DB2 security works and how to grant and revoke privileges; describe DB2 locking and isolation mechanisms; and use DB2 utilities such as Reorg, Run stats, Check data, etc.

Instruction: Major topics covered in the course are DB2 catalog and directory; logical database design; physical database design; data definition language; backup and recovery; DB2 object management; DB2 security; and DB2 performance. Methods of instruction include lecture, discussion, workshop problems, and classroom exercises.

Credit Recommendation: In the upper division baccalaureate degree category, 2 semester hours in Computer Science, Computer Information Systems, or Data Processing (10/93).

DB2 Application Programming (5520)

Location: St. Louis, MO.

Length: 32.5 hours (1 week).

Dates: January 1989-Present.

Objective: To prepare students to write programs which access DB2 databases with such preparation to include the use of SQL and how to embed SQL in COBOL and PL/1 programs.

Learning Outcome: Upon successful completion of this course, the student will be able to write SQL statements to retrieve data from a DB2 table; write SQL statements to update DB2 tables; code application programs with embedded SQL statements; understand how dynamic SQL works; precompile, compile, link, bind, and execute application programs; and use the DB2 EXPLAIN facility to evaluate SQL statement performance.

Instruction: Major topics covered in the course are introduction to DB2; SQL statements including SELECT, data and time handling; accessing multiple tables; updating; embedding SQL; dynamic SQL; bind; and applications development guidelines. Methods of instruction include lecture, discussion, and workshops.

Credit Recommendation: In the upper division baccalaureate degree category, 2 semester hours in Computer Science, Computer Information Systems, or Computer Information Systems, or Data Processing (10/93).

DB2, SQL, and QMF for Information Systems Personnel (5550)

Location: St. Louis, MO.

Length: 21 hours (3 days).

Dates: January 1989-Present.

Objective: To prepare the student to use the QMF and DB2; use QMF screen panels to submit SQL queries; use QMF report formatting panels; use the QMF commands Reset, Draw, Save, Display, List, Run; and use QMF application support facilities.

Learning Outcome: Upon successful completion of this course, the student will understand the relationship between QMF and DB2; use QMF screen panels to submit SQL queries; use QMF report formatting panels; use the QMF commands Reset, Draw, Save, Display, List, and Run; and QMF application support facilities.

Instruction: Major topics covered in the course are basic SQL Select statements; QMF fundamentals; control breaks; QMF object management; advanced QMF formatting; SQL joins and unions; SQL summarization; and SQL updating. Methods of instruction include lecture; discussion; and workshops in coding, debugging, executing SQL statements, QMF formatting panels, commands, procedures, and application support facilities.

Credit Recommendation: In the upper division baccalaureate degree category, 1 semester hour in Computer Science, Computer Information Systems, or Data Processing (10/93).

Design Center Engineering (D-651)

Location: Advanced Education System, Irving, TX.

Length: 52 hours (7 days).

Dates: June 1981-March 1994.

Objective: To give the student a fundamental overview of telephone in communications network/facility planning and design.

Learning Outcome: Upon successful completion of this course, the student will be able to define telephone engineering terminology; use telephone planning documents; and describe the telephone network planning organization and process.

Instruction: Major topics covered in the course are the organization of telephone engineering function, definition of engineering terms, engineering documents, and distribution planning tasks. Methods of instruction include lecture, discussion, and computer-assisted classroom projects/exercises.

Credit Recommendation: In the upper division baccalaureate degree category, 1 semester hour in Telecommunications (3/89).

Digital Circuit Technology (262)

Location: Advanced Education System, Irving, TX.

Length: 56 hours (1.5 weeks).

Dates: September 1987-March 1994.

Objective: To provide the student with the technical knowledge to install and maintain digital data circuits.

Learning Outcome: Upon successful completion of this course, the student will be able to demonstrate an understanding of basic digital terminology; identify the levels of digital hierarchy; perform the turn-up of both dataport networks and digital data banks; and locate and clear DDB circuit trouble.

Instruction: Major topics covered in the course are the theory of data communications, multiplexing, timing and synchronization issues, digital and circuit operation, and testing procedures. Methods of instruction include lecture, discussion, and laboratory exercises.

Credit Recommendation: In the lower division baccalaureate/associate degree category, 2 semester hours in Electronics Technology or Telecommunications (3/89).

Digital Synchronization Maintenance (263)

Location: Irving, TX.

Length: 24 hours (3 days).

Dates: November 1990-December 1996.

Objective: To provide students with the knowledge and skills required to install, maintain, and isolate faults on digital synchronization equipment.

Learning Outcome: Upon successful completion of this course, the student will be able to use telecom test equipment to make measurements such as frequency and phase; to isolate time errors; to install and adjust timing generators; and to analyze network synchronization.

Instruction: Major topics covered in the course are installation of a bits clock; use of an oscilloscope, test set, and other commonly used equipment; and trouble analysis of digital synchronization equipment. Methods of instruction include lecture, laboratory, and classroom exercises.

Credit Recommendation: In the lower division baccalaureate/associate degree category, 1 semester hour in Telecommunications laboratory (12/91).

Economic Study Module (ESM) (D-686)

Location: Southwestern Bell Education Centers.

Length: 18 hours (1.5 days).

Dates: February 1984-March 1994.

Objective: To give the student an understanding of the theory and application of engineering economics related to provide telecommunications transmission capacity.

Learning Outcome: Upon successful completion of this course, the student will be able to prepare input mask on the cathode ray terminal for the problem file and the user cost data file; analyze and return ESM programs for smoothed results; and evaluate the alternatives selected.

Instruction: Major topics covered in the course are economics concepts, time value of money, discounting net cash flow, present worth, and the application of economic study module software. Methods of instruction include lecture, discussion, and computer-assisted instruction.

Credit Recommendation: In the upper division baccalaureate degree category, 1 semester hour in Engineering Economics or Telecommunications (3/89). **NOTE:** Credit is awarded only if Loop Engineering Assignment Data (D-685) is successfully completed.

Effective Business Communication
1. Effective Business Writing
2. Presentation Skills

Location: St. Louis, MO; Dallas, TX; and other Southwestern Bell locations.

Length: *Version 1:* 24 hours (3 days); *Version 2:* 24 hours (2 days).

Dates: *Versions 1 and 2:* January 1986-September 1994.

Objective: *Version 1:* To provide information about the basic principles of business writing and communication in a business setting. *Version 2:* To provide the skills and confidence to stand up and speak in almost any situation.

Learning Outcome: *Version 1:* Upon successful completion of this course, the student will be able to understand and utilize effective patterns of business communication; and prepare and use several formats for business letters, memos, and newsletters. *Version 2:* Upon successful completion of this course, the student will be able to analyze the audience; organize his or her thoughts; use visual aids; field questions; use effective speaking techniques; and speak with confidence.

Instruction: *Version 1:* Major topics covered in the course are business communications patterns and principles, psychology of writing, and business writing practices and procedures. *Version 2:* Major topics covered in the course are the principles of effective speaking; how to develop and present a speech by using the presentation process of introduction, body, and conclusion; use of visual aids; and handling questions.

Credit Recommendation: *Versions 1 and 2:* In the lower division baccalaureate/associate degree category, 1 semester hour in Business Communication (9/89) (9/94). **NOTE:** Students must successfully complete both courses to receive the credit recommendation.

Effective Sales Management (ESM)

Location: Irving, TX; St. Louis, MO.

Length: 28 hours (3.5 days).

Dates: December 1987-January 1994.

Objective: To provide the student with a definition of the sales manager's role, development of attitudes, leadership, performance criteria, and evaluation standards for a sales group.

Learning Outcome: Upon successful completion of this course, the student will be able to understand the function of the sales manager; utilize a variety of motivational tools in directing subordinates; and supervise, correct, and evaluate the subordinate's selling techniques.

Instruction: Major topics covered in the course are the role of the sales manager; attitudes, motivation, and leadership principles; and setting standards, forecasting, and managing performance. Methods of instruction include lecture, case study, role play, and practical exercises.

Credit Recommendation: In the upper division baccalaureate degree category, 2 semester hours in Sales Management (1/89).

Effective Sales Management

Location: St. Louis, MO; Dallas, TX; and other Southwestern Bell locations.

Length: 32 hours (4 days).

Dates: October 1988-September 1994.

Objective: To enable the sales manager to effectively lead sales units in meeting objectives.

Learning Outcome: Upon successful completion of this course, the student will be able to understand the role of a sales manager; coach and communicate with salespeople; and provide leadership and motivation to a sales unit.

Instruction: Major topics covered in the course are the sales manager's role, attitudes, communication, leadership, motivation, performance management planning, execution, and evaluation. Methods of instruction include lecture, discussion, handouts, and role playing.

Credit Recommendation: In the upper division baccalaureate degree category, 2 semester hours in Supervisory Management (9/89) (9/94).

1. Empowering Leader
2. Unlimited Power of Team (0230)

Location: St. Louis, MO; Dallas, TX; and other Southwestern Bell locations.

Length: *Version 1:* 7 hours (1 day); *Version 2:* 28 hours (3.5 days).

Dates: *Version 1:* July 1993-Present; *Version 2:* January 1993-Present.

Objective: *Version 1:* To provide an introduction of empowerment, and review organizational arenas in which management may attempt to improve its leadership roles. *Version 2:* To describe the role of the individual in team building by use of the commitment of individuals.

Learning Outcome: *Version 1:* Upon successful completion of this course, the student will be able to identify and overcome obstacles to empowerment, and understand the role of managers in developing empowerment. *Version 2:* Upon successful completion of this course, the student will be able to communicate more effectively in the work environment, use questions to clarify communications, and develop strategies to increase team effectiveness.

Instruction: *Version 1:* Major topics covered in the course are the definition of empowerment, components of empowerment arenas, and how managers or supervisors can develop leadership ability by use of empowerment concepts. *Version 2:* Major topics covered in the course are the disciplines required for success and the importance of teamwork.

Credit Recommendation: In the lower division baccalaureate/associate degree category, 2 semester hours in Personnel Management only when both Empowering Leader and Unlimited Power of Team are taken (9/93) (9/94).

ESP (Enterprise Scheduling Processor) Overview (3033)

Location: Various locations in the United States and Great Britain.

Length: 24 hours (3 days).

Dates: January 1996-Present.

Objective: To provide an overview of the Enterprise Scheduling Processor (ESP) for students who will be doing job setup in ESP.

Learning Outcome: Upon successful completion of this course, the student will be able to create events and applications to manage and control the job flow.

Instruction: Major topics covered in the course are ESP applications, creating/scheduling events, managing dependencies, tracking jobs, controlling the job flow, symbolic variables, ESP resources, JCL tailoring, forecasting future workloads, and historical reporting. Methods of instruction include lecture, discussion, and online exercises.

Credit Recommendation: In the lower division baccalaureate/associate degree category, 1 semester hour in Management Information Systems, Computer Information Systems, or Data Processing (11/97).

External Environments of a Public Utility (Issues and Impacts)

Location: Management Development Training Centers in Arkansas, Kansas, Missouri, Oklahoma, Texas, plus suitcased throughout Texas.

Length: 16 hours (2 days).

Dates: October 1985-May 1994.

Objective: To acquaint the student with the diversification issues emanating from the divestment of the corporation; legal, financial, and regulatory environment; various clients including the investors, stakeholders, and general public; rate structure; and formulation of public opinion.

Learning Outcome: Upon successful completion of this course, the student will be able to discuss key issues that affect company earnings; locate resources to obtain information regarding the company's financial situation; respond to commonly asked questions about company finances and operations; and public image.

Instruction: Major topics covered in the course are stakeholder's relationships and issues, regulation, consumer relations, investor relations, locating and managing resources, rates, securities law, investments, financing the business, and impacts on profit/assets.

Credit Recommendation: In the lower division baccalaureate/associate degree category, 1 semester hour in External Environments of a Public Utility, or in the lower division baccalaureate/associate degree category, 3 semester hours in Personnel Management if taken in conjunction with Goal Setting and Performance Evaluation, Improving Business Relationships, Interpersonal Business Communications, Introduction to Personnel Policy, Supervisory Skills Workshop, and Understanding Managing Performance (5/89).

Farbar Comprehensive Thesis (DQ 502)

Location: Advanced Education System, Irving, TX.

Length: 32 hours (4 days).

Dates: October 1988-October 1995.

Objective: To integrate prerequisite courses taught in the Data Quest Program.

Learning Outcome: Upon successful completion of this course, the student will be able to explain the process for analyzing a multiple voice and data systems network; analyze the business and technical issues faced by a client; and determine how products and services can be integrated into a solution with other vendors, equipment and services.

Instruction: Major topics covered in the course are a capstone case study designed to integrate knowledge attained in the Data Quest Program to enhance marketing and sales performance. Methods of instruction include case study and discussion.

Credit Recommendation: In the upper division baccalaureate degree category, 2 semester hours in Marketing-Sales (10/90).

Fiber Optics (112)

Location: Advanced Education System, Irving, TX.

Length: 40 hours (1 week).

Dates: January 1989-March 1994.

Objective: To provide the student with knowledge of fiber optic theory, typical system application, use of WORD document, and hands-on technical experience in the installation and maintenance of high- and low-speed fiber optic systems.

Learning Outcome: Upon successful completion of this course, the student will have a working knowledge in the installation and maintenance of fiber optic systems using WORD documents, test equipment, and technical documentation.

Instruction: Major topics covered in the course are the basic principles of digital transmissions, fiber optic technology, digital performance testing, and low- and high-speed light-guide systems. Methods of instruction include lecture, discussion, and laboratory exercises.

Credit Recommendation: In the upper division baccalaureate degree category, 1 semester hour in Computer Science, Electronics Technology, or Telecommunications (3/89).

Financial Selling Skills

Location: Irving, TX.

Length: 32 hours (4 days).

Dates: September 1988-January 1994.

Objective: To provide the student with a foundation in fundamental concepts of finance in order to apply financial concepts to the process of selling.

Learning Outcome: Upon successful completion of this course, the student will be able to understand the major financial concepts, terms, and techniques; apply financial principles to a client's problem and situation; and use financial motivation to close a sale.

Instruction: Major topics covered in the course are a glossary of accounting and finance terminology; problems in various financial analyses and techniques; and introduction of financial criteria into a sales presentation and close.

Credit Recommendation: In the upper division baccalaureate degree category, 3 semester hours in Marketing, or in the lower division baccalaureate/associate degree category, 3 semester hours in Finance (1/89).

1. Franklin Time Management
2. Effective Meeting Skills
3. Stress Management (0222)
(Formerly Course 1: Time on My Side [0215])

Location: St. Louis, MO; Dallas, TX; and other Southwestern Bell locations.

Length: 24 hours (3 days).

Dates: *Version 1:* September 1994-Present; *Version 2:* July 1993-Present; *Version 3:* January 1990-Present.

Objective: *Version 1:* To provide an awareness of the importance of time management toward achieving professional objectives. *Version 2:* To teach critical skills for effective meeting and leadership participation. *Version 3:* To provide an overview of the topic of stress and its impact on our daily lives.

Learning Outcome: Upon successful completion of this course, (1) the student will be able to establish personal and professional goals and priorities; plan effective short-term and long-term activities that will lead to timely achievement of goals; and learn to use tools and techniques to improve levels of time management skills; (2) the student will be able to effectively participate in and lead meetings and handle difficult situations in meetings; and (3) the student will be able to identify sources and symptoms of stress and its impact on our daily lives.

Instruction: *Version 1:* Major topics covered in the course are nature of time; and the need and effective use of management materials. *Version 2:* Major topics covered in the course are principles of effective meeting leadership and participation including setting objectives, planning, personal interaction, and handling difficult situations. *Version 3:* Major topics covered in the course are stress assumptions, triggers, responses, self-assessment, and management techniques. Methods of instruction include lecture, classroom exercises, instructor-led discussion, case studies, role playing, and problem solving.

Credit Recommendation: In the lower division baccalaureate/associate degree category, 2 semester hours in Personnel Management only when Franklin Time Management, Effective Meeting Skills, and Stress Management are taken (9/93) (9/94).

Fundamental Electrical Circuits/Telephone Transmission (311)
(Fundamentals of Analog Transmission)

Location: Advanced Education System, Irving, TX.

Length: 40 hours (1 week).

Dates: February 1983-March 1994.

Objective: To train students to apply general principles of electrical circuits to telephone voice transmission.

Learning Outcome: Upon successful completion of this course, the student will be able to apply standard electrical testing techniques to telephone voice circuits; understand signaling loops; and adjust line quality to telephone standards.

Instruction: Major topics covered in the course are the use of volt/ohm meters and other specialized instruments, basic signaling techniques, including E+M, DX and SF, and line quality monitoring and adjustment. Methods of instruction include lectures and laboratory exercises.

Credit Recommendation: In the lower division baccalaureate/associate degree category, 1 semester hour in Electrical Circuits (3/89).

Fundamentals of Electricity in Telephony (D-314)

Location: St. Louis, MO; Houston, TX; and Oklahoma, OK.

Length: 16 hours (2 days).

Dates: February 1988-March 1994.

Objective: To provide the student with an understanding of elementary electrical and transmission terminology concepts.

Learning Outcome: Upon successful completion of this course, the student will be able to define basic electrical terms, symbols, and units of measure; calculate value of an unknown electrical property using Ohm's law; and recognize various factors that affect loss or gain in electrical signals.

Instruction: Major topics covered in the course are electric circuits, circuit impairments, and telephone circuits. Methods of instruction include computer-assisted instruction.

Credit Recommendation: In the lower division baccalaureate/associate degree category, 1 semester hour in Electric Technology or Physics (3/89).

Fundamentals of Selling (615001)

Location: St. Louis, MO, and Dallas, TX.

Length: 40 hours (1 week).

Dates: September 1985-July 1993.

Objective: To instruct the student in basic sales skills in communications services.

Learning Outcome: Upon successful completion of this course, the student will be able to prepare a sales approach to a customer; deliver a sales presentation; and effectively close a sale.

Instruction: Major topics covered in the course are qualifying customers, designing sales approaches, outlining sales presentations, and delivering and practicing techniques for presentations. Methods of instruction include lecture and multiple experiential exercises.

Credit Recommendation: In the lower division baccalaureate/associate degree category, 2 semester hours in Personal Selling/Salesmanship (7/88).

Fundamentals of Selling

Location: St. Louis, MO; Dallas, TX; and other Southwestern Bell locations.

Length: 40 hours (5 days).

Dates: November 1988-September 1994.

Objective: To enable the sales force to effectively sell communications solutions through preparation, approach and data gathering, solution development, proposal, presentation, handling objections, closing, and follow-through.

Learning Outcome: Upon successful completion of this course, the student will be able to identify prospects from multiple sources and gather enough information to make appointments; develop proposals that suit customer needs and present them in a persuasive manner; and handle objections and close the sale.

Instruction: Major topics covered in the course are prospecting and pre-approach information, approach and needs identification, needs analysis and solution development, writing and presenting proposals, handling objections, closing the sale, and implementation. Methods of instruction include lecture, group discussions and exercises, written exercises, role playing with feedback, videotapes, and handouts.

Credit Recommendation: In the lower division baccalaureate/associate degree category, 3 semester hours in Sales (9/89) (9/94).

General Utilities (3062)

Location: Various locations in the United States and Great Britain.

Length: 40 hours.

Dates: January 1996-Present.

Objective: To provide the student with the skills required for developing, testing, and maintaining programs to be run under an MVS operating system.

Learning Outcome: Upon successful completion of this course, the student will be able to describe a variety of ways in which utilities can be used to aid program testing and maintenance; code the JCL and utility control statements to perform common program related functions (i.e., create test datasets, move and copy datasets, list datasets, and update partitioned datasets); and describe several uses of utilities which support the operating system.

Instruction: Major topics covered in the course are IEFBR14, IEBDG, IEBPTPCH, WCSGENER, IEHPROGM, IEHLIST, IEBCOPY, SYNCSORT, YM00111A, YM88111A, YM60111A, and YM61111A. Methods of instruction include discussion, online review, and online exercises.

Credit Recommendation: In the lower division baccalaureate/associate degree category, 2 semester hours in Management Information Systems, Computer Information Systems, or Data Processing (11/97).

Goal Setting and Performance Evaluation (Joint Goal Setting)

Location: Management Development Training Centers in Arkansas, Kansas, Missouri, Oklahoma, Texas, plus suitcased throughout Texas.

Length: 8 hours (1 day).

Dates: January 1974-March 1993.

Objective: To provide the student with knowledge about the joint goal-setting process and the appraisal performance as it relates to goals.

Learning Outcome: Upon successful completion of this course, the student will be able to use the management appraisal system; develop goals that meet management appraisal system criteria; and implement the joint goal setting process with his or her supervisor.

Instruction: Major topics covered in the course are managing performance, setting goals jointly, activity versus output, the performance cycle, and measuring performance.

Credit Recommendation: In the vocational certificate category, 1 semester hour in Goal Setting and Performance Evaluation, or in the lower division baccalaureate/associate degree category, 3 semester hours in Personnel Management if taken in conjunction with External Environments of a Public Utility, Improving Business Relationships, Interpersonal Business Communications, Introduction to Personnel Policy, Supervisory Skills Workshop, and Understanding Managing Performance (5/89).

High Performance Management

Location: St. Louis, MO; Dallas, TX; and other Southwestern Bell locations.

Length: 20 hours (2.5 days).

Dates: January 1986-September 1994.

Objective: To provide general information about the basic principles of performance appraisal, career planning, and subordinate development.

Learning Outcome: Upon successful completion of this course, the student will be able to effectively document employee behavior, conduct performance appraisals, and coach and counsel employees.

Instruction: Major topics covered in the course are performance appraisal, documenting subordinate behavior, career planning and preparation, and employee development. Methods of instruction include lecture, discussion, written exercises, and role play.

Credit Recommendation: In the upper division baccalaureate degree category, 1 semester hour in Personnel Management (9/89) (9/94).

High Tech Evolution—Markets/Issues/Player (DQ 601)

Location: Advanced Education System, Irving, TX.

Length: 32 hours (4 days).

Dates: October 1988-October 1995.

Objective: To introduce recent developments, new issues, and technological advances in data communications, and review concepts previous covered in the Data Quest Program.

Learning Outcome: Upon successful completion of this course, the student will be able to: discuss telecommunications environment trends; discuss computing systems evolution; define point to point communications; discuss data network architecture updates; and define LAN and MAN technology; discuss ISDN.

Instruction: Major topics covered in the course are the telecommunications environment, computing system trends, point to point communication trends, data network architecture directions, LANs and MANs, and ISDN evolution. Methods of instruction include lecture and discussion.

Credit Recommendation: In the upper division baccalaureate degree category, 2 semester hours in Marketing-Sales (10/90).

Hiring the Experienced Manager (0205)

Location: St. Louis, MO; Dallas, TX; and other Southwestern Bell locations.

Length: 16 hours (2 days).

Dates: January 1988-Present.

Objective: To provide information about how to effectively identify, recruit, and hire management personnel.

Learning Outcome: Upon successful completion of this course, the student will be able to conduct effective selection interviews; collect and document information to make uniform, fair, and accurate employment decisions; and recruit and hire top applicants.

Instruction: Major topics covered in the course are interviewing and selection techniques and EEO/AAP policies and procedures. Methods of instruction include lecture, discussion, and exercises.

Credit Recommendation: In the lower division baccalaureate/associate degree category, 1 semester hour in Personnel Management (9/89) (9/94).

ICSC Initial Training-Customer Billing Inquiry Center (CBIC) (CBIC-IT)

Location: Various locations in Arkansas, Kansas, Missouri, Oklahoma, and Texas.

Length: 640 hours (16 weeks).

Dates: October 1983-Present.

Objective: To teach service representatives how to handle billing and collection activity for inter-exchange customer accounts.

Learning Outcome: Upon successful completion of this course, the student will be able to handle invoice billing, perform account validation procedures, investigate claims and issue adjustments on customers' accounts, perform collection and treatment activity, handle all customer contacts in an effective and businesslike manner, and use a variety of reference documents.

Instruction: Major topics covered in the course are independent exchange carriers, invoice billing, account validation, and claims investigation. Methods of instruction include class role plays, test cases, and examinations.

Credit Recommendation: In the lower division baccalaureate/associate degree category, 3 semester hours in Customer Relations (10/93).

ICSC Initial Training-Customer Point of Contact (CPOC) (CPOC-IT)

Location: Various locations in Arkansas, Kansas, Missouri, Oklahoma, and Texas.

Length: 480 hours (12 weeks).

Dates: October 1983-Present.

Objective: To teach service representatives how to handle service order activity for inter-exchange carriers.

Learning Outcome: Upon successful completion of this course, the student will be able to review customers' access service requests for accuracy and input those requests in a computerized system; coordinate with other departments to ensure a customer's order is completed on time; handle customer requests, questions, and complaints about access service; communicate with customers in an effective and businesslike manner; and use a variety of reference materials.

Instruction: Major topics covered in the course are customer contact skills, TIRKS, WATS Access service, and LEE Data terminals. Methods of instruction include class role play, test cases, and examinations.

Credit Recommendation: In the lower division baccalaureate/associate degree category, 3 semester hours in Customer Relations (10/93).

I/IA ESS Overview and Software (513)

Location: Dallas, TX.

Length: 32 hours (4 days).

Dates: May 1986-July 1993.

Objective: To provide the student with an understanding of the number one ESS processor and software documentation.

Learning Outcome: Upon successful completion of this course, the student will be able to describe the number one ESS processor and the peripheral equipment; identify and interpret input and output messages, and locate suspected faulty circuit packs; and identify software documentation.

Instruction: Major topics covered in the course are the identification of the I/IA processor, the peripheral equipment and the hardware/software documentation, and the identification of input and output messages, and alarms in order to locate faulty circuit packs. Methods of instruction include programmed, self-paced instruction.

Credit Recommendation: In the vocational certificate category, 1 semester hour in Electromechanical Troubleshooting (7/88).

Improving Business Relationships

Location: Management Development Training Centers in Arkansas, Kansas, Missouri, Oklahoma, Texas, plus suitcased throughout Texas.

Length: 24 hours (3 days).

Dates: January 1978-June 1993.

Objective: To provide the student with knowledge and skills in business communications, coaching, problem resolution, and planning and leading discussions.

Learning Outcome: Upon successful completion of this course, the student will be able to analyze interpersonal work relations requiring discussion; plan and conduct discussions with subordinates, peers, and superiors; and solve problems with maintaining self-esteem of others and self.

Instruction: Major topics covered in the course are communications, employee performance, difficult persons and situations, problem-solving and group dynamics, relationships with both subordinates and superiors.

Credit Recommendation: In the vocational certificate category, 1 semester hour in Improving Business Relationships, or in the lower division baccalaureate/associate degree category, 3 semester hours in Personnel Management if taken in conjunction with External Environments of a Public Utility, Goal Setting and Performance Evaluation, Interpersonal Business Communications, Introduction to Personnel Policy, Supervisory Skills Workshop, and Understanding Managing Performance (5/89).

Improving Customer Relations 1. Improving Customer Contact 2. Managing Customer Contact (ICC)

Location: St. Louis, MO; Dallas, TX; and other Southwestern Bell locations.

Length: 12 hours (1.5 days).

Dates: January 1988-September 1994.

Objective: *Course 1:* To provide the student with the basic communications-related skills needed to effectively interact with and serve customers in a sales setting. *Course 2:* To provide the student with basic information about how to effectively manage employees in customer contact positions.

Learning Outcome: *Course 1:* Upon successful completion of this course, the student will be able to handle interactions with customers and clients in a pleasant and courteous manner; employ effective listening and questioning skills; and identify the characteristics of dissatisfied customers and employ strategies to overcome the dissatisfaction. *Course 2:* Upon successful completion of this course, the student will be able to define and describe the characteristics of an organization's customer base and apply effective principles of communication in a customer service environment.

Instruction: *Course 1:* Major topics covered in the course are telephone courtesy, listening skills and techniques, principles of body language, questioning techniques, and problem-solving. *Course 2:* Major topics covered in the course are managing customer service employees, principles of effective service management, and listening and questioning skills. Methods of instruction include lecture, discussion, written exercises, role plays, and videotapes.

Credit Recommendation: *Courses 1 and 2:* In the lower division baccalaureate/associate degree category, 1 semester hour in Business Communications (9/89) (9/94). **NOTE:** Students must successfully complete both courses to receive the credit recommendation.

IMS Basic Data Communications Programming and Message Format Service (5035)

Location: St. Louis, MO.

Length: 40 hours (1 week).

Dates: February 1988-Present.

Objective: To teach the student how to program in an IMS data base/data communications environment.

Learning Outcome: Upon successful completion of this course, the student will be able to use an IMS online system for application development and implementation; use SWBT IMS guidelines and standards in the development of online IMS programs; and use BTS and the test IMS online systems to debug application programs.

Instruction: Major topics covered in the course are programming concepts of the IMS data base/data communications system including basic DC concepts and terminology associated with the IMS online system. Methods of instruction include lecture, in-class exercises, and workshop problems.

Credit Recommendation: In the upper division baccalaureate degree category, 2 semester hours in Computer Science, or Data Processing (7/88) (9/93).

IMS Message Format Service (ISC/TE 5050)

Location: Southwestern Bell, One Bell Center, St. Louis, MO.

Length: 56 hours (7 days).

Dates: March 1983-April 1995.

Objective: To provide students with practical experience in coding and generating MFS blocks required for message processing and in coding and executing an IMS MP program using BTS under TSO.

Learning Outcome: Upon successful completion of this course, the student will be able to code DIF/DOF, MID and MOD control blocks; design and code the MFS control statements to generate repeating fields and to use PF keys, DSCAs, system literals, logical paging, and operator logical paging; and generate MFS control blocks using the PDF MFSGEN panel.

Instruction: Major topics include operator training, MFS review, MFS screen design, using PF keys, MFS workshops, and logical paging. Methods of instruction include lecture/discussion, program coding, debugging, and execution.

Credit Recommendation: In the upper division baccalaureate degree category, 2 semester hours in Computer Science, Data Processing, or Computer Information Systems (4/90).

IMS/VS Concepts for Managers (ISC/TE 5012)

Location: Southwestern Bell, One Bell Center, St. Louis, MO.

Length: 16 hours (2 days).

Dates: February 1986-April 1995.

Objective: To teach students (managers) fundamental data base management system concepts and applications using the IBM IMS as an example.

Learning Outcome: Upon successful completion of this course, the student will be able to describe the basic properties of data base management systems; define/describe a data base schema; describe common data base utility operations such as back-up, recovery, and/or reorganization.

Instruction: Major topics include data base schemas and data definition language; data language; data base types and organization; data base utility programs and operations; and data base application program. Methods of instruction include lecture and classroom exercises.

Credit Recommendation: In the lower division baccalaureate/associate degree category, 1 semester hour in Business Data Processing or Management Information Systems (4/90).

IMS/VS: DL/I Programming (ICS/TE 5022)

Location: St. Louis, MO.

Length: 64 hours (8 days).

Dates: March 1983-Present.

Objective: To teach the student to program in an IMS batch environment using DL/I coding.

Learning Outcome: Upon successful completion of this course, the student will be able to describe DL/I terminology and its relationship within the database; code and test programs to access a DL/I database to do sequential searches; and replace segments, delete segments, and execute path cells.

Instruction: Major topics covered in the course is how to use programming code to alter and control the IMS data bases. Methods of instruction include lecture and programming laboratory.

Credit Recommendation: In the upper division baccalaureate degree category, 2 semester hours in Computer Science or Data Processing (7/88) (10/93).

Influence Management

Location: Management Development Training Centers in Arkansas, Kansas, Missouri, Oklahoma, Texas, plus suitcased throughout Texas.

Length: 24 hours (3 days).

Dates: August 1988-May 1994.

Objective: To provide the student with the knowledge necessary to identify a person's influence role in a group and to develop his or her ability to influence in leading.

Learning Outcome: Upon successful completion of this course, students will have an awareness of the influence process; a plan for improvement in performing high priority influence practices; improved influence practices and tactics to allow them to implement their plan; a system for tracking the progress of their plan; and plans for involving others in their improvement efforts.

Instruction: Major topics covered in the course are identification of the manager's influence environment, conflict anticipation and management in working relationships, methods of enhancing rapport in the work group, and the effective use of influence to make high-quality decisions. Methods of Instruction Include a precourse computerized feedback on the participant's influence skills as compared to the top managers in the Fortune 500 companies. Methods of instruction include lectures, audiovisual materials, group exercises, and role playing.

Credit Recommendation: In the upper division baccalaureate degree category, 1 semester hour in Organizational Behavior (5/89).

Integrated Information and Connection (DQ 501, 501.5)

Location: Advanced Education System, Irving, TX.

Length: 32 hours (4 days).

Dates: October 1988-October 1995.

Objective: To introduce digital transmission technology, including network interconnectivity.

Learning Outcome: Upon successful completion of this course, the student will be able to describe the purpose and function of channel banks and digital cross-connect systems; discuss several major issues concerning digital transmissions including framing, formats, and clear channel techniques; and compare and contrast various alternate techniques for digitizing speech.

Instruction: Major topics covered in the course are voice, data, and image integration; T carrier fundamentals; data network alternatives; transmission systems; and computer networking.

Credit Recommendation: In the upper division baccalaureate degree category, 2 semester hours in Telecommunications (10/90).

Interaction Management (0219)

Location: St. Louis, MO; Dallas, TX; and other locations in Missouri, Texas, Oklahoma, Arkansas, and Kansas.

Length: 30 hours (4 days).

Dates: August 1990-Present.

Objective: To develop effective supervisory and leadership skills.

Learning Outcome: Upon successful completion of this course, the student will be able to understand and apply the principles of supervisory leadership; build better relationships with subordinates; and more effectively communicate, motivate, coach, and apply disciplinary skills.

Instruction: Major topics covered in the course are the principles of leadership and the day-to-day measurement skills of communications, coaching, motivation, problem-solving, and disciplinary techniques. Methods of instruction include lecture, discussion, classroom exercises, case studies, role playing, and problem-solving.

Credit Recommendation: In the lower division baccalaureate/associate degree category, 2 semester hours in Supervisory Management (9/90) (9/94).

Interpersonal Business Communications (Interpersonal Communications Workshop)

Location: Management Development Training Centers in Arkansas, Kansas, Missouri, Oklahoma, Texas, plus suitcased throughout Texas.

Length: 16 hours (2 days).

Dates: January 1972-May 1994.

Objective: To improve the student's interpersonal communications in the work environment.

Learning Outcome: Upon successful completion of this course, the student will be able to identify roadblocks to business communications; use and interpret effective verbal and nonverbal communications; and develop assertive expression, conflict resolution skills, and practice their use.

Instruction: Major topics covered in the course are barriers to communication and the communication process, skills in developing communicational content and styles, assertive behavior and self-assessment, listening, and handling conflict.

Credit Recommendation: In the vocational certificate category, 1 semester hour in Interpersonal Business Communications, or in the lower division baccalaureate/associate degree category, 3 semester hours in Personnel Management if taken in conjunction with External Environments of a Public Utility, Goal Setting and Performance Evaluation, Improving Business Relationships, Introduction to Personnel Policy, Supervisory Skills Workshop, and Understanding Managing Performance (5/89).

Introduction to C Programming/UNIX (8550)

Location: St. Louis, MO and Dallas, TX.

Length: 40 hours (5 days).

Dates: January 1986-Present.

Objective: To provide the experienced programmer with knowledge of the basic structure and syntax of the C programming language.

Learning Outcome: Upon successful completion of this course, the student will be able to create, compile, and execute basic C programs in the UNIX environment; describe how a C program interfaces with the UNIX system; and describe the use of arithmetic, logical, and relational operators in the C language.

Instruction: Major topics covered in the course are fundamental data types, operators and data conversion, control structures and statements, decimal data types and functions, storage classifications, pointers, and libraries. Methods of instruction include lecture, discussion, classroom exercises, and problem-solving.

Credit Recommendation: In the lower division baccalaureate/associate degree category, 2 semester hours in Computer Information Systems, Computer Science, or Data Processing (1/89) (10/93) **NOTE:** Duplicate credit cannot be given for course 8550D or 8556.

Introduction to Data Base Systems and Programming (D-954, D-555)

Location: Southwestern Bell at St. Louis, San Antonio, Mission, Topeka, Wichita, and Oklahoma City.

Length: 32 hours (4 days).

Dates: January 1986-April 1995.

Objective: To teach the student fundamental data base management system concepts and programming techniques.

Learning Outcome: Upon successful completion of this course, the student will be able to perform fundamental data base operations such as building entry forms, updating records and creating data base reports; and write data base programs including query, update, and report programs.

Instruction: Major topics covered in the course are creation and modification of data base structures, data base principles and organization, program flow control, data base program concepts, input processing, output report, and program debugging. Methods of instruction include lecture, computer-assisted instruction, video, and laboratory.

Credit Recommendation: In the lower division baccalaureate/associate degree category, 1 semester hour in Data Processing (4/90).

Introduction to DOS/C Programming (8550D)

Location: St. Louis, MO.

Length: 40 hours (5 days).

Dates: January 1992-Present.

Objective: To provide the experienced programmer with knowledge of the basic structure and syntax of the C Programming language.

Learning Outcome: Upon successful completion of this course, the student will be able to create, compile, and execute basic C programs in the DOS environment; describe how a C program interfaces with the DOS system; and describe the use of arithmetic, and logical and relational operators in the C language.

Instruction: Major topics covered in the course are fundamental data types, operators and data conversion, control structures and statements, decimal data types and functions, storage classifications, pointers, and libraries. Methods of instruction include lecture, discussion, classroom exercises, and problem solving.

Credit Recommendation: In the lower division baccalaureate/associate degree category, 2 semester hours in Computer Information Systems, Computer Science, or Data Processing (10/93). **NOTE:** Duplicate credit should not be given for 8550 or 8556.

Introduction to ESS and Minicomputer Fundamentals (511)

Location: Dallas, TX.

Length: 80 hours (10 days).

Dates: December 1983-July 1993.

Objective: To provide the student with general knowledge in computer fundamentals as used in the stored program switching system.

Learning Outcome: Upon successful completion of this course, the student will be able to understand the binary, octal, and hexidecimal numbering systems; describe the operation of diodes and transistors and applications in logic and computer fundamentals; and describe the use of the oscilloscope in analyzing the equipment and communication busses.

Instruction: Major topics covered in the course are basic electronic component operation in the digital logic application area. Number bases are covered with application to computers. Taught are oscilloscope and its application to troubleshooting the computer and the communication busses. Methods of instruction include self-paced, programmed instruction.

Credit Recommendation: In the lower division baccalaureate/associate degree category, 2 semester hours in Electronics Technology (7/88).

Introduction to IPT/PET (ISC/TE 40501) and SWBT Test Complex (ISC/TE 3010) and ISPF/PDF (ISC/TE 6091) and Basic JCL Workshop (ISC/TE 3031)

Location: Southwestern Bell, One Bell Center, St. Louis, MO.

Length: 56 hours (7 days).

Dates: January 1982-April 1995.

Objective: General introduction to the major components of a computing environment, along with some basic principles of user interaction with large computer systems.

Learning Outcome: Upon successful completion of this course, the student will be able to describe the basic principles of the way a computer stores information; describe the complexity of large computing environments and explain where each component fits into the global picture; explain the advantages of program development tools, and demonstrate the use of ISPF/PDF programs and the use of Basic Job Control Language.

Instruction: Major topics include machine representation of information, including various number systems and code; understanding the functions of each of the major components of a large computing environment; learning the facilities provided by the ISPF/PDF group of programs; and studying the MVS/XA job control language in an MVS/XA environment. Methods of instruction include lecture, discussion, classroom exercises, case studies, role playing, problem-solving programming, debugging, and execution.

Credit Recommendation: In the lower division baccalaureate/associate degree category, 2 semester hours in Computer Science, Computer Information Systems, Management Information Systems, or Data Processing (4/90).

Introduction to Microcomputers (D-950 and D-956 or D-957)

Location: Southwestern Bell at St. Louis, San Antonio, Mission, Topeka, Wichita, and Oklahoma City.

Length: 32 hours (4 days).

Dates: January 1986-December 1996.

Objective: To provide students with a comprehensive understanding of fundamental microcomputer hardware and software, including the use of word processors.

Learning Outcome: Upon successful completion of this course, the student will be able to describe the fundamental components and organization of a microcomputer system; operate a microcomputer system, including booting, creating files, performing backup, etc.; and operate the disk operating system, DOS, and word processing application software.

Instruction: Major topics covered in the course include microcomputer hardware components, disk operating system concepts, disk operation procedures, fundamental text editor operation, fundamental file system concepts and operations, and word processing operation. Methods of instruction include lecture, laboratory, problem-solving, and computer-assisted video.

Credit Recommendation: In the lower division baccalaureate/associate degree category, 1 semester hour in Data Processing, Management Information Systems, or Computer Science (4/90) (12/91). **NOTE:** D-950 and D-956 or D-957 must be completed.

Introduction to MVS/C Programming (8556)

Location: St. Louis, MO.

Length: 75 hours (2 weeks).

Dates: July 1991-Present.

Objective: To provide the experienced programmer with knowledge of the basic structure and syntax of the C programming language.

Learning Outcome: Upon successful completion of this course, the student will be able to create, compile, and execute basic C programs in the MVS environment; describe how a C program interfaces with the MVS system; and describe the use of arithmetic, logical, and relational operators in the C language.

Instruction: Major topics covered in the course are fundamental data types;

operators and data conversion; control structures and statements; decimal data types and functions; and storage classifications, pointers, and libraries. Methods of instruction include lecture, discussion, classroom exercises, and problem solving.

Credit Recommendation: In the lower division baccalaureate/associate degree category, 2 semester hours in Computer Information Systems, Computer Science, or Data Processing (10/93). **NOTE**: Duplicate credit cannot be given for 8550 or 8550D.

Introduction to Personnel Policy (Initial Management Training)

Location: Management Development Training Centers in Arkansas, Kansas, Missouri, Oklahoma, and Texas.

Length: 16 hours (2 days).

Dates: July 1980-May 1994.

Objective: To provide the student with the skills and knowledge to enable him or her to master specific administrative procedures.

Learning Outcome: Upon successful completion of this course, the student will be able to interpret and apply corporate missions, goals, and policies; and implement correctly personnel policies and procedures, including salary administration, EEO, affirmative action, and privacy.

Instruction: Major topics covered in the course are corporate mission, goals and policies, how the job fits into the scope of Southwestern Bell Telephone Company, resources available that enable performance of administrative responsibilities, equal employment opportunity, affirmative action program, and privacy program.

Credit Recommendation: In the vocational certificate category, 1 semester hour in Personnel Management, or in the lower division baccalaureate/associate degree category, 3 semester hours in Personnel Management if taken in conjunction with External Environments of a Public Utility, Goal Setting and Performance Evaluation, Improving Business Relationships, Interpersonal Business Communications, Supervisory Skills Workshop, and Understanding Managing Performance (5/89).

Introduction to Relational Databases (DB2 Overview [5510]) (DB2 SQL & QMF for End Users [5540])

Location: St. Louis, MO.

Length: 26 hours (4 days).

Dates: February 1989-Present.

Objective: To introduce the student to the concepts of a relational database, a structured query language, and a query facility through the study of DB2, SQL, and QMF.

Learning Outcome: Upon successful completion of this course, the student will be able to define a relational database; explain how such databases store and access data; understand the relationship between a query management facility and an associated database; write SQL statements to access and update the data; and use QMF panels for formatting reports.

Instruction: Major topics covered in the course are introduction to DB2; relationship between QMF and DB2; statements; QMF panels; QMF commands; and QMF procedures. Methods of instruction include lecture, discussion, and classroom exercises in SQL coding, debugging, and execution; and QMF report formatting.

Credit Recommendation: In the lower division baccalaureate/associate degree category, 1 semester hour in Computer Science, Computer Information Systems, or Data Processing (10/93).

Introduction to Sales Training Supervision (Supervisory Consultant Selling Skills [615002])

Location: St. Louis, MO; Irving, TX.

Length: 24 hours (3 days).

Dates: January 1988-January 1994.

Objective: To provide the student with a basis for evaluating and advising sales people in making an initial sales contact, and developing and using effective selling skills.

Learning Outcome: Upon successful completion of this course, the student will be able to identify and use the steps in making an initial contact with a client; determine whether the sales person's activity and sales technique are effective; and identify ways of developing improved selling skills.

Instruction: Major topics covered in the course are a review of selling fundamentals, coaching and development of selling skills, and practice and evaluation of sales technique. Methods of instruction include lecture, group discussion, group exercises, written exercises, role playing, and videotape/slides.

Credit Recommendation: In the upper division baccalaureate degree category, 1 semester hour in Sales Supervision (1/89).

Introduction to Telephony (SWBT II)/Data Communications (SWGT12)

Location: Advanced Education System, Irving, TX.

Length: 32 hours (4 days).

Dates: October 1988-October 1995.

Objective: To introduce basic vocabulary of telephony and data communications.

Learning Outcome: Upon successful completion of this course, the student will be able to trace the sequence of events that must occur to provide a telephone circuit; differentiate between space and time division switching; describe the structure of frequency and time division carrier systems; discuss the fundamental structure of a computer and the mechanisms for information storage; and relate the bandwidth of a link to its information-carrying capacity.

Instruction: Major topics covered in the course are fundamentals of networks, switching systems, traffic engineering, signaling, carrier systems, data communications, protocols, and applications. Methods of instruction include lecture and discussion.

Credit Recommendation: In the lower division baccalaureate/associate degree category, 2 semester hours in Telecommunications (10/90).

Introduction to UNIX Operating Systems and Shell Programming 1. UNIX Orientation (8500) 2. The Shell and Editing (8510) 3. Tools (8540) 4. Shell Programming (8580)

Location: St. Louis, MO; and training centers in Kansas, Arkansas, Oklahoma, and Texas.

Length: 1. 7.5 hours (1 day); 2. 22.5 hours (3 days); 3. 7.5 hours (1 day); 4. 32 hours (4 days).

Dates: January 1986-Present.

Objective: To give the student a general awareness of data processing, basic concepts, and some elementary hands-on experience with hardware and software systems.

Learning Outcome: Upon successful completion of this course, the student will be able to access the UNIX system and use system communications; build a personal file system that includes directions; use basic shell commands and control structures; use shell quoting mechanisms to escape the meaning of special characters; use redirection of input and output in conjunction with shell programs; use special shell variables and parameters and user-defined variables within a shell program; and use interactive execution of a shell program as well as commands and facilities.

Instruction: Major topics covered in the course are orientation to the UNIX system, basic shell commands, use of the UNIX system for program development, documentation, and data processing, and programming language capabilities of the UNIX shell. Methods of instruction include lecture, discussion, and classroom exercises.

Credit Recommendation: In the lower division baccalaureate/associate degree category, 3 semester hours in Computer Information Systems, Computer Science, or Data Processing (1/89) (10/93). **NOTE**: Students must complete all four courses to receive the credit.

Introduction to Windows 3.1 (1580/PC1580/1560)
Introduction to Word for Windows (1584/PC1584)
Intermediate Word for Windows (1586/PC1586)
Introduction to Excel for Windows (1588/PC1588)

Location: St. Louis, MO.

Length: 26.5 hours (4 days).

Dates: January 1993-Present.

Objective: To teach students how to use the features of graphical user interface (Windows 3.1), a word processor tool (Word for Windows), and a spreadsheet tool (Excel for Windows).

Learning Outcome: Upon successful completion of this course, the student will be able to use the mouse, select a menu, open and close a group of windows, and use the program manager and file manager programs; and learn how to use most of the features of a windows-based word processor tool and those of a windows-based spreadsheet tool.

Instruction: Major topics covered in the course are communicating with windows; multiple windows; using an application; managing files and directories; use of style sheets; formatting; creating headers and footers; editing documents; enhancing a worksheet; creating a chart document; and using functions and macros. Methods of instruction include lecture, discussion, computer-assisted videotapes, and laboratory exercises.

Credit Recommendation: In the lower division baccalaureate/associate degree category, 2 semester hours Computer Information Systems, Computer Science, or Data Processing (10/93). **NOTE**: All four courses must by completed to receive the credit recommendation. Students should not receive additional credit upon completion of other courses with similar course content.

ISDN (DQ 303)

Location: Advanced Education System, Irving, TX.

Length: 32 hours (4 days).

Dates: October 1988-October 1995.

Objective: To provide an introduction to the evolution of digital networks and ISDN.

Learning Outcome: Upon successful completion of this course, the student will be able to describe the evolution of the network to an all-digital environment; discuss physical, data link, and signaling protocols for ISDN; and identify possible ISDN applications.

Instruction: Major topics covered in the course are ISDN evolution, overview, the D channel, physical layer, and signaling system. Methods of instruction include lecture, discussion, and laboratory exercises.

Credit Recommendation: In the upper division baccalaureate degree category, 2 semester hours in Telecommunications (10/90).

ISDN Fundamentals (1033)

Location: Irving, TX.

Length: 40 hours (1 week).

Dates: November 1990-December 1996.

Objective: To provide an overview of basic ISDN concepts, including functional groupings of equipment, reference points, and transmission concepts.

Learning Outcome: Upon successful completion of this course, the student will have a working knowledge of the architecture and services of ISDN to include installation options, management of power supplier, as well as ISDN configurations related to terminal displays, coaxial eliminators, circuits connectivity, and testing procedures.

Instruction: Major topics covered in the course are basic ISDN concepts; physical layer hardware; physical layer transmission concepts; data link construction and maintenance, and network layer construction and maintenance. Methods of instruction include lecture, discussion, and laboratory.

Credit Recommendation: In the upper division baccalaureate degree category, 2 semester hours in Telecommunications (12/91).

Leadership and Teamwork (0218)

Location: St. Louis, MO; Dallas, TX; and other locations in Missouri, Texas, Oklahoma, Arkansas, and Kansas.

Length: 24 hours (3 days).

Dates: August 1990-Present.

Objective: To learn and apply the skills of leadership.

Learning Outcome: Upon successful completion of this course, the student will be able to improve his or her supervisory skills by selling ideas, negotiating differences, and obtaining agreements and the support of subordinates.

Instruction: Major topics covered in the course are effective listening; building interpersonal rapport skills; analytical problem-solving; managing resistance; and obtaining commitments. Methods of instruction include lecture, discussion, classroom exercises, case studies, role playing, and problem-solving.

Credit Recommendation: In the lower division baccalaureate/associate degree category, 2 semester hours in Management or Communications (9/90) (9/94).

Leadership Skills Workshop

Location: Management Development Training Centers in Arkansas, Kansas, Missouri, Oklahoma, and 3 centers in Texas.

Length: 24 hours (3 days).

Dates: October 1972-July 1993.

Objective: To introduce the student to functions and responsibilities of first-level managers and to introduce the student to various leadership decision styles and explore their impact on work group dynamics.

Learning Outcome: Upon successful completion of this course, the student will be able to identify, choose, and develop a flexible personal leadership style and create an effective and productive small work group.

Instruction: Major topics covered in the course are time management, planning and implementation, problem-solving, decision-making, communication feedback, small group dynamics, decision styles, conducting meetings, formal presentations, and moving operations from one location to another. Methods of instruction include lecture and multiple experiential methods.

Credit Recommendation: In the upper division baccalaureate degree category, 1 semester hour in Introduction to Supervision or Leadership (7/88).

Light Guide Design (D-680)

Location: Advanced Education System, Irving, TX.

Length: 40 hours (1 week).

Dates: January 1983-March 1994.

Objective: To teach the student to design fiber optic transmission systems and study the latest technology in design criteria.

Learning Outcome: Upon successful completion of this course, the student will be able to describe properties of lightwave and fiber optic transmission systems; design fiber optic transmission loops; and specify test criteria and procedures for fiber optic transmission systems.

Instruction: Major topics covered in the course are principles of lightwave transmission, fiber optic technology, digital data transmission, and multiplexing/demultiplexing. Methods of instruction include lecture, discussion, classroom exercises, and computer-assisted instruction.

Credit Recommendation: In the upper division baccalaureate degree category, 1 semester hour in Telecommunications (3/89).

Local Area Network: Installation and Maintenance (CO LAN/1032)

Location: Irving, TX.

Length: 40 hours (1 week).

Dates: January 1991-December 1996.

Objective: To provide students with a working knowledge of Local Area Networks (LAN) and Central Office Networks (CO-LAN). Emphasis is placed on the hardware installation and maintenance of LAN equipment.

Learning Outcome: Upon successful completion of this course, the student will be able to test and locate faults on coaxial and fiber optic media; install communications servers and transceivers on an Ethernet Bus; use a LAN analyzer to identify faulty stations; load user addresses in the communication server; test wideband transmission facilities for CO-LAN; and perform routine maintenance and installation.

Instruction: Major topics covered in the course are the foundation for implementation of an Ethernet LAN using 3Com/bridge equipment; coax and fiber are the media used in conjunction with the LAN implementation; CO-LAN will demonstrate installation of central office and customer-based voice data multiplexers; emphasis is placed on the AT&T Datakit II as the data switch; and hardware implementation of the Datakit is covered in detail. Methods of instruction include lecture, discussion, exercises, and laboratory.

Credit Recommendation: In the lower division baccalaureate/associate degree category, 2 semester hours in Telecom--munication (12/91).

Local Area Networks (DQ 203)

Location: Advanced Education System, Irving, TX.

Length: 16 hours (2 days).

Dates: October 1988-October 1995.

Objective: To overview Local Area Network (LAN) technology and applications.

Learning Outcome: Upon successful completion of this course, the student will be able to enumerate the taxonomic variable for classifying LANs; compare and contrast various premises, wiring plans; explain the structure and function of bridges, gateways, and routers; and discuss methods of interconnecting LANs.

Instruction: Major topics covered in the course are LAN technology, topology and media, logical link control, central office local area network, and network performance. Methods of instruction include lecture and discussion.

Credit Recommendation: In the upper division baccalaureate degree category, 1 semester hour in Computer Science or Telecommunications (10/90).

Loop Electronics Design (D-663)

Location: Irving, TX; St. Louis, MO; and Oklahoma City, OK.

Length: 40 hours (1 week).

Dates: January 1984-March 1994.

Objective: To teach the student to produce detailed technical design of digital carrier systems.

Learning Outcome: Upon successful completion of this course, the student will be able to design communications loop remote terminal and repeater locations; produce detailed network testing and conditioning specifications; and describe digital communication loop design requirements.

Instruction: Major topics covered in the course are basic analog and digital switching, basic signal impairment, and digital loop design. Methods of instruction include lecture, discussion, and computer-assisted design projects.

Credit Recommendation: In the upper division baccalaureate degree category, 1 semester hour in Telecommunications (3/89).

Loop Engineering Assignment Data (D-685)

Location: Southwestern Bell Education Centers.

Length: 24 hours (3 days).

Dates: April 1982-March 1994.

Objective: To teach the student the development, structure, and application of Loop Engineering Information Systems (LEIS).

Learning Outcome: Upon successful completion of this course, the student will be able to state the purpose and describe the operation of an automated data collection analysis program; use automated planning reports to complete loop technology planning activities; and use the UNIX operating system to create, edit, and print automated planning documents and reports.

Instruction: Major topics covered in the course are the fundamentals of Loop Engineering Information System (LEIS), UNIX operating system, use of the UNIX editor (vi), use of data base reports, and generation and use of Loop Engineering Reports. Methods of instruction include lecture, discussion, computer-assisted instruction, and laboratory projects.

Credit Recommendation: In the upper division baccalaureate degree category, 1 semester hour in Telecommunications (3/89). **NOTE:** Students may receive credit only if Economic Study Workshop (D-686) has been successfully completed.

Loop Technology Planning Fundamentals (D-694)

Location: Advanced Education System, Irving, TX.

Length: 40 hours (1 week).

Dates: August 1988-March 1994.

Objective: To teach the student fundamental communications loop technology planning skills.

Learning Outcome: Upon successful completion of this course, the student will be able to establish network planning areas; gather necessary design and planning data; and analyze existing loop technology plans.

Instruction: Major topics covered in the course are loop technology planning fundamentals, long-range planning consideration, planning software tools, and loop technology planning tasks. Methods of instruction include lecture, discussion, case studies, and computer/video-assisted instruction.

Credit Recommendation: In the upper division baccalaureate degree category, 1 semester hour in Telecommunications (3/89).

Lotus 1-2-3 Spreadsheet and Advanced Lotus 1-2-3 (D-952, D-953)

Location: Southwestern Bell at St. Louis, San Antonio, Mission, Topeka, Wichita, and Oklahoma City.

Length: 32 hours (4 days).

Dates: January 1986-April 1995.

Objective: To teach students to use microcomputer spreadsheet software, Lotus 1-2-3.

Learning Outcome: Upon successful completion of this course, the student will be able to describe typical electronic spreadsheet operations and program functions; create, update, and modify electronic spreadsheets; and extract, combine, import, and translate data files using advanced file commands.

Instruction: Major topics include fundamental spreadsheet concepts, fundamental spreadsheet operations, file processing, spreadsheet functions and programs, graphing and graph commands. Methods of instruction include lecture, laboratory, computer-assisted videotape, and classroom exercises.

Credit Recommendation: In the lower division baccalaureate/associate degree category, 1 semester hour in Computer Science or Data Processing (4/90). **NOTE:** Both courses must be completed for this credit.

Management Career Development

Location: Management Development Training Centers in Arkansas, Kansas, Missouri, Oklahoma, and Texas.

Length: 8 hours (1 day).

Dates: March 1989-May 1989.

Objective: To identify the student's specific roles and responsibilities in the management career development process.

Learning Outcome: Upon successful completion of this course, the student will be able to utilize resources to develop and evaluate realistic career plans; prepare for a career development discussion and update the MISS employee profile; evaluate risks and benefits associated with the process; support subordinates' participation in the career development process; provide career guidance to subordinates; and manage the career development of subordinates.

Instruction: Major topics covered in the course are career development, guidance and MISS, supervisor's responsibilities, career guidance, employee development, risks, and administration of the system.

Credit Recommendation: In the upper division baccalaureate degree category, 2 semester hours in Career Counseling, Distributive Education, or Personnel Management (5/89). **NOTE:** In order to receive credit, the student must successfully complete this course in conjunction with Managing Professional Growth and Understanding Managing Performance.

Management Orientation

Location: St. Louis, MO; Dallas, TX; and other Southwestern Bell locations.

Length: 16 hours (2 days).

Dates: January 1984-Present.

Objective: To provide an introduction to human resource management concepts and policies required to be understood and administered at the supervisory management level.

Learning Outcome: Upon successful completion of this course, the student will be familiar with personnel policies and procedures at the operational level of an organization; knowledgeable regarding sources of additional information of organizational policies and procedures; and able to initiate problem-solving procedures when job performance is not satisfactory.

Instruction: Major topics covered in the course are employee benefit policies and procedures, fundamental personnel policies, procedures for handling employee performance problems, and surveys of identifying and handling procedures of EEOC, affirmative action, and sexual harassment issues. Methods of instruction include lecture, role playing, and laboratory instruction.

Credit Recommendation: In the lower division baccalaureate/associate degree category, 1 semester hour in Human Resources Management or Personnel Management (2/90) (9/94).

Manager's Camp (WRLSS-MGMT)

Location: Various locations in the United States and Great Britain.

Length: 36 hours.

Dates: July 1996-Present.

Objective: To provide wireless management employees with SBC's expectations of skills and actions, knowledge of laws that affect conduct and employment practices, procedures for necessary supervisory tasks such as performance appraisals and techniques for effective leadership.

Learning Outcome: Upon completion of this course, the student will be able to understand the importance of share owner value, administrative requirements of key company policies, management, and interpersonal skills needed to build internal partnerships and meet external customer requirements; and effectively coach and counsel employees on the advantages of a positive labor environment.

Instruction: Major topics covered in the course are SBC corporate overview, leadership and teamwork, establishing dialogue, taking a positive approach, providing feedback, motivating improved performance, coaching for commitment, equal employment opportunity/affirmative action, staffing and interviewing skills, sexual harassment in the workplace, positive discipline, performance appraisal, conducting lawful termination, and employee assistance program. Methods of instruction include lecture, video presentations, role playing, group discussions, and examinations.

Credit Recommendation: In the upper division baccalaureate degree category, 2 semester hours in Supervision or Management (11/97).

1. Managing Change
2. Managing Personal Crisis in the Workplace

Location: Missouri, Arkansas, Texas, Oklahoma, Kansas and selected other locations.

Length: *Versions 1 and 2:* 8 hours (1 day).

Dates: *Version 1:* January 1992-Present; *Version 2:* January 1991-Present.

Objective: *Version 1:* To assist managers in understanding and implementing change in their respective organizations. *Version 2:* To enable understanding personal behavior patterns in a crisis and to manage self and others in coping and healing.

Learning Outcome: *Version 1:* Upon successful completion of this course, the student will be able to better manage the implementation of change within an organization; understand his/her personal role in the change process; provide a role model for implementing change; avoid failure paths in dealing with change. *Version 2:* Upon successful completion of this course, the student will be able to help others cope with a personal crisis; understand the grieving/healing process; and cope with one's personal reactions to a crisis.

Instruction: *Version 1:* Major topics covered in the course are strategies for managing change; model for managing change; techniques for selling change and coping with change. *Version 2:* Major topics covered in the course are self-management in a crisis situation; the healing process for self and others; and leadership techniques to transcend the crisis. Methods of instruction for both courses include lecture, discussion, classroom exercises, case studies, role playing, and problem solving.

Credit Recommendation: In the lower division baccalaureate/associate degree category, 1 semester hour in Organizational Behavior or Personnel Management only when both Managing Change and Managing Personal Crisis in the Workplace are taken (9/92) (9/94).

1. Managing Diversity
2. Women and Men: Partners in the Workplace (0223)

Location: Various Southwestern Bell locations.

Length: *Versions 1 and 2:* 16 hours (2 days).

Dates: *Version 1:* January 1991-Present; *Version 2:* January 1990-Present.

Objective: To increase awareness of various issues present in today's increasingly diverse workforce.

Learning Outcome: Upon successful completion of this course, the student will be able to recognize and understand human and cultural differences in the workplace; take concrete behavioral steps to improve communications between men and women; better manage uncomfortable situations with the other sex; and understand the impact of language and behavior on others.

Instruction: Major topics covered in the course are awareness of intercultural differences, gender stereotypes, and behavioral skill development. Methods of instruction include lecture, cases, role playing, and videotape.

Credit Recommendation: In the lower division baccalaureate/associate degree category, 2 semester hours in Management or Human Resource Development only when both Managing Diversity and Women and Men: Partners in the Work-place are taken (9/91) (9/94).

Managing Interpersonal Relationships

Location: St. Louis, MO; Dallas, TX; and other Southwestern Bell locations.

Length: 20 hours (2.5 days).

Dates: January 1986-September 1994.

Objective: To improve communication skills and overcome barriers to effective communications.

Learning Outcome: Upon successful completion of this course, the student will be able to understand the fundamental need for effective communications; identify situations of ineffective communications; and use knowledge of social styles to overcome barriers to effective communications.

Instruction: Major topics covered in the course are behavior observation, awareness, and formulation of communication strategy. Methods of instruction include lecture, group discussion, role play, and videotapes.

Credit Recommendation: In the lower division baccalaureate/associate degree category, 1 semester hour in Organizational Behavior (9/89) (9/94).

Managing Labor Relations I

Location: Management Development Training Centers in Arkansas, Kansas, Missouri, Oklahoma, Texas, plus suitcased throughout Texas.

Length: 16 hours (2 days).

Dates: August 1983-May 1994.

Objective: To allow the student to acquire knowledge and skills in the discussion and application of labor policies, agreements, and contracts with the Communication Workers of America.

Learning Outcome: Upon successful completion of this course, the student will be able to discuss and apply policies, legal aspects, and labor contracts of the company; interpret and manage job responsibilities related to labor relations and provide documentation; and apply the labor agreement provisions in day-to-day employee problems.

Instruction: Major topics covered in the course are union organization and collective bargaining, Communication Workers of America contracts and labor relations, employee classifications and compensation, hours of work and work schedules, holidays, vacations and excused work days, absence from duty, correcting people/performance problems, responding to employee complaints, separation from service, job changes, and travel and transportation.

Credit Recommendation: In the upper division baccalaureate degree category, 1 semester hour in Personnel Management and Supervision (5/89).

Managing Labor Relations II

Location: Management Development Training Centers in Arkansas, Kansas, Missouri, Oklahoma, Texas, plus suitcased throughout Texas.

Length: 16 hours (2 days).

Dates: August 1983-May 1994.

Objective: To allow the student to acquire knowledge and skills in the discussion and application of labor policies, agreements and contracts with the Communication Workers of America, and problem-solving in personnel development, documentation, insubordination, and grievances.

Learning Outcome: Upon successful completion of this course, the student will be able to interpret problems and devise solutions relating to CWA contracts and follow satisfactory procedures relating to all aspects of labor contracts and relations with CWA.

Instruction: Major topics covered in the course are settling grievances, developing managers, handling insubordination, and documentation.

Credit Recommendation: In the upper division baccalaureate degree category, 1 semester hour in Labor Relations or Personnel Management and Supervision (5/89).

Managing Professional Growth

Location: Management Development Training Centers in Arkansas, Kansas, Missouri, Oklahoma, Texas, plus suitcased throughout Texas.

Length: 16 hours (2 days).

Dates: May 1987-May 1994.

Objective: To design an individual professional growth/development plan.

Learning Outcome: Upon successful completion of this course, the student will be able to clarify performance expectations; improve effectiveness on current job; capitalize on individual strengths; and lead a discussion with his or her supervisor about the professional development plan.

Instruction: Major topics covered in the course are completing a questionnaire describing the skills required in the current job and the current strengths and weaknesses of the individual, and developing a process for comparing the individual's perceptions with those of the supervisor's.

Credit Recommendation: In the upper division baccalaureate degree category, 2 semester hours in Career Counseling, Distributive Education, or Personnel Management (5/89). **NOTE:** In order to receive credit, the student must successfully complete this course in conjunction with Management Career Development and Understanding Managing Performance.

Managing Professional Growth (0208)

Location: St. Louis, MO; Dallas, TX; and other Southwestern Bell locations.

Length: 16 hours (2 days).

Dates: January 1986-Present.

Objective: To enable the student to perform a self-evaluation of values, resources, and goals in order to develop career expectations.

Learning Outcome: Upon successful completion of this course, the student will be able to determine and evaluate personal values; analyze talents and deficiencies as they pertain to job satisfaction; and develop a plan to maximize the student's potential capacity for growth.

Instruction: Major topics covered in the course are the determination of values, establishing personal priorities, ascertaining talents and educational or training deficiencies, managing job satisfaction, and preparing for personal career growth.

Credit Recommendation: In the lower division baccalaureate/associate degree category, 1 semester hour in Personnel Management (9/89) (9/94).

Managing Sales Performance

Location: Various locations in the United States and Great Britain.

Length: 16 hours (2 days).

Dates: January 1995-Present.

Objective: To provide the sales manager with the language, values and skills to improve the potential of the sales team.

Learning Outcome: Upon successful completion of this course, the student will be able to improve, maintain and enhance the performance of sales people; coach to improve performance and reinforce successful performance; counsel and direct sales processes and principles and create developmental action plans for achieving maximum performance in the sales force.

Instruction: Major topics covered in the course are sales manager as coach; coaching process; coaching techniques for relating; coaching techniques for discovering; coaching techniques for advocating and supporting.

Credit Recommendation: In the lower division baccalaureate/associate degree category, 1 hour in Sales Management (9/95).

Managing Sales Productivity

Location: Various locations in the United States and Great Britain.

Length: 24 hours (3 days).

Dates: January 1995-Present.

Objective: To provide sales managers with the core competencies and skills to improve productivity, model competence and creative direction for the sales force.

Learning Outcome: Upon successful completion of this course, the student will be able to develop the skills necessary for effective daily interaction with sales people; assess and strengthen coaching skills; handle objections from sales people more effectively; establish meaningful performance objectives with sales people; efficiently prepare for and conduct joint sales calls; prepare and conduct effective sales meetings; effectively manage both time and territory.

Instruction: Major topics covered in the course are coaching for sales productivity; principles of effective selling; fundamental communication skills handling objections; establishing performance objectives; guidelines for effective sales meetings; and planning for performance improvement. Methods of instruction include lecture, discussion classroom exercises, a/v material, computer assisted instruction.

Credit Recommendation: In the upper division baccalaureate degree category, 1 hour in Sales Management (9/95).

Managing Sales Professionals (MSPROFS)

Location: Irving, TX.

Length: 80 hours (2 weeks).

Dates: October 1990-Present.

Objective: To equip the student with the necessary knowledge, skills, and tools needed by a newly assigned first-level manager in a sales/service center environment.

Learning Outcome: Upon successful completion of this course, the student will be able to effectively manage a staff of sales professionals.

Instruction: Major topics covered in the course are leadership, professionalism, integrity, ethics, team building, customer service, customer satisfaction, and managing sales professionals. Methods of instruction include lecture, discussion, classroom exercises, and case studies.

Credit Recommendation: In the lower division baccalaureate/associate degree category, 3 semester hours in Sales Management (10/93).

Managing the Appraisal Cycle

Location: St. Louis, MO; Dallas, TX; and other Southwestern Bell locations.

Length: 16 hours (2 days).

Dates: July 1993-Present.

Objective: To help students learn how to plan and set employee expectations and conduct effective performance reviews.

Learning Outcome: Upon successful completion of this course, the student will be able to develop performance expectations, recognize performance trends, conduct performance reviews, and handle difficult situations.

Instruction: Major topics covered in the course are identifying performance expectations, tracking and providing feedback on expectations, and conducting the performance review. Methods of instruction include lecture, discussion, classroom exercises, case studies, problem solving, and role playing.

Credit Recommendation: In the upper division baccalaureate degree category, 1 semester hour in Personnel Management or Organizational Behavior (9/93) (9/94).

Negotiating Successfully (NS)

Location: Irving, TX; St. Louis, MO.

Length: 24 hours (3 days).

Dates: February 1987-January 1994.

Objective: To provide the student with a basis for planning and participating in a negotiation session by defining interests and issues, confronting differences, and achieving agreement or consensus.

Learning Outcome: Upon successful completion of this course, the student will be able to plan and participate in a negotiation; analyze the positions and disagreements; and assist in resolution of conflicts.

Instruction: Major topics covered in the course are analysis and planning of a negotiation; listening skills; body language; analysis of differences and conflict; and methods of achieving agreement or consensus. Methods of instruction include class book, flip charts, videotape, practice in role playing, and discussion.

Credit Recommendation: In the lower division baccalaureate/associate degree category, 1 semester hour in Interpersonal Skills or Sales (1/89).

Negotiation Skills

Location: St. Louis, MO; Dallas, TX; and other Southwestern Bell locations.

Length: *Version 1:* 28 hours (3.5 days); *Version 2:* 24 hours (3 days).

Dates: *Version 1:* January 1986-December 1994; *Version 2:* January 1995-Present.

Objective: To improve the manager's negotiation skills whether within the daily business environment or in formal bargaining situations.

Learning Outcome: Upon successful completion of this course, the student will be able to understand the negotiation process; plan for and conduct negotiations; identify and handle conflicts arising in negotiation; identify shared outcomes; and handle the "dirty tricks" of the negotiation process.

Instruction: Major topics covered in the course are the definition of negotiation, elements of the negotiation environment, recognizing conflict, achieving rapport, the "dirty tricks" that arise, and selecting negotiating style. Methods of instruction include lecture, discussion, class exercises, cases, problem-solving, videotapes, and role play.

Credit Recommendation: *Version 1:* In the upper division baccalaureate degree category, 2 semester hours in Management or Communications (9/89) (9/94). *Version 2:* In the lower division baccalaureate/ associate degree category, 1 semester hour in Management or Communications (9/95).

Network Data Link Lab and Protocol (1029) or (1029M)

Location: Irving, TX.

Length: 1029: 80 hours (2 weeks); 1029M: 50 hours (1 week).

Dates: October 1989-December 1996.

Objective: To provide students with a comprehensive understanding of data communication with special emphasis on protocols and data link layers.

Learning Outcome: Upon successful completion of this course, the student will be able to install and maintain various types of modems and data service units; use a data line monitor to observe and analyze data; understand modulation and multiplexing schemes; and understand various data communications protocols.

Instruction: Major topics covered in the course are numbering systems; digital logic; data codes; error checking; modulation; multiplexing; and transmission protocols. Methods of instruction include precourse and homework assignments.

Credit Recommendation: In the upper division baccalaureate degree category, 3 semester hours in Computer Science and Telecommunications (12/91).

Network Distribution Services-Basic Engineering (D-650)

Location: Irving, TX.

Length: 80 hours (2 weeks).

Dates: January 1986-Present.

Objective: To prepare students to function in outside plant design center engineering.

Learning Outcome: Upon successful completion of this course, the student will have a basic knowledge of the responsibilities of the outside plant design center engineer; design work orders for aerial, underground, and buried facilities; and identify and understand the importance and functions of engineering tools and associated records.

Instruction: Major topics covered in the course are accounting, work prints, clearances, electrical protection, tools, resistance design, serving area concept, T-1 digital, light guide, and highway print reading. Methods of instruction include lecture, discussion, classroom exercises, computer-assisted videotapes, and self-paced instruction.

Credit Recommendation: In the lower division baccalaureate/associate degree category, 3 semester hours in Telecommunications Technology (10/93).

Noise Reduction (D-313)

Location: St. Louis, MO; Houston, TX; and Oklahoma City, OK.

Length: 12 hours (1.5 days).

Dates: January 1987-March 1994.

Objective: To provide the student with knowledge of the basic electrical circuit characteristics and techniques for noise reduction on such a circuit.

Learning Outcome: Upon successful completion of this course, the student will be able to trace current flow through a DC circuit; define circuit loss and its effect on transmission; and determine the source of noise in a circuit.

Instruction: Major topics covered in the course are basic DC circuits, basic AC circuits, and noise reduction. Methods of instruction include computer-assisted instruction.

Credit Recommendation: In the lower division baccalaureate/associate degree category, 1 semester hour in Electric Technology or Physics (3/89).

Overview of Data Communications (DQ 101)

Overview of Data Communications for Managers (DQ100)

Location: Advanced Education System, Irving, TX.

Length: 40 hours (1 week).

Dates: October 1988-October 1995.

Objective: To introduce the basic structure and functions of data communications.

Learning Outcome: Upon successful completion of this course, the student will be able to list and describe the differences between parallel and serial communications; discuss both asynchronous transmission and synchronous transmission; describe the need for link layer protocols; and explain the concept of layering.

Instruction: Major topics covered in the course are data communications theory, data link protocols, networking, open systems, SNA, ISDN, packet switching, and LANs.

Credit Recommendation: In the upper division baccalaureate degree category, 2 semester hours in Data Communications (10/90). **NOTE:** Credit should be awarded for completion of either course. The information presented in both of these courses is similar. Credit in either but not both is applicable.

PAR Sales

Location: Missouri, Arkansas, Texas, Oklahoma, Kansas and selected other locations.

Length: 24 hours (3 days).

Dates: January 1992-Present.

Objective: To utilize leadership ability to develop professional and effective selling skills.

Learning Outcome: Upon successful completion of this course, the student will be able to use listening skills to establish commonality, qualify the prospect, determine client's perception of needs, offer appropriate products or services to meet their needs, overcome objectives and close the sale to the customer's long term satisfaction.

Instruction: Major topics covered in the course are reading the customer, establishing rapport, learning how to effectively offer your product and closing the sale. Methods of instruction include interactive video and workbooks.

Credit Recommendation: In the lower division baccalaureate/associate degree category, 2 semester hours in Professional Selling or Communications (9/92) (9/94).

Performance Advantage (WRLSS-PA)

Location: Various locations in the United States and Great Britain.
Length: 14 hours (2 days).
Dates: May 1996-Present.
Objective: To provide the student with the skills and knowledge needed to perform successfully as representatives in a call center that is providing service to customers who are calling with questions, problems, concerns and complaints about their wireless telephone service.
Learning Outcome: Upon successful completion of this course, the student will be able to describe the role that service plays in maintaining and building customer relationships in a competitive environment; and demonstrate the specific service skills that are needed to build loyalty by meeting and exceeding the customer's expectations.
Instruction: Major topics covered in the course are professional telephone techniques, establishing rapport, asking effective questions to gather information and determine the customer's need, presenting recommendations and solutions in clear and simple terms, handling objections and concerns, and managing high risk situations in a way that maintains customer loyalty and closes the contact effectively. Methods of instruction include lecture, group presentations, discussion, case studies, role playing, written exercises, analysis of sample audio-tape contacts, and examinations.
Credit Recommendation: In the vocational certificate category, 1 semester hour in Customer Relations or Business Communication (11/97).

Performing Arts (WRLSS-ARTS)

Location: Various locations in the United States and Great Britain.
Length: 12 hours (2 days).
Dates: April 1996-Present.
Objective: To provide participants with the skills and knowledge necessary to build customer relationships by proactively selling value-added products to wireless telephone customers.
Learning Outcome: Upon successful completion of this course, the student will be able to describe the differences between product selling and consultative selling and explain the role that each plays in their company's product line in terms of features, applications, and benefits; and demonstrate the specific sales skills needed to sell products to customers.
Instruction: Major topics covered in the course are questioning and listening for clues to identify customers' needs; making effective product recommendations; handling customers' questions, concerns, and objections and determining customer's needs; and asking for the sale and gaining the customer's agreement. Methods of instruction include lecture, group presentations, group discussions, role playing, written exercises, and examinations.
Credit Recommendation: In the upper division baccalaureate degree category, 1 semester hour in Marketing or Salesmanship (11/97).

Personnel Management Issues
1. Time on My Side (0215)
2. Supporting Victims of Abuse (0216)
3. Stress Management (0222) (0222)

Location: St. Louis, MO; Dallas, TX; and other locations in Missouri, Texas, Oklahoma, Arkansas, and Kansas.
Length: 24 hours (3 days).
Dates: January 1990-September 1994.
Objective: (1). To provide an awareness of the importance of time management toward achieving professional objectives. (2). To provide information on how to provide sensitive and informed support to victims of physical abuse. (3). To provide an overview of the topic of stress and its impact on our daily lives.
Learning Outcome: Upon successful completion of this course, the student will be able to (1).establish personal and professional goals and priorities; plan effective short-term and long-term activities that will lead to timely achievement of goals; and learn to utilize tools and techniques to improve levels of time management skills. (2). Learn how to provide sensitive and informed support to employees who are victims of physical assault. (3). Identify sources and symptoms of stress; assess personality and life style habits that contribute to stress levels; and learn a variety of stress management techniques.
Instruction: (1). Major topics covered in the course are nature of time; need for time management; and how to effectively use time on my side materials. (2). Overview of rape; women's view of risk of rape; coercion and effects; and manager's role in support of victims. (3). Stress assumptions; triggers; responses; self-assessment; and management techniques.
Credit Recommendation: In the lower division baccalaureate/associate degree category, 2 semester hours in Current Issues in Personnel Management (9/90) (9/94). **NOTE:** Students must satisfactorily complete all three courses to receive credit.

Phone Trunk Testing (512) (SCC Trunk Tester)

Location: Advanced Education System, Irving, TX.
Length: 65 hours (1.5 weeks).
Dates: January 1983-March 1994.
Objective: To familiarize the student with the Switching Control Center (SCC) and phone trunk workstation as well as SCC procedures as they apply to phone trunk installation and maintenance functions.
Learning Outcome: Upon successful completion of this course, the student will be able to perform basic phone trunk testing; phone trunk installation; and phone trunk field maintenance.
Instruction: Major topics covered in the course are the switching control center activities of trunking and facilities, interoffice signaling, transmission, trunk orders, trunk testing, administration, and full maintenance. Method of instruction includes self-instruction.
Credit Recommendation: In the lower division baccalaureate/associate degree category, 2 semester hours in Data Communications, Teleprocessing, or as a technical elective (3/89).

PL/I Language and Case Study (ISC/TE I4050L and I4050C or L4051L and L4051C)

Location: Southwestern Bell, One Bell Center, St. Louis, MO.
Length: 160 hours (20 days).
Dates: January 1982-April 1995.
Objective: The course teaches students to write programs in PL/I and teaches use of the language in user applications.
Learning Outcome: Upon successful completion of this course, the student will be able to design, code, compile, and execute PL/I programs; perform arithmetic operations, data manipulation, and condition-testing in PL/I; and structure programs using external/internal procedures.
Instruction: Major topics include overview of the PL/I language, compiling and executing PL/I programs, data representation, conversion, and movement; file declaration; record I/O; table programming logic; and arrays. Methods of instruction include lecture, discussion, classroom exercises, and linear video.
Credit Recommendation: In the lower division baccalaureate/associate degree category, 3 semester hours in Data Processing, Computer Information Systems,

Management Information Systems, or Computer Science (4/90). **NOTE:** All course numbers listed in course title must be completed to receive the credit recommendation.

Positive Discipline (0058)

Location: Management Development Training Centers in Arkansas, Kansas, Missouri, Oklahoma, and Texas.

Length: 8 hours (1 day).

Dates: March 1986-Present.

Objective: To provide the student with an understanding of the key concepts of positive discipline with an identification of typical performance and disciplinary problems.

Learning Outcome: Upon successful completion of this course, the student will be to define the core concepts of positive discipline; recognize the positive discipline process; state beneficial results of the process; utilize tools required by the process; know the techniques for gaining agreement and for employee interviews with union representation; and execute reliable documentation for actions in the process.

Instruction: Major topics covered in the course are the positive discipline approach, encouraging positive performance, correcting performance problems, conducting disciplinary meetings, recognizing disciplinary situations, and documentation. Methods of instruction include lectures with print and non-print media support and application exercises.

Credit Recommendation: In the vocational certificate category, 1 semester hour (10/93). **NOTE:** In order to receive 1 hour credit in the vocational certificate category, the student must successfully complete this course in conjunction with Supervisory Skills Workshop (0005).

Positive Discipline

Location: Management Development Training Centers in Arkansas, Kansas, Missouri, Oklahoma, Texas, plus suitcased throughout Texas.

Length: 8 hours (1 day).

Dates: *Version 1:* March 1986-December 1989; *Version 2:* January 1990-Present.

Objective: *Version 1:* To provide the student with the development of managerial ways of encouraging high performance and correcting deficient performance through positive discipline. *Version 2:* To provide the student with an understanding of the key concepts of positive discipline with an identification of typical performance and disciplinary problems.

Learning Outcome: *Version 1:* Upon successful completion of this course, the student will be able to gain individual commitment to company goals and respect for other employees; focus on the problem needing correction; make the individual responsible for correcting of his or her problems with supervisory assistance; treat employees as adults and maintain open relationships; and emphasize the use of early problem identification and coaching to correct problems. *Version 2:* Upon successful completion of this course, the student will be able to define the core concepts of positive discipline; recognize the positive discipline process; state beneficial results of the process; utilize tools required by the process; know the techniques for gaining agreement and for employee interviews with union representation; and execute reliable documentation for actions in the process.

Instruction: *Version 1:* Major topics covered in the course are the positive discipline approach, encouraging positive performance, correcting performance problems, conducting disciplinary meetings, and documentation. *Version 2:* Major topics covered in the course are the positive discipline approach, encouraging positive performance, correcting performance problems, conducting disciplinary meetings, recognizing disciplinary situations, and documentation. Methods of instruction include lectures with print and non-print media support and application exercises.

Credit Recommendation: *Version 1:* In the upper division baccalaureate degree category, 3 semester hours in Organizational Behavior (5/89). **NOTE:** In order to receive credit, the student must successfully complete this course in conjunction with Creating High Performance Teams and Situational Leadership. *Version 2:* In the lower division baccalaureate/associate degree category, 1 semester hour in Supervision (10/93). **NOTE:** In order to receive credit, the student must successfully complete this course in conjunction with Supervisory Skills Workshop (0005).

Powertalk

Location: Various locations in the United States and Great Britain.

Length: 16.5 hours (2 days).

Dates: January 1991-Present.

Objective: To develop skills required to stand up in front of any group and make effective presentations and to increase effectiveness in group meetings.

Learning Outcome: Upon successful completion of this course, the student will be able to analyze an audience and create and deliver an effective presentation; effectively use visual aids; change the tempo and timbre of the voice to suit the audience; and channel nervous energy toward more effective presentations.

Instruction: Major topics covered in the course are audience analysis, creating an effective talk using a 5 point outline, tips from theater to maximize audience acceptance and buy-in, creating sincerity and authenticity, effective use of visual aids, dramatic persuasion and when to use metaphors for impact and retention. Methods of instruction include lecture, discussion, role playing, classroom exercises, audio/visual taping, learner presentations, observations, and papers.

Credit Recommendation: In the lower division baccalaureate/associate degree category, 1 semester hour in Speech or Communications (11/97).

Presentation Skills (0201)

Location: Missouri, Arkansas, Texas, Oklahoma, Kansas, and other selected locations.

Length: 16 hours (2 days).

Dates: January 1986-Present.

Objective: To provide the skills and confidence to stand up and speak in almost any situation.

Learning Outcome: Upon successful completion of this course, the student will be able to analyze the audience, organize his/her thoughts, prepare and use visual aids, field questions, use effective speaking techniques, and speak with confidence.

Instruction: Major topics covered in the course are principles of effective speaking, preparation and the use of visual aids, and handling questions. Methods of instruction include lecture, classroom exercises, audio/visual material, and learner presentations/reports.

Credit Recommendation: In the lower division baccalaureate/associate degree category, 1 semester hour in Business Communication (9/94) (9/95).

Principles of Digital Transmission (260) (260M)

Location: Irving, TX.

Length: 40 hours (5-8 days).

Dates: January 1990-December 1996.

Objective: To provide an introduction to the basic theory and concepts regarding services and systems of digital communications.

Learning Outcome: Upon successful completion of this course, the student will be able to understand basic digital theory and demonstrate that understanding; understand basic digital network concepts and demonstrate that understanding; and be familiar with the services available in the digital data transmission arena.

Instruction: Major topics covered in the course are identifying the advantages of digital transmissions; explaining analog to digital conversion using appropriate digital terminology; describing the functions and applications of digital multiplexers to include hierarchy; identifying the uses and advantages of generic digital loop carrier systems; listing the primary components and their purpose and operation in digital data transmission; and performing set-up and operation of digital test equipment. Methods of instruction include lecture, discussion, exercises, and laboratory.

Credit Recommendation: In the upper division baccalaureate degree category, 2 semester hours in Telecommunications (12/91).

Principles of Management

Location: St. Louis, MO; Dallas, TX; and other Southwestern Bell locations.

Length: 16 hours (2 days).

Dates: January 1986-Present.

Objective: To develop understanding of interpersonal management functions and how to apply them.

Learning Outcome: Upon successful completion of this course, the student will be able to define and set goals with other people; get things done through others; evaluate performance and give constructive feedback; and effectively manage time.

Instruction: Major topics covered in the course are the management functions of planning, leading, organizing, and controlling; the "One Minute Manager" functions of goal setting and control; interpersonal communications skills that include listening and effective expression; time management; delegation of authority; motivation; and leadership. Methods of instruction include instructor-led lecture and discussion, classroom exercises, case studies, role playing, and use of videotapes.

Credit Recommendation: In the upper division baccalaureate degree category, 1 semester hour in Management (9/89) (9/94) (9/95).

Problem Solving and Decision Making (0219)

Location: St. Louis, MO; Dallas, TX; and other locations in Missouri, Texas, Oklahoma, Arkansas, and Kansas.

Length: *Version 1:* 24 hours (3 days); *Version 2:* 16 hours (2 days).

Dates: *Version 1:* January 1990-December 1994; *Version 2:* January 1995-Present.

Objective: To provide the skills and knowledge needed to make effective business decisions and solve business problems.

Learning Outcome: Upon successful completion of this course, the student will be able to understand and implement a variety of techniques related to effectively solving business problems; utilize and understand the practices associated with effective group and teamwork interactions and operations; and demonstrate knowledge through practical case work and job-related exercises.

Instruction: Major topics covered in the course are problem-solving and decision-making models and techniques; group effectiveness and teamwork skills; and situation analysis. Methods of instruction include lecture, discussion, classroom exercises, case studies, role playing, problem-solving, computer-assisted/video taped instruction, projects, presentations, and examinations.

Credit Recommendation: *Version 1:* In the lower division baccalaureate/associate degree category, 2 semester hours in Management (9/90) (9/94). *Version 2:* In the lower division baccalaureate/associate degree category, 1 semester hour in Management (9/95).

Producing Results With Others

Location: Management Development Training Centers in Arkansas, Kansas, Missouri, Oklahoma, Texas, plus suitcased throughout Texas.

Length: 16 hours (2 days).

Dates: December 1983-May 1994.

Objective: To provide the student with the behavioral approach of information processing when applied to teaching.

Learning Outcome: Upon successful completion of this course, the student will be able to observe people by what they say and what they do; identify what a person's comfort zone is, that person's preferred method of handling a problem, and his or her approach to handling a task; understand how these behaviors may assist the instructor in teaching; and how to master the social style approach to interpersonal relationships.

Instruction: Major topics covered in the course are the observation of others, basics of behavior, social style model, earning social endorsement, interpretation of the social style report, and recommendations for using style.

Credit Recommendation: In the upper division baccalaureate degree category, 1 semester hour in Organizational Behavior (5/89).

Professional Residence Initial Marketing Education Service Order Center (PRIME-SOC)

Location: Various locations in Arkansas, Kansas, Oklahoma, Missouri, and Texas.

Length: 388 hours (48.5 days).

Dates: October 1983-Present.

Objective: To teach service representatives how to negotiate all orders for residence telephone service.

Learning Outcome: Upon successful completion of this course, the student will be able to recommend and sell complete service to new customers; market services to existing customers; handle customer requests, questions and complaints about telephone service; communicate with customers in an effective and businesslike manner; type service orders; and use a variety of reference documents.

Instruction: Major topics covered in the course are sales dialogue, negotiating new connects and disconnects, billing inquiries, and number change orders. Methods of instruction include simulated role play, on-job contact handling, drills, and exercises.

Credit Recommendation: In the lower division baccalaureate/associate degree category, 3 semester hours in Customer Relations (10/93).

Professional Residence Initial Marketing Education-Billing Inquiry Center (PRIME-BIC)

Location: Various locations in Arkansas, Kansas, Oklahoma, Missouri, and Texas.

Length: 264 hours (33 days).

Dates: October 1983-Present.

Objective: To teach service representatives how to handle billing matters concerning monthly accounts and long distance charges.

Learning Outcome: Upon successful completion of this course, the student will be able to handle customer requests, questions, and complaints about their telephone billing matters; communicate with customers in an effective and businesslike manner; market services as appropriate; update accounts; type service orders; and use a variety of reference documents.

Instruction: Major topics covered in the course are customer billing records, billing inquiries, credit information, and revenue protection procedures. Methods of instruction include simulated role play, on-job contact handling, and drills and exercises within individual lessons.

Credit Recommendation: In the lower division baccalaureate/associate degree category, 3 semester hours in Customer Relations (10/93). **NOTE:** Students should not receive credit for both this course and the PRIME-RMC course.

Professional Residence Initial Marketing Education-Revenue Management Center (PRIME-RMC)

Location: Various locations in Arkansas, Kansas, Oklahoma, Missouri, and Texas.

Length: 160 hours (20 days).

Dates: October 1983-Present.

Objective: To teach service representatives how to handle collections, monthly accounts; long distance matters concerning monthly accounts; and long distance charges for live and final accounts.

Learning Outcome: Upon successful completion of this course, the student will be able to handle customer requests, questions, and complaints about their past due accounts; communicate with customers in an effective and business manner; update accounts; type service orders for disconnect non-pays, suspends, and restorals; and use a variety of reference documents.

Instruction: Major topics covered in the course are customer billing records, billing inquiries, credit information, and revenue protection procedures. Methods of instruction include simulated role play, on-job contact handling, and drills/exercises within individual lessons.

Credit Recommendation: In the lower division baccalaureate/associate degree category, 3 semester hours in Customer Relations (10/93). **NOTE**: Students should not receive credit for both this course and the PRIME-BIC course.

Professional Sales Negotiations (0228)

Location: Missouri, Arkansas, Texas, Oklahoma, Kansas and selected other locations.

Length: 24 hours (3 days).

Dates: January 1991-Present.

Objective: To be able to use the art of negotiation to close the sale to the mutual satisfaction of both parties.

Learning Outcome: Upon successful completion of this course, the student will be able to understand the definition of "negotiation," and determine when and how to use it to meet customer needs.

Instruction: Major topics covered in the course are key issues in negotiating, preparing to negotiate, and managing negotiations. Methods of instruction include independent review of prerequisite knowledge, readings, videos, case studies, group discussions, interactive exercises, review of practical applications, and role playing.

Credit Recommendation: In the upper division baccalaureate degree category, 2 semester hours in Advanced Professional Selling, Negotiations, or Communications (9/92) (9/94).

Program Design (ISC/TE 4060)

Location: Southwestern Bell, One Bell Center, St. Louis, MO.

Length: 40 hours (5 days).

Dates: January 1983-April 1995.

Objective: To enhance the student's ability to design algorithms in a language-independent environment and develop their general documentation skills.

Learning Outcome: Upon successful completion of this course, the student will be able to produce a modular breakdown of a given user problem specification; verify that each module in the breakdown is complete and consistent; and produce complete documentation describing the design and how it conforms to the stated requirements.

Instruction: Major topics include basic problem-solving techniques; organization of various types of data items and how they are incorporated into an overall design; and grouping a number of data items into one entity (EX'ARRAY), and how this can be used to enhance a design. Methods of instruction include lecture, discussion, classroom exercises, case studies, and problem-solving.

Credit Recommendation: In the lower division baccalaureate/associate degree category, 2 semester hours in Computer Science, Computer Information Systems, Management Information Systems, or Data Processing (4/90).

Program Maintenance and Testing (ISC/TE 4110) and Problem Analysis Using ABEND-AID (ISC/TE 3051)

Location: Southwestern Bell, One Bell Center, St. Louis, MO.

Length: 24 hours (3 days).

Dates: September 1983-April 1995.

Objective: To develop a general understanding of the requirements of maintaining and testing computer programs, together with an insight into a more specialized diagnostic tool.

Learning Outcome: Upon successful completion of this course, the student will be able to state the importance and requirements of program maintenance and testing; use general techniques of problem diagnosis, modification of code, and revalidation of programs; and use the ABEND-AID tool for problem diagnostics.

Instruction: Major topics include general techniques for program maintenance and testing; modifying and revalidating program after fault discovery; and use of ABEND-AID system to enhance the efficiency of the process of problem analysis and correction. Methods of instruction include lecture, discussion, classroom exercises, case studies/role playing, and problem-solving.

Credit Recommendation: In the lower division baccalaureate/associate degree category, 1 semester hour in Computer Science, Computer Information Systems, Management Information Systems, or Data Processing (4/90).

Project Management Workshop (0216)

Location: St. Louis, MO; Dallas, TX; and other locations in Missouri, Texas, Oklahoma, Arkansas, and Kansas.

Length: 24 hours (3 days).

Dates: January 1990-Present.

Objective: To provide an opportunity to understand the basic principles of the project management and relate them to a variety of on-the-job issues.

Learning Outcome: Upon successful completion of this course, the student will be able to understand the process of and techniques utilized in effective project management; apply the knowledge of the project management process to individual work situations; and recall and understand the key factors to consider in selecting and utilizing project management software.

Instruction: Major topics covered in the course are project management models and systems; project management skills (technical- and people-oriented); project management software (selection and utilization); and project management evaluation. Methods of instruction include lecture, discussion, case studies, and role play.

Credit Recommendation: In the upper division baccalaureate degree category, 2

semester hours in Management (9/90) (9/94).

Public Packet Switching and X.25 (DQ 202)

Location: Advanced Education System, Irving, TX.

Length: 40 hours (1 week).

Dates: October 1988-October 1995.

Objective: To introduce and overview packet switching with an in-depth discussion and analysis of X.25 packet technology.

Learning Outcome: Upon successful completion of this course, the student will be able to explain the structure of the X.25 recommendation; describe the x.75 internetworking protocol; explain how a synchronous device can be interfaced to a PDN; and monitor and debug X.25 and X.28 links.

Instruction: Major topics covered in the course are OSI and packet switching, public data networks, X.25 physical layer, X.25 data link layer protocol, and X.25 packet layer protocol. Methods of instruction include lecture, discussion, laboratory, examinations, and case study.

Credit Recommendation: In the upper division baccalaureate degree category, 2 semester hours in Data Communications, Computer Science, or Telecommunications (10/90).

RADAR Selling Skills (RADAR)

Location: Irving, TX; Houston, TX; and St. Louis, MO.

Length: 40 hours (1 week).

Dates: September 1990-Present.

Objective: To teach students the core sales skills necessary to be successful in a selling environment.

Learning Outcome: Upon successful completion of this course, the student will be able to demonstrate an understanding of the selling process and to demonstrate knowledge and skill in the planning and execution of the selling process.

Instruction: Major topics covered in the course are the selling environment, selling techniques, and dealing with objections. Methods of instruction include lecture, discussion, classroom exercises, and a written final examination.

Credit Recommendation: In the lower division baccalaureate/associate degree category, 2 semester hours in Salesmanship or Marketing (10/93).

Report Writing Using the Fourth Generation Language (4GL)

1. FOCUS Report Writing (5305)
2. FOCUS Advanced Reporting Techniques (5330)

Location: St. Louis, MO; Dallas, TX; and various locations in the five-state Southwestern Bell area.

Length: 23 hours (4 days).

Dates: April 1987-Present.

Objective: To instruct the student in the techniques of creating reports from existing data bases using the 4GL FOCUS.

Learning Outcome: Upon successful completion of this course, the student will be able to generate and format reports that select certain data base fields, sort these fields as needed, and summarize the selected fields; join FOCUS files; use multiple verbs, sort phrases, and "if tests" in multiple reports; and merge subsets of two or more data bases into a new hold file.

Instruction: Major topics covered in the course are FOCUS overview, report requests, data selection, summarization, and computation, report formatting, join command, table command option, and setting the environment. Methods of instruction include lecture, discussion, and laboratory exercises.

Credit Recommendation: In the lower division baccalaureate/associate degree category, 1 semester hour in Computer Information Systems (CIS), Computer Science, or Data Processing (3/89) (10/93). **NOTE:** In order for the student to receive credit, both courses must be successfully completed. Credit should be awarded for either this course sequence (5305, 5330) or course sequence (5310, 5320, and 5330), but not for both.

Revenue Management New Hire Training (MO-WRLSRM)

Location: Various locations in the United States and Great Britain.

Length: 144 hours (18 days).

Dates: July 1997-Present.

Objective: To develop a working knowledge of the responsibilities, personal characteristics and effective strategies needed to service customers.

Learning Outcome: Upon completion of this course, students will be able to define the responsibilities and character qualities of the customer service representative; use verbal and nonverbal (tone) positive messaging; employ active listening skills; and practice effective telephone techniques.

Instruction: Major topics covered in the course are the customer service professional, building customer relations, telephone etiquette, and negotiating skills. Methods of instruction include lecture, discussion, classroom exercises, role playing, quizzes, observation, and final examination.

Credit Recommendation: In the lower division baccalaureate/associate degree category, 1 semester hour in Customer Relations or Business (11/97).

Sales Center Initial Training Curriculum (SDC-SRC-IT)

Location: Various locations in Arkansas, Kansas, Missouri, Oklahoma, and Texas.

Length: 672 hours (16.8 weeks).

Dates: January 1993-Present.

Objective: To teach students the sales model and product applications to service customer needs, how to handle inquiries, and how to process service orders.

Learning Outcome: Upon successful completion of this course, the student will be able to recommend and sell telecommunications network services and equipment, process service orders, quote applicable charges, handle customer questions and/or complaints, and use a variety of reference documents.

Instruction: Major topics covered in the course are interpersonal skills, communications, and salesmanship. Methods of instruction include lecture, discussion, classroom exercises, verbal sales presentations, and written examinations.

Credit Recommendation: In the lower division baccalaureate/associate degree category, 3 semester hours in Salesmanship or Marketing (10/93).

Sales Presentation Skills; Communispond Effective Presentation Skills; Versatile Sales Person

Location: Irving, TX.

Length: 1. 20 hours (2.1/2 days); 2. 16 hours (2 days); 3.

Dates: March 1987-January 1994.

Objective: To provide the student with the ability to identify and practice the selling skills that minimize interference and noise in sales presentation delivery, and create a physical environment and an appropriate format, and deliver a sales presentation with different media.

Learning Outcome: Upon successful completion of this course, the student will be able to develop confidence in the development and delivery of a sales presentation; use visual aids effectively in making sales; and use techniques of various audio and visual media.

Instruction: Major topics covered in the course are audience analysis, planning of physical arrangements, choice and use of visual aids, and effective delivery and dialog.

Credit Recommendation: In the lower division baccalaureate/associate degree category, 2 semester hours in Sales (1/89). **NOTE:** Students must complete all three courses to receive the credit.

Sales Strategies and Tactics

Location: St. Louis, MO; Dallas, TX; and other Southwestern Bell locations.

Length: 40 hours (5 days).

Dates: May 1989-September 1994.

Objective: To enable senior account managers to effectively sell communication solutions through identification of strategic directions, territory management, account planning, call planning, approach and data gathering, presentation, closing, and maintaining goodwill.

Learning Outcome: Upon successful completion of this course, the student will be able to analyze a territory, prioritize potential accounts, develop and implement a plan to realize territorial sales potential; and sell to and maintain positive relationships with complex organizations.

Instruction: Major topics covered in the course are strategy planning, territory management, account management, call planning, approach, presentation, and closing. Methods of instruction include lecture, discussion, readings, written assignments, videotapes, and role playing with feedback.

Credit Recommendation: In the upper division baccalaureate degree category, 2 semester hours in Industrial Sales (9/89) (9/94).

Sales Strategies and Tactics: Account Executive (SS&T-AE)

Location: St. Louis, MO; Irving, TX; Kansas City, MO.

Length: 40 hours (5 days).

Dates: October 1987-January 1994.

Objective: To develop the skills of the student, sales account executive, or other manager in reaching sales objectives, teaching and supervisory sales planning, developing effective relationship to the sales territory, and leadership of a sales group.

Learning Outcome: Upon successful completion of this course, the student will be able to lead a sales team; teach and reinforce sales planning; become a role model for the sales force; and help sales people develop self-confidence and competence in selling.

Instruction: Major topics covered in the course are strategic sales planning, territory management, opportunity management, and sales call development and delivery. Methods of instruction include lecture, exercises, and role playing.

Credit Recommendation: In the upper division baccalaureate degree category, 3 semester hours in Sales Management (1/89).

Sales Strategies and Tactics: Management

Location: St. Louis, MO; Irving, TX; and Kansas City, MO.

Length: 40 hours (5 days).

Dates: October 1987-May 1994.

Objective: To develop the skills of the student, sales account executive, or other manager, in reaching sales objectives, teaching and supervisory sales planning, developing effective relationship to the sales territory, and leadership of a sales group.

Learning Outcome: Upon successful completion of this course, the student will be able to lead a sales team, teach and reinforce sales planning; become a role model for the sales force; and help sales people develop self-confidence and competence in selling.

Instruction: Major topics covered in the course are strategic sales planning, territory management, opportunity management, and sales call development and delivery. Methods of instruction include lecture, exercises, and role playing.

Credit Recommendation: In the upper division baccalaureate degree category, 3 semester hours in Sales Management (5/89).

Seven Basic Habits of Highly Effective People (0232)

Location: St. Louis, MO; Dallas, TX; and other Southwestern Bell locations.

Length: 28 hours (3.5 days).

Dates: January 1989-Present.

Objective: To empower people and organizations to significantly increase their performance by working together to achieve common goals.

Learning Outcome: Upon successful completion of this course, the student will be able to understand and apply the seven basic habits in order to enhance his or her personal effectiveness and that of the organization.

Instruction: Major topics covered in the course are the seven basic habits that lead to the results noted above. The seven habits include: be proactive; begin with the end in mind; put first things first; think win/win; seek first to understand, then be understood; synergize; and sharpen the saw. Methods of instruction include lecture and discussion, classroom exercises, case studies, role playing, and videotapes.

Credit Recommendation: In the lower division baccalaureate/associate degree category, 2 semester hours in Management or as a General Elective (9/89) (9/94).

Seven Basic Habits of Highly Effective People, Part I Sharpen the Saw, Part II

Location: St. Louis, MO; Dallas, TX; and other Southwestern Bell locations.

Length: Part I: 32 hours (4 days); Part II: 8 hours (1 day).

Dates: Part I: January 1989-Present; Part II: January 1992-Present.

Objective: Part I: To empower people and organizations to significantly increase their performance by working together to achieve common goals. Part II: To build on seven basic habits and allow students to improve learned skills.

Learning Outcome: Upon successful completion of Part I, the student will be able to understand and apply the seven basic habits in order to enhance his or her personal effectiveness and that of the organizations; Part 2: the student will be able to enhance knowledge of work habits of effective people and apply these habits to personal, management, and organizational environments.

Instruction: Part 1: Major topics covered in the course are the seven basic habits: be proactive; begin with the end in mind; put first things first; think win/win; seek first to understand, then be understood; synergize; and sharpen the saw. Part 2: Major topics covered in the course are seven basic habits of effective people; and enhanced skill building and utilization of knowledge found in these seven basic habits. Methods of instruction for Part 1 include lecture, discussion, classroom exercises, case studies, role playing, and videotapes. Methods of instruction for Part 2 include lecture, discussion, classroom exercises, and videos.

Credit Recommendation: Part 1: In the lower division baccalaureate/associate degree category, 2 semester hours in Personnel Management (9/89). Part 2: In the lower division baccalaureate/associate degree category, 1 additional semester hour in Management or as a General Elective if the student has also completed the course Sharpening the Saw (9/93) (9/94).

Situational Leadership

Location: Management Development Training Centers in Arkansas, Kansas, Missouri, Oklahoma, Texas, plus suitcased throughout Texas.

Length: 16 hours (2 days).

Dates: January 1984-October 1990.

Objective: To present the situational leadership theory to help the student choose an appropriate style of leadership for the many different situations encountered on the job.

Learning Outcome: Upon successful completion of this course, the student will be able to identify employee development potential; apply situational leadership theory to work environments; choose an appropriate leadership style; and manage motivation using situational leadership; and develop strategies for change.

Instruction: Major topics covered in the course are situational leadership theory, developing employees, classic motivation concepts, and managing change.

Credit Recommendation: In the upper division baccalaureate degree category, 3 semester hours in Organizational Behavior (5/89). **NOTE:** Credit is awarded only if the student successfully completes this course in conjunction with Creating High Performance Teams and Positive Discipline.

SNA, Network Performance and Management (DQ 401/401.5)

Location: Advanced Education System, Irving, TX.

Length: 48 hours (6 days).

Dates: October 1988-October 1995.

Objective: To introduce SNA, other network architectures, and typical user configurations.

Learning Outcome: Upon successful completion of this course, the student will be able to describe various approaches to computer network architecture; draw the SNA layers and relate the function of each layer; explain typical user configurations based on manufacturer's components; and discuss fundamental concepts employed in other architectures.

Instruction: Major topics covered in the course are SNA overview, synchronous data link control (SDLC), path control, transmission, SNA messages, error handling, network management and design, SNA introduction, SNA physical and data link layers and communication, and Unisys network architectures. Methods of instruction include lecture, discussion, and a case study.

Credit Recommendation: In the upper division baccalaureate degree category, 3 semester hours in Computer Science-Telecommunications (10/90).

Social Styles Managing Interpersonal Relationships

Location: Missouri, Arkansas, Texas, Oklahoma, Kansas, and other selected locations.

Length: 16 hours (2 days).

Dates: January 1994-Present.

Objective: To improve interpersonal skills and overcome barriers to effective job performance.

Learning Outcome: Upon successful completion of this course, the student will be able to recognize the variety of social styles inherent in people; build on social style differences; and manage the conflicts that occur.

Instruction: Major topics covered in the course are the behavioral dimensions of individual social styles, techniques for building on individual differences in style, and techniques for handling conflicts that occur. Methods of instruction include lecture, discussion, classroom exercises, audio/visual material, computer-assisted instruction, and learner presentations/ reports.

Credit Recommendation: In the lower division baccalaureate/associate degree category, 1 semester hour in Organizational Behavior or Management (9/94).

Specialized Computer Peripheral Maintenance (515.1) (1/1A ESS Peripheral Maintenance)

Location: Advanced Education System, Irving, TX.

Length: 90 hours (2.5 weeks).

Dates: January 1983-March 1994.

Objective: To teach the student to diagnose problems and make fixes to specialized telephone peripheral equipment.

Learning Outcome: Upon successful completion of this course, the student will be able to diagnose malfunctions in computer switching peripheral units; analyze the cause of a computer switching peripheral malfunction; and correct a computer peripheral malfunction.

Instruction: Major topics covered in the course are peripheral maintenance in 1/1A common remreed frames, combined miscellaneous and miniaturized universal trunk frames, 1/1A peripheral unit controller, and 1/1 digital carrier trunk. Methods of instruction include self-paced instruction.

Credit Recommendation: In the lower division baccalaureate/associate degree category, 2 semester hours in Electronics (3/89). **NOTE:** This course combined with Computer CPU Maintenance (515.2) and Attached Processor Maintenance (515.4) comprise the course Computer CPU and Peripheral Maintenance (515.0) for 5 semester hours. Credit should be awarded for either this sequence of courses or for course 515.0, but not both.

Specialized Telephone Software Applications (514) (1/1A ESS SCC Translations)

Location: Advanced Education System, Irving, TX.

Length: 72.5 hours (1*3/4 weeks).

Dates: January 1983-March 1994.

Objective: To teach the student to use specialized telephone software that analyzes incoming phone requests digit by digit.

Learning Outcome: Upon successful completion of this course, the student will be able to understand specialized telephone translation software, implement changes to the system through specialized telephone translation software, and recover from malfunctions of specialized telephone translation software.

Instruction: Major topics covered in the course are simulator training in specialized telephone translation software, including updating a translation data base and debugging software malfunctions. Methods of instruction include computer-assisted self-instruction.

Credit Recommendation: In the lower division baccalaureate/associate degree category, 2 semester hours in Computer Software (3/89).

Subscriber Loop Carrier 96 (D-407)

Location: Dallas, TX; Houston, TX; Oklahoma City, OK; and St. Louis, MO.

Length: 40 hours (1 week).

Dates: April 1987-June 1993.

Objective: To introduce the student to subscriber loop systems, such as the SLC-96, including the input and output signals.

Learning Outcome: Upon successful completion of this course, the student will be able to maintain a SLC-96 system; set up and test a central office and a remote terminal; and be able to use the task-oriented practice (TOP) flow chart system.

Instruction: Course teaches the installation, startup, and troubleshooting of the Subscriber Loop Carrier 97 (SLC 96) system. The course includes both the central office terminal and the remote terminal. Methods of instruction include programmed instruction, discussion, lecture, and video. Half the course is hands-on laboratory experience.

Credit Recommendation: In the vocational certificate category, 1 semester hour in Telecommunications (7/88).

Supervisory Skills Workshop (0005) (Formerly Supervisory Skills Workshop)

Location: Management Training Centers in Texas, Kansas, Missouri, Oklahoma, and 3 locations in Texas.

Length: 8 hours (1 day).

Dates: June 1990-Present.

Objective: To provide the student with supervisory knowledge and skills in dealing with non-management employees in the measurement of their work performance and behavior.

Learning Outcome: Upon successful completion of this course, the student will be able to evaluate a non-management employee using a standardized performance appraisal procedure; understand the monitoring process; document and accurately appraise work performance and behavior; direct work performance relating to quantity and quality of work and safety; provide feedback and coaching; and communicate the elements of the career planning process.

Instruction: Major topics covered in the course are definitions of performance areas, documentation, written and verbal performance appraisals, monitoring processes, feedback, coaching, and career development. Methods of instruction include lectures with print and non-print media support and application exercises.

Credit Recommendation: In the vocational certificate category, 1 semester hour in Supervisory Skills (10/93). **NOTE:** In order to receive 1 semester hour in the vocational certificate category, the student must successfully complete this course in conjunction with Positive Discipline (0058).

Supervisory Skills Workshop

Location: Management Training Centers in Arkansas, Kansas, Missouri, Oklahoma, and 3 locations in Texas.

Length: 16 hours (2 days).

Dates: April 1987-June 1990.

Objective: To provide the student with supervisory knowledge and skills in dealing with employees and procedures in the work environment.

Learning Outcome: Upon successful completion of this course, the student will be able to organize on-the-job training; evaluate a nonmanagement employee using a standardized performance appraisal procedure; and solve supervisory problems and recommend decisions concerning employees.

Instruction: Major topics covered in the course are interpersonal skills including training and evaluating employees, conflict resolution, union-management relations, and decision-making. Methods of instruction include lecture and multiple experiential methods.

Credit Recommendation: In the upper division baccalaureate degree category, 1 semester hour in Introduction to Supervision, or in the lower division baccalaureate/associate degree category, 3 semester hours in Personnel Management if taken in conjunction with External Environments of a Public Utility, Goal Setting and Performance Evaluation, Improving Business Relationships, Interpersonal Business Communications, Introduction to Personnel Policy, and Understanding Managing Performance (7/88) (5/89).

Supporting Service Excellence (0224)

Location: Various Southwestern Bell locations.

Length: 16 hours (2 days).

Dates: January 1991-Present.

Objective: To provide an understanding of the principles and value of providing effective service beyond customer expectations.

Learning Outcome: Upon successful completion of this course, the student will be able to provide excellent customer service; determine how to coach and reinforce skills in others; and recognize and deal with barriers to providing exceptional customer service.

Instruction: Major topics covered in the course are key principles of effective customer service; enhancing customer service interactions; identifying and providing extraordinary service opportunities; leading by example; and support of contact persons. Methods of instruction in-clude lecture, discussion, cases, and videotape.

Credit Recommendation: In the vocational certificate category, 1 semester hour in General Business (9/91) (9/94). **NOTE:** One hour of credit is recommended for either Supporting Service Excel-lence or Beyond Customer Expectations but not for both.

SWBT BMP Programming (ISC/TE 5025)

Location: Southwestern Bell, One Bell Center, St. Louis, MO.

Length: 24 hours (3 days).

Dates: October 1987-April 1995.

Objective: To teach COBOL or PL/1 programmers who have experience with IMS batch applications the fundamentals of BMP programming in the SWBT environment.

Learning Outcome: Upon successful completion of this course, the student will be able to identify the special characteristics of a BMP; identify changes necessary to convert a batch program to a BMP; describe sync-point processing; use extended restart; and use BTS for testing IMS BMP programs.

Instruction: Major topics include MVS/IMS environment changes, language coding changes, BTS changes, symbolic checkpoint call, SWBT CHKP frequency checker, and XRST call format. Methods of instruction include lecture, discussion, and workshop exercises.

Credit Recommendation: In the upper division baccalaureate degree category, 1 semester hour in Computer Science or Computer Information Systems or Data Processing (4/90).

The Counselor Salesperson

Location: Missouri, Arkansas, Texas, Oklahoma, Kansas, and other selected locations.

Length: 24 hours (3 days).

Dates: September 1994-Present.

Objective: To train beginning sales representatives in selling from the buyer's point of view.

Learning Outcome: Upon successful completion of this course, the student will be able to approach buyers with a problem-solving attitude; use client feedback to improve personal sales skills; open sales calls with customer orientation, asking effective questions; listen with a focus on the buyer; close the sale; and follow-up after the sale.

Instruction: Major topics covered in the course are identification of buying obstacles, overcoming obstacles, techniques of opening sales calls, building credibility, effective questioning, five techniques for asking for the business, managing the implementation, dealing with dissatisfaction, and enhancing the buyer/seller relationship. Methods of instruction include lecture, discussion, classroom exercises, case studies, audio/visual material, and role plays.

Credit Recommendation: In the lower division baccalaureate/associate degree category, 2 semester hours in Selling or Communications (9/94).

Train the Trainer (0221)

Location: St. Louis, MO; Dallas, TX; and other locations in Missouri, Texas, Oklahoma, Arkansas, and Kansas.

Length: 40 hours (5 days).

Dates: January 1990-Present.

Objective: To provide information about basic principles and practices of the training process and to allow demonstration of these skills through simulated teaching/training sessions.

Learning Outcome: Upon successful completion of this course, the student will be able to identify characteristics of adult learners and implement effective instructional practices based on this knowledge; select and utilize effective instructional methods; and practice effective individual and group-oriented communication patterns and practices.

Instruction: Major topics covered in the course are instructional methods and techniques; communication skills, group and individual roles and functions of trainers; and adult learning theory.

Credit Recommendation: In the upper division baccalaureate degree category, 3 semester hours in Management or Human Resource Management (9/90) (9/94).

Trainer Skills Workshop (0006) (Formerly Trainer Skills Workshop)

Location: St. Louis, MO, and Dallas, TX.

Length: 64 hours (8 days).

Dates: November 1993-Present.

Objective: To orient the student the student to the training function and uses of instructional methodologies for the purpose of developing and practicing instructional skills.

Learning Outcome: Upon successful completion of this course, the student will be able to develop a training course using multiple instructional methodologies; conduct a training course; and evaluate the effectiveness of training skills and of a training course.

Instruction: Major topics covered in the course are purpose and functions of the trainer, learning processes and characteristics of adults, and instructional methods, and presentation skills. Methods of instruction include lecture and multiple experiential exercises.

Credit Recommendation: In the upper division baccalaureate degree category, 3 semester hours in Instructional Methods (7/88) (10/93).

Understanding Managing Performance

Location: Management Development Training Centers in Arkansas, Kansas, Missouri, Oklahoma, Texas, plus suitcased throughout Texas.

Length: 8 hours (1 day).

Dates: October 1978-October 1990.

Objective: To provide the student with an understanding of performance management procedure toward the effective direction of subordinate managers and their appraisal and future development.

Learning Outcome: Upon successful completion of this course, the student will be able to participate with manager employees in planning work and setting goals; develop performance expectations and gather objective data for evaluation; make key decisions on compensation, promotion, and termination; and develop performance appraisals and potential appraisals for future development.

Instruction: Major topics covered in the course are work planning and joint goal setting, performance appraisal process, salary plans, appraisal of employee potential, and recommendation for future staffing assignments.

Credit Recommendation: In the upper division baccalaureate degree category, 2 semester hours in Career Counseling, Distributive Education, or Personnel Management if taken in conjunction with Management Career Development and Managing Professional Growth, or in the lower division baccalaureate/associate degree category, 3 semester hours in Personnel Management if taken in conjunction with External Environments of a Public Utility, Goal Setting and Perfor-mance Evaluation, Improving Business Relationships, Interpersonal Business Communications, Introduction to Person-nel Policy, and Supervisory Skills Workshop (5/89).

UNIX Security (8597)

Location: Various locations in the United States and Great Britain.

Length: 12 hours (2 days).

Dates: December 1997-Present.

Objective: To provide training on basic UNIX security terminology, policy administration, and various tools with an emphasis on the completion of the SW-908 Security Review.

Learning Outcome: Upon successful completion of this course, the student will be able to outline security responsibilities of a system administrator; discuss UNIX security issues and implement basic techniques for securing system software and hardware; discuss the completion of the SW-908 Security Review; and locate and use reference information and materials.

Instruction: Major topics covered in the course are SW908 overview, protection of resources, access control, access procedures, and completion of the 10-point checklist. Methods of instruction include lecture, discussion, and review and lab exercises.

Credit Recommendation: In the lower division baccalaureate/associate degree category, 2 semester hours in Computer Science or Management Information Systems (11/97).

UNIX System Administration - Advanced (8591)

Location: Various locations in the United States and Great Britain.

Length: 12 hours (2 days).

Dates: November 1997-Present.

Objective: To provide training on hardware capabilities, system performance and tuning, access control, system debugging, and internals for the system administrator who performs monitoring, maintenance, security, and installation functions on small to mid-size UNIX systems.

Learning Outcome: Upon successful completion of this course, the student will be able to outline examples of system administrator responsibilities; administer disks and file systems; discuss UNIX security issues and implement basic techniques for securing system software and hardware; reconfigure the UNIX kernel to handle new peripherals or add-on software packages; monitor the performance of a multi-user UNIX system and do simple performance tuning operations; perform basic process and memory management techniques; discuss system-troubleshooting procedures; and locate and use reference information and materials.

Instruction: Major topics covered in the course are management of UNIX file systems, kernel configuration and patch application, memory management, backup strategies and tools, system performance and tuning, handling system crashes, security basics, and system activity monitoring. Methods of instruction include lecture, discussion, and review and lab exercises.

Credit Recommendation: In the lower division baccalaureate/associate degree category, 1 semester hour in Management Information Systems (11/97).

UNIX System Administration - Fundamentals (8590)

Location: Various locations in the United States and Great Britain.

Length: 18 hours (3 days).

Dates: February 1997-Present.

Objective: To provide knowledge of the basic non-programming skills required to be an effective UNIX System Administrator.

Learning Outcome: Upon successful completion of this course, the student will be able to outline examples of system administrator responsibilities; discuss UNIX related policies and guidelines; describe the design and operation of UNIX file systems; manage user accounts: adding/deleting users, changing user account attributes, and controlling password requirements; manage UNIX processes (starting and killing jobs and scheduling jobs); describe backup strategies and tools; startup and shutdown UNIX systems; administer printers and the print spool system; discuss basic networking issues and the process for obtaining new IP's; and locate and use reference information and materials.

Instruction: Major topics covered in the course are UNIX related policies and guidelines; UNIX file systems; managing user accounts: adding/deleting users, changing user account attributes, and controlling password requirements per company guidelines; managing UNIX processes (starting and killing jobs and scheduling jobs); backup strategies and tools; starting up and shutting down of UNIX systems; administering printers and the print spool system; basic networking issues; and the process for obtaining new IP's. Methods of instruction include lecture, discussion, and review and lab exercises.

Credit Recommendation: In the lower division baccalaureate/associate degree category, 1 semester hour in Computer Science or Management Information Systems (11/97).

UNIX Systems Programming
1. C UNIX Interface (8555)
2. Advanced Shell Programming (8585)

Location: St. Louis, MO.

Length: 1. 40 hours (5 days); 2. 24 hours (3 days).

Dates: August 1988-Present.

Objective: To enable the experienced C programmer to perform routine systems programming tasks using C language system calls as well as to perform some of these tasks using the UNIX operating systems shell language.

Learning Outcome: Upon successful completion of this course, the student will be able to use the C libraries to develop C interfaces to the UNIX operating system and understand and use the system's programming capabilities of the shell language.

Instruction: Major topics covered in the course are advanced aspects of the C programming language, fiber and I/O, process creation and management, creating and customizing a shell environment, and monitoring and controlling processes through the shell language. Methods of instruction include lecture, discussion, and classroom exercises. Prerequisite: The student is assumed to be an experienced C language programmer and has a working knowledge of the internals of the UNIX operating system.

Credit Recommendation: In the upper division baccalaureate degree category, 3 semester hours in Computer Information Systems, Computer Science, or Data Processing (1/89) (9/93). **NOTE:** Students must complete both courses to receive the credit.

Use of Fourth Generation Language (4GL)
1. FOCUS Report Preparation, File Design, and Maintenance (5310)
2. FOCUS Application Development Techniques (5320)
3. FOCUS Advanced Reporting Techniques (5330)

Location: St. Louis, MO.

Length: 52 hours (8 days).

Dates: August 1986-Present.

Objective: To introduce the student to the basic techniques of creating reports and defining, creating, and updating data bases using FOCUS.

Learning Outcome: Upon successful completion of this course, the student will be able to generate reports from selected fields in a data base and sort and summarize report fields; create master file descriptions and new files or update existing ones; and understand the differences in the summary functions of subtotal, summarize, and recompute.

Instruction: Major topics covered in the course are an introduction to FOCUS, basic report formats, arithmetic and grouping functions, file design and maintenance, joining files, modifying data bases, prompt transactions, table command review, define command, match command and alternate file views. Methods of instruction include lecture, discussion, and laboratory exercises.

Credit Recommendation: In the lower division baccalaureate/associate degree category, 2 semester hours in Computer Information Systems (CIS), Computer Science, or Data Processing (3/89) (10/93). **NOTE:** Credit should be awarded for this course sequence (5310, 5320, 5330) or course sequence (5305 and 5330), but not for both.

Utilities and Library Control Systems (ISC/TE 3062 and 3042 or ISC/TE 3062, 3043, and 3044)

Location: Southwestern Bell, One Bell Center, St. Louis, MO.

Length: 72 hours (9 days).

Dates: February 1984-April 1995.

Objective: To enable the student to use compilers and link-loaders using a library system (Panvalet and Panexec) and to make use of general utilities available in an IBM MVS operating system environment.

Learning Outcome: Upon successful completion of this course, the student will be able to describe a variety of ways in which general utilities can be used in program testing and maintenance; code JCL and utility control statements to perform common program functions; and access Panvalet and Panexec through TSO, Batch, and PDF environments.

Instruction: Major topics include compiling and link-editing using TSO datasets; panvalet batch commands; fundamentals of catalogued procedure usage; IBM linkage editor control statements; and coding JCL and utility control statements to create test data sets, move and copy data sets, list data sets, and update partitioned data sets. Methods of instruction include lecture, discussion, classroom exercises, and computer terminal exercises.

Credit Recommendation: In the lower division baccalaureate/associate degree category, 3 semester hours in Computer Science, Computer Information Systems, Data Processing, or Management Information Systems (4/90).

Versatile Sales Person

Location: St. Louis, MO; Irving, TX.

Length: 16 hours (2 days).

Dates: June 1981-January 1994.

Objective: To provide the student with a basis for evaluating human behavior and interaction. Social style analysis is used to differentiate clients and define differentiated responses and tactics to sell heterogeneous clientele.

Learning Outcome: Upon successful completion of this course, the student will be able to classify customers according to assertiveness and responsiveness; analyze mannerisms, speech, work areas, and social styles; and use social style in the design of sales strategy.

Instruction: Major topics covered in the course are social style awareness, analysis, and application, analysis of mannerisms, speech, and work areas; and practice in application of social style theory in setting. Methods of instruction include class discussions, exercises, role playing, examinations, projects, and presentations.

Credit Recommendation: In the lower division baccalaureate/associate degree category, 1 semester hour in Human Behavior in Organizations or Salesmanship (1/89).

Versatile Sales Person (0213)

Location: St. Louis, MO; Dallas, TX; and other Southwestern Bell locations.

Length: 16 hours (2 days).

Dates: November 1988-Present.

Objective: To provide an understanding of social style analysis to classify clients and develop effective coping skills.

Learning Outcome: Upon successful completion of this course, the student will be able to classify clients as analytical, amiable, driving, or expressive; manage tension during the sales process; and develop sales strategies appropriate for the buyer's classification.

Instruction: Major topics covered in the course are social styles and coping strategies. Methods of instruction include class discussion, exercises, videotapes, role playing, projects, and presentations.

Credit Recommendation: In the lower division baccalaureate/associate degree category, 1 semester hour in Selling or Communication (9/89) (9/94).

Wiring Specialized Telephone Circuits (A) (901) (Installation and Maintenance of Special Circuits)

Location: Advanced Education System, Irving, TX.

Length: 160 hours (4 weeks).

Dates: January 1980-March 1994.

Objective: To provide the student with in-depth instruction in the use and maintenance of specially designed telephone circuits.

Learning Outcome: Upon successful completion of this course, the student will be able to install new specially designed telephone circuits and isolate and repair trouble in specially designed telephone circuits.

Instruction: Major topics covered in the course are the installation and repair of specially designed telephone circuits for use in WATS lines, ATM lines, and others. Methods of instruction include lecture, discussion, and laboratory exercises.

Credit Recommendation: In the lower division baccalaureate/associate degree category, 4 semester hours in Electrical Circuits (3/89). **NOTE:** This course is the same as course 20002 in content; however, it is twice as long and contains many more practice exercises.

School of Engineering and Logistics

The School was established in 1956 as the Intern Training Center at the Red River Army Depot. The first class entered in 1957 and graduated in 1958. Since that time, the mission has greatly diversified and the name was changed to the School of Engineering and Logistics (SEL). Since the school's beginning, over 5,500 have graduated from the intern programs and more than that number from short courses.

The present missions are to provide training in nine different career fields of specialization, perform research and consulting services, participate in writing publications, and present a large number and variety of short courses. In 1993 SEL started conducting a number of one to four week courses for the Defense Acquisition University. All intern programs prepare the students for journeyman level positions for various career fields in the government. The intern programs are Supply Management, Maintenance Management, Quality and Reliability Assurance, Maintainability Engineering, Safety Engineering, Product/ Production Engineering, Quality and Product Assurance Engineering, Software Engineering, and Test and Evaluation Engineering.

Source of official student records: Chief, Department of Engineering or Chief, Department of Logistics, School of Engineering and Logistics, Red River Army Depot, Texarkana, TX 75507-5000, 903-334-2168.

Additional information about the courses: College Credit Recommendation Service, American Council on Education, One Dupont Circle, Washington, DC 20036-1193.

Acquisition and Contracting (50190)

Location: School of Engineering and Logistics, Red River Army Depot.

Length: 20 hours (3 weeks).

Dates: January 1975-Present.

Objective: To comprehend the acquisition process for military equipment, procurement law, and relationships to all logistics areas.

Learning Outcome: Upon successful completion of this course, the student will be able to describe the contracting process, understand the roles/responsibilities of contracting participants, describe various contracting methods and contract types, understand the relationship between logistics and the contracting function, and discuss current issues in contracting.

Instruction: Major topics covered in the course are an introduction to acquisition negotiations, types of contracts, and contracting officers' responsibilities. Methods of instruction include lecture, discussion, and an examination.

Credit Recommendation: In the graduate degree category, 1 semester hour in Public Administration (6/84) (6/95).

Administrative Systems Analysis and Design (50030)
(Formerly Administrative Systems and Design)

Location: School of Engineering and Logistics, Red River Army Depot.

Length: *Version 1:* 50 hours (2.5 weeks); *Version 2:* 40 hours.

Dates: *Version 1:* June 1980-December 1993; *Version 2:* January 1994-Present.

Objective: *Version 1:* To teach the student the planning procedures for office communications and paperwork flow in an organization. *Version 2:* To provide the student with knowledge of systems and procedures and the skills to analyze and make recommendations for improvements in existing organizations.

Learning Outcome: Upon successful completion of this course, the student will be able to know the definition of management terms, construct and interpret charts depicting differences in proposals, analyze the existing organizational structure, recommend improvements in efficiency, and give an oral presentation of recommendations.

Instruction: *Version 1:* Major topics covered in the course are functions of management, the role of administrative systems, and management analysis techniques, including forms of analysis and layout planning. Methods of instruction include lecture, a student project, and a project presentation is critiqued. *Version 2:* Major topics covered in the course are management analysis techniques such as forms analysis and layout planning and project presentation. Methods of instruction include lecture, student project, and project presentation (critiqued).

Credit Recommendation: *Version 1:* In the graduate degree category, 2 semester hours in Management (6/84). *Version 2:* In the upper division baccalaureate degree category, 2 semester hours in Office Management (6/95).

Advance Test Design and Evaluation (66021)
(Formerly Test Design and Analysis II [87021])

Location: School of Engineering and Logistics, Red River Army Depot.

Length: *Version 1:* 60 hours (10 weeks); *Version 2:* 100 hours (10 weeks).

Dates: *Version 1:* June 1989-June 1995; *Version 2:* June 1995-Present.

Objective: To provide the student with advanced knowledge of experimental design methods, analysis of variance, and model-building techniques.

Learning Outcome: *Version 1:* Upon successful completion of this course, the student will be able to work with fixed level multivariate designs; perform specifically tailored data-gathering procedures to include layout and analysis strategies for nested, split plot, lattice, and crossover designs; and perform advanced design strategies. *Version 2:* Upon successful completion of this course, the student will be able to apply, formulate, and contrast various advanced test designs, building on the prerequisite course, Engineering Test Design and Analysis; formulate testing plans using fixed level mulltivariate designs, higher order composite and nested designs; and apply the concepts of design resolution and augmentation when applicable.

Instruction: *Version 1:* Major topics covered in the course are factorial designs for ANOVA models, model diagnostics and transformations, confounding in two-level experiments, special design strategies, and sequential test strategies. Methods of instruction include lecture and problem laboratory. *Version 2:* Major topics covered in the course are fixed level design, special designs, and sequential test strategies. Methods of instruction include lecture, laboratory, practical exercises, and written examinations.

Credit Recommendation: *Version 1:* In the graduate degree category, 3 semester hours in Statistics (2/90) (6/95). *Version 2:* In the graduate degree category, 3 semester hours in Statistics (2/90) (6/95).

Advanced Microprocessors (65541)
(Formerly Advanced Microprocessors [81541])

Location: School of Engineering and Logistics, Red River Army Depot.

Length: *Version 1:* 50 hours (10 weeks); *Version 2:* 100 hours (10 weeks).

Dates: *Version 1:* August 1986-June 1995; *Version 2:* June 1995-Present.

Objective: To provide the student with hands-on experience using an INTEL 80286 microprocessor. Programming and interfacing are emphasized.

Learning Outcome: *Version 1:* Upon successful completion of this course, the student will be able to program using assembler language, measure and convert signals, and know bus communication protocols. *Version 2:* Upon successful completion of this course, the student will be able to explain and illustrate the commonalities and differences between several different microprocessors; program these microprocessors and interface these assembly language programs written in Ada; and apply these Ada/assembly programs to real-time situations.

Instruction: *Version 1:* Major topics covered in the course are an in-depth study of programming techniques and details for currently utilized processors; applications of microprocessors for robotics, process control, and process inspection; process automation, measurement, signal generation, and conversion; and interfacing, programming techniques, and application. *Version 2:* Major topics covered in the course are an introduction to the 80X86 and 680X0 families, Ada/assembly language interface, and real-time applications. Methods of instruction include five hours of lecture and laboratory per week.

Credit Recommendation: *Version 1:* In the graduate degree category, 2 semester hours in Electrical Engineering or Software Engineering (9/87). *Version 2:* In the upper division baccalaureate degree category, 3 semester hours in Computer Science or Engineering; or in the graduate degree category, 3 semester hours in Industrial or Manufacturing Engineering (6/95).

Advanced Reliability, Availability, and Maintainability (60545) (Formerly Advanced Topics in Reliability and Maintainability Engineering [82545])

Location: School of Engineering and Logistics, Red River Army Depot.

Length: *Version 1:* 60 hours (10 weeks); *Version 2:* 100 hours.

Dates: *Version 1:* February 1981-June 1995; *Version 2:* June 1995-Present.

Objective: To give students an in-depth study of advanced topics in reliability and maintainability.

Learning Outcome: Upon successful completion of this course, the student will be able to estimate reliability, availability, and maintainability parameters from life testing data and predict and allocate reliability and maintainability characteristics of systems during their early development as well as account for reliability-centered maintenance and repairable systems.

Instruction: *Version 1:* Major topics covered in the course are reliability estimation, reliability growth, software reliability, and reliability-centered maintenance. Methods of instruction include five hours of lecture per week and one hour of laboratory per week. *Version 2:* Major topics covered in the course are reliability estimation, RAM prediction & allocation, reliability-centered maintenance, renewal processes and Markov chains, and repairable systems. Methods of instruction include five hours lecture and laboratory per week.

Credit Recommendation: *Version 1:* In the graduate degree category, 3 semester hours in Industrial Engineering (12/84). *Version 2:* In the graduate degree category, 4 semester hours in Industrial Engineering (6/95).

Aircraft

Location: School of Engineering and Logistics, Red River Army Depot.

Length: 26 hours (2 weeks).

Dates: January 1975-December 1993.

Objective: To give the student a knowledge of the principles of flight, aircraft parts and functions, and Army aircraft uses, normally required of a maintenance manager.

Instruction: Major topics covered in the course are characteristics of both fixed wing and rotary wing aircraft, aircraft engines, hydraulics, transmissions, and a description of Army aircraft. Methods of instruction include lecture, discussion, and weekly examinations.

Credit Recommendation: In the lower division baccalaureate/associate degree category, 1 semester hour in Military Science (6/84).

Automotive Principles

Location: School of Engineering and Logistics, Red River Army Depot.

Length: 60 hours (4 weeks).

Dates: February 1982-December 1993.

Objective: To provide the student with a basic understanding of how all systems on an automotive vehicle operate.

Instruction: Major topics covered in the course are engines, fuel systems, cooling systems, lubrication, brakes, power train, steering, and electrical systems. Methods of instruction include lecture and weekly examinations.

Credit Recommendation: In the vocational certificate degree category, 2 semester hours in Automotive or Mechanical Engineering (6/84).

Blueprint Reading

Location: School of Engineering and Logistics, Red River Army Depot.

Length: 40 hours (2 weeks).

Dates: February 1982-December 1993.

Objective: To provide the student with a knowledge of drafting principles so that students will be able to read prints.

Instruction: Major topics covered in the course are how to complete drawings, extract data from prints, and sketch various geometrical shapes. Methods of instruction include lecture, laboratory, and weekly tests.

Credit Recommendation: In the lower division baccalaureate/associate degree category, 2 semester hours in Drafting (6/84).

Cataloging

Location: School of Engineering and Logistics, Red River Army Depot.

Length: 20 hours (1 week).

Dates: January 1975-December 1993.

Objective: To enable the student to comprehend the federal and Army cataloging procedures.

Instruction: Major topics covered in the course are application of federal and Army cataloging procedures to management of cataloging-related problems. Methods of instruction include lecture, discussion, laboratory exercises, and an examination.

Credit Recommendation: In the lower division baccalaureate/associate degree category, 1 semester hour in Management (6/84).

Communication Control and Interface Techniques (87017)

Location: School of Engineering and Logistics, Red River Army Depot.

Length: 60 hours (10 weeks).

Dates: August 1989-September 1993.

Objective: To provide the student with an understanding of data (hardware/software) communication systems.

Learning Outcome: Upon successful completion of this course, the student will be able to understand interface techniques for data reception and transmission signal conditioning and control; understand architecture requirements for networking of distributed computer systems; and identify various protocols used in data communication systems.

Instruction: Major topics covered in the course are data communication methods, distributed computer systems, and applications. Methods of instruction include lecture and problem laboratory.

Credit Recommendation: In the upper division baccalaureate degree category, 3 semester hours in Electrical Engineering (2/90).

Computer Applications for Engineering (87014)

Location: School of Engineering and Logistics, Red River Army Depot.

Length: 90 hours (10 weeks).

Dates: January 1989-September 1993.

Objective: To provide the student with an introduction to the Ada programming language.

Learning Outcome: Upon successful completion of this course, the student will be able to describe the situations that led to the development and use of Ada; describe how the use of Ada enforces the use of software engineering principles such as abstracting, information hiding, and modularity; and write programs in Ada using statements and constructs such as array slices and attributes, unconstrained arrays, text characters/string I/O, and aggregates.

Instruction: Major topics covered in the course are a software engineering overview, Ada programming language and coding, Ada statements, programming and microcomputer I/O, and Ada programming support environment. Methods of instruction include lecture, discussion, and laboratory exercises.

Credit Recommendation: In the upper division baccalaureate degree category, 3 semester hours in Computer Science (2/90). **NOTE:** Credit should not be granted for both this course and Software Engineering Using Ada I (81520).

Computer Integrated Manufacturing and Automated Assembly (62555)

Location: School of Engineering and Logistics, Red River Army Depot.

Length: 100 hours.

Dates: June 1995-Present.

Objective: To provide the student with a knowledge of computer systems used to control integrated manufacturing systems.

Learning Outcome: Upon successful completion of this course, the student will be able to create an architecture of a computer system for control of an integrated manufacturing system and demonstrate knowledge of the different welding processes used in CAM.

Instruction: Major topics covered in the course are hardware, software, database systems, and local area networks; computer frameworks; artificial intelligence and expert systems; fixed automation; and automated assembly and welding. Methods of instruction include lecture, laboratory, practical exercises, and written examinations.

Credit Recommendation: In the graduate degree category, 4 semester hours in Industrial Engineering (6/95).

Computer Integrated Manufacturing Tools (62554) (Formerly Computers in Manufacturing [83554])

Location: School of Engineering and Logistics, Red River Army Depot.

Length: *Version 1:* 90 hours (20 weeks); *Version 2:* 100 hours.

Dates: *Version 1:* December 1984-June 1995; *Version 2:* June 1995-Present.

Objective: To provide the student with an understanding of how computers function in manufacturing and manufacturing support.

Learning Outcome: Upon successful completion of this course, the student will be able to use computers for the control of industrial processes and formulate adaptive control strategies that will optimize use of manufacturing resources.

Instruction: *Version 1:* Major topics covered in the course are simulations, random number generation, numerical control, computer-aided manufacturing, and integrated manufacturing. Methods of instruction include six one-hour meetings per week for the first ten weeks, then three one-hour meetings per week for second ten weeks; lecture; laboratory; and written examinations. *Version 2:* Major topics covered in the course are robotics, CAM, adaptive controls, and integrated manufacturing support systems. Methods of instruction include five hours lecture and three hours of laboratory per week, practical exercises, and written examinations.

Credit Recommendation: *Versions 1 and 2:* In the graduate degree category, 4 semester hours in Industrial Engineering (12/84) (6/95).

Computer Science (84558)

Location: School of Engineering and Logistics, Red River Army Depot.

Length: 70 hours (10 weeks).

Dates: January 1974-September 1993.

Objective: To provide students with an understanding of scientific computer programming theory and application.

Instruction: Major topics covered in the course are an introduction to FORTRAN, COBOL, and other programming languages, and discussion of scientific and engineering applications. Methods of instruction include five hours of lecture per week, two hours of laboratory per week, and written examinations.

Credit Recommendation: In the lower division baccalaureate/associate degree category, 3 semester hours in Computer Science (12/84).

Computer Science (83558)

Location: School of Engineering and Logistics, Red River Army Depot.

Length: 70 hours (10 weeks).

Dates: January 1980-September 1993.

Objective: To provide the student with an understanding of scientific computer programming theory, FORTRAN programming language, and scientific and engineering applications.

Instruction: Major topics covered in the course are computer fundamentals, basic FORTRAN, advanced FORTRAN, and brief sessions on other programming languages.

Credit Recommendation: In the upper division baccalaureate degree category, 4 semester hours in Computer Science (12/84).

Computer Simulation and Communication Techniques (81559)

Location: School of Engineering and Logistics, Red River Army Depot.

Length: 80 hours (10 weeks: five 1-hour lectures/week; one 3-hour lab/week).

Dates: August 1986-September 1993.

Objective: To teach the student analysis and design methods used in simulation and communication networks.

Learning Outcome: Upon successful completion of this course, the student will be able to work with simulation methods (Monte Carlo method) and program with GASP IV; understand and use hardware and interface standards and protocols; and understand distributed computing systems.

Instruction: Major topics are digital simulation techniques, data communications techniques, and distributed computing systems, and computer networking methods. Emphasis is placed on utilization of presented materials as tools in development and testing of real-time distributed software systems. Methods of instruction include examinations (65 percent), homework (15 percent), and laboratory (20 percent).

Credit Recommendation: In the graduate degree category, 3 semester hours in Computer Engineering or Computer Science (9/87).

Computer Simulation for System Design (82559)

Location: School of Engineering and Logistics, Red River Army Depot.

Length: 70 hours (10 weeks); seven 1-hour meetings per week.

Dates: February 1977-September 1993.

Objective: To provide students with an understanding of the theory of generating random numbers.

Instruction: Major topics covered in the course are detailed studies of simulation languages and practical experience with simulator languages. Methods of instruction include five hours of lecture per week, two hours of laboratory per week, and a written examination.

Credit Recommendation: In the graduate degree category, 3 semester hours in Computer Science (12/84).

Computer Simulation Techniques (88559)

Location: School of Engineering and Logistics, Red River Army Depot.

Length: 70 hours (10 weeks).

Dates: February 1981-September 1993.

Objective: To give the student a knowledge of modeling, simulation techniques, and computer-aided technology.

Instruction: Major topics covered in the course are generation of random numbers, Monte Carlo simulations, GASP IV simulation language, and numerical control and computer-aided design in manufacturing. Methods of instruction include lectures, laboratory, research, examinations, and written reports.

Credit Recommendation: In the graduate degree category, 4 semester hours in Industrial Engineering (6/84).

Computer Techniques for Engineers (81558)

Location: School of Engineering and Logistics, Red River Army Depot.

Length: 70 hours (10 weeks: five 1-hour lectures/week; two 1-hour labs/week).

Dates: August 1986-September 1997.

Objective: To teach the student some important elements concerning systems architecture and selected programming languages (high level).

Learning Outcome: Upon successful completion of this course, the student will be able to read and understand operation of programs written in FORTRAN, COBOL, PASCAL, and C languages, and understand language design characteristics such as structures, data types, run-time considerations, interpretative languages, lexical analysis, and passing.

Instruction: Major topics covered in the course are computer system architecture, programming languages/operating systems, FORTRAN programming, computer systems architecture, programming languages, operating systems used within the Army for engineering applications, business applications, and real-time applications. A brief introduction to FORTRAN syntax and programming concepts emphasizing engineering applications is provided. Methods of instruction include hourly examinations and laboratory exercises.

Credit Recommendation: In the graduate degree category, 3 semester hours in Computer Engineering or Computer Science (9/87).

Corps/Intermediate Level Supply (51330) (Formerly Standard Army Intermediate Level Supply Subsystem [SAILS])

Location: School of Engineering and Logistics, Red River Army Depot.

Length: *Version 1:* 24 hours (8 days); *Version 2:* 32 hours (11 days).

Dates: *Version 1:* January 1975-March 1994; *Version 2:* March 1994-Present.

Objective: To show the student how Standard Army Intermediate Level Supply Subsystem (SAILS) operates and its importance to the operation of the retail system/wholesale system of Inventory Management.

Learning Outcome: Upon successful completion of this course, the student will be able to know common terms and specific facts about the SAILS and SARSS-O supply systems; understand and recognize the basic processes of the SAILS and SARSS-O systems; interpret information input and output from SAILS and SARSS-O; and apply concepts needed to research output products from SAILS and SARSS-O.

Instruction: *Version 1:* Major topics covered in the course are the basic computer files and selected input documents and output products of the SAILS system. Methods of instruction include lecture, laboratory, and multiple choice examinations. *Version 2:* Major topics covered in the course are the basic computer files and selected input documents and output products of the SAILS system and coverage of the SARSS-O system. Methods of instruction include lecture, practical exercises, and written examinations.

Credit Recommendation: *Version 1:* In the upper division baccalaureate degree category, 1 semester hour in Management (6/84). *Version 2:* In the upper division baccalaureate degree category, 2 semester hours in Supply Management (6/95).

Cost Estimating for Engineering

Location: School of Engineering and Logistics, Red River Army Depot.

Length: 40 hours (1 week).

Dates: January 1976-September 1993.

Objective: To aid students involved in weapon systems cost estimating at research and development activities.

Instruction: Major topics covered in the course are design to cost estimating, statistics, economic analysis, and trace. Methods of instruction include case studies, twenty-two and one-half hours of lecture per week, and seventeen and one-half hours of workshop per week. A seminar approach is used.

Credit Recommendation: In the upper division baccalaureate degree category, 2 semester hours and in the graduate degree category, 1 semester hour in Military Science (12/84).

Current Topics in Software Engineering (81590)

Location: School of Engineering and Logistics, Red River Army Depot.

Length: 90 hours (10 weeks: one 1-hour lecture/week; 80 hours of conference attendance).

Dates: August 1986-September 1993.

Objective: To provide the student with an understanding of current concerns and developments in software engineering.

Learning Outcome: Upon successful completion of this course, the student will have an understanding of the current happenings and developments in software engineering.

Instruction: Major topics covered in the course are an understanding of current happenings and developments in software engineering, and software engineering components. Methods of instruction include guest lectures and attendance at nationally recognized software symposia.

Credit Recommendation: In the graduate degree category, 3 semester hours in

Computer Engineering, Computer Science, or Software Engineering (9/87).

Current Topics in Test and Evaluation (66020) (Formerly Advanced Methods in Test and Evaluation [87020])

Location: School of Engineering and Logistics, Red River Army Depot.

Length: *Version 1:* 60 hours (10 weeks); *Version 2:* 100 hour (10 weeks).

Dates: *Version 1:* October 1989-June 1995; *Version 2:* June 1995-Present.

Objective: *Version 1:* To provide the student with advanced topics in quantitative data analysis and optimization techniques. *Version 2:* To provide the student with an in-depth understanding of management principles that affect test and evaluation program.

Learning Outcome: *Version 1:* Upon successful completion of this course, the student will be able to demonstrate the ability to apply the methods learned to solving advanced engineering problems in the areas of data collection, design strategy, and optimization techniques. *Version 2:* Upon successful completion of this course, the student will be able to investigate and assess current and projected developments in test and evaluation through researching topics published in leading technical journals and presentations of current topics by experts from government and industry.

Instruction: *Version 1:* Major topics covered in the course are statistical analysis of non-random samples and linear programming. Methods of instruction include lecture, conferences, practical exercises, and written examinations. *Version 2:* Major topics covered in the course are communication skills, research sources, and current developments. Methods of instruction include lecture, research, reports, oral presentations, and written examinations.

Credit Recommendation: *Versions 1 and 2:* In the graduate degree category, 3 semester hours in Optimization Theory (Industrial Engineering) (2/90) (6/95).

Defense Inventory Management Simulation (DIMSIM) (50183) (Formerly Defense Inventory Management Simulation [DIMSIM])

Location: School of Engineering and Logistics, Red River Army Depot.

Length: 50 hours (2 weeks).

Dates: January 1975-Present.

Objective: A computer simulation that requires students to analyze complex logistical data and to make decisions on various logistics functions.

Learning Outcome: Upon successful completion of this course, the student will be able to analyze logistics data and make logical management decisions about requirements determination, budgeting, programming, procurement direction, rebuilding direction, distribution planning, and disposal direction functions as they relate to the operation of a MSC.

Instruction: *Version 1:* Major topics covered in the course are practical application of management tools and techniques such as inventory policies, variables safety levels, moving average, exponential smoothing, and planned overhaul program. Methods of instruction include lecture, simulation exercises, and simulation performance. *Version 2:* Major topic covered in the course is inventory management. Methods of instruction include lecture, simulation exercises, and evaluation by simulation performance.

Credit Recommendation: *Version 1:* In the graduate degree category, 2 semester hours in Management (6/84). *Version 2:* In the graduate degree category, 2 semester hours in Management or Logistics (6/95).

Department of Army Publications (50080) (Formerly Department of the Army Publication)

Location: School of Engineering and Logistics, Red River Army Depot.

Length: 40 hours (2 weeks).

Dates: *Version 1:* January 1975-June 1995; *Version 2:* June 1995-Present.

Objective: To teach the student the policies, responsibility, and procedures governing official publications and forms used by the Army.

Learning Outcome: Upon successful completion of this course, the student will be able to identify general policies, responsibilities, and procedures governing preparation, approval, and production of official publications and blank forms; identify the use and purpose of various types of military publications, understand numbering systems of military forms and publications, and define design use and purpose of the stock numbering system.

Instruction: *Version 1:* Major topics covered in the course are military and federal specifications and stock standards. Methods of instruction include lecture, laboratory, workshops, exercises, and examinations. *Version 2:* Major topics covered in the course are National/NATO Stock Numbering System, introduction to AR25-30, introduction to administrative publications, blank forms, training publications, technical publications, supply type publications, modification work orders, DA PAM 108-1, AMC 310-1 and 7, and specification standards. Methods of instruction include lecture, laboratory, workshops, exercises, and examinations.

Credit Recommendation: *Version 1:* In the upper division baccalaureate degree category, 2 semester hours in Management (6/84). *Version 2:* In the lower division baccalaureate/associate degree category, 2 semester hours in Office Administration (6/95).

Direct Support/General Support Supply Procedures (51320) (Formerly Direct Support/General Support Supply Procedures)

Location: School of Engineering and Logistics, Red River Army Depot.

Length: *Version 1:* 30 hours (2 weeks); *Version 2:* 32 hours.

Dates: *Version 1:* January 1975-January 1994; *Version 2:* January 1994-Present.

Objective: To teach the student what the Direct Support/General Support Supply Procedures system is and to calculate supply performance of a Direct Supply Unit in terms of supply satisfaction and accommodation.

Learning Outcome: Upon successful completion of this course, the student will be able to know common terms associated with this level of supply, know the property accountability, storage, and stockage procedures at this level of supply, understand the development and use of ASL, both automated and the stockage policy basis, apply concept of demand supported stockage, and understand the impact of changing concepts of management.

Instruction: *Versions 1 and 2:* Major topics covered in the course are concepts of demand-supported stockage and economic order quantity; requisitioning objectives, reorder points, safety levels, order ship times, operating levels at the Direct Support Unit level; retention policy; stock record-keeping policy and procedures; replenishment, issue and receiving; air lines of communication; location survey/ inventory procedures; alternate methods of supply; methods of measuring supply support and performance; and class of supply structure. Methods of instruction include lecture, practical exercises, and written examinations.

Credit Recommendation: *Version 1:* In the upper division baccalaureate degree category, 1 semester hour in Management (6/84). *Version 2:* In the upper division baccalaureate degree category, 2 semester hours in Supply Management (6/95).

Distributive Management Information Systems (50090) (Formerly Management Information Systems)

Location: School of Engineering and Logistics, Red River Army Depot.

Length: *Versions 1 and 2:* 80 hours (4 weeks).

Dates: *Version 1:* January 1975-January 1993; *Version 2:* January 1993-Present.

Objective: *Version 1:* To provide the student with a knowledge of advanced data processing (ADP) systems so that students will be able to program a computer, understand computer terminology, and develop automated systems. *Version 2:* To provide the student with the fundamentals of computer systems and technologies to provide the tools and techniques used to process and analyze data.

Learning Outcome: Upon successful completion of this course, the student will be able to use spreadsheets, program in BASIC, demonstrate a working knowledge of XENIX, and use word processing and electronic mail.

Instruction: *Version 1:* Major topics covered in the course are FORTRAN statements: input/output statements, control statements, subscripted variables, DO loops; basic FORTRAN program operation; and disk input/output. An overview of computer technology is also given. Methods of instruction include lecture, laboratory, and weekly examinations. *Version 2:* Major topics covered in the course are spreadsheets, programming in BASIC, XENIX, word processing, and electronic mail. Methods of instruction include lecture, laboratory, and weekly examinations.

Credit Recommendation: *Version 1:* In the graduate degree category, 3 semester hours in Data Processing (6/84). *Version 2:* In the lower division baccalaureate/associate degree category, 3 semester hours in Computer Information Systems (6/95).

Economic Analysis (83507)

Location: School of Engineering and Logistics, Red River Army Depot.

Length: 60 hours (6 weeks).

Dates: January 1976-September 1993.

Objective: To give students concepts concerning economic considerations and problems that will improve their decision-making skills and abilities. Analytic techniques used in cost estimating are stressed.

Instruction: Major topics covered in the course are interest and economic equivalence, evaluating replacement alternatives and public activities, and risk, uncertainty, and economic modeling. Methods of instruction include seven hours of lecture per week, three hours of laboratory per week, written examinations, in-class exercises, and homework.

Credit Recommendation: In the graduate degree category, 3 semester hours in Economic Analysis (12/84).

Economic Analysis and Software Life-Cycle Costs (81566)

Location: School of Engineering and Logistics, Red River Army Depot.

Length: 60 hours (6 weeks: five 1-hour lectures/week; five 1-hour labs/week).

Dates: August 1986-September 1993.

Objective: To provide the student with an understanding of economic considerations, concepts, and problems designed to improve decision-making, analytical abilities, and methods of evaluation.

Learning Outcome: Upon successful completion of this course, the student will be able to demonstrate an understanding of interest and economic equivalence, replacement alternatives and public activities, risks, uncertainty, economic modeling, and software life-cycle cost evaluation.

Instruction: Major topics covered in the course are interest and economic equivalence; evaluating replacement alternatives and public activities; risk, uncertainty, and economic modeling; and software life-cycle cost evaluation.

Credit Recommendation: In the graduate degree category, 3 semester hours in Economics, Computer Engineering, Computer Software, or Software Engineering (9/87).

Electrical Fields and Circuits (87504)

Location: School of Engineering and Logistics, Red River Army Depot.

Length: 91 hours (6.5 weeks).

Dates: January 1975-September 1993.

Objective: To enable the student to analyze and design electrical systems.

Instruction: Major topics covered in the course are basic concepts of electrical fields and circuits. Methods of instruction include lecture, practical exercises, research, and an examination.

Credit Recommendation: In the upper division baccalaureate degree category, 4 semester hours in Electrical Engineering (6/84).

Electronic/Polymeric Materials and Production Processes (62600) (Formerly Product/Production Engineering III [83600])

Location: School of Engineering and Logistics, Red River Army Depot.

Length: *Version 1:* 60 hours (10 weeks); *Version 2:* 100 hours.

Dates: *Version 1:* January 1983-June 1995; *Version 2:* June 1995-Present.

Objective: *Version 1:* To give students an in-depth exposure to manufacturing and testing of electronic devices and nonmetals such as various plastics. *Version 2:* To provide the student with an in-depth exposure to manufacturing and testing of various electronic devices. Non-metals such as different plastics are also investigated.

Learning Outcome: Upon successful completion of this course, the student will be able to design an efficient manufactory system using the most appropriate manufacturing process for production of electronic and polymeric products and analyze designs of weapons systems and recommend design changes that will enhance producibility of polymeric and electronic components.

Instruction: *Version 1:* Major topics covered in the course are material characteristics, nonmetal production processes, and electronic production processes. Methods of instruction include five hours of lecture per week, one hour of laboratory, and written examinations. *Version 2:* Major topics covered in the course are electronic and polymeric materials, manufacturing of polymeric material, and manufacturing of electronic material. Methods of instruction include lecture, practical exercises, and written examinations.

Credit Recommendation: *Version 1:* In the graduate degree category, 3 semester hours in Mechanical Engineering (12/84). *Version 2:* In the graduate degree category, 3 semester hours in Industrial Engineering (6/95).

Electronics

Location: School of Engineering and Logistics, Red River Army Depot.

Length: 40 hours (3 weeks).

Dates: February 1982-December 1993.

Objective: To teach the student how to recognize various electrical/electronic components, know what their function is in a circuit, and analyze circuits using test equipment to identify faculty components.

Instruction: Major topics covered in the course are basic principles of electricity and its use in Army equipment. Methods of instruction include lecture; laboratory, five projects are worked in laboratory; and an examination.

Credit Recommendation: In the lower division baccalaureate/associate degree category, 1 semester hour in Electrical/ Electronics Technology or Industrial Arts (6/84).

Embedded Algorithms (65550) (Formerly Embedded Computer Algorithms [81550])

Location: School of Engineering and Logistics, Red River Army Depot.

Length: *Version 1:* 60 hours (10 weeks); *Version 2:* 100 hours (10 weeks).

Dates: *Version 1:* August 1986-December 1994; *Version 2:* January 1995-Present.

Objective: To teach the student theory and application of information structures and algorithms to design, implement, and maintain real-time systems.

Learning Outcome: *Version 1:* Upon successful completion of this course, the student will be able to apply theory of structures and algorithms to real-time applications such as data acquisition, process control, and interfacing. *Version 2:* Upon successful completion of this course, the student will be able explain and illustrate the use of discrete mathematics and linear algebra to the field of embedded algorithms and design and create computer algorithms for application in embedded real-time systems.

Instruction: *Version 1:* Major topics covered in the course are an introduction to the theory of information structures and algorithms and their application to design implementation of real-time systems; linear, tree, and graph structures; memory management; algorithm design and analysis; and real-time applications. Methods of instruction include three examinations (90 percent) and selected programs (10 percent). *Version 2:* Major topics covered in the course are discrete mathematics and linear algebra, fundamental data structures, sorting algorithms, and dynamic information structures. Methods of instruction include five hours of lecture and laboratory per week.

Credit Recommendation: *Versions 1 and 2:* In the graduate degree category, 3 semester hours in Computer Engineering, Computer Science, or Software Engineering (9/87) (6/95).

Engineering Applications for Computers (88558)

Location: School of Engineering and Logistics, Red River Army Depot.

Length: 70 hours (10 weeks).

Dates: January 1980-September 1993.

Objective: To teach the student scientific computer programming theory.

Instruction: Major topics covered in the course are FORTRAN statements, FORTRAN programming, and disk input/ output. Methods of instruction include lecture, laboratory with outside assignments, a examination, and research papers.

Credit Recommendation: In the upper division baccalaureate degree category, 4 semester hours in Computer Science (6/84).

Engineering Management

Location: School of Engineering and Logistics, Red River Army Depot.

Length: 50 hours (10 weeks).

Dates: September 1976-September 1993.

Objective: To provide students with management techniques.

Instruction: Major topics covered in the course are the study of top-level decision-making structures, analysis of economic and social forces affecting defense decisions, and study of various management system philosophies and theories. Methods of instruction include study of staff studies and engineering reports, five hours of lecture per week, and written examinations and reports.

Credit Recommendation: In the upper division baccalaureate degree category, 3 semester hours in Management (12/84).

Engineering Materials (87503)

Location: School of Engineering and Logistics, Red River Army Depot.

Length: 74 hours (6 weeks).

Dates: January 1975-September 1993.

Objective: To enable the student to select appropriate materials for engineering applications after considering service life, corrosion, and environmental effects.

Instruction: Major topics covered in the course are metals, polymers, and ceramics. Methods of instruction include lecture, practical exercises, research, and an examination.

Credit Recommendation: In the upper division baccalaureate degree category, 3 semester hours in Mechanical Engineering (6/84).

Engineering Statistics (60511) (Formerly Engineering Statistics [84511])

Location: School of Engineering and Logistics, Red River Army Depot.

Length: *Version 1:* 60 hours (10 weeks); *Version 2:* 90 hours (10 weeks).

Dates: January 1974-Present.

Objective: To provide students with knowledge of probability and statistical methods, and their application to engineering problems.

Learning Outcome: Upon successful completion of this course, the student will be able to model, analyze, and evaluate events and parameters which are nondeterministic; determine probabilities of composite and conditional events; utilize appropriate discrete and continuous probability distribution models or to derive the distribution of a given function of variables; determine and calculate appropriate numerical measures of central tendency and dispersion; and determine the appropriate sampling technique to utilize, how to conduct sampling and evaluate results.

Instruction: Major topics covered in the course are probability theory, random variables and probability distributions, expected values, and sampling statistics. Methods of instruction include written examinations, practical exercises, lecture, and laboratory.

Credit Recommendation: In the graduate degree category, 3 semester hours in Statistics (12/84) (6/95).

Engineering Test Design and Analysis (60519) (Formerly Design of Engineering Experiments [82519])

Location: School of Engineering and Logistics, Red River Army Depot.

Length: *Version 1:* 60 hours (10 weeks); *Version 2:* 90 hours (10 weeks).

Dates: *Version 1:* February 1977-June 1995; *Version 2:* June 1995-Present.

Objective: *Version 1:* To provide students with an understanding of statistical model-building technology so that students can use data collection and analysis skills. Planning is emphasized to optimize information and cost of experiments. *Version 2:* To provide the student with knowledge of experimental design methods, analysis of variance, and regression methods.

Learning Outcome: Upon successful completion of this course, the student will

be able to apply, formulate, and contrast various statistical models used in designing collection, analyzing, and evaluation of engineering test data, formulate data collection systems to obtain the maximum amount of information of the effect of one or more variables on a response, and construct multivariable prediction equations for response measurements.

Instruction: *Version 1:* Major topics covered in the course are linear regression, multiple regression, nonlinear regression, one-way analysis of variance, and blocked designs. Methods of instruction include five hours of lecture per week, one hour of laboratory per week, and written examinations. *Version 2:* Major topics covered in the course are introduction to design of experiments, analysis of variance techniques, design and analysis of factorial designs, regression methods, and special experimental designs. Methods of instruction include five hours of lecture and four hours of laboratory which includes computer applications.

Credit Recommendation: *Versions 1 and 2:* In the graduate degree category, 3 semester hours in Industrial Engineering (12/84) (6/95).

Experimental Design (84519)

Location: School of Engineering and Logistics, Red River Army Depot.

Length: 60 hours (10 weeks).

Dates: January 1977-September 1993.

Objective: To provide students with information on model-building technology and engineering experimentation methods.

Instruction: Major topics covered in the course are data collection and analysis, empirical development of parameters, and time-dependent models. The applications of experimental design to safety research are stressed. Methods of instruction include dive hours of lecture per week, one hour of laboratory per week, and written examinations.

Credit Recommendation: In the graduate degree category, 3 semester hours in Industrial Engineering (12/84).

Financial Management (50070)
(Formerly Financial Management)

Location: School of Engineering and Logistics, Red River Army Depot.

Length: 20 hours (1 week).

Dates: January 1975-Present.

Objective: To provide the student with a knowledge of the overall DOD and Army financial management structure.

Learning Outcome: Upon successful completion of this course, the student will be able to recognize policies and laws that have determined DoD's organizational and financial structure, recognize the Army's budget formulation and the external factors that influence the formulation process, recognize the Congressional Appropriation and Authorization processes, and recognize the review and audit function used to assure compliance with the law and established policies.

Instruction: Major topics covered in the course are aspects of financial management, such as the stock funds, that are most affected by the actions of graduate interns. Methods of instruction include lecture, classroom exercises, and an examination.

Credit Recommendation: In the graduate degree category, 1 semester hour in Financial Management or Public Finance (6/84) (6/95).

Human Factors in System Design (60568)
(Formerly Human Factors Engineering in Systems Design [84568])

Location: School of Engineering and Logistics, Red River Army Depot.

Length: *Version 1:* 50 hours (10 weeks); *Version 2:* 100 hours (10 weeks).

Dates: *Version 1:* June 1982-June 1995; *Version 2:* June 1995-Present.

Objective: To provide students with an understanding of an industrially oriented human engineering tool for systematic analysis.

Learning Outcome: Upon successful completion of this course, the student will be able to understand how human physiological and environmental factors affect human/system performance; develop and apply human engineering tools for systematic analysis; evaluate man-machine systems along with complex equipment operation and maintenance procedures; and identify the physical and design factors for design, protection, installation, maintenance, inspection, and operation of hardware, personnel subsystems, and system procedures.

Instruction: *Version 1:* Major topics covered in the course are an identification and evaluation of man-machine systems leading to the development of human factors data design and hardware, personnel subsystems, and system procedures for operations and maintenance. Methods of instruction include lecture and written examinations. *Version 2:* Major topics covered in the course are human factors in system development, information input activities, man-machine dynamics, layout of workplaces, and anthropometry. Methods of instruction include five hours lecture and laboratory per week, practical exercises, and written examinations.

Credit Recommendation: *Versions 1 and 2:* In the graduate degree category, 3 semester hours in Industrial Engineering (12/84) (6/95).

Human Operations in Complex Systems (82560)

Location: School of Engineering and Logistics, Red River Army Depot.

Length: 60 hours (10 weeks); six 1-hour meetings per week.

Dates: September 1976-September 1993.

Objective: To provide students with an understanding of how human physiological and environmental factors affect system performance.

Instruction: Major topics covered in the course are human engineering tools for systematic analysis identification and evaluation of man-machine systems and the development of human factors and system procedures for operation and maintenance of complex equipment. Methods of instruction include five hours of lecture per week, one hour of laboratory per week, and written examinations.

Credit Recommendation: In the graduate degree category, 3 semester hours in Industrial Engineering (12/84).

Integrated Logistics Support (50150)
(Formerly Integrated Logistics Support)

Location: School of Engineering and Logistics, Red River Army Depot.

Length: 60 hours (3 weeks).

Dates: January 1975-Present.

Objective: To learn the phases and possible problem areas in the life cycle of an end item, including the interfaces that occur internally within AMC and externally with other elements in the Department of the Army and the Department of Defense.

Learning Outcome: Upon successful completion of this course, the student will be able to identify and understand ILS as it applies to Life Cycle Management, possess an understanding for the relationship of events and the responsible parties, possess a working knowledge of organizational linkage for Army Materiel Acquisition, and understand the materiel need process and alternative methods to satisfy army materiel needs under the elements of ILS.

Instruction: Major topics covered in the course are the development of the maintenance concept of the materiel need and progresses through the feasibility, design, development, testing, evaluation, procurement, and production phases. Methods of instruction include lecture, discussion, and an examination.

Credit Recommendation: In the graduate degree category, 3 semester hours in Management or Industrial Management (6/84) (6/95).

Introduction to AMC Commodity Command Standard Systems (51360) (Formerly Introduction to CCSS Commodity Command Standard System)

Location: School of Engineering and Logistics, Red River Army Depot.

Length: 20 hours (1 week).

Dates: January 1975-Present.

Objective: To provide the student with a knowledge of the Commodity Command Standard System for Inventory Management.

Learning Outcome: Upon successful completion of this course, the student will be able to understand the CCSS process, the seven major functional areas, documentation, structure, and file system and analyze, interpret, and apply data extracted from the documents and files.

Instruction: Major topics covered in the course are how provisioning, cataloging, supply control, maintenance, and international logistics are performed within the Commodity Command Standard System. Methods of instruction include lecture, discussion, laboratory exercises, and an examination.

Credit Recommendation: In the upper division baccalaureate degree category, 1 semester hour in Management (6/84) (6/95).

Introduction to Reliability, Availability, and Maintainability (50239) (Formerly Reliability, Availability, and Maintainability)

Location: School of Engineering and Logistics, Red River Army Depot.

Length: 20 hours (1 week).

Dates: January 1975-Present.

Objective: To teach the student the basic elements, theory, and practical application of reliability engineering.

Learning Outcome: Upon successful completion of this course, the student will be able to calculate and understand redundant circuits (series, parallel, and combinations of both), understand reliability prediction and analysis of failure rate data, calculate system effectiveness (availability, MTTF, MTBF, MTTR, MDT, MAMDT, etc.), understand and apply definitions and concepts, and apply probability theory and influencing factors.

Instruction: Major topics covered in the course are the theories and techniques pertinent to the evaluation of engineering problems in system reliability, maintainability, and other measures of system effectiveness. Methods of instruction include lecture, practical exercises, and written examinations.

Credit Recommendation: In the graduate degree category, 1 semester hour in Industrial Engineering (6/84) (6/95).

Introduction to the Army in the Field/Organization of the Army (50203) (Formerly Introduction to the Army in the Field)

Location: School of Engineering and Logistics, Red River Army Depot.

Length: *Version 1:* 24 hours (1 week); *Version 2:* 20 hours (1 week).

Dates: *Version 1:* January 1975-June 1995; *Version 2:* June 1995-Present.

Objective: To teach the student how the Army and supporting government agencies are organized and relate to each other.

Learning Outcome: Upon successful completion of this course, the student will be able to discuss the chain of command from the President to the unit level within the Department of the Army, understand the organization, mission, and functions of the major army commands, and describe the interrelationships of the General Services Administration, the Defense Logistics Agency, and the Army Materiel Command.

Instruction: Major topics covered in the course are the operational and technical chains of command. Methods of instruction include lecture and an examination.

Credit Recommendation: *Versions 1 and 2:* In the upper division baccalaureate degree category, 1 semester hour in Military Science (6/84) (6/95).

Issues (51410)

Location: School of Engineering and Logistics, Red River Army Depot.

Length: 20 hours (1 week).

Dates: January 1975-Present.

Objective: To provide the student with a comprehensive study of the standard depot system stock control procedures used in processing materiel release orders and related supply documents and issuing materiel within the AMC distribution system.

Learning Outcome: Upon successful completion of this course, the student will be able to identify MRO computer processing, key concepts, and materiel documentation flow; identify management reports used to monitor performance in the issue function; and identify issue problems and recommend solutions.

Instruction: Major topics covered in the course are terms, policies, responsibilities, and procedures used for materiel release order processing of general supplies; shipment planning; stock selection; issues and warehouse details consolidation; packing and marking; outloading operations; special processing; related documentation; performance reporting; Depot Direct Support System (DSS) procedures; containerization; and preparation of materiel for Consolidation Containerization Points (CCP). Methods of instruction include lecture, discussion, laboratory exercises, research, and an examination.

Credit Recommendation: In the upper division baccalaureate degree category, 1 semester hour in Industrial Management (6/84) (6/95).

Logistic Support Exercise (LOGEX) (50223) (Formerly Logistic Support Exercise)

Location: School of Engineering and Logistics, Red River Army Depot.

Length: 40 hours (1 week).

Dates: *Version 1:* January 1975-May 1995; *Version 2:* June 1995-Present.

Objective: To allow the student to test management skills in the initial and follow-up support of a weapon system.

Learning Outcome: *Version 2:* Upon successful completion of this course, the student will be able to function in a support role, apply logistics knowledge, and participate as a "team player".

Instruction: *Version 1:* Major topics covered in this course are a management decision-making exercises in which the student plays a particular role in support of an end item; the roles the student must play are maintenance manager, item manager, comptroller, and battalion supply manager. Costs are affixed to all decisions made by the student. Methods of instruction include lecture, extensive use of practical exercises, and analyzing exercise results. *Version 2:* Major topics covered in the course are development of a prototype weapon system, its initial fielding and provisioning, and its logistics support for 36 months. Costs are affixed to all decisions made by the student. Methods of instruction include lecture, extensive use of practical exercises, and evaluation by analyzing exercise results.

Credit Recommendation: *Version 1:* In the graduate degree category, 3 semester hours in Management (6/84). *Version 2:* In the graduate degree category, 3 semester hours in Management or Military Science (6/95).

Logistics Support Analysis (61518) (Formerly Logistics Support Analysis [82518])

Location: School of Engineering and Logistics, Red River Army Depot.

Length: *Version 1:* 70 hours (10 weeks); *Version 2:* 100 hours.

Dates: *Version 1:* February 1981-June 1995; *Version 2:* June 1995-Present.

Objective: To provide the student with an orientation to the Army Logistics Support System.

Learning Outcome: Upon successful completion of this course, the student will be able to apply systems engineering approaches to the Army acquisition and logistic support processes, use methods and techniques for analysis and assessment of acquisition and support systems designing, and use Integrated Logistics Support (ILS) to ensure compatibility between support systems and equipment.

Instruction: *Version 1:* Major topics covered in the course are methods and techniques for analyzing and assessing the effectiveness of the support system and on ILS in ensuring the compatibility of equipment and its support system. Methods of instruction include five hours of lecture per week, one hour discussion per week, one hour of laboratory per week, and a written examination. *Version 2:* Major topics covered in the course are introduction to integrated logistics support, logistics engineering principles, logistics support analysis, and computer-aided acquisition. Methods of instruction include lecture, laboratory, practical exercises, and written examinations.

Credit Recommendation: *Versions 1 and 2:* In the upper division baccalaureate degree category, 3 semester hours in Industrial Engineering (12/84) (6/95).

Maintainability Analysis (60517) (Formerly Maintainability Analysis [82517])

Location: School of Engineering and Logistics, Red River Army Depot.

Length: *Version 1:* 60 hours (10 weeks); *Version 2:* 100 hours (10 weeks).

Dates: *Version 1:* February 1977-June 1995; *Version 2:* June 1995-Present.

Objective: To provide students with techniques that can be used for system analysis relative to maintainability areas.

Learning Outcome: Upon successful completion of this course, the student will be able to apply systems engineering principles, statistics, and current military standards to analyze systems for maintainability considerations; derive and specify maintainability requirements based on the overall system functional requirements; utilize various testing procedure to demonstrate accomplishment of system goals; predict and allocate maintainability parameters to subsystem levels, and evaluate systems for effectiveness of maintainability accomplishment.

Instruction: *Versions 1 and 2:* Major topics covered in the course are maintainability in quantitative and qualitative terms, maintainability as a system characteristic, maintainability demonstration techniques, maintainability allocation and prediction, and maintainability design factors. Methods of instruction include five hours of lecture per week, one hour of laboratory per week, and written examinations.

Credit Recommendation: *Versions 1 and 2:* In the graduate degree category, 3 semester hours in Industrial Engineering (12/84) (6/95).

Maintainability Analysis and Design (88517)

Location: School of Engineering and Logistics, Red River Army Depot.

Length: 60 hours (10 weeks).

Dates: May 1981-September 1993.

Objective: To provide the student with techniques in maintainability that are used in product quality assurance.

Instruction: Major topics covered in the course are quantitative and qualitative terms, system requirements and characteristics, demonstration techniques, allocation and prediction, and design factors. Methods of instruction include lecture, laboratory exercises, and an examination.

Credit Recommendation: In the graduate degree category, 3 semester hours in Industrial Management (6/84).

Maintainability Case Studies (61516) (Formerly Maintainability Case Studies [82516])

Location: School of Engineering and Logistics, Red River Army Depot.

Length: *Version 1:* 60 hours (10 weeks) (6 one-hour meetings per week); *Version 2:* 100 hours (10 weeks).

Dates: *Version 1:* February 1981-June 1995; *Version 2:* June 1995-Present.

Objective: To provide students with examples of specific applications of reliability and maintainability principles in acquisition of Army equipment by following selected items through the development cycle to monitor maintainability inputs and accomplishments.

Learning Outcome: Upon successful completion of this course, the student will be able to develop and evaluate solutions to specific problems in the field of maintainability, especially as related to DoD problem areas; application of RAM principles in acquisition of Army equipment will be demonstrated by following selected items through the development cycle to monitor maintainability inputs and accomplishments; and attend and report on tutorials, presentations, and conferences at the Annual Reliability and Maintainability Symposium.

Instruction: *Version 1:* Major topics covered in the course are U.S. Army equipment's research and development cycle, selected current systems, and state-of-the-art developments in reliability and maintainability. Methods of instruction include five hours of lecture per week, one hour of laboratory per week, and written examinations. *Version 2:* Major topics covered in the course are the U.S. Army Equipment R&D Cycle Workshop, R&M programs for current system development, system development, and annual R&M Symposium. Methods of instruction include five hours of lecture and five hours of laboratory per week, practical exercises, and written examinations.

Credit Recommendation: *Versions 1 and 2:* In the upper division baccalaureate degree category, 3 semester hours in Military Science (12/84) (6/95).

Maintainability Research Project (61585) (Formerly Problems in Maintainability Engineering II [82585])

Location: School of Engineering and Logistics, Red River Army Depot.

Length: *Version 1:* 60 hours (10 weeks); *Version 2:* 100 hours (10 weeks).

Dates: *Version 1:* May 1977-June 1995; *Version 2:* June 1995-Present.

Objective: To demonstrate to students advanced engineering capability through resolution of one or two problems by professional problem-solving and documentation techniques.

Learning Outcome: Upon successful completion of this course, the student will be able to accomplish advanced study and research in the field of maintainability, especially as related to DoD problem areas and demonstrate professional problem-solving skills by choosing a manageable problem, evaluating pertinent background data and reference materials, performance of current literature survey and critical analysis, and formulation of a formal research proposal.

Instruction: *Versions 1 and 2:* Major topics covered in the course are research requirements and sources, research techniques and topic selection, and research problem and report. Methods of instruction include each student does original research on an Army problem area, one hour of lecture per week, five hours of research per week, and research reports.

Credit Recommendation: *Versions 1 and 2:* In the graduate degree category, 3 semester hours in Industrial Engineering (12/84) (6/95).

Maintenance Management (51470)

Location: School of Engineering and Logistics, Red River Army Depot.

Length: *Version 1:* 23 hours (1 week); *Version 2:* 30 hours.

Dates: *Version 1:* January 1975-October 1992; *Version 2:* October 1992-Present.

Objective: To provide the student with the knowledge of the entire Army maintenance system.

Learning Outcome: Upon successful completion of this course, the student will be able to be familiar with common terms and terminologies, compute maintenance expenditure limits, and be familiar with methods and procedures applicable to wholesale maintenance operations.

Instruction: Major topics covered in the course are the varied aspects of equipment maintenance from the types of maintenance accomplished, the organizations involved and responsibilities at each level, the proper initiation of a maintenance program, through the financial and procedural means of controlling maintenance costs and production; Army maintenance systems; and coding procedures. Methods of instruction include lecture, discussion, laboratory, and an examination.

Credit Recommendation: *Version 1:* In the upper division baccalaureate degree category, 1 semester hour in Management (6/84). *Version 2:* In the upper division baccalaureate degree category, 1 semester hour in Maintenance Management (6/95).

Management Analysis

Location: School of Engineering and Logistics, Red River Army Depot.

Length: 64 hours (2 weeks).

Dates: January 1975-June 1997.

Objective: To provide the student with the theory and application of qualitative and quantitative methods that can be used in conducting a decision risk analysis.

Instruction: Major topics covered in the course are analytical techniques, decision analysis, subjective estimating network techniques, and simulation. Methods of instruction include lecture, laboratory, case studies, and an examination.

Credit Recommendation: In the upper division baccalaureate degree category, 2 semester hours in Management and in the graduate degree category, 1 semester hour in Management (6/84).

Management Information Systems

Location: School of Engineering and Logistics, Red River Army Depot.

Length: 80 hours (4 weeks).

Dates: January 1975-June 1997.

Objective: To provide the student with a knowledge of advanced data processing systems so that students will be able to program a computer, understand computer terminology, and develop automated systems.

Instruction: Major topics covered in the course are FORTRAN statements, FORTRAN program, disk input/output, and general information on computer technology. Methods of instruction include lecture, laboratory, and weekly examinations.

Credit Recommendation: In the graduate degree category, 3 semester hours in Data Processing (6/84).

Management of Major Items (51380)

Location: School of Engineering and Logistics, Red River Army Depot.

Length: 40 hours (1 week).

Dates: June 1980-Present.

Objective: To introduce the student to methods used in managing major items.

Learning Outcome: Upon successful completion of this course, the student will be able to know common terminology and specific facts relevant to the management of major items; interpret computer output and apply the necessary concepts needed in the management of major items; evaluate the relevancy of data; and know methods used in SACS, CBS-X, SSN System, TAEDP, and the ERPS.

Instruction: Major topics covered in the course are funding, computing requirements, and the Army Materiel Plan. Methods of instruction include lecture, laboratory, and an examination.

Credit Recommendation: In the upper division baccalaureate degree category, 2 semester hours in Management (6/84) (6/95).

Management of Secondary Items (51370)

Location: School of Engineering and Logistics, Red River Army Depot.

Length: *Version 1:* 120 hours (6 weeks); *Version 2:* 100 hours.

Dates: *Version 1:* January 1975-January 1993; *Version 2:* January 1993-Present.

Objective: To introduce the student to the techniques of inventory management of secondary items at the wholesale level.

Learning Outcome: Upon successful completion of this course, the student will be able to understand the theory of inventory management and the Army's method of categorizing, obtaining information, and supporting data and analyze data and interpret the results from forecasting demand data, asset data, requirements determination, supply control studies, funding, and distribution management.

Instruction: *Version 1:* Major topics covered in the course are management of secondary items; organization for inventory management; selective item management; data integration and standardization; Commodity Command Standard System structures; and return disposal, output products, and file structure. Methods of instruction include lecture, laboratory exercises, and weekly examinations. *Version 2:* Major topics covered in the course are Defense Integrated Materiel Management System (DIMMS), Supply Management Grouping Designator (SMGD), the Study Method Code (SMG), inventory management processing code, and other systems. Methods of instruction include lecture, classroom exercises, audio/visual material, and an examination.

Credit Recommendation: *Versions 1 and 2:* In the graduate degree category, 3 semester hours in Management (6/84) (6/95).

Management Techniques: Parts I and II (82508,82509)

Location: School of Engineering and Logistics, Red River Army Depot.

Length: 70 hours (10 weeks); seven 1-hour meetings per week.
Dates: September 1980-September 1993.
Objective: To make the student proficient in those management techniques that will be required in their civil service center.
Instruction: Major topics covered in the course are managerial processes, management information systems, and personnel processes. Methods of instruction include five hours of lecture per week, one hour of discussion per week, one hour of laboratory per week, and a written examination.
Credit Recommendation: In the upper division baccalaureate degree category, 3 semester hours in Management (12/84).

Material Acquisition and Total Quality Management (60506) (Formerly Army Systems Management and Engineering [82506])

Location: School of Engineering and Logistics, Red River Army Depot.
Length: *Version 1:* 60 hours (10 weeks); *Version 2:* 90 hours (10 weeks).
Dates: *Version 1:* September 1976-June 1995; *Version 2:* June 1995-Present.
Objective: To provide the student with a comprehensive study of the organization, management tools, and procedures used to develop DoD equipment.
Learning Outcome: Upon successful completion of this course, the student will be able to explain the role of various DoD organizations in the Materiel Acquisition process; identify milestones, documents, and procedures used during each phase of weapon system development; demonstrate knowledge of environmental considerations in equipment design and acquisition; know the importance of continuous improvement using TQM principles in the team approach; and assess his oral communicative skills through student presentations.
Instruction: *Version 1:* Major topics covered in the course are defense management organizations, level of army maintenance, materiel acquisition management, Army planning and budgeting for system development, and acquisition of Army systems. Methods of instruction include five hours of lecture per week, one hour of laboratory per week, and written examinations. *Version 2:* Major topics covered in the course are DoD organizational structure, life cycle management, Army acquisition pollution prevention, total quality management (TQM), and communication techniques. Methods of instruction include five hours of lecture and four hours of laboratory per week, practical exercises, and written examinations.
Credit Recommendation: *Versions 1 and 2:* In the upper division baccalaureate degree category, 3 semester hours in Military Science (12/84) (6/95).

Material Technology (64532) (Formerly Army Manufacturing and Testing Technology [88532])

Location: School of Engineering and Logistics, Red River Army Depot.
Length: *Version 1:* 50 hours (5 weeks); *Version 2:* 100 hours (10 weeks).
Dates: *Version 1:* July 1980-June 1995; *Version 2:* June 1995-Present.
Objective: *Version 1:* To provide the student with information on the Army's Manufacturing Methods and Technology Program. *Version 2:* To provide the student with knowledge of potential quality problems connected with materials and how to prevent or detect the problems.
Learning Outcome: Upon successful completion of this course, the student will be able to recognize the potential of introducing discontinuities in materials due to manufacturing processes and methods of detecting the discontinuities; recognize potential corrosion problems and recommend possible solutions to alleviate them; and formulate a checklist for auditing a manufacturing process or product design for materials and methods utilized.
Instruction: *Version 1:* Major topics covered in the course are concepts and methods with emphasis on procedures and techniques associated with AMC Manufacturing Methods and Technology Program and Materials Testing Program; and nondestructive testing and special acceptance inspection equipment. Methods of instruction include lecture, outside work, and an examination. *Version 2:* Major topics covered in the course are material characteristics, material processes, nondestructive testing, and corrosion control. Methods of instruction include five hours of lecture and laboratory per week, oral presentations, and a written examination.
Credit Recommendation: *Version 1:* In the lower division baccalaureate/associate degree category, 3 semester hours in Engineering Technology (6/84). *Version 2:* In the upper division baccalaureate degree category, 3 semester hours in Engineering Technology (6/95).

Materials and Primary Production (62502) (Formerly Product/Production Engineering I [83502])

Location: School of Engineering and Logistics, Red River Army Depot.
Length: *Version 1:* 80 hours (13 weeks); *Version 2:* 100 hours (10 weeks).
Dates: *Version 1:* January 1976-June 1995; *Version 2:* June 1995-Present.
Objective: To provide students with an understanding of the scope of AMC product/production engineering. Activities concerning interrelationships among materials, production, and selection for uses in design.
Learning Outcome: Upon successful completion of this course, the student will be able to identify the role of PPE in selecting manufacturing materials and processes; analyze the relationship between material microstructure, alloy content, and material properties; compare the capabilities of various manufacturing processes in the areas of casting, powder metallurgy, and hot forming; and assess the productivity of systems during early stages of design and recommend changes to lower costs and enhance producibility. This course includes "hands-on" experience with a Computer-Aided Design (CAD) system.
Instruction: *Version 1:* Major topics covered in the course are a product/production engineering overview; covers research, development and acquisition policies and procedures, materiel characteristics, and uses production processes. Methods of instruction include lecture, laboratory, and a written examination. *Version 2:* Major topics covered in the course are material properties and structures, alloys and heat treatment, primary production processes, and introduction to CAD. Methods of instruction include five hours of lecture per week, two hours of laboratory per week, three hours practical exercises per week, and written and laboratory examinations.
Credit Recommendation: *Versions 1 and 2:* In the upper division baccalaureate degree category, 3 semester hours in Mechanical Engineering (12/84) (6/95).

Materiel Acquisition Management (83509)

Location: School of Engineering and Logistics, Red River Army Depot.
Length: 60 hours (10 weeks).

Dates: January 1976-September 1993.

Objective: To give students an understanding of materiel acquisition management and its application to Army materiel.

Instruction: Major topics covered in the course are life-cycle model, configuration management, force modernization process, weapon system and equipment support analysis, and financial management. Methods of instruction include five hours of lecture per week, one hour of laboratory per week, and written examinations.

Credit Recommendation: In the lower division baccalaureate/associate degree category, 3 semester hours in Military Science (12/84).

Mathematical Statistics (81511)

Location: School of Engineering and Logistics, Red River Army Depot.

Length: *Version 1:* 66 hours (11 weeks); *Version 2:* 80 hours (10 weeks) .

Dates: *Version 1:* August 1986-December 1988; *Version 2:* January 1989-September 1993.

Objective: To provide the student with knowledge of basic probability and statistics and their application to engineering problems.

Learning Outcome: Upon successful completion of this course, the student will be able to solve basic engineering problems of a probabilistic or statistical nature; apply statistical techniques to problems in software engineering; and communicate the techniques developed with other engineers and managers.

Instruction: Major topics covered in the course are mathematical statistics, probability, random variables, probability distributions, mathematical expectations, sampling distributions, central limit theorem, integral estimation, and hypothesis testing. Methods of instruction include lecture and problem-solving.

Credit Recommendation: *Version 1:* In the upper division baccalaureate degree category, 3 semester hours in Mathematical Statistics (9/87). *Version 2:* In the graduate degree category, 3 semester hours in Statistical Methods (2/90).

Mathematical Statistics for Product Assurance (88511)

Location: School of Engineering and Logistics, Red River Army Depot.

Length: 60 hours (10 weeks).

Dates: January 1980-September 1993.

Objective: To teach the student probability theory, random variables and probability distribution, expected values, and related statistical techniques.

Instruction: Major topics covered in the course are statistical concepts required for product assurance. Methods of instruction include lecture, practical exercises, research, examinations, and a research paper.

Credit Recommendation: In the graduate degree category, 3 semester hours in Statistics (6/84).

Mathematical Statistics I (87006)

Location: School of Engineering and Logistics, Red River Army Depot.

Length: 60 hours (10 weeks).

Dates: January 1989-September 1993.

Objective: To provide the student with an understanding of various statistical methods.

Learning Outcome: Upon successful completion of this course, the student will be able to successfully perform in future courses oriented toward the application of advanced statistical concepts.

Instruction: Major topics covered in the course are probability theory, random variables, expectation, distribution, and transformations of random variable functions. Methods of instruction include lecture, conference, practical exercises, and examinations.

Credit Recommendation: In the graduate degree category, 3 semester hours in Statistics (2/90). **NOTE:** Students should not receive credit for both this course and Mathematical Statistics I (82511).

Mathematical Statistics I (82511)

Location: School of Engineering and Logistics, Red River Army Depot.

Length: 60 hours (10 weeks); six 1-hour meetings per week.

Dates: September 1976-September 1993.

Objective: To provide the student with an understanding of various statistical methods.

Instruction: Major topics covered in the course are basic probability theory, random variables, sums of random variables, and expected values. Methods of instruction include five hours of lecture per week, one hour of laboratory per week, and written examinations.

Credit Recommendation: In the graduate degree category, 3 semester hours in Statistics (12/84).

Mathematical Statistics II (87007)

Location: School of Engineering and Logistics, Red River Army Depot.

Length: 65 hours (5 weeks).

Dates: February 1989-September 1993.

Objective: To provide the student with an understanding of sampling distributions, hypothesis testing, nonparametric evaluation techniques, and point and interval estimation using maximum likelihood and minimum variance techniques.

Learning Outcome: Upon successful completion of this course, the student will be able to successfully perform in future courses oriented toward application of more advanced statistical concepts.

Instruction: Major topics covered in the course are sampling distributions, hypothesis testing, nonparametric evaluation techniques, and point and interval estimation. Methods of instruction include lecture, conference, practical exercises, and examinations.

Credit Recommendation: In the graduate degree category, 3 semester hours in Statistics (2/90). **NOTE:** Students should not receive credit for both this course and Mathematical Statistics II (85215).

Mathematical Statistics II (82512)

Location: School of Engineering and Logistics, Red River Army Depot.

Length: 60 hours (10 weeks); six 1-hour meetings per week.

Dates: November 1976-September 1993.

Objective: To provide students with an understanding of sampling distribution, parameter estimation, hypothesis testing, and statistical experimental design.

Instruction: Major topics covered in the course are sampling statistics and distributions, estimation of parameters, and application of hypotheses. Methods of instruction include five hours of lecture per week, one hour of laboratory per week, and a written examination.

Credit Recommendation: In the graduate degree category, 3 semester hours in Statistics (12/84).

Microprocessor Controls (60540) (Formerly Microprocessor Controls [81540])

Location: School of Engineering and Logistics, Red River Army Depot.

Length: *Version 1:* 140 hours (10 weeks; three 1-hour lectures/week; one 2-hour lab/week); *Version 2:* 90 hours.

Dates: *Version 1:* January 1983-June 1995; *Version 2:* June 1995-Present.

Objective: *Version 1:* To give the student an understanding of microprocessor architecture, numbers, computer codes and arithmetic, and assembly language programming. *Version 2:* To provide students with a working knowledge of the use of microprocessor systems for monitoring and controlling physical processes.

Learning Outcome: *Version 2:* Upon successful completion of this course, the student will be able to demonstrate an understanding of the operation of a microprocessor and program a microprocessor in assembly language.

Instruction: *Version 1:* Major topics covered in the course are microcomputer operations and architecture, memory technology, peripheral support, and microcomputer applications in control. Methods of instruction include lecture, laboratory, and written examinations. *Version 2:* Major topics covered in the course are microprocessor fundamentals, internal operation, memory, and peripheral support. Methods of instruction include five hours lecture and four hours laboratory per week, and examination.

Credit Recommendation: *Version 1:* In the upper division baccalaureate degree category, 3 semester hours in Computer Engineering (9/87). *Version 2:* In the upper division baccalaureate degree category, 2 semester hours in Computer Science or Computer Engineering (6/95).

Military Standard Data Systems (51490) (Formerly Military Standard Data Systems [MSDS])

Location: School of Engineering and Logistics, Red River Army Depot.

Length: 60 hours (3 weeks).

Dates: January 1975-Present.

Objective: To define and discuss the current Military Standard Data Systems used by the Department of Defense, to include the development, scope, interface, and use of each.

Learning Outcome: Upon successful completion of this course, the student will be able to identify the various Military Standard Data Systems used by the logistics elements of the Department of Defense and describe the logistic function of each; demonstrate proficiency in the interpretation and use of code used by the various systems; understand the use of the forms used by the systems; and understand the procedures of each system and be able to select various documents to be used in various situations.

Instruction: Major topics covered in the course are the development, scope, and relationship of Military Standard Data Systems. Methods of instruction include lecture, group and individual practical exercises, application and analysis of practical exercises, presentations, projects, and examinations.

Credit Recommendation: In the upper division baccalaureate degree category, 1 semester hour in Military Science (6/84) (6/95).

Missiles and Rockets

Location: School of Engineering and Logistics, Red River Army Depot.

Length: 25 hours (1 week).

Dates: February 1982-December 1993.

Objective: To familiarize the student with basic principles of missiles and rockets.

Instruction: Major topics covered in the course are maintenance problems. Methods of instruction include lecture and an examination.

Credit Recommendation: In the lower division baccalaureate/associate degree category, 1 semester hour in Military Science (6/84).

Non-Destructive Testing (53850)

Location: School of Engineering and Logistics, Red River Army Depot.

Length: 40 hours (10 days).

Dates: January 1995-Present.

Objective: To provide students with the skills to compare and demonstrate nondestructive testing methods used by the Army including liquid penetrant, magnetic particle, radiography, ultrasonic, and Eddy current testing. Discussion of certification of N.D.T. personnel.

Learning Outcome: Upon successful completion of this course, the student will be able to know the various nondestructive testing methods, understand how the various methods work, and know which methods are applicable under given circumstances.

Instruction: Major topics covered in the course are nondestructive testing methods and discussion of certification of N.D.T. personnel. Methods of instruction include lecture and practical exercises.

Credit Recommendation: In the upper division baccalaureate degree category, 2 semester hours in Industrial Engineering (6/95).

Operating Systems (65576) (Formerly Software Configuration Management [51576])

Location: School of Engineering and Logistics, Red River Army Depot.

Length: *Version 1:* 50 hours (10 weeks); *Version 2:* 100 hours (10 weeks).

Dates: *Version 1:* August 1986-December 1994; *Version 2:* January 1995-Present.

Objective: *Version 1:* To present the student with the concepts, policies, and administrative requirements of configuration management. *Version 2:* To provide the student with knowledge of the concepts of various computer operating systems currently in use.

Learning Outcome: *Version 1:* Upon successful completion of this course, the student will be able to explain hardware configuration management practices; explain software configuration management practices; and apply configuration management principles of configuration identification, configuration control, configuration status accounting, and configuration auditing to a software development project. *Version 2:* Upon successful completion of this course, the student will be able to explain and illustrate the commonalities and differences between several different types of operating systems and relate the differences between operating systems to the need for different approaches to utilize these systems.

Instruction: *Version 1:* Major topics covered in the course are management aspects, specifications and engineering drawing, and configuration control. *Version 2:* Major topics covered in the course are an overview, process management, storage management, files and protection, and distributed systems. Methods of instruction include five hours of lecture and laboratory per week.

Credit Recommendation: *Versions 1 and 2:* In the graduate degree category, 3 semester hours in Computer Information Systems, Computer Science, or Software Engineering (9/87) (6/95).

Operational Analysis for Production Systems (83520)

Location: School of Engineering and Logistics, Red River Army Depot.

Length: 60 hours (10 weeks).

Dates: September 1976-September 1993.

Objective: To provide a survey of uses of operations research techniques.

Instruction: Methods of instruction include five hours of lecture per week, one hour of laboratory per week, and a written examination.

Credit Recommendation: In the graduate degree category, 3 semester hours in Industrial Management (12/84).

Oral Communications

Location: School of Engineering and Logistics, Red River Army Depot.

Length: 60 hours (3 weeks).

Dates: January 1975-December 1993.

Objective: To provide students with an awareness of the importance of effective communications within any organization and to provide practice in making prepared presentations and briefings.

Instruction: Major topics covered in the course are key points on proper presentations such as vocal, physical, emotional, and intellectual behavior on the platform. Methods of instruction include lecture, student presentations, evaluation of student presentations, and weekly examinations.

Credit Recommendation: In the lower division baccalaureate/associate degree category, 3 semester hours in Speech (6/84).

Physical Inventory (51420)

Location: School of Engineering and Logistics, Red River Army Depot.

Length: 20 hours (1 week).

Dates: January 1975-Present.

Objective: To provide the student with a knowledge of the physical inventory system, with interface between the depots and accountable supply distribution activities.

Learning Outcome: Upon successful completion of this course, the student will be able to identify the actions required in a physical inventory; identify the types of physical inventories prescribed by DoD; identify the conditions that require a physical inventory; and identify and present solutions to major problems associated with planning scheduling, and the actual conduct of a physical inventory.

Instruction: Major topics covered in the course are terms and definitions applicable to the physical inventory at all supply levels for general supplies and ammunition; location survey procedures; types of inventories; location record audit/match procedures; adjustments of records; performance reporting; registration of small arms; Materiel Release Details; and Physical Inventory Quality Control. Methods of instruction include lecture, discussion, laboratory exercises, research, satellite in-struction, computer simulation, and an examination.

Credit Recommendation: In the upper division baccalaureate degree category, 1 semester hour in Industrial Management (6/84) (6/95).

Pollution Prevention Engineering (60024)

Location: School of Engineering and Logistics, Red River Army Depot.

Length: 100 hours.

Dates: June 1995-Present.

Objective: To provide the student with the knowledge of manufacturing processes which generate pollution products, and techniques to minimize and control pollution.

Learning Outcome: Upon successful completion of this course, the student will be able to evaluate manufacturing processes, materials, and treatments for environmental consequences and identify pollutants and codes applicable.

Instruction: Major topics covered in the course are manufacturing process technology, air pollution, hazardous waste minimization, and systems engineering for pollution prevention. Methods of instruction include lecture and laboratory.

Credit Recommendation: In the graduate degree category, 3 semester hours in Environmental Science or Industrial Engineering (6/95).

Preservation and Packaging (50286)

Location: School of Engineering and Logistics, Red River Army Depot.

Length: 20 hours (1 week).

Dates: January 1975-Present.

Objective: To provide the student with the capability for working as a preservation and packaging specialist in the GS-2032 career field and related areas.

Learning Outcome: Upon successful completion of this course, the student will be able to know common terms applicable to preservation and packaging; understand the specification and standardization system in the DoD; apply packaging, preservation, and cleaning concepts of future work situations; know the types of preservations and methods of packaging, packing, cleaning, and marking military supplies; and recognize the relationship of preservation and packaging to receiving, storage, shipping, maintenance, production planning and control, and Army readiness.

Instruction: Major topics covered in the course are methods of cleaning, preservation, and packaging in accordance with military and civilian specifications. Methods of instruction include lecture, laboratory exercises, and an examination.

Credit Recommendation: In the upper division baccalaureate degree category, 1 semester hour in Industrial Management (6/84) (6/95).

Principles of Management (84508)

Location: School of Engineering and Logistics, Red River Army Depot.

Length: 50 hours (5 weeks).

Dates: September 1976-September 1993.

Objective: To make the student proficient in those management techniques necessary for managers during career progression.

Instruction: Major topics covered in the course are studying top-level decision-making structures; identifying and assessing the economic and social forces affecting defense decisions; analyzing various management systems, philosophies, and theories and their applications, limitations, and values to the Army; and presenting oral and written solutions of specified management problems. The structure of staff studies and engineering reports are given special emphasis. Methods of in-struction include nine hours of lecture per week, one hour of laboratory per week, written examinations, reports, and presentations.

Credit Recommendation: In the upper division baccalaureate degree category, 3 semester hours in Management (12/84).

Principles of Radiological Safety Engineering (84549)

Location: School of Engineering and Logistics, Red River Army Depot.

Length: 60 hours (10 weeks).

Dates: January 1978-September 1993.

Objective: To provide students with an understanding of the basic theory of nuclear reactions, radioactivity, and sources of radiation and their interaction with matter.

Instruction: Major topics covered in the course are atomic structure and radiation, radiation effects and dosimetry, radioactive materiel transportation, radioactive commodity system safety, internal and external permissible exposure limits, and protection against external radiation. Methods of instruction include five hours of lecture per week, one hour of laboratory per week, written examinations, and project presentations.

Credit Recommendation: In the graduate degree category, 3 semester hours in Safety Engineering (12/84).

Problems in Maintainability Engineering I

Location: School of Engineering and Logistics, Red River Army Depot.

Length: 60 hours (10 weeks); six 1-hour meetings per week.

Dates: February 1977-September 1993.

Objective: To give students advanced study and research in the field of maintainability engineering.

Instruction: Major topics covered in the course are research sources, research techniques, and topic selection. Methods of instruction include two hours of lecture per week, four hours of research per week, and research reports.

Credit Recommendation: In the graduate degree category, 3 semester hours in Industrial Engineering (12/84).

Problem-Solving Techniques (61570) (Formerly Problem-Solving Techniques [82570])

Location: School of Engineering and Logistics, Red River Army Depot.

Length: *Version 1:* 60 hours (10 weeks); *Version 2:* 100 hours (10 weeks).

Dates: *Version 1:* February 1974-June 1995; *Version 2:* June 1995-Present.

Objective: To provide students with scientific and engineering approaches to problem-solving and decision-making.

Learning Outcome: Upon successful completion of this course, the student will be able to apply scientific and engineering approaches to problem-solving and decision-making, optimize methods to be used to determine resource allocations to maximize efficiency and output, synthesize Markov models for stochastic systems, determine and analyze risk associated with various program approaches, and formulate and solve goal programming problems.

Instruction: *Version 1:* Major topics covered in the course are presentations of optimization problems, Markov decision processes, decision risk analysis, and dynamic programming. Methods of instruction include five hours of lecture per week, one hour of laboratory per week, and an examination. *Version 2:* Major topics covered in the course are optimization problems, Markov decision processes, decision risk analysis, and advanced linear and goal programming. Methods of instruction include five hours lecture and laboratory per week, practical exercises, and written examinations.

Credit Recommendation: *Versions 1 and 2:* In the graduate degree category, 3 semester hours in Operations Research (12/84) (6/95).

Procurement Policies and Procedures for Engineers (87005)

Location: School of Engineering and Logistics, Red River Army Depot.

Length: 50 hours (10 weeks).

Dates: October 1989-September 1993.

Objective: To provide the student with a working knowledge of the defense procurement system for technical personnel, including the legal aspects, policies, and procedures.

Learning Outcome: Upon successful completion of this course, the student will be able to compare the formal advertising and negotiation methods of government procedure, evaluation of technical proposals, and cost and price analysis; discuss contract law, work statements, specifications, and other aspects of acquisition management; and identify items of concern in contract administration, including taxes, insurance, patents, modification, and termination procedures.

Instruction: Major topics covered in the course are initial planning in acquisition management, preparation and award of contracts, contract administration and negotiations, and test and evaluation contracting. Methods of instruction include lecture.

Credit Recommendation: In the graduate degree category, 1 semester hour in Contract Law (2/90).

Procurement Policies and Procedures for Engineers (88506)

Location: School of Engineering and Logistics, Red River Army Depot.

Length: 50 hours (5 weeks).

Dates: July 1980-September 1993.

Objective: To give the student a working knowledge of the defense procurement system for technical personnel.

Instruction: Major topics covered in the course are legal aspects, policies, and procedures. Methods of instruction include lecture, practical assignments, written examinations, and reports.

Credit Recommendation: In the upper division baccalaureate degree category, 3 semester hours in Business Administration (6/84).

Product Assurance Management (64507) (Formerly Product Assurance Management and Engineering II)

Location: School of Engineering and Logistics, Red River Army Depot.

Length: *Version 1:* 50 hours (5 weeks); *Version 2:* 100 hours.

Dates: *Version 1:* January 1980-June 1995; *Version 2:* June 1995-Present.

Objective: *Version 1:* To provide the student with a knowledge of product assurance and engineering with increasing emphasis on the management of product assurance and its interface with other functional areas. *Version 2:* To provide the student with an understanding of the role of product assurance with emphasis on the management of product assurance functions and techniques.

Learning Outcome: Upon successful completion of this course, the student will be able to identify role and terminology of product assurance; prepare quality cost studies, analyze and present cost information to support/quality functions; formulate management plans to control quality based on knowledge of product assurance tools and philosophy, and identify situations in which an expert system can be used to increase productivity.

Instruction: *Version 1:* Major topics covered in the course are maintenance, logistics, laboratories, and design items, how quality affects design practices, and review quality design techniques available to the engineer. Methods of instruction include lecture, outside work, examinations, and written reports. *Version 2:* Major topics covered in the course are product assurance policies, objectives, and organization; quality costs; product assurance management; and quality improvement and expert systems. Methods of instruction include lecture, laboratory, practical exercises, and written examinations.

Credit Recommendation: *Version 1:* In the lower division baccalaureate/associate degree category, 3 semester hours in Industrial Management (6/84). *Version 2:* In the upper division baccalaureate degree category, 4 semester hours in Industrial Engineering (6/95).

Product Assurance Management and Engineering I (88503)

Location: School of Engineering and Logistics, Red River Army Depot.

Length: 60 hours (10 weeks).

Dates: January 1980-September 1993.

Objective: To give the student a survey of the various product assurance management and technical tools, techniques, and technical guidance (including Army regulations, standards, pamphlets, directives, and other published material).

Instruction: Major topics covered in the course are the Army equipment life cycle and its relationship to product assurance and tests. Methods of instruction include lecture, laboratory, examinations, and written reports.

Credit Recommendation: In the lower division baccalaureate/associate degree category, 3 semester hours in Military Science (6/84).

Production Engineering Programs (62506) (Formerly Army Manufacturing Technology [83506])

Location: School of Engineering and Logistics, Red River Army Depot.

Length: *Version 1:* 60 hours (10 weeks); *Version 2:* 100 hours (10 weeks).

Dates: *Version 1:* January 1976-June 1995; *Version 2:* June 1995-Present.

Objective: *Version 1:* To give students an introduction to Army producibility engineering programs. *Version 2:* To provide students with an introduction to production engineering as related to Army manufacturing.

Learning Outcome: Upon successful completion of this course, the student will be able to be familiar with a wide variety of production engineering programs in AMC, explain the relationship among these programs and how these programs function in the concurrent engineering scheme, become familiar with the regulatory requirements, purposes, documentation, and responsibilities of these programs, and examine the requirements for cost/schedule control systems used in acquisitions and program management. A variety of production facilities will be toured.

Instruction: *Version 1:* Major topics covered in the course are producibility, producibility engineering and planning, military adaptation of commercial items, manufacturing methods and technology, value engineering, and productivity. Six hours of lecture per week. Evaluation through written examination. *Version 2:* Major topics covered in the course are concurrent engineering, production support programs, mobilization planning, cost/schedule (CSCS), and product facility tours. Methods of instruction include case studies, field trips, and five hours of lecture and laboratory per week.

Credit Recommendation: *Version 1:* In the upper division baccalaureate degree category, 3 semester hours in Military Science (12/84). *Version 2:* In the upper division baccalaureate degree category, 3 semester hours in Industrial or Manufacturing Technology (6/95).

Production Modeling Techniques (83576)

Location: School of Engineering and Logistics, Red River Army Depot.

Length: 60 hours (10 weeks).

Dates: January 1983-September 1993.

Objective: To provide students with an understanding of scientific and engineering approaches to the modeling of production systems.

Instruction: Major topics covered in the course are Markov processes, forecasting techniques, and munitions production systems. Methods of instruction include five hours of lecture per week, one hour of laboratory per week, and written examinations.

Credit Recommendation: In the graduate degree category, 3 semester hours in Industrial Engineering (12/84).

Production Planning and Control (51440)

Location: School of Engineering and Logistics, Red River Army Depot.

Length: *Version 1:* 78 hours (7 weeks); *Version 2:* 40 hours (2 weeks).

Dates: *Version 1:* January 1975-June 1995; *Version 2:* June 1995-Present.

Objective: *Version 1:* To teach the student how to plot a production schedule that will meet a production deadline when placed in a production control situation. *Version 2:* To instruct the student in missions and functions of an Army production planning and control organization.

Learning Outcome: Upon successful completion of this course, the student will be able to discuss the purpose and functions of a depot supply production planning and control organization and its relationship with the Materiel Readiness Commands (MRCs) and the Depot Systems Command (DESCOM).

Instruction: *Version 1:* Major topics covered in the course are principles and fundamentals of program planning and control as applied to various types of activities. Methods of instruction include lecture, discussion, and an examination. *Version 2:* Major topics covered in the course are the purpose and functions of a depot supply product planning and control organization. Methods of instruction include lecture, laboratory, research, and an examination.

Credit Recommendation: *Version 1:* In the graduate degree category, 4 semester hours in Industrial Management (6/84). *Version 2:* In the upper division baccalaureate degree category, 2 semester hours in Industrial Management (6/95).

Production Planning and Control (52620)

Location: School of Engineering and Logistics, Red River Army Depot.

Length: *Version 1:* 40 hours (2 weeks); *Version 2:* 104 hours .

Dates: *Version 1:* January 1975-June 1995; *Version 2:* June 1995-Present.

Objective: To instruct the student in missions and functions of an Army production planning and control organization.

Learning Outcome: Upon successful completion of this course, the student will be able to understand and use forecasting models, apply various review techniques for tracking and costing production, understand and manage the five M's (manpower, money, machines, methods, and materials), and understand work authorization, product and process planning, routing, material management, and scheduling.

Instruction: *Version 1:* Major topics covered in the course are the purpose and functions of a depot supply product planning and control organization and its relationship with Materiel Readiness Command and the Depot System Command. Methods of instruction include a product planning and control related group project, lecture, laboratory, research, and an examination. *Version 2:* Major topics covered in the course are principles and design of production control systems, planning and forecasting, and specific methods and techniques used by the Army. Methods of instruction include lecture, classroom exercises, audio/visual material, case studies, laboratory, research, and examinations.

Credit Recommendation: *Version 1:* In the graduate degree category, 1 semester hour in Industrial Management (6/84). *Version 2:* In the upper division baccalaureate degree category, 3 semester hours in Management, or in the graduate degree category, 2 semester hours in Management (6/95).

Production Processes (62505) (Formerly Product/Production Engineering II [83505])

Location: School of Engineering and Logistics, Red River Army Depot.

Length: *Version 1:* 100 hours (11 weeks); *Version 2:* 100 hours (10 weeks).

Dates: *Version 1:* January 1976-June 1995; *Version 2:* June 1995-Present.

Objective: *Version 1:* To further students' understanding of principles learned in Product/Production Engineering I. *Version 2:* To provide students with an in-depth understanding of cold working and machining processes from the standpoint of producibility, capabilities, limitations, and economics.

Learning Outcome: Upon successful completion of this course, the student will be able to design manufacturing processes for cold working and machining of metal parts based on capabilities, limitations, and economics of these processes; prepare detailed process plans for machining of metal parts; use SEL's Production Lab for "hands-on" experience with the principles of machining and numerical control, including a demonstration of computer process through construction of numerical control programs; and create three dimensional part designs using CAD techniques.

Instruction: *Version 1:* Major topics covered in the course are inspection, machining process, and production equipment; joining processes; and finishing and surface treatments. Also includes plant visits in Dallas. Methods of instruction include lecture, laboratory, and a written examination. *Version 2:* Major topics covered in the course are cold working processes, metal removal processes, numerical control (NC), and advanced computer-aided design (CAD). Methods of instruction include five hours of lecture per week, three hours of laboratory per week, two hours of practical exercises per week, and written and laboratory examinations.

Credit Recommendation: *Versions 1 and 2:* In the graduate degree category, 3 semester hours in Mechanical Engineering (12/84) (6/95).

Production Quality Control (83514)

Location: School of Engineering and Logistics, Red River Army Depot.

Length: 60 hours (10 weeks).

Dates: January 1975-September 1993.

Objective: To teach students statistical methods as used in industrial quality control.

Instruction: Major topics covered in the course are process control theory, sampling plans, and military standards for inspection. Methods of instruction include five hours of lecture per week, one hour of laboratory per week, written examinations, and reports.

Credit Recommendation: In the graduate degree category, 3 semester hours in Quality Control (12/84).

Production Systems Design (62516) (Formerly Production Systems Design [83516])

Location: School of Engineering and Logistics, Red River Army Depot.

Length: *Version 1:* 60 hours (10 weeks); *Version 2:* 100 hours (10 weeks).

Dates: *Version 1:* January 1976-June 1995; *Version 2:* June 1995-September 1993.

Objective: *Version 1:* To teach students the techniques and considerations involved in planning, designing, and modernizing production systems. *Version 2:* To provide the student with an understanding of the basic theory and principles used in design and layout planning for manufacturing plants and materials handling.

Learning Outcome: Upon successful completion of this course, the student will be able to apply the basic theory and principles of systematic layout planning to develop alternative design plans for a manufacturing facility; compare alternative designs to determine the optimal approach, considering a variety of parameters such as material flow, space requirements, and activity relationships; employ the principles of material handling to analyze materials handling problems and develop strategies; and participate in a team to develop alternative designs, analyze and evaluate these alternative layouts and material handling systems, and select the most efficient design.

Instruction: *Version 1:* Major topics covered in the course are introduction to plant layout, system engineering of production lines and equipment, production lead-time estimating, and production planning and control. Methods of instruction include five hours of lecture per week, one hour of laboratory per week, and written examinations. *Version 2:* Major topics covered in the course are introduction to plant layout, system engineering of production lines, materials handling, and team projects. Methods of instruction include five hours of lecture and laboratory per week, practical exercises, and written examinations.

Credit Recommendation: *Versions 1 and 2:* In the upper division baccalaureate degree category, 3 semester hours in Industrial Engineering (12/84) (6/95).

Product/Production Engineering Research Project (62585) (Formerly Problems in Product/Production Engineering I and II [83585])

Location: School of Engineering and Logistics, Red River Army Depot.

Length: *Version 1:* 120 hours (20 weeks); *Version 2:* 100 hours.

Dates: *Version 1:* January 1976-June 1995; *Version 2:* June 1995-Present.

Objective: *Version 1:* To allow students to research and study assigned problems. Techniques concerning documentation and professional problem solving are stressed. *Version 2:* To allow the student to research a problem that pertains to production engineering. Documentation and professional problem solving are emphasized.

Learning Outcome: Upon successful completion of this course, the student will be able to perform advanced study and research in the fields of production (emphasis on DoD problem areas), select a manageable problem, evaluate pertinent background data and reference materials, perform a literature survey and critical analysis, and formulate a research proposal.

Instruction: *Version 1: Section I:* Major topics covered in the course are familiarization of library, research proposals, and topic selection. Methods of instruction include two 2.5-hour meetings per week and one hour of laboratory per week. *Section II:* Major topics covered in the course are writing and presenting the research results. Methods of instruction include two 2.5-hour meetings per week and one hour of laboratory per week. *Version 2:* Major topics covered in the course are research requirements and sources, research techniques and topic selection, and research problem and report. Methods of instruction include two hours lecture per week, eight hours independent research per week, oral presentations, and written reports.

Credit Recommendation: *Version 1:* In the graduate degree category, 6 semester hours in Graduate Research (12/84). **NOTE:** Students must complete both I and II to receive any credit. *Version 2:* In the graduate degree category, 4 semester hours in Industrial Engineering (6/95).

Product/Production Planning and Control (83508)

Location: School of Engineering and Logistics, Red River Army Depot.

Length: 60 hours (10 weeks).

Dates: January 1976-January 1993.

Objective: To familiarize students with management role, concept, and techniques used in the Department of Defense and related commercial facilities.

Instruction: Major topics covered in the course are cost/schedule control system, network-based management techniques, line of balance, plant operations management, project management, and production management. Methods of instruction include five hours of lecture per week, one hour of laboratory per week, and written examinations.

Credit Recommendation: In the upper division baccalaureate degree category, 3 semester hours in Management (12/84).

Program Evaluation and Economic Analysis (60566) (Formerly Techniques in Cost Estimation [82566])

Location: School of Engineering and Logistics, Red River Army Depot.

Length: *Version 1:* 60 hours (10 weeks); *Version 2:* 90 (10 weeks).

Dates: *Version 1:* November 1976-June 1995; *Version 2:* June 1995-Present.

Objective: *Version 1:* To provide students with an understanding of the theories and techniques pertinent to the solution of engineering problems in system reliability, maintainability, and other measures of effectiveness. *Version 2:* To provide the student with methods to consider economics when alternatives are evaluated and selected.

Learning Outcome: Upon successful completion of this course, the student will be able to evaluate programs which are competing for limited resources and select those which are of greatest benefit to DoD, formulate cost estimates by the application of various techniques, make decisions based on cost estimates arrived at by using economic analysis techniques including rate of return, payback potential, economic life, and break even analysis, and examine how the techniques are utilized within the framework of DoD's fiscal structure.

Instruction: *Version 1:* Major topics covered in the course are interest and economic equivalence; evaluating replacement alternative and public activities; and risk, uncertainty, and economic modeling. Methods of instruction include five hours of lecture per week, one hour of laboratory per week, and written examinations. *Version 2:* Major topics covered in the course are cost estimation techniques, economic analysis, replacement alternatives, army financial management, and environment policy. Methods of instruction include five hours lecture per week, four hours of laboratory per week, practical exercises, and written examinations.

Credit Recommendation: *Version 1:* In the graduate degree category, 3 semester hours in Economic Analysis (12/84). *Version 2:* In the graduate degree category, 3 semesters hours in Industrial Engineering (6/95).

Programming Languages (60558) (Formerly Computer Science [82558])

Location: School of Engineering and Logistics, Red River Army Depot.

Length: *Version 1:* 70 hours (10 weeks); *Version 2:* 90 hours (10 weeks).

Dates: *Version 1:* September 1976-December 1994; *Version 2:* January 1995-Present.

Objective: *Version 1:* To provide students with an understanding of scientific computer programming theory and application, introduce FORTRAN, and discuss scientific and engineering applications. *Version 2:* To provide students with an understanding of computer programming languages and applications.

Learning Outcome: Upon successful completion of this course, the student will be able to explain and illustrate the commonalities and differences between several programming languages, relate the differences in the languages to the need for different approaches to program design meeting the requirements of DoD-STD-2167A, and write the same program in several languages and point out the commonalities and differences between the programs.

Instruction: *Version 1:* Major topics covered in the course are an introduction to FORTRAN and discussion of scientific and engineering applications. Methods of instruction include five hours of lecture per week, two hours of laboratory per week, and a written examination. *Version 2:* Major topics covered in the course are software goals and principles, Ada programming language, programming languages, and BASIC programming language. Methods of instruction include five hours of lecture and four hours of laboratory per week.

Credit Recommendation: *Version 1:* In the lower division baccalaureate/associate degree category, 3 semester hours in Computer Science (12/84). *Version 2:* In the upper division baccalaureate or graduate degree category, 3 semester hours in Computer Science (6/95).

Project Analysis and Planning (60520) (Formerly Techniques in Operations Research [82520])

Location: School of Engineering and Logistics, Red River Army Depot.

Length: *Version 1:* 60 hours (10 weeks); *Version 2:* 90 hours (10 weeks).

Dates: *Version 1:* September 1976-June 1995; *Version 2:* June 1995-Present.

Objective: *Version 1:* To provide students with specific capabilities in operations research. *Version 2:* To provide students with techniques used in performing project analysis and planning activities.

Learning Outcome: Upon successful completion of this course, the student will be able to formulate and assess project plans to optimize the use of constrained resources, prepare forecasts, determine levels of inventory to minimize cost, design service facilities which balances demand for services and the cost of providing the services, allocate scarce resources efficiently to achieve important organizational objectives, and to prepare plans, schedules, and monitoring system for complex projects.

Instruction: *Version 1:* Major topics covered in the course are operations research techniques such as production and inventory control; linear programming; queuing theory, game theory, and dynamic programming. Methods of instruction include five hours of lecture per week, one hour of laboratory per week, and written examinations. *Version 2:* Major topics covered in the course are inventory analysis/planning, queuing analysis/planning, allocation analysis/planning, and project planning techniques. Methods of instruction include five hours of lecture per week, four hours of laboratory per week, practical exercises, and written examinations.

Credit Recommendation: *Version 1:* In the graduate degree category, 3 semester hours in Operations Research (12/84) (6/95). *Version 2:* In the graduate degree category, 3 semester hours in Operations Research (12/84) (6/95).

Project Management (81508)

Location: School of Engineering and Logistics, Red River Army Depot.

Length: 60 hours (10 weeks: six 1-hour lectures/week).

Dates: August 1986-September 1993.

Objective: To give the student an introduction to the concept of project/system management organizations, the general operating procedures and funding criteria for project management, and the roles and responsibilities of project managers.

Learning Outcome: Upon successful completion of this course, the student will be able to trace the history of the development of modern management thought; exhibit a working knowledge of personnel administration in a federal service; describe the work of modern management theorists including (but not limited to) Maslow, McGregor, Herzberg, and McClellan; discuss in detail the functions of management: planning, organizing, controlling, and conducting; and apply the techniques of PERT and CPM.

Instruction: Major topics covered in the course are a history of management thought, personnel administration in the federal service, the works of modern management theorists, the functions of management, and the techniques of PERT and CPM.

Credit Recommendation: In the upper division baccalaureate degree category, 3 semester hours in Business Administration or Management (9/87).

Properties of Hazardous Materials (63569) (Formerly Chemical Safety in the Industrial Environment [84569])

Location: School of Engineering and Logistics, Red River Army Depot.

Length: *Version 1:* 60 hours (10 weeks); *Version 2:* 90 hours (10 weeks).

Dates: *Version 1:* March 1979-June 1995; *Version 2:* June 1995-Present.

Objective: *Version 1:* To introduce students to the chemical compounds and solutions used in the Army-industrial complex and review their properties, use, and limitations. *Version 2:* To introduce students to the hazardous properties of chemical compounds and methods of assessment and control applicable to the Army-industrial complex.

Learning Outcome: Upon successful completion of this course, the student will be able to identify and categorize various hazardous materials that are present in military/industrial environments; apply generalized safety and human factors principles included in the prerequisite courses to specific problems related to hazardous material control; and analyze facilities and equipment design from the viewpoint of identifying, eliminating, and minimizing the risks associated with hazardous materials.

Instruction: *Version 1:* Major topics covered in the course are the effect of chemical compounds on the human body and methods of protection against them; specific techniques for use in recognition and control of chemical hazards; and safety engineering techniques, methods, and criteria for selecting, testing, and using special protective equipment in situations where hazards cannot be eliminated. Methods of instruction include five hours of lecture per week, one hour of laboratory per week, written examinations, projects, and a presentation. *Version 2:* Major topics covered in the course are flammable liquids, gases, and solids; explosive and reactive compounds; cryogenic gases; chemical health hazards; and consequence analysis. Methods of instruction include five hours of lecture per week, four hours of laboratory per week, practical exercises, and written examinations.

Credit Recommendation: *Version 1:* In the graduate degree category, 3 semester hours in Industrial Safety or Engineering (12/84). *Version 2:* In the upper division baccalaureate degree category, 3 semester hours in Industrial Engineering or Safety Engineering (6/95).

Provisioning (50170)

Location: School of Engineering and Logistics, Red River Army Depot.

Length: 40 hours (10 days).

Dates: January 1995-Present.

Objective: To convey to the student the importance and necessity of logistically supporting the system during the phases of the Acquisition Life Cycle.

Learning Outcome: Upon successful completion of this course, the student will be able to define the common Provisioning terms, recognize the differences in the activities performed during the stages of the life cycle, and give an oral presentation to their peers on a topic related to Provisioning.

Instruction: Major topics covered in the course are review of current provisioning policies and management procedures, emphasizing interrelationships and interdependencies of logistic functions with a focus on management of Provisioning. Methods of instruction include audio/visual material, handouts, and an examination.

Credit Recommendation: In the upper division baccalaureate degree category, 3 semester hours in Industrial Management (6/95).

Quality Assurance (52640) (Formerly Quality Assurance)

Location: School of Engineering and Logistics, Red River Army Depot.

Length: 20 hours (1 week).

Dates: January 1975-Present.

Objective: To provide the student with a knowledge of quality control/assurance and how it relates to other logistics and management activities.

Learning Outcome: Upon successful completion of this course, the student will be able to know the definitions of Quality related terms, understand the interdependencies of the functional areas of Logistics, give an oral presentation to their peers on relevant Quality topics, and distinguish between the responsibilities of the Quality Assurance specialist at the various managerial levels in DoD.

Instruction: *Version 1:* Major topics covered in the course are basic methods used in cleaning, drying, preserving, wrapping, packaging, and marking. Methods of instruction include lecture, research, practical exercises, and an examination. *Version 2:* Major topics covered in the course are Quality related terms, functional areas of Logistics, public speaking, and the responsibilities of Quality Assurance specialist at various managerial levels. Methods of instruction include lecture, research, practical exercises, and an examination.

Credit Recommendation: *Version 1:* In the upper division baccalaureate degree category, 1 semester hour in Business Management (6/84). *Version 2:* In the upper division baccalaureate degree category, 1 semester hour in Introduction to Business Management or Introduction to Quality Management (6/95).

Quality/Product Assurance Research Project (64585) (Formerly Problems in Quality and Reliability Engineering II [88585])

Location: School of Engineering and Logistics, Red River Army Depot.

Length: *Version 1:* 120 hours (20 weeks); *Version 2:* 100 hours.

Dates: *Version 1:* May 1981-June 1995; *Version 2:* June 1995-Present.

Objective: *Version 1:* To provide the student with advanced study and research in the field of Quality and Reliability Engineering. *Version 2:* To provide the student with experience in doing advance study and research in the field of Quality/Product Assurance Engineering.

Learning Outcome: Upon successful completion of this course, the student will be able to perform advanced study and research in the field of Quality/Product Assurance, especially as related to DoD problem areas and show professional problem solving skills by choosing a manageable problem, evaluating pertinent background data and reference materials, performance of a current literature survey and critical analysis, and formulation of a formal research project.

Instruction: *Version 1:* Major topics covered in the course are original research and analysis, writing, reporting, and publication in an Army problem area. Methods of instruction include lecture, research, and a research project. *Version 2:* Major topics covered in the course are research requirements and sources, research techniques and topic selection, and research problems and report. Methods of instruction include two hours of lecture per week, eight hours independent research per week, oral presentations, and written reports.

Credit Recommendation: *Version 1:* In the graduate degree category, 6 hours in Graduate Research (6/84). *Version 2:* In the graduate degree category, 4 semester hours in Industrial Engineering (6/95).

Radiological Safety and Hazards Evaluation (84550)

Location: School of Engineering and Logistics, Red River Army Depot.

Length: 60 hours (10 weeks).

Dates: April 1978-September 1993.

Objective: To present students with pertinent information concerning the evaluation and control of various ionizing and nonionizing radiations. Safety control techniques are of primary importance.

Instruction: Major topics covered in the course are X-ray safety, protection against internal radiation, nuclear reactor safety, handling and disposal of radioactive materiel, radiation detection and measurement, and radiation control and licensing requirements. Methods of instruction include five hours of lecture per week, one hour of laboratory per week, and written examinations.

Credit Recommendation: In the graduate degree category, 3 semester hours in Safety Engineering (12/84).

Receiving (51390)

Location: School of Engineering and Logistics, Red River Army Depot.

Length: 20 hours (1 week).

Dates: January 1975-Present.

Objective: To provide an in-depth understanding of the policies and step-by-step procedures for processing material through the receiving function of a major distribution depot.

Learning Outcome: Upon successful completion of this course, the student will be able to understand the importance and use of materiel prepositioned materiel receipt documents; identify the three basic categories of receipt discrepancies and wgat reporting action is required; discuss management information systems and tools used to monitor and control receiving operations; understand the uses of receipt control numbers; and identify receiving performance indicators and determine causes of and recommend corrections for substandard performance.

Instruction: Major topics covered in the course are the function of depots and the receiving function as a central point of receipt in the supply system. Methods of instruction include lecture, videocassettes, a field trip, computer simulation, student-centered learning, and an examination.

Credit Recommendation: In the upper division baccalaureate degree category, 1 semester hour in Industrial Management (6/84) (6/95).

Reliability Design and Evaluation (87013)

Location: School of Engineering and Logistics, Red River Army Depot.

Length: 60 hours (10 weeks).

Dates: June 1989-September 1993.

Objective: To provide the student with an understanding of quantitative reliability and system effectiveness evaluation techniques that can be used in engineering design and development.

Learning Outcome: Upon successful completion of this course, the student will be able to determine proper parameters to track system changes in reliability and effectiveness; perform reliability allocation; and develop a statistically valid test for system evaluation of RAM characteristics.

Instruction: Major topics covered in the course are system effectiveness, reliability allocation, reliability prediction and growth, reliability testing, maintenance systems, and RAM evaluation methodologies. Methods of instruction include lecture, laboratory exercises, and written assignments.

Credit Recommendation: In the graduate degree category, 3 semester hours in Reliability Design and Analysis (2/90).

Reliability Engineering (84525)

Location: School of Engineering and Logistics, Red River Army Depot.

Length: 60 hours (10 weeks).

Dates: April 1981-September 1993.

Objective: To provide students with an understanding of the theories and techniques pertinent to the solution of engineering problems in system reliability.

Instruction: Major topics covered in the course are statistical techniques for predicting and assessing reliability, reliability measures, and probabilistic design. Methods of instruction include five hours of lecture per week, one hour of laboratory, and written examinations.

Credit Recommendation: In the graduate degree category, 3 semester hours in Industrial Engineering (12/84).

Reliability Engineering Design and Analysis (60526) (Formerly Reliability Analysis and Design [88526])

Location: School of Engineering and Logistics, Red River Army Depot.

Length: *Version 1:* 60 hours (10 weeks); *Version 2:* 90 hours (10 weeks).

Dates: *Version 1:* February 1981-June 1995; *Version 2:* June 1995-Present.

Objective: To provide the student with quantitative reliability analysis techniques used in engineering design.

Learning Outcome: Upon successful completion of this course, the student will be able to quantify reliability system design and testing plus construct and test reliability models, determine effects of redundancy, stress and strength, and failure modes on reliability; and plan and manage reliability growth programs.

Instruction: *Version 1:* Major topics covered in the course are system effectiveness parameters, reliability growth, reliability prediction and allocation, and reliability modeling techniques for systems. Methods of instruction include lecture, laboratory, and written tests. *Version 2:* Major topics covered in the course are measures and terminology, analysis or strength and stresses, reliability, models analysis of failure modes and effects, and estimates of reliability and reliability growth. Methods of instruction include five hours of lecture per week and four hours of laboratory per week.

Credit Recommendation: *Version 1:* In the graduate degree category, 3 semester hours in Industrial Engineering (6/84). *Version 2:* In the graduate degree category, 4 semester hours in Industrial Engineering (6/95).

Research Project (50140) (Formerly Maintenance Management Program: Research Project)

Location: School of Engineering and Logistics, Red River Army Depot.

Length: 40 hours (2 weeks).

Dates: January 1975-Present.

Objective: To allow the student to develop a research paper on a topic related to logistics.

Learning Outcome: Upon successful completion of this course, the student will be able to design, conduct, and present the results of a research project on a topic related to logistics.

Instruction: Major topics covered in the course are logistics, student reports, and conference. Methods of instruction include lecture, discussion, and student reports.

Credit Recommendation: In the graduate degree category, 2 semester hours in Directed Research Management or Management (6/84) (6/95).

Safety Aspects of Facilities Design (84562)

Location: School of Engineering and Logistics, Red River Army Depot.

Length: 60 hours (10 weeks).

Dates: September 1977-September 1993.

Objective: To provide students with an understanding of specialized training in the design of buildings and similar facilities from the standpoint of accident elimination.

Instruction: Major topics covered in the course are the generalized safety and human factors principles included in the prerequisite courses are used in specific problems of safety related to facilities designed for use by human beings, environmental effects and control, flow of traffic (human and materiel), and access to facilities. Methods of instruction include five hours of lecture per week, one hour of laboratory per week, written examinations, projects, and presentations.

Credit Recommendation: In the upper division baccalaureate degree category, 3 semester hours in Safety Engineering (12/84).

Safety Considerations in Electrical/Electronic Systems Design (84531)

Location: School of Engineering and Logistics, Red River Army Depot.

Length: 60 hours (10 weeks).

Dates: April 1983-September 1993.

Objective: To provide students with the knowledge and understanding of electricalenergy hazards and appropriate control measures to minimize personnel injury and equipment damage.

Instruction: Major topics covered in the course are a review of electrical circuits, hazards, created by electrical and electromagnetic energy, effect of current flow on personnel, and abnormal circuit conditions. Methods of instruction include dive hours lecture per week, one hour laboratory per week, written examinations, project, and a presentation.

Credit Recommendation: In the lower division baccalaureate/associate degree category, 3 semester hours in Technology (12/84).

Safety Engineering Concepts (63540) (Formerly Principles of Safety [84540])

Location: School of Engineering and Logistics, Red River Army Depot.

Length: *Version 1:* 50 hours (5 weeks); *Version 2:* 90 hours (10 weeks).

Dates: *Version 1:* December 1984-June 1995; *Version 2:* June 1995-Present.

Objective: To provide students with a foundation in the field of safety and the discipline of safety engineering.

Learning Outcome: Upon successful completion of this course, the student will be able to understand and comprehend basic concepts of the field of safety and the discipline of safety engineering and demonstrate knowledge of the evolution of safety and safety engineering, theories of safety management, accident causation, risk management concepts, and AMC's Safety Program.

Instruction: *Version 1:* Major topics covered in the course are evolution of safety and safety engineering, theories of accident causation, safety standards, and codes, and the Occupational Safety and Health Act. Methods of instruction include ten hours of lecture per week, written examinations, projects, and presentations. *Version 2:* Major topics covered in the course are background and historical perspective, theories of accident causation, theories of safety management, risk management concepts, and the AMC Safety Program. Methods of instruction include five hours of lecture per week, four hours of laboratory per week, practical exercises, and written examinations.

Credit Recommendation: *Versions 1 and 2:* In the upper division baccalaureate degree category, 3 semester hours in Industrial Safety or Safety Engineering (12/84) (6/95).

Safety Engineering Research Project (63585) (Formerly Problems in Safety Engineering [84585])

Location: School of Engineering and Logistics, Red River Army Depot.

Length: *Version 1:* 60 hours (10 weeks); *Version 2:* 100 hours (10 weeks).

Dates: *Version 1:* June 1985-June 1995; *Version 2:* June 1995-Present.

Objective: *Version 1:* To test the students' understanding of important concerns in safety engineering. *Version 2:* To study and research a significant problem in the safety engineering field.

Learning Outcome: Upon successful completion of this course, the student will be able to accomplish advanced study and research in the field of safety, especially as related to DoD problem areas and demonstrate professional problem-solving skills by choosing a manageable problem, evaluating pertinent background data and reference materials, performance of current literature survey and critical analysis, and formulation of a formal research proposal.

Instruction: *Version 1:* Major topic covered in the course is a research paper in safety engineering. Methods of instruction include lecture and laboratory. *Version 2:* Major topics covered in the course are research requirements and sources, research techniques and topic selection, and research problem and report. Methods of instruction include two hours of lecture per week, eight hours of independent research per week, oral presentations, and written reports (findings and results required).

Credit Recommendation: *Version 1:* In the graduate degree category, 3 semester hours in Safety Engineering (12/84) (6/95). *Version 2:* In the graduate degree category, 3 semester hours in Safety Engineering (12/84) (6/95).

Safety Engineering Tools and Techniques

Location: School of Engineering and Logistics, Red River Army Depot.

Length: 60 hours (10 weeks).

Dates: April 1984-September 1993.

Objective: To provide students with an understanding of the basic tools and techniques developed to use in applying management information systems programs to safety management and engineering functions.

Instruction: Major topics covered in the course are development of a safety data file program and a safety management control technique program. Students also develop and run a computer simulation of a safety engineering problem. Methods of instruction include lecture, laboratory, exercises, simulations, problem-solving, and examinations.

Credit Recommendation: In the upper division baccalaureate degree category, 3

semester hours in Industrial Management (12/84).

Security Assistance Management (50233) (Formerly Security Assistance Management)

Location: School of Engineering and Logistics, Red River Army Depot.

Length: 32 hours (2 weeks).

Dates: January 1975-Present.

Objective: To enable the student to comprehend the history, role, and operation of the U.S. Security Assistance Management Program.

Learning Outcome: Upon successful completion of this course, the student will be able to define security assistance; identify and relate major security assistance programs; identify the authorization for security assistance; define roles and responsibilities of security assistance personnel; describe how CCSS and security assistance programs relate and assist FMS; understand the report of discrepancy system, including all files; and understand the transportation system associated with security assistance programs.

Instruction: Major topics covered in the course are military assistance through grant aid and international military education and training; foreign military sales; the role of organization in the Department of Defense; financial requirements; quality assurance terms; North Atlantic Treaty and multi-national programs; and the role of major subordinate command organizations and responsibilities. Methods of instruction include lecture, discussion, and an examination.

Credit Recommendation: In the graduate degree category, 1 semester hour in Management or Military Science (6/84) (6/95).

Software Development and Test (87010)

Location: School of Engineering and Logistics, Red River Army Depot.

Length: 60 hours (10 weeks).

Dates: April 1989-September 1993.

Objective: To provide students with a knowledge of design measures, strategies, and technical tools and techniques for software development.

Learning Outcome: Upon successful completion of this course, the student will be able to develop and test computer software.

Instruction: Major topics covered in the course are software design methodology, software systems requirements definition and design methodologies, software project planning, and computer system architectures and operating systems. Methods of instruction include lecture, conference, laboratory projects, and written examinations.

Credit Recommendation: In the graduate degree category, 3 semester hours in Software Engineering (2/90).

Software Engineering Assurance Research Project (65585) (Formerly Problems in Software Engineering I and II [81585])

Location: School of Engineering and Logistics, Red River Army Depot.

Length: *Version 1:* 60 hours (10 weeks); *Version 2:* 100 hours (10 weeks).

Dates: *Version 1:* August 1986-December 1994; *Version 2:* January 1995-Present.

Objective: To provide the student with advanced study and research in the field of software engineering. Emphasis is placed on the role of communication skills such as organizing ideas, writing, structure and content of proposals, technical reports, manuals, and other software project documentation.

Learning Outcome: *Version 1:* Upon successful completion of this course, the student will be to recognize research sources and demonstrate research techniques, select a research topic, do research, develop a research proposal, prepare a formal research report, and present and defend a completed report. *Version 2:* Upon successful completion of this course, the student will be accomplish advanced study and research in the field of Software Engineering, especially as related to DoD problem areas and demonstrate professional problem-solving skills by choosing a manageable problem, evaluating pertinent background data and reference materials, performance of current literature survey and critical analysis, and formulation of a formal research proposal.

Instruction: *Version 1:* Major topics covered in the course are familiarization with research sources, research techniques and topic selection, research problem selection and proposal development, performance of research, preparation of formal research report, and report presentation and defense. *Version 2:* Major topics covered in the course are research requirements and sources, research techniques and topic selection, and research problem and report. Methods of instruction include two hours of lecture per week, eight hours of independent research per week, and oral and written presentations, findings and results are required.

Credit Recommendation: *Version 1:* In the graduate degree category, 6 semester hours in General Studies or Interdisci-plinary Studies (9/87). **NOTE:** Three semester hours should be applied to Introduction to Graduate Studies and three semester hours should be applied to Thesis Writing. *Version 2:* In the graduate degree category, 4 semester hours in Software Engineering, or Computer Information Systems (6/95).

Software Engineering Concepts (60530) (Formerly Software Engineering Concepts I [81530])

Location: School of Engineering and Logistics, Red River Army Depot.

Length: *Version 1:* 66 hours (11 weeks); *Version 2:* 90 hours (10 weeks).

Dates: *Version 1:* August 1986-December 1994; *Version 2:* January 1995-Present.

Objective: To provide the student with a set of design measures, strategies, technical tools, and techniques for software development.

Learning Outcome: *Version 1:* Upon successful completion of this course, the student will be able to use the tools, techniques, and methodologies appropriate for use during analysis, design, and coding activities and implement management controls that will lend traceability and visibility to software development and maintenance activities. *Version 2:* Upon successful completion of this course, the student will be able to perform a software requirements analysis, construct a software design, prepare a software quality assurance plan, plan for software maintenance, integrate software configuration management into all aspects of software development, discuss and describe different software development methodologies and models and their appropriate uses, and describe the traditional System Development Life Cycle (SDLC) and its management implications.

Instruction: *Version 1:* Major topics covered in the course are software systems analysis, system design methodology, and programming methodology. *Version 2:* Major topics covered in the course are management of software development, software requirements analysis, software design, software quality assurance, software maintenance, and software configuration management. Methods of instruction include five hours of lecture per week, four hours of laboratory per week, team assignments, and case studies, involving analysis and design of computer applications where team members perform and present the results of the case studies to other members of the class.

Credit Recommendation: *Versions 1 and 2:* In the upper division baccalaureate degree category, 3 semester hours in Computer Information Systems, Computer Science, or Software Engineering (9/87) (6/95).

Software Engineering With Ada I (65520) (Formerly Software Engineering Using Ada I [81520])

Location: School of Engineering and Logistics, Red River Army Depot.

Length: *Version 1:* 99 hours (11 weeks); *Version 2:* 100 hours (10 weeks).

Dates: *Version 1:* August 1986-December 1994; *Version 2:* January 1995-Present.

Objective: To provide the student with an introduction to the Ada programming language. Topics include data abstraction and types, packages, generic program units, and input/output.

Learning Outcome: *Version 1:* Upon successful completion of this course, the student will be able to describe the situations that led to the development and use of Ada; describe how the use of Ada enforces the use of software engineering principles such as abstraction, information hiding, and modularity; and write programs in Ada using statements and constructs such as array slices and attributes, unconstrained arrays, text/character/string IO, and aggregates. *Version 2:* Upon successful completion of this course, the student will be able to write advanced programs in Ada using abstraction, strong typing, generic program units, and various I/O techniques, write these program using good software engineering practices, and defend their design approach and methodology.

Instruction: *Version 1:* Major topics covered in the course are software engineering overview; Ada programming language and coding; and Ada programming support environment. *Version 2:* Major topics covered in the course are data abstractions and strong typing, advanced package, generic program units, and input/output techniques. Methods of instruction include five hours of lecture and laboratory per week.

Credit Recommendation: *Version 1:* In the upper division baccalaureate degree category, 3 semester hours in Computer Science (9/87). *Version 2:* In the lower division baccalaureate/associate degree category (sophomore level), 3 semester hours in Computer Information Systems, Computer Science, or Software Engineering (6/95).

Software Engineering With Ada II (65521) (Formerly Software Engineering Using Ada II [81521])

Location: School of Engineering and Logistics, Red River Army Depot.

Length: *Version 1:* 99 hours (11 weeks); *Version 2:* 100 hours (10 weeks).

Dates: *Version 1:* August 1986-December 1994; *Version 2:* January 1995-Present.

Objective: To provide the student with an understanding of how Ada programming deals with exception handling and concurrent programming, as related to real-time processing problems.

Learning Outcome: *Version 1:* Upon successful completion of this course, the student will be able to demonstrate exception handling programming and demonstrate concurrent programming of real-time processing problems. *Version 2:* Upon successful completion of this course, the student will be able to write advanced programs in Ada using record types, discriminated records, private types and generics, concurrency and tasking, and real-time constraints.

Instruction: *Version 1:* Major topics covered in the course are advanced features of Ada programming language, tasks, exception handling, and concurrent programming as relating to real-time processing problems. Methods of instruction include lecture, laboratory, examinations, and performance testing in the laboratory. *Version 2:* Major topics covered in the course are record types and discriminated records, private types and generics, concurrency and tasking, and real-time considerations. Methods of instruction include five hours of lecture and laboratory per week.

Credit Recommendation: *Version 1:* In the graduate degree category, 3 semester hours in Computer Engineering, Computer Science, or Software Engineering (9/87). *Version 2:* In the upper division baccalaureate degree category, 3 semester hours in Computer Engineering, Computer Information Systems, Computer Science, or Software Engineering (6/95).

Software Engineering Workshop (65586) (Formerly Software Engineering Workshop [81586])

Location: School of Engineering and Logistics, Red River Army Depot.

Length: *Version 1:* 60 hours (10 weeks); *Version 2:* 100 hours (10 weeks).

Dates: *Version 1:* August 1986-December 1994; *Version 2:* January 1995-Present.

Objective: To give the student the opportunity to participate as a team member in a complete software development project. The size and scope of the project are such that the software development tools and techniques presented in the previous course will be used.

Learning Outcome: *Version 1:* Upon successful completion of this course, the student will be able to design and develop a software system. *Version 2:* Upon successful completion of this course, the student will be able to participate in and contribute to the development of a "large scale" software development project and apply the software development tools and techniques learned in previous courses in the Software Engineering Program.

Instruction: *Version 1:* Major topics covered in the course are project teams that design and develop a software system. *Version 2:* Major topics covered in the course are project introduction and software development. Methods of instruction include five hours of lecture, laboratory, and software development per week.

Credit Recommendation: *Versions 1 and 2:* In the graduate degree category, 3 semester hours in Computer Engineering, Computer Information Systems, Computer Science, or Software Engineering (9/87) (6/95).

Software Quality (88586)

Location: School of Engineering and Logistics, Red River Army Depot.

Length: 50 hours (10 weeks).

Dates: July 1983-September 1993.

Objective: To give the student a set of design measures, strategies, management and technical tools, techniques, and technical guidance.

Instruction: Major topics covered in the course are regulations, standards, pamphlets, and directives. Methods of instruction include lecture, outside study, and an examination.

Credit Recommendation: In the upper division baccalaureate degree category, 3 semester hours in Industrial Management (6/84).

Software Systems Acquisition (65504) (Formerly Software Technical Data Package Development [81504])

Location: School of Engineering and Logistics, Red River Army Depot.

Length: *Version 1:* 50 hours (10 weeks); *Version 2:* 100 hours (10 weeks).

Dates: *Version 1:* August 1986-December 1994; *Version 2:* January 1995-Present.

Objective: *Version 1:* To familiarize the student with policies, procedures, and responsibilities for the acquisition, review, preparation, proofing, maintenance, control, and transmission of a technical data package. *Version 2:* To familiarize the student with policies, procedures, and responsibilities for the acquisition of software systems.

Learning Outcome: *Version 1:* Upon successful completion of this course, the student will be able to use the methodology required by the Army Materials Command for developing a technical data package; introduce this methodology for development of software technical data packages; and demonstrate technical data package development through individual and group projects. *Version 2:* Upon successful completion of this course, the student will be able to explain the concepts, policies, and administrative requirements of a software development project and devise a software system acquisition plan including cost estimates, a configuration management plan, and documentation requirements.

Instruction: *Version 1:* Major topics covered in the course are the components of a technical data package and the steps used to develop a technical data package. Methods of instruction include homework, quizzes (10 percent), group project(s) (30 percent), and written exams (60 percent). *Version 2:* Major topics covered in the course are software project planning, cost and schedule estimation models, software cost estimation, and configuration management. Methods of instruction include five hours of lecture and laboratory per week.

Credit Recommendation: *Version 1:* In the upper division baccalaureate degree category, 3 semester hours in Military Science (9/87). **NOTE:** While similar material is covered in public education—this material appears to be too closely tied to DOD STD-2167 to be generally applicable. *Version 2:* In the upper division baccalaureate degree category, 3 semester hours in Computer Information Systems, Military Science, or Software Engineering (6/95).

Software Test and Evaluation (87023)

Location: School of Engineering and Logistics, Red River Army Depot.

Length: 60 hours (10 weeks).

Dates: October 1989-February 1995.

Objective: To provide the student with software test and evaluation strategies, technical tools, and techniques.

Learning Outcome: Upon successful completion of this course, the student will be able to describe the role of software testing in the software development cycle and the functions, responsibilities, and activities of a software testing organization; apply different types of software testing techniques using different types of software testing and evaluation tools; and describe and utilize appropriate military regulations, policies, standards, and methodologies pertaining to software test and evaluation.

Instruction: Major topics covered in the course are software testing and evaluation methods, tools, validation and evaluation, software quality assurance, techniques and testing, and Department of Defense software test and evaluation practices. Methods of instruction include lecture, laboratory exercises, and scenario simulation.

Credit Recommendation: In the graduate degree category, 2 semester hours in Software Engineering (2/90).

Software Test and Evaluation (60531) (Formerly Software Engineering Concepts II [81531])

Location: School of Engineering and Logistics, Red River Army Depot.

Length: *Version 1:* 66 hours (11 weeks); *Version 2:* 100 hours (10 weeks).

Dates: *Version 1:* August 1986-December 1994; *Version 2:* January 1995-Present.

Objective: To present the student with principles of design, implementation, debugging, testing, documentation, and maintenance of team-oriented software projects.

Learning Outcome: *Version 1:* Upon successful completion of this course, the student will be able to identify problems associated with team-oriented software projects; use software testing and debugging techniques; and employ methods of measuring software quality. *Version 2:* Upon successful completion of this course, the student will be able to develop software test plans and test utilizing various software testing techniques; apply these software tests to computer programs for the purpose of debugging, verification, and validation; determine the appropriateness of a particular test for a computer program; and utilize software reliability models during development and testing of software.

Instruction: *Version 1:* Major topics covered in the course are software quality assurance and software testing. Methods of instruction include examination and lectures. *Version 2:* Major topics covered in the course are introduction to software testing, software testing techniques, unit testing, integration testing, system testing, independent verification and validation, SQA, software metrics, and software reliability. Methods of instruction include five hours of lecture and laboratory per week.

Credit Recommendation: *Version 1:* In the graduate degree category, 3 semester hours in Computer Engineering, Computer Science, or Software Engineering (9/87). *Version 2:* In the graduate degree category, 3 semester hours in Computer Information Systems, Computer Science, or Software Engineering (6/95).

Special Topics in Product Assurance (64587) (Formerly Design by Reliability [88587] and End of Course Projects [88586])

Location: School of Engineering and Logistics, Red River Army Depot.

Length: *Version 1:* 60 hours (10 weeks); *Version 2:* 100 hours (10 weeks).

Dates: *Version 1:* May 1981-June 1995; *Version 2:* June 1995-Present.

Objective: *Version 1:* To provide the student with methods applicable to design optimization. *Version 2:* To provide the student with methods applicable to design optimization and to allow the students to apply what they have learned during their Product/Assurance Engineering Training Program.

Learning Outcome: Upon successful completion of this course, the student will be able to prepare product assurance inputs to contracts, such as contract data requirement lists, statements of work, etc.; formulate and evaluate reliability allocation models using dynamic and nonlinear programming techniques; evaluate designs of controls and displays, for ease of maintenance and operation using knowledge of human capabilities and anthropmetry data; and use workshops to demonstrate applications of principles in acquisition of systems.

Instruction: *Version 1:* Major topics covered in the course are stress/strength analysis, failure modes and effects analysis, fault tree analysis, probabilistic design, and optimization techniques. Methods of instruction include lecture, laboratory exercises, and an examination. *Version 2:*

Major topics covered in the course are product assurance and contracting, reliability optimization using dynamic programming, reliability using nonlinear programming, human/machine interfaces, and U.S. Army Equipment R&D Cycle Workshop. Methods of instruction include five hours lecture and laboratory per week, practical exercises, and written examinations.

Credit Recommendation: *Version 1:* In the graduate degree category, 3 semester hours in Industrial Engineering (6/84). *Version 2:* In the graduate degree category, 3 semester hours in Management (6/95).

Specifications and Standards (53870)

Location: School of Engineering and Logistics, Red River Army Depot.

Length: 20 hours (1 week).

Dates: January 1995-Present.

Objective: To provide the students with the ability to use specifications and standards in contracts with emphasis on development and writing of different levels of specifications.

Learning Outcome: Upon successful completion of this course, the student will be able to know the definition of key terms, understand the purpose of specifications and standards, and demonstrate a knowledge of effective application of specifications and standards.

Instruction: Major topics covered in the course are specifications and standards in contracts and definitions of key terms. Methods of instruction include lecture and practical application.

Credit Recommendation: In the upper division baccalaureate degree category, 1 semester hour in Industrial Engineering (6/95).

Statics and Dynamics (87501)

Location: School of Engineering and Logistics, Red River Army Depot.

Length: 93 hours (13 weeks).

Dates: January 1975-September 1993.

Objective: To give the student an understanding of the relationships of basic force, mass, and acceleration; to apply these relationships in solving engineering problems; and to use vector methods to analyze the kinematic and dynamic behavior of solid bodies.

Instruction: Major topics covered in the course are the fundamental concepts and principal units, methods of problem solution, and the importance of numerical accuracy. Methods of instruction include lecture, practical exercises, research, and an examination.

Credit Recommendation: In the lower division baccalaureate/associate degree category, 4 semester hours in Mechanical Engineering (6/84).

Statistical Analysis (50100)

Location: School of Engineering and Logistics, Red River Army Depot.

Length: *Version 1:* 60 hours (3 weeks); *Version 2:* 80 hours.

Dates: January 1975-Present.

Objective: To provide the student with a basic knowledge of statistical techniques and procedures for collecting, describing, analyzing, and interpreting data.

Learning Outcome: Upon successful completion of this course, the student will be able to collect, analyze, and interpret numerical data and utilize the results in decision making and research design.

Instruction: *Version 1:* Major topics covered in the course are introduction to probability, probability distributions, and statistical inference; testing of hypothesis using f and t tests; and use of test methods for independence, single regression, and analysis of variance. Methods of instruction include lecture, problem-solving, and examinations. *Version 2:* Major topics covered in the course are descriptive graphs, descriptive measures, probability concepts, probability distributions, statistical inference and sampling, hypothesis tests, applications of the chi-square statistic, analysis of variance, simple and multiple linear regression, and nonparametric statistic. Methods of instruction include lecture, classroom exercises, computer-assisted instruction, problem-solving, and an examination.

Credit Recommendation: *Version 1:* In the graduate degree category, 3 semester hours in Business Statistics (6/84). *Version 2:* In the graduate degree category, 3 semester hours in Statistics (6/95).

Statistical Methods and Systems Reliability (83525)

Location: School of Engineering and Logistics, Red River Army Depot.

Length: 60 hours (10 weeks); six 1-hour meetings per week.

Dates: February 1977-September 1993.

Objective: To provide students with an understanding of statistical methods used in industrial quality control.

Instruction: Major topics covered in the course are aspects of the physical application of the process control theory and techniques, significant tests, sampling plans, and military standards for inspection. Methods of instruction include five hours of lecture per week, one hour of laboratory per week, and written examinations.

Credit Recommendation: In the graduate degree category, 3 semester hours in Industrial Engineering (12/84).

Statistical Methods in Reliability (88525)

Location: School of Engineering and Logistics, Red River Army Depot.

Length: 60 hours (10 weeks).

Dates: November 1980-September 1993.

Objective: To provide the student with the theories and techniques pertinent to the solution of engineering problems in system reliability, maintainability, and other measures of effectiveness.

Instruction: Major topics covered in the course are reliability, reliability measurements, static reliability models, probabilistic design, and dynamic probability models. Methods of instruction include lecture, laboratory, written examinations, and reports.

Credit Recommendation: In the graduate degree category, 3 semester hours in Industrial Engineering (6/84).

Statistical Methods in Reliability and Maintainability (82525)

Location: School of Engineering and Logistics, Red River Army Depot.

Length: 60 hours (10 weeks); six 1-hour meetings per week.

Dates: February 1977-September 1993.

Objective: To provide students with an understanding of statistical methods used in industrial quality control.

Instruction: Major topics covered in the course are aspects of the physical application of the process control theory and techniques, significant tests, sampling plans, and military standards for inspection. Methods of instruction include five hours of lecture per week, one hour of laboratory per week, and written examinations.

Credit Recommendation: In the graduate degree category, 3 semester hours in Industrial Engineering (12/84).

Statistical Process Control (60514) (Formerly Statistical Quality Control [88514])

Location: School of Engineering and Logistics, Red River Army Depot.

Length: *Version 1:* 60 hours (10 weeks); *Version 2:* 90 hours (10 weeks).

Dates: *Version 1:* January 1975-June 1995; *Version 2:* June 1995-Present.

Objective: *Version 1:* To provide the student with statistical methods used in industrial quality control. *Version 2:* To provide the student with statistical methods used in industrial process control.

Learning Outcome: Upon successful completion of this course, the student will be able to determine, analyze, and evaluate point and confidence interval estimators for means, variances, differences, and proportions; demonstrate the ability to develop and utilize hypothesis tests in various sampling applications; understand and apply statistical process control tools and techniques in appropriate processes, and conduct statistical analysis and evaluation of various systems.

Instruction: *Version 1:* Major topics covered in the course are aspects of the physical application of the process control theory and techniques, sampling plans, and military standards for inspection. Methods of instruction include lecture, laboratory, written examinations, and reports. *Version 2:* Major topics covered in the course are estimation techniques, hypothesis testing, control charts, and problem identification techniques. Methods of instruction include five hours of lecture per week, four hours of laboratory per week, practical exercises, and written examinations.

Credit Recommendation: *Versions 1 and 2:* In the graduate degree category, 3 semester hours in Reliability (Industrial Engineering) (6/84) (6/95).

Statistical Process Control/Quality Assurance (50175)

Location: School of Engineering and Logistics, Red River Army Depot.

Length: 60 hours.

Dates: January 1995-Present.

Objective: To learn techniques and procedures for conducting process capacity and process improvement studies.

Learning Outcome: Upon successful completion of this course, the student will be able to utilize SPC techniques in making recommendations for process capacity and process improvement.

Instruction: Major topics covered in the course are data collection and analysis, graphic tools, control charts, and quality assurance. Methods of instruction include lecture, discussion, exercises, case studies, and presentations.

Credit Recommendation: In the graduate degree category, 3 semester hours in Business Statistics or I.E. Statistics (6/95).

Statistical Quality Control (84514)

Location: School of Engineering and Logistics, Red River Army Depot.

Length: 60 hours (10 weeks).

Dates: May 1974-September 1993.

Objective: To provide students with an understanding of statistical methods use in industrial quality control.

Instruction: Major topics covered in the course are aspects of physical application of the process control theory and technique, significance tests, sampling plans, and military standards for inspection. Methods of instruction include five hours of lecture per week, one hour of laboratory per week, examinations, projects, and presentations.

Credit Recommendation: In the graduate degree category, 3 semester hours in Quality Control (12/84).

Statistical Quality Control (82514)

Location: School of Engineering and Logistics, Red River Army Depot.

Length: 60 hours (10 weeks).

Dates: January 1975-February 1995.

Objective: To provide the student with knowledge of statistical methods used in industrial quality control, including aspects of physical applications of control theory and techniques, significance tests, sampling plans, and military standards for inspection.

Learning Outcome: Upon successful completion of this course, the student will be able to construct and use control charts; select appropriate sampling plans to meet specific objectives; and apply military standards for inspection and sampling.

Instruction: Major topics covered in the course are central tendency, graphical techniques, chi-square and Kolmorgov-Smirnoff tests, theory and use of control charts, sampling plans, and military standards for inspection and sampling. Methods of instruction include lectures.

Credit Recommendation: In the graduate degree category, 3 semester hours in Reliability (Industrial Engineering) (2/90).

Stratification

Location: School of Engineering and Logistics, Red River Army Depot.

Length: 20 hours (1 week).

Dates: June 1984-June 1997.

Objective: To show the student the concept of "time-phased simulation of buy."

Instruction: Major topics covered in the course are principles of demand-supported stockage and their relationship to secondary items budget process. Methods of instruction include lecture, discussion, and an examination.

Credit Recommendation: In the upper division baccalaureate degree category, 1 semester hour in Management (6/84).

Strength of Materials (87502)

Location: School of Engineering and Logistics, Red River Army Depot.

Length: 73 hours (five 2-hour meetings and one individual problem session per week for 65 weeks).

Dates: January 1975-September 1993.

Objective: To enable the student to analyze forces on materials to ascertain required strengths and design parameters.

Instruction: Major topics covered in the course are stress and strain, torsion on circular shafts, torsion shear flow, deflection of beams, statically indeterminate beams, buckling, and combination stress. Methods of instruction include lecture, practical exercises, research, and an examination.

Credit Recommendation: In the upper division baccalaureate degree category, 3 semester hours in Mechanical Engineering (6/84).

Supply Management (52730) (Formerly Supply, Storage, and Transportation Procedures)

Location: School of Engineering and Logistics, Red River Army Depot.

Length: *Version 1:* 80 hours (4 weeks); *Version 2:* 70 hours (4 weeks).

Dates: *Version 1:* January 1975-January 1993; *Version 2:* January 1993-Present.

Objective: *Version 1:* To introduce the student to inventory management and the Army supply system. *Version 2:* To introduce the student to Department of the Army retail and wholesale level supply system, to include storage management, transportation management, and inventory management.

Learning Outcome: Upon successful completion of this course, the student will be able to understand the role of the retail supply system as it relates as a customer of the army wholesale supply system, understand the overall concept of the army wholesale supply system, identify and define the terms and definitions related to the army supply system, understand the flow of documentation in the army supply system, and prepare documentation related to the requisitioning and issue of military supplies.

Instruction: *Version 1:* Major topic covered in the course is the Commodity Command Standard System structure, capabilities, and functions. Methods of instruction include lecture and laboratory.

Version 2: Major topics covered in the course are the retail supply system, army wholesale supply system, documentation used in the army supply system, and requisitioning and issue of military supplies. Methods of instruction include group projects, practical exercises, and computer simulation.

Credit Recommendation: *Versions 1 and 2:* In the upper division baccalaureate degree category, 1 semester hour in Military Science (6/84) (6/95).

Supply Simulation (51340) (Formerly Supply Simulation [SUPSIM])

Location: School of Engineering and Logistics, Red River Army Depot.

Length: 20 hours (1 week).

Dates: January 1975-Present.

Objective: To provide the students with a knowledge of system requirements of DS/DS and SAILS, using a computer simulation of Stock Control and Inventory Management.

Learning Outcome: Upon successful completion of this course, the student will be able to apply the concepts and principles learned in unit and intermediate level supply courses and the computer simulation to solve mathematical problems involving stockage levels and construct charts and graphs if necessary and demonstrate correct usage of computer input and output.

Instruction: Major topics covered in the course are unit and organization supply, direct and general support supply, and Standard Army Intermediate Supply subsystem in making supply management decisions typical of those required at this level of supply. Methods of instruction include computer-assisted exercises and computer simulation.

Credit Recommendation: In the graduate degree category, 1 semester hour in Inventory Management (6/84) (6/95).

System Assessment Techniques (88571)

Location: School of Engineering and Logistics, Red River Army Depot.

Length: 60 hours (10 weeks).

Dates: November 1980-September 1993.

Objective: To provide the student with a detailed discussion of system assessment techniques and the Army's Assessment Program.

Instruction: Major topics covered in the course are studies of Army discipline reviews, the Standard Army Maintenance System, sample data collection, and industries assessment programs. Methods of instruction include lecture, practical exercises, and an examination.

Credit Recommendation: In the graduate degree category, 3 semester hours in Statistics (6/84).

System Effectiveness Evaluation (66018) (Formerly Theory of Maintained Systems [87018])

Location: School of Engineering and Logistics, Red River Army Depot.

Length: *Version 1:* 60 hours (10 weeks); *Version 2:* 100 hours (10 weeks).

Dates: *Version 1:* August 1989-June 1995; *Version 2:* June 1995-Present.

Objective: To provide the student with the theory and quantitative techniques for the design and application of complex repairable statistical models.

Learning Outcome: *Version 1:* Upon successful completion of this course, the student will be able to draw Markov diagrams, set up the transition matrix, and evaluate the probabilities; model repairable systems using the Markov process and use the model to calculate estimates; and solve problems modeled with a Poisson process. *Version 2:* Upon successful completion of this course, the student will be able to formulate evaluation programs to assess operational effectiveness and suitability of systems in development and formulate programs that will enable decision makers to answer critical system issues and track development progress in meeting system effectiveness goals.

Instruction: *Version 1:* Major topics covered in the course are Markov chains, Poisson processes, renewal theory, and repairable systems. Methods of instruction include lecture and problem laboratory. *Version 2:* Major topics covered in the course are system effectiveness, maintainability concepts and evaluation, logistics supportability evaluation, and repairable systems. Methods of instruction include lecture, laboratory, practical exercises, and written examinations.

Credit Recommendation: *Versions 1 and 2:* In the graduate degree category, 3 semester hours in Industrial Engineering or Statistics (2/90) (6/95).

System Engineering in Material Acquisition (60509) (Formerly Procurement Policies and Procedures for Engineers [83503] and Technical Data Package Development/Preparation [83504])

Location: School of Engineering and Logistics, Red River Army Depot.

Length: *Version 1:* 50 hours (5 weeks); *Version 2:* 90 hours (10 weeks).

Dates: *Version 1:* January 1976-June 1995; *Version 2:* June 1995-Present.

Objective: *Version 1:* To give students a working knowledge of the defense procurement system. *Version 2:* To provide students with knowledge of the defense materiel acquisition system.

Learning Outcome: Upon successful completion of this course, the student will be able to demonstrate knowledge of the procedures, responsibilities, and management controls for development of technical product data, compare and contrast sealed bidding, negotiation, and small purchases methods of acquisition to determine the type of acquisition process and type of contract that should be used in procurement of defense material, and apply risk assessment and hazard analysis techniques to analyze impact of military pollution source.

Instruction: *Version 1:* Major topics covered in the course are legal aspects, procedures, and policies concerning contracts are studied. Methods of instruction include lecture, practical assignments, a written examination, and reports. *Version 2:* Major topics covered in the course are technical data package (TDP), configuration management, procurement policies and procedures, current acquisition tools, and hazard analysis and risk assessment. Methods of instruction include five hours of lecture per week, four hours of laboratory per week, practical exercises, and written examinations.

Credit Recommendation: *Version 1:* In the upper division baccalaureate degree category, 3 semester hours in Management (12/84). *Version 2:* In the upper division baccalaureate degree category, 3 semester hours in Military Science (6/95).

System Safety Analysis I (63566) (Formerly Product Reliability and Safety [84566])

Location: School of Engineering and Logistics, Red River Army Depot.

Length: *Version 1:* 60 hours (10 weeks); *Version 2:* 90 hours (10 weeks).

Dates: *Version 1:* September 1977-June 1995; *Version 2:* June 1995-Present.

Objective: *Version 1:* To provide students with an understanding of the specialized emphasis required to develop the ability to function in the product design process as a specialist in safety engineering. *Version 2:* To provide students with an understanding of the specialized tools required to evaluate complex systems for the existence of safety problems during the product design process.

Learning Outcome: Upon successful completion of this course, the student will be able to understand basic concepts of the various system safety analyses that are utilized in the development of a new operational system; demonstrate preliminary analyses by application to example systems; conduct failure modes and effects analyses; define and demonstrate operational analyses; construct and evaluate fault trees; attend and report on tutorials, presentations, and conferences at a system safety symposium.

Instruction: *Version 1:* Major topics covered in the course are accident prevention and human factor principles are brought to focus on specific problems of accident elimination as related to product liability and safety. Methods of instruction include five hours of lecture per week, one hour of laboratory per week, written examinations, projects, and presentations. *Version 2:* Major topics covered in the course are preliminary analyses, failure modes and effects analyses, operational analyses, fault tree analysis, and Annual Safety Symposium. Methods of instruction include five hours of lecture per week, four hours of laboratory per week, practical exercises, and written examinations.

Credit Recommendation: *Version 1:* In the graduate degree category, 3 semester hours in Industrial Management (12/84). *Version 2:* In the graduate degree category, 3 semester hours in Industrial Safety or Safety Engineering (6/95).

System Simulation (60559) (Formerly Computer Simulation and Modeling [87015])

Location: School of Engineering and Logistics, Red River Army Depot.

Length: *Version 1:* 80 hours (10 weeks); *Version 2:* 90 hours (10 weeks).

Dates: *Version 1:* June 1989-June 1995; *Version 2:* June 1995-Present.

Objective: *Version 1:* To provide the student with digital simulation and modeling techniques useful in assessing the data validity and accuracy resulting from small samples, aggregated test data, differing test lengths, and differing sample sizes. *Version 2:* To give the student a knowledge of simulation techniques and simulation modeling applications.

Learning Outcome: *Version 1:* Upon successful completion of this course, the student will be able to write random number generations in Ada for continuous functions, discrete functions, normal distributions, and various statistical tests; perform I/O analysis on simulations; and utilize Ada-based packages to write several simulations. *Version 2:* Upon successful completion of this course, the student will be able to explain the use of system simulation as a problem-solving tool; describe the basic elements of a simulation language or modeler; compare and contrast the capabilities of various simulation languages and modelers; and write a system simulation utilizing a modern simulation language or modeler.

Instruction: *Version 1:* Major topics covered in the course are basic simulation modeling, I/O data analysis, random numbers generators (using and testing), alternate system comparisons, validation of simulation models, stochastic modeling, Monte Carlo simulation, and exploratory analysis. Methods of instruction include lecture, discussion, and laboratory exercises. *Version 2:* Major topics covered in the course are introduction to simulation, random deviate generation/testing, simulation language survey, and system modeling using simulation. Methods of instruction include five hours lecture and four hours laboratory per week, practical exercises, and written examinations.

Credit Recommendation: *Versions 1 and 2:* In the graduate degree category, 3 semester hours in Computer Science (2/90) (6/95).

Systems Acquisition Management (87008)

Location: School of Engineering and Logistics, Red River Army Depot.

Length: 60 hours (10 weeks).

Dates: April 1989-September 1993.

Objective: To provide the student with a knowledge of the structure and function of the government and the mechanisms involved in weapon system acquisition.

Learning Outcome: Upon successful completion of this course, the student will be able to describe the organization and function of the various governmental levels from the federal government down to the MSC level, and describe how these governmental agencies work together during the weapon system acquisition process.

Instruction: Major topics covered in the course are Department of Defense management organization, materiel acquisition management, planning and budgeting for system development, force modernization, and the Army industrial base. Methods of instruction include lecture and classroom exercises.

Credit Recommendation: In the upper division baccalaureate degree category, 2 semester hours in Military Science (2/90).

Systems Engineering (81515)

Location: School of Engineering and Logistics, Red River Army Depot.

Length: 50 hours (10 weeks: five 1-hour lectures/week).

Dates: August 1986-September 1997.

Objective: To give the student an introduction to the processes and patterns of systems engineering and the planning, organization, and management of programs for developing large, highly complex systems, with special emphasis on problems of embedded computers and relationships between hardware and software.

Learning Outcome: Upon successful completion of this course, the student will be able to identify and practice methods of overcoming conceptual blocks to problem-solving; define the basic concepts of general systems thinking as applied to complex system development; define and use systems engineering tools and techniques as aids in the development of large, complex systems; and relate systems engineering techniques to the development of systems with embedded computer resources.

Instruction: Major topics are systems concepts, systems engineering methods, and embedded computer systems principles.

Credit Recommendation: In the graduate degree category, 3 semester hours in Business Administration, Computer Engineering, Computer Science, or Software Engineering (9/87).

Systems Hazards I (63564) (Formerly Safety in the Occupational Environment I [84564])

Location: School of Engineering and Logistics, Red River Army Depot.

Length: *Version 1:* 60 hours (10 weeks); *Version 2:* 80 hours (10 weeks).

Dates: *Version 1:* September 1981-June 1995; *Version 2:* June 1995-Present.

Objective: To provide students with the knowledge and understanding of materials and techniques essential to the detection, evaluation, and control of certain known physical occupational hazards with emphasis on hazards most common in industrial environments.

Learning Outcome: Upon successful completion of this course, the student will be able to understand and apply basic human physiological principles to study problems associated with noise, vibration, hot and cold environments, and ionizing radiation; demonstrate methods of monitoring these hazardous environments; study and analyze methods for controlling hazardous environments; and identify potentially hazardous systems and recommend methods and procedures for protecting personnel.

Instruction: *Version 1:* Major topics covered in the course are ventilation, heat stress, noise control and hearing conversion, vibration, and illumination. Methods of instruction include five hours of lecture per week, one hour of laboratory per week, written examinations, projects, and presentations. *Version 2:* Major topics covered in the course are noise control and hearing conservation, vibration, heat and cold stress, and ionizing radiation. Methods of instruction include five hours of lecture per week, three hours of laboratory per week, practical exercises, and written examinations.

Credit Recommendation: *Versions 1 and 2:* In the upper division baccalaureate degree category, 3 semester hours in Industrial Safety or Safety Engineering (12/84) (6/95).

Systems Hazards II (63572) (Formerly Safety in the Occupational Environment II [84572])

Location: School of Engineering and Logistics, Red River Army Depot.

Length: *Version 1:* 60 hours (10 weeks); *Version 2:* 80 hours (10 weeks).

Dates: *Version 1:* November 1981-June 1995; *Version 2:* June 1995-Present.

Objective: *Version 1:* To enable students to apply OSHA and AMC safety standards to practices and methods used in industrial operations. *Version 2:* To recognize and control major hazards common in most military systems and industrial processes.

Learning Outcome: Upon successful completion of this course, the student will be able to understand and apply basic human physiological principles to study problems associated with electrical/electronic systems, radar/microwave systems, laser devices, and mechanical hazards; demonstrate methods for controlling these hazardous environments; study and analyze methods for controlling these hazardous environments; and identify potentially hazardous systems and recommend methods and procedures for protecting personnel.

Instruction: *Version 1:* Major topics covered in the course are industrial manufacturing and maintenance process, principles of machine guarding, safety in welding operations, materiel handling safety, OSHA standards and safety surveys, and industrial hygiene. Methods of instruction include five hours of lecture per week, one hour of laboratory per week, and written examinations. *Version 2:* Major topics covered in the course are electrical/electronic systems, radar/microwave systems, laser devices, and mechanical hazards. Methods of instruction include five hours of lecture per week, three hours of laboratory per week, practical exercises, and written examinations.

Credit Recommendation: *Versions 1 and 2:* In the upper division baccalaureate degree category, 3 semester hours in Industrial Safety or Safety Engineering (12/84) (6/95).

Systems Reliability (81525)

Location: School of Engineering and Logistics, Red River Army Depot.

Length: 60 hours (five 1-hour lectures/week; one 1-hour lab/week).

Dates: August 1986-September 1993.

Objective: To enable the student to make reliability calculations, perform reliability tests, and apply reliability management techniques.

Learning Outcome: Upon successful completion of this course, the student will be able to identify reliability parameters; make system reliability calculations; and use reliability management techniques in allocation, prediction, and growth.

Instruction: Major topics covered in the course are reliability measures, static and dynamic reliability models, and reliability estimation. Methods of instruction include lecture, problem-solving laboratories, homework (15 percent), examinations (10 percent), and a final examination (25 percent).

Credit Recommendation: In the upper division baccalaureate degree category, 3 semester hours in Engineering Systems Reliability (9/87).

Systems Safety Analysis II (63567) (Formerly Systems Safety Engineering [84567])

Location: School of Engineering and Logistics, Red River Army Depot.

Length: *Version 1:* 60 hours (10 weeks); *Version 2:* 90 hours (10 weeks).

Dates: *Version 1:* April 1977-June 1995; *Version 2:* June 1995-Present.

Objective: *Version 1:* To provide students with information on the tools and techniques required to provide safety engineering output in various stages during system design. *Version 2:* To provide students with a background in quantitative tools and techniques required to conduct probabilistic risk assessment and tools used to evaluate software for potential safety problems.

Learning Outcome: Upon successful completion of this course, the student will be able to understand and apply advanced concepts of specific system safety analyses that are utilized in the development of a new operational system; construct, solve, and evaluate quantitative fault trees; apply event tree approach and cause-consequence analysis for specific systems; and demonstrate the hazards potential of software associated with operational systems through software analyses.

Instruction: *Version 1:* Major topics covered in the course are the relationship of safety with the reliability and maintainability disciplines and the management of an effective system safety program. Methods of instruction include five hours of lecture per week, one hour of laboratory per week, examinations, projects, and presentations. *Version 2:* Major topics covered in the course are quantitative fault tree analyses, event tree analyses, cause-consequence analysis, and software analysis. Methods of instruction include five hours of lecture per week, four hours of laboratory per week, practical exercises, and written examinations.

Credit Recommendation: *Versions 1 and 2:* In the graduate degree category, 3 semester hours in Industrial Safety or Safety Engineering (12/84) (6/95).

Systems Safety in Materiel Acquisition (63571) (Formerly Systems Safety Management [84571])

Location: School of Engineering and Logistics, Red River Army Depot.

Length: *Version 1:* 60 hours (10 weeks); *Version 2:* 80 hours (10 weeks).

Dates: *Version 1:* January 1980-June 1995; *Version 2:* June 1995-Present.

Objective: To give students a comprehensive study of the role of the Army System Safety Program in overall systems management.

Learning Outcome: Upon successful completion of this course, the student will be able to understand the role of the Army System Safety Program in overall systems management; integrate system safety efforts in the system acquisition model by providing system safety inputs at appropriate points in the life cycle; and demonstrate flexibility and effectiveness in applying techniques for organization for system safety.

Instruction: *Version 1:* Major topics covered in the course are the integration of the Army System Safety effort in the overall system management model and establishment of a system safety organization that allows flexibility and procedures. The student must complete a project for developing system safety input and present the results to the class. Methods of instruction include five hours of lecture per week, one hour of laboratory per week, written examinations, projects, and presentations. *Version 2:* Major topics covered in the course are system safety requirements, life cycle system safety program, and tasks of the system safety engineer. Methods of instruction include five hours of lecture per week, three hours of laboratory per week, practical exercises, and written examinations.

Credit Recommendation: *Versions 1 and 2:* In the upper division baccalaureate degree category, 3 semester hours in Military Science (12/84) (6/95).

Technical Data Package Development (88504)

Location: School of Engineering and Logistics, Red River Army Depot.

Length: 40 hours (1 week).

Dates: May 1981-September 1993.

Objective: To introduce the student to the policies, procedures, and responsibilities for the acquisition, preparation, review, proofing, maintenance, improvement, control, and transmission of the technical data package for procurement and production purposes.

Instruction: Major topics covered in the course are history and controls, technical data package, management and control systems; information storage retrieval, specifications and standardization, product assurance, and technical documentation. Methods of instruction include lecture and an examination.

Credit Recommendation: In the upper division baccalaureate degree category, 2 semester hours in Military Science (6/84).

Techniques in Operations Research (88520)

Location: School of Engineering and Logistics, Red River Army Depot.

Length: 60 hours (10 weeks).

Dates: January 1980-September 1993.

Objective: To teach the student the operations research field and operations research techniques.

Instruction: Major topics covered in the course are production and inventory control, linear programming, game theory, and dynamic programming. Methods of instruction include lecture, laboratory exercises, examinations, and written reports.

Credit Recommendation: In the graduate degree category, 3 semester hours in Industrial Engineering (6/84).

Techniques of Management

Location: School of Engineering and Logistics, Red River Army Depot.

Length: 40 hours (1 week).

Dates: January 1975-September 1993.

Objective: To provide the student with an understanding of widely used principles, philosophies, tools, and applications of management.

Instruction: Methods of instruction include lecture, discussion, in-basket exercises, research, and an examination.

Credit Recommendation: In the upper division baccalaureate degree category, 3 semester hours in Management (6/84).

Test and Evaluation Laboratory (66022)
(Formerly Test and Evaluation Laboratory [87022])

Location: School of Engineering and Logistics, Red River Army Depot.

Length: *Version 1:* 60 hours (10 weeks); *Version 2:* 100 hours (10 weeks).

Dates: *Version 1:* October 1989-June 1995; *Version 2:* June 1995-Present.

Objective: To provide the student with a functional knowledge of documentation, testing, and time phasing involved in the research and development portion of the acquisition cycle.

Learning Outcome: *Version 1:* Upon successful completion of this course, the student will be able to bring other materials from other courses into a final form. *Version 2:* Upon successful completion of this course, the student will be able to apply concepts learned in other courses in developing an integrated strategy for test and evaluation; develop, schedule, coordinate, and evaluate Army testing of a hypothetical Army system; and participate in working groups considering testing issues and conduct briefings at key review points.

Instruction: *Version 1:* Major topics covered in the course are pre-concept exploration (written communications), concept exploration (documents and reviews), demonstration (documents and reviews), and development (documents and reviews). *Version 2:* Major topics covered in the course are test and evaluation in systems acquisition, test design and evaluation, and lessons learned. Methods of instruction include lecture, laboratory, practical exercises, and written examinations.

Credit Recommendation: *Versions 1 and 2:* In the graduate degree category, 3 semester hours in Industrial Engineering (Seminar or Special Problems) (2/90) (6/95).

Test and Evaluation Management (88530)

Location: School of Engineering and Logistics, Red River Army Depot.

Length: 60 hours (10 weeks).

Dates: January 1980-September 1993.

Objective: To give the student an understanding of the testing procedures occurring during the development of new materiel system, and the evaluations that are performed to determine the technical and military worth of the materiel under test.

Instruction: Major topics covered in the course are the interrelationship of development and operational tests and their evaluations, the coordinated test program, test schedule, review committees, and the development of the test and evaluation master plan. Methods of instruction include lectures, laboratory, examinations, and written reports.

Credit Recommendation: In the upper division baccalaureate degree category, 3 semester hours in Industrial Engineering (6/84).

Test and Evaluation Management (60012)
(Formerly Test and Evaluation Management I [87012])

Location: School of Engineering and Logistics, Red River Army Depot.

Length: *Version 1:* 60 hours (10 weeks); *Version 2:* 100 hours (10 weeks).

Dates: *Version 1:* June 1989-June 1995; *Version 2:* June 1995-Present.

Objective: To provide the student with an understanding of the organization, regulations, responsibilities, and policies of the developer, tester, and evaluator at each step in the process of materiel acquisition.

Learning Outcome: *Version 1:* Upon successful completion of this course, the student will be able to discuss organization and policies specific to each phase of materiel acquisition; work with plans, reviews, and documents with emphasis on the Test and Evaluation Master Plan (TEMP); and evaluate systems with emphasis on scheduling and planning of critical tests. *Version 2:* Upon successful completion of this course, the student will be able to formulate and manage testing programs for Army systems; determine which regulations apply to the program, how to implement required actions, and how to document results; recognize the importance of the efforts; and convince other organizations to support testing requirements when competing for constrained resources.

Instruction: *Version 1:* Major topics covered in the course are management theory, force integration, the role of the program manager, types of tests used in life cycle testing, systems engineering management, study of Test and Evaluation Master Plan, and plans, reviews, and documents. Methods of instruction include lecture and problem laboratory. *Version 2:* Major topics covered in the course are organization and responsibilities; life cycle test and evaluation; continuous evaluation; and test and evaluation issues. Methods of instruction include lecture, laboratory, practical exercises, and written examinations.

Credit Recommendation: *Versions 1 and 2:* In the graduate degree category, 3 semester hours in Industrial Engineering (2/90) (6/95).

Test and Evaluation Management II (87016)

Location: School of Engineering and Logistics, Red River Army Depot.

Length: 60 hours (10 weeks).

Dates: August 1989-September 1993.

Objective: To provide the student with an in-depth understanding of management principles that affect test and evaluation programs.

Learning Outcome: Upon successful completion of this course, the student will be able to generate requirements for preparation of rationale reports and translate these requirements into a test and evaluation program; apply principles of Total Quality Management (TQM); and apply statistical techniques in decision analysis and estimation.

Instruction: Major topics covered in the course are requirements generation, reliability, availability and maintainability, integrated logistics support, Total Quality Management, and test and evaluation funding and contracts. Methods of instruction include lecture and problem laboratory.

Credit Recommendation: In the graduate degree category, 3 semester hours in Industrial Engineering (2/90).

Test and Evaluation Research Project (66585) (Formerly Current Research in Test and Evaluation [87019])

Location: School of Engineering and Logistics, Red River Army Depot.

Length: *Version 1:* 60 hours (10 weeks); *Version 2:* 100 hours (10 weeks).

Dates: *Version 1:* August 1989-June 1995; *Version 2:* June 1995-Present.

Objective: *Version 1:* To enable the student to independently isolate, research, document, and report current real-world problems in the field of test and evaluation. *Version 2:* To allow students to research and study a problem pertinent to test and evaluation engineering. Techniques concerning documentation and professional problem-solving are stressed.

Learning Outcome: *Version 1:* Upon successful completion of this course, the student will be able to develop a research proposal. *Version 2:* Upon successful completion of this course, the student will be able to accomplish advanced study and research in the field of test and evaluation, especially as relate to DoD problem areas; and demonstrate professional problem-solving skills by choosing a manageable problem, evaluating pertinent background data and reference materials, performance of current literature survey and critical analysis, and formulation of a formal research proposal.

Instruction: *Version 1:* Major topics covered in the course are research sources, research techniques, research topic selection, and research methodology. Methods of instruction include independent research under faculty guidance. *Version 2:* Major topics covered in the course are research requirements and sources, research techniques and topic selection, and research problem and report. Methods of instruction include lecture, independent research, oral presentations, and written reports. Oral and written presentation of work-in-progress, findings and results required.

Credit Recommendation: *Versions 1 and 2:* In the graduate degree category, 3 semester hours in Research Techniques (2/90) (6/95).

Test Design and Analysis I (87011)

Location: School of Engineering and Logistics, Red River Army Depot.

Length: 60 hours (10 weeks).

Dates: April 1989-Present.

Objective: To provide the student with statistical model-building techniques and data collection strategies.

Learning Outcome: Upon successful completion of this course, the student will be able to evaluate and use factorial test designs; use diagnostic methods for checking model validity; and use predictive statistics (regression methods).

Instruction: Major topics covered in the course are factorial experiments, model diagnostics and transformation, and regression methods. Methods of instruction include lecture and problem laboratory.

Credit Recommendation: In the graduate degree category, 3 semester hours in Statistics (2/90). **NOTE:** Students should not receive credit for both this course and Test Engineering and Analysis (88531).

Test Engineering (66004) (Formerly Test Engineering and Management [87004])

Location: School of Engineering and Logistics, Red River Army Depot.

Length: *Version 1:* 60 hours (10 weeks); *Version 2:* 100 hours (10 weeks).

Dates: *Version 1:* January 1989-June 1995; *Version 2:* June 1995-Present.

Objective: To provide the student with an understanding of engineering management, test issues, and types of testing conducted at Army facilities.

Learning Outcome: *Version 1:* Upon successful completion of this course, the student will be able to list various types of instrumentation commonly used within military tests; describe the basic Army Test and Evaluation Process and the major test plans and reports; and list the organizations within AMC and TRADOC that take part in the test and evaluation process. *Version 2:* Upon successful completion of this course, the student will be able to identify necessary test equipment to measure Army equipment characteristics and determine what test facilities could be utilized for testing of a particular Army system, how to plan and schedule the particular tests, and what necessary documents and reports should be generated, including what information should be contained in the document.

Instruction: *Version 1:* Major topics covered in the course are specific planning, scheduling and reporting documents, considerations for detailed testing, equipment used for engineering measurements, and Army testing and test facilities. Methods of instruction include lecture and laboratory exercises. *Version 2:* Major topics covered in the course are engineering measurements, Army testing and test facilities, test planning, and test documents and reports. Methods of instruction include lecture, laboratory, practical exercises, and written examinations.

Credit Recommendation: *Versions 1 and 2:* In the upper division baccalaureate degree category, 1 semester hour in Measurements and Testing (2/90) (6/95).

Test Engineering and Analysis (88531)

Location: School of Engineering and Logistics, Red River Army Depot.

Length: 60 hours (10 weeks).

Dates: February 1981-September 1993.

Objective: To provide the student with the statistical model-building technology.

Instruction: Major topics covered in the course are the design and evaluation of tests, methods of collecting test data, and test evaluation techniques used within the Army. Methods of instruction include lecture, laboratory, examinations, and written reports.

Credit Recommendation: In the graduate degree category, 3 semester hours in Statistics (6/84).

Theory of Life Testing and Reliability (87009)

Location: School of Engineering and Logistics, Red River Army Depot.

Length: 60 hours (10 weeks).

Dates: April 1989-September 1993.

Objective: To provide the student with an understanding of the theory of life testing and quantitative reliability design analysis.

Learning Outcome: Upon successful completion of this course, the student will be able to apply quantitative techniques of life testing and reliability to effectively model and predict system life and effectiveness.

Instruction: Major topics covered in the course are system reliability modeling, prediction, assessment through the use of fault tests, stress strength analyses, probabilistic mechanical design, and failure mode analysis. Methods of instruction include lecture, conference, and practical exercises.

Credit Recommendation: In the graduate degree category, 3 semester hours in Design Reliability (Industrial Engineering) (2/90).

Thermodynamics (87505)

Location: School of Engineering and Logistics, Red River Army Depot.

Length: 76 hours (five 2-hour meetings and two 1-hour individual problem sessions per week for 6.5 weeks).

Dates: January 1975-September 1993.

Objective: To enable the student to apply thermodynamics principles in solving practical problems.

Instruction: Major topics covered in the course are the principles of work and heat transfer and the laws of thermodynamics. Methods of instruction include lecture, practical exercises, research, and an examination.

Credit Recommendation: In the upper division baccalaureate degree category, 3 semester hours in Mechanical Engineering (6/84).

Total Quality Management: Techniques of Management (50113) (Formerly Techniques of Management)

Location: School of Engineering and Logistics, Red River Army Depot.

Length: *Version 1:* 20 hours (3 weeks); *Version 2:* 40 hours.

Dates: January 1975-Present.

Objective: To review the principles of management, to learn the philosophy of Total Quality Management, the cultural changes required to support continuous improvement, and to develop a model for implementation.

Learning Outcome: Upon successful completion of this course, the student will be able to evaluate management practices, identify problem areas, and develop a model and course of action to create a "Total Quality Organization".

Instruction: Major topics covered in the course are principles of management, leadership, TQM, philosophy, systems theory and implementation, and team learning. Methods of instruction include lecture, discussion, classroom exercises, case studies, learner presentations/reports, an examination, and study teams.

Credit Recommendation: *Version 1:* In the upper division baccalaureate degree category, 2 semester hours in Management (6/84). *Version 2:* In the upper division baccalaureate degree category, 3 semester hours in Management (6/95).

Transportation Management (51460)

Location: School of Engineering and Logistics, Red River Army Depot.

Length: 20 hours (1 week).

Dates: January 1975-Present.

Objective: To provide the student with a basic knowledge of transportation management and its relationship to other areas of management and logistics.

Learning Outcome: Upon successful completion of this course, the student will be able to define and discuss traffic management as it relates to other areas of distribution management; discuss freight services, rates and tariffs, freight classification, routing and documentation of freight; be familiar with procedures for loss and damage in shipments; and understand trends in transportation.

Instruction: Major topics covered in the course are an introduction to transportation and traffic management agencies; freight services; classifications; rates and tariffs; routing and documentation of freight; loss and damage in shipment; household goods and personal baggage; containerizations; and trends in transportation. Methods of instruction include lecture, computer simulation, student-centered learning through group projects, and an examination.

Credit Recommendation: In the upper division baccalaureate degree category, 1 semester hour in Transportation Management (6/84) (6/95).

Unit and Organization Supply Procedures (51310) (Formerly Unit and Organization Supply Procedures)

Location: School of Engineering and Logistics, Red River Army Depot.

Length: 26 hours (2 weeks).

Dates: January 1975-Present.

Objective: To teach the student policies and procedures used at the unit and organizational level of supply in the United States Army.

Learning Outcome: Upon successful completion of this course, the student will be able to know common terms applying to this level of supply; understand the TAADS and the authorization document concept; know automated procedures for request, followup, cancellation, and modification of supplies; demonstrate correct use of property books, automated management of PLL, sources of supply for a unit, and IMPL's; and demonstrate proper use of technical manuals.

Instruction: Major topics covered in the course are the organization for supply at the user/direct supply level; the Army Authorizations Documents System and its impact on supply; preparation and maintenance of property books; preparation of a request for issue, follow-up, and cancellation; maintenance of the Document Register; sources of supply available to the unit; use of repair parts technical manuals; prescribed load list procedures; and applicable supply terminology. Methods of instruction include lecture, laboratory, discussion, classroom exercises, and written examinations.

Credit Recommendation: In the upper division baccalaureate degree category, 1 semester hour in Military Science (6/84) (6/95).

Warehousing and Materials Handling (51430)

Location: School of Engineering and Logistics, Red River Army Depot.

Length: 20 hours (1 week).

Dates: January 1975-Present.

Objective: To teach the student types of materiel stored, types of storage facilities, safety, policies, and storage management systems used in warehousing.

Learning Outcome: Upon successful completion of this course, the student will be able to state the objectives of storage; list the basic resources needed for effective storage; distinguish between categories of storage space; describe the characteristics, advantages, and limitations of the various types of storage facilities; list and discuss the commodity and capacity factors to be considered in space planning and layout; list and discuss various types of storage aids; compute gross, net, and actual storage space; explain the design of the stock location number, and give basic rules of effective storage.

Instruction: Major topics covered in the course are planning storage; space requirement factors; effective use of storage space; stock location system; storage procedures; commingled storage; storage for other services; types and application of Materials Handling Equipment (MHE); planning materials handling operations; selection of Materials Handling Equipment; computing MHE requirements; and innovations in materials handling and its interface with the Depot Modernization Program. Methods of instruction include lecture, laboratory, student-centered learning through group participation and computer simulation, and an examination.

Credit Recommendation: In the upper division baccalaureate degree category, 1 semester hour in Industrial Management or Storage Management (6/84) (6/95).

Written Communications (50060)

Location: School of Engineering and Logistics, Red River Army Depot.

Length: 40 hours (2 weeks).

Dates: January 1975-Present.

Objective: To give the student an understanding of communication models and analysis of group communication, with emphasis on organizational communications.

Learning Outcome: Upon successful completion of this course, the student will be able to evaluate language skills, compose memoranda and letters in accordance with Army regulations, and make formal presentations.

Instruction: Major topics covered in the course are effective writing and research techniques and staff studies. Methods of instruction include lecture, classroom exercises, learner presentations/reports, an examination, and problem-solving.

Credit Recommendation: In the upper division baccalaureate degree category, 3 semester hours in Communications or Technical Writing (6/84) (6/95).

Seafarers Harry Lundeberg School of Seamanship

The Seafarers Harry Lundeberg School of Seamanship, founded in 1967, provides academic and career programs for boatmen and unlicensed seafarers. The purpose of the school is to train, guide, and encourage young people to pursue careers on the seas or on America's network of inland and coastal waterways, as well as to upgrade seafarers and boatmen to higher ratings. The school is administered by a joint board of trustees representing private American shipowners and the Seafarers International Union.

The school conducts both academic and vocational programs. The academic program consists of an adult basic education program, a high school equivalency program, and a two-year college program. Vocational programs are developed and expanded as changes in industry or in Coast Guard regulations occur.

The courses listed below are part of the training or upgrading programs. Many of the courses include hands-on experience aboard vessels as well as in the school's laboratories.

Source of official student records: Director of Vocational Education, Seafarers Harry Lundeberg School of Seamanship, Piney Point, MD 20674.

Additional information about the courses: College Credit Recommendation Service, American Council on Education, One Dupont Circle, Washington, DC 20036-1193.

Able Seaman (NST 221)
Part 1: Basic Seamanship
Part 2: Navigation
Part 3: First Aid and Safety
(Formerly Lifeboat and Able Seaman)

Location: Seafarers Harry Lundeberg School of Seamanship, Piney Point, MD.

Length: *Version 1:* Approximately 240 hours (5 weeks, 5 days), residential; *Part 1:* 144 hours; *Part 2:* 36 hours; *Part 3:* 22 hours; *Version 2:* Approximately 320 hours (8 weeks); *Version 3:* 110 hours (4 weeks); *Version 4:* 140 hours (4 weeks).

Dates: *Version 1:* October 1975-December 1984; *Version 2:* January 1982-October 1986; *Version 3:* January 1985-December 1994; *Version 4:* January 1995-Present.

Objective: To provide the student with a sufficient understanding of lifesaving and seamanship skills to prepare for endorsement by the Coast Guard as an Able Seaman.

Learning Outcome: Upon successful completion of this course, the student will acquire working knowledge of the following subjects to enable the student to perform duties as qualified Able Seaman Unlimited, Able Seaman Limited, or Able Seaman Special: rules of the road; use of the magnetic and gyro compasses; use of booms; running rigging; winches; CPR; first aid; firefighting; manila and wire splicing; rigging and using stages; hitches and boatswains chairs; lifesaving equipment; aids to navigation; helmsmanship and lookout duties; and splices used aboard ship.

Instruction: *Version 1: Part 1:* Major topics covered in the course are lifeboat handling, deck seamanship, marlinspike seamanship, helmsmanship, cargo handling, and rigging. *Part 2:* Major topics covered in the course are the rules of the road, bearings, aids to navigation, magnetic compass, and radio use. *Part 3:* Major topics covered in the course are treatment of wounds, shock, fractures, and burns; artificial respiration; toxic substances; survival measures; prevention and treatment of diseases; introduction to use of shipboard safety equipment; proper storage and handling of hazardous materials; fire prevention; and shipboard fire fighting. *Version 2: Part 1:* Major topics covered in the course are lifeboat handling, deck seamanship, marlinspike seamanship, helmsmanship, cargo handling, and rigging. *Part 2:* Major topics covered in the course are the rules of the road, bearings, aids to navigation, magnetic compass, and radio use. *Part 3:* Major topics covered in the course are treatment of wounds, shock, fractures, and burns; artificial respiration; toxic substances; survival measures; prevention and treatment of diseases; introduction to use of shipboard safety equipment; proper storage and handling of hazardous materials; fire prevention; and shipboard fire fighting. *Version 3:* Major topics covered in the course are duties of Able Seaman aboard ship, ship construction and terminology, characteristics of SIU contracted ships, ship's organization, ship's control, bridge equipment and instruments, helmsmanship, basic fix plotting, compass (magnetic and gyro), aids to navigation (bouyage), rules of the nautical road, and firefighting. *Version 4:* Major topics covered in the course are duties of Able Seaman aboard ship, ship construction and terminology, characteristics of SIU contracted ships, ship's organization, ship's control, bridge equipment and instruments, helmsmanship, basic fix plotting, compass (magnetic and gyro), aids to navigation (bouyage), rules of the nautical road, and firefighting.

Credit Recommendation: *Version 1: Part 1:* In the lower division baccalaureate/associate degree category, 6 semester hours in Seamanship. *Part 2:* In the lower division baccalaureate/associate degree category, 2 semester hours in Coastwise Navigation and Piloting. *Part 3:* In the lower division baccalaureate/associate degree category, 1 semester hour in First Aid and Safety (11/77) (6/82). **NOTE:** Further credit may be granted for Part 3 upon institutional evaluation. *Version 2: Part 1:* In the lower division baccalaureate/associate degree category, 6 semester hours in Seamanship. *Part 2:* In the lower division baccalaureate/associate degree category, 2 semester hours in Coastwise Navigation and Piloting. *Part 3:* In the lower division baccalaureate/associate degree category, 1 semester hour in First Aid and Safety (11/77) (6/82). **NOTE:** Further credit may be granted for Part 3 upon institutional evaluation. *Version 3:* In the lower division baccalaureate/associate degree category, 3 semester hours in Seamanship, 2 semester hours in Coastwise Navigation and Piloting, and 1 semester hour in First Aid and Safety (2/88). *Version 4:* In the lower division baccalaureate/associate degree category, 6 semester hours in Seamanship (12/94).

Advanced Seamanship
(Formerly Advanced Deck-Inland and Oceans)

Location: Seafarers Harry Lundeberg School of Seamanship, Piney Point, MD.

Length: *Version 1:* 80 hours (2 weeks); *Version 2:* 70 hours (2 weeks).

Dates: *Version 1:* May 1975-January 1988; *Version 2:* February 1988-February 1991.

Objective: To provide students with the skills required to perform the entry rating jobs in the deck and engine department on board merchant ships and towing vessels.

Instruction: *Version 1:* Major topics covered in the course are deck and engine skills and their practical application, work habits on board ship, and actual shipboard work. Methods of instruction include lecture, discussion, and laboratory, with an emphasis on on-the-job training. *Version 2:* Major topics covered in the course are deck department watches, pneumatic tools, electrical tools, priming and painting, maintain lines, heaving line, lock and lines, and safety aboard ships, and electrical safety. Methods of instruction include lecture, discussion, and laboratory, with an emphasis on on-the-job training.

Credit Recommendation: *Version 1:* In the lower division baccalaureate/associate degree category, 2 semester hours in Seamanship (6/82) (2/88). *Version 2:* In the lower division baccalaureate/associate degree category, 2 semester hours in Seamanship (6/82) (2/88).

Assistant Cook Utility (Formerly Assistant Cook)

Location: Seafarers Harry Lundeberg School of Seamanship, Piney Point, MD.

Length: *Version 1:* 208 hours (6 weeks); residential; 42 hours lecture and discussion, 30 hours laboratory, and 136 hours workshop; *Version 2:* 280 hours (7 weeks); *Version 3:* 245 hours (7 weeks).

Dates: *Version 1:* September 1976-December 1985; *Version 2:* January 1986-December 1993; *Version 3:* January 1994-September 1996.

Objective: *Version 1:* To develop the skills of food service workers and enable them to perform the duties of assistant cook. *Version 2:* To develop the skills of food service workers and enable them to perform the duties of assistant cook with special emphasis on food production. *Version 3:* To develop the skills of food service workers and enable them to perform the duties of assistant cook with special emphasis on food production.

Learning Outcome: *Version 1:* Upon successful completion of this course, the student will be able to maintain the ship galley in a sanitary condition; prepare salads in a ship galley; prepare pasta and rice in a ship galley; prepare vegetables in a ship galley; prepare breakfast in a ship galley; and prepare a night luncheon in a ship galley. *Version 2:* Upon successful completion of this course, the student will be able to maintain the ship galley in a sanitary condition; prepare salads in a ship galley; prepare pasta and rice in a ship galley; prepare vegetables in a ship galley; prepare breakfast in a ship galley; and prepare a night luncheon in a ship galley. *Version 3:* Upon successful completion of this course, the student will be able to prepare salads, pasta and rice, vegetables, breakfast, and night luncheons in a ship galley and maintain the galley in a sanitary manner.

Instruction: Major topics covered in the course are preparation, cooking, and serving of vegetables (fresh, canned, and frozen), cooked salads, sandwiches, and breakfast foods; and the basics of food preparation, including sanitation, dietary values, work organization, and the use of recipes, are emphasized. Methods of instruction include lecture, discussion, audio/visual material, demonstrations, practical exercises, and final examination.

Credit Recommendation: *Version 1:* In the lower division baccalaureate/associate degree category, 3 semester hours in Quantity Food Production and 3 semester hours in Food Preparation (9/78). *Version 2:* In the lower division baccalaureate/associate degree category, 3 semester hours in Quantity Food Production, 4 semester hours in Food Preparation, and 1 semester hour in Kitchen Supervision (2/88). *Version 3:* In the lower division baccalaureate/associate degree category, 7 semester hours in Food Preparation and Production (12/94).

Basic Deck

Location: Seafarers Harry Lundeberg School of Seamanship, Piney Point, MD.

Length: *Version 1:* 36 hours (2 weeks); *Version 2:* 70 hours (2 weeks).

Dates: *Version 1:* June 1972-December 1993; *Version 2:* January 1994-March 1997.

Objective: To provide the skills required to perform the entry rating jobs aboard merchant ship and towing vessels.

Learning Outcome: Upon successful completion of this course, the student will be able to tie knots, use shipboard terminology, and stand shipboard watches.

Instruction: Major topics covered in the course are nautical time, standing watch, knot tying, and shipboard functions. Methods of instruction include lecture, discussion, audio/visual material, practical experience, quizzes, and final examination.

Credit Recommendation: *Version 1:* In the lower division baccalaureate/associate degree category, 2 semester hours in Seamanship (6/82) (2/88) (12/94). *Version 2:* In the lower division baccalaureate/associate degree category, 2 semester hours in Seamanship (6/82) (2/88) (12/94).

Basic Engine

Location: Seafarers Harry Lundeberg School of Seamanship, Piney Point, MD.

Length: *Version 1:* 46 hours (2 weeks); *Version 2:* 40 hours (2 weeks).

Dates: *Version 1:* May 1975-January 1988; *Version 2:* February 1988-March 1997.

Objective: To familiarize the student with steam and diesel engine plants, their operation, systems, and associated parts. Students also learn the care and use of hand and power tools through actual machine shop practice.

Learning Outcome: Upon successful completion of this course, the student will be able to utilize basic hand tools and be familiar with basic ships engine systems (steam and diesel).

Instruction: Major topics covered in the course are the theory of operation, construction, hand tools, routine maintenance of diesel and steam power plants, boilers and their operation, steam turbines and auxiliary equipment, and basic operation of the steam and water cycle. Methods of instruction include lecture, discussion, audio/visual material, practical experiences aboard vessels, quizzes, and final examination.

Credit Recommendation: *Version 1:* In the lower division baccalaureate/associate degree category, 3 semester hours in Marine Engineering (6/82). *Version 2:* In the lower division baccalaureate/associate degree category, 3 semester hours in Marine Engineering (2/88) (12/94).

Basic Steward

Location: Seafarers Harry Lundeberg School of Seamanship, Piney Point, MD.

Length: *Version 1:* 70 hours (2 weeks), residential, 10 hours lecture and laboratory and 25 hours workshop per week; *Version 2:* 140 hours (4 weeks).

Dates: *Version 1:* May 1975-January 1988; *Version 2:* February 1988-December 1996.

Objective: *Version 1:* To develop the skills required to perform entry-level jobs in maritime food service departments. *Version 2:* To develop skills required to perform entry-level jobs in maritime food service departments with emphasis on food preparation and production.

Learning Outcome: Upon successful completion of this course, the student will be able to perform entry-level jobs in merchant vessel steward departments; prepare basic salads, vegetables, and breakfast cooking; understand the units of measure; identify galley equipment; and correctly use knives.

Instruction: *Version 1:* Major topics covered in the course are food service operations, kitchen responsibilities and safety, use of kitchen utensils and tools, use of measurements and recipes, and quantity food preparation. *Version 2:* Major topics covered in the course are food service operations, kitchen responsibilities and safety, use of kitchen utensils and tools, use of measurements and recipes, and quantity food preparation and production. Methods of instruction include lecture, discussion, audio/visual material, practical exercises, and a final examination.

Credit Recommendation: *Version 1:* In the lower division baccalaureate/associate degree category, 2 semester hours in Introductory Food Service Operations (9/78). *Version 2:* In the lower division baccalaureate/associate degree category, 4 semester hours in Introductory Food Service Operations (2/88) (12/94).

Celestial Navigation (NST 233)

Location: Seafarers Harry Lundeberg School of Seamanship, Piney Point, MD.

Length: *Version 1:* 186 hours (5 weeks); *Version 2:* 157 hours (5 weeks); *Version 3:* 168 hours (5 weeks).

Dates: *Version 1:* September 1979-January 1988; *Version 2:* February 1988-December 1993; *Version 3:* January 1994-Present.

Objective: *Version 1:* To provide the student with a knowledge of all aspects of celestial navigation that are required for licensing as Towboat Operation-Oceans, Master/Mate of Uninspected Vessels not over 300 gross tons, Master/Mate of Freight and Towing Vessels, and Third Mate candidate. *Version 2:* To enable the student to understand all aspects of celestial navigation that are required for licensing as Towboat Operator-Oceans, Master/Mate of Uninspected Vessels not over 300 gross tons, Master/Mate of Freight and Towing Vessels, Third Mate Unlimited, and Second Mate Unlimited. *Version 3:* To enable the student to understand all aspects of celestial navigation that are required for licensing as Towboat Operator-Oceans, Master/Mate of Uninspected Vessels not over 300 gross tons, Master/Mate of Freight and Towing Vessels, Third Mate Unlimited, and Second Mate Unlimited.

Learning Outcome: Upon successful completion of this course, the student will be able to have basic knowledge of theory of nautical astronomy and time; determine sunrise, sunset, moonrise, moonset, and civil twilight; determine latitude by polaris; determine time of LAN; determine latitude by meridian altitude; determine compass error using amplitudes and azimuths of celestial bodies; have basic knowledge of marine sextant, sextant errors, and practical use; and determine position using LOP's of sun, moon, planets, and stars and plotting same.

Instruction: *Version 1:* Major topics covered in the course are computing time of sunrise, sunset, twilight, moonrise and moonset, determining compass error by amplitude and azimuth, latitude by polaris, determining time of meridian passage of the sun, latitude by meridian altitude of the sun, position by sun line, use and adjustments of the sextant, underway practical experience in celestial navigation, and review of the international and inland rules of the road. Methods of instruction include lecture, discussion, and lab. *Version 2:* Major topics covered in the course are nautical astronomy; time; sunrise, sunset, moonrise, and moonset; Greenwich Hour angle and declination; latitude by polaris observation; time of local apparent noon; sextant corrections; latitude by observation at local apparent noon; and sunlines. Methods of instruction include lecture, discussion, laboratory exercises, quizzes, and Coast Guard licensing examination. *Version 3:* Major topics covered in the course are nautical astronomy; time; sunrise, sunset, moonrise, and moonset; Greenwich Hour angle and declination; latitude by polaris observation; time of local apparent noon; sextant corrections; latitude by observation at local apparent noon; and sunlines. Methods of instruction include lecture, discussion, laboratory exercises, quizzes, and Coast Guard licensing examination.

Credit Recommendation: *Version 1:* In the lower division baccalaureate/associate degree category, 8 semester hours in Celestial Navigation, 1 semester hour in First Aid and Safety, and 1 semester hour in Rules of the Road (6/82) (2/88). *Version 2:* In the lower division baccalaureate/associate degree category, 8 semester hours in Celestial Navigation, 1 semester hour in First Aid and Safety, and 1 semester hour in Rules of the Road (6/82) (2/88). *Version 3:* In the lower division baccalaureate/associate degree category, 8 semester hours in Celestial Navigation (12/94).

Chief Cook

Location: Seafarers Harry Lundeberg School of Seamanship, Piney Point, MD.

Length: *Version 1:* Approximately 242 hours (8 weeks); residential; 50 hours lecture and discussion, 54 hours laboratory, and 138 hours workshop; *Version 2:* 333 hours (9 weeks); *Version 3:* 310 hours (9 weeks).

Dates: *Version 1:* September 1976-January 1988; *Version 2:* February 1988-December 1993; *Version 3:* January 1994-June 1996.

Objective: *Version 1:* To teach a cook and baker (second cook) to serve as chief cook. *Version 2:* To upgrade qualified members of the steward's department to chief cook. *Version 3:* To upgrade qualified members of the steward's department to chief cook.

Learning Outcome: Upon successful completion of this course, the student will be able to operate galley equipment; satisfy general and specific sanitation and safety requirements; operate most cutting equipment and identify cuts of meat; maintain inventory control records; prepare meats, seafood, poultry, soups, sauces, and gravies; supervise galley personnel; and produce menus and meals aboard ship.

Instruction: *Version 1:* Major topics covered in the course are principles of preparation of meats, poultry, seafood, soups, sauces, and gravies; quantity preparation of these foods; identification of meat cuts by the use of charts; work organization; sanitation; and the use of recipes. *Version 2:* Major topics covered in the course are principles of preparation of meats, poultry, seafood, soups, sauces, and gravies; quantity preparation of these foods; identification of meat cuts by the use of charts; work organization; sanitation; use of recipes; work supervision; and maintaining inventory control. Methods of instruction include lecture, audio/visual material, practical experiences, demonstration, classroom work, practical tests, and a final examination. *Version 3:* Major topics covered in the course are principles of preparation of meats, poultry, seafood, soups, sauces, and gravies; quantity preparation of these foods; identification of meat cuts by the use of charts; work organization; sanitation; use of recipes; work supervision; and maintaining inventory control. Methods of instruction include lecture, audio/visual material, practical experiences, demonstration, classroom work, practical tests, and final examination.

Credit Recommendation: *Version 1:* In the lower division baccalaureate/associate degree category, 3 semester hours in Food Preparation and 3 semester hours in Quantity Food Production (9/78). *Version 2:* In the lower division baccalaureate/associate degree category, 4 semester hours in Food Preparation, 3 semester hours in Quantity Food Production, and 3 semester hours in Kitchen Supervision (2/88). *Version 3:* In the lower division baccalaureate/associate degree category, 4 semester hours in Food Preparation, 3 semester hours in Quantity Food Production, and 3 semester hours in Kitchen Supervision (12/94).

Chief Steward

Location: Seafarers Harry Lundeberg School of Seamanship, Piney Point, MD.

Length: *Version 1:* Approximately 232.5 hours (8 weeks) residential, 72 hours lecture and discussion, 86 hours laboratory, and 74.5 hours workshop; *Versions 2 and 3:* 324 hours (9 weeks).

Dates: *Version 1:* September 1975-January 1988; *Version 2:* February 1988-December 1993; *Version 3:* January 1994-December 1996.

Objective: *Version 1:* To teach chief cooks the duties of mess steward. *Version 2:* To enhance cooking skills and to provide the management and operational skills necessary for successful operation of the stewards department aboard ship. *Version 3:* To enhance cooking skills and to provide the management and operational skills necessary for successful operation of the stewards department aboard ship.

Learning Outcome: Upon successful completion of this course, the student will be able to plan menus; supervise subordinates; organize and operate the steward department; and cook, type, and conduct an inventory control system.

Instruction: *Version 1:* Major topics covered in the course are organization, work supervision, menu planning, inventory control, requisitioning procedures, sanitation, all aspects of food production, nutrition, typing, first aid, CPR, and safety. *Version 2:* Major topics covered in the course are organization, work supervision, menu planning, inventory control, requisitioning procedures, sanitation, all aspects of food production, nutrition, typing, and safety. Methods of instruction include lecture, audio/visual material, practical exercises, quizzes, and final examination. *Version 3:* Major topics covered in the course are organization, work supervision, menu planning, inventory control, requisitioning procedures, sanitation, all aspects of food production, nutrition, typing, and safety. Methods of instruction include lecture, audio/visual material, practical exercises, quizzes, and a final examination.

Credit Recommendation: *Version 1:* In the lower division baccalaureate/associate degree category, 2 semester hours in First Aid and Cardiopulmonary Resuscitation, 4 semester hours in Food Service Organization and Supervision, and 2 semester hours in Quantity Food Production (9/78). **NOTE:** Credit for typing on the basis of institutional assessment. *Version 2:* In the lower division baccalaureate/associate degree category, 2 semester hours in Nutrition, 6 semester hours in Food Management, and 2 semester hours in Quantity Food Production (2/88). *Version 3:* In the lower division baccalaureate/associate degree category, 2 semester hours in Nutrition, 5 semester hours in Food Management, and 1 semester hour in Quantity Food Production (12/94).

Designated Duty Engineer (IMET 241)
(Formerly Chief/Assistant Engineer: Uninspected Motor Vessels and License Diesel Engineer: Uninspected)

Location: Seafarers Harry Lundeberg School of Seamanship, Piney Point, MD.

Length: *Version 1:* 235 hours (8 weeks); *Versions 2 and 3:* 320 hours (10 weeks).

Dates: *Version 1:* January 1978-January 1988; *Version 2:* February 1988-December 1993; *Version 3:* January 1994-Present.

Objective: To provide the student with sufficient knowledge to pass the U.S. Coast Guard Chief Engineer or Assistant Engineer Diesel License of specified horsepower on uninspected vessels.

Learning Outcome: *Version 1:* Upon successful completion of this course, the student will be able to sit for United States Coast Guard Chief or Assistant Engineer Uninspected Motor Vessels. *Version 2:* Upon successful completion of this course, the student will be able to sit for United States Coast Guard Chief or Assistant Engineer Uninspected Motor Vessels. *Version 3:* Upon successful completion of this course, the student will be able to perform the duties and functions of a diesel power plant operating engineer.

Instruction: Major topics covered in the course are training in pumps, compressors, heat exchanges, propellers, shafting, steering systems, valves, instruments, lubrication, inspections, ship construction, damage control, reduction gears, diesel construction, diesel principles, fuel injection, starting systems, governors, boilers, direct current components, alternating current components, batteries, refrigeration, fire fighting, emergency equipment, Coast Guard regulations, pollution laws, sanitary systems, and first aid; and practical engine training which includes extensive operation of maintenance on the school's tugs and in the engine shop. In addition, an applicant must hold a first aid and CPR certificate, which is offered at the school. Methods of instruction include lecture, discussion, practical exercises, quizzes, and Coast Guard licensing examinations.

Credit Recommendation: *Version 1:* In the lower division baccalaureate/associate degree category, 9 semester hours in Diesel Engine Technology (6/82). *Version 2:* In the lower division baccalaureate/associate degree category, 9 semester hours in Diesel Engine Technology, 1 semester hour in Electricity, 1 semester hour in First Aid/CPR, and 1 semester hour in Industrial Safety (2/88). *Version 3:* In the lower division baccalaureate/associate degree category, 9 semester hours in Diesel Engine Technology, 1 semester hour in Electricity, 1 semester hour in First Aid/CPR, and 1 semester hour in Industrial Safety (12/94).

Coastwise Navigation and Piloting (Quartermaster)

Location: Seafarers Harry Lundeberg School of Seamanship, Piney Point, MD.

Length: *Version 1:* 64 hours (2 weeks), residential; *Version 2:* 132 hours (3 weeks), residential; *Version 3:* 168 hours (8 weeks).

Dates: *Version 1:* October 1972-March 1977; *Version 2:* April 1977-October 1985; *Version 3:* June 1982-December 1985.

Objective: To provide the student with a working knowledge of marine navigation.

Instruction: *Version 1:* Same as Version 2 (below) but coverage is less complete. Tides and currents, electronic aids to navigation, and sounding are not covered. *Version 2: Version 2:* Major topics covered in the course are the use of magnetic and gyro compass; rules of the road; international codes and signals; bridge publications and instruments; aids to navigation; use of radar; loran, fathometers, and RDF; and tides and currents. *Version 3:* Same as Version 2, but includes more practical training.

Credit Recommendation: *Version 1:* In the lower division baccalaureate/associate degree category, 3 semester hours in Navigation (11/77). *Version 2:* In the lower division baccalaureate/associate degree category, 6 semester hour in Navigation (11/77). *Version 3:* In the lower division baccalaureate/associate degree category, 7 semester hours in Navigation (6/82). *Prerequisite:* Lifeboatman and Able Seaman course or Coast Guard endorsement as Able Seaman Unlimited Any Waters.

Conveyorman

Location: Seafarers Harry Lundeberg School of Seamanship, Piney Point, MD.

Length: *Version 1:* 34 hours (indicates number of hours devoted to instruction in welding; *Version 2:* 100 hours (4 weeks); *Version 3:* 103 hours (4 weeks).

Dates: *Version 1:* February 1980-January 1988; *Version 2:* February 1988-December 1993; *Version 3:* January 1994-Present.

Objective: To teach the student the use, maintenance, and repair of marine conveyor systems.

Learning Outcome: Upon successful completion of this course, the student will be able to operate cargo handling equipment aboard bulk carriers and perform basic gas and air welding functions.

Instruction: Major topics covered in the course are an introduction to types and developments of self-unloaders, conveyorman belt construction and types, belt adjustments, belt splicing procedures and practical application, related electrical AC and DC systems, practical electrical troubleshooting, electrical test equipment, power failure testing, hydraulic ram theory, practical hydraulic troubleshooting, pipe fitting and threading, gate construction, maintenance and operation, oxy-acetylene cutting, and electric and welding shop practical training. Methods of instruction include lecture, discussion, audio/visual material, practical exercises, quizzes, and final examination.

Credit Recommendation: *Version 1:* In the lower division baccalaureate/associate degree category, 2 semester hours in Welding (6/82). **NOTE:** While this course is at the postsecondary level, it does not equate directly to standard collegiate course offerings. Institutional evaluation of the applicability of this course and of appropriate credit is recommended. *Version 2:* In the vocational certificate category, 3 semester hours in Conveyor Operation and Maintenance (2/88). *Version 3:* In the vocational certificate category, 3 semester hours in Conveyor Operation and Maintenance (12/94).

Cook and Baker

Location: Seafarers Harry Lundeberg School of Seamanship, Piney Point, MD.

Length: *Version 1:* 208 hours (6 weeks), residential, 40 hours lecture and discussion, 22 hours laboratory, and 146 hours workshop; *Versions 2 and 3:* 302 hours (9 weeks).

Dates: *Version 1:* September 1976-January 1988; *Version 2:* February 1988-December 1993; *Version 3:* January 1994-April 1997.

Objective: *Version 1:* To teach assistant cooks to bake. *Version 2:* To provide the skills required to perform shipboard baking and breakfast preparation. *Version 3:* To provide the skills required to perform shipboard baking and breakfast preparation.

Learning Outcome: Upon successful completion of this course, the student will be able to operate the equipment found in the bake shop; understand the different methods of measuring in a bake shop; prepare pastry, pies, gelatins, puddings, custards, cookies, icings, bread, and rolls; be familiar with safety and sanitation procedures in the bake shop; and be able to name and explain functions of different ingredients used in baking.

Instruction: *Version 1:* Major topics covered in the course are baking breads, rolls, pies, cakes, cookies, breakfast pastries, desserts, breakfast preparations, sanitation, work organization, and recipe requirements. *Version 2:* Major topics covered in the course are baking breads, rolls, pies, cakes, cookies, breakfast pastries, desserts, breakfast preparations, sanitation, work organization, recipe requirements, baking theory, and on-the-job preparation and production of bread and rolls, pastries, cakes, pie doughs and fillings, cookies, and icings. Methods of instruction include lecture, audio/visual material, practical exercises and demonstrations, topic quizzes, and final examination. *Version 3:* Major topics covered in the course are baking breads, rolls, pies, cakes, cookies, breakfast pastries, desserts, breakfast preparations, sanitation, work organization, recipe requirements, baking theory, and on-the-job preparation and production of bread and rolls, pastries, cakes, pie doughs and fillings, cookies, and icings. Methods of instruction include lecture, audio/visual material, practical exercises and demonstrations, topic quizzes, and final examination.

Credit Recommendation: *Version 1:* In the lower division baccalaureate/associate degree category, 3 semester hours in Baking and 3 semester hours in Quantity Food Production (9/78). *Version 2:* In the lower division baccalaureate/associate degree category, 6 semester hours in baking and 3 semester hours in Quantity Food Production (2/88). *Version 3:* In the lower division baccalaureate/associate degree category, 6 semester hours in baking and 3 semester hours in Quantity Food Production (12/94).

Diesel Engines (MET 209)

Location: Seafarers Harry Lundeberg School of Seamanship, Piney Point, MD.

Length: *Version 1:* 128 hours (3 weeks, 4 days), residential, 34 hours lecture/discussion and 6 hours laboratory/workshop per week; *Version 2:* 180 hours (6 weeks), including approximately 50 hours laboratory/workshop; *Version 3:* 185 hours (6 weeks).

Dates: *Version 1:* January 1975-January 1988; *Version 2:* February 1988-December 1993; *Version 3:* January 1994-Present.

Objective: To provide the knowledge to operate small diesel engines.

Learning Outcome: Upon successful completion of this course, the student will be able to disassemble, diagnose, repair, reassemble, and tune-up a high speed diesel engine; perform maintenance on diesel engine air intake systems; and troubleshoot low, medium, and high speed performing diesel engines.

Instruction: *Version 1:* Major topics covered in the course are types, design, construction, and characteristics of various diesel engines; diesel nomenclature and principles of operation; introduction to the fuel, air, lubrication, and exhaust systems; the use of various gauges, meters, and instruments used on diesel engines; the care, operation, maintenance, and recording of diesel engine performance signals used between bridge and engine room; basic fire fighting; and first aid and safety. *Version 2:* Major topics covered in the course are more in-depth coverage of air intake systems, fuel injectors, lubrication systems, governors, and plant automation. Methods of instruction include lecture, discussion, practical exercises, and final examination. *Version 3:* Major topics covered in the course are more in-depth coverage of air intake systems, fuel injectors, lubrication systems, governors, and plant automation. Methods of instruction include lecture, discussion, practical exercises, and final examination.

Credit Recommendation: *Version 1:* In the lower division baccalaureate/associate degree category, 6 semester hours in Diesel Engines (11/77) (6/82). *Version 2:* In the lower division baccalaureate/associate degree category, 9 semester hours in Diesel Engine Technology (2/88). *Version 3:* In the lower division baccalaureate/associate degree category, 9 semester hours in Diesel Engine Technology (12/94).

Electro-Hydraulic System Maintenance (MET 228) (Hagglund Crane Maintenance)

Location: Seafarers Harry Lundeberg School of Seamanship, Piney Point, MD.

Length: *Versions 1 and 2:* 180 hours (6 weeks).

Dates: *Version 1:* February 1988-December 1993; *Version 2:* January 1994-Present.

Objective: To provide the electro-hydraulic technician with the theoretical knowledge and practical skills to maintain, troubleshoot, and repair complex electrically-controlled hydraulic systems.

Learning Outcome: Upon successful completion of this course, the student will be able to read and interpret manufacturer's instructions, diagrams, operations and maintenance manuals; perform routine tests and inspections; and train operator in routine maintenance and inspection procedures.

Instruction: Major topics covered in the course are basic hydraulics, electrical control of hydraulic systems, and deck cranes (specifically Hagglunds type TAP 1626, TG3632, TG2432). Methods of instruction include lecture, classroom exercises, audio/visual material, graded practical exercises, quizzes, and final examination.

Credit Recommendation: *Version 1:* In the vocational certificate category, 6 semester hours in Electro-Hydraulic Control Systems (2/88). *Version 2:* In the vocational certificate category, 6 semester hours in Electro-Hydraulic Control Systems (12/94).

Fireman, Oiler, and Watertender (MET 221) (Formerly Fireman, Watertender, and Oiler)

Location: Seafarers Harry Lundeberg School of Seamanship, Piney Point, MD.

Length: *Version 1:* 56 hours (2 weeks); *Version 2:* 84 hours (3 weeks); *Version 3:* Approximately 144 hours (4-6 weeks); residential, includes 14 hours supervised independent study; *Version 4:* 180 homes (8 weeks); *Version 5:* 194 hours (8 weeks).

Dates: *Version 1:* June 1972-August 1975; *Version 2:* September 1975-September 1976; *Version 3:* October 1976-January 1988; *Version 4:* February 1988-December 1993; *Version 5:* January 1994-Present.

Objective: *Version 1:* To review the theoretical and practical knowledge required to perform the job of fireman/watertender or oiler aboard ship. *Version 2:* To review the theoretical and practical knowledge required to perform the job of fireman/watertender or oiler aboard ship. *Version 3:* To provide students with the theoretical and practical knowledge required to perform the job of fireman/watertender or oiler aboard ship. *Version 4:* To provide students with the theoretical and practical knowledge required to perform the job of fireman/ watertender or oiler aboard ship. *Version 5:* To provide students with the theoretical and practical knowledge required to perform the job of fireman/watertender or oiler aboard ship.

Learning Outcome: Upon successful completion of this course, the student will be able to sit for the United States Coast Guard Unlicensed rating as Fireman, Oiler, Watertender (FOWT).

Instruction: *Version 1:* Same as Version 3 except coverage is less in-depth. *Version 2:* Same as Version 3 except coverage is less in-depth. *Version 3:* Major topics covered in the course are parts of a boiler and their functions; the steam and water cycle; fuel oil and lube oil systems; fire-fighting and emergency procedures; use of a simulator in putting boilers on the line; changing burners; operating auxiliary equipment; and starting and securing main engines. *Version 4:* Major topics covered in the course are parts of a boiler and their functions; the steam and water cycle; fuel oil and lube oil systems; fire-fighting and emergency procedures; use of a simulator in putting boilers on the line; changing burners; operating auxiliary equipment; starting and securing main engines; and diesels, refrigeration, and auxiliary systems. Methods of instruction include lecture, discussion, classroom exercises, audio/visual material, and the Coast Guard licensing examination. *Version 5:* Major topics covered in the course are parts of a boiler and their functions; the steam and water cycle; fuel oil and lube oil systems; fire-fighting and emergency procedures; use of a simulator in putting boilers on the line; changing burners; operating auxiliary equipment; starting and securing main engines; and diesels, refrigeration, and auxiliary systems. Methods of instruction include lecture, discussion, classroom exercises, audio/visual material, and the Coast Guard licensing examination.

Credit Recommendation: *Version 1:* In the lower division baccalaureate/associate degree category, 2 semester hours in Marine Engineering (11/77). *Version 2:* In the lower division baccalaureate/associate degree category, 2 semester hours in Marine Engineering (11/77). *Version 3:* In the lower division baccalaureate/associate degree category, 6 semester hours in Marine Engineering (6/82). *Version 4:* In the lower division baccalaureate/associate degree category, 6 semester hours in Basic Marine Engineering, 1 semester hour in Diesel Technology, and 1 semester hour in Refrigeration Technology (2/88). *Version 5:* In the lower division baccalaureate/associate degree category, 6 semester hours in Basic Marine Engineering, 1 semester hour in Diesel Technology, and 1 semester hour in Refrigeration Technology (12/94).

First Class Pilot (NST 229)

Location: Seafarers Harry Lundeberg School of Seamanship, Piney Point, MD.

Length: *Versions 1 and 2:* 197 hours (7 weeks); *Version 3:* 245 hours (7 weeks).

Dates: *Version 1:* June 1973-December 1993; *Version 2:* June 1973-December 1993; *Version 3:* January 1994-Present.

Objective: To prepare for successful completion of the U.S. Coast Guard First Class Pilot examination.

Learning Outcome: Upon successful completion of this course, the student will be able to adequately perform all functions of a First Class Pilot.

Instruction: *Version 1:* Major topics covered in the course are first aid and lifesaving, piloting and coastwise navigation, rules of the road, electronic aids to navigation, marine meteorology, advanced seamanship, and marine investigation regulations. Methods of instruction include lecture, discussion, and laboratory. *Version 2:* Major topics covered in the course are rules of the road, local area knowledge, chart sketching, instruments and accessories, piloting, tides and currents, ship handling, weather, first aid, CPR, and fire fighting. *Version 3:* Major topics covered in the course are rules of the road, local area knowledge, chart sketching, instruments and accessories, piloting, tides and currents, ship handling, maritime regulations, weather, first aid, CPR, and fire fighting. Methods of instruction include lecture, classroom exercises, audio/visual material, laboratory exercises, demonstrations, quizzes, and the Coast Guard licensing examination.

Credit Recommendation: *Version 1:* In the lower division baccalaureate/associate degree category, 1 semester hour in First Aid and Life Saving, 5 semester hours in Piloting and Coastwise Navigation, 2 semester hours in Rules of the Road; 1 semester hour in Electronic Aids to Navigation; 1 semester hour in Marine Meteorology; 1 semester hour in Advanced Seamanship; and 1 semester hour in Marine Investigation/Regulations (6/82) (2/88). *Version 2:* In the lower division baccalaureate/associate degree category, 1 semester hour in First Aid and Life Saving, 5 semester hours in Piloting and Coastwise Navigation, 2 semester hours in Rules of the Road; 1 semester hour in Electronic Aids to Navigation; 1 semester hour in Marine Meteorology; 1 semester hour in Advanced Seamanship; and 1 semester hour in Marine Investigation/ Regulations (6/82) (2/88). *Version 3:* In the lower division baccalaureate/associate degree category, 5 semester hours in Piloting and Coastwise Navigation, 2 semester hour in Rules of the Road, 1 semester hour in Electronic Aids to Navigation, 1 semester hour in Meteorology, 1 semester hour in Maritime Regulations, and 1 semester hour in First Aid/CPR (12/94).

Hydraulics (MET 218)

Location: Seafarers Harry Lundeberg School of Seamanship, Piney Point, MD.

Length: *Version 1:* 82 hours (4 weeks); *Version 2:* 86 hours (4 weeks).

Dates: *Version 1:* September 1987-December 1993; *Version 2:* January 1994-Present.

Objective: To provide a basic understanding and troubleshooting knowledge of hydraulic systems.

Learning Outcome: Upon successful completion of this course, the student will be able to read a hydraulic system design; understand how a hydraulic system works; and troubleshoot and repair hydraulic systems, particularly as they relate to the shipping industry.

Instruction: Major topics covered in the course are a general introduction to the principles and applications of fluid dynamics relating to cargo handling systems, and hydraulic troubleshooting and repair procedures. Methods of instruction include lecture, classroom exercises, practical exercises, audio/visual material, laboratory exercises, quizzes, and a final examination.

Credit Recommendation: *Version 1:* In the lower division baccalaureate/associate degree category, 4 semester hours in Introduction to Hydraulics (2/88). *Version 2:* In the lower division baccalaureate/ associate degree category, 4 semester hours in Introduction to Hydraulics (12/94).

Limited Master or Mate: Inland and Near Coastal (Formerly Master/Mate Freight and Towing)

Location: Seafarers Harry Lundeberg School of Seamanship, Piney Point, MD.

Length: 315 hours (10 weeks).

Dates: *Version 1:* February 1988-December 1993; *Version 2:* January 1994-Present.

Objective: To offer classroom instruction leading to United States Coast Guard certification as Master/Mate of Freight and Towing vessels of not more than 1,600 gross tons.

Learning Outcome: Upon successful completion of this course, the student will have basic knowledge of tugboat use and operation; tows, types of barges, terminal operations, safety, fire fighting capability, and off-shore supply; marine meteorology; rules of the road; electronic aids to navigation; advanced seamanship; first aid and lifesaving; piloting and coastwise navigation; and marine resuscitation (CPR).

Instruction: Major topics covered in the course are rules of the road, ship construction, cargo gear, ship handling, tides and currents, instruments and accessories, weather, rules and regulations, stability, ships business, charts, and piloting, first aid, CPR, and fire fighting. Methods of instruction include lecture, discussion, case studies, audio/visual material, demonstrations, quizzes, and the Coast Guard licensing examination.

Credit Recommendation: *Version 1:* In the lower division baccalaureate/associate degree category, 1 semester hour in First Aid and Lifesaving (CPR), 5 semester hours in Piloting and Coastwise Navigation, 2 semester hours in Rules of the Road, 1 semester hour in Electronic Aids to Navigation, 1 semester hour in Marine Meteorology, 1 semester hour in Advanced Seamanship, and 1 semester hour in Rules and Regulations (2/88). *Version 2:* In the lower division baccalaureate/associate degree category, 1 semester hour in First Aid and Lifesaving (CPR), 5 semester hours in Piloting and Coastwise Navigation, 1 semester hours in Rules of the Road, 1 semester hour in Electronic Aids to Navigation,2 semester hours in Marine Meteorology, 1 semester hour in Advanced Seamanship, and 1 semester hour in Rules and Regulations (12/94).

Liquid Cargo Operations (MET 213) (Pump Room Operations and Maintenance)

Location: Seafarers Harry Lundeberg School of Seamanship, Piney Point, MD.

Length: *Version 1:* Approximately 222 hours (6 weeks); *Version 2:* 180 hours (6 weeks).

Dates: *Version 1:* April 1979-January 1988; *Version 2:* February 1988-Present.

Objective: *Version 1:* To train the student in pumpman operation and maintenance and liquid cargo operations. *Version 2:* To provide knowledge needed to operate, maintain, troubleshoot, and repair liquid cargo handling equipment aboard ship; and to efficiently load and discharge liquid cargo in compliance with environmental regulations.

Learning Outcome: Upon successful completion of this course, the student will be able to perform the duties of pumpman; perform valve and pump repair; and operate loading and discharging procedures.

Instruction: Major topics covered in the course are fire fighting and safety, first aid, cargo properties and emergency procedures, tanker development and construction, operation and maintenance of valves and pumps, loading procedures, cargo pump operation, cargo measurement, discharging procedures, ballasting procedures, tank cleaning, inert gas systems, pollution control, cargo control system, and hydraulics and machine shop. Methods of instruction include lecture, discussion, classroom exercises, audio/visual material laboratory exercises, on-the-job training, quizzes, and final examination.

Credit Recommendation: *Version 1:* In the lower division baccalaureate/associate degree category, 3 semester hours in Machine Shop Practices and 4 semester hours in Liquid Cargo Operations (6/82). *Version 2:* In the lower division baccalaureate/associate degree category, 3 semester hours in Machine Shop Practices and 4 semester hours in Liquid Cargo Operations (2/88) (12/94).

Marine Electrical Maintenance I (MET 215)

Location: Seafarers Harry Lundeberg School of Seamanship, Piney Point, MD.

Length: *Version 1:* 198 hours (5 weeks, 2 days), residential; *Versions 2 and 3:* 240 hours (8 weeks).

Dates: *Version 1:* October 1975-May 1982; *Version 2:* June 1982-December 1993; *Version 3:* January 1994-Present.

Objective: To provide the student with the theoretical and practical knowledge required to act as a troubleshooter and to repair motors, generators, controllers, and signal appliances.

Learning Outcome: Upon successful completion of this course, the student will be able to perform routine maintenance and repair and troubleshoot in the areas of rotating electrical machinery, lighting systems, galley equipment, cargo handling equipment, and ships interior communications.

Instruction: *Version 1:* Major topics covered in the course are electrical theory and power systems; electrical measuring instruments; classroom and practical training in the control, operation, maintenance, troubleshooting, and repair of AC and DC motors and generators; controllers and solid-state motor control. *Version 2:* Same as Version 1, but includes more practical training. Methods of instruction include lecture, classroom exercises, audio/visual material, laboratory and practical exercises, quizzes, and final examination. *Version 3:* Same as Version 1, but includes more practical training. Methods of instruction include lecture, classroom exercises, audio/visual material, laboratory and practical exercises, quizzes, and final examination.

Credit Recommendation: *Version 1:* In the lower division baccalaureate/associate degree category, 8 semester hours in Electricity (11/77). **NOTE:** If student has completed QMED course, a maximum of 8 semester hours in Electricity should be granted. *Version 2:* In the lower division baccalaureate/associate degree category, 9 semester hours in Electricity (6/82) (2/88). *Version 3:* In the lower division baccalaureate/associate degree category, 9 semester hours in Electricity (12/94). *Prerequisite:* Qualified Marine Engine Department, endorsement, or endorsement as Electrician.

Marine Electrical Maintenance II (MET 225)
(Formerly Variable Speed DC Drives)

Location: Seafarers Harry Lundeberg School of Seamanship, Piney Point, MD.

Length: 180 hours (6 weeks).

Dates: February 1988-Present.

Objective: To provide the electrical maintenance technician with the theory of DC drive systems and the construction, operation, maintenance, and repair of electronic DC motor drive systems.

Learning Outcome: Upon successful completion of this course, the student will be able to perform routine tests and inspections; conduct routine maintenance of electronic DC motor drive systems; and read and interpret manufacturers' operations and maintenance instructions and diagrams.

Instruction: Major topics covered in the course are DC motors and generators; operation and maintenance; power electronics; diodes SCR's; power modules; crane electrical distribution; relay logic and operation; LASH I and II systems; and electronic component alignment. Methods of instruction include lecture, classroom exercises, field trips, audio/visual material, laboratory and practical exercises, quizzes, and final examination.

Credit Recommendation: In the lower division baccalaureate/associate degree category, 4 semester hours in Industrial Electronics Laboratory (2/88) (12/94).

Original Third or Second Assistant Engineer: Steam and/or Motor-Inspected (MET 241)
(Formerly Third Assistant Engineer Steam and/or Motor-Inspected)

Location: Seafarers Harry Lundeberg School of Seamanship, Piney Point, MD.

Length: *Version 1:* 248 hours (10 weeks); *Version 2:* 278 hours (11 weeks); *Version 3:* 311 hours (10 weeks).

Dates: *Version 1:* January 1981-January 1988; *Version 2:* February 1988-December 1993; *Version 3:* January 1994-Present.

Objective: To provide sufficient knowledge to pass the U.S. Coast Guard Third Assistant Engineer Unlimited License Examination.

Learning Outcome: *Version 1:* Upon successful completion of this course, the student will be able to sit for Original Third Assistant Engineer's License. *Version 2:* Upon successful completion of this course, the student will be able to sit for Original Third Assistant Engineer's License. *Version 3:* Upon successful completion of this course, the student will be able to operate and maintain engine room equipment for steam and diesel power plant and shipboard systems; and perform watch standing operations including normal, emergency, and personal emergency situations.

Instruction: Major topics covered in the course are engine room watching aboard deep sea ships, and operation and maintenance of all machinery located in the engine spaces including advanced electricity, electronics, propulsion and steering systems, boilers, turbines, diesels, safety, hydraulics, air conductors, and refrigeration and distilling units. Methods of instruction include lecture, discussion, classroom exercises, audio/visual material, quizzes, and the Coast Guard licensing examination.

Credit Recommendation: *Version 1:* In the lower division baccalaureate/associate degree category, 3 semester hours in Electricity, 2 semester hours in Industrial Safety, 2 semester hours in Diesel Power, 1 semester hour in First Aid and CPR, and 4 semester hours in Ship Systems and Auxiliary Equipment (6/82). *Version 2:* In the lower division baccalaureate/associate degree category, 3 semester hours in Electricity, 2 semester hours in Industrial Safety, 2 semester hours in Diesel Engine Technology, 1 semester hour in First Aid and CPR, and 4 semester hours in Ship Systems and Auxiliary Equipment or Power Plant Technology (2/88). *Version 3:* In the lower division baccalaureate/ associate degree category, 3 semester hours in Electricity, 2 semester hour in Industrial Safety, 2 semester hour in Diesel Engine Technology, 1 semester hour in First Aid/CPR, 4 semester hour in Ship Systems and Auxiliary Equipment or Power Plant Technology (12/94).

Process Control Instrumentation: Automation

Location: Seafarers Harry Lundeberg School of Seamanship, Piney Point, MD.

Length: *Version 1:* 106 hours (3 weeks and 4 days); *Version 2:* Approximately 120 hours (4 weeks).

Dates: *Version 1:* November 1979-January 1988; *Version 2:* February 1988-June 1989.

Objective: To teach process control instrumentation for automated vessels.

Learning Outcome: Upon successful completion of this course, the student will be able to operate and maintain marine type combustion control equipment; operate and maintain marine type feedwater regulation equipment; and operate and maintain drilling plant control equipment.

Instruction: Major topics covered in the course are process control instrumentation including automated boiler equipment, pneumatics, systems analysis, and the operation of remote controls for all components in the steam and water cycle; level, temperature, flow, force, weight and motion measurement; final control elements; safety calibration; and testing procedures. Methods of instruction include lecture, laboratory, and classroom and practical training.

Credit Recommendation: *Version 1:* In the lower division baccalaureate/associate degree category, 7 semester hours in Process Control Instrumentation (6/82) (2/88). *Version 2:* In the lower division baccalaureate/associate degree category, 7 semester hours in Process Control Instrumentation (6/82) (2/88).

Qualified Members of the Engine Department (QMED) (MET 231)
Part 1: Principles of Electricity
Part 2: Principles of Refrigeration
Part 3: Principles of Steam Generation Systems
Part 4: First Aid and Safety

Location: Seafarers Harry Lundeberg School of Seamanship, Piney Point, MD.

Length: 336 hours (12 weeks), residential; *Part 1:* 76 hours; *Part 2:* 74 hours; *Part 3:* 162 hours; *Part 4:* 24 hours.

Dates: *Version 1:* June 1977-December 1993; *Version 2:* June 1977-December 1993; *Version 3:* January 1994-Present.

Objective: To provide the knowledge required for certification for Qualified Marine Engine Department (QMED), and to provide a thorough understanding of industrial steam generation systems.

Learning Outcome: *Version 1:* Upon successful completion of this course, the student will be able to obtain ratings for pumpman, refrigeration engineer, machinist, electrician, deck engineer, junior engineer, and deck engine mechanic (DEMAC). *Version 2:* Upon successful completion of this course, the student will be able to obtain ratings for pumpman, refrigeration engineer, machinist, electrician, deck engineer, junior engineer, and deck engine mechanic (DEMAC). *Version 3:* Upon successful completion of this course, the student will be able to operate and repair equipment associated with pumpman, refrigeration engineer, machinist, electrician, deck engineer, junior engineer, and deck engine mechanic (DEMAC).

Instruction: *Part 1:* Major topics covered in the course are fundamental concepts of electricity; batteries; electrical circuits; magnetism and electromagnetic circuits; transformers; AC motors and generators; use and care of electrical instruments; troubleshooting of electrical equipment; starting, securing, and paralleling turbo generators; placing electrical measuring instruments; soldering, brazing, and welding; and fire-fighting and emergency procedures. *Part 2:* Major topics covered in the course are principles of refrigeration; compressors; receivers; dehydrators; valves (solenoids, therm-expansion, packless); evaporators; and testing for and repairing leaks. Emphasizes troubleshooting and refrigeration problems. *Part 3:* Major topics covered in the course are operation, use, and repair of pumps; boiler theory and boiler water treatment; piping, tubing, and valves; automation principles; evaporators; and fuels. *Part 4:* Major topics covered in the course are preparation for emergency at sea; work safety; emergency first aid and procedures; and controlling and extinguishing shipboard fires. Methods of instruction include lecture, classroom exercises, audio/visual material, laboratory exercises, and the Coast Guard licensing examination.

Credit Recommendation: *Version 1: Part 1:* In the lower division baccalaureate/associate degree category, 4 semester hours in Electricity. *Part 2:* In the lower division baccalaureate/associate degree category, 4 semester hours in Refrigeration. *Part 3:* In the lower division baccalaureate/associate degree category, 9 semester hours in Steam Generation Systems. *Part 4:* In the lower division baccalaureate/associate degree category, 1 semester hour in First Aid and Safety (11/77) (6/82). *Version 2: Part 1:* In the lower division baccalaureate/associate degree category, 4 semester hours in Electricity. *Part 2:* In the lower division baccalaureate/associate degree category, 4 semester hours in Refrigeration. *Part 3:* In the lower division baccalaureate/associate degree category, 9 semester hours in Power Plant Technology or Steam Generation Systems. *Part 4:* In the lower division baccalaureate/associate degree category, 1 semester hour in First Aid and Safety (2/88). *Version 3: Part 1:* In the lower division baccalaureate/associate degree category, 4 semester hours in Basic Electricity. *Part 2:* In the lower division baccalaureate/associate degree category, 4 semester hours in Refrigeration. *Part 3:* In the lower division baccalaureate/associate degree category, 9 semester hours in Power Plant Technology or Steam Generation Systems. *Part 4:* In the lower division baccalaureate/associate degree category, 1 semester hour in Industrial Safety (12/94).

Qualified Members of the Engine Department (QMED)
Part 1: Principles of Electricity
Part 2: Principles of Refrigeration
Part 3: Principles of Steam Generation Systems

Location: Seafarers Harry Lundeberg School of Seamanship, Piney Point, MD.

Length: 242 hours (8 weeks); residential. *Part 1:* 66 hours; *Part 2:* 64 hours; *Part 3:* 112 hours.

Dates: October 1973-May 1977.

Objective: To provide the student with the knowledge required for certification for QMED and to operate industrial steam generation systems.

Instruction: *Part 1:* Same as 12-week version, with less time devoted to placed electrical measuring instruments, soldering, brazing, and welding. *Part 2:* Same as 12-week version, with less time devoted to troubleshooting procedures. *Part 3:* Same as 12-week version, with less time devoted to fuels.

Credit Recommendation: *Part 1:* In the lower division baccalaureate/associate degree category, 3 semester hours in Electricity (11/77). *Part 2:* In the lower division baccalaureate/associate degree category, 3 semester hours in Refrigeration (11/77). *Part 3:* In the lower division baccalaureate/associate degree category, 6 semester hours in Steam Generation Systems (11/77).

Qualified Members of the Engine Department (QMED)
Part 1: Principles of Electricity
Part 2: Principles of Refrigeration
Part 3: Principles of Steam Generation Systems

Location: Seafarers Harry Lundeberg School of Seamanship, Piney Point, MD.

Length: 124 hours (6 weeks), residential; *Part 1:* 48 hours; *Part 2:* 46 hours; *Part 3:* 30 hours.

Dates: November 1972-October 1973.

Objective: To provide the student with the knowledge required for certification for Qualified Marine Engine Department (QMED) and to operate and repair refrigeration and electrical equipment and to introduce the student to the operation of industrial steam generation systems.

Instruction: *Part 1:* Same as eight-week version except less time is devoted to AC and DC electricity. *Part 2:* Same as eight-week version except less time is devoted to review. *Part 3:* Major topic covered in the course is boiler theory.

Credit Recommendation: *Part 1:* In the lower division baccalaureate/associate degree category, 2 semester hours in Electricity. *Part 2:* In the lower division baccalaureate/associate degree category, 2 semester hours in Refrigeration. *Part 3:* In the lower division baccalaureate/associate degree category, 1 semester hour in Steam Generation Systems (11/77) (6/82).

Qualified Members of the Engine Department (QMED)
Part 1: Principles of Electricity
Part 2. Principles of Refrigeration

Location: Seafarers Harry Lundeberg School of Seamanship, Piney Point, MD.

Length: 98 hours (4 weeks), residential; *Part 1:* 48 hours; *Part 2:* 46 hours.

Dates: October 1972-June 1982.

Objective: To provide the student with the knowledge required for certification for Qualified Marine Engine Department (QMED) and to operate and repair refrigeration and electrical equipment.

Instruction: *Parts 1 and 2:* Same as six-week version.

Credit Recommendation: *Part 1:* In the lower division baccalaureate/associate degree category, 2 semester hours in Electricity. *Part 2:* In the lower division baccalaureate/associate degree category, 2 semester hours in Refrigeration (11/77).

Refrigerated Containers/Advanced Maintenance (MET 227)

Location: Seafarers Harry Lundeberg School of Seamanship, Piney Point, MD.

Length: 210 hours (6 weeks).

Dates: *Version 1:* February 1988-December 1993; *Version 2:* January 1994-Present.

Objective: To provide theoretical background and practical experience in the construction, operation, maintenance, and repair of refrigerated container systems including engine, refrigeration, and electrical systems.

Learning Outcome: Upon successful completion of this course, the student will be able to perform standard refrigeration service techniques and system diagnosis; perform electrical troubleshooting on refrigerated container units; conduct a compressor overhaul; and assume the duties of a maintenance electrician aboard container ships relative to refrigerated containers.

Instruction: Major topics covered in the course are review of refrigeration systems; capacity control; refrigerants; applied electricity; wiring diagrams, motors and diesel engines; and systems operation, maintenance and troubleshooting. Methods of instruction include lecture, classroom exercises, audio/visual material practical exercises, quizzes, and final examination.

Credit Recommendation: *Version 1:* In the lower division baccalaureate/associate degree category, 2 semester hours in Refrigeration Technology, 2 semester hours in Diesel Technology, and 1 semester hour in Electrical Maintenance (2/88). *Version 2:* In the lower division baccalaureate/associate degree category, 3 semester hours in Refrigeration Technology, 1 semester hour in Electrical Maintenance, and 1 semester hour in Diesel Engines (12/94).

Refrigeration Systems Maintenance and Operation (MET 217) (Formerly Maintenance of Shipboard Refrigeration Systems)

Location: Seafarers Harry Lundeberg School of Seamanship, Piney Point, MD.

Length: *Version 1:* 248 hours (5 weeks); *Version 2:* 210 hours (6 weeks).

Dates: *Version 1:* December 1975-December 1993; *Version 2:* January 1994-Present.

Objective: To provide the theoretical and practical knowledge required to repair a refrigeration system.

Learning Outcome: Upon successful completion of this course, the student will be able to perform routine maintenance on ship stores, and refrigeration and air conditioning plants; and troubleshoot shipboard refrigeration equipment.

Instruction: Major topics covered in the course are basic refrigeration, refrigeration components, maintenance of refrigeration systems, parts of replacement and overhaul, electrical circuitry, and electrical wiring and troubleshooting. Methods of instruction include lecture, discussion, audio/visual material, practical training, and final examination.

Credit Recommendation: *Version 1:* In the lower division baccalaureate/associate degree category, 10 semester hours in Refrigeration (11/77) (6/82) (2/88). *Version 2:* In the lower division baccalaureate/associate degree category, 8 semester hours in Refrigeration/Air Conditioning Technology (12/94). **NOTE:** If student has completed QMED course, the maximum of 10 semester hours in Refrigeration should be granted. *Prerequisite:* Qualified Marine Engine Department, any rating endorsement, or endorsement as Refrigeration Engineer and Electrician.

Third Mate: Inspected Vessels (NST 227)

Location: Seafarers Harry Lundeberg School of Seamanship, Piney Point, MD.

Length: *Versions 1 and 2:* 311 hours (10 weeks).

Dates: *Version 1:* January 1981-December 1993; *Version 2:* January 1994-Present.

Objective: To provide sufficient knowledge to pass the U.S. Coast Guard Third Mate Unlimited License Examination.

Learning Outcome: Upon successful completion of this course, the student will be able to execute the duties of a Third Mate-Inspected Vessels in a satisfactory manner.

Instruction: *Version 1:* Major topics covered in the course are celestial navigation, coastwise navigation, rules of the road, marine meteorology, seamanship, and cargo handling. Methods of instruction include lecture, discussion, and laboratory. *Version 2:* Major topics covered in the course are rules of the road, ship construction, cargo gear, ship handling, tides and currents, instruments and accessories, weather, rules and regulations (CFR), stability, ships business, charts and piloting, first aid, CPR, and fire fighting. Methods of instruction include lecture, discussion, classroom exercises, case studies, audio/visual material, quizzes, and the Coast Guard licensing examination.

Credit Recommendation: *Version 1:* In the lower division baccalaureate/associate degree category, 3 semester hours in Celestial Navigation, 4 semester hours in Coastwise Navigation, 3 semester hours in Rules of the Road, 1 semester hour in Marine Meteorology, 2 semester hours in Seamanship, and 2 semester hours in Cargo Handling (6/82) (2/88). *Version 2:* In the lower division baccalaureate/associate degree category, 4 semester hours in Coastwise Navigation, 3 semester hours in Rules of the Road, 2 semester hours in Seamanship, 2 semester hours in Cargo Handling, and 1 semester hour in Meteorology (12/94).

Towboat Cook

Location: Seafarers Harry Lundeberg School of Seamanship, Piney Point, MD.

Length: *Version 1:* 277 hours (6 weeks), residential, 29 hours lecture and discussion, 24 hours laboratory, and 224 hours workshop; *Version 2:* 240 hours (6 weeks).

Dates: *Version 1:* September 1976-December 1979; *Version 2:* January 1980-December 1993.

Objective: To develop the skills required to independently operate a food service kitchen serving up to twelve people.

Learning Outcome: Upon successful completion of this course, the student will be able to perform as cook onboard tugs and towboats.

Instruction: Major topics covered in the course are food principles and preparation of baked goods, breakfast foods, vegetables, sandwiches, salads, meats, fish, beverages, soups, and sauces; work scheduling and organization; menu planning; purchasing and storing supplies; and sanitation.

Credit Recommendation: In the lower division baccalaureate/associate degree category, 7 semester hours in Food Preparation (9/78) (2/88).

Towboat Operator: Inland and Oceans, 200 Miles

Location: Seafarers Harry Lundeberg School of Seamanship, Piney Point, MD.

Length: *Version 1:* 210 hours (5 weeks, 4 days), residential, includes 20 hours supervised independent study and 24 hours license preparation review; *Version 2:*

244 hours (7 weeks); *Version 3:* 238 hours (7 weeks).

Dates: *Version 1:* April 1973-May 1982; *Version 2:* June 1982-January 1988; *Version 3:* February 1988-February 1993.

Objective: To provide the student with a sufficient understanding of the principles of towboat operation, U.S. Coast Guard rules and regulations, and rules of the road (inland and international) to obtain a license as a towboat operator.

Instruction: *Version 1:* Major topics covered in the course are the rules of the road; use of magnetic compass; operation and use of navigational instruments and accessories; tides and currents; emergency signals; use of charts in navigation; aids to navigation; lifesaving and simple first aid; fire fighting; regulations and laws applicable to the operation of a towing vessel; pollution prevention and control. Course leads to licensing as 1st or 2nd class operator of uninspected towing vessels on inland waters or on oceans (not more than 200 miles off shore). *Version 2:* Same as Version 1, but includes more practical training. *Version 3:* Major topics covered in the course are earth coordinates and charts; instruments and accessories; compasses, dead reckoning, and piloting; aids to navigation (buoys and lights); navigation publications; electronic navigation; tides and currents; weather; rules of the road; seamanship and safety; and rules and regulations.

Credit Recommendation: *Version 1:* In the lower division baccalaureate/associate degree category, 8 semester hours in Navigation (11/77). *Version 2:* In the lower division baccalaureate/associate degree category, 9 semester hours in Navigation (6/82). *Version 3:* In the lower division baccalaureate/associate degree category, 9 semester hours in Towboat Operations (2/88).

Towboat Operator: Western Rivers

Location: Seafarers Harry Lundeberg School of Seamanship, Piney Point, MD.

Length: 108 hours (2 weeks, 4 days), residential, includes 10 hours supervised independent study and 16 hours license preparation review; 33 hours lecture/discussion and 7 hours laboratory/workshop per week.

Dates: May 1973-November 1980.

Objective: To provide the student with a sufficient understanding of towboat operation, U.S. Coast Guard rules and regulations, and rules of the road for western rivers to obtain a license as a towboat operator.

Instruction: Major topics covered in the course are the rules of the road; operation and use of river piloting instruments and accessories; emergency signals; use of river charts; aids to piloting; boatmanship for western rivers; regulations and laws applicable to the operation of a towing vessel; and pollution prevention and control. Course leads to licensing as 1st or 2nd class operator of uninspected vessels on western rivers. Methods of instruction include lecture, discussion, and hands-on exercises.

Credit Recommendation: In the lower division baccalaureate/associate degree category, 5 semester hours in River Piloting (11/77) (6/82).

Union Education

Location: Seafarers Harry Lundeberg School of Seamanship, Piney Point, MD.

Length: 40 hours (five 1-hour meetings for 8 weeks).

Dates: May 1975-February 1988.

Objective: To provide the student with a foundation on which to establish ideas about unions and to help the student gain an understanding of the history of the labor movement in America.

Instruction: Major topics covered in the course are growth of the labor movement from 1894 to the present, changes that have taken place in unions, relationships with management and government, vacation, pension and welfare plans, politics, and law. Methods of instruction include lecture and discussion.

Credit Recommendation: In the lower division baccalaureate/associate degree category, 1 semester hour in Labor Education (11/82).

Union Leadership (Alternative Title: Union History)

Location: Seafarers Harry Lundeberg School of Seamanship, Piney Point, MD.

Length: 160 hours (4 weeks).

Dates: April 1978-February 1988.

Objective: To provide students with a working knowledge of union matters so that they can act as union representatives, officials, or shop stewards aboard ship.

Instruction: Major topics covered in the course are the historical, economic, and social development of the Seafarers' Union; the history of the labor movement from 1884 to present; the formation, organization, constitution, and contract functions are examined in relation to the members' responsibilities; and the backgrounds of international and local maritime unions and their associations. Methods of instruction include lecture, discussion, and field trips.

Credit Recommendation: In the lower division baccalaureate/associate degree category, 2 semester hours in Labor Studies or Labor Relations (11/82).

Water Survival (NST 102) (Formerly Lifeboat [NST 102])

Location: Seafarers Harry Lundeberg School of Seamanship, Piney Point, MD.

Length: *Version 1:* 60 hours (2 weeks); *Version 2:* 70 hours (2 weeks).

Dates: *Version 1:* June 1972-January 1988; *Version 2:* February 1988-Present.

Objective: *Version 1:* To give knowledge of the nomenclature of lifeboats and liferafts, and survival and abandon ship procedures including 30 hours of actual rowing experience. *Version 2:* To provide sufficient understanding of lifesaving techniques, equipment, and practical boat handling procedures to pass the United States Coast Guard examination and receive an endorsement.

Learning Outcome: *Version 1:* Upon successful completion of this course, the student will be able to pass United States Coast Guard examination and receive an endorsement as Lifeboatman. *Version 2:* Upon successful completion of this course, the student will have sufficient knowledge and experience to function as a life boatman.

Instruction: *Version 1:* Major topics covered in the course are emergency duties, lifeboat construction, lifeboat launching and recovery, basic compass in navigation, life raft construction, life raft launching and maintenance, use of all lifeboat and life raft equipment, survival methods such as abandon ship procedures, hypothermia prevention, eating and drinking to survive, helicopter rescue procedures, and use of the emergency radio and signals to attract attention. Methods of instruction include laboratory experience both indoor and on the water. *Version 2:* Major topics covered in the course are emergency duties, lifeboat construction, lifeboat launching and recovery, basic compass in navigation, life raft construction, life raft launching and maintenance, use of all lifeboat and life raft equipment, survival methods such as abandon ship procedures, hypothermia prevention, eating and drinking to survive, helicopter rescue procedures, and use of the emergency radio and signals to attract attention. Methods of instruction include lecture, discussion, classroom exercises, audio/ visual material, practical exercises, laboratory experience both indoor and on the water including 30 hours of actual rowing experience, quizzes, and the Coast Guard licensing examination.

Credit Recommendation: *Version 1:* In the lower division baccalaureate/associate degree category, 2 semester hours in Seamanship (6/82) (2/88) (12/94). *Version 2:* In the lower division baccalaureate/associate degree category, 2 semester hours in Seamanship (6/82) (2/88) (12/94).

Welding (MET 210)
(Formerly Welding [MET 102])

Location: Seafarers Harry Lundeberg School of Seamanship, Piney Point, MD.

Length: 120 hours (4 weeks).

Dates: *Version 1:* September 1973-December 1993; *Version 2:* January 1994-Present.

Objective: To provide the skills required to perform basic welding and cutting jobs aboard ship.

Learning Outcome: Upon successful completion of this course, the student will be able to perform basic welding and cutting including flat, horizontal, vertical, and pipe welds, and flat brazing and oxyacetylene cutting.

Instruction: Major topics covered in the course are training in electric welding and oxyacetylene cutting and brazing. Methods of instruction include lecture, discussion, audio/visual material, practical exercises and projects, quizzes, and final examination.

Credit Recommendation: *Version 1:* In the lower division baccalaureate/associate degree category, 4 semester hours in Welding (6/82) (2/88) (12/94). *Version 2:* In the lower division baccalaureate/associate degree category, 4 semester hours in Welding (6/82) (2/88) (12/94).

Seminary Extension

Seminary Extension is an external theological education program of the six theological seminaries of the Southern Baptist Convention: Southern Baptist Theological Seminary, Southwestern Baptist Theological Seminary, Golden Gate Baptist Theological Seminary, New Orleans Baptist Theological Seminary, Southeastern Baptist Theological Seminary, and Midwestern Baptist Theological Seminary. Each of these institutions is accredited by its regional accrediting agency and by the Association of Theological Schools.

The program of Seminary Extension includes two delivery systems: The Independent Study Institute, which offers correspondence courses and other forms of home study, and a network of more than 300 extension centers.

To meet the needs of students with a wide range of educational backgrounds, Seminary Extension offers courses on two levels of difficulty. Basic Curriculum courses (in English and Spanish) are designed for pastors who have had only limited formal education. Courses in the diploma-level curriculum are for pastors and lay persons who are qualified to perform satisfactorily on a college level. The courses listed below are in the diploma or college-level curriculum.

Source of official student records: Seminary Extension, Southern Baptist Convention Building, 901 Commerce Street, Suite 500, Nashville, TN 37203.

Additional information about the courses: College Credit Recommendation Service, American Council on Education, One Dupont Circle, Washington, DC 20036-1193.

A Study of Matthew's Gospel (NT 3170) (Formerly [NT 0170])

Location: Seminary Extension Centers throughout the U. S. or the Independent Study Institute.

Length: 17 lessons (2.5 hours each).

Dates: January 1991-Present.

Objective: To become familiar with the sequence of events in the ministry of Jesus as presented by Matthew and to be able to state the purpose of Matthew's gospel.

Learning Outcome: Upon successful completion of this course, the student will be familiar with sequence of events in Jesus' ministry, be able to identify theological themes in Matthew's gospel, recognize Matthew's distinctive purpose in writing a gospel.

Instruction: Major topics covered in the course are Introduction to Matthew's Gospel; Sermon on the Mount; Jesus' Ministry in Galilee; and Jesus' Ministry in Jerusalem. Methods of instruction include classroom lecture and discussion or through independent study.

Credit Recommendation: In the upper division baccalaureate degree category, 3 semester hours in Religion (3/93).

Biblical Backgrounds (BB 3101) (Formerly [BB 0101])

Location: Seminary Extension Centers throughout the U. S. or the Independent Study Institute.

Length: 16 lessons.

Dates: *Version 1:* January 1978-May 1993; *Version 2:* June 1993-Present.

Objective: To survey systematically the historical geography and archaeology of Bible lands and peoples as a prerequisite to interpreting the Bible's meaning for today.

Instruction: Major topics covered in the course are events from the time of the patriarchs to the time of the apostolic church; the world of the Bible in its historical context; and political, cultural, economic, and religious factors influencing biblical figures. Methods of instruction include classroom lecture and discussion or through independent study.

Credit Recommendation: *Version 1:* In the lower division baccalaureate/associate degree category, 1-3 semester hour(s) in History or Religion (11/77) (9/82). *Version 2:* In the lower division baccalaureate/associate degree category, 1 semester hour in History or Religion (3/93).

Contemporary Christian Preaching (PM 3257) (Formerly [PM 0257])

Location: Seminary Extension Centers throughout the U. S. or the Independent Study Institute.

Length: *Version 1*: 16 lessons; *Version 2*: 17 lessons.

Dates: *Version 1:* January 1978-May 1993; *Version 2:* June 1993-Present.

Objective: To prepare the student to develop, deliver, and evaluate sermons.

Instruction: Major topics covered in the course are an understanding and appreciation of the work of preaching; extensive written work in conception, outlining, and drafting of oral presentations; using resources for ideas, texts, and topics in various appropriate methods of oral presentations; instruction in long-range preaching plans. Methods of instruction include classroom lecture and discussion or through independent study.

Credit Recommendation: *Version 1:* In the upper division baccalaureate degree category, 1-3 semester hour(s) in Communications or Homiletics (2/77) (9/82). *Version 2:* In the upper division baccalaureate degree category, 3 semester hours in Communications or Homiletics (3/93).

Dynamics of Teaching (RE 3264) (Formerly [RE 0264])

Location: Seminary Extension Centers throughout the U. S. or the Independent Study Institute.

Length: *Version 1*: 16 lessons; *Version 2*: 17 lessons.

Dates: *Version 1:* January 1978-May 1993; *Version 2:* June 1993-Present.

Objective: *Version 1:* To introduce students to some basic principles of the teaching-learning process and to develop students' teaching skills. *Version 2:* To provide students with skills needed to become effective Sunday School teachers.

Instruction: Major topics covered in the course are a survey of the nature of the relation of the teacher to the teaching task; the steps in lesson-plan development; and the use of teaching aids. Methods of instruction include classroom lecture and discussion or independent study.

Credit Recommendation: *Version 1:* In the lower division baccalaureate/associate degree category, 3 semester hours in Education (11/77) (9/82). *Version 2:* In the lower division baccalaureate/associate degree category, 3 semester hours in Religious Education or Specialized Education elective (3/93).

Formation for Ministry (GM 3500) (Formerly [GM 0500])

Location: Seminary Extension Centers throughout the U. S. or the Independent Study Institute.

Length: 17 lessons (2.5 hours each).

Dates: January 1989-Present.

Objective: To come to an understanding of basic information about Christian spirituality, personhood, and ministerial skills as these influence the student's practice of ministry.

Learning Outcome: Upon successful completion of this course, the student will be able to more thoroughly integrate his or her call to Christian service with personal life history, and begin to develop biblical and theological resources to understand his or her calling.

Instruction: Major topics covered in the course are spiritual discipline; vocational discernment; theology of ministry. Methods of instruction include classroom lecture and discussion or through independent study.

Credit Recommendation: In the upper division baccalaureate degree category, 3 semester hours in Religion (3/93).

History of Christian Thought (CH 3212) (Formerly [CH 0212])

Location: Seminary Extension Centers throughout the U. S. or the Independent Study Institute.

Length: 16 lessons.

Dates: *Version 1:* January 1978-May 1993; *Version 2:* June 1993-Present.

Objective: Using primary documents, to present the widely influential components of Christian thought from the Apostolic Age to the English Reformation.

Instruction: Major topics covered in the course are an examination and interpretation of numerous historical sources, using a broad chronological framework. In the study of the English Reformation, particular emphasis is given to Baptist thought. Methods of instruction include classroom lecture and discussion or independent study.

Credit Recommendation: *Version 1:* In the graduate or upper division baccalaureate degree category, 1-3 semester hour(s) in History of Religion, Religion, or Theology (11/77) (9/82). *Version 2:* In the upper division baccalaureate degree category, 3 semester hours in History of Religion, Religion, or Theology (3/93).

History of Christianity (CH 3211) (Formerly [CH 0211])

Location: Seminary Extension Centers throughout the U. S. or the Independent Study Institute.

Length: *Version 1:* 16 lessons; *Version 2:* 17 lessons.

Dates: *Version 1:* January 1978-May 1993; *Version 2:* June 1993-Present.

Objective: To introduce the major historical periods and movements of Christianity.

Instruction: *Version 1:* Major topics include perspectives on the great movements and heresies in Christian history. *Version 2:* Heavy emphasis on selected aspects of Baptist and free church history. Methods of instruction include classroom lecture and discussion or independent study.

Credit Recommendation: *Version 1:* In the upper division baccalaureate degree category, 1-3 semester hours in History of Religion (11/77) (9/82). *Version 2:* In the upper division baccalaureate degree category, 3 semester hours in History of Religion (3/93).

How to Understand the Bible (BB 3100)

Location: Seminary Extension Centers throughout the U. S. or the Independent Study Institute.

Length: 17 lessons.

Dates: June 1993-Present.

Objective: To introduce the student to the nature, purpose, and interpretation of the Bible.

Learning Outcome: Upon successful completion of this course, the student will be able to understand the Bible as a whole, how it developed, and how it should be interpreted and applied to life.

Instruction: Major topics covered in the course are introduction to doctrinal, historical, literary and other general questions involved in reading the Bible with understanding; the authority, purpose and message of the Bible; the history reflected in or narrated by the Old Testament and the New literary forms; text, canon and versions; principles of interpretation. Methods of instruction include classroom lecture and discussion or through independent study.

Credit Recommendation: In the lower division baccalaureate/associate degree or in the upper division baccalaureate degree category, 3 semester hours in Humanities or Religion (3/93).

How to Understand the Bible (BB 0100)

Location: Seminary Extension Centers throughout the U. S. or the Independent Study Institute.

Length: 16 lessons.

Dates: January 1978-May 1993.

Objective: To introduce the student to the nature, purpose, and interpretation of the Bible.

Instruction: Begins with a basic survey of the Bible and progresses through the Bible as literature, principles of biblical interpretation, canonical development, form criticism, placement in the world of sacred scriptures.

Credit Recommendation: In the lower division baccalaureate/associate degree category or in the upper division baccalaureate degree category, 1-3 semester hours in History, Humanities, or Religion (11/77) (9/82).

Introduction to Christian Ethics (CE 3231) (Formerly [CE 0231])

Location: Seminary Extension Centers throughout the U. S. or the Independent Study Institute.

Length: *Version 1*: 16 lessons; *Version 2*: 17 lessons.

Dates: *Version 1:* January 1978-May 1993; *Version 2:* June 1993-Present.

Objective: To introduce the ethical teaching of the Bible as a foundation for the responsibilities of marriage and family living, race relations, and economic and political life.

Learning Outcome: Upon successful completion of this course, the student will be acquainted with general ethical theory; identify key ethical issues; use the Bible as a basic resource in dealing with ethical issues; working knowledge and understanding of a variety of theological and historical perspectives in relation to Christian ethics; resources for continuing interest and involvement with Christian ethics; and able to articulate, with improved skill, ethical concerns to others.

Instruction: Major topics covered in the course are a comprehensive exploration of Old and New Testament ethics and an examination of contemporary social, economic, and political issues as they relate to personal ethics. Methods of instruction include classroom lecture and discussion or independent study.

Credit Recommendation: *Version 1:* In the upper division baccalaureate degree category, 1-3 semester hours in Ethics, Philosophy, Religion, or Sociology (11/77) (9/82). *Version 2:* In the upper division baccalaureate degree category, 3 semester hours in Ethics, Philosophy, or Religion (3/93).

Luke (NT 0172)

Location: At certified teaching sites of the Southern Baptist Seminaries.

Length: 26 hours (17 weeks).

Dates: September 1997-Present.

Objective: To provide the student with an understanding of the life and teachings of Jesus in the Gospel of Luke in the New Testament with special emphasis on the parables of Jesus that are unique to Luke.

Learning Outcome: Upon successful completion of this course, the student will be able to understand and outline the historical circumstances that gave rise to the Gospel of Luke, including the theological significance of the birth stories, parables, and ministries of John the Baptist and Jesus as they are recorded in the Gospel of Luke.

Instruction: Major topics covered in the course are sessions on the birth of John and Jesus; the setting of the ministry of Jesus; mixed reactions to Jesus' early ministry; the good news of Jesus; mixed responses to the ministry of Jesus; the teaching of discipleship and prayer; warnings to disciples and the call for commitment; an introduction to the parables of Jesus; the good Samaritan and the great banquet; a lost sheep, a lost coin, and prodigal son; the dishonest steward and the rich man and Lazarus; the widow and the unjust judge and the Pharisee and the tax collector; Jesus' ministry just before Jerusalem; the events of the last week; and the death and resurrection of Jesus. Methods of instruction include lecture, projects, presentations, team work, video, and interactive computer.

Credit Recommendation: In the upper division baccalaureate degree category, 3 semester hours in Religion or Humanities (11/97).

New Testament Survey Part I: Background and Introduction (NT 3165) (Formerly [NT 0165])

Location: Seminary Extension Centers throughout the U. S. or the Independent Study Institute.

Length: 17 lessons (2.5 hours each).

Dates: January 1987-Present.

Objective: To come to know the historical and cultural background of the New Testament through the study of several of the primary literary sources.

Learning Outcome: Upon successful completion of this course, the student will be able to understand the historical and cultural background of the New Testament; identify major religious and cultural influences on the New Testament; and understand the process of producing and translating the New Testament canon.

Instruction: Major topics covered in the course are historical and political study of Palestinian Judaism; cultural and religious study of Palestinian Judaism; Hellenistic influences on Judaism and the early Church; and canon, text, and translations of the New Testament. Methods of instruction include classroom lecture and discussion or independent study.

Credit Recommendation: In the lower division baccalaureate/associate degree category, 3 semester hours in Religion or Humanities (3/93).

New Testament Survey Part II: The Gospels (NT 3166) (Formerly [NT 0166])

Location: Seminary Extension Centers throughout the U. S. or the Independent Study Institute.

Length: 17 lessons (2.5 hours each).

Dates: March 1983-Present.

Objective: To learn how to interpret and apply the teachings of Jesus and the teachings about Jesus that are found in the gospels of Matthew, Mark, Luke, and John.

Learning Outcome: Upon successful completion of this course, the student will be able to recognize the distinctions between synoptic and Johannine gospels; understand the story of the life of Jesus; be familiar with the teachings of Jesus.

Instruction: Major topics covered in the course are introduction to the Gospels; study of Synoptic Stories of Jesus; and study of John's story of Jesus. Methods of instruction include classroom lecture and discussion or independent study.

Credit Recommendation: In the lower division baccalaureate/associate degree category, 3 semester hours in Religion or Humanities (3/93).

New Testament Survey Part III: The Early Church (NT 3107) (Formerly New Testament Survey, The Early Church: Version 1: NT 0167, Version 2: NT 3167)

Location: Seminary Extension Centers throughout the U. S. or the Independent Study Institute.

Length: 16 lessons.

Dates: *Version 1:* January 1978-May 1993; *Version 2:* June 1993-Present.

Objective: To introduce the student to an historical survey of the New Testament documents, stressing why these books were chosen for the canon and how the authors selected their contents.

Instruction: Major topics covered in the course are the New Testament, book by book, from the Acts of the Apostles through the Revelation of John. Methods of instruction include classroom lecture and discussion or independent study.

Credit Recommendation: *Version 1:* In the lower division baccalaureate/associate degree category, 1-3 semester hour(s) in Humanities or Religion (11/77) (9/82). *Version 2:* In the upper division baccalaureate degree category, 3 semester hours in Humanities or Religion (but not at a senior seminar level) (3/93).

New Testament Theology (TH 3201) (Formerly [TH 0201])

Location: Seminary Extension Centers throughout the U. S. or the Independent Study Institute.

Length: 16 lessons.

Dates: *Version 1:* January 1978-May 1993; *Version 2:* June 1993-Present.

Objective: To present thematically the teaching of the New Testament based upon exegesis.

Instruction: Major topics covered in the course are teachings of the New Testament, including the Bible, God, humanity, sin, salvation, the church, the ordinances, the ministry, the Christian life, the kingdom, and the ultimate goal of humanity, and of history. Methods of instruction include lecture and discussion or through independent study.

Credit Recommendation: *Version 1:* In the graduate degree category, 1-3 semester hour(s) in History of Religion, Religion, or Theology (11/77) (9/82). *Version 2:* In the upper division baccalaureate degree category, 3 semester hours in Religion or Humanities (3/93).

Old Testament Survey Part I (OT 3103) (Formerly [OT 0103])

Location: Seminary Extension Centers throughout the U. S. or the Independent Study Institute.

Length: 17 lessons (2.5 hours each).

Dates: March 1983-Present.

Objective: To introduce the student to facts and methods necessary to understand the Old Testament; to study the historical books from Genesis through 2 Samuel.

Learning Outcome: Upon successful completion of this course, the student will be familiar with the biblical text and its antecedents; will know the various authors and schools that produced these books; and will be familiar with the history of Israel's forebears in Canaan and with the history of the people of Israel from Moses to David.

Instruction: Major topics covered in the course are basic introductory questions (the Old Testament world, canon, text, etc.) and then it works from Genesis through 2 Samuel, book by book. Methods of instruction include classroom lecture and discussion or through independent study.

Credit Recommendation: In the lower division baccalaureate/associate degree

category, 3 semester hours in Humanities or Religion (3/93).

Old Testament Survey Part II (OT 3104) (Formerly [OT 0104])

Location: Seminary Extension Centers throughout the U. S. or the Independent Study Institute.

Length: 17 lessons (2.5 hours each).

Dates: March 1983-Present.

Objective: To review foundational questions of biblical studies, as in Part I, and to introduce the students to the pre-exilic historical and prophetic books, beginning with I Kings.

Learning Outcome: Upon successful completion of this course, the student will be more familiar with introductory matters of Old Testament study; will know the individual collections of oracles of the Major Prophets and three of the Minor Prophets; and will be familiar with Israelite history from Solomon to the Exile.

Instruction: Major topics covered in the course are 1-2 Kings, 1-2 Chronicles; the Eighth Century Prophets (Amos, Hosea, Micah, Isaiah); and Jeremiah and Ezekiel. Methods of instruction include classroom lecture and discussion or through independent study.

Credit Recommendation: In the lower division baccalaureate/associate degree category, 3 semester hours in Humanities or Religion (3/93).

Old Testament Survey Part III (OT 3105) (Formerly [OT 0105])

Location: Seminary Extension Centers throughout the U. S. or the Independent Study Institute.

Length: 17 lessons (2.5 hours each).

Dates: March 1983-Present.

Objective: To introduce the student to works reflective of Jewish life and experience in the post-exilic period; to summarize and reflect on what has been learned in this survey (Parts I, II, and III).

Learning Outcome: Upon successful completion of this course, the student will be familiar with the history of the Jewish people from the sixth to the first century B.C., and with the writings reflective of that history.

Instruction: Major topics covered in the course are Ezra-Nehemiah, Esther, the Late Minor prophets, the Wisdom Books, and Apocalyptic. Methods of instruction include classroom lecture and discussion or through independent study.

Credit Recommendation: In the lower division baccalaureate/associate degree category, 3 semester hours in Humanities or Religion (3/93).

Pastoral Care (PM 3251) (Formerly [PM 0251])

Location: Seminary Extension Centers throughout the U. S. or the Independent Study Institute.

Length: 16 lessons.

Dates: *Version 1:* January 1978-May 1993; *Version 2:* June 1993-Present.

Objective: To provide an understanding of the processes of caring for and counseling church members and others.

Instruction: Major topics covered in the course are the pastor's role as counselor; personal problems and self-definition; and dealing with issues such as grief, marriage conflict, vocational choice, and child-parent relationships. Methods of instruction include classroom lecture and discussion or through independent study.

Credit Recommendation: *Version 1:* In the graduate degree category, 1-3 semester hour(s) in Pastoral Counseling (1/77) (9/82). *Version 2:* In the upper division baccalaureate degree category, 3 semester hours in Pastoral Counseling (3/93).

Pastoral Care in a Hospital Setting (PM 3300) (Formerly [PM 0300])

Location: Seminary Extension Centers throughout the U.S.

Length: 10 lessons (3 hours each).

Dates: January 1985-Present.

Objective: To examine the foundations, principles, and procedures of a shepherding ministry to persons in times of developmental change and emergency crises by focusing on ministry to persons when they are hospitalized.

Learning Outcome: Upon successful completion of this course, the student will be able to begin to develop theologically sound and clinically informed strategies of pastoral care given in the hospital setting.

Instruction: Major topics covered in the course are basic approaches to crisis care in hospital settings; care of adults, youth and children; ministry in situations of grief conflict. Methods of instruction include classroom lecture and discussion, videotaped lectures by senior professor and supervised on-site experience.

Credit Recommendation: In the upper division baccalaureate degree category, 3 semester hours in Religion, or (Counseling) Psychology (3/93). **NOTE**: This course is not a substitute for a course in clinical pastoral education.

Pastoral Leadership in a Small Church (PM 3258) (Formerly [PM 0258])

Location: Seminary Extension Centers throughout the U. S. or the Independent Study Institute.

Length: 17 lessons (2.5 hours each).

Dates: January 1991-Present.

Objective: To become aware of the distinctives and uniqueness of the small church in order to serve more effectively as a pastor in a small church setting.

Learning Outcome: Upon successful completion of this course, the student will be able to better understand and appreciate dynamics of small churches, develop leadership/pastoral strategies which address the unique concerns of small churches.

Instruction: Major topics covered in the course are theological and sociological understandings of small churches; leadership in the small church; the ministry of the small church; and the pastoral care of the small church. Methods of instruction include classroom lecture and discussion or independent study.

Credit Recommendation: In the upper division baccalaureate degree category, 3 semester hours in Religion (3/93).

Pastoral Ministries (PM 0252) (Formerly PM 133)

Location: Seminary Extension Centers throughout the U. S. or the Independent Study Institute.

Length: 16 lessons.

Dates: January 1978-May 1993.

Objective: To provide an understanding of the life and work of the pastor in relation to the church's total mission, with attention to the minister's various roles and functions.

Instruction: A guide to the main functions of the parish pastor, such as leading in worship, visiting, counseling, conducting weddings and funerals, and financial management. Attention is also given to the minister's own growth.

Credit Recommendation: In the graduate degree category, 3 semester hours in Pastoral Ministries (11/77) (9/82).

Philosophy of Religion (TH 3202)

Location: Seminary Extension Centers throughout the U. S. or the Independent Study Institute.

Length: 17 lessons (2.5 hours each).

Dates: September 1993-Present.

Objective: To understand and deal with some of the great philosophical questions of life and to learn the history of these various questions.

Learning Outcome: Upon successful completion of this course, the student will be familiar with major issues of philosophy of religion; be able to discuss issues critically; understand how to think about issues philosophically.

Instruction: Major topics covered in the course are various approaches to question of meaning; discussion of good and evil; questions of relating faith and reason; relationship of science and religion. Methods of instruction include classroom lecture and discussion or independent study.

Credit Recommendation: In the upper division baccalaureate degree category, 3 semester hours in Religion, Philosophy, or Humanities (3/93).

Principles of Church Administration (CA 3281)

Location: Seminary Extension Centers throughout the U. S. or the Independent Study Institute.

Length: 17 lessons (2.5 hours each).

Dates: June 1993-Present.

Objective: To introduce the student to the ends, means, and resources of church administration; from both a managerial and a biblical perspective.

Learning Outcome: Upon successful completion of this course, the student will see administration in terms of biblical understandings of church and ministry, and will learn practical and helpful ways to envision and execute the tasks of church administration.

Instruction: Major topics covered in the course are the purpose and objectives of church administration, the planning, organizing, and use of physical and financial resources; and human resources (volunteer, staff). Methods of instruction include textbook; audio tape with listening guide, classroom lecture and discussion or independent study.

Credit Recommendation: In the lower division baccalaureate/associate degree category, 3 semester hours in Religion (3/93).

Public Worship (PM 3254) (Formerly [PM 0254])

Location: Seminary Extension Centers throughout the U. S. or the Independent Study Institute.

Length: *Version 1*: 16 lessons; *Version 2*: 17 lessons.

Dates: *Version 1:* January 1978-May 1993; *Version 2:* June 1993-Present.

Objective: *Version 1:* To consider the nature, history, and purpose of corporate worship. *Version 2:* To develop students as effective leaders of worship.

Instruction: Major topics covered in the course are an examination of worship from the perspectives of personal experience, theology, psychology, Bible, Christian history, music, and various elements in public worship. Special attention is given to developing skill in planning and conducting public worship. Methods of instruction include classroom lecture and discussion or independent study.

Credit Recommendation: *Version 1:* In the upper division baccalaureate degree category, 1-3 semester hour(s) in Religion (11/77) (9/82). *Version 2:* In the upper division baccalaureate degree category, 2 semester hours in Religion (3/93).

Systematic Theology (TH 3200) (Formerly [TH 0200])

Location: Seminary Extension Centers throughout the U. S. or the Independent Study Institute.

Length: *Versions 1 and 2:* 16 lessons; *Version 3:* 17 lessons.

Dates: *Version 1:* January 1978-August 1982; *Version 2:* September 1982-May 1993; *Version 3:* June 1993-Present.

Objective: To provide a comprehensive presentation of the methodical interpretation and organization of the teachings of Christianity.

Instruction: Major topics covered in the course are Christian doctrines, with emphasis on revelation, God, creation of humanity, the person and work of Jesus Christ, the church, the Christian life, and the Christian hope. Methods of instruction include classroom lecture and discussion or independent study.

Credit Recommendation: *Version 1:* In the graduate or upper level baccalaureate degree category, 6 semester hour(s) in History of Religion, Religion, or Theology (11/77). *Version 2:* In the graduate or upper level baccalaureate degree category, 1-6 semester hours in the same subject areas as noted above (9/82). *Version 3:* In the upper division baccalaureate degree category, 3 semester hours in History of Religion, Religion, or Theology (3/93).

Teaching the Bible to Adults (RE 3304) (Formerly [RE 0304])

Location: Seminary Extension Centers throughout the U. S. or the Independent Study Institute.

Length: 10 lessons (3 hours each).

Dates: January 1989-Present.

Objective: For students to grow in their ability to teach the Bible to adults.

Learning Outcome: Upon successful completion of this course, the student will be able to articulate and perform the role of teacher in an adult education Bible class, prepare course and lesson plans for these classes, and develop study habits commensurate with the teaching role.

Instruction: Major topics covered in the course are the importance of the teaching ministry of the church, with special emphasis on the preparation of teachers in their personal study, teaching preparation, and facilitation of student learning. Methods of instruction include classroom lecture and discussion or through independent study.

Credit Recommendation: In the lower division baccalaureate/associate degree category, 3 semester hours in Religion, Education (3/93).

The Pastor as a Person (PM 3250) (Formerly [PM 0250])

Location: Seminary Extension Centers throughout the U. S. or the Independent Study Institute.

Length: 16 lessons.

Dates: *Version 1:* January 1978-May 1993; *Version 2:* June 1993-Present.

Objective: To introduce the student to the nature of the pastor's life and ministry in today's world.

Instruction: Major topics covered in the course are an exploration of the essential factors of the pastor's personal function, with attention to role fulfillment, personal investment, value systems, and growth potential. Methods of instruction include classroom lecture and discussion or through independent study.

Credit Recommendation: *Version 1:* In the graduate or upper division baccalaureate degree category, 1-3 semester hour(s) in Pastoral Ministries (11/77) (9/82). *Version 2:* In the upper division baccalaureate degree category, 3 semester hours in Pastoral Ministries (3/93).

Shen School dba Appraiser Licensing School

Shen School dba Appraiser Licensing School has offered California Department of Real Estate approved college level correspondence courses since 1986. This was the first year in which California law required all prospective salesperson licensees to complete a 45 hour course in Real Estate Principles. Upon issuance of the license, the licensee must complete 2 additional college level 3 unit (45 hour) courses within 8 months in order to keep the license active. Appraisal Licensing School has three 45 hour courses approved by the Department of Real Estate.

Shen School dba Appraiser Licensing School is approved by the California Council for Private Postsecondary and Vocational Education as a private vocational school.

APPRAISAL PROGRAM

A new appraisal license law went into effect on January 1, 1992, requiring all applicants to complete a minimum number hours of education prior to licensure.

Shen School dba Appraiser Licensing School has been approved by the California Office of Real Estate Appraisers to offer a Prelicense program that consists of two 45 hours correspondence courses. The two prelicense courses are designed to cover specific topics required by the Appraiser Qualification Board and to prepare the applicant to pass the State License Examination. The school also has the OREA's approval for a 56 hour of Continuing Education program. This includes the mandated 7 hour course in Uniform Standards of Professional Appraisal Practice and the 4 hour course on Federal State Regulations. The balance of the 45 hours consists of a 3 unit course in Real Estate Finance.

All courses have been developed by Thomas E. Felde and are updated each year to reflect all of the latest changes in the law and regulations. Mr. Felde has devoted over 30 years to writing, teaching and publishing on the subjects of real estate, appraisal and legal aspects.

Source of official student records: Registry of Credit Recommendations, American Council on Education, One Dupont Circle, Washington, DC 20036-1193.

Additional information about the courses: College Credit Recommendation Service, American Council on Education, One Dupont Circle, Washington, DC 20036-1193.

Elements of California Real Estate Finance and Appraisal Regulations (Formerly Continuing Education for Appraiser Licensees)

Location: Independent study by correspondence.

Length: 56 hours.

Dates: January 1996-Present.

Objective: To provide the student with an overview of the Uniform Standards for Professional Appraisal Practices (USPAP) and real estate finance in California.

Learning Outcome: Upon successful completion of this course, the student will be able to demonstrate familiarity with generally accepted appraisal theory and practice.

Instruction: Major topics covered in the course are documentation, Federal Reserve, and federal agencies; institutional lenders; disclosure and anti-discrimination laws; Truth in Lending and RESPA; conventional, FHA, VA, and CAL-VET loans; real estate math; the secondary markets; FIRREA loan underwriting; junior loans and leverage; loan processing and closing; construction financing; investment property financing; and federal and California regulations applying to real property. Methods of instruction include correspondence study involving directed text readings, special projects, and a proctored final examination.

Credit Recommendation: In the lower division baccalaureate/associate degree category, 2 semester hours in Real Estate Finance or Business Administration (5/97).

Introduction to Real Estate Appraisal (Formerly License Qualification Program)

Location: Independent study by correspondence.

Length: 90 hours.

Dates: January 1992-Present.

Objective: To provide the student with an overview of appraisal principles, real property law and real estate financing.

Learning Outcome: Upon successful completion of this course, the student will be able to demonstrate familiarity with generally accepted appraisal theory and practice.

Instruction: Major topics covered in the course are real property ownership and encumbrances; business opportunities, land descriptions, and real estate financing; real estate law; real estate contracts; Uniform Standards of Professional Appraisal Practice (USPAP); real property valuation and appraisal; the appraisal process and neighborhood analysis; site inspection; property inspection; three methods of property valuation; capitalization rates; and appraising special interests. Methods of instruction include correspondence study involving directed text readings, special projects, and a proctored final examination.

Credit Recommendation: In the lower division baccalaureate/associate degree category, 3 semester hours in Real Estate or Business Administration (5/97).

Showboat Casino Hotel

Showboat, Inc., through its subsidiaries, operates in Las Vegas, Nevada and Atlantic City, New Jersey, and Sidney, Australia. Their operations feature casino gambling, bowling, special events, and other attractions.

In the area of training, Atlantic City Showboat has excelled. Education is encouraged at all levels of the organization, and is available for all departments in the company. Programs are designed to meet the learning and developmental needs of adults in today's business world. Classroom facilities, audiovisual support, and library are available to ensure an atmosphere of continued learning and professional and personal growth.

Source of official student records: Registry of Credit Recommendations, American Council on Education, One Dupont Circle, Washington, DC 20036-1193.

Additional information about the courses: Office of Corporate-Higher Education, Thomas Edison State College, 101 W. State Street, Trenton, NJ 08608-1176.

Effective Supervision I and II

Location: Showboat Hotel/Casino, Atlantic City, NJ.

Length: *Effective Supervision I:* (22.5 hours); *Effective Supervision II:* (13.75 hours).

Dates: *Effective Supervision I*: April 1989-Present; *Effective Supervision II*: February 1991-Present.

Objective: To develop the administrative, cognitive, and interpersonal skills needed to effectively supervise the work unit.

Learning Outcome: Upon successful completion of this course, the student will be able to process information effectively to learn new material; identify and define problems and make decisions; interact with others by utilizing methods that enhance understanding and respect; develop mutually beneficial working relationships; structure one's own activities and the activities of others; and coordinate the use of resources to maximize productivity and efficiency.

Instruction: *Effective Supervision I*: Major topics covered in the course are development of a participant's understanding and abilities as a leader, and in coaching and motivating their employees, sexual harassment issues, corporate policy, and procedure administration.

Effective Supervision II: Major topics covered in the course are development of the skills necessary to address the more complex problems facing supervisors including cost reduction, managing change, problem solving and cultural diversity issues.

Credit Recommendation: In the lower division baccalaureate/associate degree category, 3 semester hours in Principles of Supervision or as a Business elective (12/91) (10/96). **NOTE**: Students must successfully complete both Modules "I" and "II" to be eligible for the credit recommendation.

Management Development Sequence
1. Management Development I
2. Management Development II

Location: Atlantic City, NJ.

Length: *Course I*: 24 hours (3 days); *Course II*: 24 hours (3 days).

Dates: April 1990-March 1992.

Objective: To increase understanding and ability to manage the crucial aspects of the actions and interactions that take place within the organization, develop managerial judgement, and enhance skills to enable managers to effectively manage themselves and others.

Learning Outcome: Upon successful completion of this course, students will be able to identify the communication style(s) of themselves and others and choose the appropriate communications pattern for dealing with specific problems and the people involved; understand the patterns and appearances of organizational conflict, and know the options and alternatives available for dealing with conflict; understand and demonstrate appropriate procedures for handling inadequate performers while acting in a lawful manner and maintaining employee dignity and respect; understand and demonstrate appropriate management principles, and develop and apply critical thinking skills for effective decision making, and prepare for unexpected problems; understand critical management imperatives and demonstrate how to apply successful service techniques to the management of the organization; Build work teams to establish trusting, credible and cooperative internal relationships; develop and apply critical thinking skills, and successfully motivate and manage a culturally diverse workforce and identify, and stop and prevent sexual harassment.

Instruction: Major topics covered in the course are communication; conflict management; decision making; team building; and issues in the management of employees including motivation, performance, delegation, and prevention of sexual harassment. Methods of instruction include discussion, lecture, lab, simulation, collaborative learning, role playing, use of video, exercises, a paper on a job related project, and an end-of-course examination.

Credit Recommendation: In the upper division baccalaureate degree category, 3 semester hours in Organizational Behavior or Management elective (10/96). **NOTE**: Students must successfully complete both Courses 1 and 2 to be eligible for the credit recommendation.

Public Speaking: Building Delivery Skills

Location: Atlantic City, NJ.

Length: 16 hours (2 days).

Dates: August 1995-Present.

Objective: To provide the attendee with increased confidence in speaking ability and with a format for delivering concise presentations.

Learning Outcome: Upon successful completion of this course, the student will be able to develop material for a presentation in an organized method; utilize the room space effectively while presenting; use visual aids effectively; control breathing in order to strengthen vocal power; and increase confidence level while speaking in front of a group.

Instruction: Major topics covered in the course are all the elements of effective communication through the art of public speaking, posture, vocal variety, movement, and eye communication, creating a presentation in an organized, concise method. Methods of instruction include delivering extemporaneous and prepared speeches; presentations and which are video taped; and private feedback sessions.

Credit Recommendation: In the lower division baccalaureate/associate degree category, 1 semester hour in Public Speaking (10/96).

Snelling and Snelling, Inc.

Snelling University is composed of a group of highly experienced professionals who are responsible for assisting in the development of profitable Snelling personnel services franchises. Snelling and Snelling, Inc. was founded in 1951 and operates personnel services franchises in the United States and internationally.

The university's mission is to provide the knowledge and skills new and existing franchises need to run a profitable and successful business. Snelling University supports this function by offering critical sales and operational classes to train new franchise owners how to run their business. This training takes place at the state-of-the-art facility in Dallas, Texas, which includes live telephone labs, computer-based instruction, and a spectacular 50-seat amphitheater-style auditorium with a unique computer display projection system. Snelling University also offers challenging continuing education courses to further enhance the skills of franchise owners and their staff. These ongoing educational sessions concentrate on introductory and advanced sales and management training and are conducted at various meeting facilities across the United States.

Instructional design is completed at Snelling International in Dallas and involves content experts along with experienced course developers. The instructional team includes individuals who have strong platform skills and extensive experience in the personnel services profession. Most are degreed professionals.

Source of official student records: Snelling and Snelling, Inc., Suite 700, 12801 N. Central Expressway, Dallas, TX 75243, Attn: William F. Hamrick.

Additional information about the courses: College Credit Recommendation Service, American Council on Education, One Dupont Circle, Washington, DC 20036-1193.

Introduction to Sales

Location: Various locations nationwide.

Length: 71 hours (10 days).

Dates: September 1987-Present.

Objective: To enable participants to make in-person sales calls to secure new and repeat business.

Learning Outcome: Upon successful completion of this course, the student will be able to qualify prospects on the telephone and in person; uncover specific needs during sales visits; demonstrate their ability to make sales calls through role plays and actual client visits; and make outgoing telemarketing calls to make appointments for in-person calls.

Instruction: Major topics covered in the course are qualifying prospects; telemarketing; outside sales; features/benefits; closing; follow-up; and organization. Methods of instruction include role plays; written exercises; on-the-job observation by manager; and a final examination.

Credit Recommendation: In the vocational certificate category, 3 semester hours or in the lower division baccalaureate/associate degree category, 2 semester hours in Introduction to Sales or Business elective (5/91).

Managing a Personnel Service Office (Business Administration—FSC Snelling Personnel Services Training Program—Week 2)

Location: Snelling and Snelling, Snelling International, Dallas, TX.

Length: 50 hours (5.5 days).

Dates: January 1989-Present.

Objective: To train participants to successfully operate a personnel services office.

Learning Outcome: Upon successful completion of this course, the student will be able to conduct performance reviews; develop staff; manage the financial aspects of the business; and design appropriate business and marketing plans.

Instruction: Major topics covered in the course are hiring and selection of staff; communication and leadership styles; performance reviews; accounting for small business: break-even, financials, pricing structure; business and marketing planning; training staff; career pathing; performance problems; and compensation. Methods of instruction include questions and answer review sessions; role play; small group activities; case studies; and final exam.

Credit Recommendation: In the lower division baccalaureate/associate degree category, 3 semester hours in Personnel Services Office Management or Business elective; or in the upper division baccalaureate degree category, 2 semester hours in Personnel Management (5/91).

Marketing Personnel Services (Marketing—FSC Snelling Personnel Services Training Program—Week 1)

Location: Snelling and Snelling, Snelling International, Dallas, TX.

Length: 49.75 hours (5 days).

Dates: January 1989-Present.

Objective: To apply the placement and assignment process by making outgoing telemarketing calls, securing job and assignment orders, interviewing candidates, and placing the candidate with the appropriate job/assignment.

Learning Outcome: Upon successful completion of this course, the student will be able to make telemarketing calls to secure job orders; qualify clients; prepare an applicant for an interview; overcome objections raised by clients during a sales presentation; and gain information to match the applicant with the appropriate job opening.

Instruction: Major topics covered in the course are telemarketing; sales; features/benefits; taking orders; classified advertising; direct mail; interviewing; closing techniques; outside sales; territory management; account penetration; and account development. Methods of instruction include question and answer reviews; role play; small group activities; case studies; jeopardy/game problem-solving activity; live and semi-live phone labs; and final exam.

Credit Recommendation: In the lower division baccalaureate/associate degree category, 3 semester hours in Marketing Personnel Services or Business elective (5/91).

Sales Techniques (Principles of Salesmanship: Video Course)

Location: Various locations nationwide.

Length: 15.5 hours.

Dates: January 1991-Present.

Objective: To teach participants how to write classified ads to attract applicants, set goals, stay organized, and increase sales.

Learning Outcome: Upon successful completion of this course, the student will be able to write classified ads effectively; list techniques used to uncover client's needs; make a recruiting action call; and set goals.

Instruction: Major topics covered in the course are key components of marketing; desk organization; classified advertising; telemarketing calls; advanced sales techniques; and goal setting. Methods of instruction include written exercises—answer to instructor-led discussions.

Credit Recommendation: In the vocational certificate category, 1 semester hour in Sales Techniques or Business elective (5/91).

Supervisory Management (Sales Management)

Location: Various locations nationwide.

Length: 24 hours (3 days).

Dates: February 1990-Present.

Objective: To teach managers how to supervise employees; improve employee performance; and improve marketing techniques.

Learning Outcome: Upon successful completion of this course, the student will be able to employ effective communication techniques; reinforce and motivate employees; assist employees in goal setting; review performances for employees; recognize the vital signs for a successful operation; and utilize various methods of marketing the business.

Instruction: Major topics covered in the course are Sales Management: communication skills; active listening; focusing on behavior and giving specific advice; reinforcement/motivational techniques; goal setting; reviewing a sales call made by an employee; and weekly sales performance review. Marketing Your Business: analyzing the performance of the business; performance reviews with employees; market research; methods of marketing; and marketing calendars. Methods of instruction include written exercises; role plays; instructor observation; case studies; and small group activities.

Credit Recommendation: In the upper division baccalaureate degree category, 1 semester hour in Supervision, Supervisory Management, or Business elective (5/91).

Telemarketing (Advanced Marketing Theory)

Location: Dallas, TX, and nationwide.

Length: 24 hours (3 days).

Dates: May 1990-Present.

Objective: To teach participants how to write telemarketing scripts to gain job orders and names of qualified applicants, and, to research the marketplace, target accounts, develop customer relationships, and gain new business from existing clients.

Learning Outcome: Upon successful completion of this course, the student will be able to write telemarketing scripts; obtain prospects through telemarketing; qualify accounts; develop customer relationships; and gain new business from existing clients.

Instruction: Major topics covered in the course are Prospecting and Telemarketing Segment: types of telemarketing calls; prospecting sources; benefits; telemarketing scripts; objection handling; and goal setting. Recruiting: advantages to recruiting; recruiting telemarketing calls; new ideas for recruiting; and direct and indirect recruiting. Account Development: developing repeat business; researching the marketplace; account usage levels; problems: solving/customer service; and follow-up. Methods of instruction include role-plays; case studies/group problem solving; and instructor-led question/answer session.

Credit Recommendation: In the lower division baccalaureate/associate degree category, 1 semester hour in Telemarketing or Business elective (5/91).

Telemarketing: Field Course (Introduction to Marketing-Field Course)

Location: Various locations nationwide.

Length: 69.5 hours (10 days).

Dates: October 1988-Present.

Objective: To train participants to telemarket effectively to uncover job openings and gain new business.

Learning Outcome: Upon successful completion of this course, the student will be able to interview, match, and orient applicants and temporaries to prepare them for permanent placement or temporary assignments, and to close the applicant and employer on interviews and placements.

Instruction: Major topics covered in the course are writing telemarketing scripts; taking thorough job/assignment orders; interviewing; features/benefits; closing the sale; and reference checking. Methods of instruction include role plays; written exercises; on-the-job observation by manager; and final examination.

Credit Recommendation: In the vocational certificate category, 3 semester hours or in the lower division baccalaureate/associate degree category, 2 semester hours in Telemarketing or Business elective (5/91).

Society For Human Resource Management

The Society for Human Resource Management (SHRM) is the leading voice of the human resource profession, representing the interests of more than 85,000 professional and student members from around the world. SHRM provides its membership with education and information services, conferences and seminars, government and media representation, and publications that equip human resource professionals for their roles as leaders and decision makers within their organizations. The Society is a founding member and Secretariat of the World Federation of Personnel Management Associations (WFPMA) which links human resource associations in 55 nations.

Source of official student records: Registry of Credit Recommendations, American Council on Education, One Dupont Circle, Washington, DC 20036-1193.

Additional information about the courses: College Credit Recommendation Service, American Council on Education, One Dupont Circle, Washington, DC 20036-1193.

Overview of Human Resource Management SHRM Learning System

Location: Various sites in the United States.

Length: 30 hours (10 weeks).

Dates: January 1996-Present.

Objective: To provide knowledge of the major human resource management functions needed to be an effective human resource professional.

Learning Outcome: Upon successful completion of this course, the student will be able to describe human resource management planning and practices, including recruitment, selection, and placement of employees; understand techniques of analyzing training needs and selecting appropriate training methods; understand various aspects of labor relations, including due process and critical employee relations practices; and identify requirements for total compensation, strategies and methods of job evaluation.

Instruction: Major topics covered in the course are management practices; selection and placement; training and development; compensation and benefits; employee and labor relations; and health, safety and security. Methods of instruction include lecture, discussion, classroom exercises, case studies, audio-visual material, module tests, and final examination.

Credit Recommendation: In the upper division baccalaureate degree category, 3 semester hours in Human Resource Development, Management, or Business Administration (1/96).

Overview of Human Resource Management The SHRM Learning System

Location: Independent Study.

Length: Self-paced learning, six modules (est. 50-60 hours).

Dates: January 1996-Present.

Objective: To provide knowledge of the major human resource management function needed to be an effective human resource professional.

Learning Outcome: Upon successful completion of this course, the student will be able to describe human resource management planning and practices, including recruitment, selection, and placement of employees; understand techniques of analyzing training needs and selecting appropriate training methods; understand various aspects of labor relations, including due process and critical employee relations practices; identify requirements for total compensation, strategies and methods of job evaluation.

Instruction: Major topics covered in the course are management practices; selection and placement; training and development; compensation and benefits; employee and labor relations; and health, safety and security. Methods of instruction include computer-assisted pretest and final examination.

Credit Recommendation: In the upper division baccalaureate degree category, 3 semester hours in Human Resource Development, Management, or Business Administration (1/96).

Strategic Human Resource Management Series

Employee Relations: Managing Employees in a Dynamic Work Environment

Location: Various sites in the United States.

Length: 26 hours (9 weeks).

Dates: January 1996-Present.

Objective: To provide knowledge of employee relations trends and skills in adopting and incorporating these practices to address these trends.

Learning Outcome: Upon successful completion of this course, the student will be able to describe changes affecting the workplace and in the workforce; demonstrate sensitivity to gender issues that occur in the workplace; apply performance appraisal systems in identifying and addressing performance problems; identify workplace diversity issues and strategies to enhance workplace experiences; identify alternative dispute resolution techniques and their benefits; understand and apply appropriate employee involvement techniques; and identify potential sources of risk and approaches to minimize/eliminate risk; and identify strategies for improving work/life balance.

Instruction: Major topics covered in the course are diversity in the workplace; management and worker relations; reducing risk at work; resolving workplace disputes; and managing work/life issues. Methods of instruction include lecture, discussion, classroom exercises, audio-visual material, learning outcome assessment by instructor observation, and final examination.

Credit Recommendation: In the upper division baccalaureate degree category, or graduate degree category, 2 semester hours in Human Resource Management, Management, Organizational Behavior, Organizational Development, or Business Administration (1/96).

Management Practices: The Strategic Management of Human Resources

Location: Various sites in the United States.

Length: 26 hours (9 weeks).

Dates: January 1996-Present.

Objective: To provide knowledge of and skills for applying contemporary management practices.

Learning Outcome: Upon successful completion of this course, the student will be able to recognize how strategic HRM and systems thinking can facilitate organizational change; identify core elements of an organizational strategy that effectively support values and ethics; identify approaches for the successful implementation of change; understand the role of HRM in a reengineering effort; identify alternative organizational design structures; identify quality indicators and the approaches to achieving quality; identify technologies that meet HR needs; and recognize how HR leaders can help achieve competitive success.

Instruction: Major topics covered in the course are human resource's strategic role in an organization; redirecting organizational values and ethics; organizational transformation; re-evolutionizing work; and organizational design. Methods of instruction include lecture, discussion, classroom exercises, case studies, audio-visual material, learning outcome assessment by instructor observation, and final examination.

Credit Recommendation: In the upper division baccalaureate degree category, or in the graduate degree category, 2 semester hours in Human Resource Management, Management, Organizational Behavior, Organizational Development, or Business Administration (1/96).

Software Technology Group

Software Technology Group (STG) founded in 1993 with a mission-to provide world class consulting, training, and integration services to Corporate Clients worldwide. STG's courses cater to the needs of both practicing and aspiring professionals. STG has trained over 10,000 satisfied participants worldwide, in 1996.

STG's training-full time and part time - is delivered through course material developed in-house. The courseware developed in-house is continually updated based on instructor/participant feedback and software release updates. Currently we offer public and private courses on Oracle 7.1 and Developer 2000, Unix and 'C', OOP and C++, Structured System Analysis and Design (SSAD), Analysis and Design of Client/Server Programming, PowerBuilder 4.0 etc.

STG's classroom instruction is heavily lab oriented with one personal computer per participant i.e., each participant has a computer available all of the time. Our courses are offered in San Jose, California, and New Delhi, Bangalore, Chennai, Calcutta and Hyderabad in India.

Source of official student records: Registry of Credit Recommendations, American Council on Education, One Dupont Circle, Washington, DC 20036-1193.

Additional information about the courses: College Credit Recommendation Service, American Council on Education, One Dupont Circle, Washington, DC 20036-1193.

Excel Program

Client/Server Computing: Overview, Analysis, and Design

Location: San Jose, CA and multiple locations in Asia.

Length: 36 hours (5 weeks; three 2.5 hour meetings per week).

Dates: January 1994-Present.

Objective: To provide an understanding of client/server architecture and an overview of system analysis and design technologies.

Learning Outcome: Upon successful completion of this course, the student will be able to understand client/server technology and the current system analysis and design methodologies.

Instruction: Major topics covered in the course are an introduction to client/server and distributed data processing, introduction to networking, client/server architecture and application development, graphical user interface, analysis and design of client/server systems, data modeling, process modeling, process design, and transaction design. Methods of instruction include lecture, audio/visual material, discussion, computer-assisted instruction, classroom exercises, learner presentations/reports, tests, a weekly teacher/student conference, and final examination.

Credit Recommendation: In the vocational certificate category or in the lower division baccalaureate/associate degree category, 2 semester hours in Information Systems (1/97).

Data Communication and Networking

Location: San Jose CA, and multiple locations in Asia.

Length: 36 hours (5 weeks; three 2.5 hour meetings per week).

Dates: January 1994-Present.

Objective: To provide the student with an overview and understanding of computers and the networks which attach them and to understand how various networks function.

Learning Outcome: Upon successful completion of this course, the student will be able to understand the various types of networks, the functionality of networks, and the service they provide.

Instruction: Major topics covered in the course are network type, transmission media, topologies, network service, OSI function and layers, and network servers. Methods of instruction include lecture, audio/visual material, discussion, computer-assisted instruction, classroom exercises, learner presentations/reports, quizzes, observations, tests, reports, papers, a lab project, and final examination.

Credit Recommendation: In the vocational certificate category or the lower division baccalaureate/associate degree category, 2 semester hours in Information Systems (1/97).

Database Administration in Oracle

Location: San Jose, CA and multiple locations in Asia.

Length: 30 hours (4 weeks; three 2.5 hour meetings per week).

Dates: January 1994-Present.

Objective: To prepare professionals to understand Oracle7 Database Administration and to perform some typical DBA tasks.

Learning Outcome: Upon successful completion of this course, the student will be able to perform Oracle7 startup and shutdown and Oracle7 application tuning; secure backup/recovery; coordinate Oracle7 DBA management and control; and create an Oracle7 database.

Instruction: Major topics covered in the course are Oracle architecture, managing rollback segment, database startup and shutdown, DB creation procedure, application tuning, backup and recovery, managing users, database privileges and auditing, and SQL*NET. Methods of instruction include lecture, audio/visual material, discussion, computer-assisted instruction, classroom exercises, learner presentations/reports, computer lab exercises, tests, a weekly teacher/student conference, and final examination.

Credit Recommendation: In the vocational certificate category or in the lower division baccalaureate/associate degree category, 2 semester hours in Information Systems (1/97).

Design of RDBMS Systems Using Oracle Forms and Report Tools

Location: San Jose and multiple locations in Asia.

Length: 35 hours (5 weeks; three 2.5 hour meetings per week).

Dates: January 1994-Present.

Objective: To train professionals to use Oracle Developer/2000, Oracle Forms Version 4.5, and Reports 2.5.

Learning Outcome: Upon successful completion of this course, the student will be able to implement forms, menus, and reports using Oracle Developer/2000.

Instruction: Major topics covered in the course are Oracle Forms 4.5 and Oracle Reports 2.5. Methods of instruction include lecture, audio/visual material, discussion, computer-assisted instruction, classroom exercises, learner presentations/reports, computer lab exercises, quizzes, observations, tests, reports, papers, weekly teacher/student conferences, and final examination.

Credit Recommendation: In the vocational certificate category or the lower division baccalaureate/associate degree category, 2 semester hours in Information Systems (1/97).

Object Oriented Programming and C++

Location: San Jose and multiple locations in Asia.

Length: 35 hours (9 weeks; three 2.5 hour meetings per week).

Dates: January 1994-Present.

Objective: To introduce the student to Object-Oriented Programming (OOP) using the C++ programming language.

Learning Outcome: Upon successful completion of this course, the student will be able to write simple programs in C++ and have a general overview of the Object-Oriented methodology.

Instruction: Major topics covered in the course are C++ language basics, control structures, functions, references, classes and objects, overloading, inheritance, polymorphism, type conversions, input/output streams, templates, exception handling, and object-oriented design. Methods of instruction include lecture, classroom exercises, tests, a lab project, and final examination.

Credit Recommendation: In the vocational certificate category or the lower division baccalaureate/associate degree category, 2 semester hours in Information Systems (1/97).

Principles of RDBMS and Application Development in Oracle

Location: San Jose and multiple locations in Asia.

Length: 35 hours (5 weeks; three 2.5 hour meetings per week).

Dates: January 1994-Present.

Objective: To prepare professionals in the fundamentals of DBMS, provide an understanding of RDBMS and concepts of client/server technology, and to deliver an overview of Oracle7, SQL concepts, PL/SQL concepts, and Oracle7 architecture and administration.

Learning Outcome: Upon successful completion of this course, the student will be able to use SQL, SQL*PLUS, PL/SQL, and SQL*Loader in small applications; prototype a RDBMS in Oracle; and understand Oracle7 architecture and administration.

Instruction: Major topics covered in the course are an introduction to RDBMS and client/server technology, SQL, SQL*PLUS, PL/SQL, and ORACLE7 utilities. Methods of instruction include lecture, audio/visual material, discussion, computer-assisted instruction, classroom exercises, learner presentations/reports, computer lab exercises, tests, reports, papers, weekly teacher/student conferences, and final examination.

Credit Recommendation: In the vocational certificate category or the lower division baccalaureate/associate degree category, 2 semester hours in Information Systems (1/97).

Programming in "C"

Location: San Jose, CA and multiple locations in Asia.

Length: 35 hours (5 weeks, three 2.5 hour meetings per week).

Dates: January 1994-Present.

Objective: To instruct the student on the basics of the "C" programming language, including an overview of the "C" language.

Learning Outcome: Upon successful completion of this course, the student will be able to write simple programs in the "C" language; and have a general overview of more complicated aspects of the language, such as multidimensional arrays, linked lists, and pointers.

Instruction: Major topics covered in the course are types, constant, operators, control structures, functions, arrays, files, structures, pointers, bitwise operators, and linked lists. Methods of instruction include lecture, audio/visual material, discussion, computer-assisted instruction, classroom exercises, learner presentations/reports, case studies, tests, lab work, and final examination.

Credit Recommendation: In the vocational certificate category or the lower division baccalaureate/associate degree category, 2 semester hours in Information Systems (1/97).

Structured Systems Analysis and Design

Location: San Jose, CA and multiple locations in Asia.

Length: 42 hours (6 weeks; three 2.5 hour meetings per week).

Dates: January 1994-Present.

Objective: To prepare entry level professionals to conduct systems analysis using structured techniques.

Learning Outcome: Upon successful completion of this course, the student will be able to use techniques like data flow diagrams, data modeling, normalization, process design, structure charts, program coding techniques, and overview of the system development life cycle.

Instruction: Major topics covered in the course are system development life cycle, data flow diagrams, data modeling, normalization, process modeling, structure charts, program coding techniques, and module testing. Methods of instruction include lecture, audio/visual material, discussion, computer-assisted instruction, classroom exercises, learner presentations/reports, computer lab assignments, quizzes, observations, tests, weekly teacher/student conferences, and final examination.

Credit Recommendation: In the vocational certificate category or the lower division baccalaureate/associate degree category, 2 semester hours in Information Systems (1/97).

UNIX Operating System

Location: San Jose and multiple locations in Asia.

Length: 35 hours (5 weeks; three 2.5 hour meetings per week).

Dates: January 1994-Present.

Objective: To teach students how to become a productive user of the UNIX operating system.

Learning Outcome: Upon successful completion of this course, the student will be able to effectively use the UNIX environment to manage their files and directories; and write simple shell scripts.

Instruction: Major topics covered in the course are introductory commands, files and directories, file manipulations, redirection and filters, visual editor, introduction to processes, and introduction to shell programming. Methods of instruction include lecture, audio/visual material, classroom exercises, learner presentations/reports, tests, and final examination.

Credit Recommendation: In the vocational certificate category or the lower division baccalaureate/associate degree category, 1 semester hour in Information Systems (1/97).

Windows Programming Using MFC

Location: San Jose, CA and multiple locations in Asia.

Length: 35 hours (5 weeks; three 2.5 hour meetings per week).

Dates: January 1994-Present.

Objective: To provide an overview to Windows programming using MFC.

Learning Outcome: Upon successful completion of this course, the student will be able to perform simple Windows programming using MFC and understand Open Database Connectivity (ODBC).

Instruction: Major topics covered in the course are Windows fundamentals and architecture, MFC fundamentals and architecture, fonts, dialog boxes, menus, toolbars, serialization, printing, database, and management with Microsoft ODBC. Methods of instruction include lecture, audio/visual material, classroom exercises, learner presentations/reports, tests, UB assignments, and final examination.

Credit Recommendation: In the vocational certificate category or in the lower division baccalaureate/associate degree category, 2 semester hours in Information Systems (1/97).

Somerset School of Massage Therapy

Somerset School of Massage Therapy (SSMT) began offering courses in massage therapy and related subjects in 1987. Approved by the New Jersey Department of Education for post-secondary vocational training in 1991, SSMT quickly became the leader in massage therapy education in New Jersey. The program received accreditation in 1993 from COMTA (Commission on Massage Therapy Accreditation). SSMT remains on the leading edge of the fastest growing health care profession of the 1990's.

The Somerset School of Massage Therapy exists in order to provide the highest quality education in the field of massage therapy. Our mission is to graduate massage therapists who can be therapeutic as well as nurturing, who can be anatomically specific as well as intuitive, and to provide the business skills necessary for success in today's job market.

SSMT offers a 564 hour training program in various forms of therapeutic massage, anatomy and physiology, and business and professional ethics. In addition, electives in Shiatsu and Advanced Myofascial Massage Therapy are also offered. The School employs two curriculum writers who work continuously to update and revise the curriculum. Revisions are based on current research in the profession and anatomy and physiology, and feedback from faculty and students.

Our student body is comprised primarily of career-changing individuals. While massage therapy has traditionally attracted the female population, we now have a male student population of 30%. The average student age is 30.

The full massage therapy vocational training program is offered five times yearly: three part-time programs (one year in length), and two full-time programs (six months in length). Shiatsu and Advanced Myofascial Massage Therapy are offered once per year. All courses are held at the School's facility in central New Jersey.

Source of official student records: Registry of Credit Recommendations, American Council on Education, One Dupont Circle, Washington, DC 20036-1193.

Additional information about the courses: Office of Corporate Higher-Education Programs, Thomas Edison State College, 101 West State Street, Trenton, New Jersey 08608-1176.

Advanced Myofascial Massage Therapy

Location: Somerset, NJ.

Length: 38 hours (two 3-day weekends).

Dates: September 1994-Present.

Objective: To instruct the student in advanced myofascial massage strategies and skills and to provide an understanding of fascia and its role in postural distortion.

Learning Outcome: Upon successful completion of this course, the student will be able to perform segmental and full body postural analysis, have a working clinical understanding of fascia, demonstrate competency in the application of myofascial massage therapy, and demonstrate self-care methods.

Instruction: Major topics covered in the course are structural analysis and postural assessment, myofascial anatomy and physiology, body psychology, massage therapy boundaries and safety issues, the biomechanical aspects of strain, and comparative review of deep tissue approaches. Methods of instruction include lecture, discussion, overhead projections, demonstrations, and hands-on practice with a partner. Students are evaluated by clinical applications, a take home test, and an in-class hands-on evaluation for certification.

Credit Recommendation: In the lower division baccalaureate/associate degree category, 1 semester hour in Myofascial Massage Therapy (11/97).

Anatomy, Physiology and Pathology I (AP101)

Location: Somerset, NJ.

Length: 83 hours.

Dates: January 1994-Present.

Objective: To instruct the student in a detailed study of musculo/skeletal anatomy, physiology, and pathology.

Learning Outcome: Upon successful completion of this course, the student will be able to understand and use basic anatomical terminology; name, identify, and palpate the bones of the body including major processes; identify different types of joints and their movements; have a working understanding of the muscular system including palpatory skills; and understand basic pathologies of the skeletal and muscular systems.

Instruction: Major topics covered in the course are introduction to anatomy and physiology, basic anatomical terminology, study of the anatomy, physiology, and pathology of the skeletal and muscular systems. Methods of instruction include lecture, discussion, overhead projections, lab work (building muscles with clay on miniature skeletons), and palpatory anatomy. Students are evaluated through written examinations.

Credit Recommendation: In the lower division baccalaureate/associate degree category, 4 semester hours in Human Biology when taken with Course AP201 Anatomy, Physiology and Pathology II (11/97).

Anatomy, Physiology and Pathology II (AP201)

Location: Somerset, NJ.

Length: 29 hours.

Dates: January 1994-Present.

Objective: To instruct the student in the nervous and circulatory systems as they relate to massage therapy, as well as provide and overview of the respiratory, digestive, and endocrine systems.

Learning Outcome: Upon successful completion of this course, the student will be able to understand the structure and function of the nervous and circulatory systems and associated pathologies, understand the physiology of the nervous system and how it works with the muscular system to produce movement and sensation, and know the general overview of the structure and function of the respiratory, digestive, and endocrine systems.

Instruction: Major topics covered in the course are a study of the nervous system, including the central and peripheral nervous systems, the reflex arc, the stretch reflex and golgi tendon organ. Study of the circulatory system includes blood, vessels, and blood pressure, the structure and function of the heart, and diseases associated with the system. Structure and function of the respiratory, digestive, and endocrine systems are also discussed. Methods of instruction include lecture, discussion, and overhead projections. Students are evaluated through written examinations.

Credit Recommendation: In the lower division baccalaureate/associate degree category, 4 semester hours in Human Biology when taken with Course AP101 Anatomy, Physiology and Pathology I (11/97).

Myofascial and Deep Tissue Techniques (MT201)

Location: Somerset, NJ.

Length: 46 hours.

Dates: January 1994-Present.

Objective: To teach the student gentle, yet specific ways to treat myofasical pain by working beyond superficial layers of tissue.

Learning Outcome: Upon successful completion of this course, the student will be able to understand fascia and its role in pain and postural distortion, perform a full body postural analysis and develop treatment plans, perform myofascial stretches and deep tissue massage on the neck, back, and limbs.

Instruction: Major topics covered in the course are detailed study of postural distortions, proper body mechanics for the therapist facilitating ease of movement, subjective and objective assessment skills, and a system of stretches and deep tissue techniques. Methods of instruction include lecture, discussion, overhead projection, demonstrations, and hands-on practice with a partner. Students are evaluated through written clinical applications and practical examinations.

Credit Recommendation: In the lower division baccalaureate/associate degree category, 5 semester hours in Theory and Practice of Massage Therapy and related modalities when taken with Courses MT101 Therapeutic Massage and Related Modalities; and MT202/OC201 Sports Massage, Hydrotherapy, CPR and First Aid (11/97).

Neuromuscular Therapy/Anatomy (AP301/MT301)

Location: Somerset, NJ.

Length: 94 hours (3 full weekends plus 6 four-hour classes).

Dates: September 1995-Present.

Objective: To teach the student how to work with chronic myofascial pain, how to assess and treat specific muscles and tendons, and how to address and reduce the causal factors contributing to chronic pain.

Learning Outcome: Upon successful completion of this course, the student will be able to understand myofascial trigger points and pain referral points, understand and treat chronic myofascial pain, identify and treat bellies and attachments of specific muscles, identify stressors and perpetuating factors contributing to chronic pain, understand corrective actions to relieve chronic pain, and perform self care techniques for TMJ.

Instruction: Major topics covered in the course are detailed study of the neuromuscular system including trigger points, pain referral patterns, assessment and treatment of muscle, tendon, and periosteal attachments, and addressing and reducing the causal factors contributing to chronic pain. Methods of instruction include lecture, discussion, overhead projections and slides, hands-on demonstrations with the aid of live video, and hands-on practice with a partner. Students are evaluated by written and practical examinations.

Credit Recommendation: In the lower division baccalaureate/associate degree category, 3 semester hours in Applied Neuromuscular Therapy & Anatomy (11/97).

Shiatsu

Location: Somerset, NJ.

Length: 105-120 hours (24 weeks/ plus two weekends).

Dates: September 1995-Present.

Objective: To teach the student the theory and philosophy of Shiatsu (oriental massage), as well as techniques for manually stimulating the acupuncture points of the body.

Learning Outcome: Upon successful completion of this course, the student will be able to know the acupuncture "map" of the surface of the body, feel an acupoint from the perspective of both the giver and receiver of the technique, use pressure and stretching to treat the acupoints of the body, use assessment techniques to ensure that appropriate areas of the body are treated, and understand introductory Traditional Chinese/Japanese Medicine.

Instruction: Major topics covered in the course are Chinese/Japanese medical theory, meridian and point location, five phase theory, and oriental evaluation. Methods of instruction include lecture, discussion, demonstrations and hands-on practice with a partner. Students are evaluated by written and practical examinations and at home self-evaluations.

Credit Recommendation: In the lower division baccalaureate/associate degree category, 3 semester hours in Theory and Practice of Shiatsu (11/97).

Sports Massage, Hydrotherapy, CPR, First Aid (MT202/OC201)

Location: Somerset, NJ.

Length: 48 hours.

Dates: January 1994-Present.

Objective: To teach the student pre- and post-event sports massage, active/assisted and self-care stretching, Adult CPR and First Aid, and the therapeutic use of ice and moist heat.

Learning Outcome: Upon successful completion of this course, the student will be able to perform pre- and post-event massage and know contraindications for same, understand the physiology of stretching, perform self-care and active/assisted stretches, know how and when to use ice and moist heat, and perform Adult CPR and First Aid.

Instruction: Major topics covered in the course are a detailed study of the physiology and benefits of stretching, working with a variety of athletes at sports events, clinical applications of sports massage, hydrotherapy, Adult CPR and First Aid. Methods of instruction include lecture, discussion, demonstrations and hands-on experience with a partner. Students are evaluated by written and practical examinations.

Credit Recommendation: In the lower division baccalaureate/associate degree category, 5 semester hours in Theory and Practice of Massage Therapy and related modalities when taken with Courses MT101 Therapeutic Massage and Related Modalities; and MT201 Myofascial and Deep Tissue Techniques (11/97).

Student Client Internship (MT102)

Location: Somerset, NJ.

Length: 100 hours (25 weeks/ part-time; 125 weeks/ full-time).

Dates: November 1997-Present.

Objective: To teach the student how to set up and operate a private practice in massage therapy.

Learning Outcome: Upon successful completion of this course, the student will be able to keep an appointment book, schedule appointments, track cancellations, and handle payments; keep client files including intake forms, SOAP charts, and records of appointments; know the appropriate therapy to administer on a client and when to refer to another health care professional; have developed sophisticated public relation and telephone skills necessary for running a small business; and use and understand universal precautions in treating all clients.

Instruction: Major topics covered in the course are performing massage on the public and other students, client history and SOAP charting, helping in the office and running the front desk, setting up and cleaning rooms, and participating in round table discussions. Methods of instruction include the clinic director or supervisor giving the student direction during each clinic shift based on the client load for that day. The director can observe the massage and is available for advice and support throughout the internship. Staff-supervised off-site events can also be added to the internship when available. The student keeps a log book of experiences which is evaluated by the clinic director. In addition, clients have the opportunity to fill out feedback sheets after their massages.

Credit Recommendation: In the lower division baccalaureate/associate degree

category, 1 semester hour in Student Internship in Massage Therapy (11/97).

Therapeutic Massage & Related Modalities (MT101)

Location: Somerset, NJ.

Length: 164 hours.

Dates: January 1994-Present.

Objective: To teach the student therapeutic Swedish massage, on-site massage, prenatal massage, and foot reflexology, with emphasis on professional ethics, body mechanics, and business management skills.

Learning Outcome: Upon successful completion of this course, the student will be able to use proper body mechanics, universal precautions, and professional ethics in performing: a one-hour therapeutic Swedish Massage, a fifteen minute on-site massage, a prenatal massage, and a thirty minute foot reflexology session; and know the basics for setting up a massage practice.

Instruction: Major topics covered in the course are benefits and contraindications, and history of massage therapy, therapeutic Swedish massage, on-site massage, prenatal massage, foot reflexology, HIV/AIDS awareness, business management and professional ethics, and Tai Chi. Methods of instruction include lecture, discussion, overhead projection, demonstrations and hands-on practice with a partner. Students are evaluated by written and practical examinations.

Credit Recommendation: In the lower division baccalaureate/associate degree category, 5 semester hours in Theory and Practice of Massage Therapy and related modalities when taken with Courses MT201 Myofascial and Deep Tissue Techniques and Course MT202/OC201 Sports Massage, Hydrotherapy, CPR, First Aid (11/97).

St. Louis Police Academy

The St. Louis Police Academy, a part of the St. Louis Metropolitan Police Department, was established in 1869 as the nation's first formalized police recruit training program. In 1947 it was reorganized and patterned after the FBI National Academy. In addition to classes attended by police recruits, the Academy provides in-service classes for continuing education and seminars and training in various law enforcement topics to interested police agencies.

Instructors are commissioned officers or other experts in their field who are able to provide the highest quality training. Courses are conducted at the Police Academy. Subjects include: law, firearms, criminal investigation, patrol, and defensive tactics.

Source of official student records: Registry of Credit Recommendations, American Council on Education, One Dupont Circle, Washington, DC 20036-1193.

Additional information about the courses: College Credit Recommendation Service, American Council on Education, One Dupont Circle, Washington, DC 20036-1193.

Basic Police Recruit Training

Location: St. Louis Police Academy, St. Louis, Missouri.

Length: *Version 1:* 648 hours (16.5 weeks); *Version 2:* 880 hours (22 weeks).

Dates: *Version 1:* January 1987-October 1995; *Version 2:* September 1995-Present.

Objective: *Versions 1 and 2:* To provide the students with the skills and knowledge necessary to serve effectively at the entry level for a police officer.

Learning Outcome: *Versions 1 and 2:* Upon successful completion of this course, the student will be able to perform all routine police duties at the entry level.

Instruction: *Versions 1 and 2: Part I:* Major topics covered in the course are Behavioral Studies. These courses provide the student with a basic knowledge necessary to deal with people in a culturally diverse community. *Part II:* Major topics covered in the course are legal studies and fundamental knowledge of substantive and procedural criminal and constitutional law necessary to perform police functions in accordance with municipal, state, and federal laws. *Part III:* Major topics covered in the course are skill development, defensive tactics, firearms, drivers training, physical training, and role playing. *Part IV:* Major topics covered in the course are supplemental programs and community oriented policing. *Part V:* Major topics covered in the course are technical studies, extensive training in investigative methods and techniques, first aid, CPR, juvenile procedures, patrol procedures, traffic control functions, and domestic violence investigations. Methods of instruction include lectures, practical demonstrations, role playing, and proficiency and written examinations.

Credit Recommendation: *Versions 1 and 2:* Part I: In the lower division baccalaureate/associate degree category, 3 semester hours in Human Relations. *Part II:* In the lower division baccalaureate/associate degree category, 3 semester hours in Arrest, Search, and Seizure and 3 semester hours in Criminal Law. *Part III:* In the lower division baccalaureate/associate degree category, 3 semester hours in Physical Education. *Part V:* In the lower division baccalaureate/associate category, 4 semester hours in Criminal Investigation, 3 semester hours in First Aid, 2 semester hours in Police Report Writing, 3 semester hours in Traffic Law and Investigation, and 3 semester hours in Patrol Procedures (9/95).

Stonier Graduate School of Banking

The mission of the American Bankers Association is to enhance the ability of America's banks and bankers to serve the needs and desires of the American public. With more than 1,000 bankers who volunteer their time on councils and committees, and a national staff of about 400, ABA serves this mission through activities in government relations, communications, education, and other activities targeted to the specific needs of banks.

The Professional and Development Council, made up of senior-level bankers from around the country, guides the work of the Bank Programs and Professional Development (BP&PD) group within ABA. The Bank Programs and Professional Development group's missions include banker education, research, evaluation, and program development.

The BP&PD Group studies new developments in banking that will affect bank employees and analyzes the educational resources banks currently use. This analysis identifies future opportunities for training and development.

The Bank Programs and Professional Development Group also evaluates ABA's ongoing banking education program with the goal of pinpointing strengths and weaknesses and providing better coordination of existing programs. Based on this evaluation, BP&PD develops new educational materials and revises programs where needed.

The BP&PD Group is responsible for a variety of educational programs. These include 15 national schools which serve some 3,000 mid- and senior-level bankers each year. These schools range in duration from one to six weeks. BP&PD also sponsors BankSim, a computer-based bank management training tool.

One of the largest adult education programs in the world, the American Institute of Banking (AIB), is also part of BP&PD. Over 250,000 students take courses each year through 600 local AIB chapters.

ABA's concern for education extends to the general public as well. The Education Foundation, operated by ABA, helps the American public understand the economic system through the Personal Economics Program (PEP). Effort is directed as well toward the development of materials in the area of economic education.

The Stonier Graduate School of Banking is the largest single program offered by ABA. General policies and direction are set by the Stonier Advisory Board under the overall review of the Professional Development Council described above. The Stonier Advisory Board is made up of 12 to 15 senior bankers and one or more academic advisors. The board members include Stonier faculty members, human resource and development specialists from user banks, and line bank executives. The board is responsible for setting general policies and direction for the Stonier Graduate School of Banking.

The director of the Stonier Graduate School of Banking is the director of the Programs and Products group within the BP&PD Group. Staff support for the program is provided by seven individuals, all of whom are employees of the BP&PD Group and who work on Stonier as well as on other educational programs.

Source of official student records: Stonier Graduate School of Banking, American Bankers Association, 1120 Connecticut Avenue, N.W., Washington, DC 20036

Additional information about the courses: College Credit Recommendation Service, American Council on Education, One Dupont Circle, Washington, DC 20036-1193.

Business Policy

Location: University of Delaware—Newark, DE.

Length: 37.5 hours; 22 hours independent study.

Dates: June 1988-April 1995.

Objective: To provide skills in formulating decision and developing strategies for managing a financial institution in a competitive environment.

Learning Outcome: Upon successful completion of this course, the student will be able to analyze complex situations and make policy decision which will affect the future of an organization; work effectively with other members of senior management in setting and achieving goals; and understand the importance of effective leadership and planning in a dynamic environment.

Instruction: Major topics covered in the course are business policy, leadership, asset and liability management, cost control, loan pricing, and business ethics. Methods of instruction include bank simulation exercises, class lecture, and discussion.

Credit Recommendation: In the upper division baccalaureate or in the graduate degree category, 3 semester hours in Management or Business Policy (4/90).

NOTE: The entire three-year program must be completed to receive credit.

Directed Studies/Thesis

Location: University of Delaware—Newark, DE.

Length: 150 hours of independent study.

Dates: June 1988-April 1995.

Objective: To provide the student with the skills needed to conduct and present original research.

Learning Outcome: Upon successful completion of this course, the student will be able to analyze a business problem or development or public policy issue; locate and effectively use all sources of information related to this topic; courses of action; evaluate the effect on that situation of various courses of action based on some specified criteria; and communicate all of this effectively in a written report.

Instruction: Between their second and third years, participants complete a thesis or a strategic leadership project.

Participants writing a thesis select a topic of importance to the banking industry. The thesis must make a significant contribution to the existing body of knowledge and must be supported by extensive research. Participants must successfully defend their thesis in front of a board of three thesis examiners.

The strategic leadership project is designed to provide participants an opportunity to solve a problem their bank is facing or to exploit some opportunity. The student develops and presents a solution to the problem as well as a plan for implementing their solution, which is detailed in a written report. They defend their analysis and plan before a panel of banker-experts.

Credit Recommendation: In the graduate degree category, 3 semester hours to satisfy thesis or independent study (4/90).

Financial Economics

Location: University of Delaware—Newark, DE.

Length: 22.5 hours; approximately 80 hours of independent study.

Dates: June 1988-April 1995.

Objective: To provide the student with an understanding of the basic economic principles which affect the economy and managing a firm within this economy.

Learning Outcome: Upon successful completion of this course, the student will be able to understand the effects of various monetary policy decisions on our financial systems; analyze money and capital market conditions and the factors affecting interest rates and international capital flows; and apply tools of financial analysis in business decision making.

Instruction: Major topics covered in the course are monetary economics money and capital markets; and management economics (i.e., topics such as capital budgeting, cost of capital and leasing). Methods of instruction include lecture, discussion, and extension problems.

Credit Recommendation: In the upper division baccalaureate or in the graduate degree category, 3 semester hours in Finance or Economics (4/90). **NOTE:** The entire three-year program must be completed to receive credit.

Investments and Bank Funds Management

Location: University of Delaware—Newark, DE.

Length: 21 hours; 80 hours independent study project.

Dates: June 1988-April 1995.

Objective: To learn and understand the basic tools of asset/liability management with particular emphasis on the role of the investment function.

Learning Outcome: Upon successful completion of this course, the student will be able to understand how to use the basic tools of asset/liability management; be able to analyze bank financial performance; recognize different kinds of risk and the tools for managing risk; understand the role of the investment portfolio in asset/liability management; and relate the bank's financial strategy to its strategic plan.

Instruction: Major topics covered in the course are asset/liability management; investment portfolio management; asset/liability management simulation exercises; and financial management of commercial banks. Methods of instruction include lecture, discussion, cases, extension problems, and simulations.

Credit Recommendation: In the upper division baccalaureate or in the graduate degree category, 3 semester hours in Finance (4/90). **NOTE:** The entire three-year program must be completed to receive credit.

Management (Bank Management I and Bank Management II)

Location: University of Delaware—Newark, DE.

Length: 48 hours; 80 hours independent study.

Dates: June 1988-April 1995.

Objective: To provide the knowledge and skills one needs to become an effective management of human and nonhuman resources within an organization.

Learning Outcome: Upon successful completion of this course, the student will be able to understand and apply basic principles in managing human resources; analyze an organizational structure; cope better with changing management culture; apply marketing tools and concepts to banking operations; analyze and manage the commercial lending function; and understand the factors that impact retail bank management.

Instruction: Major topics covered in this course are human resources management; managing with impact; general management as well as the specialized topics of bank marketing management; commercial loan portfolio management; and retail bank management. Methods of instruction include lecture, discussion, classroom exercises, and case method/extension problems.

Credit Recommendation: In the upper division baccalaureate or in the graduate degree category, 3 semester hours in Management (4/90). **NOTE:** The entire three-year program must be completed to receive credit.

Selected Topics in Business and Finance

Location: University of Delaware—Newark, DE.

Length: 45 hours.

Dates: June 1988-April 1995.

Objective: To understand and apply the principles involved in particular functional areas of finance.

Learning Outcome: Upon successful completion of this course, the student will be able to analyze, understand, and solve specific problems in finance; and know where to obtain and utilize additional information on problem solving.

Instruction: Students select up to eight electives from a broad range of offerings that are generally grouped as follows: asset/liability management, pricing and quality of services, strategic planning, mergers and acquisitions, sales and investment management, and loan administration. Methods of instruction include lecture, discussion, classroom exercises, and cases.

Credit Recommendation: In the upper division baccalaureate or in the graduate degree category, 3 semester hours in Finance (4/90). **NOTE:** The entire three-year program must be completed to receive credit.

Synergistics, Inc.

Synergistics, Inc. provides corporations and institutions of higher education quality training and educational degree-completion programs while enhancing individual and organizational learning. We represent a synthesis of several decades of consulting and training experience in both the corporate and educational fields. Through our cooperative partnerships, organizations become true learning systems where adults recognize their status as lifelong learners and where organizations reap the benefits through excellence in learning systems.

Our clients range from over 50 colleges and universities, to national and international corporate site locations where we have established fully functional Synergistics Learning Centers. We offer multiple curriculum lines in areas such as Organizational Management, Criminal Justice Administration, and Early Childhood Education. In each program the greatest success story is that of the individual adult learner who regains a passion for learning and reinvestment into organizational life.

The corporate headquarters for Synergistics, Inc. is located in Rochester, New York. This location houses our curriculum development center where new curriculum lines are constantly researched and current curriculum is maintained and expanded. All of our curriculum is offered in modular fashion where a learner-centric model prevails. The program in Organizational Management has been successfully placed in all six regional, academic, accreditation areas. All of our modules are facilitated by individuals carrying a minimum of a master's degree in their area of expertise.

Our advanced corporate training module is offered at locations nationally as well as internationally where it has gained the applause of adult learners and corporations alike. Our evaluation and delivery systems are consistent with andragogical methodologies designed to enhance adult learning. We provide the link between corporate training and institutions of higher education where ACE recommendations are accepted and academic degrees can be awarded.

Source of official student records: Registry of Credit Recommendations, American Council on Education, One Dupont Circle, Washington, DC 20036-1193.

Additional information about the courses: College Credit Recommendation Service, American Council on Education, One Dupont Circle, Washington, DC 20036-1193.

Organizational Management

Accounting Basics (Bus 345)

Location: Various locations throughout the United States.

Length: 28 hours (7 weeks).

Dates: September 1986-Present.

Objective: To introduce students to accounting concepts and the key components used as information and communication guides, and as the basis for decision-making. Some financial concepts are presented.

Learning Outcome: Upon successful completion of this course, the student will be able to read and analyze financial statements, especially income statements; balance sheets; statements of cash flows; use the fundamental "bookkeeping" tools of accounting and understand how these tools are used to compile financial information; be familiar with internal cost concepts and how to make managerial decisions based on the sue of this accounting information; develop various types of operating budgets and know their implications; and understand how not-for-profit organizations differ in terms of accounting structure and operating approach.

Instruction: Major topics covered in the course are accounting principles, financial statement analysis, managerial and cost accounting, budgeting, and capital budgeting. Methods of instruction include discussion, lecture, classroom exercises, short presentations, and final project.

Credit Recommendation: In the lower division baccalaureate/associate degree category, 3 semester hours in Accounting or Business Administration (8/96).

Adult Development and Life Assessment

Location: Various locations throughout the United States.

Length: 24 hours (6 weeks).

Dates: September 1996-Present.

Objective: To evaluate career development in light of adult development theory, various learning styles, and their application to the work environment.

Learning Outcome: Upon successful completion of this course, the student will be able to identify critical career experiences; examine developmental workplace skills; and document findings in a portfolio for review for career assessment credit.

Instruction: Major topics covered in the course are basic writing and library skills, career assessment, adult learning and developmental styles, and Kolb's model of experiential learning. Methods of instruction include discussion, classroom exercises, lecture, learner presentations, homework assignments, reports, and a summary paper.

Credit Recommendation: In the lower division baccalaureate/associate degree category, 3 semester hours in Adult Learning, Career Development, Psychology, or Organizational Behavior (8/96).

An Introduction to Research and Analysis Using Statistics

Location: Various locations throughout the United States.

Length: 20 hours (5 weeks).

Dates: September 1986-Present.

Objective: To introduce statistical research methodology and tools that will help students complete their research projects.

Learning Outcome: Upon successful completion of this course, the student will be able to use the appropriate descriptive statistics to describe a set of data, including measures of central tendency and measures of variability; select the appropriate statistical test for making inferences about a population based on a sample, including confidence intervals, the independent t-test, and chi-square tests; define, research, analyze, and evaluate a problem relevant to his or her own interests; and interpret and document the results of a statistical analysis as part of a research paper.

Instruction: Major topics covered in the course are descriptive and differential statics, collecting samples, central tendency, normal dispersion, and estimation. Methods of instruction include discussion, classroom exercises, lecture, learner presentations, reports, and weekly problem sets.

Credit Recommendation: In the lower division baccalaureate/associate degree category, 3 semester hours in Business Administration or Statistics (8/96).

Business Law (Bus 420)

Location: New York, New Jersey, Seattle, WA.

Length: 28 hours (7 weeks).

Dates: February 1997-Present.

Objective: To provide the adult learner with an overview of the legal issues affecting businesses so that he or she will understand the fundamentals of Business Law sufficiently to make the majority of his or her business relating to legal matters without assistance.

Learning Outcome: Upon successful completion of this course, the student will be able to understand the legal rights and social forces inherent in our American legal environment; understand the rules governing the principal-agent relationship; understand the nature of contractual arrangements, their elements, the rights and duties of contractual parties, and the remedies for their breach; understand the various forms of business organizations; understand the various security devices and their effects on debtors and creditors in and out of bankruptcy; and develop the skills and methods needed to analyze a given set of facts for the purpose of identifying the legal issues of problems involved and applying the appropriate rule of law in resolving the issue.

Instruction: Major topics covered in the course are Business Law studies in history, background, sources, and influences of our modern day law as it pertains to the business activities of individuals, corporations, and other legal entities with particular emphasis upon business litigation; legal liabilities, alternative dispute resolution techniques, and the laws governing contracts; creditors' rights; secured transactions; bankruptcy; agency; partnerships; and corporations. Methods of instruction include lecture, discussion, computer-assisted instruction, simulation or role play, reports, papers, journals, attendance, homework, and projects.

Credit Recommendation: In the upper division baccalaureate degree category, 4 semester hours in Business Law, Business Law Government, or Ethics and Society (4/97).

Group and Organizational Dynamics

Location: Various locations throughout the United States.

Length: 20 hours (5 weeks).

Dates: September 1986-Present.

Objective: To help students develop effective strategies for efficient and productive group management.

Learning Outcome: Upon successful completion of this course, the student will be able to demonstrate knowledge of types of group processes and relationship of groups to organizations; examine the Strength Development Inventory and a variety of motivational patterns that influence small group dynamics; analyze group and individual decision-making techniques; demonstrate an awareness of organizational complexity; and identify the nature, management, and significance of group and organizational conflict.

Instruction: Major topics covered in the course are portfolio review, time management, strength bombardment, individual and group decision-making, small group interaction, group size and structure, brainstorming, and conflict resolution. Methods of instruction include discussion, classroom exercises, lecture, case studies, learner presentations, summary papers, reports, and homework assignments.

Credit Recommendation: In the upper division baccalaureate degree category, 3 semester hours in Group Dynamics, Organizational Behavior, or Management (8/96).

Human Resource Management (Orgd 445)

Location: Various locations throughout the United States.

Length: 20 hours (5 weeks).

Dates: September 1986-Present.

Objective: To provide a practical approach to the function and practices of human resource management in the achievement of organizational objectives.

Learning Outcome: Upon successful completion of this course, the student will be able to understand the role of the personnel function; know the difference between Equal Employment Opportunity (EEO) and Affirmative Action Planning; be familiar with the components of a personnel planning and forecasting process; identify the advantages/disadvantages of various internal/external recruiting sources; be aware of the elements of effective performance appraisal; and become familiar with unions, and elements of labor relations, including grievance procedures, arbitration and mediation.

Instruction: Major topics covered in the course are Government regulation of Human Resource Management including EEO and Affirmative Action; recruitment, selection, orientation, and compensation of employees; performance appraisal practices; and unions, grievances, arbitration, and mediation. Methods of instruction include discussion, classroom exercises, lecture, case studies, role playing, summary papers, reports, and homework assignments.

Credit Recommendation: In the upper division baccalaureate degree category, 3 semester hours in Human Resource Management or Business Administration (8/96).

Issues in Management (Bus 330)

Location: Various locations throughout the United States.

Length: 20 hours (5 weeks).

Dates: September 1986-Present.

Objective: To introduce the student to concepts of management as they pertain to the dynamics of leadership, motivation, strategic planning, and controlling.

Learning Outcome: Upon successful completion of this course, the student will be able to understand and apply various management concepts including motivation, leadership styles and effectiveness, strategic planning, organizing principles, negotiation, and the principles of TQM.

Instruction: Major topics covered in the course are management theories, strategic planning, employee motivation, organization structure and design, leadership, conflict resolution, and the distinction between MBO and TQM. Methods of instruction include discussion, classroom exercises, case studies, lecture, learner presentations, reports, self-assessment surveys, observations, and a summary paper.

Credit Recommendation: In the upper division baccalaureate degree category, 3 semester hours in Management or Business Administration (8/96).

Managerial Accounting (Bus 340)

Location: New York, New Jersey, and Seattle, WA.

Length: 20 hours (5 weeks).

Dates: February 1997-Present.

Objective: To understand the use of financial accounting, budgeting, and financial analysis.

Learning Outcome: Upon successful completion of this course, the student will be able to understand financial and cost accounting; and complete problems as applied to assets, bonds, financial statement analysis, and cost accounting.

Instruction: Major topics covered in the course are financial statement analysis; accounting for assets; liabilities and equity; present value analysis; standard costs; and a final research project on how a company applies generally accepted accounting principals, including financial analysis and cost accounting. Methods of instruction include discussion, classroom exercises, case studies, reports, and papers.

Credit Recommendation: In the upper division baccalaureate degree category, 3 semester hours in Accounting or Business Administration (4/97).

Managerial Economics (Bus 335)

Location: Various locations throughout the United States.

Length: 20 hours (5 weeks).

Dates: September 1986-Present.

Objective: To provide students with a foundation of economic principles and theory that can be used in making managerial decisions that relate to resource allocation.

Learning Outcome: Upon successful completion of this course, the student will be able to apply economic principles to business situations; predict outcomes of managerial economic decisions; use the logic of economics when making personal decisions and when solving business problems; and use terms correctly when describing economic principles.

Instruction: Major topics covered in the course are supply and demand, elasticities, present value analysis, production and costs, perfect competition, monopolistic competition, monopoly, oligopoly, and game theory. Methods of instruction include lecture, discussion, classroom exercises, learner presentations, homework assignments, and a final project.

Credit Recommendation: In the lower division baccalaureate/associate degree category, 3 semester hours in Microeconomics or Managerial Economics (8/96).

Managerial Finance (Bus 350)

Location: New York, New Jersey, and Seattle, WA.

Length: 20 hours (5 weeks).

Dates: February 1997-Present.

Objective: To introduce the students to issues in managerial finance.

Learning Outcome: Upon successful completion of this course, the student will be able to develop a firm understanding of the field of corporate finance: short term finance, capital budgeting, and long term finance; use traditional financial statements and related accounting data for broad based financial planning; and apply capital budgeting techniques to the analysis of investment opportunities.

Instruction: Major topics covered in the course are the organization wide use of financial planning within the firm and corporate finance, the importance of short-term finance in current operations, use of capital budgeting tools for investment analysis, and the foundation of long-term finance for defining the organization's cost of capital and optimal capital structure. Methods of instruction include lecture, discussion, simulation or role play, homework, class participation, and projects.

Credit Recommendation: In the upper division baccalaureate degree category, 3 semester hours in Managerial Finance (4/97).

Marketing

Location: Various locations throughout the United States.

Length: 20 hours (5 weeks).

Dates: September 1986-Present.

Objective: To understand the role and skills of marketing and apply these concepts to organizational planning and strategies.

Learning Outcome: Upon successful completion of this course, the student will be able to discuss the evolution of marketing; develop a personal selling plan; apply the functions of marketing to business situations; develop marketing programs; and understand the international implications for marketing.

Instruction: Major topics covered in the course are the evolution and nature of marketing; role of marketing; marketing functions; and marketing concepts, theory, and terminology. Methods of instruction include discussion, classroom exercises, lecture, case studies, audio/visual material, learner presentations, homework, and a summary paper.

Credit Recommendation: In the upper division baccalaureate degree category, 3 semester hours in Marketing or Business Administration (8/96).

Organizational Communication

Location: Various locations throughout the United States.

Length: 60 hours (20 weeks) .

Dates: September 1986-Present.

Objective: To investigate communication and relationships in creating a productive work environment.

Learning Outcome: Upon successful completion of this course, the student will be able to understand the importance of communication and methods of communicating effectively in organizations; identify and analyze facilitating and hindering forces in effective communications; practice developing and delivering effective interpersonal communications; understand theory and practice team-building, conflict resolution, and problem solving; understand how communication and organizational cultures relate to one another; and understand the role of verbal and nonverbal messages and how to use them effectively.

Instruction: Major topics covered in the course are the communication process and media, team building, and conflict resolution. Methods of instruction include discussion, classroom exercises, lecture, audio/visual material, role play, classroom participation, homework assignments, and a summary paper.

Credit Recommendation: In the upper division baccalaureate degree category, 3 semester hours in Organizational Communication or Business Administration (8/96).

Personal Values and Organizational Ethics

Location: Various locations throughout the United States.

Length: 20 hours (5 weeks).

Dates: September 1986-Present.

Objective: To help students better understand their own values and how such values relate to the "business world" in which they function.

Learning Outcome: Upon successful completion of this course, the student will be able to differentiate among the three basic types of ethical systems; understand how human values interface with organizational ethics; and identify implications and resolutions to ethical problems in the workplace.

Instruction: Major topics covered in the course are ethical principles in business; ethics in consumer production and marketing; and human value perspectives of four basic world views that dominate western cultures, include Christianity, Marxism, Skinner's Conditional Behaviorism, and Existentialism. Methods of instruction include discussion, classroom exercises, lecture, case studies, learner presentations, reports, homework assignments, and summary reports.

Credit Recommendation: In the upper division baccalaureate degree category, 3 semester hours in Business Ethics or Philosophy (8/96).

Research Project Seminar

Location: Various locations throughout the United States.

Length: 200-250 hours (77 weeks).

Dates: October 1986-Present.

Objective: To provide the student with the necessary skills to research, write, and present a final written project.

Learning Outcome: Upon successful completion of this course, the student will be able to demonstrate research writing skills; and make an oral presentation covering the process of a project.

Instruction: Major topics covered in the course are research writing and oral presentations. Method of instruction includes independent study, which is reviewed chapter by chapter by an advisor who provides continual feedback, evaluation, and a final grade.

Credit Recommendation: In the upper division baccalaureate degree category, 5

semester hours in Research Methods or Business Administration (8/96).

Social Problems and Their Impact On the Workplace (Soc 402)

Location: Various locations throughout the United States.

Length: 20 hours (5 weeks).

Dates: September 1986-Present.

Objective: To gain insight and broaden the student perception of social problems affecting the workplace and to increase awareness of how the workplace can respond positively to them.

Learning Outcome: Upon successful completion of this course, the student will be able to identify and analyze the causes, conditions, and consequences, and propose strategies to alleviate social problems in five specific areas: poverty, racism, sexism, drug/alcohol abuse, and illiteracy.

Instruction: Major topics covered in the course are a sociological and systematic approach to problem analysis and solution via a seven-stage task force, experiential process, identification of six critical social problems that challenge the Workforce 2000 model, and introduces six perspectives of social problems. Methods of instruction include discussion, classroom exercises, lecture, learner presentations, reports, observation papers, homework assignments, and summary reports.

Credit Recommendation: In the upper division baccalaureate degree category, 3 semester hours in Sociology or Business Administration (8/96).

Strategic Planning (Bus 450)

Location: Various locations throughout the United States.

Length: 20 hours (5 weeks).

Dates: October 1986-Present.

Objective: To introduce the student to strategic planning methodology and its implications.

Learning Outcome: Upon successful completion of this course, the student will be able to understand the strategic planning process, the role of mission statements, and strength, weakness, opportunities, and threats (SWOT) analysis; and the role of "corporate-level" strategies and their implementation in an organization.

Instruction: Major topics covered in the course are mission statement development, internal and external environmental analysis, SWOT analysis, and strategy formulation. Methods of instruction include discussion, case studies, lecture, homework assignments, class participation, and a take-home final.

Credit Recommendation: In the upper division baccalaureate degree category, 3 semester hours in Management or Business Administration (8/96).

Systems Approach to Organizational Change

Location: Various locations throughout the United States.

Length: 20 hours (5 weeks).

Dates: September 1986-Present.

Objective: To examine the formal and informal functions of organizations and analyze an agency or organization based on a systems model.

Learning Outcome: Upon successful completion of this course, the student will be able to understand organizational concepts; apply concepts of systems theory problem-solving and decision-making to a research project; understand implementation and management of change in organizations; use a systems model to examine his or her organization; and recognize major theorists and researchers.

Instruction: Major topics covered in the course are organizational concepts, implementation and management of change, systems theory problem solving, and systems analysis of organizations. Methods of instruction include discussion, classroom exercises, case studies, lecture, learner presentations, homework, and a summary paper.

Credit Recommendation: In the upper division baccalaureate degree category, 3 semester hours in Organizational Behavior or Management (8/96).

Technical Education & Development Corporation

Technical Education & Development Corporation was incorporated in August 1989, commencing business on January 2, 1990. While the primary mission of this company is to provide training to business and industry, TEDCo. also intends to continue to offer quality educational programs to the general public including basic skills training, apprentice and journeyman upgrade, on-site training, self-improvement courses, college credit courses, current technological advancements, customized training courses, performance-based training, job deficit training, employee enhancement programs, and immediate course delivery.

TED Co. is fulfilling the training needs that are not readily available from the two-year and four-year post-secondary institutions. Training programs may be customized to assure skill deficits are addressed and to fulfill exact training needs for specialized programs.

Technical Education & Development Corporation is built on a philosophy of education and service, which focuses on the needs of the community. The training it provides to business, industry, and the general public is designed to improve individual knowledge, skills (performance), and attitude. Technical Education & Development Corporation provides students with a comprehensive, yet practical, education through skill-based curricula. Employees conscientiously strive to implement basic adult education principles.

Faculty requirements:

A. A post-secondary degree in a field related to the course topic, and/or,

B. Work experience in a related field (either holding a current position, or two or more years of related experience) and/or

C. Teaching experience in a related field (either holding a current teaching license or two or more years of teaching experience).

ACE/PONSI-evaluated courses are typically selected by business and industry to be offered by Technical Education & Development Corporation at its Kokomo, Indiana, sites or at the customers' sites, therefore; ACE/PONSI-evaluated courses allow business/industrial and/or general public students to apply for college credit at recognized colleges or universities.

Source of official student records: Registry of Credit Recommendations, American Council on Education, One Dupont Circle, Washington, DC 20036-1193.

Additional information about the courses: College Credit Recommendation Service, American Council on Education, One Dupont Circle, Washington, DC 20036-1193.

Arc Welding I

Location: Technical Education & Development Corporation Facilities, Leased Facilities, and Customer Sites.

Length: 44 hours (11 weeks).

Dates: March 1990-December 1997.

Objective: To acquire the knowledge and skills for oxyacetylene welding, cutting, brazing, and shielded metal Arc welding.

Learning Outcome: Upon successful completion of this course, the student will be able to follow correct safety procedures; demonstrate knowledge of OAW and SMAW theory; accurately set up and adjust a shielded metal Arc welder; demonstrate skills for running beads in flat positions for both processes; and accurately set up and adjust an oxyacetylene torch for welding, brazing, and cutting.

Instruction: Major topics covered in the course are policy, procedure, and principles; safety; oxyacetylene and Arc setup and shutdown; fuel gases, electrode selection; running leads, tee, butt, and corner joints; and cutting and brazing techniques.

Credit Recommendation: In the lower division baccalaureate/associate degree category or vocational certificate category, 2 semester hours in Welding Technology I (12/91).

Arc Welding II

Location: Technical Education & Development Corporation Facilities, Leased Facilities, and Customer Sites.

Length: 44 hours (11 weeks).

Dates: March 1990-December 1997.

Objective: To acquire the knowledge and skills needed to complete SMAW vertical and overhead positions, as well as advanced joint designs.

Learning Outcome: Upon successful completion of this course, the student will be able to follow correct safety procedures and demonstrate correct technique for welding steel plate in vertical and overhead positions with F3 and F4 electrodes.

Instruction: Major topics covered in the course are policy, procedure, and principles; safety; SMAW skills in vertical and overhead positions; application of advanced joint designs; demonstration and practice of F3 and F4 electrode group; and destructive and nondestructive testing of welds.

Credit Recommendation: In the vocational certificate category or in the lower division baccalaureate/associate degree category, 2 semester hours in Welding Technology II (12/91).

Basic Mathematics (Developmental/Remedial)

Location: Technical Education & Development Corporation facilities.

Length: 32 hours (8 weeks).

Dates: January 1991-December 1997.

Objective: To train in basic mathematics from computations with numbers through basic algebra.

Learning Outcome: Upon successful completion of this course, the student will be able to perform the fundamental operations in mathematics with a high degree of accuracy.

Instruction: Major topics covered in the course are addition, subtraction, multiplication, and division of whole numbers; algebraic equations; fractions; decimals; percentages; and measurements. Methods of instruction include lecture, discussion, and classroom exercises.

Credit Recommendation: In the lower division baccalaureate/associate degree category, 2 semester hours in Developmental, Basic, or Remedial Mathematics (12/91).

Cabinetry I

Location: Technical Education & Development Corporation Facilities, Leased Facilities, and Customer Sites.

Length: 44 hours (15 weeks).

Dates: August 1991-December 1997.

Objective: To acquire the knowledge in the construction of casework, joint design, and material selection.

Learning Outcome: Upon successful completion of this course, the student will understand wood product lay out for kitchens, bathrooms, and other built-in cabinet casework.

Instruction: Major topics covered in the course are tool safety; work-site housekeeping; materials and utilization of wood products including blueprint materials; labor; sketching; cost estimating of materials and construction problems to include cabinet-making procedures; and tool use.

Credit Recommendation: In the lower division baccalaureate/associate degree category, 2 semester hours in Industrial Technology/Cabinetry Design I (12/91).

Cabinetry II

Location: Technical Education & Development Corporation Facilities, Leased Facilities, and Customer Sites.

Length: 44 hours (15 weeks).

Dates: August 1991-December 1997.

Objective: To acquire the knowledge in the advanced layout and construction of cabinets.

Learning Outcome: Upon successful completion of this course, the student will be able to layout and construct casework including cabinet frame construction.

Instruction: Major topics covered in the course are policies, procedures, and techniques related to case and kitchen cabinet construction and installation; cabinet shelves and interiors; fasteners and hardware and wood finish techniques.

Credit Recommendation: In the lower division baccalaureate/associate degree category, 2 semester hours in Industrial Technology/Cabinetry Design II (12/91).

Computer Awareness

Location: Technical Education & Development Corporation Facilities, Leased Facilities, and Customer Sites.

Length: 30 hours (11 weeks); one 3-hour meeting per week.

Dates: January 1990-December 1997.

Objective: To give a brief overview of computers and DOS V5.0, WordPerfect V5.1, Lotus 1-2-3 V3.3, DBASE III Plus, and Harvard Graphics V2.3.

Learning Outcome: Upon successful completion of this course, the student will be able to understand base components of personal computers; basic computer terminology, DOS commands, disk operating functions such as booting up the computer, cleaning screen, formatting disks, copying files and disks, adding and deleting files; and have an awareness of basic word processing, spreadsheets, graphs, data bases, and graphic packages.

Instruction: Major topics covered in the course are DOS basic commands and functions; introduction to Word Perfect 5.1; introduction to Lotus 1-2-3; and introduction to Harvard graphics. Methods of instruction include lecture, and hands-on exercises in the computer lab.

Credit Recommendation: In the lower division baccalaureate/associate degree category, 1 semester hour in Personal Computer Literacy and Awareness (12/91).

Fundamentals of Accounting

Location: Technical Education & Development Corporation Facilities, Leased Facilities, and Customer Sites.

Length: 48 hours (8 weeks); two 3-hour meetings per week.

Dates: January 1991-December 1997.

Objective: To introduce the student to the basic principles and practices of the generally accepted accounting procedures for a service business, including the completion of financial reports.

Learning Outcome: Upon successful completion of this course, the student will be able to open an accounting system; analyze and record business transactions in journals and ledgers; prepare standard financial reports; and know definitions of accounting terms and concepts.

Instruction: Major topics covered in the course are starting an accounting system; changes caused by business transactions; balance sheet; analyzing and recording business transactions in journals; posting to general ledger; analyzing transactions affecting assets; liabilities and capital; recording transactions in journals; developing income statement; adjustments and closing entries; general ledger and posting; and checking account and reconciling a bank statement. Methods of instruction include lecture, discussion, and student workbook.

Credit Recommendation: In the lower division baccalaureate/associate degree category, 3 semester hours in Bookkeeping/Accounting (12/91).

Fundamentals of Accounting II

Location: Technical Education & Development Corporation Facilities, Leased Facilities, and Customer Sites.

Length: 48 hours (8 weeks); two 3-hour sessions per week.

Dates: January 1992-December 1997.

Objective: To build on the basic accounting principles and practices by introducing the student to the accounting practices for a merchandising business, including payables and receivables. Also, to offer a basic introduction to automated accounting.

Learning Outcome: Upon successful completion of this course, the student will be able to analyze and record partnership transactions in an expanded journal, general ledger, and subsidiary ledgers; perform period-end adjustments and closing entries; prepare standard financial reports and schedules; know and understand accounting terms as they apply to a merchandising partnership; know the basic differences of and terms and procedures for cost, managerial, not-for-profit, and automated accounting.

Instruction: Major topics covered in the course include analysis of business transactions; recording transactions in an expanded journal; general and subsidiary ledgers; end-of-period work; and resulting financial statements and schedules. A complete accounting cycle for a merchandising partnership is presented. Methods of instruction include lecture/discussion with demonstration by instructor, in-class exercises, independent assignments, and completion of class project.

Credit Recommendation: In the lower division baccalaureate/associate degree category, 3 semester hours in Bookkeeping/Accounting (12/91).

Furniture I

Location: Technical Education & Development Corporation Facilities, Leased Facilities, and Customer Sites.

Length: 44 hours (15 weeks).

Dates: August 1991-December 1997.

Objective: To acquire the skills in the design, layout, and materials used to construct basic furniture

Learning Outcome: Upon successful completion of this course, the student will be able to effectively utilize wood materials and tools in the production of furniture styles; joint construction; and layout of chairs and tables.

Instruction: Major topics covered in the course are wood selections and properties of fine furniture; ordering material for furniture; and procedures and problems in furniture design and finishing.

Credit Recommendation: In the lower division baccalaureate/associate degree category, 2 semester hours in Industrial Technology/Furniture I (12/91).

Furniture Repair

Location: Technical Education & Development Corporation Facilities, Leased Facilities, and Customer Sites.

Length: 44 hours (15 weeks).

Dates: August 1997-December 1997.

Objective: To acquire the technical skills in the design, layout, and material used in the construction of furniture.

Learning Outcome: Upon successful completion of this course, the student will be able to effectively utilize furniture stripper, stains, and sealers; repair, manufacture or replace problem parts or fixtures; select proper woods, and apply proper finish.

Instruction: Major topics covered in the course are knowledge and selection of furniture woods; stripping and preparing furniture for finish; finishing procedures to include staining, filling, distressing, glazing, protective coating, and final finishing.

Credit Recommendation: In the lower division baccalaureate/associate degree category, 2 semester hours in Industrial Technology/Furniture I (12/91).

Interpersonal Communication

Location: Technical Education & Development Corporation Facilities, Leased Facilities, and Customer Sites.

Length: 48 hours (16 weeks); 3 hours per week.

Dates: January 1991-December 1997.

Objective: To provide the student with the ability to promote and sustain better communication with others.

Learning Outcome: Upon successful completion of this course, the student will be able to demonstrate an understanding of theoretical models of communication and various roles, rules, strategies and games of interpersonal communication.

Instruction: Major topics covered in the course are understanding of action and inaction models of communication; various roles, rules, strategies, and games of interpersonal communication; the ecological nature of interpersonal communication; the role of self in interpersonal communication; primary message systems: language, gesture, space, sexuality; and patterns of interpersonal communication. Methods of instruction include instructor-led lecture and discussion with in-class application exercises and independent assignments.

Credit Recommendation: In the lower division baccalaureate/associate degree category, 3 semester hours in Interpersonal Communication (12/91).

Interviewing Skills

Location: Technical Education & Development Corporation Facilities, Leased Facilities, and Customer Sites.

Length: 16 weeks; one 3-hour meeting per week.

Dates: January 1990-December 1997.

Objective: To provide a basic understanding of the job interview process, including resume construction and letters of application.

Learning Outcome: Upon successful completion of this course, the student will be able to interview effectively; write a viable resume; and write a letter of application that is clear and concise.

Instruction: Major topics covered in the course are interview process from both the interviewee and interviewer perspectives; letters of application; resumes; and legal ramifications of various questions asked in the interview. Methods of instruction include lecture, handouts, and classroom exercises such as mock interviews.

Credit Recommendation: In the lower division baccalaureate/associate degree category, 1 semester hour in Interviewing Skills (12/91).

Money Management

Location: Technical Education & Development Corporation Facilities and Customer Sites.

Length: 48 hours (16 weeks); one 3-hour meeting per week.

Dates: January 1991-December 1997.

Objective: To introduce students to the fundamentals of money management and personal finance.

Learning Outcome: Upon successful completion of this course, the student will be able to discuss different forms of investments and the risks associated with each; discuss the advantages and disadvantages of permanent and temporary life insurance; decide on the type of will needed; and make retirement investment choices.

Instruction: Major topics covered in the course are payroll savings plans; estate planning; investments; insurance; and taxes and how to reduce them. Methods of instruction include lecture, class exercises, and projects.

Credit Recommendation: In the lower division baccalaureate/associate degree category, 2 semester hours in Personal Money Management (12/91).

Personal Income Tax Accounting

Location: Technical Education & Development Corporation Facilities, Leased Facilities and Customer Sites.

Length: 30 hours.

Dates: December 1990-December 1997.

Objective: To assist the student in the preparation of his personal income tax return.

Learning Outcome: Upon successful completion of this course, the student will be able to understand most of the parts involved in the preparation of his personal federal and state tax return and understand the filing requirements.

Instruction: Major topics covered in the course are federal revenue system; taxation of individuals; personal exemptions and itemized deductions; and business expenses.

Credit Recommendation: In the lower division baccalaureate/associate degree category, 2 semester hours in Personal Income Tax (12/91).

Public Speaking

Location: Technical Education & Development Corporation Facilities.

Length: 48 hours (16 weeks).

Dates: January 1991-December 1997.

Objective: To improve student's verbal skills in dialogue and public speaking.

Learning Outcome: Upon successful completion of this course, the student will be able to demonstrate the practice of active listening, effectively communicate one-to-one and one-to-group, and incorporate visual aids with extemporaneous presentations.

Instruction: Major topics covered in the course are impromptu speeches; audience analysis; communication process; and organization of speeches. Methods of instruction include lecture, discussion, and student presentations.

Credit Recommendation: In the lower division baccalaureate/associate degree category, 3 semester hours in Introduction to Public Speaking (12/91).

Reading Effectiveness

Location: Technical Education & Development Corporation, Kokomo, IN.

Length: 48 hours (16 weeks).

Dates: January 1991-December 1997.

Objective: To improve students' reading comprehension.

Learning Outcome: Upon successful completion of this course, the student will be able to more efficiently and effectively master the content of textbooks, technical articles, newspapers and magazine stories, editorials and other expressions of opinion; to use more effectively an increased vocabulary; and to read faster.

Instruction: Major topics covered in the course are determining and distinguishing among the meanings of words; techniques to improve the recall of details; and techniques to improve the rate of reading. Methods of instruction include lecture, discussion, and in-class exercises.

Credit Recommendation: In the lower division baccalaureate/associate degree category, 1 semester hour in Remedial or Developmental Reading (12/91).

Residential and Light Commercial Wiring

Location: Technical Education & Development Corporation Facilities, Leased Facilities, and Customer Sites.

Length: 48 hours (16 weeks).

Dates: August 1990-December 1997.

Objective: To acquire skills in general and appliance circuits and wiring methods, according to National Electrical Codes and local codes, as they pertain to housing and basic commercial wiring.

Learning Outcome: Upon successful completion of this course, the student will be able to read blueprints; plan; and obtain and install appropriate devices to ensure safe operations of the circuits in homes and basic commercial wiring according to established codes.

Instruction: Major topics covered in the course are planning, installing, and connecting circuits and components required for a workable and acceptable residence and commercial establishments, according to national and local codes.

Credit Recommendation: In the vocational certificate or in the lower division baccalaureate/associate degree category , 3 semester hours in Electrical Wiring, Electrical Engineering Technology, or Building Materials Technology (12/91).

Residential Plumbing

Location: Technical Education & Development Corporation Facilities, Leased Facilities, and Customer Sites.

Length: 30 hours (15 weeks).

Dates: March 1990-December 1997.

Objective: To familiarize and introduce student to residential plumbing.

Learning Outcome: Upon successful completion of this course, the student will be able to demonstrate the ability to maintain, repair, and replace residential plumbing pipes, valves, and related plumbing accessories; develop an understanding of technical knowledge of basic residential plumbing including zoning, building codes, water supplies, drainage systems, and operation of related fixtures; and demonstrates practical knowledge of usage of appropriate tools and equipment and their safe operation.

Instruction: Major topics covered in the course are safety; plumbing problems and procedures; repair or replacement of residential plumbing, pipes, drains, vents and fixtures; and study of plumbing drawings to included pipe layout and blueprint symbols.

Credit Recommendation: In the lower division baccalaureate/associate degree category, 2 semester hours in Industrial Technology/Residential Plumbing (12/91).

Stress Management

Location: Technical Education & Development Corporation Facilities.

Length: 11 weeks; one 3-hour meeting per week.

Dates: January 1990-December 1997.

Objective: To provide students with basic stress management skills.

Learning Outcome: Upon successful completion of this course, the student will be able to recognize stress; identify underlying causes of stress; identify symptoms of stress; and incorporate techniques for coping with stress including diet and exercise.

Instruction: Major topics covered in the course are stress and effects of stress; coping skills, including stress reduction through diet; types of personalities; products of negative thinking; and stress management through exercise. Methods of instruction include lecture, in-class exercises and assignments, and use of handout materials.

Credit Recommendation: In the lower division baccalaureate/associate degree category, 2 semester hours in Stress Management (12/91).

Study Skills

Location: Technical Education & Development Corporation Facilities, Leased Facilities, and Customer Sites.

Length: 33 hours (11 weeks); one 3-hour meeting per week.

Dates: January 1991-December 1997.

Objective: To provide the student an opportunity to improve basic reading, study, note-taking, test-taking, and time-management skills.

Learning Outcome: Upon successful completion of this course, the student will be able to understand and apply effective techniques for reading, studying, note-taking, test-taking and time-management skills required for college-level work.

Instruction: Major topics covered in the course are effective scheduling and organization of time; effective taking, organizing, and studying of classroom notes; reading and studying textbooks; identification of necessary skills to improve memory; and identification and use of test-taking techniques. Methods of instruction include instructor lecture and demonstration, in-class discussions, supplemental exercises/handouts, and homework assignments.

Credit Recommendation: In the lower division baccalaureate/associate degree category, 1 semester hour in Study Skills (12/91).

Time Management

Location: Technical Education & Development Corporation Facilities, Leased Facilities, and Customer Sites.

Length: 30 hours.

Dates: January 1992-December 1997.

Objective: To assist participants to develop an understanding of how to make more effective and efficient use of time.

Learning Outcome: Upon successful completion of this course, the student will be able to identify problems that cause ineffective use of time; set priorities; identify time wasters; explore the causes and payoffs of procrastination; identify means of starting and completing overwhelming or distasteful tasks; and explore creative and effective use of time.

Instruction: Major topics covered in the course are inventory of time management; setting priorities; time wasters; how to eliminate time wasters; planning your time; and goal setting.

Credit Recommendation: In the lower division baccalaureate/associate degree category, 2 semester hours in Time Management (12/91).

Tool Skills

Location: Technical Education & Development Corporation Facilities, Leased Facilities, and Customer Sites.

Length: 44 hours (15 weeks).

Dates: August 1990-December 1997.

Objective: To learn to operate power tools in a safe manner in construction and cabinet shops.

Learning Outcome: Upon successful completion of this course, the student will be able to operate power tools safely in a shop or on the job.

Instruction: Major topics covered in the course are safety in the use of stationary and portable tools related to construction and cabinet shops.

Credit Recommendation: In the vocational certificate or in the lower division baccalaureate/associate degree category , 3 semester hours in Industrial Education/Shop Safety (12/91).

Understanding Wood

Location: Technical Education & Development Corporation Facilities, Leased Facilities, and Customer Sites.

Length: 44 hours (15 weeks).

Dates: October 1991-December 1997.

Objective: To acquire the skills to identify, grade, and use proper types of wood for a given project.

Learning Outcome: Upon successful completion of this course, the student will

be able to identify by type, grade, and use of wood different requirements of the specific job in industry.

Instruction: Major topics covered in the course are identifying grades and uses of a particular type of wood to meet industrial/building requirements.

Credit Recommendation: In the vocational certificate or in the lower division baccalaureate/associate degree category , 2 semester hours in Manufacturing Technology, Introduction to Wood, or Working/Woodworking I (12/91).

Welding Certification

Location: Technical Education & Development Corporation Facilities, Leased Facilities, and Customer Sites.

Length: 48 hours (16 weeks).

Dates: March 1990-December 1997.

Objective: To acquire the knowledge and skills to enable students to take the welding certification examination.

Learning Outcome: Upon successful completion of this course, the student will be able to define the scope of the AWS code D1.1-90; demonstrate competencies to pass a certification test on 3/8" steel plate; prepare test coupons for testing; perform a root and face bend test and analyze results; understand the scope of the API code 1104; and understand the scope of the ASME code section IX.

Instruction: Major topics covered in the course are policy, procedure, and principles; safety; scope of code D1.1-90 (performance standards, testing criteria, limits of certification); skills to certify for all positions with F-4 electrodes on mild steel

Technical Training Project, Inc.

Technical Training Project, Inc. (TTP) was created by a consortium of eleven pharmaceutical companies in the New Jersey-New York area as a private non-profit organization.

The project's purpose was to combat the problems of unemployment and underemployment among minority groups and disadvantaged people. To do this, TTP created its own curriculum and training schedule, so that within a twenty-week work-study period, the trainee would acquire technical competence, discipline, motivation, and skills to qualify for an entry-level laboratory technician position.

The trainee goes through an intensive academic course of study taught by the staff of TTP. In addition, scientists from various companies provide lectures to supplement the training process.

TTP uses the laboratories of the sponsoring companies for the on-the-job-training phase of the program. Here a trainee works in the laboratory under the supervision of a skilled professional and is exposed to state-of-the-art scientific equipment.

Through the years TTP has continuously reviewed its curriculum to ensure it is keeping pace with the needs of industry. This is accomplished through a technical Advisory Committee, comprised of scientists from the companies meeting with the staff. Areas of academic and laboratory concentrations are discussed as are choice of textbooks.

Source of official student records: Registry of Credit Recommendations, American Council on Education, One Dupont Circle, Washington, DC 20036-1193.

Additional information about the courses: Office of Corporate-Higher Education, Thomas Edison State College, 101 West State Street, Trenton, NJ 08608-1176.

Laboratory Technician Program

Location: Newark, NJ.

Length: 800 hours (20 weeks).

Dates: July 1978-Present.

Objective: To provide classroom and technical training for entry-level chemical laboratory technicians.

Learning Outcome: Upon successful completion of this training program, the student will be able to understand the basic principles of organic and inorganic chemistry; use chemicals, materials, and laboratory equipment; handle mathematical calculations and general concepts of normality, dilution, weighing samples, and use of laboratory equipment; demonstrate a basic understanding of selected concepts in the life sciences as related to laboratory work, i.e., bacterial culture, soil sampling, human anatomy, and cell biology; maintain laboratory reports on all experiments; perform various techniques of wet and dry analysis; and apply theory to work experience in the laboratories of sponsoring companies.

Instruction: Major topics covered in the course are basic organic and inorganic chemistry; mathematics; an introduction to several areas of the biological sciences; career and educational planning; and how to use laboratory equipment. Methods of instruction include classroom exercises, laboratory experiments, an internship in a laboratory, lecture, and discussion.

Credit Recommendation: In the lower division baccalaureate/associate degree category, 4 semester hours in College Chemistry I, 4 in College Chemistry II, 3 in Chemistry Seminar, 3 in Chemical Calculations, 5 in Instrumental Methods, 4 in Fundamentals of Organic Chemistry, 3 in Technical Mathematics, and 3 in Chemical Technology Internship, for a grand total of 29 semester hours (7/88) (1/95).

Tel-A-Train

Since 1973 Tel-A-Train has produced technical training courses and training products for manufacturing, industry and vocational education institutions worldwide. Tel-A-Train's standards of excellence in performance-based instructional design and video production quality have made us a recognized leader in video training for mechanical and electrical maintenance, hydraulics and pneumatics, solid state electronics, Total Productive Maintenance and industrial safety.

To complement a comprehensive video library, Tel-A-Train also produces hands-on training hardware to support practical skills development in the areas of Mechanical Maintenance, Pneumatics, Precision Mechanical Measuring and Arc Welding.

In 1994 Tel-A-Train was purchased by Westcott Communication of Dallas, Texas, owner of a variety of satellite training networks. In May of 1996, Westcott was acquired by PRIMEDIA (formerly K-III Communications) of New York, a multi-billion dollar information, education, and media company that shares Tel-A-Trains long-standing commitment to develop and produce the most effective technical and industrial training on the market.

In 1997 Tel-A-Train introduced its interactive multimedia simulations, delivered on CD-ROM. This format presents a virtual workplace, in which Trainees must evaluate Electrical equipment condition, make decisions and apply skills. The realism of the environment significantly increases the effectiveness of technical training. Development is underway to add mechanical applications to the Tel-A-Train CD library and to offer web-based training solutions.

Source of official student records: Registry of Credit Recommendations, American Council on Education, One Dupont Circle, Washington, DC 20036-1193.

Additional information about the courses: College Credit Recommendation Service, American Council on Education, One Dupont Circle, Washington, DC 20036-1193.

Applied Electricity

Location: Customers' plants/facilities.

Length: 75 hours (7 sessions).

Dates: December 1995-Present.

Objective: To provide the student with an understanding of basic electricity; its generation, transmission, and usage.

Learning Outcome: Upon successful completion of this course, the student will be able to understand and use control schematics and diagrams; describe basic electrical principles, terminology, and symbols; and apply these concepts to electrical equipment and systems.

Instruction: Major topics covered in the course are electrical generation, plant distribution, electrical auxiliaries, electrical symbols, reading ladder diagrams, and electrical troubleshooting. Methods of instruction include video programs, study guide, lecture, lab exercises, quizzes, homework assignments, lab practice, module review examinations, and final examination.

Credit Recommendation: In the vocational certificate category or lower division baccalaureate/associate degree category, 2 semester hours in Basic Electricity (11/97).

Industrial Safety

Location: Customers' plants/facilities.

Length: 75 hours (10 sessions).

Dates: November 1995-Present.

Objective: To create awareness of the safety issues and hazards inherent in industrial and manufacturing environments, and to provide information on protective equipment and safe practices that ensure personal protection in the course of job performance.

Learning Outcome: Upon successful completion of this course, the student will be able to demonstrate safe workplace practices in industrial and manufacturing environments; recognize potential safety hazards; resolve dangerous conditions; and identify standard safety operating procedures.

Instruction: Major topics covered in the course are safety—general, occupational,and hazardous communications; electrical lockout; shop; confined space entry; drug-free workplace; sexual harassment; blood-borne pathogens and first aid safety; student presentations; and examination. Methods of instruction include video programs, study guide, lecture, lab exercises, quizzes, completion of lab exercises, research paper, and final examination.

Credit Recommendation: In the vocational certificate category or lower division baccalaureate/associate degree category, 3 semester hours in Industrial Safety (11/97).

Industrial Welding

Location: Customers' plants/facilities.

Length: 120 hours (15 sessions).

Dates: August 1994-Present.

Objective: To provide welding and weld safety training for industrial applications— oxygen/acetylene gas cutting and electric arc welding(including shielded metal, gas tungsten and gas metal welding) and their applications (carbon and stainless pipe and miscellaneous steel); and air carbon arc cutting.

Learning Outcome: Upon successful completion of this course, the student will be able to use the terminology of welding; make welds of basic joints safely; and be certified on oxygen/acetylene gas cutting procedures.

Instruction: Major topics covered in the course are welding safety, introduction to SM arc welding, 6010 and 7018 welding rods, stringer beads, weave beads/restarts, tips and techniques, square groove welds, air carbon arc, carbon steel pipe, low alloy pipe, GT and GM arc welding, stainless steel pipe, practice, and examination. Methods of instruction include video programs, study guide, lecture, lab exercises, quizzes, homework assignments, lab practice, and final examination.

Credit Recommendation: In the vocational certificate category or lower division baccalaureate/associate degree category, 4 semester hours in Industrial Welding (11/97).

Managing Employee Safety and Health

Location: Various customers' plants/facilities.

Length: 40 hours.

Dates: January 1992-Present.

Objective: To prepare supervisors to proactively and systematically manage health and safety issues in the workplace.

Learning Outcome: Upon successful completion of this course, the student will be able to coordinate and manage an occupational safety program.

Instruction: Major topics covered in the course are job hazard analysis, compliance issues, ergonomics, accident investigation, hazardous conditions, managing safety and health, effective communications, safety meetings, and improving employee safety performance. Methods of instruction include video programs, study guide, lecture, lab exercises, quizzes, case studies, and final examination.

Credit Recommendation: In the vocational certificate category or lower division baccalaureate/associate degree category, 2 semester hours in Occupational Safety (11/97).

Mechanical Maintenance

Location: Customers' plants/facilities.

Length: 105 hours (10 or more sessions).

Dates: November 1995-Present.

Objective: To provide comprehensive training in installation, maintenance and trouble-shooting of industrial mechanical equipment, including identification of specific components and how they are used in an industrial or manufacturing system.

Learning Outcome: Upon successful completion of this course, the student will be able to install and adjust equipment components; monitor performance; perform diagnostic troubleshooting procedures; and perform preventative maintenance of industrial mechanical equipment.

Instruction: Major topics covered in the course are basic terms, lubrication techniques, bearings, gears and reducers, flexible drives, positive drives, coupling alignment, brakes and clutches, valves, and centrifugal pumps. Methods of instruction include video programs, study guide, lecture, lab exercises, quizzes, completion of lab exercises, and final examination.

Credit Recommendation: In the vocational certificate category or lower division baccalaureate/associate degree category, 4 semester hours in Industrial Equipment Maintenance (11/97).

Precision Mechanical Measuring

Location: Customers' plants/facilities.

Length: 45 hours (5 sessions).

Dates: December 1989-Present.

Objective: To provide training in methods of obtaining measurements in fractional, decimal and metric scales and reading/recording surface dimensions using precision instruments (dial caliper and Vernier micrometer).

Learning Outcome: Upon successful completion of this course, the student will be able to make precision measurements in the English and metric systems using basic mechanical measuring devices (rulers, micrometers & calipers) and relate measurements to print specifications.

Instruction: Major topics covered in the course are introduction to measurements, micrometers, calipers, applied measurement skills, and advanced technology. Methods of instruction include video programs, study guide, lecture, lab exercises utilizing Precision Mechanical Measuring Kit, quizzes, homework assignments, lab practice, and final examination.

Credit Recommendation: In the vocational certificate category or lower division baccalaureate/associate degree category, 2 semester hours in Precision Measurement (11/97).

Total Productive Maintenance

Location: Customers' plants/facilities.

Length: 75 hours (5 sessions).

Dates: November 1995-Present.

Objective: To provide the student with an understanding of total productive maintenance and methods of improving overall equipment effectiveness.

Learning Outcome: Upon successful completion of this course, the student will be able to understand and implement key elements of total productive maintenance; evaluate and improve overall equipment effectiveness; and apply preventive and predictive maintenance practices.

Instruction: Major topics covered in the course are the five key elements of total productive maintenance, determination of overall equipment effectiveness, principles of preventative and predictive maintenance. Methods of instruction include video programs, study guide, lecture, lab exercises, quizzes, homework assignments, lab practice, and final examination.

Credit Recommendation: In the vocational certificate category or lower division baccalaureate/associate degree category, 2 semester hours in Industrial Maintenance Technology (11/97).

Telecommunications Research Associates

Since 1985, TRA has provided the highest-quality telecommunications training available, globally, to more than 138,000 communications professionals. TRA provides public, private, and custom instructor-led training as well as; live video, distance learning production, and support media such as LexiCAT (a hypertext glossary of over 3,000 telecommunications terms and acronyms with upwards of 30,000 hyperlinks). But the single greatest distinguishing factor separating TRA from other training companies is our faculty. They have helped create the very technologies they teach. The TRA faculty currently hold over 30 patents in communications and information-processing technologies, and have served in the industry's leading research and development facilities (such as Bell Labs). They are or have been "frontline engineers" in developing learning materials and deploying new technologies.

Students receive a TRA course book that contains exact copies of the graphics used by the instructor to illustrate technical concepts. Also contained in the course book are instructor-written Section Summaries and student Reinforcement Exercises.

Source of official student records: Registry of Credit Recommendation, American Council on Education, One Dupont Circle, Washington, DC 20036-1193.

Additional information about the courses: College Credit Recommendation Service, American Council on Education, One Dupont Circle, Washington, DC 20036-1193.

(3-Day) Understanding Emerging Technologies in 1998™

Location: Various sites in the United States, Canada, Europe, and Asia.

Length: 19 hours (3 days).

Dates: April 1991-Present.

Objective: To provide students with a broad overview of the most significant new communications technologies affecting them today.

Learning Outcome: Upon successful completion of this course, the student will be able to conceptualize the fundamentals of the technologies and applications taught; and understand the "where and why" to utilize these new technologies.

Instruction: Major topics covered in the course are network signaling systems, Signaling System Number 7 (SS7) and the Advanced Intelligent Network (AIN); the concepts and technologies supporting wireless communication, and the Internet; Competitive Access Providers (CAPs); access technologies as well as the key players and today's regulatory environment; detailed sections on SONET, Frame Relay, ATM, and SMDS; Computer/ Telephony Integration (CTI), and what's in store for communications in the near future. Methods of instruction include lecture, audio/visual material, discussion, classroom exercises, case studies, and final examination.

Credit Recommendation: In the upper division baccalaureate degree category, 1 semester hour in Telecommunications, Networking, Computer Engineering, or Electrical Engineering (10/97).

Understanding AIN™

Location: Various sites in the United States, Canada, Europe, and Asia.

Length: 15 hours (2 days).

Dates: December 1994-Present.

Objective: To provide a practical understanding of the concepts behind the Advanced Intelligent Network (AIN), the network capabilities required to provide AIN services, and the mechanisms which will allow AIN services to co-exist with non-AIN services; and examines the AIN services currently being deployed, and the issues these deployments are facing.

Learning Outcome: Upon successful completion of this course, the student will be able to understand AIN's goals and architecture and how the AIN will be used to provide new, flexible services, such as individualized call management and Personal Communications Service.

Instruction: Major topics covered in the course are how AIN enables the delivery of flexible new services more quickly and affordably, AIN's long-term goals, the AIN architecture, basic call model and trigger processing, feature design and interactions, how PCS providers use wireline AIN capabilities to offer flexible new services, and how many are preparing to build their own private Wireless Intelligent Networks. Methods of instruction include lecture, audio/visual material, discussion, classroom exercises, case studies, and final examination.

Credit Recommendation: In the upper division baccalaureate degree category, 1 semester hour in Telecommunications, Networking, Computer Engineering, or Electrical Engineering (10/97). **NOTE:** Student should receive credit for this course or "Understanding SS7, AIN, and LNP", but not for both.

Understanding ATM Implementations™

Location: Various sites in the United States, Canada, Europe, and Asia.

Length: 15 hours (2 days).

Dates: August 1995-Present.

Objective: To provide students with an excellent understanding of current ATM technologies, including business perspectives, switch designs, and protocols, as well as how networks are evolving to ATM.

Learning Outcome: Upon successful completion of this course, the student will have an understanding of Asynchronous Transfer Mode and its potential, as well as how the major broadband components complement and compete with one another.

Instruction: Major topics covered in the course are the implementation issues surrounding Asynchronous Transfer Mode (ATM) for three near-term applications: ATM Local Area Networks (LANs), ATM Wide Area Networks (WANs), and ATM Video Networks; the equipment, services, and issues surrounding implementation of ATM with special case studies; up-to-date information about the activities of the ATM Forum's technical committees; services available from the major public carriers; and real-world applications, network management, quality-of-service issues, and interworking with other technologies. Methods of instruction include lecture, audio/visual material, discussion, classroom exercises, case studies, and final examination.

Credit Recommendation: In the upper division baccalaureate degree category, 1 semester hour in Telecommunications, Networking, Computer Engineering, or Electrical Engineering (10/97).

Understanding ATM™

Location: Various sites in the United States, Canada, Europe, and Asia.

Length: 15 hours (2 days).

Dates: November 1992-Present.

Objective: To familiarize students with the evolution from today's non-ATM networks and applications to a practical implementation of ATM.

Learning Outcome: Upon successful completion of this course, the student will be able to recognize which customer networks are likely to benefit most from ATM and in which applications; have an idea about how to advise customers and proceed with application; and understand the alternatives to ATM to lead a customer to the overall best decision for broadband networking.

Instruction: Major topics covered in the course are the foundation for ATM; the evolution to an ATM network; the business perspective on how ATM compares with alternative technologies; the many interfaces and the protocol; and voice over ATM, Private Network/Network Interface (PNNI), congestion control, the adaptation layer, and ATM standard interfaces and switch design. Methods of instruction include lecture, audio/visual material, discussion, classroom exercises, case studies, and final examination.

Credit Recommendation: In the upper division baccalaureate degree category, 1 semester hour in Telecommunications, Networking, Computer Engineering, or Electrical Engineering (10/97).

Understanding CDMA™

Location: Various sites in the United States, Canada, Europe, and Asia.

Length: 15 hours (2 days).

Dates: December 1996-Present.

Objective: To provide students with an introduction and examination of IS-95 Based CDMA for PCS and Digital Cellular Networks.

Learning Outcome: Upon successful completion of this course, the student will thoroughly understand PCS and CDMA.

Instruction: Major topics covered in the course are IS-95-based Code Division Multiple Access (CDMA) for Personal Communications Service (PCS); Digital Cellular Networks; which Service Providers are deploying CDMA; alternative technologies; technologies supporting CDMA; the key parameters which characterize a CDMA system; and the parameters which affect system capacity and engineering decisions (such as Eb/I0, Cell Loading, Forward, Reverse Capacity Limits, and system Coverage and Capacity), as well as detailed examination of the functions and components of forward and reverse CDMA radio links. Methods of instruction include lecture, slide presentations, discussion, classroom exercises, case studies, pre/post tests, and final examination.

Credit Recommendation: In the upper division baccalaureate degree category, 1 semester hour in Telecommunications, Computer Engineering, or Electronic Engineering (10/97).

Understanding Competitive Local Access™ Wired and Wireless

Location: Various sites in the United States, Canada, Europe, and Asia.

Length: 15 hours (2 days).

Dates: March 1994-Present.

Objective: To give students an understanding of the current and future of cable, enabling them to make the right choices in this fiercely competitive market.

Learning Outcome: Upon successful completion of this course, the student will be able to identify the major players and gain insight into their strategies, as well as the business applications that will drive their battle over market share.

Instruction: Major topics covered in the course are the multi-billion dollar revolution in the market to deliver cable, wireless, and voice communications to businesses and homes; the competitors, the Regional Bell Operating Companies (RBOCs), Telcos, Cable Operators, Interexchange Carriers (IECs), Competitive Local Exchange Carriers (CLECs), Cellular Operators, International Communications Companies, and the vertically-integrated communications companies which may evolve from combinations of these players. Methods of instruction include lecture, audio/visual material, discussion, classroom exercises, case studies, and final examination.

Credit Recommendation: In the upper division baccalaureate degree category, 1 semester hour in Telecommunications, Networking, Computer Engineering, or Electrical Engineering (10/97).

Understanding Emerging Technologies in 1998™

Location: Various sites in the United States, Canada, Europe, and Asia.

Length: 15 hours (2 days).

Dates: January 1997-Present.

Objective: To provide students with a broad overview of the most significant new communications technologies affecting them today. Real-world examples and technology implementation scenarios describe and explain these new technologies.

Learning Outcome: Upon successful completion of this course, the student will be able to state and/or discuss the fundamentals of the technologies and applications taught; and discuss "where and why" to utilize these new technologies.

Instruction: Major topics covered in the course are fundamental technologies forming today's communications networks; their effect on the marketplace; backbone network technologies such as Advanced Intelligent Network (AIN) and Signaling System Number 7 (SS7), Frame Relay, and Asynchronous Transfer Mode (ATM); the Internet; Hybrid Fiber/Coax (HFC); and Wireless. Methods of instruction include lecture, audio/visual material, discussion, classroom exercises, case studies, and final examination.

Credit Recommendation: In the upper division baccalaureate degree category, 1 semester hour in Telecommunications, Networking, Computer Engineering, or Electrical Engineering (10/97).

Understanding Emerging Technologies™ "ET Lite"

Location: Various sites in the United States, Canada, Europe, and Asia.

Length: 15 hours (2 days).

Dates: January 1997-Present.

Objective: To provide students with an overview of the most significant new communications technologies affecting them today. This class addresses the business issues surrounding these technologies and does not go into the network operations detail.

Learning Outcome: Upon successful completion of this course, the student will be able to explain the primary functions of the technologies presented and applications for them; and discuss the business reasons for and against deploying these services and what vendor products are available.

Instruction: Major topics covered in the course are similar to the regular Emerging Technologies course, but without the more extensive detail. Methods of instruction include lecture, audio/visual material, discussion, classroom exercises, case studies, and final examination.

Credit Recommendation: In the upper division baccalaureate degree category, 1 semester hour in Telecommunications, Networking, Computer Engineering, or Electrical Engineering (10/97).

Understanding Emerging Wireless Technologies™

Location: Various sites in the United States, Canada, Europe, and Asia.

Length: 15 hours (2 days).

Dates: January 1997-Present.

Objective: To explore the wide range of wireless data capabilities and opportunities currently available.

Learning Outcome: Upon successful completion of this course, the student will be able to compare and contrast the alternatives currently available and emerging for wireless data; and determine which alternatives are best-suited to their own or their customers' needs.

Instruction: Major topics covered in the course are an overview of basic radio concepts which apply to all wireless applications; a review of the providers of wireless voice and data services, covering the technologies and business plans of Cellular; Personal Communications Service (PSC); and Enhanced Special Mobile Radio (ESMR) licensees. Methods of instruction include lecture, slide presentations, discussion, classroom exercises, case studies, tests, and final examination.

Credit Recommendation: In the upper division baccalaureate degree category, 1 semester hour in Telecommunications or Computer Engineering (10/97).

Understanding Frame Relay™

Location: Various sites in the United States, Canada, Europe, and Asia.

Length: 15 hours (2 days).

Dates: June 1991-Present.

Objective: To provide students with an understanding of network solutions based on Frame Relay. Students understand Frame Relay as a protocol, as well as how Frame Relay networks are designed, engineering considerations for Frame Relay solutions, and how Frame Relay networks are managed.

Learning Outcome: Upon successful completion of this course, the student will be able to discuss the fundamental concepts associated with Frame Relay as a protocol; how Frame Relay interworks with current and future LAN/WAN technologies; and discuss, develop, configure, and support a wide variety network implementations based on Frame Relay.

Instruction: Major topics covered in the course are Frame Relay from a technical and users perspective; evaluation of this fast-growing technology; Frame Relay applications such as Local Area Network (LAN) interconnection; the transport of Systems Network Architecture (SNA) and Voice Traffic; and Frame Relay network design protocols and Customer Premises Equipment (CPE). Methods of instruction include lecture, audio/visual material, discussion, classroom exercises, case studies, and final examination.

Credit Recommendation: In the upper division baccalaureate degree category, 1 semester hour in Telecommunications, Networking, Computer Engineering, or Electrical Engineering (10/97).

Understanding ISDN Interfaces and Applications™

Location: Various sites in the United States, Canada, Europe, and Asia.

Length: 15 hours (2 days).

Dates: May 1996-Present.

Objective: To provide a thorough understanding of the practical issues and benefits associated with implementing ISDN-based applications and solutions.

Learning Outcome: Upon successful completion of this course, the student will be able to discuss the applications and issues related to implementing ISDN.

Instruction: Major topics covered in the course are the important underlying concepts and technologies that contribute to ISDN's versatility; and how ISDN supports both voice, packet, and switched digital services and, the leading applications driving its adoption today. Methods of instruction include lecture, audio/visual material, discussion, classroom exercises, case studies, and final examination.

Credit Recommendation: In the upper division baccalaureate degree category, 1 semester hour in Telecommunications, Networking, Computer Engineering, or Electrical Engineering (10/97).

Understanding ISDN Interfaces, Applications, and Protocols™

Location: Various sites in the United States, Canada, Europe, and Asia.

Length: 19 hours (3 days).

Dates: September 1995-Present.

Objective: To provide a thorough understanding of the practical issues associated with implementing ISDN-based applications and solutions, from both a customer and supplier perspective. Additionally, a review of the ISDN protocol emphasizing the key components will be conducted.

Learning Outcome: Upon successful completion of this course, the student will be able to discuss the benefits, components, and issues related to implementing ISDN solutions, from both a customer and supplier perspective; and clarify the key areas associated with implementing and using ISDN.

Instruction: Major topics covered in the course are the "big picture" of today's communications marketplace and technology infrastructure; network signaling systems, Signaling System Number 7 (SS7), and the Advanced Intelligent Network (AIN); the concepts and technologies supporting wireless communication; the Internet; Competitive Access Providers (CAPs); access technologies and the key players in today's regulatory environment; detailed sections on SONET, Frame Relay, ATM, and SMDS; Computer/Telephony Integration (CTI); and what's in store for communications in the near future. Methods of instruction include lecture, audio/visual material, discussion, classroom exercises, case studies, and final examination.

Credit Recommendation: In the upper division baccalaureate degree category, 1 semester hour in Telecommunications, Networking, Computer Engineering, or Electrical Engineering (10/97).

Understanding ISDN™

Location: Various sites in the United States, Canada, Europe, and Asia.

Length: 15 hours (2 days).

Dates: September 1985-Present.

Objective: To provide a thorough understanding of the technical issues associated with implementing ISDN-based applications and solutions, primarily from a supplier perspective; and a review of the ISDN protocol emphasizing the key components.

Learning Outcome: Upon successful completion of this course, the student will be able to discuss the components and issues related to implementing ISDN solutions.

Instruction: Major topics covered in the course are the important underlying concepts and technologies contributing to ISDN's versatility; how the ISDN interface supports Voice, Video, Circuit-Switched Data, and Packet-Switched Data services; and examines the ISDN protocols (Q.921, Q.931, Q.932, X.25, I.430, I.450, I.451, and T1.601). Methods of instruction include lecture, audio/visual material, discussion, classroom exercises, case studies, and final examination.

Credit Recommendation: In the upper division baccalaureate degree category, 1 semester hour in Telecommunications, Networking, Computer Engineering, or Electrical Engineering (10/97).

Understanding LAN and TCP/IP Integration™

Location: Various sites in the United States, Canada, Europe, and Asia.

Length: 15 hours (2 days).

Dates: June 1996-Present.

Objective: To offer students an understanding of the fundamental concepts associated with LAN technologies, LAN standards, and LAN operation and internetworking, and how the TCP/IP suite is integrated into new and existing LANs.

Learning Outcome: Upon successful completion of this course, the student will be able to design, engineer, and implement TCP/IP in both existing and legacy Local Area Networks; identify various LAN standards, Media, and operational scenarios, and discuss internetworking challenges and solutions.

Instruction: Major topics covered in the course are Local Area Network (LAN) technologies and applications, LAN standards and interoperability, LAN media operations and standards, TCP/IP bridges and routers, LAN switches and virtual LANs, and routing of packets. Methods of instruction include lecture, audio/visual material, discussion, classroom exercises, case studies, and final examination.

Credit Recommendation: In the upper division baccalaureate degree category, 1 semester hour in Telecommunications Networking, Computer Engineering, or Electrical Engineering (10/97). **NOTE:** Student should receive credit for this course or "Understanding Wide Area Data Networking", but not for both.

Understanding Personal Communications Service™

Location: Various sites in the United States, Canada, Europe, and Asia.

Length: 15 hours (2 days).

Dates: April 1992-Present.

Objective: To provide students with the basic concepts behind PCS, the network capabilities required to support PCS, and the issues being decided today.

Learning Outcome: Upon successful completion of this course, the student will be able to state the technological hurdles PCS faces in deployment, early services the technology is expected to provide, and the larger overall picture of how and why PCS will have such a large impact on our society as a whole.

Instruction: Major topics covered in the course are the evolution of wireless and cellular services; the concepts behind PCS; the network capabilities required to support PCS; who the key players will be; and today's decision making processes concerning PCS deployment. Methods of instruction include lecture, slide presentation, discussion, classroom exercises, case studies, and final examination.

Credit Recommendation: In the upper division baccalaureate degree category, 1 semester hour in Telecommunications or Computer Engineering (10/97).

Understanding SONET and Other Broadband Technologies™

Location: Various sites in the United States, Canada, Europe, and Asia.

Length: 15 hours (2 days).

Dates: December 1994-Present.

Objective: To provide a practical overview of SONET, ATM, and Broadband technologies, as well as their applications, evolution, implementation and regulatory status.

Learning Outcome: Upon successful completion of this course, the student will be able to discuss high-bandwidth transport technology topics.

Instruction: Major topics covered in the course are an overview of Broadband technologies and protocols; Synchronous Optical Network (SONET) applications and implementations, including Digital Loop Carrier, Local Access, and Backbone Rings; and how Asynchronous Transfer Mode (ATM) is carried over SONET. Methods of instruction include lecture, audio/visual material, discussion, classroom exercises, case studies, and final examination.

Credit Recommendation: In the upper division baccalaureate degree category, 1 semester hour in Telecommunications, Networking, Computer Engineering, or Electrical Engineering (10/97).

Understanding SS7, AIN, and LNP™

Location: Various sites in the United States, Canada, Europe, and Asia.

Length: 15 hours (2 days).

Dates: July 1997-Present.

Objective: To provide a practical understanding of the Signaling System Number 7 (SS7) architecture, protocols and service opportunities. Building upon this SS7 foundation, we'll help students understand what it takes to build Advanced Intelligent Network (AIN) services by examining AIN's goals, architecture, call model and messaging process; why the industry is scrambling to introduce a long-term solution for Local Number Portability; and to illustrate how SS7 and AIN will support this solution.

Learning Outcome: Upon successful completion of this course, the student will be able to discuss SS7 and AIN architectures and service capabilities; and understand how SS7 and AIN will support the long-term solution for Local Number Portability.

Instruction: Major topics covered in the course are Local Number Portability; the regulatory environment; consumer and carrier perspectives; interim portability solutions; long-term portability solutions based on SS7 and AIN; detailed call flows illustrate how each layer of SS7 and the AIN application contribute to accomplishing LNP in the network; and updates on other important LNP issues such as service ordering, NPA-NXX decoupling, and cost recovery. Methods of instruction include lecture, audio/visual material, discussion, classroom exercises, case studies, and final examination.

Credit Recommendation: In the upper division baccalaureate degree category, 1 semester hour in Telecommunications, Networking, Computer Engineering, or Electrical Engineering (10/97). **NOTE:** Student should receive credit for this course or "Understanding AIN", but not for both.

Understanding the Basics of Communications Networks™

Location: Various sites in the United States, Canada, Europe, and Asia.

Length: 15 hours (2 days).

Dates: January 1997-Present.

Objective: To provide students with a broad and relatively in-depth understanding of the current and emerging communications networks: switching, signaling, transmission, and control.

Learning Outcome: Upon successful completion of this course, the student will be able to discuss the major issues in telecommunications and use correctly industry terminology; and have a very broad understanding of signaling, switching, transmission, and network control.

Instruction: Major topics covered in the course are the history of telephony from early systems to today's digital infrastructure; "switching", including the types of switches used in telephone networks; how switches interwork with one another; modern transmission systems and multiplexing techniques; wireless communications technology and devices; how wireless devices mesh with "land-line" systems; and technologies used on network backbones to control and process calls, along with high-bandwidth technologies. Methods of instruction include lecture, audio/visual material, discussion, classroom exercises, case studies, and final examination.

Credit Recommendation: In the upper division baccalaureate degree category, 1 semester hour in Telecommunications,

Networking, Computer Engineering, or Electrical Engineering (10/97).

Understanding the Internet and Electronic Commerce™ Applications and Infrastructure

Location: Various sites in the United States, Canada, Europe, and Asia.

Length: 15 hours (2 days).

Dates: June 1996-Present.

Objective: To provide students with an excellent understanding of the Internet and its expected evolution, enabling them to more clearly judge the potential business opportunities it presents as it continues to evolve.

Learning Outcome: Upon successful completion of this course, the student will be able to discuss the current state and future potential of the Internet.

Instruction: Major topics covered in the course are Internet overviews, Internet business models, Web Commerce, key security topics, comparison of Internet Service Providers (ISPs) to commercial on-line services, the features of several popular World Wide Web (WWW) authoring tools, threats and opportunities the Internet represents to communications companies, and demonstrations of the dynamic nature of the Internet. Methods of instruction include a live demonstration of Internet telephony and videoconferencing in addition to lecture, audio/visual material, discussion, classroom exercises, case studies, demonstration, and final examination.

Credit Recommendation: In the lower division baccalaureate/associate degree category, 1 semester hour in Information Technology (10/97).

Understanding Wide Area Data Networking™

Location: Various sites in the United States, Canada, Europe, and Asia.

Length: 15 hours (2 days).

Dates: July 1996-Present.

Objective: To provide students with an understanding of Wide Area Networks, TCP/IP, Frame Relay, ATM, and IP Switching.

Learning Outcome: Upon successful completion of this course, the student will be able to configure and support communication plans for internetworking options; and have the knowledge to objectively compare and contrast technology options.

Instruction: Major topics covered in the course are Wide Area Networking (WAN), Frame Relay, Switched Multimegabit Data Service (SMDS), Asynchronous Transfer Mode (ATM), IP Switching, and integration. Methods of instruction include lecture, audio/visual material, discussion, classroom exercises, case studies, and final examination.

Credit Recommendation: In the upper division baccalaureate degree category, 1 semester hour in Telecommunications, Networking, Computer Engineering, or Electrical Engineering (10/97). **NOTE:** Student should receive credit for this course or "Understanding LAN and TCP/IP Integration", but not for both.

Understanding Wireless Data™

Location: Various sites in the United States, Canada, Europe, and Asia.

Length: 15 hours (2 days).

Dates: June 1994-Present.

Objective: To explore the wide range of wireless data capabilities and opportunities - from data over paging networks to data over satellite networks - and almost everything in between, including Cellular and PCS Circuit Switched Data as well as ARDIS, RAM, and CDPD wireless packet switched data networks.

Learning Outcome: Upon successful completion of this course, the student will be able to discuss the choices available for wireless data delivery, and which alternatives are best suited for specific applications; state the driving forces for wireless data services; and proactively address network and customer demands.

Instruction: Major topics covered in the course are Wireless Data and E-Mail, Fax, and Corporate and Internet Database Access; personal computing (increasingly small but high-powered notebook, palmtop, and PDA computing devices); wireless data radio technologies; and simple extensions to Paging Networks to Satellite Data Networks. Methods of instruction include lecture, slide presentation, discussion, classroom exercises, case studies, and final examination.

Credit Recommendation: In the upper division baccalaureate degree category, 1 semester hour in Telecommunications, Computer Engineering, or Electronics Engineering (10/97).

TESST Technology Institute

TESST Technology Institute, founded in 1967, offer specialized career education programs in electronics and computer technology, drafting and design technology, software applications, and Medical Office Administration. Our mission is to provide quality career and technology education that prepares students for employment and advancement in their chosen field of study.

TESST has locations in Alexandria, Virginia; Baltimore, Maryland; and Hyattsville, Maryland. All three TESST Institutes are accredited by the Accrediting Commission for Career Schools & Colleges of Technology (ACCSCT).

For more information about TESST visit our web site at http\\www.tesst.com.

AUTHORIZED TESST TECHNOLOGY INSTITUTE SCHOOLS

Tesst Technology Institute
1808 Edison Highway
Baltimore, MD 21213
Contact: Susan Sherwood
Phone No.: 410-327-6640
Fax No.: 410-327-1908

Tesst Technology Institute
1400 Duke Street
Alexandria, VA 22314
Contact: Clete Mehringer
Phone No.: 703-548-4800
Fax No.: 703-683-2765

Source of official student records: Registry of Credit Recommendations, American Council on Education, One Dupont Circle, Washington, DC 20036-1193; or Office of the Registrar, TESST Technology Institute: 1400 Duke Street, Alexandria, VA 22314; Edison Highway, Baltimore, MD 21213, and 5122 Baltimore Avenue, Hyattsville, MD 20781

Additional information about the courses: College Credit Recommendation Service, American Council on Education, One Dupont Circle, Washington, DC 20036-1193.

AC and DC Fundamentals

Location: Hyattsville, MD; Baltimore, MD; and Alexandria, VA.

Length: 110 lecture hours/ 90 laboratory hours.

Dates: July 1996-Present.

Objective: To provide students with the basic concepts of AC and DC electrical circuits.

Learning Outcome: Upon successful completion of this course, the student will be able to demonstrate a knowledge of basic electrical circuit concepts and problem solutions, and demonstrate correct laboratory measurement techniques and safety.

Instruction: Major topics covered in the course are voltage sources; Ohm's law; power, series, parallel, and series-parallel circuits; voltage dividers; circuit theorems, including Thevenin, Norton, and superposition; magnetism; capacitance; inductance; reactance; transformers; time constants; R-C, R-L, and R-C-L circuits; resonance; band width; Q; use of analog and digital multimeters; oscilloscope; and frequency meter. Methods of instruction include lecture, laboratory exercise , tests, and final examination.

Credit Recommendation: In the lower division baccalaureate/associate degree category, 4 semesters hours in AC/DC Circuit Fundamentals and 1 semester hour in AC/DC Circuit Laboratory (11/96).

Computer Applications for Technicians

Location: Hyattsville, MD; Baltimore, MD; and Alexandria, VA.

Length: 30 laboratory hours.

Dates: July 1996-Present.

Objective: To gain an understanding of selected computer application programs and the skills to use them in various technical applications.

Learning Outcome: Upon successful completion of this course, the student will be able to skillfully use spreadsheets, graphics, and database management.

Instruction: Major topics covered in the course are spreadsheets (in business and electronics), graphics, and database management in applied electronics. Methods of instruction include laboratory exercises and quizzes.

Credit Recommendation: In the lower division baccalaureate/associate degree category, 1 semester hour in Computer Literacy or Computer Laboratory Applications (11/96).

Computer Architecture: Diagnostics and Repair

Location: Hyattsville, MD; Baltimore, MD and Alexandria, VA.

Length: 170 lecture hours/ 80 laboratory hours.

Dates: January 1997-Present.

Objective: To provide the student with the understanding of microprocessors 8085, 8088, and 80468; with the understanding of assembly language and machine language programs; and the skills necessary to identify computer parts, setup and configure software and hardware, and to diagnose and troubleshoot the personal computer.

Learning Outcome: Upon successful completion of this course, the student will be able to understand computer processing architecture including registers, system boards, circuitry, and control systems; write assembly language programs to control input/output and peripheral devices; identify computer parts, disassemble and reassemble the personal computer; use a disk operating system ; install and configure a hard disk; and install and configure a software application.

Instruction: Major topics covered in the course are architecture of microprocessors 8085, 8088, and 80486 and their internal registers; circuitry and control systems; assembly language and machine language; diagnosis and repair of computers; subsystems; computer components; the microprocessor and support; memory input/output; peripherals; hard disk installation; and the disk operating system. Methods of instruction include lecture, discussion, classroom exercises, laboratory exercises, quizzes, and final examination.

Credit Recommendation: In the lower division baccalaureate/associate degree category, 6 semester hours in Computer Systems or Computer Architecture and 2 semester hours in Computer Diagnostics and Repair; in the upper division baccalaureate degree category, 6 semester hours in Computer Systems or Computer Architecture and 2 semester hours in Computer Diagnostics and Repair (11/96).

Customer Relations

Location: Hyattsville, MD; Baltimore, MD; and Alexandria, VA.

Length: 25 lecture hours.

Dates: July 1996-Present.

Objective: To provide students with professionally developed concepts and theories to deal successfully with interactions between people and to handle customer complaints.

Learning Outcome: Upon successful completion of this course, the student will know how to deal with people, and to maintain good customer relations as required in the business world.

Instruction: Major topics covered in the course are verbal and non-verbal communication; perceptions; assertiveness and self concepts; explaining; persuasion; handling customer complaints; and interpersonal skills. Methods of instruction include lecture, discussion, case studies, quizzes, and final examination.

Credit Recommendation: In the lower division baccalaureate/associate degree category, 1 semester hour in Customer Relations, General Business, Psychology, or Basic Occupational Communication (11/96).

Digital Electronics

Location: Hyattsville, MD; Baltimore, MD; and Alexandria, VA.

Length: 120 lecture hours/100 laboratory hours.

Dates: July 1996-Present.

Objective: To prepare the student with basic concepts and applications of digital electronic devices and circuits.

Learning Outcome: Upon successful completion of this course, the student will be able to demonstrate a knowledge of basic digital electronic devices.

Instruction: Major topics covered in the course are essential of switching circuits; logic gates; Boolean algebra; Karnaugh maps; binary, BCD, and gray codes; multiplexer; logic families; flip-flop; counters; digital displays; shift register; IC timer; multivibrators; D/A, and A/D converters; RAM; programmable logic; and laboratory exercises to support theoretical concepts. Methods of instruction include lecture, laboratory exercises, tests, and final examination.

Credit Recommendation: In the lower division baccalaureate/associate degree category, 3 semester hour in Digital Electronics and 1 semester hour in Digital Electronics Laboratory (11/96).

Electronic Communications I

Location: Hyattsville, MD; Baltimore, MD; and Alexandria, VA.

Length: 100 lecture hours/80 laboratory hours.

Dates: July 1996-Present.

Objective: To provide the student with basic concepts of radio and video systems and laboratory exercises to practice troubleshooting video and systems.

Learning Outcome: Upon successful completion of this course, the student will be able to demonstrate a knowledge of video circuits and demonstrate an ability to analyze and isolate video circuit defects in the laboratory.

Instruction: Major topics covered in the course are basic theory and operation of television receivers with supporting concepts of AM, FM, and SSB transmission lines and antennas; information on VCR and computer monitor operations; laboratory exercises including construction of AM radio; and troubleshooting TV systems, VCR and computer monitor. Methods of instruction include lecture, laboratory exercises, tests, and final examination .

Credit Recommendation: In the lower division baccalaureate/associate degree category, 2 semester hour in Television Technology and 1 semester hour in Video Systems Laboratory (11/96).

Employment Preparation

Location: Hyattsville, MD; Baltimore, MD; and Alexandria, VA.

Length: 25 lecture hours.

Dates: July 1996-Present.

Objective: To prepare students for the job search upon graduation.

Learning Outcome: Upon successful completion of this course, the student will be able to search for a job using traditional and non-traditional job search methods; prepare a resume; and communicate effectively in an interview utilizing special techniques.

Instruction: Major topics covered in the course are career goals; self analysis; finding and researching prospective employers; resume writing; and preparing for the interview. Methods of instruction include lecture, mock interviews, resumes, and applications.

Credit Recommendation: In the lower division baccalaureate/associate degree category, 1 semester hour in Survival Skills, Career Advancement and Planning, Business Communication, or Technical Writing (11/96).

Mechanics for Electronic Technicians

Location: Hyattsville, MD; Baltimore, MD; and Alexandria, VA.

Length: 25 lecture hours.

Dates: January 1997-Present.

Objective: To provide students with knowledge of basic mechanical devices used on electronic equipment.

Learning Outcome: Upon successful completion of this course, the student will be able to do mechanical fabrication.

Instruction: Major topics covered in the course are basic machine principles; relays; sensors; switches; special tools; adjustments; mechanical troubleshooting; motor control; electric motors; and copiers. Methods of instruction include lecture, quizzes, tests, and final examination .

Credit Recommendation: In the vocational certificate category, 1 semester hour in Applied Mechanics (11/96).

MS DOS

Location: Hyattsville, MD; Baltimore, MD; and Alexandria, VA.

Dates: July 1996-Present.

Objective: To define DOS as a system software for IBM and compatible computers, with sufficient explanation and in enough depth for an understanding of DOS's internal, external, and advanced commands.

Learning Outcome: Upon successful completion of this course, the student will be able to identify the six units of computer systems (input, output, memory, processor, controls, and power supply) and to have a clear understanding of their operations.

Instruction: Major topics covered in the course are introduction to computer basic units; theory of DOS commands; versions of DOS commands; and applications of DOS commands as a system software. Methods of instruction include lecture, discussion, classroom exercises, and quizzes.

Credit Recommendation: In the lower division baccalaureate/associate degree category, 1 semester hour in Computer Literacy and Operating Systems (11/96).

Principles of Troubleshooting

Location: Hyattsville, MD; Baltimore, MD; and Alexandria, VA.

Length: 32 lecture hours.

Dates: July 1996-Present.

Objective: To provide the student with the basic skills in troubleshooting electronic circuits.

Learning Outcome: Upon successful completion of this course, the student will be able to perform tests on video equipment to isolate defective components using electronic test equipment, schematics, and block diagrams.

Instruction: Major topics covered in the course are electrical safety; troubleshooting principles; analyzing defects using symptoms; test equipment; use of schematic diagrams for troubleshooting; and laboratory exercises to practice troubleshooting techniques. Methods of instruction include lecture, and laboratory.

Credit Recommendation: In the lower division baccalaureate/associate degree category, 1 semester hour in Electronic Troubleshooting Laboratory (11/96).

Semiconductor Devices and Electronic Circuits

Location: Hyattsville, MD; Baltimore, MD; and Alexandria, VA.

Length: 110 lecture hours/ 100 laboratory hours.

Dates: July 1996-Present.

Objective: To provide students with an introduction to basic electronic devices and circuits.

Learning Outcome: Upon successful completion of this course, students will be able to demonstrate a knowledge of basic electronic devices and circuits, and to apply the concepts in related laboratory exercises.

Instruction: Major topics covered in the course are essentials of semiconductor devices, including diodes and transistors; solid state amplifiers, including rectifiers, biasing, small signal and power amplifiers; multistage amplifiers; thrysistor; operational amplifier circuits; and an overview of voltage regulators, active filters, oscillators and phase locked loops. Methods of instruction include lecture, laboratory exercises, quizzes, and final examination.

Credit Recommendation: In the lower division baccalaureate/associate degree category, 2 semester hours in Fundamentals of Electronic Devices and Circuits, 2 semester hours in Applications of Electronic Devices and 2 semester hours in Electronic Devices Laboratory 1 and 2 for Non-Electronic Technology Majors (11/96).

Study and Life Skills

Location: Hyattsville, MD; Baltimore, MD; and Alexandria, VA.

Length: 20 lecture hours.

Dates: January 1996-Present.

Objective: To provide students with life style skills which will give direction and enhance both their academic and personal lives.

Learning Outcome: Upon successful completion of this course, the student will be able to develop time management skills, memory techniques, test-taking skills, reading comprehensive skills, note-taking skills, and budgeting skills.

Instruction: Major topics covered in the course are time management resources, memory, relationships, money, health, writing, tests, notes, and thinking. Methods of instruction include lecture, discussion, classroom exercises, and quizzes.

Credit Recommendation: In the vocational certificate category, 1 semester hour in Survival Skills, Study Skills, or Time Management (11/96).

Technical Mathematics (Elements of Math, Intermediate Algebra, Trigonometry)

Location: Hyattsville, MD; Baltimore, MD; and Alexandria, VA.

Length: 120 lecture hours.

Dates: October 1996-Present.

Objective: To provide the student with the basic mathematical concepts required to study electronic circuits and systems.

Learning Outcome: Upon successful completion of this course, the student will be able to demonstrate knowledge of arithmetic concepts; solve basic algebraic equations; factor polynomials; employ logarithms to solve problems; and demonstrate knowledge of geometry, trigonometry, number systems, and graphing techniques.

Instruction: Major topics covered in the course are arithmetic concepts; scientific and engineering notations; algebraic equations; units of measure; geometry; linear equations and graphing; systems of linear equations; determinants and matrices; trigonometry; vectors and phasors; complex numbers; logarithms; quadratic equations; and number systems. Methods of instruction include lecture, discussion, classroom exercises, homework assignments, quizzes, laboratory exercises, and final examination .

Credit Recommendation: In the lower division baccalaureate/associate degree category, 3 semester hours in Technical Mathematics upon completion of ETTC program (11/96).

Telecommunications and LAN Systems

Location: Hyattsville, MD; Baltimore, MD; and Alexandria, VA.

Length: 125 lecture hours/ 75 laboratory hours.

Dates: January 1997-Present.

Objective: To provide the student with the technical knowledge and practical experience necessary to become an entry level technician in telecommunications.

Learning Outcome: Upon successful completion of this course, the student will be able to perform routine operation, analysis, trouble shooting, and repair of telecommunication systems, including LAN/WAN networks.

Instruction: Major topics covered in the course are pulse/digital modulation techniques; frequency and time division multiplexing; computer interfaced telecommunication networks; UARTS and modems, including modulation and compression techniques and interface standards; LAN/WAN topologies and protocols; error detection, correction and control; public switched telephone network, North American Digital MUX Hierarchy fiber: coax and copper line transmission mediums; and cellular phone system. Methods of instruction include lecture, laboratory exercises, quizzes, and final examination (11/96).

Credit Recommendation: In the lower division baccalaureate/associate degree category, 3 semester hours in Telecommunications or Networking and 2 semester hours in Telecommunications Laboratory; and in the upper division baccalaureate degree category, 3 semester hours in Telecommunications or Networking and 2 semester hours in Telecommunications Laboratory (11/96).

Training/Etc Inc.

/training/etc Inc. specializes in the design, delivery and leasing of high-end technical training courses. Our subject-matter competencies consist of onsite courses on the UNIX Operating System (Fundamentals through System Administration), Programming Languages and Design (C, C++, Perl, Java and OOAD using UML), the Internet (CGI and JavaScript Programming) and RDBMS (Oracle and Sybase).

/training/etc Inc. was formed as a collaboration of several leading software trainers specializing in the design and presentation of educational programs for the technical professional. Trainers and course developers at */training/etc Inc.* are required to have a wide variety of experience in applications, training, and "people skills." It is our belief that the instructor is the most important resource in the classroom. Therefore, it is important that they not only be subject matter experts, but that they also possess effective leadership and interpersonal skills.

Since 1981, */training/etc Inc.* has conducted hands-on on-site seminars at many leading firms, in many sectors of the economy, including information technology organizations, financial institutions, biopharmaceutical laboratories and the federal government. Please contact our office to discuss how */training/etc Inc.*, a woman owned business, may satisfy your training requirements.

Source of official student records: Registry of Credit Recommendations, American Council on Education, One Dupont Circle, Washington, DC 20036-1193.

Additional information about the courses: College Credit Recommendation Service, American Council on Education, One Dupont Circle, Washington, DC 20036-1193.

Advanced C Programming (AI 432)

Location: Various.

Length: 35 hours (5 days).

Dates: January 1997-Present.

Objective: To provide students with more sophisticated techniques utilizing the C programming language.

Learning Outcome: Upon successful completion of this course, the student will be able to use a variety of data types appropriate to specific programming problems; utilize the modular features of the language; master the use pointers; utilize optimization techniques; use bit manipulation techniques; and write system calls directly into the UNIX operating system.

Instruction: Major topics covered in the course are sorting and searching techniques, optimization techniques, resolving portability issues, advanced low level operations, and the UNIX and C interface including I/O calls and process management calls. Methods of instruction include lecture, discussion, classroom exercises, and a final examination.

Credit Recommendation: In the lower division baccalaureate/associate degree category, 1 semester hour in Computer Science, Computer Information Systems, C Programming, or Application Development (1/97).

Internetworking with TCP/IP (AI 441)

Location: Various.

Length: 35 hours (5 days).

Dates: January 1997-Present.

Objective: To provide students with an explanation and understanding of the various protocols comprising the TCP/IP suite and relate these protocols to the UNIX operating system.

Learning Outcome: Upon successful completion of this course, the student will be able to identify the seven layers of the OSI networking model and relate this to TCP/IP; configure host IP, netmask, and broadcast addresses; use operating system commands to monitor network problems; and identify the networking protocols that support the TCP/IP networking model.

Instruction: Major topics covered in the course are open vs. proprietary systems; protocol models, stacks, and suites; connecting networks with bridges, routers, and gateways; network physical layer; IP layer; transport layer protocol; domain name services; network file system; SMTP and SNMP protocols; and networking tools; remote login, and administration of a TCP/IP network. Methods of instruction include lecture, discussion, hands-on lab exercises, audio/visual material, laboratory exercises, and a final examination.

Credit Recommendation: In the lower division baccalaureate/associate degree or upper division baccalaureate degree category, 2 semester hours in Networking, Data Communications, Computer Science, or Computer Information Systems (1/97).

Introduction to C (Introduction to C Programming [AI 412] and Intermediate C Programming [AI 422])

Location: Various.

Length: 140 hours (20 days).

Dates: January 1997-Present.

Objective: To provide students with fundamental programming techniques in using the C programming languages.

Learning Outcome: Upon successful completion of this course, the student will be able to identify and utilize appropriate data structures, language structure, and syntax of C; and use various control flow constructs (arrays, pointers, and calls to the UNIX operating system) to efficiently solve programming problems.

Instruction: Major topics covered in the course are data structures, language syntax, operators, control flow, the preprocessor, functions, strings, arrays, pointers, and stream and binary file I/O. Methods of instruction include lecture, discussion, classroom exercises, and a final examination.

Credit Recommendation: In the lower division baccalaureate/associate degree category, 2 semester hours in Computer Science, Computer Information Systems, C Programming, or Application Development (1/97).

Introduction to C++ Programming (AI 442)

Location: Various.

Length: 35 hours (5 days).

Dates: January 1997-Present.

Objective: To provide students with an introduction to the C++ programming language.

Learning Outcome: Upon successful completion of this course, the student will be able to understand how object oriented software engineering enhances the software development process, identify the major elements in an object oriented programming language; implement data abstraction and encapsulation in the creation of abstract data types; implement operator overloading; derive classes using inheritance in C++; select the proper class protection mechanism; demonstrate the use of virtual functions to implement polymorphism; write programs utilizing the I/O classes in C++; and explain advanced concepts such as templates, exceptions and multiple inheritances, and modify programs which use them.

Instruction: Major topics covered in the course are creating new C data types; search and sort files; manipulating bit structures, using optimization techniques; and resolving portability issues and within object oriented programming, classes, operator overloading, inheritance, polymorphism, virtual functions, and templates. Methods of instruction include lecture, discussion, classroom exercises, and a final examination.

Credit Recommendation: In the lower division baccalaureate/associate degree category, 1 semester hour in Computer Science, Computer Information Systems, C++ Programming, or Application Development (1/97).

Introduction to PERL Programming (AI 313) (PERL Programming)

Location: Various.

Length: 35 hours (5 days).

Dates: January 1997-Present.

Objective: To provide students with an introductory study of the PERL programming language.

Learning Outcome: Upon successful completion of this course, the student will be able to manipulate files and directories; use the powerful regular expression capabilities of PERL; generate "awk-like" reports; solve problems by using PERL's associative array capability; take advantage of PERL's powerful interface to UNIX; and perform some system administration functions.

Instruction: Major topics covered in the course are I/O, PERL operators, arrays and array functions, control flow, subroutines, packages, libraries, accessing system resources, and generating basic reports. Methods of instruction include lecture, discussion, hands-on lab exercises, student assessments, and a final examination.

Credit Recommendation: In the lower division baccalaureate/associate degree category, 1 semester hour in Computer Science, Computer Information Systems, PERL Programming, or Application Development (1/97).

UNIX Fundamentals (AI 411)

Location: Various.

Length: 35 hours (5 days).

Dates: January 1997-Present.

Objective: To provide students with a basic study of the UNIX operating system including its evolution, structure, programming environment, and user interface.

Learning Outcome: Upon successful completion of this course, the student will be able to explain the UNIX shell, evolution, structure, programming environment, and user interface.

Instruction: Major topics covered in the course are login and logout of a UNIX system; recall commands for automatic execution; launch and control jobs; provide front ends to well known commands; create and use shell environment variables; customize the environment using many shell productivity aids such as aliases, variables, etc. and the startup files kshrc and cshrc; write shell functions; use the pattern matching operators of the Korn Shell; and write shell scripts incorporating features such as variables, aliases, and functions. Methods of instruction include lecture, discussion, classroom exercises, and a final assessment.

Credit Recommendation: In the lower division baccalaureate/associate degree category, 1 semester hour in Computer Science, Computer Information Systems, UNIX Programming, or Application Development (1/97).

UNIX Shell Programming (AI 421)

Location: Various.

Length: 35 hours (5 days).

Dates: January 1997-Present.

Objective: To provide students with an examination of the UNIX Korn Shell.

Learning Outcome: Upon successful completion of this course, the student will be able to use the shell as a command line interface, a programming language, and a tool for customizing the UNIX environment.

Instruction: Major topics covered in the course are shell process creation, use of a variety of shell metacharacters, commands for automatic execution, controlling jobs, front ends to well known commands, use of shell environment variables, customization of the environment using aliases and the startup files, write shell functions, use the pattern matching operators of the Korn Shell, and write shell scripts incorporating features such as variable, aliases, and functions. Methods of instruction include lecture, discussion, classroom exercises, and a final examination.

Credit Recommendation: In the lower division baccalaureate/associate degree category, 1 semester hour in Computer Science, Computer Information Systems, UNIX Programming, or Application Development (1/97).

UNIX System Administration (AI 431)

Location: Various.

Length: 35 hours (5 days).

Dates: January 1997-Present.

Objective: To provide students with the necessary tools to manage a UNIX system.

Learning Outcome: Upon successful completion of this course, the student will be able to install, startup, and shutdown the UNIX system.

Instruction: Major topics covered in the course are installation, troubleshooting, and maintenance of a UNIX system; use of the front end system administration tool (SYSADMSH, SMIT,SAM, SYSADM, ADMINTOOL, etc.) to add and delete users; add devices; partition the disk and perform other administrative functions; use the administrator files and commands in the /etc directory; check file system integrity; provide user guidance; backup and restore all or parts of the system; monitor system performance; and establish and maintain network connectivity. Methods of instruction include lecture, discussion, classroom exercises, and a final project or examination.

Credit Recommendation: In the lower division baccalaureate/associate degree or upper division baccalaureate degree category, 1 semester hour in Computer Science, Computer Information Systems, UNIX System Administration, or Application Development (1/97).

Travelers Group

The Travelers Group is one of the world's largest multiline financial services companies, focusing on insurance, and investments. Through its affiliated companies, it offers a range of products and services, including commercial property and casualty insurance, personal auto and homeowners insurance, life insurance, individual disability insurance, investment banking, annuities, pension and investment management services, private placement loans, commercial and residential mortgages, individual retirement accounts, and Keogh plans and consumer banking services.

In commercial lines, Travelers is one of the leading United States underwriters of commercial multiple-peril insurance and a major provider of workers' compensation coverage.

Travelers has seen the need for intensive workers' compensation-specific training. As a consequence, Travelers has developed the Workers' Compensation Claims Management Training Program. Travelers founded the pioneer vocational school in the insurance industry. The first session began January 5, 1903. The claim training programs continue to be an industry standard producing a long line of claim professionals.

Source of official student records: Director, Workers' Compensation, Travelers, PO Box 4416, Atlanta, GA 30302.

Additional information about the courses: College Credit Recommendation Service, American Council on Education, One Dupont Circle, Washington, DC 20036-1193.

Workers' Compensation Claim Management

Location: Atlanta, GA (Hartford, CT*; Naperville, IL*; and Brea, CA.* — *From April 1989 to January 1991)

Length: 150 hours (4 weeks).

Dates: April 1989-August 1997.

Objective: To provide instruction in workers' compensation claim management.

Learning Outcome: Upon successful completion of this course, the student will be able to handle all aspects of workers' compensation claim management from notification of claim to claim resolution.

Instruction: Major topics covered in the course are workers' compensation contract analysis, investigation techniques, cost containment, interpretation of medical reports, disability management, negotiation techniques, establishment of reserves, and claim resolution. Methods of instruction include lectures, discussion, presentation by outside experts, field observations, and use of relevant computer software.

Credit Recommendation: In the upper division baccalaureate degree category, 4 semester hours in Insurance or Business Administration (8/91).

TRO Learning, Inc.

TRO Learning, Inc. is a leading developer and marketer of microcomputer-based, interactive, self-paced instructional and testing systems used in a wide variety of settings: secondary schools, community colleges, job training programs, government-funded programs, and private industry. TRO Learning was formed in September of 1989 when certain assets of Control Data Corporation's Training and Education Group were purchased by William R. Roach, who serves as TRO Learning's Chairman of the Board and Chief Executive Officer. In December 1992, TRO Learning became a publicly held company and is traded on the NASDAQ-NMS exchange under the symbol TUTR.

For nearly 30 years, TRO's PLATO products have been the hallmark of excellence in effective computer-based education and training programs. The comprehensive PLATO courseware library includes over 5,000 hours of mastery-based instruction in reading, writing, language arts, mathematics, science, social studies, life and work skills, and technology courses. The standardized, modular structure of PLATO courseware provides maximum flexibility to design customized programs to meet both individual learner and program objectives.

A variety of PLATO Delivery System options are available to meet a wide range of program needs including Internet access, local area networks, and CD-ROM configurations.

PLATO Pathways provides capabilities to manage the entire instructional process including skill-level assessment, prescription, mastery testing, recordkeeping, and reporting. Pathways provides course performance data for submission to ACE/PONSI.

TRO Learning has domestic offices located throughout the United States, and international offices in the United Kingdom and throughout Canada. TRO Learning has international distributors located in Singapore, Malaysia, Korea, Taiwan, Dubai, and South Africa. More information on the Company and its products and services can be found on the Internet at http://www.tro.com.

Source of official student records: Registry of Credit Recommendations, American Council on Education, One Dupont Circle, Washington, DC 20036-1193.

Additional information about the courses: College Credit Recommendation Service, American Council on Education, One Dupont Circle, Washington, DC 20036-1193.

Algebra (Beginning and Intermediate)

Location: Various sites in the United States.

Length: 56 hours.

Dates: September 1994-Present.

Objective: To provide students with the fundamentals of algebra for further study in more advanced math courses, engineering, and computer sciences.

Learning Outcome: Upon successful completion of this course, the student will be able to solve algebraic problems that require the knowledge of integers, rationals, sets, exponents, absolute value, polynomials, factoring, rational expressions, equalities and inequalities, graphing, and introductory probability.

Instruction: Major topics covered in the course are sets and numbers, polynomials and factoring, math sentences, rational expressions, graphs, systems and equations, and probability. Methods of instruction include interactive computer-based tutorials, applications, and mastery tests.

Credit Recommendation: In the lower division baccalaureate/associate degree category, 1 semester hour in Algebra (10/96).

Precalculus (Advanced Algebra/Trigonometry and Geometry and Measurement)

Location: Various sites in the United States.

Length: 88 hours.

Dates: September 1994-Present.

Objective: To provide students with the fundamentals of advanced algebra, measurement, plane and solid geometry, and trigonometry necessary for the study of calculus, engineering, or computer science.

Learning Outcome: Upon successful completion of this course, the student will be able to solve algebraic problems that require the knowledge of parabolas, ellipses, hyperbolas, functions, graphing functions, exponential and logarithmic functions, trigonometric functions, identities, and equations, sines and cosines, and polar coordinates and solve measurement and geometry problems involving transformations, coordinates in two and three dimensions, distance, area, and volume.

Instruction: Major topics covered in the course are numbers and their properties, equations and inequalities, functions and their graphs, exponential functions, transformations, symmetry, coordinates and curves, solid and coordinate geometry, trigonometric functions, trigonometric identities, and equations. Methods of instruction include interactive computer-based tutorials, applications, and mastery tests.

Credit Recommendation: In the lower division baccalaureate/associate degree category, 3 semester hours in Precalculus (10/96).

U.S. Army Community and Family Support Training Center

The U.S. Army Community and Family Support (CFS) Training Center was established in Falls Church, Virginia in August 1987. It is a major organizational element of the Human Resources Directorate, U.S. Army Community and Family Support Center, a field operating agency of the Department of the Army. The mission of the Training Center is to train Morale, Welfare, and Recreation managers in the management and administration of MWR people, programs, and resources. The principal target audience is the manager of the Army's Morale, Welfare, and Recreation (MWR) programs at installations in the United States and locations in Europe, Central America, and the Pacific Rim. It also provides a limited amount of skill and technical level training to non-managerial employees. In addition, the Navy, Air Force, and Marine Corps MWR programs participate in the Army's training program to varying degrees. The courses listed in the training curriculum are a sequential and progressive approach to employee development and grow out of the Center's CFS Master Training Program. They represent a significant part of the Army Civilian Training, Education, and Development System for the MWR career field. All courses in the curriculum are based on extensive needs assessments in which the target employee plays a major role, supported by the program managers, instructional staff, and other subject matter experts as appropriate. Although a few of the courses are delivered by colleges, universities, or professional associations under contract, most are developed and delivered by the Training Center staff in Falls Church. The instructional staff are selected from the top echelon of operating managers in the Army's MWR programs. The Center believes that effective and credible trainers must have "walked a day in the shoes of the student".

For information about official student records contact The CFS Training Center, ATTN: CFSC-HRT, 6245 Leesburg Pike, Suite 400, Falls Church, VA 22044.

Source of official student records: Registry of Credit Recommendations, American Council on Education, One Dupont Circle, Washington, DC 22036-1193.

Additional information about the courses: College Credit Recommendation Service, American Council on Education, One Dupont Circle, Washington, DC 20036-1193.

Applied Financial Planning and Forecasting

Location: Various military sites worldwide.

Length: 40 hours (5 days).

Dates: January 1994-Present.

Objective: To understand the income statement and financial trend analysis in generating income and controlling expenses, and forecast for Morale Welfare and Recreation Activities utilizing financial and non-financial data.

Learning Outcome: Upon successful completion of this course, the student will be able to identify trends in revenues and expenses; prepare forecasts of operating income and expenses; and utilize pricing and break-even analysis.

Instruction: Major topics covered in the course are the income statements, trend analysis, generating income through sales, other operating income and other income, controlling labor expenses, managing expenses by controlling cost of goods sold, labor costs, other expenses, depreciation, resale inventory management, inventory management, forecast utilizing financial and non-financial data, operational standards, pricing analysis, and break-even analysis. Methods of instruction include lecture, discussion, classroom exercises, case studies, audio/visual material, learner presentations/reports, and examinations.

Credit Recommendation: In the lower division baccalaureate/associate degree category, 2 semester hours in Financial Management (7/96).

Child Development Center Directors' Course

Location: CFS Training Center, Falls Church, VA.

Length: 79 hours (2 weeks).

Dates: November 1991-Present.

Objective: To enhance the participants skills in evaluating and implementing child development center programs through practical application of management principles and assessment tools.

Learning Outcome: Upon successful completion of this course, the student will be able to demonstrate proficiency in the application of developmentally appropriate program principles, financial management, budgeting, personnel management, and communication skills.

Instruction: Major topics covered in the course are labor costs, environmental safety, child abuse, observation techniques, problem identification, food buying and preparation, developing and evaluating program planning, personnel, time, and financial management. Methods of instruction include lecture, discussion, classroom exercises, case studies, computer-assisted instruction, group presentations/reports, adult experiential mode, and a final examination.

Credit Recommendation: In the upper division baccalaureate degree category, 3 semester hours in Child Development, Day Care Administration, Personnel Management, or Social or Human Services (7/96). **NOTE:** Students must complete the Community and Family Support Management Course before enrolling in this course.

Community and Family Support Management (Correspondence) Course

Location: Correspondence except for one week residential at Falls Church, VA.

Length: 39 hours (6 months) for completion of 13 sub-courses by correspondence plus one week residential.

Dates: November 1994-Present.

Objective: To familiarize new managers with various areas of management including financial management, management controls, budgeting, personnel management, and acquisition management.

Learning Outcome: Upon successful completion of this course, the student will be able to demonstrate proficiency in practical application of financial management, budgeting, acquisition management, management controls, personnel management, marketing, and oral and written communications.

Instruction: Major topics covered in the course are financial management, budgeting, personnel management, management controls, acquisition management, marketing, and oral and written communications. Methods of instruction include lecture, discussion, classroom exercises, case studies, audio visual material, computer-assisted instruction, quizzes, reports, tests, and a final examination.

Credit Recommendation: In the lower division baccalaureate/associate degree category, 3 semester hours in Business Administration (7/96).

Community and Family Support Management (Resident Course)

Location: CFS Training Center, Falls Church, VA.

Length: 120 hours (3 weeks - 40 hours per week).

Dates: August 1987-Present.

Objective: To familiarize new managers with various areas of management including financial management, management controls, budgeting, personnel management, and acquisition management.

Learning Outcome: Upon successful completion of this course, the student will be able to demonstrate proficiency in practical application of financial management, budgeting, acquisition management, management controls, personnel management, marketing, and oral and written communications.

Instruction: Major topics covered in the course are financial management, budgeting, personnel management, management controls, acquisition management, marketing, and oral and written communications. Methods of instruction include lecture, discussion, classroom exercises, case studies, audio visual material, computer-assisted instruction, quizzes, reports, observations, tests, and a final examination.

Credit Recommendation: In the lower division baccalaureate/associate degree category, 3 semester hours in Business Administration (7/96).

Director, Personnel and Community Activities

Location: CFS Training Center, Falls Church, VA.

Length: 120 hours (3 weeks).

Dates: August 1992-Present.

Objective: To improve performance based skills in the areas of long range planning, financial management, program evaluation and developing a vision for the future.

Learning Outcome: Upon successful completion of this course, the student will be able to demonstrate proficiency in the advanced application of strategic planning financial management, cash management controls, program evaluation, personnel management and labor relations, leadership performance, and decision-making.

Instruction: Major topics covered in the course are financial management, facility, programs and services, and planning. Methods of instruction include lecture, discussion, classroom exercises, case studies, audio visual material, computer-assisted instruction, learner presentations/reports, adult experiential mode, and a final examination.

Credit Recommendation: In the upper division baccalaureate degree category, 3 semester hours in Business Administration (7/96).

Multi Program Managers' Course

Location: CFS Training Center, Falls Church, VA.

Length: 119 hours (3 weeks).

Dates: September 1995-Present.

Objective: To improve performance based skills in the areas of financial management, organization management, internal management controls, leadership, and consulting.

Learning Outcome: Upon successful completion of this course, the student will be able to demonstrate proficiency in the advanced applications of strategic planning, financial management, budgeting, management controls, personnel management, leadership, and communication skills.

Instruction: Major topics covered in the course are personnel management, financial management, and budgeting. Methods of instruction include lecture, discussion, classroom exercises, case studies, audio visual material, computer-assisted instruction, learner presentations/reports, adult experiential mode, and a final examination.

Credit Recommendation: In the upper division baccalaureate degree category, 3 semester hours in Business Administration (7/96).

NAF (Nonappropriated Fund) Contracting Advanced

Location: Various military sites worldwide.

Length: 76 hours (2 weeks).

Dates: March 1991-Present.

Objective: To introduce participants to all phases of the federal acquisition process, from acquisition planning to post award actions, and to prepare them to serve as contracting officers.

Learning Outcome: Upon successful completion of this course, the student will be able to review purchase requests for completeness and accuracy; prepare and issue solicitations; negotiate with prospective contractors; and conduct acquisition training.

Instruction: Major topics covered in the course are Nonappropriated Fund regulatory guidance; contract formation, including legal aspects; ethics; negotiation and acquisition systems; types of contracts; termination, closeout, and remedies; contract acceptance; and disputes and appeals. Methods of instruction include lecture, discussion, classroom exercises, case studies, learner presentations/reports, a mid-term examination, and a final examination.

Credit Recommendation: In the upper division baccalaureate degree category, 2 semester hours in Acquisition, General Business, Procurement, or Purchasing (7/96).

NAF (Nonappropriated Fund) Contracting Basic

Location: Various military sites worldwide.

Length: 35.5 hours (4.5 days).

Dates: January 1989-Present.

Objective: To introduce participants to the nonappropriated fund (NAF) small-purchase arena and prepare them to serve as contracting officers.

Learning Outcome: Upon successful completion of this course, the student will be able to prepare purchase request forms, requests for quotations, purchase and delivery orders, requests for proposals, or invitations for bids; issue blanket purchase agreements; and understand the technical terms used in the Nonappropriated Fund small purchase process.

Instruction: Major topics covered in the course are federal acquisition responsibility and authority; federal acquisition responsibility and authority; purchase requirements; contract methods and formats; unpriced purchase orders; blanket purchase agreements; administration of small purchases, and standards of conduct. Methods of instruction include lecture, discussion, classroom exercises, case studies, quizzes, and a final examination.

Credit Recommendation: In the lower division baccalaureate/associate degree category, 1 semester hour in Acquisition, General Business, Procurement, and Purchasing (7/96).

Supplemental Program Services and Family Child Care Directors' Course

Location: CFS Training Center, Falls Church, VA.

Length: 79 hours (2 weeks).

Dates: September 1995-Present.

Objective: To provide the basic management skills necessary to implement various child development service programs on a military installation.

Learning Outcome: Upon successful completion of this course, the student will be able to demonstrate proficiency in areas of procurement and regulatory requirements: fire, safety, health and nutrition interviewing and feedback; and parental involvement education.

Instruction: Major topics covered in the course are personnel management; financial management; interviewing and feedback; situational leadership; and parental services. Methods of instruction include lecture, discussion, classroom exercises, case studies, learner presentations/reports, adult experiential mode, and a final examination.

Credit Recommendation: In the upper division baccalaureate degree category, 3 semester hours in Business Management or Social Services Management (7/96). **NOTE:** Students must complete the Community and Family Support Management Course before enrolling in this course.

Training and Curriculum Specialist Course

Location: CFS Training Center, Falls Church, Virginia.

Length: 77 hours (2 weeks).

Dates: September 1995-Present.

Objective: To provide participants with the necessary skills to ensure quality developmental programming and the ability to deliver effective caregiver/provider training.

Learning Outcome: Upon successful completion of this course, the student will be able to demonstrate proficiency in adult training skills, basic financial management and budgeting, individual development plans, team building leadership, and communication skills.

Instruction: Major topics covered in the course are accreditation standards, individual and program developmental plans; adult learning styles; child abuse prevention, observation, relationships, and mentoring; and financial management. Methods of instruction include lecture, discussion, classroom exercises, case studies, 2 hours of outside classroom work per evening, adult experiential mode, and a final examination.

Credit Recommendation: In the upper division baccalaureate or graduate degree category, 1 semester hour in Administration, Adult Learning, Child Development, Management, Social Work, or Training and Curriculum Development (7/96). **NOTE:** Students must complete the Community and Family Support Management Course before enrolling in this course.

Youth Services Managers' Course

Location: CFS Training Center, Falls Church, VA.

Length: 78.5 hours (2 weeks) residential; or 2 hours precourse work.

Dates: August 1990-Present.

Objective: To prepare the youth services director to manage program facilities and resources.

Learning Outcome: Upon successful completion of this course, the student will be able to demonstrate proficiency in the application of financial management, budgeting, personnel management, communication skills, and integrating youth development concepts into recreation and sports programs and activities.

Instruction: Major topics covered in the course are program planning, personnel and staffing, child abuse prevention and identification, and youth development. Methods of instruction include lecture, discussion, classroom exercises, case studies, audio visual material, computer-assisted instruction, learner presentations/ reports, adult experiential mode, and a final examination.

Credit Recommendation: In the upper division baccalaureate degree category, 2 semester hours in Social Services Management (7/96). **NOTE:** The student must complete the Community and Family Support Management Course before taking this course.

U.S. Army Family Team Building

The Army Family Team Building (AFTB) Branch was established during fiscal year 1993 as a branch of the Family Support Division, U.S. Army Community and Family Support Center. The Center is located in Alexandria, Virginia.

The AFTB mission is to improve overall readiness of the force by teaching and promoting personal and family readiness through progressive and sequential education. Additionally, AFTB supports America's Army in adapting to a changing world and responding to family issues from lessons learned in recent deployments. This mission involves developing, managing, and coordinating all relative policy, funding, training studies, analysis, and research for issues related to evolving Active Reserve, and National Guard Components within America's Army.

The training courses offered by AFTB are fully coordinated, developmental, and sequential, incorporating the military environment and the Army's philosophy concerning America's Army. Students taking AFTB courses are primarily a cross level of Department of the Army civilians and family member students who may elect between two options: one for college recognition and one for a certificate of course completion. Students taking courses for college recognition undergo a proficiency evaluation (final examination) administered at the end of each course. The AFTB courses by design are exportable and can be delivered on site which allows for a wider opportunity of student participation.

Source of official student records: Registry of Credit Recommendations, American Council on Education, One Dupont Circle, Washington, DC 20036 or Community and Family Support Center, Attn: CFSC-FST, Room 1416, Hoffman I, 2461 Eisenhower Avenue, Alexandria, VA 22331

Additional information about the courses: College Credit Recommendation Service, American Council on Education, One Dupont Circle, Washington, DC 20036-1193.

Leadership and Management

Location: Various active duty Army, Army Reserve, and National Guard sites worldwide.

Length: 18 hours (5 days).

Dates: July 1994-Present.

Objective: To provide families of Army personnel with basic leadership and management skills to help them establish partnerships with the Army for the enhancement of soldiers' performance, readiness, and retention.

Learning Outcome: Upon successful completion of this course, the student will be able to employ leadership and group dynamics techniques to build cohesive teams and to manage individual and group conflict; manage crisis situations, stress, time, and meetings; motivate family members and volunteers based on an understanding of the hierarchy of human needs; and listen attentively, communicate effectively, and display skill in maintaining positive public and media relations.

Instruction: Major topics covered in the course are an introduction to effective leadership, building a cohesive team, understanding needs, group dynamics, conflict management, stress and time management, communication, and effective public/media relations. Methods of instruction include lecture, discussion, classroom exercises, audio/visual material, and final examination.

Credit Recommendation: In the upper division baccalaureate degree category, 1 semester hour in Small Group Communications, Organizational Behavior, or Human Resources Management (9/94). **NOTE:** Participants must successfully complete Personal Development or equivalent at the same time they complete Leadership and Management to receive credit for this course.

Master Trainer Course

Location: Various active duty Army, Army Reserve, and National Guard sites worldwide.

Length: 24 hours, 30 minutes (4 days).

Dates: June 1994-Present.

Objective: To provide the knowledge and skills for effectively facilitating training; to provide an overview of three AFTB programs (The Military Environment, Personal Development, and Leadership Management); and to provide the information to organize and deliver these programs.

Learning Outcome: Upon successful completion of this course, the student will be able to demonstrate effective presentation skills; describe the content of the AFTB program; develop some understanding for managing volunteers to assist in their delivery; and demonstrate skill in handling logistical matters associated with delivering these programs.

Instruction: Major topics covered in the course are presentation delivery, logistical and administrative support, marketing and promotion, "speaking on your feet," volunteer management, an implementation plan workshop, and America's Army. Methods of instruction include lecture, discussion, classroom exercises, audio/visual materials, instructional technology presentation practice and critique, and final examination.

Credit Recommendation: In the upper division baccalaureate degree category, 2 semester hours in Master Trainer (Military), Train the Trainer, or Methods of Training Adult Learners (9/94).

Personal Development

Location: Various active duty Army, Army Reserve, and National Guard sites worldwide.

Length: 19 hours (5 days).

Dates: June 1994-Present.

Objective: To provide the families of Army personnel with a broad range of skills and insights conducive to personal development in an Army culture, especially under conditions where Army personnel and their families are separated by duty assignments.

Learning Outcome: Upon successful completion of this course, the student will be able to engage in creative problem solving; communicate and supportively network effectively with others; establish supportive relationships; identify and use available resources for family support; and employ learned skills to assist others.

Instruction: Major topics covered in the course are listening, problem solving, relationship building; identification and use of resources; networking with community agencies; and adapting to change. Methods of instruction include lecture, discussion, audio/visual material, informal exercises, and final examination.

Credit Recommendation: In the lower division baccalaureate/associate degree category, 1 semester hour in Leadership Styles and Behavior, Organizational Behavior, Human Resource Management, or Presentation Skills Workshop (9/94).

The Military Environment

Location: Various active duty Army, Army Reserve, and National Guard sites worldwide.

Length: 12 hours, 20 minutes (4 days).

Dates: July 1994-Present.

Objective: To provide families of Army personnel with an introduction to the military environment's unique organizational, social, and economic structure, and an understanding of how these factors impact family life.

Learning Outcome: Upon successful completion of this course, the student will be able to use appropriate terms and acronyms to identify military personnel, activities, ranks, organizations, and command structure; exhibit sensitivity for military traditions, courtesies and protocol; and understand the resources available to military families and the demands military service places on family life.

Instruction: Major topics covered in the course are the basic and unique terms and acronyms used routinely in military life; traditions, customs, courtesies, and protocol observed by military personnel; benefits and responsibilities of military life; and the organizational structure of the Army. Methods of instruction include lecture, discussion, classroom exercises, audio/visual material, and final examination.

Credit Recommendation: In the lower division baccalaureate/associate degree category, 1 semester hour in Military Science or ROTC (9/94).

U.S. Army Management Staff College, Program in Sustaining Base Leadership and Management

The Army Management Staff College (AMSC), Program in Sustaining Base Leadership and Management, was established in 1987 by the Chief of Staff of the Army. The mission of the College is "to educate and prepare selected Army civilian and military leaders to assume more important leadership and management responsibilities by providing instruction in strategies, doctrines, and systems relating to the Total Army with emphasis on the sustaining base, and to develop doctrine, to provide consulting services, and to research with emphasis on the sustaining base."

AMSC's faculty consists of highly qualified subject matter experts in the areas of Leadership and Management, Decision Making, Resource Management, Information Management, Force Integration, National Policy, Military Forces and Doctrine, Acquisition Management, Logistics Management, Installation Management, and Personnel Management. This team of professionals provides a totally integrated curriculum, examining the Army's processes and support systems from holistic, multifunctional, and multidimensional perspectives. This results in a curriculum which is interdisciplinary and "spirals" through the skills, themes, concepts, and topics involved. The ultimate purpose is the application of these skills, themes, concepts, and topics. The College provides one program three times per year, which has been offered in 19-week, 15-week, and 14-week formats. Students are required to be resident during this intensive learning experience.

Fort Belvoir, Virginia, is the college location, provides a study campus environment for students, including a sustaining base library as well as seminar, lecture, and student service facilities. The Washington, DC area provides a "natural" location—the curriculum requires easy access to facilities such as Capitol Hill, executive and legislative organizations, Pentagon, Library of Congress, Office of Personnel Management and other government facilities. The curriculum-supporting Guest Speaker Program, one means of providing the most current and relevant perspectives in a wide variety of curriculum areas, is greatly enhanced by the College's proximity to Washington, DC.

Source of official student records: Commandant, U.S. Army Management Staff College, Program in Sustaining Base Leadership and Management, ATTN: TAPC-CPC-AAR, 5500-21st Street, Suite 1206, Fort Belvoir, VA 22060-5934.

Additional information about the courses: College Credit Recommendation Service, American Council on Education, One Dupont Circle, Washington, DC 20036-1193.

Army Management Staff College, Program in Sustaining Base Leadership and Management, Version 3
(Formerly Army Management Staff College, Version 3)

Location: Alexandria, VA; Ft. Belvoir, VA.

Length: 433 hours (12 weeks) residential, including 40 hours pre AMSC lesson.

Dates: May 1997-Present.

Objective: To educate selected Army civilian and military leaders to assume more important leadership and managerial responsibilities in the sustaining base by focusing on leadership, management and decision making.

Learning Outcome: Upon successful completion of this course, the student will be able to communicate in oral and written format with various levels of staff and management in an appropriate and effective manner; manage employee selection, evaluation and training; coordinate employee compensation and benefits, interpret labor law for the organization; counsel employees as appropriate; recognize political trends and discuss the challenges, concerns, and opportunities these trends represent for U.S. security interests, and the need for coherent national policies; manage an integrated system of procurement, inventory control and ultimate distribution from a domestic and/or global perspective, including personnel and materiel; utilize problem solving processes to stimulate the exploration of leadership, management, and decision making in large (and small) organizations; apply management principles to consideration of structure management and control of public service sector; identify an organizational culture, with similarities and differences, and manage effectively and sensitively in that environment; explore national interests in elements of power and their effects upon shaping national strategy; assess the impact of the American political culture on strategic planning; identify the major elements of government, at various levels; and be able to describe and manage a project involving the interaction between the public and private sectors.

Instruction: Major topics covered in the course are effective written and oral business and professional communications, personnel management, career development, promotion and "rif" issues; elements and procedures by which governments relate to international institutions, with emphasis on the alliances and international organizations, international law and diplomacy; planning, programming, and budgeting; materiel acquisition, inventory and distribution management; problem solving, policy making and learning facilitation in the context of group interaction and team building, within an organizational structure; and assessment of how the influence of politics, military power, geography, strategic intelligence and economic inter-dependence effects the formulation of national goals and objectives; and an understanding of the multi-faceted mission of a city or a military installation and the support, services, and facilities needed to make a "city within a city" function effectively. Methods of instruction include a balanced mix of seminars, lectures, and practical exercises. It is structured with a focus on active learning; intensive student reading, writing and oral presentations, classroom analysis, small group interaction, lectures by faculty members and prominent outside authorities on the sustaining base; and relevant practical exercises and case studies.

Credit Recommendation: In the upper division baccalaureate degree category, 3 semester hours in Business Communications; in the upper division baccalaureate degree category, 3 semester hours in Human Resources Management; in the upper division baccalaureate degree category, 3 semester hours in Public Administration; in the graduate degree category, 6 semester hours in Logistics Manage-ment; in the graduate degree category 3 semester hours in Management; in the graduate degree category 6 semester hours in Government (9/97).

Army Management Staff College, Program in Sustaining Base Leadership and Management, Non-Resident
(Formerly Army Management Staff College, Non-Resident)

Location: Alexandria, VA, Fort Belvoir, VA.

Length: 52 weeks including two one-week resident sessions.

Dates: January 1992-Present.

Objective: To educate selected Army civilian and military leaders to assume more important leadership and managerial responsibilities in the Sustaining Base by focusing on leadership, management, and decision making.

Learning Outcome: Upon successful completion of this course, the student will be able to communicate in oral and written format with various levels of staff and management in an appropriate and effective manner; provide a framework for looking at lifestyle practices relative to health and fitness in achieving greater personal and professional effectiveness; manage employee selection, evaluation, and training; coordinate employee compensation and benefits, interpret labor law for the organization; counsel employees as appropriate; recognize global trends and discuss the challenges, concerns and op-portunities these trends represent to U.S. security interests and the need for coherent national policies; manage an integrated system of procurement, inventory control and ultimate distribution from a domestic and/or global perspective, including personnel, and materiel; utilize problem-solving processes to stimulate the exploration of leadership, management, and decision making in large (and small) organizations; apply management principles to consideration of structure management and control of public service sector; identify an organizational culture, with similarities and differences, and manage effectively and sensitively in that environment; explore national interests in elements of power and their effects upon shaping national strategy; assess the impact of the American political culture on strategic planning; identify the major elements of government at various levels and be able to describe and manage a project involving the interaction between the public and private sectors.

Instruction: Major topics covered in the course are effective written and oral business and professional communications, improved personal and professional effectiveness through informed perspectives on nutrition and cardiovascular health and the tools to develop a fitness program that is safe and effective; personnel management; career development; promotion and Re-duction in Force (RIF) issues, legal and procedural; elements and procedures by which governments relate to international institutions, with emphasis on the United Nations system, international law and diplomacy; planning programming, and budgeting; materiel acquisition, inventory and distribution management; problem solving, policy making, and learning facilitation in the context of group interaction and team building within an organizational structure; an assessment of how the influence of politics, military power, geography, strategic intelligence, and economic interdependence are assessed effect the formulation of national goals and objectives; and an understanding of the multi-faceted mission of a city or a military installation and the support, services, and facilities needed to make a "city within a city" function effectively. The course is a non-resident program requiring active student participation in practical exercises at home station, in addition to intensive writing and reading requirements. Methods of instruction include a mix of readings and exercises, written essays and research papers, and oral presentations which the student delivers to leaders in his or her home station community. The program requires that the student engage in individual reflection and group interaction in both asynchronous and synchronous modes via America On Line/Military City On Line. Students actively participate in video teleconferences with prominent authorities on the sustaining base; view video-taped presentations from the resident curriculum; complete practical exercises, case studies, and assignments requiring action research, analysis, synthesis, conclusion development; and make recommendations for implementation. Evaluation mechanisms include written examinations, essays, book review, research papers, oral presentations, self-assessments, and the same Capstone Exercise required in the resident course.

Credit Recommendation: In the lower division baccalaureate/associate degree category, 3 semester hours in Health and Wellness; in the upper division baccalaureate degree category, 3 semester hours in Business Communications, in the upper division baccalaureate degree category, 3 semester hours in Human Resources Management, in the upper division baccalaureate degree category, 3 semester hours in Public Administration; in the graduate degree category, 3 semester hours in International Relations, 6 semester hours in Logistics Management, 3 semester hours in Management Strategy and Decision Making, and 3 semester hours in National Government Policy (11/95).

Army Management Staff College, Program in Sustaining Base Leadership and Management, Version 1 (Formerly Army Management Staff College, Version 1)

Location: Linthicum, MD; Alexandria, VA.

Length: 494 - 505 hours (19, 15, 14 weeks) residential.

Dates: July 1987-December 1990.

Objective: To educate selected Army civilian and military leaders to assume more important leadership and managerial responsibilities in the sustaining base by focusing on leadership, management, and decision making.

Learning Outcome: Upon successful completion of this course, the student will be able to communicate in oral and written format with various levels of staff and management in an appropriate and effective manner; provide a framework for looking at lifestyle practices relative to health and fitness in achieving greater personal and professional effectiveness; manage employee selection, evaluation, and training; coordinate employee compensation and benefits; interpret labor law for the organization, and counsel employees as appropriate; discuss the challenges, concerns, and opportunities of U.S. security interests and the need for coherent national policies; manage an integrated system of procurement, inventory control, and ultimate distribution including personnel and materiel; apply management principles to consideration of structure management and control of public service sector; identify an organizational culture, with similarities and differences, and manage effectively and sensitively in that environment; explore national interests in elements of power and their effects upon shaping national strategy; assess the impact of the American political culture on strategic planning; and identify the major elements of government at various levels, and be able to describe and manage a project involving the interaction between the public and private sectors.

Instruction: Major topics covered in the course are effective written and oral business and professional communications, improved personal and professional effectiveness through informed perspectives on nutrition and cardiovascular health with the tools to develop a fitness program that is safe and effective; personnel management, career development, and promotion—planning, programming, and budgeting; materiel acquisition, inventory, and distribution management; problem solving, policy making, and learning facilitation in the context of group interaction and team building withing an organizational structure; influence of politics, military power, geography, strategic intelligence, and economic inter-dependence are assessed as they effect the formulation of national goals and objectives; an understanding of the multi-faceted mission of a city or a military installation and the support, services, and facilities needed to make a "city within a city" function effectively. Methods of instruction include a mix of lectures, seminars, and practical exercises. Course activity includes written and oral presentations, classroom analysis, small group interaction, lectures by faculty members and prominent outside authorities on the sustaining base, and relevant practical exercise and case studies.

Credit Recommendation: In the lower division baccalaureate/associate degree category, 2 semester hours in Health and Wellness, and 1 semester hour in Computer Literacy; in the upper division baccalaureate degree category, 3 semester hours in Communication Arts, 3 semester hours in Introduction to Management, and 3 semester hours in Introduction to Statistics; and in the graduate degree category, 6 semester hours in Budgeting and Logistics Management, and 6 semester hours in Public Policy (8/94).

Army Management Staff College, Program in Sustaining Base Leadership and Management, Version 2 (Formerly Army Management Staff College, Version 2)

Location: Alexandria, VA; Ft. Belvoir, VA.

Length: 427 hours (14 weeks) residential.

Dates: January 1991-April 1997.

Objective: To educate selected Army civilian and military leaders to assume more important leadership and managerial responsibilities in the sustaining base by focusing on leadership, management and decision making.

Learning Outcome: Upon successful completion of this course, the student will be able to communicate in oral and written format with various levels of staff and management in an appropriate and effective manner; provide a framework for looking at lifestyle practices relative to health and fitness in achieving greater personal and professional effectiveness; manage employee selection, evaluation and training; coordinate employee compensation and benefits; interpret labor law for the organization, counsel employees as appropriate; recognize global trends and discuss the challenges, concerns, and opportunities these trends represent for U.S. security interests, and the need for coherent national policies; manage an integrated system of procurement, inventory control and ultimate distribution from a domestic and/or global perspective, including personnel and materiel; utilize problem-solving processes to stimulate the exploration of leadership, management, and decision making in large (and small) organizations; apply management principles to consideration of structure management and control of public service sector; identify an organizational culture, with similarities and differences, and manage effectively and sensitively in that environment; explore national interests in elements of power and their effects upon shaping national strategy; assess the impact of the American political culture on strategic planning; identify the major elements of government, at various levels, and be able to describe and manage a project involving the interaction between the public and private sectors.

Instruction: Major topics covered in the course are effective written and oral business and professional communications, improved personal and professional effectiveness through informed perspectives on nutrition and cardio-vascular health with the tools to develop a fitness program that is safe and effective; personnel management, career development, promotion and "rif" issues, legal and procedural; elements and procedures by which governments relate to international institutions, with emphasis on the United Nations system, international law and diplomacy; planning, programming, and budgeting; materiel acquisition, inventory and distribution management; problem solving, policy making and learning facilitation in the context of group interaction and team building, within an organizational structure; an assessment of how the influence of politics, military power, geography, strategic intelligence and economic interdependence effect the formulation of national goals and objectives; an understanding of the multi-faceted mission of a city or a military installation and the support, services, and facilities needed to make a "city within a city" function effectively. Methods of instruction include a balanced mix of seminars, lectures, and practical exercises. It is structured with a focus on active learning intensive student reading, writing and oral presentations, classroom analysis, small group interaction, lectures by faculty members and prominent outside authorities on the sustaining base, and relevant practical exercises and case studies.

Credit Recommendation: In the upper division baccalaureate degree category, 3 semester hours in Business Communications; in the lower division baccalaureate/associate degree category, 3 semester hours in Health and Wellness; in the upper division baccalaureate degree category, 3 semester hours in Human Resources Management; in the graduate degree category, 3 semester hours in International Relations, 6 semester hours in Logistics Management, 3 semester hours in Management Strategy and Decision Making, 3 semester hours in National Government Policy; and in the upper division baccalaureate degree category, 3 semester hours in Public Administration (11/92).

Personnel Management for Executives Program (PME)

Location: Various locations throughout the United States and abroad.

Length: *Version 1*: 65 hours (10 days); *Version 2*: 65 hours (9 days) + 2 hours homework per night + optional paper.

Dates: *Version 1:* September 1981-August 1995; *Version 2:* September 1995-Present.

Objective: To improve management within the Department of the Army (and other federal government departments) by stimulating executives to want to do a better job of managing human resources and by providing an opportunity to develop direction and understanding of management and improve management skills.

Learning Outcome: Upon successful completion of this course, the student will be able to manage cultural diversity in the workforce; engage in active listening skills; project importance of values and ethics to employees; incorporate advanced team-building skills into management style at the workplace; integrate different personality and communication styles for effective management; manage stress by incorporating total wellness (mental and physical); recognize significance/impact of (a) mission on an international level, (b) international issues on mission; and select the components of multiple management philosophies to increase efficiency, effectiveness, and readiness.

Instruction: *Version 1:* Major topics covered in the course are current and emerging management practices, management ethics, conflict management, international management, conflict resolution, and interpersonal communication skills. *Version 2:* Major topics covered in the course are current and emerging management practices in communications, managerial success, wellness and stress management, ethics, successful leadership, leadership styles, managing change, managing a culturally diverse workforce and managing with a global perspective. Methods of instruction include lecture, discussion, case studies, video presentations, small group discussion. learner presentations, self-assessments and post program evaluations.

Credit Recommendation: *Version 1:* In the graduate degree category, 2 semester hours in General Management, Human Resources Management, or Organizational Behavior or 3 semester hours for students who, in addition to the course, complete an independent case study report (8/91). *Version 2:* In the graduate degree category, 3 semester hours in General Manage-ment, Human Resource Development or Organizational Behavior or 4 semester hours for students who, in addition to the course, complete an optional research paper (11/95).

U.S. Department of Agriculture Graduate School

The Graduate School, U.S. Department of Agriculture was created in 1921 and is a nonprofit, self-supporting, continuing education institution governed by a board appointed by the Secretary of Agriculture. The school's mission is the "improvement of government service and self-development through education and training." Although classes are attended primarily by government workers, they are open to all adults who wish to update skills, prepare for a different field of employment, or fulfill personal goals.

Instructors are practitioners in their fields, trained in educational techniques, thus assuring the highest quality in training and education. Courses are conducted in Washington, DC, but can be conducted on-site anywhere. Correspondence programs naturally can be accomplished anywhere.

The Graduate School, USDA offers courses in more than 40 subject areas, including accounting, computer sciences, editing, paralegal, sciences and engineering, and foreign languages.

Source of official student records: Registrar's Office, Graduate School, USDA, Room 1101, South Agriculture Building, 1400 Independence Avenue, N.W., Washington, DC 20250-9910.

Additional information about the courses: College Credit Recommendation Service, American Council on Education, One Dupont Circle, Washington, DC 20036-1193.

Accounting, Financial Management

Advanced Accounting I (EACCT 350)

Location: Washington, DC.

Length: 30 hours (3 hours per week for 10 weeks).

Dates: January 1978-September 1987.

Objective: To provide the student with an understanding of accounting for partnerships, installment sales, and mergers and acquisitions.

Learning Outcome: Upon successful completion of this course, the student will be able to prepare a liquidation of a partnership; understand home office and branch accounting; accounting for installment sales; and understand accounting for mergers and acquisitions.

Instruction: Major topics covered in the course are formation and liquidation of partnerships, accounting for installment sales, home office and branch operations, and mergers and acquisitions. Methods of instruction include lectures, class discussions, written homework, and examinations.

Credit Recommendation: In the upper division baccalaureate degree category, 2 semester hours in Advanced Accounting (6/88) (6/93).

Advanced Accounting II (EACCT 351)

Location: Washington, DC.

Length: 30 hours (3 hours per week for 10 weeks).

Dates: January 1978-March 1997.

Objective: To provide the student with an understanding of the preparation and use of corporate consolidated financial statements.

Learning Outcome: Upon successful completion of this course, the student will know the legal and financial aspects of consolidated financial statements and understand the use of the equity and cost methods for preparing consolidated statements.

Instruction: Major topics covered in the course are the legal and financial nature of consolidated statements; working papers for preparing consolidated statements; equity and cost methods; intercompany transactions in preferred stocks and bonds; interpretation of consolidated statements, including footnotes; consolidated income statements; and foreign branches and subsidiaries. Methods of instruction include lectures, discussions, written homework, and examinations.

Credit Recommendation: In the upper division baccalaureate degree category, 2 semester hours in Advanced Accounting (6/88) (6/93).

Advanced Accounting III (EACCT 352)

Location: Washington, DC.

Length: 30 hours (3 hours per week for 10 weeks).

Dates: January 1978-March 1997.

Objective: To provide the student with an understanding of preparation of realization and liquidation statements, receivership statements, and accounting for estate and trusts.

Learning Outcome: Upon successful completion of this course, the student will be able to understand the nature of estates and trusts and how to prepare relevant financial statements; prepare a statement of realization and liquidation and a statement of affairs; and prepare financial statements for a business in receivership.

Instruction: Major topics covered in the course are accounting for estates and trusts; statement of realization and liquidation; statement of affairs and its legal purpose; accounting for a business in receivership; and an introduction to accounting for estate and local governments. Methods of instruction include lectures, discussions, written homework, and examinations.

Credit Recommendation: In the upper division baccalaureate degree category, 2 semester hours in Advanced Accounting (6/88) (6/93).

Auditing I (EAUDIT 310)

Location: Washington, DC.

Length: 30 hours (3 hours per week for 10 weeks).

Dates: January 1978-March 1997.

Objective: To introduce generally accepted auditing procedures, professional ethics, and legal liability considerations.

Learning Outcome: Upon successful completion of this course, the student will be able to know generally accepted auditing standards; standard audit reports, including unqualified opinion, qualified opinion, adverse opinion and disclaimer; importance of professional ethics; legal liability considerations; how to plan an audit; how to study and evaluate internal controls in an automatic data processing environment; how to gather audit evidence—how much and what kind; and statistical samplings used in auditing.

Instruction: Major topics covered in the course are the role of the auditor in the American economy; professional ethics and the legal liability of auditors, planning the audit, internal control, the audit of electronic data processing systems, evidence (what kind and how much), statistical sampling, audit working papers, and examination of general records. Methods of instruction include lecture, analyses of practical audit problems, and chapter examinations.

Credit Recommendation: In the upper division baccalaureate degree category, 1 semester hour in Accounting, Auditing, or Business Administration (6/88) (6/93).

Auditing II (EAUDIT 311)

Location: Washington, DC.

Length: 30 hours (3 hours per week for 10 weeks).

Dates: January 1978-March 1997.

Objective: To introduce the student to the auditing techniques for working capital accounts, property, and liability accounts.

Learning Outcome: Upon successful completion of this course, the student will be able to conduct an internal audit according to accepted auditing principles and in compliance with legal and ethical constraints; and prepare audit reports.

Instruction: Major topics covered in the course are auditing of cash, securities, and other investments; investment revenue; accounts and notes receivable; sales transactions; inventories and cost of sales; property, plant, and equipment depreciation and depletion; prepaid expenses, deferred charges, and intangible assets; accounts payable and other liabilities; interest-bearing debt and interest expense; owner's equity; and financial statements and audit reports. Methods of instruction include lecture, problem exercises, and chapter examinations.

Credit Recommendation: In the upper division baccalaureate degree category, 2 semester hours in Accounting, Auditing, or Business Administration (6/88) (6/93).

Budget Execution and Funds Control (ECNTR 416)

Location: Washington, DC.

Length: 30 hours (3 hours per week for 10 weeks).

Dates: January 1978-Present.

Objective: To provide the student with an understanding of the concepts, procedures, and practices in the administrative control under the anti-deficiency act of the problems associated with appropriation, apportionment, and obligation of the federal budget and its processes.

Learning Outcome: Upon successful completion of this course, the student will be able to understand the process of appropriation allotment and obligation of the federal budget; examine from a critical standpoint continuing legislation, special appropriations, allotments, account balances, and other special problems associated with the appropriation of the federal funding process.

Instruction: Major topics covered in the course are obligations, appropriations, apportionment, different types of appropriations—single, multiple, no year, definite year, and one-year, and continuing legislation for agencies without new budgets. Methods of Instruction Include lecture, discussion and problem solving.

Credit Recommendation: In the upper division baccalaureate degree category, 2 semester hours in Accounting, Business Administration, or Public Administration (6/88) (6/93).

Budget Planning, Development, and Presentation (ECNTR 414)

Location: Washington, DC.

Length: 30 hours (10 weeks).

Dates: September 1987-Present.

Objective: To provide the student with an overview of the federal budgetary process including the review and submissions by various government instrumentalities, Office of Management and Budget (OMB) and congressional hearings, appropriation enactments, and such budgetary changes as supplemental appropriations, budget amendments, recessions, and deferrals and sequestrations.

Learning Outcome: Upon successful completion of this course, the student will have a basic understanding of the budget appendix, including language sheets, program and financing schedules, object classification schedules, and personnel summaries; understand how a budget is formulated; and demonstrate a basic understanding of budget submissions, the review process, appeals processes, and budgetary time constraints.

Instruction: Major topics covered in the course are basic legal and administrative concepts and practices in preparing, justifying, and presenting budget estimates for an agency of the federal government. Students are introduced to the terminology and process by which an organization secures personnel and dollar resources needed to execute programmatic responsibilities. Methods of instruction include lecture, discussion, classroom exercises, problem solving activities, and objective examinations.

Credit Recommendation: In the upper division baccalaureate degree category, 2 semester hours in Accounting, Business Administration, or Public Administration (1/90) (1/95).

Capital Budgeting (REA Borrower Accounting-Telephone) (CACCT 212)

Location: Correspondence Study.

Length: 13 lessons (self-paced).

Dates: January 1978-Present.

Objective: To provide instruction and training for those students who are now or intend in the future to be employed as accountants or bookkeepers of telephone utilities financed by the Rural Electrical Administration (REA). It may also serve as a guide to directors, managers, auditors, lawyers, or engineers who are concerned with the activities of these borrowers.

Learning Outcome: Upon successful completion of this course, the student will be able to understand accounting systems applicable to the telephone industry in general, and maintain accounting records and accounting procedures applicable to telephone utilities financed by loans approved by REA and the Rural Telephone Bank.

Instruction: Major topics covered in the course are recommended books of account and basic accounting systems applicable to the telephone industry; accounting to be performed during the periods of organization, initial construction, and operations; requesting and accounting for REA and rural telephone bank loan funds; and recommended plant accounting procedures including construction and retirement work order accounting. Methods of instruction include self-paced study and proctored exams.

Credit Recommendation: In the upper division baccalaureate degree category, 1 semester hour in Accounting, Business Administration, Capital Budgeting, or Public Administration (6/88) (6/93).

Capital Budgeting (REA Borrower Accounting-Telephone) (CACCT 211)

Location: Correspondence Study.

Length: 13 lessons (self-paced).

Dates: June 1981-Present.

Objective: To train potential and current office managers, accountants, and bookkeepers for closing accounting work in offices of electric utilities financed by Rural Electrical Administration (REA).

Learning Outcome: Upon successful completion of this course, the student will be able to open, maintain, and close the accounts; understand accounting for construction costs of electrical plants; prepare financial and statistical reports; and understand requesting loan funds and accounting for their repayment.

Instruction: Major topics covered in the course are REA books of account; accounting for construction costs; meter readings, accounting, and collecting; financial and statistical statements; and calculation of depreciation rates. Methods of instruction include self-paced study, written homework, and proctored final examination.

Credit Recommendation: In the upper division baccalaureate degree category, 1 semester hour in Accounting, Business

Administration, Capital Budgeting, or Public Administration (6/88) (6/93).

Concepts of Federal Accounting I (ECNTR 420)

Location: Washington, DC.
Length: 30 hours (10 weeks).
Dates: *Version 1:* January 1987-December 1994; *Version 2:* January 1995-Present.
Objective: To provide the student with an understanding of the basic concepts of federal government accounting and how they differ from other accounting methods, and an understanding of the policies and reporting requirements of the U.S. Treasury.
Learning Outcome: Upon successful completion of this course, the student will be able to utilize accounting principles, standards, and processes as prescribed by the Controller General of the United States and understand fund accounting, budgetary accounting, accrual accounting, cost accounting, and cash basis accounting.
Instruction: Major topics covered in the course are the concepts and practices of federal accounting, federal financial management policy, the relationship between accounting and budgeting,internal controls, and the standard government-wide general ledger. Methods of instruction include lectures, instructor-led discussions, case studies, problem solving, and examinations.
Credit Recommendation: *Version 1:* In the upper division baccalaureate degree category, 2 semester hours in Federal Government Accounting (1/90). *Version 2:* In the lower division baccalaureate/associate degree category, 2 semester hours in Federal Government Accounting (1/95).

Concepts of Federal Accounting II (ECNTR 421)

Location: Washington, DC.
Length: 30 hours (10 weeks).
Dates: April 1987-Present.
Objective: To provide the student with an understanding of the concepts of federal government accounting, and how they differ from other accounting methods, and an understanding of the U.S. Treasury policies and reporting requirements.
Learning Outcome: Upon successful completion of this course, the student will be able to utilize accounting principles, standards, and processes prescribed by the Controller General of the United States, understand fund accounting, budgetary accounting, cost accounting, and basis accounting.
Instruction: Major topics covered in the course are the concepts and practices of federal accounting, federal financial management policy, the relationship between accounting and budgeting, internal controls, and the standard government-wide general ledger. Methods of instruction include lectures, instructor-led discussion, case studies, problem solving, and examinations.
Credit Recommendation: In the upper division baccalaureate degree category, 2 semester hours in Federal Government Accounting (1/90) (1/95).

Cost Accounting I (CACCT 250)

Location: Correspondence Study.
Length: 8 lessons (self-paced).
Dates: January 1982-June 1993.
Objective: To provide the student with a practical knowledge of job order cost accounting systems and procedures and the role cost accounting plays in planning and controlling operations.
Learning Outcome: Upon successful completion of this course, the student will be able to perform job order cost accounting; do accounting for purchases and storage of materials; control and value inventory; and record and control labor.
Instruction: Major topics covered in the course are job order cost accounting, inventory valuation procedures, and labor costs. Methods of instruction include self-guided study, problem-solving, case analysis, and a proctored final examination.
Credit Recommendation: In the upper division baccalaureate degree category, 1 semester hour in Accounting, Business Administration, or Cost Accounting (6/93).

Cost Accounting I (EACCT 250)

Location: Washington, DC.
Length: 30 hours (3 hours per week for 10 weeks).
Dates: January 1978-June 1993.
Objective: To provide the student with the practical knowledge of job order cost accounting systems and procedures; monitoring costs; job order cost cycle; purchase of materials; storage and issuance of materials; inventory control; timekeeping and payroll, charging labor costs into production; departmentalizing of overhead costs; setting overhead rates; applying manufacturing overhead; accounting for scrap, spoiled goods, and defective goods; and completion of the cost cycle.
Learning Outcome: Upon successful completion of this course, the student will be able to perform job order cost accounting; maintain records for purchase and storage of materials; maintain records for the control and valuation of inventory; and maintain records for the control of labor costs.
Instruction: Major topics covered in the course are job order cost accounting, inventory valuation, and labor costs. Methods of instruction include lecture, problem solving, and cost analysis.
Credit Recommendation: In the upper division baccalaureate degree category, 1 semester hour in Accounting, Business Administration, or Cost Accounting (6/88) (6/93).

Cost Accounting II (CACCT 251)

Location: Correspondence Study.
Length: 6 lessons (self-paced).
Dates: January 1982-June 1993.
Objective: To provide the student with knowledge to make entries and prepare statements for a process cost accounting system.
Learning Outcome: Upon successful completion of this course, the student will be able to record costs incurred in each step of a process manufacturing operation; prepare worksheets and costs of production reports; and make computations of equivalent units of production and unit costs.
Instruction: Major topics covered in the course are process cost systems, production reports, average cost of work in process, by-product costing, joint costing, and allocation of common costs. Methods of instruction include self-guided study, practical exercises, and a proctored final examination.
Credit Recommendation: In the upper division baccalaureate degree category, 1 semester hour in Accounting, Business Administration, or Cost Accounting (6/93).

Cost Accounting II (EACCT 251)

Location: Washington, DC.
Length: 30 hours (3 hours per week for 10 weeks).
Dates: January 1978-June 1993.
Objective: To provide the student with an understanding of how to make entries and prepare statements for a process cost accounting system, and an understanding of the use of costs, budgeting, bids, and expenditures analysis in planning and control.
Learning Outcome: Upon successful completion of this course, the student will be able to record entries for a process control system; prepare relevant cost of pro-

duction reports; and prepare budgets and analyses used for planning and control of manufacturing and non-manufacturing costs.

Instruction: Major topics covered in the course are process cost systems, production reports, budgets used in planning and control, direct costing, standard costs, and break-even analysis. Methods of instruction include lectures, class discussions, practical exercises, and examinations.

Credit Recommendation: In the upper division baccalaureate degree category, 2 semester hours in Accounting, Business Administration, or Cost Accounting (6/88) (6/93).

Cost Accounting III (CACCT 252)

Location: Correspondence Study.

Length: 6 lessons (self-paced).

Dates: January 1982-Present.

Objective: To provide the student with an understanding of the use of costs in planning and control, including the use of standard costs, the ability to prepare budgeted income statements, and use appropriate techniques for decision making.

Learning Outcome: Upon successful completion of this course, the student will be able to prepare various budgets used in planning and control; use a standard manufacturing cost system; prepare budgeted income statements; use break-even analysis and differential cost analysis; and evaluate capital expenditure proposals.

Instruction: Major topics covered in the course are planning and control involving use of cost data, budgeting manufacturing and non-manufacturing costs, standard costs, direct costing, break-even analysis, capital expenditure analysis, and computerized cost accounting in a nonprofit service center. Methods of instruction include self-guided study, practical exercises, and a proctored final examination.

Credit Recommendation: In the upper division baccalaureate degree category, 1 semester hour in Accounting, Business Administration, or Cost Accounting (6/88) (6/93).

Federal Government Accounting I (CACCT 260)

Location: Correspondence Study.

Length: 14 lessons (self-paced).

Dates: August 1982-Present.

Objective: To provide the student with the basic regulations, principles, and standards that govern accounting and financial reporting by U.S. government agencies prescribed by the Comptroller General of the United States, the General Accounting Office, and the Bureau of the Budget.

Learning Outcome: Upon successful completion of this course, the student will be able to identify terminology and concepts of federal government accounting and prepare general ledger entries.

Instruction: Major topics covered in the course are basic principles and practices of federal government accounting, concepts and method of fund control, practice with basic records, accounting working capital funds, allotment obligation, disbursements, and transfer appropriations. Methods of instruction include self-guided study, practical exercises, and a proctored examination.

Credit Recommendation: In the upper division baccalaureate degree category, 2 semester hours in Government Accounting (6/88) (6/93).

Federal Government Accounting II (CACCT 261)

Location: Correspondence Study.

Length: 12 lessons (self-paced).

Dates: August 1982-Present.

Objective: To provide the student with the ability to compile data and prepare reports based on regulations and standards of U.S. government agencies with respect to inventory and property accounting, revolving funds, and the obligation and disbursement of funds.

Learning Outcome: Upon successful completion of this course, the student will be able to record transactions involving acquisition, depreciation, and sale of property; working capital funds and cost accounting; preparation of business-type financial statements for federal government activities; and reporting of budget execution showing status of funds apportioned, obligated, and unobligated.

Instruction: Major topics covered in the course are property accounting, working capital funds, financial statements for federal government activities, budget execution reports and reports on obligations, transfer of obligating authority to field offices, and statement of financial condition for Treasury Department. Methods of instruction include self-guided instruction, written homework problems, and proctored final examination.

Credit Recommendation: In the upper division baccalaureate degree category, 2 semester hours in Governmental Accounting (6/88) (6/93).

Financial Management (NFINC 750)

Location: Washington, DC.

Length: *Version 1:* 40 hours (3 weeks); *Version 2:* 90 hours (3 weeks).

Dates: *Version 1:* September 1974-July 1989; *Version 2:* August 1989-Present.

Objective: *Version 1:* To provide the student with an understanding of financial and managerial accounting practices and procedures in governmental and business accounting. *Version 2:* To understand financial tools and techniques used in management decision making.

Learning Outcome: *Version 1:* Upon successful completion of this course, the student will be able to demonstrate skills in financial and managerial accounting; demonstrate proficiency in governmental and business accounting practices and procedures; and use accounting as a tool to make management decisions. *Version 2:* Upon successful completion of this course, the student will be able to demonstrate knowledge of financial management principles and techniques and apply financial management principles and techniques to management decision making.

Instruction: *Version 1:* Major topics covered in the course are concepts of present value and inflation; capital budgeting; optimizing investment decisions; cash budgeting in financial management; current asset management; cost of capital; dividend policies; stock; portfolio analysis; and investment theory. Methods of instruction include lecture, discussion, and case studies. *Version 2:* Major topics covered in the course are accounting and financial overview; time value of money; capital budgeting and risk analysis; cash flow estimation; capital structure and leverage; and working capital management. Methods of instruction include lecture, discussion, case studies, classroom exercises, and computer applications in Quattro Pro.

Credit Recommendation: *Version 1:* In the upper division baccalaureate degree category, 3 semester hours in Accounting (but not for Accounting majors), Business Administration, Business Management, or Finance (6/88). *Version 2:* In the upper division baccalaureate degree category, 3 semester hours in Finance or Business (6/93).

Income Tax I (EFINC 220)

Location: Washington, DC.

Length: 30 hours (10 weeks).
Dates: September 1984-Present.
Objective: To provide the student with a familiarity with income tax laws as they relate to individuals and a working knowledge of a variety of individual tax forms.
Learning Outcome: Upon successful completion of this course, the student will be able to demonstrate a minimum level of understanding of the tax laws as they pertain to individuals; have an ability to prepare moderately complex tax returns; and have sufficient knowledge to research tax questions and be reasonably sure the research is complete or exhaustive.
Instruction: Major topics covered in the course are the basic 1040 tax return and accompanying schedules-A, D, E, C, and F, forms 2119 and 2106, and others as appropriate, children's income, nonbusiness losses, educational expenses, medical expenses, interest, taxes, and standard compared with itemized deductions. Methods of instruction include lecture, discussion, case studies, and problem solving.
Credit Recommendation: In the lower division baccalaureate/associate degree category, 2 semester hours in Accounting, Banking/Booking, Business Administration, or General Business (1/90).

Internal Auditing I (CAUDT 301)

Location: Correspondence Study.
Length: 13 lessons (approx. 30 hours).
Dates: January 1990-Present.
Objective: To train students to plan and conduct internal audits.
Learning Outcome: Upon successful completion of this course, the student will be able to conduct a preliminary survey; develop standards of audits procedures that ensure objectivity; develop working papers that document audit findings; and detect and prevent fraud.
Instruction: Major topics covered in the course are professional standards and ethics, staff/line conflict relative to audits, preliminary surveys, elements that should be present for presentation of deficiency findings, use of computers for audits, and fraud prevention. Methods of instruction include written assignments and a final examination.
Credit Recommendation: In the upper division baccalaureate degree category, 3 semester hours in Auditing (1/90) (1/95).

Internal Auditing II (CAUDT 302)

Location: Correspondence Study.
Length: 15 lessons (approximately 30 hours).
Dates: January 1990-Present.
Objective: To train the student to plan and conduct internal audits using advanced concepts and procedures.
Learning Outcome: Upon successful completion of this course, the student will be able to use mathematical modeling to detect trends and predict outcomes; use computer software programs for examining automated records; and make audit report reviews and then review management replies for two-day communications during the audit process.
Instruction: Major topics covered in the course are legal requirements imposed on boards of directors relative to internal audits, coordination of internal and external audits, counseling of management based on the findings of the audit, and modern and updated audit procedures involving the use of computers and modeling. Methods of instruction include written assignments and final examination.
Credit Recommendation: In the upper division baccalaureate degree category, 3 semester hours in Auditing (1/90) (1/95).

International Finance (NFINC 813)

Location: Washington, DC.
Length: 40 hours (3 weeks).
Dates: September 1974-May 1991.
Objective: To provide the student with a knowledge of the international economic environment and its influence on corporate financial management and international business operations.
Learning Outcome: Upon successful completion of this course, the student will be able to demonstrate understanding of the international gold standard in the adjustment process of foreign exchange rates; foreign investments; capital budgeting; international financial institutions; and current issues in international finance.
Instruction: Major topics covered in the course are foreign adjustments of accounts; markets and exchange rates; international financial operations to include risk management; capital budgeting; international financial institutions and markets; current issues such as world debt problems; and balance of payments are explored. Methods of instruction include lecture, discussion, and case studies.
Credit Recommendation: In the upper division baccalaureate degree category, 3 semester hours in Business Administration, Business Management, or Finance (6/88) (6/93).

Leadership and Management Development (NMGMT 846)

Location: Washington, DC.
Length: *Version 1:* 40 hours (3 weeks); *Version 2:* 90 hours (3 weeks).
Dates: September 1974-Present.
Objective: To explore the role of leadership in the management of organizations; and to introduce basic management theories and their relationship to individuals, groups or teams, and to other organizations.
Learning Outcome: Upon successful completion of this course, the student will be able to demonstrate, explain, or give a presentation on the following leadership and management areas; the difference between leadership and management; characteristics of teamwork, membership and leadership; communication models; conflict management models and applications; problem solving model and applications; and decision making model and applications.
Instruction: Major topics covered in the course are basic functions of management, teamwork, leadership, communications, conflict management, problem solving, decision making, and human resources. Methods of instruction include lecture, discussion, written assignments, group exercises, presentations, and projects.
Credit Recommendation: In the upper division baccalaureate degree category, 3 semester hours in Business Administration, Business Management, or Public Administration (6/88) (6/93).

Principles of Accounting I (CACCT 101)

Location: Correspondence Study.
Length: 12 lessons (self-paced).
Dates: April 1982-Present.
Objective: To provide the student with the knowledge to record typical accounting transactions based on generally accepted accounting principles, summarize data, and prepare financial statements.
Learning Outcome: Upon successful completion of this course, the student will be able to understand the accounting cycle; understand the preparation and content of financial statements; understand rules for recording, accumulating, and summarizing financial transactions to include journal entries and posting to the general ledger; understand payroll accounting; and understand proper accounting for transactions affecting assets, receivables, expenses, and income, deferrals, and accruals.
Instruction: Major topics covered in the course are accounting principles and practices, including the accounting cycle, financial statements, accounting for mer-

chandise and cash transactions, procedures for periodic reporting, accounts receivable and accounts payable, deferrals and accruals, and payables. Methods of instruction include self-guided study, practical exercises, sole proprietorship practice set, and a proctored final examination.

Credit Recommendation: In the lower division baccalaureate/associate degree category, 2 semester hours in Principles of Accounting (6/88) (6/93).

Principles of Accounting I (EACCT 101)

Location: Washington, DC.

Length: 30 hours (3 hours per week for 10 weeks).

Dates: January 1978-Present.

Objective: To provide the student with the knowledge to record typical accounting transactions based on generally accepted accounting principles, to summarize data, and to prepare financial statements.

Learning Outcome: Upon successful completion of this course, the student will be able to understand the complete accounting cycle, including the use of special journals and subsidiary ledger accounts; prepare financial statements; journalize and post business transaction; and make adjusting and closing entries.

Instruction: Major topics covered in the course are accounting principles; the accounting cycle; determining cost of goods sold, gross profit, and net profit; adjusting and closing entries; deferrals and accruals; and bank reconciliation. Methods of Instruction Include lectures, proctored exercises, and examinations.

Credit Recommendation: In the lower division baccalaureate/associate degree category, 2 semester hours in Principles of Accounting (6/88) (6/93).

Principles of Accounting II (CACCT 102)

Location: Correspondence Study.

Length: 12 lessons (self-paced).

Dates: April 1982-Present.

Objective: To provide the student with the knowledge to account for plant assets, inventories, receivables and payables, and the determination of the division of partnership profits and allocation of corporate dividends.

Learning Outcome: Upon successful completion of this course, the student will be able to account for plant assets, inventories, and receivables and payables; do partnership accounting, including division of profits; do corporation accounting including payment of dividends on preferred and common stock, statement of cash flows; and financial analysis.

Instruction: Major topics covered in the course are receivables, inventories, plant assets, notes payable, partnerships, corporations, and long term debt. Methods of instruction include self-guided study, practical exercises, corporation practice set, and a proctored final examination.

Credit Recommendation: In the lower division baccalaureate/associate degree category, 2 semester hours in Principles of Accounting (6/88) (6/93).

Principles of Accounting II (EACCT 102)

Location: Washington, DC.

Length: 30 hours (3 hours per week for 10 weeks).

Dates: January 1978-Present.

Objective: To provide the student with the knowledge of how to account for plant assets, inventories, receivables and payables, division of partnership profits, and corporation equity and dividends.

Learning Outcome: Upon successful completion of this course, the student will be able to account for plant assets, inventories, receivables and payables; account for payroll, including payroll taxes; account for division of partnership profits; account for stockholders' equity, earnings, and dividends; and make entries for issuance and redemption of corporation bonds.

Instruction: Major topics covered in the course are concepts and principles, receivables and payables, plant assets and depreciation, payroll accounting, corporation accounting, and issuance and redemption of bonds. Methods of Instruction Include lecture, problems, discussion, and examination.

Credit Recommendation: In the lower division baccalaureate/associate degree category, 2 semester hours in Principles of Accounting (6/88) (6/93).

Principles of Accounting III (CACCT 103)

Location: Correspondence Study.

Length: 12 lessons (self-paced).

Dates: April 1982-Present.

Objective: To provide the student with the essentials of branch and departmental accounting, manufacturing cost accounting, standard costs and financial planning, budgeting, and the concepts of data processing systems for accounting.

Learning Outcome: Upon successful completion of this course, the student will be able to make entries and prepare statements for departmental and branch accounting and for manufacturing cost accounting; prepare budgets for a manufacturing firm, including evaluation of capital investments; solve problems involving differential analysis; and standard costs and cost revenue analysis.

Instruction: Major topics covered in the course are statement of changes in financial position; financial statement analysis; accounting for decentralized operations and manufacturing operations; job order cost accounting; process cost accounting; standard cost accounting; profit reporting for management analysis; differential analysis; and accounting for individuals and nonprofit organizations. Methods of instruction include self-guided study, practical exercises, and a proctored final examination.

Credit Recommendation: In the lower division baccalaureate/associate degree category, 2 semester hours in Principles of Accounting (6/88) (6/93).

Principles of Accounting III (EACCT 103)

Location: Washington, DC.

Length: 30 hours (3 hours per week for 10 weeks).

Dates: January 1978-Present.

Objective: To provide the student with the essentials of manufacturing cost accounting, financial statement analysis, responsibility accounting, and break-even analysis.

Learning Outcome: Upon successful completion of this course, the student will be able to make journal entries and prepare statements for manufacturing cost accounting; perform financial statement analysis, break-even analysis, and differential analysis; and understand profit and cost center accounting and accounting for nonprofit organizations.

Instruction: Major topics covered in the course are financial statement analysis; responsibility accounting (profit centers and cost centers); manufacturing cost accounting (process and job order); break-even analysis; differential analysis; and individual and nonprofit organizational accounting (introductory). Methods of Instruction Include lectures, practical exercises, discussion, and examinations.

Credit Recommendation: In the lower division baccalaureate/associate degree

category, 2 semester hours in Principles of Accounting (6/88) (6/93).

Survey of Federal Controllership (ECNTR 401)

Location: Washington, DC.

Length: 30 hours (10 weeks).

Dates: September 1986-Present.

Objective: To provide the student with an understanding of the federal budget formulation and execution process and an understanding of the relationship of the controller to other department executives.

Learning Outcome: Upon successful completion of this course, the student will be able to plan and manage the budget formulation process within the guidelines provided by the Office of Management and Budget.

Instruction: Major topics covered in the course are budget formulation and execution, survey of federal government accounting, survey of federal government finance, and a survey of federal government financial management. Methods of instruction include research papers, presentation, guided discussion, and examination.

Credit Recommendation: In the upper division baccalaureate degree category, 2 semester hours in Controllership or Business Administration (1/90).

Administration, Management, Supervision

Congressional and Parliamentary Procedures (EPUAP 365)

Location: Washington, DC or various locations throughout the U.S.

Length: 30 hours (10 weeks).

Dates: September 1987-Present.

Objective: To provide the student with an understanding of the interplay of House and Senate rules, procedures, precedents, and strategies that are vital to an understanding of how Congress works and legislation is enacted.

Learning Outcome: Upon successful completion of this course, the student will be able to understand how the Congress makes laws and how its rules and procedures shape domestic and foreign policy.

Instruction: Major topics covered in the course are overall view of the congressional process; organizational setting of and political environment of Congress; discussion of congressional budget process; steps in the legislature process; and explanation of how legislation is formed and emerges from committees, House and Senate floor action related to legislation; discussion of presidential veto power and how House and Senate legislature differences are resolved; authorization and appropriation process in the Congress; and examination of congressional oversight of its legislation and examination of use legislative histories. Methods of instruction include lectures, video instruction, quizzes, paper (includes oral presentation), and final examination.

Credit Recommendation: In the upper division baccalaureate degree category, 2 semester hours in Paralegal Studies, Political Science, or Public Administration (6/93).

Establishing and Operating a Small Business (EMGMT 223)

Location: Washington, DC.

Length: 30 hours (10 weeks).

Dates: September 1980-Present.

Objective: To provide the student with an understanding of the creation and management of small business firms.

Learning Outcome: Upon successful completion of this course, the student will be able to write and update a business plan; establish and maintain a bookkeeping system and related financial statements; develop and monitor a budget; and identify business opportunities and pitfalls.

Instruction: Major topics covered in the course are writing a business plan, establishing and maintaining a bookkeeping system, income statements and balance sheets, business records, potential market identification and setting prices, tax responsibilities, and business organization options. Methods of instruction include lecture, discussion, text and handouts, classroom exercises, case studies, and examinations.

Credit Recommendation: In the lower division baccalaureate/associate degree category, 2 semester hours in Business Administration, Economics, or Management (1/90).

Evaluating and Reporting on Internal Control Systems (CMGMT 202)

Location: Correspondence Study.

Length: 7 lessons (maximum completion time is 1 year).

Dates: August 1987-Present.

Objective: To provide the student with knowledge and skills required to develop, implement, evaluate, and report results on systems of internal controls.

Learning Outcome: Upon successful completion of this course, the student will be able to identify specific controls and describe their strengths and weaknesses; analyze programs and develop vulnerability assessments; identify and assess control techniques; and correct control problems.

Instruction: Major topics covered in the course are the scope and background of internal controls, OBM guidelines, vulnerability assessments, documenting, evaluating, and reporting on cycles and related controls, and problem-solving methodologies. Methods of instruction include independent study, study guide, written assignments, instructor feedback, and a proctored final examination.

Credit Recommendation: In the lower division baccalaureate/associate degree category, 1 semester hour in Business Administration or Management (1/90) (1/95).

Federal Health Policy (EPUAP 451)

Location: Washington, DC.

Length: 30 hours (10 weeks).

Dates: January 1987-Present.

Objective: To provide the student with an understanding of current issues in federal health policy.

Learning Outcome: Upon successful completion of this course, the student will be able to analyze health legislation and identify various options in federal health policy.

Instruction: Major topics covered in the course are history of federal health policy, Bush Administration health agenda, congressional health initiatives, including mandatory employer-provided health insurance, and the need for long-term care and other health issues. Methods of instruction include lecture, discussion, classroom exercises, student presentations, visual aids, and examinations.

Credit Recommendation: In the upper division baccalaureate degree category, 2 semester hours in Health Care Administration, Political Science, or Public Policy (1/90).

Information and Records Management (CMGMT 201)

Location: Correspondence Study.

Length: 15 lessons.

Dates: January 1990-Present.

Objective: To provide the student with knowledge of essential information and records management (IRM) concepts and methodologies.

Learning Outcome: Upon successful completion of this course, the student will be able to understand the history and role of IRM as a technique for controlling information and its costs; describe the elements of an effective IRM program (techniques, equipment, facilities, and other applicable resources); and evaluate the impact and importance of new technologies on the role of IRM.

Instruction: Major topics covered in the course are the history and role of IRM, records inventory and disposition schedules, six basic file types, file maintenance and filing equipment, effective subject filing, correspondence management, directives, mail and copier management, forms management, maintenance of inactive records, and impact and importance of technologies. Methods of instruction include independent study, study guide, written assignments, instructor feedback, and a proctored examination.

Credit Recommendation: In the lower division baccalaureate/associate degree category, 2 semester hours in Business Administration or Information Systems Management (1/90) (1/95).

Management Information Systems Certificate Program (NINFO 499)

Location: Washington, DC.

Length: 480 hours (16 weeks).

Dates: August 1989-December 1994.

Objective: To provide the student with an understanding of strategic planning and management principles and of computer technologies necessary for successful implementation of management information systems and databases.

Learning Outcome: Upon successful completion of this course, the student will be able to establish MIS strategic planning process in organizations; describe relationships between technology and MIS; use various microcomputers and software packages; understand automated office concept and how it integrates with MIS program; identify MIS criteria and staffing requirements; and employ skills needed to analyze, design, and modify MIS and databases.

Instruction: This certificate program includes three major components: leadership and management development; computer applications in management; and principles of MIS. Methods of instruction include lecture, discussion, computer laboratory, case studies, and practical exercises. **NOTE**: This component may be taken as a separate course.

Credit Recommendation: In the upper division baccalaureate degree category, 12 semester hours in Computer Science or Management (1/90) (1/95). **NOTE**: If the component on principles of management information systems (114 hours, 4 weeks) is taken separately, the credit recommendation in the upper baccalaureate degree category is 6 semester hours in Computer Science or Management.

Modern Program Manager (CMGMT 203)

Location: Correspondence Study.

Length: 16 lessons.

Dates: January 1990-Present.

Objective: To provide the student with an understanding of elementary concepts of program management.

Learning Outcome: Upon successful completion of this course, the student will be able to apply techniques of management by objectives; apply techniques of strategic planning; prepare budgets; and evaluate programs and performance of subordinates.

Instruction: Major topics covered in the course are strategic management, environmental analysis, preparation of budgets, designing program structures, the team concept, management by objectives, project planning, and evaluation. Methods of instruction include independent study, study guide, written assignments, instructor feedback, and a proctored examination.

Credit Recommendation: In the lower division baccalaureate/associate degree category, 1 semester hour in Business Administration or Management (1/90) (1/95).

Modern Supervisory Practice (CSADM 201)

Location: Correspondence Study.

Length: 16 lessons.

Dates: January 1990-Present.

Objective: To provide the student with knowledge of basic supervision principles.

Learning Outcome: Upon successful completion of this course, the student will be able to identify principles of good organizational structure; identify basic principles of supervision; and recognize importance of human relationships in a work environment.

Instruction: Major topics covered in the course are planning, communications, decision-making, problem-solving, human behavior, and supervision. Methods of instruction include independent study, study guide, written assignments, instructor feedback, and proctored examination.

Credit Recommendation: In the lower division baccalaureate/associate degree category, 2 semester hours in Business Administration, Management, Public Administration, or Supervision (1/90) (1/95).

Principles of Marketing (NMARKT 540)

Location: Washington, DC.

Length: Version 1: 40 hours (3 weeks); Version 2: 90 hours (3 weeks).

Dates: September 1974-Present.

Objective: To introduce the student to principles and concepts of marketing and the relationships between elements of marketing.

Learning Outcome: Upon successful completion of this course, the student will be able to perceive marketing problems and issues; make strategic and operational decisions responsive to problems and issues; and evaluate the proper role of the public and private sectors to control marketing practices.

Instruction: Major topics covered in the course are marketing concepts, marketing strategy, assessing marketing opportunities, buyer behavior, product and price management, channel management, promotion management, and marketing and public policy. Methods of instruction include lecture, discussion, case studies, and problem solving.

Credit Recommendation: In the upper division baccalaureate or graduate degree category, 3 semester hours in Business Administration, Business Management, or Marketing (6/88) (6/93).

Project Analysis (NMGMT 975)

Location: Washington, DC.

Length: *Version 1:* 120 hours (4 weeks); *Version 2:* 150 hours (5 weeks).

Dates: *Version 1:* September 1974-July 1989; *Version 2:* September 1989-Present.

Objective: *Version 1:* To provide the student with knowledge and understanding of project management sufficient to manage and control projects and activities. *Version 2:* To provide the student with knowledge and skill to analyze costs, benefits, and risks of projects; understanding of external factors that affect projects; and ability to develop appropriate recommendations.

Learning Outcome: *Version 1:* Upon successful completion of this course, the student will be able to understand the procedures used in analyzing projects; develop the supporting data and analyze the critical points in monitoring projects; and develop the proper tools to evaluate and estimate the benefits as well as the cost of projects. *Version 2:* Upon successful completion of this course, the student will be able to understand and apply techniques of project analysis, including the data collection process; and financial and economic analysis and formulate spreadsheets using Quattro Pro to estimate project costs and benefits.

Instruction: *Version 1:* Major topics covered in the course are benefits/cost, methods of optimization, capital budgeting, statistical methods for project management, and accounting and budgeting. Methods of instruction include lecture, discussion, case and field studies, and extensive out-of-class preparation. *Version 2:* Major topics covered in the course are preparation of project budgets; cash flow analysis and discounted cash flow; new present value; risk and return; economic valuation and computer workshop. Methods of instruction include lecture, discussion, classroom exercises, case studies, project preparation, and presentation.

Credit Recommendation: *Version 1:* In the graduate degree category, 5 semester hours in Accounting, Business Administration, Management Science, or Public Administration (6/88). *Version 2:* In the upper division baccalaureate or graduate degree category, 3 semester hours in Business Administration, Public Administration, or Project Management (6/93).

Project Management (NMGMT 960)

Location: Washington, DC.

Length: *Version 1:* 40 hours (3 weeks); *Version 2:* 150 hours (5 weeks).

Dates: *Version 1:* September 1974-September 1989; *Version 2:* October 1989-Present.

Objective: *Version 1:* To provide the student with an understanding of principles and concepts of project management and application to projects in an international environment. *Version 2:* To provide knowledge of generic elements of effective project management.

Learning Outcome: *Version 1:* Upon successful completion of this course, the student will be able to apply project management principles and concepts in management of international projects. *Version 2:* Upon successful completion of this course, the student will be able to apply project management principles and concepts in administering international projects and apply project management software tools to project management.

Instruction: *Version 1:* Major topics covered in the course are project management systems, project life cycle, time scheduling techniques, resource management, and computers as a tool for project management. Methods of instruction include lecture, discussion, and classroom projects. *Version 2:* Major topics covered in the course are principles of project management; project life cycle; project planning; time scheduling techniques; resource management; project network analysis; and project monitoring and evaluation. Methods of instruction include lecture, discussion, case studies, computer applications, and classroom projects.

Credit Recommendation: *Version 1:* In the upper division baccalaureate degree category, 3 semester hours in Administration, Business Administration, Project Management, or Public Administration (6/88). *Version 2:* In the upper division baccalaureate or graduate degree category, 3 semester hours in Management, Business Administration, Project Management, or Public Administration (6/93).

Project Management (EMGMT 120)

Location: Washington, DC.

Length: *Version 1:* 15 hours (5 weeks); *Version 2:* 30 hours (10 weeks).

Dates: *Version 1:* June 1987-September 1990; *Version 2:* September 1990-Present.

Objective: To provide the student with knowledge of generic elements of effective project management.

Learning Outcome: *Version 1:* Upon successful completion of this course, the student will be able to allocate project resources in a budget; develop a project schedule; lead project work teams; and visualize, articulate, and prioritize project goals. *Version 2:* Upon successful completion of this course, the student will be able to understand the basic concepts of project management; use practical techniques to plan, schedule, and control a project; understand and appreciate the variety of leadership behaviors required to successfully manage a project; and identify and understand their own leadership style and its impact on the project team.

Instruction: *Version 1:* Major topics covered in the course are work breakdown structure, scheduling, PERT analysis, project review, cost estimating, leadership, and work group communications. Methods of instruction include lecture, discussion, student projects, term paper, and examinations. *Version 2:* Major topics covered in the course are an introduction to project management; planning and organizing the project; organizing and staffing the project team; leadership styles and decision-making; project implementation and monitoring; project management effectiveness; conflicts in project management; project management controlling techniques; phasing out the project; and project management in the year 2000. Methods of instruction include lecture, discussion, student projects, a term paper, and examinations.

Credit Recommendation: *Version 1:* In the lower division baccalaureate/associate degree or upper division baccalaureate degree category, 1 semester hour in Business Administration, Management, or Public Administration (1/90). *Version 2:* In the lower division baccalaureate/associate degree or upper division baccalaureate degree category, 2 semester hours in Business Administration, Management, or Public Administration (1/95).

Success-Oriented Supervision (CSADM 202)

Location: Correspondence Study.

Length: 15 lessons.

Dates: January 1990-Present.

Objective: To provide the student with knowledge and use of effective supervisory skills.

Learning Outcome: Upon successful completion of this course, the student will be able to identify various leadership and management styles; understand and provide for high levels of employee motivation; utilize systematic problem-solving and decision-making methods; and perform personnel functions.

Instruction: Major topics covered in the course are leadership styles, motivation, problem-solving, decision-making, interviewing, and personnel functions. Methods of instruction include independent study, study guide, written assignments, instructor feedback, and a proctored examination.

Credit Recommendation: In the lower division baccalaureate/associate degree category, 2 semester hours in Business Administration, Management, or Public Administration (1/90) (1/95).

The Marketing Concept (EMGMT 240)

Location: Washington, DC.

Length: 30 hours (10 weeks).

Dates: January 1985-Present.

Objective: To provide the student with an understanding of the need for profit-driven programs or projects to establish clear definitions of business, competition, market position, customers, pricing, and the role of strategic planning.

Learning Outcome: Upon successful completion of this course, the student will be able to apply concepts of strategic planning; apply concepts of effective marketing; understand the research aspects of marketing; and identify various techniques for product delivery to the market.

Instruction: Major topics covered in the course are marketing mix, strategic planning, segmentation, marketing, audit plan review, and research. Methods of instruction include lecture, discussion, case studies, projects, and an examination.

Credit Recommendation: In the lower division baccalaureate/associate degree category, 2 semester hours in Business Administration, Management, or Marketing (1/90) (1/95).

The Process of Management (EMGMT 110)

Location: Washington, DC.

Length: 20 hours (10 weeks).

Dates: April 1988-January 1995.

Objective: To provide the student with an understanding of essentials of management staff members.

Learning Outcome: Upon successful completion of this course, the student will be able to define objectives of an organization and measure attainment of those objectives; recognize the effects of verbal and nonverbal communication; and apply techniques of transactional analysis.

Instruction: Major topics covered in the course are management by objectives; the role of management information, constructive communications, and transactional analysis. Methods of instruction include lecture, discussion, text and related readings, classroom exercises, student presentations, and an examination.

Credit Recommendation: In the lower division baccalaureate/associate degree category, 1 semester hour in Business Administration or Management (1/90) (1/95).

Training of Trainers (NMGMT 650)

Location: Washington, DC.

Length: 120 hours (4 weeks).

Dates: October 1989-Present.

Objective: To provide the student with an understanding of principles and techniques for designing and delivering effective adult training programs.

Learning Outcome: Upon successful completion of this course, the student will be able to understand and apply principles of adult education; conduct training needs analysis; design course curricula relevant to adult training needs; conduct training programs using a variety of delivery techniques; skillfully use training technologies, and evaluate training outcomes.

Instruction: Major topics covered in the course are learning principles; planning the learning experience; managing the learning experience; and use of advanced training technologies and aids. Methods of instruction include lecture, discussion, and classroom exercises.

Credit Recommendation: In the upper division baccalaureate degree category, 3 semester hours in Human Resources Management or Adult Education (6/93).

Computer Science

Ada Programming (ECOMP 335)

Location: Washington, DC.

Length: 30 hours (10 weeks).

Dates: January 1984-December 1993.

Objective: To provide the student with an understanding of the principles of Ada to permit the student to design and write Ada programs and teach Ada to others.

Learning Outcome: Upon successful completion of this course, the student will be able to make full use of Ada and software engineering features; write, compile, link, and execute Ada programs; employ information hiding and data obstruction; and develop concurrent programs using Ada's task facility.

Instruction: Major topics covered in the course are Ada history and basic concepts; lexical style and scalan types; control structures: IF, CASE, LOOP, and GO TO statements; composite types: array types, characters and strings, and one-dimensional array operations; subprograms, overall structure, and private types; advanced types, numeric types, and generic types; and tasking, external interfaces, string packages, and utility programs. Methods of instruction include lecture, demonstration, and lab work.

Credit Recommendation: In the lower division baccalaureate/associate degree category, 2 semester hours in Computer Science or Data Processing (6/88) (6/93).

ADP Documentation and Writing (ECOMP 254)

Location: Washington, DC.

Length: 30 hours (10 weeks).

Dates: January 1984-December 1993.

Objective: To help students understand the characteristics and uses of documentation of various computer programs.

Learning Outcome: Upon successful completion of this course, the student will be able to write and revise documentation; and evaluate and refine documentation.

Instruction: Major topics covered in the course are methods of documentation management and planning tools, charting techniques, procedures, decision processes, programs, systems, user manuals, document types and content guidelines, document uses, word processing, desktop publishing, user interface, online documentation, and self-paced training and video documentation; a number of actual documentation of packages, such as LOTUS 1-2-3, WordPerfect, and dBASE III+, communication packages, and demo packages are evaluated. Methods of instruction include lecture, discussion, and laboratory exercises.

Credit Recommendation: In the lower division baccalaureate/associate degree category, 2 semester hours in Data Processing or Information Systems Management (6/88) (6/93).

Advanced C Programming (ECOMP 376)

Location: Washington, DC.

Length: 30 hours (10 weeks).

Dates: January 1986-Present.

Objective: To provide the student with the knowledge of advanced techniques for applying the C programming language to complex computing problems.

Learning Outcome: Upon successful completion of this course, the student will be able to design, debug, and write C programs that incorporate one or more of interactive menus, graphics, text processing, file processing, and numerical algorithms.

Instruction: Major topics covered in the course are file management, graphics, interactive uses, construction of software tools, interaction of C with different hardware and operating systems, and construction of custom function libraries. Methods of instruction include lecture, demonstrations, and laboratory exercises.

Credit Recommendation: In the lower division baccalaureate/associate degree category or in the upper division baccalaureate degree category, 2 semester hours in Computer Science or Data Processing (6/88) (6/93).

BASIC Programming for Beginners (ACOMP 138)

Location: Washington, DC.

Length: 30 hours (5 days) .

Dates: *Version 1:* September 1983-August 1993; *Version 2:* September 1993-Present.

Objective: To provide the student with a rudimentary understanding of BASIC and executing programs using BASIC.

Learning Outcome: Upon successful completion of this course, the student will

be able to design, code, debug, and execute programs written in BASIC.

Instruction: Major topics covered in the course are BASIC language concepts including arithmetic operations, comparing, looping, interactive programming, arrays, menus, subroutines, and sorting. Methods of instruction include lecture, discussion, classroom exercises, and programming assignments.

Credit Recommendation: *Version 1:* In the lower division baccalaureate/associate degree category, 1 semester hour in Data Processing (6/88). *Version 2:* In the lower division baccalaureate/associate degree category, 2 semester hours in Computer Science or Information Systems (8/93).

BASIC Programming Language (ECOMP 140)

Location: Washington, DC.

Length: 30 hours (10 weeks).

Dates: January 1984-September 1992.

Objective: To provide the student with a knowledge of algorithmic solutions to practical problems in computing and data processing and other fields and the ability to program problems in BASIC with an emphasis on structured programming techniques.

Learning Outcome: Upon successful completion of this course, the student will be able to demonstrate programming capabilities by applying them to applications and will be able to move to more advanced programming.

Instruction: Major topics covered in the course are basic statements; language including arithmetic operations; logic operators; conditional statements; nesting; and arrays. Methods of instruction Include lecture, discussion, demonstration, and laboratory work.

Credit Recommendation: In the lower division baccalaureate/associate degree category or in the upper division baccalaureate degree category, 2 semester hours in Computer Science, Data Processing, or Information Systems Management (6/88) (6/93).

C Programming (ECOMP 275)

Location: Washington, DC.

Length: 30 hours (10 weeks).

Dates: September 1985-Present.

Objective: To provide the student with the knowledge and application of C language programs.

Learning Outcome: Upon successful completion of this course, the student will be able to design, write, compile, and execute C language programs.

Instruction: Major topics covered in the course are introduction to C; variables; types and constants; integer variables; elementary operators and arrays; functions; local and global variables; input and output; assignment, arithmetic and unary operators; loops and control statements; pointers, pointers in functions, arrays of structures; and recursive functions. Methods of instruction include lecture, demonstration, and laboratory exercises.

Credit Recommendation: In the lower division baccalaureate/associate degree category or in the upper division baccalaureate degree category, 2 semester hours in Computer Science or Data Processing (6/88) (6/93).

COBOL Programming I (ECOMP 145)

Location: Washington, DC.

Length: 40 hours (10 weeks).

Dates: January 1978-June 1992.

Objective: To help the student understand the basic features of COBOL programs.

Learning Outcome: Upon successful completion of this course, the student will understand the basic structure of COBOL and applications; and code, debug, and execute simple COBOL programs.

Instruction: Major topics covered in the course are COBOL structure, the four COBOL divisions, editing techniques; structured programming design; relational operators, table handling; and control break logic. Methods of instruction include lecture, discussion, and laboratory exercises.

Credit Recommendation: In the lower division baccalaureate/associate degree category or in the upper division baccalaureate degree category, 3 semester hours in Computer Science, Computer Information Systems, or Data Processing (6/88) (6/93).

COBOL Programming II (ECOMP 146)

Location: Washington, DC.

Length: 30 hours (10 weeks).

Dates: January 1978-June 1992.

Objective: To provide the student with an understanding of advanced features of moderate to complex COBOL programs using the advanced features of the language.

Learning Outcome: Upon successful completion of this course, the student will be able to explain advanced features and operation of a COBOL program within the total COBOL environment; and code, debug, and execute moderate to complex COBOL programs.

Instruction: Major topics covered in the course are sequential file processing; single and double arrays; sorting; processing ISAM files; relative file processing; and report writer. Methods of instruction include lecture, discussion, and laboratory exercises.

Credit Recommendation: In the lower division baccalaureate/associate degree category or in the upper division baccalaureate degree category, 2 semester hours in Computer Science, Computer Information Systems, or Data Processing (6/88) (6/93).

Computer Applications in Management (NCOMP 215)

Location: Washington, DC.

Length: 228 hours (8 weeks).

Dates: August 1987-December 1994.

Objective: To provide a comprehensive introduction to the practical use and integration of software applications into current computerized environments. Participants get extensive hands-on experience by assembling an IBM-compatible computer.

Learning Outcome: Upon successful completion of this course, the student will be able to apply software as a management tool and use major software packages; use and upgrade a microcomputer; and understand the capabilities of computerized systems.

Instruction: Major topics covered in the course are integration of computer applications in an organized routine. Methods of instruction include lectures, discussions, heavy emphasis on handling in exercises, and individual and continual monitoring by instructors.

Credit Recommendation: In the lower division baccalaureate/associate degree category, 4 semester hours in Data Processing (1/90) (1/95).

Data Communications Technology (CCOMM 125)

Location: Correspondence Study.

Length: 10 lessons.

Dates: June 1993-Present.

Objective: To introduce the student to data communication equipment and networks.

Learning Outcome: Upon successful completion of this course, the student will be able to develop and extend computer networks; attach various devices to a network; and interconnect various types of networks.

Instruction: Major topics covered in the course are overview of data communications; data terminals; messages; and transmission channels; asynchronous and synchronous modems; multiplexing techniques, fiber optic systems, and satellite systems; protocols and error control; local area networks; architectures and packet networks; network design and management; and wide area networks. Methods of instruction include self-paced study and proctored examination.

Credit Recommendation: In the lower division baccalaureate/associate degree category, 3 semester hours in Data Communications Technology (6/93).

Database Design (ECOMP 364)

Location: Washington, DC.

Length: 30 hours (10 weeks).

Dates: January 1984-Present.

Objective: To provide the student with the knowledge and use of various data base management systems and creation of an elementary data base system.

Learning Outcome: Upon successful completion of this course, the student will be able to review a database management system and determine what kind of data structures it can handle, and the type of DBMS model it represents; and develop an elementary conceptual database design for an application.

Instruction: Major topics covered in the course are purpose and use of a database management system; various storage devices and systems used in database work; logical relationships and several data representations; data base design and models; various database systems such as the relational model and CODASYL model; and database administration. Methods of instruction include lecture, discussion, demonstration, and laboratory exercises.

Credit Recommendation: In the lower division baccalaureate/associate degree category or in the upper division baccalaureate degree category, 2 semester hours in Computer Science, Computer Information Systems, or Data Processing (6/88) (6/93).

dBASE Programming Featuring dBASE III (ECOMP 268)

Location: Washington, DC.

Length: 30 hours (10 weeks).

Dates: September 1987-Present.

Objective: To provide the student with a working knowledge of dBASE programming, particularly with dBASE III.

Learning Outcome: Upon successful completion of this course, the student will be able to write command files and format files; search for specific records in indexed and nonindexed files; and build menus to create and use procedural files.

Instruction: Major topics covered in the course are an overview of dBASE language and operation, dBASE functions, dBASE command files, and executing. Methods of instruction include lectures and discussions. Evaluation is done in grading of homework assignments.

Credit Recommendation: In the lower division baccalaureate/associate degree category, 2 semester hours in Data Processing (1/90).

FORTRAN Programming (ACOMP 140)

Location: Washington, DC.

Length: 60 hours (10 days).

Dates: September 1984-Present.

Objective: To provide the student with the ability to write structured FORTRAN 77 programs.

Learning Outcome: Upon successful completion of this course, the student will be able to design, program, and execute structured FORTRAN 77 programs and use structured flowcharts and pseudocode.

Instruction: Major topics covered in the course are problem solution; structured programming; constants and variables; arithmetic operations; control structures; arrays; subprograms; character strings; data types; sequential and direct access data files; and sorting. Methods of instruction include lecture, discussion, laboratory exercises, quizzes.

Credit Recommendation: In the lower division baccalaureate/associate degree category, 4 semester hours in Computer Science (6/88) (8/93).

IBM 360/370 OS/VS Job Control Language (JCL) (ECOMP 242)

Location: Washington, DC.

Length: 35 hours (10 weeks).

Dates: January 1978-March 1996.

Objective: To provide the student with an understanding of the Job Control Language for the OS/MVS environment to construct the majority of job streams.

Learning Outcome: Upon successful completion of this course, the student will be able to construct job streams that cover 90 percent or more of computer applications; use catalogued procedures; and debug JCL statements.

Instruction: Major topics covered in the course are JCL syntax rules; parameters of JOB, EXEC, and DD statements; tape processing; disk processing; catalogued procedures; in-stream procedures; and utilities. Methods of instruction include lecture, discussion, and laboratory exercises.

Credit Recommendation: In the lower division baccalaureate/associate degree category, 2 semester hours in Data Processing (6/88) (6/93).

IBM System 360/370 PL/1 (ECOMP 251)

Location: Washington, DC.

Length: 37.5 hours (10 weeks).

Dates: January 1978-March 1992.

Objective: To provide the student with the knowledge and skill to develop structured PL/1 programs.

Learning Outcome: Upon successful completion of this course, the student will be able to demonstrate an understanding of the concepts and terminology of structured PL/1 programming, and write and maintain structured PL/1 programs.

Instruction: Major topics covered in the course are program definition; procedures and statements; assignments and control statements; stream and record I/O; arrays and structures; subroutines; on-conditions and built-in functions; compiled time facilities and list processing; and file structure and data definition statements. Methods of instruction include lecture, discussion, and laboratory exercises.

Credit Recommendation: In the lower division baccalaureate/associate degree category or in the upper division baccalaureate degree category, 3 semester hours in Data Processing (6/88) (6/93).

Information Storage and Retrieval (ECOMP 363)

Location: Washington, DC.

Length: 30 hours (10 weeks).

Dates: September 1989-Present.

Objective: To provide the student with a basic understanding of information retrieval theory and practice.

Learning Outcome: Upon successful completion of this course, the student will be able to understand information retrieval methodology; evaluate existing information in retrieval systems; and design and implement a basic information retrieval system.

Instruction: Major topics covered in the course are record formats, file structures, text analysis, and automatic indexing, query languages and Boolean logic, retrieval evaluation, and retrieval refinement. Methods of instruction include lecture, discussion, classroom exercises, midterm examination, final examination, and term project.

Credit Recommendation: In the upper division baccalaureate degree category, 2 semester hours in Data Processing (1/90).

Introduction to Computer Programming (CCOMP 102)

Location: Correspondence study.

Length: 10 lessons.

Dates: January 1985-Present.

Objective: To provide the student with a basis for specific programming language courses.

Learning Outcome: Upon successful completion of this course, the student will be able to understand the basic logic and techniques of computer programming; discuss the major advantages and disadvantages of the most common programming languages; and appreciate the need for structured programming techniques and the need for documentation.

Instruction: Major topics covered in the course are development of algorithms for computer programs, program development and debugging, flowcharts and decision tables, pseudocode, introduction to BASIC, introduction to FORTRAN, introduction to COBOL, system documentation and logical design, physical system design, and feasibility analysis and system implementation. Methods of instruction include extensive readings, written assignments, and examinations.

Credit Recommendation: In the lower division baccalaureate/associate degree category, 3 semester hours in Data Processing (1/90).

Introduction to Computer Programming (ECOMP 111)

Location: Washington, DC.

Length: 30 hours (10 weeks).

Dates: January 1986-Present.

Objective: To provide the student with an understanding of the principles of structured computer programming and problem solution; emphasis is placed on the algorithmic approach.

Learning Outcome: Upon successful completion of this course, the student will be able to apply the rules and guidelines of structured programming; use flowcharting concepts in problem solving; and implement a computer program in BASIC.

Instruction: Major topics covered in the course are problem definition, the programming process, solution implementation; structured programming and problem solving using the algorithmic approach; flowcharting, structure charts, pseudocode; data types and attributes; introduction to BASIC language; and writing, debugging, and running a BASIC program. Methods of instruction include lectures and demonstrations with hands-on experience.

Credit Recommendation: In the lower division baccalaureate/associate degree category, 2 semester hours in Computer Information Systems or Data Processing (6/88) (6/93).

Introduction to Data Processing (ACOMP 114)

Location: Washington, DC.

Length: *Version 1:* 24 hours (4 days); *Version 2:* 30 hours (5 days).

Dates: *Version 1:* September 1981-August 1993; *Version 2:* September 1993-Present.

Objective: *Version 1:* To provide the student with a knowledge of computers and their use. *Version 2:* To provide the student with a basic knowledge of the fundamentals of computers and information processing.

Learning Outcome: *Version 1:* Upon successful completion of this course, the student will be able to identify the components and functions of a computer system; differentiate types and uses of various hardware and software; and explain the basic concepts of data processing. *Version 2:* Upon successful completion of this course, the student will be able to recognize basic computer concepts, terminology, and components (including hardware and software) of a computer system; distinguish between micro and mainframe computing; identify the various occupational specialties in the field; and be introduced to data communications and to the BASIC programming language.

Instruction: *Version 1:* Major topics covered in the course are elements of data processing including input/output; file organization; data bases and data communications; and applications of software packages. Methods of instruction include lecture, demonstration, and field visit. *Version 2:* Major topics covered in the course are an overview of informations systems technology, basic concepts and terminology of computers, components of a system, differences between types of computers, basic concepts of data communications and an introduction to programming using the BASIC language. Methods of instruction include lecture, classroom discussion, a lab experience and field trip to a computer center, and examinations.

Credit Recommendation: *Version 1:* In the lower division baccalaureate/associate degree category, 1 semester hour in Computer Science or Data Processing (6/88). *Version 2:* In the lower division baccalaureate/associate degree category, 2 semester hours in Introduction to Data Processing; Introduction to Computers and Computing or Introduction to Computer Information Systems (8/93).

Introduction to Information Systems Technology (CCOMP 110)

Location: Correspondence study.

Length: 11 lessons.

Dates: September 1988-Present.

Objective: To provide the student with an understanding of the automatic data processing systems technology.

Learning Outcome: Upon successful completion of this course, the student will be able to understand basic automatic data processing system concepts and principles; identify and select the hardware, software, and service elements appropriate to data processing needs and requirements; and identify the functional components of a digital general purpose computer.

Instruction: Major topics covered in the course are an overview of electronic digital computer data processing, with special emphasis on the history and evaluation of data processing, data representation, arithmetic, equipment, applications software, systems development cycle, and modes of processing. Methods of instruction include readings and examinations.

Credit Recommendation: In the lower division baccalaureate/associate degree category, 2 semester hours in Data Processing (1/90).

Introduction to Information Systems Technology (ECOMP 110)

Location: Washington, DC.

Length: 30 hours (10 weeks).

Dates: January 1986-Present.

Objective: To provide the student with knowledge of the fundamentals of computers and information processing.

Learning Outcome: Upon successful completion of this course, the student will be able to recognize basic concepts, terminology and components, including hardware and software of a computer system; distinguish between the functions performed by mainframe and microcomputers; and identify the various occupational specialties in the computer field.

Instruction: Major topics covered in the course are overview of information systems technology; basic concepts and terminology of computers; primary computer components; understanding the differences between types of computers; running a simple computer program on a microcomputer; and discussion of computers in society. Methods of instruction include lectures and demonstrations with laboratory work.

Credit Recommendation: In the lower division baccalaureate/associate degree category, 2 semester hours in Data Processing or Information Systems Technology (6/88) (6/93).

Introduction to ISPF (Interactive Systems Productivity Facility) (ACOMP 346)

Location: Washington, DC.

Length: 18 hours (3 days).

Dates: September 1983-Present.

Objective: To provide the student with an understanding of the operations and applications of the ISPF.

Learning Outcome: Upon successful completion of this course, the student will be able to create and edit data sets and programs in the IBM/MVS environment.

Instruction: Major topics covered in the course are overview of ISPF; ISPF menus; managing data; editing data; partitioned data sets; data set utilities; and advanced ISPF features. Methods of instruction include lecture, presentations, classroom discussion, and examination.

Credit Recommendation: In the lower division baccalaureate/associate degree category, 1 semester hour in Computer Information Systems, Management Information Systems, or Systems Programming (6/88) (8/93).

Introduction to Job Control Language (JCL) (ACOMP347)

Location: Washington, DC.

Length: 12 hours (2 days).

Dates: January 1983-Present.

Objective: To provide the student with sufficient understanding of the job control language to construct and debug the majority of IBM/MVS job streams.

Learning Outcome: Upon successful completion of this course, the student will be able to construct job streams and debug JCL statements that cover 90 percent or more of computer applications.

Instruction: Major topics covered in the course are JCL syntax rules; parameters of JOB; EXEC and DD statements; tape and disk processing; and concepts of catalogued procedures. Methods of instruction include lecture, presentations, and student exercises.

Credit Recommendation: In the lower division baccalaureate/associate degree category, 1 semester hour in Data Processing, Computer Information Systems, or Management Information Systems (8/93).

Introduction to LAN System Administration (ECOMP 283)

Location: Washington, D.C.

Length: 30 hours (10 weeks).

Dates: September 1993-Present.

Objective: To prepare the student to design and maintain a LAN as a LAN network administrator.

Learning Outcome: Upon successful completion of this course, the student will be able to determine software needs; establish director and user security; create system and individual user login scripts; install application programs; design a custom menu, review third party software utilities for netware; configure printers, monitor network performance, and provide network security.

Instruction: Major topics covered in the course are determining software requirements; designing the directory structure; assigning and entering User and Group Trustee assignments; implementing login scripts; installing applications and configurations; implementing the menu system; and management utilities for a Novell local area network. Methods of instruction include lecture, discussion, classroom exercises, case studies, audio/visual material, computer laboratory exercises, article reviews and handouts, classroom exercises, projects, and a final examination.

Credit Recommendation: In the lower division baccalaureate/associate degree category, 2 semester hours in Computer Information Systems, Data Communications and Networking, or Management Information Systems (1/95).

Introduction to Local Area Networks (ECOMP 281)

Location: Washington, D.C.

Length: 30 hours (10 weeks).

Dates: September 1993-Present.

Objective: To provide an overview of local area fundamentals and determine its use in the organization.

Learning Outcome: Upon successful completion of this course, the student will be able to discuss defacto networking industry standards (to include the OSI Reference Model); apply these standards in the basic design and implementation of networks; explain network configurations and their application in the workplace; and execute basic Novell Netware commands in support of basic netware administration functions.

Instruction: Major topics covered in the course are an overview of networks; data communications standards; business applications using network technologies; local area network standards; Novell Netware administration fundamentals; commands and menus; and business applications using Novell Netware. Methods of instruction include lecture, discussion, classroom exercises, audio/visual material, computer-assisted instruction; video tape and hands-on exercises in a computer laboratory, and a mid-term and final examination.

Credit Recommendation: In the lower division baccalaureate/associate degree category, 2 semester hours in Computer Information Systems, Data Communications and Networking, or Management Information Systems (1/95).

Introduction to Problem-Solving (ACOMP 119) (Formerly Problem Solving for COBOL Programmers)

Location: Washington, DC.

Length: 24 hours (4 days).

Dates: September 1983-Present.

Objective: To provide the student with the knowledge of structured techniques for elementary program design and documentation.

Learning Outcome: Upon successful completion of this course, the student will be able to select appropriate structured techniques to construct charts and diagrams for depicting and documenting systems and programs.

Instruction: Major topics covered in the course are structured techniques; systems analysis; top-down approach; data flow diagrams; systems flowcharts and designs; decision tables and decision trees; pseudocode; and programming features. Methods of instruction include lecture, discussion, classroom exercises, and final examination.

Credit Recommendation: In the lower division baccalaureate/associate degree category, 1 semester hour in Computer Information Systems or Science, or Computer Science (6/88) (8/93).

Introduction to UNIX (ECOMP 130)

Location: Washington, D.C.

Length: 30 hours (10 weeks).

Dates: September 1990-Present.

Objective: To provide the student with a detailed introduction to the UNIX operating system.

Learning Outcome: Upon successful completion of this course, the student will be able to describe the major components and architecture of UNIX; log on and off of UNIX; communicate with others on the system; create and modify files; use UNIX commands for I/O redirection; and use UNIX utilities to create simple tools.

Instruction: Major topics covered in the course are an overview and history of UNIX; sending and receiving mail; using and controlling files and directories; searching text files; compiling and running a program, the shell command line; and text editor. Methods of instruction include lecture, discussion, classroom exercises, extensive hands-on exercises, quizzes, and a final examination.

Credit Recommendation: In the lower division baccalaureate/associate degree category, 2 semester hours in Computer Science, Computer Information Systems, Data Processing, or Management Informations Systems (1/95).

LAN Hardware and Troubleshooting (ECOMP 282)

Location: Washington, D.C.

Length: 30 hours (10 weeks).

Dates: April 1993-Present.

Objective: To enable participants to understand the differences between various LAN topologies, select and install hardware for a LAN, and conduct basic LAN troubleshooting.

Learning Outcome: Upon successful completion of this course, the student will be able to understand and select hardware to support ethernet, token ring, token bus, and Arcnet LANS; and understand wiring needs, cabling systems, interface cards, and the use of troubleshooting drivers such as breakout boxes, signal tracers, protocol analyzers and bit error rate testers to resolve LAN physical layer problems.

Instruction: Major topics covered in the course are pc architecture, specific hardware required for a LAN, various wiring types and schemes, troubleshooting test equipment, file servers vs. work stations, and interfacing LAN hardware. Methods of instruction include lecture, discussion, classroom exercises, audio/visual material, laboratory exercises including installation of a small LAN, and a final examination.

Credit Recommendation: In the lower division baccalaureate/associate degree category, 2 semester hours in Computer Information Systems, Data Communications and Networking, or Management Information Systems (1/95).

Microcomputer Applications (NCOMP 575) (Formerly Computer Software Operations)

Location: Washington, DC.

Length: 120 hours (4 weeks).

Dates: November 1991-Present.

Objective: To provide students with techniques which increase productivity and efficiency in database operations, programming methods, and desktop publishing methods.

Learning Outcome: Upon successful completion of this course, the student will be able to design, create, and modify databases, menus and reports using dBase IV; create integrated spreadsheets, macros, programs, and menus using Lotus 1-2-3; use string formulae, financial functions, formatting and graphs employing Quattro Pro 3.0; create flyers and reports using Wordperfect, Drawperfect, and Pagemaker; and use software integration techniques to translate files.

Instruction: Major topics covered in the course are advanced applications in Lotus and Quattro Pro; dBase applications and programming; desktop publishing and applications using Pagemaker and DrawPerfect; document preparation; and integration through peripherals and procedural techniques. Methods of instruction include lecture, discussion, and classroom exercises with assigned projects.

Credit Recommendation: In the lower division baccalaureate/associate degree category or in the upper division baccalaureate degree category, 4 semester hours in Computer Information Systems, Information Systems Management, or Data Processing (6/93).

Object Oriented Structure Analysis, Design, and Programming (ECOMP 246)

Location: Washington, D.C.

Length: 40 hours (10 weeks).

Dates: January 1992-September 1993.

Objective: To acquaint the student with object oriented data modeling, state transition diagramming, use of case scripting, data flow diagramming, and structured design and programming concepts.

Learning Outcome: Upon successful completion of this course, the student will be able to prepare object data models and state transition diagrams; use case scripts, data flow diagrams, and structured program designs; and employ the concepts of classes, relationships, inheritance, encapsulation, and similar concepts in structured design of programs.

Instruction: Major topics covered in the course are an overview of object models; evaluating design; summary of object methods; object modeling; dynamic modeling; analysis; structured design and mapping design of code in various languages (COBOL, C++, etc.). Methods of instruction include lecture, discussion, classroom exercises, and a final take-home examination.

Credit Recommendation: In the lower division baccalaureate/associate degree category, 2 semester hours in Computer Information Systems, Computer Science, Data Processing, or Management Information Systems (1/95).

Object-Oriented Structural Analysis (ECOMP 247) (Formerly Structured Design and Programming)

Location: Washington, D.C.

Length: 30 hours (10 weeks).

Dates: September 1980-Present.

Objective: To understand the characteristics of computer program documentation.

Learning Outcome: Upon successful completion of this course, the student will be able to write and revise documentation and evaluate and refine documentation.

Instruction: Major topics covered in the course are methods of ADP documentation and writing using advanced techniques and methods; current methods of structured analysis, structured design, program coding, program development, program refinement, and program quality evaluation; and history of manual typing to desktop and on-line video documentation techniques for screen capture, text scanning, word processing, and graphics. Methods of instruction include lecture, discussion, laboratory exercises, and teams made up of class members write documents and make a presentation (this has students learn to communicate ideas and form a team product in addition to learning goals).

Credit Recommendation: In the lower division baccalaureate/associate degree category, 2 semester hours in Data Processing or Information Systems Management (6/88) (6/93).

Operating Systems (ECOMP 203)

Location: Washington, DC.

Length: 30 hours (10 weeks).

Dates: September 1984-Present.

Objective: To provide the student with a fundamental understanding of an operating system's primary functions and how these functions are performed in various hardware environments.

Learning Outcome: Upon successful completion of this course, the student will be able to demonstrate an understanding of the history of the functions and purposes of an operating system and understand how operating systems are implemented and how they relate to other software systems.

Instruction: Major topics covered in the course are an overview of the history of operating systems, how various resource management routines and system input/output (I/O) routines work together, and how operating systems are implemented and relate to other software systems within the automatic data processing system. Methods of instruction include lectures, discussions, and classroom exercises.

Credit Recommendation: In the lower division baccalaureate/associate degree category, 2 semester hours in Computer Science or Data Processing (1/90).

PASCAL Programming (ACOMP 145)

Location: Washington, DC.

Length: 30 hours (5 days).

Dates: September 1983-March 1993.

Objective: To provide the student with a knowledge and application of structured PASCAL programs.

Learning Outcome: Upon successful completion of this course, the student will be able to design PASCAL programs using structured flowcharts and pseudocode and write and execute PASCAL programs.

Instruction: Major topics covered in the course are data types, arithmetic operations; assignment statements, input/output, control structures, Begin, End, For, While, Repeat, If, Case functions and procedures; one-dimensional arrays; set operations; and records and fields. Methods of instruction include lecture, demonstration, and laboratory exercises.

Credit Recommendation: In the lower division baccalaureate/associate degree category, 2 semester hours in Computer Science (6/88) (8/93).

PASCAL Programming (ECOMP 269)

Location: Washington, DC.

Length: 30 hours (10 weeks).

Dates: September 1984-Present.

Objective: To provide the student with the ability to develop algorithms necessary to solve typical computer problems and to implement the algorithms using structural, efficient PASCAL code.

Learning Outcome: Upon successful completion of this course, the student will be able to develop algorithms to solve typical computer problems; develop and implement structured, documented, and efficient PASCAL code; and understand and use ASCII and binary files.

Instruction: Major topics covered in the course are the development of algorithms, PASCAL program structure, arithmetic and logical operators, loops, functions and procedures, decision operators, single- and multidimensional arrays, sets, records, and ASCII and binary files. Methods of instruction include lecture, discussion, laboratory exercises using IBM-compatible computers, and assignments.

Credit Recommendation: In the lower division baccalaureate/associate degree category, 2 semester hours in Computer Science, Computer Information Systems, or Data Processing (1/90) (1/95).

PROLOG Programming: An Introduction with Artificial Intelligence Examples (ECOMP 380)

Location: Washington, DC.

Length: 30 hours (10 weeks).

Dates: January 1988-Present.

Objective: To enable the student to design, program, and explain the operation of an expert system or of programs in the PROLOG language of corresponding difficulty.

Learning Outcome: Upon successful completion of this course, the student will be able to solve a variety of problems using PROLOG; write an expert system in PROLOG; and demonstrate an understanding of artificial intelligence concepts and applications.

Instruction: Major topics covered in the course are an introduction to PROLOG concepts, PROLOG programming techniques, relational data base, building an expert system shell, language processing (grammar, syntax, semantics), and software engineering. Methods of instruction include lectures, projects, presentations, and examinations.

Credit Recommendation: In the upper division baccalaureate degree category, 2 semester hours in Computer Science (1/90).

Structured COBOL Programming I (ACOMP 155)

Location: Washington, DC.

Length: *Version 1:* 72 hours (12 days); *Version 2:* 60 hours (10 days).

Dates: *Version 1:* September 1983-August 1993; *Version 2:* September 1993-Present.

Objective: *Version 1:* To provide the student with an understanding and use of structured COBOL programs in elementary business reports. *Version 2:* To enable the student to write and execute documented structured COBOL programs which produce elementary business reports.

Learning Outcome: Upon successful completion of this course, the student will be able to design, code, execute, and debug elementary structured COBOL with documentation.

Instruction: *Version 1:* Methods of instruction include lecture, demonstration, and laboratory exercises. *Version 2:* Methods of instruction include lecture, discussion, workshops, programming assignments, computer laboratory, and final examination.

Credit Recommendation: *Version 1:* In the vocational certificate or lower division baccalaureate/associate degree category, 1 semester hour in Computer Science or Data Processing (6/88). *Version 2:* In the lower division baccalaureate/associate degree category, 2 semester hours in Computer Information Systems, or Computer Science (8/93).

Structured COBOL Programming II (ACOMP 156)

Location: Washington, DC.

Length: *Version 1:* 72 hours (12 days); *Version 2:* 60 hours (10 days).

Dates: *Version 1:* September 1983-August 1993; *Version 2:* September 1993-Present.

Objective: *Version 1:* To provide the student with an understanding and application of structured COBOL programs to business reports. *Version 2:* To write structured COBOL programs that use advanced techniques to produce reports.

Learning Outcome: *Version 1:* Upon successful completion of this course, the student will be able to use structured COBOL for compound logic statement such as nested IFS, control breaks, processing tables in memory and to design a menu program. *Version 2:* Upon successful completion of this course, the student will be able to use structured COBOL programming techniques to depict complex logic such as nested IFs, control breaks, and processing tables in memory; and to design a menu program.

Instruction: *Version 1:* Major topics covered in the course are nested IF statements, control break processing, multiple level control break processing, table processing, and menu programming. Methods of instruction include lecture, demonstration, and laboratory exercises. *Version 2:* Major topics covered in the course are nested IF statements; batch validation processing; SORT verb processing; control break processing; multiple level control break processing; group indication processing; and one dimension table processing. Methods of instruction include lecture, class discussion, programming assignments, and final examination.

Credit Recommendation: *Version 1:* In the vocational certificate or lower division baccalaureate/associate degree category, 1 semester hour in Computer Science or Data Processing (6/88). *Version 2:* In the lower division baccalaureate/associate degree category, 2 semester hours in Computer Information Systems or Computer Science (8/93).

Structured COBOL Programming III (ACOMP 157)

Location: Washington, DC.

Length: *Version 1:* 72 hours (12 days); *Version 2:* 60 hours (10 days).

Dates: *Version 1:* September 1983-August 1993; *Version 2:* September 1993-Present.

Objective: To provide the student with the knowledge to understand and create structured COBOL programs incorporating use of utilities, file organization, and debugging with storage dumps.

Learning Outcome: *Version 1:* Upon successful completion of this course, the student will be able to use sort verbs, utilities, and JCL; create and update sequential files; create ISAM files and access randomly; use two- and three-dimensional tables; and use report writer and strings. *Version 2:* Upon successful completion of this course, the student will to use sort verbs; manipulate character data; create and update sequential files; create and randomly access ISAM files; use two- and three-dimensional tables; and use batch and interactive file maintenance techniques.

Instruction: *Version 1:* Major topics covered in the course are sequential files, ISAM files, including randomly accessing and updating, sorting, and two and three-dimensional tables. Methods of instruction include lecture, demonstration, and laboratory exercises. *Version 2:* Major topics covered in the course are COBOL sort features; character data manipulation statements; sequential and ISAM files including the accessing and maintenance (via batch and interactive techniques) of these files; two- and three-dimensional tables; utilities; and JCL. Methods of instruction include lecture, workshop, programming assignments, and final examination.

Credit Recommendation: *Version 1:* In the vocational certificate or lower division baccalaureate/associate degree category, 1 semester hour in Computer Science or Data Processing (6/88). *Version 2:* In the lower division baccalaureate/associate degree category, 2 semester hours in Computer Information Systems or Computer Science (8/93).

Structured Systems Analysis and Design (ACOMP 713)

Location: Washington, DC.

Length: 18 hours (3 days).

Dates: September 1983-Present.

Objective: To provide the student with a basic understanding of structured systems analysis and design techniques relevant to an information systems environment.

Learning Outcome: Upon successful completion of this course, the student will be able to describe the phases of an information system analysis and design project, and explain the approach used in conducting the process.

Instruction: Major topics covered in the course are systems concepts; life cycle planning the project; information gathering; structured analysis tools; data flow diagrams; and file organization and database design. Methods of instruction include lecture, class presentations, individual, and group exercises.

Credit Recommendation: In the lower division baccalaureate/associate degree category, 1 semester hour in Computer Information Systems or Management Information Systems (6/88) (8/93).

Systems Analysis and Design (ECOMP 362)

Location: Washington, DC.

Length: 30 hours (15 weeks).

Dates: September 1980-Present.

Objective: To provide the student with a knowledge of the tools and techniques used in systems analysis.

Learning Outcome: Upon successful completion of this course, the student will be able to identify the degree and nature of participation in the systems development process required by the analyst; identify the various activities involved in systems development; and demonstrate an awareness of the tools and techniques used in systems analysis and design.

Instruction: Major topics covered in the course are systems concepts; systems development life cycle; role of the systems analyst; system planning considerations;, information gathering techniques; structured analysis tools; cost/benefit analysis; input/output considerations; file organization and database design; and system testing and quality assurance. Methods of instruction include lecture, discussion, and classroom exercises.

Credit Recommendation: In the lower division baccalaureate/associate degree category, 2 semester hours in Data Processing or Information Systems Management (6/88) (6/93).

Systems Analysis and Documentation (ACOMP 345)

Location: Washington, DC.

Length: 18 hours (3 days).

Dates: January 1983-June 1995.

Objective: To provide the student with a knowledge of the tools and techniques used in systems analysis.

Learning Outcome: Upon successful completion of this course, the student will be able to describe the phases of an information system analysis project and the tools and techniques used in the process.

Instruction: Major topics covered in the course are systems concepts, life cycle, planning the project, and information gathering; structured analysis tools; data flow diagrams; and file organization and database design. Methods of instruction include lecture, presentations, and classroom discussion.

Credit Recommendation: In the lower division baccalaureate/associate degree category, 1 semester hour in Computer Information Systems or Information Systems Management (6/88) (8/93).

Technical Writing (ACOMP 265)

Location: Washington, DC.

Length: 18 hours (3 days).

Dates: September 1983-Present.

Objective: To provide the student with the ability to write clear, direct procedures for accomplishing required technical tasks and to document computer programs.

Learning Outcome: Upon successful completion of this course, the student will be able to write and re-write documents clearly; know the steps necessary to write successfully; and know the rules of good grammar, proper punctuation, tense, and word choice.

Instruction: Major topics covered in the course are steps to successful writing; preparation, research, organization, draft writing, revision, understanding various formats such as play script, narrative and cookbook; review of and creation of user documentation, data processing terminology; and guidelines and standards for computer system documentation. Methods of instruction include lecture, class presentation, student exercises, and final examination.

Credit Recommendation: In the lower division baccalaureate/associate degree category, 1 semester hour in English or Technical Writing (6/88) (8/93).

Telecommunications Project Management (ECOMP 225)

Location: Washington, DC.

Length: 30 hours (10 weeks).

Dates: September 1988-Present.

Objective: To introduce the student to the management activities necessary to integrate telecommunications projects.

Learning Outcome: Upon successful completion of this course, the student will be able to plan, estimate resources requirements, control and schedule project activities in a telecommunications project; identify necessary automated tools used in decision making in project planning and design; and identify and understand the use of data processing staff required in project management.

Instruction: Major topics covered in the course are planning, resource estimating, controlling and scheduling a telecommunications project, process involved in the management activities necessary to successfully integrate the development, design, and application of a telecommunications project, and appropriate use and management of staff on project development, design, and implementation. Methods of instruction include lectures, discussions, and a term paper.

Credit Recommendation: In the lower division baccalaureate/associate degree category, 2 semester hours in Information Systems Management (1/90).

Teleprocessing and Data Communication Systems (ECOMP 224)

Location: Washington, DC

Length: 37.5 hours (10 weeks).

Dates: September 1984-Present.

Objective: To provide the student with an overview of fundamental concepts and current practices associated with today's teleprocessing and data communication systems.

Learning Outcome: Upon successful completion of this course, the student will be able to understand technology, concepts, and practices associated with data communications.

Instruction: Major topics covered in the course are teleprocessing and data communication hardware, fundamental communication concepts, network configuration, and network protocols and software. Methods of instruction include lectures, discussions, homework assignments, and a final examination.

Credit Recommendation: In the lower division baccalaureate/associate degree category, 2 semester hours in Data Processing (1/90).

Economics

Econometrics I (EECON 545)

Location: Washington, DC.

Length: 30 hours (10 weeks).

Dates: January 1987-Present.

Objective: To provide the student with the theory and practice of statistical methods and techniques in their application to economic applications and problems.

Learning Outcome: Upon successful completion of this course, the student will be able to understand the basic application of the linear regression and correlation model to economic data; to test and validate various models as to their usefulness and applicability to conditions and situations; understand the application of various tests of significance, confidence regions, and other methods that are applicable to the analysis of economic data.

Instruction: Major topics covered in the course are the basic theory and methods of empirical economics; the general linear model, analytical techniques such as least squares estimation, testing for significance, analysis of variance, and confidence limits; and prediction and forecasting are included as applications of the various models. Methods of instruction include lectures, discussions, problem-solving, graded homework, a term paper, and a final examination.

Credit Recommendation: In the upper division baccalaureate degree or the graduate degree category, 3 semester hours in Business Administration, Economics, or Statistics (1/90) (1/95).

Econometrics II (EECON 546)

Location: Washington, DC.

Length: 30 hours (10 weeks).

Dates: January 1989-Present.

Objective: To provide the student with the theory and practice of statistical and other quantitative methods in developing solutions to economic problems.

Learning Outcome: Upon successful completion of this course, the student will be able to develop and apply multilevel models and techniques to various economic problems and situations; use various software packages in the application of econometric methods to various economic conditions; and interpret the outcomes and draw conclusions concerning the various kinds of analysis.

Instruction: Major topics covered in the course are the analysis of complex economic problems, seasonal adjustments, autolagged variables, multiple stage least squares simulation, and policy. Methods of instruction include lectures, discussions, problem-solving, graded homework, a term paper, and a final examination.

Credit Recommendation: In the graduate degree category, 2 semester hours in Business Administration, Economics, or Statistics (1/90) (1/95).

Economics of Oil (EECON 249)

Location: Washington, DC.

Length: 30 hours (10 weeks).

Dates: April 1991-March 1997.

Objective: To understand real world economic practices in the oil industry.

Learning Outcome: Upon successful completion of this course, the student will be able to apply appropriately principles of resource economics to practices in the petroleum industry, and examine global dimensions of supply and demand conditions in the petrochemical industry.

Instruction: Major topics covered in the course are oligopoly and monopoly theories applied to oil, risk and uncertainty, regulation, cartel behavior, externalities, oil resource issues as a part of the larger energy industry. Methods of instruction are lecture, discussions, problems, student reports, term papers, and examinations.

Credit Recommendation: In the upper division baccalaureate degree category, 2 semester hours in Resource Economics,

Business, or Public Administration elective (6/93).

Environmental and Natural Resource Economics (EECON 215)

Location: Washington, DC.
Length: 30 hours (10 weeks).
Dates: July 1991-Present.
Objective: To understand the economics of resources, and apply those tools to natural resource and other public policy areas.
Learning Outcome: Upon successful completion of this course, the student will be able to explain principles of resource economics and major natural resource allocation problems; describe various resource economics applications, and present formal policy analysis work based on this knowledge.
Instruction: Major topics covered in the course are natural resource futures, key concepts and definitions, limitations of conventional economic analysis, risks and uncertainties in the environment, benefit-cost evaluation, policy criteria in energy, water and natural environmental areas. Methods of instruction include lecture, discussions, cases, problems, student reports, and examinations.
Credit Recommendation: In the upper division baccalaureate degree category, 2 semester hours in Resource Economics, Natural Resources, Business, Economics, or Public Administration elective (6/93).

International Monetary Theory (EECON 561)

Location: Washington, DC.
Length: 30 hours (10 weeks).
Dates: January 1987-Present.
Objective: To provide the student with a basic knowledge of the concepts and tools used in the analysis of the world financial system and its relation to economic conditions in the United States.
Learning Outcome: Upon successful completion of this course, the student will be able to demonstrate a knowledge of causes determining changes in balance-of-payments accounts, exchange rates, and foreign influence on domestic income and show a basic understanding of monetary and fiscal policy.
Instruction: Major topics covered in the course are domestic and international role of the dollar, foreign exchange, European currencies, exchange rates and interest arbitrage, exchange flexibility and the goal of stability, national monetary and commercial systems, monetary standards, and national currencies. Methods of instruction include lecture, discussion, projects and presentations, quizzes, and final examination.
Credit Recommendation: In the graduate degree category, 2 semester hours in Business Administration or Economics (1/90) (1/95).

International Trade and Commercial Policy (EECON 450)

Location: Washington, DC.
Length: 30 hours (10 weeks).
Dates: September 1987-Present.
Objective: To provide the student with a basic knowledge of classical and modern theories of international trade, including the economic effects of U.S. and foreign commercial policies on international trade and the application of economic theory to current developments in international trade.
Learning Outcome: Upon successful completion of this course, the student will be able to display a knowledge of classical and modern theories of international trade; demonstrate familiarity with a variety of salient topics in the field, including tariff impact, terms of trade, and general agreements on tariffs and trade, among others; and understand international transactions, balance of trade, and financial requirements of international trade.
Instruction: Major topics covered in the course are a review of classical and modern theories of international trade; economic effects of U.S. and foreign commercial policies on international trade transactions; the domestic impact of tariffs; terms of trade; antidumping and countervailing duties; preferential treatment of imports from less-developed countries; and application of economic theory to current developments in international trade. Methods of instruction include lecture, student presentation, discussion, quizzes, and an examination.
Credit Recommendation: In the upper division baccalaureate degree category, 2 semester hours in Business Administration or Economics (1/90) (1/95).

Introduction to International Economics I (EECON 310)

Location: Washington, DC.
Length: 30 hours (10 weeks).
Dates: September 1984-Present.
Objective: To provide the student with a comprehensive introduction to the field of international economics, introducing the basic principles underlying international trade as it relates to world events, trade patterns, production, and income distribution. Emphasis is placed on microeconomics.
Learning Outcome: Upon successful completion of this course, the student will be able to demonstrate an understanding of microeconomic aspects of international trade and understand the major determinants of international trading patterns, costs and benefits of trade restrictions, and the effects of income distribution on country development.
Instruction: Major topics covered in the course are Ricardian factor proportion, neoclassical and dynamic explanations of comparative advantage, examination of the impact of trade on economic growth, the theory and practice of commercial policy, and the export promotion versus import substitution development strategy controversy. Methods of instruction include lecture, discussion, classroom exercises, case studies, role playing, quizzes, and examination.
Credit Recommendation: In the upper division baccalaureate degree category, 2 semester hours in Business Administration or Economics (1/90).

Introduction to International Economics II (EECON 311)

Location: Washington, DC.
Length: 30 hours (10 weeks).
Dates: January 1985-Present.
Objective: To provide the student with a comprehensive introduction to the field of international economics, introducing analytical methods, relevant institutions, and policy problems. Emphasis is placed on macroeconomics.
Learning Outcome: Upon successful completion of this course, the student will be able to demonstrate an understanding of basic macroeconomic aspects of international trade; understand operations of the international market for foreign exchange; and intelligently discuss the macroeconomic linkages among nations influencing allocation, trade flows, international debt problems, and economic welfare and growth.
Instruction: Major topics covered in the course are the financial and monetary aspects of the international economy, providing an introduction to both the Keynesian and Monetarist paradigms of the open economy. Students are exposed to the international market and foreign exchange, as well as to those macroeconomic linkages that influence allocation, trade flows, inflation, international debt problem, and growth. Methods of instruction include lecture, discussion, classroom

exercises, case studies, role playing, quizzes, and examination.

Credit Recommendation: In the upper division baccalaureate degree category, 2 semester hours in Business Administration or Economics (1/90).

Management Economics for Developing Countries (NECON 780)

Location: Washington, DC.

Length: 40 hours (3 weeks).

Dates: September 1974-February 1990.

Objective: To allow the student to examine economic development and economic behavior of developing countries, and the dynamics of managing interdependent economics of lesser developed countries.

Learning Outcome: Upon successful completion of this course, the student will be able to demonstrate knowledge of theories of economic development in developing countries, and critically analyze goals and objectives of economic systems to include resource allocation.

Instruction: Major topics covered in the course are economic analysis of agriculture, forestry, extractive resources, population, and demographics in developing countries. Methods of instruction include lecture, discussion, and projects.

Credit Recommendation: In the upper division baccalaureate degree category, 3 semester hours in Business Administration or Economics (6/88) (6/93).

Principles of Economics I (EECON 110)

Location: Washington, DC.

Length: 30 hours (10 weeks).

Dates: September 1984-Present.

Objective: To provide the student with an understanding of the operation of the forces of demand and supply, the role of price and national income, and product accounts as they measure aggregate supply and demand. Emphasis is placed on the macro concepts of the field.

Learning Outcome: Upon successful completion of this course, the student will be able to demonstrate a basic understanding of the role of demand, supply, and price in the operation of a market economy; appreciate and understand the basic tools of basic monetary and fiscal policy; and understand basic concepts and application such as unemployment, inflation, and the role of government in regulating economic policies.

Instruction: Major topics covered in the course are demand, supply, and price interdependence; economic organization of a market economy; consumption, investment, and productivity; money and banking; fiscal policy; aggregate demand and supply; and taxes and related subjects such as unemployment and inflation. Methods of instruction include lecture, case studies, problem-solving, case presentations, and midterm and final examinations.

Credit Recommendation: In the lower division baccalaureate/associate degree category, 2 semester hours in Macroeconomics (1/90) (1/95).

Principles of Economics II (EECON 111)

Location: Washington, DC.

Length: 30 hours (10 weeks).

Dates: January 1985-Present.

Objective: To introduce the student to microeconomic concepts and theory as an explanation for the behavior of a market economy, provide basic facts that cause an economy to function, and provide a rational framework for decision-making.

Learning Outcome: Upon successful completion of this course, the student will be able to demonstrate an understanding of economic theory at the micro level; explain the effects of microeconomics as it affects consumers, producers, and public agencies; and introduce concepts such as welfare maximization and consumer surplus.

Instruction: Major topics covered in the course are opportunity cost, market structure, income effects, price determination in the short and long run, and the application of microeconomic theory to current economic issues such as tax policy, comparable worth, and labor. This course is a continuation of Principles of Economics I (EECON 110), directing most of the elements to the micro elements. Methods of instruction include lecture, case studies, problems and discussions, and midterm and final examinations.

Credit Recommendation: In the lower division baccalaureate/associate degree category, 2 semester hours in Microeconomics (1/90).

Editing, Journalism

Advanced Practice in Editing (CEDIT 310)

Location: Correspondence Study.

Length: 11 lessons (self-paced).

Dates: March 1986-Present.

Objective: To enhance editing skills and broaden editorial perspective.

Learning Outcome: Upon successful completion of this course, the student will be able to edit a variety of manuscripts in accordance with specific style guides (e.g., GPO); fit copy to available space; write an abstract; and understand basic principles of publication management.

Instruction: Major topics covered in the course are copy editing, substantive editing, writing and editing for specialized audiences, and publications management. Methods of instruction include self-paced instruction on ALF/A GRAD/Ole Computer Conferencing Center.

Credit Recommendation: In the upper division baccalaureate degree category, 3 semester hours in Business Communications, Communications, English, or Journalism (6/88) (6/93).

Applied Indexing (CEDIT 361)

Location: Correspondence Study.

Length: 10 lessons (self-paced).

Dates: March 1983-Present.

Objective: To provide the student with extensive practice in subject indexing and techniques, as applied to a variety of nonfictional texts.

Learning Outcome: Upon successful completion of this course, the student will be able to distinguish between letter-by-letter and word-by-word indexing; define "merging indexes" and understand the procedure; and make appropriate estimates of time and costs.

Instruction: Major topics covered in the course are letter-by-letter indexing; indexing style and format differences; time and cost estimates; merging indexes; hierarchical indexing; and comprehensive in-depth indexing. Methods of instruction include self-paced learning with proctored examination.

Credit Recommendation: In the upper division baccalaureate degree category, 3 semester hours in Information Systems Management or Library Science (6/88) (6/93).

Basic Indexing (CEDIT 360)

Location: Correspondence Study.

Length: 10 lessons (self-paced).

Dates: June 1987-Present.

Objective: To provide the student with the knowledge of indexing techniques and focusing on nonfictional texts.

Learning Outcome: Upon successful completion of this course, the student will be able to differentiate between material suitable for headings and subheadings; alphabetize listings accurately; and determine cross-references.

Instruction: Major topics covered in the course are index editing, index preparation, computers and indexing, and indexing as a business. Methods of instruction include self-paced learning with a proctored examination.

Credit Recommendation: In the lower division baccalaureate/associate degree category, 3 semester hours in Information Systems Management or Library Science (6/88) (6/93).

Editing Technical Manuscripts (CEDIT 350)

Location: Correspondence Study.

Length: 10 lessons (self-paced).

Dates: February 1986-Present.

Objective: To provide the student with the knowledge and skill required to help experienced general editors make the transition to technical editing.

Learning Outcome: Upon successful completion of this course, the student will be able to demonstrate constructive author-editor relationships in a variety of settings; make appropriate choices of presentation concerning tables, charts, graphs, and other illustrations; and understand the special concerns of international audiences.

Instruction: Major topics covered in the course are technical definitions, author-editor relationships, illustrations, procedures writing, international audiences, and review of camera-ready material. Methods of instruction include self-paced learning with a proctored final examination.

Credit Recommendation: In the upper division baccalaureate degree category, 3 semester hours in Business Communications, Communications, English, or Journalism (6/88) (6/93).

Feature Writing (EOURN 231)

Location: Washington, DC.

Length: 30 hours (10 weeks).

Dates: September 1983-June 1993.

Objective: To provide the student with knowledge and skill for creation and marketing of feature articles for magazines and newspapers.

Learning Outcome: Upon successful completion of this course, the student will be able to demonstrate improved work related to writing skills; analyze potential publishing markets; demonstrate skill in dealing with editors; plan, research, outline, and write feature articles; and understand legal rights and responsibilities of authors.

Instruction: Major topics covered in the course are the development of ideas for feature articles, researching materials for articles, interviewing subjects for articles, analyzing publishing markets, skills for effective writing, and improving writing on-the-job. Methods of instruction include lecture, discussion, classroom exercises, preparation of articles, and writing potential publishers.

Credit Recommendation: In the lower division baccalaureate/associate degree category, 2 semester hours in Communication Arts, English, or Journalism (1/90) (1/95).

Intermediate Editing (EEDIT 230) Style and Techniques for Editors

Location: Washington, DC.

Length: 30 hours (10 weeks).

Dates: January 1978-June 1993.

Objective: To provide the student with a knowledge of intermediate editing skills and editing methods in different settings.

Learning Outcome: Upon successful completion of this course, the student will be able to edit the substantive content of material to make it more effective; perform basic copy editing; understand the basics of electronic editing; and edit charts, graphs, and tables and reconcile them with the text.

Instruction: Major topics covered in the course are proofreading and copy editing marks, editorial style (including nondiscriminatory language), statistics, graphs, charts, and careers in editing. Methods of instruction include classroom instruction and class exercises.

Credit Recommendation: In the lower division baccalaureate/associate degree category, 2 semester hours in Business Communications, Communications, English, or Journalism (6/88).

Intermediate Editing Principles and Practices (CEDIT 230)

Location: Correspondence Study.

Length: 10 lessons (self-paced).

Dates: November 1982-Present.

Objective: To review basic editing principles and practices, and to discuss copyright laws, graphics, specialized documents, and stylistic problems emanating from particular ethnic and geographical environments.

Learning Outcome: Upon successful completion of this course, the student will be able to correct copy, noting stylistic differences; make decisions on what is or what is not copyrightable; and make decisions on effectiveness of visual displays.

Instruction: Major topics covered in the course are copy editing, graphic design, copyright, and stylistic errors. Methods of instruction include self-paced instruction with a proctored final examination.

Credit Recommendation: In the lower division baccalaureate/associate degree category, 3 semester hours in Communications, English, or Journalism (6/88) (6/93).

Intermediate Public Speaking (ESPCH 350)

Location: Washington, DC.

Length: 30 hours (1 week).

Dates: September 1987-Present.

Objective: To provide students with the skills needed to adapt public speaking and speech writing techniques to specific situations.

Learning Outcome: Upon successful completion of this course, the students will be able to make persuasive public speeches; use a variety of methods to organize, research, and write effective speeches; act as facilitator or moderator in small group communication situations; use basic communication skills to demonstrate leadership skills; and modify speech techniques to serve special needs of student in his or her work.

Instruction: Major topics covered in the course are review of basic speaking and writing techniques; review of basic types of speech; and speeches for special occasions, e.g., persuasion, argumentation, small group presentation of chosen formats (special needs above). Methods of instruction include lecture, discussion, videotape of individual speech, feedback; individual, videotape of speech/feedback; group analysis, analysis of speeches by well-known speakers, textbook readings, and videotape presentations of well-known speakers.

Credit Recommendation: In the upper division baccalaureate degree category, 2 semester hours in Speech or Communication (6/93).

Introduction to the Editing Process (CEDIT 140)

Location: Correspondence Study.

Length: 12 lessons (self-paced).

Dates: October 1988-Present.

Objective: To provide the student with a knowledge of editing techniques and publishing processes.

Learning Outcome: Upon successful completion of this course, the student will be able to perform a basic edit on a nontechnical manuscript, evidencing correct grammar, spelling, and punctuation; demonstrate various approaches to editing; and demonstrate awareness of the remainder of the publishing process after an edit is completed.

Instruction: Major topics covered in the course are editing techniques and processes, marking up copy for typesetting and determining format, composition (typesetting), and preparing front and rear matter. Methods of instruction include self-paced instruction on ALF/A Grad/Ole Computer Conferencing System.

Credit Recommendation: In the lower division baccalaureate/associate degree category, 3 semester hours in Communications, English, or Journalism (6/88) (6/93).

Newsletters, House Organs, and Specialty Publications (EJOUR 271)

Location: Washington, DC.

Length: 30 hours (10 weeks).

Dates: April 1985-June 1993.

Objective: To provide the student with the skill in producing newsletters and other publications using traditional "hands-on" methods.

Learning Outcome: Upon successful completion of this course, the student will be able to produce a newsletter and other publications; develop news and public relations sources; and handle all tasks required to prepare a publication for printing.

Instruction: Major topics covered in the course are writing, editing, illustrating, layout, typesetting, proofreading, staffing, production, and marketing. Methods of instruction include lecture, discussion, classroom exercises, student projects, and examinations.

Credit Recommendation: In the lower division baccalaureate/associate degree category, 2 semester hours in Communication Arts, English, or Journalism (1/90).

Practice in Editing (EEDIT 310)

Location: Washington, DC.

Length: 30 hours (10 weeks).

Dates: January 1985-Present.

Objective: To provide the student with a sensitivity to good writing, clear thinking and editing; a comprehension of differences between mechanical copy preparation and substantive editing; a sharpening of grammar and writing skills; and enhancement of knowledge and confidence as an editor.

Learning Outcome: Upon successful completion of this course, the student will be able to copy edit letters, memos, reports, news and feature articles using standard copyediting symbols; recognize grammatical errors; and reorganize editorial material meets specific publisher or editor criteria.

Instruction: Major topics covered in the course are rules of grammar and punctuation, and techniques for editing copy for publication in specialized journals. Methods of instruction include lecture, discussion, and classroom and take-home editing assignments.

Credit Recommendation: In the upper division baccalaureate degree category, 3 semester hours in Business Communications, Communications, English, or Journalism (6/88) (8/93).

Principles of Editing (EEDIT 140)

Location: Washington, DC.

Length: 30 hours (10 weeks).

Dates: January 1978-Present.

Objective: To introduce the student to the principles of editing and the particular tasks of an editor, and to enable the student to apply editorial principles in production.

Learning Outcome: Upon successful completion of this course, the student will be able to convey information from a writer to a reader clearly, concisely, completely, and correctly; eliminate unnecessary words and sentences from the writer's material; organize material effectively; and produce a newsletter or small publication from a blank piece of paper all the way through to the finished product.

Instruction: Major topics covered in the course are steps in publication, design and layout; and processes and techniques of printing (including desktop publishing), style and grammar, form and organization, and incorporation of photos, tables, and charts. Methods of instruction include lecture, discussion, classroom exercises, demonstrations, and a field trip.

Credit Recommendation: In the lower division baccalaureate/associate degree category, 3 semester hours in Business Communications, Communications, English, or Journalism (6/88) (8/93).

Printing, Layout, and Design (CEDIT 270)

Location: Correspondence Study.

Length: 11 lessons (self-paced).

Dates: November 1982-Present.

Objective: To provide the student with the knowledge of the process, techniques, and tools that relate to design and production of printed materials, primarily without the use of a computer program.

Learning Outcome: Upon successful completion of this course, the student will be able to identify fundamental concepts in printing, layout, and design; understand the necessary theoretical background for efficient development of projects; and apply techniques and creative approaches to the job.

Instruction: Major topics covered in the course are planning, printing, production, print media and the printing process, composition, book binding, typography and design, photographs, layout, copy editing, and design. Methods of instruction include self-paced instruction with a proctored final examination.

Credit Recommendation: In the lower division baccalaureate/associate degree category, 3 semester hours in English, Journalism, or Technical Writing (6/88) (6/93).

Printing, Layout, and Design (EEDIT 270)

Location: Washington, DC.

Length: 30 hours (10 weeks).

Dates: January 1978-Present.

Objective: To provide the student with a knowledge of production concepts and the ability to solve common production problems, primarily without the use of a computer program.

Learning Outcome: Upon successful completion of this course, the student will be able to address common production problems with increased knowledge of production concepts; develop technical vocabulary to relate in production environments; and put individual working problems in perspective, determining how they relate to others and to real life situations.

Instruction: Major topics covered in the course are printing processes, typography and design, printing types, illustration, printing for the government, and regulations for style, printing, and binding. Methods of instruction include lecture, discussion, presentations, and critiques.

Credit Recommendation: In the lower division baccalaureate/associate degree category, 3 semester hours in English, Journalism, or Technical Writing (6/88) (6/93).

Proofreading (CEDIT 160)

Location: Correspondence Study.

Length: 10 lessons (self-paced).

Dates: June 1988-Present.

Objective: To provide the student with an understanding and application of professional proofreading techniques.

Learning Outcome: Upon successful completion of this course, the student will be able to perform an accurate proofreading of narrative text, graphics, tabular material, mathematics text, foreign languages, and illustrations; identify typography variances and critically review for technique quality; and identify and use conventional marking techniques and proofreading symbols.

Instruction: Major topics covered in the course are proofreading and proofmarks, measuring types and space, alternate marking systems, production process, procedures, tasks, queries and questions, and special proofreading problems. Methods of instruction include self-paced instruction with a proctored final examination.

Credit Recommendation: In the lower division baccalaureate/associate degree category, 3 semester hours in Business English, English, Journalism, or Technical Writing (6/88) (6/93).

Proofreading (EEDIT 160)

Location: Washington, DC.

Length: 30 hours (10 weeks).

Dates: January 1984-June 1997.

Objective: To provide the student with the knowledge of proofreading skills.

Learning Outcome: Upon successful completion of this course, the student will be able to proofread narrative material in a manner that identifies and corrects errors in spelling, punctuation, and capitalization.

Instruction: Major topics covered in the course are punctuation, spelling, capitalization, and proofreading. Methods of instruction include exams, projects, presentations, and drills.

Credit Recommendation: In the lower division baccalaureate/associate degree category, 3 semester hours in Business Communications, Communications, English, or Journalism (6/88) (6/93).

Publishing Management (CEDIT 375)

Location: Correspondence Study.

Length: 9 lessons (self-paced).

Dates: November 1982-Present.

Objective: To provide the student with an understanding and application of accepted management principles to government and private printing.

Learning Outcome: Upon successful completion of this course, the student will be able to make the transition from editing to management; demonstrate understanding of management principles; and apply management principles to a publishing organization.

Instruction: Major topics covered in the course are management practice of government and private publishing style, including selection of staff; government regulations on printing; copyright laws; Freedom of Information Act and Privacy Act; clearance and review procedures for policies, quality, and content; fitting and evaluating materials for various audiences; distribution problems; reader surveys; economics of publishing; and management principles.

Credit Recommendation: In the upper division baccalaureate degree category, 3 semester hours in Business Communications, Communications, English, or Journalism (6/88) (6/93).

Publishing Management (EEDIT 375)

Location: Washington, DC.

Length: 30 hours (10 weeks).

Dates: January 1985-September 1993.

Objective: To provide the student with an understanding and application of accepted management principles to government and private publishing.

Learning Outcome: Upon successful completion of this course, the student will be able to make the transition from editing to management; demonstrate understanding of management principles; and apply management principles to a publishing organization.

Instruction: Major topics covered in the course are principles of management, government regulations on printing, copyright laws, Freedom of Information Act, Privacy Act, clearance and review procedures, reader surveys, and economics of publishing. Methods of instruction include lecture, discussion, handouts, and written assignments.

Credit Recommendation: In the upper division baccalaureate degree category, 3 semester hours in Business Communications, Communications, English, or Journalism (6/88) (6/93).

Seminar in Editing (EEDIT 580)

Location: Washington, DC.

Length: 30 hours (10 weeks).

Dates: February 1985-March 1989.

Objective: To provide the student with an understanding of the scope and complexities of editing and the skills required of a professional, along with skills for analyzing problems encountered in editing.

Learning Outcome: Upon successful completion of this course, the student will be able to critique copy for ideas, quality of writing, and logical development; demonstrate basic editing skills; and analyze editorial problems arising in the planning, preparation, production, printing, and layout of publications, emphasizing the effects of technology.

Instruction: Major topics covered in the course are editorial issues/problems, preparation, production and management of publications, research on job-related problems, and professionalism on the job. Methods of instruction include lecture, discussion, case studies, and audiovisual aids.

Credit Recommendation: In the upper division baccalaureate or graduate degree category, 3 semester hours in Business English, Communications, English, Journalism, or Technical Writing (6/88) (6/93).

Special Topics in Editing (CEDIT 425)

Location: Correspondence Study.

Length: 8 lessons (maximum completion time is 2 years).

Dates: January 1990-January 1998.

Objective: To provide the student with skill in use of state-of-the-art technology in electronic publishing by editors, writers, publication managers, and project directors.

Learning Outcome: Upon successful completion of this course, the student will be able to place the desktop publishing revolution in historical and organizational perspective; compare and contrast manual and computer-generated indexing systems; discern differences between classes and types of tables; and recognize, change, and select best presentation and production methods.

Instruction: Major topics covered in the course are abstracting, casting tables, editing with electronic equipment, indexing, and preparing charts.

Credit Recommendation: In the upper division baccalaureate degree category, 1 semester hour in Journalism (1/90) (6/93).

Thesaurus Building (CEDIT 301)

Location: Correspondence Study.

Length: 11 lessons (self-paced).

Dates: August 1987-January 1996.

Objective: To provide the student with a knowledge of the concepts behind a thesaurus and the selection and usefulness of terms.

Learning Outcome: Upon successful completion of this course, the student will know the characteristics and value of well-constructed thesauri; develop hierarchical listings; and work with existing thesauri from various sources.

Instruction: Major topics covered in the course are interrelationships among terms, structure (alphabetical versus hierarchical display), and sources of thesauri; develop hierarchical listings; and work with existing thesauri from various sources. Methods of instruction include self-paced instruction with proctored final examination.

Credit Recommendation: In the vocational certificate or lower division baccalaureate/associate degree category, 1 semester hour in Information Systems Management or Library Science (6/88) (6/93).

Engineering

Basic Electricity (CENGN 101)

Location: Correspondence Study.

Length: 16 lessons (self-paced).

Dates: July 1981-Present.

Objective: To provide the student an introduction to the fundamental concepts of electricity for beginning technicians and other interested laypersons.

Learning Outcome: Upon successful completion of this course, the student will be able to understand the fundamental concepts of electricity; differentiate between basic AC and DC circuits; and describe basic electrical components such as resistors, inductors, capacitors, and motors.

Instruction: Major topics covered in the course are fundamental concepts and safety; DC circuits; AC circuits; inductance and capacitance; electromagnetism; electrical instruction; and motors and transformers. Methods of instruction include self-paced instruction with proctored examination.

Credit Recommendation: *Version 1:* In the lower division baccalaureate/associate degree category, 2 semester hours in Electrical Technology (6/88). *Version 2:* In the lower division baccalaureate/associate degree category, 3 semester hours in Electrical or Electrical Technology (6/93).

Basic Electronics (CENGN 201)

Location: Correspondence Study.

Length: 19 lessons (self-paced).

Dates: July 1981-Present.

Objective: To provide the student with a basic knowledge of the principles of electronics at the technical level.

Learning Outcome: Upon successful completion of this course, the student will be able to describe the basic principles of electronic components; basic electronic circuits; and outline basic receiver and transmitter technology.

Instruction: Major topics covered in the course are electronic principles, diodes, transistors and electric tubes, tuned circuits, detectors, amplifiers (audio, RF, power, IF), oscillators, receivers and transmitters, and transmission lines and antennas. Methods of instruction include self-paced instruction with proctored examination.

Credit Recommendation: In the lower division baccalaureate/associate degree category, 3 semester hours in Electronics Technology (6/88) (6/93).

Electric Transmission and Distribution (CENGN 202)

Location: Correspondence Study.

Length: 16 lessons (self-paced).

Dates: March 1983-Present.

Objective: To provide the student with knowledge of the concepts, principles, and devices associated with the transmission and distribution of electric energy.

Learning Outcome: Upon successful completion of this course, the student will be able to identify the constituent parts of the total electric transmission and distribution system and perform simple computations such as power factors, regulation, efficiency, short-circuit currents, mechanical properties of lines, etc.

Instruction: Major topics covered in the course are electric transmission theory; transmission terminal facilities; transmission lines; mechanical design; primary and secondary distribution systems; capacitors, transformers, and system protection; planning and load characteristics and auxiliary equipment. Methods of instruction include self-paced instruction with proctored examination.

Credit Recommendation: In the lower division baccalaureate/associate degree category, 2 semester hours in a terminal associate degree program in Electrical Engineering Technology or Electronic Technology (6/88) (6/93).

Electrical Wiring (CENGN 203)

Location: Correspondence Study.

Length: *Version 1*: 16 lessons (self-paced); *Version 2*: 20 lessons (self-paced).

Dates: January 1982-Present.

Objective: To familiarize the student with the National Electrical Code while presenting the technical and practical aspects of electrical wiring.

Learning Outcome: Upon successful completion of this course, the student will be able to locate codes and understand and apply the National Electrical Code; read electrical blueprints; wire, according to code, single-and multiple-family dwellings, commercial structures, and industrial power installations.

Instruction: Major topics covered in the course are wiring of single- and multiple-family dwellings; services for commercial and industrial establishments; and specialized and hazardous locations; specifics include conductor sizing, grounding, panel sizing, cable types, and blueprint reading. Methods of instruction include self-paced instruction with proctored examination.

Credit Recommendation: *Version 1:* In the vocational certificate category, 2 semester hours in Electricians Apprentice Programs (6/88). *Version 2:* In the vocational certificate category, 3 semester hours in Electricians Apprentice Programs (6/93).

Engineering Mechanics I (Statics) (CENGN 208)

Location: Correspondence Study.

Length: 9 lessons (self-paced).

Dates: August 1987-Present.

Objective: To provide the student with the background, skill, concepts, and basic understanding of statics as it relates to engineering mechanics using simplified approaches and modern high school mathematics without calculus, and covers applied statics and stresses practical aspects.

Learning Outcome: Upon successful completion of this course, the student will be able to identify force systems and solve problems involving force equilibrium and direction; solve problems of coplanar, parallel force, and concurrent force systems and noncoplanar, parallel force, and nonconcurrent force systems; and calculate and locate centroids, center of gravity, and moments of inertia.

Instruction: Major topics covered in the course are basic principles, coplanar parallel and concurrent force systems, coplanar and noncoplanar nonconcurrent force systems, friction, center of gravity, centroids, and related aspects. Methods of instruction include self-paced instruction with proctored examination.

Credit Recommendation: In the lower division baccalaureate/associate degree category, 2 semester hours in Engineering Mechanics (Statics) (6/88) (6/93). **NOTE:**

Would only apply for Engineering Technology.

Engineering Mechanics II (Dynamics) (CENGN 209)

Location: Correspondence Study.

Length: 9 lessons (self-paced).

Dates: August 1987-Present.

Objective: To provide students with the background, skill, concepts, and basic understanding of dynamics as it relates to engineering mechanics using simplified approaches and modern high school mathematics without calculus, and covers applied dynamics and stresses practical aspects.

Learning Outcome: Upon successful completion of this course, the student will be able to solve problems involving rectilinear motion and kinetic forces on rigid bodies; and solve problems involving rotational motion; solve problems related to impulse and momentum.

Instruction: Major topics covered in the course are basic problems involving rectilinear motion, kinetic forces on rigid bodies, forces on bodies traveling along any path, rotational motion, forces perpendicular to the plane of motion, and forces of impulse and momentum. Methods of instruction include self-paced instruction and proctored examination.

Credit Recommendation: In the lower division baccalaureate/associate degree category, 2 semester hours in Engineering Mechanics (Dynamics) (6/88) (6/93). **NOTE:** Would only apply to Engineering Technology.

Fiber Optic Communications (CENGN 207)

Location: Correspondence Study.

Length: 13 lessons (self-paced).

Dates: August 1987-Present.

Objective: To provide the student with an understanding of the background theory and basic concepts of fiber optic communications and fiber optic communication technology.

Learning Outcome: Upon successful completion of this course, the student will be able to explain basic physical concepts of fiber optic communications; describe the elements of a fiber optic communications system; and define the system parameters that specify fiber optic communication.

Instruction: Major topics covered in the course are optics and light wave fundamentals, optical fibers, integrated optics, light sources and detectors, light couplers and detectors, modulation, noise and detection, and system design. Methods of instruction include self-paced instruction with proctored examination.

Credit Recommendation: *Version 1:* In the lower division baccalaureate/associate degree category, 2 semester hours in Electrical Engineering (6/88). *Version 2:* In the lower division baccalaureate/associate degree category, 3 semester hours in Electrical Engineering (6/93).

Hydraulics I (CENGN 204)

Location: Correspondence Study.

Length: 9 lessons (self-paced).

Dates: March 1983-Present.

Objective: To introduce the student to the basic principles of hydrostatics and their application to engineering problems.

Learning Outcome: Upon successful completion of this course, the student will be able to apply the principles of hydrostatics to engineering problems such as the calculation of pressure forces acting on hydraulic structures, stability of dams under hydrostatic forces.

Instruction: Major topics covered in the course are basic physical units; manometry and pressure head; forces and moments acting on dams due to hydrostatic pressure; and the stability of dams. Methods of instruction include self-paced instruction with proctored examination.

Credit Recommendation: In the lower division baccalaureate/associate degree category, 2 semester hours in two-year terminal degree in Engineering Technology programs (6/88) (6/93).

Hydrology I (CENGN 501)

Location: Correspondence Study.

Length: 16 lessons (self-paced).

Dates: March 1983-Present.

Objective: To provide the student with the major hydrological and pertinent meteorological elements—how these phenomena are observed and the data analyzed.

Learning Outcome: Upon successful completion of this course, the student will be able to describe the hydrologic cycles; make measurements and interpretation of streamflow, precipitation, and other basic data; and understand the physics of soil moisture and the infiltration and rainfall runoff relations.

Instruction: Major topics covered in the course are elementary meteorology and statistics; measurements and interpretation of streamflow, precipitation, and other basic data; hydrologic cycles; physics of soil moisture; infiltration theory; and rainfall runoff relations. Methods of instruction include self-paced instruction with proctored examination.

Credit Recommendation: In the upper division baccalaureate degree category, 3 semester hours in Hydrology in Civil Engineering (6/88) (6/93).

Hydrology II (CENGN 502)

Location: Correspondence Study.

Length: 16 lessons (self-paced).

Dates: March 1983-Present.

Objective: To provide the student with the ability to apply the data analysis techniques applicable to the science of hydrology.

Learning Outcome: Upon successful completion of this course, the student will be able to use hydrologic data to forecast streamflow; and estimate parameters needed in water control structure design.

Instruction: Major topics covered in the course are hydrographs and their uses; relationships between runoff, rainfall, and storm derivation; features and functions of reservoirs; and calculation of sediment load in a stream. Methods of instruction include self-paced instruction with proctored examination.

Credit Recommendation: In the upper division baccalaureate degree category, 3 semester hours in Hydrology in Civil Engineering (6/88) (6/93).

Solid State Fundamentals (CENGN 102)

Location: Correspondence Study.

Length: 14 lessons (self-paced).

Dates: August 1987-Present.

Objective: To provide the student with the knowledge required for application of solid state electronic devices.

Learning Outcome: Upon successful completion of this course, the student will be able to repair printed circuit boards; read and understand device specifications; and understand and test solid state devices and basic solid state circuits.

Instruction: Major topics covered in the course are PC boards, diodes; diode circuits; and testing of diodes; power supplies, other diodes (i.e., EDs and pressure sensors); transistors; transistor circuits; and transistor testing; SCRs and Triacs; integrated circuits; and introduction to fiber optics. Methods of instruction include self-paced instruction with proctored examination.

Credit Recommendation: In the lower division baccalaureate/associate degree

category, 2 semester hours in Electrical or Electronics Technology (6/88) (6/93).

Stormwater Management (CENGN 410)

Location: Correspondence study.
Length: 15 lessons.
Dates: August 1989-Present.
Objective: To provide the student with an understanding of practical and legal aspects of stormwater management.
Learning Outcome: Upon successful completion of this course, the student will be able to describe the process of establishing a program of stormwater management in a community; identify relevant legal issues; and identify various engineering methodologies for stormwater management.
Instruction: Major topics covered in the course are the drainage basin, legal aspects of drainage, drainage planning, analysis of rainfall, engineering methodologies, floodplain management, and water quality. Methods of instruction include independent study, study guide, written assignments, instructor feedback, and a proctored examination.
Credit Recommendation: In the upper division baccalaureate degree category, 3 semester hours in Civil Engineering or Natural Resources (1/90) (1/95).

Strength of Materials (CENGN 206)

Location: Correspondence Study.
Length: 14 lessons (self-paced).
Dates: August 1987-Present.
Objective: To provide the student with the background skills, concepts, and basic understanding of strength of materials as they relate to the design of structural members, parts, and connections by simplified approaches, and the use of modern high school mathematics without the use of calculus.
Learning Outcome: Upon successful completion of this course, the student will be able to identify basic units of measurement and terms and solve fundamental problems involving material strengths; identify forces on structural members and solve problems involving stresses; prepare shear and moment diagrams; and solve basic problems for members subject to axial and bending stress.
Instruction: Major topics covered in the course are basics of strength of materials, including stress and deformation; engineering materials and riveted joints; thin-walled pressure vessels and welded joints; torsion; centroids and moments of inertia; shear and moment in beams; stresses, design, and deflector of beams; statically indeterminate beams; combined stresses; column; and impact loading and strain energy. Methods of instruction include self-paced instruction with proctored examination.
Credit Recommendation: In the lower division baccalaureate/associate degree category, 3 semester hours in Strength of Materials (6/88) (6/93). **NOTE:** Applies to Engineering Technology programs.

English, Writing, Speech

Better Letters (CWRIT 101)

Location: Correspondence Study.
Length: 7 lessons (maximum completion time is 2 years).
Dates: January 1990-Present.
Objective: To provide the student with knowledge and skill required for writing effective letters.
Learning Outcome: Upon successful completion of this course, the student will be able to apply 17 rules for writing effective letters; understand and use the "45" writing formula and the Fog Index; and demonstrate awareness of the qualities of good letters.
Instruction: Major topics covered in the course are communication skills, rules for letter writing, measuring readability, and analyzing letters. Methods of instruction include independent study, written assignments, instructor feedback, and examination.
Credit Recommendation: In the vocational certificate category, 1 semester hour in Business English, Communications, or English (1/90) (1/95).

Effective Writing for Professionals (CWRIT 401)

Location: Correspondence Study.
Length: 15 lessons (maximum completion time is 2 years).
Dates: January 1990-Present.
Objective: To provide the student with an understanding of the application of good writing principles to reports and journal articles.
Learning Outcome: Upon successful completion of this course, the student will be able to plan, outline, and write technical reports and articles; understand the value of outlines and their use in report writing; demonstrate familiarity with correct rules of grammar; employ correct spelling and punctuation marks; and write communications directed to specific audiences.
Instruction: Major topics covered in the course are outlines and their use in writing, using grammatical reference sources, spelling and punctuation rules, writing for specific audiences, and appropriate use of active and passive voices. Methods of instruction include independent study, written assignments, instructor feedback, and examination.
Credit Recommendation: In the upper division baccalaureate degree category, 1 semester hour in Communication Arts, English, or Journalism (1/90) (1/95).

Government Writing (EWRIT 120)

Location: Washington, D.C.
Length: 30 hours (10 weeks).
Dates: September 1990-Present.
Objective: To provide students with knowledge and skills necessary for drafting and composing a variety of government, business, and technical communications.
Learning Outcome: Upon successful completion of this course, the student will be able to analyze and write for a specific audience; establish a specific writing purpose; select and organize information to fit audience and purpose; and write clear, concise, and error-free messages.
Instruction: Major topics covered in the course are audience analysis; planning process; organizational techniques; diction and tone; grammar and mechanics; and technical writing formats. Methods of instruction include lecture, discussion, classroom exercises and writing situations, critiques, graded writing assignments, quizzes, and a final examination.
Credit Recommendation: In the lower division baccalaureate/associate degree category, 1 semester hour in Business Communications, Communications, English, or Technical Writing (1/95).

Introduction to Speechwriting (CWRIT 103)

Location: Correspondence Study.
Length: 11 lessons (maximum completion time is 2 years).
Dates: January 1990-Present.
Objective: To provide the student with an understanding of and skills required for writing and delivering effective speeches.
Learning Outcome: Upon successful completion of this course, the student will be able to prepare introductions for speakers and prepare speeches of tribute and courtesy, political speeches, after-dinner speeches, and speeches for conferences and other occasions.

Instruction: Major topics covered in the course are locating speech material, developing and supporting various types of speeches, maintaining audience attention through delivery, and audience analysis. Methods of instruction include independent study, written assignments, instructor feedback, and an examination.

Credit Recommendation: In the lower division baccalaureate/associate degree category, 2 semester hours in Communication Arts, English, or Speech (1/90) (1/95).

Practical Writing (EWRIT 050)

Location: Washington, DC.

Length: 30 hours (10 weeks).

Dates: September 1987-Present.

Objective: To provide students with an understanding of the principal steps of the writing process to their own writing by the end of the course.

Learning Outcome: Upon successful completion of this course, the student will be able to draft, organize, write, and edit a report or essay that is error free.

Instruction: Major topics covered in the course are basic grammar; editing for idea development; planning; paragraph structure; and word choice. Methods of instruction include lecture, examination, questionnaire, essay, and test use.

Credit Recommendation: In the lower division baccalaureate/associate degree category, 3 semester hours in Developmental Writing (6/93). **NOTE**: Does not the replace English composition required courses. Credit should be awarded for EWRIT 030 or EWRIT 050, but not both.

Public Speaking (ESPCH 151)

Location: Washington, D.C.

Length: 30 hours (10 weeks).

Dates: September 1989-Present.

Objective: To provide the student with knowledge and skills in speech preparation and delivery, and the development of self-confidence in public speaking, group communication, and leadership.

Learning Outcome: Upon successful completion of this course, the student will be able to deliver speeches using appropriate delivery techniques; organize, research, and write speeches; apply the basic principles of oral communication to practical situations; and critically evaluate speeches and speakers.

Instruction: Major topics covered in the course are styles of public speaking; audience analysis; voice skills; preparation and delivery techniques for speeches of information, demonstration, persuasion, and special occasions. Methods of instruction include lecture, discussion, classroom exercises, audio/visual material, learner presentation/reports, graded individual speeches (written or oral), and text book exercises.

Credit Recommendation: In the lower division baccalaureate/associate degree category, 2 semester hours in Speech, Communications, or Theatre (1/95).

Report Writing (CWRIT 201)

Location: Correspondence Study.

Length: 17 lessons.

Dates: January 1990-Present.

Objective: To provide the student with skill in composing organized, informative, appropriate, and grammatically correct written reports.

Learning Outcome: Upon successful completion of this course, the student will be able to determine main topic and purpose of reports; compose grammatically correct sentences; write factually and clearly for intended audiences; compose short and long written communications; and summarize reports for executive review.

Instruction: Major topics covered in the course are sentence structure, effective word usage and correct grammar, preparing reports for specific audiences, and composing long and short reports. Methods of instruction include independent study, written assignments, instructor feedback, and an examination.

Credit Recommendation: In the lower division baccalaureate/associate degree or upper division baccalaureate degree category, 1 semester hour in Communication Arts, English, or Technical Writing (1/90) (1/95).

Technical Writing (EWRIT 305)

Location: Washington, D.C.

Length: 30 hours (10 weeks).

Dates: September 1987-Present.

Objective: To provide the student with the skills needed to plan, design, implement, and evaluate technical documents.

Learning Outcome: Upon successful completion of this course, the student will be able to understand the purpose of technical writing; conduct an audience analysis; develop a document plan; and design, implement, and evaluate a finished document.

Instruction: Major topics covered in the course are the definition of technical writing; style and organization; technical description; computer documentation; proposal; audience analysis; and document design, implementation, and evaluation. Methods of instruction include lecture, discussion, classroom exercises, writing assignments and document design, graded written assignments, in-class exercises, and mid-term and final examinations.

Credit Recommendation: In the upper division baccalaureate degree category, 2 semester hours in Business Communication, Communication, English, Professional Writing, or Technical Writing (1/95).

Voice and Diction (ESPCH 190)

Location: Washington, DC.

Length: 30 hours (1 week).

Dates: September 1987-Present.

Objective: To identify and overcome obstacles to good vocal quality and clear articulation.

Learning Outcome: Upon successful completion of this course, the student will be able to understand the physical underpinnings of good vocal quality and know how to use them; use variety in inflection and intonation; "translate" short passages from standard American English into international phonetic alphabet (IPA); use standard American diction effectively; and produce several effective speeches using theories and techniques learned in class.

Instruction: Major topics covered in the course are to produce effective; expressive sound; control articulation; and use standard American diction. Methods of instruction include lecture, discussion, class exercises, case studies, role playing, problem solving, instructor facilities student performance; peer evaluation-group or class setting; instructor comments on individual performance; self evaluation-students evaluate the tapes of their own performances; diagnostic materials; text instruction and exercises; written examination; and audio and videotape materials.

Credit Recommendation: In the lower division baccalaureate/associate degree category, 2 semester hours in Speech, Communications, or Theater (6/93).

Writing for Government and Business (CWRIT 102)

Location: Correspondence Study.

Length: 15 lessons (maximum completion time required is 2 years).

Dates: January 1990-Present.

Objective: To provide the student with skills for preparing correctly worded and punctuated and organized letters, memos, and reports.

Learning Outcome: Upon successful completion of this course, the student will be able to use an outline to organize sentences and paragraphs in a written communication; use punctuation marks correctly in a written communication; and edit communications to identify misspelled or confusing words.

Instruction: Major topics covered in the course are correct grammatical usage, rules of punctuation, spelling, and writing communications that readers can comprehend. Methods of instruction include independent study, written assignments, instructor feedback, and an examination.

Credit Recommendation: In the vocational certificate category, 1 semester hour in Business English, Communication Arts, or English (1/90) (1/95).

Environmental Studies

Animal Behavior (ENATH 151)

Location: Washington, DC.

Length: 30 hours (10 weeks of 2 hour classes plus field trips).

Dates: March 1986-Present.

Objective: To understand ethological theory, methods and study, and the measurement of animal behavior.

Learning Outcome: Upon successful completion of this course, the student will apply the fundamentals of ethological study, comprehend basics of ethological theory, assess the behavior of different animals.

Instruction: Major topics covered in the course are animal senses, communication, inheritance and experience, reproductive behavior, feeding, and evaluation of behavior. Methods of instruction include lecture, discussion, projects, field trips, and exams.

Credit Recommendation: In the lower division baccalaureate/associate degree category, 2 semester hours in Elements of Animal Behavior, Biology for Naturalists, or Biological Science elective (6/93).

Biology for Naturalists (ENATH 110)

Location: Washington, DC.

Length: 32 hours (10 classes plus field trips).

Dates: September 1984-Present.

Objective: To understand concepts of biology with emphasis on the natural history and classification of animals.

Learning Outcome: Upon successful completion of this course, the student will be able to describe biological and chemical processes that occur in organisms, list the physical constraints that limit organisms, and identify how populations change over time.

Instruction: Major topics covered in the course are cell structure and energetics, genetics, animal biology including nutrient procurement, gas exchange, coordination, homeostasis and taxonomic survey. Methods of instructions include lecture, discussion, student project and field trip, and final exam.

Credit Recommendation: In the lower division baccalaureate/associate degree category, 2 semester hours in Biology or Natural Science elective (6/93).

Environmental Policy: Waste Management (EENVS 310)

Location: Washington, DC.

Length: 30 hours (10 weeks).

Dates: September 1992-June 1995.

Objective: To provide knowledge of provisions, applications, and problem related to current waste management regulation.

Learning Outcome: Upon successful completion of this course, the student will be able to explain principles and specific rules related to the Clean Air Act, Water Act, Solid Waste Disposal Act, Resource Recovery, and Conservation Act (RCRA), and know how agencies implement the provisions of them.

Instruction: Major topics covered in the course are major federal laws affecting waste disposal, cases and problems facing industry and regulators, waste management decisions making, hazardous materials and waste, resource recovery economics, and superfund issues. Methods of instruction include lecture, discussion, student reports, guest speakers, and examinations.

Credit Recommendation: In the upper division baccalaureate degree category, 2 semester hours in Environmental, Public Policy, Business, or Economics elective (6/93).

Geology (ENATH 125)

Location: Washington, DC.

Length: 40 hours (10 weeks including 3 field trips).

Dates: March 1993-Present.

Objective: To understand the regional geology of Maryland, Virginia, Pennsylvania, Virginia, and W. Virginia, and the processes that created these conditions, and skill in rock and mineral identification.

Learning Outcome: Upon successful completion of this course, the student will be able to identify basic rocks and minerals, fundamentals of reading geological history of the region studied.

Instruction: Major topics covered in the course are identification of rocks and minerals, regional geology, and reading geological maps. Methods of instruction include lecture, discussion, labs, field trips, class exercises, and examinations.

Credit Recommendation: In the lower division baccalaureate/associate degree category, 2 semester hours in Survey, Principles of Applied Geology, or Physical Science elective (6/93).

Human Ecology (ENATH 280)

Location: Washington, DC.

Length: 30 hours (10 weeks).

Dates: September 1984-Present.

Objective: To understand the interaction of human populations growth, environmental quality and natural resource management.

Learning Outcome: Upon successful completion of this course, the student will be able to identify the impacts of human populations on air and water quality, describe the limits on available energy, mineral, water and other natural resources, and make informed decision concerning environmental issues.

Instruction: Major topics covered in the course are human population growth, air and water quality, and food production and biodiversity. Methods of instruction include lecture, discussion, field trips, and examinations.

Credit Recommendation: In the lower division baccalaureate/associate degree category, 2 semester hours in Introduction to Environmental Science, Introduction to Human Ecology, or Natural Science elective (6/93).

Introduction to Ecology (ENATH 160)

Location: Washington, DC.

Length: 30 hours (10 weeks; ten-2 hour classes plus field trips).

Dates: September 1984-Present.

Objective: To understand the principles and concepts of ecology.

Learning Outcome: Upon successful completion of this course, the student will be able to describe the principles that govern the flow of energy and cycling of materials through ecosystems, identify factors that govern population growth, and describe the changes that occur as ecosystems evolve.

Instruction: Major topics covered in the course are ecosystem energetics, global cycles, population dynamics, and evolution of ecosystems. Methods of instruction include lecture, discussion, field trips, project, and examinations.

Credit Recommendation: In the lower division baccalaureate/associate degree category, 2 semester hours in Ecology, Principles of Ecology, or Natural Science elective (6/93).

National Environmental Protection (EENVS 435)

Location: Washington, DC.

Length: 30 hours (10 weeks).

Dates: April 1993-Present.

Objective: To understand provisions in the National Environmental Policy Act (NEPA), its provisions and how these federal policies are administered.

Learning Outcome: Upon successful completion of this course, the student will be able to discuss NEPA and explain how national environmental policies are established and managed, and how changes in environmental policy are accomplished.

Instruction: Major topics covered in the course are provisions of the National Environmental Policy Act, related executive orders, activities and programs of executives agencies, departments and various commissions, Council on Environmental Quality (CEQ). Methods of instruction include lecture, discussions, student presentations, expert guest lectures, and project.

Credit Recommendation: In the upper division baccalaureate degree category, 2 semester hours in Public or Environmental Policy, Business, or Public Administration elective (6/93).

Principles of Horticulture (EHORT 160)

Location: Washington, DC.

Length: 30 hours (10 weeks).

Dates: September 1992-Present.

Objective: To understand basic principles and concepts of horticulture.

Learning Outcome: Upon successful completion of this course, the student will be able to describe the life cycle of flowering plants, identify environmental conditions that influence plant growth including pests, soil and weather conditions, and describe the procedures of plant propagation.

Instruction: Major topics covered in the course are plant morphology, plant life cycle, pest management, soil management, soil management, regulating plant growth; and plant propagation. Methods of instruction include lecture, discussion, student project, and examinations.

Credit Recommendation: In the lower division baccalaureate/associate degree category, 2 semester hours in Horticulture, Botany, or Biology elective (6/93).

The Living Soil (ENATH 175)

Location: Washington, DC.

Length: 44 hours (11 weeks; 2 hour classes plus field trips).

Dates: September 1989-Present.

Objective: To understand basic soil properties, soil ecology and uses, and management of soils.

Learning Outcome: Upon successful completion of this course, the student will be able to identify and categorize the physical properties of soils, demonstrate a general understanding of the soil classification system; describe the relationships between soil properties and the uses and management of soils, use published soil surveys as a tool in decision making about soil use and management.

Instruction: Major topics covered in the course are mineral chemistry, weathering, morphology, organic matter, physical properties, classification, fertility and nutrients, soil-water relations, and erosion and mapping. Methods of instruction include lecture, discussion, field study, student projects, and examinations.

Credit Recommendation: In the upper division baccalaureate degree category, 2 semester hours in Soil Science, Agriculture, or Natural Science elective (6/93).

Wildlife Ecology (ENATH 265)

Location: Washington, DC.

Length: 30 hours (10 weeks, 3 hour class plus 2 all-day field trips).

Dates: September 1992-Present.

Objective: To understand the many and varied aspects of field of wildlife ecology and management.

Learning Outcome: Upon successful completion of this course, the student will be able to explain the concepts of habitat and population dynamics, and the impact of institutional environment on wildlife policy; and, to discuss careers in wildlife management.

Instruction: Major topics covered in the course are importance of habitat, basic population dynamics, impacts of institutional environment on wildlife policies, and careers in wildlife. Methods of instruction include lecture, discussion, classroom exercises, laboratory, and field trips.

Credit Recommendation: In the lower division baccalaureate/associate degree category, 2 semester hours in Principles of Wildlife Ecology or Natural Science elective (6/93).

Graphic Arts, Photography

Cartography I (ECART 125)

Location: Washington, DC.

Length: 30 hours (10 weeks).

Dates: September 1987-Present.

Objective: To introduce the student to fundamental concepts and practical applications of cartography.

Learning Outcome: Upon successful completion of this course, the student will be able to understand and apply cartography required to produce maps and charts from various information sources, solve problems in the evaluation of data in the preparation of maps for distribution.

Instruction: Major topics covered in the course are map and chart production from original surveys, from compiled sources, published information, previously printed charts or maps; and apply information via standard techniques for lithographic printing. Methods of instruction include lecture, discussion, projects, exercises, and presentations.

Credit Recommendation: In the lower division baccalaureate/associate degree category, 2 semester hours in Principles of Cartography (6/93).

Creative Photography Through Composition (EPHOS 350)

Location: Washington, DC.

Length: 30 hours (10 weeks).

Dates: September 1984-Present.

Objective: To provide the student with an understanding of principles of composition and design related to using the camera in creating special effects for better visual communication.

Learning Outcome: Upon successful completion of this course, the student will be able to recognize good composition; use the camera as a tool for visual communication; apply a variety of exposure techniques in creating special effects; identify all elements of composition and design in a picture; and interpret photographs relative to elements of composition and design.

Instruction: Major topics covered in the course are composition—definition, good practices, bad practices, preparation for picture taking; elements of composition—line, geometrical shapes and forms, exposure techniques, and photograph critiques. Methods of instruction include lecture, discussion, classroom exercises, problems, and examinations.

Credit Recommendation: In the lower division baccalaureate/associate degree category, 3 semester hours in Photography (1/90).

Design and Preparation of Camera-Ready Mechanicals (EGART 218)

Location: Washington, DC.

Length: 30 hours (10 weeks).

Dates: September 1984-Present.

Objective: To provide the student with the knowledge and skills necessary to produce reproduction art for a variety of publications.

Learning Outcome: Upon successful completion of this course, the student will be able to select paper appropriate for work to be reproduced; select appropriate type; select artwork (illustrations and photographs); make art for printers; and prepare mechanicals.

Instruction: Major topics covered in the course are the selection of paper, selection of type, paste-up techniques, cropping of photos and illustrations, keying of second color, and steps in design from thumbnail to mechanical. Methods of instruction include lecture, discussion, text and handouts, classroom exercises, and examination.

Credit Recommendation: In the lower division baccalaureate/associate degree category, 2 semester hours in Communication Arts or Graphic Design (1/90).

Materials and Techniques in the Graphic Arts (EGART 210)

Location: Washington, DC.

Length: 30 hours (10 weeks).

Dates: September 1984-Present.

Objective: To provide the student with the fundamental skills and basic procedures in preparing art for print and projection.

Learning Outcome: Upon successful completion of this course, the student will be able to use basic tools in preparing a publication; specify appropriate type for publications; select appropriate chart/diagram format to display information; prepare tissue layouts; size and crop photographs; and estimate costs of design and printing of a specific piece or publication.

Instruction: Major topics covered in the course are design/paste-up tools, project requirements—quality, method, deadline, cost, and preparation of art for print or projection. Methods of instruction include lecture, discussion, text and handouts, classroom exercises, and examination.

Credit Recommendation: In the lower division baccalaureate/associate degree category, 2 semester hours in Communication Arts or Graphic Design (1/90).

Portrait Photography (EPHOS 355)

Location: Washington, DC.

Length: 30 hours (10 weeks).

Dates: January 1983-Present.

Objective: To provide the student with an understanding and use of fundamental techniques of classic portraiture using proper camera angles and lenses with male and female models.

Learning Outcome: Upon successful completion of this course, the student will be able to analyze and select proper facial features; use cameras with appropriate lenses; create basic lighting patterns; and pose male and female models.

Instruction: Major topics covered in the course are the selection of camera and camera lenses for various film formats, analysis of the face—five classic views, posing models, basic light patterns, shooting sessions, application of classic portraiture techniques, and classic portraiture techniques on location. Methods of instruction include lecture, discussion, classroom exercises, problems, and examinations.

Credit Recommendation: In the lower division baccalaureate/associate degree category, 3 semester hours in Photography (1/90).

LANGUAGES/ARABIC

Arabic Short Story (EARAB301)

Location: Washington, DC.

Length: 30 hours (10 weeks).

Dates: June 1992-Present.

Objective: To help the student understand Arab culture, society, and literary styles through a variety of works, some in Arabic and some translated into English.

Learning Outcome: Upon successful completion of this course, the student will be able to appreciate and evaluate some modern Arabic prose, its style, content, and social/political commentary.

Instruction: Major topics covered in the course are selections from seven modern works (or collections of works) by authors from a variety of Arab countries. Methods of instruction include lectures, discussions, outside classroom preparation and reading, and examinations.

Credit Recommendation: In the lower division baccalaureate/associate degree category, 2 semester hours in Literature, World Literature, Arabic Literature (not Arabic language) (8/93).

Introduction to Arabic I (EARAB151)

Location: Washington, DC.

Length: 30 hours (10 weeks).

Dates: September 1984-Present.

Objective: To introduce students to the Arabic alphabet and sound system (Modern Standard Arabic), and to teach rudiments of MSA grammar for constructing simple sentences with emphasis on communication in the context of Arab culture.

Learning Outcome: Upon successful completion of this course, the student will be able to read and write in Arabic script; compose simple sentences using basic vocabulary; engage in simple conversations; and apply knowledge of Arab culture and social values.

Instruction: Major topics covered in the course are Arabic pronunciation; alphabet; simple conversations and reading; and descriptions of Arabic-speaking countries. Methods of instruction include lectures, discussions, classroom exercises, examinations, and audio cassettes.

Credit Recommendation: In the lower division baccalaureate/associate degree category, 2 semester hours in Elementary Modern Standard Arabic (8/93).

Introduction to Arabic II (EARAB152)

Location: Washington, DC.

Length: 30 hours (10 weeks).

Dates: September 1984-Present.

Objective: To help the student improve mastery of MSA pronunciation and script; introduce verbs, nominal and verbal sentences, and use of an Arabic dictionary; and to expand oral and written communication skills.

Learning Outcome: Upon successful completion of this course, the student will be able to use Arabic verbs; construct simple sentences; use an Arabic dictionary; and communicate basic personal information.

Instruction: Major topics covered in the course are Arabic verbs and sentence structure, design of an Arabic dictionary, vocabulary relating to personal information, and major characteristics of Arab culture. Methods of instruction include lectures, discussions, classroom exercises, examinations, videos, visual aids, and audio cassettes.

Credit Recommendation: In the lower division baccalaureate/associate degree category, 2 semester hours in Elementary Modern Standard Arabic (8/93).

Introduction to Arabic III (EARAB153)

Location: Washington, DC.
Length: 30 hours (10 weeks).
Dates: September 1992-Present.
Objective: To help student's learn more complex structural patterns, expand vocabulary, and study a variety of subjects that reflect Arab culture and thought.

Learning Outcome: Upon successful completion of this course, the student will be able to use more complex structures and broader vocabulary; recognize and use pronouns and verb forms; and read and discuss a variety of texts.

Instruction: Major topics covered in the course are pronouns; question words and markers; verb forms and tenses; cases; plural categories; and negatives. Methods of instruction include lectures, discussions, classroom exercises, handouts and charts, examinations, visual aids, and audio cassettes.

Credit Recommendation: In the lower division baccalaureate/associate degree category, 2 semester hours in Elementary Modern Standard Arabic (8/93).

Introduction to Arabic IV (EARAB154) (Formerly Intermediate Arabic I [EARAB 210])

Location: Washington, DC.
Length: 30 hours (10 weeks).
Dates: January 1993-Present.
Objective: To improve the student's communication skills in speaking, reading, and writing.

Learning Outcome: Upon successful completion of this course, the student will be able to communicate with broader vocabulary and more complex structures in a wide variety of situational topics.

Instruction: Major topics covered in the course are an overview of basic MSA grammar and structure and use of Arabic with emphasis on aural comprehension. Methods of instruction include lectures, discussions, classroom exercises, handouts and charts, examinations, outside preparation (homework), visual aids, and audio cassettes.

Credit Recommendation: In the lower division baccalaureate/associate degree category, 2 semester hours in Elementary Modern Standard Arabic (not Intermediate) (8/93).

LANGUAGES/CHINESE

Advanced Chinese I (ECHIN250)

Location: Washington, DC.
Length: 30 hours (10 weeks).
Dates: January 1993-Present.
Objective: To provide the student with a continuation of study of Chinese language.

Learning Outcome: Upon successful completion of this course, the student will be able to analyze structure of Chinese sentences; engage in advanced conversation in Chinese; read Chinese texts; and write short compositions in Chinese.

Instruction: Major topics covered in the course are advanced grammar; writing new Chinese characters; study of Chinese history; economy; and their culture. Methods of instruction include lectures, films, quizzes, and examinations.

Credit Recommendation: In the lower division baccalaureate/associate degree category, 2 semester hours in Chinese (8/93).

Intermediate Chinese I (ECHIN210)

Location: Washington, DC.
Length: 30 hours (10 weeks).
Dates: September 1984-Present.
Objective: To help the student review and continue study of crucial grammatical patterns and master socially useful conversational skills.

Learning Outcome: Upon successful completion of this course, the student will be able to demonstrate more sophisticated vocabulary in conversations and comprehend simple speeches and written passages in Chinese.

Instruction: Major topics covered in the course are comparative patterns, aspect marker, and modal particle "le." Methods of instruction include lectures, oral drill and character writing, and examination.

Credit Recommendation: In the lower division baccalaureate/associate degree category, 2 semester hours in Intermediate Chinese (6/88) (8/93).

Intermediate Chinese II (ECHIN211)

Location: Washington, DC.
Length: 30 hours (10 weeks).
Dates: January 1985-Present.
Objective: To enable the student to work through intermediate level texts containing the important grammatical patterns and a fairly sophisticated content and engage in everyday conversations, and to stimulate an interest in Chinese literature.

Learning Outcome: Upon successful completion of this course, the student will be able to engage in everyday conversations and exhibit improved comprehension in reading.

Instruction: Major topics covered in the course are more advanced reading and conversation; work on sentence structure and vocabulary; read longer articles and experience a gradual transition from regular textbook Chinese to "real" modern Chinese literature. Methods of instruction include conversation and writing exercises based on reading materials.

Credit Recommendation: In the lower division baccalaureate/associate degree category, 2 semester hours in Chinese (6/88) (8/93).

Intermediate Chinese III (ECHIN212)

Location: Washington, DC.
Length: 30 hours (10 weeks).
Dates: April 1985-Present.
Objective: To help the student develop (depending on student's background) increased facility in reading and discussing texts of literary and topical interest.

Learning Outcome: Upon successful completion of this course, the student will be able to feel at ease conversing with speakers of Chinese and give speeches and tell stories in Chinese.

Instruction: Major topics covered in the course are reading selections from modern Chinese literature in the form of essays, short stories, and newspaper articles. Methods of instruction include conversation and writing exercises based on reading materials.

Credit Recommendation: In the lower division baccalaureate/associate degree category, 2 semester hours in Chinese (6/88) (8/93).

Introductory Chinese I (ECHIN151)

Location: Washington, DC.
Length: 30 hours (10 weeks).
Dates: September 1984-Present.
Objective: To help the student develop a good pronunciation of Mandarin Chinese, a foundation in basic grammar of simple verbal sentences, and an elementary vocabulary, together with some knowledge of Chinese culture and customs.

Learning Outcome: Upon successful completion of this course, the student will be able to use a vocabulary of 150 Chinese words; recognize 100 Chinese words; and reproduce 75 Chinese characters.

Instruction: Major topics covered in the course are initials and finals, including tone, stroke order in writing, and simple statements and questions. Methods of instruction include lectures, oral drill and character writing, and examination.

Credit Recommendation: *Version 1:* In the lower division baccalaureate/associate degree category, 2 semester hours in Introductory Chinese (6/88). *Version 2:* In the vocational certificate or in the lower division baccalaureate/associate degree category, 2 semester hours in Chinese (8/93).

Introductory Chinese II (ECHIN152)

Location: Washington, DC.

Length: 30 hours (10 weeks).

Dates: January 1985-Present.

Objective: To help the student maintain a good pronunciation of Mandarin Chinese, become familiar with more complex grammatical patterns, and expand vocabulary.

Learning Outcome: Upon successful completion of this course, the student will be able to use a vocabulary of 300 words; recognize 250 characters; and reproduce 300 characters.

Instruction: Major topics covered in the course are complex expressions, tag questions, and modal particles. Methods of instruction include lectures, oral drill and character writing, and examination.

Credit Recommendation: In the lower division baccalaureate/associate degree category, 2 semester hours in Introductory Chinese (6/88) (8/93).

Introductory Chinese III (ECHIN153)

Location: Washington, DC.

Length: 30 hours (10 weeks).

Dates: April 1985-Present.

Objective: To help the student maintain a pronunciation of Mandarin Chinese, become familiar with more grammatical constructions, and expand oral and written vocabulary.

Learning Outcome: Upon successful completion of this course, the student will be able to use more advanced patterns and more practical language in conversational situations and exhibit more competence in reading and writing.

Instruction: Major topics covered in the course are optative verbs and modal particle "le." Methods of instruction include lectures, oral drill and character writing, and examination.

Credit Recommendation: In the lower division baccalaureate/associate degree category, 2 semester hours in Chinese (6/88) (8/93).

LANGUAGES/CZECHOSLOVAKIAN

Intermediate Czech I (ECZEC210)

Location: Washington, DC.

Length: 30 hours (10 weeks).

Dates: April 1985-Present.

Objective: To provide the student with development and improvement in reading, writing and conversational skills in contemporary Czech above the levels of competency achieved in introductory Czech III.

Learning Outcome: Upon successful completion of this course, the student will be able to read and comprehend texts of average difficulty (easy-reading books), and demonstrate an improved level of speaking and listening comprehension using correct grammar.

Instruction: Major topics covered in the course are review of grammar presented in Introductory CZech I, II, and III; further study of noun cases, singular and plural, with special emphasis on genitive, accusative, dative, and instrumental cases; and further study of ver system. Methods of instruction include lecture, discussion, interactive oral classwork, oral presentations, readings, writing an original composition, translation of more complicated text from Czech to English, and oral and written examinations.

Credit Recommendation: In the lower division baccalaureate/associate degree category, 2 semester hours in Intermediate Czech (8/93).

Introductory Czech I (ECZEC151)

Location: Washington, DC.

Length: 30 hours (10 weeks).

Dates: September 1984-Present.

Objective: To provide the student with an introduction to sound and writing system, a basic grammatical structure, and to develop rudimentary conversation skills and vocabulary dealing with practical, personal, and social needs and situations.

Learning Outcome: Upon successful completion of this course, the student will be able to read and write Czech at a basic level; ask and respond orally to simple questions based on familiar topics and vocabulary; and form and understand basic sentences dealing with family, job, visits, and orientation in a town.

Instruction: Major topics covered in the course are alphabet and diacritical marks; sound system, noun gender; singular and plural; noun cases; pronouns; prepositions; cardinal numerals; possessives; verb conjugation; and transitive verbs. Methods of instruction include lecture, discussion, homework assignments, classroom exercises, role playing, audio tape segments, problem solving, oral and written drills and examinations.

Credit Recommendation: In the lower division baccalaureate/associate degree category, 2 semester hours in Introductory Czech I (8/93).

Introductory Czech II (ECZEC152)

Location: Washington, DC.

Length: 30 hours (10 weeks).

Dates: January 1985-Present.

Objective: To provide the student with a continuation of introduction to grammatical structure and further development of speaking, listening, reading and writing contemporary Czech, and to help students gain an understanding of the writing system to interpret written language in areas of practical need.

Learning Outcome: Upon successful completion of this course, the student will be able to read simple connected texts in Czech; grasp main ideas from more complex texts; form sentences using more advanced grammar; and carry on a simple conversation on a familiar theme or subject.

Instruction: Major topics covered in the course are further study of grammar, including nouns, pronouns, adjectives, noun cases, vocative case and verb conjugation; and additional vocabulary dealing with practical, personal, and social situations and needs. Methods of instruction include lecture, discussion, homework assignments, classroom exercises including role playing, problem solving, and dictation; and translation of Czech sentences into English, English sentences into Czech; oral and written drills; and examinations.

Credit Recommendation: In the lower division baccalaureate/associate degree category, 2 semester hours in Introductory Czech (8/93).

Introductory Czech III (ECZEC153)

Location: Washington, DC.

Length: 30 hours (10 weeks).

Dates: April 1987-Present.

Objective: To provide the student with a continuation and deeper understanding of Czech grammatical structure; enlarge active vocabulary; and further improve skills in speaking, listening, writing, and reading contemporary Czech.

Learning Outcome: Upon successful completion of this course, the student will be able to read with accurate pronunciation; comprehend texts of average difficulty (such as newspapers and magazine articles); and speak comfortably on simple topics.

Instruction: Major topics covered in the course are review and further study of declensions of nouns; adjectives; possessive adjectives; personal pronouns, and verb conjugations; and particular study of locative, accusative, and instrumental cases. Methods of instruction include lecture, discussion, homework assignments, classroom exercises including role playing, problem solving, and dictation; translation of Czech sentences into English, English sentences into Czech; oral and written drills and examinations; and creative writing.

Credit Recommendation: In the lower division baccalaureate/associate degree category, 2 semester hours in Introductory Czech (8/93).

LANGUAGES/ENGLISH AS A SECOND LANGUAGE

Better Pronunciation Skills I (EESOL 200)

Location: Washington, DC.

Length: 30 hours (10 weeks).

Dates: September 1992-Present.

Objective: To enhance the student's English pronunciation; and to increase student's ability to speak English.

Learning Outcome: Upon successful completion of this course, the student will be able to discriminate accurately English phonetic sounds; make correct phonetic choices in speaking situations; and speak more effectively and with greater confidence.

Instruction: Major topics covered in the course are English phonetics, and standard English pronunciation. Methods of instruction include pre-tests, drill exercises, oral presentations, and audio materials.

Credit Recommendation: In the lower division baccalaureate/associate degree category, 2 semester hours in Communications or Language Studies (8/93).

Better Pronunciation Skills II (EESOL 201)

Location: Washington, DC.

Length: 30 hours (10 weeks).

Dates: September 1992-Present.

Objective: To help the student diagnose speech patterns, identify and correct problems; and to develop self-confidence in speaking English.

Learning Outcome: Upon successful completion of this course, the student will be able to speak English with improved pronunciation; use English confidently in typical daily situations or in formal settings; and carry over learned skills into everyday speech.

Instruction: Major topics covered in the course are articulation and diaphragm control in speaking English; and voice, diction, inflections in English. Methods of instruction include oral presentations, audio and video diagnosis, speech drills, play-reading, and speech-reading.

Credit Recommendation: In the lower division baccalaureate/associate degree category, 2 semester hours in Communications or Language Studies (8/93).

Communication Skills II (EESOL 121)

Location: Washington, DC.

Length: 30 hours (10 weeks).

Dates: January 1990-Present.

Objective: To provide the student with strengthening of the student's listening, speaking, reading and writing skills, and introducing cultural aspects of American society.

Learning Outcome: Upon successful completion of this course, the student will be able to understand to a high degree what is being what is being said by a native speaker; recognize and use many idiomatic expressions used in every day situations; and speak English more accurately as they will be able to apply correctly the use tenses and the irregular plurals of nouns and adjectives.

Instruction: Major topics covered in the course are verbs to be, to have; nouns and pronouns; simple tenses (e.g., past, present); modal auxiliaries; comparisons; reading and conversation; and culture activity. Methods of instruction include lecture, discussion, classroom exercises, case studies, role playing, problem solving, and question and answer sessions.

Credit Recommendation: In the lower division baccalaureate/associate degree category, 2 semester hours in Communications and Language Studies (8/93).

Communications Skills II (EESOL 124)

Location: Washington, DC.

Length: 30 hours (10 weeks).

Dates: September 1992-Present.

Objective: To provide the student with development of high intermediate level speaking, reading, and writing skills in English.

Learning Outcome: Upon successful completion of this course, the student will be able to read newspapers and journals with good comprehension and minimum dictionary use; recognize and use idiomatic English; and recognize and use basic pronunciation rules of English.

Instruction: Major topics covered in the course are intensive conversational English; reading journalistic English; and writing grammatically correct English. Methods of instruction include lecture, discussion, pronunciation drills, listening comprehension, oral presentation, and weekly quizzes.

Credit Recommendation: In the lower division baccalaureate/associate degree or upper division baccalaureate degree category, 2 semester hours in Communication Skills or Language Studies (8/93).

Communications Skills III (ESOL 122)

Location: Washington, DC.

Length: 30 hours (10 weeks).

Dates: January 1990-Present.

Objective: To help the student continue to develop oral communication skills while strengthening reading and writing skills in English.

Learning Outcome: Upon successful completion of this course, the student will be able to comprehend and use more advanced grammatical structures, thus improving accuracy; understanding the contrasts between their cultures and that of the United States; read with more complete understanding; and write more accurately about familiar situations.

Instruction: Major topics covered in the course are parts of speech; continuation of simple tenses (perfect tenses, gerunds, infinitives); conditional; idioms; oral presentations; and classroom activity. Methods of instruction include classroom exercises, case studies, role playing, problem solving, and shop instruction exams.

Credit Recommendation: In the lower division baccalaureate/associate degree category, 2 semester hours in Communications or Language Studies (8/93).

Communications Skills IV (ESOL 123)

Location: Washington, DC.

Length: 30 hours (10 weeks).

Dates: January 1990-Present.

Objective: To help the student further develop oral communication skills while strengthening reading and writing skills in English.

Learning Outcome: Upon successful completion of this course, the student will be able to comprehend and use more advanced grammatical structures, and read with more complete comprehension.

Instruction: Major topics covered in the course are four communication skills listening, speaking, reading, writing; vocabulary building; and conversational English. Methods of instruction include discussion and analysis, simulation and role playing, oral presentations, and homework critiques.

Credit Recommendation: In the lower division baccalaureate/associate degree category, 2 semester hours in Communications or Language Studies (8/93).

ESOL Intensive I (EESOL 205)

Location: Washington, DC.

Length: 60 hours (5 weeks).

Dates: January 1993-Present.

Objective: To develop the student's functional command of English grammar for writing and speaking, and build confidence in speaking English in everyday situations.

Learning Outcome: Upon successful completion of this course, the student will be able to function at an elementary level of spoken English; comprehend English idiomatic expressions at a passive level; and use basic English grammatical structures satisfactorily.

Instruction: Major topics covered in the course are basic grammar, syntax and structure of English; and vocabulary building; and conversational English. Methods of instruction include oral presentations, question-response and repetition drills, homework assignments, periodic quizzes, audio and video materials, and role-playing and games.

Credit Recommendation: In the lower division baccalaureate/associate degree category, 4 semester hours in Communications and Language Studies (8/93).

ESOL Intensive II (EESOL 206)

Location: Washington, DC.

Length: 60 hours (5 weeks).

Dates: January 1993-Present.

Objective: To develop the student's further command of English grammar beyond skill level of ESOL I; and to develop greater confidence in speaking situations.

Learning Outcome: Upon successful completion of this course, the student will be able to function at better than elementary level of spoken English; comprehend English idiomatic expressions at passive level; use basic English grammatical structures effectively in speaking and writing; and read moderately difficult texts in English with satisfactory comprehension.

Instruction: Major topics covered in the course are grammar; syntax and structure of English; vocabulary building; and conversational English. Methods of instruction include oral presentations, question-response, homework assignments, periodic quizzes, audio and video materials, simulations, role playing, and games.

Credit Recommendation: In the lower division baccalaureate/associate degree category, 4 semester hours in English or Language Studies (8/93).

Reading and Writing Skills II (EESOL 126)

Location: Washington, DC.

Length: 30 hours (10 weeks).

Dates: January 1990-Present.

Objective: To help the student develop reading and writing skills in English at the low intermediate level.

Learning Outcome: Upon successful completion of this course, the student will be able to organize and read letters, descriptions, and essays; outline and write accurate paragraphs; and pronounce correctly.

Instruction: Major topics covered in the course are organizing ideas by grouping; spelling rules for noun endings, vowels, homophones and consonants; and basic paragraph development. Methods of instruction include lecture, discussion, examinations, and audiovisual.

Credit Recommendation: In the lower division baccalaureate/associate degree category, 2 semester hours in Communications or Language Studies (8/93).

Reading and Writing Skills III (EESOL 127)

Location: Washington, DC.

Length: 30 hours (10 weeks).

Dates: January 1990-Present.

Objective: To help the student develop skills to write well-structured, properly punctuated paragraphs in English; to improve reading comprehension; and to develop and improve library skills.

Learning Outcome: Upon successful completion of this course, the student will be able to read English texts with high level analytical skill; apply mechanics of English grammar to written expression; use library efficiently; and understand and interpret nuances of English usage.

Instruction: Major topics covered in the course are recognizing main ideas, understanding words in context; library as source of information; and rules of English punctuation. Methods of instruction include written presentations with emphasis on paragraph, lecture, discussion, analysis of texts, and oral presentations.

Credit Recommendation: In the lower division baccalaureate/associate degree category, 2 semester hours in Language Studies or Communications (8/93).

Reading and Writing Skills IV (EESOL 128)

Location: Washington, DC.

Length: 30 hours (10 weeks).

Dates: January 1990-Present.

Objective: To provide the student with an advanced level reading and writing skill in English.

Learning Outcome: Upon successful completion of this course, the student will be able to interpret author's point of view; extract meaning from contexts; and comprehend the structural organization of reading passages.

Instruction: Major topics covered in the course are common rhetorical styles description, comparison and contrast, and persuasion. Methods of instruction include lecture, discussion, weekly journals, in-class compositions, book report, and examinations.

Credit Recommendation: In the lower division baccalaureate/associate degree category, 2 semester hours in Language Studies or Communications (8/93).

LANGUAGES/FRENCH

Advanced French I (EFREN 250)

Location: Washington, DC.

Length: 30 hours (10 weeks).

Dates: April 1985-Present.

Objective: To provide the student with development of advanced skills (listening, speaking, reading and writing, and to review sophisticated grammar and vocabulary).

Learning Outcome: Upon successful completion of this course, the student will be able to read and comprehend advanced texts; speak French using sophisticated sentences and vocabulary; and write with limited fluency.

Instruction: Major topics covered in the course are aspects of modern France, its current patterns and literature; films to enhance class discussion; articles from French magazines and newspapers; and oral and written compositions and translations. Methods of instruction include class discussions, role playing, oral written assignments, and compositions.

Credit Recommendation: In the upper division baccalaureate degree category, 2 semester hours in French (8/93)

Advanced French II (EFREN 251)

Location: Washington, DC.

Length: 30 hours (10 weeks).

Dates: September 1992-Present.

Objective: To help the student enhance all primary language skills (listening, speaking, reading, and writing) in order to enable the student to participate in the professional, social, and cultural life of a French-speaking environment.

Learning Outcome: Upon successful completion of this course, the student will be able to comprehend the media re: subject matters within the student's range of experience; to express him/herself with clarity; to read advanced materials; and to write with ease.

Instruction: Major topics covered in the course are advanced literary texts and non-literary articles from French magazines and newspapers. Methods of instruction include extensive reading, debates, dictations, grammar exercises, exposes, oral and written translations, and compositions.

Credit Recommendation: In the upper division baccalaureate degree category, 2 semester hours in French (8/93).

Conversational French I (EFREN 110)

Location: Washington, DC.

Length: 30 hours (10 weeks).

Dates: January 1980-Present.

Objective: To provide the student with the ability to speak and understand limited French.

Learning Outcome: Upon successful completion of this course, the student will be able to understand spoken French involving limited vocabulary; express basic concepts in French; and relate to aspects of contemporary French and Francophone culture.

Instruction: Major topics covered in the course are speaking, listening, reading, and grammar, with emphasis on speaking and listening. Methods of instruction include readings, dialogues, audio/visual materials, and other oral class activities.

Credit Recommendation: In the lower division baccalaureate/associate degree category, 2 semester hours in Conversational French I (1/90) (1/95).

Conversational French II (EFREN 111)

Location: Washington, DC.

Length: 30 hours (10 weeks).

Dates: January 1980-Present.

Objective: To provide the student with the ability to speak and understand increasingly complex French.

Learning Outcome: Upon successful completion of this course, the student will be able to understand spoken French involving increasingly complex patterns and vocabulary; express increasingly elaborate concepts in French; and relate to broader aspects of contemporary French and Francophone culture.

Instruction: Major topics covered in the course are expansion of vocabulary and development of speaking and listening skills through dialogues and other oral exercises. Methods of instruction include readings, discussions, dialogues, audio/visual materials, other oral activities, and cultural outings.

Credit Recommendation: In the lower division baccalaureate/associate degree category, 28ester hours in Conversational French II (1/90) (1/95).

Conversational French III (EFREN 112)

Location: Washington, DC.

Length: 30 hours (10 weeks).

Dates: January 1980-Present.

Objective: To provide the student with the ability to speak and understand complex French.

Learning Outcome: Upon successful completion of this course, the student will be able to understand spoken French involving relatively complex patterns and vocabulary; express elaborate concepts in French; and relate with greater ease to contemporary French and Francophone culture.

Instruction: Major topics covered in the course are continued expansion and development of speaking and listening skills through class activities, individual presentations, and group discussions. Methods of instruction include readings, discussions, dialogues, audio/visual materials, individual presentations, and other oral class activities.

Credit Recommendation: In the lower division baccalaureate/associate degree category, 2 semester hours in Conversational French III (1/90) (1/95).

France and the French (EFREN 412)

Location: Washington, DC.

Length: 30 hours (10 weeks).

Dates: January 1993-Present.

Objective: To strengthen the listening, speaking, and reading skills of the student and to enhance understanding of the French people.

Learning Outcome: Upon successful completion of this course, the student will be able to comprehend lectures in French about topics dealing with economics, history and politics; to speak on a variety of topics with accuracy; and to read articles on French culture, politics, economy, and contemporary life.

Instruction: Major topics covered in the course are French stereotypes; contemporary French society; U.S. and France relations; French politics; French economy, educational system, women, and France's role in the European community; and major literary authors of the 16th, 17th, 18th, and 19th centuries. Methods of instruction include research, presentations, and preparation questions on lectures.

Credit Recommendation: In the upper division baccalaureate degree category, 2 semester hours in French (8/93).

French for Reading Knowledge (EFREN 115)

Location: Washington, DC.

Length: 30 hours (10 weeks).

Dates: September 1992-Present.

Objective: To enable students to read a variety of French texts.

Learning Outcome: Upon successful completion of this course, the student will be able to read and comprehend various texts, to recognize cognates, tenses, and to use reading strategies.

Instruction: Major topics covered in the course are grammar, reading exercises, and strategies. Methods of instruction include projects, presentations, outside work, and examinations.

Credit Recommendation: In the lower division baccalaureate/associate degree category, 2 semester hours in French (8/93).

Intensive French I (EFREN 260)

Location: Washington, DC.

Length: 60 hours (5 weeks).

Dates: January 1993-Present.

Objective: To help the student master basic French language, including grammar and idiomatic expressions, within a short period of time.

Learning Outcome: Upon successful completion of this course, the student will be able to interact in French in class and with French speaking people outside of class; to know about aspects of French culture and history; and to answer accurately questions related to videotapes viewed in class showing activities such as getting on the bus, and reading menus.

Instruction: Major topics covered in the course are presentation of key words; phrases and idiomatic expressions; "situational" French-daily occurrences in French; and conversations about everyday topics among students. Methods of instruction include situations of French daily life acted out by students; pronunciation drills; grammar explanation; readings from texts adapted from French literature; and review of homework assignments.

Credit Recommendation: In the lower division baccalaureate/associate degree category, 4 semester hours in French (8/93).

Intensive French II (EFREN 261)

Location: Washington, DC.

Length: 60 hours (5 weeks).

Dates: January 1993-Present.

Objective: To help the student improve basic French language skills with a short time.

Learning Outcome: Upon successful completion of this course, the student will be able to use more advanced communication skills, and improve reading skills.

Instruction: Major topics covered in the course are pronunciations; irregular verbs; verbs in the present, perfect ("passe compose") and imperfect; structures with the use of pronominal verbs; and the subjunctif. Methods of instruction include class discussions, quizzes and final examinations, oral and written assignments, and compositions.

Credit Recommendation: In the lower division baccalaureate/associate degree category, 4 semester hours in French (8/93).

Intermediate French I (EFREN 210)

Location: Washington, DC.

Length: 30 hours (10 weeks).

Dates: January 1984-Present.

Objective: To expand vocabulary and consolidate grammar and develop greater proficiency in all skills including translation.

Learning Outcome: Upon successful completion of this course, the student will be able to demonstrate greater proficiency in speaking, writing, reading, and translating and a broader understanding of French culture.

Instruction: Major topics covered in the course are readings about culture and society, review of grammar, writing, and speaking. Methods of instruction include grammar presentation, readings, oral and written exercises, and assignments.

Credit Recommendation: In the lower division baccalaureate/associate degree category, 2 semester hours in Intermediate French I (6/88) (8/93).

Introductory French I (EFREN 151)

Location: Washington, DC.

Length: 30 hours (10 weeks).

Dates: January 1984-Present.

Objective: To help the student understand, speak, read, and write limited basic French with relative accuracy in the context of contemporary French culture.

Learning Outcome: Upon successful completion of this course, the student will be able to understand, speak, read, and write limited basic French with relative accuracy in the context of contemporary French culture.

Instruction: Major topics covered in the course are vocabulary, listening, reading, writing, and grammar with emphasis on the latter two. Methods of instruction include grammar, presentations, oral class activities, and written and audio tape assignments.

Credit Recommendation: In the lower division baccalaureate/associate degree category, 2 semester hours in Introductory French I (6/88) (8/93).

Introductory French II (EFREN 152)

Location: Washington, DC.

Length: 30 hours (10 weeks).

Dates: January 1984-Present.

Objective: To help the student understand, speak, read, and write more complex French in the context of contemporary French culture.

Learning Outcome: Upon successful completion of this course, the student will be able to understand, speak, read, and write moderately complex French in the context of contemporary French culture.

Instruction: Major topics covered in the course are review and continuation of grammar study; expansion of vocabulary; and development of language skills through readings and dialogues. Methods of instruction include grammar presentations, oral class activities, and written and audio tape assignments.

Credit Recommendation: In the lower division baccalaureate/associate degree category, 2 semester hours in Introductory French II (6/88) (8/93).

Introductory French III (EFREN 153)

Location: Washington, DC.

Length: 30 hours (10 weeks).

Dates: January 1984-Present.

Objective: To help the student understand, speak, read, and write increasingly complex French in the context of contemporary French culture.

Learning Outcome: Upon successful completion of this course, the student will be able to understand, speak, read, and write increasingly complex French in the context of contemporary French culture.

Instruction: Major topics covered in the course are more complex structural patterns through readings and dialogues and progressive growth in the use of the language, both in oral and written work. Methods of instruction include guided conversation, oral and written exercises, group activities, and assignments.

Credit Recommendation: In the lower division baccalaureate/associate degree category, 2 semester hours in Introductory French III (6/88) (8/93).

Survey of French Literature I (EFREN 310)

Location: Washington, DC.

Length: 30 hours (10 weeks).

Dates: January 1993-Present.

Objective: To improve the student's ability to read and comprehend French and Francophone literary works.

Learning Outcome: Upon successful completion of this course, the student will be able to demonstrate an understanding of literary genres and movements, and to deal with increased ability to literary works in terms of historical context, themes, analysis, comparison, and criticism.

Instruction: Major topics covered in the course are literary works of all genres by major 19th and 20th century French and Francophone authors and the context, historic, social, linguistic, and aesthetic in which they were written. Methods of instruction include readings; instructor's introductions; instructor/student discussions in French; student's class presentations; compositions; and final presentations on essays.

Credit Recommendation: In the lower division baccalaureate/associate degree category, 2 semester hours in Survey of French Literature I (8/93).

LANGUAGES/GERMAN

Advanced German I (EGERM 250)

Location: Washington, DC.

Length: 30 hours (10 weeks).

Dates: January 1990-Present.

Objective: To provide the student with preparation to read and discuss advanced German texts and to demonstrate oral and written skills.

Learning Outcome: Upon successful completion of this course, the student will be able to interpret advanced German texts; communicate in German in formal and informal settings; and use both oral and written skills effectively.

Instruction: Major topics covered in the course are development of oral writing skills; discussion of everyday topics; and simulation of typical communication situations. Methods of instruction include grammar discussion and analysis, simulation, role playing,, oral presentations, and writing short compositions.

Credit Recommendation: In the lower division baccalaureate/associate degree category or in the upper division baccalaureate degree category, 2 semester hours in Advanced German I (8/93).

Advanced German II (EGERM 251)

Location: Washington, DC.

Length: 30 hours (10 weeks).

Dates: January 1990-Present.

Objective: To provide the student with a continuation of EGERM 250; to broaden and further student's ability to read and discuss advanced German texts.

Learning Outcome: Upon successful completion of this course, the student will be able to interpret advanced German texts more easily and accurately; communicate more effectively in German in both formal and informal settings; and use oral writing skills more effectively.

Instruction: Major topics covered in the course are further development of speaking and writing skills; discussion of everyday topics; and stimulation of typical communication situations. Methods of instruction include grammar discussion and analysis, simulation, role playing, oral presentations, and writing short compositions.

Credit Recommendation: In the lower division baccalaureate/associate degree category or in the upper division baccalaureate degree category, 2 semester hours in Advanced German II (8/93).

Conversational German III (EGERM 112)
(Formerly Advanced Conversational German (EGERM 312)

Location: Washington, DC.

Length: 30 hours (10 weeks).

Dates: January 1980-Present.

Objective: To assist the student with development of advanced speaking and comprehension skills and mastery of more advanced vocabulary in the German language.

Learning Outcome: Upon successful completion of this course, the student will be able to demonstrate a mastery of complex structures of spoken German; converse on more specific and abstract topics; and exhibit familiarity with social, political, and cultural issues facing Germany.

Instruction: Major topics covered in the course are everyday life in present day Germany, role changes of men and women in Germany, problems of German youth, and German cultural life, including literary texts. Methods of instruction include lecture, discussion, case studies, role playing, problem-solving, dialogues, presentations, group presentations, taped recordings, and examinations.

Credit Recommendation: In the upper division baccalaureate degree category, 2 semester hours in Advanced Conversational German (1/90).

Conversational German IV (EGERM 113)

Location: Washington, DC.

Length: 30 hours (10 weeks).

Dates: January 1993-Present.

Objective: To help the student develop more effective oral communication skills; and to master more complex grammatical structures.

Learning Outcome: Upon successful completion of this course, the student will be able to communicate more effectively with a native speaker in formal and informal settings; comprehend spoken German more easily; and more efficiently reproduce near-native speaking patterns more accurately.

Instruction: Major topics covered in the course are communication in typical social situations, acquiring, and providing information; and understanding German culture. Methods of instruction include discussion and analysis; video and print materials; audio materials in class and for homework; and oral presentations; and group discussions.

Credit Recommendation: In the lower division baccalaureate/associate degree category, 2 semester hours in German (8/93).

German for Business (EGERM 305)

Location: Washington, DC.

Length: 30 hours (10 weeks).

Dates: January 1991-Present.

Objective: To provide the student with specific information on the differences and similarities of German and U.S. business practices as expressed through the German language.

Learning Outcome: Upon successful completion of this course, the student will be able to use correct spoken and written business language in German; successfully conduct business meetings with German nationals; and have knowledge of German customs and habits.

Instruction: Major topics covered in the course are review of geographical and historical analysis of German speaking countries; overview of economics and trade and industry of Germany; and examination of the place of German in the common market. Methods of instruction include lectures, discussions, project presentations, assignments on readings, and discussions on common events.

Credit Recommendation: In the upper division baccalaureate or graduate degree category, 2 semester hours in Business, German, or European Studies (8/93).

German for Reading Knowledge (EGERM 115)

Location: Washington, DC.

Length: 30 hours (10 weeks).

Dates: January 1985-Present.

Objective: To provide the student with proficiency to read advanced general and technical material in German.

Learning Outcome: Upon successful completion of this course, the student will be able to read relatively difficult texts in specific disciplines with aid of dictionary; and recognize basic and more complex grammatical structures.

Instruction: Major topics covered in the course are basic German grammar; complex grammatical structures; and vocabulary building. Methods of instruction include reading and analysis of selected texts from various disciplines; question/answer format; translation exercises; and sight reading for comprehension.

Credit Recommendation: In the lower division baccalaureate/associate degree

category, 2 semester hours in German (8/93).

German Short Story (EGERM 300)

Location: Washington, DC.
Length: 30 hours (10 weeks).
Dates: January 1989-Present.
Objective: To provide the student with an introduction to German literature in 20th century; emphasis is placed on short story.
Learning Outcome: Upon successful completion of this course, the student will be able to understand and interpret contemporary German literature and relate literature to its socio-political context.
Instruction: Major topics covered in the course are German short stories; 20th century German life and culture; and analysis of short story as genre. Methods of instruction include discussion and analysis, oral presentations, and a research paper.
Credit Recommendation: In the upper division baccalaureate degree category, 2 semester hours in German Short Story (8/93).

German Women Writers (EGERM 505)

Location: Washington, DC.
Length: 30 hours (10 weeks).
Dates: January 1993-Present.
Objective: To provide the student with a broad survey of German women writers from 13th to 20th century.
Learning Outcome: Upon successful completion of this course, the student will be able to discuss role of women writers in history of German literature; appreciate role and contributions of women in historical contexts ranging from later medieval to modern period; and better understand role of literature in cultural emancipation of women.
Instruction: Major topics covered in the course are nature of literature written by women in Germany; and German social and cultural life from female perspective. Methods of instruction include lecture and discussion, oral presentations, and a research paper.
Credit Recommendation: In the lower division baccalaureate/associate degree category or upper division baccalaureate degree category, 2 semester hours in German Literature (8/93).

Intermediate German I (EGERM 210)

Location: Washington, DC.
Length: 30 hours (10 weeks).
Dates: January 1984-Present.
Objective: To provide the student with a grammar review and development of conversational, reading, and writing skills with an emphasis on contemporary style and vocabulary. This course is designed for participants with a working knowledge of German verb tenses, moods, and voices.
Learning Outcome: Upon successful completion of this course, the students will have reviewed present and past tenses, as well as four cases; gain practice in speaking German; improve their writing skills; and increased their knowledge of contemporary life in the German-speaking countries.
Instruction: Major topics covered in the course are grammar review and development of conversational, reading, and writing skills with an emphasis on contemporary style and vocabulary. This course is designed for participants with a working knowledge of German verb tenses, moods, and voices. Methods of instruction include classroom instruction, lecture, discussion, and drill exercises.
Credit Recommendation: In the lower division baccalaureate/associate degree category, 2 semester hours in Intermediate German (6/88) (8/93). *Prerequisite:* Introductory German III (EGERM 153) or equivalent.

Intermediate German II (EGERM 211)

Location: Washington, DC.
Length: 30 hours (10 weeks).
Dates: February 1985-Present.
Objective: To emphasize the student's reading and writing skills as well as develop a more varied and contemporary vocabulary through study of newspapers, magazines, and recordings.
Learning Outcome: Upon successful completion of this course, the student will have reviewed prepositions, adjectives, and subjunctive mood; gain practice in speaking German; improved writing skills; and increased knowledge of contemporary life in the German-speaking countries.
Instruction: Major topics covered in the course are emphasizing reading and writing skills as well as development of a more varied and contemporary vocabulary through study of newspapers, magazines, and recordings. Methods of instruction include lecture, discussion, and drill exercises.
Credit Recommendation: In the lower division baccalaureate/associate degree category, 2 semester hours in German (6/88) (8/93).

Intermediate German III (EGERM 212)

Location: Washington, DC.
Length: 30 hours (10 weeks).
Dates: March 1985-Present.
Objective: To emphasize the student's expanding vocabulary, idiomatic structures, and conversational fluency by using a variety of texts; and readings that stress contemporary life in Germany.
Learning Outcome: Upon successful completion of this course, the student will be able to use passive voice, relative clauses, and idioms; gain practice in speaking German; improve writing skills; and increase knowledge of contemporary life in the German-speaking countries.
Instruction: Major topics covered in the course are further development of skills in reading, writing, and vocabulary using German newspapers, magazines, and recordings.
Credit Recommendation: In the lower division baccalaureate/associate degree category, 2 semester hours in German (6/88) (8/93).

Introductory Conversational German I (EGERM 110) (Formerly Conversational German I [EGERM 110])

Location: Washington, DC.
Length: 30 hours (10 weeks).
Dates: January 1980-Present.
Objective: To provide the student with an introduction to the basic structure and vocabulary of German, with emphasis on the spoken language.
Learning Outcome: Upon successful completion of this course, the student will be able to recall basic structure and vocabulary; engage in simple conversations in the present tense; and express familiarity with aspects of everyday life in Germany.
Instruction: Major topics covered in the course are cultural content including student life, everyday life, sports, and transportation; grammatical content including cases, pronouns, prepositions, and the present tense of verbs. Methods of instruction include lecture, oral presentation, listening comprehension training, audio/visual materials, classroom exercises, graded weekly tests, and evaluation of conversation.
Credit Recommendation: In the lower division baccalaureate/associate degree category, 2 semester hours in Elementary

Conversational German I or Introductory German (1/90) (1/95).

Introductory Conversational German II (EGERM 111) (Formerly Conversational German II [EGERM 111])

Location: Washington, DC.
Length: 30 hours (10 weeks).
Dates: January 1980-Present.
Objective: To improve the students' speaking skills and expand vocabulary and to provide useful control of the structure in basic reading and writing.
Learning Outcome: Upon successful completion of this course, the student will be able to demonstrate mastery of the basic structure of spoken German; converse in several situations and about various topics; and exhibit greater understanding of German culture.
Instruction: Major topics covered in the course are the cultural content including current events, family life, work and leisure time in Germany, and customs in German-speaking countries; grammatical content including present perfect and past tenses, prepositions, and subordinate clauses. Methods of instruction include lecture, oral presentation, listening comprehension training, reading and writing exercises, audio/visual materials, graded weekly tests, and evaluation of presentations and conversation.
Credit Recommendation: In the lower division baccalaureate/associate degree category, 2 semester hours in Elementary Conversational German II or Introductory German II (1/90) (1/95).

Introductory Conversational German III (EGERM 112) (Formerly Advanced Conversational German [EGERM 312])

Location: Washington, DC.
Length: 30 hours (10 weeks).
Dates: September 1990-Present.
Objective: To further develop the student's speaking and comprehension skills, as well as to teach advanced vocabulary.
Learning Outcome: Upon successful completion of this course, the student will be able to demonstrate mastery of complex structure of spoken German and an advanced vocabulary in German.
Instruction: Major topics covered in the course are cultural content including the political and social conditions of Unified Germany; and grammatical content including adjectives, clauses, passive voice, reflexive verbs, and vocabulary building. Methods of instruction include lecture, oral presentation, discussion, listening comprehension training, graded weekly tests, and evaluation of presentations and conversation.
Credit Recommendation: In the upper division baccalaureate degree category, 2 semester hours in German (8/93) (1/95).

Introductory German I (EGERM 151)

Location: Washington, DC.
Length: 30 hours (10 weeks).
Dates: January 1984-Present.
Objective: To provide the student with the ability to speak, read, and write on an elementary level; Essential grammar skills as well as basic vocabulary are the main focus.
Learning Outcome: Upon successful completion of this course, the student will be able to understand and use basic grammatical structures; engage in simple conversations; function in the target culture; and understand basic aspects of the target culture.
Instruction: Major topics covered in the course are basic grammatical structures and vocabulary; personal information; immediate surroundings; leisure-time activities; shopping and travel; and introduction to German-speaking countries. Methods of instruction include lecture, discussion, classroom exercises, case studies, role playing, and problem solving.
Credit Recommendation: In the lower division baccalaureate/associate degree category, 2 semester hours in Introductory German I (6/88) (8/93).

Introductory German II (EGERM 152)

Location: Washington, DC.
Length: 30 hours (10 weeks).
Dates: January 1984-Present.
Objective: To introduce the student to fourth case (dative) and more complex grammatical structures.
Learning Outcome: Upon successful completion of this course, the student will be able to understand and use basic grammatical structures; engage in simple conversations; function in the target culture; understand basic aspects of the target culture; and understand and use German sentence structure.
Instruction: Major topics covered in the course are further development of grammar competence; and improvement of basic skills proficiency. Methods of instruction include lecture, discussion, classroom exercises, case studies, role playing, and problem solving.
Credit Recommendation: In the lower division baccalaureate/associate degree category, 2 semester hours in Introductory German II (6/88) (8/93).

Introductory German III (EGERM 153)

Location: Washington, DC.
Length: 30 hours (10 weeks).
Dates: February 1985-Present.
Objective: To introduce the student to complex tenses.
Learning Outcome: Upon successful completion of this course, the student will be able to use more complex structures; engage in extended conversations; and have a sounder understanding of the target culture.
Instruction: Major topics covered in the course are introduction to more complex tense forms; and further development of basic skills proficiency. Methods of instruction include lecture, discussion, classroom exercises, case studies, role playing, and problem solving.
Credit Recommendation: In the lower division baccalaureate/associate degree category, 2 semester hours in Introductory German III (6/88) (8/93).

Introductory German IV (EGERM 154)

Location: Washington, DC.
Length: 30 hours (10 weeks).
Dates: January 1993-Present.
Objective: To provide the student with complete study of basic grammar; further strengthening of four basic skills; and broadening of cultural knowledge.
Learning Outcome: Upon successful completion of this course, the student will be able to reproduce basic grammatical structures; use approximately 12,200 word vocabulary; comprehend simple spoken German; and reproduce simple German statements, questions, and commands.
Instruction: Major topics covered in the course are general knowledge of German grammar; basic speaking, reading, writing, and comprehension; and German culture and daily life. Methods of instruction include review and performance of grammar drills and exercises, oral presentations, and written work.
Credit Recommendation: In the lower division baccalaureate/associate degree category, 2 semester hours in Introductory German (8/93).

The German Novella (EGERM 401)

Location: Washington, DC.

Length: 30 hours (10 weeks).
Dates: January 1990-Present.
Objective: To provide the student with an introduction to German literature and culture (18th to early century) and emphasis is on the German Novella theories and reading of representative Novellas.
Learning Outcome: Upon successful completion of this course, the student will be able to understand German literature and culture from the 18th to early 20th century; and understand theories on the German Novella and be able to interpret and discuss such works.
Instruction: Major topics covered in the course are Representative German Novellas. Methods of instruction include lectures, discussions, oral presentations, and a research paper.
Credit Recommendation: In the upper division baccalaureate degree category, 2 semester hours in German Literature (8/93).

LANGUAGES/GREEK

Intermediate Greek I (EGREE 210)
Location: Washington, DC.
Length: 30 hours (10 weeks).
Dates: January 1984-June 1993.
Objective: To provide the student with conversational reading and writing skills, to expand vocabulary, and to provide grammar review and advanced grammar for students with a working knowledge of the basics of the language.
Learning Outcome: Upon successful completion of this course, the student will be able to demonstrate an understanding of the course material in a final take-home exam, which consists of essays and questions on grammar; write compositions with selected themes; read and understand newspaper articles; and apply knowledge learned in the course to conversation.
Instruction: Major topics covered in the course are advanced grammar; fictional prose; Greek mythology; and current events. Methods of instruction include classroom sessions with emphasis on compositions and general discussion of events and situations. Grammar drills, reading, and essay presentation are also parts of this course.
Credit Recommendation: In the lower division baccalaureate/associate degree category, 2 semester hours in Modern Greek (6/88).

Intermediate Greek II (EGREE 211)
Location: Washington, DC.
Length: 30 hours (10 weeks).
Dates: January 1985-June 1993.
Objective: To develop conversational vocabulary and writing skills, expands vocabulary, and provides grammar review and advanced grammar.
Learning Outcome: Upon successful completion of this course, the student will be able to demonstrate an understanding of the course material in a final take-home exam, which consists of essays, questions on grammar, and true and false statements; give an oral presentation in class; read and analyze newspaper articles; write compositions; and apply knowledge learned in the course to conversation.
Instruction: Major topics covered in the course are advanced grammar; fictional prose; Greek mythology; and current events. Methods of instruction include classroom instruction intended to improve the oral as well as the writing style of the student. Many topics are discussed, helping the students to increase fluency.
Credit Recommendation: In the lower division baccalaureate/associate degree category, 2 semester hours in Modern Greek (6/88).

Intermediate Greek III (EGREE 212)
Location: Washington, DC.
Length: 30 hours (10 weeks).
Dates: February 1986-June 1993.
Objective: To provide students with the opportunity to apply their advanced knowledge to conversational and writing activities.
Learning Outcome: Upon successful completion of this course, the student will be able to demonstrate an understanding of the course material in a final take-home exam, which consists of essays, questions on Greek and American history and geography; give an oral presentation in class; read and analyze newspaper articles; write compositions; and apply knowledge learned in the course to conversation.
Instruction: Major topics covered in the course are advanced grammar; fictional prose; current events; and geography and history. Methods of instruction include class instruction intended to improve the oral as well as the writing style of the student. Many topics are discussed, helping the students to increase fluency.
Credit Recommendation: In the lower division baccalaureate/associate degree category, 2 semester hours in Modern Greek (6/88).

Introduction to Classical Greek I (EGREC 151)
Location: Washington, DC.
Length: 30 hours (10 weeks).
Dates: September 1992-Present.
Objective: To develop the student's ability to read the language within the context of ancient Greek culture; and mastery of vocabulary and grammar is emphasized.
Learning Outcome: Upon successful completion of this course, the student will be able to correctly pronounce vocabulary and read and translate basic texts; use simple grammar structures; enhance English vocabulary derived from ancient Greek; and demonstrate knowledge of Greek mythology.
Instruction: Major topics covered in the course are basic grammar to include noun declensions; essential vocabulary; and ancient Greek history, culture, and daily life. Methods of instruction include lecture, discussion, reading exercises, translation practice, and weekly tests on learned vocabulary and grammar.
Credit Recommendation: In the lower division baccalaureate/associate degree category, 2 semester hours in Classics or Humanities (8/93).

Introduction to Classical Greek II (EGREC 152)
Location: Washington, DC.
Length: 30 hours (10 weeks).
Dates: January 1993-Present.
Objective: To help the student continue to develop a beginner's ability to read the language within the context of ancient Greek culture; and mastery of vocabulary and grammar is emphasized.
Learning Outcome: Upon successful completion of this course, the student will be able to demonstrate improved pronunciation of vocabulary; read and translate basic texts; correctly use more complex grammar structures; gain additional knowledge of ancient Greek culture, history, and mythology; and demonstrate enhanced English vocabulary derived from ancient Greek.
Instruction: Major topics covered in the course are grammar to include additional noun declensions; essential vocabulary; and ancient Greek history, culture, and daily life. Methods of instruction include lecture, discussion, translation practice, reading exercises, and weekly tests on learned vocabulary and grammar.

Credit Recommendation: In the lower division baccalaureate/associate degree category, 2 semester hours in Classics or Humanities (8/93).

Introduction to Classical Greek III (EGREC 153)

Location: Washington, DC.
Length: 30 hours (10 weeks).
Dates: April 1993-Present.
Objective: To help the student continue to develop ability to read the language within the context of ancient Greek culture; and mastery of vocabulary and grammar is emphasized.
Learning Outcome: Upon successful completion of this course, the student will be able to understand and translate more complex literary and historical texts; use complex grammar structures; gain additional knowledge of ancient Greek culture, history, and social life; and further enhance English vocabulary derived from ancient Greek.
Instruction: Major topics covered in the course are grammar with emphasis on verbs; essentials vocabulary; and ancient Greek history, culture, and daily life. Methods of instruction include lecture, discussions, translation practice, reading passages aloud, and weekly tests on learned vocabulary and grammar.
Credit Recommendation: In the lower division baccalaureate/associate degree category, 2 semester hours in Classics or Humanities (8/93).

Introductory Greek II (EGREE 152)

Location: Washington, DC.
Length: 30 hours (10 weeks).
Dates: February 1985-Present.
Objective: To broaden the student's knowledge of grammar, build vocabulary through reading and writing, and increase conversation skills through dialogues.
Learning Outcome: Upon successful completion of this course, the student will be able to demonstrate an understanding of the course material in a final take-home exam; construct an essay with selected words taken from the materials covered in the course; and apply knowledge learned in the course to conversation.
Instruction: Major topics covered in the course are conversation relative to more complex subjects; contracted verbs; present tense of passive voice, reflexive verbs; imperfect (i.e., past continuous tense); factors governing time and duration of an event for the use of simple past or imperfect; direct object; and possessive case of nouns. Methods of instruction include classroom instruction, which combines grammar drills, reading, dialogue presentation, and question and answer period.
Credit Recommendation: In the lower division baccalaureate/associate degree category, 2 semester hours in Modern Greek (6/88) (8/93).

Introductory Greek III (EGREE 153)

Location: Washington, DC.
Length: 30 hours (10 weeks).
Dates: March 1986-Present.
Objective: To improve the student's ability to understand and use grammar, increase vocabulary, and develop writing skills.
Learning Outcome: Upon successful completion of this course, the student will be able to demonstrate an understanding of the course material in a final take-home exam; construct an essay with selected words taken from the materials covered in the course; and apply knowledge learned in the course to conversation.
Instruction: Major topics covered in the course are the future and continuous future; comparison of adjectives and adverbs; irregular verbs and nouns; present perfect and past perfect tenses; contractions; and techniques of composition writing. Methods of instruction include classroom instruction, which combines grammar drills, reading, dialogue presentation, and question and answer period.
Credit Recommendation: In the lower division baccalaureate/associate degree category, 2 semester hours in Modern Greek (6/88) (8/93).

Introductory Greek I—Modern (EGREE 151)

Location: Washington, DC.
Length: 30 hours (10 weeks).
Dates: September 1984-Present.
Objective: To introduce students to the Greek alphabet and general structure of the language, with emphasis upon grammar, writing, basic vocabulary, and foundation work in speaking, comprehension and reading.
Learning Outcome: Upon successful completion of this course, the student will be able to demonstrate an understanding of the course material in a final take-home exam; construct an essay with selected words taken from the materials covered in the course; and apply knowledge learned in the course to conversation.
Instruction: Major topics covered in the course are conversation relative to more complex subjects; contracted verbs; present tense of passive voice; reflexive verbs; imperfect (i.e., past continuous tense); factors governing time and duration of an event for the use of simple past or imperfect; direct object; and possessive case of nouns. Methods of instruction include classroom instruction, which combines grammar drills, reading, dialogue presentation, and question and answer period.
Credit Recommendation: In the lower division baccalaureate/associate degree category, 2 semester hours in Modern Greek (6/88) (8/93).

LANGUAGES/ITALIAN

Advanced Italian I (EITAL250)

Location: Washington, DC.
Length: 30 hours (10 weeks).
Dates: April 1985-Present.
Objective: To provide the student with a general review of Italian grammar and develop greater proficiency in all skills.
Learning Outcome: Upon successful completion of this course, the student will be able to read and understand simple contemporary literary and nonliterary Italian; understand Italian spoken at normal speed; and converse and/or describe with relative accuracy.
Instruction: Major topics covered in the course are review of grammar, vocabulary and idioms; and reading and translation of literary and nonliterary materials. Methods of instruction include lecture, discussion, classroom exercises, conversation, reading aloud, and examinations.
Credit Recommendation: In the lower division baccalaureate/associate degree category, 2 semester hours in Advanced Italian I (8/93).

Advanced Italian II (EITAL251)

Location: Washington, DC.
Length: 30 hours (10 weeks).
Dates: September 1991-Present.
Objective: To continue to provide a general review of Italian grammar and develop greater proficiency in all skills.
Learning Outcome: Upon successful completion of this course, the student will be able to demonstrate a full knowledge of grammatical structure and expanded vocabulary and use of idioms in speaking, reading, and writing.
Instruction: Major topics covered in the course are review of grammar, vocabulary, and idioms; and reading and discussion of literary and nonliterary materials. Methods of instruction include lecture,

discussion, classroom exercises, conversation, compositions, and examinations.

Credit Recommendation: In the lower division baccalaureate/associate degree category, 2 semester hours in Advanced Italian II (8/93).

Conversational Italian I (EITAL 110)

Location: Washington, DC.

Length: 30 hours (10 weeks).

Dates: January 1983-Present.

Objective: To provide the student with the ability to speak and understand basic present day Italian.

Learning Outcome: Upon successful completion of this course, the student will be able to understand spoken Italian and express basic concepts in the present tense within limited everyday cultural contexts.

Instruction: Major topics covered in the course are greetings, numbers, days of the week, geographical and descriptive vocabulary; grammatical content covers personal pronouns, present tense, singular and plural, questions, agreement of adjectives. Methods of instruction include lecture, discussion, dialogues and readings, oral classroom exercises, audio cassettes, films, and examinations.

Credit Recommendation: In the lower division baccalaureate/associate degree category, 2 semester hours in Conversational Italian (8/93).

Conversational Italian II (EITAL 111)

Location: Washington, DC.

Length: 30 hours (10 weeks).

Dates: September 1984-Present.

Objective: to expand the student's ability to speak Italian and to increase facility in reading and writing.

Learning Outcome: Upon successful completion of this course, the student will be able to understand and speak Italian involving more complex grammatical patterns, past tenses, and broader vocabulary.

Instruction: Major topics covered in the course are various aspects of family life; months, seasons and temporal expressions, grammatical content covers present perfect, imperfect and imperative; reflexives, pronouns, and negatives. Methods of instruction include lecture, discussion, dialogues and readings, oral classroom activities, audio cassettes, films, and examinations.

Credit Recommendation: In the lower division baccalaureate/associate degree category, 2 semester hours in Conversational Italian II (8/93).

Intermediate Italian I (EITAL 210)

Location: Washington, DC.

Length: 30 hours (10 weeks).

Dates: January 1985-Present.

Objective: To expand the student's vocabulary and knowledge of intermediate grammar, thereby improving reading and conversation skills.

Learning Outcome: Upon successful completion of this course, the student will be able to correctly use more complex grammatical structures in conversation and to understand and discuss simple newspaper articles.

Instruction: Major topics covered in the course are sports, food, work, music, radio, and TV; grammatical content includes combined pronouns, reciprocal verbs, future and conditional, and present and past subjunctive. Methods of instruction include lecture, discussion, role playing, oral classroom exercises, and examinations.

Credit Recommendation: In the lower division baccalaureate/associate degree category, 2 semester hours in Intermediate Italian I (8/93).

Intermediate Italian II (EITAL211)

Location: Washington, DC.

Length: 30 hours (10 weeks).

Dates: September 1984-Present.

Objective: To expand the student's knowledge of intermediate grammar and vocabulary and to develop writing skills and to enhance reading and conversational skills.

Learning Outcome: Upon successful completion of this course, the student will be able to demonstrate mastery of additional complex grammatical structures in speaking and writing.

Instruction: Major topics covered in the course are music, work, newspapers, transportation, professions; grammatical content includes all tense of subjunctive, past conditional, comparative, and superlative. Methods of instruction include lecture, discussion, role playing, oral classroom exercises, student presentations, and examinations.

Credit Recommendation: In the lower division baccalaureate/associate degree category, 2 semester hours in Intermediate Italian II (8/93).

Intermediate Italian III (EITAL212)

Location: Washington, DC.

Length: 30 hours (10 weeks).

Dates: April 1987-Present.

Objective: To further expand the student's knowledge of intermediate grammar structures and vocabulary and to enable the student to read, comprehend, and discuss simple short stories from Italian literature.

Learning Outcome: Upon successful completion of this course, the student will be able to apply more advanced grammar and expanded vocabulary to the discussion of literary works and aspects of contemporary Italian culture.

Instruction: Major topics covered in the course are Italian literature, politics and government, pollution; grammatical content includes literary past tense, relative pronouns, imperative with pronouns, interrogatives, passive voice, and impersonal construction. Methods of instruction include lecture, discussion, role playing, oral classroom exercises, and examinations.

Credit Recommendation: In the lower division baccalaureate/associate degree category, 2 semester hours in Intermediate Italian III (8/93).

LANGUAGES/JAPANESE

Advanced Japanese I (EJAPN 250)

Location: Washington, DC.

Length: 30 hours (10 weeks).

Dates: September 1986-Present.

Objective: To sharpen the student's reading, translation, and speaking skills.

Learning Outcome: Upon successful completion of this course, the student will be able to read and translate Japanese articles and stories of moderate difficulty.

Instruction: Major topics covered in the course are reading and translation. Methods of instruction include lectures, discussion, exercises, quizzes, and examinations.

Credit Recommendation: In the upper division baccalaureate degree category, 2 semester hours in Advanced Japanese (6/88) (8/93).

Advanced Japanese II (EJAPN 251)

Location: Washington, DC.

Length: 30 hours (10 weeks).

Dates: January 1987-Present.

Objective: To prepare the student to accurately translate Japanese materials and practice summarizing in Japanese.

Learning Outcome: Upon successful completion of this course, the student will be able to read and translate accurately

Japanese of moderate difficulty; start reading newspapers; and know up to 700 kanji.

Instruction: Major topics covered in the course are reading and translating. Methods of instruction include lecture, discussion, exercises, quizzes, and examination.

Credit Recommendation: In the upper division baccalaureate degree category, 2 semester hours in Advanced Japanese (6/88) (8/93).

Advanced Japanese III (EJAPN 252)

Location: Washington, DC.

Length: 30 hours (10 weeks).

Dates: April 1987-Present.

Objective: To further sharpen the students reading and translating skills and improve ability to speak Japanese.

Learning Outcome: Upon successful completion of this course, the students will be able to read current materials, newspapers and periodicals, with a dictionary and assistance from the instructor; and will know 881 kanji.

Instruction: Major topics covered in the course are reading and translating. Methods of instruction include lecture, discussion, exercises, quizzes, and examination.

Credit Recommendation: In the upper division baccalaureate degree category, 2 semester hours in Advanced Japanese (6/88) (8/93).

Intermediate Japanese I (EJAPN 210)

Location: Washington, DC.

Length: 30 hours (10 weeks).

Dates: September 1985-Present.

Objective: To introduce the student to an additional 50 kanji; learn to use a kanji dictionary; read a Japanese story; and write a Japanese letter.

Learning Outcome: Upon successful completion of this course, the student will be able to use superlatives, comparatives, conditionals, quotatives, and other verbal and adjectival constructions; be familiar with various levels and styles of speaking; and recognize and write 150-200 kanji and within limitations, use a kanji dictionary.

Instruction: Major topics covered in the course are superlatives, comparatives, conditionals, quotatives, and other verbal and adjectival constructions; ways to express obligation (i.e., must, should, etc.) in the linguistic and cultural context; speech styles and levels; and use of dictionaries. Methods of instruction include home study, free conversation, quizzes, and examination.

Credit Recommendation: In the lower division baccalaureate/associate degree category, 2 semester hours in Intermediate Japanese (6/88) (8/93).

Intermediate Japanese II (EJAPN 211)

Location: Washington, DC.

Length: 30 hours (10 weeks).

Dates: January 1986-Present.

Objective: To introduce the student to 75 more kanji.

Learning Outcome: Upon successful completion of this course, the student will be able to handle more complex Japanese patterns such as the extended predicate rashii, nagara, and tearu; handle guided conversation; and recognize and write 200-275 kanji.

Instruction: Major topics covered in the course are extended predicate; supposition; and auxiliary verbs. Methods of instruction include lecture, discussion, exercises, extracurricular activities, quizzes, and examinations.

Credit Recommendation: In the lower division baccalaureate/associate degree category, 2 semester hours in Intermediate Japanese (6/88) (8/93).

Intermediate Japanese III (EJAPN 212)

Location: Washington, DC.

Length: 30 hours (10 weeks).

Dates: April 1986-Present.

Objective: To introduce the student to 75 more kanji.

Learning Outcome: Upon successful completion of this course, the student will be able to handle complex Japanese sentences and verbal patterns, including tehishii, te kureru, te morau, hodo, and tameni; handle elementary nontechnical conversations; and recognize and write 350 kanji.

Instruction: Major topics covered in the course are adjectival and copular gerund; more expressions using auxiliary verbs; degree; complex sentences, and quotatives. Methods of instruction include home study, translation, quizzes, and examination.

Credit Recommendation: In the lower division baccalaureate/associate degree category, 2 semester hours in Intermediate Japanese (6/88) (8/93).

Introductory Japanese I (EJAPN 151)

Location: Washington, DC.

Length: 30 hours (10 weeks).

Dates: September 1984-Present.

Objective: To provide the student with a basic knowledge of the Japanese language and culture and also learn "hiragana".

Learning Outcome: Upon successful completion of this course, the student will be able to read and write hiragana; use and understand simple copular and adjectival sentences, including negative sentences; and use roughly 40 useful expressions.

Instruction: Major topics covered in the course are hiragana; simple copular sentences, simple adjectival sentences, basic sentence particles, negation; and culture and general background information. Methods of instruction include lecture, discussion, exercises, and examination.

Credit Recommendation: In the lower division baccalaureate/associate degree category, 2 semester hours in Introductory Japanese (6/88) (8/93).

Introductory Japanese II (EJAPN 152)

Location: Washington, DC.

Length: 30 hours (10 weeks).

Dates: January 1985-Present.

Objective: To introduce the student to katakana and 50-75 kanji.

Learning Outcome: Upon successful completion of this course, the student will be able to read and write hiragana and katakana; recognize 50-75 kanji; write 25-50 kanji; use and understand simple verbal sentences, including commands and continuatives; know verbs of giving and receiving; and use and understand simple noun modification.

Instruction: Major topics covered in the course are katakana; 50-75 kanji; simple verbal sentences; and verbal gerunds. Methods of instruction include lecture, discussion, exercises, and examinations.

Credit Recommendation: In the lower division baccalaureate/associate degree category, 2 semester hours in Introductory Japanese (6/88) (8/93).

Introductory Japanese III (EJAPN 153)

Location: Washington, DC.

Length: 30 hours (10 weeks).

Dates: April 1985-Present.

Objective: To introduce the student to an additional 75 kanji and read a simple children's story.

Learning Outcome: Upon successful completion of this course, the student will be able to use compound sentences and noun clause modifiers; handle permission and prohibition and potential expressions;

use direct-style verbal forms in discourse; read simple passages written in Japanese; and write 150 kanji.

Instruction: Major topics covered in the course are noun clause modification; potential expressions; "because" expressions, expressions of intention and probability; direct-style verbal forms; and 75 kanji. Methods of instruction include lecture, discussion, exercise, extra-curricular activities, and examination.

Credit Recommendation: In the lower division baccalaureate/associate degree category, 2 semester hours in Introductory Japanese (6/88) (8/93).

LANGUAGES/KOREAN

Conversational Korean I (EKORN 110)

Location: Washington, DC.

Length: 30 hours (10 weeks).

Dates: September 1992-Present.

Objective: To provide the student with a rudimentary introduction to spoken Korean and to the Korean alphabet.

Learning Outcome: Upon successful completion of this course, the student will be able to use approximately 50 useful Korean expressions and phrases; form simple copula and verbal sentences; write the letters of the Korean alphabet; and encode simple words and phrases in Korean.

Instruction: Major topics covered in the course are the sound system of Korean; the orthographic principles of written Korean; the structure of simple sentences (verb inflection, particle use, etc.); the cultural and social-linguistic factors and speech styles; and general background information on Korea. Methods of instruction include lecture, drill, audiovisual aids, and examinations.

Credit Recommendation: In the lower division baccalaureate/associate degree category, 2 semester hours in Introductory Korean (9/93).

Conversational Korean II (EKORN 111)

Location: Washington, DC.

Length: 30 hours (10 weeks).

Dates: January 1992-Present.

Objective: To improve student pronunciation and understanding of basic Korean grammar, useful expressions, and the Korean alphabet.

Learning Outcome: Upon successful completion of this course, the student will be able to use approximately 100 useful Korean expressions and phrases; distinguish between positive and negative verbal forms; use a few familiar and polite verbal and nominal forms; and recognize readily sounds and combinations of sounds associated with the letters of the Korean alphabet.

Instruction: Major topics covered in the course are verbal inflection; phrase particles, numbers, and noun modifiers; alphabet practice; and additional information about Korea. Methods of instruction include lecture, drill and examinations.

Credit Recommendation: In the lower division baccalaureate/associate degree category, 2 semester hours in Introductory Korean (9/93).

Conversational Korean III (EKORN 112)

Location: Washington, DC.

Length: 30 hours (10 weeks).

Dates: April 1993-Present.

Objective: To further improve student pronunciation and understanding of basic Korean grammar and useful expressions, as well as to read and write longer phrases and some short sentences.

Learning Outcome: Upon successful completion of this course, the student will be able to use approximately 150 useful Korean expressions and phrases; understand and use some verbal inflection marking tense; use imperatives and declarative sentences; link simple sentences into more complex expressions; and recognize and write additional simple sentences using the Korean alphabet.

Instruction: Major topics covered in the course are verbal tense marking, conjunctions and verbal connectives, complex expressions combining verbal forms, time words and their use, and further background and cultural information. Methods of instruction include lecture, drill, and examinations.

Credit Recommendation: In the lower division baccalaureate/associate degree category, 2 semester hours in Introductory Korean (9/93).

LANGUAGES/LATIN

Introductory Latin I (ELATN151)

Location: Washington, DC.

Length: 30 hours (10 weeks).

Dates: September 1985-Present.

Objective: To provide the student with an ability to pronounce, read, and translate Latin at an elementary level; emphasis is placed on vocabulary and grammar skills for the student who is interested in studying Latin literature or enriching their knowledge of English and European languages.

Learning Outcome: Upon successful completion of this course, the student will be able to read basic texts and understand essential grammar and vocabulary; and have an expanded English vocabulary from the study of Latin derivatives, and an awakened interest in the Classical tradition.

Instruction: Major topics covered in the course are basic grammatical structure; vocabulary and word order; literary texts based on mythology; and political and historical readings. Methods of instruction include lecture and discussion; translation exercises; pronunciation practice; and weekly tests based on learned vocabulary and grammar skills.

Credit Recommendation: In the lower division baccalaureate/associate degree category, 2 semester hours in Classics or Humanities (8/93).

Introductory Latin II (ELATN 152)

Location: Washington, DC.

Length: 30 hours (10 weeks).

Dates: January 1986-Present.

Objective: To help improve and expand a beginner's ability to pronounce, read, and translate the language used in literary, political and historical texts; emphasis is placed on vocabulary development and grammar.

Learning Outcome: Upon successful completion of this course, the student will be able to read texts that are syntactically more complex; have a greater knowledge of the grammar and an expanded vocabulary; and have gained practice translating literary texts.

Instruction: Major topics covered in the course are basic grammatical structures to include additional declensions and passive voice; literary texts based mythology; and political and historical readings. Methods of instruction include lecture, discussion, translation exercises, pronunciation practice, and weekly tests based on learned vocabulary and grammar skills.

Credit Recommendation: In the lower division baccalaureate/associate degree category, 2 semester hours in Classics or Humanities (8/93).

Introductory Latin III (ELATN 153)

Location: Washington, DC.

Length: 30 hours (10 weeks).

Dates: April 1987-Present.

Objective: To continue to improve the beginning student's knowledge of the language and to further enhance the student's ability to pronounce, read, and translate literary, political, and historical texts; emphasis is placed upon vocabulary development and grammar.

Learning Outcome: Upon successful completion of this course, the student will have an overall knowledge of how the language is structured; an expanded vocabulary to read and perform on-sight translations; further developed English vocabulary derived from Latin; and possess a sounder appreciation and understanding of the Latin literary tradition.

Instruction: Major topics covered in the course are complex grammar items to include the subjunctive; advanced vocabulary; and readings from classical medieval literature. Methods of instruction include lecture, discussion, translation exercises, pronunciation practice, and weekly tests based on learned vocabulary and grammar skills.

Credit Recommendation: In the lower division baccalaureate/associate degree category, 2 semester hours in Classics or Humanities (8/93).

LANGUAGES/LITHUANIAN

Conversational Lithuanian I (ELITH110)

Location: Washington, DC.

Length: 30 hours (10 weeks).

Dates: April 1990-Present.

Objective: To introduce the student to sound system, basic grammatical structure of Lithuanian, and initiate the development of speaking, listening, reading, and writing skills.

Learning Outcome: Upon successful completion of this course, the student will be able to converse in the present tense using nominative, accusative, locative, and vocative cases of basic first, second, and third declension nouns.

Instruction: Major topics covered in the course are alphabet; sound system; basic grammatical structure of Lithuanian including four noun cases, verb conjugation, numbers, singular and plural, first and last names, cities, profession, and telling time; and culture and history of Lithuania (incorporated in textbook). Methods of instruction include lecture, discussion, and oral, role playing, teacher-led conversations, free conversation, written exercises, and examinations.

Credit Recommendation: In the lower division baccalaureate/associate degree category, 2 semester hours in Conversational Lithuanian I (8/93).

Conversational Lithuanian II (ELITH111)

Location: Washington, DC.

Length: 30 hours (10 weeks).

Dates: September 1990-Present.

Objective: To continue to introduce the student to grammatical structure including all seven noun cases, the present, past, and future verb tenses, expand basic vocabulary; and improve their speaking, listening comprehension, and writing skills.

Learning Outcome: Upon successful completion of this course, the student will be able to carry on a simple conversation in Lithuanian using all seven noun cases and present, past, and future verb tenses.

Instruction: Major topics covered in the course are all noun cases, present, past, and future verb tenses; time expression; and culture and history of Lithuania (incorporated in textbook). Methods of instruction include lecture; discussion; and oral, role playing, teacher-led conversations, free conversation, written exercises, and examinations.

Credit Recommendation: In the lower division baccalaureate/associate degree category, 2 semester hours in Conversational Lithuanian II (8/93).

Conversational Lithuanian III (ELITH 112)

Location: Washington, DC.

Length: 30 hours (10 weeks).

Dates: January 1991-Present.

Objective: To continue to introduce the student to grammatical structure, expansion of vocabulary, and improved mastery of speaking, listening, comprehension, and writing skills.

Learning Outcome: Upon successful completion of this course, the student will be able to carry on a simple conversation in Lithuanian using all seven noun cases and verb tenses; and demonstrate improved pronuniciation, listening, and writing skills and expanded vocabulary.

Instruction: Major topics covered in the course are all noun cases; fourth and fifth declension nouns; verb tenses; imperatives; reflexive verbs; cardinal and ordinal numbers; adjectives; and culture and history in Lithuania (incorporated in textbook). Methods of instruction include lecture, discussion; and oral, role playing, teacher-led conversations, free conversation, classwork; oral quizzes; and oral report; and written homework.

Credit Recommendation: In the lower division baccalaureate/associate degree category, 2 semester hours in Conversational Lithuanian III (8/93).

LANGUAGES/POLISH

Introductory Polish I (EPOLH151)

Location: Washington, DC.

Length: 30 hours (10 weeks).

Dates: September 1984-Present.

Objective: To provide the beginning student with basic elements of Polish grammar and to develop elementary level skills in reading, speaking, writing, and comprehending Polish; and to introduce student to Polish culture.

Learning Outcome: Upon successful completion of this course, the student will be able to give basic personal information; make requests; get information; speak about specific familiar topics; understand basic concepts of Polish grammar; pronounce words with a fair degree of accuracy; read selected everyday materials for gist; and write simple sentences.

Instruction: Major topics covered in the course are basic vocabulary; alphabet; sound system; introduction to grammar, including noun gender and cases, adjectives, verb system, numbers and time expressions; Polish culture; social context of everyday Polish; vocabulary of advertisements in newspapers; and most common expressions. Methods of instruction include lecture, discussion, classroom exercises involving oral and written work, dictations, assigned readings, video segments on Poland; mid-term and final exams; instructor uses Polish to address students, give instructions, and speak on simple topics; and uses English to introduce and explain grammar.

Credit Recommendation: In the lower division baccalaureate/associate degree category, 2 semester hours in Introductory Polish I (8/93).

Introductory Polish II (EPOLH152)

Location: Washington, DC.

Length: 30 hours (10 weeks).

Dates: January 1985-Present.

Objective: To develop further the student's knowledge and mastery of basic grammar and to broaden familiarity with and appreciation of Polish culture.

Learning Outcome: Upon successful completion of this course, the student will be able to participate in a conversation related to everyday topics as well as talk about their jobs, hobbies, and discuss familiar topics; understand basic concepts of Polish grammar covered in course; read newspaper articles for gist; increase familiarity with Polish culture; and continue to enlarge vocabulary and knowledge of common expressions.

Instruction: Major topics covered in the course are continuation of study of verb system, noun cases, and numbers; study of adjectives, adverbs, and comparatives; pronunciation; everyday topics from Polish culture; common expressions; and reading authentic materials. Methods of instruction include lecture, discussion, classroom exercises involving oral and written work, dictations, songs, assigned readings, videotape, a final class presentation, midterm and final exam; instructor uses Polish to address students, give instructions and speak in everyday topics; and uses English to introduce and explain grammar.

Credit Recommendation: In the lower division baccalaureate/associate degree category, 2 semester hours in Introductory Polish II (8/93).

Introductory Polish III (EPOLH153)

Location: Washington, DC.

Length: 30 hours (10 weeks).

Dates: April 1987-Present.

Objective: To complete the student's survey of Polish grammar begun in EPOL 151/152 and to develop further mastery of elementary speaking, reading, and writing skills.

Learning Outcome: Upon successful completion of this course, the student will be able to converse in Polish on elementary level; read simple texts in Polish; comprehend spoken Polish in a general way; and manipulate basic grammatical structures satisfactorily.

Instruction: Major topics covered in the course are continuation of study of grammatical structure of Polish, including noun cases, verbs of motion; continuation of developing conversation skills; and further introduction of topics related to Polish culture and daily life and associated vocabulary. Methods of instruction include lecture, discussion, oral and written work, videotaped segments of Polish TV news programs, classroom exercises, daily videotapes presenting Polish culture and society, newspaper articles, and lectures conducted in Polish only, with some explanation of grammar points in English.

Credit Recommendation: In the lower division baccalaureate/associate degree category, 2 semester hours in Introductory Polish III (8/93).

LANGUAGES/PORTUGUESE

Intermediate Portuguese I (EPORT 210)

Location: Washington, DC.

Length: 30 hours (10 weeks).

Dates: *Version 1:* January 1980-December 1994; *Version 2:* January 1995-Present.

Objective: *Version 1:* To enhance the student's fluency in oral and written use of the Portuguese language. *Version 2:* To enhance and further apply new modes of grammar topics; talk at length on the phone; and read newspapers, short stories, and chronicles by renowned Brazilian contemporary authors.

Learning Outcome: *Version 1:* Upon successful completion of the course, the student will be able to conduct a fluent conversation in Portuguese using all verb tenses; write short compositions in Portuguese; discuss current topics of interest reported in the Brazilian press; and summarize Portuguese newspaper and magazine articles. *Version 2:* Upon successful completion of the course, the student will be able to write lengthy compositions and speak fluently on any topic about urban life; read and understand complex texts; and understand elliptic forms usually appearing in poetry and folk songs.

Instruction: *Version 1:* Major topics covered in the course are a review of vocabulary, grammar, and idiomatic expressions, aspects of Brazilian history, prepositions "a," "para," and "pos," use of "presente composts," and reflexive pronouns. Methods of instruction include texts, audiotapes, visual aids, and examinations. *Version 2:* Major topics covered in the course are written assignments, communication skills using idiomatic expressions, irregular and less used verbs, command forms, past and future of the subjunctive tense, short stories and chronicles, compound tenses, talks on the phone, indirect speech, and the passive voice. Methods of instruction include lecture, discussion, and classroom exercises.

Credit Recommendation: *Versions 1 and 2:* In the lower division baccalaureate/associate degree category, 2 semester hours in Intermediate Portuguese I (1/90) (1/95).

Introductory Portuguese I (EPORT 151)

Location: Washington, DC.

Length: 30 hours (10 weeks).

Dates: *Version 1:* January 1980-December 1994; *Version 2:* January 1995-Present.

Objective: *Version 1:* To provide the student with the use of the Portuguese language by speaking and writing simple sentences that express common needs in everyday life. *Version 2:* To introduce students to the basic grammatical structure of Portuguese; provide them with basic skills (listening, speaking, reading, and writing) used in Brazil; and teach them some Brazilian cultural traits.

Learning Outcome: *Version 1:* Upon successful completion of the course, the student will be able to identify basic structural patterns of grammar; participate in short dialogues or conversations; recognize time, numbers, and days of the week; and describe some aspects of Brazilian culture. *Version 2:* Upon successful completion of the course, the student will be able to interact in simple conversation, using short sentences, related to everyday situations in an urban environment.

Instruction: *Version 1:* Major topics covered in the course are phonetics, introduction to grammar, basic sentence patterns, basic vocabulary, oral comprehension, and aspects of Brazilian culture. Methods of instruction include texts, audiotapes, visual aids, and examinations. *Version 2:* Major topics covered in the course are present and past tenses of most frequently used indicative verbs ending in -ar, -er, and -ir; some irregular verbs; the possessives; specific expressions with verbs ir, estar, and precisar; prepositions perto de, longe de, etras, etc.; means of transportation; plural forms; and the Brazilian Carnival and food. Methods of instruction include lecture, discussion, and classroom exercises.

Credit Recommendation: *Versions 1 and 2:* In the lower division baccalaureate/associate degree category, 2 semester hours in Introductory Portuguese I (1/90) (1/95).

Introductory Portuguese II (EPORT 152)

Location: Washington, DC.

Length: 30 hours (10 weeks).

Dates: *Version 1:* January 1980-January 1995; *Version 2:* February 1995-Present.

Objective: *Version 1:* To provide the student with use of compound sentences in the Portuguese language in spoken and written communications. *Version 2:* To increase vocabulary and oral competency; to teach students to use more complex grammatical structures; and to deepen their knowledge of some aspects of Brazilian culture.

Learning Outcome: *Version 1:* Upon successful completion of the course, the student will be able to use regular verbs with "ar" and "er" endings in independent sentences; use present, past, future, imperfect, and gerund tenses; know degrees of comparison; and describe more complicated aspects of Brazilian culture. *Version 2:* Upon successful completion of the course, the student will be able to interact in a conversation on subjects related to simple, everyday activities in a city; exchange ideas on simple aspects of Brazilian urban culture; use expressions to indicate the hour; identify colors and days of the week; and talk about personal activities using verbs in the past tense.

Instruction: *Version 1:* Major topics covered in the course are phonetics (second stage) auxiliary verbs, idiomatic expressions, colors, the verbs "saber," "querer," "dizer," and "ver," demonstrative pronouns, and prepositions "em" and "de." Methods of instruction include texts, audiotapes, visual aids, and examinations. *Version 2:* Major topics covered in the course are present and past (perfect and imperfect) tenses of regular and irregular verbs (querer, poer, ver, ser, estar por, dizer, etc.); numbers; colors; hours and days of the week; differences of usage between formal and informal Portuguese; and some aspects of Brazilian culture. Methods of instruction include lecture, discussion, classroom exercises, and audio/visual material.

Credit Recommendation: *Versions 1 and 2:* In the lower division baccalaureate/associate degree category, 2 semester hours in Introductory Portuguese II (1/90) (1/95).

Introductory Portuguese III (EPORT 153)

Location: Washington, DC.

Length: 30 hours (10 weeks).

Dates: *Version 1:* January 1980-December 1994; *Version 2:* January 1995-Present.

Objective: *Version 1:* To provide the student with use of more complex structural patterns of the Portuguese language in both oral and written communications. *Version 2:* To help students understand, speak, read, and write increasingly complex Portuguese structure; to teach students to read longer articles and narratives; and to write compositions on topics presented in class.

Learning Outcome: *Version 1:* Upon successful completion of the course, the student will be able to understand short articles in Portuguese language publications; hold a conversation in Portuguese at a more sophisticated level; and demonstrate understanding of oral and written Portuguese communications. *Version 2:* Upon successful completion of the course, the student will be able to use the future and the present subjunctive tenses in a variety of situations; read long texts and speak at length about the text; apply, in writing, more sophisticated vocabulary; and understand more fully special traits of Brazilian culture.

Instruction: *Version 1:* Major topics covered in the course are relative pronouns, the verbs "vir," "ver," "fazer," "dar," and verbs with "ir" endings, present subjunctive, selected adverbs, and the conditional tense. Methods of instruction include texts, audiotapes, visual aids, and examinations. *Version 2:* Major topics covered in the course are future of regular and irregular verbs; use of indefinite such as 'algum'; uses of diminutive and affectionate language; ordinal numbers; past participle of main verbs; verbs and nouns that are interrelated; the present subjunctive; adverbs; typical expressions; and narratives on Brazilian culture, poetry, and folk songs. Methods of instruction include lecture, discussion, and classroom exercises.

Credit Recommendation: *Versions 1 and 2:* In the lower division baccalaureate/associate degree category, 2 semester hours in Introductory Portuguese III (1/90) (1/95).

LANGUAGES/RUSSIAN

Advanced Conversation, Reading and Composition in Russian (ERUSS254)

Location: Washington, DC.

Length: 30 hours (10 weeks).

Dates: September 1991-Present.

Objective: To provide the student with development in analytical skills and ability to recognize stylistic and grammatical structures in Russian literary and journalistic texts.

Learning Outcome: Upon successful completion of this course, the student will be able to analyze various styles of writing with full comprehension of vocabulary and idiomatic expression; express interpretive ideas effectively in Russian, orally and in writing; and discuss and analyze current events through the use of Russian newspapers.

Instruction: Major topics covered in the course are reading and discussion of contemporary texts; and style and character of literary texts. Methods of instruction include written homework, oral presentations, quizzes, translations of English into Russian and Russian into English, discussion, and examinations.

Credit Recommendation: In the upper division baccalaureate degree category, 2 semester hours in Russian (8/93).

Advanced Russian Grammar (ERUSS253)

Location: Washington, DC.

Length: 30 hours (10 weeks).

Dates: January 1993-Present.

Objective: To provide the student with a review of Russian grammar, and increase proficiency in spoken Russian through reading and discussion of contemporary texts dealing with Russian life and culture.

Learning Outcome: Upon successful completion of this course, the student will be able to use effectively all elements of basic Russian grammar; and to read, discuss, and write about various aspects of Russian life and culture.

Instruction: Major topics covered in the course are general grammar review; discussion of typical daily life situations in Russia; and readings, and discussion on Russian culture. Methods of instruction include lecture, discussions, grammar drills and exercises, role playing, dictation, compositions (homework), quizzes, and examinations.

Credit Recommendation: In the upper division baccalaureate degree category, 2 semester hours in Russian (8/93).

Advanced Russian I (ERUSS250)

Location: Washington, DC.

Length: 30 hours (10 weeks).

Dates: April 1985-Present.

Objective: To provide the student with further development of the knowledge and mastery of Russian grammar through reading, speaking, and writing about Russian current events and Russian culture, in Russian.

Learning Outcome: Upon successful completion of this course, the student will be able to communicate orally and in writing on a higher proficiency level; comprehend lectures and discussions in Russian; and read newspaper articles and material of similar difficulty with ease.

Instruction: Major topics covered in the course are grammar review and analysis; reading journalistic, popular, and literary texts; and discussion and conversation in Russian. Methods of instruction include lecture, discussion, question-answer format, use of newspapers, videos, quizzes, tests, compositions, and grammar exercises.

Credit Recommendation: In the lower division baccalaureate/associate degree category, 2 semester hours in Russian (8/93).

Advanced Russian II (ERUSS251)

Location: Washington, DC.

Length: 30 hours (10 weeks).

Dates: January 1993-Present.

Objective: To provide the student with continued development of knowledge and mastery of Russian grammar through reading, speaking, and writing about Russian current events and Russian culture, in Russian.

Learning Outcome: Upon successful completion of this course, the student will be able to reproduce simple and complex grammatical structures orally and in writing; read relatively difficult texts with greater proficiency; and converse and comprehend spoken Russian on a higher level of proficiency.

Instruction: Major topics covered in the course are advanced grammar, moods, aspects, adverbs, verbal adverb; aspects of Russian culture; and Russian current events (TV news). Methods of instruction include grammar exercises, translations and compositions, dictations, weekly quizzes, role playing, homework, lecture, and discussion.

Credit Recommendation: In the lower division baccalaureate/associate degree category, 2 semester hours in Russian (8/93).

Advanced Russian III (ERUSS252)

Location: Washington, DC.

Length: 30 hours (10 weeks).

Dates: January 1993-Present.

Objective: To expand the student's vocabulary and increase proficiency in use of standard and idiomatic Russian orally and in writing; and provide an overview of Russian verb conjugation.

Learning Outcome: Upon successful completion of this course, the student will be able to read and comprehend contemporary Russian texts with high level of understanding; enhance Russian conversation through increased use of idiomatic expressions; and translate proficiently from Russian to English and English to Russian.

Instruction: Major topics covered in the course are novel and movie "The Twelve Chairs", basis of discussion; continuation of grammar review with emphasis on verb conjugation; and idiomatic expressions. Methods of instruction include discussion, oral and written presentations, quizzes, exams, homework, print, and video materials.

Credit Recommendation: In the lower division baccalaureate/associate degree category, 2 semester hours in Russian (8/93).

Intermediate Russian I (ERUSS 210)

Location: Washington, DC.

Length: 30 hours (10 weeks).

Dates: January 1984-Present.

Objective: To provide the student with vocabulary expansion through the study of word formation and usage and development of cultural awareness through reading and commentary; emphasis is on grammatical control.

Learning Outcome: Upon successful completion of this course, the student will be able to show greater grammatical accuracy in basic constructions; initiate and sustain a conversational exchange on familiar topics; write short compositions; and translate simple texts.

Instruction: Major topics covered in the course are grammar; case usage with emphasis on genitive and instrumental (nouns, adjectives, pronouns, numerals); verbs (reflexive, motion, and conditional constructions); impersonal constructions; time expressions; and reading and translation. Methods of instruction include lecture, discussion, oral and written drills.

Credit Recommendation: In the lower division baccalaureate/associate degree category, 2 semester hours in Russian (6/88) (8/93).

Intermediate Russian II (ERUSS211)

Location: Washington, DC.

Length: 30 hours (10 weeks).

Dates: January 1985-Present.

Objective: To provide the student with further development of basic vocabulary; and to increase reading and writing proficiency in Russian.

Learning Outcome: Upon successful completion of this course, the student will be able to use effectively all basic and some more complex grammatical structures; to conduct simple conversations in Russian; to read standard moderately difficult texts in Russian; and to reproduce written statements with grammatical and idiomatic accuracy.

Instruction: Major topics covered in the course are continuation of basic grammar; further development of reading and writing skills; and basic conversational Russian. Methods of instruction include lecture, discussion, classroom exercises, role playing, oral presentations, audio-video supplements, newspaper articles, and frequent quizzes.

Credit Recommendation: In the lower division baccalaureate/associate degree category, 2 semester hours in Russian (8/93).

Intermediate Russian III (ERUSS212)

Location: Washington, DC.

Length: 30 hours (10 weeks).

Dates: April 1987-Present.

Objective: To provide the student with a completion of basic grammar; and further development and improvement of proficiency in speaking, reading, writing, and understanding Russian.

Learning Outcome: Upon successful completion of this course, the student will be able to demonstrate significant improvement of oral and written skills; demonstrate proficiency in reading Russian and translating from English to Russian, and Russian to English.

Instruction: Major topics covered in the course are general grammar review; exposure to more complex grammatical structures; exposure to journalistic Russian style and vocabulary; and oral expression. Methods of instruction include lecture, discussion, written and oral examinations, homework, grammar exercises, and translations.

Credit Recommendation: In the lower division baccalaureate/associate degree category, 2 semester hours in Russian (8/93).

Introductory Russian I (ERUSS 151)

Location: Washington, DC.

Length: 30 hours (10 weeks).

Dates: January 1984-Present.

Objective: To introduce the student to the sound and writing systems of contemporary Russian; and emphasis on the development of the basic skills—listening, speaking, reading, and writing.

Learning Outcome: Upon successful completion of this course, the student will be able to ask and respond to simple questions orally and in writing about his or herself and familiar topics and understand simple phrases in a printed text.

Instruction: Major topics covered in the course are sound system (pronunciation and intonation); writing system (printed and cursive); and grammar—verb conjugation, case system (prepositional-singular, nominative-singular and plural, accusative-singular); and motion verbs, possessive adjectives, and telling time. Methods of instruction include oral and written drills, lecture, and discussion.

Credit Recommendation: In the lower division baccalaureate/associate degree category, 2 semester hours in Russian (6/88) (8/93).

Introductory Russian II (ERUSS152)

Location: Washington, DC.

Length: 30 hours (10 weeks).

Dates: January 1984-Present.

Objective: To continue to introduce the student to grammatical structure and further development in listening, speaking, reading, and writing of contemporary Russian.

Learning Outcome: Upon successful completion of this course, the student will be able to carry on simple conversation on familiar topics; have conceptual understanding of verbal aspects and tenses as well as noun cases; and read simple narrative.

Instruction: Major topics covered in the course are grammatical case (accusative, dative, and genitive) of nouns, adjectives, and pronouns; verbs (past and future tenses, concept of aspect, imperatives); and time expressions. Methods of instruction include lecture, discussion, and oral and written drills.

Credit Recommendation: In the lower division baccalaureate/associate degree category, 2 semester hours in Russian (6/88) (8/93).

Introductory Russian III (ERUSS153)

Location: Washington, DC.

Length: 30 hours (10 weeks).

Dates: January 1984-Present.

Objective: To provide the student with continued instruction in Russian grammar as well as further improvement in speaking, understanding, reading, and writing.

Learning Outcome: Upon successful completion of this course, the student will be able to use the dative and genitive cases of nouns; understand and use the prepositional and dative case of personal pronouns and special modifiers; understand and use the prepositional case of adjective endings in the singular; understand and use the accusative case of relative adjectives; have a comfortable use of the imperfective future and imperative forms; and understand to a greater extent verb aspects and multidirectional "going" verbs.

Instruction: Major topics covered in the course are the introduction to Russian grammar and provide further improvement in speaking and understanding with increased emphasis on reading and writing; and designed for beginners who have had an extensive formal or information introduction to Russian. Methods of instruction include lecture, discussion, and oral and written drills.

Credit Recommendation: In the lower division baccalaureate/associate degree category, 2 semester hours in Russian (6/88) (8/93). *Prerequisite:* Introductory Russian I (ERUSS152) or equivalent.

Russian Business Culture (ERUSS300)

Location: Washington, DC.

Length: 30 hours (10 weeks).

Dates: September 1992-Present.

Objective: To acquaint the student with current situation in economic and business life in Russia.

Learning Outcome: Upon successful completion of this course, the student will be able to find and utilize business opportunities in Russia; use "survival" language skills in Russian; and know traits of Socialist Economics still prevailing in today's Russia and characteristics of New Reform Government.

Instruction: Major topics covered in the course are business culture in Russia and Russian Business Law; current events in Russian from economic perspective; and "survival" Russian for business travelers. Methods of instruction include lecture, analysis, discussion, and a research paper.

Credit Recommendation: In the upper division baccalaureate or graduate degree category, 2 semester hours in Business (8/93).

Russian for Reading Knowledge (ERUSS115)

Location: Washington, DC.

Length: 30 hours (10 weeks).

Dates: January 1993-Present.

Objective: To prepare the student to read Russian.

Learning Outcome: Upon successful completion of this course, the student will be able to read standard literary or journalistic Russian texts with aid of dictionary; recognize basic grammatical structures; and recognize basic grammatical forms and differentiate by number and gender.

Instruction: Major topics covered in the course are outline of Russian grammar and sentence structure; and use of the dictionary to decipher Russian texts. Methods of instruction include reading Russian texts, discussion in English of Russian reading selections, and questions-answer format.

Credit Recommendation: In the lower division baccalaureate/associate degree category, 2 semester hours in Russian (8/93).

LANGUAGES/SERBO-CROATIAN

Conversational Serbian and Croatian I (ESERB110) (Formerly Conversational Serbo-Croatian I)

Location: Washington, DC.

Length: 30 hours (10 weeks).

Dates: September 1992-Present.

Objective: To introduce the student to the sound and writing systems of contemporary Serbo-Croatian (including Cryllic alphabet for Serbian and Latin Alphabet for Croatian) and the basics of Serbo-Croatian grammar and conversation; emphasis on developing reading, speaking, listening, and writing skills.

Learning Outcome: Upon successful completion of this course, the student will be able to read both the cryllic and Latin alphabets, translate and read simple text, ask and respond to simple questions on familiar topics using vocabulary and expressions from everyday conversation; and recognize basic grammatical forms and form simple sentences.

Instruction: Major topics covered in the course are daily, as well as travel and business vocabulary; phrases and expressions in everyday conversation in Serbian and Croatian; Cryllic and Latin alphabets, pronunciation and intonation patterns and differences between the various Serbo-Croatian dialects; cultures of the various regions, and observations on recent history of the various regions. Methods of instruction include lecture, discussion, aural, oral, written classroom exercises, and examinations.

Credit Recommendation: In the lower division baccalaureate/associate degree category, 2 semester hours in Conversational Serbian and Croatian I (8/93).

Conversational Serbian and Croatian II (ESERB111) (Formerly Conversational Serbo-Croatian II)

Location: Washington, DC.
Length: 30 hours (10 weeks).
Dates: April 1993-Present.
Objective: To help the student continue introduction to vocabulary and basis of Serbo-Croatian grammar and conversation.
Learning Outcome: Upon successful completion of this course, the student will be able to achieve improved command of reading, writing, and conversational skills in Serbo-Croatian; and will gain a better understanding of the differences between the two languages.
Instruction: Major topics covered in the course are focusing upon increasing vocabulary; improving reading, writing, and conversational skills through further study of Serbo-Croatian grammar with continued examination of differences between the two languages; and continue the study of the cultures and political and economic affairs of the various regions. Methods of instruction include lecture, discussion, aural, oral, and written classroom exercises, and examinations.
Credit Recommendation: In the lower division baccalaureate/associate degree category, 2 semester hours in Conversational Serbian and Croatian II (8/93).

LANGUAGES/SIGN LANGUAGE

Introduction to American Sign Language I (ESIGN200)

Location: Washington, DC.
Length: 30 hours (10 weeks).
Dates: January 1993-Present.
Objective: To provide the student with an introduction to the basics of American Sign Languages (ASL); and to present information about Deaf culture so that students are more culturally sensitive and to understand the Deaf community.
Learning Outcome: Upon successful completion of this course, the student will be able to demonstrate ability to use ASL introduced in the course; and develop an awareness of Deaf culture.
Instruction: Major topics covered in the course are exchanging personal information; talking about surroundings; telling where you live; family; basic numbers; giving directions; yes/no questions; wh-questions; and other basic statements. Methods of instruction include classroom exercises, videotapes, classroom activities, and examinations.
Credit Recommendation: In the lower division baccalaureate/associate degree category, 2 semester hours in Basic American Sign Language (ASL) (8/93).

Introduction to American Sign Language II (ESIGN201)

Location: Washington, DC.
Length: 30 hours (10 weeks).
Dates: January 1993-Present.
Objective: To continue to provide the student with an introduction to the basics of American Sign Language (ASL); to present information about Deaf culture so that students are more culturally sensitive; and understand the Deaf community.
Learning Outcome: Upon successful completion of this course, the student will be able to demonstrate ability to use ASL introduced in the course; have improved comprehension in ASL; and demonstrate an increase in awareness of Deaf culture.
Instruction: Major topics covered in the course are describing others, making requests; attributing qualities to others; talking about routines; clock numbers; and other communicative skills. Methods of instruction include classroom exercises, videotapes, classroom activities, and examinations.
Credit Recommendation: In the lower division baccalaureate/associate degree category, 2 semester hours in Basic American Sign Language (ASL) (8/93).

Introduction to American Sign Language III (ESIGN202)

Location: Washington, DC.
Length: 30 hours (10 weeks).
Dates: January 1993-Present.
Objective: To broaden the basic knowledge of and skill in using American Sign Language (ASL).
Learning Outcome: Upon successful completion of this course, the student will be able to exhibit further awareness of deaf culture; demonstrate improved comprehension in ASL; and demonstrate increased knowledge about Deaf culture.
Instruction: Major topics covered in the course are describing others; making requests; attributing qualities to others; talking about routines; clock numbers; and other communicative skills. Methods of instruction include classroom exercises, videotapes, classroom activities, and examinations.
Credit Recommendation: In the lower division baccalaureate/associate degree category, 2 semester hours in Basic American Sign Language (ASL) (8/93).

LANGUAGES/SPANISH

Advanced Spanish Grammar (ESPAN253)

Location: Washington, DC.
Length: 30 hours (10 weeks).
Dates: April 1993-Present.
Objective: To provide the student with advanced studies in Spanish grammar within the framework of modern grammatical theory.
Learning Outcome: Upon successful completion of this course, the student will be able to demonstrate, through written compositions, a high degree of accuracy and flexibility in Spanish.
Instruction: Major topics covered in the course are review of Spanish language grammatical structures with emphasis on the most difficult and advanced. Methods of instruction include lecture, discussion, and oral and written classroom exercises.
Credit Recommendation: In the upper division baccalaureate degree category, 2 semester hours in Spanish (8/93).

Advanced Spanish I (ESPAN250)

Location: Washington, DC.
Length: 30 hours (10 weeks).
Dates: September 1984-Present.
Objective: To enable students to read and understand a variety of topics as published in newspapers and periodicals and to increase their oral competence as listeners and speakers.
Learning Outcome: Upon successful completion of this course, the student will be able to read articles at an advanced level of comprehension; to exchange ideas in a conversation involving everyday expressions; and use more advanced vocabulary.
Instruction: Major topics covered in the course are acquisition of advanced vocabulary; review of key points in grammar; applied grammar in readings from different sources on a variety of topics. Methods of instruction include exercises and practice on conversation, videotapes, discussions, and homework on grammar exercises.
Credit Recommendation: In the upper division baccalaureate degree category, 2 semester hours in Spanish (8/93).

Advanced Spanish II (ESPAN251)

Location: Washington, DC.
Length: 30 hours (10 weeks).
Dates: January 1989-Present.

Objective: To increase the student's oral comprehension and improve oral performance.

Learning Outcome: Upon successful completion of this course, the student will be able to speak on subjects ranging from everyday topics to moderate discussions on various themes.

Instruction: Major topics covered in the course are subjects related to articles published in newspapers and periodicals, seen in videotapes, and discussed orally, and emphasis on oral achievement. Methods of instruction include exercises and practice in conversation, videotapes, presentations, and writing of short composition in class or as homework.

Credit Recommendation: In the upper division baccalaureate degree category, 2 semester hours in Spanish (8/93).

Advanced Spanish III (ESPAN252)

Location: Washington, DC.

Length: 30 hours (10 weeks).

Dates: January 1989-Present.

Objective: To enhance the student's aural comprehension and oral performance through extensive reading.

Learning Outcome: Upon successful completion of this course, the student will be able to command advanced vocabulary, and converse on subjects of general interest, based on present day publications (newspapers, and periodicals).

Instruction: Major topics covered in the course are reading of articles on contemporary subjects published in leading periodicals from Spanish America; acquisition of vocabulary pertinent to advanced readings and conversation. Methods of instruction include exercises, practice in conversation, review of major points of grammar, presentations, and writing of short composition in class or as homework.

Credit Recommendation: In the upper division baccalaureate degree category, 2 semester hours in Spanish (8/93).

Conversational Spanish I (ESPAN110)

Location: Washington, DC.

Length: 30 hours (10 weeks).

Dates: January 1984-Present.

Objective: To provide the student with a limited ability to speak and understand Spanish.

Learning Outcome: Upon successful completion of this course, the student will be able to understand spoken Spanish involving limited vocabulary; express basic concepts in Spanish; and understand aspects of contemporary Hispanic cultures.

Instruction: Major topics covered in the course are present indicative verb forms; negative and interrogative sentences; numbers; present progressive; comparison of adjective and adverbs; months and seasons of the year; and direct and indirect object pronouns. Methods of instruction include lecture, discussions, oral classroom exercises, and examinations.

Credit Recommendation: In the lower division baccalaureate/associate degree category, 2 semester hours in Elementary Spanish (8/93).

Conversational Spanish II (ESPAN111)

Location: Washington, DC.

Length: 30 hours (10 weeks).

Dates: September 1984-Present.

Objective: To provide the student with a limited ability to speak and understand Spanish.

Learning Outcome: Upon successful completion of this course, the student will be able to understand spoken Spanish involving limited vocabulary; express basic concepts in Spanish; and understand aspects of contemporary Hispanic cultures.

Instruction: Major topics covered in the course are verb tenses (preterit, imperfect); direct and indirect object pronouns; Por and Para; time expressions with hacer; reflexive and possessive pronouns; and uses of the definite article. Methods of instruction include oral drills, dialogues, simulations, songs, games, and examinations.

Credit Recommendation: In the lower division baccalaureate/associate degree category, 2 semester hours in Elementary Spanish (8/93).

Conversational Spanish III (ESPAN112)

Location: Washington, DC.

Length: 30 hours (10 weeks).

Dates: January 1990-Present.

Objective: To provide the student with a limited ability to speak and understand Spanish.

Learning Outcome: Upon successful completion of this course, the student will be able to understand spoken Spanish involving limited vocabulary; express basic concepts in Spanish; and understand aspects of contemporary Hispanic cultures.

Instruction: Major topics covered in the course are relative pronouns; subjunctive, command forms; uses of sino and pero; past particle; and past perfect. Methods of instruction include lecture, discussion, oral drills, presentation, and examinations.

Credit Recommendation: In the lower division baccalaureate/associate degree category, 2 semester hours in Elementary Spanish (8/93).

Intensive Spanish I (ESPAN205)

Location: Washington, DC.

Length: 60 hours (5 weeks).

Dates: January 1993-Present.

Objective: To provide the student with an intensive introduction to speaking, reading, and writing Spanish.

Learning Outcome: Upon successful completion of this course, the student will be able to understand spoken Spanish involving vocabulary covered; express basic concepts in Spanish; and understand aspects of contemporary Hispanic cultures.

Instruction: Major topics covered in the course are vocabulary for greetings and courtesy, classroom expressions, family and numbers, colors, dates, clothing, weather, time, food, travelling and health; verb tenses including present, preterit, and imperfect. Methods of instruction include lecture, discussion, oral and written classroom activities, and examinations.

Credit Recommendation: In the lower division baccalaureate/associate degree category, 4 semester hours in Elementary Spanish (8/93).

Intensive Spanish II (ESPAN206)

Location: Washington, DC.

Length: 60 hours (5 weeks).

Dates: January 1993-Present.

Objective: To provide the student with a continued intensive practice in speaking, reading, and writing Spanish.

Learning Outcome: Upon successful completion of this course, the student will be able to understand spoken Spanish involving vocabulary covered; express basic concepts in Spanish; and understand aspects of contemporary Hispanic cultures.

Instruction: Major topics covered in the course are vocabulary related to daily occurrences, running errands, asking for information, renting an apartment, clothing and shopping, dealing with road emergencies, weekend activities; and verb tenses including preterit, imperfect, perfect tenses, future, conditional and all forms of the subjunctive. Methods of instruction include lecture, discussion, oral and written classroom activities, and examinations.

Credit Recommendation: In the lower division baccalaureate/associate degree

category, 4 semester hours in Intermediate Spanish (8/93).

Intermediate Spanish I (ESPAN 210)

Location: Washington, DC.
Length: 30 hours (10 weeks).
Dates: January 1980-Present.
Objective: To provide the student with a review of Spanish grammar and introduction to Hispanic civilization, culture, literature, and art to extend reading, writing, and conversational skills.
Learning Outcome: Upon successful completion of this course, the student will be able to demonstrate appreciation for Hispanic literature and art; and make oral and written presentations about aspects of Hispanic culture.
Instruction: Major topics covered in the course are European and American origins of contemporary Hispanic culture, the role of religion in Hispanic culture, review of selected aspects of Spanish grammar, and readings dealing with themes from both Spain and Latin America. Methods of instruction include lecture, discussion, oral and written reports, and examinations.
Credit Recommendation: In the lower division baccalaureate/associate degree category, 2 semester hours in Intermediate Spanish I (1/90) (1/95).

Intermediate Spanish II (ESPAN 211)

Location: Washington, DC.
Length: 30 hours (10 weeks).
Dates: January 1980-Present.
Objective: To provide the student with further Spanish grammar review and additional topics in Hispanic civilization, culture, literature, and art to extend reading, writing, and conversational skills.
Learning Outcome: Upon successful completion of this course, the student will be able to demonstrate appreciation for Hispanic literature and art and make oral and written presentations about Hispanic culture.
Instruction: Major topics covered in the course are a review of selected aspects of Spanish grammar, socioeconomic and modern historical aspects of Hispanic culture, and selected readings dealing with topics from Spain and Latin America. Methods of instruction include lecture, discussion, oral and written reports, and examinations.
Credit Recommendation: In the lower division baccalaureate/associate degree category, 2 semester hours in Intermediate Spanish II (1/90) (1/95).

Intermediate Spanish III (ESPAN 212)

Location: Washington, DC.
Length: 30 hours (10 weeks).
Dates: January 1980-Present.
Objective: To provide the student with continued Spanish grammar review and acquaintance with more complex topics in Hispanic civilization, culture, literature, and art to further extend reading, writing, and conversational skills.
Learning Outcome: Upon successful completion of this course, the student will be able to demonstrate appreciation of Hispanic literature and art and make oral and written presentations in Spanish, using a more sophisticated level of vocabulary and fluency, on topics about Hispanic culture.
Instruction: Major topics covered in the course are a review of selected aspects of Spanish grammar, the role of Hispanic countries in the contemporary world, and selected readings dealing with topics from Spain and Latin America. Methods of instruction include lecture, discussion, oral and written presentations, and examinations.
Credit Recommendation: In the lower division baccalaureate/associate degree category, 2 semester hours in Intermediate Spanish III (1/90) (1/95).

Introductory Spanish I (ESPAN 151)

Location: Washington, DC.
Length: 30 hours (10 weeks).
Dates: January 1980-Present.
Objective: To enhance the student's understanding, speaking, reading, and writing of limited basic Spanish in the context of contemporary Hispanic culture.
Learning Outcome: Upon successful completion of this course, the student will be able to carry on simple conversations in Spanish; read simple texts in Spanish and deduce meaning of new words from context; express simple ideas written in Spanish; and demonstrate elementary familiarity with cultures of Spanish-speaking countries.
Instruction: Major topics covered in the course are vocabulary for greetings and courtesy, classroom expressions, family, numbers, colors, dates, clothing, weather, time, and food, past tense of regular and irregular verbs, gender and number agreement, comparison, personal pronouns, and the relationship between pronunciation and spelling. Methods of instruction include grammar presentations, group conversation, listening practice, and examinations.
Credit Recommendation: In the lower division baccalaureate/associate degree category, 2 semester hours in Introductory Spanish I (1/90) (1/95).

Introductory Spanish II (ESPAN 152)

Location: Washington, DC.
Length: 30 hours (10 weeks).
Dates: January 1980-Present.
Objective: To enhance the student's understanding, speaking, reading, and writing of basic Spanish in the context of contemporary Hispanic culture.
Learning Outcome: Upon successful completion of this course, the student will be able to converse about travel, home, daily routines, holidays, health, and cars; express likes and dislikes, desires, requests, and feelings; narrate events that occurred in the past; and read more varied texts and express a greater variety of ideas in written Spanish.
Instruction: Major topics covered in the course are vocabulary related to travel and vacations, houses, furniture, daily chores, holidays, emotions, parts of the body, health, cars, and ordinal numbers, object pronouns, present subjunctive, and perfect and imperfect tenses. Methods of instruction include grammar presentations, group conversation, listening practice, and examinations.
Credit Recommendation: In the lower division baccalaureate/associate degree category, 2 semester hours in Introductory Spanish II (1/90) (1/95).

Introductory Spanish III (ESPAN 153)

Location: Washington, DC.
Length: 30 hours (10 weeks).
Dates: January 1980-Present.
Objective: To enhance the student's understanding, speaking, reading, and writing of expanded basic Spanish in the context of contemporary Hispanic culture.
Learning Outcome: Upon successful completion of this course, the student will be able to converse about technology, the environment, entertainment, sports, government and politics, professions, and living and working abroad; express hypothetical situations; read more difficult texts, and express a greater variety of ideas in written Spanish.
Instruction: Major topics covered in the course are vocabulary regarding tech-

nology, the environment, entertainment, sports, government and civic responsibility, money, careers, travel and living abroad, perfect tenses, past subjunctive mood and tense in complex sentences, future tense and the conditional tense. Methods of instruction include grammar presentations, group conversation, listening practice, and examinations.

Credit Recommendation: In the lower division baccalaureate/associate degree category, 2 semester hours in Introductory Spanish III (1/90) (1/95).

Introductory Spanish IV (ESPAN154)

Location: Washington, DC.

Length: 30 hours (10 weeks).

Dates: April 1982-Present.

Objective: To provide the student with continued instruction in Spanish grammar as well as further improvement in speaking, understanding, reading, and writing.

Learning Outcome: Upon successful completion of this course, the student will be able to converse about hobbies, sports, the government and its responsibilities, professions, housing, and traveling; express hypothetical situations; read more difficult texts; and express a greater variety of ideas in written Spanish.

Instruction: Major topics covered in the course are commands; subjunctive; stressed possessives; future tense; conditional tense; uses of prepositions; and Por and Para. Methods of instruction include lecture, discussions, oral drills and exercises, and examinations.

Credit Recommendation: In the lower division baccalaureate/associate degree category, 2 semester hours in Intermediate Spanish (8/93).

Spanish Business Correspondence (ESPAN300)

Location: Washington, DC.

Length: 30 hours (10 weeks).

Dates: September 1989-Present.

Objective: To acquaint the student with general practice and special rules of business terminology in Spanish.

Learning Outcome: Upon successful completion of this course, the student will be able to understand and communicate business needs in the Spanish forma to correspondence by applying the language of contemporary international markets.

Instruction: Major topics covered in the course are business and commercial terminology; writing of letters in the areas of real estate, banking, and advertising; review of main points of grammar, acquisition of specific vocabulary and verb conjugation. Methods of instruction include presentation of "case brief," written compositions and letters, and examination.

Credit Recommendation: In the upper division baccalaureate degree category, 2 semester hours in Spanish (8/93).

Spanish Business Cultures (ESPAN301)

Location: Washington, DC.

Length: 30 hours (10 weeks).

Dates: September 1993-Present.

Objective: To help the student understand written and unwritten guidelines for business interaction in Spanish-speaking countries.

Learning Outcome: Upon successful completion of this course, the student will be able to demonstrate an understanding of the course material through an oral and written analysis of a particular country selected at the beginning of the course. The projects revolve around "risk analysis."

Instruction: Major topics covered in the course are review of geographical and historical analysis of Latin American countries; overview of economics in Latin American and Spain; and examination of international markets and organizations and regional economic blocks including NAFTA, TEFTA, etc. Methods of instruction include project presentation, assignments on reading, and discussion about current events on country of interest.

Credit Recommendation: In the upper division baccalaureate or graduate degree category, 2 semester hours in Business or Latin American Studies (8/93).

Survey of Latin American Literature (ESPAN291)

Location: Washington, DC.

Length: 30 hours (10 weeks).

Dates: January 1989-Present.

Objective: To provide the student with an overview of Spanish American literature from the Colonial to contemporary periods.

Learning Outcome: Upon successful completion of this course, the student will be able to analyze and evaluate literary collections by the most representative authors of the periods covered.

Instruction: Major topics covered in the course are literary trends of Spanish America through representative authors and their works. Methods of instruction include primarily lecture, discussion, and final examination.

Credit Recommendation: In the upper division baccalaureate degree category, 2 semester hours in Spanish/American Literature (8/93).

Survey of Spanish Literature (ESPAN290)

Location: Washington, DC.

Length: 30 hours (10 weeks).

Dates: January 1985-Present.

Objective: To provide the student with an overview of Spanish literature from the Middle Ages to the contemporary period.

Learning Outcome: Upon successful completion of this course, the student will be able to analyze and evaluate literary discourses by the most representative authors of the periods covered.

Instruction: Major topics covered in the course are literary trends of Spain through representative authors and their works. Methods of instruction include lecture, discussion, classroom exercises, and final examination.

Credit Recommendation: In the upper division baccalaureate degree category, 2 semester hours in Survey of Spanish Literature (8/93).

LANGUAGES/SWAHILI

Intermediate Swahili I (ESWAH210)

Location: Washington, DC.

Length: 30 hours (10 weeks).

Dates: January 1988-Present.

Objective: To provide the student with advanced conversational reading and writing skills, expand vocabulary, provide more grammatical structures, and increase student's fluency both orally and in the written form.

Learning Outcome: Upon successful completion of this course, the student will be able to engage in fluent conversation using more grammatical structures; demonstrate greater grammatical accuracy in more complex constructions and a sounder understanding of the target culture; read with noticeable feeling for the language; initiate and sustain a conversational exchange on general subjects taking place in everyday life; write short compositions in Swahili; and be able to discuss current topics of interest with a much sounder understanding of the target culture.

Instruction: Major topics covered in the course are more grammatical structures; various forms of relative pronouns; forms of verbs, causative (-sha/-za), stative (-ka) and reciprocal (-na) reflexive-ji- (verbs with double suffixes the modal meaning of hu-indicating a possibility; the use of verbs of deterrence (e.g. kataza "forbid", zuia "prevent"); more situational applications (e.g. at Football game); and short stories reflecting east African culture which will help prepare the student for more advanced reading material. Methods of instruction include lecture, discussion, classroom exercises, case studies, role playing, problem solving, and examinations.

Credit Recommendation: In the lower division baccalaureate/associate degree category, 2 semester hours in Swahili (8/93).

Introductory Swahili I (ESWAH151)

Location: Washington, DC.

Length: 30 hours (10 weeks).

Dates: September 1987-Present.

Objective: To prepare the student to demonstrate an understanding of the grammatical rules and patterns involved in the Swahili language and develop an elementary vocabulary to be used in simple conversations.

Learning Outcome: Upon successful completion of this course, the student will be able to feel at ease engaging in simple conversation with speakers of Swahili; write simple sentences and read Swahili; have an understanding and perception of Swahili grammatical structure; and have some knowledge of Swahili culture and customs.

Instruction: Major topics covered in the course are simple conversations (e.g., greetings, simple requests, inquiries of health, workplace); basic grammatical structures (e.g. verbal markers na and negative, li, and ta); noun classes (ki-vi, m-mi); simple imperative (sema, rudi, ingia); concordial agreement of various noun classes; verb roots; prefixes, suffixes, sentence patterns; verbs (to have and to be); infinitive verbs; few numbers; and Swahili culture through situational applications (e.g. market scene, kitchen scene, etc.). Methods of instruction include lecture, discussion, classroom exercises, case studies, role playing, problem solving, and examinations.

Credit Recommendation: In the lower division baccalaureate/associate degree category, 2 semester hours in Swahili (8/93).

Introductory Swahili II (ESWAH152)

Location: Washington, DC.

Length: 30 hours (10 weeks).

Dates: January 1988-Present.

Objective: To improve the student's pronunciation of Swahili, familiarize students with more complex grammatical structure and expand vocabulary.

Learning Outcome: Upon successful completion of this course, the student will be able to understand, speak, read, and write moderately complex material with relative accuracy in the context of Swahili culture (current social, political, or economic) events taking place around them.

Instruction: Major topics covered in the course are more grammar structures (e.g. tense marker me- and ka, Hu tense, negative of tense markers me, li and ta); imperative with object prefixes, subjunctives together with their negatives; telling time and age; verbs suffixes (e.g. pikia and pikiwa); object prefixes of various noun classes; numbers, and numerical adjectives, simple math; and more situational applications to expand vocabulary (such as prices of market items and bargaining at the market). Methods of instruction include lecture, discussion, classroom exercises, case studies, role playing, problem solving, and examinations.

Credit Recommendation: In the lower division baccalaureate/associate degree category, 2 semester hours in Swahili (8/93).

Introductory Swahili III (ESWAH153)

Location: Washington, DC.

Length: 30 hours (10 weeks).

Dates: January 1988-Present.

Objective: To help the student understand, speak, read, and write complex Swahili with relative accuracy in the context of East African culture.

Learning Outcome: Upon successful completion of this course, the student will be able to use more complex structures, speak better and engage in extended conversations; understand various verb forms in speech patterns; read with better intonation with better understanding; and write simple communications.

Instruction: Major topics covered in the course are more complex structures (e.g. conditional tenses); different functions of KU; prefixes indicating place Po, Ko, Mo, directions and places where things and places are located; adjectives with unusual feature (e.g. -ote [all, whole]; another form of subjunctive —niende? [should I go?]); situational applications (road scene). Methods of instruction include lecture, discussion, classroom exercises, case studies, role playing, problem solving, and examinations.

Credit Recommendation: In the lower division baccalaureate/associate degree category, 2 semester hours in Swahili (8/93).

LANGUAGES/SWEDISH

Introductory Swedish I (ESWED 151)

Location: Washington, DC.

Length: 30 hours (10 weeks).

Dates: January 1985-Present.

Objective: To provide the student with and introduction to Swedish pronunciation, grammar, and vocabulary; and teach the students to express themselves on a very elementary level.

Learning Outcome: Upon successful completion of this course, the student will be able to form simple sentences and ask simple questions in the present and past tenses; read and write on a very elementary level; and show some acquaintance with Swedish culture and customs.

Instruction: Major topics covered in the course are foundation in speaking, reading, and writing Swedish; and covers the basics in grammar drills, and emphasis is placed on speaking. Methods of instruction include lecture, discussion, classroom instruction, and examination.

Credit Recommendation: In the lower division baccalaureate/associate degree category, 2 semester hours in Swedish (6/88) (8/93).

Introductory Swedish II (ESWED 152)

Location: Washington, DC.

Length: 30 hours (10 weeks).

Dates: January 1985-Present.

Objective: To provide the student with continued development of basic language skills-comprehension, reading, speaking, and writing.

Learning Outcome: Upon successful completion of this course, the student will be able to form sentences in all tenses, using a broader vocabulary and with a distinct pronunciation; read simple texts and write simple narrative; and know more about Swedish culture and customs.

Instruction: Major topics covered in the course are expansion of vocabulary and knowledge of grammar; pronunciation; writing; emphasis placed on speaking. Methods of instruction include lectures, discussions, classroom exercises, and examination.

Credit Recommendation: In the lower division baccalaureate/associate degree category, 2 semester hours in Swedish (6/88) (8/93).

Introductory Swedish III (ESWED 153)

Location: Washington, DC.
Length: 30 hours (10 weeks).
Dates: January 1985-Present.
Objective: To provide the student with further study of basic language skills—comprehension, reading, speaking, and writing.
Learning Outcome: Upon successful completion of this course, the student will be able to have a conversation in Swedish with teacher or patient native speaker; read easier Swedish texts; write a letter or simple narrative with more complicated sentence structure than in ESWED 152; and show increased familiarity with contemporary Swedish culture and customs.
Instruction: Major topics covered in the course are further improvement in speaking, writing, and comprehension. (Designed for those with a good knowledge of basic Swedish).
Credit Recommendation: In the lower division baccalaureate/associate degree category, 2 semester hours in Swedish (6/88) (8/93).

LANGUAGES/UKRAINIAN

Conversational Ukrainian I (EUKRA110)

Location: Washington, DC.
Length: 30 hours (10 weeks).
Dates: January 1993-Present.
Objective: To introduce the student to the sound and writing systems of contemporary Ukrainian and to Ukrainian culture, emphasis is on the development of the basic skills of reading, speaking, listening, and writing; and to help students learn language through a conversationally-based text.
Learning Outcome: Upon successful completion of this course, the student will be able to pronounce Ukrainian words written in the Cryllic alphabet, ask and respond to simple questions on familiar topics orally and in writing, and understand simple phrases in printed text.
Instruction: Major topics covered in the course are the Cryllic alphabet; sound system; basic vocabulary; introduction of verbs (including "to have", "to be") in present, past, future tenses; introduction to gender, cases, number, and useful expressions; and Ukrainian culture. Methods of instruction include lectures in English and Ukrainian; classroom exercises and drills; written homework and class preparation assignments; language lab instruction (audiotape listening practice); guest presentations on Ukrainian culture, and examinations.
Credit Recommendation: In the lower division baccalaureate/associate degree category, 2 semester hours in Introductory Ukrainian I (8/93).

Conversational Ukrainian II (EUKRA111)

Location: Washington, DC.
Length: 30 hours (10 weeks).
Dates: January 1993-Present.
Objective: To provide the student with continued introduction to grammatical structure of Ukrainian and to Ukrainian culture; and further development of the basic skills of reading, speaking, listening, and writing of contemporary Ukrainian presented through a conversationally-based textbook.
Learning Outcome: Upon successful completion of this course, the student will be able to ask and respond to simple questions orally and in writing; have a larger working vocabulary; an improved conceptual understanding of verbal aspects, tenses, and noun cases; read simple narrative text; and have expanded knowledge of Ukrainian culture.
Instruction: Major topics covered in the course are continued presentation of verbs, including aspect, tense, reflexive verbs and verbs of motion; and further study of noun cases, pronouns, adjectives, prepositions, time expressions, and idiomatic expressions. Methods of instruction include lectures in English and Ukrainian, classroom exercises and drills, written homework and class preparation assignments, language lab instruction (audiotape listening practice), guest presentations on Ukrainian culture, and examinations.
Credit Recommendation: In the lower division baccalaureate/associate degree category, 2 semester hours in Introductory Ukrainian II (8/93).

LIBRARY TECHNIQUES

Basic Reference Services and Reference Tools (CLIBT 245)

Location: Correspondence Study.
Length: 10 lessons.
Dates: January 1990-Present.
Objective: To provide the student with an understanding of reference services in libraries, including the types of questions and types of reference materials and their usage in meeting information needs of patrons.
Learning Outcome: Upon successful completion of this course, the student will be able to know functions of reference services; demonstrate a working knowledge of basic reference tools; and answer elementary questions.
Instruction: Major topics covered in the course are the functions of a reference service; reference role of library technicians; characteristics of reference materials; analysis of questions; types of sources—dictionaries, encyclopedias, indexes and abstracts, bibliographies, U.S. government documents, geographical information sources, and nonprint media reference sources. Methods of instruction include independent study, graded written assignments, and a final examination.
Credit Recommendation: In the lower division baccalaureate/associate degree category, 1 semester hour in Library Science (1/90) (1/95).

Basic Reference Services and Reference Tools (ELIBT 245)

Location: Washington, DC.
Length: 30 hours (10 weeks) or two to three two-hour sessions per week (5 weeks).
Dates: September 1989-Present.
Objective: To provide the student with an understanding of reference services in libraries, including information gathering behavior, question characteristics, and reference sources.
Learning Outcome: Upon successful completion of this course, the student will be able to know function of reference services; assist users to use libraries effectively; answer elementary questions; and know the characteristics of a range of basic reference sources.
Instruction: Major topics covered in the course are the functions and organization of reference services, reference roles of library techniques, types and characteristics of questions, procedures used to answer questions, characteristics and use of reference sources, computer-assisted reference services, and library cooperation and interlibrary loans. Methods of instruction include lecture, discussions, question and problem sets, classroom exercises, role playing, and midterm, and final examinations.

Credit Recommendation: In the upper division baccalaureate degree category, 2 semester hours in Library Services (1/90).

Cataloging and Classification I (ELIBT 120)

Location: Washington, DC.
Length: 30 hours (10 weeks).
Dates: September 1984-Present.
Objective: To provide the student with fundamentals of serial and monographic descriptive cataloging.
Learning Outcome: Upon successful completion of this course, the student will be able to recognize AACR2 cataloging, as applied to several formats (books, serials, sound recordings); use AACR2 to elementary bibliographic description; select MARC tags for each bibliographic format; and perform copy cataloging or elementary original cataloging.
Instruction: Major topics covered in the course are an introduction to general bibliographic procedures, an overview to bibliographic utilities, elements of monographic bibliographic description, including title, statement of responsibility, edition, publication place, date, publisher, rules for serials description, access points and form of entry, and technical reading of a book. Methods of instruction include readings in textbook, handouts, exercises, lecture, and discussion.
Credit Recommendation: In the lower division baccalaureate/associate or in the upper division baccalaureate degree category, 2 semester hours in Library Science (1/90).

Cataloging and Classification II (ELIBT 220)

Location: Washington, DC.
Length: 30 hours (10 weeks).
Dates: September 1980-Present.
Objective: To provide the fundamentals of subject cataloging and classification, with emphasis on monographs.
Learning Outcome: Upon successful completion of this course, the student will be able to explain how to assign subject headings and classification number; and understand the importance to library users of subject access to information.
Instruction: Major topics covered in the course are the basic concepts of subject arrangement of library materials, subject heading lists and classification schedules, classification systems LCC, DCC, UDC, SuDoc, LCSH, Sears, TEST, MESH, PRECIS; and automation in subject cataloging. Methods of instruction include lectures and readings in textbook.
Credit Recommendation: In the lower division baccalaureate/associate or in the upper division baccalaureate degree category, 2 semester hours in Library Science (1/90).

Descriptive Cataloging (CLIBT 120) (Formerly Cataloging and Classification I (Descriptive Cataloging)[CLIBT 120])

Location: Correspondence Study.
Length: 14 assignments (approximately 45 hours).
Dates: *Version 1:* January 1990-August 1994; *Version 2:* September 1994-Present.
Objective: To provide the student with the fundamentals of descriptive cataloging functions, rules, and procedures.
Learning Outcome: Upon successful completion of this course, the student will be able to describe the basic functions of descriptive book cataloging; demonstrate a working knowledge of cataloging rules and procedures for monographs, serials, and nonprint materials; describe the structure and content of library catalogs and catalog records; and understand the relationship between catalog and the physical materials they represent.
Instruction: Major topics covered in the course are an overview of cataloging functions in libraries; catalogs, cataloging records, and authority files; technical reading of a book; introduction to AACR2/AACR2R; access points and forms of entry; and elements of bibliographic description: title, statement of responsibility, edition, publication place, date, publisher, physical description, and descriptive cataloging aids. Methods of instruction include independent study, graded written assignments, and a final examination.
Credit Recommendation: *Version 1:* In the lower division baccalaureate/associate degree or upper division baccalaureate degree category, 2 semester hours in Library Science (1/90). *Version 2:* In the lower division baccalaureate/associate degree or upper division baccalaureate degree category, 3 semester hours in Library Science (1/95).

Introduction to Bibliographies (CLIBT 325)

Location: Correspondence Study.
Length: 9 lessons (approximately 30 hours).
Dates: January 1990-January 1995.
Objective: To provide the student with the knowledge to apply principles for developing and organizing bibliographies.
Learning Outcome: Upon successful completion of this course, the student will be able to use library resources to select materials to be included in bibliographies; establish appropriate bibliographical citations according to standard style sheets; organize a bibliography; and develop an appreciation for bibliographical theory and techniques.
Instruction: Major topics covered in the course are the history of bibliographic systems in the United States, types of bibliographies, library resources used for identifying books, periodicals, newspapers, and nonprint materials, format and design of reports and bibliographies, and bibliographic citation procedures and styles. Methods of instruction include readings in textbook and final examination.
Credit Recommendation: In the upper division baccalaureate degree category, 2 semester hours in Library Science (1/90) (1/95).

Introduction to Library Techniques (ELIBT 110)

Location: Washington, DC.
Length: 30 hours (10 weeks).
Dates: September 1980-January 1995.
Objective: To provide the student with an understanding of the general organization of a library.
Learning Outcome: Upon successful completion of this course, the student will be able to describe the basics of library organization; describe the role of library paraprofessionals and their career opportunities; describe the future trends in library automation; and describe the use of computers in libraries.
Instruction: Major topics covered in the course are library administration, organization, basic services, and automation. Methods of instruction include lecture, discussion, reading assignments, and final examination.
Credit Recommendation: In the lower division baccalaureate/associate degree category, 2 semester hours in Library Technology-Technicians (1/90).

Introduction to Library Techniques (CLIBT 110)

Location: Correspondence Study.
Length: 10 lessons.
Dates: September 1987-Present.
Objective: To introduce students to the library as an institution, the role it serves within its community, its internal organization and operations, and the role of the library technician.

Learning Outcome: Upon successful completion of this course, the student will be able to describe the various types of libraries in the United States today; describe the purpose of these libraries; describe the functions common to all libraries; understand the basic library terminology, and describe the major responsibilities of a library technician.

Instruction: Major topics covered in the course are the role of the library technician, different types of library resources, and basic library organization services. Methods of instruction include independent study, graded written assignments, and a final examination.

Credit Recommendation: In the lower division baccalaureate/associate degree category, 2 semester hours in Library Technology-Technician (1/90) (1/95).

Library Media Services (CLIBT 210)

Location: Correspondence Study.

Length: 10 lessons.

Dates: January 1990-Present.

Objective: To provide the student with an understanding of the various types of media in library collections and the selection, processing, storage, access, and use of these materials.

Learning Outcome: Upon successful completion of this course, the student will be able to understand the characteristics of various types of nonprint media; know selection principles and sources for each type; understand methods of accessing, storing, and circulating these media; understand staff and service policies and procedures; and understand trends and intellectual property issues related to nonprint media.

Instruction: Major topics covered in the course are administration, selection, evaluation, processing, and organization and maintenance of nonprint materials. Methods of instruction include independent study, graded written assignments, and a final examination.

Credit Recommendation: In the lower division baccalaureate/associate degree category, 2 semester hours in Library Technology-Technician (1/90) (1/95).

New Information Technology (ELIBT 402)

Location: Washington, DC.

Length: 30 hours (10 weeks).

Dates: September 1988-Present.

Objective: To provide the student with an understanding of new technology trends and of vaporware and computer viruses.

Learning Outcome: Upon successful completion of this course, the student will be able to demonstrate an understanding of how new technology could be used information storage, retrieval, presentation, or dissemination.

Instruction: Major topics covered in the course are artificial intelligence and expert systems, electronic bulletin boards, CD-ROM technology and applications, WORM (Write-Once-Read-Many) optical storage, full-test scanning, optional character recognition, interactive videodisc for training, photographic storage an retrieval and optical media, and hypermedia applicability for information. Methods of instruction include lecture, discussion, hands-on experience, and research paper.

Credit Recommendation: In the upper division baccalaureate degree category, 2 semester hours in Library Technology and Information Services (1/90).

Subject Cataloging and Classification (CLIBT 220) (Formerly Cataloging and Classification II (Subject Cataloging)[CLIBT 220])

Location: Correspondence Study.

Length: 12 lessons.

Dates: January 1990-Present.

Objective: To provide the student with fundamentals of subject cataloging and classification.

Learning Outcome: Upon successful completion of this course, the student will be able to explain the basic concepts of subject headings and classification numbers and how they are assigned; understand the importance to library users of subject access to information; and identify the tools of subject cataloging.

Instruction: Major topics covered in the course are basic concepts of subject cataloging and classification, specific classification schemes, which include DDC, LCC, Cutter Expansive, Brown's, Colon Classification, SuDoc, Guelph, book numbers, LC and Sears Subject Headings lists, coordinate indexing, PRECIS, and MARC and bibliographic networks. Methods of instruction include independent study, graded written assignments, and a final examination.

Credit Recommendation: In the lower division baccalaureate/associate degree or in the upper division baccalaureate degree category, 2 semester hours in Library Science (1/90) (1/95).

The Use of Archives and Manuscripts (CLIBT 511)

Location: Correspondence Study.

Length: 9 lessons (approximately 45 hours).

Dates: January 1990-Present.

Objective: To provide the student with an understanding of the functions and characteristics of archives and manuscripts and how to use them effectively.

Learning Outcome: Upon successful completion of this course, the student will become familiar with the history, functions, and methods of archival institutions; know resources of major archival and manuscript collections; and be able to explain these resources through pertinent reference books, guides, and finding aids.

Instruction: Major topics covered in the course are the history and types of archives, techniques for describing and using archives, archival resources in federal, state, local history, genealogy and church, university, and private institution archives, reference and finding aids, and special archives—maps, audiovisual materials, and machine-readable files. Methods of instruction include readings in textbook, a special project, and final examination.

Credit Recommendation: In the graduate degree category, 3 semester hours in History or Library Science (1/90) (1/95).

Mathematics, Statistics

Advanced Agricultural Statistics (CSTAT 401)

Location: Correspondence Study.

Length: 18 lessons (maximum course length is 1 year; however, the student may apply for an extension of another year).

Dates: January 1985-Present.

Objective: To provide the student with an understanding and uses of agricultural statistics.

Learning Outcome: Upon successful completion of this course, the student will be able to use statistical tables and properly set up and conduct moment correlation coefficient analyses.

Instruction: Major topics covered in the course are normal distribution, binomial distribution, student distribution, hypothesis testing and confidence intervals, regression, correlation, chi-square tests, analysis of variance, multiple regression, and sample surveys. Methods of instruction include lecture and discussion.

Credit Recommendation: In the upper division baccalaureate degree category, 3

semester hours in Education or Social Science (1/90) (1/95).

Analytic Geometry (CMATH 105)

Location: Correspondence Study.
Length: 14 lessons.
Dates: January 1995-Present.
Objective: To provide students with the ability to solve algebraic equations.
Learning Outcome: Upon successful completion of this course, the student will be able to determine the equations of lines, circles, and other geometric forms and graph them based on a coordinate system.
Instruction: Major topics covered in the course are equations of lines, circles, parabolas, ellipses, and other geometric forms. Methods of instruction include independent study, graded assignments, and a final examination.
Credit Recommendation: In the lower division baccalaureate/associate degree category, 1 semester hour in Mathematics (1/95).

Basic Mathematics (CMATH 101)

Location: Correspondence Study.
Length: 15 lessons.
Dates: January 1995-Present.
Objective: To provide a basis for further study in the principles and applications of arithmetic, algebra, logarithms, geometry, and trigonometry.
Learning Outcome: Upon successful completion of this course, the student will be able to solve problems involving algebraic fractions, plane geometry, trigonometry, and basic electric circuits.
Instruction: Major topics covered in the course are percentage, ratio, and proportion; powers and roots; algebra; factoring; equations; quadratic equations; graphs; logarithms; geometry; trigonometry; and radians. Methods of instruction include independent study, graded written assignments, quizzes, and a final examination.
Credit Recommendation: In the lower division baccalaureate/associate degree category, 2 semester hours in Mathematics (1/95).

Basic Technical Mathematics (Pre-Calculus Algebra) (EMATH 128) (Formerly Precalculus Algebra)

Location: Washington, DC.
Length: 30 hours (10 weeks).
Dates: September 1982-Present.
Objective: To provide the student with the ability to solve algebraic precalculus problems.
Learning Outcome: Upon successful completion of this course, the student will be able to solve a system of linear equations; plot two-variable equations on Cartesian coordinates; add, subtract, and multiply complex numbers; evaluate expressions involving functional notation; and understand the concept of linear interpolation.
Instruction: Major topics covered in the course are linear algebraic equations, quadratic equations, laws of components, analytic geometry, graphs, Cartesian and other coordinate systems, trigonometry, simultaneous equations, factoring, logarithms, complex numbers, and exponentials. Methods of instruction include homework, lectures, problem review sessions, and midterm and final examinations.
Credit Recommendation: In the lower division baccalaureate/associate degree category, 2 semester hours in Mathematics (1/90) (1/95).

Calculus I (CMATH 210)

Location: Correspondence Study.
Length: 10 lessons (self-paced).
Dates: November 1982-Present.
Objective: To provide the student with an understanding of the meaning and use of the derivatives of mathematical functions.
Learning Outcome: Upon successful completion of this course, the student will be able to understand the meaning of the derivative, and its relationship to the slope of the tangent line, and determine the maximum and minimum points of a curve.
Instruction: Major topics covered in the course are variables; functions; limits, continuity; derivatives; maxima and minima; mean value theorem; and approximation methods of finding roots. Methods of instruction include self-guided instruction, guided homework problems, and a proctored final examination.
Credit Recommendation: In the lower division baccalaureate/associate degree category, 2 semester hours in Differential Calculus or Mathematics (6/88) (6/93).

Calculus I (EMATH 210)

Location: Washington, DC.
Length: 30 hours (10 weeks).
Dates: January 1978-Present.
Objective: To provide the student with an understanding of the meaning and use of the derivative of mathematical functions.
Learning Outcome: Upon successful completion of this course, the student will be able to understand the meaning of the derivative and its relationship to the slope of the tangent line; and determine the maximum and minimum points of a curve.
Instruction: Major topics covered in the course are variables; functions; limits; continuity; derivatives; maxima and minima; mean value theorem; Newton's approximation of roots; and derivatives of transcendental functions. Methods of instruction include lectures, class exercises, and written homework.
Credit Recommendation: In the lower division baccalaureate/associate degree category, 2 semester hours in Differential Calculus or Mathematics (6/88) (6/93).

Calculus II (CMATH 211)

Location: Correspondence Study.
Length: 11 lessons (self-paced).
Dates: March 1983-Present.
Objective: To provide the student with an understanding of the concepts and applications of the integration of mathematical functions.
Learning Outcome: Upon successful completion of this course, the student will be able to understand concepts of integration, and apply integration to the development of the area under a curve.
Instruction: Major topics covered in the course are simple integration; the definite integral; approximation methods of integration; and integration of trigonometric functions. Methods of instruction include self-guided instruction, graded homework problems, and a proctored final examination.
Credit Recommendation: In the lower division baccalaureate/associate degree category, 2 semester hours in Integral Calculus or Mathematics (6/88) (6/93).

Calculus II (EMATH 211)

Location: Washington, DC.
Length: 30 hours (10 weeks).
Dates: January 1978-Present.
Objective: To provide the student with an understanding of the concepts and applications of the integration of mathematical functions.
Learning Outcome: Upon successful completion of this course, the student will be able to understand concepts of integration; and apply integration to the development of the area under a curve.
Instruction: Major topics covered in the course are simple integration; the definite integral; approximate methods of integration; trigonometric substitutions; and estimation methods. Methods of instruction include lectures, class exercises, and written homework.
Credit Recommendation: In the lower division baccalaureate/associate degree

category, 2 semester hours in Integral Calculus or Mathematics (6/88) (6/93).

Calculus III (EMATH 212)

Location: Washington, DC.

Length: 30 hours (10 weeks).

Dates: January 1978-Present.

Objective: To provide the student with the knowledge to develop and solve differential equations.

Learning Outcome: Upon successful completion of this course, the student will be able to use derivatives and integrals to solve differential equations; and solve special functions, such as Fourier series and Laplace transformations.

Instruction: Major topics covered in the course are first order differential equations; Euler's equation; Lagrange's method; partial derivatives; Fourier analysis; and Laplace transforms. Methods of instruction include lectures, class exercises, and graded homework problems.

Credit Recommendation: In the lower division baccalaureate/associate degree category, 2 semester hours in Differential Equations or Mathematics (6/88) (6/93).

College Algebra (CMATH 250)

Location: Correspondence Study.

Length: 15 lessons.

Dates: January 1995-Present.

Objective: To provide the student with the algebra skills necessary for doing applied calculus.

Learning Outcome: Upon successful completion of this course, the student will be able to solve and graph equations and inequalities, to graph algebraic functions, and solve systems of equations using determinants.

Instruction: Major topics covered in the course are equations and inequalities; functions; ratio, exponential and logarithmic functions; and determinants and systems of equations. Methods of instruction include independent study, graded written assignments, and a final examination.

Credit Recommendation: In the lower division baccalaureate/associate degree category, 3 semester hours in Finite Mathematics (1/95).

College Math (Finite Mathematics) (CMATH 101, CMATH 103)

Location: Correspondence Study.

Length: 60 lessons (course length is 1 year per course; however, the student may apply for an extension of another year).

Dates: January 1980-December 1994.

Objective: To provide the student with an understanding of the basic principles and applications of arithmetic, algebra, logarithms, geometry, and trigonometry.

Learning Outcome: Upon successful completion of this course, the student will be able to graph functions, solve systems of equations using determinants, understand basic trigonometric theory and functions; use matrix addition, subtraction, and multiplication; and use algebra and analytic geometry.

Instruction: Major topics covered in the course are determinants, powers and roots, vectors, algebraic equations and fractions, scientific notations, analytic geometry, graphs, functions, trigonometry, and basic electric circuits. Methods of instruction include assignments with final examination.

Credit Recommendation: In the lower division baccalaureate/associate degree category, 3 semester hours in Basic College Mathematics (1/90) (1/95).

Elements of Statistics (CSTAT 350)

Location: Correspondence Study.

Length: 14 lessons (self-paced).

Dates: February 1989-Present.

Objective: To provide a basic understanding of the fundamental concepts and logic of statistical methods and computational techniques.

Learning Outcome: Upon successful completion of this course, the student will be able to calculate the common statistical parameters of a sample population; apply tests of significance to statistical data; calculate chi-square statistics and apply goodness of fit tests; calculate regression equations and correlation coefficients; and utilize simple nonparametric methods to compare samples.

Instruction: Major topics covered in the course are empirical frequency distributions, measures of central tendency, measures of variation, probability, sampling distributions estimation, tests of significance, regression and correlation, and nonparametric methods. Methods of instruction include self-paced lessons and a proctored open-book examination.

Credit Recommendation: In the lower division baccalaureate/associate degree category, 2 semester hours in Applied Statistics, Mathematics, or Physical Sciences or in the upper division baccalaureate degree category, 3 semester hours in Social Sciences (1/90).

Introduction to Sample Surveys (ESTAT 350)

Location: Washington, DC.

Length: 30 hours (10 weeks).

Dates: January 1984-Present.

Objective: To introduce the student to various aspects of survey, including planning and managing a survey, designs, and statistical formulae.

Learning Outcome: Upon successful completion of this course, the student will be able to design and summarize basic surveys and critique surveys for major problems.

Instruction: Major topics covered in the course are simple, random, stratified, cluster, and systematic sampling; methods of estimation; summation notation; simple unbiased estimates; and the economic design of surveys. Methods of instruction include lecture.

Credit Recommendation: In the upper division baccalaureate degree category, 2 semester hours in Applied Statistics, Evaluation, or Social Science (1/90) (1/95). **NOTE:** Students can only receive credit for this course or CSTAT 350 (correspondence course).

Introductory Statistics I (ESTAT 101)

Location: Washington, DC.

Length: 30 hours (3 hours per week for 10 weeks).

Dates: January 1978-Present.

Objective: To provide the student with the knowledge of basic statistical concepts and measurement tools in collecting, analyzing, and presenting various kinds of data in various formats.

Learning Outcome: Upon successful completion of this course, the student will be able to determine and use measures of central tendency and dispension for discrete and continuous contribution; understand and be familiar with the concepts of probability, and the use of probability distributions such as the normal, binomial, and chi-square; and be able to perform low level statistical analysis and prepare interpretations.

Instruction: Major topics covered in the course are construction of various presentations of data; central tendency; probability; and probability distributions. Methods of instruction include lecture, discussion, problems, and examinations.

Credit Recommendation: In the upper division baccalaureate degree category, 2 semester hours in Business Administration, Management Science, or Statistics (6/88) (6/93).

Introductory Statistics II (ESTAT 102)

Location: Washington, DC.
Length: 30 hours (3 hours per week for 10 weeks).
Dates: January 1978-Present.
Objective: To provide the student with an understanding of statistical sampling and sampling distributions for real world applications, and comparison of means and development of inferences from statistics about populations. This course is a continuation of Introductory Statistics I (ESTAT 101).
Learning Outcome: Upon successful completion of this course, the student will be able to use and apply sampling distributions to various kinds of problems and applications; compare various means, develop sample designs, test for significance, and perform analysis of variance; and introduce the concepts of regression and correlation.
Instruction: Major topics covered in the course are sampling, sample design, various tests of significance, inference analysis of variance, and design of simple experiments. Methods of instruction include lecture, discussion, problems, and examinations.
Credit Recommendation: In the upper division baccalaureate degree category, 2 semester hours in Business Administration, Management Science, or Statistics (6/88) (6/93).

Introductory Statistics III (ESTAT 103) (Correlation and Regression Analysis)

Location: Washington, DC.
Length: 30 hours (3 hours per week for 10 weeks).
Dates: January 1978-Present.
Objective: To teach the student the methods and techniques of correlation and regression, in both linear and nonlinear applications; and nonparametric statistical measures.
Learning Outcome: Upon successful completion of this course, the student will be able to demonstrate an understanding and apply linear correlation and regression analysis to data sets of various kinds, and to understand the strengths, weaknesses, and uses of correlation and regression analysis in both linear and non-linear cases.
Instruction: Major topics covered in the course are correlation and regression analysis and application of nonparametric statistics. Methods of instruction include lecture, discussion, problems, and examinations.
Credit Recommendation: In the upper division baccalaureate degree category, 2 semester hours in Business Administration, Management Science, or Statistics (6/88) (6/93).

Managerial Statistics (NSTAT 550)

Location: Washington, DC.
Length: 40 hours (3 weeks).
Dates: September 1974-February 1990.
Objective: To allow the student to understand and apply relevant principles and concepts of basic statistics to managerial situations and positions.
Learning Outcome: Upon successful completion of this course, the student will be able to use accurate and reliable statistical measures of data; use various statistical techniques such as forecasting models; correlation; regression; sampling and risk analysis; and understand probability as a basis for using and applying statistical measures to data.
Instruction: Major topics covered in the course are scientific method; sources of statistics; measures of central tendency; sampling; probability; correlation; and regression analysis. Methods of instruction include lecture, discussion, and problem solving.
Credit Recommendation: In the upper division baccalaureate or graduate degree category (for students not majoring in Statistics), 3 semester hours in Business Administration, Management Science, or Statistics (6/88) (6/93).

Mathematics for Economists I (EMATH 475)

Location: Washington, DC.
Length: 30 hours (10 weeks).
Dates: April 1985-Present.
Objective: To provide the student with a basic understanding of the application of basic mathematics, sets, functions, differential calculus, and matrices to simple economic problems.
Learning Outcome: Upon successful completion of this course, the student will be able to understand the concepts and operations of the differential calculus, set theory, functions and matrices and apply the methods of differential calculus, set theory, functions, and matrices to analyze economic problems.
Instruction: Major topics covered in the course are set theory, functions, differential calculus and matrices, and equilibrium analysis. Methods of instruction include lecture, problem sets, and examinations.
Credit Recommendation: In the upper division baccalaureate degree category, 2 semester hours in Economics (1/90) (1/95).

Mathematics for Economists II (EMATH 476)

Location: Washington, DC.
Length: 30 hours (10 weeks).
Dates: January 1985-Present.
Objective: To provide the student with a basic understanding of the concept of optimization and the use of exponential and logarithmic functions and Lagrange multiplier methods.
Learning Outcome: Upon successful completion of this course, the student will be able to understand the concepts of optimization and exponential and logarithmic functions and apply exponential and logarithmic functions and Lagrange multiplier methods in the analysis of economic problems.
Instruction: Major topics covered in the course are optimization concepts, maxima and minima, Lagrange multiplier methods, exponential and logarithmic functions, and utility optimization. Methods of instruction include lecture, problem sets, and examinations.
Credit Recommendation: In the upper division baccalaureate degree category, 2 semester hours in Economics (1/90) (1/95).

Sample Survey Methods (CSTAT 501)

Location: Correspondence Study.
Length: 17 lessons.
Dates: January 1980-Present.
Objective: To ensure the student's ability to choose a proper sample survey design and estimation techniques when planning a sample survey.
Learning Outcome: Upon successful completion of this course, the student will be able to design efficient sample surveys that controls sampling errors and survey costs.
Instruction: Major topics covered in the course are the principles of sample design, biases and nonsampling errors, simple random sampling, stratified simple random sampling, duster sampling, stratified cluster sampling, multi-stage sampling, double sampling, systematic sam-

pling, sampling frames, and multiframe sampling. Methods of instruction include practical exercises.

Credit Recommendation: In the graduate degree category, 4 semester hours in Applied Statistics or Elements of Statistics (1/90) (1/95).

Theory of Sample Surveys (ESTAT 426) *(Elements of Statistics)*

Location: Washington, DC.

Length: 30 hours (10 weeks).

Dates: September 1980-Present.

Objective: To provide the student with a comprehensive understanding of the theory of samples as it has been developed to provide a background for good sampling methods.

Learning Outcome: Upon successful completion of this course, the student will be able to determine the required size and sample allocation methods for a cost-efficient sample and compare the sampling efficiency of various survey designs.

Instruction: Major topics covered in the course are simple random sampling, sampling for proportions, estimation of sample size, stratified sampling, ration estimate, regression estimates, systematic sampling, cluster sampling, and double sampling. Methods of instruction include lecture, discussion, problem sets, and examinations.

Credit Recommendation: In the upper division baccalaureate degree category, 5 semester hours in Applied Statistics, or in the graduate degree category, 3 semester hours in Applied Statistics (1/90).

Trigonometry (CMATH 103)

Location: Correspondence Study.

Length: 15 lessons.

Dates: January 1995-Present.

Objective: To provide an understanding of basic trigonometric theory and functions.

Learning Outcome: Upon successful completion of this course, the student will be able to use knowledge of trigonometry to solve problems which involve determining heights, distances, and angles.

Instruction: Major topics covered in the course are measurement of angles, solutions of triangles, vectors, and imaginary and complex numbers. Methods of instruction include independent study, graded written assignments, and a final examination.

Credit Recommendation: In the lower division baccalaureate/associate degree category, 1 semester hour in Mathematics (1/95).

Paralegal

Administrative Law and Procedure (CLAWS 310)

Location: Correspondence Study.

Length: 10 lessons (self-paced).

Dates: February 1985-Present.

Objective: To provide the student with an understanding of the workings of administrative agencies within the federal government.

Learning Outcome: Upon successful completion of this course, the student will be able to appreciate the interdependent role of the three branches of the federal government and understand the role and function of federal administrative agencies.

Instruction: Major topics covered in the course are principles and practice of administrative law in the federal field; provisions of Administrative Procedure Act dealing with formal and informal rulemaking and adjudication; notice, hearing, evidence, findings, and control by the courts, with a discussion of pertinent and applicable principles of constitutional law. Methods of instruction include self-paced learning with proctored examination.

Credit Recommendation: In the lower division baccalaureate/associate degree category, 2 semester hours in Paralegal Studies (6/88) (6/93).

Administrative Law and Procedure (ELAWS 310)

Location: Washington, DC.

Length: 30 hours (10 weeks).

Dates: January 1984-Present.

Objective: To provide the student with the understanding of the legal basis of constitutional limitations and procedural limitations on agency authority.

Learning Outcome: Upon successful completion of this course, the student will be able to appreciate the interdependence of the three branches of government and understand the role and function of administrative agencies.

Instruction: Major topics covered in the course are principles and practice of administrative law in the federal field, provisions of the Administrative Procedure Act dealing with formal and informal rulemaking and adjudication; notice, hearing, evidence, findings, and control by the courts; and pertinent principles of constitutional law. Methods of instruction include lecture, discussion, and case studies.

Credit Recommendation: In the lower division baccalaureate/associate degree category, 2 semester hours in Paralegal Studies (6/88) (6/93).

Alternative Dispute Resolution (ELAWS 315)

Location: Washington, DC, or various locations throughout the U.S.

Length: 30 hours (10 weeks).

Dates: June 1993-Present.

Objective: To provide the student with a knowledge of alternatives to litigation for resolving legal disputes, including negotiation, mediation, and arbitration.

Learning Outcome: Upon successful completion of this course, the student will be able to understand what Alternative Dispute Resolution (ADR) is, and what are its benefits and drawbacks vis-a-vis litigation; what it means to negotiate based on interests rather than positions; what mediation is, including the stages of mediation, the role of the mediator, the qualifications and ethical obligations of the mediator, confidentiality; students must play the mediator in a mock mediation; and what arbitration is; what the hybrid ADR processes are (med-arb; mini-trial, early neutral valuation, fact finding).

Instruction: Major topics covered in the course are alternatives to litigation as a means for resolving legal disputes, including mediation, outcome prediction methods, and arbitration; additional topics include confidentiality; degree of central parties have over the process and outcome; acceptance/rejection of ADR by clients and attorneys; and ADR in disputes involving the federal government. Methods of instruction include lectures, role-playing, and final project (paper, oral presentation, or both).

Credit Recommendation: In the lower division baccalaureate/associate degree category, 2 semester hours in Paralegal Studies (6/93).

Business Law I (CLAWS 120)

Location: Correspondence.

Length: 15 lessons (self-paced).

Dates: February 1985-Present.

Objective: To provide the student with knowledge of certain aspects of the substantive law applicable to many business transactions.

Learning Outcome: Upon successful completion of this course, the student will be able to apply knowledge of law to business relationships.

Instruction: Major topics covered in the course are aspects of law essential to conduct of modern business including contracts, bailments, sales, and warranties. Methods of instruction include self-paced instruction with proctored examinations.

Credit Recommendation: *Version 1:* In the lower division baccalaureate/associate degree category, 2 semester hours in Business Administration or Paralegal Studies (6/88). *Version 2:* In the lower division baccalaureate/associate degree category, 3 semester hours in Business Administration or Paralegal Studies (6/93).

Business Law I (ELAWS 120)

Location: Washington, DC.

Length: 30 hours (10 weeks).

Dates: January 1984-Present.

Objective: To provide the student with an understanding of legal principles involved in contracts, sales, Uniform Commercial Code, and torts.

Learning Outcome: Upon successful completion of this course, the student will be able to understand the basic elements of contract law; understand Article 2 of the Uniform Commercial Code (sales); identify the major difference between contract law and Article 2 of the Uniform Commercial Code; determine when one incurs contractual liability and when one does not incur this liability; and identify and describe those areas of criminal and tort law that are of particular concern to business.

Instruction: Major topics covered in the course are business torts and crimes; contracts;, sales and warranties; and topics that relate to current legal developments. Methods of instruction include lecture, discussion, and case studies.

Credit Recommendation: In the lower division baccalaureate/associate degree category, 2 semester hours in Business Administration or Paralegal Studies (6/88) (6/93).

Business Law II (CLAWS 121)

Location: Correspondence Study.

Length: 11 lessons (self-paced).

Dates: February 1986-Present.

Objective: To provide the student with the knowledge of advanced aspects of substantive law applicable to business.

Learning Outcome: Upon successful completion of this course, the student will be able to apply knowledge of law to business relationships.

Instruction: Major topics covered in the course are aspects of law essential to conduct of modern business: agency, partnerships, corporations, corporate stock and shareholders; personal and real property; leases; and estates and trusts. Methods of instruction include self-paced instruction with proctored examinations.

Credit Recommendation: In the lower division baccalaureate/associate degree category, 2 semester hours in Business Administration or Paralegal Studies (6/88) (6/93).

Business Law II (ELAWS 220)

Location: Washington, DC.

Length: 30 hours (10 weeks).

Dates: January 1986-Present.

Objective: To provide the student with an understanding of legal principles involved in personal and real property, agency, corporations, and partnerships.

Learning Outcome: Upon successful completion of this course, the student will be able to understand the basic elements of personal and real property law and understand the basic elements of the law of agency, partnerships, and corporations.

Instruction: Major topics covered in the course are real and personal property law; agency; partnerships; and corporations. Methods of instruction include lecture, discussion, and case studies.

Credit Recommendation: In the lower division baccalaureate/associate degree category, 2 semester hours in Business Administration or Paralegal Studies (6/88) (6/93).

Civil Litigation for Paralegals (ELAWS 245)

Location: Washington, DC.

Length: 30 hours (10 weeks).

Dates: January 1985-Present.

Objective: To provide the student with an understanding of the principles and procedures of civil litigation for preparation of legal documents necessary to take a case through the court system.

Learning Outcome: Upon successful completion of this course, the student will be able to understand the principles and procedures of civil litigation and assist attorneys in document preparation, case preparation, and evaluation.

Instruction: Major topics covered in the course are types of jurisdiction, steps in the litigation process, discovery, trial preparation, and enforcement of judgments. Methods of instruction include lecture, discussion, texts and handouts, and an examination.

Credit Recommendation: In the lower division baccalaureate/associate degree category, 2 semester hours in Legal Assisting or Paralegal Studies (1/90) (1/95).

Constitutional Law (CLAWS 251)

Location: Correspondence Study.

Length: 16 lessons (self-paced).

Dates: February 1985-Present.

Objective: To provide the student with the knowledge of the Constitution and its provisions relevant to understanding the process of constitutional decision-making.

Learning Outcome: Upon successful completion of this course, the student will be able to apply constitutional principles to the full range of substantive and procedural areas.

Instruction: Major topics covered in the course are source and scope of judicial power; federal power to regulate interstate commerce; federal taxing and spending power; the state's exercise of police power; equal protection: racial discrimination, state action, economic, social discrimination; due process; the individual's right to privacy; freedom of speech, press, and religion; standing, mootness, and ripeness; political questions; and advisory opinions. Methods of instruction include self-paced instruction with proctored examinations.

Credit Recommendation: *Version 1:* In the lower division baccalaureate/associate degree category, 2 semester hours in Government and Politics/Political Science or Paralegal Studies (6/88). *Version 2:* In the lower division baccalaureate/associate degree category, 3 semester hours in Government and Politics or Political Science, or Paralegal Studies (6/93).

Criminal Law (CLAWS 135)

Location: Correspondence Study.

Length: 9 lessons (self-paced).

Dates: June 1988-Present.

Objective: To provide the student with knowledge of substantive areas of criminal laws.

Learning Outcome: Upon successful completion of this course, the student will be able to understand basic principles of criminal law.

Instruction: Major topics covered in the course are legal aspects of criminal law: elements of specific crimes, common defenses, and the proof necessary to convict persons of crimes. Methods of instruction include self-paced instruction with proctored examinations.

Credit Recommendation: In the lower division baccalaureate/associate degree category, 2 semester hours in Administration of Justice, Criminology, or Paralegal Studies (6/88) (6/93). **NOTE:** Credit for this course should not be awarded as credit for a course in Criminal Procedures and Evidence.

Environmental Law (ELAWS 145)

Location: Washington, DC.
Length: 30 hours (10 weeks).
Dates: January 1984-Present.
Objective: To provide the student with an understanding of the basic thrust of each of the environmental statutes and implementation of regulations and how they relate to other areas of law.
Learning Outcome: Upon successful completion of this course, the student will be able to understand the environmental concerns and policies that led to passage of the major (and some minor) environmental statutes, with concentration on the past two decades, and understand the implementation of the environmental statutes by federal agencies.
Instruction: Major topics covered in the course are land use planning; environmental planning; legislation; pollution; hazardous wastes; land use; clean air and water; and the processes under the National Environmental Protection Act. Methods of instruction include lecture, discussion, and case studies.
Credit Recommendation: In the lower division baccalaureate/associate degree category, 2 semester hours in Environmental Science or Paralegal Studies (6/88) (6/93).

Family Law (CLAWS 150)

Location: Correspondence Study.
Length: 14 lessons (self-paced).
Dates: June 1988-Present.
Objective: To introduce the student to substantive and procedural aspects of domestic relations law.
Learning Outcome: Upon successful completion of this course, the student will be able to apply knowledge of domestic relations law to client interview and case preparation.
Instruction: Major topics covered in the course are legal aspects of divorce; annulment; separation; adoption; legitimization; alimony; and child support, as well as related tax consequences of divorce and separation. Methods of instruction include self-paced instruction with proctored examinations.
Credit Recommendation: *Version 1:* In the lower division baccalaureate/associate degree category, 2 semester hours in Paralegal Studies (6/88). *Version 2:* In the lower division baccalaureate/associate degree category, 3 semester hours in Paralegal Studies or Human Development Counseling (6/93).

Family Law (ELAWS 150)

Location: Washington, DC.
Length: 30 hours (10 weeks).
Dates: January 1984-Present.
Objective: To provide the student with knowledge of substantive and procedural aspects of domestic relations law.
Learning Outcome: Upon successful completion of this course, the student will be able to demonstrate skills in interviewing, investigation, writing, research, pleadings, relevant case law (limited), and legal analysis; and identify the issues in a case, prepare a case for trial, negotiate agreements, and assist in the trial.
Instruction: Major topics covered in the course are legal aspects of divorce and annulment; separation; defense; adoption; legitimation; custody; habeas corpus; support; alimony; tax consulting; out-of-state divorces; validity; and jurisdiction service; analysis of separation and custody agreements as well as other documents in divorce proceedings. Methods of instruction include lecture, discussion, and case studies.
Credit Recommendation: In the lower division baccalaureate/associate degree category, 2 semester hours in Paralegal Studies, or Human Development Counseling (6/88) (6/93).

Financing Long-Term Health Care (LLAWS 325)

Location: Correspondence Study.
Length: 9 lessons (self-paced including final examination).
Dates: May 1993-Present.
Objective: To provide the student with an understanding of the structure and operation of the "medicaid" program, financial eligibility requirements, services covered, the appeals process, and private long-term care insurance.
Learning Outcome: Upon successful completion of this course, the student will be able to understand Medicaid structure and operation; and explain and resolve the complex issues of Medicare financial eligibility, the Medicaid appeals process, state-specific regulations, and legal issues of private long-term care insurance for those who are ineligible for Medicaid coverage.
Instruction: Major topics covered in the course are introduction to Medicaid administration of Medicaid; notice and hearing rights eligibility categories; financial eligibility including spousal impoverishment rules; Medicaid planning; residency and services; and long-term care insurance policies. Methods of instruction include self-paced instruction with proctored examination.
Credit Recommendation: In the upper division baccalaureate degree category, 2 semester hours in Paralegal Studies (6/93).

FOIA and the Privacy Act (CLAWS 335)

Location: Correspondence Study.
Length: 9 lessons (self-paced).
Dates: February 1986-Present.
Objective: To provide the student with an understanding of the Freedom of Information and Privacy Acts and their case interpretation.
Learning Outcome: Upon successful completion of this course, the student will be able to analyze substantive and procedural problems relating to Freedom of Information and Privacy Acts.
Instruction: Major topics covered in the course are the Freedom of Information Act: legislative history, publication; requirements; procedures and processing requests; exemptions and fees; and the Privacy Act definitions, limitations of disclosure; access to records; publication requirements; exemptions; and new systems reports. Methods of instruction include self-paced instruction with proctored examinations.
Credit Recommendation: In the lower division baccalaureate/associate degree category, 2 semester hours in Paralegal Studies (6/88) (6/93).

FOIA and the Privacy Act (ELAWS 335)

Location: Washington, DC.
Length: 30 hours (10 weeks).
Dates: January 1984-Present.
Objective: To provide the student with an understanding of the FOIA and Privacy Acts and apply the appropriate legal principles in solving relevant problems.
Learning Outcome: Upon successful completion of this course, the students will be able to understand the FOIA and Privacy Act that would enable them to file a request under either act or respond to a request if they are employed by a federal agency; appreciate how these statutes are administered by federal agencies; understand how litigation concerning these acts is handled in federal courts; demonstrate skills in researching and analyzing federal court cases; and appreciate the historical and legal foundation of these statutes in Anglo-American jurisprudence.

Instruction: Major topics covered in the course are the Freedom of Information Act: legislative history, publication requirements, procedures and processing request; exemptions, and fees, and the Privacy Act definitions; limitations of disclosure; access to records; publication and other requirements; exemptions; and new system reports. Methods of instruction include lecture, discussion, and case studies.

Credit Recommendation: In the lower division baccalaureate/associate degree category, 2 semester hours in Paralegal Studies (6/88) (6/93).

Immigration Law (ELAWS 252)

Location: Washington, DC or various locations throughout the United States.

Length: 30 hours (10 weeks).

Dates: September 1991-Present.

Objective: To train students to work with the Immigration and Nationality Act by focusing on specific procedures encountered by an alien in the United States that require legal assistance.

Learning Outcome: Upon successful completion of this course, the student will be able to understand major points of immigration law and procedures, and apply the Immigration and Nationality Act to specific fact patterns, including the completion of a claim for asylum.

Instruction: Major topics covered in the course are history and sources of immigration law; administrative structure of immigration law; concepts of alienage, citizenship and entry into the United States; requirements for immigrant and nonimmigrant visas; understanding of exclusion/deportation proceedings; and issues surrounding granting of asylum. Methods of instruction include lectures, examination, projects, and field trips.

Credit Recommendation: In the lower division baccalaureate/associate degree category, 3 semester hours in Paralegal Studies (6/93).

Introduction to Elderlaw (ELAWS 114)

Location: Washington, DC or various locations throughout the U.S.

Length: 30 hours (10 weeks).

Dates: March 1992-March 1997.

Objective: To provide the student with an introduction to the newly expanding legal specialty of Elderlaw.

Learning Outcome: Upon successful completion of this course, the student will be able to apply the various laws and regulations to resolve legal problems of clients or their family members; explain principles and issues; identify advantages and disadvantages of various legal procedures and documents; and to use efficient resources and sources of assistance.

Instruction: Major topics covered in the course are substantive law topics that highlight the key elements of governmental programs of particular interest to older persons including Social Security Retirement and Disability, Supplement Security Income, Medicaid and Medicare; issues in nursing home admissions contracts; elder abuse and consumer law; protective services; and surrogate decision making, including living will, powers of attorney, and guardianship. Methods of instruction include lectures by a team of experts, case-study analysis, oral discussion, and final examination.

Credit Recommendation: In the lower division baccalaureate/associate degree category, 3 semester hours in Paralegal Studies (6/93). **NOTE**: Credit for ELAWS 114 excludes credit for CLAWS 115.

Introduction to Elderlaw (LLAWS 115)

Location: Correspondence Study.

Length: 10 lessons (including final examination).

Dates: March 1992-Present.

Objective: To provide the student with an introduction to the newly-expanding legal specialty of Elderlaw.

Learning Outcome: Upon successful completion of this course, the student will be able to apply the various laws and regulations to resolve legal problems of clients or their family members; explain principles and issues; identify advantages and disadvantages of various legal procedures and documents; and to use efficient resources and sources of assistance.

Instruction: Major topics covered in the course are that substantive law topics highlight the key elements of governmental programs of particular interest to older persons including Social Security, retirement, and disability; supplement security income, Medicaid and Medicare; issues in nursing home admissions contracts; elder abuse and consumer law; protective services and surrogate decision making, including living will; and powers of attorney and guardianship. Methods of instruction include self-paced instruction with proctored examination.

Credit Recommendation: In the lower division baccalaureate/associate degree category, 3 semester hours in Paralegal Studies (6/93). **NOTE**: Credit for LLAWS 115 excludes credit for ELAWS 114.

Introduction to Law for Paralegals (CLAWS 110/LLAWS 110)

Location: Correspondence Study.

Length: 11 lessons (self-paced).

Dates: *Version 1:* February 1985-February 1992; *Version 2:* March 1992-Present.

Objective: To provide the student with a general introduction to the role paralegals play in the legal system.

Learning Outcome: *Version 1:* Upon successful completion of this course, the student will be able to understand the role of a paralegal in a lawyer's office and understand fundamental principles of legal writing. *Version 2:* Upon successful completion of this course, the student will be able to understand the various sources of law and legal principles applicable to a wide variety of situations; and students will be provided with a practical guide to the skills, duties, and responsibilities necessary for a paralegal profession.

Instruction: *Version 1:* Major topics covered in the course are constitutional law, criminal law, contracts law, tort law, wills and trusts law, real estate law, consumer protection law, skills of case analysis, and components of an opinion. Methods of instruction include self-paced instruction with proctored examination. *Version 2:* Major topics covered in the course are reading/briefing court opinions; legal analysis and writing skills; legal research; professional responsibilities; civil procedure; discovery; property; and family law. Methods of instruction include self-paced instruction with proctored examination.

Credit Recommendation: *Version 1:* In the lower division baccalaureate/associate degree category, 2 semester hours in Paralegal Studies (6/88). *Version 2:* In the lower division baccalaureate/associate degree category, 3 semester hours in Paralegal Studies (6/93). **NOTE:** Credit for one CLAWS 110 or LLAWS 110 excludes credit for the other.

Introduction to Law for Paralegals (ELAWS 110)

Location: Washington, DC.

Length: 30 hours (10 weeks).

Dates: January 1985-Present.

Objective: To provide the student with knowledge of the legal profession and the role of paralegals in that profession.

Learning Outcome: Upon successful completion of this course, the student will

be able to understand the elements of the American judicial system and concepts basic to various areas of substantive law.

Instruction: Major topics covered in the course are the court system, torts, contracts, domestic relations, legal research, administrative law, property law, and criminal law. Methods of instruction include lecture, discussion, texts, classroom exercises, case studies, and examinations.

Credit Recommendation: In the lower division baccalaureate/associate degree category, 2 semester hours legal Assisting or Paralegal Studies (1/90) (1/95).

Legal Ethics and Law Office Systems (CLAWS 116)

Location: Correspondence Study.

Length: 12 lessons.

Dates: January 1995-Present.

Objective: To provide the student with a thorough understanding of basic ethical principles and their applications to specific situations in the law as well as to management systems which are unique to law offices.

Learning Outcome: Upon successful completion of this course, the student will be able to identify a problem of legal ethics (as distinct from a question of law or pure ethics), and identify the authoritative canon, ethical considerations, and disciplinary rule (if extant) which apply; and weigh the facts of the problem against the canon and form a reasoned opinion

Instruction: Major topics covered in the course are integrity and competence; making legal services available; the unauthorized practice; preserving confidences and secrets; representing adverse interests; competence and professional negligence; zealous representation within the bonds of the law; work to improve the legal system; avoid the appearance of impropriety; regulating the profession; the business side of law; time billing and accounting; recordkeeping and automated systems; managing a fictitious case; opening the case; and protecting the client's interests during discovery. Methods of instruction include independent study by correspondence, graded assignments, a term paper, and a final examination.

Credit Recommendation: In the lower division baccalaureate/associate degree category, 3 semester hours in Paralegal Studies (1/95).

Legal Ethics and Law Office Systems (ELAWS 115)

Location: Washington, DC.

Length: 30 hours (10 weeks).

Dates: September 1980-Present.

Objective: To provide the student with an understanding of basic ethical principles and their application to specific situations in a law office, and understanding of the basic principles and procedures of law office management.

Learning Outcome: Upon successful completion of this course, the student will be able to identify and avoid potential breaches of legal ethics; research ethical precedents in evaluating and resolving specific ethical problems; and choose the most appropriate office management system for a specific law office.

Instruction: Major topics covered in the course are client and case file confidentiality, ethical obligations as an officer of the court, ethics as applicable to the paralegal, automated office systems, and time management. Methods of instruction include lecture, discussion, texts, term paper, case studies, and examination.

Credit Recommendation: In the lower division baccalaureate/associate degree category, 2 semester hours in Legal Assisting or Paralegal Studies (1/90) (1/95).

Legal Literature (CLAWS 210/LLAWS 210)

Location: Correspondence Study.

Length: 13 lessons.

Dates: January 1994-Present.

Objective: To provide students a basic legal literature vocabulary and skills in locating legal information from primary and secondary sources.

Learning Outcome: Upon successful completion of this course, the student will be able to find, access, and interpret primary and secondary sources of the law, including but not limited to the American legal system, court structure and court reporting, utilize West digests, ALR, Shepard's citations, looseleaf services, and other sources of relevant information.

Instruction: Major topics covered in the course are the structure of the law and its sources; dissecting a court opinion; federal court reporters; state court reporters and the national reporter system; reporter digests; annotated law reports (ALR); Shepard's citations; the federal and state constitution; sources of federal legislation; sources of federal legislative histories; administrative law resources; sources of looseleaf services; and secondary sources of the law. Methods of instruction include independent study by correspondence, graded assignments, and a final examination.`

Credit Recommendation: In the lower division baccalaureate/associate degree category, 3 semester hours in Paralegal Studies (1/95).

Legal Research (CLAWS 215/LLAWS 215) (Formerly Legal Research II [CLAWS 552])

Location: Correspondence Study.

Length: *Version 1:* 12 lessons (self-paced); *Versions 2 and 3:* 15 lessons (self-paced).

Dates: *Version 1:* June 1988-March 1992; *Version 2:* March 1992-June 1992; *Version 3:* July 1992-Present.

Objective: To provide the student with knowledge of basic concepts for effective research and research materials required to assist attorneys in general or government practice.

Learning Outcome: Upon successful completion of this course, the student will be able to assist lawyers in research required for various legal activities and express results of research in clearly written memoranda, client letters, and other legal communications.

Instruction: Major topics covered in the course are statutory materials; court cases; administrative law materials; various secondary sources; use of the computer in legal research; updating materials; and writing memoranda and briefs. Methods of instruction include self-paced instruction with proctored examination.

Credit Recommendation: *Version 1:* In the lower division baccalaureate/associate degree category, 2 semester hours in Paralegal Studies (6/88). *Version 2:* In the lower division baccalaureate/associate degree category, 2 semester hours in Paralegal Studies (6/88). *Version 3:* In the lower division baccalaureate/associate degree category, 3 semester hours in Paralegal Studies (6/93). **NOTE:** Credit for one CLAWS 215 or LLAWS 215 excludes credit for the other.

Legal Research I: Legal Literature (CLAWS 551)

Location: Correspondence Study.

Length: 13 lessons (self-paced).

Dates: June 1988-Present.

Objective: To provide the student with knowledge of legal materials used in researching statutory and judicial publications, their utility, contents, and currency for the libraries, library technician, and paralegal.

Learning Outcome: Upon successful completion of this course, the student will

be able to identify materials in the legislative history; identify and recover published opinions; identify administrative law materials; sherpardize; and identify and recover law journal articles.

Instruction: Major topics covered in the course are statutory materials; court cases; administrative law materials; various secondary sources; use of the computer in legal research;and updating materials. Methods of instruction include self-paced instruction with proctored examination.

Credit Recommendation: In the lower division baccalaureate/associate degree category, 2 semester hours in Paralegal Studies (6/88) (6/93).

Legal Research I: Legal Literature (ELAWS 551)

Location: Washington, DC.

Length: 30 hours (10 weeks).

Dates: January 1987-Present.

Objective: To provide the student with knowledge of legal materials used in researching statutory and judicial publications with emphasis on their utility, contents, and currency for the paralegal.

Learning Outcome: Upon successful completion of this course, the student will be able to identify materials in the legislative history; identify and recover published opinions; identify administrative law materials; shepardize; and identify and recover law journal articles.

Instruction: Major topics covered in the course are statutory materials; court cases; administrative law materials; various secondary sources; use of the computer in legal research; and updating materials. Methods of instruction include lecture, discussion, and case studies.

Credit Recommendation: In the lower division baccalaureate/associate degree category, 2 semester hours in Paralegal Studies (6/88) (6/93).

Legal Research II (ELAWS 552)

Location: Washington, DC.

Length: 30 hours (10 weeks).

Dates: December 1988-Present.

Objective: To provide the student with instruction covering the rules of legal writing, statutory interpretation, case analysis, citation checking, shepardizing techniques, reviewing unpublished legal materials, and preparing office memoranda.

Learning Outcome: Upon successful completion of this course, the student will be able to apply rules for statutory interpretation; compile legislative histories; prepare office briefs for attorneys; check cities; shepardize cases and states; and weigh authorities.

Instruction: Major topics covered in the course are basic concepts for effective research and surveys the research materials required to assist attorneys in general and government practice; applies materials in solving problems and writing memoranda and briefs; and emphasizes writing skills and research.

Credit Recommendation: In the lower division baccalaureate/associate degree category, 2 semester hours in Paralegal Studies (6/88) (6/93).

Legal Writing (CLAWS 220/LLAWS 220)

Location: Washington, DC.

Length: 30 hours (10 weeks).

Dates: September 1945-Present.

Objective: To provide the student with skill in preparing accurate, concise, and logical memoranda and arguments in various legal documents.

Learning Outcome: Upon successful completion of this course, the student will be able to summarize case opinions and legal arguments of opponents; identify legal issues; and draft persuasive arguments in a logical manner.

Instruction: Major topics covered in the course are types of legal documents, memoranda, and case briefs. Methods of instruction include lecture, discussion, texts, classroom exercises, written assignments, and examinations.

Credit Recommendation: In the lower division baccalaureate/associate degree category, 2 semester hours in Communication Arts, Legal Assisting, or Paralegal Studies (1/90) (1/95).

Legal Writing I (CLAWS 555)

Location: Correspondence Study.

Length: *Version 1:* 12 lessons (self-paced); *Version 2:* 13 lessons (self-paced).

Dates: *Version 1:* February 1986-May 1992; *Version 2:* June 1992-Present.

Objective: To provide the student with knowledge of techniques for clear and effective legal writing.

Learning Outcome: Upon successful completion of this course, the student will be able to understand and use appropriate legal forms and communicate effectively in legal writing.

Instruction: *Version 1:* Major topics covered in the course are leases, employment contracts, wills, case briefs, and interoffice memoranda. Methods of instruction include self-paced instruction with proctored examinations. *Version 2:* Major topics covered in the course are wills; legal memoranda; real estate contracts; leases; consumer credit agreements; legal complaints; opinion letters; and legal citations. Methods of instruction include self-paced instruction with proctored examination.

Credit Recommendation: *Version 1:* In the lower division baccalaureate/associate degree category, 2 semester hours in Communication Arts, Journalism, or Paralegal Studies (6/88). *Version 2:* In the lower division baccalaureate/associate degree category, 3 semester hours in Paralegal Studies (6/93). **NOTE:** CDt for one CLAWS 220 or LLAWS 220 excludes credit for the other.

Legal Writing II (CLAWS 556)

Location: Correspondence Study.

Length: 11 lessons (self-paced).

Dates: August 1987-January 1998.

Objective: To provide the student with advanced knowledge of techniques for clear and effective legal writing.

Learning Outcome: Upon successful completion of this course, the student will be able to understand and use appropriate legal forms and communicate effectively in legal writing.

Instruction: Major topics covered in the course are pretrial writing in the form of a memorandum and pleadings; a trial brief; legal correspondence of various types; and legislative drafting. Methods of instruction include self-paced instruction with proctored examination.

Credit Recommendation: In the lower division baccalaureate/associate degree category, 2 semester hours in Communication Arts, Journalism, or Paralegal Studies (6/88) (6/93).

Litigation (CLAWS 345)

Location: Correspondence Study.

Length: *Version 1:* 11 lessons (self-paced); *Version 2:* 12 lessons (self-paced including a mid-term and final examination).

Dates: *Version 1:* August 1987-April 1993; *Version 2:* May 1993-Present.

Objective: To acquaint the student with procedural aspects of the litigation process.

Learning Outcome: Upon successful completion of this course, the student will be able to understand the litigation process and assist attorneys in case investigation, evaluation, and preparation of litigation documents.

Instruction: Major topics covered in the course are the process of civil litigation for paralegals; factual investigation of the client's case; preparation of pleadings and pretrial motions that are necessary to commence and defend a lawsuit; discovery devices available for obtaining relevant information from opposing and third parties and what to do with that information in preparing for trial; and, finally, post-trial proceedings and settlement documents. Methods of instruction include self-paced instruction with proctored examination.

Credit Recommendation: In the lower division baccalaureate/associate degree category, 2 semester hours in Paralegal Studies (6/88) (6/93).

Medicare and Medigap Law (LLAWS 320)

Location: Correspondence Study.

Length: 9 lessons (self-paced including final).

Dates: June 1993-Present.

Objective: To provide the student with a knowledge of Medicare rules and regulations regarding eligibility, coverage, and appeals procedures; and private "Medigap" policies.

Learning Outcome: Upon successful completion of this course, the student will be able to understand the structure of the Medicare program; identify services covered by Medicare Parts "A" and "B"; comprehend special issues regarding Medicare HMO's; be familiar with the shapes of the administrative appeals process; and identify the provision of standard "Medigap" policies.

Instruction: Major topics covered in the course are Medicare structure and operation; Medicare coverage of hospital care; skilled nursing home health care; hospice and health maintenance organizations (HMO's); Medicare appeals; private insurance; and "Medigap." Methods of instruction include self-paced instruction with proctored examination.

Credit Recommendation: In the upper division baccalaureate degree category, 2 semester hours in Paralegal Studies (6/93).

Nursing Home Law (LLAWS 225)

Location: Correspondence Study.

Length: 10 lessons (self-paced including final examination).

Dates: February 1993-Present.

Objective: To provide the student with an understanding of issues and questions facing older persons and their families in regard to nursing home care, alternative long-term care, and financial aspects.

Learning Outcome: Upon successful completion of this course, the student will be able to answer the questions asked by older persons and their family and resolve the problems that may develop involving nursing homes; identify alternative to nursing home care; and plan for the cost of long-term care.

Instruction: Major topics covered in the course are nursing home facilities; quality-of-care standards; resident rights; admission and discharge issues; financing (Medicare, Medicaid, private insurance); alternative to nursing home care; and advance planning for financial and health-care decisions. Methods of instruction include self-paced instruction with proctored examination; the emphasis is on practical and legal remedies.

Credit Recommendation: In the lower division baccalaureate/associate degree category, 3 semester hours in Paralegal Studies (6/93).

Protective Services Law (LLAWS 315)

Location: Correspondence Study.

Length: 10 lessons (self-paced including final examination).

Dates: June 1992-Present.

Objective: To provide the student with the comprehension and practical knowledge of the legal tools available to protect the person or property of individuals in case of incapacity.

Learning Outcome: Upon successful completion of this course, the student will be able to understand the advantages and disadvantages of powers of attorney for both financial and medical decisions and living wills; gain experience in drafting such documents; and understand the law and issues involving representative payees, guardians, and conservators, adult protective services, and long-term care placement.

Instruction: Major topics covered in the course are powers of attorney; advance medical directives; health care decision making; representative payee programs; financial planning; guardians and conservators; adult abuse protective statutes; and pre-admission screening to nursing homes. Methods of instruction include self-paced instruction with proctored examination.

Credit Recommendation: In the upper division baccalaureate degree category, 2 semester hours in Paralegal Studies (6/93).

Public Benefits (LLAWS 355)

Location: Correspondence Study.

Length: 9 lessons.

Dates: August 1994-Present.

Objective: To become familiar with laws and regulations for railroad, retirements, food stamps, VA benefits, and energy assistance programs; and become familiar with Social Security retirement, Medicaid, supplemental security incomes, and disability benefit programs.

Learning Outcome: Upon successful completion of this course, the student will be able to comprehend the scope of poverty for senior citizens including eligibility for benefits, and examine and interpret the role of administrative hearings and procedural rights.

Instruction: Major topics covered in the course are an introduction to public benefits, food stamps, veterans benefits, railroad retirement, low-income home energy assistance program, supplemental security income, Medicaid, Medicare, and administrative appeals. Methods of instruction include independent study by correspondence, graded assignments, and a final examination.

Credit Recommendation: In the lower division baccalaureate/associate degree category, 2 semester hours in Paralegal Studies (1/95).

Real Estate Principles (ELAWS 250)

Location: Washington, DC.

Length: 30 hours (10 weeks).

Dates: January 1986-Present.

Objective: To provide the student with an understanding of fundamental principles and theories relevant to real estate transactions.

Learning Outcome: Upon successful completion of this course, the student will be able to use in appropriate ways the basic terminology of real estate transactions; understand legal principles relevant to real estate transactions; and assist attorneys in document preparation and interpretation.

Instruction: Major topics covered in the course are types of ownership, recording and transferring of title, contract law as applicable to real estate, financing, taxation, and appraisals. Methods of instruction include lecture, discussion, text and handouts, and examinations.

Credit Recommendation: In the lower division baccalaureate/associate degree category, 2 semester hours in Business Administration, Legal Assisting, Paralegal Studies, or Real Estate (1/90) (1/95).

Real Estate Transaction (CLAWS 350)

Location: Correspondence Study.

Length: 16 lessons (self-paced).

Dates: August 1987-Present.
Objective: To provide the student with the comprehension and practical knowledge of real estate laws and procedures.
Learning Outcome: Upon successful completion of this course, the student will be able to assist the lawyer in preparing documents for various real estate transactions.
Instruction: Major topics covered in the course are property rights and interests; legal aspects of real estate transactions and settlement; and drafting of a real estate sales contract and settlement documents. Methods of instruction include self-paced instruction with proctored examination.
Credit Recommendation: *Version 1:* In the lower division baccalaureate/associate degree category, 2 semester hours in Business Administration or Paralegal Studies (6/88). *Version 2:* In the lower division baccalaureate/associate degree category, 3 semester hours in Business Administration, Paralegal Studies, or Urban Studies (6/93).

Social Security and Supplemental Income Law (LLAWS 300)

Location: Correspondence Study.
Length: 10 lessons.
Dates: March 1994-Present.
Objective: To acquaint the student with aspects of the Social Security Act and its programs, including the process of determining appropriate entitlements and methods of compliance.
Learning Outcome: Upon successful completion of this course, the student will be able to understand the history and administration of the Social Security Act including benefit calculations and determinations as well as the necessary methods of enforcing benefit entitlements.
Instruction: Major topics covered in the course are Social Security Act; supplemental security income overview; disability program overview; authorized representatives; sequential evaluation; gathering evidence; notices and appeals; administrative hearings; and overpayment and medical improvement. Methods of instruction include independent study by correspondence, graded assignments, and a final examination.
Credit Recommendation: In the lower division baccalaureate/associate degree category, 3 semester hours in Paralegal Studies (1/95).

Tort Law (CLAWS 240)

Location: Correspondence Study.
Length: 12 lessons.
Dates: April 1987-Present.
Objective: To provide the student with an understanding of the principles of tort law and application of these principles to specific situations.
Learning Outcome: Upon successful completion of this course, the student will be able to identify the bases of tort liability in both intentional and unintentional torts and the various defenses available in given tort situations.
Instruction: Major topics covered in the course are duty owed, proximate cause, defenses, negligence, vicatious liability, product liability, strict liability, and defamation. Methods of instruction include independent study, study guide, written assignments, instructor feedback, and a proctored examination.
Credit Recommendation: In the lower division baccalaureate/associate degree category, 3 semester hours in Legal Assisting or Paralegal Studies (1/90) (1/95).

Tort Law (ELAWS 240)

Location: Washington, DC.
Length: 30 hours (10 weeks).
Dates: January 1987-Present.
Objective: To provide the student with an understanding of the fundamental principles of substantive tort law.
Learning Outcome: Upon successful completion of this course, the student will be able to define torts and distinguish them from contracts and from crimes; explain the basis of tort liability, describe intentional torts; define negligence; define strict liability; identify defenses to intentional torts; identify defense to an action in negligence; identify defenses to an action in strict liability; and identify recoverable damages for negligence, intentional torts, and strict liability.
Instruction: Major topics covered in the course are fundamental principles of torts, including consideration of liability based on negligence; intentional torts, and strict liability; the relationship of tort to contract, with special attention given to recoverable damages; and trespass, conversion, false imprisonment, assault, fraud, defamation, mental distress, and misuse of legal process. Methods of instruction include lecture, discussion, and case studies.
Credit Recommendation: In the lower division baccalaureate/associate degree category, 2 semester hours in Paralegal Studies (6/88) (6/93).

Wills and Probate (ELAWS 166)

Location: Washington, DC.
Length: 30 hours (10 weeks).
Dates: January 1987-Present.
Objective: To provide the student with knowledge of wills and estates from planning to administration.
Learning Outcome: Upon successful completion of this course, the student will be able to understand interstate distribution; taxes relevant to decedents and heirs; how to title property to avoid probate; how wills and trusts are drafted and the different types of each; and the process of probate and estate administration.
Instruction: Major topics covered in the course are how to administer the estate of a decedent and the basics of creating wills, trusts, and other instruments (deeds, joint accounts, etc.) that transfer monetary interests at death. Methods of instruction include lecture, discussion, and case studies.
Credit Recommendation: In the lower division baccalaureate/associate degree category, 2 semester hours in Paralegal Studies (6/88) (6/93).

Wills, Trusts, and Estate Administration (CLAWS 275)

Location: Correspondence Study.
Length: 10 lessons (self-paced).
Dates: August 1987-Present.
Objective: To provide the student with knowledge of wills and estates from planning to administration.
Learning Outcome: Upon successful completion of this course, the student will be able to provide effective assistance to attorneys and agencies involved in probate.
Instruction: Major topics covered in the course are client interview; tax considerations; intestacy; distribution by operation of law; elements of a will; trusts; complex wills; execution and other formalities; revocations; codicils and other means of changing a will; will substitutes; and probate. Methods of instruction include self-paced instruction with proctored examination.
Credit Recommendation: *Version 1:* In the lower division baccalaureate/associate degree category, 2 semester hours in Paralegal Studies (6/88). *Version 2:* In the lower division baccalaureate/associate degree category, 3 semester hours in Paralegal Studies (6/93).

PERSONNEL

Basic Labor-Management Relations (EPERS 450)

Location: Washington, DC.

Length: 30 hours (10 weeks).

Dates: September 1984-Present.

Objective: To provide the student with an understanding of the law and practice of labor relations, particularly in the federal sector.

Learning Outcome: Upon successful completion of this course, the student will be able to describe legal framework of federal sector labor relations; describe labor relations practices in the federal sector; and compare labor relations in federal, state, local, and private sectors.

Instruction: Major topics covered in the course are the history of federal sector labor relations, functions and roles of the Federal Labor Relations Authority and other relevant federal agencies, the process by which unions win representation rights in the federal agencies, the process by which unions win representation rights in the federal sector, and practice of federal sector labor relations and comparison with state, local, and private sector labor relations. Methods of instruction include lecture, discussion, classroom exercises, and examinations.

Credit Recommendation: In the lower division baccalaureate/associate degree category, 2 semester hours in Business Administration, Labor Studies, or Public Administration (1/90) (1/95).

Federal Personnel Procedures (CPERS 130)

Location: Correspondence Study.

Length: 15 lessons (maximum completion time is 1 year).

Dates: January 1980-Present.

Objective: To provide the student with an understanding and application of government personnel policies and regulations to areas of labor-management relations.

Learning Outcome: Upon successful completion of this course, the student will be able to identify major components of the federal personnel system and explain the importance of each; recognize and explain management's personnel responsibilities to employees; provide assistance to management in carrying out these responsibilities; and analyze personnel problems and select appropriate policies and procedures for resolution.

Instruction: Major topics covered in the course are the background of the federal personnel system, using the federal personnel manual, processing personnel actions, position classification, staffing and placement, affirmative employment, adverse actions, grievance and appeals, retirement, reductions in force, training, labor-management relations, and benefits and leave. Methods of instruction include independent study, study guide, written assignments, instructor feedback, and proctored examination.

Credit Recommendation: In the lower division baccalaureate/associate degree category, 2 semester hours in Business Administration, Management, Personnel Administration, or Public Administration (1/90).

Federal Personnel Procedures (EPERS 130)

Location: Washington, DC.

Length: 30 hours (10 weeks).

Dates: September 1984-Present.

Objective: To provide the student with an understanding and application of federal government personnel policies and regulations to areas of labor-management relations.

Learning Outcome: Upon successful completion of this course, the student will be able to identify major components of the federal personnel system and explain the importance of each; recognize and explain management's personnel responsibilities to employees; provide assistance to management in carrying out these responsibilities; and analyze personnel problems and select appropriate policies and procedures for resolution.

Instruction: Major topics covered in the course are the background of federal personnel system, using the federal personnel manual, processing personnel actions, position classification, staffing and placement, affirmative employment, adverse actions, grievance and appeals, retirement, reductions in force, training, labor-management relations, and benefits and leave. Methods of instruction include lecture, discussion, text and Federal Personnel Manual, classroom exercises, case studies, and an examination.

Credit Recommendation: In the lower division baccalaureate/associate degree category, 2 semester hours in Business Administration, Management, Personnel Administration, or Public Administration (1/90) (1/95).

Human Resource Development (NPERS 516)

Location: Washington, DC.

Length: 120 hours (4 weeks).

Dates: October 1989-Present.

Objective: To provide the student with identification and analysis of human resource development principles, issues, and approaches; and, identification of criteria for assessing HRD training needs; and establishing and maintaining HRD support programs.

Learning Outcome: Upon successful completion of this course, the student will be able to apply HRD principles and approaches to organizations and cultures in which students will work; plan and deliver training programs that orientate line managers to HRD principles and approaches; conduct comprehensive assessments of HRD training needs; and develop training curricula to meet training needs.

Instruction: Major topics covered in the course are human resources effectiveness in economic and social paradigm shift; critical elements of HRD effectiveness; and HRD management tools (e.g., performance management and total quality management). Methods of instruction include lecture, discussion, case studies, models, and projects.

Credit Recommendation: In the upper division baccalaureate or graduate degree category, 3 semester hours in Human Resources Management or Business Administration (6/93).

Personnel Recruitment Principles and Practices (EPERS 230)

Location: Washington, DC.

Length: 20 hours (10 weeks).

Dates: January 1985-Present.

Objective: To provide the student with an understanding of various recruitment techniques for personnel administrators.

Learning Outcome: Upon successful completion of this course, the student will be able to understand the role of recruiters; describe recruitment processes; prepare and conduct an employment interview; and understand Equal Employment Opportunity recruitment regulations.

Instruction: Major topics covered in the course are job interview techniques, recruitment planning, special emphasis recruitment, and recruitment regulations. Methods of instruction include lecture, discussion, case studies, term paper, and examinations.

Credit Recommendation: In the lower division baccalaureate/associate degree category, 1 semester hour in Business Administration, Management, Personnel

Administration, or Public Administration (1/90) (1/95).

Position Classification (EPERS 340)

Location: Washington, DC.
Length: 30 hours (10 weeks).
Dates: September 1984-Present.
Objective: To provide the student with an understanding of policies and practices relevant to position classification in the federal sector.
Learning Outcome: Upon successful completion of this course, the student will be able to apply federal government policies and regulations in all aspects of position management.
Instruction: Major topics covered in the course are the Civil Service Reform Act of 1978, classes of positions, qualifications and classifications, techniques of classification, position analysis, factor evaluation system, position management and conflict, and wage grade classification system. Methods of instruction include lecture, discussion, classroom exercises, class studies, and examinations.
Credit Recommendation: In the lower division baccalaureate/associate degree category, 2 semester hours in Business Administration, Personnel Administration, or Public Administration (1/90).

Staffing and Placement (EPERS 250)

Location: Washington, DC.
Length: 30 hours (10 weeks).
Dates: September 1984-January 1995.
Objective: To provide the student with a knowledge of general principles and background of federal service staffing.
Learning Outcome: Upon successful completion of this course, the student will be able to identify the processes involved in selecting personnel for promotion; identify employee recruitment and placement regulations; understand basic principles involved in conducting effective interviews; and understand roles of employees, supervisors, and personnel officers in the recruitment process.
Instruction: Major topics covered in the course are placement records, Equal Employment Opportunity/special employment programs, candidate evaluation, recruitment process, and staffing functions. Methods of instruction include lecture, discussion, case studies, and examinations.
Credit Recommendation: In the lower division baccalaureate/associate degree category, 2 semester hours in Business Administration, Management, Personnel Administration, or Public Administration (1/90) (1/95).

SCIENCES

Dynamic Meteorology I (CMETO 361)

Location: Correspondence Study.
Length: 16 lessons (self-paced).
Dates: April 1982-Present.
Objective: To provide the student with the fundamentals of general meteorology.
Learning Outcome: Upon successful completion of this course, the student will be able to understand the concepts of dynamics as applied to weather analysis and to weather forecasting.
Instruction: Major topics covered in the course are fundamental concepts, thermodynamics, thermodynamics of water vapor, hydrostatic equilibrium and geopotential, and stability. Methods of instruction include self-paced instruction with proctored examination.
Credit Recommendation: In the upper division baccalaureate degree category, 3 semester hours in Meteorology (6/88) (6/93).

Dynamic Meteorology II (CMETO 362)

Location: Correspondence study.
Length: 10 lessons (self-paced).
Dates: August 1982-Present.
Objective: To provide the student with a continuation of Dynamic Meteorology I, covering the application of the general principles of mechanics and fluid motion to the study of the atmosphere and its movement.
Learning Outcome: Upon successful completion of this course, the student will be able to apply concepts of mechanics and fluid motion to the study of the atmosphere; apply concepts of mechanics and fluid motion to weather analysis; and apply concepts of mechanics and fluid motion to weather forecasting.
Instruction: Major topics covered in the course are vector analysis; equations of motion; horizontal motion; variations of wind, pressure, and thermal fields in the vertical; mechanism of pressure change; and weather prediction. Methods of instruction include self-paced instruction with proctored examination.
Credit Recommendation: In the upper division baccalaureate degree category, 3 semester hours in Meteorology (6/88) (6/93).

General Physics I (CPHYS 201)

Location: Correspondence Study.
Length: 13 lessons (self-paced).
Dates: June 1988-Present.
Objective: To provide the student with a working knowledge of basic physical concepts, applying the acquired principles of physics to fields of study, or employment.
Learning Outcome: Upon successful completion of this course, the student will be able to exhibit a working knowledge of certain basic physical concepts; relate the knowledge acquired to classes of problems in areas such as pollution, energy, water quality and describe physical phenomena in a manner universally understood by other physical scientists.
Instruction: Major topics covered in the course are kinematics, dynamics, gravitation, equilibrium, energy, fluids, temperature, kinetic theory, heat, thermodynamics, waves, and sound. Methods of instruction include self-paced instruction with proctored examination.
Credit Recommendation: In the lower division baccalaureate/associate degree category, 3 semester hours in noncalculus-based Physics or Physical Science (6/88) (6/93).

General Physics II (CPHYS 202)

Location: Correspondence Study.
Length: 11 lessons (self-paced).
Dates: June 1988-Present.
Objective: To provide the student with a working knowledge of physical concepts such that those principles may be applied.
Learning Outcome: Upon successful completion of this course, the student will be able to exhibit a working knowledge of key physical concepts; relate the knowledge acquired to certain classes of problems which impact society (i.e., energy needs, radioactivity, nuclear effects).
Instruction: Major topics covered in the course are a continuation of General Physics I and includes the introduction of electric field, magnetism, circuits, light and electromagnetic waves, relativity, quantum theory and quantum mechanics, atoms, radioactivity, and nuclear energy. Methods of instruction include self-paced instruction with proctored examination.
Credit Recommendation: In the lower division baccalaureate/associate degree category, 3 semester hours in noncalculus-

based Physics or Physical Science (6/88) (6/93).

Introduction to Meteorology (CMETO 160)

Location: Home study correspondence course.

Length: 11 lessons (1 year limit with possible extension for a fee).

Dates: September 1995-Present.

Objective: To provide a comprehensive survey of atmospheric processes for those interested and those wishing to become meteorologists.

Learning Outcome: Upon successful completion of this course, the student will be able to understand the basic dynamic nature of the atmosphere, give a preliminary evaluation of a weather map, and discuss intelligently weather parameters and atmospheric variables, as well as apply this knowledge to the betterment of mankind.

Instruction: Major topics covered in the course are basic in nature and include a study of the atmosphere, solar and terrestrial radiation, temperature, moisture and atmospheric stability, forms of condensation and precipitation, air pressure and winds, circulation, air masses, weather patterns, and weather forecasting. Methods of instruction include self-pace independent study, written learner presentations/reports, written assignments graded by an instructor, a mid-term examination, and a final proctored examination.

Credit Recommendation: In the lower division baccalaureate/associate degree category, 3 semester hours in Introduction to Meteorology or Introduction to Atmospheric Sciences (3/96).

Physical Meteorology (CMETO 260)

Location: Home study correspondence course.

Length: 10 lessons (1 year limit with possible extension for a fee).

Dates: September 1995-Present.

Objective: To provide the student with a fundamental knowledge of the physical parameters of the Earth's atmosphere.

Learning Outcome: Upon successful completion of this course, the student will be able to understand and utilize knowledge of the physical processes within the atmosphere and know the relationships between these processes and various environmental factors.

Instruction: Major topics covered in the course are basic physics of the atmosphere and, in particular, include basic cloud processes, radiation transfer, gravitational effects, atmospheric gases, physical processes in the atmosphere, atmospheric electricity, laws relative to radiational physics, solar radiation, terrestrial radiation, radiational balance of the Earth, atmospheric optics, air pollution, and global climates. Methods of instruction include self-paced independent study, written learner presentations/reports, written assignment graded by an instructor, and a final proctored examination.

Credit Recommendation: In the lower division baccalaureate/associate degree category, 3 semester hours in Physical Meteorology or Atmospheric Physics (3/96).

Synoptic Meteorology I (CMETO 461)

Location: Home study correspondence course.

Length: 12 lessons (1 year limit with possible extension for a fee).

Dates: September 1995-Present.

Objective: To provide the student with the fundamental knowledge necessary to derive horizontal and vertical parameters of synoptic or large areas of the atmosphere from surface analyses.

Learning Outcome: Upon successful completion of this course, the student will be able to understand the three-dimensional nature and non-linearity of the atmosphere; utilize the tools of the meteorologist, such as surface and satellite analyses, Nested Grid Methods, Skew T-Log P Diagrams, National Weather Service Models, and concepts of vorticity and stability and derive synoptic atmospheric variables.

Instruction: Major topics covered in the course are instruction in the general principles of synoptic meteorology; various techniques of atmospheric observation such as surface, upper-air, radar, and satellite observations; and the analysis of atmospheric circulation, various analytical procedures, and an introduction to kinematics as applied to the atmosphere, vorticity, vertical structures, Skew T-Log P Diagrams, thermal structures of the atmosphere, isentropic analysis, vertical motions, and the derived forces and resultant winds. Methods of instruction include self-paced independent study, written learner presentations/reports, written assignments graded by an instructor, a mid-term examination, and a final proctored examination.

Credit Recommendation: In the upper division baccalaureate degree category, 3 semester hours in Synoptic Meteorology (3/96).

Synoptic Meteorology II (CMETO 462)

Location: Home study correspondence course.

Length: 11 lessons (1 year limit with possible extension for a fee).

Dates: September 1995-Present.

Objective: This course is designed to follow Synoptic Meteorology I or CMETO 461. The emphasis is on the study of air masses; global weather patterns; surface analysis and pressure-pattern recognition, as well as further study of the vertical structures of the atmosphere.

Learning Outcome: Upon successful completion of this course, the student will be able to utilize applicable data to analyze surface maps; identify air masses, patterns, mesoscale features as well as analyze vertical structures such as cell and supercell convective complexes and with the aid of surface, radar, and satellite data; and determine the various features of the atmosphere.

Instruction: Major topics covered in the course are air mass patterns, surface analysis, pressure-pattern recognition, and the evolution of cyclones and anticyclones. Portions of the course covers features such as global weather patterns, further study of the vertical structure of the atmosphere, isentropic analyses, jet streams, squall lines, development of supercells, tornadoes, dry lines, satellite analysis, as well as tropical weather systems. Methods of instruction include self-paced independent study, written learner presentations/reports, written assignments graded by an instructor, a mid-term examination, and a final proctored examination.

Credit Recommendation: In the upper division baccalaureate/associate degree category, 3 semester hours in Synoptic Meteorology (3/96).

U.S. Department of Defense Security Institute

The U.S. Department of Defense Security Institute (DoDSI) is an activity established by the Secretary of Defense. The Institute is under the management oversight, policy direction, and technical guidance of the Deputy Assistant Secretary of Defense (Intelligence and Security).

The Institute serves as the Department of Defense focal point for promoting activities supporting DoD security programs in education and training, awareness, and career development. The Institute presents courses of instruction, including independent study, resident, and field extension, relating to the Department of Defense Security Programs. These courses are designed for U.S. Government personnel, plus selected employees and representatives of U.S. industry.

Five teams manage and provide the education, training, and special publications and products for DoDSI. The Security Education and Awareness Team primarily produces or coordinates production of the DoDSI recurring and special publications and products. These publications include a topical bulletin on security and a periodical of news clippings of security interest. The Industrial Security Team produces and conducts courses and special training in the National Industrial Security program as well as personnel security investigations and interviews. The Personnel Security Team produces and conducts courses and special training in the DoD personnel security, administration, management, and adjudications. The Systems Protection Training Team offers training in special access programs security, acquisitions systems protection, AIS security and security briefings. Finally, the Information Security Team produces and conducts courses and special training in the DoD information security program, classification management, international security, and in general security requirements and management.

Selection procedures for faculty members must conform to requirements by the Federal Government's Office of Personnel Management (OPM). Applicants must submit a personal qualification statement which is reviewed by panel members selected for their expertise in the subject area. Knowledge, skills, abilities, education, work experience, and other pertinent qualifying information is used to determine the rating of an applicant. The instructors are evaluated twice yearly by team members who provide feedback and critique on their performances.

To receive a course diploma, students must demonstrate mastery of course content through formal examination, formally evaluated criterion exercises, the completion of graded written exercises, faculty observation and evaluation, and graded homework assignments or some combination thereof. Students who do not meet minimum academic or performance standards are given a letter of attendance in lieu of a course diploma. All students are assigned to faculty advisors, and when students develop academic or performance problems, their advisor works with them in free time to improve their mastery of the required knowledge or skills.

Source of official student records: Registrar, Department of Defense Security Institute, c/o Defense General Supply Center, 8000 Jefferson Davis Highway, Richmond, VA 23297-5091.

Additional information about the courses: College Credit Recommendation Service, American Council on Education, One Dupont Circle, Washington, DC 20036-1193.

Advanced Personnel Security Adjudications (5220.12)

Location: Richmond, VA.

Length: 37 hours (1 week).

Dates: March 1993-Present.

Objective: To train senior personnel security adjudicators in the advanced skills required to make final adjudicative determinations for security eligibility and administer due process procedures when necessary.

Learning Outcome: Upon successful completion of this course, the student will be able to identify significant derogatory information in cases during initial, post-adjudicative and reconsideration reviews; adjudicate significant derogatory information in cases during initial, post-adjudicative and reconsideration review; prepare Statement of Reasons; review replies to and make final determinations; review reconsideration requests to determine presence of new mitigating information; and obtain additional investigation necessary and make recommendations to sustain or overturn initial determinations.

Instruction: Major topics covered in the course are review of significant derogatory information; requesting additional information, to include any medical evaluation necessary; evaluation of significant derogatory and/or additional information; writing Statement of Reasons; reviewing rebuttals; final determinations; reconsideration requests. Methods of instruction include lecture/discussion, computer assisted videos, laboratory, and an examination.

Credit Recommendation: In the lower division baccalaureate/associate degree category, 2 semester hours in Personnel Management (9/95). **NOTE:** DoD Personnel Security Adjudications Course (5220.11) is a prerequisite for this course.

Basic Personnel Security Investigations (5220.16)

Location: Richmond, VA and various locations nationally.

Length: 67 hours (2 weeks).

Dates: January 1993-Present.

Objective: To provide security personnel within the Department of Defense, and from other federal agencies, with training on the elements and techniques of conducting personnel security investigations.

Learning Outcome: Upon successful completion of this course, the student will be able to conduct interviews and record checks; report information from confidential sources; obtain statements; and write reports of investigation and identify fundamentals of effective case management.

Instruction: Major topics covered in the course are conducting personnel security investigations; the background investigations process; techniques and procedures for record reviews and interviews; development and resolution of derogatory issue information; fundamentals of report writing; essentials of effective case management; adjudicative procedures; the uses and types of subject interviews in personnel security investigations; and the relevance of polygraph examinations in the personnel security investigations process. Methods of instruction include lecture, discussion, interviews, practical exercises, and examinations.

Credit Recommendation: In the lower division baccalaureate/associate degree category, 3 semester hours in Basic Personnel Security Investigations (9/95).

Information Systems Security Basics (5220.22)

Location: Richmond, VA.

Length: 36 hours (4.5 days).

Dates: April 1994-Present.

Objective: To present basic computer security skills training to entry level personnel so that they may successfully perform their duties as Information Systems Security Officers.

Learning Outcome: Upon successful completion of this course, the student will

be able to explain the threat to and vulnerabilities of information systems; discuss the history of information systems security laws and policy and their impact on the responsibilities of an information systems security officer and practitioner; employ appropriate security countermeasures and safeguards to manage threats and minimize vulnerabilities; and identify required physical, personnel, and procedural security procedures to protect information and the systems on which it is processed.

Instruction: Major topics covered in the course are computer security skills to support the protection of information and information systems as they relate to defensive information warfare. Methods of instruction include lecture, projects, presentations, team work, videos, and interactive computer.

Credit Recommendation: In the lower division baccalaureate/associate degree category, 2 semester hours in Security Systems (9/95).

International Program Security (5220.03)

Location: Richmond, VA.

Length: 33.6 hours (1 week, plus approximately 2 hours per night of additional reading.

Dates: November 1993-Present.

Objective: To provide a basis for personnel to identify the applicable security requirements of an international program, how to implement international program security requirements, and how to provide the security support necessary to assist in properly carrying out the objectives of an international program at command or organizational level, and in industry.

Learning Outcome: Upon successful completion of this course, the student will be able to recognize and identify the security implications of various types of government sponsored international programs and commercial sales.

Instruction: Major topics covered in the course are the security implications of international programs, to include government programs and commercial sales; the interrelationship of the information disclosure and technology transfer decision process; the National Disclosure Policy (NDP); the International Traffic in Arms Regulation (ITAR); and the Export Administration Regulations (EAR). Methods of instruction include lecture, projects, presentations, team work, videos, and interactive computer.

Credit Recommendation: In the lower division baccalaureate/associate degree category, 3 semester hours in Security (9/95).

Introduction to Personnel Security Adjudications (DoD Personnel Security Adjudications Independent Study Course [DS 1102])

Location: Student's work site or home.

Length: Self-study (approximately 50 hours).

Dates: *Version 1:* July 1988-August 1995; *Version 2:* September 1995-Present.

Objective: To prepare DoD personnel security adjudicators for attendance in the DoD Personnel Security Adjudications Course (resident phase) by introducing students to the DoD Personnel Security Program and the process of making personnel security determinations.

Learning Outcome: Upon successful completion of this course, the student will be able to identify appropriate national security threats; demonstrate an understanding of methods, policies, and procedures employed by the Defense Investigative Service, Office of Personnel Management, and other investigative agencies in the conduct of security investigations; and demonstrate an ability to analyze, weigh, decide, and act on given personnel security information.

Instruction: Major topics covered in the course are an introduction to the personnel security program; employing activities' initial responsibilities; personnel security investigations; central adjudication; adjudicative issues; continuous evaluation; the history, foundation, and scope of the personnel security program; the responsibilities and methods of the various agencies involved in the personnel security program; the investigations used in the personnel security program, with explanation of their uses, elements, and idiosyncrasies; the adjudicator's responsibilities; and the adjudication policy guidelines.

Credit Recommendation: *Version 1:* In the vocational certificate category, 2 semester hours in Personnel Security Adjudications (10/88) (9/95). *Version 2:* In the vocational certificate category, 3 semester hours in Personnel Security Adjudications (9/95). **NOTE:** This course is a prerequisite for DoD Personnel Security Adjudications Course.

Introduction to Security Administration (5220.09) (DoD Security Specialist Course)

Location: Richmond, VA and various locations nationally.

Length: 112 hours (3 weeks).

Dates: September 1986-Present.

Objective: To provide the student with an introduction to security programs, policies, and procedures as they apply to the security specialist field.

Learning Outcome: Upon successful completion of this course, the student will be able to identify major security programs for safeguarding classified and sensitive government information; demonstrate a basic knowledge of policies and principles inherent in each program; and apply the basic principles of security to development, implementation, and evaluation of programs within home agencies.

Instruction: Major topics covered in the course are information, physical, industrial, personnel, computer, communications, operations security programs, security management, inspections and oversight, and education and training. Methods of instruction include lectures, discussion, study, examinations, and exercises.

Credit Recommendation: In the lower division baccalaureate/associate degree category, 3 semester hours in Introduction to Security Administration (10/88) (9/95).

Personnel Security Adjudications (5220.11)

Location: Richmond, VA or various locations nationally.

Length: 67 hours (2 weeks).

Dates: June 1989-Present.

Objective: To provide the student with a structured approach to personnel security adjudication and evaluation of investigation results. Emphasis is on the practical application involving student decision making and "how to do" exercises.

Learning Outcome: Upon successful completion of this course, the student will be able to process personnel security information (i.e., analyze, weigh, and decide on personnel security investigation); evaluate the results of investigations and reports of derogatory information against the current adjudicative criteria to determine necessary actions warranted and the adequacy of the investigation on information; and differentiate between position sensitivity and security determination requirements and involved agencies, rules, and procedures.

Instruction: Major topics covered in the course are basic skills and knowledge required of an adjudicator working in a DoD or non DoD Central Adjudication Facility; how to review personnel security investigations and other sources of information for completeness, validity, and required action; and applying the DoD adjudication policy when reviewing investigations to make personnel security determinations. Methods of instruction include lectures, discussions, and extensive classroom exercises. Case studies are used throughout to illustrate issues discussed. Exercises provide practice in using the Defense Clearance and Investigations Index (DCII), summarizing investigations, identifying adjudicative issues, and applying each of the adjudication guidelines.

Credit Recommendation: In the lower division baccalaureate/associate degree category, 3 semester hours in Personnel Security Adjudications (10/88) (9/95). **NOTE:** The DoD Personnel Security Adjudications Independent Study Course is a prerequisite.

Personnel Security Investigations Course (5220.08)

Location: Richmond, VA.

Length: 131 hours (4 weeks).

Dates: January 1984-August 1995.

Objective: To provide newly assigned special agents with introductory training in investigative policies and procedures.

Learning Outcome: Upon successful completion of this course, the student will be able to demonstrate an understanding of Defense Investigative Service (DIS) jurisdiction, investigative procedure, legislation; demonstrate practical knowledge of interviewing techniques, including nonverbal communication and techniques of effective listening as applied to DIS duties; and demonstrate an understanding of DIS policy and procedures as applied in background investigation/periodic reinvestigation procedures.

Instruction: Major topics covered in the course are the basic skills and knowledge necessary for competent performance by individuals new to the personnel security investigative field and an intense, performance-oriented experience covering all aspects of personnel security investigations from origin of the investigation with an authorized requester, through case handling, investigative methods and techniques, administrative requirements of proper, accurate, and complete report writing to processing and return of the comprehensive investigation to the requester. Methods of instruction include lectures, demonstrations, group activities, extensive practical application. Through observation and videotaping, student performance is evaluated and feedback provided to enable the individual to attain a satisfactory performance level directly related to the job.

Credit Recommendation: In the lower division baccalaureate/associate degree category, 3 semester hours in Principles of Personnel Security, or in the lower division baccalaureate/associate degree category, 2 semester hours in Principles of Personnel Security; or in the lower division baccalaureate/associate degree category, 1 semester hour in Personnel Security Investigations (10/88) (9/95).

Personnel Security Management (5220.18)

Location: Richmond, VA and various locations nationally.

Length: *Version 1:* 30 hours (4 days); *Version 2:* 21 hours.

Dates: *Version 1:* December 1993-February 1996; *Version 2:* February 1996-Present.

Objective: To prepare personnel security specialists and other personnel performing substantial personnel security duties to implement and maintain the Personnel Security program at the base/installation level.

Learning Outcome: Upon successful completion of this course, the student will be able to manage the implementation of a personnel security program; perform investigative requirements and prepare/submit requests for personnel security investigations; evaluate derogatory information for the granting of interim security clearances and/or temporary suspension of access to classified information; and administer a continuous evaluation program.

Instruction: Major topics covered in the course are personnel security investigations and agencies; administrative procedures; preparing and submitting investigation requests; using the personnel security adjudication guidelines; evaluation of information; operating the continuous evaluation program; sources of information granting; interim security clearances; temporarily suspending access; and procedures for implementing denial or revocation of security clearances. Methods of instruction include lecture, directed discussions, videos, projects, and examinations.

Credit Recommendation: In the vocational certificate degree category, 2 semester hours in Security Management (9/95) (7/96).

Principles of Industrial Security (5220.02) (Industrial Security Specialist Course)

Location: Richmond, VA.

Length: 227.5 hours (6.5 weeks).

Dates: July 1986-August 1995.

Objective: To provide comprehensive and formal classroom education and training for national industrial security representatives assigned to positions in the National Industrial Security Program, including the conduct of surveys, security assessments, education and training functions, and administrative inquiries.

Learning Outcome: Upon successful completion of this course, the student will be able to perform the functions of an industrial security representative; accomplish facility security assessments; provide guidance on internal security controls and security violations; and evaluate and certify computer systems for processing classified information.

Instruction: Major topics covered in the course are the necessary skills and program knowledge required to evaluate effectively the implementation of the National Industrial Security Program in industry. The underlying focus of discussions and practical exercises is to direct the students' attention to the main purpose of the National Industrial Security Program, i.e., protection of classified information. This discourages the industrial security representative from having a narrow view to the "requirements" set forth in the National Industrial Security Program Operating Manual, and permits effective program implementation in varying environments. The course is intended for persons serving as Department of Defense Industrial Security Representatives. Methods of instruction include lecture, discussions, and practical exercises.

Credit Recommendation: In the lower division baccalaureate/associate degree category, 3 semester hours in Principles of Industrial Security or Industrial Security Administration, and 1 semester hour in Practicum in Industrial Security (10/88) (9/95). **NOTE:** Structures of Industrial Security, Essentials of Industrial Security Management, and Protecting Secret and Confidential Documents (Independent Study Courses) are prerequisites.

Principles of Information Security Management (5220.07) (Information Security Management [5220.7])

Location: Richmond, VA and various locations nationally.

Length: 67 hours (2 weeks).

Dates: *Version 1:* October 1987-August 1995; *Version 2:* September 1995-Present.

Objective: To provide the student with a comprehensive understanding of the

Defense Information Security Program, including proper classification, downgrading and declassification of information, and safeguarding of classified information.

Learning Outcome: Upon successful completion of this course, the student will be able to demonstrate a basic understanding of the principles of information security management and have the ability to apply them within their employing activities; demonstrate an awareness of organizations involved in the DoD Information Security Program; and identify and utilize the official literature in the field of information security program.

Instruction: Major topics covered in the course are the basic skills and knowledge required to effectively implement the Department of Defense Information Security Program in an organization. Students are encouraged to focus on the purpose and goals underlying requirements—rather than viewing them simply as "rules"—to permit effective program implementation in widely varying environments. Key policy developers from the Information Security Oversight Office and Office of the Secretary of Defense lecture on current program developments and discuss issues of concern with students. The course is primarily intended for persons serving as Security Managers within the meaning of the Department of Defense Information Security Regulation. People in similar positions in other Executive Branch organizations and persons working in related disciplines would also benefit from the course. The first week of the course (which focuses on classification management) is open to employees of contractors participating in the Defense Industrial Security Program. Program policies and requirements are presented in lectures and quizzes. Methods of instruction include classroom discussions and practical exercises which demonstrate the application of policies and requirements in a variety of specific situations.

Credit Recommendation: *Version 1:* In the lower division baccalaureate/associate degree category, 2 semester hours in Principles of Information Security (10/88) (9/95). *Version 2:* In the vocational certificate degree category, 3 semester hours in Principles of Information Security Management, or in the lower division baccalaureate/associate degree category, 2 semester hours in Principles of Information Security Management (9/95).

Security for Special Programs (5220.14)

Location: Richmond, VA.

Length: 80 hours (2 weeks).

Dates: October 1991-Present.

Objective: To provide personnel assigned to support special access programs, mid-level security management training focusing on enhanced security throughout the program's lifecycle.

Learning Outcome: Upon successful completion of this course, the student will be able to prepare and present justification and reports for a model special access program; identify activities, regulations, sources, and references that contribute to security management; identify the role of oversight agencies involved with special access programs; and develop a security program that will be tailored to achieve enhanced security and satisfy agency policy and congressional reporting requirements.

Instruction: Major topics covered in the course are an introduction to decision-making factors applicable in most acquisition-based special access programs. Methods of instruction include lecture, discussion, computer assisted videos, and examinations.

Credit Recommendation: In the lower division baccalaureate/associate degree category, 3 semester hours in Security for Special Access Programs (9/95).

Structures of Industrial Security
Essentials of Industrial Security Management
Protecting SECRET and CONFIDENTIAL Documents
Automated Data Processing Concepts and Terms
Physical Security

Location: Student's work site or home.

Length: Self-study (approximately 72 hours).

Dates: January 1986-August 1995.

Objective: To provide the student with an overview of the Industrial Security Program and Defense Investigative Service, physical security, and AIS processing.

Learning Outcome: Upon successful completion of these courses, the student will be able to demonstrate an understanding of organization, missions, functions, and history of Defense Investigative Service and National Industrial Security Program; demonstrate an understanding of industrial personnel security clearance program and process; demonstrate a basic understanding of National Industrial Security Program structure and function; demonstrate a basic understanding of protective barriers, lighting, locks, and security process in physical security administration; and identify functions and characteristics of computer systems.

Instruction: Major topics covered in the course are Defense Investigative Service structure and functions, National Industrial Security Program structure and functions, processing of government clearances, facility security administration, principles and criteria of physical security, and basic concepts of automated data processing.

Credit Recommendation: In the vocational certificate category, 3 semester hours in Principles of Industrial Security (10/88).

U.S. Department of Justice, Federal Bureau of Prisons

The Federal Bureau of Prisons Staff Training Academy at the Federal Law Enforcement Training Academy provides introductory correctional training for all new Bureau of Prisons employees, regardless of their job specialty. This in-depth three week training program prepares employees to supervise inmates and maintain the security of all federal prisons. The program consists of three major components: academics, firearms, and self-defense. Major academic subject areas include: interpersonal communication skills, inmate supervision, correctional law, sexual issues, managing diversity and inmate profiles. A varied instructional program including lecture, role-playing, physical training, and practical exercises enable the Academy to provide a quality training experience for all employees.

Source of official student records: Registrar, Federal Bureau of Prisons, Staff Training Academy, Building 21, FLETC, Glynco, GA 31524.

Additional information about the courses: College Credit Recommendation Service, American Council on Education, One Dupont Circle, Washington, DC 20036-1193.

Bureau of Prisons Basic Training (Formerly Introduction to Correctional Techniques)

Location: Federal Law Enforcement Training Center, Glynco, GA.

Length: 135 hours (3 weeks).

Dates: August 1993-Present.

Objective: To train new federal employees in common core correctional skills and knowledge. This program provides an in-depth study of common core correctional skills and knowledge that must be possessed by all new Federal Bureau of Prison employees regardless of their job specialty. The course consists of three weeks of training in academics, firearms, and self-defense.

Learning Outcome: Upon successful completion of this course, the student will be able to apply specific facts, skills, and knowledge in determining the best solutions or most appropriate course of action in response to job-relevant scenarios and situations within the work environment of the federal prison system.

Instruction: Major topics covered in the course are fundamentals of correctional law, correctional supervision, use of force, weapons handling, qualifying, interpersonal communications, inmate related situations, cultural and religious diversity, and self-defense training. Methods of instruction include lecture, role plays, practical exercises, and performance training.

Credit Recommendation: In the lower division baccalaureate/associate degree category, 2 semester hours in Introduction to Corrections (7/93).

U.S. Department of Justice, Immigration and Naturalization

The Federal Law Enforcement Training Center of the U.S. Immigration and Naturalization Service provides basic training for border patrol agents through the Border Patrol Academy and for immigration inspectors, immigration examiners, criminal investigators, and deportation officers through the Immigration Officer Academy. The Academic Specialities Staff serves as a resource to both academies in educational technology and methodology. The staff also maintains liaison with area colleges and universities and with the FLETC Training Operations Division. The Administrative Office sets up and operates all administrative systems and procedures to serve the instructional staff and students. Varied administrative and academic activities enable the Immigration and Naturalization Service to provide a quality learning experience for trainees.

Source of official student records: Chief, Academic Specialities Staff, U.S. Immigration and Naturalization Service, Federal Law Enforcement Training Center, Glynco, GA 31520.

Additional information about the courses: College Credit Recommendation Service, American Council on Education, One Dupont Circle, Washington, DC 20036-1193.

BORDER PATROL ACADEMY

Border Patrol Agent Basic Training Part 1: Immigration and Nationality Law Part 2: Criminal Investigation Part 3: Human Relations Part 4: Physical Education Part 5: Spanish Language (Formerly Border Patrol Academy)

Location: U.S. Immigration and Naturalization Service, Officer Development and Training Facility, Federal Law Enforcement Training Facility, Glynco, GA.

Length: *Version 1*: 648 hours (16 weeks), residential; consisting of the following: *Part 1*: 148 hours; *Part 2*: 71 hours; *Part 3*: 64 hours; *Part 4*: 150 hours; *Part 5*: 198 hours (140 hours of classroom instruction plus 58 hours of supervised language laboratory). *Version 2:* 700 hours (17 weeks), residential, consisting of the following: *Part 1:* 148 hours; *Part 2:* 73 hours; *Part 3:* 63 hours; *Part 4:* 200 hours; *Part 5:* 216 hours (150 hours of classroom instruction plus 66 hours of supervised language laboratory).

Dates: *Version 1:* January 1970-May 1985; *Version 2:* June 1985-June 1993.

Objective: To provide prospective border patrol agents the skills and knowledge necessary to serve effectively in the basic law enforcement role at the entry level with the United States Immigration and Naturalization Service.

Instruction: *Part 1:* **Immigration and Nationality Law:** Major topics covered in the course are detailed exploration of nationality, immigration, and other areas of criminal law of major importance to border patrol agents and other federal law enforcement personnel; discussion of the constitutional aspects of arrest, search and seizure, interrogation, and confessions, and identification of civil liability issues. Methods of instruction include lecture and discussion. *Part 2:* **Criminal Investigation:** Major topics covered in the course are investigative methods and techniques, interviewing and interrogation, collection, preservation, reporting and disclosure of information, and recognition and handling of specific offenses. *Part 3:* **Human Relations:** Major topics covered in the course are interpersonal communications. Methods of instruction include role playing. *Part 4:* **Physical Education:** Major topics covered in the course are firearms, driving, physical conditioning, defensive tactics, trauma management, survival swimming, and CPR. *Part 5:* **Spanish Language:** Major topics covered in the course are basic grammar structure, up to and including the subjunctive mood, and the formation of complex sentences; and emphasis on vocabulary building and on oral and aural skills. Methods of instruction include formal grammar presentations, translation exercises, dictation exercises, oral drill, and reading exercises supplemented by daily, supervised language laboratory use.

Credit Recommendation: *Version 1:* Part 1: In the lower division baccalaureate/associate degree category or in the upper division baccalaureate degree category, 3 semester hours in Immigration and Nationality Law. *Part 2:* In the lower division baccalaureate/associate degree category or in the upper division baccalaureate degree category, 3 semester hours in Immigration and Nationality Law. *Part 3:* In the lower division baccalaureate/associate degree category, 3 semester hours in Human Relations. *Part 4:* In the lower division baccalaureate/associate degree category, 4 semester hours in Physical Education (11/79). *Part 5:* In the lower division baccalaureate/associate degree category, 8 semester hours in Spanish Language (2/81). *Version 2:* Part 1: In the lower division baccalaureate/associate degree category or in the upper division baccalaureate degree category, 3 semester hours in Immigration and Nationality Law. *Part 2:* In the lower division baccalaureate/associate degree category or in the upper division baccalaureate degree category, 3 semester hours in Criminal Investigation. *Part 3:* In the lower division baccalaureate/associate degree category, 3 semester hours in Human Relations. *Part 4:* In the lower division baccalaureate/associate degree category, 7 semester hours in Physical Education. *Part 5:* In the lower division baccalaureate/associate degree category, 12 semester hours in Spanish Language (7/87).

Border Patrol Agent Basic Training Part 1: Immigration and Nationality Law Part 2: Criminal Investigation Part 3: Human Relations Part 4: Physical Education Part 5: Spanish Language

Location: Border Patrol Academy, Federal Law Enforcement Training Facility, Glynco, GA.

Length: *Version 3:* 736 hours (18 weeks).

Dates: *Version 3:* July 1993-Present.

Objective: To provide border patrol agents the skills and knowledge necessary to serve effectively in the basic law enforcement role at the entry level with the U.S. Immigration and Naturalization Service.

Learning Outcome: Upon successful completion of this course, the student will be able to understand and apply Immigration and Nationality Law as it pertains to border patrol and perform all routine duties of an entry level border patrol officer.

Instruction: Major topics covered in the course are Immigration and Nationality Law; criminal law; all alien related activities (apprehension, detention/arrest, interrogation, surveillance, search and seizure); firearms, physical conditioning; and driver training. Methods of instruction include lecture, discussion, laboratory, and practical exercises.

Credit Recommendation: *Version 3:* In the lower division baccalaureate/associate degree category or upper division baccalaureate degree category, 4 semester hours in Immigration and Nationality Law, 2 semester hours in Basic Law Enforcement; and in the lower division baccalaureate/associate degree category, 6 semester hours in Spanish, and 4 semester hours of Physical Education (7/93). **NOTE:** For credit recommendations for a course taken before July 1993, consult the 1993 National Guide or prior National Guide editions. Also, dual credit for other similar FLETC course should not be given.

IMMIGRATION OFFICER ACADEMY

Immigration Detention Enforcement Officer Basic Program (IDEOB)

Location: Immigration Officer Academy, Federal Law Enforcement Training Center, Glynco, GA.

Length: 279 hours (7 weeks).

Dates: January 1988-Present.

Objective: To provide students with the skills and knowledge necessary to perform effectively as an entry level detention officer.

Learning Outcome: Upon successful completion of this course, the student will be able to carry out duties related to the detention, care, transporting, supervision, and deportation of aliens.

Instruction: Major topics covered in the course are detention regulations and procedures, immigrant status, driver training, physical conditioning, firearms usage and care, and transportation of prisoners. Methods of instruction include lecture, discussion, and practical exercises.

Credit Recommendation: In the lower division baccalaureate/associate degree category or upper division baccalaureate degree category, 3 semester hours in Prisoner Supervision (7/93).

Immigration Officer Basic Training Course (IOBTC) (IOBTC) Version 1: Part 1: Immigration and Nationality Law Part 2: Criminal Investigation Part 3: Human Relations Part 4: Physical Education Part 5: Spanish Language Version 2: Part 1: Immigration and Nationality Law Part 2: Specialized Training Part 3: Physical Education Part 4: Spanish Language Part 5: Introduction to Federal Immigration and Naturalization

Location: Immigration Officer Academy, Federal Law Enforcement Training Center, Glynco. GA.

Length: *Version 3:* 632 hours (15 weeks).

Dates: *Version 3:* July 1993-Present.

Objective: To provide prospective immigration officers with the skills and knowledge necessary to specialize in one of four positions: special agent, deportation officer, immigration inspector, or immigration examiner.

Learning Outcome: Upon successful completion of this course, the student will be able to perform routine duties in an assigned specialization which usually includes classification of aliens; deportation procedure and activities; criminal investigations; drug interdiction; surveillance; execution of search warrants; detention and arrest; vehicular pursuit; search and seizure; and terrorism.

Instruction: Major topics covered in the course are Nationality and Immigration Law; aspects of arrest, search and seizure, interrogation and confessions; investigative methods and techniques; interviewing and collection; preservation; reporting and disclosure of information; interpersonal communication; firearms; driving; physical conditioning, and defensive tactics; and basic instruction in beginning Spanish. Methods of instruction include lecture, discussion, laboratory, and practical exercises.

Credit Recommendation: *Version 3:* In the lower division baccalaureate/associate degree category or upper division baccalaureate degree category, 4 semester hours in Immigration and Nationality Law; and in the lower division baccalaureate/associate degree category, 6 semester hours in Spanish and 2 semester hours in Physical Education (7/93). **NOTE:** For credit recommendations for a course taken before July 1993, consult the 1993 National Guide or prior National Guide editions. Also, dual credit for other similar FLETC courses should not be given.

Immigration Officer Basic Training Course (IOBTC) (IOBTC) Version 1: Part 1: Immigration and Nationality Law Part 2: Criminal Investigation Part 3: Human Relations Part 4: Physical Education Part 5: Spanish Language Version 2: Part 1: Immigration and Nationality Law Part 2: Specialized Training Part 3: Physical Education Part 4: Spanish Language Part 5: Introduction to Federal Immigration and Naturalization (Formerly Immigration Officer Academy)

Location: U.S. Immigration and Naturalization Service, Officer Development and Training Facility, Federal Law Enforcement Training Center, Glynco, GA.

Length: *Version 1:* 560 hours (14 weeks), residential; including the following: *Part 1*: 132 hours; *Part 2:* 64 hours; *Part 3*: 33 hours; *Part 4*: 128 hours; *Part 5*: 177 hours (134 hours of language instruction plus 43 hours of supervised language laboratory). *Version 2:* 560-687.5 hours (14-18 weeks), residential; including the following: *Part 1*: 88 hours; *Part 2*: 64 hours; *Part 3*: 128 hours; *Part 4*: 177 hours (136 hours of language instruction plus 41 hours of supervised language laboratory); *Part 5*: 103 hours.

Dates: *Version 1:* January 1980-May 1985; *Version 2:* June 1985-June 1993.

Objective: To provide prospective immigration officers with the skills and knowledge necessary to specialize in one of four positions: special agent, deportation officer, immigration inspector, or immigration examiner.

Instruction: *Version 1:* Part 1: **Immigration and Nationality Law:** Major topics covered in the course are detailed exploration of nationality, immigration, and other areas of criminal law of major importance to immigration officers; discussion of the constitutional aspects of arrest, search and seizure, interrogation, and confessions; and identification of civil liability issues. Methods of instruction include lecture and discussion. *Part 2:* **Criminal Investigation:** Major topics covered in the course are investigative methods and techniques, interviewing, and interrogation; collection, preservation, reporting and disclosure of information; and recognition and handling of specific issues. *Part 3:* **Human Relations:** Major topics covered in the course are Interpersonal communications. *Part 4:* **Physical Education:** Major topics covered in the course are firearms, driving, physical conditioning, and defensive tactics. *Part 5:* **Spanish Language:** Major topics covered in the course are basic grammatical structure, up to and including the subjunctive mood, and the formation of complex sentences; and emphasis on vocabulary building and oral and aural skills. Methods of instruction include formal grammar presentations and translation exercises supplemented by daily, supervised language laboratory use. *Version 2:* Part 1: **Immigration and Nationality Law:** Major topics covered in the course are detailed exploration of nationality, immigration, and other areas of criminal law of major importance to immigration officers; discussion of the constitutional aspects of arrest, search and seizure, interrogation, and confessions; and identification of civil liability issues. *Part 2:* **Specialized Training:** Major topics covered in the course are immigration officers receive an applied, awareness-oriented, training course designed to develop the ability to apply theoretical and practical aspects of their specific job requirements. *Part 3:* **Physical Education:** Major topics covered in the course are firearms, driving, physical conditioning, and defensive tactics. *Part 4:* **Spanish Language:** Major topics covered in the course are basic grammatical structure, up to and including the subjunctive mood, and the formation of complex sentences; and emphasis on vocabulary building and oral and aural skills. Methods of instruction include formal grammar presentations and translation exercises supplemented by daily, supervised language laboratory use. *Part 5:* **Introduction to Federal Immigration and Naturalization:** Major topics covered in the course are agency organization, authority, records, and internal policies governing immigration and naturalization.

Credit Recommendation: *Version 1:* Part 1: In the lower division baccalaureate/associate degree category or in the upper division baccalaureate degree category, 3 semester hours in Immigration and Nationality Law. *Part 2:* In the lower division baccalaureate/associate degree category or in the upper division baccalaureate degree category, 3 semester hours in Criminal Investigation. *Part 3:* In the lower division baccalaureate/associate degree category, 2 semester hours in Human Relations. *Part 4:* In the lower division baccalaureate/associate degree category, 4 semester hours in Physical Education (11/79). *Part 5:* In the lower division baccalaureate/associate degree category, 8 semester hours in Spanish Language. *Version 2:* Part 1: In the lower division baccalaureate/associate degree category or in the upper division baccalaureate degree category, 3 semester hours in Immigration and Nationality Law. *Part 2:* In the lower division baccalaureate/associate degree category or in the upper division baccalaureate degree category, 3 semester hours in Federal Law Enforcement. *Part 3:* In the lower division baccalaureate/associate degree category, 5 semester hours in Physical Education. *Part 4:* In the lower division baccalaureate/associate degree category, 8 semester hours in Spanish Language. *Part 5:* In the lower division baccalaureate/ associate degree category, 3 semester hours in Federal Law Enforce-ment (2/81) (7/87).

Integrated Immigration Special Agent Basic Training Program

Location: Immigration Officer Academy, FLETC, Glynco, GA.

Length: 842 hours (18 weeks).

Dates: January 1994-Present.

Objective: To provide immigration officers with the skills and knowledge of a special agent.

Learning Outcome: Upon successful completion of this course, the student will be able to perform routine duties in an assigned specialization which usually includes classification of aliens; deportation procedure and activities; criminal investigations; drug interdiction; surveillance; execution of search warrants; detention and arrest; vehicular pursuit; search and seizure; and terrorism.

Instruction: Major topics covered in the course are Nationality and Immigration Law; legal aspects of arrest, search and seizure, interrogation and confessions; investigative methods and techniques; interviewing and collection; preservation; reporting and disclosure of information; interpersonal communication; firearms; driving; physical conditioning and defensive tactics; and basic instruction in beginning Spanish. Methods of instruction include lecture, discussion, laboratory, and practical exercises.

Credit Recommendation: In the lower division baccalaureate/associate degree category or upper division baccalaureate degree category, 4 semester hours in Immigration and Nationality Law; 4 semester hours in Criminal Investigation, and 3 semester hours in Criminal Law and Procedures; and in the lower division baccalaureate/associate degree category, 6 semester hours in Spanish and 2 semester hours in Physical Education (7/93).

U.S. Department of Justice, Immigration and Naturalization, Leadership Development Center

Recognizing the need for enhanced administrative training for Service managers and supervisors, the Leadership Development Center, Immigration and Naturalization Service, Dallas, Texas, was created in 1995 to serve this need. The Center's courses, the first of which was conducted in March 1996, provide consistency and quality in the training of Service managers and supervisors. Historically, the Service has concentrated its greatest training efforts on the law enforcement training and operational needs of the Service, and these are provided for at the Border Patrol Academy in Glynco, Georgia, and at the Immigration Officer Basic Training courses provided at Glynco, Artesia, New Mexico and Charleston, South Carolina.

As specialists in the field of managerial and supervisory training, the Center staff understands the special needs of adult learners and offers programs which nurture their talents and experience. Their staff focuses on motivating students toward success by sharing expertise in team building, stress management, communications, leadership, ethics, values, motivation, and management styles. In addition, the Center focuses on Immigration and Naturalization Service-specific cases relating to disciplinary actions, labor-management relations, performance management and leave administration. The majority of the Center's courses are site-based in Dallas.

The student population consists of both newly appointed and experienced supervisors, managers and executives from throughout the Service who are stationed all over the world.

Source of official student records: Registry of Credit Recommendations, American Council on Education, One Dupont Circle, Washington, DC 20036-1193.

Additional information about the courses: College Credit Recommendation Service, American Council on Education, One Dupont Circle, Washington, DC 20036-1193.

Advanced Management

Location: Dallas, TX.

Length: 84 hours (36 contact, 2 pre-work, 6 homework, 40 post-work).

Dates: July 1996-Present.

Objective: To provide high level managers with the knowledge, skills, and abilities to successfully manage departments within an organization.

Learning Outcome: Upon successful completion of this course, the student will be able to better deal with stress, know how to manage change, recognize and understand visioning and purpose, and create a learning organization.

Instruction: Major topics covered in the course are stress management, feedback, management styles, value systems and integrity, interviewing, managing change, visioning, creating purpose, valuing diversity, sexual harassment, decision making, creating a learning organization, budgeting, time management, improving systems, case study utilizing skills learned during the course. Methods of instruction include lecture, discussion, audio/video materials, learner presentations, reports, observations, and peer and instructor evaluations.

Credit Recommendation: In the upper division baccalaureate degree category, 3 semester hours in Management or Human Resource Development (1/97).

Advanced Supervision

Location: Dallas, TX.

Length: 75 hours (36 contact, 5 homework, 2 pre-work, 32 post-work).

Dates: May 1996-Present.

Objective: To enhance supervisory skills of course participants.

Learning Outcome: Upon successful completion of this course, the student will be able to deal with anger, resolve conflict, mediate disputes, administer leave, speak publicly, and manage stress.

Instruction: Major topics covered in the course are creating an open, honest, work place; communication; public speaking; leave administration; managing anger; negotiating; managing stress; managing media relations; team building; motivating and persuading; ethics; personal mastery; and time management. Methods of instruction include lecture, discussion, classroom exercises, audio/visual material, role playing, reports, observations, and peer/instructor evaluations.

Credit Recommendation: In the upper division baccalaureate degree category, 3 semester hours in Supervision, Management, or Business Administration (1/97).

Balanced Leadership

Location: Dallas, TX.

Length: 83 hours (36 contact, 1 pre-work, 6 homework, 40 post-work).

Dates: December 1996-Present.

Objective: To develop an awareness of the value of diversity in the work force, manage time and meetings, utilize 360 degree feedback on value systems, work through ethical dilemmas, review ethics and integrity, engage in strategic thinking, and develop policies for the future.

Learning Outcome: Upon successful completion of this course, the student will be able to increase leadership effectiveness.

Instruction: Major topics covered in the course are the value of diversity, managing time and meetings, feedback, ethics and integrity, strategic thinking, and "what is good staff work?." Methods of instruction include lecture, discussion, classroom exercises, audio/visual material, learner presentation, reports , and observations.

Credit Recommendation: In the upper division baccalaureate degree category, 3 semester hours in Supervision, Management, or Business Administration (1/97).

Basic Management

Location: Dallas, TX.

Length: 66 hours (36 contact, 4 pre-work, 26 homework).

Dates: March 1996-Present.

Objective: To enhance the knowledge, skills, and abilities of new managers through instruction and interaction and interaction relating to how best to manage people and resources.

Learning Outcome: Upon successful completion of this course, the student will be able to understand management style and how best to accomplish the mission of an organization through self and others.

Instruction: Major topics covered in the course are life style management, vision, process redesign facilitating change, coaching, diversity, leading teams, management styles, feedback, values, leading with and through others, motivating, managing resources, discipline, and Merit Systems Protection Board case law. Methods of instruction include lecture, discussion, classroom exercises, audio/visual material, role playing, reports, observation, and follow-up evaluations.

Credit Recommendation: In the upper division baccalaureate degree category, 3 semester hours in Management or Human Resource Management (1/97).

Basic Supervision

Location: Dallas, TX.

Length: 98 hours (36 contact, 42 correspondence, 20 post-work).

Dates: March 1996-Present.

Objective: To give first line supervision an understanding of desired supervisory techniques in handling day-to-day situations.

Learning Outcome: Upon successful completion of this course, the student will be able to supervise subordinates utilizing the tools and skills provided by the course.

Instruction: Major topics covered in the course are stress management, feedback, management styles, team building, diversity, sexual harassment, labor-management relations, discipline, performance appraisals, communications, leadership, and motivation. Methods of instruction include lecture, discussion, classroom exercises, audio/visual material, role playing, reports, and observations.

Credit Recommendation: In the lower division baccalaureate/associate degree category, 3 semester hours in Supervision, Management, or Business Administration (1/97).

Impact Leadership

Location: Dallas, TX.

Length: 52 hours (36 contact, 10 prework, 6 homework).

Dates: July 1996-Present.

Objective: To help middle and upper level managers explore and deepen their understanding and implementation of sound leadership principles and practices.

Learning Outcome: Upon successful completion of this course, the student will be able to identify personal guiding principles of leadership and sense of purpose as they establish their leadership priorities and practices; identify and remove success barriers in the systems and culture of organizations to create a work environment that fosters greater productivity; build effective teams that are united by clarity of purpose, that are mobilized by empowerment, and that deliver value through teamwork; define personal strengths and weaknesses as leaders and use that information to improve leadership effectiveness; effectively communicate with others; and plan and implement strategies and tactics for improving personal, organization, and interpersonal leadership.

Instruction: Major topics covered in the course are stress management, self-management, feedback from the organization, reflection on organizational and personal values, managing the chaos that accompanies change, empowerment, team building, and stewardship of resources and systems. Methods of instruction include lecture, discussion, classroom exercises, case studies, audio/visual material, learner presentations, reports, and observations.

Credit Recommendation: In the upper division baccalaureate degree category, 3 semester hours in Supervision, Management, or Business Administration (1/97).

U.S. Department of Justice, U.S. Marshals Service

The Basic Deputy U.S. Marshal Training Course provides an in-depth study of law enforcement and administrative concepts that applicants must possess upon entry into the U.S. Marshals Service. The Basic Deputy Course is the third and final segment of a comprehensive 15 week program which includes a 2 day Pre-Basic orientation and an intensive 9 week Criminal Investigator School, presented by Federal Law Enforcement Training Center at Glynco, Georgia.

The Basic Training School consists of 6 weeks of training which is devoted to classroom instruction, practical exercises, and administrative support time. Basic Training serves as an enhancement to several subjects that were initiated in the Criminal Investigator School, e.g., warrant investigations and firearms. Instruction is also offered in operational and administrative areas, most of which are unique to the United States Marshals Service, and include witness security, court security, personal protection, process, and the handling of prisoners.

The objective of this course is to provide the most extensive, complete, and meaningful curriculum on matters directly related to the mission of the Service. In this regard, every effort is made to research and develop a curriculum of primary concern to subject areas contained in this course.

It also provides new deputies with the knowledge and skills necessary to equip them for street work. The Marshals Service Training Academy is considered to be a leader in this field. A great emphasis is placed on "hands on" training and follows a system of periodically rotating its staff in order to keep abreast of field operations and to bring in fresh new ideas.

The importance of sound formal training for Deputy U.S. Marshals cannot be overstated, in that, it follows a program which ensures that new personnel are fully prepared to meet the pressures and conditions of the career environment in which they are expected to operate.

To successfully graduate from Basic Deputy Training an individual must complete the 2 day Pre-Basic orientation, the 9 week Criminal Investigator School and all phases of Basic Training.

Source of official student records: Training Coordinator, U.S. Marshals Service, Federal Law Enforcement Training Center, Building 20, Glynco, GA 31524.

Additional information about the courses: College Credit Recommendation Service, American Council on Education, One Dupont Circle, Washington, DC 20036-1193.

Deputy U.S. Marshals Basic Training School

Location: Federal Law Enforcement Training Center, Glynco, GA.

Length: *Version 1:* 205 hours (5 weeks); *Version 2:* 242 hours (6 weeks).

Dates: *Version 1:* January 1980-June 1993; *Version 2:* July 1993-Present.

Objective: To give students an in-depth treatment of skills and knowledge necessary for proficiency in the job of Deputy U.S. Marshal.

Learning Outcome: Upon successful completion of this course, the student will be able to describe, discuss, and utilize the specialized training to become a proficient and competent Deputy U.S. Marshal.

Instruction: Major topics covered in the course are prisoner handling; courtroom security; witness/personal protection; criminal investigations; firearms training; driver training; and physical conditioning. Methods of instruction include lecture, discussion, laboratory, and practical exercises.

Credit Recommendation: *Version 1:* In the lower division baccalaureate/associate degree category, 2 semester hours in Physical Education, 1 semester hour in Criminal Intelligence, 2 semester hours in Court Security Procedures or Personal Security, but not both (7/87). *Version 2:* In the lower division baccalaureate/associate degree category or in the upper division baccalaureate degree category, 3 semester hours in Court Security Procedures or Personal Security, but not both, and 1 semester hour in Criminal Intelligence (7/93).

U.S. Department of Labor, Office of Job Corps

Job Corps is a national training and employment program administered by the United States Department of Labor, Employment and Training Administration, to address the multiple barriers to employment facing disadvantaged youth throughout the United States. Job Corps was originally established by the Economic Opportunity Act of 1964, and is currently funded through Title IV-B of the Job Training Partnership Act.

The purpose of Job Corps is to assist young people who need and can benefit from an unusually intensive program, operated primarily in the residential setting of Job Corps center, to become more responsible, employable, and productive citizens. The program is highly targeted to the most severely disadvantaged youth facing various barriers to employment.

Source of official student records: Registry of Credit Recommendations, American Council on Education, One Dupont Circle, Washington, DC 20036-1193.

Additional information about the courses: College Credit Recommendation Service, American Council on Education, One Dupont Circle, Washington, DC 20036-1193.

Accounting Clerk Trade

Applied Accounting

Location: Tongue Point Job Corps Center, Astoria, OR and at various sites across the nation.

Length: 400-600 hours. Note: Since this a competency-based, open-entry, and open exit course, students who meet the competency requirements may complete the program in varied periods of time.

Dates: January 1992-Present.

Objective: To develop an understanding of the accounting cycle to perform effectively as a control, billing, payroll, or accounting clerk.

Learning Outcome: Upon successful completion of this course, the student will be able to learn accounting vouchers and procedures emphasizing the basic accounting equation; analyze and record business transactions using double-entry bookkeeping procedures; journalize and post business transactions; produce trial balances, worksheets, and financial reports; complete the accounting cycle with adjusting and closing entries and post closing trial balances; use special journals for sales, cash receipts, purchases and cash payments; analyze, record, and manage banking transactions relating to deposits, banking accounts, and maintain a petty cash fund; prepare and maintain payroll records; establish and maintain an inventory control system; and use practical techniques for verifying accuracy for all data including coding, journalizing, posting, and auditing data.

Instruction: Major topics covered in the course are theory and practice of accounting; the complete accounting cycle to include the double-entry process, accounts receivable and accounts payable; journals and ledgers, preparation of year-end financial statements; adjusting, correcting, and closing entries; payroll preparation and taxes; bank transactions and reconciliation; calculation of interest and discounts; managing petty cash; auditing accounts; preparing purchase orders; inventory control and managing accounting records. Methods of instruction include lecture, discussion, hands-on demonstrations, classroom exercises, case studies, audiovisual material, computer-assisted instruction, learner presentations, projects, reports, quizzes, final examination, observations, tests, papers, extensive training achievement records (TARS), progress performance evaluation panel, and weekly productivity charts.

Credit Recommendation: In the vocational certificate category or the lower division baccalaureate/associate degree category, 3 semester hours in Accounting or Business Administration (11/96).

Clerical Occupations Trade

Introduction to Computer Applications

Location: Tongue Point Job Corps Center, Astoria, OR, and at various sites across the nation.

Length: 400-600 hours (6-9 Months) Note: Since this a competency-based, open entry and open exit course, students who meet the competency requirements may complete the program in varied periods of time.

Dates: December 1994-Present.

Objective: To develop understanding of and ability to apply computer skills required to perform efficiently as a receptionist, information processor, or secretary.

Learning Outcome: Upon successful completion of this course, the student will be able to perform the basic operating systems in MS-DOS and Windows environments, demonstrating mastery of the menu tools, key commands, and file and print managers; create and modify database; sort and query a database and create a report; master commands of various word processing software functions; manage files using directories and sub-directories, and produce quality business documents; use spreadsheet functions to perform basic and complex formulas; specify and format name ranges; and create and print spreadsheets and graphs.

Instruction: Major topics covered in the course are keyboard skills and procedures, computer skills and procedures, database software, word processing software, operating systems and file management, spreadsheet software, desktop publishing software, and computer networks. Methods of instruction include individual study with faculty mentoring and peer tutoring, classroom exercises, audio/visual material, quizzes, competency tests, and extensive training achievement records (TAR's).

Credit Recommendation: In the vocational certificate category or the lower division baccalaureate/associate degree category, 3 semester hours in Computer Information Systems (6/95).

Office Procedures

Location: Tongue Point Job Corps Center, Astoria, OR, and at various sites across the nation.

Length: 400-600 hours (6-9 Months) Note: Since this a competency-based, open-entry, and open exit course, students who meet the competency requirements may complete the program in varied periods of time.

Dates: December 1994-Present.

Objective: To develop understanding of and ability to apply office procedures required to perform efficiently as a receptionist, information processor, or secretary.

Learning Outcome: Upon successful completion of this course, the student will be able to demonstrate professionalism, including grooming, hygiene, and positive attitudes; demonstrate mastery of basic Business English in written and oral communication; utilize office references and equipment; manage time; utilize basic mathematics and calculator skills; and apply ARMA (American Records Management Association) rules.

Instruction: Major topics covered in the course are Business English, telephone procedures, office procedures and resources, photocopier, calculators, transcription, preparing and processing mail, record keeping, business mathematics, filing systems; grooming hygiene, and personal and interpersonal habits. Methods of instruction include individual study with faculty mentoring and peer tutoring, lecture, discussion, classroom exercises, quizzes, competency tests, and extensive training achievement records (TAR's).

Credit Recommendation: In the vocational certificate category or the lower division baccalaureate/associate degree category , 3 semester hours in Office Procedures or Office Administration (6/95).

Work Experience

Location: Tongue Point Job Corps Center, Astoria, OR, and at various sites across the nation.

Length: 210 hours (6-Weeks).

Dates: December 1994-Present.

Objective: To demonstrate general office skills in a workplace assignment.

Learning Outcome: Upon successful completion of this course, the student will be able to apply general office skills.

Instruction: Major topics covered in the course are various clerical skills. Workplace experience and employer checklist of tasks performed.

Credit Recommendation: In the vocational certificate category, 1 semester hour in Field Experience (6/95).

NURSES AIDE PROGRAM

Nursing Assistant (Nurse Aide)

Location: Clearfield Job Corps Center, Utah.

Length: 850 hours (6 months) of classroom instruction plus 6 weeks of clinical practice. Note: Since this is competency - based, open-entry and open-exit program, students who meet the competency requirements may complete the program in a shorter period of time.

Dates: July 1992-Present.

Objective: To provide knowledge and skills needed by nursing assistants (nurse aides) to provide quality basic care for people in the health care system.

Learning Outcome: Upon successful completion of this course, the student will be able to recognize the importance of the nurse assistant's role in improving the quality of life for patients; encourage patients to be independent; support and maintain the rights of patients; demonstrate sensitivity to the physical and psychological needs of patients; communicate effectively with staff, patients and significant others; provide quality basic patient care; reduce the potential negative effects of the health care system; observe and document patients' physical condition and overall well-being; and work well as a team member.

Instruction: Major topics covered in the course are an introduction to the health care system; rights of individuals in the health care system; role and responsibilities of nursing assistants; maintaining infection control; safety and emergency procedures; the human body and the aging process; assisting and moving patients; environmental care; assisting patients with personal care; oral hygiene; nutrition; elimination care needs; taking and recording vital signs; admission/discharge/transfer of patients; death and dying; care for patients with special needs; restorative nursing; planning and prioritizing work; acute care; and home health care. Methods of instruction include lecture, discussion, classroom exercises, case studies, audio/visual material, in addition to the classroom instruction, 2 weeks of clinical practice supervised by a Job Corps clinical instructor and 6 weeks at a health care facility under supervision of a preceptor, computerized tests, extensive training achievement records (TARs) based on industry certified task lists, quizzes, and a final examination which must be passed at the 80% level.

Credit Recommendation: In the vocational certificate category or the lower division baccalaureate/associate degree category , 6 semester hours for classroom instruction and 2 semester hours for clinical experience in Nursing Assistant (Nurse Aide) (5/95).

RETAIL SALES TRADE

Fundamentals of Business Math

Location: Sacramento, CA and various sites across the nation.

Length: 24 weeks. Note: Since this a competency-based, open-entry, and open exit course, students who meet the competency requirements may complete the program in varied periods of time.

Dates: February 1996-Present.

Objective: To understand the fundamentals of business math; to provide mathematical principles, concepts and applications necessary to acquire the knowledge and skills essential to perform a variety of problem-solving and application activities.

Learning Outcome: Upon successful completion of this course, the student will be able to understand fundamental mathematical concepts and demonstrate such by solving addition, subtraction, multiplication, and division problems, fractions, decimals, percentages, weights, measures, sales transactions and graphics.

Instruction: Major topics covered in the course are addition, subtraction, multiplication, division, decimals, fractions, calculating percentages and interest, sales inventory valuation and depreciation. Methods of instruction include lecture, discussion, hands-on demonstrations, classroom exercises, case studies, audiovisual materials, tests, quizzes, projects, work experience evaluation, observations, weekly productivity charts, and extensive training achievement records (TARs).

Credit Recommendation: In the vocational certificate category or in the lower division baccalaureate/associate degree category, 3 semester hours in Business (10/96).

Introduction to Communication and Interpersonal Skills

Location: Sacramento, CA and various sites across the nation.

Length: 24 weeks. Note: Since this a competency-based, open-entry, and open exit course, students who meet the competency requirements may complete the program in varied periods of time.

Dates: February 1996-Present.

Objective: To develop effective written and oral communication skills including transformation of behavior through positive attitude, sending and receiving of verbal and nonverbal messages, employment of active listening skills, and demonstration of written abilities through preemployment paperwork, and customer-service documents.

Learning Outcome: Upon successful completion of this course, the student will be able to exhibit positive, enthusiastic customer-service attitudes by identifying needed behavior changes and setting goals for reaching the new behavior patterns; demonstrating active listening skills for following oral directions, assessing customer needs, assisting in training new employees, and handling customer inquiries and complaints; communicate effectively with co-workers and customers by sending and receiving verbal and nonverbal messages (including appropriate grooming and dress) and using feedback to determine level of effectiveness; establish a customer-service manner for positively interacting with customers in person or by phone from first contact through sale including merchandise selection assistance; and use effective written communication skills in the pre-employment paperwork and customer-service documents.

Instruction: Major topics covered in the course are self-development including raising personal and career success; communication skills including active listening, using the telephone, and demonstration of customer-service attitude and behavior patterns; positive customer interaction including handling inquiries and complaints by phone or in person; merchandise selection assistance, making of sale, and satisfactory handling of difficult customers; and use of effective writing skills. Methods of instruction include lecture, discussion, hands-on demonstrations, classroom exercises, case studies, audiovisual materials, tests, quizzes, projects, work experience evaluation, observations, weekly productivity charts, and extensive training achievement records (TARs).

Credit Recommendation: In the vocational certificate category or in the lower division baccalaureate/associate degree category, 3 semester hours in Business (10/96).

Practical Retailing

Location: Sacramento, CA and various sites across the nation.

Length: 24 weeks. Note: Since this a competency-based, open-entry, and open exit course, students who meet the competency requirements may complete the program in varied periods of time.

Dates: February 1996-Present.

Objective: To provide understanding of and ability to apply retail marketing concepts and skills required to perform effectively and efficiently as a retail sales clerk, merchandiser, or other retail worker.

Learning Outcome: Upon successful completion of this course, the student will be able to demonstrate entry level knowledge of and proficiency in receiving and checking merchandise, calculating prices, marking and stockkeeping, positive approach at helping customers make buying decisions, recording sales transactions, demonstrating features and related buyers benefits, creating effective displays, developing and monitoring attractive visual store merchandise.

Instruction: Major topics covered in the course are understanding of customers and their wants and needs, personal selling, customer service and satisfaction, sales promotion, receiving, pricing, marking, display, merchandising, sales entry, inventory control, ethics and regulations of sales and marketing strategies, identifying opportunities and developing and implementing retail marketing plans. Methods of instruction include lecture, discussion, hands-on demonstrations, classroom exercises, case studies, audiovisual materials, tests, quizzes, projects, work experience evaluation, observations, weekly productivity charts, and extensive training achievement records (TARs).

Credit Recommendation: In the vocational certificate category or in the lower division baccalaureate/associate degree category, 3 semester hours in Business (10/96).

U.S. Department of the Navy

The Department of the Navy, Child Development Program provides quality child care to 25,974 children in military child development centers and family child care homes world-wide. The Navy Child Development Training Program has been recognized as a leading source of quality training since 1986. The Navy trains 2,675 caregivers and 1,495 family child care providers in techniques for planning and conducting effective, quality child growth and development activities. Knowledge and skills are acquired through on the job training where caregivers and providers demonstrate competency as defined by the Council for Early Childhood Professional Recognition. Training is self-instructional and caregivers and providers proceed through each of the thirteen modules at their own pace with the assistance of Training Curriculum Specialists and FCC Monitored Directors. Completion of the training is a condition of employment for all caregiving personnel after they have completed a required orientation program which includes CPR, Standard First Aid, and Fire and Safety techniques. Each Training Curriculum Specialist in the Navy Standardized Program meets the professional qualifications of the National Academy of Early Childhood Program Specialists and they are responsible for ensuring that development and revision remain relevant and current.

Source of official student records: Registry of Credit Recommendations, American Council on Education, One Dupont Circle, Washington, DC 20036-1193.

Additional information about the courses: College Credit Recommendation Service, American Council on Education, One Dupont Circle, Washington, DC 20036-1193.

Family Child Care Providers Training Program

Location: Military Family Child Care facilities worldwide.

Length: Thirteen self-paced instructional modules. Military policy requires completion in 18-24 months.

Dates: January 1994-Present.

Objective: To develop qualified in-home child-care providers at Family Child Care homes worldwide.

Learning Outcome: Upon successful completion of this course, the student will be able to understand the developmental differences among children of different ages and apply this knowledge in their care of children; identify, enhance, and develop new skills as home child-care providers; plan, conduct, and evaluate an effective and quality child development program to meet the physical, social and emotional and intellectual needs of each child in the program; and understand the principles behind preventing and reporting child abuse and become familiar with the Family Day Care Environment Rating Scale.

Instruction: Major topics covered in the course are keeping children safe, promoting good health and nutrition,the learning environment, promoting physical development, promoting cognitive development, promoting communication, promoting creativity, building childrens' self-esteem, promoting social development, providing positive guidance, working with families, program management, maintaining a commitment to professionalism. Methods of instruction include self-instructional, paper-based materials supplemented with printed material, audiovisual materials, practical applications, one-on-one interaction with the Family Child Care Monitor/Director, written tests, observations, and competency assessments.

Credit Recommendation: In the vocational certificate category or the lower division baccalaureate/associate degree category, 3 semester hours in Child Development or Early Childhood Education (12/96). **NOTE**: Students must complete all thirteen modules to receive credit for this course.

Navy Standardized Child Development Training: Infants (PERS-659)

Location: Navy Child Development Centers located at Naval installations worldwide.

Length: Thirteen self-paced instructional modules. Navy policy requires completion in 18-24 months.

Dates: January 1986-Present.

Objective: To develop qualified caregivers of Infants (0-12 months) for Child Development Centers.

Learning Outcome: Upon successful completion of this course, the student will be able to identify, enhance, and develop new skills as caregivers of infants; plan, conduct and evaluate an effective and quality child development program to meet the physical, social, emotional, and intellectual needs of each infant in the program, and become familiar with the Infant and Toddler Environment Rating Scale (ITERS).

Instruction: Major topics covered in the course are keeping children safe, promoting good health and nutrition, creating and using an environment for learning, promoting physical development, promoting cognitive development, promoting communication, promoting creativity, building childrens' self-esteem, promoting social development, providing positive guidance, working with families, being an effective manager, and maintaining a commitment to professionalism. Methods of instruction include self-instructional, paper-based materials supplemented with printed material, audiovisual materials, practical applications, one-on-one coaching, written tests, observations, and competency assessments.

Credit Recommendation: In the vocational certificate category or the lower division baccalaureate/associate degree category, 3 semester hours in Child Development or Early Childhood Education (12/96). **NOTE**: Students must complete all thirteen modules of this course in order to receive credit.

Navy Standardized Child Development Training: Preschoolers (PERS-659)

Location: Navy Child Development Centers located at Naval installations worldwide.

Length: Thirteen self-paced instructional modules. Navy policy requires completion in 18-24 months.

Dates: January 1986-Present.

Objective: To develop qualified caregivers of Preschoolers (3-5 years) for Child Development Centers.

Learning Outcome: Upon successful completion of this course, the student will be able to identify, enhance, and develop new skills as caregivers of preschoolers; plan, conduct and evaluate an effective and quality child development program to meet the physical, social, and emotional and intellectual needs of each in the program, and become familiar with the Early Childhood Environment Rating Scale (ECERS).

Instruction: Major topics covered in the course are keeping children safe, promoting good health and nutrition, the learning environment, promoting physical development, promoting cognitive development, promoting communication, promoting creativity, building childrens' self-esteem, promoting social development, providing positive guidance, working with families, being an effective manager, and maintaining a commitment to professionalism. Methods of instruction include self-instructional, paper-based materials supplemented with printed material, audiovisual materials, practical applications, one-on-one coaching, written tests, observations, and competency assessments.

Credit Recommendation: In the vocational certificate category or the lower division baccalaureate/associate degree category, 3 semester hours in Child Development or Early Childhood Education (12/96). **NOTE**: A student must complete all thirteen modules to receive credit for this course.

Navy Standardized Child Development Training:Pretoddlers (PERS-659)

Location: Navy Child Development Centers located at Naval installations worldwide.

Length: Thirteen self-paced instructional modules. The Navy policy requires completion in 18-24 months.

Dates: August 1996-Present.

Objective: To develop qualified caregivers of Pretoddlers (12-24 months) for Child Development Centers.

Learning Outcome: Upon successful completion of this course the student will be able to identify, enhance, and develop new skills as caregivers of pretoddlers; plan, conduct and evaluate an effective and quality child development program to meet the physical, social and emotional and intellectual needs of each pretoddler in the program, and become familiar with the Infant and Toddler Environment Rating Scale (ITERS).

Instruction: Major topics covered in the course are keeping children safe, promoting good health and nutrition, the learning environment, promoting physical development, promoting cognitive development, promoting communication, promoting creativity, building childrens' self-esteem, promoting social development, providing positive guidance, working with families, being an effective manager, and maintaining a commitment to professionalism. Methods of instruction include self-instructional, paper-based materials supplemented with printed material, audiovisual material, practical application exercises, one-on-one coaching, written tests, observations, and competency assessments.

Credit Recommendation: In the vocational certificate category or the lower division baccalaureate/associate degree category, 3 semester hours in Child Development or Early Childhood Education (12/96). **NOTE**: A student must complete all thirteen modules to receive credit for this course.

Navy Standardized Child Development Training: Toddlers (PERS-659)

Location: Navy Child Development Centers located at Naval installations worldwide.

Length: Thirteen self-paced instructional modules. Navy policy requires completion in 18-24 months.

Dates: January 1986-Present.

Objective: To develop qualified caregivers of Toddlers (24-36 months) for Child Development Centers.

Learning Outcome: Upon successful completion of this course, the student will be able to identify, enhance, and develop new skills as caregivers of toddlers; plan, conduct, and evaluate an effective and quality child development program to meet the physical, social, emotional, and intellectual needs of each toddler in the program, and become familiar with the Infant and Toddler Environment Rating Scale (ITERS).

Instruction: Major topics covered in the course are keeping children safe, promoting good health and nutrition, the learning environment, promoting physical development, promoting cognitive development, promoting communication, promoting creativity, building children s' self-esteem, promoting social development, providing positive guidance, working with families, being an effective manager, and maintaining a commitment to professionalism. Methods of instruction include self-instructional, paper-based materials supplemented with printed material, audiovisual materials, practical application exercises, one-on-one coaching, written tests, observations, and competency assessments.

Credit Recommendation: In the vocational certificate category or the lower division baccalaureate/associate degree category, 3 semester hours in Child Development or Early Childhood Education (12/96). **NOTE**: A student must complete all thirteen modules to receive credit for this course.

U.S. Department of the Treasury

The Federal Law Enforcement Training Center, established in 1970 in the Department of the Treasury, is a consolidated interagency training facility. The center provides basic and advanced training for law enforcement personnel of more than 70 participating federal agencies. The center conducts research in law enforcement training, methods, and curriculum content and develops such methods and content for use in its training programs. The center assists participating agencies in determining their needs for law enforcement training and in developing curriculum, course content, and teaching methods and techniques for the specialized courses that the agencies conduct at the center. The center also provides facilities, equipment, and support services necessary for the center's numerous law enforcement training programs.

Source of official student records: Registrar's Office, Program Support Division, Federal Law Enforcement Training Center, Building 68, Room 1A15, Glynco, GA 31520.

Additional information about the courses: College Credit Recommendation Service, American Council on Education, One Dupont Circle, Washington, DC 20036-1193.

FEDERAL LAW ENFORCEMENT TRAINING CENTER

Criminal Investigator Training Program (CITP) (8CI)
Version 1: Part 1: Criminal Law, Procedure and Evidence
Part 2: Criminal Investigation
Part 3: Physical Education
Version 2: Part 1: Criminal Investigation
Part 2: Physical Skills Development
Version 3: Part 1: Criminal Investigation
Part 2: Physical Skills
(Formerly Criminal Investigator Training Program [8CI])

Location: Federal Law Enforcement Training Center, Glynco, GA.

Length: *Version 1:* 256.5 hours (8 weeks); *Version 2:* 304-357 hours (8 weeks); *Version 3:* 357 hours (8 weeks).

Dates: *Version 1:* July 1970-May 1985; *Version 2:* June 1985-June 1991; *Version 3:* July 1991-Present.

Objective: To provide criminal investigators with skills and knowledge to perform the investigative role effectively.

Learning Outcome: Upon successful completion of this course, the student will be able to conduct full comprehensive investigations of criminal offenses within the jurisdiction of their assigned responsibilities.

Instruction: *Version 1: Part 1:* Major topics covered in the course are assault, conspiracy, parties to criminal offenses, organized and white-collar crime, civil rights, evidence (including self-incriminations), constitutional law, entrapment, federal court procedures, arrest, search and seizure, pretrial conference and witness briefs, tactics of defendants, and mock trial. *Part 2:* Major topics covered in the course are crime investigation, fingerprints, photographs, questioned documents, car stop/search, informants, surveillance, undercover operations. *Part 3:* Major topics covered in the course are firearms, defensive driving, cardiopulmonary resuscitation, and defensive tactics. Methods of instruction include lecture, discussion, workshops, and practical exercises. *Version 2: Part 1:* Major topics covered in the course are behavorial science topics such as ethics and conduct, stress management, interviewing, investigator operations and techniques including execution of search warrants, use of informants, surveillance, undercover operations, crime scene investigation, photography, introduction to computers, and link analysis; legal topics such as constitutional law, detention and arrest, evidence, court procedures, search and seizure, and federal statutes. *Part 2:* Major topics covered in the course are defensive driving, firearms usage, marksmanship, CPR, defensive tactics, and arrest techniques. *Version 3: Parts 1 and 2:* Major topics covered in the course are criminal law and procedures; interviewing; execution of search warrants; use of informants; surveillance; undercover operations; crime scene investigation; detention and arrest; search and seizure; firearms usage; defensive driving; and physical conditioning. Methods of instruction include lecture, discussion, laboratory, and practical exercises.

Credit Recommendation: *Version 1: Part 1:* In the lower division baccalaureate/associate degree category or upper division baccalaureate degree category, 3 semester hours in Criminal Law and Procedure and Evidence. *Part 2:* In the lower division baccalaureate/associate degree category or upper division baccalaureate degree category, 3 semester hours in Criminal Investigation. *Part 3:* In the lower division baccalaureate/associate degree category, 2 semester hours in Physical Education (11/78). *Version 2: Part 1:* In the lower division baccalaureate/associate degree category or upper division baccalaureate degree category, 7 semester hours in Criminal Justice. *Part 2:* In the lower division baccalaureate/ associate degree category, 2 semester hours in Physical Education (7/87). *Version 3: Parts 1 and 2:* In the lower division baccalaureate/associate degree category or upper division baccalaureate degree category, 4 semester hours in Criminal Investigation, 3 semester hours in Criminal Law and Procedures; and in the lower division baccalaureate/associate degree category, 2 semester hours in Physical Education (7/93). **NOTE:** Dual credit for similar FLETC courses should not be given.

Land Management Training Program (LMTP) (11LM) (Formerly Police Training Program [11LM] and prior to 1994, Formerly Police Training Program [9PT])

Location: Federal Law Enforcement Training Center, Glynco, GA.

Length: *Course 1:* 386 hours (9 weeks); *Course 2:* 478 hours (11.2 weeks).

Dates: *Course 1:* July 1993-December 1993; *Course 2:* January 1994-Present.

Objective: *Courses 1 and 2:* To provide non-urban or isolated law enforcement officers from the federal land management community with the skills and knowledge to serve effectively in the basic law enforcement and criminal investigation roles at the entry level.

Learning Outcome: *Courses 1 and 2:* Upon successful completion of this course, the student will be able to apply law enforcement policy and techniques related to the investigation, apprehension, or detention of criminal offenders in a field situation.

Instruction: *Courses 1 and 2:* Major topics covered in the course are criminal law and procedure, interviewing, execution of warrants, crime scene processing, report writing, detention and arrest of suspects, firearms usage, and high performance driver training, and physical techniques and conditioning. Methods of instruction include lecture, discussion, laboratory, and practical exercises.

Credit Recommendation: *Course 1:* In the lower division baccalaureate/associate degree category or upper division baccalaureate degree category, 3 semester hours in Criminal Law and Procedure; and in the lower division baccalaureate/associate degree category, 3 semester hours in

Basic Law Enforcement and 2 semester hours in Physical Education (7/93). *Course 2:* In the lower division baccalaureate/associate degree category or in the upper division baccalaureate degree category, 3 semester hours in Criminal Investigation, 3 semester hours in Criminal Law and Pro-cedures, and in the lower division baccalaureate/associate degree category, 3 semester hours in Basic Law Enforcement and 3 semester hours in Physical Education (7/93). **NOTE:** Dual credit for other similar FLETC courses should not be given.

Mixed Basic Police Training Program (MBPTP) (Formerly Police Training Program [8PT])

Location: Federal Law Enforcement Training Center, Glynco, GA.

Length: *Version 4:* 367 hours (8 weeks).

Dates: November 1990-Present.

Objective: *Version 4:* To provide federal uniformed law enforcement officers with the skills and knowledge to serve effectively in the basic law enforcement role at the entry level.

Learning Outcome: *Version 4:* Upon successful completion of this course, the student will be able to apply law enforcement policy and techniques related to criminal offenses.

Instruction: *Version 4:* Major topics covered in the course are criminal law and procedure, interviewing, crime scene processing, report writing, radio communications, detention and arrest of suspects, firearms usage, driver training, and physical techniques and conditioning. Methods of instruction include lecture, discussion, laboratory, and practical exercises.

Credit Recommendation: *Version 4:* In the lower division baccalaureate/associate degree category or upper division baccalaureate degree category, 3 semester hours in Criminal Law and Procedure; and in the lower division baccalaureate/ associate degree category, 3 semester hours in Basic Law Enforcement and 2 semester hours in Physical Education (7/93). **NOTE:** Dual credit for other similar FLETC courses should not be given. For credit recommendations for course taken before July 1993 consult 1993 National Guide or prior National Guide editions.

U.S. CUSTOMS SERVICE ACADEMY

Customs Inspector Basic Training Program (USCSI) (Formerly 11PI or 9PI Program)

Location: U.S. Customs Service Academy, FLETC, Glynco, GA.

Length: *Version 1:* 416 hours (11 weeks); *Version 2:* 424 hours (12 weeks).

Dates: January 1992-Present.

Objective: To prepare trainee inspectors to function as federal law enforcement officers and as decision-makers in the selective examination environment.

Learning Outcome: Upon successful completion of this course, the student will be able to function in all areas of customs inspector responsibility at the entry level.

Instruction: Major topics covered in the course are detention regulations and procedures, immigrant status, driver training, physical conditioning, firearms usage and care, and transportation of prisoners. Methods of instruction include lecture, discussion, and practical exercises.

Credit Recommendation: In the lower division baccalaureate/associate degree category or upper division baccalaureate degree category, 4 semester hours in Customs Law Enforcement, 2 semester hours in Customs Law, and 2 semester hours in Physical Education (7/93).

U.S. Drug Enforcement Administration

The United States Drug Enforcement Administration (DEA) of the Department of Justice has overall responsibility for enforcing the provisions of the federal drug statutes. Through enforcement strategy, the gathering of drug intelligence, the use of science and technology research, close narcotics enforcement coordination with foreign countries, and the sponsorship of specialized drug training schools, the Drug Enforcement Administration exerts a unified effort designed to curb the worldwide illicit distribution of narcotics and dangerous drugs.

The Office of Training (TR) is the educational arm of the Drug Enforcement Administration. TR conducts programs for special agent personnel and compliance investigators; directs an ongoing executive, mid-management, and supervisory program for personnel assigned to higher-level positions; and conducts inservice programs for DEA personnel in such areas as conspiracy investigations and specialized enforcement techniques.

Source of official student records: Drug Enforcement Administration, Office of Training, FBI Academy Field Training Unit, Quantico, VA 22135

Additional information about the courses: College Credit Recommendation Service, American Council on Education, One Dupont Circle, Washington, DC 20036-1193.

Basic Narcotic and Dangerous Drug Law Enforcement School for State and Local Drug Enforcement Officers (Formerly Criminal Investigation-Drug Abuse Two-Week Drug Law Enforcement Training School)

Location: The Federal Law Enforcement Center (FLETC), Brunswick, Ga., and at various sites in the U.S.

Length: 77 hours (2 weeks); residential.

Dates: April 1968-Present.

Objective: To introduce state and local drug law enforcement officers to the principles of criminal investigation as they relate to enforcement techniques.

Learning Outcome: Upon successful completion of this course, the student will be able to identify major classifications of psychoactive drugs including dominant pharmachological effects and user/abuser recognition within the context of drug law enforcement; demonstrate fundamental concepts of effective interviewing techniques, informant handling, and basic undercover techniques; describe fundamental concepts of asset removal; identify essential safety issues in clandestine laboratory investigation; explain elements of effective evidence handling and diversion investigation; and demonstrate basic principles of surveillance, criminal conspiracy investigation, and raid planning.

Instruction: Major topics covered in the course are drug law enforcement principles and techniques including clandestine laboratories, informants, surveillance, undercover techniques, technical equipment raid planning, intelligence, drug officer stress, and diversion investigation; drug traffic patterns and drug abuse education; pharmacology stressing drug identification and field testing; and legal procedures stressing evidence, trial techniques, and conspiracy investigation. Methods of instruction include lecture, discussion, classroom exercises, audio/visual material, practical exercises, and final examination.

Credit Recommendation: In the lower division baccalaureate/associate degree category, 4 semester hours in Law Enforcement (1/76) (11/94).

Drug Enforcement Officers Academy Part 1: Criminal Investigation Part 2: Internship and Field Service Training Part 3: Drug Abuse Part 4: Criminal Procedures Part 5: Communications Part 6: Physical Education Part 7: Police Administration

Location: National Training Institute, Washington, DC

Length: 407 hours (10 weeks), residential, *Part 1:* 131 hours, *Part 2:* 130 hours, *Part 3*: 39 hours, *Part 4*: 37 hours, *Part 5*: 20 hours, *Part 6:* 22 hours, *Part 7:* 28 hours.

Dates: *Version 1:* October 1970-December 1985; *Version 2:* February 1988-December 1993.

Objective: To provide state and local enforcement officers with in-depth knowledge of the most current techniques in narcotics and dangerous drugs enforcement, and with the expertise needed to provide leadership in combating drug abuse.

Instruction: *Part 1:* Major topics covered in the course are clandestine laboratories; informants; surveillance; undercover, drug smuggling, and conspiracy investigations; technical investigative aids; photography; interview and interrogation; initiation and development of a case; raid planning and execution; concealment; field testing; determining drug-related deaths; role of intelligence information; and value of news media in investigation. Methods of instruction include lectures, discussions, classroom demonstrations, and practical and field training exercises. *Part 2:* Major topics covered in the course are simulated transactions and practical exercises in fact finding and intelligence gathering are used to apply principles and techniques learned in the classroom. Involves planning, use of equipment, conducting raids, arrest procedures, and surveillance. Field training is reviewed through preparation of critiques and detailed reports and use of videotaped exercises. Students are supervised by staff instructors. *Part 3:* Major topics covered in the course are drug identification, characteristics of various types of drugs, effects of drugs, methadone programs, national and international drug traffic patterns, social and psychological aspects of drug abuse, and drug research programs. Methods of instruction include lecture, discussion, demonstration, and field testing exercises. *Part 4:* Major topics covered in the course are the constitutional restrictions, limitations, and safeguards relative to the conduct of searches and seizures under the Fourth Amendment; forfeitures; rules of evidence; Uniform Controlled Substances Act; rules of Federal Criminal Procedure; trial techniques; mock hearings; legal aspects of electronic surveillance; identification and interrogation; conspiracy; and possession with intent to distribute to others. Methods of instruction include lectures and discussions. *Part 5:* Major topics covered in the course are several theories of communications and develops requirements for effective communication; applies these principles to the presentation of formal instruction. Oral presentation of a lesson is a course requirement. Methods of instruction include lecture, discussion, demonstration, and class participation. *Part 6:* Major topics covered in the course are developing the physical stamina of the student through calisthenics and endurance tests. Methods of instruction include lectures, demonstration, and class participation. *Part 7:* Major topics covered in the course are the managerial procedures needed to operate a narcotics unit within an agency's organizational structure. Covers the managerial functions of planning, supervising, and directing. Methods of instruction include lectures and discussion.

Credit Recommendation: *Part 1:* In the lower division baccalaureate/associate degree category, 4 semester hours in

Criminal Justice or Law Enforcement (1/76). **NOTE:** This section duplicates the material covered in the *Two-Week Law Enforcement* course (see above). *Part 2:* In the lower division baccalaureate/associate degree category or in the upper division baccalaureate degree category, 3 semester hours in Criminal Justice or Law Enforcement (1/76). *Part 3:* In the lower division baccalaureate/associate degree category or in the upper division baccalaureate degree category, 2 semester hours in Criminal Justice or Law Enforcement (1/76). *Part 4:* In the lower division baccalaureate/associate degree category or in the upper division baccalaureate degree category, 3 semester hours in Criminal Justice or Law Enforcement (1/76). *Part 5:* In the lower division baccalaureate/associate degree category, 1 semester hour in Communications (1/76). *Part 6:* In the lower division baccalaureate/associate degree category, 2 semester hours in Physical Education (1/76). *Part 7:* In the lower division baccalaureate/associate degree category, 2 semester hours in Criminal Justice or Law Enforcement (1/76) (11/94).

State and Local Drug Law Enforcement Officers Academy (Drug Enforcement Officers Academy)

Location: Drug Enforcement Administration Office of Training, FBI Academy, Quantico, VA.

Length: 320 hours (8 weeks); *Part 1*: Administration - 40 hours; *Part 2*: Investigations - 200 hours; *Part 3*: Firearms and Defensive Tactics - 80 hours.

Dates: January 1994-Present.

Objective: To provide state and local drug law enforcement officers with knowledge of current techniques in narcotics and dangerous drug law enforcement.

Learning Outcome: Upon successful completion of this course, the student will be able to apply drug law enforcement techniques including drug identification, undercover operations, and surveillance in furthering drug investigations; and apply safe tactical techniques to drug law enforcement situations.

Instruction: Major topics covered in the course are *Part 1 , Administration*: leadership, integrity, ethics, stress management, risk management, critical incident management, asset forfeiture and management, case management, and liability issues; *Part 2 , Investigations*: interviewing, drug laws, undercover operations, raids, surveillance, informant handling, drug identification and trends, drug trafficking, criminal organizations, drug evidence, and drug handling; *Part 3* , Firearms and Defensive Tactics . Methods of instruction include lecture, discussion, classroom exercises, audio/visual material, practical exercises, and final examinations.

Credit Recommendation: In the lower division baccalaureate/associate degree category, 2 semester hours in Police Administration; 4 semester hours in Criminal Investigation; and 4 semester hours in Physical Education or Firearms Training (11/94).

U.S. General Services Administration Interagency Training Center

The U.S. General Services Administration (GSA) created the Interagency Training Center in 1963 to teach employees how to perform functions for which GSA has governmentwide responsibility. Those functions include the areas of procurement, real and personal property, supply, travel and transportation management.

Classes are open to all Federal, State and local government employees as well as cost-reimbursable contractors who perform these duties. Each year, approximately 1,000 classes are conducted worldwide from among the 65 different courses that are offered. Approximately 15,000 students attend these classes in major centers of Federal employment around the country and overseas.

Courses are developed in cooperation with the GSA Federal Acquisition Institute and other governmentwide program offices. New courses are "field-tested" by experts from around government, and our instructors are experienced practititioners with years of on-the-job experience in their respective fields. In addition to the technical proficiency required of all instructors, they must have a minimum of a bachelors degree and some form of instructor training to ensure their use of optimum delivery techniques in the classroom.

Students register through their employing agencies, and are issued a formal certificate upon successful completion of the course.

Source of official student records: Registry of Credit Recommendation, American Council on Education, One Dupont Circle, Washington, DC 20036-1193 or [Program Manager], GSA Interagency Training Center, P.O. Box 15608, Arlington, VA 22215-0608.

Additional information about the courses: College Credit Recommendation Service, American Council on Education, One Dupont Circle, Washington, DC 20036-1193.

Basic Contract Administration (2256)

Location: Albuquerque, NM, Atlanta, Boston, Chicago, Denver, Fort Worth, TX, Kansas City, MO, New York, Philadelphia, San Francisco, Seattle, Washington, D. C. and additional national and international sites.

Length: 33 hours, plus a minimum of 7 hours outside reading (5 days).

Dates: October 1996-Present.

Objective: To provide the student with the knowledge to administer, and to close-out a contract for supplies and services.

Learning Outcome: Upon successful completion of this course, the student will be able to prepare a contract administration plan; conduct a post-award orientation; place delivery orders; monitor performance of contractors; resolve problems; select and pursue a formal contract remedy; process contractor invoices; and close out contracts.

Instruction: Major topics covered in the course are contract administration planning; postaward orientation; performance monitoring; problem resolution, contract modification, options and remedies; payment; contract closeout; and disputes, claims, and terminations. Methods of instruction include lecture, discussion, case studies, student activities, visual aids, and directed out-of-class reading. Evaluation methods used are evaluated by a proctored final examination.

Credit Recommendation: In the lower division baccalaureate/associate degree category, 1 semester hour in Acquisition Management, Business Administration, Management, Procurement Management, Public Administration, or Purchasing and Supply Management (8/97).

Construction Contracting (2232)

Location: Atlanta, Boston, Chicago, Denver, Fort Worth, TX, Kansas City, MO, New York, Philadelphia, San Francisco, Seattle, Washington, D. C. and additional national and international sites.

Length: 75 hours, plus a minimum of 10 hours outside reading (2 weeks).

Dates: October 1996-Present.

Objective: To provide the student with the knowledge to process all phases of a construction contract, including initial planning, specification development, award, modification, and contract administration.

Learning Outcome: Upon successful completion of this course, the student will be able to describe the identification of construction projects and the criteria to determine the type of acquisition and design plans; review the procurement request, identify and issue the solicitation; evaluate and award contracts; identify and develop a contract administration team and monitoring system, and conduct the pre-construction conference; review, and monitor Schedule of Prices, specifications and drawings, subcontracting plans, labor compliance, and various construction contract clauses; analyze delays, their effect on time and cost, and process delay claims; identify reasons, sources and types of modifications and document change orders; process disputes and claims, select remedies and process terminations.

Instruction: Major topics covered in the course are presolicitation stage; solicitation phase; bid evaluation and award; contract administration planning; contract administration clauses; day-to-day contract administration; delays; modifications; and remedies in construction contracting. Methods of instruction include lecture, discussion, case studies, student activities, visual aids, and directed out-of-class reading. Evaluation methods used is evaluated by proctored mid-term and final examinations.

Credit Recommendation: In the lower division baccalaureate/associate degree category, 3 semester hours in Acquisition Management, Business Administration, Management, Procurement Management, Public Administration, or Purchasing and Supply Management (8/97). **NOTE:** This credit recommendation only applies if this course is taken in combination with Introduction to Contracting and Procurement Planning.

Contracting by Negotiation (2236)

Location: Atlanta, Boston, Chicago, Fort Worth, TX, Kansas City, MO, New York, Philadelphia, San Francisco, Seattle, Washington, D. C. and additional national and international sites.

Length: 33 hours, plus a minimum of 7 hours outside reading (5 days).

Dates: October 1996-Present.

Objective: To provide the student with the knowledge and skills to critique, process, evaluate, amend, price and negotiate contracts.

Learning Outcome: Upon successful completion of this course, the student will be able to critique a Statement of Work and technical evaluation factors; prepare RFPs; conduct a preproposal conference; process proposals; obtain cost and pricing data and/or audits; review technical evaluation reports; perform cost analyses; determine a competitive range; develop negotiation strategies; conduct negotiations; award contracts; and conduct debriefings.

Instruction: Major topics covered in the course are Statement of Work; technical evaluation, source selection, and contract types; government furnished property, bonds, and RFPs; preproposal conferences, processing proposals; price objectives, cost analysis, and competitive ranges; negotiation strategies, and errors; award preparation, awards, and debriefing. Methods of instruction include lecture, discussion, case studies, student activities, visual aids, and directed out-of-class reading. Evaluation methods used is evaluated by a proctored final examination.

Credit Recommendation: In the lower division baccalaureate/associate degree category, 1 semester hour in Acquisition Management, Business Administration, Management, Procurement Management, Public Administration, or Purchasing and Supply Management (8/97).

Contracting by Sealed Bidding (2238)

Location: Atlanta, Boston, Chicago, Fort Worth, TX, Kansas City, MO, New York, Philadelphia, San Francisco, Seattle, St. Louis, MO, Washington, D. C. and additional national and international sites.

Length: 33 hours, plus a minimum of 7 hours outside reading (5 days).

Dates: October 1996-Present.

Objective: To provide the student with the knowledge and skills to solicit, amend, process and evaluate sealed bids so that the responsible conforming bidder may be selected.

Learning Outcome: Upon successful completion of this course, the student will be able to prepare and publicize an Invitation for Bid; respond to preaward inquiries; amend and cancel a bid; control and abstract bids to safeguard the sealed bidding process; evaluate bids for responsiveness; calculate the evaluated price; apply price-related factors; process late bids; identify, resolve, and process mistakes in bids; determine responsibility; and make final award decisions.

Instruction: Major topics covered in the course are a review of procurement planning; bid solicitation; publicizing proposed procurement; amending and cancelling IFBs; processing bids; identifying and resolving mistakes in bids; determining responsibility of proposed contractors; awarding of contracts; and contract award protests. Methods of instruction include lecture, discussion, case studies, student activities, visual aids, and directed out-of-class reading. Evaluation methods used is evaluated by a proctored final examination.

Credit Recommendation: In the lower division baccalaureate/associate degree category, 2 semester hours in Acquisition Management, Business Administration, Management, Procurement Management, Public Administration, or Purchasing and Supply Management (8/97). **NOTE:** This credit recommendation only applies if this course is taken in combination with Introduction to Contracting and Procurement Planning.

Contracting for Architect and Engineer Services (2240)

Location: Atlanta, Boston, Chicago, Denver, Fort Worth, TX, Kansas City, MO, New York, Philadelphia, San Francisco, Seattle, Washington, D. C. and additional national and international sites.

Length: 33 hours, plus a minimum of 7 hours outside reading (5 days).

Dates: October 1996-Present.

Objective: To provide the student with the knowledge and skills to contract for architect and engineering services.

Learning Outcome: Upon successful completion of this course, the student will be able to process contracts for architect/engineering (A/E) services from initial planning through specification development, award, modification, and contract administration.

Instruction: Major topics covered in the course are forecasting requirements for A/E services; the Brooks Act; the selection process including the scope of work, evaluation board procedures and report; evaluation and negotiation of A/E proposals; contract award, administration and modifications; evaluation of A/E performance; and closeout. Methods of instruction include lecture, discussion, case studies, student activities, visual aids, and directed out-of-class reading. Evaluation Methods Used is evaluated by a proctored final examination.

Credit Recommendation: In the lower division baccalaureate/associate degree category, 2 semester hours in Acquisition Management, Business Administration, Management, Procurement Management, Public Administration, or Purchasing and Supply Management (8/97). **NOTE:** This credit recommendation only applies if this course is taken in combination with Introduction to Contracting and Procurement Planning.

Cost Analysis (2298)

Location: Atlanta, Boston, Chicago, Denver, Fort Worth, TX, Kansas City, MO, New York, Philadelphia, San Francisco, Seattle, Washington, D. C. and additional national and international sites.

Length: 33 hours, plus a minimum of 7 to 8 hours outside reading (5 days).

Dates: October 1996-Present.

Objective: To provide the student with the knowledge and skills to conduct a cost analysis based either on certified cost or pricing data or on data other than cost or pricing data.

Learning Outcome: Upon successful completion of this course, the student will be able to evaluate cost and pricing data; allowability of proposed cost data collection for cost analysis; quantitative techniques for estimating costs; direct and indirect costs; facilities cost of capital; prenegotiation objectives on the overall price, profit or fee; cost analysis documentation; and "best and final offers."

Instruction: Major topics covered in the course are costs and cost analysis; obtaining offeror information; identifying considerations affecting cost allowability; collecting information; defining and evaluating work design for contract performance; improvement curves; analyzing direct material, labor and other costs, analyzing indirect costs, facilities capital cost of money and analyzing for profit or fee; preparing for negotiation. Methods of instruction include lecture, discussion, case studies, student activities, visual aids, and directed out-of-class reading. Evaluation methods used is evaluated by an applied quiz and a proctored final examination.

Credit Recommendation: In the upper division baccalaureate category, 3 semester hours in Acquisition Management, Business Administration, Management, Procurement Management, Public Administration, or Purchasing and Supply Management (8/97). **NOTE:** To receive credit for this course, students also must complete Price Analysis.

Introduction to Contracting (1200)

Location: Albuquerque, NM, Atlanta, Boston, Chicago, Denver, Fort Worth, TX, Hines, IL, Kansas City, MO, Los Angeles, Minneapolis, New Orleans, New York, Norfolk, Orlando, Philadelphia, Portland, Salt Lake City, San Antonio, San Diego, San Francisco, Seattle, St. Louis, MO, Washington, D. C. and additional national and international sites.

Length: 33 hours, plus a minimum of 7 hours outside reading (5 days).

Dates: October 1996-Present.

Objective: To provide the student with a basic overview of the federal acquisition process, and the principal duties of contracting personnel.

Learning Outcome: Upon successful completion of this course, the student will be able to identify and define the basic components of the Federal acquisition process, its goals, and the principal sources of Federal Contract Law; describe typical approaches to organizing the acquisition function; identify and define the roles and responsibilities of contracting personnel; identify the principal contracting functions, and the standards of conduct that apply to the acquisition process.

Instruction: Major topics covered in the course are the federal acquisition process and its goals; basic statutes and regulations affecting acquisition; roles and responsibilities of contracting officer representatives; stages (presolicitation, solicitation, award, post-award administration, modifications, terminations, claims) of the acquisition process; and standards of conduct. Methods of instruction include lecture, discussion, case studies, student activities, visual aids, and directed out-of-class reading. Evaluation methods used is evaluated by a proctored final examination.

Credit Recommendation: In the lower division baccalaureate/associate degree category, 2 semester hours in Acquisition Management, Business Administration, Management, Procurement Management, Public Administration, or Purchasing and Supply Management (8/97). **NOTE:** This credit recommendation only applies if this course is taken in combination with Procurement Planning and Contracting by Sealed Bidding or Procurement Planning and Contracting for Architect Engineer Services. Students may receive a credit recommendation of 3 semester hours if this course is taken in combination with Procurement Planning and Construction Contracting.

Price Analysis (2299)

Location: Atlanta, Boston, Chicago, Denver, Fort Worth, TX, Kansas City, MO, New York, Philadelphia, San Francisco, Seattle, Washington, D. C. and additional national and international sites.

Length: 33 hours, plus a minimum of 7 hours outside reading (5 days).

Dates: October 1996-Present.

Objective: To provide contract specialists with the knowledge to prepare for contract pricing analysis, to analyze contract prices, and to make price-related decisions in simplified acquisitions, sealed bidding and in negotiated procurements.

Learning Outcome: Upon successful completion of this course, contract specialists will be able to conduct price analysis; make price-related decisions; evaluate sealed bids; and prepare for negotiations under Parts 12,13, 14 and 15 of the Federal Acquisition Regulation (FAR).

Instruction: Major topics covered in the course are elements and approaches to contract pricing; solicitation, terms and publicity to maximize price competition; identification of contract actions and conditions for which cost or pricing data are required; development of award criteria for pricing; cost factors related to contract administration; use of price indexing in analyzing contract costs; cost-volume-profit analysis; comparison and analysis of price differences; sealed bidding price decisions; determination of need to negotiate; and identification of the principle elements of a price negotiation. Methods of instruction include lecture, discussion, case studies, student activities, visual aids, and directed out-of-class reading. Evaluation methods used is evaluated by a proctored final examination.

Credit Recommendation: In the upper division baccalaureate category, 3 semester hours in Acquisition Management, Business Administration, Management, Procurement Management, Public Administration, or Purchasing and Supply Management (8/97). **NOTE:** To receive credit for this course, students also must complete Cost Analysis.

Procurement Planning (2218)

Location: Atlanta, Boston, Chicago, Denver, Fort Worth, TX, Kansas City, MO, New York, Philadelphia, San Francisco, Seattle, Washington, D. C. and additional national and international sites.

Length: 33 hours, plus a minimum of 7 hours outside reading (5 days).

Dates: October 1996-Present.

Objective: To provide the student with the knowledge and skills to perform the planning and presolicitation activities of the procurement process.

Learning Outcome: Upon successful completion of this course, the student will be able to review procurement requests; perform market research; identify sources, set-aside requirements, and type of competition needed; formulate evaluation factors; and prepare a procurement plan.

Instruction: Major topics covered in the course are the review of purchase requests and funding availability; market research; specifications and Statements of Work (SOW); role of the Service Contract Act; identification of sources, set asides and 8A programs; determination of type of competition needed; analysis of lease vs. purchase issues; identification of evaluation factors; methods of procurement; and the procurement plan. Methods of instruction include lecture, discussion, case studies, student activities, role playing, visual aids, and directed out-of-class reading. Evaluation Methods Used is evaluated by a proctored final examination.

Credit Recommendation: In the lower division baccalaureate/associate degree category, 2 semester hours in Acquisition Management, Business Administration, Management, Procurement Management, Public Administration, or Purchasing and Supply Management (8/97). **NOTE:** This credit recommendation only applies if this course is taken in combination with Introduction to Contracting and Contracting by Sealed Bidding or Introduction to Contracting and Contracting for Architect Engineer Services. Students may receive a credit recommendation of 3 semester hours if this course is taken in combination with Introduction to Contracting and Construction Contracting.

Source Selection (2269)

Location: Atlanta, Boston, Chicago, Fort Worth, TX, Kansas City, MO, New York, Philadelphia, San Francisco, Seattle, Washington, D. C. and additional national and international sites.

Length: 33 hours, plus a minimum of 7 to 8 hours outside reading (5 days).

Dates: October 1996-Present.

Objective: To provide the student with the knowledge and skills to make sound source selection decisions in a competitive negotiations environment.

Learning Outcome: Upon successful completion of this course, the student will be able to plan source selection, including developing evaluation criteria and evaluating proposals, and use the "best value" approach to source selection award decisions.

Instruction: Major topics covered in the course are the source selection process, source selection planning, developing evaluation factors, technical evaluation, establishing the competitive range, best and final offers, and selection and award of contracts. Methods of instruction include lecture, discussion, case studies, student activities, visual aids, and directed out-of-class reading. Evaluation methods used is evaluated by a proctored final examination.

Credit Recommendation: In the lower division baccalaureate/associate degree category, 1 semester hour in Acquisition Management, Business Administration, Management, Procurement Management, Public Administration, or Purchasing and Supply Management (8/97).

U.S. Naval Facilities Contracts Training Center

The Naval Facilities Contracts Training center (NFCTC) is a school under the command of the Naval Facilities Engineering Command Deputy Director of Contracting. NFCTC is also a component school of the Defense Acquisition University (DAU) for the Department of Defense (DOD). It is co-located with the United States Navy's Civil Engineer corps Officers School at the Naval Facilities Institute (NFI), Port Hueneme, California. NFCTC provides specialized and mandatory quality education and training for military and civilian procurement professionals involved in various aspects of facilities services, and course designed to meet new or unique construction acquisition program requirements.

Source of official student records: Registry of Credit Recommendations, American Council on Education, One Dupont Circle, Washington, DC 20036-1193.

Additional information about the courses: College Credit Recommendation Service, American Council on Education, One Dupont Circle, Washington, DC 20036-1193.

Advanced Contract Management

Location: Naval Facilities Institute, Port Hueneme, CA and various locations throughout the U.S., Europe, and the Pacific Rim.

Length: 66 hours (10 days).

Dates: April 1986-June 1991.

Objective: To develop a comprehensive management philosophy about contract management which emphasizes responsibility and accountability in facilities related contracting.

Learning Outcome: Upon successful completion of this course, the student will be able to identify techniques of quality assurance which can be applied to contract administration; articulate the essential nature of contract administration services with outside agencies; describe the functional components of contract administration and acquisitions; and understand the importance of overhead cost and be able to compute fail value ratios.

Instruction: Major topics covered in the course are ethics, acquisition planning, source selection, "Brooks Act", options, day to day administration, modifications, administration of costs contracts, and acceptance and remedies. Methods of instruction include lecture, discussion, case studies, visual aids, and examinations.

Credit Recommendation: In the upper division baccalaureate degree category or graduate degree category, 3 semester hours in Procurement and Contracting, Business Administration, or Logistics and Material Management elective (11/92).

Architect-Engineer Contract Management (CTC 366)

Location: Naval Facilities Institute, Port Hueneme, CA and various locations throughout the U.S., Europe, and the Pacific Rim.

Length: 36 hours (4.5 days).

Dates: November 1985-Present.

Objective: To secure a basic understanding of the architect/engineer contracting requirements, including a specific focus on the "Brooks Act", i.e. the acquisition of technical and professional services by the Federal government.

Learning Outcome: Upon successful completion of this course, the student will be able to recognize the need for team participation in the architect/engineer acquisition process; specificity of scope of work and synopsis and Slate Board actions; basic cost/price analysis techniques; negotiation strategy design; law and regulations unique to architect/engineer contracting; and contract (program) management and administration.

Instruction: Major topics covered in the course are scope of work (need for definition, accuracy and exclusiveness); source selection criteria/process leading to award, cost/price analysis; negotiation/strategies and fee negotiation concepts; and contract management (program) and administration. Methods of instruction include lecture, discussion, classroom exercises, outside reading, visual aids, student handbook, and resource materials.

Credit Recommendation: In the lower division baccalaureate/associate degree category or upper division baccalaureate degree category, 3 semester hours in Civil Engineering or Business elective (11/92).

Construction Contract Management (CON 223) (Formerly Advanced Contract Management [CTC 542] and [CON 211])

Location: Naval Facilities Institute, Port Hueneme, CA and various locations throughout the U.S., Europe, and the Pacific Rim.

Length: 88 hours (13.5 days).

Dates: February 1992-Present.

Objective: To develop a comprehensive management philosophy about contract management which emphasizes responsibility and accountability in facilities related contracting.

Learning Outcome: Upon successful completion of this course, the student will be able to describe the functional components of contract administration; identify techniques of quality assurance which can be applied to construction contract administration; and articulate the essential nature of contract administration services with outside agencies, including the importance of direct and indirect costs and applied to construction.

Instruction: Major topics covered in the course are ethics, acquisition planning, source selection, "Brooks Act", options, day to day administration, modifications, administration of costs contracts, and acceptance and remedies. Methods of instruction include lecture, discussion, case studies, visual aids, and examinations.

Credit Recommendation: In the upper division baccalaureate degree category or graduate degree category, 3 semester hours in Procurement and Contracting, Business Administration, or Logistics and Material Management elective (11/92).

Construction Contract MODS (CTC 343)

Location: Naval Facilities Institute, Port Hueneme, CA and various locations throughout the U.S., Europe, and the Pacific Rim.

Length: 36 hours (4.5 days).

Dates: October 1985-Present.

Objective: To enable the student to apply and use correct procedures and sound judgement in administering construction contract modifications and be able to advise the contracting officer on correct courses of action and achieve settlements with construction contracts in accordance with the FAR, DFARS, and basic statutes.

Learning Outcome: Upon successful completion of this course, the student will be able to identify sources of potential modifications; prepare and apply the correct modification clauses to address contract problems; develop and maintain techniques for quantifying and monitoring contract performance; and determine equitable adjustments to the contract cost and time terms as a result of contract modification.

Instruction: Major topics covered in the course are modification theory and authority; types of modifications; entitlement guidance; principles of clause analysis; written records; bar charts; critical path method; types of delays; unilateral modifications; trends; preventions; acceleration concepts and types; loss of efficiency impacts; entitlement studies; bilateral modifications; business clearances; and ethics in contracting. Methods of instruction include lecture, discussion, case studies, workshops, and examinations.

Credit Recommendation: In the lower division baccalaureate/associate degree category or upper division baccalaureate degree category, 3 semester hours in Civil Engineering or Business elective (11/92).

Construction Contract Pricing (CON 104) (Formerly Contract Pricing and Negotiation)

Location: Naval Facilities Institute, Port Hueneme, CA and various locations throughout the U.S., Europe, and the Pacific Rim.

Length: 92 hours (3 weeks).

Dates: October 1992-Present.

Objective: To introduce the student to the environment, goals, and basic principles of cost and price analysis and contract negotiations.

Learning Outcome: Upon successful completion of this course, the student will be able to comprehend the environment of contract pricing; use the fundamentals of graphing, elementary math, and algebra; comprehend the relationship between the variable cost, volume, profit, and various contract compensation arrangements; apply selected techniques and approaches used in the evaluation of direct costs and profit analysis; apply selected techniques and develop the Government's prenegotiation position (Government Estimate); apply and integrate the various techniques utilizing a case study; and learn and practice the fundamentals of contract negotiation.

Instruction: Major topics covered in the course are introduction to pricing; cost-volume-profit analysis; labor rate and hour analysis; direct and indirect cost analysis; ethics; a government negotiations workshop; cost estimating and a contractor profit workshop. Methods of instruction include lecture, workshops, videotapes and visual aids.

Credit Recommendation: In the lower division baccalaureate/associate degree category or upper division baccalaureate degree category, 4 semester hours in Contract Pricing and Negotiation, Cost and Price Analysis and Contract Negotiation, Government Contract Cost and Price Analysis, or Business elective (11/92).

Construction Contracting Fundamentals (CON 101) (Formerly Management of Defense Acquisition-Basic[CTC 142] and [CON 103])

Location: Naval Facilities Institute, Port Hueneme, CA and various locations throughout the U.S., Europe, and the Pacific Rim.

Length: 120 hours (4 weeks).

Dates: June 1980-Present.

Objective: To give the student an introduction and expansion of basic knowledge and skills of government contracts management with an emphasis on facilities related contracting.

Learning Outcome: Upon successful completion of this course, the student will be have knowledge of basic contracting functions and responsibilities, and skills techniques in solving operational problems of contract management within the restraints of statutory and regulatory authority.

Instruction: Major topics covered in the course are statutes, regulations, and policies; elements of a contract; qualifying potential contractors; pre-solicitation considerations; patents and data; purchase by negotiation and sealed bidding; contract types and purposes; cost and pricing techniques; clauses and provisions; contract administration; modifications; quality assurance; terminations; disputes and appeals; ethical considerations of contracting personnel; and related contracting functions. Methods of instruction include lecture, discussion, examinations, and out-of-class readings.

Credit Recommendation: In the lower division baccalaureate/associate degree category or upper division baccalaureate degree category, 3 semester hours in Acquisitions Contracting or Management elective (11/92).

Contracting Negotiating Workshop (CTC 315)

Location: Naval Facilities Institute, Port Hueneme, CA and various locations throughout the U.S., Europe, and the Pacific Rim.

Length: 27 hours (4 days).

Dates: November 1985-September 1992.

Objective: To provide the student with knowledge of negotiation issues, strategies, and tactics and application of this knowledge in negotiation workshop sessions.

Instruction: Major topics covered in the course are techniques for negotiating prime contracts; contract modifications; and contract terminations. Methods of instruction include lecture, discussion, out-of-class readings, case studies, visual aids and group exercises.

Credit Recommendation: In the lower division baccalaureate/associate degree category, 1 semester hour in Acquisitions Contracting, Business or Management elective (11/92).

Cost and Price Analysis (CTC 331) (Contract Cost and Price Analysis)

Location: Naval Facilities Institute, Port Hueneme, CA and various locations throughout the U.S., Europe, and the Pacific Rim.

Length: 63 hours (2 weeks).

Dates: November 1985-September 1992.

Objective: To introduce the student to the environment, goal and basic principles of cost analysis.

Learning Outcome: Upon successful completion of this course, the student will have knowledge of cost and price theory and an ability to appropriately apply this knowledge in cost/price analysis of contractor proposals.

Instruction: Major topics covered in the course are pricing, cost estimates and analysis, cost projection, effects of learning rates on costs, and the role of buyers in evaluating bid proposals including profit analysis, depreciation, and legal implications. Methods of instruction include lecture, discussion, out-of-class readings, and problem solving exercises.

Credit Recommendation: In the upper division baccalaureate degree category, 3 semester hours in Acquisitions Contracting, Business or Management elective (11/92). **NOTE**: Contract Cost and Price Analysis (CTC 331) and Contracting Negotiating Workshop (CTC 315) combined to form the new course Construction Contract Pricing (CON 106).

Facilities Support Contracts (CTC 337)

Location: Naval Facilities Institute, Port Hueneme, CA and various locations throughout the U.S., Europe, and the Pacific Rim.

Length: 37 hours (4.5 days).

Dates: October 1985-Present.

Objective: To provide the student with a general overview of procurement, and detailed instruction of NAVFACENCOM contracting for base operations, maintenance and support.

Learning Outcome: Upon successful completion of this course, the student will be able to understand the procurement, policy procedures, laws and regulations that impact the planning, specification, development and award of contracts for base operations, maintenance, and support.

Instruction: Major topics covered in the course are contract types; acquisition planning and specification preparation; solicitation and award; Facilities Support contract clauses; funding; modification pricing and execution; exercising options to extend; and payments and quality assurance methods. Methods of instruction include lecture, discussion, in-class exercises, case studies, and examinations.

Credit Recommendation: In the lower division baccalaureate/associate degree category, 3 semester hours in Procurement and Contracting or Government Contracting or Business elective (11/92).

Facilities Support Contracts Seminar and Workshop (CTC 337) [Facilities Support Contracts II (CTC 437)]

Location: Naval Facilities Institute, Port Hueneme, CA and various locations throughout the U.S., Europe, and the Pacific Rim.

Length: 32 hours (4.5 days).

Dates: November 1989-Present.

Objective: To integrate knowledge gained in Facilities Support Contracts I course with individual/group responsibilities and dynamics, in a seminar/workshop setting.

Learning Outcome: Upon successful completion of this course, the student will be able to understand and describe individual/group roles, responsibilities and interactions; role of consultants; team planning skills in accomplishment of objectives; team approach in problem solving and potential for increased quality; the development of a bid structure, technical specifications, and quality analysis; possible solutions to problems in day-to-day contract administration using acquired knowledge; and using available resources.

Instruction: Major topics covered in the course are roles and responsibilities; group dynamics; quality and the acquisition process; fixed price award fee; and administrative survival skills. Methods of instruction include lecture, team assignments, class case studies, and seminar/workshop participation.

Credit Recommendation: In the lower division baccalaureate/associate degree category or upper division baccalaureate degree category, 1 semester hour in Procurement and Contracting, Government Contracting, or Business elective (11/92). **NOTE**: Credit given if student successfully completes Facilities Support Contracts I (CTC 337).

Government Contract Law (CON 210) (Formerly Government Law [CON 201] and Government Contract Law [CTC 302])

Location: Naval Facilities Institute, Port Hueneme, CA and various locations throughout the U.S., Europe, and the Pacific Rim.

Length: 75 hours (2 weeks).

Dates: October 1985-Present.

Objective: To provide the student with the knowledge and understanding of the legal aspects of contracting.

Learning Outcome: Upon successful completion of this course, the student will be able to identify legislation that is relevant to contracting law; understand basic legal principles and sources of contracting law; interpret contract language, including modification, terminations, remedies, and awards; and recognize the major elements of contracting, procurement, bid procedures, subcontracting, and funding.

Instruction: Major topics covered in the course are contract formation and modifications, essential elements of a contract, specifications and inspection/acceptances, equitable adjustments, labor law, and termination for default and convenience. Methods of instruction include lecture, discussion, case studies, visual aids, and examinations.

Credit Recommendation: In the upper division baccalaureate degree category or graduate degree category, 3 semester hours in Government Contract Law or Procurement/Management elective (11/92).

U.S. Postal Service Corporate Training and Development

Training and development of 750,000 postal employees programs provided by several organizations within the U.S. Postal Service. Courses are offered at the William F. Bolger Center for Leadership Development, the Technical Training Center, and at other designated postal installations.

The Center for Leadership Development consists of the main facility in Potomac, Maryland. The Technical Training Center is located on the University of Oklahoma campus in Norman, Oklahoma. Postal Employee Development Centers are located in approximately 186 locations throughout the country.

Source of official student records: Registry of Credit Recommendations, American Council on Education, One Dupont Circle, Washington, DC 20036-1193 or Center for Leadership Development Courses, Office of the Registrar, William F. Bolger Center for Leadership Development, 10000 Kentsdale Drive, Potomac, MD 20858-4320.

Technical Training Center Courses, Office of the Registrar, Technical Training Center, P.O. Box 1400, Norman, OK 73070-7810.

Postal Employee Development Center Courses, Corporate Training and Develop--ment, U.S. Postal Service, 475 L'Enfant Plaza, SW, Washington, DC 20260-4215.

Additional information about the courses: College Credit Recommendation Service, American Council on Education, One Dupont Circle, Washington, DC 20036-1193.

Administration of Maintenance Programs: Module I (56170-00)

Location: Correspondence.

Length: Approximately 40 hours.

Dates: January 1975-June 1981.

Objective: To provide an understanding of the principles of managing a maintenance organization.

Instruction: Major topics covered in the course are an introduction to the management elements of planning, organizing, controlling, and directing. Also covers staffing, scheduling, human interaction, motivation, safety, and communications.

Credit Recommendation: In the lower division baccalaureate/associate degree category or in the upper division baccalaureate degree category, 2 semester hours in General Management (2/78).

Associate Supervisor Program (17590-00)

Location: Local field sites.

Length: 40 hours (16 weeks).

Dates: May 1996-Present.

Objective: To provide basic knowledge and skills in leadership, management, communication, processing and distribution, and customer service.

Learning Outcome: Upon successful completion of this course, the student will be able to understand corporate goals and mission; analyze leadership styles; develop effective communications techniques; set and evaluate performance goals; promote team building, develop positive customer relationships; supervise employees; and manage processing and distribution equipment.

Instruction: Major topics covered in the course are team building, supervision, performance management, leadership, customer service, administration, skills building, safety, and labor relations. Methods of instruction include lecture, discussion, classroom exercises, case studies, audio/visual material, presentations and reports, final examination, observations, and on-site performance evaluations.

Credit Recommendation: In the lower division baccalaureate/associate degree category, 3 semester hours in Supervision (8/96).

Basic Diesel Mechanics Module I: Basic Diesel Maintenance (56160-00)

Location: Correspondence.

Length: Approximately 51 hours.

Dates: March 1975-June 1981.

Objective: To provide a foundation in the principles of diesel engines, electrical systems, and transmissions.

Instruction: Basic diesel principles; engine structure; fuel, air intake, exhaust, lubricating, cooling electrical, and transmission systems; and clutches.

Credit Recommendation: In the vocational certificate category, 3 semester hours, or in the lower division baccalaureate/associate degree category, 2 semester hours in Diesel Mechanics (2/78).

Basic Diesel Mechanics Module II: Mack-Diesel Maintenance (56161-00)

Location: Correspondence.

Length: Approximately 40 hours.

Dates: March 1975-June 1981.

Objective: To enable the student to describe the parts, functions, and operating principles of the Mack ENDT 673A, B, and C engines.

Instruction: Major topics covered in the course are topics related to the Mack-diesel engine, including engine structure, fuel, air intake, exhaust, lubricating, cooling, and electrical systems; engine operation; engine testing and run-in; troubleshooting and failure analysis; and shop manual organization.

Credit Recommendation: In the lower division baccalaureate/associate degree category, 1 semester hour or in the vocational certificate category, 2 semester hours in Diesel Mechanics (2/78).

Basic Electricity (56150-00)

Location: Correspondence.

Length: Approximately 150 hours.

Dates: January 1972-June 1981.

Objective: To enable students to analyze and solve problems associated with AC and DC circuitry.

Instruction: Major topics covered in the course are fundamental principles of electricity, including the behavior of AC and DC electrical circuits. Use of formulas and equations essential to an understanding of electricity; fundamentals of magnetism, resistance, inductance, and capacitance. No laboratory experiences included.

Credit Recommendation: In the lower division baccalaureate/associate degree category, 2 semester hours in Electricity (2/78).

Basic Pneumatics and Hydraulics (56147-00)

Location: Correspondence.

Length: Approximately 80 hours.

Dates: October 1972-April 1984.

Objective: To develop a basic theoretical understanding of hydraulic and pneumatic systems.

Instruction: Major topics covered in the course are, in logical sequence, the fundamentals of hydraulics and pneumatics and the operation of fluid power components. Topics include physics of fluids, basic systems and circuit diagrams, control and measurement of flow, and component equipment functions.

Credit Recommendation: In the lower division baccalaureate/associate degree

category, 2 semester hours in Mechanical Technology (2/78).

Communication Skills for Managers (11278-00) (Formerly [11451-00] or [11251-00])

Location: Potomac, MD, and Field Centers.

Length: 40 hours (5 days).

Dates: October 1982-March 1992.

Objective: To provide students with a knowledge of basic communication skills and concepts of reading, speaking, and listening and their application.

Learning Outcome: Upon successful completion of this course, the student will be able to identify course entry- level proficiency of reading, listening, writing, and speaking skills; identify barriers and aids to effective reading, listening, writing, and speaking; demonstrate principles of effective reading, listening, talking, writing, and speaking; give and receive feedback on principles of effective listening, writing, and speaking; identify four characteristics of effective interpersonal communication; and demonstrate principles of effective briefings.

Instruction: Training consists of instructor-led lectures, exercises, and the application of theories, concepts, and principles used in the communication process of speaking, listening, reading, and writing. Methods of instruction include videocassettes, videotaping, slides, graphics, and audiocassettes.

Credit Recommendation: In the lower division baccalaureate/associate degree category, 1 semester hour in Human Relations, Business Communications (3/87). **NOTE:** Students who receive credit for Communication Skills for Supervisors should not receive credit for this course.

Communication Skills for Supervisors (11281-00)

Location: Potomac, MD, and Field Centers.

Length: 40 hours (5 days).

Dates: October 1982-March 1992.

Objective: To provide students with oral, listening, writing, and reading skills and concepts necessary to establish a foundation for effective communication in the workplace.

Learning Outcome: Upon successful completion of this course, the student will be able to identify course entry- level proficiency of reading, listening, writing, and speaking skills; identify barriers and aids to effective reading, listening, writing, and speaking; demonstrate principles of effective reading, listening, talking, writing, and speaking; give and receive feedback on principles of effective listening, writing, and speaking; and identify four characteristics of effective interpersonal communication and compare pre- and post-course attitude toward these characteristics.

Instruction: The training consists of lectures, role play exercises, and the application of theories and concepts to the communication process. Methods of instruction include the use of videocassettes, videotaping, graphics, and audiocassettes.

Credit Recommendation: In the lower division baccalaureate/associate degree or vocational certificate category, 1 semester hour in Business Communications, Human Relations (3/87). **NOTE:** Students who receive credit for Communication Skills for Managers should not receive credit for this course.

Constructive Conflict Resolution (11220-00)

Location: Potomac, MD, Field Centers, and on-site.

Length: 24 hours (3 days).

Dates: *Version 1:* September 1985-July 1989; *Version 2:* August 1989-Present.

Objective: To enable the student to identify sources of interpersonal conflict and techniques for resolving them.

Learning Outcome: Upon successful completion of this course, the student will be able to recognize and employ effective communication styles; listen more effectively; deal with personal, conflict-generating challenges; and identify and employ productive approaches to conflict resolution.

Instruction: Major topics covered in the course are interpersonal problem recognition and solution by instruction in human relations and classroom exercises in which students practice interviewing, counseling, and conflict resolution.

Credit Recommendation: *Version 1:* In the lower division baccalaureate/associate degree category, 1 semester hour in Human Relations (3/87). *Version 2:* In the lower division baccalaureate/associate degree category or in the upper division baccalaureate degree category, 1 semester hour in Conflict Resolution, Human Relations, or Organizational Behavior (8/89). **NOTE:** To receive credit student must have completed 11222-00 and 11223-00.

Customer Service Representative (42151-00)

Location: Correspondence.

Length: Approximately 40 hours.

Dates: February 1978-April 1984.

Objective: To provide an overview of knowledge, skills, and techniques of effective salesmanship/sales management and to enable students to design customized user service.

Instruction: Major topics covered in the course are the role of the customer service representative; product knowledge and customized service programs; sales processes, including precall planning and use of visual sales aids; time and territory management; customer relations and psychology of selling. Major topics covered in the course are same material that Customer Service Representation MAS (10068-10) covers but does not provide classroom application of principles.

Credit Recommendation: In the lower division baccalaureate/associate degree category, 1 semester hour in Sales Management or Salesmanship (2/78).

Customer Services Managers (MAS)

Location: Potomac, MD.

Length: 80 hours (10 days).

Dates: October 1982-March 1992.

Objective: To provide the student with an understanding of the various subunits of operation in the post office and how a knowledge of these units contributes to effective management.

Learning Outcome: Upon successful completion of this course, the student will be able to manage an associate office.

Instruction: Major topics covered in the course are customer services management data system; unit and route reviews; growth management, staffing and scheduling, financial operations, labor relations, and safety and budget responsibilities.

Credit Recommendation: In the lower division baccalaureate/associate degree category, 1 semester hour in General Supervision (3/87).

Digital Electronics (56548-00)

Location: Correspondence.

Length: Approximately 30 hours.

Dates: February 1976-April 1984.

Objective: To introduce the principles of digital electronics.

Instruction: Major topics covered in the course are the basics of numbering systems, including methods of conversions between systems; various coding schemes; circuit introduction to Boolean algebra; and elements of digital electronics.

Credit Recommendation: In the lower division baccalaureate/associate degree category, 1 semester hour in Digital Electronics (2/78).

Financial Management (17261-00)

Location: Potomac, MD.

Length: 104 hours (32 weeks).

Dates: August 1989-August 1994.

Objective: To provide the student with introductory knowledge of and familiarity with U.S.P.S. managerial accounting functions, mission, objectives, and procedures as well as an understanding of basic personnel functions and human relations skills.

Learning Outcome: Upon successful completion of this course, the student will be able to analyze financial and labor utilization reports used by the U.S.P.S.; prepare a variety of financial activity reports according to U.S.P.S. accounting system; and be familiar with individual and group interaction options or strategies.

Instruction: Major topics covered in the course are preparation of financial data and reports, budget preparation and analysis, labor utilization analysis, assessment and impact on worker performance, communication and feedback strategies, and group processes and leadership.

Credit Recommendation: In the lower division baccalaureate/associate degree category, 1 semester hour in Human Behavior and in the lower division baccalaureate/associate degree category, 2 semester hours in Accounting, Bookkeeping, or Managerial Accounting for a total of 3 semester hours (8/89).

Hearing Officers' Training (21275-00)

Location: Potomac, MD.

Length: 24 hours (3 days).

Dates: January 1981-March 1992.

Objective: To provide participant with knowledge of several legal terms and the procedures for investigating the validity of various allegations.

Learning Outcome: Upon successful completion of this course, the student will be able to perform completely and thoroughly the administrative duties of a hearing officer to assure appellant and management rights are not violated; conduct a pre-hearing conference consistent with regulations; conduct a formal hearing, when the appellant is not subject to the provisions of a collective bargaining agreement, in such a manner that all pertinent and valid evidence is surfaced; analyze factual materials as they relate to Step One Hearing Procedures; and write clear and concise findings of fact after conducting the hearing.

Instruction: Major topics covered in the course are to prepare hearing officers to conduct hearings in appeals from adverse actions and disciplinary sanctions filed by employees not subject to the provisions of a collective bargaining agreement. It clarifies the functions and responsibilities of hearing officers by setting forth guidelines for use in preparing for the hearing. It also suggests what should be done before, during, and after the hearing to assure that all of the facts are developed and recorded, proper procedures are used, and the hearing is conducted in an efficient and productive manner.

Credit Recommendation: In the lower division baccalaureate/associate degree category, 1 semester hour in Paralegal Training (3/87).

Improving Group Performance (112200-00, 11222-00) 1. Management Styles and Employee Motivation (11223-00)

Location: Potomac, MD, Field Centers, and on-site.

Length: 1. 16 hours (2 days); 2. 16 hours (2 days).

Dates: August 1986-March 1992.

Objective: To provide managers and supervisors with information on adversarial work relationships, individual and group motivational theories, management styles and management behavior modification techniques for self and subordinate development.

Learning Outcome: Upon successful completion of this course, students will be able to recognize the roots of the management-labor adversarial relationship, the assumptions underlying these roots, and the resulting impact on productivity; compare and contrast one's management style and the style of others in order to develop a greater understanding of individual management styles; compare and contrast major motivational theories underlying group motivation and group dynamics by applying the concepts to practical, work-related situations; and apply the newly learned and enhanced concepts of managerial behavior modification, which emphasize a humanistic approach to developing one's full potential and the fullest potential of one's subordinates.

Instruction: Major topics covered in the course are designed to facilitate the learning and application of alternative approaches to management styles and employee motivation as a means of increasing organizational effectiveness. The course utilizes instrumentation to identify management styles and fine-tune people skills with exercises that have direct applicability to on-the-job activities. Principal theories and concepts are discussed in small group activities that are designed to promote feedback through a free flow of ideas. Introductions to and closure for each module are facilitated by lecturettes appropriate video. A student workbook is provided to ensure a sequential, progressive flow of the material as the subject matter moves from textbook concept to back-home application with the use of a training transfer strategy.

Credit Recommendation: In the lower division baccalaureate/associate degree category, 1 semester hour in Human Relations (3/87). **NOTE:** To receive credit students must take both courses.

Introduction to Basic Mathematics and Electricity (56123-00)

Location: Correspondence.

Length: Approximately 50 hours.

Dates: January 1972-June 1981.

Objective: To provide an understanding of the fundamentals of mathematics necessary in the study of electricity and to introduce the principles of electricity.

Instruction: A refresher in basic arithmetic operations such as addition, subtraction, multiplication, and division. Positive and negative numbers, fractions, square roots, and powers of ten. Also includes an introduction to electrical units and prefixes, elementary algebraic equations, formulas, rectangular coordinates, trigonometric relations, and vectors.

Credit Recommendation: In the vocational certificate category, 3 semester hours in Basic Mathematics and Electricity (2/78).

Introduction to Health and Safety Management (21218-00) (Formerly Introduction to Safety Management)

Location: Potomac, MD, and Field Centers.

Length: 80 hours (10 days).

Dates: *Version 1:* February 1987-July 1989; *Version 2:* August 1989-Present.

Objective: To acquaint health and safety personnel with the technical, analytical, and managerial skills necessary to perform work tasks effectively.

Learning Outcome: Upon successful completion of this course, the student will be able to perform the duties and responsibilities required of health and safety personnel.

Instruction: Major topics covered in the course are basic health and safety management activities and procedures including administration, planning and coordination, reviewing, monitoring, consulting, investigating, supervising, organizing, and promoting within a postal safety management program.

Credit Recommendation: *Version 1:* In the vocational certificate category, 1 semester hour in Occupational Safety (3/87). *Version 2:* In the upper division baccalaureate degree category, 3 semester hours in Industrial Engineering, Industrial Hygiene, Production and Operations Management, or Occupational Health and Safety (8/89).

Mail Processing Basics (17501-00)

Location: Local field sites.

Length: 37 hours (4-12 days).

Dates: January 1994-Present.

Objective: To identify and explain the elements of a mail processing operation including mail flow; mail handling categories and equipment; and personnel scheduling and grievance handling.

Learning Outcome: Upon successful completion of the course, the student will be able to identify and explain the elements of a mail processing operation including mail flow; mail handling categories and equipment; and personnel scheduling and grievance handling.

Instruction: Major topics covered in the course are mail facility operating plans; mail reporting and tracing systems; automated, mechanical, and manual mail operations; mail flow of a letter from collection box to delivery point; work week scheduling and leave control; and anticipating and responding to grievances. Methods of instruction include lecture, discussion, classroom exercises, case studies, and quizzes.

Credit Recommendation: In the vocational certificate category, 1 semester hour in Mail Transportation (8/96).

Managing Personal Effectiveness (11221-00)

Location: Potomac, MD, Field Centers, and on-site.

Length: 24 hours (3 days).

Dates: July 1985-March 1992.

Objective: To assist managers in acquiring principles for use at their present and higher level endeavors.

Learning Outcome: Upon successful completion of this course, the student will be able to recognize the optimal stress level that causes high performance; demonstrate the ability to identify sources and symptoms of stress; develop an understanding and awareness of holistic living; analyze the physical dimension of holistic living; develop strategies to combat stress internally; develop strategies to manage nonwork, psychological dimensions of holistic living; analyze work-related stress and develop strategies to effectively manage stress; demonstrate an understanding of crucial elements in time management that contribute to stress and ineffective use of time; develop skills that enable a manager to exercise effective control of individual and employee time; and develop a comprehensive individual strategy for maintaining personal effectiveness that integrates both time and stress management techniques.

Instruction: Major topics covered in the course are selected strategies which are used to assist managers deal effectively with stress. The instructor uses exercises, questionnaires, lectures, and workbooks.

Credit Recommendation: In the lower division baccalaureate/associate degree category, 1 semester hour in Human Relations (3/87).

Power Transistors (56143-00)

Location: Correspondence.

Length: Approximately 20 hours.

Dates: January 1972-June 1981.

Objective: To develop awareness of thermal, frequency, and size problems associated with power transistors.

Instruction: Considers compromises that enable both low and high frequency power transistors to operate at high temperatures and currents. Includes regulator circuits and overload protection.

Credit Recommendation: In the lower division baccalaureate/associate degree category, 1 semester hour in Electronics (2/78).

Report Writing for Postal Managers (33530-00) (Formerly Report Writing for Postal Managers [33150-00])

Location: Correspondence.

Length: Approximately 40 hours.

Dates: February 1978-July 1988.

Objective: To provide an understanding of the mechanics of report writing.

Instruction: Major topics covered in the course are a review of grammar; spelling; word mechanics; usage; editing and proofreading; planning, preparation, and evaluation of written reports.

Credit Recommendation: In the lower division baccalaureate/associate degree category, 1 semester hour in Communications (2/78).

Secretary to the Postal Executive (33130-00)

Location: Correspondence.

Length: Approximately 40 hours.

Dates: February 1978-April 1984.

Objective: To provide an overview of the principles of management and business communications.

Instruction: Major topics covered in the course are principles and applications of effective communication, with emphasis on making the secretary an effective office manager.

Credit Recommendation: In the lower division baccalaureate/associate degree category, 1 semester hour in Secretarial Science (2/78).

Supervisory Leadership (17224-00)

Location: Potomac, MD, Southern, Midwest, and Western Field Centers.

Length: 40 hours (5 days).

Dates: *Version 1:* January 1986-July 1989; *Version 2:* August 1989-Present.

Objective: To provide the student with the skills to become an effective leader.

Learning Outcome: Upon successful completion of this course, the student will have familiarity with different leadership styles and know more about his or her own personality and that of his or her subordinates.

Instruction: Major topics covered in the course are having the learners assess their preferred leadership style, utilizing instrumentation that was introduced in Supervisory Skills Building. The learners have evaluated their supervisory behavior during the intervening months of actual on-the-job experience. They now explore the barriers encountered on the job and discuss strategies to overcome these barriers. The main focus of the course is self-analysis; each learner evaluates his managerial behavioral style, its effectiveness in various situations with various types of subordinates, and prepares a practical change strategy. Particular emphasis is given to optimizing the learner's leadership success in the work environment. Methods of instruction include lecture, discussion, and class exercises.

Credit Recommendation: *Version 1:* In the lower division baccalaureate/associate degree category, 1 semester hour in Human Relations (3/87). *Version 2:* In the lower division baccalaureate/associate degree category, 2 semester hours in Human Relations (8/89). **NOTE:** Students who receive credit for this course should not receive credit for Supervisory Leadership: General Management #11203-00.

Supervisory Leadership: General Management (11203-00)

Location: Potomac, MD, and Field Centers.

Length: 40 hours (5 days).

Dates: *Version 1:* September 1986-July 1989; *Version 2:* August 1989-Present.

Objective: To provide the student with the skills to become an effective leader.

Learning Outcome: Upon successful completion of this course, the student will have a familiarity with different leadership styles and know more about his or her own personality and that of his or her subordinates.

Instruction: Major topics covered in the course are having the learners assess their preferred leadership style, utilizing carefully selected instrumentation to disclose relative information. The learners relate their supervisory behavior to actual on-the-job experiences. They explore the barriers encountered on the job and discuss strategies for overcoming these barriers. The main focus of the course is self-analysis; each learner evaluates his or her managerial behavioral style, its effectiveness in various situations with various types of subordinates, and prepares a practical change strategy. Particular emphasis is given to optimizing probabilities for the learner's leadership success in the work environment. Methods of instruction include lecture, discussion, and class exercises.

Credit Recommendation: *Version 1:* In the lower division baccalaureate/associate degree category, 1 semester hour in Human Relations (3/87). *Version 2:* In the lower division baccalaureate/associate degree category, 2 semester hours in Human Relations (8/89). **NOTE:** Students who receive credit for this course should not receive credit for Supervisory Leadership #17224-00.

Transistors and Transistor Applications (56142-00)

Location: Correspondence.

Length: Approximately 75 hours.

Dates: January 1972-June 1981.

Objective: To develop a theoretical understanding of transistors and their use in common electronic circuits.

Instruction: Major topic covered in the course is an in-depth study of solid-state theory, transistor amplifiers, load line analysis, equivalent circuit analysis, feedback, tuned circuits, multivibrators, and modulation.

Credit Recommendation: In the lower division baccalaureate/associate degree category, 3 semester hours in Electronics (2/78).

Vehicle Accident Investigation (51159-00)

Location: Correspondence.

Length: Approximately 40 hours.

Dates: February 1978-April 1984.

Objective: To develop skills in reporting, investigating, and analyzing vehicle accidents.

Instruction: Major topics covered in the course are data collecting, interviewing, calculations, highway and human factors, road and tire evidence, vehicular evidence, forms, and analysis of accidents.

Credit Recommendation: In the lower division baccalaureate/associate degree category, 1 semester hour in Industrial or Public Safety (2/78).

Vehicle Maintenance Management Skills Building (17259-00)

Location: Potomac, MD.

Length: 80 hours (10 days).

Dates: April 1987-March 1992.

Objective: To train maintenance supervisors to understand and utilize principles of human relations for more productive vehicle maintenance.

Learning Outcome: Upon successful completion of this course, the student will recognize the importance of self-esteem, giving and receiving feedback, on-the-job improvement, and employee motivation.

Instruction: Major topics covered in the course are principles of human relations, human motivation, motivation of employees, and developing team work; the second half covers maintenance training that is industry specific.

Credit Recommendation: In the vocational certificate category, 3 semester hours in Automotive Science Supervision (3/87).

Vehicle Operations Management Skills Building (17252-00)

Location: Potomac, MD.

Length: 80 hours (10 days).

Dates: March 1987-March 1992.

Objective: To train postal supervisors in the performance of supervising functions in report writing, safety, record keeping, budgeting, labor relations.

Learning Outcome: Upon successful completion of this course, students will be able to understand the organization structure in which he/she operates and prepare standardized reports, keep records, prepare budget estimates and comply with union requirements in the vehicle operations area.

Instruction: Major topics covered in the course are industry specific management functions in report writing, record keeping, labor relations, safety and budgeting.

Credit Recommendation: In the vocational certificate category, 3 semester hours in Management of a Vehicle Operation Service (3/87).

Women's Program Coordinator (21271-00) (Formerly Equal Employment Opportunity Administration, Woman's Program Coordinator—Special Emphasis Series)

Location: Potomac, MD.

Length: 80 hours (10 days).

Dates: January 1978-March 1992.

Objective: To furnish the students with basic managerial skills necessary to perform effectively as coordinator of an equal opportunity employment program.

Learning Outcome: Upon successful completion of this course, the student will understand the relationships and organizational structure; gather, analyze, and interpret data; identify the needs of women that are unique; assist employees by career counseling, job applications, filing of grievances; and speak and write effectively.

Instruction: Major topics covered in the course are organizational relationships within the Postal Service, recruitment of women, career counseling, identification of the needs of women, development of training workshops, development and delivery of special material, and the conduct of meetings.

Credit Recommendation: In the lower division baccalaureate/associate degree category, 1 semester hour in Personnel Management (3/87).

Inspection Service

The courses listed below are part of the Postal Inspection Training Program of the Career Development Branch, located in Potomac, Maryland. The program's purpose is to train law enforcement officers of the U.S. Postal Service.

Introduction to Law Enforcement Security Force Training (12252)

Location: Potomac, MD.

Length: *Version 1:* 48 hours (3 weeks), residential; *Version 2:* 140 hours (4 weeks), residential.

Dates: *Version 1:* October 1972-December 1980; *Version 2:* January 1981-December 1985.

Objective: To develop the skills, knowledge, and attitudes required to perform as security police officers and supervisors.

Instruction: Major topics covered in the course are various aspects of law and legal procedures applicable to the security aspects of law enforcement. Emphasis is given to principles of security such as building control; bomb threats; building search; narcotics and dangerous drugs; arson and fire prevention; emergency medical aid; defensive tactics; and crowds, mobs, and social disorders. Program includes firearms training, a study of individual behavior and human relations, and basics of improved oral and written communications. Lectures, discussions, practical exercises, and audio- visual equipment are used.

Credit Recommendation: In the lower division baccalaureate/associate degree category, 3 semester hours in Law Enforcement (2/75).

Postal Inspector Basic Training (12251)
Part 1: Audit Procedures I
Part 2. Audit Procedures II
Part 3: Criminal Law I
Part 4: Basic Criminal Investigation
Part 5: Advanced Criminal Investigation
Part 6: Administrative Practice
Part 7: Personal Defense

Location: Potomac, MD.

Length: *Version 1:* 404 hours (16 weeks), residential. *Part 1:* 50 hours; *Part 2*: 53 hours; *Part 3*: 45 hours; *Part 4*: 69 hours; *Part 5*: 71 hours; *Part 6*: 64 hours; *Part 7*: 52 hours; *Version 2*: 473 hours.

Dates: *Version 1:* October 1972-January 1981; *Version 2:* February 1981-December 1985.

Objective: To train postal inspectors in all aspects of inspection service work and to prepare them to assume the responsibilities of their first duty assignments.

Instruction: *Part 1:* Major topic covered in the course is a study of types of funds and accounts, types of audits and financial investigations, and audit standards. *Part 2:* Major topic covered in the course is a study of audit writing and working papers; economic analysis; service, operational, and financial audits. A practical exercise is included. *Part 3:* Major topics covered in the course are the theory, evolution, and current status of presenting evidence in criminal cases; the laws of arrest, search and seizure, and entrapment; statements and affidavits; problems of legality in presenting various kinds of physical evidence. *Part 4:* Major topics covered in the course are principles of investigation, investigative techniques, legal practices and procedures, security operations, and preparation of case reports. *Part 5:* Major topics covered in the course are the instructional content of the Basic Criminal Investigation block. Stress is on use of advanced techniques and advanced technology, nonroutine methods, preventive analysis, and control operations. *Part 6:* Major topics covered in the course are general administrative principles; report writing; case study approaches; technical, analytical, and managerial skills; and policy development. *Part 7:* Major topics covered in the course are theory and practice of selected defense skills and their application to coping successfully with situations in which the student encounters personal attack.

Credit Recommendation: *Part 1:* In the upper division baccalaureate degree category or in the graduate degree category, 3 semester hours in Auditing, Business Administration or Public Administration (2/75) (1/81). *Part 2:* In the upper division baccalaureate degree category or in the graduate degree category, 3 semester hours in Auditing, Business Administration or Public Administration (2/75) (1/81). *Part 3:* In the graduate degree category, 3 semester hours in Criminal Law (2/75) (1/81). *Part 4:* In the lower division baccalaureate/associate degree category, 3 semester hours in Criminal Justice (2/75) (1/81). *Part 5:* In the upper division baccalaureate degree category, 3 semester hours in Criminal Justice (2/75) (1/81). *Part 6:* In the upper division baccalaureate degree category, 3 semester hours in Business Administration, Management or Public Administration (2/75) (1/81). *Part 7:* In the lower division baccalaureate/associate degree category, 1 semester hour in Physical Education (2/75) (1/81). **NOTE:** *Version 1:* All participants complete Parts 1, 3, 4, 6, and 7. Trainees specializing in auditing complete Part 2 (Audit Procedures II), and those specializing in criminal investigation complete Part 5 (Advanced Criminal Investigation). *Version 2:* All participants complete Parts 1 through 7.

Management Training Series (MTS)

Associate Office Management MTS (13589)

Location: PEDC Centers.

Length: Self-study.

Dates: February 1978-March 1984.

Objective: To enhance the supervisory and personnel management skills of incumbent associate office managers.

Instruction: Major topics covered in the course are activities of an associate office with urban delivery responsibilities, including delivery and collection services, mail processing, window services, and financial procedures.

Credit Recommendation: In the lower division baccalaureate/associate degree category, 1 semester hour in Personnel Administration or Supervision (3/79). **NOTE:** Credit should not be granted for both this course and Associate Office Management MAS (10205-00).

Associate Office Postmaster MTS (13590)

Location: PEDC Centers.

Length: Self-study.

Dates: May 1978-March 1984.

Objective: To strengthen the supervisory and management skills of incumbent associate office postmasters.

Instruction: Major topics covered in the course are financial operations, employee and labor relations, mail processing and delivery systems, and communications.

Credit Recommendation: In the lower division baccalaureate/associate degree category, 1 semester hour in Personnel Administration or Supervision (3/79).

Building Equipment Maintenance Supervisor MTS (55583)

Location: PEDC Centers.

Length: Self-study.

Dates: May 1978-March 1984.

Objective: To enhance the supervisory knowledge and skills of first-line supervisors of building equipment maintenance personnel.

Instruction: Major topics covered in the course are maintenance of building facilities, including determination of manpower requirements, scheduling of maintenance, custodial functions, energy conservation, working environment considerations, safety practices, communications, and employee relations.

Credit Recommendation: In the lower division baccalaureate/associate degree category, 1 semester hour in Personnel Administration or Supervision (3/79). **NOTE:** Credit should not be granted for both this course and Building Equipment Maintenance Supervisors MAS (10217-00).

Building Services Maintenance Supervisor MTS (55585)

Location: PEDC Centers.

Length: Self-study.

Dates: May 1978-March 1984.

Objective: To enhance the supervisory knowledge and skills of incumbent first-line supervisors of building services maintenance personnel.

Instruction: Major topics covered in the course are supervision of custodial personnel, determination of manpower requirements, scheduling of custodial services, energy conservation, safety practices, communications, and employee relations.

Credit Recommendation: In the lower division baccalaureate/associate degree category, 1 semester hour in Personnel Administration or Supervision (3/79). **NOTE:** Credit should not be granted for both this course and Building Services Maintenance Supervisors MAS (10218-00).

Customer Services Representative MTS (42590)

Location: PEDC Centers.

Length: Self-study.

Dates: January 1977-March 1984.

Objective: To provide customer services representatives with knowledge, skills, and techniques of effective salesmanship and sales management and to enable them to design customized user services.

Instruction: Major topics covered in the course are role of the customer services representative; product knowledge and customized service programs; sales processes, including pre-call planning and use of visual sales aids; time and territory management; customer relations, and the psychology of selling.

Credit Recommendation: In the lower division baccalaureate/associate degree category, 2 semester hours in Sales Management or Salesmanship (3/79). **NOTE:** Credit should not be granted for both this course and Customer Service Representative MAS (10268-00).

Delivery Service Supervisor MTS (44585)

Location: PEDC Centers.

Length: Self-study.

Dates: January 1978-March 1984.

Objective: To strengthen the supervisory skills of incumbent delivery services supervisors.

Instruction: Major topics covered in the course are day-to-day supervision of delivery services and collections, mail count, and route inspections; evaluation of route inspection data; scheduling and staffing; revenue-producing programs; financial procedures; and employee and labor relations activities.

Credit Recommendation: In the lower division baccalaureate/associate degree category, 1 semester hour in Personnel Administration or Supervision (3/79). **NOTE:** Credit should not be granted for both this course and Delivery Service Supervisors MAS (10210-00).

Employee Relations Management MTS (21581)

Location: PEDC Centers.

Length: Self-study.

Dates: July 1978-March 1984.

Objective: To improve the managerial performance of incumbent personnel in major employee relations functions.

Instruction: Major topics covered in the course are the role and responsibilities of employee relations personnel with emphasis on recruitment, selection, placement, compensation and benefits, career development, records maintenance, budget, and developing action plans.

Credit Recommendation: In the lower division baccalaureate/associate degree category or in the upper division baccalaureate degree category, 2 semester hours in Industrial Relations, Personnel Administration, or Supervision (3/79). **NOTE:** Credit should not be granted for both this course and Employee Relations Management MAS (10270-00).

Labor Relations Management MTS (22590)

Location: PEDC Centers.

Length: Self-study.

Dates: April 1978-March 1984.

Objective: To help postal service managers and postal service labor relations specialists understand labor relations.

Instruction: Major topics covered in the course are contract analysis, grievance procedures, employee representation, discipline, and mediation/arbitration. Also includes the evolution of labor law, local implementation, and procedures for dealing with employees and union representatives.

Credit Recommendation: In the lower division baccalaureate/associate degree category or in the upper division baccalaureate degree category, 2 semester hours in Collective Bargaining, Industrial Relations, Labor Relations, or Personnel Administration (3/79).

Mail Processing Equipment Maintenance Supervisor MTS (55596)

Location: PEDC Centers.

Length: Self-study.

Dates: May 1978-March 1984.

Objective: To enhance the personnel supervision knowledge and skills of incumbent first-line supervisors of mail processing equipment maintenance personnel.

Instruction: Major topics covered in the course are supervision of the maintenance of mail processing equipment during mail transportation, preparation, and sorting; safety practices; communications; work environment considerations; and employee relations.

Credit Recommendation: In the lower division baccalaureate/associate degree category, 1 semester hour in Personnel Administration or Supervision (3/79). **NOTE:** Credit should not be granted for both this course and Mail Processing Equipment Maintenance Supervisors MAS (10216-00).

Mail Processing for Managers MTS (52596)

Location: PEDC Centers.

Length: Self-study.

Dates: January 1976-March 1984.

Objective: To provide management training for incumbent mail processing managers.

Instruction: Major topics covered in the course are mail processing operations emphasizing management reporting systems used in the daily operations of Mail Processing Centers; methods improvement and plant layout to improve mail flow, enhanced employee performance with respect to performance appraisal, disciplinary actions, and grievances; and proper planning and control techniques for use in mechanized and manual mail processing operations.

Credit Recommendation: In the lower division baccalaureate/associate degree category, 3 semester hours in Business Administration or Management (3/79). **NOTE:** Credit should not be granted for both this course and Mail Processing for Supervisors MTS (52595).

Mail Processing for Supervisors MTS (52595)

Location: PEDC Centers.

Length: Self-study.

Dates: January 1976-March 1984.

Objective: To provide management training for incumbent mail processing supervisors.

Instruction: Major topics covered in the course are mail processing operations, emphasizing management reporting systems used in the daily operations of mail processing centers; methods improvement and plant layout to improve the flow of mail; enhanced employee performance with respect to performance appraisal, disciplinary actions, and grievances; and proper planning control procedures for use in manual and mechanized mail processing operations.

Credit Recommendation: In the lower division baccalaureate/associate degree category, 3 semester hours in Business Administration or Management (3/79). **NOTE:** Credit should not be granted for both this course and Mail Processing for Managers MTS (52596).

PEDC Managers MTS (21590)

Location: PEDC Centers.

Length: Self-study.

Dates: July 1978-March 1984.

Objective: To improve the performance of incumbent managers in the administration of training and development activities.

Instruction: Major topics covered in the course are the Postal Employee Development Center (PEDC), the roles and responsibilities of the PEDC manager-supervisor, planning and budgeting for employee training programs, and employee development programs and considerations.

Credit Recommendation: In the lower division baccalaureate/associate degree category, 2 semester hours in Personnel Administration or Supervision (3/79).

Presentation Skills (21530-00)

Location: PEDC Centers.

Length: 24 hours (3 days).

Dates: August 1989-August 1994.

Objective: To assist the students in developing the necessary skills for effective oral presentations, to develop the knowledge necessary to help them "think on their feet," and assist in the development of effective presentations.

Learning Outcome: Upon successful completion of this course, the student will be able to make high quality job-related presentations of varying types; interact successfully with adults of differing learning backgrounds; demonstrate sensitivity to audience needs and feelings; assign and follow appropriate presentation formats; and utilize visual aids effectively.

Instruction: Major topics covered in the course are effective measures for presenting instructional material in classroom or group settings, the role and importance of the speaker, speaker image and confidence, effective presentation methods and strategies, and the use of presentation visual aids. Students take a major responsibility for presenting course content as a means for practicing presentation skills. Each student is responsible for several presentations, which are videotaped and evaluated.

Credit Recommendation: In the lower division baccalaureate/associate degree category, 1 semester hour in Business Communications, Public Speaking, or Instructional Methodology in a Teacher Education Program (8/89).

Retail Sales and Services Management MTS (42591)

Location: PEDC Centers.

Length: Self-study.

Dates: April 1977-March 1984.

Objective: To improve the performance of incumbent managers of retail sales and services activities.

Instruction: Major topics covered in the course are cost reduction and control techniques; revenue generations; interaction between managers, subordinates, and customers; and principles of retail sales management.

Credit Recommendation: In the lower division baccalaureate/associate degree category or in the upper division baccalaureate degree category, 2 semester hours in Retail Management, Sales Management, or Supervision (3/79). **NOTE:** Credit should not be granted for both this course and Retail Sales and Services Management MAS (10274-10).

Window Services Management MTS (41590)

Location: PEDC Centers

Length: Self-study.

Dates: March 1978-March 1984.

Objective: To provide management training for incumbent window services supervisors.

Instruction: Major topics covered in the course are covers postal products and services; retail programs; management of window service operations; and scheduling, staffing, and supervision of the sales force.

Credit Recommendation: In the lower division baccalaureate/associate degree category, 1 semester hour in Personnel Administration or Supervision (3/79). **NOTE:** Credit should not be granted for both this course and Window Service for Managers MAS (10273-00).

Postal Employee Development Centers

The courses listed below are self-instructional. Students applying for credit must pass a proctored final examination, successful completion of which will be indicated on the student's record.

Accounting I (31591-00)

Location: Self-instruction; PEDC Centers.

Length: 60 hours programmed instruction and approximately 120 hours outside problem-solving.

Dates: November 1976-August 1989.

Objective: To provide an understanding of basic accounting theory and practice, including the preparation of financial statements.

Instruction: Major topics covered in the course are fundamentals of accounting theory, including use of journals and ledgers, preparation of financial statements, and accounting for job order and process systems.

Credit Recommendation: In the lower division baccalaureate/associate degree category, 3 semester hours in Accounting (2/78) (4/84).

Accounting II (31592-00)

Location: Self-instruction; PEDC Centers.

Length: 60 hours programmed instruction and approximately 120 hours outside problem-solving.

Dates: November 1976-April 1989.

Objective: To provide a further understanding of accounting principles and practices, including corporate accounting.

Instruction: Major topics covered in the course are a continuation of Accounting I, including notes and interest, voucher system, partnership equity, budgeting, income tax, and corporate accounting.

Credit Recommendation: In the lower division baccalaureate/associate degree category, 3 semester hours in Accounting (2/78) (4/84).

Basic Electronics (56545-00) (Formerly Electronics I [56517-00])

Location: Self-instruction; PEDC Centers.

Length: *Version 1*: Approximately 40 hours; *Version 2*: Approximately 39 hours.

Dates: *Version 1:* April 1977-February 1983; *Version 2:* March 1983-Present.

Objective: To provide a basic understanding of electrical and electronic circuits, measuring instruments and components, and to develop basic skills in laboratory measurement techniques.

Instruction: Major topics covered in the course are elements and concepts of electricity and electronics, including types and measurement of electrical components and values. Inductance, capacitance, and resistance circuitry; components and component value determination; electrical measurement utilizing the volt-ohm meter; and the oscilloscope.

Credit Recommendation: In the vocational certificate category, 3 semester hours in Basic Electricity/Electronics or in the lower division baccalaureate/associate degree category, 1 semester hour lecture and 1 semester hour laboratory in Industrial Arts (2/78).

Basic Industrial Electricity (56540-00)

Location: Self-instruction; PEDC Centers.

Length: Approximately 36 hours.

Dates: December 1975-June 1981.

Objective: To provide introductory training in the basic theory of operation of fundamental industrial electrical circuitry.

Instruction: Major topics covered in the course are basic principles of electricity and magnetism; series and parallel circuits; secondary cells; meters; transistors; motors and motor control; circuit protective devices. Self-instruction is augmented with an electrical training device.

Credit Recommendation: In the vocational certificate category, 1 hour lecture and 1 hour laboratory in Basic Electricity or in the lower division baccalaureate/associate degree category, 1 semester hour in Industrial Arts (2/78).

Bulk Conveyor Systems (55501-00)

Location: Self-instruction; PEDC Centers.

Length: Approximately 36 hours.

Dates: October 1974-April 1989.

Objective: To give students a basic knowledge of the fundamentals and operating principles of bulk conveyors necessary for proper maintenance.

Instruction: Major topics covered in the course are bulk conveyor maintenance functions, safety considerations, use of tools, conveyor components, belt adjustments and repairs, bearing installation, maintenance of motors and drive parts, electrical principles, and motor control circuits.

Credit Recommendation: In the vocational certificate category, 2 semester hours in Electromechanics or in the lower division baccalaureate/associate degree category, 1 semester hour in Electromechanics (2/78) (4/84).

Digital Electronics II (56549-00)

Location: Self-instruction; PEDC Centers.

Length: Approximately 64 hours.

Dates: January 1974-June 1981.

Objective: To provide a study of logic circuits through the application of logic principles.

Instruction: Major topics covered in the course are principles of logic functions; gates; and encoding, decoding, and basic flip-flop circuits.

Credit Recommendation: In the lower division baccalaureate/associate degree category, 2 semester hours in Digital Electronics (2/78).

Electronics II (56518-00)

Location: Self-instruction; PEDC Centers.

Length: Approximately 40 hours.

Dates: January 1978-June 1981.

Objective: To provide the basic knowledge and skills required to troubleshoot simple electronic equipment and to use necessary test equipment.

Instruction: Major topics covered in the course are electronic operation and troubleshooting analysis of electronic equipment at the component level, integrated circuit level, and card level.

Credit Recommendation: In the lower division baccalaureate/associate degree category, 1 semester hour lecture and 2 semester hours laboratory in Electronics (2/78) (4/84).

Introduction to Digital Computer Systems (Formerly Digital Electronics [56548-00])

Location: Self-instruction; PEDC Centers.

Length: *Version 1:* Approximately 36 hours; *Version 2:* Approximately 49 hours.

Dates: *Version 1:* February 1974-April 1986; *Version 2:* May 1986-Present.

Objective: To introduce the principles of digital electronics.

Instruction: Major topics covered in the course are basics of numbering systems, including methods of conversion between systems; various coding schemes; circuit introduction to Boolean algebra; and elements of digital electronics.

Credit Recommendation: In the lower division baccalaureate/associate degree category, 1 semester hour in Digital Electronics (2/78).

Introduction to Postal Supervision (11561-00) Introduction to Postal Management

Location: *Version 1: Courses 1 and 3*, Self-instruction; *Course 2*, Postal Employee Development Centers. *Version 2: Course 1,* Postal Employee Development Centers; *Course 2,* Correspondence.

Length: *Version 1:* total of approximately 40 hours; *Version 2:* Approximately 30 hours.

Dates: *Version 1:* February 1978-February 1989; *Version 2:* March 1989-Present.

Objective: *Versions 1 and 2:* To introduce supervisory personnel to the fundamentals of supervision.

Instruction: *Versions 1 and 2:* Major topics covered in the course are the role of the supervisor, tools of a manager, personnel management, applied principles of management, and general management functions and responsibilities.

Credit Recommendation: *Version 1: Courses 1, 2, or 3*: In the lower division baccalaureate/associate degree category, 1 semester hour in Business Administration (2/78). *Version 2: Courses 1 and 2*: In the lower division baccalaureate/associate degree category, 1 semester hour in Business Administration (4/84).

TECHNICAL TRAINING DIVISION

The courses listed below are offered by the Institute's Technical Training Center in Norman, Oklahoma, where more than 100,000 Postal Service employees have completed resident courses in a broad variety of technical disciplines since 1969.

Accident Investigation (55646-00) (55646-10) (55646-05) (Formerly [10011-10] and [10211-00])

Location: Technical Training Center, Norman, OK.

Length: 120 hours (3 weeks), residential.

Dates: June 1977-September 1987.

Objective: To develop the investigative and reporting skill of newly assigned claims officers.

Instruction: Major topics covered in the course are all aspects of accident investigation for both vehicle and nonvehicle accidents, preparation of accident reports, knowledge of the Federal Tort Claims Act, technical investigation skills, and preparation of exhibits and data.

Credit Recommendation: In the lower division baccalaureate/associate degree category, 3 semester hours in Industrial or Public Safety (12/77) (4/84).

Advanced Digital Applications (55698-00) (Formerly Digital Electronics)

Location: Technical Training Center, Norman, OK.

Length: 120 hours (3 weeks), residential, 20 hours lecture/discussion and 20 hours of laboratory per week.

Dates: September 1975-June 1985.

Objective: To provide students with the basic concepts of digital circuit analysis, troubleshooting techniques, and the knowledge to prepare them to take courses associated with digital equipment maintenance at the electronic technical level.

Instruction: Major topics covered in the course are applications and circuit configurations of registers, counters, multiplexers, converters (A/D, D/A), delay lines, and multivibrators. Includes instruction on the use of logic probes and oscilloscopes to troubleshoot IC circuits. The concepts of core and solid state memory circuits are an integral part of the program.

Credit Recommendation: In the lower division baccalaureate/associate degree category, 3 semester hours in Digital Electronics (9/77) (4/84).

Air Brakes: FMVSS121 (55619-00)

Location: Technical Training Center, Norman, OK.

Length: 80 hours (2 weeks), residential, 16 hours lecture/discussion and 24 hours of laboratory/workshop per week.

Dates: October 1975-May 1986.

Objective: To develop skills and knowledge in troubleshooting and maintenance of basic air brakes systems and antiskid systems in conformance with Federal Motor Vehicle Service (DOT) Standard #121 for fleet vehicles.

Instruction: Major topics covered in the course are classroom theory and practical laboratory exercises on compressors, brake valves (single and dual), governors, treadle valve, brake chambers, spring brake chambers, relay valves, safety valves, control valves, modulator assemblies, fail-safe monitors, tractor and trailer ratio relay valves, wheel speed sensors, electronic systems, and service brakes used in heavy duty vehicles.

Credit Recommendation: In the lower division baccalaureate/associate degree category or in the upper division baccalaureate degree category, 3 semester hours in Automotive Technology, Diesel Mechanics, Industrial Education, or Transportation Technology (9/77) (4/84).

Allison Automatic Transmissions (55620-00)

Location: Technical Training Center, Norman, OK.

Length: 80 hours (2 weeks), residential, 18 hours of lecture/discussion and 22 hours of laboratory/workshop per week.

Dates: January 1975-April 1986.

Objective: To develop an understanding of the operation and overhaul procedures of Allison automatic transmissions.

Instruction: Major topics covered in the course are torque converters, hydraulic pumps, valve bodies, circuits, planetary gears, powerflows, internal and external inspection, disassembly and reassembly, adjustment, and diagnostic procedures.

Credit Recommendation: In the upper division baccalaureate degree category, 2 semester hours in Automotive Technology, Diesel Mechanics, Heavy Equipment Operations, or Mechanical Technology (9/77) (4/84).

Automatic Business Mail Process Systems (55657-00)

Location: Technical Training Center, Norman, OK.

Length: 336 hours (8.5 weeks), residential, 16 hours lecture/discussion and 24 hours of laboratory per week.

Dates: April 1975-March 1982.

Objective: To develop the knowledge and skills necessary for performing preventive maintenance, system fault isolation, and repair maintenance of the Automatic Business Mail Processing System.

Instruction: Major topics covered in the course are an in-depth study of programming and hardware associated with the PDP8E computer, including Power Fail/Auto Restart (KP-8E), Positive I/O Business Interface (KA-8E), Extended Memory Controller (KM08E), High Speed Reader/Punch (PC-04), High Speed Reader/Punch Controller (PC-8E), Data Break Interface (KD-8E), Disk File (DF32DP), Postal and Data Systems Bar/Half-Bar Code Reader (CR3000), Fairchild LSM and Power Fail/Auto Restart (KP-8E), Computer Interface, UBM/SPLSM, ABMPS software, system troubleshooting, and system maintenance.

Credit Recommendation: In the upper division baccalaureate degree category, 3 semester hours in Computer Systems Architecture and Peripheral Devices; and in the lower division baccalaureate/associate degree category or in the upper division baccalaureate degree category, 3 semester hours in Assembly Language for a total of 6 semester hours (9/77) (4/84).

Automatic Transmission Overhaul (55627-00)

Location: Technical Training Center, Norman, OK.

Length: 80 hours (2 weeks), residential, 15 hours of lecture/discussion and 25 hours of laboratory/workshop per week.

Dates: October 1970-August 1986.

Objective: To develop student's understanding of automatic transmission overhaul procedures; to increase effectiveness, confidence, and skills in diagnosing, disassembling, inspecting, reassembling, and adjusting automatic transmissions and components.

Instruction: Major topics covered in the course are operation and service of torque converters, hydraulic pumps, valve bodies, circuits, clutches, planetary gears, power flows, and internal and external inspection, adjustment, and diagnosis procedures. Includes units of instruction and workshop experiences in use of special tools and equipment. Covers the Borg Warner M-11 and M-43, Ford C-4, GM Turbohydramatic 400, and Chrysler 727 and 904 transmissions.

Credit Recommendation: In the lower division baccalaureate/associate degree category, 3 semester hours in Automotive Technology, Industrial Education, or Mechanical Technology (12/74) (3/81).

Automotive Diesel Mechanics (55639-00) (Postal Diesel [55639-00])

Location: Technical Training Center, Norman, OK.

Length: 120 hours (3 weeks), residential, 15 hours of lecture/discussion and 25 hours of laboratory/workshop per week.

Dates: July 1973-October 1983.

Objective: To enable students to become proficient in troubleshooting, diagnosing, servicing, and repairing components in systems described below, performing diesel engine tune-ups, using test equipment, and analyzing engine performance.

Instruction: Major topics covered in the course are classroom presentations and shop work experiences on diesel engine systems, including fuel, air induction, exhaust, cooling, lubricating, and engine clutch; tune-up procedures; use of analyzing equipment, including the pressure prover, nozzle pop tester, and diesel timing light; proper use of shop and parts manuals, vehicle record cards, technical bulletins, measuring devices, troubleshooting charts, and preventive maintenance schedules.

Credit Recommendation: In the lower division baccalaureate/associate degree category or in the upper division baccalaureate degree category, 5 semester hours in Automotive Technology, Diesel Mechanics, Industrial Arts, Industrial Education, or Power Technology (12/74) (3/81). **NOTE:** The courses Automotive Diesel Mechanics, Caterpillar Diesel (55618-00), Cummins Diesel I (55617-01), and Cummins Diesel II (55617-02) have some overlap in course material. It is therefore recommended that a maximum of 6 credits be granted for completion of two or more of these courses.

Automotive Electrical Systems (55625-02)

Location: Technical Training Center, Norman, OK.

Length: 80 hours (2 weeks), residential, 15 hours of lecture/discussion and 25 hours of laboratory/workshop per week.

Dates: *Version 1:* July 1970-September 1983; *Version 2:* October 1983-Present.

Objective: To provide students with technical knowledge in the maintenance and repair of automotive electrical systems and in the use and care of automotive testing equipment, and to increase the students' proficiency in analyzing, diagnosing, and repairing various automotive electrical systems.

Instruction: Major topics covered in the course are automotive electricity and the construction, repair, and adjustment of automotive electrical systems. Includes use of automotive test equipment; battery testing; and the troubleshooting and repair of starting, charging, ignition, lighting, and instrument systems.

Credit Recommendation: In the lower division baccalaureate/associate degree category, 3 semester hours in Automotive Technology or Industrial Electrical Technology (12/74) (4/84).

Automotive Mechanic Fundamentals (55622-00)

Location: Technical Training Center, Norman, OK.

Length: 80 hours (2 weeks), residential, 24 hours lecture/discussion and 16 hours of laboratory/workshop per week.

Dates: January 1970-December 1985.

Objective: To develop a basic understanding of the major components and systems of motor vehicles; and of the care and use of shop equipment, hand tools, diagnostic equipment, special tools, and preventive maintenance techniques. To provide a broad foundation for continued education in the automotive field.

Instruction: Major topics covered in the course are the basics of automotive mechanics, including shop safety, shop equipment, tire examination and maintenance, brake and suspension systems, engine operation, cooling and fuel systems, automotive electrical circuits (cranking, charging, ignition, instruments), and the testing of electrical circuits. Includes familiarization with clutches, transmissions (manual and automatic), drive lines, and rear axles.

Credit Recommendation: In the lower division baccalaureate/associate degree category, 3 semester hours in Automotive Technology (9/77) (4/84).

Bar Code Printer Maintenance: CBT (55660-42)

Location: Technical Training Center, Norman, OK.

Length: 36 hours (4.5 days).

Dates: August 1988-September 1994.

Objective: To provide the student with basic knowledge and skills in bar code printing techniques focused on the Model 9140, BCP.

Learning Outcome: Upon successful completion of this course, the student will be able to start up and analyze for faulty operations on the BCP, Model 9140; isolate mechanical or electrical causes of faulty operations and repair the system; and align and adjust the BCP for proper operation.

Instruction: Major topics covered in the course are orientation to all system components and start, stop, and adjust controls, and repair and maintenance procedures for electrical and mechanical adjustments and repairs of the Model 9140. Methods of instruction include lecture and laboratory exercises on the Model 9140.

Credit Recommendation: In the vocational certificate category, 1 semester hour in Electromechanical Machinery (9/89).

Bar Code Sorter (Bell & Howell): BCS (55662-10)

Location: Technical Training Center, Norman, OK.

Length: 76 hours (2 weeks).

Dates: August 1983-September 1994.

Objective: To provide the student with knowledge and skill in preventive maintenance, troubleshooting, analysis, and repair maintenance of the RA-9, Bar Code Sorter (BCS).

Learning Outcome: Upon successful completion of this course, the student will be able to analyze the operation of the RA-9 BCS in fault isolation mode to perform preventive and repair maintenance tasks, and align and adjust the RA-9 BCS.

Instruction: Major topics covered in the course are orientation to all start, stop, and adjusting controls for the BCS system, and necessary skills in proper load, unload, align, adjust, and repair procedures for the

Bell & Howell RA-9 Bar Code Sorter. Methods of instruction include lecture and laboratory exercises on the RA-9.

Credit Recommendation: In the vocational certificate category, 2 semester hours in Electromechanical Machinery (9/89).

Basic Conveyors and Controls (55666-01)

Location: Technical Training Center, Norman, OK.

Length: 76 hours (2 weeks).

Dates: August 1989-September 1994.

Objective: To teach the student maintenance and repair of U.S.P.S. conveyors and their control circuits.

Learning Outcome: Upon successful completion of this course, the student will be able to do routine preventive maintenance on conveyor systems; know the theory of operation of the parts of a conveyor system, including power circuits, sensors, fluid power, chains, drive shaft, couplings, belts, bearings, pulleys and adjustors; and troubleshoot the system and do corrective maintenance as needed.

Instruction: Major topics covered in the course are mechanical systems such as fluid power, shaft drive systems, couplings, chain drives, pulleys, gear reductions, bearings; care and repair are covered. Motor control switching, the electrical system, including fuses and breakers; system troubleshooting; and safety are also included. Methods of instruction include lecture and hands-on laboratory exercises.

Credit Recommendation: In the lower division baccalaureate/associate degree category, 2 semester hours in Electromechanical Systems (9/89).

Basic Conveyors and Controls (55666-00)

Location: Technical Training Center, Norman, OK.

Length: 116 hours (3 weeks).

Dates: September 1985-September 1994.

Objective: To develop the ability to operate and maintain programmable controlled conveyor systems.

Instruction: Major topics covered in the course are the basic understanding of the operation of programmable controllers; the interpretation of ladder logic diagrams; the installation and troubleshooting of conveyor systems, using such test instruments as: DUM's, P.C. LED indicators and CRT programming. In addition, principles of basic fluid power and electromechanical assemblies associated with large belt conveying systems are taught.

Credit Recommendation: In the vocational certificate category, 4 semester hours in Electromechanical Troubleshooting or in the lower division baccalaureate/associate degree category, 2 semester hours in Electromechanical Systems Technology, and 1 semester hour in Programmable Controllers (6/86).

Basic Programmable Controllers: GE Series I (55666-10)

Location: Technical Training Center, Norman, OK.

Length: 38 hours (1 week).

Dates: January 1988-September 1994.

Objective: To provide the student with the fundamental knowledge and experience in the operation, maintenance, and troubleshooting of programmable controlled equipment utilizing the GE Series I programmable controller.

Learning Outcome: Upon successful completion of this course, the student will be able to install, power-up, and perform operational tests on the Series I PC and the programmable controlled equipment, and upload a program from magnetic tape, verify CPU memory, make timer adjustments, and perform system analysis to detect defective I/O modules, power supplies, and associated wiring using manufacturer's documentation, a hand-held programmer, and a digital voltmeter.

Instruction: Major topics covered in the course are the basic operation and components of a GE Series I programmable controller, unloading a program from magnetic tape, verification of program operation, and troubleshooting of controlled conveyor systems.

Credit Recommendation: In the vocational certificate category, 1 semester hour in Basic Programmable Controllers (9/89).

BMC Building Equipment Mechanic (55672-00)

Location: Technical Training Center, Norman, OK.

Length: 160 hours (4 weeks), residential, 20 hours of lecture and 20 hours of laboratory per week.

Dates: March 1976-October 1981.

Objective: To provide an understanding of air conditioning and heating systems utilized in large installations and develop skills in operating and performing preventive and repair maintenance on air conditioning and heating equipment.

Instruction: Major topics covered in the course are operation and maintenance of basic heating, ventilating, and air conditioning systems, including hot water heating systems, direct expansion and chilled water systems, centrifugal compressors, automatic controls, and central automated building monitoring systems.

Credit Recommendation: In the upper division baccalaureate degree category, 6 semester hours in Building and Construction Management, Building Maintenance, Building Operations Management, or Electromechanical Technology (9/77).

BMC Electrical Power Mechanics (55677-00)

Location: Technical Training Center, Norman, OK.

Length: 160 hours (4 weeks), residential, 20 hours of lecture/discussion and 20 hours of laboratory.

Dates: April 1976-June 1982.

Objective: To provide a theoretical and practical background in basic electricity.

Instruction: Major topics covered in the course are basic principles of electricity; electrical power distribution; motors and motor controls; solid state devices and control circuits; electrical diagrams; instruments; troubleshooting techniques; and familiarization with and utilization of basic electronic laboratory equipment.

Credit Recommendation: In the lower division baccalaureate/associate degree category, 3 semester hours in Basic Electricity and 1 semester hour in Basic Electronic Laboratory (9/77).

BMC Mail Processing Mechanics (55671-04) (Formerly 55671-00)

Location: Technical Training Center, Norman, OK.

Length: *Version 1:* 160 hours (4 weeks), residential, 24 hours of lecture and 16 hours of laboratory per week; *Version 2:* 200 hours (5 weeks); *Version 3:* 192 hours (5 weeks).

Dates: *Version 1:* January 1976-August 1982; *Version 2:* September 1982-August 1989; *Version 3:* September 1989-Present.

Objective: To provide students with the abilities to operate, troubleshoot, adjust, and repair mechanical, electrical, electromechanical, and electronic equipment. The equipment consists of conveyors, motors, reducers, relay logic, integrated circuit logic, and pneumatic and hydraulic systems.

Instruction: Major topics covered in the course are basic and complex mechanical mechanisms; drive configurations; conveyor components; analysis and troubleshooting of electrical control systems; basic and complex mechanical, pneumatic, and electrical assemblies of sortation equipment, including drive assemblies, conveying assemblies, motors and motor controls, as well as the associated digital electronic control systems.

Credit Recommendation: In the upper division baccalaureate degree category, 6 semester hours in Electromechanical Technology (9/77) (4/84) (9/89). **NOTE:** (8/82: This course was changed to a 5-week course. The change was such as not to affect the course description or credit recommendation.)

Brakes and Suspension Systems (55623-00)

Location: Technical Training Center, Norman, OK.

Length: 80 hours (2 weeks), residential, 20 hours of lecture/discussion and 20 hours of laboratory/workshop per week.

Dates: January 1974-September 1986.

Objective: To develop skills and knowledge in troubleshooting and maintaining hydraulic brake systems, drum and disc, and their components and to provide an understanding of front-end suspension components and geometry.

Instruction: Major topics covered in the course are shop safety, front suspension systems, wheel alignment, steering gears, wheel bearings, steering linkage, wheel balancing, springs, and attaching parts, sway control mechanisms, single and dual master cylinders, pressure differential switches, drum and caliper components, metering valves, proportional valves, brake hoses and lines, brake drums, and rotors.

Credit Recommendation: In the lower division baccalaureate/associate degree category, 3 semester hours in Automotive Technology, Industrial Education, or Transportation Technology (9/77) (4/84).

Burroughs MLOCR/CS Maintenance Training (55660-19) (Formerly Burroughs OCR/CS Maintenance Training [55660-18])

Location: Technical Training Center, Norman, OK.

Length: *Version 1:* 228 hours (6 weeks); *Version 2:* 272 hours (7 weeks, 4 days).

Dates: *Version 1:* September 1986-May 1989; *Version 2:* June 1989-Present.

Objective: To teach the student the operation, maintenance, and repair of the Burroughs Optical Character Reader/Channel Sorter.

Learning Outcome: Upon successful completion of this course, the student will be able to explain the overall operation of the system, including the mechanical, electrical, and electronic subsystems; perform preventive maintenance and do adjustments such as transport system, prescanning system, bar code reader and mainscan alignment; and locate and repair faults in the system.

Instruction: Major topics covered in the course are overall operation of the system and safety considerations; the control panels, transport control unit, scanning system, bar code reader and printers; the mechanical, electromechanical, and electronic components of the computerized optical character reader; and general information on thyristors, photoelectric scanning, optical electronics, and digital systems. Methods of instruction include lecture and hands-on laboratory exercises.

Credit Recommendation: In the lower division baccalaureate/associate degree category, 3 semester hours in Digital Electronic Systems (9/89).

Caterpillar Diesel (55618-00)

Location: Technical Training Center, Norman, OK.

Length: 120 hours (3 weeks), residential, 15 hours of lecture and 25 hours of laboratory/workshop per week.

Dates: July 1975-April 1985.

Objective: To provide an understanding of the principles of operation of the 1150 and 3208 Series Caterpillar diesel engines. To develop skill in troubleshooting, diagnosing, servicing, and repairing components; performing tune-ups; and using test equipment.

Instruction: Major topics covered in the course are the following diesel systems: fuel, air induction, exhaust, cooling, and lubricating. Also covers tune-up procedures, use of analyzing equipment for fuel systems, troubleshooting charts, use of manuals and bulletins, and use of measuring devices.

Credit Recommendation: In the lower division baccalaureate/associate degree category or in the upper division baccalaureate degree category, 4 semester hours in Automotive Technology, Diesel Mechanics, Industrial Arts, Industrial Education, or Power Technology (9/77) (4/84). **NOTE:** The courses Automotive Diesel Mechanics, Caterpillar Diesel (55618-00), Cummins Diesel I (55617-01), and Cummins Diesel II (55617-02) have some overlap in course material. It is therefore recommended that a maximum of 6 credits be granted for completion of two or more of these courses.

Computer Forwarding System Maintenance (55669-20) (Formerly 55669-03)

Location: Technical Training Center, Norman, OK.

Length: *Version 1:* 152 hours (4 weeks); *Version 2:* 69 hours (2 weeks).

Dates: *Version 1:* June 1985-June 1988; *Version 2:* July 1988-Present.

Objective: To provide the student with knowledge, skills, and abilities to accomplish electronic, electrical, and electromechanical repairs to a microcomputer, dual floppy disk drives, printer, and CRT display.

Learning Outcome: Upon successful completion of this course, the student will be able to diagnose and repair internal and interactive faults in and between the computer subsystems. This includes powering-up, operating the system, troubleshooting the operation, performing preventive maintenance, alignments and adjustments, and board/assembly replacement of faulty components.

Instruction: Major topics covered in the course are electromechanical and electrical adjustments, digital electronic circuitry, and concepts pertinent to the Computer Forwarding System. Emphasizes use of diagnostic routines for fault isolation to the printed circuit board level and use of common test equipment to locate faults to the major component level.

Credit Recommendation: *Version 1:* In the lower division baccalaureate/associate degree category, 3 semester hours in Digital Computer Systems Troubleshooting (6/86). *Version 2:* In the lower division baccalaureate/associate degree category, 2 semester hours in Digital Computer Systems Troubleshooting (9/89).

Consolidated MPLSM Training (55658-10)

Location: Technical Training Center, Norman, OK.

Length: 92 hours (2 weeks, 1.5 days).

Dates: March 1983-January 1986.

Objective: To teach maintenance personnel to troubleshoot and repair the various models of the Multi-Position Letter Sorting Machine.

Learning Outcome: The course produces maintenance and repair people for the MPLSM.

Instruction: Major topics covered in the course are safety and the operation, documentation, preventive maintenance, and repair of several models of the MPLSM. Approximately half the time is spent in class and half on demonstration and laboratory experience.

Credit Recommendation: In the vocational certificate category, 3 semester hours in Electromechanical Troubleshooting Procedures (6/86).

Cummins Diesel I (55617-01)

Location: Technical Training Center, Norman, OK.

Length: 80 hours (2 weeks), residential, 15 hours of lecture and 25 hours of laboratory/workshop per week.

Dates: June 1976-May 1980.

Objective: To provide an understanding of the principles of operation of the NTC 230 PT Model Cummins diesel engine. To develop skill in troubleshooting, diagnosing, servicing, and repairing components; performing tune-ups; and using test equipment.

Instruction: Major topics covered in the course are the following diesel systems: fuel, air induction, exhaust, cooling, and lubricating. Also covers tune-up procedures, use of analyzing equipment for fuel systems, and troubleshooting charts.

Credit Recommendation: In the lower division baccalaureate/associate degree category or in the upper division baccalaureate degree category, 3 semester hours in Automotive Technology, Diesel Mechanics, Industrial Arts, Industrial Education, or Power Technology (9/77). **NOTE:** The courses Automotive Diesel Mechanics, Caterpillar Diesel (55618-00), Cummins Diesel I (55617-01), and Cummins Diesel II (55617-02) have some overlap in course material. It is therefore recommended that a maximum of 6 credits be granted for completion of two or more of these courses. *Prerequisite:* Automotive Diesel Mechanics or Caterpillar Diesel.

Cummins Diesel III (55617-03) (Formerly Cummins Diesel II [55617-02])

Location: Technical Training Center, Norman, OK.

Length: 120 hours (3 weeks), residential, 15 hours of lecture and 25 hours of laboratory/workshop per week.

Dates: *Version 1:* January 1977-March 1983; *Version 2:* April 1983-June 1986.

Objective: To provide an understanding of the principles of operation of the NTC 230 PT Model Cummins diesel engine. To develop skill in troubleshooting, diagnosing, servicing, and repairing components; performing tune-ups; and using test equipment.

Instruction: Major topics covered in the course are the following diesel systems: fuel, air induction, exhaust cooling, and lubricating. Also covers tune-up procedures, use of analyzing equipment for fuel systems, troubleshooting charts, use of manuals and bulletins, and use of measuring devices.

Credit Recommendation: In the lower division baccalaureate/associate degree category or in the upper division baccalaureate degree category, 4 semester hours in Automotive Technology, Diesel Mechanics, Industrial Arts, Industrial Education, or Power Technology (9/77) (4/84). **NOTE:** The courses Automotive Diesel Mechanics, Caterpillar Diesel (55618-00), Cummins Diesel I (55617-01), and Cummins Diesel II (55617-02) have some overlap in course material. It is therefore recommended that a maximum of 6 credits be granted for completion of two or more of these courses. This course has been reevaluated and continues to meet the requirements for credit recommendations. (The Cummins Diesel II course was discontinued in 1983 and replaced with the Cummins Diesel III course. The change was made because of an equipment change. This change does not affect the course description or credit recommendation.)

Customer Service and Postal Machines (55603-01)

Location: Technical Training Center, Norman, OK.

Length: 52 hours (1.5 weeks) residential; 20 hours of lecture and 32 hours of laboratory/workshop.

Dates: June 1977-September 1985.

Objective: To develop skill in preventive maintenance, troubleshooting, analysis, and repair maintenance of postage meters.

Instruction: Major topics covered in the course are troubleshooting, preventive maintenance, and repair maintenance of the Pitney Bowes Meter Machine Bases 4000 Series (R Line) and 5400 Series, Friden Meter Machine Base Model 9010, and Model 14-75 Data Recorder.

Credit Recommendation: In the vocational certificate category, 1 semester hour in Mechanical Devices (9/77) (4/84).

Customer Vending Machines (55610-01)

Location: Technical Training Center, Norman, OK.

Length: 68 hours (1.5 weeks) residential; 34 hours of lecture and 34 hours of laboratory/workshop.

Dates: July 1977-May 1982.

Objective: To develop skill in reading schematics, understanding nomenclature, and disassembly and assembly of electromechanical vending equipment.

Instruction: Major topics covered in the course are use of manuals, in-line drawings, schematics, and test equipment to troubleshoot, repair, and make periodic preventive maintenance checks on vending equipment.

Credit Recommendation: In the lower division baccalaureate/associate degree category, 2 semester hours in Electromechanical Technology (9/77).

Digital Computer Concepts: DCC (55699-05)

Location: Technical Training Center, Norman, OK.

Length: 108 hours (3 weeks).

Dates: September 1985-June 1991.

Objective: This course enables the student to acquire basic computer concepts, including the applications of various peripheral devices.

Instruction: Major topics covered in the course are safety; introduction to computer systems; Introduction to system software; introduction to system hardware; functional analysis of system operations; and Multi-user operations, such as commands, media handling and media installation, file protections schemes; diagnostic operating system; and computer maintenance.

Credit Recommendation: In the lower division baccalaureate/associate degree category, 2 semester hours in Computer Maintenance (6/86).

Digital Computer Systems Conversion (55699-02)

Location: Technical Training Center, Norman, OK.

Length: 80 hours (10 days).

Dates: January 1986-January 1988.

Objective: To teach the basic skills and knowledge of computers to enable the student to attend more advanced specific computer equipment courses.

Learning Outcome: Upon successful completion of this course, the student will know basic digital computer theory and the application of equipment, firmware, and software. The concepts of maintenance and repair are stressed.

Instruction: Major topics covered in the course are generic computer training includes system operation, block diagram, programming, port location, diagnostics, preventive maintenance, and corrective maintenance. The course is half classroom work, and half laboratory.

Credit Recommendation: In the vocational certificate category, 2 semester hours in Basic Computer Theory (6/86).

Digital Computer Technology (55694-00)

Location: Technical Training Center, Norman, OK.

Length: *Version 1:* 240 hours (6 weeks), residential, 24 hours of lecture/discussion and 16 hours of laboratory/workshop per week; *Version 2:* 320 hours (8 weeks).

Dates: *Version 1:* July 1972-July 1975; *Version 2:* July 1975-November 1981.

Objective: To provide programming knowledge needed to train on sophisticated digital computerized systems; to provide in-depth knowledge of the theory, operation, troubleshooting, maintenance, and repair of the PDP-8 digital computer; and to familiarize the student with associated peripheral devices commonly used to communicate with high-speed computers.

Instruction: Major topics covered in the course are safety, operator and maintenance documentation, theory of operation, power distribution, motor control, and jam/fault circuitry.

Credit Recommendation: In the lower division baccalaureate/associate degree category, 2 semester hours in Electromechanical Troubleshooting (6/86).

Digital Electronics (55693-00) (Formerly Logic Circuits)

Location: Technical Training Center, Norman, OK.

Length: 160 hours (4 weeks), residential, 30 hours of lecture/discussion and 10 hours of laboratory/workshop per week.

Dates: July 1970-March 1976.

Objective: To provide students with a background in digital logic in order to prepare them for advanced training on sophisticated digital electronics equipment.

Instruction: Major topics covered in the course are the basic principles of number systems, Boolean algebra, and logic circuits such as gates, encoders, decoders, flip-flops, shift registers, and various counters found in sophisticated digital equipment. Utilizes both theory and equipment hardware.

Credit Recommendation: In the lower division baccalaureate/associate degree category, 4 semester hours in Computer Systems, Electronics, or Optical Data Processing (12/74) (3/81).

Electric Vehicle: DJ5E (55629-00)

Location: Technical Training Center, Norman, OK.

Length: 140 hours (3 weeks), residential, 15 hours of lecture and 25 hours of laboratory/workshop per week.

Dates: March 1977-September 1981.

Objective: To develop the knowledge and skills necessary to achieve proficiency in diagnostic troubleshooting, preventive maintenance, use of applicable test equipment, removal and replacement of defective components, and calibration of printed circuit boards on the Gould Electric Vehicle Propulsion System.

Instruction: Major topics covered in the course are principles of operation and the technical knowledge required to perform preventive and repair maintenance of Gould Electric Powered Vehicle; electrical and electronic theory; use of test equipment, including the oscilloscope and D.V.M. schematic interpretation and laboratory exercises on the electrical/electronic propulsion system.

Credit Recommendation: In the lower division baccalaureate/associate degree category, 2 semester hours in Automotive Technology, Industrial Education, or Transportation Technology (9/77).

Electrical Power Mechanic: EPM (55677-00)

Location: Technical Training Center, Norman, OK.

Length: 160 hours (4 weeks), residential, 20 hours of lecture/discussion and 20 hours of laboratory per week.

Dates: April 1976-December 1985.

Objective: To provide a theoretical and practical background in basic electricity.

Instruction: Major topics covered in the course are basic principles of electricity; electrical power distribution; motors and motor controls; solid state devices and control circuits; electrical diagrams; instruments; troubleshooting techniques; and familiarization with and utilization of basic electronic laboratory equipment.

Credit Recommendation: In the lower division baccalaureate/associate degree category, 3 semester hours in Basic Electricity and 1 semester hour in Basic Electronic Laboratory (9/77).

Electronic Sort Processor: ESP (55659-05) (Formerly [55659-00; 55659-01])

Location: Technical Training Center, Norman, OK.

Length: 280 hours (7 weeks).

Dates: April 1976-September 1987.

Objective: To enable maintenance personnel to perform preventive maintenance, troubleshooting analysis, and repair maintenance required to maintain the Electronic Sort Processor.

Instruction: Major topics covered in the course are detailed principles of operations; circuit analysis; diagnosis, analysis, and correction of electronic faults within the Electronic Sort Processor system and associated interface module and the peripheral control board; system adjustment and alignment and associated procedures; and use of operation and maintenance manuals. Requires previous formal training on electromechanical systems, logic systems, and advanced digital applications.

Credit Recommendation: In the lower division baccalaureate/associate degree category, 3 semester hours as a technical elective in Electronics; or in the upper division baccalaureate degree category, 2 semester hours as a technical elective in Electronics (9/77) (4/84).

Engine Tune-up and Air Pollution Control Devices (55624-00)

Location: Technical Training Center, Norman, OK.

Length: 80 hours (2 weeks), residential, 15 hours of lecture/discussion and 25 hours of laboratory/workshop per week.

Dates: August 1973-October 1985.

Objective: To provide students with an understanding of automotive air pollution control; to train them to maintain motor vehicles equipped with air pollution control devices; and to develop the students' skill in preventive maintenance and engine tune-up, use of engine analyzing and tune-up equipment, analyzing engine performance, and testing and servicing air pollution control devices.

Instruction: Major topics covered in the course are vehicle air pollution terminology; compression; ignition; carburation; tune-up procedures; use of analyzing equipment, including the oscilloscope; and inspection, testing, and servicing of air pollution control devices in current use.

Credit Recommendation: In the lower division baccalaureate/associate degree category, 3 semester hours in Automotive Technology, Industrial Arts, or Industrial Education (12/74) (3/81).

Environmental Control I (55686-00)

Location: Technical Training Center, Norman, OK.

Length: 80 hours (2 weeks), residential, 20 hours of lecture and 20 hours of laboratory/workshop per week.

Dates: February 1970-August 1989.

Objective: To provide a basic understanding of air conditioning and heating systems used in commercial buildings, and to develop skills in operating and performing preventive and repair maintenance on air conditioning and heating equipment.

Instruction: Major topics covered in the course are operation and maintenance of forced-air systems, direct-fired heating systems, natural-draft low-pressure hot water and steam boilers, direct-expansion systems (including all reciprocating compressors), and controls for small/medium systems. Special emphasis is placed on energy conservation and safety.

Credit Recommendation: In the lower division baccalaureate/associate degree category, 3 semester hours in Building and Construction Management, Building Maintenance, or Building Operations Management (9/77) (4/84).

Environmental Control II (55689-31, 32, 33, 34)

Location: Technical Training Center, Norman, OK.

Length: 160 hours (4 weeks), residential, 20 hours of lecture and 20 hours of laboratory per week.

Dates: July 1971-December 1984.

Objective: To develop the technician's ability to operate, maintain, troubleshoot, and repair large capacity, year-round environmental control systems and to acquaint the technician with the tools and procedures used to calibrate, test, and adjust HVAC equipment and systems.

Instruction: Major topics covered in the course are operation and maintenance of large HVAC systems, including mechanical draft low - and high-pressure steam and hot water boilers, fuels, combustion, burners, boiler controls, pumps, hot water and steam distribution systems, air handlers, air distribution, water and air balancing, centrifugal water chillers, controls for large tonnage condensing units, and system controls. System controls include maintenance and calibration of electric, pneumatic, and electronic control equipment of the major manufacturers. Control system components are thermostats, relays, transducers, masters and submasters, single and dual input controllers, discriminators, amplifiers, and actuators. Coverage also includes total control system functions and sequence of operation of the year-round environmental control systems with use of central control units.

Credit Recommendation: In the upper division baccalaureate degree category, 6 semester hours in Building and Construction Management, Building Maintenance, Building Operations Management, or Electromechanical Technology (9/77) (4/84).

Environmental Control III: HVAC Heating (55689-05)

Location: Technical Training Center, Norman, OK.

Length: 36 hours (1 week).

Dates: September 1980-March 1986.

Objective: To develop students' ability to operate, provide preventive maintenance of, troubleshoot, and perform inspection procedure on heating equipment.

Instruction: Major topics covered in the course are operation, maintenance, and troubleshooting of heating systems, including steam and hot water tube boilers, cast iron boilers, natural gas or oil fired burners, float controls, combustion control, air handling units, pumps, air separators, strainers, valves, air balancing, expansion tanks, steam traps, and condensate pumps. Lecture, discussion, and laboratory are used.

Credit Recommendation: In the lower division baccalaureate/associate degree category, 1 semester hour in Environmental Control Technology (3/81).

Environmental Control IV: Advanced Air Conditioning (55689-08) (Formerly Environmental Control IV (Advanced Air Conditioning) [55689-06])

Location: Technical Training Center, Norman, OK.

Length: *Versions 1 and 2:* 38 hours (3 weeks).

Dates: *Version 1:* October 1980-September 1984; *Version 2:* October 1984-Present.

Objective: To train students to perform preventive maintenance, troubleshooting, and minor repairs on large-capacity refrigeration equipment for air conditioning and acquaint them with the tools, procedures, and techniques for full service of large air conditioning systems.

Instruction: Major topics covered in the course are troubleshooting and minor repair of large-tonnage refrigeration equipment. Repair of reciprocating compressors is emphasized. Control system maintenance and maintenance of cooling towers are also covered. Lecture and laboratory are used.

Credit Recommendation: In the lower division baccalaureate/associate degree category, 2 semester hours in Air Conditioning, Environmental Technology, or Refrigeration (3/81).

Environmental Control V: HVAC and Energy Conservation Analysis (55689-07)

Location: Technical Training Center, Norman, OK.

Length: 36 hours (1 week).

Dates: November 1980-September 1988.

Objective: To provide training in the operation of HVAC equipment so that energy costs are kept to a minimum and the equipment is properly maintained.

Instruction: Major topics covered in the course are heating and cooling load calculations; psychometric procedures for energy conservation; use of central control systems; interrelationships of the chiller, tower, pumps, air handling units, controls, boiler, and auxiliary equipment, and the interdependency of units; and total system troubleshooting. Lecture, discussion, and laboratory are used.

Credit Recommendation: In the lower division baccalaureate/associate degree category, 1 semester hour in Environmental Control Technology (3/81).

Fundamentals of Automatic Transmissions (55626-00)

Location: Technical Training Center, Norman, OK.

Length: 40 hours (1 week), residential, 24 hours of lecture/discussion and 16 hours of laboratory/workshop.

Dates: March 1971-September 1985.

Objective: To provide an understanding of power flows and the maintenance and adjustment of automatic transmissions.

Instruction: Major topics covered in the course are principles of operation and functions of transmission components; familiarization with parts; use of special tools; use of technical manuals; and adjustments and scheduled maintenance.

Credit Recommendation: In the lower division baccalaureate/associate degree category, 1 semester hour in Automotive Technology, Industrial Education, or Mechanical Technology (9/77) (4/84).

Industrial Electrical Services (55687-03) (Formerly Industrial Electrical Services (55687-00, 55687-01 or 55687-02)

Location: Technical Training Center, Norman, OK.

Length: 120 hours (3 weeks), residential, 20 hours of lecture/discussion and 20 hours of laboratory per week.

Dates: *Version 1:* January 1972-November 1982; *Version 2:* January 1983-October 1984; *Version 3:* October 1984-Present.

Objective: To provide the student with theoretical and practical knowledge of electricity and standard electrical circuits, and the basic skills of electrical wiring in a power distribution system.

Instruction: Major topics covered in the course are principles of electricity, magnetism, direct current, alternating current, motors, generators, transformers, electrical power distribution, motor controls, equipment wiring, electrical lighting, and repair and preventive maintenance of a complete electrical system.

Credit Recommendation: In the lower division baccalaureate/associate degree category, 1 semester hour in Industrial Electronics and 2 semester hours in Power Distribution Technology (9/77) (4/84).

M36/M500B Direct Feed Facer Canceler System (55654-01)

Location: Technical Training Center, Norman, OK.

Length: 114 hours (4 weeks).

Dates: January 1981-July 1990.

Objective: To teach maintenance mechanics to maintain, troubleshoot, and repair the Direct Feed Facer Canceler System.

Learning Outcome: Upon successful completion of this course, the student will be able to recognize system malfunctions and do adjustment/alignment replacement as necessary to restore the equipment to operating condition.

Instruction: Major topics covered in the course are safety, operator and maintenance documentation, theory of operation, power distribution, motor control, and jam/fault circuitry.

Credit Recommendation: In the lower division baccalaureate/associate degree category, 2 semester hours in Electromechanical Troubleshooting (6/86).

Mark II Facer-Canceler and Feeder Machine (55653-00)

Location: Technical Training Center, Norman, OK.

Length: 160 hours (4 weeks), residential, 25 hours of lecture/discussion and 15 hours of laboratory/workshop per week.

Dates: July 1969-October 1983.

Objective: To train maintenance personnel to maintain, troubleshoot, and repair facer-canceler and feeder systems.

Instruction: Major topics covered in the course are component assembly identification, location, and function; repair and parts replacement; troubleshooting analysis techniques; adjustment, alignment, and preventive maintenance of an electromechanical system. Utilizes appropriate technical manuals and data, diagnostic test equipment (oscilloscopes, volt-ohm meters, etc.), and regular and special tools.

Credit Recommendation: In the lower division baccalaureate/associate degree category, 3 semester hours in Electromechanical Technology or Mechanical Technology (12/74).

Microprocessor-Controlled Mark II: Micro-Mark II (55653-08)

Location: Technical Training Center, Norman, OK.

Length: 60 hours (8 days).

Dates: January 1983-December 1987.

Objective: To train maintenance mechanics to troubleshoot and repair the microprocessor-controlled Mark II facer canceler system.

Learning Outcome: Upon successful completion of this course, the maintenance mechanic is able to do routine maintenance, troubleshoot, and repair the microprocessor-controlled facer-canceler system.

Instruction: Major topics covered in the course are provides instruction on the facer canceler operation consisting of these major blocks: (1) familiarization, documentation, and operation, (2) the equipment power distribution and motor control, and (3) machine indicia recognition gating and canceling functions. Routine preventive maintenance is stressed throughout the course.

Credit Recommendation: In the vocational certificate category, 2 semester hours in Electromechanical Troubleshooting (6/86).

Model 120/121 MPLSM/ZMT On-Site Maintenance Certification (OSMC) Program (55655-02)

Location: Each postal facility maintaining Model 120/121 MPLSM/ZMT equipment.

Length: 85 hours (8.5 weeks), five 2-hour sessions per week.

Dates: August 1970-September 1987.

Objective: To provide supplemental and supportive training for students who have completed related, prerequisite training and bring them to an adequate level of proficiency in the repair and maintenance of Multi-Position Letter-Sorter/Zip-Mail Translator Systems.

Instruction: Major topics covered in the course are detailed circuit analysis of all circuits in the ZMT; detailed troubleshooting techniques and peculiarities of equipment. Also includes some theory of operation and minor maintenance of peripheral equipment: Model 33 AST Teletype, Mohawk Data Sciences Digital Printer Series 800, EDIT, Sorensen and Lambda power supplies, and the Sequential-Chordal Trainer Console.

Credit Recommendation: In the lower division baccalaureate/associate degree category, 1 semester hour in Electromechanical Laboratory and 1 semester hour in Electronic Troubleshooting Laboratory (9/77) (4/84). **NOTE:** Credit should not be granted for both this course and Model 140/141 MPLSM OSMC Program, degree category I (55658-05) or Model 140/141 MPLSM OSMC Program, degree category II (55659-02). *Prerequisite:* Zip-Mail Translator (55655-01) resident training.

Model 140/141 MPLSM On-Site Maintenance Certification (OSMC) Program, Category I (55658-05)

Location: Each postal facility maintaining Model 140/141 MPLSM/ZMT equipment.

Length: 190 hours (19 weeks), consisting of 22 programmed modules.

Dates: November 1976-April 1989.

Objective: To train maintenance personnel to perform preventive maintenance, exercise diagnostic fault isolation techniques, and perform corrective maintenance on the Model 140/141 Multi-Position Letter-Sorting System within minimum time frames.

Instruction: Major topics covered in the course are detailed training in the principles and theory of operation for the 140/141 Multi-Position Letter-Sorter, the Zip-Mail Translator, and the Electronic Sort Processor. Detailed circuit analysis, alignment procedures, and corrective maintenance techniques are included for each subassembly of the system. Electronic "model" concepts are covered as they relate to the 140/141 system. All interfacing and control functions between the Letter Sorter, the ZMT, and ESP are taught in detail. Additional training in the principles and theory of operation of keyboards, teletypes, and associate electrical circuitry.

Credit Recommendation: In the lower division baccalaureate/associate degree category, 1 semester hour in Electromechanical Laboratory and 1 semester hour in Electronic Troubleshooting Laboratory (9/77) (4/84). **NOTE:** Credit should not be granted for Electromechanical Laboratory for both this course and Model 140/141 MPLSM OSMC Program, degree category II (55659-02). Also, credit should not be granted for both this course and Model 120/121 MPLSM/ZMT OSMC Program (55655-02).

Model 140/141 MPLSM On-Site Maintenance Certification (OSMC) Program, Category II (55659-02)

Location: Each postal facility maintaining Model 140/141 MPLSM/ZMT equipment.

Length: 140 hours (14 weeks), consisting of 12 programmed modules.

Dates: November 1976-April 1989.

Objective: To train maintenance personnel to perform preventive maintenance, exercise diagnostic fault isolation techniques, and perform corrective maintenance on the Model 140/141 letter-sorting system within minimal time frames.

Instruction: Major topics covered in the course are detailed training in the practical application and theory of operation for the 140/141 Multi-Position Letter-Sorter, the Zip-Mail Translator, and the Electronic Sort Processor. Detailed circuit analysis, alignment procedures, and corrective maintenance techniques are included for each subassembly of the system. Electronic "model" concepts are covered as they relate to the 140/141 system. All interfacing and control functions between the Letter Sorter, the ZMT, and the ESP are taught in detail.

Credit Recommendation: In the lower division baccalaureate/associate degree category, 1 semester hour in Electromechanical Laboratory (9/77) (4/84). **NOTE:** Credit should not be granted for Electromechanical Laboratory for both this course and Model 140/141 MPLSM OSMC Program, degree category I (55658-05) or Model 120/121 MPLSM/ZMT OSMC Program (55655-02). Credit may be granted for this course and the Electronic Troubleshooting Laboratory portion of 55655-02.

Model 140/141 MPLSM/ZMT/ESP (55658-00) (Comprised of 55658-01 and 55658-24)

Location: Technical Training Center, Norman, OK.

Length: 600 hours (15 weeks).

Dates: January 1977-November 1987.

Objective: To train maintenance personnel to perform preventive and corrective maintenance, and exercise diagnostic fault isolation techniques on the Model 140/141 letter-sorting system (including the Multi-Position Letter-Sorter Machine, Zip-Mail Translator, and Electronic Sort Processor).

Instruction: Refer to instruction sections of Multi-Position Letter-Sorter Machine (55651-00), Zip-Mail Translator (55655-01), and Electronic Sort Processor (55659-00).

Credit Recommendation: In the lower division baccalaureate/associate degree category, 3 semester hours in Computer Maintenance Technology, and 3 semester hours in Electromechanical Technology, and either 3 semester hours as a technical elective in Electronics in the lower division baccalaureate/associate degree category or 2 semester hours as a technical elective in the upper division baccalaureate degree category (for a total of 9 or 8 semester hours) (9/77) (4/84). **NOTE:** If credit is granted for one or more of the courses cited in the Instruction section, the credit granted for this course should be reduced accordingly. If all the courses cited above are taken, no credit should be granted for this course. This course is also given as an eleven-week course for students who have completed Model 140/141 Multi-Position Letter-Sorter Machine (55658-01).

Model 140/141 Multi-Position Letter-Sorter Machine (55658-01)

Location: Technical Training Center, Norman, OK.

Length: 80 hours (2 weeks), residential, 20 hours of lecture/discussion and 20 hours of laboratory/workshop per week.

Dates: January 1977-March 1983.

Objective: To train maintenance personnel to troubleshoot, repair, and perform normal preventive maintenance on the multi-position letter-sorter machine.

Instruction: Major topics covered in the course are operating principles; component assembly identification, location, and function; alignment and adjustment procedures; repair and parts replacement; analysis, diagnosis, and correction of electrical and mechanical equipment malfunctions; and preventive maintenance practices.

Credit Recommendation: In the lower division baccalaureate/associate degree category, 3 semester hours in Electromechanical Technology (9/77). **NOTE:** This course is made up of a two-week session from Model 140/141 MPLSM/ZMT/ESP (55658-00), which is sometimes taken independently.

Multi-Position Letter-Sorter Machine: MPLSM (55651-00)

Location: Technical Training Center, Norman, OK.

Length: 120 hours (3 weeks), residential, 20 hours of lecture/discussion and 20 hours of workshop per week.

Dates: May 1970-June 1983.

Objective: To train maintenance personnel to troubleshoot, repair, and perform normal preventive maintenance on the multi-position letter-sorter machine.

Instruction: Major topics covered in the course are operating principles, component assembly identification, location, and function; alignment and adjustment procedures; repair and parts replacement; analysis, diagnosis, and correction of electrical and mechanical equipment malfunctions; and preventive maintenance practices.

Credit Recommendation: In the lower division baccalaureate/associate degree category, 3 semester hours in Electromechanical Technology or Mechanical Technology (12/74) (3/81).

Multi-Position Letter-Sorter Machines 140/141 (55658-20)

Location: Technical Training Center, Norman, OK.

Length: 76 hours (2 weeks).

Dates: January 1986-November 1986.

Objective: To train maintenance personnel to troubleshoot, repair, and perform preventive maintenance on Models 140/141 (MPLSM).

Instruction: Major topics covered in the course are operating principles; component assembly identification, location, and function; alignment and adjustment procedures; repair and parts replacement; analysis and correction of electrical and mechanical equipment malfunctions; and preventive maintenance practices of the Models 140/141 Multi-Position Letter-Sorter Machines.

Credit Recommendation: In the vocational certificate category, 3 semester hours in Electromechanical Troubleshooting (6/86).

Optical Character Reader I (55656-01)

Location: Technical Training Center, Norman, OK.

Length: 640 hours (16 weeks), residential, 30 hours of lecture/discussion and 10 hours of laboratory per week.

Dates: July 1971-June 1979.

Objective: To prepare electronic technicians to perform preventive and corrective maintenance on the computer-assisted Optical Character Reader I by providing the necessary theoretical background.

Instruction: Major topics covered in the course are a unit-by-unit analysis of the logical circuitry required for the Optical Character Reader to perform its functions. The latest modifications to the system (including bar code reader) are incorporated. Covers the relationship of all the separate component units and their integration into a complete system, including the OCR, the line printer, the magnetic tape memory system, channel multiplexers, the PDP8-L computer, and interface control circuits.

Credit Recommendation: In the lower division baccalaureate/associate degree category, 1 semester hour in Physics, and in the upper division baccalaureate degree category, 3 semester hours in Computer Technology and 5 semester hours in Computer Peripheral Devices (9/77).

Optical Character Reader I: On-Site Maintenance Certification Program (55656-02)

Location: Each postal facility utilizing the Optical Character Reader.

Length: 183 hours (minimum of 3 months), approximately 20 hours of laboratory per week.

Dates: July 1971-June 1979.

Objective: To provide the electronic technician with supplemental training in the troubleshooting and repair skills necessary to maintain and repair the computer-assisted Optical Character Reader.

Instruction: Major topics covered in the course are theoretical and hands-on training in preventive and corrective maintenance and troubleshooting techniques for use with major sections of the Optical Character Reader, including optical systems, vacuum systems, mechanical systems, electronic recognition systems, peripheral devices, and associated interfaces. Also covers the PDP8-L computer.

Credit Recommendation: In the lower division baccalaureate/associate degree category, 2 semester hours in Electromechanical Laboratory (9/77) (4/84).

Perimeter Office Fleet Maintenance (55638-11) (Formerly Perimeter Office Fleet Maintenance [55638-00], [55638-10], and [55638-05])

Location: Technical Training Center, Norman, OK.

Length: 80 hours (9 days), residential, 28 hours of lecture and 12 hours of laboratory/workshop per week.

Dates: *Version 1:* February 1970-November 1988; *Version 2:* December 1988-Present.

Objective: To provide knowledge of the objectives of a vehicle maintenance program with emphasis on procedure relating to reports and records, inspecting vehicles, and administering maintenance programs.

Instruction: Major topics covered in the course are vehicle maintenance handbooks, vehicle operations handbooks, position description handbooks, maintenance bulletins, modification orders, contract work orders, and contract maintenance. Also covers scheduled and repair maintenance, records and reports, and safety.

Credit Recommendation: In the lower division baccalaureate/associate degree category, 2 semester hours in Automotive Service Management, Automotive Technology, or Transportation Technology (9/77) (4/84).

Pitney-Bowes OCR/CS Maintenance Training (55660-28)

Location: Technical Training Center, Norman, OK.

Length: 228 hours (6 weeks).

Dates: September 1986-September 1994.

Objective: To teach the student proficiency-level operation maintenance and repair procedures for the Pitney-Bowes Character Reader/Channel Sorter (OCR/CS).

Learning Outcome: Upon successful completion of this course, the student will be able to understand the overall system operation, including the mechanical, electrical, electronic, and basic computer components of the system; be able to perform preventive maintenance and system adjustment/adjustment procedures on subsystems, including transport, bar code reader, and scanning units; and be able to locate, isolate, and repair system faults.

Instruction: Major topics covered in the course are overall system operation and safety aspects, the control panel operations, and transporter, bar code reader, and printer unit operation and maintenance. The course also covers repair and maintenance of electrical, mechanical, electronic, and computerized optical components at the PC board level, covering general information on the character recognition and computer interpretation of printed matter. Methods of instruction include lecture and laboratory exercises on the Pitney-Bowes OCR/CS System.

Credit Recommendation: In the lower division baccalaureate/associate degree category, 3 semester hours in Digital Electronic Systems (9/89).

Postal Scales (55605-01)

Location: Technical Training Center, Norman, OK.

Length: 40 hours (1 week), residential, 15 hours of lecture and 25 hours of laboratory/workshop.

Dates: September 1977-September 1986.

Objective: To develop skill in testing, adjusting, preventive maintenance, troubleshooting, analysis, and repair maintenance of mechanical scales.

Instruction: Major topics covered in the course are testing, adjusting, troubleshooting, preventive maintenance, and repair maintenance of such scales as Pitney Bowes, Pennsylvania, and Triner.

Credit Recommendation: In the vocational certificate category, 1 semester hour in Mechanical Devices (9/77) (4/84).

Postal Source Data System On-Site Maintenance Certification Program (55641-02)

Location: Each postal facility utilizing the Postal Service Data Source.

Length: 240 hours; self-paced.

Dates: May 1973-April 1984.

Objective: To provide the electronic technician with supplemental training in the diagnostic and repair skills necessary to maintain and repair in the Postal Source Data System.

Instruction: Major topics covered in the course are comprehensive theoretical and practical training in troubleshooting and repair of the following types of electronic circuits: relays, digital logic, communications, programming logic, and special purpose circuits. The technician must perform preventive maintenance, adjustment, and repair of the following mechanical devices: drive belts, gears, chains, cam shafts, clutches, brakes, and associated linkages.

Credit Recommendation: In the upper division baccalaureate degree category, 2 semester hours in Systems Troubleshooting and Maintenance Laboratory (9/77) (4/84).

Postal Source Data Systems (55641-01)

Location: Technical Training Center, Norman, OK.

Length: 520 hours (13 weeks).

Dates: *Version 1:* July 1972-May 1986; *Version 2:* June 1986-September 1988.

Objective: To provide students with knowledge and techniques required to maintain the PSDS system.

Instruction: Major topics covered in the course are familiarization with the entire system, including input, output, and control devices; decimal, binary, and octal number systems, including the manipulation of the three systems and application of the principles to the system; electrical, mechanical, electromechanical, and electronic theory in detail sufficient for effective maintenance of the devices involved; theory of operation of input, output, and control devices; study and application of necessary test equipment; corrective maintenance procedures, based on symptom analysis and effective troubleshooting techniques; and routine preventive maintenance procedures.

Credit Recommendation: *Version 1:* In the lower division baccalaureate/associate degree category, 3 semester hours in Electromechanical Technology, 6 semester hours in Computer System Analysis, and 3 semester hours in Electronic and Electromechanical Fundamentals (12/74) (3/81). *Version 2:* In the lower division baccalaureate/associate degree category, 3 semester hours in Electromechanical Theory and 6 semester hours in Computer System Analysis (6/86).

Process Control System Basic (55670-36) (Formerly Basic Process Control System [55670-10])

Location: Technical Training Center, Norman, OK.

Length: *Version 1:* 480 hours (12 weeks); *Version 2:* 360 hours (9 weeks).

Dates: *Version 1:* January 1981-March 1985; *Version 2:* July 1985-March 1986.

Objective: To prepare qualified personnel to interact with a computer and its peripherals and to program in assembly language, use diagnostic routines, and repair peripheral equipment.

Instruction: Major topics covered in the course are an introduction to computers with assembly language programming, computer architecture, and peripherals. Major topics covered in the course are flowcharting, developing logic commands, machine language programming, and use of an editor-assembler in program development. Disk systems, magnetic tape systems, and line printers are covered. Lecture, discussion, and laboratory are used.

Credit Recommendation: In the upper division baccalaureate degree category, 3 semester hours in Introduction to Computers, and in the lower division baccalaureate/associate degree category, 3 semester hours in Computer Circuit Diagnostics and Repair or Electromech-anical Technology (3/81).

Process Control System Line Printer (55670-31)

Location: Technical Training Center, Norman, OK.

Length: 120 hours (3 weeks).

Dates: *Version 1:* April 1986-May 1986; *Version 2:* June 1986-June 1990.

Objective: To provide electronic technicians with an in-depth understanding of functional operations, logic circuitry, diagnostic routines, and corrective maintenance procedures for the DPC Model V-306 Line Printer and interface electronics.

Instruction: Major topics covered in the course are electromechanical, electrical, and digital concepts pertinent to the V-306 Line Printer. Half the student's time is spent in lecture-discussion and half is spent in laboratory and directed study.

Credit Recommendation: *Version 1:* In the lower division baccalaureate/associate degree category, 3 semester hours in Electromechanical Technology (3/81). *Version 2:* In the lower division baccalaureate/associate degree category, 2 semester hours in Electromechanical Technology (6/86).

Process Control System Magnetic Tape Unit (55670-32)

Location: Technical Training Center, Norman, OK.

Length: 120 hours (3 weeks).

Dates: May 1978-June 1989.

Objective: To provide electronic technicians with an in-depth understanding of functional operations, logic circuitry, and diagnostic and maintenance techniques for the Wangco Model 1025 magnetic tape unit.

Instruction: Major topics covered in the course are specifics of the Wangco magnetic tape unit Model1025 using lecture-discussion and laboratory. The material is presented in a format broad enough to be of general value to an electromechanical technician maintaining complex computer peripheral equipment. Lecture, discussion, laboratory, and directed study time are used.

Credit Recommendation: In the lower division baccalaureate/associate degree category, 1 semester hour in Computer Peripheral Maintenance or Electromechanical Equipment (3/81). *Prerequisite:* Basic Process Control System (55670-10).

Process Control System Mail Processing Peripherals (55670-34)

Location: Technical Training Center, Norman, OK.

Length: 160 hours (4 weeks).

Dates: May 1981-July 1987.

Objective: To provide electronic technicians with an understanding of functional operations, logic circuitry, diagnostic routines, and corrective maintenance procedures for mail processing equipment, PCS interface, and peripherals.

Instruction: Major topics covered in the course are operating theory, logic circuit analysis, component function and location, troubleshooting techniques, corrective maintenance, and preventive maintenance routines. Methods of instruction include lecture, discussion, laboratory, and directed self-study.

Credit Recommendation: In the lower division baccalaureate/associate degree category, 2 semester hours in Electromechanical Technology (3/81).

Process Control System NOVA 800 (55670-30)

Location: Technical Training Center, Norman, OK.

Length: 240 hours (6 weeks).

Dates: July 1978-May 1985.

Objective: To provide electronic technicians with an in-depth understanding of functional operations and logic circuitry associated with the NOVA 800 computer, Centronics 761 printer, and high-speed paper tape reader.

Instruction: Major topics covered in the course are detailed hardware and logic analysis for the NOVA 800 computer. Includes the timing generator, core memory, CPU, I/O, and programmed data channels. Instruction on the Centronics 761 printer and high-speed paper tape reader covers principles of operation, logic analysis, controller software, and corrective maintenance. Lecture, discussion, laboratory, and directed study time are used.

Credit Recommendation: In the upper division baccalaureate degree category, 3 semester hours in Computer Maintenance Technology (3/81). *Prerequisite:* Basic Process Control System (55670-10).

Security Equipment (55606-01)

Location: Technical Training Center, Norman, OK.

Length: 40 hours (1 week), residential, 15 hours of lecture and 25 hours of laboratory/workshop.

Dates: July 1977-September 1986.

Objective: To develop skill in maintenance and repair of combination locks and lock boxes.

Instruction: Major topics covered in the course are troubleshooting, preventive maintenance, and repair maintenance of safe and vault combination locks and lock boxes.

Credit Recommendation: In the vocational certificate category, 1 semester hour in Maintenance Mechanics or Security (9/77) (4/84).

Self-Service Postal Center Equipment Program (55607-00)

Location: Technical Training Center, Norman, OK.

Length: 264 hours (6.5 weeks).

Dates: July 1977-October 1979.

Objective: To develop skill in troubleshooting, servicing, and repairing of components of a number of independent mechanical and electromechanical systems.

Instruction: Major topics covered in the course are burglar alarms, self-service postal scales, coin handling units and packaging machine, currency coin changer, rejectors dollar bill validators, multicommodity vending machines, multidenominational stamp vending machines, Scribe 906 multidenominational stamp vendor, and GSMC-76 multicommodity vendor.

Credit Recommendation: In the lower division baccalaureate/associate degree category, 5 semester hours in Electromechanical Technology or Mechanical Technology (9/77).

Single-Position Letter-Sorter Machine (55652-00)

Location: Field, Dallas, TX.

Length: *Version 1:* 92 hours (2 weeks, 2 days); *Version 2:* 76 hours (2 weeks).

Dates: *Version 1:* January 1974-January 1984; *Version 2:* February 1984-Present.

Objective: To train technicians responsible for the preventive maintenance, troubleshooting, repair, and installation of digitally controlled electromechanical equipment.

Instruction: Major topics covered in the course are equipment orientation; use of maintenance manuals; system control; signal data flow; logic circuit and mechanical analysis; component assembly, identification, and replacement procedures for the single-position letter-sorter machine.

Credit Recommendation: In the lower division baccalaureate/associate degree category, 1 semester hour in Digital Systems and 1 semester hour in Electromechanical Systems (9/77) (4/84). *Prerequisite*: Satisfactory completion of Introduction to Burroughs Single Position LSM (56559-00).

Teletype Maintenance (55685-00)

Location: Technical Training Center, Norman, OK.

Length: 80 hours (2 weeks).

Dates: April 1979-September 1983.

Objective: To teach students preventive maintenance and corrective repair of Teletype Model 33 terminals.

Instruction: Major topics covered in the course are theory followed by extensive hands-on laboratory work with the Teletype Model 33. Electrical and mechanical operation, adjustments, and maintenance of the four major units of the Model 33—the typing unit, the keyboard, the call control unit, and the tape punch/reader. Course entails complete disassembly and reassembly of the terminal. Lecture, discussion, and laboratory are used.

Credit Recommendation: In the vocational certificate category, 2 semester hours in Basic Electromechanics or Teletype Repair (3/81).

Vehicle Maintenance Analysis and Diagnosis (55628-00) (Formerly Vehicle Maintenance Analyst)

Location: Technical Training Center, Norman, OK.

Length: 80 hours (2 weeks), residential, 24 hours of lecture and 16 hours of laboratory per week.

Dates: September 1970-April 1989.

Objective: To provide the student with an understanding of the duties and responsibilities in the technical areas of vehicle inspection, maintenance analysis, corrective measures, and work interpretation, and to introduce the proper methods of preparing detailed directive work orders.

Instruction: Major topics covered in the course are vehicle maintenance records; manufacturers' publications; headquarters' maintenance bulletins; modification work orders; cost and safety; preparing and analyzing work orders; use of automotive diagnostic test equipment; troubleshooting techniques; methods of analyzing vehicles; repair procedures; interim maintenance programs; the vehicle maintenance analyst's duties, responsibilities, and working relationships; the organization structure of vehicle maintenance.

Credit Recommendation: In the lower division baccalaureate/associate degree category, 2 semester hours in Automotive Technology or Transportation Technology (9/77) (4/84).

Vehicle Maintenance Facility Control (55634-00)

Location: Technical Training Center, Norman, OK.

Length: 80 hours (2 weeks), residential, 25 hours of lecture/discussion and 15 hours of laboratory per week.

Dates: February 1971-September 1985.

Objective: To provide the student with an understanding of a vehicle maintenance facility's operating policies and procedures and to develop skills in the application of these procedures to daily operations.

Instruction: Major topics covered in the course are topics related to the operation of a vehicle maintenance facility, emphasizing the efficient application of management techniques to manpower control; problem identification and solving; stockroom control; and fleet maintenance record and report use; shop safety; fleet-oriented programs.

Credit Recommendation: In the lower division baccalaureate/associate degree category, or in the upper division baccalaureate degree category, 3 semester hours in Automotive Service Management,

Automotive Technology, or Transportation Technology (9/77) (4/84).

Vehicle Maintenance Facility Utilization (55633-00)

Location: Technical Training Center, Norman, OK.

Length: 80 hours (2 weeks), residential, 25 hours of lecture/discussion and 15 hours of laboratory/workshop per week.

Dates: September 1970-October 1985.

Objective: To provide participants with techniques for a vehicle maintenance facility, emphasizing selection of appropriate corrective action to obtain maximum utilization of space, parts, personnel, and equipment.

Instruction: Major topics covered in the course are work evaluation; repair order analysis; ratio of parts costs to labor costs; estimating; job analysis; vehicle maintenance programs; and communication skills.

Credit Recommendation: In the lower division baccalaureate/associate degree category or in the upper division baccalaureate degree category, 3 semester hours in Automotive Service Management, Automotive Technology, and Transportation Technology (9/77) (4/84).

ZIP-Mail Translator (55655-05) (Formerly ZIP-Mail Translator [55655-01])

Location: Technical Training Center, Norman, OK.

Length: 280 hours (7 weeks).

Dates: August 1970-September 1987.

Objective: To train students to troubleshoot, repair, and perform preventive maintenance on the ZIP-mail translator system of the letter-sorter machine.

Instruction: Major topics covered in the course are component assembly identification, location, and function; repair and parts replacement; troubleshooting analysis techniques; adjustment, alignment, and preventive maintenance procedures. Teaches the proper use of appropriate technical manuals and data, diagnostic test equipment, and regular and special tools.

Credit Recommendation: In the lower division baccalaureate/associate degree category, 3 semester hours in Data Processing System Analysis and 3 semester hours in Computer Maintenance Technology, Data Processing Technology, or Electronics Technology (12/74) (3/81).

U.S. Postal Service Purchasing and Materials

Purchasing and Materials is responsible for buying and supplying one of the largest service organizations in the world. Postal Service purchasing policies and procedures are a mix of the best of public and private buying practices. This policy retains the best aspects of the Federal procurement system while giving contracting officers the discretion of using market awareness and business judgment when awarding contracts.

The U.S. Postal Service is headquartered in Washington, DC. Purchasing and Materials awards and manages nationwide and large-dollar value contracts. Field offices are strategically placed to provide field customer support. The material management function manages the acquisition, stocking, and distribution of all postal-specific repair parts, supplies, and equipment; operates three material distribution centers totaling more than 1.7 million square feet; and distributes more than 23,000 line items (worth $200 million) to some 38,000 internal customers a year.

Professional Development staff is a small group of professionals dedicated to helping Purchasing and Materials to achieve its goals and objectives by ensuring that contracting professionals have the necessary knowledge, skills, and abilities to perform at the highest professional standards. The mission of Professional Development is to coordinate the planning, development, and implementation of Purchasing and Materials functional training and professional development programs for purchasing and materiel management professionals system wide. Core functions include workforce development and the design and delivery of high-quality, cost-effective instructional systems and other behavioral interventions designed to help optimize purchasing performance, productivity, and quality of purchasing actions. Professional development is responsible for contracting officer certification and maintains a contracting officer database to ensure that they have a highly effective cadre of contracting officers.

A student population of approximately 1200 employees from Postal Service Headquarters and affiliated field units throughout the country attend training at two locations. While students generally come from two major functional areas, purchasing and material management, employees from other organizational functions who have purchasing or materiel management responsibilities also attend their classes. Professional Development sponsors approximately 50-100 individual course offerings within a given fiscal year.

Source of official student records: Registry of Credit Recommendations, American Council on Education, One Dupont Circle, Washington, DC 20036-1193 or Program Manager, Professional Development, Policies, Planning, and Diversity, U.S. Postal Service, 475 L'Enfant Plaza SW, Room 4130, Washington, DC 20260-6201.

Additional information about the courses: College Credit Recommendation Service, American Council on Education, One Dupont Circle, Washington, DC 20036-1193.

Advanced Contract Administration (34280-00)

Location: Various locations.

Length: 36 hours (1 week).

Dates: January 1987-November 1996.

Objective: To provide insight into exceptions to the general rules of contract administration.

Learning Outcome: Upon successful completion of this course, the student will be able to demonstrate knowledge of the essential elements of a contract and of contract administration; identify contract terms and conditions; prepare a contract administration plan; and apply knowledge of rules and circumstances associated with post-award contract administration.

Instruction: Major topics covered in the course are elements of a contract, authority to contract, contract compliance, contract administration, planning, evaluation of performance, changes, determinations, claims, and acceptance. Methods of instruction include lecture, discussion, classroom exercises, case studies, and examinations.

Credit Recommendation: In the upper division baccalaureate degree category, 1 semester hour in Business Administration, Public Administration, Purchasing, or Procurement Management (5/94).

Advanced Purchasing (31270-00)

Location: Potomac, MD and Norman, OK.

Length: 36 hours (1week).

Dates: January 1997-Present.

Objective: To provide students with an understanding of all the steps involved in forming a purchase contract using custom buying methods from purchase planning through contract award.

Learning Outcome: Upon successful completion of this course, the student will be able to discuss purchasing strategies and practices; form purchasing teams; draft complex purchase plans; hold contract award sessions; discuss contract administration and dispute resolution issues; conduct closeout; and apply standards of ethical conduct to purchasing situations.

Instruction: Major topics covered in this course are individual purchase plans; developing a solicitation; proposal evaluation; pre-award, contract award and notification; debriefing; protests; and ethics. Methods of instruction include lecture, discussion, outside reading, role playing, small group activities, and a final examination.

Credit Recommendation: In the lower division baccalaureate/associate degree or upper division baccalaureate degree category, 3 semester hours in Public Administration, Procurement, or Business Administration (4/97). **NOTE:** Students must have successfully completed: Principles of Purchasing (34260-00) or (34560-00) or Fundamentals of Purchasing: Theory and Practice (34268-00) to receive credit for this course.

Basic Contract Administration (34264-00)

Location: Various locations.

Length: *Version 1*: 36 hours (1 week); *Version 2*: 36 hours plus 8 hours outside reading (1 week).

Dates: *Version 1:* January 1987-August 1995; *Version 2:* September 1995-Present.

Objective: To provide knowledge of post-award management practices necessary for oversight and administration of contractor performance.

Learning Outcome: *Version 1:* Upon successful completion of this course, the student will be able to observe and direct start-up activities to initiate new contracts, conduct continuing surveillance of contractor activity, interpret contract documents, process invoices, modify contract procedures, monitor progress of contractors, initiate actions to overcome delays, and determine actions needed to effect terminations. *Version 2:* Upon successful completion of this course, the student will be able to develop a plan for monitoring a specific contract and provide notice of individual responsibilities; conduct post award orientation of postal service contractors; monitor contract performance, costs, and modifications; and close out contracts.

Instruction: *Version 1:* Major topics covered in the course are contract interpretation, post-award orientation, monitoring contract progress, quality inspection and acceptance, subcontract reviews, contract change process, constructional changes, and financial administration and payment. Methods of instruction include lecture, discussion, classroom exercises, case studies, videotapes, handouts, and examinations. *Version 2:* Major topics covered in the course are procurement planning, contract interpretation, post-award activities; performance monitoring, modifications and changes, closeouts, and contractor remedies. Methods of instruction include lecture, discussion, classroom exercises, case studies, videotapes, handouts and examinations.

Credit Recommendation: *Version 1:* In the upper division baccalaureate degree category, 1 semester hour in Business Administration, Public Administration, Purchasing, or Procurement Management (5/94). *Version 2:* In the upper division baccalaureate category, 2 semester hours in Business Administration, Public Administration, Purchasing, or Procurement Management (9/95). **NOTE:** Students must have successfully completed Principles of Purchasing (34260-00) or (34560-00) to receive credit for this course (5/94).

Commercial Purchasing (34269-00)

Location: Potomac, MD and Norman OK.

Length: 36 hours (1 week).

Dates: December 1996-Present.

Objective: To provide students with knowledge of the steps involved in forming a contract with commercial vendors, from purchase planning through contract award.

Learning Outcome: Upon successful completion of this course, the student will be able to define purchasing from commercial vendors; the components, and phases of the process; describe contract administration, dispute resolution, market research, prequalification, solicitation, proposal development, compliance monitoring, and contract termination in a commercial purchasing environment.

Instruction: Major topics covered in this course are overview of the commercial purchasing process; market research; purchase planning; prequalification; preparing a commercial solicitation; evaluating proposals and awarding a contract; debriefings and protests; ethics. Methods of instruction include lecture, discussion, outside readings, and a final examination.

Credit Recommendation: In the upper division baccalaureate degree category, 2 semester hours in Public Administration, Procurement, or Business Administration (4/97). **NOTE:** Students must have successfully completed: Principles of Purchasing (34260-00) or (34560-00) or Fundamentals of Purchasing: Theory and Practice (34268-00) to receive credit for this course.

Contract Administration (34266-00)

Location: Potomac MD, Norman OK, and other sites.

Length: 36 hours plus 8 hours outside reading (1 week).

Dates: April 1997-Present.

Objective: To provide understanding of the basic steps in the contract administration process, from initial planning through contract closeout, including claims, disputes and contract modification.

Learning Outcome: Upon successful completion of this course, the student will be able to identify essential elements of a contract; develop a contract administration plan; provide oversight and administration of contractor performance; monitor contract performance, cost and modification; and closeout.

Instruction: Major topics covered in the course are post-award orientation; contracting language; performance monitoring; quality assurance; payments and financing; contract termination; contract claims and disputes; contract modifications; contract closeouts; and fraud, debarment and ethics. Methods of instruction include lecture, discussion, classroom exercises, case studies, learner presentations, outside reading, and homework assignments. Methods of evaluating learning outcomes include class participation and a proctored final examination.

Credit Recommendation: In the upper division baccalaureate degree category, 3 semester hours in Business Administration, Public Administration, Procurement, or Purchasing (11/97). **NOTE:** Students must have successfully completed Fundamentals of Purchasing (34268-00) and Commercial Purchasing (34269-00) to receive credit for this course.

Contract Formation (34263-00)

Location: Various locations.

Length: *Version 1:* 76 hours (2 weeks); *Version 2:* 80 hours plus outside reading (2 weeks).

Dates: September 1986-November 1996.

Objective: To provide an understanding of steps involved in forming a contract, from purchase planning through contract award.

Learning Outcome: *Version 1:* Upon successful completion of this course, the student will be able to justify awards on a sole-source basis when appropriate; evaluate proposals, negotiate necessary revisions, and develop a sound contract; determine contract types that most appropriately allocate the risk performance and provide incentives for contractor performance; determine what, if any, labor laws and regulations apply; prepare all required documentation and wage related determinations prior to solicitation; and determine whether direct costs for labor and materials, indirect costs, and profit or fees are proper and reasonable. *Version 2:* Upon successful completion of this course, the student will be able to plan procurements; develop and issue solicitations; and evaluate and award contracts.

Instruction: *Version 1:* Major topics covered in the course are advance planning, requisition reviewing, and selecting appropriate contract type; developing and implementing individual purchase plans; developing solicitation documents; communicating with offerer, establishing competitive range, and requesting last and final range; selecting contractor and awarding documentation; and handling protest and freedom of information requests. *Version 2:* Major topics covered in the course are market research, procurement planning, developing and issuing solicitations, monitoring the solicitation process, evaluating results, negotiating contracts, conducting debriefings, and handling contractor remedies. Methods of instruction include lecture, discussion, classroom exercises, case studies, role playing, videotapes, and final examination.

Credit Recommendation: *Version 1:* In the upper division baccalaureate degree category, 2 semester hours in Business Administration, Public Administration, Purchasing, or Procurement Management (5/94). *Version 2:* In the upper division baccalaureate degree category, 3 semester hours in Business Administration, Public Administration, Purchasing, or Procurement Management (9/95).

Contract Law (34284-00)

Location: Potomac MD, Norman OK, and other sites.

Length: *Version 1:* 36 hours (1 week); *Version 2:* 36 hours plus 8 hours outside reading (1 week).

Dates: January 1987-Present.

Objective: To provide understanding of the legal aspects of contracting.

Learning Outcome: *Version 1:* Upon successful completion of this course, the student will be able to understand the constitutional origin of contracting authority, the role of Congress, and the various legal aspects of the purchasing process. *Version 2:* Upon successful completion of this course, the student will be able to understand the origin of contract law, the role of Congress, and the various legal aspects of the purchasing process in the federal government and commercial sector.

Instruction: *Version 1:* Major topics covered in the course are federal government authority and role in procurement, procurement systems, contracts, inspection, modification, terminations, claims, and remedies. Methods of instruction include lecture, discussion, classroom exercises, case studies and examinations. *Version 2:* Major topics covered in the course are federal government authority and role in procurement; procurement systems; contracts; policies and procedures; inspection, modification, terminations, claims and remedies of contracts; contractor's role; bidding process; postal service policy; and the overall laws that guide the contracting industry. Methods of instruction include lecture, discussion, classroom exercises, case studies, participation and a proctored final examination.

Credit Recommendation: *Version 1:* In the upper division baccalaureate degree category or in the graduate degree category, 1 semester hour in Business Administration, Public Administration, Purchasing or Procurement Management (5/94). **NOTE:** Students must have successfully completed Principles of Purchasing (34260-00) or (34560-00) and Contract Formation (34263-00) to receive credit for this course. *Version 2:* In the lower division baccalaureate/associate degree category or in the upper division baccalaureate degree category, 3 semester hours in Business Law or Business Administration (11/97). **NOTE:** Students must have successfully completed Fundamentals of Purchasing (34268-00), Commercial Purchasing (34269-00), and Contract Administration (34266-00) to receive credit for this course.

Contracting Officer's Representative

Location: Various locations.

Length: 28 hours (35 days).

Dates: September 1995-Present.

Objective: To provide an overview of the roles and responsibilities of a contracting officer's representative, including what the representative should do in all phases of the purchasing process from requirements to contract close-out.

Learning Outcome: Upon successful completion of this course, contracting officer representatives will be able to understand and use fundamental principles involved in the purchasing process, including contract formation and administration.

Instruction: Major topics covered in the course are roles and responsibilities of the contracting officer's representative, basic purchasing principles and practices, ethical practices, contract formation procedures, types of contracts, source selection, contract administration, contract changes, quality assurance, and contract closeout. Methods of instruction include lecture, discussion, classroom exercises, and a final examination.

Credit Recommendation: In the lower division baccalaureate/associate degree category or in the upper division baccalaureate category, 1 semester hour in Acquisition Management, Business Administration, Procurement, Public Administration, or Purchasing (9/95).

Cost and Price Analysis (Price Analysis) (34285-00)

Location: Potomac MD, Norman OK, and other sites.

Length: *Version 1:* 35 hours (1 week); *Version 2:* 36 hours plus 8 hours outside reading (1 week).

Dates: January 1992-Present.

Objective: To provide an overview of cost and price analysis and an understanding of the relationship between these concepts and the concept of "best value".

Learning Outcome: Upon successful completion of this course, the student will be able to determine the fair and reasonable price based on analysis and comparison of pricing factors; and display an understanding of price analysis, cost analysis, market-based pricing, and performance price analysis.

Instruction: *Version 1:* Major topics covered in the course are procurement planning and pricing, price theory, techniques of price analysis, cost analysis, profit analysis, documentation of negotiations, and best value analysis techniques. Methods of instruction include lecture, discussion, student presentations, classroom projects, and examinations. *Version 2:* Major topics covered in the course are procurement planning and pricing, price theory, price analysis, indexing, pricing data, cost analysis, and best value analysis techniques. Methods of instruction include lecture, discussion, student presentations, case analysis, outside reading and exercises, classroom projects, and a proctored final examination.

Credit Recommendation: *Version 1:* In the upper division baccalaureate degree category, 1 semester hour in Business Administration, Public Administration, Purchasing, or Procurement Management (5/94). **NOTE:** Students must have successfully completed Principles of Purchasing (34260-00) or (34560-00) and Contract Formation (34262-00) to receive credit for this course. *Version 2:* In the upper division baccalaureate degree category, 2 semester hours in Business Administration, Purchasing, or Procurement Management (11/97). **NOTE:** Students must have successfully completed Fundamentals of Purchasing (34268-00), Commercial Purchasing (34269-00), and Contract Administration (34266-00) to receive credit for this course.

Fundamentals of USPS Purchasing (Fundamentals of Purchasing: Theory and Practice)

Location: Potomac MD and Norman OK.

Length: 36 hours (1 week).

Dates: January 1997-Present.

Objective: To provide an overview of the Postal Service buying process with emphasis on the use of the USPS Purchasing Manual.

Learning Outcome: Upon successful completion of this course, the student will be able to define purchasing terminology and concepts; explain USPS organizational structure, and the roles of the contract ing officer and purchasing team; select appropriate market research methods; discuss ethical issues and standards; and identify elements of a contract and the factors to be considered in prequalification, solicitation, proposal development, compliance monitoring, and contract termination.

Instruction: Major topics covered in this course are overview of USPS purchasing process including planning considerations; market research; contracts; supplier selection, qualification and solicitations; evaluation of proposals; contract award, administration, modification, and termination processes; and purchasing ethics. Methods of instruction include lecture, discussion, outside readings, activities, and a final examination.

Credit Recommendation: In the lower division baccalaureate/associate or upper division baccalaureate degree category, 2 semester hours in Public Administration,

Procurement, or Business Administration (4/97).

Introduction to Procurement for Project Officers (34267)

Location: Various locations.
Length: 28 hours (1 week).
Dates: January 1987-August 1995.
Objective: To provide an understanding of the purchasing process.
Learning Outcome: Upon successful completion of this course, the student will be able to demonstrate understanding of the basic principles of contract formation and administration.
Instruction: Major topics covered in the course are purchasing systems, including planning, protests, terminations, disputes, acceptance and payment, quality assurance, modifications, COR duties, ethical conduct, and contract fraud. Methods of instruction include lecture, discussion, classroom exercises, case studies, and final examination.
Credit Recommendation: In the upper division baccalaureate degree category, 1 semester hour in Business Administration, Public Administration, Purchasing, or Procurement Management (5/94).

Inventory Management (34273-00)

Location: Various locations.
Length: 68 hours (2 weeks).
Dates: January 1987-Present.
Objective: To provide knowledge of basic inventory management principles and practices applicable to the USPS.
Learning Outcome: Upon successful completion of this course, the student will be able to demonstrate understanding of USPS inventory management system policies, procedures, and organization, and its relationship to other key purchasing functions; and utilize basic management concepts including the requirements stack, optimum order quantity, forecasting systems, USPS reports, and effectiveness of inventory management under USPS standards.
Instruction: Major topics covered in the course are why inventories exist, USPS structure, automated systems, functions of inventory management, requirements determination, safety levels, basic math review, EOQ, forecasting, and reparables planning and tracking. Methods of instruction include lecture, discussion, classroom exercises, case studies, role playing, and final examination.
Credit Recommendation: In the upper division baccalaureate degree category, 2 semester hour in Business Administration, Public Administration, Purchasing, or Procurement Management (5/94). **NOTE**: Students may not receive credit for this course and Inventory Management Self-Study (34556-00).

Inventory Management Self-Study (34556-00)

Location: Correspondence.
Length: 79 estimated hours (2-7 units).
Dates: November 1993-August 1997.
Objective: To provide knowledge of basic inventory management principles and practices applicable to the USPS.
Learning Outcome: Upon successful completion of this course, the student will be able to demonstrate understanding of USPS inventory management system policies, procedures, and organization, and its relationship to other key purchasing functions; to utilize basic management concepts including the requirements stack, optimum order quantity, forecasting systems, USPS reports, and effectiveness of inventory management under USPS standards.
Instruction: Major topics covered in the course are why inventories exist, USPS structure, automated systems, functions of inventory management, requirements determination, safety levels, basic math review, EOQ, forecasting, and reparables planning and tracking. Methods of instruction include independent study by correspondence and final examination.
Credit Recommendation: In the upper division baccalaureate degree category, 2 semester hours in Business Administration, Public Administration, Purchasing, or Procurement Management (5/94). **NOTE**: Students may not receive credit for this course and Inventory Management (34273-00).

Materiel Accountability and Control (34282-00)

Location: Various locations.
Length: 36 hours (1 week).
Dates: July 1988-Present.
Objective: To provide basic concepts of materiel accountability and control.
Learning Outcome: Upon successful completion of this course, the student will be able to relate the concepts of accountability and control to materiel management; determine when different levels of control and location audits are needed; conduct location audits and physical inventories; identify critical points in the physical distribution process at which control and accountability may be lost; and assess the performance of materiel management functions.
Instruction: Major topics covered in the course are control and accountability and the need for these concepts; requirements planning; MAO responsibilities, attributes, and interactions; inventory accuracy requirements; conducting location audits; physical distribution, automated data processing system, and types of controls; and review and evaluation of system performance. Methods of instruction include lecture, discussion, case studies, role playing, videotapes, and examinations.
Credit Recommendation: In the upper division baccalaureate degree category, 1 semester hour in Business Administration, Public Administration, Purchasing, or Procurement Management (5/94).

Materiel Management Principles and Practices (3426l-00)

Location: Various locations.
Length: 76 hours (2 weeks).
Dates: February 1987-Present.
Objective: To provide an understanding of materiel management including requirements planning, warehousing, distribution, and inventory.
Learning Outcome: Upon successful completion of this course, the student will be able to understand and operate within the USPS materiel management system and demonstrate skill in item identification, requirements planning, inventory management, property management using the EXSEL system, preparation of documents, and forecasting on a fiscal year basis.
Instruction: Major topics covered in the course are the USPS materiel management system, financial and budget implications of materiel management, performance measurement and review, provisioning and cataloging, procurement process overview, inventory management principles, requisition preparation, materiel disposition, ethics and standards of conduct, and managing distribution of materiel. Methods of instruction include lecture, discussion, classroom exercises, case studies, and final examination.
Credit Recommendation: In the upper division baccalaureate degree category, 2 semester hours in Business Administration, Public Administration, Purchasing, Procurement Management, or Logistics Management (5/94).

Negotiation Strategies and Techniques (3428l-00)

Location: Various locations.

Length: *Version 1*: 36 hours (1 week); *Version 2*: 36 hours plus 8 hours outside reading (1 week).

Dates: *Version 1:* January 1987-September 1994; *Version 2:* October 1994-Present.

Objective: *Version 1:* To provide methodology that can be applied to the negotiation process, emphasizing the relationship between theory and practice. *Version 2:* To provide participants with a practical and organized system to apply to the negotiation process emphasizing the relationship between the theory and practice of negotiation.

Learning Outcome: *Version 1:* Upon successful completion of this course, the student will be able to prepare for a negotiation by setting objectives, converting objectives into primary and secondary issues, and prioritizing primary issues; compare and contrast competitive techniques and negotiation stages; identify both competitive and collaborative processes; and identify tension relievers, attitudinal shifts, and emotional postures relevant to managing a negotiation. *Version 2:* Upon successful completion of this course, the student will be able to prepare and conduct a negotiation by setting objectives and converting objectives into primary and secondary issues. Students will be able to identify personal characteristics that relate to their personal negotiation styles and demonstrate their skills in a series of practical exercises.

Instruction: *Version 1:* Major topics covered in the course are developing issues and positions, competitive techniques, analyzing individual negotiation styles, negotiation strategies, attitude shifts and steps of the collaborative negotiator, one-on-one videotaping and preparation, and themes of negotiation (structural analysis and profile development). Methods of instruction include lecture, discussion, classroom exercises, case studies, role playing, videotapes, and examinations. *Version 2:* Major topics covered in the course are preparing for negotiations, conducting negotiations, influencing the other party, and identifying and applying your style to the negotiation process.

Credit Recommendation: *Version 1:* In the upper division baccalaureate category, 1 semester hour in Purchasing or Procurement (5/94). *Version 2:* In the upper division baccalaureate category, 2 semester hours in Business Administration, Public Administration, Purchasing or Procurement (9/95). **NOTE**: Students must have successfully completed Principles of Purchasing (34260-00) or Principles of Purchasing Self-Study (34560-00) and Contract Formation (34263-00) to receive credit for this course (5/94).

Principles of Purchasing (34260-00)

Location: Various locations.

Length: 36 hours (1 week).

Dates: January 1987-November 1996.

Objective: To provide an introduction to purchasing which includes a broad survey of the purchasing process.

Learning Outcome: Upon successful completion of this course, the student will be able to demonstrate an understanding of business practices and ethical standards in the purchasing system.

Instruction: Major topics covered in the course are purchasing systems, contract law, procurement planning, requisition preparation and review, procurement manuals, contract types, price analysis, contract modifications and disputes, inspection and acceptance, and contract fraud. Methods of instruction include lecture, discussion, classroom exercises, and final examination.

Credit Recommendation: In the upper division baccalaureate degree category, 1 semester hour in Purchasing or Procurement Management (5/94). **NOTE**: Students may not receive credit for this course and Principles of Purchasing Self-Study (34560-00).

Principles of Purchasing Self-Study (34560-00)

Location: Correspondence.

Length: 20 lessons.

Dates: March 1994-June 1997.

Objective: To provide an introduction to purchasing which includes a broad survey of the purchasing process.

Learning Outcome: Upon successful completion of this course, the student will be able to demonstrate an understanding of business practices and ethical standards in the purchasing system.

Instruction: Major topics covered in the course are purchasing systems, contract law, procurement planning, requisition preparation and review, procurement manuals, contract types, price analysis, contract modifications and disputes, inspection and acceptance, and contract fraud. Methods of instruction include independent study by correspondence and final examination.

Credit Recommendation: In the upper division baccalaureate degree category, 1 semester hour in Purchasing or Procurement Management (5/94). **NOTE**: Students may not receive credit for this course and Principles of Purchasing (31260-00).

Simplified Purchasing (34262-00)

Location: Various locations.

Length: 36 hours (1 week).

Dates: January 1987-November 1996.

Objective: To provide the ability to place orders with sources of supply established by the Postal Service or the federal government, and to make direct, open-market buys from commercial sources under stipulated dollar amounts, using simplified procedures.

Learning Outcome: Upon successful completion of this course, the student will be able to state the rationals for using established sources and simplified procedures for small purchases; cite basic principals of good buying and explain the importance of their application to even the smallest purchase; identify appropriate sources of supply for most items required by USPS; identify appropriate purchasing procedures for fulfilling small requirements; and determine the most advantageous quotation, taking into account price and other factors.

Instruction: Major topics covered in the course are how USPS obtains what it needs; reviewing requisitions; established sources of supply; ordering from various sources; holding discussions with vendors; establishing and using basic pricing agreement; handling inspection, acceptance, and rejection; and interacting with vendors and offerers. Methods of instruction include lecture, discussion, classroom exercises, case studies, role playing, videotapes, and final examination.

Credit Recommendation: In the upper division baccalaureate degree category, 1 semester hour in Purchasing or Procurement Management (5/94). **NOTE:** Students may not receive credit for this course and Simplified Purchasing Self-Study (34562-00).

Simplified Purchasing Self-Study (34562-00)

Location: Correspondence.

Length: 20 lessons.

Dates: May 1994-June 1997.

Objective: To provide the ability to place orders with sources of supply established by the Postal Service or the federal government, and to make direct, open-market buys from commercial sources under stipulated dollar amounts, using simplified procedures.

Learning Outcome: Upon successful completion of this course, the student will

be able to state the rationale for using established sources and simplified procedures for small purchases; cite basic principals of good buying and explain the importance of their application to even the smallest purchase; identify appropriate sources of supply for most items required by USPS; identify appropriate purchasing procedures for fulfilling small requirements; and determine the most advantageous quotation, taking into account price and other factors.

Instruction: Major topics covered in the course are how USPS obtains what it needs; reviewing requisitions; established sources of supply; ordering from various sources; holding discussions with vendors; establishing and using basic pricing agreement; handling inspection, acceptance, and rejection; and interacting with vendors and offerers. Methods of instruction include independent study by correspondence and final examination.

Credit Recommendation: In the upper division baccalaureate degree category, 1 semester hour in Purchasing or Procurement Management (5/94). **NOTE:** Students may not receive credit for this course and Simplified Purchasing (34262-00).

Storage and Distribution (34274-00)

Location: Various locations.

Length: 36 hours (1 week).

Dates: January 1987-Present.

Objective: To provide understanding of the principles and techniques of storage and distribution.

Learning Outcome: Upon successful completion of this course, the student will be able to apply appropriate techniques to receiving, storage, and issuing materiel including sensitive and hazardous materiel, storage and locator systems, inventories and audits, and transportation.

Instruction: Major topics covered in the course are basic principles; facilities and equipment; receiving, storing, issuing and shipping; transportation management; modern systems; inventory, accuracy, and performance measures; and reparables. Methods of instruction include lecture, discussion, classroom exercises, case studies, field trip, audio-visual aids, and examinations.

Credit Recommendation: In the upper division baccalaureate degree category, 1 semester hour in Business Administration, Public Administration, Purchasing, or Procurement Management (5/94). **NOTE:** Students may not receive credit for this course and Storage and Distribution Self-Study (34555-00).

Storage and Distribution Self-Study (34555-00)

Location: Correspondence.

Length: 2-5 units.

Dates: May 1992-August 1997.

Objective: To provide understanding of the principles and techniques of storage and distribution.

Learning Outcome: Upon successful completion of this course, the student will be able to apply appropriate techniques to receiving, storage, and issuing materiel including sensitive and hazardous materiel, storage and locator systems, inventories and audits, and transportation.

Instruction: Major topics covered in the course are basic principles; facilities and equipment; receiving, storing, issuing and shipping; transportation management; modern systems; inventory, accuracy, and performance measures; and reparables. Methods of instruction include independent study by correspondence and final examination.

Credit Recommendation: In the upper division baccalaureate degree category, 1 semester hour in Business Administration, Public Administration, Purchasing, or Procurement Management (5/94). **NOTE:** Students may not receive credit for this course and Storage and Distribution (34274-00).

Strategic Issues in Purchasing and Materials (34286-00) (Formerly Strategic Issues in Purchasing [34286-00])

Location: Potomac, MD.

Length: *Version 1:* 36 hours (1 week); *Version 2:* 36 hours plus 8 hours outside reading (1 week); *Version 3:* 35 hours (1 week).

Dates: *Version 1:* June 1992-October 1994; *Version 2:* November 1994-January 1996; *Version 3:* January 1996-Present.

Objective: *Version 1:* To provide knowledge of the changing environment of purchasing, techniques to analyze corporate strategies, and techniques to examine traditional purchasing approaches. *Versions 2 and 3:* To provide students with strategic purchasing concepts applicable in purchasing actions throughout the USPS.

Learning Outcome: *Version 1:* Upon successful completion of this course, the student will be able to engage in strategic planning and purchasing; and display an understanding of the total supply management process. *Version 2:* Upon successful completion of this course, the student will be able to formulate purchasing policies and procedures that contribute to reaching the USPS objectives; investigate corporate and product strategies employed elsewhere to identify promising improvements; examine Postal Service purchasing strategies and challenge those in need of change; and devise integrated purchasing approaches with customers and suppliers that work smoothly within the organization. *Version 3:* Upon successful completion of this course, the student will be able to formulate purchasing policies and procedures for USPS objectives; evaluate effective purchasing policies and procedures; examine Postal Service purchasing strategies and challenge those in need of change; and devise appropriate integrated purchasing approaches with customers and suppliers.

Instruction: *Version 1:* Major topics covered in the course are purchasing and USPS strategic planning, scope of purchasing activities, creative thinking, the why and how of partnerships with vendors, internal partnering, and strategic purchasing operations. *Version 2:* Major topics covered in the course are the importance of strategic purchasing, professionalism, supplier management, organization and evolving purchasing strategies. *Version 3:* Major topics covered in the course are the importance of strategic purchasing; policy issues; impact of customer on the perfect purchasing process, improving supplier management; JIT; determining requirements and buying best value; evolving purchasing strategies; competition and socioeconomic considerations; and ethics. Methods of instruction include lecture, discussion, outside readings, exercises, and a final examination.

Credit Recommendation: *Versions 1, 2, and 3:* In the upper division baccalaureate degree category, 2 semester hours in Public Administration, Procurement, or Business Administration (2/97).

U.S. Public Health Service

The Indian Health Service (IHS) is a component of the Public Health Service, Department of Health and Human Services, whose efforts are directed toward improving health services and promoting better health for all Americans. IHS serves the health needs of some 700,000 Indians and Alaska Natives who look to the federal government for assistance. The majority of the Native Americans live on federal Indian reservations in 24 states mostly west of the Mississippi and in villages of Alaska.

The Training Center program was established in 1968 to help achieve the mission of IHS by identifying the training needs of Indian and Alaska Native people and to develop specific training programs designed to meet those needs. Training is offered in the areas of health awareness, health skills, and health management, with emphasis on development of tribal capacity to function independently.

These courses were designed for the community health representatives and other tribal health workers who, as liaisons between the Native American communities, the health facilities, and the tribes, provide health services to their people.

Source of official student records: National CHR Training Office, 3200 Canyon Lake Drive, Rapid City, SD 57002.

Additional information about the courses: College Credit Recommendation Service, American Council on Education, One Dupont Circle, Washington, DC 20036-1193.

Community Health Representative Basic Training Course (CHR 100) Community Health Representative (CHR 100)

Location: Rapid City, SD; field locations in the United States.

Length: *Versions 1 and 2*: 88.5 hours (3 weeks); *Version 3*: 120 hours (3 weeks).

Dates: *Version 1:* May 1977-August 1990; *Version 2:* September 1990-September 1995; *Version 3:* October 1995-Present.

Objective: *Version 1:* To introduce basic concepts of health and disease, communication skills, health planning, and community organization. *Version 2:* To introduce basic concepts of health and disease, communication skills, health planning, and community organization. *Version 3:* To provide community outreach workers with an introduction to basic concepts of health and disease, wellness techniques, and communication skills.

Learning Outcome: *Version 3*: Upon successful completion of this course, the student will be able to understand objectives of personal and community health programs and the role of community health representatives in health education, contracting, and reporting; effectively communicate health education information to individuals and groups and comprehend communications from others; deliver health promotion programs using available resources and identify at-risk clients; introduce concepts of disease prevention based on knowledge of diseases, anatomy, and functions of body systems that help clients seek to be healthy; explain in nontechnical language information about family planning, health, and wellness; assist community members in understanding environmental health issues and maintaining a healthy environment; and introduce concepts and interventions of mental illness, alcoholism, chemical dependency, and dysfunctional families.

Instruction: *Version 1:* Major topics covered in the course are an introduction to the tasks required of community outreach workers as related to community health problems and community resources; basic concepts of health and disease including physical and mental health, nutrition, maternal and child health, dental health, and environmental health; and the skills required in effective communication, first aid, safe driving, and community development. Methods of instruction include lecture, discussion, laboratory, and field trips. *Version 2:* Major topics covered in the course are an introduction to the tasks required of community outreach workers as related to community health problems and community resources; basic concepts of health and disease including physical and mental health, nutrition, maternal and child health, dental health, and environmental health; and the skills required in effective communication, first aid, safe driving, and community development. Methods of instruction include lecture, discussion, laboratory, and field trips. *Version 3:* Major topics covered in the course are community health and wellness, anatomy and physiology, disease concepts, mental health, nutrition, pre-natal and child health, dental health, environmental health, sexually transmitted diseases, basic home health care, and communication skills. Methods of instruction include lecture, discussion, audio-visual aids, individualized and group projects, student presentations, role playing, laboratory and written exercises, and unit examinations.

Credit Recommendation: *Version 1:* In the lower division baccalaureate/associate degree category, 4 semester hours in Allied Health, Community Health, or Public Health (9/78) (9/83) (9/90). *Version 2:* In the lower division baccalaureate/associate degree category, 5 semester hours in Allied Health, Community Health, or Public Health (7/90). *Version 3:* In the lower division baccalaureate/associate degree category, 3 semester hours in Community Health, 1 semester hour in Introduction to Home Health Care, 1 semester hour in Mental Health, and 1 semester hour in Communications Skills (7/95).

U.S. West Learning Systems

The mission of U.S. West Learning Systems is to provide learning opportunities for all employees of U.S. West.

Learning Systems personnel work as a team sharing knowledge to create formal and informal learning opportunities and experiences, recognizing that learning occurs under many circumstances, outside the realm of institutions as well as inside.

Source of official student records: Registry of Credit Recommendations, American Council on Education, One Dupont Circle, Washington, DC 20036-1193 or U.S. West Learning Systems, 3898 South Teller, Lakewood, CO 80235.

Additional information about the courses: College Credit Recommendation Service, American Council on Education, One Dupont Circle, Washington, DC 20036-1193.

Management Courses

Applied New Product Development (4040)

Location: Denver, Seattle, Phoenix, Omaha, Minneapolis.

Length: 20 hours (2 days).

Dates: June 1992-August 1997.

Objective: To give participants the knowledge and skill necessary to develop a new product or service. To understand the issues and challenges facing new product development teams.

Learning Outcome: Upon successful completion of this course, the student will be able to evaluate new ideas and concepts; translate market research into customer needs; screen new product opportunities; understand the difference between product enhancements versus new product development; and set prices for new products and manage product teams.

Instruction: Major topics covered in the course are importance of new products; new product development process; idea generation; concept development; prototype development and performance testing; testing new products in the market; and commercializing new products. Methods of instruction include lecture, case studies, and group exercises.

Credit Recommendation: In the upper division baccalaureate degree category, 1 semester hour in Product Development Process or Marketing Elective (8/92).

Applied Product and Market Management (4030)

Location: Denver, Seattle, Phoenix, Omaha, Minneapolis.

Length: 20 hours (2 days).

Dates: June 1992-August 1997.

Objective: To focus on the participant's understanding and applying the product management process.

Learning Outcome: Upon successful completion of this course, the student will be able to understand the product/market life cycle; understand the product planning process; manage products in different phases of the life cycle; and develop strategies for declining products and services.

Instruction: Major topics covered in the course are product planning; product life cycle; marketing mix; product pricing including cross elasticity; promotion; and channel management. Methods of instruction include lecture, classroom exercises, case studies, and simulation.

Credit Recommendation: In the upper division baccalaureate degree category, 1 semester hour in Product Management or Marketing Elective (8/92).

Basic Telephone Accounting (7470000)

Location: Various locations throughout the United States.

Length: *Version 1*: 32 hours (4 days); *Version 2*: 24 hours (3 days).

Dates: *Version 1:* March 1981-August 1989; *Version 2:* June 1992-Present.

Objective: To provide the student with an understanding of the principles and processes of financial accounting and the ability to apply these processes to telephone accounting.

Learning Outcome: Upon successful completion of this course, the student will be able to recognize and use the basic language of financial accounting; describe the accounting process; describe functional telephone accounting and its relationship to the FCC uniform accounting system; understand concepts and principles of financial accounting; describe balance sheet equation and apply it to accounting transactions; classify and record financial transactions in journal entry form; establish, post, and balance ledger accounts; and prepare ledger accounting reports, worksheets, and workbooks.

Instruction: Major topics covered in the course are balance sheet elements, income statement elements, FCC uniform system of accounts, statement of cash flow, balance sheet equation, the account, journal entries and functional accounting, and the eight-step accounting process. Methods of instruction include lecture, discussion, practical classroom exercises, case studies, pre-course assignments including a pre-test, quizzes, and a self-graded final examination.

Credit Recommendation: In the lower division baccalaureate/associate degree category, 2 semester hours in Accounting (4/94).

Coaching Skills

Location: Independent study by correspondence.

Length: 10 self-paced lessons.

Dates: September 1992-Present.

Objective: To enable students to read, write, and talk about chemistry; to understand chemical formulas and equations; to set up and solve routine chemical problems; and to think chemistry on atomic or molecular levels, visualizing what happens in a chemical change.

Learning Outcome: Upon successful completion of this course, the student will be able to define and give examples of mass, matter, and chemical property and physical property; distinguish between physical change and chemical change and give examples of each; define and give examples of an element atom compound and mixture; distinguish between the units of measurement used in the english, metric, and si systems; define density, mass, and volume; use scientific notation; define mole and recognize its uses in calculating chemical formulas; give percent composition; calculate the empirical formula of a compound; identify structural or chemical properties that can be changed when an ion is formed; distinguish between the solute and solvent components of a solution; identify the characteristics of water-soluble compounds; define and give examples of conjugate acid-base pairs; define organic chemistry and biochemistry; and understand the significance of amino acids to protein structure.

Instruction: Major topics covered in the course are atomic and molecular structure, chemical formulas and calculations, acid-base chemistry, and biochemistry. Methods of instruction include independent study, textbook, course manual, self-administered unit quizzes, and a proctored final examination.

Credit Recommendation: In the lower division baccalaureate/associate degree, 3 semester hours in Chemistry (11/95).

Conflict Resolution and Problem-Solving (81600000)

Location: Lakewood, CO.

Length: 24 hours (3 days).

Dates: May 1989-Present.

Objective: Identify causes of conflict and develop strategies to deal with various elements of conflict.

Learning Outcome: Upon successful completion of this course, the student will be able to provide managers with the skills to make and resolve differences using the collaborative and alternative approach to resolving contact.

Instruction: Major topics covered in the course are decision-making and conflict management principles, negotiation and bargaining procedures, strategies for conflict management, and communication and facilitated decision-making. Methods of instruction include instructor-led lectures and discussions, case negotiation exercises, experiential exercises in conducting meetings, role playing, and decision-making.

Credit Recommendation: In the upper division baccalaureate degree category, 1 semester hour in Human Resource Development or Personnel Management (8/89) (10/95).

Cornerstones of Learning (4000)

Location: All USWC Learning Systems Training Sites.

Length: 22-26 hours (3 days).

Dates: June 1991-August 1997.

Objective: To identify principles of human learning, instruction, and curriculum development associated with the dynamics of psychology and education.

Learning Outcome: Upon successful completion of this course, the student will be able to demonstrate mechanism of enhancing human memory; demonstrate principles of instruction; and demonstrate components of system approach to curriculum development.

Instruction: Major topics covered in the course are various kinds of memory; motivation; learning styles; organizational and systems analysis; teaching and retention methods; curriculum development, evaluation, and standardization. Methods of instruction include lecture, discussion, classroom exercises, case studies, problem solving, and video and media instructional material.

Credit Recommendation: In the upper division baccalaureate degree category, 1 semester hour in Learning Theory or Psychology of Learning (8/92).

Dynamics of Professional Development for Minority Corporate Professionals
1. Efficacy Seminar for Minority Corporate Professionals (8320A000/8320B000)
2. Risk Taking for Professional Development (83600000)

Location: Phoenix, AZ; Lakewood, CO; Des Moines, IA; Minneapolis, MN; Albuquerque, NM; Omaha, NE; Portland, OR; Salt Lake City, UT; Seattle, WA; and suitcase locations.

Length: 64 hours (8 days).

Dates: April 1986-December 1995.

Objective: To assist the minority professional in developing a more effective behavior in the pursuit of life and career aspirations and objectives, offer insight and strategy for career advancement and higher-level job performance, provide a study of the relationship between psychological and intellectual risk as related to personal and professional change and development, and provides guidance and process for accepting uncertainty in risk and change.

Learning Outcome: Upon successful completion of this course, the student will be able to analyze and evaluate his or her pattern of motivation and the psychological dimensions of achievement and performance; identify the critical factors in achieving higher performance advancement and reward; improve the ability to influence outcomes and product results; access his or her capacity for and reaction to personal risk, uncertainty, and intellectual change; plan a personal program for confidence and development; and set a series of development goals for career planning and advancement.

Instruction: Major topics covered in the course are personal assessment of motivation structure; racial factors affecting performance and group dynamics; adaptive responses to internally and externally imposed obstacles to minority professional development; appreciation of well-known motivational and behavioral theories; risk taking inventory; Survey of Risk Taking (SORT); simulation of risk-taking (Ring Toss Analysis); case study involving a project and its analysis; management of personal and professional development; and the Attribution Theory. Methods of instruction include instructor-led lectures and discussions, risk-oriented games and simulations, visual exhibits, handouts, self-assessment exercises, and exercises in goal setting.

Credit Recommendation: In the lower division baccalaureate/associate degree category, 3 semester hours in Human Resource Development (8/89) (10/95). **NOTE**: Students must successfully complete both courses to receive the credit recommendation.

Dynamics of Professional Development for Women
1. Efficacy Seminar for Women (8330A000/8330B000)
2. Risk Taking for Professional Development (83600000)

Location: Phoenix, AZ; Lakewood, CO; Des Moines, IA; Minneapolis, MN; Albuquerque, NM; Omaha, NE; Portland, OR; Salt Lake City, UT; and Seattle, WA.

Length: 48 hours (6 days).

Dates: July 1987-December 1995.

Objective: To assist women in developing more effective behavior in pursuit of life and career objectives by bridging the gap between potential for performance and actual on-the-job effectiveness, and to study the relationship between psychological and intellectual risk as related to personal and professional change and development, and provide guidance and process for accepting uncertainty of risk and change.

Learning Outcome: Upon successful completion of this course, the student will be able to analyze and evaluate his or her pattern of motivation and the psychological dimensions of achievement and performance; identify the critical factors in achieving higher performance advancement and reward; improve the ability to influence outcomes and product results; access his or her capacity for and reaction to personal risk, uncertainty, and intellectual change; plan a personal program for confidence and development; and set a series of development goals for career planning and advancement.

Instruction: Major topics covered in the course are personal assessment of motivation structure; racial factors affecting performance and group dynamics; adaptive response to internally and externally imposed obstacles to minority professional development; appreciation of well-known motivational and behavioral theories; risk taking inventory; Survey or Risk Taking (SORT); simulation of risk-taking (Ring Toss Analysis); case study involving a project and its analysis; management of personal and professional development; and the Attribution Theory. Methods of instruction include instructor-led lectures and discussion, risk-oriented games and simulations, visual exhibits, handouts, self-assessment exercises, and exercises in goal setting.

Credit Recommendation: In the lower division baccalaureate/associate degree category, 3 semester hours in Human Resource Management (8/89) (10/95). **NOTE**: Students must successfully complete both courses to receive the credit recommendation.

Efficacy Seminar for Professionals of Color

Location: Phoenix, AZ; Lakewood, CO; Des Moines, IA; Minneapolis, MN; Albuquerque, NM; Omaha, NE; Portland, OR; Salt Lake City, UT; Seattle, WA; and suitcase locations.

Length: 32 contact hours (4 days).

Dates: April 1986-Present.

Objective: To identify the psychological factors that influence performance; map obstacles to achieve goals and develop strategies to overcome barriers; and understand the motivation process and how it impacts behavior.

Learning Outcome: Upon successful completion of this course, the student will be able to identify needs and specific skills for attaining career goals and develop a clearer understanding of organizational behavior and the work environment.

Instruction: Major topics covered in the course are models of development; goal setting; living a quality life; power/politics; types of confidence; and personal strengths inventory. Methods of instruction include performance tests, etc.

Credit Recommendation: In the lower division baccalaureate/associate degree category, 2 semester hours in Human Resource Development (10/95).

Efficacy Seminar for Women

Location: Phoenix, AZ; Lakewood, CO; Des Moines, IA; Minneapolis, MN; Albuquerque, NM; Omaha, NE; Portland, OR; Salt Lake City, UT; Seattle, WA; and suitcase locations.

Length: 4 days (32 contact hours).

Dates: July 1987-Present.

Objective: To assist women in developing more effective behavior in pursuit of life and career objectives by bridging the gap between potential for performance and actual on-the-job effectiveness.

Learning Outcome: Upon successful completion of this course, the student will be able to analyze and evaluate his or her pattern of motivation and the psychological dimensions of achievement and performance; identify the critical factors in achieving higher performance advancement and reward; improve the ability to influence outcomes and product results; access his our her capacity for and reaction to personal risk, uncertainty, and intellectual change; plan a personal program for confidence and development; and set a series of development goals for career planning and advancement.

Instruction: Major topics covered in the course are personal assessment of motivation structure; racial factors affecting performance and group dynamics; adaptive responses to internally and externally imposed obstacles to minority professional development; appreciation of well-known motivational and behavioral theories; risk taking inventory; Survey of Risk Taking (SORT); simulation of risk-taking (Ring Toss Analysis); case study involving a project and its analysis; management of personal and professional development; and the Attribution theory. Methods of instruction include instructor-led lectures and discussions, risk-oriented games and simulations, visual exhibits, handouts, self-assessment exercises, and exercises in goal setting.

Credit Recommendation: In the lower division baccalaureate/associate degree category, 2 semester hours in Human Resource Development (10/95).

Evaluation of Learning (9760000)

Location: Lakewood, CO; Seattle, WA; Omaha, NE; Minneapolis, MN.

Length: 30.75 hours (4 days).

Dates: February 1992-August 1997.

Objective: To provide classroom instructors with information and knowledge to design, construct, and implement an appropriate evaluation instrument which will measure learning in a competency based environment.

Learning Outcome: Upon successful completion of this course, the student will be able to discuss the advantages and limitations of various knowledge and performance based evaluation instruments; select and construct testing instruments and documents to measure learning outcomes; distinguish between outcome and content validity; and edit performance and knowledge based instruments.

Instruction: Major topics covered in the course are advantages and limitations of testing instruments, design of knowledge and performance evaluation documents, editing testing practices, validation strategies, and Federal laws in testing practices and procedures. Methods of instruction include motivation, guidance and practices using group discussion, in-class exercises, individual presentations and oral questions, and audio-visual presentations.

Credit Recommendation: In the upper division baccalaureate degree category, 2 semester hours in Education Tests and Measurements (8/92).

Front End Analysis (9750) (Training Needs Assessment)

Location: Denver, Seattle, Omaha, Minneapolis.

Length: 28 hours (4 days).

Dates: July 1991-August 1997.

Objective: To provide an understanding of the training needs assessment process.

Learning Outcome: Upon successful completion of this course, the student will be able to identify the characteristics of training needs assessment; planning a training needs assessment project; produce an interview guide for assessing training needs; and produce a task analysis document.

Instruction: Major topics covered in the course are training needs assessment (TNA) characteristics; techniques for planning a TNA; produce an interview guide; purpose and components of a task analysis document; and participate in "jury of peers" sessions. Methods of instruction include lecture, workbook, classroom exercises, projects, presentations, and exams.

Credit Recommendation: In the upper division baccalaureate degree category, 1 semester hour in Training Needs Assessment (8/92).

Instructional Design (97450000)

Location: Denver, Seattle, Omaha, Minneapolis.

Length: 37.5 hours (5 days).

Dates: June 1991-August 1997.

Objective: To provide the student with the theory and structure of instructional design concepts and practices in a competency based learning approach.

Learning Outcome: Upon successful completion of this course, the student will be able to explain the theories of learning and instruction; create and implement designed instructional documents; develop course introduction materials, write instructional objectives; identify instructional resources; and produce an instructional guide.

Instruction: Major topics covered in the course are the theory of learning and instruction; the production of program, course, objective, and task outlines; the implementation of course schedules; and day previews and course evaluations. Pluralism and respect for the individual will also be a topic of discussion. Methods of instruction include motivation, guidance and practice which emphasizes group discussion and exercises, and audio and visual presentation. Individual student presentations will also be expected.

Credit Recommendation: In the upper division baccalaureate degree category, 2 semester hours in Instructional Design (8/92).

Instructional Management I (97350000)

Location: All USWC training sites any suitcase location.

Length: 40 hours (5 days).

Dates: July 1991-August 1997.

Objective: To provide classroom instructors with the principles and practices of a competency based instructional delivery system. Presentation skills, classroom management, and learning theory will be emphasized.

Learning Outcome: Upon successful completion of this course, the student will be able to plan for an effective delivery of educational information; use flexible teaching methods to accommodate different learning styles; inform students of available learning resources; provide feedback to students on learning progress; and develop an appropriate student evaluation instrument.

Instruction: Major topics covered in the course are learning agreements and outcomes, presentation methods and styles, group activities, pluralism, audiovisual techniques, listening and questioning activities, feedback on performance, professional classroom ethics and performance evaluation. Methods of instruction include motivation, guidance and practice which emphasizes explanation and informing techniques, demonstrations, brainstorming, role-playing, drilling, case studies, and simulations.

Credit Recommendation: In the upper division baccalaureate degree category, 3 semester hours in Instruction Methods and Management (8/92).

Labor Relations (80300WT)

Location: Phoenix, AZ; Lakewood, CO; Des Moines, IA; Minneapolis, MN; Albuquerque, NM; Omaha, NE; Portland, OR; Salt Lake City, UT; and Seattle, WA.

Length: 40 hours (5 days).

Dates: September 1987-August 1995.

Objective: To provide management, union officers, and stewards with a better understanding of the labor movement, labor relations within the firm, and use of the labor contract to resolve labor/management problems.

Learning Outcome: Upon successful completion of this course, the student will be able to recognize federal laws regulating management/union activities; state management and union rights and responsibilities; analyze and resolve labor/management problems; identify "just cause" factors and burden of proof; document all data relative to a contract problem; and explain the grievance and arbitration processes.

Instruction: Major topics covered in the course are labor history and laws, management and worker rights under the contract, discipline, suspensions and dismissal, grievance procedures, and arbitration. Methods of instruction include lecture, class discussion, role playing, videos, and team analysis.

Credit Recommendation: In the upper division baccalaureate degree category, 2 semester hours in Labor Relations (8/89) (10/95).

LAN Components (2005AC00)
LAN Interconnection (2007AC00)

Location: Learning Systems and Employee Development, Lakewood, CO.

Length: *Course 1*: 40 hours (5 days); *Course 2*: 40 hours (5 days).

Dates: April 1992-August 1997.

Objective: *Course 1*: To understand hardware and software components of bus and ring Local Area Networks. *Course 2*: To understand hardware, software, and routing protocols in connecting two or more ring or bus LANs.

Learning Outcome: *Course 1*: Upon successful completion of this course, the student will be able to understand microcomputer attributes, LAN hardware and software, installation procedures, protocol analysis, LAN architectures, and troubleshooting of IEEE 802.3 and 802.5 networks. *Course 2*: Upon successful completion of this course, the student will be able to use hardware devices and applications software to connect one ring or bus network to another, troubleshoot networks, network protocols (e.g. TCP/IP, UDP), and routing in single and multi-protocol networks.

Instruction: *Course 1*: Major topics covered in the course are Intel based microcomputer architecture, LAN hardware installation, NetWare workstation generation, NetWare server configuration, familiarization with protocol analysis, IEEE 802.3 overview and analysis, IEEE 802.5 overview and analysis, and troubleshooting LANS. *Course 2*: Major topics covered in the course are bridges, routers, and repeaters; local bridging with IEEE 802.3; remote bridging with IEEE 802.3; spanning tree protocol; troubleshooting bridged IEEE 802.3 networks; open data-link interface; token ring and source routing; troubleshooting bridged token ring networks; source routing transparently; Internet protocol; Internet packet exchange protocol; routing protocols-RIP; other routing protocols; and troubleshooting internet works and multi-protocol networks. Methods of instruction include lectures, classroom activities (case studies), laboratory work, and outside class preparation.

Credit Recommendation: In the upper division baccalaureate degree category, 3 semester hours in Telecommunications, Data Communications, or CIS. (8/92). **NOTE**: Student must complete both courses to receive credit.

LAN/WAN Design (2006AC00)
LAN Components (2005AC00)

Location: Learning Systems and Employee Development, Lakewood, CO.

Length: *Course 1*: 22 hours (3 days); *Course 2*: 40 hours (5 days).

Dates: April 1992-August 1997.

Objective: *Course 1*: To understand data communications network design requirements for LANS and WANS. *Course 2*: To understand hardware and software components of BUS and ring Local Area Networks.

Learning Outcome: *Course 1*: Upon successful completion of this course, the student will be able to understand interconnected LANS and WANS; basic traffic engineering, and T-1 backbone networks, bridges, and routers. *Course 2*: Upon successful completion of this course, the student will be able to understand microcomputer attributes, LAN hardware and software, installation procedures, protocol analysis, LAN architectures and troubleshooting of IEEE 802.3 and 802.5 networks.

Instruction: *Course 1*: Major topics covered in the course are evolution of enterprise networks, theory of network design, building T-carrier backbones, applied network design, traffic assessment, and application of bridgers and routers. *Course 2*: Major topics covered in the course are microcomputer attributes, LAN hardware installation, NetWare workstation generation, NetWare server configuration, familiarization with protocol analysis, IEEE 802.3 overview and analysis, IEEE 802.5 overview and analysis, and troubleshooting LANS. Methods of instruction include lectures, classroom exercises (case studies), laboratory work, and outside class preparation.

Credit Recommendation: In the upper division baccalaureate degree category, 2 semester hours in Telecommunications, Data Communications, or CIS. (8/92). **NOTE**: Student must complete both courses to receive credit.

Leader-Manager (81550000)

Location: Lakewood, CO, and suitcase locations.

Length: 24 hours (3 days).

Dates: May 1989-June 1994.

Objective: To develop in the student an understanding of influences and trends in business required of contemporary leaders in business management.

Learning Outcome: Upon successful completion of this course, the student will be able to identify and understand changing influences on businesses and work units (i.e., enhancers of management principles); develop strategies to become a leader manager (i.e., styles and processes of leaders who manage); establish personal and business goals and objectives for leader-managers; and stimulate and manage high performance of teams (motivation, communications, power, etc.).

Instruction: Major topics covered in the course are strategies for developing leadership skills and attributes among business managers in a changing work force and work environment; it enhances managers' skills in creating a work environment that encourages adaptability and new learning among a work force facing new and increasingly complex challenges. Methods of instruction include lecture and discussion.

Credit Recommendation: In the upper division baccalaureate degree category, 2 semester hours in Management (8/89).

Leading a Diverse Work Force The Value of Human Diversity (8940/8945)

Location: Phoenix, AZ; Lakewood, CO; Des Moines, IA; Minneapolis, MN; Albuquerque, NM; Omaha, NE; Portland, OR; Salt Lake City, UT; Seattle, WA; and suitcase locations.

Length: 4 days (33 contact hours).

Dates: January 1989-Present.

Objective: To examine leadership in a pluralistic work force and identify pluralistic leadership qualities; examine one's own values, attitudes and behavior and understand effects of socialization on values and behaviors. Participants develop a personal action plan designed to improve effectiveness as manager of a diverse work force, dealing with issues such as race, gender, sexual orientation and physical disabilities.

Learning Outcome: Upon successful completion of this course, the student will be able to exercise leadership to promote change in the perceptions, emotions and behaviors of employees towards valuing differences among people and leading them to be assets to the corporation and optimize corporate ability to compete in the marketplace.

Instruction: Major topics covered in the course are leadership, pluralism/diversity/socialization. Methods of instruction include lecture, discussion, classroom exercises, audio/visual material, learner reports.

Credit Recommendation: In the upper division baccalaureate/associate degree category, 2 semester hours in Human Resource Development, Personnel Management, or Leadership (10/95). **NOTE:** Student must successfully complete both courses to receive the credit recommendations.

Leading a Diverse Workforce (89400000)

Location: Various locations throughout the United States.

Length: 32 hours (3 days).

Dates: February 1989-Present.

Objective: To promote valuing differences and facilitating constructive changes in the perceptions, emotions, and behaviors of participants, leading them to be unique assets to the corporation.

Learning Outcome: Upon successful completion of this course, students will be able to increase their understanding of systems impact on pluralism, corporate values and personal values; and increase their understanding of the role of power dynamics or establishing, maintaining, and changing perceptions, myths, stereotypes, opportunities, and job related behaviors and attitudes in a pluralistic work environment.

Instruction: Major topics covered in the course are applying pluralism, philosophy among various aspects of leadership activities in the work environment; recognizing and developing values, perceptions, and behaviors supporting system change towards a pluralistic society; and self assessment and social systems power dynamics. Methods of instruction include lecture, exercises, experiential self-assessment, group activities, video presentations, and discussions.

Credit Recommendation: In the graduate degree category, 1 semester hour in Personnel Management, Social Science, or Education (6/93).

Management of Professional Development
1. Managing Diversity (80400000)
2. Managing Risk (80550000)
3. Risk Taking for Professional Development (83600000)

Location: Phoenix, AZ; Lakewood, CO; Des Moines, IA; Minneapolis, MN; Albuquerque, NM; Omaha, NE; Portland, OR; Salt Lake City, IA; Seattle, WA; and suitcase locations.

Length: 40 hours (5 days).

Dates: November 1987-December 1995.

Objective: This course provides the student with the leadership capabilities to deal with rapid social change and performance from a pluralistic work group; explains the relationship between psychological and intellectual risk as related to personal and professional change and development; provides guidance and process for accepting uncertainty in risk and changes; and prepares the manager for his or her role in fostering innovation and successfully developing creative, imaginative people ready to accept risk and personal development.

Learning Outcome: Upon successful completion of this course, the student will be able to understand the psychological implications of managing a diverse workforce; assess his or her capacity for and reaction to personal risk, uncertainty, and intellectual change; plan a personal program for confidence and development; set a series of development goals for career planning and advancement; understand the ways in which risk takers and innovators may be encouraged, managed, and rewarded; identify and plan techniques for developing innovative people; and provide support and commitment to risk acceptance and development.

Instruction: Major topics covered in the course are what good management is, analysis of the issues managers face in a multicultural work force, problem-solving, goal setting, risk taking inventory, Survey of Risk Taking (SORT), a simulation of risk taking (Ring Toss Analysis), a case study involving a project and its analysis, management of personal and professional development, the Attribution Theory, the psychology of risk in personal and professional development, management encouragement and reward systems used in dealing with innovators, relationship of expectations to performance, and a behavioral simulation game: *Tower Building*. Methods of Instruction include instructor-led lectures and discussion, self-assessment exercises, risk-oriented games, simulations and exercises in goal setting and risk management, problem-solving, case study, and career development.

Credit Recommendation: In the lower division baccalaureate/associate degree category, 2 semester hours in Human Resource Development or Personnel Management (8/89) (10/95). **NOTE**: Student must successfully complete all three courses to receive the credit recommendation.

Managing Development and Diversity (8331)

Location: U.S. West Centers for Professional Development.

Length: 16 hours (2 days).

Dates: September 1990-August 1997.

Objective: To give the trainee a rationale and developmental framework for identifying, understanding, and managing the potentially problematic and underdeveloped resources associated with managing a diverse workforce.

Learning Outcome: Upon successful completion of this course, the student will be able to increase the knowledge of the psychology of personal worth and performance common to all people in an organizational culture; increase the knowledge of employment and personal situations that render people of color and women vulnerable to conditions that decrease work performance and personal worth; increase one's skills and ability to create action plans that enhance the organization's ability to advance cultural diversity from a developmental perspective.

Instruction: Major topics covered in the course are understanding management of workers as a developmental process rather than merely a discreet product of outcome; understanding how the process of development is critical to resolving and enhancing issues of diversity; and understanding how attribution theory, learned helplessness, learning theory, and stereotypes impact cultural diversity. Methods of instruction include lecture, discussion, and action plans with specific knowledge and skills to a problem solving situation; group exercises in clarifying organizational norms and overcoming obstacles to organizational changes via power dynamics; and structured exercises.

Credit Recommendation: In the upper division baccalaureate or graduate degree category, 1 semester hour in Business Administration, Personnel Management, or Social Science (8/92).

Managing in a Changing Environment (81500000)

Location: Lakewood, CO, and suitcase locations.

Length: 16 hours (2 days).

Dates: May 1989-June 1994.

Objective: To provide the students with a set of strategies and skills managers can use to manage the change process and to maximize the new opportunities that change presents for managers and their employees.

Learning Outcome: Upon successful completion of this course, the students will be able to understand the change process and its effects on people; distinguish reactions to change; and deal with themselves and their employees in working through change issues.

Instruction: Major topics covered in the course are the changing environment, things that might end when the old environment changes, transition from the old to the new environment, and the challenges that occur with the advent of the new environment. Methods of instruction include lecture, instructor-led discussion, case studies, and role playing.

Credit Recommendation: In the lower division baccalaureate/associate degree category, 1 semester hour as an elective in Management (8/89).

Marketing Challenges (4000)

Location: Denver, Seattle, Phoenix, Omaha, Minneapolis.

Length: 24 hours (3 days).

Dates: March 1992-August 1997.

Objective: To develop a pragmatic understanding of the total marketing process for those who must manage and/or contribute to it. To build a foundation of marketing fundamentals.

Learning Outcome: Upon successful completion of this course, the student will be able to understand the marketing process; know the process through which customers pass in deciding to purchase-customer buying behavior; understand how to obtain marketplace intelligence; segment markets, to position products; and understand key factors that impact the ability to develop new products.

Instruction: Major topics covered in the course are marketing process; consumer buying behavior; marketing research; target markets and segmentation; new product development; and pricing and promotion. Methods of instruction include lecture, films, and guest speakers.

Credit Recommendation: In the upper division baccalaureate degree category, 1 semester hour in Principles of Marketing (8/92).

Marketing Decisions (4020)

Location: Denver, Seattle, Phoenix, Omaha, Minneapolis.

Length: 30 hours (3 days).

Dates: April 1992-August 1997.

Objective: To help participants understand the integral relationship between marketing decisions and economics, finance, accounting, and business strategy.

Learning Outcome: Upon successful completion of this course, the student will be able to demonstrate how marketing decisions affect corporate profitability and shareholder value; present a business case outlining marketing decisions; and to understand capital budgeting, present value, and IRR.

Instruction: Major topics covered in the course are economic impact of marketing strategy; capital budgeting; market analysis; measuring business performance; pricing and channel management. Methods of instruction include lecture, cases, and simulation.

Credit Recommendation: In the upper division baccalaureate degree category, 2 semester hours in Marketing Management, Marketing Decisions, or Marketing Elective (8/92).

Risk Taking for Professional Development (8360)

Location: Phoenix, AZ; Lakewood, CO; Des Moines, IA; Minneapolis, MN; Albuquerque, NM; Omaha, NE; Portland, OR; Salt Lake City, UT; Seattle, WA; and suitcase locations.

Length: 2 days (16 contact hours).

Dates: April 1986-Present.

Objective: To introduce participants to the concept of risk taking in the work environment. Lecture presentation and practical application exercises will allow participants to develop a framework for making effective risk decisions.

Learning Outcome: Upon successful completion of this course, the student will be able to create an atmosphere that encourages effective risk-taking and creativity; increase individual and departmental productivity; improve job satisfaction and team morale; use a common language for discussing goals and objectives; respond to failure in a way that increases the likelihood of future success; make full use of the capabilities of all employees.

Instruction: Major topics covered in the course are define the nature of intelligent risk; explaining the relationship between risk-taking and professional DEU; analyzing influences on risk tendencies; developing action plans. Methods of instruction include classroom activity with large and small group interaction and self-analysis of current management styles. Simulation games are used to emphasize the content theory of risk taking.

Credit Recommendation: In the lower division baccalaureate/associate degree category, 1 semester hour in Human Resource Development (10/95).

Trainer Skills Workshops A and B (96570000 and 9658000)

Location: Lakewood, CO, and 14-state U.S. West region.

Length: 72 hours (9 days).

Dates: January 1980-December 1995.

Objective: To introduce new trainers to teaching techniques and skills.

Learning Outcome: Upon successful completion of this course, the student will be able to deliver presentations in a variety of instructional modes, including lecture, discussion, case study, role playing, and self-paced instruction, and apply and perform the following training skills: oral presentation, media usage, questioning, listening, nonverbal communications, helping and counseling, and group dynamic management.

Instruction: Major topics covered in the course are the self-assessment of trainer skills, techniques of instructional delivery, the weaknesses and strengths of common instructional techniques, the characteristics of adult learning, professional and ethical considerations in training, and the key role of the trainer in a rapidly changing environment. Methods of instruction include lecture, instructor-led discussion, case studies, role playing, videos, and instructional laboratory.

Credit Recommendation: In the upper division baccalaureate degree category, 3 semester hours in Introduction to Teaching Methods (8/89).

Writing Procedures and Users Guides (96590000)

Location: Denver, CO; Portland, OR; Seattle, WA; and Bellevue, WA.

Length: 32 hours (4 days).

Dates: June 1986-August 1994.

Objective: To teach the student effective writing skills for improved formatting, communication, and illustration of data.

Learning Outcome: Upon successful completion of this course, the student will be able to identify the various types of technical written communication and the appropriate formats for each; write clearly and concisely using appropriate figures, charts, and exhibits for complex or numerical data; and develop the ways of controlling the quality of written communications.

Instruction: Major topics covered in the course are clarity in written communications, formats for various types of writing, writing with computers, quality control, and left brain-right brain concepts and their relation to writing and communication skills. Methods of instruction include instructor-led discussions, lectures, visual aids, group exercises, and writing exercises.

Credit Recommendation: In the upper division baccalaureate degree category, 1 semester hour in Business Communications or Technical Writing (8/89).

A, B, C: Leadership Skills for the 90's (8860)

Location: Phoenix, AZ; Lakewood, CO; Des Moines, IA; Minneapolis, MN; Albuquerque, NM; Omaha, NE; Portland, OR; Salt Lake City, UT; Seattle, WA; and suitcase locations.

Length: 4 days (32 contact hours).

Dates: January 1994-Present.

Objective: This learning program focuses on the four leadership styles; Directing, Coaching, Supporting, and Delegating. Delivery of theory is followed by practical application in the workplace. Participants will establish learning goals aimed at developing the vital skills of people development and leadership.

Learning Outcome: Upon successful completion of the course, the student will be able to define Directing, Coaching, Supporting, and Delegating; Determine which style is most appropriate for any given situation; carry on a one-on-one coaching session; develop an action plan for implementation within their work group.

Instruction: Major topics covered in the course are personal assessment of trust in the organization; communications that promote effective, supportive and directive supervisory skills and behaviors; linking employee satisfaction to performance; linking situational leadership to the core skills of Directing, Coaching, Supporting and Delegating; handling performance problems.- No formal prerequisite - pre course activity required.

Credit Recommendation: In the lower division baccalaureate/associate degree category, 2 semester hours in Business Management, Leadership, Human Resource Development, or Human Potential (10/95).

Communispond (8305)

Location: Phoenix, AZ; Lakewood, CO; Des Moines, IA; Minneapolis, MN; Albuquerque, NM; Omaha, NE; Portland, OR; Salt Lake City, UT; Seattle, WA; and suitcase locations.

Length: 2 days (16 hours).

Dates: March 1988-Present.

Objective: To provide the student with a communications skills system to handle any kind of business presentation or public speech.

Learning Outcome: Upon successful completion of this course, the student will be able to make more persuasive business presentations, public speeches, better sales calls and productive business meetings.

Instruction: Major topics covered in the course are physical skills in communications, organization methods of presentation, visual aid processes and question and answer controls. Methods of instruction include discussion, classroom, audio/visual material, learner presentations.

Credit Recommendation: In the upper division baccalaureate degree category, 1 semester hour in Speech or Communication (10/95).

Positive Power and Influence (8350)

Location: Phoenix, AZ; Lakewood, CO; Des Moines, IA; Minneapolis, MN; Albuquerque, NM, Omaha, NE; Portland, OR; Salt Lake City, UT; Seattle, WA; and suitcase locations.

Length: 3 days (26 contact hours).

Dates: October 1988-Present.

Objective: To provide student with a skills development program focusing on influence and leadership skills. Participants learn an influence model for analyzing face-to-face situations and assess which influence styles they under-use or avoid.

Learning Outcome: Upon successful completion of this course, the student will learn how to influence others to achieve desired results without positional authority. Present ideas with a stronger and more convincing approach, resulting in greater impact on the decision-making process. Enter potentially confrontational situations and create a positive atmosphere. Increase levels of enthusiasm and motivation surrounding individual assignments, department goals, and company vision.

Instruction: Major topics covered in the course are positive and negative power and positional and personal power, influence styles in management or leadership situations, style flexibility tracks, setting clear personal learning goals and formulating effective strategies for leadership situations. Methods of instruction include lecture, discussion, classroom exercises, audio/visual material, case studies, learner presentations/reports.

Credit Recommendation: In the upper division baccalaureate degree category, 2 semester hours in Personnel Management, Leadership, or Social Science (10/95).

Network Institute

Advanced Communications: Module 1 (2001AC00)

Location: Lakewood, CO.

Length: 73 hours (2 weeks).

Dates: November 1991-December 1995.

Objective: To survey the basic concepts of data communications and data processing to include the roles and strategies of major data communication equipment distributors and to introduce fundamental architecture concepts of computer systems including operating systems, common software packages and OSI layers.

Learning Outcome: Upon successful completion of this course, the student will be able to define basic terms associated with data communications; differentiate among circuit, message and packet switching; discuss requirements for network protocols; explain the concepts of clear channels, out of band signaling and disassociated signaling network; discuss the concept of an integrated services network and the basic structure of ISDN; in addition, the student will be able to develop algorithms and write BASIC programs to implement these algorithms; identify the principle components of a computing system; describe a bus architecture; compare and contrast various types of DBMS and explain the importance of fourth generation languages; and explain the concept of protocol transparency.

Instruction: Major topics covered in the course are evolution of distributed computing; point to point communications; switching evolution; open systems interconnection trends; SNA and DEC; network management; local area networks; ISDN; introduction to programming; database management systems; software development tools; computer architecture (introduction); operating systems (introduction); memory management; processor management; and the file system. Methods of instruction include lecture, discussion, laboratory, and problem solving.

Credit Recommendation: In the lower division baccalaureate/associate degree category, 3 semester hours in Data Processing, Computer Science, or Telecommunication Management and 3 semester hours in Electronics Technology (12/90).

Advanced Communications: Module 2 (2002AC00)

Location: Lakewood, CO.

Length: 73 hours (2 weeks).

Dates: November 1991-December 1995.

Objective: To explore the lower layers of the OSI Model and its interaction with major vendor systems.

Learning Outcome: Upon successful completion of this course, the student will be able to differentiate between design based on blocking probability and design based on delay considerations; state the network design problem; explain the effects of various routing strategies on network costs and performance; differentiate between connection based networks and connectionless systems; describe the routing algorithm used in each of the example networks.

Instruction: Major topics covered in the course are physical layer protocols; DTE/DEC Interface; Transmission Media; Binary Synchronous Communications; Digital Data Communications Message Protocol; Introduction to Network Design; Designing Local Access Networks; Designing Packet Networks. Methods of instruction include lecture, discussion, and laboratory.

Credit Recommendation: In the graduate degree category, 6 semester hours in Data Processing, Computer Science, or MBA/Telecom Management (12/90). **NOTE**: Student must complete this course plus Module 3 (Advanced Communications [2003AC00] and Module 4 (Advanced Communications [2004AC00] to receive credit.

Advanced Communications: Module 3 (2003AC00)

Location: Lakewood, CO.

Length: 73 hours (2 weeks).

Dates: November 1991-December 1995.

Objective: To explore the middle layers of the OSI Model and its interaction with major vendor systems.

Learning Outcome: Upon successful completion of this course, the student will be able to describe and discuss the three major areas of computer network architectures; describe and discuss Packet Switching from the perspective of the technology; and describe and discuss computer net architecture of major vendors.

Instruction: Major topics covered in the course are Packet Switching; X.25 recommendation; SNA; DNA; and Unisys. Methods of instruction include lecture, discussion, laboratory, computer-assisted videotape, and classroom exercises.

Credit Recommendation: In the graduate degree category, 6 semester hours in Data Processing, Computer Science or MBA/Telecom Management (12/90). **NOTE**: Student must complete this course plus Module 2 (Advanced Communications [2002AC00]) and Module 4 (Advanced Communications [2004AC00]) to receive credit.

Advanced Communications: Module 4 (2004AC00)

Location: Lakewood, CO.

Length: 73 hours (2 weeks).

Dates: November 1991-December 1995.

Objective: To explore the upper layers of the OSI Model and its interaction with major vendor systems.

Learning Outcome: Upon successful completion of this course, the student will be able to compare LAN topologies; compare methodologies of using Base Band and Broad Band systems; explain the importance of IEEE 802.3; explain how a central office-based LAN may be structured; and describe the capabilities of CPET carrier multiplexing equipment.

Instruction: Major topics covered in the course are LAN technology and standards; LAN Operating Systems and Products; MANS; T-Carrier fundamentals; Switching Systems; Network evolution to ISDN; and ISDN. Methods of instruction include lecture, discussion, and laboratory.

Credit Recommendation: In the graduate degree category, 6 semester hours in Data Processing, Computer Science or MBA/Telecom Management (12/90). **NOTE**: Student must complete this course plus Module 2 (Advanced Communications [2002AC00]) and Module 3 (Advanced Communications [2003AC00]) to receive credit.

Technical Courses

1/1A ESS Method of Operation (33740000)

Location: Des Moines, IA; and suitcase locations.

Length: 36 hours (5 days).

Dates: January 1977-December 1995.

Objective: To provide the student with the appropriate No. 1 ESS terminology and the knowledge needed to trace an outgoing, incoming, intra-office, or tandem call through the system.

Learning Outcome: Upon successful completion of this course, the student will be able to utilize appropriate No. 1 ESS terminology; trace calls through the system; and identify the principal hardware and software components.

Instruction: Major topics covered in the course are operation, features, and documentation of the No. 1 ESS. Methods of instruction include lecture, discussion, and laboratory exercises.

Credit Recommendation: In the vocational certificate or in the lower division baccalaureate/associate degree category, 1 semester hour in Electronic Switching Systems (8/89).

1A ESS Peripheral Units (33600000) (Curriculum 5BA)

Location: Phoenix, AZ; Lakewood, CO; Minneapolis, MN; Albuquerque, NM; Salt Lake City, UT; and Seattle, WA.

Length: 408 hours (10 weeks).

Dates: August 1985-December 1995.

Objective: To provide the student with fundamental and advanced training for the maintenance of peripheral units for first and second generation electronic switching systems.

Learning Outcome: Upon successful completion of this course, the student will be able to understand ESS and microprocessor fundamentals; maintain second generation peripheral units; and maintain peripheral units common to 1/1A ESS.

Instruction: Major topics covered in the course are digital electronics fundamentals, test equipment, 1A basic call processing, Bell System practices, computer concepts and system configuration, ESS switch communication buses, scanners, switching networks, line and trunk switching circuits, and peripheral unit controllers. Methods of instruction include self-paced, practical exercises under direct supervision of an administrator.

Credit Recommendation: In the vocational certificate category, 6 semester hours in Digital Switching Systems Maintenance or in the lower division baccalaureate/associate degree category, 3 semester hours in Computer Systems, Digital Electronics, or Logic Circuit Fundamentals (8/89) (10/95).

1A ESS Processor Maintenance (33700000)

Location: Phoenix, AZ; Lakewood, CO; Minneapolis, MN; Albuquerque, NM; Salt Lake City, UT; and Seattle, WA.

Length: 248 hours (6 weeks).

Dates: August 1985-December 1995.

Objective: To provide the student with training enabling use of standard reference sources, test equipment, and access terminals to locate and correct hardware and software problems in 1A ESS processor units.

Learning Outcome: Upon successful completion of this course, the student will be able to use access terminals to interrogate 1A ESS processor for problem data; use documentation to analyze problem data; and locate the associated software or hardware defect and take appropriate corrective action.

Instruction: Major topics covered in the course are 1A ESS processor hardware fundamentals and maintenance procedures and 1A ESS system operation and maintenance. Methods of instruction include self-paced instruction and problem-solving.

Credit Recommendation: In the vocational certificate category, 6 semester hours in Digital Switching Systems Maintenance (8/89) (10/95).

5ESS BRCS-CTX Translations (32370000)

Location: Phoenix, AZ; Lakewood, CO; Minneapolis, MN; and Salt Lake City, UT.

Length: 40 hours (1 week).

Dates: January 1988-Present.

Objective: To provide students with information necessary to build and maintain the database to add 5ESS switch Business and Residential Custom Services and Centrex Customers.

Learning Outcome: Upon successful completion of this course, the student will be able to exhibit competence in all #5ESS business and residential custom service and centrex service translation related problems.

Instruction: Major topics covered in the course are features, capabilities, and troubleshooting procedures for the BRCS/CTX. Methods of instruction include computer-assisted instruction under the direct supervision of an instructor (CBT).

Credit Recommendation: In the vocational certificate or lower division baccalaureate/associate degree category, 1 semester hour in Digital Switching Systems Maintenance (8/89) (10/95).

5ESS Introduction (32320000)

Location: Phoenix, AZ; Lakewood, CO; Minneapolis, MN; and Salt Lake City, UT.

Length: 40 hours (1 week).

Dates: July 1987-Present.

Objective: To allow the student to become familiar with the 5ESS components, interfaces and subsystems, supporting maintenance facilities, and documentation.

Learning Outcome: Upon successful completion of this course, the student will be able to use all 5ESS system documentation; understand all system hardware and operating system software; understand interconnecting modules; and use digital switching and distributed processing concepts.

Instruction: Major topics covered in the course are an overview of the major subsystem modules comprising the 5ESS, digital transmission and switching concepts including ISDN, documentation for maintenance and repair of the 5ESS, and local and remote facilities maintenance for the 5ESS. Methods of instruction include computer-assisted instruction under the direct supervision of an administrator.

Credit Recommendation: In the vocational certificate category, 2 semester hours or in the lower division baccalaureate/associate degree category, 1 semester hour in Telecommunications (8/89) (10/95).

5ESS ISDN Maintenance (32400000)

Location: All U.S. West locations.

Length: 24 hours (3 days).

Dates: March 1988-December 1995.

Objective: To familiarize the student with modern communication networks that enable both circuit and packet switched services and communications protocols that apply to ISDN and the 5ESS switch.

Learning Outcome: Upon successful completion of this course, the student will be able to recognize protocols and standards as they apply to the 5ESS switch and to maintain and repair both hardware and software.

Instruction: Major topics covered in the course are the advantages of packet switching versus circuit switching, standards used in ISDN, and major components of Integrated Services Line Unit. Methods of instruction include lecture and discussion.

Credit Recommendation: In the upper division baccalaureate degree category, 1 semester hour in Computer Science or Telecommunications (8/89).

5ESS Maintenance (32350000)

Location: Phoenix, AZ; Lakewood, CO; Minneapolis, MN; and Salt Lake City, UT.

Length: 64 hours (8 days).

Dates: July 1987-Present.

Objective: To enable the student to recognize and correct fault conditions on the 5ESS switch and perform routine maintenance.

Learning Outcome: Upon successful completion of this course, the student will be able to respond to alarms caused by diagnostic failures; perform line maintenance and clear network failures; and perform ongoing ESS switch software maintenance.

Instruction: Major topics covered in the course are self-maintenance, software backup and maintenance, use of the 5ESS Master Control Center, how to perform network measurements; and use of maintenance documentation and diagnostic reports. Methods of instruction include computer-assisted instruction under direct supervision of an instructor (CBT).

Credit Recommendation: In the vocational certificate category, 3 semester hours or in the lower division baccalaureate/associate degree category, 1 semester hour in Digital Switching System Maintenance (8/89) (10/95).

5ESS Overview (32310000)

Location: Phoenix, AZ; Lakewood, CO; Minneapolis, MN; and Salt Lake City, UT.

Length: 24 hours (3 days).

Dates: July 1987-August 1994.

Objective: To provide the student with basic knowledge of the functional units, system architecture, and maintenance facilities of the 5ESS.

Learning Outcome: Upon successful completion of this course, the student will be able to use all 5ESS system documentation; understand all system hardware and operating system software; and understand digital switching concepts and distributed processing concepts.

Instruction: Major topics covered in the course are a functional description of 5ESS modules, a description of the software architecture, and an overview of maintenance facilities. Methods of instruction include computer-assisted instruction and the use of videotapes.

Credit Recommendation: In the lower division baccalaureate/associate degree category, 1 semester hour in Computer Technology (8/89).

5ESS Remote Switching System Operation and Maintenance (32390000)

Location: Phoenix, AZ; Lakewood, CO; Minneapolis, MN; and Salt Lake City, UT.

Length: 40 hours (1 week).

Dates: July 1987-Present.

Objective: To provide the student with an understanding of the three modules of a 5ESS switch, major self-maintenance features, and adding or modifying switch data.

Learning Outcome: Upon successful completion of this course, the student will be able to maintain 5ESS remote switching modules; maintain hardware and software; and respond to system alarms.

Instruction: Major topics covered in the course are resolving diagnostic failures and the operation of the Master Control Center for solving system problems and performing recent changes. Methods of instruction include computer-assisted instruction under direct supervision of an instructor (CBT).

Credit Recommendation: In the vocational certificate category, 2 semester hours in Digital Switching Systems Maintenance or in the lower division baccalaureate/associate degree category, 1 semester hour in Digital Switching Systems Maintenance (8/89) (10/95).

5ESS Switch Analyzation (32380000)

Location: Phoenix, AZ; Lakewood, CO; Minneapolis, MN; and Salt Lake City, UT.

Length: 56 hours (7 days).

Dates: February 1989-Present.

Objective: To provide the student with an understanding of initialization/maintenance procedures and how to perform file system maintenance and storage media updates.

Learning Outcome: Upon successful completion of this course, the student will be able to solve system initialization problems; add memory to switching modules; analyze office monitoring system reports; and manage office-dependent data.

Instruction: Major topics covered in the course are use of the file system and application programs, audits, asserts and initialization procedures, system recovery procedures, log files, and transaction reports. Methods of instruction include computer-assisted instruction under direct supervision of an instructor (CBT).

Credit Recommendation: In the vocational certificate category or in the lower division baccalaureate/associate degree category, 3 semester hours in Digital Switching Systems Software (8/89) (10/95).

5ESS Switch Surveillance (32330000)

Location: Phoenix, AZ; Lakewood, CO; Minneapolis, MN; and Salt Lake City, UT.

Length: 24 hours (3 days).

Dates: July 1987-Present.

Objective: To provide the student with practical experience using the Master Control Center, system documentation, and job aids to respond to 5ESS switch alarms and system failures.

Learning Outcome: Upon successful completion of this course, the student will be able to respond to alarms; perform emergency call traces; and prioritize machine-generated output messages.

Instruction: Major topics covered in the course are the major self-maintenance features of the 5ESS switch, the 5ESS switch documentation, functions of the Master Control Center components, response to maintenance alarm, and determining proper response to diagnostic system status reports. Methods of instruction include computer-assisted instruction under the direct supervision of an administrator (CBT).

Credit Recommendation: In the vocational certificate category, 1 semester hour in Digital Switching Systems Maintenance (8/89) (10/95).

5ESS Switch Translations (32360000)

Location: Phoenix, AZ; Lakewood, CO; Minneapolis, MN; and Salt Lake City, UT.

Length: 40 hours (1 week).

Dates: July 1987-Present.

Objective: To provide the student with knowledge necessary to manipulate translation data to locate, create, correct, and check translation troubles in the 5ESS switch.

Learning Outcome: Upon successful completion of this course, the student will

be able to exhibit competence in all 5ESS switch translation procedures and locate and repair 5ESS switch split translations by using the Office Data Base Editor (ODBE).

Instruction: Major topics covered in the course are major self-maintenance features of the 5ESS switch, text interface and menu modes of change menus and views (RC/V), office-dependent data, problems with digital analysis, routing, and line/trunk translations, and terms associated with office-based relations. Methods of instruction include computer-assisted instruction (CBT).

Credit Recommendation: In the vocational certificate category or in the lower division baccalaureate/associate degree category, 1 semester hour in Digital Switching Systems Maintenance (8/89) (10/95).

5ESS Trunk Maintenance (32340000)

Location: Phoenix, AZ; Lakewood, CO; Minneapolis, MN; and Salt Lake City, UT.

Length: 16 hours (2 days).

Dates: July 1987-Present.

Objective: To provide the student with information necessary to perform routine maintenance tests on new trunk groups and service groups.

Learning Outcome: Upon successful completion of this course, the student will be able to resolve trunk and subscriber line troubles using the Trunk Line Work Station (TLWS).

Instruction: Major topics covered in the course are computer emulation of the functions and responses of the 5ESS switch, and use of the Trunk Line Work Station (TLWS) to test trunks and resolve trunk-related equipment problems. Methods of instruction include computer-assisted instruction (CBT).

Credit Recommendation: In the vocational certificate category, 1 semester hour in Digital Switching Systems Maintenance (8/89) (10/95).

Air Leak Locating (1663000)

Location: Phoenix, AZ; Lakewood, CO; Des Moines, IA; Minneapolis, MN; and Portland, OR.

Length: 36-40 hours (5 days).

Dates: April 1988-December 1993.

Objective: To provide the student with knowledge to become familiar with the major parts of an air pressure system, the tools and techniques used in measuring such a system, and the methods used in finding leaks in pressurized systems.

Learning Outcome: Upon successful completion of this course, the student will be able to identify the parts of a pressurized system and the tools to measure these systems; compute flow rate and pressure drop; and determine basic calculations of fluid and pressure flow and use them in leak detection.

Instruction: Major topics covered in the course are tools used in pressurized system measurements, hardware components of systems, cable pressurization and calculations of pressurization and flow, and use of gradient method and helium method of locating leaks. Methods of instruction include self-paced laboratory and cassette tapes.

Credit Recommendation: In the vocational certificate or lower division baccalaureate/associate degree category, 1 semester hour in Air Pressure Systems (8/89).

Basic Carrier for Outside Forces (17060000)

Location: Phoenix, AZ; Lakewood, CO; and Des Moines, IA.

Length: 32 hours (1 week).

Dates: April 1982-December 1994.

Objective: To provide the student with the fundamentals of both analog and digital carrier systems.

Learning Outcome: Upon successful completion of this course, the student will be able to demonstrate knowledge of analog carrier operation and of analog equipment; identify the major components of two basic analog equipment configurations; perform voltage and loss measurements; and isolate reported trouble in a defective analog system with the necessary tools/test sets.

Instruction: Major topics covered in the course are frequency combining and separating, multichannel operation, signal loss and loss measurements, analog troubleshooting, digital carriers, encoding and decoding, and specialized digital operations. Methods of instruction include lecture, discussion, and laboratory exercises.

Credit Recommendation: In the lower division baccalaureate/associate degree category, 1 semester hour in Communication Systems Practices (8/89).

Basic Electricity (32800000 and 3611000)

Location: Phoenix, AZ; Lakewood, CO; Minneapolis, MN; Albuquerque, NM; Salt LakeCity, UT; and Seattle, WA.

Length: 32 hours (1 week).

Dates: September 1979-December 1994.

Objective: To teach the student the basic principles of simple electrical circuits.

Learning Outcome: Upon successful completion of this course, the student will be able to solve fundamental electrical problems; apply proper safety precautions in work settings; adjust and use basic test equipment in electrical circuit measurements; and explain basic current, voltage, resistance, and power relationship in DC and AC circuits.

Instruction: Major topics covered in the course are voltage, current, resistance series and parallel components, and AC components. Methods of instruction include lecture, discussion, and laboratory.

Credit Recommendation: In the vocational certificate category, 2 semester hours in Basic Electricity (8/89).

Basic Electricity (10310000)

Location: Phoenix, AZ; Lakewood, CO; and Salt Lake City, UT.

Length: 64-80 hours (8-10 days).

Dates: March 1986-December 1994.

Objective: To acquaint the student with the fundamental principles of electricity and electronics.

Learning Outcome: Upon successful completion of this course, the student will be able to make simple DC and AC circuit calculations; identify the symbols for simple passive and active components; and describe certain electrical/electronic concepts, such as resonance, rectification, amplification, transformer ratio, etc.

Instruction: Major topics covered in the course are DC components and relationships, AC components and relationships, and single semiconductor devices. Methods of instruction include lecture, laboratory, and self-paced reading/instruction.

Credit Recommendation: In the lower division baccalaureate/associate degree category, 4 semester hours in Electronics Technology (8/89).

Basic Electronics (10300000)

Location: Phoenix, AZ; Lakewood, CO; and Salt Lake City, UT.

Length: 102-120 hours (13-15 days).

Dates: March 1986-December 1994.

Objective: To acquaint the student with the fundamental principles of electricity and electronics and digital logic.

Learning Outcome: Upon successful completion of this course, the student will be able to make simple DC and AC circuit calculations; describe the operation of several semiconductor devices; make simple digital logic/Boolean algebra calculations; and describe many electrical/electronic concepts, such as resonance, transformer operation, rectification, etc.

Instruction: Major topics covered in the course are DC components and relationships, AC components and relationships, active semiconductor devices, and digital logic concepts. Methods of instruction include lecture, laboratory, and self-paced reading/instruction.

Credit Recommendation: In the lower division baccalaureate/associate degree category, 6 semester hours in Electronics Technology (8/89).

Basic Transmission and Signaling Principles (1605A000)

Location: Phoenix, AZ; Lakewood, CO; and suitcase locations.

Length: 32 hours (4 days).

Dates: January 1986-December 1994.

Objective: To acquaint the student with the fundamental principles of signaling and signal transmissions.

Learning Outcome: Upon successful completion of this course, the student will be able to describe and define transmission fundamentals; describe the function of several types of devices used in signal transmission/teleplay; calculate gains and losses for a typical network; and describe typical transmission impairments and their remedies.

Instruction: Major topics covered in the course are communications and signal-noise considerations, basic circuit elements, measurement of transmission, transmission line concepts, and telephone system considerations. Methods of instruction include discussions and self-paced instruction.

Credit Recommendation: In the vocational certificate category, 1 semester hour in Data Communications or in the upper division baccalaureate degree category, 1 semester hour in Communications, Electronics Technology, or Transmission Lines (8/89).

Cable Fault Locating (16620000)

Location: Phoenix, AZ; Lakewood, CO; Des Moines, IA; Minneapolis, MN; and Seattle, WA.

Length: 40 hours (1 week).

Dates: July 1980-August 1994.

Objective: To provide students with knowledge in the use and application of various fault-locating equipment.

Learning Outcome: Upon successful completion of this course, the student will be able to identify various fault types and the affected conductors; measure the characteristics of a conductor; and estimate the approximate distance to a fault.

Instruction: Major topics covered in the course are conductor and fault characteristics, use of various fault-locating sets, and choice of appropriate measuring set. Methods of instruction include self-paced instruction.

Credit Recommendation: In the vocational certificate category, 1 semester hour in Electrical Technology (8/89).

Centron Chain Curriculum
1. Introduction to Telecommunications (50950000)
2. Centron Custom-System and Station Features (Central Territory) (5002AOCT)
3. Centron Custom-System and Station Features (Eastern Territory) (5002AOET)
4. Centraflex I, II, III, IV/Centron (Western Territory) (5003OOWT)
5. Centron Custom-Sales Application (50080000)

Location: All U.S. West locations with territorial customization for Eastern, Central, and Western customers.

Length: 32 hours (4 days).

Dates: June 1988-December 1994.

Objective: To provide the student with a brief introduction to telecommunications concepts and analyze the Custom Centron system station features and sales applications.

Learning Outcome: Upon successful completion of this course, the student will be able to describe different telecommunications systems; describe Centron Custom Sales Application System; describe the implementation, features, and services of this system; and describe a plan for evaluating the system it services, and sales and marketing features among the competition in the public sector.

Instruction: Major topics covered in the course are telecommunications terminology and concepts, transmission media, Centron standard and optical features and product benefits, Centron Sales Application System and service mechanisms, quality control, and sales and marketing procedures for applications of this system. Methods of instruction include lecture and discussion.

Credit Recommendation: In the lower division baccalaureate/associate degree category, 2 semester hours in Telecommunications (8/89). **NOTE:** Students must successfully complete course 50950000, and either 5002AOCT, 5002AOET, or 5003OOWT, and 50080000 to receive the credit recommendation. Students who receive credit for this curriculum should not receive credit for the Fiber-Carrier, Fiber-End User, or Network Sizing and Control Curricula.

Circuit Reading (12200000 and 3182000)

Location: Phoenix, AZ; Lakewood, CO; Des Moines, IA; and suitcase locations.

Length: 37-40 hours (1 week).

Dates: August 1979-December 1995.

Objective: To enable students to read standard schematic diagrams and drawings.

Learning Outcome: Upon successful completion of this course, the student will be able to identify and interpret terms and abbreviations used on standard drawings and understand the circuit drawing from end to end.

Instruction: Major topics covered in the course are symbology and various standard types of drawings. Methods of instruction include self-paced instruction.

Credit Recommendation: In the lower division baccalaureate/associate degree category, 1 semester hour in Basic Circuit Reading (8/89).

Computer Network Architectures Continued: Module 5 (55050000)

Location: U.S. West Learning Systems and Employee Development Center, Lakewood, CO.

Length: 73 hours (2 weeks).

Dates: December 1990-December 1993.

Objective: To explore the upper layers of the OSI model and its interaction with major vendor systems.

Learning Outcome: Upon successful completion of this course, the student will be able to compare LAN topologies; compare methodologies of using base band and broad band systems; explain the importance of IEEE 802.2; explain how a central office-based LAN may be structured; and describe the capabilities of CPET carrier multiplexing equipment.

Instruction: Major topics covered in the course are LAN technology and standards; LAN operating systems and products; MANS; T-Carrier fundamentals; switching systems; network evolution to ISDN; and ISDN. Methods of instruction include lecture/discussion, and laboratory.

Credit Recommendation: In the graduate degree category, 6 semester hours in Data Processing, Computer Science, or MBA/Telecom Management (12/90). **NOTE:** Student must complete this course plus Module 3 (The Chained Layers [55030000] and Module 4 (Computer Network Architectures [55040000) to receive credit.

Computer Network Architectures: Module 4 (55040000)

Location: U.S. West Learning Systems and Employee Development Center, Lakewood, CO.

Length: 73 hours (2 weeks).

Dates: October 1990-December 1993.

Objective: To explore the middle layers of the OSI model and its interaction with major vendor systems.

Learning Outcome: Upon successful completion of this course, the student will be able to describe and discuss the three major areas of computer network architectures; describe and discuss packet switching from the perspective of technology; and describe and discuss computer network architecture of major vendors.

Instruction: Major topics covered in the course are packet switching; X.25 recommendation; SNA; DNA; and UNISYS. Methods of instruction include lecture/discussion, laboratory, computer-assisted/videotape, and classroom exercises.

Credit Recommendation: In the graduate degree category, 6 semester hours in Data Processing, Computer Science, or MBA/Telecom Management (12/90). **NOTE:** Student must complete this course plus Module 3 (The Chained Layers [55030000]) and Module 5 (Computer Network Architectures Continued [55050000]) to receive credit.

Computing Systems and the OSI Model: Module 2 (55020000)

Location: U.S. West Learning Systems and Employee Development Center, Lakewood, CO.

Length: 73 hours (2 weeks).

Dates: August 1990-December 1993.

Objective: To introduce fundamental architecture concepts of computer systems including operating systems, common software packages, and OSI layers.

Learning Outcome: Upon successful completion of this course, the student will be able to develop algorithms and write BASIC programs to implement these algorithms; identify the principal components of a computing system; describe a bus architecture; compare and contrast various types of data base management systems and explain the importance of fourth-generation languages; and explain the concept of protocol transparency.

Instruction: Major topics covered in the course are introduction to programming; data base management systems; software development tools; computer architecture (introduction); operating systems (introduction); memory management; processor management; and the file system. Methods of instruction include lecture/discussion, laboratory, and problem-solving.

Credit Recommendation: In the lower division baccalaureate/associate degree category, 3 semester hours in Electronics Technology (12/90).

(1) Data Communications Introduction (33000000)
(2) Data Communication Protocols (33010000)

Location: All U.S. West locations.

Length: 1. 16 hours (2 days). 2. 24 hours (3 days).

Dates: July 1989-December 1994.

Objective: (1) To provide the student with a foundation for further study in the data communications series. (2) To enable the student to examine the reasons for and the advantages of a layered structure for protocols.

Learning Outcome: Upon successful completion of this course, the student will be able to understand the impact of data speed, transmission impairments, and service degradation on communication systems; understand the significance of several protocols; and recognize the need for protocol compatibility in multivendor equipment environments.

Instruction: Major topics covered in the course are data signals, modulation techniques, transmission media, multiplexing techniques, and transmission impairments. Methods of instruction include lecture and the use of videotapes.

Credit Recommendation: In the lower division baccalaureate/associate degree category, 1 semester hour in Data Communications Technology or Telecommunications Technology (8/89). **NOTE:** Students must successfully complete both courses to receive the credit recommendation.

Data Communications ISDN (33020000)

Location: All U.S. West locations.

Length: 24 hours (3 days).

Dates: July 1989-December 1994.

Objective: To provide the student with an understanding of major concepts about ISDN, a telephone network architecture that includes voice, circuit and packet switched data, and video.

Learning Outcome: Upon successful completion of this course, the student will be able to understand ISDN user to network interfaces, call path, and switch architecture; understand packet switching versus circuit switching; understand channel protocols for ISDN; understand ISO 7 layer model; and understand Common Channel Signaling System Seven.

Instruction: Major topics covered in the course are ISDN attributes, standard interfaces and protocols, capabilities, and switch architectures. Methods of instruction include lecture and discussion and use of videotapes.

Credit Recommendation: In the upper division baccalaureate degree category, 2 semester hours in Computer Science, Information Systems, or Telecommunications (8/89).

Data Communications Packet Switching (33030000)

Location: All U.S. West locations.

Length: 20 hours (2.5 days).

Dates: July 1989-December 1994.

Objective: To provide the student with an understanding of packet switching concepts and the specific features of DIGIPAC, a packet switching service.

Learning Outcome: Upon successful completion of this course, the student will be able to compare methods of data transmission, including hardware and software aspects, and understand DIGIPAC pricing, applications, and benefits.

Instruction: Major topics covered in the course are packet switching standards, protocols, hardware, DIGIPAC features, pricing, and selling to the customer. Methods of instruction include lecture and discussion.

Credit Recommendation: In the lower division baccalaureate/associate degree category, 1 semester hour in Computer Technology, Information Systems, or Telecommunications (8/89).

Data Communications Signaling System 7 (33040000)

Location: All U.S. West locations.

Length: 20 hours (2.5 days).

Dates: July 1989-December 1994.

Objective: To provide the student with an understanding of the principles and applications of common channel signaling network elements.

Learning Outcome: Upon successful completion of this course, the student will be able to understand principles and applications of common channel signaling networks; recognize the major elements in the common channel signaling network architecture; and understand support systems such as SMS and SEAS.

Instruction: Major topics covered in the course are evaluation of intelligent networks, architecture, and operations of SS7 networks, 800 service features and operation, and maintenance philosophy of CCS/SS7 networks. Methods of instruction include lecture and demonstration.

Credit Recommendation: In the upper division baccalaureate degree category, 1 semester hour in Computer Science or Telecommunications (8/89).

Design Center Engineering (30700000)

Location: Phoenix, AZ; Lakewood, CO; Minneapolis, MN; Albuquerque, NM; Salt Lake City, UT; and Seattle, WA.

Length: 80 hours (2 weeks).

Dates: September 1982-August 1994.

Objective: To train the student in the design and planning of a communications distribution center.

Learning Outcome: Upon successful completion of this course, the student will be able to implement and maintain the design engineer's portion of plans; implement, maintain, and change distribution area plans; and schedule and track the design engineer's work load.

Instruction: Major topics covered in the course are design criteria for distribution facility. Methods of instruction include lecture, laboratory work, and discussion.

Credit Recommendation: In the vocational certificate category, 1 semester hour in Communications Network Design (8/89).

DMS100 and #5ESS Curriculum (Western Territory On)
1. DMS 100 Hands-On (50040000)
2. #5 ESS Overview (50070000)
3. DMS 100 System Design (50050000)
4. DMS 100 Provisioning (50060000)

Location: Portland, OR, and Seattle, WA.

Length: 32 hours (3 days).

Dates: November 1988-December 1995.

Objective: To provide the student with an understanding of services, features, and architecture of the DMS100 digital switch.

Learning Outcome: Upon successful completion of this course, the student will be able to understand architecture and features of DMS100; configure DMS100 system to present understandable feature interactions; complete relevant implementation forms; and understand basic features of #5ESS.

Instruction: Major topics covered in the course are #5ESS overview, DMS100 system design, and DMS100 provisioning. Methods of instruction include lecture, discussion, and laboratory exercises.

Credit Recommendation: In the vocational certificate or lower division baccalaureate/associate degree category, 1 semester hour in Telecommunications Theory (8/89). **NOTE:** Students must successfully complete all four courses to receive the credit recommendation.

Fiber-Carrier Curriculum
1. Introduction to Telecommunications (50950000)
2. Fiber Optics Technology and Service Carrier Marketing (50820000)

Location: All U.S. West locations.

Length: 24 hours (3 days).

Dates: June 1988-December 1994.

Objective: To provide the student with a brief introduction to telecommunications concepts and fiber optic technology.

Learning Outcome: Upon successful completion of this course, the student will be able to describe different telecommunications systems; accurately describe fiber optic service and components of a typical lightwave system; and explain equipment requirements, protection, options, and applications of DS3 service.

Instruction: Major topics covered in the course are telecommunications terminology and concepts, transmission media, basic fiber optic technology, advantages of fiber optic systems, and customer premises requirements and protection options. Methods of instruction include lecture and discussion.

Credit Recommendation: In the lower division baccalaureate/associate degree category, 1 semester hour in Telecommunications Technology (8/89). **NOTE:** Student must successfully complete both courses to receive the credit recommendation. Students who receive credit for this curriculum should not receive credit for Centron Chain, Fiber-End User, or Network Sizing and Control Curricula.

Fiber-End User Curriculum
Introduction to Telecommunications (50950000) (1)
Lightway 1 — Sales Applications (50810000) (2)

Location: All U.S. West locations.

Length: 24 hours (3 days).

Dates: June 1988-December 1994.

Objective: To provide the student with a brief introduction to telecommunications and fiber optic concepts used in selling the Lightway 1 system of high speed digital transmission systems.

Learning Outcome: Upon successful completion of this course, the student will be able to describe different telecommunications systems; understand the Lightway 1 leased bandwidth service including compatabilities, benefits, and operation; recognize competing systems and identify a set of issues important to prospects; and determine which customers are good prospects for using the system and identify a set of issues important to prospects.

Instruction: Major topics covered in the course are telecommunications terminology and concepts, transmission media, description of Lightway 1 system technology, interface, power, and space requirements, analysis of competitive systems, and customer analysis, approaches, appeals, and decision factors. Methods of instruction include lecture and discussion.

Credit Recommendation: In the lower division baccalaureate/associate degree category, 1 semester hour in Telecommunications Technology (8/89). **NOTE:** Students must successfully complete both courses to receive the credit recommendation. Students who receive credit for this curriculum should not receive credit for the Centron Chain, Fiber-Carrier, or Network Sizing and Control Curricula.

Fundamentals of Electricity and Transmission (16200000)

Location: Phoenix, AZ; Lakewood, CO; Des Moines, IA; Minneapolis, MN; and Portland, OR.

Length: 24 hours (3 days).

Dates: January 1988-December 1994.

Objective: To provide the student with a brief introduction to the principles of electricity and telephony.

Learning Outcome: Upon successful completion of this course, the student will be able to answer questions regarding the concepts covered.

Instruction: Major topics covered in the course are electricity fundamentals. Methods of instruction include lecture, self-paced reading, and experiments.

Credit Recommendation: In the vocational certificate category, 2 semester hours in Basic Electricity (8/89).

General Transmission Concepts (10320000)

Location: Phoenix, AZ; Lakewood, CO; and Salt Lake City, UT.

Length: 80 hours (10 days).

Dates: March 1986-December 1994.

Objective: To provide the student with the general transmission concepts and the knowledge required to identify the applications and components of communication systems.

Learning Outcome: Upon successful completion of this course, the student will be able to recognize and describe the characteristics of several different transmission networks.

Instruction: Major topics covered in the course are introduction to electrical signals, telephone switching concepts, customer loop design, carrier fundamentals, and data fundamentals. Methods of instruction include lecture and demonstration.

Credit Recommendation: In the upper division baccalaureate degree category, 3 semester hours in Introduction to Telecommunications (8/89).

IMS/VS DL/1 Batch Programming and BTS (766000WT)
1. IMS/VS DL/1 TP Programming and MFS (767500WT)
2. IMS Debugging Considerations (7680000WT)
3. IMS Checkpoint/Restart (768500WT)

Location: Denver, CO; Portland, OR; and Bellevue, WA.

Length: 72 hours (9 days).

Dates: June 1980-October 1994.

Objective: This series of basic courses provides the student with knowledge in IMS batch application coding, TP application coding, Message Format Services components, debugging techniques, and program system restarts.

Learning Outcome: Upon successful completion of this course, the student will be able to retrieve segments from a data base; provide linkages between Data Language/1 and COBOL; retrieve and respond to messages in the message queues; describe the facilities of the Message Format Service and the IMS functions peculiar to MFS; find information about the last eight user calls in a batch/online IMS dump; and identify types of failures and recovery mechanisms in an IMS/VS batch environment.

Instruction: Major topics covered in the course are Data Language/1, the program communication block, data base description, IMS batch processing region, region controller, DL/1-application program interface, IMS batch terminal simulation, IMS message processing control region, debugging, and system failures. Methods of instruction include tutor assistance, self-paced instruction, PC computer-based training, case problems, and the use of videotapes.

Credit Recommendation: In the upper division baccalaureate degree category, 3 semester hours in Computer Information Systems, Computer Science, or Data Processing (8/89). **NOTE:** Students must successfully complete all four courses to receive the credit recommendation.

Integrated Curriculum
Data Communications Fundamentals (50970000) (1)
ISDN—An Overview (50550000) (2)
ISDN—Total Solutions Sales Course (50560000) (3)

Location: All U.S. West locations.

Length: 64 hours (8 weeks).

Dates: July 1988-December 1994.

Objective: To provide the student with an understanding of basic data communication system concepts, ISDN network architecture, and the process of selling ISDN services to business customers.

Learning Outcome: Upon successful completion of this course, the student will be able to recognize, describe, and discuss the components of a data communication system, identify transmission impairments and signal improvement techniques; describe the integrated services digital network architecture; describe the ISDN products and services; analyze customer needs and propose system configurations for a client; and utilize company personnel in the sales effort.

Instruction: Major topics covered in the course are data processing hardware, data processing software, systems/networks, ISDN capabilities, applications and network interfaces, customer premise equipment and network architecture, identifying and preparing approaches to target prospects, following a pricing strategy methodology, and using company resources in the sales presentation and follow-up. Methods of instruction include lecture and discussion with case study analysis.

Credit Recommendation: In the lower division baccalaureate/associate degree category, 2 semester hours in Computer Technology, Information Systems, or Telecommunications (8/89). **NOTE:** Students who receive credit for this curriculum should not receive credit for the Packet Curriculum. Students must successfully complete all three courses to receive the credit recommendation.

Introduction to Communications and the Marketplace (Module 1) (55010000)

Location: U.S. West Learning Systems and Employee Development Center, Lakewood, CO.

Length: 73 hours (2 weeks).

Dates: June 1990-December 1993.

Objective: To survey the basic concepts of data communications and data processing to include the roles and strategies of major data communication equipment distributors.

Learning Outcome: Upon successful completion of this course, the student will be able to define basic terms associated with data communications; differentiate among circuit, message, and packet switching; and discuss requirements for network protocols; explain the concepts of clear channels, out of band signaling, and disassociated signaling networks; and discuss the concept of an integrated services network, and the basic structure of ISDN.

Instruction: Major topics covered in the course are evolution of distributed computing; point to point communications; switching evolution; open systems interconnection trends; SNA and DEC; network management; local area networks; and ISDN. Methods of instruction include lecture/discussion, laboratory, role playing, and case studies.

Credit Recommendation: In the lower division baccalaureate/associate degree category, 3 semester hours in Data Processing, Computer Science, or Telecommunications Management (12/90).

Introduction to Signaling and Supervision (10330000)

Location: Phoenix, AZ; Lakewood, CO; and Salt Lake City, UT.

Length: 40 hours (5 days).

Dates: March 1986-July 1995.

Objective: To provide the student with the basic concepts of signaling and signaling systems.

Learning Outcome: Upon successful completion of this course, the student will be able to identify the options required for signaling compatibility on all circuits and identify and resolve any compatible problems in the system.

Instruction: Major topics covered in the course are relays, DC loop signaling, single frequency signaling, and multiple frequency signaling. Methods of instruction include lecture and laboratory exercises.

Credit Recommendation: In the lower division baccalaureate/associate degree category, 2 semester hours in Communication Systems Practices (8/89).

Network Sizing and Control Curriculum
Introduction to Telecommunications (50950000) (1)
Network Engineering (50990000) (2)
Command-A-Link (50270000) (3)

Location: All U.S. West locations.

Length: 32 hours (4 days).

Dates: June 1988-December 1995.

Objective: To provide the student with a brief introduction to telecommunication concepts, network engineering, and the Command-A-Link sales application.

Learning Outcome: Upon successful completion of this course, the student will be able to describe different telecommunications systems; understand basic communications engineering terms and formulas used in traffic engineering; and understand the rules of the company-specific Command-A-Link sales application.

Instruction: Major topics covered in the course are telecommunications terminology and concepts, transmission media, Erlang B and C communication engineering tables, review of WATS pricing and rules, components of Command-A-Link, and rules for Command-A-Link sales. Methods of instruction include lecture, discussion, and laboratory exercises.

Credit Recommendation: In the lower division baccalaureate/associate degree category, 2 semester hours in Telecommunications (8/89). **NOTE:** Students must successfully complete all three courses to receive the credit recommendation. Students who receive credit for this curriculum should not receive credit for the Centron Chain, Fiber-End User, or Fiber-Carrier Curricula.

Packet Curriculum
Data Communication Fundamentals (50970000) (1)
DIGIPAC 101—Basic Packet Switching Service (50400000) (2)
DIGIPAC Applications (50420000) (3)
4. Total Solutions Sales Course (50560000)

Location: All U.S. West locations.

Length: 72 hours (9 days).

Dates: July 1988-December 1994.

Objective: To provide the student with an understanding of basic data system concepts, how packet switched networks work, and the DIGIPAC system offering.

Learning Outcome: Upon successful completion of this course, the student will be able to recognize, describe, and discuss the components of a data communication system; identify transmission impairments and signal improvement techniques; describe packet switching hardware, standards, and protocols; understand DIGIPAC features, pricing, and how to apply to customer needs; and prepare a DIGIPAC sales proposal.

Instruction: Major topics covered in the course are data processing hardware, data processing software, systems/networks, standards and protocols used in packet-switched networks, selling DIGIPAC, including characteristics and benefits, analysis of target customers and prospects, and pricing and sales procedures for DIGIPAC. Methods of instruction include lecture and discussion with case study.

Credit Recommendation: In the lower division baccalaureate/associate degree category, 2 semester hours in Computer Technology, Information Systems, or Telecommunications (8/89). **NOTE:** Students must successfully complete all four courses to receive the credit recommendation. Students who receive credit for this curriculum should not receive credit for the Integrated Curriculum.

Special Services Circuit Design (10360000)

Location: Phoenix, AZ; Lakewood, CO; and Salt Lake City, UT.

Length: 176 hours (22 days).

Dates: March 1986-December 1995.

Objective: To teach the student voice frequency special service circuit design in the areas of nonswitched circuits, switched circuits, data circuits, and access service circuits.

Learning Outcome: Upon successful completion of this course, the student will be able to design and construct a two-point private line data circuit using available hardware and information, and design and construct an Inter Tandem PBX Tie Trunk using available hardware and information.

Instruction: Major topics covered in the course are two-point private line, switched special services, PBX services, "T" carrier services, data circuits, and dial Tie Trunks. Methods of instruction include lecture, discussion, and laboratory exercises.

Credit Recommendation: In the upper division baccalaureate degree category, 8 semester hours in Communications Circuit Design (8/89).

The Chained Layers: Module 3 (55030000)

Location: U.S. West Learning Systems and Employee Development Center, Lakewood, CO.

Length: 73 hours (2 weeks).

Dates: September 1990-December 1993.

Objective: To explore the lower layers of the OSI model and its interaction with major vendor systems.

Learning Outcome: Upon successful completion of this course, the student will be able to differentiate between design based on blocking probability and design based on delay considerations; state the network design problem; explain the effects of various routing strategies on network costs and performance; differentiate between connection-based networks and connectionless systems; and describe the routing algorithm used in each of the example networks.

Instruction: Major topics covered in the course are physical layer protocols; DTE/DEC interface; transmission media; binary synchronous communications; digital data communications message protocol; introduction to network design; designing local access networks; and designing packet networks. Method of instruction include lecture, discussion, and laboratory.

Credit Recommendation: In the graduate degree category, 6 semester hours in Data Processing, Computer Science, or MBA/Telecom Management (12/90). **NOTE:** Student must complete this course plus Module 4 (Computer Network Architectures [55040000]) and Module 5 (Computer Network Architectures Continued [55050000]) to receive credit.

Understanding Digital Communication (32110000)

Location: All U.S. West locations.

Length: 20 hours (2.5 days).

Dates: January 1989-December 1995.

Objective: To provide the student with an awareness of digital technology used in the telecommunications industry.

Learning Outcome: Upon successful completion of this course, the student will be able to describe and discuss digital theory and applications in telecommunications.

Instruction: Major topics covered in the course are pulse code modulation theory, digital transmission network theory, and digital switching theory. Methods of instruction include lecture and use of video tapes.

Credit Recommendation: In the lower division baccalaureate/associate degree category, 1 semester hour in Digital Communications or Electronics Technology (8/89) (10/95).

UAW-Chrysler Technology Training Center

The UAW-Chrysler Technology Training Center (TTC) is a jointly planned and executed program and training facility of the UAW-Chrysler National Training Center (NTC). The NTC is independently incorporated as an educational organization and is responsible for the training provided at the TTC for both skilled trades and production workers of Chrysler Corporation who are represented by the United Auto Workers (UAW). All decisions are made jointly by UAW and Chrysler representatives.

Classes are conducted at the TTC in Detroit, Michigan in a facility of over 120,000 sq. ft. dedicated to training. It includes classrooms and labs with the latest technological equipment available for production facilities. It provides a centralized location for UAW-represented Chrysler workers to train on new equipment and to upgrade their skills.

Courses emphasize a mix of hands-on training with enough theory so that participants understand the technical systems, operations, and equipment. Class sizes are intentionally kept small (around 8) to ensure optimum instructor-student interaction and adequate hands-on experience. Courses are designed and developed by a Technology Training Committee of UAW and Chrysler representatives responsible for addressing the technical training needs of the company, in conjunction with the TTC staff and selected training providers with expertise in the technical area of each course.

Classes are conducted by highly qualified instructors of training providers who have subject expertise and training experience in the technical subject area. Successful completion of courses is based on obtaining a passing test score, completing all assigned laboratory exercises, and meeting minimum attendance requirements.

Source of official student records: Registry of Credit Recommendations, American Council on Education, One Dupont Circle, Washington, DC 20036-1193 or UAW-Chrysler Technology Training Center, Registration Desk, 3675 E. Outer Drive, Detroit, Michigan 48234, 1-800-683-8840.

Additional information about the courses: College Credit Recommendation Service, American Council on Education, One Dupont Circle, Washington, DC 20036-1193.

Advanced Geometric Dimensioning and Tolerancing for Manufacturing (GDT 300)

Location: UAW Chrysler Technology Training Center.

Length: 40 hours (1 week).

Dates: April 1997-Present.

Objective: To train the students how to identify and apply geometrical characteristics and tolerances as they relate to a part feature.

Learning Outcome: Upon successful completion of this course, the student will be able to verify features, features of size, and features of location.

Instruction: Major topics covered in the course are clearance; transition and/or interference fit; maximum material condition, least material condition, and tolerance zones on internal and external parts; and positional and bonus tolerances. Methods of instruction include lecture, discussion, written exercises, and hands-on labs.

Credit Recommendation: In the vocational certificate category or in the lower division baccalaureate/associate degree category, 2 semester hours in Geometric Dimensioning and Tolerancing (7/97).

Advanced Troubleshooting Hydraulic Equipment (HYT 300)

Location: UAW-Chrysler Technology Training Center, Detroit, Michigan.

Length: 40 hours (1 week).

Dates: April 1997-Present.

Objective: To provide the students with the ability to troubleshoot industrial hydraulic systems.

Learning Outcome: Upon successful completion of this course, the student will be able to troubleshoot hydraulic systems using prints of the equipment found in their plants; identify the pitfalls of installation procedures; determine why proportional valves fail and how to prevent failure; interpret from schematics the operation of logic and cartridge technology; read and interpret schematics to aid in troubleshooting; and demonstrate an understanding of servo valve technology and how to properly set up various types of servos.

Instruction: Major topics covered in the course are safety, troubleshooting techniques, formulas, directional valves, rectifier circuits, relief valves, check valves, modular stacks, mounting configuration, actuators, proportional valves technology, servo valves, pumps and control technology, logic control forces, filtration, fluid power graphical symbols, fluid power formulas, and definition of terms. Methods of instruction include lecture, discussion, classroom exercises, observations, lab exercises, a pre-test, and final examination.

Credit Recommendation: In the lower division baccalaureate/associate degree category, 2 semester hours in Fluid Power Technology (11/97).

Bearing Life Improvement (BLT 101)

Location: UAW Chrysler Technology Training Center.

Length: 24 hours (3 days).

Dates: April 1997-Present.

Objective: To provide the student with the ability to diagnose the root cause of bearing failure, and to properly repair failed bearings.

Learning Outcome: Upon successful completion of this course, the student will be able to determine proper sizes of shafts and housings; measure straight and tapered shafts; perform mounting and dismounting of bearings; properly lubricate rolling bearings; monitor rolling bearings to prevent catastrophic failure; identify all types of bearing failures and how to prevent future failures; and rework large bearings.

Instruction: Major topics covered in the course are bearing fundamentals, bearing types, bearing seals, bearing shafts and housing fits, bearing mounting and dismounting, bearing lubrication, and bearing failures. Methods of instruction include lecture, discussion, problem solving exercises, and hands-on labs.

Credit Recommendation: In the lower division baccalaureate/associate degree category, 1 semester hour in Bearing Life Improvement or Mechanical Engineering (7/97).

CATIA Fundamentals (CTT 200)

Location: UAW-Chrysler Technology Training Center, Detroit, Michigan.

Length: 40 hours (1 week).

Dates: November 1997-Present.

Objective: To teach the student how to log on to CATIA, move around inside of CATIA models, view multiple CATIA models, cut a section, and perform simple analysis and plotting using CATIA.

Learning Outcome: Upon successful completion of this course, the student will be able to identify key hardware; log on to CATIA; explain and identify key elements of an active CATIA window; create and store a Palette; cut a section using surface geometry; identify and explain the difference between Space and Draw Modes; manipulate geometry; and create, apply, verify and analyze a Filter.

Instruction: Major topics covered in the course are introduction to CATIA, logging on to CATIA, inside of CATIA, create and storing a Palette, interacting with CATIA, data structure, /M Find, REF-MODEL, working with CATIA, layer function, overlay tool, plotting, analysis function, and section cutting. Methods of instruction include lecture, discussion, classroom exercises, computer-aided instruction, and pre and post testing.

Credit Recommendation: In the lower division baccalaureate/associate degree category, 2 semester hours in Computer Aided Design (11/97).

CATIA Fundamentals for Die Makers (CTT 300)

Location: UAW-Chrysler Technology Training Center, Detroit, Michigan.

Length: 40 hours (1 week).

Dates: November 1997-Present.

Objective: To teach the student how to log on to CATIA, move around inside of CATIA models, view multiple CATIA models, cut a section, and perform simple analysis and plotting using CATIA with specific applications to die manufacturing.

Learning Outcome: Upon successful completion of this course, the student will be able to identify key hardware; log on to CATIA; explain and identify key elements of an active CATIA window; create and store a Palette; cut a Section using solid geometry; identify and explain the difference between Space and Draw Modes as they relate to solid geometry; manipulate geometry; and create, apply, verify and analyze a Filter.

Instruction: Major topics covered in the course are introduction to CATIA, logging onto CATIA, inside of CATIA, create and storing a Palette, interacting with CATIA, data structure, /M Find, REF-MODEL, working with CATIA, layer function, overlay tool, plotting, analysis function, section cutting, and simple geometric analysis specifically applied to die construction. Methods of instruction include lecture, discussion, classroom exercises, computer-aided instruction, and pre and post testing.

Credit Recommendation: In the lower division baccalaureate/associate degree category, 2 semester hours in Computer Aided Design (11/97).

Computerized Numerical Control: Advanced Troubleshooting the GE-FANUC Series 15 CNC (CNT 308)

Location: UAW Chrysler Technology Training Center.

Length: 40 hours (1 week).

Dates: April 1997-Present.

Objective: To train students on how to diagnose problems with the GE-Fanuc Series 15 CNC, and to get it back on line quickly.

Learning Outcome: Upon successful completion of this course, the student will be able to restart by using both the short and long methods; format data; analyze circuit flow; recognize danger areas when working with memory; access key functions; upload and download parts programs; set-up communications between a PC and the CNC; and troubleshoot.

Instruction: Major topics covered in the course are a refresher of keep relays, Basic Machine Interface (BMI), communications between the PC and CNC, deadload, and troubleshooting. Methods of instruction include lecture, discussion, problem solving exercises, hands-on labs, and an application project.

Credit Recommendation: In the lower division baccalaureate/associate degree category, 2 semester hours in Industrial Controls (7/97).

Computerized Numerical Control: Basic Operator Training for the GE FANUC Series 16/18A CNT (CNT 150)

Location: UAW Chrysler Technology Training Center.

Length: 16 hours (2 days).

Dates: April 1997-Present.

Objective: To provide the student with the skills needed to operate a GE Fanuc Series 16/18A control.

Learning Outcome: Upon successful completion of this course, the student will be able to identify the hardware components of the Series 16/18A control; understand the various CRT/MDI units and their functions; identify the components of a simple part program; interpret, edit, and register a part program; apply the operator panel functions; understand the decode process of M-Codes; recognize and describe the safety functions; and locate and interpret alarms and messages generated by the CNC.

Instruction: Major topics covered in the course are the fundamental concepts and safety measures that are implemented on the Series 16/18 control. Methods of instruction include hands-on lab exercises, lecture, and discussion sessions.

Credit Recommendation: In the vocational certificate category or in the lower division baccalaureate/associate degree category, 2 semester hours in Computerized Numerical Control (CNC) after completion of both Computerized Numerical Control: Basic Operator Training for the GE FANUC Series 16/18A CNC (CNT 150) and Computerized Numerical Control: Basic Operator Training for the GE FANUC Series 16/18B CNC (CNT 175) (7/97).

Computerized Numerical Control: Basic Operator Training for the GE FANUC Series 16/18B CNC (CNT 175)

Location: UAW Chrysler Technology Training Center.

Length: 16 hours (2 days).

Dates: April 1997-Present.

Objective: To provide the student with the skills needed to operate a GE Fanuc Series 16/18B control.

Learning Outcome: Upon successful completion of this course, the student will be able to identify the hardware components of the Series 16/18B control; understand the various CRT/MDI units and their functions; identify the components of a simple part program; interpret, edit, and register a part program; apply the operator panel functions; understand the decode process of M-Codes; recognize and describe the safety functions; and locate and interpret alarms and messages generated by the CNC.

Instruction: Major topics covered in the course are the fundamental concepts and safety measures that are implemented on the Series 16/18 control. Methods of instruction include hands-on lab exercises, lecture, and discussion sessions.

Credit Recommendation: In the vocational certificate category or in the lower division baccalaureate/associate degree category, 2 semester hours in CNC after completion of both Computerized Numerical Control: Basic Operator Training for the GE FANUC Series 16/18A CNC (CNT 150) and Computerized Numerical Control: Basic Operator Training for the GE FANUC Series 16/18B CNC (CNT 175) (7/97).

Computerized Numerical Control: Basic Operator Training for the GE-FANUC Series 15 CNC (CNT 100)

Location: UAW Chrysler Technology Training Center.

Length: 40 hours (1 week).

Dates: April 1997-Present.

Objective: To train skilled workers responsible for the GE-Fanuc Series 15 CNC how to properly operate this controller.

Learning Outcome: Upon successful completion of this course, the student will be able to select and use the automatic and manual modes of operation of the GE-Fanuc Series 15 CNC; read a parts program; and use signaling commands.

Instruction: Major topics covered in the course are automatic modes such as EDIT, MEM, MDI, and TAPE; manual modes such as JOG, INC, and DRN; optional skip block; axis operation; code systems; programs; and troubleshooting parameters and diagnostics. Methods of instruction include lecture, discussion, problem solving exercises, hands- on labs, and an application project.

Credit Recommendation: In the lower division baccalaureate/associate degree category, 2 semester hours in Basic CNC Operations (7/97).

Computerized Numerical Control: Basic Programmer Training for the GE-FANUC Series 15 CNC (CNT 400)

Location: UAW Chrysler Technology Training Center.

Length: 40 hours (1 week).

Dates: April 1997-Present.

Objective: To train skilled workers responsible for the GE-Fanuc Series 15 CNC how to properly program this controller.

Learning Outcome: Upon successful completion of this course, the student will be able to use, program, and troubleshoot the GE-Fanuc Series 15 CNC.

Instruction: Major topics covered in the course are practical functions and programs, operation, optional block skip, axis operation, code systems, programs, reading and saving programs, and troubleshooting parameters and diagnostics. Methods of instruction include lecture, discussion, problem solving exercises, hands-on labs, and an application project.

Credit Recommendation: In the lower division baccalaureate/associate degree category, 2 semester hours in Industrial Controls (7/97).

Computerized Numerical Control: Maintenance and Troubleshooting the GE FANUC Series Powermate D CNC (CNT 310)

Location: UAW Chrysler Technology Training Center.

Length: 32 hours (4 days).

Dates: April 1997-Present.

Objective: The purpose of this course is to provide the active participant the skills needed to operate and troubleshoot the GE Fanuc Powermate D.

Learning Outcome: Upon successful completion of this course, the student will be able to identify the hardware components of the Powermate D; understand the various CRT/MDI units and their functions; identify, interpret, edit, and register a simple part program; interpret and understand the purpose of functional instructions; identify PMC diagnostic tools; recommend corrective action by recognizing the state of the LED's, Model A I/O, and diagnostic page; locate and interpret alarms and messages generated by the CNC; and utilize Procomm Plus software to save and restore files.

Instruction: Major topics covered in the course are the fundamental concepts, components, ladder diagramming, and practical applications of the Powermate D control. Methods of instruction include hands-on lab exercises, lecture, and discussion sessions.

Credit Recommendation: In the vocational certificate category or in the lower division baccalaureate/associate degree category, 2 semester hours in Computerized Numerical Control (7/97).

Computerized Numerical Control: Maintenance and Troubleshooting the GE FANUC Series 16/18A CNC (CNT 350)

Location: UAW Chrysler Technology Training Center.

Length: 36 hours (4 days).

Dates: April 1997-Present.

Objective: To provide the student with the skills needed to operate and troubleshoot the GE Fanuc Series 16/18A control.

Learning Outcome: Upon successful completion of this course, the student will be able to identify the hardware components of the Series 16/18A control; understand the various CRT/MDI units and their functions; identify, interpret, edit, and register a simple part program; interpret and understand the purpose of functional instructions; identify PMC diagnostic tools; recommend corrective action by recognizing the state of the LED's, Model A I/O, and diagnostic page; locate and interpret alarms and messages generated by the CNC; and utilize Procomm Plus software to save and restore files.

Instruction: Major topics covered in the course are the fundamental concepts, components, ladder diagramming, and practical applications of the Series 16/18A control. Methods of instruction include hands-on lab exercises, lecture, and discussion sessions.

Credit Recommendation: In the vocational certificate category or in the lower division baccalaureate/associate degree category, 2 semester hours in Computerized Numerical Control (CNC) (7/97).

Computerized Numerical Control: Maintenance and Troubleshooting the GE FANUC Series 16/18B CNC (CNT 375)

Location: UAW Chrysler Technology Training Center.

Length: 36 hours (4.5 days).

Dates: April 1997-Present.

Objective: To provide the student with the skills needed to operate and troubleshoot the GE Fanuc Series 16/18B control.

Learning Outcome: Upon successful completion of this course, the student will be able to identify the hardware components of the Series 16/18B control; understand the various CRT/MDI units and their functions; identify, interpret, edit, and register a simple part program; interpret and understand the purpose of functional instructions; identify PMC diagnostic tools; recommend corrective action by recognizing the state of the LED's, Model A I/O, and diagnostic page; locate and interpret alarms and messages generated by the CNC; and utilize Procomm Plus software to save and restore files.

Instruction: Major topics covered in the course are the fundamental concepts, components, ladder diagramming, and practical applications of the Series 16/18B control. Methods of instruction include hands-on lab exercises, lecture, and discussion sessions.

Credit Recommendation: In the vocational certificate category or in the lower division baccalaureate/associate degree category, 2 semester hours in Computerized Numerical Control (CNC) (7/97).

Computerized Numerical Control: Troubleshooting GE-FANUC Digital Servo Alpha Series Drives (CNT 205)

Location: UAW Chrysler Technology Training Center.

Length: 24 hours (2 days).

Dates: April 1997-Present.

Objective: To provide the student with the skills needed to effectively troubleshoot GE-Fanuc drives.

Learning Outcome: Upon successful completion of this course, the student will be able to identify parts for ordering replacements; basic servo theory; automatic downloading of Servo parameters; GE-Fanuc DC link; handshaking between CNC and Servo amplifier; alarm Identification; and location of Servo components within the system.

Instruction: Major topics covered in the course are the fundamentals of troubleshooting, components, and practical applications of the GE Digital Servo Alpha Drives. Methods of instruction include hands-on lab exercises, lecture, and discussion sessions.

Credit Recommendation: In the vocational certificate category or in the lower division baccalaureate/associate degree category, 1 semester hour in Industrial Controls (7/97).

Computerized Numerical Control: Troubleshooting GE-FANUC Digital Servo C Series Drives (CNT 210)

Location: UAW Chrysler Technology Training Center.

Length: 24 hours (2 days).

Dates: April 1997-Present.

Objective: To provide the student with the skills needed to effectively troubleshoot GE-Fanuc drives.

Learning Outcome: Upon successful completion of this course, the student will be able to identify parts for ordering replacements; basic servo theory; automatic downloading of Servo parameters; GE-Fanuc DC link; handshaking between CNC and Servo amplifier; alarm identification; and location of Servo components within the system.

Instruction: Major topics covered in the course are the fundamentals of troubleshooting, components, and practical applications of the GE Digital Servo C Drives. Methods of instruction include hands-on lab exercises, lecture, and discussion sessions.

Credit Recommendation: In the vocational certificate category or in the lower division baccalaureate/associate degree category, 1 semester hour in Industrial Controls (7/97).

Computerized Numerical Control: Troubleshooting GE-FANUC Digital Servo S Series Drives (CNT 215)

Location: UAW Chrysler Technology Training Center.

Length: 24 hours (2 days).

Dates: April 1997-Present.

Objective: To provide the student with the skills needed to effectively troubleshoot GE-Fanuc drives.

Learning Outcome: Upon successful completion of this course, the student will be able to identify parts for ordering replacements; basic servo theory; automatic downloading of Servo parameters; GE-Fanuc DC link; handshaking between CNC and Servo amplifier; alarm identification; and location of Servo components within the system.

Instruction: Major topics covered in the course are the fundamentals of troubleshooting, components, and practical applications of the GE Digital Servo S Drives. Methods of instruction include hands-on lab exercises, lecture, and discussion sessions.

Credit Recommendation: In the vocational certificate category or in the lower division baccalaureate/associate degree category, 1 semester hour in Industrial Controls (7/97).

Computerized Numerical Control: Troubleshooting the GE-FANUC Series 15 CNC (CNT 300)

Location: UAW Chrysler Technology Training Center.

Length: 40 hours (1 week).

Dates: April 1997-Present.

Objective: To make technicians proficient troubleshooters of problems encountered in the GE-Fanuc Series 15 CNC Controller.

Learning Outcome: Upon successful completion of this course, the student will be able to identify key terms; enter and manipulate data; identify, locate, and trace basic machine interface signals from external sources through the system; select and set machine parameters; upload and download parts programs and parameters with a PC; and troubleshoot.

Instruction: Major topics covered in the course are nomenclatures, descriptions, and functional relationships of printed circuit boards; BMI signaling; sequence programming; softkey main menu screens; reading and saving programs; troubleshooting; and parts programming. Methods of instruction include lecture, discussion, problem solving exercises, hands-on labs, and an application project.

Credit Recommendation: In the lower division baccalaureate/associate degree category, 2 semester hours in Industrial Controls (7/97).

Die Making Technology (MDT 100)

Location: UAW-Chrysler Technology Training Center, Detroit, Michigan.

Length: 40 hours (1 week).

Dates: April 1997-Present.

Objective: To introduce students to the current and new technologies directly affecting die making at the Chrysler Corporation.

Learning Outcome: Upon successful completion of this course, the student will be able to understand and implement technologies used during the entire die construction process.

Instruction: Major topics covered in the course are the basic instructions on the technologies used for die design, CNC cutter path programming, die construction, die tryout, production tryout, metallurgy, heat treatment, welding, and preventive maintenance. Methods of instruction include lecture, discussion, lab exercises, and post test.

Credit Recommendation: In the lower division baccalaureate/associate degree category, 2 semester hours in Die Making Technology (11/97).

Electrical/Electronic Fundamentals for Mechanical Crafts (IET 105)

Location: UAW Chrysler Technology Training Center.

Length: 40 hours (1 week).

Dates: April 1997-Present.

Objective: To provide a skilled tradesperson from crafts other than the electrical and electronic crafts with a knowledge of the fundamentals of electrical and electronic technology, and to train them in basic electrical and electronic troubleshooting and repair procedures.

Learning Outcome: Upon successful completion of this course, the student will be able to use a multimeter to make voltage and current readings; read a resister value from three color code; use Ohm's law to calculate voltage drops, current, resistance, and power; calculate RC time for resister capacitor circuits, test relays, solenoids, contacters, switches, and motor starters; understand basic principles of AC and DC motors; work safely with electricity; and identify component parts in schematics and ladder diagrams.

Instruction: Major topics covered in the course are fundamental concepts, practical applications, units of measurement, circuits, components, circuit parts, ladder diagramming, and AC and DC motors. Methods of instruction include lecture, discussion, problem solving exercises, hands-on labs, and an application project.

Credit Recommendation: In the lower division baccalaureate/associate degree

category, 2 semester hours in Electrical/ Electronic Fundamentals (7/97).

Electronic Maintenance-Electrical Controls (IET 200A)

Location: Chrysler locations worldwide.

Length: 40 hours (1 week).

Dates: April 1997-Present.

Objective: To provide the student with the knowledge of the fundamentals of electrical and electronic technology, and to train them in basic electrical and electronic troubleshooting and repair procedures.

Learning Outcome: Upon successful completion of this course, the student will be able to work safely with electricity; use instruments to take and calculate electrical readings; read and interpret electrical drawings and ladder diagrams; identify and test electrical components; and understand the basic principles of AC and DC motors.

Instruction: Major topics covered in the course are fundamental concepts, practical applications, units of measurement, circuits, components, circuit parts, ladder diagramming, and AC and DC motors. Methods of instruction include lecture, discussion, problem solving exercises, and hands-on labs.

Credit Recommendation: In the lower division baccalaureate/associate degree category, 2 semester hours in Basic Industrial Electronics or Industrial Electricity (7/97).

Electronic Maintenance-Troubleshooting AC Motor Drives (IET 200D)

Location: UAW Chrysler Technology Training Center.

Length: 40 hours (1 week).

Dates: April 1997-Present.

Objective: To provide the student with the skill to set-up, troubleshoot, and repair AC motor drives.

Learning Outcome: Upon successful completion of this course, the student will be able to troubleshoot and perform tests on both P.W.M. and V.V.V.F. motor drives.

Instruction: Major topics covered in the course are variable-voltage, variable-frequency, pulse-width modulated types of AC motor drive types, and basic troubleshooting and repair techniques. Methods of instruction include lecture, discussion, problem solving exercises, and hands-on labs.

Credit Recommendation: In the lower division baccalaureate/associate degree category, 2 semester hours in Electronic Maintenance Troubleshooting AC Motor Drive (7/97).

Electronic Maintenance-Troubleshooting Electronics to the Board Level (IET 200B)

Location: UAW Chrysler Technology Training Center.

Length: 40 hours (1 week).

Dates: April 1997-Present.

Objective: To provide the student with the skill to troubleshoot electronic equipment to the board level.

Learning Outcome: Upon successful completion of this course, the student will be able to use test equipment to identify which board needs to be replaced or repaired in an electronic system.

Instruction: Major topics covered in the course are basic math, fundamental concepts, circuits, test equipment, solid state switches, op amps, power supplies, digital logic devices, measurement techniques, and troubleshooting. Methods of instruction include lecture, discussion, problem solving exercises, hands-on labs, and an application project.

Credit Recommendation: In the lower division baccalaureate/associate degree category, 2 semester hours in Survey of Electronics Fundamentals (7/97).

Electronic Maintenance-Troubleshooting Electronics to the Component Level (IET 200C)

Location: UAW Chrysler Technology Training Center.

Length: 40 hours (1 week).

Dates: April 1997-Present.

Objective: To provide the student with the skills necessary to troubleshoot electronic equipment to the component level.

Learning Outcome: Upon successful completion of this course, the student will be able to identify circuit boards in need of replacement and to use test equipment to identify defective components in a board.

Instruction: Major topics covered in the course are math review, electronic concepts, circuits, semiconductors, op amp circuits, power supplies, digital logic systems, and troubleshooting techniques. Methods of instruction include lecture, discussion, problem solving exercises, hands-on labs, and an application project.

Credit Recommendation: In the lower division baccalaureate/associate degree category, 2 semester hours in Electronic Troubleshooting (7/97).

Electronics for Material Handling Equipment (EMT 200)

Location: UAW Chrysler Technology Training Center

Length: 40 hours (1 week).

Dates: April 1997-Present.

Objective: To provide the student with the ability to troubleshoot and repair electric vehicles, such as, forklifts.

Learning Outcome: Upon successful completion of this course, the student will be able to effectively troubleshoot the electrical/electronic controls of electric powered vehicles; read single line drawings; read and interpret control circuit ladder diagrams; identify which circuit components need to be replaced in a control circuit; understand digital circuits well enough to identify defective components; test components; understand basic principles of DC motors; take voltage and current readings; and use a megger to test motors.

Instruction: Major topics covered in the course are proper use of test equipment, fundamental concepts of electricity, practical applications and calculations, circuits, basic electrical components, single line diagrams, control components, motors, drive train control components, ladder diagrams, and troubleshooting techniques. Methods of instruction include lecture, discussion, problem solving exercises, hands-on labs, and an application project.

Credit Recommendation: In the lower division baccalaureate/associate degree category, 2 semester hours in Survey of Electronics Fundamentals (7/97).

Fundamentals of Metallurgy (WLT 200)

Location: UAW Chrysler Technology Training Center.

Length: 40 hours (1 week).

Dates: April 1997-Present.

Objective: To provide the student with practical information regarding the manufacture, processing, and use of six important metals that are used in the automotive industry.

Learning Outcome: Upon successful completion of this course, the student will be able to identify common metals used in auto plants; determine a metals repair characteristics for welding or machining; quench and flame harden metals; perform hardness tests; and prepare metal for repair welding procedures.

Instruction: Major topics covered in the course are properties of metals; metal identification; material specifications; crystal structures; effects of plastic deformation and heat treatment; and applications of tool steels, cast irons, stainless steel, copper alloys, and aluminum. Methods of instruction include lecture, discussion, hands-on labs, and instructor demonstrations.

Credit Recommendation: In the lower division baccalaureate/associate degree category, 2 semester hours in Metallurgy (7/97).

Geometric Dimensioning and Tolerancing for Manufacturing (GDT 100)

Location: UAW Chrysler Technology Training Center.

Length: 40 hours (1 week).

Dates: April 1997-Present.

Objective: To train the students how to interpret blueprint drawings used in manufacturing and inspection of parts.

Learning Outcome: Upon successful completion of this course, the student will be able to recognize and sketch part views; and apply and interpret symbology, dimensioning, and tolerancing part features in order to provide a more thorough understanding.

Instruction: Major topics covered in the course are sketch part views, symbology, and dimensioning and tolerancing part features. Methods of instruction include lecture, discussion, written exercises, and hands-on labs.

Credit Recommendation: In the vocational certificate category or in the lower division baccalaureate/associate degree category, 2 semester hours in Blueprint Reading (7/97).

Industrial Air Logic (ALT 101)

Location: UAW Chrysler Technology Training Center.

Length: 40 hours (1 week).

Dates: April 1997-Present.

Objective: To train the students how to identify, size, and troubleshoot Air Logic systems.

Learning Outcome: Upon successful completion of this course, the student will be able to match circuit functions of air logic components to their symbols; fabricate, operate, and analyze various air logic circuits; and identify basic air logic circuits and the sequence of operation of the system.

Instruction: Major topics covered in the course are the fundamentals of compressed air, power valve symbology, comparison of electrical relays verses pneumatic air logic components and functions, ladder diagrams, and troubleshooting procedures and techniques. Methods of instruction include lecture, discussion, troubleshooting exercises, and hands-on labs.

Credit Recommendation: In the lower division baccalaureate/associate degree category, 2 semester hours in Pneumatic Logic Controls (7/97).

Industrial Gear Box Repair (GRT 300)

Location: UAW Chrysler Technology Training Center.

Length: 40 hours (1 week).

Dates: April 1997-Present.

Objective: To provide the student with the skills required to troubleshoot, align, install, and rebuild gear boxes.

Learning Outcome: Upon successful completion of this course, the student will be able to correctly rebuild gear boxes; troubleshoot failed gear boxes; select the proper gear box; properly install a speed reducer; correctly replace seals and bearings; and correctly set up a gear box using shims.

Instruction: Major topics covered in the course are alignment, installation, and rebuilding of gearboxes, including worm, helical, herringbone, and spur gear; selection of lubricants; and application of service ratings. Methods of instruction include lecture, discussion, problem solving exercises, and hands-on labs.

Credit Recommendation: In the lower division baccalaureate/associate degree category, 2 semester hours in Industrial Gear Box Repair or Mechanical Engineering (7/97).

Industrial Rigging (IMT 300)

Location: UAW Chrysler Technology Training Center.

Length: 40 hours (1 week).

Dates: April 1997-Present.

Objective: To train the student involved in rigging to do so efficiently, and above all, safely.

Learning Outcome: Upon successful completion of this course, the student will be able to inspect various equipment for safety; determine safe load limits; figure balance point of loads; and apply the techniques of a skilled rigger.

Instruction: Major topics covered in the course are how to inspect, select, and safely use hooks; nylon slings; wire rope slings; wire rope; chains; chain slings; hoist chain; metal mesh; and metal mesh slings. Methods of instruction include lecture, discussion, problem solving exercises, hands-on labs, and an application project.

Credit Recommendation: In the lower division baccalaureate/associate degree category, 2 semester hours in Industrial Rigging or Mechanical Engineering (7/97).

Mig and Flux Cored Arc Welding (WMF 200)

Location: UAW Chrysler Technology Training Center.

Length: 40 hours (1 week).

Dates: April 1997-Present.

Objective: To provide the student with the skills necessary to produce acceptable quality welds on automotive sheet metal and underbody chassis components.

Learning Outcome: Upon successful completion of this course, the student will be able to set-up/adjust production arc welding equipment; weld automotive sheet metal components with both welding processes to Chrysler Engineering processes standards; and inspect completed welds for quality.

Instruction: Major topics covered in the course are the fundamentals of both processes, set up and adjustment of equipment, selection of shielding gases, electrode wire specifications, and variables that affect weld quality and safe practices. Methods of instruction include lecture, discussion, instructor demonstrations, and hands-on lab exercises to enable students to produce quality fillet and groove welds.

Credit Recommendation: In the lower division baccalaureate/associate degree category, 2 semester hours in Welding (GMAW-FCAW) (7/97).

Overview of Mig and Tig Welding Processes (WMT 200)

Location: UAW Chrysler Technology Training Center.

Length: 40 hours (1 week).

Dates: April 1997-Present.

Objective: To provide the student with experience necessary to set up, adjust, and troubleshoot MIG and TIG welding equipment.

Learning Outcome: Upon successful completion of this course, the student will be able to perform welds on mild steel plate materials using the MIG and TIG welding processes; and select the proper filler metals and shielding gases.

Instruction: Major topics covered in the course are the fundamentals of both processes, set up and adjustment of equipment, selection of electrodes and filler metals shielding gases, process variations, and safety. Methods of instruction include lecture, discussion, instructor demonstration, and hands-on lab practice.

Credit Recommendation: In the lower division baccalaureate/associate degree category, 2 semester hours in Welding (GMAW-GTAW) (7/97).

Pipe and Tube Welding, MIG (WXT 200)

Location: UAW Chrysler Technology Training Center.

Length: 80 hours (2 weeks).

Dates: April 1997-Present.

Objective: To provide the student with skills necessary to produce acceptable quality welds on pipe and tubing.

Learning Outcome: Upon successful completion of this course, the student will be able to prepare, fit, and tack weld pipe joints; weld pipe in all positions using the gas metal arc welding process; and inspect completed welds for quality.

Instruction: Major topics covered in the course are set up and adjustment of MIG equipment for welding pipe; manual techniques to perform quality welds in the 2F, 5F, IGR, 2G, 5G, and fixed positions; and review of prequalified welding procedure specifications. Methods of instruction include lecture, discussion, instructor demonstrations, and hands-on lab practice.

Credit Recommendation: In the lower division baccalaureate/associate degree category, 3 semester hours in Steel Pipe Welding with GMAW (7/97).

Pipe and Tube Welding, SMAW (WXT 201)

Location: UAW Chrysler Technology Training Center.

Length: 80 hours (2 week).

Dates: April 1997-Present.

Objective: To provide the student with skills necessary to produce acceptable quality welds on pipe and tubing.

Learning Outcome: Upon successful completion of this course, the student will be able to prepare, fit, and tack weld pipe joints; weld pipe in all positions using the gas metal arc welding process (STICK); and inspect completed welds for quality.

Instruction: Major topics covered in the course are set up and adjustment of shielded metal arc equipment for welding pipe and manual techniques to perform quality fillet and groove welds in the 2F, 5F, IGR, 2G, and 5G positions. Methods of instruction include lecture, discussion, instructor demonstrations, and hands-on lab practice.

Credit Recommendation: In the lower division baccalaureate/associate degree category, 3 semester hours in Steel Pipe Welding with SMAW (7/97).

Pipe and Tube Welding, TIG (WXT 202)

Location: UAW Chrysler Technology Training Center.

Length: 80 hours (2 weeks).

Dates: April 1997-Present.

Objective: To provide the student with skills necessary to produce acceptable quality welds on pipe and tubing.

Learning Outcome: Upon successful completion of this course, the student will be able to prepare, fit, and tack weld pipe joints; weld pipe in all positions using the gas tungsten welding process; and inspect completed welds for quality.

Instruction: Major topics covered in the course are a review of the TIG welding process and electric arc safety; welding codes and specifications; joint designs and variables that affect quality; and manual techniques needed to weld in 1GR, 2G, 5G, and 6G positions. Methods of instruction include lecture, discussion, instructor demonstrations, and hands-on lab practice.

Credit Recommendation: In the lower division baccalaureate/associate degree category, 3 semester hours in Steel Pipe Welding using GTAW (7/97).

Programmable Logic Controllers: Advanced Allen Bradley PLC-5 Family/6200 Software (BAT 205)

Location: UAW Chrysler Technology Training Center.

Length: 40 hours (1 week).

Dates: April 1997-Present.

Objective: To train the students how to program, edit, and troubleshoot Allen Bradley PLC-5 Programmable Logic Controllers.

Learning Outcome: Upon successful completion of this course, the student will be able to enter, edit, and troubleshoot automation systems using the Allen Bradley PLC-5 Programmable Logic Controller.

Instruction: Major topics covered in the course are basic instructions using Allen Bradley 6200 software, hardware, and troubleshooting techniques. Methods of instruction include lecture, discussion, troubleshooting exercises, and hands-on labs.

Credit Recommendation: In the vocational certificate category or in the lower division baccalaureate/associate degree category, 2 semester hours in Industrial/Electrical Controls (7/97).

Programmable Logic Controllers: Advanced Allen Bradley PLC-5 Family/ICOM Software (BAT 255)

Location: UAW Chrysler Technology Training Center.

Length: 40 hours (1 week).

Dates: April 1997-Present.

Objective: To train the students how to program, edit, and troubleshoot Allen Bradley PLC-5 Programmable Logic Controllers.

Learning Outcome: Upon successful completion of this course, the student will be able to enter, edit, and troubleshoot automation systems using the Allen Bradley PLC-5 Programmable Logic Controller.

Instruction: Major topics covered in the course are basic instructions using Allen Bradley ICOM software, hardware, and troubleshooting techniques. Methods of instruction include lecture, discussion, troubleshooting exercises, and hands-on labs.

Credit Recommendation: In the vocational certificate category or in the lower division baccalaureate/associate degree category, 2 semester hours in the Industrial/Electrical Controls (7/97).

Programmable Logic Controllers: Allen Bradley 1336 Plus Family Variable Speed AC Drives (BAT 400)

Location: UAW Chrysler Technology Training Center.

Length: 40 hours (1week).

Dates: April 1997-Present.

Objective: To provide the student with operation and hands-on experience in the setup, installation, editing, and troubleshooting of the 1336-Plus Variable Frequency AC Drive.

Learning Outcome: Upon successful completion of this course, the student will be able to setup, install, edit, and troubleshoot the 1336-Plus Variable Frequency AC Drive.

Instruction: Major topics covered in the course are both the manual (stand alone) and remote I/O (with the PLC-5 Programmable Controller) operation of this drive, the HIM (Human Interface Module), the Drive Manager, and the Drive Monitor Software. Methods of instruction include lectures, hands-on experience, and labs.

Credit Recommendation: In the vocational certificate category or in the lower division baccalaureate/associate degree category, 2 semester hours in Industrial Maintenance (7/97).

Programmable Logic Controllers: Allen Bradley PLC-5 Family Panelview 1200 (BAT 300)

Location: UAW Chrysler Technology Training Center

Length: 40 hours (1 week).

Dates: April 1997-Present.

Objective: To provide the student with the operation and hands-on experience in setup, installation, editing, communications, and troubleshooting of the Allen Bradley PanelView 1200 operator terminal.

Learning Outcome: Upon successful completion of this course, the student will be able to setup, install, and edit the Allen Bradley 1200 operator terminal.

Instruction: Major topics covered in the course are PanelView 1200 operator terminal set up, configuration, DH+ and serial communications, standard programming techniques, the Allen Bradley Panel View 1200 operator terminal, Panel Builder software, and AB 5/40 PLC processors and software. Methods of instruction include lectures, hands-on experience, and labs.

Credit Recommendation: In the vocational certificate category or in the lower division baccalaureate/associate degree category, 2 semester hours in Industrial Electrical Controls (7/97).

Programmable Logic Controllers: Allen Bradley PLC-5 Family/6200 Software (BAT 105)

Location: UAW Chrysler Technology Training Center.

Length: 80 hours (2 weeks).

Dates: April 1997-Present.

Objective: To train the students how to program, edit, and troubleshoot Allen Bradley PLC-5 Programmable Logic Controllers.

Learning Outcome: Upon successful completion of this course, the student will be able to enter, edit, and troubleshoot automation systems using the Allen Bradley PLC-5 Programmable Logic Controller.

Instruction: Major topics covered in the course are basic instructions using Allen Bradley 6200 software, hardware, and troubleshooting techniques. Methods of instruction include lecture, discussion, troubleshooting exercises, and hands-on labs.

Credit Recommendation: In the vocational certificate category or in the lower division baccalaureate/associate degree category, 4 semester hours in Industrial/Electrical Controls (7/97).

Programmable Logic Controllers: Allen Bradley PLC-5 Family/ICOM Software (BAT 155)

Location: UAW Chrysler Technology Training Center.

Length: 80 hours (2 week).

Dates: April 1997-Present.

Objective: To train the students how to program, edit, and troubleshoot Allen Bradley PLC-5 Programmable Logic Controllers.

Learning Outcome: Upon successful completion of this course, the student will be able to enter, edit, and troubleshoot automation systems using the Allen Bradley PLC-5 Programmable Logic Controller.

Instruction: Major topics covered in the course are basic instructions using Allen Bradley ICOM software, hardware, and troubleshooting techniques. Methods of instruction include lecture, discussion, troubleshooting exercises, and hands-on labs.

Credit Recommendation: In the vocational certificate category or in the lower division baccalaureate/associate degree category, 4 semester hours in Industrial/Electrical Controls (7/97).

Qualification/Certification of Welding Skills for Pipe and Tube (TIG and GTAW) (WQT 404)

Location: UAW Chrysler Technology Training Center.

Length: 40 hours (1 week).

Dates: April 1997-Present.

Objective: To provide the student with the opportunity to demonstrate welding skills by completing welder qualification test(s) specified by the American Welding Society, American Society of Mechanical Engineers, and/or the Canadian Welding Bureau.

Learning Outcome: Upon successful completion of this course, the student will be able to receive a welder qualification certificate for passing a visual inspection and passing a guided bend test or fillet break test.

Instruction: Major topics covered in the course are welding codes and qualifications, material preparation, and fit-up. Methods of instruction include lecture, discussion, problem solving, and extensive performance tests that measure the level of skills needed to meet industrial code requirements for welding pipe and tube.

Credit Recommendation: In the lower division baccalaureate/associate degree category, 2 semester hours in Steel Pipe Welding (7/97).

Qualification/Certification of Welding Skills for Sheet Metal, Aluminum (WQT 407)

Location: UAW Chrysler Technology Training Center.

Length: 40 hours (1 week).

Dates: April 1997-Present.

Objective: To provide the student with the opportunity to demonstrate welding skills by completing welder qualification test(s) specified by the American Welding Society, American Society of Mechanical Engineers, and/or the Canadian Welding Bureau.

Learning Outcome: Upon successful completion of this course, the student will be able to receive a welder qualification certificate for passing a visual inspection and passing a guided bend test or fillet break test.

Instruction: Major topics covered in the course are a review of welding codes and specifications, material preparation and joint designs, distortion control, selection of electrodes, filler metals, and shielding gases. Methods of instruction include lecture, discussion, problem solving, and performance testing that measure the level of skills needed to meet American Welding Society (AWS) Sheet Metal Welding Code - D9.1.

Credit Recommendation: In the lower division baccalaureate/associate degree category, 2 semester hours in Aluminum Sheet Metal with GMAW and GTAW (7/97).

Qualification/Certification of Welding Skills for Sheet Metal, Steel, and Stainless (WQT 406)

Location: UAW Chrysler Technology Training Center.

Length: 40 hours (1 week).

Dates: April 1997-Present.

Objective: To provide the student with the opportunity to demonstrate welding skills by completing welder qualification test(s) specified by the American Welding Society, American Society of Mechanical Engineers, and/or the Canadian Welding Bureau.

Learning Outcome: Upon successful completion of this course, the student will be eligible to receive a welder qualification certificate for passing a visual inspection and passing a guided bend test or fillet break test.

Instruction: Major topics covered in the course are a review of welding codes and specifications, material preparation and joint fit-up, distortion control, selection of electrodes, filler metals, and shielding gases. Methods of instruction include lecture, discussion, problem solving exercises, and performance tests that measure the level of skills needed to meet AWS Sheet Metal Welding Code D9.1 requirements.

Credit Recommendation: In the lower division baccalaureate/associate degree category, 2 semester hours in General Welding Qualification (GMAW, FCAW, GTAW, and SMAW) (7/97).

Qualification/Certification of Welding Skills for Steel Pipe (MIG) (GMAW) (WQT 402)

Location: UAW Chrysler Technology Training Center.

Length: 40 hours (1 week).

Dates: April 1997-Present.

Objective: To provide the student with the opportunity to demonstrate welding skills by completing welder qualification test(s) specified by the American Welding Society, American Society of Mechanical Engineers, and/or the Canadian Welding Bureau.

Learning Outcome: Upon successful completion of this course, the student will be able to receive a welder qualification certificate for passing a visual inspection and passing a guided bend test or fillet break test.

Instruction: Major topics covered in the course are welding codes and qualifications, a review of safe practices, material preparation, and fit up of joint details. Methods of instruction include lecture, discussion, problem solving, and extensive performance tests that measure the level of skills needed to meet industrial welding code requirements.

Credit Recommendation: In the lower division baccalaureate/degree category, 2 semester hours in Steel Pipe Welding (GMAW) (7/97).

Qualification/Certification of Welding Skills for Steel Pipe (SMAW) (WQT 403)

Location: UAW Chrysler Technology Training Center.

Length: 40 hours (1 week).

Dates: April 1997-Present.

Objective: To provide the student with the opportunity to demonstrate welding skills by completing welder qualification test(s) specified by the American Welding Society, American Society of Mechanical Engineers, and/or the Canadian Welding Bureau.

Learning Outcome: Upon successful completion of this course, the student will be able to receive a welder qualification certificate for passing a visual inspection and passing a guided bend test or fillet break test.

Instruction: Major topics covered in the course are welding codes and qualifications, a review of safe practice, and material preparation. Methods of instruction include lecture, discussion, problem solving, and extensive performance tests that measure the level of skills needed to meet industrial welding code requirements.

Credit Recommendation: In the lower division baccalaureate/degree category, 2 semester hours in Steel Pipe Welding (GMAW) (7/97).

Qualification/Certification of Welding Skills for Structural Aluminum (WQT 401)

Location: UAW Chrysler Technology Training Center.

Length: 40 hours (1 week).

Dates: April 1997-Present.

Objective: To provide the student with the opportunity to demonstrate welding skills by completing welder qualification test(s) as specified by the American Welding Society, American Society of Mechanical Engineers, and/or the Canadian Welding Bureau.

Learning Outcome: Upon successful completion of this course, the student will be able to receive a welder qualification certificate for passing a visual inspection and passing a guided bend test or fillet break test.

Instruction: Major topics covered in the course are a review of welding procedure specifications, variables that affect weld quality, and preparation of metal coupons for destructive testing. Methods of instruction include lecture, discussion, problem solving exercises, and extensive performance tests that measure the level of skills needed to meet the AWS D1.2 Aluminum Welding Code.

Credit Recommendation: In the lower division baccalaureate/associate degree category, 2 semester hours in Structural Aluminum Welding with GMAW and GTAW (7/97).

Qualification/Certification of Welding Skills for Structural Steel (WQT 400)

Location: UAW Chrysler Technology Training Center.

Length: 40 hours (1 week).

Dates: April 1997-Present.

Objective: To provide the student with the opportunity to demonstrate welding skills by completing welder qualification test(s) as specified by the American Welding Society, American Society of Mechanical Engineers, and/or the Canadian Welding Bureau.

Learning Outcome: Upon successful completion of this course, the student will be able to receive a welder qualification certificate for passing a visual inspection and passing a guided bend test or fillet break test.

Instruction: Major topics covered in the course are a review of welding procedure specifications, variables that affect weld quality, and preparation of metal coupons for destructive testing. Methods of instruction include lecture, discussion, problem solving exercises, and welding performance tests on ASTM A-36 structural steel plate in 2F, 3G, and 4G positions.

Credit Recommendation: In the lower division baccalaureate/associate degree category, 2 semester hours in Structural Steel Welding (7/97).

Qualification/Certification of Welding Skills for Tool and Die (WQT 405)

Location: UAW Chrysler Technology Training Center.

Length: 40 hours (1 week).

Dates: April 1997-Present.

Objective: To provide the student with the opportunity to demonstrate welding skills by completing welder qualification test(s) as specified by the Chrysler Die Engineering process standards.

Learning Outcome: Upon successful completion of this course, the student will be able to receive a welder qualification certificate for passing a visual inspection; passing a cross section and etch test; and passing a die penetrant test inspection.

Instruction: Major topics covered in the course are allowable repairs, problem solving exercises, and acceptance criteria per Die Engineering process standards. Method of instruction includes extensive performance testing to measure the level of skills and competency required to weld tool and die materials.

Credit Recommendation: In the lower division baccalaureate/associate degree category, 2 semester hours in Tool and Die Welding (7/97).

Robotics: ABB Electrical Maintenance (ABT 350)

Location: UAW Chrysler Technology Training Center.

Length: 40 hours (1 week).

Dates: April 1997-Present.

Objective: To provide the student with the ability to identify the electrical components and theory of operation, and apply proper troubleshooting procedures to the IRB 2000, 3000/3200 and 6000 robots.

Learning Outcome: Upon successful completion of this course, the students should be able to operate the control panel and programming unit; read ABB circuit diagrams; set up commutation resolvers, limit, and sync switches; analyze and interpret system fault indications and codes; diagnose and repair basic electrical faults and servo-systems data; make basic adjustments, diagnose and rectify emergency stop conditions; make I/O connections to peripheral equipment and safety devices; and repair and replace system components.

Instruction: Major topics covered in the course are the operation of robot control and mechanical unit, safety precautions used while troubleshooting the electrical system, description of components in the robot controller, principles of logical troubleshooting from Power-up through Emergency stop loop, and the Servo system. Methods of instruction include lecture, discussion, problem solving exercises, and hands-on labs.

Credit Recommendation: In the vocational certificate category or in the lower division baccalaureate/associate degree category, 2 semester hours in Industrial Maintenance (7/97).

Robotics: ABB Operation/Programming (ABT 300)

Location: UAW Chrysler Technology Training Center.

Length: 40 hours (1 week).

Dates: April 1997-Present.

Objective: To provide the student with the ability to operate and program the robot using the teach pendant.

Learning Outcome: Upon successful completion of this course, the student will be able to understand Basic Robot Safety principles, control panel, and program unit operation; understand programming structure and language; create programs including function, positioning, and conditional programs; use of subprograms and basic adaptive programming; perform manual functions and system setup; transfer programs to and from disks; edit programs or instructions; interpret system diagnostic messages; and clear minor operation faults.

Instruction: Major topics covered in the course are the operating controls and indicators on the Robot Controller; safety precautions used while programming and program execution; selecting proper menus from the program unit for programming and program execution; positioning the robot by use of joystick control; and advanced programming principles including: Subprogramming, Reference point program control, Storing Positional Locations, and Palletizing. Methods of instruction include lecture, discussion, problem solving exercises, and hands-on labs.

Credit Recommendation: In the vocational certificate category or in the lower division baccalaureate/associate degree category, 2 semester hours in Industrial Maintenance (7/97).

Robotics: Nachi Electrical Maintenance (RNT 350)

Location: UAW Chrysler Technology Training Center.

Length: 40 hours (1 week).

Dates: April 1997-Present.

Objective: To provide the student with the ability to effectively maintain, diagnose, troubleshoot, and repair the base AR Nachi control cabinet and Nachi robot arm.

Learning Outcome: Upon successful completion of this course, the student will be able to electrically maintain, diagnose, troubleshoot, and repair the base AR11 Nachi control cabinet and Nachi robot arm.

Instruction: Major topics covered in the course are robot safety, system components, control system overview, power supply distribution, encoder system, servo drive system, pc board/function, schematic diagram analysis, error codes, I/O monitoring, component replacement procedures, hands-on troubleshooting, arm wiring, motor replacement, and cabinet maintenance. Methods of instruction include hands-on labs, pre-tests, and post tests.

Credit Recommendation: In the vocational certificate category or in the lower division baccalaureate/associate degree category, 2 semester hours in Industrial Maintenance (7/97).

Robotics: Nachi Operation/Programming (RNT 300)

Location: UAW Chrysler Technology Training Center.

Length: 40 hours (1 week).

Dates: April 1997-Present.

Objective: To provide the student with the ability to effectively operate, program, make program modifications, and prepare or maintain the Nachi robot.

Learning Outcome: Upon successful completion of this course, the student will be able to effectively operate and program the Nachi AR1 controller/robot arm.

Instruction: Major topics covered in the course are fundamental robot concepts, operation, programming system, screen displays, mode selections, writing/editing robot programs, communication with external equipment, and error reporting/recovery and practical applications. Methods of instruction include lecture, discussion, problem solving exercises, and hands-on labs utilizing all material covered.

Credit Recommendation: In the vocational certificate category or in the lower division baccalaureate/associate degree category, 2 semester hours in Industrial Robotics (7/97).

Structural Steel Welding (WTT 200)

Location: UAW Chrysler Technology Training Center.

Length: 40 hours (1 week).

Dates: April 1997-Present.

Objective: To enable the student to produce acceptable quality welds on structural steel using the shielded metal arc and flux-cored arc welding processes.

Learning Outcome: Upon successful completion of this course, the student will be able to prepare structural steel for welding; set up and adjust welding equipment; and weld structural steel in all positions.

Instruction: Major topics covered in the course are material specification, weld joint design, tacking and fit up, filler metal selection and storage of low hydrogen electrodes, set up and adjustment of equipment, and welding techniques. Methods of instruction include lecture, discussion, problem solving exercises, hands-on labs, and an application project.

Credit Recommendation: In the lower division baccalaureate/associate degree category, 2 semester hours in Welding

Structural Steel with SMAW and FCAW (7/97).

Troubleshooting Fluid Power Equipment (FLT 100)

Location: UAW Chrysler Technology Training Center.

Length: 40 hours (1 week).

Dates: April 1997-Present.

Objective: To provide the student with the knowledge of how to effectively and efficiently troubleshoot, repair, and maintain fluid power equipment.

Learning Outcome: Upon successful completion of this course, the student will be able to read pneumatic schematics; identify and understand common hydraulic and pneumatic components; understand common circuit applications; troubleshoot fluid power circuits; perform preventive maintenance; and remove, clean, and replace fluid power components.

Instruction: Major topics covered in the course are basic concepts of compressed air, hydraulics, hydraulic directional control valves, pressure control valves, volume controls, cylinder applications, pumps, and pneumatic power supply systems. Methods of instruction include lecture, discussion, problem solving exercises, hands-on labs, and an application project.

Credit Recommendation: In the lower division baccalaureate/associate degree category, 2 semester hours in Survey of Fluid Power (7/97).

Troubleshooting Industrial Hydraulic Equipment (HYT 100)

Location: UAW Chrysler Technology Training Center.

Length: 40 hours (1 week).

Dates: April 1997-Present.

Objective: To provide the student with the ability to troubleshoot industrial hydraulic equipment.

Learning Outcome: Upon successful completion of this course, the student will be able to read hydraulic schematics; identify and understand common hydraulic components; troubleshoot hydraulic power circuits; perform preventive maintenance on hydraulic systems; and remove, clean, and replace hydraulic power components.

Instruction: Major topics covered in the course are an introduction to fluid power and hydraulics; directional control valves; manual overrides; pressure control valves; volume controls; rapid advance, feed speed, and rapid return circuits; cylinder applications; pumps; servo hydraulic systems; and industrial hydraulic circuits and applications. Methods of instruction include lecture, discussion, problem solving exercises, hands-on labs, and an application project.

Credit Recommendation: In the vocational certificate category or in the lower division baccalaureate/associate degree category, 2 semester hours in Basic Hydraulics (7/97).

Troubleshooting Pneumatic Controls and Equipment (PNT 101)

Location: UAW Chrysler Technology Training Center.

Length: 40 hours (1 week).

Dates: April 1997-Present.

Objective: To provide the student with the ability to troubleshoot pneumatic controls and equipment.

Learning Outcome: Upon successful completion of this course, the student will be able to read pneumatic schematics; identify and understand pneumatic components; troubleshoot pneumatic control circuits and programmable logic controllers; read and interpret ladder diagrams; understand common circuit applications; perform preventive maintenance on pneumatic systems; and remove, clean, and replace pneumatic components.

Instruction: Major topics covered in the course are basic concepts of compressed air, cylinders, control valves, volume controls, compressors, plant distribution systems, control circuitry, ladder diagramming, and troubleshooting and repair techniques. Methods of instruction include lecture, discussion, problem solving exercises, hands-on labs, and an application project.

Credit Recommendation: In the lower division baccalaureate/associate degree category, 2 semester hours in Mechanical Engineering (7/97).

Vibration Analysis, Alignment, and Balancing (VAT 100)

Location: UAW Chrysler Technology Training Center.

Length: 40 hours (1 week).

Dates: April 1997-Present.

Objective: To provide the student with the ability to troubleshoot vibration problems encountered in rotating equipment using vibration analysis. Also, learn how to properly align and balance rotating equipment.

Learning Outcome: Upon successful completion of this course, the student will be able to diagnose vibration problems; measure phase and vibration; analyze a spectrum; choose transducers; use spike energy; determine resonance; do reverse indicator alignment; compensate for thermal growth; determine balance weight; and perform correct balancing.

Instruction: Major topics covered in the course are basic vibration concepts as they relate to problems with rotating equipment, single channel FFT analysis, proper alignment procedures, and single and dual plane balancing. Methods of instruction include lecture, discussion, problem solving exercises, hands-on labs, and an application project.

Credit Recommendation: In the lower division baccalaureate/associate degree category, 2 semester hours in Survey of Vibration Analysis, Alignment, and Balancing or Mechanical Engineering (7/97).

Welding Aluminum Alloys (WAT 200)

Location: UAW Chrysler Technology Training Center.

Length: 40 hours (1 week).

Dates: April 1997-Present.

Objective: To provide the student with skills necessary to weld aluminum alloys using recommended welding processes and filler metals.

Learning Outcome: Upon successful completion of this course, the student will be able to select the appropriate welding process for aluminum; select the appropriate filler metal; set up and adjust the welding equipment; and produce acceptable quality welds on aluminum alloys.

Instruction: Major topics covered in the course are aluminum material specifications, selection of welding filler metals, surface preparation prior to welding, shielding gas selection, AC and DC, and DCEN. Methods of instruction include lecture, discussion, problem solving, instructor demonstration, hands-on labs, and an application project.

Credit Recommendation: In the lower division baccalaureate/associate degree category, 2 semester hours in Welding Aluminum (7/97).

Welding Safety and Overview of Processes (WPT 100)

Location: UAW Chrysler Technology Training Center.

Length: 40 hours (1 week).

Dates: April 1997-Present.

Objective: To provide the student with a general understanding of manual and semi-automatic welding processes used in metal working industries. In addition, the course will prepare the student to safely operate oxy-fuel gas and electric arc welding equipment per Chrysler MTI SMI-116.

Learning Outcome: Upon successful completion of this course, the student will be able to safely set-up and operate oxy-fuel cutting and electric arc welding equipment.

Instruction: Major topics covered in the courses are related hazards and safety precautions; proper set up adjustment of oxy-fuel gas and electric arc welding and cutting equipment; and the following welding processes: shielded metal arc, gas metal arc, gas tungsten arc, plasma arc, and oxy fuel gas cutting. Methods of instruction include lecture, discussion, instructor demonstrations, hands-on lab practices, problem solving, and a performance test.

Credit Recommendation: In the lower division baccalaureate/associate degree category, 2 semester hours in Welding Safety (7/97).

Welding Sheet Metal (WSM 200)

Location: UAW Chrysler Technology Training Center.

Length: 40 hours (1 week).

Dates: April 1997-Present.

Objective: To enable the student to produce acceptable quality welds on sheet metal using the shielded metal arc (STICK), gas metal arc (MIG), and gas tungsten arc welding process (TIG).

Learning Outcome: Upon successful completion of this course, the student will be able to identify the welding processes to use; set up and adjust welding equipment; and weld sheet metal in flat, horizontal, and vertical down welding positions.

Instruction: Major topics covered in the course are material specifications, weld joint designs, techniques for quality welds, process selection, filler metal selection, and distortion control. Methods of instruction include lecture, discussion, instructor demonstrations, and hands-on labs.

Credit Recommendation: In the lower division baccalaureate/associate degree category, 2 semester hours in Sheet Metal Welding using SMAW, GMAW, and GTAW (7/97).

Welding Tool and Die Steels (WDT 200)

Location: UAW Chrysler Technology Training Center.

Length: 40 hours (1 week).

Dates: April 1997-Present.

Objective: To enable the student to successfully repair weld tool and die steels using approved welding processes and procedures.

Learning Outcome: Upon successful completion of this course, the student will be able to identify various tool steels; apply the appropriate preheat; weld repair-worn or broken tools; and apply the appropriate post weld heat treatment.

Instruction: Major topics covered in the course are welding repair procedures for tool steels and cast die materials, material identification, hardness testing, preparation of material surfaces for welding, and preheat and postheat schedules. Methods of instruction include lecture, discussion, problem solving exercises, hands-on labs, and an application project.

Credit Recommendation: In the lower division baccalaureate/associate degree category, 2 semester hours in Tool and Die Welding (7/97).

UAW-Ford

The United Auto Workers and Ford Motor Company established the Education, Development and Training Program in the 1982 Collective Bargaining Agreement. The agreement charters the program to be responsive to the personal, educational, and training needs of UAW-represented hourly employees of Ford Motor Company.

The program is administered by the UAW-Ford National Development and Training Center (N.E.D.T.C.) located in Dearborn, Michigan, under the direction of a Joint Governing Body consisting of company and UAW Representatives.

The UAW serves more than 1,500,000 active and retired workers throughout the United States and Canada. Ford Motor Company manufactures, assembles, and markets its cars, trucks, tractors, and related automotive products through independent dealerships in the United State and Canada. The company has approximately 100,000 hourly, UAQ-represented workers in 20 states. In all, there are over 70 locations serviced by the UAW-Ford N.E.D.T.C.

Source of official student records: UAW-Ford National Development and Training Center, P.O. Box 6002, Dearborn, MI 48121.

Additional information about the courses: College Credit Recommendation Service, American Council on Education, One Dupont Circle, Washington, DC 20036-1193.

Employee Development

Successful Retirement Planning: Instructor Training

Location: UAW—Ford National Education, Development and Training Center.

Length: 44 hours (6 days).

Dates: August 1984-February 1990.

Objective: To train participants to deliver retirement planning programs.

Instruction: Major topics covered in the course are a review of the instructional skills necessary and the information base required to deliver a program on retirement planning that includes the following units: Planning, Health, Medication and Drugs, Social Security, Benefits, Money, Legal, and Leisure.

Credit Recommendation: In the lower division baccalaureate/associate degree or upper division baccalaureate degree category, 3 semester hours in Human Services Related Programs or Labor Studies (2/85).

UAW-GM Center for Human Resources

The Center for Human Resources Joint Skill Development and Training Department is located in the UAW-GM Center for Human Resources in Auburn Hills, Michigan. The Center for Human Resources (CHR) provides administrative, consultative, and training related services for the benefit of 200,000 UAW-represented GM employees throughout the country.

The CHR is also responsible for training and staff development for local union and management training representatives and joint committees throughout the United States.

Courses offered by the CHR are focused on preparing local training professionals to deliver training to UAW-represented employees at their plant locations. These courses are developed internally by course development specialists or are purchased from outside vendors and are revised as needed.

Source of official student records: Registry of Credit Recommendations, American Council on Education, One Dupont Circle, Washington, DC 20036-1193 or Joint Skill Development and Training Department, Program Development and Delivery Group, UAW-GM Center for Human Resources, 2630 Featherstone Road, Auburn Hills, MI 48326.

Additional information about the courses: College Credit Recommendation Service, American Council on Education, One Dupont Circle, Washington, DC 20036-1193.

Conflict Resolution Through Mediation

Location: UAW-GM Center for Human Resources in Auburn Hills MI, and regional sites at Decatur GA, Indianapolis IN, Royal Oak, MI, Saginaw MI, Flint MI, O'Fallon MO, and Cheektowago NY.

Length: 22 hours (3 days).

Dates: August 1995-Present.

Objective: To teach the mediation process as a conflict resolution technique.

Learning Outcome: Upon successful completion of this course, the student will be able to describe several causes and effects of conflict; distinguish mediation from other forms of dispute resolution; demonstrate effective mediation skills; be aware of the implications of a mediator's behavior; and identify advantages of co-mediation.

Instruction: Major topics covered in the course are understanding and dealing with conflict; preparation for, data gathering, and conducting mediation; power and influence; caucus; co-mediation; mediation ethics; and mediation closure. Methods of instruction include lecture, discussion, case studies, and role-playing.

Credit Recommendation: In the lower division baccalaureate/associate degree category, 1 semester hour in Human Resource Management (12/97).

Data Collection and Analysis

Location: UAW-GM Center for Human Resources in Auburn Hills MI, and regional sites at Decatur GA, Indianapolis IN, Royal Oak, MI, Saginaw MI, Flint MI, O'Fallon MO, and Cheektowago NY.

Length: 36 hours (5 days).

Dates: March 1996-Present.

Objective: To provide the participants with the skills needed for collection and analysis of data gathered through interviews, questionnaires and focus groups.

Learning Outcome: Upon successful completion of this course, the student will be able to identify the advantages and disadvantages of interviews, questionnaires, and focus groups; plan and develop a written questionnaire; plan and conduct an interview; and a focus group; and interpret and report on survey findings.

Instruction: Major topics covered in the course are methods and purpose of data collection; sampling; written questionnaires including data collection, data entry, and content analysis; developing and conducting interviews; focus groups; and use of MS Word, MS Excel, and QN survey design software to facilitate the data collection and analysis process. Methods of instruction include classroom exercises, case studies, computer software exercises, lecture and audio/visual materials.

Credit Recommendation: In the lower division baccalaureate/associate degree category, 2 semester hours in Research Methods (12/97).

Effective Business Writing

Location: UAW-GM Center for Human Resources in Auburn Hills MI, and regional sites at Decatur GA, Indianapolis IN, Royal Oak, MI, Saginaw MI, Flint MI, O'Fallon MO, and Cheektowago NY.

Length: 16 hours (2 days).

Dates: September 1993-Present.

Objective: To provide participants with a process to learn to write more effective documents.

Learning Outcome: Upon successful completion of this course, the student will be able to prepare and revise documents using a five-step writing process.

Instruction: Major topics covered in the course are planning the writing task; brainstorming; organizing ideas; drafting the document; and revising for clarity, emphasis. Methods of instruction include classroom exercises, activities, lecture, discussion, and audio visual materials.

Credit Recommendation: In the vocational certificate category or the lower division baccalaureate/associate degree category, 1 semester hour in Writing Skills (12/97).

Effective Classroom Instruction

Location: Center for Human Resources, Auburn Hills, MI and various locations throughout the U.S.

Length: 36 hours (4.5 days).

Dates: October 1988-Present.

Objective: To provide the participant with an understanding of the basic principles of effective instruction for use with adult learners.

Learning Outcome: Upon successful completion of this course, the student will be able to develop effective instructional delivery techniques, and select and use appropriate instructional methods and media.

Instruction: Major topics covered in the course are adult learning theory, instruction techniques and methods, and instructional media applications. Methods of instruction include examinations, projects, presentations, role play, demonstrations, programmed notes, small groups, and case studies.

Credit Recommendation: In the lower division baccalaureate/associate degree category, 1 semester hour in Teaching/Training Techniques (2/93).

Facilitator Skills

Location: Center for Human Resources, Auburn Hills, MI and various locations throughout the U.S.

Length: 36 hours (5 days).

Dates: February 1985-Present.

Objective: To provide the participant with an understanding of basic facilitation skills and principles.

Learning Outcome: Upon successful completion of this course, the student will be able to facilitate group activities, plan and conduct productive meetings, and communicate with groups more effectively.

Credit Recommendation: In the lower division baccalaureate/associate degree

category, 1 semester hour in Communication (2/93).

Human Resource Development: Roles and Responsibilities

Location: Center for Human Resources, Auburn Hills, MI and various locations throughout the U.S.

Length: 38 hours (4.75 days).

Dates: January 1992-Present.

Objective: To provide an overview of the principles and processes of personal and organizational change and development in a labor and management setting.

Learning Outcome: Upon successful completion of this course, the student will be able to describe roles and responsibilities of personal and organizational change, explain the role of change in a labor and management setting, and identify opportunities for labor and management integration toward change.

Instruction: Major topics covered in the course are personal change, organizational change, organizational development, and human resource development. Methods of instruction include examinations, projects, presentations, role plays, small group exercises, and personal assessment tools.

Credit Recommendation: In the lower division baccalaureate/associate degree category, 2 semester hours in Management, Public Administration, or Human Resources Development (2/93).

Implementing Innovation

Location: Center for Human Resources, Auburn Hills, MI and various locations throughout the U.S.

Length: 24 hours (3 days).

Dates: May 1992-Present.

Objective: To learn the skills and techniques essential for implementing innovation within an organization.

Learning Outcome: Upon successful completion of this course, the student will be able to identify the skills needed for implementing an organizational innovation, apply a process for introducing innovations within an organization, and recognize and deal with resistance to innovation.

Instruction: Major topics covered in the course are the process of consulting, techniques for implementing organizational change, and techniques for handling resistance to change. Methods of instruction include examinations, projects, presentations, process models, and structured exercises.

Credit Recommendation: In the lower division baccalaureate/associate degree category, 1 semester hour in Organization Dynamics (2/93).

Internal Consultant Curriculum CORE Series

Location: Center for Human Resources, Auburn Hills, MI and various locations throughout the U.S.

Length: *Part A*: 72 hours (2 weeks); *Part B*: 72 hours (2 weeks); *Part C*: 72 hours (2 weeks).

Dates: August 1985-Present.

Objective: To increase participants' ability to consult with individuals, groups, and organizations; to assess their current skills, learn consulting techniques, and acquire an understanding of organizational development techniques. *Part A*: To provide participants with an in-depth understanding of their values and beliefs and to use application of behavioral sciences to provide participants with an understanding of themselves in relation to the consulting role. *Part B*: To provide participants with a basic understanding of the theories, tools, methods, and instruments used in consulting. *Part C*: To provide participants with an understanding of the organizational environment and the ability to analyze the total organization as a system.

Learning Outcome: Upon successful completion of *Part A*, the student will be able to apply the experiential learning cycle to promote individual learning; document learning experiences; apply the PAC survey as a means of personal interpretation; describe various personality factors using the Myers-Briggs Type Indicator model; discuss transactional analysis; and describe the application of Gestalt theory within the organization. Upon successful completion of *Part B*, the student will be able to describe the aspects of giving and receiving feedback; demonstrate the process used to identify the consultant role to a client; describe the ethical considerations of the consultant/client relationship; perform a diagnosis of an organization and design an intervention; and identify primary and alternative consulting styles. Upon successful completion of *Part C*, the student will be able to describe the major foundations of organizational theory using systems concepts; describe four types of cultures that may prevail in an organization; describe the change models for organizations; and develop a strategic change plan using case studies and other information.

Instruction: Major topics covered in *Part A* are experiential learning, Theory X and Theory Y, hierarchy of needs, Myers-Briggs, transactional analysis, Gestalt Theory, and personal values. Methods of instruction include examinations, projects, presentations, visual aids, practice activities, problem solving models, and small group projects. Major topics covered in *Part B* are feedback, consultant identification, consultant/client relationships, ethics, interventions and style. Methods of instruction include examinations, projects, presentations, visual aids, practice activities, problem solving models, and small group projects. Major topics covered in *Part C* are general systems theory, organizational structure, change models, organizational culture, and strategic planning. Methods of instruction include examinations, projects, presentations, visual aids, practice activities, problem solving models, and small group projects.

Credit Recommendation: *Part A*: In the lower division baccalaureate/associate degree category, 3 semester hours in Interpersonal Processes or Communication. *Part B*: In the upper division baccalaureate degree category, 3 semester hours in Consultation or Consulting Techniques. *Part C*: In the upper division baccalaureate degree category, 3 semester hours in Organizational Change (2/93).

Introductory Presentation Skills

Location: Center for Human Resources, Auburn Hills, MI and various locations throughout the U.S.

Length: 20 hours (2.5 days).

Dates: August 1991-Present.

Objective: To provide the participant with a process model to plan, develop, and deliver group presentations.

Learning Outcome: Upon successful completion of this course, the student will be able to use a defined model to plan, develop and deliver presentations, recognize and address fears involved in making presentations, use a variety of presentation types, visual aids, and audio-visual equipment to enhance presentations and give and receive effective feedback.

Instruction: Major topics covered in the course are the presentation process model, message preparation, conquering fear, physical delivery skills, audience analysis, and environmental analysis. Methods of instruction include examinations, projects, presentations, process models, video-tape and audio visuals, and video-tape feedback.

Credit Recommendation: In the lower division baccalaureate/associate degree

category, 1 semester hour in Communication (2/93).

Planning for Joint Activities

Location: Center for Human Resources, Auburn Hills, MI and various locations throughout the U.S.

Length: 36 hours (4.5 days).

Dates: July 1992-Present.

Objective: To learn and apply principles of teamwork and interpersonal skills in facilitating labor/management activities.

Learning Outcome: Upon successful completion of this course, the student will be able to identify primary activities of labor and management representatives, recognize characteristics of effective joint labor and management teams, and determine natural labor and management integration opportunities.

Instruction: Major topics covered in the course are communication, personal development, labor/management action plans, and Myers-Briggs Type Indicators. Methods of instruction include structured exercises, self-assessment, role play, examinations, projects, and presentations.

Credit Recommendation: In the upper division baccalaureate degree category, 2 semester hours in Labor and Industrial Relations (2/93).

Principles of Training

Location: Center for Human Resources in Auburn Hills, MI and various locations throughout the U.S.

Length: 36 hours (1 week).

Dates: May 1986-March 1997.

Objective: Participants will be able to identify, understand, and apply the basic principles and techniques of training program design and administration.

Learning Outcome: Upon successful completion of this course, the student will be able to design and implement a plan for a comprehensive training program; monitor and evaluate training program effectiveness; and administer the training function as part of the total organization.

Instruction: Major topics covered in the course are integration of training, diagnostic tools, program design, administration, and action planning. Methods of instruction include lecture, discussion, role playing, and problem solving exercises.

Credit Recommendation: In the lower division baccalaureate/associate degree category, 3 semester hours in Human Resource Development, Training, or Personnel Management (3/92).

Training Needs Analysis

Location: Center for Human Resources in Auburn Hills, MI and various locations throughout the U.S.

Length: 14 hours (2 days).

Dates: April 1987-March 1997.

Objective: Participants will be able to identify, understand how to conduct a training needs analysis, and utilize its findings.

Learning Outcome: Upon successful completion of this course, the participant will be able to identify and define organizational training problems; develop a data based strategy for conducting a training needs analysis; and collect and analyze data and report on the findings of a training needs analysis.

Instruction: Major topics covered in the course are identification of organizational problems addressed by training; planning and designing a problem based training needs analysis; gathering, analyzing and interpreting data; and report writing. Methods of instruction include case studies, role playing, scenarios, lecture, discussion, and group activities.

Credit Recommendation: In the upper division baccalaureate degree category, 1 semester hour in Human Resource Development or Training and Personnel Management (3/92).

Ultrasound Diagnostic School

Ultrasound Diagnostic Schools (UDS), operated by Ultrasound Technical Services, a wholly owned subsidiary of Whitman Medical Corporation, are proprietary educational institutions devoted only to the training of Imaging technologists for the medical field. Established in 1977, UDS currently has school locations positioned along the Eastern seaboard of the United States from the Boston area to that of Miami, Florida and additional locations in Texas and Ohio. Locations are in the following cities: Marlborough, MA; Carle Place, NY; Elmsford, NY; New York, NY; Iselin, NJ; Philadelphia, PA; Pittsburgh, PA; Silver Spring, MD; Atlanta, GA; Tampa, FL; Jacksonville, FL; Pompano Beach, FL; Bellaire, TX; Irving, TX; and Independence, Ohio.

Two types of ultrasound training are offered by UDS: a basic program and a program of continuing medical education courses in diagnostic medical ultrasound. The basic training program is a 40 week didactic and laboratory instructional experience capped with an additional three and a half month, full-time, clinical externship in a hospital or clinical setting. The objective of the program is to train individuals in human anatomy, physiology and pathology, medical terminology, physics of ultrasound and doppler techniques, and evaluations in order that they may qualify as diagnostic medical sonographers. The continuing medical education course components are designed for practicing medical sonographers, physicians, and other medical personnel in imaging fields. Each facility conducts four sessions of the basic program each year: two during the day and two at night.

Each of the UDS institutions is accredited by the Accrediting Bureau of Health Education Schools, a U.S. Department of Education approved allied health accrediting body for private and public postsecondary institutions. Also each facility is licensed by its respective home state. All institutions are eligible to participate in the U.S. Department of Education Stafford Loan, Supplemental Loan for Students, and Pell Grant Program.

Source of official student records: Registry of Credit Recommendations, American Council on Education, One Dupont Circle, Washington, DC 20036-1193.

Additional information about the courses: Office of Corporate-Higher Education Programs, Thomas Edison State College, 101 West State Street, Trenton, NJ 08608-1176.

Adult Echocardiography

Location: Atlanta, GA; Bellaire, TX; Carle Place, NY; Elmsford, NY; Independence, OH; Irving, TX; Iselin, NJ; Jacksonville, FL; Marlborough, MA; New York, NY; Philadelphia, PA; Pittsburgh, PA; Pompano Beach, FL; Silver Spring, MD; and Tampa, FL.

Length: 48 hours (16 weeks).

Dates: September 1983-Present.

Objective: To perform basic adult echocardiographic exams on patients.

Learning Outcome: Upon successful completion of this course, the student will be able to perform basic echocardiographic examinations using ultrasound and recognizing common anomalies and pathology.

Instruction: Major topics covered in the course are basic cardiac anatomy and physiology; pathophysiology; hemodynamic changes; cardipmyopathy; great vessel diseases; physical principals; and instrumentation. Methods of instruction include lecture, discussion, and classroom exercises.

Credit Recommendation: In the lower division baccalaureate/associate degree or in the upper division baccalaureate degree category , 3 semester hours in Adult Echocardiography (3/90) (1/95).

Diagnostic Ultrasound Basic Program
Abdominal Sonography
Clinical Experience
Embryology
Human Anatomy and Physiology I
Human Anatomy and Physiology II
Medical Terminology
Obstetrical/Gynecological Sonography
Pathophysiology
Scanning Laboratory
Sonography Lab
Ultrasound Physics

Location: Ultrasound Diagnostic Schools in locations along the Eastern seaboard of the United States, Texas, and Ohio.

Length: *Version 1:* 484 hours (class and laboratory) (9 months); 480 hours externship (3 months); *Version 2:* 1,205 hours (54 weeks); 645 hours (class and laboratory) and 560 hours (clinical experience); *Version 3:* 1,340 hours (700 hours class and laboratory) (640 hours clinical study).

Dates: *Version 1:* September 1983-October 1994; *Version 2:* November 1993-Present; *Version 3:* January 1997-Present.

Objective: *Versions 1 and 2:* To provide students with the knowledge and skills necessary to achieve the competence level required for entry-level positions in applied ultrasound. *Version 3:* To enable the student to perform complex ultrasound exams on a variety of patients.

Learning Outcome: *Version 1:* Upon successful completion of *Section 1*, the student will be able to retain the knowledge of medical root, prefix and suffix, and be able to apply this knowledge to all new medical language encountered; and understand the pulse-echo principles of sound interaction with tissues and be able to begin to operate ultrasound equipment, choose proper transducers, and regulate equipment mechanisms. Upon successful completion of *Section 2*, the student will be able to identify the structure of the arterial and venous systems; distinguish between normal and pathological states by using patient scans and slides; identify the anatomical structure of the digestive system; define clinical symptoms of disorders; produce quality ultrasound studies of the accessory organs; identify the major structures associated with the urinary system, their functions and abnormalities, and differentiate them using ultrasonograms; identify the features of the adrenal glands, their relationship to surrounding structures, and their function as part of the endocrine system; define clinical symptoms of disorders and produce ultrasound studies of these glands; identify the features of the spleen, describe its role as part of the immune system, and distinguish abnormal states using patient scans and slides; and describe the anatomy and physiology of the lymphatic system and produce ultrasound studies for lymph node assessment. Upon the successful completion of *Section 3*, the student will be able to identify anatomical features of the female reproductive system, reproductive physiology of the female, identify pathological states, and produce ultrasound studies; understand gamete production, the fertilization process, early cell division, embryo implantation, fetal development, and recognition of birth defects; identify physiologic changes during pregnancy, identify and describe fetal anatomical development, and using ultrasound scans to distinguish normal and abnormal conditions. Upon successful completion of *Section 4*, the student will be able to describe the anatomy, physiology, and pathology of the parts studied and conduct ultrasound studies to detect pathological conditions. Upon successful completion of *Section 5*, the student will have knowledge of standard operating procedures for the performance of ultrasound studies in clinical settings and have achieved the competence required for entry-level positions in applied ultrasound. *Version 2:* Upon successful completion of *Section 1:*, the student will be retain the knowledge of medical root, prefix and suffix, and be able to apply this knowledge to all new medical language encountered; and understand the pulse-echo principles of sound interaction with tissues and be able to begin to operate ultrasound equipment, choose proper transducers, regulate equipment mechanisms, doppler principles, and spectral tracings. Upon successful completion of *Section 2*, the student will be able to identify the structure of the arterial and venous systems; distinguish between normal and pathological states by using patient scans and slides; drop Doppler into vessels to determine blood flow; identify the anatomical structure of the digestive system; define clinical symptoms of disorders; produce quality ultrasound of the accessory organs; identify hepatic vessels through Doppler techniques; identify the major structures associated with the urinary system, their functions and abnormalities, and differentiate them using ultrasonograms; identify renal veins and monitor renal transplants through Doppler techniques; identify the features of the adrenal glands, their relationship to surrounding structures, and their function as part of the endocrine system; define clinical symptoms of disorders and produce ultrasound studies of these glands; identify the features of the spleen, describe its role as part of the immune system, and distinguish abnormal states using patient scans and slides; identify blood flow in pathological masses through Doppler techniques; describe the anatomy and physiology of the lymphatic system and produce ultrasound studies for lymph node assessment. Upon successful completion of *Section 3*, the student will be able to identify anatomical features of the female reproductive system, reproductive physiology of the female, identify pathological states, and produce ultrasound studies; identify associated vasculature cyclical changes in blood flow; understand gamete production, the fertilization process, early cell division, embryo implantation, fetal development, and recognition of birth defects; identify physiologic changes during pregnancy, identify and describe fetal anatomical development, and using ultrasound scans to distinguish normal and abnormal conditions, and identify umbilical flow through Doppler and ectopic pregnancies. Upon successful completion of *Section 4*, the student will be able to describe the anatomy, physiology, and pathology of the parts studied and conduct ultrasound studies to detect pathological conditions; and identify neovascularity associated with pathology. Upon successful completion of *Section 5*, the student will have knowledge of standard operating procedures for the performance of ultrasound studies in clinical settings and have achieved the competence required for entry-level positions in applied ultrasound. *Version 3:* Upon successful completion of this course, the student will be able to perform ultrasound procedures; understand anatomy and physiology while evaluating patients; and provide physicians with reports and images to be interpreted for diagnostic results.

Instruction: *Version 1:* The program is divided into four sections, followed by a clinical experience (Section 5). In the first four sections, students have regular quizzes and examinations at the conclusion of each course segment for both lecture and lab. *Section 1:* Major topics covered in this unit are introduction to medical terminology, scanning techniques, and the basic physical principles of ultrasound. The unit develops a working knowledge of medical terminology, including a survey of diagnostic, disease, and therapeutic terminology for major body systems and processes. Further, this unit also covers the basic mathematical and physical principles of ultrasound. Topics include ultrasound propagation, interaction of sound with tissue, sound generation and detection, instrumentation, imaging artifacts, and performance measurements. There are 17 classes and 5 laboratory sessions. (Each class or lab period, anywhere in the program, is scheduled for 4 hours.) *Section 2:* Major topics covered in this unit are the anatomy, physiology, pathology, and sonographic interpretation and techniques of the cardiovascular system; the gastrointestinal tract and accessory organs; the renals, adrenals, spleen, and retroperitoneum. This unit extends for 32 lecture and 11 laboratory classes. Patho-logical states are presented using tapes, slides, and ultrasound studies. The heart, arteries, and veins are studied both in normal and pathological states. Also covered is the gastrointestinal tract with special emphasis on the liver, gallbladder, pancreas, and biliary system. The urinary system is studied with emphasis on the kidney. The endocrine system is examined, with special emphasis on the adrenals. There is a study of the spleen and its relationship to the lymphatic system; and finally, there is a study of the retroperitoneal structures and the lymphatic system. *Section 3:* Major topics covered in this unit are anatomy, physiology, pathology, and sonographic interpretations for gynecology, embryology, and obstetrics. This unit extends for 22 lecture and 12 lab classes. Pathological states are presented using tapes, slides, and ultrasound studies. Topics include a detailed examination of all the organs of the female reproductive system; the processes of reproduction, normal embryonic development, fetal development, and genetic defects; and a detailed study of fetal development including the female anatomical and physiological changes; specific emphasis is given to ultrasonographic studies of fetal development at each trimester. *Section 4:* Major topics covered in this unit are the anatomy, physiology, pathology, and sonographic interpretations for the extremities, thyroid, urinary bladder, breast, and male reproductive system. This unit extends for 8 lecture and 5 laboratory classes. Topics covered include the anatomy of the lower extremities (legs), the thyroid and parathyroid glands, urinary bladder, mammary glands, and the male reproductive system. *Section 5:* Major topics covered in this unit are a 12-week clinical experience under the supervision of the clinical professional performing the complete range of ultrasound diagnostic scans, developing clinical diagnosis, presenting case studies, and learning clinical setting protocols. *Version 2:* The program is divided into four sections, followed by a clinical experience (Section 5). In the first four sections, students have regular quizzes and examinations at the conclusion of each course segment for both lecture and lab. *Section 1:* Major topics covered in this unit are introduction to medical terminology, scanning techniques, and the physical principles of Spectral Doppler and color flow. The unit develops a working knowledge of medical terminology, including a survey of diagnostic, disease, and therapeutic terminology for major body systems and processes. Further, this unit also covers the basic mathematical and physical principles of ultrasound. Topics include ultrasound propagation, interaction of sound with tissue, sound generation and detection, instrumentation, imaging artifacts, and performance measurements. There are 21 classes and 9 laboratory sessions. (Each class or lab period, anywhere in the program, is scheduled for 4 hours.) *Section 2:* Major topics covered in this unit are the anatomy, physiology, pathology, and sonographic interpretation and techniques of the cardiovascular system; the gastrointestinal tract and accessory organs; the renals, adrenals, spleen, and retroperitoneum. This unit extends for 39 lecture and 17 laboratory classes. Pathological states are presented using tapes, slides, and general ultrasound and Doppler studies. The heart, arteries, and veins are studied both in normal and pathological states. Spectral Doppler and color flow studies are included. Also covered is the gastrointestinal tract with special emphasis on the liver, gallbladder, pancreas, and biliary system. The urinary system is studied with emphasis on the kidney and kidney vasculature. The endocrine system is examined, with special emphasis on the adrenals. There is a study of the spleen and its relationship to the lymphatic system; and finally, there is a study of the retroperitoneal structures and the lymphatic system. *Section 3:* Major topics covered in this unit are the anatomy, physiology, pathology, and sonographic interpretations for gynecology, embryology, and obstetrics. This unit extends for 28 lecture and 17 lab classes. Pathological states are presented using tapes, slides, and ultrasound studies. Topics include a detailed examination of all the organs of the female reproductive system; the processes of reproduction, normal embryonic development, fetal development, and genetic defects; and a detailed study of fetal development including the female anatomical and physiological changes; specific emphasis is given to ultrasonographic studies of fetal development at each trimester. Doppler studies of pelvic vasculature and fetal vessel integration are included. *Section 4:* Major topics covered in this unit are the anatomy, physiology, pathology, and sonographic interpretations for the extremities with emphasis on Doppler studies, thyroid, urinary bladder, breast, and male reproductive system. This unit extends for 11 lecture and 7 laboratory classes. Topics covered include the anatomy of the lower extremities (legs), the thyroid and parathyroid glands, urinary bladder, mammary glands, and the male reproductive system. *Section 5:* Students participate in a 14 week clinical experience under the supervision of the clinical professional. They will perform the complete range of ultrasound diagnostic scans including Doppler studies, developing clinical diagnosis, presenting case studies, and learning clinical setting protocols. *Version 3:* Major topic covered in this program is how a to become diagnostic medical sonographer. The program is divided into seven areas or segments, followed by a clinical experience. In each of the first 7 areas, students have regular quizzes and examination at the conclusion of each course segment for both lecture and lab. *Ultrasound Physics and Instrumentation:* Major topics covered in the course are the basic mathematical and physical principles and instrumentation of ultrasound such as the pulse-echo principle, propagation, attenuation, image generation, artifacts, and quality assurance; Doppler Physics and instrumentation, Spectral Analysis, and an introductory career workshop. *General Ultrasound I:* Major topics covered in the course are a brief introduction to medical terminology in order to develop a working knowledge of anatomic, pathologic, and ultrasonic descriptives; organs of the gastrointestinal tract; the upper abdominal vasculature and liver; anatomy; physiology; relevant pathologies; sonographic interpretation; scan techniques for the afore mentioned organs and structures; and Career Services Workshop #2. *General Ultrasound II:* Major topics covered in the course are the biliary system, pancreas, renal tract, anatomy, physiology, relevant pathologies, sonographic interpretation, scan techniques relevant to the afore mentioned organs and body systems, and Career Services Workshop #3. *General Ultra-sound III:* Major topics covered in the course are the urinary bladder, adrenal glands and reticulo-endothelial system are examined in detail to complete the programs studied of the abdominal soft tissues, ultrasound of the extremities including the popliteal fossa and lower limb venous Doppler and Cartoid imaging, sonography of the thyroid gland, breast ultrasound, anatomy, physiology, relevant pathologies, sonographic interpretation, and scan techniques for each organ and structure. *General Ultrasound IV:* Major topics covered in the course are the male and female reproductive organs, anatomy, physiology, relevant pathologies of each organ or structure, scan technique and sonographic interpretation for each system, and Career Services Workshop #4. *Obstetric Ultrasound I:* Major topics covered in the course are the processes of fertilization and early embryological development, first trimester normal development and complications, normal development of the fetus and placenta into the second trimester, and Career Services Workshop #5. *Obstetric Ultrasound II:* Major topics covered in the course are second and third trimester complications of pregnancy, both maternal and fetal; fetal congenital abnormalities; fetal well-being studies including the biophysical profile and fetal Doppler; Doppler applications for general abdominal, gynecological, and small parts ultrasound; and Career Services Workshop #6. *Ultrasound Externship:* Major topics covered in the course are an externship at a medical facility during which students are expected to observe and record all cases and perform examinations with and without assistance under the supervision of a clinical instructor, maintain logs of studies observed and performed, and prepare case studies for presentation to senior faculty and students.

Credit Recommendation: *Version 1: Section 1:* In the lower division baccalaureate/associate degree category, 3 semester hours in Medical Terminology; and in the lower division baccalaureate/associate or upper division baccalaureate degree category, 3 semester hours in Ultrasound Physics. *Section 2:* In the lower division baccalaureate/associate degree category, 3 semester hours in Human Anatomy and Physiology I and 3 semester hours in Human Anatomy and Physiology II. **NOTE:** These two courses are both non-laboratory courses. *Section 3:* In the lower division baccalaureate/associate or upper division baccalaureate degree category, 2 semester hours in Embryology, 3 semester hours in Pathophysiology, 3 semester hours in OB/GYN Sonography, and 1 semester hour in Scanning Lab. *Section 4:* In the lower division baccalaureate/associate or upper division baccalaureate degree category, 4 semester hours in Abdominal Sonography and 2 semester hours in Sonography Lab. *Section 5:* In the lower division baccalaureate/associate or upper division baccalaureate degree category, 3 semester hours in Clinical Experience. Therefore, for successful completion of all five SECTIONS of the program, a student would be eligible for a cumulative total of 36 semester hours of credit (3/90). *Version 2:* In the lower division baccalaureate/associate degree category, 4 semester hours in Medical Terminology; and in the lower division baccalaureate/associate or upper division baccalaureate degree category, 4 semester hours in Ultrasound Physics. *Section 2:* In the lower division baccalaureate/associate or upper division baccalaureate degree category, 5 semester hours in Abdominal Sonography and 3 semester hours in Sonography Lab. *Section 3:* In the lower division baccalaureate/associate or upper division baccalaureate degree category, 2 semester hours in Embryology, 3 semester hours in Pathophysiology and OB/GYN Sonography, and 2 semester hours in Scanning Lab. *Section 4:* In the lower division baccalaureate/associate degree category, 3 semester hours in Human Anatomy and Physiology I and 3 semester hours in Human Anatomy and Physiology II. **NOTE:** These two courses are both non-laboratory courses. *Section 5:* In the lower division baccalaureate/associate or upper division baccalaureate degree category, 4 semester hours in Clinical Experience. Therefore, for successful completion of all 5 Sections of the program, a student would be eligible for a cumulative total of 36 semester hours of credit (4/94). *Ultrasound Physics and Instrumentation/General Ultrasound I:* In the lower division baccalaureate/associate degree category, 4 semester hours in Medical Term-inology; and in the lower division baccalaureate/associate or upper division baccalaureate degree category, 4 semester hours in Ultrasound Physics and Instru-mentation. *General Ultrasound II:* In the lower division baccalaureate/associate or upper division baccalaureate degree category, 5 semester hours in Abdominal Sonography and 3 semester hours in Sonography Lab. *General Ultrasound III:* In the lower division baccalaureate/associate degree category, 3 semester hours in Human Anatomy and Physiology I, 3 semester hours in Human Anatomy and Physiology II. **NOTE:** These two courses are both non-laboratory courses., and 3 semester hours in Cross-Sectional Anatomy. *General Ultrasound IV/Obstetric Ultrasound I/Obstetric Ultrasound II:* In the lower division baccalaureate/associate or upper division baccalaureate degree category, 5 semester hours in OB/GYN Sonography and 3 semester hours in Scanning Lab. *Ultrasound Externship:* In the lower division baccalaureate/associate or upper division baccalaureate degree category, 4 semester hours in Clinical Experience. Therefore, for successful completion of all program areas, a student is eligible for a cumulative total of 37 semester hours (3/97).

Medical Assistant Program
MA100 Introduction to Medical Assistance
MA101 Medical Law and Ethics
MA102 Basic Assisting Skills
MA103 Human Relations
MA104 Terminology
MA105 Secretarial Skills
MA106 Health Insurance
MA107 Business Procedures
MA108 Anatomy and Pysiology
MA109 Clinical Skills
MA110 Management Skills
MA111 Laboratory Skills
MA112 Advanced Skills
MA113 Professional Development
MA114 Final/Externship

Location: Atlanta, GA; Bellaire, TX; Carle Place, NY; Elmsford, NY; Independence, OH; Irving, TX; Iselin, NJ; Jacksonville, FL; Marlborough, MA; New York, NY; Philadelphia, PA; Pittsburgh, PA; Pompano Beach, FL; Silver Spring, MD; and Tampa, FL.

Length: 900 hours (42 weeks).

Dates: November 1994-Present.

Objective: To train the student to become a medical assistant with front office and clinical medical office skills.

Learning Outcome: Upon successful completion of this course, the student will be able to perform medical office billing and scheduling; conduct general medical front office business; and perform clinical medical office procedures, such as blood collection and vital signs, and assist the physician.

Instruction: Major topics covered in the course are medical practice, law, medical communications, medical records, insurance, patient preparation, basic laboratory procedures and tests, and skill development. Methods of instruction include lecture, laboratory exercises, and a hospital externship.

Credit Recommendation: In the lower division baccalaureate/associate degree category, 3 semester hours in non-lab Anatomy and Physiology, 3 semester hours in Medical Office Procedures, 2 semester hours in Introduction to Medical Assistant, 1 semester hour in Interpersonal Skills, 2 semester hours in CPR and First Aid, 2 semester hours in Advanced Clinical Skills for Medical Assistants, 2 semester hours in Clinical Skills for Medical Assistants, 1 semester hour in Medical Assistant Lab Skills, and 2 semester hours in Medical Assistant Externship, a total of 18 semester hours (1/95).

Noninvasive Cardiovascular Technology Program

Location: Atlanta, GA; Bellaire, TX; Carle Place, NY; Elmsford, NY; Independence, OH; Irving, TX; Iselin, NJ; Jacksonville, FL; Marlborough, MA; New York, NY; Philadelphia, PA; Pittsburgh, PA; Pompano Beach, FL; Silver Spring, MD; and Tampa, FL.

Length: 1,024 hours (52 weeks).

Dates: September 1994-Present.

Objective: To train the student to become a cardiovascular technologist.

Learning Outcome: Upon successful completion of this course, the student will be able to perform EKG, stress, and Holter examinations on patients; perform adult echocardiographic examinations with color flow on patients; and perform vascular Doppler examinations on patients.

Instruction: Major topics covered in the course are skill development; extensive cardiovascular anatomy and physiology; normal and pathologic states of the cardiovascular systems; and sonographic imaging and electrocardiographic methods. Methods of instruction include lecture, laboratory exercises, and a hospital externship.

Credit Recommendation: In the lower division baccalaureate/associate degree category, 3 semester hours in Cardiovascular Anatomy and Physiology, 3 semester hours in Cardiovascular Pathophysiology, 1 semester hour in Physics of Instrumentation, 3 semester hours in EKG Technology, 4 semester hours in Echocardiography and Lab, 5 semester hours in Vascular Technology, 4 semester hours in Clinical Externship, and 1 semester hour in CPR, for a total of 24 semester hours (1/95).

Registry Review Course

Location: Ultrasound Diagnostic Schools sites in locations along Eastern seaboard of the U.S. and TX.

Length: 23 hours (over the course of several weeks).

Dates: September 1986-January 1994.

Objective: To provide the participant with a review of material in preparation for the certification examination of the American Registry of Diagnostic Medical Sonographers.

Learning Outcome: At the conclusion of this course the participant will be well versed in the topics of adult echocardiography and obstetrics, gynecology, and ultrasonic physics and instrumentation. The student will be prepared to sit for the examination of the American Registry of Diagnostic Medical Sonographers.

Instruction: Major topics covered in the course are four units: ultrasonic physics and instrumentation; abdomen and small parts; obstetrics and gynecology; and adult echocardiography.

Credit Recommendation: In the upper division baccalaureate degree category, 1 semester hour in Registry Review (3/90).

Vascular Doppler (Formerly Peripheral and Cerebrovascular Doppler)

Location: Atlanta, GA; Bellaire, TX; Carle Place, NY; Elmsford, NY; Independence, OH; Irving, TX; Iselin, NJ; Jacksonville, FL; Marlborough, MA; New York, NY; Philadelphia, PA; Pittsburgh, PA; Pompano Beach, FL; Silver Spring, MD; and Tampa, FL.

Length: 42 hours (13 weeks).

Dates: September 1983-Present.

Objective: To perform vascular studies using ultrasound.

Learning Outcome: Upon successful completion of this course, the student will be able to perform basic vascular examinations on extremities and carotids and recognize common anomalies and pathology.

Instruction: Major topics covered in the course are instruction in the pathophysiology of arterial and venous diseases; testing procedures in noninvasive care prevention and in clinical laboratory organization; Doppler Physics; peripheral duplex scanning; and disease states. Methods of instruction include lecture, case study evaluations, and lab for demonstration and practice.

Credit Recommendation: In the lower division baccalaureate/associate degree or in the upper division baccalaureate degree category, 3 semester hours in Peripheral and Cerebrovascular Doppler (3/90) (1/95).

Union Pacific Railroad Company

Union Pacific focuses on quality throughout its Management Training Program. Employees are offered a rich selection of professionally designed, and professionally taught, management training courses. The course help employees develop efficient management and leadership skills; grow personally and careerwise; and focus on achieving business results by meeting the ever-increasing, customer-driven demand for top notch service and satisfaction. Union Pacific prepares its employees through hands-on, real-life educational experiences, that often only can be simulated in college classrooms.

Union Pacific is dedicated to educating its employees so they can meet the challenges of the 21st century. Courses go beyond teaching employees what to do, for they also teach them how to think, how to apply their learning on the job, how to interface with others, and how to be effective, empowered, and involved business leaders.

Source of official student records: Registry of Credit Recommendations, American Council on Education, One Dupont Circle, Washington, DC 20036-1193.

Additional information about the courses: College Credit Recommendation Service, American Council on Education, One Dupont Circle, Washington, DC 20036-1993.

Basics of Communications and Listening (PXBF)
Making Presentations (PXBW)

Location: Various locations throughout the United States.

Length: *Course 1:* 7.75 hours (1 day); *Course 2:* 14.5 hours (2 days).

Dates: January 1987-December 1997.

Objective: *Course 1:* To provide the student with the basic tools necessary for effectively communicating in a organizational setting. *Course 2:* To provide the student with the skills necessary to deliver presentation to various audiences.

Learning Outcome: *Course 1:* Upon successful completion of this course, the student will be able to explain the communication process; identify barriers to effective communication; overcome barriers to the communication process; and demonstrate communication skills. *Course 2:* Upon successful completion of this course, the student will be able to prepare a presentation to the level of the audience; effectively make use of visual aids during presentations; interact with audiences; achieve an awareness of and be able to demonstrate proficiency in making presentations.

Instruction: *Course 1:* Major topics covered in the course are the communication process; barriers to communication; listening techniques; and communication delivery techniques. Methods of instruction include lecture, video presentation, discussion, and structured experiences. *Course 2:* Major topics covered in the course are visual aids; effective audience interaction; and effective delivery techniques. Methods of instruction include lecture, video presentation, discussion, and structured experiences.

Credit Recommendation: In the upper division baccalaureate degree category, 1 semester hour in Business Communication or Communicative Arts elective (4/93). **NOTE:** Student must complete both courses to receive credit.

Building Effective Work Teams (PXBH)

Location: Various locations throughout the United States.

Length: 7.5 hours (1 day).

Dates: January 1988-December 1997.

Objective: To focus on the effectiveness of a functional team, its dynamics, productivity, and function.

Learning Outcome: Upon successful completion of this course, the student will be able to plan effective teams; coordinate team members' activities and meetings; and understand importance of teamwork for meeting quality goals and business objectives.

Instruction: Major topics covered in the course are principles of building effective work teams; conducting meetings; and principles of quality management. Methods of instruction include lecture, video presentation, discussion, and structured experiences.

Credit Recommendation: In the upper division baccalaureate degree category, 1 semester hour in Supervision or Management (4/93) (9/95). **NOTE:** Student must complete Delegation (PXB1) or Recognizing Employee Performance (PXEP) to receive credit.

Building Teams Advanced Support Management (PXM6), Team Leader (PXCA), Team Member (PXCB), and Building Teams (PXJ8)

Location: Various sites throughout the United States.

Length: 54.5 (8 days).

Dates: June 1993-Present.

Objective: To provide the student with the skills important for leading, managing and participating in Quality Improvement Teams.

Learning Outcome: Upon successful completion of this course, the student will be able to start, monitor, work on and review improvement teams.

Instruction: Major topics covered in the course are problem solving, team development, leadership, group dynamics, conducting meetings, quality and customer satisfaction. Methods of instruction include lecture, discussion, classroom exercises, audio-visual material, case studies, computer-assisted instruction, learner presentations, reports, examinations and other.

Credit Recommendation: In the upper division baccalaureate degree category, 3 semester hours for successful completion of Team Leader; 4 semester hours for successful completion of all four courses; or 1 semester hour for successful completion of Building Teams Advanced Support Management (PXM6), Team Member (PXCB), and Building Teams (PXJ8) in Management or Total Quality Management (9/95).

Business Letter Writing (PXLW)

Location: Various sites throughout the United States.

Length: 26 hours (3 days).

Dates: January 1992-Present.

Objective: To provide the student with a focus on the skills necessary to draft, edit, and produce written business correspondence.

Learning Outcome: Upon successful completion of this course, the student will be able to organize ideas in a logical manner; prepare draft memos and letters using appropriate formats; use proper punctuation and grammar; and revise documents into a final form.

Instruction: Major topics covered in the course are planning, brainstorming and organizing business correspondence; preparing draft correspondence; revising drafts, and preparing final copies or correspondence. Methods of instruction include lecture, video presentation, discussion, and structured experiences.

Credit Recommendation: In the upper division baccalaureate degree category, 1 semester hour in Business Communication or Communicative Arts elective (4/93).

Coaching Employee Performance (PXCM or PXDQ)

Location: Various locations throughout the United States.

Length: 14 hours (2 days).
Dates: January 1992-December 1996.
Objective: To emphasize how superiors and managers can raise employees confidence and competence levels through advice and input; and demonstrate how to identify coaching opportunities to enhance employee success.
Learning Outcome: Upon successful completion of this course, the student will be able to identify coaching opportunities; develop or improve coaching opportunities; develop or improve coaching skills and abilities; and raise employee confidence and competence.
Instruction: Major topics covered in the course are planning; building commitment; establishing direction; coaching; and providing feedback. Methods of instruction include lecture, video presentation, discussion, and structured experiences.
Credit Recommendation: In the upper division baccalaureate degree category, 1 semester hour in Supervision or Management (4/93) (9/95).

Delegation (PXB1)

Location: Various locations throughout the United States.
Length: 7.5 hours (1 day).
Dates: January 1988-December 1997.
Objective: To review the content and sequence for developing a delegation plan.
Learning Outcome: Upon successful completion of this course, the student will be able to apply delegation skills; seek employee input and ideas; communicate parameters of delegated tasks; identify restrictions; and resources and time frame.
Instruction: Major topics covered in the course are recognizing delegation opportunities; identifying the appropriate level of authority to delegate; and developing a delegation plan. Methods of instruction include lecture, video presentation, discussion, and structured experiences.
Credit Recommendation: In the upper division baccalaureate degree category, 1 semester hour in Supervision or Management (4/93). **NOTE:** Students must complete Recognizing Employee Performance (PXER) or Building Effective Work Teams (PXBH) to receive credit.

Franklin Personal Productivity Program (PXFP)

Location: Various locations throughout the United States.
Length: 7 hours (1 day).
Dates: January 1991-Present.
Objective: To help students integrate time management principles and techniques to increase their productivity by using Franklin Day Planner.
Learning Outcome: Upon successful completion of this course, the student will be able to use the Franklin Day Planner; increase personal productivity; store information for record retrieval; and reduce unpredictable demands on time.
Instruction: Major topics covered in the course are time management, goal setting; and productivity pyramid. Methods of instruction include lecture, video presentation, discussion, and structured experiences.
Credit Recommendation: In the lower division baccalaureate/associate degree category, 1 semester hour in General Business, Management, or Business elective (4/93). **NOTE:** Student must complete Time Management: Handling Priorities (PXBV) and Project Management for Beginners (PX14) to receive credit.

Instructional Methodology (Instructional Design for New Designers: PXIU)

Location: Various sites throughout the United States.
Length: PXIU 22 hours (3 days); PXED: 30 hours (4 days) - Total 52 hours (7 days).
Dates: January 1995-Present.
Objective: To provide student with the skills necessary to design an effective training course and to analyze, organize & present manual-length document based on Information Mapping Methodology.
Learning Outcome: Upon successful completion of this course, the student will bel able to set up a work plant to design a training course; write objectives, design tests and exercises, select instructional methods, develop course materials and evaluate course; analyze, build, organize and apply critical information into manual-length documents.
Instruction: Major topics covered in the course are project planning, analyzing tasks, writing unique, research based approach to classifying information. Methods of instruction include lecture, discussion, classroom exercises, audio-visual material case studies, computer-assisted instruction, learner presentations, reports and examinations.
Credit Recommendation: In the upper division baccalaureate degree category, 3 semester hours for successful completion of both courses or 1 semester hour for successful completion of one course in Education or Management (9/95).

Leadership Development Program (PXLD)

Location: Various locations throughout the United States.
Length: 48 hours (6 days).
Dates: January 1985-Present.
Objective: To provide middle and upper level management with a focus on advanced development of the individual's management skills.
Learning Outcome: Upon successful completion of this course, the student will be able to effectively use his or her individual characteristics and leadership style to effectively manage functional and/or cross-functional work groups.
Instruction: Major topics covered in the course are assessment of individual characteristics using the Myers-Briggs type indicators, identification of individual styles; and application to cases, problems, and project management. Methods of instruction include lecture, role play, exercises, and video tape feed-back.
Credit Recommendation: In the upper division baccalaureate degree category, 3 semester hours or in the graduate degree category, 2 semester hours in Leadership or Management (4/93).

Leadership Program (Project Cheyenne Delta Series Leadership Program) (PXP1, PXP2, PXP5, PXP7)

Location: Various locations throughout the United States.
Length: 19.5 hours (3 days).
Dates: January 1992-Present.
Objective: To provide the student with the leadership skills of communication, motivation, and working well with others.
Learning Outcome: Upon successful completion of this course, the student will be able to actively seek and take into account the ideas and opinions of others; deal with conflicts between individual goals and organizational priorities; redirect the inefficient efforts of others; and provide credit for the good work of others.
Instruction: Major topics covered in the course are communicating needs and expectation, listening for understanding, criticizing constructively, discussion skills, managing conflict, and giving credit. Methods of instruction include lecture, exercises, role play, and video presentation.
Credit Recommendation: In the upper division baccalaureate degree category, 1

semester hour in Management, Supervision, or Communication elective (4/93).

Leadership School (PXLL)

Location: Various sites throughout the United States.

Length: 24 hours (3 days).

Dates: March 1995-Present.

Objective: To provide participants with leadership theory and application experiences enabling them to model, encourage and apply leadership skills on the job.

Learning Outcome: Upon successful completion of this course, the student will be able to describe the behaviors of leadership; improve an identified area of leadership effectiveness during the leadership school and on the job; apply leadership tools, processes, and concepts when making decisions in a business case simulation; explain the synergistic approach to Total Quality Management; explain the links between leadership and business success; and model and encourage leadership skills on the job.

Instruction: Major topics covered in the course are leadership theory and behavior; job agreements; customer focused service; ethics and culture; managing data; benchmarking; and change model action plans. Methods of instruction include lecture, discussion, classroom exercises, audio-visual material, case studies, roll plays, computer-assisted instruction, learner presentations, and examinations.

Credit Recommendation: In the upper division baccalaureate degree category, 1 semester hour in Management or Public Administration (9/95).

Making a Personal Development Plan (PXCE)

Location: Various locations throughout the United States.

Length: 4 hours (5 days).

Dates: January 1991-Present.

Objective: To help the student prepare a personal development plan by assessing strengths, weaknesses, and career development interests.

Learning Outcome: Upon successful completion of this course, the student will be able to develop long and short range career development plans; and assess strengths, weaknesses, and abilities.

Instruction: Major topics covered in the course are definitions of personal development, personal development process, and personal development plan. Method of instruction includes workshops.

Credit Recommendation: In the lower division baccalaureate/associate degree category, 1 semester hour in Management or Business elective (4/93). **NOTE:** Student must complete Conducting Effective Performance Appraisals (PXBP) and Writing the Job Agreement (PXCD) to receive credit.

Management Simulation (Workshop in Management Action) (Looking Glass) (PX87)

Location: Kansas City, MO and Omaha, NE.

Length: 27.25 hours (3.5 days).

Dates: January 1983-Present.

Objective: To provide the student with experience using leadership skills of teamwork, decisiveness, delegation, and communication through a management simulation

Learning Outcome: Upon successful completion of this course, the student will be able to understand personal management behaviors, time management, and interpersonal styles as measured by standardized questionnaires; and develop an appreciation of cross-functional activities within an organization.

Instruction: Major topics covered in the course are a simulation of issues facing the top management of Looking Glass, Inc., a simulated corporation with $200 million in sales and 4,000 employees; participants are given information on the company, a job description, and an office setting; they run through the normal work day; the managers struggle with issues and crisis, actions and reactions, and their relationships with one another - just like the real world; after participating as senior management in this corporation, participants examine their decisions and actions in detail. Methods of instruction include hands-on simulation, discussion, role playing, and video.

Credit Recommendation: In the upper division baccalaureate degree or graduate category, 1 semester hour in Business or Management (4/93).

Positive Leadership (PXCF)

Location: Various locations throughout the United States.

Length: 14.5 hours (2 days).

Dates: January 1990-December 1997.

Objective: To help the student develop the leadership skills of supervisors and managers so that they feel comfortable, confident, and competent in leading teams.

Learning Outcome: Upon successful completion of this course, the student will be able to build and maintain trust and mutual respect among member of a work team; enable work teams to function efficiently and effectively with a minimum of management intervention; and support and encourage performance that contributes to the organization's competitiveness in the marketplace.

Instruction: Major topics covered in the course are leadership, developing trust, communication skills, improvement, direction, motivation, guidance, and problem solving. Methods of instruction include lecture, video presentations, discussion, and structured experiences.

Credit Recommendation: In the upper division baccalaureate degree category, 1 semester hour in Supervision or Management (4/93).

Process Improvement (PXSP)

Location: Various locations throughout the United States.

Length: 22 hours (3 days).

Dates: April 1994-Present.

Objective: To provide information and build skills in advanced problem-solving methodology as it relates to examining business processes and targeting for improvement.

Learning Outcome: Upon successful completion of this course, the student will be able to identify variation; document process flow; collect and analyze data; identify improvement opportunities in processes; and use problem solving tools to improve a process.

Instruction: Major topics covered in the course are process theory, data collection and analysis, problem solving methodologies. Methods of instruction include lecture, discussion, classroom exercises, audio-visual material, case studies, role plays computer-assisted instruction, learner presentation, and examinations.

Credit Recommendation: In the upper division baccalaureate degree category, 1 semester hour in Total Quality Management or Decision Science (9/95).

Recognizing Employee Performance (PXEP)

Location: Various locations throughout the United States.

Length: 6.25 hours (1 day).

Dates: January 1990-December 1997.

Objective: To raise supervisors awareness of situations and instances that lend themselves to recognition.

Learning Outcome: Upon successful completion of this course, the student will be able to make a distinction between reward and recognition; distinguish between types and degrees of recognition; and effectively provide recognition to employees.

Instruction: Major topics covered in the course are rewards, recognition, and guidelines for giving recognition. Methods of instruction include lecture, video presentation, discussion, and structured experiences.

Credit Recommendation: In the upper division baccalaureate degree category, 1 semester hour in Supervision or Management (4/93). **NOTE:** Student must complete Delegation (PXB1) or Building Effective Work Teams (PXBH) to receive credit.

Staff Performance Development (Coaching Employee Performance [PXDQ], Performance Development Review [PX13])

Location: Various sites throughout the United States.

Length: 21.5 hours (3 days).

Dates: June 1993-Present.

Objective: To provide the student with the skills and practice needed to build and maintain improved staff performance.

Learning Outcome: Upon successful completion of this course, the student will be able to create developmental action plans and job agreements to achieve long-term goals and to communicate in a way that motivates people to improve their performance.

Instruction: Major topics covered in the course are performance reviews, job agreements, development plans, coaching, and communication. Methods of instruction include lecture, discussion, classroom exercises, audio-visual material, case studies, role plays, computer-assisted instruction, learner presentation, reports, and examinations.

Credit Recommendation: In the upper division baccalaureate degree category, 1 semester hour in Management, Human Resource Management, Communications, or Supervision (9/95).

Time Management: Handling Multiple Priorities (PXBV)

Location: Various locations throughout the United States.

Length: 7.5 hours (1 day).

Dates: January 1990-December 1997.

Objective: To provide the student with an understanding of the value of goal setting, setting priorities, time management, practice with timelines, Gantt charts, and using monitoring tools.

Learning Outcome: Upon successful completion of this course, the student will be able to understand principles of time management; schedule time; and set priorities.

Instruction: Major topics covered in the course are time management, setting objectives, planning, and prioritizing. Methods of instruction include lecture, video presentation, discussion, and structured experiences.

Credit Recommendation: In the lower division baccalaureate/associate degree category, 1 semester hour in General Business, Management, or Business elective (4/93). **NOTE:** Student must complete Franklin Personal Productivity Program (PXFP) or Project Management for Beginners (PX14) to receive credit.

TQMS (Total Quality Management System) Basic Project Management (PXMJ)

Location: Omaha, NE.

Length: 26 hours (3 days).

Dates: January 1990-Present.

Objective: To provide the student with the tools and techniques of project management to enable them to plan, schedule, and control projects.

Learning Outcome: Upon successful completion of this course, the student will be able to form, coordinated, and manage a project team; allocate resources and make budgets; and report project status and where corrective action can be used.

Instruction: Major topics covered in the course are the planning cycle, network planning tools and techniques, modern planning and control systems, and control and monitoring. Methods of instruction include lecture, video presentation, discussion, and structured experience.

Credit Recommendation: In the upper division baccalaureate degree category, 2 semester hours in Project Management or Business elective (4/93).

TQMS (Total Quality Management System) Facilitator Training (PXCC)

Location: Various locations throughout the United States.

Length: 37.5 hours (5 days).

Dates: January 1990-Present.

Objective: To provide the student with the fundamental skills needed to develop and facilitate Quality Improvement Teams.

Learning Outcome: Upon successful completion of this course, the student will be able to assess and advise team leaders; observe group processes and dynamics; understand various communication and leadership styles; and teach quality improvement processes and advise supporting managers.

Instruction: Major topics covered in the course are establishing, supporting, advising, and evaluating Quality Improvement and maintenance and reporting of Quality Improvement Team records. Methods of instruction include lecture, video presentation, discussion, and structured experiences.

Credit Recommendation: In the upper division baccalaureate degree category, 2 semester hours in Quality Management, Management, or Business elective (4/93).

TQMS (Total Quality Management System) Manager Support (PXM1), (PXM2), (PXM3)

Location: Various locations throughout the United States.

Length: 8.5 hours (1 day).

Dates: January 1991-December 1997.

Objective: To provide the student with instruction on the procedures for establishing Quality Improvement Teams, techniques to lead a quality improvement teams, and methods for ensuring that a team is effectively accomplishing its goals.

Learning Outcome: Upon successful completion of this course, the student will be able to establish a quality improvement team; guide a team in their application of the problem solving process; identify the manager's role in making quality improvement teams successful; and evaluate quality team effectiveness.

Instruction: Major topics covered in the course are establishing quality improvement teams, working with quality improvement teams, and evaluating quality improvement team effectiveness. Methods of instruction include lecture, video presentation, discussion, and structured experience.

Credit Recommendation: In the upper division baccalaureate degree category, 1 semester hour in Quality Management, Management, or Business elective (4/93). **NOTE:** Student must complete Total Quality Management System (TQMS) Problem Solving (PXCS) to receive credit.

TQMS (Total Quality Management System) Manager Training (PXQM)

Location: Various locations throughout the United States.

Length: 14 hours (2 days).

Dates: January 1988-Present.

Objective: To establish the basic foundation for implementing the quality process. It relates the business objectives and action plans for meeting them to the individual manager in their area of responsibility.

Learning Outcome: Upon successful completion of this course, the student will be able to understand and explain how all of the elements of quality fit together to achieve business objectives; communicate support for business objectives and why these objectives are important to the future of the organization; and translate business objectives into specific action plans which can be measured, controlled, and improved.

Instruction: Major topics covered in the course are an introduction to the total quality management system, the need for a quality improvement process, linking job responsibilities to business objectives, using quality system procedures, the four principles of quality management, and working through quality improvement teams. Methods of instruction include lecture, video presentation, discussion, and structured experience.

Credit Recommendation: In the upper division baccalaureate degree category, 1 semester hour in Quality Management, Management, or Business elective (4/93).

TQMS (Total Quality Management System) Problem Solving (PXCS)

Location: Various locations throughout the United States.

Length: 7.5 hours (1 day).

Dates: January 1987-Present.

Objective: To provide the student with an understanding of problem solving process and provides practice in the use of basic analytical tools used to solve problems.

Learning Outcome: Upon successful completion of this course, the student will be able to apply the problem solving process to situations to improve the quality commitment to business solutions; become more proficient in techniques of collecting, analyzing, and applying data to generate effective problem solving alternatives; and recognize the interpersonal dynamics and roles played in successful group problem solving sessions.

Instruction: Major topics covered in the course are the problem solving process, collecting and analyzing data, and dynamics and skills in group problem solving. Methods of instruction include lecture, video presentation, discussion, and structured experience.

Credit Recommendation: In the upper division baccalaureate degree category, 1 semester hour in Quality Management or as a Management or Business elective (4/93). **NOTE:** Students must complete Total Quality Management System (TQMS) Manager Support (PXM1), (PXM2), (PXM3) to receive credit.

TQMS (Total Quality Management System) Project Management for Beginners (PX14)

Location: Various locations throughout the United States.

Length: 10.5 hours (1.5 days).

Dates: January 1993-December 1997.

Objective: To give students a basic understanding of project planning techniques and tools.

Learning Outcome: Upon successful completion of this course, the student will be able to use a mind map to identify project elements; define a project; identify expected results; complete a Gantt chart; and use the tools to develop a Gantt chart.

Instruction: Major topics covered in the course are mind mapping, brain storming, Gantt charts, and major and minor elements of a project. Methods of instruction include lecture, video presentation, discussion, and structured experiences.

Credit Recommendation: In the lower division baccalaureate/associate degree category, 1 semester hour in Management or Supervision (4/93). **NOTE:** Student must complete Total Quality Management System (TQMS) Team Leader Training (PXCA) to receive credit (p/95).

TQMS (Total Quality Management System) Team Leader Training (PXCA)

Location: Various locations throughout the United States.

Length: *Version 1:* 38.5 hours (4.5 days); *Version 2:* 35 hours (1 week).

Dates: *Version 1:* January 1988-May 1993; *Version 2:* June 1993-Present.

Objective: *Version 1:* To help the student teach and lead members of a quality improvement team through the steps o the problem solving story so they will be able to make presentations of team activities to management. *Version 2:* To build skills important to leading and managing improvement teams.

Learning Outcome: *Version 1:* Upon successful completion of this course, the student will be able to communicate the total quality management system to team members; lead the team in application of the problem solving process; use the tools and techniques necessary to work opportunities; recognize Cost of Quality issues; deliver presentations; and teach problem solving and statistical tools to team members. *Version 2:* Upon successful completion of this course, the student will be able to complete team administration requirements for improvement of team activities, use group dynamics to conduct effective team meetings, use problem-solving steps and tools to develop an improvement team story, teach problem-solving tools to team members, conduct meetings with the support manager, develop and execute meeting agendas, and explain failure and control costs to team members.

Instruction: *Version 1:* Major topics covered in the course are leading a team, problem solving for quality improvement, developing and selecting alternative solutions, implementation and future plans, and problem solving and statistical tools. Methods of instruction include lecture, video presentation, discussion, and structured experience. *Version 2:* Major topics covered in the course are how to teach and lead members of an improvement team through the steps of the problem-solving story so they will be able to make presentations of team activities to management. Methods of instruction include lecture, discussion (instructor led), classroom exercises, case studies, role playing, problem-solving, prepare a presentation, teach a problem solving tool, and computer-assisted videotape.

Credit Recommendation: *Version 1:* In the upper baccalaureate degree category, 3 semester hours in Quality Management, Management, Business, or Communications elective (4/93). *Version 2:* In the upper baccalaureate degree category, 3 semester hours in Quality Management, Management, Business, or Communications elective (9/95). **NOTE:** Student must complete both this course and TQMS (Total Quality Management System) Team Member Training to receive the credit recommendation.

TQMS (Total Quality Management System) Team Member Training (PXCB)

Location: Various locations throughout the United States.

Length: 8 hours (1 days).

Dates: January 1990-Present.

Objective: To provide information and build skills in preparation for participants' involvement on Quality Improvement Teams.

Learning Outcome: Upon successful completion of this course, the student will be able to understand team-oriented problem solving steps, tools, and techniques;

and develop the ability to participate in quality teams.

Instruction: Major topics covered in the course are to provide the prospective team member of quality improvement team information and experiences, and provide a hands-on overview of the six step problem solving process and tools, problem statements, and roles and responsibilities of team members.

Credit Recommendation: In the upper division baccalaureate degree category, 3 semester hours in Quality Management, Management, or Business elective (9/95). **NOTE:** Student must complete Total Quality Management System (TQMS) Team Leader Training (PXCA) to receive the credit recommendation.

TQMS (Total Quality Management System) Team Member Training (PXTM)

Location: Various locations throughout the United States.

Length: 8 hours (1 day).

Dates: July 1994-Present.

Objective: To provide information and build skills in preparation for participants' involvement on Quality Improvement Teams.

Learning Outcome: Upon successful completion of this course, the student will be able to define terms associated with quality and customer satisfaction; identify the purpose and benefits of quality improvement teams; recognize how the problem solving process is used to improve business processes and customer satisfaction; identify the purpose of each step in the problem solving process; and participate as an effective improvement team member using their knowledge of team member roles and meeting guidelines.

Instruction: Major topics covered in the course are quality improvement team information and experiences, a hands on overview of the six step problem solving process and tools, problem statements, and roles and responsibilities of team members. Methods of instruction include lecture, video presentation, discussion, and structured experiences.

Credit Recommendation: In the upper division baccalaureate degree category, 3 semester hours in Quality Management, Management, or Business elective (9/95). **NOTE:** Student must complete Total Quality Management System (TQMS) Team Leader Training (PXCA) to receive the credit recommendation (9/95).

Train-the Trainer/Team Leader (PXQI)

Location: Omaha, NE.

Length: 140 hours.

Dates: January 1991-Present.

Objective: To provide participants an in-depth learning experience in Quality Improvement Processes, principles of adult learning, and group dynamics in the context of knowledge and skill-building for teaching adult learners.

Learning Outcome: Upon successful completion of this course, the student will be able to communicate the rationale for quality improvement as a way of doing business in competitive environments; describe Total Quality Management System and its relationship to business objectives; teach the problem solving process and tools; teacher group dynamics; and demonstrate principles of adult learning.

Instruction: Major topics covered in the course are quality improvement, adult learning, group dynamics, and problem-solving.

Credit Recommendation: In the upper division baccalaureate degree category, 3 semester hours in Education or Management (9/95).

Train-the Trainer/Team Member (PXQ1)

Location: Omaha, NE; St. Louis, MO; No. Little Rock, AR; and Houston, TX.

Length: 35 hours (1 week).

Dates: September 1994-Present.

Objective: To build content and instructional skills important to effectively provide training to the adult learner.

Learning Outcome: Upon successful completion of this course, the student will be able to use the principles of adult learning; outline and explain the six problem solving steps; and teach an adult learner course.

Instruction: Major topics covered in the course are problem solving methodologies, adult learning strategies, and pedagogy of teaching. Methods of instruction include lecture, discussion, classroom exercises, audio-visual material, case studies, learner presentations, and examinations.

Credit Recommendation: In the upper division baccalaureate degree category, 3 semester hours in Education or Management (9/95).

Writing the Job Agreement (PXCD)

Location: Various locations throughout the United States.

Length: 4 hours (.5 day).

Dates: January 1991-Present.

Objective: To provide the student with a focus on writing and improving job agreements using performance development review procedures.

Learning Outcome: Upon successful completion of this course, the student will bel able to develop clear and accurate job responsibility statements; write performance requirements; and test and refine performance requirements against criteria for effectiveness.

Instruction: Major topics covered in the course are job agreements, job responsibilities, performance requirements, and job agreement discussion. Methods of instruction include workshops.

Credit Recommendation: In the lower division baccalaureate/associate degree category, 1 semester hour in Management or Business elective (4/93). **NOTE:** Student must complete Making a Personal Development Plan (PXCE) and Conducting Effective Performance Appraisals (PXBP) to receive credit.

United Nations Institute for Training and Research

Established in 1995, The United Nations Institute For Training and Research Programme of Correspondence Instruction (UNITAR POCI) is one of the training programs offered by the United Nations Institute for Training and Research (UNITAR). It is the purpose of UNITAR POLIC to provide standard training to students world-wide to prepare them to serve on humanitarian and peace-keeping missions.

UNITAR POCI offers eight separate self-paced correspondence courses. Topics include Principles of Peace Support, Refuge Assistance, Demining, Military Peace-keeping, and others. All courses are available in English, two are available in French, and three are in Spanish. Courses range from 4 to 12 lessons and from 20 to 60 clock hours of study time. Students may enroll any time and proceed at a speed that suits them. Each lesson contains objectives, study material, and a self-scoring quiz. At the end of each course is an Examination the student mails to UNITAR POCI for grading. If they pass with a score of 75% they are awarded a Certificate-of-Completion.

The primary student population consists of military officers who may serve on UN peace-keeping missions but additional students include enlisted personnel, diplomats, civilians, academics, and serious citizens. Many nations endorse correspondence courses from UNITAR POCI as part of their own national training programs and also award points for course completion that are applied for selection, assignment, or promotion.

Courses are drafted by recognized experts and experienced peacekeepers from many nations and reviewed within the UN Department of Peace-keeping Operations to ensure consistency with established practices. Courses are revised to reflect changes in political developments and operational requirements.

Students may enroll and submit their exams at any time by mail, fax, e-mail, or through UNITAR POCI's home page http://www.wm.edu/unpeacek/index.html. Courses are delivered through the mail immediately following enrollment.

Source of official student records: Registry of Credit Recommendations, American Council on Education, One Dupont Circle, Washington, DC 20036-1193.

Additional information about the courses: College Credit Recommendation Service, American Council on Education, One Dupont Circle, Washington, DC 20036-1193.

Principles for the Conduct of Peace Support Operations

Location: Independent study by correspondence.

Length: Approximately 40 hours of independent study divided over seven lessons and 165 pages.

Dates: October 1996-Present.

Objective: To provide an historical and operational framework with which the student may assess or participate in the full-range of peace support operations, applying techniques and planning methodologies developed for peace operations.

Learning Outcome: Upon successful completion of this course the student will understand the different types of peace operations and distinguish the political and military environments that call for different types of peace operations.

Instruction: Major topics covered in the course are The UN Charter and Peace Support Operations (PSO), PSOs During the Cold War, Present-day Peace Support Operations, Conceptual Approaches, Development of Peace Support Operations, The Nature of Conflict, Peace Support Tasks, The Nature of Peace Support Operations, The Significance of Consent, Operational Tasks, Peace-keeping Tasks, Peace Enforcement Tasks, Principles That Promote Consent, Operational Techniques, Application and Incident Management, Techniques That Promote Consent, Planning Process of UN PSOs, Mission Analysis, Functions in Combat, Command and Control, Control of the Electro-magnetic Spectrum, Information and Intelligence, Maneuver, Protection, Fire Support, Deployability, Combat Service Support.

Credit Recommendation: In the lower division baccalaureate/associate degree category, 1 semester hour in Military Science or Political Science (12/97).

Serving as a United Nations Military Observer:Methods and Procedures

Location: Independent study by correspondence.

Length: Approximately 42 hours of independent study divided over nine lessons and 152 pages.

Dates: March 1997-Present.

Objective: To help students develop an understanding of how to serve as a United Nations Military Observer (MILOBS), deal with culture shock, and understand social customs.

Learning Outcome: Upon successful completion of this course the student will understand the structure of the United Nations and the role of peacekeeping within the UN.

Instruction: Major topics covered in the course are United Nations Peace-keeping, Principles for Peace-keeping, Operational and Tactical Considerations, Composition of Peace-keeping Operations, Demands and Duties, Military Observer Duties, Observation and Information Gathering, Communication with the Media, Liaison, Negotiation, Mediation, Written Communications, Report Writing Style Guide, Communications, Regulations Affecting UN Use of Communications, Procedures for Radio Communication, Security and Safety, Detainment, Mines, Sniper Fire, Lost Radio Contact, Notes for the Guidance of Military Observers on Appointment, Medical Situations Requiring First Aid Assistance, Casevac/medevac Requests, and Driving Safety. Methods of instruction include a self-paced correspondence course with End-of-Lesson Quizzes and an End-of-Course Examination.

Credit Recommendation: In the lower division baccalaureate/associate degree category, 1 semester hour in Military Science (12/97). **NOTE:** Credit cannot be received for both this course and UNITED Nations Civilian Police: Restoring Order Following Hostilities.

The Global Landmine Problem: Preventing Casualties to Peacekeepers and the Civilian Population (Formerly Demining in the Aftermath of War: Preventing Casualties to Peacekeepers and The Civilian Population)

Location: Independent study by correspondence.

Length: Approximately 40 hours of independent study divided over 12 lessons and 170 pages.

Dates: December 1996-Present.

Objective: To develop an understanding of the global problem of land mines, and the differences between humanitarian and military demining.

Learning Outcome: Upon successful completion of this course the student will understand the scope and extent of the current world-wide problem with land mines and the role of the United Nations in addressing this problem. The student will be able to differentiate between military and humanitarian mine clearance and the different priorities of each. The student will be able to list the ten commandments of conduct in mine-affected areas and will be familiar with methods for marking mines. The student will be able to take proper action upon the discovery of a mine and be familiar with the possible consequences of encounters with mines.

Instruction: Major topics covered in the course are the United Nations and The Global Landmine Problem, The Scope of The Problem, Current UN Mine Clearance Programs, The Demining Data Base, The Distinction Between Humanitarian and Military Mine Clearance, Methods of Mine Clearance, Problems of Humanitarian Mine Clearance, The Threat of Mines in Peace-keeping Operations, The Functioning And Use of Mines, Duration of the Mine Threat, Modern Mines, Military Minelaying, Nuisance Mining, Irregular Minelaying, Use of Booby Traps, Principles of Booby Traps, Types of Booby Traps, Clearance of Booby Traps, Conduct in Mine-affected Areas, The Ten Commandments of Conduct in Mine-Affected Areas, Common Signs And Markings of Mines And Minefields, Principles of Military Marking, NATO Minefield Markings, Former Soviet Union (FSU) Minefield Markings, Humanitarian Marking Systems, Action on Accidentally Discovering Mines, Action Before Entering Potentially Mined Areas, The Treatment and Consequences of Mine Injuries, Impact on Society, Military Mine Clearance, Minefield Clearance Drills, Action on Finding a Tripwire, Mine Information, The UN Database, Combatant Mine Records, Mine Awareness Training. Methods of instruction include a self-paced correspondence course with End-of-Lesson Quizzes and an End-of-Course Examination.

Credit Recommendation: In the vocational certificate category, 1 semester hour in Military Science or Military Field Engineering (12/97).

United Nations Civilian Police: Restoring Order Following Hostilities

Location: Independent study by correspondence.

Length: Approximately 44 hours of independent study divided over 10 lessons and 170 pages.

Dates: July 1997-Present.

Objective: To help students develop an understanding of the roles and duties of United Nations Civilian Police in restoring civil order following chaos.

Learning Outcome: Upon successful completion of this course the student will be able to trace the history of UN Civilian Police; understand the roles and duties of UN Civilian Police; and the Do's and Don't of UN CIVPOL.

Instruction: Major topics covered in the course are The History of Civilian Police Operations; Role and Duties, Privileges, Immunities and Responsibilities; Cultural and Social Relations, Interaction with the Media; Organization and Staff Duties, Do's and Don'ts; United Nations Peace-keeping, Liaison, Negotiation, Mediation, Use of Interpreters, Staff Duties And Reporting; General Security Measures; Administrative and Logistics Matters, Notes for the Guidance of UN CIVPOLs on Assignment, First Aid and Health Precautions; Winter and Desert Driving. Methods of instruction include a self-paced correspondence course with End-of-Lesson Quizzes and an End-of-Course Examination.

Credit Recommendation: In the lower division baccalaureate/associate degree category, 1 semester hour in Law Enforcement or Criminal Justice (12/97). **NOTE:** Credit may not be received for both this course and United Nations Military Observer: Methods and Techniques for Serving on a UN Observer Mission.

United Nations Peace-Keeping Operations: Commanding United Nations Peace-keeping Operations:Methods and Techniques for Peace-keeping on the Ground

Location: Independent study by correspondence.

Length: Approximately 55 hours of independent study divided over 12 lessons and 170 pages.

Dates: April 1996-Present.

Objective: To acquaint Officers and NCOs with the responsibilities of leadership for UN Peace-keeping Operations.

Learning Outcome: Upon successful completion of this course the student will understand the various tasks associated with peacekeeping operations.

Instruction: Major topics in the course are General Institutional and Legal Framework of Operations; Framework of Peace-keeping Operations; Conduct of Action in Peace-keeping Operations; Missions and Operational Techniques in Peace-keeping Operations; and Rules of Engagement and Behavior in a Peace-keeping Operation; Media Behavior towards civilian populations and cooperation with humanitarian agencies. Methods of instruction include a self-paced correspondence course and an End-of-Course Examination.

Credit Recommendation: In the lower division baccalaureate/associate degree category, 1 semester hour in Military Science (12/97). **NOTE:** United Nations Peace-Keeping Operations: Peacekeeping Logistics must also be completed.

United Nations Peace-keeping Operations: UN Peacekeeping Logistics

Location: Independent study by correspondence.

Length: Approximately 25 hours of independent study divided over four lessons and 89 pages.

Dates: February 1995-Present.

Objective: To provide the student an institutional framework, appreciation of relevant principles, and functional guidelines to assess and direct international logistics in support of UN PeaceKeeping operations.

Learning Outcome: This course is designed to provide the student with a conceptual foundation and background in UN logistical operations. Upon successful completion the student will be able to understand accepted United Nations logistical doctrine, procedures, and policies; and will be familiar with the fundamental concepts, principles, and tenets that comprise UN logistical operations.

Instruction: Major topics in the course are United Nations Logistics System; Principles of International Logistics; Phases of Logistic Planning, and Financial Arrangements. Methods of instruction include a self-paced correspondence course an End-of-Course Examination.

Credit Recommendation: In the lower division baccalaureate/associate degree category, 1 semester hour in Military Science, Logistics Management, or Resource Management (12/97).

University Affiliated Program of New Jersey

The University Affiliated Program of New Jersey is a component of the University of Medicine and Dentistry of New Jersey-Robert Wood Johnson Medical School.

This program works collaboratively with two- and four-year colleges and universities throughout the state to develop and strengthen developmental disability concentrations and courses and to promote the inclusion of information about developmental disabilities in standard curricula. It provides training and technical assistance to a variety of public and private agencies and organizations, sponsors seminars and lecture series, conducts field research and assists in the development of model/demonstration services serving varying age and disability groups.

University Affiliated Programs are funded by the Administration on Developmental Disabilities (ADD), Administration on Children and Families, U.S. Department of Health and Human Services. There are over forty such programs nationwide, each of which is located in, or affiliated with, major universities or teaching hospitals. In addition to the core funding received from ADD, programs receive support from federal, state, and local grants and contracts designed to address specific research, training, or service needs. Each program has four major components: interdisciplinary training, exemplary service, technical assistance, and dissemination of information and applied research.

Source of official student records: Registry of Credit Recommendations, American Council on Education, One Dupont Circle, Washington, DC 20036-1193.

Additional information about the courses: Office of Corporate-Higher Education Programs, Thomas Edison State College, 101 W. State Street, Trenton, NJ 08608-1176, (609) 633-6271.

Building Person-Centered Supports

Location: Six agencies throughout New Jersey—Association for Retarded Citizens/Atlantic County; United Cerebral Palsy Association Atlantic and Cape May Counties; Our House, Inc.; Association for Retarded Citizens/Union County; United Cerebral Palsy Association, Morris/Somerset Counties.

Length: 40 hours (1 week).

Dates: December 1990-June 1993.

Objective: To train middle managers to increase the opportunities for empowerment, contribution, and integration for persons with developmental disabilities by shifting service delivery from a program paradigm to an individualized support paradigm.

Learning Outcome: Upon successful completion of this course, the student will be able to describe the differences between system-centered and person-centered approaches; identify implications of new relationships between agency/staff and individuals with developmental disabilities, their families, friends, and community; list service options in residential, vocational, and family support areas; describe the pivotal role of the middle manager in the new service paradigm; identify adult learning strategies that facilitate the transfer of learning; explain the integration of functional goals, personal preferences, natural environments, and participation in the context of state-of-the-art services vs. "the readiness theory"; finalize a Personal Futures Plan incorporating the values and philosophies of person-centered planning, functional goals, personal preferences, natural environments, and consumer participation.

Instruction: Major topics covered in the course are values and philosophy of a person-centered development approach, Personal Futures Planning, shaping and designing state-of-the-art services and individualized support approaches to service delivery to people with developmental disabilities. The course will increase the management and supervisory skills of participants and enhance their ability to communicate and collaborate in developing a plan for organizational change. The training will assist community provider agencies in shifting service delivery from a program model to a more person-centered approach. Methods of instruction include a ten-hour practicum and outside course work.

Credit Recommendation: In the lower division baccalaureate/associate degree category, 3 semester hours in Human Services or Education elective (4/92).

Partnership and Collaboration: Supported Employment Service Coordination

Location: Locations throughout New Jersey.

Length: 40 hours (5 days over 3 weeks).

Dates: February 1994-Present.

Objective: To enable service coordination professionals to assist consumers to access meaningful employment services.

Learning Outcome: Upon successful completion of this course, the student will be able to understand the right to supported employment service, assist a person with a disability to plan for a career in the context of whole life planning, develop a collaborative team for service planning and delivery, and support consumer decision-making through advocacy and ongoing service support.

Instruction: Major topics covered in the course are historic and current thinking, technologies, and legislation which influence development and facilitation of collaborative teams, consumer empowerment, service provision, and service evaluation; person-centered planning; building partnerships; team facilitation; and evaluating consumer satisfaction. Methods of instruction include lecture, discussion, activities, and an appropriate graduate project.

Credit Recommendation: In the graduate degree category, 3 semester hours in Human Resource Management, Special Education, or Rehabilitation Counseling (11/95).

Supported Employment Leadership: A Manager's Guide to Supported Employment Services

Location: Locations throughout New Jersey.

Length: 40 hours (5 days over 3 weeks).

Dates: July 1995-Present.

Objective: To enable SE program managers to ensure quality service provision by providing skills development in the areas of staff recruitment and supervision, program development, and evaluation and change management.

Learning Outcome: Upon successful completion of this course, the student will be able to identify qualified employee candidates, develop and manage a team of staff, effectively supervise staff, identify quality service indicators, and understand the process of systems change.

Instruction: Major topics covered in the course are the current thinking in leadership and management skills and systems change strategies, recruiting, hiring, supervising and keeping quality staff, developing collaborative partnerships, evaluating services and ensuring quality, and influencing and implementing change. Methods of instruction include lecture, discussion, activities, and an appropriate graduate project.

Credit Recommendation: In the graduate degree category, 3 semester hours in Human Resource Management, Special Education, or Rehabilitation Counseling (11/95).

Supported Employment Training

Location: Locations throughout the state.

Length: 48 hours.

Dates: February 1992-Present.

Objective: To provide education to support employment specialists in order to increase the career and employment opportunities for people with severe disabilities by educating and empowering participants in the individualized choose/get/keep methodology of supported employment and promoting a systems change in vocational services from a train/place service paradigm to a place/train individual support paradigm.

Learning Outcome: Upon successful completion of this course, the student will be able to describe the factors which led to the emergence of supported employment; the legal frameworks and regulations affecting supported employment; the elements and values which contribute to quality in supported employment; and the roles of all critical stakeholders in facilitating supported employment; identify the limitations of traditional vocational assessment; develop a personal career profile for a target consumer (focus person); list strategies for facilitating a career planning meeting and promoting an individualized planning process; develop a marketing plan for job development services and create incentives; conduct a job analysis at a work site, identify and develop supportive behavior techniques, explain the role of technology and job modification and adaptation in solving job challenges, describe effective learning strategies and methods of adapting technological job challenges; describe concepts related to consumer empowerment, strategies for family involvement, utilization of social security incentives and benefits; and effectively participate in the management of organizational change within a traditional, vocational facility in its evolution toward a more community based, individualized supported employment service.

Instruction: Major topics covered in the course are provides training in the implementation of comprehensive supported employment services and the individualized support approach to lifelong career development and support when working with people with severe disabilities. This training is appropriate for personnel working with consumers who experience mental illness, traumatic brain injury, dual sensory impairment, physical disabilities, mental retardation, autism, epilepsy, cerebral palsy, spina bifida and other developmental disabilities. The training will also assist agencies in shifting service delivery from a program model to an individualized person-centered approach using a systems change technology. This training is based on the choose/get/keep methodology of supported employment and incorporates such state of the art practices as personal career profiles, marketing and job development, job carving and adaptation, assistive technology and worksite modification, positive behavioral supports, co-worker natural supports, consumer empowerment, corporate initiatives, social security work incentives, reasonable accommodations and continuous quality improvement for assessing service outcomes. Methods of instruction include six classroom days and two field days.

Credit Recommendation: In the lower division baccalaureate/associate degree category, 3 semester hours in Introduction to Special Education or Rehabilitation Counseling (2/93).

University of California, University Extension

Since 1891, UC Berkeley Extension has been creating bridges between the public and the University of California at Berkeley. Our comprehensive and self-supporting educational programs and services reflect the high academic standards of one of the world's finest universities. By providing lifelong learning opportunities for personal and professional growth, we are a catalyst for positive change in individual lives and in local, national, and global communities.

These programs are designed for professionals with mid-level managerial experience, but are available to all adults who are interested in advancing their education. Instructors are practitioners in their fields, trained in educational techniques. All credit courses and the Extension instructors who teach them are reviewed and approved by the appropriate academic department on the Berkeley campus and by the Committee an Courses of the Academic Senate. In addition, campus faculty review some non-credit courses and serve as consultants in curriculum development. This oversight by Univer-sity faculty is your assurance of excellence in course content and quality of instruction. UC Berkeley Extension is accredited by the Western Association of Schools and Colleges.

Source of official student records: Registry of Credit Recommendations, American Council on Education, One Dupont Circle, Washington, DC 20036-1193 or Registration and Student Services, Record Unit, University Extension, 1995 University Avenue, Suite 110, Berkeley, CA 94720-7020.

Additional information about the courses: College Credit Recommendation Service, American Council on Education, One Dupont Circle, Washington, DC 20036-1193.

Business Negotiating (X 451.3)

Location: Berkeley, San Francisco, Atherton, Contra Costa, Oakland, Rohnert Park, and Fremont, CA (potentially to be delivered abroad).

Length: 30 hours (15 weeks).

Dates: January 1988-Present.

Objective: To teach the student the skills and techniques used to conduct successful negotiations.

Learning Outcome: Upon successful completion of this course, the student will be able to identify the basic terms, principles, and concepts involved with negotiations; gain knowledge, insight, and understanding regarding the environments in which negotiations are conducted; learn and develop skill utilizing analytical techniques useful in negotiations; cognitively understand emotions within negotiations and develop techniques for incorporating those emotions into the negotiation strategy; build linkages to the knowledge base necessary for more advanced negotiations; and develop skills necessary to identify and resolve negotiating problems within work settings.

Instruction: Major topics covered in the course are the basic theories, research, and methodology of effective business negotiations and practice applying theory and technique in typical negotiating situations. Methods of instruction include both seminar and lecture/discussion format, selected audiovisual materials, case studies, and other educational aids.

Credit Recommendation: In the upper division baccalaureate degree category, 2 semester hours in Negotiating or Management (8/96).

Consumer Buying Behavior (X 461.7)

Location: Berkeley, San Francisco, Atherton, Contra Costa, Oakland, Rohnert Park, and Fremont, CA.

Length: 30 hours (15 weeks).

Dates: January 1988-Present.

Objective: To develop the student's ability to identify the major internal and external factors that influence an individual's buying behavior and translate buyer behavior information into marketing strategy.

Learning Outcome: Upon successful completion of this course, the student will be able to identify the major internal and external factors that influence an individual's buying behavior and translate buyer behavior information into marketing strategy.

Instruction: Major topics covered in the course are how successful firms use their knowledge or consumer attitudes and behavior to segment markets; how to design marketing strategies; how to measure market performance; and analysis of the consumer as the basis for the development of the marketing mix for your product, service, or company (economics, social, psychological and cultural factors are considered); types of consumer research methods; and types of marketing issues. Methods of instruction include lecture, reading, case studies, class discussions, homework assignments, guest lecturers, and a short final examination. **NOTE**: Potentially to be delivered abroad.

Credit Recommendation: In the upper division baccalaureate degree category, 2 semester hours in Marketing or Consumer Behavior (8/96).

Corporate Finance (X 430.1)

Location: Berkeley, San Francisco, Atherton, Contra Costa, Oakland, Rohnert Park, and Fremont, CA.

Length: 30 hours (15 weeks).

Dates: January 1988-Present.

Objective: To provide students with some of the financial decision-making concepts and skills used in business corporations.

Learning Outcome: Upon successful completion of this course, the student will be able to perform basic financial analysis utilizing financial tools (e.g. cash flow analysis, ratios, etc.) which will facilitate management decision-making.

Instruction: Major topics covered in the course are modern financial theories, the strategies and tools of decision-making, and how corporate finance works, the range of issues involved, and how to perform the basic calculations required for financial analysis. Methods of instruction include lecture, class discussions, case studies, and application exercises. **NOTE**: Potentially to be delivered abroad.

Credit Recommendation: In the upper division baccalaureate degree category, 2 semester hours in Finance (8/96).

Essentials of Advertising (X 401.7)

Location: Berkeley, San Francisco, Atherton, Contra Costa, Oakland, Rohnert Park, and Fremont, CA.

Length: 30 hours (15 Weeks).

Dates: January 1988-Present.

Objective: To provide an understanding of the vocabulary and methods used in advertising and an understanding of advertising account management.

Learning Outcome: Upon successful completion of this class, the student will be able to research and develop a successful advertising campaign.

Instruction: Major topics covered in the course are an overview of the essential methods, strategies, and vocabulary necessary for a fundamental understanding of the advertising process. Examples are drawn from high-tech, industrial, consumer, and service areas. Methods of instruction include readings, lectures, case studies, and small group assignments. **NOTE**: Potentially to be delivered abroad.

Credit Recommendation: In the upper division baccalaureate degree category, 2 semester hours in Advertising (8/96).

Essentials of Economics (X 402.8)

Location: Berkeley, San Francisco, Atherton, Contra Costa, Oakland, Rohnert Park, and Fremont, CA.

Length: 30 hours (15 weeks).

Dates: January 1988-Present.

Objective: To enable students to think "like economists", understand the powerful lessons of the economic approach, and feel very comfortable with the business sections of any newspaper.

Learning Outcome: Upon successful completion of this course, students will be able to recognize how theory works; demonstrate a thorough understanding of microeconomic and macroeconomic concepts such as scarcity, opportunity costs, economic profit, cost-push and demand-pull inflation, comparative advantage, concentration ratios, etc.; apply economic theory to the material that will be discussed in class; and appreciate and understand the business section of the San Francisco Chronicle and Examiner and the Wall Street Journal.

Instruction: Major topics covered in the course are an overview of general economic issues, theories, and concepts in both microeconomics and macroeconomics, such as, supply and demand, externalities, elasticity, unemployment, inflation, gross national product, and gross domestic product, etc.; money and monetary policies, the relationship between the price level and inflation, how to evaluate the various market structures, market concentration ratios, and anti-trust laws in the United States; and International trade. Methods of instruction include lectures, class discussions, assigned problem sets, required project, and readings. **NOTE**: Potentially to be delivered abroad.

Credit Recommendation: In the lower division baccalaureate/associate degree category, 2 semester hours in Economics (8/96).

Essentials of Marketing (X 460.1)

Location: Berkeley, San Francisco, Atherton, Contra Costa, Oakland, Rohnert Park, and Fremont, CA.

Length: 30 hours (15 weeks).

Dates: January 1988-Present.

Objective: To provide an overview of the principles of marketing and an understanding of the role of marketing in an organization's strategic plan.

Learning Outcome: Upon successful completion of this course, the student will be able to understand the marketing concept and how marketing can affect the profitability and image of a company.

Instruction: Major topics covered in the course are a study of the evolution of markets and marketing; market structure, organization, and behavior; marketing functions; pricing and price policy; marketing costs and efficiency; public and private regulations; service marketing; consumer demographics; distribution; promotion; personal selling; international marketing; and careers in marketing. Methods of instruction include readings, lectures, case studies, and small group assignments. **NOTE**: Potentially to be delivered abroad.

Credit Recommendation: In the upper division baccalaureate degree category, 2 semester hours in Marketing (8/96).

Implementing an Integrated Marketing Communications Approach (X 466.1)

Location: Berkeley, San Francisco, Atherton, Contra Costa, Oakland, Rohnert Park, and Fremont, CA.

Length: 30 hours (15 weeks).

Dates: January 1988-Present.

Objective: To provide an understanding of the methods that exist in the marketing communications mix, to provide an understanding of the integration of various marketing communications methods, and to develop an integrated marketing communications plan.

Learning Outcome: Upon successful completion of this course, the student will be able to develop advertising, public relations, personal selling sales promotions, and direct marketing into an integrated marketing communications plan.

Instruction: Major topics covered in the course are an overview of marketing communications methods such as promotion, advertising, public relations, direct marketing and personal sales and how to design an integrated marketing communications plan. Methods of instruction include lecture, small group discussion, and group projects. **NOTE**: Potentially to be delivered abroad.

Credit Recommendation: In the upper division baccalaureate degree category, 2 semester hours in Marketing or Marketing Communications (8/96).

International Marketing (X 495.4)

Location: Berkeley, San Francisco, Atherton, Contra Costa, Oakland, Rohnert Park, and Fremont, CA.

Length: 30 hours (15 weeks).

Dates: January 1988-Present.

Objective: To develop an awareness of the importance of international marketing to the modern corporation and to participate in the development of a marketing plan for a small company wishing to develop international sales of a new or existing product.

Learning Outcome: Upon successful completion of this course, the student will be able to create a marketing plan for a small company wishing to develop international sales of a new or existing product.

Instruction: Major topics covered in the course are the similarities between domestic and international marketing; international marketing, and the various factors that differentiate it from domestic marketing; the effects of different cultural, legal, economic, and political factors on international marketing; and corporate organizations for international marketing and sales. Methods of instruction include lectures, discussions, and class exercises. **NOTE**: Potentially to be delivered abroad.

Credit Recommendation: In the upper division baccalaureate degree category, 2 semester hours in International Marketing (8/96).

Management Accounting (X 420.4)

Location: Berkeley, San Francisco, Atherton, Contra Costa, Oakland, Rohnert Park, and Fremont, CA.

Length: 30 hours (15 weeks).

Dates: January 1988-Present.

Objective: To teach the student the fundamental concepts and techniques of managerial accounting with an emphasis on how financial data can be used for management.

Learning Outcome: Upon successful completion of this course, the student will be able to identify and record business events correctly, produce financial statements appropriate for information purposes, analyze and interpret business financial statements, and make business decisions using relevant accounting data.

Instruction: Major topics covered in the course are an introduction to financial and managerial accounting designed specifically for international students with no accounting background, basic accounting concepts, and how accounting information is used to help managers make decisions. Methods of instruction include lecture, out-of-class assignments (specifically readings and accounting problems), and class discussion. **NOTE**: Potentially to be delivered abroad.

Credit Recommendation: In the lower division baccalaureate/associate degree

category, 2 semester hours in Accounting (8/96).

Management of Human Resources (X 450.1)

Location: Berkeley, San Francisco, Atherton, Contra Costa, Oakland, Rohnert Park, and Fremont, CA.

Length: 30 hours (15 weeks).

Dates: January 1988-Present.

Objective: To develop an understanding of basic human resources principles and practices, discuss and learn more about various human resource policies and procedures in an organizational setting, discuss and recognize many of the major human resource regulated Federal and State laws and regulations, and provide a broad base for further study in human resources.

Learning Outcome: Upon successful completion of this course, the student will be able to develop an understanding of basic human resource principles and practices, discuss and learn more about various human resource policies and procedures in an organizational setting, discuss and recognize many of the major human resource regulated Federal and State laws and regulations, and provide a broad base for further study in human resource.

Instruction: Major topics covered in the course are the professional practice of human resource management and a general overview of human resource management and its major functional areas. Methods of instruction include lecture, class discussion, and assigned readings. **NOTE**: Potentially to be delivered abroad.

Credit Recommendation: In the upper division baccalaureate degree category, 2 semester hours in Management or Human Resources (8/96).

Marketing Planning (X 405.5)

Location: Berkeley, San Francisco, Atherton, Contra Costa, Oakland, Rohnert Park, and Fremont, CA.

Length: 30 hours (15 weeks).

Dates: January 1988-Present.

Objective: To provide students with an understanding and use of marketing plans; to develop an understanding of marketing plan components; and to develop a marketing plan including a situation analysis, company's goals and constraints, objectives, and programs.

Learning Outcome: Upon successful completion of this course, the student will be able to develop, write, and implement a marketing plan.

Instruction: Major topics covered in the course are an overview and understanding of the principles and practices involved in developing and writing an effective marketing plan and integrating it with an organization's business goals; the marketing plan's critical components including competitive and company situation analysis, objectives, strategies and tactics, and forecasting; plan implementation; controls; and measurements. Methods of instruction include assigned readings, lectures, case studies and analyses, a market plan, and class/team discussions. **NOTE**: Potentially to be delivered abroad.

Credit Recommendation: In the upper division baccalaureate degree category, 2 semester hours in Marketing Planning (8/96).

Marketing Research: Concepts and Techniques (X 460.6)

Location: Berkeley, San Francisco, Atherton, Contra Costa, Oakland, Rohnert Park, and Fremont, CA.

Length: 30 hours (15 weeks).

Dates: January 1988-Present.

Objective: To provide students with an overview of market research concepts and techniques and an opportunity to apply concepts and techniques through an individual project.

Learning Outcome: Upon successful completion of this course, the student will be able to understand marketing research methods available to address her/his company's needs.

Instruction: Major topics covered in the course are methods and techniques for conducting market research, an overview of market research, the nature and types of basic data sources, effective questionnaire design, and interpreting and applying findings to marketing decisions. Methods of instruction include lectures, discussions, case studies, individual projects, and presentations. **NOTE**: Potentially to be delivered abroad.

Credit Recommendation: In the upper division baccalaureate degree category, 2 semester hours in Marketing or Marketing Research (8/96).

Organization and Management (X 490.1)

Location: Berkeley, San Francisco, Atherton, Contra Costa, Oakland, Rohnert Park, and Fremont, CA.

Length: 30 hours (15 weeks).

Dates: January 1988-Present.

Objective: To explore theories of organizational structure and style along with practical examples of how they operate in today's business environment. Case materials drawn from the literature as well as student's own organizational experience will be presented for analysis.

Learning Outcome: Upon successful completion of this course, the student will be able to understand how and why organizational structure and management styles evolve and affect one another.

Instruction: Major topics covered in the course are how and why organizational structure and management styles evolve and affect one another, major theories of management practice, organizational structure, planning, strategy , and leadership. Methods of instruction include tests, projects, essays, and in-class presentations. **NOTE**: Potentially to be delivered abroad.

Credit Recommendation: In the upper division baccalaureate degree category, 2 semester hours in Management (8/96).

Strategic Marketing (X 460.2)

Location: Berkeley, San Francisco, Atherton, Contra Costa, Oakland, Rohnert Park, and Fremont, CA.

Length: 30 hours (15 weeks).

Dates: January 1988-Present.

Objective: To provide students with an understanding of strategic marketing concepts and processes; to help students identify opportunities for competitive advantage and the key marketing elements that lead to meeting customers' needs and organizational objectives; to provide an opportunity for students to work together as teams to apply concepts through the identification, analysis, and significance of the major components that incorporate the elements required of a strategic market analysis.

Learning Outcome: Upon successful completion of this course, the student will be able to identify opportunities for competitive advantage and the key marketing elements that lead to meeting customers' needs and organizational objectives.

Instruction: Major topics covered in the course are how strategic marketing relates to marketing and business and the process of strategic versus the tactical nature of marketing which will include conducting a strategic marketing analysis that identifies a company's specific objectives and opportunities, analyzing data, and selecting winning strategies. Methods of instruction include assigned readings, lectures, case studies and analyses, class exercises, and class/team discussions. **NOTE**: Potentially to be delivered abroad.

Credit Recommendation: In the upper division baccalaureate degree category, 2 semester hours in Marketing (8/96).

University of St. Thomas

Founded in 1885, the University of St. Thomas is the largest private university in Minnesota. St. Thomas offers twenty-five master's and three doctoral programs in addition to its fifty-four undergraduate programs. It is a comprehensive liberal arts university that emphasizes value-centered, career-oriented education.

Now the fifth-largest graduate business school in the United States, the University of St. Thomas Graduate School of Business offers a complete array of educational resources and programs, including eight degree programs and nine professional development centers.

The Master of International Management Program (MIM) was founded in 1984 and is the second largest program in the Graduate School of Business. As a graduate program in international business, it is designed to provide students with training in international business, intercultural understanding, and proficiency in a foreign language. The MIM program is offered through partnerships in Canada, Taiwan, and Uruguay, and is affiliated with over 20 universities worldwide.

MIM students represent over 35 countries worldwide. There are approximately 500 registered students in the MIM program.

Source of official student records: Registry of Credit Recommendations, American Council on Education, One Dupont Circle, Washington, DC 20036-1193.

Additional information about the courses: College Credit Recommendation Service, American Council on Education, One Dupont Circle, Washington, DC 20036-1193.

Business Spanish I (INSP600)

Location: St. Paul, Minnesota.
Length: 42 hours (14 weeks).
Dates: February 1987-Present.
Objective: To develop effective and professional Spanish communication skills necessary for success in an international business community.
Learning Outcome: Upon successful completion of this course, the student will be able to demonstrate day-to-day use of the language in business situations.
Instruction: Major topics covered in the course are grammar, regional studies of Latin countries, and marketing strategies. Methods of instruction include lecture, discussion, classroom exercises, audio/visual presentations, quizzes, and examinations. **NOTE:** Graduate students are evaluated through a combination of papers, quizzes, and examinations. Three absences or more from class can reduce a student's final grade.
Credit Recommendation: In the graduate degree category, 3 semester hours in Business Spanish I (2/97).

Business Spanish II (INSP601)

Location: St. Paul, Minnesota.
Length: 42 hours (14 weeks).
Dates: February 1987-Present.
Objective: To master the elements of business communication required at the executive level of international business conducted in Spanish.
Learning Outcome: Upon successful completion of this course, the student will be able to demonstrate an improved practical use of the language in a business setting and an enhanced knowledge of the language itself.
Instruction: Major topics covered in the course are grammar and regional economies. Methods of instruction include lecture, discussion, classroom exercises, audio/visual, reports, papers, and examinations. **NOTE:** Graduate students are evaluated through a combination of papers and examinations. Three absences or more from class can reduce a student's final grade.
Credit Recommendation: In the graduate degree category, 3 semester hours in Business Spanish II (2/97).

Intercultural Communications and Management (INMG600)

Location: St. Paul, Minnesota.
Length: 42 hours (14 weeks).
Dates: February 1987-Present.
Objective: To train the international manager to be aware of cross-cultural nuances in order to facilitate effective communication and mutual understanding in a business environment.
Learning Outcome: Upon successful completion of this course, the student will be able to develop a broader framework for making judgments in an international setting by developing a general concept of cultural differences.
Instruction: Major topics covered in the course are the shaping of culture, the impact of culture on management, sexual harassment and the law, and cultural communication. Methods of instruction include lecture, discussion, case studies, readings, papers, presentations, group projects, and examinations. **NOTE:** Graduate students are evaluated through a combination of papers, oral presentations, group projects, and examinations. Three absences or more from class can reduce a student's final grade.
Credit Recommendation: In the graduate degree category, 3 semester hours in Intercultural Communications (2/97).

International Economics (INEC600)

Location: Minneapolis, Minnesota.
Length: 42 hours (14 weeks).
Dates: February 1987-Present.
Objective: To provide students the knowledge to analyze fundamental economic forces and circumstances that effect the flow of resources across national borders.
Learning Outcome: Upon successful completion of this course, the student, as managers, will be able to help students understand the role of technological change and government in altering economic relationships among nation-states.
Instruction: Major topics covered in the course are trade policy and agreements, international monetary economics, exchange rates and economic integration, environmental problems, and immigration policy. Methods of instruction include lecture, discussion, case studies, readings, papers and examinations. **NOTE:** Graduate students are evaluated through a combination of papers and examinations. Three absences or more from class can reduce a student's final grade.
Credit Recommendation: In the graduate degree category, 3 semester hours in International Economics (2/97).

International Personnel Management (INHR700)

Location: Minneapolis, Minnesota.
Length: 42 hours (14 weeks).
Dates: February 1987-Present.
Objective: To understand the impact of diverse cultures and different value systems on the major functions of human resource management.
Learning Outcome: Upon successful completion of this course, the student will be able to more thoroughly appreciate the dynamics of human behavior within multinational organizations; gain a frame of reference for cross-cultural business leadership and managing human resources in a multicultural setting; and gain knowledge and skills in specific human resource functions unique to international business operations.
Instruction: Major topics covered in the course are the expatriation process,

theories of motivation, labor relations, fundamental human resource structures in various countries, and compensation and benefits systems. Methods of instruction include lecture, discussion, case studies, readings, papers, projects, and examinations. **NOTE:** Graduate students are evaluated through a combination of papers, projects, case study, mid-term, and final examinations.

Credit Recommendation: In the graduate degree category, 3 semester hours in International Personnel Management or International Human Resources (2/97).

International Planning, Organization, and Control (INMG800)

Location: Minneapolis, Minnesota.
Length: 42 hours (14 weeks).
Dates: February 1987-Present.

Objective: To apply knowledge acquired in the other international business disciplines to develop company objectives, organization policy, and managerial and financial strategies.

Learning Outcome: Upon successful completion of this course, the student will be able to make managerial decisions due to better training based on real life situations simulated in class and make timely, thoughtful decisions in circumstances that simulate real-life situations.

Instruction: Major topics covered in the course are strategic management, leadership issues, marketing and manufacturing management, operating environment, labor climate, and distinctive competencies. Methods of instruction include lecture, discussion, case studies, readings, papers, presentations, projects, and examinations. **NOTE:** Graduate students are evaluated through a combination of papers, student presentations, examinations, and projects.

Credit Recommendation: In the graduate degree category, 3 semester hours in International Strategic Management (2/97).

Multinational Business Finance (INFC700)

Location: St. Paul, Minnesota.
Length: 42 hours (14 weeks).
Dates: February 1987-Present.

Objective: To analyze in depth an assortment of complex questions concerning international trade and finance.

Learning Outcome: Upon successful completion of this course, the student will be able to recommend actions for the management of translations and transactions; design policies for multinational working capital management; understand the idea of adjusted present value; and determine comparative advantages and international financial models.

Instruction: Major topics covered in the course are government influence on exchange rate relations between inflation, interest and exchange rates, managing transaction exposure, direct foreign investment, country risk analysis, and the international debt crisis. Methods of instruction include lecture, discussion, case studies, readings, papers and examinations. **NOTE:** Graduate students are evaluated through a combination of papers and examinations. Three absences or more from class can reduce a student's final grade.

Credit Recommendation: In the graduate degree category, 3 semester hours in Finance (2/97).

UOL Publishing, Inc.

UOL Publishing, Inc., formerly University Online, Inc. (UOL), headquartered in Falls Church, Virginia, purchased the computer-based instruction component from Control Data in January 1994 and continues to provide education products and services from the internet.

The computer-assisted and computer-managed instruction is supplemented by texts or workbooks and multimedia presentations.

Procedures followed by Army Education Service Centers are designed in accordance with guidelines established by UOL Publishing, Inc. Every Army Education Service Center that delivers ACE credit-recommended courses published by UOL Publishing, Inc. maintains a formal liaison with UOL Publishing and delivers UOL Publishing courses, grades (if such is the case), and certificates of completion in accordance with UOL Publishing administrative requirements. These requirements are based on UOL Publishing's adherence to policies and procedures of ACE/CREDIT.

Source of official student records: Registry of Credit Recommendations, American Council on Education, One Dupont Circle, Washington, DC 20036-1193 or Registrar, CYBIS Support, University Online, Inc., 12372 River Ridge Boulevard, Burnsville, MN 55337-1665.

Additional information about the courses: College Credit Recommendation Service, American Council on Education, One Dupont Circle, Washington, DC 20036-1193.

Business/Management Curriculum

Accounts Receivable Collection Techniques

Location: Various sites around the country.

Length: Approximately 16 hours (computer-based instruction).

Dates: October 1979-Present.

Objective: To recognize the importance of accounts receivable collections and to apply various collections skills (letters, telephone, customer visits) to job situations.

Learning Outcome: Upon successful completion of this course, the student will be able to handle collection more efficiently.

Instruction: Major topics covered in the course are basic accounts receivable files and reports with the three primary collection techniques: written, telephone, and personal visits. Methods of instruction include simulation exercises, multimedia presentations, and drill and practice.

Credit Recommendation: In the lower division baccalaureate/associate degree category, 1 semester hour in Accounts Receivable Collection Techniques (11/81) (6/86) (10/95).

Basic Management (Resource Management, Supervisory Success, Time Management, Effective Supervision) (Formerly Resource Management, Supervisory Success, Time Management)

Location: Various sites around the country.

Length: *Version 1*: Approximately 28 hours (computer-based instruction); *Version 2*: Approximately 36 hours (computer-based instruction).

Dates: May 1980-Present.

Objective: To enable the participant to understand lower-level management concepts that deal with effective supervision, communication, planning, motivation, and resource and time management.

Learning Outcome: Upon successful completion of this course, the student will understand management and personnel dynamics at the first level of supervision.

Instruction: Major topic covered in the course is lower-level management concepts. Methods of instruction include simulation exercises, multimedia presentations, and drill and practice.

Credit Recommendation: In the lower division baccalaureate/associate degree category, 1 semester hour in Basic Management (11/81) (6/86) (10/95).

Better Business Letters

Location: Various sites around the country.

Length: Approximately 13 hours (computer-based instruction).

Dates: October 1979-Present.

Objective: To increase efficiency and effectiveness by producing low-cost business letters that communicate persuasively, enthusiastically, and effectively.

Learning Outcome: Upon successful completion of this course, the student will have enhanced written communication skills.

Instruction: Major topics covered in the course are techniques for producing business letters and memoranda that communicate in an effective manner. Methods of instruction include simulation exercises, multimedia presentations, drill and practice.

Credit Recommendation: In the vocational certificate category, 1 semester hour in Business Communication (11/81) (6/86) (10/95).

Building Your Own Business and Obtaining Financing (Version 2) (Formerly Building Your Own Business - Version 1)

Location: Various sites around the country.

Length: *Version 1*: Approximately 39 hours (computer-based instruction); *Version 2*: Approximately 43 hours (computer-based instruction).

Dates: *Version 1:* October 1979-May 1986; *Version 2:* June 1986-Present.

Objective: To enable the participant to understand and readily identify the primary considerations that must be addressed in founding or expanding a small business.

Learning Outcome: Upon successful completion of this course, the student will be able to integrate the various activities necessary to found or expand a small business.

Instruction: Major topics covered in the course are starting, improving, and expanding a business. Methods of instruction include simulation exercises, multimedia presentations, and drill and practice are used.

Credit Recommendation: *Version 1:* In the lower division baccalaureate/associate degree category, 1 semester hour in Introduction to Small Business Management (11/81). *Version 2:* In the lower division baccalaureate/associate degree category, 2 semester hours in Introduction to Small Business Management (6/86) (10/95).

Business Systems Analyst Sequence

Location: Various sites around the country.

Length: Approximately 117 hours (computer-based instruction).

Dates: October 1979-Present.

Objective: To help prepare the student to become a business systems analyst in terms of computer concepts and the business environment.

Learning Outcome: Upon successful completion of this course, the student will understand the basic tasks involved in successfully designing, developing, implementing, and evaluating a business information system and will be able to apply that understanding to case studies.

Instruction: Major topics covered in the course are the basic tools of the systems analyst and with the procedures needed to design, develop, and implement a business information system; computer system hardware, basic elements of COBOL programming; introduction to computer systems and data base management systems. Methods of instruction include simulation exercises, multimedia presentations, drill, and practice.

Credit Recommendation: In the lower division baccalaureate/associate degree category, 3 semester hours in Business Systems Analysis (11/81) (6/86) (10/95).

Communications and Consulting Skills Sequence (Communication Skills, Consulting Skills, The Helping Relationship)

Location: Various sites around the country.

Length: Approximately 27 hours (computer-based instruction).

Dates: May 1983-Present.

Objective: To provide the student with the basic skills pertaining to communication, consulting, cooperation, and listening.

Learning Outcome: Upon successful completion of this course, the student will have more effective interpersonal relations.

Instruction: Major topics covered in the course are identification and improvement of communication styles; improvement of listening; and establishing cooperative relationships in personal and professional settings.

Credit Recommendation: In the lower division baccalaureate/associate degree category, 1 semester hour in Communications (6/86) (10/95).

CREATE Curriculum

Location: Various sites around the country.

Length: Approximately 250 hours (computer-based instruction).

Dates: October 1979-Present.

Objective: To provide training in the design, development, and implementation of CAI and CMI courseware.

Learning Outcome: Upon successful completion of this course, the student will understand the fundamentals of curriculum design and its implementation through CAI and CMI.

Instruction: Major topics covered in the course are providing training in the skills required for designing, developing, and managing the development of individualized instruction; CREATE fundamentals; design; development; Tutor Author Language; CAI; CMI; and management. Methods of instruction include simulation exercises, multimedia presentations, drill, and practice. *Prerequisite:* Introduction to Computer-Based Education.

Credit Recommendation: In the graduate degree category, 8 semester hours in Development and Design of CAI and CMI using CREATE (CYBIS) (11/81) (6/86) (10/95).

Foundations of Corporate Financial Management (Capital Budgeting, Financing for Long-Term Growth, Short-Term Financial Planning Sequences)

Location: Various sites around the country.

Length: Approximately 82 hours (computer-based instruction).

Dates: September 1979-Present.

Objective: To provide a thorough understanding of the principles of corporate financial management.

Learning Outcome: Upon successful completion of this course, the student will understand the basic processes for financial management of a corporation.

Instruction: Major topics covered in the course are an introduction to capital budgeting, the effect of taxes and the uncertain economy on budgeting, capital structure and financial leverage, cost of capital, dividend policy and retention of earnings, issuance of capital stock, intermediate and long-term financing, leasing, mergers and acquisitions, and inventory control. Methods of instruction include simulation exercises, multimedia presentations, drill and practice.

Credit Recommendation: In the upper division baccalaureate degree category, 3 semester hours in Foundations of Corporate Financial Management (6/86) (9/90) (10/95).

Introduction to Programming in BASIC (Introduction to Programming in BASIC, BASIC Programming Techniques)

Location: Various sites around the country.

Length: Approximately 45 hours (computer-based instruction).

Dates: August 1980-Present.

Objective: To provide a practical introduction to programming techniques through the use of the BASIC language.

Learning Outcome: Upon successful completion of this course, the student will have an elementary knowledge of the function of computers and the vocabulary and syntax of the BASIC programming language.

Instruction: Major topics covered in the course are an introduction to advanced programming techniques through use of the BASIC language; structured programming fundamentals, interactive and logical loop programming, array handling techniques, function and subroutine use, and file processing methods. Methods of instruction include simulation exercises, multimedia presentations, drill and practice.

Credit Recommendation: In the lower division baccalaureate/associate degree category, 1 semester hour in Computer Programming (11/81) (6/86) (10/95). **NOTE:** If taken with Introduction to Computers, then 2 semester hours are recommended in the same degree category. (No credit is recommended for Introduction to Computers if taken separately.)

Managerial Accounting (Financial Management Sequence, Understanding Financial Statements Sequence)

Location: Various sites around the country.

Length: Approximately 72 hours (computer-based instruction).

Dates: June 1979-Present.

Objective: To provide a background in managerial accounting techniques and practices.

Learning Outcome: Upon successful completion of this course, the student will understand the basic techniques and vocabulary of accounting, especially cost accounting.

Instruction: Major topics covered in the course are a review of accounting fundamentals; basics of income statements and balance sheets; cost systems, cost reporting, classification of costs, burden costs, cost standards and variances, determination of profits, valuation of inventories, long-range planning, budgeting, budget control; basics of financial statement analysis and the basics of constructing pro forma financial statements.

Credit Recommendation: In the lower division baccalaureate/associate degree category or in the upper division baccalaureate degree category, 3 semester hours in

Managerial Accounting (6/86) (9/90) (10/95).

Managerial Planning, Organizing, and Controlling Curriculum

Location: Various sites around the country.

Length: Approximately 35 hours (computer-based instruction).

Dates: October 1979-Present.

Objective: To enable the participant to improve managerial skills in planning and budgeting, organizing, and controlling work flow.

Learning Outcome: Upon successful completion of this course, the student will be able to plan the reorganization of a department to form an effective work group.

Instruction: Major topics covered in the course are management issues and tasks relevant to the interrelated responsibilities of planning and budgeting, the use of principles of organizing structures, interrelated communication systems, management-by-objectives, and the achievement of departmental plans. Methods of instruction include simulation exercises, multimedia presentations, drill and practice.

Credit Recommendation: In the upper division baccalaureate degree category, 2 semester hours in Management (11/81) (10/95).

Managerial Success Curriculum

Location: Various sites around the country.

Length: Approximately 26 hours (computer-based instruction).

Dates: May 1980-Present.

Objective: To enable the participants to improve managerial effectiveness and their personal roles as a change agent.

Learning Outcome: Upon successful completion of this course, the student will better understand the role of the effective middle manager.

Instruction: Major topics covered in the course are middle management, the expansion of managerial perspective, motivation, communication, the setting of objectives, and performance appraisal. Methods of instruction include simulation exercises, multimedia presentations, drill, and practice.

Credit Recommendation: In the lower division baccalaureate/associate degree category, 1 semester hour in Management and Supervision (11/81) (6/86) (10/95).

Office Communication and Behavior: Success (Formerly Office Communication and Behavior [Excel])

Location: Various sites around the country.

Length: Approximately 21 hours (computer-based instruction).

Dates: June 1979-Present.

Objective: To improve proficiency in handling office problems and in supporting the activities of managers.

Learning Outcome: Upon successful completion of this course, the student will understand the political and social forces present in the work environment.

Instruction: Major topics covered in the course are the manager's job, managerial styles, coping with change, successful communications, developing a professional approach, criticism and job responsibilities, setting performance standards, effective use of time, and career goal considerations.

Credit Recommendation: In the vocational certificate category, 1 semester hour in Secretarial Science or Paralegal Studies (6/86) (9/90) (10/95).

Problem Analysis and Decision-Making

Location: Various sites around the country.

Length: Approximately 24 hours (computer-based instruction).

Dates: October 1979-Present.

Objective: To enable the participant to develop an understanding of a systematic approach to problem analysis and decision-making and be able to apply effective decision-making skills.

Learning Outcome: Upon successful completion of this course, the student will be able to examine the factors involved in analyzing a problem and will better understand the decision-making process.

Instruction: Major topics covered in the course are the decision-making process, including its relationship to problem analysis with emphasis on the Alpha-Omega method, included are the factors involved in making a choice and followup on that choice. Methods of instruction include simulation exercises, multimedia presentations, drill and practice.

Credit Recommendation: In the upper division baccalaureate degree category, 1 semester hour in Problem Analysis and Decision-Making (11/81) (10/95).

Selling: The Psychological Sequence (Effective Sales Calls, Selling: The Psychological Approach, Telephone as a Sales Tool, Value Selling) (Version 2) (Formerly Effective Sales Calls, Selling: The Psychological Approach, Telephone as a Sales Tool) (Version 1)

Location: Various sites around the country.

Length: *Version 1:* Approximately 25.5 hours (computer-based instruction); *Version 2:* Approximately 42.5 hours (computer-based instruction).

Dates: *Version 1:* October 1979-May 1986; *Version 2:* June 1986-Present.

Objective: To enable the participant to develop a psychological approach to selling.

Learning Outcome: Upon successful completion of this course, the student will become a better salesperson and be able to prepare a value selling presentation.

Instruction: Major topics covered in the course are a basic psychological approach to selling; development of the psychological approach to selling; using the telephone as a sales tool; effective sales calls; and organizing a sales strategy. Methods of instruction include simulation exercises, multimedia presentations, drill, and practice .

Credit Recommendation: *Version 1:* In the lower division baccalaureate/associate degree category, 1 semester hour in Basic Selling or Introduction to Sales (11/81). *Version 2:* In the lower division baccalaureate/associate degree category, 2 semester hours in Basic Selling or Introduction to Sales (6/86) (10/95). **NOTE:** The student should not receive credit for both Selling: The Psychological Sequence and Selling: The Strategic Approach Sequence.

Selling: The Strategic Approach Sequence (The Strategic Process; Time and Territory Management; Account Control, Executive Selling; The Telephone as a Sales Tool; Value Selling)

Location: Various sites around the country.

Length: Approximately 39.5 hours (computer-assisted instruction).

Dates: November 1983-Present.

Objective: To provide a framework for selling.

Learning Outcome: Upon successful completion of this course, the student will be able to organize a sales presentation incorporating a value selling analysis.

Instruction: Major topics covered in the course are developing a strategic process, effective time and territory management, maintaining control of accounts, and executive and value selling.

Credit Recommendation: In the lower division baccalaureate/associate degree category, 2 semester hours in Basic Selling or Introduction to Sales (6/86) (10/95). **NOTE:** The student should not receive credit for both Selling: The Strategic Approach Sequence and Selling: The Psychological Sequence.

Computer Science/Mathematics Curriculum

Ada Programming Fundamentals (Ada Overview, Ada Programming: Fundamentals)

Location: Various sites around the country.

Length: Approximately 40 hours (computer-based instruction).

Dates: August 1985-Present.

Objective: To understand the Ada programming environment and to learn the basics of Ada and introduce effective design and development methods.

Learning Outcome: Upon successful completion of this course, the student will be able to understand the rationale of the design and development of the Ada programming language, the effective use of Ada to improve cost efficiency and productivity throughout the software life cycle; to write and compile Ada programs encompassing basic features such as objects, subprograms and packages; and to use Ada program structure concepts.

Instruction: Major topics covered in the course are the development of the understanding of productivity, reliability, and the economics of problem-solving associated with the development and maintenance of computer software, the effective use of Ada concepts and terminology, the impact of Ada on software design and development, the basic Ada program units and structure concepts, syntax and types, and central structure. *Prerequisite:* The ability to program in a higher level language (e.g., PASCAL, FORTRAN, COBOL, JOVIAL).

Credit Recommendation: In the lower division baccalaureate/associate degree category, 1 semester hour in Computer Science (6/86) (10/95).

Advanced Ada and Software Engineering (Ada Programming: Advanced Features; Ada Programming: Software Engineering)

Location: Various sites around the country.

Length: Approximately 60 hours (computer-based instruction).

Dates: November 1985-Present.

Objective: To identify attributes of numeric and private types, the syntax and use of unconstrained arrays, and the concept and use of exception processing capabilities; and to use these concepts in software engineering.

Learning Outcome: Upon successful completion of this course, the student will be able to write and compile Ada programs, making use of numeric and private types, the syntax for unconstrained arrays, the exception processing capabilities, the syntax of composite types, the characteristics of access types, the use of explicit type conversions, the use of discriminated records and variant records and generics, and the use of the Ada programming environment for the design and development of major software.

Instruction: Major topics covered in the course are the development of Ada programs using numeric and private types, data structures, type conversion, and unconstrained arrays; discriminated records and generics; library issues and exceptions; concurrency; issues of portability; machine dependency; and library routines, design, and program structure. *Prerequisite:* Ada Programming Fundamentals.

Credit Recommendation: In the upper division baccalaureate degree category, 2 semester hours in Computer Science (6/86) (10/95). **NOTE:** If the course is supplemented with programming assignments, the credit recommendation is 3 semester hours Computer Science in the upper division baccalaureate degree category.

Algebra

Location: Various sites around the country.

Length: Approximately 75 hours (computer-based instruction).

Dates: April 1983-Present.

Objective: To provide practice, workbook exercises, tutorials, and testing on topics normally found in a one-year (elementary or beginning) algebra course.

Learning Outcome: Upon successful completion of this course, the student will be able to solve algebraic problems (nonverbal and verbal) that require the knowledge of integers, rationals, and real numbers, sets and set notation, exponents (integer and rational), absolute value, variables, polynomials, factoring, rational expressions, equalities and inequalities, graphing (one and two dimensional), and introductory probability.

Instruction: Major topics covered in the course are sets and numbers, exponents (integer and rational), polynomials, and factoring; solutions of first and second (quadratic) degree equations, first degree inequalities, systems of two linear equations, and first and second degree verbal problems; rational expressions, graphs (one and two dimensional); and a brief introduction to elementary probability. *Prerequisites:* Mastery of basic mathematics (i.e., addition, subtraction, multiplication, division, fractions, decimals, ratio/proportion/percent).

Credit Recommendation: In the lower division baccalaureate/associate degree category, 2 semester hours in Mathematics (6/86) (10/95).

Calculus 1

Location: Various sites around the country.

Length: Approximately 125 hours (computer-based instruction).

Dates: June 1984-Present.

Objective: To introduce students to the fundamentals of differential and integral calculus, equivalent to the first semester of college calculus, and to prepare them for study in the physical sciences, engineering, or further study in calculus.

Learning Outcome: Upon successful completion of this course, the student will understand the basic concepts and theories of calculus and will be able to apply this knowledge to the analysis and accurate solution of graphical, geometrical, and physical problems utilizing differentiation and integration.

Instruction: Major topics covered in the course are limits and limit theories, continuity, definition and applications of the derivative including related rates, maxima-minima theory, graphical analysis, the chain rule, techniques of differentiation, the indefinite and definite integral, fundamental theorem of calculus, applications of the definite integral to geometric, and physical problems. Topics covered correspond to a first semester college calculus course. Methods of instruction include individualized instruction consisting of textbook reading and practice problems and computer-assisted lessons with problem-solving and self-testing, delivered by the CYBIS computer-based educational system.

Credit Recommendation: In the lower division baccalaureate/associate degree category, 4 semester hours in Mathematics (6/86) (10/95). *Prerequisite:* Precalculus or equivalent.

Calculus 2

Location: Various sites around the country.

Length: Approximately 90 hours (computer-based instruction).

Dates: August 1985-Present.

Objective: To provide instruction equivalent to second semester calculus with emphasis on transcendental functions, techniques and applications of the integral, and sequences and series.

Learning Outcome: Upon successful completion of this course, the student will be able to diagnose and solve calculus problems involving inverse functions, integration techniques, and applications, and will be able to apply the appropriate theories to test for convergence of infinite series.

Instruction: Major topics covered in the course are properties of inverse functions; differentiation and integration of transcendental functions; L'Hopital's Rule; and indeterminate forms, applications of the integral, numerical integration, improper integrals, and test for convergence of sequences and series. Topics covered correspond to a second semester college calculus course. Methods of instruction include individualized instruction consisting of textbook reading and practice problems and computer-assisted lessons with problem solving and self-testing delivered by the CYBIS computer-based educational system.

Credit Recommendation: In the lower division baccalaureate/associate degree category, 4 semester hours in Calculus (6/86) (10/95). *Prerequisite:* Calculus 1 or equivalent.

Chemistry 1

Location: Various sites around the country.

Length: Approximately 90 hours (computer-based instruction).

Dates: July 1983-Present.

Objective: To give the student a basic introduction to chemistry, exclusive of laboratory, and to prepare the student for further study in chemistry.

Learning Outcome: Upon successful completion of this course, the student will be able to convert units and dimensions used for measured quantities; identify chemical symbols, their masses and atomic numbers; calculate atomic masses; and determine the molecular and empirical formulas when given percent-by-mass composition; calculate the total enthalpy changes when given the heat of atomization and formation values; select a potential source of energy for a given energy-yield requirement; use the ideal gas law to calculate molar mass and density of a gas, and solve problems using the van de Walls equations; understand the electronic structure of atoms and bonding; write net ionic equations when given a chemical reaction; and identify the differences between solutions and colloids.

Instruction: Major topics covered in the course are measurement and calculations; classification of matter; atoms, molecules, and ions; chemical formulas and equations; thermochemistry; physical behavior of gases; electronic structure of atoms; chemical bonding; liquids and solids; intermolecular forces; and properties of solutions. Methods of instruction include individualized instruction consisting of assigned reading and computer-assisted lessons involving drill, practice, and testing delivered by the CYBIS computer-based education system. *Prerequisite:* 2 years of high school algebra and 1 year high school chemistry.

Credit Recommendation: In the lower division baccalaureate/associate degree category, 3 semester hours in Chemistry (7/83) (9/90) (10/95).

Chemistry 2

Location: Various sites around the country.

Length: Approximately 95 hours (computer-based instruction).

Dates: January 1986-Present.

Objective: To provide instruction equivalent to second semester of college chemistry, exclusive of laboratory. Emphasis is on kinetics, thermodynamics, and gaseous and aqueous equilibria.

Learning Outcome: Upon successful completion of this course, students will be able to apply their understanding of chemical concepts to solve problems involving reaction kinetics, gas phase equilibria, acid-base chemistry, solution equilibria, electrochemistry, thermodynamics, and coordination chemistry.

Instruction: Major topics covered in the course are reaction rates and mechanisms, gas phase equilibria, equilibrium calculations, acid-base definitions, acid-base and solubility equilibria, applications of thermodynamics, electrochemistry, chemistry of the representative elements, and coordination chemistry. Topics covered correspond to a second semester non-laboratory college chemistry course. Methods of instruction include individualized instruction consisting of textbook reading and practice problems with computer-assisted lessons and self-tests delivered by the CYBIS computer-based education system.

Credit Recommendation: In the lower division baccalaureate/associate degree category, 3 semester hours in Chemistry (6/86) (10/95). **NOTE:** This is a nonlaboratory course. *Prerequisite:* Chemistry 1 or equivalent.

Computer Literacy

Location: Various sites around the country.

Length: Approximately 50 hours (computer-based instruction).

Dates: August 1985-Present.

Objective: To overcome "computer anxiety," understand computer life skills, and become informed on public policy concerning computers and computer-related products. Achieve computer skills in word processing, spreadsheets, and simple data analysis.

Learning Outcome: Upon successful completion of this course, students will understand how to use the computer to improve study and work skills, how computers affect their lives directly or indirectly, and how to be effective consumers of computer products and services.

Instruction: Major topics covered in the course are computer careers, computers in the classroom, history of computers, computer crime, robotics, computers and government, electronic funds transfer, human factors, privacy, social values, artificial intelligence, supercalc, data file fundamentals, word processing fundamentals, spreadsheet, and computers and the future.

Credit Recommendation: In the lower division baccalaureate/associate degree category, 2 semester hours in Computer Science (6/86) (10/95). **NOTE:** If the course material is supplemented by laboratory exercises using word processing, supercalc, spreadsheets, then the credit recommendation is 3 semester hours in

Computer Science in the lower division baccalaureate/associate degree category.

Data Communications

Location: Various sites around the country.

Length: Approximately 16 hours (computer-based instruction).

Dates: March 1982-Present.

Objective: To study how computer systems interconnect through common carrier communications networks.

Learning Outcome: Upon successful completion of this course, the student will be able to understand terminology commonly used in describing data communication systems, recognize the types of data communication services available, identify data communication hardware and their operational characteristics, recognize types of data transmission techniques, and recognize typical problems and failures.

Instruction: Major topics covered in the course are introduction to communication, basic communication systems, communication facilities and common carriers, data communication hardware, communication problems, and systems maintenance. *Prerequisite:* Basic electronics and computer fundamentals.

Credit Recommendation: In the lower division baccalaureate/associate degree category, 1 semester hour in Computer Science (6/86) (10/95). **NOTE:** If the course material is supplemented by a laboratory, the credit recommendation is 2 semester hours in Computer Science in the lower division baccalaureate/associate degree category.

Data Processing Concepts

Location: Various sites around the country.

Length: Approximately 38 hours (computer-based instruction).

Dates: September 1985-Present.

Objective: To provide the student with an understanding of how computers are used by modern organizations in their day-to-day operations.

Learning Outcome: Upon successful completion of this course, the student will be able to describe the role of computers in daily business operations; describe keypunching and the use of punched cards in a data processing system; identify the principles of magnetic tape and magnetic disk for storage outside of central memory; describe record layouts, printer report layouts, and system flowcharts; and describe program flowcharts, computer language, and operating systems.

Instruction: Major topics covered in the course are introduction to data processing systems; card data processing systems and keypunching; auxiliary storage; introduction to system analysis and design; and introduction to program design and development.

Credit Recommendation: In the lower division baccalaureate/associate degree category, 1 semester hour in Elementary Computer Concepts (9/90) (10/95). **NOTE:** This course is not designed for computer science majors.

Geometry

Location: Various sites around the country.

Length: Approximately 45 hours (computer-based instruction).

Dates: January 1987-Present.

Objective: To teach students the topics generally taught in first-year geometry and prepare them for more advanced mathematical studies.

Learning Outcome: Upon successful completion of this course, the student will be able to identify parallels between basic geometric concepts and their applications to real-life situations.

Instruction: Major topics covered in the course are introduction to geometry, angles, introduction to triangles, perpendicular and parallel lines, right triangles, polygons, quadrilaterals, transformations, measuring area, introduction to circles, geometric solids, and coordinate geometry. *Prerequisite:* Completion of one year of high school algebra or equivalent.

Credit Recommendation: In the lower division baccalaureate/associate degree category, 1 semester hour in Geometry (9/90) (10/95).

Introduction to Microprocessors (Microprocessors: A Short Course)

Location: Various sites around the country.

Length: Approximately 75 hours (computer-based instruction).

Dates: July 1980-Present.

Objective: To give the student a working knowledge of the concepts, terminology, and analysis of basic microprocessor circuits.

Learning Outcome: Upon successful completion of this course, the student will be able to understand the basics of microprocessors, operate and program microprocessors (machine language); and understand microprocessor components, circuitry for external interfaces, and simple machine language programming.

Instruction: Major topics covered in the course are introduction to fundamental information on computer systems, logic fundamentals, microprocessor introduction, microprocessor fundamentals, machine language, instruction flow, memory and microprocessor interfacing, D/A and A/D, serial and parallel, troubleshooting, and introduction to high level languages. *Prerequisite:* Basic electronics or equivalent.

Credit Recommendation: In the lower division baccalaureate/associate degree category, 3 semester hours in Computer Science or Computer Engineering (6/86) (10/95). **NOTE:** Recommendation requires lab activities.

Introduction to RPG II Programming

Location: Various sites around the country.

Length: Approximately 48 hours (computer-based instruction).

Dates: *Version 1:* March 1982-August 1990; *Version 2:* September 1990-Present.

Objective: To train students in Introductory RPG II Programming.

Learning Outcome: Upon successful completion of this course, the student will be able to write RPG II programs that use input/output; perform arithmetic operations; produce reports that contain edited data, control breaks, and total lines; process files containing multiple record types; and use advanced operations (Look Ahead, SETON, SETOFF, and MOVE) for processing.

Instruction: Major topics covered in the course are both the theory and practical applications of the RPG II language. A total of five major RPG II programs are written. The programs are specifically designed to provide experience in printing elementary reports, calculations and comparisons, multiple records, move operations, and control level indicators. Methods of instruction include a series of simulation exercises, multimedia presentations, drill and practice.

Credit Recommendation: *Version 1:* In the lower division baccalaureate/associate degree category, 1 semester hour in RPG II Programming (7/83). *Version 2:* In the lower division baccalaureate/associate degree category, 2 semester hours in RPG II Programming (9/90) (10/95).

PASCAL

Location: Various sites around the country.

Length: Approximately 90 hours (computer-based instruction).

Dates: June 1984-Present.

Objective: To teach students to use a modular approach and basic control structure in the design and writing of programs in the PASCAL language.

Learning Outcome: Upon successful completion of this course, the student will understand the modular top-down approach and basic control structure in the design and writing of programs in the PASCAL language.

Instruction: Major topics covered in the course are computer concepts, PASCAL structures, problem-solving, control structure, attributes of data, modularity, and introduction to data structure. Emphasis is on algorithm development. Programming assignments are not included in the course.

Credit Recommendation: In the lower division baccalaureate/associate degree category, 2 semester hours in Computer Science (6/86) (10/95). **NOTE:** If the course material is supplemented with programming assignments, then the credit recommendation is 3 semester hours in Computer Science in the lower division baccalaureate/associate degree category.

Physics I

Location: Various sites around the country.

Length: Approximately 90 hours (computer-based instruction).

Dates: July 1983-Present.

Objective: To enable the student to understand and explain the fundamental concepts, definitions, and relations of elementary Newtonian mechanics and apply them to solve problems in mechanics.

Learning Outcome: Upon successful completion of this course, the student will be able to state and explain the fundamental concepts, definitions, and relations of mechanics and apply them to solving problems in Newtonian mechanics.

Instruction: Major topics covered in the course are subject areas basic to the understanding of mechanics including kinematics in one and two dimensions, force, particle statics and dynamics, work and energy, impulse and momentum, rotational motion and angular momentum rigid body motion, conservation of energy and momentum, and simple harmonic motion. Methods of instruction include personalized self-instruction using CYBIS computer-based education. *Prerequisite:* Mathematics through differential calculus and coregistration in integral calculus.

Credit Recommendation: In the lower division baccalaureate/associate degree category, 4 semester hours in Physics (7/83) (9/90) (10/95). **NOTE:** This is a calculus-based physics course not including laboratory.

Physics II

Location: Various sites around the country.

Length: Approximately 90 hours (computer-based instruction).

Dates: December 1986-Present.

Objective: To enable the student to understand and explain the fundamental concepts, definitions and relations of electric and magnetic fields and electrical and magnetic properties of matter.

Learning Outcome: Upon successful completion of this course, the student will be able to state and explain the fundamental concepts, definitions, and relations of electric and magnetic fields and forces; calculate the magnetic field and potential from simple charge distributions; calculate the magnetic field from currents; solve problems in DC electric circuits; and describe magnetic properties of matter.

Instruction: Major topics covered in the course are subject areas basic to the understanding of electricity and magnetism including Coulomb's law, electric fields and potentials, Gauss' law, capacitance, DC circuits, magnetic fields, forces on charges in magnetic fields, Ampere's law, Biot-Savart law, Faraday's law, inductance, and magnetic properties of matter. Methods of instruction include personalized self-instruction using CYBIS computer-based education.

Credit Recommendation: In the lower division baccalaureate/associate degree category, 4 semester hours in Physics (10/95). **NOTE:** This is a calculus-based physics course not including laboratory. *Prerequisite:* Differential and Integral Calculus.

Precalculus

Location: Various sites around the country.

Length: Approximately 120 hours (computer-based instruction).

Dates: September 1984-Present.

Objective: To provide the student with the understanding and skills in college algebra and trigonometry functional analysis and analytic geometry necessary for the study of calculus.

Learning Outcome: Upon successful completion of this course, the student will be able to formulate and solve problems in elementary functional analysis; trigonometric, logarithmic, and exponential functions; and in analytic geometry of second degree curves.

Instruction: Major topics covered in the course are elementary functions designed to prepare students for successful study of calculus; properties of real numbers; algebraic operations; equations and inequalities; graphical representation of algebraic relations; analysis of second degree curves; logarithmic, exponential, and trigonometric functions and their graphs; trigonometric identities and equations; and applications of trigonometry. Methods of instruction include individualized instruction consisting of textbook reading, practice problems, and computer-assisted lessons with self-tests delivered by the CYBIS computer-based educational system. *Prerequisite:* 3 years of high school mathematics or equivalent.

Credit Recommendation: In the lower division baccalaureate/associate degree category, 4 semester hours in Precalculus Mathematics (6/86) (10/95).

Structured COBOL Programming

Location: Various sites around the country.

Length: Approximately 295 hours (computer-based instruction).

Dates: March 1982-Present.

Objective: To train students in elementary and advanced structured COBOL programming.

Learning Outcome: Upon successful completion of this course, the student will be able to describe control structures, compilation procedures, records and files, and COBOL arithmetic and editing features; understand programming techniques and documentation; format reports and understand control breaks and table handling; describe techniques used to design structured programs; and validate, sort, and update sequential files.

Instruction: Major topics covered in the course are the structure of the COBOL language and its use in a variety of practical problems; structured documentation; COBOL reports and table;, structured analysis and design; and validating, sorting, and updating sequential files. Methods of instruction include a series of simulation exercises, multimedia presentations, drill, and practice.

Credit Recommendation: In the lower division baccalaureate/associate degree category, 3 semester hours in COBOL Programming and 2 semester hours in Advanced COBOL Programming (7/83) (9/90) (10/95).

Structured Programming with FORTRAN 77

Location: Various sites around the country.

Length: Approximately 90 hours (computer-based instruction).

Dates: July 1983-Present.

Objective: To provide the student with the skills and knowledge necessary to solve problems using structured programs and modular techniques using the FORTRAN 77 programming language.

Learning Outcome: Upon successful completion of this course, the student will be able to use a modular top-down approach and basic control structures to design and write programs in the FORTRAN 77 language.

Instruction: Major topics covered in the course are developing computer programs using the top-down design and structured programming of the FORTRAN language; programming and computers; basic sequential programs; modular design; control structures; repetition and arrays; character data; subprograms; and formulated input and output. Methods of instruction include exercises, simulation, and computer-based modules.

Credit Recommendation: In the lower division baccalaureate/associate degree category, 3 semester hours in Structured Programming (7/83) (9/90) (10/95).

Mechanical Engineering Curriculum

Fluid Power Systems
a. Hydraulic Power Fundamentals
b. Pneumatic Power Fundamentals

Location: Various sites around the country.

Length: a. 65 hours; b. 47 hours (computer-based instruction).

Dates: September 1983-Present.

Objective: To learn the importance and functioning of fluid power and control systems and to interpret fluid circuit diagrams.

Learning Outcome: Upon successful completion of this course, the student will understand fluid power transfer and have the ability to select components and assemble into fluid power systems.

Instruction: Major topics covered in course "a" are basic hydraulic relations, hydraulic components and circuits, and hydraulic system maintenance and troubleshooting. Major topics covered in course "b" are preparation and distribution of air in pneumatic systems, use of compressed air in pneumatic systems, safety in pneumatic systems, and pneumatic system maintenance and troubleshooting.

Credit Recommendation: In the vocational certificate category, 3 semester hours as a technical elective for engineering students (6/86) (10/95). **NOTE:** Students may receive 1 semester hour for course "a" and 2 semester hours for course "b."

Industrial Electronics

Location: Various sites around the country.

Length: 345 hours (computer-based instruction).

Dates: November 1982-Present.

Objective: To understand and apply number systems such as binary, octal, decimal, and hexadecimal and to understand and apply principles of semiconductors, circuit analysis, and essential measuring instruments.

Learning Outcome: Upon successful completion of this course, the student will have a working knowledge of electronic circuits and components and the logic of computer operation, understand basic computer components and logic circuits, and be capable of troubleshooting practices.

Instruction: Major topics covered in the course are basic electronics, semiconductor electronics, and digital electronics.

Credit Recommendation: In the vocational certificate category, 5 semester hours as a technical elective (6/86) (10/95).

Mechanisms

Location: Various sites around the country.

Length: 91 hours (computer-based instruction).

Dates: June 1981-Present.

Objective: To identify and study proper installation, operation, and maintenance of common mechanisms including gears, belt drives, bearings, and shafts.

Learning Outcome: Upon successful completion of this course, the student will have the ability to successfully install the mechanisms studied.

Instruction: Major topics covered in the course are machine elements, gear drive systems, gear maintenance, belt drive systems, chain drive systems, bearing types, shaft drives, bearing maintenance, troubleshooting, and preventive maintenance.

Credit Recommendation: In the lower division baccalaureate/associate degree category, 1 semester hour in Engineering for Non-Engineering and Non-Science majors (6/86) (10/95).

Robotics Sequence (Introduction to Robotics, Robotics Literacy, Robotics Safety, Working with Robots, Robot Drive Systems, Teach Mode Programming, Troubleshooting)

Location: Various sites around the country.

Length: Approximately 25 hours (computer-based instruction).

Dates: August 1983-Present.

Objective: Describe robots and robotic functions; define commonly used robot terminology and functions; delineate equipment, procedures, and legal requirements for safe robot operation; identify kinds of robots with applications and information resources; functioning and maintenance of typical pneumatic, hydraulic, and electric drive and positioning systems; learn techniques for programming and checking by teach mode process; and diagnose and solve robot problems and by using maintenance manuals.

Learning Outcome: Upon successful completion of this course, the student will have limited skills in selection, safe installation, operation, and routine maintenance of robotic systems.

Instruction: Major topics covered in the course are industrial robots, robot components, robotic terminology, positioning and control limitations, end of arm tooling-grippers, drive systems, servo and non-servo control, robot communications, safety-hazard elimination, manipulator specification and operation, teach mode programming, and troubleshooting and maintenance.

Credit Recommendation: In the vocational certificate or lower division baccalaureate/associate degree category, 1 semester hour as a technical elective (6/86) (10/95). **NOTE:** Students must complete all modules to receive credit.

Vanguard Schools

CompuTaught, Inc. was incorporated in 1989 as a for-profit educational entity. It is a developer of educational courseware and a proprietary school that offers courses to the general public. The company's mission is to provide cost-effective education solutions in professional content areas. Its courses are designed to produce accelerated learning and enhanced retention using computer-based instruction.

CompuTaught currently offers courses in the field of real estate, with offerings that are appropriate for those interested in either real estate brokerage or real estate appraisal. Its courses are offered in selected states for continuing education credit to licensed professionals in real estate brokerage and to licensed and/or certified professionals in real estate appraisal. They are also offered in selected states in satisfaction of state education requirements for obtaining a real estate brokerage license. However, enrollment is open to anyone, regardless of whether they are seeking a license or currently have a license or certificate in one of these areas.

All courses are offered on a correspondence or independent study basis and students can enroll by mail or by telephone. All required coursework is completed on a personal computer using courseware supplied by CompuTaught. The courses are self-contained tutorials that provide everything a student needs to complete a course. Once a course is completed, the disk containing the course and the student's records are returned to CompuTaught to obtain credit for course completion. The courses are designed by teams of professionals with advanced degrees in various fields of educational methods and technology as well as expertise in the subject matter. The courses are based on highly effective teaching techniques that teach to mastery on an individualized basis, thus insuring that the student understands the course material.

Inquiries concerning enrollment and/or student records should be directed to CompuTaught, Inc., 1395 S. Marietta Parkway, Building 400, Suite 107, Marietta, GA 30067.

Source of official student records: Registry of Credit Recommendations, American Council on Education, One Dupont Circle, Washington, DC 20036-1193.

Additional information about the courses: College Credit Recommendation Service, American Council on Education, One Dupont Circle, Washington, DC 20036-1193.

Professional Development Series in Real Estate:
ADA and Fair Housing
Consensual Dual Agency
Pricing Property to Sell
Homeowner's Tax Breaks
Tax Free Exchange
Basic Real Estate Finance
Methods of Residential Finance
Real Estate Math
Business Management in a Real Estate Office

Location: United States.

Length: 42 hours (9 real estate modules of varying length) (self-paced).

Dates: November 1995-Present.

Objective: An electronic module course that provides continuing post-licensure real estate education.

Learning Outcome: Upon successful completion of this course, the student will be able to demonstrate knowledge of fair housing laws and practices; disability laws and provisions; consensual dual agency; pricing sale property; tax breaks for homeowners; tax free exchange; basic and residential finance; real estate math; and real estate office business management.

Instruction: Major topics covered in the course are laws, practices, and provisions pertaining to fair housing; Ameri-cans with Disabilities Act; dual agency, as well as evaluation of property values, tax implications of home ownership and exchange; and real estate finance and of-fice management. Methods of instruction include self-paced, computer-based, and interactive learning.

Credit Recommendation: In the lower division baccalaureate/associate degree category or upper division baccalaureate degree category, 2 semester hours in Real Estate, if student has taken all 9 modules (42 hours) of the Professional Development Series in Real Estate (11/95).

Virginia Insurance Reciprocal

The Virginia Insurance Reciprocal (TVIR), licensed March 17, 1977 as Virginia Hospital Insurance Reciprocal (VHIR), is rated A (Excellent) by A.M. Best Company. Products include professional and general liability insurance, managed care organization liability insurance, umbrella, pollution, and excess hospital liability coverage.

The mission of the education department is to provide high quality programs to TVIR insureds and others by: 1) assisting participants to improve quality of care with resultant risk reduction in a cost effective manner, and 2) specifically addressing risk management issues with the outcome of reducing financial losses through malpractice claims.

The education department accesses resources of the risk management, claims, underwriting, and actuarial departments of TVIR. Two full-time dedicated staff are involved in the program design, development, and presentations.

Participants in the classes hold positions such as risk manager, quality manager, department head, and consultant.

Each course is beta tested by a select group of 13 risk managers prior to being offered to all subscribers. New courses, chosen by review of literature, discussions with the pilot group, discussions with current faculty, and everyday exposure to the risk management environment are the responsibility of the second vice president of education. Discussions are held with instructors to assure all information is updated and relevant to the healthcare environment. On-line literature searches are also used to assure timely, accurate information is included.

Classroom sessions, presented multiple times per year, are limited to 25 students per session, and include both on-site and independent course work. Three and one-half on-site classes combine classroom instruction and group projects. The independent study focuses on projects applicable to daily risk management functions.

Instructors for the courses include specially chosen professionals with national recognition and responsibility for risk management programs, as well as, TVIR staff professionals with backgrounds in insurance and claims management.

Source of official student records: Registry of Credit Recommendations, American Council on Education, One Dupont Circle, Washington, DC 20036-1193.

Additional information about the courses: College Credit Recommendation Service, American Council on Education, One Dupont Circle, Washington, DC 20036-1193.

The Educational Approach to Changing Healthcare (TEACH™).

An Overview of Regulation in Health Care (201)
(Regulatory Issues [201])

Location: The Virginia Insurance Reciprocal, Glen Allen, VA.

Length: 21.25 hours, plus an additional 12 hours independent study project.

Dates: June 1995-Present.

Objective: To provide an overview of external regulatory requirements in the health care industry.

Learning Outcome: Upon successful completion of this course, the student will be familiar with state and local legal requirements, restrictions, and opportunities with respect to any proposed risk financing program; types of tort reform available in jurisdictions; and legal liabilities from the pursuit of new or additional services or marketing strategies.

Instruction: Major topics covered in the course are Healthcare Quality Improvement Act, peer review procedure, National Practitioner Data Bank, Tort Reform, Consolidated Omnibus Budget Reconciliation Act of 1985, Patient Self Determination Act of 1990, Safe Medical Devices Act of 1990, Americans with Disabilities Act, JCAHO Guidelines, and OSHA regulations. Methods of instruction include lecture, discussion, audiovisuals, course competency tests, and an independent project or paper.

Credit Recommendation: In the lower division baccalaureate/associate degree category, 1 semester hour in Regulation or Health Care (6/96).

Claims Administration in Healthcare Facilities (301)
(Claims Administration [301])

Location: The Virginia Insurance Reciprocal, Glen Allen, VA.

Length: 21.25 hours, plus an additional 12 hours independent study project.

Dates: December 1995-Present.

Objective: To enable the student to describe proper claims administration and management processes for both insured and retained claims.

Learning Outcome: Upon successful completion of this course, the student will be able to define or explain key words and phrases of claims administration, describe purposes of and steps in the claims administration process, explain the importance of implementing and monitoring each step for claims administration, describe how an institution's claim cost can be properly reduced, describe circumstances and procedures appropriate for resolving disputes through alternative dispute resolution, describe causes and specific methods of controlling rising costs of medical claims, and describe purposes and steps of a claims management program.

Instruction: Major topics covered in the course are potentially compensable events, fileaways, and integration of all entities. Methods of instruction include lecture, discussion, audiovisuals, course competency tests, and an independent paper.

Credit Recommendation: In the lower division baccalaureate/associate degree category, 1 semester hour in Claims Administration (6/96).

Insurance (601)

Location: The Virginia Insurance Reciprocal, Glen Allen, VA.

Length: 21.25 hours, plus an additional 12 hours independent study project.

Dates: June 1996-Present.

Objective: To identify retaining and insurance exposures, the procurement of insurance as an integral step in the risk management process, insurance principles, and the technical aspects of insurance.

Learning Outcome: Upon successful completion of this course, the student will be able to define or explain key words and phrases and types of insurance; describe mechanics for using insurance, both in planning for and in obtaining funds after a loss; describe benefits, costs, and limitations of insurance as a risk financing technique; identify components of insurance contracts; apply to insurance documents a framework for analyzing insurance coverage in terms of events covered, limitations on amount of recovery, and actions after a loss to secure recovery; identify insurance financing options; describe the competitive bidding process; describe risk management applications for HMO/physician purchase, managed care, workers' compensation, and employee benefits; and evaluate insurance requirements for new healthcare risks.

Instruction: Major topics covered in the course are types of insurance, types of insurance financing, protection of the insureds' organizational rights under contract, depriving the organization of its coverage through an inadvertent error, losses of policy coverage, policy limits, selection of a broker or agent, and use of competitive bidding. Methods of instruction include lecture, discussion, group projects, audiovisuals, course competency tests, and an independent paper/project.

Credit Recommendation: In the upper division baccalaureate degree category, 1 semester hour in Insurance (6/96).

Introduction to Total Quality Management for Hospitals (501) (Total Quality Management [501])

Location: The Virginia Insurance Reciprocal, Glen Allen, VA.

Length: 21.25 hours, plus an additional 12 hours independent study project.

Dates: December 1996-Present.

Objective: To give students an understanding of the evolving development of Total Quality Management (TQM) philosophy, origin, tools, and capabilities for Risk Management cultures.

Learning Outcome: Upon successful completion of this course, the student will be able to define and explain key words and concepts for TQM; explain reasons for paradigm shift to TQM in a risk management culture; explain and describe basic tenets for implementing TQM; identify and discuss TQM tools; explain customer focus of TQM; explain enlightened leadership; understand flow charting, Gantt charting, and PERT.

Instruction: Major topics covered in the course are behavioral theory, managing chaos, benchmarking, flow charting, program and report technique, Gantt chart, quality management vs. quality improvement, leadership vs. management, motivating people, employee training and involvement, critical path method tool, and statistics. Methods of instruction include lecture, discussion, group projects, audiovisuals, course competency tests, and an independent study.

Credit Recommendation: In the upper division baccalaureate degree category, 1 semester hour in Quality Management, Business Administration, or Public Administration (6/96).

Risk Financing (701)

Location: The Virginia Insurance Reciprocal, Glen Allen, VA.

Length: 21.25 hours.

Dates: September 1996-Present.

Objective: To identify the differences among the full range of risk financing techniques and explain appropriate criteria for choosing among or combining these varied techniques.

Learning Outcome: Upon successful completion of this course, the student will be able to define or explain each of the key words and phrases for risk financing; distinguish among risk financing techniques; explain how an organization's choice of risk financing to pay for particular types of losses should be influenced by characteristics of the organization, exposures that may generate its losses, and risk financing markets in which the institution operates; and apply risk financing basics to new healthcare ventures.

Instruction: Major topics covered in the course are current program assessment, risks of new ventures, basic elements of risks, commercial insurance purchase, mechanisms for self-funding, formula for allocation of premium, and rate setting for practices. Methods of instruction include lecture, discussion, audiovisuals, and course competency tests.

Credit Recommendation: In the upper division baccalaureate degree category, 1 semester hour in Risk Financing in Health Care Administration (6/96).

Selected Topics in Quality Management in Health Care Organizations (401) (Quality Management [401])

Location: The Virginia Insurance Reciprocal, Glen Allen, VA.

Length: 21.25 hours, plus an additional 12 hours independent study project.

Dates: March 1996-Present.

Objective: To give students an understanding of operational length between risk management functions and quality management functions, as well as access of quality management functions to risk management information in identifying and correcting potential risks in patient care and safety, focusing on integrating these functions into a collaborative process.

Learning Outcome: Upon successful completion of this course, the student will be able to define or explain key words and phrases of quality management; describe and illustrate similarities and differences between risk management and quality management; develop credentialing policies; develop credentialing processes; incorporating Joint Commission guidelines; describe and illustrate privilege delineation processes; and expand credentialing.

Instruction: Major topics covered in the course are initial staff credentialing, privilege delineation, reappointment process, Joint Commission guidelines, the role of the National Practitioner Data Bank, and document control. Methods of instruction include lecture, discussion, group projects, audiovisuals, course competency tests, and an independent study.

Credit Recommendation: In the upper division baccalaureate degree category, 1 semester hour in Quality Management, Business Administration, or Public Administration (6/96).

Survey of Risk Management (101)

Location: The Virginia Insurance Reciprocal, Glen Allen, VA.

Length: 21.25 hours, plus an additional 12 hours independent study project.

Dates: March 1995-Present.

Objective: To give students an overview of the risk management process, with an emphasis of the administrative aspects of risk management.

Learning Outcome: Upon successful completion of this course, the student will be able to explain the nature, purposes, and steps in risk management; identify the exposures to accidental losses facing individuals and organizations; describe and apply alternative risk management techniques; and develop, justify, and apply decision rules for choosing risk management techniques.

Instruction: Major topics covered in the course are policy and procedures, reports, contracts, benchmarking, and specific applications for healthcare. Methods of instruction include lecture, discussion, audiovisuals, course competency tests, and an independent paper.

Credit Recommendation: In the lower division baccalaureate/associate degree category, 1 semester hour in Risk Management or Public Administration (6/96).

VITAL LEARNING

VITAL LEARNING Corporation is dedicated to enhancing its clients' productivity by providing the best, measurable training and development solutions. Founded in 1989, VITAL LEARNING has sales offices in major cities throughout the United States, and on five continents. Their diverse team of experienced program designers have merged exceptional research talent with the creative flair required to develop courses. VITAL LEARNING programs have met the needs of half a million participants in seven languages. VITAL LEARNING also has the complete in-house capability to produce video, audio and print materials for customization to meet specific customer needs.

Source of official student records: Registry of Credit Recommendations, American Council on Education, One Dupont Circle, Washington, DC 20036-1193.

Additional information about the courses: College Credit Recommendation Service, American Council on Education, One Dupont Circle, Washington, DC 20036-1193.

Communications
1. Fundamental Skills of Communicating
2. Communicating with Your Manager
3. Building Commitment through Communication

Location: Various locations worldwide.

Length: 16 hours (2 half-days, 1 full day).

Dates: February 1989-Present.

Objective: To provide the student with basic communication skills important in today's business environment.

Learning Outcome: Upon successful completion of this course, the student will be able to understand and apply the theories of communication in relevant work situations.

Instruction: Major topics covered in the course are communication process, use of non-verbal and verbal factors, listening skills, and barriers to communication. Methods of instruction include lecture, discussions, audio video, presentations, role playing, problem solving, and hands-on and practical applications.

Credit Recommendation: In the lower division baccalaureate/associate degree category, 1 semester hour in Communication or Business Communication (9/95). **NOTE:** All three courses must be successfully completed to receive credit.

Management
Group A: Fundamental Skills of Managing , Delegating Effectively, Preparing for Change, Assigning Tasks Effectively, Performance Assessment, Coaching for Improved Performance, Developing Performance Standards, Positive Reinforcement for Improved Employee Performance, and Leading Productive Meetings
Group B: Achieving Results Through Leadership, Developing Productive Partnerships, and Challenging the Workflow for Continuous Improvement

Location: Various sites worldwide.

Length: 60 hours (3 full days and 9 half-days).

Dates: February 1989-Present.

Objective: To provide the student with basic business management skills.

Learning Outcome: Upon successful completion of this course, the student will be able to demonstrate an understanding of the basic managerial tasks.

Instruction: Major topics covered in the course are managing employee performance, developing management skills, team building, and continuous improvement. Methods of instruction include lecture, discussions, audio video, presentations, role playing, problem solving, and hands-on practical applications.

Credit Recommendation: In the lower division baccalaureate/associate degree category, 1 semester hour for successful completion of any four Group A courses, 1 semester hour for successful completion of any two Group B courses, 1 semester hour for successful completion of any two Group A courses plus any one Group B course (9/95). **NOTE:** No course(s) may be counted toward more than one semester hour total.

Management
1. Planning
2. Organizing
3. Directing
4. Controlling

Location: Various sites worldwide.

Length: 16 hours (4 half-days).

Dates: February 1989-Present.

Objective: To provide the student with basic business management skills.

Learning Outcome: Upon successful completion of this course, the student will be able to demonstrate an understanding of the basic managerial functions: planning, organizing, directing, and controlling.

Instruction: Major topics covered in the course are managing employee performance, developing management skills, team building, and continuous improvement. Methods of instruction include lecture, discussions, audio video, presentations, role playing, problem solving, and hands-on practical applications.

Credit Recommendation: In the lower division baccalaureate/associate degree category, 1 semester hour in Management (9/95). **NOTE:** All four courses must be successfully completed to receive credit.

Personnel Management
1. Improving Employee Work Habits
2. Using Positive Discipline
3. Dealing with Complaints
4. Dealing with Conflicts
5. Dealing with Employee Response to Controls
6. Motivating the Productive Employee
7. Management Orientation
8. Reinforcement and Support

Location: Various locations worldwide.

Length: 28 hours (7 half-days).

Dates: February 1989-Present.

Objective: To provide the student with basic personnel management skills.

Learning Outcome: Upon successful completion of this course, the student will be able to effectively manage the interpersonal aspects of personnel management.

Instruction: Major topics covered in the course are conflict resolution, motivation, discipline, and change. Methods of instruction include lecture, discussions, audio video, presentations, role playing, problem solving, and hands-on and practical applications.

Credit Recommendation: In the lower division baccalaureate/associate degree category, 1 semester hour for successful completion of any four courses listed above in Personnel Management (9/95). **NOTE:** If all seven courses are successfully completed, the student should be awarded 2 semester hours in the lower division baccalaureate/associate degree category in Personnel Management.

Sales
1. Customer-Oriented Selling
2. Telephone Prospecting and Qualifying

Location: Various locations worldwide.

Length: 32 hours (4 full days).

Dates: February 1989-Present.

Objective: To provide the student with the skills necessary for telephone prospecting and qualification of sales leads and presentation, negotiation, and communication to complete the sales transaction.

Learning Outcome: Upon successful completion of this course, the student will be able to prospect and qualify sales leads and conduct a sales call using a customer-oriented selling technique.

Instruction: Major topics covered in the course are prospecting, qualifying, communications, planning, the sales cycle, and negotiation techniques. Methods of instruction include lecture, discussions, audio video, presentations, role playing, problem solving, and hands-on and practical applications.

Credit Recommendation: In the lower division baccalaureate/associate degree category, 1 semester hour in Marketing, Business Administration, or Management for successful completion of only *Customer-Oriented Selling* (9/95). **NOTE:** Student should be awarded 2 semester hours in the lower division baccalaureate/associate degree category in Marketing, Business Administration, or Management if *Customer-Oriented Selling* and *Telephone Prospecting and Qualifying* are successfully completed.

Wackenhut Corporation

The Wackenhut Corporation was founded in 1954 by George R. Wackenhut, a former educator and FBI agent, as a private sector security services company. Wackenhut has grown to over 45,000 employees in the United States and 54 other nations. Wackenhut Training Institute (WTI) is the training division of the company. Its purpose is to conduct security-related research, analyze security training needs at client companies, and design and conduct training. All WTI courses support the organization's mission and the missions of client companies vis-a-vis the security function. The course development process begins with an in-depth job-task analysis in which security personnel are observed doing their daily tasks. Thereafter, one-on-one interviews are conducted in which security officers describe their tasks and suggest what is not being done that needs to be done. Supervisors, security managers, and security customers are also interviewed. A tentative class outline is then drafted. Next, everyone who was interviewed is asked to fill out a questionnaire that is designed to assess findings from the interviews. Then, a curriculum decision tree is developed in which job-task training elements are prioritized for difficulty, consequence, and frequency, the course is modified as necessary and finalized. Many programs are then sent to the University of Maryland University College for evaluation and awarding of continuing education units (CEUs). WTI's education programs are presented to security personnel (security officers and supervisors) throughout the United States. Participants are high school graduates; some have college experience or degrees. Delivery methods include lecture, discussion, demonstration, interaction using learning games, case studies, role plays, etc., or mixtures thereof-all presented through Malcom Knowles' model of adult learning. Instructors are qualified through one of three instructor training seminars that lead to WTI certification, or academic degrees in security or subject-related disciplines. The Vice President, Training, WTI makes unannounced visits to classrooms to assess instructors; reviews student critiques, and solicits and reviews comments regarding instructor effect from Wackenhut management, clients, and others.

Source of official student records: Registry of Credit Recommendations, American Council on Education, One Dupont Circle, Washington, DC 20036-1193.

Additional information about the courses: College Credit Recommendation Service, American Council on Education, One Dupont Circle, Washington, DC 20036-1193.

Certification Course for Armed Private Security Personnel (WTI-05)

Location: Smithsonian Institution and various locations.

Length: 40 hours (1 week).

Dates: March 1997-Present.

Objective: To reduce the civil and criminal liability associated with the use of deadly and non-deadly force by armed security personnel.

Learning Outcome: Upon successful completion of this course, the student will be able to achieve a qualifying score on a firearms qualification course. Qualifying scores on the firearms segment will vary from state to state, depending upon legislated requirements.

Instruction: Major topics covered in the course are use of force civil and criminal liability, use of force continuum, self defense techniques and practice, OC sprays, handcuff techniques and practice, firearms federal and state requirements, firearm safety, firearm nomenclature, firearm misfires, firearm grip and stance techniques and practice, breathing and aiming techniques and practice, and firearms qualification. Methods of instruction include lecture, discussion, classroom exercises, case studies, audiovisual material, laboratory, and final examination.

Credit Recommendation: In the vocational certificate or in the lower division baccalaureate/associate degree category, 3 semester hours in Criminal Justice, Law Enforcement, or Security Administration (5/97).

Introduction to Facility Security Officers Duties and Responsibilities (WT1-03)

Location: Smithsonian Institution, Catholic University of America, and various work sites of Wackenhut contracts and other industrial clients worldwide.

Length: 80 hours (2 weeks).

Dates: June 1997-Present.

Objective: To provide the prospective and newly assigned security persons the tools necessary to understand the responsibilities and performance expectations of their assignments and to uniformly perform the associated tasks.

Learning Outcome: Upon successful completion of this course, the student will be able to perform the basic tasks necessary to effectively assume his or her duties assigned within the protective services industry.

Instruction: Major topics covered in the course are the introduction to the security mission, access control, report writing, diversity, legal authority, use of force, emergency response and medical emergencies, human relations, patrol procedures, alarm response, interpersonal communication, and conflict resolution. Methods of instruction include lecture, discussion, classroom exercises, case studies, audiovisual material, and final examination.

Credit Recommendation: In the lower division baccalaureate/associate degree category, 4 semester hours in Private Security or Security Administration (3/97).

Leadership Skills for Security Supervisors (WT1-01)

Location: Smithsonian Institution, Catholic University of America, and various work sites of Wackenhut contracts and other industrial clients worldwide.

Length: 40 hours (1 week).

Dates: March 1997-Present.

Objective: To familiarize the security supervisory students with basic theories and applications of personnel and organizational management in the context of their role in the security organization; to provide an opportunity for them to assess their present supervisory skills; and to enhance them through learning and practice.

Learning Outcome: Upon successful completion of this course, the student will be able to produce an action plan that clearly charts the supervisor's present state of readiness for supervisory tasks and supervisory skill assessment instruments; identify specific actions to bring deficiencies into line with the ideals present; and perform the role of managing people in a more professional and sensitive manner.

Instruction: Major topics covered in the course are the leadership role of security supervisors, ethics, decision making, time and task management, report writing, note talking, motivation, coaching and counseling, discipline, performance appraisal, change management, abnormal behavior and violence in the workplace, interpersonal communication, and administration of contractual requirements. Methods of instruction include lecture, discussion, classroom exercises, case studies, audiovisual material, learner presentations, reports, self assessments, and final examination.

Credit Recommendation: In the upper division baccalaureate degree category, 3 semester hours in Management (3/97).

Patrol Procedures (WTI-04-A) Facility Security Refresher

Location: Smithsonian Institution and various locations.

Length: 40 hours (1 week).

Dates: March 1997-Present.

Objective: To assure quality and consistency in providing security functions to a myriad of facilities worldwide. This course is offered to security officers who provide such services to contracted sites. The objective of this course is to provide a refresher in topics that relate to the high civil liability areas as well as in topics that relate to customer service, ethics, and the general duties of security personnel. The first three days of this course of instruction will cover topics common to both line and supervisory security personnel. On the remaining two days, the supervisory and line personnel will be given separate training topics that are specific to their respective duties.

Learning Outcome: Upon successful completion of this course, the student will be able to demonstrate continuance of improved performance in the areas of basic security, customer service, firearms, and other high liability areas for security officers.

Instruction: Major topics covered in the course are range safety rules and procedures, live fire practice and qualification, legal authority law review, legal authority federal and constitutional law, constitutional restrictions on use of force, arrest procedures, crime scene and evidence preservation, facility rules and regulations update, courtroom testimony, communication skills practice and review, customer service review, dealing with difficult people, sexual harassment, EEO and diversity, report writing practice and review, access and key control, patrol techniques, alcohol and drug abuse prevention, safety and accident prevention, interview techniques and practice, field note-taking review and practice, security for special events, using and responding to alarms, fire and life safety, and crowd control and emergency evacuation. Methods of instruction include lecture, discussion, classroom exercises, case studies, audiovisual material, learner presentations, reports, self assessments, and final examination.

Credit Recommendation: In the lower division baccalaureate/associate degree category, 3 semester hours in Criminal Justice, Law Enforcement, or Security Administration (5/97). **NOTE:** Individuals who take this course are not eligible to take and receive credit for Patrol Supervision, WTI-04-B.

Patrol Supervision (WTI-04-B) Facility Security Refresher

Location: Smithsonian Institution and various locations.

Length: 40 hours (1 week).

Dates: March 1997-Present.

Objective: To assure quality and consistency in providing security functions to a myriad of facilities worldwide. This course is offered to security supervisors who provide such services to contracted sites. The objective of this course is to provide a refresher in topics that relate to the high civil liability areas as well as in topics that relate to customer service, ethics, and the general duties of security leaders. The first three days of this course of instruction will cover topics common to both line and supervisory security personnel. On the remaining two days, the supervisory and line personnel will be given separate training topics that are specific to their respective duties.

Learning Outcome: Upon successful completion of this course, the student will be able to demonstrate in the continuance of improved performance in the areas of basic security, customer service, firearms and other high liability areas for security supervisors.

Instruction: Major topics covered in the course are range safety rules and procedures, live fire practice and qualification, legal authority law review, legal authority federal and constitutional law, constitutional restrictions on use of force, arrest procedures, crime scene and evidence preservation, facility rules and regulations update, courtroom testimony, communication skills practice and review, customer service review, dealing with difficult people, sexual harassment, EEO and diversity, report writing practice and review, communication skills practice and review, practice in criticizing and disciplining employees, constructive criticism practice, coaching and counseling practice, practice in identifying worker interactive styles, motivating for good performance, evaluating performance, incident reporting and practice, roll call training development and practice, emergency response review, roundtable discussion identifying and solving leadership challenges specific to the supervisor's contract security site. Methods of instruction include lecture, discussion, classroom exercises, case studies, audiovisual material, learner presentations, reports, self assessments, and final examination.

Credit Recommendation: In the upper division baccalaureate degree category, 3 semester hours in Criminal Justice, Law Enforcement, or Security Administration (5/97). **NOTE:** Individuals who take this course are not eligible to take and receive credit for Patrol Procedures, WTI-04-A.

Technical Skills for Security Supervisors (WTI-02)

Location: Smithsonian Institution and various locations.

Length: 40 hours (1 week).

Dates: March 1997-Present.

Objective: To assure quality and consistency in providing supervisory security functions to a myriad of facilities worldwide, the course is offered to security supervisors who provide such services to contracted sites and to train security supervisors in the basic technical skills necessary to successfully perform the duties and responsibilities of a security supervisor.

Learning Outcome: Upon successful completion of this course, the student will be involved in product produced as a result of the training and in supervisory behavioral improvements demonstrated on the job. The key product emanating from this course is the production of an action plan that clearly charts the supervisor's present state of readiness for technical supervisory tasks as deduced from feedback from facilitators and technical skills assessment instruments, and specific actions the learner will take to bring deficiencies into line with the ideals presented in the course. The supervisor will be expected to perform the technical aspects of managing people in a more professional and proficient manner than was the case for that individual before the course, as measured by his or her management.

Instruction: Major topics covered in this course are the introduction to computer software for security operations, software uses for the reporting function, understanding and using e-mail, advanced arrest procedures, local law enforcement arrest documentation, fingerprinting techniques, local booking procedures, principles of adult learning, identifying when a performance problem can be resolved by training, instruction techniques for security leaders, developing roll call and OJT training, using case studies and visuals, testing for application of training, how to conduct security surveys and practice, supervisor's response to bomb threats, supervisor's response to medical and non-medical emergencies, supervisor's response to dealing with the homeless and other special groups, supervisor's response to alarms, de-escalation techniques for hostile situations, supervisory communication with management, dealing with contract vendors, supervisor's response to access control, supervisor's response to evacuation, and recognizing contract-related security threats. Methods of instruction include lecture, discussion, classroom exercises, use of a computer, case studies, audiovisual material, learner presentations, reports, and final examination.

Credit Recommendation: In the upper division baccalaureate degree category, 3 semester hours in Criminal Justice or Security Administration (5/97).

Western CUNA Management School

Western CUNA Management School serves credit union employees in thirteen western states. Overall authority for school policies belongs to a board of trustees composed of credit union presidents and industry officials. The board of trustees receives input from a council of advisors which consists of industry officials from the sponsoring states.

Because the school is located at Pomona College, it draws upon the college's resources, including faculty and classrooms. The California Credit Union League provides administrative support and supplies all requested audiovisual and other equipment.

Source of official student records: Vice President of Education and Training, Western CUNA Management School, California Credit Union League, 2350 S. Garey Avenue, Pomona, CA 91766.

Additional information about the courses: College Credit Recommendation Service, American Council on Education, One Dupont Circle, Washington, DC 20036-1193.

Western CUNA Management School

Location: Pomona, CA.

Length: 165 hours (three 2-week sessions over 3 years)

Dates: *Version 1:* August 1979-August 1981; *Version 2:* August 1982-Present; *Version 3:* September 1989-Present.

Objective: To provide credit union personnel with an introduction to basic knowledge and technical skills related to the management of financial institutions.

Learning Outcome: Upon successful completion of this course, the student will be able to apply strategic management principles to administration of financial institutions; apply principles and techniques of financial management to administration of credit unions; demonstrate understanding of total quality management as a management tool; understand and comply with current legal thinking in employment law and lending practices; and demonstrate appropriate interpersonal skills in the management of human resources.

Instruction: *Area 1:* Business Management: principles, methods, and procedures essential to successful management with a focus on the major functions of management. (1) Planning: the decision-making process, goal setting, and organizational policies; (2) Organizing: structure, hierarchy, and roles; (3) Leading/Directing: leadership styles, motivating, and time management; and (4) Controlling: the controlling process and evaluating budgeting. *Area 2:* Personnel Administration: staffing process, record keeping, evaluation and appraisal, compensation, discipline and conflict resolution, training and development, and work analysis. *Area 3:* Marketing and Advertising: marketing functions, practice, and research, advertising policy and problems germane to the credit union industry; and economic principles and sociological factors underlying these areas. *Area 4:* Financial Management: cash management, budgeting, money and banking, payment systems, forecasting, portfolio management, risk management, business law, and legal and regulatory problems. *Area 5:* Communications: effective oral and written communication. The following skills are emphasized: listening, providing feedback, understanding others, public speaking, and business writing. *Area 6:* Human Relations: the development of productive and satisfying work relationships. The following skills are emphasized: nonverbal communication, building a relationship, decision-making, problem-solving, stress diagnosis and management, and time management. Methods of instruction include lectures, cases, small-group discussion, survey/questionnaire grids, and interactive group experiences. *Version 3:* Major topics covered in the course are financial management, labor law, total quality management, marketing, managerial functions, organizational behavior and communication, environmental scanning, and strategic planning. Methods of instruction include lecture, discussion, classroom exercises, case studies, audio/visual material, computer-assisted instruction, learner presentations, reports, 2 major graded projects, and final examinations.

Credit Recommendation: *Version 1:* In the lower division baccalaureate/associate degree category, 9 semester hours as follows: Same as Version 2 (below) except that there are no semester hours for Area 2. *Version 2:* In the lower division baccalaureate/associate degree category, 10 semester hours as follows: *Area 1:* 3 semester hours in Business Administration, Management, or Supervision; *Area 2:* 1 semester hour in Business Administration or Personnel Management; *Area 3:* 1 semester hour in Business Administration or Marketing; *Area 4:* 3 semester hours in Finance or Business Administration; *Area 5:* 1 semester hour in Business Administration, Communications, or Psychology; *Area 6:* 1 semester hour in Business Administration, Behavioral Sciences, or Psychology. *Version 3:* Year 1: In the lower division baccalaureate/associate degree category, 2 semester hours in Introduction to Business; Year 2: In the upper division baccalaureate degree category, 4 semester hours in Business Administration or Management; and Year 3: In the upper division baccalaureate degree category, 4 semester hours in Finance or Business Administration (1/82) (12/94).

Westinghouse Savannah River Company

Westinghouse Savannah River Company (WSRC) Site Operations Training was organized in 1995 to provide training services to the more than 11,000 employees of WSRC who are assigned to production, operating, and technical divisions at the Savannah River Site. Site Operations Training services include these programs:

- Fundamentals Training Program,
- Technical Staff Training Program,
- Quality Assurance Training Program, and
- Emergency Response Organization Training.

Each program is designed around specific skill and knowledge needs as identified by Site management.

Participants in the Fundamentals Training Program receive instruction in a variety of science and mathematics topics, including Principles of Electricity, Classical Physics, Instrument and Control, Fluid Flow, Mechanical Science, Algebra, Trigonometry, and numerous others. These courses are developed in accordance with performance-based training concepts in use throughout the military and in numerous manufacturing organizations, and are conducted by a highly qualified instructional staff. All courses are conducted in modern facilities located at the Savannah River Site. Trainee mastery of subject matter is determined through a rigorous examination process. Upon successful completion of Fundamentals Training, the employees are equipped to cope with the demands of highly technical job-specific training in accordance with particular job assignments.

Source of official student records: Registry of Credit Recommendations, American Council on Education, One Dupont Circle, Washington, DC 20036-1193.

Additional information about the courses: College Credit Recommendation Service, American Council on Education, One Dupont Circle, Washington, DC 20036-1193.

Fluid Flow

Location: Savannah River Site, Aiken, SC.

Length: 64 hours (1.6 weeks).

Dates: September 1993-Present.

Objective: To provide essential knowledge of general engineering principles and mathematics associated with fluid systems, including conditions affecting fluid flow in a system, the effects on the operation of a system, and assessments to prevent accidents.

Learning Outcome: Upon successful completion of this course, the student will be able to explain essential principles of fluid flow; identify general danger situations and their solutions; and perform essential mathematical calculations.

Instruction: Major topics covered in the course are pressure, fluid statics, conservation of mass and energy, Bernouilli's principle, fluid friction, static and dynamic heads, energy transfers in ideal and real fluids, compression and decompression, water hammer, pipe whip, siphoning, and cross connections. Methods of instruction include lecture, discussion, classroom exercises, case studies, problem solving, videotapes, quizzes, and final examination.

Credit Recommendation: In the lower division baccalaureate/associate degree category, 2 semester hours in Fluid Mechanics or General Physics non-calculus based (3/97).

General Chemistry

Location: Savannah River Site, Aiken, SC.

Length: 120 hours (3 weeks).

Dates: September 1993-Present.

Objective: To provide a knowledge of basic inorganic chemistry and chemical principles.

Learning Outcome: Upon successful completion of this course, the student will be able to describe the characteristics of matter; calculate molecular weight, gram molecular weight, and perform mass/mole conversions; describe chemical bonding; write chemical formulas and balance chemical equations; describe solutions and solve solution concentration problems involving molarity, normality, parts-per-million, parts-per-billion, weight percent, mole percent, volume percent; calculate unknown concentrations and volumes; describes acids, bases, and salts; solve pH problems; explain ion exchangers; describe causes, effects, and minimization of corrosion, stress, thermal shock, and fracture; describe behavior of gases and solve problems using the combined gas law and ideal gas law; describe hazards associated with chemicals; and apply appropriate safety precautions and procedures.

Instruction: Major topics covered in the course are principles of matter; atomic structure; chemical bonding; solutions and chemical concentrations; acids, bases, and salts; water chemistry and ion exchange; oxidation-reduction, corrosion, and material stress; the behavior of gases; and chemical safety. Methods of instruction include lecture, discussion, practical exercises and worksheets, classroom demonstrations, audio-visual demonstrations and explanations, supervised study, quizzes, and final examination.

Credit Recommendation: In the lower division baccalaureate/associate degree category, 4 semester hours in Chemistry (3/97).

General Physics

Location: Savannah River Site, Aiken, SC.

Length: 96 hours.

Dates: September 1993-Present.

Objective: To provide a knowledge of classical physics principles required to be successful in an advanced technical training program.

Learning Outcome: Upon successful completion of this course, the student will be able to have an understanding of physics concepts of force, work, energy, momentum, weight, power, and properties of matter.

Instruction: Major topics covered in the course are force, work, energy, momentum, acceleration, weight, power, simple machines, and properties of matter. Methods of instruction include lecture, classroom exercises, practical demonstrations, videotape, and final examination.

Credit Recommendation: In the lower division baccalaureate/associate degree category, 3 semester hours in Engineering Technology or General Physics (5/97).

Heat Transfer

Location: Savannah River Site, Aiken, SC.

Length: 72 hours (1.8 weeks).

Dates: September 1993-Present.

Objective: To provide a knowledge of thermodynamic and heat transfer principles as they apply to nuclear facilities.

Learning Outcome: Upon successful completion of this course, the student will be able to explain and/or work applicable problems concerning the states of matter, the types and rates of heat transfer, the laws of thermodynamics, latent heat, heat exchange, energy conversions, and heating and cooling.

Instruction: Major topics covered in the course are the effects of heat on solids, liquids, and gases; modes of heat transfer; use of heat to do work; rate of heat transfer by conduction and convection; change of phase; sensible heat and latent heat; evaporation, boiling, and condensation; the laws of thermodynamics; general energy equation and Bernoulli's equation; heat engines; entropy; heat exchangers and their operation; thermodynamic systems and properties; forms of energy; energy conversions in fluid systems; and heating and cooling processes in fluids. Methods of instruction include lecture, classroom exercises, practical demonstrations, and final examination.

Credit Recommendation: In the lower division baccalaureate/associate degree category, 2 semester hours in Engineering Technology (3/97).

Instrumentation and Controls

Location: Savannah River Site, Aiken, SC.

Length: 56 hours (1.4 weeks).

Dates: September 1993-Present.

Objective: To provide a basic knowledge of the theory and operation of various instruments and control systems.

Learning Outcome: Upon successful completion of this course, the student will be able to understand and describe the principles of operation of instruments and devices to measure temperature, pressure, fluid level, fluid flow, position, and radiation.

Instruction: Major topics covered in the course are measurement fundamentals, principle of control systems, temperature measurements, pressure measurements, level measurements, flow measurements, position measurements, measurement and sensing devices, radiation detection, piping and instrumentation diagrams, and engineering logic diagrams. Methods of instruction include lecture, discussion, classroom exercises, practical demonstrations, case studies, audio-visual material, quizzes, and final examination.

Credit Recommendation: In the lower division baccalaureate/associate degree category, 2 semester hours in Instrumentation and Control Technology (3/97).

Mathematics

Location: Savannah River Site, Aiken, SC.

Length: 80 hours (2 weeks).

Dates: September 1993-Present.

Objective: To provide a basic foundation in mathematics, particularly in the areas of geometry and algebraic functions.

Learning Outcome: Upon successful completion of this course, the student will be able to apply mathematical principles to perform basic mathematical manipulations and solve problems in geometry and algebra.

Instruction: Major topics covered in the course are exponents; scientific notation; shapes, figures, and volumes; algebraic laws, equations, and word problems; graphs; units; and conversions. Methods of instruction include lecture, classroom exercises, discussion, audio-visual material, quizzes, and final examination.

Credit Recommendation: In the lower division baccalaureate/associate degree category, 3 semester hours in Mathematics (3/97).

Mechanical Technology (Mechanical Science)

Location: Savannah River Site, Aiken, SC.

Length: 88 hours (2.2 weeks).

Dates: September 1993-Present.

Objective: To provide a knowledge of mechanical technology principles required to understand fluid systems.

Learning Outcome: Upon successful completion of this course, the student will be able to demonstrate knowledge and skill of safe operation and control of valves, valve actuators, pumps, heat exchangers, systems, and piping; and demonstrate the ability to understand and interpret blueprints, system diagrams, and piping diagrams.

Instruction: Major topics covered in the course are valves, valve actuators and positioners, positive displacement pumps, centrifugal pumps, jet pumps, filters and strainers, heat exchangers, compressed air systems, ventilation systems, steam systems, introduction to print reading, piping and instrumentation diagrams, pump laws, and refrigeration systems. Methods of instruction include lecture, discussion, classroom exercises, case studies, audio-visual material, quizzes, and final examination.

Credit Recommendation: In the lower division baccalaureate/associate degree category, 2 semester hours in Engineering Technology (3/97).

Nuclear Science

Location: Savannah River Site, Aiken, SC.

Length: 40 hours (1 week).

Dates: September 1993-Present.

Objective: To provide a basic knowledge of nuclear science principles.

Learning Outcome: Upon successful completion of this course, the student will be able to describe atomic structure and nuclear forces; describe various modes of radioactive decay including the interactions of radiation with matter; and describe nuclear fission including neutron interactions and energy levels, critical mass, and the factors that affect critical mass.

Instruction: Major topics covered in the course are atomic structure and nuclear forces; radioactive decay and interactions of radiation with matter; fissionability and criticality; and critical mass, including the factors that affect critical mass. Methods of instruction include lecture, discussion, audio-visual demonstrations and explanations, supervised study, periodic quizzes, and final examination.

Credit Recommendation: In the lower division baccalaureate/associate degree category, 2 semester hours in General Science or Engineering Technology (3/97).

Principles and Practice of Radiation Detection and Monitoring (Principles of Radiation Detection)

Location: Westinghouse Savannah River Company.

Length: 62 hours.

Dates: January 1990-Present.

Objective: To prepare the student with the necessary knowledge to perform radiological surveys and assessments of radiological conditions in the workplace. The student must be able to distinguish the characteristics and the theory of operation of various radiation detection instruments and monitors and their advantages and limitations in radiological monitoring. The student must understand and be able to apply the statistical processes and concepts that are used in a nuclear counting environment.

Learning Outcome: Upon successful completion of this course, the student will know and be able to explain the radiological survey processes used in the workplace, radiation detector theory and its application to specific radiation survey and contamination monitoring instrumentation, and counting errors and statistical applications in nuclear counting operations.

Instruction: Major topics covered in the course address radiological surveys and monitoring; radiation detector theory; portable radiation and contamination monitoring instrumentation; air sampling methods and equipment; and counting errors & statistics as applied in count room operations and sample analysis. Methods of instruction include lecture, demonstrations, discussion, classroom exercises and problem solving, and course examination.

Credit Recommendation: In the upper division baccalaureate degree category, 3

semester hours in Engineering Technology or Nuclear Science (11/97).

Principles of Electricity

Location: Savannah River Site, Aiken, SC.

Length: 88 hours (2.2 weeks).

Dates: September 1993-Present.

Objective: To provide a knowledge of principles of electricity, magnetism, electrical circuits, and components.

Learning Outcome: Upon successful completion of this course, the student will be able to demonstrate an understanding of electricity, magnetism, AC and DC circuits, motors, generators, and electrical safety systems.

Instruction: Major topics covered in the course are electrical forces, electrical terminology, units of measurement pertaining to electricity, magnetism and magnetic induction, DC sources, DC circuits, Kirchloff's laws, batteries, AC generation and analysis, three-phase circuits, AC motor theory, transformers, system components and protection devices, motor controllers, switches, indicating devices, drawings and schematics, electrical hazards, circuit breakers, system definitions and groundings, AC generator components, uninterruptible power supplies, and variable speed drives. Methods of instruction include lecture, discussion, classroom exercises, video materials, quizzes, and final examination.

Credit Recommendation: In the lower division baccalaureate/associate degree category, 3 semester hours in non-calculus based General Physics or Electrical Engineering Technology (3/97).

Principles of Health Physics

Location: Westinghouse Savannah River Company.

Length: 50 hours.

Dates: January 1990-Present.

Objective: To provide the student with fundamental health physics principles and concepts in the areas of respiratory protection controls, biological effects of radiation, ALARA, dosimetry, and internal and external exposure control.

Learning Outcome: Upon course completion, the student will know and be able to discuss the biological effects of radiation and relative risk; the application of ALARA principles to radiological work; the measurement of radiation exposure through dosimetry; and the applications employed for internal and external exposure control.

Instruction: Major topics covered in the course are biological effects of radiation, ALARA, dosimetry, internal and external exposure control, and respiratory protection. Methods of instruction include lecture, discussion, classroom exercises, audio-visual material, and written examinations.

Credit Recommendation: In the upper division baccalaureate degree category, 3 semester hours in Engineering Technology, Radiological Technology, or Health Physics (11/97).

Principles of Nuclear Physics

Location: Westinghouse Savannah River Company.

Length: 50 hours.

Dates: January 1990-Present.

Objective: To provide the student with an understanding of fundamental principles of radioactivity and radioactive decay including sources of radiation and radioactive decay schemes, sources of radioactivity (natural and man-made), interactions of radiation with matter, and fission and criticality processes. Principles of radioactivity are applied in discussions of the uses of uranium, plutonium, and tritium and their respective hazards.

Learning Outcome: Upon successful completion of this course, the student can describe sources of radiation, the processes of radioactive decay including performing activity calculations, interactions of radiation with matter, and the fission process including factors affecting reactivity and criticality control.

Instruction: Major topics covered in this course are sources of radiation, radioactivity and radioactive decay, interactions of radiation, fission and criticality, and uranium, plutonium, and tritium hazards. Methods of instruction include lecture, discussion, classroom exercises, and module tests.

Credit Recommendation: In the lower division baccalaureate/associate degree category, 3 semester hours in General Science, Nuclear Science, or Engineering Technology (11/97).

Principles of Radiological Controls

Location: Westinghouse Savannah River Company.

Length: 64 hours.

Dates: January 1990-Present.

Objective: To provide the student with important principles and considerations used in the control of radioactive materials in the workplace. The student must demonstrate knowledge of principles of radioactive waste management; control of radioactive contamination including decontamination of equipment and personnel; shipment and receipt of radioactive materials including radioactive source control; and access control and work area setup techniques used to implement effective work practices that minimize radioactive waste and worker exposures to radiation and radioactive contamination.

Learning Outcome: Upon successful completion of this course, the student will be able to explain and summarize principles and techniques used to control radioactive material in the workplace with emphasis on radioactive waste management; shipping and receipt of radioactive material; control of contamination and decontamination techniques; and access control and work area set-up.

Instruction: Major topics covered in this course are principles of waste management; radioactive material control; shipment and receipt of radioactive materials; contamination control and personnel decontamination; source control; and access control & work area setup.

Credit Recommendation: In the upper division baccalaureate degree category, 3 semester hours in Nuclear Technology or Health Physics Technology (12/97).

Radiation Detection Laboratory I

Location: Westinghouse Savannah River Company.

Length: 81 hours.

Dates: January 1990-Present.

Objective: Through performance-based assessments, ensure that the radiological control inspector has and can apply the technical knowledge and skills needed to perform radiological surveys of radiation and contamination levels in the workplace using appropriate instrumentation.

Learning Outcome: Upon successful completion of this course, the student will be able to describe the theory and principles of operation of radiological instrumentation used in workplace monitoring; conduct radiological assessments and surveys of radiological conditions in the workplace; and analyze and interpret radiological survey results to determine appropriate radiological controls for worker protection.

Instruction: Major topics covered in this course are the theory and use of survey meters, air samplers, tritium meters and other instruments needed for detection of alpha, beta, and gamma radiation and neutrons; methods employed to decontaminate survey instruments and personal effects; techniques used in the performance of radiation and contamination surveys; how to obtain and analyze air samples using various types of air sampling equipment; and determining proper radiological controls through posting, containment or surveys (e.g., controlling radioactive sources, tracking contaminated equipment, or the elimination or minimization of radioactive waste). Methods of instruction include guided discussion to support and clarify previous lecture topics using one on one or small group settings; analogies and examples that will assist the student's understanding; laboratory exercises and demonstrations with student practice to learn and demonstrate acceptable performance using pre-identified criteria; and a final evaluation combining technical knowledge questions and required skill demonstrations.

Credit Recommendation: In the upper division baccalaureate degree category, 2 semester hours in Nuclear Science or Health Physics (11/97).

Radiation Detection Laboratory II

Location: Westinghouse Savannah River Company.

Length: 67.5 hours.

Dates: January 1990-Present.

Objective: Through performance-based assessments, ensure that the student is knowledgeable and has the necessary technical expertise needed to make an effective radiological control inspector who can assess and respond to both routine and abnormal radiological conditions in the work place.

Learning Outcome: Upon successful completion of this course, the student will acquire the skills and knowledge, and the ability to manipulate or apply various concepts and techniques needed for the conduct of work involving different levels and types of radiation and radioactive contamination.

Instruction: Major topics covered in this course are methods employed in conducting personnel skin decontamination for alpha, beta-gamma and tritium contamination; the operation and calibration of gasflow proportional counting systems, tritium bubbler, and other types of radiological equipment; environmental radiological assessments of soil, air, and water; radiological containment inspection/certification of huts, windbreaks, polybottles and glovebags; and responses to radiological monitor alarms and follow-up actions for personnel protection and monitoring. Methods of instruction include guided discussion to support and clarify previous lecture topics using one on one or small group settings; analogies and examples that will assist the student's understanding; laboratory exercises and demonstrations with student practice to learn and demonstrate acceptable performance using pre-identified criteria; and a final evaluation combining technical knowledge questions and required skill demonstrations.

Credit Recommendation: In the upper division baccalaureate degree category, 2 semester hours in Nuclear Science or Health Physics (11/97).

Radiation Detection Laboratory III

Location: Westinghouse Savannah River Company.

Length: 70 hours.

Dates: January 1990-Present.

Objective: To provide direct hands-on experience and student evaluations of the operation and calibration of nuclear counting systems including Geiger-Mueller and scintillation detectors used in scaler systems, and a gas flow proportional counting system. The student must demonstrate satisfactory skills in performing radiological surveys including control of radiological jobs in a mock-up training facility.

Learning Outcome: Upon successful completion of this course, the student will be able to operate and calibrate nuclear counting systems in accordance with procedures and pre identified criteria; and demonstrate satisfactory control of radiological work in a typical job setting minimizing radiological exposures to himself and assigned workers and controlling or minimizing radioactive waste generation.

Instruction: Major topics covered in the course emphasize the operation and calibration of Geiger-Mueller and scintillation detectors connected to Eberline or Ludlum scalers; operation and calibration of a NMC PC-5 gas flow proportional counting system; and a job coverage lab in a mock-up laboratory facility. Methods of instruction include lecture, instructor demonstrations, student hands-on practice and demonstrations, group activities, with a written examination and required performance evaluations with pre established criteria.

Credit Recommendation: In the upper division baccalaureate degree category, 2 semester hours in Nuclear Science or Health Physics (11/97).

Wisconsin Public Service Corporation

Wisconsin Public Service Corporation's Nuclear Department is charged with the responsibility of providing such scientific, engineering, technical, managerial, and operations educational and training programs to department personnel as are required for the safe and economic operation of the Kewaunee Nuclear Power Plant.

The training aspects of the various programs are provided by the Nuclear Training Group which is composed of individuals with extensive knowledge in a cadre of disciplines; some with degrees in science or engineering, others with many years of experience in nuclear power generation who hold United States Nuclear Regulatory Commission Senior Reactor Operator Licenses on the facility, and some with technical credentials in electronics or the various crafts. Appropriate support personnel assist in program delivery.

The education component is provided by the availability of study programs leading to Baccalaureate Degrees in Nuclear Science and Technology Management through a major university, and Associate Degrees in various disciplines through local technical colleges. These university and college programs are managed by corporate personnel holding terminal degrees and professorial credentials in appropriate disciplines. The courses recommended for academic credit by the American Council on Education's College Credit Recommendation Service, are an integral part of these advanced educational programs.

The corporation has also provided a library of scientific, engineering, technical and operations supporting materials for study use. A full scale, plant-specific training simulator is located at the nuclear facility for use by operator trainees, licensed plant operators, and engineering staff. This instrument is capable of generating hundreds of instrument and equipment failures and accident scenarios on which the operators can practice and master plant operations under normal, abnormal and emergency conditions.

Source of official student records: Director of Nuclear Education, Nuclear Department, Wisconsin Public Service Corporation, P.O. Box 19002, Green Bay, WI 54307-9002.

Additional information about the courses: College Credit Recommendation Service, American Council on Education, One Dupont Circle, Washington, DC 20036-1193.

Accident and Transient Analysis

Location: Kewaunee Nuclear Training Center, WI.

Length: 94 hours (2 weeks).

Dates: August 1984-Present.

Objective: To provide the student with instruction for detecting the symptoms associated with the various accident categories, their impact on the critical safety functions, and the automatic and operator actions necessary to mitigate their consequences.

Learning Outcome: Upon successful completion of this course, the student will be able to evaluate the various transients and accident conditions that cause abnormal and emergency situations; understand the impact of these conditions on safety; and respond properly with a recovery/restoration technique to correct the emergency situations.

Instruction: Major topics covered in the course are the theory, causes, and responses to increased and decreased secondary heat removal events, increased and decreased reactor coolant events, and decreased reactor coolant flow. After classroom instruction, events are presented to students using the control room simulator and the student's response to the situation is evaluated. Methods of instruction include classroom lectures, classroom discussions, hands-on control room simulations of symptom-based reactor events, self-study, and examinations.

Credit Recommendation: In the upper division baccalaureate or graduate degree category, 3 semester hours in Nuclear Engineering (11/89) (12/94).

Nuclear Systems Overview - Version 1

Location: Kewaunee Nuclear Training Center, WI.

Length: 73.5 hours (2 weeks).

Dates: January 1984-November 1994.

Objective: To provide students with an understanding of the operation of nuclear power plant systems.

Learning Outcome: Upon successful completion of this course, students will be able to demonstrate a knowledge of nomenclature; understand concepts; and define and describe operating systems of nuclear power plants.

Instruction: Major topics covered in the course are reactor coolant; chemical volume control; rod control; main steam; main turbine; main feedwater; main generator; electrical; radioactive waste; radiation monitoring systems; and instrumentation and accident analysis. Methods of instruction include lecture.

Credit Recommendation: In the lower division baccalaureate/associate degree category, 2 semester hours in Nuclear Engineering Technology (12/86). **NOTE:** Credit should not be awarded for this course if participants have completed the Reactor Operator Fundamentals course.

Nuclear Systems Overview - Version 2

Location: Kewaunee Nuclear Training Center, WI.

Length: 99 hours (2.5 weeks).

Dates: December 1994-Present.

Objective: To provide an understanding of the operation of nuclear power plant systems.

Learning Outcome: Upon successful completion of this course, the student will be able to demonstrate a knowledge of nomenclature; understand concepts; and define and describe operating systems of nuclear power plants.

Instruction: Major topics covered in the course are reactor coolant; chemical volume control; rod control; main stream; main turbine; main feedwater; main generator; electrical; radioactive waste; and radiation monitoring systems and instrumentation. Methods of instruction include lecture.

Credit Recommendation: In the lower division baccalaureate/associate degree category, 3 semester hours in Nuclear Engineering Technology (12/94). **NOTE:** Credit should not be awarded for this course if participants have completed the Reactor Operator Fundamentals course.

Radiation Monitoring Systems - Version 1

Location: Kewaunee Nuclear Training Center, WI.

Length: 62 hours (5 weeks).

Dates: January 1985-November 1994.

Objective: To provide the student with a knowledge of radiation monitoring systems.

Learning Outcome: Upon successful completion of this course, the student will understand the function and characteristics of radiation monitoring systems and the chemistry relevant to the primary sampling system.

Instruction: Major topics covered in the course are purpose, operations, and equipment of radiation monitoring and primary sampling systems. The chemistry relevant to the primary sampling system such as deposits and corrosion is discussed. Methods of instruction include lecture and discussion.

Credit Recommendation: In the lower division baccalaureate/associate degree category, 1 semester hour in Nuclear Engineering Technology (8/86).

Radiation Monitoring Systems - Version 2

Location: Kewaunee Nuclear Training Center, WI.

Length: 62 hours (5 weeks).

Dates: December 1994-Present.

Objective: To provide the student with a knowledge of radiation monitoring systems.

Learning Outcome: Upon successful completion of this course, the student will be able to understand the function and characteristics of radiation monitoring systems and the chemistry relevant to the primary sampling system.

Instruction: Major topics covered in the course are the purpose, operations, and equipment of a radiation monitoring system and the chemistry relevant to the primary sampling system such as deposits and corrosion. Methods of instruction include lecture and discussion.

Credit Recommendation: In the lower division baccalaureate/associate degree category, 1 semester hour in Nuclear Engineering Technology (12/94).

Reactor Operator Fundamentals: Chemistry

Location: Kewaunee Nuclear Training Center, WI.

Length: 40 hours (1 week).

Dates: January 1981-Present.

Objective: To give the student instruction in fundamentals of chemistry.

Learning Outcome: Upon successful completion of this course, the student will understand the fundamentals of chemistry and be able to perform stoichiometric calculations.

Instruction: Major topics covered in the course are fundamentals and principles of chemistry including atomic theory, law of mass action, bonding, solution concentrations, pH, and electrochemistry (nonlaboratory). Methods of instruction include lectures.

Credit Recommendation: In the lower division baccalaureate/associate degree category, 1 semester hour in General Chemistry (8/86) (12/94).

Reactor Operator Fundamentals: Core Physics - Version 1

Location: Kewaunee Nuclear Training Center, WI.

Length: 150 hours (4 weeks).

Dates: January 1981-December 1992.

Objective: To provide a survey of plant-specific reactor core components and coolant flow, the effects of various coefficients on core reactivity, and core power distribution and reactivity control during reactor operation.

Learning Outcome: Upon successful completion of this course, the student will be able to describe, define, and calculate reactor components, the multiplication factor, reactivity and reactivity changes, the effects of various coefficients (Doppler, temperature, void, etc.), fission product poisoning, lumped and distributed poisons, power distribution, and reactivity control often contrasting parameters at BOL with EOL.

Instruction: Major topics covered in the course are reactor core construction, reactivity and fuel effects, moderator temperature effects and power defect, fission product poisoning, chemical shim control, control rod reactivity effect, estimated critical condition and shutdown, reactivity considerations, nuclear power distribution in a PWR core, and reactivity control during power operation. Methods of instruction include lecture, discussion, and classroom exercises.

Credit Recommendation: In the lower division baccalaureate/associate degree category, 3 semester hours in Nuclear Engineering/Nuclear Engineering Technology (8/86).

Reactor Operator Fundamentals: Core Physics - Version 2

Location: Kewaunee Nuclear Training Center, WI.

Length: 65 hours (8 days).

Dates: January 1993-Present.

Objective: To provide a survey of plant-specific reactor core components and coolant flow, the effects of various coefficients on core reactivity, and core power distribution and reactivity control during reactor operation.

Learning Outcome: Upon successful completion of this course, the student will be able to describe, define, and calculate reactor components, the multiplication factor, reactivity and reactivity changes; the effects of various coefficients (Doppler, temperature, void, etc.), fission product poisoning, lumped and distributed poisons, power distribution, and reactivity control often contrasting parameters at BOL with EOL.

Instruction: Major topics covered in the course are reactor core construction; reactivity and fuel effects; moderator temperature effects and power defect; fission product poisoning; chemical shim control; control rod reactivity effect; estimated critical condition and shutdown; reactivity considerations; nuclear power distribution in a PWR core; and reactivity control during power operation. Methods of instruction include lecture, discussion, and classroom exercises.

Credit Recommendation: In the lower division baccalaureate/associate degree category, 2 semester hours in Nuclear Engineering/Nuclear Engineering Technology (12/94).

Reactor Operator Fundamentals: Heat Transfer and Fluid Flow - Version 1

Location: Kewaunee Nuclear Training Center, WI.

Length: 160 hours (4 weeks).

Dates: January 1981-December 1992.

Objective: To provide the student with an understanding of basic concepts of heat transfer and fluid mechanics as applied to pressurized water reactors.

Learning Outcome: Upon successful completion of this course, the student will be able to understand the basic laws of heat transfer, thermodynamics, and fluid mechanics and apply these concepts to the operation of a pressurized water reactor.

Instruction: Major topics covered in the course are properties of water, reactor heat transfer, reactor thermodynamics, heat exchangers, steam generator thermodynamics, turbine thermodynamics and the rankine cycle, fluid mechanics in the turbine, condensor/tertiary thermodynamics, piping and pump fluid mechanics instrumentation, steady state and normal transients, and core thermal parameters and limits. Methods of instruction include lecture and classroom exercises.

Credit Recommendation: In the upper division baccalaureate degree category, 2 semester hours in Heat Transfer and Fluid Mechanics (8/86).

Reactor Operator Fundamentals: Heat Transfer and Fluid Flow - Version 2

Location: Kewaunee Nuclear Training Center, WI.

Length: 65 hours (8 days).

Dates: January 1993-Present.

Objective: To provide the student with an understanding of basic concepts of heat transfer and fluid mechanics as applied to pressurized water reactors.

Learning Outcome: Upon successful completion of this course, the student will

be able to understand the basic laws of heat transfer, thermodynamics, and fluid mechanics and apply these concepts to the operation of a pressurized water reactor.

Instruction: Major topics covered in the course are properties of water; reactor heat transfer; reactor thermodynamics; heat exchanges; steam generator thermodynamics, turbine thermodynamics and the rankine cycle; fluid mechanics in the turbine; condensor/tertiary thermodynamics; piping and pump fluid mechanics instrumentation; steady state and normal transients; and core thermal parameters and limits. Methods of instruction include lecture and classroom exercises.

Credit Recommendation: In the upper division baccalaureate degree category, 2 semester hours in Heat Transfer and Fluid Mechanics (12/94).

Reactor Operator Fundamentals: Mathematics

Location: Kewaunee Nuclear Training Center, WI.

Length: 37 hours (1 week).

Dates: January 1981-December 1992.

Objective: To develop skills in solving linear and quadratic equations, use of mensuration formulae, exponents, logarithms, graphs, and to introduce basic concepts of calculus.

Learning Outcome: Upon successful completion of this course, the student will be able to solve linear, quadratic, and exponential equations; construct graphs; find slopes and intercepts; and calculate basic trigonometric functions using a calculator.

Instruction: Major topics covered in the course are fundamentals of algebra, exponentials, logarithms, graphs, and an introduction to calculus concepts of integrals and derivatives. Methods of instruction include lecture and classroom discussions.

Credit Recommendation: In the lower division baccalaureate/associate degree category, 1 semester hour in Mathematics (Algebra and Trigonometry) (8/86) (12/94).

Reactor Operator Fundamentals: Mathematics and Basic Physics (Formerly Reactor Operator Fundamentals: Mathematics)

Location: Kewaunee Nuclear Training Center, WI.

Length: 54 hours (7 days).

Dates: January 1993-Present.

Objective: To develop skills in solving linear and quadratic equations; use of mensuration formulae; exponents; logarithms; graphs; and to introduce the basic concepts of calculus and physics.

Learning Outcome: Upon successful completion of this course, the student will be able to solve linear, quadratic, and exponential equations; construct graphs; find slopes and intercepts; calculate basic trigonometric functions using a calculator; describe and discuss properties of matter, energy, fluids, electricity, and magnetism; and perform basic calculations related to work, energy, and power.

Instruction: Major topics covered in the course are the fundamentals of algebra; exponentials; logarithms; graphs; an introduction to calculus concepts of integrals and derivatives; and an overview of work, energy, power, fluids, electricity, and magnetism. Methods of instruction include lecture, classroom exercises, and written or oral examinations.

Credit Recommendation: In the lower division baccalaureate/associate degree category, 1 semester hour in Mathematics (Algebra and Trigonometry) and 1 semester hour in General Physics for a total of 2 semester hours (12/94).

Reactor Operator Fundamentals: Radiation - Version 1

Location: Kewaunee Nuclear Training Center, WI.

Length: 80 hours (2 weeks).

Dates: January 1981-December 1992.

Objective: To provide a fundamental knowledge of the properties and effects of nuclear radiation.

Learning Outcome: Upon successful completion of this course, the student will be able to understand the physical and biological effects of nuclear radiation, radiation detection and protection and perform determinations of half-lives and activities.

Instruction: Major topics covered in the course are radioactive decay, interaction of radiation with matter, biological effects of radiation, radiation detectors, and radiation protection and regulations. Methods of instruction include lecture, self-study, and examinations.

Credit Recommendation: In the upper division baccalaureate degree category, 3 semester hours in Nuclear Science (Radiology/Health Physics) (8/86).

Reactor Operator Fundamentals: Radiation - Version 2

Location: Kewaunee Nuclear Training Center, WI.

Length: 39 hours (1 week).

Dates: January 1993-Present.

Objective: To provide fundamental knowledge of the properties and effects of nuclear radiation.

Learning Outcome: Upon successful completion of this course, the student will be able to understand the physical and biological effects of nuclear radiation; radiation detection and protection; and perform determinations of half-lives and activities.

Instruction: Major topics covered in the course are radioactive decay, interaction of radiation with matter, biological effects of radiation, radiation detectors, and radiation protection and regulations. Methods of instruction include lecture, self-study, and examinations.

Credit Recommendation: In the upper division baccalaureate degree category, 2 semester hours in Nuclear Science/Health Physics (12/94).

Reactor Operator Fundamentals: Reactor Theory

Location: Kewaunee Nuclear Training Centers, WI.

Length: *Version 1:* 112 hours (3 weeks); *Version 2:* 68 hours (2 weeks).

Dates: *Version 1:* January 1981-November 1994; *Version 2:* December 1994-Present.

Objective: To provide a survey of information on the structure of the atom, properties of the neutron, nuclear interactions, radioactive decay, and static and kinetic reactor behavior.

Learning Outcome: Upon successful completion of this course, the student will be able to describe, define, and calculate basic properties of the atom, the neutron, and radioisotopes as they relate to the steady state or dynamic behavior of a reactor core.

Instruction: *Version 1:* Major topics covered in the course are the properties of energy and matter, atomic physics, nuclear reactions, neutron physics, reactor statics, reactor kinetics, and subcritical reactor behavior. Methods of instruction include lecture, discussion, problem solution, and supervised self-study. *Version 2:* Major topics covered in the course are nuclear physics including nuclear reaction, neutron physics, reactor physics, reactor kinetics, and subcritical reactor theory. Methods of instruction include lecture, discussion, classroom exercises, and examination.

Credit Recommendation: *Version 1:* In the lower division baccalaureate/associate degree category, 2 semester hours in Nuclear Engineering/Nuclear Engineering Technology (8/86) (12/94). *Version 2:* In the lower division baccalaureate/associate degree category, 2 semester hours in

Nuclear Engineering/Nuclear Engineering Technology (8/86) (12/94).

Reactor Operator Simulator Training (Normal Operations; A) - Version 1

Location: Kewaunee Nuclear Training Center, WI.

Length: 440 hours (11 weeks).

Dates: January 1991-November 1994.

Objective: To provide students with knowledge of normal, abnormal, and emergency nuclear power plant operation.

Learning Outcome: Upon successful completion of this course, students will have the knowledge and skill for startup, normal operation, and shutdown of nuclear power plants, and the ability to diagnose and mitigate malfunctions and to institute appropriate emergency operating procedures in nuclear power plants.

Instruction: Major topics covered in the course are normal startup, shutdown, and full power operation of a nuclear power plant; occasional expected malfunctions; rare abnormal/emergency malfunctions; and emergency operating procedures for taking appropriate corrective action when malfunctions occur in nuclear power plants. Methods of instruction include lecture, classroom discussions, and extensive laboratory training utilizing a simulator.

Credit Recommendation: In the upper division baccalaureate degree category, 3 semester hours in Nuclear Engineering Technology (12/86).

Reactor Operator Simulator Training (Normal Operations; A) - Version 2

Location: Kewaunee Nuclear Training Center, WI.

Length: 440 hours (11 weeks).

Dates: December 1994-Present.

Objective: To provide students with knowledge of normal, abnormal, and emergency nuclear power plant operation.

Learning Outcome: Upon successful completion of this course, the student will be able to demonstrate the knowledge and skill for startup, normal operation, and shutdown of nuclear power plants; diagnose and mitigate malfunctions; and institute appropriate emergency operating procedures in nuclear power plants.

Instruction: Major topics covered in the course are normal startup, shutdown, and full power operation of a nuclear power plant; occasional expected malfunctions; rare abnormal/emergency malfunctions; and emergency operating procedures for taking appropriate corrective action when malfunctions occur in nuclear power plants. Methods of instruction include lecture, classroom discussions, and extensive laboratory training utilizing a simulator.

Credit Recommendation: In the upper division baccalaureate degree category, 5 semester hours in Nuclear Engineering Technology (12/94).

Reactor Operator Systems: Administration and Emergency Planning

Location: Kewaunee Nuclear Training Center, WI.

Length: 173.5 hours (4.5 weeks).

Dates: January 1981-Present.

Objective: To provide the student with instruction in nuclear plant management as it relates to compliance with technical specifications, selected portions of Title 10 of the Code of Federal Regulations and Emergency Planning and Fire Protection.

Learning Outcome: Upon successful completion of this course, the student will be able to describe and explain the implications, definitions, limitations, compliance, and basis for the various sections of technical specifications; and describe and interpret the interrelationships of emergency planning with off-site organizations.

Instruction: Major topics covered in the course are subjects related to administration and emergency planning as described in technical specifications, administrative control directives, and Title 10 Code of Federal Regulations; and emergency planning and integrated plant emergency operating procedures. Methods of instruction include lecture, classroom discussion, and on-the-job training.

Credit Recommendation: In the upper division baccalaureate degree category, 2 semester hours in Nuclear Plant Management (8/86) (12/94).

Reactor Operator Systems: Electrical Generation and Distribution Systems

Location: Kewaunee Nuclear Training Center, WI.

Length: 105 hours (9 days).

Dates: January 1981-Present.

Objective: To provide the student with instruction on power plant electrical generation and distribution systems—design, components, instrumentation, and functions—as they apply to a reactor operator.

Learning Outcome: Upon successful completion of this course, the student will have an understanding of the electrical generation and distribution system of a power plant.

Instruction: Major topics covered in the course are main generator and generator auxiliaries, protection relating, substation and electrical distribution, 4160 volt electrical system, 480 volt electrical system, and emergency systems. Methods of instruction include lectures, classroom discussions and on-the-job training.

Credit Recommendation: In the lower division baccalaureate/associate degree category, 1 semester hour in Electrical or Nuclear Engineering Technology (8/86) (12/94).

Reactor Operator Systems: Emergency Diesel Generator Mechanical/Electrical Systems

Location: Kewaunee Nuclear Training Center, WI.

Length: 51 hours (7 days).

Dates: January 1981-Present.

Objective: To provide the student with instruction on the diesel generator mechanical/electrical systems of a nuclear power plant as they apply to a reactor operator.

Learning Outcome: Upon successful completion of this course, the student will have an understanding of the diesel generator mechanical/electrical systems of a nuclear power plant and relate these systems to technical specifications.

Instruction: Major topics covered in the course are diesel generator—mechanical, diesel generator—electrical, and load shedding and sequencing. Methods of instruction include lectures, on-the-job training, self-study, and examinations.

Credit Recommendation: In the lower division baccalaureate/associate degree category, 1 semester hour in Nuclear Engineering Technology (8/86) (12/94).

Reactor Operator Systems: Integrated Reactor Protection and Safety Features

Location: Kewaunee Nuclear Training Center, WI.

Length: 58 hours.

Dates: January 1981-Present.

Objective: To provide the student with descriptions, purposes, operating limits, interlocks, alarms, and associated procedures for reactor protection systems and engineered safeguards systems.

Learning Outcome: Upon successful completion of this course, the student will be able to describe and become familiar with the operation, functions, locations, operating limits, instrumentation, procedures, and technical specification implications of all the system components.

Instruction: Major topics covered in the course are subjects related to integrated reactor protection and safety features including the integrated safety features and the reactor protection and safeguards logic. Methods of instruction include lectures, self-study, on-the-job-training, simulator demonstrations and examinations.

Credit Recommendation: In the lower division baccalaureate/associate degree category, 1 semester hour in Nuclear Engineering Technology (8/86) (12/94).

Reactor Operator Systems: Plant Secondary Coolant and Auxiliary Systems

Location: Kewaunee Nuclear Training Center, WI.

Length: 189 hours (24 days).

Dates: January 1981-Present.

Objective: To provide the student with instruction on the plant secondary coolant and auxiliary systems of a nuclear power plant as they apply to a reactor operator.

Learning Outcome: Upon successful completion of this course, the student will have an understanding of the plant secondary coolant and auxiliary systems and relate these systems to technical specifications; and be able to describe and explain the principles of fire protection and the associated alarm responses and the implications of these responses to technical specifications.

Instruction: Major topics covered in the course are station and instrument air, main steam and steam pumps, steam pump control, bleed steam, feedwater heaters, heater drains, circulating water, main turbine and auxiliaries, turbine control system, air removal, condensate system, main feed water, makeup water, secondary sampling system, and secondary chemistry control. Methods of instruction include lectures, classroom discussions, on-the-job training, self-study, simulator demonstrations, and examinations.

Credit Recommendation: In the lower division baccalaureate/associate degree category, 3 semester hours in Nuclear Engineering Technology (8/86) (12/94).

Reactor Operator Systems: Plant Ventilation Systems

Location: Kewaunee Nuclear Training Center, WI.

Length: 84 hours (2 weeks and 1 day).

Dates: January 1981-Present.

Objective: To provide the student with instruction on the plant ventilation systems of a nuclear power plant as they apply to a reactor operator.

Learning Outcome: Upon successful completion of this course, the student will understand the various ventilation systems of a nuclear power plant and be able to relate these systems to technical specifications.

Instruction: Major topics covered in the course are turbine building and screenhouse, auxiliary building, shield building, reactor building, containment building, and post LOCA hydrogen control, and control room air conditioning. Methods of instruction include lectures, classroom discussions, classroom exercises, and on-the-job-training.

Credit Recommendation: In the lower division baccalaureate/associate degree category, 1 semester hour in Nuclear Engineering Technology (8/86) (12/94).

Reactor Operator Systems: Reactor Core Design, Components, Instrumentation, and Functions

Location: Kewaunee Nuclear Training Center, WI.

Length: 54 hours (1.5 weeks).

Dates: January 1981-Present.

Objective: To provide a description and familiarization of reactor vessel internal components and incore and excore nuclear instrumentation.

Learning Outcome: Upon successful completion of this course, the student will be able to locate and describe the function of reactor vessel internals and explain safety limits associated with these components; to understand some basic instrumentation theory and explain functions of the instrumentation and the associated readouts and interlocks; and to understand the relationship with other plant components and technical specification limits.

Instruction: Major topics covered in the course are subjects related to design, components, instrumentation, and functions of the reactor core including the reactor vessel and internals and excore and incore instrumentation. Methods of instruction include lectures, self-study, and on-the-job-training.

Credit Recommendation: In the lower division baccalaureate/associate degree category, 1 semester hour in Nuclear Engineering Technology (8/86) (12/94).

Reactor Operator Systems: Reactor Emergency and Auxiliary Coolant Systems

Location: Kewaunee Nuclear Training Center, WI.

Length: 138 hours (4 weeks).

Dates: January 1981-Present.

Objective: To provide the student with descriptions, purposes, associated interlocks and alarms, and procedures for all system components.

Learning Outcome: Upon successful completion of this course, the student will be able to describe and become familiar with the operation, functions, locations, interconnections, interactions, limits, precautions, and procedures where applicable of all the system components.

Instruction: Major topics covered in the course are chemical and volume control, component cooling, residual heat removal, internal containment spray, and safety injection. Methods of instruction include lecture, on-the-job-training, self-study, and simulator demonstrations.

Credit Recommendation: In the lower division baccalaureate/associate degree category, 2 semester hours in Nuclear Engineering Technology (8/86) (12/94).

Reactor Operator Systems: Reactor Primary Coolant Systems

Location: Kewaunee Nuclear Training Center, WI.

Length: 123.5 hours (3.5 weeks).

Dates: January 1981-November 1994.

Objective: To provide the student with descriptions, purposes, flow paths, arrangements, indications, and normal and abnormal procedures for all system components.

Learning Outcome: Upon successful completion of this course, the student will be able to describe and become familiar with the operation, functions, locations, interconnections, interaction tests, instrumentation, and limits and procedures (normal and abnormal) for all the components of the primary coolant system.

Instruction: Major topics covered in the course are reactor coolant systems, pressurizer and pressure relief tank, pressurizer pressure instrumentation and pressure control, pressurizer level control, reactor coolant pumps, and steam generators and level control. Methods of instruction include lecture, classroom discussions, and classroom exercises.

Credit Recommendation: In the lower division baccalaureate/associate degree category, 2 semester hours in Nuclear Engineering Technology (8/86) (12/94).

Reactor Operator Systems: Rod Control

Location: Kewaunee Nuclear Training Center, WI.

Length: 59 hours (1.5 weeks).

Dates: January 1981-Present.

Objective: To provide a description and familiarization with the rod control system, rod position indications and the rod insertion limit, and temperature instrumentation.

Learning Outcome: Upon successful completion of this course, the student will be able to locate and describe the functions of rod control system, position indicators, and temperature instrumentation; and relate the system to technical specifications.

Instruction: Major topics covered in the course are the full length control rods, rod position indication, RCS temperature monitoring, and rod insertion limits. Methods of instruction include lectures, classroom discussions, classroom exercises, and on-the-job-training.

Credit Recommendation: In the lower division baccalaureate/associate degree category, 1 semester hour in Nuclear Engineering Technology (8/86) (12/94).

Reactor Operator Systems: Special Auxiliary Systems

Location: Kewaunee Nuclear Training Center, WI.

Length: 82 hours (4 weeks).

Dates: January 1981-Present.

Objective: To provide the student with instruction on the special auxiliary systems of a nuclear power plant as they apply to a reactor operator.

Learning Outcome: Upon successful completion of this course, the student will have an understanding of the special auxiliary systems of a nuclear power plant and relate these systems to technical specifications.

Instruction: Major topics covered in the course are auxiliary feedwater system, source water system, and refueling and spent fuel pool system. Methods of instruction include lectures, classroom discussions, classroom exercises, and on-the-job-training.

Credit Recommendation: In the lower division baccalaureate/associate degree category, 1 semester hour in Nuclear Engineering Technology (8/86) (12/94).

Senior Reactor Operator: Operational Administration

Location: Kewaunee Nuclear Training Center, WI.

Length: 98 hours (3 weeks).

Dates: January 1981-Present.

Objective: To provide in-depth knowledge of nuclear plant operational administration.

Learning Outcome: Upon successful completion of this course, the student will be able to describe the organizational responsibilities, supervisor responsibilities, and duties of plant personnel from plant manager to radiation protection personnel as outlined in the course description.

Instruction: Major topics covered in the course are supervisor training, plant organization, operations, reactor engineering and corporate engineering organization, maintenance and supply, chemistry, radiation, radiological protection, plant safety organization, plant emergencies, plant security, project and program control techniques, operational quality assurance program, regulatory requirements, and plant shutdown and special activities. Methods of instruction include lectures and self-study.

Credit Recommendation: In the upper division baccalaureate degree category, 3 semester hours in Nuclear Engineering or Management (8/86) (12/94).

Senior Reactor Operator: Plant Systems Review and Upgrade

Location: Kewaunee Nuclear Training Center, WI.

Length: 160 hours(4 weeks).

Dates: January 1981-Present.

Objective: To provide in-depth and integrated knowledge of all plant systems.

Learning Outcome: Upon successful completion of this course, the student will be able to describe, explain, and analyze the bases, design requirements, precautions, limitations, procedures, and technical specification implications of all plant systems.

Instruction: Major topics covered in the course are reactor core, rod control system, reactor primary coolant system, reactor emergency and auxiliary coolant systems, plant ventilation systems, special auxiliary systems, emergency diesel generator mechanical/electrical systems, integrated reactor protection and safety features, radiological and nonradiological waste disposal systems, radiation monitoring systems, plant secondary coolant and auxiliary systems, electrical generation and distribution systems, and fire emergencies. Methods of instruction include lectures, case studies, self-study, and simulator demonstrations.

Credit Recommendation: In the upper division baccalaureate degree category, 3 semester hours in Nuclear Engineering (8/86) (12/94).

Senior Reactor Operator: Simulator Training (Abnormal Operations)

Location: Kewaunee Nuclear Training Center, WI.

Length: 440 hours (11 weeks) in two separate course modules.

Dates: January 1991-Present.

Objective: To provide conceptual understanding of nuclear power plant design and operation and of abnormal/ emergency operating conditions, and understanding of interaction among various nuclear power plant operating systems.

Learning Outcome: Upon successful completion of this course, students will have technical, operational, and conceptual understanding of nuclear power plant operations and ability to diagnose and solve problems encountered in abnormal/ emergency nuclear power plant operation.

Instruction: Major topics covered in the course are performance of routine water power plant operation, response to selected abnormal events, and diagnosis and mitigation of nuclear power plant malfunctions. Methods of instruction include lecture, classroom discussions, and hands-on training using a simulator.

Credit Recommendation: In the upper division baccalaureate degree category, 5 semester hours in Nuclear Engineering Technology (12/86) (12/94).

Zaidner Institute

The Neve Yerushalayim College was founded in 1970 to offer women with a limited background in Jewish studies an intensive education with an appreciation of the Land of Israel and its history. Its subsequent development has seen the introduction of additional academic programs designed to meet the changing needs of contemporary Jewish women.

The Zaidner Institute, formerly known as Ma'alot Yerushalayim College, was established in Jerusalem in 1984 as an affiliate school of Neve Yerushalayim College. The institute provides a post-high school, college level, career-oriented education. The student body consists of young Jewish women with substantial prior Judaic and secular education, as well as women adult learners.

Zaidner's mission is to provide young women in Israel the opportunity of pursuing advanced Jewish studies, while at the same time, achieving a level of secular education enabling entry into the job markets of both Israel and the United States. Zaidner also seeks to meet the needs of adult women who must balance their desire for educationally valid study with family obligations.

At the time of its first class in 1984, Ma'alot offered courses in Computer Science and Business, in addition to Judaic Studies. From 1985, a fourth area of study, Education/Psychology, was offered. In 1995, a program in graphic arts was introduced. An integrated set of courses in Speech Pathology was made available in Fall 1996. These courses are designed to enable students to satisfy the prerequisites for admission to the University of North Texas graduate program in Speech Pathology which will be offered at Neve Yerushalayim College beginning with the Spring 1998 term.

Students matriculating to accredited institutions of higher learning have been able to receive college credits for some, if not all, of their Zaidner course work. Currently, students who choose to earn a college diploma may select from seven available tracks developed to articulate with degree programs offered through Thomas A. Edison State College of New Jersey. There are Baccalaureate degrees with specializations in: Art, Business Administration, Computer Science, Humanities, Liberal Studies, Psychology and Social Sciences.

For all courses taught at the Zaidner Institute, the hours listed are each a full 60 minutes of instruction, not the academic hour of 45-50 minutes.

Source of official student records: Registrar, Zaidner Institute, Neve Yerushalayim, P.O. Box 16020, Jerusalem, Israel.

Additional information about the courses: College Credit Recommendation Service, American Council on Education, One Dupont Circle, Washington, DC 20036-1193.

Abnormal Psychology (PSY 430)

Location: The Zaidner Institute, Neve Yerushalayim, Jerusalem.

Length: *Version 1:* 42 hours (14 weeks); *Version 2:* 39 hours (13 weeks).

Dates: *Version 1:* February 1992-January 1997; *Version 2:* February 1997-Present.

Objective: To introduce the student to the concept of normal vs. abnormal behavior and to understand its causes, manifestations, and treatment.

Learning Outcome: Upon successful completion of this course, the student will be able to understand historical perspectives toward abnormal behavior; be familiar with all the major DSM-IV classifications of abnormal behavior — their causes, manifestations, and treatment (neuroses, psychosomatic disorders, personality disorders, addictive disorders, psychoses, organic disorders, eating disorders, suicide, and developmental disorders of childhood); understand the psychoanalytic, environmental, behavioral, and humanistic theories about mental illness; and be familiar with the major forms of treatment available today.

Instruction: Major topics covered in the course are historical perspective, major psychiatric (DSM-IV) categories, causes and treatment, and three major therapeutic orientations: Psychoanalytical, Behavioral, and Humanistic. Methods of instruction include lecture and case study analysis.

Credit Recommendation: In the upper division baccalaureate degree category, 3 semester hours in Abnormal Psychology (12/91) (2/97). *Prerequisites:* Introduction to Psychology and Theories of Personality.

Accounting Theory (ACC 480)

Location: The Zaidner Institute, Neve Yerushalayim, Jerusalem.

Length: *Version 1:* 42 hours (14 weeks); *Version 2:* 39 hours (13 weeks).

Dates: *Version 1:* September 1991-January 1997; *Version 2:* February 1997-Present.

Objective: To give the student an understanding of the nature of the theoretical considerations that underpin generally accepted accounting principles (GAAP).

Learning Outcome: Upon successful completion of this course, the student will be able to understand the difficulties of measuring income and expense; understand the difficulties of valuation; and understand contemporary issues in accounting theory.

Instruction: Major topics covered in the course are consolidation; installment sales, interim reporting, bankruptcy — liquidation and reorganization; estates and trusts; earnings per share; and statement of cash flows. Methods of instruction include lecture and discussion.

Credit Recommendation: In the upper division baccalaureate degree category, 3 semester hours in Accounting Theory (12/91) (2/97).

Advanced Accounting I (ACC 460) (Formerly Advanced Accounting [ACC 460])

Location: The Zaidner Institute, Neve Yerushalayim, Jerusalem.

Length: *Version 1:* 42 hours (14 weeks); *Version 2:* 39 hours (13 weeks).

Dates: *Version 1:* September 1991-January 1997; *Version 2:* February 1997-Present.

Objective: To give the student an understanding of accounting principles and procedures of consolidated financial statements including purchase versus pooling method of consolidation and partnerships.

Learning Outcome: Upon successful completion of this course, the student will be able to identify and resolve contemporary accounting issues; account for consolidations using both the purchase and pooling method; discuss interpretative problems in consolidations; account for all phases of partnerships; and understand branch accounting.

Instruction: Major topics covered in the course are partnership organization and liquidations; branch accounting — inventories, interbranch billings; equity method of purchase accounting; consolidated statements; and pooling method. Methods of instruction include lecture and discussion.

Credit Recommendation: In the upper division baccalaureate degree category, 3 semester hours in Advanced Accounting I (12/91) (2/97).

Advanced COBOL (CMP 240)

Location: The Zaidner Institute, Neve Yerushalayim, Jerusalem.

Length: *Version 1:* 42 hours (14 weeks); *Version 2:* 39 hours (13 weeks).

Dates: *Version 1:* February 1985-January 1997; *Version 2:* February 1997-Present.

Objective: To teach the student the advanced concepts and various options of COBOL.

Learning Outcome: Upon successful completion of this course, the student will be able to successfully apply advanced topics in COBOL.

Instruction: Major topics covered in the course are tables, linear and binary searches, sorting, multiple record types, subroutines, control breaks, sequential file processing, indexed file processing, and menus and screen building. Methods of instruction include lectures, labs, examinations, and programs.

Credit Recommendation: In the upper division baccalaureate degree category, 3 semester hours in Advanced COBOL (12/91) (2/97). *Prerequisite:* COBOL.

Analysis of Hebrew Scriptures: Deuteronomy (REL 260)

Location: The Zaidner Institute, Neve Yerushalayim, Jerusalem.

Length: 39 hours (13 weeks).

Dates: September 1984-Present.

Objective: To examine the Book of Deuteronomy in the original Hebrew with the 11th century commentary of Rashi.

Learning Outcome: Upon successful completion of this course, the student will be able to articulate an in-depth understanding of the major religious and historical elements of the Book of Deuteronomy.

Instruction: Major topics covered in the course are Jewish creed declarations and their philosophical implications, the Decalogue, charity, Biblical poetry, and Moses' farewell oration. Methods of instruction include lecture, discussion, and textual analysis.

Credit Recommendation: In the lower division baccalaureate/associate degree category or in the upper division baccalaureate degree category, 3 semester hours in Analysis of Hebrew Scriptures: Deuteronomy, Religious Studies, or Hebraic/Judaic Studies (12/91) (2/97).

Analysis of Hebrew Scriptures: Exodus (REL 230)

Location: The Zaidner Institute, Neve Yerushalayim, Jerusalem.

Length: 39 hours (13 weeks).

Dates: September 1984-Present.

Objective: To examine the Book of Exodus in the original Hebrew with the 11th century commentary of Rashi.

Learning Outcome: Upon successful completion of this course, the student will be able to articulate an in-depth understanding of the major religious, historical, and legal elements of the Book of Exodus.

Instruction: Major topics covered in the course are enslavement and the redemption, Revelation, the Tabernacle, and laws of the festivals. Methods of instruction include lecture, discussion, and textual analysis.

Credit Recommendation: In the lower division baccalaureate/associate degree category or in the upper division baccalaureate degree category, 3 semester hours in Analysis of Hebrew Scriptures: Exodus, Religious Studies, or Hebraic/Judaic Studies (12/91) (2/97).

Analysis of Hebrew Scriptures: Genesis (REL 220)

Location: The Zaidner Institute, Neve Yerushalayim, Jerusalem.

Length: 39 hours (13 weeks).

Dates: September 1984-Present.

Objective: To examine the Book of Genesis in the original Hebrew with the 11th century commentary of Rashi.

Learning Outcome: Upon successful completion of this course, the student will be able to articulate an in-depth understanding of the major religious and historical elements of the Book of Genesis.

Instruction: Major topics covered in the course are account of creation, the Sabbath day, the nature of man, deluge and dispersion, the covenant with Abraham, and the patriarchs. Methods of instruction include lecture, discussion, and textual analysis.

Credit Recommendation: In the lower division baccalaureate/associate degree category or in the upper division baccalaureate degree category, 3 semester hours in Analysis of Hebrew Scriptures: Genesis, Religious Studies, or Hebraic/Judaic Studies (12/91) (2/97).

Analysis of Hebrew Scriptures: Leviticus (REL 240)

Location: The Zaidner Institute, Neve Yerushalayim, Jerusalem.

Length: 39 hours (13 weeks).

Dates: September 1984-Present.

Objective: To examine the Book of Leviticus in the original Hebrew with the 11th century commentary of Rashi.

Learning Outcome: Upon successful completion of this course, the student will be able to articulate an in-depth understanding of the major religious elements of the Book of Leviticus.

Instruction: Major topics covered in the course are sacrificial rite, rationale for sacrifices, identification of ritually pure and impure animals, ritual defilement, laws of sexual relationship, business and social behavior, and priestly code. Methods of instruction include lecture, discussion, and textual analysis.

Credit Recommendation: In the lower division baccalaureate/associate degree category or in the upper division baccalaureate degree category, 3 semester hours in Analysis of Hebrew Scriptures: Leviticus, Religious Studies, or Hebraic/Judaic Studies (12/91) (2/97).

Analysis of Hebrew Scriptures: Numbers (REL 250)

Location: The Zaidner Institute, Neve Yerushalayim, Jerusalem.

Length: 39 hours (13 weeks).

Dates: September 1984-Present.

Objective: To examine the Book of Numbers in the original Hebrew with the 11th century commentary of Rashi.

Learning Outcome: Upon successful completion of this course, the student will be able to articulate an in-depth understanding of the major religious and historical elements of the Book of Numbers.

Instruction: Major topics covered in the course are laws of vows, tithes and inheritance as well as narrative sections including the episodes of the spies, Korah's rebellion, and Balaam's curse/blessing. Methods of instruction include lecture, discussion, and textual analysis.

Credit Recommendation: In the lower division baccalaureate/associate degree category or in the upper division baccalaureate degree category, 3 semester hours in Analysis of Hebrew Scriptures: Numbers, Religious Studies, or Hebraic/Judaic Studies (12/91) (2/97).

Anatomical and Physiological Bases of Speech (SPS 401)

Location: The Zaidner Institute, Neve Yerushalayim, Jerusalem.

Length: 39 hours (13 weeks).

Dates: October 1996-Present.

Objective: To provide students with a working knowledge of the anatomical structure and physiological functioning of the human respiratory, phonatory, articulatory, and resonance systems.

Learning Outcome: Upon successful completion of this course, the student will be able to define and use relevant terminology and understand the anatomical structure and physiological functioning of the human respiratory system, phonatory system, and articulatory and resonance system.

Instruction: Major topic covered in the course is a study of the structure of the human body as it relates to the speech process. Methods of instruction include lecture and tests.

Credit Recommendation: In the upper division baccalaureate degree category, 3 semester hours in Speech and Hearing Science (2/97). *Prerequisite:* Introduction to Communication Disorders.

Assembly Language (CMP 160)

Location: The Zaidner Institute, Neve Yerushalayim, Jerusalem.

Length: *Version 1:* 42 hours (14 weeks); *Version 2:* 39 hours (13 weeks).

Dates: *Version 1:* February 1987-January 1997; *Version 2:* February 1997-Present.

Objective: To provide proficiency in Assembly Language Programming, as well as an insight into how the computer performs high level instruction by understanding the low level operations of which they consist.

Learning Outcome: Upon successful completion of this course, the student will be able to write an assembler source program using a standard editor; compile and correct errors; link the object code into an executable program; and execute the program directly or through the Debug facility.

Instruction: Major topics covered in the course are an introduction to number systems, a description of register sets, memory storage and addressing, the basic fetch-decode-execute cycle of a computer, and Assembly Language with emphasis on understanding the effect of each instruction. Methods of instruction include lecture, labs, examinations, and programs.

Credit Recommendation: In the lower division baccalaureate/associate degree category, 3 semester hours in Assembly Language or Computer Science elective (12/91) (2/97).

Audiology (SPS 410)

Location: The Zaidner Institute, Neve Yerushalayim, Jerusalem.

Length: 39 hours (13 weeks).

Dates: February 1997-Present.

Objective: To provide students with knowledge on the history of audiology and to familiarize them with the pathologies and etiologies of hearing loss. In addition, students will gain a working knowledge of pure tone audiometry, speech audiometry, and acoustic emmitance.

Learning Outcome: Upon successful completion of this course, the student will be able to identify types of hearing loss and know their etiology; perform pure tone hearing threshold screenings; interpret basic audiometric data and make appropriate referrals; and understand in depth the anatomical and physiological components of the hearing mechanism.

Instruction: Major topics covered in the course are anatomical and physiological aspects of the hearing mechanism, types of hearing losses and their etiologies, performance of pure tone hearing threshold screenings, and interpretation of audiometric data. Methods of instruction include lecture, examination, audiology labs, and supervisor observation.

Credit Recommendation: In the upper division baccalaureate degree category, 3 semester hours in Speech and Hearing Science (2/97). *Prerequisites:* Introduction to Communication Disorders and Speech and Hearing Science.

Auditing of Financial Statements (ACC 320)

Location: The Zaidner Institute, Neve Yerushalayim, Jerusalem.

Length: *Version 1:* 42 hours (14 weeks); *Version 2:* 39 hours (13 weeks).

Dates: *Version 1:* September 1991-January 1997; *Version 2:* February 1997-Present.

Objective: To give the student an understanding of the nature of the audit process and the procedures related to conducting an audit, with special reference to the role of the external auditor.

Learning Outcome: Upon successful completion of this course, the student will be able to conduct a review of internal control; prepare an audit work plan; prepare audit work papers; understand the nature of materiality; understand the nature of evidential matters; conduct and audit major balance sheet items; and understand the nature of auditing in the EDP environment.

Instruction: Major topics covered in the course are professional ethics, legal responsibilities, audit report, audit planning and analytical procedures, study of internal control, audit program, and audit sampling. Methods of instruction include lecture, discussion, and problem solving.

Credit Recommendation: In the upper division baccalaureate degree category, 3 semester hours in Auditing of Financial Statements or Auditing (12/91) (2/97).

Business and Society (BUS 420)

Location: The Zaidner Institute, Neve Yerushalayim, Jerusalem.

Length: *Version 1:* 42 hours (14 weeks); *Version 2:* 39 hours (13 weeks).

Dates: *Version 1:* September 1984-January 1997; *Version 2:* February 1997-Present.

Objective: To give the student an integrated approach to the complexities and trade-offs that exist when business organizations operate in an ambient society.

Learning Outcome: Upon successful completion of this course, the student will be able to reflect on the nature of doing business; identify values and expectations in the ambient culture; identify different sets of claims made on the business; identify the political and economic patterns of the society; arrive at a functional definition of ethical behavior; appreciate problems of trade-offs; reflect constructively on business ethics; and appreciate the need for corporate awareness.

Instruction: Major topics covered in the course are the corporation in society; government activity, regulation, policy, and politics; corporate responsibility and consumer protection; social impacts of science and technology; ecology, environment, and business; and global concerns. Methods of instruction include lecture and discussion.

Credit Recommendation: In the upper division baccalaureate degree category, 3 semester hours in Business and Society, Legal Environment of Business, or Business elective (12/91) (2/97).

Business Law I (BUS 330)

Location: The Zaidner Institute, Neve Yerushalayim, Jerusalem.

Length: *Version 1:* 42 hours (14 weeks); *Version 2:* 39 hours (13 weeks).

Dates: *Version 1:* September 1984-January 1997; *Version 2:* February 1997-Present.

Objective: To explore the nature and practice of the law as it applies to business transactions.

Learning Outcome: Upon successful completion of this course, the student will be able to appreciate the legal environment of business; recognize torts as they are encountered in business; recognize when a contract has been established; recognize duties under contracts; and know appropriate remedies for contractual breach.

Instruction: Major topics covered in the course are legal environment, torts, contract and criminal law, frauds, breach and remedy, intellectual property, computer law and computer crime, the legal environment of business, and a rigorous analysis of contract law. Methods of instruction include lecture and discussion.

Credit Recommendation: In the lower division baccalaureate/associate degree category or in the upper division baccalaureate degree category, 3 semester hours in Business Law I (12/91) (2/97).

Business Law II (BUS 340)

Location: The Zaidner Institute, Neve Yerushalayim, Jerusalem.

Length: *Version 1:* 42 hours (14 weeks); *Version 2:* 39 hours (13 weeks).

Dates: *Version 1:* September 1985-January 1997; *Version 2:* February 1997-Present.

Objective: To give the successful student an understanding of the nature and practice of the law as it applies to business transactions. The student is expected to gain a solid understanding of sales law, the UCC, warranties, product liability, commercial paper, partnership and corporation law, and other legal issues affecting the business world.

Learning Outcome: Upon successful completion of this course, the student will be able to understand the issuance of commercial paper; understand endorsement and holder in due course concepts; understand the legal duties of corporations; understand the formation and nature of partnerships; and know the law related to agency.

Instruction: Major topics covered in the course are sales law; the UCC; warranties; product liability; commercial paper; secured transactions; agency law; partnerships and corporations, directors, managers, and shareholders; and regulation, mergers, and acquisition. Methods of instruction include lecture, case study, and discussion.

Credit Recommendation: In the lower division baccalaureate/associate degree category or in the upper division baccalaureate degree category, 3 semester hours in Business Law II (12/91) (2/97).

Business Policy (BUS 470)

Location: The Zaidner Institute, Neve Yerushalayim, Jerusalem.

Length: *Version 1:* 42 hours (14 weeks); *Version 2:* 39 hours (13 weeks).

Dates: *Version 1:* January 1989-January 1997; *Version 2:* February 1997-Present.

Objective: To give the student an integrated approach to the strategic planning process, including the range of strategies open to the organization.

Learning Outcome: Upon successful completion of this course, the student will be able to identify corporate strengths and weaknesses; identify environmental opportunities and strengths; match internal and external factors; determine appropriate strategy options; develop a viable strategy; appreciate problems in organizational structure; appreciate problems of strategy implementation; identify resource requirements; and measure success of strategy choice.

Instruction: Major topics covered in the course are strategic planning; goals and mission; integrative strategies; functional area interrelationships; input and matching states and matrices; and goals, evaluation, and strategic planning processes. Methods of instruction include lecture, discussion, laboratory, cases, and projects.

Credit Recommendation: In the upper division baccalaureate degree category, 3 semester hours in Business Policy or Business Strategy (12/91) (2/97).

Calculus I (MAT 111)

Location: The Zaidner Institute, Neve Yerushalayim, Jerusalem.

Length: *Version 1:* 42 hours (14 weeks); *Version 2:* 39 hours (13 weeks).

Dates: *Version 1:* February 1988-January 1997; *Version 2:* February 1997-Present.

Objective: To offer to the student an introduction to calculus, in particular differential calculus. The course will provide the student with the ability to continue to integral calculus.

Learning Outcome: Upon successful completion of this course, the student will be able to understand limits; understand and apply concepts of derivatives; and understand the importance of core theories such as Rolle's Theorem, the Mean Value Theorem, etc.

Instruction: Major topics covered in the course are number systems, elements of analytical geometry, functions and function theory, limits, differentiation, and applications of derivatives. Methods of instruction include lectures, examinations, quizzes, and homework.

Credit Recommendation: In the lower division baccalaureate/associate degree category, 3 semester hours in Calculus I (12/91) (2/97).

Calculus II (MAT 112)

Location: The Zaidner Institute, Neve Yerushalayim, Jerusalem.

Length: *Version 1:* 42 hours (14 weeks); *Version 2:* 39 hours (13 weeks).

Dates: *Version 1:* February 1988-January 1997; *Version 2:* February 1997-Present.

Objective: To provide an understanding of integral calculus and its applications.

Learning Outcome: Upon successful completion of this course, the student will be able to understand and apply integration including definite integrals; understand limits; understand integration of logs, exponential functions, trigonometric functions, and hyperbolic functions; and integrate by parts.

Instruction: Major topics covered in the course are a continuation of Calculus I; antiderivatives; integration by u-substitution; areas as limits; the definite integral; area between two curves; volumes; length of plane curves; area of surface of revolution; logarithms and exponential functions; hyperbolic functions; first-order differential equations; inverse functions; inverse trigonometric and hyperbolic functions and their derivatives; integration by parts; and integration of powers of sine, cosine, secant, and tangent. Methods of instruction include lectures, examinations, quizzes, and homework.

Credit Recommendation: *Version 1:* In the lower division baccalaureate/associate degree category or in the upper division baccalaureate degree category (depending upon math background of students), 3 semester hours in Calculus II (12/91). *Version 2:* In the lower division baccalaureate/associate degree category, 3 semester hours in Calculus II (2/97). *Prerequisite:* Calculus I.

Calligraphy I (ART 210)

Location: The Zaidner Institute, Neve Yerushalayim, Jerusalem.

Length: 39 hours (13 weeks).

Dates: September 1995-Present.

Objective: To learn the fundamentals of Hebrew calligraphy with broad-edge pen; layout and design principles.

Learning Outcome: Upon successful completion of this course, the student will be able to take on elementary commissions in Hebrew lettering and carry them out.

Instruction: Major topics covered in the course are the fundamentals of Hebrew calligraphy, layout and design, the Dead Sea Scrolls and their scripts with developing a modern hand, and color theory and exercises. Methods of instruction include lecture, demonstration, and group critique, color exercise, and projects.

Credit Recommendation: In the lower division baccalaureate/associate degree category, 3 semester hours in Calligraphy I (2/97).

Calligraphy II (ART 211)

Location: The Zaidner Institute, Neve Yerushalayim, Jerusalem.

Length: 39 hours (13 weeks).

Dates: September 1995-Present.

Objective: To analyze historical scripts. Redeveloping towards modernization, more sophisticated design problems and solutions. In short to give the student the necessary tools to undertake original lettering commissions.

Learning Outcome: Upon successful completion of this course, the student will be able to carry out calligraphic commissions with a repertoire of scripts in both Hebrew and Latin alphabets; prepare material for printing and reproducing; and draw letter forms for use in logos, etc.

Instruction: Major topics covered in the course are a continuation of Calligraphy I: study of medieval Sephardi and Ashkenazi scripts, introduction to Roman and Italic, and experimental writing. Methods of instruction include lectures, demonstrations, and group critiques.

Credit Recommendation: In the upper division baccalaureate degree category, 3 semester hours in Calligraphy II (2/97). *Prerequisite:* Calligraphy I.

Clinical Methods and Observation in Speech and Language Pathology (SPS 490)

Location: The Zaidner Institute, Neve Yerushalayim, Jerusalem.

Length: 39 hours (13 weeks).

Dates: August 1996-Present.

Objective: To help students develop an understanding of, and experiential feeling for, the diagnostic and therapeutic process.

Learning Outcome: Upon successful completion of this course, the student will be able to present principles and elements of the diagnostic and therapeutic process; select target behaviors for remediation and demonstrate knowledge with regard to increasing and decreasing these target behaviors; understand the impact of cultural diversity upon the diagnostic and therapeutic process; and better appreciate diagnostic and therapeutic procedures through direct and video-taped observation.

Instruction: Major topics covered in the course are various types of clinical methods, evaluation and practices, actual remediation and evaluation coupled with treatment maintenance and selection of target behaviors, multi-cultural issues, knowledge of professional issues, and the ASHA code of ethics. Methods of instruction include lecture, examination, videotapes, labs, and student presentations.

Credit Recommendation: In the upper division baccalaureate degree category, 3 semester hours in Speech and Hearing Science (2/97). *Prerequisite:* Introduction to Communication Disorders.

COBOL (CMP 140)

Location: The Zaidner Institute, Neve Yerushalayim, Jerusalem.

Length: *Version 1:* 42 hours (14 weeks); *Version 2:* 39 hours (13 weeks).

Dates: *Version 1:* February 1985-January 1997; *Version 2:* February 1997-Present.

Objective: To teach students how to program in COBOL and to familiarize them with typical business applications.

Learning Outcome: Upon successful completion of this course, students will be able to code an efficient COBOL program and prepare reports compatible to specifications given to them.

Instruction: Major topics covered in the course are programming in COBOL language, program structure, data description, arithmetic operations, Input/Output operations, control structures (including Perform, GoTo), tables, searching, sorting, table look-ups, and editing reports. Methods of instruction include lectures, labs, examinations, and programs.

Credit Recommendation: In the lower division baccalaureate/associate degree category, 3 semester hours in COBOL (12/91) (2/97).

College Algebra (MAT 101)

Location: The Zaidner Institute, Neve Yerushalayim, Jerusalem.

Length: 39 hours (13 weeks).

Dates: December 1987-Present.

Objective: To provide students with algebra skills and problem solving skills.

Learning Outcome: Upon successful completion of this course, the student will be able to solve verbal problems algebraically; understand the real and complex number system; and graph linear equations and inequalities.

Instruction: Major topics covered in the course are algebraic expressions, real and complex numbers, equations and inequalities, algebraic and graphic solutions, and verbal applications. Method of instruction includes lecture.

Credit Recommendation: In the lower division baccalaureate/associate degree category, 3 semester hours in College Algebra or Mathematics (2/97).

Computer Graphics I (ART 240)

Location: The Zaidner Institute, Neve Yerushalayim, Jerusalem.

Length: 39 hours (13 weeks).

Dates: October 1995-Present.

Objective: To introduce the student to the basics of MAC computers and to achieve competence in the communication between the MAC and IBM systems. To obtain fluency in the Freehand 6.5 System.

Learning Outcome: Upon successful completion of this course, the student will be able to use the graphic programs of the computer competently and efficiently for their graphic needs; use the mouse and keyboard skillfully; gain a basic understanding of computers and concepts in computers; and develop almost unlimited creative options.

Instruction: Major topics covered in the course are how to produce lines, shapes and other graphics needs, and learn about the computer and its functions. Methods of instruction include lecture, practical assignments, and practical work.

Credit Recommendation: In the lower division baccalaureate/associate degree category, 4 semester hours in Computer Graphics I (2/97).

Computer Graphics II (ART 310)

Location: The Zaidner Institute, Neve Yerushalayim, Jerusalem.

Length: 39 hours (13 weeks).

Dates: February 1996-Present.

Objective: To allow for the student to develop skills in the application of image processing and painting using various computer programs, to enable them to perform those tasks essential to graphic design work.

Learning Outcome: Upon successful completion of this course, the student will be able to use PhotoShop for image editing and painting; understand the difference between various computerized graphics methods; understand image processing and color terminology; scan and create an image; and edit, enhance, and print or export it for use in other applications.

Instruction: Major topics covered in the course are computerized image editing and painting, the attainment of the correct terminology and skills to facilitate the processes of creating and scanning an image, and enhancing an image and its future printing and exporting. Methods of instruction include lecture and practical work.

Credit Recommendation: In the lower division baccalaureate/associate degree or in the upper division baccalaureate degree category category, 4 semester hours in Computer Graphics II (2/97).

Computer Graphics III (ART 320)

Location: The Zaidner Institute, Neve Yerushalayim, Jerusalem.

Length: 39 hours (13 weeks).

Dates: February 1996-Present.

Objective: To teach students the advanced study of layout application, enabling them to complete layout tasks within the realm of graphic design.

Learning Outcome: Upon successful completion of this course, the student will be able to use Quark Xpress for layout tasks such as creating a newspaper, brochure, book, or poster and understand layout terminology.

Instruction: Major topics covered in the course are computerized layout and its relevant applications and terminology and how to complete various layout tasks skillfully and creatively. Methods of instruction include lecture and lab.

Credit Recommendation: In the upper division baccalaureate degree category, 4 semester hours in Computer Graphics III (2/97).

Computer Graphics IV (ART 410)

Location: The Zaidner Institute, Neve Yerushalayim, Jerusalem.

Length: 39 hours (13 weeks).

Dates: October 1996-Present.

Objective: To instruct the student in a variety of multi-media creative applications in order to enable them to design multi-media projects for use in the field of graphics.

Learning Outcome: Upon successful completion of this course, the student will be able to use "director" to create a multimedia project by creating or importing objects; combine images to design a screen; and use timing.

Instruction: Major topics covered in the course are multi-media creation and processing and the application of text and image combinations using illustrations, annotations, video, and sound. Methods of instruction include lecture and lab.

Credit Recommendation: In the upper division baccalaureate degree category, 4 semester hours in Computer Graphics IV (2/97).

Computer Systems Architecture (CMP 380)

Location: The Zaidner Institute, Neve Yerushalayim, Jerusalem.

Length: *Version 1:* 42 hours (14 weeks); *Version 2:* 39 hours (13 weeks).

Dates: *Version 1:* February 1990-January 1997; *Version 2:* February 1997-Present.

Objective: To provide the students with an understanding of how computers function at the hardware level.

Learning Outcome: Upon successful completion of this course, the student will be able to understand the implementation of internal memory devices, methods of data transfer, microcoding, timing mechanisms, and the functioning of parallel processors.

Instruction: Major topics covered in the course are historical perspective, hardware technology, microprogramming, I/O devices, memory systems, and parallel machines. Methods of instruction include lectures, labs, examinations, and programs.

Credit Recommendation: In the upper division baccalaureate degree category, 3 semester hours in Computer Systems Architecture (12/91) (2/97).

Cost Accounting (ACC 201)

Location: The Zaidner Institute, Neve Yerushalayim, Jerusalem.

Length: *Version 1:* 42 hours (14 weeks); *Version 2:* 39 hours (13 weeks).

Dates: *Version 1:* January 1985-January 1997; *Version 2:* February 1997-Present.

Objective: To give the student an understanding of the nature and practice of the accumulation and presentation of costs in manufacturing industries, and to enable the student to generate budgets and report budget variance for management in a way that is meaningful to managers.

Learning Outcome: Upon successful completion of this course, the student will be able to differentiate between fixed and variable costs; describe cost behavior; use job costing techniques; use standard costing systems; determine variances from standard; design budgets; determine cost/volume relationships; be aware of behavioral aspects of cost determination; and be able to apply cost concepts to financial statements.

Instruction: Major topics covered in the course are fixed and variable cost; cost, volume, and price relationships; job costing systems; standard and variable costs; budgets and variances; cost accounting; and financial statement reporting. Methods of instruction include lecture, discussions, and problems.

Credit Recommendation: In the lower division baccalaureate/associate degree category or in the upper division baccalaureate degree category, 3 semester hours in Cost Accounting (12/91) (2/97).

Daniel (REL 450)

Location: The Zaidner Institute, Neve Yerushalayim, Jerusalem.

Length: 39 hours (13 weeks).

Dates: September 1984-Present.

Objective: To examine the Book of Daniel in the original Hebrew and Aramaic, with English translations and with the 11th century commentary of Rashi and other classical commentaries.

Learning Outcome: Upon successful completion of this course, the student will be able to articulate an in-depth understanding of the major religious, moral, and apocalyptic themes of the Book of Daniel.

Instruction: Major topics covered in the course are literary structure, language, and history of the book of Daniel; structures of history; apocalyptic revelations and their interpretations; redemption; theodicy; and eschatology. Methods of instruction include lecture, discussion, and textual analysis.

Credit Recommendation: In the upper division baccalaureate degree category, 3 semester hours in The Book of Daniel, Religious Studies elective, or Hebraic/Judaic Studies (12/91) (2/97).

Data Processing (CMP 201)

Location: The Zaidner Institute, Neve Yerushalayim, Jerusalem.

Length: *Version 1:* 42 hours (14 weeks); *Version 2:* 39 hours (13 weeks).

Dates: *Version 1:* September 1991-January 1997; *Version 2:* February 1997-Present.

Objective: To provide the students with an understanding of how companies and institutions use computers to process information and to gain meaningful output; the course takes an overall view of the data processing systems.

Learning Outcome: Upon successful completion of this course, the student will be able to understand computer and data processing terminology; gain an understanding of software and hardware systems; design records and files; and design input forms and output reports.

Instruction: Major topics covered in the course are the nature and utility of computers, explanations of basic hardware, explanations of basic software, design of data base, design of input forms, and design of output reports. Methods of instruction include lectures, examinations, and projects.

Credit Recommendation: In the lower division baccalaureate/associate degree

category, 3 semester hours in Data Processing (12/91) (2/97).

Data Structures (CMP 275)

Location: The Zaidner Institute, Neve Yerushalayim, Jerusalem.

Length: *Version 1:* 42 hours (14 weeks); *Version 2:* 39 hours (13 weeks).

Dates: *Version 1:* February 1987-January 1997; *Version 2:* February 1997-Present.

Objective: To give the student an understanding of the various abstract data structures and the means to implement them.

Learning Outcome: Upon successful completion of this course, the student will be able to understand what different data structures are, how they aid us in problem-solving, and how to actually create and use them in a program (included are queues, stacks, linked lists, circular lists, doubly-linked lists, binary trees, genealogical trees, and graphs).

Instruction: Major topics covered in the course are dynamic storage allocation, linked lists, recursion, stacks, queues, other list structures, binary trees, graphs, and sorting and searching methods. Methods of instruction include lectures, labs, examinations, and programs.

Credit Recommendation: In the lower division baccalaureate/associate degree category or in the upper division baccalaureate degree category, 3 semester hours in Data Structures or Computer Science elective (12/91) (2/97).

Database (CMP 440)

Location: The Zaidner Institute, Neve Yerushalayim, Jerusalem.

Length: *Version 1:* 42 hours (14 weeks); *Version 2:* 39 hours (13 weeks).

Dates: *Version 1:* February 1989-January 1997; *Version 2:* February 1997-Present.

Objective: *Version 1:* To provide the student with a general introduction of the concepts of databases, hands-on experience in developing a database. *Version 2:* To provide the student with a general introduction of the concepts of database management systems, relational database, and data warehousing.

Learning Outcome: *Version 1:* Upon successful completion of this course, the student will be able to demonstrate a thorough understanding of database systems; create indexed files; and design a working database system. *Version 2:* Upon successful completion of this course, the student will be able to understand the various kinds of databases and work with a database.

Instruction: *Version 1:* Major topics covered in the course are an introduction to databases (utilities, advantages, types of databases), construction of a simple database that allows users to structure database records, how to enter data into the records, and how to retrieve the information as desired. Methods of instruction include lectures, labs, examinations, and programs. *Version 2:* Major topics covered in the course are database concepts and definitions, physical organization, components of databases, data modeling, data normalization, data description and query languages, SQL, query processing, transaction processing, database integrity, database designs, C/S environment, and data warehousing. Methods of instruction include lecture, discussion, demonstration of hardware, and lab.

Credit Recommendation: *Version 1:* In the upper division baccalaureate degree category, 3 semester hours in Databases or Computer Science elective (12/91). *Version 2:* In the upper division baccalaureate degree category, 3 semester hours in Computer Science or Computer Informa-tion Systems elective (2/97).

Developmental Psychology I (PSY 210)

Location: The Zaidner Institute, Neve Yerushalayim, Jerusalem.

Length: *Version 1:* 42 hours (14 weeks); *Version 2:* 39 hours (13 weeks).

Dates: *Version 1:* September 1985-January 1997; *Version 2:* February 1997-Present.

Objective: To provide the student with an in-depth understanding of the growth and development of human beings from conception through middle childhood, focusing on physical, intellectual, emotional, and social components.

Learning Outcome: Upon successful completion of this course, the student will be able to understand the physiology of conception, prenatal development, and birth; have a working knowledge of Piaget's theory of cognitive development; apply Piaget's principles to develop a practical understanding of how children think and learn; be familiar with Erikson's theory of psychosocial development and be able to apply it to understanding human behavior; learn to recognize the various social and emotional states a child passes through from birth to adolescence; learn about the physical capabilities of neonates and the changes they undergo in the first year; learn about the concept of intelligence — what it is, how it is measured, and nature vs. nurture controversy; understand the role and importance of attachment in normal development; and comprehend the major types of abnormal development — autism, schizophrenia, mental retardation, depression, etc.

Instruction: Major topics covered in the course are theory and research on physical, mental, emotional, and social development from birth through mid-childhood; Erikson's stages of psychosocial development; language development; intellectual development; and Piaget's theory. Methods of instruction include lectures and individual projects.

Credit Recommendation: In the lower division baccalaureate/associate degree category, 3 semester hours in Child Developmental Psychology (12/91) (2/97). *Prerequisite:* Introduction to Psychology.

Developmental Psychology II (PSY 211)

Location: The Zaidner Institute, Neve Yerushalayim, Jerusalem.

Length: *Version 1:* 42 hours (14 weeks); *Version 2:* 39 hours (13 weeks).

Dates: *Version 1:* September 1991-January 1997; *Version 2:* February 1997-Present.

Objective: To give students an in-depth understanding of the physical, emotional, social, and intellectual changes one undergoes in adolescence, adulthood, and life span development.

Learning Outcome: Upon successful completion of this course, the student will be able to understand such factors in adolescence as a stormy period, physical and cognitive changes over the life span, Erikson's psychosocial stages 5-8, mid-life crises, death and dying, and Kubler-Ross stages.

Instruction: Major topics covered in the course are physical, cognitive, emotional, and social aspects of various stages of adult development; transition from child to adult; marriage; career; raising a family; growing old; and facing death. Methods of instruction include lectures, field observations, and projects.

Credit Recommendation: In the lower division baccalaureate/associate degree category, 3 semester hours in Adolescent and Adult Developmental Psychology (12/91) (2/97). *Co-requisite:* Introduction to Psychology and Developmental Psychology I.

Disorders of Articulation and Phonology (SPS402) (SPS 402)

Location: The Zaidner Institute, Neve Yerushalayim, Jerusalem.

Length: 39 hours (13 weeks).

Dates: February 1997-Present.

Objective: To provide an understanding of phonology, articulation and speech perception. In addition, the students will have a working knowledge of the various assessment procedures and intervention techniques.

Learning Outcome: Upon successful completion of this course, the student will be able to identify errors in the sound system and describe them in relation to speech sound segments, distinctive features, and phonological processes; understand the development of the sound system and phonology; describe various types of articulation tests and techniques for assessment; and discuss various approaches to treatment of articulation disorders.

Instruction: Major topics covered in the course are diagnostic and remediation procedures used with people who have articulation disorders, the overall sequence of acquisition of speech, and identification of errors in the sound system. Methods of instruction include lecture and examination.

Credit Recommendation: In the upper division baccalaureate degree category, 3 semester hours in Speech and Hearing Science (2/97). *Prerequisites:* Introduction to Communication Disorders and Phonetics.

Drawing I (ART 101)

Location: The Zaidner Institute, Neve Yerushalayim, Jerusalem.

Length: 39 hours (13 weeks).

Dates: October 1995-Present.

Objective: To develop the students' basic ability to draw correctly from nature in various black and white media to give them a fundamental understanding of the components of a successful illustration and the use of illustration on the printed page. The course will provide a groundwork from which students may continue to develop sophistication of style and expression of ideas.

Learning Outcome: Upon successful completion of this course, the student will be able to draw from observation in a variety of black-white media; understand the appropriateness of specific media and/or style of execution to the subject; compose a page that uses illustration with type; and understand basic elements of pictorial symbolism as it is used in illustration.

Instruction: Major topics covered in the course are a basic understanding of natural forms and light and shadow through drawing from observation with various black and white media, skills in basic concepts in illustration, symbolism of ideas, graphic impact, uses of images with type, use of works by old and contemporary masters of art, and contemporary illustrators as teaching devices. Methods of instruction include demonstration, discussion, studio practice, and critiques.

Credit Recommendation: In the lower division baccalaureate/associate degree category, 3 semester hours in Drawing I (2/97).

Drawing II (ART 102)

Location: The Zaidner Institute, Neve Yerushalayim, Jerusalem.

Length: 39 hours (13 weeks).

Dates: October 1995-Present.

Objective: To further develop the students' basic ability to draw correctly from nature in various black and white media to give them a fundamental understanding of the components of a successful illustration and the use of illustration on the printed page.

Learning Outcome: Upon successful completion of this course, the student will have a continued growth in skills and understanding following Drawing I.

Instruction: Major topics covered in the course are a deeper understanding of natural forms and light and shadow through drawing from observation with various black and white media, skills in deeper concepts in illustration, symbolism of ideas, graphic impact, uses of images with type, use of works by old and contemporary masters of art, and contemporary illustrators as teaching devices. Methods of instruction include demonstration, discussion, studio practice, and critiques.

Credit Recommendation: In the upper division baccalaureate degree category, 3 semester hours in Drawing II (2/97). *Prerequisite:* Drawing I.

English Composition I (ENG 101)

Location: The Zaidner Institute, Neve Yerushalayim, Jerusalem.

Length: *Version 1:* 42 hours (14 weeks); *Version 2:* 39 hours (13 weeks).

Dates: *Version 1:* February 1987-January 1997; *Version 2:* February 1997-Present.

Objective: To enable students to prepare correct and effective expository writing.

Learning Outcome: Upon successful completion of this course, the student will be able to display a proficiency in English written expression; demonstrate basic research techniques applicable for written material; and write objective-based essays and reports.

Instruction: Major topics covered in the course are correct and effective grammar of the English language, sentence structure, paragraph structure and types of expositional development, and the short essay a genre and as a prelude to the research essay. Methods of instruction include lecture, discussion, and responses to student writing.

Credit Recommendation: In the lower division baccalaureate/associate degree category, 3 semester hours in English Composition I (2/97).

English Composition II (ENG 102)

Location: The Zaidner Institute, Neve Yerushalayim, Jerusalem.

Length: *Version 1:* 42 hours (14 weeks); *Version 2:* 39 hours (13 weeks).

Dates: *Version 1:* February 1987-January 1997; *Version 2:* February 1997-Present.

Objective: To further develop students' skills in effective writing and to prepare them in good research paper techniques.

Learning Outcome: Upon successful completion of this course, the student will be able to display further proficiency in English written expression; utilize basic research paper techniques; cull essential information by accessing existing storage and retrieval (non-electronic) systems; and critically read professional literature.

Instruction: *Version 1:* Major topics covered in the course are the continued development of their proficiency in English expression and to use basic research paper techniques. Methods of instruction include writing assignments, short essays, and a research essay. *Version 2:* Major topics covered in the course are expository writing and basic techniques of the research paper. Methods of instruction include lecture, discussion, and responses to many written assignments including the staged development of a research project from decision upon topic, through note-taking, outlining, drafting, to final writing.

Credit Recommendation: In the lower division baccalaureate/associate degree category, 3 semester hours in English Composition II (2/97).

Esther (REL 255)

Location: The Zaidner Institute, Neve Yerushalayim, Jerusalem.

Length: 39 hours (13 weeks).

Dates: February 1997-Present.

Objective: To examine the Book of Esther in the original Hebrew text together with the commentary of Rashi; to explicate major themes as well as provide answers to questions of detail, sequence, and syntactical analysis; to review the Talmudic and Midrashic statements regarding the matter as a source for additional detail and amplification of the text; to refer to the commentary of Ibn Ezra for concomitant interpretation when necessary; and to study The Book of Esther narrative in light of its historical referents.

Learning Outcome: Upon successful completion of this course, the student will be able to correctly identify the authorship and sequence of events recorded in the Book of Esther; analyze the central philosophical and theological themes in the Book of Esther; and articulate the laws of Purim.

Instruction: Major topics covered in the course are a close reading of the Book of Esther focusing on its homiletic interpretation and the theological implications. Methods of instruction include lecture and discussion.

Credit Recommendation: In the lower division baccalaureate/associate degree category or in the upper division baccalaureate degree category, 3 semester hours in The Book of Esther, Religious Studies, or Hebraic/Judaic Studies (2/97).

Ethics of the Fathers (PHI 250)

Location: The Zaidner Institute, Neve Yerushalayim, Jerusalem.

Length: 39 hours (13 weeks).

Dates: October 1992-Present.

Objective: To examine the ethical, moral and theological teachings of the Mishnaic tract, Avot, utilizing various schools of interpretation.

Learning Outcome: Upon successful completion of this course, the student will be able to analyze the ethical, moral, and theological teachings represented in the Avot tract and the various interpretations reflected in the accompanying Avot commentaries.

Instruction: Major topics covered in the course are charity, altruism and selfishness, humility, asceticism, spirituality, judicial ethics, theodicy, and eschatology. Methods of instruction include lecture and discussion.

Credit Recommendation: In the lower division baccalaureate/associate degree category, 3 semester hours in Ethics of the Fathers, Religious Studies, or Philosophy (2/97).

Feminism and Jewish Perspectives on Women (REL 410)

Location: The Zaidner Institute, Neve Yerushalayim, Jerusalem.

Length: 39 hours (13 weeks).

Dates: September 1992-Present.

Objective: To examine major issues of feminism with an emphasis on the role of women in Jewish law and thought.

Learning Outcome: Upon successful completion of this course, the student will be able to articulate the underlying concerns motivating the broader feminist movement; understand the specific concerns felt by Jewish feminists seeking to reconcile their sense of independence with an authentic Jewish connection; and understand the feminist concerns as formulated in primary and secondary traditional sources.

Instruction: Major topics covered in the course are contemporary feminism, social position of women in the bible, historical perspectives, love, marriage, purity, motherhood and career, sexuality, divorce and widowhood, and women and ritual law. Methods of instruction include lecture and discussion.

Credit Recommendation: In the lower division baccalaureate/associate degree category or in the upper division baccalaureate degree category, 3 semester hours in Feminism and Jewish Perspectives on Women, Women's Studies, Religious Studies, or Judaic Studies (2/97).

File Management and Processing (CMP 340)

Location: The Zaidner Institute, Neve Yerushalayim, Jerusalem.

Length: *Version 1:* 42 hours (14 weeks); *Version 2:* 39 hours (13 weeks).

Dates: *Version 1:* February 1986-January 1997; *Version 2:* February 1997-Present.

Objective: To teach the student about the various types of files, their use, and how to work with them.

Learning Outcome: Upon successful completion of this course, the student will be able to decide which type of file is most suitable for an application and write programs using the files.

Instruction: Major topics covered in the course are sequential file processing — creation of files, adding, deleting, and updating records, merging two or more files, and searches in sorted and unsorted files; direct file processing; creation of files, adding, deleting, and updating records; and backup procedures, storage devices, ISAM, VSAM, relative files, inverted files, and familiarity with data bases. Methods of instruction include lectures, labs, examinations, and programs.

Credit Recommendation: In the upper division baccalaureate degree category, 3 semester hours in File Management and Processing or Computer Science elective (12/91) (2/97).

Financial Institutions and Markets (BUS 150)

Location: The Zaidner Institute, Neve Yerushalayim, Jerusalem.

Length: *Version 1:* 42 hours (14 weeks): *Version 2:* 39 hours (13 weeks).

Dates: *Version 1:* September 1987-January 1997; *Version 2:* February 1997-Present.

Objective: To give the successful student an understanding of the nature and practice of finance as it affects the corporate sector.

Learning Outcome: Upon successful completion of this course, the student will be able to understand the role of financial intermediation; appreciate risk; appreciate present and future value; understand the importance of capital structuring; appreciate the dynamics of debt financing; appreciate the dynamics of equity financing; and reflect on ethical behavior in the financial markets.

Instruction: Major topics covered in the course are U.S. financial institutions; short-term financial management; government and consumer financing; monetary, fiscal, and debt-managing policies. Methods of instruction include lecture and discussion.

Credit Recommendation: In the upper division baccalaureate degree category, 3 semester hours in Financial Institutions and Markets (12/91) (2/97). **NOTE:** This is an elective course in Finance not equivalent to Principles to Finance.

Fundamentals of Speech (COM 101)

Location: The Zaidner Institute, Neve Yerushalayim, Jerusalem.

Length: *Version 1:* 42 hours (14 weeks); *Version 2:* 39 hours (13 weeks).

Dates: November 1986-Present.

Objective: To enhance students' communication skills in the area of public speaking, emphasis is placed on practical situations that they are likely to face in employment or social interaction. Also, the course strives to develop skills in public speaking in an environment of controlled criticism.

Learning Outcome: Upon successful completion of this course, the students will be able to more effectively define and articulate the objective they seek to achieve by speaking; better evaluate the nature of the audience and its effect on basic types of speeches; compose a speech appropriate to achieve a given objective for a given audience; deliver a speech with greater confidence; appreciate the speeches of others and more precisely analyze the elements of their speeches; chair an informal business meeting; participate more constructively in informal business meetings; and recognize other forms and applications of oral communication (radio, television, etc.).

Instruction: Major topics covered in the course are principles of and obstacles to public communication, basic types of speeches, use of audiovisual aids, communication in meetings, interviewing techniques, print and audiovisual media, and role of criticism. Methods of instruction include lecture, discussion, student presentations and criticism, role-playing, and analysis of recorded speeches.

Credit Recommendation: In the lower division baccalaureate/associate degree category, 3 semester hours in Communication, Rhetoric, or Speech (12/91) (2/97).

Graphic Design I (ART 201)

Location: The Zaidner Institute, Neve Yerushalayim, Jerusalem.

Length: 39 hours (13 weeks).

Dates: November 1995-Present.

Objective: To explore the fundamentals of visual communication through the use of symbols and typography and to provide the student with the basic skills for further advancement in the area of graphic design.

Learning Outcome: Upon successful completion of this course, the student will be able to approach problem solving visually; develop conceptual skills; achieve a broad understanding of typography and its place in the design process; use typography in a creative and exciting manner; create an acute awareness of how design problems have been solved successfully by other graphic designers; and visually communicate intended message effectively.

Instruction: Major topics covered in the course are an introduction to typography and graphic design, knowledge of typefaces and their application in design, effective versus ineffective graphic communication, the relation of symbols to design problems, and the logic behind design solutions. A strong emphasis is placed on familiarity with current graphic design publications and how to examine carefully the transition from conceptualization to execution emphasizing concept rather than technique. Methods of instruction include studio practice, demonstration and discussion, and critiques.

Credit Recommendation: In the lower division baccalaureate/associate degree category, 3 semester hours in Graphic Design I (2/97).

Graphic Design II (ART 202)

Location: The Zaidner Institute, Neve Yerushalayim, Jerusalem.

Length: 39 hours (13 weeks).

Dates: November 1995-Present.

Objective: To explore the fundamentals of visual communication through the use of symbols and typography and to provide the student with the basic skills for further advancement in the area of graphic design.

Learning Outcome: Upon successful completion of this course, the student will be able to approach problem solving visually; develop conceptual skills; achieve a broad understanding of typography and its place in the design process; use typography in a creative and exciting manner; create an acute awareness of how design problems have been solved successfully by other graphic designers; and visually communicate intended message effectively.

Instruction: Major topics covered in the course are further application of skills learned in Graphic Design I and refinement of techniques in new areas of design. Methods of instruction include studio practice, demonstration and discussion, and critiques.

Credit Recommendation: In the upper division baccalaureate degree category, 3 semester hours in Graphic Design II (2/97). *Prerequisite:* Graphic Design I.

Group Dynamics (SOC 320)

Location: The Zaidner Institute, Neve Yerushalayim, Jerusalem.

Length: *Version 1:* 42 hours (14 weeks); *Version 2:* 39 hours (13 weeks).

Dates: *Version 1:* December 1991-January 1997; *Version 2:* February 1997-Present.

Objective: To provide an understanding of group processes and social skill development as group members or leaders.

Learning Outcome: Upon successful completion of this course, the student will be able to read, discuss, and understand a sample of the theoretically significant literature in group dynamics; discover general principles of group behavior concerning what conditions and factors produce what effects; and develop an appreciation and understanding of the applicability of principles of group dynamics to the functioning of groups and the experiences of group members.

Instruction: Major topics covered in the course are groups and group formation and development, emergent group structures, mediating group processes, interpersonal power within groups, status and role, group tasks and group goals, groups in action, effective participation in groups, and the physical environment of groups. Methods of instruction include lecture, discussion, observations of groups, and student reports.

Credit Recommendation: In the upper division baccalaureate degree category, 3 semester hours in Group Dynamics (12/91) (2/97). *Prerequisite:* Introduction to Sociology or Introduction to Psychology.

Intermediate Accounting I (ACC 301)

Location: The Zaidner Institute, Neve Yerushalayim, Jerusalem.

Length: 39 hours (13 weeks).

Dates: February 1997-Present.

Objective: To provide the student with a greater understanding of financial statement preparation and utilization.

Learning Outcome: Upon successful completion of this course, the student will be able to appreciate contemporary issues in financial statement preparation; understand issues in the preparation of financial statements; and appreciate specific issues in the balance sheet and income statement.

Instruction: Major topics covered in the course are elements of a financial statement packet, financial statements, issues related to cash, internal control, notes receivable, inventory system, acquisition of property, depreciation and depletion, intangibles, and generally accepted accounting principles and their consistent application in the collection and the presentation of financial information. Methods of instruction include lecture, discussion, and practice sets.

Credit Recommendation: In the lower division baccalaureate/associate degree category, 3 semester hours in Intermediate Accounting I (2/97).

Intermediate Accounting I (ACC 301) (ACC 302)
Intermediate Accounting II

Location: The Zaidner Institute, Neve Yerushalayim, Jerusalem.

Length: 50 hours (30 weeks).

Dates: January 1985-January 1997.

Objective: To teach the student to consolidate his or her prior learning in accounting, and to develop an ongoing awareness of the issues, complexities, and accepted alternatives within financial accounting.

Learning Outcome: Upon successful completion of this course, the student will be able to identify and resolve issues of accounting theory; present financial statements reflecting GAAP; account for changes in price level and exchange rate; and account for pensions and leases.

Instruction: Major topics covered in the course are statement of income and retained earnings (intraperiod tax allocation); statement of cash flows; time value of money; annuities; balance sheet analysis, accounting for current assets and current liabilities; accounting for bonds and long-term debt; corporate accounting: formation, contributed capital, dividends; and accounting for leases. Generally accepted accounting principles and their consistent application in the collection and the presentation of financial information are stressed. Methods of instruction include lecture, discussion, and practice sets.

Credit Recommendation: In the upper division baccalaureate degree category, 6 semester hours in Intermediate Accounting (12/91) (2/97). **NOTE:** Student may receive 3 hours of credit upon successful completion of Intermediate Accounting I.

Intermediate Accounting II (ACC 302)

Location: The Zaidner Institute, Neve Yerushalayim, Jerusalem.

Length: 39 hours (13 weeks).

Dates: February 1997-Present.

Objective: To teach students a greater understanding of financial statement preparation and utilization. This course is a continuation of Intermediate Accounting I.

Learning Outcome: Upon successful completion of this course, the student will be able to identify and resolve issues of accounting theory; present financial statements reflecting GAAP; account for changes in price level and exchange rate; and account for pensions and leases.

Instruction: Major topics covered in the course are current liabilities and contingencies, the corporation, classes of stock issued, earning per share calculations, investments, accounting for income taxes, accounting changes, statement of cash flow, basic analytical techniques in financial analysis, full disclosure issues in financial accounting, and generally accepted accounting principles and their consistent application in the collection and the presentation of financial information. Methods of instruction include lecture, discussion, and practice sets.

Credit Recommendation: In the lower division baccalaureate/associate degree category, 3 semester hours in Intermediate Accounting II (2/97). *Prerequisite:* Intermediate Accounting I.

International Business (BUS 440)

Location: The Zaidner Institute, Neve Yerushalayim, Jerusalem.

Length: *Version 1:* 42 hours (14 weeks); *Version 2:* 39 hours (13 weeks).

Dates: *Version 1:* September 1991-January 1997; *Version 2:* February 1997-Present.

Objective: *Version 1:* To give the student an integrated approach to the environments of international business and the operations of multinational enterprises. *Version 2:* To provide a broad approach to international business, with the objective of exposing students to the fullest possible range of issues on an introductory level, including physical, societal, economic and competitive factors which influence the objectives and operational decisions of small, mid-sized and large businesses seeking to expand operations beyond their domestic borders and/or to adjust their domestic operations in the face of increasing international competition at home.

Learning Outcome: *Version 1:* Upon successful completion of this course, the student will be able to identify elements of international environments; identify international opportunities and strengths; understand the elements of trade theory; identify the role of the multi-national enterprise; formulate currency exchange variables; appreciate problems in international management; appreciate problems of international market strategy; understand cultural difference in business settings; and evaluate significant components in international cases. *Version 2:* Upon successful completion of this course, the student will understand the means of conducting international business, with an emphasis on what makes international businesses different from domestic businesses; understand the effects of social systems within countries on the conduct of international businesses; understand the major theories explaining national and regional patterns of international businesses and the institutions influencing those activities; gain introduction to the financial exchange systems and institutions that measure and facilitate international transactions; and examine some of the management issues and concerns which arise within specific functional disciplines of business organizations when firms conduct operations in multi-national settings.

Instruction: *Version 1:* Major topics covered in the course are international business patterns and theories, financial risk assessment in an international context, currency exchange, international financial systems, trade and investment, political risk assessment, nation-state firm interactions, government policies and their influence on production and trade, international legal environments, cross-cultural management, motivation issues, corporate communication, and technology transfer. Methods of instruction include lecture, case study, and discussion. *Version 2:* Major topics covered in the course are a very broad approach to International Business and the physical, societal, economic, and competitive factors that influence corporate decision-making. Methods of instruction include lecture, extensive outside reading from business periodicals and journals linking theory and techniques discussed in class to real world of business, and introduction to the case method.

Credit Recommendation: *Versions 1 and 2:* In the upper division baccalaureate degree category, 3 semester hours in International Business (12/91) (2/97).

Introduction to Communication Disorders (SPS 110)

Location: The Zaidner Institute, Neve Yerushalayim, Jerusalem.

Length: 39 hours (13 weeks).

Dates: August 1996-Present.

Objective: To provide an overview of speech, language and hearing disorders in children and adults by introducing students to the physical mechanisms of communication and to the identification and treatment of communication disorders.

Learning Outcome: Upon successful completion of this course, the student will be able to understand basic speech, language and hearing disorders in children and adults, and how they pertain to the speech and language pathologist.

Instruction: Major topics covered in the course are an introduction to the common types of communication disorders including the various disorders of hearing, articulation, language, voice, and fluency juxtaposed against normal speech and language development. Methods of instruction include lecture, tests, videos, student presentations, and lab work.

Credit Recommendation: In the lower division baccalaureate/associate degree category, 3 semester hours in Speech and Hearing Science (2/97).

Introduction to Computers (CMP 101)

Location: The Zaidner Institute, Neve Yerushalayim, Jerusalem.

Length: *Version 1:* 42 hours (14 weeks); *Version 2:* 39 hours (13 weeks).

Dates: *Version 1:* September 1987-January 1997; *Version 2:* February 1997-Present.

Objective: To introduce the elementary programming concepts to the student and develop proficiency in programming in BASIC.

Learning Outcome: Upon successful completion of this course, the student will be able to analyze a problem, write an algorithm for it, and code its solution in BASIC; debug and thoroughly test the program; and decide which sort or search methods are most efficient for a particular case and implement the methods.

Instruction: Major topics covered in the course are processing numeric and character information, debugging and testing (verification) of programs, program structure, arithmetic operations, looping, input/output operations, arrays, subroutines, character string manipulation, and sorting and searching. Methods of instruction include lectures, lab, examinations, and programs.

Credit Recommendation: In the lower division baccalaureate/associate degree category, 3 semester hours in Computer Science or as a Computer Science elective (12/91) (2/97).

Introduction to Counseling (PSY 250)

Location: The Zaidner Institute, Neve Yerushalayim, Jerusalem.

Length: *Version 1:* 42 hours (14 weeks); *Version 2:* 39 hours (13 weeks).

Dates: *Version 1:* September 1991-January 1997; *Version 2:* February 1997-Present.

Objective: To provide an introduction to the dynamics of the counseling relationship.

Learning Outcome: Upon successful completion of this course, the student will be able to define and structure the counseling situation; identify the elements of effective helping; conduct initial, fact-finding interviews for a mental-status examination; use the Carkhuff model of helping and problem-solving; understand the effective use of self in the counseling process; understand Roger's theory of counseling; use specific skills that facilitate good communication; and deal with hostile and resistant clients.

Instruction: Major topics covered in the course are the nature of helping relationships, goals in counseling, counseling skills and techniques, ethics in counseling, and the necessary components of effective helping in a theoretical as well as a practical framework. Methods of instruction include lecture, role play, and video.

Credit Recommendation: In the upper division baccalaureate degree category, 3 semester hours in Introduction to Counseling (12/91) (2/97). *Prerequisite:* Introduction to Psychology. Theories of Personality is suggested.

Introduction to Jewish Philosophy (PHI 385)

Location: The Zaidner Institute, Neve Yerushalayim, Jerusalem.

Length: 39 hours (13 weeks).

Dates: September 1984-Present.

Objective: To examine and analyze the major philosophical/theological issues in medieval Jewish thought from a variety of conceptual perspectives.

Learning Outcome: Upon successful completion of this course, the student will be able to analyze the central questions underlying each issue and their broader conceptual implications; analyze the dialectic subtleties separating diverse positions and their identification with larger schools of opposing ideological thought; and analyze the Hebrew text of selected readings drawn from the medieval philosophic/theological literature.

Instruction: Major topics covered in the course are free will, Divine Providence, eschatology, philosophy of Mitzvot, faith and reason, and prophecy and existence of God. Methods of instruction include lecture, discussion, and textual analysis.

Credit Recommendation: In the lower division baccalaureate/associate degree category, 3 semester hours in Introduction to Jewish Philosophy or Liberal Arts elective (12/91) (2/97).

Introduction to Linguistics (LAN 410)

Location: The Zaidner Institute, Neve Yerushalayim, Jerusalem.

Length: *Version 1:* 42 hours (14 weeks); *Version 2:* 39 hours (13 weeks).

Dates: *Version 1:* February 1991-December 1996; *Version 2:* January 1997-Present.

Objective: To give students an overview of the field of linguistics past and present (its history; development, current challenges and the methodology used to meet them); and to impart to students the basic concepts, terminology, and interesting nature of the field, in order to facilitate their desire and ability to continue to read independently on the subject after course completion.

Learning Outcome: Upon successful completion of this course, the student will be able to comprehend and apply linguistic theory relevant to their niche (e.g., teaching English as a second language); interpret phonetic transcription currently used in dictionaries and encyclopedias; understand past and current research in the field; value the relevance of applied linguistics and psycholinguistics; benefit from following the progress in identification of issues in language acquisition and bilingualism, which will have been sharply defined; and appreciate the linguistic environment in Israel and its special problems and challenges.

Instruction: Major topics covered in the course are conceptualization of linguistics, morphology and phonology, semantics, syntax, sentences and transformational grammar, language acquisition, bilingualism, sociolinguistics and psycholinguistics, and linguistics and modern Hebrew. Methods of instruction include lecture, discussion, audio-visual presentations, student projects, critical review of journal articles, and examinations.

Credit Recommendation: *Version 1:* In the upper division baccalaureate degree category, 3 semester hours in Linguistics, Speech and Hearing, or Communication (12/91). *Version 2:* In the lower division baccalaureate/associate degree category, 3 semester hours in Linguistics, Speech and Hearing, or Communication (2/97).

Introduction to Marketing (BUS 360)

Location: The Zaidner Institute, Neve Yerushalayim, Jerusalem.

Length: *Version 1:* 42 hours (14 weeks); *Version 2:* 39 hours (13 weeks).

Dates: *Version 1:* January 1988-January 1997; *Version 2:* February 1997-Present.

Objective: To give the student an understanding of the nature and practice of marketing within the business organization and the larger societal environment.

Learning Outcome: Upon successful completion of this course, the student will be able to appreciate the marketing concept; determine marketing segments, targets, and positioning; determine an optimal marketing mix; appreciate brand decisions; understand institutional marketing considerations; understand the significance of marketing channels; understand advertising and public relations; and recognize the social/consumer interest in marketing.

Instruction: Major topics covered in the course are the marketing role; management imperatives; marketing's role in the firms' strategic planning; forecasting, market structure, and segmentation; targeting, market segments, and product positioning; branding, packaging, advertising, and promotion; and pricing and distribution channels. Methods of instruction include discussion, lecture, and case studies.

Credit Recommendation: In the upper division baccalaureate degree category, 3 semester hours in Introduction to Marketing (12/91) (2/97).

Introduction to Psychology (PSY 101)

Location: The Zaidner Institute, Neve Yerushalayim, Jerusalem.

Length: *Version 1:* 42 hours (14 weeks); *Version 2:* 39 hours (13 weeks).

Dates: *Version 1:* September 1985-January 1997; *Version 2:* February 1997-Present.

Objective: To provide an overview of the various theories, methods, and fields of basic and applied psychology.

Learning Outcome: Upon successful completion of this course, the student will be able to demonstrate familiarity with biological and physiological influences on psychology (sensation and perception) and with major personality theories, mental health/illness, and social influences upon people.

Instruction: Major topics covered in the course are biological bases of behavior, human intellect, personality, mental health, psychodevelopment, and social psychology. Method of instruction includes lecture.

Credit Recommendation: In the lower division baccalaureate/associate degree category, 3 semester hours in Introduction to Psychology or Principles of Psychology (12/91) (2/97).

Introduction to Sociology (SOC 101)

Location: The Zaidner Institute, Neve Yerushalayim, Jerusalem.

Length: *Version 1:* 42 hours (14 weeks); *Version 2:* 39 hours (13 weeks).

Dates: *Version 1:* December 1987-January 1997; *Version 2:* February 1997-Present.

Objective: To present basic sociological concepts and methods through understandable definitions and contemporary examples and to familiarize students with the main theoretical approaches, enabling them to use sociological theories and concepts in evaluating human interactions and institutions.

Learning Outcome: Upon successful completion of this course, the student will be able to contrast the sociological perspective with that of other social science disciplines; explain the sociological processes of social organization, socialization, conformity and deviance, social stratification, bureaucratization, discrimination, collective behavior, and social change; understand and apply sociological theories and methods; and identify the critical social institutions of human societies and describe their functions, patterns of organization, and differential treatment of individuals and groups.

Instruction: Major topics covered in the course are the nature and perspectives of sociology; methods of sociological research; organization of social life; socialization; groups; social stratification; deviance and social control; racial and cultural minorities; formal organizations; collective behavior and social movements; role, position, and identity; and social change. Methods of instruction include lecture, discussion, exercises, and presentations.

Credit Recommendation: In the lower division baccalaureate/associate degree category, 3 semester hours in Introduction to Sociology (12/91) (2/97).

Introduction to Statistics (MAT 201)

Location: The Zaidner Institute, Neve Yerushalayim, Jerusalem.

Length: *Version 1:* 42 hours (14 weeks); *Version 2:* 39 hours (13 weeks).

Dates: *Version 1:* February 1985-January 1997; *Version 2:* February 1997-Present.

Objective: To give the student an appreciation of statistical methods and techniques and the ability to use these methods in varied business data contexts.

Learning Outcome: Upon successful completion of this course, the student will be able to describe a given data set in statistical terms; calculate all standard statistical parameters; use simple probability notions; handle normal distribution problems; appreciate the techniques of comparative statistics; identify problems requiring advanced statistics; and convey statistical information to decision-makers.

Instruction: Major topics covered in the course are measurement scales, sources of data, descriptive statistics, data display, univariate measure of location and variability, basic probability, normal curve and applications, correlation and regression, inferential statistics, probability theory, binomial distribution, and parametric and nonparametric tests of significant difference. Methods of instruction include lectures, analytic lab, examinations, and presentations.

Credit Recommendation: In the lower division baccalaureate/associate degree category or in the upper division baccalaureate degree category, 3 semester hours in Statistics (12/91) (2/97).

Jewish Philosophy: Interpersonal Relationships (PHI 380)

Location: The Zaidner Institute, Neve Yerushalayim, Jerusalem.

Length: 39 hours (13 weeks).

Dates: September 1984-Present.

Objective: To examine and analyze the biblical and rabbinic perspectives on the ethico-legal dynamic of interpersonal relations.

Learning Outcome: Upon successful completion of this course, the student will be able to demonstrate an understanding of the substance of the ethico-legal teachings addressing the interpersonal dynamic and the Hebrew linguistic and literary elements characteristic of the relevant biblical and rabbinic text materials.

Instruction: Major topics covered in the course are examining issues of hatred, reproof, revenge, cynical and deceptive abuse, friendship, greed, and charity. Methods of instruction include lecture, discussion, and textual analysis.

Credit Recommendation: In the lower division baccalaureate/associate degree category or in the upper division baccalaureate degree category, 3 semester hours in Jewish Philosophy: Interpersonal Relationships or Hebraic/Judaic Studies elective (12/91) (2/97).

Job (REL 355)

Location: The Zaidner Institute, Neve Yerushalayim, Jerusalem.

Length: 39 hours (13 weeks).

Dates: September 1984-Present.

Objective: To examine the Book of Job in the original Hebrew with the 11th century commentary of Rashi and other classical commentaries.

Learning Outcome: Upon successful completion of this course, the student will be able to articulate an in-depth understanding of the major religious and moral elements of the Book of Job, in particular biblical theodicy.

Instruction: Major topics covered in the course are Job as a literary figure — allegory and history; Theodicy in its Biblical and post-Biblical perspectives; a Just God and the problem of Evil; classical commentaries from Job; and God and Man — reaching out and response. Methods of instruction include lecture, discussion, and textual analysis.

Credit Recommendation: In the upper division baccalaureate degree category, 3 semester hours in The Book of Job, Religious Studies elective, or Hebraic/Judaic Studies (12/91) (2/97).

Jonah (REL 270)

Location: The Zaidner Institute, Neve Yerushalayim, Jerusalem.

Length: 39 hours (13 weeks).

Dates: September 1992-Present.

Objective: To examine the original Hebrew text of the Book of Jonah, its narrative motifs and its social, ethical and theological messages from a variety of interpretive perspectives.

Learning Outcome: Upon successful completion of this course, the student will be able to demonstrate an understanding of the linguistic and literary elements in the Book of Jonah; demonstrate an understanding of the social, ethical, and theological concepts; and demonstrate an understanding of the various Talmudic, midrashic, and exegetical interpretations.

Instruction: Major topics covered in the course are the historical Jonah literary structure, the prophet's mission, and universalism. Methods of instruction include lecture and discussion.

Credit Recommendation: In the lower division baccalaureate/associate degree category or in the upper division baccalaureate degree category, 3 semester hours in The Book of Jonah, Religious Studies, or Hebraic/Judaic Studies (2/97).

Language Disorders (SPS 420)

Location: The Zaidner Institute, Neve Yerushalayim, Jerusalem.

Length: 39 hours (13 weeks).

Dates: February 1997-Present.

Objective: To provide the student with an understanding and working knowledge of the assessment and intervention strategies used for a language-disordered population.

Learning Outcome: Upon successful completion of this course, the student will be able to identify and utilize normal language theories in assessment and therapeutic procedures; identify language disorders by their characteristics and classify language disorders by using differential diagnosis; and interpret basic diagnostic data to develop appropriate therapeutic goals.

Instruction: Major topic covered in the course is the exploration of assessment and intervention strategies and procedures used with a language-disordered population. Methods of instruction include lecture and examination.

Credit Recommendation: In the upper division baccalaureate degree category, 3 semester hours in Speech and Hearing Science (2/97). *Prerequisites:* Introduction to Communication Disorders and Normal Speech and Language Development.

Linear Algebra (MAT 221)

Location: The Zaidner Institute, Neve Yerushalayim, Jerusalem.

Length: *Version 1:* 42 hours (14 weeks); *Version 2:* 39 hours (13 weeks).

Dates: *Version 1:* September 1991-January 1997; *Version 2:* February 1997-Present.

Objective: To teach the student linear algebra and to expand the student's theoretical background in linear systems and linear operators to facilitate education in future courses such as differential equations, numerical analysis, and linear programming.

Learning Outcome: Upon successful completion of this course, the student will be able to understand vectors and vector spaces; solve systems of linear equations; perform multiplication of matrices and inverse matrices; solve equations involving matrices; understand determinants, minors, cofactors, classical adjoints, eigenvalues, and eigenvectors of matrices; understand the Cayley-Hamilton Theorem, canonical form of matrices, and invariant subspaces; and use inner products to compute norms.

Instruction: Major topics covered in the course are vectors, linear equations and systems of linear equations, matrices, vector spaces, basis and dimension, linear transformations, determinants, eigenvalues and eigenvectors, characteristic equation, canonical forms, diagonalization, invariant subspaces, linear functionals, and inner product spaces. Methods of instruction include lectures, examinations, quizzes, and homework.

Credit Recommendation: In the upper division baccalaureate degree category, 3 semester hours in Linear Algebra (12/91) (2/97).

Literature and History of the Mussar Movement (REL 340)

Location: The Zaidner Institute, Neve Yerushalayim, Jerusalem.

Length: 39 hours (13 weeks).

Dates: September 1984-Present.

Objective: To examine the historical context, central personalities, and ideological and methodological principles of the Mussar movement.

Learning Outcome: Upon successful completion of this course, the student will be able to demonstrate a knowledge of the historical and cultural setting in which the Mussar movement arose and of the central Mussar figures and their ideological and pedagogical profiles.

Instruction: Major topics covered in the course are the nineteenth century Jewish cultural climate, biographies of major Mussar figures, analysis of the ethical system, and ideology and methodology of major Mussar figures. Methods of instruction include lecture and discussion.

Credit Recommendation: In the upper division baccalaureate degree category, 3 semester hours in Literature and History of the Mussar Movement, Religious Studies elective, or Hebraic/Judaic Studies (12/91) (2/97).

Macroeconomics (BUS 260)

Location: The Zaidner Institute, Neve Yerushalayim, Jerusalem.

Length: *Version 1:* 42 hours (14 weeks); *Version 2:* 39 hours (13 weeks).

Dates: *Version 1:* September 1985-January 1997; *Version 2:* February 1997-Present.

Objective: To give the student an understanding of the nature of macroeconomics theory as applied to economic output, price levels, and unemployment.

Learning Outcome: Upon successful completion of this course, the student will be able to appreciate the circular flows in economic environments; understand the history and nature of macroeconomics; understand the means of determining economic outputs; appreciate the role of government and fiscal policy; understand the banking system and monetary policy; relate to the issues of unemployment; relate to the issues of inflation; and appreciate the interrelation between economic and political considerations.

Instruction: Major topics covered in the course are macroelements of supply and demand; measuring national output; consumption and investment; government fiscal and monetary policy (FRB); income distribution and wealth; and inflation and unemployment. Methods of instruction include lecture, discussion, case studies, and presentations.

Credit Recommendation: In the lower division baccalaureate/associate degree category, 3 semester hours in Principles of Macroeconomics (12/91) (2/97).

Managerial Finance (BUS 350)

Location: The Zaidner Institute, Neve Yerushalayim, Jerusalem.

Length: *Version 1:* 42 hours (14 weeks); *Version 2:* 39 hours (13 weeks).

Dates: *Version 1:* January 1992-January 1997; *Version 2:* February 1997-Present.

Objective: To provide students with the theoretical and practical problem-solving skills used in the major functions of business finance.

Learning Outcome: Upon successful completion of this course, the student will be able to understand and apply a variety of quantitative and nonquantitative concepts in financial management situations, including present value, net present value, discounted cash flow analysis, internal rate of return, the portfolio theory of risk assessment, the capital asset pricing model, and the cost of capital.

Instruction: Major topics covered in the course are the concepts and tools used in business financial decision-making; valuation, capital budgeting, risk analysis, corporate structuring, and short- and long-term business financing and cash management; introduction to corporate finance; the time value of money; valuation of bonds; valuation of stocks; deriving cash flows in capital budgets; capital budgeting and risk; capital structure; leverage; financial statements; financial forecasting; managing current assets; long-term financing statements; financial forecasting; managing current assets; long-term financing; and special topics. Methods of instruction include lecture and problem-solving.

Credit Recommendation: In the upper division baccalaureate degree category, 3 semester hours in Managerial Finance or Principles of Finance (1/92) (2/97).

Megillot I: Ruth, Esther (REL 265)

Location: The Zaidner Institute, Neve Yerushalayim, Jerusalem.

Length: 50 hours (30 weeks).

Dates: September 1984-January 1997.

Objective: To provide the student with the knowledge of the Books of Ruth and Esther in the original Hebrew with the 11th century commentary of Rashi and other classical commentaries.

Learning Outcome: Upon successful completion of this course, the student will be able to articulate an in-depth understanding of the major religious and historical elements of the Books of Ruth and Esther.

Instruction: Major topics covered in the course are religious conversion in the Bible, Levirate marriage, the meta-historical implications of the Book of Ruth, historical and religious context of the story of Esther, analysis of Biblical narrative, legal implications of the Book of Esther, and Divine Providence in human affairs. Methods of instruction include lecture, discussion, and textual analysis.

Credit Recommendation: In the lower division baccalaureate/associate degree category or in the upper division baccalaureate degree category, 3 semester hours in The Book of Ruth and The Book of Esther, Religious Studies elective, or Hebraic/Judaic Studies (12/91) (2/97).

Megillot II: Song of Songs, Ecclesiastes, Lamentations (REL 365)

Location: The Zaidner Institute, Neve Yerushalayim, Jerusalem.

Length: 39 hours (13 weeks).

Dates: September 1984-Present.

Objective: To examine the Books of Song of Songs, Ecclesiastes, and Lamentations in the original Hebrew with the 11th century commentary of Rashi and other classical commentaries.

Learning Outcome: Upon successful completion of this course, the student will be able to articulate an understanding of the major religious, literary, and moral symbolic elements of the Books of Song of Songs, Ecclesiastics, and Lamentations.

Instruction: Major topics covered in the course are Song of Songs — issues of authorship, literary issues (allegorical interpretation, structure, and style); Ecclesiastics — authorship, canonic issues, wisdom, wisdom literature, pessimism, and optimism; Lamentations — historical context; the role of Jerusalem; and Theodicy. Methods of instruction include lecture, discussion, and textual analysis.

Credit Recommendation: In the lower division baccalaureate/associate degree category or in the upper division baccalaureate degree category, 3 semester hours in Song of Songs, Ecclesiastes, Lamentations, Religious Studies elective, or Hebraic/Judaic Studies (12/91) (2/97).

Methods of Biblical Analysis (REL 480)

Location: The Zaidner Institute, Neve Yerushalayim, Jerusalem.

Length: 39 hours (13 weeks).

Dates: September 1984-Present.

Objective: To examine selected moral/legal/religious motifs, derived from the text of the Pentateuch through a variety of hermeneutical/exegetical methodologies.

Learning Outcome: Upon successful completion of this course, the student will be able to articulate an understanding of various classical exegetical approaches to the Bible; articulate the moral, legal, and religious implications of exegetical insights; and demonstrate skills in Biblical research.

Instruction: Major topics covered in the course are analysis of exegetical approaches to parallels in Biblical literature, the 13 hermeneutical principles, exegetical approaches to identifying Biblical commandments, and classical Biblical translations and their exegetical implications. Methods of instruction include lecture, discussion, textual preparation and analysis, and independent research.

Credit Recommendation: In the upper division baccalaureate degree category, 3 semester hours in Methods of Biblical Analysis or elective in Hebraic/Judaic Studies (12/91) (2/97).

Microeconomics (BUS 250)

Location: The Zaidner Institute, Neve Yerushalayim, Jerusalem.

Length: *Version 1:* 42 hours (14 weeks); *Version 2:* 39 hours (13 weeks).

Dates: *Version 1:* September 1985-January 1997; *Version 2:* February 1997-Present.

Objective: To give the successful student an understanding of the nature and practice of the function of the market, price, production, and the economic behavior of the firm.

Learning Outcome: Upon successful completion of this course, the student will be able to understand utility and demand theory; analyze cost; recognize imperfect competition in the market place; understand the firm and the labor market; understand the role of government in the markets; and appreciate the elements of international trade.

Instruction: Major topics covered in the course are output and price and supply and demand; theories of utility and demand; production cost analysis and marginal products, marginal costs; pricing input factors: land, resources, wages, salaries, and the labor market; competition — perfect and imperfect, oligopoly, monopoly, regulation, and antitrust policy; and government policy and public choice, economic growth, and international trade. Methods of instruction include lecture and discussion.

Credit Recommendation: In the lower division baccalaureate/associate degree category, 3 semester hours in Microeconomics (12/91) (2/97).

Midrashic and Aggadic Literature (REL 440)

Location: The Zaidner Institute, Neve Yerushalayim, Jerusalem.

Length: 39 hours (13 weeks).

Dates: September 1984-Present.

Objective: To enable the student to examine the distinctive characteristics of midrashic literature.

Learning Outcome: Upon successful completion of this course, the student will be able to demonstrate an understanding of linguistic and literary elements of midrashic literature and identify various midrashic types and historical approaches to the interpretation of aggadah and midrash.

Instruction: Major topics covered in the course are attitudes toward midrashic and aggadic literature, literary forms in aggadic literature, rabbinic theology as reflected in the midrash, esotericism and exotericism in aggadic literature, and a survey of major works of aggadic literature. Methods of instruction include lecture and discussion.

Credit Recommendation: In the lower division baccalaureate/associate degree category or in the upper division baccalaureate degree category, 3 semester hours in Midrashic and Aggadic Literature, Religious Studies elective, or Hebraic/Judaic Studies elective (12/91) (2/97).

Minor Prophets: Hosea and Zacharia (REL 375)

Location: The Zaidner Institute, Neve Yerushalayim, Jerusalem.

Length: 39 hours (13 weeks).

Dates: September 1984-Present.

Objective: To examine the original Hebrew text of the prophetic books of Hosea and Zacharia, their poetic figure and lyrical style, and their moral/political/theological messages from various exegetical perspectives.

Learning Outcome: Upon successful completion of this course, the student will be able to articulate an understanding of the lyrical quality and figurative references of the minor prophets; the moral, political, and theological message of the books; and the variety of talmudic, midrashic, and exegetical interpretations.

Instruction: Major topics covered in the course are a general introduction to the minor prophets, geopolitical cultural context of the message, repentance and reconciliation, knowledge of God, the prophetic experience, and poetic and literary conceptions. Methods of instruction include lecture, discussion, and textual analysis.

Credit Recommendation: In the lower division baccalaureate/associate degree category or in the upper division baccalaureate degree category, 3 semester hours in Minor Prophets: Hosea and Zacharia, Religious Studies elective, or Hebraic/Judaic Studies (12/91) (2/97).

Neurological Bases of Communication (SPS 430)

Location: The Zaidner Institute, Neve Yerushalayim, Jerusalem.

Length: 39 hours (13 weeks).

Dates: February 1997-Present.

Objective: To introduce students to the bases of communication within the central and peripheral nervous systems.

Learning Outcome: Upon successful completion of this course, the student will be able to describe the gross neuroanatomy related to language abilities in central and peripheral nervous systems; explain basic cellular physiology related to transfer of information within the central and peripheral nervous systems; describe and understand language development associated with normal nervous system development; and understand the impact of various neuropathological conditions upon speech and language functions.

Instruction: Major topics covered in the course are neuroanatomy, cellular physiology, and cortical organization responsible for the development and use of verbal and non-verbal language in humans. Methods of instruction include lecture and examination.

Credit Recommendation: In the upper division baccalaureate degree category, 3 semester hours in Speech and Hearing Science (2/97). *Prerequisite:* Introduction to Communication Disorders.

Normal Speech and Language Development (SPS 320)

Location: The Zaidner Institute, Neve Yerushalayim, Jerusalem.

Length: 39 hours (13 weeks).

Dates: October 1996-Present.

Objective: To give students a basic understanding of normal speech and language development from pre-school through adolescence, through an introduction to the theories and components of language and experience with language sampling.

Learning Outcome: Upon successful completion of this course, the student will be able to understand the components of language; know the stages and various aspects of normal language development; analyze a language sample in a pre-school child; and have a command of professional terminology connected with language development.

Instruction: Major topics covered in the course are theories of language development, language milestones, cognitive and sociological bases for development of language, language development during pre-school through adolescence, and social contexts of interpersonal communication. Methods of instruction include lecture, examinations, and language sample analysis.

Credit Recommendation: In the upper division baccalaureate degree category, 3 semester hours in Speech and Hearing Science (2/97). *Prerequisite:* Introduction to Communication Disorders.

Object Oriented Programming Using C++ (CMP 450)

Location: The Zaidner Institute, Neve Yerushalayim, Jerusalem.

Length: 39 hours (13 weeks).

Dates: February 1997-Present.

Objective: To give students a thorough knowledge of how to use C++ for object oriented programming.

Learning Outcome: Upon successful completion of this course, the student will be able to design object oriented solutions to programming problems using C++.

Instruction: Major topics covered in the course are the key concepts associated with object oriented design and programming: classes, abstract data types, objects, encapsulation, inheritance, implementation hiding, polymorphism, and others; the C++ language, and examples that illustrate the ideas involved in object oriented programming and the syntax of C++. Methods of instruction include lecture and discussion.

Credit Recommendation: In the upper division baccalaureate degree category, 3 semester hours in Object Oriented Programming or Computer Science elective (2/97).

Operating Systems (CMP 460)

Location: The Zaidner Institute, Neve Yerushalayim, Jerusalem.

Length: *Version 1:* 42 hours (14 weeks); *Version 2:* 39 hours (13 weeks).

Dates: *Version 1:* February 1989-January 1997; *Version 2:* February 1997-Present.

Objective: To provide students with a thorough understanding of operating systems, the services provided to users, how the services are provided and how problems are handled such as deadlock and process co-ordination.

Learning Outcome: Upon successful completion of this course, the student will be able to demonstrate knowledge of the details of operating systems for multi-user, multi-program environments.

Instruction: Major topics covered in the course are a general introduction to operating systems; the services provided to users and how users can request services through system calls; algorithms for and approaches to CPU scheduling; disk scheduling; file management; memory management; input/output handling; concurrent programming; and problems such as critical sections, process co-ordination, and deadlock and solutions to these problems. Methods of instruction include lectures, labs, examinations, and programs.

Credit Recommendation: In the upper division baccalaureate degree category, 3 semester hours in Operating Systems or Computer Science elective (12/91) (2/97).

Operations Management (BUS 380)

Location: The Zaidner Institute, Neve Yerushalayim, Jerusalem.

Length: *Version 1:* 42 hours (14 weeks); *Version 2:* 39 hours (13 weeks).

Dates: *Version 1:* September 1991-January 1997; *Version 2:* February 1997-Present.

Objective: To give the student an understanding of the nature and scope of production and operations management and the ability to apply such techniques to supply and capacity problems in a business environment.

Learning Outcome: Upon successful completion of this course, the student will be able to understand the role of job design and productivity; appreciate quality management; determine demand for products; organize inventory control systems; and successfully use an array of statistical and mathematical techniques to assist in planning and control.

Instruction: Major topics covered in the course are operations and productivity, systems design, facility location, forecasting demands and trends, material management, inventory analyses, and PEPT and CPM. Methods of instruction include lecture, discussion, and problem sets/computer modeling.

Credit Recommendation: In the upper division baccalaureate degree category, 3 semester hours in Operations Management (12/91) (2/97).

Pascal (CMP 120)

Location: The Zaidner Institute, Neve Yerushalayim, Jerusalem.

Length: *Version 1:* 42 hours (14 weeks); *Version 2:* 39 hours (13 weeks).

Dates: *Version 1:* February 1986-January 1997; *Version 2:* February 1997-Present.

Objective: To teach the student how to program in PASCAL while improving programming techniques and practices.

Learning Outcome: Upon successful completion of this course, the student will be able to write programs in PASCAL in an organized, systematic manner.

Instruction: Major topics covered in the course are programming in the PASCAL language; integer, real, character, and Boolean data types; user-defined data types through enumeration and subrange; control structures; input-output operations; arrays; multidimensional arrays; procedures and functions; scope; records; variants; sets; PASCAL files; and menus. Methods of instruction include lectures, labs, examinations, and programs.

Credit Recommendation: In the lower division baccalaureate/associate degree category, 3 semester hours in PASCAL (12/91) (2/97).

Philosophical and Theological Foundations of Jewish Prayer (PHI 180)

Location: The Zaidner Institute, Neve Yerushalayim, Jerusalem.

Length: 39 hours (13 weeks).

Dates: September 1984-Present.

Objective: To examine the philosophical and theological underpinnings of Jewish prayer.

Learning Outcome: Upon successful completion of this course, the student will be able to analyze the philosophical and theological centrality of prayer in Judaism; identify central themes in specific parts of the prayers; and define central terms and activities connected with prayer and their conceptual implications.

Instruction: Major topics covered in the course are examinations of the texts of prayers; the setting of prayer; preparation for prayer; intention and devotion during prayer; and the silent prayer (Shemonah Esreh) — its components, themes, laws, and explanation of those items. Methods of instruction include lecture, discussion, and textual preparation.

Credit Recommendation: In the lower division baccalaureate/associate degree category or in the upper division baccalaureate degree category, 3 semester hours in Philosophical and Theological Foundations of Jewish Prayer, Religious Studies, or Theology (12/91) (2/97).

Philosophy of Jewish Education (PHI 245)

Location: The Zaidner Institute, Neve Yerushalayim, Jerusalem.

Length: 39 hours (13 weeks).

Dates: September 1984-Present.

Objective: To examine traditional Jewish educational philosophies representing a variety of historical periods and religious ideologies.

Learning Outcome: Upon successful completion of this course, the student will be able to articulate an in depth understanding of the ideological orientation underlying each school's particular educational philosophy; the points of ideological and didactic disagreement separating the various schools; and the diversity of interpretative posture, represented by the various schools, in their treatment of classic talmudic sources.

Instruction: Major topics covered in the course are attitudes toward Jewish education and educational philosophy as reflected in the following periods: talmudic, Eastern Europe in the 16th century, 18th century hasidic ideology, mitnagdic thought, and 19th century Western Europe. Methods of instruction include lecture, discussion, and textual analysis.

Credit Recommendation: In the upper division baccalaureate degree category, 3 semester hours in Philosophy of Jewish Education or Education elective (12/91) (2/97).

Phonetics (SPS 301)

Location: The Zaidner Institute, Neve Yerushalayim, Jerusalem.

Length: 39 hours (13 weeks).

Dates: October 1996-Present.

Objective: To provide students with an in-depth understanding of clinical phonetics and to equip them with the skills necessary to produce phonetic transcriptions.

Learning Outcome: Upon successful completion of this course, the student will be able to perceive, describe, and categorize sounds of normal and disordered speech; and transcribe a speech sample using the IPA system of phonetic notation.

Instruction: Major topics covered in the course are the sound system of spoken American English; the basic types of sounds and their related physiology, aerodynamics, and acoustic properties; and how to develop the ability to perceive, describe, and categorize the sounds of normal and disordered speech. Methods of instruction include lecture, testing, analytical lab work, and transcription assignments.

Credit Recommendation: In the upper division baccalaureate degree category, 3 semester hours in Speech and Hearing Science (2/97). *Prerequisite:* Introduction to Communication Disorders.

Photography (ART 300)

Location: The Zaidner Institute, Neve Yerushalayim, Jerusalem.

Length: 39 hours (13 weeks).

Dates: February 1992-Present.

Objective: To teach the students the basics of photography and the knowledge that is necessary for a graphic artist to work with a photographer.

Learning Outcome: Upon successful completion of this course, the student will be able to carry a production project through, involving photography in the most successful manner.

Instruction: Major topics covered in the course are the basics of photography and how to ascertain the necessary skills to enable a graphic artist to work with a photographer. Methods of instruction include lectures, lab, projects, and field trips.

Credit Recommendation: In the lower division baccalaureate/associate degree category, 3 semester hours in Photography (2/97).

Preparation for Print (ART 400)

Location: The Zaidner Institute, Neve Yerushalayim, Jerusalem.

Length: 39 hours (13 weeks).

Dates: February 1996-Present.

Objective: To give student the ability to execute an idea in graphic design.

Learning Outcome: Upon successful completion of this course, the student will be able to prepare projects for print in an efficient manner and deal with problems that arise with films, plates, and color.

Instruction: Major topics covered in the course are the subject of printing and an understanding of the techniques and preparation for practical application in a manner which will enable students to prepare projects for print. Methods of instruction include lecture and practical work.

Credit Recommendation: In the lower division baccalaureate/associate degree category, 3 semester hours in Preparation for Print (2/97).

Principles of Accounting I (ACC 101)

Location: The Zaidner Institute, Neve Yerushalayim, Jerusalem.

Length: 39 hours (13 weeks).

Dates: February 1997-Present.

Objective: To introduce the student to the key issues in the preparation of financial statements.

Learning Outcome: Upon successful completion of this course, the student will be able to analyze economic transactions; record economic transactions in the accounting system; prepare necessary adjusting and closing entries; maintain the general ledger; prepare financial statements (Income Statement, Statement of Owner's Equity, Balance Sheet); and appreciate generally accepted accounting principles (GAAP).

Instruction: Major topics covered in the course are the environment of accounting, debit/credit notation, adjustments, closing entries, accounting issued in a merchandise enterprise, design of an accounting system, internal control, current accounts, examination of different inventory methods, and long term assets - valuation and depreciation. Methods of instruction include lecture, discussion, problems, computer simulation and projects, and practice sets.

Credit Recommendation: In the lower division baccalaureate/associate degree category, 3 semester hours in Principles of Accounting I (2/97).

Principles of Accounting I (ACC 101) (ACC 102)
Principles of Accounting II

Location: The Zaidner Institute, Neve Yerushalayim, Jerusalem.

Length: 84 hours (42 hours per course) (28 weeks, 14 weeks per course).

Dates: September 1984-January 1997.

Objective: To give the student an understanding of the nature and practice of financial accounting.

Learning Outcome: Upon successful completion of this course, the student will be able to analyze economic transactions; record economic transactions in the accounting system; prepare necessary adjusting and closing entries; maintain the general ledger; prepare financial statements (Income Statement, Statement of Owners' Equity, Balance Sheet, and Statement of Change in Financial Position); and appreciate generally accepted accounting principles (GAAP).

Instruction: Major topics covered in the course are the accounting cycle, accounting for enterprises, deferrals and accruals, accounting system design, asset accounts/inventory methods, liability accounts, GAAP and accounting theory, partnerships and corporate accounting, equity accounts, and statement of changes. Methods of instruction include lecture, discussion, problems, computer simulation and projects, and practice sets.

Credit Recommendation: In the lower division baccalaureate/associate degree category, 3 semester hours in Principles of Accounting I and II (12/91) (2/97). **NOTE:** The first half of this course is equivalent to Principles of Accounting I. On successful completion of the first half coursework and mid-term examination, the student should receive 3 semester hours for Accounting I.

Principles of Accounting II (ACC 102)

Location: The Zaidner Institute, Neve Yerushalayim, Jerusalem.

Length: 39 hours (13 weeks).

Dates: February 1997-Present.

Objective: To provide the student with a further introduction to the key issues in the preparation of financial statements.

Learning Outcome: Upon successful completion of this course, the student will be able to appreciate complexities in asset, liability accounts; appreciate capital structure and owner's equity accounts; have an integral knowledge of GAAP; conduct a basic financial analysis of statements; prepare a cash flow statement; understand the needs of users of financial statements; and recognize fundamental cost accounting issues.

Instruction: Major topics covered in the course are payroll accounting, establishment of a broad framework of generally accepted accounting principles, examination of partnerships, examination of corporations, present and future value of money, consolidation accounting, analysis of financial statements, statement of cash flow, and an introduction to manufacturing concerns. Methods of instruction include lecture, discussion, problems, computer simulation and projects, and practice sets.

Credit Recommendation: In the lower division baccalaureate/associate degree category, 3 semester hours in Principles of Accounting II (2/97). *Prerequisite:* Principles of Accounting I.

Principles of Jewish Belief: Polemics (PHI 410)

Location: The Zaidner Institute, Neve Yerushalayim, Jerusalem.

Length: 39 hours (13 weeks).

Dates: September 1992-Present.

Objective: To examine rationalist approaches to aspects of traditional Jewish faith doctrine.

Learning Outcome: Upon successful completion of this course, the student will be able to analyze the case for the existence of G-d and attendant aspects of the Jewish faith doctrine argued in rationalist terms; the substantive argumentation of opposing positions; and the problematic ramifications of a faith commitment untempered by the rationalistic dimension.

Instruction: Major topics covered in the course are arguments for the belief in G-d and arguments for Divine origin of Torah. Methods of instruction include lecture and discussion.

Credit Recommendation: In the lower division baccalaureate/associate degree category or in the upper division baccalaureate degree category, 3 semester hours in The Principles of Jewish Belief: Polemics, Philosophy, Theology, or Religious Studies (2/97).

Principles of Management (BUS 370)

Location: The Zaidner Institute, Neve Yerushalayim, Jerusalem.

Length: *Version 1:* 42 hours (14 weeks); *Version 2:* 39 hours (13 weeks).

Dates: *Version 1:* January 1987-December 1996; *Version 2:* February 1997-Present.

Objective: *Version 1:* To give the student an understanding of the nature and practice of management, the elements of strategy formation, and the requirements of leadership. *Version 2:* To give the student an understanding of the importance of the firm to modern society, role and tasks of management, the impact of rapid change on managers and businesses.

Learning Outcome: *Version 1:* Upon successful completion of this course, the student will be able to understand the functions of management including the fundamentals of planning, organization design, leadership, and control/information systems; appreciate the varied meanings of work; understand motivation; understand the elements of individual differences; appreciate the dynamics and synergism of groups; understand the structure of organizations; understand the problems of organizational form and function; and reflect upon appropriate personal management styles. *Version 2:* Upon successful completion of this course, the student will be able to understand the profound changes in current worldwide markets and competition and the requirements for firms and their leaders in the new era; understand the role and process of planning in a contemporary business; be familiar with issues of ethics, culture, organization, and design in large businesses and corporations; have a basic understanding of the principles of organization behavior, motivation, communication, and decision making in contemporary business organizations; be stimulated to think about their own personal and professional goals; and consider what type of professional settings they might find the most satisfactory.

Instruction: *Version 1:* Major topics covered in the course are work and the role of managers; individuals and attributes and theories of motivation; group attributes and dynamics; organization structure and function; decision-making and strategic planning; budgeting and control processes; and leadership, power, and authority. Methods of instruction include lecture, case study, and discussion. *Version 2:* Major topics covered in the course are the importance of the firm to modern society, role and tasks of management, ethical issues and societal responsibility of the firm, decision making, international business, importance and process of planning, individual and group behavior, theories of motivation, control, managing for quality, leadership, and the impact of rapid change on managers and businesses. Methods of instruction include lecture with extensive outside reading from business periodicals and journals linking theory and techniques discussed in class to the real world of business.

Credit Recommendation: *Version 1:* In the upper division baccalaureate degree category, 3 semester hours in Principles of Management (12/91). *Version 2:* In the lower division baccalaureate/associate degree category, 3 semester hours in Principles of Management (2/97).

Programming C++ (CMP 250)

Location: The Zaidner Institute, Neve Yerushalayim, Jerusalem.

Length: 39 hours (13 weeks).

Dates: February 1997-Present.

Objective: To teach the student how to program in C++ with an understanding of the features of the language. The course covers theory as well as practical applications.

Learning Outcome: Upon successful completion of this course, the student will be able to write programs in C++ using most of the features of the language.

Instruction: Major topics covered in the course are an introduction to object oriented programming, data types, arrays, strings, enumerations, pointers, pointer arithmetic, dynamic storage, loops and other control structures, function prototyping, function calls, recursion, pointers to functions, and an introduction to inheritance and polymorphism. Methods of instruction include lecture, labs, examinations, and programs.

Credit Recommendation: In the lower division baccalaureate/associate degree category, 3 semester hours in Programming (2/97).

Programming in FORTRAN (CMP 150)

Location: The Zaidner Institute, Neve Yerushalayim, Jerusalem.

Length: *Version 1:* 42 hours (14 weeks); *Version 2:* 39 hours (13 weeks).

Dates: *Version 1:* September 1984-January 1997; *Version 2:* February 1997-Present.

Objective: To teach the students to program in FORTRAN and familiarize them with common scientific applications.

Learning Outcome: Upon successful completion of this course, the student will be able to write FORTRAN programs and competently refer to manuals for assistance when needed.

Instruction: Major topics covered in the course are programming in the FORTRAN language, integer and real arithmetic, character and logical data types, control statements, built-in functions, arrays, formatting, subprograms, and sequential files. Methods of instruction include lectures, labs, examinations, and programs.

Credit Recommendation: In the lower division baccalaureate/associate degree category, 3 semester hours in Programming in FORTRAN (12/91) (2/97).

Programming Language One (CMP 130)

Location: The Zaidner Institute, Neve Yerushalayim, Jerusalem.

Length: 42 hours (14 weeks).

Dates: September 1984-May 1995.

Objective: To teach the student the material necessary to write programs in PL/1.

Learning Outcome: Upon successful completion of this course, the student will be able to write PL/1 programs and competently refer to manuals for assistance when needed.

Instruction: Major topics covered in the course are programming in the PL/1 language; data types and attributes, arithmetic data, string data, label data, mathematical expressions, operators, and precedence; stream input/output (lists, edit, data), control statements, built-in functions, one-dimensional arrays, multidimensional arrays, do loops with its various forms, structures, character string manipulations, subroutines, functions, block structure, record input/output, and direct files. Methods of instruction include lectures, labs, examinations, and programs.

Credit Recommendation: In the lower division baccalaureate/associate degree category, 3 semester hours in Programming in PL/1 or Computer Science elective (12/91) (2/97).

Programming Languages (CMP 330)

Location: The Zaidner Institute, Neve Yerushalayim, Jerusalem.

Length: *Version 1:* 42 hours (14 weeks); *Version 2:* 39 hours (13 weeks).

Dates: *Version 1:* February 1990-January 1997; *Version 2:* February 1997-Present.

Objective: To give the student an understanding of the components of com puter languages to know which languages are used for which applications.

Learning Outcome: Upon successful completion of this course, the student will be able to write programs in the various languages covered; be familiar with the special features in specific languages; and understand various aspects of language implementations.

Instruction: Major topics covered in the course are formal definitions of programming languages and specification of syntax and semantics; global properties and algorithmic languages, including scopes of declaration, storage allocation, binding time, subroutines, and co-routines; list processing; string manipulation; data description; and simulation languages. Methods of instruction include lectures, labs, examinations, and programs.

Credit Recommendation: In the upper division baccalaureate degree category, 3 semester hours in Programming Languages or Computer Science elective (12/91) (2/97).

Prophecy and the Early Prophets (REL 455)

Location: The Zaidner Institute, Neve Yerushalayim, Jerusalem.

Length: 39 hours (13 weeks).

Dates: September 1994-Present.

Objective: To examine selected passages drawn from the Early Prophets, emphasizing concepts of prophecy and symbolic action.

Learning Outcome: Upon successful completion of this course, the student will be able to demonstrate an understanding of difficult passages involving the element of prophetic signs; the phenomena of prophecy and royalty, with particular emphasis on the period of Saul and David; and the laws and customs associated with the above passages.

Instruction: Major topics covered in the course are concepts of prophecy, the nature of prophetic signs, selected prophetic symbols, prophetic symbols of royalty, Satan and power of evil, false prophecy, and ritual acts. Methods of instruction include lecture, discussion, and textual analysis.

Credit Recommendation: In the lower division baccalaureate/associate degree or in the upper division baccalaureate degree category, 3 semester hours in Religious Studies, Hebraic/Judaic Studies, or Theology (2/97).

Proverbs (REL 350)

Location: The Zaidner Institute, Neve Yerushalayim, Jerusalem.

Length: 39 hours (13 weeks).

Dates: September 1984-Present.

Objective: To examine the Book of Proverbs in the original Hebrew with the classical commentaries.

Learning Outcome: Upon successful completion of this course, the student will be able to articulate an in-depth understanding of the major religious and moral themes of the Book of Proverbs, with its major talmudic, midrashic, and medieval exegetical commentaries.

Instruction: Major topics covered in the course are authorship, literary form and use of metaphor, wisdom and its didactic influence, virtue, issues of youth and age, and Providence. Methods of instruction include lecture, discussion, and textual analysis.

Credit Recommendation: In the lower division baccalaureate/associate degree category or in the upper division baccalaureate degree category, 3 semester hours in The Book of Proverbs, Religious Studies elective, or Hebraic/Judaic Studies (12/91) (2/97).

Psalms (LIT 150)

Location: The Zaidner Institute, Neve Yerushalayim, Jerusalem.

Length: 39 hours (13 weeks).

Dates: September 1984-Present.

Objective: To examine representative passages from the Book of Psalms in the original Hebrew with classical commentaries and rabbinic sources.

Learning Outcome: Upon successful completion of this course, the student will be able to articulate an understanding of major categories of Psalms, their themes, motifs, and historical context.

Instruction: Major topics covered in the course are form and literary style, authorship, introductory phrases, and themes and motifs as reflected in classical commentaries and rabbinic sources. Methods of instruction include lecture, discussion, and textual analysis.

Credit Recommendation: In the upper division baccalaureate degree category, 3 semester hours in Psalms, Religious Studies, Theology, or Hebraic/Judaic Studies (12/91) (2/97).

Psychological Foundations of Education (PSY 260)

Location: The Zaidner Institute, Neve Yerushalayim, Jerusalem.

Length: *Version 1:* 42 hours (14 weeks); *Version 2:* 39 hours (13 weeks).

Dates: *Version 1:* September 1985-April 1997; *Version 2:* May 1997-Present.

Objective: To provide the necessary information concerning the philosophies and psychological processes associated with the educational experience.

Learning Outcome: Upon successful completion of this course, the student will be able to formulate a personal definition of a teacher, student, and classroom; devise and utilize behavioral objectives in support of a teaching task and construct taxonomies of objectives; comprehend contemporary learning theories, cognitive theories, and information processing models; understand theories of motivation and apply them to classroom management; assess and effectively relate to pupil variability in terms of stage theories of normal development and typical age-level characteristics; and demonstrate familiarity with different means of evaluating classroom learning.

Instruction: Major topics covered in the course are theoretical perspectives and research pertinent to classroom teaching; how children develop, interact, and learn within educational settings; and psychological evaluation of school achievement. Methods of instruction include lecture and discussion.

Credit Recommendation: *Version 1:* In the lower division baccalaureate/associate degree category, 3 semester hours in Psychological Foundations of Education (12/91). *Version 2:* In the upper division baccalaureate degree category, 3 semester hours in Psychological Foundations of Education (2/97). *Prerequisites:* Introduction to Psychology and Developmental Psychology I.

Psychological Testing and Measurement (PSY 410)

Location: The Zaidner Institute, Neve Yerushalayim, Jerusalem.

Length: *Version 1:* 42 hours (14 weeks); *Version 2:* 39 hours (13 weeks).

Dates: *Version 1:* January 1986-January 1997; *Version 2:* February 1997-Present.

Objective: To provide the theoretical and practical information necessary to competently understand and evaluate the major psychological tests used today.

Learning Outcome: Upon successful completion of this course, the student will be able to interpret psychiatric test results; understand statistical analysis of tests; know major components of I.Q. tests; understand the nature of personality tests and the difference between projective and standardized tests; and be aware of ethical issues in testing.

Instruction: Major topics covered in the course are the characteristics of psychological tests, intelligence tests, aptitude and interest tests, and personality tests. Methods of instruction include lecture and class demonstration.

Credit Recommendation: In the upper division baccalaureate degree category, 3 semester hours in Psychological Tests and Measurements (12/91) (2/97). *Prerequisite:* Introduction to Psychology, and Developmental Psychology I and/or Theories of Personality are suggested.

Ruth (REL 265)

Location: The Zaidner Institute, Neve Yerushalayim, Jerusalem.

Length: 39 hours (13 weeks).

Dates: February 1997-Present.

Objective: To examine the Book of Ruth in the original Hebrew text together with the commentary of Rashi and Ibn Ezra.

Learning Outcome: Upon successful completion of this course, the student will be able to identify the authorship and sequence of events recorded in the Book of Ruth; define the minimal requirements for conversion to Judaism; identify the generations that existed between Judah the son of Jacob and King David; and describe the laws governing the redemption and acquisition of property.

Instruction: Major topics covered in the course are historic referents, laws of conversion, laws of Levirate marriage, and the contemporary relevance of the themes in Ruth to Jewish belief. Methods of instruction include lecture and discussion.

Credit Recommendation: In the lower division baccalaureate/associate degree category or in the upper division baccalaureate degree category, 3 semester hours in The Book of Ruth, Religious Studies, or Hebraic/Judaic Studies (2/97).

Social Psychology (PSY 340)

Location: The Zaidner Institute, Neve Yerushalayim, Jerusalem.

Length: *Version 1:* 42 hours (14 weeks); *Version 2:* 39 hours (13 weeks).

Dates: *Version 1:* January 1986-January 1997; *Version 2:* February 1997-Present.

Objective: To evaluate the theoretic and scientific methods of how people perceive, influence, and relate to one another.

Learning Outcome: Upon successful completion of this course, the student will be able to know the experimental method in social psychology, causes and effects of prejudice, learned social behavior, competition and cooperation in social situations, and altruism in human behavior.

Instruction: Major topics covered in the course are theory and research on how an individual affects and is affected by his or her social environment; membership in groups, both formal and informal; conformity, prejudice, competition, and cooperation; and a basic understanding of the major principles and theories regarding how an individual is affected by the groups of which he or she is a part. Methods of instruction include lecture, discussion, and written examinations.

Credit Recommendation: In the upper division baccalaureate degree category, 3 semester hours in Social Psychology (12/91) (2/97). *Prerequisite:* Introduction to Sociology or Introduction to Psychology.

Sociology of Education (SOC 210)

Location: The Zaidner Institute, Neve Yerushalayim, Jerusalem.

Length: *Version 1:* 42 hours (14 weeks); *Version 2:* 39 hours (13 weeks).

Dates: *Version 1:* December 1984-January 1997; *Version 2:* February 1997-Present.

Objective: To explore the educational process through the discipline of sociology and the related discipline of social psychology, and to examine the organization and effects of education in industrial society.

Learning Outcome: Upon successful completion of this course, the student will be able to distinguish between socialization, learning, and education, between peer group and reference group, between manifest and latent functions of education, and between social class caste, culture, status, and prestige; discuss the effects of bureaucracy in formal education; identify factors that contribute to inequality in educational opportunities and conflict within the educational system; discuss proposals for educational reform; and apply principles of group dynamics to the analysis of classroom behavior.

Instruction: Major topics covered in the course are learning in a social setting, functions of education, classroom as a social system, schools and student subcultures, controversy amidst educational research, organization of the educational enterprise, teachers as employees or professionals, conflict and legitimacy in school, education and inequality, emerging issues in modern education, and proposals for educational reform. Methods of instruction include discussion, lecture, and field observation.

Credit Recommendation: In the lower division baccalaureate/associate degree category, 3 semester hours in The Sociology of Education (12/91) (2/97). *Prerequisite:* Introduction to Sociology or Introduction to Psychology.

Sociology of the Community (SOC 310)

Location: The Zaidner Institute, Neve Yerushalayim, Jerusalem.

Length: *Version 1:* 42 hours (14 weeks); *Version 2:* 39 hours (13 weeks).

Dates: *Version 1:* February 1989-January 1997; *Version 2:* February 1997-Present.

Objective: To examine the different approaches to the concept of community and analyze the relationship between community dynamics and social policy.

Learning Outcome: Upon successful completion of this course, the student will be able to provide varying definitions of the concept "community" and their historical and ideological backgrounds; explain the functions provided by communities; discuss and contrast models of community development and attachment; analyze patterns of community life; and discuss social policy implications arising from an understanding of the sociology of the community.

Instruction: Major topics covered in the course are the concept of community, community types, theories of community, social system theory, conflict theory, community power structure and leadership, methods of community study and research, community development and dynamics, the Jewish community, and the future of "community". Methods of instruction include lecture, discussion, and student presentations.

Credit Recommendation: In the upper division baccalaureate degree category, 3 semester hours in the Sociology of Community or Social Science elective (12/91) (2/97). *Prerequisite:* Introduction to Sociology.

Sociology of the Family (SOC 410)

Location: The Zaidner Institute, Neve Yerushalayim, Jerusalem.

Length: 39 hours (13 weeks).

Dates: October 1994-Present.

Objective: To consider contemporary family roles and functions in the light of cross-cultural and historical comparisons and as they are influenced by the social forces that impinge on them.

Learning Outcome: Upon successful completion of this course, the student will be able to indicate how sociologists approach the study of the family; distinguish this approach from descriptive, historical, and therapeutic approaches; place her own family in a larger cross-cultural and historical context; distinguish several definitions of family, showing how they emerge from different ways of looking at families; summarize the major theories on explanations of family life and changes; clarify and specify family roles and relationships including grandparents and extended relatives and the functions they serve in different societies; discuss the processes by which families form (the institution of marriage), terminate, and reconstruct; identify and discuss the stressors, response factors and processes whereby families adjust to situations of change; and examine functional alternatives to the family.

Instruction: Major topics covered in the course are an examination of definitions and varieties of families, family roles, relationships, and functions, problems facing the contemporary family, mate selection, divorce, death and remarriage, stress and conflict in family life, alternatives to the family, and aging and the family. Theoretical perspectives provide a framework for studying families. Methods of instruction include lecture and case studies.

Credit Recommendation: In the upper division baccalaureate degree category, 3 semester hours in Sociology of the Family or Social Science (2/97). *Prerequisite:* Introduction to Sociology and/or Introduction to Psychology.

Speech and Hearing Science (SPS 310)

Location: The Zaidner Institute, Neve Yerushalayim, Jerusalem.

Length: 39 hours (13 weeks).

Dates: February 1997-Present.

Objective: To have students gain an in-depth understanding of the physical principles of speech and hearing with an emphasis upon theoretical models of speech production and hearing perception, and to introduce students to the basic principles of diagnostic equipment and its operation.

Learning Outcome: Upon successful completion of this course, the student will be able to possess a working knowledge of the physical principles of speech and hearing; be better able to understand and evaluate speech and hearing problems; and be equipped to evaluate basic test results and their practical application.

Instruction: Major topics covered in the course are an introduction to the physics of sound; the physical properties of the outer, middle, and inner ear; the process of signal detection and speech production; basic principles of audiometry; functioning of ABR, OAE equipment; and evaluation of test results. Methods of instruction include lecture and lab.

Credit Recommendation: In the upper division baccalaureate degree category, 3 semester hours in Speech and Hearing Science (2/97). *Prerequisite:* Introduction to Communication Disorders.

Studies in Jewish Law: Agriculture in the Land of Israel (REL 320)

Location: The Zaidner Institute, Neve Yerushalayim, Jerusalem.

Length: 39 hours (13 weeks).

Dates: September 1984-Present.

Objective: To equip the student with the knowledge of the concepts and applications of Jewish legal principles relating to agricultural activity.

Learning Outcome: Upon successful completion of this course, the student will be able to articulate certain agricultural laws and practices and their underlying rationale.

Instruction: Major topics covered in the course are the laws of tithes and the laws of the Sabbatical year. Methods of instruction include lecture, discussion, and textual analysis.

Credit Recommendation: In the lower division baccalaureate/associate degree category or in the upper division baccalaureate degree category, 3 semester hours in Studies in Jewish Law: Agriculture in the Land of Israel, Religious Studies, or Hebraic/Judaic Studies elective (12/91) (2/97).

Studies in Jewish Law: Blessings (REL 210)

Location: The Zaidner Institute, Neve Yerushalayim, Jerusalem.

Length: 39 hours (13 weeks).

Dates: September 1984-Present.

Objective: To equip the student with the knowledge of the Laws of Blessings and their underlying rationale.

Learning Outcome: Upon successful completion of this course, the student will be able to demonstrate a knowledge of the laws of blessings and their halakhic sources.

Instruction: Major topics covered in the course are general principles of blessings, formal structures of blessings, biblical and talmudic sources of blessings, sequence of blessings, diverse types of blessings, and blessings for life cycle events. Methods of instruction include lecture, discussion, and textual analysis.

Credit Recommendation: In the lower division baccalaureate/associate degree category or in the upper division baccalaureate degree category, 3 semester hours in Studies in Jewish Law: Blessings, Hebraic/Judaic Studies elective, or Religious Studies (12/91) (2/97).

Studies in Jewish Law: Dietary Law (REL 110)

Location: The Zaidner Institute, Neve Yerushalayim, Jerusalem.

Length: 39 hours (13 weeks).

Dates: September 1984-Present.

Objective: To provide the student with the knowledge of the practical aspects of

Jewish dietary law and their halakhic underpinnings.

Learning Outcome: Upon successful completion of this course, the student will be able to demonstrate a knowledge of criteria for determining forbidden and permissible food and correct procedures for ascertaining and providing for Kashrut.

Instruction: Major topics covered in the course are classical laws of Kashrut with particular emphasis on the modern technological impact on Kashrut observance. Methods of instruction include lecture and discussion.

Credit Recommendation: In the lower division baccalaureate/associate degree category, 3 semester hours in Studies in Jewish Law: Dietary Law, Hebraic/Judaic Studies, or Religious Studies elective (12/91) (2/97).

Studies in Jewish Law: Economics and Business Relationships (REL 310)

Location: The Zaidner Institute, Neve Yerushalayim, Jerusalem.

Length: 39 hours (13 weeks).

Dates: September 1984-Present.

Objective: To provide the student with the knowledge of selected themes in Jewish law and ethics related to business and finance.

Learning Outcome: Upon successful completion of this course, the student will be able to analyze the underlying Jewish legal, ethical, and theological principles implicit in commercial activity, as well as their practical manifestations.

Instruction: Major topics covered in the course are Judaic business ethics, advertising and promotional activity, usury prohibitions and their contemporary applications, employer-employee relations, and copyright. Methods of instruction include lecture, discussion, and textual analysis.

Credit Recommendation: In the lower division baccalaureate/associate degree category or in the upper division baccalaureate degree category, 3 semester hours in Studies in Jewish Law: Economics and Business Relationships, Hebraic/Judaic Studies elective, or Business Law elective (12/91) (2/97).

Studies in Jewish Law: Interpersonal Communication (REL 315)

Location: The Zaidner Institute, Neve Yerushalayim, Jerusalem.

Length: 39 hours (13 weeks).

Dates: September 1987-Present.

Objective: To examine the issues of interpersonal relations in Jewish law.

Learning Outcome: Upon successful completion of this course, the student will be able to demonstrate an understanding of the laws of interpersonal communication and of their biblical and rabbinic sources.

Instruction: Major topics covered in the course are biblical and rabbinic sources on verbal abuse and laws of slander, gossip, and the private and public exchange of information in Jewish Law. Methods of instruction include lecture and discussion.

Credit Recommendation: In the lower division baccalaureate/associate degree category or in the upper division baccalaureate degree category, 3 semester hours in Studies in Jewish Law: Interpersonal Communication, Religious Studies, or Hebraic/Judaic Studies (2/97).

Studies in Jewish Law: Interpersonal Relationships (REL 335)

Location: The Zaidner Institute, Neve Yerushalayim, Jerusalem.

Length: 39 hours (13 weeks).

Dates: March 1996-Present.

Objective: To examine the biblical and halakhic texts dealing with various interpersonal relationships.

Learning Outcome: Upon successful completion of this course, the student will be able to demonstrate an understanding of diverse Rabbinic approaches to complex psychological, social, moral, and theological issues of interpersonal relationships.

Instruction: Major topics covered in the course are respect in family relationships, adoption, love for fellow humans, care for the ill, and labor relations. Methods of instruction include textual analysis, lecture, and discussion.

Credit Recommendation: In the lower division baccalaureate/associate degree category or in the upper division baccalaureate degree category, 3 semester hours in Studies in Jewish Law: Interpersonal Relationships, Religious Studies elective, Hebraic/Judaic Studies, or Liberal Arts (2/97).

Studies in Jewish Law: Laws and Customs of the Shabbat I (REL 120)

Location: The Zaidner Institute, Neve Yerushalayim, Jerusalem.

Length: 39 hours (13 weeks).

Dates: September 1984-Present.

Objective: To equip the student with the knowledge of the laws of the Sabbath and their biblical and rabbinic sources.

Learning Outcome: Upon successful completion of this course, the student will be able to articulate the philosophical-theological basis for the Sabbath and its centrality to the faith of the traditional Jew; the cultural significance of Sabbath symbols; and the motifs of Sabbath prayer.

Instruction: Major topics covered in the course are biblical and rabbinic sources for Sabbath observance, including concepts of labor and rest. Methods of instruction include lecture, discussion, and textual analysis.

Credit Recommendation: In the lower division baccalaureate/associate degree category, 3 semester hours in Studies and Jewish Law: Laws and Customs of the Sabbath I or Hebraic/Judaic Studies elective (12/91) (2/97).

Studies in Jewish Law: Laws and Customs of the Shabbat II (REL 215)

Location: The Zaidner Institute, Neve Yerushalayim, Jerusalem.

Length: 39 hours (13 weeks).

Dates: February 1992-Present.

Objective: To analyze the major categories of the prohibition of melakhah (work) on the Sabbath.

Learning Outcome: Upon successful completion of this course, the student will be able to demonstrate an understanding of the major categories of melakhah and their rabbinic boundaries; and the application of Sabbath laws to medical emergencies.

Instruction: Major topics covered in the course are the full range of the 39 categories of melakha and their contemporary application. Methods of instruction include lecture and discussion.

Credit Recommendation: In the lower division baccalaureate/associate degree category or in the upper division baccalaureate degree category, 3 semester hours in Studies in Jewish Law: Laws and Customs of the Shabbat II, Religious Studies elective, or Hebraic/Judaic Studies (2/97).

Studies in Jewish Law: Prayer (REL 325)

Location: The Zaidner Institute, Neve Yerushalayim, Jerusalem.

Length: 39 hours (13 weeks).

Dates: September 1992-Present.

Objective: To examine the halakhic texts governing the practice of Jewish daily prayer, its structure and substance.

Learning Outcome: Upon successful completion of this course, the student will be able to demonstrate an understanding of the laws, practices, content, and structure of Jewish prayer as derived from their halakhic sources; demonstrate a familiarity with textual materials bearing on the requirements of prayer; and demonstrate a familiarity with the cross-cultural diversity of prayer traditions as represented in a variety of rabbinic textual source materials.

Instruction: Major topics covered in the course are the prayer obligation, framework, traditions, and laws governing central elements of daily prayers. Methods of instruction include lecture and discussion.

Credit Recommendation: In the lower division baccalaureate/associate degree category or in the upper division baccalaureate degree category, 3 semester hours in Studies in Jewish Law: Prayer, Religious Studies, Theology, or Hebraic/Judaic Studies (2/97).

Studies in Jewish Philosophy and Ethics (PHI 455)

Location: The Zaidner Institute, Neve Yerushalayim, Jerusalem.

Length: 39 hours (13 weeks).

Dates: September 1984-Present.

Objective: To examine selected ethical/philosophical themes from the text of Pirkei Avot, a moralistic Mishnaic text, with the accompanying sixteenth century Derekh Hayyim gloss of Judah Loew ben Bezalel (Maharal of Prague).

Learning Outcome: Upon successful completion of this course, the student will be able to analyze the ethical/philosophic thematics addressed in the mishnaic and accompanying Derekh Hayyim texts, as well as talmudic source references cited and exposited in the Derekh Hayyim gloss.

Instruction: Major topics covered in the course are the ideas of R. Judah Loew of Prague vis a vis judicial integrity, the learning process, political leadership, definition of virtue, and a wide selection of ethical and philosophical ideas. Methods of instruction include lecture, discussion, and textual analysis.

Credit Recommendation: In the lower division baccalaureate/associate degree category or in the upper division baccalaureate degree category, 3 semester hours in Jewish Philosophy and Ethics or Philosophy elective (12/91) (2/97).

Studies in the Writings of Luzatto (PHI 370)

Location: The Zaidner Institute, Neve Yerushalayim, Jerusalem.

Length: 39 hours (13 weeks).

Dates: September 1992-Present.

Objective: To systematically analyze Rabbi Luzatto's ethical system and exposition of the biblical and rabbinic sources.

Learning Outcome: Upon successful completion of this course, the student will be able to appreciate the major themes in the author's ethical teaching and the author's particular methodology in interpretation of supportive biblical and rabbinic references cited within the work.

Instruction: Major topics covered in the course are the moral values of vigilance, diligence, cleanliness, self-denial, purification, piety, humility, fear of sin, and holiness. Methods of instruction include lecture and discussion.

Credit Recommendation: In the lower division baccalaureate/associate degree category or in the upper division baccalaureate degree category, 3 semester hours in Ethics/Philosophy, Religious Studies, or Hebraic/Judaic Studies (2/97).

Studies in the Writings of the Maharal of Prague (PHI 360)

Location: The Zaidner Institute, Neve Yerushalayim, Jerusalem.

Length: 39 hours (13 weeks).

Dates: September 1992-Present.

Objective: To examine the ethical/theological system of the Maharal of Prague.

Learning Outcome: Upon successful completion of this course, the student will be able to demonstrate an understanding of the fundamental substance of the author's writings; the terminology characteristic of the author's literary style, with its philosophic/mystical connotations; and the author's distinctive methodology in interpretation of biblical and rabbinic sources.

Instruction: Major topics covered in the course are a reflection of the specific text which will be studied comprehensively. Text selections will vary. Methods of instruction include lecture and discussion.

Credit Recommendation: In the upper division baccalaureate degree category, 3 semester hours in Studies in the Writings of the Maharal of Prague, Hebraic/Judaic Studies, Theology, or Religious Studies (2/97).

Survey of Biblical Themes (REL 385)

Location: The Zaidner Institute, Neve Yerushalayim, Jerusalem.

Length: 39 hours (13 weeks).

Dates: February 1994-Present.

Objective: To examine selected Biblical topics with their classical commentaries.

Learning Outcome: Upon successful completion of this course, the student will be able to demonstrate an understanding of the breadth of ethical, moral, and theological motifs implicit in the given narratives; and the diversity of interpretive positions reflected in the accompanying talmudic, midrashic, and exegetical sources.

Instruction: Major topics covered in the course are selected ethical, moral, and theological themes from the Books of Genesis and Exodus. Methods of instruction include lecture and discussion.

Credit Recommendation: In the lower division baccalaureate/associate degree category or in the upper division baccalaureate degree category, 3 semester hours in Survey of Biblical Themes, Hebraic/Judaic Studies, or Religious Studies (2/97).

Survey of Exceptional Children (PSY 310)

Location: The Zaidner Institute, Neve Yerushalayim, Jerusalem.

Length: *Version 1:* 42 hours (14 weeks); *Version 2:* 39 hours (13 weeks).

Dates: *Version 1:* January 1990-January 1997; *Version 2:* February 1997-Present.

Objective: To provide the student with a brief overview of all the major exceptionalities dealt with in the school environment.

Learning Outcome: Upon successful completion of this course, for each of the exceptionalities presented, the student will be able to identify its symptoms in pupils in the classroom; understand basic diagnostic procedures; understand relevant terms (i.e., decibels, adventitious deafness, etc.); read and interpret IEPs; understand the necessary physiology; understand the causative factors; and know basic treatment techniques and specific classroom management techniques.

Instruction: Major topics covered in the course are an introduction to the study of exceptional children, hearing impaired, visually impaired, mental retardation, emotionally disturbed (behavior disordered), physically handicapped, speech and language disorders, gifted, and normalization; incidence; causation; diagnosis; treatment; behavior management; and suggestions for the classroom teacher. Methods of instruction include lecture, observation, and discussion.

Credit Recommendation: In the upper division baccalaureate degree category, 3 semester hours in Survey of Exceptional Children (12/91) (2/97).

Systems Analysis (CMP 480)

Location: The Zaidner Institute, Neve Yerushalayim, Jerusalem.

Length: *Version 1:* 42 hours (14 weeks); *Version 2:* 39 hours (13 weeks).

Dates: *Version 1:* February 1989-January 1997; *Version 2:* February 1997-Present.

Objective: To provide the students with an understanding of how major computer systems are designed, coded, tested, and implemented.

Learning Outcome: Upon successful completion of this course, the student will be able to understand and use various system design tools and translate the design tools into a working implementation.

Instruction: Major topics covered in the course are methods of system design, system designer tools, design of user interface, data base design, issues of security and integrity, and system integration. Methods of instruction include lectures, labs, examinations, and programs.

Credit Recommendation: *Versions 1 and 2:* In the upper division baccalaureate degree category, 3 semester hours in Systems Analysis or Computer Science elective (12/91) (2/97).

Tax Accounting (ACC 330)

Location: The Zaidner Institute, Neve Yerushalayim, Jerusalem.

Length: 42 hours (14 weeks).

Dates: September 1991-February 1997.

Objective: To give the student an understanding of the nature and practice of individual, partnership, and corporate taxation.

Learning Outcome: Upon successful completion of this course, the student will be able to determine an individual's correct gross income; determine deductions and tax accounting for individuals, partnerships, and corporations; determine tax credits; and complete sets of appropriate individual, partnership, and corporate tax returns.

Instruction: Major topics covered in the course are individuals — gross income, exclusions, property transactions, capital gains and losses, personal deductions, and tax shelter; partnerships — formation, inclusion and exclusion of new partners, and distributions; corporations — income and expenses, profit and loss, capital and dividends, sub "S" corporations, depreciation, leases, pensions, and tax. Methods of instruction include lecture, discussions, and problem-solving.

Credit Recommendation: In the upper division baccalaureate degree category, 3 semester hours in Tax Accounting (12/91) (2/97).

Tax Accounting - Individual (ACC 330) (Formerly Tax Accounting [ACC 330])

Location: The Zaidner Institute, Neve Yerushalayim, Jerusalem.

Length: 39 hours (13 weeks).

Dates: February 1997-Present.

Objective: To give the student an understanding of the nature and practice of individual taxation.

Learning Outcome: Upon successful completion of this course, the student will be able to determine an individual's correct gross income; determine deductions and tax accounting for individuals; determine tax credits; and complete sets of appropriate tax returns.

Instruction: Major topics covered in the course are gross income, exclusions, property transactions, capital gains and losses, personal deductions, and tax shelter. Methods of instruction include lecture, discussions, and problem-solving.

Credit Recommendation: In the upper division baccalaureate degree category, 3 semester hours in Individual Tax Accounting (2/97).

Teaching English as a Foreign Language I (EDU 213)

Location: The Zaidner Institute, Neve Yerushalayim, Jerusalem.

Length: *Version 1:* 42 hours (14 weeks); *Version 2:* 39 hours (13 weeks).

Dates: *Version 1:* January 1986-January 1997; *Version 2:* February 1997-Present.

Objective: To provide an understanding of the methodological principles and techniques necessary for teaching English as a foreign language to elementary school students.

Learning Outcome: Upon successful completion of this course, the student will be able to demonstrate an understanding of the structure of an English lesson and the application of the principles of lesson planning; the ability to design lesson plans for teaching the four basic skills necessary for mastery of a language: comprehension, speech, reading, and writing; how to manage the classroom environment when teaching English language acquisition; and the ability to critically evaluate classroom situations devoted to teaching English.

Instruction: Major topics covered in the course are effective classroom routines, listening comprehension, speech techniques in the classroom, development of reading skills, Israel Board of Education requirements on English competency, and issues and problems in the teaching of writing. Methods of instruction include lecture, discussion, role-playing, audio/visual presentations, group processes, laboratory work, and practical experience through classroom observation, teaching, model lessons, and extensive study of sample curricula and teaching aids.

Credit Recommendation: In the lower division baccalaureate/associate degree category, 3 semester hours in The Teaching of Reading as a Foreign Language (12/91) (2/97). *Co-requisite:* Developmental Psychology I or Psychological Foundations of Education.

Teaching English as a Foreign Language II (EDU 214)

Location: The Zaidner Institute, Neve Yerushalayim, Jerusalem.

Length: *Version 1:* 42 hours (14 weeks); *Version 2:* 39 hours (13 weeks).

Dates: *Version 1:* January 1986-January 1997; *Version 2:* February 1997-Present.

Objective: To extend the theoretical and practical understanding of TEFL that students have already acquired in TEFL I through further examination of specific topics that are essential for effective language teaching. In addition to discussion of theoretical issues, emphasis is placed on analyzing a variety of educational materials, extensive classroom observations, and preparation of sample materials and lesson plans, culminating in a supervised student teaching experience.

Learning Outcome: Upon successful completion of this course, the student will be able to demonstrate a greater understanding of the issues involved in teaching English as a foreign language; the ability to create and utilize a variety of visual aids for the classroom; the ability to critically evaluate available texts in the field of teaching English as a foreign language; the function of testing and familiarity with a variety of ways of testing proficiency in English language acquisition; and the ability to plan and execute an effective lesson for teaching English as a foreign language to elementary school students.

Instruction: Major topics covered in the course are issues and problems in the teaching of vocabulary, evaluating textbooks for TEFL, pattern practices and group learning, testing language skills, and evaluating various comprehension tests. Methods of instruction include lecture, discussion, role playing, audio/visual presentations, group processes, and language laboratory work.

Credit Recommendation: In the lower division baccalaureate/associate degree category, 3 semester hours in The Teaching of English as a Foreign Language II

(12/91) (2/97). *Prerequisite:* Teaching English as a Foreign Language 1.

Teaching Reading to Young Children (EDUC 204)

Location: The Zaidner Institute, Neve Yerushalayim, Jerusalem.

Length: 42 hours (14 weeks).

Dates: January 1986-December 1996.

Objective: To provide students with an understanding of the theoretical issues and practical considerations relevant to teaching reading successfully, as well as some experience in preparing educational materials for this purpose.

Learning Outcome: Upon successful completion of this course, the student will be able to understand the theoretical background to various methods of teaching reading and know which are most effective based on the evidence from current research in the field; and implement an effective reading program at pre-reading, initial, or advanced levels, as well as for foreign language learners. This involves selecting the most appropriate materials from those available in packaged programs and designing supplementary materials (e.g., games, tests) on their own, and understand research reports relating to teaching reading (e.g., be familiar with the concepts "correlation" and "significance") and understanding the practical ramifications of such studies.

Instruction: Major topics covered in the course are an overview of language development and its relationship to beginning reading, promoting and elevating reading readiness, theoretical background and empirical support for popular methods of reading instruction, development and evaluation of reading comprehension, teaching reading as a foreign language, and recognizing and EDU of reading disabilities. Methods of instruction include lecture, discussion, and simulation.

Credit Recommendation: In the lower division baccalaureate/associate degree category, 3 semester hours in Teaching Reading or Teaching Reading to Young Children (12/91) (2/97).

The Early Prophets: Joshua (REL 170)
(Formerly The Early Prophets: The Book of Joshua [REL 170])

Location: The Zaidner Institute, Neve Yerushalayim, Jerusalem.

Length: 39 hours (13 weeks).

Dates: September 1984-Present.

Objective: To examine the Book of Joshua in the original Hebrew with the 11th century commentary of Rashi and other classical commentaries.

Learning Outcome: Upon successful completion of this course, the student will be able to articulate an in-depth understanding of the major religious, historical, and geographical elements of the Book of Joshua.

Instruction: Major topics covered in the course are conquest of the Land of Israel, division of land, tribal boundaries, the charge to Joshua, and a review of the laws governing cities of refuge. Methods of instruction include lecture, discussion, textual analysis, and use of maps.

Credit Recommendation: In the lower division baccalaureate/associate degree category or in the upper division baccalaureate degree category, 3 semester hours in The Book of Joshua, Religious Studies elective, or Hebraic/Judaic Studies (12/91) (2/97).

The Early Prophets: Judges (REL 175)
(Formerly The Early Prophets: The Book of Judges [REL 175])

Location: The Zaidner Institute, Neve Yerushalayim, Jerusalem.

Length: 39 hours (13 weeks).

Dates: September 1984-Present.

Objective: To examine the Book of Judges in the original Hebrew with classical commentaries.

Learning Outcome: Upon successful completion of this course, the student will be able to articulate an in-depth understanding of the major historical and religious elements of the Book of Judges.

Instruction: Major topics covered in the course are the role of the judge and the king, the judgeship and Song of Deborah, Gideon's test of G-d, Jephtha's vow, the personality of Samson and the Nazarite laws, and the idol of Micha. Methods of instruction include lecture, discussion, and textual analysis.

Credit Recommendation: In the lower division baccalaureate/associate degree category or in the upper division baccalaureate degree category, 3 semester hours in The Book of Judges, Religious Studies elective, or Hebraic/Judaic Studies (12/91) (2/97).

The Early Prophets: Kings I and II (REL 275)
(Formerly The Early Prophets: Book of Kings I and II [REL 275])

Location: The Zaidner Institute, Neve Yerushalayim, Jerusalem.

Length: 39 hours (13 weeks).

Dates: September 1984-Present.

Objective: To examine of the Book of Kings in the original Hebrew with the 11th century commentary of Rashi and other classical commentaries.

Learning Outcome: Upon successful completion of this course, the student will be able to articulate an in-depth understanding of the major religious and historical elements of the Book of Kings.

Instruction: Major topics covered in the course are biographies of the Kings of Judah and Israel, the split in the kingdoms, the personalities of Elijah and Elisha, the exile of ten tribes, and the destruction of the first Temple. Methods of instruction include lecture, discussion, and textual analysis.

Credit Recommendation: In the lower division baccalaureate/associate degree category or in the upper division baccalaureate degree category, 3 semester hours in The Book of Kings I and II, Religious Studies elective, or elective in Hebraic/Judaic Studies (12/91) (2/97).

The Early Prophets: Samuel I and II (REL 271)
(Formerly The Early Prophets: The Book of Samuel I and II [REL 270])

Location: The Zaidner Institute, Neve Yerushalayim, Jerusalem.

Length: 39 hours (13 weeks).

Dates: September 1984-Present.

Objective: To examine the Book of Samuel in the original Hebrew with the 11th century commentary of Rashi and rabbinic sources.

Learning Outcome: Upon successful completion of this course, the student will be able to articulate an in-depth understanding of the major personalities and events of the period.

Instruction: Major topics covered in the course the narrative of Samuel I and II; the personalities of Samuel, Saul, David, and other biblical figures; and moral and religious teachings implicit in the biblical text. Methods of instruction include lecture, discussion, and textual analysis.

Credit Recommendation: In the lower division baccalaureate/associate degree category or in the upper division baccalaureate degree category, 3 semester hours in The Book of Samuel I and II, Religious Studies elective, or Hebraic/Judaic Studies (12/91) (2/97).

The Later Prophets: Isaiah (REL 370)
(Formerly Isaiah [REL 370])

Location: The Zaidner Institute, Neve Yerushalayim, Jerusalem.

Length: 39 hours (13 weeks).
Dates: September 1984-Present.
Objective: To examine the Book of Isaiah in the original Hebrew with the 11th century commentary of Rashi and other classical commentaries.
Learning Outcome: Upon successful completion of this course, the student will be able to articulate an in-depth understanding of the historical, religious, and moral elements of the book of Isaiah.
Instruction: Major topics covered in the course are geopolitical context, Israel as the suffering servant, political prophecies, literary motifs, Theophany, ceremonial duty and ethical character, theodicy, and eschatology. Methods of instruction include lecture, discussion, and textual analysis.
Credit Recommendation: In the lower division baccalaureate/associate degree category or in the upper division baccalaureate degree category, 3 semester hours in The Book of Isaiah, Religious Studies elective, or elective in Hebraic/Judaic Studies (12/91) (2/97).

The Later Prophets: Jeremiah (REL 470)
(Formerly Jeremiah [REL 470])

Location: The Zaidner Institute, Neve Yerushalayim, Jerusalem.
Length: 39 hours (13 weeks).
Dates: September 1984-Present.
Objective: To examine the Book of Jeremiah in the original Hebrew with 11th century commentary of Rashi and other classical commentaries.
Learning Outcome: Upon successful completion of this course, the student will be able to articulate an in-depth understanding of the major moral, religious, political, historical, and theological elements of the Book of Jeremiah.
Instruction: Major topics covered in the course are historical and geopolitical context, Jeremiah's biography, false prophecy, symbolic prophecy, consolation, eschatology, and universalism. Methods of instruction include lecture, discussion, and textual analysis.
Credit Recommendation: In the lower division baccalaureate/associate degree category or in the upper division baccalaureate degree category, 3 semester hours in The Book of Jeremiah, Religious Studies elective, or Hebraic/Judaic Studies (12/91) (2/97).

Theories of Personality (PSY 420)

Location: The Zaidner Institute, Neve Yerushalayim, Jerusalem.
Length: *Version 1:* 42 hours (14 weeks); *Version 2:* 39 hours (13 weeks).
Dates: *Version 1:* January 1986-January 1997; *Version 2:* February 1997-Present.
Objective: To give the student an understanding of and appreciation for the historical process in the development of modern psychology, comparing the major theories of personality, with an emphasis on practical application.
Learning Outcome: Upon successful completion of this course, the student will be able to understand the theoretical underpinnings of each major personality theory based on the impact of historical and social influences upon its originator; be conversant with all the major theories that have contributed to and shaped modern psychological thought; and be able to evaluate the contributions of each theory and to assess the current status of each theory.
Instruction: Major topics covered in the course are major personality theories, development of normal and abnormal behavior, and historical influences on the development of various personality theories. The course provides a comprehensive view of the development of personality theory over the last 100 years. Methods of instruction include lectures, video presentations, reading of selected literature, and workshop discussions.
Credit Recommendation: In the upper division baccalaureate degree category, 3 semester hours in Theories of Personality (12/91) (2/97). *Prerequisite:* Introduction to Psychology.

Topics in Chassidic Thought (PHI 420)

Location: The Zaidner Institute, Neve Yerushalayim, Jerusalem.
Length: 39 hours (13 weeks).
Dates: September 1992-Present.
Objective: To analyze the fundamental concepts of chassidic thought, through the examination of primary and secondary source materials.
Learning Outcome: Upon successful completion of this course, the student will be able to demonstrate an understanding of the fundamental concepts of the chassidic world view; and the ideological conflict separating Chassidim and Mitnagdim.
Instruction: Major topics covered in the course are worship, prayer, Torah study, ritual performance, the righteous master, and conceptions of G-d. Methods of instruction include lecture and discussion.
Credit Recommendation: In the lower division baccalaureate/associate degree category or in the upper division baccalaureate degree category, 3 semester hours in Topics in Chassidic Thought, Religious Studies, Theology, or Hebrew/Judaic Studies (2/97).

Topics in Jewish Philosophy (PHI 485)

Location: The Zaidner Institute, Neve Yerushalayim, Jerusalem.
Length: 39 hours (13 weeks).
Dates: September 1984-Present.
Objective: To provide the advanced student with an insight into selected Jewish philosophical and theological topics.
Learning Outcome: Upon successful completion of this course, the student will be able to demonstrate an understanding of differing classical approaches to a variety of Jewish theological and philosophical topics.
Instruction: Major topics covered in the course are the approach of various schools of Jewish thought and their biblical/rabbinic roots, Maimonidean rationalism, Safed pietism, East European mystical-rationalism, Lurianic mysticism, and chassidic thought. Methods of instruction include lecture, discussion, and textual analysis.
Credit Recommendation: In the upper division baccalaureate degree category, 3 semester hours in Topics in Jewish Philosophy (12/91) (2/97).

Zaidner Institute of Montreal

Maalot-Montreal, a division of the Zaidner Institute in Israel, was established in 1997 to provide a quality college level education in an Orthodox Jewish environment. Currently the student population consists of young women with a strong background in Jewish studies who are pursuing a degree in Liberal Arts with a view to meeting the degree requirements of the Thomas A. Edison State College of New Jersey.

The course selection reflects the students' career interests in Jewish studies, in the social sciences related to education, and in computer science.

A highly qualified and experienced faculty teaches the courses which are congruent with those of the Zaidner Institute in Israel. The close association between the Montreal and Israel divisions ensures consistency and ongoing monitoring for course development and revision.

Source of official student records: Registry of Credit Recommendations, American Council on Education, One Dupont Circle, Washington, DC 20036-1193.

Additional information about the courses: College Credit Recommendation Service, American Council on Education, One Dupont Circle, Washington, DC 20036-1193.

Abnormal Psychology (PSY 430)

Location: The Zaidner Institute, Neve Yerushalayim, Jerusalem.

Length: 39 hours (13 weeks)..

Dates: February 1997-Present.

Objective: To introduce the student to the concept of normal vs. abnormal behavior and to understand its causes, manifestations, and treatment.

Learning Outcome: Upon successful completion of the course, the student will be able to understand historical perspectives toward abnormal behavior; be familiar with all the major DSM-IV classifications of abnormal behavior — their causes, manifestations, and treatment (neuroses, psychosomatic disorders, personality disorders, addictive disorders, psychoses, organic disorders, eating disorders, suicide, and developmental disorders of childhood); understand the psychoanalytic, environmental, behavioral, and humanistic theories about mental illness; and be familiar with the major forms of treatment available today.

Instruction: Major topics covered in the course are historical perspective, major psychiatric (DSM-IV) categories, causes and treatment, and three major therapeutic orientations: Psychoanalytical, Behavioral, and Humanistic. Methods of instruction include lecture and case study analysis.

Credit Recommendation: In the upper division baccalaureate degree category, 3 semester hours in Abnormal Psychology (2/97). *Prerequisites:* Introduction to Psychology and Theories of Personality.

Calculus I (MAT 111)

Location: Zaidner Institute of Montreal.

Length: 39 hours (13 weeks).

Dates: February 1997-Present.

Objective: To offer to the student an introduction to calculus, in particular differential calculus. The course will provide the student with the ability to continue to integral calculus.

Learning Outcome: Upon successful completion of this course, the student will be able to understand limits; understand and apply concepts of derivations; and understand the importance of core theories such as Rolle's Theorem, the Mean Value Theorem, etc.

Instruction: Major topics covered in the course are number systems, elements of analytical geometry, functions and function theory, limits, differentiation, and applications of derivatives. Methods of instruction include lectures, examinations, quizzes, and homework.

Credit Recommendation: In the lower division baccalaureate/associate degree category, 3 semester hours in Calculus I (2/97).

College Algebra (MAT 101)

Location: Zaidner Institute of Montreal.

Length: 39 hours (13 weeks).

Dates: February 1997-Present.

Objective: To provide students with algebra skills and problem solving skills.

Learning Outcome: Upon successful completion of this course, the student will be able to solve verbal problems algebraically; understand the real and complex number system; and graph linear equations and inequalities.

Instruction: Major topics covered in the course are algebraic expressions, real and complex numbers, equations and inequalities, algebraic and graphic solutions, and verbal applications. Method of instruction includes lecture.

Credit Recommendation: In the lower division baccalaureate/associate degree category, 3 semester hours in College Algebra or Mathematics (2/97).

Computer Graphics I (ART 240)

Location: The Zaidner Institute, Neve Yerushalayim, Jerusalem.

Length: 39 hours (13 weeks)..

Dates: October 1995-Present.

Objective: To introduce the student to the basics of MAC computers and to achieve competence in the communication between the MAC and IBM systems. To obtain fluency in the Freehand 6.5 System.

Learning Outcome: Upon successful completion of this course, the student will be able to use the graphic programs of the computer competently and efficiently enough for their graphic needs; use the mouse and keyboard skillfully; gain a basic understanding of computers and concepts in computers; and develop almost unlimited creative options.

Instruction: Major topics covered in the course are how to produce lines, shapes and other graphics needs, and learn about the computer and its functions. Methods of instruction include lecture, practical assignments, and practical work.

Credit Recommendation: In the lower division baccalaureate/associate degree category, 4 semester hours in Computer Graphics I (2/97).

Computer Graphics II (ART 310)

Location: Zaidner Institute of Montreal.

Length: 39 hours (13 weeks).

Dates: February 1996-Present.

Objective: To allow for the student to develop skills in the application of image processing and painting using various computer programs, to enable them to perform those tasks essential to graphic design work.

Learning Outcome: Upon successful completion of this course, the student will be able to use PhotoShop for image editing and painting; understand the difference between various computerized graphics methods; understand image processing and color terminology; scan and create an image; and edit, enhance, and print or export it for use in other applications.

Instruction: Major topics covered in the course are computerized image editing and painting, the attainment of the correct terminology and skills to facilitate the processes of creating and scanning an image, and enhancing an image and its future printing and exporting. Methods of instruction include lecture and practical work.

Credit Recommendation: In the lower division baccalaureate/associate or upper division baccalaureate degree category, 4 semester hours in Computer Graphics II (2/97).

Computer Graphics III (ART 320)

Location: Zaidner Institute of Montreal.

Length: 39 hours (13 weeks).

Dates: February 1996-Present.

Objective: To teach students the advanced study of layout application, enabling them to complete layout tasks within the realm of graphic design.

Learning Outcome: Upon successful completion of this course, the student will be able to use Quark Xpress for layout tasks such as creating a newspaper, brochure, books, or poster and understand layout terminology.

Instruction: Major topics covered in the course are computerized layout and its relevant applications and terminology and how to complete various layout tasks skillfully and creatively. Methods of instruction include lecture and lab.

Credit Recommendation: In the upper division baccalaureate degree category, 4 semester hours in Computer Graphics III (2/97).

Data Processing (CMP 201)

Location: Zaidner Institute of Montreal.

Length: 39 hours (13 weeks).

Dates: February 1997-Present.

Objective: To provide the students with an understanding of how companies and institutions use computers to process information and to gain meaningful output; the course takes an overall view of the data processing systems.

Learning Outcome: Upon successful completion of this course, the student will be able to understand computer and data processing terminology; gain an understanding of software and hardware systems; design records and files; and design input forms and output records.

Instruction: Major topics covered in the course are the nature and utility of computers, explanations of basic hardware, explanations of basic software, design of a database, design of input forms, and design of output reports. Methods of instruction include lectures, examinations, and projects.

Credit Recommendation: In the lower division baccalaureate/associate degree category, 3 semester hours in Data Processing (2/97).

Database (CMP 440)

Location: Zaidner Institute of Montreal.

Length: 39 hours (13 weeks).

Dates: February 1997-Present.

Objective: To provide the student with a general introduction of the concepts of database management systems, relational database, and data warehousing.

Learning Outcome: Upon successful completion of this course, the student will be able to understand the various kinds of databases and work with a database.

Instruction: Major topics covered in the course are database concepts and definitions, physical organization, components of databases, data modeling, data normalization, data description and query languages, SQL, query processing, transaction processing, database integrity, database designs, C/S environment, and data warehousing. Methods of instruction include lecture, discussion, demonstration of hardware, and lab.

Credit Recommendation: In the upper division baccalaureate degree category, 3 semester hours in Computer Science or Computer Information Systems elective (2/97).

Introduction to Computers (CMP 101)

Location: Zaidner Institute of Montreal.

Length: 39 hours (13 weeks).

Dates: February 1997-Present.

Objective: To introduce the elementary programming concepts to the student and develop proficiency in programming in BASIC.

Learning Outcome: Upon successful completion of this course, the student will be able to analyze a problem, write an algorithm for it, and code its solution in BASIC; debug and thoroughly test the program; and decide which sort or search methods are most efficient for a particular case and implement the method.

Instruction: Major topics covered in the course are processing numeric and character information, debugging and testing (verification) of programs, program structure, arithmetic operations, looping, input/output operations, arrays, subroutines, character string manipulation, and sorting and searching. Methods of instruction include lectures, lab, examinations, and programs.

Credit Recommendation: In the lower division baccalaureate/associate degree category, 3 semester hours in Computer Science or as a Computer Science elective (2/97).

Introduction to Psychology (PSY 101)

Location: Zaidner Institute of Montreal.

Length: 39 hours (13 weeks).

Dates: February 1997-Present.

Objective: To provide an overview of the various theories, methods, and fields of basic and applied psychology.

Learning Outcome: Upon successful completion of this course, the student will be able to demonstrate familiarity with biological and physiological influences on psychology (sensation and perception) and with major personality theories, mental health/illness, and social influences upon people.

Instruction: Major topics covered in the course are biological bases of behavior, human intellect, personality, mental health, pscyhodevelopment, and social psychology. Method of instruction includes lecture.

Credit Recommendation: In the lower division baccalaureate/associate degree category, 3 semester hours in Introduction to Psychology or Principles of Psychology (2/97).

Introduction to Sociology (SOC 101)

Location: Zaidner Institute of Montreal.

Length: 39 hours (13 weeks).

Dates: February 1997-Present.

Objective: To present basic sociological concepts and methods through understandable definitions and contemporary examples and to familiarize students with the main theoretical approaches, enabling them to use sociological theories and concepts in evaluating human interactions and institutions.

Learning Outcome: Upon successful completion of this course, the student will be able to contrast the sociological perspective with that of other social science disciplines; explain the sociological processes of social organization, socialization, conformity and deviance, social stratification, bureaucratization, discrimination, collective behavior, and social change; understand and apply sociological theories and methods; and identify the critical social instructions of human societies and describe their functions, patterns of organization, and differential treatment of individuals and groups.

Instruction: Major topics covered in the course are the nature and perspectives of sociology; methods of sociological research; organization of social life; socialization; groups; social stratification; deviance and social control; racial and cultural minorities; formal organizations; collective behavior and social movements; role, position, and identity; and social change. Methods of instruction include lecture, discussion, exercises, and presentations.

Credit Recommendation: In the lower division baccalaureate/associate degree category, 3 semester hours in Introduction to Sociology (2/97).

Isaiah (REL 370)

Location: Zaidner Institute of Montreal.
Length: 39 hours (13 weeks).
Dates: February 1987-Present.
Objective: To examine the Book of Isaiah in the original Hebrew with the 11th century commentary of Rashi and other classical commentaries.
Learning Outcome: Upon successful completion of this course, the student will be able to articulate an in-depth understanding of the historical, religious, and moral elements of the book of Isaiah.
Instruction: Major topics covered in the course are geopolitical context; Israel as the suffering servant; political prophecies; literary motifs; Theophany, ceremonial duty, and ethical character; Theodicy; and Eschatology. Methods of instruction include lecture, discussion, and textual analysis.
Credit Recommendation: In the lower division baccalaureate/associate or upper division baccalaureate degree category, 3 semester hours in The Book of Isaiah, Religious Studies elective, or elective in Hebraic/Judaic Studies (2/97).

Jeremiah (REL 470)

Location: Zaidner Institute of Montreal.
Length: 39 hours (13 weeks).
Dates: February 1987-Present.
Objective: To examine the Book of Jeremiah in the original Hebrew with 11th century commentary of Rashi and other classical commentaries.
Learning Outcome: Upon successful completion of this course, the student will be able to articulate an in-depth understanding of the major moral, religious, political, historical, and theological elements of the Book of Jeremiah.
Instruction: Major topics covered in the course are historical and geopolitical context, Jeremiah's biography, false prophecy, symbolic prophecy, consolation, Eschatology, and universalism. Methods of instruction include lecture, discussion, and textual analysis.
Credit Recommendation: In the lower division baccalaureate/associate or upper division baccalaureate degree category, 3 semester hours in The Book of Jeremiah, Religious Studies elective, or Hebraic/ Judaic Studies (2/97).

Job (REL 355)

Location: Zaidner Institute of Montreal.
Length: 39 hours (13 weeks).
Dates: February 1987-Present.
Objective: To examine the Book of Job in the original Hebrew with the 11th century commentary of Rashi and other classical commentaries.
Learning Outcome: Upon successful completion of this course, the student will be able to articulate an in-depth understanding of the major religious and moral elements of the Book of Job, in particular Biblical Theodicy.
Instruction: Major topics covered in the course are Job as a literary figure – allegory and history; Theodicy in its Biblical and post-Biblical perspectives; a Just God and the problem of Evil; classical commentaries from Job; and God and Man - reaching out response. Methods of instruction include lecture, discussion, and textual analysis.
Credit Recommendation: In the upper division baccalaureate degree category, 3 semester hours of The Book of Job, Religious Studies elective, or Hebraic/Judaic Studies (2/97).

Linear Algebra (MAT 221)

Location: Zaidner Institute of Montreal.
Length: 39 hours (13 weeks).
Dates: February 1997-Present.
Objective: To teach the student linear algebra and to expand the student's theoretical background in linear systems and linear operators to facilitate education in future courses such as differential equations, numerical analysis, and linear programming.
Learning Outcome: Upon successful completion of this course, the student will be able to understand vectors and vector spaces; solve systems of linear equations; perform multiplication of matrices and inverse matrices; solve equations involving matrices; understand determinants, minors, cofactors, classical adjoints, eigenvalues, and eigenvectors of matrices; understand the Cayley-Hamilton Theorem, canonical form of matrices, and invariant subspaces; and use inner products to compute norms.
Instruction: Major topics covered in the course are vectors, linear equations and systems of linear equations, matrices, vector spaces, basis and dimension, linear transformations, determinants, eigenvalues and eigenvectors, characteristic equation, canonical forms, diagonalization, invariant subspaces, linear functionals, and inner product spaces. Methods of instruction include lectures, examinations, quizzes, and homework.
Credit Recommendation: In the upper division baccalaureate degree category, 3 semester hours in Linear Algebra (2/97).

Macroeconomics (BUS 260)

Location: Zaidner Institute of Montreal.
Length: 39 hours (13 weeks).
Dates: February 1997-Present.
Objective: To give the student an understanding of the nature of macroeconomics theory as applied to economic output, price levels, and unemployment.
Learning Outcome: Upon successful completion of this course, the student will be able to appreciate the circular flows in economic environments; understand the history and nature of macroeconomics; understand the means of determining economic outputs; appreciate the role of government and fiscal policy; understand the banking system and monetary policy; relate to the issues of unemployment; relate to the issues of inflation; and appreciate the interrelation between economic and political considerations.
Instruction: Major topics covered in the course are macroelements of supply and demand; measuring national output; consumption and investment; government fiscal and monetary policy (FRB); income distribution and wealth; and inflation and unemployment. Methods of instruction include lecture, discussion, case studies, and presentations.
Credit Recommendation: In the lower division baccalaureate/associate degree category, 3 semester hours in Principles of Macroeconomics (2/97).

Megillot II: Song of Songs, Ecclesiastes, Lamentations (REL 365)

Location: The Zaidner Institute, Neve Yerushalayim, Jerusalem.
Length: 39 hours (13 weeks)..
Dates: September 1984-Present.
Objective: To examine the Book of Song of Songs, Ecclesiastes, and Lamentations in the original Hebrew with the 11th century commentary of Rashi and other classical commentaries.
Learning Outcome: Upon successful completion of this course, the student will be able to articulate an understanding of the major religious, literary, and moral symbolic elements of the Books of Song of Songs, Ecclesiastes, and Lamentations.
Instruction: Major topics covered in the course are Song of Songs — issues of authorship, literary issues (allegorical interpretation, structure, and style); Ecclesiastes — authorship, canonic issues, wisdom, wisdom literature, pessimism, and optimism; Lamentations — historical context; the role of Jerusalem; and Theodicy. Methods of instruction include lecture, discussion, and textual analysis.
Credit Recommendation: In the lower division baccalaureate/associate degree category or in the upper division baccalau-

reate degree category, 3 semester hours in Song of Songs, Ecclesiastes, Lamentations, Religious Studies elective, or Hebraic/Judaic Studies (2/97).

Microeconomics (BUS 250)

Location: Zaidner Institute of Montreal.
Length: 39 hours (13 weeks).
Dates: February 1997-Present.
Objective: To give the successful student an understanding of the nature and practice of the function of the market, price, production, and the economic behavior of the firm.
Learning Outcome: Upon successful completion of this course, the student will be able to understand utility and demand theory; analyze cost; recognize imperfect completion in the market place; understand the firm and the labor market; understand the role of government in the markets; and appreciate the elements of international trade.
Instruction: Major topics covered in the course are output and price and supply and demand; theories of utility and demand; production cost analysis and marginal products; marginal costs; pricing input factors; land, resources, wages, salaries, and the labor market; competition – perfect and imperfect, oligopoly, monopoly, regulation, and antitrust policy; and government policy and public choice, economic growth, and international trade. Methods of instruction include lecture and discussion.
Credit Recommendation: In the lower division baccalaureate/associate degree category, 3 semester hours in Microeconomics (2/97).

Minor Prophets: Hosea and Zacharia (REL 375)

Location: Zaidner Institute of Montreal.
Length: 39 hours (13 weeks).
Dates: February 1987-Present.
Objective: To examine the original Hebrew text of the prophetic books of Hosea and Zacharia, their poetic figure and lyrical style, and their moral/political/theological messages from various exegetical perspectives.
Learning Outcome: Upon successful completion of this course, the student will be able to articulate an understanding of the lyrical quality and figurative references of the minor prophets; the moral, political, and theological message of the books; and the variety of Talmudic, midrashic, and exegetical interpretations.
Instruction: Major topics covered in the course are a general introduction to the minor prophets, geopolitical cultural context of the message, repentance and reconciliation, knowledge of God, the prophetic experience, and poetic and literary conceptions. Methods of instruction include lecture, discussion, and textual analysis.
Credit Recommendation: In the lower division baccalaureate/associate or upper division baccalaureate degree category, 3 semester hours in Minor Prophets: Hosea and Zacharia, Religious Studies elective, or Hebraic/Judaic Studies (2/97).

Programming C++ (CMP 250)

Location: Zaidner Institute of Montreal.
Length: 39 hours (13 weeks).
Dates: February 1997-Present.
Objective: To teach the student how to program in C++ with an understanding of the features of the language. The course covers theory as well as practical applications.
Learning Outcome: Upon successful completion of this course, the student will be able to write programs in C++ using most of the features of the language.
Instruction: Major topics covered in the course are an introduction to object-oriented programming, data types, arrays, strings, enumerations, pointers, pointer arithmetic, dynamic storage, loops and other control structures, function prototyping, function calls, recursion, pointers to functions, and an introduction to inheritance and polymophism. Methods of instruction include lecture, labs, examinations, and programs.
Credit Recommendation: In the lower division baccalaureate/associate degree category, 3 semester hours in Programming (2/97).

Psychological Testing and Measurement (PSY 410)

Location: Zaidner Institute of Montreal.
Length: 39 hours (13 weeks).
Dates: February 1997-Present.
Objective: To provide the theoretical and practical information necessary to competently understand and evaluate the major psychological tests used today.
Learning Outcome: Upon successful completion of this course, the student will be able to interpret psychiatric test results; understand statistical analysis of tests; know major components of I.Q. tests; understand the nature of personality tests and the difference between projective and standardized tests; and be aware of ethical issues in testing.
Instruction: Major topics covered in the course are the characteristics of psychological tests, intelligence tests, aptitude, and interest tests; and personality tests. Methods of instruction include lecture and class demonstration.
Credit Recommendation: In the upper division baccalaureate degree category, 3 semester hours in Psychological Tests and Measurements (2/97). *Prerequisite:* Introduction to Psychology, Developmental Psychology I, and/or Theories of Personality are suggested.

Social Psychology (PSY 340)

Location: The Zaidner Institute, Neve Yerushalayim, Jerusalem.
Length: 39 hours (13 weeks).
Dates: February 1997-Present.
Objective: To evaluate the theoretic and scientific methods of how people perceive, influence, and relate to one another.
Learning Outcome: Upon successful completion of this course, the student will be able to know the experimental method in social psychology, causes and effects of prejudice, learned social behavior, competition and cooperation in social situations, and altruism in human behavior.
Instruction: Major topics covered in the course are theory and research on how an individual affects and is affected by his or her social environment; membership in groups, both formal and informal; conformity, prejudice, competition, and cooperation; and a basic understanding of the major principles and theories regarding how an individual is affected by the groups of which he or she is a part. Methods of instruction include lecture, discussion, and written examinations.
Credit Recommendation: In the upper division baccalaureate degree category, 3 semester hours in Social Psychology (2/97). *Prerequisite:* Introduction to Sociology or Instruction to Psychology.

Sociology of Education (SOC 210)

Location: Zaidner Institute of Montreal.
Length: 39 hours (13 weeks).
Dates: February 1997-Present.
Objective: To explore the educational process through the discipline of sociology and the related discipline of social psychology, and to examine the organization and effects of education in industrial society.
Learning Outcome: Upon successful completion of this course, the student will be able to distinguish between socialization, learning, and education, between peer group and reference group, between manifest and latent functions of education, and between social class caste, culture, status, and prestige; discuss the effects of bureaucracy in formal education; identify factors that contribute to inequality in educational opportunities and conflict within the educational system; dis-

cuss proposals for educational reform; and apply principles of group dynamics to the analysis of classroom behavior.

Instruction: Major topics covered in the course are learning in a social setting, functions of education, classroom as a social system, schools and student subcultures, controversy amidst educational research, organization of the educational enterprise, teachers as employees or professionals, conflict and legitimacy in school, education and inequality, emerging issues in modern education, and proposals for educational reform. Methods of instruction include discussion, lecture, and field observation.

Credit Recommendation: In the lower division baccalaureate/associate degree category, 3 semester hours in The Sociology of Education (2/97). *Prerequisite:* Introduction to Sociology or Introduction to Psychology.

Sociology of the Community (SOC 310)

Location: Zaidner Institute of Montreal.

Length: 39 hours (13 weeks).

Dates: February 1997-Present.

Objective: To examine the different approaches to the concept of community and analyze the relationship between community dynamics and social policy.

Learning Outcome: Upon successful completion of this course, the student will be able to provide varying definitions of the concept "community" and their historical and ideological backgrounds; explain the functions provided by communities; discuss and contrast models of community development and attachment; analyze patterns of community life; and discuss social policy implications arising from an understanding of the sociology of the community.

Instruction: Major topics covered in the course are the concept of community, community types, theories of community, social system theory, conflict theory, community power structure and leadership, methods of community study and research, community development and dynamics, the Jewish community, and the future of "community". Methods of instruction include lecture, discussion, and student presentations.

Credit Recommendation: In the upper division baccalaureate degree category, 3 semester hours in the Sociology of Community or Social Science elective (2/97). *Prerequisite:* Introduction to Sociology.

Theories of Personality (PSY 420)

Location: Zaidner Institute of Montreal.

Length: 39 hours (13 weeks).

Dates: February 1997-Present.

Objective: To give the student an understanding of and appreciation for the historical process in the development of modern psychology, comparing the major theories of personality, with an emphasis on practical application.

Learning Outcome: Upon successful completion of this course, the student will be able to understand the theoretical underpinnings of each major personality theory based on the impact of historical and social influences upon its originator; be conversant with all the major theories that have contributed to and shaped modern psychological thought; and evaluate the contributions of each theory and to assess the current status of each theory.

Instruction: Major topics covered in the course are major personality theories, development of normal and abnormal behavior, and historical influences on the development of various personality theories. The course provides a comprehensive view of the development of personality theory over the last 100 years. Methods of instruction include lectures, video presentations, reading of selected literature, and workshop discussions.

Credit Recommendation: In the upper division baccalaureate degree category, 3 semester hours in Theories of Personality (2/97). *Prerequisite:* Introduction to Psychology.

Evaluation Process:

Procedures
and
Criteria

The Evaluation Process: Procedures and Criteria

The credit recommendations in this guide are established on the basis of a thorough evaluation process. Organizations participate in the program on a voluntary basis. Each organization selects courses for review with the assistance of ACE/CREDIT staff.

Eligibility

1. Organizations eligible to submit educational programs for review are private industry, government agencies, labor unions, and associations that offer courses to their employees, members, or customers. Also eligible are professional, trade, or industrial associations whose primary or exclusive purpose is to provide occupationally oriented educational programs to members or to employees of member organizations.

2. Only educational programs or courses conducted on a formal basis and with official approval of the organization are considered. Courses must be under the control of the participating organization. Informal on-the-job training and job experience usually are not reviewed.

   Although learning outcomes are the most important basis for making credit recommendations, the following factors must also be considered when selecting courses or programs for review. The course:

   - content and rigor must be at the postsecondary level.
   - material presented must be at the postsecondary level.
   - must have a prescribed program of instruction.
   - instructors should be selected on the basis of their qualifications, including formal education and experience, to teach the subject matter.
   - should serve people who can use the credit recommendations toward a postsecondary credential or who can use it for employment or advancement purposes.
   - must use appropriate procedures (tests, projects, oral quizzes, etc.) to evaluate student performance. Correspondence, distance learning, and independent study courses must include a proctored examination administered under secure conditions.
   - courses must be currently offered or newly developed courses, which have not been offered to regular classes, must first be offered to student pilot test groups.

Documentation

3. Prior to the review, organizations submit information concerning the administration of their educational programs. This information helps ACE/CREDIT determine whether the organization demonstrates sufficient stability and control to present its courses for review.

   Administrative information submitted includes:

   - A description of the administration of the training program;
   - Procedures for selecting and evaluating instructional staff;
   - Procedures for course development, evaluation, and revision; and
   - Procedures for ensuring consistent quality in programs delivered at multiple locations.

   This submission becomes part of ACE/CREDIT's permanent record on the participating organization.

4. Course information submitted includes:

   - Course syllabus describing the objectives and content.
   - Instructional materials (textbooks, audiovisual materials, case studies, problems, etc.) used for the course.
   - Required or suggested qualifications of course participants.
   - Qualifications of instructional staff.
   - Techniques (including samples, if available) used to evaluate student performance.
   - Duration of the course.

5. For courses and programs involving other instructional approaches, e.g., videotapes, computers, or independent study courses, some of the foregoing information is not appropriate to the process. However, appropriate and available items must be provided in sufficient detail to allow each course to be judged by the review team. (See *Distance Learning Evaluation Guide*)

6. Each participating organization must maintain permanent and official records of students' participation and perfor-

mance in any course which is reviewed. The organization must demonstrate the capability to store and retrieve student records for the period covered by the credit recommendations and must participate in the Registry of Credit Recommendations.

Selection of Reviewers

7. To conduct initial course reviews, no fewer than two subject matter specialists are used. The names of potential reviewers are solicited from postsecondary institutions, professional and educational associations, accrediting agencies, and noncollegiate organizations. Among criteria considered in selecting course evaluators are:

- Reviewer competence as evidenced by formal training and experience in area of courses being reviewed.
- Credibility and reputation among colleagues.
- Teaching experience and other aspects of experience in postsecondary settings, including knowledge of curriculum and instruction as evidenced, for example, by having served on a curriculum committee.

The Course Review

8. Review sessions usually are conducted at the location of the organization offering the courses. Organizational staff members familiar with the courses are available to answer questions that may arise during the review of course materials.

After a thorough review of all the information and materials supplied by the organization, the team members first decide if a course is at the college level. If it is, they then determine the category of credit (described in the section "How to Use This Guide,"), the number of credit hours, and the appropriate subject area(s) in which credit can be recommended. Whenever the team establishes a credit recommendation for a course, it has determined that the method of assessment is adequate to judge that students successfully completing the course have mastered the subject matter. The team members also review each course exhibit (the description of the course that will appear in *The National Guide*) to ensure that it adequately describes the course.

If the team recommends that no academic credit be granted the course will not appear in the guide.

Evaluative Criteria

9. When exercising their professional judgment to determine a credit recommendation, experienced review team members consider the following factors while comparing college courses they teach with those being reviewed:

- The content of a course, its level of difficulty, its applicability to a range of postsecondary programs, and its learning outcomes are of primary importance.
- Distinctive aspects of workplace education, including the background and selection of both instructors and students, the duration of a course, ongoing application of classroom and outside learning in the student's work, and motivational factors.
- For independent study courses and courses delivered by computers, internet, television, and other means, the quality and technical merits of the assessment instruments must be exemplary because of their key role in determining the acquisition of desired learning outcomes. (See *Distance Learning Evaluation Guide*)

Credit recommendations made by reviewers are not derived by a simple arithmetic conversion. Intensive courses offered by participating organizations do not necessarily require as much outside preparation as many regular college courses. Reviewers consider the factors of pre- and post-course assignments, prior work-related experience, the concentrated nature of the learning experience, and course material reinforcement in the subsequent work setting.

In some cases, the team may cluster a group of two or more related courses which individually are too short to be eligible for review. Courses are combined for review only if they form a coherent sequence and can be viewed as components of a larger course. If appropriate, a single credit recommendation is established for the group of courses; in such cases, the recommendation applies only when a student has completed all courses.

Reasons for failing to recommend credit have included:

- The course is too limited in scope or too narrowly focused to be comparable to those in college programs.
- The material presented in the course is not comparable to courses offered by colleges and universities.
- Adequate evaluation of student performance is lacking.

- The material presented is insufficient for a judgment to be based upon it.

Updating Recommendations

10. Credit recommendations are kept current by the following procedures:

- On an annual basis, participating organizations must submit information on each course for which a credit recommendation has been established. Any indication of a substantive change in a course will result in a re-evaluation of the course.
- At three-year intervals, each course is reviewed by a team of subject matter specialists to determine if the credit recommendation is still applicable. Ideally, this team will consist of at least one member of the team that established the initial recommendation. The course materials will be compared with those used at the time of the last review and with changes in the subject area field.

The course evaluation procedures used by the American Council on Education in the development of credit recommendations for apprenticeship programs and for independent-study courses are substantially the same as those described above. Descriptions of policies and procedures for the evaluation of apprenticeship programs and independent study are available on request from CREDIT.

Registry of Credit Recommendations

Registry of Credit Recommendations

The American Council on Education administers the Registry of Credit Recommendations for organizations participating in the ACE/CREDIT Program. The Registry offers individuals a permanent, computerized record of all courses evaluated by the ACE/CREDIT program.

The Registry enhances the probability of an individual receiving college credit for training courses by providing colleges and universities with a transcript formatted in a manner similar to most collegiate transcripts and carrying the seal of the American Council on Education. The transcript eliminates the need for an explanation of organization certificates of completion and organization-issued documents. In addition, it relieves organizations of the burden of handling transcript requests and issuing transcripts and provides individuals continuous access to their records.

Inclusion on the Registry transcript service is required of all ACE/CREDIT-participating organizations for a small fee per course.

How the Registry Works

- The American Council on Education's CREDIT Program or one of the ACE/CREDIT State Affiliate Offices conducts a course review.
- Course descriptions with credit recommendations are sent to participating organizations and to course review team members for verification.
- The finalized course exhibits are then published in *The National Guide to Educational Credit for Training Programs* and are entered into the Registry's computer file.
- A Registry welcome packet is sent to the participating organization and the method of participation is finalized.

How the Registry Is Used

- The ACECREDIT-participating organization informs course participants of ACE's credit recommendations.
- Individuals who successfully complete a course and are interested in establishing a record of their educational accomplishments must submit the required forms, or information signed by the participating organization's designated education representative, to the Registry with the $25.00 processing fee (a one-time fee for establishing and updating the individual's record).
- Individuals receive a course verification document that includes a cumulative course listing and a transcript request form. The participating organization also receives a verification document.
- An individual seeking college credit for ACE-evaluated courses requests in writing that the ACE Registry send a transcript to a designated college or university.
- ACE sends the requested transcript within five days of receiving the request.
- ACE sends an individual a confirmation card indicating the transcript has been sent.

For more information, call (202) 939-9434 and ask specifically for the Registry office, or write the Center for Adult Learning and Educational Credentials, American Council on Education, One Dupont Circle, Suite 250, Washington, DC 20036-1193; ATTN: Registries. (A sample Registry transcript appears on the following page.)

Sample Transcript

Registry of Credit Recommendations
American Council on Education
One Dupont Circle • Washington, D.C. 20036-1193
(202) 939-9434

VALIDATION NUMBER 8700117874

11/17/94

CANISIUS COLLEGE
ATTN REGISTRAR
2001 MAIN STREET
BUFFALO, NY 14208

SEND AT THE REQUEST OF

CLAVEN, CLIFFORD

BOSTON, MA 02116

IDENTIFICATION #: 000-00-0503
Birth Date: 08/08/45

		COURSE TITLE AND DESCRIPTION
CCHS-0008	02/15/93	**HUMAN ANATOMY AND PHYSIOLOGY (BIO 110)** **CALIFORNIA COLLEGE FOR HEALTH SCIENCES** **LD BACC/ASSOC-3 SH: HUMAN ANATOMY AND PHYSIOLOGY OR HUMAN BIOLOGY. IF BIO 110 AND BIO 120 COMPLETED, STUDENT COULD SEEK 6 SH: HEALTH SCIENCES** 9 LESSONS (125 HRS) STUDENT WILL BE ABLE TO DESCRIBE THE STRUCTURE AND FUNCTION OF ALL MAJOR ORGAN SYSTEMS OF THE HUMAN BODY.
CCHS-0015	07/15/93	**FUNDAMENTALS OF CHILD DEVELOPMENT (ECE 100)** **CALIFORNIA COLLEGE FOR HEALTH SCIENCES** **LD BACC/ASSOC-3 SH: EARLY CHILDHOOD EDUCATION** 7 SELF-PACED LESSONS (15 LEARNING EXERCISES) STUDENT WILL BE ABLE TO IDENTIFY & DESCRIBE SEVERAL LEARNING THEORIES; ANALYZE PHYSICAL, SOCIAL, COGNITIVE, & EMOTIONAL DEVELOPMENT.
CCHS-0020	08/08/94	**INFANT AND TODDLER CARE (ECE 120)** **CALIFORNIA COLLEGE FOR HEALTH SCIENCES** **LD BACC/ASSOC-3 SH: EARLY CHILDHOOD EDUCATION** 13 SELF-PACED MODULES STUDENT WILL UNDERSTAND THE DEVELOPMENT OF INFANTS & TODDLERS & PROVIDE THEM WITH AN ENRICHING ENVIRONMENT THAT WILL ENCOURAGE THEM TO REACH THEIR OPTIMAL POTENTIAL.
--------	--------- 3	Educational Activities on File -------------------------

Users are urged to consult the current issues of *The National Guide to Educational Credit for Training Programs* which is available from Oryx Press (800-279-ORYX) and *The Guide to Credit by Examination* which is available from the Credit by Examination Program of the American Council on Education (202-939-9434).

Awarding Credit for Extrainstitutional Learning

Awarding Credit for Extrainstitutional Learning[1]

The following statement by the ACE Commission on Educational Credit and Credentials has been approved by the ACE Board of Directors and endorsed by the Commission on Recognition of Postsecondary Accreditation.

The American Council on Education recommends that postsecondary educational institutions develop policies and procedures for measuring and awarding credit for learning attained outside their sponsorship.

American society abounds in resources for learning at the postsecondary level. Public, private, and proprietary educational institutions exercise the central but not exclusive responsibility for instruction and learning. Associations, business, government, industry, the military, and unions sponsor formal instruction. In addition, independent study and reading, work experiences, the mass media, and social interaction contribute to learning and competency.

Full and effective use of all educational resources is a worthy educational and social goal. Achieving this goal will depend to a large extent on providing equitable recognition for extrainstitutional learning.

- Educational credentials have a significant bearing on the economic, professional, and social status of the individual. Thus, social equity requires that equivalent learning, regardless of where or how it is achieved, be incorporated into the system of rewards for learning and competency; and

- Recognition encourages learning and contributes to pedagogical effectiveness. Teaching students what they already know is both stultifying to them and wasteful of educational and personal resources.

Postsecondary educational institutions legally authorized and accredited to award degrees and other educational credentials have a special responsibility to assess extrainstitutional learning as part of their credentialing function.

In the development of institutional policies and procedures, the American Council on Education recommends the following guidelines and resources.

Guidelines

1. Reliable and valid evaluation of student achievement is the *sine qua non* in awarding credit. Experience, whether acquired at work, in social settings, in the library, at home, or in the formal classroom, is in itself an inadequate basis for awarding credit. Increased attention to evaluation procedures and techniques is necessary when learning has been attained without participation in a program of study prescribed by an educational institution.

2. In determining whether it is appropriate to accept a student's extrainstitutional learning for credit, the governing consideration should be the student's educational objective, including requirements for graduation. Learning should be articulated, documented, and measured in the context of the institution's role and the student's educational objective.

3. Institutions should evaluate extrainstitutional learning and award credit only in subject-matter fields in which they have available faculty expertise or where they can rely on nationally validated examinations or other procedures for establishing credit equivalencies. Normally, institutions should evaluate learning and award credit only in subject fields in which they offer comparable courses or curricula; however, elective credit should be accepted appropriately.

4. Institutions awarding credit for extrainstitutional learning should develop clearly stated policies and other information related to administrative responsibility, student eligibility, means of assessment, recording of results on transcripts, storage of documentation, student fees, and maximum number of credits allowable.

5. Institutional policy should include the provision that the institution's policies and procedures for awarding credit for extrainstitutional learning be subject to periodic re-evaluation.

[1] "Extrainstitutional learning" is defined as learning that is attained outside the sponsorship of legally authorized and accredited postsecondary educational institutions. The term applies to learning acquired from work and life experiences, independent reading and study, the mass media, and participation in formal courses sponsored by associations, business, government, industry, the military, and unions.

Resources

1. *Guide to the Evaluation of Educational Experiences in the Armed Services*, published by the American Council on Education.

2. *The National Guide to Educational Credit for Training Programs*, published by the American Council on Education.

3. *Credentialing Educational Accomplishments*, published by the American Council on Education.

4. *Guide to Educational Credit by Examination*, published by the American Council on Education and available from the ACE Credit by Examination Program.

5. Publications of the Council for Adult and Experiential Learning, 223 W. Jackson Blvd., Suite 510, Chicago, IL 60606.

American Council on Education

ACE Board of Directors

Commission on Educational Credit and Credentials

ACE/PONSI Staff

ACE Board of Directors

EXECUTIVE COMMITTEE

Lois B. DeFleur, President
State University of New York
at Binghamton
Chair

John A. DiBiaggio, President
Tufts University
Vice Chair/Chair Elect

Michele Tolela Myers, President
Denison University
Immediate Past Chair

Vernon O. Crawley, President
Moraine Valley Community College
Secretary

Edward B. Fort, Chancellor
North Carolina Agricultural &
Technical State University

Freeman A. Hrabowski, III, President
University of Maryland
Baltimore County

Kenneth A. Shaw, President/
Chancellor
Syracuse University, NY

Elisabeth Zinser, Chancellor
University of Kentucky
Lexington Campus

Stanley O. Ikenberry, President
American Council on Education

CLASS OF 1998

Raymond C. Bowen, President
LaGuardia Community College
City University of New York

Edward B. Fort, Chancellor
North Carolina Agricultural &
Technical State University

Janet L. Holmgren, President
Mills College

Martin C. Jischke, President
Iowa State University

Steven S. Koblik, President
Reed College

Michele Tolela Myers, President
Denison University

Eduardo J. Padrón, President
Miami-Dade Community College

Elisabeth Zinser, Chancellor
University of Kentucky
Lexington Campus

CLASS OF 1999

Vernon O. Crawley, President
Moraine Valley Community College

Lois B. DeFleur, President
State University of New York
at Binghamton

John V. Lombardi, President
University of Florida

Walter E. Massey, President
Morehouse College

Anne S. McNutt, President
Technical College of the Lowcountry

Miguel A. Nevarez, President
University of Texas–Pan American

Kenneth A. Shaw, President/
Chancellor
Syracuse University

Julianne Still Thrift, President
Salem College

CLASS OF 2000

Michael F. Adams, President
University of Georgia

Robert M. Berdahl, Chancellor
University of California, Berkeley

Philip R. Day, Jr., President
Daytona Beach Community College

John A. DiBiaggio, President
Tufts University

Vera King Farris, President
Richard Stockton College
of New Jersey

Freeman A. Hrabowski, III, President
University of Maryland
Baltimore County

Neil Rudenstine, President
Harvard University

William Segura, Chancellor
Texas State Technical College System

ASSOCIATION REPRESENTATIVES

*Association of American Colleges
& Universities*
Harold W. Eickhoff, President
The College of New Jersey

*American Association of
Community Colleges*
Augustine P. Gallego, Chancellor
San Diego Community College District

*American Association of State
Colleges & Universities*
Ed M. Elliott, President
Central Missouri State University

Association of American Universities
Francis L. Lawrence, President
Rutgers, The State University
of New Jersey

*Association of Catholic Colleges
& Universities*
Karen M. Kennelly, CSJ, President
Mount St. Mary's College

*Association of Jesuit Colleges
& Universities*
Harold Ridley, SJ., President
Loyola College of Maryland

Council of Independent Colleges
Harold M. Kolenbrander, President
Mount Union College

*National Association for Equal
Opportunity in Higher Education*
(To be announced)

*National Association of Independent
Colleges & Universities*
Ann H. Die, President
Hendrix College

*National Association of State
Universities & Land-Grant Colleges*
Peter McPherson, President
Michigan State University

*American Association of Colleges
for Teacher Education*
Allen D. Glenn, Dean
College of Education, University
of Washington

*National Association of College
and University Attorneys*
Sheila Trice Bell, Executive Director
and Chief Executive Officer
National Association of College
and University Attorneys

*Washington Higher Education
Secretariat*
James E. Morley, Jr., President
National Association of College
and University Business Officers

Program Offices

American Council on Education

The American Council on Education is nationally recognized as a major coordinating body for postsecondary education. Within the council, the College Credit Recommendation Service (ACE/CREDIT) is administered by the Center for Adult Learning and Educational Credentials. The role of the center and its policy-making and advisory arm, the Commission on Educational Credit and Credentials, is to give attention to educational credit and credentialing policies for postsecondary education; to foster and operate programs to establish credit equivalencies among educational alternatives; to assist agencies and institutions in providing persons with due recognition for competency, knowledge, and skills, wherever and however obtained; and to provide individuals with an alternative means of demonstrating high school graduation competencies. The center makes credit recommendations for testing programs such as the College-Level Examination Program (CLEP) and administers the General Educational Development (GED) Testing Service and the National External Diploma Program (EDP). Other activities of the center include the evaluation of military formal courses and Army military occupational specialties (MOSs), selected Marine Corps MOSs, and Navy and Coast Guard ratings.

1998 Board of Directors

Executive Committee

Michele Tolela Myers, President, Denison University, *Chair*
Lois DeFleur, *Vice Chair/Chair Elect*
Eduardo J. Padrón, *Secretary*
Francis T. Borkowski
Rita Bornstein
Freeman A. Hrabowski, III
Manuel T. Pacheco
Kenneth A. Shaw
Elisabeth Zinser
Stanley O. Ikenberry, President, American Council on Education

Class of 1998

Raymond C. Bowen, President, LaGuardia Community College, City University of New York
John A. DiBiaggio, President, Tufts University (MA)
Edward B. Fort, Chancellor, North Carolina Agricultural & Technical State University
Martin C. Jischke, President, Iowa State University
Steven S. Koblik, President, Reed College (OR)
Michele Tolela Myers, President, Denison University (OH)
Eduardo J. Padrón, President, Miami-Dade Community College
Elisabeth Zinser, Chancellor, University of Kentucky

Class of 1999

Vernon O. Crawley, President, Moraine Valley Community College
Lois B. DeFleur, President, State University of New York at Binghamton
John V. Lombardi, President, University of Florida
Walter E. Massey, President, Morehouse College
Anne S. McNutt, President, Technical College of the Lowcountry
Miguel A. Nevarez, President, University of Texas-Pan American
Kenneth A. Shaw, President/Chancellor, Syracuse University
Julianne Still Thrift, President, Salem College

Elected Officers of Associations—Ex officio for three-year terms:

Harold W. Eickhoff, President, The College of New Jersey, *Association of American Colleges and Universities*
Augustine P. Gallego, President, San Diego Community College District, *American Association of Community Colleges*
Ed M. Elliott, President, Central Missouri State University, *American Association of State Colleges and Universities*
F. Patrick Ellis, FSC, President, The Catholic University of America, *Association of American Universities*
Karen M. Kennelly, CSJ, President, Mount St. Mary's College, *Association of Catholic Colleges and Universities*

John P. Schlegel, SJ, President, University of San Francisco, *Association of Jesuit Colleges and Universities*
John L. Henderson, President, Wilberforce University, *Council of Independent Colleges*
Earl S. Richardson, President, Morgan State University, *National Association for Equal Opportunity in Higher Education*
Ann H. Die, President, Hendrix College, *National Association of Independent Colleges and Universities*
Peter McPherson, President, Michigan State University, *National Association of State Universities and Land-Grant Colleges*

Elected Officers of Associations—Ex officio for one-year terms:
Mary Louise Reid, Chair, AGB Board of Directors, *Association of Governing Boards of Universities and Colleges*
Tomas A. Arciniega, President, California State University-Bakersfield, *Hispanic Association of Colleges and Universities*
James E. Morley, Jr., President, National Association of College and University Business Officers, *Washington Higher Education Secretariat*

Commission on Educational Credit and Credentials

Terms Ending December 31, 1998
Dennis M. Faber, Director, DACUM Resource Center, Dundalk Community College
Merle W. Harris, President, Charter Oak State College
Mary S. Knudten, Dean, University of Wisconsin Center-Waukesha County
Sigfredo Maestas, President, Northern New Mexico Community College
Donald J. MacIntyre, President, Fielding Institute
*Gregory S. Prince, Jr., President, Hampshire College

Terms Ending December 31, 1999
Franklin C. Ashby, Vice President for Instruction, Dale Carnegie & Associates
Zerrie D. Campbell, President, Malcolm X College
Robert L. Caret, President, San Jose State University
Robert G. Elkins, Manager, Union Pacific Railroad Company
Jerry Evans, Assistant Executive Director for Programs, Institute for Career Development, Inc.
Leon Flancher, Vice President for Extended Campus, Embry-Riddle Aeronautical University
Bonnie Gordon, Vice President for College Relations, Ithaca College
James W. Hall, President, Empire State College-SUNY
Edison O. Jackson, President, Medgar Evers College
Roberto Marrero-Corletto, Chancellor, University of Puerto Rico-Humacao Campus
John W. Moore, President, Indiana State University
Jerry Moskus, President, Lane Community College
Leslie N. Purdy, President, Coastline Community College
Allan Quigley, Professor of Adult Education, The Pennsylvania State University
Michael Sheeran, S.J., President, Regis University
Ronald Taylor, DeVry Institute
David Voight, Director, Small Business Center, U.S. Chamber of Commerce
David J. Ward, Sr., Vice President for Academic Affairs, University of Wisconsin System
Gregory Weidemann, Graduate Dean, Towson State University
Larry L. Whitworth, President, Tidewater Community College
*Chairperson

STAFF OFFICER
Susan Porter Robinson, ACE Vice President and Director
The Center for Adult Learning and Educational Credentials
American Council on Education

1998 ACE/CREDIT Advisory Committee

Rick Adamson, Executive Vice President, Learning Tree International
Richard J. Armbruster, Vice President, TESST Technology Institute
James L. Boyd, Director of Curriculum Development and Training, National Joint Apprenticeship and Training Committee for the Electrical Industry
Margaret Carty, Ex officio Member, BOMI Institute
Adrienne Cox, Program Services Coordinator, UAW-Ford
Steven T. Edwards, Director, Maryland Fire and Rescue Institute
Robert G. Elkins, Manager, Omaha Training Center, Union Pacific Railroad Company, *Chair*
George M. Flattery, President, ICI University
Jerry R. Foster, Director, Graduate School of Banking at Colorado
Larry Lottier, Dean, Dana Corporation
Nina Omelchenko, Vice President of University Services, University of Phoenix
Diane L. Rhodes, Service Quality Director, Business Customer Care, AT&T
Delbert Ringquist, Dean, College of Extended Learning, Central Michigan University
Remedios del Rosario, Commissioner of Water, City of Atlanta Water Department
Barbara Sadek, Director of Education, Society of Human Resource Management
Kenneth Scheiderman, Ex officio Member, California College for Health Sciences
Mary Lou Vainisi, Director, Learning and Development, McDonald's Corporation
Phyllis Walls, Director, Oklahoma Affiliate Office of ACE, The University of Oklahoma
Richard Wellins, Senior Vice President, Programs and Marketing, Development Dimensions International

Staff

Stanley O. Ikenberry, President, American Council on Education
Susan P. Robinson, ACE Vice President and Director, Center for Adult Learning and Educational Credentials
Stephen C. Sattler, Director, Marketing and Communications, Center for Adult Learning and Educational Credentials
Richard Kraus, Marketing Services Coordinator, Marketing and Communications, Center for Adult Learning and Educational Credentials

Jo Ann Robinson, Director, ACE/CREDIT and Corporate Programs
Jacqueline Taylor, Program Operations Manager
Nancy Musick, Accounts Manager
Theresa Watts, Assistant Director, ACE/CREDIT
Ben Hulan, Interim State Coordinator

Tina Brewington, Registries Coordinator
Mary Cowan, Staff Assistant
Kimblyn Short, Registries Assistant

Special thanks for guide production to Jennifer Brown and for editorial assistance to Janza Pullen.

National Educational Association Endorsements

ACE/CREDIT Endorsements

- AACSB-The International Association for Management Education
- ACT
- American Association of Colleges for Teacher Education
- American Association of Colleges of Nursing
- American Association of Collegiate Registrars and Admissions Officers
- American Association of Community Colleges
- American Association of State Colleges and Universities
- American Association of University Professors
- Association for Continuing Higher Education
- Association of American Colleges and Universities
- Association of Community College Trustees
- Association of Jesuit Colleges and Universities
- National Association of Independent Colleges and Universities
- National Association of State Universities and Land-Grant Colleges
- The College Board
- The University of Oklahoma
- University Continuing Education Association

Statement to Members by the American Association of Collegiate Registrars and Admissions Officers

The American Association of Collegiate Registrars and Admissions Officers (AACRAO) welcomes the efforts of the Center for Adult Learning and Educational Credentials in publishing *The National Guide to Educational Credit for Training Programs*.

The National Guide is a valuable tool for extending the concept of awarding credit for learning acquired outside the traditional framework of colleges and universities and is being used more widely than ever before by colleges and universities throughout the country.

Over the years, AACRAO has supported and endorsed the Center's companion evaluation activity, which gives us guidance for credit recommendations sponsored by the armed services. The *Guide to the Evaluation of Experiences in the Armed Services* is an equally valuable resource for AACRAO's members.

The National Guide will continue to gain a wider audience and will prove extremely useful to our member institutions. AACRAO commends this series to them as they formulate policies and make decisions on the awarding of credit for coursework offered through nontraditional methods.

Wayne E. Becraft
Executive Director
American Association of Collegiate Registrars and Admissions Officers

Statement from the AACSB-The International Association for Management Education

The AACSB-The International Association for Management Education supports the Center for Adult Learning and Educational Credentials of the American Council on Education in its efforts to enable learners to receive formal recognition for their educational accomplishments attained outside the college and university classroom. *The National Guide to Educational Credit for Training Programs* can be a useful tool and resource for information in awarding academic credit acquired in nontraditional settings.

Sharon Barber
Director of Communications
AACSB-The International Association for Management Education

Statement from ACT

The Center for Adult Learning and Educational Credentials of the American Council on Education is commended for its important work of establishing credit recommendations for organized learning experiences offered outside of traditional settings. Listings in *The National Guide to Educational Credit for Training Programs* include courses sponsored by business, industry, labor unions, and government; and by voluntary, professional, and religious associations. The ACT commends The Center for its efforts in publishing *The National Guide* and receives our full endorsement for its evaluation activity, which gives guidance to our member institutions that award academic credit for nontraditional learning.

David A. Lutz
Director of Postsecondary Services
ACT

Statement from the American Association of Colleges for Teacher Education

The American Association of Colleges for Teacher Education welcomes the efforts of ACE/CREDIT for its efforts in publishing *The National Guide to Educational Credit for Training Programs*. The National Guide is a valuable tool for awarding credit for learning acquired outside the traditional framework of colleges and universities and is being used widely throughout the country by registrars and other collegiate officials. We support the Center for Adult Learning and Educational Credentials in publishing *The National Guide*.

David G. Imig
Executive Director
American Association of Colleges for Teacher Education

Statement from the American Association of Colleges of Nursing

The American Association of Colleges of Nursing welcomes the efforts of ACE/CREDIT for its efforts in publishing *The National Guide to Educational Credit for Training Programs. The National Guide* is a valuable tool for awarding credit for learning acquired outside the traditional framework of colleges and universities and is being used widely throughout the country by registrars and other collegiate officials. We support the Center for Adult Learning and Educational Credentials in publishing *The National Guide.*

Carole A. Anderson
President
American Association of Colleges of Nursing

Statement from the American Association of Community Colleges

The Center for Adult Learning and Educational Credentials of the American Council on Education is commended for its important work of establishing credit recommendations for organized learning experiences offered outside of traditional settings. Listings in *The National Guide to Educational Credit for Training Programs* include courses sponsored by business, industry, labor unions, and religious associations. The American Association of Community Colleges commends The Center for its efforts in publishing *The National Guide* and receives our full endorsement for its evaluation activity, which gives guidance to our member institutions that award academic credit for nontraditional learning.

David R. Pierce
President
American Association of Community Colleges

Statement from the American Association of State Colleges and Universities

The American Association of State Colleges and Universities supports the Center for Adult Learning and Educational Credentials of the American Council on Education in its efforts to enable learners to receive formal recognition for their educational accomplishments attained outside the college and university classroom. The American Association of State Colleges and Universities recognizes *The National Guide to Educational Credit for Training Programs* as a valuable tool and resource for reliable information in awarding academic credit for learning acquired in nontraditional settings.

James B. Appleberry
President
American Association of State Colleges and Universities

Statement from the American Association of University Professors

The American Association of University Professors supports the Center for Adult Learning and Educational Credentials of the American Council on Education in its efforts to enable learners to receive formal recognition for their educational accomplishments attained outside the college and university classroom. The American Association of of University Professors recognizes *The National Guide to Educational Credit for Training Programs* as a valuable tool and resource for reliable information in awarding academic credit for learning acquired in nontraditional settings.

Mary Burgan
General Secretary
American Association of University Professors

Statement from the Association for Continuing Higher Education

The Association for Continuing Higher Education (ACHE) is pleased to endorse the American Council on Education's *National Guide to Educational Credit for Training Programs* produced by the College Credit Recommendation Service (CREDIT). We believe that the CREDIT program and the *Guide* provide a service which is critical for adult learners who wish to advance in their careers through continuing their collegiate education. By setting high standards for the recognition of extra-institutional learning, and providing a mechanism for colleges and universities across the country to recognize that learning with consistency and integrity, the American Council on Education is leading the way toward a lifelong learning society.

On this we congratulate you and wish you continued success. We pledge our support to the endeavor and will encourage our membership to recognize the CREDIT program at their institutions.

Paula E. Peinovich, PhD
President
Association for Continuing Higher Education

Statement from the Association of American Colleges and Universities

The Association of American Colleges and Universities supports the Center for Adult Learning and Educational Credentials of the American Council on Education in its efforts to enable learners to receive formal recognition for their educational accomplishments attained outside the college and university classroom.

Paula P. Brownlee
President
Association of American Colleges and Universities

Statement from the Association of Community College Trustees

The Association of Community College Trustees supports the Center for Adult Learning and Educational Credentials of the American Council on Education in its efforts to enable learners to receive formal recognition for their educational accomplishments attained outside the college and university classroom. The Association of Community College Trustees recognizes *The National Guide to Educational Credit for Training Programs* as a valuable tool and resource for reliable information in awarding academic credit for learning acquired in nontraditional settings.

Ray Taylor
President
Association of Community College Trustees

Statement from the Association of Jesuit Colleges and Universities

The Association of Jesuit Colleges and Universities supports the Center for Adult Learning and Educational Credentials of the American Council on Education in its efforts to enable learners to receive formal recognition for their educational accomplishments attained outside the college and university classroom. The Association of Jesuit Colleges and Universities recognizes *The National Guide to Educational Credit for Training Programs* as a valuable tool and resource for reliable information in awarding academic credit for learning acquired in nontraditional settings.

Paul S. Tipton, S.J.
President
Association of Jesuit Colleges and Universities

Statement from the National Association of Independent Colleges and Universities

The National Association of Independent Colleges and Universities supports the Center for Adult Learning and Educational Credentials of the American Council on Education in its efforts to enable learners to receive formal recognition for their educational accomplishments attained outside the college and university classroom. The National Association of Independent Colleges and Universities recognizes *The National Guide to Educational Credit for Training Programs* as a valuable tool and resource for reliable information in awarding academic credit for learning acquired in nontraditional settings.

David L. Warren
President
National Association of Independent Colleges and Universities

Statement from the National Association of State Universities and Land-Grant Colleges

The National Association of State Universities and Land-Grant Colleges welcomes the efforts of ACE/CREDIT for its efforts in publishing *The National Guide to Educational Credit for Training Programs. The National Guide* is a valuable tool for awarding credit for learning acquired outside the traditional framework of colleges and universities and is being used widely throughout the country by registrars and other collegiate officials. We support the Center for Adult Learning and Educational Credentials in publishing *The National Guide.*

C. Peter Magrath
President
National Association of State Universities and Land-Grant Colleges

Statement from The College Board

The College Board supports the Center for Adult Learning and Educational Credentials of the American Council on Education in its efforts to enable learners to receive formal recognition for their educational accomplishments attained outside the college and university classroom. The College Board recognizes *The National Guide to Educational Credit for Training Programs* as a valuable tool and resource for reliable information in awarding academic credit for learning acquired in nontraditional settings.

Donald M. Stewart
President
The College Board

Statement from The University of Oklahoma

In keeping with the mission of The University of Oklahoma, we are committed to providing the best possible educational experience for our student, including awarding credit in recognition of the need to evaluate learning which has taken place outside the formal higher education structure. This applies to work experiences and participation in formal courses sponsored by associations, businesses, government, industry, the military, and unions. The University of Oklahoma commends the Center for Adult Learning and Educational Credentials of the American Council on Education in its efforts in publishing *The National Guide to Educational Credit for Training Programs*. We recognize their publications and methods as an valuable tool for validating extra-institutional learning.

David L. Boren
President
The University of Oklahoma

Statement from University Continuing Education Association

The University Continuing Education Association supports the Center for Adult Learning and Educational Credentials of the American Council on Education in its efforts to enable learners to receive formal recognition for their educational accomplishments attained outside the college and university classroom. The University Continuing Education Association recognizes *The National Guide to Educational Credit for Training Programs* as a valuable tool and resource for reliable information in awarding academic credit for learning acquired in nontraditional settings.

Kay J. Kohl
Executive Director
University Continuing Education Association

ACE/PONSI
Review Team Coordinators

ACE/CREDIT Review Team Coordinators

Edward L. Angus
Professor
Department of Political Science
Fort Lewis College
Durango, CO 81391-3999
(1995)

Eugene W. Bartell
Professor
Robotics Insitute
Carnegie-Mellon University
Pittsburgh, PA 15213
(1994)

Lowell N. Ballew
Associate Professor
Computer Science Department
East Texas State University
Commerce, TX 75428
(1995)

Frances N. Beckles
Professor
Social Science Department
Morgan State University
Baltimore, MD 21239
(1995)

George W. Boulware
Chairman and Professor
Department of Business Administration
Lipscomb University
Nashville, TN 37204-3951
(1995)

Melanie A. Brown
Assistant to the Dean and Professor
University of the District of Columbia
College of Professional Studies
Washington, DC 20008
(1996)

Sarah K. Bryant
Department Chair
Finance and IB
Johns Hopkins University
Columbia, MD 21046
(1996)

Sam Chapman
Chair
Management Studies Department
Diablo Valley College
Pleasant Hill, CA 94523
(1995)

James E. Couch
Associate Professor Emeritus
Department of Communication
Florida International University
8700 SW 55th Street
Cooper City, FL 33328
(1995)

Lansing J. Davis
Office of Workforce Development
New Jersey Department of Labor
Trenton, NJ 08625-0933
(1995)

Larry R. Davis
Head and Professor
Division of Business Administration
East Texas State University
Texarkana, TX 75505
(1995)

Sylvia W. Galloway
Director of Private Sector Programs
Association of Governing Boards of
Universities and Colleges
Washington, DC 20036
(1995)

Mattie Giles
Professor
Department of Social Work
University of the District of Columbia
Washington, DC 20008
(1995)

James W. Koerlin
Chairman
Department of Telecommunications Management
Golden Gate University
San Francisco, CA 94105
(1995)

John E. McAllister
Deputy Secretary for Administration
Department of Labor and Industry
Commonwealth of Pennsylvania
Harrisburg, PA 17120
(1994)

Dorothy E. McNutt
Chair and Professor Emeritus
Division of Business
College of the Mainland
Texas City, TX 77591
(1995)

Dr. Joseph Migliaccio
Professor
Northern Virginia Community College
Alexandria, VA 22301
(1996)

Daniel Negron, Jr.
Assistant Director
Office of Corporate-Higher Education Programs
Thomas Edison State College
Trenton, NJ 08608-1176
(1995)

Richard Profozich
Professor
Prince George's Community College
Largo, MD 20774
(1996)

James A. Ratigan
Director
Office of Corporate-Higher Education Programs
Thomas Edison State College
Trenton, NJ 08608-1176
(1995)

Robert E. Scully
Assistant Professor
School of Adult & Continuing Education
Barry University
Miami Shores, FL 33161-6695
(1995)

Celeste M. Sichenze
Professor Emeritus
Business Management
Northern Virginia Community College
Annandale, VA 22003
(1995)

Ned J. Sifferlen
Provost
Sinclair Community College
Dayton, OH 45402
(1995)

W. Franklin Spikes
Professor
Department of Foundations and Adult Education
Kansas State University
Manhattan, KS 66506-5305
(1995)

Phyllis Walls
Director
Oklahoma Affiliate Office of ACE/PONSI
College of Continuing Education
The University of Oklahoma
1700 Asp
Norman, OK 73072-6400
(1996)

Sally Jo Wright
Chair and Professor Emeritus
Business Administration Department
Sangamon State University
Springfield, IL 62794-9243
(1995)

Review Team Evaluators

Review Team Evaluators in Alphabetical Order

Tom Abbott
Dean
Learning Resources and University Development
University of Maine at Augusta
Augusta, ME (1995)

Said I. Abdel-Khalik
Professor
Nuclear Engineering Program
School of Mechanical Engineering
Georgia Institute of Technology
Atlanta, GA (1997)

Don Adams
Professor
Oklahoma State University
Stillwater, OK

Joseph D. Adams
Assistant Division Chairman
Northern Virginia Community College
Annandale, VA

Muriel H. Adams
Director
Medical Record Technology
Prince George's Community College
Largo, MD (1993)

Robert F. Adick
Edison State Community College
Raymond Walters General & Technical College
Cincinnati, OH (1994)

Richard August Ahrens
Professor
College of Human Ecology
University of Maryland
College Park, MD (1996)

Frank Alberico
Director
Law Enforcement Program
Joliet Junior College
Joliet, IL (1997)

Louis Albert
Director
Professional Services
American Association for Higher Education
Washington, DC

Leonard Alberts
Professor
Drafting and Design Department
Pennsylvania Institute of Technology
Upper Darby, PA

Don A. Albright
Professor
Mathematics and Chemistry
Northwestern College
St. Paul, MN

Charles Alexander
Professor
Signal Analysis and Communications
George Washington University
Washington, DC

David G. Alexander
Senior Staff Associate
George Meany Center for Labor Studies
Silver Spring, MD

Richard L. Allen
Assistant Dean
Career Education and Community Service
Northern Oklahoma College
Tonkawa, OK

Gemmy S. Allen
Marketing and Management Instructor
Mountain View College
Dallas, TX

Eugene Alm
University of Wisconsin
Madison, WI (1994)

Richard A. Almonte
Consultant
Department of Education
Bureau of Vocational-Technical Education
Providence, RI

Dr. Ramon C. Alonso
Professor
Business Strategy of International Management
University of Oklahoma
Norman, OK (1997)

Roy Alvarez
Cornell University
Ithaca, NY

Clinton L. Anderson
Senior Consultant
Servicemembers Opportunity Colleges
Washington, DC (1996)

James M. Anderson
Professor
Department of Civil Engineering
University of California
Berkeley, CA

Edwin L. Andrews
Chairman
Division of Arts and Sciences
SUNY Agricultural and Technical College
Cobleskill, NY

Joseph G. Andritzky
Associate Professor
Management/Criminal Justice Operations
Concordia University
Mequon, WI (1995)

Frank Angell
Professor of Insurance and Finance
New York University
New York, NY

Roanne Angiello
Dean
Business Technologies Division
Bergen Community College
Paramus, NJ

Edward L. Angus
Professor
Fort Lewis College
Durango, CO (1995)

Richard G. Anthony
Associate Professor
Engineering Technology
Cuyahoga Community College
Cleveland, OH (1997)

Charles Ardolino
Faculty Member and Administrator
Coastline Community College
Fountain Valley, CA

Alfred Arkley
Professor
Management Program
Sangamon State University
Springfield, IL

Alfred Armand
President
A-H and Associates
Burlingame, CA (1994)

Dr. George Arnovick
Professor
Computer Science Dept.
CSU
Chico, CA (1997)

George E. Arnstein
Fellow
American Association for the Advancement of Science
Washington, DC (1993)

Gerald Arsenault
Professor of Social Sciences
Education Coordinator
Cumberland County College
Vineland, NJ

Roy Ashley
Professor Emeritus
Industrial Education
University of Maryland
College Park, MD (1995)

William F. Atchison
Professor Emeritus
University of Maryland
College Park, MD (1994)

Roger Atherton
Director
College of Business Administration
University of Oklahoma
Norman, OK

Joseph R. Avella
Academic Dean
American Military U.
Manassas Park, VA (1997)

Clarence Avery
Professor
School of Accounting
University of Central Florida
Orlando, FL

Alexander W. Avtgis
Dean
Wentworth Institute of Technology
Boston, MA (1993)

Robert C. Azar
Chairman
Department of Mechanical Engineering
Western New England College
Springfield, MA

Dale Babione
Retired Deputy Assistant Secretary of Defense
Vice President
Boeing
Fairfax, VA (1994)

Robert Baden
Freetrade Union Institute
Washington, DC (1996)

Adedeji Badiru
Professor
School of Industrial Engineering
University of Oklahoma
Norman, OK (1995)

Prabir K. Bagchi
Associate Professor
Department of Management Science
School of Business and Public Management
George Washington University
Washington, DC (1994)

W.E. Bailey
Automotive Center Coordinator
Oklahoma State University
Okmulgee, OK

Sandra O. Bailey
Program Head
Medical Records Technology Program
Northern Virginia Community College
Annandale, VA (1995)

Carl D. Baird
Professor
Agricultural Engineering Department
University of Florida
Gainesville, FL

Barry Baker
Assistant Chief
City of Fairfax Fire and Rescue
Fairfax, VA (1996)

James Baker
Mentor
Thomas Edison State College
Trenton, NJ (1995 NJ)

James R. Baker
Professor
Imaging Systems
Virginia Polytechnic Institute
and State University
Blacksburg, VA

John R. Baker, Sr.
Adjunct Faculty
Technology Programs
Johns Hopkins University (1997)

Dennis M. Bakewicz
Assistant Professor of Biology
New York City Technical College (CUNY)
New York, NY

Joseph Balabon
Director of MIS
Mercer County Community College
Trenton, NJ

Lewis Baldwin
Associate Professor
Department of Religious Studies
Vanderbilt University
Nashville, TN

Gary E. Ballman
Associate Dean of Curriculum Services
Medical Laboratory Technology
Northern Virginia Community College
Annandale, VA (1996)

Ajeyo Banerjee
Assistant Professor
Graduate School of Business Administration
University of Colorado
Denver, CO (1995)

Paul Bankit
Faculty Advisor
Embry-Riddle Aeronautical University
Ft. Eustis, VA

Guy R. Banville
Associate Dean
School of Business
St. Louis University
St. Louis, MO

Daniel G. Barbee
Director
Graduate Program
Pembroke State University
Lumberton, ND

Thomas C. Barker
Dean
School of Allied Health Professions
Virginia Commonwealth University
Richmond, VA

Joan Barnacle
Instructor of Medical Assisting
Indian Valley College
Novato, CA

Frank Barnes
Professor
Electrical and Computer Engineering
University of Colorado
Boulder, CO (1996)

William Barnes
Associate Professor and Coordinator
Electrical Engineering Technology
New Jersey Institute of Technology
Newark, NJ (1995 NJ)

Raymond Barrall
Director
Environmental Health/Radiation Safety
University of Illinois at Chicago
Chicago, IL (1996)

Eugene W. Bartel
Senior Research Associate
Carnegie-Melon University
Pittsburgh, PA

Richard A. Bassler
Director
Computer Systems Applications Program
American University
Washington, DC

Harish Batra
Associate Dean
College of Business and Economics
University of Wisconsin
Whitewater, WI

Colin Battle
Director of Curriculum
Broward Community College
Ft. Lauderdale, FL

Jon Bauman
Professor of Music
Frostburg State University
Frostburg, MD

Dale K. Bean
Vice President
Education and Programs Director
California College for Health Sciences
National City, CA (1996)

John R. Beaton
Dean
College of Human Ecology
University of Maryland
College Park, MD (1994)

Frances N. Beckles
Associate Professor
Social Work Department
Morgan State University
Baltimore, MD (1997)

Floyd C. Begin
Professor
St. Ambrose University
Davenport, IA (1994)

Norris Bell
Director of Continuing Education
Graduate Center
Virginia Polytechnic Institute
and State University
Falls Church, VA (1994)

Dr. John Belveal
Engineering Technologies and Aeronautics
Midwest City, OK (1997)

Patricia Benjamin
Director of Education
Connecticut Center for Massage Therapy
Newington, CT (1996)

Susanne Bensel
Professor
Modern Language Department
Johns Hopkins University
Washington, DC

Kenneth R. Benson
Chairman
Health, Urban and Outdoor Recreation
Kean College of New Jersey
Union, NJ

Katherine Benz-Campbell
Instructor of Ultrasound
Bergen Community College
Paramus, NJ (1996)

Lila Bergman
Director
Department of Economics
Hunter College, CUNY
New York, NY

Adele Berlin
Professor
University of Maryland
College Park, MD

Zvi Bernstein
Jerusalem, Israel

Thomas Berry
Professor
Department of Slavic Languages
University of Maryland
College Park, MD

John C. Bessee
Chair
Bible Department
East Texas State University
Commerce, TX (1995)

Constance Beutel
Distance Education
Learning Evaluation Center
Stanford University
Instructional Television Network
Benicia, CA (1996)

Don Biederman
Director
Telecommunications Technical Program
Skyline College
San Bruno, CA

Patrick Biesty
Dean
Business and Social Studies
County College of Morris
Randolph, NJ

Shirley A. Biggs
Associate Professor
University of Pittsburgh
Pittsburgh, PA

George E. Biles
Dean
School of Management
Robert Morris College
Coraopolis, PA (1995)

Charles Billman
Director
Vocational Programs
Rockvalley College
Rockford, IL (1996)

Dan Bintz
Consultant
MSTC/MATC
Sun Prairie, WI (1997)

Beatrice Black
University of the District of Columbia
Washington, DC

Bishop B. Blackwell
Professor
Aeronautical Science Department
Embry-Riddle Aeronautical University
Daytona Beach, FL

H. Joseph Blair
Chair and Professor
Department of Christianity and Philosophy
Houston Baptist University
Houston, TX (1996)

Russell R. Blankenfeld
Instructor
Rochester Community College
Rochester, MN

Arthur H. Boisselle
Coordinator
Pikes Peak Community College
Colorado Springs, CO

Zvigdor Boncheck
Jerusalem, Israel

Byron D. Bond
Dean
Extended Instruction Services
Vincennes University
Vincennes, IN (1995)

T. W. Bonham
Associate Dean
College of Business
Virginia Polytechnic Institute
and State University
Blacksky, VA (1996)

William Boras
Associate Professor
School of Business
Ferris State College
Big Rapids, MI

Vera Z. Borkovec
Associate Professor Emerita
Language and Foreign Studies
American University
Washington, DC

Don Boren
Chairman
Department of Legal Studies
Bowling Green University
Bowling Green, OH (1994)

George W. Boulware
Professor and Chair
Department of Business Administration
David Lipscomb University
Nashville, TN (1997)

Edward K. Bowdon
Professor and Head
Department of Engineering Technology
Texas A&M University
Tyler, TX

Dr. Jack Bower
Assistant Professor of Accounting
Eastern College
St. David, PA

Robert L. Bowers
Chairman
Division of Business and Public Services
J. Sargeant Reynolds Community College
Richmond, VA

Doreen Boyce
Chairman
Department of Economics and Management
Hood College
Frederick, MD

Jean Ann Boyce
Assistant Professor
Computer Science Department
University of Maryland University College
College Park, MD (1997)

Paul Boyd
Chairman
Electronics Department
University of the District of Columbia
Washington, DC

Patricia Bradley
Chair and Associate Professor
American Studies
Temple University
Philadelphia, PA (1995)

William Brant
Professor of Management
Rider University
Lawrenceville, NJ (1993 NJ)

Martha Bravnig
Vice President
Executive Security International
Aspen, CO

Eugene Brill
Coordinator
Grossmont College
El Cajon, CA

James Broman
Management Consultant
Alexandria, VA (1994)

Audrey Bronson
Professor of Psychology
Cheyney State College
Cheyney, PA

Glenn E. Brooks
Professor
Political Sciences
Colorado College
Colorado Springs, CO (1996)

John R. Brooks
Professor of Marketing
College of Business and Economics
Houston Baptist University
Houston, TX

Rick Brooks
Coordinator
Engineering Technologies
Rosa State College
Midwest City, OK (1997)

Jacqueline Brophy
Director
Labor Liberal Arts Program
Cornell University
New York, NY

George D. Brower
Associate Professor of Economics and Business
Moravian College
Bethehem, PA

Melanie A. Brown
Professor
Management and Office Systems
University of the District of Columbia
Washington, DC (1996)

Janice Brown-Glasgow
Bowie State University
School of Business
Bowie, MD (1997)

Robert Brucker
Field Consultant
Bureau of Vocational/Educational Education
Pennsylvania Department of Education
Harrisburg, PA

Sarah K. Bryant
Department Chair
Finance and International Business
Johns Hopkins University
Columbia, MD (1996)

Hanita Brumfield
Chair
Department of Political and Social Sciences
Mount Vernon College
Washington, DC (1993)

Jerome Buescher
Instructor of Microbiology
College of Graduate Studies
Thomas Jefferson University
Philadelphia, PA (1995 NJ)

Paul Burkhart
Professor of Speech
Shippensburg University
Shippensburg, PA

Edward Burns
Adjunct Professor
County College of Morris
Randolph, NJ

Herbert J. Burrows
Instructor
Nuclear Science Program
University of Maryland
College Park, MD (1993)

Jack D. Burson
Professor
Technology Department
McNeese State University
Lake Charles, LA (1995)

Rosemary Burton
Minnieland, Inc.
Woodbridge, VA (1997)

Stanley Bush
Professor
Telecommunications Department
University of Colorado at Boulder
Boulder, CO (1996)

Roy Byrd
Chairman
Department of Technology
Cameron University
Lawton, OK

Wayne Camara
Director
Scientific Affairs
American Psychological Association
Washington, DC

Damon Davis Camp, Jr.
Professor
Department of Criminal Justice
Georgia State University
Atlanta, GA (1993)

Gerald R. Camp
Associate Professor
Business and Technology Department
University of Akron
Akron, OH

Raymond Campbell
Chair
Department of General Education
Thomas Jefferson University
Philadelphia, PA (1995)

Louis Campo
Professor
Engineering Department
Union County College
Elizabeth, NJ (1996)

Lou Cantori
Professor
Department of Political Science
University of Maryland Baltimore County
Baltimore, MD (1997)

Perry Caranicas
Community Faculty
Metropolitan State University
Minneapolis, MN

Deb Carlson
Professor and Director
Audiology and Speech Pathology
University of Texas Medical Center
Galveston, TX (1994)

Patrick Carlton
Professor
Youngstown State University
Youngstown, OH (1995)

John Carmichael
Senior Professor
Business Department
Union County College
Crawford, NJ (1997)

Dr. David G. Carnevale
Associate Professor
Political Science Department
University of Oklahoma
Norman, OK (1997)

Michael Carr
Program Director
Respiratory Therapy
East Los Angeles College
Monterey Park, CA (1996)

Paula Carroll
Associate Director
Administrative Computer Center
University of Maryland
College Park, MD

Alfred Carter
Professor
Social Science Division
Manchester College
Manchester, CT (1993)

Charles Cassady
Instructor
Technology Department
Gwinnett Technical Institute
Lawrenceville, GA (1996)

Frank H. Cassell
Professor Emeritus
Kellogg Graduate School of Management
Northwestern University
Evanston, IL

Joseph F. Castellano
Professor
Accounting Department
Wright State University
Dayton, OH

Jerrold Casway
Chair, Division of Social Sciences
Howard Community College
Columbia, MD (1997)

Dorothy Cavagnaro
Professor Emeritus
Department of HRIM
Northern Virginia Community College
Annandale, VA (1996)

Albert Cawns
Professor
Webster University
St. Louis, MO

Joseph Celauro
Adjunct Professor
College of New Jersey
Trenton, NJ

Herman Cember
Professor
Northwestern University
Evanston, IL

Neal Chalofsky
Visiting Assistant Professor
School of Education and Human Development
George Washington University
Washington, DC

Harlan L. Chaney
Professor Emeritus
Business, Economics, and Finance Department
University of the District of Columbia
Washington, DC (1996)

Miriam Chaplin
Associate Professor
School of Education
Rutgers University
Camden, NJ

Sam Chapman
Chairman
Management Studies Department
Diablo Valley Community College
Pleasant Hills, CA (1997)

James J. Chastain
Professor
Insurance Education
Howard University
Washington, DC

Frank Cheng
Industrial Eletronic Technology Dept.
Central Michigan University
Mt. Pleasant, MI (1997)

Robert Chenoweth
Department Chairman
Data Processing
County College of Morris
Randolph, NJ

Robert Childs
ACE Fellow Assistant to Provost
George Mason University
Fairfax, VA

Robert J. Chinnis
Associate Professor
American University
Washington, DC

Richard Christensen
Associate Professor
Nuclear Engineering Department
Ohio State University
Columbus, OH (1995)

Gen Sen Chu
Director
Learning Resources Center
Northern Virginia Community College
Alexandria, VA

Vincent P. Cieri
Chief
Training Development
Fort Monmouth, NJ

Joseph J. Cioch
Professor and Department Head
Restaurant, Hotel, and Institutional Management
Purdue University
West Lafayette, IN

Samuel Cipollo
Professor
Department of Physics
Creighton University
Omaha, NE (1994)

Joseph Cirrincione
Associate Professor
Department of Geography
University of Maryland
College Park, MD

William A. Clarey
Professor
Business Administration
Bradley University
Peoria, IL (1997)

Donald J. Clark, Jr.
Professor and Director
Language Lab
Johns Hopkins University
Baltimore, MD (1995)

Edward Clark
Associate Professor of Electronics Technology
Atlantic Community College
Mays Landing, NJ (1993 NJ)

Gary S. Clark
Assistant Professor and Program Coordinator
Department of Management
Sinclair Community College
Dayton, OH (1994)

Jacqueline Clark, Esquire
Wallingford, PA (1994)

William Clark
Associate Professor
Tidewater Community College
Portsmouth, VA (1995)

Alvin Clay
Dean and Professor Emeritus
Commerce and Finance
Villanova University
Villanova, PA (1995)

Lonnie Cleaver
Chair
Religious Studies Department
Southern Methodist University
Dallas, TX (1995)

Preston Clement
Professor
Mercer County Community College
Trenton, NJ

Alexander Cloner
Dean
School of Public Administration
University of Southern California, Sacramento
Sacramento, CA

William Clontz
Director, Program Support
MFRI International Group
Alexandria, VA (1997)

Mary Ann Coffland
Chair
Department of Italian
George Washington University
Springfield, VA (1993)

Jerry S. Cohen
Associate Professor
Raritan Valley Community College
Somerville, NJ

Don Coleman
Chairman
Department of Systems and Computer Science
Howard University
Washington, DC

Gary Collins
Instructor
Public Services Department (Fire Sciences)
San Joaquin Delta College
Stockton, CA

James Comer
Associate Professor
University of Cincinnati
Cincinnati, OH

Frank W. Connolly
Director
Academic Computing Services
American University
Washington, DC

Thomas J. Connolly
Chairman and Professor
Embry-Riddle Aeronautical University
Bunnell, FL

Dr. Steven Cornelius
Chair, Hospitality Management
Sinclair Community College
Dayton, OH (1997)

William L. Corsover
Adjunct Professor
Division of Continuing Education
Florida International University
North Miami, FL (1996)

Robert W. Cosgriff
Associate Academic Dean
Mirus University
Springfield, VA (1996)

Dr. Miro Costa
Associate Professor
Golden Gate University
San Francisco, CA (1997)

Leval Cothran
Chairman, Physiology
College of Medicine
Howard University
Washington, DC (1997)

Robert Cotner
Chairman
English and Philosophy Department
Montgomery College
Rockville, MD

Amy Coury
Professor
Nursing
Los Angeles Harbor College
Los Angeles, CA

John R. Cox
Professor
Finance
California State University, Los Angeles
Los Angeles, CA

Virgil G. Cox
Dean
Engineering Technology, Math, & Physics
Gaston College
Dallas, NC (1994)

Constance Craft
President
Learning Tree of America
Carrollton, GA (1995)

Kenneth Crawford
Professor
Department of Meteorology
University of Oklahoma
Norman, OK (1993)

Michael Crone
DeVry Institute of Technology
Atlanta, GA

John P. Crossley
University of Southern California
School of Religion
Los Angeles, CA (1997)

Constance Crowley
Assistant Clinical Professor
Family Health Care Nursing
University of California
San Francisco, CA

Joseph Crowley
Professor
Department of Marketing and Management
Community College of Philadelphia
Philadelphia, PA

David Cummins
Assistant Professor
Insurance Department
Wharton School
University of Pennsylvania
Philadelphia, PA

Wayne Cunningham
School of Management
University of Scranton
Scranton, PA

Anthony Cupo
Associate Professor of Business
County College of Morris
Randolph, NJ (1995 NJ)

Nancy Curry
Chairperson
University of Pittsburgh
Pittsburgh, PA

Alan Czarapata
Professor
Engineering Technology
Montgomery College
Rockville, MD (1997)

Joseph Dahms
Chairperson
Department of Economics and Management
Hood College
Frederick, MD (1993)

Nell Dale
University of Texas
Department of Computer Science
Austin, TX

Jerome C. Darnell
Professor of Finance
College of Business Administration
University of Colorado, Boulder
Boulder, CO

Gordon Darkenwald
Professor of Adult Development
School of Education
Rutgers University
New Brunswick, NJ

James Daschbach
Professor
Department of Industrial Engineering
University of Toledo
Toledo, OH (1995)

Sister Ellen Dauwer
Associate Dean
Adult Undergraduate Programs
College of Saint Elizabeth
Morristown, NJ (1993)

Bill Davies
Director of END Training Program
Naval School of Health
Bethesda, MD (1995)

Dan A. Davis
Associate Dean of Liberal Studies
University of Oklahoma
Norman, OK

Herbert J. Davis
Program Director
Business Management
School of Government and
Business Administration
George Washington University
Washington, DC

James J. Davis
Associate Professor
Romance Languages Department
Howard University
Washington, DC (1993)

Lansing Davis
Office of Workforce Development
Trenton, NJ (1997)

Larry R. Davis
Division Head
Business Administration Division
Texas A&M University at Texarkana
Texarkana, TX (1997)

Laura A. Davis
Consultant
Alexandria, VA (1997)

Leonard Davis
Professor
West Virginia University
Morgantown, WV

Monte Davis
Professor
Nuclear Research Center
Georgia Institute of Technology
Atlanta, GA (1997)

Ralph G. Davis
California Maritime Academy
Vallejo, CA (1994)

Robert L. Davis
Dean
University of Missouri
Rolla, MO

Roscoe K. Davis
Professor
Management Science and Information Technology
College of Business Administration
University of Georgia
Athens, GA

Nancy Dawson
Lecturer
African and African American Studies
State University of New York, Albany
Albany, NY

Robert de Iongh
Business Department
San Francisco City College
San Francisco, CA

Brenda De La Mare
Program Director
Nurse Aide Training/Competency Evaluation
Utah Registry
Kaysville, UT (1995)

Lloyd M. DeBoer
Chairman
George Mason University
Fairfax, VA

Rev. Paul F. deLadurantaue
Diocesan Secretary for Religious Studies
Diocese of Arlington
Arlington, VA (1996)

Lynne Delay
Professor
Graduate Program for Administrators
Rider University
Lawrenceville, NJ

Eugene Deloatch
School of Engineering
Howard University
Washington, DC

William DeLone
Associate Professor of Management
Kogod College of Business
American University
Washington, DC (1996)

Thomas G. DeLutis
President
Information Systems Architects, Inc.
Fairfax, VA (1997)

Donald A. Dermody
Professor
Cornell University
Ithaca, NY

George DeSain
Department Head
Industrial Education and Technology
Western Carolina University
Cullowhee, NC (1997)

Donald Devers
Assistant Professor
Social Science and Public Service Division
Northern Virginia Community College
Annandale, VA

Louise Dieterle
Vice President
Leadership Development Association
Naperville, IL

Terry P. Dixon
Vice President and Professor
Academic Affairs/Computer Science
Clarkson College
Omaha, NE (1995)

Dr. Andrew Do
Professor
Dept. of Finance
San Diego State University
San Diego, CA (1997)

Joseph Dobson
Assistant Professor
Department of Management
Western Illinois University
Macomb, IL

Helen Doerpinghaus
Professor
College of Business
University of South Carolina
Columbia, SC

Michael Donahue
Adjunct Professor
Fire Service Training and Hazardous Materials
Montgomery College
Rockville, MD (1995)

Shawn Riva Donaldson
Assistant Professor of Sociology
Richard Stockton College of New Jersey
Pomona, NJ (1995 NJ)

Carole Donavan
Professor
Montclair State University
Upper Montclair, NJ

R.D. Draper
Psychology Department
Montclair State University
Upper Montclair, NJ

Leslie Dreiling
Adjunct Professor
Computational Sciences
George Mason University
Washington, DC

Dr. Donald Dudziak
Head
Department of Nuclear Engineering
North Carolina State University
Raleigh, NC (1997)

Li-Chuange Duke
Professor of Chinese
School of Advanced International Studies
Johns Hopkins University
Washington, DC

John Duncan
Instructor
School of Technology
Kent State University
Kent, OH (1993)

Howard Dunn
Professor
Mercer County Community College
Trenton, NJ (1997)

Margaret Dunn
Associate Professor of English
Kean College of New Jersey
Union, NJ

William J. Dunne
Associate Dean
College of Business Administration
University of Illinois
Chicago, IL

John M. Dwyer
Associate Professor
Department of Mathematics
and Computer Science
University of Detroit Mercy
Detroit, MI (1995)

Kenneth J. Dwyer
Hudson County Community College
Belleville, NJ

Alice F. Dyer
Director
Educational Development and Training
General Hospital Center
Passaic, NJ (1996)

Dr. Dineen Ebert
Professor-Information Office Systems Dept.
St. Louis Community College at Meramec
Kirkwood, MO (1997)

N. Dean Eckhoff
Professor
Department of Nuclear Engineering
Kansas State University
Manhattan, KS (1994)

Charles Edelson
Assistant Dean
College of Business and Management
University of Maryland
College Park, MD

Robert Edmister
Professor of Finance
College of Business and Management
University of Maryland
College Park, MD

Bill Edwards
Chairman
Aerospace Department
Southeastern State University
Durant, OK (1997)

Steven T. Edwards
Director
Maryland Fire and Rescue Institute
College Park, MD (1997)

Steven A. Egger
Associate Professor
Sangamon State University
Springfield, IL

William D. Eglinton
Director
Vocational Education
Seafarers Harry Lundeberg School of Seamanship
Pincy Point, MD (1996)

Matt Eichor
Chairman
Criminal Justice Systems Program
Northeast Missouri State University
Kirksviolle, MO (1995)

Warren Eidsness
Professor Emeritus
Mathematics Department
Normandale Community College
Bloomington, MN (1995)

Joel Eigne
Professor
Sociology Department
Franklin and Marshall College
Lancaster, PA

Adel I. El-Ansary
Professor
School of Government and Business Administration
George Washington University
Washington, DC

Norb Elbert
Professor
Department of Business Administration
Bellarmine College
Louisville, KY

Thomas S. Elleman
Professor Emeritus
Department of Nuclear Engineering
North Carolina State University
Raleigh, NC (1995)

Larry Elowitz
Professor and Chairman
Department of Government and Sociology
Georgia College
Milledgeville, GA (1993)

Bois Elwell
Productive Business Results
Long Beach, CA

William Enslin
Chairman
Department of Management
Rowan University
Glassboro, NJ

Ali Etili
Consultant
Arlington, VA (1994)

John B. Eubanks
Professor
School of Religions
Howard University
Washington, DC

Henry Ernsthal
Associate Professor
Department of Public Administration
George Washington University
Washington, DC

Michael Evans
Associate Professor
Virginia Polytechnic Institute and State University
Blacksburg, VA

Marvin Eyler
Dean
College of Physical Education, Recreation, and Health
University of Maryland
College Park, MD

Gary W. Falkenberg
Professor of Management
Oakland Community College, Auburn Hills
Auburn Heights, MI

Julian Wade Farrior
Chairman and Associate Professor
Natural Science/Mathematics Division
Gwynedd-Mercy College
Gwynedd Valley, PA (1993)

Richard Faw
Professor
Nuclear Engineering
Kansas State University
Manhattan, KS

Dale Feinauer
Associate Professor
College of Business
University of Wisconsin, Oshkosh
Oshkosh, WI

M. Ali Fekrat
Professor
School of Business
Georgetown University
Washington, DC (1994)

Carol Felder
Assistant Professor
Raritan Valley Community College
Somerville, NJ

Emanual Feldman
Jerusalem, Israel

Bernard M. Ferreri
Associate Vice Chancellor
City Colleges of Chicago
Chicago, IL

Mayer Fialkoff
Adjunct Professor
Touro Graduate School of Jewish Studies
Jerusalem, Israel (1997)

Lewis R. Fibel
Vice President and Dean of Faculty
Sullivan County Community College
Loch Sheldrake, NY

Carl Fields
Chairman
Nuclear Engineering Technology Program
Pennsylvania State University
Monaca, PA

George Fieo
Freeman & Fieo Public Accountants
Philadelphia, PA (1994)

Arnold Finchum
Chairman
Technology Department
California Polytechnic State University, San Luis Obispo
San Luis Obispo, CA

Rudolph J. Fiorillo
Chairman
Visual and Performing Arts Division
Northern Virginia Community College
Alexandria, VA (1994)

Chana M. Firestone
Art History
Touro College
Jerusalem, Israel (1997)

Diana Fischer
Computer Technology
Prince George's Community College
Largo, MD

Gary Fischer
Associate Professor
Industrial Engineering
University of Iowa
Iowa City, IA

Naftali Fish
Adjunct Professor of Psychology
Touro College
Jerusalem, Israel (1997)

James Fisk
Department of Chemistry
Stanford University
Birmingham, AL

Stevenson W. Fletcher
Head
Hotel, Restaurant, and Travel Administration
University of Massachusetts
Amherst, MA

John Flynn
Associate Professor
Montgomery County Community College
Blue Bell, PA (1996)

Joseph Flynn
Professor
College of New Jersey
Trenton, NJ (1993)

William Ford
Chief Juvenile Probation Officer
Bucks County Courthouse
Doylestown, PA

Ernest Foreman
Professor
Management and Information Science
George Washington University
Washington, DC

Roger Formissano
Graduate School of Banking
University of Wisconsin
Madison, WI

Phyllis Forrest
Education Consultant
Washington, DC

Edward L. Foss
Chair
Marine Technology
Cape Fear Community College
Wilmington, NC (1996)

Marion Fox
Professor
Rose State University
Midwest City, OK (1995)

Marvin Franson
Trade & Industry Division
Chippewa Valley Technical College
Eau Claire, WI (1997)

Nevin R. Frantz, Jr.
Professor and Director
Division of Vocational and Technical Education
Virginia Polytechnic Institute and State University
Blacksburg, VA

Donald D. Fraser
Professor
Department of Chemistry
Essex County College
Newark, NJ (1995 NJ)

Howard Freas
Professor
Bucks County Community College
Newtown, PA

Robert O. Freedman
Dean of Graduate Studies
Baltimore Hebrew College
Baltimore, MD

Stuart Freedman
University of Lowell
Lowell, MA

Marlowe Froke
Professor Emeritus
Pennsylvania State University
State College, PA (1996)

Paul Fugazzotto
Director
Urinary Research Center
Rapid City, SD

Dennis D. Fulk
Department Head
Civil Engineering Technology
Stark Technical College
Canton, OH (1996)

James J. Fyfe
Associate Professor
School of Justice
American University
Washington, DC

Robert Gagnon
Adjunct Professor
Department of Fire Protection Engineering
University of Maryland
College Park, MD (1994)

Ken Gaiser
Program Specialist
Dept. of Fire & Rescue Services
Emergency Management
Rockville, MD (1997)

Daniel J. Gallagher
Sangamon State University
Business Administration Program
Springfield, IL (1997)

Margaret Galligan
Smeal College of Business Administration
Pennsylvania State University
Mont Alto, PA (1997)

Joel D. Galloway
Dean
Ferris State University
Big Rapids, MI

Ivan Galtman
Executive Director
Philadelphia Chapter of American Institute of Banking
Philadelphia, PA (1996)

Kenneth L. Gann
Former Assistant Professor
Austin Peay State University
Fort Campbell, KY

Cara Gargano
Chairperson
Department of Theater, Film, and Dance
Long Island University
Brookville, NY

Linda W. Garner
Staff Training Specialist
Exxon Production Research Co.
Houston, TX

Leonard Garrett
Professor
Temple University
Philadelphia, PA

Patrick Garrett
Chairman
Electrical Engineering Technology
Ohio College of Applied Science
University of Cincinnati
Cincinnati, OH

H. Donald Garrison
Associate Professor
Technology Department
University of Texas
Tyler, TX

Sr. Patricia Geary
Assistant Dean and Assistant Professor of Education
Georgean Court College
Lakewood, NJ (1995)

Neil J. George
Academic Dean
Webster University
St. Louis, MO

William George
Associate Professor
College of Commerce and Finance
Villanova University
Villanova, PA

Ronald Gepner
Associate Professor
Mercer County Community College
Trenton, NJ

Victor Gerdes
Academic Vice President (Retired)
College of Insurance
New York, NY

Michael Gerli
Associate Professor
School of Languages and Linguistics
Georgetown University
Washington, DC

Mattie Giles
Professor and Coordinator
Social Work Practicum
University of the District of Columbia
Washington, DC (1996)

John B. Gifford
Professor of Marketing
School of Business Administration
Miami University
Oxford, OH (1993)

Alan Gilbreth
Air Force Institute of Technology
W-PAFB, OH (1994)

Dr. Mattie Giles
Professor
University of the District of Columbia
Washington, DC (1997)

David Giltinan
Professor
Physics Department
Edinboro State College
Edinboro, PA

Dolores C. Gioffre
Assistant Professor
Montclair State University
Upper Montclair, NJ

Dorothy Gleckner
Associate Professor
Bergen County Community College
Paramus, NJ (1995)

Richard Glenn
Chair And Associate Professor
Automotive Service Technology
Catonsville Community College.
Catonsville, MD (1996)

Jacob M. Glickman
Senior Economist
State of Israel, Ministry of Finance
Income Tax Commission
Jerusalem, Israel (1997)

Helmut Golatz
Head
Department of Labor Studies
Pennsylvania State University
University Park, PA

Joel Goldberg
Professor Emeritus
Macomb Community College
Warren, MI (1997)

Tom Golder
Security Analyst
Albuquerque, NM (1995)

Aaron Goldman
Los Alamos, NM (1994)

Karina Golden
Assistant Professor
Department of Education
Bowie State University
Bowie, MD (1996)

Mark G. Goldin
Associate Professor
George Mason University
Fairfax, VA (1997)

Barry M. Goldstone
Lecturer
Business Division
Northern Virginia Community College
Annandale, VA (1996)

Roxanne Gonzales
Chairperson
Electronics Engineering Technology
Sinclair Community College
Dayton, OH (1997)

S.K. Gosh
Associate Professor
Department of Civil Engineering, Mechanics, and Metallurgy
University of Illinois
Chicago, IL

Menachem Gottesman
Efrat, Israel

John W. Gould
Associate Professor
Graduate School of Business
University of Southern California
Los Angeles, CA

Steele Gow
Dean
School of General Studies
University of Pittsburgh
Pittsburgh, PA

Raghava Gowda
Professor
Department of Computer Science
University of Dayton
Dayton, OH (1997)

Shail Gowda
Adjunct Professor
Sinclair Community College
Dayton, OH (1997)

David Grant
Professor
Department of Religion
Texas Christian University
Fort Worth, TX (1994)

George Graves
Professor
Aerospace Engineering
California State Polytechnic University, Pomona
Pomona, CA

David E. Gray
Vice President
Administration and Staff Coordination
California State University, Long Beach
Long Beach, CA

Marion Green
Director
Early Childhood Development
Montgomery College
Rockville, MD (1994)

Alton L. Greenfield
Reading Specialist
Minnesota Department of Education
St. Paul, MN

Blaine Greenfield
Senior Professor of Business
Bucks County Community College
Newtown, PA (1993 NJ)

Robert Gregg
Dean of Technology
Southeastern Illinois College
Harrisburg, IL

Johnnie Griffin
President
Secretarial Evaluation Clinic
Washington, DC (1996)

Elihu Grossmann
Professor
Department of Chemical Engineering
Drexel University
Philadelphia, PA

Albert Grubbs, Jr.
Associate Professor
Engineering Technology
Texas A&M University
College Station, TX

John D. Guilfoil
Associate Dean
College of Business and Public Administration
New York University
New York, NY

Virginia Guilford
Interim Associate VP, Academic Affairs
Bowie State University
Upper Marlborom MD (1997)

Manak C. Gupta
Professor of Finance
Temple University
Philadelphia, PA (1995)

Sandra Gustavson
Chair
Department of Insurance, Legal Studies,
and Real Estate
University of Georgia
Athens, GA

John Gutowski
Chairperson
Psychology and Learning
Development Department
Middlesex County College
Edison, NJ

Effie Hacklander
Associate Dean
College of Human Ecology
University of Maryland
College Park, MD

William Haeberle
Professor
Graduate School of Business
Indiana University
Bloomington, IN

Trudi Bellardo Hahn
Associate Professor
Catholic University of America
Washington, DC

Radwan Hakim
Professor
Arab American Translators
Falls Church, VA

William Halal
Associate Professor
School of Business
American University
Washington, DC

Kay Hale
Director, Instruction Program
Texas Higher Education Coordinating Board
Austin, TX (1995)

Nancy Lynch Hale
Chairperson
Business Education Office
Pace University
New York, NY

Charles P. Hall, Jr.
Professor
Insurance and Risk and Health Administration
Temple University
Philadelphia, PA

James C. Hall
Associate Professor of Management
Pace University
New York, NY

Jim Hall
Associate Professor of Management
Pace University
New York, NY (1996)

John W. Hall
Professor and Chairman
Risk Management and Insurance Department
Georgia State University
Atlanta, GA

G. Victor Hallman
Department of Insurance
Wharton School
University of Pennsylvania
Philadelphia, PA (1995)

Howard Hamilton
Professor
Electrical Engineering
University of Pittsburgh
Pittsburgh, PA

Richard J. Hammel
Assistant Professor
Pharmacy Administration
University of Arizona
Tucson, AZ

David Hampton
Professor
Management Department
San Diego State University
San Diego, CA (1997)

Steven Hampton
Professor
Flight Technology
Embry-Riddle Aeronautical University
Daytona Beach, FL

Thomas Handler
Professor
Electrical Engineering Technology Department
Middlesex County College
Edison, NJ

Lyman Handy
Chair
Department of Petroleum Engineering
School of Engineering
University of Southern California
Los Angeles, CA

Carolyn Hannah
Professor
Sinclair Community College
Dayton, OH (1994)

Dr. Lymen Hannah
Dept. of Manufacturing & Construction
Central Missouri State University
Warrensburg, MO (1997)

Richard Hanson
Professor Emeritus
Raritan Valley Community College
Somerville, NJ

Sally Ann Hanson
Professor
Information Systems
Mercer County Community College
Trenton, NJ (1996)

Muhammad Haque
Associate Professor
Department of Civil, Mechanical,
and Environmental Engineering
George Washington University
Washington, DC (1993)

Dave Harding
Ohio University
Chillicothe, OH (1996)

R.L. Hardy
Civil Engineering Department
Iowa State University
Ames, IA

Andrew Hargrove
Professor Electrical Engineering Department
Norfolk State University
Norfolk, VA (1996)

Mahrash S. Hariri
Persian Instructor
Middle East Institute
Washington, DC (1994)

John Harrington
Professor
Seton Hall University
South Orange, NJ

Gary Harris
Associate Professor
Electrical Engineering Department
Howard University
Washington, DC (1994)

Marilyn Hart
Professor
Educational Psychology
Kean College of New Jersey
Union, NJ (1993)

Ronald Hart
Director of MIS
Essex County College
Newark, NJ

Sharon Yvonne Hart
Vice President for Academic Affairs
Northcentral Technical Center
Wausau, WI (1997)

Richard M. Harter
Assistant Professor of Electronics
Champlain College
Burlington, VT

Adele Hartig
Instructor
Bergen Community College
Paramus, NJ

John Hartmann
Professor
Northern Illinois University
DeKalb, IL

Barron Harvey
Associate Professor
Business Administration
Howard University
Washington, DC

Carol Harvey
Assistant Professor
Management and Marketing
Assumption College
Worcester, MA (1995)

Mike Harvey
Chairman
Department of Marketing
Southern Methodist University
Dallas, TX

Roger W. Haskell
Professor
Department of Human Resource Development
University of Tennessee
Knoxville, TN (1997)

Harold Hatchett
Professor
Management Department
Texas A&M University
Texarkana, TX (1997)

Lynda S. Hatfield
Dean
Professional Technical Education
Clatsop Community College
Astoria, OR (1995)

Howard Hauck
Adjunct Professor
Data Processing
Passaic County College
Patterson, NJ

Francis J. Haughey
Professor of Radiation Science
Rutgers University
New Brunswick, NJ (1995 NJ)

John C. Hawley
Hawley Insurance Agency
Montrose, PA (1995)

Rev. Jack Healy, O.Carm.
Rochester, NY

Sean Healy
Professor
Kean College of New Jersey
Union, NJ

Peter Hechler
Associate Professor
School of Business and Economics
California State University, Los Angeles
Los Angeles, CA

Linda Hefferin
Professor
Office of Admissions and Technology
Elgin Community College
Elgin, IL (1997)

Rabbi Chaim Solomon Heifetz
Adjunct Professor
Women's Adult Education Program
Jerusalem, Israel (1997)

Russell Heiserman
Professor
School of Technology
Oklahoma State University
Stillwater, OK

Andrew Heitzman
Associate Professor
Special Education
State University College of Arts and Sciences
Geneseo, NY

Michael Gary Helliwell
Associate Professor
Department of Management Science
Kean College of New Jersey
Union, NJ (1995)

Gary A. Hemphill
Chairman
Aviation Department
Delta State University
Cleveland, MS (1997)

Eric Hepburn
Dean
Social Sciences and Humanities
Middlesex County College
Edison, NJ (1997)

Richard Herbstritt
Professor
Gannon University
Erie, PA

William Heuson
Professor
School of Business Administration
University of Miami
Coral Gables, FL

John P. Hill
Professor and Academic Dean
Public Services Technologies Division
Thomas Nelson Community College
Hampton, VA (1996)

Leo Hilton
Coordinator
William Patterson University
Wayne, NJ

Rodney Hinkle
Dean
Fisher College
Boston, MA

Clete Hinton
Director
Weekend College
William Rainey Harper College
Palatine, IL

John F. Hitchcock
Bridgewater, NJ

Mary J. Hitchcock
Professor
Food Science, Nutrition, and Food Systems Administration Department
University of Tennessee
Knoxville, TN

William J. Hoben
Dean
University of Dayton
Dayton, OH

JoAnn Hoiles
Associate Professor (Retired)
Management
Raritan Valley Community College
Somerset, NJ (1993)

Van Holladay
Adjunct Professor
Administration of Justice Department
Northern Virginia Community College
Woodbridge, VA (1997)

Jerry J. Holman
President
Qualifications Evaluation Systems Corporation
Gaithersburg, MD

Milton C. Holmen
Professor
School of Business Administration
University of Southern California, Los Angeles
Los Angeles, CA

Robert K. Holz
Professor
University of Texas at Austin
Austin, TX

Kathryn L. Hoover
Morton, PA (1995)

Cecilia Hopkins
Director
Division Business
College of San Mateo
San Mateo, CA

Patrick J. Hopkins
Professor
Harrisburg Area Community College
Harrisburg, PA (1995)

Peter Horn
Professor
Department of Management
College of Business
Arizona State University
Tempe, AZ (1996)

Carmi Horowitz
Touro Graduate School of Jewish Studies
Jerusalem, Israel (1997)

Rosalie Howell
District Manager
Children's World Learning Centers
Atlanta, GA (1997)

Marianne Hoy
Professor
Nursing Division
Cumberland County College
Vineland, NJ (1993)

Gregory Lee Hricenak
President
Dragon's Teeth Design
Greensburg, PA

George L. Huebner
Professor Emeritus
Department of Meteorology
Texas A&M University
College Station, TX (1996)

Thomas E. Hulbert
Associate Dean and Director
School of Engineering Technology
Northeastern University
Boston, MA

M. Gweneth Humphreys
Chairman
Mathematics Department
Randolph Macon Woman's College
Lynchburg, VA

Margaret Humphreys
Assistant Professor and Director
Early Childhood Development Center
School of Education
College of Charleston
Charleston, SC (1995)

Bobby R. Hunt
Professor
Computer Science
University of Arizona
Tucson, AZ

William Hunter
Associate Professor of Biology
County College of Morris
Randolph, NJ

Robert Hurley
Professor
Criminal Justice
California State University, Sacramento
Sacramento, CA

James F. Huston
Professor
Edinboro State College
Edinboro, PA

John P. Hyde
Director of Instruction
Career Tech Center
Holland, MI

John Hyland
Chairman
Social Sciences Department
LaGuardia Community College
Long Island City, NY

Elizabeth Iannizzi
Professor
Department of Secretarial Science
New York Community College
Brooklyn, NY

Regina Igel
Associate Professor
Spanish and Portuguese Department
University of Maryland
College Park, MD (1997)

Emilio Iodice
Director
Office of Consumer Goods and Service
U.S. Department of Commerce
Washington, DC

Betty Ipock
Director
Associate Degree Nursing Program
Missouri Southern State College
Joplin, MO

J.R. Isaac
Professor
Indian Institute of Technology
Powai, Bombay, India

Parthasarathy Iyengar
Associate Professor
County College of Morris
Randolph, NJ (1993)

Keith Jackson
Department o Electrical Engineering
Howard University
Washington, DC

David Jacobs
Assistant Professor
Department of Management, Personnel, and Industrial Relations
American University
Washington, DC (1993)

Rhoda Jacobs
Associate Professor
Business Administration
County College of Morris
Randolph, NJ

John Jaeck
Consultant
Fox Island, WA (1994)

Surinder M. Jain
Chairperson, EET
Sinclair Community College
Dayton, OH (1997)

Thomas L. Jamison
Professor
SUNY College of Technology
Wellsville, NY (1997)

Dr. Thomas A. Janke
V.P. Emeritus
University of Maryland University College
College Park, MD (1997)

Robert W. Jefferson
Professor and Chairperson
Western Illinois University
Macomb, IL

Betty Jehn
Adjunct Professor
Computer Science
University of Dayton
Dayton, OH

Lawrence A. Jehn
Professor Emeritus
Computer Science
University of Dayton
Dayton, OH

William Jensen
Attorney/Instructor
Office of General Counsel
USDA Graduate School
Washington, DC (1996)

James John
Dean of Engineering
University of Massachusetts
Amherst, MA

Clarence Johns
Coordinator
Business and Industry Services
University of Kentucky
Lexington, KY (1994)

Dale Johnson
Associate Professor
MIS Department
University of Wisconsin, Eau Claire
Eau Claire, WI

James Johnson
Professor and Chair
Howard University
Washington, DC

Joyce Nichols Johnson
Satellite Television Instructor
Oklahoma State University
Stillwater, OK

Thomas Johnson
Dean
William Rainey Harper College
Palatine, IL

Edward V. Jones
Associate Professor and Director
Office of Adult Learning and
Professional Development
Graduate School of Education
George Mason University
Fairfax, VA (1997)

Gail P. Jones
Professor
Technology Department
Cameron University
Lawton, OK (1997)

Maryhelen Jones
Director
Off-Campus Library Service
Central Michigan University
Mount Pleasant, MI (1995)

Ethel K. Jorgensen
Professor
Department of Business Administration
Los Angeles Valley College
Van Nuys, CA

Rodney Jurist
Chairman
Department of Business Education
Rider University
Lawrenceville, NJ

Thomas Jurkanin
Assistant Manager
Illinois Local Government Law
Enforcement Officers Training Board
Springfield, IL

Joseph M. Kanyan
Professor
Department of Music
George Mason University
Fairfax, VA

Martin Kaplan
Professor
Drexel University
Philadelphia, PA (1994)

Leonard Kapochus
Associate Professor of Business
Cumberland County College
Vineland, NJ

Charles Kardon
Miami Valley Pension
Dayton, OH

Janice Karlen
Associate Professor of Management &
Accounting
LaGuardia Community College (CUNY)
New York, NY (1993)

Ralph Katerberg
Associate Professor
College of Business Administration
University of Cincinnati
Cincinnati, OH (1996)

Adolph Katz
Professor
School of Business
Fairfield University
Fairfield, CT

Saul W. Katz
Associate Dean
Kingsborough Community College
Brooklyn, NY

Larry G. Keating
Associate Professor
Department of Electrical Engineering Technology
Metropolitan State College
Denver, CO

James R. Keiser
Associate Professor
Hotel and Institutional Administration
Pennsylvania State University
University Park, PA (1994)

J. Roland Kelley
Chairman
Business Admi nistration
Tarrant County Junior College System, Northeast
Hurst, TX

Nancy Kelly
Professor of Social Work
Rutgers University
Camden, NJ (1993)

Robert A. Kemp
Professor of Management
Drake University
Des Moines, IA

Kenneth Kent
Division Chair (Retired)
DeKalb Technical Institute
Clarkston, GA (1996)

Clyde Kesler
Professor
Civil Engineering and Theoretical and Applied Mechanics
University of Illinois
Urbana, IL

Judy Kieffer
Associate Professor of Nursing
University of Louisville
Louisville, KY

Patricia Yoshiko Kidd
Professor
U.S. Department of Agriculture Graduate School
Washington, DC (1996)

James E. Killorin
Denver University
Telecommunications Division
Denver, CO

Geoffrey King
Chair
Department of Management
California State University, Fullerton
Fullerton, CA

Jerry King
Dean
Trinity Valley Community College
Athens, TX

Paul Kinney
Dean
Business School
California State University
Chico, CA

Donna J. Kizzier
Associate Professor
Vocational and Adult Education
University of Nebraska-Lincoln
Lincoln, NE (1995)

Lonnie D. Kliver
Professor
Department of Religious Studies
Southern Methodist University
Dallas, TX (1997)

Julius Kline
Jerusalem, Israel

Russell Kline
Professor of Technology
Oklahoma State University
Oklahoma City, OK

Wallace C. Knapp
Director
Computer Services Department
Catonsville Community College
Baltimore, MD (1997)

George W. Knight
Director of Educational Materials
Seminary Extension
Nashville, TN (1995)

Melvin Knight
Professor Emeritus
School of Education
University of Alabama at Birmingham
Birmingham, AL (1997)

Ronald Knipfer
Dean
Sinclair Community College
Dayton, OH

Glenn Knudsvig
Director
English Board
University of Michigan
Ann Arbor, MI

Bert Kobayashi
Chairman
Department of Health and Physical Education
University of California, San Diego
La Jolla, CA

George Kocher
Director
Mining Resource Center
Wabash Valley College
Mt. Carmel, IL

James Koerlin
Dean
School of Technology and Industry
Golden Gate University
San Francisco, CA (1997)

John Kokus
Professor and Director
Real Estate Center
Kogod College of Business Administration
American University
Washington, DC (1997)

Michael Kolesnick
Coordinator
Community College of Vermont
Rutland, VT

Michael Kolivosky
Dean
Hillsdale College
Hillsdale, MI

Ric Koonce
Program Head
Fire Science Program
J. Sargeant Reynolds Community College
Richmond, VA (1994)

David Korn
Chairman
German and Russian Department
Howard University
Washington, DC

Stanley Kossen
Instructor
Business and Economics
Merritt College
Oakland, CA

Joseph Kossik
Director
Business Studies
Community College of Denver
Denver, CO (1996)

Ronald Kostar
Professor of Intelectual Heritage
Temple University
Philadelphia, PA

Kenneth Kovach
Professor
School of Business Administration
George Mason University
Fairfax, VA (1996)

Ernest Kovacs, Jr.
Research Scientist
New Jersey Department of Transportation
Trenton, NJ

Anthony Kowalski
Director
American Bankers Association
Washington, DC

Connie Kraft
President
Learning Tree of America, Inc.
Carrollton, GA (1994)

Paul Krasucki
Assistant Professor of Computer Science
Rutgers University
New Brunswick, NJ

Sanford Kravitz
Professor
School of Public Affairs and Services
Florida International University
North Miami, FL

Eugene J. Kray
Dean of Community Education
Delaware County Community College
Media, PA

A.C. Krizan
Associate Professor
Murray State University
Murray, KY

Dr. Galen Kroeck
Associate Professor
College of Business Administration
Florida International University
Miami, FL (1997)

Charles Kroncke
Associate Professor
University of Wisconsin, Madison
Madison, WI

Steven Kubriki
Professor
Richard Stockon College of New Jersey
Stockton, NJ

Dr. Arun Kumar
Assistant Professor of Information and Decision Sciences
Montclair University
Upper Montclair, NJ

Robert Lager
Chairman
Department of Russian
Georgetown University
Washington, DC

Marilyn Lair
Associate Professor of Business
Cameron University
Lawton, OK

Betty G. Lall
Director
Union University Urban Affairs Program
Cornell University
New York, NY

David R. Lambert
Associate Professor
Suffolk University
Boston, MA

Edward N. Lambremont
Chair, Nuclear Science & Engineering
Louisiana State University
Baton Rouge, LA (1997)

Gerald E. Lampe
Professor and Director
Language Studies
School of Advanced International Studies
Johns Hopkins University
Washington, DC (1996)

Jack Landers
Dept. of Manufacturing and Construction
Central Missouri State University
Warrensburg, MO (1997)

Eric A. Larson
Dean
Business and Allied Health
Elgin Community College
Elgin, IL (1996)

Carol J. LaSasso
Professor
Department of Education
Gallaudet University
Washington, DC (1996)

Deborah Laster
Teacher/Mentor
Teacher Mentor Program
New York City Board of Education
Bronx, NY

Kenneth R. Lauer
Professor of Civil Engineering
University of Notre Dame
Notre Dame, IN

William C. Lauer
Rider University
Lawrenceville, NJ

Arthur C. Laufer
Professor of Management
California State University, Long Beach
Long Beach, CA

Joseph Launie
Department of Finance, Insurance, and Real Estate
California State University
Northridge, CA

Judith Laux
Associate Professor and Chair
Department of Economics
Colorado College
Colorado Springs, CO (1995)

Richard Lechowich
Professor and Head
Department of Food Science and Technology
Virginia Polytechnic Institute and State University
Blacksburg, VA

C.W. Lee
Professor
Department of Accounting and Data Processing
California State University, Dominguez Hills
Carson, CA

Davis Lee
Professor of Japanese
George Washington University
Washington, DC (1993)

Edward L. Lee II
President
The Lee Group, Inc.
Falls Church, VA (1996)

Fred E. Lee
Associate Director
Professional Development Institute
College of Business
North Texas State University
Richardson, TX

Maureen Lee-Locke
Instructor
Katharine Gibbs School
Boston, MA (1996)

Arch Leean
Chairman
Art Department
St. Olaf College
Northfield, MN

Claudette Lefebre
Associate Professor
Department of Leisure Studies
New York University
New York, NY

Richard Leininger
Associate Professor
School of Business and Management
Saginaw Valley State College
University Center, MI

Frank J. Lembo
Professor
Department of Real Estate
Northern Virginia Community College
Annandale, VA (1995)

Linda Lengyel
Professor
Law and Justice
Trenton State College
Trenton, NJ

William J. Lenicka
Associate Vice President for Academic Affairs
Georgia Institute of Technology
Atlanta, GA

Mary M. Leonard
Assistant Professor and Psychologist
University of Maryland
College Park, MD

Thomas Leonard
Chairman
Aeronautics Department
San Jose State University
San Jose, CA

Ann St. Clair Lesman
Professor of Spanish
Northern Virginia Community College
Alexandria, VA

Edward Leven
Golden Gate University
San Francisco, CA

James Levine
Chair and Professor
Department of Foreign Languages
George Mason University
Fairfax, VA (1994)

Viola Levitt
Associate Dean
Health Technology Department
Prince George's Community College
Largo, MD

Tamara Lewis
Professor
Davenport College, South Bend
Granger, IN

Bruce E. Libby
Manager
Occupational Safety and Health
Scientech, Inc.
Rockville, MD (1995)

Charles Libera
Coordinator
Business and Public Administration
Metropolitan State University
St. Paul, MN

Marilyn Liebrenz-Himes
Associate Professor
School of Government and Business
George Washington University
Washington, DC (1997)

Diana Linton
Assessment Specialist
George Meany Center for Labor Studies
Silver Spring, MD (1994)

M.A. Littlejohn
North Carolina State University
Raleigh, NC

L. H. Livingston
Senior Staff
Science Applications International Corporation
Aiken, SC (1996)

Linwood Livingston
Aiken, SC (1994)

Anne Lloyd
Professor
Department of Urban Education
Temple University
Philadelphia, PA

Jim Lock
Assistant Professor
Accounting and Finance
Northern Virginia community College
Alexandria, VA (1995

Dr. David L. Loebach
Sangamon State University
Springfield, IL (1997)

Dan A. Lookadoo
Professor
Electronics Department
New River Community College
Dublin, VA (1997)

David Lopez
Professor, Industrial Engineering
Central Michigan University
Mt. Pleasant, MI (1997)

Robert Losey
Associate Professor
Finance and Real Estate
Kogod College of Business Administration
The American University
Washington, DC (1995)

Joseph P. Longo, Jr.
Dean
School of Intelligence Information Systems
Defense Intelligence College
Washington, DC

Paul Lou
Instructor
Diablo Valley College
Pleasant Hill, CA

David Lucht
Vice President
Firepro, Inc.
Wellesley Hills, MA

Norbert Ludkey
Program Coordinator
Computer and Information Science
City College of San Francisco
San Francisco, CA

John A. Ludrick
Assistant to the Dean
School of Education
Southwestern Oklahoma State University
Weatherford, OK

John Ludwig
Lincoln Electric Co.
Southfield, MI (1997)

Donald Lundberg
Chairman
Hotel and Restaurant Management
California State Polytechnic University
Pomona, CA

Jack Luskin
Associate Director for Education and Training
Toxics Use Reduction Institute
University of Massachusetts
Lowell, MA

M. Kamburi Lyabaugh
Professor
Department of African Studies
Howard University
Washington, DC (1993)

Keith MacDonald
Associate Professor
Ferris State College
Big Rapids, MI

William C. MacDonald
Dean
Management Division
Lesley Graduate School
Lesley College
Cambridge, MA

Donald I. MacInnes
Director
Teacher Education Laboratory
Presbyterian School of Christian Education
Richmond, VA

John R. MacKenzie
Associate Professor
University of the District of Columbia
Washington, DC

Miles MacMahon
Professor
Essex County College
Newark, NJ

John Magnotti
Director and Professor Emeritus
Procurement Management Program
American University
Washington, DC (1997)

Haydee Magro
Professor of Portuguese
Brazilian-American Cultural Institute
Washington, DC

Peter Maher
Assistant Professor
Department of Math and Computer Science
University of Missouri, St. Louis
St. Louis, MO

Robert Main
Professor
College of Communications
California State University
Chico, CA

David Mair
Associate Professor
Department of English
University of Oklahoma
Norman, OK (1995)

Patricia Malone
Assistant Professor
Rider University
Lawrenceville, NJ

Anthony Maltese
Chairman
Department of Communications
William Patterson University
Wayne, NJ

Louis Mangione
Professor of Chinese
Department of Critical Languages
Temple University
Philadelphia, PA

Anthony Mann
Chairman
Computer Information Systems
Sinclair Community College
Dayton, OH (1997)

Barbara Marantz
Empire State College
Hartsdale, NY (1995)

William March
Professor
Aeronautics and Business Administration
Embry-Riddle Aeronautical University
Bunnell, FL (1997)

Julius Mariasis
Associate Professor
Massachusetts Bay Community College
Wellesley Hills, MA

Reed Markham
Professor
California State Polytechnic University
Pomona, CA

Leonard Marks
Instructor
Santa Ana College
Santa Ana, CA

Cynthia Martin
Associate Professor
Asian and East European Language Departments
University of Maryland
College Park, MD (1997)

Joseph H. Martin
President
Martin & Benner Appraisal Co.
Lawrenceville, NJ

Mel Martin
Administrative Director
Respiratory Care Pulmonary Function
St. Joseph's Hospital
Towson, MD (1995)

Thomas Martin
Professor
Department of Management
College of Business Administration
University of Nebraska
Omaha, NE (1993)

William R. Martin
Professor
School of Education
George Mason University
Fairfax, VA

Santo Marzullo
Chairman
Washington Technical Institute
Washington, DC

Dana Massey
Assistant Professor
Professional Studies Department
Bellevue University
Bellevue, NE (1995)

Lance Masters
Chair
School of Business
California State University
Hayward, CA (1996)

Rocci S. Mastroberti
Chairman
Anne Arundel Community College
Arnold, MD

William J. Mathias
Dean
University of South Carolina
Columbia, SC

Charles Maxey
Assistant Professor
School of Business Administration
University of Southern California
Los Angeles, CA

Lee Maxwell
Professor
Colorado State University
Fort Collins, CO

Paul D. Maxwell
Assistant Dean
Northeastern University
Boston, MA

Brigitte May
Professor
University of Maryland—Baltimore County
Catonsville, MD

John Mayer
Associate Professor
Worcester Polytechnic Institute
Worcester, MA

Patricia Mayer
Associate Professor
Rutgers University, Douglas College
New Brunswick, NJ

Edward Mazze
Professor
Temple University
Philadelphia, PA (1993 NJ)

John E. McAllister
Deputy Secretary for Administration
Dept. of Labor and Industry
Commonwealth of Pennsylvania
Harrisburg, PA (1997)

Barnaby McAusian
Assistant Professor
Burlington County College
Pemberton, NJ

Mary McBride
Professor
New York University
New York, NY (1993)

Neal McBryde
Dean
Bee County College
Beeville, TX

Herbert E. McCartney
Automotive Program Head
Northern Virginia Community College
Alexandria, VA

Michael McCaskey
School of Languages and Linguistics
Georgetown University
Washington, DC

Dr. Jim McClullen
Social Science Dept.
Northern Virginia Community College
Alexandria, VA (1997)

Kenneth McCreedy
Assistant Professor
School of Community Services
Virginia Commonwealth University
Richmond, VA

William E. McDonald
Senior Art Advisor (Retired)
U.S. Department of Education
Washington, DC (1994)

Garnett McDonough
Chair
Real Estate and Legal Assisting
Sinclair Community College
Dayton, OH

James A. McDonough
Professor of Civil Engineering
Virginia Military Institute
Lexington, VA

Paul E. McDuffee
Director
Airline Operators Certificate Program
Embry-Riddle Aeronautical University
Bunnell, FL

Robert Barlow McEwen
Research Physical Scientist
National Mapping Division
U.S. Geological Society
Reston, VA (1993)

Phil McGee
Director
Greenville Technical College
Greenville, SC

Robert McGowan
Associate Professor
Department of Management
University of Denver
Denver, CO

Robert McIntosh
Professor of Tourism
School of Hotel, Restaurant,
and Institutional Management
Michigan State University
East Lansing, MI

Ronald L. McKeen
Professor Emeritus
Virginia Polytechnical Institute &
State University
Falls Church, VA (1997)

Charles McKenny
Chair
United States Marine Staff College
Quantico, VA (1993)

George W. McKinney, Jr.
Virginia Bankers' Professor of Bank Management
University of Virginia
Charlottesville, VA

Robert L. McLeod
Director of Regional Operations
National Fire Sprinkler Association
Patterson, NY

Dale McNabb
Associate Director for Small Business
Andrews Air Force Base
Washington, DC

James McNeill
Consultant
Olney, MD (1994)

Dorothy McNutt
Chairperson and Professor Emeritus
Business ad Computer Science Department
College of the Mainland
Texas City, TX (1997)

Robert McVicker
Director
Cooperative Education
University of Lowell
Lowell, MA

Charles Medler
Chair
California State University, Sacramento
Sacramento, CA

Karen L. Medsker
Professor
Human Resources
Marymount University
Arlington, VA (1995)

John S. Megerson
Director
District Security
Southwest Texas State University
San Marcos, TX (1996)

Dr. John Mellon
Associate Professor of Hospitality
Management
Teikyo Post University
Waterbury, CT

William Melnicoe
Chair
California State University, Sacramento
Sacramento, CA

Arnold Meltzer
Professor
George Washington University
Washington, DC

Steven J. Meltzer
Chief
Internal Revenue Service
Washington, DC

Paul Mercado
Chairman
Pennsylvania Institute of Technology
Upper Darby, PA

John Mercier
Professor
Rowan University
Glassboro, NJ

Sidney Messer
Professor
City College of San Francisco
San Francisco, CA

Paul A. Meyer
Associate Professor
Economics Department
University of Maryland
College Park, MD (1997)

Richard L. Meyer
Professor
College of Business Administration
University of South Florida
Tampa, FL (1994)

David Michaels
Professor
Northern Virginia Community College
Annandale, VA

James Middleman
Professor
Department of comparative and Regional Studies
School of International Service
American University
Washington, DC (1995)

Jacqueline Middleton
Adjunct Professor
Department of Management
Montgomery College
Germantown, MD (1997)

Walter Mietus
Professor Emeritus
Applied Technologies Department
University of Maryland
College Park, MD (1995)

Joseph Migliaccio
Professor
Science and Technology Department
Northern Virginia Community College
Alexandria, VA (1997)

Raymond Mignogna
Chair
Math, Physics, and Engineering
Charles County Community College
La Plata, MD

Wilbert L. Miles
Faculty and Managerial Consultant
University of Colorado
Denver, CO (1997)

Dr. Allen Miller
Golden Gate University
School of Technology & Industry
San Francisco, CA (1997)

Lawrence F. Miller
Professor
Nuclear Engineering
University of Tennessee
Knoxville, TN (1997)

Peter Miller
Assistant Professor
Philadelphia College of Pharmacy and Sciences
Philadelphia, PA (1996)

Vergil V. Miller
Dean
Oklahoma State University
Stillwater, OK

Jake Milliones
Assistant Professor
University of Pittsburgh
Pittsburgh, PA

Sam Mills
Assistant Director
J. Sargeant Reynolds Community College
Richmond, VA

Stuart Milner
Assistant Professor
School of Education
Catholic University of America
Washington, DC

Robert Minter
Chairman
University of Denver
Denver, CO

Gerald Mitchell
Professor
Telecommunications Department
University of Colorado at Boulder
Boulder, CO (1995)

Herbert Mitchell
Dean
Virginia Polytechnic Institute and State University
Blacksburg, VA

Dr. James H. Mittleman
Division of Componative & Regional Studies
School of International Service
The American University
Washington, DC (1997)

Jan L. Mize
Director
Georgia State University
Atlanta, GA

Nancy Moeller
Associate Dean
Hiram Weekend College
Hiram, OH

Francis H. Moffitt
Professor
Civil Engineering Department
University of California
Berkeley, CA

Robeson S. Moise
Associate Professor
Department of Power and Transportation
Central Missouri State University
Warrensburg, MO

Morris Mokowitz
Chair
Rutgers University
New Brunswick, NJ

Richard A. Molenaar
Assistant Professor
University of North Dakota
Grand Forks, ND

Joanne Moncrief
Chief Copy Editor
National Journal Magazine
Washington, DC

Geroald Monigold
Director
Fire Service Institute
University of Illinois
Champaign, IL (1995)

Jack R. Monks
Professor
Technology Department
McNeese State University
Lake Charles, LA

Jose G. Montero
Associate Professor
Northern Virginia Community College
Annandale, VA

A. Thompson Montgomery
Associate Professor
San Francisco State University
San Francisco, CA

Cathleen Moore
Associate Professor of Psychology
Philadelphia College of Pharmacy and Sciences
Philadelphia, PA (1997)

James M. Moore
Professor
Virginia Polytechnic Institute and State University
Blacksburg, VA

R. Kevin Moore
Assistant Professor
Christian Studies Department
Union University
Jackson, TN (1996)

Rudy Moore
Professor
Rosemont College
Rosemont, PA

Harry More
Professor
San Jose State University
San Jose, CA

Russell Morey
Chairperson
Western Illinois University
Macomb, IL

Jim Lee Morgan
Professor
West Los Angeles College
Culver City, CA

Michael Morgan
Professor
College of Environmental Sciences
University of Wisconsin, Green Bay
Green Bay, WI (1993)

W.J. Morgan, Jr.
Professor
Florida International University
Miami, FL

Joseph M. Moricz
Dean
Robert Morris College
Coraopolis, PA

Richard Mortimer
Chairman
Drexel University
Philadelphia, PA

George Mostoller
Professor of Engineering Technology
University of Pittsburgh at Johnstown
Johnstown, PA (1995)

Tim Mott
Union Institute
Cincinnati, OH

Homer J. Mottice
Professor
Florida State University
Tallahassee, FL

Rafael Moure-Eraso
Associate Professor
Work Environment Department
College of Engineering
University of Massachusetts
Lowell, MA

Mel Moyer
Associate Professor of Psychology
Rowan University
Glassboro, NJ (1995 NJ)

J. Robert Mueller
Director of Nuclear Education
Wisconsin Public Service Corporation
Green Bay, WI (1997)

George Muhlberg
Adjunct Professor
School of Management
Robert Morris College
Coraopolis, PA (1994)

Eiko Muira
Professor
University of Maryland
College Park, MD

William J. Mulkeen
Adjunct Professor of Criminal Justice
Warren County Community College
Washington, NJ (1995)

Joseph J. Mulligan
Division General Manager
General Dynamics
Avenel, NJ
Adjunct Professor
Middlesex County College
Edison, NJ

Donald J. Mullineaux
Associate Dean
College of Business and Economics
University of Kentucky
Lexington, KY

Gary Murdock
Research Assistant Professor
Washington University School of Medicine
St. Louis, MO (1995)

Richard J. Murphy
Professor
Northeastern University
Boston, MA

Patricia Murrell
Director
Center for the Study of Higher Education
Memphis State University
Memphis, TN

Dr. Morris Muskovitz
Chair, Hebraic Studies Dept.
Rutgers University
New Brunswick, NJ (1997)

Phyllis Myers
Professor
School of Business
Virginia Commonwealth University
Richmond, VA

Richard A. Myren
Dean and Professor
American University
Washington, DC

Noel Myricks
Associate Professor
University of Maryland
College Park, MD (1995)

Sumiko Nagasawa
Professor
Chinese and Japanese Department
Georgetown University
Washington, DC (1993)

John Nagohosian
Director
Henry Ford Community College
Dearborn, MI

Velma C. Nance
Coordinator
Distance Learning
Peralta Community College
Oakland, CA (1997)

Anthony Natale
Adjunct Professor
Bucks County Community College
Newtown, PA (1994)

Prabhaker Nayak
Professor of Economics and Business
William Paterson University
Wayne, NJ (1993 NJ)

Richard G. Nehrbass
Assistant Professor
School of Management
California State University, Dominguez Hills
Carson, CA

Edward A. Nelson
Professor
School of Business and Economics
California State University
Los Angeles, CA

Ray A. Nelson
Chair
Department of Professional Education
Bemidji State University
Bemidji, MN (1995)

Richard S. Nelson
Professor
San Francisco State University
San Francisco, CA

Glen Nemecek
Coordinator, Aviation Education
Oklahoma State University
Stillwater, OK (1997)

Charles P. Nemeth
Professor
Wilmington, DE

Art Newberry
Assistant Director of Academics
MEBA Engineering School
Easton, MD (1997)

Clarence Newhouse
Assistant Dean
School of Divinity
Howard University
Washington, DC

Joe M. Newton
Coordinator
Bakersfield College
Bakersfield, CA

Marilyn L. Nicholas
Professor
Towson State University
Towson, MD (1996)

James Nielsen
Professor of Finance
College of Business Administration
Oregon State University
Corvallis, OR

Thomas Niles
Director
Monmouth University
West Long Beach, NJ

Gerard Nistal
Professor and Chair
Holly Cross College
New Orleans, LA

G. Joseph Norwood
Professor and Chair
Division of Pharmacy Administration
School of Pharmacy
University of North Carolina Chapel Hill
Chapel Hill, NC (1994)

David Novicki
Division Director
Michigan State University
East Lansing, MI

James Null
Dean
University of Colorado at Colorado Springs
Colorado Springs, CO

Margaret Nydell
Professor
Arabic Dialect Project
Georgetown University
Washington, DC (1994)

Dr. Alfred Obernberger
Associate Professor
Georgetown University
Washington, DC (1997)

Michael O'Brien
Chairman
Thomas Nelson Community College
Hampton, VA

Rev. Richard O'Brien, SJ
Jesuit Community
Georgetown University
Washington, DC (1996)

Colleen O'Brien-Thorpe
Professor
Northern Virginia Community College
Annandale, VA (1994)

David O'Gorman
Professor
Business Administration
Sangamon State University
Springfield, IL (1994)

Bryan O'Neil
Middlesex Community College
Bedford, NH

Charles O'Rear
Professor and Chair
Department of Forensic Sciences
George Washington University
Washington, DC (1994)

Robert Oberg
Department of Computer Sciences
Framingham State College
Framingham, MA

Alfred Obernbereger
Chairman
German Department
Georgetown University
Washington, DC

Herbert Oestreich
School of Business
San Jose State University
San Jose, CA

Martin Oettinger
Associate Professor
University of California, Davis
Davis, CA

Godwin Ohiwerei
Associate Professor of Sociology
Jersey City State College
Jersey City, NJ (1995 NJ)

Frank Oldham
President and Chief Operating Officer
Worthen National Bank of Conway
Conway, AR

Van N. Oliphant
Professor of Management
Memphis State University
Memphis, TN

Harold Oliver
Educational Advisor
U.S. Army Ordnance Center and School
Aberdeen Proving Ground, MD

Alan Oppenheim
Professor and Director of M.B.A. Program
Montclair State University
Upper Montclair, NJ

Rosa Oppenheim
Associate Professor
Graduate School of Management
Rutgers University
New Brunswick, NJ

Carl Van Orden
Professor Emeritus
Business and Economics
Belmont Abbey College
Belmont, NC (1994)

Bill Osborn
Director
Industrial Technology Program
Johnson County Community College
Overland Park, KS (1995)

Howard P. Osborn
Director
Maryland Casualty Company
Baltimore, MD

Rose Marie Oster
Professor
Department of German and Slavic Languages
University of Maryland
College Park, MD (1993)

Leo B. Osterhaus
Dean
St. Edwards University
Austin, TX

Dula Pacquiao
Edison, NJ

Ivor P. Page
Erik Jonsson School of Engineering & Computer Science
University of Texas-Dallas
Richardson, TX (1997)

Jim Painter
Durham Technical Institute
Durham, NC

Naomi Palmer
Speech & Language Pathologist
Los Angeles, CA (1997)

Ray Palmer
Vice Chairman
Milwaukee School of Engineering
Milwaukee, WI

Paul A. Palumbo
Associate Director
Police Training Institute
University of Illinois
Champaign, IL (1997)

Yvonne Panaro
Professor
Georgetown University
Washington, DC

Frank Paone
President
Detroit College of Business
Dearborn, MI

Salvatore Paratore
Associate Professor
George Washington University
Washington, DC

Esther Parnes
Chairman, Dept. of Computer Science
Emunah College for Women
Jerusalem, Israel (1997)

Kenneth Parzych
Professor of Economics and Management Sciences
Eastern Connecticut State University
Willimantis, CT

Phillip Pastras
Professor
Middlesex County College
Edison, NJ

Thomas Patrick
Chair
Department of Business Administration
College of New Jersey
Trenton, NJ (1993)

Walter Pauk
Director
Cornell University
Ithaca, NY

John Paulson
Arizona Division of Emergency Services
Phoenix, AZ

Fred B. Paxton
Director
Fort Campbell Extended Campus
University of Kentucky
Hopkinsville, KY

George Payne
Professor
Gudelsky Institute for Technical Education
Montgomery College
Rockville, MD (1997)

A.J. Pearson
Executive Director
NJATC
Upper Marlboro, MD

James Pellegrino
Associate Professor
School of Education
University of Pittsburgh
Pittsburgh, PA

John L. Penkala
State College, PA

Michael Pepper
Chairman of Business and Economics Division
and Program Director of Hotel, Restaurant,
and Tourism
Transylvania University
Lexington, KY (1995 NJ)

Eng. Jorge E. Pereira
San Juan, Puerto Rico (1997)

Everett Perkins
Director
Fire Service Extension
West Virginia University
Morgantown, WV (1994)

Lawrence Hobdy Perkins
Director
University of Western Florida
Pensacola, FL

David A. Perreault
Coordinator
School of Engineering
Boston University
Boston, MA

Frances Peterson
Chair
Rio Hondo College
Whittier, CA

Jackie Pflaum
Associate Professor
College of Nursing and Health Sciences
University of Alaska, Anchorage
Anchorage, AK

Deepak B. Phatak
Professor
Indian Institute of Technology, Bombay
Bombay, India

James Phelps
Professor
University of Lowell
Lowell, MA

Chuck Philip
Dean of Instruction
Health and Sciences Department
Kalamazoo Valley Community College
Kalamazoo, MI (1997)

Kenneth Phillips
Chair
California State University, Los Angeles
Los Angeles, CA

Lawrence C. Phillips
Professor
School of Management
Case Western Reserve University
Cleveland, OH (1993)

Marylou Phillips
Associate Professor of Medical Imaging
Holy Family College
Philadelphia, PA

John Phipps
Chairman
Flight Technology Department
Embry-Riddle Aeronautical University
Daytona Beach, FL

Valerie Brown Pickard
President
Collaborations, Inc.
Indianapolis, IN (1995)

Bruce R. Piringer
Director
Fire and Rescue Training Institute
University of Missouri
Columbia, MO (1995)

Rosemary Pittman
Director
School of Nursing
University of Washington
Seattle, WA

William Pivar
Director
Business Education
College of the Desert
Palm Desert, CA

Joseph Pizzillo
Professor
Secondary Education/Foundations of Education
Rowan University
Glassboro, NJ (1993)

Chester C. Platt
Associate Dean for Area 8
Coastline Community College
Mountain Valley, CA

Robert Pleasure
Executive Director
George Meany Center for Labor Studies
Silver Spring, MD

Mark S. Plovnick
Dean
School of Business and Public Administration
University of the Pacific
Stockton, CA

Richard Podlesnik
School of Business Administration
Fort Lewis College
Durango, CO (1993 NJ)

Francis Polk
Assistant Dean of Instruction
Ocean County College
Toms River, NJ

Richard Pontinen
Chairman and Professor
Hamline University
St. Paul, MN

Thomas Poppendieck
Director
Hamline University
St. Paul, MN

Samuel I. Porrath
Chairman
Niagara University
Niagara, NY

Daniel E. Porter
Chairperson
Departments of Fire Science and
Safety Risk Management
Sinclair Community College
Dayton, OH (1995)

Jacquelyn Porter
Professor
Philosophy and Religion Department
Marymount University
Arlington, VA (1995)

Russell Pounds
Professor Emeritus
Iowa State University
Ames, IA (1996)

Robert A. Powell
Electronics
Oakland Community College
Auburn Hills, MI (1997)

Walter M. Presz, Jr.
Professor
Western New England College
Springfield, MA

Glenn Pribbenow
Field Systems Manager
Fire Service Institute
Iowa State University Extension
Ames, IA (1995)

Gene Hill Price
Lecturer
Department of Computer Sciences
Old Dominion University
Norfolk, VA (1996)

Stanley D. Price
Dean
Golden Gate University
San Francisco, CA

Thomas Price
Head
Business Assistance and Training Center
Joliet Junior College
Joliet, IL (1995)

Paul Prins
Executive Director
Ferris State University
Big Rapids, MI

Travis S. Pritchett
Professor
College of Business Administration
University of South Carolina
Columbia, SC

Preston Probasco
Acting Director
Cybernetic Systems
School of Social Science
San Jose State University
San Jose, CA

Richard Profozich
Professor and Director
Writing Center
Prince George's Community College
Largo, MD (1997)

Patricia Protho-Shepherd
Associate Chief Nurse/Education
Philadelphia V.A. Medical Center
Philadelphia, PA (1995)

Mark S. Puclik
Associate Professor
Business Administration Department
University of Illinois
Springfield, IL (1997)

Simin Pulat
Professor
School of Industrial Engineering
University of Oklahoma
Norman, OK (1995)

Miguel Pulido
Academic Coordinator
Eastern College
Wynnewood, PA (1995 NJ)

Jeanette Purdy
Professor of Business
Mercer County Community College
Trenton, NJ (1996)

Enrico Puzzudi
Chairman, Manufacturing Engineering Technology
Henry Ford Community College
Dearborn, MI (1997)

Sister Rose Ann Quinn
Director of Montessori
Chestnut Hill College
Philadelphia, PA

Samuel Rabinowitz
Professor of Management
Rutgers University
Camden, NJ

Ronald Racster
Associate Dean/Professor
College of Business
Ohio State University
Columbus, OH

Denis T. Raihall
Professor
Drexel University
Philadelphia, PA (1994)

Louise S. Rainis
Consultant
Washington, DC

William L. Raley
Director
College of the Mainland
Texas City, TX

Margarete Ralston
Associate Professor
Electronics Engineering Technology
Metropolitan State College of Denver
Denver, CO

Felicenne Ramey
Assistant Professor
School Business and Public Administration
California State University
Sacramento, CA

Hamideh P. Ramjerdi-Shirazi
Professor of Economics
Kean College of New Jersey
Union, NJ (1995 NJ)

Wayne Ramp
Professor
Southern Illinois University
Carbondale, IL

S. Robert Ramsey
Professor
Department of Hebrew and East
Asian Languages
University of Maryland
College Park, MD (1996)

Richard L. Rath
Senior Editor
Yachting Magazine
Cos Cob, CT

Virginia Ratigan
Associate Professor
Religious Studies Department
Rosemont College
Rosemont, PA (1997)

Gayle Rayburn
Professor of Accounting
College of Business Administration
Memphis State University
Memphis, TN

Mohammed Razani
University of California Extension
Daly City, CA (1994)

Cheryl Isaacs Redmon
Instructor
Business Office Technology Department
Santa Rosa Junior College
Santa Rosa, CA (1996)

Irving S. Reed
Professor of Electrical Engineering
University of Southern California
Los Angeles, CA

Larry Reed
Executive Vice President
Navarro College
Corsicana, TX

Robert Reed
Director
Emergency Administration
University of North Texas
Denton, TX

T. Zane Reeves
Professor
Division of Public Administration
University of New Mexico
Albuquerque, NM (1993)

Laureen Regan
Assistant Professor
Department of Risk Management and Insurance
Temple University
Philadelphia, PA (1995)

Howard Reichbart
Program Head
Northern Virginia Community College
Annandale, VA (1997)

Robert Reid
Dean
Technical Division
Broome Community College
Binghamton, NY

Wallace Reiff
Associate Dean and Professor of Finance
Florida Technical College
Orlando, FL

Mary E. Reilly
Chair
Secretarial Science Department
Middlesex County College
Edison, NJ

Matt Reiser
Professor Emeritus
Cleveland State College
Cleveland, TN

James Renick
Associate Provost
George Mason University
Fairfax, VA

Benjamin Resnick
Academic Advisement Coordinator
Communications Department
Rowan University
Glassboro, NJ

Charles Rhyner
Professor
Physics Department
University of Wisconsin, Green Bay
Green Bay, WI (1997)

Harriett Rice
Associate Professor
Business Administration Department
Los Angeles City College
Los Angeles, CA

George Rich
Professor
Department of Physical Education
California State University, Northridge
Northridge, CA

Delia R. Richards
Professor and Chair
Early Childhood Education Program
Prince George's Community College
Largo, MD (1997)

Jack Richards
Director
Automotive Technician Program
Ferris State University
Big Rapids, MI

Lester J. Richards
Automotive Program Director
Ferris State University
Big Rapids, MI

Marc Riedel
Research Associate
University of Pennsylvania
Philadelphia, PA

Ervine M. Rips
Professor
New Jersey Institute of Technology
Newark, NJ

Albert D. Robinson
Coordinator
Washtenaw Community College
Ann Arbor, MI

Gerald D. Robinson
Professor
Macomb Community College
Warren, MI

Gordon Robinson
Professor
Pennsylvania State University
University Park, PA

James A. Robinson
Associate Professor
Department of English, American Literature and Drama
University of Maryland
College Park, MD (1996)

Newton Rochte
Professor Emeritus
University of Toledo
Toledo, OH

Yvonne Rodgers
Business Teacher
C.A. Fredd State Technical College
Tuscaloosa, AL

Stewart Rodnon
Professor
Rider University
Lawrenceville, NJ

Derrill C. Rohlfs
Department
George Washington University
Washington, DC

Dwight Rogers
Assistant Professor and Chair
Industrial Technology
Eastern New Mexico University
Portales, NM (1995)

Lloyd Rogers
Assistant Dean
Sacramento City College
Sacramento, CA

Johnson Roney III
Director
Mercer County Community College
Trenton, NJ

James F. Rooney
Professor
Catholic University of America
Washington, DC

Theresa Rosania
Associate Professor
Kean College of New Jersey
Union, NJ

Shifra Rosen
Jerusalem, Israel

Theodore Rosen
Bethesda, MD

William E. Rosenbach
Professor
Leadership Development Center
Gettysburg College
Gettysburg, PA (1994)

Lee Rosenthal
Professor
Electrical Engineering Technology
Fairleigh Dickinson University
Teaneck, NJ (1993 NJ)

Peter Burton Ross
Professor
Department of English Studies
University of District of Columbia
Washington, DC (1993)

Daniel Rota
Professor
Robert Morris College
Pittsburg, PA (1994)

Gene Roth
Professor
Idaho State University
Pocatello, ID

John Rouselle
Purdue University
West Lafayette, IN

Walter F. Rowe
Professor
Department of Forensic Science
George Washington University
Washington, DC (1995)

Lenore Rubin
Director
NYNEX Mobile Communications
Orangeburg, NY

Patrick Runde
Associate Dean
University of Wisconsin
Madison, WI

Robert A. Rupen
Professor of Political Science
University of North Carolina-Chapel Hill (1997)

John E. Ryan
Associate Dean
McGeorge School of Law
Sacramento, CA

Charles Sabatino
Assistant Director
Commission Legal Problems of the Elderly
American Bar Association
Washington, DC (1993)

Steve Saffron
Director
American Indian Program
Scottsdale Community College
Scottsdale, AZ

Charles Sahrbeck
Director (Retired)
Management Training
General Motors Corporation
Flint, MI

Ann Barbara Sakurai
Chair and Professor
Math and Science Department
Webster University
St. Louis, MO

Robert Saladarini
Professor of Information Systems
Bergen Community College
Paramus, NJ (1996)

Octavio Salati
Professor
University of Pennsylvania
Philadelphia, PA

Tom S. Sale
Chairman
Department of Finance and Economics
Louisiana Tech University
Ruston, LA

Harrylyn Sallis
Dean
Adult Learning
Millsaps College
Jackson, MS

Richard Sandhusen
Assistant Professor of Marketing Department
Rider University
Lawrenceville, NJ

Mel Sandler
Associate Professor
University of New Hampshire
Durham, NH

Robert Sandlin
Sandlin and Associates
San Diego, CA (1994)

Joseph Santora
Professor of Management and Humanities
Essex County College
Newark, NJ

Rajib Sanyal
Assistant Professor
College of New Jersey
Trenton, NJ (1993)

Rebecca J. Sartin
Health Technologies
Pima Community College
Tucson, AZ

Annabelle Sartore
Chair
Department of Management
California State University, Long Beach
Long Beach, CA

Henry Sauer
Program Manager
Chemical Manufacturers Association
Washington, DC

Charles R. Sayre
Commissioner
Kentucky Police Training Academy
Richmond, KY (1995)

Ralph M. Scarrow
Professor
California Polytechnic Institute, Pomona
Pomona, CA

Susan Schaefer
Associate Professor
Management Science Department
California State University
Hayward, CA

Reiner Schaeffer
Director of Academy Libraries
U.S. Air Force Academy
Colorado Springs, CO

John Schillinger
Chair and Professor
Department of Languages
and Foreign Study
American University
Washington, DC (1994)

Daniel J. Schleef
Professor
Department of Mechanical and Industrial Engineering
University of Cincinnati
Cincinnati, OH

John Schmeling
President
Education Connection
Vincennes, IN

Donald Schmidt
Professor
Hudson Valley Community College
Troy, NY

William Schmitt
Associate Professor
Computer Science Department
Temple University
Philadelphia, PA (1993 NJ)

Stephen Schneider
Assistant Dean
Suffolk County Community College
Brentwood, NY

Penelope S. Schott
Assistant Professor of English
Raritan Valley Community College
Somerville, NJ

Charles Schuler
Professor
Industrial Arts Department
California State College
California, PA

Helene Schwarberg
Assistant Department Head
University of Cincinnati
Cincinnati, OH

Susan Scoboria
Director of Admissions
New Center College
Long Island, NY

Barbara Williams Scott
Consultant
Alexandria, VA (1996)

Robert E. Scully
Assistant Professor
School of Adult and Continuing Education
Barry University
Miami, FL (1997)

John H. Seabrook
Westfield, NJ

Jennie Seaton
Virginia Commonwealth University
Richmond, VA

William Seaton
Director of DIAL
Directed Independent Adult Learning
Thomas Edison State College
Trenton, NJ

Gabriella Sechi
Assistant Professor
Department of Engineering Technology
College of New Jersey
Trenton, NJ

Ronald L. Seeber
Associate Dean
New York State School of Industrial and Labor Relations
Cornell University
Ithaca, NY

James Seeck
Associate Professor of Business and Social Science
Harper College
Palatine, IL

Richard Selden
New School for Social Research
New York, NY

Steven Selden
Professor
Department of Education Policy, Planning, and Administration
College of Education
University of MD
College Park, MD (1993)

Genevieve Semple
Belmar, NJ

Walter Senska
Apprenticeship Coordinator
Macomb Community College
Warren, MI

Oscar N. Serbein
Professor Emeritus of Insurance
Graduate School of Business
Stanford University
Stanford, CA

Mohammed Sesay
Professor
Department of Mathematics
University of the District of Columbia
Washington, DC (1995)

Robert Settlage
Director
Maternity and Infant Care Project
University of Southern California
Los Angeles, CA

David Setser
Electronics Instructor
Engineering Technology Program
Johnson County Community College
Overland Park, KS (1995)

Tom Seymour
Professor
Business Administration
Minot State University
Minot, ND (1995)

Donald Shaffer
Associate Professor
Continuing Education
Dundalk Community College
Baltimore, MD

John Shaffer
Director of Aviation
University of Albuquerque
Albuquerque, NM

Wallace Shakun
Dean of Technology
Director of Technical and Adult Education Programs
Clayton State College
Morrow, GA (1995)

Glen Shamburg
Director, Aviation
College of Continuing Education
Norman, OK (1997)

Hugh M. Shane
Chairperson
Western Illinois University
Macomb, IL

Bill Shannon
Professor of Paralegal Studies
Northern Virginia Community College
Alexandria, VA

Renee H. Shea
Professor
Department of English
University of the District of Columbia
Washington, DC (1996)

Harry Sheater
Professor of Chemistry
Union County College
Cransford, NJ (1996 NJ)

Larry Short
Director of Graduate Program
Management Department
Drake University
Des Moines, IA

Phillip Shrotman
District Coordinator
Cooperative Work Experience Education
Long Beach City College
Long Beach, CA

Milton Shuch
Chairman
Department of Management
Simmons College
Boston, MA

S. Cabell Shull
Chairman
University of Mississippi
University, MS

Louis Shuster
Professor of Management
School of Business and Public Administration
California State College
Bakersfield, CA

Celeste M. Sichenze
Professor Emeritus
Business Management
Northern Virginia Community College
Annandale, VA (1997)

Jerrold Siegel
Professor
Department of Math and Computer Science
University of Missouri-St. Louis
St. Louis, MO

Kemp Sigmon
Dean
Industrial Division
Spartansburg Technical College
Spartansburg, SC

Shirley Silvers
Professor
Queensborough Community College
Bayside, NY

Eugene Simko
School of Business Administration
Monmouth University
West Long Branch, NJ

Gale Simons
Associate Dean for Research
Director, Engineering Experiment Station
Kansas State University
Manhattan, KS (1994)

Don Simonson
Professor of Finance
University of Oklahoma
Norman, OK

Steven H. Simpler
Dean or Professor
School of Religion
Belmont University
Nashville, TN (1993)

Dennis Simpson
SPADA
Western Michigan University
Kalamazoo, MI (1993)

Richard W. Simpson
Director
Bureau of Regulations, Rates, and Policies
Pennsylvania Insurance Department
Harrisburg, PA

John H. Sims
Chairman
Management Science Department
California State University
Hayward, CA

Delavan Sipes
Associate Professor of Electronics
Biomedical Engineering Technology Coordinator
Schoolcraft College
Livonia, MI

S. Jay Sklar
Assistant Professor
Law and Real Estate
Temple University
Bala Cynwyd, PA (1993)

James B. Smathers
Professor
University of California, Los Angeles
Los Angeles, CA

In-Soon Shin Smeenk
Asian Studies Consultant
Washington, DC (1996)

Wayne Smeltz
Associate Professor of Business
Rider University
Lawrenceville, NJ (1993 NJ)

Ann Smith
Dean
Career and Technical Education
Charles County Community College
LaPlata, MD

Gerald Smith
Chairman
Business Division
Vincennes University
Vincennes, IN

James W. Smith
Professor
School of Business
St. Regis University
Denver, CO (1993)

Joshua W. Smith, Jr.
Instructor and Assistant Program Director
Geneva College Extension Program at CUTS - Center for Urban Theological Studies
Philadelphia, PA

Paul L. Smith, Jr.
Research Professor
Institute of Atmospheric Sciences
South Dakota School of Mines and Technology
Rapid City, SD (1994)

Robert J. Smith
Professor
Management Department
School of Business Administration
California State University, Long Beach
Long Beach, CA

Walter S. Smith
Department Head
Oklahoma State Technical Institute
Okmulgee, OK

Clinton H. Smoke, Jr.
Director
Fire Science Institute
Northern Virginia Community College
Annandale, VA (1997)

Andrew Snow
Associate Professor of Information Systems
University of Pittsburgh
Pittsburgh, PA

Roberto Socas
Professor of Social Science/Bilingual
Essex County College
Newark, NJ (1993)

Monterrat Sola-Sole
Associate Professor
Department of Spanish
University of District of Columbia
Washington, DC (1996)

Ed Solinski
Indiana University, Purdue
Indianapolis, IN

Wilbur H. Somerton
Professor
Department of Mechanical Engineering
University of California
Berkeley, CA

Judy Sparks
Professor
Department of Management and Organization
University of Southern California
Los Angeles, CA

Patrick M. Sparks
Assistant Professor
School of Business and Public Administration
California State University
Sacramento, CA

Suzanna Spears
Dean
Division of Extended Studies
Pikes Peak Community College
Colorado Springs, CO (1995)

Michael G. Spencer
Associate Professor
Materials Science Center
Howard University
Washington, DC

Ronald Spicer
Coordinator
Insurance Program
Pikes Peak Community College
Colorado Springs, CO (1995)

Arvid Sponberg
Professor of English
Valparaiso University
Valparaiso, IN

W. Franklin Spikes
Professor and Chair
Department of Adult and Continuing Education
Kansas State University
Manhattan, KS (1995)

Terry Spradley
Professor
Technical Education Division
Cameron University
Lawton, OK

Langley Spurlock
Director
Chemical Manufacturers Association
Washington, DC

Jerrold F. Stach
Assistant Professor
Computer Science/Telecommunication
University of Missouri, Kansas City
Kansas City, MO (1993 NJ)

John Stachler
Sinclair Community College
Dayton, OH (1994)

John J. Staczek
Professor
Department of Linguistics
Georgetown University
Washington, DC

Robert Stafford
Professor
Computer Information Systems Department
Temple University
Philadelphia, PA

Jan Stalder
President
Rescue Evolutions
Piano, TX (1995)

Martin Stamm
Adjunct Professor of Sociology
Middlesex County College
Edison, NJ (1993 NJ)

Sally Newman Standiford
Professor and Director
Educational Technology Center
Ames Teacher Education Center
University of Wisconsin
River Falls, WI (1996)

James Starkey
Professor of Economics
Chafee Social Science Center
University of Rhode Island
Kingston, RI

Joseph Stencel
Health Physicist
Princeton University
Princeton, NJ

Henry Stick
Professor
Department of Economics and Finance
University of Dayton
Dayton, OH (1995)

James Stinchcomb
Director
School of Justice and Safety Administration
Miami-Dade Community College
North Campus
Miami, FL

John Stinson
Professor of Management
Ohio University
Athens, OH

Michael Stinson
Professor
Computer Science Department
Central Michigan University
Mount Pleasant, MI (1995)

John W. Stockman
Professor
Department of Organizational Behavior and Environment
California State University
Sacramento, CA

Ernie Stolpe
Silver Consolidated Schools
Silver City, NM (1996)

James B. Stone
Chairman
Division of Specialized Allied Studies
Mining Occupational and Transportation Safety
Marshall University
Huntington, WV

Stanton Stone
Rockford Police Department
Rockford, IL

Kenneth Stough
Professor Emeritus
Industrial Education
University of Maryland
College Park, MD (1995)

Susan Strasinger
Director and Professor
Medical Technology Program
Northern Virginia Community College
Annandale, VA (1997)

Steve Strawderman
Captain
EMS Supervision
Prince William County Department of Fire and Rescue
Prince William, VA (1997)

John C. Strayer
Director
Pennsylvania Institute of Technology
Upper Darby, PA

George B. Strother
Professor (Retired)
University of Wisconsin, Madison
Madison, WI

Allen Stubberud
Associate Dean
School of Engineering
University of California, Irvine
Irvine, CA

Susan Studds
Professor
IRM College
National Defense University
Washington, DC (1997)

Dr. Alan T. Stutts
Dean
Conrad Hilton College of Hotels & Restaurant Mgmt.
Houston, TX (1997)

Carolyn Stumpf
Professor of Management
Georgian Court College
Lakewood, NJ

Thomas F. Sullivan
Professor
Business Department
Fisher College
Boston, MA

Paul Sultan
Professor of Economics and Management
Southern Illinois University
Edwardsville, IL

Ronald Sundberg
Dean of Continuing Education
Elmira College
Elmira, NY

Vaidy Sunderam
Professor
Math and Computer Science
Emory University
Atlanta, GA

Tom Sutherlin
Professor of Technology
Cameron University
Lawton, OK

Dr. John R. Sutton
Chair, Manufacturing & Construction
Central Missouri University
Warrensburg, MO (1997)

William Swyter
Dean of the Faculty
Montgomery College
Rockville, MD

Jesse Symms
Chairman
Electronics Department
College of the Mainland
Texas City, TX

Richard Szukalski
Business Department
City College of San Francisco
San Francisco, CA

Tom Tahnk
Instructor
Metropolitan State University
St. Paul, MN

Connie Talbert
Dean
College of Business
Arkansas State University
State University, AR

Edward Tangman
Chairman
Engineering Technologies Division
Northern Virginia Community College
Annandale, VA

Charlotte M. Tatro
Director
Institute for Women's Research and Studies
Florida International University
Miami, FL

Estelle Taylor
Chairperson
Howard University
Washington, DC

Harvey Taylor
Attorney-Professor
Paralegal Studies
Barclay Career School
Washington, DC (1993)

James C. Taylor
Dean
School of Hotel and Restaurant Management
University of Houston
Houston, TX

Russell E. Taylor
Director and Associate Professor
Automotive Department
Northern Virginia Community College
Alexandria, VA (1996)

John TenBrook
Professor of Business
Camden County College
Blackwood, NJ

Melvin C. Terrell
Vice President for Student Affairs
Northeastern Illinois University
Chicago, IL

Gerald Thebeau
Adjunct Professor
Department of Management
Webster College
St. Louis, MO (1995)

Barbara N. Thomas
President/Owner
BNT Academy
Lanham, MD (1996)

Thomas Thomas
St. Johns University
Staten Island, NY

Bonnie Thomas-Moore
Assistant Professor and Coordinator
Food Service Management Program
University of Akron
Akron, OH

Duly H. Thompson
Director of Law Enforcement
Anne Arundel Community College
Arnold, MD

A.L. Thurman
Associate Chairman
Department of American Thought and Language
University College
Michigan State University
East Lansing, MI

Martha Tilmann
Professor
College of San Mateo
San Mateo, CA (1997)

Terry J. Tinney
Associate Professor
St. Louis University
Glen Carbon, IL

Judyth Tinsley
Executive Director
Washington Hearing and Speech Society
Washington, DC (1996)

Ralph Todd
Chairman
Management Education Department
American River College
Sacramento, CA

Leon J. Tolle, Jr.
Professor
Our Lady of the Lake University
San Antonio, TX

John Toller
Assistant Executive Director
Human Resources and Affirmative Action
University of Michigan
Ann Arbor, MI (1996)

Donald F. Tonge
Certified Public Accountant
Brookhaven, PA (1994)

W. Sanford Topham
Associate Professor/Clinical Engineering Administrator
Department of Biomedical Engineering
Case Western Reserve University
Cleveland, OH

John S. Townsend
Director
Radioactive and Hazardous Material
Technology Program
New Mexico State University—Carlsbad
Carlsbad, NM (1994)

Lazar Trachtenberg
Professor of Computer Science
Drexel University
Philadelphia, PA (1995)

Joseph Tramutola
Professor
Fairleigh Dickinson University
Rutherford, NJ (1993)

Stuart J. Travis
Associate Professor and Head
Ferris State College
Big Rapids, MI

M'Kean Tredway
Director
Office of Continuing Education
Northern Virginia Community College, Manassas
Manassas, VA

Konstantinos Triantis
Assistant Professor
Department of Industrial Engineering
and Operations Research
Virginia Tech
Falls Church, VA

Kellee Trice
Program Director
School of CNP
Upland, PA (1995)

James S. Trieschmann
Associate Dean
University of Georgia
Athens, GA

Angelo Tritini
Department of Criminal Justice
Passaic County College
Peterson, NJ (1993 NJ)

Edward F. Troicke
Professor Emeritus
Department of Electrical Engineering
Technology
Broome County Community College
Binghamton, NY (1997)

Donald Trucksess
Assistant Director of DIAL
Thomas Edison State College
Trenton, NJ

Harold Dean Trulear
Dean
First Professional Programs
New York Theological Seminary
New York, NY (1995)

Tai-Ching Tuan
Assistant Professor
School of Electrical Engineering and
Computer Science
University of Oklahoma
Norman, OK

Gary Tucker
Sinclair Community College
Dayton, OH (1996)

Norma Jean Tucker
Dean of Instruction
Merritt College
Oakland, CA

Woodie L. Tucker
Professor
Virginia Commonwealth University
Richmond, VA

Robert E. Tumelty
Professor and Director
Health Care Administration Program
California State University
Long Beach, CA

Frederick Turner
Professor of Communications
Rider University
Lawrenceville, NJ

Hester Turner
Attorney
New York, NY

Robert Turrill
Assistant Dean
Graduate Programs
University of Southern California
Los Angeles, CA

Dr. Richard K. Tworek
Riverside Community College
Moreno Valley, CA (1997)

Charles E. Tychsen
Professor
Business Division
Northern Virginia Community College
Annandale, VA (1997)

Thomas Tynan
Associate Director
Connecticut Department of Higher Education
Hartford, CT

David Tyrell
Middlesex Community College
Edison, NJ

Don Uhlenberg
Professor
University of North Dakota
Grand Forks, ND

Stan Urban
Professor
Macomb Community College
Warren, MI (1995)

Joseph G. Uy
Lecturer
Department of Engineering and
Engineering Technology
Montgomery College
Rockville, MD

Clayton Lewis Vaclli
Professor of Linguistics and Interpretation
Gallaudet University
Washington, DC (1993)

Thomas Vakos
Instructor
Gateway Technical College

Joe Valencic
Professor
Marine Science
Mission Viejo, CA (1994)

Luis Valle
Coordinator of Special Programs
Department of Curriculum Development
and Education
Trant County Junior College
Ft. Worth, TX (1995)

Charles Vanderbosh
Director of Education and Training
Baltimore City Police Department
Baltimore, MD

Wesley R. Van Pelt
Visiting Scientist
Department of Environmental Sciences
Rutgers University
New Brunswick, NJ

Juanita Vertress
Departments of Fire Science and
Safety Risk Management
Sinclair Community College
Dayton, OH (1995)

Jack Vernon
Professor of Otolaryngology
Oregon Health Sciences University
Portland, OR

Tim Vogelsberg
Associate Professor
Psychological Studies in Education
Temple University
Philadelphia, PA (1993)

Anthony Voce, Esquire
Lansdale, PA (1994)

Paul D. VonHoltz
Assistant Professor
Industrial Education and Technology
Rowan University
Glassboro, NJ

L.W. VonTersch
Dean
Michigan State University
East Lansing, MI

Hiroko Fukuda Wagner
Senior Lecturer
Japanese Dept.
Johns Hopkins University
Washington, DC (1997)

Joseph A. Wagner
Associate Professor
Ohio State University
Mansville, OH

Samuel Wagner
Associate Dean
School of Business Administration
Temple University
Philadelphia, PA

Arthur Wainer
Professor
Department of Chemistry
Edinsboro State College
Edinsboro, PA

John Wakelin
Adjunct Faculty
Computer Science
College for Lifelong Learning
University System of New Hampshire
Concord, NH (1997)

Henry Walbasser
Professor of Education and Director of Graduate Studies
University of Maryland
Baltimore, MD

Dr. Alan G. Walker
Director, Fireman Training Program
Louisiana State University
Baton Rouge, LA (1997)

Richard Ernest Walker
Chairman
Department of German and Russian
University of Maryland
College Park, MD

Richard Walls
Professor of Educational Psychology
West Virginia University
Morgantown, WV

James P.M. Walsh, SJ
Associate Professor
Theology Department
Georgetown University
Washington, DC (1993)

Harold R. Walt
Dean
College of Business
University of San Francisco
San Francisco, CA

David J. Ward
Senior Vice President for Academic Affairs
Department of Finance
University of Wisconsin System
Oshkosh, WI (1996)

Jean Warner
Associate Professor
Rider University
Lawrenceville, NJ

Beth I. Warren
Fellow
Industrial and Labor Relations School
Cornell University
Ithaca, NY (1996)

Clay Warren
Professor and Director
Communications Program
George Washington University
Washington, DC (1997)

Nick Washienko
Professor of Administration
Boston University
Boston, MA (1994)

Craig Washington
Chairman
Automotive Engineering and Public Service Division
Northern Virginia Community College
Alexandria, VA

Myma Wasserman
Adjunct Professor of Education
Seton Hall University
East Orange, NJ (1995 NJ)

Richard Waters
Coordinator
Hotel, Restaurant Management, and Food Services
Long Beach City College
Long Beach, CA

Jack Waxman
Chairman of Business Education Division
Diablo Valley College
Pleasant Hill, CA

K. Mark Weaver
Associate Professor of Management
University of Alabama
University, AL

Carol Weber
Assistant Professor of Business/
Office Systems Technology
Mercer County Community College
Trenton, NJ

Steven Weibart
Assistant Professor
Department of Insurance
Georgia State University
Atlanta, GA

Richard Weid
Manchester, MI (1995)

Robert S. Weinbeck
Assistant Professor
State University of New York-Brockport
Brockport, NY

Devora Weiner
Adjunct Instructor
Computer & Accounting Departments
Empire State College-SUNY
Jerusalem, Israel (1997)

Howard Weiner
Assistant Professor of Data Processing
Business Division
Northern Virginia Community College
Annandale, VA

James Weisbecker
Professor
Computer Science Department
Pennsylvania State University
Malver, PA (1995)

Marvin Weiss
Dean
New York Institute of Technology
New York, NY

Inge B. Wekerle
Department of Foreign Language
and Literature
George Mason University
Fairfax, VA

David Y. Wen
Professor and Chairman
Diablo Valley College
Pleasant Valley, CA

Terrence W. West
Professor
County College of Morris
Hackettstown, NJ

Dr. K. Cy Whaley
Associate Professor of Diagnostic Imaging
Thomas Jefferson University
Philadelphia, PA

Glenn Whan
Professor of Chemical and Nuclear
Engineering
University of New Mexico
Albuquerque, NM

Valerie J. Wheat
Instructor of Romance Languages
Howard University
Washington, DC

Dr. Edith Wheeler
Assistant Professor
Early Childhood Education
Towson University
Towson, MD (1997)

Robert A. Wheeler
Director
Associate Degree Program
Dickinson State College
Dickinson, ND

Ladylease Goodridge White
Professor
Essex County College
Newark, NJ (1993)

Marilyn Domas White
Associate Professor
College of Library and Information Sciences
University of Maryland
College Park, MD (1997)

Richmond White
Chairman
Division of Engineering, Physics, Math,
and Technology
Texarkana Community College
Texarkana, TX

Gerald Whitlock
Professor of Management and Psychology
University of Tennessee
Knoxville, TN

William E. Whitsell
Professor
Department of Economics
Franklin and Marshall University
Lancaster, PA

Kimberly Whittaker
Electronics Instructor
Dept. of Engineering Technology-Telecommunications
Johnson County Community College
Overland Park, KS (1997)

Lurline Whittaker
Acting Chairperson
Human Ecology Department
Morgan State University
Baltimore, MD (1996)

Dr. Rolf T. Wigand
Professor and Director
Graduate Program in Information
Resources Management
Syracuse University
Syracuse, NY

Michael Wiggins
Assistant Department Chair
Embry-Riddle Aeronautics University
Daytona Beach, FL

Sheila Wiggins
Instructor
Computer Science Department
Morgan State University
Baltimore, MD (1994)

Garland Wiggs
Crumpler, NC

Gary Wilcox
Dean of Arts and Sciences
Des Moines Area Community College
Ankeny, IA

Lawrence Wilcox
Professor
Department of Computer Science and
Information Systems
Southeastern Oklahoma State University
Durant, OK (1995)

Elsie Wilkens
Assistant Director of Education
St. John's Mercy Medical Center
St. Louis, MO

Robert Wilkins
Director
Department of Cardiopulmonary Sciences
Loma Linda University
Loma Linda, CA (1996)

John C. Wilkinson
Director of Military Programs
Southern Illinois University at Carbondale
Carbondale, IL (1994)

Alvin Williams
Coordinator of Computer Sciences and
Engineering Technologies
Essex County College
Newark, NJ (1996)

Gene Williams
Assistant Vice Chancellor
University of Kentucky
Lexington, KY

James F. Williams
Associate Professor
Computer Science Department
Montgomery Community College
Rockville, MD

Ronald J. Williams
Professor
Del Mar College
Corpus Christie, TX

Margaret Williams-Betlyn
President
Community College of Beaver County
Monaca, PA

Maria Wilmeth
Program Manager
U.S. Department of Agriculture
Graduate School
Washington, DC (1996)

Arthur Wilson
Professor of Finance
George Washington University
Washington, DC (1995)

Hugh H. Wilson
Professor
Department of Ceramic Engineering
Clemson University
Clemson, SC

Kennedy Wilson
Former Professor of Commerce
University of Virginia
Falls Church, VA

Kennedy L. Wilson
Intelligence Officer
Central Intelligence Agency
Washington, DC

Robert R. Wilson
Assistant Director of Extension Service and Director of Independent Study
University of Michigan
Ann Arbor, MI

Wayne Wilson
Professor
School of Business
Cameron University
Lawton, OK

Richard Winchell
Center for Public Affairs
Arizona State University
Temple, AZ

Doris Witherspoon
Director
Industrial Technology Division
Henry Ford Community College
Dearborn, MI

F. Stanton Woerth
Director of Industrial Relations
Temple University
Philadelphia, PA

Mary Joan Wogan
Consultant
Arlington, VA

Fancher Wolfe
Professor of Math, Statistics, and Economics
Metropolitan State University
Minneapolis, MN

John Wolfe
Assistant Dean of Continuing Education
University of Kansas
Lawrence, KS

Ronald Wolfe
Georgetown University
Washington, DC

Glenn L. Wood
Professor of Finance
School of Business and Public Administration
California State College
Bakersfield, CA

Victoria M. Wood
Nutritional Consultant
Vienna, VA (1994)

Wendell Wood
Manager
Management Development and Training Department
International Harvester Company
Chicago, IL

Richard Woodring
Dean
College of Engineering
Drexel University
Philadelphia, PA

Janice E. Woods
Associate Dean
Des Moines Area Community College
Des Moines, IA (1993)

Nell Woodward
Associate Professor
Orange Coast College
Costa Mesa, CA

Donald Woolf
Professor Emeritus
Department of Management
University of Oklahoma
Norman, OK (1995)

Ronald Woolf
Professor of Management
College of Business Administration
University of Oklahoma
Norman, OK

Dr. Bruce Worsham
Associate Professor of Insurance and Taxation
American College
Bryn-Mawr, PA (1995)

George Wright
Lecturer
Engineering Technology
Texas A&M University
College Station, TX

George B. Wright
Assistant Professor
Texas A&M University
College Station, TX

John D. Wright
Associate Professor
Engineering Technology
Frederick Community College
Frederick, MD

Raymond E. Wright
Chairman
Roosevelt University
Chicago, IL (1994)

Sally Jo Wright
Professor and Chair
Business Administration Department
Sangamon State University
Sangamon, IL (1994)

Emily Wughalter
Professor
New York University
New York, NY

Martin Wuollet
Coordinator
College of DuPage
Glen Ellyn, IL

Paul E. Wyant
Dean
Business Technologies
Sinclair Community College
Dayton, OH (1995)

La Monte Wyche
Associate Professor
Howard University
Washington, DC

Barbara Ann Wyles
Associate Dean of Curriculum Services
Northern Virginia Community College
Annandale, VA

Chen D. Yang
Program Manager, International Programs
George Mason University
Arlington, VA (1997)

Raymond Yarbrough
Associate Professor
Electrical Engineering and Computer Science
University of Santa Clara
Santa Clara, CA

Dewey Yeager
Division Head of Engineering and
Professor Emeritus
Department of Engineering Technology
Oklahoma State University
Oklahoma City, OK (1997)

Stanley B. Yeldell
Assistant Professor
Law and Justice Department (1997)
Rowan University
Glassboro, NJ (1996)

Charles Young
Adjunct Instructor
Electronics Technology
Dekalb Technical Institute
Clarkston, GA (1996)

Charles Young
Project Manager
Naval Surface Weapons Center
Silver Spring, MD

Darroch Young
Chair
Business Division
Santa Monica City College
Santa Monica, CA

James Young
Counselor/VA Coordinator
Wallace Community College-Selma
Selma, AL

Steve Zabetakis
Professor
Hagerstown Community College
Hagerstown, MD (1995)

Thomas Zepf
Professor
Department of Physics
Creighton University
Omaha, NE (1994)

Review Team Evaluators by State

ALABAMA

James Fisk
Department of Chemistry
Stanford University
Birmingham, AL

Melvin Knight
Professor
School of Education
University of Alabama
Birmingham, AL (1997)

K. Mark Weaver
Associate Professor of Management
University of Alabama
University, AL

James Young
Counselor/VA Coordinator
Wallace Community College
Selma, AL

ALASKA

Jackie Pflaum
Associate Professor
College of Nursing and Health Sciences
University of Alaska
Anchorage, AK

ARIZONA

Richard J. Hammel
Assistant Professor
Pharmacy Administration
University of Arizona
Tucson, AZ

Peter Horn
Professor
Department of Management
College of Business
Arizona State University
Tempe, AZ (1996)

Bobby R. Hunt
Professor
Computer Science
University of Arizona
Tucson, AZ

John Paulson
Arizona Division of Emergency Services
Phoenix, AZ

Steve Saffron
Director
American Indian Program
Scottsdale Community College
Scottsdale, AZ

Rebecca J. Sartin
Health Technologies
Pima Community College
Tucson, AZ

Richard Winchell
Center for Public Affairs
Arizona State University
Temple, AZ

ARKANSAS

Frank Oldham
President and Chief Operating Officer
Worthen National Bank of Conway
Conway, AR

Connie Talbert
Dean
College of Business
Arkansas State University
State University, AR

CALIFORNIA

James M. Anderson
Professor
Department of Civil Engineering
University of California
Berkeley, CA

Charles Ardolino
Faculty Member and Administrator
Coastline Community College
Fountain Valley, CA

Alfred Armand
President
A-H and Associates
Burlingame, CA (1994)

George Arnovick
Professor
Computer Science Dept.
CSU
Chico, CA (1997)

Joan Barnacle
Instructor of Medical Assisting
Indian Valley College
Novato, CA

Dale K. Bean
Vice President
Education and Programs Director
California College for Health Sciences
National City, CA (1996)

Constance Beutel
Distance Education
Learning Evaluation Center
Stanford University
Instructional Television Network
Benicia, CA (1996)

Don Biederman
Director
Telecommunications Technical Program
Skyline College
San Bruno, CA

Eugene Brill
Coordinator
Grossmont College
El Cajon, CA

Michael Carr
Program Director
Respiratory Therapy
East Los Angeles College
Monterey Park, CA (1996)

Sam Chapman
Chairman
Business Management Department
Diablo Valley Community College
Pleasant Hills, CA (1997)

Alexander Cloner
Dean
School of Public Administration
University of Southern California
Sacramento, CA

Gary Collins
Instructor
Public Services Department
San Joaquin Delta College
Stockton, CA

Miro Costa
Associate Professor
Golden Gate University
San Francisco, CA (1997)

Amy Coury
Professor
Department of Nursing
Los Angeles Harbor College
Los Angeles, CA

John R. Cox
Professor
Department of Finance
California State University
Los Angeles, CA

Constance Crowley
Assistant Clinical Professor
Family Health Care Nursing
University of California
San Francisco, CA

Ralph G. Davis
California Maritime Academy
Vallejo, CA (1994)

Robert de Iongh
Business Department
San Francisco City College
San Francisco, CA

Bois Elwell
Productive Business Results
Long Beach, CA

Arnold Finchum
Chairman
Technology Department
California Polytechnic State University
San Luis Obispo, CA

John P. Gossley
University of Southern California
School of Religion
Los Angeles, CA (1997)

John W. Gould
Associate Professor
Graduate School of Business
University of Southern California
Los Angeles, CA

George Graves
Professor
Aeorspace Engineering
California State Polytechnic University
Pomona, CA

David E. Gray
Vice President
Administration and Staff Coordination
California State University
Long Beach, CA

David W. Hampton
Professor
Management Department
San Diego State University
San Diego, CA (1997)

Lyman Handy
Chair
Department of Petroleum Engineering
School of Engineering
University of Southern California
Los Angeles, CA

Peter Hechler
Associate Professor
School of Business and Economics
California State University
Los Angeles, CA

Milton C. Holmen
Professor
School of Business Administration
University of Southern California, Los Angeles
Los Angeles, CA

Cecilia Hopkins
Director
Division Business
College of San Mateo
San Mateo, CA

Robert Hurley
Professor
Criminal Justice
California State University
Sacramento, CA

Ethel K. Jorgensen
Professor
Department of Business Administration
Los Angeles Valley College
Van Nuys, CA

Geoffrey King
Chair
Department of Management
California State University
Fullerton, CA

Paul Kinney
Dean
Business School
California State University
Chico, CA

Bert Kobayashi
Chairman
Department of Health and Physical Education
University of California, San Diego
La Jolla, CA

James Koerlin
Dean
School of Technology and Industry
Golden Gate University
San Francisco, CA (1997)

Stanley Kossen
Instructor
Business and Economics
Merritt College
Oakland, CA

Arthur C. Laufer
Professor of Management
California State University
Long Beach, CA

Joseph Launie
Department of Finance, Insurance, and Real Estate
California State University
Northridge, CA

C.W. Lee
Professor
Department of Accounting and Data Processing
California State University
Carson, CA

Thomas Leonard
Chairman
Aeronautics Department
San Jose State University
San Jose, CA

Edward Leven
Golden Gate University
San Francisco, CA

Paul Lou
Instructor
Diablo Valley College
Pleasant Hill, CA

Norbert Ludkey
Program Coordinator
Computer and Information Science
City College of San Francisco
San Francisco, CA

Donald Lundberg
Chairman
Hotel and Restaurant Management
California State Polytechnic University
Pomona, CA

Robert Main
Professor
College of Communications
California State University
Chico, CA

Michael Maloon
Certified Financial Planner
California Financial Advisory
San Ramon, CA (1995)

Reed Markham
Professor
California State Polytechnic University
Pomona, CA

Leonard Marks
Instructor
Santa Ana College
Santa Ana, CA

Lance Masters
Chair
School of Business
California State University
Hayward, CA (1996)

Charles Maxey
Assistant Professor
School of Business Administration
University of Southern California
Los Angeles, CA

Charles Medler
Chair
California State University
Sacramento, CA

William Melnicoe
Chair
California State University
Sacramento, CA

Sidney Messer
Professor
City College of San Francisco
San Francisco, CA

Allen Miller
Golden Gate University
School of Technology & Industry
San Francisco, CA (1997)

Francis H. Moffitt
Professor
Civil Engineering Department
University of California
Berkeley, CA

A. Thompson Montgomery
Associate Professor
San Francisco State University
San Francisco, CA

Harry More
Professor
San Jose State University
San Jose, CA

Jim Lee Morgan
Professor
West Los Angeles College
Culver City, CA

Velma C. Nance
Coordinator
Distance Learning
Peralta Community College
Oakland, CA (1997)

Richard G. Nehrbass
Assistant Professor
School of Management
California State University
Carson, CA

Edward A. Nelson
Professor
School of Business and Economics
California State University
Los Angeles, CA

Richard S. Nelson
Professor
San Francisco State University
San Francisco, CA

Joe M. Newton
Coordinator
Bakersfield College
Bakersfield, CA

Herbert Oestreich
School of Business
San Jose State University
San Jose, CA

Martin Oettinger
Associate Professor
University of California
Davis, CA

Naomi Palmer
Speech and Language Pathologist
Los Angeles, CA (1997)

Frances Peterson
Chair
Rio Hondo College
Whittier, CA

Kenneth Phillips
Chair
California State University
Los Angeles, CA

Mark Pitre
Certified Financial Planner
California Financial Advisory
San Ramon, CA (1995)

William Pivar
Director
Business Education
College of the Desert
Palm Desert, CA

Chester C. Platt
Associate Dean
Coastline Community College
Mountain Valley, CA

Mark S. Plovnick
Dean
School of Business and Public Administration
University of the Pacific
Stockton, CA

Stanley D. Price
Dean
Golden Gate University
San Francisco, CA

Preston Probasco
Acting Director
Cybernetic Systems
School of Social Science
San Jose State University
San Jose, CA

Felicenne Ramey
Assistant Professor
School Business and Public Administration
California State University
Sacramento, CA

Mohammed Razani
University of California Extension
Daly City, CA (1994)

Cheryl Isaacs Redmon
Instructor
Business Office Technology Department
Santa Rosa Junior College
Santa Rosa, CA (1996)

Irving S. Reed
Professor of Electrical Engineering
University of Southern California
Los Angeles, CA

Harriett Rice
Associate Professor
Business Administration Department
Los Angeles City College
Los Angeles, CA

George Rich
Professor
Department of Physical Education
California State University
Northridge, CA

Lloyd Rogers
Assistant Dean
Sacramento City College
Sacramento, CA

John E. Ryan
Associate Dean
McGeorge School of Law
Sacramento, CA

Robert Sandlin
Sandlin and Associates
San Diego, CA (1994)

Annabelle Sartore
Chair
Department of Management
California State University
Long Beach, CA

Ralph M. Scarrow
Professor
California Polytechnic Institute
Pomona, CA

Susan Schaefer
Associate Professor
Management Science Department
California State University
Hayward, CA

Oscar N. Serbein
Professor Emeritus of Insurance
Graduate School of Business
Stanford University
Stanford, CA

Robert Settlage
Director
Maternity and Infant Care Project
University of Southern California
Los Angeles, CA

Phillip Shrotman
District Coordinator
Cooperative Work Experience Education
Long Beach City College
Long Beach, CA

Louis Shuster
Professor of Management
School of Business and Public Administration
California State College
Bakersfield, CA

John H. Sims
Chairman
Management Science Department
California State University
Hayward, CA

James B. Smathers
Professor
University of California
Los Angeles, CA

Robert J. Smith
Professor
Management Department
School of Business Administration
California State University
Long Beach, CA

Wilbur H. Somerton
Professor
Department of Mechanical Engineering
University of California
Berkeley, CA

Judy Sparks
Professor
Department of Management and Organization
University of Southern California
Los Angeles, CA

Patrick M. Sparks
Assistant Professor
School of Business and Public Administration
California State University
Sacramento, CA

John W. Stockman
Professor
Department of Organizational Behavior
and Environment
California State University
Sacramento, CA

Richard Streid
Professor
California State University
Northridge, CA (1994)

Allen Stubberud
Associate Dean
School of Engineering
University of California
Irvine, CA

Richard Szukalski
Business Department
City College of San Francisco
San Francisco, CA

Martha Tilmann
Professor
College of San Mateo
San Mateo, CA (1997)

Ralph Todd
Chairman
Management Education Department
American River College
Sacramento, CA

Norma Jean Tucker
Dean of Instruction
Merritt College
Oakland, CA

Robert E. Tumelty
Professor and Director
Health Care Administration Program
California State University
Long Beach, CA

Robert Turrill
Assistant Dean
Graduate Programs
University of Southern California
Los Angeles, CA

Richard K. Tworek
Riverside Community College
Moreno Valley, CA (1997)

Joe Valencic
Professor
Marine Science
Saddleback Community College
Mission Viejo, CA (1994)

Harold R. Walt
Dean
College of Business
University of San Francisco
San Francisco, CA

Richard Waters
Coordinator
Hotel, Restauant Management, and Food Services
Long Beach City College
Long Beach, CA

Jack Waxman
Chairman
Business Education Division
Diablo Valley College
Pleasant Hill, CA

David Y. Wen
Professor and Chairman
Diablo Valley College
Pleasant Valley, CA

Robert Wilkins
Director
Department of Cardiopulmonary Sciences
Loma Linda University
Loma Linda, CA (1996)

Glenn L. Wood
Professor of Finance
School of Business and Public Administration
California State College
Bakersfield, CA

Nell Woodward
Associate Professor
Orange Coast College
Costa Mesa, CA

Raymond Yarbrough
Associate Professor
Electrical Engineering and Computer Science
University of Santa Clara
Santa Clara, CA

Darroch Young
Chair
Business Division
Santa Monica City College
Santa Monica, CA

COLORADO

Ajeyo Banerjee
Assistant Professor
University of Colorado
Denver, CO

Frank Barnes
Professor
Electrical and Computer Engineering
University of Colorado
Boulder, CO (1996)

Arthur H. Boisselle
Coordinator
Pikes Peak Community College
Colorado Springs, CO

Martha Bravnig
Vice President
Executive Security International
Aspen, CO

Glenn E. Brooks
Professor
Political Sciences
Colorado College
Colorado Springs, CO (1996)

Stanley Bush
Professor
Telecommunications Department
University of Colorado at Boulder
Boulder, CO (1996)

Jerome C. Darnell
Professor
Department of Finance
College of Business Administration
University of Colorado
Boulder, CO

Larry G. Keating
Associate Professor
Department of Electrical Engineering Technology
Metropolitan State College
Denver, CO

James E. Killorin
Denver University
Telecommunications Division
Denver, CO

Joseph Kossik
Director
Business Studies
Community College of Denver
Denver, CO (1996)

Judith Laux
Associate Professor and Chair
Department of Economics
Colorado College
Colorado Springs, CO (1995)

Lee Maxwell
Professor
Colorado State University
Fort Collins, CO

Robert McGowan
Associate Professor
Department of Management
University of Denver
Denver, CO

Wilbert L. Miles
Faculty and Managerial Consultant
University of Colorado
Denver, CO (1997)

Robert Minter
Chairman
University of Denver
Denver, CO

James Null
Dean
University of Colorado
Colorado Springs, CO

Richard Podlesnik
School of Business Administration
Fort Lewis College
Durango, CO (1993 NJ)

Margarete Ralston
Associate Professor
Electronics Engineering Technology
Metropolitan State College of Denver
Denver, CO

Reiner Schaeffer
Director of Academy Libraries
U.S. Air Force Academy
Colorado Springs, CO

James W. Smith
Professor
School of Business
St. Regis University
Denver, CO (1993)

Ronald Spicer
Coordinator
Insurance Program
Pikes Peak Community College
Colorado Springs, CO (1995)

CONNECTICUT

Patricia Benjamin
Director of Education
Connecticut Center for Massage Therapy
Newington, CT (1996)

Alfred Carter
Professor
Social Science Division
Manchester College
Manchester, CT (1993)

Adolph Katz
Professor
School of Business
Fairfield University
Fairfield, CT

Dr. John Mellon
Associate Professor of Hospitality Management
Teikyo Post University
Waterbury, CT

Kenneth Parzych
Professor
Economics and Management Sciences
Eastern Connecticut State University
Willimantis, CT

Richard L. Rath
Senior Editor
Yachting Magazine
Cos Cob, CT

Thomas Tynan
Associate Director
Connecticut Department of Higher Education
Hartford, CT

DISTRICT OF COLUMBIA

Louis Albert
Director
Professional Services
American Association for Higher Education
Washington, DC

Charles Alexander
Professor
Signal Analysis and Communications
George Washington University
Washington, DC

Clinton L. Anderson
Senior Consultant
Servicemembers Opportunity Colleges
Washington, DC (1996)

George E. Arnstein
Fellow
American Association for the Advancement of Science
Washington, DC (1993)

Robert Baden
Freetrade Union Institute
Washington, DC (1996)

Prabir K. Bagchi
Associate Professor
Department of Management Science
School of Business and Public Management
George Washington University
Washington, DC (1994)

Richard A. Bassler
Director
Computer Systems Applications Program
American University
Washington, DC

Susanne Bensel
Professor
Modern Language Department
Johns Hopkins University
Washington, DC

Beatrice Black
University of the District of Columbia
Washington, DC

Vera Z. Borkovec
Associate Professor Emerita
Language and Foreign Studies
American University
Washington, DC

Paul Boyd
Chairman
Electronics Department
University of the District of Columbia
Washington, DC

Melanie A. Brown
Professor
Management and Office Systems
University of the District of Columbia
Washington, DC (1996)

Hanita Brumfield
Chair
Department of Political and Social Sciences
Mount Vernon College
Washington, DC (1993)

Wayne Camara
Director
Scientific Affairs
American Psychological Association
Washington, DC

Neal Chalofsky
Visiting Assistant Professor
School of Education and Human Development
George Washington University
Washington, DC

Harlan L. Chaney
Professor Emeritus
Business, Economics, and Finance Department
University of the District of Columbia
Washington, DC (1996)

James J. Chastain
Professor
Insurance Education
Howard University
Washington, DC

Robert J. Chinnis
Associate Professor
American University
Washington, DC

Don Coleman
Chairman
Department of Systems and Computer Science
Howard University
Washington, DC

Frank W. Connolly
Director
Academic Computing Services
American University
Washington, DC

Leval Cothran
Chairman, Physiology
College of Medicine
Howard University
Washington, DC (1997)

Herbert J. Davis
Program Director
Business Management
School of Government and Business Adminstration
George Washington University
Washington, DC

James J. Davis
Associate Professor
Romance Languages Department
Howard University
Washington, DC (1993)

Eugene Deloatch
School of Engineering
Howard University
Washington, DC

William DeLone
Associate Professor of Management
Kogod College of Business
American University
Washington, DC (1996)

Andrew Do
Professor
Dept. of Finance
San Diego State University
San Diego, CA (1997)

Leslie Dreiling
Adjunct Professor
Computational Sciences
George Mason University
Washington, DC

Li-Chuange Duke
Professor of Chinese
School of Advanced International Studies
Johns Hopkins University
Washington, DC

Adel I. El-Ansary
Professor
School of Government and
Business Administration
George Washington University
Washington, DC

John B. Eubanks
Professor
School of Religions
Howard University
Washington, DC

Henry Ernsthal
Associate Professor
Department of Public Administration
George Washington University
Washington, DC

M. Ali Fekrat
Professor
School of Business
Georgetown University
Washington, DC (1994)

Ernest Foreman
Professor
Management and Information Science
George Washington University
Washington, DC

Phyllis Forrest
Education Consultant
Washington, DC

James J. Fyfe
Associate Professor
School of Justice
American University
Washington, DC

Michael Gerli
Associate Professor
School of Languages and Linguistics
Georgetown University
Washington, DC

Mattie Giles
Professor and Coordinator
Social Work Practicum
University of the District of Columbia
Washington, DC (1997)

Johnnie Griffin
President
Secretarial Evaluation Clinic
Washington, DC (1996)

Trudi Bellardo Hahn
Associate Professor
Catholic University of America
Washington, DC

William Halal
Associate Professor
School of Business
American University
Washington, DC

Muhammad Haque
Associate Professor
Department of Civil, Mechanical,
and Environmental Engineering
George Washington University
Washington, DC (1993)

Mahrash S. Hariri
Persian Instructor
Language Department
Middle East Institute
Washington, DC (1994)

Gary Harris
Professor
Electrical Engineering Department
Howard University
Washington, DC (1994)

Barron Harvey
Associate Professor
Business Administration
Howard University
Washington, DC

Emilio Iodice
Director
Office of Consumer Goods and Service
U.S. Department of Commerce
Washington, DC

Keith Jackson
Department of Electrical Engineering
Howard University
Washington, DC

David Jacobs
Assistant Professor
Department of Management, Personnel,
and Industrial Relations
American University
Washington, DC (1993)

William Jensen
Attorney and Instructor
Office of General Counsel
U.S. Department of Agriculture Graduate School
Washington, DC (1996)

James Johnson
Professor and Chair
Howard University
Washington, DC

Patricia Yoshiko Kidd
Professor
U.S. Department of Agriculture Graduate School
Washington, DC (1996)

John Kokus
Professor and Director
Real Estate Center
Kogood College of Business Administration
American University
Washington, DC (1997)

David Korn
Chairman
German and Russian Department
Howard University
Washington, DC

Anthony Kowalski
Director
American Bankers Association
Washington, DC

Robert Lager
Chairman
Department of Russian
Georgetown University
Washington, DC

Gerald E. Lampe
Professor and Director
Language Studies
School of Advanced International Studies
Johns Hopkins University
Washington, DC (1993)

Carol J. LaSasso
Professor
Department of Education
Gallaudet University
Washington, DC (1996)

Davis Lee
Professor of Japanese
George Washington University
Washington, DC (1993)

Marilyn Liebrenz-Himes
Associate Professor
School of Government and Business
George Washington University
Washington, DC (1997)

Joseph P. Longo, Jr.
Dean
School of Intelligence Information Systems
Defense Intelligence College
Washington, DC

Robert Losey
Associate Professor
Department of Finance and Real Estate
Kogood College of Business Administration
American University, DC (1995)

M. Kamburi Lyabaugh
Professor
Department of African Studies
Howard University
Washington, DC (1993)

John R. MacKenzie
Associate Professor
University of the District of Columbia
Washington, DC

John Magnotti
Director and Professor Emeritus
Procurement Management Program
American University
Washington, DC (1997)

Haydee Magro
Professor of Portuguese
Brazilian-American Cultural Institute
Washington, DC

David Martin
Professor
Kogod School of Business
American University
Washington, DC (1995)

Santo Marzullo
Chairman
Washington Technical Institute
Washington, DC

Michael McCaskey
School of Languages and Linguistics
Georgetown University
Washington, DC

William E. McDonald
Senior Art Advisor (Retired)
U.S. Department of Education
Washington, DC (1994)

Dale McNabb
Associate Director for Small Business
Andrews Air Force Base
Washington, DC

Arnold Meltzer
Professor
George Washington University
Washington, DC

Steven J. Meltzer
Chief
Internal Revenue Service
Washington, DC

Stuart Milner
Assistant Professor
School of Education
Catholic University of America
Washington, DC

James Mittleman
Division of Componative & Regional Studies
School of International Service
The American University
Washington, DC (1997)

Joanne Moncrief
Chief Copy Editor
National Journal Magazine
Washington, DC

Richard A. Myren
Dean and Professor
American University
Washington, DC

Sumiko Nagasawa
Professor
Chinese and Japanese Department
Georgetown University
Washington, DC (1993)

Clarence Newhouse
Assistant Dean
School of Divinity
Howard University
Washington, DC

Rev. Richard O'Brien, SJ
Jesuit Community
Georgetown University
Washington, DC (1996)

Charles O'Rear
Professor and Chair
Department of Forensic Sciences
George Washington University
Washington, DC (1994)

Alfred Obernberger
Associate Professor
Georgetown University
Washington, DC (1997)

Yvonne Panaro
Professor
Georgetown University
Washington, DC

Salvatore Paratore
Associate Professor
George Washington University
Washington, DC

Louise S. Rainis
Consultant
Washington, DC

Derrill C. Rohlfs
Department
George Washington University
Washington, DC

James F. Rooney
Professor
Catholic University of America
Washington, DC

Peter Burton Ross
Professor
Department of English Studies
University of District of Columbia
Washington, DC (1993)

Walter F. Rowe
Professor
Department of Forensic Science
George Washington University
Washington, DC (1995)

Charles Sabatino
Assistant Director
Commission Legal Problems of the Elderly
American Bar Association
Washington, DC (1993)

Henry Sauer
Program Manager
Chemical Manufacturers Association
Washington, DC

John Schillinger
Chair and Professor
Department of Languages and Foreign Studies
American University
Washington, DC (1994)

Morley Segal
Professor
School of Government and Public Administration
American University
Washington, DC

Mohammed Sesay
Professor
Department of Mathematics
University of the District of Columbia
Washington, DC (1995)

Renee H. Shea
Professor
Department of English
University of the District of Columbia
Washington, DC (1996)

Stanley W. Sherman
Professor
School of Business and Public Management
George Washington University
Washington, DC (1994)

In-Soon Shin Smeenk
Asian Studies Consultant
Washington, DC (1996)

Monterrat Sola-Sole
Associate Professor
Department of Spanish
University of District of Columbia
Washington, DC (1996)

Michael G. Spencer
Associate Professor
Materials Science Center
Howard University
Washington, DC

Langley Spurlock
Director
Chemical Manufacturers Association
Washington, DC

John J. Staczek
Professor
Department of Linguistics
Georgetown University
Washington, DC

Susan Studds
Professor
IRM College
National Defense University
Washington, DC (1997)

Estelle Taylor
Chairperson
Howard University
Washington, DC

Harvey Taylor
Attorney-Professor
Paralegal Studies
Barclay Career School
Washington, DC (1993)

Judyth Tinsley
Executive Director
Washington Hearing and Speech Society
Washington, DC (1996)

Clayton Lewis Vaclli
Professor of Linguistics and Interpretation
Gallaudet University
Washington, DC (1993)

Hiroko F. Wagner
Senior Lecturer
Japanese Dept.
Johns Hopkins University
Washington, DC (1997)

James P.M. Walsh, SJ
Associate Professor
Theology Department
Georgetown University
Washington, DC (1993)

Clay Warren
Professor and Director
Communications Program
George Washington University
Washington, DC (1997)

Valerie J. Wheat
Instructor of Romance Languages
Howard University
Washington, DC

Maria Wilmeth
Program Manager
U.S. Department of Agriculture Graduate School
Washington, DC (1996)

Arthur Wilson
Professor
Finance Department
George Washington University
Washington, DC (1995)

Kennedy L. Wilson
Intelligence Officer
Central Intelligence Agency
Washington, DC

Ronald Wolfe
Georgetown University
Washington, DC

La Monte Wyche
Associate Professor
Howard University
Washington, DC

DELAWARE

Charles P. Nemeth
Professor
Wilmington, DE

FLORIDA

Clarence Avery
Professor
School of Accounting
University of Central Florida
Orlando, FL

Carl D. Baird
Professor
Agricultural Engineering Deparatment
University of Florida
Gainesville, FL

Colin Battle
Director of Curriculum
Broward Community College
Ft. Lauderdale, FL

Bishop B. Blackwell
Professor
Aeronautical Science Department
Embry-Riddle Aeronautical University
Daytona Beach, FL

Thomas J. Connolly
Chairman and Professor
Embry-Riddle Aeronautical University
Bunnell, FL

William L. Corsover
Adjunct Professor
Division of Continuing Education
Florida International University
North Miami, FL (1996)

Steven Hampton
Professor
Flight Technology
Embry-Riddle Aeronautical University
Daytona Beach, FL

William Heuson
Professor
School of Business Adminstation
University of Miami
Coral Gables, FL

Sanford Kravitz
Professor
School of Public Affairs and Services
Florida International University
North Miami, FL

Galen Kroeck
Associate Professor
College of Business Administration
Florida International University
Miami, FL (1997)

William March
Dean and Professor
Embry-Riddle Aeronautical University
Bunnell, FL (1997)

Paul E. McDuffee
Director
Airline Operators Certificate Program
Embry-Riddle Aeronautical University
Bunnell, FL

Richard L. Meyer
Professor
College of Business Administration
University of South Florida
Tampa, FL (1994)

W.J. Morgan, Jr.
Professor
Florida International University
Miami, FL

Homer J. Mottice
Professor
Florida State University
Tallahassee, FL

Lawrence Hobdy Perkins
Director
University of Western Florida
Pensacola, FL

John Phipps
Chairman
Flight Technology Department
Embry-Riddle Aeronautical University
Daytona Beach, FL

Wallace Reiff
Associate Dean and Professor of Finance
Florida Technical College
Orlando, FL

Robert E. Scully
Assistant Professor
School of Adult and Continuing Education
Barry University
Miami, FL (1997)

James Stinchcomb
Director
School of Justice and Safety Administration
Miami-Dade Community College
North Campus
Miami, FL

Charlotte M. Tatro
Director
Institute for Women's Research and Studies
Florida International University
Miami, FL

Michael Wiggins
Assistant Department Chair
Embry-Riddle Aeronautics University
Daytona Beach, FL

GEORGIA

Said I. Abdel-Khalik
Professor of Nuclear Engineering Program
School of Mechanical Engineering
Georgia Institute of Technology
Atlanta, GA (1997)

Damon Davis Camp, Jr.
Professor
Department of Criminal Justice
Georgia State University
Atlanta, GA (1993)

Charles Cassady
Instructor
Technology Department
Gwinnett Technical Institute
Lawrenceville, GA (1996)

Constance Craft
President
Learning Tree of America
Childhood and Early Learning Centers
Carrollton, GA (1995)

Michael Crone
DeVry Institute of Technology
Atlanta, GA

Monte Davis
Professor
Nuclear Research Center
Georgia Institute of Technology
Atlanta, GA (1997)

Roscoe K. Davis
Professor
Management Science and Information Technology
College of Business Administration
University of Georgia
Athens, GA

Larry Elowitz
Professor and Chairman
Department of Government and Sociooogy
Georgia College
Milledgeville, GA (1993)

Sandra Gustavson
Chair
Department of Insutance, Legal Studies, and Real Estate
University of Georgia
Athens, GA

John W. Hall
Professor and Chairman
Risk Management and Insurance Department
Georgia State University
Atlanta, GA

Rosalie Howell
District Manager
Children's World Learning Centers
Atlanta, GA (1997)

Kenneth Kent
Division Chair (Retired)
DeKalb Technical Institute
Clarkston, GA (1996)

William J. Lenicka
Associate Vice President for Academic Affairs
Georgia Institute of Technology
Atlanta, GA

Jan L. Mize
Director
Georgia State University
Atlanta, GA

Wallace Shukun
Dean of Technology
Director
Tecnical and Adult Educational Programs
Clayton State College
Morrow, GA (1995)

Vaidy Sunderam
Professor
Math and Computer Science
Emory University
Atlanta, GA

James S. Trieschmann
Associate Dean
University of Georgia
Athens, GA

Steven Weibart
Assistant Professor
Department of Insurance
Georgia State University
Atlanta, GA

Charles Young
Adjunct Instructor
Electronics Technology
Dekalb Technical Institute
Clarkston, GA (1996)

IDAHO

Gene Roth
Professor
Idaho State University
Pocatello, ID

ILLINOIS

Frank Alberico
Director
Law Enforcement Program
Joliet Junior College
Joliet, IL (1997)

Alfred Arkley
Professor
Management Program
Sangamon State University
Springfield, IL

Raymond Barrall
Director
Environmental Health and Radiation Safety
University of Illinois at Chicago
Chicago, IL (1996)

Charles Billman
Director
Vocational Programs
Rockvalley College
Rockford, IL (1996)

Frank H. Cassell
Professor Emeritus
Kellogg Graduate School of Management
Northwestern University
Evanston, IL

Herman Cember
Professor
Northwestern University
Evanston, IL

William A. Clarey
Professor
Business Administration
Bradley University
Peoria, IL (1997)

Louise Dieterle
Vice President
Leadership Development Association
Naperville, IL

Joseph Dobson
Assistant Professor
Department of Management
Western Illinois University
Macomb, IL

William J. Dunne
Associate Dean
College of Business Administration
University of Illinois
Chicago, IL

Steven A. Egger
Associate Professor
Sangamon State University
Springfield, IL

Bernard M. Ferreri
Associate Vice Chancellor
City Colleges of Chicago
Chicago, IL

Daniel J. Gallagher
Sangamon State University
Business Administration Program
Springfield, IL (1997)

S.K. Gosh
Associate Professor
Department of Civil Engineering, Mechanics, and Metallurgy
University of Illinois
Chicago, IL

Robert Gregg
Dean of Technology
Southeastern Illinois College
Harrisburg, IL

John Hartmann
Professor
Northern Illinois University
DeKalb, IL

Linda Hefferin
Professor
Office of Admissions and Technology
Elgin Community College
Elgin, IL (1997)

Clete Hinton
Director
Weekend College
William Rainey Harper College
Palatine, IL

Robert W. Jefferson
Professor and Chairperson
Western Illinois University
Macomb, IL

Thomas Johnson
Dean
William Rainey Harper College
Palatine, IL

Thomas Jurkanin
Assistant Manager
Illinois Local Government Law
Enforcement Officers Training Board
Springfield, IL

Clyde Kesler
Professor
Civil Engineering and Theoretical /AppliedMechanics
University of Illinois
Urbana, IL

George Kocher
Director
Mining Resource Center
Wabash Valley College
Mt. Carmel, IL

Eric A. Larson
Dean
Business and Allied Health
Elgin Community College
Elgin, IL (1996)

David L. Loebach
Sangamon State University
Springfield, IL (1997)

Russell Morey
Chairperson
Western Illinois University
Macomb, IL

David O'Gorman
Professor
Business Administration
Sangamon State University
Springfield, IL (1994)

Paul A. Palumbo
Associate Director
Police Training Institute
University of Illinois
Champaign, IL (1997)

Mark S. Puclik
Associate Professor
Business Administration Department
University of Illinois
Springfield, IL (1997)

Wayne Ramp
Professor
Southern Illinois University
Carbondale, IL

James Seeck
Associate Professor
Business and Social Science
Harper College
Palatine, IL

Hugh M. Shane
Chairperson
Western Illinois University
Macomb, IL

Stanton Stone
Rockford Police Department
Rockford, IL

Paul Sultan
Professor
Department of Economics and Management
Southern Illinois University
Edwardsville, IL

Melvin C. Terrell
Vice President for Student Affairs
Northeastern Illinois University
Chicago, IL

Terry J. Tinney
Associate Professor
St. Louis University
Glen Carbon, IL

John C. Wilkinson
Director
Military Programs
Southern Illinois University
Carbondale, IL (1994)

Wendell Wood
Manager
Management Development and Training Department
International Harvester Company
Chicago, IL

Raymond E. Wright
Chairman and Professor
Roosevelt University
Arlington Heights, IL (1994)

Martin Wuollet
Coordinator
College of DuPage
Glen Ellyn, IL

INDIANA

Joseph J. Cioch
Professor and Department Head
Restaurant, Hotel, and Institutional Management
Purdue University
West Lafayette, IN

James Daschbach
Professor
Department of Aerospace and Mechanical Engineering
Notre Dame University
Notre Dame, IN (1995)

William Haeberle
Professor
Gruaduate School of Business
Indiana University
Bloomington, IN

Kenneth R. Lauer
Professor of Civil Engineering
University of Notre Dame
Notre Dame, IN

Tamara Lewis
Professor
Davenport College, South Bend
Granger, IN

Valerie Brown Pickard
President
Collaborations, Inc.
Indianapolis, IN (1995)

John Rouselle
Purdue University
West Lafayette, IN

John Schmeling
President
Education Connection
Vincennes, IN

Gerald Smith
Chairman
Business Division
Vincennes University
Vincennes, IN

Ed Solinski
Indiana University, Purdue
Indianapolis, IN

Arvid Sponberg
Professor of English
Valparaiso University
Valparaiso, IN

IOWA

Floyd C. Begin
Professor
St. Ambrose University
Davenport, IA (1994)

Gary Fischer
Associate Professor
Industrial Engineering
University of Iowa
Iowa City, IA

R.L. Hardy
Civil Engineering Department
Iowa State University
Ames, IA

Robert A. Kemp
Professor of Management
Drake University
Des Moines, IA

Russell Pounds
Professor Emeritus
Iowa State University
Ames, IA (1996)

Glenn Pribbenow
Field Systems Manager
Fire Service Department
Ames, IA (1994)

Larry Short
Director of Graduate Program
Management Department
Drake University
Des Moines, IA

Gary Wilcox
Dean of Arts and Sciences
Des Moines Area Community College
Ankeny, IA

Janice E. Woods
Associate Dean
Des Moines Area Community College
Des Moines, IA (1993)

KANSAS

N. Dean Eckhoff
Professor
Department of Nuclear Engineering
Kansas State University
Manhattan, KS

Richard Faw
Professor
Nuclear Engineering
Kansas State University
Manhattan, KS

Gale Simons
Professor and Associate Dean
Department of Nuclear Engineering
Kansas State University
Manhattan, KS (1995)

W. Franklin Spikes
Professor and Chair
Department of Adult and Continuing Education
Kansas State University
Manhattan, KS (1995)

Kimberly Whittaker
Electronics Instructor
Dept. of Engineering Technology-Telecommunications
Johnson County Community College
Overland Park, KS (1997)

John Wolfe
Assistant Dean
Division of Continuing Education
University of Kansas
Lawrence, KS (1994)

KENTUCKY

Norb Elbert
Professor
Department of Business Administration
Bellarmine College
Louisville, KY

Kenneth L. Gann
Former Assistant Professor
Austin Peay State University
Fort Campbell, KY

Clarence Johns
Coordinator
Business and Industry Services
University of Kentucky
Lexington, KY (1994)

Judy Kieffer
Associate Professor of Nursing
University of Louisville
Louisville, KY

A.C. Krizan
Associate Professor
Murray State University
Murray, KY

Donald J. Mullineaux
Associate Dean
College of Business and Economics
University of Kentucky
Lexington, KY

Fred B. Paxton
Director
Fort Campbell Extended Campus
University of Kentucky
Hopkinsville, KY

Michael Pepper
Chairman of Business and Economics
Division and Program Director of Hotel,
Restaurant, and Tourism
Transylvania University
Lexington, KY (1995 NJ)

Charles R. Sayre
Commissioner
Kentucky Police Training Academy
Richmond, KY (1995)

Gene Williams
Assistant Vice Chancellor
University of Kentucky
Lexington, KY

LOUISIANA

Jack D. Burson
Professor
Technology Department
McNeese State University
Lake Charles, LA (1995)

Edward N. Lambremont
Chair
Nuclear Science & Engineering
Louisiana State University
Baton Rouge, LA (1997)

Jack R. Monks
Professor
Technology Department
McNeese State University
Lake Charles, LA

Gerard Nistal
Professor and Chair
Holly Cross College
New Orleans, LA

Tom S. Sale
Chairman
Department of Finance and Economics
Louisiana Tech University
Ruston, LA

Alan G. Walker
Director
Fireman Training Program
Louisiana State University
Baton Rouge, LA (1997)

MAINE

Tom Abbott
Dean
Learning Resources and University Development
University of Maine at Augusta
Augusta, ME (1995)

MARYLAND

Muriel H. Adams
Director
Medical Record Technology
Prince Georges Community College
Largo, MD (1993)

Richard August Ahrens
Professor
Department of Nutrition and Food
College of Human Ecology
University of Maryland
College Park, MD (1996)

David G. Alexander
Senior Staff Associate
George Meany Center for Labor Studies
Silver Spring, MD

Roy Ashley
Adjunct Professor
Department of Industrial Education
University of Maryland
College Park, MD (1995)

William F. Atchison
Professor Emeritus
University of Maryland
College Park, MD (1994)

John R. Baker, Sr.
Adjunct Faculty
Technology Programs
Johns Hopkins University (1997)

Jon Bauman
Professor of Music
Frostburg State University
Frostburg, MD

John R. Beaton
Dean and Professor Emeritus
College of Human Ecology
University of Maryland
College Park, MD (1994)

Frances N. Beckles
Associate Professor
Social Work Department
Morgan State University
Baltimore, MD (1997)

Adele Berlin
Professor
University of Maryland
College Park, MD

Thomas Berry
Professor
Department of Slavic Languages
University of Maryland
College Park, MD

Doreen Boyce, Chairman
Department of Economics and Management
Hood College
Frederick, MD

Jean Ann Boyce
Assistant Professor of Computer Science
University of Maryland University College
College Park, MD (1997)

Janice Brown-Glasgow
Bowie State University
School of Business
Bowie, MD (1997)

Sarah K. Bryant
Professor and Chair
Department of Finance and International Business
Johns Hopkins University
Columbia, MD (1996)

Herbert J. Burrows
Instructor
Nuclear Science Program
University of Maryland
College Park, MD (1993)

Lou Cantori
Professor
Department of Political Science
University of Maryland Baltimore County
Baltimore, MD (1997)

Paula Carroll
Associate Director
Administrative Computer Center
University of Maryland
College Park, MD

Jerrold Casway
Chair
Division of Social Sciences
Howard Community College
Columbia, MD (1997)

Joseph Cirrincione
Associate Professor
Department of Geography
University of Maryland
College Park, MD

Donald J. Clark, Jr.
Director and Professor
Language Lab
Johns Hopkins University
Baltimore, MD (1995)

Robert Cotner
Chairman
English and Philosophy Department
Montgomery College
Rockville, MD

Alan Czarapata
Professor
Engineering Technology
Montgomery College
Rockville, MD (1997)

Joseph Dahms
Chairperson
Department of Economics and Management
Hood College
Frederick, MD (1993)

Bill Davies
Director
END Training Progam
END School
Naval School of Health
Bethesda, MD (1995)

Michael Donahue
Adjunct Professor
Fire Service Department and Hazardous Materials
Montgomery College
Rockville, MD (1995)

Charles Edelson
Assistant Dean
College of Business and Management
University of Maryland
College Park, MD

Robert Edmister
Professor of Finance
College of Business and Management
University of Maryland
College Park, MD

Steven T. Edwards
Director
Maryland Fire and Rescue Institute
College Park, MD (1997)

William D. Eglinton
Director
Vocational Education
Seafarers Harry Lundeberg School of Seamanship
Pincy Point, MD (1996)

Marvin Eyler
Dean
College of Physical Education, Recreation, and Health
University of Maryland
College Park, MD

Diana Fischer
Computer Technology
Prince Georges Community College
Largo, MD

Robert O. Freedman
Dean of Graduate Studies
Baltimore Hebrew College
Baltimore, MD

Robert Gagnon
Adjunct Professor
Department of Fire Protection Engineering
University of Maryland
College Park, MD (1994)

Richard Glenn
Chair and Associate Professor
Automotive Service Technology
Catonsville Community College
Catonsville, MD (1996)

Karina Golden
Assistant Professor
Department of Education
Bowie State University
Bowie, MD (1996)

Ken Gaiser
Program Specialist
Dept. of Fire and Rescue Services
Emergency Management
Rockville, MD (1997)

Marion Green
Director
Early Childhood Development Program
Montgomery College
Rockville, MD (1994)

Virginia Guilford
Interim Associate Vice President, Academic Affairs
Bowie State University
Upper Marlboro, MD (1997)

Effie Hacklander
Associate Dean
College of Human Ecology
University of Maryland
College Park, MD

Jerry J. Holman
President
Qualifications Evaluation Systems Corporation
Gaithersburg, MD

Regina Igel
Associate Professor
Spanish and Portuguese Department
University of Maryland
College Park, MD (1997)

Thomas A. Janke
Vice President Emeritus
University of Maryland University College
College Park, MD (1997)

Wallace Knapp
Director
Computer Services Department
Catonsville Community College
Baltimore, MD (1997)

Mary M. Leonard
Assistant Professor and Psychologist
University of Maryland
College Park, MD

Viola Levitt
Associate Dean
Health Technology Department
Prince Georges Community College
Largo, MD

Diana Linton
Assessment Specialist
George Meany Center for Labor Studies
Silver Spring, MD (1994)

Bruce E. Lippy
Manager
Occupational Safety and Health
Scientech, Inc.
Rockville, MD (1995)

Cynthia Martin
Associate Professor
Asian and East European Language Departments
University of Maryland
College Park, MD (1997)

Mel Martin
Administrative Director
Respiratory Care Pulmonary Function
St. Joseph's Hospital
Towson, MD (1995)

Rocci S. Mastroberti
Anne Arundel Community College
Arnold, MD

Brigitte May
Professor
University of Maryland—Baltimore County
Catonsville, MD

James McNeill
Consultant
Olney, MD (1994)

Paul A. Meyer
Associate Professor
Economics Department
University of Maryland
College Park, MD (1997)

Jacqueline Middleton
Professor
Department of Management
Montgomery College
Germantown, MD (1997)

Walter Mietus
Professor
Department of Industrial Education
University of Maryland
College Park, MD (1995)

Raymond Mignogna
Chair
Department of Math, Physics, and Engineering
Charles County Community College
La Plata, MD

Eiko Muira
Professor
University of Maryland
College Park, MD

Noel Myricks
Associate Professor
University of Maryland
College Park, MD (1995)

Art Newberry
Assistant Director of Academics
MEBA Engineering School
Easton, MD (1997)

Marilyn L. Nicholas
Professor
Towson State University
Towson, MD (1996)

Harold Oliver
Educational Advisor
U.S. Army Ordnance Center and School
Aberdeen Proving Ground, MD

Howard P. Osborn
Director
Maryland Casualty Company
Baltimore, MD

Rose Marie Oster
Professor
Department of German and Slavic Languages
University of Maryland
College Park, MD (1993)

George Payne
Professor
Gudelsky Institute for Technical Education
Montgomery College
Rockville, MD (1997)

Robert Pleasure
Executive Director
George Meany Center for Labor Studies
Silver Spring, MD

Richard Profozich
Professor and Director
Writing Center
Prince Georges Community College
Largo, MD (1997)

S. Robert Ramsey
Professor
Department of Hebrew and East Asian Languages
University of Maryland
College Park, MD (1996)

Delia R. Richards
Professor and Chair
Early Childhood Education Program
Prince Georges Community College
Largo, MD (1997)

James A. Robinson
Associate Professor
Department of English, American Literature, and Drama
University of Maryland
College Park, MD (1996)

Steven Selden
Professor
Department of Education Policy, Planning, and Administration
College of Education
University of MD
College Park, MD (1993)

Donald Shaffer
Associate Professor
Continuing Education
Dundalk Community College
Baltimore, MD

Andrea L. Smith
Dean
Career and Technical Education
Charles County Community College
LaPlata, MD (1995)

Kenneth Stough
Professor of Industrial Education
University of Maryland
College Park, MD (1995)

William Swyter
Dean of the Faculty
Montgomery College
Rockville, MD

Barbara N. Thomas
President/Owner
BNT Academy
Lanham, MD (1996)

Duly H. Thompson
Director of Law Enforcement
Anne Arundel Community College
Arnold, MD

Joseph G. Uy
Lecturer
Department of Engineering and Engineering Tehnology
Montgomery College
Rockville, MD

Charles Vanderbosh
Director of Education and Training
Baltimore City Police Department
Baltimore, MD

Henry Walbasser
Professor of Education and Director of Graduate Studies
University of Maryland
Baltimore, MD

Richard Ernest Walker
Chairman
Department of German and Russian
University of Maryland
College Park, MD

Edith Wheeler
Assistant Professor
Early Childhood Education
Towson University
Towson, MD (1997)

Marilyn Domas White
Associate Professor
College of Library and Information Sciences
University of Maryland
College Park, MD (1997)

Lurline Whittaker
Acting Chairperson
Human Ecology Department
Morgan State University
Baltimore, MD (1996)

Sheila Wiggins
Instructor
Computer Science Department
Morgan State University
Baltimore, MD (1994)

James F. Williams
Associate Professor
Computer Science Department
Montgomery Community College
Rockville, MD

John D. Wright
Associate Professor of Engineering Technology
Frederick Community College
Frederick, MD

Charles Young
Project Manager
Naval Surface Weapons Center
Silver Spring, MD

Steve Zabetakis
Professor
Hagerstown Community College
Hagerstown, MD (1995)

MASSACHUSETTS

Alexander W. Avtgis
Dean
Wentworth Institute of Technology
Boston, MA (1993)

Robert C. Azar
Chairman
Department of Mechanical Engineering
Western New England College
Springfield, MA

Stevenson W. Fletcher
Head
Hotel, Restaurant, and Travel Administration
University of Massachusetts
Amherst, MA

Stuart Freedman
University of Lowell
Lowell, MA

Carol Harvey
Assistant Professor
Management and Marketing Department
Assumption College
Worcester, MA (1995)

Rodney Hinkle
Dean
Fisher College
Boston, MA

Thomas E. Hulbert
Associate Dean and Director
School of Engineering Technology
Northeastern University
Boston, MA

James John
Dean of Engineering
University of Massachusetts
Amherst, MA

David R. Lambert
Associate Professor
Suffolk University
Boston, MA

Maureen Lee-Locke
Instructor
Katharine Gibbs School
Boston, MA (1996)

David Lucht
Vice President
Firepro, Inc.
Wellesley Hills, MA

Jack Luskin
Associate Director for Education and Training
Toxics Use Reduction Institute
University of Massachusetts
Lowell, MA

William C. MacDonald
Dean
Management Division
Lesley Graudate School
Lesley College
Cambridge, MA

Julius Mariasis
Associate Professor
Massachusetts Bay Community College
Wellesley Hills, MA

Paul D. Maxwell
Assistant Dean
Northeastern University
Boston, MA

John Mayer
Associate Professor
Worcester Polytechnic Institute
Worcester, MA

Robert McVicker
Director
Cooperative Education
University of Lowell
Lowell, MA

Rafael Moure-Eraso
Associate Professor
Work Environment Department
College of Engineering
University of Massachusetts
Lowell, MA

Richard J. Murphy
Professor
Northeastern University
Boston, MA

Robert Oberg
Department of Computer Sciences
Framingham State College
Framingham, MA

David A. Perreault
Coordinator
School of Engineering
Boston University
Boston, MA

James Phelps
Professor
University of Lowell
Lowell, MA

Walter M. Presz, Jr.
Professor
Western New England College
Springfield, MA

Milton Shuch
Chairman
Department of Management
Simmons College
Boston, MA

Thomas F. Sullivan
Professor
Business Department
Fisher College
Boston, MA

Nick Washienko
Professor of Business Administration
Boston University
Boston, MA (1994)

MICHIGAN

William Boras
Associate Professor
School of Business
Ferris State College
Big Rapids, MI

Frank Cheng
Industrial Electronic Technology Department
Central Michigan University
Mt. Pleasant, MI (1997)

John M. Dwyer
Associate Professor
Department of Mathematics and Computer Science
University of Detroit Mercy
Detroit, MI (1995)

Gary W. Falkenberg
Professor of Management
Oakland Community College, Auburn Hills
Auburn Heights, MI

Joel D. Galloway
Dean
Ferris State University
Big Rapids, MI

Joel Goldberg
Professor Emeritus
Macomb Community College
Warren, MI (1997)

John P. Hyde
Director of Instruction
Career Tech Center
Holland, MI

Maryhelen Jones
Director
Off-Campus Library Services
Central Michigan University
Mount Pleasant, MI (1995)

Glenn Knudsvig
Director
English Board
University of Michigan
Ann Arbor, MI

Michael Kolivosky
Dean
Hillsdale College
Hillsdale, MI

Richard Leininger
Associate Professor
School of Business and Management
Saginaw Valley State College
University Center, MI

David Lopez
Professor, Industrial Engineering
Central Michigan University
Mt. Pleasant, MI (1997)

John Ludwig
Lincoln Electric Co.
Southfield, MI (1997)

Keith MacDonald
Associate Professor
Ferris State College
Big Rapids, MI

Robert McIntosh
Professor of Tourism
School of Hotel, Restaurant,
and Institutional Management
Michigan State University
East Lansing, MI

John Nagohosian
Director
Henry Ford Community College
Dearborn, MI

David Novicki
Division Director
Michigan State University
East Lansing, MI

Frank Paone
President
Detroit College of Business
Dearborn, MI

Chuck Philip
Dean of Instruction
Health and Sciences Department
Kalamazoo Valley Community College
Kalamazoo, MI (1997)

Robert A. Powell
Electronics
Oakland Community College
Auburn Hills, MI (1997)

Paul Prins
Executive Director
Ferris State University
Big Rapids, MI

Enrico Puzzudi
Chairman
Manufacturing Engineering Technology
Henry Ford Community College
Dearborn, MI (1997)

Jack Richards
Director
Automotive Technician Program
Ferris State University
Big Rapids, MI

Lester J. Richards
Automotive Program Director
Ferris State University
Big Rapids, MI

Albert D. Robinson
Coordinator
Washtenaw Community College
Ann Arbor, MI

Gerald D. Robinson
Professor
Macomb Community College
Warren, MI

Walter Senska
Apprenticeship Coordinator
Macomb Community College
Warren, MI

Dennis Simpson
SPADA
Western Michigan University
Kalamazoo, MI (1993)

Delavan Sipes
Associate Professor of Electronics
Biomedical Engineering Technology Coordinator
Schoolcraft College
Livonia, MI

Michael Stinson
Professor
Computer Sciences Department
Central Michigan University
Mount Pleasant, MI (1995)

A.L. Thurman
Associate Chairman
Department of American Thought and Language
University College
Michigan State University
East Lansing, MI

John Toller
Assistant Executive Director
Human Resources and Affirmative Action
University of Michigan
Ann Arbor, MI (1996)

Stuart J. Travis
Associate Professor and Head
Ferris State College
Big Rapids, MI

Stan Urban
Professor
School of Technology
Macomb Community College
Warren, MI (1995)

L.W. VonTersch
Dean
Michigan State University
East Lansing, MI

Richard Weid
Manchester, MI (1995)

Robert R. Wilson
Assistant Director of Extension Service and
Director of Independent Study
University of Michigan
Ann Arbor, MI

Doris Witherspoon
Director
Industrial Technology Division
Henry Ford Community College
Dearborn, MI

MINNESOTA

Don A. Albright
Professor
Mathematics and Chemistry
Northwestern College
St. Paul, MN

Russell R. Blankenfeld
Instructor
Rochester Community College
Rochester, MN

Perry Caranicas
Community Faculty
Metropolitan State University
Minneapolis, MN

Warren Eidness
Professor and Chairman
Department of Mathematics
Normandale Community College
Bloomington, MN (1995)

Alton L. Greenfield
Reading Specialist
Minnesota Department of Education
St. Paul, MN

Arch Leean
Chairman
Art Department
St. Olaf College
Northfield, MN

Charles Libera
Coordinator
Business and Public Administration
Metropolitan State University
St. Paul, MN

Ray A. Nelson
Professor and Chair
Department of Professional Education
Bemidji State University
Bemidji, MN (1995)

Richard Pontinen
Chairman and Professor
Hamline University
St. Paul, MN

Thomas Poppendieck
Director
Hamline University
St. Paul, MN

Tom Tahnk
Instructor
Metropolitan State University
St. Paul, MN

Fancher Wolfe
Professor of Math, Statistics, and Economics
Metropolitan State University
Minneapolis, MN

MISSISSIPPI

Gary A. Hemphill
Chair
Commercial Aviation Department
Delta State University
Cleveland, MS (1997)

Harrylyn Sallis
Dean
Adult Learning
Millsaps College
Jackson, MS

S. Cabell Shull
Chairman
University of Mississippi
University, MS

MISSOURI

Guy R. Banville
Associate Dean
School of Business
St. Louis University
St. Louis, MO

Albert Cawns
Professor
Webster University
St. Louis, MO

Robert L. Davis
Dean
University of Missouri
Rolla, MO

Dineen Ebert
Professor-Information Office Systems Department
St. Louis Community College at Meramec
Kirkwood, MO (1997)

Matt Eichor
Chairman
Criminal Justice Systems Program
Northeast Missouri State University
Kirksville, MO (1995)

Rod Gelatt
Professor
School of Journalism
University of Missouri
Columbia, MO (1994)

Neil J. George
Academic Dean
Webster University
St. Louis, MO

Lymen Hannah
Dept. of Manufacturing and Construction
Central Missouri State University
Warrensburg, MO (1997)

Betty Ipock
Director
Associate Degree Nursing Program
Missouri Southern State College
Joplin, MO

Jack Landers
Department of Manufacturing and Construction
Central Missouri State University
Warrensburg, MO (1997)

Peter Maher
Assistant Professor
Department of Math and Computer Science
University of Missouri, St. Louis
St. Louis, MO

Robeson S. Moise
Associate Professor
Department of Power and Transportation
Central Missouri State University
Warrensburg, MO

Gary Murdock
Assistant Professor
Department of OB/GYN
Washington University School of Medicine
St. Louis, MO (1995)

Bruce R. Piringer
Director
Fire and Rescue Training Institute
University of Missouri
Columbia, MO (1994)

Ann Barbara Sakurai
Chair and Professor
Math and Science Department
Webster University
St. Louis, MO

Jerrold Siegel
Professor
Department of Math and Computer Science
University of Missouri-St. Louis
St. Louis, MO

Gerry F. Stach
Assistant Professor of Computer Science/
Telecommunication
University of Missouri, Kansas City
Kansas City, MO (1993 NJ)

John R. Sutton
Chair, Manufacturing and Construction
Central Missouri University
Warrensburg, MO (1997)

Gerald Thebeau
Adjunct Professor
Department of Management
Webster University
St. Louis, MO (1995)

Elsie Wilkens
Assistant Director of Education
St. John's Mercy Medical Center
St. Louis, MO

NEBRASKA

Samuel Cipolla
Professor
Department of Physics
Creighton University
Omaha, NE (1994)

Terry P. Dixon
Vice President and Professor
Academic Affairs and Computer Science
Clarkson College
Omaha, NE (1995)

Donna J. Kizzier
Assistant Professor
Vocational and Adult Education
University of Nebraska
Lincoln, NE (1995)

Thomas Martin
Professor
Department of Management
College of Business Administration
University of Nebraska
Omaha, NE (1993)

Dana Massey
Assistant Professor
Professional Studies Department
Bellevue University
Bellevue, NE (1995)

Thomas Zepf
Professor
Department of Physics
Creighton University
Omaha, NE (1994)

NEW HAMPSHIRE

Bryan O'Neil
Middlesex Community College
Bedford, NH

Mel Sandler
Associate Professor
University of New Hampshire
Durham, NH

John Wakelin
Adjunct Faculty
Computer Science
College for Lifelong Learning/University System of New Hampshire
Concord, NH (1997)

NEW JERSEY

Roanne Angiello
Dean
Business Technologies Division
Bergen Community College
Paramus, NJ

Gerald Arsenault
Professor of Social Sciences
Education Coordinator
Cumberland County College
Vineland, NJ

James Baker
Mentor
Thomas Edison State College
Trenton, NJ (1995 NJ)

Joseph Balabon
Director of MIS
Mercer County Community College
Trenton, NJ

William Barnes
Associate Professor of Engineering Technology
and Coordinator, Electrical Engineering Technology
New Jersey Institute of Technology
Newark, NJ (1995 NJ)

Kenneth R. Benson
Chairman
Health, Urban and Outdoor Recreation
Kean College of New Jersey
Union, NJ

Katherine Benz-Campbell
Instructor of Ultrasound
Bergen Community College
Paramus, NJ (1996)

Patrick Biesty
Dean
Business and Social Studies
County College of Morris
Randolph, NJ

William Brant
Professor of Management
Rider University
Lawrenceville, NJ (1993 NJ)

Edward Burns
Adjunct Professor
County College of Morris
Randolph, NJ

Louis Campo
Professor
Engineering Department
Union County College
Elizabeth, NJ (1996)

John Carmichael
Senior Professor
Business Department
Union County College
Crawford, NJ (1997)

Joseph Celauro
Adjunct Professor
College of New Jersey
Trenton, NJ

Miriam Chaplin
Associate Professor
School of Education
Rutgers University
Camden, NJ

Robert Chenoweth
Department Chairman
Data Processing
County College of Morris
Randolph, NJ

Vincent P. Cieri
Chief of Training Development
Fort Monmouth, NJ

Edward Clark
Associate Professor of Electronics Technology
Atlantic Community College
Mays Landing, NJ (1993 NJ)

Preston Clement
Professor
Mercer County Community College
Trenton, NJ

Jerry S. Cohen
Associate Professor
Raritan Valley Community College
Somerville, NJ

Anthony Cupo
Associate Professor of Business
County College of Morris
Randolph, NJ (1995 NJ)

Gordon Darkenwald
Professor of Adult Development
School of Education
Rutgers University
New Brunswick, NJ

Sister Ellen M. Dauwer
Associate Dean
Adult Undergraduate Programs
College of St. Elizabeth
Morristown, NJ (1993)

Lansing Davis
Office of Workforce Development
Trenton, NJ (1997)

Lynne Delay
Professor
Graduate Program for Administrators
Rider University
Lawrenceville, NJ

Shawn Riva Donaldson
Assistant Professor of Sociology
Richard Stockton College of New Jersey
Pomona, NJ (1995 NJ)

Carole Donavan
Professor
Montclair State University
Upper Montclair, NJ

R.D. Draper
Psychology Department
Montclair State University
Upper Montclair, NJ

Howard Dunn
Professor
Mercer County Community College
Trenton, NJ (1997)

Margaret Dunn
Associate Professor of English
Kean College of New Jersey
Union, NJ

Kenneth J. Dwyer
Hudson County Community College
Belleville, NJ

Alice F. Dyer
Director
Educational Development and Training
General Hospital Center
Passaic, NJ (1996)

William Enslin
Chairman
Department of Management
Rowan University
Glassboro, NJ

Carol Felder
Assistant Professor
Raritan Valley Community College
Somerville, NJ

Joseph Flynn
Professor
College of New Jersey
Trenton, NJ (1993)

Donald D. Fraser
Professor of Chemistry
Essex County College
Newark, NJ (1995 NJ)

Sr. Patricia Geary
Assistant Dean and Assistant Professor of Education
Georgean Court College
Lakewood, NJ (1995 NJ)

Ronald Gepner
Associate Professor
Mercer County Community College
Trenton, NJ

Victor Gerdes
Professor of Finance (Retired)
Rider University
Lawrenceville, NJ

Dolores C. Gioffre
Assistant Professor
Montclair State University
Upper Montclair, NJ

Dorothy S. Gleckner
Associate Professor
Bergen County Community College
Paramus, NJ (1995)

John Gutowski
Chairperson
Psychology and Learning Development Department
Middlesex County College
Edison, NJ

Thomas Handler
Professor
Electrical Engineering Technology Department
Middlesex County College
Edison, NJ (1993)

Richard Hanson
Professor Emeritus
Raritan Valley Community College
Somerville, NJ

Sally Ann Hanson
Professor of Information Systems
Mercer County Community College
Trenton, NJ (1996)

John Harrington
Professor
Seton Hall University
South Orange, NJ

Marilyn Hart
Professor
Educational Psychology
Kean College of New Jersey
Union, NJ (1993)

Ronald Hart
Director of MIS
Essex County College
Newark, NJ

Adele Hartig
Instructor
Bergen Community College
Paramus, NJ

Howard Hauck
Adjunct Professor
Data Processing
Passaic County College
Patterson, NJ

Francis J. Haughey
Professor of Radiation Science
Rutgers University
New Brunswick, NJ (1995 NJ)

Sean Healy
Professor
Kean College of New Jersey
Union, NJ

Michael Gary Helliwell
Associate Professor
Department of Management Science
Kean College of New Jersey
Union, NJ (1995)

Eric Hepburn
Dean
Social Sciences and Humanities
Middlesex County College
Edison, NJ (1997)

Leo Hilton
Coordinator
William Patterson University
Wayne, NJ

JoAnn Hoiles
Associate Professor (Retired)
Management
Raritan Valley Community College
Somerset, NJ (1993)

Marianne Hoy
Professor
Nursing Division
Cumberland County College
Vineland, NJ (1993)

William Hunter
Associate Professor of Biology
County College of Morris
Randolph, NJ

Parthasarathy Iyengar
Associate Professor
County College of Morris
Randolph, NJ (1993)

Rhoda Jacobs
Associate Professor
Business Administration
County College of Morris
Randolph, NJ

Rodney Jurist
Chairman
Department of Business Education
Rider University
Lawrenceville, NJ

Leonard Kapochus
Associate Professor of Business
Cumberland County College
Vineland, NJ

Nancy Kelly
Professor of Social Work
Rutgers University
Camden, NJ (1993)

Ernest Kovacs, Jr.
Research Scientist
New Jersey Department of Transportation
Trenton, NJ

Paul Krasucki
Assistant Professor of Computer Science
Rutgers University
New Brunswick, NJ

Steven Kubriki
Professor
Richard Stockon College of New Jersey
Stockton, NJ

Arun Kumar
Assistant Professor of Information and Decision Sciences
Montclair University
Upper Montclair, NJ

William C. Lauer
Rider University
Lawrenceville, NJ

Linda Lengyel
Professor of Law and Justice
Trenton State College
Trenton, NJ

Miles MacMahon
Professor
Essex County College
Newark, NJ

Patricia Malone
Assistant Professor
Rider University
Lawrenceville, NJ

Anthony Maltese
Chairman
Department of Communications
William Patterson University
Wayne, NJ

Joseph H. Martin
President
Martin & Benner Appraisal Co.
Lawrenceville, NJ

Patricia Mayer
Associate Professor
Rutgers University, Douglas College
New Brunswick, NJ

Barnaby McAusian
Assistant Professor
Burlington County College
Pemberton, NJ

Thomas J. McCoy
Business Division
Middlesex County College
Edison, NJ

John Mercier
Professor
Rowan University
Glassboro, NJ

Morris Mokowitz
Chair
Rutgers University
New Brunswick, NJ

Mel Moyer
Associate Professor of Psychology
Rowan University
Glassboro, NJ (1995 NJ)

William J. Mulkeen
Adjunct Professor
Criminal Justice Department
Warren County Community College
Washington, NJ (1995)

Joseph Mulligan
Division General Manager
General Dynamics
Avenel, NJ
and Adjunct Professor at Middlesex County College
Edison, NJ

Morris Muskovitz
Chair, Hebraic Studies Dept.
Rutgers University
New Brunswick, NJ

Prabhaker Nayak
Professor of Marketing
William Paterson University
Wayne, NJ (1993 NJ)

Thomas Niles
Director
Monmouth University
West Long Beach, NJ

Godwin Ohiwerei
Associate Professor of Sociology
Jersey City State College
Jersey City, NJ (1995 NJ)

Alan Oppenheim
Professor and Director M.B.A. Program
Montclair State University
Upper Montclair, NJ

Rosa Oppenheim
Associate Professor
Graduate School of Management
Rutgers University
New Brunswick, NJ

Dula Pacquiao
Edison, NJ

Phillip Pastras
Professor
Middlesex County College
Edison, NJ

Thomas Patrick
Chair
Department of Business Administration
College of New Jersey
Trenton, NJ (1993)

Joseph Pizzillo
Professor of Secondary Education
Foundations of Education
Rowan University
Glassboro, NJ (1993)

Francis Polk
Assistant Dean of Instruction
Ocean County College
Toms River, NJ

Jeanette Purdy
Professor of Business
Mercer County Community College
Trenton, NJ (1996)

Samuel Rabinowitz
Professor of Management
Rutgers University
Camden, NJ

Denis Railhall
Professor
Seton Hall Univsity
South Orange, NJ (1994)

Hamideh P. Ramjerdi-Shirazi
Professor of Economics
Kean College of New Jersey
Union, NJ (1995 NJ)

Mary E. Reilly
Chair
Secretarial Science Department
Middlesex County College
Edison, NJ

Benjamin Resnick
Academic Advisement Coordinator
Communications Department
Rowan University
Glassboro, NJ

Ervine M. Rips
Professor
New Jersey Institute of Technology
Newark, NJ

Stewart Rodnon
Professor
Rider University
Lawrenceville, NJ

Johnson Roney III
Director
Mercer County Community College
Trenton, NJ

Theresa Rosania
Associate Professor of Marketing
Kean Collegeof New Jersey
Union, NJ

Lee Rosenthal
Professor of Electrical Engineering Technology
Fairleigh Dickinson University
Teaneck, NJ (1993 NJ)

Robert Saladarini
Professor of Information Systems
Bergen Community College
Paramus, NJ (1996)

Richard Sandhusen
Assistant Professor
Marketing Department
Rider University
Lawrenceville, NJ

Joseph Santora
Professor of Management and Humanities
Essex County College
Newark, NJ

Rajib Sanyal
Assistant Professor
College of New Jersey
Trenton, NJ (1993)

Penelope S. Schott
Assistant Professor of English
Raritan Valley Community College
Somerville, NJ

William Seaton
Director
Directed Independent Adult Learning
Thomas Edison State College
Trenton, NJ

Gabriella Sechi
Assistant Professor
Department of Engineering Technology
College of New Jersey
Trenton, NJ

Harry Sheater
Professor of Chemistry
Union County College
Cransford, NJ (1996 NJ)

Eugene Simko
School of Business Administration
Monmouth University
West Long Branch, NJ

Wayne Smeltz
Associate Professor of Business
Rider University
Lawrenceville, NJ (1993)

Roberto Socas
Professor of Social Science/Bilingual
Essex County College
Newark, NJ (1993)

Martin Stamm
Adjunct Professor of Sociology
Middlesex County College
Edison, NJ (1993 NJ)

Joseph Stencel
Health Physicist
Princeton University
Princeton, NJ

Carolyn Stumpf
Professor of Business Administration
Georgian Court College
Lakewood, NJ

Ronald Sundberg
Dean of Continuing Education
Elmira College
Elmira, NY

John TenBrook
Professor of Business
Camden County College
Blackwood, NJ

Joseph Tramutola
Professor
Fairleigh Dickinson University
Rutherford, NJ (1993)

Angelo Tritini
Department of Criminal Justice
Passaic County College
Peterson, NJ (1993 NJ)

Donald Trucksess
Assistant Director of DIAL
Thomas Edison State College
Trenton, NJ

Frederick Turner
Professor of Communications
Rider University
Lawrenceville, NJ

David Tyrell
Middlesex Community College
Edison, NJ

Wesley R. Van Pelt
Visiting Scientist
Department of Environmental Sciences
Rutgers University
New Brunswick, NJ

Paul D. VonHoltz
Assistant Professor
Industrial Education and Technology
Rowan University
Glassboro, NJ

Jean Warner
Associate Professor
Rider University
Lawrenceville, NJ

Myra Wasserman
Adjunct Professor of Education
Seton Hall University
East Orange, NJ (1995 NJ)

Carol Weber
Assistant Professor of Business/
Office Systems Technology
Mercer County Community College
Trenton, NJ

Terrence W. West
Professor
County College of Morris
Hackettstown, NJ

Ladylease Goodridge White
Professor
Essex County College
Newark, NJ (1993)

Alvin Williams
Coordinator of Computer Science and Engineering
Technologies
Essex County College
Newark, NJ (1996)

Stanley B. Yeldell
Assistant Professor
Law and Justice Department
Rowan University
Glassboro, NJ (1997)

NEW MEXICO

Tom Golder
Security Analyst
Albuquerque, NM (1995)

Aaron Goldman
Los Alamos, NM (1994)

T. Zane Reeves
Professor
Division of Public Administration
University of New Mexico
Albuquerque, NM (1993)

Dwight Rogers
Assistant Professor and Chair
Industrial Technology
Eastern New Mexico University
Portales, NM (1995)

John Shaffer
Director of Aviation
University of Albuquerque
Albuquerque, NM

Ernie Stolpe
Silver Consolidated Schools
Silver City, NM (1996)

John Townsend
Director
Radioactive and Hazardous Material
Technology Program
New Mexico State University
Carlsbad, NM (1994)

Glenn Whan
Professor of Chemical and Nuclear Engineering
University of New Mexico
Albuquerque, NM

NEW YORK

Roy Alvarez
Cornell University
Ithaca, NY

Edwin L. Andrews
Chairman
Division of Arts and Sciences
SUNY Agricultural and Technical College
Cobleskill, NY

Frank Angell
Professor of Insurance and Finance
New York University
New York, NY

Dennis M. Bakewicz
Assistant Professor of Biology
New York City Technical College (CUNY)
New York, NY

Lila Bergman
Director
Department of Economics
Hunter College, CUNY
New York, NY

Jacqueline Brophy
Director
Labor Liberal Arts Program
Cornell University
New York, NY

Nancy Dawson
Lecturer
African and African American Studies
State University of New York, Albany
Albany, NY

Donald A. Dermody
Professor
Cornell University
Ithaca, NY

Lewis R. Fibel
Vice President and Dean of Faculty
Sullivan County Community College
Loch Sheldrake, NY

Cara Gargano
Chairperson
Deparatment of Theater, Film, and Dance
Long Island University
Brookville, NY

John D. Guilfoil
Associate Dean
College of Business and Public Administration
New York University
New York, NY

Nancy Lynch Hale
Chairperson
Business Education Office
Pace University
New York, NY

James C. Hall
Associate Professor
Pace University
Brooklyn, NY

Jim Hall
Associate Professor of Management
Pace University
New York, NY (1996)

Rev. Jack Healy, O.Carm.
Rochester, NY

Andrew Heitzman
Associate Professor
Special Education
State University College of Arts and Sciences
Geneseo, NY

John Hyland
Chairman
Social Sciences Deparatment
LaGuardia Community College
Long Island City, NY

Elizabeth Iannizzi
Professor
Department of Secretarial Science
New York Community College
Brooklyn, NY

Thomas L. Jamison
Professor
SUNY College of Technology
Wellsville, NY (1997)

Janice Karlen
Associate Professor of Management & Accounting
LaGuardia Community College CUNY
New York, NY (1993)

Saul W. Katz
Associate Dean
Kingsborough Community College
Brooklyn, NY

Betty G. Lall
Director
Union University Urban Affairs Program
Cornell University
New York, NY

Deborah Laster
Teacher/Mentor
Teacher Mentor Program
New York City Board of Education
Bronx, NY

Claudette Lefebre
Associate Professor
Department of Leisure Studies
New York University
New York, NY

Barbara Marantz
Computer Science Department
Empire State College
Hartsdale, NY (1995)

Mary McBride
Professor
New York University
New York, NY (1993)

Robert L. McLeod
Director of Regional Operations
National Fire Sprinkler Association
Patterson, NY

Walter Pauk
Director
Cornell University
Ithaca, NY

Donald Schmidt
Professor
Hudson Valley Community College
Troy, NY

Stephen Schneider
Assistant Dean
Suffolk County Community College
Brentwood, NY

Susan Scoboria
Director of Admissions
New Center College
Long Island, NY

Ronald L. Seeber
Associate Dean
New York State School of Industrial and Labor Relations
Cornell University
Ithaca, NY

Richard Selden
Adjunct Professor
New York University
New York, NY

Shirley Silvers
Professor
Queensborough Community College
Bayside, NY

Edward Troicke
Associate Professor
Department of Electrical Engineering Technology
Broome County Community College
McDonough, NY (1997)

Harold Dean Trulear
Professor and Dean
First Professional Programs
New York Theological Seminary
New York, NY (1995)

Thomas Thomas
St. Johns University
Staten Island, NY

Beth I. Warren
Fellow
Industrial and Labor Relations School
Cornell University
Ithaca, NY (1996)

Robert S. Weinbeck
Assistant Professor
State University of New York
Brockport, NY

Devora Weiner
Adjunct Instructor
Computer & Accounting Departments
Empire State College
SUNY (1997)

Dr. Rolf T. Wigand
Professor and Director
Graduate Program in Information
Resources Management
Syracuse University
Syracuse, NY

Emily Wughalter
Professor
New York University
New York, NY

NORTH CAROLINA

Steve Chapman
Professor
Department of Business Management
North Carolina State University
Raleigh, NC (1995)

Virgil G. Cox
Dean
Engineering Technology, Math, and
Physics Department
Gaston College
Dallas, NC (1994)

George DeSain
Department Head and Professor
Industrial Engineering
Western Carolina University
Cullowhee, NC (1997)

Donald Dudziak
Professor
Department of Nuclear Engineering
North Carolina State University
Raleigh, NC (1997)

Thomas S. Elleman
Professor Emeritus
Department of Nuclear Engineering
North Carolina State University
Raleigh, NC (1995)

Edward L. Foss
Chair
Marine Technology
Cape Fear Community College
Wilmington, NC (1996)

M.A. Littlejohn
North Carolina State University
Raleigh, NC

Carl Van Orden
Associate Professor Emertius
Business and Economics
Belmont Abbey College
Belmont, NC (1994)

G. Joseph Norwood
Chairman and Professor
Division of Pharmacy Administration
School of Pharmacy
University of North Carolina
Chapel Hill, NC (1994)

Jim Painter
Durham Technical Institute
Durham, NC

Robert A. Rupen
Professor of Political Science
University of North Carolina-Chapel Hill
Chapel Hill, NC (1997)

NORTH DAKOTA

Daniel G. Barbee
Director
Graduate Program
Pembroke State University
Lumberton, ND

Richard A. Molenaar
Assistant Professor
University of North Dakota
Grand Forks, ND

Tom Seymour
Professor
Business Administration Department
Minot State University
Minot, ND (1995)

Don Uhlenberg
Professor
University of North Dakota
Grand Forks, ND

Robert A. Wheeler
Director
Associate Degree Program
Dickinson State College
Dickinson, ND

OHIO

Robert F. Adick
Edison State Community and
Raymond Walters General and Technical College
Cincinatti, OH (1994 OH)

Richard G. Anthony
Associate Professor
Engineering Technology
Cuyahoga Community College
Cleveland, OH (1997)

Don Boron
Chairman
Department of Legal Studies
Bowling Green University
Bowling Green, OH (1994)

Gerald R. Camp
Associate Professor
Business and Technolgoy Department
University of Akron
Akron, OH

Patrick Carlton
Professor
Youngstown State University
Youngstown, OH

Joseph F. Castellano
Professor
Accounting Department
Wright State University
Dayton, OH

Richard Christensen
Professor
Nuclear Engineering Department
Ohio State University
Columbus, OH (1995)

Gary S. Clark
Professor and Coordinator
Department of Aviation Management
Sinclair Community College
Dayton, OH (1994)

James Comer
Associate Professor
University of Cincinnati
Cincinnati, OH

Steven Cornelius
Chair, Hospitality Management
Sinclair Community College
Dayton, OH (1997)

James M. Daschbach
Professor
Department of Industrial Engineering
University of Toledo
Toledo, OH (1995)

John Duncan
Instructor
School of Technology
Kent State University
Kent, OH (1993)

Dennis D. Fulk
Department Head
Civil Engineering Technology
Stark Technical College
Canton, OH (1996)

Patrick Garrett
Chairman
Electrical Engineering Technology
Ohio College of Applied Science
University of Cincinnati
Cincinnati, OH

John B. Gifford
Professor of Marketing
School of Business Administration
Miami University
Oxford, OH (1993)

Alan Gilbrath
School of Systems and Logistics
Air Force Institute of Technology
Wright Patterson Air Force Base, OH (1994 OH)

Roxanne Gonzales
Chairperson
Electronics Engineering Technology
Sinclair Community College
Dayton, OH (1997)

Raghava Gowda
Professor
Department of Computer Science
University of Dayton
Dayton, OH (1997)

Shail Gowda
Adjunct Professor
Sinclair Community College
Dayton, OH (1997)

Carolyn Hannah
Professor
Sinclair Community College
Dayton, OH (1994)

William J. Hoben
Dean
University of Dayton
Dayton, OH

Surinder M. Jain
Chairperson, EET
Sinclair Community College
Dayton, OH (1997)

Betty Jehn
Adjunct Professor
Computer Science
University of Dayton
Dayton, OH

Lawrence A. Jehn
Professor Emeritus
Computer Science
University of Dayton
Dayton, OH

Charles Kardon
Miami Valley Pension
Dayton, OH

Ralph Katerberg
Associate Professor
College of Business Administration
University of Cincinnati
Cincinnati, OH (1996)

Ronald Knipfer
Dean
Sinclair Community College
Dayton, OH

Anthony Mann
Professor and Chairman
Computer Information Systems
Sinclair Community College
Dayton, OH (1997)

Garnett McDonough
Chair
Real Estate and Legal Assisting
Sinclair Community College
Dayton, OH

Karen Meyer
Wright State University
Dayton, OH (1994)

Nancy Moeller
Associate Dean
Hiram Weekend College
Hiram, OH

Tim Mott
Union Institute
Cincinnati, OH

Dan Parker
Professor
Sinclair Community College
Dayton, OH (1994)

Lawrence C. Phillips
Professor
School of Management
Case Western Reserve University
Cleveland, OH (1993)

Daniel E. Porter
Chair
Departments of Fire Science
and Safety Risk Management
Sinclair Community College
Dayton, OH (1995 OH)

Newton Rochte
Professor Emeritus
University of Toledo
Toledo, OH

Daniel J. Schleef
Professor
Department of Mechanical and Industrial Engineering
University of Cincinnati
Cincinnati, OH

Helene Schwarberg
Assistant Department Head
University of Cincinnati
Cincinnati, OH

John Stackler
Sinclair Community College
Dayton, OH (1994 OH)

Henry Stick
Professor of Economics and Finance
University of Dayton
Dayton, OH (1995)

John Stinson
Professor of Management
Ohio University
Athens, OH

Bonnie Thomas-Moore
Assistant Professor and Coordinator
Food Service Management Program
University of Akron
Akron, OH

W. Sanford Topham
Associate Professor and Clinical
Engineering Administrator
Department of Biomedical Engineering
Case Western Reserve University
Cleveland, OH

Gary Tucker
Sinclair Community College
Dayton, OH (1996)

Juanita Ventress
Department of Fire Science and
Safety Risk Management
Sinclair Community College
Dayton, OH (1995 OH)

Joseph A. Wagner
Associate Professor
Ohio State University
Mansville, OH

Paul E. Wyant
Dean
Business Technologies
Sinclair Community College
Dayton, OH (1995)

OKLAHOMA

Don Adams
Professor
Oklahoma State University
Stillwater, OK

Richard L. Allen
Assistant Dean
Career Education and Community Service
Northern Oklahoma College
Tonkawa, OK

Ramon C. Alonso
Professor
Business Strategy & International Management
University of Oklahoma
Norman, OK (1997)

Roger Atherton
Director
College of Business Administration
University of Oklahoma
Norman, OK

Adedeji B. Badiru
Professor
School of Industrial Engineering
University of Oklahoma
Norman, OK (1997)

W.E. Bailey
Automotive Center Coordinator
Oklahoma State University
Okmulgee, OK

John Belveal
Engineering Technologies and Aeronautics
Midwest City, OK (1997)

Rick Brooks
Coordinator
Engineering Technologies
Rosa State College
Midwest City, OK (1997)

Roy Byrd
Chairman
Department of Technology
Cameron University
Lawton, OK

David G. Carnevale
Associate Professor
Political Science Department
University of Oklahoma
Norman, OK (1997)

Kenneth Crawford
Professor of Meteorology
University of Oklahoma
Norman, OK (1993)

Dan A. Davis
Associate Dean of Liberal Studies
University of Oklahoma
Norman, OK

Bill Edwards
Chair
Aerospace Department
Southeastern Oklahoma State University
Durant, OK (1997)

Marion Fox
Professor
Rose State University
Midwest City, OK (1995)

Russell Heiserman
Professor
School of Technology
Oklahoma State University
Stillwater, OK

Joyce Nichols Johnson
Satellite Television Instructor
Oklahoma State University
Stillwater, OK

Gail P. Jones
Professor
Technology Deparatment
Cameron University
Lawton, OK (1997)

Russell Kline
Professor of Technology
Oklahoma State University
Oklahoma City, OK

Marilyn Lair
Associate Professor of Business
Cameron University
Lawton, OK

John A. Ludrick
Assistant to the Dean
School of Education
Southwestern Oklahoma State University
Weatherford, OK

David Mair
Associate Professor of English
University of Oklahoma
Norman, OK (1995)

Vergil V. Miller
Dean
Oklahoma State University
Stillwater, OK

Glen Nemecek
Coordinator, Aviation Education
Oklahoma State University
Stillwater, OK (1997)

Simin Pulat
Professor
School of Industrial Engineering
University of Oklahoma
Norman, OK (1995)

Mr. Glen Shamburg
Director
Aviation College of Continuing Education
Norman, OK (1997)

Don Simonson
Professor of Finance
University of Oklahoma
Norman, OK

Walter S. Smith
Department Head
Oklahoma State Technical Institute
Okmulgee, OK

Terry Spradley
Professor
Technical Education Division
Cameron University
Lawton, OK

Tom Sutherlin
Professor of Technology
Cameron University
Lawton, OK

Tai-Ching Tuan
Assistant Professor
School of Electrical Engineering
and Computer Science
University of Oklahoma
Norman, OK

Lawrence Wilcox
Professor
Department of Computer Science and
Information Systems
Southeastern Oklahoma State University
Durant, OK (1995)

Wayne Wilson
Professor
School of Business
Cameron University
Lawton, OK

Donald Woolf
Professor
Department of Management
College of Business Administration
University of Oklahoma
Norman, OK

Dewey Yeager
Division Head of Engineering and Professor Emeritus
Department of Engineering Technology
Oklahoma State University
Oklahoma City, OK (1997)

OREGON

Lynda S. Hatfield
Dean
Professional Technical Education
Clatsop Community College
Astoria, OR (1995)

James Nielsen
Professor of Finance
College of Business Administration
Oregon State University
Corvallis, OR

Jack Vernon
Professor of Otolaryngology
Oregon Health Sciences University
Portland, OR

PENNSYLVANIA

Leonard Alberts
Professor
Drafting and Design Department
Pennsylvania Institute of Technology
Upper Darby, PA

Eugene W. Bartel
Senior Research Associate
Carnegie-Melon University
Pittsburgh, PA

Shirley A. Biggs
Associate Professor
University of Pittsburgh
Pittsburgh, PA

George E. Biles
Dean and Professor
School of Management
Robert Morris College
Coraopolis, PA (1995)

Dr. Jack Bower
Assistant Professor of Accounting
Eastern College
St. David, PA

Patricia Bradley
Chair and Associate Professor
American Studies
Temple University
Philadelphia, PA (1995)

Audrey Bronson
Professor of Psychology
Cheyney State College
Cheyney, PA

George D. Brower
Associate Professor of Economics and Business
Moravian College
Bethehem, PA

Robert Brucker
Field Consultant
Bureau of Vocational/Educational Education
Pennsylvania Department of Education
Harrisburg, PA

Jerome Buescher
Instructor of Microbiology
College of Graduate Studies
Thomas Jefferson University
Philadelphia, PA (1995 NJ)

Paul Burkhart
Professor of Speech
Shippensburg University
Shippensburg, PA

Raymond Campbell
Chair
Department of General Education
Thomas Jefferson University
Philadelphia, PA (1995)

Alvin A. Clay
Professor and Dean
College of Commerce
Villanova University
Villanova, PA (1995)

Joseph Crowley
Professor
Department of Marketing and Management
Community College of Philadelphia
Philadelphia, PA

David Cummins
Assistant Professor
Insurance Department
Wharton School
University of Pennsylvania
Philadelphia, PA

Wayne Cunningham
School of Management
University of Scranton
Scranton, PA

Nancy Curry
Chairperson
University of Pittsburgh
Pittsburgh, PA

Joel Eigne
Professor
Sociology Department
Franklin and Marshall College
Lancaster, PA

Julian Wade Farrior
Chairman and Associate Professor
Natural Science/Mathematics Division
Gwynedd-Mercy College
Gwynedd Valley, PA (1993)

Carl Fields
Chairman
Nuclear Engineering Technology
Pennsylvania State University
Monaca, PA

George Fieo
Freeman and Fieo Public Accountants
Philadelphia, PA (1994)

John Flynn
Associate Professor
Montgomery County Community College
Blue Bell, PA (1996)

William Ford
Chief Juvenile Probation Officer
Bucks County Courthouse
Doylestown, PA

Howard Freas
Professor
Buck County Community College
Newton, PA

Marlowe Froke
Professor Emeritus
Pennsylvania State University
State College, PA (1996)

Margaret Galligan
Smeal College of Business Administration
Pennsylvania State University
Mont Alto, PA (1997)

Ivan Galtman
Executive Director
Philadelphia Chapter of American Institute of Banking
Philadelphia, PA (1996)

Leonard Garrett
Professor
Temple University
Philadelphia, PA

William George
Associate Professor
College of Commerce and Finance
Villanova University
Villanova, PA

David Giltinan
Professor
Physics Department
Edinboro State College
Edinboro, PA

Helmut Golatz
Head
Department of Labor Studies
Pennsylvania State University
University Park, PA

Steele Gow
Dean
School of General Studies
University of Pittsburgh
Pittsburgh, PA

Blaine Greenfield
Senior Professor of Business
Bucks County Community College
Newtown, PA (1993 NJ)

Elihu Grossmann
Professor
Department of Chemical Engineering
Drexel University
Philadelphia, PA

Manak C. Gupta
Professor of Finance
Temple University
Philadelphia, PA

Charles P. Hall, Jr.
Professor
Insurance and Risk and Health Adminstration
Temple University
Philadelphia, PA

G. Victor Hallman
Professor
Department of Insurance
Wharton School
University of Pennsylvania
Philadelphia, PA (1995)

Howard Hamilton
Professor
Electrical Engineering
University of Pittsburgh
Pittsburgh, PA

John C. Hawley
Hawley Insurance Agency
Montrose, PA 18801 (1995)

Richard Herbstritt
Professor
Gannon University
Erie, PA

Kathleen L. Hoover
Consultant
Morton, PA (1995)

Patrick J. Hopkins
Professor
Harrisburg Area Community College
Harrisburg, PA (1995)

Gregory Lee Hricenak
President
Dragon's Teeth Design
Greensburg, PA

James F. Huston
Professor
Edinboro State College
Edinboro, PA

Martin Kaplan
Professor
ECE Department
Drexel University
Philadelphia, PA (1994)

James R. Keiser
Assistant Professor Emeritus
Hotel and Institutional Administration
Pennsylvania State University
University Park, PA (1994)

Ronald Kostar
Professor of Intelectual Heritage
Temple University
Philadelphia, PA

Eugene J. Kray
Dean of Community Education
Delaware County Community College
Media, PA

Anne Lloyd
Professor
Department of Urban Education
Temple University
Philadelphia, PA

Louis Mangione
Professor of Chinese
Department of Critical Languages
Temple University
Philadelphia, PA

Edward Mazze
Professor
Temple University
Philadelphia, PA (1993 NJ)

John E. McAllister
Deputy Secretary for Administration
Dept. of Labor & Industry
Commonwealth of Pennsylvania
Harrisburg, PA (1997)

Paul Mercado
Chairman
Pennsylvania Institute of Technology
Upper Darby, PA

Peter Miller
Assistant Professor
Philadelphia College of Pharmacy and Sciences
Philadelphia, PA (1996)

Jake Milliones
Assistant Professor
University of Pittsburgh
Pittsburgh, PA

Cathleen Moore
Associate Professor of Psychology
Philadelphia College of Pharmacy and Sciences
Philadelphia, PA (1997)

Rudy Moore
Professor
Rosemont College
Rosemont, PA

Joseph M. Moricz
Dean
Robert Morris College
Coraopolis, PA

Richard Mortimer
Chairman
Drexel University
Philadelphia, PA

George Mostoller
Professor
Engineering Technology Department
University of Pittsburgh at Johnstown
Johnstown, PA (1995)

George K. Muhlberg
Adjunct Professor
School of Management
Robert Morris College
Coraopolis, PA (1994)

Anthony Natale
Adjunct Professor
Bucks County Community College
Newtown, PA (1995)

James Pellegrino
Associate Professor
School of Education
University of Pittsburgh
Pittsburgh, PA

John L. Penkala
State College, PA

Marylou Phillips
Associate Professor of Medical Imaging
Holy Family College
Philadelphia, PA

Patricia Prothno-Shepherd
Associate Chief Nurse/Education
Philadelphia V.A. Medical Center
Philadelphia, PA (1995)

Miguel Pulido
Academic Coordinator
Eastern College
Waynnewood, PA (1995 NJ)

Sister Rose Ann Quinn
Director of Montessori
Chestnut Hill College
Philadelphia, PA

Denis T. Raihall
Professor
Drexel University
Philadelphia, PA

Virginia Ratigan
Associate Professor
Religious Studies Department
Rosemont College
Rosemont, PA (1997)

Laureen Regan
Assistant Professor
Department of Risk Management and Insurance
Temple University
Philadelphia, PA (1995)

Marc Riedel
Research Associate
University of Pennsylvania
Philadelphia, PA

Gordon Robinson
Professor
Pennsylvania State University
University Park, PA

William E. Rosenbach
Professor
Leadership Development Center
Gettysburg College
Gettysburg, PA (1994)

Col. Daniel Rota
Professor
Robert Morris College
Pittsburgh, PA (1994)

Octavio Salati
Professor
University of Pennsylvania
Philadelphia, PA

William Schmitt
Associate Professor
Computer Science Department
Temple University
Philadelphia, PA (1993 NJ)

Charles Schuler
Professor
Industrial Arts Department
California State College
California, PA

Richard W. Simpson
Director
Bureau of Regulations, Rates, and Policies
Pennsylvania Insurance Department
Harrisburg, PA

S. Jay Sklar
Assistant Professor
Law and Real Estate
Temple University
Bala Cynwyd, PA (1993)

Joshua W. Smith, Jr.
Instructor and Assitant Program Director
Geneva College Extension Program at CUTS-
Center for Urban Theological Studies
Philadelphia, PA

Andrew Snow
Associate Professor of Information Systems
University of Pittsburgh
Pittsburgh, PA

Robert Stafford
Professor
Computer Information Systems Department
Temple University
Philadelphia, PA

John C. Strayer
Director
Pennsylvania Institute of Technology
Upper Darby, PA

Donald F. Tonge
Certified Public Accountant
Brookhaven, PA (1994)

Lazar Trachtenberg
Professor
Computer Science Department
Drexel University
Philadelphia, PA (1995)

Kellee Trice
Program Director
School of CNP
Upland, PA (1995)

Anthony Voci
Attorney at Law
Lansdale, PA (1994)

Tim Vogelsberg
Associate Professor
Psychological Studies in Education
Temple University
Philadelphia, PA (1993)

Samuel Wagner
Associate Dean
School of Business Administration
Temple University
Philadelphia, PA

Arthur Wainer
Professor of Chemistry
Edinsboro State College
Edinsboro, PA

James Weisbecker
Professor
Computer Science Department
Great Valley Graduate Center
Pennsylvania State University
Malvern, PA (1995)

K. Cy Whaley
Associate Professor of Diagnostic Imaging
Thomas Jefferson University
Philadelphia, PA

William E. Whitsell
Professor
Department of Economics
Franklin and Marshall University
Lancaster, PA

Margaret Williams-Betlyn
President
Community College of Beaver County
Monaca, PA

F. Stanton Woerth
Director of Industrial Relations
Temple University
Philadelphia, PA

Richard Woodring
Dean, College of Engineering
Drexel University
Philadelphia, PA

C. Bruce Worsham
Associate Vice President and Director
Hubner School
American College
Bryn-Mawr, PA (1995)

RHODE ISLAND

Richard A. Almonte
Consultant
Department of Education
Bureau of Vocational-Technical Education
Providence, RI

James Starkey
Professor of Economics
Chafee Social Science Center
University of Rhode Island
Kingston, RI

SOUTH CAROLINA

Helen Doerpinghaus
Professor
College of Business
University of South Carolina
Columbia, SC

Margaret Humphreys
Assistant Professor and Director
Early Childhood Development Center
School of Education
College of Charleston
Charleston, SC (1995)

L. H. Livingston
Senior Staff
Science Applications International Corporation
Aiken, SC (1996)

Linwood Livingston
Aiken, SC (1994)

William J. Mathias
Dean
University of South Carolina
Columbia, SC

Phil McGee
Director
Greenville Technical College
Greenville, SC

Travis S. Pritchett
Professor
College of Business Administration
University of South Carolina
Columbia, SC

Kemp Sigmon
Dean of Industrial Division
Spartansburg Technical College
Spartansburg, SC

Hugh H. Wilson
Professor
Department of Ceramic Engineering
Clemson University
Clemson, SC

SOUTH DAKOTA

Paul Fugazzotto
Director
Urinary Research Center
Rapid City, SD

Paul L. Smith, Jr.
Research Professor
Institute of Atmospheric Sciences
South Dakota School of Mines and Technology
Rapid City, SD (1994)

TENNESSEE

Lewis Baldwin
Associate Professor
Department of Religious Studies
Vanderbilt University
Nashville, TN

George Boulware
Professor and Chair
Department of Business
Lipscomb University
Nashville, TN (1997)

Roger W. Haskell
Professor
Department of Human Resource Development
University of Tennessee
Knoxville, TN (1997)

Mary J. Hitchcock
Professor
Food Science, Nutrition, and Food
Systems Administration Deparatment
University of Tennessee
Knoxville, TN

George W. Knight
Director
Education Materials
Seminary Extension
Nashville, TN (1995)

Lawrence F. Miller
Professor
Department of Nuclear Engineering
University of Tennessee
Knoxville, TN (1997)

R. Kevin Moore
Assistant Professor
Christian Studies Department
Union University
Jackson, TN (1996)

Patricia Murrell
Director
Center for the Study of Higher Education
Memphis State University
Memphis, TN

Van N. Oliphant
Professor of Management
Memphis State University
Memphis, TN

Gayle Rayburn
Professor of Accounting
College of Business Administration
Memphis State University
Memphis, TN

Matt Reiser
Professor Emeritus
Cleveland State College
Cleveland, TN

Steven H. Simpler
Dean or Professor
School of Religion
Belmont University
Nashville, TN (1993)

Gerald Whitlock
Professor of Management and Psychology
University of Tennessee
Knoxville, TN

TEXAS

Gemmy S. Allen
Marketing and Management Instructor
Mountain View College
Dallas, TX

Lowell Ballew
Associate Professor
Computer Science Department
East Texas State University
Commerce, TX (1995)

John C. Besse
Chair
Bible Department
East Texas State University
Commerce, TX (1995)

H. Joseph Blair
Chair and Professor
Department of Christianity and Philosophy
Houston Baptist University
Houston, TX (1996)

Edward K. Bowdon
Professor and Head
Department of Engineering Technology
Texas A&M University
Tyler, TX

John R. Brooks
Professor of Marketing
College of Business and Economics
Houston Baptist University
Houston, TX

Deb Carlson
Director and Professor
Audiology and Speech Pathology
University of Texas Medical Center
Galveston, TX (1994)

Nell Dale
University of Texas
Department of Computer Science
Austin, TX

Larry R. Davis
Head
Business Administration Division
Texas A&M University
Texarkana, TX (1997)

Linda W. Garner
Staff Training Specialist
Exxon Production Research Co.
Houston, TX

H. Donald Garrison
Associate Professor
Technology Department
University of Texas
Tyler, TX

David Grant
Professor
Department of Religion
Texas Christian University
Forth Worth, TX (1994)

Albert Grubbs, Jr.
Associate Professor
Engineering Technology
Texas A&M University
College Station, TX

Kay Hale
Director
Instructional Program
Community and Technical College Division
Texas Higher Education Coordinating Board
Austin, TX (1995)

Mike Harvey
Chairman
Department of Marketing
Southern Methodist University
Dallas, TX

Harold Hatchett
Professor
Management Department
Texas A&M University
Texarkana, TX (1997)

Robert K. Holz
Professor
University of Texas at Austin
Austin, TX

George L. Huebner
Professor Emeritus
Department of Meteorology
Texas A&M University
College Station, TX (1996)

J. Roland Kelley
Chairman
Business Administration
Tarrant County Junior College System, Northeast
Hurst, TX

Jerry King
Dean
Trinity Valley Community College
Athens, TX

Lonnie D. Kliver
Professor
Department of Religious Studies
Southern Methodist University
Dallas, TX (1997)

Fred E. Lee
Associate Director
Professional Development Institute
College of Business
North Texas State University
Richardson, TX

Neal McBryde
Dean
Bee County College
Beeville, TX

Dorothy McNutt
Chairperson and Professor Emeritus
Business and Computer Science Department
College of the Mainland
Texas City, TX (1997)

John S. Megerson
Director
District Security
Southwest Texas State University
San Marcos, TX (1996)

Leo B. Osterhaus
Dean
St. Edwards University
Austin, TX

Ivor P. Page
Erik Jonsson School of Engineering&
Computer Science
University of Texas-Dallas
Richardson, TX (1997)

William L. Raley
Director
College of the Mainland
Texas City, TX

Larry Reed
Executive Vice President
Navarro College
Corsicana, TX

Robert Reed
Director
Emergency Administration
University of North Texas
Denton, TX

Jan Stalder
President
Rescue Evloutions
Plano, TX (1995)

Alan T. Stutts
Dean, Conrad N. Hilton College of Hotels and Restaurant Management
Houston, TX (1997)

Jesse Symms
Chairman
Electonics Department
College of the Mainland
Texas City, TX

James C. Taylor
Dean
School of Hotel and Restaurant Management
University of Houston
Houston, TX

Leon J. Tolle, Jr.
Professor
Our Lady of the Lake University
San Antonio, TX

Richmond White
Chairman
Division of Engineering, Physics, Math, and Technology
Texarkana Community College
Texarkana, TX

Ronald J. Williams
Professor
Del Mar College
Corpus Christie, TX

George B. Wright
Assistant Professor
Engineering Technology
Texas A&M University
College Station, TX

UTAH

Brenda De La Mare
Program Director
Nurse Aide Training/Competency Evaluation
Utah Registry
Kaysville, UT (1995)

VERMONT

Richard M. Harter
Assistant Professor of Electronics
Champlain College
Burlington, VT

Michael Kolesnick
Coordinator
Community College of Vermont
Rutland, VT

VIRGINIA

Joseph D. Adams
Assistant Division Chairman
Northern Virginia Community College
Annandale, VA

Joseph R. Avella
Academic Dean
American Military U.
Manassas Park, VA (1997)

Dale Babione
Deputy Assistant Secretary of Defense
Fairfax, VA (1994)

Sandra O. Bailey
Program Head
Medical Records Technology Program
Northern Virginia Community College
Annandale, VA (1995)

Barry Baker
Assistant Chief
City of Fairfax Fire and Rescue
Fairfax, VA (1996)

James R. Baker
Professor
Imaging Systems
Virginia Polytechnic Institute and State University
Blacksburg, VA

Gary E. Ballman
Associate Dean of Curriculum Services and Professor
Medical Laboratory Technology
Northern Virginia Community College
Annandale, VA (1996)

Paul Bankit
Faculty Advisor
Embry-Riddle Aeronautical University
Ft. Eustis, VA

Thomas C. Barker
Dean
School of Allied Health Professions
Virginia Commonwealth University
Richmond, VA

Norris Bell
Director of Continuing Education
Graduate Center
Virginia Polytechnic Institute and
State University
Falls Church, VA (1994)

T. W. Bonham
Associate Dean
College of Business
Virginia Polytechnic Institute and
State University
Blacksky, VA (1996)

Robert L. Bowers
Chairman
Division of Business and Public Services
J. Sargeant Reynolds Community College
Richmond, VA

James Brohan
Management Consultant
Alexandria, VA (1994)

Rosemary Burton
Minnieland, Inc.
Woodbridge, VA (1997)

Dorothy Cavagnaro
Professor Emeritus
Department of HRIM
Northern Virginia Community College
Annandale, VA (1996)

Robert Childs
ACE Fellow Assistant to Provost
George Mason University
Fairfax, VA

Gen Sen Chu
Director
Learning Resources Center
Northern Virginia Community College
Alexandria, VA

William Clark
Professor
Tidewater Community College
Portsmouth, VA (1995)

William Clontz
Director
Program Support
MFRI International Group
Alexandria, VA (1997)

Mary Ann Coffland
Chair
Department of Italian
George Washington University
Springfield, VA (1993)

Robert W. Cosgriff
Associate Academic Dean
Mirus University
Springfield, VA (1996)

Laura A. Davis
Consultant
Alexandria, VA (1997)

Lloyd M. DeBoer
Chairman
George Mason University
Fairfax, VA

Rev. Paul F. deLadurantaue
Diocesan Secretary for Religious Studies
Diocese of Arlington
Arlington, VA (1996)

Thomas G. DeLutis
President
Information Systems Architects, Inc.
Fairfax, VA (1997)

Donald Devers
Assistant Professor
Social Science and Public Service Division
Northern Virginia Community College
Annandale, VA

Ali Etili
Consultant
Arlington, VA (1994)

Michael Evans
Associate Professor
Virginia Polytechnic Institute and State University
Blacksburg, VA

Rudolph J. Fiorillo
Chairman
Visual and Performing Arts Division
Northern Virginia Community College
Alexandria, VA (1994)

Nevin R. Frantz, Jr.
Professor and Director
Division of Vocational and Technical Education
Virginia Polytechnic Institute and State University
Blacksburg, VA

Mark G. Goldin
Associate Professor
George Mason University
Fairfax, VA (1997)

Barry M. Goldstone
Lecturer
Business Division
Northern Virginia Community College
Annandale, VA (1996)

Radwan Hakim
Professor
Arab American Translators
Falls Church, VA

Andrew Hargrove
Professor Electrical Engineering Department
Norfolk State University
Norfolk, VA (1996)

John P. Hill
Professor and Academic Dean
Public Services Technologies Division
Thomas Nelson Community College
Hampton, VA (1996)

Van Holladay
Adjunct Professor
Administrator of Justice Department
Northern Virginia Community College
Woodbridge, VA (1997)

M. Gweneth Humphreys
Chairman
Mathematics Department
Randolph Macon Woman's College
Lynchburg, VA

Edward V. Jones
Director and Associate Professor
Office of Adult Learning and
Professional Management
Graduate School of Education
George Mason University
Fairfax, VA (1997)

Joseph M. Kanyan
Professor
Department of Music
George Mason University
Fairfax, VA

Ric Koonce
Program Head
Fire Science Department
J. Sargeant Reynolds Community College
Richmond, VA (1994)

Kenneth Kovach
Professor
School of Business Administration
George Mason University
Fairfax, VA (1996)

Richard Lechowich
Professor and Head
Department of Food Science
and Technology
Virginia Polytechnic Institute and
State University
Blacksburg, VA

Edward L. Lee II
President
The Lee Group, Inc.
Falls Church, VA (1996)

Frank Lembo
Professor
Real Estate
Northern Virginia Community College
Annandale, VA (1994)

Ann St. Clair Lesman
Professor of Spanish
Northern Virginia Community College
Alexandria, VA

James Levine
Chair and Professor
Foreign Languages and Literatures
George Mason University
Fairfax, VA (1994)

Jim Lock
Assistant Professor
Department of Accounting and Finance
Northern Virginia Communtiy College
Alexandria, VA (1995)

Dan A. Lookadoo
Professor
Electronics Department
New River Community College
Dublin, VA (1997)

Donald I. MacInnes
Director
Teacher Education Laboratory
Presbyterian School of Christian Education
Richmond, VA

William R. Martin
Professor
School of Education
George Mason University
Fairfax, VA

Herbert E. McCartney
Automotive Program Head
Northern Virginia Community College
Alexandria, VA

Kenneth McCreedy
Assistant Professor
School of Community Services
Virginia Commonwealth University
Richmond, VA

Jim McClullen
Social Science Department
Northern Virginia Community College
Alexandria, VA (1997)

James A. McDonough
Professor of Civil Engineering
Virginia Military Institute
Lexington, VA

Robert Barlow McEwen
Research Physical Scientist
National Mapping Division
U.S. Geological Society
Reston, VA (1993)

Ronald L. McKeen
Professor Emeritus
Virginia Polytechnical Institute and State University
Falls Church, VA (1997)

Charles McKenny
Chair
United States Marine Staff College
Quantico, VA (1993)

George W. McKinney, Jr.
Virginia Bankers' Professor of Bank Management
University of Virginia
Charlottesville, VA

Karen L. Medsker
Professor
Human Resources Department
Marymount University
Arlington, VA (1995)

David Michaels
Professor
Northern Virginia Community College
Annandale, VA

Joseph Migliaccio
Professor
Science and Technology Department
Northern Virginia Community College
Alexandria, VA (1997)

Sam Mills
Assistant Director
J. Sargeant Reynolds Community College
Richmond, VA

Herbert Mitchell
Dean
Virginia Polytechnic Institute and State University
Blacksburg, VA

Jose G. Montero
Associate Professor
Northern Virginia Community College
Annandale, VA

James M. Moore
Professor
Virginia Polytechnic Institute and State University
Blacksburg, VA

Phyllis Myers
Professor
School of Business
Virginia Commonwealth University
Richmond, VA

Margaret Nydell
Director
Arabic Dialect Project
Georgetown University
Diplomatic Language Sciences, Inc.
Arlington, VA (1994)

Michael O'Brien
Chairman
Thomas Nelson Community College
Hampton, VA

Colleen O'Brien-Thorpe
Professor
Northern Virginia Community College
Annandale, VA (1994)

Sister Jacquelyn Porter
Professor
Philosophy and Religion Department
Marymount University
Arlington, VA (1995)

Gene Hill Price
Lecturer
Department of Computer Sciences
Old Dominion University
Norfolk, VA (1996)

Howard Reichbart
Program Head
Hotel, Restaurant, and Institutional Management
Northern Virginia Community College
Annandale, VA (1997)

James Renick
Associate Provost
George Mason University
Fairfax, VA

Barbara Williams Scott
Consultant
Alexandria, VA (1996)

Jennie Seaton
Virginia Commonwealth University
Richmond, VA

Bill Shannon
Professor of Paralegal Studies
Northern Virginia Community College
Alexandria, VA

Celeste M. Sichenze
Professor Emeritus
Department of Management
Northern Virginia Communiuty College
Annandale, VA (1997)

Clinton H. Smoke, Jr.
Director of Fire Science Institute
Northern Virginia Community College
Annandale, VA (1997)

Susan Strasinger
Director and Professor
Medical Technology Program
Northern Virginia Community College
Annandale, VA (1997)

Steve Strawderman
Captain
EMS Supervision
Prince William County Department of Fire and Rescue
Prince William, VA (1997)

Edward Tangman
Chairman
Engineering Technologies Division
Northern Virginia Community College
Annandale, VA

Russell E. Taylor
Director and Associate Professor
Automotive Department
Northern Virginia Community College
Alexandria, VA (1996)

M'Kean Tredway
Director
Office of Continuing Educaton
Northern Virginia Community College, Manassas
Manassas, VA

Konstantinos Triantis
Assistant Professor
Department of Industrial Engineering
and Operations Research
Virginia Tech
Falls Church, VA

Woodie L. Tucker
Professor
Virginia Commonwealth University
Richmond, VA

Charles E. Tychsen
Professor
Business Division
Northern Virginia Community College
Annandale, VA (1997)

Craig Washington
Chairman
Automotive Engineering and Public Service Division
Northern Virginia Community College
Alexandria, VA

Howard Weiner
Assistant Professor of Data Processing
Business Division
Northern Virginia Community College
Annandale, VA

Inge B. Wekerle
Department of Foreign Language and Literature
George Mason University
Fairfax, VA

Kennedy Wilson
Former Professor of Commerce
University of Virginia
Falls Church, VA

Victoria M. Wood
Nutritional Consultant
Vienna, VA (1994)

Barbara Ann Wyles
Associate Dean of Curriculum Services
Northern Virginia Community College
Annandale, VA

Chen D. Yang
Program Manager, International Programs
George Mason University
Arlington, VA (1997)

WASHINGTON

John Jaeck
Consultant
Fox Island, WA (1994)

Rosemary Pittman
Director
School of Nursing
University of Washington
Seattle, WA

WEST VIRGINIA

Leonard Davis
Professor
West Virginia University
Morgantown, WV

Everett Perkins
Director of Fire Service Extension
West Virginia University
Morgantown, WV (1994)

James B. Stone
Chairman
Division of Specialized Allied Studies
Mining Occupational and Transportation Safety
Marshall University
Huntington, WV

Richard Walls
Professor of Educational Psychology
West Virginia University
Morgantown, WV

WISCONSIN

Eugene Alm
University of Wisconsin
Hales Corners, WI (1994)

Joseph G. Andritzky
Associate Professor
Management/Criminal Justice Operations
Concordia University
Mequon, WI (1995)

Harish Batra
Associate Dean
College of Business and Economics
University of Wisconsin
Whitewater, WI

Dan Bintz
Consultant
MSTC/MATC
Sun Prairie, WI (1997)

Dale Feinauer
Associate Professor
College of Business
University of Wisconsin
Oshkosh, WI

Roger Formissano
Graduate School of Banking
University of Wisconsin
Madison, WI

Marvin Franson
Trade & Industry Division
Chippewa Valley Technical College
Eau Claire, WI (1997)

Sharon Yvonne Hart
Vice President
Northcentral Technical College
Wausau, WI (1997)

Dale Johnson
Associate Professor
MIS Department
University of Wisconsin
Eau Claire, WI

Charles Kroncke
Associate Professor
University of Wisconsin
Madison, WI

Michael Morgan
Professor
College of Environmental Sciences
University of Wisconsin
Green Bay, WI (1993)

J. Robert Mueller
Director of Nuclear Education
Wisconsin Public Service Corporation
Green Bay, WI (1997)

Ray Palmer
Vice Chairman
Milwaukee School of Engineering
Milwaukee, WI

Charles Rhyner
Professor
Physics Department
University of Wisconsin, Green Bay
Green Bay, WI (1997)

Patrick Runde
Associate Dean
University of Wisconsin
Madison, WI

Sally Newman Standiford
Professor and Director
Educational Technology Center
Ames Teacher Education Center
University of Wisconsin
River Falls, WI (1996)

George B. Strother
Professor (Retired)
University of Wisconsin
Madison, WI

David J. Ward
Senior Vice President for Academic Affairs
Department of Finance
University of Wisconsin System
Oshkosh, WI (1996)

ISRAEL

Zvi Bernstein
Jerusalem, Israel

Zvigdor Boncheck
Jerusalem, Israel

Emanual Feldman
Jerusalem, Israel

Mayer Fialkoff
Adjunct Professor
Touro Graduate School of Jewish Studies
Jerusalem, Israel (1997)

Chana M. Firestone
Touro College
Art History
Jerusalem, Israel (1997)

Naftali Fish
Adjunct Professor of Psychology
Touro College
Jerusalem, Israel (1997)

Jacob M. Glickman
Senior Economist
State of Israel, Ministry of Finance
Income Tax Commission
Jerusalem, Israel (1997)

Menachem Gottesman
Efrat, Israel

Rabbi Chaim Solomon Heifetz
Adjunct Professor
Women's Adult Education Program
Jerusalem, Israel (1997)

Carmi Horowitz
Touro Graduate School of Jewish Studies
Jerusalem, Israel (1997)

Julius Kline
Jerusalem, Israel

Esther Parnes
Chairman, Department of Computer Science
Emunah College for Women
Jerusalem, Israel (1997)

Shifra Rosen
Jerusalem, Israel

INDIA

J.R. Isaac
Professor
Indian Institute of Technology
Powai, Bombay, India

Deepak B. Phatak
Professor
Indian Institute of Technology, Bombay
Bombay, India

S.K. Wasan
Professor and Registrar
Delhi University
New Delhi, India (1995)

ACE/PONSI
Course Index

Accounting

Advance Learning Network
- *Managerial Accounting (Bus 340)*

American Bankers Association
- *Accounting (1000)*
- *Accounting II (1010)*
- *Analyzing Financial Statements (6920)*
- *Bank Accounting (6000)*
- *Bank Control and Audit (6150)*

American Compensation Association
- *Principles of Accounting and Finance (T2)*

American Institute for Chartered Property Casualty Underwriters, Insurance Institute of America
- *AIAF 111: Statutory Accounting for Property and Liability Insurers*
- *APA 91: Principles of Premium Auditing*
- *APA 92: Premium Auditing Applications*
- *CPCU 08: Accounting and Finance*
- *CPCU V: Management, Accounting, and Finance*

American Institute of Banking of New Jersey
- *Accounting I (ACC101)*
- *Accounting II (ACC102)*
- *Analyzing Financial Statements (CRL101)*
- *Bank Control and Audit (SUP 101)*

American Institute of Banking, Mid-Atlantic Chapter
- *Accounting I (201)*
- *Accounting II (202)*
- *Analyzing Financial Statements (205)*

AT&T School of Business and Technology
- *A Cost Model for Communications*
- *Auditing Standards and Principles (FE0601)*
- *Cash Flow Analysis I (AT&T 401A)*
- *Contemporary Accounting and Financial Concepts (FE0200)*
- *Cost Analysis and Cost Reduction (FE0104)*
- *Finance and Accounting for Business Managers (FEO103)*
- *Financial Leadership Program (Module 1): Accounting and Reporting*
- *Financial Leadership Program (Module 2): Managing Risk*
- *Financial Leadership Program (Module 4): Business Analysis and Decision Support*
- *Financial Management in Telecommunications*
- *Financial Management in Telecommunications (SE3000)*
- *Financial Planning Control and Decision Making (UMMD and SG1010)*
- *Financial Statement Analysis*
- *Fundamentals of Finance and Accounting (UPFF or SE2000)*
- *Introduction to Accounting (FE0100)*
- *Lease Versus Buy Decision (FE0460)*

Bell Atlantic Corporation
- *Basic Accounting*
- *Basic Telephone Accounting*
- *Cost and Accounting Systems*
- *Fundamentals of Revenue Accounting*
- *Introduction to Property and Cost Accounting*
- *Payroll Accounting (2666)*

Bisk-Totaltape Publishing Company
- *Accounting and Reporting - Taxation, Managerial, and Governmental and Not-for-Profit Organizations (Self-Study)*
- *Accounting and Reporting - Taxation, Managerial, and Governmental and Not-for-Profit Organizations (Online)*
- *Financial Accounting and Reporting - Business Enterprises (Online)*
- *Financial Accounting and Reporting - Business Enterprises (Self-Study)*

BOMI Institute
- *Real Property Accounting (11031)*

California College for Health Sciences
- *Accounting I (ACC 220)*

College for Financial Planning, Inc.
- *Basic Tax Preparation (Accredited Tax Preparer Program)*
- *Income Tax Planning (CFP III)*

Acquisition

Bankruptcy

Behavioral Science

Biology

Business Management

Advance Learning Network
Adult Development and Life Assessment

American Institute for Chartered Property Casualty Underwriters, Insurance Institute of America
AIS 25: Delivering Insurance Services

Ameritech
Building the Distributor Partnership (A10037)

AT&T School of Business and Technology
Information Mapping, Structured Writing (IE1202)
Interpersonal Management Skills for Information Systems (IE1800)
Statistics I: Introduction to Statistics and Probability (QU1135)

Computer Learning Centers, Inc. (National)
Principles of Accounting (GE 104)

Educational Services Institute
Global Strategic Planning
Managing Projects in Organizations

Hampton Group, Inc.
Managing Project Teams (0009)
Project and Program Management: Software, People, and Budgets

Institute of Management Sciences
Introduction to Management (PMT 102)

International Association of Machinists and Aerospace Workers
Labor Leadership I
Labor Leadership II

Lucent Technologies, Inc., Learning and Performance Center
Cost of Quality Workshop (LQM302L)
Mini-MBA in General Management (LBM025L)

Mercantile Stores, Inc.
Business Analysis and Application II

National Emergency Training Center (NFA)
Fire Service Supervision: Personal Effectiveness (F310)

NRI Schools/A Division of The McGraw-Hill Companies
Business Management I (MG101)
Business Management II (MG102)
Entrepreneurship (MG210)

OmniTech® Consulting Group, Inc.
Choosing and Managing Your Telecom Supplies

Paychex, Inc.
Level 1: Paychex Management Essentials
Level 2: The Developing Paychex Manager
Level 2: The Developing Paychex Sales Manager
Level 2: The Developing Paychex Supervisor
Level 2.5: The Developing Paychex Client Services Manager
Level 3: Innovative Leadership Skills

TESST Technology Institute
Study and Life Skills

U.S. Army Community and Family Support Training Center
Supplemental Program Services and Family Child Care Directors' Course

U.S. Army Management Staff College, Program in Sustaining Base Leadership and Management
Army Management Staff College, Program in Sustaining Base Leadership and Management, Version 3

Business Technology

AT&T School of Business and Technology
Initial Analyst Training (IE 2500)

Computer Learning Centers, Inc. (National)
Introduction to Business Mathematics (Statistics) (GE 107)
UNIX Administration Program
1. UNIX Administration I (OS 101)
2. UNIX Administration II (OS 201)

National Institute for Paralegal Arts and Sciences
- *Legal Communications for Paralegals (English Composition)*

National Management Association
- *Supervisory and Management Skills Program*

National Mine Health and Safety Academy
- *Applied Communication Techniques*
- *Communication Skills I or Communication, Interpersonal, Small Group*
- *Effective Writing*
- *Public Speaking and Briefing Techniques*
- *National Weather Service Training Center*
- *Writing and Broadcast Seminar (WBS01)*

Omega Institute
- *Business Communications (326,327,328)*

Pacific Bell
- *Active Communicating, Stage II (20579)*
- *Active Communicating: Maintaining Customer Focus (20399C)*
- *Basic Business Writing (01010A)*
- *Basic Negotiation Skills (41427)*
- *Effective Business Presentations (42211)*
- *Effective Business Writing (01048)*
- *High Gain Listening (01059)*
- *High Impact Presenting (01095)*
- *System Design Consultant Communication Skills (02138)*
- *The Versatile Organization (42000 or 42000P)*
- *Writing Management Reports (01266)*

Public Service Electric & Gas
- *Oral Presentation Skills*
- *Systematic Analysis of Ideas*

Qualtec Institute for Competitive Advantage
- *TQM: Facilitator Skills Instructor Training (FL310T)*

Safeguards and Security Central Training Academy
- *Security Education Coordinators Training (CTA-110)*

SBC Center for Learning
- *Communispond Effective Presentation Skills (CEPS)*
- *Effective Business Communication*
- *1. Effective Business Writing*
- *2. Presentation Skills*
- *Improving Business Relationships*
- *Negotiation Skills*
- *Overview of Data Communications (DQ 101)*
- *Presentation Skills (0201)*

School of Engineering and Logistics
- *Oral Communications*
- *Written Communications* (50060)

Technical Education & Development Corporation
- *Interpersonal Communication*
- *Public Speaking*

U.S. Army Management Staff College, Program in Sustaining Base Leadership and Management
- *Army Management Staff College, Program in Sustaining Base Leadership and Management, Non-Resident*
- *Army Management Staff College, Program in Sustaining Base Leadership and Management, Version 2*

U.S. Department of Agriculture Graduate School
- *Better Pronunciation Skills I (EESOL 200)*
- *Better Pronunciation Skills II (EESOL 201)*
- *Communication Skills II (EESOL 121)*
- *Communications Skills II (EESOL 124)*
- *Communications Skills III (ESOL 122)*
- *Communications Skills IV (ESOL 123)*
- *Intermediate Public Speaking (ESPCH 350)*
- *Introduction to Speechwriting (CWRIT 103)*
- *Practical Writing (EWRIT 050)*
- *Reading and Writing Skills II (EESOL 126)*
- *Reading and Writing Skills III (EESOL 127)*
- *Reading and Writing Skills IV (EESOL 128)*

Construction Technology

Education

Zaidner Institute
Psychological Foundations of Education (PSY 260)
Psychological Testing and Measurement (PSY 410)
Sociology of Education (SOC 210)
Survey of Exceptional Children (PSY 310)
Teaching Reading to Young Children (EDUC 204)
Zaidner Institute of Montreal
Sociology of Education (SOC 210)

Educational Administration
Independent School of Management
Developing and Applying Your Leadership Style
Heading the Small School
Leading the Effective Elementary School
Leading the Successful Preschool Division
Leading the Successful Upper School
Leading Today's Changing Middle School
Managing Your Curriculum
Renewing Your Administrative Perspective
Scheduling the Elementary School Program
Scheduling the Middle School Program
Scheduling Without Conflict
The Assistant Headship
The Board Presidency
The Role of the Director of Parent Relations

Electrical Technology
AT&T Network and Computing Services/Network Operations and Engineering Training
DR4 Digital Radio System Maintenance (OF-0305)
AT&T School of Business and Technology
Introduction to Technical Mathematics and Electricity and Electronics
Bell Atlantic Corporation
Advanced Peripheral Processor Maintenance
Advanced Peripheral Processor Maintenance
Basic Electricity and Electronics Course (492)
Data Management for Switching Networks
Digital Technology
Feeder Administration
Fiber Optics Design/Loop Electronics Design (EN4121)
General Transmission Concepts
Interoffice Facilities Current Planning (EN2100)
Light Wave Design (Fiber Optics Design)
Loop Electronics Design
Loop Electronics Planning
Repair Transmission (224)
Subscriber Carrier: Lightwave Design (NE31OIC)
Calhoon MEBA Engineering School
Electrical Troubleshooting
Electricity
Carolina Power & Light Company
COC: Electrical Science, Instrumentation, and Control (COB01N-EL, IC)
Reactor Operator Theory: Electrical Sciences (RO6C02H-ELEC)
Senior Reactor Operator Theory: Electrical Science S06C00H-ELEC; Version A
Senior Reactor Operator Theory: Electrical Science S06C00H-ELEC; Version B
Chrysler Corporation Advanced Technical Training
Hydraulic Systems Analysis (HSA 201)
Industrial Electrical Controls (IEC 101)
Programmable Controllers PLC-2 Family (BAB 102)
Programmable Controllers PLC-2 Family Advanced Program (AAB 202)
Programmable Controllers PLC-3 and PLC-3/10 Advanced Program (AAB 203)
Programmable Controllers PLC-3 and PLC-3/10 (BAB 103)
Programmable Controllers PLC-5 Family (BAB 105)
Programmable Controllers—Modicon 484 (MOD 104)

Financial Management

Health Care Administration

Health Education

Human Resource Management

Law Enforcement

Management

Management Information Systems

Mathematics

Nuclear Materials

Nuclear Technology

Political Science

Power Plant Technology

Procurement

Production Management

Project Management

Public Administration

Radiation

Recreation

Religious Studies

Sales

Supervision

Systems

Technology

ACE/PONSI
Participating Organizations
Index

Participating Organizations Index

Apprenticeship/Lab

Automatic Sprinkler Apprenticeship Program
Carpenters Health and Safety Fund of North America
I.B.E.W. Local Union 269
International Union of Operating Engineers
Laborers-AGC
National Joint Apprenticeship and Training Committee for the Electrical Industry
National Training Fund for the Sheet Metal and Air Conditioning Industry
UAW-Ford
UAW-GM Center for Human Resources

Association

America's Community Bankers
American Association of Direct Human Service Personnel
American Bankers Association
American Compensation Association
American Health Information Management Association
American Institute for Chartered Property Casualty Underwriters, Insurance Institute of America
American Society of Safety Engineers
Certified Employee Benefit Specialist Program
College for Financial Planning, Inc.
Credit Union National Association
Health Insurance Association of America
Insurance Data Management Association
Insurance Educational Association
International Association of Fire Fighters
International Association of Machinists and Aerospace Workers
International Hearing Society
Language Matters, Inc.
Massachusetts Bankers Association, Inc.
National Association Medical Staff Services
National Association of Independent Fee Appraisers
National Association of Power Engineers Educational Foundation
National Association of Securities Dealers, Inc.
National Certified Public Manager Consortium
National Child Care Association
National Management Association
National Registry of Radiation Protection Technologists (NRRPT)
New Jersey Association of Realtors
New Jersey Council for the Humanities
PADI International, Inc.
Society For Human Resource Management
Stonier Graduate School of Banking

Corporation

Ameritech
AT&T Network and Computing Services/Network Operations and Engineering Training
AT&T School of Business and Technology
Baltimore Gas & Electric Company
Bell Atlantic Corporation
Bisk-Totaltape Publishing Company
Caesars Atlantic City
Carolina Power & Light Company
Case Corporation
Central States Health and Life Company
Chrysler Corporation Advanced Technical Training
Commerce Bank N.A.
Commonwealth Edison Company
CoreStates New Jersey National Bank
Dana Corporation
Dollar Rent A Car Systems, Inc.
Duquesne Light Company
EG&G Mound Applied Technologies
Entergy Operations, Inc.
Entergy Operations, Inc., River Bend
First Data Card Services Group
Florida Power and Light Company
JR Electronics And Pneumatics, Corp.
Knight-Ridder, Inc.
Land Rover University
Lockheed Martin Utility Services, Inc.
Lucent Technologies, Customer Training & Information Products
Lucent Technologies, Inc., Business Communications Systems Education & Training
Lucent Technologies, Learning and Performance Center
Lucent Technologies, Technical Services Company
McDonald's Corporation
Mercantile Stores, Inc.
Omaha Public Power District
Pacific Bell
Paychex, Inc.
Peachbottom Atomic Power Station
Positive Child Development Training, Inc.
Public Service Electric & Gas
SBC Center for Learning
Showboat Casino Hotel
Snelling and Snelling, Inc.
Technical Education & Development Corporation
Travelers Group
U.S. West Learning Systems
UAW-Chrysler Technology Training Center
Union Pacific Railroad Company
Virginia Insurance Reciprocal
Westinghouse Savannah River Company

Government

Institute/School

Training Supplier

ACE/PONSI
State/Country Index

State/Country Index

New Mexico

New York

North Carolina

Ohio

Oklahoma

Pennsylvania

South Carolina

Tennessee

Texas

Virginia

ACE/PONSI Subject Index

Subject Index

Health Care/Safety

Human Resources

Insurance

Law Enforcement/Security

Legal/Paralegal

Management

Manufacturing

Nutrition

Public Administration

Real Estate

Recreation

Religious Studies

Technology

Telecommunications

Transportation

Utilities

Cooperating Colleges and Universities by State

Cooperating Colleges and Universities by State

The acceptance of ACE Credit Recommendations by accredited colleges and universities is crucial to the usefulness of this Guide. The list which follows gives the names of many academic institutions that use the National Guide to consider awarding college credit to adult learners. However, the listing of a particular academic institution provides no guarantee that credit will be awarded without exception. Acceptance of our credit recommendations is at the discretion of each institution and depends on such variables as the institution's overall policy toward extra-institutional learning, the specific department or school where acceptance of the credit recommendations is being sought, and the major and minor areas of concentration. Nonetheless, the ACE list of academic institutions will be useful to organizations and adult learners in their efforts to achieve academic recognition.

Accredited Colleges and Universities who would like to be included in future editions of the National Guide may complete and return the removable postcard located on the last page of this guide.

ALABAMA

Alabama Aviation and Technical College
Ozark, AL
334/774-5113

Athens State College
Athens, AL 35611
205/233-8214

Community College of the Air Force
Maxwell Air Force Base, AL 36112-6613
334/953-6436

International Bible College
Florence, AL 35630
205/766-6610

John C. Calhoun State Community College
Decatur, AL 35609-2216
205/306-2596

Lawson State Community College
Burmingham, AL 35221
205/929-6312

Northeast Alabama Community College
Rainsville, AL 35986
205/638-4418

Spring Hill College
Mobile, AL 36608
334/380-2240

Troy State University
Troy, AL 36082
334/670-3616

Troy State University at Dothan
Fort Rucker, AL 36362-0457
334/983-6556
334/598-2443

Troy State University in Montgomery
Montgomery, AL 36103-4419
334/241-9532

University of Alabama
Tuscaloosa, AL 35487-0388
205/348-6330

University of Alabama at Huntsville
Huntsville, AL 35899
205/890-6750

University of South Alabama
Mobile, AL 36688-0002
334/460-7718

Wallace Community College, Aviation Campus
Ozark, AL 36361-1209
334/774-5113, ext. 640

Wallace State Community College
Henceville, AL 35077-2000
205/352-8125

ALASKA

Alaska Pacific University
Anchorage, AK 99508
907/562-2337

University of Alaska, Fairbanks
Fairbanks, AK 99775
907/474-7522

University of Alaska, Southeast
Ketchican, AK 99901
907/225-6177

ARIZONA

Arizona Institute of Business and Technology
Phoenix, AZ 85033
602/849-7830

Central Arizona College
Coolidge, AZ 85228
520/426-4444

Cochise College
Douglas, AZ 85607
520/364-0350

Gate Way Community College
Phoenix, AZ 85034-1795
602/392-5194

ITT Technical Institute
Phoenix, AZ 85008
602/231-0871

Mohave Community College
Kingman, AZ 86401
520/757-4331

Northland Pioneer College
Holbrook, AZ 86025
520/537-2976, ext. 329

Ottawa University
Phoenix, AZ 85021
602/371-1188, ext. 168

Rio Salado College
Tempe, AZ 85281
602/517-8140

University of Phoenix
Phoenix, AZ 85044
602/966-5394

ARKANSAS

Arkansas State University - Beebe
Beebe, AR 72012
501/882-8280

Arkansas Tech University
Russellville, AR 72801-2222
501/968-0234

Garland County Community College
Hot Springs, AR 71913
501/760-4222

Harding University
Searcy, AR 72149-0001
501/279-4404

Mississippi County Community College
Blytheville, AR 72316
870/762-1020

University of Central Arkansas
Conway, AR 72035
501/450-5200

CALIFORNIA

Allan Hancock College
Santa Maria, CA 93454
805/922-6966, ext. 3407 or 3512

California State Polytechnic University
Pomona, CA 91768
909/ 869-2290

California State University, Bakersfield
Bakersfield, CA 93309
805/664-3420

California State University, Chico
Chico, CA 95929-0725
530/898-5712

California State University, Dominguez Hills
Carson, CA 90704-0005
310/243-3307

California State University, Fresno
Fresno, CA 93740-8026
209/278-2191

California State University at Hayward
Hayward, CA 94542
510/885-3716

California State University at Los Angeles
Los Angeles, CA 90032
213/343-2730

California State University at Stanislaus
Turlock, CA 95382
209/667-3256

Cogswell Polytechnical College
Sunnyvale, CA 94089
408/541-0100, ext. 131

Columbia College
Sonora, CA 95310
209/588-5234

De Anza College
Cupertino, CA 95014
408/864-8321

Diablo Valley College
Pleasant Hill, CA 94523
925/685-1230, ext. 330

Don Bosco Technical Institute
Rosemead, CA 91770-4299
626/301-6500, ext. 22

Golden Gate University
San Francisco, CA 94105
415/442-7200

Golden West College
Huntington Beach, CA 92647
714/895-8121

John F. Kennedy University
Orinda, CA 94563
510/258-2212

La Sierra University
Riverside, CA 92515
909/785-2006

Los Angeles Harbor College
Wilmington, CA 90744
310/522-8200

Menlo College
Atherton, CA 94027-4301
650/324-2347

Monterey Peninsula College
Monterey, CA 93940
408/645-1372

Mount St. Mary's College
Los Angeles, CA 90049
310/954-4010

National University
La Jolla, CA 92037
619/642-8181

Palomar College
San Marcos, CA 92069-1487
760/744-1150

Patten College
Oakland, CA 94601
510/533-8300

Point Loma Nazarene College
San Diego, CA 92106-2899
619/849-2548

San Diego State University
San Diego, CA 92182-7455
619/594-7800

University of La Verne
La Verne, CA 91750
909/593-3511, ext. 4007

University of Redlands
Redlands, CA 92374
909/793-2121, ext. 3234

University of San Francisco
San Francisco, CA 94117-1080
415/422-6143

COLORADO

Arapahoe Community College
Littleton, CO 80160
303/794-1550

Colorado Aero Tech
Broomfield, CO 80021
303/466-1714

Colorado Community College and Occupational Education System
Denver, CO 80204-2554
303/620-4000

Colorado State University
Fort Collins, CO 80523-8021
970/491-2712

Colorado Technical University
Colorado Springs, CO 80907
719/598-0200

Community College of Aurora
Aurora, CO 80231
303/360-4703

Community College of Denver
Denver, CO 80217-3363
303/556-2413

Morgan Community College
Fort Morgan, CO 80701
970/867-3081

Northeastern Junior College
Sterling, CO 80751
970/522-6600, ext. 6676

Pikes Peak Community College
Colorado Springs, CO 80906-5498
719/540-7225; 800/777-9446

Regis University
Denver, CO 80221-1099
303/458-1844

Trinidad State Junior College
Trinidad, CO 81082
719/846-5680

CONNECTICUT

Albertus Magnus College
New Haven, CT
203/773-8514

Charter Oak State College
Newington, CT 06111
860/666-4595, ext. 17

Eastern Connecticut State University
Willimantic, CT 06226
860/465-5286

Middlesex Community College
Middletown, CT 06457-4889
860/343-5719

Naugatuck Valley Community-Technical College
Waterbury, CT 06708
203/575-8083

Norwalk Community-Technical College
Norwalk, CT 06854
203/857-7035

Quinebaug Valley Community College
Danielson, CT 06239
860/774-1130

Sacred Heart University
Fairfield, CT 06432
203/371-7910

Southern Connecticut State University
New Haven, CT 06515
203/392-5656

University of New Haven
West Haven, CT 06516
203/934-7305

DELAWARE

Wesley College
Dover, DE 19901-3875
302/736-2439

DISTRICT OF COLUMBIA

Georgetown University
School for Summer & Continuing Education
Washington, DC 20057
202/687-5706

Southeastern University
Washington, DC 20024
202/488-8162

Strayer College
Washington, DC 20005
202/408-2424

Trinity College
Washington, DC 20017
202/884-9200

University of the District of Columbia
Washington, DC 20008
202/274-5100

FLORIDA

Barry University
Miami Shores, FL 33161
305/899-3143

Brevard Community College
Cocoa, FL 32922
407/634-3700

Broward Community College
Fort Lauderdale, FL 33301
954/761-7465

Chipola Junior College
Marianna, FL 32446
850/718-2397

Daytona Beach Community College
Daytona Beach, FL 32114
904/254-4414

Edison Community College
Fort Meyers, FL
941/489-9349

Embry-Riddle Aeronautical University
Extended Campus
Daytona Beach, FL 32114-3900
904/226-6961

Florida Community College at Jacksonville
Jacksonville, FL 32202
904/633-8359

Florida International University
North Miami, FL 33181
305/919-5669

Florida Metropolitan University System
Tampa College
Clearwater, FL 34619
813/725-2688

Florida Metropolitan University
Tampa College, West Hillsborough
Tampa, FL 33614
813/879-6000

Florida State University
Tallahassee, FL 32306-2480
850/644-5887

Jacksonville University
Jacksonville, FL 3221
904/745-7090

Jones College
Jacksonville, FL 32211
904/743-1122

Manatee Community College
Bradenton, FL 34206
941/755-1511, ext. 4200

Nova Southeastern University
Fort Lauderdale, FL 33314
954/262-8414

Palm Beach Community College
Lake Worth, FL 33461
561/439-8080

St. Petersburg Junior College
St. Petersburg, FL 33733
813/341-3170

GEORGIA

Albany State University
Albany, GA 31705
912/430-4605

Armstrong Atlantic State University
Savannah, GA 31419-1997
912/921-5432

Brenau University
Gainesville, GA 30501
770/534-6119

Coastal Georgia Community College
Bruswick, GA 31520-3644
912/262-3075

Columbus State University
Columbus, GA 31993
706/568-2237

Darton College
Albany, GA 31707-3098
912/430-6729

DeKalb Technical Institute
Clarkston, GA 30021
404/297-9522, ext. 1237

Emmanuel College
Franklin Springs, GA 30639
706/245-7226

Georgia State University
Atlanta, GA 30302-4044
404/651-3450

Oglethorpe University
Atlanta, GA 30319
404/364-8315

Shorter College
Marietta, GA 30067
770/989-5671

Valdosta State University
Valdosta, GA 31698
912/333-5791

HAWAII

Chaminade University of Honolulu
Honolulu, HI 96816
808/735-4722

Hawaii Pacific University
Honolulu, HI 96813
808/544-1129

IDAHO

Boise State University
Boise, ID 83725
208/385-1418

ILLINOIS

Barat College
Lake Forest, IL 60045
847/604-6275

Carl Sandburg College
Galesburg, IL 61401
309/341-5234

College of DuPage
Glen Ellyn, IL 60137
630/942-2481

Concordia University
River Forest, IL 60305
708/209-3535

DeVry Institutes of Technology
Oakbrook Terrace, IL 60181
630/571-7700

Eastern Illinois University
Charleston, IL 61920
217/581-5618

Governors State University
University Park, IL 60466
708/534-4092

Greenville College
Greenville, IL 62246
618/664-2800, ext. 4593

Illinois Community College System
Springfield, IL 62701-1874
217/785-5003

Illinois Valley Community College
Oglesby, IL 61348-9692
815/224-2720, ext. 437

John Wood Community College
Quincy, IL 62301
217/224-6500, ext. 4336

Joliet Junior College
Joliet, IL 60431
815/729-9020, ext. 2245

Kaskaskia College
Centralia, IL 62801
618-532-1981

Kishwaukee College
Malta, IL 60150-9699
815/825-2086, ext. 218

Lake Land Community College
Mattoon, IL 61938
217/234-5378

Lewis and Clark Community College
Godfrey, IL 62035
618/466-3411, ext. 5000

Lewis University
Romeoville, IL 60446
815/838-0500, ext. 5212 or 800/897-9000, ext. 5250

MacMurray College
Jacksonville, IL 62650
217/479-7014

McKendree College
Lebanon, IL 62254
618/537-6817

Midstate College
Peoria, IL 61614
309/692-4092

North Park University
Chicago, IL 60625
773/244-5767

Olivet Nazerene University
Kankakee, IL 60901
815/939-5201

Parkland College
Champaign, IL 61821
217/351-2482

University of Illinois at Springfield
Springfield, IL
217/786-6626

Waubonsee Community College
Sugar Grove, IL 60554-9799
630/466-7900, ext. 0373

Western Illinois University
Macomb, IL 61455
309/298-1929

INDIANA

Bethel College
Mishawaka, IN 46545
219/257-3302

Calumet College of Saint Joseph
Whiting, IN 46394
219/473-4211

Franklin College of Indiana
Franklin, IN 46131
317/736-8441

Goshen College
Goshen, IN 46526
219/535-7515

Huntington College
Huntington, IN 46750
219/359-4160

Indiana Institute of Technology
Fort Wayne, IN 46803
219/422-5561, ext. 276

Indiana University
Bloomington, IN 47405
812/855-3341

Indiana University-Purdue University at Indianapolis
Indianapolis, IN 46202-5143
317/274-1505

Ivy Tech State College
Indianapolis, IN 46202
317/921-4936

Ivy Tech State College
Madison, IN 47250-1881
812/265-2580

Ivy Tech State College, Northwest
Gary, IN 46409
219/981-1111

Ivy Tech State College, Sellersburg
Sellersburg, IN 47172
812/246-3301

Ivy Tech State College, South Bend
South Bend, IN 46619
219/289-7001

Ivy Tech State College, Terre Haute
Terre Haute, IN 47802
812/299-1121, ext. 203

Marian College
Indianapolis, IN 46222-1997
317/955-6041

Oakland City University
Oakland, IN 47660
812/749-1238

St. Mary-of-the-Woods College
St. Mary-of-the-Wood, IN 47876
812/535-5181

Tri-State University at South Bend
South Bend, IN 46601
219/234-4810

University of Indianapolis
Indianapolis, IN 46227
317/788-3262

University of St. Francis
Fort Wayne, IN 46808
219/434-3294

Valparaiso University
Valparaiso, IN 46383
219/464-5212

IOWA

Briar Cliff College
Sioux City, IA 51104
712/279-5446

Buena Vista University
Storm Lake, IA 50588
712/749-2634

Clarke College
Dubuque, IA 52001
319/588-6354

Clinton Community College
Clinton, IA 52732
319/244-7006

Des Moines Area Community College
Ankeny, IA 50021
515/964-6332

Graceland College
Lamoni, IA 50140
515/784-5111

Iowa Lakes Community College
Estherville, IA 51334
712/362-7922

Iowa Wesleyan College
Mt. Pleasant, IA 52641
319/385-6227

Iowa Western Community College
Council Bluffs, IA 51502
712/325-3400

Kirkwood Community College
Cedar Rapids, IA 52406
319/398-5603

Loras College
Dubuque, IA 52004-0178
319/588-7139

Marycrest International University
Davenport, IA 52804
319/326-9219

Muscatine Community College
Muscatine, IA 52761
319/288-6004

St. Ambrose University
Davenport, IA 52803
319/333-6477

Scott Community College
Bettendorf, IA 52722
319/441-4001

Simpson College
Indianola, IA 50125
515/961-1644

Southwestern Community College
Creston, IA 50801
515/782-7081

University of Dubuque
Dubuque, IA 52001
319/589-3270

University of Iowa
Iowa City, IA 52242
319/335-1549

University of Northern Iowa
Cedar Falls, IA 50614-0006
319/273-2244

Upper Iowa University
Fayette, IA 52142
319/425-5283

Wartburg College
Waverly, IA 50677
319/352-8272

KANSAS

Allen County Community College
Iola, KS 66749
316/365-5116, ext. 221

Baker University
School of Professional & Graduate Studies
Overland Park, KS 66211
913/491-4432

Barclay College
Havilad, KS 67059
316/862-5252

Benedictine College
Atchison, KS 66002
913/367-5340, ext. 2550

Bethel College
North Newton, KS 67117
316/283-2500

Colby Community College
Colby, KS 67701
785/462-3984

Cowley County Community College
Arkansas City, KS 67005
316/442-0430

Donnelly College
Kansas City, KS 66102
913/621-6070

Emporia State University
Emporia, KS 66801
316/341-5171

Fort Hays State University
Hays, KS 67601
785/628-4531

Garden City Community College
Garden City, KS 67846
316/276-9597

Independence Community College
Independence, KS 67301
316/331-4100, ext 4295

Kansas City Kansas Community College
Kansas City, KS 66112
913/334-1100, ext. 201

Kansas Newman College
Wichita, KS
316/942-4291, ext. 121

Ottawa University
Ottawa, KS 66067
785/242-5200

Pittsburg State University
Pittsburg, KS 66762
316/235-4253

Pratt Community College
Pratt, KS 67124
316/672-9800

St. Mary College
Leavenworth, KS 66048
913/682-5151

Seward County Community College
Liberal, KS 67905-1137
316/629-2616

Southwestern College
Winfield, KS 67156-2499
316/221-8208

Sterling College
Sterling, KS 67579-0098
316/278-2173

Tabor College
Hillsboro, KS 67063
316/947-3121

KENTUCKY

Bellarmine College
Louisville, KY 40205
502/452-8133

Brescia College
Owensboro, KY 42301
502/686-4248

Cumberland College
Williamsburg, KY 40769
606/539-4316

Hazard Community College
Hazard, KY 41701
606/436-5721

Hopkinsville Community College
Hopkinsville, KY 42241-2100
502/886-3921, ext. 100

Kentucky Wesleyan College
Owensboro, KY 42301
502/926-3111

Owensboro Community College
Owensboro, KY 42303
606/336-5082

Prestonsburg Community College
Prestonsburg, KY 41653
606/886-3863

St. Catherine College
St. Catherine, KY 40061
606/336-5082, ext. 213

Spalding University
Louisville, KY 40203-2188
502/585-7110

Thomas More College
Fort Mitchell, KY 41017
606/341-4554

LOUISIANA

The American College of Prehospital Medicine
New Orleans, LA 70130-1135
800/735-ACPM

Delgado Community College
New Orleans, LA 70119
504/483-4143

Our Lady of Holy Cross College
New Orleans, LA
504/394-7744

University of New Orleans
New Orleans, LA 70148-2135
504/280-6595

MAINE

Casco Bay College
Portland, ME 04101
207/772-0196

Central Maine Technical College
Auburn, ME 04210
207/784-2385

Eastern Maine Technical College
Bangor, ME 04401
207/941-4623

Husson College
Bangor, ME 04401
207/947-1121
1/800/4Husson

Kennebec Valley Technical College
Fairfield, ME 04937-1367
207/453-5000

Maine College of Art
Portland, ME 04101
207/775-5098

Maine Maritime Academy
Castine, ME 04420
207/326-2426

Northern Maine Technical College
Presque Isle, ME 04769
207/768-2792

St. Joseph's College
Standish, ME 04084
207/892-6766

Southern Maine Technical College
South Portland, ME 04106
207/767-9520

University of Maine at Farmington
Farmington, ME 04938
207/778-2050

University of Maine at Fort Kent
Fort Kent, ME 44743
207/834-7521

University of Maine at Presque Isle
Presque, ME 04769
207/768-9525

University of Southern Maine
Portland, ME 04104-9300
207/780-4683

Washington County Technical College
Calais, ME 04619
207/454-1002

MARYLAND

Allegany College of Maryland
Maryland, MD 21502
301/784-5211

Anne Arundel Community College
Arnold, MD 21012
410/541-2243

Catonsville Community College
Catonsville, MD 21228
410/455-4380

Charles County Community College
LaPlata, MD 20646
301/934-2251, ext. 7523

Chesapeake College
Wye Mills, MD 21679
410/827-5846

College of Notre Dame of Maryland
Baltimore, MD 21210
410/532-5320

Columbia Union College
Takoma Park, MD 20912
301/891-4119

Dundalk Community College
Baltimore, MD 21222
410/285-9802

Frederick Community College
Frederick, MD 21702
301/846-2492

Garrett Community College
McHenry, MD 21541
301/387-3059

Griggs University
Silver Spring, MD 20904
301/680-6586

Hagerstown Junior College
Hagerstown, MD 21742-6590
301/790-2800

Harford Community College
Bel Air, MD 21015-1698
410/836-4139

Howard Community College
Columbia, MD 21044
410/772-4856

Johns Hopkins University
Baltimore, MD 21218-2691
410/516-6053

Maryland College of Art & Design
Silver Spring, MD 20902
301/649-4454

Montgomery College
Rockville, MD 20850
301/279-5000

Montgomery College, Takoma Park Campus
Takoma Park, MD 20912
301/650-1501

Prince George's Community College
Largo, MD 20774-2199
301/322-0801

Towson State University
Towson, MD 21252-0001
410/830-2078

University of Baltimore
Baltimore, MD 21201
410/837-4796

University of Maryland University College
College Park, MD 20742
301/985-7289

MASSACHUSETTS

Anna Maria College
Paxton, MA 01612-1198
508/849-3359

Assumption College
Worcester, MA 01609
508/767-7355

Bunker Hill Community College
Boston, MA 02129
617/228-2000

Cambridge College
Cambridge, MA 02138
617/868-1000, ext. 181

Cape Cod Community College
West Barnstable, MA 02668
508/362-2131, ext. 4709

College of Our Lady of the Elms
Chicopee, MA 01013
413/598-8520

Fisher College
Boston, MA 02116
617/236-8829

Greenfield Community College
Greenfield, MA 01301
413/774-3131

Holyoke Community College
Holyoke, MA 01040
413/552-2550

Massasoit Community College
Brockton, MA 02402
508/855-9100

Nichols College
Dudley, MA 01571
508/943-1560

North Shore Community College
Danvers, MA 01923-0340
508/762-4000, ext. 5429

Quinsigamond Community College
Worcester, MA 01606
508/854-4380

University of Massachusetts, Amherst
Amherst, MA 01003
413/545-0222

MICHIGAN

Central Michigan University
Mt. Pleasant, MI 48859
517/774-4456

Cornerstone College
Grand Rapids, MI 49525
616/222-1431

Davenport College of Business
Grand Rapids, MI 49503
616/732-1202

Delta College
University Center, MI 48710
517/686-9291

Gogebic Community College
Ironwood, MI 49938
906/932-4231, ext. 212

Kalamazoo Valley Community College
Kalamazoo, MI 49003-4070
616/372-5205

Kellogg Community College
Battle Creek, MI 49017-3397
616/965-3931

Northwood University
Midland, MI 48640
517/837-4455

Siena Heights College
Adrian, MI 49221
517/264-7122

MINNESOTA

Alexandria Technical College
Alexandria, MN 56308
320/762-4470

Anoka Ramsey Community College
Coon Rapids, MN 55433
612/422-3424

Century Community and Technical College
White Bear Lake, MN 55110
612/779-3288

College of St. Catherine
St. Paul, MN 55105
612/690-6531

College of St. Scholastica
Duluth, MN 55811-4199
218/723-6562

Concordia University
St. Paul, MN 55104-5494
612/641-8211

Metropolitan State University
St. Paul, MN 55101
612/772-7776

Minnesota West Community and Technical College
Worthington, MN 56187
507-372-3406

North Central Bible College
Minneapolis, MN 55404
612/343-4788

North Hennepin Community College
Minneapolis, MN 55445
612/424-0713

Northland Community College
Thief River Falls, MN 56701
218/681-0701

Ridgewater College
Willmar, MN 56201
320/231-2917

St. Cloud State University
St. Cloud, MN 56301-4498
320/255-2111

St. Cloud Technical College
St. Cloud, MN 56303
320/654-5075

Saint Mary's University
Minneapolis, MN 55404-4403
612/874-9877

MISSISSIPPI

Alcorn State University
Lorman, MS 39096
601/877-6143

Belhaven College
Jackson, MS 39211
601/968-8880

Delta State University
Cleveland, MS 38733
601/846-4010

Hinds Junior College District
Raymond, MS 39154
601/857-3280

Jones County Junior College
Ellisville, MS 39437
601/477-4025

Mississippi Gulf Cost Community College
Perkinston, MS 39573
601/928-6280

Mississippi State University
Mississippi State, MS 39759
601/325-3742

Mississippi Valley State University
Itta Bena, MS 38941
601/254-3435

William Carey College
Hattiesburg, MS 39401-5499
601/582-6196

MISSOURI

Central Missouri State University
Warrensburg, MO 64093
660/543-4811

Columbia College
Columbia, MO 65216
573/875-7200

Culver-Stockton College
Canton, MO 63435
217/231-6339

Jefferson College
Hillsboro, MO 63050
314/797-3000, ext. 210

Lindenwood College
St. Charles, MO 63301
314/949-2000

Maple Woods Community College
Kansas City, MO 64119
816/436-3100

Maryville University of St. Louis
St. Louis, MO 63141-7299
314/529-9370

Moberly Junior College
Moberly, MO 65270
660/263-4110, ext. 282

North Central Missouri College
Trenton, MO 64683
660/359-3948, ext. 400

Park College
Parkville, MO 64152-3792
816/741-2000

St. Louis University
St. Louis, MO 63103
314/977-2330

State Fair Community College
Sedalia, MO 65301
660/530-5800

Stephens College
Columbia, MO 65215
573/876-7277

Webster University
St. Louis, MO 63119
314/968-6910

MONTANA

Flathead Valley Community College
Kalispell, MT 59901
406/756-3846

Fort Peck Community College
Poplar, MT 59255
406/768-5551

Montana State University, Billings
Billings, MT 59101-0298
406/657-2158

Montana State University, Bozeman
Bozeman, MT 59717-2180
406/994-6617

Montana State University, Northern
Havre, MT 59501
406/265-3703

Montana Tech College of Technology
Butte, MT 59701
406/496-4689

Montana Tech of the University of Montana
Butte, MT 59701
406/496-4689

Rocky Mountain College
Billings, MT 59102
406/657-1030

University of Great Falls
Great Falls, MT 59405
406/791-5200

University of Montana
Missoula, MT 59812-1265
406/243-0211

NEBRASKA

Central Community College
Grand Island, NE 68802-4903
308/389-6305

Chadron State College
Chadron, NE 69337
308/432-6221

Clarkson College
Omaha, NE 68131-2739
800/647-5500

College of St. Mary
Omaha, NE 68124
402/399-2441

Creighton University
Omaha, NE 68178
402/280-2702

Dana College
Blair, NE 68008
402/426-7209

Doane College
Lincoln, NE 68504
402/466-4774

Grace University
Omaha, NE 68108
402/449-2800

Midland Lutheran College
Fremont, NE 68025
402/721-5480

Nebraska Christian College
Norfolk, NE 68701
402/379-5000

Nebraska College of Technical Agriculture
Curtis, NE 69025
308/367-4124

Northeast Community College
Norfolk, NE 68702-0469
402/644-0524

Southeast Community College
Linclon, NE 68520
402/437-2619

University of Nebraska, Omaha
Omaha, NE 68182-0331
402/554-2347

Wayne State College
Wayne, NE 68787
402/375-7239

York College
York, NE 68467-2699
402/363-5677 or 5678

NEVADA

Career College of Northern Nevada
Reno, NV 89502
702/856-2266

Great Basin College
Elko, NV 89801
702/753-2272

Truckee Meadows Community College
Reno, NV 89512
702/673-7042

Western Nevada Community College
Carson City, NV 89703
702/887-3138

NEW HAMPSHIRE

College for Lifelong Learning
Concord, NH 03301
603/228-3000

McIntosh College
Dover, NH 03820
603/742-1234

New Hampshire College
Manchester, NH 03106
603/668-2211, ext. 2113

Rivier College
Nashua, NH 03060
603/888-1311

White Pines College
White Pines, NH
603/887-4401

NEW JERSEY

Atlantic Community College
Mays Landing, NJ 08330
609/625-1111

Berkeley College
West Pagebrun, NJ 07424
973/278-5400

Bloomfield College
Bloomfield, NJ 07003
201/748-9000, ext. 230

Brookdale Community College
Lincroft, NJ 07738
732/224-2368

Caldwell College
Caldwell, NJ 07006
973/228-4424

Centenary College
Hackettstown, NJ 07840
908/852-1400

College of Saint Elizabeth
Morristown, NJ 07960-6989
973/290-4601

Cumberland County College
Vineland, NJ 08362-0517
609/691-8600, ext. 201

Fairleigh Dickinson University
Teaneck, NJ 07666
201/692-7080

Georgian Court College
Lakewood, NJ 08701-2697
732/364-8218, ext. 249

Gloucester County College
Sewell, NJ 08080
609/468-5000

Jersey City State College
Jersey City, NJ 07305
201/200-3005

Mercer County Community College
Trenton, NJ 08690
609/586-4800, ext. 3240

Monmouth University
West Long Beach, NJ 07764
732/571-4495

Ocean County College
Toms River, NJ 08754-2001
732/255-0400, ext. 2018

Ramapo College of New Jersey
Mahwah, NJ 07430
201/529-6482

Rider University
Lawrenceville, NJ 08648
609/896-5033

St. Peter's College
Jersey City, NJ 07306-5997
201/915-9022

Salem Community College
Carneys Point, NJ 08069
609/351-2642

Thomas Edison State College
Trenton, NJ 08608
609/633-6271

William Paterson University
Wayne, NJ 07470
973/720-3093, ext. 2121

NEW MEXICO

College of Santa Fe
Santa Fe, NM 87505
505/473-6317

College of the Southwest
Hobbs, NM 88240
505/392-6561

San Juan College
Farmington, NM 87402
505/599-0300

University of New Mexico
Albuquerque, NM 87131
505/277-2446

NEW YORK

Adirondack Community College
Queensbury, NY 12804
518/743-2275

Broome Community College
Binghamton, NY 13901
607/778-5138

Buffalo State College
Buffalo, NY 14222
716/878-4017

Cayuga County Community College
Auburn, NY 13021
315/255-1743

Clinton Community College
Plattsburgh, NY 12901
518/562-4100

College of Staten Island
Staten Island, NY 10314
718/982-2012

Corning Community College
Corning, NY 14830
607/962-9220

Dominican College of Blauvelt
Orangeburg, NY 10962
914/359-7800

Dowling College
Long Island, NY 11769-1999
516/244-3036

Dutchess Community College
Poughkeepsie, NY 12601
914/431-8099

Elmira College
Elmira, NY 14901
607/735-1825

Erie Community College
Buffalo, NY 14203
716/851-1100

Five Towns College
Dix Hills, NY 11746
516/424-7000

Fulton-Montgomery Community College
Johnstown, NY 12095
518/762-5302

Hartwick College
Oneonta, NY 13820
607/431-4460

Herbert H. Lehman College
Bronx, NY 10468
718/960-8104

Hilbert College
Hamburg, NY 14075
716/649-7900, ext. 341

Hudson Valley Community College
Troy, NY 12180-1573
518/270-1573

Jefferson Community College
Watertown, NY 13601
315/786-2230

John Jay College of Criminal Justice
New York, NY 10019
212/237-8878

Keuka College
Keuka Park, NY 14478
315/536-4411, ext. 5204

Kingsborough Community College
Brooklyn, NY 11235
718/368-5136

Laboratory Institute of Merchandising
New York, NY 10022
212/752-1530

Long Island University
C.W. Post Campus
Brookville, NY 11548
516/299-3230

Long Island University
Center Brooklyn Campus
Brooklyn, NY 11201
718/488-1292

Long Island University
Center Southampton Campus
Southampton, NY 11968
516/287-8341

Mater Dei College
Ogdensburg, NY 13669
315/393-5930, ext. 426

Medaille College
Buffalo, NY 14214-2695
716/884-3281

Monroe Community College
Rochester, NY 14623
716/292-2243

Mount St. Mary College
Newburgh, NY 12550
914/569-3258

Nassau Community College
Garden City, NY 11530-6793
516/572-7205

Nazareth College of Rochester
Rochester, NY 14618-3790
716/389-2873

New School University
New York, NY 10011
212/229-5119

Pace University
Pleasantville, NY 10570
914/773-3424

Pace University, Midtown Center
New York, NY 10176-0899
212/346-1770

Regents College
Albany, NY 12230
518/474-3703

Roberts Wesleyan College
Rochester, NY 14624-1997
716/594-6220

Rochester Institute of Technology
Rochester, NY 14623-0887
716/475-2607

St. Francis College
Brooklyn, NY 11201
718/489-5340

St. John Fisher College
Rochester, NY 14618
716/385-8015

St. Joseph's College
Patchogue, NY 11772
516/447-3257

St. Thomas Aquinas College
Sparkill, NY 10976-1050
914/398-4012

Skidmore College
University Without Walls
Saratoga Springs, NY 12866
518/584-5450

SUNY College at Cortland
Cortland, NY 13045
607/753-4712

SUNY College at Oswego
Oswego, NY 13126
315/341-3613

SUNY College of Technology at Morrisville
Morrisville, NY 13408
315/684-6270

SUNY Empire State College
Saratoga Springs, NY 12866
518/587-2100

SUNY Institute of Technology at Utica-Rome
Utica, NY 13504
800/786-9832

SUNY at Stony Brook
Stony Brook, NY 11794-1909
516/632-7028

Suffolk County Community College
Selden, NY 11784
516/451-4035

Tompkins Cortland Community College
Dryden, NY 13053
607/844-8211

Trocaire College
Buffalo, NY 14220-2094
716/827-2425

Ulster County Community College
Stone Ridge, NY 12484
914/687-5022

Villa Maria College of Buffalo
Buffalo, NY 14225
716/896-0700

Westchester Community College
Valhalla, NY 10595
914/785-6931

NORTH CAROLINA

Belmont Abbey College
Belmont, NC 28012
704/825-6732

Campbell University
Buie's Creek, NC 27506
910/893-1211

Chowan College
Murfreesboro, NC 27855
919/398-6280, 6281

Cleveland Technical College
Shelby, NC 28152
704/484-4099

Craven Community College
New Bern, NC 28562
919/638-4131

East Coast Bible College
Charlotte, NC 28214
704/394-2307

Fayetteville Technical Community College
Fayetteville, NC 28303
910/497-1112

Greensboro College
Greensboro, NC 27401-1875
336/272-7102, ext. 209

Isothermal Community College
Spindale, NC 28160
704/286-3636, ext. 238

John Wesley College
High Point, NC 27265
336/889-2262

Louisburg College
Louisburg, NC 27549-2399
919/496-2521

Mars Hill College
Mars Hill, NC 28754
704/689-1141

Meredith College
Raleigh, NC 27607
919/829-8593

Mitchell Community College
Statesville, NC 28677
704/878-3200

Mount Olive College
Mount Olive, NC 28365
919/658-7165

North Carolina Wesleyan College
Rocky Mount, NC 27804
919/985-5123

Pfeiffer University
Misenheimer, NC 28109
704/463-1360, ext. 2057

Rockingham Community College
Wentworth, NC 27375-0038
910/342-4261, ext. 137

Rowan-Cabarrus Community College
Salisbury, NC 28145-1595
704/637-0760, ext. 214

Saint Andrew's Presbyterian College
Laurinburg, NC 28352
910/277-5221

Sand Hills Community College
Pinehurst, NC 28387
910/692-6185

Surry Community College
Dobson, NC 27017
919/386-8121

Vance-Granville Community College
Henderson, NC 27536
919/492-2061

Wilson Technical Community College
Wilson, NC 27893
919/291-1195

Wingate University
Wingate, NC 28174
704/233-8000

NORTH DAKOTA

North Dakota State College of Science
Wahpeton, ND 58076
701/671-2203

University of Mary
Bismrack, ND 58504-9652
701/255-7500

University of North Dakota
Grand Forks, ND 58202-8357
701/777-3821

University of North Dakota
Williston, ND 58802-1326
701/774-4200

Valley City State University
Valley City, ND 58072
701/845-7431

OHIO

Antioch College/Antioch University
Yellow Springs, OH 45387
937/767-6328

Ashland University
Ashland, OH 44805
419/289-5030

Bluffton College
Bluffton, OH 45817
419/358-3311

Bowling Green State University
Bowling Green, OH 43403-0020
419/372-2915

Capital University
Columbus, OH 43209
614/236-6327

Cincinnati Bible College & Seminary
Cincinnati, OH 45204
513/244-8171

Cleveland State University
Cleveland, OH 44118
216/523-7244

Cuyahoga Community College
Cleveland, OH 44115
216/987-4778

Cuyahoga Community College, Eastern Campus
Warrensville Township, OH 44122
216/987-2013

David N. Myers College
Cleveland, OH 44115
216/523-3824

Davis College
Toledo, OH 43623
419/473-2700

Edison Community College
Piqua, OH 45356
937/778-8600

Franklin University
Columbus, OH 43215-5399
614/341-6357

Heidleberg College
Tiffin, OH 44883
419/448-2090

Kent State University
Kent, OH 44242-0001
330/672-9292

Lake Erie College
Painesville, OH 44077
440/639-7825

Lakeland Community College
Kirtland, OH 44094
216/953-7118

Lorain County Community College
Elyria, OH 44035
440/365-5222

Lourdes College
Sylvania, OH 43560-2898
419/885-3211

Malone College
Canton, OH 44709
330/471-0800

North Central Technical College
Mansfield, OH 44901
419/755-4800

Northwestern College
Lima, OH 45805
419/998-3163

Ohio University
Athens, OH 45701
614/593-4211

Otterbein College
Westerville, OH 43081
614/823-1154

Shawnee State University
Portsmouth, OH 45662
614/355-2593

Sinclair Community College
Dayton, OH 45402
937/512-2940

Southern State Community College
Hillsboro, OH 45133
937/393-3431, ext. 2615

Terra Community College
Fremont, OH 43420
419/334-8400

The Union Institute
Cincinnati, OH 45206
513/861-6400

The University of Findlay
Findlay, OH 45840
419/424-4556

Tiffin University
Tiffin, OH 44883
419/447-6442

University of Cincinnati
College of Evening & Continuing Education
Cincinnati, OH 45221-0146
513/556-9192

Urbana University
Urbana, OH 43078
937/484-1316

Washington State Community College
Marietta, OH 45750
614/374-8716

Wilmington College
Wilmington, OH 45177
937/382-6661

Wright State University
Dayton, OH 45435
937/775-5588

Xavier University
Cincinnati, OH 45207
513/745-3358

OKLAHOMA

Bartlesville Wesleyan College
Bartlesville, OK 74006
918/335-6200

Cameron University
Lawton, OK 73505
405/581-2288

Mid-America Bible College
Oklahoma City, OK 73170
405/697-3800

Northeastern Oklahoma A&M College
Miami, OK 74354
918/540-6211

Northeastern State University
Tahlequah, OK 74653
918/456-5511

Northern Oklahoma College
Tonkawa, OK 74653-0310
580/628-6201

Oklahoma Baptist University
Shawnee, OK 74801
405/878-2025

Oklahoma City Community College
Oklahoma City, OK 73159
405/682-7512, ext. 7512

Oklahoma State University
Stillwater, OK 74078
405/744-7679

Oklahoma State University, Oklahoma City
Oklahoma City, OK 73106
405/956-3252

Oklahoma State University, Ormulgee
Ormulgee, OK 74447
918/756-6211

Oral Roberts University
Tulsa, OK 74133
918/495-6549

Phillips University
Enid, OK 73701
580/548-2296

Rogers University
Claremore, OK 74017
918/343-7539

Rose State College
Midwest City, OK 73110-2799
405/733-7300

Seminole State College
Seminole, OK 74868
405/382-9950

Southeastern Oklahoma State University
Durant, OK 74701-0609
580/924-0121

Southern Nazarene University
Bethany, OK 73008
405/491-6386

Southwestern Oklahoma State University
Weatherford, OK 73096
580/774-3777

The University of Oklahoma
Norman, OK 73037-0001
405/325-2252

Tulsa Community College
Tulsa, OK 74135
918/595-7526

University of Oklahoma Health Sciences Center
Oklahoma City, OK 73190
405/271-2347

University of Science and Arts of Oklahoma
Chickasha, OK 73018
405/224-3140

OREGON

Concordia University
Portland, OR 97211
503/493-6512

Northwest Christian College
Eugene, OR 97401
541/684-7201

Rogue Community College
Grants Pass, OR 97527
541/471-3500, ext. 317

Southwestern Oregon Community College
Coos Bay, OR 97420
541/888-7246

Western Baptist College
Salem, OR 97301
503/375-7590 or 800/764-1383

Western Oregon University
Monmouth, OR 97361
503/838-8180

PANAMA

Panama Canal College
APO AA 34002
507/272-3107

PENNSYLVANIA

Allentown College of St. Francis DeSales
Center Valley, PA 18034
610/282-1100, ext. 1342

Alvernia College
Reading, PA 19607
610/796-8201

Cabrini College
Radnor, PA 19087-3698
610/902-8302

Clarion University of Pennsylvania
Clarion, PA 16214
814/226-2000

Community College of Allegheny County
Pittsburgh, PA 15233-1895
412/237-3185

Delaware County Community College
Media, PA 19063-1094
610/359-5043

Eastern College
St. Davids, PA 19087
610/341-5854

Harrisburg Area Community College
Harrisburg, PA 17110
717/780-2370

Immaculata College
Immaculata, PA 19087-0300
610/647-4400, ext. 3235

King's College
Wilkes-Barre, PA 18711
717/208-5970

Lackawanna Junior College
Scranton, PA 18509
717/961-7840

Lancaster Bible College
Lancaster, PA 17601
717/560-8258

LaSalle University
Philadelphia, PA 19141
215/951-1020

Lehigh Carbon Community College
Schnecksville, PA 18078-2598
610/799-1195

Muhlenberg College
Allentown, PA 18104
610/821-3300

Neumann College
Aston, PA 19014-1298
610/558-5608

Pennsylvania College of Technology
Williamsport, PA 17701
717/326-3761

Pennsylvania Institute of Technology
Media, PA 19063
610/565-7900

Pennsylvania State University
University Park, PA 16802
814/865-4700

Point Park College
Pittsburgh, PA 15222
412/392-3907

Reading Area Community College
Reading, PA 19601
610/373-1525

St. Francis College of Pennsylvania
Loretto, PA 15940
814/472-3100

Seton Hill College
Greensburg, PA 15601
412/838-4218

Thiel College
Greenville, PA 16125
724/589-2110

University of Scranton, A Jesuit University
Scranton, PA 18510-4592
717/941-7580

Valley Forge Christian College
Pheonixville, PA 19460
610/935-0450

Westmoreland County Community College
Youngwood, PA 15697
412/925-4212

PUERTO RICO

Humacao University College, UPR
Humacao, PR 00791-4300
787/850-9374

RHODE ISLAND

Community College of Rhode Island
Warwick, RI 02886-1807
401/825-2147

Johnson and Wales College
Providence, RI 02903
401/598-1841

Providence College School of Continuing Education
Providence, RI 02918
401/865-1487

Rhode Island College
Providence, RI 02809
401/456-8234

Roger Williams University
Bristol, RI 02809
401/254-3062

Salve Regina University
Newport, RI 02840
401/847-6650

SOUTH CAROLINA

Claflin College
Orangeburg, SC 29115
803/535-5244

Coker College
Hartsville, SC 29550
803/383-8022

College of Charleston
Charleston, SC 29424
803/953-5527

Limestone College
Gaffney, SC 29340
864/488-4540

Midlands Technical College
Columbia, SC 29902
803/738-7699

Newberry College
Newberry, SC 29108
803/321-5112

Orangeburg - Calhoun Technical College
Orangeburg, SC 29118
803/535-1220

Southern Wesleyan University
Central, SC 29630-1020
846/639-2453, ext. 388

Spartanburg Technical College
Spartanburg, SC 29305-4386
864/591-3613

Technical College of the Lowcountry
Beaufort, SC 29901
803/525-8247

Trident Technical College
Charleston, SC 29423-8067
803/574-3277

University of South Carolina, Beaufort
Beaufort, SC 29902
803/522-7497

Williamsburg Technical College
Kingstree, SC 29556
803/354-2021

SOUTH DAKOTA

Huron University
Huron, SD 57350
605/352-8721

Kilian Community College
Sioux Falls, SD 57104-6014
605/336-1711

Mount Marty College
Yankton, SD 57078
605/668-1515

National American University
Rapid City, SD 57701
605/394-4990

Northern State University
Aberdeen, SD 57401
605/626-2012

TENNESSEE

Austin Peay State University
Clarksville, TN 37044-4448
931/648-7121

Bethel College
McKenzie, TN 38201
901/352-4003

Carson-Newman College
Jefferson City, TN 37760
423/471-3240

Chattanooga State Technical Community College
Chattanooga, TN 37402
423/697-2478

Dyersburg State Community College
Dyersburg, TN 38024
901/286-3300

Jackson State Community College
Jackson, TN 38301
901/425-2631

Lincoln Memorial University
Harrogate, TN 37752
423/869-6280

Martin Methodist College
Pulaski, TN 38478
615/363-9801

Milligan College
Milligan College, TN 37682
423/461-8782

Middle Tennessee State University
Murfreesboro, TN 37132
615/898-2111

Nashville State Technical Institute
Nashville, TN 37209
615/353-3217

Northeast State Technical Community College
Blountville, TN 37617-0246
423/323-0201

Roane State Community College
Harriman, TN 37748
423/882-4513

Shelby State Community College
Memphis, TN 38134
901/544-5025

Tennessee Wesleyan College
Athens, TN 37371
423/745-7504, ext. 5201

Tusculum College
Greenville, TN 37745
423/636-7300

Union University
Jackson, TN 38305
901/661-5040

University of Memphis
Memphis, TN 38152-6626
901/678-3995

University of Tennessee, Chattanooga
Chattanooga, TN 37401
423/755-4111

University of Tennessee, Martin
Martin, TN 38238
901/587-7053

TEXAS

Abilene Christian University
Abilene, TX 79699
915/674-2355

Angelina College
Lifkin, TX 75902
409/659-1301

College of The Mainland
Texas City, TX 77591
409/938-1211

Concordia University of Austin
Austin, TX 78705
512/452-7661

Dallas Baptist University
Dallas, TX 75211-9990
214/333-5122

Dallas County Community College District
Dallas, TX 75202
214/860-2129

Del Mar College
Corpus Christi, TX 78404
512/886-1248

El Centro College
Dallas, TX 75202
214/860-2019

El Paso County Community College District
El Paso, TX 79998
915/831-2204

Howard Payne University
Brownwood, TX 76801
915/649-8002

Lamar University
Beaumont, TX 77710
409/880-8400

Laredo Community College
Laredo, TX 78040
956/721-5177

Lubbock Christian University
Lubbock, TX 79407-2099
806/796-8800

MTI College of Business and Technology
Houston, TX 77036
713/974-7181

Odessa College
Odessa, TX 79764
915/335-6409

Our Lady of the Lake University
San Antonio, TX 78207-4689
210/431-3949

St. Edward's University
Austin, TX 78704-6489
512/448-8715

Saint Mary's University
San Antonio, TX 78228-8576
210/431-2299, ext. 1103

Southwest Texas State University
San Marcos, TX 78666
512/245-2115

Southwestern Adventist College
Keene, TX 76059
817/556-4721

Sul Ross State University
Alpine, TX 79832
915/837-8050

Texas Lutheran University
Seguin, TX 78155
830/372-8041

Texas State Technical College
Harlingen, TX 78550
956/425-0665

Texas State Technical College, Sweetwater
Sweetwater, TX 79556
915/235-7374

Texas A&M University, Corpus Christi
Corpus Christi, TX 78412
512/994-5952

Texas A&M University, Kingsville
Kingsville, TX 78363
512/593-2811

University of Central Texas
Killeen, TX 76540-1416
254/526-8262, ext. 261

University of North Texas
Denton, TX 76203-1277
940/565-2681

Vernon Regional Junior College
Vernon, TX 76384
940/552-6291

Wayland Baptist University
Plainview, TX 79072
806/296-4708

UTAH

College of Eastern Utah
Price, UT 84501
435/637-2120, ext. 5205

Hawthorne University
Salt Lake City, UT 84109-0327
801/485-1801

Snow College
Ephraim, UT 84627
435/283-7140

Salt Lake Community College
Salt Lake City, UT 84310
801/957-4249

Weber State University
Ogden, UT 84408-1137
801/626-7670

VERMONT

Community College of Vermont
Waterbury, VT 05676
802/241-1191

Norwich University
Northfield, VT 05663
802/468-6679

Vermont Technical College
Randolph Center, VT 05061
802/728-1302

VIRGINIA

American Military University
Manassas Park, VA 20111
703/330-5398

Averett College
Danville, VA 24541
804/791-5739

Blue Ridge Community College
Weyers Cave, VA 24486
540/234-9261

Central Virginia Community College
Lynchburg, VA 24502
804/832-7630

Christopher Newport University
Newport News, VA 23606
757/594-7155

George Mason University
Fairfax, VA 22030-4444
703/993-2302

Germanna Community College
Locust Grove, VA 22508
540/727-3027

James Madison University
Harrisonburg, VA 22807
540/568-6824

John Tyler Community College
Chester, VA 23831
804/796-4151

Liberty University
Lynchburg, VA 24506-1803
804/582-7709

Lynchburg College
Lynchburg, VA 24501-3199
804/544-8218

Mary Washington College
Fredericksburg, VA 22401
540/654-1038

Northern Virginia Community College
Annadale, VA 22003
703/323-3198

Paul D. Camp Community College
Franklin, VA 23851
757/569-6725

Piedmont Virginia Community College
Charlottesville, VA 22902
804/961-5411

Radford University
Radford, VA 24142
540/831-5952

Richard Bland College
Petersberg, VA 23805
804/862-6220

Shenandoah University
Winchester, VA 22601
540/665-4506

Southwest Virginia Community College
Richlands, VA 24641
540/964-7200

Thomas Nelson Community College
Hampton, VA 23670
757/825-3517

Tidewater Community College
Norfolk, VA 23510
757/822-1068

Virginia Wesleyan College
Norfolk, VA 23502
757/455-3386

WASHINGTON

City University
Renton, WA 98055
425/637-1010; 800/426-5596

Eastern Washington University
Cheney, WA 99004
509/359-2201

Pierce College
Tacoma, WA 98498-1999
253/964-6621

Renton Technical College
Renton, WA 98056
425/235-5840

Skagit Valley College, Mt. Vernon Campus
Mt. Vernon, WA 98273-5899
360/416-7600

University Colleges
Bellingham, WA 98227-5211
360/738-0336

Whitworth College
Spokane, WA 99251
509/777-4313

Yakima Valley Community College
Yakima, WA 98907-1647
509/574-4635

WEST VIRGINIA

Bluefield State College
Bluefield, WV 24701
304/327-4060

The College of West Virginia
Beckley, WV 25801
304/253-7351, ext. 448

Davis & Elkins College
Elkins, WV 26241
304/637-1261

Fairmont State College
Fairmont, WV 26554
304/367-4141

Glenville State College
Glenville, WV 26351
304/462-7361

Southern West Virginia Community
and Technical College
Mount Gay, WV 25637
304/792-7040

University of Charleston
Charleston, WV 25304
304/357-4737

West Liberty State College
West Liberty, WV 26074
304/336-8007

West Virginia State College
Institute, WV 25112-1000
304/766-3144

West Virginia University
Morgantown, WV 26506
304/293-5441

West Virginia Wesleyan College
Buckhannon, WV 26201
304/473-8470

WISCONSIN

Alverno College
Milwaukee, WI 53215
414/382-6029

Cardinal Stritch University
Milwaukee, WI 53217-3985
414/410-4092

Carroll College
Waukesha, WI 53186
414/524-7215

Gateway Technical College
Kensoha, WI 53144-1690
414/656-6929

Marian College
Fond du Lac, WI 54935
920/923-7618

Mount Senario College
Ladysmith, WI 54848
715/532-5511, ext. 121

Northland College
Ashland, WI 54806
715/682-1227

Silver Lake College
Manitowoc, WI 54220-9319
920/686-6231

Southwest Wisconsin Technical College
Fennimore, WI 53809
608/822-3262

Stratton College
Milwaukee, WI 53202
414/276-5200

University of Wisconsin, Platteville
Platteville, WI 53818
608/342-1321

University of Wisconsin, Stevens Point
Stevens Point, WI 54481
715/346-2441

WYOMING

Casper College
Casper, WY 82601
307/268-2110

Laramie County Community College
Cheyenne, WY 82001
307/778-1242

Western Wyoming Community College
Rock Springs, WY 82902
307/383-1639

Cooperating Colleges and Universities in Alphabetical Order

Cooperating Colleges and Universities in Alphabetical Order

Abilene Christian University
Abilene, TX 79699
915/674-2355

Adirondack Community College
Queensbury, NY 12804
518/743-2275

Alabama Aviation and Technical College
Ozark, AL 36361-1209
334/774-5113

Alaska Pacific University
Anchorage, AK 99508
907/562-2337

Albany State University
Albany, GA 31705
912/430-4605

Albertus Magnus College
New Haven, CT 06511
203/773-8514

Alcorn State University
Lorman, MS 39096
601/877-6143

Alexandria Technical College
Alexandria, MN 56308
320/762-4470

Allan Hancock College
Santa Maria, CA 93454
805/922-6966, ext. 3407 or 3512

Allegany College of Maryland
Maryland, MD 21502
301/784-5211

Allen County Community College
Iola, KS 66749
316/365-5116, ext. 221

Allentown College of St. Francis DeSales
Center Valley, PA 18034
610/282-1100, ext. 1342

Alvernia College
Reading, PA 19607
610/796-8201

Alverno College
Milwaukee, WI 53215
414/382-6029

The American College of Prehospital Medicine
New Orleans, LA 70130-1135
800/735-ACPM

American Military University
Manassas Park, VA 20111
703/330-5398

Angelina College
Lifkin, TX 75902
409/659-1301

Anna Maria College
Paxton, MA 01612-1198
508/849-3359

Anne Arundel Community College
Arnold, MD 21012
410/541-2243

Anoka Ramsey Community College
Coon Rapids, MN 55433
612/422-3424

Antioch College/Antioch University
Yellow Springs, OH 45387
937/767-6328

Arapahoe Community College
Littleton, CO 80160
303/794-1550

Arizona Institute of Business and Technology
Phoenix, AZ 85033
602/849-7830

Arkansas State University - Beebe
Beebe, AR 72012
501/882-8280

Arkansas Tech University
Russellville, AR 72801-2222
501/968-0234

Armstrong Atlantic State University
Savannah, GA 31419-1997
912/921-5432

Ashland University
Ashland, OH 44805
419/289-5030

Assumption College
Worcester, MA 01609
508/767-7355

Athens State College
Athens, AL 35611
205/233-8214

Atlantic Community College
Mays Landing, NJ 08330
609/625-1111

Austin Peay State University
Clarksville, TN 37044-4448
931/648-7121

Averett College
Danville, VA 24541
804/791-5739

Baker University
School of Professional & Graduate Studies
Overland Park, KS 66211
913/491-4432

Barat College
Lake Forest, IL 60045
847/604-6275

Barclay College
Havilad, KS 67059
316/862-5252

Barry University
Miami Shores, FL 33161
305/899-3143

Bartlesville Wesleyan College
Bartlesville, OK 74006
918/335-6200

Belhaven College
Jackson, MS 39211
601/968-8880

Bellarmine College
Louisville, KY 40205
502/452-8133

Belmont Abbey College
Belmont, NC 28012
704/825-6732

Benedictine College
Atchison, KS 66002
913/367-5340, ext. 2550

Berkeley College
West Pagebrun, NJ 07424
973/278-5400

Bethel College
Mishawaka, IN 46545
219/257-3302

Bethel College
North Newton, KS 67117
316/283-2500

Bethel College
McKenzie, TN 38201
901/352-4003

Bloomfield College
Bloomfield, NJ 07003
201/748-9000, ext. 230

Blue Ridge Community College
Weyers Cave, VA 24486
540/234-9261

Bluefield State College
Bluefield, WV 24701
304/327-4060

Bluffton College
Bluffton, OH 45817
419/358-3311

Boise State University
Boise, ID 83725
208/385-1418

Bowling Green State University
Bowling Green, OH 43403-0020
419/372-2915

Brenau University
Gainesville, GA 30501
770/534-6119

Brescia College
Owensboro, KY 42301
502/686-4248

Brevard Community College
Cocoa, FL 32922
407/634-3700

Briar Cliff College
Sioux City, IA 51104
712/279-5446

Brookdale Community College
Lincroft, NJ 07738
732/224-2368

Broome Community College
Binghamton, NY 13901
607/778-5138

Broward Community College
Fort Lauderdale, FL 33301
954/761-7465

Buena Vista University
Storm Lake, IA 50588
712/749-2634

Buffalo State College
Buffalo, NY 14222
716/878-4017

Bunker Hill Community College
Boston, MA 02129
617/228-2000

Cabrini College
Radnor, PA 19087-3698
610/902-8302

Caldwell College
Caldwell, NJ 07006
973/228-4424

California State Polytechnic University
Pomona, CA 91768
909/ 869-2290

California State University, Bakersfield
Bakersfield, CA 93309
805/664-3420

California State University, Chico
Chico, CA 95929-0725
530/898-5712

California State University, Dominguez Hills
Carson, CA 90704-0005
310/243-3307

California State University, Fresno
Fresno, CA 93740-8026
209/278-2191

California State University at Hayward
Hayward, CA 94542
510/885-3716

California State University at Los Angeles
Los Angeles, CA 90032
213/343-2730

California State University at Stanislaus
Turlock, CA 95382
209/667-3256

Calumet College of Saint Joseph
Whiting, IN 46394
219/473-4211

Cambridge College
Cambridge, MA 02138
617/868-1000, ext. 181

Cameron University
Lawton, OK 73505
405/581-2288

Campbell University
Buie's Creek, NC 27506
910/893-1211

Cape Cod Community College
West Barnstable, MA 02668
508/362-2131, ext. 4709

Capital University
Columbus, OH 43209
614/236-6327

Cardinal Stritch University
Milwaukee, WI 53217-3985
414/410-4092

Career College of Northern Nevada
Reno, NV 89502
702/856-2266

Carl Sandburg College
Galesburg, IL 61401
309/341-5234

Carroll College
Waukesha, WI 53186
414/524-7215

Carson-Newman College
Jefferson City, TN 37760
423/471-3240

Casco Bay College
Portland, ME 04101
207/772-0196

Casper College
Casper, WY 82601
307/268-2110

Catonsville Community College
Catonsville, MD 21228
410/455-4380

Cayuga County Community College
Auburn, NY 13021
315/255-1743

Centenary College
Hackettstown, NJ 07840
908/852-1400

Central Arizona College
Coolidge, AZ 85228
520/426-4444

Central Community College
Grand Island, NE 68802-4903
308/389-6305

Central Maine Technical College
Auburn, ME 04210
207/784-2385

Central Michigan University
Mt. Pleasant, MI 48859
517/774-4456

Central Missouri State University
Warrensburg, MO 64093
816/543-4111

Central Virginia Community College
Lynchburg, VA 24502
804/832-7630

Century Community and Technical College
White Bear Lake, MN 55110
612/779-3288

Chadron State College
Chadron, NE 69337
308/432-6221

Chaminade University of Honolulu
Honolulu, HI 96816
808/735-4722

Charles County Community College
LaPlata, MD 20646
301/934-2251, ext. 7523

Charter Oak State College
Newington, CT 06111
860/666-4595, ext. 17

Chattanooga State Technical Community College
Chattanooga, TN 37402
423/697-2478

Chesapeake College
Wye Mills, MD 21679
410/827-5846

Chipola Junior College
Marianna, FL 32446
850/718-2397

Chowan College
Murfreesboro, NC 27855
919/398-6280, 6281

Christopher Newport University
Newport News, VA 23606
757/594-7155

Cincinnati Bible College & Seminary
Cincinnati, OH 45204
513/244-8171

City University
Renton, WA 98055
425/637-1010 or 800/426-5596

Claflin College
Orangeburg, SC 29115
803/535-5244

Clarion University of Pennsylvania
Clarion, PA 16214
814/226-2000

Clarke College
Dubuque, IA 52001
319/588-6354

Clarkson College
Omaha, NE 68131
402/552-6119

Cleveland State University
Cleveland, OH 44118
216/523-7244

Cleveland Technical College
Shelby, NC 28152
704/484-4099

Clinton Community College
Clinton, IA 52732
319/244-7006

Clinton Community College
Plattsburgh, NY 12901
518/562-4100

Coastal Georgia Community College
Bruswick, GA 31520-3644
912/262-3075

Cochise College
Douglas, AZ 85607
520/364-0350

Cogswell Polytechnical College
Sunnyvale, CA 94089
408/541-0100, ext. 131

Coker College
Hartsville, SC 29550
803/383-8022

Colby Community College
Colby, KS 67701
785/462-3984

College for Lifelong Learning
Concord, NH 03301
603/228-3000

College of Charleston
Charleston, SC 29424
803/953-7031

College of DuPage
Glen Ellyn, IL 60137
630/942-2481

College of Eastern Utah
Price, UT 84501
435/637-2120, ext. 5205

College of Notre Dame of Maryland
Baltimore, MD 21210
410/532-5320

College of Our Lady of the Elms
Chicopee, MA 01013
413/598-8520

College of Santa Fe
Santa Fe, NM 87505
505/473-6317

College of St. Catherine
St. Paul, MN 55105
612/690-6531

College of St. Elizabeth
Convent Station, NJ 07961
973/290-4055

College of St. Mary
Omaha, NE 68124
402/399-2441

College of St. Scholastica
Duluth, MN 55811-4199
218/723-6562

College of Staten Island
Staten Island, NY 10314
718/982-2012

College of The Mainland
Texas City, TX 77591
409/938-1211

College of the Southwest
Hobbs, NM 88240
505/392-6561

Colorado Aero Tech
Broomfield, CO 80021
303/466-1714

Colorado Community College and
Occupational Education System
Denver, CO 80204-2554
303/620-4000

Colorado State University
Fort Collins, CO 80523-8021
970/491-2712

Colorado Technical University
Colorado Springs, CO 80907
719/598-0200

Columbia College
Sonora, CA 95310
209/588-5234

Columbia College
Columbia, MO 65216
573/875-7200

Columbia Union College
Takoma Park, MD 20912-7796
301/891-4000

Columbus State University
Columbus, GA 31993
706/568-2237

Community College of Allegheny County
Pittsburgh, PA 15233-1895
412/237-3185

Community College of Aurora
Aurora, CO 80231
303/360-4703

Community College of Denver
Denver, CO 80217-3363
303/556-2413

Community College of Rhode Island
Warwick, RI 02886-1807
401/825-2147

Community College of the Air Force
Maxwell Air Force Base, AL 36112-6613
334/953-6436

Community College of Vermont
Waterbury, VT 05676
802/241-1191

Concordia University
River Forest, IL 60305
708/209-3535

Concordia University
St. Paul, MN 55104-5494
612/641-8211

Concordia University
Portland, OR 97211
503/493-6512

Concordia University of Austin
Austin, TX 78705
512/452-7661

Cornerstone College
Grand Rapids, MI 49525
616/222-1431

Corning Community College
Corning, NY 14830
607/962-9220

Cowley County Community College
Arkansas City, KS 67005
316/442-0430

Craven Community College
New Bern, NC 28562
919/638-4131

Creighton University
Omaha, NE 68178
402/280-2702

Culver-Stockton College
Canton, MO 63435
217/231-6339

Cumberland College
Williamsburg, KY 40769
606/539-4316

Cumberland County College
Vineland, NJ 08362-0517
609/691-8600, ext. 201

Cuyahoga Community College
Cleveland, OH 44115
216/987-4778

Cuyahoga Community College-Eastern Campus
Warrensville Township, OH 44122
216/987-2013

Dallas Baptist University
Dallas, TX 75211-9990
214/333-5122

Dallas County Community College District
Dallas, TX 75202
214/860-2129

Dana College
Blair, NE 68008
402/426-7209

Darton College
Albany, GA 31707-3098
912/430-6729

Davenport College of Business
Grand Rapids, MI 49503
616/732-1202

David N. Myers College
Cleveland, OH 44115
216/523-3824

Davis & Elkins College
Elkins, WV 26241
800/624-3157

Davis College
Toledo, OH 43623
419/473-2700

Daytona Beach Community College
Daytona Beach, FL 32114
904/254-4414

De Anza College
Cupertino, CA 95014
408/864-8321

DeKalb Technical Institute
Clarkston, GA 30021
404/297-9522, ext. 1237

Del Mar College
Corpus Christi, TX 78404
512/886-1248

Delaware County Community College
Media, PA 19063-1094
610/359-5043

Delgado Community College
New Orleans, LA 70119
504/483-4143

Delta College
University Center, MI 48710
517/686-9291

Delta State University
Cleveland, MS 38733
601/846-4010

Des Moines Area Community College
Ankeny, IA 50021
515/964-6332

DeVry Institutes of Technology
Oakbrook Terrace, IL 60181
630/571-7700

Diablo Valley College
Pleasant Hill, CA 94523
925/685-1230, ext. 330

Doane College
Lincoln, NE 68504
402/466-4774

Dominican College of Blauvelt
Orangeburg, NY 10962
914/359-7800

Don Bosco Technical Institute
Rosemead, CA 91770-4299
626/301-6500, ext. 22

Donnelly College
Kansas City, KS 66102
913/621-6070

Dowling College
Long Island, NY 11769-1999
516/244-3036

Dundalk Community College
Baltimore, MD 21222
410/285-9802

Dutchess Community College
Poughkeepsie, NY 12601
914/431-8099

Dyersburg State Community College
Dyersburg, TN 38024
901/286-3300

East Coast Bible College
Charlotte, NC 28214
704/394-2307

Eastern College
St. Davids, PA 19087
610/341-5854

Eastern Connecticut State University
Willimantic, CT 06226
860/465-5286

Eastern Illinois University
Charleston, IL 61920
217/581-5618

Eastern Maine Technical College
Bangor, ME 04401
207/941-4623

Eastern Washington University
Cheney, WA 99004
509/359-2201

Edison Community College
Fort Meyers, FL
941/489-9349

Edison Community College
Piqua, OH 45356
937/778-8600

El Centro College
Dallas, TX 75202
214/860-2019

El Paso County Community College District
El Paso, TX 79998
915/831-2204

Elmira College
Elmira, NY 14901
607/735-1825

Embry-Riddle Aeronautical University
Extended Campus
Daytona Beach, FL 32114-3900
904/226-6961

Emmanuel College
Franklin Springs, GA 30639
706/245-7226

Emporia State University
Emporia, KS 66801
316/341-5171

Erie Community College
Buffalo, NY 14203
716/851-1100

Fairleigh Dickinson University
Teaneck, NJ 07666
201/692-7080

Fairmont State College
Fairmont, WV 26554
304/367-4141

Fayetteville Technical Community College
Fayetteville, NC 28303
910/497-1112

Fisher College
Boston, MA 02116
617/236-8829

Five Towns College
Dix Hills, NY 11746
516/424-7000

Flathead Valley Community College
Kalispell, MT 59901
406/756-3846

Florida Community College at Jacksonville
Jacksonville, FL 32202
904/633-8359

Florida International University
Miami, FL 33199
305/348-3662

Florida Metropolitan University System
Tampa College
Clearwater, FL 34619
813/725-2688

Florida Metropolitan University
Tampa College, West Hillsborough
Tampa, FL 33614
813/879-6000

Florida State University
Tallahassee, FL 32306-2480
850/644-5887

Fort Hays State University
Hays, KS 67601
785/628-4531

Fort Peck Community College
Poplar, MT 59255
406/768-5551

Franklin College of Indiana
Franklin, IN 46131
317/736-8441

Franklin University
Columbus, OH 43215-5399
614/341-6357

Frederick Community College
Frederick, MD 21702
301/846-2492

Fulton-Montgomery Community College
Johnstown, NY 12095
518/762-5302

Garden City Community College
Garden City, KS 67846
316/276-9597

Garland County Community College
Hot Springs, AR 71913
501/760-4222

Garrett Community College
McHenry, MD 21541
301/387-3059

Gate Way Community College
Phoenix, AZ 85034-1795
602/392-5194

Gateway Technical College
Kensoha, WI 53144-1690
414/656-6929

George Mason University
Fairfax, VA 22030-4444
703/993-2302

Georgetown University
School for Summer & Continuing Education
Washington, DC 20057
202/687-5706

Georgia State University
Atlanta, GA 30302-4044
404/651-4145

Georgian Court College
Lakewood, NJ 08701-2697
732/364-8218, ext. 249

Germanna Community College
Locust Grove, VA 22508
540/727-3027

Glenville State College
Glenville, WV 26351
304/462-7361

Gloucester County College
Sewell, NJ 08080
609/468-5000

Gogebic Community College
Ironwood, MI 49938
906/932-4231, ext. 212

Golden Gate University
San Francisco, CA 94105
415/442-7200

Golden West College
Huntington Beach, CA 92647
714/895-8121

Goshen College
Goshen, IN 46526
219/535-7515

Governors State University
University Park, IL 60466
708/534-4092

Grace University
Omaha, NE 68108
402/449-2800

Graceland College
Lamoni, IA 50140
515/784-5111

Great Basin College
Elko, NV 89801
702/753-2272

Greenfield Community College
Greenfield, MA 01301
413/774-3131

Greensboro College
Greensboro, NC 27401-1875
336/272-7102, ext. 209

Greenville College
Greenville, IL 62246
618/664-2800, ext. 4593

Griggs University
Silver Spring, MD 20904
301/680-6586

Hagerstown Junior College
Hagerstown, MD 21742-6590
301/790-2800

Harding University
Searcy, AR 72149-0001
501/279-4404

Harford Community College
Bel Air, MD 21015-1698
410/836-4139

Harrisburg Area Community College
Harrisburg, PA 17110
717/780-2370

Hartwick College
Oneonta, NY 13820
607/431-4460

Hawaii Pacific University
Honolulu, HI 96813
808/544-1129

Hawthorne University
Salt Lake City, UT 84109-0327
801/485-1801

Hazard Community College
Hazard, KY 41701
606/436-5721

Heidleberg College
Tiffin, OH 44883
419/448-2090

Herbert H. Lehman College
Bronx, NY 10468
718/960-8104

Hilbert College
Hamburg, NY 14075
716/649-7900, ext. 341

Hinds Junior College District
Raymond, MS 39154
601/857-3280

Holyoke Community College
Holyoke, MA 01040
413/552-2550

Hopkinsville Community College
Hopkinsville, KY 42241-2100
502/886-3921, ext. 100

Howard Community College
Columbia, MD 21044
410/772-4856

Howard Payne University
Brownwood, TX 76801
915/649-8002

Hudson Valley Community College
Troy, NY 12180-1573
518/270-1573

Humacao University College, UPR
Humacao, PR 00791-4300
787/850-9374

Huntington College
Huntington, IN 46750
219/359-4160

Huron University
Huron, SD 57350
605/352-8721

Husson College
Bangor, ME 04401
207/947-1121
1/800/4Husson

Illinois Community College System
Springfield, IL 62701-1874
217/785-5003

Illinois Valley Community College
Oglesby, IL 61348-9692
815/224-2720, ext. 437

Immaculata College
Immaculata, PA 19087-0300
610/647-4400, ext. 3235

Independence Community College
Independence, KS 67301
316/331-4100, ext. 4295

Indiana Institute of Technology
Fort Wayne, IN 46803
219/422-5561, ext. 276

Indiana University
Bloomington, IN 47405
812/855-3341

Indiana University-Purdue University at Indianapolis
Indianapolis, IN 46202-5143
317/274-1505

International Bible College
Florence, AL 35630
205/766-6610

Iowa Lakes Community College
Estherville, IA 51334
712/362-7922

Iowa Wesleyan College
Mt. Pleasant, IA 52641
319/385-6227

Iowa Western Community College
Council Bluffs, IA 51502
712/325-3400

Isothermal Community College
Spindale, NC 28160
704/286-3636, ext. 238

ITT Technical Institute
Phoenix, AZ 85008
602/231-0871

Ivy Tech State College
Indianapolis, IN 46202
317/921-4936

Ivy Tech State College
Madison, IN 47250-1881
812/265-2580

Ivy Tech State College, Northwest
Gary, IN 46409
219/981-1111

Ivy Tech State College, Sellersburg
Sellersburg, IN 47172
812/246-3301

Ivy Tech State College, South Bend
South Bend, IN 46619
219/289-7001

Ivy Tech State College, Terre Haute
Terre Haute, IN 47802
812/299-1121, ext. 203

Jackson State Community College
Jackson, TN 38301
901/425-2631

Jacksonville University
Jacksonville, FL 3221
904/745-7090

James Madison University
Harrisonburg, VA 22807
540/568-6824

Jefferson College
Hillsboro, MO 63050
314/797-3000, ext. 210

Jefferson Community College
Watertown, NY 13601
315/786-2230

Jersey City State College
Jersey City, NJ 07305
201/200-3005

John C. Calhoun State Community College
Decatur, AL 35609-2216
205/306-2596

John F. Kennedy University
Orinda, CA 94563
510/258-2212

John Jay College of Criminal Justice
New York, NY 10019
212/237-8878

John Tyler Community College
Chester, VA 23831
804/796-4151

John Wesley College
High Point, NC 27265
336/889-2262

John Wood Community College
Quincy, IL 62301
217/224-6500, ext. 4336

Johns Hopkins University
Baltimore, MD 21218-2691
410/516-6053

Johnson and Wales College
Providence, RI 02903
401/598-1841

Joliet Junior College
Joliet, IL 60431
815/729-9020, ext. 2245

Jones College
Jacksonville, FL 32211
904/743-1122

Jones County Junior College
Ellisville, MS 39437
601/477-4025

Kalamazoo Valley Community College
Kalamazoo, MI 49003-4070
616/372-5205

Kansas City Kansas Community College
Kansas City, KS 66112
913/334-1100, ext. 201

Kansas Newman College
Wichita, KS
316/942-4291, ext. 121

Kaskaskia College
Centralia, IL 62801
618-532-1981

Kellogg Community College
Battle Creek, MI 49017-3397
616/965-3931

Kennebec Valley Technical College
Fairfield, ME 04937-1367
207/453-5000

Kent State University
Kent, OH 44242-0001
330/672-9292

Kentucky Wesleyan College
Owensboro, KY 42301
502/926-3111

Keuka College
Keuka Park, NY 14478
315/536-4411, ext. 5204

Kilian Community College
Sioux Falls, SD 57104-6014
605/336-1711

King' s College
Wilkes-Barre, PA 18711
717/208-5970

Kingsborough Community College
Brooklyn, NY 11235
718/368-5136

Kirkwood Community College
Cedar Rapids, IA 52406
319/398-5603

Kishwaukee College
Malta, IL 60150-9699
815/825-2086, ext. 218

La Sierra University
Riverside, CA 92515
909/785-2006

Laboratory Institute of Merchandising
New York, NY 10022
212/752-1530

Lackawanna Junior College
Scranton, PA 18509
717/961-7840

Lake Erie College
Painesville, OH 44077
440/639-7825

Lake Land Community College
Mattoon, IL 61938
217/234-5378

Lakeland Community College
Kirtland, OH 44094
216/953-7118

Lamar University
Beaumont, TX 77710
409/880-8400

Lancaster Bible College
Lancaster, PA 17601
717/560-8258

Laramie County Community College
Cheyenne, WY 82001
307/778-1242

Laredo Community College
Laredo, TX 78040
956/721-5177

LaSalle University
Philadelphia, PA 19141
215/951-1020

Lawson State Community College
Burmingham, AL 35221
205/929-6312

Lehigh Carbon Community College
Schnecksville, PA 18078-2598
610/799-1195

Lewis and Clark Community College
Godfrey, IL 62035
618/466-3411, ext. 5000

Lewis University
Romeoville, IL 60446
815/838-0500, ext. 5212 or
800/897-9000, ext. 5250

Liberty University
Lynchburg, VA 24506-1803
804/582-7709

Limestone College
Gaffney, SC 29340
864/488-4540

Lincoln Memorial University
Harrogate, TN 37752
423/869-6280

Lindenwood College
St. Charles, MO 63301
314/949-2000

Long Island University C.W. Post Campus
Brookville, NY 11548
516/299-3230

Long Island University Center Brooklyn Campus
Brooklyn, NY 11201
718/488-1292

Long Island University Center Southampton Campus
Southampton, NY 11968
516/287-8341

Lorain County Community College
Elyria, OH 44035
440/365-5222

Loras College
Dubuque, IA 52004-0178
319/588-7139

Los Angeles Harbor College
Wilmington, CA 90744
310/522-8200

Louisburg College
Louisburg, NC 27549-2399
919/496-2521

Lourdes College
Sylvania, OH 43560-2898
419/885-3211

Lubbock Christian University
Lubbock, TX 79407-2099
806/796-8800

Lynchburg College
Lynchburg, VA 24501-3199
804/544-8218

MacMurray College
Jacksonville, IL 62650
217/479-7014

Maine College of Art
Portland, ME 04101
207/775-5098

Maine Maritime Academy
Castine, ME 04420
207/326-2426

Malone College
Canton, OH 44709
330/471-0800

Manatee Community College
Bradenton, FL 34206
941/755-1511, ext. 4200

Maple Woods Community College
Kansas City, MO 64119
816/436-3100

Marian College
Indianapolis, IN 46222-1997
317/955-6041

Marian College
Fond du Lac, WI 54935
920/923-7618

Mars Hill College
Mars Hill, NC 28754
704/689-1141

Martin Methodist College
Pulaski, TN 38478
615/363-9801

Mary Washington College
Fredericksburg, VA 22401
540/654-1038

Marycrest International University
Davenport, IA 52804
319/326-9219

Maryland College of Art & Design
Silver Spring, MD 20902
301/649-4454

Maryville University of St. Louis
St. Louis, MO 63141-7299
314/529-9370

Massasoit Community College
Brockton, MA 02402
508/855-9100

Mater Dei College
Ogdensburg, NY 13669
315/393-5930ext. 426

McIntosh College
Dover, NH 03820
603/742-1234

McKendree College
Lebanon, IL 62254
618/537-6817

Medaille College
Buffalo, NY 14214-2695
716/884-3281

Menlo College
Atherton, CA 94027-4301
650/324-2347

Mercer County Community College
Trenton, NJ 08690
609/586-4800, ext. 3240

Meredith College
Raleigh, NC 27607
919/829-8593

Metropolitan State University
St. Paul, MN 55101
612/772-7776

Mid-America Bible College
Oklahoma City, OK 73170
405/697-3800

Middle Tennessee State University
Murfreesboro, TN 37132
615/898-2111

Middlesex Community College
Middletown, CT 06457-4889
860/343-5719

Midland Lutheran College
Fremont, NE 68025
402/721-5480

Midlands Technical College
Columbia, SC 29902
803/738-7699

Midstate College
Peoria, IL 61614
309/692-4092

Milligan College
Milligan College, TN 37682
423/461-8782

Minnesota West Comm. and Tech. College, Worthington
Worthington, MN 56187
507-372-3406

Mississippi County Community College
Blytheville, AR 72316
870/762-1020

Mississippi Gulf Cost Community College
Perkinston, MS 39573
601/928-6280

Mississippi State University
Mississippi State, MS 39759
601/325-3742

Mississippi Valley State University
Itta Bena, MS 38941
601/254-3435

Mitchell Community College
Statesville, NC 28677
704/878-3200

Moberly Junior College
Moberly, MO 65270
660/263-4110, ext.282

Mohave Community College
Kingman, AZ 86401
520/757-4331

Monmouth University
West Long Beach, NJ 07764
732/571-4495

Monroe Community College
Rochester, NY 14623
716/292-2243

Montana State University - Billings
Billings, MT 59101-0298
406/657-2158

Montana State University - Northern
Havre, MT 59501
406/265-3703

Montana State University, Bozeman
Bozeman, MT 59717-2180
406/994-6617

Montana Tech College of Technology
Butte, MT 59701
406/496-4689

Montana Tech of the University of Montana
Butte, MT 59701
406/496-4689

Monterey Peninsula College
Monterey, CA 93940
408/645-1372

Montgomery College
Rockville, MD 20850
301/279-5000

Montgomery College-Takoma Park Campus
Takoma Park, MD 20912
301/650-1501

Morgan Community College
Fort Morgan, CO 80701
970/867-3081

Mount Marty College
Yankton, SD 57078
605/668-1515

Mount Olive College
Mount Olive, NC 28365
919/658-7165

Mount Senario College
Ladysmith, WI 54848
715/532-5511, ext. 121

Mount St. Mary College
Newburgh, NY 12550
914/569-3258

Mount St. Mary's College
Los Angeles, CA 90049
310/954-4010

MTI College of Business and Technology
Houston, TX 77036
713/974-7181

Muhlenberg College
Allentown, PA 18104
610/821-3300

Muscatine Community College
Muscatine, IA 52761
319/288-6004

Nashville State Technical Institue
Nashville, TN 37209
615/353-3217

Nassau Community College
Garden City, NY 11530-6793
516/572-7205

National American University
Rapid City, SD 57701
605/394-4990

National University
La Jolla, CA 92037
619/642-8181

Naugatuck Valley Community-Technical College
Waterbury, CT 06708
203/575-8083

Nazareth College of Rochester
Rochester, NY 14618-3790
716/389-2873

Nebraska Christian College
Norfolk, NE 68701
402/379-5000

Nebraska College of Technical Agriculture
Curtis, NE 69025
308/367-4124

Neumann College
Aston, PA 19014-1298
610/558-5608

New Hampshire College
Manchester, NH 03106
603/668-2211, ext. 2113

New School University
New York, NY 10011
212/229-5119

Newberry College
Newberry, SC 29108
803/321-5112

Nichols College
Dudley, MA 01571
508/943-1560

North Carolina Wesleyan College
Rocky Mount, NC 27804
919/985-5123

North Central Bible College
Minneapolis, MN 55404
612/343-4788

North Central Missouri College
Trenton, MO 64683
660/359-3948, ext. 400

North Central Technical College
Mansfield, OH 44901
419/755-4800

North Dakota State College of Science
Wahpeton, ND 58076
701/671-2203

North Hennepin Community College
Minneapolis, MN 55445
612/424-0713

North Park University
Chicago, IL 60625
773/244-5767

North Shore Community College
Danvers, MA 01923-0340
508/762-4000, ext. 5429

Northeast Alabama Community College
Rainsville, AL 35986
205/638-4418

Northeast Community College
Norfolk, NE 68702-0469
402/644-0524

Northeast State Technical Community College
Blountville, TN 37617-0246
423/323-0201

Northeastern Junior College
Sterling, CO 80751
970/522-6600, ext. 6676

Northeastern Oklahoma A&M College
Miami, OK 74354
918/540-6211

Northeastern State University
Tahlequah, OK 74653
918/456-5511

Northern Maine Technical College
Presque Isle, ME 04769
207/768-2792

Northern Oklahoma College
Tonkawa, OK 74653-0310
580/628-6201

Northern State University
Aberdeen, SD 57401
605/626-2012

Northern Virginia Community College
Alexandria, VA 22311
703/323-3198

Northland College
Ashland, WI 54806
715/682-1227

Northland Community College
Thief River Falls, MN 56701
218/681-0701

Northland Pioneer College
Holbrook, AZ 86025
520/537-2976, ext. 329

Northwest Christian College
Eugene, OR 97401
541/684-7201

Northwestern College
Lima, OH 45805
419/998-3163

Northwood University
Midland, MI 48640
517/837-4455

Norwalk Community-Technical College
Norwalk, CT 06854
203/857-7035

Norwich University
Northfield, VT 05663
802/468-6679

Nova Southeastern University
Fort Lauderdale, FL 33314
954/262-8414

Oakland City University
Oakland, IN 47660
812/749-1238

Ocean County College
Toms River, NJ 08754-2001
732/255-0400, ext. -2018

Odessa College
Odessa, TX 79764
915/335-6409

Oglethorpe University
Atlanta, GA 30319
404/364-8315, ext. 0315

Ohio University
Athens, OH 45701
614/593-4211

Oklahoma Baptist University
Shawnee, OK 74801
405/878-2025

Oklahoma City Community College
Oklahoma City, OK 73159
405/682-7512, ext. 7512

Oklahoma State University
Stillwater, OK 74078
405/744-7679

Oklahoma State University, Oklahoma City
Oklahoma City, OK 73106
405/956-3252

Oklahoma State University at Ormulgee
Ormulgee, OK 74447
918/756-6211

Olivet Nazerene University
Kankakee, IL 60901
815/939-5201

Oral Roberts University
Tulsa, OK 74133
918/495-6549

Orangeburg - Calhoun Technical College
Orangeburg, SC 29118
803/535-1220

Ottawa University
Phoenix, AZ 85021
602/371-1188, ext. 168

Ottawa University
Ottawa, KS 66067
785/242-5200

Otterbein College
Westerville, OH 43081
614/823-1154

Our Lady of Holy Cross College
New Orleans, LA
504/394-7744

Our Lady of the Lake University
San Antonio, TX 78207-4689
210/431-3949

Owensboro Community College
Owensboro, KY 42303
606/336-5082

Pace University
Pleasantville, NY 10570
914/773-3424

Pace University (Midtown Center)
New York, NY 10176-0899
212/346-1770

Palm Beach Community College
Lake Worth, FL 33461
561/439-8080

Palomar College
San Marcos, CA 92069-1487
760/744-1150

Panama Canal College
APO AA 34002
507/272-3107

Park College
Parkville, MO 64152-3792
816/741-2000

Parkland College
Champaign, IL 61821
217/351-2482

Patten College
Oakland, CA 94601
510/533-8300

Paul D. Camp Community College
Franklin, VA 23851
757/569-6725

Pennsylvania College of Technology
Williamsport, PA 17701
717/326-3761

Pennsylvania Institute of Technology
Media, PA 19063
610/565-7900

Pennsylvania State University Main Campus
University Park, PA 16802
814/865-4700

Pfeiffer University at Charlotte
Charlotte, NC
704/463-1360, ext. 2057

Phillips University
Enid, OK 73701
580/548-2296

Piedmont Virginia Community College
Charlottesville, VA 22902
804/961-5411

Pierce College
Tacoma, WA 98498-1999
253/964-6621

Pikes Peak Community College
Colorado Springs, CO 80906-5498
719/540-7225 or 800/777-9446

Pittsburg State University
Pittsburg, KS 66762
316/235-4253

Point Loma Nazarene College
San Diego, CA 92106-2899
619/849-2548

Point Park College
Pittsburgh, PA 15222
412/392-3907

Pratt Community College
Pratt, KS 67124
316/672-9800

Prestonsburg Community College
Prestonsburg, KY 41653
606/886-3863

Prince George's Community College
Largo, MD 20774-2199
301/322-0801

Providence College School of Continuing Education
Providence, RI 02918
401/865-1487

Quinebaug Valley Community College
Danielson, CT 06708
203/575-8083

Quinsigamond Community College
Worcester, MA 01606
508/854-4380

Radford University
Radford, VA
540/831-5952

Ramapo College of New Jersey
Mahwah, NJ 07430
201/529-6482

Reading Area Community College
Reading, PA 19601
610/373-1525

Regents College
Albany, NY 12230
518/474-3703

Regis University
Denver, CO 80221-1099
303/458-1844

Renton Technical College
Renton, WA 98056
425/235-5840

Rhode Island College
Providence, RI 02809
401/456-8234

Richard Bland College
Petersberg, VA 23805
804/862-6220

Rider University
Lawrenceville, NJ 08648
609/896-5033

Ridgewater College
Willmar, MN 56201
320/231-2917

Rio Salado College
Tempe, AZ 85281
602/517-8140

Rivier College
Nashua, NH 03060
603/888-1311

Roane State Community College
Harriman, TN 37748
423/882-4513

Roberts Wesleyan College
Rochester, NY 14624-1997
716/594-6220

Rochester Institute of Technology
Rochester, NY 14623-0887
716/475-2607

Rockingham Community College
Wentworth, NC 27375-0038
910/342-4261, ext. 137

Rocky Mountain College
Billings, MT 59102
406/657-1030

Roger Williams University
Bristol, RI 02809
401/254-3062

Rogers University
Claremore, OK 74017
918/343-7539

Rogue Community College
Grants Pass, OR 97527
541/471-3500, ext. 317

Rose State College
Midwest City, OK 73110-2799
405/733-7300

Rowan-Cabarrus Community College
Salisbury, NC 28145-1595
704/637-0760, ext. 214

Sacred Heart University
Fairfield, CT 06432
203/371-7910

Saint Mary's University
San Antonio, TX 78228-8576
210/431-2299, ext. 1103

Saint Mary's University
Minneapolis, MN 55404-4403
612/874-9877

Salem Community College
Carneys Point, NJ 08069
609/351-2642

Salt Lake Community College
Salt Lake City, UT 84310
801/957-4249

Salve Regina University
Newport, RI 02840
401/847-6650

San Diego State University
San Diego, CA 92182-7455
619/594-7800

San Juan College
Farmington, NM 87402
505/599-0300

Sand Hills Community College
Pinehurst, NC 28387
910/692-6185

Scott Community College
Bettendorf, IA 52722
319/441-4001

Seminole State College
Seminole, OK 74868
405/382-9950

Seton Hill College
Greensburg, PA 15601
412/838-4218

Seward County Community College
Liberal, KS 67905-1137
316/629-2616

Shawnee State University
Portsmouth, OH 45662
614/355-2593

Shelby State Community College
Memphis, TN 38134
901/544-5025

Shenandoah College
Winchester, VA 22601
540/665-4506

Shorter College
Marietta, GA 30067
770/989-5671

Siena Heights College
Adrian, MI 49221
517/264-7122

Silver Lake College
Manitowoc, WI 54220-9319
920/686-6231

Simpson College
Indianola, IA 50125
515/961-1644

Sinclair Community College
Dayton, OH 45402
937/512-2940

Skagit Valley College - Whidbey Campus
Oak Harbor, WA 98277-3099
360/679-5330

Skidmore College/ University Without Walls
Saratoga Springs, NY 12866
518/584-5450

Snow College
Ephraim, UT 84627
435/283-7140

Southeast Community College
Lincoln, NE 68505
402/437-2619

Southeastern Oklahoma State University
Durant, OK 74701-0609
580/924-0121

Southeastern University
Washington, DC 20024
202/488-8162

Southern Connecticut State University
New Haven, CT 06515
203/392-5656

Southern Maine Technical College
South Portland, ME 04106
207/767-9520

Southern Nazarene University
Bethany, OK 73008
405/491-6386

Southern State Community College
Hillsboro, OH 45133
937/393-3431, ext. 2615

Southern Wesleyan University
Central, SC 29630-1020
846/639-2453, ext. 388

Southern West Virginia Community and Technical College
Mount Gay, WV 25637
304/792-7040

Southwest Texas State University
San Marcos, TX 78666
512/245-2115

Southwest Virginia Community College
Richllands, VA 24641
540/964-7200

Southwest Wisconsin Technical College
Fennimore, WI 53809
608/822-3262

Southwestern Adventist College
Keene, TX 76059
817/556-4721

Southwestern College
Winfield, KS 67156-2499
316/221-8208

Southwestern Community College
Creston, IA 50801
515/782-7081

Southwestern Oklahoma State University
Weatherford, OK 73096
580/774-3777

Southwestern Oregon Community College
Coos Bay, OR 97420
541/888-7246

Spalding University
Louisville, KY 40203-2188
502/585-7110

Spartanburg Technical College
Spartanburg, SC 29305-4386
864/591-3613

Spring Hill College
Mobile, AL 36608
334/380-2240

St. Ambrose University
Davenport, IA 52803
319/333-6477

St. Andrews Presbyterian College
Laurinburg, NC 28352
910/277-5000

St. Catharine College
St. Catharine, KY 40061
606/336-9304

St. Cloud State University
St. Cloud, MN 56301-4498
320/255-2111

St. Cloud Technical College
St. Cloud, MN 56303
320/654-5075

St. Edward's University
Austin, TX 78704-6489
512/448-8715

St. Francis College
Brooklyn, NY 11201
718/489-5340

St. Francis College of Pennsylvania
Loretto, PA 15940
814/472-3100

St. John Fisher College
Rochester, NY 14618
716/385-8015

St. Joseph's College
Standish, ME 04084
207/892-6766

St. Joseph's College
Patchogue, NY 11772
516/447-3257

St. Louis University
St. Louis, MO 63103
314/977-2330

St. Mary College
Leavenworth, KS 66048
913/682-5151

St. Mary-of-the-Woods College
St. Mary-of-the-Wood, IN 47876
812/535-5181

St. Peter's College
Jersey City, NJ 07306-5997
201/915-9022

St. Petersburg Junior College
St. Petersburg, FL 33733
813/341-3170

St. Thomas Aquinas College
Sparkill, NY 10976-1050
914/398-4012

State Fair Community College
Sedalia, MO 65301
660/530-5800

Stephens College
Columbia, MO 65215
573/876-7277

Sterling College
Sterling, KS 67579-0098
316/278-2173

Stratton College
Milwaukee, WI 53202
414/276-5200

Strayer College
Washington, DC 20005
202/408-2424

Suffolk County Community College
Selden, NY 11784
516/451-4035

Sul Ross State University
Alpine, TX 79832
915/837-8050

SUNY - Empire State College
Saratoga Springs, NY 12866
518/587-2100

SUNY at Stony Brook
Stony Brook, NY 11794-1909
516/632-7028

SUNY College at Cortland
Cortland, NY 13045
607/753-4712

SUNY College at Oswego
Oswego, NY 13126
315/341-3613

SUNY College of Technology at Morrisville
Morrisville, NY 13408
315/684-6270

SUNY Institute of Technology at Utica-Rome
Utica, NY 13504
800/786-9832

Surry Community College
Dobson, NC 27017
919/386-8121

Tabor College
Hillsboro, KS 67063
316/947-3121

Technical College of the Lowcountry
Beaufort, SC 29901
803/525-8247

Tennessee Wesleyan College
Athens, TN 37371
423/745-7504, ext. 5201

Terra Community College
Fremont, OH 43420
419/334-8400

Texas A&M University - Corpus Christi
Corpus Christi, TX 78412
512/994-5952

Texas A&M University - Kingsville
Kingsville, TX 78363
512/593-2811

Texas Lutheran University
Seguin, TX 78155
830/372-8041

Texas State Technical College
Harlingen, TX 78550
956/425-0665

Texas State Technical College - Sweetwater
Sweetwater, TX 79556
915/235-7374

The College of West Virginia
Beckley, WV 25801
304/253-7351, ext. 448

The Union Institute
Cincinnati, OH 45206
513/861-6400

The Universtiy of Findlay
Findlay, OH 45840
419/424-4556

Thiel College
Greenville, PA 16125
724/589-2110

Thomas Edison State College
Trenton, NJ 08608
609/984-1150

Thomas More College
Fort Mitchell, KY 41017
606/341-4554

Thomas Nelson Community College
Hampton, VA 23670
757/825-3517

Tidewater Community College
Norfolk, VA 23510
757/822-1068

Tiffin University
Tiffin, OH 44883
419/447-6442

Tompkins Cortland Community College
Dryden, NY 13053
607/844-8211

Towson State University
Towson, MD 21252-0001
410/830-2078

Trident Technical College
Charleston, SC 29423-8067
803/574-3277

Trinidad State Junior College
Trinidad, CO 81082
719/846-5680

Trinity College
Washington, DC 20017
202/884-9200

Tri-State University at South Bend
South Bend, IN 46601
219/234-4810

Trocaire College
Buffalo, NY 14220
716/826-1200

Troy State University
Troy, AL 36082
334/670-3616

Troy State University at Dothan
Fort Rucker, AL 36362-0457
334/983-6556
334/598-2443

Troy State University in Montgomery
Montgomery, AL 36103-4419
334/241-9532

Truckee Meadows Community College
Reno, NV 89512
702/673-7042

Tulsa Community College
Tulsa, OK 74135
918/595-7526

Tusculum College
Greenville, TN 37745
423/636-7300

Ulster County Community College
Stone Ridge, NY 12484
914/687-5022

Union University
Jackson, TN 38305
901/661-5040

University Colleges
Bellingham, WA 98227-5211
360/738-0336

University of Alabama
Tuscaloosa, AL 35487-0388
205/348-6330

University of Alabama at Huntsville
Huntsville, AL 35899
205/890-6750

University of Alaska, Fairbanks
Fairbanks, AK 99775
907/474-7522

University of Alaska, Southeast
Juneau, AK 99801
907/465-6458

University of Baltimore
Baltimore, MD 21201
410/837-4796

University of Central Arkansas
Conway, AR 72035
501/450-5200

University of Central Texas
Killeen, TX 76540-1416
254/526-8262 , ext. 261

University of Charleston
Charleston, WV 25304
304/357-4737

University of Cincinnati
College of Evening and Continuing Education
Cincinnati, OH 45221-0146
513/556-9192

University of Dubuque
Dubuque, IA 52001
319/589-3270

University of Great Falls
Great Falls, MT 59405
406/791-5200

University of Illinios at Springfield
Springfield, IL
217/786-6626

University of Indianapolis
Indianapolis, IN 46227
317/788-3262

University of Iowa
Iowa City, IA 52242
319/335-1549

University of La Verne
La Verne, CA 91750
909/593-3511, ext. 4007

University of Maine at Farmington
Farmington, ME 04938
207/778-2050

University of Maine at Fort Kent
Fort Kent, ME 44743
207/834-7521

University of Maine at Presque Isle
Presque, ME 04769
207/768-9525

University of Mary
Bismrack, ND 58504-9652
701/255-7500

University of Maryland University College
College Park, MD 20742
301/985-7289

University of Massachusetts - Amherst
Amherst, MA 01003
413/545-0222

University of Memphis
Memphis, TN 38152-6626
901/678-3995

University of Montana
Missoula, MT 598121265
406/243-0211

University of Nebraska-Omaha
Omaha, NE 68182-0331
402/554-2347

University of New Haven
West Haven, CT 06516
203/934-7305

University of New Mexico
Albuquerque, NM 87131
505/277-2446

University of New Orleans
New Orleans, LA 70148-2135
504/280-6595

University of North Dakota
Grand Forks, ND 58202-8357
701/777-3821

University of North Dakota
Williston, ND 58802-1326
701/774-4200

University of North Texas
Denton, TX 76203-1277
940/565-2681

University of Northern Iowa
Cedar Falls, IA 50614-0006
319/273-2244

University of Oklahoma
Norman, OK 73037-0001
405/325-2252

University of Oklahoma Health Sciences Center
Oklahoma City, OK 73190
405/271-2347

University of Phoenix
Phoenix, AZ 85044
602/966-5394

University of Redlands
Redlands, CA 92374
909/793-2121, ext. 3234

University of San Francisco
San Francisco, CA 94117-1080
415/422-6143

University of Science and Arts of Oklahoma
Chickasha, OK 73018
405/224-3140

University of Scranton, A Jesuit University
Scranton, PA 18510-4592
717/941-7580

University of South Alabama
Mobile, AL 36688-0002
334/460-7718

University of South Carolina- Beaufort
Beaufort, SC 29902
803/522-7497

University of Southern Maine
Portland, ME 04104-9300
207/780-4683

University of St. Francis
Fort Wayne, IN 46808
219/434-3294

University of Tennessee-Chattanooga
Chattanooga, TN 37401
423/755-4111

University of Tennessee at Martin
Martin, TN 38238
901/587-7053

University of the District of Columbia
Washington, DC 20008
202/274-5100

University of Wisconsin-Platteville
Platteville, WI 53818
608/342-1321

University of Wisconsin-Stevens Point
Stevens Point, WI 54481
715/346-2441

Upper Iowa University
Fayette, IA 52142
319/425-5283

Urbana University
Urbana, OH 43078
937/484-1316

Valdosta State University
Valdosta, GA 31698
912/333-5791

Valley City State University
Valley City, ND 58072
701/845-7431

Valley Forge Christian College
Pheonixville, PA 19460
610/935-0450

Valparaiso University
Valparaiso, IN 46383
219/464-5212

Vance-Granville Community College
Henderson, NC 27536
919/492-2061

Vermont Technical College
Randolph Center, VT 05061
802/728-1302

Vernon Regional Junior College
Vernon, TX 76384
940/552-6291

Villa Maria College of Buffalo
Buffalo, NY 14225
716/896-0700

Virginia Wesleyan College
Norfolk, VA 23502
757/455-3386

Wallace Community College - Aviation Campus
Ozark, AL 36361-1209
334/774-5113, ext. 640

Wallace State Community College
Henceville, AL 35077-2000
205/352-8125

Wartburg College
Waverly, IA 50677
319/352-8272

Washington County Technical College
Calais, ME 04619
207/454-1002

Washington State Community College
Marietta, OH 45750
614/374-8716

Waubonsee Community College
Sugar Grove, IL 60554-9799
630/466-7900, ext. 0373

Wayland Baptist University
Plainview, TX 79072
806/296-4708

Wayne State College
Wayne, NE 68787
402/375-7239

Weber State College
Ogden, UT 84408-1137
801/626-7670

Webster University
St. Louis, MO 63119
314/968-6910

Wesley College
Dover, DE 19901-3875
302/736-2439

West Liberty State College
West Liberty, WV 26074
304/336-8007

West Virginia State College
Institute, WV 25112-1000
304/766-3144

West Virginia University
Morgantown, WV 26506
304/293-5441

West Virginia Wesleyan College
Buckhannon, WV 26201
304/473-8470

Westchester Community College
Valhalla, NY 10595
914/785-6931

Western Baptist College
Salem, OR 97301
503/375-7590, or 800/764-1383

Western Illinois University
Macomb, IL 61455
309/298-1929

Western Nevada Community College
Carson City, NV 89703
702/887-3138

Western Oregon University
Monmouth, OR 97361
503/838-8180

Western Wyoming Community College
Rock Springs, WY 82902
307/383-1639

Westmoreland County Community College
Youngwood, PA 15697
412/925-4212

White Pines College
White Pines, NH
603/887-4401

Whitworth College
Spokane, WA 99251
509/466-1000

William Carey College
Hattiesburg, MS 39401-5499
601/582-6196

William Paterson University
Wayne, NJ 07470
973/720-3093, ext. 2121

Williamsburg Technical College
Kingstree, SC 29556
803/354-2021

Wilmington College
Wilmington, OH 45177
937/382-6661
800/341-9318

Wilson Technical Community College
Wilson, NC 27893
919/291-1195

Wingate University
Wingate, NC 28174
704/233-8000

Wright State University
Dayton, OH 45435
937/775-5588

Xavier University
Cincinnati, OH 45207
513/745-3358

Yakima Valley Community College
Yakima, WA 98907-1647
509/574-4635

York College
York, NE 68467-2699
402/363-5677 or 5678